OXFORD ADVANCED LEARNER'S DICTIONARY OF CURRENT ENGLISH

OXFORD ADVANCED LEARNER'S DICTIONARY OF CURRENT ENGLISH

A S HORNBY

with
A P Cowie
A C Gimson

Berlin
Cornelsen & Oxford University Press

Alleinberechtigte Ausgabe für die Bundesrepublik Deutschland einschl. Berlin (West) und für Österreich.

© der Originalausgabe:
Oxford University Press 1974
1. Auflage 1948 (12 Drucke)
2. Auflage 1963 (19 Drucke)
3. Auflage 1974
11. überarbeiteter Druck 1980
13. Druck 1982

Computer typeset in
Times and Univers by
George Overs Ltd,
Oxford University Press,
Unwin Brothers Ltd
and Tradespools Ltd.
Printed in Great Britain
at the University Press, Oxford
by Eric Buckley
Printer to the University.

ISBN 3-8109-0048-6

Bestellnummer 486

Vertrieb für die Bundesrepublik Deutschland einschl. Berlin (West), für Österreich und die Schweiz:
Cornelsen-Velhagen & Klasing Verlagsgesellschaft, Bielefeld.

The publishers are grateful to the following for permission to reproduce the photographs:

Aerofilms Ltd; The Associated Press Ltd; Atkin, Grant & Lang Ltd; The Australian High Commission; Babcock Weitz; Barnaby's Picture Library; The British Aircraft Corporation; The British Leyland Motor Corporation Ltd; The British Oxygen Co Ltd; The British Petroleum Co Ltd; British Rail; The British Tourist Authority; Camera Press Ltd; The Canadian High Commission; J Allan Cash Ltd; The Controller of Her Majesty's Stationery Office (British Crown Copyright); Coventry Climax Engines Ltd; De Beers Ltd; Arnold Dolmetsch Ltd; The Electricity Council of Great Britain; Fox Photos Ltd; Gillette Industries Ltd; Gravity-Randall Ltd; The Greek State Tourist Office; Will Green Ltd; John M Henderson & Co Ltd; The International Harvester Co Ltd; The Japanese Embassy; Jarrold & Sons Ltd; Kelvin Hughes; The Keystone Press Agency Ltd; Kodak Ltd; Quentin Lloyd; The London Museum; Madame Tussaud's Ltd; The Mansell Collection; Massey-Ferguson (UK) Ltd; Messerschmitt-Bölkow-Blohm; Myford Ltd; The National Cash Register Co Ltd; The National Portrait Gallery, London; James Neill (Sheffield) Ltd; The New Charing Cross Hospital, London; The Novosti Press Agency; Philips Electrical Ltd; Pifco Ltd; The Rev C E Pocknee; The Post Office; The Progress Gyroscope Co Ltd; Prout Catamarans; Pye TVT; The Radio Times Hulton Picture Library; Rana Båtfabrikk; Ransomes, Sims & Jeffries Ltd; Record-Marples-Ridgway Ltd; The Royal National Institute for the Blind; St George's Hospital Medical School, London; The Science Museum, London (British Crown Copyright); Walter Scott (Bradford) Ltd; Scottish Aviation Ltd; Shure Electronics Ltd; The Singer Co Ltd; Thomas Smith & Sons (Rodley) Ltd; Spear & Jackson Ltd; The Sport & General Press Agency Ltd; Stanley Tools Ltd; Steinway & Sons; John Topham Ltd; The Trustees of the British Museum; The Trustees of the British Museum (Natural History); The Trustees of the Wallace Collection, London; The Union-Castle Mail Steamship Co Ltd; The United States Information Service; Vespa Scooters; Vickers Ltd; The Victoria & Albert Museum, London (British Crown Copyright); Wilkinson Sword Ltd; Wolf Electric Tools Ltd; Carl Zeiss Ltd.

Contents

Contributors

General Editor
A S Hornby
with
A P Cowie

Pronunciation
Professor A C Gimson
Dr S M Ramsaran

Specialist Editor
Dr L Todd

Illustrations
Roger Gorringe
Carl James
Richard Lewington
Sean Milne
Colin Newman
Vyvyan Thomas
David Woodroffe

Acknowledgements

I continue to be indebted to correspondents in many parts of the world for calling attention to occasional misprints and errors, and for suggestions on possible additions. These suggestions have been carefully considered and acted on where I felt in agreement with them.

Professor V Gatenby and Mr H Wakefield shared the work of compiling the first edition (1942). The value of their contributions remains, although these were extensively revised and added to in the second edition (1963) and in this third edition.

I pay tribute to the editors of the English Language Teaching Department of the Oxford University Press, especially Christina Ruse and Jonathan Price, and to the staff of the computer type-setting section, for their work on the text of this edition.

A S HORNBY

General preface

This is a completely revised, up-dated and re-set impression of the third edition. It combines the traditions of the Oxford Dictionaries with the language-teaching skills of A S Hornby. It provides the student or teacher of the English language with the most practically useful and comprehensive record of the language as it is spoken and written today.

There are four new features of this revised impression:

1 A simple but detailed *Introduction*, which not only explains what is in the Dictionary, but also suggests how the Dictionary can be used.
2 A phonetic interpretation and transcription by Professor A C Gimson, editor of the *English Pronouncing Dictionary*.
3 An Appendix on *Punctuation*, explaining how all the English punctuation marks are used.
4 A *Key to the verb patterns* inside the back cover, for constant easy reference.

Preface to the phonetic information

In this revised impression, the representation of pronunciation differs somewhat from that shown previously. The phonetic notation now conforms to that to be found in the majority of important English dictionaries used by non-native learners of English, and in particular to the latest (14th) edition of the *English Pronouncing Dictionary* (Dent, 1977). As a consequence, the length mark associated with certain vowels has been restored, though in strict phonological terms this mark may be considered redundant if the chosen vowel symbols distinguish qualitative differences. Nevertheless, the reactions of users of the Dictionary have suggested that an indication of length is widely held to be pedagogically useful, there being many occasions when quantitative as well as qualitative features provide significant cues to meaning. In addition, the simple vertical primary stress mark has been restored in place of the previous slanting mark, which was judged by many to be too readily suggestive of a specific tone.

The pronunciations recommended differ little from those shown previously. However, certain highly-elided forms have been replaced by others of a more careful style, judged to be more useful for even the advanced learner of English. Similarly, the marking of syllabic consonants in non-final positions has been abandoned, an expanded solution involving the insertion of a weak vowel being preferred.

The task of making these and other changes has been shared between my colleague Dr S M Ramsaran and myself.

A C GIMSON
University College London

Key to entries

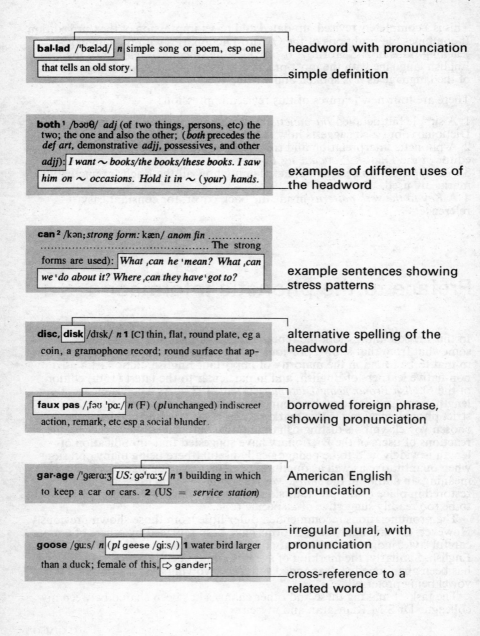

bal·lad /'bæləd/ n simple song or poem, esp one that tells an old story. — headword with pronunciation / simple definition

both¹ /bəʊθ/ adj (of two things, persons, etc) the two; the one and also the other; (both precedes the def art, demonstrative adjj, possessives, and other adjj): I want ~ books/the books/these books. I saw him on ~ occasions. Hold it in ~ (your) hands. — examples of different uses of the headword

can² /kən; strong form: kæn/ anom fin .... The strong forms are used): What ,can he 'mean? What ,can we 'do about it? Where ,can they have 'got to? — example sentences showing stress patterns

disc, disk /dɪsk/ n 1 [C] thin, flat, round plate, eg a coin, a gramophone record; round surface that ap- — alternative spelling of the headword

faux pas /ˌfəʊ 'pɑː/ n (F) (pl unchanged) indiscreet action, remark, etc esp a social blunder. — borrowed foreign phrase, showing pronunciation

gar·age /'gærɑːʒ US: gə'rɑːʒ/ n 1 building in which to keep a car or cars. 2 (US = service station) — American English pronunciation

goose /guːs/ n (pl geese /giːs/) 1 water bird larger than a duck; female of this, ⇨ gander; — irregular plural, with pronunciation / cross-reference to a related word

hon·our² (US = **honor**) /'ɒnə(r)/ vt [VP6A] **1** respect highly, feel honour for; confer honour on:

American English spelling

lazy /'leɪzɪ/ adj (-ier, -iest) unwilling to work; doing little work; suitable for, causing, inducing, inactivity: a ~ fellow; a ~ afternoon. ⇨ idle. '~-bones n ~ person. lazi·ly adv lazi·ness n

comparative and superlative forms of an adjective

compound, with stress pattern

leap /liːp/ vi,vt (pt,pp leapt /lept/ or leaped /liːpt/) **1** [VP2A,C,3A] jump (jump is the usu word;

irregular form of a verb, with pronunciation

li·able /'laɪəbl/ adj (usu pred) **1** ~ for, responsible according to law: Is a man ~ for his wife's debts in your country? **2** be ~ to sth, be subject to: If you drive a car to the danger of the public, you make yourself ~ to a heavy fine, or even to imprisonment. He is ~ to seasickness. **3** be ~ to do sth,

special uses of an adjective with a preposition

mean·time /'miːntaɪm/ adv, n (in the) ~, meanwhile.

special grammatical way in which the headword is used

pave·ment /'peɪvmənt/ n **1** (GB) paved way at the side of a street for people on foot (US = sidewalk).

where to divide the headword at the end of a line

different word used in American English

people /'piːpl/ n [U] (collective, with pl v. Note that for one human being, it is preferable to use man, woman, boy, girl and not person, which, although useful in definitions, may be derogatory or formal). **1** persons in general: streets crowded with

special note on problems of usage or grammar

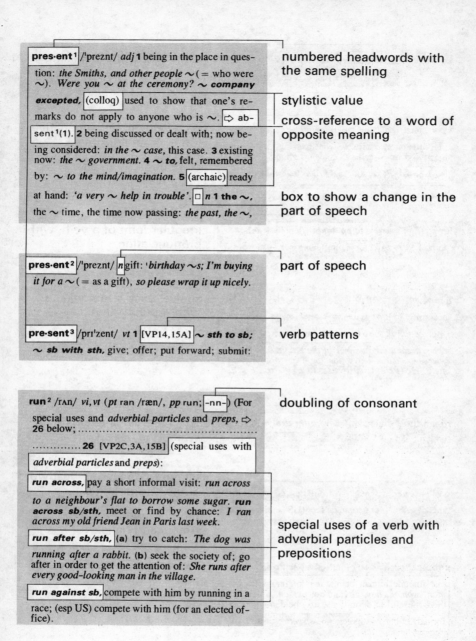

pres·ent¹ /'preznt/ adj **1** being in the place in question: *the Smiths, and other people* ∼ (= *who were* ∼). *Were you* ∼ *at the ceremony?* ∼ *company excepted,* (colloq) used to show that one's remarks do not apply to anyone who is ∼. ⇨ absent¹(1). **2** being discussed or dealt with; now being considered: *in the* ∼ *case,* this case. **3** existing now: *the* ∼ *government.* **4** ∼ *to,* felt, remembered by: ∼ *to the mind/imagination.* **5** (archaic) ready at hand: *'a very* ∼ *help in trouble'.* □ *n* **1 the** ∼, the ∼ time, the time now passing: *the past, the* ∼,

numbered headwords with the same spelling

stylistic value

cross-reference to a word of opposite meaning

box to show a change in the part of speech

pres·ent² /'preznt/ *n* gift: '*birthday* ∼*s; I'm buying it for a* ∼ (= as a gift), *so please wrap it up nicely.*

part of speech

pre·sent³ /prɪ'zent/ *vt* **1** [VP14,15A] ∼ *sth to sb;* ∼ *sb with sth,* give; offer; put forward; submit:

verb patterns

run² /rʌn/ *vi,vt* (*pt* ran /ræn/, *pp* run; -nn-) (For special uses and *adverbial particles* and *preps*, ⇨ 26 below; ....
.... **26** [VP2C,3A,15B] (special uses with *adverbial particles* and *preps*):

run across, pay a short informal visit: *run across to a neighbour's flat to borrow some sugar.* **run across sb/sth,** meet or find by chance: *I ran across my old friend Jean in Paris last week.*

run after sb/sth, (a) try to catch: *The dog was running after a rabbit.* (b) seek the society of; go after in order to get the attention of: *She runs after every good-looking man in the village.*

run against sb, compete with him by running in a race; (esp US) compete with him (for an elected office).

doubling of consonant

special uses of a verb with adverbial particles and prepositions

shot[1] /ʃɒt/ n **1** [C] (sound of the) firing of a gun, etc: *hear ~s in the distance;* ....

.... **a 'long ~,** an attempt to solve a problem, etc with little evidence, few facts to go on: *It's a long ~ but I think John must have known about the murder.* **,not by a 'long ~,** not even if circumstances were most favourable. **3** [C]

idioms, showing stress patterns

tibia /'tɪbɪə/ n (*pl ~e* /-bɪiː/) (anat) shin-bone; inner and thicker of the two bones between the knee and the foot. ⇨ the illus at skeleton.

specialist English usage

cross-reference to an illustration

vi·o·late /'vaɪəleɪt/ vt [VP6A] **1** break (an oath, a treaty, etc); act contrary to (what one's conscience tells one to do, etc). **2** act towards (a sacred place, sb's seclusion, etc) without proper respect: *~ sb's privacy.* **3** rape. **vi·o·la·tion** /ˌvaɪə'leɪʃn/ n [U] violating or being ~d: *act in violation of a treaty;* [C] instance of this: *violations of the rights of the citizens/the right of free speech, etc.*

derivative, with pronunciation

uncountable and countable uses of the noun

Using the Dictionary

Who is this Dictionary for?

This is a Dictionary that has been specially prepared for the learner of the English language. All its parts have been designed and put together to give the learner the most *practical* help in developing the three language skills: speaking, writing, and reading.

This is a Dictionary for the learner of English who has mastered the rules of English grammar and pronunciation, and has acquired a vocabulary that enables him to read and understand English of moderate difficulty. It is for the learner who wants to develop further his knowledge of how English words, compounds, and idiomatic expressions are used, what they mean, how they are pronounced, and how they are spelt.

What is in this Dictionary?

The Introduction

The Introduction has 3 aspects.

1 It explains, in simple, clear language, all the different parts that go to make up the entries for the words in the Dictionary. It also contains examples of all these different parts of a dictionary entry.

2 It contains useful information about *spelling* (for example, how to spell the plurals of nouns), about *pronunciation* (for example, how to pronounce the inflections of nouns, verbs and adjectives), about *grammar* (for example, how to use a 'phrasal verb' like **take off**) and about *style* (for example, how to use idioms and proverbs).

3 It has 4 important lists, which the learner will find constantly useful: (i) Verb patterns (p xxix); (ii) The forms of the anomalous verbs (e g *can, could*) (p xxxix); (iii) The strong and weak spoken forms of common words (e g *and, from*) (p xxxix); (iv) The written and spoken forms of the common English contractions (e g *we're, wasn't*) (p xli).

The Dictionary

This is a Dictionary of the English Language as it is written and spoken today by educated British men and women. It lists words, compound words and idiomatic expressions that the learner is likely to come across in everyday English speech, in official and informal writing, and in the literature of the 20th and 19th centuries. For all the listed items there is information on (i) spelling, (ii) pronunciation, (iii) grammatical use, (iv) meaning (or meanings). In addition, there are examples showing their use in current English. Guidance is also given, wherever necessary or helpful, on difficult points of meaning, spelling and pronunciation. All special American English spellings and pronunciations are given.

The Illustrations

There are a large number of illustrations, because a drawing is often a more useful way of showing a meaning than a written explanation. Many of these illustrations are found in groups, for example, *insects, wild cats* and *flowers*. Others are of systems that have many related parts, for example, *the respiratory system, the eye, the motor-car, football*. The learner is guided by a cross-reference from a word that is illustrated to the page where the illustration is found.

finding words and meanings

The Appendices

There are 10 Appendices at the end of the book, containing useful information for the learner of English. There are 3 that the learner is particularly recommended to use:

Appendix 3 *Affixes*. These are the small items of the language that are used to build up many English words. They are divided into *prefixes*, which come at the beginning of a word (for example *ex-*, *extra-*, and *under-*, as in *ex-president*, *extra-thin*, and *underestimate*), and *suffixes*, which come at the end of a word (for example *-ee*, *-ish*, *-ize*, as in *employee*, *childish* and *criticize*). Notes on how these affixes are used to form words, their pronunciations, and examples of their use, are also given.

Appendix 4 *Numerical Expressions*. This is a unique and comprehensive guide on how to use numbers and expressions that contain numbers. For example, there are sections on how to express *distance*, *temperature*, *sports scores*, *the time*, *the date*, *amounts of money* and *telephone numbers*. Notes on pronunciation, and many examples of usage, are also given.

Appendix 9 *Punctuation*. This is a detailed guide, with examples, on how to use all the English punctuation marks, for example *the comma*, *the colon*, *quotation marks*, *parentheses*, *the apostrophe*. There are also sections on the punctuation of *Abbreviations*, *Conversation*, *Quotations* and *Letters*.

How is this Dictionary to be used?

There are two chief ways in which the Dictionary can be used.

1 It can be used to help the learner *understand* the meanings of words, compounds and idioms, when he meets them for the first time in spoken or written English.

2 It can also help the learner to *use* words correctly in sentences of his own, (i) by giving their spelling and pronunciation, (ii) by showing their grammatical patterns and forms, (iii) by indicating (through examples) the contexts in which they are generally used.

If this *Introduction* is carefully studied, the user will come to understand the many different features of English words which are covered in the Dictionary. He will then be able to use the Dictionary regularly and successfully in reading, writing and speaking English.

The user of the Dictionary should also work carefully through the companion Practice Book, *Use Your Dictionary*. By doing all the exercises in *Use Your Dictionary*, the learner will increase his understanding of what is contained in the Dictionary, and of how it can be fully used.

Finding words and meanings

How to find a word in the Dictionary

A headword

In the Dictionary the words explained are arranged in alphabetical order and printed in **bold** type. They are called *headwords*. The information explaining the meanings and uses of a headword is called an *entry*. Sometimes two or more headwords have the same spelling. These are numbered, for example **die¹**, **die²**. These headwords have the same spelling but they either have different meanings or they are different parts of speech.

When you meet a word for the first time, in a book or paper, you will often find that its spelling is not the same as the headword to which it belongs, and which you need to refer to. This may be because it is the plural form of a *noun* (for example, *boxes, oxen, phenomena*). In the case of these three examples, the headword that you need to look up is the singular form of the nouns (**box**, **ox**, **phenomenon**) and you should refer to that. Note, however, that when a plural is very irregular (for example *brethren*), it will have an entry of its own.

Sometimes, too, you will meet the irregular past tense or past participle forms of *verbs* (for example *sprang, sprung*, or *bore, borne*, or *spoke, spoken*). In all these cases, the headwords are the infinitives (**spring, bear, speak**), and those are the words to look up. To help you, though, the Dictionary has special entries for all of the irregular forms *sprang, sprung*, etc and these refer you to the full entries for the verbs:

sprang...*pt* of spring³.
sprung...*pp* of spring³.

Note, too, that if you meet the comparative (*faster*) or superlative (*fastest*) of an adjective (here, *fast*), it is the headword **fast** that you must refer to. Once again, irregular forms, such as *better* or *best*, have their own entries.

A derivative

A *derivative* is a word formed by adding an ending (called a *suffix*) to a headword, for example *-able, -ness, -ance, -ly, -ment*, as in *acceptable, dryness, acceptance, yearly, amazement*. Derivatives are printed in **bold** type, and are listed alphabetically at the end of an entry. Some may be written ~·**ness**, ~·**ly**, ~·**ment**, etc (where the tilde ~ represents the headword). Others are printed in full because the spelling has changed, for example **amazing, mag·nifi·cence**. (⇨ Appendix 3 for a list and explanation of endings such as *-able, -ness*, etc.)

Sometimes a derivative of a word has its own separate entry. This may be because its spelling is very different: compare **adhere** with its derivative **adhesion**. It may also be because its meaning is very different. For example, the derivative **scarcely** has a quite different meaning from that of its parent word **scarce**.

A compound

A *compound* is a word formed by adding another word to a headword. It is written as one word (**nightdress**), or as two words separated by a hyphen (**night-time**), or as two separate words (**night life**). The same compound may be found, in different books, newspapers, notices etc, written sometimes with a hyphen, sometimes as one word, sometimes as two words. Compare, for example, **head-master, headmaster, head master**. This indicates that there is no general agreement amongst the users of the language about how that compound is written. The form given in the Dictionary is the most common in modern British English usage. Compounds are printed in **bold** type, and are listed alphabetically at the end of an entry, but before derivatives. In the longer entries, they are placed at the end of the numbered sections to whose meanings they are most closely related.

finding words and meanings

An idiom

An *idiom* (also called an *idiomatic expression*) is a phrase or sentence of two or more words that has a special meaning of its own. Idioms are printed in **bold italic** type, and are listed alphabetically at the end of an entry, but before both compounds and derivatives. In the longer entries, they are placed at the end of the numbered sections to whose meanings they are most closely related. To find an idiom, look for it in the entry for the most important word in the phrase or sentence (usually a *noun*, *verb* or *adjective*). For example, **pick holes in** is found in the entry for **hole**; **get hold of the wrong end of the stick** is found in the entry for **stick**. (⇨ *Using idiomatic English* on page xxvi of this Introduction.)

A verb with a particle or a preposition

English contains many phrases made up of a *verb* and an *adverbial particle*, for example **go back**, **run away**, **take sth down**, or of a *verb* and a *preposition*, for example, **go through sth**, **run into sb**, **take after sb**. Many of these phrases are idiomatic, and are printed and listed in the same way as other idioms.

In the entries for the very common verbs like **go**, **make**, **put**, **take**, these verbal phrases are all gathered together in alphabetical order at the end of the verb's entry. They are called 'special uses with *adverbial particles* and *prepositions*'. For example, at the end of the entry for the verb **take** you will find **take after sb**, **take sth apart**, **take (away) from sth**, **take sth back**, etc. (⇨ *How to use a verb with the correct adverbial particle or preposition* on page xxv of this Introduction.)

When you meet a *verb* + *particle* in speech or writing, it may take one of several forms. Compare *He took down the curtains*; *He took the curtains down*; *He took them down*. These are different ways of using **take sth down** and this is the phrase you should look up in the Dictionary. On the other hand, *go through John's pockets*, *go through them* are the two possible ways of using the *verb* + *preposition* **go through sth**, and that is the form which should be looked up.

How to find the meaning of a word

Definition numbers

Many entries are divided into sections numbered in bold type, i.e. **1**, **2**, **3**, **4** etc. These numbers show the different meanings or usages that the headword has. For example, the verb **decorate** has three meanings: **1** to adorn, to make attractive. **2** to give a building paint, plaster, wallpaper, carpets, etc. **3** to award someone a medal. Definitions are listed in order of meanings from the most common or most simple to the most rare or most complicated.

If you are faced with **decorate** used with one of these meanings you will want to have some way of deciding which of the numbered definitions is the right one. This is one of those occasions when the *example phrases and sentences* will prove of great value. Suppose that you have this sentence in front of you: *Two airmen were decorated for their heroism*. This will suggest that meaning **3** is the right one, as the sentence closely resembles the example provided in the entry: *Several soldiers were decorated for bravery*. It is by matching the sentence you have with the example sentences in the Dictionary entry that you are able to decide which definition is the right one.

Writing English

How to check the spelling of a word In order to learn how to spell a word you must find it in the Dictionary. It is important to know the alphabet well. You should be able to judge quickly whether any word comes before or after another one. Remember that if the first letters of two words are the same, you must look at the next letters to decide where to find the words in the Dictionary. In **care** and **cart** 'e' comes before 't' in the alphabet, so **care** comes before **cart** in the Dictionary.

How to find a word on any page of the Dictionary To help you quickly find a word in the Dictionary, the *first* and *last* headword are printed together in large bold type in the top left-hand or right-hand corner of that page. These two words are divided by a slant mark, for example **hold/home**. Suppose you want to check the spelling of the word **holiday**. Since it comes alphabetically between **hold** and **home**, immediately you see **hold/home** at the top of the page you know that that is the page where **holiday** is to be found.

How to spell the plural of a noun The plural of a noun is formed by adding -*s* to the end of the noun. For example *boat*, plural *boats*; *apple*, plural *apples*; *idea*, plural *ideas*. But if the noun ends in -*s*, -*z*, -*x*, -*ch* or -*sh*, then the plural is formed by adding -*es* to the noun. For example *bus*, plural *buses*; *box*, plural *boxes*; *dish*, plural *dishes*.

How to spell the plural of a noun ending in -*y* Nouns ending in -*y*, if the -*y* is preceded by a consonant, form the plural by changing the -*y* into -*ies*. For example *city*, plural *cities*. If the -*y* is preceded by a vowel, the plural is -*ys*. For example *monkey*, plural *monkeys*. This spelling information is given in the Dictionary for all nouns ending in -*y*.

How to spell the plural of a noun ending in -*o* Some nouns that end in -*o* add -*s* to form the plural. For example *piano*, plural *pianos*. Some add -*es* to form the plural. For example *tomato*, plural *tomatoes*. Some add either -*s* or -*es*. For example *volcano*, plural *volcanos* or *volcanoes*. This spelling information is given in the Dictionary for all nouns ending in -*o*.

How to spell the forms of a verb The third person present singular of a verb is formed by adding -*s* to the end of the verb. For example *fit*, *it fits*; *write*, *she writes*; *see*, *he sees*. But if the verb ends in -*s*, -*z*, -*x*, -*ch* or -*sh*, then the third person present singular is formed by adding -*es* to the verb. For example *miss*, *she misses*; *mix*, *it mixes*; *touch*, *he touches*.

The past tense and the past participle of a verb are formed by adding -*ed* to the end of the verb. For example *pull*, *pulled*; *push*, *pushed*; *follow*, *followed*. But if the verb ends in -*e* or -*ee*, then the past tense and past participle are formed by adding -*d* to the end of the verb. For example *smile*, *smiled*; *agree*, *agreed*.

The present participle of a verb is formed by adding -*ing* to the end of the verb. For example *think*, *thinking*; *go*, *going*; *be*, *being*; *see*, *seeing*. But if the verb ends in a 'silent' -*e*, then the present participle is formed by dropping this -*e* from the end of the verb and then adding -*ing*. For example *love*, *loving*; *owe*, *owing*; *tire*, *tiring*.

How to spell the forms of a verb ending in -*y* Verbs that end in -*y* form the past tense and the past participle by changing the -*y* into -*ied*. For example *carry*, past tense and past participle *carried*. This spelling information is given in the Dictionary for all verbs that end in -*y*.

The third person present singular of verbs ending in -*y* is formed by changing the -*y* to -*ies*. For example *you carry*, but *she carries*.

The present participle of verbs ending in -*y* is formed by adding -*ing* to the end of the verb. For example *carry*, present participle *carrying*.

Doubled consonants Many verbs that end with a single consonant have this letter repeated in the spelling for the present and past participles and the past tense. For example, *drop* has *dropping* and *dropped*. In the same way, some adjectives repeat the last consonant in the spelling for the comparative and superlative. For example, *hot* has *hotter* and *hottest*. If the consonant is doubled, the Dictionary shows this by printing the repeated letter in brackets, for example, **drop** (-pp-); **hot** (-tt-). (⇨ *How American English is written*, below.)

How to divide a word when writing or typing When writing or typing it is sometimes necessary to divide a word at the end of the line because there is not enough space for the complete word. This division is always shown by adding a hyphen (-) immediately after the first part of the divided word at the end of the line. Many people prefer not to divide words at all (especially when writing by hand), but if you do, here are three considerations to help you.

1 By syllable

This means dividing the word into syllables or units of sound. For example, the word **kind** has one syllable, **kind·ly** has two, **un·kind·ly** has three and **un·kind·li·ness** has four.

2 By structure

This means dividing the word into the smaller units of meaning from which the word is built up. It may have a beginning (a prefix) such as *anti-*, *dis-*, *un-*, etc (as in **anti·sep·tic**, **dis·ap·pear**, **un·able**) or an ending (a suffix) such as -*age*, -*able*, -*fully* (as in **post·age**, **agree·able**, **grate·fully**).

3 By meaning

This means deciding whether each part of the divided word can be understood or spoken so that the complete word is easily recognised from the two parts. For example, it may be a compound word made up of two different words, such as *spot* and *light* in **spot·light**.

All three considerations must be used to decide whether and where you can divide a word. Here are six useful rules to help you:

1 Never divide a word within a syllable.
2 Never divide an ending (a suffix) of two syllables such as -*able*, -*ably*, -*fully*.
3 With the exception of -*ly*, never divide a word so that an ending of two letters such as -*ed*, -*er*, -*ic* begins the next line.
4 Never divide a word so that one of the parts is a single letter.
5 Never divide a word of one syllable.
6 Never divide a word of less than five letters.

The bold dot . The recommended places of word-division are given in the Dictionary for all headwords, derivatives and compounds. A bold dot (·) is printed where division is recommended, for example **sep·ar·ate**; **~·ly**. This means that these divisions are all possible:

sep- arate	separ- ate	separate- ly

How American English is written When American spelling is different from British English, it is given in the Dictionary in brackets immediately after the headword, for example

col·our (US = color), **py·ja·mas** (US = pa·ja·mas).

The main differences in spelling are:

British	American
-our (*honour*)	-or (*honor*)
-re (*centre*)	-er (*center*)
-ogue (*dialogue*)	-og (*dialog*)
-ence (*defence*)	-ense (*defense*)
-ize} (*realize*) -ise} (*realise*)	-ize (*realize*)
ae (*anaemia*)	e (*anemia*)

Sometimes American English spelling does not double the consonant at the end of a word, while British English spelling does, especially when the consonant is an 'l'. For example, *travel* has (GB) *travelling* and *traveller*, and (US) *traveling* and *traveler*. The Dictionary tells you these facts by putting (-ll-; US -l-) in the entry.

Speaking English

How a word is pronounced

In written English one letter can often be pronounced in different ways. For example, the letter *a* is pronounced differently in *hat, pass, came, water, dare, ago*. Phonetic spelling is a way of writing a word so that one symbol always represents only one sound. Two words may be spelt differently in ordinary spelling, but if they sound the same, then the phonetic spelling is the same. For example, *key* and *quay* have the same phonetic spelling /ki:/. Each headword and derivative has a phonetic spelling after the ordinary spelling. Inside the cover of the Dictionary there is a list of all the letters (*phonetic symbols*) used in the phonetic spelling.

Models of pronunciation

A British English pronunciation is given for each word, and, in those cases where there is a marked difference, the American version is also shown. The British English form is that which has been called *Received Pronunciation* or *General British*. The forms recommended correspond to those given in the *English Pronouncing Dictionary* (Dent), but the pronunciation shown may not always be that which appears first in *EPD*. Where there is a choice between several acceptable forms, that form is selected which is likely to be easiest for learners. The American pronunciation given is that which is widely acceptable in the United States and has been called *General American*.

In spoken British English an *r* at the end of a written word (either as the final letter or in an *re* ending as in *fire*) is not sounded unless another word that begins with a vowel sound follows in the same sentence. For example, the *r* is not heard in *His car was sold* but it is heard in *His car isn't old*. To show this, words which end in *r* or *re* have (r) at the end of the phonetic spelling in the dictionary, for example **car** /kɑ:(r)/.

How American English is pronounced

Whenever Americans pronounce a word in a very different way from British speakers, the Dictionary gives the phonetic spelling of the American pronunciation after the British one, for example **half** /hɑ:f US: hæf/; **address** /ə'dres US: 'ædres/. If only part of the pronunciation changes, only that part is given for the American pronunciation in order to save space, for example **attitude** /'ætɪtju:d US: -tu:d/.

American English forms are shown with the same phonetic symbols as are used for British English. However, particularly in the case of vowels, the same symbol will often mean somewhat different qualities in the British and American varieties. For example, in American English, the /ɒ/ in *hot* is similar to the British English /ɑ:/ sound, and the /ʌ/ of *cut* is similar to a stressed /ə/ sound.

There is one difference between British and American pronunciation that is *not* given in the Dictionary. This is the use of the /r/ sound in American English in words where British English does not use it, for example in the words **arm** and **poor**. The British pronunciations of these words are /ɑ:m/ and /pʊə(r)/ (the symbol (r) is explained in *Models of Pronunciation* above); the American pronunciations are /ɑ:rm/ and /pʊər/. The rule to follow in the case of the /r/ sound in American English is to sound the /r/ *whenever* it occurs in the spelling of a word.

Syllabic consonants
The consonants /n/ and /l/ often form a syllable by themselves, i e without a vowel, especially at the end of words. Thus, when *sudden*, *middle*, *nation*, *final*, for instance, are shown as /'sʌdn/, /'mɪdl/, /'neɪʃn/, /'faɪnl/, this means that /n/ and /l/ are syllabic. But syllabic /n/ and /l/ may also occur before a vowel within a word. When this happens, /ən/ and /əl/ are usually given in the Dictionary, representing an equally acceptable pronunciation which many learners may find easier. Thus we have *final* /'faɪnl/ and *finally* /'faɪnəlɪ/, where /-əl-/ may be said as a syllabic /l/ if preferred (so that in any case it is distinct from *finely* /'faɪnlɪ/).

How a word is stressed
When a word has more than one syllable, one of them is spoken with more force than the rest. This force is called *stress*, and the syllable which is stressed is shown with the stress-mark /'/ before it in the Dictionary. For example, *any* /'enɪ/ has a stress on the first syllable, *depend* /dɪ'pend/ has a stress on the second syllable.

In some words, usually long ones, other syllables may also be spoken with more force than the rest, but with a stress that is not as strong as for those syllables marked /'/. The stress-mark /ˌ/ is used to show this.

So, /'/ is used to show the strongest or *primary* stress, and /ˌ/ is used to show the less strong or *secondary* stress, as in **pronunciation** /prəˌnʌnsɪ'eɪʃn/.

How a two-word compound is stressed
A compound that is made up of two separately written words, for example **national park**, is normally spoken with the strong stress in the second word: ˌnational 'park. If a compound does not have stress marks indicated, then it follows this normal pattern. Sometimes, however, a compound is spoken with the strong stress on the first word, for example 'post office. In this case, the stress mark is always shown.

How an idiom is stressed
One of the words in any idiom is always spoken with more force than the other words. Normally, this stressed word is the last 'important' word in that idiom, that is, the last word that is either a *noun*, a *verb*, an *adjective* or an *adverb*. For example, in the idiom **separate the sheep from the goats**, the word *goats* carries the strong stress, because it is the last important word (in this case a *noun*) in the idiom. In the idiom **play fast and loose with** the word *loose* carries the strong stress, because it is the last *adverb* in the idiom.

In some idioms, however, a word that comes before the last important word in the idiom carries the strong stress. In this case, the word that is stressed is always shown with a stress mark. For example, **at 'any rate** and **for the 'most part**.

How an inflection is pronounced An *inflection* is the changed form a word takes when it is used in a particular grammatical way, for example, in the plural (*sky, skies*), in the past tense (*smile, smiled*), in the comparative (*wild, wilder*). Inflections are usually made by changing the ending of a word.

The plural of nouns, and the third person singular present of verbs

1 If the final sound of the noun's singular or the verb's infinitive is a *vowel* or /b, d, g, v, ð, m, n, ŋ, l/, the ending is formed by the addition of /-z/. For example *city* /'sɪtɪ/, *cities* /'sɪtɪz/; *ring* /rɪŋ/, *rings* /rɪŋz/.

2 If the final sound of the noun's singular or the verb's infinitive is /p, t, k, f, θ/, the ending is formed by the addition of /-s/. For example *work* /wɜːk/, *works* /wɜːks/.

3 If the final sound of the noun's singular or the verb's infinitive is /s, z, ʃ, ʒ, tʃ, dʒ/, the ending is formed by addition of /-ɪz/. For example *match* /mætʃ/, *matches* /'mætʃɪz/.

The past tense and past participle of verbs

1 If the final sound of the verb's infinitive is a *vowel* or /b, g, v, ð, z, ʒ, dʒ, m, n, ŋ, l/, the past tense and the past participle are formed by the addition of /-d/. For example *hurry* /'hʌrɪ/, *hurried* /'hʌrɪd/; *judge* /dʒʌdʒ/, *judged* /dʒʌdʒd/.

2 If the final sound of the verb's infinitive is /p, k, f, θ, s, ʃ, tʃ/, the past tense and the past participle are formed by the addition of /-t/. For example *stop* /stɒp/, *stopped* /stɒpt/.

3 If the final sound of the verb's infinitive is /t, d/, the past tense and the past participle are formed by the addition of /-ɪd/. For example *paint* /peɪnt/, *painted* /'peɪntɪd/.

The comparative and superlative of adjectives

1 The comparative is formed by the addition of /-ə(r)/ to the final sound of the adjective. For example *high* /haɪ/, *higher* /'haɪə(r)/; *wild* /waɪld/, *wilder* /'waɪldə(r)/.

2 The superlative is formed by the addition of /-ɪst/ to the final sound of the adjective. For example *low* /ləʊ/, *lowest* /'ləʊɪst/; *green* /griːn/, *greenest* /'griːnɪst/.

In the Dictionary, phonetic spelling is given for inflections only if the forms do not follow the ordinary rules, for example, the plural of **basis**: bases /'beɪsiːz/; the past tense of **read**: read /red/; the comparative of **young**: younger /'jʌŋgə(r)/.

How a derivative is pronounced Most derivatives are formed by adding a *suffix* to the end of a word. The pronunciation of these suffixes is given in the special list of prefixes and suffixes found in Appendix 3, pages 1012–1015. These derivatives are pronounced simply by saying the suffix after the word. For example, the adverb **slowly** /'sləʊlɪ/ is made by joining the word **slow** /sləʊ/ to the suffix -*ly* /lɪ/.

However, whenever there is doubt about how a suffix or a derivative is pronounced, the phonetic spelling is given. For example **mouthful** /-fʊl/, **regretful** /-fl/. Also, if a change of stress is caused by adding a suffix to a word, then the pronunciation of the derivative is given in full, for example, **photograph** /'fəʊtəgrɑːf/, but **photographer** /fə'tɒgrəfə(r)/, **photographic** /ˌfəʊtə'græfɪk/.

How French words are pronounced in English

Some French words used in English are completely anglicized (ie no longer considered to be foreign words, and given a completely English pronunciation), for example *café* /ˈkæfeɪ/, *restaurant* /ˈrestrɒnt/. There are other French words and phrases which are still regarded as foreign but which are normally given a completely English pronunciation, for example *à la carte* /ˌɑː lɑː ˈkɑːt/, *table d'hôte* /ˌtɑːbl ˈdəʊt/. A difficulty arises with the pronunciation of French nasalized vowels, as in *salon, en route*. Native speakers of English use different pronunciations in such cases, varying from total anglicization to a more or less successful imitation of the French. This Dictionary gives the anglicized form, /ˈsælɒn/, /ˌɒn ˈruːt/.

Grammar

Irregular forms of nouns, verbs and adjectives

An *irregular* form of a word is one that is not made in the normal (or *regular*) way. For example, the normal way of forming the plural of an English noun in writing is to add *-s* or *-es*, and the normal way of forming a past tense or past participle of a verb is to add *-d* or *-ed*. Whenever a form is made in any other way, then this is given (together with the pronunciation if necessary), at the beginning of the entry. For example, **axis** /ˈæksɪs/ *n* (*pl* axes /ˈæksiːz/); **choose** /tʃuːz/ *vt*, *vi* (*pt* chose /tʃəʊz/, *pp* chosen /ˈtʃəʊzn/); **bad** /bæd/ *adj* (worse, worst).

Comparative and superlative forms of adjectives

The comparative and superlative forms of all adjectives of two or more syllables are made by using the words *more* and *most* before the adjective. For example, the comparative form of *interesting* is *more interesting*; the superlative form of *pleasant* is *most pleasant*.

All adjectives of one syllable, and many adjectives of two syllables, make the comparative and superlative forms by adding *-r*, *-st* or *-er*, *-est* or *-ier*, *-iest* to the end of the adjective. For example, the comparative forms of *gentle*, *cold* and *happy* are *gentler*, *colder* and *happier*; the superlative forms are *gentlest*, *coldest* and *happiest*. In the Dictionary, an adjective that has a comparative and superlative form of this sort has (-r, -st) or (-er, -est) or (-ier, -iest) printed in the entry.

Countable and uncountable nouns

The correct use of the *noun* is a very important but difficult skill to acquire when learning English. For example, some nouns can be used in the plural form, while others cannot. In addition, many nouns have several meanings, some of which may have a plural form, and some of which may not. This Dictionary gives the learner special help in this area, by the use of the symbols [C], [U] or [C,U] in an entry for a noun.

[C] means that the noun has both a singular and a plural form. It can be used in the singular with *a*, *an*, *another* (*a bottle*, *an apple*, *another boy*), in the plural with *many* (*many bottles*) and in the singular or plural with numbers (*one apple*, *six apples*). Nouns that can be used in these ways are *countable*. [C] in the entry tells you this. When no information is given in a noun entry, it is an obvious countable noun.

[U] means that the noun does not have a plural form. It can be used in the singular with words like *some*, *enough*, *much*, *more* (*some information*, *enough money*, *much noise*). It cannot be used with *a*, *an*, *another*, or with *many*, or with numbers. Nouns that are used in this way are *uncountable*. [U] in the entry tells you this.

[C,U] means that the noun can be used either as countable or uncountable. For example, *coffee* is used as [C] in *Two coffees, please*, and as [U] in *Have some more coffee*.

Some nouns (or some meanings of some nouns) are only used with the definite article *the*, or only with the indefinite article *a/an*. The Dictionary shows this by putting *the* or *a/an* + the noun in **bold** type at the beginning of the definition. For example **the sun**, **a sleep**.

How to use a verb with the correct adverbial particle or preposition	Phrases like **take off** (a *verb* with an *adverbial particle*), **go with** (a *verb* with a *preposition*), and **make up to** (a *verb* with both an *adverbial particle* and a *preposition*) are very important in English because they are so common. They are treated with special care in the Dictionary. The correct particle or preposition is printed with the verb in **bold italic** type in the entry so that you can find it easily.

It is important to know why the dictionary uses the brackets ( ) and the slant / in providing this information. Brackets ( ) round a preposition or particle mean that the verb can be used with or without it. For example, **prepare (for)** can be used as in *prepare a meal*, or as in *prepare for an examination*. A slant / means that you can choose any of the words listed to make a sentence. For example, **move along/down/up** shows that *move along the bus*, *move down the bus*, *move up the bus* are all correct.

It is also important to know why and how the words *sb* (somebody) and *sth* (something) are used in these phrases.

Consider the phrase **take off** (*verb + particle*). This is found in the dictionary in both the forms **take off** and **take sth off**. **take off** means that the phrase can be used without an object, for example *The aeroplane took off*. **take sth off** means that the phrase can be used with an object (in this case a thing), for example *She took her hat off* or *She took off her hat*.

Consider the phrase **go with** (*verb + preposition*). This is found in the dictionary only in the form **go with sb/sth**. This means that the phrase must be used with an object (in this case either a person or a thing) after the preposition, for example *Paul went with* (= accompanied) *Peter to Rome*, or *Your shirt doesn't go with* (= match) *your trousers*.

You will notice that some verbs (*get, give, go*, etc) are used with a large number of prepositions and particles. Because many of these combinations (for example **make up**) have a large number of meanings, you will find a section at the end of each of these verb entries called 'special uses with *adverbial particles* and *prepositions*'. In this section, these combinations are listed in bold italic type in alphabetical order (**make after**, **make at**, **make away**, **make for**, etc).

How to use an adjective with the correct preposition	Many adjectives in English must, or may, be followed by a preposition, for example **conversant with** (where the preposition must be used), and **distinct from** (where *from* is optional). To help the learner to form correct sentences using these adjectives, the prepositions are included in bold print at the beginning of the entry. For example,

conversant...*adj* ~ **with**,
distinct...*adj* ~ **(from)**,

Note that brackets ( ) are used when the preposition is optional.

Style

How to choose
the words that
the headword
usually
combines with

Speaking and writing correct English is not only a matter of pronunciation, spelling or grammar. You must also know the kinds of context in which the headword is normally used. The example phrases and sentences are especially valuable in this respect, because they show the words (or kinds of words) that the headword often combines with. For example, at **regular(1)** there is *regular teeth/features*; at **regular(2)** there is *regular hours/habits*; at **regulate(1)** there is *regulate one's conduct/ expenditure*; at **regulate(2)** there is *regulate a clock* and *regulate speed*.

The learner wishing to make up sentences of his own will find examples containing the slant / particularly useful. For example, *inspired poets/ artists* and *inspire sb with hope/enthusiasm/confidence*. He can compose different sentences using those alternatives; but they will also help him to guess other words that can be used. For example, *inspired musicians/ dancers/painters* and *inspire sb with new faith/passion/devotion*.

How to use the
more usual
or more suitable
word

You should also be confident that the kind or style of English you are using is right in that particular context: that it is not too *formal* or *colloquial*, that it will not offend the listener or reader, or that it is not *dated* (old-fashioned), or *archaic* (no longer used). To help you, there is information in an entry when the word is to be used only in a particular style or context. For example, formal words are not used in everyday conversation, or in letters to friends and relations; while colloquial words are not used in business letters, or in conversation with a person whom you do not know well or who is your superior.

Sometimes the Dictionary will warn you that a word is both a *dated* word and a *slang* word (dated sl), or both a *modern* word and a *colloquial* word (modern colloq).

Sometimes the Dictionary will tell you what the more usual word is, particularly in entries for *formal* or *dated* vocabulary.

Remember that *slang* vocabulary is not popular for very long and that such words should only be used if you are sure that they are not dated, that they will sound quite natural when you use them, and that they will not cause offence.

How to use
specialist
English words

Some words are used only by a group of speakers or writers because of the work they do, the way they live, the activity they are enjoying, the subject they are studying, etc. These are 'specialist' areas such as *business, science, law, sport, music, medicine,* etc. Trying to use specialist words outside the contexts where they belong can make your English seem unnatural. To help you, the Dictionary gives the specialist English area in brackets at the beginning of the explanation of the meaning.

How to use
idiomatic
English

An important sign of a person who has learnt English from a native-speaker (or a person who has a native-speaker's command of the language) is his knowledge of the meaning and correct use of expressions such as **make up one's mind, be all ears, with all one's heart**, etc. These are called *idioms* or *idiomatic expressions*. They are groups of two or more words which must be learnt as a whole because the meaning of the expression may be different from the meanings of its parts. An example is **hit the nail on the head**, which means 'guess right'. In the Dictionary, these expressions are printed in **bold italic** type.

Like the style for verbs with prepositions or particles (which are themselves types of idioms), brackets are used for words which can be omitted, as in **make (both) ends meet** and slants for alternatives as in *begin/start at the wrong end*. When there are no brackets or slants, the expression cannot be changed. For example, the idiom *have an ear to the ground* cannot be changed to *have a head to the ground* or *have an ear to the floor*. But the idiom *bear/keep something in mind* can be either *bear something in mind* or *keep something in mind*.

An exception to this is when *etc* is used after two or more words that are divided from one another by the slant mark. This means that *only words of a similar sort* to the words that are given (divided by the slant mark) may be used in the idiom. For example, the idiom *be pushing thirty/forty, etc*, means that only number words that express someone's age in years may be used in this idiom.

When two or more idioms are divided from one another by a semi-colon *(;)*, this means that the idioms *have the same meaning*. For example, *take it from me* and *take my word for it*, which are listed together, separated only by a semicolon *(;)*, in the entry for the verb *take*, have the same meaning, 'believe me when I say'.

Native speakers use these expressions naturally and unconsciously. You will need to learn them before using them. The more you use them, the more they will become a natural part of your English. Unless you use them, your English will always be 'foreign'. But you must be very careful not to use the idioms you know too often, and not to use them one after another in the same sentence, or in sentence after sentence. An idiom must be used with care and thought, only when your meaning can best be expressed with the idiom's special 'strength', 'flavour' or 'style'.

Proverbs
You should note that *proverbs* are seldom used in ordinary speech or writing. Although the native speaker knows the meaning of most English proverbs, he will actually use one rarely, and then only when he is wanting to be humorous, or by referring to the proverb in an indirect way (for example by quoting only half of it), or by introducing it by saying something like 'You know what they say, . . .' or 'As the old saying goes, . . .' The reason is this. English proverbs are phrases or sentences containing advice, warning or truth. Although they are expressed in striking language, in their meanings they are rather obvious remarks to make about human experience. They are thought of as the sort of remark that would be made by someone who is rather dull, someone who cannot express in his own words what he thinks or feels, but who has to borrow a proverb from the language to do this. A *proverb*, a *cliché*, a *truism*, a *hackneyed phrase*, and a *trite remark* are all the sorts of expressions that someone who wants to express himself clearly, carefully and honestly will try to avoid.

The sign △
Some words in the Dictionary are followed by the sign △. These are *taboo* words. They are words used when the speaker wishes to swear, or be indecent, or be offensive. They are all words that are likely to cause embarrassment or anger if they are used in the wrong situation. The learner of English is strongly advised to avoid using them.

Verb patterns

For anyone who is learning to speak or write correct English, the most important word in a sentence is the *verb*. For this reason the compilers of the Dictionary have paid particular attention to *verb patterns*. These show the learner how to use verbs to form correct sentences.

A person learning English as a foreign language may be tempted to form sentences by *analogy*. For example, he hears or sees such sentences as *Please tell me the meaning* and *Please show me the way* (an indirect object followed by a direct object). By analogy he forms the incorrect sentence *Please explain me the meaning* (instead of *Please explain the meaning to me*). He hears or sees such sentences as *I intend to come, I propose to come*, and *I want to come*, and by analogy he forms the incorrect sentences as *I suggest to come* (instead of *I suggest that I should come*). He hears or sees such sentences as *I asked him to come, I told him to come*, and *I wanted him to come*, and by analogy he forms such incorrect sentences as *I proposed him to come* and *I suggested him to come* (instead of *I proposed/suggested that he should come*). He notes that *He began to talk about the matter* means the same as *He began talking about the matter* and supposes, wrongly, that *He stopped to talk about the matter* means the same as *He stopped talking about the matter*.

To help the learner to avoid such mistakes, the compilers of the Dictionary have provided a set of tables (on pages xxix–xxxviii) in which various Verb Patterns are set out with examples. Each pattern has a numbered code (for example, [VP5], [VP6A], [VP21]), and this provides a link between the tables and the verb entries in the Dictionary, because every verb entry has its own code (or several codes if there are several meanings).

A few examples will show how the learner can refer from the [VP] codes in entries to the [VP] tables in the Introduction. One of the patterns given in the Dictionary for **congratulate** is [VP14], and this verb is also used in one of the examples in the [VP] table for [VP14]: *We congratulated him on his success*. The pattern provided for the second meaning of **consider** is [VP6A]. If the learner turns to that table he will find several examples based on that pattern, for example *We all enjoyed the film*. This will help him to form a correct sentence with **consider** in [VP6A], for example *He considered the problem*.

Sometimes extra information is given in an entry to help the learner to learn the right pattern. For example, in the entry for **absolve**, he will find the verb + preposition ~ *(from)*, placed after the codes [VP6A,14]. This shows that the verb can be used as in *absolve a man from a vow*. In the entry for **accede** there are the codes [VP2A,3A], followed by ~ *(to)*, showing that the verb may be used as in *accede to a proposal*.

It is important to note that the learner is not expected to memorize these verb patterns. They are a simple reference system, a practical tool to guide the learner who wants to form correct sentences. They are a way of helping the learner who will benefit from a list of the grammatical rules that underlie the different sorts of example sentences that are given in the entries for verbs.

A full treatment of these verb patterns is found in *Guide to Patterns and Usage in English*, by A S Hornby (Oxford University Press).

Note: The use of the asterisk * indicates that the phrase or sentence is an example of *incorrect* usage.

[VP1] This pattern is for the verb *be*. The subject complement may be a noun, a pronoun, an adjective, an adjective phrase (e g a prepositional group). There may be an adverbial adjunct or an infinitive phrase.

Subject + BE	subject complement/adjunct
1 *This is*	*a book.*
2 *This suitcase is*	*mine.*
3 *The children are*	*asleep.*
4 *This book is*	*for you.*
5 *This is*	*where I work.*

There are variations with introductory *there/it*.

There/It + BE	subject
1 *There was*	*a large crowd.*
2 *It was impossible*	*to go further.*
3 *It was a pity*	*the weather was so bad.*

[VP2A] This pattern is for verbs which may be used without a complement. Such verbs are called complete intransitive verbs. Adjuncts are possible but not essential.

Subject	*vi*
1 *We all*	*breathe, drink and eat.*
2 *The moon*	*rose.*
3 *A period of political unrest*	*followed.*

There are variations with introductory *there/it*.

1 *There followed*	*a long period of political unrest.*
2 *It doesn't matter*	*whether we start now or later.*

That-clauses are possible after *seem, appear, happen, chance* and *follow*.

1 *It seemed*	*(that) the day would never end.*
2 *It so chanced/happened*	*(that) we were out when she called.*
3 *It doesn't follow*	*(that) they are husband and wife.*

[VP2B] Verbs in this pattern are used with an adverbial adjunct of distance, duration, weight, cost, etc. *For* may occur before adverbials of distance and duration. An indirect object may occur after *cost, last* and *take* (meaning 'require').

Subject + *vi*	*(for)* + adverbial adjunct
1 *We walked*	*(for) five miles.*
2 *The meeting lasted*	*(for) two hours.*
3 *The book cost (me)*	*£1.20.*
4 *This box weighs*	*five kilos.*

[VP2C] Many intransitive verbs are used with an adverbial adjunct (including an adverbial particle alone, or an adverbial particle followed by a preposition).

Subject + *vi*	adverbial adjunct
1 *Go*	*away!*
2 *Please come*	*in.*
3 *I'll soon catch*	*up with you.*
4 *It's getting*	*on for midnight.*
5 *It looks*	*like rain/as if it were going to rain.*

verb patterns

[VP2D] Verbs in this pattern are followed by an adjective, a noun or, in the case of a reflexive verb, a pronoun. Inchoative verbs (e g *become*, *come*, *get*) and verbs of the senses (e g *smell*, *taste*, *feel*) are among the many verbs used in this pattern.

Subject + *vi*	adjective/noun/pronoun
1 *Her dreams have come*	*true.*
2 *The fire has burnt*	*low.*
3 *She married*	*young.*
4 *He died*	*a millionaire.*
5 *Later he became*	*an acrobat.*
6 *You're not looking*	*yourself.*

[VP2E] In this pattern the predicative adjunct is a present participle.

Subject + *vi*	present participle
1 *She lay*	*smiling at me.*
2 *Do you like to go*	*dancing?*
3 *The children came*	*running to meet us.*

[VP3A] Verbs in this pattern are followed by a preposition and its object (which may be a noun, pronoun, gerund, phrase, or clause). The verb and preposition function as a unit.

Subject + *vi*	preposition + noun/pronoun
1 *You may rely*	*on that man/his discretion/his being discreet.*
2 *Can I count*	*on your help?*
3 *What has happened*	*to them?*

An infinitive phrase may follow the noun/pronoun.

1 *We're waiting*	*for our new car to be delivered.*
2 *I rely*	*on you to be discreet.*
3 *She pleaded*	*with the judge to have mercy.*

[VP3B] The preposition is omitted before a *that*-clause, thus producing the same word order as in [VP9] (for transitive verbs).

> *He insisted on his innocence.*   [VP3A]
> *He insisted that he was innocent.*   [VP3B]
> Cf   *He declared that he was innocent.*   [VP9]

The preposition may be retained if its object is a dependent question, or if a preceding 'preposition + *it*' construction is used.

Subject + *vi*	(preposition (+ *it*))	clause
1 *I agree*		*that it was a mistake.*
2 *You must see*	*(to it)*	*that this sort of thing never occurs again.*
3 *I hesitated*	*(about)*	*whether to accept your offer.*
4 *Have you decided*	*(upon)*	*where you will go for your holidays?*
5 *Don't worry*	*(about)*	*how the money was lost.*

[VP4A]   In this pattern the verb is followed by a *to*-infinitive of purpose, outcome, or result.

Subject + *vi*	*to*-infinitive
1 *We stopped*	*to rest/to have a rest.*
2 *How did you come*	*to know her?*
3 *Will he live*	*to be ninety?*
4 *Someone has called*	*to see you.*

[VP4B]   The infinitive may be equivalent to a co-ordinate clause.

Subject + *vi*	*to*-infinitive
1 *He awoke*	*to find the house on fire.*
2 *The good old days have gone*	*never to return.*
3 *Electronic music has clearly come*	*to stay.*
4 *He looked round*	*to see the door slowly opening.*

[VP4C]   The infinitive adjunct is used after some verbs which, in [VP3A], are used with prepositions.
 Don't trouble/bother about that.
 Don't trouble/bother to meet me.

Subject + *vi*	*to*-infinitive
1 *She hesitated*	*to tell anyone.*
2 *She was longing*	*to see her family again.*
3 *He agreed*	*to come at once.*

[VP4D]   The verbs *seem* and *appear* are used in this pattern. If the infinitive is *be* with an adjective or noun as complement, *to be* may be omitted (unless the adjective is one that is used only predicatively, as in [VP4E].

Subject + SEEM/APPEAR	*(to be)* + adjective/noun
1 *He seemed*	*(to be) surprised at the news.*
2 *This seems*	*(to be) a serious matter.*
3 *I seem*	*(to be) unable to enjoy myself.*

There is a variation of this pattern with introductory *it*, when the subject is an infinitive or gerund, or a clause.

It + SEEM/APPEAR	adjective/noun	subject
1 *It seemed*	*reasonable*	*to try again.*
2 *It seems*	*a pity*	*to waste all that food.*
3 *It doesn't seem*	*much use*	*going on.*
4 *It appears*	*unlikely*	*that we'll arrive on time.*

[VP4E]   If the adjective after *seem/appear* is used only predicatively (e g *awake, asleep, afraid*), *to be* is obligatory. *Happen* and *chance* are also used in this pattern.

Subject + SEEM/APPEAR HAPPEN/CHANCE	*to*-infinitive
1 *The baby seems*	*to be asleep/to be sleeping.*
2 *My enquiries seem*	*to have been resented.*
3 *She happened*	*to be out when I called.*
4 *We chanced*	*to meet in the park.*
5 *There seems*	*to have been some mistake.*

verb patterns

[VP4F] The finites of *be* are used with a *to*-infinitive to convey a variety of meanings, ⇨ *be*[4](3).

Subject + BE	*to*-infinitive
1 *We're*	*to be married in May.*
2 *At what time am I*	*to come?*
3 *How am I*	*to pay my debts?*

[VP5] In this pattern the auxiliary verbs or anomalous finites *will/would, shall/should, can/could, must, dare, need* are followed by a bare infinitive (i e without *to*). The phrases *had better, had/would rather* and *would sooner* fit into this pattern.

Subject + anomalous finite	infinitive
1 *You may*	*leave now.*
2 *You needn't*	*wait.*
3 *You'll*	*find it in that box.*
4 *I didn't dare*	*tell anyone.*
5 *You'd better*	*start at once.*

[VP6A] The verbs in this pattern have a noun or pronoun as direct object. Conversion to the passive voice is possible.

Subject + *vt*	noun/pronoun
1 *Did you enjoy*	*the film?*
2 *We all had*	*a good time.*
3 *Everyone likes*	*her.*

[VP6B] The verbs in this pattern have a noun or pronoun as direct object, but conversion to the passive voice is not possible. *Have*, meaning 'possess/take/eat/drink', follows this pattern. Reflexive verbs, and verbs with cognate objects, follow this pattern.

Subject + *vt*	noun/pronoun
1 *Have you had*	*breakfast yet?*
2 *She has*	*green eyes.*
3 *Have you hurt*	*yourself?*
4 *She smiled*	*her thanks.*
5 *He dreamed*	*a very odd dream.*

[VP6C] In this pattern the object is a gerund, not replaceable by a *to*-infinitive.

Subject + *vt*	gerund
1 *She enjoys*	*playing tennis.*
2 *Have you finished*	*talking?*
3 *I resent*	*being spoken to so rudely.*

[VP6D] In this pattern the object is a gerund. This may be replaced by a *to*-infinitive. For the difference between *like swimming* and *like to swim*, see the notes on [VP6D] in *Guide to Patterns and Usage*.

Subject + *vt*	gerund
1 *She loves*	*going to the cinema.*
2 *I'll continue*	*working while my health is good.*
3 *He began*	*talking about his clever children.*

[VP6E]   After *need, want* (= need) and *won't/wouldn't bear*, the gerund is equivalent to a passive infinitive.

Subject + NEED/WANT/BEAR	gerund
1 *He'll need*	*looking after* (= to be looked after).
2 *My shoes want*	*mending* (= to be mended).
3 *His language wouldn't bear*	*repeating* (= was too bad to be repeated).

[VP7A]   In this pattern the object of the verb is a *to*-infinitive. (For intransitive verbs with the same word order, see [VP4].)

Subject + *vt*	(*not*) + *to*-infinitive
1 *Do they want*	*to go?*
2 *He pretended*	*not to see me.*
3 *We hope/exptect/intend*	*to climb Mount Everest.*
4 *I forgot/remembered*	*to post your letters.*

[VP7B]   *Ought*, and the finites of *have* in this pattern indicate obligation. In colloquial style *have got to* is more usual than *have to*.

Subject + HAVE/OUGHT	(*not*) + *to*-infinitive
1 *Do you often have*	*to work overtime?*
2 *You don't have*	*to leave yet, do you?*
3 *You ought*	*not to waste your money there.*

[VP8]   In this pattern the object of the verb is an interrogative pronoun or adverb (except *why* or *whether*), followed by a *to*-infinitive.

Subject + *vt*	interrogative pronoun/adverb + *to*-infinitive
1 *Do you know/see*	*how to do it?*
2 *I couldn't decide*	*what to do next.*
3 *I've discovered*	*where to find him.*
4 *You must learn*	*when to give advice and when to be silent.*

[VP9]   The object of the verb is a *that*-clause. *That* is often omitted, except after more formal verbs (e g *decide, intend*).

Subject + *vt*	*that*-clause
1 *I suppose*	*you'll be leaving soon.*
2 *I wish*	*you wouldn't interrupt.*
3 *Do you think*	*it'll rain?*
4 *The workers decided*	*that they would go on strike.*
5 *We intended*	*that John should be invited.*

[VP10]   In this pattern the object of the verb is a dependent clause or question. The clause is introduced by a relative adverb or pronoun, *what*, or *whether/if*.

Subject + *vt*	dependent clause/question
1 *Does anyone know*	*how it happened?*
2 *Come and see*	*what I've done!*
3 *I wonder*	*whether/if he'll come.*
4 *She asked*	*why I was late.*

verb patterns

[VP11]   The verb is followed by a noun or pronoun and a *that*-clause.

Subject + *vt*	noun/pronoun	*that*-clause
1 *He warned*	*us*	*that the roads were icy.*
2 *I convinced*	*the policeman*	*that I was innocent.*
3 *We satisfied*	*ourselves*	*that the plan would work.*

[VP12A]   The verb is followed by an indirect object (I O) and a direct object (D O). The indirect object is equivalent to a prepositional object with *to*, as in [VP13A].

Subject + *vt*	I O	D O
1 *Won't you lend*	*him*	*your car?*
2 *He doesn't owe*	*me*	*anything.*
3 *He denied/grudged*	*her*	*nothing.*

[VP12B]   In this pattern the indirect object is equivalent to a prepositional object with *for*, as in [VP13B].

Subject + *vt*	I O	D O
1 *She made*	*herself*	*a new dress.*
2 *Will you do*	*me*	*a favour?*
3 *She cooked*	*her husband*	*some sausages.*

[VP12C]   Verbs in this pattern are rarely or never convertible to [VP13]. The labels I O and D O are not used.

Subject + *vt*	noun/pronoun	noun/pronoun
1 *Ask*	*him*	*his name.*
2 *I envy*	*you*	*your fine garden.*
3 *He struck*	*the door*	*a heavy blow.*

[VP13A]   In this pattern the verb is followed by a direct object, the preposition *to*, and the prepositional object. It is convertible to [VP12A].

Subject + *vt*	D O	*to* + noun/pronoun
1 *She told*	*the news*	*to everyone in the village.*
2 *He sold*	*his old car*	*to one of his neighbours.*
3 *I've sent*	*presents*	*to everyone in my family.*

[VP13B]   In this pattern the preposition is *for*. It is convertible to [VP12B].

Subject + *vt*	D O	*for* + noun/pronoun
1 *She made*	*a new dress*	*for her daughter.*
2 *Will you do*	*a favour*	*for a friend of mine?*
3 *Can you cash*	*this cheque*	*for me?*

[VP14]   In this pattern the verb is followed by a direct object and a preposition and its object. This pattern is not convertible to [VP12], as are [VP13A] and [VP13B]. 'Give something to somebody' [VP12A] may be converted to 'Give somebody something' [VP13A]. 'Explain something to somebody' cannot be converted to '*Explain somebody something'.

    The preposition is linked to the verb and they must be learnt together, e g 'congratulate somebody *on* something', 'compare one thing *to/with* another'. In [VP15] however the prepositional phrase is variable, e g 'put something *on/under the table, in the drawer*'.

Subject + *vt*	DO	prep	noun
1 *We congratulated*	*him*	*on*	*his success.*
2 *Compare*	*the copy*	*with*	*the original.*
3 *He compared*	*the heart*	*to*	*a pump.*
4 *I explained*	*my difficulty*	*to*	*him.*

Variations are possible. If the DO is long, the prepositional phrase may precede it. Introductory *it* may be used when there is an infinitive phrase or a clause.

Subject + *vt*	prep + noun	DO
1 *I explained*	*to him*	*the impossibility of granting his request.*
2 *I must leave it*	*to your own ‹ judgement*	*to decide whether you should offer your resignation.*

Compare:	Subject + *vt*	DO	prep + noun
	1 *I explained*	*the problem*	*to him.*
	2 *I must leave*	*the decision*	*to you.*

[VP15A] In [VP15] the DO is followed by an adverbial phrase of place, duration, distance, etc which is obligatory. 'I read the book' [VP6] is a complete sentence, but '*I put the book' is not. *Put* needs an adjunct. e g 'I put the book *down/away/on the shelf*'. With verbs marked [VP15A] the adverbial is a prepositional phrase, which is variable (unlike [VP14]).

Subject + *vt*	DO	adverbial phrase
1 *Don't let the child put*	*his head*	*out of the car window/into the plastic bag.*
2 *The secretary showed*	*me*	*to the door/into the reception room.*
3 *Please put*	*these papers*	*on that desk/in that file/in my briefcase.*

[VP15B] In this pattern adverbial particles are used. When the DO is a personal pronoun, the adverbial particle follows. When the DO is a noun or noun phrase, the adverbial particle may either follow or precede. If the DO is long, the adverbial particle usually precedes.

Subject + *vt*	DO	adverbial particle
1 *Take*	*them/your shoes*	*off.*
2 *Don't throw*	*it/that old hat*	*away.*
3 *Did you wind*	*it/the clock*	*up?*

Subject + *vt*	adverbial particle	DO
1 *Lock*	*up*	*all your valuables.*
2 *She gave*	*away*	*all her old clothes.*
3 *Don't forget to switch*	*off*	*the lights in all the rooms downstairs.*

[VP16A] In this pattern there is an adverbial adjunct which is an infinitive phrase. This may be introduced by *in order to* or *so as to*. [VP16A] is to be distinguished from [VP17] (with the same word order).

verb patterns

Cf *I sent*   *Tom*   *to buy some fruit.* [VP16A]
    I want   *Tom*   *to buy some fruit.* [VP17]

In [VP16A] the infinitive is one of purpose or intended result. In [VP17] the infinitive is part of the direct object.

Subject + *vt*	D O	*to*-infinitive
1 *He brought*	*his brother*	*to see me.*
2 *He opened*	*the door*	*to let the cat out.*
3 *They left*	*me*	*to do all the dirty work.*

[VP16B] The D O is followed by a noun introduced by *as* or *like*, or a clause introduced by *as if* or *as though*.

Subject + *vt*	D O	*as/like* + noun *as if/though* + clause
1 *I can't see*	*myself*	*as a pop singer.*
2 *Her parents spoilt*	*her*	*as a child.*
3 *He carries*	*himself*	*like a soldier.*
4 *You mustn't treat*	*your wife*	*as if she were a servant.*

[VP17] In this pattern the verb is followed by a noun or pronoun and a *to*-infinitive. The noun/pronoun + *to*-infinitive is the object of the verb.

Subject + *vt*	noun/pronoun	(*not*) + *to*-infinitive
1 *He likes*	*his wife*	*to dress colourfully.*
2 *They warned*	*us*	*not to be late.*
3 *Do you want/wish*	*me*	*to stay?*

[VP18A] In this pattern the verb is used with a noun or pronoun and a bare infinitive. The verbs indicate physical perceptions. These verbs are also used in [VP19]. [VP18] indicates completed activity and [VP19] activity in progress.

Subject + *vt*	noun/pronoun	infinitive
1 *Did you see/notice*	*anyone*	*leave the house?*
2 *We felt*	*the house*	*shake.*
3 *I once heard*	*her*	*sing the part of Aida.*

[VP18B] A small number of verbs which do not indicate physical perceptions are used in this pattern. *Make* and *let* are examples. Compare *force/compel* and *allow/permit*, which are used in [VP17].

Please let   *me*   *go.* [VP18B]
Please allow/permit   *me*   *to go.* [VP17]

Subject + *vt*	noun/pronoun	infinitive
1 *What makes*	*you*	*think so?*
2 *Let*	*me*	*go!*
3 *I've never known*	*him*	*behave so badly before.*

[VP18C] *Have* is used in this pattern when it means 'wish', 'experience' or 'cause'.

Subject + HAVE	noun/pronoun	infinitive
1 *What would you have*	*me*	*do?*
2 *Have*	*the visitors*	*shown in, please.*
3 *I had*	*a frightening thing*	*happen to me yesterday.*
4 *We often have*	*our friends*	*visit us on Sundays.*

[VP19A] The verb is followed by a noun or pronoun and a present participle. The verbs indicate physical perceptions and are those used in [VP18A].

Subject + *vt*	noun/pronoun	present participle
1 *Can you smell*	*something*	*burning?*
2 *She could feel*	*her heart*	*beating wildly.*
3 *Did you notice*	*anyone*	*standing at the gate?*
4 *Didn't you hear*	*me*	*knocking?*

[VP19B] This pattern is used for some verbs which do not indicate physical perceptions.

Subject + *vt*	noun/pronoun	present participle
1 *I found*	*John*	*working at his desk.*
2 *They left*	*me*	*waiting outside.*
3 *This set*	*me*	*thinking.*
4 *Please start*	*the clock*	*going.*
5 *He soon had*	*them all*	*laughing.*

[VP19C] In this pattern the noun or pronoun is followed by the *-ing* form of a verb, and this may be either the present participle or the gerund, depending upon whether it is preceded by a noun or pronoun, or a possessive. For fuller notes , see [VP19C] in *Guide to Patterns and Usage*.

Subject + *vt*	noun/pronoun/ possessive	*-ing* form of the verb
1 *I can't understand*	*him/his*	*behaving so foolishly.*
2 *Can you imagine*	*me/my*	*being so stupid?*
3 *Does this justify*	*you/your*	*taking legal action?*
4 *I can't remember*	*my parents/their*	*ever being unkind to me.*
5 *I admire*	*Tom('s)/him/his*	*standing his ground.*

[VP20] In this pattern the verb is followed by a noun or pronoun, an interrogative adverb (except *why*) or pronoun, and a *to*-infinitive. The pattern may be compared to [VP12A].

| *Tell* | *me* | *your name.* [VP12A] |
| *Tell* | *me* | *what to call you.* [VP20] |

Subject + *vt*	noun/pronoun	interrogative + *to*-infinitive
1 *I showed*	*them*	*how to do it.*
2 *Tell*	*him*	*where to put it.*
3 *Ask*	*your teacher*	*how to pronounce the word.*

[VP21] This pattern is similar to [VP20]. An interrogative clause follows the noun or pronoun.

Subject + *vt*	noun/pronoun	interrogative clause
1 *Tell*	*me*	*what your name is.*
2 *Ask*	*him*	*where he put it.*
3 *Show*	*me*	*what you have in your pockets.*

verb patterns

[VP22] The D O is followed by an adjective which indicates result or manner.

Subject + *vt*	D O	adjective
1 *We painted*	*the ceiling*	*green.*
2 *The sun keeps*	*us*	*warm.*
3 *The mud made*	*walking*	*difficult.*

[VP23] The D O is followed by a noun (the object complement).

Subject + *vt*	D O	noun
1 *They made*	*Newton*	*President of the Royal Society.*
2 *They named*	*the baby*	*Richard.*
3 *They usually call*	*him*	*Dick.*

[VP24A] The D O is followed by a past participle.

Subject + *vt*	D O	past participle
1 *You must make*	*your views*	*known.*
2 *Have you ever heard*	*this opera*	*sung in Italian?*
3 *We want*	*the work*	*finished by Saturday.*

[VP24B] *Have* is used in this pattern to indicate what the subject of the sentence experiences, undergoes, or suffers (as in Nos 1 and 2), or what is held or possessed (as in No 3).

Subject + HAVE	D O	past participle
1 *King Charles had*	*his head*	*cut off.*
2 *I've recently had*	*my appendix*	*removed.*
3 *They have*	*scarcely any money*	*saved for their old age.*

[VP24C] *Have* and *get* are used in this pattern meaning 'cause to be'.

Subject + HAVE/GET	D O	past participle
1 *Can we have/get*	*the programme*	*changed?*
2 *Please have/get*	*these letters*	*translated into English.*
3 *I'll have/get*	*the matter*	*seen to.*

[VP25] The D O is followed by *to be* (often omitted) and an adjective or a noun. In spoken English [VP9] (i e with a *that*-clause) is preferred.

Subject + *vt*	D O	(*to be*) + adjective/noun
1 *Most people considered*	*him*	*(to be) innocent.*
2 *They all felt*	*the plan*	*to be unwise.*
3 *I've always found*	*Jonathan*	*friendly/a good friend.*
4 *In Britain we presume*	*a man*	*(to be) innocent until he is proved guilty.*

For 1, *Most people consider that he was innocent* [VP9] is more usual. Introductory *it* is used if, instead of a noun, there is a clause, infinitive phrase, etc.
Cf *Do you consider long hair for men strange?*
   Do you consider it strange for men to let their hair grow long?

Anomalous verbs

Some of the verbs in the Dictionary carry the description *anomalous verb* (abbreviated *anom v*), or *anomalous finite* (abbreviated *anom fin*). A verb is an *anomalous finite* if it forms its negative by adding the word *not* (or its contraction *-n't*) after the verb. For example, the negative of *must* is *must not* or *mustn't*. All the forms of the English anomalous verbs are set out in the table below.

	Non-finite forms		Finite forms	
Infinitive	Present Participle	Past Participle	Present Tense	Past Tense
be	*being*	*been*	*am, is, are*	*was, were*
have	*having*	*had*	*have, has*	*had*
do	*doing*	*done*	*do, does*	*did*
—	—	—	*shall*	*should*
—	—	—	*will*	*would*
—	—	—	*can*	*could*
—	—	—	*may*	*might*
—	—	—	*must*	—
—	—	—	*ought*	—
—	—	—	*need*	—
—	—	—	*dare*	—
—	—	—	—	*used*

Strong and weak forms

The words listed below all have two or more different pronunciations: a *strong* form and one or more *weak* forms. It is the weak forms which occur most frequently in connected speech. For example, *from* is /frəm/ in *He ˌcomes from 'Spain.*

The strong form occurs when a word is said in isolation, or when it is given special emphasis in connected speech. For instance, *from* is /frɒm/ in *This ˌpresent's not 'from John; it's 'for him.* In addition, when prepositions and auxiliary verbs come at the end of a clause they generally take their strong form, whether or not they are stressed. For example, *ˌWhere do you 'come from?* has /frɒm/ (*not* /frəm/).

The words below are very common in ordinary speech, and it is only by understanding the different forms and using them correctly that the learner will develop a mastery of natural, conversational English.

	STRONG FORM	WEAK FORM	NOTES ON THE WEAK FORM
DETERMINER			
a	/eɪ/	/ə/	
an	/æn/	/ən/	
his	/hɪz/	/ɪz/	Not used to begin a sentence
our	/'aʊə(r)/	/ɑː(r)/	
some	/sʌm/	/səm/	Used only when *some* means 'an undefined amount or number of'
the	/ðiː/	/ðə/, /ðɪ/	/ðɪ/ before vowels
your	/jɔː(r)/	/jə(r)/	

strong and weak forms

	STRONG FORM	WEAK FORM	NOTES ON THE WEAK FORM
CONJUNCTION			
and	/ænd/	/ən/	
as	/æz/	/əz/	
but	/bʌt/	/bət/	
than	/ðæn/	/ðən/	
that	/ðæt/	/ðət/	Also used when *that* is a relative pronoun
PREPOSITION			
at	/æt/	/ət/	
for	/fɔː(r)/	/fə(r)/, /fr/	/fr/ before vowels
from	/frɒm/	/frəm/	
of	/ɒv/	/əv/	
to	/tuː/	/tə/	Not used before vowels
PRONOUN			
he	/hiː/	/iː/	Not used to begin a sentence
her	/hɜː(r)/	/ɜː(r)/, /ə(r)/	Not used to begin a sentence; /ə(r)/ in rapid speech
him	/hɪm/	/ɪm/	
them	/ðem/	/ðəm/	
us	/ʌs/	/əs/	
VERB			
am	/æm/	/əm/	
are	/ɑː(r)/	/ə(r)/	
can	/kæn/	/kən/	
do	/duː/	/də/	Not used before vowels
does	/dʌz/	/dəz/	
had	/hæd/	/həd/, /əd/	Auxiliary use only; /həd/ used to begin a sentence
has	/hæz/	/həz/, /əz/, /z/, /s/	Auxiliary use only; /əz/ used after the consonants /s, z, ʃ, ʒ, tʃ, dʒ/; /həz/ used to begin a sentence
have	/hæv/	/həv/, /əv/	Auxiliary use only; /həv/ used to begin a sentence
is	/ɪz/	/z/, /s/	Not used to begin or end a sentence
must	/mʌst/	/məst/	
shall	/ʃæl/	/ʃəl/	
was	/wɒz/	/wəz/	
were	/wɜː(r)/	/wə(r)/	
will	/wɪl/	/əl/	Not used to begin or end a sentence
would	/wʊd/	/əd/	Not used to begin or end a sentence

Contractions

In English there are a number of contractions of words which are used in speech, and in writing which reproduces spoken language, for example drama, direct speech in novels and short stories, personal letters. It is important that the learner should learn and make use of these contracted forms if he wants his English to sound natural.

When contractions are written, the two words are shortened by omitting one or two letters and joining the words together. The letters that are omitted are represented by an apostrophe (').

When contractions are spoken, the two words are shortened by omitting some sounds and pronouncing the two words as one.

PERSONAL PRONOUN + VERB

I'm	/aɪm/	I am		*she'll*	/ʃiːl/	she will
I've	/aɪv/	I have		*she'd*	/ʃiːd/	she would; she had
I'll	/aɪl/	I shall/will				
I'd	/aɪd/	I would; I had		*it's*	/ɪts/	it is; it has
				it'll	/'ɪtl/	it will
you're	/jʊə(r)/	you are				
you've	/juːv/	you have		*we're*	/wɪə(r)/	we are
you'll	/juːl/	you will		*we've*	/wiːv/	we have
you'd	/juːd/	you would; you had		*we'll*	/wiːl/	we shall/will
				we'd	/wiːd/	we would; we had
he's	/hiːz/	he is; he has				
he'll	/hiːl/	he will		*they're*	/'ðeɪə(r)/	they are
he'd	/hiːd/	he would; he had		*they've*	/ðeɪv/	they have
				they'll	/ðeɪl/	they will
she's	/ʃiːz/	she is; she has		*they'd*	/ðeɪd/	they would; they had

VERB + NOT

aren't	/ɑːnt/	are not		*mayn't*	/'meɪənt/	may not
can't	/kɑːnt/	cannot		*mightn't*	/'maɪtnt/	might not
couldn't	/'kʊdnt/	could not		*mustn't*	/'mʌsnt/	must not
daren't	/deənt/	dare not		*needn't*	/'niːdnt/	need not
didn't	/'dɪdnt/	did not		*oughtn't*	/'ɔːtnt/	ought not
doesn't	/'dʌznt/	does not		*shan't*	/ʃɑːnt/	shall not
don't	/dəʊnt/	do not		*shouldn't*	/'ʃʊdnt/	should not
hasn't	/'hæznt/	has not		*wasn't*	/'wɒznt/	was not
haven't	/'hævnt/	have not		*weren't*	/wɜːnt/	were not
hadn't	/'hædnt/	had not		*won't*	/wəʊnt/	will not
isn't	/'ɪznt/	is not		*wouldn't*	/'wʊdnt/	would not

OTHER COMMON CONTRACTIONS

here's	/hɪəz/	here is		*what's*	/wɒts/	what is?
how's	/haʊz/	how is?		*when's*	/wenz/	when is?
that'd	/'ðætəd/	that would		*where's*	/weəz/	where is?
that'll	/'ðætl/	that will		*who'd*	/huːd/	who would?
that's	/ðæts/	that is		*who'll*	/huːl/	who will?
there's	/ðeəz/	there is		*who's*	/huːz/	who is?
what'll	/'wɒtl/	what will				

Aa

A¹, a /eɪ/ (*pl* A's, a's /eɪz/) the first letter of the English alphabet: *He knows the subject from A to Z,* knows it thoroughly. **A1** /ˌeɪ 'wʌn/ (**a**) (of ships) classified as first class. ⇨ Lloyd's. (**b**) (colloq) excellent: *an A1 dinner; feeling A1,* in excellent health.

a² /ə; *strong form:* eɪ/, **an** /ən; *strong form:* æn/ *indef art* **1** one: *I said 'a train was coming, not 'the train. I have a pen (pl some pens). Have you a pen (pl any pens)?* Cf *some, any, several, a few* with *pl nn.* **2** (used in the pattern **a** + *adj* or *pron* of number and quantity): *a lot of money; a great many friends; a few books; a little more.* **3** (with possessives): *a friend of my father's,* one of my father's friends; *a book of John's,* one of John's books. **4** (used in the pattern **many/such/what** + **a**): *Many a man would be glad of the opportunity/such an opportunity. What an opportunity you missed!* **5** (used in the pattern **half** + **a** + **n**): *half a dozen; half an hour;* (before 1971) *half a crown,* the sum of 2s 6d. Cf *a half-crown,* former coin worth 2s 6d (= 12½p). **6** (used in the pattern **as/how/so/too** + *adj* + **a**): *He's not so big a fool as he looks. She's as clever a girl as you can wish to meet. It's too difficult a book for me.* **7** that which is called; any; every (no *article* in *pl*): *A horse is an animal.* Cf *Horses are animals.* **8** (When two objects, articles, etc naturally go together and are thought of as a unit, the *indef art* is not repeated): *a cup and saucer; a knife and fork.* **9** (used with a person's name, and the title *Mr, Mrs,* etc to indicate that the person is perhaps unknown to the person addressed): *A Mr White has called. A Mrs Green is asking to see you.* **10** one like: *He thinks he's a Napoleon,* a man like Napoleon. **11** *of/at a,* (in some phrases) the same: *They're all of a size. Carry them three at a time.* **Birds of a feather flock together,** (prov) people of the same kind like to be together. **12** (used distributively): *twice a month; 20p a pound; 50p an hour; sixty miles an hour.*

aback /ə'bæk/ *adv* backwards. **be ˌtaken a'back,** be startled, disconcerted.

an abacus

aba·cus /'æbəkəs/ (*pl* -cuses /-kəsɪz/ or -ci /'æbəsaɪ/) *n* frame with beads or balls sliding on rods, for teaching numbers to children, or (still in the East) for calculating; early form of digital computer.

abaft /ə'bɑːft *US:* ə'bæft/ *adv, prep* (naut) at, in, toward, the stern half of a ship; nearer the stern

than; behind.

aban·don¹ /ə'bændən/ *vt* **1** [VP6A] go away from, not intending to return to; forsake: *The order was given to ~ ship,* for all on board to leave the (sinking) ship. *The cruel man ~ed his wife and child.* **2** [VP6A] give up: *They ~ed the attempt,* stopped trying. *They had ~ed all hope,* no longer had any hope. *The new engine design had to be ~ed for lack of financial support.* **3** [VP14] **~ oneself to,** give oneself up completely to, eg passions, impulses: *He ~ed himself to despair.* **~ed** *part adj* **1** given up to bad ways; depraved; profligate: *You ~ed wretch!* **2** deserted; forsaken. **~·ment** *n* [U].

aban·don² /ə'bændən/ *n* [U] careless freedom, as when one gives way to impulses: *waving their arms with ~.*

abase /ə'beɪs/ *vt* [VP6B] **~ oneself,** humiliate or degrade oneself: *~ oneself so far as to do sth,* lower oneself in dignity to the extent of doing sth. **~·ment** *n* [U].

abash /ə'bæʃ/ *vt* [VP6A] (passive only) cause to feel self-conscious or embarrassed: *The poor man stood/felt ~ed at this display of wealth,* was confused, not knowing what to do or say.

abate /ə'beɪt/ *vt, vi* [VP6A,2A] (liter) (of winds, storms, floods, pain, etc) make or become less: *The ship sailed when the storm ~d.* **2** [VP6A] (legal) bring to an end; abolish: *We must ~ the smoke nuisance in our big cities.* **~·ment** *n* [U] abating; decrease.

ab·at·toir /'æbətwɑː(r) *US:* ˌæbə'twɑːr/ *n* slaughter-house (for cattle, sheep, etc).

abbé /'æbeɪ *US:* æ'beɪ/ *n* (courtesy title for a) French priest, esp one without official duties.

ab·bess /'æbes/ *n* woman (*Mother Superior*) at the head of a convent or nunnery.

ab·bey /'æbɪ/ *n* (*pl* -beys) **1** building(s) in which men (*monks*) or women (*nuns*) live as a community in the service of God. **2** the whole number of monks or nuns in an ~. **3** church or house which was once an ~ or part of an ~. **the A~,** often used of Westminster A~, London.

ab·bot /'æbət/ *n* man (*Father Superior*) at the head of the monks in an abbey or monastery.

ab·brevi·ate /ə'briːvɪeɪt/ *vt* [VP6A,14] shorten (a word, title, etc): *~ January to Jan.* ⇨ abridge. **ab·brevi·ation** /əˌbriːvɪ'eɪʃn/ *n* **1** [U] abbreviating or being ~d. **2** [C] shortened form (esp of a word). ⇨ App 2,9.

ABC /ˌeɪ biː 'siː/ *n* **1** the letters A to Z of the (Roman) alphabet. **2** simplest facts of a subject, to be learnt first.

ab·di·cate /'æbdɪkeɪt/ *vt, vi* **1** [VP6A] give up, renounce, a high office, authority or control, responsibility. **2** [VP2A] give up the throne: *King Edward VIII ~d in 1936 and was created Duke of Windsor.* **ab·di·ca·tion** /ˌæbdɪ'keɪʃn/ *n* **1** [U] abdicating. **2** [C] instance of this.

ab·do·men /'æbdəmən/ *n* **1** (colloq = *belly*) part of the body that includes the stomach and bowels. ⇨ the illus at trunk. **2** last of the three divisions of an insect, spider, etc. ⇨ the illus at insect.

ab·domi·nal /æb'dɒmɪnl/ *adj* in, of, for, the abdomen: *~ pains; an ~ operation.* ⇨ intestinal.

ab·duct /æb'dʌkt/ vt [VP6A] take or lead (esp a woman or child) away unlawfully, by force or fraud. ⇨ kidnap. **ab·duc·tion** /æb'dʌkʃn/ n

abeam /ə'bi:m/ adv (naut) on a line at a right angle to the length of a ship or aircraft: *The lighthouse was ~ of the ship.*

abed /ə'bed/ adv (old use) in bed.

ab·er·ra·tion /ˌæbə'reɪʃn/ n 1 [U] (usu fig) straying away from the right path, from what is normal: *stealing sth in a moment of ~.* 2 [C] instance of this; defect: *The delay was caused by an ~ in the computer.* **ab·er·rant** /æ'berənt/ adj straying away from what is normal, expected or usual; not true to type.

abet /ə'bet/ vt (-tt-) [VP6A,14] (legal) help (sb) (in doing wrong); encourage (vice, crime): *~ sb in a crime.* **aid and ~ sb,** (legal) be an accomplice in his wrongdoing.

abey·ance /ə'beɪəns/ n [U] (formal) condition of not being in force or in use for a time: *The question is in ~,* is suspended, eg until more information is obtained. *fall/go into ~,* (legal) (of a law, rule, custom, etc) be suspended; be no longer observed.

ab·hor /əb'hɔː(r)/ vt (-rr-) [VP6A] think of with hatred and disgust; detest: *~ cruelty to animals.* **~·rence** /əb'hɒrəns US: -'hɔːr-/ n [U] hatred and disgust: *hold sth in ~rence; his ~rence of flattery.* **~·rent** /əb'hɒrənt US: -'hɔːr-/ adj hateful; causing horror (to sb, to his feelings).

abide /ə'baɪd/ vt,vi (pt,pp (1,2,4) ~d, (3) abode /ə'bəʊd/) 1 [VP3A] ~ **by,** (formal) be faithful to; keep: *~ by a promise/decision. I ~ by* (colloq 'stick to') *what I said. You'll have to ~ by the consequences,* endure them. (Used only of undesirable consequences.) 2 [VP6A] (esp with *can't* or *couldn't*) endure; bear: *She can't ~ that man.* 3 [VP2C] (in old or liter use) rest, remain, stay: *~ at/in a place; ~ with sb.* 4 [VP6A] (liter) wait for: *~ the event; ~ sb's coming.* **abid·ing** adj (liter) never-ending; lasting.

abil·ity /ə'bɪlətɪ/ n 1 [U] (potential) capacity or power (to do sth physical or mental): *to the best of my ~,* as well as I can. *I do not doubt your ~ to do the work.* 2 [U] cleverness; intelligence: *a man of great ~.* 3 [C] (pl -ties) special natural power to do sth well; talent: *a man of many abilities.*

ab initio /ˌæb ɪ'nɪʃɪəʊ/ adv (Lat) from the beginning.

ab·ject /'æbdʒekt/ adj 1 (of conditions) wretched; miserable: *living in ~ poverty.* 2 (of persons, their actions, behaviour) degraded; deserving contempt because cowardly or self-abasing: *~ behaviour; an ~ apology.* **~·ly** adv **ab·jec·tion** /æb'dʒekʃn/ n

ab·jure /əb'dʒʊə(r)/ vt [VP6A] (formal) promise or swear solemnly on oath or in public to give up, eg a belief, a right, evil ways: *~ one's religion.* **ab·jur·ation** /ˌæbdʒʊə'reɪʃn/ n [U] abjuring; state of having been ~d: [C] action of this: *an abjuration of faith.*

ab·la·tive /'æblətɪv/ adj, n (gram) name of a form in Latin nouns indicating an agent, instrument or cause. **the ~ case,** ⇨ case¹(3).

ab·laut /'æblaʊt/ n (ling) systematic vowel changes in verb forms of Indo-European languages (as in drive, drove, driven).

ablaze /ə'bleɪz/ pred adj, adv 1 on fire, in a blaze: *set it ~. The whole building was soon ~.* 2 (fig) shining; bright; excited: *The streets were ~ with lights. Her face was ~ with anger.*

able /'eɪbl/ adj 1 be ~ *to do sth,* have the power, means or opportunity to do sth: *Shall/Will you be ~ to come? You are better ~ to do it than I am.* ⇨ can², could. 2 (-r, -st) clever; capable; having or showing knowledge or skill: *an ~ lawyer; an ~ speech; the ~st/most ~ man I know.* **~-'bodied** /-'bɒdɪd/ adj physically strong. **~ 'seaman,** **~-,bodied 'seaman** n (GB abbr = **AB**) seaman trained and certified for all duties. **ably** /'eɪblɪ/ adv in an ~ manner.

ab·lu·tion /ə'bluːʃn/ n (usu pl) (formal) ceremonial washing of the hands or the body, esp as an act of religion: *perform one's ~s,* (often joc or fac) wash oneself.

ab·ne·ga·tion /ˌæbnɪ'geɪʃn/ n [U] (formal) self-denial; (often ,self-'~) self-sacrifice.

ab·nor·mal /æb'nɔːml/ adj different, often in an undesirable way, from what is normal, ordinary or expected. **~·ly** adv **~·ity** /ˌæbnɔː'mælətɪ/ n [U] quality of being ~; [C] (pl -ties) sth that is ~.

Abo /'æbəʊ/ n (pl Abos) ⚠ (derog) = Aborigine.

aboard /ə'bɔːd/ adv, prep on (to) or in(to) a ship, aircraft, or (US) a train or motor-coach: *It's time to go ~. All ~!* (ie Go or come ~.) *Welcome ~!* (eg as a greeting by a stewardess on an aircraft.)

abode¹ /ə'bəʊd/ n 1 (old or liter use) house; dwelling-place: *take up one's ~ with one's parents-in-law,* go and live with them. 2 (legal) *place of ~,* domicile. *of/with no fixed ~,* having no fixed dwelling-place.

abode² /ə'bəʊd/ pt,pp of abide.

abol·ish /ə'bɒlɪʃ/ vt [VP6A] put an end to, do away with, eg war, slavery, an old custom. **abol·ition** /ˌæbə'lɪʃn/ n [U] ~ing or being ~ed (esp used, in the 18th and 19th cc, of Negro slavery). **abol·ition·ist** /ˌæbə'lɪʃənɪst/ n (esp) person who wished to ~ Negro slavery.

A-bomb /'eɪ bɒm/ n ⇨ atomic.

abom·in·able /ə'bɒmɪnəbl/ adj 1 causing hatred and disgust (to sb). 2 (colloq) unpleasant; bad: *~ weather/food.* **~ 'snowman,** = yeti. **abom·in·ably** /-əblɪ/ adv

abom·in·ate /ə'bɒmɪneɪt/ vt [VP6A,C] detest; feel hatred or disgust for; (colloq) dislike. **abom·in·ation** /əˌbɒmɪ'neɪʃn/ 1 [U] horror and disgust: *hold sth in abomination.* 2 [C] sth that arouses horror and disgust (to sb).

abo·rig·inal /ˌæbə'rɪdʒənl/ adj (of races of people, living creatures, etc) belonging to, existing in, a region from earliest times, or from the time when the region was first known. □ n ~ inhabitant, plant, etc of a region. **abo·rig·ines** /ˌæbə'rɪdʒəniːz/ n pl the ~, the ~ inhabitants. **Abo·rig·ine** /ˌæbə'rɪdʒənɪ/ n Australian ~ person.

abort /ə'bɔːt/ vt,vi [VP6A,2A] come to nothing; miscarry; terminate prematurely: *~ a space mission,* cancel it in space, eg because of mechanical trouble.

abor·tion /ə'bɔːʃn/ n 1 [U] (legal) expulsion of the foetus from the womb during the first 28 weeks of pregnancy; helping or causing this: *A~ was formerly a crime in Britain.* 2 [C] instance of this; miscarriage of birth: *have/procure an ~.* 3 [C] creature produced by ~; dwarfed or mis-shapen creature; (fig) plan, effort, etc that has failed to develop. **~·ist** /-ɪst/ n person who brings about an ~; person who favours and supports legal ~.

abort·ive /ə'bɔːtɪv/ adj coming to nothing; unsuccessful; arrested in development: *plans that proved ~; an ~ rebellion.* **~·ly** adv

abound /ə'baʊnd/ *vi* [VP3A] ~ *in/with,* have, exist, in great numbers or quantities: *The river ~s in fish. Fish ~ in the river. The hut ~ed with vermin. Vermin ~ed in the hut.*

about[1] /ə'baʊt/ *adv of degree* (contrasted with *just* or *exactly*) a little more or less than; a little before or after: ~ *as high as that tree; for ~ three miles; ~ six o'clock; on or ~ the fifth of May. I've had just ~ enough* (colloq understatement for 'quite enough'). *It's ~ time you stopped being so rude* (colloq understatement for 'quite time'). *That's ~ (the size of) it,* (colloq) That is how I assess it, how I see it.

about[2] /ə'baʊt/ *adv part* (may usu be replaced by *around* in 1, 2 and 3) **1** (with *vv* of movement) here and there, in no particular direction: *The children were rushing ~. The boys were climbing ~ on the rocks. Don't drop cigarette ash ~. Don't leave waste paper and empty bottles ~ in the park. He's taking Jane ~ a lot these days,* eg to dances, cinemas, theatres. **2** (with other *vv,* indicating position, etc): *There were books lying ~ on the floor/people sitting ~ on the grass.* **3** (with *be*): *There was no one ~,* no one to be seen. *There's a lot of influenza ~,* many people have it. *be (out and) ~,* be able to get out, work, etc after eg an illness. *be up and ~,* be out of bed and active. **4** *bring sth ~,* ⇨ bring(4). *come ~,* ⇨ come(11). **5** facing round; in the opposite direction: *It's the wrong way ~. A~ turn!* (GB), *A~ face!* (US), (mil commands) turn round to face the other way. **,~-'face** *vi* turn and face the other way. □ *n* complete reversal of views, actions, etc: *He did a complete ~-face.* **6** (of two or more persons or groups) *take turns ~; (do sth) turn and turn ~,* ⇨ turn [1](4).

about[3] /ə'baʊt/ *prep* (may usu be replaced by *around* or *round* in 1, 2 and 3) **1** (with *vv* of movement) here and there, in no particular direction: *walking ~ the town; travelling ~ the world.* **2** (with other *vv,* indicating position, state, etc): *idle men standing ~ on street corners; books and papers lying ~ the room. I haven't any money ~ me,* ie with me, in my pockets. **3** near to: *I dropped the key somewhere ~ here.* **4** concerning; regarding; in connection with: *He is careless ~ his personal appearance. What do you know ~ him? What is he so angry ~? Tell me all ~ it. How/What ~...,* used to ask for information, to make a suggestion or to get sb's opinion: *What ~ his qualifications for the position? How ~ going to France for our holidays?* **5** concerned or occupied with: *What are you ~?* (= colloq 'up to?'). *And while you're ~ it...,* while you're doing that.... *Mind what you're ~,* Be careful what you do. *go/set ~ sth,* deal with it: *Do you know how to go ~ it,* deal with the task? **6** round (which is now more usu preferred): *the fields ~ Oxford. She hung ~ his shoulders. He has his wits ~ him,* ⇨ wit. **7** ~ *to* + *inf,* on the point of (doing sth), just going to (do sth): *As I was ~ to say, when you interrupted me... He was ~ to start.*

above[1] /ə'bʌv/ *adv* (contrasted with *below*[1], *under*[1](1) and *underneath*) **1** at a higher point; overhead; on high: *My bedroom is just ~. Seen from ~, the fields looked like a geometrical pattern. A voice from ~ shouted a welcome.* **2** earlier (in a book, article, etc): *As was stated ~...; See the statement ~/the ~ statement.* **3** in Heaven: *the Powers ~,* the heavenly powers. **,~ 'board** *adv* without deception or concealment; honourably. □

pred adj frank; open. ⇨ **underhand.** **,~-'mentioned,** **,~-'named** *adjj* mentioned, named, ~ (or earlier) in this book, article, etc.

above[2] /ə'bʌv/ *prep* (contrasted with *below*[2], *under*[2] and *underneath;* ~ may sometimes be replaced by *over* or *beyond*) **1** higher than: *The sun rose ~ the horizon. We were flying ~ the clouds.* Cf We flew *over/across* the Sahara. *The water came ~ our knees. A captain in the Navy ranks ~ a captain in the Army.* **2** greater in number, price, weight, etc: *The temperature has been ~ the average recently. There is nothing in this shop ~/over fifty cents. It weighs ~/over ten tons. Applicants must be ~/over the age of 21.* **3** more than: *A soldier should value honour ~ life. ~ all,* more than anything else. *over and ~,* in addition to. **4** too great, good, difficult, etc for: *If you want to learn, you must not be ~ asking* (= not be too proud to ask) *questions. He is ~ meanness and deceit,* does not show meanness or practise deceit. *This book is ~* (now more usu *beyond*) *me,* too difficult for me. **5** out of reach of (because too great, good, etc): *His heroism was ~/beyond all praise. His conduct has always been ~ suspicion.* **6** (various uses): *the waterfall ~* (= up stream from) *the bridge; live ~/beyond one's means,* in a style too expensive for one's income; *be ~ oneself,* in high spirits; *get ~ oneself,* become conceited, too self-satisfied and lacking in self-control; *She married ~ her station,* married sb from a higher social class.

ab·ra·ca·dabra /,æbrəkə'dæbrə/ *n* [U] magic jargon; gibberish.

abrade /ə'breɪd/ *vt* [VP6A] rub or scrape off, wear away (skin, etc) by friction or hard rubbing.

ab·ra·sion /ə'breɪʒn/ *n* [U] rubbing, scraping, or wearing off; [C] area where sth has been worn or scraped away: *an ~ of the skin.*

ab·ras·ive /ə'breɪsɪv/ *n* [U] substance (eg *emery*) used for rubbing or grinding down surfaces; [C] particular type of ~. □ *adj* causing abrasion; (fig) harsh, rough: *an ~ voice/character.*

abreast /ə'brest/ *adv* (of persons, ships, etc) on a level, side by side, and facing the same way: *walking three ~; warships in line ~. be/keep ~ (of/ with),* level with, not behind: *You should read the newspapers to keep ~ of the times,* to be informed of the latest events, ideas, discoveries, etc.

abridge /ə'brɪdʒ/ *vt* [VP6A] make shorter, esp by using fewer words: *an ~d edition of 'David Copperfield';* shorten (an interview, the time sth lasts). ⇨ abbreviate. *~-ment,* **abridg·ment** *n* [U] abridging; [C] sth, eg a book, that is ~d.

abroad /ə'brɔːd/ *adv* **1** in or to a foreign country or countries; away from one's own country: *be/go/ live/travel ~; visitors who have come from ~. Do you like it ~/being ~?* **2** far and wide; everywhere: *There's a rumour ~ that...,* People are saying that.... **3** (old use) out of doors: *You were ~ early this morning.*

ab·ro·gate /'æbrəgeɪt/ *vt* [VP6A] (formal) repeal or annul by authority. **ab·ro·ga·tion** /,æbrə'geɪʃn/ *n*

abrupt /ə'brʌpt/ *adj* **1** unexpectedly sudden: *The road is full of ~ turns.* **2** (of speech, writing, behaviour) rough; brusque; disconnected: *a man with an ~ manner,* ie rather impolite, gruff, blunt; *an ~ style,* eg of speaking or writing. **3** (of a slope) steep. *~·ly adv ~·ness n*

ab·scess /'æbses/ *n* [C] collection of thick yellowish-white liquid (called *pus*) formed in a cavity in the body: *~es on the gums.*

ab·scond /əb'skɒnd/ vi [VP2A,3A] ~ (with) (from), go away suddenly, secretly, and aware of having done wrong, esp to avoid arrest.

ab·sence /'æbsəns/ n 1 [U] being away (from): ~ from school; during his ~ in America, while he was there. In the ~ of the Manager (ie while he is away) Mr X is in charge of the business. **leave of** ~, ⇨ leave²(1). 2 [C] occasion or time of being away: numerous ~s from school; a long ~; after an ~ of three months. 3 [U] lack; non-existence: in the ~ of definite information. Cold is the ~ of heat. 4 ~ **of mind**, absent-mindedness (⇨ below).

ab·sent¹ /'æbsənt/ adj 1 ~ (from), not present (at): ~ from school/work. 2 lost in thought; abstracted: When I spoke to him he looked at me in an ~ way but did not answer. ~·ly adv (rare) = ~-mindedly. ˌ~-'minded adj so deep or far away in thought that one is unaware of what one is doing, what is happening around one, etc. ~-**mind·ed·ly** adv ~-**minded-ness** n

ab·sent² /əb'sent/ vt [VP6B,14] ~ **oneself (from),** stay away (from): Why did you ~ yourself (from school) yesterday?

ab·sen·tee /ˌæbsən'ti:/ n person who is absent. ~ **landlord,** land or house owner who habitually lives away from the place he owns. ~·**ism** /-ɪzəm/ n [U] habitual failure to be present, eg the practice of being absent from work or regular duty frequently and without good reason.

ab·sinthe, ab·sinth /'æbsɪnθ/ n [U] bitter, green alcoholic drink made with wormwood and other herbs.

ab·so·lute /'æbsəlu:t/ adj 1 complete; perfect: A child usually has ~ trust in its mother. When giving evidence in a law court, we must tell the ~ truth. 2 unlimited; having complete or arbitrary power: An ~ ruler need not ask anyone for permission to do anything. 3 real; undoubted: It is an ~ fact. He must not be punished unless you have ~ proof of his guilt. 4 unconditional; unqualified: An ~ promise must be kept whatever happens. 5 not relative; not dependent on or measured by other things. ~ **zero,** lowest temperature theoretically possible, = −273·15°C. ⇨ App 5. ~·ly adv 1 completely; ~ly impossible; ~ly right. 2 unconditionally: He refused ~ly. 3 /ˌæbsə'lu:tlɪ/ (colloq, in answer to a question, or as a comment) quite so; certainly. **ab·so·lut·ism** /'æbsəlu:tɪzəm/ n (pol) ~(2) government; despotism.

ab·sol·ution /ˌæbsə'lu:ʃn/ n [U] (RC Church) freeing (esp by a priest in the sacrament of penance) from the consequences of sin: grant, pronounce ~ from sin. ⇨ penance.

ab·solve /əb'zɒlv/ vt [VP6A,14] ~ (from), declare free (from sin, guilt, a promise, duty, etc): I ~ you from all blame/from your vows.

ab·sorb /əb'sɔːb/ vt 1 [VP6A] take or suck in, eg a liquid; take in, eg heat, light, (fig) knowledge, etc: Paper that ~s ink is called blotting-paper. Dry sand ~s water. The clever boy ~ed all the knowledge his teachers could give him. 2 [VP6A] use up much of the attention, interest or time of: His business ~s him. He is completely ~ed in his business. He was ~ed in a book. ~·ent /-ənt/ adj, n (substance) capable of ~ing: ~ent cotton wool. **ab·sorp·tion** /əb'sɔːpʃn/ n [U] ~ing or being ~ed; engrossment: Complete absorption in sport interferred with his studies.

ab·stain /əb'steɪn/ vi [VP3A,2A] ~ (from), hold oneself back, refrain: His doctor told him to ~

from beer and wine. At the last election he ~ed (from voting). ~·er n person who ~s, esp total ~er, one who never takes alcoholic drinks.

ab·stemi·ous /əb'sti:mɪəs/ adj sparing or moderate, esp in taking food and drink; frugal: ~ habits; an ~ meal. ~·ly adv ~-**ness** n

ab·sten·tion /əb'stenʃn/ n [U] ~ (from), abstaining, esp not using one's vote at an election, etc; [C] instance of this: six votes for, three against and two ~s.

ab·sti·nence /'æbstɪnəns/ n [U] ~ (from), abstaining, eg from food, enjoyment, esp alcoholic drink. ˌtotal '~, refraining completely from alcoholic drink.

ab·stract¹ /'æbstrækt/ adj 1 separated from what is real or concrete; thought of separately from facts, objects or particular examples: A flower is beautiful, but beauty itself is ~. ~ 'art, art which does not represent objects, scenes, etc in an obvious way, but abstracts and isolates features of reality. ⇨ realism(1). ~ 'noun, (gram) one that is the name of a quality or state, eg length, goodness, virtue. 2 **in the** ~, regarded in an ideal or theoretical way.

ab·stract² /əb'strækt/ vt [VP6A,14] ~ (from), take out; separate: ~ metal from ore; (colloq) steal: ~ a wallet from sb's pocket. ~ed adj not paying attention; withdrawn in thought. ~·ed·ly adv in an absent-minded way.

ab·stract³ /'æbstrækt/ n [C] short account, eg of the chief points of a piece of writing, a book, speech, etc: an ~ of a sermon.

ab·strac·tion /əb'strækʃn/ n 1 [U] abstracting or being abstracted. 2 [U] absent-mindedness: in a moment of ~; with an air of ~. 3 [C] visionary idea; idea of a quality apart from its material accompaniments: Whiteness is an ~. Don't lose yourself in ~s, ie keep a firm hold on reality. 4 [U] formation of such an idea or ideas.

ab·struse /əb'stru:s/ adj whose meaning or answer is hidden or difficult to understand; profound. ~·ly adv ~-**ness** n

ab·surd /əb'sɜːd/ adj unreasonable; foolish; ridiculous: What an ~ suggestion! It was ~ of you to suggest such a thing. ~·ly adv ~-**ity** n (pl -ties) 1 [U] state of being ~; unreasonableness. 2 [C] ~ act or statement.

abun·dance /ə'bʌndəns/ n 1 [U] great plenty: food and drink in ~; live in ~, have plenty of those things that make life enjoyable. 2 (with indef art) quantity that is more than enough: an ~ of good things.

abun·dant /ə'bʌndənt/ adj 1 more than enough; plentiful: We have ~ proof of his guilt. 2 ~ **in,** rich in; well supplied with: a land ~ in minerals (with an abundance of or abounding in are more usu). ~·ly adv: I've made my views ~ly clear.

abuse¹ /ə'bju:s/ n 1 [U] ~ (of), wrong use; [C] instance of this; an ~ of trust. 2 [C] unjust custom or practice that has become established: remedy an ~; put an end to ~s. 3 [U] angry or violent attack in words; bad language; cursing: greet sb with a stream of ~; shower ~ on sb.

abuse² /ə'bju:z/ vt [VP6A] 1 make a bad or wrong use of: Don't ~ your authority/the confidence they have placed in you. 2 say severe, cruel or unjust things to sb or about sb. 3 (old use) ill-treat. 4 (old use, esp in the passive) deceive: She has been much ~d.

abus·ive /ə'bju:sɪv/ adj using, containing, insults

äussere Erscheinung - outward appearance (handwritten annotation)

and curses: *use* ~ *language to sb; become* ~, begin to insult and curse. ~·**ly** *adv*

abut /ə'bʌt/ *vi* (-tt-) [VP3A] ~ **on,** (of land) have a common boundary with; border on. ~·**ment** *n* (eng) structure that bears the weight of a bridge or an arch.

abysm /ə'bɪzəm/ *n* [C] (poet) abyss.

abys·mal /ə'bɪzməl/ *adj* (esp fig and colloq) bottomless; extreme: ~ *ignorance,* (colloq) complete absence of knowledge. ~·**ly** *adv*

abyss /ə'bɪs/ *n* hole so deep as to appear bottomless: (fig) *the* ~ *of despair.* **the** ~, hell, or the lower world.

aca·cia /ə'keɪʃə/ *n* [C] **1** (sorts of) tree from which gum is obtained. **2** (*false* ~ or *locust tree*) (sorts of) similar tree grown as an ornament in parks and gardens.

aca·demic /ˌækə'demɪk/ *adj* **1** of teaching, studying; of schools, colleges, etc; scholarly, literary or classical (contrasted with technical or scientific): ~ *subjects; the* ~ *year,* (usu Oct to June in GB and US). ~ **freedom,** liberty to teach and to discuss problems without outside, eg Government, interference. **2** too much concerned with theory and logic; not sufficiently practical: *The question/issue is* ~, is of no practical consequence. **3** of an academy: ~ *rank/costume.* □ *n* [C] university teacher; professional scholar. **aca·demi·cally** /-klɪ/ *adv*

aca·dem·icals /ˌækə'demɪklz/ *n pl* academic costume (cap and gown), as worn on ceremonial occasions.

acad·emy /ə'kædəmɪ/ *n* (*pl* -mies) **1** school for higher learning, usu for a special purpose: *a* '*naval/military* ~; *an* ~ *of* '*music; a* '*riding/* '*fencing* ~. **2** society of distinguished scholars; society for cultivating art, literature, etc, of which membership is an honour: *The Royal A*~ *of Arts.* **aca·dem·ician** /əˌkædə'mɪʃn US: ˌækədə'mɪʃn/ *n* member of an ~(2), eg of the Royal A~ in GB or of the French A~.

ac·cede /ək'siːd/ *vi* [VP2A,3A] ~ (**to**), (formal) **1** assent or agree, eg to a request or proposal. **2** take up or succeed to, eg an office, a post, a position of authority.

ac·cel·er·ando /ækˌselə'rændəʊ/ *n, adv, adj* (music) (direction for) increasing speed gradually. ⇨ **rallentando.**

ac·cel·er·ate /ək'seləreɪt/ *vt,vi* **1** [VP6A] increase the speed of; cause to move faster or happen earlier. **2** [VP2A] (of a motion or process) become faster. **ac·cel·er·ation** /əkˌselə'reɪʃn/ *n* [U] making or being made quicker; rate of increase; of speed per unit of time: *a car with good acceleration.*

ac·cel·er·ator /ək'seləreɪtə(r)/ *n* **1** device, eg the pedal in a car, for controlling speed. ⇨ the illus at motor. **2** (phys) device for accelerating particles or nuclei, also called (colloq) an 'atom-smasher'.

ac·cent /'æksənt US: 'æksent/ *n* [C] **1** prominence (by means of stress or intonation) given to a syllable: *In the word 'today' the* ~ *is on the second syllable.* **2** mark or symbol, usu above a letter, used in writing and printing to indicate the quality of a vowel sound or syllabic stress. ⇨ acute(5), circumflex and grave[3]. **3** [sometimes U] individual, local or national way of pronouncing: *a Cockney* ~; *speaking English with a foreign* ~; *speak without an* ~. **4** (*pl*) way of speaking which indicates a particular quality, etc: *in the tender* ~*s of love.* **5** (colloq) emphasis given to some aspect of a

display, performance, etc: *At this year's Motor Show the* ~ *is on sports cars.* □ *vt* /æk'sent/ [VP6A] pronounce with an ~; put emphasis on (a syllable or word); make prominent or conspicuous.

ac·cen·tu·ate /ək'sentʃʊeɪt/ *vt* [VP6A] give more force or importance to; draw attention to. **ac·cen·tu·ation** /əkˌsentʃʊ'eɪʃn/ *n*

ac·cept /ək'sept/ *vt,vi* [VP6A,9,16B,2A] **1** (consent to) receive (sth offered): ~ *a gift/an invitation. He asked her to marry him and she* ~*ed him/his proposal. I cannot* ~ *your apology.* **2** agree; recognize; regard with favour or approval: *I* ~ *that the change may take some time. It is an* ~*ed truth/ fact,* sth that everyone believes. **3** (comm) take responsibility for: ~ *a bill of exchange;* ~ *delivery of goods.* ~·**able** /-əbl/ *adj* worth ~ing; welcome: *if this proposal is* ~*able to you.* **ac·cepta·bil·ity** /əkˌseptə'bɪlətɪ/ *n* **ac·cept·ance** /-əns/ *n* [U] **1** ~ing or being ~ed. **2** approval; favourable reception: *The proposal met with/found general* ~*ance.* **3** (comm) agreement to pay; (legal) contract, bill of exchange, which has been offered and ~ed. **ac·cep·ta·tion** /ˌæksep'teɪʃn/ *n* generally ~ed meaning of a word or expression.

ac·cess /'ækses/ *n* [U] **1** way (in) to a place: *easy/ difficult of* ~; (attrib) *good* ~ *roads,* roads giving good ~. *The only* ~ *to the farmhouse is across the fields.* '~**-road,** (US) *slip-road,* ⇨ slip[2](8). **2** ~ **to,** right, opportunity or means of reaching, using or approaching: *Students must have* ~ *to good books. Only high officials had* ~ *to the Emperor.* **3** *an* ~ *of,* (old use) attack (of fever, etc); sudden attack, outburst (of anger, rage, despair, etc). ~·**ible** /ək'sesəbl/ *adj* ~ (**to**), able to be reached, used, visited, etc: *facts that are* ~*ible to all; a collection of paintings not* ~*ible to the public;* that can be influenced by: *a man who is not* ~*ible to argument.* **ac·ces·si·bil·ity** /əkˌsesə'bɪlətɪ/ *n* [U].

ac·ces·sary /ək'sesərɪ/ *n* (*pl* -ries), *pred adj* (= US *accessory*(1)) (legal) person who helps in any act, esp a crime: *an* ~ *to a crime; He was made* ~ *to the crime.* ~ *before/after the* **fact,** ⇨ fact(1).

ac·ces·sion /æk'seʃn/ *n* ~ **to,** **1** [U] reaching a rank, position or state: *the Queen's* ~ *to the throne; on his* ~ *to the estate/to manhood.* **2** [U] addition; increase; [C] example of this: *recent* ~*s to the school library; the* ~ *of new members to a political party.*

ac·ces·sory /ək'sesərɪ/ *n* (*pl* -ries) **1** accessary. **2** sth helpful, useful, but not an essential part of: *the accessories of a bicycle,* eg the lamp, a pump; *the accessories of a woman's dress,* eg gloves, a handbag.

ac·ci·dence /'æksɪdəns/ *n* [U] (gram) that part of grammar which deals with meaningful differences in the form of a word, eg have, has, had; foot, feet, etc. The more usu term is now *morphology.* ⇨ syntax.

ac·ci·dent /'æksɪdənt/ *n* **1** [C] sth that happens without a cause that can be seen at once, usu sth unfortunate and undesirable: *There have been many railway* ~*s this year. He was killed in a road/motoring* ~. *There has been an* ~ *to... A* ~*s will happen,* (prov) Some unfortunate events must be accepted as inevitable. **meet with/have an** ~, experience one: *I had a slight* ~ *on the way to work this morning.* '~**-prone,** ⇨ prone. **2** [U] chance; fortune: *by* ~ *of birth.* **by** ~, by chance: *You might cut yourself by* ~; *you would not cut yourself on purpose.* **without** ~, safely. '~ **insur-**

ance, against injury, damage or death which is the result of an ~.

ac·ci·den·tal /ˌæksɪ'dentl/ adj happening unexpectedly and by chance: an ~ meeting with a friend. **~·ly** /-təlɪ/ adv

ac·claim /ə'kleɪm/ vt 1 [VP6A,16B] welcome with shouts of approval; applaud loudly: ~ the winner of a race; ~ sb as a great actor. 2 [VP23] make (sb) ruler, salute (sb) by ~ing: They ~ed him King. □ n [U] applause; approval: The play received great critical ~.

ac·cla·ma·tion /ˌæklə'meɪʃn/ n 1 [U] loud and enthusiastic approval of a proposal, etc: elected/carried by ~, without voting. 2 (usu pl) shouts or applause of welcome, acceptance: the ~s of the crowd.

ac·cli·mate /'æklɪmeɪt/ vt,vi (= acclimatize). **ac·cli·ma·tion** /ˌæklaɪ'meɪʃn/ n

ac·cli·mat·ize /ə'klaɪmətaɪz/ vt,vi [VP14,2A] ~ (to), get (oneself, animals, plants, etc) used to a new climate, or (fig) to a new environment, new conditions, etc: You will soon get ~d. **ac·cli·mat·iz·ation** /əˌklaɪmətaɪ'zeɪʃn US: -tɪ'z-/ n

ac·cliv·ity /ə'klɪvətɪ/ n (pl -ties) [C] upward slope. ⇨ declivity.

ac·col·ade /'ækəleɪd US: ˌækə'leɪd/ n [C] 1 bestowal of a knighthood by a tap on the shoulder with the flat of a sword. 2 (fig) praise; approval: the ~s of the literary critics.

ac·com·mo·date /ə'kɒmədeɪt/ vt [VP6A,14] 1 have, provide, lodging for: This hotel can ~ 600 guests. 2 ~ sb (with sth), grant sth to sb; do sb a favour: The bank will ~ you with a loan. 3 ~ sth to, change sth so that it fits with or is in harmony with (sth else): I will ~ my plans to yours. **ac·com·mo·dat·ing** adj willing to oblige others; easy to deal with.

ac·com·mo·da·tion /əˌkɒmə'deɪʃn/ n 1 [U] (GB) furnished, unfurnished room(s), eg in a flat, house, hostel or in a hotel, etc: Wanted, ~ for a married couple with small child, in London, eg as in a newspaper advertisement. Hotel ~ was scarce during the Olympic Games. 2 (pl, US) lodgings; room(s) and food. 3 [C] sth that helps; sth for convenience: an '~ ladder, (attrib) a portable one hung from the side of a ship. 4 [U] (formal) compromise; settlement or adjustment (of one thing to another); [C] example of this: come to an ~, reach a compromise, eg in a dispute. ⇨ agreement.

ac·com·pani·ment /ə'kʌmpənɪmənt/ n [C] 1 sth that naturally or often goes with another thing: Disease is often an ~ of famine. 2 (music) (usu) instrumental part to support a voice, choir or solo instrument: a song with a piano ~. **ac·com·pan·ist** /ə'kʌmpənɪst/ n person who plays a musical ~.

ac·com·pany /ə'kʌmpənɪ/ vt (pt,pp -nied) [VP6A,14] 1 go with: Warships will ~ the convoy across the Atlantic. He was accompanied by his secretary. 2 attend; characterize: fever accompanied with delirium; lightning accompanied with thunder. 3 occur or do at the same time as: ~ one's words with blows. 4 (music) play an accompaniment to: The singer was accompanied at the piano by Gerald Moore.

ac·com·plice /ə'kʌmplɪs US: ə'kɒm-/ n [C] helper or companion (in, esp, wrongdoing).

ac·com·plish /ə'kʌmplɪʃ US: ə'kɒm-/ vt [VP6A] perform; succeed in doing; finish successfully: ~ a task; a man who will never ~ anything. **an ~ed fact**, sth already done. **~ed** adj clever; skilled

(in): an ~ed dancer; well trained or educated in such social arts as conversation, art and music: an ~ed young lady. **~·ment** n 1 [U] completion; finishing: the ~ment of their aims; difficult of ~ment. 2 [C] sth ~ed, esp sth well done. 3 [C] skill in a social or domestic art: Among her ~ments were dancing, playing the piano, sewing and cooking.

ac·cord¹ /ə'kɔːd/ n 1 [U] of one's own ~, without being asked or forced; willingly. **in/out of ~ (with)**, in/out of harmony (with), agreeing/not agreeing with. **with one ~**, everybody consenting. 2 [C] treaty, agreement (between countries; with a country).

ac·cord² /ə'kɔːd/ vi,vt 1 [VP2A,2C,3A] ~ (with), match, agree (with); be in agreement or harmony (with): His behaviour and his principles do not ~ (well together). His behaviour does not ~ with his principles. What you say does not ~ with the previous evidence. 2 [VP13A,12A] (formal style) give; grant: ~ sb permission; ~ permission to sb. He was ~ed a warm welcome.

ac·cord·ance /ə'kɔːdəns/ n in ~ with, in agreement or conformity with: in ~ with your wishes; in ~ with custom/the regulations.

ac·cord·ing /ə'kɔːdɪŋ/ 1 ~ as, conj in proportion as; in a manner that depends upon: You will be praised or blamed ~ as your work is good or bad. 2 ~ to, prep (a) on the authority of: A~ to the Bible, God created the world in six days. (b) in a degree in proportion to: He will be punished ~ to the seriousness of his crime. (c) in a manner consistent with: The books are placed on the shelves ~ to authors. **~·ly** adv 1 for that reason; therefore. 2 as the (stated) circumstances suggest: I have told you the circumstances, so you must act ~ly.

ac·cord·ion /ə'kɔːdɪən/ n (also piano ~) portable musical instrument with a bellows, metal reeds and a keyboard; (attrib) having narrow folds like the bellows of an ~: ~ pleats in a skirt.

ac·cost /ə'kɒst US: ə'kɔːst/ vt [VP6A] go up to and speak to first, esp a stranger in a public place; (of a prostitute) solicit: I was ~ed by a beggar/a prostitute.

ac·couche·ment /ə'kuːʃmɒŋ/ n (F) lying in; confinement; childbirth. ⇨ lie in at lie²(1).

ac·count¹ /ə'kaʊnt/ n 1 [C] (comm) statement of money (to be) paid or received (for goods, services, etc): I have an ~ with the Midland Bank, keep my money with that Bank, pay my debts, etc by means of cheques from that Bank, etc. **open an ~; open a bank/post office, etc ~**, start to keep one's money at a bank, etc. **ask a shop/shopkeeper/store to put sth down to one's ~**, ask him to note the price of what is bought, for payment later. **settle one's ~ (with)**, pay what one owes (to a tradesman, etc); (fig) avenge oneself for an injury, etc. **send in/render an ~**, send a written statement of what is owed. Hence, **~ 'rendered**, an ~ previously sent in but not yet paid. **balance/square ~s (with sb)**, receive or pay the difference between debit and credit; (fig) remove moral grievances between people by giving or taking punishment. **'budget ~**, (with a shop) one used for buying goods, paying bills, etc by making regular payments to the shop; (with a bank) special ~ with a bank which makes regular deductions for bills paid. **'current ~, de'posit ~, 'joint ~, 'private ~, 'savings ~**, ⇨ current¹(3), deposit¹(1), joint², private(1) and save¹(2). 2 (archaic) counting; calculation. **money of ~**, used of sums of money, not of coins or banknotes. ⇨ guinea. **3** (*sing* only) benefit; profit: *invest one's money to good* ∿. **turn/put sth to** *(good)* ∿, use money, abilities, talent, etc profitably: *He turned/ put his knowledge of Spanish to good* ∿. **work on one's own** ∿, for one's own purposes and profit, and at one's own risk. **4** [U] **call/bring sb to** ∿, require him to justify or explain his conduct; state that he is answerable for sth. **5** [C] **give a good** ∿ **of oneself**, do well; act in a way that brings credit, eg by defeating opponents in contests. **6** [C] report; description; narrative: *Don't always believe newspaper* ∿s *of events. by one's own* ∿, according to what one oneself says. **by/from all** ∿s, according to what everybody, all the papers, etc say. **7** [U] estimation. **be** *(reckoned) of some/small* ∿, be (considered) of some/low value. **take sth into** ∿; **take** ∿ **of sth**, note or consider it; pay attention to it. **leave sth out of** ∿, **take no** ∿ **of sth**, pay no attention to it. **8** [U] reason; cause. **on** ∿ **of**, because of. **on this/that** ∿, for this/that reason: *He's angry on that* ∿. *Don't stay away on* ∿ *of John/on John's* ∿. **on no** ∿; **not on any** ∿, in no case; not for any reason: *Don't on any* ∿ *leave the baby alone in the house.*

ac·count[2] /ə'kaʊnt/ *vt, vi* **1** [VP3A] ∿ **for,** (a) serve as an explanation of; explain the cause of: *His illness* ∿s *for his absence. Ah, that* ∿s *for it! He has been asked to* ∿ *for his conduct,* explain why he acted as he did. **There's no** ∿**ing for tastes,** We cannot explain why people have different likes and dislikes. (b) give a reckoning of (money that has been entrusted to one): *The boy has to* ∿ (*to his parents*) *for the money they give him for school expenses.* (c) destroy; kill; capture: *We* ∿*ed for a fine brace of partridges.* **2** [VP25] consider: *In English law a man is* ∿*ed innocent until he is proved guilty.* ∿**able** /-əbl/ *adj* ∿**able** *(to sb) (for sth)*, responsible; expected to give an explanation: *I'll hold you* ∿*able. A madman is not* ∿*able for his actions.*

ac·count·an·cy /ə'kaʊntənsɪ/ *n* [U] profession of an accountant.

ac·count·ant /ə'kaʊntənt/ *n* [C] (in GB) person whose profession is to keep and examine business accounts[1]. **chartered** ∿, (abbr **CA**) ⇨ **charter** *v*(1) (US = **certified public** ∿, abbr **CPA**).

ac·coutre·ments (US = **ac·cou·ter·ments**) /ə'ku:təmənts/ *n pl* equipment; trappings; (mil) soldier's kit excluding clothes and weapons.

ac·credit /ə'kredɪt/ *vt* [VP14] (usu passive) **1** appoint or send (sb) as an ambassador, with official letters of introduction: *He was* ∿*ed to/at Lisbon.* **2** = credit[2]. ∿**ed** *part adj* officially recognized (person); generally accepted (belief, opinion, etc); guaranteed to be of an approved quality.

ac·cretion /ə'kri:ʃn/ *n* **1** [U] increase by organic addition or growth; the growing of separate things into one. **2** [C] sth added; sth resulting from ∿.

ac·crue /ə'kru:/ *vi* [VP2A,3A] ∿ *(to sb) (from sth),* come as a natural growth or development: *If you keep your money in the Savings Bank, interest* ∿s. *A* ∿*d interest is interest due, but not yet paid or received.*

ac·cu·mu·late /ə'kju:mjʊleɪt/ *vt, vi* [VP6A,2A] make or become greater in number or quantity; come or gather together; heap up: *By buying ten books every month, he soon* ∿*d a library. Dust soon* ∿s *if the rooms are not swept. By working hard you may* ∿ *a fortune.*

ac·cu·mu·la·tion /ə,kju:mjʊ'leɪʃn/ *n* **1** [U] accumulating; collection: *the* ∿ *of money/useful knowledge.* **2** [C] material, etc accumulated: *an* ∿ *of books/evidence/rubbish.* **ac·cu·mu·lat·ive** /ə'kju:mjʊlətɪv US: -leɪtɪv/ *adj* arising from ∿; growing by a succession of additions.

ac·cu·mu·la·tor /ə'kju:mjʊleɪtə(r)/ *n* [C] **1** (GB) storage battery, eg for a motor vehicle: *charge/ discharge/an* ∿, cause a current to flow into/out of it. **2** (in a computer) device which stores numbers and progressively adds numbers.

ac·cu·rate /'ækjərət/ *adj* **1** careful and exact: *be* ∿ *in one's work/in what one says; quick and* ∿ *at figures; take* ∿ *aim.* **2** free from error: ∿ *scales. Clocks in railway stations should be* ∿. ∿**·ly** *adv* **ac·cu·racy** /'ækjərəsɪ/ *n* [U] exactness; correctness.

ac·cursed /ə'kɜ:sɪd/, **ac·curst** /ə'kɜ:st/ *adj* (poetic) under a curse; detestable; hateful.

ac·cu·sa·tion /,ækju:'zeɪʃn/ *n* **1** [U] accusing or being accused. **2** [C] charge of doing wrong, of having broken the law: *bring an* ∿ *of theft against sb; be under an* ∿ *of theft.*

ac·cus·ative /ə'kju:zətɪv/ *adj, n* (gram) (of the) form of a word when it is the direct object of a verb or preposition. **the** ∿ **case,** ⇨ case[1](3).

ac·cuse /ə'kju:z/ *vt* [VP6A,14] ∿ **sb (of sth),** say that (sb) has done wrong, broken the law, is to be blamed: ∿ *sb of theft/cowardice; be* ∿*d of sth.* **the** ∿**d,** the person(s) charged in a criminal case. **ac·cuser** *n* **ac·cus·ing·ly** /ə'kju:zɪŋlɪ/ *adv* in an accusing manner: *He pointed accusingly at me.*

ac·cus·tom /ə'kʌstəm/ *vt* [VP14] ∿ *(oneself) to,* make used to: *When he became a soldier, he had to* ∿ *himself to long marches.* **become/be** ∿**ed to,** become/be used to: *The boy soon became* ∿*ed to hard work and poor food. This is not the kind of treatment I am* ∿*ed to,* not the kind I usually receive. ∿**ed** *part adj* usual; habitual: *in his* ∿*ed seat.*

ace /eɪs/ *n* [C] **1** the one on dice, on (playing-)cards or dominoes (⇨ these words); card so marked: *the* ∿ *of spades.* **an ace in the hole,** (US sl, from the game of poker) sth held in reserve, likely to turn failure into success. **2** (colloq) person who is first-rate or expert at sth, esp an airman or a driver of racing cars. **3** *within an ace of,* failing, escaping, by a narrow margin: *within an ace of death/of being killed.*

acerb·ity /ə'sɜ:bətɪ/ *n* **1** [U] (formal) bitterness of speech, manner, temper. **2** [C] (*pl* -ties) instance of this; bitter remark, etc.

acetic /ə'si:tɪk/ *adj* of vinegar or ∿ acid. ∿ **'acid,** the acid contained in vinegar. **acet·ate** /'æsɪteɪt/ *n* salt of ∿ acid: *acetate silk,* artificial silk made from cellulose acetate.

acety·lene /ə'setəli:n/ *n* [U] (chem) colourless gas (C_2H_2) which burns with a bright light, used in carbide lamps and for welding and cutting metal. ⇨ oxyacetylene.

ache /eɪk/ *n* [C] (*sing,* with or without the *def art*) dull continuous pain: *have* ∿s *and pains all over.* (∿ is only combined with *back, ear, head, heart, stomach, tummy* and *tooth,* as in *back∿.* For other parts of the body *a pain/* ∿ *in my/his/the foot, etc* is used): *have a* 'head∿; *suffer from* 'back∿s/*from* (*the*) 'tooth ∿. 'heart∿, ⇨ heart(7). □ *vi* **1** [VP2A] have a steady or continuous dull pain: *My head* ∿s/*is aching. After climbing the mountain, he* ∿*d all over. It makes my heart* ∿, makes me sad. 2 [VP3A,4A] ~ *(for),* have a longing: *His heart ~ed for her. He was aching for home. He ~d to be free.*

achieve /ə'tʃiːv/ *vt* [VP6A] **1** complete; accomplish; get (sth) done: *He will never ~ anything, will not do anything successfully. I've ~d only half of what I hoped to do.* **2** gain or reach by effort: ~ *one's purpose;* ~ *success/distinction in public life.* **achiev·able** /-əbl/ *adj* that can be ~d. ~**ment** *n* **1** [U] achieving: *the ~ment of an undertaking/of one's aims; impossible of ~ment; an ~ment test* (of skills, etc). **2** [C] sth ~d; sth done successfully, with effort and skill: *The inventor was rewarded by the Government for his scientific ~ments.*

Achilles /ə'kɪliːz/ *n* **the heel of ~**; ~' **heel,** (fig) small but weak or vulnerable point, eg in sb's character: *Spelling is my ~' heel.*

acid¹ /'æsɪd/ *adj* **1** sour; sharp to the taste: *A lemon is an ~ fruit. Vinegar has an ~ taste.* '~ **drops,** sweets of boiled sugar with an ~ flavour. **2** (fig) sharp; sarcastic: *an ~ wit; ~ remarks.*

acid² /'æsɪd/ *n* **1** [U] (chem) substance that contains hydrogen, which may be replaced by a metal to form a salt: *Vinegar contains acetic ~. H₂SO₄ stands for sulphuric ~;* [C] example of this: *Some ~s burn holes in wood and cloth.* ~ **test** *n* (fig) test that gives conclusive proof of the value or worth of sth. **2** [U] (sl) **LSD.** ⇨ **App 2.** ~**ify** /ə'sɪdɪfaɪ/ *vt,vi* (*pt,pp* -fied) [VP6A,2] make or become ~. ~**ity** /ə'sɪdətɪ/ *n* [U] state or quality of being ~. ~**ic** /ə'sɪdɪk/ *adj* ~**u·lated** /ə'sɪdjʊleɪtɪd US:* -ɪdʒʊl-/ *adj* made slightly ~. ~**u·lous** /ə'sɪdjʊləs *US:* -dʒʊl-/ *adj* (lit or fig) somewhat sour in taste or manner; sharp; bitter: *an ~ulous drink/tone of voice.*

ack-ack /,æk 'æk/ *n* (mil sl) anti-aircraft gun/fire, etc.

ac·knowl·edge /ək'nɒlɪdʒ/ *vt* **1** [VP6A,C,9A,24A] confess; admit the truth, existence or reality of: *He refused to ~ defeat/that he was defeated. He would not ~ his mistake. He won't ~ himself beaten. He ~d having been frightened. Does he ~ the signature,* agree or admit that it is his? [VP25] (liter style): *We praise thee, O God, we ~ Thee to be the Lord.* [VP16B] *Stephen ~d Henry as his heir,* recognized his claim to be heir. [VP25] *They all ~d him master,* agreed that he was their master. **2** [VP6A] report that one has received (sth): ~ *(receipt of) a letter.* **3** [VP6A] express thanks for: *We must not fail to ~ his services to the town. We should always ~ gifts promptly.* **4** [VP6A] indicate that one recognizes (sb) by giving a greeting, a smile, a nod of the head, etc: *I passed her in the street but she didn't even ~ me when I smiled.* ~**ment, ac·knowl·edg·ment** *n* **1** [U] act of acknowledging: *We are sending you a small sum of money in ~ment of your valuable help.* **2** [C] sth given or done to ~ sth: *We have had no ~ment of our letter,* no reply. *This basket of fruit is a slight ~ment of your kindness.*

acme /'ækmɪ/ *n* **the ~,** summit; highest point of development; point of perfection: *the ~ of his desires/skill.*

acne /'æknɪ/ *n* [U] disease (common among adolescents) in which there are pimples and blackheads on the face and neck.

aco·lyte /'ækəlaɪt/ *n* person who helps a priest in some religious services, esp the celebration of Mass.

ac·on·ite /'ækənaɪt/ *n* (bot) (sorts of) plant with blue or purple flowers; monkshood; drug from the dried poisonous root of one of these kinds, used to slow down the action of the heart.

acorn /'eɪkɔːn/ *n* seed or fruit of the oak tree. ⇨ the illus at tree. '~-**cup** *n* cuplike holder of an ~.

acous·tic /ə'kuːstɪk/ *adj* of sound, the science of sound and the sense of hearing. □ *n* [C] studio, hall, etc from the consideration of its ~s (⇨ **2** below): *Try recording the music in a better ~.* **acous·tics** *n* **1** (with *sing v*) the scientific study of sound. **2** (with *pl v*) the physical properties of sound; the properties of a hall, etc, that make it good, poor, etc for hearing music, speeches, etc: *The ~s of the new concert hall are excellent.*

ac·quaint /ə'kweɪnt/ *vt* [VP14] **1** ~ *sb/oneself with,* make familiar with, reveal to: ~ *sb with the facts of the case;* ~ *oneself/become ~ed/make oneself ~ed with one's new duties.* **2** *be ~ed (with sb),* have met (sb) personally: *I am not ~ed with the lady. We are not ~ed.*

ac·quaint·ance /ə'kweɪntəns/ *n* **1** [U] knowledge or information gained through experience: *He has some ~ with German, but does not speak it fluently.* *have a bowing/nodding ~ with,* have some ~ with (a person, a subject). *make sb's ~,* make *the ~ of sb,* get to know sb, eg by being introduced. *(up)on (further) ~,* when known for a (further) period of time. **2** [C] person with whom one is acquainted; person whom one knows (less intimately than a friend): *He has a wide circle of ~s.* **3** (older English, collective): *He has a wide ~,* many ~s. ~**·ship** /-ʃɪp/ *n* (circle of) ~s(2).

ac·quiesce /,ækwɪ'es/ *vi* **1** [VP2A] agree; accept silently or without protest. **2** [VP3A] ~ *in,* accept an arrangement, a conclusion, etc without protest: *Her parents will never ~ in such an unsuitable marriage.* **ac·qui·es·cence** /,ækwɪ'esns/ *n* (act of) acquiescing. **ac·qui·es·cent** /-'esnt/ *adj* disposed to ~.

ac·quire /ə'kwaɪə(r)/ *vt* [VP6A] gain by skill or ability, by one's own efforts or behaviour: ~ *a good knowledge of English/a reputation for dishonesty/a taste for brandy. an ~d taste,* one that comes when one has experimented with sth and, in the end, comes to like it: *Retsina* (= the resin-flavoured Gk wine) *is an ~d taste for British people.* ~**·ment** *n* **1** [U] acquisition (now the more usu word). **2** [C] accomplishment(3) (now the more usu word).

ac·qui·si·tion /,ækwɪ'zɪʃn/ *n* **1** [U] acquiring: *He devotes his time to the ~ of knowledge.* **2** [C] sth acquired: *my most recent ~s,* eg books I have bought recently. *Mr A will be a valuable ~ to* (= a valuable new member of) *the teaching staff of our school.*

ac·quis·itive /ə'kwɪzətɪv/ *adj* fond of, in the habit of, acquiring: ~ *of new ideas.* *the ~ society,* that values the possession of more and more material things.

ac·quit /ə'kwɪt/ *vt* (-tt-) **1** [VP6A,14] ~ *sb (of/on sth),* give a legal decision that (sb) is not guilty, eg of an offence: *He was ~ted of the crime/~ted on two of the charges.* **2** [VP16B] conduct (oneself): *He ~ted himself well/like a hero.* ~**·tal** /ə'kwɪtl/ *n* [U] judgement that a person is not guilty: *a sentence of ~tal;* [C] instance of this: *three convictions and two ~tals.*

acre /'eɪkə(r)/ *n* [C] measure of land, 4840 sq yds or about 4000 sq metres. **God's ~,** churchyard (for burials). ~**·age** /'eɪkərɪdʒ/ *n* [U] area of land measured in ∼s: *What is the ∼age of the London parks?*

ac·rid /'ækrɪd/ *adj* (of smell or taste) sharp; biting: *the ∼ smell of burning feathers;* (fig) bitter in temper or manner.

ac·ri·mony /'ækrɪmənɪ *US:* -məʊnɪ/ *n* [U] (formal) bitterness of temper, manner, language. **ac·ri·moni·ous** /ˌækrɪ'məʊnɪəs/ *adj* (of arguments, quarrels, words) bitter.

ac·ro·bat /'ækrəbæt/ *n* person who can perform difficult or unusual physical acts with skill, eg on a tightrope or trapeze. **∼·ic** /ˌækrə'bætɪk/ *adj* of or like an ∼: *∼ic feats.* **∼·ics** *n pl* (used with *sing v*) ∼ic tricks or feats: *aircraft ∼ics.*

acrobats

ac·ro·nym /'ækrənɪm/ *n* [C] word formed from the initial letters of a name, eg **NASA** /'næsə/, National Aeronautics and Space Administration. ⇨ App 2.

acrop·olis /ə'krɒpəlɪs/ *n* fortified part of a Gk city in ancient times, esp **the A∼,** that of Athens.

across¹ /ə'krɒs *US:* ə'krɔːs/ *adv* (used with *vv* in the senses of the *prep*): *Can you swim ∼? Will you row me ∼? I helped the blind man ∼. Come ∼ to my office this afternoon. The river is half a mile ∼,* = wide. **∼ from,** (US) opposite: *The bank is just ∼ from the school.*

across² /ə'krɒs *US:* ə'krɔːs/ *prep* **1** from one side to the other side of: *walk ∼ the street; draw a line ∼ a sheet of paper; a bridge ∼ the river; row sb ∼ a lake.* **∼-the-'board,** including all groups, members, etc esp in an occupation or industry: *an ∼-the-board wage increase.* **2** on the other side of: *My house is just ∼ the street. We shall soon be ∼ the Channel. He addressed me from ∼ the room.* **3** so as to form a cross; so as to cross or intersect: *He sat with his arms ∼ his chest. The two lines pass ∼ each other at right angles.* **4** (with *vv*) ⇨ come(15), drop²(13), get(17), put¹(11) and run¹(28).

acros·tic /ə'krɒstɪk *US:* -'krɔːs-/ *n* word puzzle, word arrangement, in which the first, or the first and last, letters of the lines make a word or words.

acryl·ic /ə'krɪlɪk/ *n* (comm) **∼ 'fibre,** (kinds of) synthetic fibre used for making dress materials, etc. **∼ 'resin,** (kinds of) transparent colourless plastic widely used in industry, eg for plastic lenses, aircraft windows.

act¹ /ækt/ *n* [C] **1** sth done: *To kick a cat is a cruel act. It is an act of kindness to help a blind man across the street.* **Acts (of the Apostles),** (NT) accounts of the missionary work of the Apostles. **2** process of, instant of, doing; action. *(catch sb) in the (very) act (of doing sth),* while performing the action: *The thief was caught in the act of breaking into the house. In the act of* (= While) *picking up the ball, he slipped and fell.* **Act of God,** sth which is the result of uncontrollable natural forces,

eg storms, floods, earthquakes. ⇨ also grace(3). **3** law made by a legislative body: *an Act of Parliament: the Acts of Congress.* **£4** main division of a play: *a play in five acts; Hamlet, Act 1, Scene 3.* ⇨ scene(5). **5** one of a series of short performances in a programme: *a circus/variety act.* **6** (colloq) pretence: *Don't take him seriously—it's just an ∼.* *put on an act,* (colloq) pretend; behave in an affected way (to get one's own way, etc).

act² /ækt/ *vi,vt* **1** [VP2A,3A] perform actions, do sth: *The time for talking is past; we must act at once. The girl's life was saved because the doctors acted so promptly. You have acted* (= behaved) *generously.* *act (up)on (a suggestion/sb's advice/an order),* do what is suggested, advised, etc. **2** [VP2A,3A] do what is required; function normally: *The brakes wouldn't act, so there was an accident. The pump is not acting well,* not performing its proper function. *act (up)on,* have an effect (up)on: *This medicine acts on the heart/the bowels.* **3** [VP2A,C,3A] perform in a professional or official capacity: *The police refused to act,* would not interfere. *act as,* be, perform, as an interpreter, mediator, etc. *act for/on behalf of,* represent (sb) as a solicitor, barrister in a legal case: *A solicitor acts for his clients.* **4** [VP2A,C,6A] take part in a play on the stage; take the part of, eg a character in a play or cinema film, or in real life: *Who is acting (the part of) Hamlet? She acts well. Don't act the fool/ass/idiot,* don't behave foolishly. *Browning's plays won't act,* are not suitable for the stage. *She's not really crying; she's only acting* (= pretending) *in order to gain your sympathy.* [VP15B] *act sth out,* perform actions which represent, and may help to release, the fears, inhibitions, etc of a neurotic person. *act up,* (colloq) behave badly so as to attract attention; cause pain, irritation, annoyance by functioning badly: *My leg/car/TV, etc has been acting* (now more usu *playing*) *up all week.*

act·ing /'æktɪŋ/ *adj* doing the duties of another person for a time: *The A∼ Manager/Headmaster; A∼ Captain.* □ *n* [U] (art of) performing in a play for the theatre, cinema, TV, etc: *She did a lot of ∼ while she was at college.* **'∼ copy,** (of a script) one for the use of an actor or actress.

ac·tin·ism /'æktɪnɪzəm/ *n* [U] property of light rays that produces chemical activity and changes (as in photographic films). **ac·tinic** /æk'tɪnɪk/ *adj* of ∼: *actinic rays,* component of the sun's radiation.

ac·tion /'ækʃn/ *n* **1** [U] process of doing things; movement; (way of) using energy, influence, etc: *The time has come for ∼, We must act now. A man of ∼ is not content just to talk.* *bring/call sth into ∼,* cause it to operate. *put/set sth in ∼,* cause it to start acting. *put sth out of ∼,* stop it working; make it unfit for use. *take ∼,* begin to act. **'∼ painting,** form of abstract painting in which paint is splashed, dribbled, etc on to the canvas. **2** [C] thing done; act: *We shall judge you by your ∼s, not by your promises. She is impulsive in her ∼s,* does things impulsively. *A∼s speak louder than words,* Doing sth is more convincing than talking about it. **3** [C] **(a)** mechanism of a piano, gun or other instrument. **(b)** manner of bodily movement, eg of a horse when jumping, of an athlete. **4** [C] legal process. *bring an ∼ against sb,* seek judgement against him in a law court. **5** [U] fighting between bodies of troops, between warships, etc: *go into ∼,* start fighting; *killed in*

~. [C] instance of this: *break off the* ~, stop fighting. '~ **stations,** (mil) positions to which soldiers, etc go when fighting is expected to begin. ~**·able** /-əbl/ *adj* giving just cause for legal ~.

ac·ti·vate /'æktɪveɪt/ *vt* [VP6A] make active; (chem) accelerate a reaction in, eg by heat; (phys) cause radiation from. **ac·ti·va·tion** /ˌæktɪ'veɪʃn/ *n*

ac·tive /'æktɪv/ *adj* **1** doing things; able to do things; in the habit of doing things; energetic; characterized by activity: *He's over 90 and not very* ~. *A boy with an* ~ *brain will be more successful than a dull boy. Mount Vesuvius is an* ~ *volcano,* is one that erupts. *She has an* ~ (= lively) *imagination. He takes an* ~ *part in school affairs. on* ~ **service,** (Navy, Army, Air Force) (GB) engaged in actual military service, esp in fighting during a war; (US) on full duty, not in the reserves. *under* ~ *consideration,* being considered or canvassed. **2** (gram) **the** ~ **(voice),** (a) form of a *v phrase* not containing *be* + *pp,* as in: *He was driving.* Cf *He was being driven.* ⇨ passive. **(b)** sentence containing a *vt* in which the *n* or *pron* preceding the *v,* and agreeing with it (the grammatical subject), refers to the doer of the action, ie the agent: *The children finished the cake* (active). Cf *The cake was finished by the children*(passive). ~**·ly** *adv*

ac·tiv·ist /'æktɪvɪst/ *n* [C] person taking an active part, eg in a political movement.

ac·tiv·ity /æk'tɪvəti/ *n* (*pl* -ties) **1** [U] being active or lively: *When a man is over 70, his time of full* ~ *is usually past.* **2** [C] thing (to be) done; occupation: *Classroom activities are things done by pupils in the classroom; outdoor activities are things done outside. My numerous activities leave me little leisure.*

ac·tor /'æktə(r)/ *n* **1** man who acts on the stage, TV or in films. **2** person who takes part in a notable event, etc.

ac·tress /'æktrɪs/ *n* woman actor(1).

ac·tual /'æktʃʊəl/ *adj* existing in fact; real: *It's an* ~ *fact; I haven't invented or imagined it. Can you give me the* ~ *figures,* the real figures, not an estimate or a guess? *What is the* ~ *position of affairs?* ~**·ly** /'æktʃʊlɪ/ *adv* **1** in ~ fact; really: *the political party* ~ly *in power. He looks honest, but* ~ly *he's a rogue.* **2** strange or surprising as it may seem: *He* ~ly *expected me to do his work for him! He not only ran in the race; he* ~ly *won it!* ~**·ity** /ˌæktʃʊ'ælətɪ/ *n* (*pl* -ties) **1** [U] ~ existence; reality. **2** [C, usu *pl*] ~ conditions or facts; realities.

ac·tu·ary /'æktʃʊərɪ/ *US*: -tʃʊerɪ/ *n* (*pl* -ries) expert who calculates insurance premiums (by studying rates of mortality, frequency of fires, thefts, accidents, etc). **ac·tu·ar·ial** /ˌæktʃʊ'eərɪəl/ *adj* of an ~ or his work.

ac·tu·ate /'æktʃʊeɪt/ *vt* [VP6A] (formal) cause to act: *A great statesman is* ~d *by love of his country, not by love of power.*

acu·ity /ə'kjuːəti/ *n* [U] (formal) acuteness.

acu·men /ə'kjuːmen/ *n* [U] sharpness and accuracy of judgement; ability to understand clearly: *business* ~.

acu·punc·ture /'ækjʊpʌŋktʃə(r)/ *n* [U] (med) pricking or puncturing of the living tissues of the human body with fine needles to cure disease, to relieve pain and as a local anaesthetic.

acute /ə'kjuːt/ *adj* **1** (of the senses, sensations, intellect) keen, sharp, quick: *Dogs have an* ~ *sense of smell. Our anxiety became more* ~. *He felt* ~ *remorse for his wrongdoing. A bad tooth can cause* ~ *pain. He is an* ~ *observer.* **2** (of diseases) coming sharply to a crisis: *The patient has reached the* ~ *stage of the disease,* the brief period during which the disease is severe and at a turning point. *Pneumonia is an* ~ *disease,* one that comes quickly to a turning-point. ⇨ chronic. **3** (of sounds) high; shrill. **4** ~ **angle,** angle of less than 90°. ⇨ the illus at angle. **5** ~ **accent,** mark over a vowel ('), as over *e* in *café.* ~**·ly** *adv* ~**·ness** *n*

ad /æd/ *n* [C] (colloq abbr for) advertisement: *'Want ads',* in newspapers, etc.

ad·age /'ædɪdʒ/ *n* [C] old and wise saying; proverb.

adagio /ə'dɑːdʒɪəʊ/ *n* (*pl* -gios /-dʒɪəʊz/) *adj, adv* (music) (passage played) gracefully and in slow time.

Adam /'ædəm/ *n* ~**'s 'apple,** part that projects in the front of the throat, esp in men, and moves up and down when one speaks. ⇨ the illus at head. **the old** ~, (facet) the immoral, selfish side of human nature. *not know sb from* ~, not know him at all. ⇨ know(2).

ada·mant /'ædəmənt/ *n* [C] kind of stone that, it is said, cannot be cut or broken. □ *pred adj* unyielding; firm in purpose: *He was* ~ *to their pleas. On this point I am* ~, Nothing can change my decision. *I only wish he were less* ~. **ada·man·tine** /ˌædə'mæntaɪn/ *adj* unyielding; inflexible.

adapt /ə'dæpt/ *vt* [VP6A, 14] make suitable for a new use, need, situation, etc: *When you go to a new country, you must* ~ *yourself to new manners and customs. Difficult books are sometimes* ~ed *for use in schools. This book is* ~ed *to the needs of beginners/*~ed *for beginners. The play has been* ~ed *from the French,* ie translated and changed to suit English audiences. *Novels are often* ~ed *for the stage, television and radio.* ~**er,** ~**or** /-tə(r)/ *nn* person who ~s sth; device that enables sth to be used for a purpose, or in a way, different from that for which it was designed, eg a fitting for taking electric current from an outlet so that more than one piece of apparatus may be used. ~**·able** /-əbl/ *adj* able to ~ oneself; able to be ~ed: *an* ~*able man,* one who can ~ himself to circumstances, etc. ~**a·bil·ity** /əˌdæptə'bɪlətɪ/ *n* [U] power of ~ing or being ~ed. **ad·ap·ta·tion** /ˌædæp'teɪʃn/ *n* ~**ation (of sth) (for/to sth),** **1** [U] state of being ~ed; ~ing. **2** [C] sth made by ~ing: *an* ~*ation (of a novel) for the stage/for broadcasting.*

add /æd/ *vt, vi* **1** [VP6A, 14] *add sth (to sth),* join, unite, put (one thing together with another): *If you add 5 and/to 5 you get 10. The house has been added to from time to time,* new rooms, etc have been built on to it. *If the tea is too strong, add some hot water.* '**adding–machine** *n* machine for calculating mechanically. **2** [VP6A, 9A] say further; go on to say: *'and I hope you'll come early,' he added. She added that….* **3** [VP15B, 3A, 2C] (special uses with *adverbial particles* and *preps*):

add sth in, include.

add to, increase: *This adds to our difficulties.*

add sth together, combine two or more things.

add sth up, find the sum of: *add up a column of figures; add up ten figures; add them up.*

add up (to), **(a)** give as a result, when joined: *The figures add up to 365.* **(b)** (colloq) mean; indicate; amount to: *All that this adds up to is that you don't want to help, so why not say so at once?* **(c)** (colloq) make sense; be plausible: *It just doesn't add up.*

ad·den·dum /ə'dendəm/ n (pl -da /-də/) thing (omitted) that is to be added.

ad·der /'ædə(r)/ n viper; any of several small poisonous snakes common in Europe, Africa (eg the puff-∿) and Asia. ⇨ the illus at snake.

ad·dict /ə'dɪkt/ vt (usu passive) **be ∿ed to,** be given to, habitually or compulsively: He is ∿ed to alcohol/smoking/lying/study/drugs. □ n /'ædɪkt/ person who is ∿ed, esp to sth harmful: a 'drug ∿. **ad·dic·tion** /ə'dɪkʃn/ n [U] being ∿ed; [C] instance of this. **ad·dic·tive** /ə'dɪktɪv/ adj causing ∿ion: ∿ive drugs.

ad·di·tion /ə'dɪʃn/ n 1 [U] process of adding: The sign + stands for ∿. **in** ∿ **(to),** as well (as). 2 [C] sth added or joined: They've just had an ∿ to the family, another child. He will be a useful ∿ to the staff of the school, a useful new teacher. ∿**al** /-ʃənl/ adj extra; added: ∿al charges. ∿**ally** /-ʃənəlɪ/ adv

ad·di·tive /'ædɪtɪv/ n [C] substance added in small amounts for a special purpose: food ∿s, eg to add colour; petrol ∿s, eg to reduce engine knocking.

addle /'ædl/ adj (usu in compounds) confused; muddled. '∿**-brained,** '∿**-pated** /-peɪtɪd/ adjj having confused ideas. '∿**-head** n person with confused ideas. □ vt, vi 1 [VP6A] confuse: ∿ one's head/brains. 2 [VP2A] (of eggs) become rotten: ∿d eggs.

ad·dress[1] /ə'dres US: 'ædres/ n 1 details of where a person may be found and where letters, etc may be delivered: What's your home/business ∿? Let me know if you change your ∿. 2 speech or talk (to an audience). ,**public** '∿ **system,** system using microphones, loudspeakers, etc for amplifying speeches. 3 [U] (old use) manner or behaviour, esp in conversation: a man of pleasing ∿. 4 [U] **form of** ∿, style of written or spoken communication: polite forms of ∿. 5 (pl) (old use) polite attentions or courtship: pay one's ∿es to a lady, seek to win her hand in marriage; reject sb's ∿es, show that one does not welcome sb's wishes to be friendly. ∿**ee** /,ædre'si:/ n person to whom sth is ∿ed(2). A∿o·**graph** /ə'dresəʊɡrɑ:f US: -ɡræf/ n (P) machine for printing ∿es(1) on circulars, etc.

ad·dress[2] /ə'dres/ vt 1 [VP6A,16B] make a speech to; speak to, using a title: Mr Green will now ∿ the meeting. Don't ∿ me as 'Colonel'; I'm only a major. 2 [VP6A] write a destination on (with the name of the person to whom sth is to be delivered): The letter was wrongly ∿ed. 3 [VP14] ∿ **sth to,** send (a remark, complaint, etc) to: Please ∿ all enquiries to this office. Please ∿ complaints to the manager, not to me. 4 [VP14] ∿ **oneself to,** (formal) work at, apply oneself to, be busy with (a task, etc): It's time we ∿ed ourselves to the business in hand, time we got busy with the business we are here for.

ad·duce /ə'dju:s US: ə'du:s/ vt [VP6A] (formal) put forward (as proof, as an example): ∿ reasons/ proof/authority.

ad·en·oids /'ædɪnɔɪdz US: -dən-/ n pl (anat) soft, sponge-like growth between the back of the nose and the throat, in some cases making breathing and speech difficult: have one's ∿ out, ie by a surgical operation. She's got ∿, (colloq) is suffering from inflammation of the ∿. ⇨ the illus at head. **ad·en·oidal** /,ædɪ'nɔɪdl/ adj of the ∿: an adenoidal youth, one suffering from diseased ∿.

adept /'ædept/ adj expert, skilled (in sth; at or in doing sth). □ n expert: I'm not an ∿ in photo-

graphy.

ad·equate /'ædɪkwət/ adj satisfactory; sufficient; satisfying a requirement: £10 a week is not ∿ to support a family. Are you getting an ∿ wage for the work you're doing? ∿**ly** adv **ad·equacy** /'ædɪkwəsɪ/ n [U] state of being ∿: He often doubts his adequacy as a husband and father.

ad·here /əd'hɪə(r)/ vi [VP2A,3A] ∿ **(to),** (formal) 1 stick fast (to): Glue and paste are used to make one surface ∿ to another. 2 remain faithful (to); support firmly: ∿ to one's plans/to an opinion/to a political party/to a promise. We decided to ∿ to the programme. (Cf depart from). **ad·her·ence** /-rəns/ n: adherence to a plan.

ad·her·ent /əd'hɪərənt/ n supporter (of a party, etc, but not necessarily a member): The proposal is gaining more and more ∿s.

ad·hesion /əd'hi:ʒn/ n 1 [U] adhering; being or becoming attached or united. 2 [U] support: give one's ∿ to a plan. 3 [U] (path) joining together of tissues in the body, eg after an injury; [C] instance of this: painful ∿s resulting from a wound that did not heal.

ad·hes·ive /əd'hi:sɪv/ adj having the property of sticking: ∿ tape/plaster. □ n [C,U] ∿ substance, eg gum.

ad hoc /,æd 'hɒk/ adj,adv (Lat) arranged for a particular purpose; not pre-arranged; informal: an ∿ committee meeting.

adieu /ə'dju: US: ə'du:/ n, int (pl -s or -x /ə'dju:z US: ə'du:z/) (F) goodbye: bid sb ∿; make one's ∿/∿s, say goodbye.

ad in·fi·nitum /,æd ,ɪnfɪ'naɪtəm/ adv (Lat) without limit; for ever.

ad inter·im /,æd 'ɪntərɪm/ (Lat) in the meantime.

adi·pose /'ædɪpəʊs/ adj of animal fat; fatty: ∿ tissue.

ad·jac·ent /ə'dʒeɪsnt/ adj next (to), lying near (to) but not necessarily touching: ∿ rooms; ∿ angles, ⇨ the illus at angle. The house ∿ to the church is the vicarage.

ad·jec·tive /'ædʒɪktɪv/ n (gram) word that names a quality, or that defines or limits a noun. **ad·jec·ti·val** /,ædʒɪk'taɪvl/ adj of or like an ∿: an adjectival phrase/clause.

ad·join /ə'dʒɔɪn/ vt,vi [VP6A,2A] ∿ **(to),** be next or nearest to: The playing-field ∿s the school. The two houses ∿. ∿**-ing** part adj: ∿ing bedrooms.

ad·journ /ə'dʒɜ:n/ vt,vi 1 [VP6A] break off, eg proceedings of a meeting, etc for a time: The meeting was ∿ed for a week/until the following week. 2 [VP2C] (of a meeting, etc) be broken off in this way: The meeting ∿ed at five o'clock. 3 [VP2A,C] (colloq, of persons who have met together) (a) break off proceedings and separate. (b) go to another place: When dinner was over they ∿ed to the sitting-room. ∿**-ment** n∿ing or being ∿ed.

ad·judge /ə'dʒʌdʒ/ vt 1 [VP25,9] decide officially, by law: ∿ sb (to be) guilty; ∿ that a man is insane. 2 [VP14] award: ∿ land and property to sb; ∿ a prize/legal damages to sb.

ad·ju·di·cate /ə'dʒu:dɪkeɪt/ vt,vi 1 [VP6A,14] (of a judge or court) give a judgement or decision upon: ∿ a claim for damages. 2 [VP2A,3A] sit in judgement in order to decide: ∿ (up)on a question. 3 [VP25] declare (sb to be): ∿ sb bankrupt. **ad·ju·di·ca·tion** /ə,dʒu:dɪ'keɪʃn/ n **ad·ju·di·ca·tor** /-tə(r)/ n judge; member of a jury, eg in a musical competition.

ad·junct /'ædʒʌŋkt/ n 1 sth extra but subordinate. 2

(gram) word(s) or phrase added to qualify or define another word in a sentence.

ad·jure /ə'dʒʊə(r)/ vt [VP17A] (formal) ask (sb) earnestly or solemnly; require (sb) to do sth as though on oath or under penalty: *I ~ you to tell the truth.* **ad·jur·ation** /ˌædʒʊə'reɪʃn/ n [U] adjuring; [C] earnest or solemn request.

ad·just /ə'dʒʌst/ vt [VP6A,14] ~ **oneself/sth (to)**, set right; put in order; regulate; make suitable or convenient for use: *The body ~s itself to changes in temperature. You can't see well through a telescope unless it is ~ed correctly to your sight. She will have to ~ herself to new conditions,* change her ways of living, thinking, etc. *Please do not ~ your sets,* warning on a TV screen that the controls need not be changed. *You should ~ your expenditure to your income.* ,well-'~ed, (psych) in harmonious relations with other persons: *a well ~ed child.* ~·**able** /-əbl/ adj that can be ~ed. ~·**er** n (comm) person from an insurance company whose business it is to settle amounts due when claims are made, eg for loss. ~·**ment** n 1 [U] ~ing; settling of, eg insurance, claims; [C] act of ~ing. 2 [C] means of ~ing sth; part of an apparatus for ~ing sth.

ad·ju·tant /'ædʒʊtənt/ n 1 (mil) army officer responsible for general administration and discipline in a battalion. 2 (also ~ **bird**) large Indian stork.

ad lib /ˌæd 'lɪb/ adv (abbr of *ad libitum*) (colloq) freely; without restraint. □ **ad-lib** vi (-bb-) [VP2A] (colloq) improvise, eg by making additions to one's part in a play. □ *attrib adj* made by ~bing: ~ *comments.*

ad libitum /ˌæd 'lɪbɪtəm/ adv (Lat; abbr *ad lib*) (music) (to be) performed with omissions as desired. ⇨ **obbligato**(2).

ad-man /'æd mæn/ n (colloq) man who composes commercial advertisements.

ad·mass /'ædmæs/ n [U] that part of the public easily influenced by the mass media. ⇨ **media**.

ad·min·is·ter /əd'mɪnɪstə(r)/ vt, vi 1 [VP6A] control, manage, look after business affairs; a household, etc: ~ *a country,* govern it. 2 [VP6A,14] apply; put into operation; hand out; give: ~ *the law;* ~ *punishment to sb;* ~ *relief/help to people who are suffering from floods;* ~ *a severe blow to the enemy;* ~ *justice,* do the work of a judge. 3 [VP6A,14] cause to take: ~ *the last sacraments,* ie to a dying man. *The oath was ~ed to him.* 4 ~ **to,** ⇨ **minister**(2).

ad·min·is·tra·tion /əd,mɪnɪ'streɪʃn/ n 1 [U] management of affairs, etc, esp public affairs, government policy, etc. 2 [C] (often A~) (esp US) that part of the Government which manages public affairs: *Successive A~s failed to solve the country's problems.* 3 [U] the administering of justice, an oath, a sacrament, relief, a remedy, a punishment. ⇨ **ministration**.

ad·min·is·tra·tive /əd'mɪnɪstrətɪv US: -streɪtɪv/ adj of the management of affairs; of an administration(2): *an ~ post; lacking in ~ ability.*

ad·min·is·tra·tor /əd'mɪnɪstreɪtə(r)/ n person who administers; person with ability to organize; (legal) person officially appointed to manage the property of others, to take charge of an estate, etc.

ad·mir·able /'ædmərəbl/ adj excellent; causing admiration. **ad·mir·ably** /-əblɪ/ adv

ad·miral /'ædmərəl/ n officer in command of a country's warships, or of a fleet or squadron; naval rank above vice-~ and below (GB) ~ of the fleet

or (US) fleet ~. ~·ty /'ædmərəltɪ/ n 1 office of ~. 2 that branch of Government which controls the Navy. **the A~ty,** (GB) headquarters of the naval administration. ,**Court of 'A~ty,** court for deciding law questions concerning shipping.

ad·mir·ation /ˌædmə'reɪʃn/ n [U] 1 feeling of pleasure, satisfaction, respect (or, formerly) wonder: *She speaks English so well that her friends are filled with ~. Everyone cried out in ~. We were lost in ~ of the scenery. My ~ for your skill is great.* 2 (*sing* with *indef art*) object that arouses ~.

ad·mire /əd'maɪə(r)/ vt [VP6A] 1 look at with pleasure or satisfaction; have a high regard for: *Come and ~ the view! Visitors to Britain usually ~ our policemen.* 2 express admiration of: *Don't forget to ~ the baby.* **ad·mirer** n person who ~s; man who finds a woman attractive: *Mary and her many ~s.* **ad·mir·ing** adj showing or feeling admiration: *admiring glances; an admiring crowd.* **ad·mir·ing·ly** adv

ad·miss·ible /əd'mɪsəbl/ adj 1 (legal) that can be allowed as judicial proof: ~ *evidence.* 2 (formal) that can be allowed or considered. **ad·missi·bil·ity** /əd,mɪsə'bɪlətɪ/ n [U].

ad·mis·sion /əd'mɪʃn/ n 1 [U] admitting, being admitted, to a society, a school, a building such as a theatre, a museum, etc; fee, charge or condition for this: *A~ to the school is by examination only. Price of ~, 10p. A~ free.* 2 [C] statement admitting sth; confession or acknowledgement: *make an ~ of guilt; an ~ that one has done wrong. To resign now would be an ~ of failure.* **by/on his own ~,** as he himself admitted.

ad·mit /əd'mɪt/ vt, vi (-tt-) 1 [VP6A,14] ~ **sb (into/in),** allow (sb or sth) to enter; let in: *The servant opened the door and ~ted me (into the house). Only one hundred boys are ~ted to the school each year. I ordered that he was not to be ~ted. Children not ~ted. The windows are small and do not ~ enough light and air.* 2 [VP6A] (of enclosed spaces) have room enough for: *The harbour ~s large liners and cargo boats. The theatre is small and ~s only 300 people.* 3 [VP6A] acknowledge, confess, accept, as true or valid: ~ *a claim/an assumption.* 4 [VP6A,C,9,14,25] acknowledge; confess: *The accused man ~ted his guilt. I ~ my mistake/that I was mistaken. He ~ted having done wrong. You must ~ the task to be difficult* (more usu. *that the task is difficult*). *It is generally ~ted that...,* Most people acknowledge or agree that.... 5 [VP3A] ~ **of,** (formal) leave room for: *The words ~ of* (= can have) *no other meaning. It ~s of no excuse,* There can be no excuse for it. ~ **to,** make an acknowledgement; confess: *I must ~ to feeling ashamed of my conduct.* ~·**ted·ly** /əd'mɪtɪdlɪ/ adv 1 without denial; by general admission: *He is ~tedly an atheist.* 2 (usu in initial position) = 'I acknowledge, agree': *A~tedly I've never actually been there.*

ad·mit·tance /əd'mɪtns/ n [U] act of admitting, being admitted (esp to a place that is not public); right of entry: *I called at his house but was refused ~,* was not allowed to enter. *No ~ except on business.*

ad·mix /æd'mɪks/ vt, vi [VP6A,2A] mix; become mixed; add as an ingredient.

ad·mix·ture /æd'mɪkstʃə(r)/ n (formal) = mixture.

ad·mon·ish /əd'mɒnɪʃ/ vt [VP6A,14] (formal) give a mild warning or a gentle reproof to: *The teacher ~ed the boys for being lazy/~ed them against* *smoking.* **ad·mo·ni·tion** /ˌædməˈnɪʃn/ *n* [U] ~ing, warning; [C] instance of this. **ad·moni·tory** /ədˈmɒnɪtrɪ *US:* -tɔːrɪ/ *adj* containing admonition: *an admonitory letter.*

ad nauseam /ˌæd ˈnɔːzɪæm/ *adv* (Lat) to the point of being disgusted; (colloq) to a degree so as to cause annoyance, eg because of length or repetition.

ado /əˈduː/ *n* [U] (archaic) fuss; trouble and excitement: *Without more/much/further ado, he signed the agreement.*

adobe /əˈdəʊbɪ/ *n* [U] sun-dried brick (not fired in a kiln), of clay and straw: (attrib) *an ~ house.*

adobe houses

ado·les·cence /ˌædəˈlesns/ *n* [U] period of life between childhood and maturity; growth during this period. **ado·les·cent** /-ˈlesnt/ *adj*, *n* (person) growing up from childhood (age 12 or 13 to 18).

adopt /əˈdɒpt/ *vt* [VP6A] **1** take (sb) into one's family as a relation, esp as a son or daughter, with legal guardianship: *As they had no children of their own, they ~ed an orphan.* ⇨ foster. **2** take, eg an idea or custom, and use: *European dress has been ~ed by people in many parts of the world.* **3** accept, eg a report or recommendation: *Congress ~ed the new measures.* **adop·tion** /əˈdɒpʃn/ *n* ~ing or being ~ed: *the country of his ~ion.* **adop·tive** *adj* taken by ~ion: *his ~ive parents.*

adore /əˈdɔː(r)/ *vt* **1** [VP6A] worship (God); love deeply and respect highly. **2** [VP6A,C] (colloq; not in progressive tenses) like very much: *The baby ~s being tickled.* **ador·able** /-əbl/ *adj* lovable; delightful. **ador·ably** /-əblɪ/ *adv* **ador·ation** /ˌædəˈreɪʃn/ *n* [U] worship; love: *his adoration for Jane.* **adorer** *n* person who ~s (sb). **ador·ing** *adj* showing love: *adoring looks.* **ador·ing·ly** *adv*

adorn /əˈdɔːn/ *vt* [VP6A,14] add beauty or ornament(s) to; decorate (oneself *with* jewels, etc); add distinction to. **~·ment** *n* [U] ~ing; [C] sth used for ~ing; ornament; decoration.

ad·renal /əˈdriːnl/ *adj* (anat) of or near the kidneys: *~ glands.*

ad·ren·alin /əˈdrenəlɪn/ *n* [U] (med) hormones secreted by the adrenal glands, prepared as a substance used in the treatment of heart failure, etc.

adrift /əˈdrɪft/ *adv*, *pred adj* (of ships and boats) afloat, not under control and driven by wind and water; loose: *cut a boat ~ from its moorings;* (fig) at the mercy of circumstances: *turn sb ~,* send him away, eg from home, without money or means of livelihood.

adroit /əˈdrɔɪt/ *adj* ~ *(at/in),* clever; skilful; ingenious or resourceful when dealing with problems. **~·ly** *adv* **~·ness** *n*

adu·la·tion /ˌædjʊˈleɪʃn *US:* -dʒʊˈl-/ *n* [U] (the giving of) excessive praise or respect, esp to win favour.

adult /ˈædʌlt/ *adj* grown to full size or strength; (of

persons) intellectually and emotionally mature. □ *n* person or animal grown to full size and strength; (legal) person old enough to vote, marry, etc: *education for ~s; ~ education.* **~·hood** /-hʊd/ *n* the state of being ~.

adul·ter·ate /əˈdʌltəreɪt/ *vt* [VP6A,14] make impure, make poorer in quality, by adding sth of less value: *~d milk,* milk with water added. **adul·ter·ant** /əˈdʌltərənt/ *n* sth used for adulterating. **adul·ter·ation** /əˌdʌltəˈreɪʃn/ *n*

adul·tery /əˈdʌltərɪ/ *n* [U] voluntary sexual intercourse of a married person with sb who is not the person to whom he or she is married; [C] (*pl* -ries) instance of this. **adul·terer** /əˈdʌltərə(r)/ *n* man who commits ~. **adul·ter·ess** /əˈdʌltərɪs/ *n* woman who commits ~. **adul·ter·ous** /əˈdʌltərəs/ *adj* of ~.

ad·um·brate /ˈædʌmbreɪt/ *vt* [VP6A] (formal) indicate vaguely or briefly; foreshadow (a coming event).

ad valorem /ˌæd vəˈlɔːrəm/ *adv* (Lat) (of taxes) in proportion to the estimated value of the goods.

ad·vance¹ /ədˈvɑːns *US:* -ˈvæns/ *n* **1** [U] forward movement; progress; [C] instance of this: *With the ~ of old age, he could no longer do the work well. Science has made great ~s during the last fifty years. The country's industrial ~ has been remarkable. Has there been an ~ in civilization during the 20th century? in ~ (of),* before(hand): *Send your luggage in ~,* before you yourself leave. *It's unwise to spend your income in ~. Galileo's ideas were (well) in ~ of the age in which he lived.* **2** (attrib use) in ~: *an ~ copy of a new book,* one supplied before publication; *an ~ party,* party, eg of explorers, soldiers, sent in ~; *have ~ notice,* eg of sb's arrival. **3** [C] money paid before it is due, or for work only partially completed. *~ 'booking,* reservation (of a room in a hotel, a seat in a theatre, etc) in ~ of the time when it is needed.

ad·vance² /ədˈvɑːns *US:* -ˈvæns/ *vi,vt* **1** [VP2A,B,3A] come or go forward: *Our troops have ~d two miles. He ~d (up) on me in a threatening manner. Has civilization ~d during this century? The forces of the enemy ~d against us.* **2** [VP2A] (of costs, values, prices) rise: *Stock market prices/Property values continue to ~.* **3** [VP6A,14] move, put or help forward: *The date of the meeting was ~d from the 10th to the 3rd June.* ⇨ postpone. *May I ~ my opinion on the matter? He worked so well that he was soon ~d (= promoted) to the position of manager. Such behaviour is not likely to ~ your interests.* **4** [VP6A] increase, raise (prices); (= colloq, *put up*): *The shopkeepers ~d their prices.* **5** [VP12A,13A] pay (money) before the due date: *He asked his employer to ~ him a month's salary. The banks often ~ money to farmers for seed and fertilizer.* **ad·vanced** *part adj* far on in life or progress, etc: *~d in years,* very old; *~d courses of study. The professor is engaged in ~d studies.* ⇨ elementary. *He has ~d ideas,* ideas that are new and not generally accepted. *~d level* (abbr **A level**) (of examinations of the General Certificate of Education), securing admission, in GB, to a college or university. **~·ment** *n* [U] promotion; preferment; improvement: *The aim of a university should be the ~ment of learning.*

ad·van·tage /ədˈvɑːntɪdʒ *US:* -ˈvæn-/ *n* **1** [C] sth useful or helpful, sth likely to bring success, esp in competition: *the ~s of a good education. Living in a big town has many ~s, such as good schools,* *libraries and theatres.* **have/gain/win an** ~ **(over); give sb an** ~ **(over),** (have, give, etc) a better position or opportunity: *Tom's university education gave him an* ~ *over boys who had not been to a university.* **have the** ~ **of sb,** know sb or sth that he does not know. **2** [U] benefit; profit: *He gained little* ~ *from his visit to London.* **take** ~ **of sb,** deceive him, play a trick on him. **take (full)** ~ **of sth,** use it profitably, for one's own benefit: *He always takes full* ~ *of the mistakes made by his rivals.* **to** ~, in a way that enables sth to be seen, used, etc in the best way: *The painting is seen to better* ~ *from a distance. You should lay out your money* (= decide how to spend or invest it) *to the best* ~. **be/prove to sb's** ~, be profitable or helpful to him. **turn sth to** ~, make the most of it; use it profitably. **3** (tennis) the first point scored after deuce. □ *vt* [VP6A] benefit.

ad·van·tage·ous /ˌædvən'teɪdʒəs/ *adj* profitable; helpful. ~**·ly** *adv*

ad·vent /'ædvənt/ *n* **1** (usu *sing* with *def art*) coming or arrival (of an important development, season, etc): *Since the* ~ *of atomic power, there have been great changes in industry.* **2 A**~, (eccles) the coming of Christ; the season (with four Sundays) before Christmas Day. **3** the second coming of Christ at the Last Judgement. **Ad·vent·ist** /'ædvəntɪst *US:* əd'ventɪst/ *n* person who believes that Christ's second coming and the end of the world are near.

ad·ven·ti·tious /ˌædven'tɪʃəs/ *adj* (formal) coming by chance; accidental: ~ *aid.*

ad·ven·ture /əd'ventʃə(r)/ *n* **1** [C] strange or unusual happening, esp an exciting or dangerous journey or activity: *A flight in an aeroplane used to be quite an* ~. *The explorer told the boys about his* ~*s in the Arctic.* ~ **playground,** playground with large wooden, metal, etc materials and structures for children to play with, in or on. **2** [U] risk; danger, eg in travel and exploration: *fond of* ~; *a story of* ~; *Robin Hood lived a life of* ~. □ *vt* (= *venture,* the usu word). **ad·ven·turer** *n* **1** person who seeks ~. **2** person who is ready to make a profit for himself by risky or unscrupulous methods. **ad·ven·tur·ess** /-ɪs/ *n* woman ~r, esp one who is ready to use guile to obtain benefits. **ad·ven·tur·ous** /-əs/ *adj* **1** fond of, eager for, ~s. **2** full of danger and excitement: *an adventurous voyage.* ~**·some** /-səm/ *adj* (rare or liter) = adventurous.

ad·verb /'ædvɜːb/ *n* (gram) word that answers questions with *how, when, where* and modifies *vv, adjj* and other *advv,* etc, eg *soon, here, well, quickly.* **ad·verb·ial** /æd'vɜːbɪəl/ *adj* of the nature of an ~. □ *n* ~ or ~ial phrase. **ad·verbi·ally** /æd'vɜːbɪəlɪ/ *adv*

ad·ver·sary /'ædvəsərɪ *US:* -serɪ/ *n* (*pl* -ries) enemy; opponent (in any kind of contest).

ad·verse /'ædvɜːs/ *adj* unfavourable; contrary or hostile (*to*): ~ *weather conditions;* ~ *winds,* eg for a sailing-ship; *developments* ~ *to our interests.* ~**·ly** *adv*

ad·ver·sity /əd'vɜːsətɪ/ *n* (*pl* -ties). **1** [U] condition of adverse fortune; trouble: *be patient/cheerful in* ~. *A brave man smiles in the face of* ~. **2** [C] misfortune; affliction.

ad·vert[1] /əd'vɜːt/ *vi* [VP3A] (formal) ~ *to,* refer to (in speech or writing): ~ *to a problem.*

ad·vert[2] /'ædvɜːt/ *n* (GB colloq abbr for) advertisement(2).

ad·ver·tise /'ædvətaɪz/ *vt, vi* [VP6A,2A,3A] make known to people (by printing notices in newspapers, etc or by other means, eg TV): ~ *one's goods;* ~ *in all the newspapers;* ~ *for an assistant in the local newspapers,* announce that one wishes to engage an assistant. **ad·ver·tiser** *n* person who ~s. ~**·ment** /əd'vɜːtɪsmənt *US:* ˌædvər'taɪzmənt/ *n* **1** [U] advertising: (attrib) *the* ~*ment manager,* eg of a newspaper. *A* ~*ment helps to sell goods.* **2** [C] public announcement (in the press, TV, etc): *If you want to sell your piano, put an* ~ *in the newspaper.* ⇨ commercial *n.*

ad·vice /əd'vaɪs/ *n* **1** [U] (informed) opinion about what to do, how to behave: *You won't get well unless you follow your doctor's* ~. *If you take my* ~ *and study hard, you'll pass the examination. You should take legal* ~, consult a lawyer. **act on sb's** ~, do what he suggests. **(give sb) a piece/bit/ word/few words of** ~, (give) an opinion about what to do, etc. **2** [C] (comm) (usu *pl*) news from a distance, esp commercial: ~*s from our Tokyo branch.* '~**-note, letter of** ~, (comm) formal notice of delivery of goods, a business call, etc.

ad·vis·able /əd'vaɪzəbl/ *adj* wise; sensible; to be advised or recommended: *Do you think it* ~ *to wait?* **ad·visa·bil·ity** /əd,vaɪzə'bɪlətɪ/ *n* [U].

ad·vise /əd'vaɪz/ *vt, vi* **1** [VP6A,C,17,20,21,14] give advice to; recommend: *The doctor* ~*d a complete rest. What do you* ~ *me to do? Please* ~ *me whether I should accept the offer. We* ~*d an early start/their starting early/them to start early. Her father* ~*d her against marrying in haste. Who is the best man to* ~ *me on this question?* **2** [VP6A,21,14] (comm) inform; notify: *Please* ~ *us when the goods are dispatched/* ~ *us of the dispatch of the goods.* **3** [VP3A] ~ **with (sb),** (old use) consult; take counsel with. **ad·viser** *n* person who gives advice, esp one who is habitually consulted: ~*r to the Government.* **ad·vised** *adj* (old use) considered; carefully thought out; deliberate. **ill** ~*d,* unwise; injudicious. **well** ~*d,* wise; judicious. **ad·vis·ed·ly** /əd'vaɪzɪdlɪ/ *adv* after careful thought. **ad·vis·ory** /əd'vaɪzərɪ/ *adj* of advice; having the power to ~: *an advisory committee/ council/panel.*

ad·vo·cate /'ædvəkət/ *n* **1** person who speaks in favour of sb or sth (esp a cause): *an* ~ *of equal pay for men and women.* **2** (legal) person who does this professionally in a court of law in Scotland (= *barrister* in England and Wales): **the Faculty of A**~**s,** the Scots Bar. **Lord A**~, principal law officer in Scotland. □ *vt* /'ædvəkeɪt/ [VP6A,C] support; speak publicly in support of: *Do you* ~ *keeping all children at school till the age of sixteen?* **ad·vo·cacy** /'ædvəkəsɪ/ *n* [U] pleading in support (*of* a cause or sb).

adze, adz /ædz/ *n* carpenter's tool (with a blade at right angles to the handle) for cutting or shaping wood.

aegis, egis /'iːdʒɪs/ *n* protection; sponsorship. **under the** ~ **of,** with the patronage or support of.

aeon, eon /'iːən/ *n* [C] period of time too long to be measured.

aer·ate /'eəreɪt/ *vt* [VP6A] charge (a liquid) with air or gas; expose to the chemical purifying action of air: ~ *the soil by digging. Blood is* ~*d in the lungs.* **aer·ation** /eə'reɪʃn/ *n*

aer·ial /'eərɪəl/ *adj* **1** existing in, moving through, the air: *an* ~ *railway/ropeway,* a system of overhead suspension for transport. **2** (archaic) of or like air; immaterial. □ *n* that part of a radio or TV system which receives or sends out signals, usu a wire or rod, or number of wires or rods (= US *antenna*).

aerie, aery, eyrie, eyry /'eərɪ/ *n* eagle's nest; nest of other birds of prey which are built high up among rocks; eagle's brood.

aero·bat·ics /ˌeərəʊ'bætɪks/ *n* (*sing v*) [U] the performance of acrobatic feats by airmen, eg flying upside down.

aero·drome /'eərədrəʊm/ *n* (= US *airdrome*) (dated) ground for the arrival and departure and servicing of aircraft, with hangars, workshops, etc (*airfield* and *airport* are the more usu words).

aero·dy·nam·ics /ˌeərəʊdaɪ'næmɪks/ *n pl* (*sing v*) [U] science dealing with the flow of air and the motion of aircraft, bullets, etc through air.

aero·naut /'eərənɔ:t/ *n* person who pilots or travels in a balloon, airship or other aircraft.

aero·naut·ics /ˌeərə'nɔ:tɪks/ *n* (*sing v*) [U] science and practice of aviation (the more usu word).

aero·plane /'eərəpleɪn/ *n* (US = *airplane*) heavier-than-air flying machine with one or more engines. ⇨ *aircraft*, *air-liner* at air¹(7).

aero·sol /'eərəsɒl *US*: -sɔ:l/ *n* [U] dispersion of fine solid or liquid particles, eg of scent, paint, insecticide, detergent, released (in a mist) by pressure from a container with compressed gas from a valve; [C] (P) the container itself.

aero·space /'eərəʊspeɪs/ *n* the earth's atmosphere and the space beyond, considered as area available to air- or space-craft: *the* ∼ *industry*.

aery /'eərɪ/ *n* ⇨ aerie.

aer·tex /'eəteks/ *n* (P) kind of loosely woven textile material (as used for underwear).

aes·thete, es·thete /'i:sθi:t *US*: 'esθi:t/ *n* person who has or claims to have great love of and understanding of what is beautiful, esp in the arts.

aes·thetic, es·thetic /i:s'θetɪk *US*: es-/ *adj* of the appreciation of the beautiful, esp in the arts; (of persons) having such appreciation: ∼ *standards*. □ *n* [U] particular set of ∼ principles: *the* ∼ *to which he remained faithful*. **aes·thet·ical, es·thet·ical** /-kl/ *adj* = aesthetic. **aes·thet·ically** /-klɪ/ *adv* **aes·thet·ics, es·thet·ics** *n* (*sing v*) [U] branch of philosophy which tries to make clear the laws and principles of beauty (contrasted with morality and utility).

aether /'i:θə(r)/ *n* ⇨ ether.

aeti·ol·ogy /ˌi:tɪ'ɒlədʒɪ/ ⇨ etiology.

afar /ə'fɑ:(r)/ *adv* (poet) far off or away. *from* ∼, from a distance.

af·fable /'æfəbl/ *adj* polite and friendly; pleasant and easy to talk to: ∼ *to everybody*; *an* ∼ *reply*. **af·fably** /-əblɪ/ *adv* **affa·bil·ity** /ˌæfə'bɪlətɪ/ *n* quality of being ∼ (*to* or *towards*).

af·fair /ə'feə(r)/ *n* [C] **1** concern; sth (to be) done; business: *That's my* ∼, *not yours*. **2** (*pl*) business of any kind; day-to-day concerns of organization, etc: *A prime minister is kept busy with* ∼*s of state*, the task of government. *When he asked me how much I earned, I told him to mind his own* ∼*s*, not to ask questions about my business, etc. *We can't afford a holiday in the present state of* ∼*s*, while things remain as they are now. **Secretary of State for Foreign/Home/Welsh, etc A**∼**s,** titles of Government Ministers in GB. **3 have an** ∼ **(with sb),** have an emotional (and sexual) relationship with sb to whom one is not married: *The doctor, they say, is having an* ∼ *with the rector's wife.* ∼

of honour, duel. **4** (colloq) occurrence; event; object: *The railway accident was a terrible* ∼. *Her hat was a wonderful* ∼. *What a ramshackle* ∼ *your old car is!*

af·fect¹ /ə'fekt/ *vt* [VP6A] **1** have an influence or impression on; act on: *The climate* ∼*ed his health,* injured it. *Some plants are quickly* ∼*ed by cold. Will the changes in taxation* ∼ *you personally,* Will you have to pay more (or less) in taxes? *The rise in the price of bread will* ∼ *us all.* **2** move the feelings of: *He was much* ∼*ed by the sad news. His death* ∼*ed us deeply.* **3** (of diseases) attack; cause a particular condition in: *The left lung is* ∼*ed, eg by cancer, tuberculosis.* **4 well/ill** ∼**ed (towards),** well/ill disposed (the more usu word) or inclined (towards). ∼**ing** *adj* moving or touching (the feelings): *an* ∼*ing sight.* ∼**ing·ly** *adv* tenderly; pathetically.

af·fect² /ə'fekt/ *vt* **1** [VP6A,7A] pretend to have or feel (ignorance, indifference); pretend (to do, etc): *She* ∼*s an American accent. He* ∼*ed not to hear me.* **2** [VP6A] have a liking for and use (esp for ostentation): *He* ∼*s long and learned words,* uses them instead of short and simple words. *She* ∼*s bright colours,* wears brightly coloured clothes, etc. ∼**ed** *adj* pretended; not natural or genuine: *an* ∼*ed politeness;* ∼*ed manners; with an* ∼*ed cheerfulness; written in an* ∼*ed style,* showing a liking for an artificial style.

af·fec·ta·tion /ˌæfek'teɪʃn/ *n* **1** [U] behaviour that is not natural or genuine: *Keep clear of all* ∼, Do not behave unnaturally; [C] instance of this: *Her little* ∼*s annoyed me.* **2** [C] pretence (made on purpose, for effect): *an* ∼ *of interest/indifference/ ignorance.*

af·fec·tion /ə'fekʃn/ *n* **1** [U] kindly feeling; love: *Every mother has* ∼ *for/feels* ∼ *toward her children. He is held in great* ∼, is much loved. **2** [U or *pl*] **gain/win sb's** ∼(**s**), win the love of. **3** [C] (old use) disease; unhealthy condition: *an* ∼ *of the throat.*

af·fec·tion·ate /ə'fekʃənət/ *adj* loving; fond; showing love (*to* sb): *an* ∼ *wife;* ∼ *looks.* ∼**ly** *adv* **Yours** ∼**ly,** used at the close of a letter, eg from a man to his sister.

af·fi·ance /ə'faɪəns/ *vt* [VP6A] (usu passive; liter or old use) promise in marriage: *be* ∼*d to* (sb), be engaged to marry him/her.

af·fi·da·vit /ˌæfɪ'deɪvɪt/ *n* (legal) written statement, made on oath, (to be) used as legal proof or evidence: *swear/make/take an* ∼.

af·fili·ate /ə'fɪlɪeɪt/ *vt,vi* [VP6A,14,2A] ∼ **(to/ with),** (of a society or institution, or a member) enter into association: *The College is* ∼*d to the University. Is the Mineworkers' Union* ∼*d with the TUC?*

af·fili·ation /əˌfɪlɪ'eɪʃn/ *n* [U] affiliating or being affiliated; [C] connection made by affiliating. '∼ **order,** (GB, legal) order made by a magistrate, determining the paternity of an illegitimate child and requiring the father to contribute towards its support.

af·fin·ity /ə'fɪnətɪ/ *n* (*pl* -ties) ∼ **(between/to/ for), 1** [C] close connection, structural resemblance (between animals and plants, languages, etc) (or of one thing to/with another). **2** [U] relationship; [C] relation (by marriage); similarity of character suggesting relationship. **3** [C] strong liking or attraction: *She feels a strong* ∼ *to/for him.* **4** chemical or physical attraction: *the* ∼ *of common salt for wat-*

er.

af·firm /ə'fɜːm/ *vt,vi* **1** [VP6A,9,14] declare positively: ~ *the truth of a statement/*~ *that it is true;* ~ *to sb that....* ⇨ **deny. 2** [VP2A] (legal) (of a person who has conscientious objections to swearing on the Bible) declare solemnly but not on oath. ~·**ation** /ˌæfə'meɪʃn/ *n* **1** [U] ~ing. **2** [C] sth ~ed; (legal) declaration made by ~ing(2). ~·**ative** /ə'fɜːmətɪv/ *adj n* (answering) 'yes': *an* ~*ative answer. The answer is in the* ~*ative,* is 'Yes'. ⇨ negative(1).

af·fix¹ /ə'fɪks/ *vt* [VP6A,14] ~ *sth (to),* (formal) fix; fasten; attach: ~ *a seal/stamp to a document;* add in writing: ~ *your signature to an agreement.*

af·fix² /'æfɪks/ *n* suffix or prefix, eg *-ly, -able, un-, co-.* ⇨ App 3.

af·fla·tus /ə'fleɪtəs/ *n* [U] (formal) divine revelation; inspiration.

af·flict /ə'flɪkt/ *vt* [VP6A,14] cause bodily or mental trouble to: ~ed *with rheumatism; feel much* ~ed *at/by the news.*

af·flic·tion /ə'flɪkʃn/ *n* **1** [U] suffering; distress: *help people in* ~. **2** [C] cause or occasion of suffering: *the* ~s *of old age,* eg deafness, blindness.

af·flu·ence /'æfluəns/ *n* [U] wealth; abundance: *living in* ~; *rise to* ~, become wealthy.

af·flu·ent¹ /'æfluənt/ *adj* wealthy; abundant: *in* ~ *circumstances.* **the** ~ **society,** society which is prosperous and whose members are concerned with material improvement.

af·flu·ent² /'æfluənt/ *n* [C] stream flowing into a larger one (*tributary* is the usu word).

af·ford /ə'fɔːd/ *vt* **1** [VP6A,7] (usu with *can/could, be able to*) spare or find enough time or money for: *We can't* ~ *a holiday/can't* ~ *to go away this summer. Are you able to* ~ *the time for a holiday?* **2** [VP7] (with *can/could*) run a risk by doing sth: *I can't* ~ *to neglect my work. She couldn't* ~ *to displease her boss.* **3** [VP12A,13A,6A] (formal) provide; give: *The trees* ~ *a pleasant shade. It will* ~ *me great pleasure to have dinner with you.*

af·for·est /ə'fɒrɪst US: ə'fɔːr-/ *vt* [VP6A] make into forest land. **af·for·est·ation** /əˌfɒrɪ'steɪʃn US: əˌfɔːr-/ *n:* ~*ation projects,* projects for planting large areas with trees.

af·fran·chise /ə'fræntʃaɪz/ *vt* [VP6A] free from servitude.

af·fray /ə'freɪ/ *n* [C] fight in a public place, causing or likely to cause a disturbance of the peace: *The men were charged with causing an* ~.

af·front /ə'frʌnt/ *vt* [VP6A] insult on purpose; hurt sb's feelings or self-respect, esp in public: *feel* ~ed *at having one's word doubted.* □ *n* [C] public insult; deliberate show of disrespect: *an* ~ *to his pride; suffer an* ~; *offer an* ~ *to sb.*

afield /ə'fiːld/ *adv* far away from home; to or at a distance: *Don't go too far* ~.

afire /ə'faɪə(r)/ *pred adj* (poet) on fire.

aflame /ə'fleɪm/ *pred adj* (poet) in flames; burning; red as if burning: (fig) ~ *with passion. The autumn woods were* ~ *with colour.*

afloat /ə'fləʊt/ *pred adj* **1** floating; borne up, carried along, on air or water: *The ship stuck fast on the rocks and we couldn't get it* ~ *again.* **2** at sea; on board ship: *life* ~, the life of a sailor. **3** awash; flooded. **4** (business) started; solvent: *get a new periodical* ~, launch it. **5** (of stories, rumours) current; in circulation.

afoot /ə'fʊt/ *pred adj* **1** in progress or operation; being prepared: *There's mischief* ~. *There's a*

scheme ~ *to improve the roads.* **2** (old use) on foot; walking.

afore /ə'fɔː(r)/ *adv, prep* (naut) before. ~ **the mast,** as an unlicensed seaman with quarters in the forecastle. '~-**said** *pron, adj* (legal) (that has been) said or mentioned before. '~-**thought,** ⇨ malice.

a fortiori /ˌeɪ ˌfɔːtɪ'ɔːraɪ/ *adv* (Lat) by a more convincing argument.

afoul /ə'faʊl/ *adv* run/fall ~ of, (more usu *run/fall foul of*) come into collision with; get mixed up with.

afraid /ə'freɪd/ *pred adj* **1** ~ (of), frightened (of): *There's nothing to be* ~ *of. Are you* ~ *of snakes?* **2** ~ *of ... gerund;* ~ **that,** doubtful or anxious about consequences: *I was* ~ *of hurting his feelings/that I might hurt his feelings. She was* ~ *of waking her husband,* didn't want to wake him, perhaps because he was ill or in need of sleep. **3** ~ **to** ... *inf,* worried, filled with apprehension: *She was* ~ *to wake her husband,* feared that he might be angry with her. *Don't be* ~ (= Don't hesitate) *to ask for my help.* **4** ~ **(that),** (*that* usu omitted) (a polite formula used with a statement that may be unwelcome): *I'm* ~ (that) *we shall be late. We missed the last train, I'm* ~. *I'm* ~ *I can't help.*

afresh /ə'freʃ/ *adv* again; in a new way: *Let's start* ~.

Af·ri·can /'æfrɪkən/ *n, adj* (indigenous inhabitant) of Africa.

Af·ri·kaans /ˌæfrɪ'kɑːns/ *n* language developed from Dutch, one of the two official European languages in the Republic of South Africa. □ *adj* of this language or the people who speak it. **Afri·kaner** /-'kɑːnə(r)/ *n, adj* (of) a native ~ speaker.

Afro- /ˌæfrəʊ/ *pref* (in compounds) of Africa or Africans: *an A*~*-hairstyle.* ~-'**Asian** *adj* of Africa and Asia. ~-**A'merican** *n* American of African descent. ~-'**wig** *n* wig in the style of hairdressing of some African women.

aft /ɑːft US: æft/ *adv* (naut) at or near the stern of a ship, ⇨ the illus at ship: *go aft; fore and aft,* ⇨ fore.

after¹ /'ɑːftə(r) US: 'æf-/ *adj* (attrib only) **1** later; following: *in* ~ *years.* **2** (naut) toward the stern of a ship: *the'*~ *cabin; the'*~*mast.*

after² /'ɑːftə(r) US: 'æf-/ *adv* later in time; behind in place: *He fell ill on Monday and died three days* ~ (*later* is more usu). *What comes* ~*? Soon* ~ (*afterwards* is more usu), *he went to live in Wales.*

after³ /'ɑːftə(r) US: 'æf-/ *conj* at or during a time later than: *I arrived* ~ *he* (*had*) *left. I shall arrive* ~ *you leave/have left.*

after⁴ /'ɑːftə(r) US: æf-/ *prep* **1** following in time; later than: ~ *dinner;* ~ *dark;* ~ *two o'clock; soon/shortly* ~ *six.* Cf *a little before* six. ~ *that,* then; next; *the day* ~ *tomorrow; the week* ~ *next;* (US) *half* ~ (= GB past) *seven.* **2** next in order to; following: *Put the direct object* ~ *the verb. 'Against' comes* ~ *'again' in the dictionary.* **3** behind: *Shut the door* ~ *you when you leave the room.* **4** in view of; as a result of: *I shall never speak to him again* ~ *what he has said about me.* **5** ~ **all,** (a) in spite of all: *A*~ *all my care, it was broken.* (b) nevertheless: *He failed* ~ *all,* in spite of all that had been done, etc. **6** (in the pattern: *n* ~ *n,* indicating succession): *day* ~ *day; week* ~ *week; time* ~ *time,* repeatedly, very often; *shot* ~ *shot.* **one (damned) thing** ~ **another,** succession of unpleasant happenings, etc. **7** (indicating manner) in the style of; in imitation of: *a painting* ~ *Rembrandt*. *(do sth)* ~ *a fashion; a man* ~ *my own heart,* ⇨ fashion(1), heart(2). **8** (with *vv*, indicating pursuit, search, inquiry): *The policeman ran* ~ *the thief. Did they inquire* ~ *me,* ask for news of me? *be/get* ~ *sb,* look for, in order to reprimand, punish, etc according to context: *The police are* ~ *him. They'll be* ~ *you if you steal apples from this orchard.* ⇨ *look* ~, *name sb* ~, *take* ~, at look¹(6), name²(1) and take(16). **9** (Irish usage) preceding a gerund, making an equivalent of a perfect tense: *He's* ~ *drinking,* has been drinking.

after- /ˈɑːftə(r) *US:* ˈæf-/ *pref* second or later. '~-**care** *n* further treatment given to a person or class of persons, eg sb who has been ill or offenders discharged from prison. '~-**damp** *n* poisonous mixture of gases after the explosion of firedamp in a coal-mine. '~-**effect** *n* effect that occurs afterwards, eg a delayed effect of a drug used medically. '~-**glow** *n* glow in the sky after sunset. **(the)** '~-**life** *n* **(a)** the life believed to follow death. **(b)** the later part of sb's lifetime (esp after a particular event). '~-**math** /-mæθ/ *n* (of grass) crop from a second growth (after the hay harvest); (fig) outcome; consequence: *Misery is usually the ~math of war.* '~-**thought** *n* [U] reflection afterwards; [C] thought that comes afterwards.

after·noon /ˌɑːftəˈnuːn *US:* ˌæf-/ *n* [U,C] time between morning and evening: *in/during the* ~; *this/yesterday/tomorrow* ~; *every* ~; *on Sunday* ~; *on the* ~ *of May 1st; one* ~ *last week; on several* ~*s;* (attrib) *an* ~ *sleep/concert.*

afters /ˈɑːftəz *US:* ˈæf-/ *n pl* (colloq) last (usu sweet) course at a meal: *What's for* ~? *Is it fruit and custard?*

after·wards /ˈɑːftəwədz *US:* ˈæf-/ *adv* after; later.

again /əˈgen/ *adv* **1** once more: *If you fail the first time, try* ~. *Say it* ~, *please. Do you think she will marry* ~, *remarry? You must type this letter* ~, retype it. *now and* ~, occasionally. ~ *and* ~; *time and (time)* ~, repeatedly; very often. *(the) same* ~, formula for re-ordering, eg a drink. **2** (with *not, never*) any more: *This must never happen* ~. *Don't do that* ~. **3** to or in the original condition, position, etc: *You'll soon be well* ~. *He was glad to be home* ~. *You won't get the money back* ~, won't regain it. *be oneself* ~, be restored to a normal (physical or mental) condition. **4** *as many/much* ~, **(a)** the same number/quantity. **(b)** twice as many/much; the same in addition. *half as many/much/long, etc* ~, half as many/much, etc in addition. **5** (often preceded by *and* or *and then*) furthermore, besides: *Then* ~, *I feel doubtful whether....*

against /əˈgenst/ *prep* **1** (indicating opposition): *Public opinion was* ~ *the proposal.* Cf *for, in favour of. We were rowing* ~ *the current.* Cf *with. It was a race* ~ *time,* an attempt to finish before a certain time, before a possible happening, etc. *She was married* ~ *her will. Is there a law* ~ *spitting in the streets in this country? His appearance is* ~ *him,* is such that people are unlikely to favour or support him. **2** (with *vv* indicating protest): *vote/ cry out/write/raise one's voice* ~ *a proposal.* **3** (with *vv*, to indicate collision or impact): *The rain was beating* ~ *the windows. He hit his head* ~ *the wall in the dark cellar.* ⇨ *run against* at run¹(21). **4** in contrast to: *The pine trees were black* ~ *the morning sky.* **5** in preparation for; in anticipation

of: *take precautions* ~ *fire; an injection* ~ *rabies; save money* ~ *a rainy day,* (prov) for a time of possible need. **6** (indicating support or close proximity): *Place the ladder* ~ *the tree. Put the piano with its back* ~ *the wall. He was leaning* ~ *a post.* **7** *over* ~, (a) facing, opposite to. **(b)** (fig) in contrast with, in addition to.

agape /əˈgeɪp/ *pred adj* (facet) with the mouth wide open (owing to wonder, surprise, or a yawn).

agar-agar /ˌeɪgɑːr ˈeɪgɑː(r) *US:* ˌɑːg- ˈɑːg-/ *n* [U] (jelly-like substance prepared from) seaweed.

ag·ate /ˈægət/ *n* (sorts of) very hard stone, a form of silica, with bands or patches of colour.

agave /əˈgeɪvɪ *US:* əˈgɑːvɪ/ *n* (bot) (kinds of) tropical fleshy-leaved plant (including *sisal*), cultivated for their fibres and as a source of intoxicating drinks, eg *pulque.*

age¹ /eɪdʒ/ *n* **1** [C] length of time a person has lived or a thing has existed: *What's his age,* How old is he? *Their ages are 4, 7 and 9. At what age do children start school in your country? What's the age of that old church? When I was your age... I have a son your age,* a son the same age as you. *She ought to be earning her own living at her age,* She's old enough now to do this. *be/come of age,* be/become old enough to be responsible in law. ⇨ *age of consent* at consent. *be of an age,* reach a stage in life when one ought to do sth: *He's of an age when he ought to be settling down,* eg get a good job, marry. *over age,* having passed a certain age or age limit: *He won't be called up for military service; he's over age.* ⇨ *age limit* at limit¹. *under age,* too young; not yet of age. '**age-bracket** *n* period of life between two specified ages, eg between 20 and 30. '**age-group** *n* number of persons of the same age. **2** [U] later part of life (contrasted with *youth*): *His back was bent with age. If we could have the strength of youth and the wisdom of age,....* **3** [C] great or long period of time, with special characteristics or events: *the age of machinery; the atomic age; the Elizabethan Age,* the time of Queen Elizabeth I of England (1558—1603). ⇨ *golden age, middle age, the Middle Ages, the Stone Age* at golden(2), middle(3), stone(1). **4** [C] (colloq) very long time: *We've been waiting an age/for ages.*

age² /eɪdʒ/ *vt,vi* (*pres part* ageing or aging, *pp* aged /eɪdʒd/) [VP6A,2A] (cause to) grow old: *He's ag(e)ing fast. I found him greatly aged,* looking much older. **aged.** ⇨ *age(d) pred adj* of the age of: *a boy aged ten.* □ *attrib adj* /ˈeɪdʒɪd/ very old: *an aged man; the poor and the aged,* those who are poor and old. '**aging,** '**age·ing** *n* [U] process of growing old; changes that occur as the result of the passing of time. '**age·less** *adj* eternal; always young; not affected by time. '**age-long** *adj* lasting for centuries; handed down the ages. ˌ**age-'old** *adj* that has been known, practised, etc for a long time: *age-old customs/ceremonies.*

agency /ˈeɪdʒənsɪ/ *n* (*pl* -cies) **1** business, place of business, of an agent(1): *The Company has agencies in all parts of Africa. He found a job through an employment* ~. *Not all travel agencies are reliable.* **2** [U] *the* ~ *of,* the operation, action of; *Rocks are worn smooth through the* ~ *of water. He obtained a position in a government office through/by the* ~ (= with the help or influence) *of friends.*

agenda /əˈdʒendə/ *n* [C] **1** (list of) things to be done, business to be discussed, eg by a committee:

the next item on the ~; *item No 5 on the* ~. **2**
(comp) set of operations which form a procedure
for solving a problem.

agent /'eɪdʒənt/ *n* **1** person who acts for, or who
manages the business affairs of, another or others:
a '*house*-~, one who buys, sells, lets and rents
houses for the owners; *a' literary* ~, one who helps
authors to find a publisher; *a' shipping or' forwarding* ~, one who sends goods by rail, sea, road, etc
for merchants, manufacturers, etc. '**law** ~, (in
Scotland) solicitor. ⇨ free¹(1), secret(1). **2** person
used to achieve sth, to get a result; (science) substance, natural phenomenon, etc producing an effect: *Rain and frost are natural* ~*s that wear away
rocks.*

agent pro·vo·ca·teur /ˌæʒɒn prəˌvɒkə'tɜː(r)/ *n* (*pl
agents provocateurs*, pronunciation unchanged)
(F) person employed to find suspected criminals or
offenders by tempting them to commit an offence
openly.

ag·glom·er·ate /ə'ɡlɒməreɪt/ *vt, vi* [VP6A,2A]
gather, collect, into a mass. □ *adj* /ə'ɡlɒmərət/ collected into, forming or growing into, a mass. **ag-
glom·er·ation** /əˌɡlɒmə'reɪʃn/ *n* [U] action of ag-
glomerating; [C] (esp untidy) heap or collection of
~d objects, eg a sprawl of untidy suburbs.

ag·glu·tin·ate /ə'ɡluːtɪneɪt/ *vt* [VP6A,2A] join
together as with glue; combine. **ag·glu·ti·nat·ive**
/ə'ɡluːtɪnətɪv *US:* -təneɪtɪv/ *adj* (of languages) that
combine simple words into compounds without
change of form or loss of meaning.

ag·grand·ize /ə'ɡrændaɪz/ *vt* [VP6A] (formal) increase (in power, rank, wealth, importance). **ag-
grand·ize·ment** /ə'ɡrændɪzmənt/ *n*: *a man bent on
personal* ~.

ag·gra·vate /'æɡrəveɪt/ *vt* [VP6A] **1** make worse or
more serious: ~ *an illness/offence.* **2** (colloq) irritate; exasperate: *He* ~*s her beyond endurance.
How aggravating,* annoying! **ag·gra·va·tion**
/ˌæɡrə'veɪʃn/ *n* [U] aggravating or being ~d; [C]
sth that ~s.

ag·gre·gate /'æɡrɪɡeɪt/ *vt, vi* **1** [VP6A,2A] bring or
come together in a mass. **2** [VP2E] amount to (specified total). □ *n* /'æɡrɪɡət/ **1** total obtained by addition; mass or amount brought together. *in the* ~,
as a whole; collectively. **2** materials (sand, gravel,
etc) mixed with cement to make concrete. **ag·gre-
ga·tion** /ˌæɡrɪ'ɡeɪʃn/ *n* [U] number of separate
things, materials, brought together into a mass or
group.

ag·gres·sion /ə'ɡreʃn/ *n* **1** [U] unprovoked hostility, often beginning a quarrel or war: *It was difficult to decide which country was guilty of* ~ (*on/
upon the other*). **2** [C] instance of this.

ag·gres·sive /ə'ɡresɪv/ *adj* **1** quarrelsome; disposed to attack: *an* ~ *man; a man with an* ~ *disposition.* **2** offensive; of or for attack: ~ *weapons.*
3 pushing; not afraid of resistance: *A man who
goes from door to door selling things has to be* ~ *if
he wants to succeed.* ~·**ly** *adv* ~·**ness** *n* **ag·gres-
sor** /-sə(r)/ *n* person, country, making an ~ attack: (attrib) *the aggressor nation.*

ag·grieve /ə'ɡriːv/ *vt* (usu passive) grieve: *be* ~*d.
feel* (**oneself**) **much** ~*d* (**at/over sth**), feel that
one has been treated unjustly; be hurt in one's feelings.

ag·gro /'æɡrəʊ/ *n* [U] (GB sl) aggression as shown
by gangs of teenagers towards other gangs, racial
minorities, etc.

aghast /ə'ɡɑːst *US:* ə'ɡæst/ *pred adj* filled with fear

or surprise: *He stood* ~ *at the terrible sight.*

agile /'ædʒaɪl *US:* 'ædʒl/ *adj* (of living things)
quick-moving; active. ~·**ly** *adv* **agil·ity** /ə'dʒɪlətɪ/
n [U].

agin /ə'ɡɪn/ *prep* (used jocularly for) against.

ag·ing *n* = ageing. ⇨ age ².

agi·tate /'ædʒɪteɪt/ *vt, vi* **1** [VP6A] move or shake
(aliquid); stir up (the surface of a liquid). **2** [VP6A]
disturb; cause anxiety to (a person, his mind or
feelings): *She was deeply* ~*d until she learnt that
her husband was among the survivors. He was* ~*d
about his wife's health.* **3** [VP3A] ~ *for,* argue
publicly in favour of, take part in a campaign for:
~ *for the repeal of a law; workers who* ~*d for
higher wages.* **agi·tated** *part adj* troubled. **agi-
tat·ing** *part adj* causing anxiety. **agi·ta·tion**
/ˌædʒɪ'teɪʃn/ *n* **1** [U] moving or shaking (of a
liquid). **2** [U] excitement of the mind or feelings;
anxiety: *She was in a state of agitation.* **3** [C,U]
discussion or debate (for the purpose of bringing
about a change); [U] social or political unrest or
trouble caused by such discussion: *Small shopkeepers carried on a long agitation against the big
department stores.* **agi·ta·tor** /-tə(r)/ *n* person who
~s, esp politically.

aglow /ə'ɡləʊ/ *pred adj* **1** bright with colour; in a
glow: *The sky was* ~ *with the setting sun.* **2** (of
persons) showing warmth from exercise or excitement: ~ *with pleasure;* shining: *a face* ~ *with
health.*

ag·nail /'æɡneɪl/ *n* [U] torn skin at the base of a
finger-nail.

ag·nos·tic /æɡ'nɒstɪk/ *n* person who believes that
nothing can be known about God or of anything
except material things. □ *adj* of this belief. **ag-
nos·ti·cism** /æɡ'nɒstɪsɪzəm/ *n* [U] this belief.

ago /ə'ɡəʊ/ *adv* (used to indicate time measured
back to a point in the past; always placed after the
word or words it modifies; used with the simple
pt): *The train left a few minutes ago/not long ago.
That was many years/a long while ago. How long
ago is it that you last saw her? I met Mary no longer ago than* (= as recently as) *last Sunday. It was
seven years ago that my brother died.* Cf It *is* seven
years *since* my brother died.

agog /ə'ɡɒɡ/ *pred adj* eager; excited: ~ *for news;*
~ *to hear the news. The whole village was* ~. *His
unexpected return set the town* ~, eg was the cause
of many rumours about the reasons for his return.

ag·ony /'æɡənɪ/ *n* (*pl* -nies) [U,C] great pain or
suffering (of mind or body): *She looked on in* ~ *at
her child's sufferings. I've suffered agonies/have
been in agonies with toothache. He was in an* ~ *of
remorse.* '~ **column,** newspaper column with advertisements for news of missing friends, etc. *pile
on the* ~, (colloq) ⇨ pile³(1). **ag·on·ized**
/'æɡənaɪzd/ *adj* expressing ~: *agonized shrieks.*
ag·on·iz·ing /'æɡənaɪzɪŋ/ *adj* causing ~.

agora /'æɡərə/ *n* (in ancient Greece) (place of) assembly; market-place. ~·**phobia** /ˌæɡərə'fəʊbɪə/ *n*
[U] fear of (crossing) open spaces.

agrar·ian /ə'ɡreərɪən/ *adj* of land (esp farmland) or
land ownership: ~ *laws/problems/reforms/
disputes.*

agree /ə'ɡriː/ *vi, vt* **1** [VP2A,3A,B] ~ (*to*), say
'Yes'; consent: *I asked him to help me and he* ~*d.
Mary's father has* ~*d to her marrying John. He
*~*d to my proposal.* **2** [VP3A,B,4C,7A] (also with
an *inf* or a *that*-clause without a *prep*) be of the
same opinion(s); be in harmony (*with sb on/about*

sth, *as to* how to do sth, etc): *We ~d to start early.
I hope you will ~ with me that our teacher's advice
is excellent. We all ~d on the terms. We ~d on an
early start/on making an early start/that we should
start early/to start early. We met at the ~d time*, at
the time we had ~d on. *We are* (= have) *all ~d
on finding the accused man innocent. We are all
~d that the proposal is a good one. We could not
~* (*as to*) *how it should be done. Have you ~d
about the price yet?* **3** [VP2A,C] (of two or more
persons) be happy together; get on well with one
another (without arguing, etc): *We shall never ~.
Why can't you children ~* (*together*)? **4** [VP3A] *~
(with)*, match, conform (with): *Your story ~s with
what I had already heard. This bill does not ~ with
your original estimate*, the two are different. **5**
[VP3A] *~ with*, suit, eg the health or constitution
of: *The climate doesn't ~ with me. The mussels I
had for lunch haven't ~d with me*, have upset my
stomach. **6** [VP3A] *~ with*, (gram) correspond in
number, person, etc with: *The verb ~s with its
subject in number and person.* **7** [VP6A] (of figures, accounts, proposals, etc) accept or approve
(as being correct): *The Inspector of Taxes has ~d
your return of income.*

agree·able /ə'griːəbl/ *adj* **1** pleasing; giving
pleasure: *She has an ~ voice.* **2** ready to agree:
*Are you ~ to the proposal? I'm ~ to doing what
you suggest.* **agree·ably** /-əblɪ/ *adv. I was
agreeably surprised*, surprised and pleased.

agree·ment /ə'griːmənt/ *n* **1** [U] having the same
opinion(s); thinking in the same way: *We are in ~
on that point. I'm quite in ~ with what you say.
There is no ~ upon/about what should be done.* **2**
[C] arrangement or understanding (spoken or written) made by two or more persons, groups, business companies, governments, etc: *sign an ~*; *an
~ to rent a house.* **come to/arrive at/make/
reach an ~ (with sb)**, reach an understanding.

ag·ri·cul·ture /'ægrɪkʌltʃə(r)/ *n* [U] science or
practice of farming; cultivation of the soil. **ag·ri·
cul·tural** /ˌægrɪ'kʌltʃərəl/ *adj* of *~: agricultural
workers.*

aground /ə'graʊnd/ *adv, pred adj* (of ships) touching the bottom in shallow water: *The ship went
~/was fast ~/ran ~.*

ah /ɑː/ *int* cry of surprise, pity, etc.

aha /ɑː'hɑː/ *int* cry of surprise, triumph, satisfaction, etc, according to context.

ahead /ə'hed/ *adv ~ (of)*, in front; in advance:
*Tom was a quick walker and soon got ~ of the
others. He ran on ~. Standard time in Turkey is
two hours ~ of Greenwich Mean Time.* **Full speed
~!** Go forward at full speed! *go ~*, (a) make progress: *Things are going ~.* (b) (colloq, also *fire
~*) continue (with what you're about to say or do).
in line ~, (of warships) moving forward, anchored, in a column or file. *look ~*, (fig) think of
and prepare for future needs.

ahem /ə'həm/ *int* (usu spelling form of the) noise
made when clearing the throat; noise made to give
a slight warning or to call sb's attention.

ahoy /ə'hɔɪ/ *int* greeting or warning cry used by
seamen.

aid /eɪd/ *vt* [VP6A,17B,14] help: *aid one another;
aid sb to do sth; aid sb with money.* □ *n* **1** [U] help: *in
aid programmes*, those designed to give help, eg to
developing countries. *He came to my aid*, came to
help me. *What is the collection in aid of*, What is
the money to be used for? ⇨ **first ¹(2)**, **legal.** **2** [C]

sth that helps. **visual aids**, pictures, films, film-
strips, etc used in teaching. **'hearing-aid**, appliance that helps a deaf person to hear.

aide–de–camp /ˌeɪd də 'kɒm *US:* 'kæmp/ *n* (*pl
aides-de-camp* pronunciation unchanged) naval
or military officer who helps a superior by carrying
orders, etc.

aide–mémoire /ˌeɪd mem'wɑː(r)/ *n* **1** (in diplomacy) memorandum. **2** document, list etc to remind sb of sth.

aigrette, aigret /'eɪgret *US:* ˌeɪ'gret/ *n* tuft of
feathers worn as an ornament on the head; spray of
gems or jewels in imitation of this.

ail /eɪl/ *vt,vi* **1** [VP6A] (old use) trouble: *What ails
him*, What's wrong with him, What's troubling
him? **2** [VP2A,B] be ill: *The children are always
ailing*, always in poor health.

ail·ment /'eɪlmənt/ *n* [C] illness.

aileron /'eɪlərɒn/ *n* hinged part of the wing of an
aircraft that helps to balance the aircraft and control
ascent and descent. ⇨ the illus at aircraft.

aim ¹ /eɪm/ *vt,vi* **1** [VP6A,14,2A] *aim (at)*, (a) point
(a gun, etc) towards: *aim a gun at sb. He aimed
(his gun) at the lion, fired and missed.* (b) send,
direct, eg a blow, object (*at* sb or sth): *Tom got
angry with his brother and aimed a heavy book at
his head.* (fig) *My remarks were not aimed at you.*
2 [VP3A, *aim at doing sth*; US VP4A, *aim to do
sth*] have as a plan or intention: *Harry aims at
becoming/to become a doctor. What are you aiming at?*

aim ² /eɪm/ *n* **1** [U] act of aiming, eg with a gun:
Take careful aim at the target. He missed his aim,
did not hit the target. **2** [C] purpose; object: *What's
your aim in life*, What do you want to do or be? *He
has only one aim in life—to be a millionaire.*
aim·less *adj* having no purpose: *an aimless
life/task/journey.* **aim·less·ly** *adv*: *wandering aimlessly about the town.*

ain't /eɪnt/ *int* (vulg) contracted form of *are/is/am not*,
and *have/has not*: *I ~ going. We ~ got any.*

air ¹ /eə(r)/ *n* **1** [U] the mixture of gases that surrounds the earth and which we breathe: *Let's go
out and have some fresh air.* *in the air*, (a) uncertain: *My plans are still quite in the air.* (b) (of
opinions, etc) spreading about: *There are rumours
in the air that....* (c) (mil) uncovered, unprotected:
Their left flank was left in the air. *clear the air*, (a)
make the air (in a room, etc) fresh again. (b) (fig)
get rid of suspicion, doubt, etc by giving facts, etc.
⇨ also *castle, hot ¹(8).* **2** [U] the atmosphere as a
place for aircraft to fly in; (attrib) of flying, aircraft,
etc: *air freight/transport/travel.* *by air*, in (an)
aircraft: *travel by air; send goods by air.* **3** [U]
(radio) *on the air*, broadcasting: *Radio Lichtenburg
is on the air 24 hours a day.* *off the air*, not
broadcasting. *come/go on the air*, start broadcasting. *come/go off the air*, stop broadcasting: *Why
has that station gone off the air?* **4** [C] (liter, naut)
breeze, light wind. **5** [C] (old use) tune, melody. **6**
[C] (a) appearance; manner: *He has an air of importance*, seems to be, looks, important. *The house
has an air of comfort.* (b) (usu *pl*) *give oneself/
put on airs*, behave in an unnatural way in the
hope of impressing people. *airs and graces*, foolish, exaggerated ways of behaving. **7** (compounds
and attrib uses) **'air·bed** *n* mattress inflated with
air. **'air-bladder** *n* (in animals and plants, esp seaweed) bladder filled with air. **'air-borne** *adj* (a)
transported by air. (b) (of an aircraft) having taken

off; in flight: *We were soon airborne.* (c) (of troops) specially trained for air operations: *an airborne division.* **'air-brake** *n* brake worked by compressed air. **Air (Chief) 'Marshal, Air 'Commodore** *nn* highest ranks in the RAF. **'air-conditioned** *adj* (of a room, building, railway coach, etc) supplied with air that is purified and kept at a certain temperature and degree of humidity. **'air-conditioning** *n* this process. **air-'cooled** *adj* cooled by a current of air. **'air cover** *n* force of aircraft used to protect a military or naval operation, eg an invasion. **'air-craft** *n* (*sing* or collective *pl*) aeroplane(s); airship(s). ⇨ the illus at the end of air[1]. **'air-craft car-rier** *n* ship built to carry aircraft, with a long, wide deck for taking off and landing. **'air-craft-man** /-mən/ *n* lowest noncommissioned rank in the RAF. **'air-crew** *n* crew of an aircraft. **'air cushion** *n* one inflated with air. **'air-cushion vehicle** *n* vehicle or craft of the hovercraft type. ⇨ the illus at hovercraft. **'air-drome** *n* (US) aerodrome. **'air drop** *n* dropping (of men, supplies) by parachutes from aircraft. **'air duct** *n* device, eg in an aircraft or a ship's cabin, for directing a flow of air for the comfort of passengers. **'air-field** *n* area of open, level ground, with hangars, workshops, offices, etc for operations of (esp military) aircraft. **'air-flow** *n* flow of air over the surfaces of an aircraft in flight. **(an/the) 'air force** *n* (with *sing* or *pl v*) the part of a country's military forces that is organized for fighting in aircraft: (GB) *the Royal Air Force (RAF).* **'air-frame** *n* complete structure of an aircraft without the engine(s). **'air gun** *n* gun in which compressed air is used to propel the charge. **'air hostess** *n* stewardess in an airliner. **'air letter** *n* sheet of light paper (to be) folded and sent, without an envelope, cheaply by airmail. **'air lift** *n* large-scale transport of persons or supplies by air, esp in an emergency. **'air-line** *n* regular service of aircraft for public use.

'air-liner *n* passenger-carrying aircraft. **'air lock** *n* (a) (bubble of air in a pipe causing) stoppage in the flow of liquid. (b) compartment with air-tight doors at each end. **'air-mail** *n* [U] mail (to be) carried by air: *'airmail edition,* (of newspapers, periodicals) printed on thin light paper for sending by airmail. **'air-man** /-mən/ *n* man who flies in an aircraft as a member of the crew, esp a pilot; (RAF) man of any rank up to and including a Warrant Officer. **air-'minded** *adj* looking upon flying as a normal and necessary method of transport. **'air pillow** *n* air cushion. **'air-plane** *n* (US) aeroplane. **'air pocket** *n* atmospheric condition (partial vacuum) causing an aircraft to drop some distance: *We had a bumpy flight because of air pockets.* **'air-port** *n* public flying ground for commercial use by airliners. **'air-pump** *n* pump for exhausting a vessel of its air. **'air-raid** *n* attack by aircraft that drop bombs; (attrib, with hyphen): *air-raid warnings/ precautions; air-raid warden,* person in charge of air-raid precautions. **'air rifle** *n* = air gun. **'air-screw** *n* aircraft propeller. ⇨ the illus at screw. **air-sea 'rescue** *n* organization for, work of, rescuing airmen and passengers from the sea, eg by the use of motor-boats or helicopters. **'air-shaft** *n* passage for air into a mine. **'air-ship** *n* gas-filled flying-machine with engine(s). ⇨ balloon, dirigible. **'air space** *n* part of the earth's atmosphere above a country: *violation of our air space by military aircraft.* **'air speed** *n* speed of an aircraft relative to the air through which it is moving. **'air-strip** *n* strip of ground for the use of aircraft, esp one made for use in war or in an emergency. **'air terminal** *n* terminus (in a town or city centre) to or from which passengers, etc travel to or from an airport. **'air-tight** *adj* not allowing air to enter or escape. **'air umbrella** *n* = air cover. **'air-way** *n* route regularly followed by airliners; (*pl*) company operating a service of airliners: *British Airways.*

aircraft

LIGHT AIRCRAFT

COMBAT AIRCRAFT (jet-fighter and bomber)

AIRLINER

'air·woman n (WRAF) woman of any rank up to and including a Warrant Officer. **'air·worthy** adj (of aircraft) fit to fly; in good working order. **'air·worthi·ness** n ,air-to-'air adj (of missiles) fired from one aircraft against another. ,air-to-'ground adj fired from an aircraft to hit a target on the ground.

air² /eə(r)/ vt [VP6A] **1** put (clothing, bedding, etc) into the open air or into a warm place to make it quite dry: *The mattress needs to be aired.* **2** let air into (a room, etc). **3** cause others to know (one's opinions, a grievance, etc): *He likes to air his knowledge,* let people see how much he knows. **air·ing** /'eərɪŋ/ n: give sth an airing, expose it to the air or to a fire; *go for an airing, take the children for an airing,* out in the fresh air. **'airing-cupboard** n warmed cupboard in which to keep bed-linen, towels, etc.

Aire·dale /'eədeɪl/ n large rough-coated terrier (kind of dog).

air·less /'eəlɪs/ adj **1** not having enough fresh air; stuffy: *an ~ room.* **2** (of the weather) calm; still: *Isn't it ~ this evening!*

airy /'eərɪ/ adj **1** having plenty of fresh air moving through it: *a nice ~ room.* **2** of or like air; immaterial. **3** not sincere; superficial: *~ promises,* unlikely to be kept; *an ~ manner,* careless and light-hearted. **air·ily** /'eərəlɪ/ adv

aisle /aɪl/ n **1** passage in a church, esp one that is divided by a row of columns from the nave; (in a small church) passage between rows of pews (= seats). ⇨ the illus at church. **2** (US) passage between any rows of seats, eg in a theatre or railway coach; any long and narrow passageway.

aitch /eɪtʃ/ n the letter H. *drop one's ~s,* fail to utter the sound /h/ at the beginning of a word, eg by saying *'at* for *hat.* **'~-bone** n (cut of beef over the) bone of the rump.

ajar /ə'dʒɑː(r)/ pred adj (of doors) slightly open.

akim·bo /ə'kɪmbəʊ/ adv *with arms ~,* with the hands on the hips and elbows bent outwards.

akin /ə'kɪn/ pred adj *~ (to),* of similar character; like: *Pity is often ~ to love.*

ala·bas·ter /'æləbɑːstə(r) US: -bæs-/ n [U] soft, white stone like marble in appearance, used for ornaments. □ adj like *~* in smoothness and whiteness.

à la carte /ˌɑː lɑː 'kɑːt/ adv (F) (of meals) ordered from a list, course by course, not at a fixed price for the complete meal (as for *table d'hôte*).

alack /ə'læk/ int (old use) cry of regret or sorrow.

alac·rity /ə'lækrətɪ/ n [U] eager and cheerful readiness.

à la mode /ˌɑː lɑː 'məʊd/ adv (F) according to the latest fashion, ideas, etc; (US) served with ice-cream: *apple pie ~.*

alarm /ə'lɑːm/ n **1** [C] (sound or signal giving a) warning of danger; apparatus used to give such a warning: *a 'fire ~. give/raise/sound the ~,* ring a bell or in other ways send out a warning signal. **'~(-clock)** n clock that can be set to ring a bell or sound a buzzer at a fixed time to waken a sleeping person: *set the ~(-clock) for six o'clock.* **2** [U] fear and excitement caused by the expectation of danger: *He jumped up in ~. I hope you didn't take/feel ~ at the news.* □ vt [VP6A] give a warning or feeling of danger to; cause anxiety to: *The noise of the shot ~ed hundreds of birds. Everybody was ~ed at the news that war might break out.* **~·ing** part adj causing *~.* **~·ist** /-ɪst/ adj, n (person)

raising *~s* with little cause.

alas /ə'læs/ int cry of sorrow or regret.

alb /ælb/ n white vestment reaching to the feet, worn by some Christian priests at ceremonies. ⇨ the illus at vestment.

al·ba·tross /'ælbətrɒs/ n large, white, web-footed seabird, common in the Pacific and Southern Oceans. ⇨ the illus at water.

al·beit /ɔːl'biːɪt/ conj (formal) though (1).

al·bino /æl'biːnəʊ US: -'baɪ-/ n (pl ~s /-nəʊz/) animal or human being born without natural colouring matter in the skin and hair (which are white) and the eyes (which are pink).

al·bum /'ælbəm/ n **1** blank book in which a collection of photographs, autographs, postage stamps, etc can be kept. **2** holder for a set of discs; long-playing record with several pieces by the same musician(s), singer(s).

al·bu·men /'ælbjʊmɪn/ n [U] **1** white of egg. ⇨ the illus at fowl. **2** substance as in white of egg, part of animal and vegetable matter.

al·chem·ist /'ælkɪmɪst/ n person who studied or practised alchemy.

al·chemy /'ælkɪmɪ/ n [U] chemistry of the Middle Ages, the chief aim of which was to discover how to change ordinary metals into gold.

al·co·hol /'ælkəhɒl US: -hɔːl/ n **1** [U] (pure, colourless liquid present in) such drinks as beer, wine, brandy, whisky. **2** [U,C] (chem) large group of compounds of the same type as *~(1).* **~·ic** /ˌælkə'hɒlɪk US: -'hɔːl-/ adj of or containing *~.* □ n person addicted to *~ic* drink. *~·ism* /-ɪzəm/ n [U] addiction to *~ic* drink; diseased condition caused by this.

al·cove /'ælkəʊv/ n recess; partially enclosed extension of a room, often occupied by a bed or by seats; similar space within a garden enclosure.

al·der /'ɔːldə(r)/ n tree of the birch family, usu growing in marshy places.

al·der·man /'ɔːldəmən/ n (pl -men /-mən/) senior member of a city or borough council in England and Ireland, next in rank to a mayor, elected by fellow councillors. *~·ic* /ˌɔːldə'mænɪk/ adj

ale /eɪl/ n [U] (GB) (kind of) beer; (old use) = beer. ⇨ also ginger. **'ale-house** n (old name for) public house.

alee /ə'liː/ adv, pred adj (naut) at, on, towards the lee or sheltered side of a ship.

alert /ə'lɜːt/ adj watchful; fully awake; lively: *~ in answering questions.* □ n **1** *on the ~,* on the look-out (*for* sth, *against* an attack, etc, *to do* sth). **2** [C] (period of) watchfulness under enemy attack, esp an air raid. **3** [C] notice to stand ready: *They received the ~ at 10am.* □ vt [VP6A] put (troops, etc) on the *~. ~·ly* adv *~·ness* n being *~* or prompt (*in* doing sth).

alex·an·drine /ˌælɪg'zændraɪn/ n (of verse rhythm) iambic line of six feet or twelve syllables.

alexia /ə'leksɪə/ n [U] (path) disease in which cerebral lesions cause inability to read (popularly called 'word blindness'). **alexic** /ə'leksɪk/ adj of *~: alexic* children.

al·falfa /æl'fælfə/ n [U] (US) = lucerne.

al·fresco /ˌæl'freskəʊ/ adj, adv (of meals) in the open air; out of doors: *an ~ lunch; lunching ~.*

alga /'ælgə/ n (pl alga e /'ældʒiː/) (bot) water plant of very simple structure.

al·ge·bra /'ældʒɪbrə/ n branch of mathematics in which signs and letters are used to represent quantities. *~·ic* /ˌældʒɪ'breɪk/, *~·ical* /-kl/ adj of *~.*

~·ic·al·ly /-klɪ/ *adv*

alias /'eɪlɪəs/ *n* (*pl* ~es /-sɪz/) name by which a person is called on other occasions: *The criminal had several ~es.* □ *adv* also called.

alibi /'ælɪbaɪ/ *n* (*pl* ~s /-baɪz/) **1** (legal) plea that one was in another place at the time of an alleged act, esp a crime: *The accused man was able to establish/prove an ~.* **2** (colloq) excuse (for failure, etc).

alien /'eɪlɪən/ *n* (legal or official use) foreigner who is not a subject of the country in which he lives: *An Englishman is an ~ in the United States.* □ *adj* **1** foreign: *an ~ environment.* **2** ~ *(to)*, differing in nature or character: *These principles are ~ to our religion.* **3** contrary or opposed (*to*): *Cruelty was quite ~ to his nature.*

alien·ate /'eɪlɪəneɪt/ *vt* [VP6A,14] ~ *sb (from)*, **1** estrange; cause (sb previously friendly) to become unfriendly or indifferent (by unpopular or distasteful actions): *The Prime Minister's policy ~d many of his followers. At various times artists have felt ~d from society,* felt shut out from society. **2** transfer ownership of (property): *Enemy property is often ~d in time of war,* ie seized by the Government. **alien·ation** /ˌeɪlɪə'neɪʃn/ *n* alienating or being ~d; estrangement; (theatre) critical detachment (of actors and audience) from, emotional non-involvement in, problems presented by a drama.

the alimentary canal

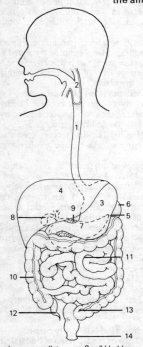

1 esophagus or gullet
2 pharynx
3 stomach
4 liver
5 pancreas
6 spleen
7 duodenum
8 gall bladder
9 bile-ducts
10 colon or large intestine
11 small intestine
12 vermiform appendix
13 rectum
14 anus

alien·ist /'eɪlɪənɪst/ *n* **1** (US) expert on the mental competence of witnesses in a law court. **2** (old use) specialist in mental illness (now called a *psychiatrist*).

alight¹ /ə'laɪt/ *pred adj* on fire; lighted up: *The sticks were damp and wouldn't catch ~.* (fig) *Their faces were ~* (= bright, cheerful) *with happiness.*

alight² /ə'laɪt/ *vi* [VP2A,3A] **1** get down (*from* a horse, bus, etc). **2** (of a bird) come down from the air and settle (*on* a branch, etc). **3** ~ *on*, (formal) (fig) find by chance.

align /ə'laɪn/ *vt,vi* **1** [VP6A,2A] arrange in a line; bring into line (esp three or more points into a straight line); eg of soldiers, form in line: ~ *the sights of a rifle.* **2** [VP14,3A] bring, come, into agreement, close co-operation, etc (*with*): *They ~ed themselves with us.* ~·ment *n* [C,U] (an) arrangement in a straight line: *The desks are in/out of ~ment. There was a new ~ment of European powers,* a new grouping (colloq, *line-up*) of powers.

No 2 is out of alignment

alike /ə'laɪk/ *pred adj* similar; like one another: *The two sisters are very much ~. All music is ~ to him,* He has no ear for music, cannot distinguish one kind from other kinds. □ *adv* in the same way: *treat everybody ~;* the same: *summer and winter ~.*

ali·men·tary /ˌælɪ'mentərɪ/ *adj* of food and digestion. **the ~ canal,** parts of the body through which food passes (from the mouth to the anus).

ali·mony /'ælɪmənɪ US: -məʊnɪ/ *n* [U] money allowance (to be) paid by a man to his wife, or former wife, by a judge's order, eg after a legal separation or divorce.

alive /ə'laɪv/ *pred adj* **1** living: *Who's the greatest man ~? You wouldn't like to be buried ~.* **2** in force; in existence: *If a claim is kept ~, it is more likely to be recognized. An awareness of the dangers of air-pollution should be kept ~ by the press and TV.* **3** ~ *to,* conscious or aware of: *He is fully ~ to the dangers of the situation/public opinion.* **4** active; lively: *He is very much ~.* **Look** ~! Hurry up! Get busy! **5** ~ *with,* full of (living or moving things): *The lake was ~ with fish.*

al·kali /'ælkəlaɪ/ *n* (*pl* ~s /-laɪz/) (chem) one of a number of substances (such as soda, potash, ammonia) that combine with acids to form salts. **al·ka·line** /'ælkəlaɪn/ *adj* of ~s: *soil of alkaline peat.*

all¹ /ɔːl/ *adj* **1** (with *pl nn*) the whole number of; (with *sing* material or abstract *nn*) the whole extent or amount of; (followed by the *def art,* demonstratives, possessives, and cardinal numbers): *All horses are animals but not all animals are horses. All five men/All five of them are hard workers. All you boys need to work harder. You've had all the fun and I've had all the hard work. He has lived all his life in London.* **of¹all people,** specially; particularly: *Of all people he should be the last to complain,* there is a strong reason why he shouldn't. *Why ask 'me to help, of'all people?* I am the least likely person to be able to help, or the person to whom the speaker has the least right to apply for help. *of all the idiots/nitwits,* an expression of annoyance with sb who has behaved foolishly. *on all fours,* ⇨ four. **2** *He spent all (of) that year* (= the whole of that year) *in London.* ⇨ whole(3). **3** (Cf *all* and *every.* *All* suggests the whole; *every* points to each member of a group individually): *All (of) the boys enjoyed themselves.* Cf *Every one of the boys enjoyed himself.* **4** *with all speed/haste,* the utmost possible. **5** any: *beyond all doubt/ argument/question,* there can't be any doubt, etc. *He hates all* (= any) *criticism of his work.* **6** ,All 'Fools' Day, 1 Apr; ,All 'Hallows', ,All 'Saints' Day, 1 Nov; ,All 'Souls' Day, 2 Nov.

all² /ɔːl/ *adv* **1** quite; entirely: *They were dressed all in black.* Cf *They were all dressed* (= All of them were dressed) *in black. Your hands are all tar,* (colloq) covered with tar. *She was all* (colloq = greatly) *excited. be all about sth,* (colloq) be concerned with it. *all alone,* (a) not in the company of others. (b) without the help and company of other persons. *all along,* (a) for the whole length of: *There are trees all along the road.* (b) (colloq) all the time; from the start: *But I knew that all along! all clear,* ⇨ clear¹(4). *all for,* (colloq) strongly in favour of; anxious to have, etc: *I'm all for accepting the offer. all the same,* yet, nevertheless. *all the same to,* a matter not causing inconvenience to; a matter of indifference to: *If it's all the same to you...; It's all the same to me whether you go or stay. all one to,* a matter of indifference to: *Do as you like; it's all one to me. all in,* (a) (colloq) exhausted; *He was all in at the end of the race.* (b) *(all-in)* inclusive of everything: *an all-in price; all-in wrestling,* with no restrictions about methods or holds. *all-out,* (colloq) using all possible strength, energy, etc: *He was going all out/was making an all-out effort. all over,* (a) in every part of: *He has travelled all over the world.* (b) at an end. *all right,* (US) *all-right* (a) satisfactory, satisfactorily; safe and sound; in good order: *Are you feeling all right?* (b) (as a response to a suggestion, etc) Yes, I consent. *all there,* (colloq) having one's wits about one; mentally alert. *not all there,* (colloq) not quite sane; mentally deficient. *all told,* altogether; as the total: *There were six people all told* (= in all). *all up (with),* at an end, over (with): *It's all up with him now,* He's likely to be ruined, to die, etc. **2** *all the* + *comp adj,* much; so much: *You'll be all the better for a holiday.*

all³ /ɔːl/ *n my/his/their, etc all,* all that I/he/they, etc possess, value most, etc: *We must stake our all in this struggle. He had lost his all.*

all⁴ /ɔːl/ (in compounds) **1** (prefixed to many *adjj* and *pres participles*) in the highest degree; without limit: ,all-'merciful; ,all-'powerful; ,all-em'bracing. **2** ,all-'mains *attrib adj* (of a radio receiver) adaptable to all voltages: *an all-mains set.* ,all-'round *adj* having ability in many different ways: *an all-round sportsman,* good at many different games and sports. Hence, ,all-'rounder *n an* ,all-,star 'cast, (for a play, etc) one with star performers for all the chief parts. ,all-,time 'high/'low *n* (colloq) highest/lowest figure, level, etc on record. ,all-,up 'weight, total weight of an aircraft, including crew, passengers, cargo, when in the air.

all⁵ /ɔːl/ *pron* **1** everything: *He wanted all or nothing.* **2** *all of,* every one, the whole: *All of us want to go. Take all of it.* **3** (used in apposition, in the same way as *both* and *each*): *We all want to go. Take it all. They were all broken.* **4** (followed by a relative clause, *that* being omitted): *All I want is peace and quiet. He took all there was.* **5** (in prepositional phrases): *above all,* ⇨ above²(3). *after all,* ⇨ after. *(not) at all, /ə 'tɔːl/* (not) in any way, in the least degree: *if you are at all worried; not at all suitable for the post. Not at all,* polite formula in answer to an expression of thanks. Cf US: You're welcome. *for all* (*his wealth/great learning),* in spite of. *for all I know/care, etc,* (used to show ignorance or indifference): *He may be dead for all I know. in all,* ⇨ in²(13). *and all,* as well; including: *The dog ate the whole rabbit, head, bones and all. once (and) for all,* now and for the last or only time. *It was all I/he, etc could not do to (laugh, etc),* I/he, etc could hardly refrain from (laughing, etc). *all in all,* of supreme or exclusive importance, interest, etc: *They were all in all to each other. (taking it) all in all,* considering everything. *not as/so* + *adj/adv* + *as all that,* to that extent; in that degree: *It's not so difficult as all that,* as is suggested, supposed, etc. *not all that* + *adj/adv,* (colloq or vulg): *It isn't all that cheap,* not cheap if all things are considered.

Allah /'ælə/ *n* name of God among Muslims.

al·lay /ə'leɪ/ *vt (pt,pp* -layed) [VP6A] make sth (eg pain, trouble, excitement, fears) less.

al·lege /ə'ledʒ/ *vt* [VP6A,9] declare; put forward, esp as a reason or excuse, in support of a claim or in denial of a charge: *In your statement you ∼ that the accused man was seen at the scene of the crime. The statement ∼d to have been made by the accused is clearly untrue. An ∼d thief,* person who is declared to be a thief. **al·le·ga·tion** /,ælɪ'geɪʃn/ *n* [U] alleging; [C] statement, esp one made without proof: *You have made serious allegations, but can you substantiate them?* **al·leg·edly** /-ɪdlɪ/ *adv*

al·le·giance /ə'liːdʒəns/ *n* [U] duty, support, loyalty, due (to a ruler or government): *Members of Parliament took the oath of ∼ to the Queen.*

al·le·gory /'æləgərɪ *US:* -gɔːrɪ/ *n* [C] (*pl* -ries) story, painting or description in which ideas such as patience, purity and truth are symbolized by persons who are characters in the story, eg Bunyan's *Pilgrim's Progress.* **al·le·goric** /,ælɪ'gɒrɪk *US:* -'gɔːr-/, **al·le·gori·cal** /-kl/ *adj*

al·le·gretto /,ælɪ'gretəʊ/ *n, adj, adv* (I; music) (passage played) fast and lively, but not so brisk as allegro.

al·legro /ə'leɪgrəʊ/ *n, adj, adv* (I; music) (passage played) in quick time; fast and lively.

al·le·luia /,ælɪ'luːjə/ *int* = hallelujah.

al·lergy /'æledʒɪ/ *n* [C] (*pl*-gies) (med) (condition of) being unusually sensitive to particular foods, kinds of pollen, insect stings, etc (as in the case of a person who begins to suffer from asthma when he gets a certain kind of dust or pollen into his nose or mouth). **al·ler·gen** /'æledʒen/ *n* (med, science) anything that causes an ∼. **al·ler·gic** /ə'lɜːdʒɪk/ *adj* of ∼. *allergic to,* having an ∼ to (sth); (colloq) having a dislike of; unable to get on well with.

al·levi·ate /ə'liːvɪeɪt/ *vt* [VP6A] make (pain, suffering) less or easier to bear. **al·levi·ation** /ə,liːvɪ'eɪʃn/ *n*

al·ley /'ælɪ/ *n* [C] (*pl* ∼s) (also '∼-way) **1** narrow passage between houses or other buildings (often a narrow street in a slum quarter). ,blind '∼, ∼ closed at one end; (fig) occupation, eg that of an errand boy, that does not teach a trade or lead to a profession. **2** path or walk in a garden or park. **3** narrow enclosure for such games as bowls and skittles.

al·liance /ə'laɪəns/ n **1** [U] association or connection. **in ~ (with)**, joined or united (with). **2** [C] union of persons, families, eg by marriage, or states (by treaty): enter into an ~ with a country.
al·lied /ə'laɪd/ ⇨ ally.

al·li·ga·tor /'ælɪgeɪtə(r)/ n reptile (like a crocodile but with a shorter snout) living in the lakes and rivers of southeastern US, ⇨ the illus at reptile; leather made from its skin. **~ pear**, avocado.

al·li·ter·ation /ə,lɪtə'reɪʃn/ n [U] repetition of the first sound or letter of a succession of words, eg safe and sound; apt ~'s artful aid. **al·lit·er·ative** /ə'lɪtrətɪv US: -təreɪtɪv/ adj **al·lit·er·ative·ly** adv

al·lo·cate /'æləkeɪt/ vt [VP6A,14] **~ (to/for)**, give, put on one side, as a share or for a purpose: ~ duties to sb; ~ a sum of money among several persons; ~ a sum of money to education. **al·lo·ca·tion** /,ælə'keɪʃn/ n **1** [U] allocating or distributing. **2** [C] **~ (to/for)**, sth ~d or assigned (to or for a purpose, etc).

al·lot /ə'lɒt/ vt (-tt-) [VP6A,12A,13A,14] **~ sth (to)**, make a distribution of; decide a person's share of: ~ sth to sb for a purpose; ~ duties (to sb). Can we do the work within the time they have ~ted (to) us? They were ~ted a house to live in. **~·ment** n **1** [U] division; distribution (of shares). **2** [C] part or share, esp (in GB) small area of public land rented as a vegetable garden.

allow /ə'laʊ/ vt,vi **1** [VP6A,C,17,15B] permit: Smoking is not ~ed here. No dogs ~ed, It is forbidden to bring dogs into this place (building, park, etc). Please ~ me to carry your bag. She is not ~ed out after dark. **2** [VP12A,13A,14] give, let (sb or sth) have; agree to give: How much money does your father ~ you for books? He ~s his wife £100 a year for clothes. She ~ed her imagination full play, did nothing to control it. The bank ~s 5 per cent interest on deposits. We can ~ (= take off, deduct) 5 per cent for cash payment. **3** [VP6A] (legal) agree that sth is right or just: The judge ~ed the claim. **4** [VP25,9] admit (now the more usu word): We must ~ him to be a genius/~ that he is a genius. **5** [VP3A] **~ for**, take into consideration: It will take thirty minutes to get to the station, ~ing for traffic delays. **~ of**, admit of (now more usu): The situation ~s of no delay. **~·able** /-əbl/ adj that is or can be ~ed (by law, the rules, etc).

allow·ance /ə'laʊəns/ n **1** [C] sum of money, amount of sth, allowed to sb: a dress ~ of £70 a year. The Director has an entertainment ~, money for entertaining important customers, etc. **2** [C] (comm, fin) deduction or discount. **3** (sing or pl) **make ~(s) for**, allow for, ⇨ allow(5). We must make ~(s) for his youth, remember that he is young, and not be too severe, etc.

alloy /'ælɔɪ/ n [C,U] mixture of metals, esp a metal of low value mixed with a metal of higher value: (used attrib) ~ steel. □ vt /ə'lɔɪ/ [VP6A] mix (one metal) with a metal or metals of lower value; (fig) spoil; impair.

all·spice /'ɔːlspaɪs/ n [U] spice made from the dried berries of a W Indian tree called the pimento.

allude /ə'luːd/ vi [VP3A] **~ to**, refer (indirectly) to; mention (now the more usu word): In your remarks you ~ to certain sinister developments.

allure /ə'lʊə(r)/ vt [VP6A,14,17A] tempt; entice; lure (now the more usu word). □ n [C,U] (liter) power to ~; fascination. **allur·ing** part adj charming; fascinating. **~·ment** n [C,U] that which ~s;

charm, attraction (now the more usu words).

al·lu·sion /ə'luːʒn/ n [C] **~ (to)**, indirect reference to: His speeches are full of classical ~s which few people understand. That man has a glass eye but he doesn't like people to make any ~ to it. **al·lus·ive** /ə'luːsɪv/ adj containing ~s.

al·luv·ial /ə'luːvɪəl/ adj made of sand, earth, etc, left by rivers or floods: ~ soil/deposits.

ally /ə'laɪ/ vt (pt,pp -lied) **1** [VP14] **~ (oneself) with/to**, unite by treaty, marriage, etc: Great Britain was allied with the United States in both World Wars; Hence: the Allied /'ælaɪd/ Powers. **2 allied to**, (of things) connected with: The English language is allied to the German language. □ n /'ælaɪ/ (pl -lies) person, state, etc, allied to another; person who gives help or support.

Alma Mater /,ælmə 'mɑːtə(r)/ n (Lat) name used for the university or school that a person attended; (US) school song or anthem.

al·ma·nac /'ɔːlmənæk/ n annual book or calendar of months and days, with information about the sun, moon, tides, anniversaries, etc.

al·mighty /ɔːl'maɪtɪ/ adj having all power; powerful beyond measure, esp A~ God. □ n the A~, God.

almond /'ɑːmənd/ n (nut inside the) hard seed (stone-fruit) of a tree allied to the peach and plum: ground ~s, ~ nuts ground to powder. shelled ~s, ~ nuts removed from the shell or hard cover. **~·eyed** adj having eyes that appear to slant upwards and become narrower.

almoner /'ɑːmənə(r) US: 'ælm-/ n **1** (formerly) official who distributed money and help to the poor. **2** (GB) hospital official in charge of social service work for patients.

al·most /'ɔːlməʊst/ adv **1** (with vv, advv, adjj, nn; replaceable by nearly): He slipped and ~ fell. That's a mistake he ~ always makes. Dinner's ~ ready. It's ~ time to start. **2** (with no, none, nothing, never, not replaceable by nearly; often replaced by hardly or scarcely with any): A~ no one (= Hardly anyone) believed her. The speaker said ~ nothing (= scarcely anything) worth listening to.

alms /ɑːmz/ n (sing or pl) money, clothes, food, etc given to the poor: give ~ to sb; ask/beg (an) ~ of sb. **'~-box** n **'~-giving** n **'~-house** n (old use) house, founded by charity, in which poor people, no longer able to earn money, may live without paying rent.

aloe /'æləʊ/ n **1** plant with thick, sharp-pointed leaves. **2** (also **bitter ~s**) juice from this plant, used in medicine.

aloft /ə'lɒft US: ə'lɔːft/ adv high up, esp at the masthead of a ship, or up in the rigging.

alone /ə'ləʊn/ pred adj, adv **1** (= by oneself/itself) without the company or help of others or other things: He likes living ~, by himself. The house stands on the hillside all ~, with no other houses near it. You can't lift the piano ~, without help. His silence ~ is proof of his guilt. **2** (following a n or pron) and no other: Smith ~ (= Smith and no one else) knows what happened. You ~ (= You and no other person) can help me in this task. **3** (in the pred, with in): We are not ~ in thinking (= not the only persons who think) that. **4** **let ~**, without referring to or considering: He cannot find money for necessities, let ~ such luxuries as wine and tobacco. **let/leave sb/sth ~**, abstain from touching, moving, interfering with: You had *better leave that dog* ~; *it will bite you if you tease it.* **let well** ~, do not go further than what is already satisfactory.

along /ə'lɒŋ *US:* ə'lɔːŋ/ *adv* **1** (used with *vv* to indicate onward movement, often with the same sense as *on*): *Come* ~! *The dog was running* ~ *behind its master.* **Move** ~ **please!** eg a request by a policeman to people who are holding up the movement of others. **2** (used, as are *over, across, up, down,* in informal requests): *Come* ~ *and see me some time.* **3** *all* ~, ⇨ all²(1). **get** ~, ⇨ get(17). □ *prep* **1** from one end of to the other end of; through any part of the length of: *We walked* ~ *the road. There are trees all* ~ *the river banks. Pass* ~ *the bus please!* (a request that passengers should move on so as to leave the entrance clear). **2** ~ **here,** in this direction. ~**side** /ə,lɒŋ'saɪd/ *adv, prep* close to, parallel with, the side of (a ship, pier, wharf).

aloof /ə'luːf/ *adv* apart. **stand/hold/keep (oneself)** ~ **(from),** keep away from, take no part in sth: *Buyers are holding* ~, making no offers to buy. □ *adj* cool; remote (by nature): *I find him rather* ~. *He's a very* ~ *character.* ~**-ness** *n*

aloud /ə'laʊd/ *adv* **1** in a voice loud enough to be heard, not in a whisper: *Please read the story* ~. **2** loudly, so as to be heard at a distance: *He called* ~ *for help.*

alp /ælp/ *n* **1** high mountain, esp one of those (**the Alps**) between France and Italy. **2** (in Switzerland) green pasture-land on a mountain-side.

al·paca /æl'pækə/ *n* **1** [C] sheep-like animal, kind of llama, of Peru. **2** [U] (cloth made from) its wool, often mixed with silk or cotton: *an* ~ *coat.*

alpen·stock /'ælpənstɒk/ *n* long, iron-tipped stick used in climbing mountains.

al·pha /'ælfə/ *n* the first letter (A, α) in the Gk alphabet. **A**~ **and Omega,** the beginning and the end. ⇨ App 4. '~ **particle,** helium nucleus given off by a radio-active substance. ~ **plus,** (of marks in an examination) very good indeed.

al·pha·bet /'ælfəbet/ *n* the letters used in writing a language, arranged in order: *the Greek* ~; *the ABC.* ⇨ App 4. ~**i·cal** /ˌælfə'betɪkl/ *adj* in the order of the ~: *The words in a dictionary are in* ~*ical order.* ~**i·cally** /-klɪ/ *adv*

al·pine /'ælpaɪn/ *adj* of the Alps; of alps: ~ *plants; an* ~ *hut.* **al·pin·ist** /'ælpɪnɪst/ ~ climber.

al·ready /ɔːl'redɪ/ *adv* (usu with *v*, but may be placed elsewhere for emphasis) **1** by this/that time: *The postman has* ~ *been/has been* ~. *When I called, Tom was* ~ *dressed.* **2** (Cf *yet* which usu replaces *already* in neg and interr sentences. In neg and interr sentences *already* is used to show surprise.): *Have you had breakfast* ~? *Is it 10 o'clock* ~? *You're not leaving us* ~, *are you?* **3** previously; before now: *I've been there* ~, *so I don't want to go again.*

al·right /ɔːl'raɪt/ = all right, ⇨ all²(1).

Al·sa·tian /æl'seɪʃn/ *n* (US = *German shepherd*) large breed of dog, like a wolf, often trained for police work. ⇨ the illus at dog.

also /'ɔːlsəʊ/ *adv* too; besides; as well. (In spoken English, *too* and *as well* are often preferred to *also*. *Also* in an affirm sentence is replaced by *either* in a neg sentence.): *Tom has been to Canada. Harry has* ~ *been to Canada.* Cf *Tom has not been to Brazil. Harry has not been to Brazil, either.* **not only... but...** ~, both... and: *He not only read the book but* ~ *remembered what he had read.* '~**-ran** *n* (racing) horse not among the first three at the

winning post; (fig) unsuccessful person in a contest.

al·tar /'ɔːltə(r)/ *n* **1** raised place (flat-topped table or platform) on which offerings are made to a god. **2** (in Christian churches) the Communion table, ⇨ the illus at church. **lead (a woman) to the** ~, marry her. '~**-piece** *n* painting or sculpture placed behind an ~.

al·ter /'ɔːltə(r)/ *vt,vi* [VP6A,2A] make or become different; change in character, appearance, etc: *The ship* ~*ed course. That* ~*s matters/the case,* makes the situation different. *These clothes are too large; they must be* ~*ed. He has* ~*ed a great deal since I saw him a year ago.* ~**·able** /-əbl/ *adj* that ~s or that can be ~ed. ~**·ation** /ˌɔːltə'reɪʃn/ *n* [U] ~ing; making a change; [C] act of changing; change that is the result of ~ing: *There isn't much* ~*ation in the village; it's almost the same as it was twenty years ago. For making* ~*ations to a suit of clothes, £1.20.*

al·ter·ca·tion /ˌɔːltə'keɪʃn/ *n* (formal) [U] quarrelling; [C] quarrel; noisy argument.

al·ter ego /ˌæltər 'egəʊ *US:* 'iːgəʊ/ *n* (Lat) one's other self; very intimate friend.

al·ter·nate¹ /ɔːl'tɜːnət/ *adj* **1** (of things of two kinds) by turns, first the one and then the other: ~ *laughter and tears. Tom and Harry do the work on* ~ *days,* eg Tom on Monday, Harry on Tuesday, Tom on Wednesday, etc. **2** (of leaves along a stem) not opposite. ~**·ly** *adv*

al·ter·nate² /'ɔːltəneɪt/ *vt,vi* **1** [VP6A,14] arrange or perform by turns; cause to take place, appear, one after the other: *He* ~*d kindness with severity,* was kind, then severe, then kind again, etc. *Most farmers* ~ *crops.* ⇨ rotation(2). **2** [VP3A] ~ **between,** pass from one state, etc to a second, then back to the first, etc: *He* ~*d between high spirits and low spirits.* ~ **with,** come one after the other, by turns: *Wet days* ~*d with fine days.* ,**alternating 'current,** current that reverses its direction at regular intervals, the cycle being repeated continuously, the number of complete cycles per second being known as the *frequency.* ⇨ direct¹(5). **al·ter·na·tion** /ˌɔːltə'neɪʃn/ *n*

al·ter·na·tive /ɔːl'tɜːnətɪv/ *adj* (of two things) that may be had, used, etc in place of sth else: *'Either' and 'or' are* ~ *conjunctions. There are* ~ *answers to* $x^2 = 16$ (ie x = +4 or x = −4). □ *n* [C] **1** choice between two things: *You have the* ~ *of working hard and being successful or of not working hard and being unsuccessful. Is there no* ~ *to what you propose?* **2** one of more than two possibilities. ~**·ly** *adv* as an ~: *a fine of £10 or* ~*ly six weeks imprisonment.*

altho /ɔːl'ðəʊ/ (US spelling for) although.

al·though /ɔːl'ðəʊ/ *conj* ⇨ though.

al·tim·eter /'æltɪmiːtə(r) *US:* æl'tɪmɪtər/ *n* barometer, eg as used in aircraft, for showing height above sea-level.

al·ti·tude /'æltɪtjuːd *US:* -tuːd/ *n* **1** (not of living things) height, esp above sea-level. **2** (usu *pl*) place high above sea-level: *It is difficult to breathe at these* ~*s.* **3** (astron) angular distance of a celestial object above the horizon.

alto /'æltəʊ/ *n* (*pl* ~s /-təʊz/) **1** (musical part for, a person having a) male singing voice between tenor and treble; counter tenor; female voice of similar range (*contralto*). **2** instrument with the same range: ~**-saxophone.**

al·to·gether /ˌɔːltə'geðə(r)/ *adv* **1** entirely; wholly:

I don't ~ agree with him. It's ~ out of the question. **2** (of a total quantity) taken as a whole: *You owe me £3 ~.* **3** (modifying a complete sentence) on the whole; considering everything: *The weather was bad and the trains were crowded—~, it wasn't a very satisfactory excursion.*

al·tru·ism /'æltruːɪzəm/ *n* [U] principle of considering the well-being and happiness of others first; unselfishness; [C] instance of this. **al·tru·ist** /'æltruːɪst/ *n* person who follows ~. **al·tru·is·tic** /ˌæltruːˈɪstɪk/ *adj* **al·tru·is·ti·cally** /-klɪ/ *adv*

alum /'æləm/ *n* [U] white mineral salt, used medically, in dyeing, etc.

alu·min·ium /ˌæljuˈmɪnɪəm/ (US = **alu·mi·num** /əˈluːmɪnəm/) *n* [U] light white metal (symbol **Al**) extracted chiefly from bauxite, used for making hard, light alloys for cooking utensils, electrical apparatus, etc.

alumna /əˈlʌmnə/ *n* (*pl* ~e /-niː/) (US) girl or woman who was a pupil or student of a school, college or university.

alum·nus /əˈlʌmnəs/ *n* (*pl* -ni /-naɪ/) (US) boy or man who was a pupil or student of a school, college or university.

al·veolar /ælˈvɪələ(r)/ *n, adj* (phon) (consonant) made by the tongue against the gum behind the upper front teeth, eg /t, d, s/.

al·ways /'ɔːlweɪz/ *adv* **1** at all times; without exception: *The sun ~ rises in the east.* (*Always* may be modified by *almost, nearly* or *not.*) *He's nearly ~ at home in the evening.* Cf *not ~* and *hardly ever. I'm not ~ at home on Sundays,* ie I'm occasionally away from home. *I'm hardly ever* (= very seldom) *at home on Sundays.* **2** (usu with the continuous tenses) again and again; repeatedly: *He was ~ asking for money. Why are you ~ finding fault?*

am /*after* 'I': m; *otherwise*: əm; *strong form*: æm/ ⇨ **be**[1].

amah /'ɑːmə/ *n* (in the East) nursemaid; maidservant.

amain /əˈmeɪn/ *adv* (old use, or poet) **1** violently. **2** in haste.

amal·gam /əˈmælgəm/ *n* **1** alloy of mercury. **2** soft mixture, eg one used for filling holes in decayed teeth.

amal·ga·mate /əˈmælgəmeɪt/ *vt, vi* [VP6A,2A] (of classes, societies, races of people, business companies) mix; combine; unite. **amal·ga·ma·tion** /əˌmælgəˈmeɪʃn/ *n* [U] mixing; combining. [C] combination; union.

am·anu·en·sis /əˌmænjʊˈensɪs/ *n* (*pl* -ses /-siːz/) person who writes from dictation or copies what sb else has written.

ama·ryl·lis /ˌæməˈrɪlɪs/ *n* (kinds of) lily-like plant growing from a bulb.

amass /əˈmæs/ *vt* [VP6A] pile or heap up; collect: ~ *riches/a fortune.*

ama·teur /'æmətə(r)/ *n* **1** person who paints pictures, performs music, acts in plays, etc, for the love of it, not for money; person playing a game, taking part in sports, etc, without receiving payment: (attrib) *an ~ painter/photographer.* ⇨ professional. ~**·ish** /-rɪʃ/ *adj* inexpert; imperfect. ~**·ism** /-rɪzəm/ *n*

ama·tory /'æmətərɪ US: -tɔːrɪ/ *adj* (formal) of or causing (esp sexual) love; of lovers; of making love.

amaze /əˈmeɪz/ *vt* [VP6A] fill with great surprise or wonder: *You ~ me! I was ~d at the news/~d to*

hear that.... **amaz·ing** *part adj* **amaz·ing·ly** *adv. He's doing amazingly well.* ~**-ment** *n* [U] *I heard with ~ment that...; His ~ment at the news was immense. He looked at me in ~ment.*

Ama·zon /'æməzən US: -zɒn/ *n* **1** (in old Gk stories) female warrior. **2** (small *a*) tall, vigorous woman.

am·bas·sa·dor /æmˈbæsədə(r)/ *n* **1** minister representing the Government of his country in a foreign country: *the British A~ to Greece.* **2** (often *A~ Extraordinary*) minister sent by the Government of one State to the Government of another on a special mission. **3** authorized representative. **am·bas·sa·dress** /æmˈbæsədrɪs/ *n* female ~. ~**-ial** /æmˌbæsəˈdɔːrɪəl/ *adj* ⇨ diplomat, embassy.

am·ber /'æmbə(r)/ *n* [U] hard, clear yellowish-brown gum used for making ornaments, etc; its colour (seen in traffic lights between red and green).

am·ber·gris /'æmbəgriːs US: -grɪs/ *n* [U] wax-like substance present in the intestines of whales and found floating in tropical seas, used as a fixative in perfumes.

am·bi·dex·trous /ˌæmbɪˈdekstrəs/ *adj* able to use the left hand or the right equally well.

am·bi·ence /'æmbɪəns/ *n* environment; atmosphere.

am·bi·ent /'æmbɪənt/ *adj* (formal) (of air, etc) on all sides; surrounding.

am·bi·guity /ˌæmbɪˈgjuːətɪ/ *n* (*pl* -ties) **1** [U] state of being ambiguous. **2** [C] expression, etc that can have more than one meaning: *Let's clear up the ~ in this paragraph.*

am·bigu·ous /æmˈbɪgjʊəs/ *adj* **1** having more than one meaning: *'More' is ~ in 'Ask me more difficult questions.'* **2** of uncertain meaning or intention: *He gave me an ~ glance.* ~**·ly** *adv*

am·bit /'æmbɪt/ *n* (often *pl*) bounds; extent; range of power or authority.

am·bi·tion /æmˈbɪʃn/ *n* **1** [U] strong desire (*to be* or *do* sth, *for* sth): *A boy who is filled with ~ usually works hard. His ~ to become prime minister is likely to be realized.* **2** [C] particular desire of this kind: *He has great ~s.* **3** [C] object of such a desire: *achieve one's ~(s).*

am·bi·tious /æmˈbɪʃəs/ *adj* **1** full of ambition: *an ~ boy; ~ for fame; ~ for one's children; ~ to succeed in life.* **2** showing or needing ambition: *~ plans; an ~ attempt.* ~**·ly** *adv*

am·biva·lent /æmˈbɪvələnt/ *adj* having either or both of two contrary or similar values, meanings, etc. **am·biva·lence** /-ləns/ *n*

amble /'æmbl/ *vi* [VP2A,C] (of a horse) move along without hurrying, lifting the two feet on one side together; (of a person) ride or walk at an easy pace. □ *n* slow, easy, pace: *He was coming along at an ~.*

am·bro·sia /æmˈbrəʊzɪə US: -əʊʒə/ *n* [U] (Gk myth) the food of the gods; anything that has a delightful taste or smell.

am·bu·lance /'æmbjʊləns/ *n* closed vehicle for carrying people who are ill, wounded in war or hurt in accidents.

am·bus·cade /ˌæmbəˈskeɪd/ *n, vt* = ambush.

am·bush /'æmbʊʃ/ *n* [C,U] (the placing of) troops, etc, waiting to make a surprise attack: *fall into an ~; be attacked from (an) ~.* **lie/wait in ~ (for),** be hidden waiting to attack. □ *vt* [VP6A] attack from such a position.

ameba /ə'miːbə/ n = amoeba.

ameer /ə'mɪə(r)/ n = amir.

ameli·or·ate /ə'miːlɪəreɪt/ vt, vi [VP6A,2A] (formal) (cause to) become better. **ameli·or·ation** /ə‚miːlɪə'reɪʃn/ n

amen /ɑː'men US: eɪ'men/ int (eccles) word used at the end of a prayer or hymn and meaning 'May it be so'.

amen·able /ə'miːnəbl/ adj ~ (to), **1** (of persons) responsive; willing to be guided or controlled: ~ to kindness/advice/reason. Do you find your wife ~? **2** (legal) (of persons) responsible (to); in a position where one must do certain things or be punished for not doing them: We are all ~ to the law. **3** (of cases, situations) able to be tested or dealt with: The case is not ~ to ordinary rules.

amend /ə'mend/ vt, vi **1** [VP6A,2A] make or become better; improve; free from faults or errors: He'll have to ~ his style of living. **2** [VP6A] make changes in the wording of a rule, a proposed law, etc. ~·able /-əbl/ adj ~·ment n [U] ~ing; [C] change proposed or made (to a rule, regulation, etc).

amends /ə'mendz/ n pl **make ~/all possible ~ (to sb) (for sth)**, give compensation: make ~ to sb for an injury.

amen·ity /ə'miːnətɪ/ n (pl -ties) **1** (pl) things, circumstances, surroundings, that make life easy or pleasant: an exchange of amenities, of courtesies, polite expressions; a town with many amenities, eg a park, a public library, playing fields; the amenities offered by a Bank, eg the provision of travel cheques, payment of standing orders. **2** (sing) pleasantness: the ~ of the climate.

Amer·ica /ə'merɪkə/ n the United States of ~.

Ameri·can /ə'merɪkən/ adj of N or S America, esp the US. '~ **organ**, small organ with reeds but no pipes. '~ **plan**, (at hotels) system of charges including room, all meals and service. □ n native or inhabitant of America; citizen of the US. ~·ism /-ɪzəm/ n [C] word or phrase typical of ~ English; [U] loyalty to the US or to things typically ~.

am·ethyst /'æmɪθɪst/ n precious stone, purple or violet.

ami·able /'eɪmɪəbl/ adj good-tempered; kind-hearted; easy and pleasant to talk to: I've always found him a most ~ fellow. **amia·bil·ity** /‚eɪmɪə'bɪlətɪ/ n **1** [U] friendliness. **2** (pl) (-ties) friendly remarks: after a few amiabilities. **ami·ably** /-əblɪ/ adv

amic·able /'æmɪkəbl/ adj peaceable; done in a friendly way: When countries cannot settle a dispute in an ~ way, they should settle it by arbitration. **amica·bil·ity** /‚æmɪkə'bɪlətɪ/ n **amic·ably** /-əblɪ/ adv: live together amicably, peacefully, in a friendly way.

amid /ə'mɪd/, **amidst** /ə'mɪdst/ preps (poet) among; in or into the middle of.

amid·ships /ə'mɪdʃɪps/ adv (naut) half-way between the bows and stern of a ship: Our cabin is ~.

amir, ameer, emir /ə'mɪə(r)/ n title used by some Muslim rulers.

amiss /ə'mɪs/ pred adj, adv wrong(ly); out of order: There's not much ~ with it. Nothing comes ~ to him, (colloq) He's ready to welcome, is able to use, anything that comes to him. **take sth ~**, take offence at it, be hurt in one's feelings: Don't take it ~ if I point out your errors.

am·ity /'æmətɪ/ n [U] friendship; friendly relations (between persons or countries): live in ~ with sb; a

treaty of ~.

am·me·ter /'æmɪtə(r)/ n meter that measures electric current in amperes.

am·mo·nia /ə'məʊnɪə/ n [U] strong, colourless gas (**NH₃**) with a sharp smell, used in refrigeration and for the manufacture of explosives and fertilizers; solution of this gas in water. **am·mo·ni·ated** /ə'məʊnɪeɪtɪd/ adj combined with ~.

am·mon·ite /'æmənaɪt/ n coiled shell of an extinct mollusc.

am·mu·ni·tion /‚æmjʊ'nɪʃn/ n [U] military stores, esp of explosives (shells, bombs, etc) to be used against the enemy.

am·nesia /æm'niːzɪə US: -'niːʒə/ n [U] (path) partial or total loss of memory.

am·nesty /'æmnəstɪ/ n (pl -ties) [C] general pardon, esp for offences against the State: The rebels returned home under an ~.

amoeba /ə'miːbə/ n (pl ~s or ~e /-biː/) (zool) simple microscopic form of living matter, found in water, soil and animal parasites, always changing shape and too small to be seen except with the help of a microscope. **amoebic** /ə'miːbɪk/ adj of, caused by, amoebae: amoebic dysentery.

amok /ə'mɒk/ adv (also **amuck**) **run ~**, run about wildly and act violently.

among /ə'mʌŋ/, **amongst** /ə'mʌŋst/ preps **1** (showing position) surrounded by; in the middle of: a village ~ the hills; sitting ~ her children; hiding ~ the bushes. (Note that the n or pron after among must be pl) Cf Switzerland is situated between France, Italy, Austria and W Germany. **2** (also with a pl n or pron, or a collective n, to show inclusion, association, connection): You are only one ~ many who need help. A~ those present were the Prime Minister, the Bishop of Barchester and Mrs Proudie. I saw him ~ the crowd. **3** (followed by a superl) one of: Leeds is ~ the largest industrial towns in England. **4** (indicating division, distribution, possession or joint activity to, for or by more than two persons): He divided his property ~ his sons. You must settle the matter ~ yourselves. They had less than £10 ~ them, all of them together had less than £10. ⇨ between ²(7). **5** (after a prep): Choose one from ~ these.

amoral /‚eɪ'mɒrəl US: -'mɔːrəl/ adj non-moral; not concerned with morals.

am·or·ous /'æmərəs/ adj easily moved to love; showing love; of (esp sexual) love: ~ looks; an ~ young man; ~ poetry. ~·ly adv

amor·phous /ə'mɔːfəs/ adj having no definite shape or form.

amor·tize /ə'mɔːtaɪz US: 'æmərt-/ vt [VP6A] (legal) end (a debt) by setting aside money regularly for future payments. ⇨ sinking fund at sink¹(7). **amor·ti·za·tion** /ə‚mɔːtɪ'zeɪʃn US: ‚æmɜːtɪ-/ n

amount /ə'maʊnt/ vi [VP3A] ~ **to**, add up to; be equal to: His debts ~ to £5000. What he said ~ed to very little indeed, didn't mean much, wasn't important. Riding on a bus without paying the fare ~s to (= is the same thing as) cheating the bus company. It ~s to this, that…, It means that…. □ n **1** total; whole: He owed me £100 but could pay only half that ~, could only pay £50. **2** [C] quantity: A large ~ of money is spent on tobacco every year. There is still quite an ~ of prejudice against him. **any ~ of**, large quantity: He has any ~ of money, is very rich. **in large/small, etc ~s**, large/small, etc quantities at a time.

amour /ə'mʊə(r)/ n [C] (fac) love affair: Don't

bore us with accounts of your ~s.

amour-propre /ˌæmʊə ˈprɒprə/ *n* (F) self-respect; self-esteem.

amp /æmp/ *n* (abbr) = ampere.

am·pere /ˈæmpeə(r) *US:* ˈæmpɪər/ *n* unit for measuring electric current.

am·pheta·mine /æmˈfetəmiːn/ *n* [C,U] (med) (trade name *Benzedrine*) (variety of) drug used medically, eg for slimming, and by drug addicts seeking euphoria.

am·phib·ian /æmˈfɪbɪən/ *n* **1** animal able to live both on land and in water, eg a frog. **2** aircraft designed to take off from and alight on either land or water. **3** flat-bottomed vehicle able to move in water and on land: (attrib) ~ *tank*.

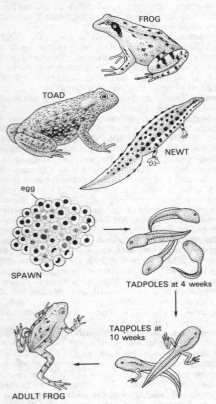

FROG

TOAD

NEWT

egg

SPAWN

TADPOLES at 4 weeks

TADPOLES at 10 weeks

ADULT FROG

amphibians

am·phibi·ous /æmˈfɪbɪəs/ *adj* adapted for both land and water: ~ *vehicles*, vehicles that can cross rivers, etc as well as move on land; ~ *operations*, military operations in which land forces use ~ vehicles when making an invasion from the sea.

amphi·theatre (US = -ter) /ˈæmfɪθɪətə(r)/ *n* **1** round or oval unroofed building with rows of seats rising behind and above each other round an open space used for public games and amusements. **2** (not US) rows of seats similarly arranged in a half-circle in a theatre. **3** (*natural* ~) level space with hills rising on all sides.

am·phora /ˈæmfərə/ *n* (*pl* ~s or ~e /-riː/) two-handled jar, used in ancient Greece and Rome for holding wine or oil.

ample /ˈæmpl/ *adj* (-r, -st) **1** large-sized; with plenty of space: *This new car has an* ~ *boot. There's* ~ *room for the children on the back seat.* **2** plentiful: *He has* ~ *resources*, is wealthy. **3** sufficient; quite enough: *£5 will be* ~ *for my needs.* **am·ply** /ˈæmplɪ/ *adv*: *amply supplied with money*, having more than is needed; *amply rewarded*, well rewarded.

am·plify /ˈæmplɪfaɪ/ *vt* (*pt,pp* -fied) [VP6A] **1** make larger or fuller, esp give fuller information, more details, etc, about: ~ *a story/an account.* **2** increase the strength of (voltage or current, etc). **am·pli·fi·ca·tion** /ˌæmplɪfɪˈkeɪʃn/ *n* **am·pli·fier** /ˈæmplɪfaɪə(r)/ *n* appliance for ~ing.

am·pli·tude /ˈæmplɪtjuːd *US:* -tuːd/ *n* [U] (formal) breadth; largeness; abundance.

am·poule (US also **am·pule**) /ˈæmpuːl/ *n* small container, esp for a hypodermic injection.

am·pu·tate /ˈæmpjʊteɪt/ *vt* [VP6A] cut off, eg an arm, a leg, by surgery. **am·pu·ta·tion** /ˌæmpjʊˈteɪʃn/ *n*

amuck /əˈmʌk/ *adv* ⇨ amok.

amu·let /ˈæmjʊlɪt/ *n* sth worn in the belief or hope that it will protect the wearer (*against* evil, etc).

amuse /əˈmjuːz/ *vt* [VP6A] **1** make time pass pleasantly for: *The boys* ~*d themselves* (*by*) *drawing caricatures of their teacher. Keep the baby* ~*d with these toys.* **2** make (sb) laugh or smile: *His foolish mistakes* ~*d all of us. The children were* ~*d at/by the storyteller's jokes. We were* ~*d to learn that....* **amus·ing** *part adj* causing laughter or smiles: *an amusing story/storyteller.* ~**·ment** *n* **1** [U] state of being ~d: *She couldn't hide her* ~*ment at his foolish mistake. To the great* ~*ment of everybody, the actor's beard fell off. He looked at me in* ~*ment.* **2** [C] sth that makes time pass pleasantly: *There are plenty of* ~*ments here—cinemas, theatres concerts, football matches, and so on.* ˈ~**·ment arcade**, room or hall containing pin-tables, gambling machines, etc, esp in large towns, seaside resorts, etc. ˈ~**·ment park/grounds**, place with swings, roundabouts, shooting galleries, and other means of amusing oneself. *places of* ~*ment*, cinemas, theatres, etc. *do sth for* ~*ment*, do it as a means of passing time pleasantly, not for a serious purpose.

an[1] /ən; *strong form:* æn/ *indef art* ⇨ a[2].

an[2] /æn/ *conj* (old use) if.

anach·ron·ism /əˈnækrənɪzəm/ *n* [C] **1** mistake in dating sth; sth out of date now or in a description of past events: *In the sentence 'Julius Caesar looked at his wrist-watch and lifted the telephone receiver' there are two* ~*s.* **2** person, custom, attitude, etc regarded (unfavourably) as out of date: *Most young people in Britain regard Tory politicians who shoot grouse in Scotland as dreadful* ~*s.* **anach·ron·is·tic** /əˌnækrəˈnɪstɪk/ *adj*

arena

an amphitheatre

ana·conda /ˌænəˈkɒndə/ n large snake of tropical S America, esp the kind that crushes its prey.

anae·mia (US = **ane·mia**) /əˈniːmɪə/ n [U] lack of enough blood; poor condition of the blood, causing paleness. **anaemic** (US = **anemic**) /əˈniːmɪk/ adj suffering from ∼.

an·aes·thesia (US = **an·es·thesia**) /ˌænɪsˈθiːzɪə US: -ˈθiːʒə/ n [U] state of being unable to feel (pain, heat, cold, etc); branch of chemistry concerned with substances producing this state. **anaes·thetic** (US = **an·es·thetic**) /ˌænɪsˈθetɪk/ n [C] substance (eg ether, chloroform), technique, that produces ∼: *under an anaesthetic.* **general anaesthetic,** one affecting the whole body, usu administered in hospital. **local anaesthetic,** one administered by injection and affecting only part of the body, eg into the gums by a dentist. **an·aes·the·tize** (US = **an·es·the·tize**) /əˈniːsθətaɪz/ vt [VP6A] make insensible to pain, etc. **an·aes·the·tist** (US = **an·es·the·tist**) /əˈniːsθətɪst/ n person trained to administer anaesthetics.

ana·gram /ˈænəgræm/ n word made by changing the order of the letters in another word (eg plum—lump): *Let's play ∼s,* make words of this kind.

anal /ˈeɪnl/ adj (anat) of the anus.

ana·lects /ˈænəlekts/ (also **ana·lecta** /ˌænəˈlektə/) n pl collection of pieces of literature: *Confucian ∼.*

an·al·gesia /ˌænælˈdʒiːzɪə US: -ʒə/ n [U] (med) absence of, condition of not feeling, pain. **an·al·ges·ic** /ˌænælˈdʒiːsɪk/ n substance, eg an ointment, which relieves pain.

anal·og·ous /əˈnæləgəs/ adj ∼ **(with),** similar or parallel (to): *The two processes are not ∼ (with each other),* ∼·**ly** adv

ana·logue (also **-log**) /ˈænəlɒg US: -lɔːg/ n 1 sth that is similar to another thing: *meat ∼,* artificial prepared substitute for meat (usu of soya beans). 2 '∼ **computer** n one which can perform operations on numbers, the numbers being represented by some physical quantity or electrical signal. ⇨ *digital computer* at digit.

anal·ogy /əˈnælədʒɪ/ n (pl -gies) 1 [C] partial likeness or agreement. **draw an ∼ between,** describe the similarities: *The teacher drew an ∼ between the human heart and a pump.* 2 [U] **by/from ∼; on the ∼ of,** by a process of reasoning between parallel cases: *argue by ∼; argument by/from ∼.*

ana·lyse (US = **-lyze**) /ˈænəlaɪz/ vt [VP6A] 1 examine (sth) in order to learn what it is made up of: *If we ∼ water, we find that it is made up of two parts of hydrogen and one part of oxygen.* 2 (gram) split up (a sentence) into its grammatical parts. 3 study or examine in order to learn about: *The leader tried to ∼ the causes of our failure.* 4 = psycho∼.

analy·sis /əˈnæləsɪs/ n (pl -yses /-əsiːz/) 1 [U] (eg of a book, a character, a situation) separation into parts possibly with comment and judgement: *critical ∼ of literary texts; expert ∼ of market trends,* ie of how prices, sales, etc are likely to go; [C] instance of this; statement of the result of doing this. ⇨ synthesis. 2 = psycho∼. **ana·lytic** /ˌænəˈlɪtɪk/, **-i·cal** /-kl/ adj of ∼; using ∼. **ana·lyti·cally** /-klɪ/ adv

ana·lyst /ˈænəlɪst/ n 1 person skilled in making (esp chemical) analyses: *a food ∼.* 2 = psycho∼. **ana·lyze** ⇨ analyse.

ana·paest (US = **-pest**) /ˈænəpiːst US: -pest/ n (of verse rhythm) foot consisting of two unaccented

syllables followed by one accented syllable, (◡◡—) as in eg 'I am 'mon/arch of 'all/I sur'vey'. **ana·paes·tic,** (US = **-pestic**) /ˌænəˈpiːstɪk US: -ˈpest-/ adj

an·archy /ˈænəkɪ/ n [U] absence of government or control; disorder; confusion. **an·arch·ism** /-ɪzəm/ n [U] political theory that government and laws are undesirable. **an·arch·ist** /-ɪst/ n person who favours ∼; person who wishes to overthrow all established governments. **an·archic** /əˈnɑːkɪk/ adj **an·archi·cally** /-klɪ/ adv

anath·ema /əˈnæθəmə/ n 1 (eccles) formal declaration of the Church, excommunicating sb or condemning sth as evil. 2 sth that is detested. ∼·**tize** /əˈnæθəmətaɪz/ vt curse.

anat·omy /əˈnætəmɪ/ n [U] science of the structure of animal bodies; study of their structures by separation into parts. **ana·tomi·cal** /ˌænəˈtɒmɪkl/ adj **anat·om·ist** /-ɪst/ n person who dissects corpses; person who studies or teaches ∼.

an·ces·tor /ˈænsestə(r)/ n any one of those persons from whom one is descended, esp one more remote than a grandparent. ∼ **worship,** the worship of one's ∼s as spirits or gods. **an·ces·tress** /-trɪs/ n woman ∼. **an·ces·tral** /ænˈsestrəl/ adj belonging to, having come from, one's ∼s: *his ancestral home.* **an·ces·try** /ˈænsestrɪ/ n (pl -ries) line of ∼s.

an·chor /ˈæŋkə(r)/ n heavy piece of iron with a ring at one end, to which a cable is fastened, used for keeping a ship fast to the sea bottom or a balloon to the ground; anything that gives stability or security. **let go/drop/cast the ∼,** lower it. **weigh ∼,** raise it. **come to ∼; bring (a ship) to ∼,** stop sailing and lower the ∼. **lie/ride/be at ∼,** be made fast and held safe by the ∼. ∼·**man** /-mən/, one who co-ordinates the work of a group of persons who work together, eg in a radio or TV studio. □ vt, vi [VP6A] make (a ship) secure with an ∼; [VP2A] lower an ∼. ∼·**age** /-rɪdʒ/ n place where ships may ∼ safely.

an·chor·ite /ˈæŋkəraɪt/ n hermit.

an·chovy /ˈæntʃəvɪ/ n (pl -vies) small fish of the herring family; it has a strong flavour and is used for sauces, etc: (attrib) ∼ *paste/sauce.*

ancient /ˈeɪnʃənt/ adj 1 belonging to times long past: ∼ *Rome and Greece; the ∼s,* the civilized people who lived long ago. 2 (often hum) very old: *an ∼-looking hat.*

an·cil·lary /ænˈsɪlərɪ US: ˈænsəlerɪ/ adj 1 helping, providing a service to those carrying on the main business of an enterprise: *The transport corps is ∼ to the infantry.* 2 subordinate (to): ∼ *roads/ undertakings/industries.*

and /usu forms: ən, ənd; (after t,d,f,v,θ,ð,s,z,ʃ,ʒ) often n; strong form: ænd/ conj 1 (connecting words, clauses, sentences): *a table and four chairs; learning to read and write.* (When two nn stand for things or persons closely connected, the determining word is not repeated before the second n): *a knife and fork.* Cf a knife and a spoon; *my father and mother.* Cf my father and my uncle. 2 (Note *twenty-five* but *five and twenty,* sometimes used in telling the time): *five and twenty to six.* 3 (In constructions replacing an *if*-clause): *Work hard and you will pass* (= If you work hard, you will pass) *the examination.* 4 (indicating intensive repetition or continuation): *for hours and hours; for miles and miles; better and better. We knocked and knocked,* continued to knock. 5 (colloq) to: *Try* *and come early. Go and buy one.*

an·dante /æn'dæntɪ/ *n, adj, adv* (I; music) (piece of music to be played) in moderately slow time.

and·iron /'ændaɪən/ *n* iron support (usu one of a pair) for holding logs in a fireplace. Also called *firedog*.

an·ec·dote /'ænɪkdəʊt/ *n* short, usu amusing, story about some real person or event.

ane·mia, ane·mic ⇨ anaemia, anaemic.

anem·om·eter /ˌænɪ'mɒmɪtə(r)/ *n* [C] (met) instrument for measuring the force and velocity of the wind.

anem·one /ə'nemənɪ/ *n* **1** (bot) (also called *windflower*) small star-shaped woodland flower; cultivated varieties of this flower. **2** '**sea** ~, popular name of a creature living in the sea, having a tube-like body with tentacles.

an anemone   a sea anemone

anent /ə'nent/ *prep* (old use, or Scot) concerning; about.

an·er·oid /'ænərɔɪd/ *adj, n* ~ **(barometer)**, one that measures air-pressure by the action of air on the elastic lid of a box partly exhausted of air.

an·es·thesia *n*⇨ anaesthesia.

anew /ə'nju: *US:* ə'nu:/ *adv* again; in a new or different way.

angel /'eɪndʒl/ *n* **1** (esp in Christian belief) messenger from God (usu shown in pictures as a human being in white with wings). **2** lovely or innocent person. **3** (as a compliment to sb who is kind, thoughtful, etc): *Thanks, you're an* ~*!* ~**ic** /æn'dʒelɪk/ *adj* of or like an ~. ~**i·cally** /-klɪ/ *adv*

an·gelica /æn'dʒelɪkə/ *n* [U] sweet-smelling plant, esp the kind used in cooking and medicine; its stem, boiled in sugar.

an·gelus /'ændʒɪləs/ *n* (also A~) (bell rung in RC churches at morning, noon and sunset to call people to recite) prayer to the Virgin Mary.

anger /'æŋgə(r)/ *n* [U] the strong feeling that comes when one has been wronged or insulted, or when one sees cruelty or injustice; the feeling that makes people want to quarrel or fight: *filled with* ~ *at what he saw; speak in* ~*; do sth in a moment of* ~. □ *vt* [VP6A] fill (sb) with ~; make angry: *He is easily* ~*ed.*

an·gina pec·toris /ænˌdʒaɪnə 'pektərɪs/ *n* (Lat) (path) heart disease marked by sharp pain in the chest.

angle¹ /'æŋgl/ *n* **1** space between two lines or surfaces that meet. '~**-dozer** *n* mechanical scraper used for levelling roads or ground surfaces. ⇨ **bulldozer.** '~**-iron** *n* L-shaped length of iron or steel used to strengthen a framework. '~**-park** *vt, vi* park a vehicle at an angle to the side of the roadway, etc: *cars* ~*-parked as close as herringbones.* **2** (fig) point of view: *Try looking at the af-*

fair from a different ~. *What* ~ *are you writing the story from?* □ *vt* [VP6A] ~ *the news,* present it to the public in a particular way (usu to suit the bias of the writer or his employer).

angle² /'æŋgl/ *vi* [VP2A,3A] **1** fish (for trout, etc) with a rod, line, hook and bait. **2** ~ *for,* (fig) use tricks, hints, etc in order to get sth: ~ *for compliments;* ~ *for an invitation to a party.* **ang·ler** /'æŋglə(r)/ *n* person who ~s. Cf *fisherman* using nets, etc. **ang·ling** *n* [U] (art, sport of) fishing with a rod.

Ang·li·can /'æŋglɪkən/ *n, adj* (member) of the Church of England.

ang·li·cize /'æŋglɪsaɪz/ *vt* [VP6A] make English or like English: ~ *a French word.* **ang·li·cism** /'æŋglɪsɪzəm/ *n* English way of saying sth.

Anglo- /ˌæŋgləʊ/ *pref* English: ~*-French relations,* between GB and France. ˌ~*-*'**Catholic** *n, adj* (member) of the party in the Anglican Church that insists upon its unbroken connection with the early Christian Church and that objects to being called Protestant. ˌ~*-*'**Indian** *n, adj* (a) (person) of British birth, living or having lived, in India. (b) (person) of mixed British and Indian blood; Eurasian. ˌ~*-*'**Saxon** *n, adj* (person) of English descent; one of the group of people who settled in England (from NW Europe) before the Norman Conquest; their language (also called *Old English*).

Anglo·mania /ˌæŋgləʊ'meɪnɪə/ *n* excessive love of and admiration for English customs, etc.

Anglo·phile /'æŋgləʊfaɪl/ (also **-phil** /-fɪl/) *n* person who loves England or English things.

Anglo·phobe /'æŋgləʊfəʊb/ *n* person who hates or fears England or English things.

Anglo·pho·bia /ˌæŋgləʊ'fəʊbɪə/ *n* excessive hatred or fear of England and of English things.

an·gora /æn'gɔːrə/ *n* **1** [C] long-haired cat, goat or rabbit. **2** [U] material made from wool of ~ goats.

an·gos·tura /ˌæŋgə'stjʊərə/ *n* [U] bitter liquid, used as a tonic, made from the bark of a S American tree.

angry /'æŋgrɪ/ *adj* (-ier, -iest) **1** filled with anger (*with* sb, *at* what sb does or says, *about* sth): *He was* ~ *at being kept waiting. He was* ~ *with himself for having made such a foolish mistake. He will be* ~ *to learn* (= when he learns) *that you have disobeyed his orders.* **2** (of a cut, sore, wound) red; inflamed. **3** (of the sea, sky, clouds) stormy; threatening. **ang·ri·ly** /-əlɪ/ *adv*

angst /æŋst/ *n* [U] (G) feeling of anxiety (eg caused by considering the state of world affairs).

an·guish /'æŋgwɪʃ/ *n* [U] severe suffering (esp of mind): *She was in* ~ *until she knew that her husband's life had been saved.* ~**ed** *adj* expressing ~: ~*ed looks.*

angu·lar /'æŋgjʊlə(r)/ *adj* **1** having angles or sharp corners. **2** (of persons) with the shape of the bones showing under the skin; (of a person's nature, etc) rather stiff and awkward: *an* ~ *gait.* ~**·ity** /ˌæŋgjʊ'lærətɪ/ *n* (*pl* -ties).

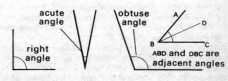

acute angle   obtuse angle   right angle   ABD and DBC are adjacent angles

angles

ani·line /'ænɪliːn *US:* 'ænəlɪn/ *n* substance obtained chemically from coal-tar, used in the manufacture of dyes, drugs, etc.

ani·mad·vert /ˌænɪmæd'vɜːt/ *vi* [VP3A] ~ *(on)*, (formal) make (esp critical) remarks (about sb's conduct). **ani·mad·version** /ˌænɪmæd'vɜːʃn *US:* -ʒn/ *n* criticism.

ani·mal /'ænɪml/ *n* **1** living thing that can feel and move about. Men, dogs, birds, flies, fish and snakes are all ~s. **the '~ kingdom,** one of three divisions (the others being *vegetable* and *mineral*). ⊏⊐ the illus at ape, bird, cat, dog, domestic, fish, insect, large, reptile, sea, small. **2** four-footed ~ (eg a dog or a horse): ~ *husbandry,* the breeding of cattle, sheep, horses, etc. **3** ~ other than man. **4** (used attrib) of the physical, not spiritual, side of man: ~ *needs,* eg food; ~ *desires.* ~ *spirits,* natural lightheartedness. **~·cule** /ˌænɪ'mælkjuːl/ *n* microscopically small ~.

ani·mate /'ænɪmət/ *adj* living; lively. □ *vt* /'ænɪmeɪt/ *v* [VP6A,14] ~ *sb/sth (to/with sth),* give life to; make lively; inspire: *A smile ~d her face. There was an ~d discussion. The news ~d us to greater efforts/with greater enthusiasm. All his life this great man was ~d by a passion for truth and justice.* ~d car'toon *n* cinema film made by photographing a series of drawings. **ani·ma·tion** /ˌænɪ'meɪʃn/ *n* [U] (esp) liveliness; ardour.

ani·mism /'ænɪmɪzəm/ *n* [U] belief that all objects (trees, stones, the wind, etc) have souls.

ani·mos·ity /ˌænɪ'mɒsətɪ/ *n* [U] ~ *(against/ towards/between),* strong dislike, active enmity; [C] *(pl* -ties) instance of this.

ani·mus /'ænɪməs/ *n* [U] animosity; (with *indef art*) instance of this: *an ~ against me.*

an·ise /'ænɪs/ *n* plant with sweet-smelling seeds. **ani·seed** /'ænɪsiːd/ *n* [U] seed of ~, used for flavouring.

ankle /'æŋkl/ *n* joint connecting the foot with the leg; thin part of the leg between this joint and the calf. ⊏⊐ the illus at leg. '~ socks, short ones just covering the ~s. **ank·let** /'æŋklɪt/ *n* ornament for the ~.

anna /'ænə/ *n* former copper coin in Pakistan and in India, a sixteenth part of a rupee.

an·nals /'ænlz/ *n pl* story of events year by year; record of new knowledge or discoveries written year by year; yearly record of the work of a learned society. **an·nal·ist** /'ænəlɪst/ *n* writer of ~.

an·neal /ə'niːl/ *vt* [VP6A] cool (metals, glass, etc) very slowly after heating, in order to toughen and temper.

an·nex[1] /ə'neks/ *vt* [VP6A,14] **1** take possession of (territory, etc). **2** ~ *(to),* add or join (sth) (as an extra part *to* sth). **~·ation** /ˌænek'seɪʃn/ *n* [U] ~ing; [U] instance of this, that which is ~ed.

an·nex[2] /'æneks/ (also **an·nexe**) *n* [C] **1** smaller building added to, or situated near, a larger one: *an ~ to a hotel.* **2** addition *(to* a document).

an·ni·hi·late /ə'naɪəleɪt/ *vt* [VP6A] destroy completely; end the existence of (eg an army, a fleet): *The invasion force was ~d.* (fig) *Radio communication has ~d space.* **an·ni·hi·la·tion** /əˌnaɪə'leɪʃn/ , *n* [U] complete destruction (of military or naval forces, etc).

an·ni·ver·sary /ˌænɪ'vɜːsərɪ/ *n* [C] *(pl* -ries) yearly return of the date of an event; celebration of this: *my wedding ~; the ~ of Shakespeare's birth; an ~ dinner,* one held to celebrate an ~.

Anno Domini /ˌænəʊ 'dɒmɪnaɪ/ (Lat) (abbr **AD** /ˌeɪ 'diː/) in the year of our Lord: *in* AD *250,* 250 years after the birth of Jesus. ⊏⊐ *before Christ* (BC) at before[3]; ⊏⊐ BC in App *2.*

an·no·tate /'ænəteɪt/ *vt* [VP6A] add notes (to a book, etc) explaining difficulties, giving opinions, etc: *an ~d text/version.* **an·no·ta·tion** /ˌænə'teɪʃn/ *n* [U] annotating; [C] note or comment.

an·nounce /ə'naʊns/ *vt* [VP6A,9,14] **1** make known: *Mr Green ~d (to his friends) his engagement to Miss White. It has been ~d that Mr Green and Miss White will be married in May. The book was ~d as in preparation. The Government ~d that the danger was past.* **2** make known the arrival of: *The secretary ~d Mr and Mrs Brown,* spoke their names as they entered. **3** say that sb is about to speak, sing, etc (eg in a TV programme). **~·ment** *n* [C] sth said, written, or printed to make known what has happened or (more often) what will happen: *a broadcast ~ment. An ~ment will be made next week. A~ments of deaths, marriages and births appear in the newspapers.* **an·noun·cer** *n* (esp) person who ~s speakers, singers, etc in a radio or TV broadcast.

an·noy /ə'nɔɪ/ *vt* [VP6A esp in passive] *be ~ed with sb/at sth/about sth,* irritate; make rather angry: *He was ~ed with his wife because the dinner was badly cooked. I felt ~ed when he refused to help. Do stop ~ing your father! He was ~ed to learn that the train would be delayed. He felt/got/ was ~ed with the boy for being so stupid/was ~ed at the boy's stupidity.* ~**ing** *part adj: It's ~ing to miss a train. How ~ing! The ~ing thing about it is that...,* What causes trouble or irritation is that.... **~·ance** /-əns/ *n* **1** [U] vexation; being ~ed: *with a look of ~ance; much to our ~ance; subject a person to ~ance,* worry him. **2** [C] sth that ~s: *All these little ~ances did not spoil her sweet temper.*

an·nual /'ænjʊəl/ *adj* **1** coming or happening every year. **2** lasting for only one year or season. **3** of one year: *his ~ income; the ~ production.* □ *n* **1** plant that lives for one year or season. **,hardy '~,** (joc) event, etc which often recurs (and is considered tiresome or monotonous). **2** book, etc that appears under the same title but with new contents every year. **~·ly** *adv*

an·nu·ity /ə'njuːətɪ *US:* -'nuː-/ *n* [C] *(pl* -ties) fixed sum of money paid to sb yearly as income during his lifetime; form of insurance to provide such a regular, annual income. **an·nui·tant** /ə'njuːɪtənt *US:* -'nuː-/ *n* person who receives an ~.

an·nul /ə'nʌl/ *vt* (-ll-) [VP6A] put an end to, eg an agreement, a law, etc; declare (that sth, eg a marriage, is) invalid, of no effect. **~·ment** *n*

an·nu·lar /'ænjʊlə(r)/ *adj* (rare) ring-like.

an·nun·ci·ate /ə'nʌnsɪeɪt/ *vt* [VP6A] (formal) announce; proclaim.

an·nun·ci·ation /əˌnʌnsɪ'eɪʃn/ *n* **the A~,** (eccles) the announcement by the angel Gabriel to Mary that she was to be the mother of Jesus Christ; festival that commemorates this, 25 Mar.

an·ode /'ænəʊd/ *n* (electr) (US also called *plate*) **1** positively charged electrode (from which current enters). ⊏⊐ cathode. **2** negative terminal of a battery.

ano·dyne /'ænədaɪn/ *n, adj* (medicine, drug) able to lessen pain; (sth) able to give comfort to the mind.

anoint /ə'nɔɪnt/ *vt* [VP6A,23,14] apply oil or ointment to (esp as a religious ceremony): ~ *sb with oil. The Lord ~ed thee King over Israel* (⇨ I Sam 15:17). ~-ment *n*

anom·al·ous /ə'nɒmələs/ *adj* irregular; different in some way from what is normal. ~ **verb**, verb that forms its interr and neg without the helping verb *do* (eg *must, ought*). ~·ly *adv* **anom·aly** /ə'nɒməlɪ/ *n* (*pl* -lies) ~ thing: *A bird that cannot fly is an anomaly.*

anon [1] /ə'nɒn/ *adv* (old use) soon. *ever and ~,* every now and then.

anon [2] /ə'nɒn/ (in footnotes, etc) short for *by an anonymous author.*

ano·nym·ity /ˌænə'nɪmətɪ/ *n* [U] state of being anonymous.

anony·mous /ə'nɒnɪməs/ *adj* without a name, or with a name that is not made known: *an ~ letter,* not signed; *an ~ gift,* from sb whose name is not known; *an author who remains ~.* ~·ly *adv*

anoph·eles /ə'nɒfɪliːz/ *n* =(zool) (kinds of) mosquito, esp the kinds that spread malaria. ⇨ the illus at **insect.**

an·or·ak /'ænəræk/ *n* [C] jacket with a hood attached, worn as protection against rain, wind and cold; wind-cheater.

an·other /ə'nʌðə(r)/ *pron, adj* ⇨ other. **1** an additional (one): *Will you have ~ cup of tea? Where shall we be in ~ ten years,* ten years from now? *I don't like this hat; please show me ~ (one).* **2** a similar (one): *This young man is very clever; he may be ~ Edison,* an inventor as clever as Edison. **3** a different (one): *We can do that ~ time. That's quite ~ matter. Taking one thing/year, etc with ~,* on the whole, taking the average (of good and bad, etc). *one ~,* ⇨ one[3](3).

answer [1] /'ɑːnsə(r) *US*: 'æn-/ *n* ~ (*to*), **1** sth done in return; reply: *Have you had an ~ to your letter? She gave no ~,* said nothing in return. *I have a complete ~ to the accusation,* can prove that it was wrongly made. *in ~ (to),* as a reply (to): *in ~ to your letter. The doctor came at once in ~ to my telephone call.* **2** solution; result of working with figures, etc: *The ~ to* 3 × 17 *is* 51. *have/know all the ~s,* know, or believe one knows, a great deal about sth.

answer [2] /'ɑːnsə(r) *US*: 'æn-/ *vt, vi* **1** [VP6A,9,12A,2A] say, write or do, sth in return (to): ~ *a question;* ~ *the teacher. He ~ed nothing. What shall I ~? Have you ~ed his letter? He ~ed that he knew nothing about it. No one ~ed. No one was able to ~ him a word* (⇨ Matt 22:48). *A~ me this question.* ~ *the door/the bell,* go to the door when sb has knocked or rung the bell. ~ *the telephone,* pick up the receiver and ~ the caller. [VP2C,15B] ~ *(sb) back,* ~ impolitely, interrupt, esp when being corrected or scolded. **2** [VP6A] fulfil; be suitable or satisfactory for: *Will this ~ your purpose?* **3** [VP2A] succeed; be satisfactory: *This plan has not ~ed; we must find a better one.* **4** [VP3A] ~ *to the name of,* (of a pet animal) have the name of: *The dog ~s to the name of Spot.* ~ *to a description,* correspond to it, be as described: *He doesn't ~ to the description of the missing man that appeared in the newspapers.* **5** [VP6A,3A] ~ *(to) the helm,* (of a ship) change course when the helm is moved: *The ship no longer ~s the helm,* cannot be steered. **6** [VP3A] ~ *for,* be responsible for: *I can't ~ for his honesty,* cannot guarantee that he is honest. *I will ~ for it* (= promise) *that the next one will be bet-*

ter. You will have to ~ for (= suffer for) *your wrongdoing one day. He has a lot to ~ for,* is responsible for, to be blamed for, many things. ~·**able** /-əbl/ *adj* **1** that can be ~ed. **2** (*pred* only) responsible (*to* sb *for* sth).

ant /ænt/ *n* small insect, proverbial for industry, that lives in highly organized societies. ⇨ the illus at **insect.** '**ant-eater** *n* name of various animals that live on ants. '**ant-hill** *n* pile of earth, etc, over an underground nest of ants; cone-shaped nest of white ants. ˌwhite 'ant *n* white ant-like insect (termite) that destroys wood, etc by eating it.

an·tag·on·ism /æn'tægənɪzəm/ *n* [C,U] (instance of) active opposition: *the ~ between the two men; feel a strong ~ for/toward sb,* find oneself strongly opposed to him.

an·tag·on·ist /æn'tægənɪst/ *n* person struggling against another; opponent.

an·tag·on·is·tic /ænˌtægə'nɪstɪk/ *adj* ~ *(to),* **1** hostile; opposed; contrary. **2** (of forces) acting against each other. **an·tag·on·is·ti·cally** /-klɪ/ *adv*

an·tag·on·ize /æn'tægənaɪz/ *vt* [VP6A] make an enemy of (sb); irritate into conflict: *I advise you not to ~ him.*

ant·arc·tic /æn'tɑːktɪk/ *adj* of the south polar regions. **the ˌA~ 'Circle,** the line of latitude 66½°S.

ante [1] /'æntɪ/ *n* stake in the game of poker that a player must put down after looking at his cards or before he can draw new cards. *raise the ~,* increase one's stake (or contribution to sth).

ante [2] /'æntɪ/ *pref* before: ~*nuptial,* before marriage.

ante·ced·ent /ˌæntɪ'siːdnt/ *adj* ~ *(to),* (formal) previous (to). □ *n* **1** preceding event or circumstance. **2** (*pl*) ancestors; past history of a person or persons. **3** (gram) noun, clause or sentence, to which a following pronoun or adverb refers. **ante·ced·ence** /-ns/ *n* priority.

ante·cham·ber /'æntɪtʃeɪmbə(r)/ *n* room leading into a large room or hall.

ante·date /ˌæntɪ'deɪt/ *vt* [VP6A] **1** put a date on, of a letter, document, etc, earlier than the true one; give an earlier date than the true one to (an event). **2** come before in time: *This event ~s the arrival of Columbus by several centuries.*

ante·di·luvian /ˌæntɪdɪ'luːvɪən/ *adj* of, suitable for, the time before the Flood, (Genesis); old-fashioned; out of date. □ *n* old-fashioned person.

ante·lope /'æntɪləʊp/ *n* deer-like, fast-running animal with thin legs. ⇨ the illus at **large.**

ante mer·id·iem /ˌæntɪ mə'rɪdɪəm/ (Lat) (abbr **am**) time between midnight and noon: *7.30am.* ⇨ *pm* at post meridiem; ⇨ App 4 (6).

ante·na·tal /ˌæntɪ'neɪtl/ *adj* existing or occurring before birth; pre-natal: ~ *clinics,* for pregnant women.

an·tenna /æn'tenə/ *n* (*pl* ~e /-niː/) **1** jointed organ found in pairs on the heads of insects and crustaceans, used for feeling, etc. ⇨ the illus at **insect.** **2** (*pl* also ~s) (esp *US*) (kind of) radio or TV aerial.

ante·nup·tial /ˌæntɪ'nʌpʃl/ *adj* before marriage: *an ~ contract.*

ante·pen·ul·ti·mate /ˌæntɪpɪ'nʌltɪmət/ *adj* last but two: *the ~ syllable.*

an·ter·ior /æn'tɪərɪə(r)/ *adj* (formal) coming before (in time or position).

ante·room /'æntɪrʊm *US*: -ruːm/ *n* antechamber; waiting-room.

an·them /'ænθəm/ *n* musical composition, usu for

choir and organ, to be sung in churches. **national** '~, song or hymn of a country, eg 'God Save the Queen'.

an·ther /'ænθə(r)/ n (bot) part of the stamen containing pollen. ⇨ the illus at **flower**.

an·thol·ogy /æn'θɒlədʒɪ/ n [C] (pl -gies) collection of poems or pieces of prose, or of both, by different writers, or a selection from the work of one writer.

an·thra·cite /'ænθrəsaɪt/ n [U] very hard form of coal that burns with little smoke or flame.

an·thrax /'ænθræks/ n [U] infectious, often fatal, disease of sheep and cattle that may be transmitted to human beings.

an·thro·poid /'ænθrəpɔɪd/ adj man-like. □ n ~ animal, esp an ape, eg a gorilla.

an·thro·pol·ogy /ˌænθrə'pɒlədʒɪ/ n [U] science of man, esp of the beginnings, development, customs and beliefs of mankind. **an·thro·pol·ogist** /ˌænθrə'pɒlədʒɪst/ n expert in ~. **an·thro·po·logi·cal** /ˌænθrəpə'lɒdʒɪkl/ adj

anti- /ænti US: ˌæntaɪ/ pref against: ˌ~-bal'listic; ˌ~-'clerical; ˌ~-'christian, opposed to Christianity.

anti–air·craft /ˌænti 'eəkrɑːft US: -kræft/ adj used against enemy aircraft: ~ guns.

anti·biotic /ˌæntibaɪ'ɒtɪk/ n, adj (med) (substance, eg penicillin) produced by moulds and bacteria, capable of destroying or preventing the growth of bacteria.

anti·body /'æntibɒdɪ/ n [C] (pl -dies) (physiol) (kinds of) substance formed in the blood tending to inhibit or destroy harmful bacteria, etc.

an·tic /'æntɪk/ n (usu pl) grotesque movement, step, attitude, intended to amuse, eg by a clown at a circus; queer behaviour.

an·tici·pate /æn'tɪsɪpeɪt/ vt [VP6A,C,9] **1** do, make use of, before the right or natural time: Don't ~ your income, order goods, etc before you receive your income. **2** do sth before sb else does it: It is said that Columbus discovered America, but he was probably ~d by sailors from Norway who reached Labrador 500 years earlier. **3** see what needs doing, what is likely to happen, etc and do what is necessary: He tries to ~ all my needs, satisfy them before I mention them. A good general tries to ~ the enemy's movements. **4** expect (which is the more usu word): We don't ~ much trouble. The directors ~d a fall in demand/that demand would fall. **an·tici·pa·tory** /ˌæn,tɪsɪ'peɪtərɪ/ adj

an·tici·pa·tion /æn,tɪsɪ'peɪʃn/ n [C,U] (in) ~ (of), action of anticipating; sth anticipated: We bought an extra supply of coal in ~ of a cold winter. Thanking you in ~, in advance and expecting you to do what I have asked.

anti–cli·max /ˌænti 'klaɪmæks/ n [C] sudden fall from sth noble, serious, important, sensible, etc; descent that contrasts with a previous rise.

anti–clock·wise /ˌænti 'klɒkwaɪz/ adv in the direction opposite to the movements of the hands of a clock.

anti·cyc·lone /ˌænti'saɪkləʊn/ n [C] (met) area in which atmospheric pressure is high compared with that of surrounding areas, with an outward flow of air; the area is characterized by quiet, settled weather. ⇨ **depression**(4).

anti·dote /'æntidəʊt/ n [C] medicine used against a poison, or to prevent a disease from having an effect: an ~ against/for/to snakebite.

anti·freeze /'æntifriːz/ n [U] substance (usu a liquid) added to another liquid to lower its freezing point, eg as used in the radiator of a motor vehicle.

anti–hero /'ænti hɪərəʊ/ n (pl ~es /-rəʊz/) (in fiction and drama) protagonist lacking the traditional characteristics of a hero, such as courage and dignity.

anti·knock /ˌænti'nɒk/ n [U] substance added to the fuel in a motor–car engine to reduce noise. ⇨ **knock**[2](3).

anti·log·ar·ithm /ˌænti'lɒgərɪðəm US: -'lɔːg-/ n number to which a logarithm belongs: 1000, 100 and 10 are the ~s of 3, 2 and 1.

anti·ma·cas·sar /ˌæntimə'kæsə(r)/ n covering to protect the back or arm of a chair or sofa from grease–marks.

anti·mony /'æntimənɪ US: -məʊnɪ/ n [U] easily broken silvery white metal, (symbol Sb) used in alloys, esp metal for type[1](3).

an·tipa·thy /æn'tɪpəθɪ/ n ~ (to/towards/ against) (between two persons), [U] strong and decided dislike; [C] (pl -thies) instance or object of this: feel/show a strong/marked ~ to a place/ against sb. **anti·pa·thetic** /ˌæntipə'θetɪk/ adj

anti·per·son·nel /ˌænti ˌpɜːsə'nel/ adj (usu of mines[2](3)) designed to kill or wound human beings (not to destroy vehicles).

an·tipo·des /æn'tɪpədiːz/ n pl (usu the ~) (two) place(s) on the opposite sides of the earth, esp the region opposite our own.

anti·quar·ian /ˌænti'kweərɪən/ adj connected with the study, collection or sale of antiquities: an ~ bookseller. □ n antiquary.

anti·quary /'æntikwərɪ US: -kwerɪ/ n (pl -ries) person who studies, collects or sells, antiquities.

anti·quated /'æntikweɪtɪd/ adj obsolete; out of date; (of persons) having old-fashioned ideas and ways.

an·tique /æn'tiːk/ adj belonging to the distant past; existing since old times; in the style of past times. □ n [C] material, (eg a piece of furniture, a work of art) of a past period (in GB at least 50 years old, in US 100 years). the ~, ~ style in art. Cf second-hand, usu of things more recent.

an·tiquity /æn'tɪkwətɪ/ n **1** [U] old times, esp before the Middle Ages; great age: the heroes of ~; a city of great ~, eg Athens; in remote ~. **2** (pl -ties) buildings, ruins, works of art, remaining from ancient times: Greek and Roman antiquities.

an·tir·rhi·num /ˌænti'raɪnəm/ n (pl ~s) (bot) genus of plants; snapdragon.

anti–Sem·ite /ˌænti 'siːmaɪt US: 'sem-/ n, adj (person) prejudiced against Jews, hating Jews. **anti–Sem·itic** /ˌænti sɪ'mɪtɪk/ adj **anti–Semi·tism** /ˌænti 'semɪtɪzəm/ n.

anti·sep·tic /ˌænti'septɪk/ n, adj (chemical substance) preventing a wound, etc from becoming septic, esp by destroying germs.

anti·so·cial /ˌænti'səʊʃl/ adj **1** opposed to social laws or to organized societies. **2** likely, tending, to interfere with or spoil public amenities: It is ~ to leave litter in public places/to play a transistor in public. **3** not sociable.

anti·tank /ˌænti'tæŋk/ attrib adj for use against military tanks: ~ guns/ditches.

an·tith·esis /æn'tɪθəsɪs/ n (pl -ses /-siːz/) **1** [U] direct opposite (of, to). **2** [U] opposition (of one thing to another, between two things); [C] instance of this; contrast of ideas vividly expressed, as in 'Give me liberty, or give me death'. **anti·thetic** /ˌænti'θetɪk/, **anti·theti·cal** /-ɪkl/ adj **anti·theti-**

cally /-klɪ/ *adv*

anti·toxin /ˌæntɪˈtɒksɪn/ *n* substance (usu a serum) able to counteract a toxin or disease.

anti·trade /ˌæntɪˈtreɪd/ *adj* '∼ **wind,** wind that blows in the opposite direction to a trade wind. □ *n* (usu *pl*) ∼ wind.

ant·ler /ˈæntlə(r)/ *n* branched horn; branch of a horn (of a stag or other deer). ⇨ the illus at large.

an·to·nym /ˈæntənɪm/ *n* [C] word that is contrary in meaning to another: *Hot is the* ∼ *of cold.* ⇨ synonym.

anus /ˈeɪnəs/ *n* (anat) opening at the end of the alimentary canal, through which waste matter passes out. ⇨ the illus at alimentary.

an·vil /ˈænvɪl/ *n* **1** large, heavy block of iron on which a smith hammers heated metal into shape. **2** (anat) bone in the ear. ⇨ the illus at ear.

anxiety /æŋˈzaɪətɪ/ *n* **1** [U] emotional condition in which there is fear and uncertainty about the future: *We waited with* ∼ *for news of her safe arrival. Tom's foolish behaviour caused his parents great* ∼. **2** [C] (*pl* -ties) instance of such a feeling: *All these anxieties made him look pale and tired. The Budget statement removed all anxieties about higher taxes.* **3** [U] keen desire: ∼ *for knowledge; his* ∼ *to please his employers.*

anxious /ˈæŋkʃəs/ *adj* **1** ∼ (about/at/for), feeling anxiety; troubled: *I am very* ∼ *about my son's health. He is* ∼ *for/about her safety/at her non-arrival.* **2** causing anxiety: *We have had an* ∼ *time. His illness has been a very* ∼ *business.* has caused us anxiety. **3** ∼ to/for/about/that, strongly wishing: *He was* ∼ *to meet you/*∼ *for his brother to meet you. We were* ∼ *that help should be sent promptly/*∼ *for help to be sent.* ∼·ly *adv*

any[1] /ˈenɪ/ *adj* **1** ⇨ some[1](1) (in neg and interr sentences, and in clauses of condition, etc) **2** (in affirm sentences, with negation implied, eg with a *v* such as '*prevent*', after the *prep* '*without*', after such *advv* as '*hardly*'): *We did the* work without any difficulty. I have hardly any leisure nowadays. Please try to prevent any loss while the goods are on the way.* **3** (usu stressed; usu in affirm sentences) no matter which: *Come any day you like. You will find me at my desk at any hour of the day, at all times. We must find an excuse, any excuse will do.* **4** in '**any case,** whatever happens, whatever the circumstances may be. **at** '**any rate,** at least. **5** (colloq; used in affirm and neg sentences, with *sing* common *nn* for *a(n)* or *one*): *This bucket is useless—it hasn't any handle.*

any[2] /ˈenɪ/ *adv of degree* (used in neg, interr and conditional sentences, in contexts where negation or doubt is indicated or implied, and with comparatives. Cf the similar use of *no* and *none*.) at all; in any degree: *Is your father any better? They were too tired to go any further. The children didn't behave any too well,* ie they behaved rather badly. *If it's any good/use, I'll buy it.* **(not) any the better/the worse (for),** (not) at all better/worse for: *He got* wet *through in the rain yesterday but isn't any the worse for it,* has not suffered in any way.

any[3] /ˈenɪ/ *pron* ⇨ some[2].

any·body /ˈenɪbɒdɪ/ *n, pron* **1** (in neg, interr, etc sentences: ⇨ somebody, someone). **2** (in affirm sentences) no matter who: *A*∼ *will tell you where the bus stop is. A*∼ *who saw the accident is asked to communicate with the police. That's* ∼'s *guess,* (colloq) is quite uncertain. ∼ *else,* ⇨ else. **3** per-

son of importance: *You must work harder if you wish to be* ∼. *Was she* ∼ *before her marriage, Had she any social position? He'll never be* ∼.

any·how /ˈenɪhaʊ/ *adv* **1** in any possible way; by any possible means: *The house was empty and I couldn't get in* ∼. **2** carelessly; without order: *The work was done all* ∼. **3** (*adv* or *conj*) in any case; at any rate: *A*∼, *you can try, even if there's not much chance of success. It's too late now,* ∼.

any·one /ˈenɪwʌn/ *n, pron* = anybody.

any·place /ˈenɪpleɪs/ *adv* (esp in US) = anywhere.

any·thing /ˈenɪθɪŋ/ *n, pron* **1** (in neg, interr, etc sentences: ⇨ something) (note the position of the *adj*): *Has* ∼ *unusual happened?* **2** no matter what: *I want something to eat;* ∼ *will do.* **be** ∼ **but,** be definitely not: *He's* ∼ *but mad.* **3** (used adverbially, to intensify a meaning): *The thief ran like* ∼ *when he saw the policeman.* **(as)** easy as ∼, (colloq) very easy.

any·way /ˈenɪweɪ/ *adv* = anyhow(3).

any·where /ˈenɪweə(r) *US:* -hweər/ *adv* **1** (in neg, interr, etc sentences: ⇨ somewhere) (note the use of ∼ with post-adjuncts): *I'll go* ∼ *(that) you suggest. Are we going* ∼ *(in) particular?* **2** (used as a *prep* object): *That leaves me without* ∼ *to keep all my books.* **3** no matter where: *Put the box down* ∼. *We'll go* ∼ *you like.*

aorta /eɪˈɔːtə/ *n* chief blood-vessel through which blood is carried from the left side of the heart. ⇨ the illus at respiratory.

apace /əˈpeɪs/ *adv* (old use, or liter) quickly: *Ill news spreads* ∼.

apache /əˈpæʃ/ *n* (in Paris) hooligan; rough.

apa·nage (also **ap·pan·age**) /ˈæpənɪdʒ/ *n* [U] **1** natural accompaniment; sth that necessarily goes with sth else. **2** property, etc coming to sb because of birth or office.

apart /əˈpɑːt/ *adv* **1** distant: *The two houses are 500 metres* ∼. *The negotiators are still miles* ∼, show no signs of agreeing. **2** to or on one side: *He took me* ∼ *in order to speak to me alone. Why does she hold herself* ∼, ie not mix with other people? **joking/jesting** ∼, speaking seriously. **set/put (sth/sb)** ∼ **(from),** put (it) on/one side; reserve it; make (sb) (appear) special: *His far-sightedness set him* ∼ *from most of his contemporaries.* **3** separate(ly): *I can't get these two things* ∼. *He was standing with his feet wide* ∼. ∼ **from,** independently of; leaving on one side: ∼ *from these reasons.* **tell/know two things or persons** ∼, distinguish one from the other. ⇨ come(15), pull[1](7), take[1](16).

apart·heid /əˈpɑːtheɪt/ *n* (S Africa) (policy of) racial segregation; separate development of Europeans and non-Europeans.

apart·ment /əˈpɑːtmənt/ *n* **1** single room in a house. **2** (*pl*) set of rooms, furnished or unfurnished, either owned or rented by the week or month, eg for a holiday at the seaside. **3** (US) set of rooms in a large building (called *an'*∼ *house*), usu on the same floor. (US ∼ = GB *flat;* US ∼ *house* = GB *block of flats;* US ∼ *hotel* = GB *service flats.*) ⇨ tenement.

apa·thy /ˈæpəθɪ/ *n* [U] absence of sympathy or interest; indifference (*towards*). **apa·thetic** /ˌæpəˈθetɪk/ *adj* showing or having ∼. **apa·theti·cally** /-klɪ/ *adv*

ape /eɪp/ *n* **1** tailless monkey (*gorilla, chimpanzee, orang-outang, gibbon*). **2** person who mimics

GIBBON
MARMOSET
RHESUS MONKEY
CHIMPANZEE
ORANG-UTAN
GORILLA
BABOON

others: *play the ape,* mimic. **3** (colloq) clumsy, ill-bred person. □ *vt* imitate (sb's behaviour, etc).
aperi·ent /ə'pɪərɪənt/ *n, adj* (formal) laxative.
aperi·tif /ə'perətɪf *US:* əˌperə'tiːf/ *n* [C] alcoholic drink, (eg *vermouth*) taken before a meal.
ap·er·ture /'æpətʃə(r)/ *n* opening, esp one that admits light, eg to a camera lens.
apex /'eɪpeks/ *n* (*pl* ∼es or apices /'eɪpɪsiːz/) top or highest point: *the ∼ of a triangle; at the ∼ of his career/fortunes.*
apha·sia /ə'feɪzɪə *US:* -ʒə/ *n* [U] (path) loss of ability to use speech or to understand speech (as the result of brain injury).
aphid /'eɪfɪd/ *n* = aphis.
aphis /'eɪfɪs/ *n* (*pl* aphides /'eɪfɪdiːz/) very small insect that lives by sucking juices from plants; plant louse.
aph·or·ism /'æfərɪzəm/ *n* [C] short, wise saying; maxim.
aph·ro·dis·iac /ˌæfrə'dɪzɪæk/ *n, adj* [C,U] (substance, drug) exciting sexual desire and activity.
api·ary /'eɪpɪərɪ *US:* -erɪ/ *n* (*pl* -ries) place with a number of hives where bees are kept. **api·ar·ist** /'eɪpɪərɪst/ *n* person who keeps bees. **api·cul·ture** /'eɪpɪkʌltʃə(r)/ *n* bee-keeping.
apiece /ə'piːs/ *adv* to, for or by, each one of a group: *They cost a penny ∼,* each.
apish /'eɪpɪʃ/ *adj* of or like an ape; foolishly imitative.
aplomb /ə'plɒm/ *n* [U] self-confidence; assurance (in speech or behaviour): *He answered with perfect ∼.*
apoca·lypse /ə'pɒkəlɪps/ *n* revelation (esp of knowledge from God). **the A∼,** the last book in the Bible, recording the revelation to St John. ⇨ App 10. **apoca·lyp·tic** /əˌpɒkə'lɪptɪk/ *adj* of or like an ∼ or the A∼.
Apoc·ry·pha /ə'pɒkrɪfə/ *n pl* (with *sing v*) those books of the Old Testament that are considered of doubtful authorship by the Jews and were excluded

from the Bible at the time of the Reformation. ⇨ App 10. **apoc·ry·phal** /ə'pɒkrɪfl/ *adj* of doubtful authority or authorship.
apo·gee /'æpədʒiː/ *n* **1** (astron) position (in the orbit of the moon or any planet) when it is at its greatest distance from the earth. **2** (fig) highest point.
apolo·getic /əˌpɒlə'dʒetɪk/ *adj* making an apology; expressing regret; excusing a fault or failure: *He was ∼ about/for arriving late. He wrote an ∼ letter.* **apolo·geti·cally** /-klɪ/ *adv* **apolo·get·ics** *n* (usu with *sing v*) the art or practice of explaining or justifying a religious belief, political creed, etc.
apolo·gist /ə'pɒlədʒɪst/ *n* person who engages in ∼s.
apolo·gize /ə'pɒlədʒaɪz/ *vi* [VP2A,3A] *∼ (to sb) (for sth),* make an apology; say one is sorry: *You must ∼ to your sister for being so rude.*
apol·ogy /ə'pɒlədʒɪ/ *n* (*pl* -gies) **1** [C] *∼ (to sb) (for sth),* statement of regret (for doing wrong, being impolite, hurting sb's feelings): *offer/make/accept/refuse an ∼; offer sb an ∼; make one's apologies (to sb),* eg for being late, for not being able to come. **2** [C] explanation or defence (of beliefs, etc). ⇨ apologetics. **3** *an ∼ for,* a poor specimen of, eg a dinner/letter.
apo·phthegm, apo·thegm /'æpəθem/ *n* [C] short, pointed or forceful saying.
apo·plexy /'æpəpleksɪ/ *n* [U] loss of power to feel, move, think, usu caused by injury to blood-vessels in the brain. **apo·plec·tic** /ˌæpə'plektɪk/ *adj* connected with, causing ∼; suffering from ∼: *an apoplectic stroke/fit;* (colloq) red in the face; easily made angry.
apos·tasy /ə'pɒstəsɪ/ *n* [U] giving up one's beliefs or faith; turning away from one's religion; [C] (*pl* -sies) instance of this. **apos·tate** /ə'pɒsteɪt/ *n, adj* (person) guilty of ∼.
a pos·teri·ori /ˌeɪ ˌpɒsterɪ'ɔːraɪ/ *adv, adj phrase* (Lat) (reasoning) from effects to causes, eg saying,

'The boys are tired so they must have walked a long way'. ⇨ a priori.

apostle /ə'pɒsl/ *n* **1** one of the twelve men (**the Twelve A~s**) chosen by Jesus to spread his teaching; missionary of the early Christian Church, eg St Paul, the A~ to the Gentiles. **2** leader or teacher of reform, of a new faith or movement. **apos·tolic** /ˌæpə'stɒlɪk/ *adj* **1** of the ~s(1) or the times when they lived. **2** of the Pope.

apos·trophe¹ /ə'pɒstrəfɪ/ *n* the sign ' used to show omission of letter(s) or number(s), (as in *can't, I'm, '05*, for *cannot, I am, 1905*), for the possessive (as in *boy's, boys'*), and for the plurals of letters (as in *There are two l's in 'Bell'*). ⇨ App 9.

apos·trophe² /ə'pɒstrəfɪ/ *n* passage in a public speech, in a poem, etc addressed to a particular person (who may be dead or absent). **apos·trophize** /ə'pɒstrəfaɪz/ *vt* make an ~ to.

apoth·ecary /ə'pɒθɪkərɪ *US:* -kerɪ/ *n* (*pl* -ries) (old use, but still in Scot) person who prepares and sells medicines and medical goods. **apothecaries' weight,** ⇨ App 5.

apo·thegm ⇨ apophthegm.

apothe·osis /əˌpɒθɪ'əʊsɪs/ *n* (*pl* -ses /-si:z/) **1** (of a human being) making or becoming a god or a saint: *the ~ of a Roman Emperor*. **2** release from earthly life. **3** glorification; glorified ideal.

ap·pal (US also **ap·pall**) /ə'pɔːl/ *vt* (-ll-) [VP6A] fill with fear or terror; dismay; shock deeply: *They were ~led at the news.* **~·ling** *adj*: *When will this ~ling war end?* **~·ling·ly** *adv*

ap·pa·nage ⇨ apanage.

ap·par·atus /ˌæpə'reɪtəs *US:* -'rætəs/ *n* [C] (*pl* ~es) (rarely *pl*; sometimes *a piece of* ~) **1** set of instruments or other mechanical appliances put together for a purpose: *a heating ~*, eg for supplying steam heat throughout a building. **2** bodily organs by which natural processes are carried on: *Your digestive ~ takes the food you eat and changes it so that it can be used to build up the body.*

ap·parel /ə'pærəl/ *n* [U] (old use, or liter) dress; clothing. □ *vt* (-ll-; US -l-) dress; clothe.

ap·par·ent /ə'pærənt/ *adj* **1** clearly seen or understood: *It was ~ to all of us...*, We all saw clearly...; *as will soon become ~*, as you will soon see. **2** seeming; according to appearances: *in spite of her ~ indifference*, although she seemed to be indifferent. **~·ly** *adv*

ap·par·ition /ˌæpə'rɪʃn/ *n* [C] the coming into view, esp of a ghost or the spirit of a dead person.

ap·peal /ə'piːl/ *vi* [VP2A,3A] ~ (*to sb*) (*against/ for/from sth*), **1** make an earnest request: *The prisoner ~ed to the judge for mercy. At Christmas people ~ to us to help the poor.* **2** (legal) take a question (to a higher court, etc) for rehearing and a new decision: *~ to another court; ~ against a decision; ~ from a judgement.* **3** go (to sb) for a decision: (football, etc) *~ to the linesman; ~ against the referee's decision;* (cricket) *The captain ~ed against the light*, said the light was too poor for further play. **4** attract; move the feelings of: *Bright colours ~ to small children. Do these paintings ~ to you?* □ *n* **1** *an ~ for*, an earnest call for: *make an ~ for help.* **2** [C] (legal) act of ~ing(2): *an ~ to a higher court; an ~ from a decision; to lodge an ~;* [U] *to give notice of ~; acquittal on ~.* **3** [C] (esp in sport) act of ~ing: *an ~ to the referee.* **4** [U] interest; (power of) attraction: *That sort of music hasn't much ~ for me/has lost its ~.* **5** [U] suppli-

cation: *with a look of ~ on her face*, asking for help or sympathy. **~·ing** *adj* **1** moving; touching the feelings or sympathy. **2** attractive. **~·ing·ly** *adv*

ap·pear /ə'pɪə(r)/ *vi* **1** [VP2A,C] come into view, become visible: *When we reached the top of the hill, the town ~ed below us. The ship ~ed on the horizon.* **2** [VP2A,C] arrive: *He promised to be here at four but didn't ~ until six.* **3** [VP2A,C] **(a)** (of an actor, singer, lecturer, etc) come before the public: *He has ~ed in every large concert hall in Europe.* **(b)** (of a book) be published: *When will your new novel ~?* **(c)** (legal) present oneself publicly: *The defendant failed to ~ before the court.* **4** [VP2A,4D,E] seem: *Why does she ~ so sad? He ~s to have many friends. You don't want to ~ a fool*, to look like a fool. *The house ~ed (to be) deserted. It would ~ that his intention was/His intention ~s to have been to arrive yesterday. There ~s to have been a mistake. So it ~s. It ~s not. It ~s to me that.../It begins to ~ that...*, It looks as though....

ap·pear·ance /ə'pɪərəns/ *n* [C] **1** act of appearing: *make an ~; make one's first ~*, (of an actor, singer, etc) appear in public for the first time. *put in an ~*, show oneself, attend (a meeting, party, etc): *I don't want to go to the garden party but I'd better put in an ~.* **2** that which shows or can be seen; what sth or sb appears to be: *The child had the ~ of being (= looked as if it were) half starved. She has a slightly foreign ~. We mustn't judge by ~s*, by what can be seen outside, by outward looks. *keep up ~s*, maintain an outward show (in order to hide what one does not wish people to see, eg by buying smart clothes and spending little on food, etc). *in ~*, so far as ~ is concerned; outwardly: *In ~ it is a strong building. to/by/from all ~(s)*, so far as can be seen: *He was to all ~(s) dead.*

ap·pease /ə'piːz/ *vt* [VP6A] make quiet or calm: ~ *sb's anger;* ~ *sb's curiosity/hunger.* **~·ment** *n* [U] appeasing, eg by making concessions to potential enemies.

ap·pel·lant /ə'pelənt/ *adj* (legal) concerned with appeals. □ *n* (legal) person who appeals to a higher court.

ap·pel·la·tion /ˌæpə'leɪʃn/ *n* [C] (formal) name or title; system of names.

ap·pend /ə'pend/ *vt* [VP6A,14] ~ *sth (to)*, (formal) add in writing or in print; add (sth) at the end: ~ *a clause to a treaty;* ~ *a seal or signature to a document.*

ap·pend·age /ə'pendɪdʒ/ *n* [C] sth added to, fastened to or forming a natural part of, a larger thing.

ap·pen·dix /ə'pendɪks/ *n* **1** [C] (*pl* -dices /-dɪsiːz/) sth added, esp at the end of a book. **2** [C] (*pl* also ~es) small out-growth on the surface of a bodily organ, esp ('vermiform ~) a worm-like appendage of the large intestine. ⇨ the illus at alimentary. **ap·pen·di·ci·tis** /əˌpendɪ'saɪtɪs/ *n* [U] diseased condition of the vermiform ~, requiring in many cases a surgical operation. **ap·pen·dec·tomy** /ˌæpen'dektəmɪ/ *n* (*pl* -mies) removal by surgery of the vermiform ~.

ap·per·tain /ˌæpə'teɪn/ *vi* [VP3A] ~ *to*, (formal) belong to as a right; be appropriate: *the duties ~ing to his office.*

ap·pe·tite /'æpɪtaɪt/ *n* [U] physical desire (esp *for* food): *She is suffering from lack of ~. If you eat a lot of chocolate before supper, it will spoil/take away your ~*, prevent you from enjoying your supper. (fig) *He had no ~ for the fight.* [C] instance of such a desire: *The long walk gave him a good* ∼.

ap·pe·tizer /'æpɪtaɪzə(r)/n sth done (eg a walk) or served (eg olives, a short alcoholic drink) in order to stimulate the ∼. **ap·pe·tiz·ing** adj pleasing to, exciting, the ∼: *an appetizing smell from the kitchen.*

ap·plaud /ə'plɔːd/ vi,vt 1 [VP6A,2A,B] show approval (of) by clapping the hands: *The audience* ∼ed (the singer) for five minutes. He was loudly ∼ed. 2 express approval of: *I* ∼ *your decision.*

ap·plause /ə'plɔːz/ n [U] loud approval; handclapping: *greeted with* ∼; *win the* ∼ *of the audience.*

apple /'æpl/ n (tree with) round fruit with firm juicy flesh and skin that is green, red or yellow when the fruit is ripe. ⇨ the illus at fruit. *the* ∼ *of one's eye,* sb or sth dearly loved. ∼ *of discord,* cause of quarrel. *upset the/sb's* '∼-*cart,* spoil the/his plans. *in* ∼-,*pie* '*order,* in perfect order, with everything in the right place. '∼-*jack* n (US) brandy distilled from fermented cider. ,∼ '*sauce,* (US = '∼-*sauce*) n (a) sliced ∼s stewed. (b) (US colloq) nonsense: insincere flattery. **Adam's** ∼, ⇨ Adam.

ap·pli·ance /ə'plaɪəns/ n [C] instrument or apparatus: *an* ∼ *for rescuing sailors from a wrecked ship,* eg a rope that can be fired from a gun; *household* ∼s, eg a washing-machine, a food-mixer.

ap·pli·cable /'æplɪkəbl/ adj ∼ (to), that can be applied; that is suitable and proper: *Is the rule* ∼ *to this case?*

ap·pli·cant /'æplɪkənt/ n ∼ (for), person who applies (esp for a position): *As the wages were low, there were no* ∼s *for the job.*

ap·pli·ca·tion /,æplɪ'keɪʃn/ n 1 [U] ∼ (to sb) (for sth), making of a request: *A list of new books may be had on* ∼ *to the publishers;* [C] request (esp in writing): *The manager received twenty* ∼s *for the position. We made an* ∼ *to the court for an enquiry.* '∼ *form,* form to be filled in when applying for sth. 2 [U] ∼ (of sth) (to sth), putting one thing on to another: *This oil is for external* ∼ *only,* to be used only on the surface; [C] substance used: *The doctor ordered an* ∼ *of ice to the forehead. Both cold and hot* ∼s *are used to help people who are in pain.* 3 [U] ∼ (of sth) (to sth), bringing a rule to bear on a case; putting to practical use: *the* ∼ *of the rule to this case; the* ∼ *of a discovery/a new process,* etc to industry. 4 [U] ∼ attention: *If you show* ∼ *in your studies* (= If you work hard) *you will succeed. My work demands close* ∼, ie I have to concentrate my thoughts on it.

ap·plied ⇨ apply.

ap·pli·qué /æ'pliːkeɪ US: ,æplɪ'keɪ/ n [U] (esp in dress-making) ornamental work made of one kind of material, or material of one colour, applied to the surface of another. □ vt ornament in this way.

ap·ply /ə'plaɪ/ vt,vi (pt,pp -lied) 1 [VP2C,3A] ∼ (to sb) (for sth), (formally) ask for: ∼ *to the Consul for a visa. You may* ∼ *in person or by letter.* 2 [VP6A,14] lay one thing on or in another; cause (sth) to serve a purpose by doing this: ∼ *a plaster to a cut;* ∼ *the brakes* (of a motor vehicle, etc); (fig) *We intend to* ∼ *economic sanctions.* 3 [VP6A,3A] ∼ (to sth), (cause to) have a bearing (on); concern: *The rule cannot be applied in every case. What I have said does not* ∼ *to you.* 4 [VP14] ∼ *oneself/one's mind/one's energies (to sth/ to doing sth),* concentrate one's thoughts, etc on a task, give all one's energy and attention to: ∼ *your*

mind to your work. We must ∼ *our energies to finding a solution.* 5 [VP14] make practical use of (research, a discovery): *We can* ∼ *his findings in new developments.* **ap·plied** part adj put to practical use: *applied mathematics,* eg as used in engineering; *applied art,* eg as used in textile designs, for pottery, etc.

ap·point /ə'pɔɪnt/ vt 1 [VP6A,14,16A] ∼ sth (for sth), choose, decide, fix (a time/date, etc): *The time* ∼ed for the meeting was 8.30pm. We must ∼ a time to meet again/a time for the next meeting. 2 [VP6A,14,16A,23,25] ∼ sb (to sth), choose for a post; set up by choosing members: *They* ∼ed White (to be) manager. Smith was ∼ed to the vacant post. The newly-∼ed officials are all expert. We must ∼ a committee. 3 [VP9] (formal or older use) give orders: ∼ *that sth shall be done.* 4 *well/ badly* ∼ed, well/badly equipped. ∼ee /əpɔɪn'tiː/ n person ∼ed to an office or position.

ap·point·ment /ə'pɔɪntmənt/ n 1 [U] appointing: *meet sb by* ∼, after fixing a time and place. 2 [C] arrangement to meet sb: *make/fix an* ∼ *with sb; keep/break an* ∼. *I have an* ∼ *with my dentist at 3pm.* 3 [C] position or office: *get a good* ∼ *in a business firm; an* ∼ *as manager.* 4 (pl) equipment; furniture.

ap·por·tion /ə'pɔːʃn/ vt [VP6A,12B,13B,14] ∼ (among/to), divide; distribute; give as a share: *I have* ∼ed you different duties each day of the week. This sum of money is to be ∼ed among the six boys.

ap·po·site /'æpəzɪt/ adj strikingly appropriate for a purpose or occasion: *an* ∼ *remark.* ∼·ly adv

ap·po·si·tion /,æpə'zɪʃn/ n [U] (gram) addition of one word or group of words to another as an explanation: *In the sentence, 'Herr Müller, our new teacher, is a German',* teacher *is in* ∼ *to* Müller; teacher *and* Müller *are in* ∼.

ap·praise /ə'preɪz/ vt [VP6A] fix a price for; say what sth is worth: ∼ *the ability of one's pupils;* ∼ *property (at a certain sum) for taxation.* **ap·prai·sal** /ə'preɪzl/ n valuation.

ap·preci·able /ə'priːʃəbl/ adj that can be seen, measured or felt: *an* ∼ *change in the temperature.* **ap·preci·ably** /-əbli/ adv

ap·preci·ate /ə'priːʃɪeɪt/ vt,vi 1 [VP6A] judge rightly the value of; understand and enjoy: *You can't* ∼ *English poetry unless you understand its rhythm. We all* ∼ *a holiday after a year of hard work.* 2 [VP6A] put a high value on: *We greatly* ∼ *all your help.* 3 [VP2B] (of land, goods, etc) increase in value: *The land has* ∼d *greatly since the new railway was built.* 4 [VP6A,9,10] realise and understand: *I* ∼ *your anxiety about your son's illness.*

ap·preci·ation /ə,priːʃɪ'eɪʃn/ n 1 [C,U] (statement giving) judgement, valuation: *Write an* ∼ *of a new symphony. She showed little or no* ∼ *of good music.* 2 [U] proper understanding and recognition: *in sincere* ∼ *of your valuable help.* 3 [U] rise in value, eg of land, business shares. **ap·preci·ative** /ə'priːʃɪətɪv/ adj feeling or showing ∼(2): *an appreciative audience; appreciative of kindness.* **ap·preci·ative·ly** /ə'priːʃɪətɪvlɪ/ adv

ap·pre·hend /,æprɪ'hend/ vt 1 [VP6A,9] (old use) understand: *You are, I* ∼, *ready to....* 2 [VP6A,9] (formal) fear: *Do you* ∼ *any difficulty/that there will be any difficulty?* 3 [VP6A] (legal) arrest, seize: ∼ *a thief.* **ap·pre·hen·sible** /,æprɪ'hensəbl/ adj capable of being ∼ed(1).

ap·pre·hen·sion /ˌæprɪ'henʃn/ n 1 [U] grasping (of ideas); understanding: *quick/slow of* ~. 2 [C,U] fear; unhappy feeling about the future: *feel* ~ *for sb's safety; filled with* ~; *entertain an* ~ *of failure*. 3 (legal) seizing: *the* ~ *of a thief/deserter*.

ap·pre·hen·sive /ˌæprɪ'hensɪv/ adj uneasy; worried: ~ *of further defeats;* ~ *for sb's safety;* ~ *that sb will be hurt.*

ap·pren·tice /ə'prentɪs/ n learner of a trade who has agreed to work for a number of years in return for being taught. □ *vt* [VP6A,14] ~ *(to),* bind as an ~: *The boy was* ~*d to a carpenter.* ~**·ship** /-tɪʃɪp/ n (time of) being an ~: *serve one's* ~*ship* (*with sb*).

ap·prise /ə'praɪz/ *vt* [VP14] ~ *of,* (formal) inform: *be* ~*d of sb's intentions; be* ~*d that....*

ap·pro /'æprəʊ/ n *on* ~, (comm sl) on approval: *goods on* ~, to be returned if not satisfactory.

ap·proach /ə'prəʊtʃ/ *vt,vi* 1 [VP6A,2A] come near-(er) (to): *A boy of eighteen is* ~*ing manhood. As winter* ~*ed the weather became colder.* (fig) *Few writers can even* ~ *Shakespeare in greatness.* 2 [VP6A] go to (sb) with a request or offer: *When is the best time to* ~ *my employer about an increase in salary? He is rather difficult to* ~, It is not easy to get on friendly terms with him. □ *n* 1 [U] act of ~ing: *The enemy ran away at our* ~. *easy/ difficult of* ~, (a) (of a place) easy/difficult to get to. (b) (of a person) easy/difficult to meet and talk to. *make* ~*es to sb,* (a) try to obtain his interest, attract his attention. (b) offer, try, to enter into personal relations with (eg of a man who wants intimate friendship with a girl or woman). 2 [C] approximation: *an* ~ *to perfection.* 3 [C] way, path, road: *All the* ~*es to the Palace were guarded by soldiers.* ~**·able** /-əbl/ adj (of a person or place) that can be ~ed; accessible.

ap·pro·ba·tion /ˌæprə'beɪʃn/ n [U] (formal) approval; sanction.

ap·pro·pri·ate¹ /ə'prəʊprɪət/ adj ~ *(for/to sth),* suited to; in keeping with: *Sports clothes are not* ~ *for a formal wedding. Write in a style* ~ *to your subject.* ~**·ly** adv

ap·pro·pri·ate² /ə'prəʊprɪeɪt/ *vt* [VP6A,14] 1 put on one side for a special purpose: *£20000 has been* ~*d for the new school buildings.* 2 take and use as one's own: *He often* ~*s my ideas.* **ap·pro·pri·ation** /əˌprəʊprɪ'eɪʃn/ n 1 [U] appropriating or being ~*d;* [C] instance of this. 2 [C] sth, esp a sum of money, that is ~*d: make an appropriation for payment of debts; Senate A*~*s Committee,* (US) one which deals with funds for defence, welfare, etc.

ap·pro·val /ə'pru:vl/ n [U] feeling, showing or saying, that one is satisfied, that sth is right, that one agrees to sth: *Your plans have my* ~. *Does what I have done meet with your* ~? *She gave a nod of* ~*/nodded her* ~. *goods on* ~, to be returned if not satisfactory.

ap·prove /ə'pru:v/ *vt,vi* 1 [VP3A] ~ *of sth/sb,* give one's approval of: *Her father will never* ~ *of her marriage to you. I cannot support a policy of which I have never* ~*d.* 2 [VP6A] confirm; agree to: *The minutes* (*of the meeting*) *were read and* ~*d. The expenditure has been* ~*d.* '~*d school,* (GB) boarding school for training and educating children under 17 who are sent there by magistrates for juvenile offences or because in need of care and protection. (US = *reformatory, reform school*).

ap·prov·ing·ly adv

ap·proxi·mate¹ /ə'prɒksɪmət/ adj ~ *(to),* very near correct; about right: *a sum of money* ~ *to what will be needed. The* ~ *area of my land is half an acre.* ~**·ly** adv

ap·proxi·mate² /ə'prɒksɪmeɪt/ *vi,vt* 1 [VP3A] ~ *to,* come near to (esp in quality or number): *His description of the event* ~*d to the truth but there were a few inaccuracies.* 2 [VP6A,3A] bring or come near to. **ap·proxi·ma·tion** /əˌprɒksɪ'meɪʃn/ n [C] almost correct amount or estimate; [U] being or getting near (in number or quality).

ap·pur·ten·ance /ə'pɜ:tɪnəns/ n (usu *pl*) (legal) sth that belongs to or usu goes with another thing: *the house and its* ~*s,* the lesser rights and privileges that go with ownership of the house.

après-ski /ˌæpreɪ 'ski:/ attrib adj of the evening period after skiing: ~ *fun and games;* ~ *clothes.*

apri·cot /'eɪprɪkɒt/ n (tree with) round, orange-yellow or orange-red fruit with soft flesh and a hard stone-like seed; colour of this fruit when ripe.

April /'eɪprəl/ n fourth month of the year. ~ **'fool,** person who is hoaxed on ˌAll 'Fools' Day (1 April).

a priori /ˌeɪ praɪ'ɔ:raɪ/ adv, adj (Lat) (reasoning) from cause to effect, eg saying, 'The boys have walked a long way so they must be tired.' ⇨ a posteriori.

apron /'eɪprən/ n 1 loose garment worn over the front part of the body to keep clothes clean; any similar covering. **tied to his mother's/wife's '**~**-strings,** too long or too much under her control. 2 hard-surfaced (tarmac, concrete, etc) area on an air-field, used for manœuvring and (un-) loading aircraft. 3 '~ **stage,** (in some theatres) part of the stage jutting out into the audience. ⇨ proscenium.

apro·pos /ˌæprə'pəʊ/ adv, pred adj to the purpose; well suited (to what is being said or done): *His suggestion is very much* ~. ~ *of prep* concerning, with reference to.

apse /æps/ n semi-circular or many-sided recess, with an arched or domed roof, esp at the east end of a church. ⇨ the illus at church.

apt /æpt/ adj (-er, est) 1 **apt** (**at doing sth**), quick-witted: *one of my aptest pupils; very apt at picking up a new subject.* 2 to the point; well suited: *an apt remark.* 3 **apt to do sth,** having a tendency, likely to do sth: *Cast iron is apt to break. He's a clever boy but apt to get into mischief.* **apt·ly** adv suitably, justly. **apt·ness** n

ap·ti·tude /'æptɪtju:d US: -tu:d/ n [U] ~ *(for),* natural or acquired talent: *He shows some* ~ *for languages.* [C] particular talent: *He has a singular* ~ *for dealing with a crisis.* '~ **test,** test to discover and assess skills.

aqua·lung /'ækwəlʌŋ/ n (P) breathing unit (face mask, valve unit and cylinder(s) of compressed air or oxygen) used for underwater swimming or diving. ⇨ the illus at frogman.

aqua·mar·ine /ˌækwəmə'ri:n/ n [C,U] bluish-green (jewel).

aqua·naut /'ækwənɔ:t/ n person trained to live for a long period, in a structure submerged in the sea, to study marine life, etc.

aqua·plane /'ækwəpleɪn/ n board on which a person stands while being pulled along by a fast motor-boat. □ *vi* ride on such a board.

aquar·ium /ə'kweərɪəm/ n (*pl* ~s, -ria /-rɪə/) (building with an) artificial pond or tank for keeping and showing living fish and water plants.

Aquar·ius /ə'kweərɪəs/ n the eleventh sign of the zodiac. ⇨ the illus at zodiac.

aqua·tic /ə'kwætɪk/ adj 1 (of plants, animals, etc) growing or living in or near water. 2 (of sports) taking place on or in water, eg rowing, swimming.

aqua·tint /'ækwətɪnt/ n [U] process of etching on copper, the picture being made by letting acid bite into a plate covered with a layer of resin dust; [C] picture made in this way.

aqua·vit /'ækwəvɪt/ n [U] strong Scandinavian liquor flavoured with caraway seed.

aque·duct /'ækwɪdʌkt/ n artificial channel for supplying water, esp one built of stone or brick and higher than the surrounding land.

an aqueduct

aque·ous /'eɪkwɪəs/ adj of or like water: an ∼ solution.

aqui·line /'ækwɪlaɪn/ adj of or like an eagle: an ∼ nose, hooked like an eagle's beak.

Arab /'ærəb/ n name applied to any of those Semitic people who speak Arabic and claim descent from the inhabitants of the Arabian Peninsula who, in the 7th c, were conquerors of N Africa, Syria and Mesopotamia: the military conquests of the ∼s; the ∼ League.

ara·besque /,ærə'besk/ n [C] (art) elaborate design of leaves, branches, scrolls, etc; (ballet) pose of a dancer on one leg, the other stretched backwards.

Ara·bian /ə'reɪbɪən/ n, adj (person) of (Saudi) Arabia or the Arabs. the ∼ Nights, famous stories of the Arabs in ancient times. the ∼ camel, the dromedary.

Ara·bic /'ærəbɪk/ adj of the Arabs. ∼ numerals, the signs 0, 1, 2, 3, etc. ⇨ App 4. □ n language of the Arabs.

Ara·bist /'ærəbɪst/ n student or specialist in Arabic culture, language, affairs, etc.

ar·able /'ærəbl/ adj (of land) suitable for ploughing; usually ploughed.

arach·nid /ə'ræknɪd/ n (zool) member of the genus including spiders, scorpions and mites.

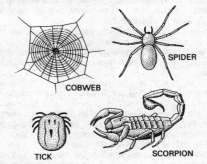

SPIDER

COBWEB

TICK   SCORPION

arachnids

ar·bi·ter /'ɑːbɪtə(r)/ n 1 ∼ (of), person with complete control (of sth): the sole ∼ of their destinies. 2 = arbitrator.

ar·bitra·ment /ɑː'bɪtrəmənt/ n [U] (formal) decid-

ing of a dispute by an arbiter; [C] decision made by an arbiter.

ar·bit·rary /'ɑːbɪtrərɪ US: -trerɪ/ adj 1 based on opinion or impulse only, not on reason. 2 dictatorial; using despotic power.

ar·bi·trate /'ɑːbɪtreɪt/ vt, vi [VP6A,2A] ∼ (between), decide by arbitration; judge between two parties to a dispute (usu at the request of the two parties): Mr X has been asked to ∼ the dispute/to ∼ between the employers and their workers. If countries would always ∼ their quarrels, wars could be avoided.

ar·bi·tra·tion /,ɑːbɪ'treɪʃn/ n [U] (attempt at a) settlement of a dispute by the decision of a person or persons chosen and accepted as judges or umpires: refer a wage dispute to ∼; submit a claim for ∼. [C] instance of such a settlement. go to ∼, arbitrate: The Union agreed to go to ∼, ie for a settlement of their claims.

ar·bi·tra·tor /'ɑːbɪtreɪtə(r)/ n (legal) arbiter; person appointed by two parties to settle a dispute.

ar·bor ⇨ arbour.

ar·bor·eal /ɑː'bɔːrɪəl/ adj (formal) of, living in, connected with trees: ∼ animals, eg squirrels, monkeys.

ar·bour (US = ar·bor) /'ɑːbə(r)/ n shady place among trees, esp one made in a garden, with climbing plants growing over a framework.

arc /ɑːk/ n part of the circumference of a circle or other curved line. ⇨ the illus at circle. **'arc-lamp**, **'arc-light** nn brilliant light produced by electric current flowing across a space between two carbon rods.

ar·cade /ɑː'keɪd/ n covered passage, usu with an arched roof, eg a passage with shops or market stalls along one or both sides; covered market. **a'muse- ment ∼**, ⇨ amusement.

Ar·cad·ian /ɑː'keɪdɪən/ adj of an ideal rustic simplicity; simple and innocent. □ n person with ∼ tastes.

ar·cane /ɑː'keɪn/ adj secret; mysterious.

arch[1] /ɑːtʃ/ n 1 curved structure supporting the weight of what is above it, as in bridges, aqueducts, gateways, etc. ⇨ the illus at aqueduct, church. 2 (also '∼·way) passageway under an ∼, built as an ornament or gateway: a triumphal ∼. 3 any curve in the shape of an ∼, eg the curved under-part of the foot, ⇨ the illus at leg; a structure for supporting climbing roses, etc. □ vt, vi 1 [VP6A] form into an ∼: The cat ∼ed its back when it saw the dog. Horses ∼ their necks. 2 [VP2C] be like an ∼: The trees ∼ over the river.

arch[2] /ɑːtʃ/ attrib adj mischievous in an innocent or playful way (esp of women and children): an ∼ glance/smile. ∼·ly adv

arch- /ɑːtʃ/ pref chief; notable; extreme: ,∼- 'enemy.

ar·chae·ol·ogy (also ar·che·ol-) /,ɑːkɪ'ɒlədʒɪ/ n [U] study of ancient things, esp remains of prehistoric times, eg tombs, buried cities. **ar·chae·ologi·cal** /,ɑːkɪə'lɒdʒɪkl/ adj of ∼. **ar·chae·ol·ogist** /,ɑːkɪ'ɒlədʒɪst/ n expert in ∼.

ar·chaic /ɑː'keɪɪk/ adj 1 (of eg a word in a language) not now used except for special purposes. 2 of ancient times. **ar·cha·ism** /'ɑːkeɪɪzəm/ n [C] ∼ word or expression; [U] use or imitation of what is ∼.

arch·angel /'ɑːkeɪndʒl/ n angel of high rank.

arch·bishop /,ɑːtʃ'bɪʃəp/ n chief bishop. **∼·ric** n position or rank of an ∼; church district governed by an ～.

arch·dea·con /ˌɑːtʃˈdiːkən/ n (in the C of E) priest next below a bishop, superintending rural deans. ～ry n (pl -ries) position, rank, residence, of an ～.

arch·dio·cese /ˌɑːtʃˈdaɪəsɪs/ n diocese of an arch-bishop.

arch·duke /ˌɑːtʃˈdjuːk US: -ˈduːk/ n (title given to) son or nephew of former Emperors of Austria.

archer /ˈɑːtʃə(r)/ n person who shoots with a bow and arrows. **arch·ery** /ˈɑːtʃərɪ/ n [U] (art of) shoot-ing with a bow and arrows.

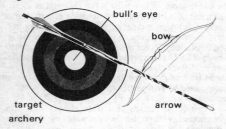

bull's eye

bow

target

arrow

archery

arche·type /ˈɑːkɪtaɪp/ n prototype; ideal form re-garded as a pattern not to be changed. **arche·typal** /ˌɑːkɪˈtaɪpl/ adj

archi·man·drite /ˌɑːkɪˈmændraɪt/ n head of a mo-nastery in the Gk Orthodox Church.

archi·pel·ago /ˌɑːkɪˈpeləgəʊ/ n (pl ～s, ～es /-gəʊz/) (sea with a) group of many islands.

archi·tect /ˈɑːkɪtekt/ n person who designs (and supervises the construction of) buildings, etc.

archi·tec·ture /ˈɑːkɪtektʃə(r)/ n [U] art and science of building; design or style of building(s). **archi-tec·tural** /ˌɑːkɪˈtektʃərəl/ adj of ～: the archi-tectural beauties of a city.

ar·chives /ˈɑːkaɪvz/ n pl (place for keeping) public or government records; other historical records. **archi·vist** /ˈɑːkɪvɪst/ n person in charge of ～.

arch·way /ˈɑːtʃweɪ/ n ⇨ arch¹(2).

arc·tic /ˈɑːktɪk/ adj of the north polar regions: the A～ Ocean; ～ weather, very cold weather. **the ,A～ 'Circle**, the line of latitude 66½°N.

ar·dent /ˈɑːdnt/ adj full of ardour: ～ supporters of the new movement. ～·ly adv

ar·dour (US = -dor) /ˈɑːdə(r)/ n ～ (for), [C,U] warm emotion; enthusiasm.

ar·du·ous /ˈɑːdjʊəs US: -dʒʊ-/ adj 1 (of work) needing and using up much energy. 2 (of a road, etc) steep; hard to climb. ～·ly adv

are¹ /ə(r); strong form: ɑː(r)/ ⇨ be¹.

are² /ɑː(r)/ n metric unit of area, = 100 square metres. ⇨ App 5.

area /ˈeərɪə/ n 1 [U] surface measure: If a room measures 3 × 5 metres, its ～ is 15 square metres/it is 15 square metres in ～. [C] instance of this measurement. ⇨ App 5. 2 [C] region of the earth's surface: desert ～s of North Africa; the postal ～s (more usu districts) into which London is divided. 3 [C] (fig) scope or range of activity: the ～ of finance. The ～s of disagreement were clearly indicated at the Board Meeting, The subjects on which members of the Board disagreed became clear. 4 [C] small courtyard giving light to the win-dows of basement rooms, eg kitchen, scullery, in an old-fashioned town house, usu with stone steps from the street pavement: sitting on the ～ steps.

areca /ˈærɪkə/ n kind of palm-tree from which

areca-nut (betel-nut) is obtained. ⇨ betel.

arena /əˈriːnə/ n (pl ～s) central part, for games and fights, of a Roman amphitheatre, ⇨ the illus at amphitheatre; (fig) any scene of competition or struggle: the ～ of politics.

aren't /ɑːnt/ = are not: aren't I? = am I not?

arête /æˈreɪt/ n (F) (esp of mountains in Switzer-land) sharp ridge. ⇨ the illus at mountain.

ar·gent /ˈɑːdʒənt/ n, adj (in heraldry and poetry) silver (colour).

ar·gon /ˈɑːgɒn/ n [U] chemically inactive gas (symbol Ar), present in the atmosphere (0·8 per cent), used in some kinds of electric lamps.

Ar·go·naut /ˈɑːgənɔːt/ n (myth) one of the heroes who sailed in the ship Argo /ˈɑːgəʊ/ with Jason in search of the Golden Fleece.

ar·gosy /ˈɑːgəsɪ/ n (pl -sies) (poet) large merchant ship, esp one with valuable cargo.

ar·got /ˈɑːgəʊ/ n [U] jargon; slang.

ar·gue /ˈɑːgjuː/ vi,vt 1 [VP2A,C,3A] ～ (with sb) (about/over sth), express disagreement; quarrel: Don't ～ with me; my decision is final. Why are they always ～ing? 2 [VP2A,3A,9] ～ (for/against/that...), maintain a case, give reasons (in support of, for, against, esp with the aim of persu-ading sb): He ～s soundly. You can ～ either way, for or against. He was arguing that poverty may be a blessing. 3 [VP14] ～ sb into/out of doing sth, persuade by giving reasons: They tried to ～ him into joining them. 4 [VP6A] debate: The lawyers ～d the case for hours. **ar·gu·able** /ˈɑːgjʊəbl/ adj that can be ～d about. **ar·gu·ably** /-əblɪ/ adv

ar·gu·ment /ˈɑːgjʊmənt/ n 1 [C] an ～ (with sb) (about/over sth), (perhaps heated) disagreement; quarrel: endless ～s about money; an ～ with the referee. 2 [U] reasoned discussion: It is beyond ～ that ...; [C] an ～ (for/against), instance of this: an ～ for not gambling; I have no wish to engage in (an) ～ with you. 3 [C] summary of the subject matter of a book, etc. **ar·gu·men·ta·tive** /ˌɑːgjʊˈmentətɪv/ adj fond of arguing(1).

ar·gu·men·ta·tion /ˌɑːgjʊmenˈteɪʃn/ n [U] process of arguing; debate.

Ar·gus /ˈɑːgəs/ n (Gk myth) monster with a hundred eyes. ～·'eyed adj observant; vigilant.

aria /ˈɑːrɪə/ n (pl ～s) song for a single voice (esp in 18th c operas and oratorios).

arid /ˈærɪd/ adj 1 (of soil, land) dry, barren; (of cli-mate, regions) having not enough rainfall to sup-port vegetation. 2 (fig) uninteresting. **arid·ity** /əˈrɪdətɪ/ n [U] dryness.

Aries /ˈeəriːz/ n the Ram, the first sign of the zo-diac. ⇨ the illus at zodiac.

aright /əˈraɪt/ adv (archaic) rightly: if I heard ～. (Before a pp use rightly, as in to be rightly inform-ed.)

arise /əˈraɪz/ vi (pt arose /əˈrəʊz/, pp arisen /əˈrɪzn/) 1 [VP2A] come into existence; come to notice; present itself: A new difficulty has ～n. If the need should ～...; Before they could start a mist arose. 2 [VP3A] ～ from, result from: Serious obligations may ～ from the proposed clause. 3 [VP2A] (old use) get up; stand up.

ar·is·toc·racy /ˌærɪˈstɒkrəsɪ/ n (pl -cies) 1 [U] government by persons of the highest social rank; [C] country or state with such a government. 2 [C] ruling body of nobles; the social class from which these nobles come. 3 [C] best representatives in any class: an ～ of talent.

ar·is·to·crat /ˈærɪstəkræt US: əˈrɪst-/ n member of

the class of nobles; person of noble birth. ~ic
/ˌærɪstə'krætɪk US: əˌrɪstə-/ adj of the aristocracy;
having the ways and manners of an ~: with an ~ic
bearing. ~i·cally /-klɪ/ adv
arith·me·tic /ə'rɪθmətɪk/ n [U] science of numbers;
working with numbers. **ar·ith·meti·cal**
/ˌærɪθ'metɪkl/ adj of ~. ~al progression, series
of numbers showing an increase, or decrease, by a
quantity that is always the same, eg 1, 2, 3, etc, or
7, 5, 3, etc. **arith·me·tician** /əˌrɪθmə'tɪʃn/ n expert
in ~.
ark /ɑːk/ n (in the Bible) **1** covered ship in which
Noah and his family were saved from the Flood. **2
Ark of the Covenant**, wooden chest in which
writings of Jewish law were kept.
arm[1] /ɑːm/ n **1** either of the two upper limbs of the
human body, from the shoulder to the hand: She
was carrying a child in her arms. He was carrying
a book under his arm, between the arm and the
body. She had a basket on her arm, with the handle
supported on her arm. **baby/child/infant in arms**,
child too young to walk. (hold, carry sth) **at arm's
length**, with the arm fully extended. **keep sb at
arm's length**, (fig) avoid becoming familiar with
him. (welcome sb/sth) **with open arms**, warmly,
with enthusiasm. **walk ˌarm-in-'arm,** (of two persons) walk side by side, with the arm of one round
the arm of the other. **'arm-band** n armlet. **'armchair** n chair with supports for the arms. **'armchair
critic**, person who offers criticism but is not actively involved. **'arm-hole** n hole (in a shirt, jacket,
etc) through which the arm is put. **'arm·let** /-lɪt/ n
band (of cloth, etc) worn round the arm (on a
sleeve). **'arm·pit** n hollow under the arm near the
shoulder. **2** sleeve: The arms of this coat are too
long. **3** large branch of a tree. **4** sth shaped like or
suggesting an arm: an arm of the sea; the arms of a
chair. **5** (fig) **the (long) arm of the law**, the authority or power of the law. **arm·ful** /'ɑːmfʊl/ n as
much as one arm, or both arms, can hold: carrying
in books by the armful.

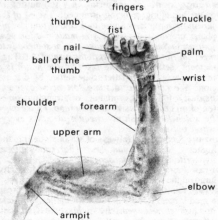

fingers
thumb
knuckle
fist
nail
palm
ball of the
thumb
wrist
shoulder
forearm
upper arm
elbow
armpit

the arm and the hand

arm[2] /ɑːm/ n branch or division of a country's armed forces: the infantry arm; the air arm.
arm[3] /ɑːm/ vt, vi [VP6A,14,2A] **arm (with)**, supply,
fit, weapons and armour; prepare for war: a warship armed with nuclear weapons; armed with a
big stick; (fig) armed with patience/with answers
to all questions. Their former enemy is arming
again (= rearming). **the armed forces/services,**
the army, navy and air force. **armed neutrality,**
policy of remaining neutral but prepared for defence against aggression.
ar·mada /ɑː'mɑːdə/ n great fleet of warships, esp
the A~, the fleet sent by King Philip II of Spain
against England in 1588.
ar·ma·dillo /ˌɑːmə'dɪləʊ/ n (pl ~s /-ləʊz/) small
burrowing animal of S America, with a body
covered with a shell of bony plates, and the habit of
rolling itself up into a ball when attacked. ⇨ the illus at small.
Ar·ma·ged·don /ˌɑːmə'gedn/ n **1** (biblical) (scene
of) the last battle to be fought between the forces of
good and evil, prophesied to happen at the end of
time. ⇨ Rev 16:16. **2** (fig) any similar dramatic
conflict.
ar·ma·ment /'ɑːməmənt/ n **1** (usu pl) military
forces and their equipment; navy, army, air force.
2 (usu pl) weapons, esp the large guns on a warship, military tank, etc: the '~s industry. **3** [U]
process of getting military forces equipped; preparation for war.
ar·ma·ture /'ɑːmətʃʊə(r)/ n (electr) that part of a
dynamo which rotates in a magnetic field and in
which the current is developed; coil(s) of an electric motor.
ar·mis·tice /'ɑːmɪstɪs/ n agreement during a war or
battle to stop fighting for a time. **'A~ Day,** 11
Nov, kept as the anniversary of the ~ that ended
fighting in the First World War (US = Veterans'
Day). ⇨ remembrance.
ar·moire /'ɑːmwɑː(r) US: ɑːm'wɑːr/ n [C] large cabinet or wardrobe.
ar·mor ⇨ armour.
ar·morial /ɑː'mɔːrɪəl/ adj of heraldry; of coats of
arms. ⇨ arms(2): ~ bearings, a coat of arms.
ar·mour (US = **ar·mor**) /'ɑːmə(r)/ n [U] **1** defensive covering, usu metal, for the body, worn in
fighting: a suit of ~. **2** metal covering (steel plates,
etc) for warships, tanks, motor vehicles, etc. **3**
(collective) tanks, motor vehicles, etc protected
with ~. '~-plate n sheet of metal used as ~. ~ed
part adj **1** covered or protected with ~: an ~ed
cruiser/car. **2** equipped with tanks, vehicles, guns,
etc, that are protected with ~: an ~ed column/
division, etc. ~er n **1** manufacturer or repairer of
arms and ~. **2** man in charge of fire-arms. ~y
/'ɑːmərɪ/ n (pl-ries) place where arms are kept.
arms /ɑːmz/ n pl **1** weapons (note, fire-arm, used
in the sing form): (attrib) an ~ depot; The soldiers
had plenty of ~ and ammunition. '~-race, competition among nations on military strength. **'fire-
~**, those requiring explosives. **'small ~**, fire-~
that can be carried by hand, eg revolvers, rifles,
light machine-guns. **lay down (one's) ~**, stop
fighting. **take up ~; rise up in ~,** (liter or fig) get
ready to fight (against). **under ~**, provided with
weapons and ready to fight. **(be) up in ~ (about-
/over),** (usu fig) be protesting vigorously. **2** (heraldry) pictorial design used by a noble family,
town, university, etc. **coat of '~**, such a design,
eg on a shield. ⇨ the illus at armour.
army /'ɑːmɪ/ n (pl-mies) **1** (a/the) ~, (with sing or
pl v) the part of a country's military forces that is
organized for fighting on land: an ~ of 100,000
soldiers; be in the ~, be a soldier; go into/join the
~, become a soldier. **'~ corps** n main subdivi-

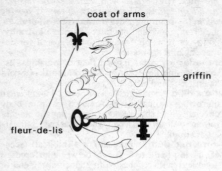

coat of arms

griffin

fleur-de-lis

escutcheon or shield

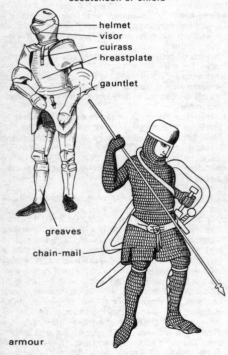

helmet
visor
cuirass
breastplate

gauntlet

greaves

chain-mail

armour

sion of an ~. '~ **list** *n* official list of commissioned officers. **2** organized body of persons: *the Salvation A*~; large number: *an* ~ *of workmen/officials/ants.*

ar·nica /'ɑːnɪkə/ *n* [U] medical substance (made from a plant) used for healing bruises and sprains.

aroma /ə'rəʊmə/ *n* **1** sweet smell, fragrance: *the* ~ *of a cigar.* **2** (fig) quality or surrounding atmosphere considered typical: *the* ~ *of wealth.* **aro·matic** /ˌærə'mætɪk/ *adj* fragrant; spicy: *the* ~*tic bark of the cinnamon tree.*

arose /ə'rəʊz/ *pt* of arise.

around¹ /ə'raʊnd/ *adv* **1** (*all*) ~, on every side; in every direction; here and there: *From all* ~ *we heard the laughter of children. Don't leave your clothes lying* ~. **2** (colloq) not far away (in place or time): *I'll be* ~ *if you should want me. I'll be se-*

eing you ~, *I expect.* **have been** ~, have travelled widely, have had experience of life and the world: *She's obviously been* ~ *a lot.* ⇨ about²(1,2,3), round², shop *v*(1), sleep²(2).

around² /ə'raʊnd/ *prep* **1** (*all*) ~, throughout: *He's been all* ~ *India.* **2** encircling (wholly or partially): *Take your arm from* ~ *my waist. Go for a run* ~ *the block.* ⇨ about³(1,2,3), round⁴.

arouse /ə'raʊz/ *vt* [VP6A,14] **1** awaken: *behaviour that might* ~ *suspicion; sufferings that* ~*d our sympathy;* ~ *sb from his sleep.* **2** cause (sb) to become active; stir (sb) up from inactivity; stimulate sexually: *fully* ~*d.*

ar·peg·gio /ɑː'pedʒɪəʊ/ *n* (*pl* ~s) (I; music) the playing of the notes of a chord(2) in (usu upwards) succession.

ar·que·bus /'ɑːkwɪbəs/ *n* early kind of portable gun, supported on a tripod or a forked rest, used before muskets were invented.

ar·rack /'æræk/ *n* [U] strong alcoholic drink made in Eastern countries.

ar·raign /ə'reɪn/ *vt* [VP6A,14] (legal) bring a criminal charge against (sb); bring (sb) before a court for trial: ~*ed on a charge of theft.* ~**·ment** *n* ~ing or being ~ed.

ar·range /ə'reɪndʒ/ *vt,vi* **1** [VP6A] put in order: *She's good at arranging flowers. I* ~*d the books on the shelves. Before going away, he* ~*d his business affairs.* **2** [VP6A,15A,3A,4C] make plans in advance, see to the details of sth: *A marriage has been* ~*d between Mr Brown and Miss White. The Tourist Bureau* ~*d everything for our journey to Rome. I have* ~*d to meet her at ten o'clock. I have* ~*d for a car to meet you at the airport. The meeting* ~*d for tomorrow has been postponed. I can't* ~ *for everything.* **3** [VP3A] ~ (**with sb**) (**for/about sth**), come to an agreement. **4** [VP6A,14] ~ (**for**), adapt (a piece of music): ~ *a piece of music for the violin.* **5** [VP6A] settle, adjust (now the more usu words): *Mrs White often has to* ~ *disputes/differences between the two boys.*

ar·range·ment /ə'reɪndʒmənt/ *n* **1** [U] putting in order; arranging or being arranged: *The* ~ *of the furniture in our new house took a long time.* **2** (*pl*) plans; preparations: *Have you made* ~s *for your journey to Scotland? I'll make* ~s *for somebody to meet you/for you to be met at the airport.* **3** [U] agreement; settlement: *The price of the house is a matter for* ~, *is a matter to be settled by discussion. We can come to some sort of* ~ *over expenses.* **4** [C] result or manner of arranging: *an* ~ (eg of orchestral music) *for the piano. I have an* ~ *by which I can cash my cheques at banks everywhere in Britain.*

ar·rant /'ærənt/ *adj* (always of sth or sb bad) in the highest degree: *an* ~ *liar/knave/dunce/hypocrite/rogue;* ~ *nonsense.*

ar·ras /'ærəs/ *n* tapestry, esp the kind formerly hung on the walls of rooms.

ar·ray /ə'reɪ/ *vt* [VP6A,15A] (liter) **1** place (esp armed forces, troops) in order for battle: *The Duke and his men* ~*ed themselves against the King*, took up arms against the King. **2** dress: ~*ed in ceremonial robes;* ~*ed like a queen.* □ *n* (liter) **1** order: *troops in battle* ~. **2** clothes: *in holiday* ~; *in bridal* ~. **3** ~ (**of**), display: *a fine* ~ *of tools; an imposing* ~ *of statistics.*

ar·rears /ə'rɪəz/ *n pl* **1** money that is owing and that ought to have been paid: ~ *of rent/wages.* **be in/ fall into** ~ (**with**), be late in paying. Cf *be behind-*

hand with. **2** work still waiting to be done: ~ *of correspondence,* letters waiting to be answered.

ar·rest /ə'rest/ *vt* [VP6A] **1** put a stop to (a process or movement): *Poor food ~s the natural growth of children.* **2** catch (sb's attention): *The bright colours of the flowers ~ed the child's attention.* **3** seize (sb) by the authority of the law: *The police ~ed the thief and put him in prison.* □ *n* act of ~ing (a wrongdoer, etc): *The police made several ~s. under ~,* held as a prisoner. **be/place/put under ~,** be/be made a prisoner: *The officer was put under ~.* **~er** *n* '**~er hook,** device for reducing the speed of aircraft as they land on the deck of an aircraft carrier. **~·ing** *adj* striking; likely to hold the attention.

ar·rière pensée /ˌærɪeə 'pɒnseɪ *US:* pɒn'seɪ/ *n* (F) ulterior motive; mental reservation.

ar·ri·val /ə'raɪvl/ *n* **1** [U] act of arriving: *on ~ home; on his ~; waiting for the ~ of news; to await ~,* (on a letter, parcel, etc) to be kept until the addressee arrives. **2** [C] sb or sth that arrives: *There are several new ~s at the hotel. The new ~* (colloq = The newborn child) *is a boy.*

ar·rive /ə'raɪv/ *vi* [VP2A,C,3A] **1** reach a place, esp the end of a journey: *~ home; ~ at a port; ~ in harbour.* **2** come: *At last the day ~d. Her baby ~d* (= was born) *yesterday.* **3** [VP3A] *~ at,* reach (a decision, a price, the age of 40, manhood, etc). **4** [VP2A] establish one's position or reputation.

ar·ro·gant /'ærəgənt/ *adj* behaving in a proud, superior manner; (of behaviour, etc) showing too much pride in oneself and too little consideration for others: *speaking in an ~ tone.* **~·ly** *adv* **ar·ro·gance** /-əns/ *n* [U].

ar·ro·gate /'ærəgeɪt/ *vt* [VP14] (formal) **1** ~ *to oneself,* claim or take without right: *He ~d to himself the dignity of a chair,* claimed to be a university professor (although he was only a lecturer). **2** attribute unjustly; ascribe: *Don't ~ evil motives to me.*

ar·row /'ærəʊ/ *n* **1** thin, pointed stick (to be) shot from a bow. ⇨ the illus at archery. **2** mark or sign (→) used to show direction or position, eg on a map or as a road sign. '**~-head** *n* pointed end of an ~.

ar·row·root /'ærəʊruːt/ *n* [U] starchy food made from the powdered root of a plant.

arse /ɑːs/ (US = **ass** /æs/) *n* (⚠, not in polite use) buttocks; anus. **silly ~,** fool. '**~-hole** (US = '**ass-hole**) *n* anus.

ar·senal /'ɑːsənl/ *n* building(s) where weapons and ammunition are made or stored; (fig) reserve of strength.

ar·senic /'ɑːsnɪk/ *n* [U] (chem) brittle, steel-grey crystalline chemical element (symbol **As**), used in glass-making, dyes, etc; white mineral compound of ~, a violent poison.

ar·son /'ɑːsn/ *n* [U] act of setting sth on fire intentionally and unlawfully, eg another person's property or one's own with the purpose of claiming under an insurance policy.

art[1] /ɑːt/ *n* **1** [U] the creation or expression of what is beautiful, esp in visual form; fine skill or aptitude in such expression: *the art of the Renaissance; children's art; the art of landscape painting. The story is developed with great art.* **the** ˌ**fine** '**arts,** drawing, painting, sculpture, architecture, music, ballet. **a** ˌ**work of** '**art,** a fine painting, piece of sculpture, etc. **an** '**art gallery,** one for the display of works of art. **an** '**art school,** one at which the arts of painting, etc are taught. **2** [C] sth in which

imagination and personal taste are more important than exact measurement and calculation: *History and literature are among the arts/the arts subjects* (contrasted with science/science subjects). *Teaching/Public speaking is an art.* ˌ**Bachelor/** ˌ**Master of** '**Arts,** (abbr **BA/MA**) person who has passed the examination and fulfilled other conditions for the award of a university degree in this branch of learning. **3** [U] cunning; trickery; [C] trick: *In spite of all her arts, the young man was not attracted to her.* **the black art,** magic (used for evil purposes). **4** (attrib) relating to art(1); of artistic design: *an* '*art historian/critic; art needlework/pottery.*

art[2] /ɑːt/ *v* (*pres t* form of *be*) (archaic) used with *thou:* *thou art,* you are.

ar·te·fact ⇨ artifact.

ar·ter·ial /ɑː'tɪərɪəl/ *adj* of or like an artery: ~ *blood:* ~ *roads,* important main roads; ~ *railways/traffic.*

ar·terio·scler·osis /ɑːˌtɪərɪəʊskləˈrəʊsɪs/ *n* [U] chronic disease with the hardening of the arteries, hindering blood circulation.

ar·tery /'ɑːtərɪ/ *n* (*pl* -ries) **1** one of the tubes carrying blood from the heart to all parts of the body. ⇨ the illus at respiratory. **2** main road or river; chief channel in a system of communications, etc: *arteries of traffic.*

ar·tesian /ɑː'tiːzɪən *US:* -ɪˈʒn/ *adj* ~ **well,** perpendicular well producing a constant supply of water rising to the surface without pumping.

art·ful /'ɑːtfl/ *adj* cunning; deceitful; clever in getting what one wants. **~·ly** /-fəlɪ/ *adv* **~·ness** *n*

ar·thri·tis /ɑː'θraɪtɪs/ *n* [U] inflammation of a joint or joints; gout. **ar·thri·tic** /ɑː'θrɪtɪk/ *adj*

ar·ti·choke /'ɑːtɪtʃəʊk/ *n* **1 globe ~,** plant like a large thistle, with a flowering head of thick, leaf-like scales used as a vegetable. ⇨ the illus at vegetable. **2 Jerusalem ~,** plant like a sunflower, with tuberous roots used as a vegetable.

ar·ticle /'ɑːtɪkl/ *n* [C] **1** particular or separate thing: ~*s of clothing,* eg shirts, coats; *toilet ~s,* eg soap, toothpaste. **2** piece of writing, complete in itself, in a newspaper or other periodical: ˌ**leading** '~, (in a newspaper) ~ expressing the views of the editor(s). **3** (legal) separate clause or item in an agreement: ~*s of apprenticeship/employment.* **4** (gram) **definite** ~, 'the'. **indefinite** ~, 'a', 'an'. □ *vt* bind, eg an apprentice by ~s(3): *an ~d clerk.*

ar·ticu·late[1] /ɑː'tɪkjʊlət/ *adj* **1** (of speech) in which the separate sounds and words are clear. **2** (of a person) able to put thoughts and feelings into clear speech: *That man is not very ~.* **3** jointed. **~·ly** *adv*

ar·ticu·late[2] /ɑː'tɪkjʊleɪt/ *vt, vi* **1** [VP6A,2C] say (words) distinctly; speak (distinctly). **2** [VP15A,2C] connect by joints: *bones that ~/are ~d with others.* **an ~d vehicle,** having parts joined in a flexible manner, eg a tractor flexibly joined to the part that carries the load.

ar·ticu·la·tion /ɑːˌtɪkjʊ'leɪʃn/ *n* [U] **1** production of speech sounds: *The speaker's ideas were good but his ~ was poor.* **2** (connection by a) joint.

ar·ti·fact, ar·te·fact /'ɑːtɪfækt/ *n* [C] artificial product; something made by human being(s), esp a simple tool or weapon of archaeological interest.

ar·ti·fice /'ɑːtɪfɪs/ *n* **1** [C] skilful way of doing sth. **2** [U] cunning; ingenuity; trickery; [C] trick.

ar·ti·fi·cer /ɑː'tɪfɪsə(r)/ *n* skilled workman. **engine-room ~,** (rank in the Navy of a) skilled mechanic.

ar·ti·fi·cial /ˌɑːtɪˈfɪʃl/ *adj* not natural or real; made by the art of man: ~ *flowers/teeth/light;* ~ *silk,* (old name for) rayon; ~ *manures,* chemical manures (not dung); ~ *tears,* not caused by genuine sorrow; ~ *manners,* affected, not natural manners. ~ **respiration,** method of forcing air into the lungs, eg to a man nearly drowned. ⇨ also **inse-mination. ar·ti·fi·ci·ally** /-ʃəlɪ/ *adv*

ar·til·lery /ɑːˈtɪlərɪ/ *n* [U] big guns (mounted on wheels, etc); branch of an army that uses these.

ar·ti·san /ˌɑːtɪˈzæn US: ˈɑːtɪzn/ *n* skilled workman in industry or trade; mechanic.

art·ist /ˈɑːtɪst/ *n* **1** person who practises one of the fine arts, esp painting. **2** person who does sth with skill and good taste: *an* ~ *in words.*

art·iste /ɑːˈtiːst/ *n* professional singer, actor, dancer, etc.

ar·tis·tic /ɑːˈtɪstɪk/ *adj* **1** done with skill and good taste, esp in the arts; able to appreciate what is beautiful. **2** having or showing good taste. **3** of art or artists. **ar·tis·ti·cally** /-klɪ/ *adv*

art·istry /ˈɑːtɪstrɪ/ *n* [U] artistic skill or work; qualities of taste and skill possessed by an artist.

art·less /ˈɑːtlɪs/ *adj* (contrasted with *artful*) natural; simple; innocent: *as* ~ *as a child of 5.* ~**·ly** *adv* ~**·ness** *n*

arty /ˈɑːtɪ/ *adj* (colloq) pretending or falsely claiming to be artistic. ~**·ˈcrafty,** (colloq) of, using, making, handmade articles, esp in a way that is considered affected.

arum /ˈeərəm/ *n* ~ **lily,** tall white lily.

Aryan /ˈeərɪən/ *adj* of the family of languages called Indo-European, ie related to Sanskrit, Persian, Greek, Latin and the Germanic and Slavonic languages; of a race using an ~ language. □ *n* person whose mother tongue is one of the ~ languages; (popular sense, now discredited) person of Germanic or Scandinavian ancestry.

as¹ /əz; *strong form:* æz/ *adv* (followed by *as, conj*) in the same degree: *I'm as tall as you. Is it as difficult as they say it is?* (In a neg sentence *as* is often replaced by *so*): *It's not so difficult as I expected.*

as² /əz; *strong form:* æz/ *conj* **1** when; while: *I saw him as he was getting off the bus. As a child, he lived in India. As he grew older he became less active.* **2** (expressing reason) since; seeing that: *As he wasn't ready in time, we went without him.* **3** (in comparisons of equality, in the patterns: *as* + *adj/adv* + *as*; *not as/so* + *adj/adv as*): *I want a box twice as large as this. It isn't as/so big as you think it is.* (Used in numerous proverbial phrases): *as easy as ABC; as heavy as lead.* (Note the *pro-nouns* in these examples): *You hate him as much as I,* ie as much as I hate him; *You hate him as much as me,* ie as much as you hate me. (When there is no ambiguity, the object form of the *pronoun* is used in speech): *At your age, you can't expect to play football as/so well as me* (= as I do). **4** (introducing a concessive clause, usu replaceable by a construction with *although*): **(a)** with an *adj* or *adv*: *I know some of the family secrets, young as I am,* although I am young. *Much as I like you* (= Although I like you much), *I will not marry you.* **(b)** (with *vv,* esp *may, might, will, would*): *Try as he would* (= Although he tried, However hard he tried), *he could not lift the rock.* **5** (introducing adverbial clauses of manner) in the way in which: *Do as I do. Do it as I do it. Leave it as it is.* **6** (introducing a complement of manner) like: *Why is he*

dressed as a woman? **7** (used to avoid repetition in the predicate): *Harry is unusually tall, as are his brothers,* and his brothers are also unusually tall. **8** in the capacity or character of: *He was respected both as a judge and as a man. Looking at Napoleon as a statesman, not as a soldier....* **9** (used in [VP16B] after *regard, view, represent, treat, ac-knowledge,* and *vv* similar in meaning but not after *consider,* to introduce a predicative): *Most people regarded him* (= looked upon him) *as a fool.* Cf *Most people considered him (to be) a fool. Do you treat all men as your equals?* **10** (used to introduce illustrations or examples; usu preceded by *such*; replaceable by *for instance, for example* or *like*): *Countries in the north of Europe, such as Finland, Norway, Sweden,....* **11** *as if; as though,* (introducing a clause of manner, with a *pt* in the clause): *He talks as if he knew all about it. He looks as if he had seen a ghost. It isn't as though he were poor.* (followed by a *to*-infinitive): *He opened his lips as if to say something.* **12** **'as for,** with reference to (sometimes suggesting indifference or contempt): *As for you, I never want to see you here again.* **'as to,** about; concerning (better avoided except when the words following *as to* are shifted to the beginning of a sentence for prominence): *As to your brother, I will deal with him later;* (with a gerund) *As to accepting their demand,....* **13** (used as a *conj* to introduce relative clauses, chiefly after *same* and *such*): *Such women as knew Tom* (= Those women who knew him) *thought he was charming. Such women as Tom knew* (= Those women whom Tom knew) *thought he was charming. You must show my wife the same respect as you show me,* the respect that you show me. *We drove out of the town by the same road as we had entered by.* **14** (introducing a non-defining relative clause, the antecedent being inferred): *Cyprus, as* (= which fact) *you all know, is in the Mediterranean. To shut your eyes to facts, as many of you do, is foolish.* **15** **'so as to, (a)** (introducing an infinitive of purpose): *He stood up so as to* (= in order to) *see better.* **(b)** (introducing an infinitive of manner): *It is foolish to behave so as to annoy* (= in ways that annoy) *your neighbours.* **16** **as good as,** the same thing as: *Will he be as good as his word?* Will he do what he promised? *He's as good as dead,* almost dead, sure to die soon. **17** **as/so long as, (a)** on condition that: *You can go where you like so long as you get back before dark.* **(b)** while: *You shall never enter this house as long as I live in it.* **18** **as much,** so; (what really amounts to) that: *I thought as much.* **19** **as far as,** ⇨ far¹(2). **as such; such as,** ⇨ such *pron.* **20** (*just*) **as soon; as soon as** (*not*), ⇨ soon(3,5). **as well (as),** ⇨ well²(8).

as·bes·tos /æzˈbestɒs/ *n* [U] soft, fibrous, grey, mineral substance that can be made into fire-proof fabrics or solid sheeting and used as a heat-insulating material.

as·cend /əˈsend/ *vt,vi* **1** [VP6A,2A,C] go or come up (a mountain, river, etc): *We watched the mists* ~*ing from the valley. The path* ~*s here.* **2** ~ **the throne,** become king or queen.

as·cend·ancy, -ency /əˈsendənsɪ/ *n* [U] (position of) having power. **gain/have the** ~ **(over sb):** *He has the* ~ *over his rivals/his party.*

as·cend·ant, -ent /əˈsendənt/ *n* **in the** ~, rising in power and influence.

as·cen·sion /əˈsenʃn/ *n* act of ascending. **the A**~,

the departure of Jesus from the earth, on the fortieth day after the Resurrection.

as·cent /ə'sent/ n [C] act of ascending; way up; upward movement: *The ~ of the mountain was not difficult. I have never made an ~* (= have never been up) *in a balloon. The last part of the ~ is steep.*

as·cer·tain /ˌæsə'teɪn/ vt [VP6A,9,8,10,17] find out (in order to be certain about); get to know: *~ the facts; ~ that the news is true; ~ whether the train stops at X; ~ what really happened.* **~·able** /-əbl/ adj that can be ~ed.

as·cetic /ə'setɪk/ adj self-denying; austere; leading a life of severe self-discipline. □ n person who (often for religious reasons) leads a severely simple life without ordinary pleasures. **as·ceti·cally** /-klɪ/ adv **as·ceti·cism** /ə'setɪsɪzəm/ n

as·cor·bic /ə'skɔːbɪk/ adj ~ **acid,** (also known as *vitamin C*) vitamin found in citrus fruits and vegetable products, used against scurvy.

as·cribe /ə'skraɪb/ vt [VP14] ~ **to, 1** consider to be the cause, origin, reason or author, of: *He ~d his failure to bad luck. This play has been ~d to Shakespeare,* it has been said that Shakespeare was the author. **2** consider as belonging to: *~ a wrong meaning to a word.* **as·crib·able** /-əbl/ adj that can be ~d: *His quick recovery is ascribable to his sound constitution.* **as·crip·tion** /ə'skrɪpʃn/ n ascribing: *The ascription of this work to Schubert may be false.*

as·dic /'æzdɪk/ n device using reflected soundwaves, for detecting submarines, etc.

asep·tic /eɪ'septɪk/ adj (of wounds, dressings, etc) free from bacteria; surgically clean. **asep·sis** /ˌeɪ'sepsɪs/ n [U] ~ condition.

asex·ual /ˌeɪ'sekʃʊəl/ adj **1** without sex or sex organs: *~ reproduction.* **2** (of a person) showing no interest in sexual relations. **~·ity** /eɪˌsekʃʊ'ælətɪ/ n

ash[1] /æʃ/ n forest-tree with silver-grey bark and hard, tough wood; [U] wood of this tree. **'ash-key** n winged seed of the ash. ⇨ the illus at tree.

ash[2] /æʃ/ n [U or pl, but not with numerals] **1** powder that remains after sth has burnt: *Don't drop cigarette ash on the carpet. Remove the ash(es) from the stove once a day. The house was burnt to ashes.* **2** (pl) the burnt (= cremated) remains of a human body. **Ash Wednesday,** first day of Lent. **'ash-bin, 'ash-can** nn (esp US; ⇨ dustbin) large rigid receptacle for ashes, cinders, kitchen waste, etc. **'ash-pan** n tray (in a fireplace, stove, etc) into which ashes drop from a fire. **'ash-tray** n small (metal, glass, etc) receptacle for tobacco ash.

ashamed /ə'ʃeɪmd/ pred adj ~ **(of/that/to do sth),** feeling shame: *You should be ~ of yourself/ of what you have done. He was/felt ~ to ask for help. He felt ~ that he had done/of having done so little. I feel ~ for you,* on your account, as if I were you. **asham·ed·ly** /ə'ʃeɪmɪdlɪ/ adv

ashen /'æʃn/ adj of ashes; pale; ash-coloured: *His face turned ~ at the news.*

ashore /ə'ʃɔː(r)/ adv on, on to, the shore. **go ~,** (of a sailor, etc) leave a ship to go on land. **run/be driven ~,** (of a ship) be forced to the shore, eg by bad weather.

ashy /'æʃɪ/ adj of or like ashes; covered with ashes; ash-coloured, pale.

Asian /'eɪʃn US: 'eɪʒn/ n, adj (native) of Asia. **Asi·atic** /ˌeɪʃɪ'ætɪk US: ˌeɪʒɪ-/ n, adj (native) of Asia (*Asian* is the preferred word).

aside /ə'saɪd/ adv on or to one side: *He laid the*

book ~, put it down and stopped reading it. *We turned ~* (= away) *from the main road. The decision/verdict was set ~,* made of no effect. *Please put this ~ for me,* reserve it. *Joking ~,* ie speaking seriously,.... □ n [C] words spoken ~, esp (on the stage) words that other persons (on the stage) are supposed not to hear.

as·in·ine /'æsɪnaɪn/ adj **1** of asses. **2** (colloq) stupid.

ask /ɑːsk US: æsk/ vt,vi (pt,pp asked) **1** [VP6A,12C,14] often with the indirect object omitted in 12C] call for an answer to; request information or service: *Did you ask the price? Ask (him) his name. May I ask (you) a question? Have I asked too much of you/asked you for too much? You asked of me more than you asked of the others. He asked a favour of me. We must ask him about it. He asked me for help.* [VP8,20] *I will ask (him) how to get there. Did you ask (her) which to buy?* [VP10,21] *They asked (me) what my name was, where I came from, and why I had come. Please ask (her) when she will be back.* [VP3A] **ask after,** ask for information about: *He asked after you/your health.* **2** [VP6A,17,15B,3A] invite: *We asked him to come again. I've been asked (out) to dinner. Mr Brown is at the door; shall I ask him in?* **ask for trouble,** (colloq) **ask for it,** behave in such a way that trouble is likely; invite trouble. **3** [VP7A,9,17,10] request to be allowed: *I must ask you to excuse me/ask to be excused. He asked permission to get up. He asked to get up/that/if he might get up.* **4** [VP6A,12C,14] demand as a price: *He asked (me) £25 a month as rent for that house. You're asking too much. What are they asking for the house?* **5 ask the banns,** (old use; now usu put up or publish) publish them.

askance /ə'skæns/ adv (only in) **look ~ at sb/ sth,** look at with suspicion.

askew /ə'skjuː/ adv, pred adj out of the straight or usual (level) position: *hang a picture ~; have one's hat on ~: cut a plank ~,* aslant.

ask·ing /'ɑːskɪŋ/ n **for the ~,** by requesting: *You may have it/It's yours for the ~,* You have only to ask for it and it will be given to you.

aslant /ə'slɑːnt US: ə'slænt/ adv, prep in a slanting direction (*to*): *The wrecked coach lay ~ the railway track.*

asleep /ə'sliːp/ adv, pred adj **1** sleeping: *He was fast ~. He fell/dropped ~ during the sermon.* **2** (of the arms or legs) without feeling (as when under pressure).

asp[1] /æsp/ n = aspen.

asp[2] /æsp/ n (zool) small poisonous snake of Egypt and Libya.

as·para·gus /ə'spærəgəs/ n [U] plant whose young shoots are cooked and eaten as a vegetable; the shoots.

as·pect /'æspekt/ n **1** look or appearance (of a person or thing): *a man of fierce ~; a man with a serious ~.* **2** front that faces a particular direction: *a house with a southern ~.* **3** (fig) particular part: *study every ~ of a subject,* study it thoroughly. **4** (gram) verb form which relates activity to passage of time. **as·pec·tual** /æ'spektʃʊəl/ adj: *There is an ~ual difference between 'I saw him cross the road' and 'I saw him crossing the road'.*

as·pen /'æspən/ n kind of poplar tree with leaves that move in the slightest wind.

as·per·ity /æ'sperətɪ/ n (pl -ties) (formal) **1** [U] roughness; harshness (of manner); severity (of weather): *speak with* ~. 2 (with *pl*) instance of one of these qualities: *the asperities of winter in Labrador; an exchange of asperities,* eg of hard or bitter words.

as·perse /ə'spɜːs/ *vt* [VP6A] (formal) slander; say false or unkind things about: ~ *sb's good name/ honour/reputation.* **as·per·sion** /ə'spɜːʃn US: -ʒn/ *n* (only in) **cast aspersions (up)on sb/sb's honour, etc,** slander him; say false things about him.

as·phalt /'æsfælt US: -fɔːlt/ *n* [U] black, sticky substance like coal-tar used for making roofs, etc waterproof, and mixed with gravel or crushed rock, for making road surfaces. □ *vt* [VP6A] surface (a road) with ~.

as·pho·del /'æsfədel/ *n* 1 sort of lily. 2 (poet) immortal flower of the Gk Elysium /ɪ'lɪːzɪəm/ (home of the dead).

as·phyxia /æs'fɪksɪə/ *n* [U] condition caused by lack of enough air in the lungs; suffocation. **as·phyxi·ate** /əs'fɪksɪeɪt/ *vt* [VP6A] make ill, cause the death of, through lack of sufficient air in the lungs: *The men in the coal-mine were* ~*ted by bad gas.* **as·phyxi·ation** /əs,fɪksɪ'eɪʃn/ *n* [U] = asphyxia; suffocation.

as·pic /'æspɪk/ *n* [U] clear meat jelly: *chicken in* ~.

as·pi·dis·tra /,æspɪ'dɪstrə/ *n* (*pl* ~s) plant with broad, pointed leaves, usually grown as a house plant.

as·pir·ant /ə'spaɪərənt/ *n* ~ *(to/after),* person who is ambitious for fame, etc: *an* ~ *to high office.*

as·pir·ate¹ /'æspərət/ *n* (phon) the sound of 'h'; sound with an 'h' in it: *Mind your* ~*s,* be careful to make the 'h' sounds where necessary.

as·pir·ate² /'æspəreɪt/ *vt* (phon) say with an 'h' sound: *The 'h' in 'honour' is not* ~*d.*

as·pir·ation /,æspə'reɪʃn/ *n* [C,U] 1 ~ *(for/after); ~ (to do/be),* aspiring; desire: *his* ~*s for fame; his* ~ *to be an actor; the* ~*s of the developing countries.* 2 aspirating.

as·pire /ə'spaɪə(r)/ *vi* [VP3A,4A] be filled with high ambition: ~ *after knowledge;* ~ *to fame;* ~ *to become an author.*

as·pirin /'æsprɪn US: -pər-/ *n* [U] (P) medicine used to relieve pain and reduce fever; [C] tablet or measure of this: *Take two* ~*s for a headache.*

ass¹ /æs/ *n* 1 animal of the horse family with long ears and a tuft at the end of its tail; donkey; stupid person. 2 **make an ass of oneself,** behave stupidly so that one is ridiculed.

ass² /æs/ *n* (US vulg) = arse.

as·sa·gai /'æsəgaɪ/ *n* = assegai.

as·sail /ə'seɪl/ *vt* [VP6A,14] ~ *(with),* attack violently; pester: ~ *sb with questions/insults; be* ~*ed with doubts.* ~**able** /-əbl/ *adj* that can be attacked. ~**ant** /-ənt/ *n* attacker.

as·sas·sin /ə'sæsɪn US: -sn/ *n* person, often one hired by others, who assassinates. ~**ate** /ə'sæsɪneɪt US: -sən-/ *vt* [VP6A] kill sb (esp an important politician, ruler) violently and treacherously, for political reasons. ~**ation** /ə,sæsɪ'neɪʃn US: ə,sæsən'eɪʃn/ *n* [U] murder of this kind; [C] instance of this.

as·sault /ə'sɔːlt/ *n* ~ *(on/upon),* violent and sudden attack: *They made an* ~ *on the enemy's positions. The sonic boom was an* ~ *on our nerves. The enemy's positions were taken by* ~. ~ *and battery,* (legal) beating or hitting sb. '~ *craft n* portable boat with an outboard motor, used for making attacks across rivers, etc. □ *vt* [VP6A] make an ~ on; attack (eg a fortress) by a sudden

rush.

as·say /ə'seɪ/ *n* [C] ~ *(of),* test of the fineness, purity, or quality (of precious metals, ores, etc): *make an* ~ *of an ore.* □ *vt* 1 [VP6A] test, eg the purity of a metal, analyse, eg an ore, etc. 2 ~ *(to do sth),* [VP6A,7A] (old use) attempt, eg sth difficult.

as·se·gai /'æsəgaɪ/ *n* throwing-spear with a wooden haft, used by S African tribes.

as·sem·blage /ə'semblɪdʒ/ *n* 1 [U] bringing or coming together; assembly (now the usu word): *the ~ of parts of a machine.* 2 [C] collection of things or (joc) persons.

as·semble /ə'sembl/ *vt,vi* 1 [VP6A,2A] gather together; collect: *The pupils* ~*d/were* ~*d in the school hall.* 2 [VP6A] fit or put together (the parts of): ~ *a watch/car.*

as·sem·bly /ə'semblɪ/ *n* (*pl* -lies) 1 [C] number of persons who have come together, esp a meeting of law-makers: *the Legislative A*~*; the school* ~, the daily ~ *of pupils and staff.* '~ **room(s),** public hall in which meetings, balls, etc take place. 2 '~ **hall,** one where a school meets for prayers, etc; workshop where parts of large machines, eg aircraft, are put together. '~ **line,** stage of mass production in which parts of a machine, vehicle, etc move along for progressive ~. 3 military call, by drum or bugle, for soldiers to assemble.

as·sent /ə'sent/ *n* ~ *(to),* official agreement, eg to a proposal; (royal) agreement (to a bill passed by Parliament). **by common** ~, everybody agreeing. **with one** ~, unanimously; nobody opposing. ⇨ accord¹(1), dissent. □ *vi* [VP2A,3A] ~ *(to),* give agreement (eg to a proposal).

as·sert /ə'sɜːt/ *vt* 1 [VP6A] make a claim to, eg one's rights. 2 [VP6A,9,25] declare: ~ *one's innocence/that one is innocent;* ~ *sth to be true.* ~ *oneself,* display authority, self-confidence.

as·ser·tion /ə'sɜːʃn/ *n* 1 [U] insisting upon the recognition of one's rights: *self-*~. 2 [C] strong statement; claim: *make an* ~.

as·sert·ive /ə'sɜːtɪv/ *adj* having or showing positive assurance: *speaking in an* ~ *tone.* ~**ly** *adv*

as·sess /ə'ses/ *vt* [VP6A,14] 1 decide or fix the amount of (eg a tax or a fine): *Damages were* ~*ed at £100.* 2 appraise; fix or decide the value of (eg property), the amount of (eg income), for purposes of taxation; (fig) test the value of: ~ *a speech at its true worth.* ~**ment** *n* [U] ~ing; [C] amount ~ed. ~**or** /-sə(r)/ *n* 1 person who ~es property, income, taxes, etc. 2 person who advises a judge, magistrate or official committee, etc on technical matters.

as·set /'æset/ *n* 1 (usu *pl*) anything owned by a person, company, etc that has money value and that may be sold to pay debts. ⇨ liability. 2 valuable or useful quality or skill: *Good health is a great* ~.

as·sev·er·ate /ə'sevəreɪt/ *vt* [VP6A,9] (formal) assert solemnly: ~ *one's innocence/that one is innocent.* **as·sev·er·ation** /ə,sevə'reɪʃn/ *n*

as·si·du·ity /,æsɪ'djuːətɪ US: -'duː-/ *n* 1 [U] constant and careful attention to what one is doing: *He plans everything with unfailing* ~. 2 (*pl*) -ties) constant attentions (*to*).

as·sidu·ous /ə'sɪdjʊəs US: -dʒʊəs/ *adj* diligent; persevering: ~ *in his duties.* ~**ly** *adv*

as·sign /ə'saɪn/ *vt* 1 [VP13A,12A] ~ *sth (to sb/ sth),* give for use or enjoyment, or as a share or part in a distribution, eg of work, duty: *Those rooms have been* ~*ed to us. Your teacher* ~*s you work to be done at home.* 2 [VP13A,B] name, put forward as a time, place, reason, etc: *Has a day been ~ed for the trial? Can one ~ a cause to these events?* **3** [VP13A,17] ~ *sb (to/to do),* appoint, name: *A~ your best man to the job. Two pupils were ~ed to sweep the classroom.* **4** [VP14] ~ *to,* (legal) transfer property, rights, etc. ~·**able** /-əbl/ *adj* that can be attributed or ~ed: ~*able to several causes.* ~·**ment** *n* [U] ~ing; [C] that which is ~ed.

as·sig·na·tion /͵æsɪg'neɪʃn/ *n* [C] appointment, eg of a time and place for a furtive meeting between lovers.

as·simi·late /ə'sɪməleɪt/ *vt,vi* **1** [VP6A,2A] absorb (food) into the body (after digestion); be thus absorbed: *We ~ some kinds of food more easily than others. Some kinds of food ~ easily.* **2** [VP6A,2A] (allow people to) become part of another social group or state: *The USA has ~d people from many countries,* has absorbed them, so that they are Americans. **3** [VP6A] absorb, eg ideas, knowledge. **4** [VP3A] ~ *to,* make or become like. **as·simi·la·tion** /ə͵sɪmə'leɪʃn/ *n* [U] assimilating or being ~d.

as·sist /ə'sɪst/ *vt,vi* [VP6A,17,14,2A,3A] ~ *(sb) (with sth/in doing sth/to do sth),* (formal) help: ~ *(sb)* with the form-filling; ~ *sb* to fill in the forms. *Two men are ~ing the police in their enquiries,* are answering questions which may lead to the arrest of the criminal(s), or perhaps their own arrest as the criminals. ~·**ance** /-əns/ *n* [U] help: *give/lend/render ~ance (to sb); come to sb's ~ance; be of ~ance (to sb).* ~·**ant** /-ənt/ *n* helper: *an ~ant to the Manager; ~ant master,* in a school; *a'shop-~ant,* one who serves customers.

as·size /ə'saɪz/ *n* **1** [U] trial by a judge and jury. **2** (*pl*) (until 1971) sessions held periodically in every English County to try civil and criminal cases before High Court Judges: (attrib, *sing*) *courts of ~; judges on ~; ~ towns.* ⇨ *Crown Court* at *court*[1](1) for the new system.

as·so·ci·ate[1] /ə'səʊʃɪət/ *adj* joined in function or dignity: *an ~ judge.* □ *n* person who has been joined with others *in* work, business or crime; person given certain limited rights in an association; companion.

as·so·ci·ate[2] /ə'səʊʃɪeɪt/ *vt,vi* ~ *with* **1** [VP14] join or connect: ~ *oneself with sb in a business undertaking;* ~ *one thing with another. We ~ Egypt with the Nile. I don't wish to ~ myself with what has been said,* don't want anyone to think that I have a part in it, or approve of it. **2** [VP3A] be often in the company of: *Don't ~ with dishonest boys.*

as·so·ci·ation /ə͵səʊsɪ'eɪʃn/ *n* **1** [U] ~ *(with),* associating; being associated; companionship: *I benefited much from my ~ with him/from our ~. His English benefited through his long ~ with British children. in ~ (with),* together (with). **2** [C] group of persons joined together for some common purpose: *the 'Automobile A~; the ͵Young Men's 'Christian A~.* **3** *͵A~* 'football, (common abbr *soccer*) game in which two teams of eleven players use a spherical ball that must not be touched with the hands except by the goalkeeper or when throwing in. ⇨ the illus at foot. **4** connection (of ideas).

as·son·ance /'æsənəns/ *n* agreement between stressed vowels in two words, but not in the following consonants, as in *sharper* and *garter.*

as·sorted /ə'sɔːtɪd/ *part adj* **1** of various sorts; mixed: *a pound of ~ toffees,* toffees of different

kinds, mixed together. **2** matched, suited, one to another: *an ill-~ couple,* husband and wife who get on badly. **as·sort·ment** /ə'sɔːtmənt/ *n* ~ collection of different examples of one class or of several classes: *This shop has a good assortment of goods to choose from.*

as·suage /æ'sweɪdʒ/ *vt* [VP6A] make (sth, eg pain, suffering, feelings, desire) less.

as·sume /ə'sjuːm *US:* ə'suːm/ *vt* **1** [VP6A,9,25] take as true before there is proof: *You ~ his innocence/him to be innocent/that he is innocent before hearing the evidence against him. He's not such a fool as you ~d* (= supposed) *him to be. Assuming this to be true....* ⇨ presume(1). **2** [VP6A] take up; undertake: ~ *the direction of a business;* ~ *office;* ~ *the reins of government,* begin to govern. **3** [VP6A] take upon or for oneself sth not genuine or sincere: ~ *a look of innocence;* ~ *a new name.*

as·sump·tion /ə'sʌmpʃn/ *n* **1** [C] sth taken for granted; sth supposed but not proved: *Their ~ that the war would end quickly was proved wrong. on the ~ that,* accepting it to be true that.... **2** [C] ~ *of,* the act of assuming(2): *his ~ of office/power/ the presidency.* **3** [C] ~ *of,* the adopting of a manner, etc which is not genuine: *with an ~ of indifference,* pretending not to be interested. **4 the A~,** reception into Heaven in bodily form of the Virgin Mary; Church feast commemorating this.

as·sur·ance /ə'ʃʊərəns/ *n* **1** [U] (often *self-~*) confidence in oneself; belief and trust in one's own powers: *He answered all the questions with ~. A businessman, to be successful, should act with perfect (self-)assurance.* **2** [C] promise; statement made to give confidence: *He gave me a definite ~ that the repairs would be finished by Friday.* **3** [U] (chiefly GB) insurance on sth that is certain: '*life ~,* because death is certain. ⇨ insurance. **4** [U] impudence (the much more usu word). **5** ~ *(in),* [U] certainty; confidence (the much more usu word). *make ~ doubly sure,* remove all possible doubt.

as·sure /ə'ʃʊə(r)/ *vt* **1** [VP11] say positively, with confidence: *I ~ you (that) there's no danger.* **2** [VP11,14] cause (sb) to be sure, to feel certain: *We tried to ~ the nervous old lady that flying was safe. He ~d me of his readiness to help.* **3** [VP6A] ensure (the more usu word): *Nothing can ~ permanent happiness.* **4** [VP6A] insure, esp against the death of sb or oneself. **as·sured** *part adj* sure; confident. *rest ~d (that),* feel confident (that). **as·sur·ed·ly** /ə'ʃʊərɪdlɪ/ *adv* surely; confidently.

as·ter /'æstə(r)/ *n* garden plant with flowers that have white, pink or purple petals round a yellow centre.

as·ter·isk /'æstərɪsk/ *n* the mark *, used to call attention to something, eg a footnote, or to show that letters are omitted, as in *Mr J***s,* for *Mr Jones.*

astern /ə'stɜːn/ *adv* **1** in or at the stern of a ship. ⇨ the illus at ship. **2** backward: *Full speed ~!* **3** *fall ~ (of),* fall behind (another ship).

as·ter·oid /'æstərɔɪd/ *n* [C] any of many small planets between the orbits of Mars and Jupiter. ⇨ the illus at planet.

asthma /'æsmə *US:* 'æzmə/ *n* [U] chronic chest disease marked by difficulty in breathing. **asth·matic** /æs'mætɪk *US:* æz-/ *adj* suffering from ~; of ~.

astig·ma·tism /ə'stɪgmətɪzəm/ *n* [U] defect in an eye or lens that prevents correct focusing. **as·tig-**

matic /ˌæstɪgˈmætɪk/ adj

astir /əˈstɜː(r)/ adv, pred adj **1** in motion; in a state of excitement: The whole village was ~ when news came that the Queen was coming. **2** (dated) out of bed and about: You're ~ early this morning.

as·ton·ish /əˈstɒnɪʃ/ vt [VP6A] surprise greatly: The news ~ed everybody. You look ~ed at the news. I was ~ed to see him there. I am ~ed that he didn't come. **~·ing** part adj very surprising: It is ~ing to me that he should be absent. **~·ment** n [U] great surprise: I heard to my ~ment that...; He looked at me in ~ment.

astound /əˈstaʊnd/ vt [VP6A] overcome with surprise; shock.

as·tra·khan /ˌæstrəˈkæn US: ˈæstrəkən/ n [U] skin of young lambs with wool in tight little curls: (used attrib) an ~ coat/cap.

as·tral /ˈæstrəl/ adj of or from the stars.

astray /əˈstreɪ/ adv, pred adj out of, off, the right path, esp (fig) into wrong-doing: The boy was led ~ by bad companions.

astride /əˈstraɪd/ adv, pred adj, prep with one leg on each side (of): riding ~; sitting ~ his father's knee.

as·trin·gent /əˈstrɪndʒənt/ n (kind of) substance that shrinks soft tissues and contracts blood-vessels, thus checking the flow of blood. □ adj of or like an ~; (fig) harsh; severe. **as·trin·gency** /əˈstrɪndʒənsɪ/ n

as·tro·dome /ˈæstrədəʊm/ n small, transparent observation dome on the top of the fuselage of an aircraft, used by the navigator.

as·tro·labe /ˈæstrəleɪb/ n instrument used in the Middle Ages to determine the height of the sun, etc. ➪ sextant.

as·trol·ogy /əˈstrɒlədʒɪ/ n [U] art of observing the positions of the stars in the belief that they influence human affairs. **as·trol·oger** /-ədʒə(r)/ n expert in ~. **as·tro·logi·cal** /ˌæstrəˈlɒdʒɪkl/ adj

as·tro·naut /ˈæstrənɔːt/ n person who travels in a spacecraft. **~·ics** /ˌæstrəˈnɔːtɪks/ n (sing v) science and technology of travel through outer space.

as·tron·omy /əˈstrɒnəmɪ/ n [U] science of the sun, moon, stars and planets. **as·tron·omer** n student of, authority on, ~. **as·tro·nomi·cal** /ˌæstrəˈnɒmɪkl/ adj of the study of ~; (colloq; of a quantity) very large: an astronomical amount.

as·tro·phys·ics /ˌæstrəʊˈfɪzɪks/ n (sing v) science of the chemical and physical conditions of the stars.

as·tute /əˈstjuːt US: əˈstuːt/ adj **1** quick at seeing how to gain an advantage. **2** shrewd; clever: an ~ lawyer/businessman. **~·ly** adv **~·ness** n

asun·der /əˈsʌndə(r)/ adv (liter) **1** (of two or more things) apart: Parents and children were driven ~ (= separated) by the war. **2** into pieces: tear sth ~.

asy·lum /əˈsaɪləm/ n **1** [U] refuge; safety; protection from persecution, etc: ask for political ~; [C] place where this is found or given. **2** [C] (formerly) institution where mentally ill people were cared for, now called a mental home/hospital/institution.

at /ət; strong form: æt/ prep **1** (place and direction) **(a)** (indicating the place in or near which sth or sb was, is or will be): at his office; at my uncle's; at the station. Cf in for countries and large towns, and places important to the speaker. **(b)** (towards; in the direction of): look at sth/sb; shoot/aim a gun at sth; rush at the enemy; laugh/growl at sb/sth; throw sth at sb, ie intending to hit him. ➪ throw to at throw[2](1); talk at sb, ie make an indirect attack on him, ➪ talk to at talk[1](1). **(c)** (indicating an attempt to get or reach sth, an uncompleted or imperfect action): The drowning man clutched at the oar, tried to seize it. He had to guess at the meaning. **(d)** (indicating distance): hold sth at arm's length. It looks better at a distance. **(e)** (indicating a point of entrance or exit) through; by: What the teacher says often goes in (at) one ear and out (at) the other. **2** (time and order) **(a)** (indicating a point of time): at 2 o'clock; at sunset; at any moment; at this (point), when this happened. **(b)** (of age): He left school at (the age of) 15. **(c)** (indicating order): at the third attempt; at first; at last. **(d)** (indicating frequency): at (all) times; at regular intervals. **3** (activity, state, manner) **(a)** (indicating occupation): at work; at play. What is he at now, What is he doing? ˌhard ˈat it, working hard. **(b)** (after adjj): busy at his tasks; good at translation. **(c)** (state, condition): at war/peace; at leisure. **(d)** (manner): at a gallop; finish something at a sitting, ie during one continuous period of activity. **4** (rate or degree, value, cost) **(a)** (rate): at full speed; at a snail's pace. **(b)** (value, cost, etc): at immense cost; sell sth at a loss; buy articles at 20p and sell them at 25p. **(c)** (with superl): at its/his/their, etc best; at least; at (the) worst. **5** (cause) **(a)** (after vv): The pupils marvelled at the extent of their teacher's knowledge. **(b)** (after adjj and pp's): impatient at the delay; delighted at the idea of going to England. ➪ also n entries for at hand, at last, in at the death and others.

ata·brine /ˈætəbriːn/ n [U] (P) bitter-tasting, antimalarial drug.

ata·vism /ˈætəvɪzəm/ n reappearance in a person of a characteristic or quality that has not shown itself for several or many generations. ➪ reversion, throwback. **ata·vis·tic** /ˌætəˈvɪstɪk/ adj

ate /et US: eɪt/ pt of eat.

atel·ier /æˈteljeɪ US: ˌætlˈjeɪ/ n (F) workshop; studio.

athe·ism /ˈeɪθɪɪzəm/ n [U] belief that there is no God. **athe·ist** /ˈeɪθɪɪst/ n person who believes that there is no God. **athe·is·tic** /ˌeɪθɪˈɪstɪk/ adj of ~ or atheists.

athirst /əˈθɜːst/ pred adj ~ (for), (liter) thirsty, eager (for news, etc).

ath·lete /ˈæθliːt/ n person trained for competing in physical exercises and outdoor games, eg a person good at running, jumping, swimming, boxing.

ath·letic /æθˈletɪk/ adj **1** of athletes. **2** physically strong, with well-balanced proportions between the trunk and limbs: an ~-looking young man.

ath·let·ics /æθˈletɪks/ n pl (usu with sing v) practice of physical exercises and sports, esp competitions in running, jumping, etc.

at·home /ət ˈhəʊm/ ➪ home[1](1).

athwart /əˈθwɔːt/ adv, prep ~ (of), (naut) from one side to the other side.

atishoo /əˈtɪʃuː/ int (hum) spelling form used to indicate a sneeze.

at·las /ˈætləs/ n book of maps.

at·mos·phere /ˈætməsfɪə(r)/ n **1** [U] esp the ~, mixture of gases surrounding the earth. **2** [U] air in any place. **3** [C] feeling, eg of good, evil, that the mind receives from a place, conditions, etc: There is an ~ of peace and calm in the country quite different from the ~ of a big city.

at·mos·pheric /ˌætməsˈferɪk/ adj of, connected with, the atmosphere: ~ conditions. ˌ~ ˈpressure,

pressure at a point due to the weight of the column of air above that point, about 14½ lb or 6·6 kg per square inch at sea level. **at·mos·pher·ics** n pl electrical discharges that occur in the atmosphere and cause crackling sounds in radio receivers.

atoll /'ætɒl/ n ring-shaped coral reef(s) almost or entirely enclosing a lagoon.

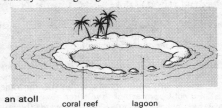

an atoll   coral reef   lagoon

atom /'ætəm/ n 1 smallest unit of an element that can take part in a chemical change: *A molecule of water* (H_2O) *is made up of two* ~s *of hydrogen and one* ~ *of oxygen.* ⇨ electron, neutron, nucleus, proton. '~ **bomb,** = atomic bomb. **2** very small bit: *blow sth to* ~s, destroy it by explosion. *There's not an* ~ *of truth* (= no truth at all) *in what he said.*

atomic /ə'tɒmɪk/ adj of an atom, or atoms. '~ **bomb,** bomb of which the destructive power comes from the release of ~ energy in the shortest possible time. ~ **'energy,** energy obtained as the result of nuclear fission. ~ **'pile,** ⇨ reactor. ~ **'weight,** weight of an atom of an element expressed on a scale in which an atom of oxygen is 16. ⇨ nuclear.

at·om·ize /'ætəmaɪz/ vt reduce to atoms. ~r n device for producing a fine spray, eg of perfume.

atonal /eɪ'təʊnl/ adj (music) not conforming to any system of key or mode. ~**ity** /ˌeɪtəʊ'nælətɪ/ n

atone /ə'təʊn/ vi [VP2A,3A] ~ **(for),** make repayment: ~ **(for)** *a fault by doing sth. How can I* ~ *for hurting your feelings? How can I* ~? ~**ment** n [U] atoning: *make* ~*ment for a fault.* **the A~ment,** the sufferings and death of Jesus.

atop /ə'tɒp/ adv ~ **(of),** (US) on top (of).

at·ra·bil·ious /ˌætrə'bɪlɪəs/ adj (rare) melancholy; acrimonious.

atro·cious /ə'trəʊʃəs/ adj 1 very wicked or cruel: *an* ~ *crime.* **2** (colloq) very bad: *an* ~ *dinner;* ~ *weather.* ~**ly** adv

atroc·ity /ə'trɒsətɪ/ n [U] wickedness; [C] (pl ties) wicked or cruel act: *the atrocities of which the enemy forces were guilty.*

atro·phy /'ætrəfɪ/ n [U] wasting away (of the body or part of it, or (fig) of a moral quality). □ vt,vi [VP6A] cause ~ in; [VP2A,B] suffer ~.

atta·boy /ˌætə'bɔɪ/ int (US colloq) (expressing encouragement or admiration) Bravo!

at·tach /ə'tætʃ/ vt,vi 1 [VP14] ~ *sth (to sth),* fasten or join: ~ *labels to the luggage;* ~ *a document to a letter; the sample* ~*ed to the letter; a house with a garage* ~*ed. A* ~*ed you will find/A* ~*ed please find...,* (business style) You will find, ~ed to this letter.... **2** [VP14] ~ *oneself to,* join eg as a junior, and perhaps unwelcome, member: ~ *oneself to a political party/to a travelling circus.* **3** *be* ~*ed to,* be bound to by love or affection: *She is deeply* ~*ed to her young brother. He is foolishly* ~*ed to old customs.* **4** [VP14] ~ *sth to sth,* consider to have; connect with: *Do you* ~ *much importance to what he says?* **5** [VP3A] ~ *to,* go with,

be joined to: *No suspicion/blame* ~*es to him,* He cannot be suspected/blamed. **6** [VP6A] (legal) seize by legal authority: *Part of his salary was* ~*ed by shopkeepers to whom he owed money.* **7** ~*ed to,* (mil) appointed to another unit for specialist duties: *a gunnery officer* ~*ed to an infantry regiment.* ~**·ment** n 1 [U] act of ~ing or joining; being ~ed. **2** [C] sth ~ed, esp an accessory ~ed to sth larger. **3** [C] affection; friendship: *have an* ~*ment for sb.* **4** legal seizing of goods, etc. **5** *on* ~*ment to,* (temporarily) appointed to.

at·taché /ə'tæʃeɪ US: ˌætə'ʃeɪ/ n person who is attached to the staff of an ambassador: *the naval/military/press* ~. ~ **case** /ə'tæʃɪ keɪs/ n small, flat, rectangular box or holder for documents.

at·tack /ə'tæk/ n 1 [C] violent attempt to hurt, overcome, defeat: *make an* ~ *upon the enemy;* [U] *The enemy came under* ~. *A* ~ *is said to be the best form of defence.* **2** [C] adverse criticism in speech or writing: *a strong* ~ *against/on the Government's policy.* **3** [C] start, occurence, eg of disease: *an* ~ *of fever; a 'liver* ~*; a 'heart* ~, pain in the region of the heart, with irregular beating. **4** [U] way of beginning an activity, eg playing the violin, playing a stroke in cricket. □ vt [VP6A] make an ~ upon: ~ *the enemy;* ~ *the Prime Minister's proposals; a disease that* ~s *children. Rust* ~s *metals.* ~**er** n person who ~s.

at·tain /ə'teɪn/ vt,vi 1 [VP6A] succeed in doing or getting: ~ *one's hopes/object/the end one has in view.* **2** [VP3A] ~ *to,* reach, arrive at: ~ *to perfection/power/prosperity;* ~ *to man's estate,* reach manhood. ~**·able** /-əbl/ adj that can be ~ed: *The goal is not yet* ~*able.* ~**·ment** n 1 [U] act of ~ing: *easy/difficult/impossible of* ~*ment,* easy, etc to ~; *for the* ~*ment of* (= in order to ~) *his purpose.* **2** [C] (usu pl) sth ~ed; skill or accomplishment in some branch of knowledge, etc: *legal/linguistic* ~*ments; a scholar of the highest* ~*ments.*

at·tain·der /ə'teɪndə(r)/ n (legal) forfeiture of property and civil rights following sentence of death or outlawry. **Bill of A~,** Parliamentary Bill imposing this penalty without trial.

at·tar /'ætə(r)/ n [U] ~ *of roses,* perfume from rose petals.

at·tempt /ə'tempt/ vt 1 [VP7A,6A] make a start at doing sth; try: *The prisoners* ~*ed to escape/an escape but failed. You have* ~*ed* (= made a start at performing) *a difficult task. Don't* ~ *impossibilities,* Don't try to do impossible things. **2** [VP6A] ~ *sb's life,* (old use) try to kill him. □ n [C] 1 ~ *to do sth;* ~ *at doing sth,* ~ing; effort to do sth: *They made no* ~ *to escape/at escaping. His first* ~ *at English composition was poor. They failed in all their* ~s *to climb the mountain.* **2** ~ *at,* sth not very well done: *Her* ~ *at a Christmas cake had to be thrown away.* **3** ~ *on/upon,* attack on: *make an* ~ *on sb's life; an* ~ *on the world speed record.*

at·tend /ə'tend/ vi,vt 1 [VP3A,2A] ~ *(to),* give care and thought (to): ~ *to one's work;* ~ *to what sb is saying,* listen carefully; ~ *to the wants of customers,* try to supply them. *Are you being* ~*ed to?* (in a shop) Is anyone serving you? *You're not* ~*ing,* not listening, not paying attention. **2** [VP6A,3A] ~ *(on/upon),* wait on; serve; look after: *Which doctor is* ~*ing you, giving you medical care? The patient has three nurses* ~*ing* (*on*) *him. She has many servants* ~*ing upon her. He had the honour of* ~*ing upon the Prince.* **3** [VP6A] go to; be present at: ~ *school/church;* ~ *a meeting/lecture. The lectures were well ~ed,* there were good audiences. **4** [VP6A] (formal) accompany: *a method that is ~ed by some risk; Our plans were ~ed with great difficulties. May good luck ~ you!,* (formal) May you have good luck!

at·tend·ance /ə'tendəns/ n **1** [U] *in ~ (on/upon),* act of attending(2): *Major X was in ~ upon the Queen. Now that the patient is out of danger, the doctor is no longer in ~.* ⇨ dance²(2). **2** [C,U] (time of) being present, at school etc: *The boy was given a prize for regular ~,* for attending school regularly. *How many ~s has he made? Is ~ at school compulsory?* **3** [C] (with *adj)* number of persons present: *There was a large ~ at church this morning.*

at·tend·ant /ə'tendənt/ n **1** servant or companion. **2** *medical ~,* doctor. **3** (*pl*) persons who accompany an important person: *the Prince and his ~s.* □ *adj* **1** accompanying: *famine and its ~ diseases,* the diseases that result from famine; *old age and its ~ evils,* eg deafness. **2** waiting upon: *an ~ nurse.*

at·ten·tion /ə'tenʃn/ n **1** [U] act of directing one's thoughts to sth: *Pay ~ to what you're doing,* Don't let your thoughts wander. *A teacher must know how to secure the ~ of his pupils. No ~ was paid to my advice,* no one took it. *Give your whole ~ to what you are doing,* ie think of nothing else. *He called/invited my ~ to some new evidence,* asked me to examine it. *He shouted to attract ~,* to make people notice him. *A~, Mr Roberts,* (in comm or official correspondence) This letter, memorandum, etc is to be dealt with by Mr Roberts. **2** (often *pl*) kind or polite act: *They showed the old lady numerous little ~s,* were kind and helpful in numerous ways. *A pretty girl usually receives more ~(s) than a plain girl,* finds men more willing to do things for her. **pay one's ~s to a lady,** (dated) court her, be polite and kind in the hope of winning her affections. **3** [U] (mil) drill position in which a man stands straight and still: *come to/stand at ~;* (as a military command): *A~!* (shortened to *'shun* /ʃʌn/).

at·tent·ive /ə'tentɪv/ *adj ~ (to),* giving or paying attention: *A speaker likes to have an ~ audience. Please be more ~ to your studies. A good host is ~ to (the needs of) his guests. She was always ~ to her young brother. ~·ly adv.* They listened ~ly to the teacher.

at·tenu·ate /ə'tenjʊeɪt/ *vt* [VP6A] (formal) make thin or slender; weaken; reduce.

at·test /ə'test/ *vt,vi* **1** [VP6A] be or give clear proof of: *The man's ability was ~ed by his rapid promotion,* His promotion was proof of his ability. *These papers ~ the fact that....* ~ *a signature,* make it legal by witnessing it. *~ed 'milk/'cattle,* certified free of disease, esp tuberculosis. **2** [VP6A] declare on oath; put (a person) on oath; cause (sb) to declare solemnly: *I have said nothing that I am not ready to ~,* to say on oath. **3** [VP2A] enrol for military service (by taking the oath of allegiance). **4** [VP3A] ~ *to,* bear witness to: *feats which ~ to his strength of will.*

at·tic /'ætɪk/ *n* space within the roof of a house: *two small rooms in the ~.*

At·tic /'ætɪk/ *adj* of ancient Athens or Attica.

at·tire /ə'taɪə(r)/ *n* [U] (liter or poet) dress: *in holiday ~.* □ *vt* [VP6A] (dated) dress: *~d in white/ satin.*

at·ti·tude /'ætɪtjuːd *US:* -tuːd/ *n* [C] **1** manner of

placing or holding the body: *He stood there in a threatening ~.* **strike an ~,** suddenly and dramatically take up an ~. **2** way of feeling, thinking or behaving: *What is your ~ towards this question,* What do you think about it, how do you propose to act? *We must maintain a firm ~,* not show signs of weakness. **at·ti·tu·din·ize** /ˌætɪ'tjuːdɪnaɪz *US:* -'tuːdən-/ *vi* [VP2A] strike ~s; speak, write, behave in an affected way.

at·tor·ney /ə'tɜːnɪ/ *n (pl ~s)* **1** person with legal authority to act for another in business or law: *letter/warrant of ~,* written authority by which a a person appoints another to act for him; *power of ~,* authority so given. **2** ,A~ 'General, (a)** legal officer with authority to act in all cases in which the State is a party, usu *district ~.* **(b)** (US, in some States) public prosecutor. **3** solicitor.

at·tract /ə'trækt/ *vt* [VP6A] **1** pull towards (by unseen force): *A magnet ~s steel.* **2** get the attention of; arouse interest or pleasure in: *Bright colours ~ babies. Bright lights ~ moths. He shouted to ~ attention. Do you feel ~ed to her,* Do you like her?

at·trac·tion /ə'trækʃn/ *n* **1** [U] power of pulling towards: *The ~ of the moon for the earth causes the tides. He cannot resist the ~ of the sea on a hot day/of a pretty girl. The cinema has little ~ for some people.* **2** [C] that which attracts: *the ~s of a big city,* eg theatres, concerts, cinemas, fine shops.

at·trac·tive /ə'træktɪv/ *adj* having the power to attract; pleasing: *a most ~ girl; goods offered at ~ prices.* ~**·ly** *adv*

at·tribute¹ /ə'trɪbjuːt/ *vt* [VP14] ~ *to,* consider as a quality of, as being the result of, as coming from: *He ~s wisdom to his teachers,* thinks they have wisdom. *He ~s his success to hard work,* says that his success is the result of hard work. *This comedy has been ~d to Shakespeare,* it has been said that Shakespeare was the author. **at·tribu·table** /ə'trɪbjʊtəbl/ *adj* that can be ~d (*to*). **at·tri·bu·tion** /ˌætrɪ'bjuːʃn/ *n* [U] act of attributing (*to*); [C] that which is ~d.

at·tribute² /'ætrɪbjuːt/ *n* [C] **1** quality looked upon as naturally or necessarily belonging to sb or sth: *Mercy is an ~ of God. Politeness is an ~ of a gentleman.* **2** material object recognized as a symbol of a person or his position: *The crown is an ~ of kingship.*

at·tribu·tive /ə'trɪbjʊtɪv/ *adj ~* **adjective,** naming a quality and used with the noun as in *'old* man', *'red* hair', and contrasted with predicative. ~**·ly** *adv*

at·tri·tion /ə'trɪʃn/ *n* [U] wearing away by rubbing: *war of ~,* war in which each side waits for the other to wear itself out.

at·tune /ə'tjuːn *US:* ə'tuːn/ *vt* [VP14] ~ *to,* bring into harmony or agreement with: *hearts ~d to worship;* make used to: *ears ~d to the sound of gunfire.*

au·ber·gine /'əʊbəʒiːn/ *n* [C] fruit of the eggplant, used as a vegetable. ⇨ the illus at vegetable.

au·brie·tia /ɔː'briːʃə/ *n* (kinds of) spring-flowering dwarf perennial grown on stone walls, rockeries, etc.

au·burn /'ɔːbən/ *adj* (usu of hair) reddish-brown.

auc·tion /'ɔːkʃn/ *n* [C,U] public sale at which goods are sold to the persons making the highest bids or offers: *sale by ~;* '~-sale; *sell goods by ~; put sth up to/for ~; attend all the local ~s; ~ bridge,* ⇨ bridge². □ *vt* [VP6A,15B] ~ *(off),* sell by ~. ~·**eer** /ˌɔːkʃə'nɪə(r)/ *n* person who conducts an ~.

aud·acious /ɔːˈdeɪʃəs/ adj 1 daring; bold. 2 foolishly bold. 3 impudent. ~·ly adv **aud·ac·ity** /ɔːˈdæsətɪ/ n

aud·ible /ˈɔːdəbl/ adj loud enough to be heard: in a scarcely ~ voice. The speaker was scarcely ~, could be heard only with difficulty. **aud·ibly** /-əblɪ/ adv **audi·bil·ity** n /ˌɔːdəˈbɪlətɪ/ n capacity for being heard.

audi·ence /ˈɔːdɪəns/ n 1 gathering of persons for the purpose of hearing a speaker, singer, etc: There was a large ~ in the theatre. He has addressed large ~s all over England. 2 persons within hearing, whether they are together or not: A broadcaster may have an ~ of several million. 3 (of a book) readers: His book has reached a wide ~. 4 formal interview given by a ruler, the Pope, etc: The Pope granted him an ~. The Prime Minister was received in ~ by the Queen.

audio- /ˈɔːdɪəʊ/ pref of hearing. ˌ~-visual ˈaids, teaching aids such as record players and film projectors. ˌ~-lingual ˈmethods, teaching methods making use of a language laboratory, tape recorders, etc. ˌ~ ˈfrequency, (radio) frequency which, when converted into sound waves by a loudspeaker, can be heard.

au·dit /ˈɔːdɪt/ n official examination of accounts to see that they are in order. □ vt [VP6A] examine, eg accounts, officially.

aud·ition /ɔːˈdɪʃn/ n 1 [C] trial hearing to test the voice of a singer, speaker, etc who is applying for employment or of an actor wishing to take part in a play. 2 [U] power of hearing; listening. □ vt [VP6A] give an ~ to.

au·di·tor /ˈɔːdɪtə(r)/ n 1 listener to a speaker, etc. 2 person who audits.

au·di·tor·ium /ˌɔːdɪˈtɔːrɪəm/ n (pl ~s) building, or part of a building, in which an audience sits.

au·di·tory /ˈɔːdɪtrɪ US: -tɔːrɪ/ adj of the sense of hearing: the ~ nerve. ⟹ the illus at ear.

au fait /ˌəʊ ˈfeɪ/ pred adj (F) instructed: put sb ~ of sth, instruct him about it.

au fond /ˌəʊ ˈfɒn/ adv (F) basically.

au·ger /ˈɔːgə(r)/ n carpenter's tool for boring large holes in wood, with a handle at right angles; instrument for boring in soil. ⟹ the illus at tool.

aught /ɔːt/ n (archaic) anything: for ~ I know/ care, used to indicate that the speaker does not know/care at all.

aug·ment /ɔːgˈment/ vt,vi [VP6A,2A] make or become greater; increase: ~ one's income by writing short stories. **aug·men·ta·tion** /ˌɔːgmenˈteɪʃn/ n [U] ~ing or being ~ed; [C] sth added.

au·gur /ˈɔːgə(r)/ n (in ancient Rome) religious official who claimed to foretell future events by omens from the entrails of birds, etc. □ vi,vt [VP6A,2A] foretell, be a sign of: Does this news ~ war? ~ well/ill (for sb/sth), be a good/bad sign for the future, for us. ~y /ˈɔːgjʊrɪ/ n (pl -ries) [C] omen; sign.

au·gust /ɔːˈgʌst/ adj majestic; causing feelings of respect or awe.

Au·gust /ˈɔːgəst/ n the eighth month.

Au·gust·an /ɔːˈgʌstən/ adj of the best period of Latin literature; classical; of the period of English Literature including Dryden, Pope and Swift.

auk /ɔːk/ n northern seabird, with short wings used in swimming.

auld lang syne /ˌɔːld læŋ ˈsaɪn/ (Scot, name of song) good times long ago.

aunt /ɑːnt US: ænt/ n sister of one's father or

mother; wife of one's uncle. ˌA~ ˈSally, wooden model of a woman's head, at which sticks are thrown, at fairs, etc; (fig) object, person, widely abused. **aun·tie, aun·ty** /ˈɑːntɪ US: ˈæntɪ/ n (familiar for) aunt.

au pair /ˌəʊ ˈpeə(r)/ n (F) (in GB) girl from overseas who, in return for light household duties, receives board and lodging, and facilities for study.

aura /ˈɔːrə/ n atmosphere surrounding a person or object and thought to come from him or it: There seemed to be an ~ of holiness about the Indian saint.

au·ral /ˈɔːrəl/ adj of the organs of hearing: an ~ surgeon.

aure·ole /ˈɔːrɪəʊl/ n halo.

au re·voir /ˌəʊ rəˈvwɑː(r)/ int (F) till we meet again; good-bye.

aur·icle /ˈɔːrɪkl/ n 1 the external part of the ear. ⟹ the illus at ear. 2 either of the two upper cavities of the heart. ⟹ the illus at respiratory.

aur·icu·lar /ɔːˈrɪkjʊlə(r)/ adj of or near the ear: ~ confession, made privately in the ear, eg of a priest.

aur·if·er·ous /ɔːˈrɪfərəs/ adj yielding gold.

aur·ora /ɔːˈrɔːrə/ n 1 A~, Roman goddess of dawn. 2 ~ bor·ea·lis /ɔːˌrɔːrə ˌbɔːrɪˈeɪlɪs/ n display of coloured light, in streamers and bands, mainly red and green, seen in the sky in the regions of the North Pole; also called Northern Lights. ~ aus·tra·lis /ɔːˌrɔːrə ɒˈstreɪlɪs/ n similar display seen in the southern hemisphere.

aus·pices /ˈɔːspɪsɪz/ n pl under (the) ~ (of), helped and favoured by: under favourable ~, with the omens in one's favour, with favourable prospects.

aus·pi·cious /ɔːˈspɪʃəs/ adj showing signs, giving promise, of future success; favourable; prosperous. ~·ly adv

Aus·sie /ˈɒzɪ/ n (sl) Australian.

aus·tere /ɔːˈstɪə(r)/ adj 1 (of a person, his behaviour) severely moral and strict. 2 (of a way of living, of places, styles) simple and plain; without ornament or comfort. ~·ly adv **aus·ter·ity** /ɔːˈsterətɪ/ n (pl -ties) 1 [U] quality of being ~. 2 (pl) ~ practices, eg fasting, living in a cell, for religious reasons.

aut·archy /ˈɔːtɑːkɪ/ n [C,U] (country under) absolute sovereignty.

aut·arky /ˈɔːtɑːkɪ/ n [U] self-sufficiency, esp of a State in its economy.

auth·en·tic /ɔːˈθentɪk/ adj genuine; known to be true: ~ news; an ~ signature. **auth·en·ti·cally** /-klɪ/ adv ~·ity /ˌɔːθenˈtɪsətɪ/ n [U] quality of being ~: feel confident of the ~ity of a signature.

auth·en·ti·cate /ɔːˈθentɪkeɪt/ vt [VP6A] prove to be genuine; prove beyond doubt the origin, authorship, etc of. **auth·en·ti·ca·tion** /ɔːˌθentɪˈkeɪʃn/ n [U] authenticating.

author /ˈɔːθə(r)/ n 1 writer of a book, play, etc: Dickens is his favourite ~. 2 person who creates or begins sth: God, the A~ of our being. ~·ess /ˈɔːθərɪs/ n woman ~. ~·ship /-ʃɪp/ n [U] 1 occupation of an ~: It's risky to take to ~ship (= begin to write books) for a living. 2 origin of a book, etc: Nothing is known of the ~ship of the book, about who wrote it.

auth·ori·tar·ian /ɔːˌθɒrɪˈteərɪən/ adj supporting or requiring obedience to authority, esp that of the State, contrasted with individual liberty. □ n supporter of this principle. ~·ism /-ɪzəm/ n

auth·ori·tat·ive /ɔːˈθɒrɪtətɪv US: -teɪtɪv/ adj 1 having, given with, authority: ~ *orders.* **2** having an air of authority; commanding: *in an ~ manner; speaking in ~ tones.* **3** that can be trusted because from a reliable source: *an ~ report; ~ information; from an ~ source.* ~**·ly** *adv*

auth·or·ity /ɔːˈθɒrətɪ/ *n* (*pl* -ties) **1** [U] power or right to give orders and make others obey: *The problem of how to cope with ~,* eg wrongdoers with the police, children with parents. *An officer has/exercises ~ over the soldiers under him. Who is in ~ here? He has made his ~ felt,* caused people to realize that he has power to make them obey. **under the ~ of; under sb's ~,** responsible(1) to: *These boys are under the ~ of their teacher/under his ~.* **2** [U] ~ **(for sth/to do sth),** right given to sb: *Only the treasurer has ~ to make payments. He had the ~ of the Governor for what he did.* **3** [U] person or (*pl*) group of persons having ~: *the City, Municipal, County, etc authorities; the health authorities; the A,tomic 'Energy A~.* **4** [C,U] person with special knowledge; book, etc that supplies reliable information or evidence: *He is a great ~ on phonetics. The 'Oxford English Dictionary' is the best ~ on English words. What is your ~ for that statement? You should quote your authorities,* give the titles of books, etc, names of persons, etc used as sources for facts.

auth·or·ize /ˈɔːθəraɪz/ *vt* **1** [VP17] give authority to: *I have ~d him to act for me while I am abroad.* **2** [VP6A] give authority for: *The Finance Committee ~d the spending of £10000 on a new sports ground. This payment has not been ~d.* ,A~d **'Version,** (common abbr **AV**) the English translation of the Bible, first published 1611. **auth·or·iz·ation** /ˌɔːθəraɪˈzeɪʃn *US:* -rɪˈz-/ *n* [U] authorizing; giving legal right (*to do* sth, *for* sth); the right given.

aut·ism /ˈɔːtɪzəm/ *n* [U] (psych) severe form of mental illness in children. **aut·is·tic** /ɔːˈtɪstɪk/ *adj* of ~: *autistic children.*

auto /ˈɔːtəʊ/ *n* (US colloq abbr of) automobile.

auto- /ˌɔːtəʊ/ *pref* (in compounds) self-, by oneself; independent(ly): ~-*intoxication,* poisoning by substances produced within the body. **'~-changer,** device (on a record-player) that plays a number of discs in succession without attention.

au·to·bahn /ˈɔːtəbɑːn/ *n* (*pl* ~s or (G) ~en /-nən/) *n*(G) motorway.

au·to·bi·ogra·phy /ˌɔːtəbaɪˈɒɡrəfɪ/ *n* (*pl*-phies) **1** [C] story of a person's life written by himself. **2** [U] the art and practice of this sort of writing. **auto·bio·graphic** /ˌɔːtəbaɪəˈɡræfɪk/, **auto·bio·graphi·cal** /-ɪkl/ *adjj* of, engaged in, ~.

au·toc·racy /ɔːˈtɒkrəsɪ/ *n* (*pl*-cies) **1** [U] government by a ruler who has unlimited power. **2** [C] (country with a) government of this kind.

au·to·crat /ˈɔːtəkræt/ *n* ruler with unlimited power; person who requires things to be done without considering the wishes of others. ~**ic** /ˌɔːtəˈkrætɪk/ *adj* of or like an ~: *Don't be so ~ic,* Don't behave as if you were an ~. **auto·crati·cally** /-klɪ/ *adv*

au·to·da·fé /ˌɔːtəʊ dɑːˈfeɪ *US:* ˌaʊtəʊ dɑː/ *n* (*pl* autos-da-fé /ˌɔːtəʊz *US:* ˌaʊtəʊz/) trial and sentence of a heretic by the Inquisition; carrying out of the sentence, esp by burning.

au·to·giro, -gyro /ˌɔːtəʊˈdʒaɪərəʊ/ *n* (P) early form of helicopter with a propeller in front and rotors above.

au·to·graph /ˈɔːtəɡrɑːf *US:* -ɡræf/ *n* person's own handwriting, esp his signature: **'~** *book/album,*

one in which signatures, eg of famous persons, are collected. □ *vt* [VP6A] write one's name on or in: *a book ~ed by the author; an ~ed photograph.*

au·to·mat /ˈɔːtəmæt/ *n* (US) restaurant at which food and drink are obtained, by the customers themselves, from coin-operated closed compartments.

au·to·mate /ˈɔːtəmeɪt/ *vt* (science, comm) convert to, control by, automation.

au·to·matic /ˌɔːtəˈmætɪk/ *adj* **1** self-acting; self-moving; (of a machine) able to work or be worked without attention: *an ~ pilot,* (on an aircraft) maintaining altitude, course, etc; ~ *gear-change* (in a motor-vehicle); ~ *weapons,* weapons that continue firing until pressure on the trigger is released. **2** (of actions) done without thought; unconscious: *Breathing is ~.* □ *n* small ~ firearm. **au·to·mati·cally** /-klɪ/ *adv*

au·to·ma·tion /ˌɔːtəˈmeɪʃn/ *n* [U] (use of) methods and machines to save human labour.

au·toma·ton /ɔːˈtɒmətən *US:* -tɒn/ *n* (*pl* ~s, -ta /-tə/) person who appears to act involuntarily or without active intelligence; robot.

au·to·mo·bile /ˈɔːtəməbiːl *US:* ˌɔːtəməˈbiːl/ *n* (esp US) motor-car.

au·ton·omous /ɔːˈtɒnəməs/ *adj* (of states) self-governing; free. **au·ton·omy** /ɔːˈtɒnəmɪ/ *n* (*pl* - mies) [U,C] (right of) self-government; freedom.

au·topsy /ˈɔːtɒpsɪ/ *n* (*pl* -sies) [C] (med) post-mortem examination of a body (by cutting it open) to learn the cause of death. ⇨ biopsy.

au·to·strada /ˌaʊtəʊˈstrɑːdə/ *n* (*pl* ~s, (I) -de /-ˈstrɑːdeɪ/) (I) = motorway.

au·tumn /ˈɔːtəm/ *n* [C] (US = *fall*) third season of the year, between summer and winter (Sept, Oct and Nov in the northern hemisphere): *in ~; in the ~ of 1980; in* (the) *early/late ~;* (fig) *in the ~ of his life;* (attrib) ~ *weather/fashions.* **au·tum·nal** /ɔːˈtʌmnəl/ *adj* of ~.

aux·ili·ary /ɔːɡˈzɪlɪərɪ/ *adj* helping; supporting: ~ *troops; an ~ verb* (eg as in *He is working; has* in *He has gone).* □ *n* (*pl*-ries) **1** ~ verb. **2** (usu *pl*) ~ troops (esp troops hired from a foreign or allied country, eg in the Roman Empire in ancient times).

avail /əˈveɪl/ *vt, vi* **1** [VP14] ~ **oneself of,** make use of, profit by, take advantage of: *You should ~ yourself of every opportunity to practise speaking English.* **2** [VP2A,3A] (liter) be of value or help: *Money does not ~ on a desert island. Nothing ~ed against the storm.* □ *n of no/little ~,* not helpful; not effective: *His intervention was of little ~. without ~; to no ~,* without result; unsuccessfully: *We pulled him out of the river and tried to revive him, but to no ~. Of what ~ is it to..., What use is it to...?*

avail·able /əˈveɪləbl/ *adj* ~ **(for)** **1** (of objects) able to be used; that may be obtained: *These tickets are ~ for one month only. The book you ordered is not ~.* **2** (of persons) able to be present: *Are you ~* (*for a meeting*) *tomorrow morning?* **avail·abil·ity** /əˌveɪləˈbɪlətɪ/ *n* [U]

ava·lanche /ˈævəlɑːnʃ *US:* -læntʃ/ *n* great mass of snow and ice at a high altitude, caused by its own weight to slide down a mountain side, often carrying with it thousands of tons of rock, and sometimes destroying forests, houses, etc in its path: (fig) *an ~ of words/letters/questions.*

avant-garde /ˌævɒn ˈɡɑːd/ *n* (F) vanguard of an army; (fig) radical leader(s) of any movement (in art, drama, literature, etc): (attrib) ~ *writers/*

artists.

av·ar·ice /ˈævərɪs/ n [U] greed (for money or possessions); great eagerness to get or keep. **av·ar·icious** /ˌævəˈrɪʃəs/ adj ∼ *(of),* greedy (of money, power, etc). **av·ar·icious·ly** adv

avast /əˈvɑːst US: əˈvæst/ int (naut) Stop!

ava·tar /ˌævəˈtɑː(r)/ n (Hindu myth) (descent to earth of a) deity in human or animal form.

avaunt /əˈvɔːnt/ int (old use) Begone; Go away!

avenge /əˈvendʒ/ vt [VP6A,14] get or take vengeance for: ∼ *an insult;* ∼ *oneself/be* ∼*d on an enemy* (for an injury, etc). *He* ∼*d his father's death upon the murderer,* punished the murderer. **aven·ger** n

av·enue /ˈævənjuː US: -nuː/ n **1** road with trees on each side, esp the private road going up to a large country house. **2** wide street with buildings on one or both sides. **3** ∼ *(to),* (fig) way (to some object or aim): ∼*s to success/promotion.*

aver /əˈvɜː(r)/ vt (-rr-) [VP6A,9] ∼ *(that),* (old use) state positively (that sth is true).

av·er·age /ˈævərɪdʒ/ n **1** [C] result of adding several quantities together and dividing the total by the number of quantities: *The* ∼ *of 4, 5 and 9 is 6.* **2** [U] standard or level regarded as ordinary or usual: *Tom's work at school is above* (*the*) ∼, *Harry's is below* (*the*) ∼ *and Jim's is about up to* (*the*) ∼. **on** *(an/the)* ∼, according to the ∼: *On* (*an/the*) *there are twenty boys present every day.* □ adj **1** found by making an ∼: *The* ∼ *age of the boys in this class is fifteen. What's the* ∼ *temperature in this town in August?* **2** of the ordinary or usual standard: *boys of* ∼ *intelligence; men of* ∼ *ability.* □ vt,vi **1** [VP6A] find the ∼ of: *If you* ∼ *7, 14 and 6, you get 9.* **2** [VP2B] amount to as an ∼; do as an ∼: ∼ *200 miles a day during a journey. The rainfall* ∼*s 36 inches a year.*

averse /əˈvɜːs/ adj ∼ *from/to,* opposed, disinclined: *He is* ∼ *to hard work. We are* ∼ *from taking action.*

aver·sion /əˈvɜːʃn US:-ʒn/ n **1** [C,U] ∼ *to,* strong dislike: *He has a strong* ∼ *to getting up early. He took an* ∼ *to me. Do you feel any* ∼ *to hard study?* **2** [C] sth or sb disliked. **pet** ∼, sth specially disliked.

avert /əˈvɜːt/ vt **1** [VP14] ∼ *(from),* turn away (one's eyes, thoughts, etc): ∼ *one's eyes/gaze from a terrible spectacle.* **2** [VP6A] prevent, avoid: ∼ *an accident;* ∼ *suspicion;.* ∼ *failure by hard work.*

avi·ary /ˈeɪvɪərɪ US: -vɪerɪ/ n (pl -ries) place for keeping birds, eg in a zoo.

avi·ation /ˌeɪvɪˈeɪʃn/ n [U] (art and science of) flying in aircraft. **'**∼ **spirit,** high-octane motor spirit used in aircraft engines. **avi·ator** /ˈeɪvɪeɪtə(r)/ n airman (now usu *pilot* or *captain*) who controls an aircraft, airship or balloon.

avid /ˈævɪd/ adj ∼ *for,* eager, greedy: ∼ *for fame/applause.* ∼**·ly** adv ∼**·ity** /əˈvɪdətɪ/ n [U] eagerness: *He accepted the offer with* ∼*ity.*

avo·cado /ˌævəˈkɑːdəʊ/ n (pl ∼s /-dəʊz/) (also *alligator pear*) pear-shaped tropical fruit. ⇨ the illus at fruit.

avo·ca·tion /ˌævəˈkeɪʃn/ n (formal) occupation that is not a person's ordinary business.

avoid /əˈvɔɪd/ vt [VP6A,C] keep or get away from; escape: *Try to* ∼ *danger. We only just* ∼*ed an accident. You can hardly* ∼ *meeting her if you both work in the same office.* ∼**·able** /-əbl/ adj that can be ∼ed. ∼**·ance** /-əns/ n [U] act of ∼ing: *the*

∼*ance of bad companions;* ∼*ance of taxation,* eg by not buying taxed goods such as tobacco and wine.

avoir·du·pois /ˌævədəˈpɔɪz/ n system of weights used, before metrication, in most English-speaking countries (1 pound = 16 ounces), used for all goods except precious metals and stones, and medicines. ⇨ App 5.

avouch /əˈvaʊtʃ/ vt,vi [VP6A,9,3A] (liter; now rare) assert; guarantee: ∼ *(for) sth.*

avow /əˈvaʊ/ vt [VP6A,25 reflex] (formal) admit; declare openly: ∼ *a fault. He* ∼*ed himself* (*to be*) *a Christian.* ∼**al** /-əl/ n [U] free and open confession; [C] instance of this: *make an* ∼*al of one's sentiments.* ∼**·ed·ly** /əˈvaʊɪdlɪ/ adv by confession; openly: *He was* ∼*edly in the wrong.*

avun·cu·lar /əˈvʌŋkjʊlə(r)/ adj (joc) of or like an uncle (esp a benevolent uncle).

await /əˈweɪt/ vt [VP6A] **1** (of persons) wait for: *I* ∼ *your instructions.* **2** be in store for; be waiting for: *A hearty welcome* ∼*s you. Death* ∼*s all men.*

awake¹ /əˈweɪk/ vi (pt awoke /əˈwəʊk/, pp (rare) awoken or ∼d) **1** [VP2A] = wake (*awake* is preferred for the fig uses, intrans, and *awaken* for the fig uses, trans) **2** [VP3A] ∼ *to,* become conscious of, realize: *He awoke to his opportunities. You must* ∼ *to the fact* (= You must realize) *that failure will mean disgrace. When he awoke to his surroundings...,* realized where he was.... [VP4B] *He awoke to find himself famous,* learnt, the next day, that he was famous.

awake² /əˈweɪk/ pred adj roused from sleep: *Is he* ∼ *or asleep?* ∼ *to,* aware of: *be* ∼ *to what is going on/to a danger/to one's own interests.*

awaken /əˈweɪkən/ vt **1** [VP6A] = awake (*awaken* is preferred for fig uses, trans). **2** [VP14] ∼ *sb to sth,* make sb aware of: ∼ *sb to a sense of his responsibility/to a sense of shame.* ∼**·ing** /əˈweɪknɪŋ/ n act of becoming aware, of realizing, esp sth unpleasant: *It was a rude* ∼*ing when he was told that he was to be dismissed for inefficiency.*

award /əˈwɔːd/ vt [VP6A,12A,13A] give or grant (by official decision): *He was* ∼*ed the first prize. The judge* ∼*ed her £200 as damages. The gold medal was* ∼*ed to Mr Brown for his fine show of vegetables.* □ n [C] **1** decision made by a judge or arbitrator. **2** sth given as the result of such a decision, eg a prize in a competition: *His horse was given the highest* ∼ *at the show.* **3** money granted to a student at a university, etc.

aware /əˈweə(r)/ pred adj ∼ *of/that,* having knowledge or realization: *Are you* ∼ *that you're sitting on my hat? We are fully* ∼ *of the gravity of the situation. Without being* ∼ *of it...; I was not* ∼ (*of*) *how deeply he had felt the death of his mother.* ∼**·ness** n [U].

awash /əˈwɒʃ/ pred adj washed over by, level with, the waves: *rocks* ∼ *at high tide. The ship's deck was* ∼.

away /əˈweɪ/ adv part **1** to or at a distance (from the place, person, etc in question): *The sea is two miles* ∼. *The shops are only a few minutes' walk* ∼. *Is our next football match at home or* ∼, on our ground or on the ground of our opponents? *It's an* ∼ *match. Take these things* ∼, remove them. *Keep the baby* ∼ *from the fire. Don't look* ∼ (ie in a different direction) *while I'm taking your photograph.* **2** ∼ *with* ..., (used in verbless exclamations): *A*∼ *with them! Take them* ∼! **3** continuously; constantly: *He was working* ∿. *He was laughing/muttering/grumbling* ∿. ⇨ grumble(1), laugh²(2), mutter. **4** (used with *vv* to indicate loss, lessening, weakening, exhaustion): *The water has all boiled* ∿, There is no water left. ⇨ blaze²(4), boil²(4), die²(3), explain(2), melt(1). **5** (in phrases): **far and** ∿, very much: *This is far and* ∿ *better.* **out and** ∿, beyond comparison: *This is out and* ∿ *the best.* **right/straight** ∿, at once, without delay.

awe¹ /ɔ:/ *n* [U] respect combined with fear and reverence: *He had a feeling of awe as he was taken before the judge. Savages often live in awe of nature. The lazy boy stood in awe of his stern teacher.* **'awe-inspiring** *adj* filling with awe: *an awe-inspiring sight.* **'awe-stricken, 'awe-struck** *adjj* suddenly filled with awe. **'awe·some** /-səm/ *adj* causing awe.

awe² /ɔ:/ *vt* [VP6A,14] **awe** (*into*), strike with awe, fill with awe: *I was awed by his solemn words. He awed them into obedience. The children were awed into silence.*

aweigh /əˈweɪ/ *adv* (naut, of an anchor) hanging just clear of the sea bottom.

aw·ful /ˈɔ:fl/ *adj* **1** terrible; dreadful: *He died an* ∿ *death. His sufferings were* ∿ *to behold.* **2** (colloq, intensive) very bad; very great; extreme of its kind: *What an* ∿ *nuisance! What* ∿ *handwriting/weather!* ∿**ly** /ˈɔ:flɪ/ *adv* (chiefly colloq) very (much): *It has been* ∿*ly hot this week. I'm* ∿*ly sorry. Thanks* ∿*ly.*

awhile /əˈwaɪl *US*: əˈhwaɪl/ *adv* for a short time: *Stay* ∿.

awk·ward /ˈɔ:kwəd/ *adj* **1** (of objects, places) not well designed for use; (of circumstances, etc) likely to cause inconvenience or difficulty: *This is an* ∿ *staircase. This is an* ∿ *corner; there have been several road accidents here. The handle of this teapot has an* ∿ *shape. The meeting was at 9 o'clock, which was an* ∿ *time for many people. It's* ∿ *that Brown should be unable to play in our team this week.* **an** ∿ **customer,** (colloq) person or animal difficult or dangerous to deal with. **2** (of living things) clumsy; having little skill: *The child is still* ∿ *with his knife and fork. Some animals are* ∿ *on land but able to move easily in the water.* **the** '∿ **age,** years when adolescents are lacking in self-confidence. **3** embarrassed: *an* ∿ *silence/pause.*

awl /ɔ:l/ *n* small pointed tool for making holes, esp in leather or wood. ⇨ the illus at tool.

awn·ing /ˈɔ:nɪŋ/ *n* canvas covering (against rain or sun), eg over a ship's deck, over or before doors or windows.

awoke ⇨ awake.

awry /əˈraɪ/ *adv, pred adj* crooked(ly); wrong(ly): *Our plans have gone* ∿, have gone wrong.

ax, axe /æks/ *n* (*pl* axes /ˈæksɪz/) tool for felling trees or splitting wood, ⇨ the illus at tool: *apply the axe to public expenditure,* reduce its cost by economies, etc. **,have an 'axe to grind,** (fig) have private interests to serve. **get the axe,** (colloq) be dismissed from one's job. □ *vt* [VP6A] (colloq) reduce, eg costs, public services; dismiss: *He's just been axed,* ie to save money.

ax·iom /ˈæksɪəm/ *n* statement accepted as true without proof or argument. **axio·matic** /ˌæksɪəˈmætɪk/ *adj* of the nature of an ∿; clear and evident without proof: *It is* ∿*atic that a whole is greater than any of its parts.*

axis /ˈæksɪs/ *n* (*pl* axes /ˈæksiːz/) **1** line round which a turning object spins. **the earth's** ∿, the imaginary line joining the North and South Poles through the centre of the earth, on which the earth rotates once in twenty-four hours. **2** line that divides a regular figure into two symmetrical parts, eg the diameter of a circle. **3** political connection (not always an alliance) between two or more states: *the Berlin—Rome—Tokyo A*∿ (before 1939); A∿ **powers.**

axle /ˈæksl/ *n* **1** rod upon or with which a wheel turns. **2** bar or rod that passes through the centres of a pair of wheels: *the back* ∿ *of a bus.*

ayah /ˈaɪə/ *n* (In India and Pakistan) native nurse-maid; lady's maid-servant.

Aya·tol·lah /ˌaɪəˈtɒlə/ *n* title of various senior Muslim leaders in Iran. ⇨ Imam.

aye¹, ay /aɪ/ *int, adv* (Scot and regional) yes; (naval) usual reply to an order: ,*Aye,* '*aye, sir!* □ *n pl* vote or person supporting a proposal: *The ayes have it,* Those for it are in the majority.

aye² /eɪ/ *adv* (old use) always: *for* ∿.

aza·lea /əˈzeɪlɪə/ *n* (kinds of) flowering shrub of the rhododendron genus.

azi·muth /ˈæzɪməθ/ *n* (astron) angular distance extending from the zenith to the horizon; (surveying) angle measured clockwise from the south or north.

az·ure /ˈæʒə(r)/ *adj, n* (poet) bright blue: *an* ∿ *sky.* ∿**·ly** *adv* ∿**·ness** *n*

Bb *behlgen über.. bei... to complain to sb. about sth*

B, b /bi:/ (*pl* B's, b's /bi:z/) the second letter of the English alphabet.

baa /bɑ:/ *n* cry of a sheep or lamb. □ *vi* (baaing, baaed or baa'd /bɑ:d/) make this cry; bleat. '∿-**lamb** *n* child's word for a sheep or lamb.

baas /bɑ:s/ *n* (S Africa) boss.

babble /ˈbæbl/ *vi,vt* **1** [VP2A,B,C] talk in a way that is difficult to understand; make sounds like a baby; (of streams, etc) murmur. **2** [VP6A,15B] ∿ (*out*), repeat foolishly; tell (a secret): ∿ (*out*) *nonsense/secrets.* □ *n* [U] **1** childish or foolish talk; confused talk not clearly to be understood (as when many people are talking at once). **2** gentle sound of water flowing over stones, etc. **bab·bler** /ˈbæblə(r)/ *n* person who ∿s, esp one who tells secrets.

babe /beɪb/ *n* **1** (liter) baby. **2** inexperienced and easily deceived person. **3** (US sl) girl or young woman.

babel /ˈbeɪbl/ *n* **1 the Tower of B**∿, tower built to reach heaven. (Gen 11). **2** (*sing* with *indef art*) scene of noisy and confused talking: *What a* ∿! *A* ∿ *of voices could be heard from the schoolroom.*

ba·boo, babu /ˈbɑ:bu:/ *n* (as Hindu title) Mr; Hindu gentleman; Hindu clerk; (old use, pej) Hindu affecting English speech and manners.

ba·boon /bəˈbu:n *US*: bæ-/ *n* large monkey (of Africa and southern Asia) with a dog-like face. ⇨ the illus at ape.

baby /ˈbeɪbɪ/ *n* (*pl* -bies) **1** very young child: *She has a* ∿-'*boy/'girl. Which of you is the* ∿ (= the youngest member) *of the family?* (*be left*)

carrying/holding/to carry/to hold the ~, (colloq) be left responsible for sth one does not wish to be responsible for (because of its difficulty or distastefulness. '~ carriage,** (US) pram. '~-faced,** looking much younger than one's age. '~-farmer,** (often pej) woman who contracts to keep (esp unwanted) babies. '~-minder,** woman paid to look after a ~ for long periods (eg while the mother is out working). '~-sit·ter,** person paid to look after a ~ for a short time (eg while its parents are at the cinema). Hence, '~-sit vi,** '~-sit·ting n** '~-talk n** kind of speech used by or to babies with distorted vocabulary and syntax. **2** (used attrib) very small of its kind: a ~ car,* a small motor-car. ~ 'grand,** small grand piano. **3** (sl) girl; sweetheart. □ vt** [VP6A] (colloq) treat like a ~: Don't ~ the boy!* '~-hood n** state of being a ~; time when one is a ~. ~·ish adj** of or like a ~: ~ish behaviour.*

bac·ca·laur·eate /ˌbækəˈlɔːrɪət/ n [C] **1** last secondary school examination in France. **2** university degree of Bachelor.

bac·ca·rat /ˈbækərɑː/ n [U] gambling game with playing cards.

bac·cha·nal /ˈbækənl/ adj **1** of or like Bacchus /ˈbækəs/ (the Gk god of wine) or his rites. **2** wild, excited, drunken: a ~ feast.* □ n** follower of Bacchus; drunken reveller. **2** dance or song in honour of Bacchus; merrymaking. **bac·cha·na·lian** /ˌbækəˈneɪlɪən/ adj of ~s; noisy and drunken.

baccy /ˈbækɪ/ n [U] (colloq) tobacco.

bach·elor /ˈbætʃələ(r)/ n **1** unmarried man, ⇨ spinster; (attrib) of, suitable for, an unmarried person: a ~ (= independent unmarried) girl; ~ flats.* **2** (man or woman who has taken the) first university degree: B~ of Arts/Science.*

ba·cil·lus /bəˈsɪləs/ n (pl -cilli /-ˈsɪlaɪ/) rod-shaped bacterium, esp one of the types that cause disease.

back¹ /bæk/ n **1** (of the human body) surface of the body from the neck to the buttocks; spine, ⇨ the illus at skeleton: If you lie on your ~, you can look up at the sky. He slipped and fell on his ~. at the ~ of sb; at sb's ~,* giving him support or protection: He knows that he has the head of the Department at his ~,* that the head is ready to support him. Cf back sb up. do/say sth behind sb's ~,** without his knowledge (always in connection with sth unpleasant, such as slander). **break one's ~,** fracture or dislocate one's spine; (fig) work (too) strenuously. **break the ~ of sth** (eg a piece of work), finish the hardest or larger part of it. **get off sb's ~,** stop being a burden or hindrance. **give sb a ~; make a ~ for sb,** bend down in the game of leapfrog, or to enable sb to climb on one's ~ in order to get over a wall, etc. **be glad to see the ~ of sb,** feel pleased to see him go away. **be with/have one's ~ to the wall,** be in a difficult position, forced to defend oneself. **be on one's ~,** (esp) be ill in bed. **put one's ~ into sth,** work at it with all one's energy. **put/get sb's ~ up,** make him angry. **turn one's ~ on sb,** turn away from him in an impolite way; avoid, shun, him. **2** upper surface of an animal's body: Fasten the saddle on the horse's ~.* **3** that part of a chair or seat on which a person's ~ rests. **4** (contrasted with front) that surface of an object that is less used, less visible or important: the ~ of one's hand,* with the nails and knuckles. You can't cut with the ~ of the knife. You can't see the ~ of your head. You write the address on the front of an envelope, not on the

~. **5** (contrasted with front) that part of a thing that is farthest from the front: a room at the ~ of the house; a garden at the ~ of a house.* **the B~s,** lawns and grounds (on the River Cam) of some Cambridge colleges. **6** break her ~,** (of a ship) break in two. **7** ('full-)~; ('half-)~,** (football, etc) player whose position is between the halfway line and the goal line. ⇨ the illus at football.

back² /bæk/ adv part **1** (contrasted with forward) to or at the rear; away from the front or the centre: Stand ~, please! The police held the crowd ~. Fasten the curtains ~. Sit ~ in your chair and be comfortable. The house stands ~* (ie at some distance) from the road. **go ~ (up)on/from one's word,** fail to keep a promise. **(in) ~ of,** (US colloq) behind: the houses ~ of the church.* **2** in(to) an earlier position or condition: Put the dictionary ~ on the shelf. Throw the ball ~ to me. Call that boy ~. We shall be ~* (= home again) before dark. Shall we walk ~ or ride ~? How far is it there and ~? My brother is just ~* (ie has just returned home) from Paris. The company is now ~ on its feet,* has re-established itself after a period of financial, etc difficulties. ~ and forth ⇨ forth.* **3** in return: If I hit you, would you hit me ~? Don't answer ~,* Don't retort or argue. When can you pay ~* (= repay) the money you borrowed? **have/get one's 'own ~ (on sb),** (colloq) have one's revenge. **4** (of time) ago; into the past: some few years ~; far ~* in the Middle Ages.

back³ /bæk/ vt,vi **1** [VP6A,15A,2A,C] go or cause to go ~ward(2): The horse ~ed suddenly. He ~ed the car into/out of the garage. The wind ~ed,* changed gradually in an anti-clockwise direction (eg from E through NE to N). ⇨ veer. ~ the oars; ~ water,** use the oars to reverse a boat's forward motion. **2** [VP6A,15B] ~ (up),** support: ~ a friend in an argument or quarrel; ~ up an argument. Hence, '~-up n** (colloq) support; spare¹. ~ a bill/note,** endorse it as a promise to pay money if necessary. **3** [VP6A] bet money on (a horse, a greyhound): The favourite was heavily ~ed,* Much money was bet on its winning the race. **4** [VP2C] '~ 'down (from),** give up a claim, etc: I see he has ~ed down from the position he took last week.* Hence, '~-down n. ~ off,** give up a claim. ~ out (of),** withdraw (from a promise or undertaking): He promised to help and then ~ed out. He's trying to ~ out of his bargain,* escape from the agreement. **5** [VP6A] put or be a lining to; put on as a surface at the ~: ~ed with sheet iron.* **6** [VP6A,3A] ~ (on) (to),** be situated at the ~ of: Our garden ~s there. Their house ~s on (to) our garden. ~er n** **1** person who ~s a horse. **2** person who gives support or help (eg to a political movement); person who gives financial support to an undertaking. ~ing n** **1** [U] help; support; [C] body of supporters: The new leader has a large ~ing.* **2** [U] material used to form a thing's ~ or support. **3** [U,C] (pop music) musical accompaniment to a singer: vocal/instrumental ~ing.*

back⁴ /bæk/ (used attrib, and in compounds, with references to the articles on the n, adv part and v above) **1** ⇨ back¹(1,2). '~-ache n** [U,C] ache or pain in the ~. '~-band n** strap over a horse's cart-saddle, supporting the shafts of a cart or carriage. '~-bone n** (a) line of bones down the middle of the ~, from the skull to the hips; spine, spinal column; ⇨ the illus at skeleton, (fig) chief support: Such men are the ~bone of the country. **(b)**

[U] (fig) strength; firmness: *He hasn't enough ~bone*, is weak in character. (c) *to the ~bone*, (fig) completely; in every way: *He's British to the ~bone.* '~-break·ing *adj* (of work) exhausting. 2 ➪ back¹(4,5). ,~·'hand(ed) *adj*: *~hand blow/ stroke*, one that is delivered with the ~ of the hand turned outwards, or in a direction different from what is usual or expected. ➪ fore·hand. Hence, (fig): *a ~handed compliment*, one that is ambiguous (eg suggesting sarcasm). '~-scratcher *n* (a) device with claws on a long handle for scratching the ~ (when there is an irritation, etc). (b) flatterer. ➪ scratch *v*(5). '~-stroke *n* (a) [U] swimming stroke done on the ~, rotating the arms alternately. (b) [C] ~-handed stroke. '~-sword *n* sword with only one cutting edge. 3 ➪ back¹(5) and back²(1). ,~-to-'~, (of housing) of two rows of terrace houses, often separated by a narrow alley, with the ~s facing. ,~·'bench(er) *n* (person occupying) one of the seats in the House of Commons (or other law-making body) used by those members, who, because they do not or have not held office, are not entitled to a front-bench seat. ➪ bench(1). '~-blocks *n pl* (in Australia) areas of land a long way from a railway, river, the sea-coast, etc and thinly populated. '~-board *n* movable board at the ~ of a cart. '~-cloth *n* painted cloth hung at the ~ of a stage in a theatre, as part of the scenery. ,~·'door *n* door at the ~ of a house or other building; (attrib, fig) secret or indirect; clandestine: *~door influence.* '~-drop *n* = ~cloth. '~-ground *n* (a) that part of a view, scene (and, fig, a description) that serves as a setting for the chief objects, persons, etc. ➪ foreground. (b) person's past experiences, education, environment. (c) contemporary condition(s): *the social and political ~ground;* (comm) details necessary to an understanding of company business: *B~ground information will be supplied at the Board meeting.* (d) *(be/keep/stay) in the ~ground,* away from publicity; hidden. (e) *~ground music/effects, etc,* music, etc that accompanies dialogue, action, etc (eg in a radio or TV programme or a cinema film) but is not essential to the story, etc. ~-less *adj* (of a dress), not covering the ~; cut to the waist at the ~: *a ~less gown.* '~-most *adj* farthest from the front. '~-room *n* room at the ~ of a building. *~room boys*, (colloq) scientists, engineers, research workers in offices and laboratories. ,~·'seat *n* seat at the ~. *take a ~seat*, (fig) behave as if one were unimportant; humble oneself. ~-seat 'driver, passenger (in a car) who corrects or advises the driver. '~-side *n* (colloq) buttocks: *give sb a kick on the ~side.* ,~·'stage *adv* (a) behind the scenes (in a theatre): *I was taken ~stage by the leading actor.* (b) (attrib): *~stage life*, of actors and actresses when not on the stage. ,~·'stair *adj* secret; underhand: *~stair influence.* '~·'stairs *n* staircase from servants' quarters: (attrib) *~stairs gossip,* ie among servants. '~-stays *n pl* (naut) set of ropes from the mast-head to the sides of a ship, sloping towards the stern. '~-wash *n* movement of water going away in waves, esp the rush of water behind a ship; (fig) unpleasant after-effects of sth done. '~-water *n* (a) part of a river not reached by its current, where the water does not flow. (b) (fig) place, condition of mind, untouched by events, progress, etc: *living in an intellectual ~water*, untouched by new ideas, etc. '~-woods *n pl* uncleared forest land; (fig) culturally backward area.

'~-woods·man /-mən/ *n* (*pl* -men) man who lives in the ~woods; (fig) old-fashioned person. ~ 'yard *n* (esp of terraced houses) (usu paved) area at the ~ of a house: *The dustbin is kept in the ~ yard.* 4 ➪ back²(1). to an earlier point in time; to a former place. ,~·'date *vt* date ~ to a time in the past: *The wage increases are to be ~dated to the first of January.* ,~·'fire *n* (sound caused by the) too early explosion of gas in an internal combustion engine, causing the piston to move in the wrong direction. □ *vi* produce, make the sound of, a ~fire; (fig) produce an unexpected or undesired result: *The plot ~fired.* '~-formation *n* [U,C] (process of making a) word that appears to be the root of a longer word (eg *televise*, from *television*). '~-log *n* accumulation of work or business (eg arrears of unfulfilled orders) not yet attended to. '~ num·ber *n* (a) issue of a periodical of an earlier date, not now on sale. (b) (fig, colloq) out-of-date or old-fashioned method, thing, person, etc. '~ pay/rent/taxes, etc, *n* pay, etc in arrears; pay, etc that is overdue. ,~·'pedal *vi* (on a bicycle, etc) pedal ~wards; (fig) retreat hurriedly from sth stated or promised. ,~·'slide *vi* [VP2A] fall back from good ways into bad old ways of living; lose interest in religious practice, morality, etc. ,~·'space *vi* move the carriage of a typewriter ~ one or more spaces by pressing the key (called the '~spacer *key*) used for this purpose. 5 ➪ back²(3). in return; in reply. '~-bite *vt,vi* slander the reputation of (sb who is absent); speak slanderously about an absent person. Hence, '~-biter *n* person who ~bites. '~-chat *n* [U] (colloq) (exchange of) impertinent remarks: *I want none of your ~chat.* '~-lash *n* [U] (a) excessive movement caused by loose connections between mechanical parts (often causing ~ward movement). (b) (fig) antagonistic reaction (esp in social or race relations). '~-talk *n* [U] = ~chat.

back·gam·mon /bæk'gæmən US: 'bæk-/ *n* [U] game for two players, played on a special double board with draughts and dice.

back·sheesh ➪ baksheesh.

back·ward /'bækwəd/ *adj* 1 towards the back or the starting-point: *a ~ glance/movement; a ~ flow of water.* 2 having made, making, less than the usual or normal progress: *This part of the country is still ~; there are no railways or roads and no electricity. Because of his long illness, Tom is ~ in his studies.* Cf *well up in. Spring is ~ this year.* 3 shy; reluctant; hesitant: *Although he is clever, he is ~ in giving his views.* □ *adv ~*(s), 1 away from one's front; towards the back: *He looked ~*(s) *over his shoulder.* 2 with the back or the end first: *It's not easy to walk ~*(s). *Can you say the alphabet ~*(s), ie ZYXWV, etc? *know sth ~ward(s),* know it perfectly; be quite familiar with it. *~*(s) *and forward(s),* first in one direction and then in the other: *travelling ~*(s) *and forward*(s) *between London and the south coast.* Cf *back and forth; to and fro.*

ba·con /'beɪkən/ *n* [U] salted or smoked meat from the back or sides of a pig. *bring home the ~,* (sl) succeed in one's undertaking. *save one's ~,* (colloq) escape death, injury, punishment.

bac·ter·ium /bæk'tɪərɪəm/ *n* (*pl* -ria /-rɪə/) (kinds of) simplest and smallest form of plant life, existing in air, water and soil, and in living and dead creatures and plants, essential to animal life and sometimes a cause of disease. **bac·ter·ial** /-rɪəl/

adj of bacteria: *bacterial contamination.* **bac·teri·ol·ogy** /bæk͵tɪərɪˈɒlədʒɪ/ *n* science or study of bacteria. **bac·teri·ol·ogist** /-dʒɪst/ *n* student of, expert in, bacteriology.

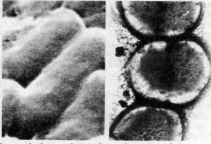

bacteria (seen through a microscope)

bad[1] /bæd/ *adj* (worse, worst) **1** wicked, evil, immoral: *It is bad to steal. He leads a bad life.* **act in bad faith,** dishonestly, insincerely. **a bad egg/ hat/lot,** (dated *sl*) morally unreliable person. **call sb bad names,** insult him. **bad language,** swear-words; (the use of) obscene or profane words merely to insult or for emphasis. **bad word,** swear-word. **2** unpleasant; disagreeable; unwelcome: *We've had some bad news. What bad weather we're having! There's a bad smell here. The way he was sacked created a bad odour,* (fig) created unpleasant feelings. **3** (of things that are in themselves undesirable) notable; noticeable; serious: *That was a bad mistake. He's had a bad accident. There's been a bad falling-off in attendance.* **4** inferior; worthless; incorrect; of poor quality: *His pronunciation is bad. He speaks bad English. What a bad drawing! You can't take photographs if the light is bad.* **be in a bad way,** be very ill or unfortunate; be in trouble or difficulty. **be in bad (with),** (US *colloq*) be in disfavour: *He's in bad with the boss.* **go from bad to worse,** become seriously worse. **with bad grace,** showing unwillingness. **not (so) bad,** (*colloq* understatement) quite good. **not half bad,** very good. **a bad business/job,** (*colloq*) an unfortunate affair. **bad debt,** one unlikely to be paid. **'bad-lands,** (US) barren, infertile regions. **bad law,** one that cannot be sustained or held to be valid. **bad shot,** (fig) wrong guess. **5** not able to be eaten; rotten: *bad eggs/meat.* **go bad,** become unfit to eat: *Don't let that fish go bad—put it in the fridge.* **6 bad for,** hurtful or injurious for; unsuitable for: *Smoking is bad for the health. Very small print is bad for the eyes. It's bad for him to live alone.* **7** in ill health, diseased: *a bad* (= sore) *finger; a bad leg,* causing pain; (*colloq*) *She feels bad today.* **be taken bad,** (*colloq*) fall ill; become more ill: *She was taken bad during the night.* **8** (*colloq*) unfortunate: *It's too bad she's so ill.* **9** (*colloq*) sorry; bothered: *I feel so bad about not being able to help you.* **bad·ly** *adv* (worse, worst) (Cf *well, better, best.*) **1** in a bad manner; roughly; untidily, etc: *badly made/ dressed/wounded.* **2** by much: *badly beaten at football; badly in need of repair.* **3** (with *want, need*) very much: *She wants it badly.* **4 badly off,** poor. **badly off for,** in need of. **bad·ness** *n* quality of being bad: *the badness of the weather/climate.* **bad**[2] /bæd/ *n* [U] that which is bad: *take the bad with the good,* take bad fortune with good fortune.

go to the bad, become completely immoral; become ruined. **to the bad,** (accounts) in loss: *I am £50 to the bad,* have lost £50 as the result (of the deal, etc).
bade /bæd/ ⇨ bid[1](3).
badge /bædʒ/ *n* **1** sth worn (usu a design on cloth or made of metal) to show a person's occupation, rank, etc or membership of a society. **2** (fig) sth that shows a quality or condition: *Chains are a ~ of slavery.*
badger[1] /ˈbædʒə(r)/ *n* small, grey animal living in holes in the earth and going about at night. ⇨ the illus at small.
badger[2] /ˈbædʒə(r)/ *vt* [VP6A,14,16A] **~ sb (with questions, etc)/(for sth)/(into doing sth),** worry or tease: *Tom has been ~ing his uncle to buy him a camera. I was ~ed into doing what she wanted.*
ba·di·nage /ˈbædɪnɑːʒ US: ͵bædənˈɑːʒ/ *n* [U] banter.
bad·min·ton /ˈbædmɪntən/ *n* game played with rackets and shuttlecocks across a high, narrow net.

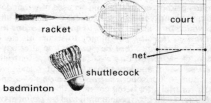

court
racket
net
shuttlecock
badminton

baffle[1] /ˈbæfl/ *vt* [VP6A] puzzle; prevent (sb) from doing sth; be too difficult to do, understand, etc: *One of the examination questions ~d me completely. They were ~d in their attempt. The scene ~d all description,* could not be described.
baffle[2] /ˈbæfl/ *n* plate, board, screen or other device, used to hinder or control the flow of a gas, a liquid or sound through an inlet or outlet.
bag[1] /bæg/ *n* **1** container made of flexible material (paper, cloth, leather) with an opening at the top, used for carrying things from place to place: *'shopping-bag; 'travelling-bag; 'handbag; 'kitbag; 'tool-bag; 'mailbag,* ⇨ these words. **bag and baggage,** with all one's belongings (used esp of sb who is expelled). **a bag of bones,** a very thin person or animal. **let the cat out of the bag,** tell a secret (without intending to do so). **pack one's bags,** pack (for a journey). **the whole bag of tricks,** (*colloq*) everything needed for a purpose; the whole lot. **2** (= *game-bag*) all the birds, animals, etc shot or caught: *They secured a good bag.* **be in the bag,** (*colloq*) (of results, outcomes, etc) be as desired: *The election is in the bag.* **3 bags of,** (*sl*) plenty of: *There's bags of room. He has bags of money.* **4 bags under the eyes,** (*colloq*) puffiness under the eyes (eg from lack of sleep). **5 old bag,** (*colloq*) fussy, unattractive, boring woman.
bag[2] /bæg/ *vt,vi* (-gg-) **1** [VP6A,15B] put into a bag or bags: *to bag* (*up*) *wheat.* **2** [VP6A] (of sportsmen) kill or catch: *They bagged nothing except a couple of rabbits.* **3** [VP6A] (*colloq*) take (sb else's property, etc without permission, but not intending to steal): *Who has bagged my matches? She bagged* (= occupied, sat in) *the most comfortable chair. Try to bag an empty table,* secure one (eg in a crowded restaurant). **4** [VP2A,C] hang loosely, looking like a cloth bag: *trousers that bag at the knees.*

baga·telle /ˌbægəˈtel/ n 1 [U] kind of game like billiards, played on a board with holes instead of pockets. 2 [C] (often *a mere* ～) sth small and of no importance. 3 [C] musical trifle.

bag·gage /ˈbægɪdʒ/ n [U] 1 (more usu, except in US, *luggage*) all the bags, trunks, etc with which a person travels. '～ room, (US) left luggage office. 2 tents, bedding, equipment, etc, of an army: '～ *animals*, '～ *train, etc*, animals, carts, trucks, etc, carrying ～. 3 (dated) (playfully) saucy girl: *You little* ～!

baggy /ˈbægɪ/ adj hanging in loose folds: *trousers* ～ *at the knees*; ～ *skin under the eyes*.

bagnio /ˈbɑːnɪəʊ/ n (old use) 1 prison. 2 brothel.

bag·pipe /ˈbægpaɪp/ n (often **the** ～s) musical instrument with air stored in a bag of wind held under one arm and pressed out through pipes in which there are reeds. ⇨ the illus at kilt.

bags /bægz/ n pl (colloq) trousers: *Oxford* ～. ⇨ debag.

bah /bɑː/ int used as a sign of contempt.

bail¹ /beɪl/ n [U] sum of money demanded by a law court, paid by or for a person accused of wrongdoing, as security that he will appear for his trial, until which time he is allowed to go free. *go/put in/ stand* ～ *(for sb)*, pay money to secure his freedom in this way. *(be) out on* ～, free after payment of ～. *forfeit one's* ～, fail to appear for trial. *refuse* ～, (of a judge) refuse to accept ～ and give freedom to a prisoner. *surrender to one's* ～, appear for trial after being out on ～. □ vt [VP15B] ～ *sb out*, obtain his freedom until trial by payment of ～. ～**ee** /ˌbeɪˈliː/ n (legal) person(s) to whom permission is given to have the goods of another (eg a laundry which accepts goods for washing or dry-cleaning). ～**·ment** n (legal) delivery of goods to a ～ee. ～**or** /ˈbeɪlɔː(r)/ n (legal) one who delivers goods to a ～ee.

bail² /beɪl/ n (cricket) either of the two cross-pieces over the three stumps. ⇨ the illus at cricket.

bail³ /beɪl/ vt, vi 1 [VP6A,15B,2A,C] ～ *(out)*, throw water out of a boat with buckets, etc: ～*ing water (out)*; ～*ing (out) the boat*. 2 (sometimes used for) bale².

bailey /ˈbeɪlɪ/ n outer wall of a castle; courtyard of a castle enclosed by strong walls. **Old B**～, London Central Criminal Court.

Bailey bridge /ˈbeɪlɪ brɪdʒ/ n bridge (in prefabricated sections) designed for speedy assembly, used for spanning rivers, etc. ⇨ the illus at bridge.

bail·iff /ˈbeɪlɪf/ n 1 law officer who helps a sheriff. 2 landowner's agent or manager.

bairn /beən/ n (Scot and N England) child.

bait¹ /beɪt/ n 1 food, or sth made in imitation, put on a hook to catch fish, or in nets, traps, etc to attract prey: *The fish took/swallowed/rose to/ nibbled at the* ～. **live** ～, small fish used as ～ to catch large fish. 2 (fig) sth that allures or tempts. *rise to the* ～, succumb to temptation.

bait² /beɪt/ vt, vi 1 [VP6A] put food, real or imitation, (on a hook, etc) to catch fish, etc: ～ *a hook with a worm*. 2 [VP6A,2A] give food to (horses on a journey); (of horses) take food. 3 [VP6A] worry (a chained animal) by making dogs attack it: 'bear-～ing; 'bull-～ing; ～ *a bear with dogs*. 4 [VP6A] torment (sb) by making cruel or insulting remarks.

baize /beɪz/ n [U] thick woollen cloth, usu green, used for covering (tables, etc): *a* '～*-covered door*; *green* ～ *for the billiard-table*.

bake /beɪk/ vt, vi [VP6A,22,2A,C] 1 cook, be cooked, by dry heat in an oven: ～ *bread/cakes*; ～*d beans. The bread is baking/being* ～*d*. 2 make or become hard by heating: *The sun* ～*d the ground hard. Bricks and earthenware articles are* ～*d in kilns*. 3 be warmed or tanned: *We are baking in the sun*. ˌ**half-**'～**d** adj (colloq) half-witted; lacking in experience or common sense: *half-*～*d ideas; a half-*～*d prophet*. ˌ**baking-**'**hot** adj very hot: *a baking-hot day*. '**baking-powder** n mixture of powders used to make bubbles of gas in cakes, etc and so cause them to be light. **baker** n person who ～s bread, etc. ～**r's dozen**, thirteen. **bak·ery** /ˈbeɪkərɪ/ n (pl -ries) place where bread is ～d for many people.

bake·lite /ˈbeɪkəlaɪt/ n [U] (P) synthetic resin compound as formerly used for fountain pens, trays, telephones, etc.

bak·sheesh /ˈbækʃiːʃ/ n [U] (in the Middle East) money given as a tip or as alms: *The porter expects* ～ *from you*.

bala·laika /ˌbæləˈlaɪkə/ n (pl ～s) guitar-like musical instrument (triangular, with three strings), popular in Russia and other countries in eastern Europe. ⇨ the illus at string.

bal·ance¹ /ˈbæləns/ vt, vi 1 [VP6A,14] weigh (a question, etc); compare (two objects, plans, etc) (in order to judge the relative weight, value, etc). 2 [VP6A,15A] keep or put (sth, oneself) in a state of balance: *Can you* ～ *a stick on the end of your nose? How long can you* ～ *(yourself) on one foot?* 3 [VP6A] (accounts) compare debits and credits and record the sum needed to make them equal. ～ *the budget*, arrange for income and expenditure to be equal. [VP2A] (of the two sides of a balance-sheet) be equal: *My accounts* ～. 4 *a* ～*d diet*, one with the quantity and variety of food needed for good health.

a balance

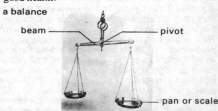

beam — pivot
pan or scale

bal·ance² /ˈbæləns/ n 1 apparatus for weighing, with a central pivot, beam and two scales or pans. *be/hang in the* ～, (fig, of a result) be still uncertain: *For a long time his fate was in the* ～. 2 regulating apparatus of a watch or clock. '～**-wheel** n wheel, in a watch, that regulates the beat. 3 [U] condition of being steady; condition that exists when two opposing forces are equal. **checks and** ～**s**, ⇨ check²(1). *hold the* ～, have the power to decide. *in the* ～, undecided. *keep one's* ～, keep steady, remain upright: *A small child has to learn to keep its* ～ *before it can walk far. Don't get excited; keep your* ～, (fig) keep calm. *lose one's* ～, become unsteady; fall; (fig) be upset mentally: *He was surrounded by so many dangers that he lost his* ～, became nervous and upset. *throw sb off his* ～, upset him; cause him to fall. ～ *of power*, condition in which no one country or group of countries is much stronger than another. 4 [U] (in art) harmony of design and proportion: *a picture lacking in* ～. 5 (accounts) difference between two columns of an account (money received and money paid out, etc). **on ~,** taking everything into consideration. **strike a ~ (between...),** find this difference; (fig) reach a solution or adjustment considered to be fair to all; (fig) compromise; find a middle course. **~ of payments,** statement (for a stated period) of the total payments to foreign countries (for imports, outflow of capital and gold) and the total receipts from foreign countries (for exports, inflow of capital and gold). **~ of trade,** difference in value between exports and imports. **'~-sheet,** written statement of this difference, with details, showing credit and debit. **6** amount still owed after a part payment: *~ to be paid within one week.* **7 the ~,** (colloq) the remainder of anything; what is left.

bal·cony /'bælkənɪ/ n (*pl* -nies) **1** platform (with a wall or rail) built on an outside wall of a building, reached from an upstairs room. **2** (in a theatre or concert hall) series of rows of seats above floor-level and (usu) rising one above the other. (US = gallery.) **bal·conied** adj having a ~ or balconies: *a balconied house.*

bald /bɔːld/ adj (-er, -est) **1** (of men) having no or not much hair on the scalp; (of animals) hairless; (of birds) featherless; (of trees) leafless; (of land, hills, etc) without trees or bushes. **2** (fig) dull; without ornament: *a ~ style of writing; a ~ statement of the facts,* one that gives the facts in an uninteresting way. **3 '~-head, '~-pate** n man with a ~ head. **go at it ,~-headed,** (colloq) attack or deal with it in a reckless manner, using all one's energy. **~·ly** adv (always fig): *speaking ~ly; to put it ~ly,* plainly, without trying to soften what one says. **~·ness** n

bal·der·dash /'bɔːldədæʃ/ n [U] foolish or meaningless talk or writing.

bal·dric /'bɔːldrɪk/ n belt (passing over the right shoulder to the left hip) for a sword, bugle, horn, etc.

bale¹ /beɪl/ n [C] heap of material pressed together and tied with rope or wire: *~s of cloth,* (usu packed in canvas); *~s of hay,* (tied in string). □ vt [VP6A] make into, pack in, *~s: to ~ hay.*

bale² /beɪl/ vt = bail³(1). **~ out (of),** (of an airman) jump with a parachute from a damaged aircraft or an aircraft out of control.

bale³ /beɪl/ n (old use, liter) evil. **~·ful** /-fʊl/ adj evil; sinister, harmful; *~ful looks/influences.* **~-fully** /-fʊlɪ/ adv

balk, baulk¹ /bɔːk/ n **1** thick, roughly squared beam of wood. **2** hindrance; obstacle; cause of delay.

balk, baulk² /bɔːk/ vt,vi **1** [VP6A,14] purposely get in the way of: *~ sb's plans,* prevent him from carrying them out; *~ sb of his prey,* prevent him from getting it; *be ~ed in one's purpose.* **2** [VP2A,3A] *~ (at),* (eg of a horse) refuse to go forward; hesitate: *The horse ~ed at the high hedge. Her husband ~ed at the expense of the plans she had made.*

ball¹ /bɔːl/ n **1** any solid or hollow sphere as used in games ('base~, 'foot~, 'tennis-~, 'cricket-~, etc. ⇨ the illus at these nn). **be on the ~,** competent (in what one is doing). **have the ~ at one's feet,** have a good chance of attaining success. **keep the ~ rolling,** keep the conversation, etc going. **play ~,** (colloq) co-operate: *The management refused to play ~.* **start/set the ~ rolling,** start sth, esp conversation, going. **The ~ is**

in his, etc court/with him, etc, The next move (in talks, etc) is his, etc. **three ~s,** pawnbroker's sign. **,~-'bearing(s),** bearings(5) in which friction is lessened by the use of small steel ~s; (*sing*) one of these ~s. **'~(-)cock** n device which regulates the supply of water in a tank or cistern by means of a floating ~ which shuts or opens a valve as the water rises and falls. **'~-pen, ,~-point-'pen,** pen in which the ink flows round a ~-bearing that rotates on contact with the paper. **2** (cricket) single delivery of the ~ by the bowler. **no ~,** delivery that breaks the rules; (baseball) any strike or throw: *a foul ~;* (football) movement of the ~ by a player: *send over a high ~.* **3** material gathered, rolled or wound, into a round mass: *a ~ of wool/string; a 'snow~; a 'meat~,* of minced meat. **4** metal missile to be fired from a gun: '*cannon-~,* (old fashioned, cf *shell*). **'~-cartridge,** one containing a bullet (contrasted with *blank cartridge*). **5** round part: *the ~ of the thumb,* near the palm, ⇨ the illus at arm; *the ~ of the foot,* near the base of the big toe, ⇨ the illus at leg. **6** ⚠ (sl) testicle. □ *int* ⚠ **~s!** (sl) Nonsense! □ *vi,vt* **1** form into a ~: *The snow ~ed under the horse's feet.* **2** wind or squeeze into a ~. **3 ~s sth up,** (sl) make a mess of it. Hence, **~s-up** n mess.

ball² /bɔːl/ n social gathering for dancing, with an organized programme, and (often) special entertainment. **'~-dress,** woman's frock to be worn at ~s. **'~-room,** large room for ~s.

bal·lad /'bæləd/ n simple song or poem, esp one that tells an old story.

bal·lade /bæ'lɑːd/ n [C] **1** poem of one or more stanzas, each with 7, 8 or 10 lines, each ending with the same refrain line, followed by an envoy. **2** musical composition of a romantic nature.

bal·last /'bæləst/ n [U] **1** heavy material (eg rock, iron, sand) loaded into a ship to keep it steady. *in ~,* carrying ~ only. **2** sand or other material carried in a balloon, to be thrown out to make the balloon go higher. **3** (fig) mental stability. **4** gravel, crushed rock, etc used to make a foundation for a road, esp a railway. □ *vt* [VP6A] supply with ~.

bal·ler·ina /ˌbælə'riːnə/ n (*pl ~s*) (I) woman ballet-dancer, esp one who takes one of the chief classical roles.

bal·let /'bæleɪ/ n **1** [C] dramatic performance, without dialogue or singing, illustrating a story by a group of dancers. **2** [U] the dancers: *a member of the ~.* **3** [U] **the ~,** this kind of stage performance as an art. **'~-dancer,** person who dances in ~s. **'~-skirt,** short skirt worn by a ~ dancer.

bal·lis·tic /bə'lɪstɪk/ adj of projectiles: *intercontinental ~ missile* (**ICBM**), long-range rocket for use in war. **bal·lis·tics** n (usu with *sing v*) study, science, of projectiles.

bal·locks /'bɒləks/ n pl ⚠ (vulg) **1** testicles. **2** nonsense.

bal·loon /bə'luːn/ n **1** bag or envelope filled with air, or with gas lighter than air: *captive ~,* one moored to the ground. **'~ barrage,** barrier of steel cables, supported by captive ~s, intended to give protection against low-flying enemy aircraft. **'bar-rage,** one of these captive ~s. **hot-'air ~,** apparatus for travel in the air with a basket or car (for the passengers, etc) suspended beneath a large bag of hot gas. **'~ tyre,** low-pressure pneumatic tyre of great width. **2** (in a strip cartoon, etc) outline for dialogue, exclamations, etc. □ *vi* [VP2A,C] swell out like a ~. **~·ist** n person who goes up in ~s.

balloons

bal·lot /'bælət/ n 1 [C] piece of paper (also '∼-paper), ticket or ball, used in secret voting; [U] secret voting; [C] instance of this. *take a* ∼, decide by voting. 2 votes so recorded. '∼-box, box into which ∼-papers are dropped by voters. □ vi [VP2A,3A] ∼ *(for)*, give a vote; draw lots.

bally /'bælɪ/ adj, adv (GB dated sl, euphem for *bloody* (3)) (used to show the speaker's strong feelings of like or dislike, etc): *What a* ∼ *nuisance!*

bally·hoo /,bælɪ'hu: US: 'bælɪhu:/ n [U] (colloq) 1 noisy publicity or advertising; vulgar or misleading ways of attracting attention. 2 uproar.

balm /bɑ:m/ n [U] 1 sweet-smelling oil or ointment obtained from certain kinds of trees, used for soothing pain or healing. 2 (fig) that which gives peace of mind; consolation. ∼y adj 1 (of air) soft and warm. 2 healing; fragrant. 3 (sl) = barmy.

bal·oney /bə'ləʊnɪ/ n = boloney.

balsa /'bɔːlsə/ n [C,U] (light-weight wood of a) tropical American tree; raft of floats fastened to a framework: (attrib) *a* ∼ *raft*.

bal·sam /'bɔːlsəm/ n 1 = balm(1). 2 tree yielding balm. 3 flowering plant grown in gardens.

bal·us·ter /'bæləstə(r)/ n one of the upright posts supporting a handrail; (pl) banisters.

bal·us·trade /,bælə'streɪd/ n row of balusters with the stonework or woodwork that joins them on top, round a balcony, terrace, flat roof, etc.

bam·bino /bæm'biːnəʊ/ n (pl ∼s) (I) 1 baby. 2 representation in art of the infant Jesus.

bam·boo /bæm'buː/ n [U] tall plant with hard, hollow, jointed stems, of the grass family; [C] (pl ∼s) stem, used as a stick or support.

bam·boozle /bæm'buːzl/ vt (colloq) [VP6A,14] 1 mystify: *You can't* ∼ *me.* 2 ∼ *sb (into/out of) (doing) (sth)* trick, cheat him.

ban /bæn/ vt (-nn-) 1 [VP6A] order with authority that sth must not be done, said, etc: *a ban-the-bomb demonstration,* one calling for nuclear disarmament. *The play was banned by the censor.* 2 [VP6A,14] ∼ *sb (from) (doing) (sth),* order with authority that sb may not do sth: *He was* ∼*ned from (attending) the meeting.* □ n (also '∼-ning-order) order that bans sth/sb: *under a ban,* banned.

ba·nal /bə'nɑːl US: 'beɪnl/ adj commonplace; uninteresting: ∼ *remarks.* ∼·ity /bə'nælətɪ/ n [U] quality of being ∼; [C] (pl -ties) ∼ remark, etc: *con-*

versation that was chiefly ∼*ities.*

ba·nana /bə'nɑːnə US: bə'nænə/ n [C] long, thick-skinned (yellow when ripe) fruit growing in bunches on the ∼-tree in tropical and semi-tropical countries. ⇨ the illus at fruit. ⇨ plantain.

band /bænd/ n 1 flat, thin strip of material, esp for fastening things together or for placing round an object to strengthen it: *iron* ∼*s round a barrel; papers kept together with a rubber* ∼. '∼-saw n (eng) machine-driven saw consisting of an endless steel belt. 2 flat, thin strip of material forming part of an article of clothing: *Some shirts have a* '*neck*∼ *and two* '*wrist*∼*s.* 3 strip or line, different from the rest in colour or design, on sth: *a white plate with a blue* ∼ *round the edge.* 4 group of persons doing sth together under a leader and with a common purpose: *a* ∼ *of robbers/fugitives/revellers.* 5 group of persons who play music together, eg of wind-instrument performers (often *brass* ∼): *the ,Regimental 'B*∼; *a* '*dance* ∼; *a* '*jazz* ∼; *a* '*steel* ∼. '∼-master /'bændmɑːstə(r)/ n conductor of a ∼. '∼s·man /-mən/ n (pl -men) member of a ∼. '∼-stand /'bændstænd/ n raised platform usu roofed, for a ∼ playing in the open air. '∼-wagon n wagon carrying the ∼ heading a march or procession (esp of a political party). *climb/jump on/aboard the* ∼*wagon,* join in what seems likely to be a successful enterprise. 6 (radio; short for '*wave*-∼) range of frequencies that may be tuned in together: *the 19-metre* ∼. □ vt,vi 1 [VP6A] put a ∼, strip or line on. 2 [VP15B,14,2C] ∼ *together/with,* unite in a group: ∼ *people together;* ∼ *with others to do sth. They* ∼*ed together to protest.*

ban·dage /'bændɪdʒ/ n strip of material for binding round a wound or injury, or for blindfolding sb. □ vt [VP6A,15B] ∼ *(up),* tie up with a ∼: ∼ *(up) a boy's leg; a man with a* ∼*d hand.*

band-aid /'bændeɪd/ n [C,U] (P) (US) type of plaster(3).

ban·danna /bæn'dænə/ n brightly coloured square of material with red or yellow spots, usu worn round the neck.

band·box /'bændbɒks/ n light, cardboard box for millinery: *She looks as if she had just come out of a* ∼, She looks extremely smart and neat.

ban·deau /'bændəʊ US: -'dəʊ/ n (pl -deaux /-dəʊz US: -'dəʊz/) band for keeping a woman's hair in place.

ban·dit /'bændɪt/ n robber, one of an armed band (eg of brigands attacking travellers in forests or mountains or, today, banks and offices). ∼·ry n [U] activity of ∼s.

ban·do·leer, ban·do·lier /,bændə'lɪə(r)/ n shoulder-belt with pockets for cartridges.

bandy[1] /'bændɪ/ vt (pt,pp -ied) [VP6A,14,15B] exchange (words, blows). *have one's name bandied about,* be talked about in an unfavourable way, be a subject for gossip. ∼ *a story about,* pass it from person to person. ∼ *words with sb,* exchange remarks quickly, esp when quarrelling.

bandy[2] /'bændɪ/ adj (of the legs) curving outwards at the knees. '∼-legged adj (of persons or animals) having ∼ legs.

bane /beɪn/ n [U] 1 (only in compounds) poison: '*rat's*-∼. 2 cause of ruin or trouble: *Drink was the* ∼ *of his life. He has been the* ∼ *of my life,* caused me constant trouble and anxiety. ∼·ful /-fʊl/ adj evil: *a* ∼*ful influence.* ∼·fully /-fʊlɪ/ adv

bang[1] /bæŋ/ n violent blow; sudden, loud noise:

He fell and got a nasty ~ on the head. He always shuts the door with a ~. The firework went off with a ~. **go (off) with a ~,** (GB colloq); **go (over) with a ~,** (US colloq) (of a performance, etc) be successful, be greatly liked. □ *vt, vi* **1** [VP6A,15B,2A,C] hit violently; give a ~ to; shut with a noise: *He ~ed at the door. He was ~ing on the door with his fist. He ~ed his fist on the table. She ~ed the keys of the piano. The teacher tried to ~ grammar into the heads of his pupils. Don't ~ the lid down. He ~ed the box down on the floor. A door was ~ing somewhere. The door ~ed shut.* **2** [VP2A,C] make a loud noise: *The fireworks ~ed. The guns ~ed away. We were ~ing away* (= firing continuously) *at the enemy. Tell the children to stop ~ing about,* being noisy. □ *adv, int:* **go ~,** burst with a loud noise; *~ in the middle,* exactly in the middle; *come ~ up* (= violently) *against sth.*

bang² /bæŋ/ *vt* cut (the front hair) squarely across the forehead: *She wears her hair ~ed.* □ *n* [C] fringe of ~ed hair.

banger /'bæŋə(r)/ *n* (sl) **1** sausage. **2** noisy firework. **3** old dilapidated car.

bangle /'bæŋgl/ *n* ornamental rigid band worn round the arm or ankle.

ban·ian, ban·yan /'bænɪən/ *n* **1** Hindu trader. **2** (also **'~-tree**) Indian fig, whose branches come down to the ground and take root.

ban·ish /'bænɪʃ/ *vt* [VP6A,14] **1** ~ *(from),* send away, esp out of the country, as a punishment: *He was ~ed from the realm.* **2** put away from, out of (the mind): ~ *care.* **~·ment** *n* [U] state of being ~ed: *go into ~ment.*

ban·is·ter /'bænɪstə(r)/ *n* post supporting the handrail of a staircase; *(pl)* posts and handrail together.

banjo /'bændʒəʊ/ *n* (*pl* ~s, ~es) musical instrument played by plucking the strings with the fingers. ⇨ the illus at string.

bank¹ /bæŋk/ *n* [C] **1** land along each side of a river or canal; ground near a river: *A river flows between its ~s. His house is on the south ~ of the river.* **2** sloping land or earth, often forming a border or division: *low ~s of earth between rice-fields. There were flowers growing on the ~s on each side of the country lanes.* **3** (also **'sand-~**) part of the sea-bed higher than its surroundings, but covered with enough water for ships except at low tide; (mining) coal-face. **4** flat-topped mass of cloud, snow, etc esp one formed by the wind: *The sun went down behind a ~ of clouds.* **5** artificial slope made to enable a car to go round a curve with less risk.

bank² /bæŋk/ *vt, vi* **1** [VP6A,15B,2C] ~ *up,* (a) make or form into ~s, ⇨ **4** above: *The snow has ~ed up.* (b) stop water (of a river, etc) from flowing by making a ~ of earth, mud, etc. (c) heap up (the fire in a fireplace or furnace) with coal-dust, etc so that the fire burns slowly for a long time. **2** [VP2A] (of a motor-car or aircraft) travel with one side higher than the other (eg when turning).

bank³ /bæŋk/ *n* **1** establishment for keeping money and valuables safely, the money being paid out on the customer's order (by means of cheques). **the B~,** the B~ of England, which is used by the British Government; *have money in the ~,* have savings; *~ clerk,* clerk working in a ~. **'~-bill** *n* bill drawn by one ~ upon another ~. **'~-book** *n* (also **'passbook**) book containing a record of a customer's ~ account. **'~ draft,** = ~*bill.* **~ 'holi-**

day *n* (GB) one of those days (not Sundays) on which ~s are closed by law, usu kept as general holidays (eg Good Friday, Easter Monday, Christmas Day); (US) any weekday on which ~s are closed. **'~-note** *n* piece of paper money issued by a ~. **'~-rate** *n* rate at which the B~ of England (or other national ~) will discount bills, ⇨ bill³(5). **'~-roll** *n* roll of paper money. **2** (gambling) sum of money held by the keeper of the gaming table, from which he pays his losses. **break the ~,** (eg at Monte Carlo) win all this money. **3** (place for storing) reserve supplies. **'blood ~** *n* place where blood or blood plasma is stored for use in hospitals, etc.

bank⁴ /bæŋk/ *vt, vi* **1** place (money) in a bank³(1): *He ~s half his salary every month.* **2** [VP3A] ~ *(with),* keep money in a bank: *Who do you ~ with,* With what firm of bankers do you keep your money? *Where do you ~?* **3** [VP3A] ~ *on/upon,* base one's hopes on: *I'm ~ing on your help.* **~er** *n* person who owns, is a partner in, or is a governor or director of, a bank³(1); (gambling) keeper of a bank³(2). **'~er's card,** card (issued by a bank) that guarantees the payment of a customer's cheque (up to a certain amount). **~er's 'order,** = *standing order.* ⇨ standing(1). **~·ing** *n* [U] the business of keeping a bank³(1): *choose ~ing as a career; ~ing hours,* eg 10am to 3.30pm.

bank⁵ /bæŋk/ *n* **1** row of keys, switches, etc: *a three-~/four-~ typewriter.* **2** bench for rowers in a galley(1). **3** row of cylinders (in an engine).

bank·rupt /'bæŋkrʌpt/ *n* (legal) person judged by a law court to be unable to pay his debts in full, his property being distributed for the benefit of his creditors. □ *adj* **1** unable to pay one's debts. **go ~,** become ~, insolvent. **2** ~ *in/of,* completely without: *The newspapers accused the Government of being ~ in ideas.* □ *vt* [VP6A] make ~. **~·cy** /'bæŋkrəpsɪ/ *n* [U] ~ condition; [C] (*pl* -cies) instance of this: *There were ten ~cies in the town last year.*

ban·ner /'bænə(r)/ *n* **1** flag (now chiefly fig): *the ~ of freedom.* **under the ~ (of),** belonging to, supporting (a particular faith or movement). **2** flag or announcement, usu on two poles, carried in (eg religious or political) processions, making known principles, slogans, etc. ~ **headline,** (in a newspaper) prominent headline in large type.

ban·nis·ter *n* = banister.

banns /bænz/ *n pl* public announcement in church that two persons are to be married: *put up/publish the ~; have one's ~ called.* **forbid the ~,** declare opposition to a proposed marriage.

ban·quet /'bæŋkwɪt/ *n* elaborate meal, usu for a special event, at which speeches are made: *a 'wedding ~.* □ *vt, vi* [VP6A] give a ~ to (sb); [VP2A] take part in a ~; feast.

ban·shee /bæn'ʃi: US: 'bænʃi:/ *n* (Ireland and the Scottish Highlands) spirit whose cry is said to mean that there will be a death in the house where the cry is heard.

bant /bænt/ *vi* [VP2A] (dated) adopt a diet designed to reduce weight (*slim* and *reduce* are the usu words). **~·ing** *n* treatment of obesity by this means.

ban·tam /'bæntəm/ *n* **1** small-sized kind of domestic fowl, esp the cock, which is a fighter. **2** boxer between 112 and 118 lb.

ban·ter /'bæntə(r)/ *vt, vi* [VP6A,2A] tease in a playful way (by joking talk). □ *n* [U] good-humoured teasing. ~·ing adj~·ing·ly adv

Ban·tu /'bæn'tu:/ US: 'bæntu:/ adj, n (member) of a group of related Central and S African peoples; of their languages.

ban·yan n = banian.

bao·bab /'beɪəbæb US: 'baʊbæb/ n tree of tropical Africa with a trunk that grows to an enormous size.

bap·tism /'bæptɪzəm/ n 1 [U] ceremony of sprinkling sb with, or immersing sb in, water, accepting him as a member of the Christian Church and (usu) giving him a name or names (in addition to the family name); [C] instance of this: *There were six ~s at this church last week.* 2 (fig) first experience of a new kind of life: *a soldier's ~ of fire,* his first experience of warfare. **bap·tis·mal** /bæp'tɪzməl/ adj of ~: ~al name/water/font.

Bap·tist /'bæptɪst/ n, adj (member) of the denomination of Christians who object to infant baptism and believe that baptism should be by immersion and at an age when a person is old enough to understand the meaning of the ceremony.

bap·tize /bæp'taɪz/ vt [VP6A,23] give baptism to (sb): *He had been ~d a Roman Catholic.*

bar[1] /bɑ:(r)/ n 1 long piece of hard, stiff material (eg metal, wood, soap, chocolate). 2 rod or rail, rigid length of wood or metal, across a door, window or gate, or forming part of a grate (in a fireplace or furnace) or grid: *He was placed behind prison bars,* put into a prison cell. 3 barrier (across a road) that could not be passed (in former times) until a sum of money (called a *toll*) was paid: *a toll bar.* 4 bank or ridge of sand, etc across the mouth of a river or the entrance to a bay, deposited by currents or tides, often hindering navigation: *The ship crossed the bar safely. We stuck fast on the bar.* 5 (fig) barrier or obstacle; sth that hinders or stops progress: *Poor health may be a bar to success in life. Poverty is not always a bar to happiness.* 6 narrow band (of colour, light, etc): *As the sun went down, there was a bar of red across the western sky.* 7 strip of metal across the ribbon of (esp a military) medal to indicate either (a) that the holder has received the same award twice, or (b) that he has served in a particular field of operations. 8 (in music) vertical line across the stave marking divisions of equal value in time; one of these divisions and the notes in it: *the opening bars of the National Anthem.* ⇨ the illus at notation. 9 railing or barrier in a law court, separating the part where the business is carried on from the part for spectators: *be tried at (the) Bar,* be tried in open court, where everyone may see and hear, not secretly. *the prisoner at the bar,* the accused person. 10 (in Parliament) railing dividing off the space to which non-members are admitted (eg for examination by members); similar place in US Senate, House of Representatives and State Legislatures. 11 (fig) sth that can be compared to a judge or examiner: *at the bar of public opinion; the bar of conscience.* 12 **the Bar,** the profession of barrister; all those who have the right to act as barristers. *be called to the Bar,* be received as a member of the Bar. *read for the Bar,* study to become a barrister. 13 (a) (in an inn or public house) room, counter, where drinks (such as beer and spirits) are served: *the Public Bar, the Private Bar,* for different classes of users. (b) (in a hotel, licensed restaurant or private house) room with such a counter. '**bar·maid** n woman who serves drinks at a bar(13). '**bar·man** /-mən/ n (pl -men) man who does this. '**bar·ten·der** n barmaid

or barman (⇨ *cocktail lounge).* 14 counter at which meals, etc are served and also eaten: *a 'milk bar; a quick-lunch bar.*

bar[2] /bɑ:(r)/ vt (-rr-) 1 [VP6A] fasten (a door, gate, etc) with a bar or bars[1](2). 2 [VP15B] keep (sb) in or out: *He barred himself in,* fastened doors, windows, etc so that no one could enter the building. 3 [VP6A] obstruct: *bar a road/path. Soldiers barred the way and we couldn't go any farther.* 4 [VP6A,14] **bar (from),** prohibit: *bar sb from a competition,* order that he shall not take part. [VP6C] (colloq): *She bars smoking in the drawing-room,* does not permit it. *We bar playing cards for money.* [VP12C] *I will bar no honest man my house,* will let any honest man visit my house. 5 [VP6A] (usu passive) mark with a stripe or stripes: *a sky barred with clouds.*

bar[3] /bɑ:(r)/, **bar·ring** /'bɑ:rɪŋ/ prep (colloq) except: *We shall arrive at noon barring accidents,* unless there are accidents. *bar none,* without exception. *bar one,* except one.

bar[4] /bɑ:(r)/ n large Mediterranean fish.

barb /bɑ:b/ n back-turning or back-curving point of an arrow, spear, fish-hook, etc. ~ed adj having a ~ or ~s. ~ed wire, wire with short, sharp points, used for fences, etc: ~ed wire entanglements, for defensive purposes in war.

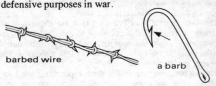

barbed wire   a barb

bar·bar·ian /bɑ:'beərɪən/ adj, n uncivilized or uncultured (person).

bar·baric /bɑ:'bærɪk/ adj of or like barbarians; uncultivated; rough and rude (esp in art and taste): *the ~ splendour of Attila's court.*

bar·bar·ism /'bɑ:bərɪzəm/ n 1 [U] state of being uncivilized, ignorant, or rude: *living in ~.* 2 [C] instance of this; (esp) misuse of language by mixing foreign or vulgar words into talk or writing.

bar·bar·ity /bɑ:'bærətɪ/ n [U] savage cruelty; [C] (pl -ties) instance of this: *the barbarities of modern warfare,* eg the bombing of towns, sinking of passenger liners.

bar·bar·ize /'bɑ:bəraɪz/ vt [VP6A] make barbarous.

bar·bar·ous /'bɑ:bərəs/ adj uncivilized; cruel; savage; unrefined in taste, conduct, or habits. ~·ly adv

bar·be·cue /'bɑ:bɪkju:/ n grill, iron framework, for cooking an animal whole; ox, pig, etc roasted whole; (outdoor) social occasion at which meat cooked over a charcoal fire is eaten. □ vt roast (meat, etc) in this way.

bar·bel /'bɑ:bl/ n large European fresh-water fish.

bar·ber /'bɑ:bə(r)/ n person whose trade is shaving and cutting men's hair (cf *hairdresser,* for both men and women). ~'s pole, pole painted in coloured spirals and used as a sign. '~'s shop, (US = '~ shop) place where a ~ does his work.

bar·bi·can /'bɑ:bɪkən/ n fortified building, esp a double tower over a gate or bridge, used in olden times as an outer defence to a city or castle.

bar·bi·tone /'bɑ:bɪtəʊn/ n [U] drug used to soothe the nerves and cause sleep; veronal.

bar·bitu·rate /bɑ:'bɪtjʊrət/ n [C,U] (chem) (kinds of) organic compound with a (possibly dangerous) soporific effect; pill for settling the nerves or inducing sleep.

bar·ca·role, bar·ca·rolle /ˌbɑːkəˈrəʊl/ n song of Venetian gondoliers.

bard /bɑːd/ n **1** (esp Celtic) minstrel. **2** (liter) poet: *the ~ of Avon,* Shakespeare. **bar·dic** adj of ~s or their songs. **bar·dol·atry** /bɑːˈdɒlətrɪ/ n [U] enthusiastic admiration of Shakespeare.

bare¹ /beə(r)/ adj (-r, -st) **1** without clothing, covering, protection, or decoration: *fight with ~ hands,* without boxing gloves; *~ to the waist,* clothed from the waist down; *with his head ~,* not wearing a hat; *~ floors,* without carpets, rugs, etc; *a ~ hillside,* without shrubs or trees; *hills ~ of vegetation; trees that are already ~,* that have already lost their leaves. *sleep on ~ boards,* without a mattress, etc. *lay ~,* uncover, expose, make known (sth secret or hidden). *in one's ~ skin,* naked. '*~-back* adv (of a horse) without a saddle: *ride ~back.* ˌ~ˈbacked adj having the back ~. □ adv = ~back. '*~-faced* adj insolent; shameless; undisguised: *It's ~faced robbery to ask £15 for such an old bicycle!* **~·faced·ly** adv '*~·foot* adv without shoes and stockings: *be/go/walk ~foot.* ˌ~ˈfooted adj with ~ feet. □ adv = ~foot. ˌ~ˈheaded adj with a ~ head; not wearing a hat. ˌ~ˈlegged adj with the legs ~; not wearing stockings. **2** empty or almost empty: *a room ~ of furniture; a larder ~ of food; ~ shelves. The garden looked ~ in winter,* had few or no flowers. **3** not more than; mere: *the ~ necessities of life,* things needed merely to keep alive; *earn a ~ living,* only just enough money to live on: *approved by a ~ majority,* a very small one; *a ~ possibility,* a mere or very slight one. **~·ly** adv **1** in a ~ way: *~ly furnished rooms,* with little furniture. **2** only just; scarcely: *We ~ly had time to catch the train. He can ~ly read and write. I ~ly know her.* **~·ness** n ~ state.

bare² /beə(r)/ vt [VP6A] uncover; reveal: *~ one's head,* take one's hat off; *~ the end of a wire,* strip off the covering of rubber, etc (before making an electrical connection). *~ one's heart,* make known one's deepest feelings. *~ its teeth,* (of an animal) show its teeth in anger.

bar·gain /ˈbɑːgɪn/ n **1** agreement to buy, sell or exchange sth, made after discussion; (in industry) agreement between management and labour over wages, hours, etc; sth obtained as the result of such an agreement. *A ~'s a ~,* When an agreement has been made, it must be kept. *drive a hard ~,* try to force an agreement favourable to oneself. *a good/bad ~,* one that favours/does not favour oneself. *into the ~,* as well; in addition; moreover. *make/strike a ~ (with sb) (over sth),* reach agreement. '*~·ing position,* (in a debate, etc) state of affairs, arrangements, etc: *The Foreign Secretary was in a good/bad ~ing position in his dealings with his opposite number in France,* was in a favourable/unfavourable position when negotiating. **2** sth offered, sold or bought cheap: *a '~ sale,* sale of goods at reduced prices; '*~-basement,* lowest floor of a shop, where goods are offered at reduced prices; '*~-counter,* counter at which ~s are displayed or sold; *~ price,* low price; '*~-hunter,* person looking for ~s. □ vi,vt **1** [VP2A,3A] *~ (with sb) (for sth),* talk for the purpose of reaching an agreement (about buying or selling sth, doing a piece of work, etc): *We ~ed with the farmer for a supply of milk and butter.* **2** [VP3A] ~

about, = ~ over. *~ for,* be ready or willing to accept or agree to: *I didn't ~ for John arriving so soon,* was surprised by this, didn't expect it. *get more than one ~s for,* (colloq) be unpleasantly surprised at the consequences. *~ over sth,* ~ with sb for sth. **3** [VP9] make a condition: *The men ~ed that they should not have to work on Saturday afternoons.* **4** [VP15B] ~ *away,* give up in return for sth; sacrifice: *~ away one's freedom,* give it up in return for some advantage or other.

barge¹ /bɑːdʒ/ n **1** large flat-bottomed boat for carrying goods and people on rivers and canals, in harbours, etc with or without sails, towed by a tug or horse; similar boat with its own engine. **2** warship's boat, for the use of the officers. **3** large rowing-boat for ceremonial occasions. '*~-pole* n long pole used for guiding a ~. *I wouldn't touch it with a ~-pole,* I dislike or distrust it extremely.

barge² /bɑːdʒ/ vi (colloq) **1** [VP3A] ~ *into/ against,* rush or bump heavily into/against (sb or sth). **2** [VP2C,3A] ~ *about,* move clumsily, without proper control of one's movements or without care (for persons or things). ~ *in/into,* intrude; make one's way in, interrupt, rudely: *Stop barging into our conversation.*

bar·gee /bɑːˈdʒiː/ n master or member of the crew of a barge. *swear like a ~,* swear forcibly, and with a great variety of swear-words.

bari·tone /ˈbærɪtəʊn/ n male voice between tenor and bass.

bar·ium /ˈbeərɪəm/ n [U] **1** soft, silvery-white metal (symbol **Ba**) of which the compounds are used in industry. **2** chemical substance (~ sulphate) introduced into the intestines before an X-ray photograph of them is taken.

bark¹ /bɑːk/ n [U] outer covering or skin on the trunks, boughs and branches of trees. ⇨ the illus at tree. □ vt [VP6A] **1** take the ~ off (a tree). **2** scrape the skin off (one's knuckles, shin, knee, etc) (by falling against sth, etc).

bark² /bɑːk/ n the cry made by dogs and foxes; (fig) sound of gunfire, or of a cough. *His ~ is worse than his bite,* He is bad-tempered but not dangerous or (fig) malicious. □ vi,vt **1** [VP2A,C,3A] (of dogs, etc) give a ~ or ~s: *The dog ~s at strangers. ~ up the wrong tree,* (fig) direct one's complaint, accusation, etc wrongly. **2** [VP6A,15B] say (sth) in a sharp, commanding voice: *The officer ~ed out his orders. 'Come here!' he ~ed (out).*

bark³, barque /bɑːk/ n **1** sailing-ship with 3 to 5 masts and sails. **2** (poet) any ship or boat.

barker /ˈbɑːkə(r)/ n (colloq) **1** person who stands outside a booth in a travelling show, or outside a shop, talking loudly to advertise the show, goods, etc. **2** (sl) pistol.

bar·ley /ˈbɑːlɪ/ n [U] grass-like plant and its seed (called grain), used for food and for making beer and whisky. ⇨ the illus at cereal. '*~-corn* n [U] grain of ~; (colloq) malt liquor. *pearl ~ n* ~ grain made smaller by grinding. '*~-water* n [U] drink made by boiling pearl ~ in water and then straining it. '*~-sugar* n [U] solid sweet substance, made from pure sugar.

barm /bɑːm/ n [U] yeast.

barmy /ˈbɑːmɪ/ adj (GB colloq) wrong in the head; foolish.

barn /bɑːn/ n **1** covered building for storing hay, grain, etc on a farm. '*~ dance* n kind of rustic dance. '*~-door* n large door of a ~; (colloq fig) target too large to miss. ˌ~ˈdoor fowl *n* ordinary kind of fowl kept on farms. '**~·storm** *vi* (US) travel rapidly through the country making political speeches, presenting plays, etc. Hence, '**~·storm·er** *n* person who does this. '**~·yard** *n* = farmyard. **2** (contemptuous) any large, plain building: *What a ~ of a house!* **3** (US) building for sheltering cattle or horses; depot for trams, buses, etc.

bar·nacle /ˈbɑːnəkl/ *n* small sea-animal that fastens itself to objects under water, rocks, the bottoms of ships, the timbers of wharves, etc.

ba·rom·eter /bəˈrɒmɪtə(r)/ *n* instrument for measuring the pressure of the atmosphere, used for forecasting the weather and measuring height above sea-level; (fig) something which forecasts changes or fluctuations (eg in public opinion, market prices). **baro·met·ric** /ˌbærəˈmetrɪk/ *adj*

bar·on /ˈbærən/ *n* **1** (in GB) nobleman; lowest rank of Peer (called *Lord* —); holder of the non-British title (called *Baron* —). **2** (orig US) great industrial leader: *oil ~s; beer ~s.* '**~·age** /-ɪdʒ/ *n* the ~s collectively; book with a list of these Peers. **~·ess** /ˈbærənɪs/ *n* ~'s wife; woman holding the rank of a ~ in her own right. **bar·o·nial** /bəˈrəʊnɪəl/ *adj* of, suitable for, ~s. **bar·ony** /ˈbærənɪ/ *n* rank of a ~: *confer a ~y on sb*, make him a ~.

bar·onet /ˈbærənɪt/ *n* member of the lowest hereditary titled order, lower in rank than a baron but above a knight; shortened to *Bart*, added to the name, as *Sir John Williams, Bart.* **~·cy** /ˈbærənɪtsɪ/ *n* rank, title, of a ~.

ba·roque /bəˈrɒk *US:* -əʊk/ *n, adj* (of the) florid or extravagant style in the arts (esp architecture) in Europe in the 17th and 18th cc.

ba·rouche /bəˈruːʃ/ *n* four-wheeled carriage, pulled by horses, with two seats facing each other and a folding top, for four occupants and a driver.

barque /bɑːk/ *n* ⇨ bark³.

bar·rack¹ /ˈbærək/ *n* **1** (usu *pl* with *indef art* and *sing v*) large building(s) for soldiers to live in: *The ~s are/is quite new.* **2** any building of plain or ugly appearance.

bar·rack² /ˈbærək/ *vt, vi* [VP6A, 2A] jeer at; make cries of protest against (eg slow play in a cricket match). **~·ing** *n* slow clapping, etc.

bar·ra·cuda /ˌbærəˈkuːdə/ *n* large, fierce Caribbean sea-fish.

bar·rage /ˈbærɑːʒ *US:* bəˈrɑːʒ/ *n* [C] **1** artificial obstacle built across a river (not across a valley) for storing water to be diverted into canals for irrigation (as on the Nile and the Indus). ⇨ dam. **2** (mil) barrier made by heavy, continuous gunfire directed onto a given area. **3** *balloon ~; ~ balloon,* ⇨ balloon.

barred /bɑːd/ *pt, pp* of bar³.

bar·rel /ˈbærəl/ *n* **1** round container, made of wooden staves with bands or hoops, or of plastic; the amount that a ~ holds. **~·roofed 'vault** *n* (semi-)cylindrical roof. **2** metal tube of a rifle, revolver or pistol. ⇨ the illus at rifle. **3** part of a fountain pen that holds the ink. **4** '**~·organ** *n* instrument from which music is produced by turning a handle and so causing a cylinder to act mechanically on keys; usu played by a man who goes round the streets, playing it for money. □ *vt* (-ll-) put in a ~ or ~s. **~·led** *part adj* stored in a ~: *~led beer.*

bar·ren /ˈbærən/ *adj* **1** (of land) not good enough to produce crops. **2** (of plants, trees) not producing fruit or seeds. **3** (of women, animals) unable to have young ones. **4** (fig) without value, interest, or result: *a ~ subject/discussion; an attempt that was ~ of results.* **~·ness** *n*

bar·ri·cade /ˌbærɪˈkeɪd/ *n* barrier of objects (eg trees, carts, overturned or burnt-out cars, barrels) made across or in front of something as a defence. □ *vt* [VP6A, 15B] ~ **(in/off)**, block (a street, etc) with a ~: *They ~d themselves in.*

bar·rier /ˈbærɪə(r)/ *n* **1** sth (eg a wall, rail, fence, turnstile) that prevents, hinders or controls, progress or movement: *The Sahara Desert is a natural ~ that separates North and Central Africa. Show your ticket at the ~*, eg in a railway station. ⇨ also crash¹(1), half(3), heat¹(5) and sound²(3). **2** (fig) hindrance: *Poor health and lack of money may both be ~s to educational progress.*

bar·ring /ˈbɑːrɪŋ/ *prep* excluding. ⇨ bar³.

bar·ris·ter /ˈbærɪstə(r)/ *n* (in England) lawyer who has the right to speak and argue as an advocate in higher law courts. ⇨ advocate, solicitor, counsel.

bar·row¹ /ˈbærəʊ/ *n* **1** = wheel-~. **2** (also '*hand-~, 'coster's ~*) small cart with two wheels, pulled or pushed by hand. '**~·boy/-man** /-mæn/ *n* costermonger. **3** (also *luggage-~*) metal frame with two wheels used by porters for luggage (at railway-stations, in hotels, etc).

bar·row² /ˈbærəʊ/ *n* mound, dating from prehistoric times, built over a burial ground. ⇨ tumulus.

bar·ter /ˈbɑːtə(r)/ *vt, vi* [VP15B, 14, 2A] ~ **(with sb/for sth);** ~ **sth away,** exchange (goods, property, etc) (for other goods, etc): *~ wheat for machinery;* (fig) *~ away one's rights/honour/freedom.* □ *n* [U] exchange made in this way. **~·er** *n*

ba·salt /ˈbæsɔːlt *US:* bəˈsɔːlt/ *n* [U] sorts of dark-coloured rock of volcanic origin.

bas·cule /ˈbæskjuːl/ *n* '**~ bridge,** (eng) kind of drawbridge of which the two halves can be raised and lowered with counter-weights.

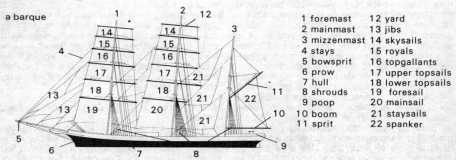

a barque

1 foremast	12 yard
2 mainmast	13 jibs
3 mizzenmast	14 skysails
4 stays	15 royals
5 bowsprit	16 topgallants
6 prow	17 upper topsails
7 hull	18 lower topsails
8 shrouds	19 foresail
9 poop	20 mainsail
10 boom	21 staysails
11 sprit	22 spanker

□ base   ● baseman

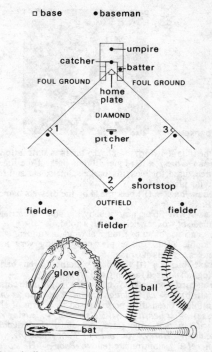

baseball

base[1] /beɪs/ *n* **1** lowest part of anything, esp the part on which sth rests or is supported: *the ~ of a pillar,* ⇨ the illus at column. '**~-board** *n* (US) skirting-board. **2** (geom) line or surface on which a figure stands or can stand: *BC is the ~ of the triangle ABC, ABCD is the ~ of the pyramid.* **3** (chem) substance capable of combining with an acid to form a salt; substance into which other things are mixed. **4** place at which armed forces, expeditions, etc have their stores, hospitals, etc: *a 'naval ~; an 'air ~; a ~ of operations; a ~ camp,* eg for an Everest expedition. **5** (maths) the number (usu 10) which is the starting point for a logarithmic system. **6** (~ball) one of four stations or positions. *get to first ~,* (US; fig) take a successful first step towards achieving sth. *~ hit n* hit on which a player gets to first ~. **7** *~-less adj* without cause or foundation: *~less fears.*

base[2] /beɪs/ *vt* [VP14] *~ sth on/upon,* build or place; use as a basis for: *Direct taxation is usually ~d upon income. I ~ my hopes on the news we had yesterday.*

base[3] /beɪs/ *adj* **1** (-r, -st) (of persons, their behaviour, thoughts, etc) dishonourable: *acting from ~ motives.* **2** *~ metals,* non-precious metals. *~ coin,* mixed with inferior metals.

base-ball /'beɪsbɔːl/ *n* national game of the US, played with a bat and ball, by two teams of nine players each, on a field with four bases[1](6).

base-ment /'beɪsmənt/ *n* lowest part of a building, partly or wholly below ground level; inhabited room(s) in this part.

bases 1 /'beɪsiːz/ *pl* of basis. **2** /'beɪsɪz/ *pl* of base[1].

bash /bæʃ/ *vt* [VP6A,15A,B] strike heavily so as to break or injure: *~ in the lid of a box; ~ sb on the head with a golf club; ~ one's head against sth in the dark.* □ *n* violent blow or knock: *give sb a ~ on the nose. have a ~ at sth,* (sl) attempt it.

bash-ful /'bæʃfl/ *adj* shy. *~-ly /-fəlɪ/ adv*

basic /'beɪsɪk/ *adj* of or at the base or foundation; fundamental: *the ~ processes of arithmetic,* eg adding, subtraction, multiplying; *the ~ vocabulary of a language,* the words that must be known. **B~ English,** artificial, simplified form of English. *~ slag n* fertilizer containing phosphates. **ba-si-cally** /-klɪ/ *adv* fundamentally.

basil /'bæzl/ *n* [U] sweet-smelling plant like mint, used in cooking.

ba-sil-ica /bə'zɪlɪkə/ *n* oblong hall with a double row of columns and an apse at one end (used in ancient Rome as a law court); building of this type used as a church: *the ~ of St Peter's in Rome.*

bas-il-isk /'bæsɪlɪsk/ *n* **1** small American lizard with a hollow crest that can swell up with air. **2** fabulous reptile able to cause death by its look or breath.

basin /'beɪsn/ *n* **1** round, open dish of metal, pottery, etc for holding liquids; contents of a ~. ⇨ **wash-~.** **2** bowl for preparing or serving food in. **3** hollow place where water collects (eg a stone structure at the base of a fountain, a deep pool at the base of a waterfall). **4** deep part of a harbour that is almost surrounded by land; dock with gates that control the inflow and outflow of water. **5** area of country drained by a river and its tributaries: *the Thames ~.*

basis /'beɪsɪs/ *n* (*pl* bases /'beɪsiːz/) **1** substance into which others are mixed; most important part of a mixture. **2** foundation (usu fig): *the ~ of morality; on a solid ~; arguments that have a firm ~,* that are founded in facts. *On the ~ of our sales forecasts* (ie From what these indicate) *we may begin to make a profit next year.*

bask /bɑːsk US: bæsk/ *vi* [VP2C] enjoy warmth and light: *sitting in the garden, ~ing in the sunshine;* (fig) *~ing in her favour/approval.*

bas-ket /'bɑːskɪt US: 'bæskɪt/ *n* **1** container, usu made of materials that bend and twist easily (eg osiers, canes, rushes) with or without a handle: *a 'shopping ~; a 'clothes ~; a waste-'paper ~.* **2** as much as a ~ holds: *They ate a ~ of plums. ~-ball* /'bɑːskɪtbɔːl US: 'bæs-/ *n* game (resembling netball), played by two teams of five players who try to throw a large inflated ball into an open-ended net fixed 10 ft above the ground. ⇨ netball.

bas-relief /,bæs rɪ'liːf/ *n* [U] (= *low relief*) form of art in which a flat surface of metal or stone is cut away so that a design or picture stands out as on a coin but often to a greater degree; [C] example of this. ⇨ the illus at church.

bass[1] /bæs/ *n* (*pl* unchanged) (zool) kinds of fish (perch) used as food, caught in rivers, lakes and in the sea.

bass[2] /beɪs/ *adj* deep-sounding; low in tone. □ *n* lowest part in music (voice and instruments); singer or instrument with lowest notes: *,~-clari'net; ,~ 'drum,* ⇨ the illus at percussion; *,double-'~,* ⇨

basketball

the illus at string; $\sim$'*clef,* $\Rightarrow$ the illus at notation.
bass[3] /bæs/ *n* [U] inner fibrous bark of the lime-tree, used for weaving baskets, mats, etc and for tying plants.
Bass /bæs/ *n* (P) beer made by the brewers named Bass.
bas·si·net /ˌbæsɪ'net/ *n* baby's cradle or carriage made of woven wicker, with a hood.
bas·soon /bə'su:n/ *n* musical wind-instrument with double reeds, made of wood, giving very low notes. $\Rightarrow$ illus at brass.
bast /bæst/ *n* [U] **1** = bass[3]. **2** other fibrous barks (eg raffia) used for tying and weaving.
bas·tard /'bɑ:stəd *US:* 'bæs-/ *n* **1** illegitimate child: (attrib) *a* $\sim$ *child/daughter/son.* **2** $\triangle$ (also as *int*) ruthless insensitive person (used as a term of abuse): *You heartless* $\sim$! *He's a real* $\sim$, *leaving his wife in that way;* (also, not abusively, friendly colloq): *Harry, you old* $\sim$! *Fancy meeting you here!* **3** $\triangle$ unfortunate fellow: *Poor* $\sim$! *He's been sacked and he won't find another job very easily;* (also of an unfortunate incident, state, etc): *this* $\sim$ *of a headache/essay.* **4** (usu attrib) (of things) not genuine or authentic; spurious. '$\sim$-**ize** *vt* **1** prove to be, pronounce as a $\sim$. **2** make spurious: *a* $\sim$*ized account of what happened.* $\sim$y *n* (legal) illegitimacy: *a* $\sim$*y order,* one (made by a magistrate) for the support of an illegitimate by its father (now called a *maintenance order*).
baste[1] /beɪst/ *vt* [VP6A,15B] (in making clothes, etc) sew pieces together with long temporary stitches (so that adjustments are possible afterwards).
baste[2] /beɪst/ *vt* [VP6A] $\sim$ *meat,* pour over it the fat, juices, etc which come from it during cooking.
baste[3] /beɪst/ *vt* [VP6A] thrash; beat.
bas·ti·nado /ˌbæstɪ'nɑ:dəʊ/ *n* (*pl* $\sim$es) caning on the soles of the feet. $\square$ *vt* [VP6A] punish by caning in this way.
bas·tion /'bæstɪən/ *n* (often five-sided) part of a fortification that stands out from the rest; (fig) military stronghold near hostile territory; (fig) sth preserved from destruction or change.
bat[1] /bæt/ *n* small mouse-like animal that flies at night and feeds on fruit and insects. $\Rightarrow$ the illus at small. **have bats in the belfry,** (sl) be eccentric, have queer ideas. **as blind as a bat,** unable to see, not seeing, clearly.
bat[2] /bæt/ *n* **1** shaped wooden implement for striking the ball in games, esp cricket and baseball. $\Rightarrow$ the illus at these entries. **carry one's bat,** (cricket) be 'not out' at the end of the innings. **do sth off one's own bat,** (fig) do it without help. **2** = batsman: *He's a useful bat.* $\square$ *vi,vt* (-tt-) **1** [VP2A,B,C] use a bat: *Green batted (for) two hours,* was at the wicket for two hours. **2** [VP6A] hit (with a bat).
bats·man /-smən/ *n* (*pl* -men) **1** (cricket) player

who bats: *He's a good batsman but no good as a bowler.* **2** (aviation) man who uses a pair of bats (like those used in table-tennis) to guide an aircraft as and after it touches down (eg on the deck of an aircraft-carrier).
bat[3] /bæt/ *n* **go off at a terrific/rare bat,** (sl) at a fast rate.
bat[4] /bæt/ *vt* (-tt-) (sl) wink. **not bat an eyelid, (a)** not sleep at all. **(b)** not show any surprise.
batch /bætʃ/ *n* **1** number of loaves, cakes, etc baked together: *baked in* $\sim$*es of twenty.* **2** number of persons or things receiving attention as a group: *a* $\sim$ *of letters to be answered; a* $\sim$ *of recruits for the army.*
bate /beɪt/ *vt* = abate. **with** $\sim$**d breath,** with the voice lowered to a whisper (in expectancy, anxiety, etc).
bath /bɑːθ *US:* bæθ/ *n* (*pl* $\sim$s /bɑːðz *US:* bæðz/) **1** washing of the body, esp by putting oneself completely in water: *I shall have a hot* $\sim$ *and go to bed. He takes a cold* $\sim$ *every morning.* '$\sim$-**robe** *n* loose-fitting robe worn before and after taking a $\sim$. **2** water for a $\sim$: *Your* $\sim$ *is ready.* '$\sim$-**tub** *n* (usu *bath* in GB except in trade use) large (usu oblong) vessel (of fibre-glass, porcelain or metal) in which $\sim$s are taken. '$\sim$-**room** *n* room in which there is a $\sim$-tub (and usu a wash-hand-basin): *Every room in the hotel has a private* $\sim$*room,* ie its own $\sim$room. **3** (container for) liquid in which sth is washed or dipped (in chemical and industrial processes): *an 'oil* $\sim$, (for parts of a machine); *a* '*hypo* $\sim$, (photography). **4** (*pl*) place where one can bath or swim: *public swimming* $\sim$*s; the Turkish* $\sim$*s.* $\square$ *vt,vi* [VP6A,2A] give a $\sim$ to: $\sim$ *the baby;* take a bath: *I* $\sim$ *every night.*
Bath /bɑːθ *US:* bæθ/ *n* (town in W England, with hot mineral springs). $\sim$-'**chair** *n* three-wheeled chair for an invalid, pushed or pulled by hand.
bathe /beɪð/ *vt,vi* **1** apply water to; soak in water; put in water: *The doctor told him to* $\sim$ *his eyes twice a day. The nurse* $\sim$*d the wound.* **2** [VP6A] **be** $\sim$*d in,* be made wet or bright all over: *Her face was* $\sim$*d in tears. The countryside was* $\sim$*d in brilliant sunshine. He was* $\sim$*d in sweat,* $\Rightarrow$ also sun(4). **3** [VP2A] go into the sea, a river, lake, etc for sport, swimming, to get cool, etc. $\square$ *n* act of swimming in the sea, a river, lake, etc: *We had an enjoyable* $\sim$ *before breakfast. Let's go for a* $\sim$. Cf *have/take a bath.* **bather** /'beɪðə(r)/ *n*
bath·ing /'beɪðɪŋ/ *n* act or practice of going into the sea, etc: *The* $\sim$ *here is safe,* It is safe to swim here. *He's fond of* $\sim$. *There have been many fatal* $\sim$ *accidents here,* Many bathers have been drowned here. '$\sim$-**cap** *n* cap to cover a woman's hair while in the water. '$\sim$-**costume/suit** *n* garment worn for swimming (cf *bikini, swimming-trunks*). '$\sim$-**machine** *n* cabin on wheels, pulled down to the water's edge and (formerly) used by bathers for dressing and undressing.
bathos /'beɪθɒs/ *n* [U] (rhet) sudden change (in writing or speech) from what is deeply moving or sublime to what is foolish or unimportant.
bathy·sphere /'bæθɪsfɪə(r)/ *n* large, strongly built, hollow sphere that can be lowered to great depths in the sea, for observation of marine life.
ba·tik /bə'tiːk/ *n* [U] method (originally in Java) of printing coloured designs on textiles by waxing the parts not to be dyed; [C] example of such a fabric.
ba·tiste /bæ'tiːst/ *n* [U] fine thin linen or cotton cloth.

bat·man /ˈbætmən/ *n* (*pl* -men /-mən/) (GB mil) army officer's personal servant.

baton /ˈbætən *US:* bəˈtɒn/ *n* **1** policeman's short, thick stick, used as a weapon: *The police made a ~ charge*, drove the crowd back by using their ~s. **2** short, thin stick used by the conductor of a band or an orchestra. **3** staff of office: *a Field-Marshal's ~*.

bats /bæts/ *pred adj* (sl) mad; eccentric. ⇨ also bat¹.

bat·tal·ion /bəˈtælɪən/ *n* army unit made up of several companies and forming part of a regiment or brigade.

bat·ten¹ /ˈbætn/ *n* long board, esp one used to keep other boards in place, or to which other boards are nailed; (on a ship) strip of wood or metal used to fasten down covers or tarpaulins over a hatch. □ *vt* [VP6A,15B] ~ *sth (down)*, make secure with ~s: *~ down the hatches.*

bat·ten² /ˈbætn/ *vi* [VP3A] ~ *on/upon*, thrive, grow fat on (esp at the expense of others, or so as to injure others).

bat·ter¹ /ˈbætə(r)/ *vt,vi* [VP6A,15A,B,2C] strike hard and often; beat out of shape: *The heavy waves ~ed the wrecked ship to pieces. Let's ~ the door down. Someone was ~ing (away) at the door. He was driving a badly ~ed old car and wearing a ~ed old hat.* '~·ing ram *n* /-tərɪŋ/ (mil) big, heavy log with an iron head used in olden times for ~ing down walls.

bat·ter² /ˈbætə(r)/ *n* [U] beaten mixture of flour, eggs, milk, etc for cooking.

bat·tery /ˈbætərɪ/ *n* (*pl* -ries) **1** army unit of big guns, with men and vehicles. **2** group of big guns on a warship, or for coastal defence. **3** portable cell for supplying electricity: *a 'car ~. This transistor has four small batteries.* ⇨ cell(3). **4** set of similar utensils or instruments used together: *a ~ of lenses/ovens.* **5** *assault and ~*, (legal) attack upon or threatening touch (to sb). **6** series of boxes, etc in which hens are kept for laying eggs or for fattening. ~ 'farm *n* farm for hens kept in batteries. '~ hen *n* hen kept in a ~. ⇨ *free-range* at free¹(3).

bat·ting /ˈbætɪŋ/ *n* [U] cotton wool in flat wads.

battle /ˈbætl/ *n* **1** [C] fight, esp between organized and armed forces (armies, navies, aircraft); (fig) any struggle: *the ~ of life.* **2** [U] victory; success: *The ~ is to the strong*, The strong are likely to win. *Youth is half the ~*, Youthful strength brings likelihood of success. **3** [U] *die in ~*, die fighting. *give/offer ~*, show readiness to fight. *refuse ~*, refuse to fight. □ *vi* [VP3A] ~ *(with/against sth) (for sth)*, struggle: *battling against adversity. They ~d with the winds and waves.* '~-axe *n* (a) heavy axe with a long handle, formerly used as a weapon. (b) (colloq) domineering and assertive woman. '~-cruiser *n* large fast cruiser with heavy guns and lighter armour than a ~ship. '~-dress *n* soldier's uniform of belted blouse and trousers. '~-field *n* place where a ~ is or was fought. '~-ground *n* ~field. '~-ship *n* large kind of warship, with big guns and heavy armour.

battle·dore /ˈbætldɔː(r)/ *n* bat or small racket used in the game called ~ and shuttlecock. ⇨ the illus at badminton.

battle·ments /ˈbætlmənts/ *n pl* flat roof of a tower or castle enclosed by parapets with openings through which to shoot.

bat·tue /bæˈtuː/ *n* [C] driving of game¹(6) (by beating bushes, etc) towards the sportsmen; occasion

when this is done.

batty /ˈbætɪ/ *adj* (sl) (of a person) crazy; slightly mad. ⇨ bats.

bauble /ˈbɔːbl/ *n* pretty, bright and pleasing ornament of little value.

baulk /bɔːk/ ⇨ balk.

baux·ite /ˈbɔːksaɪt/ *n* [U] clay-like substance from which aluminium is obtained.

baw·bee /ˈbɔːbiː/ *n* (Scot) halfpenny.

bawd /bɔːd/ *n* (old use) woman who keeps a brothel. ~y *adj* (of talk, persons) vulgar; humorously coarse: *~y talk/stories; a ~y old man.* □ *n* ~y talk, etc. ~·ily *adv*

bawl /bɔːl/ *vt,vi* [VP6A,15A,2C,3A] shout or cry loudly: *He ~ed out a curse. He ~ed to me across the street. The frightened child ~ed for help. ~ sb out*, (US, sl) scold severely.

bay¹ /beɪ/ *n* **1** (also 'bay-tree, 'bay laurel) kind of tree or shrub with leaves that are used in cooking and are spicy when crushed. **2 bays, 'bay-wreath**, laurel wreath given in olden times to poets and heroes, victors in war and athletic contests; (fig) honour; glory. **3 bay rum**, hair lotion, made from the leaves of a W Indian tree.

bay² /beɪ/ *n* part of the sea or of a large lake, enclosed by a wide curve of the shore: *the Bay of Biscay; Hudson Bay.*

bay³ /beɪ/ *n* **1** compartment between columns and pillars that divide a building into regular parts. **2** extensions of a room beyond the line of one or two of its walls; recess. ˌbay 'window, window, usu with glass on three sides, built in such a recess. ⇨ the illus at window. **3** side-line and platform in a railway station, used as a starting-point and terminus for local trains, separate from the main lines. **4** compartment in the fuselage of an aircraft: *the 'bomb bay;* part of a warship, college campus, etc for those who are ill or injured: *the'sick-bay;* compartment in a warehouse, barn etc for storing things: *Put the equipment in No 3 bay.*

bay⁴ /beɪ/ *n* deep bark, esp of hounds while hunting. *at bay*, (of a hunted animal) forced to face its attackers and show defiance; (fig) in a desperate position, compelled to struggle fiercely. *keep/hold sb at bay*, keep an enemy, etc at a distance; prevent him from coming too near. *bring (a stag, an enemy) to bay*, force (it, him) to make a final resistance; come to close quarters so that escape is impossible. □ *vi* [VP2A] (esp of large dogs, hounds) bark with a deep note, esp continuously, when hunting.

bay⁵ /beɪ/ *adj, n* reddish-brown (horse): *He was riding a dark bay.*

bay·onet /ˈbeɪənɪt/ *n* dagger-like blade that can be fixed to the muzzle of a rifle and used in hand-to-hand fighting. □ *vt* [VP6A] stab with a ~.

a bayonet

bayou /ˈbaɪuː/ *n* (in N America) marshy offshoot of a river.

ba·zaar /bəˈzɑː(r)/ *n* **1** (in Iran, India and other Eastern countries) street of workshops and shops; that part of a town where the markets and shopping streets are. **2** (in GB, US) shop for the sale of cheap goods of great variety. **3** (place where there is a)

sale of goods for charitable purposes: *a church* ~.
ba·zoo·ka /bə'zu:kə/ *n* (*pl* ~s) portable weapon
for firing armour-piercing rockets.
be¹ /bi:/ *vi* (*pres t* am /*after* 'I':m; *otherwise:* əm;
strong form: æm/, is /z/; *but* s *after* p, t, k, f, θ;
strong form: ɪz/, are /ə(r)/; *strong form:* ɑ:(r)/; *pt*
was /wəz/; *strong form:* wɒz/, were /wə(r)/; *strong
form:* wɜ:(r)/; contracted forms, I'm /aɪm/, he's
/hi:z/, she's /ʃi:z/, it's /ɪts/, we're /wɪə(r)/,
you're /jʊə(r)/, they're /ðeə(r)/; *neg* isn't/'ɪznt/,
aren't /ɑ:nt/, wasn't /'wɒznt/, weren't /wɜ:nt/;
Am I not is contracted to *aren't I* /'ɑ:nt aɪ *US:*
'ænt/; *pres p* being /'bi:ɪŋ/; *pp* been /bi:n *US:*
bɪn/) [VP1] (linking *v* (or *copula*), between the
subject and various complements) **1** (with a *n* or
pron, identifying or asking about the subject): *Today is Monday. Peter is a teacher/a Catholic. Who
is that? It's me/him/her/the postman.* **2** (with an
adj or a *prep*, indicating a quality, an attribute):
*The world is round. He is ten years old. Short
skirts are in/out of fashion.* ⇨ **fashionable, unfashionable. 3** (with a *prep* or *adverbial particle*,
indicating a place): *The lamp is on the table.
John's out in the garden. Mary's upstairs. The station is a mile away.* **4** (with a *n* or a *prep*, indicating possession, actual or intended): *The money's
not yours, it's John's. The parcel is for you.*
be² /bi:/ *vi* ⇨ be¹ [VP1] (linking *v*, indicating a
change from one quality, place, etc to another): *He
wants to be* (= become) *a fireman when he grows
up. Give me a pound, and the skirt is* (= will be)
yours. You can be (= get) *there in five minutes.
Once more he was* (= again became) *the old John
we used to know. Suddenly his face was* (= became) *scarlet.*
be³ /bi:/ *vi* ⇨ be¹ [VP1] **1** (with introductory *there*):
*There's a bus-stop down the road. There were six
of us. There are some stamps in that drawer.
There's a letter for you,* A letter has come for you.
(Cf *One of the letters is for you*). **2** (also with introductory *there*, meaning 'exist'): *There is a God.
For there to be life there must be air and water.* **3**
go; come (esp the *pp* been): *I've been to see* (=
have paid a visit to) *my uncle. Have you ever been
to Cairo? He has been to Paris.* (Cf *He's gone to
Paris,* ie is now either in Paris or on the way
there.) *Has the postman been* (ie called) *yet?* **4
the ,be-all and 'end-all (of sth),** the
most important part (of it). **been and...,** (vulg or
hum) (used to express surprise, protest, etc):
*You've been and bought a new hat! Who's been
and taken my dictionary?* **for the time being,** until
some other arrangement. ⇨ also being. **the ...-
to-be,** the future ...: *the bride/mother-to-be.*
'would-be *adj* who wishes to be or imagines himself to be: *a would-be poet.* **might-have been** *n*
[C] past possibility.
be⁴ /bi:/ *aux v* ⇨ be¹ **1** (used with *pres p* to form
the progressive or continuous tenses): *They are/
were reading. I shall be seeing him soon. What
have you been doing this week?* **2** (used with a *pp*
to form the passive voice): *He was killed in the
war. Where were they made? He is to be pitied.* **3**
[VP4F] (used with a *to*-infinitive) **(a)** (equivalent to
must or *ought,* to indicate duty, necessity, etc): *I
am to inform you* (= I have been told to inform
you) *that... You are* (= ought, deserve) *to be congratulated.* **(b)** intention: *They are to be married in
May.* **(c)** possibility: *The book was not to be* (=
could not be) *found.* **(d)** a supposition or unreal

condition: *If I were to tell you/Were I to tell you...;
If it were to rain* (= If it rained) *tomorrow....* **(e)**
(chiefly *pt*) destiny: *He was never to see his wife
and family again,* Although he did not know this at
the time, he did not see them again. **(f)** mutual arrangement: *We are to be married in May. Every
member of the party was to pay his own expenses.*
(g) the expressed wish of another person: *At what
time am I* (= do you want me) *to be there?* **(h)** purpose: *The telegram was to say that she had been
delayed.*
be- /bɪ-/ *pref* **1** all over; in every direction **(a)**
(making *vv* from *vv*): *besmear,* smear all over
(with sth). **(b)** (making *vv from nn*): *bedew,* cover
with dew. **2** (making an intransitive *v* transitive):
bemoan. Cf *bemoan one's fate,* moan about one's
fate. **3** (making *adjj* in *-ed* from *nn*) wearing: *be-
wigged;* covered with: *bejewelled.* **4** (intensifying):
begrudge; belabour.
beach /bi:tʃ/ *n* shore between high- and low-water
mark, covered with sand or water-worn pebbles.
'~ **ball** *n* very large light-weight one used for
games on the ~. '~ **buggy** *n* small motorized vehicle, used for racing on waste ground, beaches,
etc. '~·**comber** /-kəʊmə(r)/ *n* **(a)** long wave rolling in from the sea. **(b)** man who makes a poor living on the waterfront in ports in the Pacific. '~·
head *n* fortified position established on a ~ by an
invading army. ⇨ bridgehead. '~·**wear** *n* [U]
clothes for sunbathing, swimming, playing games,
etc on the ~. □ *vt* [VP6A] push or pull (a boat, a
ship) up on to the shore or ~.
bea·con /'bi:kən/ *n* **1** (old use; also '~-**fire**) fire lit
on a hill-top as a signal. **2** light on a hill or mountain, or on the coast, on rocks, etc to give warning
of danger or for the guidance of ships, etc. **3** (also
'~-**light**) fixed lantern to warn or guide ships;
flashing light to warn aircraft of high mountains,
etc. **4** (in GB) seven-foot high post with a lamp,
used to indicate a street-crossing for pedestrians:
flashing ~ or *Belisha* /bə'li:ʃə/ ~, one with a light
that flashes, to warn motorists that pedestrians have
priority over wheeled traffic. **5** (US) = beam(4).
bead /bi:d/ *n* **1** small ball of wood, glass, etc with a
hole through it, for threading with others on a
string or wire; (*pl*) necklace of ~s. **2 tell one's
~s,** (old use) say one's prayers (while counting ~s
on a rosary). **3** drop of liquid: *His face was covered
with* ~s *of sweat.* ~·**ing** *n* wooden strip with a pattern of ~s, used for ornament; similar pattern on
stonework; lace trimmings, etc with ~s on the
threads.
beadle /'bi:dl/ *n* (formerly) parish officer who
helped the priest by keeping order in church, giving
out money to the poor, etc.
beady /'bi:dɪ/ *adj* (of eyes) small, round and bright.
beagle /'bi:gl/ *n* small, short-legged hound used for
hunting hares when those who take part are on foot,
not on horse-back. **beag·ling** /-glɪŋ/ *n* hunting
hares with ~s.
beak¹ /bi:k/ *n* **1** hard, horny part of a bird's mouth,
esp when curved. ⇨ the illus at prey. **2** ram at the
prow of a warship in ancient times.
beak² /bi:k/ *n* **1** (sl) magistrate: *brought up before
the* ~. **2** (old use; sl) schoolmaster.
beaker /'bi:kə(r)/ *n* **1** open glass vessel with a lip
(as used for chemical experiments, etc). **2** (liter or
archaic) large drinking vessel; goblet. **3** plastic
vessel, shaped like and used as a drinking glass.
beam /bi:m/ *n* **1** long horizontal piece of squared

timber, or of steel, light alloy, concrete, supported at both ends, used to carry the weight of a building, etc. **2** horizontal cross-timber in a ship, joining the sides and supporting the deck(s); the greatest width of a ship, ⇨ the illus at ship. **on/off the port/ starboard** ∼, on/at a distance from either side. **on her** ∼-**ends,** (of a ship) lying over to one side; almost capsizing. **be on one's** ∼-**ends,** (of a person) at the end of one's financial resources; destitute. **broad in the** ∼, (colloq, of a person) wide and stocky. **3** (a) crosspiece of a balance, from which the scales hang. ⇨ the illus at balance. (b) chief piece of timber. in an old-style plough, to which the share is fastened. **4** (a) ray or stream of light (eg from a lamp or lighthouse, the sun or moon); (fig) bright look or smile, showing happiness, etc: *with a* ∼ *of delight.* (b) directed electromagnetic waves: *the* ∼ *system,* by which short waves are directed to a specific target. (c) radio signal used to direct an aircraft on its course. **on/ off the** ∼, (of an aircraft) following/not following the radio ∼; (colloq) on the right/wrong track; behaving in a way likely/unlikely to be right. □ *vt,vi* **1** [VP2C] (of the sun, etc) send out light and warmth; (fig) smile happily and cheerfully: ∼*ing on his friends;* ∼*ing with satisfaction.* **2** [VP6A,15] ∼ **sth (to),** (telegraphy) broadcast (a message, radio programme, etc) in a particular direction: ∼*ed from Britain to S America.*

bean /biːn/ *n* **1** (any of several plants bearing) seed in long pods (all used as vegetables): *broad* ∼*s,* 'kidney ∼*s,* 'soya ∼*s.* ⇨ the illus at vegetable. '∼-**stalk** *n* stalk of tall-growing varieties of ∼. **2** seed similar in shape of other plants (esp 'coffee-∼*s,* also called *berries*). **3** (sl uses) **be without/ not have a** ∼, be without any money. **full of** ∼*s,* lively; in high spirits or vigour. **give sb** ∼*s,* punish or scold him. **old** ∼, (dated sl, as a familiar form of address) old boy/fellow. **spill the** ∼*s,* give away information, esp sth not intended to be made known. '∼-**feast; beano** /'biːnəʊ/ *nn* (dated colloq) feast; celebration; jolly time.

bear¹ /beə(r)/ *n* **1** large, heavy animal with thick fur. ⇨ cub, whelp. '∼-**skin** *n* tall military headdress of black fur (worn by the Brigade of Guards in Britain). **2** rough, clumsy ill-mannered person. **3 the Great/Little B**∼, names of two constellations in the northern hemisphere. **4** (stock exchange) person who sells stock for future delivery hoping before then to buy it cheap. ⇨ bull¹(3). ∼**ish** *adj* rough; clumsy.

POLAR BEAR

GRIZZLY BEAR

bears

bear² /beə(r)/ *vt,vi* (*pt* bore /bɔː(r)/, *pp* borne /bɔːn/) **1** [VP6A,15B] carry: ∼ *a heavy load.* ∼ **away,** (now usu *carry off*): ∼ *away the palm,* ex-

cel in competition, by winning a prize, etc; ∼ *away* (ie win) *the prize.* **2** [VP6A] have; show: ∼ *the marks/signs/traces of blows/wounds/ punishment; a document that* ∼*s your signature;* ∼ *arms,* be provided with weapons; ∼ *no/some/not much/little resemblance to sb or sth.* **3** [VP6A] have; be known by: ∼ *a good character; a family that bore an ancient and honoured name.* **4** [VP16B] ∼ **oneself, (a)** carry oneself in a specified way: *He* ∼*s himself like a soldier,* stands, walks, etc like one. **(b)** behave; conduct oneself: *He bore himself with dignity in these difficult circumstances.* **5** [VP14,12C] ∼ **(against/towards),** have in the heart or mind: ∼ *a grudge against sb;* ∼ *no malice towards sb; bear sb no malice; the love/ hatred she bore him,* felt towards him. **6** [VP6A,14,11] bring; provide. ∼ *a hand,* help. ∼ **witness (to sth),** (fig) provide evidence; speak in support: *actions that* ∼ *witness to his courage. Will you* ∼ *witness (for me) that I am innocent?* ∼ **false witness (against sb),** give false evidence. **7** [VP6A,2A] support; sustain: *The ice is too thin to* ∼ *your weight. The ice doesn't* ∼ *yet. Who will* ∼ *the responsibility/expense?* **8** [VP6A,6D,7A,17] (usu with *can/could,* and esp in neg and interr) endure; tolerate; put up with: *I can't* ∼ *(the sight of) that old man. The pain was almost more than he could* ∼. *There's no* ∼*ing* (= It's impossible to ∼) *such rude fellows. She couldn't* ∼ *to see animals treated cruelly. She can't* ∼ *to be laughed at/can't* ∼ *being laughed at.* **9** [VP6E] be fit for: *His language won't* ∼ *repeating. Your joke will* ∼ *repeating,* is amusing enough to be heard again. **10** [VP6A,12C] give birth to: ∼ *a child. She has borne him six sons.* Cf *born:* The eldest son was born in 1932. **11** [VP2C] ∼ **(to the),** (of direction) turn, incline: *When you reach the top of the hill,* ∼ *(to the) right.* **12** [VP15B,2C,3A] (with *adverbial particles* and *preps*): **bear down,** overcome; defeat: ∼ *down the enemy;* ∼ *down all resistance.* ∼ *down on/upon,* (esp of a ship, car) move quickly towards. **be borne 'in on/upon sb,** (of sb) be made to realize: *The terrible truth was borne in on him,* he had to realize it. *It was gradually borne in on me that…, The idea that… was one that I gradually had to accept.* **bear on/upon,** have relation to, have influence on, be relevant to: *How does this* ∼ *upon the problem? These are matters that* ∼ *upon the welfare of the community.* **bring to** ∼ *on/upon,* make (sth) relate to, have influence on: *bring all one's energies to* ∼ *upon a task; bring pressure to* ∼ *on sb.* ∼ *hard/heavily/severely, etc on/upon,* be a burden on: *Taxation* ∼*s heavily on all classes in Britain.* **bear (sth or sb) out,** confirm (sth); support (sb): ∼ *out a statement. John will* ∼ *me out/*∼ *out what I've said.* **bear up (against/under sth),** be strong in the face of (sorrow, etc): *He bore up well against all these misfortunes. Tell her to* ∼ *up,* to have courage, not give way. **bear with sb,** treat him patiently or indulgently: *If you will* ∼ *with me* (ie listen patiently to me) *a little longer….* **bear·able** /'beərəbl/ *adj* (from bear²(8)) that can be borne or endured.

beard¹ /bɪəd/ *n* **1** hair of the lower part of the face (excluding the moustache): *a man with a* ∼; *a week's (growth of)* ∼; similar growth of hair on an animal: *a billy-goat's* ~. **2** ~-like sheath on the grain of barley, oats, etc. ~**ed** *adj* having a ~. ~**·less** *adj* having no ~: *a* ~*less youth.*

beard² /bɪəd/ *vt* [VP6A] defy openly, oppose: ~ *the lion in his den,* (fig) defy sb in his own stronghold.

bearer /'beərə(r)/ *n* **1** person who brings a letter or message: *the* ~ *of good news; the* ~ *of this letter.* **2** person who helps to carry a coffin to a grave, who carries a stretcher, flag, etc. **3** person employed to carry sth. **4** person who presents, at a bank, a cheque payable on demand. '~ **bonds** *n pl* bonds, interest on which is payable to the ~, the owner's name not being written on them. **5** (with *adjj*) plant, tree, etc that produces fruit, crops, etc: *a good/poor* ~.

bear·ing /'beərɪŋ/ *n* **1** [U] way of behaving; way of standing, walking, etc: *a man of noble/soldierly* ~. *His kindly* ~ *caused all the children to like him.* ⇨ bear²(4). **2** [C,U] relation, aspect: *We must consider the question in all its* ~*s. What he said has no/not much* ~ *on* (ie is not connected with) *the subject.* ⇨ bear²(12). **3** [U] possibility of being endured; endurance: *His conduct was beyond* (*all*) ~. ⇨ bear²(8). **4** [C] direction in which a place, etc, lies (as measured, eg in degrees): *take a compass* ~ *on a lighthouse;* (*pl*) relative position; direction. **get/take one's** ~**s,** find the direction of a ship's course; find one's position by looking round for landmarks, etc. **lose/be out of one's** ~**s,** be lost; (fig) be puzzled. **5** (usu *pl*) (in a machine) device that supports moving parts and reduces friction: *ball/roller* ~*s.* **6** [U] (of a tree, etc): *in full* ~, producing fruit well. ⇨ child-~.

bear·ish /'beərɪʃ/ *adj* ⇨ bear¹.

beast /biːst/ *n* **1** four-footed animal (*animal* is the usu word; *beast* is used in fables). **2** (farming) cow or bullock; animal for riding or driving. **3** cruel or disgusting person. **4** (reproachfully or playfully) person who behaves badly: *They hate that* ~ *of a foreman!* (eg of a foreman who is very strict). ~**·ly** *adj* **1** like a ~ or its ways; unfit for human use. **2** (colloq) nasty: *What* ~*ly weather!* □ *adv* (colloq; used to intensify *adjj* and *advv* used in a bad sense) very; unpleasantly: *He was* ~*ly drunk.* ⇨ jolly. *It was* ~*ly cold.* ~**·li·ness** /-lɪnɪs/ *n* [U]

beat¹ /biːt/ *vt,vi* (*pt* beat, *pp* ~en /'biːtn/) (**a**) [VP6A,14,2A,C] hit repeatedly (esp with a stick): *She was* ~*ing the carpet/* ~*ing the dust out of the carpet. He was* ~*ing a drum. We heard the drums* ~*ing/being* ~*en. The boy was* ~*en until he was black and blue,* covered with bruises. *The hunters had to* ~ *a way through the undergrowth,* make a path by forcing the branches, etc down. *Somebody was* ~*ing at/upon the door.* ~ **one's brains,** ⇨ brain(4). ~ **a retreat,** give the signal (by drum) to retreat; (fig) go back, retire. ~ **the woods,** go into them to drive out game (for sport, shooting). ~**·ing** *n* (**a**) punishment, esp by hitting repeatedly: *give sb/get a good* ~*ing.* (**b**) (colloq) defeat: *Our team got a sound* ~*ing.* **2** [VP2C] (of the sun, rain, wind, etc) strike: *The rain was* ~*ing against the windows.* **3** [VP6A,14] mix thoroughly and let air into by using a fork or similar utensil: ~ *eggs;* ~ *cream* (to a froth); ~ *flour and eggs, etc,* (to a paste). ⇨ whip²(2). **4** [VP6A,22,15B] hammer, change the shape of by blows: ~ *sth flat;* ~ *out gold,* hammer it flat; ~ *the door in,* break in by hammering down the door. **5** [VP6A,14,15A] defeat; do better than: *Our army was* ~*en. I'll* ~ *you*

to the top of that hill, race you and get there first. *He* ~ *me at chess.* ~ **the record,** break the record, make a new and better record. **6** [VP6A] be too difficult for; perplex: *That problem has* ~*en me.* **7** [VP6A,14] move up and down regularly: *The bird was* ~*ing its wings against the sides of the cage. His heart was still* ~*ing. Her heart was* ~*ing with joy.* ~ **time,** measure time (in music) by making regular movements (with the hands, etc). **8** (various uses): ~ **about the bush,** approach a subject without coming to the point. **dead** ~, tired out. ~ **it,** (sl) go away. **9** [VP2C,15B] (with *adverbial particles* and *preps*):

beat down (on), *The sun was* ~*ing down on our heads,* shining with great heat. ~ **sb/sth down:** *He wanted £800 for the car but I* ~ *him down* (= made him lower his price) *to £600. I* ~ *down his price,* made him lower it. *The wheat had been* ~*en down* (= flattened) *by the rain.*

beat sb/sth off, *The attacker/attack was* ~*en off,* repulsed.

beat sth out, *The dry grass caught fire, but we* ~ *it out,* extinguished the fire by ~*ing the burning grass. He* ~ *out* (= drummed) *a tune on a tin can.*

beat sb up, *He was badly* ~*en up* (= beaten severely with cudgels, etc) *in a back alley.* ~ **sth up (into/to),** mix thoroughly and let air into by using a fork or other utensil: ~ *the mixture up to a creamy consistency;* ~ *the flour and eggs* (*up*) *to a paste.*

beat² /biːt/ *n* **1** regular repeated stroke, or sound of this: *We heard the* ~ *of a drum. His heart* ~*s were getting weaker.* **2** recurring emphasis marking rhythm in music or poetry. **3** route over which sb goes regularly; appointed course of a sentinel or policeman: *The policeman was on his* ~, on the route he was ordered to patrol. **be off/out of one's** ~, (fig) be doing sth with which one is not familiar, sth different from one's usual work, etc.

beat³ /biːt/ *attrib adj* of or like beatniks: *the* ~ *generation.* □ *n* = beatnik.

beaten /'biːtn/ *adj* (esp) **1** shaped by beating: ~ *silver.* **2** (of a path) worn hard by use: *a well-* ~ *path.* **go off/keep to the** ~ **track,** do sth/not do anything unusual.

beater /'biːtə(r)/ *n* **1** utensil used for beating, such as: '**carpet-**~, '**egg-**~. **2** man employed to drive birds, etc to those waiting with guns to shoot them.

bea·tif·ic /bɪə'tɪfɪk/ *adj* showing great happiness; making blessed.

be·atify /bɪ'ætɪfaɪ/ *vt* [VP6A] (in the RC church) announce that a dead person is among the Blessed (ie those who will live for ever with God in a state of supreme happiness). **be·ati·fi·ca·tion** /bɪˌætɪfɪ'keɪʃn/ *n* ~ing or being beatified; first step before canonization. ⇨ canonize.

be·ati·tude /bɪ'ætɪtjuːd *US:* -tuːd/ *n* [U] great happiness; blessedness. **The B**~**s,** Christ's sermon on blessedness (in the Bible, Matt 5: 3-11).

beat·nik /'biːtnɪk/ *n* (1950's) person adopting unconventional manners and dress as a defiant protest against current morality and as a means of self-expression. Cf *hippy,* a later word.

beau /bəʊ/ *n* (*pl* ~x /bəʊz/) **1** (old use) rather old man who is greatly interested in the fashion of his clothes. **2** (now usu fac) man who pays great attention to women. **3** (now usu fac) girl's admirer or lover. **4** ~ **ideal,** one's idea of what is most excellent or beautiful. **the** ~ **monde** /ˌbəʊ 'mɔːnd/ (F) fashionable society.

Beau·jo·lais /'bəʊʒəleɪ *US:* ˌbəʊʒə'leɪ/ *n* [U] (F) light wine (usu red) of Burgundy.

beau·te·ous /'bjuːtɪəs/ *adj* (poet) beautiful.

beau·ti·cian /bjuː'tɪʃn/ *n* person who runs a beauty-parlour.

beau·ti·ful /'bjuːtɪfl/ *adj* giving pleasure or delight to the mind or senses: *a ~ face/flower/voice; ~ weather/music*. *~ly /-flɪ/ adv* in a ~ manner: *She sings ~ly. That will do ~ly*, will be most satisfactory. **beau·tify** /'bjuːtɪfaɪ/ *vt* [VP6A] make ~.

beauty /'bjuːtɪ/ *n* **1** [U] combination of qualities that give pleasure to the senses (esp the eye and ear) or to the moral sense or the intellect: *Everyone must admire the ~ of a tropical sunset/a mother's love*. *B~ is only skin deep*, (prov) We must not judge by outward appearance only. **2** [C] (*pl* -ties) person, thing, specimen, feature, characteristic, that is beautiful or particularly good: *Isn't she a ~! Her smile is one of her beauties. Look at this rose—isn't it a ~! I'm always finding new beauties in Shakespeare's poetry. That's the ~ of it*, the point that gives satisfaction. **'~-parlour** *n* establishment (now usu **'~-salon**) in which women receive treatment (of the skin, hair, etc) to increase their ~. **'~ queen** *n* girl voted the most beautiful in a ~ contest. **'~-salon**, = ~-parlour. **'~-sleep** *n* sleep before midnight. **'~-spot** *n* **1** place with beautiful scenery. **2** birthmark or artificial patch on the face, said to heighten ~.

bea·ver¹ /'biːvə(r)/ *n* **1** fur-coated animal that lives both on land and in water, with strong teeth with which it cuts down trees and makes dams across rivers. ⇨ the illus at small. **2** [U] its fur. **3** [U] heavy woollen cloth that looks like ~ fur. **4** [C] high hat made of ~ fur, formerly worn by men.

bea·ver² /'biːvə(r)/ *n* (on the helmet worn by soldiers in olden times) movable lower part that guarded the lips and chin.

bea·ver³ /'biːvə(r)/ *vi* [VP2A,C] ~ *away (at sth)*, (colloq) work hard.

be·bop /'biːbɒp/ = bop.

be·calmed /bɪ'kɑːmd/ *pred adj* (of a sailing-ship) stopped because there is no wind.

be·came *pt* of become.

be·cause /bɪ'kɒz/ *conj* **1** for the reason that: *I did it ~ they asked me to do it. Just ~ I don't complain, you mustn't suppose that I'm satisfied.* (Note that when the reason is obvious, or is thought to be known, it is preferable to use *as*, or a construction with *so: As it's raining, you'd better take a taxi. It's raining so you'd better take a taxi.* After the noun *reason*, *that* is preferred to ~: *The reason why we were late is that...*) **2** ~ *of*, *prep* by reason of; on account of: *B~ of his bad leg, he couldn't walk so fast as the others. I said nothing about it, ~ of his wife('s) being there.*

beck¹ /bek/ *n* (N England) mountain stream or brook.

beck² /bek/ *n* movement of the head, hand or arm, as a signal or sign, used only in: *be at sb's ~ and call*, be bound to obey his orders, to come and go, all the time. *have sb at one's ~ and call*, have sb always waiting to obey one's orders.

beckon /'bekən/ *vt, vi* [VP6A,15B,16A,2A] call sb's attention by a movement of the hand or arm, usu to show that he is to come nearer or to follow: *He ~ed (to) me to follow. He ~ed me on/in.*

be·come /bɪ'kʌm/ *vi, vt* (*pt* became /bɪ'keɪm/, *pp* become) **1** [VP2D] come or grow to be; begin to be: *He became a doctor. He has ~ a famous man.*

The custom has now ~ a rule. He has ~ accustomed to his new duties. It's becoming much more expensive to travel abroad. **2** [VP3A] ~ *of*, happen to: *What will ~ of the children if their father dies? I don't know what has ~ of him.* **3** [VP6A] be well suited to: *Her new hat ~s her.* **4** [VP6A] be right or fitting; befit: *He used language (eg insulting language) that does not ~ a man of his education.* **be·com·ing** *adj* ~ *(to)*, **1** (of dress, etc) well suited to the wearer: *a becoming hat/dress/style of hairdressing.* **2** suitable, appropriate: *with a modesty becoming to his low rank.* **be·com·ing·ly** *adv*

bed¹ /bed/ *n* **1** piece of furniture, or other arrangement, on which to sleep (Note omission and use of the articles): *go to bed; be in bed; get into/out of bed; put the children to bed; sit on the bed; find a bed for sb;* (fig) love-making: *He thinks of nothing but bed.* **single bed**, for one person. **double bed**, for two persons: *I want a room with two single beds/a double bed.* **twin beds**, two exactly similar single beds. **spare bed(room)**, one that is kept for an occasional visitor. **bed and board**, food and lodging; entertainment (at an inn, etc). *make the beds*, put the bedclothes (sheets, blankets, etc) in order, ready for use. *As you make your bed so you must lie on it*, (prov) you must accept the consequences of your acts. *He got out of bed on the wrong side*, said of sb who is bad-tempered for the day. *take to/keep to one's bed*, stay in bed because of illness. **2** mattress: *a feather bed; a spring-bed.* **3** flat base on which sth rests: *The machine rests on a bed of concrete.* **4** bottom of the sea, a river, lake, etc; layer of rock, stone, etc, as a foundation for a road or railway; layer of clay, rock, etc, below the surface soil: *If you dig here, you will find a bed of clay.* **'bed-rock**, solid rock below the soil, found at different depths in different places; (fig) ultimate facts or principles on which a theory, etc, is based: *reach/get down to bed-rock.* **5** garden plot, piece of ground (for flowers, vegetables, etc): *'seed-bed;* '*onion-bed;* '*flower beds.* **6** (compounds) **'bed-bug** *n* wingless, blood-sucking insect. **'bed-clothes** *n pl* sheets, blankets, etc for a bed. **'bed-fellow** *n* person with whom one shares a bed; (fig) companion. **'bed·pan** *n* vessel for waste matter from the body, used by an invalid in bed. **'bed·post** *n* upright support of a bedstead (esp the old-fashioned sort). **'bed·ridden** *adj* confined to bed by weakness or old age. **'bed·roll** *n* portable roll of bedding (eg as used by campers). **'bed·room** /*with* -dr- *as in* '*dry*', not separated as in '*head-room*'/ *n* room for sleeping in. **'bed·side** *n* side of (esp a sick person's) bed: *Dr Green has a good bedside manner*, is tactful, knows how to fill his patients with confidence in himself; (attrib) *bedside table; bedside books.* **bed·'sit(ter)** (colloq for) ˌbed·'sitting-room *n* room used (eg by students, single persons away from home) for both living in and sleeping in. **'bed·sore** *n* sore on the back, etc of an invalid, caused by lying in bed for a long time. **'bed·spread** *n* covering spread over a bed during the day. **'bed·stead** *n* framework of wood and metal to support the mattress. **'bed·time** *n* time for going to bed: *His usual bedtime is eleven o'clock.*

bed² /bed/ *vt* (-dd-) [VP6A,15A,B] **1** *bed (in/out)*, plant (seedlings, etc): *He was bedding out some young cabbage plants. He bedded the seedlings (in).* **2** *bed (in)*, place or fix in a foundation: *Bricks and stones are bedded in mortar or con-*

crete. The bullet bedded itself in (= went deep into) *the wall. Heavy guns have to be bedded* (*in*) *before they will fire accurately.* **3 bed down,** provide with a bed or bedding: *bed down a horse,* provide it with straw, etc on which to rest; *bed down a soldier/traveller, etc.* **-bed·ded,** having the specified type or number of bed(s): *a single-/double-/twin-bedded room.* **'bed·ding** *n* [U] **1** bedclothes, eg blankets. **2** straw, etc, for animals to sleep on.

be·daubed /bɪ'dɔːbd/ *pred adj* ~ **with,** smeared (with sth dirty, wet, sticky, etc).

bed·ding /'bedɪŋ/ *n* [U] ⇨ bed².

be·decked /bɪ'dekt/ *pred adj* ~ **with,** adorned, decorated (with flowers, jewels, etc).

be·dev·il /bɪ'devl/ *vt* (-ll-, US: -l-) (usu passive) confuse; complicate: *The issue is* ~*led by Smith's refusal to co-operate with us.* ~**·ment** *n*

be·dewed /bɪ'djuːd US: -'duːd/ *pred adj* ~ **with,** (liter) sprinkled with, made wet with: *a face* ~ *with tears.*

be·dim·med /bɪ'dɪmd/ *pred adj* ~ **with,** (liter) (of the eyes, mind) made dim: *eyes* ~ *with tears; a mind* ~ *with sorrow.*

bed·lam /'bedləm/ *n* **1** (old use) asylum for mad people. **2** scene of noisy confusion: *When the teacher was called away the classroom was a regular* ~.

Bed·ouin, Bed·uin /'beduɪn/ *n* (*pl* unchanged) nomadic Arab of the desert.

be·drag·gled /bɪ'drægld/ *pred adj* (esp of clothing) made wet or dirty by rain, mud, etc.

bee /biː/ *n* **1** small, four-winged, stinging insect that produces wax and honey after gathering nectar from flowers. ⇨ the illus at insect. **have a bee in one's bonnet,** be obsessed by an idea. **make a 'bee-line for,** go towards by the shortest way, go quickly towards. **'bee-hive** *n* ⇨ hive(1). **2** (chiefly US) meeting for combined work and amusement (esp of neighbours and friends). **'spelling bee,** competition in spelling.

beech /biːtʃ/ *n* [C] forest tree with smooth bark and shiny dark-green leaves and small triangular nuts; [U] its wood. **'**~ **mast** *n* [U] ~ nuts.

beef /biːf/ *n* **1** [U] flesh of an ox, bull or cow, used as meat. **'**~ **cattle,** bred and reared for ~. ⇨ **dairy** cattle. ~ **tea,** stewed juice from ~ (for people who are ill). **'**~**-steak** *n* ⇨ steak. **'**~**-eater** *n* yeoman of the guard; one of the warders of the Tower of London, dressed as in the days of the Tudor kings. **2** [U] (in men) muscle: *He's got plenty of* ~. **3** [C] (*pl* beeves /biːvz/) fattened ox, considered as food. □ *vi* (sl) complain: *Stop* ~*ing so much!* ~**y** *adj* (of a person) well covered with flesh; strong.

been ⇨ be¹.

beep /biːp/ *n* repeated signal (as during a phone conversation, indicating that it is being recorded).

beer /bɪə(r)/ *n* [U] alcoholic drink made from malt and flavoured with hops; other drinks made from roots, etc: ,ginger-'~, 'nettle-~. **small** ~, sth trifling and unimportant: *He thinks no small* ~ *of himself,* has a high opinion of himself. ~**y** *adj* like ~ in taste or smell; (eg of a person) smelling of ~.

bees·wax /'biːzwæks/ *n* [U] wax made by bees for honeycomb, used for polishing wood. □ *vt* polish with ~.

beet /biːt/ *n* sorts of plant with a sweet root. **'red** ~, used as a vegetable, esp in salads. **'white** ~, used for making sugar. ,~ **'sugar,** sugar made from ~s, identical with cane sugar. **'**~**-root**

/'biːtruːt *with tr as in 'try'*/ *n* [C,U] root of ~; red ~.

beetle¹ /'biːtl/ *n* tool with a heavy head and handle, used for crushing, ramming and smoothing.

beetle² /'biːtl/ *n* insect with hard, shiny wing-covers. ⇨ the illus at insect.

beetle³ /'biːtl/ *vi* [VP2A] overhang; project: *beetling cliffs.* **'**~**-browed** *adj* having shaggy or projecting eyebrows.

beeves ⇨ beef(3).

be·fall /bɪ'fɔːl/ *vt,vi* (*pt* befell /bɪ'fel/ *pp* befallen /bɪ'fɔːlən/) [VP6A] (used only in the 3rd person) (old use) happen (to): *What has* ~*en him?*

be·fit /bɪ'fɪt/ *vt* (-tt-) [VP6A] (used only in 3rd person) (formal) be fitted for; be right and suitable for: *It does not* ~ *a man in your position to....* ~**·ting** *adj* right and proper. ~**·ting·ly** *adv*

be·fog·ged /bɪ'fɒgd US: -'fɔːgd/ *pred adj* (fig, of a person) puzzled; muddle-headed.

be·fore¹ /bɪ'fɔː(r)/ *adv* **1** (contrasted with *afterwards*) at an earlier time; in the past; already: *I've seen that film* ~. *It had been fine the day* ~, the previous day. *You should have told me so* ~, earlier. *That happened long* ~, a long time earlier. **2** (of space or position): *They have gone on* ~, in advance.

be·fore² /bɪ'fɔː(r)/ *conj* (contrasted with *after*) previous to the time when: *I must finish my work* ~ *I go home. Do it now* ~ *you forget. It will be five years* ~ *we meet again* (note the use of the *present t* here). Cf *We shall not meet again* until five years from now.

be·fore³ /bɪ'fɔː(r)/ *prep* **1** (contrasted with *after*) earlier than: *the day* ~ *yesterday; the year* ~ *last; two days* ~ *Christmas;* ~ *the holidays; since* ~ *the war;* ~ *now/then;* ~ *long,* soon. ~ **Christ** (abbr **BC**): *in 55*BC, 55 years before the birth of Christ. **2** (contrasted with *after*) in front of (esp with reference to order or arrangement): *B comes* ~ *C. Ladies* ~ *gentlemen,* ladies first. *Your name comes* ~ *mine on the list.* **3** (contrasted with *behind*) in front of (with reference to position). (Except in a few phrases *in front of* is preferred to *before* in this sense, eg There are some trees *in front of* the house.) *carry all* ~ *one,* be successful in everything one attempts. *sail* ~ *the mast,* as an ordinary seaman, not as an officer. *sail* ~ *the wind,* with the wind behind. **4** in the presence of; face to face with: *He was brought* ~ *the judge. Don't hesitate to speak out* ~ *everyone* (ie in public) *about the way you've been treated.* **5** rather than; in preference to: *Death* ~ *dishonour.*

be·fore·hand /bɪ'fɔːhænd/ *adv* earlier; before¹(1): *I knew what he would need, so I made preparations* ~, in advance, in readiness. *Please let me know* ~. *You ought to have told me* ~. □ *pred adj* ~ (*with*), early; in advance: *When you go on a journey, it's a good thing to be* ~ *with your packing. She's always* ~ *with the rent,* pays it, or is ready to pay it, before it is due.

be·foul /bɪ'faʊl/ *vt* (liter) make dirty.

be·friend /bɪ'frend/ *vt* [VP6A] make a friend of; be kind and helpful to (esp sb younger and needing help).

beg /beg/ *vt,vi* (-gg-) **1** [VP6A,2A,C,3A,14] **beg (for) (sth) (from/of sb),** ask for (food, money, clothes, etc); make a living by asking for money (in the streets, etc): *He begged a meal. He was so poor that he had to beg (for) his bread. He made a living by begging from the rich.* **a begging letter,**

one that asks for help, esp money. **2** [VP6A,7A,17,9,2C,14] ~ **(sth) (of sb)**, ask earnestly, or with deep feeling: *beg a favour of sb*, ask him to help to do sth; *beg (of) sb to do sth. They begged us not to punish them. I beg (of) you not to take any risks. I begged (of) him to stay/that he would stay. The children begged to come with us/ that they might come with us.* **beg the question**, assume (usu unjustifiably) the truth of the matter that is in question. **go begging**, (of things) be unwanted: *If these things are going begging* (= if nobody wants them), *I'll take them.* **beg off**, ask to be excused. *He promised to come and help but has since begged off.* **beg sb off**, ask that sb may be excused or forgiven. ⇨ pardon. **3** [VP7A] take the liberty of (saying or doing sth): *I beg to differ. I beg to state/observe, etc that....*

be-gad /bɪˈgæd/ *int* (old use) by God!

be-gan ⇨ begin.

be-get /bɪˈget/ *vt* (-tt-) (*pt* begot /bɪˈgɒt/, old use begat /bɪˈgæt/, *pp* begotten /bɪˈgɒtn/) [VP6A] **1** (archaic) give existence to (as father): (Bible) *Abraham begat Isaac. The only begotten of the Father,* the only Son of God the Father. **2** (liter) be the cause of: *War ~s misery and ruin.* **~-ter** *n* one who ~s.

beg-gar /ˈbegə(r)/ *n* **1** (also '~**man**, '~**woman**) person who lives by begging, eg for money, food; poor person. **B~s can't be choosers**, must take whatever is offered them. **2** person who begs for others, for charities, etc: *He's a good ~*, successful in collecting money for charity, etc. **3** (colloq; playful or friendly use) person; fellow: *You lucky ~!* □ *vt* **1** [VP6A] make poor, ruin: *You'll ~ your family if you spend so much money on drink.* **2** ~ **description**, make words seem poor and inadequate: *The scenery ~ed description.* **~-ly** *adj* very poor; mean; deserving contempt: *What a ~ly salary to offer me!* **~-y** *n* [U] extreme poverty: *He complained that taxation was reducing him to ~y.*

be-gin /bɪˈgɪn/ *vt,vi* (-nn-, *pt* began /bɪˈgæn/, *pp* begun /bɪˈgʌn/) (For notes on the use of *begin* and *start*, ⇨ start.) **1** [VP6A,2A] start: *When did you ~ English,* learn your first English words? *It's time to ~ work. We shall ~ the meeting at seven o'clock. The meeting will ~ at seven o'clock. He has begun a new book,* is reading (or writing) the first few pages. **~ (on)**, [VP3A the *v* being understood] *He has begun on* (= is reading, writing) *a new book. Has he begun (on) another bottle,* begun to drink another bottle? **2** [VP7A,6D] (used of activities and states that come into existence. The *inf* is preferred when the *pred* denotes a state of mind or a mental activity): *She began to feel dizzy/afraid. I'm ~ning to understand. I began to think you were never coming.* (The *inf* is preferred when the grammatical subject is lifeless, not a person): *The plaster was ~ning to fall from the walls. The barometer began to fall. The water is ~ning to boil. The snow began to melt when the sun came out.* (Either the *inf* or the *gerund* is used when the grammatical subject is a person and when the *pred* indicates an activity or process, not a state. Alternatives are given in the examples. Note that if *begin* is used in one of the progressive tenses, an *inf* follows, not a *gerund*): *When did you begin learning/to learn German? She began crying/to cry. It began raining/to rain. It is ~ning to rain* (not *~ning raining*). **3** ~ **at**, start from: *Today we ~ at page 30, line 12.* **to ~ with**, in the first

place: *We can't give Smith the position; to ~ with, he's too young; secondly, I want my son to have the job.* ~ **life as**, start one's life or career as: *He began life as a builder's labourer.* ~ **the world**, (old use; liter) start in life, enter upon one's career. **~-ner** *n* (esp) person still learning and without much experience. **~-ning** *n* starting point: *I've read the book from ~ning to end. When learning a foreign language, it's important to make a good ~ning. Did democracy have its ~nings in Athens?*

be-gone /bɪˈgɒn *US*: -ˈgɔːn/ *v* (imper only) (liter) go away (stronger than 'Go!'): *B~! B~ dull care!* ⇨ also woe~.

be-gonia /bɪˈgəʊnɪə/ *n* [C] garden plant with brightly coloured leaves and flowers.

be-gorra /bɪˈgɒrə/ *int* (Irish form of) by God!

be-got, be-got-ten ⇨ beget.

be-grimed /bɪˈgraɪmd/ *pred adj* made grimy: *hands ~ with oil and dirt.*

be-grudge /bɪˈgrʌdʒ/ *vt* (intensive form of *grudge*) [VP13A,12A,6C] feel or show dissatisfaction or envy at: *No one ~s you your good fortune. We don't ~ your going to Italy.*

be-guile /bɪˈgaɪl/ **1** [VP6A,14] ~ *sb* **(into)**, cheat, deceive: *They were ~d into forming an unwise alliance.* **2** [VP6A,14] ~ **(with)**, cause (time, etc) to pass pleasantly: *Our journey was ~d with pleasant talk.* **3** [VP6A,14] ~ **(with)**, amuse: *We ~d the children with fairy tales.*

be-gum /ˈbeɪgəm/ *n* Muslim princess or lady of high rank.

be-gun ⇨ begin.

be-half /bɪˈhɑːf *US*: -ˈhæf/ *n in* ~ **of**, (US) in the interest of. **on** ~ **of**, for, in the interest of, on account of, as the representative of. **on my/his/ our/John's, etc** ~, for me/him/us/John, etc: *On ~ of my colleagues and myself,* speaking for them and me. *Don't be uneasy on my ~,* about me.

be-have /bɪˈheɪv/ *vi, reflex* **1** [VP2A,C,6B] act; conduct oneself: *He has ~d shamefully towards his wife,* has treated her in a shameful way. *Can't you make your little boy ~* (*himself*), show good manners, be polite? *The troops ~d gallantly under fire.* **2** [VP2A,C] (of machines, etc) work; function: *How's your new car behaving?* **be-haved** *adj* (in compounds) ,**well-/,badly-'~d**, behaving well/ badly. *What badly ~d children!*

be-hav-iour (*US* = **-ior**) /bɪˈheɪvɪə(r)/ *n* [U] way of behaving; manners (good or bad); treatment shown towards others: *His ~ towards me shows that he does not like me. Tom won a prize for good ~ at school.* **be on one's best ~**, take great care to behave well. **put sb on his best ~**, advise or warn him to behave well. **~-ism** /-ɪzəm/ *n* [U] (psych) doctrine that all human actions could, if full knowledge were available, be analysed into stimulus and response. **~-ist** /-ɪst/ *n* believer in this doctrine.

be-head /bɪˈhed/ *vt* [VP6A] cut off the head of (as a punishment).

be-held ⇨ behold.

be-hest /bɪˈhest/ *n* (old use; only in) **at sb's ~**, on sb's orders: *at the King's ~.*

be-hind[1] /bɪˈhaɪnd/ *adv* (contrasted with *ahead* or *in front*) **1** in the rear: *The dog was running ~. The others are a long way ~. The enemy attacked us from ~.* **fall/lag ~**, fail to keep up: *Keith was tired and fell ~.* **stay/remain ~**, stay after others have left. **2** **be ~ with/in**, be in arrears with: *Are you ~ with your work/studies, etc,* Have you done less than you ought to have done? *He was ~ in his payments*, had not made payments (eg of rent) when they were due.

be·hind² /bɪ'haɪnd/ *n* (colloq) buttocks: *He kicked the boy's ~. He fell on his ~*.

be·hind³ /bɪ'haɪnd/ *prep* 1 (contrasted with *in front of*) to the rear of: *The boy was hiding ~ a tree. Come out from ~ the door. There is an orchard ~ the house. The sun was ~ (= hidden by) the clouds. Walk close ~ me. He put the idea ~ him*, (fig) refused to consider it. ⇨ also back¹(1), scene(6) and leave¹(3). 2 (contrasted with *ahead of*) not having made so much progress as: *~ other boys of his age; a country far ~ its neighbours. Mary is ~ the other girls in sewing*. 3 **leave ~**, leave remaining after: *He left nothing but debts ~ him. The storm left a trail of destruction ~ it*. 4 **be ~ one**, (of time) be in the past: *My schooldays are far ~ me. ~ time; ~ the times*, ⇨ time¹(3,10). 5 **be/lie ~ sth**, be the cause of, explanation for, it: *What's ~ Guy's strange behaviour? B~ her harsh remarks lay a guilty and unhappy spirit*.

be·hind·hand /bɪ'haɪndhænd/ *pred adj* 1 **be/get ~ (with/in)**, be in arrears: *be ~ with the rent; get ~ in one's work*. 2 late; after others: *He did not want to be ~ in generosity*, later than others in being generous.

be·hold /bɪ'həʊld/ *vt* (*pt,pp* beheld /bɪ'held/) [VP6A] (old or liter use) take notice; see (esp sth unusual or striking). **lo and ~**, ⇨ lo. **~er** *n* spectator.

be·holden /bɪ'həʊldən/ *pred adj* **~ (to)**, under an obligation; owing thanks: *We are much ~ to you for your help*.

be·hove /bɪ'həʊv/ (US = **be·hoove** /bɪ'huːv/) *vt* (impers) *it ~s one to do sth*, (old formal use) it is right or necessary for one to do sth: *It ~s you to*, It is your duty to, You ought to...; *It does not ~ you to*, You must not or ought not to....

beige /beɪʒ/ *n* [U] colour of sandstone (brown, brownish grey or greyish yellow); soft fabric of undyed and unbleached wool.

be·ing /'biːɪŋ/ *n* 1 [U] existence. *bring/call sth into ~*, cause it to have reality or existence. *come into ~*, begin to exist: *We do not know when this world came into ~. in ~*, existing. 2 [C] living creature. *human ~*, human creature: *Men, women and children are human ~s*. 3 **the Supreme B~**, God.

be·jew·elled (US = -eled) /bɪ'dʒuːəld/ *part adj* decorated, adorned, with jewels.

be·labour (US = -bor) /bɪ'leɪbə(r)/ *vt* [VP6A] (archaic) beat hard, give hard blows to: *The robbers ~ed him soundly*.

be·lated /bɪ'leɪtɪd/ *adj* 1 coming very late or too late: *a ~ apology/explanation*. 2 (old use) overtaken by darkness: *The ~ travellers lost their way in the forest. ~·ly adv*

be·lay /bɪ'leɪ/ *vt* [VP6A] (naut and mountaineering) make secure (a rope) round sth or sb. **be'lay·ing-pin** *n* fixed wooden or iron pin or cleat for ~ing. □ *n* turn of a rope in ~ing.

belch /beltʃ/ *vt,vi* 1 [VP6A,15B] **~ (out)**, send, eg smoke, flames, out: *A volcano ~es out smoke and ashes*. 2 [VP2A] send out gas from the stomach noisily through the mouth. □ *n* act or sound of ~ing; sth ~ed out (eg a burst of flame).

be·leaguer /bɪ'liːgə(r)/ *vt* [VP6A] besiege.

bel·fry /'belfrɪ/ *n* tower for bells; part of a church tower in which bells hang. ⇨ the illus at church.

bats in the ~, ⇨ bat¹.

be·lie /bɪ'laɪ/ *vt* [VP6A] 1 give a wrong or untrue idea of: *His cheerful appearance ~d his feelings*. 2 fail to justify or be equal to (what is hoped for or promised).

be·lief /bɪ'liːf/ *n* 1 [U] **~ (in)**, the feeling that sth is real and true; trust; confidence: *I haven't much ~ in his honesty*, cannot feel sure that he is honest. *He had no great ~ in his doctor*, had little confidence that his doctor could cure him. *He has lost his ~ in God*, no longer accepts the existence of God as true. *It is my ~ that*, I feel confident that.... *in the ~ that*, feeling confident that: *He came to me in the ~ that I could help him*. *to the best of my ~*, in my genuine opinion. 2 [C] sth accepted as true or real; sth taught as part of a religion; religion: *the ~s of the Christian Church*.

be·lieve /bɪ'liːv/ *vt,vi* 1 [VP6A,9,10,25] feel sure of the truth of sth, that sb is telling the truth; be of the opinion (that): *I ~ that man. I ~ what that man says. People used to ~ (that) the world was flat. They ~d him to be/~d (that) he was insane. I ~ it to have been a mistake. Nobody will ~ what difficulty there has been over this question/how difficult this question has been. Will they be ready tomorrow? Yes, I ~ so. No, I ~ not. ~ (you) me*, I assure you. 2 [VP3A] **~ in**, (a) have trust in: *I ~ in that man*. (b) feel sure of the existence of: *~ in God*. (c) feel sure of the value or worth of: *He ~s in getting plenty of exercise. He ~s in old-fashioned remedies*. 3 **make ~**, pretend: *The boys made ~ that they were/made ~ to be explorers in the African forests*. Hence, **'make-~** *n*. *Don't be frightened, it's all make-~*, is all pretence. **be·liever** *n* person who ~s, esp a person with religious faith. **be·liev·able** *adj* that can be ~d. **be·liev·ing** *n* *seeing is believing*, you may ~ sth if you see it.

be·like /bɪ'laɪk/ *adv* (old use) possibly.

be·little /bɪ'lɪtl/ *vt* [VP6A] cause to seem unimportant or of small value: *Don't ~ yourself*, be too modest about your abilities, etc.

bell /bel/ *n* 1 hollow vessel of cast metal, usu shaped like a cup, that makes a ringing sound when struck (usu by a tongue or clapper inside the ~ or, in an electric ~, by a small hammer). **~, book and candle**, ecclesiastical curse of excommunication. *as sound as a ~*, (fig) in first-rate condition. *ring a ~*, (colloq) recall to memory sth half forgotten. 2 (naut) time signal in the form of a bell rung from one to eight times every half hour, eg: *eight ~s*, 12, 4 or 8 o'clock; *four ~s*, 2, 6 or 10 o'clock. 3 **'~-boy, '~-hop** *n* (US) boy or man employed in a hotel to carry luggage, messages, etc. ⇨ buttons(4) (GB). **'~-bottomed** *adj* (of trousers) made very wide at the bottom of the leg (eg as worn by some sailors). **'~-bottoms** *n pl* trousers made this way. **'~-buoy** *n* buoy with a ~ that is made to ring by the movement of the waves. **'~-flower** *n* any plant of the genus *campanula*. **'~-founder** *n* person whose trade is the casting of ~s. **'~-foundry** *n* place where large ~s (for churches, etc) are cast. **'~-metal** *n* [U] alloy of copper and tin used for making ~s. **'~-push** *n* button pressed to ring an electric ~. **'~-ringer** *n* person who rings church ~s. **'~-tent** *n* ~-shaped tent. **'~-wether** *n* leading male sheep of a flock, with a ~ on its neck; (fig) ringleader. □ *vt* **~ the cat**, (prov) do something dangerous in order to save others (from the fable of the mouse that suggested

fastening a ～ round the cat's neck).
bella·donna /ˌbeləˈdɒnə/ n (drug prepared from) poisonous plant with red flowers and black berries.
belle /bel/ n beautiful girl or woman: *the ～ of the ball*, the most beautiful woman present.
belles–lettres /ˌbel ˈletrə/ n pl (with *sing v*) (F) literary studies and writings (contrasted with commercial, technical, scientific, etc).
bel·li·cose /ˈbelɪkəʊs/ adj (liter) inclined to fighting; anxious to fight.
-bel·lied /-belɪd/ ⇨ belly.
bel·liger·ency /bɪˈlɪdʒərənsɪ/ n [U] being warlike; state of being at war.
bel·liger·ent /bɪˈlɪdʒərənt/ adj, n (person, nation, etc) waging war: *the ～ Powers*, those that are waging war.
bel·low /ˈbeləʊ/ vi,vt 1 [VP2A] make a loud, deep noise (like a bull); roar; shout: *He ～ed before the dentist had even started.* 2 [VP6A,15B] ～ *(out)* utter loudly or angrily: *They ～ed out a drinking song.*
bel·lows /ˈbeləʊz/ n pl *a pair of ～*, sometimes *a ～* 1 apparatus for blowing air into a fire, eg in a forge. 2 apparatus for forcing air through the pipes of an organ, eg in a church.
belly¹ /ˈbelɪ/ n 1 (colloq) abdomen. '~-flop n (colloq) clumsy dive, landing in the water on the front of the body. '~-laugh n loud, coarse laugh. □ vi give such a laugh. 2 the stomach: *with an empty ～*, hungry. '~-ache n (colloq) pain in the stomach or bowels □ vi (colloq) grumble or complain bitterly, esp without good reason. '~ button n (colloq) navel. 3 bulging part (concave or convex) of anything, eg the surface of a violin across which the strings pass. '~ landing n landing made on the hull of an aircraft (when the under-carriage fails to operate). Hence, '~-land vi. -bellied adj: ˌbig-'bellied, having a big ～. '~-ful /-fʊl/ n as much as one wants of anything: *He's had his ～ful of fighting*, doesn't want any more.
belly² /ˈbelɪ/ vi,vt [VP6A,15B,2A,C] ～ *(out)*, (cause to) swell out: *The wind bellied (out) the sails. The sails bellied (out).*
be·long /bɪˈlɒŋ US: -ˈlɔːŋ/ vi 1 [VP3A] ～ *to*, (a) be the property of: *These books ～ to me*, are mine. (b) be a member of, be connected with: *Which club do you ～ to?* 2 [VP2C] have as a right or proper place. *Do you ～ here*, live here? *Does this item of expenditure ～ under the head of office expenses*, is it rightly placed there? ～·ings n pl movable possessions (not land, buildings, a business, etc): *personal ～ings; I hope you've left none of your ～ings in the hotel.*
be·loved /bɪˈlʌvd/ pp, pred adj dearly loved: ～ *by all;* ～ *of all who knew her.* □ adj, n /bɪˈlʌvɪd/ (person) dearly loved; darling: *his ～ wife.*
be·low¹ /bɪˈləʊ/ adv (contrasted with *above¹*; also ⇨ under¹, underneath, over¹(2)) 1 (sometimes used after *from*, as if it were a n) at or to a lower level: *From the hilltop we saw the blue ocean ～. The people in the rooms ～ are very noisy. We heard voices from ～. be/go ～*, (in a ship) be/go ～ deck in (to) a cabin, saloon, etc. 2 at the foot of a page, etc; later (in a book, article, etc): *see paragraph six ～. Please affix your signature ～.* 3 *down ～*, in the lower part of a building, in a ship's hold, etc (according to context). *here ～*, on earth.
be·low² /bɪˈləʊ/ prep (contrasted with *above²*; also ⇨ under², over¹(2); *below* can sometimes, but

not always, be replaced by *under*; when *under* is possible, it is given in the examples) 1 lower than: *Skirts this year reach just ～ the knees. When the sun sets it goes ～ the horizon. Shall I write my name on, above or ～ the line? The temperature was five degrees ～ freezing-point. There is nothing ～/under 50p*, costing less than this. *The Dead Sea is ～ sea level. A captain in the army ranks ～ a captain in the Navy. Your work is ～ the average. He can't be much ～/under sixty*, ie years of age. ⇨ also belt(1), mark¹(8). 2 down stream from: *a few yards ～ the bridge.* 3 *(speak) ～ one's breath* (more usu *under*), in a whisper. 4 (replaceable by *beneath*) unworthy of: ～ *one's dignity.*
belt /belt/ n 1 adjustable band or strip of cloth, leather, etc worn round the waist or over one shoulder to support or keep in place clothes or weapons, or, like a corset, to support the abdomen: *He ate so much that he had to loosen his ～ two holes. hit below the ～*, give an unfair blow, fight unfairly. *tighten one's ～*, ⇨ tight(8). 2 endless strap, used to connect wheels and so drive machinery. 'fan-belt, in the engine of a car. 3 any wide strip or band, surrounding area, etc. **the com'muter belt**, residential area outside a large town, eg London, from which people commute to and from work. **the 'Cotton ～**, (US) area in which cotton is extensively grown. **'green ～**, area of grassland, parks, etc, round a town. □ vt 1 [VP6A,15B] fasten with a ～: *The officer ～ed his sword on.* 2 [VP6A] thrash with a ～; (colloq) strike with the fist(s): *If you don't shut up, I'll ～ you.* ～ing n: *give the boy a good ～ing*, thrash him well. 3 [VP2C,3A] ～ *along*, (colloq) move fast. 4 [VP15B] ～ *out*, (colloq) sing loudly and forcefully: *No one can ～ out those old songs like she can.* 5 [VP2C] ～ *up*, (sl) stop talking.
be·moan /bɪˈməʊn/ vt [VP6A] (poet) moan for; show great sorrow for: ～ *one's sad fate; ～ing the loss of all her money.*
be·mused /bɪˈmjuːzd/ pred adj preoccupied; confused, bewildered.
ben¹ /ben/ n (Scot) inner room (usu of a two-roomed house).
ben² /ben/ n (Scot) mountain peak (used with names as *Ben Nevis*).
bench /bentʃ/ n 1 long seat of wood or stone, eg in a public park, or across a rowing-boat; (in the House of Commons) seat occupied by certain classes of members. 'back-～es, for members not entitled to a front ～. 'cross-～es, for independent members who do not vote with either of the two main political parties. 'front-～es, reserved for ministers or ex-ministers. Hence, ˌback-/ˌcross-/ ˌfront-'bencher, one of the above people. **the 'Treasury B～**, for Ministers. '～ seat, (in a car) seat (for 2 or 3 persons) extending the width of the car. ⇨ bucket seat. 2 [U] (collective, with *def art*, often **the B～**) judges; magistrates; judge's seat or office; law court. *be raised to the B～*, be made a judge or a bishop. **the ˌKing's 'B～ Division**, of the High Court of Justice. 3 work-table at which a shoemaker, carpenter, etc, works.
bend¹ /bend/ vt,vi (pt,pp bent /bent/) 1 [VP6A,15A,B] cause (sth rigid) to be out of a straight line or surface; force into a curve or angle: *It isn't easy to ～ a bar of iron. He heated the iron rod and bent it into a right angle. B～ the end of the wire up/down/back. Rheumatism prevents him*

from ~ing his back. Her head was bent over her book. ~ **the knee (to)**, (rhet) bow, pray. **on** ~**ed knees,** (liter) kneeling; in an attitude of prayer or entreaty. ~ **a rule,** (colloq) interpret it loosely (to suit the circumstances). **2** [VP2A,C] become curved or angular; bow; stoop: *The branches were* ~*ing (down) with the weight of the fruit. The branch bent but didn't break when the boy climbed on to it. Can you* ~ *down and touch your toes without* ~*ing your knees? The tall man bent forward to listen to the little girl. Sit up straight: don't* ~ *over your desk. The river* ~*s* (= turns) *several times before reaching the sea. The road* ~*s to the left here.* **3** [VP15A] direct: *It's time for us to* ~ *our steps homeward,* turn towards home. *All eyes were bent on me,* every one was looking at me. *She stood there with eyes bent on the ground,* looking down. *He couldn't* ~ *his mind* (= give his attention) *to his studies.* **4** [VP2C,15A] ~ **(sb) to,** submit: ~ *to sb's will;* make (sb) submit: ~ *sb to one's will.* **5** [VP6A] curve (a bow) in order to string it: *None of the suitors could* ~ *the bow of Odysseus.* **6** *be bent on,* have the mind set on, have a fixed purpose: *He is bent on mastering English,* determined to learn it thoroughly. *He is bent on mischief,* has plans to do sth mischievous. **bent** *pred adj* (sl) dishonest; corrupt; mad.
bend² /bend/ *n* **1** curve or turn: *a sharp* ~ *in the road.* **round the bend,** (sl) mad. **2** sailor's knot (in a rope). **3** *the* ~*s,* (colloq) pains in the joints, caused by working in compressed air, eg in a caisson(2).
be-neath /bɪ'ni:θ/ *prep, adv* **1** (old use, or liter) below, under(neath). **2** not worthy of: *His accusations are* ~ *contempt/notice,* should be ignored. *It is* ~ *you to complain,* unworthy of you to do so.
ben-edick /'benɪdɪk/ (US = **ben-e-dict** /'benɪdɪkt/) *n* recently married man, esp one who has been a bachelor for many years.
Bene-dic-tine /ˌbenɪ'dɪktɪn/ *n, adj* **1** [C] (monk or nun) of the religious order founded in AD 529 by St Benedict. **2** [U] /-ti:n/ liqueur made by monks of this order.
bene-dic-tion /ˌbenɪ'dɪkʃn/ *n* blessing (esp one given by a priest at the end of a church service): *pronounce the* ~.
bene-fac-tion /ˌbenɪ'fækʃn/ *n* [U] doing good; [C] good deed (esp the giving of money for charity); charitable gift: *That man's* ~*s now amount to 10000.*
bene-fac-tor /'benɪfæktə(r)/ *n* person who has given friendly help, esp financial help, to a school, hospital or charitable institution. **bene-fac-tress** /'benɪfæktrɪs/ *n* woman ~.
bene-fice /'benɪfɪs/ *n* income-producing property (called a *church living*) held by a priest or clergyman (esp a vicar or rector). **bene-ficed** /-fɪst/ *adj* having a ~: *a* ~*d clergyman.*
be-nefi-cence /bɪ'nefɪsns/ *n* [U] (formal) doing good; active kindness. **be-nefi-cent** /bɪ'nefɪsnt/ *adj* (formal) doing good; kind.
bene-fi-cial /ˌbenɪ'fɪʃl/ *adj* (formal) having good effect, helpful: *Fresh air and good food are* ~ *to the health. I hope your holiday will be* ~, do you good. ~**·ly** *adv*
bene-fi-ci-ary /ˌbenɪ'fɪʃərɪ US: -'fɪʃɪerɪ/ *n* [C] (*pl* -ries) person who receives a benefit, esp one who receives money, property, etc under a will (at sb's death).
bene-fit /'benɪfɪt/ *n* **1** [U] advantage; profit; help:

Did you get much ~ *from your holiday,* did you feel better afterwards? *The book wasn't of much* ~ *to me,* didn't help me much. *The money is to be used for the* ~ *of the poor,* to help poor people. *It was done for your* ~, to help you. **give sb the** ~ **of the doubt,** assume that he is innocent because there is insufficient evidence that he is guilty. ~ *in kind,* ⇨ kind¹(4). ~ **performance/concert/match,** theatrical performance/concert/cricket or football match, etc, money for which is for the ~ of a charity, a particular player, etc. **2** [C] act of kindness; favour; advantage: *the* ~*s of a good education; the* ~*s we receive from our parents and teachers.* **3** [C] allowance of money to which a person is entitled as a citizen or as a member of an insurance society, etc: *medical/unemployment/sickness* ~*s.* □ *vt, vi* **1** [VP6A] do good to: *The new railway will* ~ *the district. The sea air will* ~ *you.* **2** [VP3A] ~ *from/by,* receive ~ from/by: *You will* ~ *by a holiday.*
ben-ev-ol-ence /bɪ'nevələns/ *n* [U] wish to do good; activity in doing good: *His* ~ *made it possible for many poor boys to attend college.*
ben-ev-ol-ent /bɪ'nevələnt/ *adj* ~ **to/towards,** kind and helpful. ~**·ly** *adv*
be-nighted /bɪ'naɪtɪd/ *part adj* **1** (liter or old use) without the light of knowledge; in moral darkness. **2** (old use, of travellers) overtaken by darkness.
be-nign /bɪ'naɪn/ *adj* **1** (of persons) kind and gentle. **2** (of soil, climate) mild, favourable. **3** (of a disease, tumour) not dangerous. ⇨ malignant(2). ~**·ly** *adv*
be-nig-nant /bɪ'nɪgnənt/ *adj* (formal) kind, gracious. ~**·ly** *adv*
be-nig-nity /bɪ'nɪgnətɪ/ *n* (*formal*) [U] kindness of heart; [C] kind act, favour.
beni-son /'benɪzn/ *n* [C] (old use) blessing.
bent¹ /bent/ *n* ~ **(for),** inclination or aptitude; natural skill in and liking: *She has a* ~ *for sewing/music.* **follow one's** ~, do what one is interested in and what one enjoys doing. **to the top of one's** ~, to one's heart's desire.
bent² ⇨ bend¹ esp (6).
be-numbed /bɪ'nʌmd/ *pred adj* made numb; with all feelings taken away: *My fingers were* ~ *with cold.*
Ben-ze-drine /'benzədri:n/ *n* (P) brand of amphetamine.
ben-zene /'benzi:n/ *n* [U] colourless liquid (C_6H_6) obtained from petroleum and coal-tar, used in the manufacture of numerous chemical products.
ben-zine /'benzi:n/ *n* [U] colourless liquid (mixture of hydrocarbons) obtained from mineral oil, used for cleaning, etc.
ben-zol /'benzɒl US: -zɔ:l/ *n* [U] = benzene.
be-queath /bɪ'kwi:ð/ *vt* [VP6A,12A,13A] ~ **(to),** **1** arrange (by making a will) to give (property, etc to sb) at death: *He has* ~*ed me his gold watch.* **2** (fig) hand down to those who come after: *discoveries* ~*ed to us by the scientists of the last century.*
be-quest /bɪ'kwest/ *n* **1** [U] bequeathing. **2** [C] sth bequeathed: *He left* ~*s of money to all his servants.*
be-rate /bɪ'reɪt/ *vt* [VP6A] scold sharply.
be-reave /bɪ'ri:v/ *vt* (*pt, pp* bereft /bɪ'reft/ or bereaved; usu bereft in (1) and bereaved in (2)) [VP14] ~ **of 1** rob or dispossess (of sth immaterial): *bereft of hope,* without hope; *bereft of reason,* mad. *Indignation bereft him of speech,* took away his power to speak. **2** (of death) leave

sad by taking away (a relation, etc): *the accident that ~d him of his wife and child; the ~d husband,* the man whose wife had died. **~·ment** *n* [U] being ~d; loss by death: *We all sympathize with you in your ~ment;* [C] instance of this: *Owing to a recent ~ment she did not attend the concert.*

be·reft ⇨ bereave.

be·ret /'bereɪ US: bə'reɪ/ *n* flat, round cap of felt or cloth, worn with sports and holiday clothes, and as military head-dress.

berg /bɜːg/ *n* = iceberg.

beri-beri /ˌberɪ 'berɪ/ *n* [U] disease, common in oriental and tropical countries, caused by lack of vitamins, etc, essential to health.

berry /'berɪ/ *n* (*pl* -ries) **1** small seedy fruit: *holly berries; straw~; black~; rasp~.* ⇨ the illus at fruit. **2** coffee bean.

ber·serk /bə'sɜːk/ *pred adj* **be/go/send sb ~,** be, go, cause sb to go uncontrollably wild: *He suddenly went ~ with rage.*

berth /bɜːθ/ *n* **1** sleeping-place in a train, a ship or an aircraft. **2** place at a wharf where a ship can be tied up; place for a ship to swing at anchor. **give a wide ~ to,** (fig) keep well away from, at a safe distance from. **3** (dated colloq) job. **find a snug ~,** an easy or pleasant job. □ *vt, vi* **1** [VP15A,2C] (naut) find, have, a sleeping-place (for): *Six passengers can be ~ed amidships.* **2** [VP6A] moor (a ship) in harbour, tie up (a ship) at a wharf, etc.

beryl /'berəl/ *n* precious stone (usu green).

be·seech /bɪ'siːtʃ/ *vt* (*pt, pp* besought /bɪ'sɔːt/) [VP6A,17A,11,13B] (old use, or liter) ask earnestly or urgently: *He besought an interview. The prisoner besought the judge to be merciful/besought him for mercy. Spare him, I ~ you.* **~·ing** *adj* (of a person's look, tone of voice, etc) entreating, appealing. **~·ing·ly** *adv*

be·seem /bɪ'siːm/ *vt* (liter, old use) (only impers, in the 3rd person) be fitting or suitable: *It ill ~s you to refuse,* It is not fitting that you should refuse.

be·set /bɪ'set/ *vt* (-tt-, *pt, pp* beset) [VP6A] close in on all sides, have on all sides: *the temptations that ~ young people,* by which they are faced on all sides: *a problem ~ with difficulties; ~ by doubts,* troubled by doubts. **~·ting sin,** sin that most frequently tempts a person: *His ~ting sin is laziness.*

be·shrew /bɪ'ʃruː/ *vt* (archaic): *B~ me!* May evil fall upon me!

be·side /bɪ'saɪd/ *prep* **1** at the side of; close to: *Come and sit ~ me. She would like to live ~ the sea,* at the sea-side. **2** compared with: *You're quite tall ~ your sister.* **set ~,** put against; compare with: *There's no one to set ~ him as a general.* **3 ~ the point/mark/question,** wide of, having nothing to do with (what is being discussed, etc). **4 ~ oneself,** at the end of one's self-control: *He was ~ himself with joy/anger.*

be·sides /bɪ'saɪdz/ *adv* moreover; also: *I don't like that new dictionary; ~, it's too expensive. It's too late to go for a walk now; ~, it's beginning to rain.* □ *prep* in addition to; as well as: *I have three other hats ~ this. There were five of us ~ John,* not including John. *He hadn't time to prepare his lecture, ~ which, he was unwell.*

be·siege /bɪ'siːdʒ/ *vt* **1** [VP6A] surround (a place) with armed forces and keep them there; attack from all sides: *Troy was ~d by the Greeks for ten years.* **2** [VP14] **~ with,** crowd round (with requests, etc): *The teacher was ~d with questions and re-*

quests *from her pupils.* **be·sieger** *n*

be·smear /bɪ'smɪə(r)/ *vt* **~ with,** smear all over, eg with grease.

be·smirch /bɪ'smɜːtʃ/ *vt* make dirty: (fig) *His reputation was ~ed.*

be·som /'biːzəm/ *n* broom made by tying a bundle of twigs to a long handle.

be·sot·ted /bɪ'sɒtɪd/ *part adj* **~ by/with,** stupefied (by alcoholic drink, drugs, love, etc).

be·sought ⇨ beseech.

be·spangled /bɪ'spæŋgld/ *pred adj* **~ with,** covered, decorated, with spangles.

be·spat·tered /bɪ'spætəd/ *pred adj* **~ with,** covered with spots of mud, etc.

be·speak /bɪ'spiːk/ *vt* (*pt* bespoke /bɪ'spəʊk/, *pp* bespoke or bespoken /bɪ'spəʊkən/) **1** [VP6A] (old use) order in advance; engage or reserve (a table in a restaurant, a room in a hotel). **bespoke shoemaker/tailor,** one who makes goods to order (contrasted with a seller of ready-made shoes, etc). ⇨ *custom-built* at custom(5). **2** [VP6A,25] (formal) be evidence of: *His polite manners ~ the gentleman.*

best¹ /best/ *adj* (independent *superl*; ⇨ good, better) of the most excellent kind: *the ~ poetry/ poets; the ~ dinner I have ever had; the ~* (= quickest, most convenient, etc) *way from London to Paris. the '~ part of,* most of; the greater part of: *I've been waiting the ~ part of an hour.* **the ~ thing to do,** that which is most likely to bring about the desired result. **make the ~ use of one's time/gifts/opportunities, etc,** use one's time, etc in the most useful way. **put one's ~ foot forward,** ⇨ foot(1). **with the '~ will in the world,** even making every effort to be fair, etc. **~ 'man,** bridegroom's friend, supporting him at his wedding.

best² /best/ *adv* (independent *superl*; ⇨ well, better) **1** in the most excellent way: *He works ~ in the morning. She was the ~-dressed woman in the village.* **as ~ one may/can,** in the ~ way possible to one. **think ~,** judge to be the ~ way of acting: *Do as you think ~.* **2** most: *He is the ~-hated man in the village.* **~-'seller** *n* book that is sold in very large numbers: *His new novel is one of the season's ~-sellers.* **3 had ~,** = had better. ⇨ better²(2).

best³ /best/ *pron* (independent *superl*; ⇨ better³) the outstanding person, thing, etc among several; the most excellent part, aspect, of sth: *He's the ~ of husbands,* is distinguished among husbands for good qualities. *We're the ~ of friends,* very close friends. **be all for the ~,** be good in the end (although not at first seeming to be good). **do sth all for the ~,** act with good intentions (although it may not seem so). **be/dress in one's (Sunday) ~,** wear one's finest clothes: *They were (dressed) in their ~ for the wedding.* **All the ~!** (used when parting from sb) With warmest wishes! **the '~ of it/the joke/etc,** the amusing part (of what happened): *And the ~ of it/the ~ part of it was that....* **at ~,** taking the most hopeful view: *We can't arrive before Friday at ~.* **at its/their/his, etc ~,** in the ~ condition: *The garden is at its best this month,* looking most beautiful. *He was at his ~ yesterday evening and kept us all amused,* talked in his most amusing way. **(even) at the '~ of times,** (even) when circumstances are most favourable. **have/get the ~ of it/of the fight/ quarrel/deal/bargain, etc,** win; gain the advantage. **have/get the ~ of everything,** enjoy the ~

food, housing, etc. **with the ~,** as well as anyone: *Although he's nearly fifty, he can still play tennis with the ~.* **with the¹~ of intentions,** intending only to help. **do one's ~/the ~ one can,** do one's utmost. **(do sth) to the ~ of one's ability/ power,** use all one's ability/power when doing it. **make the ~ of a bad job/business,** do what one can, in spite of failure, misfortune, etc. **make the ~ of one's way home,** return home as quickly as possible, in spite of difficulties. **make the ~ of things,** be contented (although things are not satisfactory). **to the ~ of my knowledge/belief/ recollection,** so far as I know/believe/recollect (though my knowledge, etc may be imperfect).

best⁴ /best/ *vt* [VP6A] (colloq) get the better of; defeat.

bes·tial /'bestɪəl/ *adj* of or like a beast; brutish; savage. **~ly** *adv* **bes·ti·al·ity** /ˌbestɪ'ælətɪ/ *n* (*pl*-ties) [U] quality of being ~; [C] ~ or brutal act.

bes·ti·ary /'bestɪərɪ US: -tɪerɪ/ *n* medieval collection of moral stories about animals.

be·stir /bɪ'stɜ:(r)/ *vt* (-rr-) [VP6A,17] **~ oneself,** (old use or joc) busy oneself, be active.

be·stow /bɪ'stəʊ/ *vt* **1** [VP6A,14] **~ (on/upon),** give as an offering: **~** *an honour/a title on sb; the praise that has been ~ed upon him.* **2** [VP6A] (old use) put, place. **~al** *n* **~ing.**

be·strew /bɪ'stru:/ *vt* (*pt* ~ed, *pp* bestrewn /-'stru:n/ or ~ed) [VP6A,14] **~ (with),** (poet) strew (a surface); scatter (things) about.

be·stride /bɪ'straɪd/ *vt* (*pt* bestrode /bɪ'strəʊd/, *pp* bestridden /bɪ'strɪdn/, bestrid /bɪ'strɪd/, bestrode) [VP6A] (formal) sit, stand, with one leg on each side of: **~** *a horse/chair/bidet/ditch/fence, etc;* (fig) dominate: *Caesar bestrode the Roman Empire.* ⇨ astride.

bet /bet/ *vt,vi* (-tt-, *pt,pp* bet or betted) [VP9,11,12C,2A,3A] **1 bet on sth, bet (sb) that...,** risk money on a race or on some other event of which the result is doubtful: *He bet me a pound that Hyperion would win. It's foolish to bet on horses. Do you ever bet?* **2** (colloq uses): *I bet,* I'm certain; *you bet,* you may be certain. □ *n* [C] agreement to risk money, etc on an event of which the result is doubtful; the money, etc offered: *make a bet; win/lose a bet; accept/take up a bet.*

beta /'bi:tə US: 'beɪtə/ *n* second letter (B, β) of the Greek alphabet. ⇨ App 4.

be·take /bɪ'teɪk/ *vt* (*pt* betook /bɪ'tʊk/, *pp* betaken /bɪ'teɪkən/) [VP14, reflex] **~ oneself to,** (old use) go to, apply oneself to.

betel /'bi:tl/ *n* leaf which is wrapped round bits of areca-nut and used by some Indians for chewing. '**~-nut,** areca-nut.

bête noire /ˌbeɪt 'nwɑ:(r)/ *n* (F) thing or person one dislikes greatly.

bethel /'beθl/ *n* nonconformist chapel; (esp US) chapel for seamen.

be·think /bɪ'θɪŋk/ *vt* (*pt,pp* bethought /bɪ'θɔ:t/) [VP11,14,17,20,21] **~ oneself (of),** (old use) reflect, consider.

be·tide /bɪ'taɪd/ *vt* (only in) **woe ~ him/you, etc** *(if...),* may misfortune come to him/you, etc (if...).

be·times /bɪ'taɪmz/ *adv* (old use) early; in good time: *We must be up ~ tomorrow.*

be·token /bɪ'təʊkən/ *vt* [VP6A] (old use) indicate, suggest: *Those black clouds ~ rain.*

be·took ⇨ betake.

be·tray /bɪ'treɪ/ *vt* **1** [VP6A] be disloyal to; act deceitfully towards: *He ~ed his principles.* **2**

[VP6A,14] **~ (to),** give away or make known or sell treacherously: *Judas ~ed Jesus to his enemies.* **3** [VP6A] allow (a secret) to become known, either by accident or on purpose. **4** [VP6A,25] be or give a sign of, show: *The boy's face ~ed the fact that he had been eating jam. His accent at once ~ed the fact that he was/~ed him to be a foreigner.* **~ oneself,** show what one really is, etc: *He had a good disguise, but as soon as he spoke he ~ed himself,* ie he was recognized by his voice. **~al** /bɪ'treɪəl/ *n* [U] ~ing or being ~ed; [C] instance of this. **~er** *n*

be·troth /bɪ'trəʊð/ *vt* (old formal use) **~ to,** [VP6A,14] engage (a woman) in contract of marriage (usu in *pp*): *His daughter was ~ed to a banker.* **~ed** *n* person engaged to be married. **~al** *n* engagement (the usual word) to be married.

bet·ter¹ /'betə(r)/ *adj* (independent *comp;* ⇨ good, best) **1** *This is good but that is ~. He's a ~ man than his brother.* **~ than one's word,** more generous than one's promise. **(do sth) against one's ~ judgement,** despite feelings that it may be unwise. **no ~ than,** practically the same as: *He's no ~ than a beggar,* is, in spite of appearances, etc, almost a beggar. **be no ~ than she should be,** (old use) be a woman of low regard or easy virtue. ⇨ virtue(2). **the ~ part of,** the larger part of: *Discretion is the ~ part of valour,* ⇨ discretion(1). **see ~ days,** be not so poor or unfortunate as at present: *He has seen ~ days.* **one's ~ feelings,** one's moral nature. **his ~ half,** (colloq) his wife. **2** (of health) recovering from illness (often contrasted with *ill* and related to *well*): *The patient is ~ today but is still not well enough to get up. I'm quite ~ now,* am fully recovered.

bet·ter² /'betə(r)/ *adv* (independent *comp;* ⇨ well, best) **1** *The ~* (= The more) *I know her the more I admire her abilities. You would write ~ if you had a good pen. You play tennis ~ than I do. You'll like it ~* (= more) *when you understand it more.* **be ~ off,** richer; more comfortable. **be ~ off without,** happier; more at ease: *We'd be ~ off without all that din from the children's room.* **know ~,** (a) be wise or experienced enough not to do sth: *You ought to know ~ than to go out without an overcoat on such a cold day.* (b) refuse to accept a statement (because one knows it is not true): *He says he didn't cheat, but I know ~,* feel sure that he did. **think (all) the ~ of sb,** have a higher opinion of him: *I shall think all the ~ of you after seeing you bear these misfortunes so bravely.* **think ~ of sth/of doing sth,** decide, after thought, not to do it. **2** (used in [VP5]) **had ~,** would find it more suitable, more to your advantage, etc: *You had ~ mind your own business. You'd ~ not say that,* I advise you not to say that. *I had ~ begin by explaining...,* It will be useful if I begin by...; *Hadn't you ~ take an umbrella?*

bet·ter³ /'betə(r)/ *n* **one's (elders and) ~s,** older, wiser, more experienced people: *Don't ignore the advice of your elders and ~s.* Cf *superior,* as in: *He's my superior at chess.* **get the ~ of sb or sth,** overcome; defeat; win (an argument, etc): *His shyness got the ~ of him,* he was overcome by shyness, was too shy to speak out. *She always gets the ~ of these quarrels.* **for ~ (or) for worse,** in both good and bad fortune. Cf *for good or ill.*

bet·ter⁴ /'betə(r)/ *vt* **1** [VP6A] improve; do better than: *The Government hopes to ~ the conditions of the peasants. Your work last year was good; I hope* *you will* ~ *it, this year.* ~ *oneself,* get a ~ position, higher wages, etc. ~**·ment** *n* [U] making or becoming ~.

bet·ter⁵, bet·tor /'betə(r)/ *n* person who bets; punter (the more usu word).

be·tween¹ /bɪ'twi:n/ *adv (in)* ~, in(to) a place or time that is before the one (place or time) but after the other: *We visited the Museum in the morning and the Art Gallery later, with a hurried lunch* ~. **far** ~, at wide intervals. **few and far** ~, few and widely scattered or separate: *In this part of Canada houses are few and far* ~.

be·tween² /bɪ'twi:n/ *prep* **1** (of place) *The letter B comes* ~ *A and C,* ie *after* A but *before* C. *The Mediterranean Sea is* ~ *Europe and Africa. A river flows* ~ *its banks.* (*Between* usu involves only two limits, but when boundaries are concerned, there may be more than two limits. *Switzerland lies* ~ *France, Italy, Austria and Germany.* ⇨ among.) **2** (of order, rank, etc): *An army major ranks* ~ *a captain and a colonel.* **3** (of time): ~ *the two world wars;* ~ *1 o'clock and 2 o'clock;* ~ *youth and middle age.* **4** (of distance, amount, etc): ~ *five and six miles;* ~ *thirty and forty tons;* ~ *5p and 10p;* ~ *freezing-point and boiling-point.* **5** (of movement) to and from: *This liner sails* ~ *Southampton and New York.* **6** (showing connection): *after all there has been* ~ *us,* in view of our past friendship, the experiences we have shared, etc. **There is ,no ' love lost** ~ **them,** They dislike each other. **There's nothing to choose** ~ **them,** They are (both or all) alike. **7** (to show sharing; used of two only): *Divide/Share the money* ~ *you.* ~ **ourselves;** ~ **you, me and the gatepost;** ~ **you and me,** in confidence. **8** (to show combination, used of two, or more than two to show several and independent relationships): *The first five batsmen scored 253 runs* ~ *them. We* (two or more) *saved up for a year and bought a second-hand car* ~ *us. B*~ *them* (ie as the result of their combined efforts) *they soon finished the work.* **9** ~ **sth and sth,** with these things combined: *B*~ *astonishment and despair she hardly knew what to do. My time is fully taken up* ~ *writing and lecturing.* **10** (showing relationship): *the relation* ~ *teacher and pupil; the distinction* ~ *right and wrong; a comparison* ~ *two things; quarrels/wars/ill-feeling/rivalries/ friendships, etc* ~ *nations.*

be·twixt /bɪ'twɪkst/ *prep, adv* (old or liter use) between. ~ **and between,** (colloq) in an intermediate state; neither one thing nor the other.

bevel /'bevl/ *n* sloping edge; surface with such a slope, eg at the side of a picture frame or a sheet of plate glass. '~ **gear,** either of a pair of gears with ~led teeth surfaces. □ *vt* (-ll-, US = -l-) give a sloping edge to.

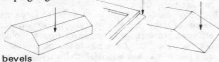

bevels

bev·er·age /'bevərɪdʒ/ *n* [C] (formal) any sort of drink except water, eg milk, tea, wine, beer.

bevy /'bevɪ/ *n* **1** company or gathering. **2** flock (*of* birds, esp quail).

be·wail /bɪ'weɪl/ *vt* [VP6A] (poet) express sorrow over; mourn for.

be·ware /bɪ'weə(r)/ *vi,vt* [VP2A,3A,10 in the im-

perative and infinitive only] ~ *(of),* be on guard, take care: *B*~ *of the dog! B*~ *of pickpockets! B*~ *(of) how you attempt it. B*~, *sir, (of) what you do.*

be·wil·der /bɪ'wɪldə(r)/ *vt* [VP6A] puzzle; confuse: *The old woman from the country was* ~ed *by the crowds and traffic in the big city. Tom was* ~ed *by the examination questions.* ~·**ing** *adj* ~s: *find sth* ~*ing.* ~·**ment** *n* [U] state of being ~ed: *He looked at me in open-mouthed* ~ment.

be·witch /bɪ'wɪtʃ/ *vt* [VP6A] **1** work magic on; put a magic spell on: *The old woman* ~ed *the cows so that they gave no milk.* **2** charm; delight very much: *She danced so well that she* ~ed *all the young men.* ~·**ing** *adj* ~es: *a* ~*ing smile.* ~·**ing·ly** *adv: She smiled at him* ~*ingly.*

bey /beɪ/ *n* (Turkish word meaning) governor: *the Bey of Tunis.*

be·yond¹ /bɪ'jɒnd/ *adv* at or to a distance; farther on: *India and the lands* ~. *What is* ~?

be·yond² /bɪ'jɒnd/ *prep* **1** at, on or to, the farther side of: *The house is* ~ *the bridge. Don't go* ~ *the town boundary. We saw peak* ~ *peak,* a succession of peaks. **2** (of time) later than: *Don't stay out* ~ (*after* is the more usu word) *10 o'clock. He never sees* ~ *the present.* **3** surpassing, exceeding; out of reach of: *Your work is* ~ *all praise,* so good that it cannot be praised enough. *We succeeded* ~ *our hopes,* were more successful than we had hoped to be. *That's going* ~ *a joke,* passes the limits of what is reasonable as a joke. *He lives* ~ *his income,* spends more than he earns. *It's quite* ~ *me,* is more than I can understand. **4** (in neg and interr) except: *He has nothing* ~ *his pension.*

be·zique /bɪ'zi:k/ *n* [U] card-game for two or four players.

bhang /bæŋ/ *n* (kinds of) narcotic made from hemp.

bi- /ˌbaɪ/ *pref* **1** appearing twice (in the period given): ˌ*bi-*'*monthly; bi-annual.* **2** lasting for two, appearing every two: *biennial.* **3** having two: *bilateral; bilingual; biped, biplane.* **4** in two ways; doubly: *bi-concave.*

bias /'baɪəs/ *n* **1** leaning of the mind towards or away from sth; predisposition: *He has a* ~ *towards/against the plan,* is in favour of it/ opposed to it without having full knowledge of it. *He is without* ~, is impartial, unprejudiced. **2** *cut on the* ~, (dress-making, etc) cut across, slantingly. **3** (esp of a ball in the game of bowls) tendency to swerve; the weighting causing this tendency. □ *vt* (*pt,pp* ~ed or ~sed) [VP6A,14] ~ *(towards/against),* give a ~ to; influence (usu unfairly): *The government used newspapers and the radio to* ~ *the opinions of the people. He is* ~(*s*)*ed towards/against the plan,* is prejudiced. *He's clearly* ~(*s*)*ed.*

bib¹ /bɪb/ *n* **1** piece of cloth tied under a child's chin. **bib and tucker,** ⇨ tucker. **2** upper part of an apron.

bib² /bɪb/ *vi* (-bb-) drink too much or too often (rare except in *wine-bibbing, wine-bibber*).

Bible /'baɪbl/ *n* sacred writings of the Jews and the Christian Church. '~ **puncher,** (colloq) evangelical preacher. **bib·li·cal** /'bɪblɪkl/ *adj* of, concerning, contained in, the ~: '*biblical style,* the style used in (esp the Authorized Version of) the ~.

bib·li·ogra·phy /ˌbɪblɪ'ɒɡrəfɪ/ *n* **1** [C] (*pl* -phies) list of books and writings of one author or about one subject. **2** [U] study of the authorship, editions, etc of books. **bib·li·ogra·pher** /ˌbɪblɪ'ɒɡrəfə(r)/ *n*

a bicycle

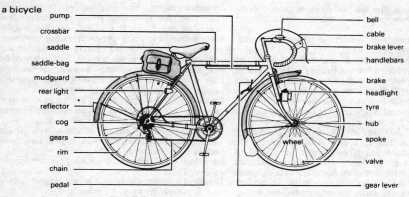

person who writes or studies bibliographies.
bib·lio·phile /'bɪblɪəfaɪl/ n person who loves and
collects books.
bibu·lous /'bɪbjʊləs/ adj (joc) fond of much alcoholic drink.
bi·cam·eral /ˌbaɪ'kæmərəl/ adj (of a legislature)
having two chambers, eg House of Commons,
House of Lords.
bi·car·bon·ate /ˌbaɪ'kɑːbənət/ n [U] acid salt of carbonic acid. ~ **of soda** (= sodium ~) (NaHCO₃),
used in cooking and in medicine.
bi·cen·ten·ary /ˌbaɪsen'tiːnərɪ US: -'sentənerɪ/ n
(celebration of the) 200th anniversary of an event.
bi·cen·ten·nial /ˌbaɪsen'tenɪəl/ adj 1 happening
once in 200 years. 2 lasting for 200 years. 3 of a
200th anniversary. □ n 200th anniversary.
bi·ceps /'baɪseps/ n (pl unchanged) large muscle in
the front part of the upper arm: His ~ is/are impressive.
bicker /'bɪkə(r)/ vi [VP2A,C,3A] ~ (with sb)
(over/about sth), quarrel about sth unimportant:
Stop ~ing!
bi·cycle /'baɪsɪkl/ n two-wheeled machine for riding on, propelled by using pedals. □ vi (usu shortened to cycle /'saɪkl/) [VP2A,C] ride a ~.
bid¹ /bɪd/ vt,vi (-dd-) 1 (pt,pp bid)
[VP6A,14,2A,3A] **bid (for)**, (at an auction sale)
make an offer of money; offer (a certain price):
Will anyone bid £5 for this painting? Mr X bid £20
for the horse so I bid £21. Is nobody else going to
bid? What shall I bid? I hoped to get the house but
a rich man was bidding against me, offering higher
prices. ⇨ **outbid**. The politicians are bidding for
popular support, making offers, eg of tax reductions, in order to get support from the public. **bid
up**, [VP15B] make the price higher by offering
more money: The goods were bid up far beyond
their real value. 2 (pt,pp bid) [VP3A] **bid for**,
(colloq) attempt to attain: The army bid for power
and succeeded. 3 (pt,pp bid) [VP2A,3A] **bid on**,
(US) state a price (for doing sth); put in a tender
for: The firm decided to bid on the new bridge. ⇨
tender³. 4 (old use) (pt bade /bæd/, pp bidden
/'bɪdn/, bid) [VP17,18B] (a) command; tell: He
bade me (to) come in. Do as you are bid. Soldiers
must do as they are bidden. Bid him come in. (b)
invite: the bidden guests; bid sb to a wedding. (c)
[VP12A,13A] say (as a greeting, etc): bid farewell
(= say goodbye) to sb; bid sb good morning. 5
bid fair to, seem likely to: Our plan bids fair to
succeed. **bid defiance to**, (old use) announce that

one defies (the enemy, etc). 6 (cards, bridge) make
a bid: bid 2 hearts. ⇨ bid²(4). **bid·dable** adj
(colloq) docile; ready to obey. **bid·ding** n [U] (a)
command. **do sb's bidding**, do what he commands. (b) act of offering a price at an auction sale:
Bidding was brisk, There were many bids, quickly
made. (c) (at cards) the making of bids(5). **bid·der**
n person who bids.
bid² /bɪd/ n 1 (at an auction sale) offer of a price:
Are there no bids for this very fine painting? Will
no one make a higher/further bid? 2 (US) statement of price for a piece of work, etc: Bids were
invited for the construction of a swimming-pool. ⇨
tender³. 3 **make a bid for**, (colloq) try to obtain:
make a bid for power/popular support. 4 (card
games, esp bridge) statement of the number of
tricks a player proposes to win: a bid of 2 hearts/3
no-trumps; raise the bid.
bide /baɪd/ vt (liter; old use) abide. (rare except in)
~ **one's time**, wait for a favourable opportunity.
bidet /'biːdeɪ US: biː'deɪ/ n (F) raised narrow bath
(to be straddled) for washing the genitals and bottom.
bi·en·nial /baɪ'enɪəl/ adj lasting for two years; happening every alternate year. □ n plant that lives two
years and has flowers and seeds in the second year.
~**·ly** adv
bier /bɪə(r)/ n movable wooden stand for a coffin or
a dead body.
biff /bɪf/ n (sl) sharp blow. □ vt (sl) strike: ~ sb on
the nose.
bi·focal /ˌbaɪ'fəʊkl/ adj (esp of lenses in spectacles
for the eyes) designed for both distant and near vision. **bi·focals** n pl spectacles with ~ lenses.
bi·fur·cate /'baɪfɜːkeɪt/ vt,vi [VP6A,2A] (formal) (of
roads, rivers, boughs of trees, etc) divide into two
branches, etc; fork. □ adj (also ~d) forked. **bi·
fur·ca·tion** /ˌbaɪfə'keɪʃn/ n
big /bɪg/ adj (-gg-) (antonym little; cf large, and
small) of large size, extent, capacity, importance,
etc. **get/grow too big for one's boots**, (colloq)
become conceited. **have big ideas**, be ambitious.
talk big, boast. **'big bug** n (sl) ⇨ bug(4). **big bu·
siness**, commerce on a ~ financial scale. **big
game**, ⇨ game¹(6). **big end** n (eng) part of a
connecting shaft that bears on a crankshaft. **big
noise** n (sl) ⇨ noise. **'big shot** n (sl) ⇨ shot¹(8).
'big stick, = ~ shot. the **'big time**, (sl) highest
level. **'big·wig** n (sl) important person.
big·amy /'bɪgəmɪ/ n [U] having two wives or husbands living. **'big·am·ous** /'bɪgəməs/ adj guilty of,

involving, ~: *a bigamous marriage.* **'big·am·ist** /'bɪgəmɪst/ *n* person guilty of ~.

bight /baɪt/ *n* **1** loop made in a rope. **2** curve in a coast, larger than, or with not so much curve as, a bay.

bigot /'bɪgət/ *n* person who holds strongly to an opinion or belief in defiance of reason or argument. ~**ed** /-ɪd/ *adj* intolerant and narrow-minded (in religion, etc). ~**ry** /-rɪ/ *n* [U] state of being ~ed; [C] act, etc, of a ~.

bi·jou /'biːʒuː/ *n* (F) jewel. □ *adj* small and elegant: ~ *villas.*

bike /baɪk/ *n,vi* (colloq and common abbr for) bicycle.

bi·kini /bɪ'kiːnɪ/ *n* scanty two-piece garment (bra and briefs) worn by girls and women for swimming and sun-bathing: ~ *top* (= bra); ~ *briefs,* ⇨ briefs.

bi·lab·ial /ˌbaɪ'leɪbɪəl/ *adj, n* (phon) (consonant) pronounced with both lips, eg /b, p, m, w/.

bi·lat·eral /ˌbaɪ'lætərəl/ *adj* of, on, with two sides; (legal) (of an agreement, etc) made between two (persons, governments). ~**·ly** *adv* ~**·ism** /-ɪzəm/ *n* principle based upon ~ agreements, esp of trade and financial agreements between countries.

bil·berry /'bɪlbərɪ/ *US:* -berɪ/ *n* (*pl* -ries) fruit of a dwarf hardy shrub growing on heaths, etc in N Europe (also called *blaeberry, whortleberry*).

bile /baɪl/ *n* [U] brownish-yellow bitter liquid produced by the liver to help in digesting food; (med) disorder of the ~; (fig) peevishness, bad temper. **'~-duct,** (anat) tube carrying ~ to the duodenum. ⇨ the illus at alimentary.

bilge /bɪldʒ/ *n* [U] **1** almost flat part of a ship's bottom, inside or outside; (also '~-water) the dirty water that collects in a ship's ~. **2** (sl) foolish or worthless talk or writing.

bil·har·zia /ˌbɪl'hɑːzɪə/ *n* tropical disease caused by parasites, flatworms in the blood and bladder.

bi·lin·gual /baɪ'lɪŋgwəl/ *adj* **1** speaking, using, two languages (esp when these are learnt together in childhood): *a* ~ *country,* one in which two languages are used officially. **2** written, printed, in two languages: *a* ~ *dictionary.* □ *n* ~ person.

bil·ious /'bɪlɪəs/ *adj* **1** caused by too much bile: *a* ~ *complaint/headache/attack;* suffering from such complaints: ~ *patients.* **2** peevish; taking a gloomy view of life. ~**·ness** *n*

bilk /bɪlk/ *vt* [VP6A,14] ~ *sb (out) of,* escape paying money to; cheat (esp by running away): *He* ~*ed us out of the money.*

bill¹ /bɪl/ *n* (also '~-hook) long-handled tool with a curved blade used for cutting off branches of trees.

bill² /bɪl/ *n* horny part of the mouth of some birds. ⇨ the illus at bird. □ *vi* (of doves) stroke ~ with ~. ~ *and coo,* (fig) exchange caresses.

bill³ /bɪl/ *n* **1** written statement of charges for goods delivered or services rendered: *It's wrong to leave a hotel without paying all your* ~*s. There are some* ~*s to pay/to be paid.* ⇨ estimate², quotation(3). *foot the* ~, ⇨ foot². **2** written or printed notice, poster, placard: *a theatre/concert* ~, giving information about a play, concert, etc. *fill/fit the* ~, be, do, all that is required or expected. *head/top the* ~, be advertised at the head of the list, in large type, etc. ~ *of fare,* list of dishes to be served at a hotel, restaurant, etc; menu. **'~-board** *n* (US) structure for the display of advertisements, eg at the roadside (GB = *hoarding*). **'~-poster, '~-**

sticker *nn* person who pastes up ~s or placards (on walls, hoardings, etc). **3** (legal) proposed law, to be discussed by a parliament (and called an *Act* when passed). **4** (US) banknote: *a ten-dollar* ~. **'~-fold** *n* (US) wallet for banknotes. **5 B**~ **of Exchange,** order to a bank to pay a sum of money on a given date. ~**s payable,** ~s of exchange due for payment by the holder. ~**s receivable,** such ~s due for payment to the holder. **6** certificate. ~ *of entry,* (comm) certificate from the Customs to indicate final clearance of imported goods. ~ *of health,* (naut) certificate regarding infectious disease in a ship's crew. *clean* ~ *of health,* (a) one certifying that there is no such disease. (b) (fig) assurance of good health. ~ *of lading,* ⇨ lading. ~ *of quantities,* ⇨ quantity(4). ~ *of sale,* ⇨ sale(1). □ *vt* **1** [VP6A] make known by means of ~s(2) or placards; announce, put, in a programme: *Olivier was* ~*ed to appear as Lear,* It was announced that he would play the part of Lear. **2** [VP14] ~ *sb for sth,* submit a ~(1) to: ~ *a client for services rendered.*

bil·let¹ /'bɪlɪt/ *n* **1** place (usu a private house) where soldiers are boarded and lodged: *The troops are in* ~*s,* in ordinary homes, not in camp or barracks. **2** (colloq) appointment or situation; job: *a soft/cushy* ~, one not needing much effort. □ *vt* [VP6A,14] ~ *(on),* place (troops) in ~s: ~ *soldiers on sb/on a town/on the villagers.*

bil·let² /'bɪlɪt/ *n* thick piece of firewood.

bil·let-doux /ˌbɪleɪ 'duː/ *n* (*pl* billets-doux, pronunciation unchanged) (F) (joc) love-letter.

bill-hook /'bɪlhʊk/ *n* ⇨ bill¹.

bil·liards /'bɪlɪədz/ *n* (with *sing v*) game played with small, hard, heavy balls and long tapering sticks (called *cues*) on an oblong, cloth-covered table: *play* ~; *have a game of* ~. *B*~ *is played by women as well as by men.* **'billiard-player/room/-table/-marker** *nn* (*sing* in compounds).

bil·lings·gate /'bɪlɪŋzgeɪt/ *n* [U] (from the name of a London fish-market) abusive language full of swear-words.

bil·lion /'bɪlɪən/ *n* (GB) million millions or 10¹²; (US) thousand millions or 10⁹. ⇨ App 4.

bil·low /'bɪləʊ/ *n* (liter) great wave; (*pl,* poet) the sea; (fig) anything that sweeps along like a great wave. □ *vi* [VP2C] rise or roll like waves: *The flames* ~*ed over the prairie.* ~**y** *adj* rising or moving like ~s.

billy /'bɪlɪ/ *n* [C] (*pl* -lies) (esp in Australia) tin can (sometimes called a *billy-can*) with a lid and a wire handle, used as a kettle or cooking pot, esp in camping out.

billy-goat /'bɪlɪ gəʊt/ *n* male goat. ⇨ nanny-goat.

billy-(h)o /'bɪlɪ (h)əʊ/ *n* (dated sl) *like* ~, vigorously: *raining/fighting like* ~.

bil·tong /'bɪltɒŋ/ *n* [U] (in S Africa) sun-dried salted meat cut into strips.

bi·met·al·lism /ˌbaɪ'metəlɪzəm/ *n* [U] system of having two metals, eg gold and silver, with a fixed ratio to each other as legal tender. **bi·met·al·lic** /ˌbaɪmɪ'tælɪk/ *adj*

bin /bɪn/ *n* large rigid container or enclosed space, usu with a lid, for storing coal, grain, flour, bread, etc: '*dustbin,* bin for rubbish, ashes, etc; '*litter bin.*

bi·nary /'baɪnərɪ/ *adj* of or involving a pair or pairs: *a* '~ *system,* (astron) two stars revolving round a common centre or one round the other. *the* ~ *scale,* (maths) with two digits, 0 and 1, as the base of the notation:

1　2　3　4　5　6　7　8　9　10
1　10　11　100　101　110　111　1000　1001　1010

bind /baɪnd/ *vt,vi* (*pt,pp* bound /baʊnd/) **1**
[VP6A,15B,14] ∼ *(to)*; ∼ *(together) (with)*, tie
or fasten, with rope, etc: *They bound his legs
(together) so that he shouldn't escape. Joan of Arc
was bound to the stake and burnt to death. The prisoner was bound hand and foot,* His arms and legs
were tied. (fig): *Commerce* ∼*s the two countries
together. We are bound to him by gratitude/by a
close friendship.* **2** [VP6A,14] ∼ *(with)*, secure the
edge of sth with tape, braid, etc: ∼ *the edge of a
carpet,* to prevent fraying; ∼ *the cuffs of a jacket
with leather.* **3** [VP6A,15B] ∼ *(up)*, tie or wind sth
round: ∼ *up a wound. Before sweeping the house
she bound up her hair in a large handkerchief.* **4**
[VP6A,15A,B] ∼ *(up)*, fasten (sheets of paper) into
a cover: ∼ *a book; a well-bound book; bound in
leather;* ∼ *up two books into one volume.* [VP2A in
progressive tenses only] *The new impression is
∼ing,* is being bound. **5** [VP6A,15B,2A] ∼ *(up/
together)*, hold or stick together in a solid mass:
Frost ∼*s the soil. The ground is frost-bound,*
frozen hard. *Clay* ∼*s* (= becomes hard) *when it is
baked. Stones bound together with cement make
good roads. Some kinds of food* ∼ *the bowels/are
∼ing,* cause constipation. **6** [VP17,14,15B,16B] ∼
sb to do sth/to sth, hold (sb) (by legal agreement,
a promise, or under penalty) to a certain course of
action: ∼ *sb to pay a debt;* ∼ *sb to secrecy,* make
him promise to keep sth secret. ∼ **oneself to do
sth,** promise, undertake, guarantee, to do it. ∼ *sb
over* (to keep the peace, etc), order that he must
appear before the judge again (if he fails to keep the
peace, etc). ∼ *sb over (as an apprentice) (to
sb)*, make an agreement that he shall be one: *The
boy was bound over as an apprentice to a carpenter.* **7** [VP2A] (dated sl) complain; carp: *Oh, do stop
∼ing!* **8** ⇨ bound⁵ for special uses of the *pp*. ∼**er**
n **1** person who ∼s, esp *a* '*book-∼er.* **2** thing that
ties or holds things together, eg a machine, or part
of a machine, that cuts and ∼s grain; loose cover
for unbound magazines; substance such as cement
or bitumen for joining things. '∼**ery** *n* place where
books are bound. ∼**ing** *adj be* ∼*ing on/upon,*
∼(6) or oblige sb to do sth: *an agreement that is

∼*ing on/upon all parties.* ⇨ also bind(5). □ *n*
[C,U] (esp) **1** book-cover. **2** strip, braid, etc for
protecting an edge or a seam (of a garment, etc).
bind·weed /'baɪndwiːd/ *n* [U] kinds of wild convolvulus.
bine /baɪn/ *n* flexible stem of various kinds of
climbing plants, eg hops.
binge /bɪndʒ/ *n* (sl) *have a* ∼; *go on the* ∼, drink
and make merry.
bingo /'bɪŋgəʊ/ *n* [U] popular gambling game,
played with cards on which numbered squares are
covered as the numbers are called at random: (attrib) ∼ *halls.*
bin·nacle /'bɪnəkl/ *n* (naut) non-magnetic stand for
a ship's compass (usu in front of the helm).
bin·ocu·lars /bɪ'nɒkjʊləz/ *n pl* field-glasses; instrument with lenses for both eyes, making distant
objects seem nearer.

lens

a pair of binoculars

bi·nomial /baɪ'nəʊmɪəl/ *adj* (maths) made up of
two numbers or algebraic expressions joined by +
or − (eg $a^2 − 3b$).
bio·chem·is·try /ˌbaɪəʊ'kemɪstrɪ/ *n* [U] chemistry
of living organisms.
bio·de·grad·able /ˌbaɪəʊdɪ'greɪdəbl/ *adj* (of substances) that can be broken down by bacteria: *Are
plastic bags indestructible or* ∼?
bi·ogra·phy /baɪ'ɒgrəfɪ/ *n* **1** [C] person's life-
history written by another. **2** [U] branch of literature dealing with the lives of persons. **bi·ogra·pher**
/baɪ'ɒgrəfə(r)/ *n* person who writes a ∼. **bio-
graphic, -i·cal** /ˌbaɪə'græfɪk, -ɪkl/ *adj* of ∼.
bi·ol·ogy /baɪ'ɒlədʒɪ/ *n* [U] science of the physical
life of animals (= *zoology*) and plants (= *botany*).
bi·ol·ogist /baɪ'ɒlədʒɪst/ *n* student of, expert in,
∼. **bio·logi·cal** /ˌbaɪə'lɒdʒɪkl/ *adj* of ∼: *a biological laboratory/experiment.* **bio,logical 'warfare**,
deliberate use of bacteria to spread disease.

KINGFISHER

GREAT TIT

NIGHTINGALE

bill

feather

breast

tail

wing

leg

claw

SKYLARK

foot

small land birds

SPARROW

ROBIN

bi·opsy /'baɪɒpsɪ/ n (pl -sies) [C] (med) removal and examination of tissue or fluid from a living body. ⇨ autopsy.

bio·scope /'baɪəskəʊp/ n (S Africa) cinema.

bi·par·ti·san /ˌbaɪpɑːtɪ'zæn US: ˌbaɪ'pɑːrtɪzn/ adj of, supported by, consisting of, two otherwise opposed (esp political) parties: a ~ foreign policy.

bi·ped /'baɪped/ n animal with only two feet.

bi·plane /'baɪpleɪn/ n aircraft with two pairs of wings, one above the other.

birch /bɜːtʃ/ n 1 [C] (kinds of) forest tree growing in northern countries; it has smooth bark and slender branches. 2 [U] its wood, eg as used for making canoes. 3 [C] (also '~-rod) bundle of ~ twigs tied together and used formerly for punishing schoolboys. □ vt [VP6A] punish with a ~-rod.

bird /bɜːd/ n 1 feathered creature with two legs and two wings, usu able to fly. ⇨ the illus below and at **fowl, prey, rare, water**. *A ~ in the hand is worth two in the bush,* (prov) Sth which one has, though small, is better than sth larger, which one has not. *(strictly) for the ~s,* (sl) bad; worthless. *get the ~,* (sl) be hissed, scorned or rejected. *give sb the ~,* (sl) hiss, scorn or reject him. *kill two ~s with one stone,* achieve two aims at once. '~-cage n cage for a ~ or ~s. '~-fancier n person who knows about, collects, breeds or sells ~s. '~-lime n sticky substance put on branches to catch ~s. ~'s-ˌeye 'view n wide view seen from high up; (fig) general survey of a subject. '~-nesting n hunting for birds' nests to get the eggs). '~-watch vi [VP2A] study birds in their natural state; hence '~-watcher n person who does this; hence '~-watching n [U]. ⇨ also feather[1], passage(1), prey. 2 (colloq) person: an odd/wise ~; a cunning old ~. 3 (GB sl) young woman.

bir·etta /bɪ'retə/ n [C] (pl ~s) square cap worn by RC and some Anglican priests.

biro /'baɪərəʊ/ n [C] (pl ~s) (P) (kind of) ball-pen.

birth /bɜːθ/ n 1 [U] (process of) being born, coming into the world; [C] instance of this: *The baby weighed seven pounds at ~,* when it was born. *The boy has been delicate from* (his) ~, has been weak in health since he was born. *Cats sometimes have four or five young at a ~. There were 167 more ~s than deaths in the town last year. give ~ to,* bring into the world; (fig) produce: *give ~ to a child/a poem/a dispute.* 2 [U] origin, descent: *She is Russian by ~ and British by marriage. be of good ~,* (old use) come of an acceptable family. '~-control n [U] (method of) preventing unwanted conception(2). '~-day n (anniversary of the) day of one's ~. '~-mark n mark on the body at or from ~. '~-place n house or district in which one was born. '~-rate n number of ~s in one year for every 1000 persons. '~-right n any of various rights, privileges and properties to which a person has a right as a member of his family, a citizen of his country, etc.

bis·cuit /'bɪskɪt/ n [C] 1 flat, thin, crisp cake of many kinds, sweetened or unsweetened. *take the ~,* (sl) be the best/worst at something; be surprising. 2 (US) bread dough baked in small shapes. 3 light-brown.

bi·sect /baɪ'sekt/ vt [VP6A] cut or divide into two (usu equal) parts. **bi·sec·tion** /baɪ'sekʃn/ n [U] division into two (equal) parts.

bi·sex·ual /ˌbaɪ'sekʃʊəl/ adj of two sexes; having both male and female sexual organs; sexually attracted to either sex. □ n individual showing one of these characteristics. ~·ity /ˌbaɪsekʃʊ'ælətɪ/ n [U] condition of being ~.

bishop /'bɪʃəp/ n 1 Christian clergyman of high rank who organizes the work of the Church in a city or district. ⇨ the illus at **vestment**. ⇨ **diocese**. ~·ric /-rɪk/ n office of a ~; district under a ~. 2 chess piece, ⇨ the illus at **chess**.

bis·muth /'bɪzməθ/ n [U] reddish-white metal (symbol **Bi**), used in alloys; compound of this used medically, eg for stomach troubles.

bi·son /'baɪsn/ n (pl unchanged) European wild ox; American buffalo. ⇨ the illus at **large**.

bis·tro /'biːstrəʊ/ n [C] (pl ~s) small, cheap restaurant; (in France) small bar[1](13) or nightclub.

bit[1] /bɪt/ n 1 mouth-piece (metal bar) forming part of a horse's bridle. ⇨ the illus at **harness**. *take the bit between one's teeth,* (of a horse) run away out of control; (fig) apply oneself to sth difficult or risky or distasteful. 2 part of a tool that cuts or grips when twisted; tool for boring or drilling holes, fitted into a *drill* or a *brace*. ⇨ the illus at **drill, brace**.

SWIFT

SWALLOW

CROW

CUCKOO

PIGEON

bit² /bɪt/ n 1 small piece of anything: *He took some paper and a few bits of wood and soon made a fire. He ate every bit of*(= all) *his dinner. He has saved a nice bit* (= a good sum) *of money. bit by bit*, slowly, gradually. *a bit at a time*, by degrees. *every bit as (good, etc)*, equally (good, etc). *do one's bit*, perform one's share of a task; give as much help as is expected of one. *wait a bit*, a short time. *a bit*, rather: *She's feeling a bit tired. a bit of a*, rather a: *He's a bit of a coward. a bit of all right*, (GB sl) very fine. *not a bit*, not at all; not in the least: *He's not a bit better. He doesn't care a bit. It's not a bit of use*, It's quite useless. *not a bit of it*, not at all (used as a strong denial): *You'd think she'd be tired after such a long journey, but not a bit of it! pull/cut/tear sth to bits*, into small pieces. *go/come to bits*, into small pieces. **2** (used colloq, like *piece*, with *news, advice, luck*): *a bit of good advice.* **3** (a) small coin: *threepenny bit*, (former) coin (GB) worth threepence. (b) (US) 12½ cents. **4** (colloq, esp US) area common to a group of subjects, attitudes, etc: *She couldn't accept the whole drug-culture bit.*

bit³ /bɪt/ n (comp) unit of information expressed as a choice between two possibilities.

bit⁴ /bɪt/ ⇨ bite¹.

bitch /bɪtʃ/ n 1 female dog, fox, otter or wolf. 2 ⚠ (derog sl) spiteful woman. □ vi [VP2A] (colloq) complain in a sour way; speak spitefully to or about sb or sth. ~y adj(colloq) spiteful.

bite¹ /baɪt/ vt,vi (pt bit /bɪt/, pp bitten /'bɪtn/). **1** [VP6A,15B,2A,3A] ~ (into), cut into with the teeth: *The dog bit me in the leg. Does your dog* ~, is it in the habit of biting people? *He bit into the peach.* ~ *at sth*, try to get it with the teeth; snap at. ~ *off*, cut off with the teeth: *He bit off a large piece of the apple.* ~ *off more than one can chew*, attempt too much. *(have) sth to* ~ *on*, sth to get one's teeth into; (fig) sth definite to do, examine, etc. ~ *the dust*, (colloq) (fig) fall to the ground; be killed. ~ *one's lips*, try to conceal one's anger or annoyance. *once bitten twice shy*, (prov) a person who has been cheated, hurt, etc is likely to be cautious afterwards. *the biter bitten*, the person who intended to cheat was himself cheated. **2** [VP6A] (a) (of fleas, mosquitoes, etc) sting: *He was badly bitten by the mosquitoes.* (b) (of fish) accept the bait: *The fish wouldn't* ~. *I tried to sell him my old car but he wouldn't* ~, (fig) would not consider the suggestion. **3** [VP6A,2A,3A] ~ (into), cause a smarting pain to; injure: *His fingers were bitten by the frost/were frost-bitten. Mustard and pepper* ~ *the tongue. Strong acids* ~ (into) *metals*, make holes in them. **4** [VP6A,2A] take strong hold of; grip: *The rails were covered with ice and the wheels did not* ~. **bit·ing** adj sharp; cutting: *a biting wind; biting words.* **bit·ing·ly** adv

bite² /baɪt/ n 1 act of biting: *eating sth at one* ~. **2** injury resulting from a ~ or sting: *His face was covered with insect* ~s. **3** piece cut off by biting. **4** (colloq) food to eat: *I haven't had a* ~ *since morning*, have eaten nothing. **5** taking bait from a hook by fish: *He had been fishing all morning but hadn't had a* ~. **6** [U] sharpness; sting: *There's a* ~ *in the air this morning.* **7** [U] grip; hold: *a file/screw with plenty of* ~.

bit·ten /'bɪtn/ ⇨ bite¹.

bit·ter /'bɪtə(r)/ adj 1 tasting like beer or unsweetened coffee. *,~-'sweet adj* sweet but with a ~ taste at the end; (fig) pleasant but with a mixture of sth unpleasant. **2** unwelcome to the mind; hard to bear; causing sorrow: ~ *hardships/experiences. His failure to pass the examination was a* ~ *disappointment. a* ~ *pill to swallow*, sth unpleasant to accept. **3** filled with, showing, caused by, envy, hate, remorse, or disappointment: ~ *quarrels/ words/enemies/reproaches/tears.* **4** piercingly cold: *a* ~ *wind.* **5** *to the* ~ *end*, until all that is possible has been done: *fight to the* ~ *end.* □ n **1** bitterness. *take the* ~ *with the sweet*, accept misfortune as well as good fortune. Cf *take the rough with the smooth*, which is more usu. **2** [U] ~ beer, ie heavily flavoured with hops: *a pint of* ~. **3** (pl) liquor made from herbs, fruits, etc taken to help digestion or used to flavour gin, etc: *orange* ~s; *gin and* ~s. **~·ly** adv**~·ness** n

bit·tern /'bɪtən/ n any of several kinds of wading birds that live on marshes, esp the kind known for its booming note. ⇨ the illus at water.

bitu·men /'bɪtjʊmən/ n [U] black, sticky substance (from petroleum), used for making roads, etc; mineral pitch; asphalt. **bit·umi·nous** /bɪ'tjuːmɪnəs US: -'tuː-/ adj containing ~ or tar: *bituminous coal*, burning with smoky yellow flames.

bi·valve /'baɪvælv/ n (zool) mollusc with a hinged double shell, eg an oyster, a mussel, a clam.

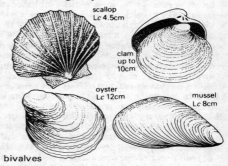

scallop Lc 4.5cm

clam up to 10cm

oyster Lc 12cm

mussel Lc 8cm

bivalves

biv·ouac /'bɪvʊæk/ n soldiers' temporary camp without tents or other cover. □ vi (pt,pp bivouacked) [VP2A] make a ~; stay in a ~.

biz /bɪz/ n (sl) business: *Good biz!* Well done! **'show·biz**, (sl) (providing and managing) popular entertainment.

bi·zarre /bɪ'zɑː(r)/ adj grotesque; odd.

bi·zonal /,baɪ'zəʊnl/ adjof two zones.

blab /blæb/ vt,vi (-bb-) [VP6A,15B,2A] (colloq) talk foolishly or indiscreetly: *Don't* ~! ~ *(out)*, tell (a secret): ~ *out a secret.*

blab·ber /'blæbə(r)/ vt,vi = blab. **'~·mouth** n person who ~s.

black /blæk/ adj (-er, -est) **1** without light or almost without light; the colour of this printing-ink; opposite to white. *be* ~ *and blue*, covered with bruises. ~ *in the face*, dark red or purple (with anger or because of making great efforts). *be in sb's* ~ *book(s)*, ⇨ book¹(6). *look* ~ *at sb; give sb a* ~ *look*, look at him angrily. *not so* ~ *as one is painted*, not so bad as one is said to be. **2** (various uses, mostly to intensify the meaning of the n): ~ *despair*, deep, dismal; ~ *tidings*, sad news, causing despair; ~ *deeds*, wicked; *in one of his* ~ *moods*, silent and bad-tempered. **3** (of work in a factory, shipyard, etc during a strike; of the materials, etc) not to be done, handled, etc: *The strikers declared the work/cargo ~*. **4** (compounds, etc) *~ and white,* ink drawing. *(have sth down) in ~ and white,* (have it) recorded in writing or print. *~ art,* magic, used for evil purposes. '*~-ball* vt prevent (sb) from being elected a member of a club by voting against him at a secret ballot. '*~-beetle* n cockroach. '*~-berry* /'blækbərı US: -berı/ n (pl -ries) small berry, ~ when ripe, growing wild on bushes (called *brambles*): *go ~berrying* /-berıŋ/, go out gathering *~berries.* ⇨ the illus at fruit. '*~-bird* n common European songbird. '*~-board* n board used in schools for writing and drawing on with chalk. *~* '*box* n device for recording information about the performance of an aircraft. *~* '*coffee* n coffee without milk, usu strong. *~* '*comedy* n (theatre) comedy with a tragic element or basic pessimism, usu heavily ironical. cf *sick joke.* **the** '*B~ Country,* the smoky, industrial area in Staffordshire and Warwickshire. *~'-cur-rant* n kind of currant with ~ fruit. ⇨ currant(2). **the** *,~* '*flag,* flag formerly used by pirates (sea-robbers); flag once used at prisons as a signal that a murderer had been executed by hanging. *,~* '*frost* n hard frost without rime. '*~-guard* /'blægɑ:d/ n person who is quite without honour; scoundrel. □ vt call (sb) a ~guard; use very bad language about or to (sb). '*~-guard·ly* /'blægədlı/ adj dishonest and immoral: *a ~guardly trick.* '*~-head* n (kind of) pimple on the skin, the top being ~. *,~* '*hole* n (astron) region in space from which no matter or radiation (eg light) can escape. *,~* '*ice* n ice, esp on a road surface, which is almost invisible and dangerous to drive on. *~-'lead* n [U] soft, grey-black solid (plumbago, or graphite) used for lead pencils, polishing and as a lubricant. □ vt polish, eg a fireplace, with ~-lead. '*~-leg* n person who offers to work when the regular workers are on strike. □ *vi,vt* (-gg-) act as ~leg; betray (fellow workers) by doing this. '*~-list* n list of persons who are considered dangerous or who are to be punished. □ vt enter the name of (sb) on a ~list. *,~* '*magic* n witchcraft. '*~-mail* vt, n [U] (force sb to make a) payment of money for not making known sth discreditable about him. Hence, '*~-mailer* n person who does this. *,~* **Ma'ria** /mə'raıə/ n van for taking prisoners from and to jail. *,~* '*mark* n (fig) mark(4) of bad conduct, failure, etc: *Her continual lateness was a ~ mark against her promotion.* *,~* '*market* n unlawful buying and selling of goods, currencies, etc that are officially controlled; place where such trading is carried on. *,~* ,*marke'teer* /,mɑ:kı'tıə(r)/ n person carrying on this trade. *,~* '*mass* n travesty of the RC Mass, for Satan instead of God. '*~-out* n (a) (during wartime) the keeping of all buildings, etc, dark (by curtains, etc, in windows, by having no street-lighting, etc) in order to prevent any light being seen, esp from the air. **(b)** temporary complete failure of the memory or consciousness; (esp flying) temporary blindness caused by a sudden turn or a change in speed. **(c)** extinguishing of all lights on the stage of a theatre, eg for a change of scenery. □ *~ out, vt,vi* [VP15B,2A] cause a ~out ((a) and (c) above); lose one's memory, etc, temporarily. ,*B~* '*Panther* n (US, 1960's) member of a militant B~ Power group. ,*B~* '*Power* n (US, 1960's) militant movement for civil rights for Negroes. *,~* '*pudding* n sausage made of blood, suet, barley, etc. ,*B~*

'*Sash* n (S Africa) women's anti-apartheid organisation. *,~* '*sheep* n good-for-nothing person. '*B~-shirt* n member of the former Italian Fascist party. '*~-smith* n man who makes and repairs things of iron, esp a shoer of horses. '*~ spot* n place (eg on a road) where accidents often happen. '*~-thorn* n thorny shrub which has white blossom before the leaves appear and purple fruit (*sloe*) like a small plum. *,~-water* '*fever,* n tropical disease with bloody urine. □ n **1** [U] ~ colour: *He was dressed in ~,* in ~ clothes. **2** [U] ~ paint or dye. **3** [C] particle of soot. **4** [C] Negro (formerly derog, but now widely used). **5 the ~,** credit side of business accounts. *be in/get into the ~,* have/get assets that exceed liabilities. ⇨ red n(4). □ vt [VP6A] **1** make ~, polish (boots, etc), with blacking. **2** declare ~(3): *The strikers ~ed the ship/the cargo. ~ out,* ⇨ ~out above.

black·a·moor /'blækəmʊə(r)/ n (old use, hum or derog) black person.

blacken /'blækən/ vt,vi **1** [VP6A,2A] make or become black. **2** [VP6A] ~ *(sb's name),* speak evil of (sb's character).

black·ing /'blækıŋ/ n [U] black paste or liquid for polishing shoes (now usu *shoe polish*).

blad·der /'blædə(r)/ n **1** bag of skin in which urine collects in human and animal bodies. ⇨ the illus at kidney. **2** such a bag, or a bag of rubber, etc, that can be filled with air, eg the rubber ~ in a football.

blade /bleıd/ n **1** flattened cutting part of a knife, sword, chisel, etc: *a pocket-knife with two ~s; a packet of five razor ~s.* ⇨ the illus at razor. **2** sword; swordsman. **3** flat wide part of an oar (the part that goes into the water), bat, propeller, etc. **4** flat, long, narrow leaf, esp of grass and cereals (wheat, barley, etc).

blae·berry /'bleıbərı US: -berı/ n = bilberry.

blah /blɑ:/ n [U] (colloq) ˙ high-sounding but meaningless talk or writing.

blame /bleım/ vt [VP6A,14] ~ *sb (for sth); ~ sth on sb,* fix on sb the responsibility for sth done (badly or wrongly) or not done: *Bad workmen often ~ their tools. He ~d his teacher for his failure. He ~d his failure on his teacher. I have nothing to ~ myself for. be to ~,* deserve censure: *Who is to ~ for starting the fire,* Whom have we to find fault with? *I am in no way to ~,* am not in any way responsible. □ n [U] **1** responsibility for sth done (badly or wrongly) or not done: *Where does the ~ lie for our failure,* Who or what is responsible? *bear/take the ~ (for sth),* take the responsibility. *put/lay the ~ on sb (for sth),* make him responsible. **2** finding fault: *If you don't do the work well, you will incur ~,* people will find fault. *~-less* adj free from ~ or faults; innocent: *I am ~less in this matter. ~-less·ly* adv *~-worthy* /'bleımwɜ:ðı/ adj deserving ~.

blanch /blɑ:ntʃ US: blæntʃ/ vt,vi [VP6A,2A] make or become pale or white, eg by taking the skin off almonds, by not letting light get to plants; make or become pale with fear, cold, etc.

blanc·mange /blə'mɒnʒ/ n [C,U] jelly made in a mould with milk: *~ powder,* mixture of powdered milk, powdered gelatine, etc to make kinds of ~.

bland /blænd/ adj **1** gentle or polite in manner or talk (usu in order to ingratiate oneself). **2** (of air, food, drink) mild; comforting. **3** featureless; uninteresting. *~-ly* adv *~-ness* n

bland·ish·ment /'blændıʃmənt/ n (usu pl) (formal) soft and gentle ways and speech intended to make sb do sth; flattery; coaxing.

blank /blæŋk/ adj 1 (of paper, parts of a document, etc) with nothing written, printed or drawn on it: *a ~ sheet of paper; a ~ page/space.* ,~ **'bill,** Bill of Exchange on which the name of the person to be paid is not stated. ,~ **'cheque,** one with the amount left for the payee to fill in. **give sb a ~ cheque,** (fig) full power to act as he thinks best. **2** empty; without interest or expression: *There was a ~ look on his face,* He seemed not to be interested, not to understand, etc. *He looked ~,* puzzled. *His future looks ~,* seems to be empty and dull. *My mind went ~,* I could not recall things, esp things I needed to be aware of. ,~ **'cartridge,** with a charge of powder, but no bullet. ,~ **'verse,** (usu lines of ten syllables) without rhyme. ,~ **'wall,** one with no door, window or other opening. **come up against a ~ wall,** (fig) be unable to find support, information, etc. □ *n* **1** space left empty or to be filled (in sth printed or written): *In a telegraph form there are ~s for the name and address, the message, etc. When Tom was doing his French translation, he left ~s for all the words he did not know.* **2** lottery ticket that does not win a prize. **draw a ~,** get nothing (after hoping to win or find sth). **3** empty surface; emptiness: *His mind/memory was a complete ~,* he could remember nothing. *The death of her husband in the war left a big ~ in her life.* **4** [C,U] ~ cartridge: *They fired twenty rounds of ~/twenty ~s.* ~**·ly** *adv*

blan·ket /'blæŋkɪt/ *n* **1** thick, woollen covering used on beds, or for keeping a horse warm in a stable, etc: (fig) *a ~ of snow.* **wet ~,** (colloq) person who, by being gloomy himself, prevents others from enjoying themselves. **2** (used attrib) covering all cases or classes: *a ~* (= comprehensive) *insurance policy; ~ instructions,* intended to provide for everything. □ *vt* [VP6A,14] ~ **(in/with),** cover thickly: *The valley was ~ed with fog.*

blare /bleə(r)/ *n* [U] sound or noise (of trumpets or horns): *the ~ of a brass band.* ~ *vi,vt* **1** [VP2A,C] ~ **(out),** make such sounds: *The trumpets ~d out.* **2** [VP15B] ~ **out,** produce with such sounds; utter loudly: *The band ~d out a current hit. He ~d out a warning.*

blar·ney /'blɑːnɪ/ *n* [U] *vt,vi* (dated) (use) the kind of talk that flatters and deceives people: *Not so much of your ~!*

blasé /'blɑːzeɪ US: blɑː'zeɪ/ *adj* ~ **(about),** not showing signs of enjoying (sth) or being pleased (about sth): *~ about her success.*

blas·pheme /blæs'fiːm/ *vi,vt* [VP2A,6A] speak in an irreverent way about God and sacred things; use violent language about (sb or sth): *~ the name of God.* ~**er** *n* person who ~s. **blas·phem·ous** /'blæsfəməs/ *adj* (of persons) using blasphemy; (of language) containing blasphemy. **blas·phem·ous·ly** *adv* **blas·phemy** /'blæsfəmɪ/ *n* [U] contemptuous or irreverent talk about God and sacred things; [C] instance of this.

blast /blɑːst US: blæst/ *n* **1** strong, sudden rush of wind: *A ~ of hot air came from the furnace. When the window was opened an icy ~ came into the room.* **2** (often [U]) strong rush of air or gas spreading outwards from an explosion: *Thousands of windows were broken by ~ during the air raids.* '~**-off,** ⇨ blast ⅴ(3). **3** stream of air used to intensify the heat in a furnace, etc. **at full ~,** (colloq) with the maximum activity. **in/out of ~,** (of a furnace) working/not working. '~**-furnace** *n* furnace

for melting iron ore by forcing into it a current of heated air. **4** sound made by a wind-instrument: *The hunter blew a ~ on his horn. The ship sounded a prolonged ~ on the siren.* **5** quantity of explosive (eg dynamite) used at one time (eg in a quarry). □ *vt* **1** [VP6A,2A] blow up (rocks, etc) with explosives: *Danger! B~ing in progress!* **2** [VP6A] cause (sth) to come to nothing; shrivel; injure: *blossom ~ed by frost. The tree had been ~ed by lightning. His hopes were ~ed.* **3** [VP15B,2C] ~ **off,** (of spacecraft, etc) force, be forced, upwards by expanding gases. Hence, '~**-off** *n* (time of) launching of such a spacecraft: *the count-down to ~-off.* **4** [VP6A] (sl) reproach sb severely: *be ~ed by one's boss; get a ~ing from sb.* **5** (in curses, with *May God* understood) *b~ it/you! ~ed* /'blɑːstɪd US: 'blæ-/ *attrib adj* (in curses) damnable.

bla·tant /'bleɪtnt/ *adj* noisy and rough; attracting attention in a vulgar and shameless way; too obvious. ~**·ly** *adv*

blather /'blæðə(r)/ *n, v* ⇨ blether.

blaze¹ /bleɪz/ *n* [C] **1** bright flame or fire: *We could see the ~ of a cheerful fire through the window. I put more wood on the fire and it soon burst into a ~,* began to burn brightly. **2** fire; burning building(s): *It took the firemen two hours to put the ~ out.* **3** (*pl*) (sl) hell: *Go to ~s! He was working like ~s,* working furiously. **4** glow of colour; bright light: *The red tulips made a ~ of colour in the garden. The main street of the town is a ~ of light(s) in the evening.* **5** violent outburst: *in a ~ of anger.*

blaze² /bleɪz/ *vi,vt* **1** [VP2A,C] burn with flame: *There was a fire blazing on the hearth. When the firemen arrived the whole building was blazing. ~ up,* burst into flames. **2** [VP2A,C] be bright with colour; shine brightly or with warmth: *The garden was blazing with colour. The sun ~d down on us.* **3** [VP2A,C] burst out with strong feeling: *He was blazing with anger/indignation.* **4** [VP2C,15B] ~ **away,** fire continuously with rifles, etc: *They ~d away at the enemy. He ~d away all his ammunition.* **blaz·ing** *adj: a blazing fire;* (fig) conspicuous: *a blazing indiscretion;* (foxhunting) *a blazing* (= very strong) *scent.*

blaze³ /bleɪz/ *n* white mark on a horse's or an ox's face; mark made on a tree by cutting the bark. □ *vt* [VP6A] mark (a tree) by cutting off part of the bark. ~ **a trail,** mark trees to show a path through a forest; (fig) do sth for the first time and show others how to do it.

blaze⁴ /bleɪz/ *vt* [VP6A,15B] ~ **(abroad),** make known far and wide: *~ the news (abroad).*

blazer /'bleɪzə(r)/ *n* loose-fitting jacket (sometimes in the colours of a school, club, team, etc) for informal wear.

bla·zon /'bleɪzn/ *n* coat of arms, esp on a shield. ⇨ the illus at armour. □ *vt* = blaze⁴. ~**ry** *n* bright display.

bleach /bliːtʃ/ *vt,vi* [VP6A,2A] make or become white (by chemical action or sunlight): *~ linen; bones of animals ~ing on the desert sand.* '~**ing-powder** *n* (eg chloride of lime) substance used to remove colour from dyed materials. □ *n* chemical for ~ing and sterilizing: *household ~.*

bleach·ers /'bliːtʃəz/ *n pl* (US) unroofed seats/planks at sports grounds.

bleak /bliːk/ *adj* **1** (of the weather) cold and cheerless; (of a place) bare, swept by cold winds: *a ~ hillside.* **2** (fig) dreary: *~ prospects.* ~**·ly** *adv*

bleary /'blɪərɪ/ adj dim; blurred. ˏ~-'eyed /ˌblɪərɪ'aɪd/ adj having ~ eyes: *He got out of bed all ~-eyed.*

bleat /bliːt/ n cry of a sheep, goat or calf. □ *vi,vt* [VP2A] make a cry of this kind; [VP6A,15B] ~ *(out),* speak, say (sth) feebly: *He ~ed (out) a complaint.*

bleed /bliːd/ *vi,vt* (*pt,pp* bled /bled/) 1 [VP2A,C] lose, send out, blood: *If you cut your finger it will ~. He was slowly ~ing to death.* 2 [VP2A,C,3A simple tenses only] ~ *(for),* feel great distress: *Our hearts ~ for homeless people during this cold winter.* 3 [VP6A] draw blood from: *Doctors used to ~ people when they were ill.* 4 [VP6A,14] force (sb) to pay money unjustly: *The blackmailers bled him for £500.* 5 [VP2A] (of a plant, tree, etc) lose sap or juice.

bleep /bliːp/ n high-pitched sound or signal sent out by radio, used eg as a summoning or warning device. □ *vi* emit such sounds.

blem·ish /'blemɪʃ/ n [C,U] mark, etc that spoils the beauty or perfection of sb or sth; moral defect: *without ~,* faultless. □ *vt* [VP6A] spoil the perfection of.

blench /blentʃ/ *vi* [VP2A] make a quick movement of fear.

blend /blend/ *vt,vi* (*pt,pp* ~ed or, liter, blent /blent/) 1 [VP6A] mix together, esp sorts of tea, tobacco, spirits, etc, to get a certain quality: *~ed whisky. A grocer used to need to know how to ~ tea. Our coffees* (ie varieties of coffee) *are carefully ~ed.* 2 [VP2A,3A] mix, form a mixture: *Oil and water do not ~. Oil does not ~ with water.* 3 [VP2A] go well together; have no sharp or unpleasant contrast: (esp of colours) pass by degrees into each other: *These two colours ~ well. How well their voices ~!* □ n [C] mixture made of various sorts (of tea, tobacco, etc): *This coffee is a ~ of Java and Brazil.*

blent ⇨ blend.

bless /bles/ *vt* (*pt,pp* ~ed /blest/ and blest, as in (6) below) [VP6A] 1 ask God's favour for: *They brought the children to Jesus and he ~ed them. The priest ~ed the people/the crops.* 2 wish happiness or favour to: *B~ you, my boy!* 3 consecrate; make sacred or holy: *bread ~ed at the altar.* 4 **be ~ed with,** be fortunate in having: *I am not greatly ~ed with worldly goods,* am not rich. *May you always be ~ed with good health.* 5 call (God) holy: *'We praise Thee, we ~ Thee,' 'We ~ Thy Holy Name.'* 6 (colloq, in exclamations, expressing surprise): *B~ me! B~ my soul! Well, I'm blest! I'm blest if I know!* ie I don't know at all. **~ed** /'blesɪd/ adj 1 holy, sacred. **the B~ed Virgin,** the mother of Jesus. **the B~ed Sacrament,** Holy Communion. 2 fortunate: *B~ed are the poor in spirit.* 3 **the B~ed,** those who are with God in paradise. 4 (sl, mild swearing) cursed: *I've broken the whole ~ed lot!* **~ed·ness** /'blesɪdnɪs/ n [U] happiness. **~·ing** n 1 the favour of God; prayer for God's favour; thanks to God before or after a meal: *ask a ~ing.* ⇨ grace(5). 2 sth that one is glad of; sth that brings comfort or happiness: *What a ~ing it is you didn't get caught in the storm yesterday!* **a ~ing in disguise,** sth that seems unfortunate, but that is seen later to be fortunate.

blether /'bleðə(r)/, **blather** /'blæðə(r)/ n [U] foolish talk. □ *vi* [VP2A,C] talk nonsense.

blew /bluː/ ⇨ blow¹.

blight /blaɪt/ n 1 [U] (sorts of) plant disease; mil-

dew. 2 [C] evil influence of obscure origin: *a ~ upon his hopes.* □ *vt* [VP6A] be a ~ on: *His hopes were ~ed. Her life was ~ed by constant illness.* **~er** n (dated sl) 1 annoying person. 2 fellow: *You lucky ~er!*

Blighty /'blaɪtɪ/ n (GB 1st world war sl) home (during service abroad). **a ~ wound,** one severe enough for a soldier to be returned to GB.

bli·mey /'blaɪmɪ/ int (vulg) expressing surprise.

blimp /blɪmp/ n 1 small non-rigid airship. 2 **(Colonel) B~,** pompous-looking reactionary person.

blind¹ /blaɪnd/ adj 1 without the power to see: *Tom helped the ~ man across the road. He is ~ in the right eye.* **turn a/one's ~ eye to sth,** pretend not to see it. **~ spot,** point on the retina insensible to light; (fig) inability to recognize, understand or sympathize with sth. 2 ~ *(to),* unable to see effects, to judge or understand well: *Mothers are sometimes ~ to the faults of their children. A man would be ~ not to see that difficulty.* 3 reckless; thoughtless: *In his ~ haste he almost ran into the river.* 4 not ruled by purpose: *Some people think that the world is governed by ~ forces.* 5 (sl) drunk (also ~ *drunk*). 6 ~ *alley,* ⇨ alley(1). **~ date,** ⇨ date¹(4). **~ flying,** navigation, eg in cloud, fog, with the aid of instruments only. **~ turning,** (in a road) one that cannot easily be seen by drivers. ˏ~·man's 'buff n game in which one player, who is blindfolded, tries to catch and identify one of the others who push him about.

blind² /blaɪnd/ *vt* [VP6A,14] ~ *sb (to),* make ~; (fig) take away the power of judgement: *a ~ing light. The soldier had been ~ed in the war. His feelings for her ~ed him to her faults.* **~·ers** n pl (US) blinkers. **~·ly** adv **~ness** n

blind³ /blaɪnd/ n [C] 1 roll of cloth (usu strong linen) fixed on a roller and pulled down to cover a window (US = *window-shade*): *pull down/lower, draw up/raise the ~s.* 2 (fig) deception: *It was only a ~,* sth intended to hide the reality. 3 (US) hide¹ n

blind·fold /'blaɪndfəʊld/ *vt* [VP6A] cover the eyes of (sb) with a bandage so that he cannot see. □ n [C] such a cover. □ adj with the eyes bandaged, covered with a handkerchief, etc.

blink /blɪŋk/ *vi,vt* 1 [VP2A,C,6A,15B] shut and open the eyes quickly: ~ *the eyes;* ~ *away a tear.* 2 [VP6A] ~ *the fact that,* (fig) refuse to consider; ignore: *There's no ~ing the fact that....* 3 [VP2C] (of lights, esp when in the distance) come and go; shine in an unsteady way: *We saw the lights of a steamer ~ing on the horizon.* □ n [C] instance of ~ing. **~·ing** adj (colloq euphem for) bloody(3): *It's a ~ing nuisance.*

blink·ers /'blɪŋkəz/ n pl (US = *blinders*) leather squares to prevent a horse from seeing sideways. ⇨ the illus at harness.

blip /blɪp/ n spot of light on a radar screen.

bliss /blɪs/ n [U] perfect happiness; great joy. **~·ful** /-fʊl/ adj **~·fully** /-fʊlɪ/ adv

blis·ter /'blɪstə(r)/ n [C] 1 small bag-like swelling under the skin, filled with liquid (caused by rubbing, burning, etc): *If your shoes are too tight, you may get ~s on your feet.* 2 similar swelling on the surface of metal, painted or varnished wood, a plant, etc. □ *vt,vi* [VP6A,2A] cause, get, a ~ or ~s on: *He is not used to manual work and his hands ~ easily. The hot sun has ~ed the paint on the door.*

blithe, blithe·some /blaɪð, -səm/ adj (chiefly poet) gay and joyous. **~·ly** adv

blith·er·ing /'blɪðərɪŋ/ adj (colloq) utter; contemptible (esp in): ~ idiot.

blitz /blɪts/ n rapid, violent attack (esp from the air). □ vt [VP6A] damage or destroy in this way (esp in pp): ~ed areas/towns, destroyed by bombing during air-raids.

bliz·zard /'blɪzəd/ n [C] violent and heavy snowstorm.

bloated /'bləʊtɪd/ adj swollen; fat and large in an unhealthy way: a ~ face; a fat, ugly man, ~ with over-eating; (fig) ~ with pride, puffed up with pride.

bloater /'bləʊtə(r)/ n kind of salted and smoked herring: ~ paste, paste made from ~s. ⇨ kipper.

blob /blɒb/ n drop of liquid, eg paint; small round mass, eg of wax; spot of colour.

bloc /blɒk/ n combination of parties, groups, states, etc with a special interest: the sterling ~, those countries with currencies related to sterling.

block¹ /blɒk/ n 1 large, solid piece of wood, stone, etc: A butcher cuts up his meat on a large ~ of wood. The ~s of stone in the Pyramids are five or six feet high. The statue is to be carved out of a ~ of marble. Children play with building ~s, cubes of wood put together to make toy houses, etc. ⇨ chip(1). 2 main part of a petrol engine, consisting of the cylinders and valves. 3 the ~, (in olden times) large piece of wood on which a person put his neck to have his head cut off as a punishment. go/be sent to the ~, to death in this way. 4 shaped piece of wood on which hats are moulded. 5 pulley, or system of pulleys, in a case (often ~ and tackle). 6 piece of wood or metal with designs, etc, cut (engraved) on it for printing. 7 mass of buildings (shops, offices, apartments, etc) joined together; (esp US) area of buildings bounded by four streets; the length of one side of such an area: To reach the post-office, walk two ~s east and then turn left. ~-buster /'blɒkbʌstə(r)/ n powerful explosive to demolish buildings; (fig) forceful person or thing bringing about a sudden effect, eg in a dispute. 8 division of seats in a theatre, concert hall, etc; large quantity of shares in a business. 9 obstruction; sth that makes movement or flow difficult or impossible: There was a ~ in the pipe and the water couldn't flow away. 'road ~, barrier across a road at which documents, etc are checked. 'traffic ~, (usu traffic jam) large number of buses, cars, vans, trams, etc held up and unable to move on. 10 '~ grant, fixed and non-recurring subsidy. ~ 'capitals/'letters/'writing, with each letter separate and in capitals: Write your name in ~ letters. 11 (cricket) spot on which a batsman rests his bat before playing a ball. 12 (sl) (person's) head: I'll knock your ~ off!

block² /blɒk/ vt 1 [VP6A,15B] ~ (up), make movement difficult or impossible in (by sth being in the way); obstruct: All roads were ~ed by the heavy snowfall. They ~ed up (= entirely covered) the entrance to the cave with big rocks. My cold gave me a ~ed-up nose. 2 [VP6A] obstruct (progress); make (action) difficult or impossible: The general succeeded in ~ing the enemy's plans. 3 [VP6A] (chiefly in pp) restrict the use or expenditure of (currency, assets, etc): ~ed sterling. 4 [VP6A] shape (eg hats) on a ~. ⇨ block¹(4). 5 ~ in/out, make a rough sketch or plan of the general arrangement (of objects in a drawing, etc). 6 (cricket) stop (the ball) with the bat (kept upright in front of the wicket).

block·ade /blɒ'keɪd/ n the enclosing or surrounding of a place, eg by armies or warships, to keep goods or people from entering or leaving. run the ~, evade and get through the forces that are surrounding a place. raise the ~, end it. '~-runner n ship, etc that gets through or past a ~. □ vt [VP6A] make a ~ around, eg a town, fort, etc.

block·age /'blɒkɪdʒ/ n [C] state of being blocked; sth that blocks: There's a ~ in the drain-pipe.

block·head /'blɒkhed/ n slow and stupid person.

block·house /'blɒkhaʊs/ n military strongpoint with openings through which to shoot.

bloke /bləʊk/ n (sl) man.

blond /blɒnd/ n, adj (man) having fair¹(5) complexion and hair.

blonde /blɒnd/ n, adj (woman) blond.

blood¹ /blʌd/ n [U] 1 red liquid flowing throughout the body of man and the higher animals: The soldiers shed their ~ (= died) for their country. It was more than flesh and ~ (= human nature) could stand. He gave his ~ to help his sister, gave ~ to be injected into his sister after a surgical operation or an accident. infuse new ~ (into sth), (fig) revive business, etc by introducing new talent. let ~, draw off ~ from a vein. ⇨ 7 below. 2 passion; temper: His ~ is up, he is angry, filled with passion. His ~ ran cold, he was filled with terror or horror. (kill sb) in cold ~, when one is not feeling angry or excited; deliberately. make bad ~ between persons, cause them to feel ill will towards one another. make one's ~ boil, make one very angry. make one's ~ run cold, fill one with fear or horror. 3 relationships; family: They are of the same ~, have ancestors in common. ,blue '~ n aristocratic descent. of the (royal) ~, of royal family. one's (own) flesh and ~, one's relations. B~ is thicker than water, (prov) The ties of family relationship are real. '~ feud n deadly feud between families. '~-relation n person related by ~, not by marriage. 4 ~ and iron, (fig) relentless use of force. 5 [C] (old colloq use) man of fashion; rich, pleasure-loving young man. 6 ~ and thunder attrib adj (of stories, dramas) melodramatic; full of exciting incidents. 7 (compounds) '~ bank n ⇨ bank¹(3). '~-bath n large-scale slaughter, eg in battle, or during a revolution. '~ brother, one who swears to treat another as a brother (perhaps by the symbolic act of mixing his ~ with the other person). '~ count n (counting of the) number of red and white corpuscles in a certain volume of ~. '~-curdling adj sending feelings of horror through the body. '~-donor n person who gives ~ for ~ transfusions. '~-group/type n any of several distinct classes of human ~. ~-'heat n the normal temperature of human ~ (about 98·5°F, 37°C). '~-hound n large dog able to trace a person by scent. ⇨ the illus at dog. '~-letting n surgical drawing off of some of a patient's ~. '~-lust, desire for killing sb. '~-money n money obtained at the cost of a life, eg received by a murderer for killing someone or as a reward for betraying sb who is to be put to death. '~-poisoning n condition that results when poisonous germs enter the ~, esp through a cut or wound. '~ pressure n the force exerted by ~ within the arteries. ~ 'red, having the colour of ~. '~-shed n killing or wounding of people; putting to death: There was great ~shed in Paris during the years after the Revolution in 1789. '~-shot adj (of the white of the eyes) red. '~-sports n pl outdoor sports in which animals or birds are killed. '~-**stained** adj (a) stained with ~: a ~stained shirt. (b) disgraced by ~shed. '~-**stock** n (collective) thoroughbred horses. '~-**sucker** n (a) creature that sucks ~, esp a leech. (b) (fig) person who unjustly forces another or others to give him as much money as possible. '~-**thirsty** adj cruel and eager to take life; taking pleasure in killing. '~-**thirsti-ness** n '~-**transfusion** n transfer of ~ (originally taken) from the veins of one person to those of another. '~-**vessel** n tube (vein or artery) through which ~ flows in the body. ⇨ the illus at respiratory. ~-**less** adj 1 without ~shed: a ~less victory. 2 pale; unfeeling and coldhearted. ~-**less·ly** adv

blood² /blʌd/ vt [VP6A] allow the first taste of ~ to (foxhounds, etc).

bloody /'blʌdɪ/ adj 1 bleeding; covered with blood: a ~ nose. 2 with much bloodshed: a ~ battle. 3 (vulg intensive): What a ~ shame! (derog) You're a ~ fool! (laud) You're a ~ genius! ,~-'**minded,** (sl) obstructive; unwilling to co-operate. □ adv (vulg sl): Not ~ likely! (= not at all likely). ~ **well,** (vulg sl) certainly.

bloom /blu:m/ n 1 [C] flower, esp of plants admired chiefly for their flowers (eg roses, tulips, chrysanthemums). in ~, (of plants) flowering: The tulips are in full ~ now. Cf in blossom for shrubs and trees. 2 [U] (time of) greatest beauty or perfection: She was in the ~ of youth. 3 [U] covering of fine dust or powder on plums, grapes, etc when they are at their best. **take the ~ off sth,** cause it to seem stale. □ vi [VP2A,C] 1 be in flower; bear flowers: The roses have been ~ing all summer. 2 (fig) be in full beauty and perfection. ~-**ing** adj 1 (in the senses of the v) 2 /'blʊmɪŋ/ (colloq euphem for bloody(3)): You ~ing idiot!

bloomer /'blu:mə(r)/ n (sl) blunder: He made a tremendous ~.

bloom·ers /'blu:məz/ n pl loose garment covering each leg to the knee and hanging from the waist, formerly worn by girls and women for games, cycling, etc, with or without a skirt.

blos·som /'blɒsəm/ n [C] flower, esp of a fruittree; [U] mass of flowers on a bush or tree. ⇨ the illus at flower. in ~, (of bushes and trees) having flowers: The apple-trees are in ~. ⇨ bloom(1). □ vi 1 [VP2A] open into flowers: The cherry-trees will ~ next month. 2 [VP2C] ~ out, develop: He ~ed out as a first-rate athlete.

blot /blɒt/ n 1 mark caused by ink spilt on paper. 2 fault; disgrace; sth that takes away from the beauty or goodness of sth: a ~ on his character; a ~ on the landscape, eg an ugly building or advertisement. □ vt (-tt-) 1 [VP6A] make a ~ or ~s on (paper with ink). ~ **one's copy-book,** (colloq) do sth that spoils one's good record. 2 [VP6A] dry up (wet ink) with ~ting-paper. '~-**ting-paper** n absorbent paper used to dry up wet ink quickly. 3 [VP15B] ~ **out,** (a) make a ~ over (words that have been written): Several words in his letter had been ~ted out. (b) hide from view: The mist came down and ~ted out the view. (c) destroy, exterminate (enemies, etc). ~-**ter** n 1 book containing sheets of writing-paper interleaved with sheets of ~ting-paper. **police** ~-**ter,** (US) book in which the police enter records, eg of lost and found articles, missing persons. 2 piece or pad of ~ting-paper.

blotch /blɒtʃ/ n large, discoloured mark, usu irregular in shape (eg on the skin, or of ink on paper).

blotto /'blɒtəʊ/ pred adj (sl) fuddled or intoxicated

with alcoholic drink.

blouse /blaʊz US: blaʊs/ n 1 outer garment from neck to waist, worn by women and girls (US = shirtwaist). 2 loose-fitting garment, often with a belt at the waist, worn by some workmen. 3 tunic as worn by some sailors and soldiers.

blow¹ /bləʊ/ vi,vt (pt blew /blu:/, pp blown /bləʊn/, or, (11) below, ~ed) 1 [VP2A,C] (with air, wind, or it as the subject) move along, flow as a current of air: It was ~ing hard, there was a strong wind. It was ~ing a gale/~ing great guns, there was a (violent) gale. The wind was ~ing round the street-corners. It's ~ing up for rain, the wind seems likely to bring rain soon. 2 [VP15A,B] (of the wind) cause to move: The wind blew my hat off. I was almost ~n over by the wind. The ship was ~n out of its course/on to the rocks. The wind blew the papers out of my hand. [VP12A] **It's an ill wind that ~s nobody any good,** ⇨ ill(2). 3 [VP2,C,E] (of objects, etc) be moved or carried by the wind or other air current: My hat blew off. The door blew open. The dust has ~n into the house. 4 [VP6A,15B,2C] send or force a strong current of air upon, into or through: ~ (on) one's food (to cool it); ~ the dust off a book; ~ (up) the fire, make it burn better (eg by using a pair of bellows). ~ **hot and cold,** (fig) vacillate. ~ **one's nose,** in order to clear it. 5 [VP6A] make by ~ing: ~ bubbles, by sending air through a pipe with soapy water, etc; shape by ~ing: ~ glass, by sending a current of air into molten glass. 6 [VP6A] use (sth) to produce a current of air: ~ bellows; work the bellows of: ~ an organ. 7 [VP6A,2A] produce sound from (a trumpet, etc) by sending air into it; (of a windinstrument, etc) produce sound: The referee blew his whistle. Stop work when the whistle ~s. The huntsman blew his horn. We heard the bugles ~ing. 8 [VP2A] breathe hard and quickly: The old man was puffing and ~ing when he got to the top of the hill. 9 [VP2A] (of whales) force up a stream of air and water: There she ~s! There is the fountain sent up by the whale! 10 [VP2A,C,6A,15B] ~ (out), (of a fuse) melt because the electric current is too strong; cause to do this: The fuse has ~n. The fuse blew out. Don't ~ (out) the fuse. 11 (sl uses) spend (money) recklessly or extravagantly: ~ £10 on a dinner with a girl friend. ⇨ blue³. B~ the expense, Don't worry about it. I'll be ~ed if.../be ~ed if I will..., I will certainly not... Well, I'm ~ed! (indicating surprise). ~ **one's top,** lose one's temper; explode into angry words, etc. 12 (compounds from the v) '~-**dry** vt [VP6A] dry (sth, esp hair) by passing a current of warm air over (it). '~-**fly** n common meat fly. '~-**hole** n (a) opening for air, smoke, etc, in a tunnel. (b) hole (in rocks, etc near the seashore) through which air and water are forced by rising tides. '~-**lamp,** '~**torch** nn lamp for directing an intensely hot flame on to a surface. '~-**pipe** n (a) tube for increasing the heat of a flame by forcing air into it. (b) tube through which some primitive people ~ poisoned darts. 13 [VP2C,3A,15B] (special uses with adverbial particles and preps):

blow back, (of gas in a tube, etc) explode. Hence, '~-**back** n explosion of gas in a tube, etc.

blow in/into, (colloq) arrive noisily, cheerfully, etc: The door opened and John blew in/blew into the room.

blow off steam, release tension by arguing, being noisy, etc: Parents must let children ~ off steam *sometimes.*

blow out; ~ *sth out*, (be) put out by ~ing: *The candle was ~n out by the wind. The flame blew out.* ~ *itself out*, exhaust itself: *The gale had ~n itself out.* ~ *one's brains out*, kill oneself by shooting in the head. '~·out *n* (a) sudden (often violent) escape of air, steam, etc; (esp) bursting of a tyre. (b) ~ing out of an electric fuse. (c) (sl) abundant meal; feast.

blow over, pass by; be forgotten: *The storm/ scandal will soon ~ over.*

blow up, (a) explode: *The barrel of gunpowder blew up.* (b) arise: *A storm is ~ing up.* (c) lose one's temper; work up to a crisis: *I'm sorry I blew up at you.* ~ *sb up*, (colloq) scold severely: *The teacher blew John up for not doing his homework.* Hence, ¸~·ing-'up *n* scolding. ~ *sth up*, (a) break or destroy by explosion: *The soldiers blew up the bridge.* (b) inflate with air or gas: ~ *up a tyre.* (c) enlarge greatly: ~ *up a photograph.* Hence, '~-up *n* greatly enlarged photograph: *The men in the procession carried ~-ups of their leader.* (d) exaggerate: *His abilities have been greatly ~n up by the newspapers.*

blow² /bləʊ/ *n* blowing: *Give your nose a good ~,* clear it thoroughly. *have/go for a ~,* go outdoors for fresh air.

blow³ /bləʊ/ *n* 1 hard stroke (given with the hand, a stick, etc): *He struck his enemy a heavy ~ on the head. at one ~; at a (single) ~,* in a single effort: *I killed six flies at a ~. come to ~s; exchange ~s,* fight. *get a ~ in,* succeed in placing a ~. *strike a ~ for,* perform a single act of support for; struggle for. *without striking a ~,* without having to fight. *a ~-by-~ account,* a detailed account (eg of a boxing match). 2 shock; disaster: *His wife's death was a great ~ to him. It was a ~ to our hopes.*

blow⁴ /bləʊ/ *vi* (*pp* ~n /bləʊn/) (chiefly in *pp* as) *full-blown roses,* wide open, with petals about to fall; *She has a complexion like a new-blown rose,* a delicate pink complexion.

blower /'bləʊə(r)/ *n* 1 apparatus for forcing air, etc into or through sth. 2 person who makes things by blowing (eg *a 'glass-~*) or who pumps air into sth (eg *an 'organ-~*). 3 (colloq) speaking-tube; (GB sl) telephone: *Get Jones on the ~ for me.*

blown /bləʊn/ *pp* of blow¹. ⟹ also blow⁴. □ *adj* breathless (as the result of effort).

blowzy /'blaʊzɪ/ *adj* (usu of a woman) red-faced, dirty-looking and untidily dressed.

blub·ber¹ /'blʌbə(r)/ *n* [U] fat of whales and other sea-animals from which oil is obtained.

blub·ber² /'blʌbə(r)/ *vi,vt* [VP2A] weep noisily; [VP15B] ~ *(sth) out,* say with sobs.

bludgeon /'blʌdʒən/ *n* short, thick stick with a heavy end, used as a weapon. □ *vt* [VP6A,14] strike repeatedly with a ~: *He had been ~ed to death.* ~ *sb into doing sth,* (fig) compel him to do it.

blue¹ /blu:/ *adj* (-r, -st) coloured like the sky on a clear day or the deep sea when the sun is shining: ~ *eyes. His face was ~ with cold.* ¸~ 'blood(ed) *adj, n* (of) aristocratic birth. ¸~ 'chips, (fin) industrial shares considered valuable because of past records. ¸~ 'film, obscene film. ¸~ 'jokes, improper jokes. ¸B~ 'Peter, ~ flag with a white square in the centre, used to show that a ship is about to sail. ¸~ 'ribbon, sign of special distinction: *the ~ ribbon of the Atlantic,* held by the liner that has the record for the fastest crossing. *look ~,* (colloq) be sad or

depressed. *(Things are) looking ~,* depressing. *once in a ~ moon,* very rarely.

blue² /blu:/ *n* 1 ~ colour: *dressed in ~; Oxford ~,* dark ~; *Cambridge ~,* light ~. 2 (the) sky. *appear/come out of the ~,* unexpectedly. *a bolt from the ~,* sth quite unexpected. 3 *win/get one's ~ (for sth),* (at Oxford or Cambridge University) gain the right to wear a ~ cap, scarf etc because one has represented the University in a sport: *She got her ~ for tennis.* Hence, person with this right: *He's a rowing ~.* 4 (poet) (the) sea. 5 *a true ~,* a loyal member (of a political party, esp the Conservative). 6 (*pl*) (dances, dance tunes, for) haunting jazz melodies originally of Negroes in the southern US. *the ~s,* (colloq) condition of being sad, melancholy. 7 (compounds) '~·bell *n* (Scotland and N England) = harebell; (S England) wild hyacinth with ~ or white flowers growing in moist places and flowering in spring. '~ book *n* book published by the Government containing a report. '~·bottle *n* meat fly or blowfly. ¸~·'collar *adj* of workers in factories, etc, who wear overalls (contrasted with *white-collar* workers). '~·jacket *n* seaman in the Navy. ¸~·'pencil *vt* mark, censor, with a ~ pencil. '~·print *n* photographic print, white on ~ paper, usu for building plans; (fig) plan, scheme: (attrib) *the ~print stage.* '~·stocking *n* woman who is regarded as having superior literary tastes and intellectual interests. **blu·ish** /'blu:ɪʃ/ *adj* tending towards ~: *bluish green.*

blue³ /blu:/ *vt* 1 make blue. 2 ~ *one's money,* (sl) spend it recklessly.

bluff¹ /blʌf/ *n* headland with a broad and very steep face. □ *adj* 1 (of headlands, cliffs, a ship's bows) with a broad, perpendicular front. 2 (of a person, his manner, etc) abrupt; rough but honest and kind, simple and good-natured. ~·ly *adv* ~·ness *n*

bluff² /blʌf/ *vt,vi* [VP6A,14,15B,2A] deceive sb by pretending. ~ *sb into doing sth,* lead sb to do sth or believe sth by deceiving him: *They were ~ed into supposing we were ill prepared.* ~ *it out,* survive a difficult situation by pretence. ~ *one's way out of sth,* escape from a situation by pretence. □ *n* [U,C] deception of this kind; (the use of) threats that are intended to get results without being carried out. *call sb's ~,* invite him to do what he threatened to do. ~·er *n* person who tries to ~ people.

blun·der /'blʌndə(r)/ *vi,vt* 1 [VP2A,C,3A] move about uncertainly, as if blind: ~ *into a wall.* 2 [VP2A] make foolish mistakes: *Our leaders have ~ed again.* □ *n* [C] stupid or careless mistake. ~·er *n* person who commits a ~.

blun·der·buss /'blʌndəbʌs/ *n* old-fashioned gun with a wide mouth, firing many bullets or small shot at once at short range.

blunt /blʌnt/ *adj* (-er, -est) 1 without a point or sharp edge: *a ~ knife.* 2 (of a person, what he says) plain; not troubling to be polite: *He's a ~ man. The ~ fact is that....* □ *vt* [VP6A] make ~: *If you try to cut stone with a knife, you will ~ the edge.* ~·ly *adv:* *to speak ~ly,* plainly, without ceremony. ~·ness *n*

blur /blɜ:(r)/ *n* 1 dirty spot or mark; smear of ink. 2 confused or indistinct effect: *If, when you try to read small print, you see only a ~, you probably need glasses.* □ *vt,vi* (-rr-) [VP6A,2A] make a dirty mark or smear on (sth); make or become unclear, confused in appearance: *Tears ~red her eyes. Mists ~red the view. The writing was ~red. Rain*

~red the windows of our car.

blurb /blɜːb/ n publisher's description of the contents of a book, printed on the paper jacket, etc.

blurt /blɜːt/ vt [VP15B] ~ **sth out,** tell sth, eg a secret, suddenly, often thoughtlessly.

blush /blʌʃ/ vi 1 [VP2A,C,3A] become red (in the face) from shame or confusion: *She ~ed for/with shame. She ~ed at the thought of...; He ~ed as red as a peony.* 2 [VP4B] (fig) be ashamed: ~ *to confess that....* □ n 1 reddening of the face, from shame, etc: *She turned away to hide her ~es.* 2 (old use) glimpse: *at first ~,* at the first look. ~**·ing** adj ~**·ing·ly** adv

blus·ter /ˈblʌstə(r)/ vi,vt 1 [VP2A,C] (of the wind, waves, etc) storm; be rough or violent. 2 [VP2A] (of persons) act and speak in a forceful but rather unsteady, often rather boastful way. 3 [VP15B] ~ **out,** utter in this way: ~ *out threats.* □ n [U] 1 noise of violent wind or waves. 2 ~ing talk and behaviour; noisy threats. ~**y** adj (of the weather) rough and blowy.

bo(h) /bəʊ/ int ⇨ boo.

boa /ˈbəʊə/ n 1 (also '~**-constrictor**) large non-poisonous snake that kills by crushing its prey. ⇨ the illus at snake. 2 (also '**feather-boa**) feather stole (formerly) worn by women.

boar /bɔː(r)/ n 1 wild male pig. 2 uncastrated male domestic pig. ⇨ hog, sow².

board¹ /bɔːd/ n 1 long, thin, flat piece of wood with squared edges, used in building walls, floors, boats, ship's decks, etc. 2 flat piece of wood or other material for a special purpose, sometimes bare, sometimes covered with cloth, leather, etc: '*sign~*'; '*notice~*; *a* '*diving-~.* 3 flat surface with patterns, etc on which games, eg chess, are played. ⇨ the illus at chess. 4 (from the ~s that form the stage of a theatre) **the ~s,** the theatre: *on the ~s,* employed as an actor; on the stage. 5 (from the ~s that form the deck of a ship) **on ~,** in a ship. **go on ~,** go on to a ship or into an airliner (in US, also of trains). **go by the ~,** (of masts, etc) fall over the ship's side; (fig, of plans, hopes, etc) be given up or abandoned; fail completely. 6 (from the idea of *table,* used for gambling). **above ~,** openly, without deception. **sweep the ~,** win all the cards or the money staked; (fig) be completely successful. 7 (from the idea of *table*) council-table; councillors; committee; group of persons controlling a business, or a government department: *the* '*B~ of* '*Governors,* eg of a school; *the* ,*B~ of* '*Trade; Local* '*Government B~;* '*School B~,* (in England until 1902) controlling elementary schools known as '*b~-schools; a Se'lection B~,* one that selects from applicants or candidates. **across the ~,** ⇨ across²(1). 8 [U] food served at table, esp meals supplied by the week or month (eg at a lodging-house) or as part payment for service: *The hotel porter gets £40 a week and free ~. B~ and lodging £45 weekly.* 9 thick, stiff paper, sometimes cloth-covered, used for book covers: *bound in cloth ~s.* ⇨ also card~, paste~. 10 (compounds) '~**·room** n room in which meetings (of a B~ of Directors, etc) are held. '~**·walk** n (US) promenade, originally made of planks, esp along a beach.

board² /bɔːd/ vt,vi 1 [VP6A,15B] make or cover with boards(1): ~ *up a window;* ~ (*over*) *the stern of a boat,* cover it with boards to make a deck. *The floor was ~ed.* 2 (⇨ board¹(8)) [VP6A,3A,E] ~ (*at sth/with sb*), get (from), supply (with), meals for a fixed weekly/monthly etc payment: *Mrs Jones*

makes a living by ~ing students. Jim ~s at 'The Willows'/with Mrs Jones. ~ **out,** take meals at a different place from that in which one lives. 3 [VP6A] get on or into (a ship, train, plane, bus, etc). ~**er** n (a) person who ~s(2) with sb. (b) boy or girl at a ~ing-school (⇨ below). ~**·ing** n [U] (a) structure of ~s(1). (b) the providing or receiving of ~¹(8). '~**·ing-card** n card allowing one to ~(3) (esp) a ship or plane. '~**·ing-house** n private house that provides ~¹(8) and lodging. '~**·ing-school** n school where pupils receive ~¹(8) and lodging as well as lessons.

boast /bəʊst/ n [C] 1 words used in praise of oneself, one's acts, belongings, etc: *It was the enemy's ~ that they could never be defeated.* 2 cause for satisfaction; sth of which one may rightly be proud: *It was his ~ that he had never failed in an examination.* □ vt,vi 1 [VP2A,3A,B] ~ (*of/ about*), make a ~ or ~s: *He ~s of being/~s that he is the best tennis-player in the town. That's nothing to ~ of. He often ~s to his neighbours about the successes of his children.* 2 [VP6A] possess with pride: *Our school ~s a fine swimming-pool.* ~**er** n person who ~s. ~**·ful** /-fʊl/ adj (of persons) fond of ~ing; (of words, etc) full of self-praise. ~**·fully** /-fəli/ adv

boat /bəʊt/ n 1 small open vessel for travelling in on water, esp the kind moved with oars ('*rowing ~*), sails ('*sailing ~*), or petrol or oil engines ('*motor-~*); also used of fishing-vessels and small steamers: *We crossed the river by ~/in a ~. B~s for hire—£2 an hour.* **be (all) in the same ~,** have the same dangers to face. **burn one's ~s,** do sth that makes it impossible to retreat, to change one's plans, etc. **take to the ~s,** (of the crew and passengers of a ship) use the ship's ~s to escape, eg when the ship is sinking. '~**-hook** n long pole for fending off or holding a ~, eg at a landing-stage. '~**-house** n shed in which ~s are stored. '~**-man** /-mən/ n (pl ~men) man who rows or sails a small ~ for pay; man from whom rowing-~s may be hired. '~**-race** n race between rowing-~s. '~**-train** n train that takes people to or from a passenger ship, eg between London and Dover. ⇨ ferry, house¹(7), life(14), mail²(1). 2 ~-shaped dish used at table for gravy or sauce. □ vi [VP2A,C] travel in a ~, esp for pleasure: *We ~ed down the river.* **go ~ing,** go out (esp in a rowing-~) for pleasure.

boater /ˈbəʊtə(r)/ n hard straw hat (formerly worn in summer for boating).

boat·swain /ˈbəʊsn/ n senior seaman who controls the work of other seamen and is in charge of a ship's rigging, boats, anchors, etc.

bob¹ /bɒb/ vi (-bb-) [VP2C] 1 move up and down: *The cork on his fishing-line was bobbing on the water.* **bob up,** (fig) carry on again; reappear: *That fellow bobs up like a cork,* cannot be 'kept down', always becomes active again after being in trouble, etc. *That question often bobs up* (*crops up* is more usu), is often asked. 2 **bob to sb,** also [VP6A] **bob a curtsy,** curtsy. □ n quick up and down movement; curtsy.

bob² /bɒb/ vt (-bb-) (dated) cut (a woman's or girl's hair) so that it hangs loosely and short of the shoulders: *She wears her hair bobbed. I shall have my hair bobbed.* □ n bobbed hair.

bob³ /bɒb/ n (pl unchanged; sl) former British coin, called 'shilling' (replaced by the 5p coin).

bob·bin /ˈbɒbɪn/ n small roller or spool for holding

thread, yarn, wire, etc in a machine.

bobby /'bɒbɪ/ n (GB colloq) policeman.

bobby pin /'bɒbɪ pɪn/ n (US) tight metal hair clip.

bobby-socks, -sox /'bɒbɪ sɒks/ n pl (US, comm) girls' ankle socks.

bobby-soxer /'bɒbɪ sɒksə(r)/ n (US sl during the 1940's) teenage or adolescent girl.

bobo-link /'bɒbəlɪŋk/ n N American songbird.

bob-sled, bob-sleigh /'bɒbsled, -sleɪ/ n 1 sleigh made by joining two short sleighs, used in tobogganing. 2 large, long sleigh with brake and steering wheel, used for racing.

a racing bobsleigh

bob-tail /'bɒbteɪl/ n (horse or dog with a) docked tail. *the rag-tag and ~*, the rabble.

bode /bəʊd/ vt,vi (old use or poet) 1 [VP12B,13B] be a sign of; foretell: *This ~s us no good.* 2 ~ *well/ill for*, be of good/bad promise for: *His idle habits ~ ill for his future*, suggest that his future career will be a failure. **bod-ing** n feeling of coming evil.

bod-ice /'bɒdɪs/ n close-fitting part of a woman's dress or of an under-garment from the shoulders to the waist.

-bodied /-bɒdɪd/ adj (with adjj): '*big-~*, '*strong-~*, having a big/strong body: *able-~*, ⇨ able.

bod-ily /'bɒdəlɪ/ adj of or in the human body or physical nature: *supply a person's ~ wants* (eg food); *~ (= physical) assault.* □ adv 1 as a whole or mass; completely: *The audience rose ~ (=* everyone rose at the same moment) *to cheer the speaker. The building was transported ~ (=* as a whole, without being pulled down) *one hundred yards down the street.* 2 in person; in the body.

bod-kin /'bɒdkɪn/ n blunt, thick needle with a large eye (used for drawing tape, etc through a hem).

body /'bɒdɪ/ n (pl -dies) 1 The whole physical structure of a man or animal: *We wear clothes to keep our bodies warm.* ⇨ the illus at arm, head, leg, skeleton, trunk. ⇨ mind, soul, spirit. *keep ~ and soul together*, remain alive: *He earns scarcely enough to keep ~ and soul together.* 2 dead ~; corpse: *His ~ was brought back to England for burial.* 3 main portion of a man or animal without the head, arms and legs: *He received one wound in the left leg and another in the ~.* 4 main part of a structure: *the ~ of a motor-car; the ~ of a concert hall*, the central part where the seats are. 5 group of persons who do sth together or who are united in some way: *Large bodies of unemployed men marched through the streets demanding work. The affairs of the school are managed by the Governing B~. A legislative ~ is a group of persons who make laws. the ,~ 'politic*, ⇨ politic(3). *in a ~*, all together; as a whole: *The staff resigned in a ~.* 6 (colloq) person; human being: *She's a nice old ~.* (in compounds): *every~, any~,*

some~, no~. 7 mass, quantity, collection: *A lake is a ~ of water. He has a large ~ of facts to prove his statements.* 8 distinct piece of matter: *the heavenly bodies*, the sun, moon and stars; *a foreign ~ (=* a speck of dirt) *in the eye.* 9 [U] (of wine, etc) full, strong quality: *wine of good ~.* 10 (compounds) '*~-guard* n group of men (sometimes a single man) guarding an important person. '*~ language* n interpreting the way sb sits, stands, moves etc as expressing his feelings. '*~-snatcher* n (formerly) person who (illegally) dug up corpses and sold them for dissection. '*~-work* n [U] main outside structure of a motor vehicle.

Boer /bɔː(r)/ n (old use) South African of Dutch descent; Afrikaner. □ adj (old use) of Dutch South Africa; Afrikaans. ~ *war*, between the ~s and the British (1899—1902).

bof-fin /'bɒfɪn/ n (sl) technician or scientist (esp one engaged in research).

bog /bɒg/ n 1 (area of) soft, wet, spongy ground (chiefly decayed or decaying vegetable matter). 2 (vulg sl) latrine. □ vt,vi (-gg-) [VP15,2E] ~ *down*, (cause) to be stuck fast, unable to make progress: *The tanks (got) ~ged down in the mud. Our discussions have ~ged down.* **boggy** /'bɒgɪ/ adj (of land) soft and wet.

bo-gey¹ ⇨ bogy.

bo-gey² /'bəʊgɪ/ n (golf) score that a good player makes for a hole (or the whole course) and that other players try to equal. ⇨ par¹(2).

boggle /'bɒgl/ vi [VP2A,3A] ~ *(at sth)*, be unwilling, hesitate; be alarmed, amazed: *The mind/ imagination ~s (at the idea).*

bo-gie /'bəʊgɪ/ n (also **bogey, bogy**) 1 trolley. 2 four-wheeled undercarriage fitted under (the end of) a railway engine or wagon to enable it to go round curves.

bo-gus /'bəʊgəs/ adj sham; counterfeit.

bogy, bo-gey /'bəʊgɪ/ n (pl -gies, -geys) evil spirit; sb or sth that causes fear.

bo-he-mi-an /bəʊ'hiːmɪən/ n, adj (person) not living in ways considered socially normal or conventional.

boil¹ /bɔɪl/ n hard (usu red, often painful) poisoned swelling under the skin, which bursts when ripe.

boil² /bɔɪl/ vi,vt 1 [VP2A,B,C,D] (of water or other liquid, also of the vessel that contains it and of what is in the water) reach the temperature at which change to gas occurs; bubble up: *When water ~s it changes into steam. The kettle is ~ing. The potatoes are ~ing. Don't let the kettle ~ dry. Let the vegetables ~ gently. keep the pot ~ing*, (fig) earn or otherwise find enough money for food, etc. '*~ing-point* n temperature at which a liquid ~s. *~ing hot*, (colloq) very hot: *a ~ing hot day.* 2 [VP2A,C] (of the sea, of a person's feelings, etc) be agitated like ~ing water: *The boat was swallowed up by the ~ing waves. He was ~ing (over) with indignation. Cruelty to animals makes her blood ~.* 3 [VP6A,22] cause water or other liquid to ~; cook in ~ing water: *We ~ eggs, fish and vegetables. Please ~ my egg for three minutes. I like my eggs ~ed hard. My brother prefers soft-~ed eggs.* 4 [VP2C,15B] ~ *away*, (a) continue to ~: *The kettle was ~ing away merrily on the fire.* (b) ~ until nothing remains: *The water had all ~ed away and the kettle was empty.* ~ *down*, be reduced in quantity: *It all ~s down to this...*, (colloq) The essence (of the statement, proposal, etc) is.... ~ *sth down*, make less by ~ing; (fig) condense: ∾ *down a long article to two hundred words,* make a précis of it. ∾ *over,* boil and flow over the side of a vessel: *The milk had ∾ed over.* □ *n the* ∾, ∾ing point: *be on the* ∾, be ∾ing. *bring sth to the* ∾, heat it until it ∾s. *come to the* ∾, begin to ∾.

boiler /'bɔɪlə(r)/ *n* **1** metal container in which water, etc is heated, eg for producing steam in an engine; tank forming part of a kitchen range for supplying hot water; tank for heating water for a laundry. '∾-suit *n* one-piece garment, overalls, for rough or dirty work. **2** person whose trade is boiling sth: *a* soap-∾.

bois·ter·ous /'bɔɪstərəs/ *adj* rough, violent: ∾ *weather; a* ∾ *wind/sea*; (of a person, his behaviour) noisy and cheerful. ∾·ly *adv*

bold /bəʊld/ *adj* (-er, -est) **1** without, showing no, fear; enterprising. *be/make so* ∾ *as to do sth,* allow oneself to do it: *if I may be so* ∾ *as to...,* If I may .venture or presume to.... *make* ∾ *with sth,* (more usu *make free with*) take the liberty of using it. *a* ∾ *front,* ⇨ front(4). **2** without feelings of shame; immodest. *as* ∾ *as brass,* impudent. **3** well marked; clear: *the* ∾ *outline of a mountain; a* ∾ *headland; a painting made with a few* ∾ (= free and vigorous) *strokes of the brush.* ∾·ly *adv* ∾·ness *n*

bole /bəʊl/ *n* trunk of a tree.

bol·ero /bə'leərəʊ/ *n* [C] (*pl* ∾s) **1** (music for a) Spanish dance. **2** /'bɒlərəʊ/ short jacket with no front fastening.

boll /bəʊl/ *n* round seed-vessel (of cotton and flax). ⇨ illus at cotton. ∾ 'weevil /'wiːvl/ *n* small destructive insect that infests cotton-plants.

bol·lard /'bɒləd/ *n* **1** upright post (usu of iron) on a quay or a ship's deck for making ropes secure. **2** protective post on a traffic island, or a roadway, sometimes with an arrow to direct traffic.

bol·locks /'bɒləks/ *n pl* ⚠ = ballocks.

bo·loney /bə'ləʊnɪ/ *n* [U] (US sl) nonsense; humbug.

Bol·she·vik /'bɒlʃəvɪk/ *n* (hist) follower of the revolutionary Marxist party that came to power in Russia in 1917; (colloq) supporter of the system of government by soviets; (colloq) person favouring Marxism or Communism.

bol·shy /'bɒlʃɪ/ *adj* (sl) rebellious; stubborn.

bol·ster[1] /'bəʊlstə(r)/ *n* long under-pillow for the head of a bed.

bol·ster[2] /'bəʊlstə(r)/ *vt* [VP6A,15B] ∾ *(up),* support; give (greatly needed, often undeserved) support to, eg a cause, theory, etc, that would otherwise fail.

bolt[1] /bəʊlt/ *n* **1** metal fastening for a door or window, consisting of a sliding pin or rod and a staple into which it fits. **2** metal pin with a head at one end and a thread (as on a screw) at the other, used with a nut for holding things together. **3** (old use) short heavy arrow shot from a cross-bow. *shoot one's (last)* ∾, make one's last effort. **4** discharge of lightning. ⇨ blue[2](2); ⇨ *thunder*∾ at thunder(1). **5** (as a measure of cloth, canvas, etc) roll (as it comes from the loom). □ *vt,vi* [VP6A,15B,2A] fasten with a ∾(1): ∾ *the doors and windows;* ∾ *sb in,* shut him in by ∾ing the door(s); ∾ *sb out,* keep him out by ∾ing the door(s). *The door* ∾*s on the inside.*

bolt[2] /bəʊlt/ *vi,vt* **1** [VP2A,2C] run away quickly; (esp of a horse) run off out of control: *As soon as I came downstairs the burglar* ∾*ed through the back*

door. **2** [VP6A] swallow (food) quickly: *We* ∾*ed a few mouthfuls of food and hurried on.* **3** [VP2A] (of plants) grow quickly upwards and go to seed. □ *n* act of running away. *make a* ∾ *for it,* run off quickly (usu to escape from sth). '∾-hole *n* hole or burrow into which to ∾ for safety.

bolt[3] /bəʊlt/ *vt* [VP2A] sift (flour).

bolt[4] /bəʊlt/ *adv* ∾ *upright,* (of sb's posture) quite upright.

bomb /bɒm/ *n* hollow metal ball or shell filled either with explosive for causing destruction or with smoke, gas, or incendiary material, eg dropped from aircraft; (old use) hand-grenade. *go like a* ∾, (sl) be very efficient, successful, etc: *My new car goes like a* ∾. '∾ bay *n* compartment (in an aircraft) for holding ∾s. '∾-disposal squad, squad for removing unexploded ∾s and making them harmless. '∾-proof *adj* giving protection against exploding ∾s: *a* ∾-*proof shelter.* '∾-shell *n* (fig) sth that comes as a great surprise and shock. '∾-sight *n* device (in an aircraft) for aiming ∾s. '∾-site *n* area (in a town) devastated by ∾s: *a car park on a* ∾-*site.* □ *vt,vi* **1** [VP6A,15B] attack with ∾s; drop ∾s on. ∾ *out,* drive out (of buildings, etc) with ∾s: ∾*ed out families/factories.* **2** [VP15B,2C] ∾ *up,* load (an aircraft) with ∾s. ∾*er* /'bɒmə(r)/ *n* aircraft used for ∾ing, ⇨ illus at aircraft; soldier trained in ∾ing.

bom·bard /bɒm'bɑːd/ *vt* [VP6A,14] ∾ *with,* attack with shells from big guns; (fig) worry with questions, requests, complaints, etc; (nuclear physics) send a stream of high-speed particles against (an atom, etc). ∾·ment *n* ∾ing or being ∾ed: *after a long* ∾*ment.*

bom·bar·dier /ˌbɒmbə'dɪə(r)/ *n* (in an artillery regiment) non-commissioned officer below a sergeant.

bom·bast /'bɒmbæst/ *n* [U] insincere, high-sounding talk. **bom·bas·tic** /bɒm'bæstɪk/ *adj* (of a person, his talk, behaviour) promising much but not likely to do much; using fine high-sounding words. **bom·bas·ti·cally** /-klɪ/ *adv*

bona fide /ˌbəʊnə 'faɪdɪ/ *adj, adv* (Lat) genuine(ly); sincere(ly); in good faith; (comm): *a* ∾ *buyer.* **bona fides** /ˌbəʊnə 'faɪdɪz/ *n* (legal) honest intention; sincerity.

bon·anza /bə'nænzə/ *n* [C] (*pl* ∾s) (US) sth, eg a gold-mine, an oil-well, that is prospering greatly; (attrib) bringing good luck and prosperity: *a* ∾ *year.*

bon·bon /'bɒnbɒn/ *n* sweet; sth made of sugar in a fancy shape, etc.

bond /bɒnd/ *n* **1** agreement or engagement that a person is bound to observe, esp one that has force in law; document, signed and sealed, containing such an agreement. *enter into a* ∾ *with sb,* agree to make a ∾ with sb. *His word is as good as his* ∾, He is so honest that his spoken promise is as reliable as a written agreement. **2** printed paper issued by a government or a corporation acknowledging that money has been lent to it and will be paid back with interest. '∾-holder *n* person holding ∾s. **3** sth that joins or unites (usu fig): *the* ∾*(s) of*

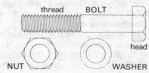

affection. Common tastes form a ~ between the two men, They are friends because they are interested in the same things. **4** the state of being joined: *Press the surfaces together to ensure a good, firm ~.* **5** (*pl*) prisoner's chains: *in ~s,* held as a prisoner or as a slave; *burst one's ~s,* win freedom. **6** (comm) *in ~,* (of goods) in a Customs warehouse (until duties are paid). *place goods in/ take goods out of ~.* □ *vt* [VP6A] **1** put (goods) into a Customs warehouse. *~ed goods,* imported and placed in ~ until duty is paid. *a ~ed warehouse,* one in which goods are stored until duties are paid. **2** join securely (with glue, etc).

bond- /bɒnd-/ *pref* in slavery, not free: '*~man,* '*bonds-man* /-mən/; '*~maid;* '*~servant;* '*~slave.*

bond·age /'bɒndɪdʒ/ *n* [U] slavery, servitude: *in hopeless ~ to his master.*

bone /bəʊn/ *n* **1** [C] one of the parts that make up the framework (ie skeleton) of an animal's body. ⊏> the illus at skeleton. *This fish has a lot of ~s in it. No ~s broken, I hope,* I hope you have not hurt yourself. *~ of contention,* subject of dispute. *feel in one's ~s that,* feel certain that. *have a '~ to pick with sb,* have sth to argue or complain about. *make no ~s about (doing) sth,* not hesitate about it, do it without scruple: *They dismissed him and made no ~s about it. (frozen) to the ~,* completely, in a penetrating way. *will not make old ~s,* will not live long. **2** [U] hard substance of which ~s are made: *Buttons are sometimes made of ~. He's all skin and ~,* is very thin. **3** (*pl,* old use) castanets; dice. **4** (compounds). *,~ 'dry adj* quite dry. '*~-head n* (sl) stupid person. *,~-'idle/ -'lazy adj* completely idle. '*~-meal n* fertilizer for crushed and powdered ~s. '*~-setter n* person who sets broken ~s. '*~-shaker n* (colloq) old bicycle without rubber tyres; old, shaky bus, car or cart. *,big-/,strong-'~d adj* having big/strong ~s. □ *vt* [VP6A] **1** take ~s out of (a chicken, a piece of meat, etc). **2** (old use) put ~s into (eg a corset). **3** (sl) steal. **4** *~ up on* (a subject), (sl) study hard.

boner /'bəʊnə(r)/ *n* (US sl) blunder.

bon·fire /'bɒnfaɪə(r)/ *n* large fire made outdoors either to celebrate some event or to burn up dead leaves, rubbish, etc: *make a ~ of,* get rid of.

bongo /'bɒŋgəʊ/ *n* (*pl ~s*) '*~ (drum),* small drum played with the hands, usu one of a pair. ⊏> illus at percussion.

bon·homie /'bɒnəmɪ/ *n* [U] (F) bluff, hearty pleasantness of manner.

bo·nito /bə'niːtəʊ/ *n* large kinds of tunny of the Atlantic Ocean, esp the striped tunny.

bon·kers /'bɒŋkəz/ *pred adj (stark, raving) ~,* (sl) raving mad; completely insane.

bon mot /,bɒn 'məʊ/ *n* (*pl bons mots* /'məʊz/) witty saying or remark.

bon·net /'bɒnɪt/ *n* **1** small, round head-dress without a hard brim, usu tied under the chin. **2** soft, flat cap worn by men in Scotland and by soldiers in some regiments. **3** protective cover of various sorts, eg over a chimney, or (US = *hood*) over the engine of a motor-car. ⊏> the illus at motor.

bonny /'bɒnɪ/ *adj* (Scot) **1** attractive, fine. **2** healthy looking; with a glow of health: *a ~ baby; her ~ face.* **bon·nily** *adj*

bo·nus /'bəʊnəs/ *n* (*pl ~es*) payment in addition to what is usual, necessary or expected, eg an extra dividend to stockholders of a business company; (insurance) a share of profits to policy-holders, or

an extra payment to workers: *cost-of-'living ~,* addition to wages or salaries because of rising prices. **no 'claims ~,** percentage reduction in an insurance premium (for a motor vehicle) if claims are not made.

bony /'bəʊnɪ/ *adj* (-ier, -iest) **1** full of bones: *a ~ fish,* eg a herring. **2** having big or prominent bones: *a tall, ~ man.* **3** with little flesh: *~ fingers.*

boo /buː/ (also **bo, boh** /bəʊ/) *int* sound made to show disapproval or contempt; exclamation used to surprise or startle: *He can't say boo to a goose,* is timid. □ *vt, vi* [VP6A,15B,2A] make such sounds: *The speaker was booed off the platform. The crowd booed and hooted.*

boob¹ /buːb/ *n* **1** = booby. **2** (colloq) silly mistake. □ *vi* (colloq) make a silly mistake.

boob² /buːb/ *n* (sl) woman's breast.

booby /'buːbɪ/ *n* silly or stupid person. '*~ prize n* prize given as a joke to the person who is last in a race or competition. '*~-trap n* sth balanced on the top of a door so that it will fall on the first person to pass through; (mil) apparently harmless object that will kill or injure sb when picked up or interfered with.

boogie /'buːgɪ *US:* 'bʊgɪ/ (also **boogie-woogie** /-'wuːgɪ *US:* -'wʊgɪ/) *n* [C,U] (instance of) highly rhythmic variety of blues²(6).

book¹ /bʊk/ *n* **1** number of sheets of paper, either printed or blank, fastened together in a cover; literary composition that would fill such a set of sheets: *write a ~.* **2 the B~,** the Bible: *swear on the B~,* take an oath. **3** main division of a large treatise or poem or the Bible: *the B~ of Genesis.* **4** packet of similar items fastened together, eg postage stamps, bus tickets, matches. **5** record of bets. ⊏> ~maker in 8 below. *make/keep a ~ (on),* take bets, etc. *not suit one's ~,* not be convenient. **6** (*pl*) business accounts, records, etc: *The firm has full order ~s,* orders for goods. *be in sb's good/bad/black ~s,* have/not have his favour or approval. *bring sb to ~ (for sth),* require him to explain his conduct. **7** libretto (of an opera). **8** (compounds): '*~-case n* piece of furniture with shelves for ~s. '*~-club n* organization that sells ~s at a discount to members who agree to buy a minimum number. '*~-ends n pl* pair of props used to keep ~s upright, eg on a table. '*~-keeper n* person who keeps accounts, eg of a business, public office. '*~-keep·ing n* (art of) keeping (business) accounts. '*~-maker n* person whose business is taking bets on horse-races. '*~-mark(er) n* sth placed between the pages of a ~ to mark the place. '*~-mobile* /-məʊbiːl/ *n* (US) truck equipped as a mobile ~ store or lending library. '*~-seller n* person who sells ~s retail. '*~-stall n* stall, kiosk, etc at which ~s, newspapers, etc are shown for sale outdoors, in a railway station, a hotel lobby, etc (US = *newsstand).* '*~ token n* ⊏> token. '*~-worm n* small maggot that eats holes in ~s; (fig) person who is very fond of reading ~s.

book² /bʊk/ *vt* [VP6A] **1** write down (orders, etc) in a notebook; (of the police) record a charge against (sb): *be ~ed for exceeding the speed limit.* **2** give or receive an order for, eg seats at a theatre, tickets for a journey; engage (sb) as a speaker, entertainer, etc: *Seats (for the theatre) can be ~ed from 10am to 6pm. Have you ~ed your passage to New York,* arranged for a cabin? *Can I ~ (a ticket) through to Naples? (fully) ~ed up,* (of a restaurant, theatre, etc) no more tables, seats, available; (of a lecturer, singer, etc) unable to accept further engagements. '∼·ing clerk *n* person who sells tickets, eg at a railway station. '∼·ing office *n* office for the sale of tickets (for travel). '∼·able /-əbl/ *adj* (of seats, etc) that can be reserved: *all seats ∼able in advance.*

bookie /'bʊkɪ/ *n* (colloq) bookmaker. ⇨ book¹(8).

book·ish /'bʊkɪʃ/ *adj* of books and studies: *a ∼ person,* one who gives much time to reading; *∼ expressions,* found in books but not colloquial; *a ∼ style,* literary, not colloquial. ∼·ness *n*

book·let /'bʊklɪt/ *n* thin book, usu in paper covers.

boom¹ /buːm/ *n* 1 long spar used to keep the bottom of a sail stretched out. ⇨ the illus at barque. 2 **derrick** ∼, pole fastened to a derrick crane, used for (un-)loading cargo. 3 heavy chain, mass of floating logs, etc held in position across a river or harbour entrance, eg as a defence in time of war, or to prevent logs from floating away. 4 long, movable arm for a microphone.

boom² /buːm/ *vt,vi* 1 [VP2A,C] (of big guns, the wind, an organ) make deep, hollow, or resonant sounds. 2 ∼ out, [VP15B] utter in a deep voice: *∼ing out Shakespearian verses.* □ *n* deep, hollow sound: *the ∼ of the guns/surf; a sonic ∼.*

boom³ /buːm/ *n* [C] sudden increase in trade activity, esp a time when money is being made quickly. ⇨ slump. '∼ town *n* town showing sudden growth and prosperity. □ *vi* [VP2A,C] have a ∼; become well known and successful: *Business is ∼ing. Jones is ∼ing as a novelist,* becoming famous.

boom·er·ang /'buːməræŋ/ *n* curved stick of hard wood (used by Australian Aborigines), which can be thrown so that, if it fails to hit anything, it returns to the thrower; (fig) argument or proposal that comes back and harms its author.

boon¹ /buːn/ *n* 1 (liter) request; favour: *ask a ∼ of sb; grant a ∼.* 2 advantage; blessing; comfort: *Parks are a great ∼ to people in big cities. A vacuum cleaner is a tremendous ∼ to busy housewives.*

boon² /buːn/ *adj* (only in) ∼ companion, jolly, congenial, companion.

boor /bʊə(r)/ *n* rough, ill-mannered person. ∼·ish /-ɪʃ/ *adj* of or like a ∼. ∼·ish·ly *adv* ∼·ish·ness *n*

boost /buːst/ *vt* [VP6A] give (sb or sth) a push up; increase the value, reputation, etc of (sb or sth): *Seeing him there ∼ed my morale.* □ *n* [C] act of ∼ing; being ∼ed. ∼·er *n* 1 thing that ∼s: *His work got a welcome ∼.* '∼·er rocket *n* rocket used to give initial speed to a missile, after which it drops and leaves the missile to continue under its own power. 2 '∼ (injection) supplementary dose of vaccine to strengthen the effect of an earlier dose; extra dose of morphine, etc (by drug addicts).

boot¹ /buːt/ *n* 1 outer covering for the foot and ankle, made of leather or rubber. ⇨ shoe. high ∼s, reaching to the knee. die with one's ∼s on; die in one's ∼s, not in bed; die while still working, etc. get the ∼, (sl) be dismissed, be kicked out. give sb the ∼, (sl) dismiss him from his job. lick sb's ∼s, behave in a servile way. put the ∼ in, (sl) kick sb, eg in a brawl; (fig) be ruthless. '∼·lace *n* string or leather strip for ∼s. 2 (GB) place for luggage in a coach or at the back of a motor-car (US = trunk). □ *vt* [VP6A,15A,B] kick. ∼ sb/sth out (of), (sl) get rid of (from); dismiss, expel (from): *He was ∼ed out of the house.* ∼ed *adj* wearing ∼s: *∼ed and spurred,* ready for a journey.

boot² /buːt/ *n to ∼,* in addition, as well.

boot³ /buːt/ *vt* (old use, usu with *it*): *What ∼s it to..., that...,* what use is it to..., that...? *It little ∼s to; It ∼s not to,* It is of little/no avail to.

bootee /buː'tiː/ *n* [C] (*pl* ∼s) infant's knitted wool boot; kind of warmly lined boot for women.

booth /buːð *US:* buːθ/ *n* 1 shelter of boards, canvas or other light materials, esp one where goods are sold at a market or a fair. 2 enclosure for a public telephone. ⇨ kiosk. 3 'polling ∼, place for voting at elections. 'listening ∼, (in a shop) enclosure where customers may listen to records.

boot·leg /'buːtleg/ *vt* make, transport or sell illicit alcoholic drinks: (attrib) ∼ liquor. ∼·ger /-legə(r)/ *n* person who does this.

boot·less /'buːtlɪs/ *adj* (liter) useless; unavailing.

booty /'buːtɪ/ *n* [U] things taken by robbers or captured from the enemy in war (and usu to be divided among those who take them).

booze /buːz/ *vi* [VP2A,C] ∼ (up), (colloq) drink alcoholic liquor, esp in excess. Hence, '∼-up, *n* [C] occasion of heavy drinking: *go on/have a ∼-up.* □ *n* [U] (colloq) alcoholic drink. go/be on the ∼, start/be in a period of heavy drinking. ∼r *n* one who ∼s; (sl) pub. boozy *adj*

bop /bɒp/ *n* (1940s) [U] style of jazz with a strong beat; [U,C] dancing/dance to this. □ *vi* [VP2A] dance to this.

bo·peep /ˌbəʊ'piːp/ *n* [U] game of hiding and suddenly showing oneself to a baby.

bor·acic /bə'ræsɪk/ *adj* of borax: ∼ acid, boric acid, ⇨ boric.

bor·age /'bɒrɪdʒ *US:* 'bɔːrɪdʒ/ *n* [U] blue-flowered, hairy-leaved plant of which the leaves are used as a seasoning.

borax /'bɔːræks/ *n* white powder used to make porcelain enamels, in glass manufacture and other industries, and for cleaning.

Bor·deaux /bɔː'dəʊ/ *n* [U] (F) (often attrib) wine from the ∼ area of France; claret.

bor·der /'bɔːdə(r)/ *n* 1 edge; part near the edge of sth: *We camped on the ∼ of a lake. A woman's handkerchief may have a lace ∼. There is a ∼ of flowers round the lawn.* 2 (land near the) line dividing two states or countries: *The criminal escaped over the ∼.* (attrib): *a ∼ town; ∼ incidents,* eg small fights between armed forces of two neighbouring states. the B∼, (esp) that between England and Scotland. '∼·land /-lænd/ *n* (a) district on either side of a ∼ or boundary. (b) (*sing* with *def art,* and attrib) condition between: *the ∼land between sleeping and waking.* '∼·line *n* line that marks a ∼. ∼line case *n* one that is dubious, eg sb who may or may not pass an examination. □ *vt,vi* [VP6A] put or be a ∼ to: *Our garden is ∼ed by a stream.* 2 [VP3A] ∼ on/upon, be next to: *My land ∼s (up)on yours. The park ∼s on the shores of the lake.* 3 ∼ on/upon, [VP3A] resemble; be almost the same as: *The proposal ∼s upon the absurd.* ∼er *n* person living on or near a frontier, esp that between England and Scotland.

bore¹ /bɔː(r)/ *vt,vi* [VP6A,14,15] make a narrow, round deep hole in sth with a revolving tool; make (a hole, one's way) by doing this or by digging out soil, etc: ∼ *a hole in wood; ∼ a well; ∼ a tunnel through a mountain; animals* (eg moles) *that ∼ their way under the ground.* □ *n* 1 (also '∼-hole) hole made by boring, eg to find water. 2 hollow inside of a gun barrel; its diameter. **borer** *n* (kind of) insect that ∼s.

bore² /bɔː(r)/ vt [VP6A] make (sb) feel tired by being dull or tedious: *I hope you're not getting ~d listening to me. I've heard all that man's stories before; they ~ me/he ~s me. ~ sb to death/ tears,* ~ him intensely. □ *n* [C] person or thing that ~s. **bor-ing** *adj*: *a boring evening.* ~-**dom** /-dəm/ *n* [U] state of being ~d.

bore³ /bɔː(r)/ *n* [C] high tidal wave, often many feet high, that advances up a narrow estuary.

bore⁴ /bɔː(r)/ *pt* of bear.

boric /'bɔːrɪk/ *adj* ~ **acid,** used as an antiseptic and a preservative.

born /bɔːn/ one of the *pp's* of bear. **1 be ~,** come into the world by birth. ~ **with a silver spoon in one's mouth,** ⇨ silver(1). **2** (with a complement) destined to be: *He was ~ a poet. He was ~ to be hanged.* **3** (attrib) by natural ability: *a ~ orator.*

borne /bɔːn/ *pp* of bear (except of birth). ⇨ bear²(10,13).

boron /'bɔːrɒn/ *n* [U] non-metallic element (symbol **B**).

bor·ough /'bʌrə *US:* -rəʊ/ *n* **1** (England) town, or part of a town, that sends one or more members to Parliament; town with a municipal corporation and rights of self-government conferred by royal charter. **2** (US) any one of the five administrative units of New York City.

bor·row /'bɒrəʊ/ *vt* [VP6A,14] ~ **(from), 1** get sth, or the use of sth, on the understanding that it is to be returned: *May I ~ your pen? Don't ~ books from me—~ them from the library! He fell into the river and had to go home in ~ed clothes. Some people are good at ~ing but bad at giving back.* ⇨ lend. **2** take and use as one's own: ~ *sb's ideas/ methods.* ~**er** *n* person who ~s.

borsch /bɔːʃ/ (US = **borscht** /bɔːʃt/) *n* [U] (kinds of) Eastern European soup, esp of beetroot.

bor·stal /'bɔːstl/ *n* ~ **(institution),** place where young offenders live and receive training designed to reform them.

bortsch /bɔːtʃ/ *n* = borsch.

bor·zoi /'bɔːzɔɪ/ *n* Russian wolf-hound.

bosh /bɒʃ/ *n, int* nonsense.

bosky /'bɒskɪ/ *adj* (liter) (of land) covered with trees and bushes.

bo'sn /'bəʊsn/ ⇨ boatswain.

bosom /'bʊzəm/ *n* [C] **1** (old use) person's chest; woman's breasts; part of dress covering these. **2** centre or inmost part, where one feels joy or sorrow; (attrib) *a ~ friend,* one who is dear and close. **3** midst: *in the ~ of one's family.*

boss¹ /bɒs/ *n* [C] (colloq) superior; person who controls or gives orders to workers: *Who's the ~ in this house,* Is the husband or the wife in control? □ *vt* [VP6A,15B] be the ~ of; give orders to: *He wants to ~ the show,* to make all the arrangements. ~ *sb about/around,* order sb here and there. ~**y** *adj* (-ier, -iest) fond of ~ing, fond of giving orders.

boss² /bɒs/ *n* round metal knob or stud on a shield or as an ornament.

boss³ /bɒs/ *n* (sl) (also '~ **shot**) bad shot or guess; bungle; *make a ~ shot at sth; make a ~ of sth.* '~**-eyed** *adj* (sl) blind in one eye; cross-eyed.

bo'sun /'bəʊsn/ ⇨ boatswain.

bot·any /'bɒtənɪ/ *n* [U] science of the structure of plants. **bot·an·ical** /bə'tænɪkl/ *adj* of ~. **botanical gardens,** park where plants and trees are grown for scientific study. **bot·an·ist** /'bɒtənɪst/ *n* student of or expert in ~. **bot·an·ize** /'bɒtənaɪz/ *vi* go out

studying and collecting wild plants.

botch /bɒtʃ/ *vt* [VP6A,15B] ~ **sth (up),** repair badly; spoil by poor, clumsy work: *a ~ed piece of work.* □ *n* piece of clumsy, badly done work; *make a ~ of sth;* clumsy patch **¹**(1) ~**er** *n* person who ~es work.

both¹ /bəʊθ/ *adj* (of two things, persons, etc) the two; the one and also the other; (*both* precedes the *def art,* demonstrative *adjj,* possessives, and other *adjj*): *I want ~ books/the books/these books. I saw him on ~ occasions. Hold it in ~ (your) hands. B~ his younger brothers are in the army. You can't have it ~ ways,* must decide on one or the other. Cf *both* and *neither: B~ these books are useful. Neither of these books is useful.* Cf *both* and *each: There are shops on ~ sides of the street. There is a butcher's shop on each side of the street.*

both² /bəʊθ/ *adv* ~... *and,* not only... but also: *Queen Anne is ~ dead and buried. He is remarkable for ~ his intelligence and his skill. He is ~ a soldier and a poet.*

both³ /bəʊθ/ *pron* **1** the two; not only the one but also the other: *B~ are good. B~ of them are good.* Cf *both* and *neither. B~ of us want to go. Neither of us wants to go.* **2** (used in apposition, in the same way as *each* and *all*): *We ~ want to go. They are ~ useful. Take them ~. You must ~ work harder.*

bother /'bɒðə(r)/ *vt,vi* **1** [VP6A,14,16A,3A] be or cause trouble to; worry: *Tell the children to stop ~ing their father. Don't ~ me with foolish questions. That man is always ~ing me to lend him money.* ~ **(oneself/one's head) (about),** be/feel anxious about: *It's not important; don't ~ your head about it. We needn't ~ (about) when it happened.* **2** [VP3A,4C,2A] ~ **(about),** take trouble: *Don't ~ about getting/~ to get dinner for me today; I'll eat out.* **3** (used as an exclamation of impatience or annoyance): *Oh, ~ (it)! B~ the flies! Oh, ~ you!* □ *n* **1** [U] worry, trouble: *Did you have much ~ (in) finding the house? It will be no ~ (to me),* won't involve much work or inconvenience. *We had quite a lot of ~ (in) getting here because of the fog. Don't put yourself to any ~,* inconvenience yourself. **2** (with *indef art*) sb or sth that gives trouble: *His lazy son is quite a ~ to him. This drawer won't shut; isn't it a ~!* ~**-ation** /ˌbɒðə'reɪʃn/ *int* What a nuisance! '~**-some** /-səm/ *adj* causing ~; troublesome or annoying.

bottle /'bɒtl/ *n* container, usu made of glass and with a narrow neck, for milk, beer, wine, medicine, ink, etc; the contents of a ~: *Mary drinks two ~s of milk a day.* '~-**fed; brought up on the ~,** (of a child) given milk from a feeding ~, not fed from its mother's breast. *too fond of the ~,* of alcoholic drinks. ~-'**green** *adj* dark green. '~-**neck** *n* (a) narrow strip of road, between two wide parts, where traffic is slowed down or held up. (b) that part of a manufacturing process, etc, where production is slowed down (eg by shortage of materials) □ *vt* [VP6A] put into, store in, ~: ~ *fruit.* ~ **up,** [VP15B] (fig) hold in, keep under control, eg anger.

bot·tom /'bɒtəm/ *n* **1** lowest part of anything, inside or outside: *There are some tea-leaves in the ~ of the cup. He fell to the ~ of the well. We were glad to reach the ~ (= foot) of the mountain. Notes are sometimes printed at the ~ (= foot) of the page.* **2** part farthest from the front or more important part: *at the ~ of the garden;* less honourable end of a table, class, etc: *The poor relations were seated at the ~ of the long table.* **3** bed of the sea, a lake, river, etc: *The ship went to the ~, sank. The lake is deep and a swimmer cannot touch ~,* touch the bed of the lake with his toes. **4** seat (of a chair); part of the body on which a person sits; buttocks: *This chair needs a new ~. She smacked the child's ~.* **5** horizontal part of a ship near the keel: *The ship was found floating ~ upwards.* **6** foundation: *We must get to the ~ of this mystery,* find out how it began. *Who's at the ~ of this business,* Who's responsible? **7** (fig uses): *The ~ has fallen out of the market,* Trade has fallen to a very low level. *at ~,* in essential character: *He's a good fellow at ~. from the ~ of my heart,* genuinely, deeply. *knock the ~ out of (an argument, etc,)* prove that it is worthless. **8** (attrib) lowest, last: *Put the book on the ~ shelf. What's your ~ price? Who's the ~ boy of the class?* ⇨ also gear(1), rock¹(6). □ *vi ~ out,* (economics) reach a low level and remain there: *The value of our oil shares on the Stock Market has now ~ed out,* ie from now on can only rise, not fall further. *~·less adj* very deep: *a ~less pit.*

botu·lism /'bɒtjʊlɪzəm/ *n* [U] type of food poisoning.

bou·doir /'bu:dwɑː(r)/ *n* woman's private sitting-room or dressing-room.

bou·gain·vil·lea /ˌbuːɡən'vɪlɪə/ *n* tropical climbing shrub with tiny flowers surrounded by red, purple, etc bracts.

bough /baʊ/ *n* large branch coming from the trunk of a tree. ⇨ the illus at tree.

bought /bɔːt/ *pt,pp* of buy.

bouil·lon /'bu:jɒn/ *n* [U] (F) clear thin soup or broth. ⇨ stock¹(9).

boul·der /'bəʊldə(r)/ *n* large piece of rock, large stone, esp one that has been rounded by water or weather.

boul·evard /'bu:ləvɑːd *US:* 'bʊl-/ *n* (F) wide city street, often with trees on each side.

bounce /baʊns/ *vi,vt* **1** [VP2A,6A] (of a ball, etc) (cause to) spring or jump back when sent against sth hard: *A rubber ball ~s well. The ball ~ed over the wall. She was bouncing a ball. ~ back,* [VP2C] (fig) recover jauntily from a setback. **2** [VP2C,6A] (cause to) move up and down violently or noisily; rush noisily or speedily: *The boy was bouncing (up and down) on the bed. He ~d into/out of the room. She ~d out of her chair. The old car ~d along the bad roads.* **3** [VP2A] (colloq) (of a cheque) be returned by a bank as worthless: *Don't worry—my cheque won't ~.* □ *n* **1** [C] (of a ball) bouncing: *catch the ball on the ~.* **2** [U] (of a person) liveliness. **bouncer** *n* = chucker-out, ⇨ chuck¹(1). **bounc·ing** *adj* (colloq) (of a person) strong and healthy.

bound¹ /baʊnd/ *n* (usu *pl*) limit: *It is beyond the ~s of human knowledge,* Man can know nothing about it. *There are no ~s to his ambition. Please keep within the ~s of reason,* do not say foolish things, attempt impracticable things. *He sets no ~s to his desires. Is it within the ~s of probability? out of ~s,* outside the limits of areas that one is allowed to enter: *Most of the bars had been placed out of ~s to troops.* (US = off limits).

bound² /baʊnd/ *vt* [VP6A, usu passive] limit (lit, fig); set bounds to; be the boundary of: *England is ~ed on the north by Scotland.*

bound³ /baʊnd/ *vt* [VP2A,C,4A] jump, spring,

bounce; move or run in jumping movements: *The ball struck the wall and ~ed back to me. His heart ~ed with joy. His dog came ~ing to meet him. Big rocks were ~ing down the hillside.* □ *n* jumping movement upward or forward: *at one ~; hit a ball on the ~* (or *rebound* /'riː'baʊnd/), after it has hit the ground and is in the air again. *by leaps and ~s,* (fig) very rapidly.

bound⁴ /baʊnd/ *part adj ~ (for),* ready to start, having started, in the direction of: *Where are you ~ (for),* Where are you going to? *The ship is ~ for Finland. If a British ship is going away from Britain, she is outward ~; if she is returning to Britain, she is homeward ~.*

bound⁵ /baʊnd/ *pp* of bind. *~ to do sth,* (a) certain to: *He hasn't got any money—so he's ~ to turn up sooner or later.* (b) obliged to: *I'm ~ to visit my grandmother every week. ~ 'up in,* much interested in, very busy with: *He is ~ up in his work. ~ 'up with,* closely connected with: *The welfare of the individual is ~ up with the welfare of the community.*

bound·ary /'baʊndrɪ/ *n* (*pl* -ries) **1** line that marks a limit; dividing line: *This stream forms a ~ between my land and his. A ~ dispute is a quarrel about where a ~ is or ought to be. If something is beyond the ~ of human knowledge, man can know nothing about it.* **2** (cricket) hit to or over the ~, scoring 4 or 6 runs.

boun·den /'baʊndən/ *adj* (only in) *my ~ duty,* (archaic) what my conscience tells me I must do.

bounder /'baʊndə(r)/ *n* (GB dated colloq) untrustworthy, ill-bred person.

bound·less /'baʊndlɪs/ *adj* without limits: *his ~ generosity. ~·ly adv*

boun·te·ous /'baʊntɪəs/ *adj* (liter) generous; giving or given freely; abundant: *a ~ harvest. ~·ly adv*

boun·ti·ful /'baʊntɪfl/ *adj* (liter) bounteous. *'~·ly /-fəlɪ/ adv*

bounty /'baʊntɪ/ *n* (*pl* -ties) **1** [U] (formal) freedom in giving; generosity. **2** [C] (formal) sth given out of kindness (esp to the poor). **3** [C] reward or payment offered (usu by a government) to encourage sb to do sth (eg increase production of goods, kill dangerous wild animals).

bou·quet /bʊ'keɪ/ *n* **1** bunch of flowers (to be) carried in the hand. **2** perfume of wine.

bour·bon /'bɜːbən/ *n* [U] kinds of whisky distilled (in the US) from maize and rye.

bour·geois /'bʊəʒwɑː *US:* ˌbʊər'ʒwɑː/ *n, adj* (person) of the class that owns property or engages in trade; (pej) (person) concerned chiefly with material prosperity and social status. *the ~ie* /ˌbʊəʒwɑː'ziː/ *n* persons of this class, collectively.

bourn(e) /bʊən/ *n* (old use) boundary; limit; goal.

bourse /bʊəs/ *n* foreign stock exchange (esp that of Paris). ⇨ stock¹(5).

bout /baʊt/ *n* **1** period of exercise, work or other activity: *a 'wrestling ~; a ~ of fighting; a 'drinking ~.* **2** fit (of illness): *a ~ of influenza; bad coughing ~s.*

bou·tique /bu:'tiːk/ *n* small shop selling articles (clothes, cosmetics, hats, etc) of the latest fashion.

bov·ine /'bəʊvaɪn/ *adj* of, like, an ox: *~ stupidity.*

bov·ril /'bɒvrɪl/ *n* [U] (P) meat extract used like beef tea.

bow¹ /bəʊ/ *n* **1** piece of wood curved by a tight string, used for shooting arrows. ⇨ the illus at archer. *have two strings to one's bow,* have more than one plan, more resources than one. **2** rod of wood with horse-hair stretched from end to end, used for playing the violin, etc. ⇨ the illus at string. **3** curve; rainbow. **4** knot made with a loop or loops; ribbon, etc, tied in this way: *Tie your shoelaces in a bow. She had a bow of pink ribbon in her hair.* ˌbow **'legged** *adj* with the legs curved outwards at the knees; bandy. ˌbow **'legs** *n pl* such legs. ˌbow **'tie** *n* necktie made into a bow. **'bow-man** /-mən/ *n* (*pl* -men) archer. □ *vt* use a bow on (a violin, etc). **bow·ing** *n*: *The violinist's bowing is excellent.*

bow² /baʊ/ *vi,vt* **1** [VP2A,C,6A,3A] bend the head or body (as a sign of respect or as a greeting, or in submission, or to indicate assent); bend (the head or body): *I raised my hat to her and she bowed in return. They bowed down to the idol. They bowed their heads in prayer. He bowed before the shrine. He bowed his thanks,* expressed his thanks by bowing. [VP15B] **bow sb in,** receive a visitor with low bows. [VP15B] **bow sb out,** bow low to sb as he leaves. **bow oneself out,** bow as one goes out. [VP2C,15A,B] **bow (oneself) out (of),** dissociate, disengage: *I'm bowing out of this scheme—I think it's a big mistake.* **bow to sb's opinion, etc,** submit to it. **have a bowing acquaintance with,** ⇨ acquaintance. **2** [VP6A,15B, usu passive] bend: *His father is bowed with age. The branches were bowed down with the weight of the snow.* □ *n* bending of the head or body (in greeting, etc): *He answered with a low bow. He made his bow to the company and left the room.*

bow³ /baʊ/ *n* **1** (often *pl*) front or forward end of a boat or ship from where it begins to curve. **on/off the (port, starboard) bow,** said of objects within 45° of the point right ahead. ⇨ the illus at ship. **2** (in a rowing-boat) oarsman nearest the bow. ⇨ stroke.

Bow Bells /ˌbaʊ 'belz/ *n pl* the bells of Bow Church, London. **born within the sound of ~,** (said of a true Cockney) born in the City of London.

bowd·ler·ize /'baʊdləraɪz/ *vt* take out of (a book, etc) words, scenes, etc that might be considered improper, unsuitable for young readers, etc.

bowel /'baʊəl/ *n* **1** (usu *pl* except in medical use and when attrib) division of the food canal below the stomach; intestine: *a ~ complaint. Keep your ~s open,* don't become constipated. ⇨ the illus at alimentary. **2** (always *pl*) innermost part: *in the ~s of the earth,* deep underground.

bower /'baʊə(r)/ *n* **1** summer-house in a garden; shady place under trees or climbing plants. **2** (liter) boudoir.

bowie knife /'baʊɪ naɪf/ *n* long knife with a blade that is double-edged at the point, used as a weapon.

bowl¹ /baʊl/ *n* **1** deep, round, hollow dish; contents of such a dish: *She ate three ~s of rice;* (compounds): *'finger-~, 'salad-~, 'sugar-~.* **2** sth shaped like a ~: *the ~ of a spoon. He filled the ~ of his pipe,* put tobacco into it. *The electric light bulb is in an alabaster ~.* **3** (esp US) amphitheatre (for open-air concerts, etc): *The Hollywood B~.*

bowl² /baʊl/ *n* **1** heavy, wooden or composition ball made so that it rolls with a bias. **2** (*pl*) game played with these balls: *have a game of ~s; play (at) ~s.*

bowl³ /baʊl/ *vi,vt* **1** [VP2A] play bowls. ⇨ bowl²(2). **'~·ing-green** *n* area of fine, smooth

grass for playing bowls. **'~·ing alley** *n* level area of wood, used for skittles, ninepins and tenpins. **2** [VP2A,6A] (cricket) send a ball to the batsman: *Smith ~ed ten overs.* ⇨ over³. **~ (out),** [VP6A,15B] dismiss (a batsman) by hitting the wicket or knocking the bails off: *The first two batsmen were ~ed (out).* **3** **~ along,** [VP2C] go quickly and smoothly on wheels: *Our car ~ed along over the smooth roads.* **4** **~ sb over,** [VP15B] **(a)** knock down. **(b)** make helpless, overcome: *He was ~ed over by the news. Her impudence ~ed me over,* left me speechless with surprise.

bowler¹ /'baʊlə(r)/ *n* **1** person who plays bowls²(2). **2** person who bowls in cricket.

bowler² /'baʊlə(r)/ *n* (also **~ 'hat**) hard, rounded, usu black hat.

bow·line /'baʊlɪn/ *n* (also **'~ knot**) simple but secure knot used by sailors, climbers, etc. ⇨ the illus at knot.

bowls /baʊlz/ *n* ⇨ bowl²(2).

bow·man /'baʊmən/ *n* (*pl* -men) archer. ⇨ bow¹(1).

bow·sprit /'baʊsprɪt/ *n* spar that extends from a ship's stem, to which ropes that support sails, etc are fastened. ⇨ the illus at barque.

bow win·dow /ˌbaʊ 'wɪndəʊ/ *n* curved bay window. ⇨ the illus at window.

bow-wow /ˌbaʊ 'waʊ/ *int* imitation of a dog's bark. □ *n* /'baʊ waʊ/ (young child's word for a) dog.

box¹ /bɒks/ *n* **1** container, usu with a lid, made of wood, cardboard, plastic, metal, etc used for holding solids: *a box of matches; a 'tool-box. Pack the books in a wooden box.* **'box-kite** *n* kite made in the form of a box (or two boxes) of light material. **'box-number** *n* number used in a newspaper advertisement as an address to which answers may be sent (and forwarded from the newspaper office). **P'O Box No** *n* number used as part of an address to which letters, etc may be directed. ⇨ also call-box, Christmas-box, letter-box, money-box, pillar-box. **2** separate compartment, with seats for several persons, in a theatre, concert hall, etc. **'box-office** *n* office for booking seats in a theatre, concert hall, etc: *The play was a box-office success, a financial success.* **3** compartment in a law court for a special purpose: *'jury-box, 'witness-box.* **4** small hut or shelter, eg for a sentry or railway signalman. **5** separate compartment in a stable or railway truck for a horse. **6** raised seat for the driver of a carriage(1) or coach(1). **box·ful** /-fʊl/ *n* full box ¹(1) (*of* sth). □ *vt* [VP6A] put into a box. **box sb/sth up,** [VP15B] shut up in a small space.

box² /bɒks/ *vt,vi* [VP6A,2A,3A] **box (with),** fight (sb) with the fists, usu with thick gloves, for sport: *Do you box, Do you fight in this way?* **box sb's ears,** give him a blow with the open hand on the ear. **'box·ing-glove** *n* padded glove (one of a pair) for use in boxing. **'box·ing-match** *n* fight between two boxers. □ *n* slap or blow with the open hand on the ear. **boxer** /'bɒksə(r)/ *n* **1** person who boxes. **2** breed of dog (like a bulldog). **box·ing** *n* [U] organised sport of fist fighting.

box³ /bɒks/ *n* [U] **1** (kinds of) small, evergreen shrub, used in garden borders. **2** (also **'box·wood**) wood of this shrub.

Box·ing Day /'bɒksɪŋ deɪ/ *n* first weekday after Christmas Day.

boy /bɔɪ/ *n* **1** male child up to the age of 17 or 18.

'boy·friend, favoured male companion of a girl or young woman. **2** son (colloq, of any age): *He has two boys and one girl.* **3** *int* (US sl) expressing enthusiasm, relief, surprise, etc. **'boy·hood** /-hʊd/ *n* [U] time when one is/was a boy. **boy·ish** *adj* of, for, like, a boy.

boy·cott /'bɔɪkɒt/ *vt* [VP6A] (join with others and) refuse to have anything to do with, to trade with (a person, business firm, country, etc); refuse to handle (goods, etc). □ *n* ~ing; treatment of this kind: *put sb/his shop/goods under a* ~; *put a* ~ *on sb, etc.*

bra /brɑ:/ *n* (colloq abbr of) brassière.

brace¹ /breɪs/ *n* **1** sth used to clasp, tighten or support, eg the roof or walls of a building. **2** revolving tool for holding another tool, eg a *bit* for boring holes, driving in screws, etc. **3** (*pl* unchanged) pair or couple (of dogs, game-birds): *five* ~ *of partridge.* **4** (*pl*) (US = *suspenders*) straps passing over the shoulders, fastened to the front and back of trousers to keep them up. **5** (often *pl*) appliance of bands and wires fastened to the teeth to correct their alignment. **6** (printing) ⇨ bracket(2).

a brace and bit

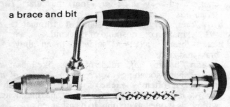

brace² /breɪs/ *vt,vi* **1** [VP6A] support; give firmness to: *The struts are firmly* ~*d.* **2** [VP6A,15B,16A] ~ *(up),* steady oneself; stand firm: *B*~ *up! He* ~*d himself to meet the blow.* **3** (usu as *part adj* in *-ing*) enliven; stimulate: *bracing air; a bracing climate.*

brace·let /'breɪslɪt/ *n* ornamental band or chain for the wrist or arm.

bracken /'brækən/ *n* [U] large fern that grows on hillsides, waste land, etc; mass of such fern.

bracket /'brækɪt/ *n* **1** wood or metal support for a shelf; support on a wall for a gas or electric lamp. **2** (printing, writing) any one of the paired marks () (*round* ~*s or parentheses*), [] (*square* ~*s*), {} (*braces*), used for enclosing words, figures etc to indicate separation from what precedes and follows. ⇨ App 9. **3** grouping; classification: *income* ~, eg of incomes from £3000 to £4500; *age* ~, eg 20 to 30 years of age. □ *vt* [VP6A,15B] put inside, join with, ~s; put together to imply connection or equality: *Jones and Smith were* ~*ed together at the top of the list.*

brack·ish /'brækɪʃ/ *adj* (of water) slightly salt; between salt and fresh water.

bract /brækt/ *n* [C] (bot) leaf-like part of a plant, often highly coloured, situated below a flower or cluster of flowers (as in bougainvillea, poinsettia).

brad /bræd/ *n* thin, flat nail with no head or a very small head.

brad·awl /'brædɔ:l/ *n* small tool for piercing holes for brads or screws. ⇨ illus at tool.

brae /breɪ/ *n* (Scot) slope; hillside.

brag /bræg/ *vi* (-gg-) ~ *(of/about),* [VP2A,3A] boast: ~ *of what one has done.* **brag·ging** *n* [U] **brag·gart** /'brægət/ *n* person who ~s.

Brah·min /'brɑ:mɪn/ *n* member of the highest Hindu priestly caste.

braid /breɪd/ *n* **1** [C] number of strands of hair woven together: *She wears her hair in* ~*s.* **2** [U] silk, linen, etc woven into a band, used for edging cloth or garments or (esp gold and silver ~) for decoration: *The uniforms of the generals were covered with gold* ~. □ *vt* [VP6A] make into ~(s); trim with ~; put (hair) into ~s.

braille /breɪl/ *n* [U] system of writing and reading (using raised dots) for blind people, to enable them to read by touch.

reading braille

brain /breɪn/ *n* **1** (*sing*) (in man and animals) the mass of soft grey matter in the head, centre of the nervous system: *The human* ~ *is a complex organ. The creature's* ~ *weighs a quarter of a kilo.* ⇨ the illus at head. **2** (colloq, usu *pl*) skull and brain(1) thought of together: *He fell and dashed his* ~*s out on the rocks.* **blow out one's** ~*s,* ⇨ blow¹(13). **3** (*pl*) animal's ~s, eaten as food: *calf's/sheep's* ~*s.* **4** (colloq, usu *sing*) mind; intellect: *have a good* ~; *use one's* ~(*s*). **beat/rack one's** ~(*s*) *(about sth),* think very hard. **have sth** *on the* ~, think constantly about it. **tax one's** ~, set oneself/be set a difficult mental task. **pick sb's** ~(*s*), learn and use his ideas. **5** [C] clever, brilliant person: *He's the* ~ *of the school staff.* **6** (compounds) **'**~**-child** *n* original idea, etc attributed to a person or group. **'**~ **drain** *n* ⇨ drain¹(2). **'**~**-fag** *n* (colloq) mental exhaustion: *suffering from* ~*-fag.* **'**~ **fever** *n* inflammation of the ~. **'**~**-storm** *n* mental upset with uncontrolled emotion, eg weeping, and violence. **'**~**-teaser** *n* difficult problem; puzzle. **'B**~**s Trust** *n* group of reputed experts giving advice, or answering questions put to them by members of an audience. **'**~**washing** *n* process of forcing a person to reject old beliefs and accept new beliefs by use of extreme mental pressure, eg persistent questioning. **'**~**wave** *n* (colloq) sudden inspiration or bright idea. □ *vt* [VP6A] kill by a heavy blow on the head: ~ *an ox.* ~**less** *adj* stupid. ~**y** *adj* (-ier, -iest) clever.

braise /breɪz/ *vt* [VP6A] cook (meat, vegetables) slowly in a covered pan or pot: ~*d beef/onions.*

brake¹ /breɪk/ *n* device for reducing speed or stopping motion, eg of a bicycle, motor-car, train, etc: *put on/apply/*(colloq) *slam on the* ~*s; act as a* ~ *upon* (*progress, initiative, etc*), hamper it; control it. ⇨ the illus at motor. □ *vt,vi* [VP6A,2A] put on the ~s: *The driver* ~*d* (*his car*) *suddenly.* **'**~**man** /-mən/ *n* (*pl* -men) (US) guard¹(5).

brake² /breɪk/ *n* area or band of brushwood, thick undergrowth or bracken.

brake³ /breɪk/ *n* large wagon or open carriage pulled by one or more horses, and with facing side seats, formerly used for pleasure outings. ⇨ shooting-brake.

bramble /'bræmbl/ *n* rough shrub with long prickly shoots; blackberry bush.

bran /bræn/ *n* [U] outer covering (husks) of grain

(wheat, rye, etc) separated from flour by sifting.

branch /brɑːntʃ US: bræntʃ/ n **1** arm-like division of a tree, growing out from the trunk, or a bough, or another ~, ⇨ the illus at tree: *He climbed up the tree and hid among the ~es.* **2** (often attrib) division or subdivision of a river, road, railway, mountain range, etc; division or subdivision of a family, subject of knowledge, organization, etc: *There is a ~ post office quite near. The bank has ~es in all parts of the country. English is a ~ of the Germanic family of languages.* **root and ~,** ⇨ root¹(1). □ *vi* [VP2A,C] send out, divide into, ~es: *The trees ~ (out) over the river. The road ~es here.* **~ off,** (of a car, road, train, etc) leave a main route and take a minor one. **~ out,** (of a person, business firm, etc) expand in a new direction, open new departments or lines of activities. **~y** *adj* with many ~es.

brand /brænd/ n **1** trademark (painted or printed on boxes, tins, packets, etc); particular kind of goods with such a mark: *the best ~s of cigars; an excellent ~ of coffee.* **~-'new** *adj* quite new (as if freshly stamped with a ~). **2** piece of burning wood. **a ~ from the burning,** person rescued from the consequences of sin; converted sinner. **3** (also '~-ing-iron), iron used red-hot, for burning a mark into a surface; mark made in this way; (in olden times) mark burned on criminals, hence, (fig) mark of guilt or disgrace: *the ~ of Cain,* of a murderer. **4** (poet) torch. □ *vt* [VP6A,16B] **1** mark (cattle, goods, etc) with a ~: *On big farms cattle are usually ~ed. Criminals used to be ~ed.* (fig) *These frightful experiences are ~ed on his memory.* **2** give (sb) a bad name: *~ sb with infamy; ~ sb (as) a heretic.*

bran·dish /'brændɪʃ/ *vt* [VP6A] wave about (to display, or before using): *~ing a sword.*

brandy /'brændɪ/ n [C,U] strong alcoholic drink distilled from wine of grapes: *two brandies and sodas,* two glasses of ~ mixed with soda water. **'~-ball** n kind of sweet. **'~-snap** n kind of gingerbread wafer.

bran-new /ˌbræn 'njuː/ *adj* = brand-new.

brash /bræʃ/ *adj* (colloq) **1** saucy; cheeky. **2** hasty; rash.

brass /brɑːs US: bræs/ n **1** [U] bright yellow metal made by mixing copper and zinc: *~ rods/buttons; a ~ foundry.* **get down to ~ tacks,** begin to talk, discuss, etc in plain, straightforward terms. ~ **'hat,** (army sl) high-ranking officer. ~ **'plate,** oblong plate of ~, on a door or gate, with the name, trade, occupation, etc, eg as used by doctors, lawyers, business firms. **,top '~,** (colloq, collective) high-ranking officers, managers, etc. **2** [U] (and *pl*) things made of ~, eg candlesticks, bowls, ornaments: *clean/do the ~/the ~es.* **3 the ~,** (collective (mus) musical instruments made of ~. ~ **'band,** band of musicians with ~ instruments. **4** [U] (GB sl) money. **5** [U] (sl) impudence. ⇨ brazen. **~y** *adj* (-ier, -iest) **1** like ~ in colour or sound. ⇨ **3** above. **2** impudent.

bras·sard /'bræsɑːd/ n (arm-band bearing a) badge worn on the sleeve.

brass-erie /'bræsərɪ/ n beer-saloon or beer-garden (usu supplying food as well as drink).

brass·iere, ·ière /'bræsɪə(r) US: brəˈzɪə(r)/ n (usu shortened to **bra**) woman's close-fitting support for the breasts.

brat /bræt/ n (derog) child.

bra·vado /brəˈvɑːdəʊ/ n **1** [U] display of boldness

or daring: *do sth out of ~,* in order to display one's courage. **2** [C] (*pl* ~es, ~s) instance of this.

brave /breɪv/ *adj* (-r, -st) **1** ready to face danger, pain or suffering; having no fear: *as ~ as a lion. Be ~! It was ~ of him to enter the burning building.* **2** needing courage: *a ~ act.* **3** (old use) fine and splendid: *this ~ new world.* □ n (poet) American Indian warrior. □ *vt* [VP6A] face, go into, meet, without showing fear: *He had ~d death a hundred times. We decided to ~ the storm,* to go out in spite of the storm. **~ it out,** [VP15B] disregard, defy, suspicion or blame. **~·ly** *adv* **brav·ery** /'breɪvərɪ/ n [U] **1** courage; being ~. **2** (old use) splendour (of dress, etc): *decked out in all their ~ry.*

bravo /ˌbrɑːˈvəʊ/ n, int (*pl* ~es, ~s) (cry of approval) Well done! Excellent!

brawl /brɔːl/ n noisy quarrel or fight. □ *vi* [VP2A] quarrel noisily; take part in a ~; (of streams) flow noisily (over stones and rocks). **~er** n person who takes part in a ~.

brawn /brɔːn/ n [U] **1** muscle; strength. **2** (not US) meat (esp pork) cut up, spiced and pickled, and compressed. **~y** *adj* (-ier, -iest) muscular: *The miner has ~y arms.*

bray /breɪ/ n cry of an ass; sound of a trumpet. □ *vt* [VP2A] make a cry or sound of this kind.

braze /breɪz/ *vt* [VP6A] solder with an alloy of brass and zinc.

brazen /'breɪzn/ *adj* **1** made of brass; like brass: *a ~ (= hard-sounding) voice; the ~ notes of a trumpet.* **2** (often '~-faced) shameless. □ *vt* (only in) ~ **it out,** behave, in spite of having done wrong, as if one has nothing to be ashamed of.

braz·ier /'breɪzɪə(r)/ n portable open metal framework (like a basket), usu on legs, for holding a charcoal or coal fire.

breach /briːtʃ/ n **1** breaking or neglect (*of* a rule, duty, agreement, etc): *a ~ of the peace,* unlawful fighting in a public place, eg the streets; *a ~ of contract* (in comm, etc); *a ~ of promise* (esp of a promise to marry); *a ~ of faith,* act of disloyalty; *a ~ of confidence; a ~ of security.* **2** opening, esp one made in a defensive wall, etc by artillery, attacking forces, etc: *step into/fill the ~,* come forward to help; *throw/fling oneself into the ~,* help those who are in trouble or danger; *stand in the ~,* bear the heaviest part of the attack; do most of the hard work. **3** broken place; gap: *The sheep got out of the field after one of them had made a ~ in the hedge. The waves made a ~ in the sea wall.* □ *vt* [VP6A] make a gap in, break through (a defensive wall, etc).

bread /bred/ n [U] food made by mixing flour with water and yeast, kneading, and baking in an oven: *a loaf/slice/piece of ~;* (sl) money: *I'm only doing it for the ~.* **~ and butter** /ˌbred n 'bʌtə(r)/, (a) slice(s) of ~ spread with butter. **~ and butter letter,** one of thanks for hospitality. **(b)** (colloq) means of living: *earn one's ~ and butter by writing.* **one's daily ~,** one's means of living. **earn one's ~,** make enough money to live on. **know which side one's ~ is buttered,** know where one may have advantages, where one's interest lies. **take the '~ out of sb's mouth,** take away his means of living, eg by business competition. **'~-crumb** n [C] tiny bit of the inner part of a loaf, esp crumbled for use in cooking. **'~-fruit** n tree with starchy fruit, grown in the South Sea Islands and W Africa. **'~-line** n line of people waiting for food

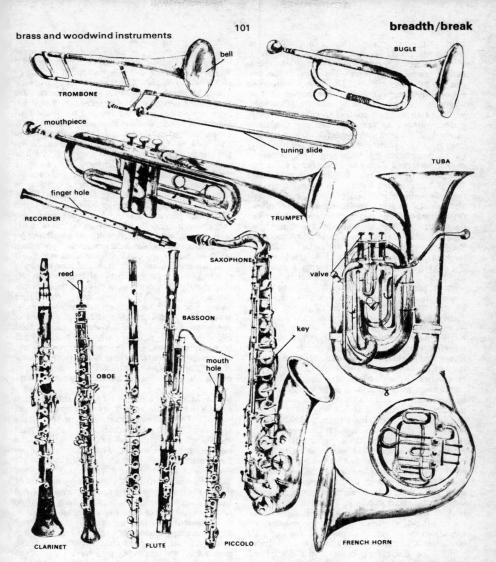

given as charity or relief; (fig): *on the ~line*, very poor. '**~·stuffs** *n pl* grain, flour. '**~·win·ner** *n* person who works to support a family.

breadth /ˈbretθ/ *n* [U] ⇨ broad¹(2). **1** distance or measure from side to side: *ten feet in ~.* ⇨ hair(2). **2** largeness (of mind or view); boldness of effect (in music or art). '**~·ways,** '**~·wise** *adv* so that the broad side is in front.

break¹ /breɪk/ *vt,vi* (*pt* broke /brəʊk/ old Eng brake /breɪk/, *pp* broken /ˈbrəʊkən/) **1** [VP6A,15B,2A,C] (of a whole thing) (cause to) go or come into two or more separate parts as the result of force, a blow or strain (but not by cutting): *When she dropped the teapot it broke. The boy fell from the tree and broke his leg. Glass ~s easily. If you pull too hard you will ~ the rope. The string broke.* **~ into/to pieces; ~ in two,** *etc,* (cause to) come or go into pieces, in two, etc parts: *He broke the box into pieces. When I hit the ball, my bat broke in two.* **2** [VP6A,15B,2A,C] (of a part or parts) (cause to) be separate or discontinuous because of force or strain: *He broke a branch from the tree. The door-handle has broken off. A large part of it broke away, came off.* **~ sb/oneself of a habit,** succeed in getting him/oneself to give it up. **3** [VP6A] make (sth) useless by injuring an essential part (of a machine, apparatus, etc): *~ a clock/a sewing-machine.* **4** [VP2D,22] (with *adjj*): *~ 'even,* make neither a profit nor a loss. **~ 'loose (from),** get or become separate: *The dog has broken loose,* got free from its chain. *All hell has broken loose,* all the devils in hell have escaped; (fig) (used to describe a scene of confusion, eg a bombardment). **~ sth open,** get it open by using force: *~ open a safe/door/the lid of a desk.* **5** [VP2A,C] (with various subjects): *The abscess/blister/bubble broke,* burst. *Day was beginning to ~,* daylight was beginning. ⇨ daybreak. *His* *voice is beginning to* ~, change in quality as he reaches manhood. *She was filled with emotion and her voice broke*, She faltered, was unable to speak clearly because of emotion. *The storm broke*, began, burst into activity. *The fine weather/The heat-wave/The frost broke*, The period of fine weather, etc ended after being settled. Cf How long will the fine weather *hold?* *The clouds broke* (= parted, showed an opening) *and the sun came through*. *The waves were* ~*ing* (= curling and falling) *over/on/against the rocks*. *The sea was* ~*ing* (= sending waves that were ~ing) *on the beach/over the wrecked ship*. *The enemy broke* (= developed gaps in their lines, fell into confusion) *and fled*. *When the bank broke* (= was unable to carry on business because of lack of funds), *many people were ruined*. *A good bowler can make the ball* ~, (in cricket) change from its course when it strikes the ground. **6** [VP6A] (with various objects): ~ *sb's back/neck/nose, etc,* cause the bone(s) of the back, etc to be out of the right position. ⇨ back¹(1). ~ *the bank,* exhaust its funds; win all the money that the person managing a gambling game has. ~ *bounds,* (mil) go out of bounds without permission or authority. ~ *one's fall,* weaken its effect, make it less violent. ~ *the force of sth,* reduce its force by bearing part of it: *The tall hedge* ~*s the force of the wind.* ⇨ windbreak. ~ *fresh/new ground,* (fig) start work at sth new; ~ *sb's heart,* reduce him to despair. ~ *a man,* ruin him; compel him to reveal a secret, etc. ~ *the news,* make it known. ~ *the (bad) news (to sb),* reveal the news in such a way that its effect is less of a shock. ~ *an officer,* dismiss him, take his commission from him. ~ *a path/way,* make one by pushing or beating aside obstacles. ~ *prison/ gaol,* escape from, make one's way out of, prison. ~ *ranks,* (of soldiers) leave the ranks without permission. ~ *a (Commonwealth/Olympic/World, etc) record,* do better than it, make a new record. ~ *a set of books/china, etc,* cause it to be incomplete by giving away or selling a part or parts of it. ~ *the skin on one's elbow/knees/ knuckles, etc,* graze it, so as to cause bleeding. ~ *step,* (of soldiers) stop marching rhythmically in step, eg to avoid excessive vibration on a weak bridge. ~ *a strike,* end it by compelling the workers to submit. ⇨ strike breaker. ~ *wind,* expel wind from the bowels or stomach. ⇨ also code(3), cover²(5), ice¹(1). **7** [VP6A,15A,B] train or discipline: ~ *a horse* (*in*), bring it to a disciplined state: *a well-broken horse;* ~ *a horse to harness/to the rein,* accustom it to wearing harness, etc. **8** [VP6A,15B] subdue, keep under, end by force: ~ *sb's spirit/will;* ~ (*down*) *the enemy's resistance;* ~ *the power of the rebel leader.* **9** [VP6A] act in opposition to; infringe: ~ *the law/the rules/a regulation;* ~ *a contract/an agreement;* ~ *the Sabbath,* do things on a Sunday that should not be done; ~ *one's word/a promise,* fail to keep a promise; ~ *an appointment,* fail to keep it; ~ *faith with sb,* betray or deceive him. **10** [VP6A] interrupt or destroy the continuity of; end the operation or duration of: ~ (*the*) *silence,* end it, eg by speaking; ~ *one's journey* (*at a place*); ~ *the peace,* cause a disturbance; ~ *one's fast,* (old use) take food after going without. ⇨ breakfast; ~ *short* (*a conversation, etc*), end it; *a broken night's sleep,* one that is disturbed or interrupted. **11** [VP15B,2C,3A] (special uses with *adverbial particles* and *preps*):

break away (*from*), go away suddenly or abruptly; give up (habits, modes of thought or belief): *The prisoner broke away* (= escaped after a struggle) *from his guards. Can't you* ~ *away from old habits? About twenty members of the Conservative Party have broken away* (= seceded). *There has been a* ~*-away from the Party. One of the provinces has broken away to form a new State.*
break 'down, (a) collapse: *His resistance will* ~ *down in time. Our plans have broken down.* Negotiations have broken down. (b) become disabled or useless: *The car/engine/machinery broke down,* ie because of a mechanical fault. *That old broken-down bus is not worth £5.* (c) suffer a physical or mental weakening: *His health broke down.* (d) be overcome by emotion, eg by bursting into tears: *She broke down when she heard the news, but quickly recovered.* ~ *sth down,* (a) get (a door, wall, etc) down by battering it. (b) overthrow by force; suppress: ~ *down all resistance/opposition.* (c) divide, analyse, classify (statistical material): ~ *down expenditure,* give details of how money is spent. (d) change the chemical composition of: *Sugar and starch are broken down in the stomach.* '~-**down** *n* (a) failure in machinery, etc: *There was a* ~*down on the railway and trains were delayed. The earthquake has caused a* ~*down of communications.* Hence: '~-**down gang,** men called to repair or remove a train, etc that has been derailed, smashed, etc. (b) collapse; weakening: *He's suffering from a nervous* ~*down.* (c) statistical analysis: *a* ~*down of expenditure.*
break forth, (esp fig, of anger, indignation) burst out.
break 'in, enter a building by force: *Burglars had broken in while we were away on holiday.* Hence, '~-**in** *n.* *The police are investigating a* ~*-in at the local bank.* ~ *sb* (esp a horse) *in,* ⇨ 7 above; train and discipline; accustom sb to a new routine. ~ *in* (*up*)*on,* disturb; interrupt: *Please don't* ~ *in on our conversation.*
break into, (a) force one's way into (a building, etc): *His house was broken into* (ie by burglars or thieves) *last week.* (b) burst suddenly into: ~ (*out*) *into a loud laugh/into loud curses/into song/into praises of sb.* (c) change one's method of movement suddenly: ~ *into a run/trot/gallop.* (d) occupy, take up, undesirably: *Social duties* ~ *into my time/leisure.* (e) (of coins and notes): ~ *into a pound note,* use one to pay for sth costing less than this sum: *I can't pay you the 50p I owe you without* ~*ing into a £5 note.* (f) open and draw upon emergency supplies: *The garrison broke into their reserves of ammunition.*
break off, (a) stop speaking: *He broke off in the middle of a sentence.* (b) pause; stop temporarily: *Let's* ~ *off for half an hour and have some tea.* ~ (*sth*) *off,* (a) (cause to) separate (a part of sth): *The mast broke off/was broken off.* (b) end abruptly: ~ *off relations* (*with sb*); ~ *off an engagement/ conversation.*
break out, ⇨ outbreak. (of fire, disease, war, rioting, violence) appear, start, suddenly: *A fire broke out during the night. The quarrel broke out afresh. Riots and disorders have broken out.* ~ *out* (*of*), escape: *Several prisoners broke out of the jail.* ~ *out in,* (a) suddenly become covered with: *His face broke out in pimples/a rash. He broke out in a cold sweat,* was struck with fear. (b) show

sudden violence in speech or behaviour: *He broke out in a rage/in curses.*
break through, make a way through (an enclosure, obstacles, etc): *The enemy's defences were strong but our soldiers broke through. The sun broke through (the clouds).* ∼ **through sth,** overcome: ∼ *through a man's reserve.* Hence, '∼-**through** *n* **(a)** (mil) piercing (of the enemy's defences). **(b)** major achievement, eg in technology: *a* ∼*through in cancer research.*
break up, (a) come to pieces; disintegrate: *The ship was* ∼*ing up on the rocks. The gathering broke up in disorder.* **(b)** (fig, of persons) go to pieces; become weak: *He broke up under the strain.* **(c)** (of a school, etc) separate at the end of term for holidays: *When do you* ∼ *'up?* **(d)** (of a couple, a relationship) come to an end: *The marriage is* ∼*ing up.* **(e)** divide: *Sentences* ∼ *up into clauses.* ∼ **sth up, (a)** smash; demolish: ∼ *up a box for firewood;* ∼ *up an old ship for scrap metal.* **(b)** (cause to) split, or divide: ∼ *up a piece of work (among several persons).* **(c)** (cause to) disperse: *The police broke up the crowd/meeting.* **(d)** bring to an end: *They broke up the alliance.* Hence, '∼-**up** *n* (end of a marriage, coalition, etc). **(e)** (esp of a period of fine weather) change for the worse; end: *The weather is* ∼*ing up.*
break with, (a) end a friendship with: ∼ *with an old friend.* **(b)** give up; make an end of: ∼ *with old habits;* ∼ *with old ties,* eg when leaving a district.
break² /breɪk/ *n* **1** breaking; broken place: *a* ∼ *in the water mains.* **2** [U] ∼ *of day (= day*∼*),* dawn. **3** interval (in space of time): *a* ∼ *in the conversation; an hour's* ∼ *for lunch; the* '*tea-*∼, eg in an office or factory; *during a* ∼ *at school,* during an interval between lessons. *without a* ∼, continuously: *He has been writing since 2 o'clock without a* ∼. **4** change, disturbance: *a* ∼ *in one's way of living; a* ∼ *in the weather.* **5** change of course of a cricket or tennis ball on first striking the ground: *a leg* ∼, (cricket) one that breaks to the left. **6** (billiards) continuous score: *make a* ∼ *of 450.* **7** *give sb a* ∼, (colloq) an opportunity (to make a new start or remedy an error). **8** (colloq) *a bad* ∼, an unfortunate remark or ill-judged action; a piece of bad luck. *a lucky* ∼, a piece of good fortune. **9** (= *break-out)* (attempt to) escape (esp from prison). *(make a) break for it,* escape.
break³ /breɪk/ *n* = brake(3).
break·able /'breɪkəbl/ *adj* easily broken. **break-ables** *n pl*∼ objects, eg glasses, cups and saucers.
break·age /'breɪkɪdʒ/ *n* **1** act of breaking. **2** place in, part of, sth that has been broken. **3** (usu *pl*) broken articles; loss by breaking: *The hotel allows £150 a year for* ∼*s,* for the cost of broken dishes, glasses, etc.
breaker /'breɪkə(r)/ *n* **1** large wave breaking into foam as it advances towards the shore; wave breaking against a rock, etc. **2** person or thing that breaks. '**ice-**∼ *n* strongly built ship used to break up ice in harbours, etc. ⇨ **house**∼ and other similar compounds.
break·fast /'brekfəst/ *n* first meal of the day: *Have a good* ∼. *He hasn't eaten much* ∼. *They were having* ∼ *when I arrived.* □ *vi* have ∼.
break·neck /'breɪknek/ *adj* (usu) *at (a)* ∼ *speed,* at a dangerous speed.
break·water /'breɪkwɔːtə(r)/ *n* sth that breaks the force of waves, esp a structure built out into the sea to shelter (part of) a harbour.

bream /briːm/ *n* (*pl* unchanged) **1** freshwater fish of the carp family. **2** (also '**sea-**∼) salt-water variety of this.
breast /brest/ *n* **1** either of the milk-producing parts of a woman: *a child at the* ∼; *give a child the* ∼. ⇨ suckle. ∼-**feed** *vi, vt* feed a baby from the breast; suckle. '∼-**fed** *adj* (of a baby) fed with milk from the ∼. Cf *bottle-fed.* **2** chest; upper front part of the human body, or of a garment covering this. '∼ **pocket** *n* one in the ∼ of a jacket, etc. '∼-**stroke,** stroke (in swimming) in which both the arms are brought at the same time from in front of the head to the sides of the body. ∼-'**high** *adv* high as the ∼: *The wheat was* ∼-*high.* ∼-'**deep** *adv* deep enough to reach the ∼: *In the middle of the stream the water was* ∼-*deep.* '∼-**plate** *n* piece of armour covering the ∼. ⇨ the illus at armour. '∼-**work** *n* low wall, eg of earth, sandbags, stones, put up as a temporary defence. **3** (fig) feelings; thoughts: *a troubled* ∼. *make a clean* ∼ *of,* confess (wrong-doing, etc). **4** part of an animal corresponding to the human ∼. □ *vt* [VP6A] present the ∼(2) to, hence (fig), face, struggle with: ∼ *the waves.*
breath /breθ/ *n* **1** [U] air taken into and sent out of the lungs; [C] single act of taking in and sending air out: *take a deep* ∼, fill the lungs with air. *bad* ∼, with an unpleasant smell. *catch/hold one's* ∼, stop breathing for a moment (from fear, excitement, etc). *get one's* ∼ *(again/back),* get back to the normal state. *in the same* ∼, at the same moment: *They are not to be mentioned in the same* ∼, cannot be compared. *lose one's* ∼, have difficulty in taking in ∼, eg while running or working hard. *out of* ∼, unable to take in ∼ quickly enough. *speak/say sth below/under one's* ∼, in a whisper. *take* ∼, get enough ∼ (after exertion): *Half-way up the mountain we stopped to take* ∼. *take sb's'* ∼ *away,* startle or surprise him. Hence, '∼-**taking,** *adj* exciting; causing awe. *waste one's* ∼, talk in vain. '∼ **test** *n* test of the alcoholic contents of a person's ∼. **2** moving air; light breeze: *There wasn't a* ∼ *of air/wind,* the air was quite still. **3** (fig) suggestion (*of*): *not a* ∼ *of suspicion/scandal.* ∼-**less** *adj* **1** out of ∼; panting; likely to cause shortness of ∼: *in a* ∼*less hurry; listening with* ∼*less attention/in* ∼*less expectation,* with the ∼ held back (in concentration or excitement). **2** unstirred by wind: *a* ∼*less (= calm) evening.* ∼-**less·ly** *adv*
breath·a·lyse /'breθəlaɪz/ *vt* [VP6A] (GB) measure the amount of alcohol in a person's breath. ∼**r** *n* instrument for breathalysing sb (usu used by the police on the driver of a car).
breathe /briːð/ *vi, vt* **1** [VP2A, C, 6A, 15B] take air into the lungs and send it out again: ∼ *in/out. He was breathing hard when he finished the race. We* ∼ *air. He* ∼*d a sigh of relief. He's still breathing,* is still alive. ∼ *again;* ∼ *freely (again),* be at ease, be relieved (after exertion, excitement, fear,

a breakwater

etc). ~ **down sb's neck,** ⇨ neck. 2 [VP6A] utter; send out, eg a scent, feeling: *Don't ~ a word of this,* keep it secret. 3 [VP6A] allow (a horse) to ~ gently and rest. **breather** n 1 short pause for rest: *take/have a ~r.* 2 short period of exercise: *go for a ~r.* **breath·ing** n [U] **breath·ing-space** n time to ~; pause; rest.

bred pt,pp of breed.

breech /bri:tʃ/ n back part of a rifle or gun barrel, where the cartridge or shell is placed: *a ,~-,loading 'gun,* loaded at the ~, not through the muzzle. '~-block n block of steel that closes the ~ of a gun.

breeches /'brɪtʃɪz/ n pl 1 'knee-~, garment fitting round the waist and below the knees. 'riding-~, garment covering the hips and thighs, buttoned below the knee, worn by men and women for riding on horseback. 2 (colloq) trousers; knicker-bockers. **wear the ~,** (said of a woman) rule her husband. '~-,buoy /'bri:tʃɪz-/ n pair of canvas ~ fastened to a lifebuoy, pulled along a rope, used for saving life at sea.

breed /bri:d/ vt,vi (pt,pp bred /bred/) 1 [VP6A] keep (animals, etc) for the purpose of producing young, esp by selection of parents: ~ *horses/ cattle.* 2 [VP2A] give birth to young; reproduce: *Rabbits ~ quickly. Birds ~ in the spring.* 3 [VP6A] train, educate, bring up: *an Englishman born and bred; a well-bred boy,* one who has been trained to behave well. **What's bred in the bone will come out in the flesh,** (prov) Hereditary characteristics always show themselves. 4 [VP6A] be the cause of: *Dirt ~s disease. War ~s misery and ruin.* ~er n 1 person who ~s animals. 2 apparatus (reactor) that produces more radio-active material than is put into it. ~·ing n [U] 1 (in verbal senses): *the ~ing of horses; the ~ing season for birds.* 2 knowledge of how to behave resulting from training: *a man of good ~ing.* ⇨ [C] kind or variety (of animals, etc) with hereditary qualities: *a good ~ of cattle.* ⇨ cross-~, half-~.

breeze¹ /bri:z/ n [C,U] wind, esp a soft, gentle wind: *a land/sea ~,* one blowing from the land/ sea at certain hours; *not much ~; not much of a ~; spring ~s.* ⇨ vi [VP2C] (colloq) ~ *in/out,* come in/go out in high spirits, or without warning, unexpectedly. **breezy** adj 1 pleasantly windy: *breezy weather.* 2 swept by ~s: *a breezy corner.* 3 (of persons) jovial; lively; good-humoured. **breez·ily** /'bri:zəlɪ/ adv **breezi·ness** /'bri:zɪnɪs/ n

breeze² /bri:z/ n [U] (not US) small coal cinders. '~ blocks, light-weight concrete building blocks made of ~ and cement.

Bren /bren/ n (also '~-gun) light-weight, semi-automatic, light machine gun. '~ carrier n small armoured vehicle that moves on tracks(3).

breth·ren /'breðrən/ n pl (old use) brothers.

breve /bri:v/ n (mus) note equal to two semibreves, now rarely used. ⇨ the illus at notation.

bre·vet /'brevɪt US: brɪ'vet/ n document that gives sb higher rank without corresponding increase in pay or authority: ~ *rank,* given by ~; ~ *major.*

brevi·ary /'bri:vɪərɪ US: -ierɪ/ n (pl -ries) book with prayers to be said daily by priests etc of the RC Church.

brev·ity /'brevətɪ/ n [U] (formal) shortness (of statements, human life and other non-material things).

brew /bru:/ vt,vi 1 [VP6A] prepare (beer, tea, etc) by soaking or boiling grain, leaves, etc; [VP2A]

make beer, etc. 2 [VP6A] (fig) bring about; [VP2A,C] gather, be forming: *Those boys are ~ing mischief. A storm is ~ing,* gathering force. *There's trouble ~ing between them,* They are likely to quarrel. ⇨ n result of ~ing; liquid made by ~ing: *the best ~s of beer; a good, strong ~ of tea.* ~er n person who ~s beer. ~ery /'brʊərɪ/ n (pl -ries) building in which ~ing of beer is carried on.

briar /'braɪə(r)/ n 1 [U] hard wood (root of a bush) used esp for making tobacco pipes. 2 [C] pipe made of this wood. 3 = brier.

bribe /braɪb/ n [C] sth given, offered or promised to sb in order to influence or persuade him (often to do sth wrong) in favour of the giver: *offer/give/ hand out/take ~s.* ⇨ vt [VP6A,17,15A] offer, give, a ~ to: ~ *a judge/witness. The child was ~d to take the nasty medicine. He had been ~d into silence/~d to say nothing.* **bri·bable** /'braɪbəbl/ adj **bri·bery** /'braɪbərɪ/ n [U] giving or taking of ~s.

bric-a-brac /'brɪk ə bræk/ n [U] bits of old furniture, china, ornaments, etc, esp old and curious, of no great value.

brick /brɪk/ n 1 [C,U] (usu rectangular block of) clay moulded and baked by fire or sun, used for building purposes: *a house made of red ~(s); a ~ wall. drop a ~,* (colloq) do or say sth indiscreet. **make ~s without straw,** attempt a difficult and fruitless task. '~-bat n piece of ~, esp as a missile: *The Minister collected a lot of ~bats,* (fig) much abuse. '~-field, '~-kiln n field, kiln, in which ~s are made. '~-layer n workman who builds with ~s. '~-work n (part of a) structure made of ~. 2 child's rectangular block (usu of wood) used for building toy houses, etc. 3 ~-shaped block of sth, eg ice-cream. 4 (colloq) generous or kind-hearted person: *You've behaved like a ~.* ⇨ vt [VP15B] ~ *up/in,* block (an opening) with ~s: ~ *up a window.*

bri·dal /'braɪdl/ n wedding-feast; wedding; (attrib) of a bride or wedding: *the '~ party,* the bride and her attendants and friends.

bride /braɪd/ n woman on her wedding-day; newly married woman. '~-cake n (old name for) wedding-cake.

bride-groom /'braɪdgrʊm/ n man on his wedding-day; newly married man.

brides·maid /'braɪdzmeɪd/ n girl or young unmarried woman (usu one of several) attending a bride at her wedding. Cf *best man* for the bridegroom.

bridge¹ /brɪdʒ/ n 1 structure of wood, stone, brick-work, steel, concrete, etc, providing a way across a river, canal, railway, etc. '~-head n defensive post or area established on the enemy's side of a river, etc; (loosely) any military position occupied in the face of the enemy. ⇨ beachhead. 2 platform over and across the deck of a ship for the use of the captain and officers. 3 upper, bony part of the nose. 4 movable part over which the strings of a violin, etc are stretched. 5 device for keeping false teeth in place, fastened to natural teeth. ⇨ vt [VP6A] join by means of a ~; build a ~ over: *a 'bridging loan,* loan (esp from a bank) to cover a period of time, eg between the purchase of one house and the sale of another; [VP15B] ~ *over,* (fig) overcome (obstacles, etc): ~ *over difficulties.*

bridge² /brɪdʒ/ n [U] card game for four players in which one player looks on while his cards, placed face up on the table, are played by his partner.

'**auction** ∼, in which the right to name the trumps goes to the player who undertakes to make the highest score. '**contract** ∼, variety of auction ∼ with penalties for failure to make the score.

bridle /'braɪdl/ n that part of a horse's harness that goes on its head, including the metal bit for the mouth, the straps and the reins. ⇨ the illus at harness. '∼-**path**, '∼-**road** n one fit for riders on horseback but not for cars, etc. □ vt, vi **1** [VP6A] put a ∼ on (a horse). **2** [VP6A] (fig) control, check: *Try to ∼ your passions*. **3** [VP2A,C] throw back the head and draw in the chin (showing pride, contempt, vanity, etc): ∼ *with anger; ∼ up; ∼ at sb's remarks*.

brief[1] /briːf/ adj (-er, -est) (of time, events, writing, speaking) lasting only for a short time: *to be ∼, to speak shortly*. ⇨ brevity. *in ∼*, in a few words. ∼·**ly** adv

brief[2] /briːf/ n [C] **1** summary of the facts of a case, drawn up for a barrister: *have plenty of ∼s*, (of a barrister) be busy with professional work. *hold a ∼ for (sb)*, (fig) argue in support or favour of. *hold no ∼ for*, (fig) not be prepared to support. '∼-**case** n flat leather or plastic case, for documents, etc. **2** (also '∼·**ing**) information, instructions, advice, etc given in advance, eg to an aircraft crew before a combat mission. **3** (comm) instructions: *My ∼ did not include the buying of new materials*. □ vt [VP6A] **1** instruct or employ (a barrister). **2** give a ∼(2) to. ⇨ debrief. **3** (comm) summarize the facts, eg of a business programme: *The Chairman will ∼ the Board on the most recent developments*.

briefs /briːfs/ n pl close-fitting pants without legs, held in position by an elastic waistband.

brier, briar /'braɪə(r)/ n thorn-covered bush, esp the wild rose.

brig /brɪg/ n two-masted ship with square sails and an extra fore-and-aft sail on the main-mast. ⇨ the illus at barque.

brig·ade /brɪ'geɪd/ n **1** army unit, usu of three battalions, forming part of an army division; corresponding armoured unit. **2** organized body of persons in uniform with special duties (eg '**fire-**∼). **Briga·dier** /ˌbrɪgə'dɪə(r)/ n (formerly ˌBrigadier-'General) officer commanding a ∼; army officer of rank between General and Colonel.

brig·and /'brɪgənd/ n member of a band of robbers, esp a band that attacks travellers in forests or mountains.

brig·an·tine /'brɪgəntiːn/ n = brig.

bright /braɪt/ adj (-er, -est) **1** giving out or reflecting much light; shining: *Sunshine is ∼. Polished steel is ∼. The leaves on the trees are ∼ green in spring*. **2** cheerful and happy; lit up with joy or hope: *∼ faces; a ∼ smile; see the ∼ side of things*. **3** quick-witted, clever: *A ∼ boy learns quickly*. □ adv (chiefly with shine) = ∼ly. ∼**en** vt, vi [VP6A,15B,2A,C] ∼**en up**, make or become ∼er or lighter, more cheerful, etc: *These flowers ∼en the classroom. The sky is ∼ening. His face ∼ened up*. ∼·**ly** adv ∼·**ness** n

brill /brɪl/ n flat fish like a turbot.

bril·liant /'brɪlɪənt/ adj very bright; sparkling; splendid, causing admiration: *a week of ∼ sunshine; a ∼ scientist; ∼ jewels*. ∼·**ly** adv **bril·liance** /'brɪlɪəns/, **bril·liancy** /'brɪlɪənsɪ/ nn [U] radiance, splendour, intelligence.

bril·lian·tine /'brɪlɪəntiːn/ n [U] cosmetic used to make the hair lie flat.

brim /brɪm/ n **1** edge of a cup, bowl, glass, etc: *full to the ∼, quite full*. **2** out-turned part (rim) of a hat, that gives shade. □ vi (-mm-) [VP2A,C] be full to the ∼. ∼ **over**, be so full that some spills over the ∼; (fig) ∼*ming over with high spirits*. ∼·**ful(l)** /ˌbrɪm'fʊl/ adj full to the ∼: *He is ∼ful of new ideas*.

brim·stone /'brɪmstəʊn/ n [U] (old name for)

bridges

a pontoon bridge

a trestle bridge

a Bailey bridge

an arch bridge

a suspension bridge

a cantilever bridge

sulphur.

brindled /'brɪndld/ adj (esp of cows and cats) brown with streaks of another colour.

brine /braɪn/ n [U] salt water, esp for pickling.

briny /'braɪnɪ/ adj salty. □ n **the briny,** (colloq) the sea.

bring /brɪŋ/ vt (pt,pp brought /brɔːt/) (For uses with adverbial particles and preps, ⇨ 6 below.) **1** ⇨ take [VP6A,15B,13,12,14] ∼ (with), come carrying sth or accompanying sb: Take this empty box away and ∼ me a full one. The soldiers came back ∼ing ten prisoners (with them). B∼ Mary to the party with you. B∼ one for me. B∼ me one. **2** [VP6A,19B,12C,14] cause to come; produce: Spring ∼s warm weather and flowers. The sad news brought tears to her eyes. His writings ∼ him £5000 a year. A phone call brought him hurrying to Leeds. **3** [VP17A] ∼ sb/oneself to do sth, persuade, induce, lead: They could not ∼ themselves to believe the news. She couldn't ∼ herself to speak about the matter. I wish I could ∼ you to see the situation from my point of view. **4** [VP14] ∼ against, (legal) start, put forward: ∼ an action/charge/an accusation against sb. **5** (phrases) ∼ sb to book, ⇨ book¹(6); ∼ sth to an end, cause it to end; ∼ sth home to sb, ⇨ home²(2); ∼ low, reduce to a low condition; ∼ sth to light, cause it to be visible or known; ∼ sth to mind; ∼ sth to pass, ⇨ pass²(3); ∼ sth into line/play, ⇨ line¹(11), play²(11); ∼ sb to his senses, ⇨ sense(2). **6** [VP15B] special uses with adverbial particles and preps):

bring about, (a) cause to happen: ∼ about a war/reforms/sb's ruin. **(b)** (naut) cause (a sailing-ship) to change direction: The helmsman brought us about.

bring back, (a) return: Please ∼ back the book tomorrow; (with indirect object): If you're going to the market, please ∼ me back ten eggs. **(b)** call to mind; cause to remember: Your newsy letter brought back many memories. **(c)** restore; reintroduce: How many MP's favour ∼ing back capital punishment? ∼ sb back to, restore to: Her stay among the mountains brought her back to health.

bring sb/sth down, (a) cause to fall; cause to be down: ∼ down a hostile aircraft, shoot it down; ∼ down prices, lower them; ∼ down (= overthrow) a tyrant. **(b)** continue (records, etc) up to: a new history of Europe, brought down to modern times, ie made up to date. **(c)** kill or wound: He aimed, fired and brought down the antelope. **(d)** (football) cause (an opponent) to fall by fouling; (Rugby) tackle. **(e)** (arith) transfer a digit from one part of a sum (from one column) to another: ∼ down the next two figures. ∼ the 'house down/∼ down the house, ⇨ house(6). ∼ down sb's wrath/fury on one's head, cause it to be aimed at oneself.

bring sth forth, produce (fruit); give birth to (young ones): What will the future ∼ forth?

bring sth forward, (a) cause to be seen, discussed, etc: Can you ∼ forward (= produce) any proof of what you say? Please ∼ the matter forward at the next meeting. **(b)** advance: The meeting has been brought forward from May 10 to May 3, is to be a week earlier. ⇨ postpone. **(c)** (abbr b/f) (bookkeeping) carry the total of a column of figures at the foot of one page to the top of the next page.

bring sth/sb in, (a) yield; (of capital, investments,

etc) produce as profit: His orchards ∼ (him) in £200 a year. He does odd jobs that ∼ him in ten to twelve pounds a week. This investment ∼s (me) in 7½ per cent. **(b)** introduce: ∼ in a new fashion/a new topic. **(c)** introduce (legislation): ∼ in a Bill on road safety. **(d)** admit (as a partner, adviser, etc): They've brought in experts to advise on the scheme. **(e)** (of the police) arrest; ∼ to a police station for questioning, etc: Two suspicious characters were brought in. **(f)** (of a jury) pronounce (a verdict): ∼ in a verdict of guilty.

bring sth/sb off, (a) rescue (esp from a wrecked ship): The passengers and crew were brought off by the Deal lifeboat. **(b)** carry (an enterprise) to success; manage to do sth successfully: It was a difficult task but we brought it off, we succeeded.

bring sth/sb on, (a) lead to, (help to) produce: He was out all day in the rain and this brought on a bad cold. **(b)** cause to develop or advance: The fine weather is ∼ing the crops on nicely. **(c)** help (a pupil, learner, etc) to develop: The coach is ∼ing on some youngsters in the reserve team.

bring sth/sb out, (a) cause to appear, show clearly: ∼ out the meaning of a poem. The sunshine will ∼ out the apple blossom, cause it to open. **(b)** publish (a book, etc): When are the publishers ∼ing out his new book? **(c)** help to lose shyness or reserve: She's a nice girl, but needs a lot of ∼ing out. **(d)** call forth (a quality): Danger ∼s out the best in him. **(e)** cause to strike: The shop-stewards brought out the foundrymen.

bring sb over (to), (esp) convert (sb) (to a different way of thinking, to a cause, etc).

bring sb/sth round, (a) cause (sb) to regain consciousness after fainting: Several girls fainted in the heat but they were soon brought round. **(b)** convert to one's views, etc: He wasn't keen on the plan, but we managed to ∼ him round. **(c)** (naut) make a boat face the opposite way: B∼ her (ie the boat) round into the wind. ∼ sb/sth round to, direct (discussion, etc) to sth new: He brought the conversation round to his favourite subject.

bring sb through, save (sb who is ill): He was very ill but good doctors and careful nursing brought him through, restored him to health.

bring sb/sth to, (a) ∼ round(a): They brought the girl to with smelling salts. They brought her to. **(b)** (naut) (cause to) stop: The ship was brought to, eg by the firing of a gun across her bows. The ship brought to, came to a stop.

bring sb/sth under, (a) subdue; discipline: The rebels were quickly brought under. **(b)** include (within a category): The various points to be dealt with can be brought under three main heads.

bring sb/sth up, (a) educate; rear: She has brought up five children. If children are badly brought up they behave badly. **(b)** vomit: ∼ up one's dinner. **(c)** call attention to: These are facts that can always be brought up against you, used as evidence against you. These are matters that you can ∼ up in committee. **(d)** (mil) summon to the front line: We need to ∼ up more tanks. **(e)** ∼ for trial: He was brought up on a charge of drunken driving. **(f)** cause to stop suddenly: His remarks brought me up short/sharp/with a jerk. ∼ up the rear, come last (in a line): The cavalry brought up the rear of the column. ∼ up at, (old use, esp of a ship) end a journey: The ship brought up at a port in Greece.

brink /brɪŋk/ n **1** upper edge of a steep place, a

sharp slope, etc; border (of water, esp when deep): *He stood shivering on the ~,* hesitating to plunge into the water. **2** (fig) edge of sth unknown, dangerous or exciting: *on the ~ of war/ruin/an exciting discovery. He's on the ~ of the grave,* will die soon. **~·man·ship** /'brɪŋkmənʃɪp/ *n* pursuit of a dangerous policy to the limits of safety.

briny ⇨ brine.

bri·oche /bri:'ɒʃ US: 'bri:əʊʃ/ *n* (F) piece of pastry baked in a circular shape.

bri·quette, bri·quet /brɪ'ket/ *n* block (brick- or egg-shaped) of compressed coal-dust.

brisk /brɪsk/ *adj* (-er, -est) (of persons and movement) active; lively; quick-moving: *a ~ walk; a ~ walker; at a ~ pace; a ~ demand for cotton goods. Trade is ~.* **~·ly** *adv*

bris·ket /'brɪskɪt/ *n* [U] breast of an animal, (sometimes eaten as a joint of meat). ⇨ the illus at dog.

bristle /'brɪsl/ *n* one of the short stiff hairs on an animal; one of the short stiff hairs in a brush: *a toothbrush with stiff ~s.* □ *vi* **1** [VP2A,C] *~ (up),* (of hair) stand up, rise on end: *The dog was angry and ~d up/its hair ~d.* **2** [VP2A,C] (fig) show rage, indignation, etc: *~ with anger.* **3** *~ with,* have in large numbers (sth difficult, sth suggesting ~s): *The battle-front ~d with bayonets. The problem ~s with difficulties.* **brist·ly** /'brɪslɪ/ *adj* like *~s;* full of *~s;* (of hair, etc) rough and coarse: *She doesn't like his bristly moustache. What a bristly, unshaven chin!*

Brit·ain /'brɪtn/ *n* (also ,Great 'B~) England, Wales and Scotland; *North B~,* Scotland. **Britan·nic** /brɪ'tænɪk/ *adj* of B~ (chiefly in *Her/His Britannic Majesty*).

Brit·ish /'brɪtɪʃ/ *adj* **1** of the ancient Britons. **2** of Great Britain, the British Commonwealth or its inhabitants: *the B~,* B~ people; *B~ citizenship; a Jamaican with a B~ passport.* **~er** *n*

Briton /'brɪtn/ *n* **1** one of the native inhabitants of S Britain at the time of the Roman invasion about 2000 years ago. **2** (liter) native of Britain.

brittle /'brɪtl/ *adj* hard but easily broken (eg coal, ice, glass): (fig) *He has a ~ temper,* quickly loses his temper.

broach¹ /brəʊtʃ/ *vt* [VP6A] make a hole in (a cask of liquor) and put in a tap in order to draw the wine, etc; (fig) begin discussion of (a topic).

broach² /brəʊtʃ/ *vi,vt* [VP2C,15B] *~ to,* (naut) veer or cause (a ship) to veer so that its side is presented to the wind and waves.

broad¹ /brɔːd/ *adj* (-er, -est) **1** wide, large across: *The river grows ~er as it nears the sea. ~ in the beam,* ⇨ beam(2). **2** (after a phrase indicating width) in breadth, from side to side: *a river fifty feet ~.* **3** extending in various or all directions: *the ~ ocean; ~ lands.* **4** full and complete. *in ~ daylight,* when it is unmistakably light: *a bank raid in ~ daylight.* **give sb a ~ hint,** a strong, unmistakable one. **5** general, not minute or detailed: *a ~ distinction. in ~ outline,* without details. **6** (of the mind and ideas) liberal; not kept within narrow limits: *a man of ~ views,* a tolerant man. *,~-* '**minded** /-'maɪndɪd/ *adj* willing to listen sympathetically to the views of others even though one cannot agree with them; having a liberal and tolerant mind. **7** (of speech) strongly marked, showing that the speaker is from a definite part of the country: *~ Scots; a ~ accent.* **8** improper; coarse: *the ~ humour of Rabelais.* **9** (phrase) *It's as ~ as it is long,* It's all the same, however you

view the problem. **10** (compounds, etc) *~ **bean*** *n* the common flattened variety, growing in large pods. **B~ Church** *n* used of churchmen who do not insist upon dogma and doctrine. *~·ly adv* (a) in a wide way. (b) in a general way: *~ly speaking,* speaking in a general way, without going into detail. *~·ness* *n* = breadth (the usu word). *~en* /'brɔːdn/ *vt,vi* [VP6A,15B,2A,C] *~en (out),* make or become *~(er): His face ~ened (out) into a grin.*

broad² /brɔːd/ *n* the *~* part (*of* sth): *the ~ of the back.* **the B~s** *n pl* name used of wide stretches of water in Norfolk, used for boating holidays and barge traffic.

broad·cast /'brɔːdkɑːst US: -kæst/ *vt,vi* (*pt,pp* broadcast or *~ed*) **1** [VP6A] send out in all directions, esp by radio or TV: *~ the news/a speech/a concert.* **2** [VP2A] speak, sing, perform music, etc for *~ing: The Prime Minister will ~ this evening.* **3** [VP6A,2A] sow (seed) by scattering it, not by sowing it in drills, etc. □ *n* (often attrib) *~ing;* sth *~: today's ~; a ~ of a football match.* ⇨ telecast. □ *adv* by *~ing: sow seed ~. ~·ing* *n, adj:* *the British B~ing Corporation,* the BBC; *a '~ing station.*

broad·cloth /'brɔːdklɒθ US: -klɔːθ/ *n* [U] fine, smooth, double-width black cloth, formerly used for men's clothes.

broad·sheet /'brɔːdʃiːt/ *n* popular ballad or tract printed on one side only of a large sheet of paper (as formerly sold in the streets).

broad·side /'brɔːdsaɪd/ *n* [C] **1** the whole of a ship's side above the water; (the firing on the same target of) all the guns on one side of a ship; (fig) strong attack of any kind made at one time against one person or group. **2** *~ on (to),* (of a ship) with one side presented to or facing: *a collision ~ on,* so that the ship's side collides with sth.

broad·ways, broad·wise /'brɔːdweɪz, -waɪz/ *adv* in the direction of the breadth.

bro·cade /brə'keɪd/ *n* [C,U] woven material richly ornamented with designs (eg in raised gold or silver thread). □ *vt* [VP6A] decorate (cloth) with raised patterns.

broc·coli /'brɒkəlɪ/ *n* [U] hardy kind of cauliflower with numerous white or purple sprouts (flowerheads), each like a small cauliflower.

bro·chure /'brəʊʃə(r) US: brəʊ'ʃʊər/ *n* short, usu descriptive, printed article in a paper cover; pamphlet: *travel/holiday~s.*

brogue¹ /brəʊg/ *n* strong, thick-soled, usu ornamented shoe for country wear.

brogue² /brəʊg/ *n* regional way of speaking, esp the Irish way of speaking English.

broil /brɔɪl/ *vt,vi* [VP6A,2A] cook, be cooked, by direct contact with fire or on a gridiron; grill; (fig) be very hot: *a ~ing day; sit ~ing in the sun. ~er* *n* bird, eg a chicken, killed at the age of 10 to 12 weeks and suitable for being *~ed* or roasted, esp one reared in a shed or concrete building (and contrasted with a *free-range* bird), ⇨ battery(6).

broke /brəʊk/ *attrib adj (stony/flat) ~,* (sl) penniless.

bro·ken /'brəʊkən/ *pp* of break: *a ~ marriage,* one that has failed; *a ~ home,* one in which the parents have separated or are divorced, so that the children lack proper care, security, etc; *~ (= imperfect) English; a ~ man,* a man reduced to despair; *~ (= uneven) ground; ~ (= disturbed, intermittent) sleep; ,~-'hearted,* crushed by grief.

bro·ker /'brəʊkə(r)/ n 1 person (eg ¹*stock*~) who buys and sells (esp stocks and shares, bonds, etc) for others. 2 official licensed to sell the goods of sb unable to pay debts. ~·age /'brəʊkərɪdʒ/ n [U] ~'s commission for services.

brolly /'brɒlɪ/ n (colloq) umbrella.

bro·mide /'brəʊmaɪd/ n 1 [U] chemical compound of bromine, eg potassium ~, esp as used in medicine to calm the nerves. 2 [C] (colloq) trite remark; dull, tiresome or boring person.

bro·mine /'brəʊmiːn/ n [U] non-metallic element (symbol **Br**), compounds of which are used in photographic and other chemicals.

bron·chi /'brɒŋkaɪ/ n pl (sing **bron·chus** /-kəs/) two main branches into which the windpipe divides before entering the lungs, also called *bronchial tubes*. ⇨ the illus at respiratory. ~al /'brɒŋkɪəl/ adj of or affecting the ~: *bronchial asthma*. **bron·chi·tic** /brɒŋ'kɪtɪk/ adj suffering from, prone to, bronchitis. **bron·chi·tis** /brɒŋ'kaɪtɪs/ n inflammation of the mucous membrane of the ~.

bronco /'brɒŋkəʊ/ n (pl -cos) wild or half-tamed horse of Western N America.

bronze /brɒnz/ n 1 [U] alloy of copper and tin: *a ~ statue; a statue in ~*. **the 'B~ Age**, period when men used tools and weapons made of ~ (between the Stone Age and the Iron Age). 2 [U] colour of ~, reddish brown. 3 [C] work of art, eg a vase, made of ~: *a fine collection of ~s and ivories*. □ vt,vi [VP6A,2A] make or become ~ colour: *faces ~d by the sun and wind*.

brooch /brəʊtʃ/ n ornamental pin for fastening or wearing on part of a woman's dress.

brood /bruːd/ n all the young birds hatched at one time in a nest; family of other egg-produced animals; (hum) young family of human beings. '~-hen n hen for breeding. '~-mare n mare for breeding. □ vi [VP2A,C] 1 (of a bird) sit on eggs to hatch them. 2 [VP3A] ~ (*on/over*), (fig) think about (troubles, etc) for a long time: *She sat there ~ing on whether life was worth living*. ~y adj (of hens) wanting to ~; (colloq, of women) feeling the desire to have children; (fig, of persons) moody; depressed.

brook¹ /brʊk/ n small stream.

brook² /brʊk/ vt [VP6A,B] (formal) (usu in neg and interr) put up with; tolerate: *He cannot ~ interference/being interfered with*.

broom¹ /bruːm/ n [U] shrub with yellow or white flowers growing on sandy banks, etc.

broom² /bruːm/ n long-handled implement for sweeping floors, etc. *a new ~*, (esp) a newly appointed official (who gets rid of old methods, traditions, etc): (prov) *a new ~ sweeps clean*. '~-stick n handle of a broom (on which witches are said to ride through the air).

Bros ⇨ App 2.

broth /brɒθ/ n [U] water in which meat has been boiled; this, flavoured and thickened with vegetables, etc, served as soup.

brothel /'brɒθl/ n house at which prostitutes may be visited.

brother /'brʌðə(r)/ n 1 son of the same parents as another person: *my elder/younger ~; the ~s Smith, the Smith ~s; Smith Brothers* or (comm style) *Smith Bros*. '~-in-law /'brʌðər ɪn lɔː/ n (pl ~s-in-law) ~ of one's husband or wife; husband of one's sister. 2 person united to others by membership of the same group, society, profession, etc; fellow member of a socialist organization, trade

union, etc: (esp attrib) *a ~ doctor; ~s in arms*, soldiers who are serving or have served together; ~ *officers*, in the same regiment. 3 (pl brethren /'breðrən/) fellow member of a religious society. **B~**, form of address: *B~ Luke*. '~·hood /-hʊd/ n 1 [U] feeling of ~ for ~. 2 [C] (members of an) association of men with common interests and aims, esp a religious society or socialist organization. ~·ly adj of or like a ~(¹s): ~ly *affection*.

brougham /'bruːəm/ n (19th c) four-wheeled closed carriage drawn by one horse.

brought pt,pp of bring.

brou·haha /'bruːhɑːhɑː/ n (dated colloq) fuss; excitement.

brow /braʊ/ n 1 (usu pl; also '**eye**-~) arch of hair above the eye: *knit one's ~s*, frown. 2 forehead. ⇨ *highbrow* at high¹(12); *lowbrow* at low¹(13). 3 top of a slope; steep slope; overhanging edge.

brow·beat /'braʊbiːt/ vt (pt browbeat, pp browbeaten) [VP6A,14] ~ (*into doing sth*), intimidate by shouting or looking stern at; bully: ~ *sb into doing sth; a poor, ~en little woman*.

brown /braʊn/ adj (-er, -est), n colour of toasted bread, or coffee mixed with milk: ~ *bread*, made with wholemeal flour; ~ *paper*, coarse kind used for parcels, etc; ~ *sugar*, half refined. *in a ~ study*, deep in thought; in a reverie. '~·stone n kinds of reddish-brown sandstone used for building. □ vt,vi [VP6A,2A] make or become ~. ~*ed off*, (sl) bored; fed up.

brownie /'braʊnɪ/ n 1 small, good-natured fairy or elf. 2 **B~** (**Guide**), (GB) junior member (age 8 to 11) of the Girl Guides.

browse /braʊz/ vi [VP2A,C] 1 feed, as animals do (on grass, etc): *cattle browsing in the fields*. 2 read (parts of a book or books) without any definite plan, for interest or enjoyment: *browsing among books in the public library*. □ n (act, period, of) browsing: *have a good ~*.

bruin /'bruːɪn/ n (pop name, eg in fairy tales, for) bear.

bruise /bruːz/ n injury by a blow or knock to the body, or to a fruit, so that the skin is discoloured but not broken: *covered with ~s after falling off his bicycle*. □ vt,vi 1 [VP6A] cause a ~ or ~s to; batter, make dents in (wood or metal): *He fell and ~d his leg. Pack the peaches carefully so that they won't get ~d*. 2 [VP2A] show the effects of a blow or knock: *A child's flesh ~s easily*. **bruiser** n tough, brutal boxer.

bruit /bruːt/ vt [VP15B] ~ *abroad*,(old use) spread (a rumour or report): ~ *it abroad*, spread the news everywhere.

brunch /brʌntʃ/ n (colloq) late morning meal instead of breakfast and lunch.

bru·nette /bruː'net/ n European with dark skin and dark-brown or black hair. ⇨ blond(e).

brunt /brʌnt/ n chief stress or strain: *bear the ~ of an attack. The main ~ of their criticism fell on us*.

brush¹ /brʌʃ/ n 1 implement of bristles, hair, wire, etc fastened in wood, bone, or other material, used for scrubbing, sweeping, cleaning (eg '*tooth*~, '*nail*~), or tidying the hair ('*hair*~); tuft of hair, etc set in a handle, used by painters and artists: *a 'paint-brush*. 2 (act of) using a ~: *He gave his clothes a good ~*, used a ~ on them. ⇨ also '~-up at brush²(1). 3 fox's tail. 4 [U] rough low-growing bushes; undergrowth: *a ~ fire*. ⇨ bush(2). 5 short, sharp fight or encounter: *a ~ with the enemy*. '~-wood n [U] = brush(4). '~-work n artist's style or way of using a paint–∿.

brush² /brʌʃ/ *vt, vi* **1** [VP6A,15B,22] use a brush on; clean, polish, make tidy or smooth: ∿ *your hat/clothes/shoes/hair/teeth;* ∿ *sth clean.* ∿ *sth away/off,* remove with a ∿: *He ∿ed away a fly from his nose,* used his hand to make the fly go away. *She ∿ed the crumbs off the tablecloth.* ∿ *sth aside/away,* (fig) pay no or little attention to (difficulties, objections, etc). ∿ *sb/sth off,* (colloq) reject, jilt; dismiss curtly: *He tries to get the girl to go out with him, but she always ∿es him off.* Hence, '∿-off *n* (colloq) rejection or dismissal: *She gave him the ∿-off.* ∿ *sth up,* use a ∿ on: ∿ *up the dust;* (fig) study or practise (sth) in order to get back skill that has been lost: *If you're going to France you'd better ∿ up your French.* Hence, '∿-up *n*: *Give your French a ∿-up.* **2** [VP2A,C,6A] touch when passing: *He ∿ed past/ by/(up) against me in a rude way. The leaves of the trees ∿ed my face as I ran through the forest.* **3** [VP2C] ∿ *off,* come off as the result of being ∿ed: *The mud will ∿ off when it dries.*

brusque /bru:sk/ *adj* (of speech or behaviour) rough and abrupt. ∿-ly *adj*∿-ness *n*

Brus·sels /'brʌslz/ *n* (attrib) of or from ∿ in Belgium: ∿ *lace/carpets.* ∿ 'sprouts, (plants with) buds growing thickly on the stem of a cabbage-like plant. ⇨ the illus at vegetable.

brutal /'bru:tl/ *adj* savage; cruel. ∿-ly /-təlɪ/ *adv* **bru·tal·ity** /bru:'tælətɪ/ *n* [U] cruelty; savagery; [C] cruel or savage act. '∿-ize *vt* [VP6A] make ∿: *Years of warfare had ∿ized the troops.*

brute /bru:t/ *n* **1** animal (except man). **2** stupid, animal-like or cruel person. **3** (attrib) animal-like; cruel and unthinking; unconscious or unreasoning; merely material; ∿ *force/strength;* ∿ *matter.* **brut·ish** /'bru:tɪʃ/ *adj* of or like a ∿: *brutish appetites.* **brut·ish·ly** *adv*

bubble /'bʌbl/ *n* **1** (in air) floating ball formed of liquid and containing air or gas: *soap ∿s; blowing ∿s.* **2** (in liquid) ball of air or gas that rises to the surface, eg in boiling water, in sparkling wines. **3** air-filled cavity in a solidified liquid, eg glass. **4** (fig) visionary plan; idea, hope, etc that is not realized: *His ∿ has burst.* **5** '∿ car *n* small car with a transparent dome as roof. '∿ gum *n* chewing gum which can be blown into bubbles on the lips. □ *vi* [VP2A,C] send up ∿s; rise in ∿s; make the sound of ∿s: *The water ∿d up through the sand. She was bubbling over with joy/high spirits/laughter.* **bub·bly** /'bʌblɪ/ *adj* full of ∿s. □ *n* (hum) champagne.

bu·bonic /bju:'bɒnɪk/ *adj* ∿ 'plague, contagious disease that spreads quickly (spread by rats, and marked by chills, fevers and swelling in the armpits and groin).

brushes

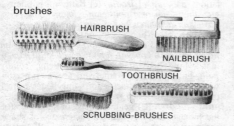

HAIRBRUSH

NAILBRUSH

TOOTHBRUSH

SCRUBBING-BRUSHES

buc·ca·neer /ˌbʌkə'nɪə(r)/ *n* pirate; unscrupulous adventurer.

buck¹ /bʌk/ *n* **1** male of a deer, hare or rabbit. ⇨ doe. '∿-skin *n* [U] soft leather made from deerskin or goatskin, used for gloves, bags, etc. '∿-shot *n* [U] large-size lead shot(4). '∿-tooth *n* (*pl* ∿teeth) (usu upper) tooth that projects. **2** (attrib) male.

buck² /bʌk/ *vi, vt* **1** [VP2A] (of a horse) jump up with the four feet together and the back arched; [VP6A] throw (the rider) to the ground by doing this. **2** ∿ *up,* [VP2C, esp in the *imperative*] (colloq) hurry. ∿ *(sb) up,* [VP15B,2C] make or become more vigorous or cheerful, ready for greater effort: *The good news ∿ed us all up. We were greatly ∿ed up by the news.*

buck³ /bʌk/ *n* (US sl) US dollar.

buck⁴ /bʌk/ *n pass the ∿ (to sb),* (sl) shift the responsibility (to). *The ∿ stops here,* The responsibility cannot be shifted further.

bucket¹ /'bʌkɪt/ *n* **1** vessel of wood, metal, canvas, plastic, etc for holding or carrying water, milk, etc; (also '∿-ful /-ful/) the amount a ∿ holds: *The rain was coming down in ∿s,* was very heavy. **2** scoop of a dredging machine, grain-elevator, etc. '∿ seat *n* (in a car or aircraft) seat with a rounded back for one person (contrasted with a *bench* seat).

bucket² /'bʌkɪt/ *vi* ride a horse hard.

buckle /'bʌkl/ *n* **1** metal, plastic or bone fastener, with one or more spikes made to go through a hole in a strap, etc, to keep sth in place. **2** ornamental clasp on a shoe. □ *vt, vi* **1** [VP6A,15] ∿ *(on),* fasten with a ∿: ∿ *a belt;* ∿ *on a sword/one's armour.* **2** [VP2C] (of a shoe, belt, etc) fasten (in a certain way). **3** [VP2C] ∿ *to/down to* (work, etc), begin (work) in earnest: ∿ *to a task. The sooner he ∿s down to it, the better.* **4** [VP2A] (of metal work, etc) bend, become twisted, crumple up from strain or heat.

buck·ler /'bʌklə(r)/ *n* small round shield, usu held by a handle or worn on the arm.

buck·ram /'bʌkrəm/ *n* [U] stiff, rough cloth (esp as used for binding books).

buck·shot /'bʌkʃɒt/ ⇨ buck¹(1).

buck·wheat /'bʌkwi:t US: -hwi:t/ *n* [U] (plant with) small triangular seed used for feeding horses and poultry. '∿ flour, flour made from this grain, used in US for breakfast cakes.

bu·colic /bju:'kɒlɪk/ *adj* of country life and farming, esp of shepherds: ∿ *verse.* **bu·col·ics** *n pl* pastoral poems.

bud /bʌd/ *n* **1** leaf, flower or branch, at the beginning of its growth. *in bud,* having buds or sending out buds: *The trees are in bud. nip sth in the bud,* put an end to sth, eg a plot, while it is in the beginning stage. **2** partly opened flower. ⇨ the illus at flower. □ *vi* (-dd-) put out buds. **bud·ding** *adj* beginning to develop: *a budding lawyer/poet.*

Bud·dhism /'bʊdɪzəm/ *n* the religion founded by Gautama /'gaʊtəmə/ or Siddartha /sɪ'dɑ:tə/ Buddha /'bʊdə/ (= teacher) in N India, in about the 6th c. **Bud·dhist** /'bʊdɪst/ *n* follower of Buddha.

buddy /'bʌdɪ/ *n* (*pl* ∿dies) (sl, as a familiar form of address) chum; mate.

budge /bʌdʒ/ *vt, vi* [VP6A, usu in *neg* and with *can, could*; VP2A,C, usu in *neg* with *won't, wouldn't*] (cause to) move very little, make the slightest movement; (fig) (cause to) change a position or attitude: *I can't ∿ it. It won't ∿ an inch.*

bud·geri·gar /'bʌdʒərɪgɑ:(r)/ *n* Australian love-

representations of Gautama Buddha

bird; kind of parakeet. ⇨ the illus at **rare**.

budget /'bʌdʒɪt/ n [C] estimate of probable future income and expenditure, esp that made by a Government; similar estimate made by a business company, society, private person, etc. '∼ **account**, account with a bank maintained by monthly transfers from a current account, so that the Bank may pay regularly recurring expenses, eg gas, electricity, rates. '∼ **plan**, system of buying goods in (large) shops by making regular monthly payments to them. □ vi [VP3A] ∼ **for**, allow or arrange for (in a ∼): ∼ for the coming year. ∼·**ary** /'bʌdʒɪtərɪ US: -terɪ/ adj of a ∼.

budgie /'bʌdʒɪ/ n (colloq abbr for a) budgerigar.

buff /bʌf/ n [U] **1** thick, strong, soft leather. **2** dull yellow colour. **3** the bare skin, esp in: stripped to the ∼, without clothing. **4** (US colloq) fan[3], enthusiast. □ vt polish (metal) with ∼(1).

buf·falo /'bʌfələʊ/ n (pl ∼s, US also ∼es) kinds of large, usu wild ox in India, Asia, Europe and Africa; N American bison: a herd of sixty ∼/∼es.

buf·fer[1] /'bʌfə(r)/ n apparatus (either spring-loaded or hydraulic) for lessening the effect of a blow or collision, eg on a railway engine or van. ∼ **state**, state situated between two or more powerful states, lessening the risk of war between them.

buf·fer[2] /'bʌfə(r)/ n (sl, usu **old** ∼) old-fashioned or foolish man.

buf·fet[1] /'bʊfeɪ US: bə'feɪ/ n counter where food and drink may be bought and consumed, eg in a railway station or (GB, in the '∼ car) on a train; sideboard or table from which food and drink are served, eg in a hotel; cold ∼, (on a menu) cold cooked meat, etc; ∼ supper, meal served to guests who do not sit at a table.

buf·fet[2] /'bʌfɪt/ n blow, generally one given with the hand; (fig) misfortune; blow delivered by fate. □ vt,vi **1** [VP6A] give a ∼ or ∼s to: flowers ∼ed by rain and wind; ∼ed by the waves/misfortunes. **2** [VP6A,3C] (rare) contend (with): ∼ (with) the waves.

buf·foon /bə'fu:n/ n clown; jester. **play the** ∼, do and say foolish things to amuse others. ∼·**ery** /-ərɪ/ n [U] clowning; clown-like behaviour; (in pl) rough jokes and actions.

bug /bʌg/ n **1** small, flat, ill-smelling, blood-sucking insect that infests dirty houses and beds. ⇨ the illus at **insect**. **2** (esp US) any small insect ('harvest bug, 'mealy-bug, etc). '**bug-hunter** n (colloq) entomologist. **3** (colloq) germ; virus infection: You've got the Asian 'flu bug. **4** (sl) **big bug**, important person. **5** (sl) defect; snag; (source of) malfunctioning, eg in a computer. **6** small hidden microphone (for listening to conversations, etc). □ vt (-gg-) [VP6A] **1** (colloq) use electronic devices (in a room, etc) in order to listen secretly to conversations: 'bugging devices. **2** (US colloq) cause to make mistakes. **3** (US sl) annoy: That man really bugs me.

buga·boo /'bʌgəbu:/ n source of annoyance or fear.

bug·bear /'bʌgbeə(r)/ n sth feared or disliked, with or without good reason: the ∼ of rising prices.

bug·ger /'bʌgə(r)/ n **1** (legal) sodomite. **2** ⚠ used as a vulgar term of abuse: You silly ∼! □ vt,vi [VP6A] commit ∼y with. ∼ **(it)!** (int, used to express irritation, anger, etc.) ∼ **off**, (esp imper) go away. ∼ **sth up**, spoil, ruin it. Hence, ∼**ed (up)**, spoilt, ruined. '∼-**all** n nothing. ∼**y** n sodomy.

buggy /'bʌgɪ/ n (pl -gies) **1** light carriage, pulled by one horse, for one or two persons: the horse and ∼ age, period before motor vehicles came into use. **2** '**beach** ∼, ⇨ beach. **3** (**baby**) ∼, (US) pram.

bugle /'bju:gl/ n musical wind instrument of copper or brass (like a small trumpet but without keys or valves), used for military signals. ⇨ the illus at **brass. bugler** n ∼ blower.

buhl /bu:l/ n [U] furniture decoration of inlaid brass, tortoise-shell and ivory: a ∼ cabinet.

build[1] /bɪld/ vt,vi (pt,pp built /bɪlt/) **1** [VP6A,12B,13B,14] ∼ **sth (of/out of)**, make by putting parts, materials, etc together (with what is made as the direct object): a house/railway. Some birds ∼ nests out of twigs. The school is built of wood. Mr Green is ∼ing a garage for me/is ∼ing me a garage. **2** [VP14] ∼ **sth into**, put parts together to form a whole (with the material as the direct object): He has built these scraps of metal into a very strange-looking sculpture. **3** [VP15B,14] ∼ **in/into**, make (sth) form a firm and permanent part of sth larger; make (sth) a fixture: Ask the carpenter to ∼ in some cupboards/to ∼ some cupboards into the walls. Hence, **built-in**: a bedroom with built-in wardrobes; a radio with a built-in aerial. **4** [VP15B,2C] ∼ **up**, (a) accumulate; form a block: Traffic is ∼ing up (= The number of vehicles is increasing steadily) along the roads to the coast. (b) come together (so as to increase or intensify): One day your books will ∼ up into a library. Their pressure on the enemy is ∼ing up. ∼ **sb/sth up**, (a) try to increase sb's reputation (through publicity, praise): Don't ∼ me up too much—I may disappoint you. (b) make, acquire, steadily and gradually: He has built up a good business/a good reputation for his goods. He went on holiday and soon built up (= strengthened) his health. (c) (passive and as adj) become covered with buildings: The district has been built up since I was last there. Hence, '**built-up areas**. (d) bring together (so as to increase or intensify): They are ∼ing up their military forces. Hence, '∼-**up** n (a) increase: a ∼-up of forces/pressure. (b) accumulation: a ∼-up of traffic. (c) flattering publicity, etc: the ∼-up of a politician's image. The press gave him a tremendous ∼-up. **5** [VP15B,3A] ∼ **on/upon**, base (hopes) on; rely on: Don't ∼ too many hopes upon his helping you. Don't ∼ on his promises. **6** (pp with advv): a well-built man, a man whose body has good proportions; solidly built, having a solid frame(work). ∼**er** n person who ∼s, esp a contractor for ∼ing houses; (fig) person who creates: a great empire ∼er.

build[2] /bɪld/ n [U] general shape or structure: (of the human body) general characteristics of shape and proportion: a man of powerful ∼. We are of the same ∼.

build·ing /'bɪldɪŋ/ n 1 [U] (art of) constructing houses, etc: '∼ *operations;* '∼ *materials;* '∼ *land,* (to be) used for houses, etc. '∼ **site,** an area of land on which an office-block, a house, etc is being built. '∼**-society,** organization for making loans to members who wish to build or buy a house, using funds supplied by its members. 2 [C] house or other structure: *Houses, schools, churches, hotels, factories and sheds are all ∼s.*

bulb /bʌlb/ n 1 almost round, thick, underground stem, sending roots downwards and leaves upwards, of such plants as the lily, onion, tulip. 2 sth like a ∼ in shape, esp an electric lamp or the swollen end of a glass tube, eg in a thermometer. **bul·bous** /'bʌlbəs/ adj of or having or like a ∼; growing from a ∼.

bulbs

bul·bul /'bʊlbʊl/ n songbird of Asia and Africa.
bulge /bʌldʒ/ n [C] irregular swelling; place where a swelling or curve shows; temporary increase in volume or numbers; (mil) salient. □ *vi,vt* [VP2A,C,6A] (cause to) swell beyond the usual size; curve outwards: *He ∼d his pockets with apples. His pockets were bulging with apples. He ∼d his cheeks.*
bulk /bʌlk/ n [U] quantity, volume, esp when large. **in ∼,** (a) in large amounts: *buy in ∼; tankers carry petroleum in ∼.* (b) loose, not packed in boxes, tins, etc. **∼ buying,** purchase at one time of a very large quantity of goods, eg by the state during a war. **the ∼ of,** the greater part or number of: *He left the ∼ of his property to his brother.* □ *vi ∼ large,* appear large or important. **∼y** adj taking up much space; clumsy to move or carry.
bulk·head /'bʌlkhed/ n [C] water-tight division or dividing wall in a ship; similar division in a tunnel, etc.
bull[1] /bʊl/ n 1 Uncastrated male of any animal of the ox family (⇨ **cow**): *a man with a neck like a ∼* (a '∼-neck), with a thick neck. *a ∼ in a 'china shop,* person who is rough and clumsy where skill and care are needed. *take the ∼ by the horns,* meet a difficulty boldly instead of trying to escape from it. '∼**-fight** n fight between men and a ∼ for public entertainment, as in Spain. '∼**-fighter** n '∼**-ring** n arena for ∼fights. '∼**-shit** n ⚠ (vulg sl) nonsense; foolish and exaggerated talk. 2 male of the whale, elephant and other large animals. 3 (Stock Exchange; ⇨ **bear**[1](4)) person who tries to raise prices with a view to selling at a profit: '∼ *market,* with rising prices. 4 (compounds) '∼**·dog** n large, powerful breed of dog, with a short, thick neck, noted for its strong grip and its courage. ⇨ the illus at dog. '∼**-doze** vt [VP6A,14] (a) remove earth, flatten obstacles with a ∼-dozer. (b) ∼*doze sb into doing sth,* force sb to do sth by using one's strength or by intimidating him. **∼-dozer** /'bʊldəʊzə(r)/ n powerful tractor that pushes a broad steel blade or sheet in front, used for levelling land, shifting large quantities of earth, etc.

'∼**·finch** n small songbird with rounded beak and brightly coloured feathers. '∼**-frog** n large American species of frog. ∼**-'headed** adj clumsy, impetuous, obstinate. '∼**'s-eye** n centre of target (for archers, etc). ⇨ the illus at archery. ∼**-'terrier** n cross between a ∼dog and a terrier.
bull[2] /bʊl/ n official order or announcement from the Pope.
bull[3] /bʊl/ n (also **Irish** ∼) foolish or amusing mistake in language, usu because there is a contradiction in terms (eg 'If you do not get this letter, please write and tell me'): *It's a lot of ∼,* nonsense.
bul·let /'bʊlɪt/ n shaped piece of lead, usu coated with another metal, (to be) fired from a rifle or revolver. Cf *shells* fired from guns. ⇨ the illus at cartridge. '∼**-headed** /-hedɪd/ adj having a small, round head. '∼**-proof** adj able to stop ∼s: a ∼-proof jacket.
bull·etin /'bʊlətɪn/ n 1 official statement of news: *a ∼ of news; a 'news ∼.* 2 printed sheet with official news or announcements.
bul·lion /'bʊlɪən/ n [U] gold or silver in bulk or bars, before manufacture.
bul·lock /'bʊlək/ n 1 young bull. 2 castrated bull.
bully[1] /'bʊlɪ/ n (pl -lies) person who uses his strength or power to frighten or hurt those who are weaker. □ vt [VP6A,14] ∼ *sb (into doing sth),* use strength, etc in this way to persuade sb to do sth.
bully[2] /'bʊlɪ/ n [U] (also '∼ **beef**) tinned beef.
bully[3] /'bʊlɪ/ n adj (sl) fine; excellent: *B∼ for you! Well done!*
bully[4] /'bʊlɪ/ n (hockey) way of putting the ball into play (beginning with two opposing players striking each others' sticks three times). □ vi [VP2C] ∼ *off,* start to play in this way.
bul·rush /'bʊlrʌʃ/ n [C] (kinds of) tall rush or reed with a thick velvety head.
bul·wark /'bʊlwək/ n 1 wall, esp one built of earth, against attack; earthwork; (fig) sth that defends or protects: *Law is the ∼ of society,* gives us security. 2 (usu pl) wall round (esp a sailing) ship's deck.
bum[1] /bʌm/ n (colloq) part of the body on which one sits; buttocks.
bum[2] /bʌm/ (sl) n habitual beggar or loafer. □ adj of poor quality; worthless. □ 1 vi (-mm-) [VP2C] ∼ *around,* loaf, wander about doing nothing. 2 vt (-mm-) [VP6A,14] ∼ *sth (off/from sb),* succeed in getting sb to give (usu reluctantly) sth to one: *He bummed a cigarette off me.*
bumble-bee /'bʌmbl biː/ n large kind of hairy bee with a loud hum.
bum-boat /'bʌmbəʊt/ n (naut) small boat carrying fresh provisions to ships lying offshore.
bump /bʌmp/ vt,vi 1 [VP6A,14,3A] ∼ *(against/ into),* come against with a blow or knock: *The room was dark and I ∼ed (my head) against the door. The blind man ∼ed into me. The car ∼ed*

a bulldozer

against the kerb/~ed into the car in front. ~
against/on, hurt (one's head, etc) by striking it on
sth. **2** [VP2C] move with a jerky, jolting motion
(like a cart on a bad road): *The heavy bus* ~*ed
along the rough mountain road.* **3** [VP15B] ~ **sb
off,** (sl) murder him. □ *adv* suddenly; violently:
Our bus ran ~ *into the wall.* □ *n* **1** blow or knock;
dull sound made by a blow (as when two things
come together with force). **2** swelling on the body
caused by such a blow; natural bulge on the skull.
⇨ **phrenology. 3** swelling on any surface. **4** (jolt
felt in an aircraft, caused by a) sudden change in
air-pressure. ~**y** *adj* (-ier, -iest) with many ~s: *a*
~*y road/ride.*
bum·per¹ /ˈbʌmpə(r)/ *n* fender (usu a horizontal
bar) on a bus, motor-car, etc (front and rear), to
lessen the effect of a collision, ⇨ the illus at motor;
(US) = **buffer¹.**
bum·per² /ˈbʌmpə(r)/ *n* **1** glass of wine, full to the
brim. **2** (attrib) sth unusually large or abundant: ~
crops; a ~ *harvest; a* ~ *edition* (of a periodical).
bum·per³ /ˈbʌmpə(r)/ *n* (cricket) ball bowled that
springs up high after striking the ground.
bump·kin /ˈbʌmpkɪn/ *n* awkward person with unpolished manners, esp from the country: *a country*
~.
bump·tious /ˈbʌmpʃəs/ *adj* conceited; self-
important: ~ *officials.* ~**·ly** *adv* ~**·ness** *n*
bun /bʌn/ *n* **1** small, round, sweet cake, usu containing currants. **2** *in a bun,* (of a woman's hair)
twisted into a knot above the back of the neck. ⇨
chignon.
bunch /bʌntʃ/ *n* **1** number of small, similar things
naturally growing together: *a* ~ *of grapes/
bananas.* **2** collection of things of the same sort
placed or fastened together: *a* ~ *of flowers/keys.* **3**
(sl) mob; gang. **4** *the best of the* ~, (colloq) the
best or pick of the lot. □ *vt, vi* [VP15B,2A,C] ~
(up/together), form into a ~; come or bring
together into a ~ or ~es, or in folds: *Don't* ~ *up,*
ie cluster together.

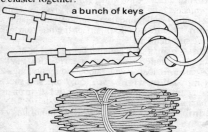

a bunch of keys

a bundle of sticks

bundle /ˈbʌndl/ *n* number of articles fastened, tied,
or wrapped together: *a* ~ *of sticks/firewood; a* ~
of old rags. The books were tied up in ~*s of
twenty.* □ *vt, vi* **1** [VP15B] ~ *up/together,* make
into a ~ or ~s: *We* ~*d everything up.* **2** [VP15A]
put together in a confused heap; put away without
order: *We* ~*d everything into a drawer.* **3**
[VP15A,B,2C] send or go in a hurry or without
ceremony: *They* ~*d him into a taxi. His mother
*~*d him off to school. They* ~*d off/out/away.*
bung /bʌŋ/ *n* large (usu wooden, rubber, cork or
plastic) stopper for closing a hole in a cask or barrel. □ *vt* [VP6A,15B] ~ *(up),* put a ~ into (the hole
in a cask). ¹~**-hole** *n* hole for filling a cask. ~*ed
up,* (of the nose) stopped up with mucus; (of

drains) clogged with dirt.
bun·ga·low /ˈbʌŋgələʊ/ *n* small house of only one
storey; (in India) such a house surrounded by a
large verandah. **bun·ga·loid** /ˈbʌŋgəlɔɪd/ *adj* of or
like ~s: *bungaloid growth,* area of unsightly
building development with many ~s.
bungle /ˈbʌŋgl/ *vt, vi* [VP6A,2A] do (a piece of
work) badly and clumsily; spoil (a task, etc) by
lack of skill. □ *n* ~*d* piece of work. **bung·ler**
/ˈbʌŋglə(r)/ *n* person who ~s.
bun·ion /ˈbʌnɪən/ *n* inflamed swelling, esp on the
large joint of the big toe.
bunk¹ /bʌŋk/ *n* narrow bed fixed on the wall, eg of
a cabin in a ship or in a train; sleeping-berth. ~
beds, pair of single beds, one fixed above the
other, usu for children.
bunk² /bʌŋk/ *vi* (GB sl) run away; play truant. □ *n*
do a ~, run away.
bunk³ /bʌŋk/ *n* [U] abbr for **bunkum.**
bunker /ˈbʌŋkə(r)/ *n* **1** that part of a ship where
coal or fuel oil is stored. **2** sandy hollow, made as
an obstacle, on a golf-course. **3** (mil) underground
shelter, fortified point, of steel and concrete. □
vt, vi **1** [VP6A,2A] fill a ship's ~s with fuel; (of a
ship) obtain supplies of fuel. **2** (usu passive) *be
*~*ed,* get one's ball into a ~ at golf; (fig) be in difficulties.
bun·kum /ˈbʌŋkəm/ *n* [U] (colloq) nonsense.
bunny /ˈbʌnɪ/ *n* (pl -nies) (child's word) rabbit.
Bun·sen /ˈbʌnsn/ *n* ~ **'burner,** burner for gas,
with an air-valve for regulating the mixture of gas
and air.
bunt·ing /ˈbʌntɪŋ/ *n* [U] (bright-coloured cloth
used for making) flags and decorations (for use in
streets and on buildings on festive occasions).
buoy /bɔɪ/ *n* **1** floating object, anchored to the bottom, used to show a navigable channel or to indicate reefs, submerged wrecks, etc. **2** (also ¹**life-**~)
sth designed to keep a person afloat in the water, eg
sth made of cork or sth that can be inflated with air.
⇨ the illus at life. □ *vi* **1** [VP6A] mark the position
of with a ~: ~ *a wreck/channel.* **2** [VP15B] ~ *up,*
keep afloat; (fig) keep up hopes, etc: ~*ed up with
new hope.*
buoy·ancy /ˈbɔɪənsɪ/ *n* [U] **1** power to float or keep
things floating: *Salt water has more* ~ *than fresh
water.* **2** (fig) lightness of spirits; power to re-
cuperate; (of the stock market) tendency of prices
to rise.
buoy·ant /ˈbɔɪənt/ *adj* able to float or to keep
things floating; (fig) light-hearted: *a* ~ *disposition;* springy: *with a* ~ *step;* (of the stock market,
etc) maintaining high prices. ~**·ly** *adv*
bur, burr /bɜː(r)/ *n* (plant with a) seed-case or
flower-head that clings to the hair or fur of animals; (fig) sth or sb that sticks like a ~, esp a person who forces his company on others and is hard
to shake off.
burble /ˈbɜːbl/ *vi* make a gentle murmuring or bubbling sound: *burbling with mirth.*
bur·den /ˈbɜːdn/ *n* **1** sth (to be) carried; load (esp
one that is heavy); (liter and fig) sth difficult to
bear: *the* ~ *of taxation (up)on industry; a* ~ *of
sorrow/grief. be a* ~ *to sb,* cause him expense
and trouble: *He was always a* ~ *to his parents.*
beast of ~, animal that carries packs on its back.
2 [U] ship's carrying capacity, tonnage; *a ship of
3000 tons* ~. **3** *the* ~ *of proof,* obligation to
prove: *The* ~ *of proof rests with him,* He must
prove the truth of his statement. **4** refrain or chorus

(of a song); (with *def art*) chief theme of a statement, speech, etc: *The ∼ of his remarks was
that....* □ *vt ∼ sb/oneself (with),* [VP6A,14] load;
put a ∼ on: ∼ *oneself with a heavy overcoat;* ∼
one's memory with useless facts; ∼*ed with taxation.* ∼**·some** /-səm/ *adj* hard to bear; making (sb)
tired; troublesome (*to* sb).

bur·dock /'bɜːdɒk/ *n* wild plant with leaves like
those of a dock and prickly flower-heads (*burrs*).

bureau /'bjʊərəʊ/ *n* (*pl* -reaux, /-rəʊz/) **1** (GB)
writing desk with drawers. **2** government or municipal department or office: *‚Infor mation B∼;*
'*Tourist B∼.* **3** (US) chest of drawers for clothes,
etc, usu with a mirror.

bureau·cracy /bjʊə'rɒkrəsɪ/ *n* [U] government by
paid officials not elected by the people, officials
who keep their positions whatever political party is
in power; (over-)complicated system of administration; [C] (*pl* -cies) instance of this system of
government; the officials as a body.

bureau·crat /'bjʊərəkræt/ *n* (often pej) official
who works in a bureau or government department,
esp one who obeys the rules of his department
without exercising much judgement. ∼**ic**
/‚bjʊərə'krætɪk/ *adj* of or like a ∼; too much attached to rules; carried on according to official
rules and habits. ∼**·i·cally** /-ɪklɪ/ *adv*

burette /bjʊə'ret/ *n* graduated glass tube with a tap
for measuring small quantities of liquid that are let
out of it.

burg /bɜːg/ *n* (US colloq) town; city.

bur·geon /'bɜːdʒən/ *vi* (poet) put out leaves; begin
to grow.

bur·ger /'bɜːgə(r)/ *n* (colloq) = hamburger.

burgh /'bʌrə/ *n* borough in Scotland.

bur·gher /'bɜːgə(r)/ *n* (old use) citizen (esp of a
Dutch, Flemish or German town).

bur·glar /'bɜːglə(r)/ *n* person who breaks into a
house in order to steal. **bur·glary** /'bɜːglərɪ/ *n* [U]
crime of breaking into a house to steal: [C] (*pl* -
ries) instance of this: *There have been numerous
∼ies in this district recently.* '∼**-alarm** *n* device to
give warning of ∼s. '∼**-proof** *adj* made so that ∼s
cannot break in or into. **burgle** /'bɜːgl/ *vt,vi*
[VP6A] break into (a building) to commit ∼y;
[VP2A] commit ∼y. ∼**·i·ous** /bɜː'gleərɪəs/ *adj*
(legal) of ∼y: *guilty of a ∼ious attempt.*

burgo·mas·ter /'bɜːgəmɑːstə(r) *US:* -mæs-/ *n*
mayor of a Dutch, Flemish or German town.

Bur·gundy /'bɜːgəndɪ/ *n* [U] kinds of (usu red)
wine of Burgundy (in Central France).

burial /'berɪəl/ *n* [U] burying, [C] instance of this.
'∼**-ground** *n* cemetery. '**B∼ Service,** the religious ceremony at a funeral.

burke /bɜːk/ *vt* [VP6A] avoid: ∼ *publicity/an issue;* suppress: ∼ *an inquiry.*

bur·lap /'bɜːlæp/ *n* [U] coarse canvas (used for
bags, wrappings, etc).

bur·lesque /bɜː'lesk/ *n* **1** [C] imitation, eg of a
book, speech, person's behaviour, for the purpose
of making fun of it or of amusing people. **2** [U] amusing imitation or parody. **3** (US) variety entertainment. ⇨ variety(5). **4** (as *adj* or attrib) intended as
a ∼. □ *vt* [VP6A] make a ∼ of; parody.

burly /'bɜːlɪ/ *adj* (of a person) big and strong; solidly built.

burn [1] /bɜːn/ *n* (Scot) small stream.

burn [2] /bɜːn/ *vt,vi* (*pt,pp* burnt /bɜːnt/ or burned
/bɜːnd/) (For uses with *adverbial particles* and
preps, ⇨ 6 below.) **1** [VP6A] use for the purpose of

lighting or heating: *Most large steamships now ∼
oil instead of coal. This lamp ∼s oil. We have ∼t
all our logs.* **2** [VP6A,14] ∼ (*to*), damage, hurt,
destroy by fire, heat or the action of acid: *Be careful not to ∼ the meat. The coffee is very hot, don't
∼ your mouth. You've ∼t my toast to a cinder!* so
that it is hard and black. *The child ∼t itself/its
fingers while playing with matches. Some acids are
strong enough to ∼ wood.* ∼ **one's fingers,** ⇨
finger. '∼**ing glass** *n* lens used to concentrate the
sun's rays (to set fire to sth). **3** [VP2A,B,C] be on
fire or alight; be capable of giving out light and
heat: *Wood ∼s easily. Stone won't ∼. All the
lights were ∼ing.* **4** [VP6A] make by heat; heat (a
material) to make (sth): ∼ *bricks/lime/charcoal;*
∼ *clay to make bricks;* ∼ *a hole in a carpet,* eg by
dropping a cigarette end. **5** [VP2A,C,4A] be hurt or
spoilt by fire or heat; scorch; be or feel warm or
hot; (fig) be filled with strong feeling: *The milk/
sauce has ∼t. She has a skin that ∼s easily,* is
quickly hurt by the sun. *Her cheeks were ∼ing
with shame. They were ∼ing to avenge the death of
their leader.* **6** [VP15B,2C] (special uses with *adverbial particles* and *preps*):
burn (sth) away, (a) continue to ∼: *The fire was
∼ing away cheerfully.* (b) make, become less, by
∼ing: destroy, be destroyed, by ∼ing: *Half the
candle had ∼t away. An area of skin on his hand
was ∼t away.*
burn sth down, be destroyed, destroy to the foundations, by fire: *The house (was) ∼t down.* ∼
(down) (low), ∼ less brightly as the material ∼s
or the fuel is used.
burn sth out, (a) become extinguished: *The fire
∼t (itself) out.* (b) (of a rocket) use up its fuel. (c)
(of an electric motor, coil) stop working because
high current has caused electrical ∼ing. (d) (usu
passive) be destroyed, be reduced to a shell, by
fire; be gutted: ∼*t-out factories/tanks.* ∼ **oneself
out,** ruin one's health by overwork, dissipation,
etc.
burn sth up, (a) burst into flames, flare up: *Put
some wood on the fire and make it ∼ up.* (b) consume, get rid of, by ∼ing: *We ∼t up all the garden
rubbish.* (c) (of a rocket, etc, re-entering the atmosphere from space) catch fire and be destroyed.
'∼**-up** *n* (GB sl) high-speed race on a public road
between young people on motor-cycles.

burn [3] /bɜːn/ *n* **1** injury, mark, made by fire, heat or
acid: *He died of the ∼s he received in the fire.* **2**
(aerospace) one firing of a rocket: *a two-minute ∼
to correct course to the moon.*

burner /'bɜːnə(r)/ *n* **1** person who burns sth or
makes sth by burning: *a 'charcoal-burner.* **2** that
part of a lamp, stove, etc from which the light or
flame comes: *a four-∼ oil-stove.*

burn·ing /'bɜːnɪŋ/ *adj* **1** intense: *a ∼ thirst/desire.*
2 exciting; hotly debated: *a ∼ question.* **3** notorious, scandalous: *a ∼ disgrace/shame.*

bur·nish /'bɜːnɪʃ/ *vt,vi* [VP6A] polish (metal) by, or
as if by, rubbing; [VP2A] take a polish: *material
that ∼es well.*

bur·nouse /bɜː'nuːs/ *n* kind of cloak with a hood,
worn by Arabs and Moors.

burp /bɜːp/ *n* [C] (colloq) belch. □ *vt,vi* [VP6A,2A]
(cause to) give a ∼: ∼ *a baby.*

burr [1] *n* ⇨ bur.

burr [2] /bɜː(r)/ *n* **1** whirring sound made by parts of
machines that turn quickly. '∼**-drill** *n* one used by
dentists. **2** marked pronunciation of 'r'; marked

(rural) accent: *speak with a soft West-country* ~.

bur·row·/'bʌrəʊ/ *n* hole made in the ground (by foxes, rabbits, etc). □ *vi, vt* [VP2A,2C,3A,6A] ~ *(into sth),* dig (a ~); (fig) investigate (sth hidden).

bur·sar /'bɜːsə(r)/ *n* **1** treasurer (esp of a college). **2** (person holding a) scholarship at a university of Scotland, or a grant for continuation of studies: *British Council* ~s *in Great Britain.* ~**y** *n* **1** college ~'s office. **2** scholarship; grant for continuation of studies.

burst¹ /bɜːst/ *vi,vt* (*pt,pp* burst) (For uses with *adverbial particles* and *preps,* ⇨ **5** below.) **1** [VP2A] (of a bomb, shell, boiler, etc) fly or break violently apart from internal pressure; explode; (of river banks, a dam, an abscess, a boil) break outwards; (of a bubble) break; (of leaf and flower buds) open out. **be** ~*ing* **to,** be eager to: *He was* ~*ing to tell us the news.* **2** [VP6A,22] cause to fly apart, explode, open suddenly, give way under pressure: ~ *a tyre/balloon; We had to* ~ *the door open. If you get much fatter you'll* ~ *your clothes. He* ~ *a blood-vessel,* suffered the ~ing of one; (fig) ~ *one's sides with laughing.* **3** ~ **(with),** [VP2A,3A] be full to over-flowing; be able to contain with difficulty: *storehouses* ~*ing with grain; sacks* ~*ing with corn. They were* ~*ing with happiness/pride/excitement/impatience/health.* **4** [VP2C] make a way or entry suddenly or by force: *He* ~ *into the room. The oil* ~ (= gushed) *out of the ground. The sun* ~ *through the clouds,* appeared through an opening in the clouds. **5** [VP2C,3A] (with *adverbial particles* and *preps*): **burst forth,** ⇨ ~ out.

burst in (on/upon), (a) interrupt: *Stop him* ~*ing in. He* ~ *in upon our conversation.* **(b)** appear or arrive suddenly: *He'll be* ~*ing in on us at any moment.*

burst into, (a) send out suddenly; break out into: *The oil-stove upset and* ~ *into flames.* **(b)** ~ *into tears/laughter, etc,* suddenly begin to cry (laugh, etc); ~ *into song,* begin to sing; ~ *into angry speech,* begin to speak angrily. **(c)** ~ *into bloom/blossom,* (of shrubs, trees) open out with blossom. **(d)** ~ *into view/sight,* (of a scene, spectacle) suddenly become visible.

burst out (into), exclaim; begin to speak: *'Why don't you behave?' he* ~ *out* (= ~ forth). *He* ~ *out into threats.* ~ *out laughing/crying,* suddenly begin to laugh/cry.

burst on/upon, come suddenly or unexpectedly to: *The view* ~ *upon our sight. The truth* ~ *upon him,* he suddenly realized it. *The cries of the mob* ~ *upon our ears.*

burst² /bɜːst/ *n* **1** bursting explosion: *the* ~ *of a shell/bomb; a* ~ *in the water main.* **2** brief, violent effort: *a* ~ *of energy/speed; work in sudden* ~s. **3** outbreak: *a* ~ *of applause/anger/tears; a* ~ *of flame.* **4** short spurt: *a* ~ *of gunfire,* eg from a machine-gun. **5** ⇨ bust².

bur·then /'bɜːðən/ *n, v*(liter) burden.

bur·ton /'bɜːtn/ *n* beer brewed at Burton-on-Trent, Derbyshire. **gone for a** ~, (GB sl) dead; missing.

bury /'berɪ/ *vt* **1** [VP6A] place (a dead body) in the ground, in a grave or in the sea; (of a clergyman) perform the Burial Service over; (of relatives) lose by death: *William Shakespeare is buried in the church at Stratford on Avon. He was buried at sea. Poor old Joe—he's dead and buried. She has buried five husbands.* **2** [VP6A,22,15A] put underground; cover with earth, leaves, etc; cover up and

forget; hide from view: *buried treasure. You wouldn't like to be buried alive. The dog buried the bone. The end of the post was buried in the ground. The house was half buried under snow. She buried* (= hid) *her.face in her hands.* ~ *oneself in the country,* go to a place in the country where one will meet few people. ~ *oneself in one's books/studies,* give all one's time and attention to them. **be buried in thoughts/memories of the past,** etc, be deep in thought, etc, paying no attention to other things. '~**ing-ground** *n* cemetery.

bus /bʌs/ *n* **1** (= *omnibus* which is now dated) public conveyance that travels along a fixed route and takes up and sets down passengers at fixed points: *Shall we walk or go by bus?* **miss the bus,** (colloq) be too late to use an opportunity. '**bus-man** /-mən/ *n* bus-driver. **,busman's 'holiday,** leisure time spent in the same kind of occupation as one's ordinary work. '~ **stop** *n* fixed stopping place for buses. **2** (sl) aeroplane; motor-car. □ *vi,vt* (-ss-) [VP2A,6A] go, take, by bus; (esp US) transport children to their schools: *the bussing of children to achieve racial integration,* eg by taking children from white areas to schools in black areas and vice versa.

busby /'bʌzbɪ/ *n* (*pl* -bies) fur cap worn for ceremonial parades by soldiers of some British regiments.

bush /bʊʃ/ *n* **1** [C] low-growing plant with several or many woody stems coming up from the root. Cf *tree,* with a single trunk: *'rose-*~; *'fruit* ~es, eg currants, gooseberries. **2** [U] (often **the** ~) wild, uncultivated land, with or without trees or bushes, esp in Africa and Australia. ⇨ also telegraph. '**B**~**man** /-mən/ *n* (*pl* -men) member of certain anciently settled tribes of West Southern Africa. ~**y** *adj* **1** covered with ~es. **2** growing thickly; thick and rough: ~*y eyebrows; a fox's* ~*y tail.*

bushed /bʊʃt/ *pred adj* (colloq) very tired.

bushel /'bʊʃl/ *n* (before metrication) measure for grain and fruit (8 gallons). ⇨ App 5. **hide one's light under a** ~, be modest about one's abilities, good qualities, etc.

busier, busiest, busily ⇨ busy.

busi·ness /'bɪznɪs/ *n* **1** [U] buying and selling; commerce; trade: *We do not do much* ~ *with them. He's in the wool* ~, buys and sells wool. *He has set up in* ~ *as a bookseller. He is in* ~ *for himself,* works on his own account, is not employed by others. *Which do you want to do, go into* ~ *or become a lawyer?* **on** ~, for the purpose of doing ~: *Are you here on* ~ *or for pleasure?* '~ **address,** address of one's shop, office, etc. Cf *home address.* '~ **hours,** hours during which ~ is done, eg 9am to 5pm. '~**like** *adj* using, showing system, promptness, care, etc. '~**man** /-mæn/ *n* (*pl* -men) man who is engaged in buying and selling, etc. **2** [C] shop; commercial enterprise, etc: *He has a good* ~ *as a greengrocer. He is the manager of three different* ~es. *The newspapers advertise many small* ~es *for sale.* **3** [U] task, duty, concern; what has to be done: *It is a teacher's* ~ *to help his pupils. I will make it my* ~ (= will undertake) *to see that the money is paid promptly. That's no* ~ *of yours,* is something about which you need not or should not trouble. **get down to** ~, start the work that must be done. **mind one's own** ~, attend to one's own duties and not interfere with those of others. **mean** ~, be in earnest. **send sb about his** ~, send him away and tell him not to interfere. **4**

[U] right: *You have no ~ to do that.* **5** (with *indef art*) difficult matter: *What a ~ it is getting the children off to school!* **6** (often contemptuous) affair; subject; device: *I'm sick of the whole ~,* tired of the affair. **7** (colloq): *the ~ end of a pin/a chisel, etc,* the sharp end, the end to be used. **8** [U] (theatre) action, facial expression, etc of the actors in interpreting their parts (as distinct from the words they speak).

busker /'bʌskə(r)/ *n* person who entertains people informally for money in public places, eg by singing or dancing to queues outside cinemas.

bust¹ /bʌst/ *n* **1** head and shoulders of a person cut in stone, or cast in bronze, gypsum, etc. **2** woman's bosom; measurement round the bosom and back.

bust² /bʌst/ *vt,vi* (sl for **burst**) ~ *sth,* smash it. **go ~,** fail; run out of money: *The business went ~.* □ *n* **have a ~; go on the ~,** a period of wild revelry. **'~-up** *n* (sl) quarrel.

bus·tard /'bʌstəd/ *n* large, swift-running bird.

bus·ter¹ /'bʌstə(r)/ *n* (in compounds) bomb or shell that wrecks completely: *'dam~; 'tank~; 'block~,* ie a bomb that may destroy a block of buildings.

bus·ter² /'bʌstə(r)/ *n* (US sl, as a form of address) fellow (= GB **mate**¹1).

bustle¹ /'bʌsl/ *vi,vt* [VP2A,C,15B] (cause to) move quickly and excitedly: *Tell him to ~,* hurry. *Everyone was bustling about/in and out,* appearing to be very busy. *She ~d the children off to school.* □ *n* [U] excited activity: *Everybody was in a ~. Why is there so much ~?*

bustle² /'bʌsl/ *n* frame formerly used to puff out a woman's skirt at the back.

busy /'bɪzɪ/ *adj* (busier, busiest) **1** working; occupied; having much to do: *The doctor is a ~ man. He was ~ with/at/over his work.* **be ~ doing sth, be in the process of doing it:** *He was ~ getting ready for his journey.* **get ~,** start: *You'd better get ~ eating.* **'~-body** *n* (*pl* ~bodies) person who interferes in the affairs of other people, esp when his help is not wanted. **2** full of activity: *a ~ day;* (of places) filled with active people, traffic, etc: *The shops are ~ before Christmas. This is one of the busiest underground stations in London.* **3** (of a telephone line) in use. □ *vt* [VP14,6A] ~ **oneself (with); ~ oneself (by/in) doing sth,** keep ~, occupy oneself with: *He busied himself with all sorts of little tasks. She busied herself by tidying up her desk.* **busi·ly** /'bɪzɪlɪ/ *adv* in a ~ way: *busily engaged in doing sth.*

but¹ /bʌt/ *adv* only (now the usu word): *We can but try. He left but an hour ago. He's but a boy.* **can not but** + *inf,* (formal) = can only + *inf: I cannot but think that...,* am compelled to...; *I could not but choose to go/I could not choose but go* (= had no alternative than to go). *I cannot but admire* (= must admire, cannot help admiring) *your decision.*

but² /bʌt; *strong form:* bʌt/ *conj* **1** (coordinating): *Tom was not there but his brother was. We tried to do it but couldn't. He's a hardworking but not very intelligent boy.* **2** (subordinating, with a neg implication): *I never go past my old school but I think* (= without thinking) *of Mr Wilkins, the headmaster. No man is so old but he may learn,* No man is too old to learn. *Never a month passes but she writes* (= in which she does not write) *to her old parents.*

but³ /bʌt; *strong form:* bʌt/ *prep* (The uses of *but* as a *prep* and as a *conj* are not always clearly to be distinguished. The subject forms of the *pers pronouns* are often used after *but* meaning 'except', as if it were a *conj.* The object forms are also used, as if *but* were a *prep*). (With negatives, eg *no one, none, nothing,* and interrogatives, eg *who,* and such words as *all, every one*) except, excluding: *Nothing but disaster would come from such a plan. They're all wrong but me. None but the brave deserve the fair* (prov)). *Who but Gloria would do such a thing?* **first/next/last but one/two/three:** *Take the next turning but one* (= the second turning) *on your left. I live in the last house but two* (= the third house from the end) *in this street. Smith was the last but one* (= second to last) *to arrive.* **'but for,** except for, without: *But for your help we should not have finished in time. But for the rain* (= If it had not rained) *we should have had a pleasant journey.* **'but that,** except that: *He would have helped us but that* (= if it had not been for the fact that) *he was short of money at the time.* **but then,** on the other hand: *London is a noisy place, but then it's also the place where you get the best entertainment.*

but⁴ /bʌt/ *rel pron* (rare; formal) who/that do/does not: *There is not one of us but wishes* (= not one of us who does not wish) *to help you. There are few of us but* (= few of us who do not) *admire your determination.*

bu·tane /'bjuːteɪn/ *n* [U] gas produced from petroleum supplied in metal containers for use in houses, etc, where there is no piped supply of gas (for cooking, heating, lighting, etc).

butch /bʊtʃ/ *adj* (colloq) (of a woman) having tendencies towards masculine behaviour and clothes; (of a man) exaggeratedly masculine. □ *n* such a person.

butcher /'bʊtʃə(r)/ *n* **1** person who kills, cuts up and sells animals for food. *~'s meat,* meat excluding poultry, game and bacon; *the ~'s,* the *~'s* shop. **2** person who has caused unnecessary death, eg a general who wastes the lives of soldiers; person who kills savagely and needlessly. □ *vt* [VP6A] kill violently, esp with a knife. *~y n* [U] **1** (attrib) *~'s* trade: *He's in the ~y business.* **2** needless and cruel killing of people.

but·ler /'bʌtlə(r)/ *n* head manservant (in charge of the wine-cellar, pantry, valuables, etc).

butt¹ /bʌt/ *n* **1** large cask for wine or ale. **2** large barrel for storing rainwater, eg from roofs.

butt² /bʌt/ *n* **1** thicker (usu wooden) end (esp of a fishing-rod or rifle). **2** unburned end of a smoked cigar or cigarette, or of a used candle.

butt³ /bʌt/ *n* **1** (usu *pl* with *def art*) shooting-range; the targets and the mound of earth behind them (used for practice in firing rifles). **2** person who is a target for ridicule, jokes, etc: *He is the ~ of the whole school.*

butt⁴ /bʌt/ *vt,vi* **1** [VP6A,15A] push with the head (as a goat does): *~ someone in the stomach.* **2** [VP2C] *~ in,* (colloq) force oneself into the conversation or company of others; interrupt sb: *May I ~ in?* [VP3A] *~ into,* run into, head or front first.

but·ter /'bʌtə(r)/ *n* [U] **1** fatty food substance made from cream by churning, used on bread, in cooking, etc. *~ will/would not melt in sb's mouth,* he has a demure and innocent appearance. **'~-bean,** large, dried haricot ~. **'~-cup** *n* wild plant with yellow flowers. **'~-fin·gers** *n* person unable to hold things well, esp one unable to catch a ball. '∼·milk *n* liquid that remains after ∼ has been separated from milk. '∼·scotch *n* [U] sweet substance made by boiling sugar and ∼ together. **2** substance similar to ∼, made from other materials: *cocoa* ∼, *peanut* ∼. □ *vt* **1** [VP6A] spread ∼ on (esp bread); cook with ∼. ⇨ also **bread**(2). **2** [VP15B] ∼ **sb up**, flatter.

but·ter·fly /'bʌtəflaɪ/ *n* (*pl* -flies) insect with four wings, often brightly coloured, and feelers. '∼ **(stroke)** *n* stroke used in swimming, both arms moving upward and outward at the same time as an up and down kick of the feet.

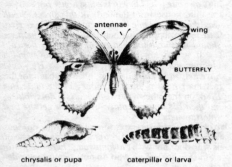

antennae — wing

BUTTERFLY

chrysalis or pupa   caterpillar or larva

three stages in the life of a butterfly

but·tery /'bʌtərɪ/ *n* (*pl* -ries) (in some GB universities) place where provisions (bread, butter, ale) are kept and from which they are served.

but·tock /'bʌtək/ *n* **1** either side of that part of the body on which a person sits: *an injection of penicillin in the left* ∼. **2** (*pl*) **the** ∼**s**, the rump, the bottom: *a smack on the* ∼*s.* ⇨ the illus at **leg**.

but·ton /'bʌtn/ *n* **1** small, usu round, bit of bone, metal, etc for fastening, on an article of clothing, or sewn on as an ornament. '∼·hole *n* hole through which a ∼ is passed; flower worn in a ∼hole (eg in the lapel of a jacket or coat). □ *vt* [VP6A] hold sb by the ∼hole (to get his attention). '∼·hook *n* hook for pulling a ∼ into place through a ∼hole. '∼·wood *n* tall tree with a ∼-shaped fruit, related to the sycamore; its wood. **2** small, round ∼-like object, esp one that, when pushed, makes an electrical contact, eg for a bell: *press/push/touch the* ∼. **3** small, unopened mushroom. **4** (*pl*) (colloq) boy wearing uniform, employed as a page in a club, hotel, etc. ⇨ **bell-hop**. □ *vt, vi* [VP6A,15B,2A] ∼ **(up/down)** fasten with a ∼ or ∼s: ∼ (*up*) *one's coat; a dress that* ∼*s down the back. My collar won't* ∼ *down*, I can't ∼ it. ∼ *up*, (colloq) complete safely, at last: *That's that job* ∼*ed up!* ∼**ed-'up** *adj* (colloq) (of a person) silent and reserved.

but·tress /'bʌtrɪs/ *n* support built against a wall. ⇨ the illus at **church**. (fig) prop; sth that supports: *the* ∼*es of society/the constitution.* □ *vt* [VP6A,15B] ∼ **(up)**, strengthen, hold up (by building a ∼); (fig) support, strengthen: ∼ *up an argument.*

buxom /'bʌksəm/ *adj* (of women) good-looking, healthy-looking and well covered with flesh.

buy /baɪ/ *vt, vi* (*pt, pp* bought /bɔːt/) **1** [VP6A,15B,12B,13B,2A,C] get in return for money, get by paying a price: *Can money buy hap-*

piness? I bought this car from Chris. Buy one for me. Buy me one. I must buy myself a new shirt. He bought it for £2. He bought them for/at 10p each. Prices are low—buy now! **buy sth back:** *He sold his house and then bought it back again.* **buy sth in,** (**a**) buy a stock of: *buy in coal for the winter.* (**b**) (at an auction sale) bid for and obtain (one's own goods) by offering a higher price than the highest offered by others (when other bids are considered too low). **buy sth off,** get rid of (an unjust claim, a blackmailer) by making a payment. **buy sb out,** pay (sb) to give up a post, property, etc or a share in one's own business. **buy sb over,** bribe or corrupt (sb). **buy sth up,** buy all or as much as possible of (sth). **2** [VP6A] obtain at a sacrifice: *He bought fame at the expense of his health and happiness. Victory was dearly bought.* □ *n* (colloq) purchase: *a good buy,* a bargain. **buyer** *n* person who buys. **buyers' market,** state of affairs when goods are plentiful and money scarce, so that low prices favour buyers.

buzz /bʌz/ *vi, vt* **1** [VP2A,C] make a humming sound (as of bees or machinery in rapid motion). **2** [VP2C] move rapidly or excitedly: ∼ *about/ around;* ∼*ing along the road.* ∼ *off,* (sl) go away. **3** [VP2A] (of the ears) be filled with a ∼ing noise: *My ears began* ∼*ing.* **4** [VP6A] (of an aircraft) fly near to or low over (another plane) in a threatening manner: *Two fighters* ∼*ed the airliner.* □ *n* humming (of bees or other insects); sound of people talking, of whirling machinery, etc. **give sb a** ∼, (sl) make a telephone call to him. ∼**er** *n* electrical device that produces a ∼ (eg to signal time, a telephone call) when the current flows.

buz·zard /'bʌzəd/ *n* kind of hawk.

by[1] /baɪ/ *adv part* **1** near: *He hid the money when nobody was by.* **standby,** ⇨ **stand**[1](13). **2** past: *He hurried by without a word. Fame passed him by. I can't get by,* can't pass. *The time has/is gone by* (= is past) *when....* **3** lay/put/set sth by, keep it, save it, for future use. **4** (in phrases) **by and by,** later on. **by the by(e), by the way,** (used to introduce a new topic, or sth that has been forgotten). **by and large,** on the whole; taking everything into consideration.

by[2] /baɪ/ *prep* **1** near; at or to the side of; beside: *Come and sit by me/by my side. My house is by the river. We had a day by the sea.* **by oneself,** alone: *He went for a holiday (all) by himself.* ⇨ **12** below. **have sth by one,** have it handy, within easy reach: *It's useful to have a good dictionary by you when you're reading.* **stand by sb,** support him. **2** (in reading the cardinal points) towards: *North by East,* one point towards the East from the North, ie between N and NNE; *East by North,* one point North of East, ie between E and ENE. ⇨ the illus at **compass**. **3** (showing direction of movement) (= *by way of*) through, along, across, over: *We came by the fields, not by the roads. Did you come by the nearest road? We travelled to Paris by Dover and Calais.* **4** past: *I go by* (= I pass) *the post office every morning on my way to work. He walked by me without speaking.* **5** (of time, esp to indicate conditions and circumstances) during: *The enemy attacked by night* (emphasizing the circumstances—under cover of darkness, etc. Cf *Everything was quiet during the night). Do you prefer travelling by night or by day? We went for a sail on the lake by moonlight. It's no use trying to escape by daylight.* **6** (of time) as soon as; not later than;

when (the time indicated) comes: *Can you finish the work by tomorrow? He ought to be here by this time/by now. They were tired out by evening. By the time (that) you get there (that* is almost always omitted) *it will be dark.* **7** (to form adverbial phrases of time, length, weight, number): *rent a house by the year; hire a bicycle by the day,* eg £5 for one day's use; *engage a clerk by the month; pay a labourer by the day/the hour; sell cloth by the yard/coal by the ton/eggs by the dozen, etc; freight charged by weight/volume; a room 20 ft by 30 ft.* **8** through the agency, means, or instrumentality of: *The streets are lighted by electricity. This church was designed by Wren. He makes a living by teaching. He was shot by a sniper. The man was killed by a falling tree/by lightning.* (Note that *by lightning* is instrumentality, not instrument. Cf The rat was killed *by* Tom *with* a stick. ⇨ with(3).) **9** (indicating path or means of travel, transport, conveyance): *travel by land/sea/air; by bus/car/boat, etc; send sth by post/hand.* **10** (indicating a part of the body that is touched, etc): *take sb by the hand,* ie take his hand; *seize sb by the hair; grab sb by the scruff of his neck.* **11** *know/learn sth by heart,* so that one can repeat it from memory. *know sb by name/reputation/sight,* know only his name, etc but not know him personally. **12** (in adverbial phrases of manner) *by accident/mistake,* accidentally, not on purpose or intentionally. *by chance/good fortune,* as the result of chance or good fortune. *by oneself,* without help. ⇨ 1 above. **13** in accordance with; in agreement with: *by request of my employer; by your leave,* with your permission; *by (the terms of) Article 3 of the Treaty.* **14** according to: *judging by appearances; by rights,* rightly. *By my watch it is 2 o'clock. That's nothing to go by,* One should not form judgements by that. **15** to the extent of: *The bullet missed me by two inches. It needs to be longer by two feet. He's too clever by half,* much too smart. ⇨ far²(2). **16** (in oaths) as surely as I believe in: *I swear by Almighty God that.... He swore by all that he held sacred that....* **17** (to express square or cubic measurement): *a carpet 30 metres by 20*

metres. **18** (arith) (to express division, = *divided by*): *15 by 3 is/equals 5.*

bye /baɪ/ n **1** sth subordinate or incidental: *by the bye.* ⇨ by¹(4). **2** (cricket) run scored on a ball that passes the batsman and the wicket-keeper.

bye-bye /'baɪ-baɪ/ n (child's word for) sleep, bed: *go to ~s* /'baɪ baɪz/. □ *int* /ˌbaɪ 'baɪ/ (colloq) goodbye.

by-elec·tion /'baɪ ɪlekʃn/ n election made necessary by the death or resignation of a member during the life of Parliament. ⇨ general election.

by·gone /'baɪgɒn *US:* -gɔːn/ *adj* past: *in ~ days,* in the time now past. □ *n (pl)* the past; past offences. *Let ~s be ~s,* Forgive and forget the past.

by-law, bye-law /'baɪlɔː/ n law or regulation made by a local, rather than a central, authority.

by-pass /'baɪpɑːs *US:* -pæs/ n new, wide road passing round a heavily populated urban area or village, to take through traffic. □ *vt* [VP6A] **1** provide with a ~: *a village/falls on a river.* **2** make a detour round (a town, etc); (fig) *Let's ~ that proposal,* ignore it.

by·path /'baɪpɑːθ *US:* -pæθ/ n less important or less direct path.

by·play /'baɪpleɪ/ n [U] (theatre) action apart from that of the main story; dumb-show of minor characters.

by-prod·uct /'baɪprɒdʌkt/ n [C] substance obtained during the manufacture of some other substance: *Ammonia, coal-tar and coke are valuable ~s obtained in the manufacture of coal-gas.*

by-road /'baɪrəʊd/ n side road; road that is not much used.

by·stander /'baɪstændə(r)/ n person standing near but not taking part in an event or activity: *She was only an innocent ~.*

by-way /'baɪweɪ/ n secondary or side road: (fig) *~s of history/literature, etc,* less known departments of history, etc.

by·word /'baɪwɜːd/ n person, place, etc regarded and spoken of as a notable example (usu bad): *She became the ~ of the village. The place was a ~ for iniquity.*

Cc

C, c /siː/ (*pl* C's, c's /siːz/) the third letter of the English alphabet; symbol for the Roman numeral 100, ⇨ App 4.

cab /kæb/ n **1** vehicle (now usu motorised, = *taxi-cab*) that may be hired for short journeys: *Shall we go by bus or take a cab?* **'cab·man** /-mən/ n (*pl* -men) driver of a cab. **'cab-rank** n row of cabs waiting to be hired. **'cab-stand** n place where cabs are authorized to wait for customers. ⇨ hansom; taxi. **2** part of a railway engine for the driver and fireman; part of a bus, lorry, etc for the driver.

ca·bal /kə'bæl/ n (group of persons who carry on) secret intrigue (esp in politics).

cab·aret /'kæbəreɪ *US:* ˌkæbə'reɪ/ n (also '~ show) entertainment (songs, dancing, etc) provided in a restaurant etc, while guests are at table.

cab·bage /'kæbɪdʒ/ n [C] (kinds of) cultivated plant with a round head (often called the *heart*) of thick greenish-white or reddish-purple leaves, ⇨ the illus at vegetable; [U] these leaves cooked as a vegetable or eaten as salad, ⇨ coleslaw.

cabby /'kæbɪ/ n (colloq) driver of a cab.

ca·ber /'keɪbə(r)/ n trunk of a roughly trimmed young fir-tree tossed in games (in the Highlands of Scotland) as a trial of strength and skill: *toss the ~.*

cabin /'kæbɪn/ n **1** room in a ship or aircraft, esp (in a ship) one for sleeping in. '~ cruiser n large motor- boat with a ~ or ~s. **2** small, usu roughly made house (eg of logs); railway signal-box.

cabi·net /'kæbɪnɪt/ n **1** piece of furniture with drawers or shelves for storing or displaying things: *a 'medicine ~; a 'filing ~,* for storing letters, documents; *a 'china ~,* often with a glass front, for displaying ornamental china. '~-maker n skilled workman who makes fine furniture. **2** plastic, wooden or metal container for radio or record-playing equipment. **3** group of men (chief ministers of state) chosen by the head of the government (the prime minister in GB) to be responsible for government administration and policy. 'C~ Minister, one of these men. **4** (old use) private room.

cable /'keɪbl/ n **1** [C,U] (length of) thick, strong

rope (of fibre or wire strands), used for making ships fast; rope or chain of an anchor. **2 '∿('s)-length** *n* 100 fathoms, one-tenth of a nautical mile. ⊏> App **5. 3** thick rope of wire strands for supporting a bridge, etc. **'∿-car, '∿-railway,** one up a steep hillside, worked by a ∿ and a stationary engine; funicular railway. **4** protected bundle of insulated wires (laid underground or on the ocean bottom) for carrying messages by electric telegraph; message so carried (= ∿gram). **5** insulated wires for conveying electric power overhead (⊏> the illus at pylon) or underground. □ *vt, vi* [VP6A,2A] send (a message), communicate, inform (sb) by ∿(4). **'∿-gram** /'keɪblgræm/ *n* ∿d telegram.

ca·boodle /kə'buːdl/ *n* (sl) **the whole ∿,** (of persons or things) all; the lot.

ca·boose /kə'buːs/ *n* **1** room on a ship's deck in which cooking is done. **2** (US) small van at the end of a freight train for the use of the train men.

ca' canny /ˌkɑː 'kænɪ/ *n* workers' policy of restricting output (by working slowly).

ca·cao /kə'kɑːəʊ/ *n* **1** (also **'∿-bean**) seed of a tropical tree from which cocoa and chocolate are made. **2** (also **'∿-tree**) the tree.

cache /kæʃ/ *n* (hiding-place for) food and stores left (eg by explorers) for later use. □ *vt* place in a ∿.

ca·chet /'kæʃeɪ *US:* kæ'ʃeɪ/ *n* distinguishing mark (to prove excellence, authenticity).

ca·chou /'kæʃuː *US:* kə'ʃuː/ *n* scented sweet formerly used by smokers to disguise the odour of tobacco in the breath.

cackle /'kækl/ *n* [U] noise made by a hen after laying an egg; [C] loud laugh; [U] foolish talk. □ *vi* (of a hen) make this noise; (of a person) talk or laugh noisily. **cack·ler** *n*

ca·coph·ony /kæ'kɒfənɪ/ *n* loud, unpleasant mixture of sounds; discord(3). **ca·coph·onous** /-nəs/ *adj*

cac·tus /'kæktəs/ (*pl* ∿es or cacti /'kæktaɪ/) (sorts of) plant from hot, dry climates with a thick, fleshy stem, usu with no leaves and covered with clusters of spines or prickles.

cactuses

cad /kæd/ *n* person guilty of or capable of dishonourable behaviour. **cad·dish** /'kædɪʃ/ *adj* of or like a cad: *a caddish trick.*

ca·daver /kə'deɪvə(r) *US:* kə'dævər/ *n* corpse. **∿·ous** /kə'dævərəs/ *adj* looking like a corpse; deadly pale.

caddy[1], **caddie** /'kædɪ/ *n* (*pl* -dies) person who is paid to carry a golfer's clubs for him round the course.

caddy[2] /'kædɪ/ *n* small box for holding the dried leaves used for making tea.

ca·dence /'keɪdns/ *n* rhythm in sound; the rise and fall of the voice in speaking; (music) sequence of sounds moving towards a pause or an end.

ca·denza /kə'denzə/ *n* ornamental passage to be played by the soloist, usu near the end of a movement, in an instrumental concerto.

ca·det /kə'det/ *n* **1** student at a naval, military or air force college. **'∿ corps** *n* (at some GB schools) organization that gives military training to older boys. **2** young person under training for a profession: **'police ∿s; British Council ∿s.**

cadge /kædʒ/ *vt, vi* [VP6A,14,2A] ∿ **(from),** beg; (try to) get by begging: ∿ *a meal from Auntie Ruby; be always cadging.* **cad·ger** *n* person who ∿s; beggar.

cad·mium /'kædmɪəm/ *n* [U] soft, silvery-white tin-like metal (symbol **Cd**).

cadre /'kɑːdə(r) *US:*'kædrɪ/ *n* **1** framework. **2** (mil) permanent establishment of a regiment, that can be expanded when necessary; hence, small group of important persons.

Caesar /'siːzə(r)/ *n* title of the Roman emperors from Augustus to Hadrian; any Roman emperor. **∿·ian** /sɪ'zeərɪən/ **('section/'birth),** delivery of a child by cutting the walls of the abdomen and uterus.

caesura /sɪ'zjʊərə *US:* -'ʒʊərə/ *n* point at which a pause naturally occurs in a line of verse.

café /'kæfeɪ *US:* kæ'feɪ/ *n* (in Europe) place where the public may buy and drink coffee, beer, wine, spirits, etc; (in GB) tea-shop, small restaurant at which meals (but not alcoholic drinks) may be bought. **∿-au-lait** /ˌkæfeɪ əʊ 'leɪ/ *n* (F) coffee with milk.

cafe·teria /ˌkæfɪ'tɪərɪə/ *n* restaurant at which customers collect their meals on trays at counters and carry them to tables.

caff /kæf/ *n* (GB sl) café.

caf·feine /'kæfiːn/ *n* [U] organic compound in tea leaves and coffee beans, used in medicine.

caf·tan /'kæftæn/ *n* long tunic with a girdle at the waist, worn by men in the Near East; woman's loosely hanging long dress.

cage /keɪdʒ/ *n* **1** framework, fixed or portable, with wires or bars, in which birds or animals may be kept. **2** camp for prisoners of war. **3** framework in which containers are lowered or raised in the shaft of a mine. □ *vt* [VP6A] put, keep, in a ∿: *a ∿d bird.*

cagey /'keɪdʒɪ/ *adj* (colloq) cautious about sharing confidences; uncommunicative; secretive. **cag·ily** *adv*

ca·goule /kə'guːl/ *n* light, waterproof garment with a hood and long sleeves, worn over clothes for protection against rain.

ca·hoots /kə'huːts/ *n pl* **be in ∿ (with),** (US sl) be planning sth (esp sth disreputable), be in league.

cai·man, cay·man /'keɪmən/ *n* S American reptile resembling an alligator.

cairn /keən/ *n* pyramid-shaped heap of rough stones set up as a landmark or a memorial.

cais·son /'keɪsn/ *n* **1** chest or wagon for ammunition, usu attached to a big gun on wheels. **2** large water-tight box or chamber in which men work under water (eg when building foundations): ∿ *disease,* ⊏> bend[2](3).

cai·tiff /'keɪtɪf/ *n* (old use) despicable or cowardly person.

ca·jole /kə'dʒəʊl/ *vt* [VPA,14] ∿ *sb* **(into/out of doing sth),** use flattery or deceit to persuade or soothe, or to get information, etc from sb. **ca·jol·ery** *n*

cake /keɪk/ *n* **1** [C,U] sweet mixture of flour, eggs, butter, etc baked in an oven: *an assortment of fancy* ~*s; a slice of* ~, ie of a large one that is cut into pieces. **a piece of** ~, (sl) sth very easy and pleasant. **(both) have one's cake and eat it,** both preserve sth unchanged and allow it to change (ie an impossibility). ~*s and ale,* merry-making. **(selling) like hot** ~*s,* very fast. **take the** ~, (colloq) be the extreme example of sth, ⇨ biscuit(1). **2** [C] mixture of other kinds of food, usu compressed and cooked in a round or ornamental shape: *'fish-*~*s;* *'oat-*~*s.* **3** [C] shaped piece of other materials or substances: *a* ~ *of soap/ tobacco.* ☐ *vt, vi* [VP6A,2A] coat thickly, become coated (*with* sth that becomes hard when dry); form into a thick hard mass: *His shoes were* ~*d with mud.*

cala·bash /'kæləbæʃ/ *n* (tree with) fruit or gourd of which the hard outer skin (or shell) is used as a container for liquids, grain, etc. ⇨ illus at **gourd.**

ca·lam·i·ty /kə'læmətɪ/ *n* (*pl* -ties) great and serious misfortune or disaster (eg a big earthquake or flood, becoming blind, the loss of all one's money). **ca·lami·tous** /kə'læmɪtəs/ *adj* marked by, causing, ~ (*to*).

cal·cify /'kælsɪfaɪ/ *vt, vi* [VP6A,2A] change, be changed, into lime; harden by deposit of lime.

cal·cine /'kælsaɪn/ *vt, vi* [VP6A,2A] make, be made, into quicklime or powder by roasting or burning; burn to ashes. **cal·ci·na·tion** /ˌkælsɪ'neɪʃn/ *n* conversion of metals into their oxides by burning.

cal·cium /'kælsɪəm/ *n* soft white metal (symbol **Ca**), the chemical basis of many compounds essential to life (occurs in bones and teeth, and forms part of limestone, marble and chalk). ~ **'carbide** *n* compound of ~ and carbon (CaC_2), used with water to make acetylene gas (C_2H_2). ~ **hydroxide** /haɪ'drɒksaɪd/ *n* slaked lime.

cal·cu·lable /'kælkjʊləbl/ *adj* that may be measured, reckoned or relied upon.

cal·cu·late /'kælkjʊleɪt/ *vt, vi* **1** [VP6A,9,8,10,2A] find out by working with numbers: ~ *the cost of a journey. Astronomers can* ~ *when there will be eclipses of the sun and moon.* **'calculating ma-chine** *n* one that works with numbers automatically. **2 be** ~**d to,** be planned or designed to: *This advertisement is* ~*d to attract the attention of housewives. a* ~*d insult,* said or done on purpose. **3** [VP3A] ~ **on,** (US) depend, bank (the usu words in GB) on: *We can't* ~ *on having fine weather for the sports meeting.* **4** [VP9] (US) suppose, believe. **5** [VP9] weigh reasons, etc and be confident (*that* sth will happen, etc); estimate. **cal·cu·lat·ing** *adj* scheming; shrewd; crafty. **cal·cu·la·tion** /ˌkælkjʊ'leɪʃn/ *n* [U] act of calculating; careful thought; [C] result of this: *After much* ~, *they decided to give Phil the position of manager. I'm out in my* ~*s,* have made a mistake in them. **calcu·la-tor** /-tə(r)/ *n* person who ~*s;* calculating machine.

cal·cu·lus /'kælkjʊləs/ *n* (*pl* -li /-laɪ/ or -luses /-ləsɪz/) **1** branch of mathematics divided into two parts, (**differential** ~ and **integral** ~), that deals with variable quantities, used to solve many mathematical problems. **2** (med) stone in some part of the human body.

cal·dron /'kɔːldrən/ *n* = cauldron.

cal·en·dar /'kælɪndə(r)/ *n* **1** list of the days, weeks, months, of a particular year; list with dates that are important to certain groups of people. **2** system by which time is divided into fixed periods, and mark-

ing the beginning and end of a year: *the Muslim* ~; *the Gregorian* ~ (with every fourth year a leap year of 366 days). '~ **month** *n* month as marked on the ~ (contrasted with a lunar month of 28 days).

cal·en·der /'kælɪndə(r)/ *n* roller-machine for pressing and smoothing cloth or paper. ☐ *vt* [VP6A] put through a ~.

cal·ends, kal·ends /'kælendz/ *n pl* first of the month in the ancient Roman calendar. **on the Greek** ~, never.

calf¹ /kɑːf *US:* kæf/ *n* **1** (*pl* calves /kɑːvz *US:* kævz)/ young of the domestic cow, ⇨ the illus at domestic; young of the seal, whale and some other animals for the first year. Cf *bull, cow, heifer, ox, steer.* **cow in** ~, pregnant cow. '~**love** *n* childish love affair; love of a young or inexperienced person. **2** [U] (also '~ **skin**) leather from the skin of a ~, esp as used in bookbinding and shoemaking.

calf² /kɑːf *US:* kæf/ *n* (*pl* **calves** /kɑːvz *US:* kævz/) fleshy part of the back of the human leg, between the knee and the ankle. ⇨ the illus at **leg.**

cali·brate /'kælɪbreɪt/ *vt* [VP6A] determine or correct the calibre or scale of a thermometer, gauge or other graduated instrument. **cali·bra·tion** /ˌkælɪ'breɪʃn/ *n* degree marks, etc on a measuring instrument.

cal·ibre (US = **cali·ber**) /'kælɪbə(r)/ *n* **1** [C] inside diameter of a tube/gun/barrel, etc. **2** [U] quality of mind or character; (person's) standing or importance: *a woman of high* ~.

cal·ico /'kælɪkəʊ/ *n* [U] cotton cloth, esp plain white cloth used for bed sheets, or with coloured designs printed on it, used for shirts, dresses, etc.

cali·pers /'kælɪpəz/ *n pl* (US) = callipers.

ca·liph, ca·lif /'keɪlɪf/ *n* title once used by rulers who were descendants and successors of Muhammad; chief civil and religious Muslim ruler: *the* **C**~ *of Baghdad.* ~·**ate** /'kælɪfeɪt/ *n* ~'s position and territory.

cal·is·then·ics /ˌkælɪs'θenɪks/ *n pl* (US) = callisthenics.

calk¹ /kɔːk/ *vt, n* [VP6A] (provide with a) sharp iron plate in a horse-shoe or boot to prevent slipping.

calk² /kɔːk/ *vt* = caulk.

call¹ /kɔːl/ *n* **1** shout; cry: *a* ~ *for help. They came at my* ~, when I shouted to them. **within** ~, within ~ing distance: *Please remain within* ~, close at hand. **2** characteristic cry of a bird; military signal (on a bugle, etc). **3** short visit (to sb's house, etc); short stop (at a place): *pay a* ~ *on a friend. I have several* ~*s to make. I must return their* ~, visit them because they visited me. **port of** ~, one at which a ship stops for a short time. **4** message; summons; invitation: *telephone* ~*s. I'll give you a* ~. *He felt the* ~ *of the sea,* i—e to be a sailor. '~**-box** *n* small cabin (in GB more usu called a *telephone kiosk*) with a public telephone. '~**-girl** *n* prostitute hired by a telephone ~. **5** demand for money (esp unpaid capital from company shareholders); claim of any kind: *I have many* ~*s on my time.* '~**-loan;** '~**-money; money on** ~; **money payable at/on** ~, money lent on condition that its return can be demanded without notice. **6** [U] (chiefly interr and neg) need; occasion: *There's no* ~ *for you to worry.* **7** player's right or turn to make a bid at bridge²; bid thus made: *Whose* ~ *is it? Was the last* ~ *two spades?*

call² /kɔːl/ *vt, vi* (For special uses with adverbial

particles and *preps,* ⇨ **9** below.) **1** [VP2A,B,3A] say sth in a loud voice; cry; speak or shout to attract attention: *Why doesn't my son come when I ∼? I thought I heard somebody ∼ing. She ∼ed to her father for help. I've been ∼ing (for) ten minutes.* ∼ **out,** cry or shout when needing help, or from surprise, pain, etc. ⇨ **9** below. **2** [VP2A,C,3A,4A] ∼ **(on sb/at a place),** pay a short visit; go to sb's house/office etc; stop at: *I ∼ed on Mr Green. I ∼ed at Mr Green's house. I ∼ed to see Mr Green. Mr Green was out when I ∼ed. A man has ∼ed to read the gas meter.* ∼ **for,** visit (a house, etc) to get sth, or to go somewhere with sb: *A man ∼s every Monday for old newspapers. I'll ∼ for you at 6 o'clock.* ∼**er** *n* person who ∼s on sb; visitor. **3** [VP23] name; describe as: *His name is Richard but we all ∼ him Dick. What are you going to ∼ the baby? He ∼s himself a colonel,* claims that he has the right to this title. *You may ∼ it what you like.* ⇨ also spade(1). ∼ **sb names,** abuse or insult him. ∼ **sth one's own,** claim as one's own property: *We have nothing that we can ∼ our own.* ∼ **into being,** create. ∼ **it a day,** ⇨ day(3). ∼ **into play,** ⇨ play²(8). **4** [VP22,23] consider; regard as: *Do you ∼ English an easy language? I ∼ that a shame. I ∼ that dishonest. Shall we ∼ it five quid,* (colloq) settle the price, sum, etc at five pounds? **5** [VP6A,15B] summon; wake; send a message to: *Please ∼ a doctor. Please ∼ me* (= wake me up) *at 6 tomorrow morning. The aircraft was ∼ing* (ie sending radio signals to) *the control station at the airport. This is London ∼ing,* is the BBC, London. *The doctor was ∼ed away to an accident. My brother ∼ed me* (*up*) (= telephoned to me) *from Leeds last night.* [VP12B,13B] (colloq): *Please ∼ me a taxi/∼ a taxi for me.* **be/feel ∼ed to do sth,** be/feel it to be one's duty to do it: *∼ed to be a doctor/to practise medicine.* ∼**-ing** *n* special duty; profession; occupation. **6** (special uses, with *nouns*) ∼ **sb's bluff,** ⇨ bluff². ∼ **a halt (to),** say that it is time to halt: ∼ *a halt to gambling,* forbid it. ∼ **a meeting,** announce that one will be held and summon people to attend. ∼ **the roll,** ⇨ roll²(4). ∼ **a strike,** order workers to come out on strike. **7** (card-games) bid or make a demand. ⇨ call¹(7). **8** (phrases) ∼ **(sb) to account,** ⇨ account¹(4). ∼ **attention to,** require (sb) to give his attention to. ∼ **the banns,** ⇨ banns. **be ∼ed to the bar,** ⇨ bar¹(12). ∼ **sth in/into question,** declare that one has doubts about it. ∼ **sb/a meeting to order,** ask for orderly behaviour, ask that attention should be paid to the rules. **9** [VP15B,3A] (special uses with *adverbial particles* and *preps*):
call by, (colloq) visit briefly (usu when passing the house, etc).
call sb down, (US sl) reprimand him severely. ∼ **sth down,** invoke, ask for it: ∼ *down curses on his head.*
call for, demand, require: *You must take such steps as seem (to be) ∼ed for,* do what seems necessary. *The occasion ∼s for prompt action.*
call sth forth, (a) be the cause of: *His behaviour ∼ed forth numerous protests.* (b) produce and use: *You will have to ∼ forth all your energy.*
call sth in, order or request the return of: *The librarian has ∼ed in all books. Gold coins were ∼ed in by the Government. He was so short of money that he had to ∼ in the loans he had made.*
call sth off, (a) ∼ away: *Please ∼ your dog off,* ∼

to your dog so that it stops worrying me. (b) decide, give orders, to stop sth: *The strike/attack was ∼ed off,* was either not started or was stopped. *You had better ∼ the deal off,* not carry out what was agreed upon.
call on/upon sb, (a) make a short visit to. ⇨ **2** above. (b) ∼ **on/upon sb (to do sth),** appeal to, invite, require him: *I ∼ed on* (= appealed to) *him to keep his promise. I now ∼ upon* (= invite) *Mr Grey to address the meeting. I feel ∼ed upon* (= feel that I ought) *to warn you that...*
call sb out, (a) summon, esp to an emergency: *The fire brigade was ∼ed out twice yesterday. Troops had to be ∼ed out.* (b) instruct (workers) to come out on strike: *The coal-miners were ∼ed out by the Union officials.*
call sth over, read (a list of names) to learn who is present. '∼**-over** *n* (also '**roll-**∼) reading of a list of names (eg in school, the army).
call sb/sth up, (a) telephone to: *I'll ∼ you up this evening.* (b) bring back to the mind: ∼ *up scenes of childhood.* (c) summon for (military, etc) service: *If war breaks out, we shall be ∼ed up at once.* Hence, '∼**-up** *n*

cal·li·gra·phy /kə'lɪgrəfɪ/ *n* [U] (art of) beautiful handwriting.
cal·li·ope /kə'laɪəpɪ/ *n* steam-organ; musical instrument with steam whistles played by pressing keys.
cal·li·pers /'kælɪpəz/ *n pl* (**pair of**) ∼, **1** instrument for measuring the diameter of round objects or the calibre of tubes, etc. **2** metal supports attached to the legs of a disabled person to enable him to walk.

for outside
measurement

for inside
measurement

callipers

cal·lis·then·ics /ˌkælɪs'θenɪks/ *n pl* (usu with a *sing v*) exercises designed to develop strong and graceful bodies.
cal·los·ity /kæ'lɒsətɪ/ *n* (*pl* -ties) area of hardened thick skin; callus.
cal·lous /'kæləs/ *adj* **1** (of the skin) made hard (by rough work, etc). **2** ∼ **(to),** (fig) unfeeling; indifferent: ∼ *to insults/his employees/the suffering of others.* ∼**·ness** *n*
cal·low /'kæləʊ/ *adj* young; unfledged; inexperienced: *a ∼ youth.* ∼**·ness** *n*
cal·lus /'kæləs/ *n* area of thick, hardened skin.
calm /kɑːm/ *adj* (-er, -est) **1** (of the weather) quiet; not windy; (of the sea) still; without large waves. **2** not excited; untroubled; quiet: *keep ∼.* □ *n a* ∼, a time when everything is quiet and peaceful. □ *vt,vi* [VP6A,15B,2C] ∼ **(down),** make or become ∼: *C∼ yourself! The sea ∼ed down.* ∼**·ly** *adv* ∼**·ness** *n* ∼ condition.
calo·mel /'kæləmel/ *n* [U] white, tasteless, insoluble substance used as a purgative.
Calor gas /'kælə gæs/ *n* [U] (P) butane.
cal·orie /'kælərɪ/ *n* unit of heat; unit of energy supplied by food: *An ounce of sugar supplies about 100 ∼s.* **cal·or·ific** /ˌkælə'rɪfɪk/ *adj* producing heat/energy: *calorific value,* (of food or fuel) quantity of heat/energy produced by a given quantity.
cal·umny /'kæləmnɪ/ *n* (*pl* -nies) (formal) [C]

false statement about a person, made to damage his character; [U] slander. **ca·lum·ni·ate** /kə'lʌmnɪeɪt/ vt [VP6A] slander.

Cal·vary /'kælvərɪ/ n hill outside Jerusalem where Jesus was crucified; carved representation of the Crucifixion.

calve /kɑːv US: kæv/ vi give birth to a calf.

Cal·vin·ism /'kælvɪnɪzəm/ n religious teaching of the French Protestant, John Calvin (1509–64). **Cal·vin·ist** n follower of Calvin's teachings.

ca·lyp·so /kə'lɪpsəʊ/ n (pl ~s /-səʊz/) improvised song, as composed by West Indians, on a subject of current interest.

ca·lyx /'keɪlɪks/ n (pl ~es or calyces /'keɪlɪsiːz/) ring of leaves (called *sepals*) forming the outer support of the petals of an unopened flower-bud. ⇨ the illus at flower.

cam /kæm/ n projection on a wheel or shaft, designed to change circular motion into up-and-down or back-and-forth motion. **cam·shaft** /'kæmʃɑːft US: -ʃæft/ n (eg in a car) shaft to which cams are attached.

cama·rad·erie /ˌkæməˈrɑːdərɪ US: -'ræd-/ n (F) [U] friendliness and mutual trust of comrades.

cam·ber /'kæmbə(r)/ n upwards slope (eg of a road surface) of a curve. □ vt, vi (of a surface) have a ~; give a ~ to.

cam·bric /'keɪmbrɪk/ n [U] fine, thin cloth of cotton or linen.

came pt of come.

camel /'kæml/ n long-necked animal, with either one (*dromedary*) or two humps on its back, used in desert countries for riding and for carrying goods. ⇨ the illus at large. '~-hair n fine hair for making the brushes used by artists; soft, heavy cloth of this hair: a ~-hair coat.

ca·mel·lia /kə'miːlɪə/ n evergreen shrub from China and Japan with shiny leaves and white, red or pink rose-like flowers; the flower.

Cam·em·bert /'kæməmbeə(r)/ n (F) rich, soft cheese (of Normandy, France).

cameo /'kæmɪəʊ/ n (pl ~s /-əʊz/) 1 piece of hard stone with a raised design, often used as a jewel or ornament. 2 short piece of writing or acting conveying the essential qualities of a person, place, event etc.

cam·era /'kæmərə/ n 1 apparatus for taking still photographs or ('film/'movie ~) moving pictures, or (T'V ~) for receiving light images and transforming them for broadcasting them or for receiving on video tape. '~-man /-mæn/ n (pl -men) person who operates a ~ for films or TV. 2 in ~, (Lat) in the judge's private room, not in court; privately.

cam·ion /'kæmɪən/ n (F) low, four-wheeled truck; lorry.

camo·mile, chamo·mile /'kæməmaɪl/ n [U] sweet-smelling plant with daisy-like flowers; the dried flowers and leaves used in medicine as a tonic.

cam·ou·flage /'kæməflɑːʒ/ n [U] 1 that which makes it difficult to recognize the presence or real nature of sth: *The white fur of the polar bear is a natural ~*, because the bear is not easily seen in the snow. 2 (in war) the use of paint, netting, boughs of trees, smoke-screens, etc to deceive the enemy by giving a false appearance to things. □ vt [VP6A] try to conceal by means of ~.

camp¹ /kæmp/ n 1 place where people (eg people on holiday, soldiers, boy scouts, explorers) live in tents or huts for a time: *be in ~; pitch a ~; strike/ break up ~*, pack up (the tents, etc). **~-'bed/ 'chair/-'stool** n one that can be folded and carried easily. **'~-fire** n one of logs, etc, made in the open air. **'~-follower** n person (not a soldier) who follows an army to sell goods or services. ⇨ also concentration ~. 2 number of people with the same ideas (esp on politics or religion): *You and I belong to different political ~s. We're in the same ~*, are in agreement, are working together. □ vi [VP2A,C] ~ (out), make, live in, a ~: *Where shall we ~ tonight? They ~ed out in the woods.* **go ~ing**, spend a holiday in tents, etc: *The boys have decided to go ~ing next summer.* **~er** n ~ing n (gerund) [U] a ~ing holiday; Do you like ~ing?

camp² /kæmp/ adj (colloq) exaggeratedly stylish: ~ acting; deliberately and amusingly old-fashioned: *those ~ old silent movies;* affectedly effeminate: *a ~ walk.* □ n exaggeration and affectation of this sort. □ vi, vt ~ (it up), behave in this way.

cam·paign /kæm'peɪn/ n [C] 1 group of military operations with a set purpose, usu in one area. 2 series of planned activities to gain a special object: *a political ~; an advertising ~; a ~ to raise funds.* □ vi [VP2A,3A] take part in, go on, a ~. □

cameras

EXPOSURE METER
TELEVISION CAMERA
FLASH LIGHT
view-finder
ground glass
mirror
spool
film
view-finder
lens
lens
CINE-CAMERA
TWIN-LENS REFLEX CAMERA
35MM CAMERA

~er *n* person who ~s or who ~ed: *He's an old ~er*, has much experience of adapting himself to circumstances.

cam·pa·nile /ˌkæmpə'niːlɪ/ *n* bell tower, usu a separate building.

cam·pan·ula /kəm'pænjʊlə/ *n* (kinds of) plant with bell-shaped flowers, usu blue or white.

cam·phor /'kæmfə(r)/ *n* [U] strong-smelling white substance used medically and in the manufacture of celluloid. '~ **ball** *n* small ball of ~, used to keep moths, etc out of clothes. ~**ated** /'kæmfəreɪtɪd/ *adj* containing ~: *~ated oil*.

cam·pion /'kæmpɪən/ *n* [U] (kinds of) common flowering plant that grows wild on roadsides and in fields.

cam·pus /'kæmpəs/ *n* (*pl* ~es /-pəsɪz/) grounds of a school, college or university.

can¹ /kæn/ *n* **1** metal container, usu with a lid, for liquids, etc: '*oil-can,* '*milk-can.* **carry the can (for sb),** (sl) take the blame. *(be) in the can,* (of film, video-tape) exposed or recorded and stored ready for use. **2** (formerly US but now also GB) tin-plated airtight container for food, drink etc; contents of such a container: *a can of beer/peaches*. ⇨ tin. **3** (US sl) prison. □ *vt* (-nn-) [VP6A] preserve (food, etc) by putting in a can(**2**) which is then hermetically sealed: *canned fish; canned music,* (sl) music recorded on discs, etc. **canned** /kænd/ *adj* (US sl) drunk. **can·nery** /'kænərɪ/ *n* place where food etc is canned.

can² /kən; *strong form:* kæn/ *anom fin* (*neg* cannot /'kænət/ or can't /kɑːnt US:* kænt/, *pt* could /kəd; *strong form:* kʊd/, *neg* couldn't /'kʊdnt/) [VP5] **1** (indicating ability or capacity to do sth) be able to; know how to: *Can you lift this box? I can't get the lid off. She can speak French.* (*Could* refers to ability or capacity in past time): *She could read Latin and Greek when she was ten.* (*Could* is used in *if*-clauses to indicate a condition, expressed or implied): *Could you lift that box* (ie now, if you tried)? *Could you have lifted that box* (ie if you had tried, eg yesterday)? (Note that *could* is not used, except in conditions, for an isolated achievement in past time. Instead, *be able to, manage to* or *succeed in* (*doing sth*) are preferred): *When the boat upset, they were able/managed to swim/succeeded in swimming to the bank* (not *they could swim to the bank* which is incorrect). **2** (*Can* is used with *vv* of perception in place of the simple tenses, which are less usual. Nothing is added to the meaning.): *I can see a sail on the horizon. I can hear people talking in the next room.* (*Could* is used for past time): *We could hear someone singing in the bathroom. She said she could smell something burning.* **3** (*Can* is used, colloquial style, to indicate permission. The use of *may* is more formal. In reported speech, *could* is used after a *v* in the *pt. Could* may also replace *can* in a tentative request in question form): *You can* (= may) *go home now. The children asked whether they could* (= might) *go for a swim. You can't travel first-class with a second-class ticket. Put that cigarette out—you can't smoke near a petrol pump!* **4** (*Can/could* are used to indicate what is possible or likely): *One of the prisoners escaped yesterday—he can/could* (= may) *be anywhere by now.* (*Can have* is used for past time): *He's an hour late—he can have been delayed by fog, of course,* that's a possibility. **5** (*Can/could* in questions (and esp with *what*(*ever*), *where, how*) indicate surprise, bewilderment, im-

patience, etc, according to context. The strong forms are used): *What ,can he 'mean? What ,can we 'do about it? Where ,can they have' got to? How ,can/,could you be so unkind?* **6** (*Can/could* indicate what is considered characteristic, what sb or sth is considered capable of being or doing. Adverbials of frequency (eg *at times, sometimes*) often occur): *Children can sometimes be very trying. It can be very cold here, even in May. The Bay of Biscay can be very rough at times. When I first knew her she could be very sarcastic, but she's more tolerant now.* **7** (*Could* is used to mean 'feel inclined to'): *I could smack your face!* **8** (*can* is used, colloquial style with imperative force, meaning 'must'): *Tell Mr Evans that he can come in now,* Tell him to come in. **9** (*can/could* are used in polite requests; ⇨ will¹(**3**)): *Do you think I could leave now/Could I leave now, do you think?* Please may I leave now? *Could you put out your cigarette, please?* Please put it out.

Ca·na·dian /kə'neɪdɪən/ *n, adj* (native) of Canada.

ca·nal /kə'næl/ *n* **1** channel cut through land for use of boats or ships (eg **the Suez** /'suːɪz/ **C~**) or to carry water to fields for irrigation. ⇨ the illus at lock. '~ **boat** *n* long, narrow boat, some of which are pulled by horses, used on ~s. **2** tube or pipe (or system of these) in a plant or animal body for food, air, etc: *the alimentary ~.* ⇨ the illus at alimentary, ear. ~**ize** /'kænəlaɪz/ [VP6A,14] make (a river) into a ~ (by straightening, building locks, etc); (fig) direct; channel: ~*ize one's energies/ efforts into charity work.* ~**iz·ation** /ˌkænəlaɪ'zeɪʃn US:* -nəlɪ'z-/ *n*

can·apé /'kænəpeɪ US:* ˌkænə'peɪ/ *n* (F) thin piece of bread or toast spread with seasoned fish, cheese, etc.

ca·nard /kæ'nɑːd/ *n* (F) false report.

ca·nary /kə'neərɪ/ *n* (*pl* -ries) **1** (also '~-**bird**) small, yellow-feathered song-bird, usu kept in a cage; [U] its colour, light yellow. **2** (also '~-**wine**) sweet white wine from the C~ Islands.

ca·nasta /kə'næstə/ *n* card game for two to six players using two packs of cards.

can·can /'kænkæn/ *n* lively high-kicking dance performed by a group of women in long skirts.

can·cel /'kænsl/ *vt,vi* (-ll-, US -l-) [VP6A] cross out, draw a line through (words or figures); make a mark on (sth, eg postage stamps, to prevent reuse): ~*led stamps.* **2** [VP6A] say that sth already arranged or decided upon will not be done, will not take place, etc: *He ~led his order for the goods,* said that he no longer wanted to receive them. *The sports meeting was ~led.* **3** [VP2C,15B] ~ **out,** (arith) (of items from the numerator and denominator) equalize each other; (fig) neutralize, make up for, each other: *The arguments ~ (each other) out.* ~**la·tion** /ˌkænsə'leɪʃn/ *n* [U] ~ling or being ~led; [C] instance of this; mark(s) used in, made by, ~ling (eg on postage stamps).

can·cer /'kænsə(r)/ *n* [C,U] diseased growth in the body, often causing death: ~ *of the throat;* '*lung ~*; (fig) pernicious evil (eg in Society). ~**ous** /'kænsərəs/ *adj* of or like ~; having ~.

Can·cer /'kænsə(r)/ *n* **Tropic of ~,** the parallel of latitude 23½°N; fourth sign of the zodiac, ⇨ the illus at zodiac.

can·de·la·brum /ˌkændɪ'lɑːbrəm/ *n* (*pl* -bra /-brə/) ornamental holder, with branches, for candles.

can·did /'kændɪd/ *adj* **1** frank, straightforward: *I* *will be quite* ∼ *with you: I think you acted foolishly.* **2** ∼ **camera,** small camera for taking informal or unposed photographs of people. ∼**·ly** *adv*

can·di·date /'kændɪdət *US:* -deɪt/ *n* **1** person who wishes, or who is put forward by others, to take an office or position (eg for election to Parliament): *The Labour* ∼ *was elected. He offered himself as a* ∼ *for the post/job/position.* **2** person taking an examination. **can·di·da·ture** /'kændɪdətʃə(r)/ *n* being a ∼(1).

can·died ⇨ candy.

candle /'kændl/ *n* round stick of wax, etc with a wick through it, which is lit to burn with a light-giving flame. *burn the* ∼ *at both ends,* use up too much energy; work very early and very late. *can't/is not fit to hold a* ∼ *to,* is not to be compared to, is not nearly so good as. *The game is not worth the* ∼, is more trouble and expense than it is worth. '∼**·light** *n* light of ∼s: *reading by* ∼*light.* '∼**·power** *n* unit of light measurement: *a ten* ∼*-power lamp.* '∼**·stick** *n* holder for (usu) a single ∼.

can·dour (*US* = -dor) /'kændə(r)/ *n* [U] quality of being candid; saying freely what one thinks.

candy /'kændɪ/ *n* **1** (also ,sugar-'∼) [U] sugar made hard by repeated boilings; [C] (*pl* -dies) piece of this. **2** [C,U] (*US* only; *GB* = *sweet(s)*) shaped piece(s) of cooked and flavoured sugar, syrup, etc usu with fruit juices, milk, nuts, etc added. □ *vt,vi* **1** [VP6A] preserve (eg fruit) by boiling or cooking in sugar: *candied plums/lemon peel.* **2** [VP2A] form into sugar crystals.

candy·tuft /'kændɪtʌft/ *n* garden plant with flat tufts of white, pink or purple flowers.

cane /keɪn/ *n* **1** long, hollow, jointed stem of tall reeds and grass-like plants (eg bamboo, sugar-∼), either [U] collectively and as material for making furniture, etc or [C] of one stem or a length of it (eg used for supporting plants, as a walking-stick): *a chair with a* ∼ *seat; raspberry* ∼*s.* '∼ *sugar n* sugar made from sugar-∼, chemically the same as beet sugar. **2** length of ∼ used as an instrument for punishing children by beating. *get the* ∼, be punished with a ∼. □ *vt* [VP6A] punish with a ∼(2).

ca·nine /'keɪnaɪn/ *adj* of, as of, a dog or dogs. '∼ *tooth n* (in a human being) one of the four pointed teeth, one on each side of the four incisors, upper and lower. ⇨ the illus at mouth.

can·is·ter /'kænɪstə(r)/ *n* **1** small box (usu metal) with a lid, used for holding tea, etc. **2** cylinder which, when thrown, or fired from a gun, bursts and scatters its contents: *a 'tear-gas* ∼.

can·ker /'kæŋkə(r)/ *n* **1** [U] disease that destroys the wood of trees; disease that causes the formation of ulcers in the human mouth, in the ears of dogs and cats, etc. **2** (fig) evil influence or tendency that causes decay. □ *vt* destroy by ∼; be a ∼ to. ∼**·ous** /'kæŋkərəs/ *adj* of or like ∼; causing ∼.

canna /'kænə/ *n* plant with large, dark leaves and bright yellow, red or orange flowers; the flower.

can·na·bis /'kænəbɪs/ *n* [U] Indian hemp, a drug also known as *hashish* and *marijuana,* smoked or chewed as an intoxicant. ⇨ hemp.

can·ned, can·nery ⇨ can ¹.

can·ni·bal /'kænɪbl/ *n* person who eats human flesh; animal that eats its own kind; (attrib) of or like ∼s: *a* ∼ *feast.* ∼**·ism** /'kænɪbəlɪzəm/ *n* practice of eating the flesh of one's own kind. ∼**·is·tic** /,kænɪbə'lɪstɪk/ *adj* of or like ∼s. ∼**·ize** /'kænɪbəlaɪz/ *vt* use (one of a number of similar

machines, engines, etc) to provide spare parts for others.

can·non /'kænən/ *n* **1** (collective; *sing* often used instead of *pl*) large, heavy gun, fixed to the ground or to a guncarriage, esp the old kind that fired a solid ball of metal (called a '∼*-ball*). (*Gun* and *shell* are the words used for the modern weapons). **2** heavy, automatic gun, firing explosive shells, used in modern aircraft in war. '∼**-fodder** *n* men regarded as expendable material in war. ∼**·ade** /,kænə'neɪd/ *n* continued firing of big guns.

muzzle ———

a cannon

can·not /'kænət/ ⇨ can ².

canny /'kænɪ/ *adj* (-ier, -iest) not prepared to take unknown risks; shrewd, esp about money matters. **can·nily** *adv*

ca·noe /kə'nuː/ *n* light boat moved by one or more paddles. □ *vt* [VP2A,C] travel by ∼. ∼**·ist** *n* person who paddles a ∼.

paddle

canoeing

canon /'kænən/ *n* **1** ecclesiastical decree: ∼ *law,* church law. **2** general standard or principle by which sth is judged: *the* ∼*s of conduct/good taste.* **3** body of writings accepted as genuine; those books of the Bible accepted as genuine by the Christian Church: *the* ∼ *of Scripture; the Chaucer* ∼. **4** official list. **5** priest (with the title *the Rev*∼) who is one of a group with duties in a cathedral. ⇨ chapter(3). **ca·noni·cal** /kə'nɒnɪkl/ *adj* according to ∼ law; authorized; regular: ∼*ical books;* ∼*ical dress,* ie of priests.

canon·ize /'kænənaɪz/ *vt* [VP6A] (R C Church) officially proclaim to be a saint(3); (colloq) authorize permanently. **canon·iz·ation** /,kænənaɪ'zeɪʃn *US:* -nɪ'z-/ *n* canonizing or being ∼d.

cañon /'kænjən/ ⇨ canyon.

can·opy /'kænəpɪ/ *n* (*pl* -pies) (usu cloth) covering above a bed, throne, etc or held (on poles) over a person; cover for the cockpit of an aircraft, ⇨ the illus at air ¹; (fig) any overhanging covering: *the* ∼ *of the heavens,* the sky; *a* ∼ *of leaves,* eg in a forest.

cant ¹ /kænt/ *n* [U] **1** insincere talk (esp implying false piety); hypocrisy. **2** special talk, words, used by a class of people, a sect, etc; jargon: *thieves'* ∼;

(attrib) *a* ~ *phrase*.

cant² /kænt/ *n* sloping or sideways surface or position. □ *vt,vi* [VP6A,15B,2A,C] give, have, a ~: ~ *a boat for repairs*.

can't /kɑːnt *US:* kænt/ = cannot, ⇨ can².

Can·tab /'kæntæb/ *adj* of Cambridge University.

can·ta·loup, -loupe /'kæntəluːp/ *n* kind of melon.

can·tank·er·ous /kæn'tæŋkərəs/ *adj* bad-tempered; quarrelsome. ~·ly *adv*

can·tata /kæn'tɑːtə/ *n* short musical work to be sung by soloists and a choir, usu a dramatic story, but not acted. ⇨ oratorio, opera.

can·teen /kæn'tiːn/ *n* **1** place (esp in factories, offices, barracks) where food and drink are sold and meals bought and eaten. **2** box or chest of table silver and cutlery (knives, forks, spoons): *a* ~ *of cutlery*. **3** soldier's eating and drinking utensils.

can·ter /'kæntə(r)/ *n* (of a horse) easy gallop: *The horse won the race at a* ~, won easily. □ *vt,vi* (cause to) gallop gently.

can·ticle /'kæntɪkl/ *n* short hymn, esp one taken from the Bible.

can·ti·lever /'kæntɪliːvə(r)/ *n* long, large, armlike bracket extending from a wall or base (eg to support a balcony). '~ **bridge** *n* one built on supports from which ~s extend and join. ⇨ the illus at **bridge**.

canto /'kæntəʊ/ *n* (*pl* ~s /-təʊz/) chief division of a long poem.

can·ton /'kæntɒn/ *n* subdivision of a country (esp of Switzerland).

can·ton·ment /kæn'tuːnmənt *US:* -'təʊn-/ *n* permanent military station; place where soldiers live.

can·tor /'kæntɔː(r)/ *n* leader of the singing in a church or synagogue.

Ca·nuck /kə'nʊk/ *n* (US sl) (French) Canadian.

can·vas /'kænvəs/ *n* [U] strong, coarse cloth used for tents, sails, bags, etc and by artists for oil-paintings; [C] (piece of this for an) oil-painting. **under** ~, **(a)** (of soldiers, scouts, etc) living in tents. **(b)** (of a ship) with sails spread.

can·vass /'kænvəs/ *vt,vi* **1** [VP2A,3A] ~ **(for)**, go from person to person and ask for votes, orders for goods, subscriptions, etc or to learn about people's views on a question: *He is* ~*ing for the Conservative candidate*. **2** [VP6A] discuss thoroughly; examine by discussion: ~ *views/opinions*. □ *n* ~ing.

can·yon, cañon /'kænjən/ *n* deep gorge (usu with a river flowing through it).

cap /kæp/ *n* **1** soft head-covering worn by boys and men, by some sailors and soldiers, without a brim, but often with a peak; special cap awarded to members of football teams, etc or worn to show rank: *a cardinal's cap*; academic head-dress with a flat top and a tassel: *wearing his cap and gown*. ⇨ mortar-board. **2** indoor head-dress worn by nurses, and formerly by old women. **3** cap-like cover (eg on a milk bottle). **4** per'cussion cap, small quantity of gunpowder in a wrapper of paper, etc, used as a detonator. **5** (phrases) *cap and bells*, cap trimmed with bells, as formerly worn by jesters. *if the cap fits*, if a person feels that the remark applies to him. *cap in hand*, humbly. *set one's cap at sb*, (of a girl or woman) try to attract as a suitor. □ *vt* (-pp-) [VP6A] **1** put a cap on; cover the top of. **2** do or say sth better than (what sb else has done or said). *cap a story/joke*, tell a more amusing one. **3** award (a player) a cap (as a member of a football team, etc): *He's been capped 36 times for England*. (Scottish universities) confer a

degree on.

ca·pa·bil·ity /ˌkeɪpə'bɪlətɪ/ *n* **1** [U] power (*of* doing things, *to do* things); fitness or capacity (*for* being improved, etc): *nuclear* ~, power, capacity, to wage nuclear war. **2** (*pl*) (-ties) undeveloped faculties; qualities, etc, that can be developed: *The boy has great capabilities*.

ca·pable /'keɪpəbl/ *adj* **1** gifted; able: *a very* ~ *doctor/nurse/teacher*. **2** ~ *of*, **(a)** (of persons) having the power, ability or inclination: *Show your teacher what you are* ~ *of*, Show him how well you can work. *He's quite* ~ *of neglecting his duty*, is the sort of man who might do so. *He's* ~ *of any crime*. **(b)** (of things, situations, etc) ready for; admitting of; open to: *The situation is* ~ *of improvement*. ca·pably *adv*

ca·pa·cious /kə'peɪʃəs/ *adj* able to hold much: *a* ~ *memory*; ~ *pockets*. ~ness *n*

ca·pac·ity /kə'pæsətɪ/ *n* [U] (and with *indef art*) ability to hold, contain, get hold of, learn things/qualities/ideas etc: *The hall has a seating* ~ *of 500*, has seats for 500 people. *The theatre was filled to* ~, was quite full. *He has a mind of great* ~, a mind well able to grasp ideas. *This book is within the* ~ *of* (= can be understood by) *young readers*. *Some persons have more* ~ *for happiness* (= a greater power of experiencing happiness) *than others*. **2** [C] (*pl* -ties) position; character. *in one's* ~ *as*, in one's position as being: *I am your friend, but in my* ~ *as an officer of the law I must take you into custody*.

cap-à-pie /ˌkæpə'piː/ *adv* **armed** ~, armed from head to foot, completely.

ca·pari·son /kə'pærɪsn/ *n* (often *pl*; old use) ornamental covering for a horse, or for a horse and the knight who rode it. □ *vt* put a ~ on (a horse).

cape¹ /keɪp/ *n* loose sleeveless garment, hanging from the shoulders.

cape² /keɪp/ *n* high point of land going out into the sea; headland. **the C~**, (S Africa) the C~ of Good Hope; C~ Province.

ca·per¹ /'keɪpə(r)/ *vi* jump about playfully. □ *n cut a* ~/~s, jump about merrily; act foolishly or fantastically.

ca·per² /'keɪpə(r)/ *n* prickly shrub; (*pl*) pickled flower-buds of this shrub, used to make ~ sauce.

cap·il·lary /kə'pɪlərɪ *US:* 'kæpələrɪ/ *n* (*pl* -ries) tube with a hair-like diameter (eg joining the arteries and veins), ⇨ the illus at **respiratory**: (attrib) ~ *attraction*, attraction of the kind that causes blotting-paper to absorb ink, or oil to rise through the wick of an oil lamp.

capi·tal¹ /'kæpɪtl/ *n* (often attrib) **1** town or city where the government of a country, state or province is carried on: *Toronto is the* ~ *of Ontario*. *London, Paris and Rome are* ~ *cities*. **2** (of letters of the alphabet) not small: *The pronoun 'I' is written and printed with a* ~ *letter*. *Write your name in* ~ *letters/in* ~*s*. **3** head, top part, of a column. ⇨ the illus at column. □ *adj* **1** punishable by death: ~ *offences*. **2** (dated colloq) excellent, first-rate: *He made a* ~ *speech*. *What a* ~ *idea!*

capi·tal² /'kæpɪtl/ *n* [U] wealth/money/property that may be used for the production of more wealth; money with which a business, etc is started (eg for building or buying factories, buying machinery. ~ **expenditure**, money spent on equipment, building, etc. ~ **gain**, profit made from the sale of investments or property. ~ **goods**, goods used to produce other goods. ~ **levy**, taking by the

State of a part of all the private wealth in the country. **'fixed** ~, machinery, buildings, etc. **'floating** ~, ~ goods. *a* ~ *of,* ~ valued at: *make* ~ *of sth,* use it to one's own advantage.

capi·tal·ism /'kæpɪtəlɪzəm/ *n* [U] economic system in which a country's trade and industry are organized and controlled by the owners of capital², the chief elements being competition, profit, supply and demand. ⇨ socialism. **capi·tal·ist** *n* 1 person who controls much capital². 2 person who supports ~. □ *adj* of, supporting ~: *a capitalist economy.* **capi·tal·is·tic** /ˌkæpɪtə'lɪstɪk/ *adj*

capi·tal·ize /'kæpɪtəlaɪz/ *vt,vi* 1 [VP6A] write or print with a capital letter. 2 convert into, use as, capital²; (fig) take advantage of; use to one's advantage or profit. 3 [VP3A] ~ *on,* profit by; exploit: ~ *on the errors of a rival firm.* **capi·tal·iz·ation** /ˌkæpɪtəlaɪ'zeɪʃn US: -ɪ'zeɪʃn/ *n*

capi·ta·tion /ˌkæpɪ'teɪʃn/ *n* (reckoning of) tax, fee, charge or grant of an equal sum per person.

Capi·tol /'kæpɪtl/ *n* building in which the United States Congress meets.

ca·pitu·late /kə'pɪtʃʊleɪt/ *vt* [VP2A] surrender (on stated conditions). **ca·pitu·la·tion** /kəˌpɪtʃʊ'leɪʃn/ *n* [U] surrendering (on stated conditions).

ca·pon /'keɪpən US: -pɒn/ *n* cock (male domestic fowl) castrated and fattened for eating.

ca·price /kə'pri:s/ *n* 1 (often sudden) change of mind or behaviour that has no obvious cause; tendency to change suddenly without apparent cause. 2 piece of music in a lively, irregular style.

ca·pri·cious /kə'prɪʃəs/ *adj* often changing; irregular; unreliable; guided by caprice: *a* ~ *breeze,* often so suddenly changing in direction. ~·ly *adv*

Cap·ri·corn /'kæprɪkɔ:n/ *n* **Tropic of** ~, the parallel of latitude 23½°S; tenth sign of the zodiac, ⇨ the illus at zodiac.

cap·si·cum /'kæpsɪkəm/ *n* kinds of plant with seed-pods containing hot-tasting seeds; such pods prepared for use in cooking, etc. ⇨ cayenne, pepper(2).

cap·size /kæp'saɪz/ *vt,vi* [VP6A,2A] (esp of a boat in the water) (cause to) overturn, upset.

cap·stan /'kæpstən/ *n* upright barrel-like object turned (formerly) by men who walk round it pushing horizontal levers, or (more usu today) by steam, etc, power, used for raising anchors, sails, etc and for pulling a ship to a wharf, etc.

cap·sule /'kæpsju:l US: 'kæpsl/ *n* 1 seed-case that opens when the seeds are ripe. 2 tiny container (eg for a dose of medicine, often soluble). 3 (recoverable or non-recoverable) receptacle (for scientific instruments, or an astronaut) which can be ejected from a spacecraft.

a space-capsule

cap·tain /'kæptɪn/ *n* 1 leader or chief commander: *the* ~ *of a ship/fire-brigade/football or cricket team.* 2 (in the army) officer (below a major and above a lieutenant) who commands a company; (in the navy) officer below an admiral and above a commander. □ *vt* [VP6A] act as ~ of (a football team, etc).

cap·tion /'kæpʃn/ *n* short title or heading of an article in a periodical, etc; words printed with a photograph or illustration, etc; word(s) on a movie film to establish the scene of the story, etc (eg Dover 1940). Cf *sub-titles.*

cap·tious /'kæpʃəs/ *adj* (formal) (fond of) finding fault, making protests, etc esp about unimportant points. ~·ly *adv*

cap·ti·vate /'kæptɪveɪt/ *vt* [VP6A] capture the fancy of; fascinate: *He was* ~*d by Helen/*~*d with her charm.*

cap·tive /'kæptɪv/ *n, adj* 1 (person, animal) taken prisoner, kept as a prisoner. *be taken/hold sb* ~, take or keep him prisoner. ~ *'audience,* one that is held to the ground by a cable. 2 ~ *'audience,* one that cannot get away easily and is, therefore, open to persuasion (eg schoolchildren watching TV). **cap·tiv·ity** /kæp'tɪvətɪ/ *n* [U] state of being held ~: *Some birds will not sing in captivity.*

cap·tor /'kæptə(r)/ *n* person who takes sb captive.

cap·ture /'kæptʃə(r)/ *vt* [VP6A] make a prisoner of; take or obtain as a prize by force, trickery, skill, etc: *Our army* ~*d 500 of the enemy. The police have not* ~*d the thief yet. This advertisement will* ~ *the attention of readers everywhere.* □ *n* [U] act of capturing: *the* ~ *of a thief;* [C] thing that is ~d.

car /kɑ:(r)/ *n* 1 motor-car. ⇨ the illus at motor. **'car-ferry** *n* ferry (sea or air) for taking cars (eg across the English Channel). **'car-port** *n* open-sided shelter for a motor-vehicle. 2 (on a railway train) (in GB) coach: *'dining-car; 'sleeping-car,* (in US also) wagon for goods: *'freight-car* (GB = *'goods-wagon*). 3 that part of a balloon, airship or lift (US = *elevator*) used by passengers. 4 (poet) wheeled vehicle; chariot: *the car of the sun-god.*

ca·rafe /kə'ræf/ *n* water-bottle, or decanter for wine, for use at table.

cara·mel /'kærəmel/ *n* 1 [U] burnt sugar used for colouring and flavouring. 2 [C] small, shaped piece of sticky boiled sugar; sweetmeat.

cara·pace /'kærəpeɪs/ *n* shell on the back of a tortoise and crustaceans. ⇨ the illus at crustacean, reptile.

carat /'kærət/ *n* 1 unit of weight (= 200 milligrams or about three and one-fifth grains) for precious stones. ⇨ App 5. 2 (US = *karat*) measure of the purity of gold, pure gold being 24 ~s: *a gold ring of 20* ~s, ie 20 parts gold, 4 parts alloy.

cara·van /'kærəvæn/ *n* 1 company of persons (eg pilgrims, merchants) making a journey together for safety, usu across desert country. 2 covered cart or wagon used for living in, eg by Gypsies or people on holiday, esp (today) the kind pulled behind a motor vehicle. ⇨ also trailer at trail(1). ~·ning *n* (the practice of) taking holidays in a ~. ~·sary, ~·serai /ˌkærə'vænsəraɪ, -səraɪ/ *n* inn with a large inner courtyard where ~s put up in Eastern countries.

cara·way /'kærəweɪ/ *n* plant with spicy seeds used to flavour bread, cakes, etc.

car·bide /'kɑ:baɪd/ *n* compound of carbon. ⇨ calcium.

car·bine /'kɑ:baɪn/ *n* short rifle (originally for soldiers on horseback).

carbo·hy·drate /ˌkɑ:bəʊ'haɪdreɪt/ *n* [C,U] (kinds of) organic compound including sugars and starches; (*pl*) starchy foods, considered to be fattening.

a caravan of camels

a gypsy caravan

a modern caravan

caravans

car·bolic acid /kɑːˌbɒlɪk ˈæsɪd/ n [U] strong-smelling, powerful liquid used as an antiseptic and disinfectant.

car·bon /ˈkɑːbən/ n 1 [U] non-metallic element (symbol **C**) that occurs in all living matter, in its pure form as diamonds and graphite and in an impure form in coal and charcoal. '~ **black** n black powder obtained by partly burning oil, wood, etc. '~ **dating**, method of dating prehistoric objects by measuring the decay of a radioactive isotope of ~. 2 [C] stick or pencil of ~ used in an electric arc-lamp. 3 [C] (also '~-**paper**) (sheet of) thin paper coated with coloured matter, used between sheets of writing paper for taking copies. 4 [C] (also ~ **copy**) copy made by the use of ~-paper. 5 ,~ **di'oxide** n gas (**CO₂**) produced by animal bodies and breathed out from the lungs; synthetic version of this used in eg canned beers and soft drinks, to give fizz. ~ **mon'oxide** n poisonous gas (**CO**) produced when ~ burns, present in the exhaust gas of petrol engines and after explosions in coal mines. ~**·ated** /ˈkɑːbəneɪtɪd/ adj containing ~ dioxide: ~ed beverages. ~**·if·er·ous** /ˌkɑːbəˈnɪfərəs/ adj (geol) producing coal: ~iferous strata. ~**·ize** vt [VP6A] convert into ~ by burning. ~**·iz·ation** /ˌkɑːbənaɪˈzeɪʃn US: -nɪˈz-/ n

car·bonic acid /kɑːˌbɒnɪk ˈæsɪd/ n [U] carbon dioxide dissolved in water (eg giving the sharp taste to soda water).

car·bor·un·dum /ˌkɑːbəˈrʌndəm/ n (P) hard compound of carbon and silicon, used for polishing and grinding.

car·boy /ˈkɑːbɔɪ/ n large, round glass or plastic bottle, usu enclosed in basketwork or a crate to protect it from being broken.

car·buncle /ˈkɑːbʌŋkl/ n 1 bright-red jewel. 2 red (usu painful) inflamed swelling under the skin.

car·bu·ret·tor (US = **-retor**) /ˌkɑːbjʊˈretə(r) US: ˈkɑːrbəreɪtər/ n that part of an internal combustion engine in which petrol and air are mixed to make an explosive mixture.

car·cass, car·case /ˈkɑːkəs/ n 1 dead body of an animal (esp one prepared for cutting up as meat): ~ meat, meat from a ~ (contrasted with tinned or corned meat). 2 (contemptuous) human body. 3 shell(2).

card¹ /kɑːd/ n 1 (usu small, oblong-shaped) piece of stiff paper or thin cardboard, as used for various purposes, eg a 'visiting-~ (US 'calling ~), with a person's name, etc on it; 'Christmas/New 'Year/ 'Birthday ~s, sent with greetings at Christmas, etc; 'record ~, one for keeping records, notes, etc, and stored in a box or drawer; ~ index, index on ~s. ~**-carrying member** n registered member of a group, political party, trade union, etc. '~ **vote** n vote taken at a trade union meeting at which each delegate has a ~ representing a certain number of workers. 2 programme for a race meeting or game, with details, and space for marking results: a 'score ~, eg for cricket. 3 (esp) one of the 52 cards (often 'playing-~) used for various games (canasta, bridge, poker, etc) and for telling fortunes. **have a ~ up one's sleeve,** have a secret plan in reserve. **hold/keep one's ~s close to one's chest,** ⇨ chest(2). **make a ~,** take a trick (⇨ trick(5)) with it. **on the ~s,** (from fortune-telling by ~s) likely or possible. **one's best/strongest ~,** one's strongest·argument, best way of getting what one wants. **play one's ~s well,** do one's business cleverly, with good judgement. **play a sure/safe/doubtful ~,** use a plan or expedient that is sure, etc. **put one's ~s on the table,** make one's plans, intentions, etc, known. '~**-sharper** n person who makes a living by swindling at ~ games. 4 (hum) person who is queer or amusing.

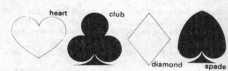

playing-card symbols

card² /kɑːd/ n toothed instrument, wire brush, for combing or cleaning wool, hemp etc. □ vt clean or comb with such an instrument.

car·da·mom /ˈkɑːdəməm/ n [U] aromatic spice from seed-capsules of various East Indian plants.

card·board /ˈkɑːdbɔːd/ n [U] thick, stiff kind of paper or pasteboard, used for making boxes, binding books, etc.

car·diac /ˈkɑːdɪæk/ adj of the heart: ~ muscle; ~ symptoms, ie of heart disease.

car·di·gan /ˈkɑːdɪɡən/ n knitted collarless woollen jacket that buttons up the front, made with sleeves.

car·di·nal /ˈkɑːdɪnl/ adj chief; most important; on which sth depends: the ~ virtues. ~ **numbers,** eg 5, 6, 7 (contrasted with ordinal numbers, eg 5th, 6th, 7th); the ~ points, of the compass (N, S, E and W). ⇨ the illus at compass. □ n bishop in the RC Church who is able to participate in the election of a Pope.

care¹ /keə(r)/ n 1 [U] serious attention or thought; watchfulness; pains: You should take more ~ over your work. This is made of glass, so take ~ not to break it. Glass, with ~! eg as a warning when goods are sent by rail. Take ~ (that) you don't get run over when you cross the street. Do your work *with more* ~. (Used with the *indef art*): *Have a* ~ (= Take ~), be cautious. **2** [U] protection; charge; responsibility: *The child was left in its sister's* ~. *The library is under the* ~ *of Mr Grey. I will leave this in your* ~, leave you responsible for it. ~ *of,* (often written **c/o**) used in addresses before the name of the person(s) to whose house, office, etc a letter is sent. **Child C**~ **officer** *n* (in GB but no longer current, now *social worker*) person appointed to look after children who are homeless or whose parents are neglectful, etc. *take into* ~, (of such an officer) take (a child lacking proper ~) to an institution. *take* ~ *of,* (colloq) deal with, be responsible for. '~-**taker** *n* person paid to take ~ of a building during the owner's absence; (US = *janitor*) person in charge of the upkeep of a public building such as a school or of a private building such as a block of flats. ~-**taker Government,** administration that continues in office until a new one is formed to take over its work. **3** [U] worry; anxiety; troubled state of mind caused by doubt or fear: *free from* ~. *C*~ *had made him look ten years older.* '~-**free** *adj* showing no worry; cheerful. '~-**laden,** '~-**worn** *adjj* showing worry; troubled. **4** [C] (usu *pl*) cause of sorrow and anxiety: *He was rich and free from* ~*s of every kind. He was poor and troubled by the* ~*s of a large family.*

care² /keə(r)/ *vi* **1** [VP2A,3A,B] (with *prep* usu omitted before a clause) ~ *(about),* feel interest, anxiety or sorrow: *He failed in the examination but I don't think he* ~*s very much/he doesn't seem to* ~. *He doesn't* ~ *much (about) what happens to me. He doesn't* ~ *what they say. I don't* ~ *who you are/how soon you leave. He doesn't* ~ *a damn,* is not in the least interested, worried, etc. *Who* ~*s?* **2** [VP3A] ~ *for,* like (to have): *Would you* ~ *for a drink? I shouldn't* ~ *for that man to be my doctor. He doesn't much* ~ *for television.* **3** [VP3A] ~ *for,* have a taste for; like: *Do you* ~ *for modern music?* **4** [VP3A] ~ *for,* look after; provide food, money, shelter etc: *Who will* ~ *for the children if their mother dies? The State must* ~ *for the families of soldiers killed in the war.* **5** [VP4C] like; be willing or desirous (inter and neg only): *Would you* ~ *to go for a walk? I don't* ~ *to be seen in his company.*

ca·reen /kə'ri:n/ *vt, vi* **1** [VP6A] turn (a ship) on one side for cleaning, repairing, etc. **2** [VP6A,2A] (cause to) tilt, lean over to one side.

ca·reer /kə'rɪə(r)/ *n* **1** [C] progress through life; development and progress of a party/principle etc: *We can learn much by reading about the* ~*s of great men.* **2** [C] way of making a living; profession: *Should all* ~*s be open to women,* Should women be allowed to enter all occupations? (attrib) professional: *a* ~ *diplomat; a* '~ *girl,* (esp) one who prefers a ~ to marriage. **3** [U] quick or violent forward movement: *in full* ~, at full speed; *stop (sb) in mid* ~. □ *vi* [VP2C,3A] ~ *about/along/past/through, etc,* rush wildly. ~-**ist** *n* person whose chief interest is personal advancement in his profession.

care·ful /'keəfl/ *adj* **1** (pred) *be* ~ *(about/of),* (of a person) taking care; cautious; thinking of, paying attention to, what one does, says, etc: *Be* ~ *not to break the eggs. Be* ~ *(about/of) what you do/what you say/where you go/how you carry it etc. Be more* ~ *with your work. Be* ~ *of your health.* **2** done with, showing care: ~ *guidance/a* ~ *guide;*

a ~ *piece of work; a* ~ *examination of the facts.* ~-**ly** /-fəlɪ/ *adv* ~-**ness** *n*

care·less /'keəlɪs/ *adj* **1** (of a person) not taking care; thoughtless: *He is* ~ *about leaving the door unlocked when he goes to bed. A* ~ *driver is a danger to the public.* **2** done or made without care: *a* ~ *mistake.* **3** (liter) light-hearted; gay: ~ *little songbirds.* **4** ~ *of,* (liter) unconcerned about; uncomplainingly accepting: *He is* ~ *of his reputation. The soldiers were* ~ *of hardship.* ~-**ly** *adv* ~-**ness** *n: a piece of* ~*ness,* a ~ act.

ca·ress /kə'res/ *n* [C] loving or affectionate touch or light stroke. □ *vt* [VP6A] give a ~ or ~es to. ~-**ing** *adj* showing love. ~-**ing·ly** *adv*

caret /'kærət/ *n* mark (‸) used (eg in correcting proofs) to show, in writing or print, where sth is to be inserted.

cargo /'kɑ:gəʊ/ *n* (*pl* ~es, US also ~s /-gəʊz/) [C,U] goods carried in a ship, aircraft or other vehicle: *a* '~ *ship/plane.* Cf *goods/freight train.*

cari·bou /'kærɪbu:/ *n* (*pl* ~s or, collective *pl* ~) N American reindeer.

cari·ca·ture /'kærɪkətjʊə(r)/ *n* **1** [C] picture of sb or sth, imitation of a person's voice, behaviour, etc, stressing certain features, to amuse or ridicule. **2** [U] art of doing this. □ *vt* [VP6A] make, give, a ~ of. **cari·ca·tur·ist** *n* expert in ~.

car·ies /'keəri:z/ *n* [U] (med) decay (of bones or teeth): *dental* ~. **cari·ous** /'keərɪəs/ *adj* (of bone) affected with ~.

car·il·lon /kə'rɪljən *US:* 'kærəlɒn/ *n* set of bells in a tower on which tunes may be played by some kind of mechanism (eg a keyboard).

Car·mel·ite /'kɑ:məlaɪt/ *n, adj* (friar or nun) of the religious order founded in 1155.

car·mine /'kɑ:maɪn/ *n, adj* deep red colour or colouring matter.

car·nage /'kɑ:nɪdʒ/ *n* [U] (liter) killing of many people: *a scene of* ~, eg a battlefield.

car·nal /'kɑ:nl/ *adj* (formal) of the body or flesh; sensual (opposite to *spiritual*): ~ *desires.* ~-**ly** *adv*

car·na·tion /kɑ:'neɪʃn/ *n* garden plant with sweet-smelling white, pink or red flowers; the flower.

car·ni·val /'kɑ:nɪvl/ *n* [U] public merrymaking and feasting, usu with processions of persons in fancy dress, esp in RC countries during the week before Lent; [C] festival of this kind.

car·ni·vore /'kɑ:nɪvɔ:(r)/ *n* flesh-eating animal. **car·ni·vor·ous** /kɑ:'nɪvərəs/ *adj* flesh-eating.

carol /'kærəl/ *n* song of joy or praise, esp a Christmas hymn: '~ *singers,* singers who visit people's houses at Christmas to sing ~s (and usu to collect money for charity). □ *vt* (-ll-, in US also -l-) sing joyfully: celebrate with ~s. ~-**ler** *n*

ca·rouse /kə'raʊz/ *vt* [VP2A] drink heavily and be merry (at a noisy meal, party etc). **ca·rousal** /kə'raʊzl/ *n* noisy drinking-party or revelry.

carp¹ /kɑ:p/ *n* (*pl* unchanged) large freshwater fish that lives in lakes and ponds.

carp² /kɑ:p/ *vt* [VP2A,3A] ~ *(at),* make unnecessary complaints about small matters: *a* ~*ing tongue;* ~*ing criticism. She's always* ~*ing at her husband.*

car·pal /'kɑ:pl/ *adj* (anat) of the wrist. □ *n* (anat) bone in the wrist, ⇨ the illus at skeleton.

car·pen·ter /'kɑ:pɪntə(r)/ *n* workman who makes and repairs (esp) the wooden parts of buildings and other structures of wood. ⇨ joiner. **car·pen·try** /-trɪ/ *n* [U] work of a ~.

car·pet /'kɑːpɪt/ n [C] **1** thick covering for floors or stairs, usu of wool, hair or synthetic fibres, often with a pattern or designs woven into it. **on the ∼,** (colloq) being reprimanded. **sweep sth under the ∼,** hide, ignore, sth, in order to delay action, escape blame, etc. '**∼-bag** n (old fashioned) travelling bag made of ∼. '**∼-bag·ger** n (US) person, during the American Civil War (1861-5), from northern USA who went to the South to seek financial or political advantage. '**∼-knight** n soldier who has not seen active service, stay-at-home soldier; ladies' man. '**∼-slippers** n pl (old-fashioned) kind of soft slippers with uppers of woollen cloth. '**∼-sweeper** n device with revolving brush(es) for sweeping ∼s and rugs. **2** sth suggesting a ∼: a ∼ of moss, eg in a garden. □ vt [VP6A] **1** cover (as) with a ∼: to ∼ the stairs; a lawn ∼ed with fallen leaves. **2** (sl) reprimand: He's been ∼ed.

car·riage /'kærɪdʒ/ n **1** [C] vehicle, esp one with four wheels, pulled by a horse or horses, for carrying people: a ∼ and pair, one pulled by two horses. ⇨ coach¹ '**∼·way** n (part of a) road used by vehicles: Cars must not park on the ∼way. **,dual '∼·way,** road divided down the centre (by a barrier, a strip of pavement or grass) for traffic in each direction (US = divided highway). **2** [C] wheeled vehicle for passengers on a railway train (US = car); coach: The first class ∼s are in front. **3** [U] (cost of) carrying of goods from place to place. ∼ **forward,** cost of ∼ to be paid by the receiver. ∼ **free/paid,** ∼ free to the receiver/paid by the sender. **4** [C] wheeled support on which a heavy object may move or be moved (eg a gun ∼); moving part of a machine, changing the position of other parts (eg the roller of a typewriter). **5** (sing only) manner of holding the head or the body (when walking, etc): She has a graceful ∼, She stands and walks gracefully. ⇨ carry(8).

a carriage

car·rier /'kærɪə(r)/ n **1** person or company that carries goods or people for payment (eg a railway, shipping or aircraft company). **2** support for luggage, etc fixed to a bicycle, motor-car, etc. **3** person, animal, etc that carries or transmits a disease without himself or itself suffering from it. **4** vehicle, ship, etc used for the transport of troops, aircraft, tanks, etc. ⇨ aircraft-∼, Bren-∼, troop-∼. **5** '**∼-bag** n strong paper or plastic bag with hand grips for eg carrying away purchases from shops. '**∼-pigeon** n pigeon used to carry messages because it can find its way home from a distant place.

car·rion /'kærɪən/ n [U] dead and decaying flesh. '**∼-crow,** crow that lives on ∼ and small animals.

car·rot /'kærət/ n (plant with) yellow or orange-red root used as a vegetable, ⇨ the illus at vegetable. **the stick and the ∼,** threats and bribes. **hold out/offer a ∼ to sb,** entice by offering a reward or advantage. ∼**y** adj (esp of hair) orange-red.

carry¹ /'kærɪ/ vt,vi (pt,pp carried) (For uses with adverbial particles and preps, ⇨ 11 below.) **1**

[VP6A,15A,B] support the weight of and move from place to place; take a person, a message, etc from one place to another: He was ∼ing a box on his shoulder. She was ∼ing the baby in her arms. Railways and ships ∼ goods. He carried (= went round and told) the news to everyone in the village. He ran off as fast as his legs could ∼ him, as fast as he could run. This bicycle has carried me 500 miles. How far will five gallons of petrol ∼ you? Some kinds of seeds are carried by the wind for great distances. The raft was carried by ocean currents to a small island. A spy carries his life in his hands, takes the risk of death. '∼-cot n light cot with handles (but no wheels) for ∼ing a baby. **2** [VP6A,15A] have with one; wear; possess: Do you always ∼ an umbrella? Ought the police to be allowed to ∼ fire-arms? I never ∼ much money with me. Can you ∼ all these figures in your head, remember them without writing them down? The wound left a scar that he will ∼ with him to the grave, that will remain for life. **3** [VP6A] support: These pillars ∼ the weight of the roof. The girders are carried on trestles. **4** [VP6A] involve; entail; have as a result: The loan carries 3½% interest. That argument does not ∼ conviction, is not convincing. Power carries responsibility with it. His word/promise carries weight, is influential. **5** [VP6A,15A] (of pipes, wires, etc) conduct; take: The oil is carried across the desert in pipe-lines. Copper carries electricity. **6** [VP15A] make longer; extend; take (to a specified point, in a specified direction, etc): ∼ a fence round a field; ∼ pipes under a street; ∼ a joke too far, be no longer amusing. Don't ∼ modesty too far. **7** [VP6A,15A] win; capture; persuade; overcome: The soldiers rushed forward and carried the enemy's position. He carried his audience with him, won their sympathy and agreement. The bill/motion/resolution was carried, there were more votes for it than against it. ∼ **the day,** be victorious. ∼ **everything before one,** be completely successful. ∼ **one's point,** win approval for it. **8** [VP6A,15A,16B] hold oneself/one's head/one's body in a specified way: He carries himself like a soldier, stands and walks like one. She carries herself badly, eg by slouching or stooping. **9** [VP2B,C] (of guns) send (a shell, etc) a certain distance; (of missiles, sounds, voices, etc) have the power to go to: Our guns do not ∼ far enough. The sound of the guns carried many miles. The shot carried 200 metres. A public speaker must have a voice that carries well. **10** [VP6A] (of a newspaper, etc) print in its pages: a newspaper that carries several pages of advertisements. **11** [VP15B,2C] (with adverbial particles and preps):

carry sb/sth away, (a) (usu passive) cause to lose self-control: He was carried away by his enthusiasm, was so enthusiastic that he was unable to judge calmly, etc. **(b)** (naut) lose (masts, etc) by breaking: The ship's masts were carried away during the storm.

carry sb back, take back in the memory: an incident that carried me back to my schooldays, caused me to recall them.

carry sth forward, (comm, book-keeping) transfer (a total of figures on a page) to the head of a new column or page.

carry sth off, win: Tom carried off all the school prizes. ∼ **it/sth off (well),** succeed in a difficult situation; cover a mistake, etc.

carry (sth) on, (a) conduct; manage: *Rising costs made it hard to ~ on the business. It's difficult to ~ on a conversation at a noisy party.* **(b)** talk volubly and complainingly; behave strangely or suspiciously: *How she does ~ on! Did you notice how they were ~ing on?* Hence, **~ings-on** *n pl: Such queer carryings-on next door*, such queer happenings! **~ on (with),** continue (doing sth): *C~ on (with your work). They decided to ~ on in spite of the weather.* **~ on (an affair) (with),** (often suggesting disapproval) flirt with; have a love affair with: *His wife is ~ing on with the postman.* **(sth) to ~ on with,** (sth) (to do or use) for the time being: *I can't give you all you need, but here's £5 to ~ on/be ~ing on with.*

carry sth out, (a) do as required or specified; fulfil; complete: *~ out a promise/threat/plan/ instruction.* **(b)** perform; conduct: *~ out experiments/tests.*

carry sb/sth through, (a) help (through difficulties, etc): *Their courage will ~ them through.* **(b)** complete; fulfil: *Having made a promise, you must ~ it through.*

carry² /'kærɪ/ *n* **1** range of a gun, etc; distance that a shell, etc, goes. **2** portage; act of carrying boats, etc, from one river or lake to another; place where this must be done.

cart /kɑːt/ *n* two-wheeled vehicle pulled by a horse. ⇨ also hand~. **be in the ~,** (sl) be in an awkward or losing position. **put the ~ before the horse,** do or put things in the wrong order, take the effect for the cause (eg by saying 'I was lazy because I didn't study'). **turn '~-wheels,** turn somersaults sideways. **'~-horse** *n* strong horse for heavy work. **'~-load** *n* as much as a ~ holds: *a ~-load of manure.* **'~-road/-track,** rough unmetalled road. □ *vt* [VP6A,15B] **1** carry in a ~: *~ing hay; ~ away the rubbish.* **2** (colloq) carry in the hands, etc: *Have you really got to ~ these parcels around for the rest of the day?* **~·age** /'kɑːtɪdʒ/ *n* [U] (cost of) carting. **~er** *n* man whose work is driving ~s; carrier(1).

a cart

carte blanche /ˌkɑːt 'blɒnʃ/ *n* (F) full authority or freedom (to use one's own judgement about how to proceed, etc).

car·tel /kɑː'tel/ *n* (comm) combination of traders, manufacturers, etc to control output, marketing, prices of goods, etc.

car·ti·lage /'kɑːtɪlɪdʒ/ *n* [C,U] (structure, part, of) tough, white tissue attached to the joints, in animal bodies; gristle. **car·ti·lagi·nous** /ˌkɑːtɪ'lædʒɪnəs/ *adj* of or like ~.

car·tog·ra·pher /kɑː'tɒgrəfə(r)/ *n* person who makes maps and charts. **car·tog·ra·phy** /kɑː'tɒgrəfɪ/ *n* [U] the drawing of maps and charts.

car·ton /'kɑːtn/ *n* cardboard box for holding goods: *a ~ of 200 cigarettes,* with 10 packets of 20.

car·toon /kɑː'tuːn/ *n* **1** drawing dealing with current (esp political) events in an amusing or satirical

way. **2** full-size preliminary drawing on paper, used as a model for a painting, a tapestry, a fresco, a mosaic, etc. **3** (= *animated* ~) cinema film made by photographing a series of drawings: *a Walt Disney ~.* □ *vt* represent (a person, etc) in a ~. **~·ist** *n* person who draws ~s(1).

car·tridge /'kɑːtrɪdʒ/ *n* **1** case (of metal, cardboard, etc) containing explosive (for blasting), or explosive with bullet or shot (for firing from a rifle or shot gun). ⇨ blank *n*(4). **'~-belt** *n* one with sockets for holding ~s. **'~-paper, (a)** paper for making ~ cases. **(b)** thick white paper for pencil and ink drawings. **2** detachable head of a pick-up (on a record-player), holding the stylus. **3** (US) cassette.

A for a rifle
B for a shotgun

case for primer   bullet

percussion cap—
for primer   shot

cartridges

carve /kɑːv/ *vt,vi* **1** [VP6A,14,15B] form (sth) by cutting away material from a piece of wood or stone: *~ a statue out of wood/a statue in oak; a figure ~d from marble; ~ out a career for oneself,* (fig) achieve one by great effort. **2** [VP6A,15A] inscribe by cutting on a surface: *~ one's initials on a tree trunk; ~ an inscription on a bench.* **3** [VP6A,15B] cut up (cooked meat) into pieces or slices at or for the table: *~ a leg of mutton/a turkey.* **'carving-knife/-fork** *n* knife, fork, used for carving meat. **carver** *n* carving-knife; person who ~s; (*pl*) carving-knife and fork. **carv·ing** *n* sth ~d in wood, etc. ⇨ sculptor, sculpture.

cary·atid /ˌkærɪ'ætɪd/ *n* (archit) draped statue of a female figure used as a support (eg a pillar) in a building.

cas·cade /kæ'skeɪd/ *n* waterfall; one section of a large, broken waterfall; wave-like fall of lace, cloth, etc. □ *vi* fall like a ~.

case¹ /keɪs/ *n* **1** instance or example of the occurrence of sth; actual state of affairs; circumstances or special conditions relating to a person or thing; (med) person suffering from a disease; instance of a diseased condition: *Is it the ~* (= Is it true) *that you have lost all your money? No, that's not the ~,* is not true. *If that's the ~* (= If the situation is as stated or suggested), *you'll have to work much harder. I can't make an exception in your ~,* for you and not for others. *Such being the ~* (= In view of, Because of, these facts, etc), *you can't go away. It's a clear ~ of cheating,* is clear that cheating has taken place. *There were five ~s of* (= five persons suffering from) *influenza. The worst ~s were sent to hospital.* **a ~ in point,** ⇨ point¹(9). **(just) in ~,** if it should happen that; because of a possibility: *It may rain—you'd better take an umbrella (just) in ~. In ~ I forget, please remind me of my promise. in ~ of,* in the event of: *In ~ of fire, ring the alarm bell.* **in 'any ~,** whatever happens or may have happened. **in 'no ~,** in no circumstances. **in 'this/that ~,** if this/ that happens, has happened, should happen. **'~-book** *n* record kept by a professional man (eg a doctor) of ~s dealt with. **~-'history** *n* record of the history of sb suffering from a disease, social or mental trouble, etc. '∼·**work** n work involving personal study of individuals or families with social problems. **2** (legal) question to be decided in a law court; the facts, arguments, etc, used on one side in a law court: *the* ∼ *for the defendant,* the statement of facts, etc in his favour. *When will the* ∼ *come before the Court? State your* ∼, Give the facts and arguments in your favour. *He has a strong* ∼. **make out a** ∼ *(for),* give arguments in favour (of) (sb, doing sth). **make out one's** ∼, prove that one is right. '∼**-law** n law based on decisions made by judges. **3** (gram) (change in the) form of a noun or pronoun that shows its relation to another word: *The first person singular personal pronoun in English has two* ∼ *forms:* 'I' (*subject* ∼), *and* 'me' (*object* ∼).

case² /keɪs/ n **1** box, bag, covering, container: '*packing*∼, large box in which goods are packed; *glass* ∼, for the display of specimens, etc (eg in a museum); *a* '*watch* ∼; *a* '*jewel* ∼, lined with velvet for keeping jewels in; *a* '*seed* ∼, on a plant, in which the seeds ripen; *a* '*pillow*∼, of cloth for covering a pillow; *a* '*dressing*∼, a case for hairbrushes, combs, razors, etc. ⇨ also suit∼, book∼. ∼**-'hardened** adj (fig) made callous by experience. **2** (printing): *upper* ∼, capital letters; *lower* ∼, small letters. □ vt [VP6A] enclose in a ∼ or casing; encase.

casein /keɪsiːn/ n [U] body-building food (protein) present in milk and forming the basis of cheese.

case·ment /keɪsmənt/ n window that opens outwards or inwards like a door, not up or down or from side to side, ⇨ sash window and the illus at window; (poet) window.

cash /kæʃ/ n [U] **1** money in coin or notes: *I have no* ∼ *with me—may I pay by cheque? We sell goods for* ∼ *only—we don't give credit.* '∼ **crops** n crops (eg coffee, sisal) to be sold for ∼ (contrasted with *subsistence crops* such as millet, beans, grown for use by the growers). '∼ **desk,** desk or counter (in a shop, etc) where payments (by ∼ or cheque) are made. '∼ **dispenser,** machine (outside some banks) which, by the use of a personal coded card, dispenses ∼. ∼ **down;** ∼ **on delivery,** payment on delivery of the goods. ⇨ credit¹(1). '∼ **price** n price for immediate payment. ∼ **register** n ∼ box with a device for recording and storing ∼ received. ∼ **and 'carry store** n one where goods are sold (usu at lower prices) for ∼ payment if the buyer takes them away with him. **2** money in any form: *be short of* ∼; *be rolling in* ∼; *out of* ∼, without money. □ vt,vi **1** [VP6A,12B,13B] give or get ∼ for: ∼ *a cheque. Can you* ∼ *this cheque for me/*∼ *me a cheque?* **2** [VP2C] ∼ **in (on),** take advantage (of); benefit (from): *shopkeepers who* ∼ *in on shortages by putting up prices.* ∼**·able** /-əbl/ adj that can be ∼ed.

a cash register   castanets

ca·shew /kæʃuː/ n (tropical American tree with) small kidney-shaped nut.

cash·ier¹ /kæʃɪə(r)/ n person who receives and pays out money in a bank, store, hotel, restaurant, etc.

cash·ier² /kəʃɪə(r)/ vt [VP6A] dismiss (eg an officer) with dishonour and disgrace.

cash·mere /kæʃmɪə(r)/ n [U] fine soft wool of Kashmir /kæʃmɪə(r)/ goats of Asia: *a* ∼ *shawl.*

cas·ing /keɪsɪŋ/ n covering; protective wrapping: *copper wire with a* ∼ *of rubber;* ∼s *for sausages.*

ca·sino /kəsiːnəʊ/ n (pl ∼s) public room or building for gambling and other amusements.

cask /kɑːsk US: kæsk/ n barrel for liquids: *a* ∼ *of cider;* amount that a ∼ holds.

cas·ket /kɑːskɪt US: kæskɪt/ n **1** small box to hold letters, jewels, cremated ashes, etc. **2** (US) coffin.

cas·sava /kəsɑːvə/ n [U] tropical plant with starchy roots from which tapioca is extracted. ⇨ the illus at vegetable.

cas·ser·ole /kæsərəʊl/ n covered heat-proof dish in which food is cooked and then served at table; food so cooked: *a* ∼ *of lamb.*

cas·sette /kəset/ n [C] (US = *cartridge*) container for magnetic tape (for use with a ∼ tape-recorder) or for photographic film (to be fitted into a camera). ⇨ the illus at tape.

cas·sock /kæsək/ n long, close-fitting outer garment, worn by some priests. ⇨ the illus at vestment.

cas·so·wary /kæsəweərɪ/ n (pl -ries) large bird of SE Asia, unable to fly, similar to, but smaller than, an emu. ⇨ illus at rare.

cast¹ /kɑːst US: kæst/ vt,vi (pt,pp cast) **1** [VP6A,15A,B] throw; allow to fall or drop: *The fisherman* ∼ *his net into the water. Snakes* ∼ *their skins. His horse* ∼ *a shoe,* one of its shoes came off. ∼ **anchor,** lower it. **be** ∼ **down,** be depressed, unhappy. ⇨ downcast. ∼ **lots;** ∼ **in one's lot with,** ⇨ lot²(1,3). ∼ **a vote,** give a vote. ∼**·ing vote** n one given (eg by the chairman) to decide a question when votes on each side are equal. ∼ **sth in sb's teeth,** ⇨ tooth(1). **2** [VP6A,15A,2C] turn or send in a particular direction: ∼ *one's eye over sth,* look at, examine, it; ∼ *a gloom/shadow on sth,* make it seem gloomy, depressing; ∼ *a new light on a problem, etc,* make it clearer, easier to understand; ∼ *a rather wary glance at sb,* look at him warily; ∼ *a slur on someone's reputation,* say things to damage it. ∼ **about for,** (anxiously) look for, try to find (eg *allies, excuses*). **3** [VP6A] pour (liquid metal) into a mould; make (eg a statue in bronze, etc) in this way: *a figure* ∼ *in bronze.* ∼ **iron** n iron in a hard, brittle form, made by shaping in moulds after melting the ore in a blast furnace, and usually converted into wrought iron or steel before being used. Hence, '∼**-iron** adj (a) made of ∼ iron. (b) (fig) hard; untiring; unyielding: *a man with a* ∼*-iron will/constitution.* **4** [VP6A,15B] ∼ **up,** add, calculate (more usu *add up* or *tot up*): ∼ *up a column of figures.* **5** [VP15B,2C] ∼ **(sb/sth) aside,** (= *cast off,* (b)) abandon; throw away as useless or unwanted. ∼ **(sth) off,** (a) unloose (a boat) and let go. (b) (fig) abandon; throw away as unwanted. Hence, ∼**-off 'clothes;** '∼**-offs** n pl clothes that the owner will not wear again. ∼ **off,** (knitting) remove the last row of stitches from the needles. ∼ **on,** (knitting) make the first row of stitches. **6** [VP6A] give (an actor) a part in a play: *He was* ∼

for the part of Hamlet. ~·ing *n* [C] sth shaped by being poured in a mould (eg a wheel or axle), ⇨ **3** above.

cast² /kɑːst *US:* kæst/ *n* **1** act of throwing (eg a net or fishing line): *stake everything on a single ~ of the dice.* **2** sth made by casting(3) or by pressing soft material into a mould: *His leg was in a plaster ~.* **3** mould where metal is poured or where soft material is pressed. **4** set of actors in a play; the distribution of the parts among these actors: *a play with an all-star ~.* **5** type or quality: *~ of features; ~ of mind.* **6** (of the eyes) slight squint.

cas·ta·nets /ˌkæstəˈnets/ *n pl* instruments of hard-wood or ivory used in pairs on the fingers to make rattling sounds as a rhythm for dancing. ⇨ the illus at cash.

cast·away /ˈkɑːstəweɪ *US:* kæst-/ *n* shipwrecked person, esp one reaching a strange country or lone-ly island.

caste /kɑːst *US:* kæst/ *n* one of the Hindu heredi-tary social classes; any exclusive social class; [U] this system. **lose ~ with/among,** lose the right to be respected; come down in social rank.

cas·tel·lated /ˈkæstəleɪtɪd/ *adj* having turrets or battlements (like a castle).

cas·ti·gate /ˈkæstɪɡeɪt/ *vt* [VP6A] punish severely with blows or by criticizing. **cas·ti·ga·tion** /ˌkæstɪˈɡeɪʃn/ *n* [C,U] (instance of) severe punish-ment.

castle /ˈkɑːsl *US:* ˈkæsl/ *n* large building or group of buildings fortified against attack, esp as in olden times; house that was once such a fortified build-ing; piece (also called *rook*) used in the game of chess, ⇨ the illus at chess. **~s in the air; ~s in Spain,** day-dreams; plans or hopes that are unlike-ly to be realized. **an Englishman's house is his ~,** his place of refuge and safety. □ *vi* (chess) move the king sideways two squares towards the ~ and place the ~ on the square the king moved across.

cas·tor, cas·ter /ˈkɑːstə(r) *US:* kæs-/ *n* **1** wheel (on a swivel) fixed to each leg of a piece of furni-ture (so that it may be turned and moved easily). **2** bottle or metal pot, with holes in the top, for sugar, salt, etc. 'Ⓗ **~ sugar** *n* white, finely powdered sugar.

cas·tor oil /ˌkɑːstə ˈɔɪl *US:* ˈkæstər ɔɪl/ *n* [U] thick, yellowish oil, made from beans of the ~ plant,

used as a purgative.

cas·trate /kæˈstreɪt *US:* ˈkæstreɪt/ *vt* [VP6A] re-move the sex glands of (a male animal); make (a male animal) useless for breeding purposes. **cas-tra·tion** /kæˈstreɪʃn/ *n* castrating.

cas·ual /ˈkæʒʊəl/ *adj* **1** happening by chance: *a ~ meeting.* **2** careless; undesigned; unmethodical; in-formal: *a ~ glance; clothes for ~ wear,* for infor-mal occasions, holidays, etc. *She's a very ~ per-son,* eg is careless and thoughtless about the con-venience of others. **3** irregular; not continued: *earn a living by ~ labour; ~ labourers,* not permanent-ly engaged by one employer. **~·ly** *adv*

casu·alty /ˈkæʒʊəltɪ/ *n* [C] **1** accident, esp one in-volving loss of life. **2** soldier or sailor who is killed, wounded or missing; person killed or seri-ously injured in an accident: *The enemy suffered heavy casualties. C~ lists were published the day after the train accident.* **'C~ Ward/Department** *n* part of a hospital to which persons injured, eg in road accidents, are taken for urgent treatment.

casu·ist /ˈkæzjʊɪst/ *n* expert in ~ry. **~ry** /-rɪ/ *n* [U] judgement of right and wrong by reference to theories, social conventions, etc, (often with false but clever reasoning); [C] false but clever argument used in this way. **casu·is·tic, -ti·cal** /ˌkæzjʊˈɪstɪk, -tɪkl/ *adj* of or like ~ry.

casus belli /ˌkeɪsəs ˈbelaɪ/ *n* (Lat) act that is held to justify war.

cat /kæt/ *n* **1** small, domestic, fur-covered animal often kept as a pet, to catch mice, etc; (= **'wild cat**) any animal of the group that includes tigers, lions, panthers and leopards. **bell the cat,** ⇨ bell(2). **let the cat out of the bag,** ⇨ bag¹(1). **like a cat on hot bricks,** very nervous or jumpy. **put/set the cat among the pigeons,** cause alarm and confusion. **wait for the cat to jump; see which way the cat jumps,** refuse to give advice, make plans, etc, until one sees what other people are thinking and doing. ˌ**cat-and-ˈdog life,** one full of quarrels. **2** (short for) ˌ**cat-o'-ˈnine-tails** *n* whip with many knotted cords, formerly used for pun-ishing wrong-doers. **room to swing a cat in,** just enough space. **3** (compounds, etc). **'cat burglar** *n* one who enters a building by climbing up walls, rainpipes, etc. **'cat-call** *n, v* (make a) loud, shrill whistle expressing disapproval (eg at a political

some wild cats

LIONESS
LEOPARD
PANTHER
LYNX
JAGUAR
LION
mane
PUMA
TIGER

meeting). '**cat·fish** *n* large fish without scales, with feelers around the mouth. '**cat-nap, 'cat-sleep** *n* short sleep (in a chair, etc, not in bed). ,**cat's 'cradle** *n* children's game with a length of string looped over the fingers of both hands and transferred between the fingers of two players. '**cat's eye** *n* reflector stud placed in roadways to guide traffic in darkness or on the rear of a vehicle (eg a bicycle). '**cat's paw** *n* person who is used as a tool by another. '**cat suit** *n* woman's or child's close-fitting one-piece garment for the whole body. '**cat-walk** *n* narrow footway along a bridge, or through a mass of machinery, engines, etc.

cata·clysm /'kætəklızəm/ *n* [C] sudden and violent change (eg a flood, an earthquake, a great war, a political or social revolution). **cata·clys·mic** /ˌkætə'klızmık/ *adj*

cata·combs /'kætəku:mz/ *n pl* series of underground galleries with openings along the sides for the burial of the dead (as in ancient Rome).

cata·falque /'kætəfælk/ *n* decorated stand or stage for a coffin at a funeral.

cata·lepsy /'kætəlepsı/ *n* [U] disease in which the sufferer has periods when he loses consciousness and sensation and his muscles become rigid. **cata·lep·tic** /ˌkætə'leptık/ *adj* of, having, ∼. □ *n* person who has ∼.

cata·logue (US also **catalog**) /'kætəlɒg *US:* -lɔːg/ *n* list of names/places/goods etc, in a special order: *a library* ∼. □ *vt* [VP6A] make a ∼ of; put in a ∼.

ca·talpa /kə'tælpə/ *n* (kinds of) tree with heart-shaped leaves and trumpet-shaped flowers.

ca·ta·ly·sis /kə'tæləsıs/ *n* the process of aiding or speeding up a chemical process by a substance that does not itself undergo any change. **cata·lyst** /'kætəlıst/ *n* [C] substance that causes ∼; (fig) sb or sth that helps to bring about a change. **cata·lyt·ic** /ˌkætə'lıtık/ *adj* of ∼; causing ∼.

cata·maran /ˌkætəmə'ræn/ *n* boat with twin hulls; two boats or canoes fastened side by side (as used in the South Seas).

a catamaran

1402

hulls

cat·a·pult /'kætəpʌlt/ *n* **1** Y-shaped stick with a piece of elastic, for shooting stones, etc from; (in ancient times) machine for throwing heavy stones in war. **2** apparatus for launching aircraft without a runway (eg from the deck of a carrier). □ *vt* launch (aircraft) with a ∼; shoot (as) from a ∼.

cata·ract /'kætərækt/ *n* [C] **1** large, steep waterfall. **2** (path) disease of the eye, in which the lens slowly clouds over, obscuring sight. ⇨ the illus at **eye**.

ca·tarrh /kə'tɑː(r)/ *n* [U] inflamation of the mucous membrane, esp of the nose and throat, causing flow of liquid, as when one has a cold; this liquid.

ca·tas·trophe /kə'tæstrəfı/ *n* [C] sudden happening that causes great suffering and destruction (eg a flood, earthquake, fire). **cata·strophic** /ˌkætə'strɒfık/ *adj*

catch[1] /kætʃ/ *vt, vi* (*pt, pp* **caught** /kɔːt/) **1** [VP6A]

stop (sth that is in motion) (eg by getting hold of it with the hands, by holding out sth into which it may come): *I threw the ball to him and he caught it. The dog caught the bit of meat in its mouth.* [VP15B] ∼ **sb out,** (cricket) dismiss a batsman by ∼ing the ball he has struck before it touches the ground. ⇨ also **3** below. **2** [VP6A] capture; seize; intercept: ∼ *a rat in a trap;* ∼ *a thief. How many fish did you* ∼*? Cats* ∼ *mice. I caught him* (= met him and stopped him) *just as he was leaving the house.* **3** [VP6A,19B,14,15B,22] come unexpectedly upon (sb) doing sth (esp sth wrong); surprise or detect: *I caught the boys stealing apples from my garden. You won't* ∼ *me* (= There's no likelihood of my being discovered) *doing that again!* ∼ *sb at it;* ∼ *sb in the act (of doing sth),* come upon him while he is actually doing it: *Just let me* ∼ *you at it again* (—then there'll be trouble)! ∼ *sb out,* detect him making a mistake. ∼ *sb napping,* ⇨ nap(1). **4** [VP6A] be in time for: ∼ *a train/the bus, etc;* ∼ *the post,* post letters before the box is emptied by the postman. **5** [VP15B,2C] ∼ *sb up;* ∼ *up (with sb),* (a) come up to sb who is going in the same direction; overtake: *Go on in front, I'll soon* ∼ *you up/*∼ *up (with you).* (b) do all the work that has not yet been done: *Tom was away from school for a month so now he's got to work hard to* ∼ *up with the rest of the class.* **6** [VP6A,2C,3A,14,15A] ∼ *(in/on),* (cause to) become fixed or prevented from moving; (cause to) be entangled: *The nail caught her dress. Her dress caught on a nail. I caught my fingers in the door,* trapped them between the door and the doorpost. *This bolt doesn't* ∼, cannot be fastened. *The latch has caught,* stuck fast. *The car was caught between two lorries. He caught his foot on a tree root and stumbled.* **7** [VP6A] get (the meaning of sth); hear (the sound of sth); receive (punishment, etc): *I don't quite* ∼ *your meaning. I didn't* ∼ *the end of the sentence. I don't quite* ∼ (= fully understand) *the idea.* [VP2C] ∼ *on (to sth),* understand. ∼ *it,* be scolded, punished, hit, etc: *You'll* ∼ *it if you're not careful! He caught it* (= was hit) *right in the eye.* ∼ *sb's attention/fancy,* succeed in getting it. ∼ *sb's eye,* look at him to attract his attention when he looks in your direction. Hence, '**eye-**∼**ing** *adj* ⇨ eye[1](3). ∼ *sight/a glimpse of,* see for a short time. **8** [VP6A] become infected with: ∼ *a disease/a fever;* ∼ *a cold.* **9** [VP3A] ∼ *at,* try to grasp: *A drowning man will* ∼ *at a straw. He will* ∼ *at* (= take eagerly) *any opportunity of practising his English.* ⇨ clutch[1]. [VP15B] ∼ *up,* grasp; seize: ∼ *up a loose end of rope. They were caught up* (fig, carried away) *in the wave of enthusiasm.* [VP15A] ∼ *hold of,* seize, grab. **10** ∼ *(fire),* begin to burn: *The wood soon caught (fire).* **11** [VP6A,12C,15A] hit: ∼ *sb a blow. She caught him one* (= gave him a blow) *on the cheek.* **12** ∼ *one's breath,* fail to breathe regularly for a moment (from surprise, etc). '∼**-crop** *n* quick-growing crop (eg lettuce) grown between rows of other crops. '∼**-penny** *adj* designed or intended merely to get sales: *a book with a* ∼*penny title.* '∼**-word** *n* (a) word placed so as to draw attention to an article, eg the subject of a paragraph; first or last word of a page in a dictionary, printed above the columns. (b) phrase or slogan in frequent current use. ∼**er** *n* (baseball) player who stands behind the batter to ∼ the ball thrown by the pitcher. ∼**·ing** *adj* (esp of diseases) infectious. ∼**y** *adj* **1** (of a tune, etc) easily remembered. **2** tricky, deceptive.

catch[2] /kætʃ/ *n* **1** act of catching (esp a ball): *That was a difficult* ∼. **2** that which is caught or worth ∼ing: *a fine* ∼ *of fish. He's a good* ∼ *for some young woman*, is a good man to get as a husband. **3** sth intended to trick or deceive; cunning question or device: *There's a* ∼ *in it somewhere. Does the teacher ever include* ∼ *questions in examination papers?* **4** device for fastening or securing a lock, door, etc. ⇨ the illus at latch. **5** song for a number of voices starting one after another.

catch·ment /'kætʃmənt/ *n* '∼(-area) land from which a river or reservoir draws its rainfall (also '∼-basin); (fig) area(s) from which a central body draws its members, eg a school its pupils, a hospital its patients; [U] amount of rainfall, etc caught.

catch·up /'kætʃəp/ *n* = ketchup.

cat·echism /'kætɪkɪzəm/ *n* [U] instruction (esp about religion) by question and answer; [C] number, succession of questions and answers designed for this purpose: *put a person through his* ∼, question him closely.

cat·echize /'kætɪkaɪz/ *vt* [VP6A] teach or examine by asking many questions.

cat·egori·cal /ˌkætɪ'gɒrɪkl/ *US:* -gɔːr-/ *adj* (of a statement) unconditional; absolute; detailed; explicit. ∼ly /-ɪklɪ/ *adv*

cat·egory /'kætɪgərɪ/ *US:* -gɔːrɪ/ *n* (*pl* -ries) division or class in a complete system or grouping. **cat·egor·ize** /'kætɪgəraɪz/ *vt* [VP6A] place in a ∼.

cater /'keɪtə(r)/ *vi* **1** [VP3A] ∼ *for*, provide food: *Weddings and parties* ∼ed *for*, The advertiser will supply food for weddings, etc. **2** [VP3A] ∼ *for/to*, make provision *for*, supply what is desired or required *to*; pander *to*: *TV programmes usually* ∼ *for all tastes. Some tabloid newspapers* ∼ *to low tastes.* ∼er *n* person who provides meals, etc brought from outside, to clubs, homes, etc; owner or manager of a hotel, restaurant, etc.

cat·er·pil·lar /'kætəpɪlə(r)/ *n* **1** larva of a butterfly or moth, ⇨ the illus at butterfly. **2** endless belt passing over toothed wheels, used to give vehicles, tanks, etc, a good grip on soft or uneven surfaces: ∼ *tractor*, one fitted with such belts.

cat·er·waul /'kætəwɔːl/ *vi*, *n* (make a) cat's howling cry.

cat·gut /'kætgʌt/ *n* [U] material used for the strings of violins, tennis rackets, etc (made by twisting the intestines of sheep and other animals).

ca·thar·sis /kə'θɑːsɪs/ *n* (*pl* -arses /-siːz/) **1** [C,U] (med) emptying of the bowels. **2** outlet for strong emotion (eg as given by the drama, or by a willing account of deep feelings given to another person). **ca·thar·tic** /kə'θɑːtɪk/ *n* (med), *adj* (substance) giving ∼.

ca·the·dral /kə'θiːdrəl/ *n* chief church in a diocese, in which is the bishop's throne, under the charge of a dean.

cath·ode /'kæθəʊd/ *n* **1** negative electrode in the form of a filament which, when hot, releases negative electrons which are attracted towards the (positive) anode. **2** negative terminal of a battery. ˌ∼'ray *n* invisible stream of electrons from the ∼ in a vacuum tube (as used in radar, television, etc), called a ˌ∼ 'ray tube.

cath·olic /'kæθəlɪk/ *adj* **1** liberal; general; including many or most things: *a man with* ∼ *tastes and interests;* ∼ *in his sympathies.* **2 the** C∼ **Church**, the whole body of Christians. **Roman** C∼ *n*, *adj* (member) of the Church that has the Pope as its chief bishop. ⇨ **Pope, Protestant, Roman(3)**. **Ca·tholicism** /kə'θɒləsɪzəm/ *n* teaching, beliefs, etc, of the Roman Catholic Church. **cath·ol·ic·ity** /ˌkæθə'lɪsətɪ/ *n* [U] quality of being ∼(1).

cat·kin /'kætkɪn/ *n* [C] tuft of soft, downy flowers hanging down from twigs of such trees as willows and birches.

cat·sup /'kætsəp/ *n* = ketchup

cat·tish, **cat·ty** /'kætɪʃ, 'kætɪ/ *adj* (esp) sly and spiteful. **cat·ti·ness** *n*

cattle /'kætl/ *n pl* oxen (bulls, bullocks, cows): *twenty head of* ∼. C∼ *were allowed to graze on the village common.* '∼-cake *n* [U] food fed to ∼, made from various materials.

Cau·casian /kɔː'keɪzɪən/ *US:* kɔː'keɪʒn/ *n*, *adj* (member) of the Indo-European group of people.

cau·cus /'kɔːkəs/ *n* (meeting of the) organization committee of a political party (making plans, decisions, etc).

caught /kɔːt/ *pt,pp* of catch.

caul /kɔːl/ *n* (physiol) thin skin enclosing a foetus, part of which, when covering a baby's head, was once thought to be a charm against drowning.

caul·dron /'kɔːldrən/ *n* large, deep, open pot in which things are boiled.

cauli·flower /'kɒlɪflaʊə(r)/ *US:* 'kɔːlɪ-/ *n* [C,U] (cabbage-like plant with a) large, white flowerhead, used as a vegetable. ⇨ the illus at vegetable.

caulk /kɔːk/ *vt* [VP6A] make (joints between planks, etc) tight with fibre or a sticky substance.

causal /'kɔːzl/ *adj* of cause and effect; of, expressing, cause. ∼·ity /kɔː'zælətɪ/ *n* [U] relation of cause and effect; the principle that nothing can happen without a cause: *the law of* ∼ity, eg cause always precedes effect. **cau·sa·tion** /kɔː'zeɪʃn/ *n* [U] ∼ity; causing or being caused. **cau·sa·tive** /'kɔːzətɪv/ *adj* acting as, expressing, cause.

cause /kɔːz/ *n* **1** [C,U] that which produces an effect; thing, event, person, etc, that makes sth happen: *The* ∼ *of the fire was carelessness. We can't get rid of war until we get rid of the* ∼s *of war.* **2** [U] reason: *There is no* ∼ *for anxiety. You have no* ∼ *for complaint/no* ∼ *to complain. Don't stay away without good* ∼. **3** [C] purpose for which efforts are being made: *work in/for a good* ∼; *fight in the* ∼ *of justice.* **make common** ∼ **with sb**, help and support him (in a political, social, etc movement). □ *vt* [VP6A,17,12A,13A] be the ∼ of; make happen: *What* ∼s *the tides? What* ∼d *his death? You've* ∼d *trouble to all of us. This has* ∼d *us much anxiety. What* ∼d *the plants to die?* (*What made them die?* is more usual.) *He* ∼d *the prisoners to be put to death.* (*He had them put to death* is more usual.) ∼·less *adj* without any natural or known ∼.

caus·erie /'kəʊzərɪ/ *n* informal discussion.

cause·way /'kɔːzweɪ/ *n* raised road or footpath, esp across wet land or swamp.

caus·tic /'kɔːstɪk/ *adj* **1** able to burn or destroy by chemical action. ∼ **soda** *n* (*Sodium Hydroxide* /haɪ'drɒksaɪd/ **NaOH**) corrosive chemical substance used in the manufacture of soap. **2** (fig) biting; sarcastic: ∼ *remarks; a* ∼ *manner.* **caus·ti·cally** /-klɪ/ *adv*

cau·ter·ize /'kɔːtəraɪz/ *vt* [VP6A] burn (eg a poisoned wound, a snake-bite) with a caustic substance or with a hot iron (to destroy infection).

cau·tion /'kɔːʃn/ *n* **1** [U] taking care; paying attention (to avoid danger or making mistakes): *When*

crossing a busy street we must use ∼. **2** [C] warning words: *A sign with 'DANGER!' on it is a* ∼. *The judge gave the prisoner a* ∼ *and set him free.* **3** (*sing* with *indef art*) (sl) person whose appearance, behaviour or conversation causes amusement. □ *vt* [VP6A,17,14] ∼ *(against)*, give a ∼ to: *I* ∼*ed him against being late. We were* ∼*ed not to drive fast. The judge* ∼*ed the prisoner*, warned and reproved him. ∼**·ary** /'kɔːʃənɪ *US:* 'kɔːʃənerɪ/ *adj* conveying advice or warning: ∼*ary tales.*
cau·tious /'kɔːʃəs/ *adj* having or showing caution: ∼ *about/of giving offence;* ∼ *not to give offence.* ∼**·ly** *adv*
cav·al·cade /ˌkævl'keɪd/ *n* [C] company or procession of persons on horseback or in carriages.
cava·lier /ˌkævə'lɪə(r)/ *n* **1** (old use) horseman or knight. **2** (in the Civil War, England, 17th c) supporter of Charles I. □ *adj* (of a person) without due seriousness; off-hand; discourteous. ∼**·ly** *adv*
cav·alry /'kævlrɪ/ *n* (usu with *pl v*, collective) soldiers who fight on horseback: (attrib) ∼ *soldier/ officer.*
cave /keɪv/ *n* hollow place in the side of a cliff or hill; large natural hollow under the ground. '∼**-dweller** *n* person living in a ∼, esp in prehistoric times. '∼**·man** /-mæn/ *n* (*pl* -men) ∼ dweller; (colloq) man of primitive instincts and behaviour. □ *vi,vt* [VP2C,15B] ∼ *in*, (cause to) fall in, give way to pressure: *The roof of the tunnel* ∼*d in.* Hence, '∼**-in** *n*
ca·veat /'keɪvɪæt/ *n* **1** (legal) process to suspend proceedings. **2** (formal) qualification; proviso: *put in/enter a* ∼ (*against*).
cav·ern /'kævən/ *n* (liter) cave. ∼**·ous** *adj* like a ∼; full of ∼s; (of a person's eyes) deepset.
caviar, cavi·are /'kævɪɑː(r)/ *n* [U] pickled roe (eggs) of the sturgeon or certain other large fish. ∼ *to the general*, too fine or delicate to be appreciated by ordinary people.
cavil /'kævl/ *vi* (-ll-, US also -l-) [VP2A,3A] ∼ *(at)*, (formal) make unnecessary complaints against, find fault with.
cav·ity /'kævɪtɪ/ *n* (*pl* -ties) empty space; small hole, within a solid body: *a* ∼ *in a tooth;* ∼ *walls*, hollow, to provide insulation.
ca·vort /kə'vɔːt/ *vi* (colloq) prance or jump about like an excited horse.
caw /kɔː/ *n* cry of a raven, rook or crow. □ *vi,vt* **1** [VP2A] make this cry. **2** [VP15B] *caw out*, utter in a cawing tone.
cay·enne /keɪ'en/ *n* (also ∼ /'keɪen/ **'pepper**) [U] very hot kind of red pepper.
cay·men ⇨ caiman.
cease /siːs/ *vt,vi* [VP6A,D,7A,2A,3A] ∼ *(from)*, (formal) come or bring to an end; stop (the more usual word): *C*∼ *fire* (= stop shooting)*! The old German Empire* ∼*d to exist in 1918. The factory has* ∼*d making bicycles. Since he* ∼*d (from) working,....* ,∼**-'fire** *n* signal to stop firing (guns); truce. □ *n* (only in) *without* ∼, incessantly. ∼**-less** *adj* never ending. ∼**·less·ly** *adv*
cedar /'siːdə(r)/ *n* [C] evergreen tree with hard, red, sweet-smelling wood used for making boxes, pencils, fences, etc; [U] the wood: *a* ∼ *cigar box.*
cede /siːd/ *vt* [VP6A,14] ∼ *(to)*, give up (rights, land, etc to another state, etc).
ce·dilla /sɪ'dɪlə/ *n* mark put under the c (ç) in the spelling of some French, Spanish and Portuguese words (as in *façade*) to show that the sound is /s/.
ceil·ing /'siːlɪŋ/ *n* **1** top inner surface of a room. **2**

cloud level; highest (practicable) level (to be) reached by an aircraft: *an aircraft with a* ∼ *of 20000 ft.* **3** maximum height, limit or level: *price* ∼*s; wage* ∼*s.*
cel·an·dine /'seləndaɪn/ *n* small, wild plant with yellow flowers.
cel·ebrant /'selɪbrənt/ *n* priest who leads the service of the Mass.
cel·ebrate /'selɪbreɪt/ *vt* [VP6A, but with the *direct object* sometimes to be understood] **1** do sth to show that a day or an event is important, or an occasion for rejoicing: ∼ *Christmas/one's birthday/a wedding anniversary/a victory;* ∼ *Mass*, lead the ceremony of the Eucharist. *It's your birthday tomorrow, so we must celebrate* (*it*). **2** praise and honour: *The names of many heroes are* ∼*d by the poets.* **cel·ebrated** (*pp* as *adj*) famous: *a* ∼*d painter;* ∼*d for its hot springs;* ∼*d as a hot spring resort.* **cel·ebra·tion** /ˌselɪ'breɪʃn/ *n* [C,U] (the act of, an occasion of) celebrating. **ce·leb·rity** /sɪ'lebrətɪ/ *n* **1** [U] being ∼d; fame and honour. **2** [C] (*pl* -ties) ∼d person: *all the celebrities of the London theatre*, all the famous actors and actresses performing in London.
ce·ler·ity /sɪ'lerətɪ/ *n* [U] (formal) quickness.
cel·ery /'selərɪ/ *n* [U] garden plant of which the stems are eaten raw as salad or cooked as a vegetable: *a bunch/stick/head of* ∼; ∼ *soup.*
ce·les·tial /sɪ'lestɪəl *US:* -tʃl/ *adj* **1** of the sky; of heaven: ∼ *bodies*, eg the sun and the stars; ∼ *joys.* **2** divinely good or beautiful.
celi·bacy /'selɪbəsɪ/ *n* [U] state of living unmarried, esp as a religious obligation. **celi·bate** /'selɪbət/ *n* [C] unmarried person (esp a priest who has taken a vow not to marry).
cell /sel/ *n* **1** small room for one person (esp in a prison or a monastery). **2** compartment in a larger structure, esp in a honeycomb, ⇨ illus at **honeycomb**. **3** unit of an apparatus for producing electric current by chemical action, eg of metal plates in acid, often part of a battery. **4** microscopic unit of living matter enclosing a nucleus with self-producing genes. **5** (of persons) centre or nucleus of (usu revolutionary) political activity: *communist* ∼*s in an industrial town.*
cel·lar /'selə(r)/ *n* underground room for storing coal, wine, etc; (person's) store of wine. ∼**·age** /'selərɪdʒ/ *n* amount of ∼ space; charge for storing sth in a ∼.
cello /'tʃeləʊ/ *n* (*pl* ∼s) bass violin, held between the player's knees, ⇨ the illus at **string**. **cel·list** /'tʃelɪst/ *n* ∼ player.
cel·lo·phane /'seləfeɪn/ *n* [U] (P) thin, moistureproof, transparent material used for wrapping and packing.
cel·lu·lar /'seljʊlə(r)/ *adj* **1** consisting of cells(4): ∼ *tissue.* **2** (of textile materials) loosely woven: ∼ *shirts.*
cel·lu·loid /'seljʊlɔɪd/ *n* [U] (P) flammable plastic substance used for making toys, toilet articles, etc (and formerly for photographic film).
cel·lu·lose /'seljʊləʊs/ *n* [U] **1** structural tissue that forms the chief part of all plants and trees, and hence of paper and many textile fibres; wood fibre. **2** (popularly, for ,∼ '*acetate*) plastic substance used for many industrial purposes (eg explosives, ornaments, toughened glass).
Celsius /'selsɪəs/ *n* (of thermometers) = centigrade.
Celt /kelt *US:* selt/ *n* member of the last group of

immigrants to settle in Britain before the coming of the Anglo-Saxons; (loosely) one of the Irish, Welsh, Gaelic or Breton people today. ~ic *n, adj* (language) of the ~s.

ce·ment /sɪ'ment/ *n* [U] **1** grey powder (made by burning lime and clay) which, after being wetted, becomes hard like stone and is used for building, etc. ⇨ concrete. '~-mixer *n* revolving drum in which ~ is mixed with other material to make concrete. **2** any similar soft substance that sets firm, used for filling holes (eg in the teeth), or for joining things. □ *vt* [VP6A,15B] put ~ on or in; join with ~; (fig) strengthen; unite firmly: ~ *a friendship.*

cem·etery /'semətrɪ *US:* 'seməterɪ/ *n* (*pl* -ries) area of land, not a churchyard, used for burials.

ceno·taph /'senətɑːf *US:* -tæf/ *n* monument put up in memory of a person or persons buried elsewhere.

cen·ser /'sensə(r)/ *n* vessel in which incense is burnt in churches.

cen·sor /'sensə(r)/ *n* **1** official with authority to examine letters, books, periodicals, plays, films, etc and to cut out anything regarded as immoral or in other ways undesirable, or, in time of war, helpful to the enemy. **2** (ancient Rome) officer who prepared a register or census of citizens and supervised public morals. □ *vt* [VP6A] examine, cut out, parts of (a book, etc); act as a ~. ~·ship /-ʃɪp/ *n* function or duties of a ~.

cen·sori·ous /sen'sɔːrɪəs/ *adj* fault-finding; severely critical: ~ *of one's neighbours.*

cen·sure /'senʃə(r)/ *vt* [VP6A,14] ~ *sb (for),* criticize unfavourably for: ~ *sb for being lazy.* □ *n* [U] rebuke; disapproval: *pass a vote of* ~ (*on sb*); *lay oneself open to public* ~; [C] expression of disapproval: *a review containing unfair* ~s *of a new book.*

cen·sus /'sensəs/ *n* (*pl* ~es) official counting of the population.

cent /sent/ *n* the 100th part of a US dollar and many other metric units of currency; metal coin of this value. *per* ~, (%) in, by or for, every 100. *(agree, etc) one hundred per* ~, completely..

cen·taur /'sentɔː(r)/ *n* (Gk myth) fabulous creature, half man and half horse. ⇨ the illus at Minotaur.

cen·ten·ar·ian /ˌsentɪ'neərɪən/ *n, adj* (person who is) 100 or more years old.

cen·ten·ary /sen'tiːnərɪ *US:* 'sentənerɪ/ *adj, n* (*pl* -ries) (having to do with a) period of 100 years; 100th anniversary.

cen·ten·nial /sen'tenɪəl/ *adj, n* = centenary. ~·ly /-nɪəlɪ/ *adv*

cen·ter /'sentə(r)/ *n* (US) = centre.

centi- /'sentɪ/ *pref* one-hundredth part of: ~*gram,* ~*metre.* ⇨ App 5.

cen·ti·grade /'sentɪɡreɪd/ *adj* in or of the temperature scale that has 100 degrees between the freezing-point and the boiling-point of water: *the* ~ *thermometer; 100°* ~ (100°C). ⇨ Fahrenheit and App 5.

cen·time /'sɒntiːm/ *n* the 100th part of a franc.

cen·ti·pede /'sentɪpiːd/ *n* small insect-like crawling creature with a long, thin body, numerous joints, and a pair of feet at each joint.

cen·tral /'sentrəl/ *adj* **1** of, at, from or near, the centre. *My house is very* ~, is in or near the middle of the town. ~ **heating,** method of warming a building by steam, hot air or water in pipes from a ~ source. **2** chief; most important: *the* ~ *idea of an argument; the* ~ *figures* (= the chief persons)

in a novel. **the** ~ **government** *n* that of the whole country. □ *n* (US) telephone exchange. ~·ly /'sentrəlɪ/ *adv*

cen·tral·ize /'sentrəlaɪz/ *vt, vi* [VP6A,2A] bring to the centre; come, put, bring, under central control: ~ *the administration of the coal mines.* **cen·tral·iz·ation** /ˌsentrəlaɪ'zeɪʃn *US:* -lɪ'z-/ *n*

centre (US = **center**) /'sentə(r)/ *n* **1** middle part or point: *the* ~ *of London; the* ~ *of a circle.* ⇨ the illus at circle. ~ *of gravity,* that point in an object about which the weight is evenly balanced in any position. '~-bit, tool for boring holes in wood. ⇨ brace. '~-board, movable board that can be raised or lowered through a slot in the keel of a sailing-boat to prevent drifting to leeward. '~-piece, ornament for the ~ of a table, ceiling, etc; (fig) most important part. **2** place of great activity, esp one to which people are attracted from surrounding districts or from which they go out: *the* '*shopping* ~ *of a town; a* ~ *of commerce.* **3** person or thing that attracts interest, attention etc: *She loves to be the* ~ *of interest.* **4** that which occupies a middle position, eg in politics, persons with moderate views, between two extremes. □ *vi, vi* **1** [VP6A,15A] place in, pass to, come to, be at, the ~: *The defender* ~*d the ball.* **2** [VP3A,14] ~ *on/upon,* focus, fix, on: *Our thoughts* ~ *upon/are* ~*d upon one idea.*

cen·tri·fu·gal /sen'trɪfjʊɡl/ *adj* moving, tending to move, away from the centre or axis: ~ *force,* the force which causes a body spinning round a centre to tend to fly off. **cen·tri·fuge** /'sentrɪfjuːdʒ/ *n* (mech) ~ machine, eg for separating small solid particles in a liquid by rotating motion.

cen·tri·pe·tal /sen'trɪpɪtl/ *adj* tending towards the centre or axis.

cen·tur·ion /sen'tjʊərɪən *US:* -'tʊər-/ *n* (in ancient Rome) leader of a unit of 100 soldiers.

cen·tury /'sentʃərɪ/ *n* [C] (*pl* -ries) **1** 100 years. **2** one of the periods of 100 years before or since the birth of Jesus Christ: *in the 20th* ~, AD 1900-1999. **3** (cricket) 100 runs made by a batsman in one innings: *make/score a* ~.

ce·ramic /sɪ'ræmɪk/ *adj* of the art of pottery. **ce·ram·ics** *n* **1** (*sing v*) art of making and decorating pottery. **2** (*pl v*) articles made of porcelain, clay, etc.

cer·eal /'sɪərɪəl/ *n* (usu *pl*) any kind of grain used for food: ~ *grasses,* eg wheat, rye, barley; food prepared from ~s: '*breakfast* ~s.

cer·ebral /'serɪbrəl *US:* sə'riːbrəl/ *adj* **1** of the brain: ~ *haemorrhage;* ~ *palsy.* ⇨ spastic. **2** intellectual; excluding the emotions.

cer·ebra·tion /ˌserɪ'breɪʃn/ *n* [U] (formal) working of the brain; thinking.

cer·emo·nial /ˌserɪ'məʊnɪəl/ *adj* formal; as used for ceremonies: ~ *dress.* □ *n* [C,U] special order of ceremony, formality, for a special event, etc: *the* ~s *of religion.* ~·ly *adv*

cer·emo·ni·ous /ˌserɪ'məʊnɪəs/ *adj* fond of, marked by, ceremony or formality. ~·ly *adv*

cer·e·mo·ny /'serɪmənɪ *US:* -məʊnɪ/ *n* (*pl* -nies) **1** [C] special act(s), religious service, etc on an occasion such as a wedding, funeral, the opening of a new public building, etc. **Master of 'Ceremonies** *n* person in charge of such formal proceedings. **2** [U] behaviour required by social customs, esp among officials, people of a special group, etc: *There's no need for* ~ *between friends. There's too much* ~ *on official occasions. stand on* ~,

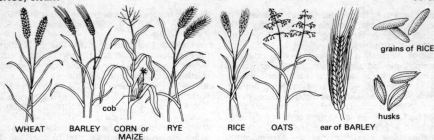

grains of RICE

husks

cob

WHEAT BARLEY CORN or RYE RICE OATS ear of BARLEY
MAIZE

pay great attention to rules of behaviour: *Please don't stand on* ~, please be natural and easy.

ce·rise /sə'riːz *US:* -iːs/ *adj, n* (of a) light, clear red.

cert /sɜːt/ *n* (sl) sth looked upon as certain to happen or that certainly has happened: *a dead* ~, an absolute certainty.

cer·tain /'sɜːtn/ *adj* **1** (pred only) settled; of which there is no doubt: *It is* ~ *that two and two make four.* **2** (pred only) ~ *(that...);* ~ *(of/about);* ~ *to do sth,* convinced; having no doubt; confident: *I'm* ~ *(that) he saw me. I'm not* ~ *(of) who he is/where he went, etc. You can be* ~ *of success. Are you* ~ *of/about that? He is* ~ *to come,* there is no doubt that he will come. *for* ~, without doubt: *I cannot say for* ~ (= with complete confidence) *when he will arrive. I don't know for* ~, have no definite knowledge. *make* ~, (a) inquire in order to be ~: *I think there's a train at 8.20 but you ought to make* ~. (b) do sth in order to be assured: *I'll go to the theatre and make* ~ *of our seats,* eg by reserving them in advance. **3** assured; reliable; sure to come or happen: *There is no* ~ *cure for this disease. The soldier faced* ~ *death.* **4** (attrib only) not named, stated or described, although it is possible to do so: *for a* ~ *reason; on* ~ *conditions; a* ~ *person I met yesterday; a person of a* ~ *age* (usu = *middle-aged).* **5** (attrib only) some, but not much: *There was a* ~ *coldness in her attitude towards me. There is a* ~ *pleasure in pointing out other people's errors.* ~**·ly** *adv* **1** without doubt: *He will* ~*ly die if you don't get a doctor.* ⇨ surely. **2** (in answer to questions) yes: *Will you pass me the towel, please? C*~*ly! Will you lend me your toothbrush? C*~*ly not* (= No)*!* ~**·ty** *n* (*pl* -ties) **1** [C] sth that is ~: *Prices have gone up—that's a* ~*ty. for a* ~*ty,* for ~, without doubt: *I know for a* ~*ty that....* **2** [U] state of being ~: *freedom from doubt: I can't say with any* ·~*ty where I shall be next week. We can have no* ~*ty of success. Would the* ~*ty of punishment deter criminals?*

cer·ti·fi·able /ˌsɜːtɪ'faɪəbl/ *adj* that can be certified: *a* ~ *lunatic,* a person who can be certified by a doctor as insane.

cer·ti·fi·cate /sə'tɪfɪkət/ *n* written or printed statement, made by sb in authority, that may be used as proof or evidence of sth: *a* '*birth/*'*marriage* ~*; a* '*health* ~, from a doctor; ~ *of origin,* (comm) document stating the country or origin of imported goods. □ *vt* provide with a ~. **cer·ti·fi·cated** /-keɪtɪd/ *adj* having the right or authority to do sth as the result of obtaining a ~: ~*d teachers,* who have obtained teaching diplomas (now called *qualified teachers).* **cer·ti·fi·ca·tion** /ˌsɜːtɪfɪ'keɪʃn/ *n* [U] act of certifying; state of being certified; [C] that which certifies.

cer·tify /'sɜːtɪfaɪ/ *vt, vi* **1** [VP6A,9,16B,25] declare (usu by giving a certificate) that one is certain of

sth, that sth is true, correct, in order: *I* ~ *(that) this is a true copy of.... I* ~ *this as/to be a true copy of.... He was certified (as) insane,* The doctor(s) wrote a certificate declaring that he was insane. *The accounts were certified (as) correct.* **certified cheque,** cheque the value of which is guaranteed by the bank. **2** [VP3A] ~ *to sth,* attest it: ~ *to sb's character,* declare that one is satisfied that it is reliable, etc.

cer·ti·tude /'sɜːtɪtjuːd *US:* -tuːd/ *n* [U] (formal) certainty (the more usu word).

ceru·lean /sɪ'ruːlɪən/ *adj* (formal) sky-blue.

cer·vix /'sɜːvɪks/ *n* (*pl* cervices /'sɜːvɪsiːz/ or ~es) (anat) narrow part of the womb. ⇨ the illus at reproduce. **cer·vi·cal** /sɜː'vaɪkl *US:* 'sɜːvɪkl/ *adj* of the ~: ~ *smear,* smear taken from the ~, to test for cancer.

Cesar·ean = Caesarean.

ces·sa·tion /se'seɪʃn/ *n* [U] (formal) ceasing: *the* ~ *of hostilities.*

ces·sion /'seʃn/ *n* [U] act of ceding (giving up lands, rights, etc by agreement); [C] sth ceded.

cess·pit /'sespɪt/, **cess·pool** /'sespuːl/ *nn* (usu covered) hole, pit or underground tank into which drains (esp for sewage) empty; (fig) filthy place.

chafe /tʃeɪf/ *vi, vt* **1** [VP6A] rub (the skin, one's hands) to get warmth. **2** [VP2A,6A] make or become rough or sore by rubbing: *A stiff collar may* ~ *your neck. Her skin* ~*s easily.* **3** [VP3A] ~ *at/ under,* feel long-continued irritation or impatience (because of sth): ~ *at the delay/hold-up/ inefficiency;* ~ *under restraints/illness.* ⇨ also chafing dish below. □ *n* ~d place on the skin.

chaff[1] /tʃɑːf *US:* tʃæf/ *n* [U] **1** outer covering (husks) of grain, removed before the grain is used as human food. **2** hay or straw cut up as food for cattle. □ *vt* [VP6A] cut up (hay, straw).

chaff[2] /tʃɑːf *US:* tʃæf/ *n* [U] good-humoured teasing or joking. □ *vt* [VP2A,C,6A,15A] make good-humoured fun (of): ~ *sb about sth.*

chaf·finch /'tʃæfɪntʃ/ *n* small European song-bird.

chaf·ing dish /'tʃeɪfɪŋ dɪʃ/ *n* vessel with a heater under it, used at table for cooking food or keeping it warm.

chag·rin /'ʃægrɪn *US:* ʃə'griːn/ *n* [U] feeling of disappointment or annoyance (at having failed, made a mistake, etc): *Much to his* ~, *he did not win the race.* □ *vt* [VP6A] (usu passive) affect with ~: *be/ feel* ~*ed at/by.*

chain /tʃeɪn/ *n* **1** flexible line of connected rings or links for connecting, continuing, restraining, ornamenting, etc, ⇨ the illus at bicycle; (*pl*) fetters of this kind, used for prisoners. *in* ~*s,* kept as a prisoner or slave. **2** number of connected things, events, etc: *a* ~ *of mountains/ideas/events/proof.* **3** measure of length (66 ft). ⇨ App 5. **4** (compounds) '~**-armour/-mail,** armour made of metal

rings linked together. ⇨ the illus at armour. '∼-
gang, gang of convicts fastened together with ∼s
while at work outside their prison. '∼-**letter,** letter
of which the recipient is asked to make copies to be
sent to other persons, who will do the same. '∼
reaction, chemical change forming products that
themselves cause more changes so that the process
is repeated again and again (as in the atomic
bomb). '∼-**smoker,** person who smokes cigarettes
in continuous succession. '∼-**stitch,** kind of sewing in which each stitch makes a loop through
which the next stitch is taken. '∼-**store,** one of
many retail shops owned and controlled by the
same company. □ *vt* [VP6A,15A,B] make fast with
a ∼ or ∼s: *The prisoners were ∼ed to the wall.*
C∼ up your dog.
chair /tʃeə(r)/ *n* **1** separate movable seat for one
person, usu with a back and in some cases with
arms (*arm∼*): *Won't you take a ∼,* sit down? '∼-
lift *n* aerial ropeway with seats for carrying persons
up and down mountain slopes, etc. Cf *ski-lift.* ⇨
also **electric, sedan. 2** [U] *the ∼,* seat, office, of a
person who presides at a meeting. *be in/take the*
∼, preside. *leave the ∼,* end the proceedings. **3**
position of professor: *the C∼ of Philosophy.* □ *vt*
[VP6A] **1** place in a ∼, raise up and carry (sb who
has won a contest): *The newly elected MP was*
∼ed by his supporters. **2** preside over: *∼ a meet-*
ing. '∼-**man** /-mən/ *n* (*pl*-men) person presiding
at a meeting; president of a company or a committee: *∼man's report,* annual report of a company,
signed by the ∼man and presented at the annual
general meeting.
chaise /ʃeɪz/ *n* low, two- or four-wheeled horse-
carriage (formerly) used by people driving for
pleasure. ∼ **'longue** /lɒŋ *US:* lɔːŋ/ *n* (*pl* ∼s
longues, pronunciation unchanged) (F) kind of
long, low chair, with an arm at one side only, for
lying on.
chalet /'ʃæleɪ/ *n* Swiss mountain hut built of wood
and with sharply sloping and overhanging roof;
summer cottage built in the same style; small hut in
a holiday camp, etc.
chal·ice /'tʃælɪs/ *n* wine-cup, esp that used for the
Eucharist.

chalices

chalk /tʃɔːk/ *n* **1** [U] soft, white, natural substance
(a kind of limestone) used for making lime. '∼-**pit**
n one from which ∼ is dug. **2** [C,U] this material,
or a material similar in texture, white or coloured,
made into sticks for writing and drawing. ⇨ blackboard. **3** *as different as ∼ and cheese; as like*
as ∼ (is) to cheese, essentially unlike. *by a 'long*
∼, by far, by much. □ *vt* write, draw, mark, with
∼; whiten with ∼. [VP15B] *∼ sth up,* write a
score or record. *∼y adj* of, containing, like, ∼.
chal·lenge /'tʃælɪndʒ/ *n* **1** invitation or call to play
a game, run a race, have a fight, etc to see who is
better, stronger, etc. **2** order given by a sentry to
stop and explain who one is: *'Who goes there?'* is

the ∼. □ *vt* [VP6A,17,14] ∼ *(to),* give, send, be, a
∼ to; ask for facts (to support a statement, etc): ∼
sb to a duel; ∼ *sb to fight;* ∼ *sb's right to do sth;*
∼ *a juryman,* (legal) object to his being a member
of the jury. **chal·len·ger** *n* one who ∼s.
cham·ber /'tʃeɪmbə(r)/ *n* **1** (old use) room, esp a
bedroom. '∼ **concert,** concert of ∼ music. ,∼ **of**
'**horrors,** place where gruesome objects are displayed. '∼-**maid,** housemaid who keeps bedrooms
in order (now chiefly in hotels). '∼ **music,** music
for a small number of players (eg a string quartet).
'∼-**pot,** vessel for urine, used in a bedroom. **2**
(*pl*) judge's room for hearing cases that need not
be taken into court; (not US) set of rooms in a large
building to live in or to use as offices. **3** (hall used
by a) group of legislators (eg in US, the Senate and
the House of Representatives), often distinguished
as the '*Upper C∼* and the '*Lower C∼.* **4** offices of
barristers, etc esp in the Inns of Court. **5** group of
persons organized for purposes of trade: *a C∼ of*
Commerce. **6** enclosed or walled space in the body
of an animal or plant: *a ∼ of the heart,* ⇨ au·ricle,
ventricle; similar cavity in some kinds of machinery; enclosed space in a gun (where a shell or
cartridge is laid).
cham·ber·lain /'tʃeɪmbəlɪn/ *n* (old use) officer
who manages the household of a king, noble, etc.
cha·mel·eon /kə'miːlɪən/ *n* small long-tongued lizard whose colour changes according to its background, ⇨ the illus at reptile; person who changes
his voice, manner, etc to match his surroundings.
chammy-leather /'ʃæmɪ leðə(r)/ *n* chamois-
leather.
cham·ois /'ʃæmwɑː *US:* 'ʃæmɪ/ *n* small goat-like
animal that lives in the high mountains of Europe
and SW Asia. ∼-**leather** /'ʃæmɪ leðə(r)/ soft
leather from the skin of goats and sheep.
chamo·mile *n* (US) = camomile.
champ[1] /tʃæmp/ *vt,vi* [VP6A,2A,C,4A] **1** (of
horses) bite (food, the bit) noisily. **2** (fig) show impatience: ∼ *with rage. The boys were ∼ing to*
start/∼ing at the bit.
champ[2] /tʃæmp/ *n* (colloq abbr of) champion(2).
cham·pagne /ʃæm'peɪn/ *n* (kinds of) white sparkling (because charged with gas) French wine.
cham·pion /'tʃæmpɪən/ *n* **1** person who fights, argues or speaks in support of another or of a cause: *a*
∼ *of free speech/of woman's rights.* **2** person,
team, animal, etc taking the first place in a competition: *a boxing/swimming/tennis, etc* ∼; (attrib):
the ∼ team; the ∼ horse. □ *adj, adv* (colloq)
splendid(ly): *That's ∼!* □ *vt* [VP6A] support; defend. ∼·**ship** /-ʃɪp/ *n* [U] act of ∼ing; [C] position
of being, or competition to decide, a ∼: *to win a*
world swimming ∼ship.
chance[1] /tʃɑːns *US:* tʃæns/ *n* **1** [U] the happening
of events without any cause that can be seen or understood; the way things happen; fortune or luck:
Let's leave it to ∼. Let ∼ decide. by ∼, by accident, not by design or on purpose. *game of ∼,*
one that is decided by luck, not by skill. *take*
one's ∼, trust to luck, take whatever happens to
come. **2** [C,U] possibility: *He has no ∼/not much*
∼/a poor ∼ of winning. I've had no ∼ to get
away/of getting away. What ∼ of success is there?
What is our ∼/are our ∼s of succeeding? What
are the ∼s that we shall succeed? The ∼s are a
hundred to one against you, It's most unlikely that
you will succeed. *If, by any ∼,..., If, by some ∼*
or other..., If it so happens that.... *on the (off)* ∼

that/of doing sth, in view of the possibility, in the hope: *I'll call at his office on the ~ that I'll see/of seeing him before he leaves.* **3** [C] opportunity; occasion when success seems very probable: *This was the ~ he had been waiting for. It's the ~ of a lifetime,* a favourable opportunity that is unlikely ever to come again. **stand a good/fair ~ (of...),** have a fair prospect (of sth). **the ,main '~** *n* opportunity of making money: *He always has an eye to the main ~,* sees when money can be made. **4** (attrib) coming or happening by ~(1): *a ~ meeting; a ~ companion.*

chance[2] /tʃɑːns *US:* tʃæns/ *vi,vt* **1** [VP3A] ~ *on/upon,* find or meet by chance. [VP4E,2A after *if*] happen by chance: *I ~d to be there. It ~d that I was out/I ~d to be out when he called.* **2** [VP6A,C] take a risk, esp ~ *it;* ~ *one's arm,* (colloq) take a chance of success although failure is probable.

chan-cel /'tʃɑːnsl *US:* 'tʃænsl/ *n* eastern part of a church, round the altar, used by the priest(s) and choir. ⇨ the illus at church.

chan-cel-lery /'tʃɑːnsəlrɪ *US:* 'tʃæns-/ *n* (*pl* -ries) **1** chancellor's position, department or residence. **2** place of business of an embassy, legation or consulate.

chan-cel-lor /'tʃɑːnsələ(r) *US:* 'tʃæns-/ *n* **1** (in some countries, eg W Germany) chief minister of state. **2** (of some universities) titular head or president (the duties being performed by the Vice-C~). **3** (GB) chief secretary of an embassy. **4** State or law official of various kinds: *the Lord C~ of England, the Lord High C~,* the highest judge (and chairman of the House of Lords); *the C~ of the Exchequer.*

chan-cery /'tʃɑːnsərɪ *US:* 'tʃæns-/ *n* (*pl* -ries) **1** (GB) Lord Chancellor's division of the High Court of Justice. **ward in ~,** person (usu a *minor(n)*) whose affairs are in charge of the Lord Chancellor (eg because of the death of the ward's parents). **2** (US) court of equity for those cases with no remedy in common law. **3** office of public records. **4** chancellery(2).

chancy /tʃɑːnsɪ *US:* 'tʃænsɪ/ *adj* (colloq) risky; uncertain.

chan-de-lier /ˌʃændə'lɪə(r)/ *n* ornamental branched holder (usu hanging from the ceiling) for a number of lights.

chan-dler /'tʃɑːndlə(r) *US:* 'tʃænd-/ *n* **1** person who makes or sells candles, oil, soap, paint, etc. **2** **ship's ~,** dealer in canvas, ropes and other supplies for ships.

change[1] /tʃeɪndʒ/ *vt,vi* **1** [VP6A,14,2A] ~ *(from/out of) (to/into);* ~ *(for),* leave one place and go to, enter, another; take off sth and put sth else on: *I must ~ these trousers—they've got oil on them. It won't take me five minutes to ~,* to put on different clothes. *He ~d out of his overalls (and into a suit). He ~ed his overalls (for a suit). We seldom ~ for dinner,* eg seldom ~ into formal evening dress. *I've ~d my address,* moved to a different house, flat, etc. *The house has ~d hands several times,* has been bought and sold several times. ~ *(trains),* leave one train and get into another during a journey: ~ *(trains) at Crewe for Stockport. Where do we ~? All ~!* (a cry heard at stations when a train is going no further). ~ *up/down,* (motoring) change to a higher/lower gear. **2** [VP6A,14] ~ *sth (for/into sth else),* give and receive in return: *Can you ~ this five-pound note, give me notes and/or coins of smaller denomina-*

tions? *He ~d his Italian money before leaving Rome. Shall we ~ seats? I ~d places with her. He ~d his car for a foreign make.* **3** [VP6A,14,2A,C] ~ *(from) (into/to),* make or become different: *That has ~d my ideas. My plans have ~d. Caterpillars ~ into butterflies or moths. The traffic lights ~d from red to green. You've ~d since I last saw you.* ~ *over (from) (to),* abandon an old system and take up a new one: *the country has ~ed over from military to democratic rule.* Hence, '~-over *n.* ~ *one's mind,* decide on a new plan, have a new opinion, etc. ~ *one's note/tune,* become more humble, sad, etc. ~ *step,* (when marching with a group) march so that the other foot is keeping time (eg with the beat of a drum). ~-**able** *adj* likely to alter; often altering; able to be ~d: ~able *weather; a ~able sort of person,* one whose moods often ~. ~-**able-ness** *n*

change[2] /tʃeɪndʒ/ *n* **1** [C] changed or different condition(s); sth used in place of another or others; move from one place to another: *a welcome ~ from town to country life. We have a new house—its a great ~ for the better. Take a ~ of clothes with you,* extra clothes to ~ into. *He had to make a quick ~* (ie of trains) *at Crewe.* **a ~ of air/climate,** eg a holiday away from home. **ring the ~s,** ⇨ ring[2](11). **2** [U] money in small(er) units; money that is the difference between the price or cost of sth and the sum offered in payment: *Can you give me ~ for a one-pound note? I have no small ~,* no coins of small value. *Don't leave your ~ on the shop counter!* **get no ~ out of (sb),** (colloq) get no help, information or advantage from. **3** [C,U] alteration; changing: *C~ is not necessarily a good thing in itself. We shall have to make a ~ in the programme. Let's hope there will be a ~ in the weather.* **for a ~,** for the sake of variety; to be different from one's routine: *I usually have breakfast at 7.30, but during the holidays I'm having it at 8.30 for a ~.* ~ **of life,** = menopause. ~-**ful** /-fʊl/ *adj* continually changing; likely to change. ~-**less** *adj* unchanging.

change-ling /'tʃeɪndʒlɪŋ/ *n* child secretly substituted for another in infancy, esp (in old stories) a strange, ugly or stupid child left by fairies in place of one they have stolen.

chan-nel /'tʃænl/ *n* **1** stretch of water joining two seas: *the English C~,* between England and England. **2** natural or artificial bed of a stream of water; passage along which a liquid may flow. **3** deeper part of a waterway: *The ~ is marked by buoys. Keep to the ~—the river is shallow at the sides.* **4** (fig) any way by which news, ideas, etc may travel: *He has secret ~s of information.* **through the usual ~s,** by the usual means of communication (between persons, groups, etc): *A debate on this question can be arranged through the usual ~s,* eg, in Parliament, through the leaders of political parties. **5** (radio, TV) band of frequencies within which signals from a transmitter must be kept (to prevent interference from other transmitters). □ *vt* (-ll-, US also -l-) [VP6A,14] **1** form a ~ or ~s in, cut out (a way): *The river had ~led its way through the soft rock.* **2** cause to go through a ~ or ~s.

chant /tʃɑːnt *US:* tʃænt/ *n* [C] often-repeated tune to which psalms and canticles are fitted; several syllables or words to one note. ⇨ hymn. □ *vi,vt* [VP2A,6A] sing; sing a ~; use a singing note (eg for a prayer in Church): ~ *sb's praises,* (fig) praise constantly.

chantey, chanty /'ʃæntɪ/ n (US) = shanty².

chaos /'keɪɒs/ n [U] complete absence of order or shape; confusion: *The room was in a state of* ~ *when the burglars had left.* **cha·otic** /keɪ'ɒtɪk/ adj in a state of ~; confused. **cha·oti·cally** /keɪ'ɒtɪklɪ/ adv

chap¹ /tʃæp/ vt,vi (-pp-) **1** [VP2A] (of the skin) become sore, rough, cracked: *My skin soon* ~*s in cold weather.* **2** [VP6A] cause to become cracked or rough: *hands and face* ~*ped by the cold.* □ n crack, esp in the skin.

chap² /tʃæp/ n (also *chop*) (*pl*) jaws, esp of animals; cheeks. '~-**fallen** adj dispirited, dejected.

chap³ /tʃæp/ n (colloq) man; boy; fellow.

chapel /'tʃæpl/ n **1** place (not a parish church) used for Christian worship, eg in a large private house, school, prison, etc. **2** small place within a Christian church, used for private prayer, with an altar, and usually named (eg a '*Lady C*~, one dedicated to Mary, the mother of Jesus). ⇨ the illus at church. **3** (GB; obsolescent use) place of worship used by those who do not belong to the established (Anglican) Church of England: *the Methodist* ~. *Are you church or* ~, Do you belong to the Church of England or to one of the Free Churches? ⇨ free¹(3). '~-**goer** /-gəʊə(r)/ n non-conformist (contrasted with a member of the Church of England). **4** [U] service held in a ~(1,3): *go to* ~.

chap·er·on /'ʃæpərəʊn/ n married or elderly person (usu a woman) in charge of a girl or young unmarried woman on social occasions. □ vt [VP6A] act as a ~ to.

chap·fallen /'tʃæpfɔːlən/ adj ⇨ chap².

chap·lain /'tʃæplɪn/ n priest or clergyman, esp in the navy, army or air force, or officiating in a chapel(1). ⇨ padre. ~-**cy** /-sɪ/ n function, area or house of a ~.

chap·let /'tʃæplɪt/ n wreath (of leaves, flowers, jewels, etc) for the head; string of beads (a short rosary) for counting prayers.

chap·man /'tʃæpmən/ n (*pl*-men) (old use) pedlar.

chap·ter /'tʃæptə(r)/ n **1** (usu numbered) main division of a book. ~ *of accidents,* number of misfortunes closely following one another. ~ *and verse,* exact reference to a passage, etc or authority (*for* a statement, etc) for. **2** period; epoch: *the most brilliant* ~ *in the history of the French court.* **3** (general meeting of the) whole number of canons of a cathedral church, or the members of a monastery or convent. '~-**house** n building used for such meetings.

char¹ /tʃɑː(r)/ vt,vi (-rr-) [VP6A,2A] (of a surface) make or become black by burning: ~*red wood.*

char² /tʃɑː(r)/ vi (-rr-) do the cleaning of offices, houses, etc with payment by the hour or the day: *go out* ~*ring.* □ n ~woman. '~-**lady,** '~-**woman** nn woman who earns money by ~ing, paid by the hour or the day.

char³ /tʃɑː(r)/ n [U] (GB sl) tea: *a cup of* ~.

char-à-banc, char·a·banc /'ʃærəbæŋ/ n (not US) (now usu called *coach*) single-decked motor-coach with all seats facing forward, used for pleasure trips.

char·ac·ter /'kærəktə(r)/ n **1** [U] (of a person, community, race, etc) mental or moral nature; mental or moral qualities that make one person, race, etc different from others: *a woman of fine/strong/ noble, etc* ~; *the* ~ *of Julius Cæsar/of the French.*

in/out of ~, appropriate/inappropriate to the actions, etc known to be in accord with a person's ~. **2** [U] moral strength: *a man of* ~. *Should* ~ *building be the chief aim of education?* **3** [U] all those qualities that make a thing, place, etc what it is and different from others: *the* ~ *of the desert areas of N Africa.* **4** [C] person who is well known: *a public* ~; person in a novel, play, etc: *the* ~*s in the novels of Charles Dickens;* person who is in some ways unusual: *He's quite a* ~, has peculiarities of his own, is not an average or typical sort of person. '~ *actor* n one who specialises in portraying unusual or eccentric people. **5** [C] (old use) description of a person's abilities and qualities, esp in a letter by an employer, that may be used when applying for a job (*testimonial* is now the usu word). **6** [C] reputation: *He has gained the* ~ *of a miser.* **7** [C] letter, sign, mark, etc used in a system of writing or printing: *Greek/Chinese, etc* ~*s.* ~-**is·tic** /ˌkærəktə'rɪstɪk/ adj forming part of, showing, the ~ of: *with his* ~*istic enthusiasm. It's* ~*istic of him,* It's what people would expect him to do, because of his ~. □ n [C] special mark or quality: *What are the* ~*istics that distinguish the Chinese from the Japanese?* ~-**is·ti·cally** /ˌkærəktə'rɪstɪklɪ/ adv. '~-**ize** vt [VP6A] show the ~ of; give ~ to; mark in a special way: *Your work is* ~*ized by lack of attention to detail. The camel is* ~*ized by the ability to go for long periods without water.* ~-**less** adj without ~; undistinguished; ordinary.

cha·rade /ʃə'rɑːd US: -'reɪd/ n [C] episode in a game in which a word is guessed by the onlookers after the word itself, and each syllable of it in turn, have been suggested by acting a little play; (*pl,* with sing *vb*) this game; (fig) action of no or sham significance; pretence.

char·coal /'tʃɑːkəʊl/ n [U] black substance, used as fuel, as a filtering material and for drawing, made by burning wood slowly in an oven with little air: *a bale/stick/piece, etc of* ~. '~-**burner** n person who makes ~; stove, etc in which ~ is used as the fuel.

chard /tʃɑːd/ n (often *Swiss* ~) variety of beet of which the leaves are used as a vegetable.

charge¹ /tʃɑːdʒ/ n **1** accusation; statement that a person has done wrong, esp that he has broken a law: *arrested on a* ~ *of theft.* **bring a** ~ **(of sth) against sb,** accuse him (of a crime, etc). **face a** ~ **(of sth),** have to answer it in court: *He faces serious* ~*s.* **lay sth to sb's** ~, bring an accusation of sth against him. '~-**sheet** n record of cases kept in a police station. **2** sudden and violent attack at high speed (by soldiers, wild animals, a football player, etc). **3** price asked for goods or services: *hotel* ~*s.* '~-**account** n (US) credit account. ⇨ credit¹(1). **4** amount of powder, etc (to be) used in a gun or for causing an explosion; amount of electricity (to be) put into an accumulator, contained in a substance, etc: *a positive/negative* ~. **5** [C] work given to sb as a duty; thing or person given or entrusted to sb to be taken care of; [U] responsibility; trust: *This ward of the hospital is in/under the* ~ *of Dr Green. I hope you'll never become a* ~ *on the public,* ie become a pauper, to be supported at public expense. **put sb/be in** ~ **(of),** be (put) in a position of responsibility (for): *Mary was (put) in* ~ *of the baby. Who's in* ~ *here?* **put sb/be in sb's** ~, be (put) in his care: *The baby was (put) in Mary's* ~. **give sb in** ~, give him up to the police. **take** ~ **of,** become responsible for. **6** directions; instructions: *the judge's* ~ *to the jury,* instructions concerning their duty (in reaching a verdict).

charge² /tʃɑːdʒ/ *vt,vi* **1** [VP6A,14] ~ *sb (with),* accuse; bring a charge(1) against: *He was* ~*d with murder. He* ~*d me with neglecting my duty.* **2** [VP6A,2A,C] make a charge(2) against; rush forward and attack: *Our soldiers* ~*d the enemy. One of our strikers* (ie in a game of football) *was violently* ~*d by the defender. The wounded lion suddenly* ~*d at me.* **3** [VP2B,14] ~ *(for),* ask as a price; ask in payment: *He* ~*d (me) fifty pence (for it). How much do you* ~ *for mending a pair of shoes?* **4** [VP14,15A,15B] ~ *to;* ~ *up;* ~ *up to,* make a record of (as a debt): *Please* ~ *these purchases to my account.* **5** [VP6A,2A] load (a gun); fill, put a charge(4) into: ~ *an accumulator. Electrons are negatively* ~*d with electricity; protons are positively* ~*d.* **6** [VP14] ~ *with,* give as a task or duty; give into sb's care: *He was* ~*d with an important mission. He* ~*d himself with* (= undertook) *the task of keeping the club's accounts in order.* **7** [VP6A,17A] (esp of a judge, or person in authority) command; instruct: *I* ~ *you not to forget what I have said. The judge* ~*d the jury,* gave them directions about how to perform their duty.
charge·able /'tʃɑːdʒəbl/ *adj* **1** that can be, is liable to be, charged: *If you steal, you are* ~ *with theft.* **2** ~ *on/to* (comm) that may be added (to an account): *sums* ~ *to a reserve;* that may be made an expense: *Costs of repairs are* ~ *on the owner of the building.*
chargé d'affaires /ˌʃɑːʒeɪ dæˈfeə(r)/ *n* (*pl* chargés d'affaires, pronunciation unchanged) official who takes the place of an ambassador or minister when the ambassador, etc is absent from his post.
charger¹ /'tʃɑːdʒə(r)/ *n* (old use) army officer's horse.
charger² /'tʃɑːdʒə(r)/ *n* (old use) large, flat dish; platter.
char·iot /'tʃærɪət/ *n* open, two-wheeled, horse-drawn carriage, used in ancient times in fighting and racing. **char·io·teer** /ˌtʃærɪə'tɪə(r)/ *n* driver of a ~.
cha·ris·ma /kə'rɪzmə/ *n* **1** (theology) spiritual grace. **2** capacity to inspire devotion and enthusiasm. **char·is·matic** /ˌkærɪz'mætɪk/ *adj*
chari·table /'tʃærɪtəbl/ *adj* showing, having, charity (*to*); for charity: ~ *institutions,* for helping poor or suffering or needy people; ~ *to all men.* **'chari·tably** /-blɪ/ *adv*
char·ity /'tʃærətɪ/ *n* **1** [U] willingness to judge other persons with kindness; neighbourly love: *judge other people with* ~. *C*~ *begins at home,* (prov) A person's first duty is to help the members of his own family. **2** (kindness in giving) help to the poor; money, food, etc so given. **live on/off** ~, live by accepting money etc from others. **3** [C] (*pl* -ties) society or organization for serving those in need: *He left all his money to charities,* to charitable institutions.
chari·vari /ˌʃɑːrɪ'vɑːrɪ US: ʃɪvə'riː/ *n* [U] hubbub; medley of noises and voices.
char·lady /'tʃɑːleɪdɪ/ *n* (*pl* -ladies) charwoman. ⇨ char².
char·la·tan /'ʃɑːlətən/ *n* person who claims to have more skill, knowledge or ability than he really has, esp one who pretends to have medical knowledge.
Charles·ton /'tʃɑːlstən/ *n* fast dance with side kicks from the knee (popular in the 1920's).

char·lock /'tʃɑːlɒk/ *n* wild mustard, a weed with yellow flowers.
charm /tʃɑːm/ *n* **1** [U] attractiveness; power to give pleasure; [C] pleasing quality or feature: *Her* ~ *of manner made her very popular. He fell a victim to her* ~*s,* her beauty, her attractive ways, etc. **2** [C] sth believed to have magic power, good or bad: *under a* ~, influenced in a magic way; ~*s against evil spirits; a* ~ *to bring good luck,* eg a trinket worn on the body. **work like a** ~, with complete success. □ *vt,vi* **1** [VP6A,2A] attract; give pleasure to: *Does goodness* ~ *more than beauty? We were* ~*ed with the scenery. I'm* ~*ed* (*pleased* is more usu) *to meet you* (used as a polite formula). **2** [VP6A,15A] use magic on; influence or protect as if by magic: *He's had a* ~*ed life,* has escaped dangers, as if protected by magic. *She* ~*ed away his sorrow,* caused him to forget his troubles. ~**ing** *adj* delightful: *a* ~*ing young lady.* ~**·ing·ly** *adv.* ~**er** *n* (usu joc) young man or woman with ~. **'snake** ~**er** *n* person able to ~(2) snakes.
char·nel house /'tʃɑːnl haʊs/ *n* place where dead human bodies or bones are stored.
chart /tʃɑːt/ *n* **1** map used by sailors, showing the coasts, depth of the sea, position of rocks, lighthouses, etc. **2** sheet of paper with information, in the form of curves, diagrams, etc (about such things as the weather, prices, business conditions, etc): *a 'weather/'temperature* ~. □ *vt* [VP6A] make a ~ of; show on a ~.
char·ter /'tʃɑːtə(r)/ *n* **1** (written or printed statement of) rights, permission to act to do sth, esp from a ruler or government (eg to a town, city or university). **2** hiring or engagement (of an aircraft, a ship, etc): *a* '~ *flight. C*~*s of oil-tankers may be by time or for the voyage.* □ *vt* [VP6A] **1** give a ~ to; grant a privilege to. ~**ed ac'countant,** (in GB) member of the Institute of Accountants (which has a royal ~). **2** hire or engage a ship, an aircraft, etc for an agreed time, purpose and payment: *travel in a* ~*ed aircraft.* '~**-party** *n* (comm) agreement between a shipowner and merchant for the use of a ship.
Chart·ism /'tʃɑːtɪzəm/ *n* early 19th c working-class movement for social and industrial reform. **Chart·ist** /-ɪst/ *n*
char·treuse /ʃɑː'trɜːz US: -'truːz/ *n* (kinds of) liqueur (green, yellow) made by Carthusian /kɑː'θjuːzɪən US: -'θuːʒn/ monks (of an austere monastic order founded in S France in 1086).
char·woman /'tʃɑːwʊmən/ *n* ⇨ char².
chary /'tʃeərɪ/ *adj* ~ *(of),* cautious, wary, careful: ~ *of catching cold; a teacher who is* ~ *of giving praise,* who seldom praises his pupils. **char·ily** *adv*
Cha·ryb·dis /kə'rɪbdɪs/ *n* ⇨ Scylla.
chase¹ /tʃeɪs/ *vt,vi* **1** [VP6A,3A,15A,B] ~ *(after),* run after in order to capture, kill, overtake or drive away: *Dogs like to* ~ *rabbits. C*~ *that dog out of the garden. The letter had been chasing after him for weeks,* eg had been following him from place to place during his travels. *This'll* ~ *away the blues!* **2** [VP2C] (colloq) hurry; rush: *The children all* ~*d off after the procession.* □ *n* act of chasing: *After a long* ~, *we caught the thief.* **give** ~ *(to),* run after; start in pursuit (of). **in** ~ *of sb/sth,* pursuing, running after. **(go on) a ,wild 'goose** ~, (embark on) a search, expedition, etc that can have no success. **chaser** *n* (in compounds) person or thing that ~s; (colloq) drink taken after another, eg a mild after a strong: *whisky with beer* ~*rs.*
chase² /tʃeɪs/ *vt* [VP6A] cut patterns or designs on

(metal or other hard material); engrave: ~d silver.

chasm /'kæzəm/ n deep opening or crack in the ground; abyss; gorge; (fig) wide difference (of feeling or interests, *between* persons, groups, nations, etc).

chas·sis /'ʃæsɪ/ n (pl spelling unchanged, but pronounced /'ʃæsɪz/) base framework of a motor-vehicle, radio or TV, on which the body and working parts are mounted.

chaste /tʃeɪst/ adj **1** virtuous in word, thought and deed; (esp) abstaining from promiscuous or all sexual intercourse. **2** (of style, taste) simple; without ornament; pure. ~·ly adv

chas·ten /'tʃeɪsn/ vt [VP6A] **1** punish in order to correct; discipline. **2** make chaste(2).

chas·tise /tʃæ'staɪz/ vt [VP6A] punish severely. ~·ment n [U] punishment.

chas·tity /'tʃæstətɪ/ n [U] state of being chaste.

chas·uble /'tʃæzjʊbl/ n (eccles) loose, sleeveless garment worn over all other vestments by a priest at the Eucharist. ⇨ the illus at **vestment**.

chat /tʃæt/ n [C] friendly talk (usu about unimportant things): *I had a long ~ with him.* □ vi, vt (-tt-) **1** [VP2A,C] have a ~: *They were ~ting (away) in the corner.* **2** [VP15B] ~ **sb up**, (colloq) ~ to in order to win friendship, or for fun: ~ *up a pretty barmaid.* ~**ty** adj fond of ~ting.

châ·teau /'ʃætəʊ/ n (pl ~x /-təʊz/) castle or large country house in France.

a chateau

chat·el·aine /'ʃætəleɪn/ n (old use) set of short chains fastened to a woman's belt for carrying keys, etc; mistress of a large country house or castle.

chat·tel /'tʃætl/ n (legal) article of personal movable property (eg a chair, a motor-car, a horse): *a person's goods and ~s.*

chat·ter /'tʃætə(r)/ vi [VP2A,C] **1** (of a person) talk quickly or foolishly; talk too much. **2** (of the cries of monkeys and some birds, of typewriter keys, of a person's upper and lower teeth striking together from cold or fear) make quick, indistinct sounds. □ n [U] sounds of the kind noted above: *the ~ of sparrows/children.* '~-box, person who ~s, esp a small child.

chauf·feur /'ʃəʊfə(r) US: ʃəʊ'fɜːr/ n man paid to drive a privately-owned motor-car. **chauf·feuse** /'ʃəʊfɜːz US: ʃəʊ'fɜːz/ n woman ~.

chau·vin·ism /'ʃəʊvɪnɪzəm/ n [U] unreasoning enthusiasm for (esp) the glory of one's own country. **chau·vin·ist** /-ɪst/ n person with such enthusiasm. **male chauvinist; chauvinist male,** (mod use) man who believes that men are superior to women and acts accordingly. **chau·vin·is·tic** /ˌʃəʊvɪ'nɪstɪk/ adj of ~ or chauvinists.

chaw /tʃɔː/ n, vt (vulg) chew. '~-bacon n ignorant bumpkin.

cheap /tʃiːp/ adj (-er, -est) **1** low in price; costing

little money: *the ~ seats in a theatre; travel by the ~est route; ~ tickets/trips,* at specially reduced fares; (used as adv): *buy/sell/get sth ~,* ie for a low price. **go ~,** be offered or bought for a low price: *Cauliflowers going ~——only 10p each!* **on the ~,** (colloq) for a low price: *buy/sell/get sth on the ~.* **2** worth more than the cost; of good value for the money. **3** of poor quality: ~ *and nasty.* '~-**jack** adj ~ and shoddy. **4** shallow; insincere: ~ *emotion;* ~ *flattery.* **5** **feel ~,** (colloq) feel ashamed. **hold sth ~,** put a low value on it, despise it. **make oneself ~,** behave so that one's reputation goes down. ~ **gibe** n unkind taunt. ~·**ly** adv for a low price: *buy/sell/get sth ~ly.* ~·**ness** n

cheapen /'tʃiːpən/ vt, vi [VP6A,2A] make or become cheap; lower the price of: *You mustn't ~ yourself,* behave so that you lower your reputation.

cheat /tʃiːt/ vi, vt [VP6A,2A,C,14] ~ **sb (out of sth);** ~ **(in/at sth),** act in a dishonest way to win an advantage or profit: ~ *the customs,* eg by not declaring dutiable goods; ~ *sb out of his money;* ~ *at cards;* ~ *in an examination.* □ n person who ~s; dishonest trick.

check¹ /tʃek/ vt, vi **1** [VP6A,15B,2C] examine in order to learn whether sth is correct: ~ *a bill;* ~ *sb's statements. Will you please ~ these figures?* ~ **sth off,** mark it as having been found correct. ~ **sth up;** ~ **up on sth,** (US = ~ **sth out**) examine or compare it to learn whether it is correct. ~ **up on sb,** examine his credentials to see whether he is what he claims to be. **2** [VP6A] hold back; restrain; cause to go slow or stop: *We have ~ed the enemy's advance. He couldn't ~ his anger. This extravagant spending must be ~ed.* **3** [VP6A] (chess) put in ~²(4). **4** [VP2C] ~ **in (at),** arrive and register at a hotel/a factory etc. ~ **out (from),** pay one's bill and leave (a hotel, supermarket etc): '~-**out time,** time at which a room etc must be vacated. '~-**out** n (esp) place (eg in a supermarket) where one pays the bill, wraps one's goods and leaves. **5** (US) [VP6A] get a ticket, a piece of wood, metal, etc that shows a right to sth (eg hat and coat at a theatre, luggage sent by train or left at a railway station): *Have you ~ed* (= got a ~²(3) for) *all your baggage?* ~**er** n person who ~s stores, orders, etc.

check² /tʃek/ n [U] **1** control; person or thing that checks or restrains: *Wind acts as a ~ upon speed. Our forces have met with a ~,* Their advance has been stopped, they have suffered a reverse. *We are keeping/holding the enemy in ~,* are preventing their advance. *I advise you to keep a ~ on* (= control) *your temper.* ~**s and 'balances** n pl (methods of) control or supervision by Government, or other authorities, to guard against misuse of power. **2** examination to make certain of accuracy; mark or tick (usu written /) to show that sth has been examined and proved to be correct: *If we both add up the figures, your result will be a ~ on mine.* '~-**list** n list of items, titles, etc, used in checking sth. '~-**out** n ⇨ check¹(5). '~-**point** n (esp) place where traffic is halted for inspection. '~-**up** n (esp a medical) examination made to certify sb/sth. **3** receipt (bit of paper, piece of wood or metal with a number on it, etc) given in return for sth handed over to sb (eg a hat and coat at a theatre, luggage sent by train). '~-**room,** (US) left-luggage office. **4** **in** ~, (chess) position of an opponent's king when it is exposed to direct attack. ⇨ check-mate. **5** (US) = cheque. '~-**book,** (US) = chequebook. **6** (US) = bill³(1): *I'll ask the waiter for my* ~.

check³ /tʃek/ *n* **1** pattern of crossed lines forming squares (often of different shades or colours); cloth with such a pattern: *Which do you want for your new dress, a stripe or a* ~? **2** (attrib) *a* ~ *tablecloth; a* ~ *pattern.* **checked** /tʃekt/ *adj* with a ~ pattern: ~*ed material.*
checker /'tʃekə(r)/ *vt* (US) = chequer.
check·ers /'tʃekəz/ (US) = draughts.
check·mate /'tʃekmeɪt/ *vt* [VP6A] **1** (chess) make a move that prevents the opponent's king from being moved away from a direct attack (and so win the game). ⇨ check²(4). **2** obstruct and defeat (a person, his plans). □ *n* complete defeat.
Ched·dar /'tʃedə(r)/ *n* [U] kind of hard yellow cheese.
cheek /tʃiːk/ *n* **1** either side of the face below the eye. ⇨ the illus at head. ~ **by jowl,** close together. **turn the other** ~, respond to violence with non-violence. ⇨ Matt 5.38. '~**bone** *n* the bone below the eye. **tongue-in-**~ ⇨ tongue. **2** [U] impudence; saucy talk or behaviour: *He had the* ~ *to ask me to do his work for him! No more of your* ~*!* □ *vt* [VP6A] be impudent to: *Stop* ~*ing your mother!* **-cheeked** *suffix* (with an *adj*): *,rosy-*~*ed 'boys,* boys with rosy ~s. ~**y** *adj* saucy; impudent. ~**·ily** *adv*
cheep /tʃiːp/ *vi, n* [VP2A,C] (make a) weak, shrill note (as young birds do).
cheer¹ /tʃɪə(r)/ *vt,vi* **1** [VP6A,15B] ~ *sb (up),* fill with gladness, hope, high spirits; comfort: *Your visit has* ~*ed (up) the sick man. Everyone was* ~*ed by the good news.* ~**·ing** *adj*: that's ~ing news. **2** [VP2C] ~ *up,* take comfort, become happy: *He* ~*ed up at once when I promised to help him.* **3** [VP6A,15B,2A,C] ~ *(on),* give shouts of joy, approval or encouragement to: *The speaker was loudly* ~*ed. Everyone* ~*ed the news that the war was over. The boys* ~*ed on their football team.* ~**·ing** *n* [U]: *The* ~*ing could be heard half a mile away.*
cheer² /tʃɪə(r)/ *n* **1** [U] (old use) state of hope, gladness: *words of* ~, of encouragement. **2** [U] **good** ~, (old use) good food and drink. **3** [C] shout of joy or encouragement: *give three* ~*s for,* cry or shout 'Hurrah!' three times. '~**-leader** *n* (US) one who leads organised cheering by a group or crowd. **4** (old use) *What* ~*? How do you feel?* **5** **C**~**s!** Word used when one drinks to sb's health.
cheer·ful /'tʃɪəfl/ *adj* **1** bringing or suggesting happiness: *a* ~ *day/room/smile;* ~ *conversation.* **2** happy and contented; willing: ~ *workers.* ~**·ly** /-fəlɪ/ *adv* ~**·ness** *n*
cheer·io /,tʃɪərɪ'əʊ/ *int* (colloq) **1** (at parting) goodbye. **2** (not US; dated) (in drinking) To your health!
cheer·less /'tʃɪəlɪs/ *adj* without comfort; gloomy; miserable: *a wet and* ~ *day; a damp, cold and* ~ *room.* ~**·ly** *adv* ~**·ness** *n*
cheery /'tʃɪərɪ/ *adj* lively; genial; merry: *a* ~ *smile/greeting.* **cheer·ily** /'tʃɪərəlɪ/ *adv*
cheese /tʃiːz/ *n* [U] solid food made from milk curds; [C] shaped and wrapped portion or ball of this: *two cream* ~*s.* '~**-cake,** **(a)** tart filled with a sweet mixture of curd, eggs, etc. **(b)** (sl) displays of a shapely female body (in a photograph, advertisement, etc). ⇨ *pin-up* at pin²(1). '~**-cloth,** thin cotton cloth (gauze) put round some kinds of ~; similar (thicker) cloth used to make shirts, etc.

'~**-paring,** excessive carefulness in the spending of money: ~*-paring economies.*
chee·tah /'tʃiːtə/ *n* kind of wild cat of Africa, resembling a leopard, which can be trained to hunt deer.
chef /ʃef/ *n* head cook in a hotel, restaurant etc.
chef-d'œuvre /,ʃeɪ 'dɜːvrə/ *n* (*pl* chefs d'œuvre, pronunciation unchanged) (F) (person's) masterpiece.
chemi·cal /'kemɪkl/ *adj* of, made by, chemistry: ~ *warfare,* using poison gas, smoke, incendiary bombs, etc. □ *n* (often *pl*) substance used in, or obtained by, chemistry. ~**·ly** /-klɪ/ *adv*
che·mise /ʃə'miːz/ *n* loose, long undergarment formerly worn by women and girls; loose beltless dress.
chem·ist /'kemɪst/ *n* **1** person trained or expert in chemistry. **2** (US = *druggist*) pharmacist; person who prepares medicines (from prescriptions) and sells medical goods, toilet articles, etc: ~*'s shop,* pharmacy.
chem·is·try /'kemɪstrɪ/ *n* [U] branch of science that deals with how substances are made up, how they (their elements) combine, how they act under different conditions.
chemo·ther·apy /,keməʊ'θerəpɪ/ *n* [U] treatment of disease by drugs that attack microbes.
che·nille /ʃə'niːl/ *n* velvety cord used for trimming dresses and furniture.
cheque /tʃek/ *n* (US = **check**) written order (usu on a printed form) to a bank to pay money: *a* ~ *for £10; pay by* ~. Cf *pay in cash.* '~**-book** *n* number of blank ~s bound together. '~ **card,** = *banker's card.* ⇨ bank⁴.
chequer /'tʃekə(r)/ *vt* (US = **checker**) (usu passive) mark with a pattern of squares or patches of different colours or shades; (fig) mark by changes of good and bad fortune, etc: *a lawn* ~*ed with sunlight and shade; a* ~*ed career,* full of ups and downs of fortune, with variety of incident.
cher·ish /'tʃerɪʃ/ *vt* [VP6A] **1** care for tenderly. **2** keep alive (hope, ambition, feelings, etc) in one's heart: *For years she* ~*ed the hope that her husband might still be alive. Don't* ~ *the illusion that your father will always pay your debts.*
che·root /ʃə'ruːt/ *n* cigar with both ends open.
cherry /'tʃerɪ/ *n* (*pl* -rries) (tree with) soft, small, round fruit, red, yellow or black when ripe and with a stone-like seed in the middle; ⇨ the illus at fruit. [U] the wood of this tree. □ *adj* red: ~ *lips.*
cherub /'tʃerəb/ *n* **1** (*pl* ~s) small beautiful child; (in art) such a child with wings. **2** (*pl* ~im /'tʃerəbɪm/) (biblical) one of the second highest order of angels. ⇨ seraph. **che·ru·bic** /tʃɪ'ruːbɪk/ *adj* (esp) sweet and innocent looking; roundfaced.
cher·vil /'tʃɜːvɪl/ *n* [U] garden herb used to flavour soups, salads, etc.
chess /tʃes/ *n* [U] game for two players with sixteen pieces each (each called a '~**-man** /-mæn/), on a board with sixty-four squares (called a '~**-board**).
chest /tʃest/ *n* **1** large, strong (usu wooden) box with a lid for storing, eg clothes, tools, money, medicine, tea, etc. ~ **of 'drawers,** large ~ with drawers for clothes. **2** (anat) upper front part of the body, enclosed by the ribs, containing the heart and lungs. ⇨ the illus at trunk. **get sth off one's** ~, (colloq) say sth one is anxious to say. **hold/keep one's cards close to one's/the** ~, be secretive. **3** (US) (funds of the) treasury of a public institution:

the community ~, for charitable purposes.

ches·ter·field /'tʃestəfiːld/ n **1** single-breasted overcoat with a flap that covers the buttonholes. **2** long padded couch with sides and a back.

chest·nut /'tʃesnʌt/ n **1** [C,U] (sorts of, wood of) tree with smooth, bright reddish-brown nut (those of the Spanish or sweet ~ being edible). ⇨ the illus at tree; ⇨ horse(4). **2** colour of the nut. **3** horse of this colour. **4** (colloq) story or joke that is too old or well known to be amusing.

cheval glass /ʃə'væl glɑːs US: glæs/ full-length mirror mounted on upright supports on which it can be tilted.

chev·ron /'ʃevrən/ n bent line or stripe (∨ or ∧) worn on the sleeve by soldiers, policemen, etc to show rank, etc.

chew /tʃuː/ vt,vi **1** [VP6A,15B,2A,C] ~ (up), work (food, etc) about between the teeth in order to crush it: C~ your food well before you swallow it. '~-ing-gum n [U] sticky substance sweetened and flavoured for ~ing. ⇨ also bite²(1) and cud. **2** [VP15B,3A] ~ sth over; ~ (up)on sth, (colloq) think over, consider. ~ the rag, (dated sl) discuss matters (esp old grievances). □ n act of ~ing; sth (to be) ~ed: a ~ of tobacco.

Chi·anti /kɪ'æntɪ/ n [U] dry red or white Italian wine.

chi·aro·scuro /kɪˌɑːrə'skʊərəʊ/ n (I) distribution of light and shade (esp in a painting).

chic /ʃiːk/ n [U] (of clothes, their wearer) style that gives an air of sophisticated elegance. □ adj stylish.

chi·can·ery /ʃɪ'keɪnərɪ/ n [U] (use of) legal trickery; [C] (pl -ries) false argument.

chi·chi /'ʃiːʃiː/ adj (colloq) pretentious; affected; vulgar.

chick /tʃɪk/ n **1** young bird just before or after hatching, esp a young chicken. '~-pea n [C] (plant with) edible yellow pea-like seed. '~-weed n [U] common small weed whose leaves and seeds are eaten by birds. **2** small child; (sl) girl.

chicken /'tʃɪkɪn/ n **1** young bird, esp a young hen: She's no ~, (fig, sl) is no longer young. ⇨ the illus at fowl. (Don't) count one's ~s before they are hatched, (Don't) be too hopeful of one's chances of success, etc. '~-feed n (fig, sl) sth of relatively small value. ~-'hearted /-hɑːtɪd/ adj lacking in courage. '~-pox n [U] disease (esp of children) accompanied by red spots on the skin. '~-run n fenced-in area for ~s to run in. **2** [U] its flesh as food. □ pred adj (sl) cowardly.

chicle /'tʃɪkl/ n [U] chief ingredient of chewing-gum.

chic·ory /'tʃɪkərɪ/ n [U] plant used as a vegetable and for salad, the root of which is roasted and made into a powder (used with or instead of coffee). ⇨ the illus at vegetable.

chide /tʃaɪd/ vt,vi (pt chided /'tʃaɪdɪd/ or chid

/tʃɪd/, pp chided, chid or chidden /'tʃɪdn/) [VP6A,14] ~ sb (for), (liter) scold; rebuke.

chief /tʃiːf/ n **1** leader or ruler: the ~ of the tribe. **2** head of a department; highest official. C~ of Staff, senior staff officer. in ~, most of all, especially: for many reasons, and this one in ~. -in-'~, supreme: the Commander-in-~. □ adj (attrib only; no comp or superl) **1** principal; most important: the ~ rivers of India; the ~ thing to remember. **2** first in rank: the C~ Justice; the ~ priest. ~·ly adv **1** above all; first of all. **2** mostly; mainly: It is ~ly composed of....

chief·tain /'tʃiːftən/ n leader of a clan or tribe; chief. ~·cy /'tʃiːftənsɪ/ n position or rank of a ~.

chif·fon /'ʃɪfɒn US: ʃɪ'fɒn/ n [U] thin, transparent silk material used for scarves, veils, etc.

chif·fon·ier /ˌʃɪfə'nɪə(r)/ n **1** (GB) movable low cupboard with a flat top used as a table. **2** (US) high chest of drawers (GB = tallboy).

chi·gnon /'ʃiːnjɒn/n (F) knot or roll of hair worn at the back of the head by women.

chil·blain /'tʃɪlbleɪn/ n [C] painful swelling, esp on the hand or foot, caused by exposure to cold. ~ed /-eɪnd/ adj having ~s.

child /tʃaɪld/ n (pl children /'tʃɪldrən/) unborn or newly born human being; boy or girl; son or daughter (of any age). '~'s play, sth very easily done. be with ~, (archaic) be pregnant. '~-birth n [U] the process of giving birth to a ~: She died in ~birth. '~-bearing n [U] giving birth to children: Ten years of ~-bearing exhausted her strength. '~-hood /-hʊd/ n [U] state of being a ~; time during which one is a ~: have a happy ~hood. sec-ond ~hood, dotage (in extreme old age). ~·ish adj of, behaving like, suitable for, a ~; not suited to an adult: ~ish games/arguments. ~·less adj having no child(ren): a ~less couple. '~·like adj simple, innocent, frank.

chile, chili /'tʃɪlɪ/ n(US) = chilli.

chill /tʃɪl/ n **1** (sing only) unpleasant feeling of coldness: There's quite a ~ in the air this morning. Take the ~ off the water, warm it a little. **2** (fig) (sing only) depressing influence; sth that causes a downhearted feeling: The bad news cast a ~ over the gathering. **3** [C] illness caused by cold and damp, with shivering of the body: catch a ~. □ adj unpleasantly cold: a ~ breeze; a ~ welcome. □ vt,vi [VP6A,2A,C] make or become cold or cool: He was ~ed to the bone. Don't ~ their enthusiasm. ~ed beef, beef preserved in cold storage at a moderately low temperature but not frozen. ~y adj (-ier, -iest) **1** rather cold: a ~y room; feel ~y. It's ~y this morning. **2** (fig) unfriendly: a ~y welcome; ~y politeness.

chilli, chilly, chile, chili /'tʃɪlɪ/ n (pl -ies) dried pod of red pepper (capsicum), often made into powder and used to give a hot flavour to sauces, etc.

chime /tʃaɪm/ n (series of notes sounded by a) tuned set of bells: a ~ of bells; ring the ~s; listen to the ~s. □ vi,vt **1** [VP6A,15A,2A,C] (of bells, a clock) make (bells) ring; ring (~s) on bells; show (the hour) by ringing: The bells/The ringers ~d out a tune. The bells are chiming. The church clock ~d midnight. **2** [VP2C] ~ in, break in on the talk of others, usu to express agreement: 'Of course,' he ~d in. ~ (in) with, be in agreement with; suit: I think your plans will ~ in with mine.

chim·era, chim·aera /kaɪ'mɪərə/ n **1** (Gk myth) monster with a lion's head, a goat's body, and a

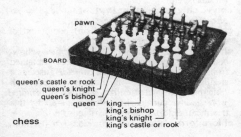

pawn

BOARD

queen's castle or rook
queen's knight
queen's bishop
queen
king
king's bishop
king's knight
chess
king's castle or rook

serpent's tail. **2** horrible creature of the imagination. **3** (fig) wild or impossible idea or fancy. **chim·eri·cal** /kaɪˈmerɪkl/ adj unreal; visionary: *chimerical ideas/schemes.*

chim·ney /ˈtʃɪmnɪ/ n **1** structure through which smoke from a fire is carried away through the wall or roof of a building. '∿·**breast** n projecting wall in a room that contains the ∿. '∿ **corner,** seat in an old-fashioned fireplace. '∿·**piece** n = mantel. '∿·**pot** n pipe (earthenware or metal) fitted to the top of a ∿. '∿·**stack** n group of ∿ tops. '∿·**sweep(er)** n man who sweeps soot from ∿s. **2** glass tube that protects the flame of an oil-lamp from draughts. **3** (mountaineering) narrow cleft or opening by which a cliff face may be climbed. ⇨ the illus at **mountain.**

chimneys

chimp /tʃɪmp/ n (colloq abbr of) chimpanzee.
chim·pan·zee /ˌtʃɪmpænˈziː/ n African ape, smaller than a gorilla. ⇨ the illus at **ape.**
chin /tʃɪn/ n part of the face below the mouth; front of the lower jaw. ⇨ the illus at **head. keep one's** '∿ **up,** (colloq) show determination to face trouble without betraying fear or sorrow. '∿-**strap** n strap (on a helmet) held on the ∿. '∿-**wagging** n (colloq) talking, gossiping.
china /ˈtʃaɪnə/ n [U] baked and glazed fine white clay; (collective) articles (eg cups, saucers, plates) made from this. '∿-**closet** n cupboard in which ∿ is kept or displayed. '∿-**ware** n [U] dishes, ornaments, etc made of ∿ clay.
chin·chil·la /tʃɪnˈtʃɪlə/ n [C] small S American animal that looks like a squirrel; [U] its soft grey fur.
chine /tʃaɪn/ n animal's backbone or part of it as a joint of meat.
chink¹ /tʃɪŋk/ n narrow opening or crack (eg between boards in the wall of a shed, through which the wind blows or through which one may peep).
chink² /tʃɪŋk/ vt,vi [VP6A,15B,2A,C] make the sound of coins, glasses, etc striking together; cause (coins, etc) to make such sounds. □ n a/the ∿ (of), this sound: *I heard the ∿ of coins.*
chintz /tʃɪnts/ n [U] kind of cotton cloth (usu glazed) with printed designs in colours, used for curtains, furniture covers, etc.
chip /tʃɪp/ n **1** small piece cut or broken off (from wood, stone, china, glass, etc). '∿-**board** n building material made from compressed ∿s of waste wood, sawdust, etc and glue. ∿ **off/of the old block,** son who is very like his father. **have a** '∿ **on one's shoulder,** have a defiant air, as if expecting and ready to accept a challenge; resent prejudice against oneself as (often incorrectly) perceived in other people. **2** strip cut from an apple, a potato, etc: *fish and* ∿s, fried fish and potato ∿s. **3** place (eg in a cup) from which a ∿ has come. **4** thin strip cut from wood, palm-leaf, etc, used in making baskets, hats, etc: (usu attrib) ∿ *bonnets;* ∿ *baskets.* **5** flat plastic counter used as a

money token (esp in gambling). **have had one's** ∿**s,** (sl) one's last chance. **(when) the** ∿**s are down,** (when) a crisis point is reached. □ vt,vi (-pp-) **1** [VP6A,15A,15B] ∿ **off/from,** cut or break a piece: ∿ *a piece off (the edge of a cup);* ∿ *old paint from the side of a ship. All the plates have* ∿*ped edges.* **2** [VP6A] make into ∿s(2): ∿*ped potatoes.* **3** [VP2A] (of things) be easily broken at the edge: *These cups* ∿ *if you are not careful.* **4** [VP2C] ∿ **in,** (colloq) **(a)** interrupt; join in (a conversation). **(b)** contribute money (to a fund). **5** [VP6A] shape (sth) by cutting the edge or surface (with an axe or a chisel). '∿·**pings** n pl bits of stone, marble, etc made by ∿ping: 'road ∿pings, for making a road surface.
chip·munk /ˈtʃɪpmʌŋk/ n small, striped N American squirrel-like rodent.
Chip·pen·dale /ˈtʃɪpəndeɪl/ n light style of drawing-room furniture (18th c in England): ∿ chairs.
chi·rop·odist /kɪˈrɒpədɪst/ n person who is expert in the treatment of troubles of the feet and toenails. **chi·rop·ody** /kɪˈrɒpədɪ/ n [U] work of a ∿.
chiro·prac·tor /ˈkaɪərəʊpræktə(r)/ n person who treats diseases by manipulating the joints (esp the spinal column).
chirp /tʃɜːp/ vi,vt, n [VP2A,C,6A] (make) short, sharp note(s) or sound(s) (as of small birds or insects); utter in this way: *the* ∿*s of the sparrows/ cicadas; grasshoppers* ∿*ing all day.*
chirpy /ˈtʃɜːpɪ/ adj (colloq) lively, cheerful. **chirp·ily** /ˈtʃɜːpɪlɪ/ adv **chirpi·ness** n
chir·rup /ˈtʃɪrəp/ vt,vi, n (make a) series of chirps.
chisel /ˈtʃɪzl/ n steel tool with a bevelled edge for shaping wood, stone or metal. ⇨ the illus at **tool.** □ vt (-ll-, also -l- in US) [VP6A,15B,14] **1** cut or shape with a ∿: ∿*led features,* (of a person's appearance) clear cut; well modelled. **2** (colloq) cheat; swindle. ∿·**ler** /ˈtʃɪzələ(r)/ n person who ∿s(2).
chit¹ /tʃɪt/ n young child; young, small, slender woman (often used rather contemptuously): *a mere* '∿ *of a child; only a* '∿ *of a woman.*
chit² /tʃɪt/ n short note or letter; note of sum of money owed (eg for drinks, etc at a hotel).
chit–chat /ˈtʃɪttʃæt/ n [U] light, informal conversation.
chiv·al·ry /ˈʃɪvlrɪ/ n [U] laws and customs (religious, moral and social) of the knights in the Middle Ages; the qualities that knights were expected to have (courage, honour, courtesy, loyalty, devotion to the weak and helpless, to the service of women). **chiv·al·rous** /ˈʃɪvlrəs/ adj of, as of, the age of ∿; of, as of, the knights of the Middle Ages; honourable; courteous.
chive /tʃaɪv/ n [U] small plant of the onion family, of which the slender leaves are used as a seasoning (in salads, etc).
chivy, chivvy /ˈtʃɪvɪ/ vt [VP15B] (colloq) ∿ **sb about/along/up,** pester; chase; harass.
chlor·ide /ˈklɔːraɪd/ n [U] (chem) compound of chlorine: ∿ *of lime/soda/potash.*
chlor·ine /ˈklɔːriːn/ n [U] (chem) greenish-yellow, bad-smelling poisonous gas (symbol Cl), obtained from common salt (= *sodium chloride*), used as a sterilizing agent and in industry. **chlor·in·ate** /ˈklɔːrɪneɪt/ vt treat, sterilize, with ∿: *chlorinated water,* water purified from disease germs by this treatment. **chlori·na·tion** /ˌklɔːrɪˈneɪʃn/ n
chloro·form /ˈklɒrəfɔːm US: ˈklɔːr-/ n [U] thin,

colourless liquid formerly given, in the form of vapour, to make a person unconscious during a surgical operation.

chloro·phyll /'klɒrəfɪl *US:* 'klɔ:r-/ *n* [U] (bot) green colouring matter in the leaves of plants.

chock /tʃɒk/ *n* block or wedge of wood used to prevent sth (eg a wheel, barrel, door) from moving. □ *vt* [VP6A,15B] ~ *(up)*, **1** make fast with, support on, a ~ or ~s. **2** (colloq): *a room ~ed up with furniture*, filled up with far too much furniture. '~-**full** (*of*); ,~-a-'**block** (*with*); ,~-a-,**block 'full** (*of*), *adjj*(pred) filled to the limit.

choc·olate /'tʃɒklət/ *n* **1** [U] substance (powder or slab) made from the crushed seeds of the cacao tree; drink made by mixing this with hot water or milk; [C,U] (colloq abbr **choc** /tʃɒk/) sweet substance made from this, usu sweetened and often flavoured: *a bar of* ~; *a box of* ~*s*; (attrib) ~ *biscuit*, covered with ~; ~ *cream*, sweet paste covered with ~. **2** the colour of this substance, dark brown. **choc-ice** /'tʃɒkaɪs/ *n* (colloq) slab of ice-cream coated with ~.

choice /tʃɔɪs/ *n* **1** act of choosing: *make a careful* ~; *be careful in your* ~; *take your* ~. **2** [U] right or possibility of choosing: *I have no* ~ *in the matter*, cannot choose, must act in this way. **for** ~, by preference; if one must select: *I should take this one for* ~. **Hobson's** ~, no ~ at all because there is only one thing to take or do. **3** variety from which to choose: *This shop has a large* ~ *of clothes*. **4** person or thing chosen: *This is my* ~. □ *adj* carefully chosen; uncommonly good: ~ *fruit*.

choir /'kwaɪə(r)/ *n* **1** company of persons trained to sing together, esp to lead the singing in church. **2** part of a church building for the ~. ⇨ illus at church. '~-**school** *n* grammar school (attached to or connected with a cathedral) for '~-**boys**.

choke[1] /tʃəʊk/ *vi,vt* **1** [VP2A,3A] be unable to breathe because of sth in the windpipe, or because of emotion: ~ *over one's food*; ~ *with anger*; ~ *to death*. **2** [VP6A,14] ~ *(with)*, stop the breathing of, by pressing the windpipe from outside or blocking it up inside, or (of smoke, etc) by being unfit to breathe: ~ *the life out of sb. The smoke almost* ~*d me. Her voice was* ~*d with sobs. Anger* ~*d his words. He swallowed a plum-stone and was almost* ~*d*, ie to death. **3** [VP3A,6A,15B] ~ *(up) (with)*, fill, partly or completely, a passage, space, etc that is usually clear: *a chimney/drain* ~*d (up) with dirt. The garden is* ~*d with weeds. Weeds have* ~*ed (up) the garden. The room was* ~*d up with useless old furniture*. **4** [VP15B] ~ *sth back/ down*, hold or keep back/down: ~ *back one's tears/indignation*; ~ *down one's anger*. ~ *sb off*, (colloq) discourage him (from doing sth); reprimand him for doing sth wrong: *He got* ~*d off for being late*. '~-**damp**, carbon dioxide gas, left after an explosion in a coal-mine.

choke[2] /tʃəʊk/ *n* valve in a petrol engine to control the intake of air: *pull out the* ~, ie the ~ control.

choker /'tʃəʊkə(r)/ *n* **1** (hum) stiff, high collar; clerical collar. **2** close-fitting necklace (eg of pearls) or scarf.

chokey, choky /'tʃəʊkɪ/ *n* (GB; dated sl) prison.

choler /'kɒlə(r)/ *n* (old use, or poet, liter) anger. ~**ic** /'kɒlərɪk/ *adj* easily made angry; often angry.

chol·era /'kɒlərə/ *n* [U] infectious and often fatal disease, common in hot countries, with vomiting and continual emptying of the bowels.

choose /tʃu:z/ *vt,vi* (*pt* **chose** /tʃəʊz/, *pp* **chosen**

/'tʃəʊzn/) **1** [VP6A,16A,B,23,2A,C,3A] ~ *(from/ out of/between)*, pick out from a greater number; show what or which one wants by taking: *She took a long time to* ~ *her new hat. The greedy boy chose the largest apple in the dish. There are only five to* ~ *from. C*~ *your friends carefully. You have chosen well. They chose me as their leader/to be their leader. I was chosen (as) leader. He had to* ~ *between death and dishonour.* **There is nothing/not much/little to** ~ **between** (two or more people or things), They are about equal, are equally good/bad, etc. **2** [VP7A,2A] decide; be pleased or determined: *I do not* ~ *to be a candidate. He chose to stay where he was. Do just as you* ~, whatever pleases you. **cannot** ~ **but**, (liter) must, have to: *He cannot* ~ *but obey*.

choosy, choosey /'tʃu:zɪ/ *adj* (-ier, -iest) (colloq, of persons) careful and cautious in choosing; difficult to please.

chop[1] /tʃɒp/ *vt,vi* (-pp-) [VP6A,15A,B] ~ *(up) (into)*, cut (into pieces) by blow(s) with an axe or other edged tool: *He was* ~*ping wood*, cutting wood into sticks. *Meat is often* ~*ped up into cubes before being cooked. He* ~*ped a branch off the tree. I'm going to* ~ *that tree down. We had to* ~ *a way* (= make a path by ~ping) *through the undergrowth*. [VP3A] ~ *at sth*, aim a cutting blow at.

chop[2] /tʃɒp/ *n* **1** chopping blow. **2** thick slice of meat with bone in it, (to be) cooked for one person. '~-**house** *n* (now usu *steak-house*) restaurant serving chops and steaks. **3** *be for/get the* ~, be about to be/be killed or sacked[2] **4** (boxing) short downward blow.

chop[3] /tʃɒp/ *n* official seal or stamp; trademark; brand of goods; (colloq) quality.

chop[4] /tʃɒp/ *vi* (-pp-) **1** [VP2A] ~ *and change*, (emphatic for *change*) be inconsistent: *He's always* ~*ping and changing*, always changing his opinions, plans, etc. **2** [VP2C] ~ *about*, (of the wind) change direction.

chop[5] /tʃɒp/ *n* ⇨ chap[2].

chop-chop /,tʃɒp 'tʃɒp/ *adv* (sl) quickly.

chop·per[1] /'tʃɒpə(r)/ *n* heavy tool with a sharp edge for chopping meat, wood, etc. ⇨ the illus at tool.

chop·per[2] /'tʃɒpə(r)/ *n* (colloq) helicopter.

choppy /'tʃɒpɪ/ *adj* (-ier, -iest) (of the sea) moving in short, broken irregular waves; (of the wind) continually changing.

chop·sticks /'tʃɒpstɪks/ *n pl* pair of tapering sticks (wood, ivory, etc) used by Chinese and Japanese for lifting food (placed on the thinnest ends) to the mouth.

chopsticks

chop suey /,tʃɒp 'su:ɪ/ *n* [U] dish of meat or chicken served with rice, onions; etc (as in a Chinese restuarant).

choral /'kɔ:rəl/ *adj* of, for, sung by or together with, a choir: *a '*~ *society; a* ~ *service; Beethoven's* ~ *symphony*.

chorale /kə'rɑ:l/ *n* simple hymn tune, usu sung by

the choir and congregation together.

chord /'kɔːd/ n **1** straight line that joins two points on the circumference of a circle or the ends of an arc. ⇨ the illus at circle. **2** (music) combination of three or more notes sounded together in harmony. ⇨ discord and also the illus at notation. **3** (now usu spelt *cord*) (anat) string-like structure, as in the throat (*the vocal* ∼*s*) or the back (*the spinal* ∼). ⇨ the illus at head. **4** string (of a harp, etc): *touch the right* ∼, (fig) appeal cleverly to emotion.

chore /tʃɔː(r)/ n small duty or piece of work, esp an ordinary everyday task (in the home, on a farm, etc); unpleasant or tiring task. Cf *char*.

chor·eogra·phy /ˌkɒrɪ'ɒgrəfɪ US: ˌkɔːr-/ n [U] art of designing and specifying the steps of ballet. **chor·eogra·pher** n

chor·is·ter /'kɒrɪstə(r) US: 'kɔːr-/ n member of a choir, esp a choir-boy.

chortle /'tʃɔːtl/ vi, n (give a) loud chuckle of glee.

chorus /'kɔːrəs/ n **1** (music for a) group of singers. '∼-girl n one of a group of girls who sing and dance in a musical play. **2** (part of a) song for all to sing (after solo verses): *Bill sang the verses and everybody joined in the* ∼. **3** sth said or cried by many people together: *The proposal was greeted with a* ∼ *of approval.* in ∼, all together: *sing/answer in* ∼. ⇨ unison. **4** (in old Gk drama) band of singers and dancers whose words and actions are a commentary on the events of the play. **5** (eg in Shakespeare's plays) actor who recites the prologue and epilogue. □ vt sing, speak, in ∼.

chose, chosen ⇨ choose.

chow /tʃaʊ/ n **1** dog of a Chinese breed. **2** (sl) food.

chow·der /'tʃaʊdə(r)/ n (US) thick soup or stew of fish or clams with vegetables.

Christ /kraɪst/ n title (= *anointed one*) given to Jesus, now used as part of (ie *Jesus* ∼) or as an alternative to his name. '∼-like adj of or like ∼; showing the spirit of ∼.

christen /'krɪsn/ vt [VP6A,23] **1** receive into the Christian church by baptism; give a name to at the baptism. *The child was* ∼*ed Mary.* **2** give a name to (eg to a new ship when it is launched). ∼-ing n ceremony of baptizing or naming: *There were ten* ∼*ings at this church last month.*

Christen·dom /'krɪsndəm/ n all Christian people and Christian countries.

Chris·tian /'krɪstʃən/ adj of Jesus and his teaching; of the religion, beliefs, church, etc based on this teaching. ∼ **era**, time reckoned from the birth of Jesus. '∼ **name**, name given at baptism. Cf *family name.* ∼ '**Science**, church and religious system of healing through spiritual means. □ n person believing in the ∼ religion. **Chris·ti·an·ity** /ˌkrɪstɪ'ænətɪ/ n [U] the ∼ faith or religion; being a ∼; ∼ character.

Christ·mas /'krɪsməs/ n (also ∼ '**Day**) yearly celebration of the birth of Jesus Christ, 25 Dec; the week beginning on 24 Dec: (attrib) *the* ∼ *holidays.*

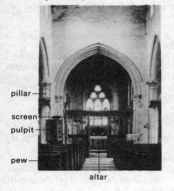

pillar
screen
pulpit
pew
altar

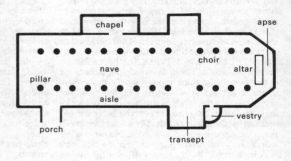

chapel
apse
choir
nave
altar
pillar
aisle
vestry
porch
transept

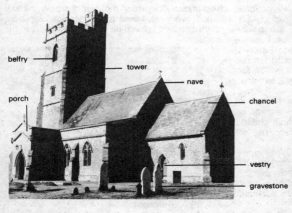

belfry
tower
nave
porch
chancel
vestry
gravestone

church architecture

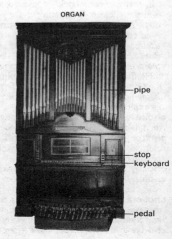

ORGAN

pipe
stop
keyboard
pedal

'**~-box** *n* (not US) money given for services during the year. '**~ card**, sent to friends at ~ to wish them 'A Merry ~ and a Happy New Year', etc. ,**Father** '**~**, traditional figure who is supposed to give children gifts at ~ (= *Santa Claus*). '**~-tide/-time**, the ~ season. '**~-tree** *n* small evergreen tree set up at ~ and decorated with tinsel, candles, presents, etc.

chro·matic /krəʊ'mætɪk/ *adj* **1** of, in, colour(s): ~ *printing*. **2** (music) of, having notes of the ~ scale, that is, the succession of semitones, twelve to the octave, normal in Western music.

chrome /krəʊm/ *n* yellow pigment, colouring matter, obtained from chromium salts, used in paints, rubber, ceramics, etc. '**~ steel** *n* alloy of steel and chromium.

chro·mium /'krəʊmɪəm/ *n* [U] element (symbol **Cr**) used for plating taps, hardware, motor-car fittings, etc and in steel alloys (including stainless steel): ~ *plating;* ~,*plated* '*fittings*.

chro·mo·some /'krəʊməsəʊm/ *n* [C] (biol) one of the minute threads in every nucleus in animal and plant cells, carrying genes.

chro·nic /'krɒnɪk/ *adj* **1** (of a disease or condition) continual, lasting for a long time: ~ *rheumatism; a* ~ *invalid*, a person with a ~ illness. ⇨ acute(2). **2** (sl) intense; severe. **chro·ni·cal·ly** /-klɪ/ *adv*

chron·icle /'krɒnɪkl/ *n* [C] record of events in the order of their happening. □ *vt* [VP6A] make a ~ of; record in a ~.

chro·no·logi·cal /ˌkrɒnə'lɒdʒɪkl/ *adj* in order of time: *Shakespeare's plays in* ~ *order*, in the order in which they were written. ~**ly** /-klɪ/ *adv*

chro·no·logy /krə'nɒlədʒɪ/ *n* [U] science of fixing dates; [C] (*pl* -**gies**) arrangement of events with dates; list or table showing this.

chro·no·meter /krə'nɒmɪtə(r)/ *n* kind of watch that keeps very accurate time, esp as used for fixing longitude at sea.

chry·sa·lis /'krɪsəlɪs/ *n* (*pl* -**lises** /-lɪsɪz/) form taken by an insect during the torpid stage of its life (ie between the time when it creeps or crawls as a larva and the time when it flies as a moth, butterfly, etc); the sheath that covers it during this time. ⇨ the illus at butterfly.

chry·san·the·mum /krɪ'sænθəməm/ *n* (flower of) garden plant blooming in autumn and early winter.

chubby /'tʃʌbɪ/ *adj* (-**ier**, -**iest**) plump: ~ *cheeks;* round-faced: *a* ~ *child*.

chuck¹ /tʃʌk/ *vt* (colloq) **1** [VP15,A,B,12A,13A] throw: ~ *away rubbish;* ~ *a drunken man out of a pub.* ,**~er-'out** *n* (sl) person whose duty it is to throw out troublesome people (from publichouses, political meetings, etc). **2** [VP6A,15B] ~ (*up*), abandon, give up (in disgust): ~ *up one's job;* ~ *work.* C~ *it,* (sl) Stop doing that! **3** ~ *sb under the chin,* touch him or her playfully with the back of the fist under the chin. □ *n the* ~, (sl) dismissal from one's job: *get the* ~; *give sb the* ~, dismiss him.

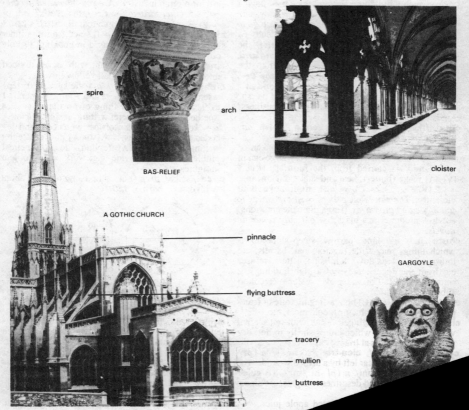

spire

arch

BAS-RELIEF

cloister

A GOTHIC CHURCH

GARGOYLE

pinnacle

flying buttress

tracery

mullion

buttress

chuck² /tʃʌk/ n that part of a lathe which grips the work to be operated on or which grips the bit on a drill. ⇨ illus at **lathe**.

chuckle /'tʃʌkl/ n low, quiet laugh with closed mouth (indicating satisfaction or amusement). □ vi [VP2A,C] laugh in this way: *He was chuckling to himself over what he was reading.*

chuffed /tʃʌft/ pred adj (GB colloq) very pleased: *be/feel/look ~.*

chug /tʃʌg/ vi (-gg-) [VP2C] make the muffled explosive sound (of an oil-engine or small petrol-engine running slowly): *The boat ~ged along.* □ n this sound.

chuk·ker /'tʃʌkə(r)/ n (polo) one of the periods into which the game is divided.

chum /tʃʌm/ n close friend (esp among boys); (Australia): *new ~*, new arrival; recent immigrant; (US) room-mate. □ vi (-mm-) [VP2C] *~ up (with sb)*, form a friendship (with). *~my* adj friendly; like a *~*.

chump /tʃʌmp/ n **1** short, thick block of wood. **2** thick piece of meat: *a ~ chop*. **3** (sl) fool; blockhead. **4** (sl) head. *off one's ~*, crazy.

chunk /tʃʌŋk/ n thick, solid piece or lump cut off a loaf, a piece of meat/cheese etc. *~y* adj (-ier, -iest) short and thick.

church /tʃɜːtʃ/ n **1** building for public Christian worship. ⇨ **chapel**. *~ register* n records of births, marriages and deaths in a parish. *'~-yard* n burial ground round a *~*. ⇨ **cemetery**. **2** [U] service in such a building: *What time does ~ begin? They're in/at ~*, attending a service. Cf *They're in the ~*, inside the building. *How often do you go to ~? '~-goer* /-gəʊə(r)/ n person who attends *~* services regularly. **3** [U] *the C~ (of Christ)*, the whole body of Christians. *the C~ of England*, England's official Protestant *~*, founded in the 16th century by King Henry VIII. *enter the C~*, become a minister¹(3) or monk/nun. *~-war·den* n elected representative of a C~ of England parish, not a priest, who helps to manage the business, funds, etc of a *~*.

churl /tʃɜːl/ n bad-tempered person. *~·ish* adv bad-tempered; ill-bred. *~·ish·ly* adv

churn /tʃɜːn/ n **1** tub in which cream is shaken or beaten to make butter. **2** (not US) very large can in which milk is carried from the farm. □ vt,vi **1** [VP6A] make (butter), beat and shake (cream) in a *~*. **2** [VP6A,15B,2A,C] *~ (up)*, stir or move about violently: *The ship's propellers ~ed the waves to foam/~ed up the waves.* (fig) agitate the emotions. *~ out*, produce in a mass: *~ out silly romantic novels.*

chute /ʃuːt/ n **1** long, narrow, steep slope down which things may slide (eg for coal, barrels, etc into a cellar, logs down a hillside, letters, refuse, etc from the upper storeys of a high building). **2** smo⸺ rapid fall of water over a slope. **3** (colloq ab⸺ ⸺rachute.

c⸺ ⸺tni/ n [U] hot-tasting mixture of fruit, ⸺n with curry, cold meat, etc.

⸺ winged insect with transparent ⸺ich chirps shrilly in hot, dry ⸺ect.

⸺ix /'sɪkətrɪks/ n (pl - ⸺healed wound.

/-niː/) (I) guide ⸺htseers places

⸺e. '~-

press n machine for pressing juice from apples.

cigar /sɪ'gɑː(r)/ n tight roll of tobacco leaves with pointed end(s) for smoking. *'~-shaped*, shaped like a cylinder with pointed ends.

ciga·rette /ˌsɪgə'ret/ US: 'sɪgəret/ n roll of shredded tobacco enclosed in thin paper for smoking. *'~-case* n one in which a supply of *~*s may be carried in the pocket or handbag. *'~-holder* n tube in which a *~* may be put for smoking. *'~-paper*, that used to make *~*s.

cinch /sɪntʃ/ n (US sl) something that is certain; something easy and sure.

cin·chona /sɪŋ'kəʊnə/ n tree from whose bark quinine is obtained.

cinc·ture /'sɪŋktʃə(r)/ n (liter) belt or girdle.

cin·der /'sɪndə(r)/ n small piece of coal, wood, etc partly burned, no longer flaming, and not yet ash. *burnt to a ~*, (of a cake, etc) cooked so that it is hard and black. *'~-track* n running track made with fine *~*s.

Cin·de·rella /ˌsɪndə'relə/ n girl or woman whose attraction, merits, etc have not been recognized; (fig) sth long neglected.

cine- /'sɪnɪ/ pref form used for *cinema* in compounds. *'~-cam·era* n camera used for taking moving pictures. ⇨ the illus at **camera**. *'~-film* n film used in *~*-cameras. *'~-pro·jec·tor* n machine for showing *~*-films on a screen.

cin·ema /'sɪnəmə/ n **1** (not US) theatre in which films are shown. **2** (the) *~*, motion pictures as an art-form or an industry: *Are you interested in (the) ~?* Cf (the) *drama*. *~-tic* /ˌsɪnə'mætɪk/ adj of *~*(2). *~-to·graphy* /ˌsɪnəmə'tɒgrəfɪ/ n [U] *~*(2).

cin·na·mon /'sɪnəmən/ n [U] spice from the inner bark of an E Indian tree, used in cooking; its colour, yellowish brown.

cinque·foil /'sɪŋkfɔɪl/ n plant with leaves divided into five parts and with small yellow flowers.

cipher, cypher /'saɪfə(r)/ n **1** the symbol 0, representing nought or zero. **2** any Arabic numeral, 1 to 9. **3** (fig) person or thing of no importance. **4** (method of, key to) secret writing: *a message in ~; a ~ key; the '~ officer*, officer who codes and decodes messages. □ vt,vi **1** [VP6A] put into secret writing. **2** [VP6A,2A] (colloq) do arithmetical problems; add up, divide, etc; work out a problem in figures.

circa /'sɜːkə/ prep (Lat, abbr *c*, *ca* or *circ*) about (with dates): *born ~ 150*BC.

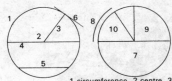

1 circumference 2 centre 3 radius
4 diameter 5 chord 6 tangent
7 semicircle 8 arc 9 quadrant
10 sector

parts of a circle

circle /'sɜːkl/ n **1** (geom) space enclosed by a curved line, every point on which is the same distance from the centre; the line enclosing this space. ⇨ also the illus at **concentric**. **2** sth round like a *~*; ring: *a ~ of trees/hills; standing in a ~*. *a vicious ~*, ⇨ **vicious**. **3** block of seats in curved rows, one above the other, between the highest part (the gallery) and the floor (the stalls) of a theatre or hall. **4** number of persons bound together by having the same or similar interests: *in theatrical ~s*, among actors, etc; *moving in fashionable ~s*, among those in fashionable society; *business ~s. He has a large ~ of friends. They are newcomers to our ~.* **5** complete series: *the ~ of the seasons*, the four seasons in succession. *come full ~*, end at the starting-point. □ *vt, vi* [VP6A,2A,C] move in a ~; go round: *The aircraft ~d (over) the landing-field. Drake ~d the globe*, sailed round the world. *The news ~d round*, was passed round.

circ·let /'sɜ:klɪt/ *n* round band (eg of gold or flowers) worn as an ornament on the head, neck or arm.

cir·cuit /'sɜ:kɪt/ *n* **1** journey round, ending where one began: *The ~ of the city walls is three miles. make a ~ of*, go round. **2** regular journey or itinerary made by judges and barristers to towns in England and Wales to county towns (*~ towns*) to hold courts to hear civil and criminal cases, replaced in 1972 by Crown Courts ⇨ **court**[1]. One of six areas in the country, each having a number of Crown Courts. *go on ~*, make this journey: *Judges go on ~ for part of the year.* **3** chain of cinemas, theatres, etc under a single management: *Some theatrical companies travel over regular ~s*, visit certain towns in succession. **4** closed path for an electric current; apparatus with a sequence of conductors, transistors, etc for carrying an electric current: *'~ diagram*, one that shows the connections in such an apparatus. *closed ~* (TV), ⇨ close[4](2). *short ~*, ⇨ short[1](1). **5** regional group of Methodist churches sharing preachers.

cir·cu·itous /sɜ:'kju:ɪtəs/ *adj* (formal) indirect; going a long way round: *a ~ route.*

cir·cu·lar /'sɜ:kjʊlə(r)/ *adj* round or curved in shape; moving round: *a ~ building; the North C~ Road*, round the north of London, for through traffic; *a ~ tour/trip*, ending at the starting-point without visiting a place more than once. *~ letter n* one sent out to many persons. *~ saw n* disc-shaped saw that revolves by machinery. □ *n* printed letter, advertisement, announcement, etc of which many copies are made and distributed. *~·ize* /'sɜ:kjʊləraɪz/ *vt* [VP6A] send ~s to.

cir·cu·late /'sɜ:kjʊleɪt/ *vi, vt* **1** [VP2A,C] go round continuously; move from place to place freely: *Blood ~s through the body. In many buildings hot water ~s through pipes to keep rooms warm. Bad news ~s quickly. In times of prosperity money ~s quickly; during a depression it ~s slowly. circulating library*, one from which books may be borrowed, usu on payment of a subscription. **2** [VP6A] cause to ~: *People who ~ false news are to be blamed.*

cir·cu·la·tion /,sɜ:kjʊ'leɪʃn/ *n* **1** [U,C] circulating or being circulated, esp the movement of the blood from and to the heart: *He has (a) good/bad ~. The ~ of rumours is common in wartime.* **2** [U] state of being circulated: *Are there many forged banknotes in ~? That book has been withdrawn from ~*, cannot now be obtained. *When were the decimal coins put into ~?* **3** [C] number of copies of a newspaper or other periodical sold to the public: *a newspaper with a (daily) ~ of more than one million.*

cir·cum·cise /'sɜ:kəmsaɪz/ *vt* remove the foreskin of (a male) or the clitoris of (a female). **cir·cum·ci·sion** /,sɜ:kəm'sɪʒn/ *n* circumcising, esp (of males) as a religious rite among Jews and Muslims.

cir·cum·fer·ence /sə'kʌmfərəns/ *n* (geom) line that marks out a circle or other curved figure; distance round sth: *The ~ of the earth is almost*

25 000 miles. ⇨ the illus at circle.

cir·cum·flex /'sɜ:kəmfleks/ *n* (also *~ accent*) mark placed over a vowel to indicate how it is to be sounded (as in French *rôle*).

cir·cum·lo·cu·tion /,sɜ:kəmlə'kju:ʃn/ *n* [C,U] (instance of) saying in many words what may be said in few words.

cir·cum·navi·gate /,sɜ:kəm'nævɪgeɪt/ *vt* [VP6A] (formal) sail round (esp the world). **cir·cum·navi·ga·tion** /,sɜ:kəm,nævɪ'geɪʃn/ *n*

cir·cum·scribe /'sɜ:kəmskraɪb/ *vt* [VP6A] (formal) draw a line round; mark the limit(s) of; narrow down, restrict: *~ one's interests.* **cir·cum·scrip·tion** /,sɜ:kəm'skrɪpʃn/ *n* **1** [U] circumscribing or being ~d. **2** [C] words inscribed round a coin.

cir·cum·spect /'sɜ:kəmspekt/ *adj* paying careful attention to everything before taking action; cautious. *~·ly adv* **cir·cum·spec·tion** /,sɜ:kəm'spekʃn/ *n* [U] prudence; caution.

cir·cum·stance /'sɜ:kəmstəns/ *n* **1** (usu *pl*) condition, fact, etc connected with an event or person: *Don't judge the crime until you know the ~s. C~s alter cases*, (prov) What may be good, wise, praiseworthy, etc in some ~s may be bad, foolish or blameworthy in other ~s. *in/under the ~s*, the ~s being so; such being the state of affairs. *in/under no ~s*, never; whatever may happen. **2** fact or detail: *There is one important ~ you have not mentioned. He has plenty of money, which is a fortunate ~.* **3** (*pl*) financial condition: *in easy/good/flourishing ~s*, having enough or plenty of money; *in reduced/straitened ~s*, poor. **4** (*sing*) (used only in) *pomp and ~*, show and ceremony.

cir·cum·stan·tial /,sɜ:kəm'stænʃl/ *adj* **1** (of a description) giving full details. **2** (of evidence) based on, consisting of details that strongly suggest sth but do not provide direct proof. *~·ly /-nʃəlɪ/ adv*

cir·cum·vent /,sɜ:kəm'vent/ *vt* [VP6A] (formal) prevent (a plan) from being carried out; find a way to get round (a law, rule, difficulty, etc). **cir·cum·ven·tion** /,sɜ:kəm'venʃn/ *n*

cir·cus /'sɜ:kəs/ *n* **1** (in ancient Rome) round or oval place with seats on all sides for public games. **2** (in modern times) a travelling show, usu given in a large tent (called *the big top*) of performing animals, clever horse-riding, etc; persons and animals giving such a show. **3** (esp in proper names) open space where a number of streets converge: *Piccadilly C~*, in London.

cir·rho·sis /sɪ'rəʊsɪs/ *n* [U] chronic (and often fatal) disease of the liver.

cir·rus /'sɪrəs/ *n* type of cloud, high in the sky, delicate and feathery in appearance.

cissy /'sɪsɪ/ *adj, n* = sissy.

cis·tern /'sɪstən/ *n* water tank, eg as above the bowl of a WC, or for storing water in a building, with pipes to taps on lower storeys.

cita·del /'sɪtədəl/ *n* fortress for protecting a town; (fig) place of refuge or safety.

cite /saɪt/ *vt* [VP6A] **1** give or mention as an example (esp by quoting from a book, to support an argument, etc). **2** (US) mention for bravery in war: *~d in dispatches.* **3** (legal) summons at law: *be ~d in divorce proceedings.* **ci·ta·tion** /saɪ'teɪʃn/ *n* [U] citing; [C] sth, esp a statement, that is ~d; (US) mention in an official record (eg for a brave act in war).

citi·zen /'sɪtɪzn/ *n* **1** person who lives in a town, not in the country: *the ~s of Paris.* **2** person who has full rights in a State, either by birth or by gaining such rights: *immigrants who have become* ~s *of the United States*, Cf *British subject;* ~ *of the world*, cosmopolitan person. ~-**ship** /-ʃɪp/ *n* being a ~; rights and duties of a ~.

cit·ric /'sɪtrɪk/ *adj* ~ **acid** *n* (chem) acid from such fruits as lemons and limes.

cit·ron /'sɪtrən/ *n* (tree with) pale yellow fruit like a lemon but larger, less acid, and thicker skinned.

cit·rous /'sɪtrəs/ *adj* of the citrus fruits.

cit·rus /'sɪtrəs/ *n* (bot) genus of trees that includes the lemon, lime, citron, orange and grapefruit; (attrib) of these trees: '~ *fruit*.

city /'sɪtɪ/ *n* (*pl* -ties) **1** large and important town; town given special rights in self-government (in GB by royal charter, in US by a charter from the State). **the C~,** the oldest part of London, now the commercial and financial centre. **2** people living in a ~. **3** (attrib): ,~'*centre*, central area of a city; ,~ '*editor*, (GB) one who deals with financial news; (US) one in charge of local news; ,~'*hall*, building for transaction of the official business of a ~; *a* 'C~ *man*, engaged in commerce or finance; ~ *state*, city that is also an independent sovereign state (eg Athens in ancient times).

civet /'sɪvɪt/ *n* **1** (also '~-**cat**) small spotted catlike animal of Africa, Asia and Europe. **2** [U] strong-smelling substance from certain glands of this animal.

civic /'sɪvɪk/ *adj* of the official life and affairs of a town or a citizen: ~ *duties;* ~ *pride; a* ~ *centre*, where the official buildings, eg the town hall, library, hospitals, etc, are grouped together. **civ·ics** *n pl* (*sing v*) study of city government, the rights and duties of citizens, etc.

civ·ies /'sɪvɪz/ *n pl* (GB sl) civilian clothes.

civil /'sɪvl/ *adj* **1** of human society; of people living together: *We all have* ~ *rights and* ~ *duties.* ,~ ,**diso'bedience**, organized refusal to obey the laws (esp as part of a political campaign). ,~ ,**en·gi'neering**, the design and building of roads, railways, canals, docks, etc. ,~ '**law**, law dealing with private rights of citizens, not with crime. ,~ '**mar·riage**, without religious ceremony but recognized by law. ,~ '**rights**, rights of a citizen to political, racial, legal, social freedom or equality. ,~ '**rights movement**, organized movement aiming to secure for all citizens the enjoyment of constitutional rights. ,~ '**war**, war between two sides in the same country, eg in the US 1861–65, in Spain 1936–39. **2** not of the armed forces. ,**C~ De'fence Corps,** organization to deal with results of attack (esp from the air). ,~ '**servant**, official in the C~ Service. **the ,C~ 'Service,** all government departments except the Navy, Army and Air Force. **3** politely helpful: *The boy gave me a* ~ *answer. Can't you be* ~? *It was* ~ *of them to offer to help us.* **4** '~ **list**, (GB) allowance of money made by Parliament for the royal household and royal pensions. ~-**ly** /'sɪvəlɪ/ *adv* politely. **ci·vil·ity** /sɪ'vɪlətɪ/ *n* [U] politeness (*to*); (*pl;* -ties) polite acts.

ci·vil·ian /sɪ'vɪljən/ *n, adj* (person) not serving with the armed forces: *I asked the soldier what he was in* ~ *life. He left the army and returned to* ~ *life. In modern wars* ~s *as well as soldiers are killed.*

civi·li·za·tion /,sɪvəlaɪ'zeɪʃn US: -əlɪ'z-/ *n* **1** [U] civilizing or being civilized; state of being civilized: *The* ~ *of mankind has taken thousands of years.* **2** [C] system, stage of, social development: *the* ~s *of ancient Egypt, Babylon and Persia.* **3** [U] civilized States collectively: *acts that horrified* ~.

civi·lize /'sɪvəlaɪz/ *vt* [VP6A] **1** bring from a savage or ignorant condition to a higher one (by giving education in methods of government, moral teaching, etc). **2** improve and educate; refine the manners of: *Many a rough man has been* ~*d by his wife.*

civ·vies /'sɪvɪz/ *n pl* = civies.

Civvy Street /'sɪvɪ striːt/ *n* (GB sl) civilian life.

clack /klæk/ *vi, n* (make the) short, sharp sound of objects struck together: *the* ~ *of her knitting needles;* ~*ing typewriters;* ~*ing tongues at the Women's Institute.*

clad /klæd/ *old pp* of clothe: *poorly* ~, dressed in poor clothes; (poet): *hills* ~ *in verdure;* (in compounds): '*steel-*~; '*iron-*~.

claim[1] /kleɪm/ *vt, vi* [VP4A,7A,9,2A] **1** demand recognition that one is, or owns, or has a right to (sth): *Does anyone* ~ *this umbrella? Every citizen in a democratic country may* ~ *the protection of the law. He* ~*ed to be the owner of/*~*ed that he owned the land. Have you* ~*ed yet*, eg made a ~ under an insurance policy. ~ *damages*, (legal) ⇨ damage. ⇨ also bonus. **2** assert; say that sth is a fact: *He* ~*ed to have/*~*ed that he had done the work without help. He* ~*ed to be the best tennis player in the school.* **3** (of things) need; deserve: *There are several matters that* ~ *my attention.*

claim[2] /kleɪm/ *n* **1** [C] assertion of a right; act of ~ing[1](1): *Does anyone make a* ~ *to* (but more usu *Does anyone* ~) *this purse*, say that it is his? *His* ~ *to own the house is invalid.* **lay** ~ **to**, demand (sth) as one's due: *If the land really belongs to you, why don't you lay* ~ *to it*, say so and try to get it? **2** [C] sum of money demanded under an insurance agreement (for loss, damage, etc): *make/put in a* ~ (*for sth*). **3** [U,C] right to ask for: *You have no* ~ *on my sympathies.* **4** [C] sth that is ~ed; piece of land (esp in a gold-bearing region) allotted to a miner: *stake out a* ~, mark boundaries to assert ownership. ~-**ant** /'kleɪmənt/ *n* person who makes a ~, esp in law.

clair·voy·ance /kleə'vɔɪəns/ *n* [U] power of perceiving what is not present to the senses; exceptional insight. ⇨ telepathy. **clair·voy·ant** /kleə'vɔɪənt/ *n* person with such power.

clam /klæm/ *n* large shell-fish, with a shell in two halves, used for food. ⇨ the illus at bivalve. ~-**bake** /'klæmbeɪk/ *n* (US) sea shore picnic at which ~s and other foods are baked. □ *vi* (-mm-) **1** [VP2A] dig for, go out for, ~s. **2** [VP2C] ~ **up**, (colloq) (suddenly) become silent; refuse to speak.

clam·ber /'klæmbə(r)/ *vi* [VP2C] climb with some difficulty, using the hands and feet: ~ *up/over a wall.* □ *n* awkward or difficult climb.

clammy /'klæmɪ/ *adj* (-ier, -iest) damp; moist; cold and sticky to the touch: ~ *hands; a face* ~ *with sweat.* **clam·mi·ly** *adv*

clam·our (US = **clam·or**) /'klæmə(r)/ *n* [C,U] loud confused noise or shout, esp of people complaining angrily or making. a demand. □ *vi,vt* [VP2A,C,4A] make a ~: *The foolish people were* ~*ing for war. The newspapers* ~*ed against the government's policy. The troops were* ~*ing to go home.* **clam·or·ous** /'klæmərəs/ *adj* noisy: *a clamorous mob.*

clamp /klæmp/ *n* **1** appliance for holding things together tightly by means of a screw. **2** band of iron, etc for strengthening or tightening. □ *vt,vi* **1** [VP6A,15B] put a ~ or ~s on; put in a ~. **2** [VP2C] ~ **down (on),** (colloq) put pressure on;

exert pressure against (in order to stop sth): *They ~ed down on the newspapers.* Hence, '~-down *n*

clan /klæn/ *n* large family group, as found in tribal communities, esp Scottish Highlanders with a common ancestor: *the Campbell ~.*

clan·des·tine /klæn'destɪn/ *adj* (formal) secret; done secretly; kept secret: *a ~ marriage.*

clang /klæŋ/ *vt,vi, n* [VP6A,2A] (make a) loud ringing sound (eg a hammer striking an anvil): *The tramdriver ~ed his bell. The ~ of the firebell alarmed the village.* ~**er** *n* (sl) **drop a ~er,** say sth indiscreet or embarrassing.

clang·our (US = **clangor**) /'klæŋə(r)/ *n* continued clanging noise; series of clangs. **clangor·ous** /'klæŋərəs/ *adj*

clank /klæŋk/ *vt,vi n* [VP6A,2A] (make a) dull metallic sound (not so loud as a clang) (eg chains or knives striking together): *prisoners ~ing their chains.*

clan·nish /'klænɪʃ/ *adj* showing clan feeling; (of people) in the habit of supporting one another against outsiders. ~·**ly** *adv*

clans·man /'klænzmən/ *n* (*pl* -men) member of a clan.

clap¹ /klæp/ *vt,vi* (-pp-) **1** [VP6A,2A,B] show approval, applaud, by striking (often) the front part of the hands together: *When the violinist finished the audience ~ped for five minutes. The baby ~ped its hands.* **2** [VP14] strike or slap lightly with the open hand, usu in a friendly way: *~ sb on the back.* **3** [VP15A,B] put quickly or energetically: *~ sb in prison;* ~ *one's hat on;* ~ *on sail,* spread more sail. ~ *eyes on sb,* (colloq, esp in neg) catch sight of: *I haven't ~ped eyes on him since 1960.* □ *n* **1** loud explosive noise (eg of thunder). **2** sound of the front of the hands brought together. (*Clapping* is the usu word for applause, not *claps*).

clap² /klæp/ *n* [U] (**the**) ~, (sl) venereal disease; (esp) gonorrhea.

clap·board /'klæpbɔːd US: 'klæbəːrd/ *n* weatherboard.

clap·per /'klæpə(r)/ *n* tongue or striker of a bell; noisy hand rattle (used, for example, to scare birds from crops). '~-**board** *n* (filming) divided, hinged and marked board which is sharply closed to mark the start of filming.

clap·trap /'klæptræp/ *n* [U] ideas, remarks, that are intended merely to attract attention or win applause; nonsense.

claque /klæk/ *n* [C] number of persons hired to applaud at a theatre, concert, etc.

claret /'klærət/ *n* [U] (kind of) red table wine from Bordeaux; (also *adj*) its colour, dark red.

clar·ify /'klærɪfaɪ/ *vt,vi* [VP6A,2A] make or become clear; make (a liquid, etc) free from impurities. **clari·fi·ca·tion** /ˌklærɪfɪ'keɪʃn/ *n* [U] ~ing or being clarified.

clari·net /ˌklærɪ'net/ *n* musical woodwind instru-

ment, with finger holes and keys. ⇨ the illus at brass. ~·**ist,** ~·**tist** *n* person who plays the ~.

clar·ion /'klærɪən/ *n* loud, shrill call made to rouse and excite; (attrib) loud and clear: *a ~ call; a ~ voice.*

clar·ity /'klærətɪ/ *n* [U] clearness.

clash /klæʃ/ *vi,vt* **1** [VP6A,15B,2A,C] make a loud, broken, confused noise (as when metal objects strike together): *Their swords ~ed. She ~ed the pans down on the stone floor. The cymbals ~ed.* **2** [VP2A,C] come suddenly together; meet in conflict: *The two armies ~ed outside the town.* **3** [VP2A,C] (of events) interfere with each other because they are (to be) at the same time on the same date: *It's a pity the two concerts ~, I want to go to both.* **4** [VP3A,2A,C] be in disagreement or at variance: *I ~ed with him/We ~ed at the last meeting of the Council. The colour of the curtains ~es with the colour of the carpet. The date of your party ~es with another engagement.* □ *n* **1** ~ing noise: *the ~ of weapons/of pots falling/of cymbals.* **2** disagreement; conflict: *a ~ of views/ opinions/colours.*

clasp /klɑːsp US: klæsp/ *n* **1** device with two parts that fasten, used to keep together two things or two parts of one thing (eg the ends of a necklace or belt). '~-**knife,** folding knife with a ~ for fixing the blade when open. **2** bar of silver, etc on a medal-ribbon (with the name of the battle, campaign, etc at which the person to whom the medal was awarded was present). **3** firm hold (with the fingers or arm); handshake; embrace. □ *vt,vi* **1** [VP6A,15A] hold tightly or closely: *~ed in each other's arms;* ~ *sb by the hand. The thief was ~ing a knife in his hand.* ~ **hands,** shake hands with sb (showing more emotion than in the usual handshake). ~ **one's hands,** press them together with the fingers interlaced: *with hands ~ed in prayer; with his hands ~ed behind him.* **2** [VP6A,15A] fasten with a clasp(1): *~ a bracelet round one's wrist.* **3** [VP2A] *This bracelet won't ~,* cannot be ~ed.

class /klɑːs US: klæs/ *n* **1** group having qualities of the same kind; kind, sort or division: *There used to be first-~, second-~ and third-~ carriages on the trains in Britain. The second highest division of the animal or vegetable kingdom is a ~.* ⇨ family, genus, order¹(15), phylum, species. *As an actor A is not in the same ~ with B,* is not so good as B. **2** [U] system of ranks in society; caste system: *It will be difficult to abolish ~;* (used attrib): *~ conflicts; the '~ struggle.* '~-**conscious,** realizing one's ~ in society and the differences between social ~es. '~-**feeling,** feeling of envy, etc of one ~ for another. ~-'**warfare,** struggle, enmity, between ~es. **3** [C] all persons in one of these ranks: *Society may be divided into upper, middle and lower ~es.* **4** group of persons taught together; their course of teaching. '~-**fellow/-mate,** present or past member of the same ~: *Jim and I were ~-mates last term.* '~-**room,** room where a ~ is taught. **5** (US) group of pupils or students who enter school or college in the same year and leave together: *the ~ of 1973,* those who finished their school course in that year. **6** all those men conscripted for service in the armed forces in a year: *the 1970 ~.* **7** (not US) grade or merit after examination: *take a first/second-~ degree.* '~-**list,** honours list issued by examiners. **8** (colloq; often attrib) distinction; excellence; style: *He's a ~ tennis*

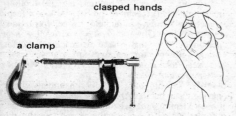

clasped hands

a clamp

player. There's not much ~ *about her.* □ *vt* [VP6A,14] place in a ~(1): *a ship* ~*ed A1; to* ~ *one thing with another.* ~**-less** *adj* without distinctions of ~(2): *Is a* ~*less society possible?*

clas·sic /'klæsɪk/ *adj* **1** of the highest quality; having a value or position recognized and unquestioned. **2** of the standard of ancient Greek and Latin literature, art and culture. **3** with qualities like those of ~(2) art, ie simple, harmonious and restrained. **4** famous because of a long history: *a* ~ *event,* eg the Oxford and Cambridge boat race or the Derby. **5** (of style in costume, etc) traditional; not new. □ *n* **1** writer, artist, book, etc of the highest class: *Milton is a* ~. *'Robinson Crusoe' is a* ~. **2** ancient Greek or Latin writer. **3 the** ~**s,** (literature of the) ancient languages of Greece and Rome. **C**~**s,** university course in these subjects: *He read C*~*s at Oxford.* **4** ~ event, ⇨ the *adj* **4** above.

clas·si·cal /'klæsɪkl/ *adj* **1** in, of ancient Gk and Roman art and literature: ~ *studies; a* ~ *education; a* '~ *scholar.* **2** of proved value because of having passed the test of time: ~ *music,* usually taking traditional, well-defined form as a concerto, symphony, etc, eg of Haydn and Mozart. **3** simple and restrained; not over-ornamented. ~**·ly** /-kəlɪ/ *adv*

clas·si·cist /'klæsɪsɪst/ *n* follower of classic style; classical scholar: *Milton was a* ~.

clas·si·fi·ca·tion /ˌklæsɪfɪ'keɪʃn/ *n* [U] classifying or being classified; [C] group into which sth is put.

clas·sify /'klæsɪfaɪ/ *vt* [VP6A] arrange in classes or groups; put into a class(1): *In a library books are usually classified by subjects.* **clas·si·fied** *adj* arranged in classes(1): *classified advertisements* (also, colloq, *classified ads*); *classified directory,* one in which the entries (eg of business firms) are entered in classes (eg builders, electricians, plumbers); (US) put in a group that is officially secret: *classified information.* **clas·si·fi·able** /'klæsɪfaɪəbl/ *adj* that can be classified.

classy /'klɑːsɪ *US:* 'klæsɪ/ *adj* (-ier, -iest) (colloq) stylish; superior; upper-class.

clat·ter /'klætə(r)/ *n* (*sing* only) **1** long, continuous, resounding noise (as of hard things falling or knocking together): *the* ~ *of a horse's hoofs on a hard road; the* ~ *of machinery; the* ~ *of cutlery.* **2** noisy talk: *The boys stopped their* ~ *when the teacher came into the classroom.* □ *vi,vt* [VP6A,2A,C] make a ~(1): *Pots and pans were* ~*ing in the kitchen. Don't* ~ *your knives and forks. Some of the dishes* ~*ed down during the earthquake.*

clause /klɔːz/ *n* **1** (gram) component of a (complex) sentence, with its own subject and predicate, esp one doing the work of a noun, adjective or adverb: *dependent/subordinate* ~. **2** (legal) complete paragraph in an agreement, legal document, etc.

claus·tro·pho·bia /ˌklɔːstrə'fəʊbɪə/ *n* [U] morbid fear of confined places (eg a lift, cave or coalmine).

clavi·chord /'klævɪkɔːd/ *n* stringed instrument with a keyboard, predecessor of the piano.

clav·icle /'klævɪkl/ *n* (anat) collar-bone. ⇨ the illus at skeleton.

claw /klɔː/ *n* **1** one of the pointed nails on the feet of some animals, reptiles and birds; foot with such nails. ⇨ the illus at bird. **2** pincers of a shell-fish (eg a lobster). ⇨ the illus at crustacean. **3** instrument or device like a ~ (eg a steel hook on a ma-

chine for lifting things). '~**-hammer** *n* hammer with one end of the head bent and divided for pulling nails out of wood. □ *vt* [VP3A,6A,15B] ~ *at;* ~ *(back),* (try to) get hold of, pull, scratch, with ~s or hands. Hence, '~**-back** *n* (colloq) regaining sth with effort and persistence.

clay /kleɪ/ *n* [U] stiff, sticky earth that becomes hard when baked; material from which bricks, pots, earthenware, etc are made: (attrib) ~ *soil; a* ~ *pipe,* tobacco pipe made of white ~. ~**ey** /'kleɪɪ/ *adj* of, like, containing, covered with, ~.

clean[1] /kliːn/ *adj* (-er, -est) **1** free from dirt: ~ *hands;* ~ *air,* free from smoke; a ~ bomb, atomic or hydrogen bomb that, it is claimed, explodes without fall-out. ⇨ **fall**[1](1). *Keep the classroom* ~. *Wash it* ~. **2** not yet used; fresh: *Put some* ~ (eg after having been washed) *sheets on the bed. Give me a* ~ *sheet of paper.* **3** pure; innocent; free from wrong-doing or indecency: *a* ~ *joke. You must lead a* ~ *life. He has a* ~ *record,* is not known to have done wrong. *Keep the party* ~, (colloq) Don't use bad language or tell improper stories. **4** well-formed; of good shape: *a motor-car/ship with* ~ *lines.* ⇨ **streamlined.** ~**-'limbed** *adj* having well-shaped limbs. **5** even; regular; with a smooth edge or surface: *A sharp knife makes a* ~ *cut. C*~ *timber has no knots in it.* **6** skilful; smart: *a* ~ *boxer;* (cricket) ~ *fielding; a* ~ *stroke/blow.* **7** having ~ habits: *a* ~ *cat.* **8** fit for food: ~*/un*~ *animals,* those that are/are not considered fit for food (by religious custom). **9** thorough, complete. *make a* ~ *sweep of,* ⇨ **sweep**[2](1). ⇨ also **breast** and **slate**(2). □ *adv* completely; entirely: *I* ~ *forgot about it. The bullet went* ~ *through his shoulder. come* ~, make a full confession. ~**-'bowled** *adj* (cricket) bowled with no possibility of doubt. ~**-'cut** *adj* sharply and pleasingly outlined: ~*-cut features.* ~**-'living** *adj* chaste. ~**-'shaven** *adj* with the hair of the face shaved off; not having a moustache or beard.

clean[2] /kliːn/ *vt,vi* **1** [VP6A] make clean (of dirt, etc): *Wash your hands and* ~ *your nails. I must have this suit* ~*ed,* sent to the dry-cleaner's. ⇨ **dry**[1](13). *C*~ *your shoes before you come into the house,* ie remove the mud, etc. ⇨ **brush, polish. 2** [VP2A] *A porcelain sink* ~*s easily,* is easy to ~. **3** [VP15B,2C] (special uses with *adverbial particles* and *preps*): ~ *sth down,* ~ by brushing or wiping: ~ *down the walls.* ~ *sb out,* win or take all the money of: *They really* ~*ed me out at Las Vegas,* I lost all my money gambling there. ~ *sth out,* ~ the inside of, remove dirt, dust, etc from: *It's time you* ~*ed out your bedroom. be* ~*ed out,* (colloq) have no money left. ~ *up,* make clean or tidy; put in order: *You should always* ~ *up after a picnic,* burn wastepaper, collect litter, empty bottles, etc. ~ *sth up,* (a) get rid of criminal and immoral elements, etc: *The mayor has decided to* ~ *up the city,* end corruption, etc. (b) (colloq) make money (as gain or profit): '~**-up** *n* (esp) (process of) ending or reducing crime, corruption, etc. □ *n* ~ing: *Give it a good* ~, ~ it well. ~**er** *n* person or thing that ~s; tool, machine, etc for ~ing; substance that removes dirt, stains, grease, etc: *send/take a suit to the* (,dry) '~*ers;* '*window-* ~*er;* '*vacuum-*~*er.*

cleanly[1] /'klenlɪ/ *adj* (-ier, -iest) habitually clean; having clean habits: *Are cats* ~ *animals?* **clean·li·ness** /'klenlɪnɪs/ *n* [U] being clean.

cleanly[2] /'kliːnlɪ/ *adv* exactly; sharply; neatly: *this* *knife doesn't cut* ~. *He caught the ball* ~, *without fumbling.*

cleanse /'klenz/ *vt* [VP6A] (formal or archaic) make thoroughly clean; make pure: ~ *of/from sin.* ~ *n* [C,U] substance that ~s (eg a synthetic detergent).

clear¹ /klɪə(r)/ *adj* **1** easy to see through: ~ *glass; the* ~ *water of a mountain lake;* free from cloud: *a* ~ *sky;* bright, pure: *a* ~ *light; a* ~ *fire,* burning without much smoke; distinct; easily seen: *a line of hills* ~ *in the morning sky; a* ~ *photograph; a* ~ *reflection in the water.* **2** free from guilt or blame: *a* ~ *conscience,* knowledge that one is innocent. **3** (of sounds, etc) easily heard; distinct; pure: *a* ~ *voice; the* ~ *note of a bell; speak so that one's words are* ~. **4** ~ *(about),* (of and to the mind) free from doubt or difficulty: *a* ~ *thinker/ statement. My memory is not* ~ *about/on that point. It was* ~ *(to everyone) that the war would not end quickly.* **make oneself/one's meaning** ~, make oneself understood: *Now, do I make myself* ~? ,~-'**headed,** having good understanding. ,~-'**sighted,** able to see, think, understand well. **5** ~ *(of),* easy or safe to pass along; free from obstacles, dangers, etc: *Is the road* ~? *The coast is* ~, (fig) There is no one about (so one can escape, etc). *Is the sea* ~ *of ice yet? The signal 'All* ~' *was sounded,* eg after an air raid, to inform people that the raiders had left. '~-**way** *n* (in GB) section of the public highway on which vehicles must not stop or park. **6** ~ *(about)* confident; certain: *I want to be quite* ~ *on this point. I am not* ~ *as to what you expect me to do.* **7** ~ *(of)* free (from debt, suspicion, a charge): *I wish I were* ~ *of debt. You are now* ~ *of suspicion.* **8** complete: *for three* ~ *days;* without limitations; with nothing (to be) deducted: *a* ~ *profit of £5; passed by a* ~ *majority of ten.* □ *n in the* ~, free from suspicion, danger, etc. ~·**ness** *n* [U] state of being ~; clarity: *the* ~*ness of the atmosphere;* ~*ness of vision.*

clear² /klɪə(r)/ *adv* **1** distinctly: *speak loud and* ~. ,~-'**cut** *adv* well defined; distinct; having ~ outlines: ~-*cut ideas/plans.* **2** quite; completely: *The prisoner got* ~ *away.* **3** ~ *(of),* apart; without touching; at or to a distance: *He jumped three inches* ~ *of the bar. Stand* ~ *of the gates of the lift.* **keep/stay** ~ *of,* avoid; have nothing to do with: *You should keep* ~ *of that fellow. You should keep* ~ *of alcohol if you're driving.*

clear³ /klɪə(r)/ *vt,vi* **1** [VP6A,14] ~ *sth (of/from),* remove, get rid of, what is unwanted or unwelcome: ~ *the streets of snow/*~ *snow from the streets;* ~ *a canal of obstructions/*~ *obstructions from a canal;* ~ *a desk,* of papers, etc; ~ *the table,* after a meal; ~ *land of trees,* esp before cultivation; ~ *one's mind of doubt;* ~ *oneself* (of a charge), prove one's innocence. ~ **the air,** ⇨ air¹(1). ~ **the decks (for action),** get a ship ready for a fight; (fig) make ready for any kind of struggle or activity. ~ **one's throat,** eg by coughing. **2** [VP6A] get past or over without touching: *The winner* ~*ed six feet,* jumped this without touching the bar. *Can your horse* ~ *that hedge? Our car only just* ~*ed the gatepost. Jack up that wheel until it* ~*s* (= no longer rests on) *the ground.* **3** [VP6A] make as a net gain or profit: ~ *£50;* ~ *expenses,* make enough money to cover them. **4** [VP6A] get (a ship or its cargo) free by doing what is necessary (signing papers, paying dues, etc) on entering or leaving a port; ~ *goods through customs,* deal with

requirements of the customs (eg by paying any necessary duties); leave (a port) after doing this. **5** [VP6A] pass a cheque/bill of exchange etc through a clearing-house. **6** [VP15B,2C] (special uses with *adverbial particles* and *preps):*

~ **away,** pass away: *The clouds have* ~*ed away.* ~ **sth away,** take away, get rid of: ~ *away the tea-things.*

~ **off,** (colloq, of a person) go away; get rid of: *they* ~*ed off/we* ~*ed them off fast.* ~ **sth off,** get rid of, make an end of: ~ *off a debt;* ~ *off arrears of work.*

~ **out,** (colloq) go away; leave: *The police are after you, you'd better* ~ *out!* ~ **sth out,** empty; make clear by taking out the contents of: ~ *out a drain/a cupboard. All these hospital expenses have* ~*ed me out,* (colloq) have left me without money.

~ **up,** become clear: *The weather/The sky is* ~*ing up.* ~ **sth up, (a)** put in order; make tidy: *C*~ *up your desk before you leave the office. Who's going to* ~ *up the mess?* **(b)** make clear; solve (a mystery, etc): ~ *up a difficulty/misunderstanding.*

clear·ance /'klɪərəns/ *n* **1** clearing up, removing, making tidy: *a* ~ *sale,* a sale to clear out unwanted or superfluous stocks of goods. *You've made a tremendous* ~ *in the flat,* made it tidy, etc by getting rid of what was unwanted. **2** [C,U] free space; space between, for moving past: *a* ~ *of only two feet,* eg for a ship moving through a canal. *There is not much/not enough* ~ *for large lorries passing under this bridge.* **3** (certificate of) clearing a ship, ⇨ clear³(4).

clear·ing /'klɪərɪŋ/ *n* open space from which trees have been cleared in a forest. '~-**house,** office at which banks exchange cheques, etc and settle accounts, the balance being paid in cash.

clear·ly /'klɪəlɪ/ *adv* **1** distinctly: *speak* ~; *state one's facts* ~. *It is too dark to see* ~. **2** obviously; undoubtedly: *'Was he mistaken?' 'C*~'.

cleat /kliːt/ *n* **1** strip of wood, etc fastened to a gangway, etc to prevent slipping. **2** piece of wood, metal, etc bolted on to sth, on which ropes may be fastened (by winding). **3** piece of material fastened to the underside of a shoe or boot (eg for football) to prevent slipping. **4** V-shaped wedge.

cleav·age /'kliːvɪdʒ/ *n* split or division; direction in which sth tends to split or divide; place where there is a split or cleft; (colloq) the cleft between a woman's breasts as seen above a low neckline of a dress.

cleave¹ /kliːv/ *vt,vi* (*pt* clove /kləʊv/, cleft /kleft/ or cleaved /kliːvd/, *pp* cloven /'kləʊvn/, cleft or cleaved) **1** [VP6A,22,15A,B] cut into two (with a blow from a heavy axe, etc); split: ~ *a block of wood in two;* ~ *a man's head open with a sword.* **2** [VP2A] come apart; split: *This wood* ~*s easily.* **3** [VP6A,14] ~ *(through),* make by cutting: ~ *one's way through the crowd;* ~ *a path through the jungle.* **in a cleft stick,** (fig) in a tight place where neither advance nor retreat is possible. ,cleft '**palate** *n* malformation in the roof of the mouth because the two sides of the palate did not join before birth. ,cloven '**hoof** *n* divided hoof of an ox, a sheep, a goat (and a devil).

cleave² /kliːv/ *vi* (*pt* ~d or, old use, clave /kleɪv/, *pp* ~d) [VP3A] ~ **to,** stick fast to; (fig) be faithful to.

cleaver /'kliːvə(r)/ *n* heavy knife used by a butcher for chopping up meat.

clef /klef/ *n* (music) symbol placed at the beginning

of a stave to show the pitch of the notes. ⇨ the illus at notation.

cleft[1] /kleft/ n crack or split (eg in the ground or in rock); opening made by a cleavage.

cleft[2] /kleft/ pt,pp of cleave[1].

cle·ma·tis /'klemətɪs/ n [U] (kinds of) climbing plant with white, yellow or purple flowers.

clem·ency /'klemənsɪ/ n [U] (formal) mercy; mildness (of temper or weather).

clem·ent /'klemənt/ adj (formal) showing mercy; (of the weather, a person's temper) mild.

clench /klentʃ/ vt 1 [VP6A] press firmly together, close tightly: ~ one's teeth/jaws; ~ one's fingers/fist; a ~ed-fist salute. 2 [VP14] grasp firmly: ~ sth in/with one's hand(s). 3 = clinch.

clere·story /'klɪəstɔːrɪ/ n (pl -ries) upper part of a wall in a large church, with windows in it above the aisle roofs. ⇨ the illus at church.

clergy /'klɜːdʒɪ/ n (collective n with pl v) persons ordained as priests or ministers of the Christian Church: Thirty of the ~ were present at the ceremony. The ~ are opposed to the plan. '~·man /-mən/ n (pl -men) (not used of a bishop) ordained minister, esp of the Church of England.

cleric /'klerɪk/ n clergyman.

cleri·cal /'klerɪkl/ adj 1 of the clergy: ~ dress; a ~ collar. 2 of, for, made by, a clerk or clerks(1): '~ work; a ~ error, one made in copying or writing.

cleri·hew /'klerɪhjuː/ n witty or nonsensical piece of verse, usu two rhyming couplets of varying length.

clerk /klɑːk US: klɜːrk/ n 1 person employed in a bank, office, shop, etc to keep records and accounts, copy letters, etc: a 'bank ~; a ,corre'spondence ~. 2 officer in charge of records, etc: the Town C~; the C~ to the Council, (usu a lawyer); ~ of the works, having charge of materials, etc for building done by contract. 3 (US) shop-assistant; salesman or saleswoman. 4 (formal or legal): ~ in holy orders, clergyman. 5 lay officer of the church with various duties: the parish ~. 6 (old use) person who can read and write: I'm no great ~, am not much good at writing. □ vi (US only) work as a ~(3).

clever /'klevə(r)/ adj (-er, -est) 1 quick in learning and understanding things; skilful: He's ~ at arithmetic/at making excuses. How ~ of you to do that! He's a ~ workman. 2 (of things done) showing ability and skill: a ~ speech/book. 3 nimble: ~ fingers. 4 smart: He was too ~ for us, he outwitted us. ~·ly adv ~·ness n

clew /kluː/ n (naut) metal loop attached to the lower corner of a sail; loop holding the strings of a hammock. □ vt (also clue) (naut) haul a sail up or down.

cliché /'kliːʃeɪ US: kliːˈʃeɪ/ n [C] idea or expression that has been too much used and is now out-dated; stereotyped phrase: a ~-ridden newspaper article.

click[1] /klɪk/ vi, n [VP6A,2A,C] (make a) short, sharp sound (like that of a key turning in a lock): The door ~ed shut. The soldier ~ed his heels and saluted. Some African languages contain several ~s, ~ing sounds.

click[2] /klɪk/ vi [VP2A] (sl; not US) strike up an acquaintance, become friends, at once.

cli·ent /'klaɪənt/ n 1 person who gets help or advice from a lawyer or any professional man: a successful lawyer with hundreds of ~s. 2 customer (at a shop). **cli·en·tele** /ˌkliːənˈtel US: ˌklaɪən-/ n (collective) customers; patrons of a restaurant, theatre, etc.

cliff /klɪf/ n steep face of rock, esp at the edge of the sea. '~-hanger n episode in a story or contest of which the end is uncertain, so that the reader or spectator is held in suspense.

cli·mac·ter·ic /klaɪˈmæktərɪk/ n critical turning-point in (the body's) physical development.

cli·mac·tic /klaɪˈmæktɪk/ adj forming a climax.

cli·mate /'klaɪmɪt/ n 1 weather conditions of a place or area; conditions of temperature, rainfall, wind, etc. 2 area or region with certain weather conditions: A drier ~ would be good for her health. 3 prevailing condition: the political ~; ~ of opinion, general attitude of people to an aspect of life, policy, etc. **cli·mat·ic** /klaɪˈmætɪk/ adj of ~. **cli·mati·cally** /-klɪ/ adv **cli·ma·tol·ogy** /ˌklaɪməˈtɒlədʒɪ/ n [U] science of ~.

cli·max /'klaɪmæks/ n event, point, of greatest interest or intensity (eg in a story or drama): bring matters to a ~; work up to a ~; as a ~ to the day's entertainment. □ vt, vi bring or come to a ~.

climb /klaɪm/ vt,vi [VP6A,2A,C] go or get up (a tree, wall, rope, mountain, etc) or down; (of aircraft) go higher, gain height; (of plants) grow upwards by turning round a support, or with the support of tendrils, etc; rise by effort in social rank, position, etc: ~ a tree; ~ up/down a tree; ~ a wall; ~ over a wall. Monkeys ~ well. ~ down, (fig) admit that one has been mistaken, unreasonable, boastful, etc. Hence, '~-down n such an admission. '~ing irons n spikes (to be) fastened to the boots for ~ing trees, ice-slopes, etc. □ n ~ing; place (to be) ~ed: a hard ~. Have you done that ~? ~er n person who ~s; person who tries to advance socially; ~ing plant.

clime /klaɪm/ n (poet) climate(2).

clinch /klɪntʃ/ vt,vi 1 [VP6A] make (a nail or rivet) fast by hammering sideways the end that protrudes. 2 [VP6A] settle (a bargain, an argument) conclusively: That ~es the argument, ends all doubt. 3 [VP2A] (boxing) come to grips, with one or both arms round the opponent's body: The boxers ~ed and the referee intervened. □ n (boxing) the act, an instance, of ~ing: get into a ~; break a ~; (colloq) embrace. ~er n (colloq) ~ing argument.

cline /klaɪn/ n graded sequence of differences. ⇨ continuum.

cling /klɪŋ/ vi (pt,pp clung /klʌŋ/) [VP2C,3A] ~ to/together, hold tight; resist separation: ~ to one's possessions; ~ to a hope of being rescued. They clung together when the time came to part. The ship clung to (= did not go far from) the coast. The child clung to its mother's skirt/ garments. She's the ~ing sort, is prone to depend upon others. ~ing clothes n showing the shape or outline of the body or limbs.

cli·nic /'klɪnɪk/ n 1 (part of a) hospital or institution where medical advice and treatment are given and where students are taught through observation of cases; teaching so given; class of students taught in this way. 2 medical establishment for a specified purpose: a 'birth-control ~; an ,ante-'natal ~; an a'bortion ~.

cli·ni·cal /'klɪnɪkl/ adj 1 (of medical teaching given) at the hospital bedside: ~ thermometer, one for measuring the temperature of the body. 2 objective(2); uninvolved: ~ judgement.

clink[1] /klɪŋk/ vi,vt, n [VP6A,2A,C] (make the) sound of small bits of metal, glass, etc knocking together: the ~ of keys/glasses. They ~ed glasses, brought their glasses together before drinking each other's health.

clink² /klɪŋk/ n (sl) prison: *be in ~; be put in ~; go to ~.*

clinker /'klɪŋkə(r)/ n [C,U] (piece of the) mass of rough, hard, slag-like material left in a stove, furnace, etc after coal has been burned.

clinker-built /'klɪŋkə bɪlt/ adj (of boats) made with the outside planks or metal plates overlapping downwards.

clip¹ /klɪp/ n [C] **1** wire or metal device for holding things (eg papers) together. **2** holder (with loops) for cartridges (to be used in a magazine rifle). □ vt (-pp-) [VP6A,15B,2C] put or keep together with a ~ or ~s: *~ papers together; ~ one paper to another.* '~-on adj (attrib) that can be attached with a ~: *a ~-on tie/brooch.*

clips

clip² /klɪp/ vt (-pp-) **1** [VP6A,22,15A,B] cut with scissors or shears; make short or neat; cut off wool from (a sheep, etc): *~ a hedge; ~ a bird's wings; ~ sb's wings,* (fig) prevent him from doing what he is ambitious to do. *~ sth out (of),* remove by ~ping: *~ an article out of a newspaper.* '~-joint n (US sl) club that over-charges; business that defrauds. **2** [VP6A] omit or abbreviate (esp the end of) sounds of (words). **3** [VP6A] punch a hole in (a bus, tram or train ticket). **4** (sl) hit or punch sharply: *~ sb's ear; ~ sb on the jaw.* □ n **1** operation of shearing. **2** amount of wool cut from (a flock of) sheep at one time. **3** smart blow: *a ~ on the jaw.* **4** (US) fast speed. **~ping** n (in verbal senses) (esp) sth ~ped off or out; *newspaper ~pings.*

clip·per /'klɪpə(r)/ n **1** (pair of) ~s, instrument for clipping: *'hair-~s; 'nail-~s.* **2** sailing ship built for speed and used formerly esp in the tea-trade, ⇨ the illus at barque; (before jet aircraft) propeller-driven air-liner.

clique /kliːk/ n group of persons united by common interests (esp in literature or art), members of which support each other and shut out others from their company. **cliquish** /'kliːkɪʃ/ adj of or like a ~; tending to form a ~.

clit·oris /'klɪtərɪs/ n (anat) erectile organ at the upper end of the vulva, analogous to the penis.

cloak /kləʊk/ n loose outer garment, without sleeves; (fig) sth used to hide or keep secret: *use patriotism as a ~ for violence; under the ~ of darkness.* *~ and dagger,* (used attrib) in the style of, concerning, espionage, melodramatic intrigue, etc. '~-room n place where hats, coats, parcels, etc may be left for a short time (eg in a theatre or a railway station); (euphem) lavatory. □ vt [VP6A] (chiefly fig) conceal (thoughts, purposes, etc).

clob·ber¹ /'klɒbə(r)/ vt [VP6A] (sl) **1** strike violently and repeatedly; hurt badly: *~ the taxpayer,* by heavy taxation. **2** defeat thoroughly: *Our team got ~ed on Saturday.*

clob·ber² /'klɒbə(r)/ n (GB sl) clothing; equipment.

cloche /klɒʃ/ n [C] **1** glass or clear plastic protection, placed in long rows over tender plants; (older use) bell-shaped glass cover for a plant. **2** woman's close-fitting hat.

clock¹ /klɒk/ n instrument (not carried or worn like a watch) for measuring and showing the time. **put the '~ back,** (a) move the hands of the ~ back (eg when Summer Time ends). **(b)** (fig) take reactionary measures. **work against the ~,** work fast to finish before a certain time. **(work) round the ~,** (work) all day and night. Hence, ,round-the-'~, (used attrib): *a round-the-~ watch/guard on sth,* all day and night. '~-face/-dial, surface of a ~ showing figures marking the hours, etc. ~-'golf, game in which a golf-ball is putted on greens arranged in a circle. '~-tower, tall structure (forming part of a building, eg a church) with a ~ high up on an outside wall. '~-watching, practice (of some workers) of thinking constantly of how soon work will end. '~-wise/,anti-'~-wise adv moving in a curve in the same direction as/in the direction opposite to that taken by the hands of a ~. '~-work, (often attrib) mechanism with wheels and springs like a ~: *~work toys; a ~work driven train; with ~work precision; like ~work,* smoothly, without trouble. □ vt,vi **1** [VP6A] measure the time of; do sth (eg run a race) in a measured period of time: *He ~ed 9.6 seconds for the 100 metres.* **2** [VP2C,15B] **~ (sb) in/out; ~ (sb) on/off,** record/have recorded the time of (eg arrival/departure): *Workers in this factory are required to ~ in and out.* **3** [VP6A] (GB sl) strike; hit: *If you don't shut up, I'll ~ you one.*

clock² /klɒk/ n design sewn or woven on the side of a sock or stocking, at the ankle.

clod /klɒd/ n lump (of earth, clay, etc). '~-hop·per /-hɒpə(r)/ n (derog) clumsy, heavy-footed person, esp a rough farm worker.

clog¹ /klɒg/ n **1** shoe with a wooden sole; shoe carved out of a block of wood. '~-dance n dance in which the dancer wears ~s or wooden-soled shoes. **2** block of wood fastened to the leg of an animal to prevent its straying; (fig) encumbrance: *a ~ on his movements.*

clogs

clog² /klɒg/ vt,vi (-gg-) [VP6A,15B,2A,C] **~ (up),** **1** (cause to) be or become blocked with waste matter, dirt, grease, etc so that movement, flow of liquid, etc is difficult or prevented: *pipes ~ged with dirt; machinery ~ged (up) with grease.* **2** encumber; burden: *Don't ~ (up) your memory with useless facts.* **~gy** adj (-ier, -iest) lumpy; sticky.

cloi·sonné /klwɑːˈzɒneɪ US: ˌklɔɪzəˈneɪ/ n [U] enamel ware, in which the colours of the design are kept apart by thin metal strips.

clois·ter /'klɔɪstə(r)/ n **1** covered walk, usu on the sides of an open court or quadrangle, with a wall on the outer side and columns or arches on the inner side, esp within a convent, cathedral or college building. ⇨ the illus at church. **2** (life in a) convent or monastery. **the ~** n the seclusion of a convent, etc. □ vt [VP6A] put in, live in, a ~(2): *live a ~ed life,* a life of seclusion.

clone /kləʊn/ n (biol) (member of a) group of organisms or plants produced non-sexually from one ancestor. □ vt [VP6A] cause to grow as a ∼.

close¹ /kləʊs/ adj (-r, -st) **1** near (in space or time): fire at ∼ range; in ∼ combat; in ∼ proximity, almost touching. **a** ∼ **call/thing,** almost an accident, disaster or failure. **a** ∼ **shave,** (fig) a narrow escape from collision or accident. **'∼-up** n (a) photograph, esp as shown on a cinema or television screen, taken at ∼ range and showing the subject on a large scale. (b) close view. **2** with little or no space in between: ∼ writing; material of ∼ texture, eg woven with the threads ∼ together. The soldiers advanced in ∼ order, with little space between them. **3** strict; severe; rigorous: a ∼ blockade/siege; in ∼ confinement; be (kept) under ∼ arrest. **keep a** ∼ **watch on sb,** watch him carefully. **4** detailed; leaving no gaps or weak points; showing each step clearly: a ∼ argument; ∼ reasoning; a ∼ reasoner. **5** thorough; concentrated: after ∼ consideration; on ∼r examination. You must give me your ∼ attention. Please make a ∼ (= faithful and exact) translation. **6** intimate: a ∼ friend/friendship. **7** restricted; limited: a ∼ scholarship, open only to a restricted category of candidates. **8** (of competitions, games, their results) in which the competitors are almost equal: a ∼ contest/match/election/finish. **9** (phonetics; of vowels) made with the tongue and the roof of the mouth fairly close together: The English vowels /i:/ and /u:/ are ∼. **10** (also ∼-'fisted) stingy; niggardly. **11 '∼ season,** time (the breeding season) during which the killing of certain wild birds and animals, and the catching of certain fish, is illegal. **12** (of the weather) stifling; (of a room, etc) unventilated; having little fresh air; (of the air) difficult to breathe because heavy: Open the windows—this room/the air here is too ∼. **13** concealed; secret; not in the habit of talking about one's affairs: keep/lie ∼ for a while, keep one's whereabouts secret, not show oneself; keep sth ∼, say nothing about it, keep it secret; be ∼ (= secretive) about sth, Cf keep sth to oneself. ∼-**ly** adv in a ∼ manner: listen ∼ly; follow an argument ∼ly; a ∼ly contested election. She ∼ly resembles her mother. ∼**-ness** n being ∼: the ∼ness of a resemblance/friendship/translation/pursuit.

close² /kləʊs/ adv in a close manner; near together; tightly: follow ∼ behind sb; stand/sit ∼ against the wall; come ∼r together; ∼ shut. ∼ **at hand,** not far away. ∼ **by (sth);** ∼ **to sth,** near (it): He lives ∼ by (the church). There's a bus-stop ∼ to the school. The ship kept ∼ to the coast. ∼ **up (to sb/sth),** very near in space (to him/it): Snuggle as ∼ up to me as you can. ∼ **on/upon** almost; very near to: He is ∼ upon sixty. It was ∼ on midnight. **sail** ∼ **to the wind,** sail almost against the wind; (fig) almost break a law or a moral principle. ∼-'**cropped/'cut** adj (of hair, grass, etc) cut very short. ∼-'**fitting** adj fitting ∼ (to the body, etc): a ∼-fitting dress. ∼-'**grained** adj (esp of wood) having a grain in which the lines in the pattern made by growth are ∼ together (eg mahogany). ∼-'**hauled** adj (of a sailing-ship) with the sails set for sailing as nearly as possible in the direction from which the wind is blowing. ∼-'**set** adj set, placed, ∼ together; ∼-set eyes/teeth.

close³ /kləʊs/ n **1** grounds round a cathedral, abbey or school, usu with its buildings (houses of the clergy, etc) round it. **2** cul-de-sac.

close⁴ /kləʊz/ vt,vi **1** [VP6A,2A] shut: If you ∼ your eyes, you can't see. Did you ∼ all the doors and windows? This box/The lid of this box doesn't ∼ properly, The lid does not fit properly. Many flowers open in the morning and ∼ at night. ∼**d book,** (fig) subject about which one knows nothing: Nuclear physics is a ∼d book to most of us. **2** [VP6A,2A] be, declare, be declared, not open: This road is ∼d to heavy motor traffic. The theatres have ∼d for the summer. It's Sunday, so the shops are ∼d. Wednesday is early-closing day here, the day on which shops ∼ for a half-holiday. When is 'closing time, the time at which shops, etc, stop doing business? The inquiry was held behind/with ∼d doors, the public being excluded. ∼**d 'circuit** n (in TV) circuit by which the current from the camera to the screen has its path along wires all the way (instead of being transmitted through the air): (attrib) ∼d-,circuit 'television. ∼**d 'shop** n trade or profession, workshop, factory, establishment, etc in which employment is open only to members of an approved trade union. **3** [VP6A,2A] bring or come to an end: ∼ a discussion; the closing days of the year; the closing (= last, final) day for applications. The chairman declared the discussion ∼d. I want to ∼ my account, settle it by paying or receiving money that is due. ∼ **a deal,** complete it, by agreeing to the terms, etc. '**closing prices,** (comm) prices of shares quoted at a Stock-Exchange at the end of a day's business. **4** [VP6A,2C] bring or come together by making less space or fewer spaces between: ∼ the ranks; ∼ up, (of soldiers, etc) come ∼r together in line or lines. **5** [VP15B,2A,3A] (special uses with adverbial particles and preps):
∼ **down,** (a) (of a factory, business, etc) stop production, shut completely: The factory (was) ∼d down because of a lack of orders. (b) (of a broadcasting station) stop transmitting: It is midnight and we are now closing down. Hence, '∼-**down** n ∼ **in,** The days are closing in, getting shorter. ∼ **in on/upon,** (a) envelop: Darkness ∼d in on us. (b) come near(er) and attack: The enemy ∼d in upon us.
∼ **with,** (a) come within striking distance of (an enemy, etc). (b) accept (an offer); make a bargain with.

close⁵ /kləʊz/ n (sing only) end (of a period of time); conclusion (of an activity, etc): at the ∼ of the day; towards the ∼ of the 17th century; (at) (the) ∼ of play, (cricket) (at the) end of play for the day. The day had reached its ∼. **draw/bring sth to a** ∼, end.

closet /'klɒzɪt/ n **1** (now chiefly US) small room for storing things. ⇨ cupboard, storeroom. **2** (old use) small room for private interviews. **3** (old use) water-closet. ⇨ water¹(7). □ attrib (colloq) acting only in private; not publicly known: I suspect he's a ∼ fascist. □ vt (usu passive) **be** ∼**ed with sb/together,** have a private meeting with: He was ∼ed with the manager/They were ∼ed together for two hours.

clo-sure /'kləʊʒə(r)/ n **1** (US = cloture) [C,U] (in Parliament) device to end a debate by taking a vote on a question: apply the ∼ to a debate; move the ∼. ⇨ guillotine. **2** [C] act of closing: pit ∼s, eg of coal-mines which are no longer economic.

clot /klɒt/ n (C) **1** half-solid lump formed from liquid, esp blood. **2** (dated schoolboy sl) idiot, fool. □ vt,vi (-tt-) [VP6A,2A] form into ∼s: ∼ted *cream*, made by scalding it; ∼*ted hair*, stuck together by dirt or blood, etc.

cloth /klɒθ *US:* klɔːθ/ *n* (*pl* ∼s /klɒθs *US:* klɔːðz/) **1** [U] material made by weaving (cotton, wool, silk, linen, etc): *three yards of* ∼; *a book with a* ∼ *binding*. **2** [C] piece of this material for a special purpose: *a* '*floor*∼; *a* '*dish*∼. **3** [U] profession as shown by the clothes worn: *the respect due to his* ∼. *the* ∼, the clergy.

clothe /kləʊð/ *vt* (*pt,pp* clothed /kləʊðd/, old style clad /klæd/) [VP6A] **1** wear clothes; put clothes on, supply clothes for: *warmly* ∼*d*; ∼*d in wool. He has to work hard in order to* ∼ *his family*, earn money for their clothes. **2** (fig) express: *His sentiments were* ∼*d in suitable language.*

clothes /kləʊðz *US:* kləʊz/ *n pl* (no *sing*; not used with numerals) **1** coverings for a person's body; dress: *a baby in long* ∼; *a* '∼*-brush*. **2** '**bed-**∼, sheets, blankets, etc, for or on a bed. '∼**-basket**, one for ∼ which are to be, or have been, washed. '∼**-horse**, frame for airing ∼ that have been washed and dried. '∼**-line**, rope (stretched between posts) on which ∼ are hung to be dried after being washed. '∼**-peg/-pin**, one used for fastening ∼ to a ∼-line. ⇨ the illus at peg.

cloth·ier /'kləʊðɪə(r)/ *n* dealer in cloth or clothes.

cloth·ing /'kləʊðɪŋ/ *n* [U] (collective) clothes: *articles of* ∼.

clo·ture /'kləʊtʃə(r)/ *n* (US) = closure(1).

cloud /klaʊd/ *n* **1** [C,U] (separate mass of) visible water vapour floating above the earth: *The top of the mountain was covered with/hidden under* ∼. *Large, black* ∼*s announced a coming storm.* '∼**-bank** *n* thick mass of low ∼. '∼**-burst** *n* sudden and violent rainstorm. '∼**-capped** *adj* (eg of mountains) having the top enveloped in ∼. '∼**-cuckoo-land** *n* imaginary and ridiculously ideal place. **2** mass of things moving together: *a* ∼ *of arrows/insects/horsemen, etc.* **3** mass (*of* smoke, dust, sand, etc) in the air. **4** vague patch on or in a liquid or a transparent object. **5** something that causes unhappiness or fear: *the* ∼*s of war; a* ∼ *of gloom. under a* ∼, out of favour, under suspicion, in disgrace. **6** (*pl*) (**have one's head**) **in the** ∼**s**, (fig) with one's thoughts far away, not paying attention (to one's surroundings, etc). □ *vi,vt* [VP2A,C,3A6A] ∼ (*over*), become, make, indistinct (as) through ∼: *The sky* ∼*ed over. Her eyes were* ∼*ed* (*over*) *with tears. All these troubles have* ∼*ed his mind*, have affected his reason. ∼**less** *adj* free from ∼s; clear: *a* ∼*less sky.* ∼**y** *adj* (-ier, -iest) **1** covered with ∼s: *a* ∼*y sky.* **2** (esp of liquids) not clear.

clout /klaʊt/ *n* **1** (colloq) blow or knock (on the head, etc, given with the hand). **2** (archaic) piece of old cloth used for housework, etc: *a* '*dish*-∼. **3** (archaic) article of clothing. □ *vt* (colloq) hit: ∼ *sb on the head.*

clove[1] ⇨ cleave[1].

clove[2] /kləʊv/ *n* dried, unopened flower-bud of a tropical tree, used as a spice. ,**oil of** '∼**s**, oil extracted from ∼s and used in medicine.

clove[3] /kləʊv/ *n* one of the small, separate sections of a compound bulb: *a* ∼ *of garlic.*

clove hitch /'kləʊv hɪtʃ/ *n* knot for fastening a rope round a pole, etc. ⇨ the illus at knot.

clo·ven ⇨ cleave[1].

clo·ver /'kləʊvə(r)/ *n* [U] low-growing plant with (usu) three leaves on each stalk, and purple, pink or white flowers, grown as food for cattle, etc. *be/*

live in ∼, in great comfort and luxury. '∼**-leaf**, highway intersection with flyovers, etc forming the pattern of a four-leaved ∼. ,**four-leaf** '∼, rare variety with four-leaved stalk, the finding of which is considered to be a good omen.

clown /klaʊn/ *n* person (esp in a circus or pantomime) who makes a living by performing amusing or foolish tricks and antics; person acting like a ∼; rude, clumsy man. □ *vi* [VP2A] behave like a ∼: *Stop all this* ∼*ing.* ∼**·ish** *adj* of or like a ∼.

cloy /klɔɪ/ *vt, vi* [VP6A,2A] make or become distasteful by excess, sweetness, richness (of food, pleasure, etc); satiate: ∼*ed with pleasure;* ∼ *the appetite by eating too much sweet food.*

club[1] /klʌb/ *n* **1** heavy stick with one thick end, used as a weapon. **2** stick with a curved head for hitting the ball in golf and hockey. □ *vt* (-bb-) [VP6A,16A] hit with a ∼: *He had been* ∼*bed to death. They* ∼*bed him with their rifles.* ∼-'**foot** *n* foot that is (from birth) thick and badly formed, hence, ,∼-'**footed** *adj*

club[2] /klʌb/ *n* one of the thirteen playing-cards with a black three-leaf design printed on it: *the ace/ten of* ∼*s; play a small* ∼; *C*∼*s are trumps.* ⇨ the illus at card.

club[3] /klʌb/ *n* **1** society of persons who subscribe money to provide themselves with sport, social entertainment, or any other shared activity, sometimes in their own grounds, buildings, etc where meals and bedrooms are available; the rooms or building(s) used by such a society (also called a '∼**house**). □ *vi* (-bb-) [VP2C] ∼ **together**, join or act (together, with others) for a common purpose: *The villagers* ∼*bed together to help the old pensioners whose house had been burnt down.* ∼**·able** /'klʌbəbl/ *adj* fit for membership of a ∼(1); sociable.

cluck /klʌk/ *vi, n* [VP2A] (make the) noise made by a hen, eg when calling her chickens.

clue /kluː/ *n* fact, idea, etc that suggests a possible answer to a problem: *get/find a* ∼ *to a mystery.* **not have a** ∼, (colloq) be completely ignorant of, unable to understand or explain (what is in question).

clump[1] /klʌmp/ *n* group or cluster (*of* trees, shrubs or plants): *growing in* ∼*s.* □ *vt* plant in ∼s.

clump[2] /klʌmp/ *vi* [VP2A,C] tread heavily: ∼ *about*, walk about putting the feet down heavily.

clumsy /'klʌmzɪ/ *adj* (-ier, -iest) **1** heavy and ungraceful in movement or construction; not well designed for its purpose: *The* ∼ *workman put his elbow through the window and broke it. An axe would be a* ∼ *tool to open a tin of jam with.* **2** tactless; unskilful: *a* ∼ *apology/forgery;* ∼ *praise.* **clum·sily** /-zəlɪ/ *adv* **clum·si·ness** *n*

clung /klʌŋ/ *pt,pp* of cling.

clunk /klʌŋk/ *vi, n* (make the) dull sound of heavy metals etc striking together.

clus·ter /'klʌstə(r)/ *n* **1** number of things of the same kind growing closely together: *a* ∼ *of flowers/berries/curls; hair growing in thick* ∼*s.* **2** number of persons, animals, objects, etc in a small, close group: *a* ∼ *of bees/spectators/islands;* consonant ∼s (in phonetics, eg *str* in strong); *houses here and there in* ∼*s.* □ *vi* [VP2A,2C,3A] ∼ (**together**) (**round**), be in, form, a close group round: *roses* ∼ *ing* (together) *round the window. The village* ∼*s round the church.*

clutch[1] /klʌtʃ/ *vt, vi* [VP2A,3A,15A] ∼ (**at**), seize; take hold of tightly with the hand(s); attempt to seize: *He ~ed (at) the rope we threw to him. A drowning man will ~ at a straw*, will make a last, desperate but hopeless attempt to be saved. *Mary ~ed her doll to her breast.* □ *n* 1 the act of ~ing: *make a ~ at sth.* 2 (esp in *pl*) control; power. **be in/out of the ~s of; get into/out of the ~es of,** eg of moneylenders. 3 device, eg a pedal, in a machine or engine for connecting and disconnecting working. parts: *let in/disengage/withdraw the ~; put the ~ in/out. The ~ is in/out.* ⇨ the illus at motor.

clutch² /klʌtʃ/ *n* set of eggs placed under a hen to hatch at one time; number of young chickens hatched from these.

clut·ter /'klʌtə(r)/ *vt* [VP6A,15B] ~ *(up),* make untidy or confused by crowding: *a desk ~ed up with papers; ~ up a room with unnecessary furniture.* □ *n* [C,U] untidy or confused state: *in a ~,* in disorder or confusion. *Get rid of all this ~!*

co- /kəʊ/ *pref* together with (another or others): *co-author; co-heir; co-exist; co-belligerents.*

coach¹ /kəʊtʃ/ *n* 1 four-wheeled carriage pulled by four or more horses, used to carry passengers and mail before railways were built ('*stage-~* and '*mail-~* for public use; '*state-~* used by a head of state on ceremonial occasions). **drive a ~ and horses through (sth),** defeat the intention of (a regulation, etc) by finding serious faults in its wording. 2 (US = *car*) railway carriage, often divided into compartments. 3 ('**motor-~**) long-distance, single-decked motor-bus: *travel by ~; a ~-tour of Europe; leave by ~ for Edinburgh.* '**~-builder** *n* craftsman who builds the body-work of motor vehicles.

a state-coach

coach² /kəʊtʃ/ *n* teacher, esp one who gives private lessons to prepare students for a public examination; person who trains athletes for contests: *a '*baseball *~.* □ *vt,vi* [VP6A,14,2A] teach or train: *~ sb for an exam; ~ the crew for the boat race.*

co·agu·late /kəʊ'ægjʊleɪt/ *vt,vi* [VP6A,2A] (of liquids) change to a thick and solid state, as blood does in air. **co·agu·lation** /kəʊˌægjʊ'leɪʃn/ *n*

coal /kəʊl/ *n* [U] black mineral that burns and supplies heat, and from which ~-gas is made; [C] piece of this material, esp (*a live ~*) one that is burning: *A hot ~ fell from the fire and burnt a hole in the carpet.* **carry ~s to Newcastle** /'nju:kɑːsl US: 'nuːkæsl/, take goods to a place where they are already plentiful. **heap ~s of fire on sb's head,** return good for evil and so induce remorse. '**~-face** *n* part of a ~ seam from which ~ is being cut. '**~-field** *n* district in which ~ is mined. '**~-gas** *n* the mixture of gases made by treating ~, used for lighting and heating. '**~-hole** *n* cellar for storing ~. '**~-house** *n* shed for storing ~. '**~-mine/-pit** *nn* mine from which ~ is dug. '**~-scuttle** *n* container for a supply of ~ near a fireside. '**~-seam** *n*

underground layer of ~. '**~-tar** *n* [U] (sometimes '*gas-tar*) thick, black, sticky substance produced when gas is made from ~. □ *vt,vi* [VP6A,2A] put ~ (into a ship, etc); take in ~: *The ship called at Gibraltar to ~. Coaling (a ship) is a dirty job.* '**~-ing-station** *n* port where ships can obtain supplies of ~.

co·alesce /ˌkəʊə'les/ *vi* come together and unite into one substance, group, etc. **co·ales·cence** /ˌkəʊə'lesns/ *n*

co·ali·tion /ˌkəʊə'lɪʃn/ *n* [U] uniting; [C] union of political parties for a special purpose: *a ~ government; the left-wing ~; form a ~.*

coam·ing /'kəʊmɪŋ/ *n* raised rim round a ship's hatches to keep water out.

coarse /kɔːs/ *adj* (-r, -st) 1 (of material) not fine and small; rough and lumpy: *~ sand/sugar;* having a rough surface or texture: *a dress made of ~ cloth; a ~ skin/complexion.* 2 (of food) common; inferior: *~ fish; ~ fishing,* eg for chub, roach, pike. 3 vulgar; not delicate or refined: *~ manners/language/words/laughter/jokes/tastes; ~ of speech.* **coarsen** /'kɔːsn/ *vt,vi* [VP6A,2A] make or become ~. **~·ly** *adv* **~·ness** *n*

coast¹ /kəʊst/ *n* [C] land bordering the sea; seashore and land near it: *The ship was wrecked on the Kent ~. There are numerous islands off the ~. The village is on the south ~.* '**~-guard** *n* officer on police duty on the ~ (to prevent or detect smuggling, report passing ships, etc). '**~-line** *n* shoreline, esp with regard to its shape: *a rugged ~line.* **~al** /'kəʊstl/ *adj* of the ~: *~al navigation.* '**~-wise** *adj, adv* along the ~.

coast² /kəʊst/ *vi,vt* 1 [VP2A,2C,3A,6A] ~ *(along),* go in, sail, a ship along the coast. 2 ride or slide down a hill or slope without using power (eg along a road on a bicycle). **~er** *n* 1 ship that sails from port to port along the coast. 2 small mat, etc (for a drinking-glass, etc) to protect a polished table, etc from drips or moisture.

coat /kəʊt/ *n* 1 long outer garment with sleeves, buttoned in the front. ⇨ *over-~; rain-~* at rain ¹(1). **turn one's ~,** change one's side or principles, desert one army or party and join the other. *~ of '*arms, ⇨ arms. *~ of '*mail, piece of armour of metal rings or plate for the upper part of the body. ⇨ the illus at armour. '**~-tails** *n pl* divided tapering part of a *tail-~,* ⇨ tail(2). 2 jacket(1). 3 any covering that can be compared to a garment, eg an animal's hair or wool. 4 layer of paint or other substance put on a surface at one time: *The woodwork has had its final ~ of paint.* □ *vt* [VP6A,14] cover with a ~ or layer: *furniture ~ed with dust; ~ pills with sugar. Tinplate is made by ~ing sheets of iron with tin.* '**~-ing** *n* 1 thin layer or covering: *two ~ings of wax.* 2 [U] cloth for ~s(1,2).

coatee /kəʊ'tiː/ *n* short coat.

coax /'kəʊks/ *vt,vi* [VP6A,17,15B,14,2A] ~ *(from/into/out of),* get sb or sth to do sth by kindness or patience: *~ a child to take its medicine; ~ a fire to burn; ~ (up) the fire; ~ sb into/out of doing sth; ~ a smile from the baby.* **~·ing** *n* [U,C] being ~ed: *give sb a ~ing. He took a lot of ~ing before he agreed to take her to the theatre.* **~·ing·ly** *adv*

cob /kɒb/ *n* 1 male swan. 2 strong short-legged horse for riding. 3 (also '**cob-nut**) large kind of hazel-nut. 4 (also '**corn-cob**) central part of an ear of maize on which the grain grows: *corn on the* *cob.* ➪ the illus at cereal.

co-balt /'kəʊbɔːlt/ *n* hard silvery-white metal (symbol **Co**) used in many alloys; deep blue colouring matter made from its compounds, used to colour glass and ceramics.

cob-ber /'kɒbə(r)/ *n* (Australia; colloq) fellow.

cobble[1] /'kɒbl/ *n* (also '∼-stone) stone worn round and smooth by water and used for paving. □ *vt* pave with these stones: ∼*d streets.*

cobble[2] /'kɒbl/ *vt* [VP6A] mend, patch (esp shoes), or put together roughly.

cob-bler /'kɒblə(r)/ *n* **1** mender of shoes. (*'shoe-repairer* is now the usu word). **2** clumsy workman. **3** (US) type of pie. *a load of (old)* ∼*s,* (GB sl) nonsense.

co-bra /'kəʊbrə/ *n* poisonous snake of Asia and Africa. ➪ the illus at snake.

cob-web /'kɒbweb/ *n* [C] fine network or single thread made by a spider. ➪ the illus at arachnid.

Coca-Cola /ˌkəʊkə 'kəʊlə/ *n* (P) popular non-alcoholic carbonated drink.

co-caine /kəʊ'keɪn/ *n* [U] product (from a shrub) used by doctors as a local anaesthetic, and also used as a stimulant by drug addicts.

cochi-neal /ˌkɒtʃɪ'niːl/ *n* [U] bright red colouring-matter made from the dried bodies of certain insects.

coch-lea /'kɒklɪə/ *n* spiral-shaped part of the inner ear. ➪ the illus at ear.

cock[1] /kɒk/ *n* **1** (used alone) adult male bird of the domestic or farmyard fowl (US = *rooster*) ➪ the illus at fowl. '∼-crow *n* early dawn. ,∼-a-'hoop *adj, adv* with boastful crowing; exultant(ly). ∼-a-doodle-doo /ˌkɒk ə ˌduːdl 'duː/ *n* the crow of the ∼(1); child's name for a ∼(1). ,∼-and-'bull story, foolish story that one should not believe. '∼-fighting *n* fighting by game-∼s as a sport for onlookers. ➪ game[1](6). *live like* '*fighting-∼s,* live on the best possible food. ∼ *of the walk,* person who dominates others. **2** (in compounds) male of other kinds of bird: '*pea*∼; ,∼-'*sparrow*; ,∼-'*robin.*

cock[2] /kɒk/ *n* **1** tap and spout for controlling the flow of a liquid or a gas, eg from a pipe, barrel. **2** lever in a gun; position of this lever when it is raised and ready to be released by the trigger. *at half/full* ∼, half ready/quite ready to be fired. *go off at half* ∼, of schemes, ceremonies, etc, begin before the arrangements are complete. **3** △ (vulg sl) penis.

cock[3] /kɒk/ *vt* [VP6A,15B] ∼ *(up),* **1** turn upwards, cause to be erect (showing attention, inquiry, defiance, etc): *The horse* ∼*ed its ears. The horse stopped with its ears* ∼*ed up. He* ∼*ed his eye at me,* glanced or winked at me knowingly, or raised his eyebrow. ,∼*ed* '*hat n* triangular hat, pointed front and back, worn with some uniforms. *knock sb/sth into a* ∼*ed hat,* knock shapeless, or so that recognition is impossible; beat thoroughly. **2** [VP6A] raise the cock of (a gun) ready for firing. ➪ cock[2](2). **3** ∼ *up,* (sl) make a mess of; upset: *They completely* ∼*ed up the arrangements for our holiday.* Hence, '∼-up *n*

cock[4] /kɒk/ *n* small, cone-shaped pile of straw or hay. □ *vt* pile (hay) in ∼s.

cock-ade /kɒ'keɪd/ *n* knot of ribbon worn on a hat as a badge.

cocka-too /ˌkɒkə'tuː/ *n* crested parrot. ➪ the illus at rare.

cock-chafer /'kɒktʃeɪfə(r)/ *n* large beetle that flies

with a loud whirring sound and is destructive to vegetation.

cocker /'kɒkə(r)/ *n* breed of spaniel.

cock-erel /'kɒkərəl/ *n* young cock[1](1), not more than one year old.

cock-eyed /'kɒkaɪd/ *adj* (sl) **1** squinting; crooked; turned or twisted to one side. **2** wild, ill-judged: *a* ∼ *scheme.*

cock-horse /ˌkɒk'hɔːs/ *n ride a* ∼, (children's word) ride on horseback or on a rocking-horse. ➪ rock(2).

cockle /'kɒkl/ *n* **1** edible shellfish; (also '∼-shell) its shell. **2** small, shallow boat. **3** *(warm, delight, etc) the* ∼*s of one's heart,* one's feelings.

cock-ney /'kɒknɪ/ *adj, n* (characteristic of a) native of the East End of London: *a* ∼ *accent;* ∼ *humour.*

cock-pit /'kɒkpɪt/ *n* **1** enclosed space where game-cocks fought. ➪ *cock-fighting* at cock[1](1); (fig) area where battles have often been fought: *Belgium, the* ∼ *of Europe.* **2** compartment in a small aircraft for the pilot. Cf *flight deck* of an airliner; driver's seat in a racing-car. ➪ the illus at air[1].

cock-roach /'kɒkrəʊtʃ/ *n* large, dark-brown insect that comes out at night in kitchens and places where food is kept. ➪ the illus at insect.

cocks-comb /'kɒkskəʊm/ *n* **1** red crest of a cock[1](1). ➪ the illus at fowl. **2** jester's cap. **3** plant with clusters of red or yellow feather-like flowers. ➪ also coxcomb.

cock-sure /ˌkɒk'ʃʊə(r)/ *adj* presumptuously or offensively sure (*of* or *about* sth); confident.

cock-tail /'kɒkteɪl/ *n* [C] **1** mixed alcoholic drink, esp one taken before a meal, eg gin and vermouth. **2** mixture of fruit juices, or spiced tomato juice, served in a glass as an appetizer; quantity of crab meat or shrimps, similarly served. **3** mixed fruit salad served in a glass.

cocky /'kɒkɪ/ *adj* (-ier, -iest) (colloq) cocksure; pert; conceited.

coco /'kəʊkəʊ/ *n* (also '∼-palm, '∼-nut palm) tropical seaside palm-tree. ∼-nut /'kəʊkənʌt/ *n* large hard-shelled seed of this palm-tree, filled with milky juice and a solid white eatable lining from which oil is extracted; ➪ copra. ➪ the illus at palm. ,∼nut 'matting, made from the tough fibre of the ∼nut's outer covering.

co-coa /'kəʊkəʊ/ *n* [U] powder of crushed cacao seeds; hot drink made from this with water or milk.

co-coon /kə'kuːn/ *n* silky covering made by a caterpillar to protect itself while it is a chrysalis, esp that of the silkworm. ➪ the illus at butterfly, silk. □ *vt* [VP6A] protect by covering completely.

co-cotte /kɒ'kɒt/ *n* (F) (dated) fashionable prostitute.

cod[1] /kɒd/ *n* **1** [C] (*pl* unchanged) (also '**cod-fish**) large sea fish. **2** [U] its flesh as food. ∼-liver oil /ˌkɒd lɪvər 'ɔɪl/ *n* [U] used as a medicine.

cod[2] /kɒd/ *vt,vi* (-dd-) [VP6A,2A] (dated colloq) hoax; make a fool of: *You're codding (me)!*

coda /'kəʊdə/ *n* passage (often elaborate in style) that completes a piece of music.

coddle /'kɒdl/ *vt* [VP6A] **1** (also '**molly-**∼) treat with great care and tenderness; pamper: ∼ *a child because it is in poor health.* **2** cook, eg eggs, in water just below boiling-point.

code /kəʊd/ *n* [C] **1** collection of laws arranged in a system. **2** system of rules and principles that has been accepted by society or a class or group of people: *a high moral* ∼; *a* ∼ *of honour. You must* *live up to the* ~ *of the school*, accept its unwritten rules of honour and conduct. **3** (also [U]) system of signs used for secrecy or brevity, eg in wartime, or for economy in sending cables, or for a computer: *send a message in* ~; *a* '*telegraph* ~; *a* ~ *telegram*; *a ,five-'letter* ~, eg one in which BXYMA stands for a phrase or sentence. **break a** ~, discover how to interpret a secret ~. **the 'Morse** ~, using dots and dashes for letters and numerals. □ *vt* (also **en**~ /en'kəʊd/) put in a ~(3); ⇨ **decode.**

co·deine /'kəʊdiːn/ *n* [U] narcotic derived from opium.

co·dex /'kəʊdeks/ *n* (*pl* **codices** /'kəʊdɪsiːz/) manuscript volume (esp of ancient texts).

codger /'kɒdʒə(r)/ *n* (colloq) queer old person; fellow.

codi·ces ⇨ **codex.**

codi·cil /'kəʊdɪsɪl US: 'kɒdəsl/ *n* appendix to a will, esp sth modifying or revoking part of it.

codi·fy /'kəʊdɪfaɪ US: 'kɒdəfaɪ/ *vt* [VP6A] put into the form of a code(1): ~ *the laws.* **codi·fi·ca·tion** /ˌkəʊdɪfɪ'keɪʃn US: ˌkɒd-/ *n*

cod·ling /'kɒdlɪŋ/ *n* young codfish.

cod·piece /'kɒdpiːs/ *n* (15th and 16th cc) bag or flap concealing the opening in the front of a man's close-fitting hose ²(2).

co-ed /'kəʊ ed/ *n* (US colloq) (girl or woman at a) co-educational school or college.

co-edu·ca·tion /ˌkəʊ ˌedʒʊ'keɪʃn/ *n* [U] education of boys and girls together. ~**al** /-'keɪʃənl/ *adj*

co-ef·fi·cient /ˌkəʊɪ'fɪʃnt/ *n* **1** (maths) number or symbol placed before and multiplying another quantity, known or unknown. (In 3xy, 3 is the ~ of xy). **2** (phys) multiplier that measures some property.

co·erce /kəʊ'ɜːs/ *vt* [VP6A,14] ~ *sb* (*into doing sth*), use force to make sb obedient, etc; compel sb (to a course of action). **co·ercion** /kəʊ'ɜːʃn US: -ʒn/ *n* [U] coercing or being ~d; government by force: *He paid the money under coercion.* **co·er·cive** /kəʊ'ɜːsɪv/ *adj* of coercion; using coercion: *coercive methods/measures.*

co·eval /ˌkəʊ'iːvl/ *adj, n* ~ (*with*), (person) of the same age; (person, things) existing at, lasting for, the same period of time.

co·exist /ˌkəʊɪɡ'zɪst/ *vi* [VP2A,3A] ~ (*with*), exist at the same time. ~·**ence** /-təns/ *n* [U] (esp) peaceful existence side by side of states with opposed political systems.

cof·fee /'kɒfɪ US: 'kɔːfɪ/ *n* [U] bush or shrub with berries containing seeds (called *beans*) which, when roasted and ground to powder, are used by infusing with boiling water for making a drink; the seeds; the powder; [C,U] the drink: *three black* ~*s*, three cups of ~ without milk; *white* ~, with milk. '~ **bar** *n* small café serving ~, beverages and light refreshments. '~**-house** *n* (formerly, in England) place frequented by literary men as a sort of club. '~**-mill** *n* device for grinding roasted ~-beans. '~**-stall** *n* movable stand selling hot ~ and food in the streets (esp at night).

cof·fer /'kɒfə(r)/ *n* **1** large, strong box, esp one for holding money or other valuables; (*pl*) place for storing valuables: *the* ~*s of a bank.* **2** ornamental panel in a ceiling, etc. **3** (also '~**-dam**) caisson(2).

cof·fin /'kɒfɪn/ *n* box or case for a dead person to be placed in and then buried. *drive a nail into sb's* ~, do sth that will bring his death or ruin nearer.

cog /kɒg/ *n* one of a series of teeth on the rim of a wheel which transfers motion by locking into the

teeth of a similar wheel. ⇨ the illus at **bicycle, gear.** *be a cog in the machine,* (fig) an unimportant part of a large enterprise. '**cog·wheel** *n* toothed wheel.

co·gent /'kəʊdʒənt/ *adj* (of arguments) strong and convincing. **co·gency** /'kəʊdʒənsɪ/ *n* [U] force or strength (of arguments).

cogi·tate /'kɒdʒɪteɪt/ *vi,vt* [VP2A,3A,6A,14] (formal or facet) meditate; think deeply: ~ *upon sth;* ~ *mischief against sb.* **cogi·ta·tion** /ˌkɒdʒɪ'teɪʃn/ *n* **1** [U] cogitating: *after much cogitation.* **2** (*pl*) thoughts; reflections.

cognac /'kɒnjæk/ *n* [U] fine French brandy.

cog·nate /'kɒgneɪt/ *adj* **1** ~ (*with*), having the same source or origin: *English, Dutch and German are* ~ *languages.* **2** related; having much in common: *Physics and astronomy are* ~ *sciences.* □ *n* [C] word, etc that is ~ with another.

cog·ni·tion /kɒg'nɪʃn/ *n* [U] (phil) knowing; awareness (including sensation but excluding emotion).

cog·ni·zance /'kɒgnɪzəns/ *n* [U] **1** (legal) being aware, having conscious knowledge (of sth). *take* ~ *of*, become officially aware of. **2** (right of) dealing with a matter legally or judicially. *fall within/ go beyond one's* ~, be sth one can/cannot deal with. **cog·ni·zant** /'kɒgnɪzənt/ *adj* ~ *of*, (phil, legal) having knowledge, being fully aware of.

cog·no·men /kɒg'nəʊmən/ *n* [C] (formal) **1** surname. **2** descriptive nickname, eg *Rusty* or *Shorty.*

co·habit /kəʊ'hæbɪt/ *vi* (formal) (usu of an unmarried couple) live together. **co·habi·ta·tion** /ˌkəʊhæbɪ'teɪʃn/ *n*

co·here /kəʊ'hɪə(r)/ *vi* [VP2A] (formal) stick together; be or remain united; (of arguments, etc) be consistent. **co·her·ence** /ˌkəʊ'hɪərəns/ *n* **co·her·en·cy** /-rənsɪ/ *n* **co·her·ent** /-rənt/ *adj* **1** sticking together. **2** consistent; (esp of speech, thought, ideas, reasoning) clear; easy to understand. **co·her·ent·ly** *adv*

co·he·sion /kəʊ'hiːʒn/ *n* cohering; tendency to stick together; force with which molecules cohere. **co·he·sive** /kəʊ'hiːsɪv/ *adj* having the power of cohering; tending to cohere.

co·hort /'kəʊhɔːt/ *n* **1** (in the ancient Roman armies) tenth part of a legion. **2** number of persons banded together.

coif /kɔɪf/ *n* (old use) close-fitting cap covering the top, back and sides of the head.

coif·feur /kwɑː'fɜː(r)/ *n* (F) hairdresser.

coif·fure /kwɑː'fjʊə(r)/ *n* style of hairdressing.

coign /kɔɪn/ *n* ~ *of* '*vantage* (formal, usu fig) place from which one has a good view of sth.

coil /kɔɪl/ *vt,vi* [VP6A,15A,B,2A,C] wind or twist into a continuous circular or spiral shape; curl round and round: ~ *a rope. The snake* ~*ed* (*itself*) *round the branch/*~*ed itself up.* □ *n* **1** sth ~*ed*; a single turn of sth ~*ed*: *the thick* ~*s of a python.* ⇨ the illus at **snake. 2** length of wire wound in a spiral to conduct electric current. **3** (colloq) an intrauterine contraceptive device in the shape of a ~.

coin /kɔɪn/ *n* [C,U] (piece of) metal money: *a small heap of* ~*s; gold and silver* ~*s; false* ~, imitation ~ in metal of low value. *the other side of the* ~, (fig) other aspect of the matter. *pay a man back in the same/his own* ~, treat him as he has treated you. □ *vt* [VP6A] make (metal) into ~*s*; invent (esp a new word). *be* '~*ing money,* be making money fast, be making large profits. *to* ~ *a phrase,* (ironic) to use a very well established idiom as if it were a new one. ~-age /'kɔɪnɪdʒ/ n 1 [U] making ~s; the ~s made; [C] system of ~s in use: *a decimal ~age*. 2 [U] inventing (of a new word); [C] newly invented word. ~er n maker of counterfeit ~s.

co-incide /ˌkəʊɪn'saɪd/ vi [VP2A,3A] ~ *(with),* 1 (of two or more objects) correspond in area and outline. 2 (of events) happen at the same time; occupy the same period of time: *They could not go to the theatre together because his free time never ~d with hers.* 3 (of ideas, etc) be in harmony or agreement: *The judges did not ~ in opinion. His tastes and habits ~ with those of his wife.*

co-inci-dence /kəʊ'ɪnsɪdəns/ n [U] the condition of coinciding; [C] instance of this, happening by chance: *by a curious ~. What a ~!* How curious, etc that these two events should come together! co-inci-dent /-dənt/ adj coinciding. co-inci-den-tal /kəʊˌɪnsɪ'dentl/ adj of the nature of a, exhibiting ~.

coir /'kɔɪə(r)/ n fibre from coconut shells, used for making ropes, matting, etc.

co-ition /kəʊ'ɪʃn/ n = coitus.

co-itus /'kəʊɪtəs/ n [U] (formal) sexual intercourse to the point of (mutual) orgasm between two human beings; the insertion of the penis into the vagina.

coke¹ /kəʊk/ n [U] rough, light substance that remains when gas has been taken out of coal by heating it in an oven, used as a fuel in stoves and furnaces. ⮐ vt turn (coal) into ~.

coke² /kəʊk/ n (P) (colloq abbr of) Coca-Cola.

coke³ /kəʊk/ n (sl) cocaine.

coker-nut /'kəʊkənʌt/ n = coconut.

col /kɒl/ n depression or pass in a mountain range. ⮕ the illus at mountain.

cola /'kəʊlə/ n = kola.

col·an·der, cul·len·der /'kʌləndə(r)/ n bowl-shaped vessel or dish with many small holes, used to drain off water from vegetables, etc in cooking.

cold¹ /kəʊld/ adj 1 of low temperature, esp when compared with the human body: ~ *weather; a ~ wind; feel ~; a hotel with hot and ~ water in every bedroom. give sb the ~ shoulder,* (fig) snub him; show distaste for his company. Hence, ˌ~-'shoulder vt [VP6A] snub. *have ~ feet,* feel afraid or reluctant (to do sth involving risk or danger). *leave one ~,* leave one unmoved, unimpressed. *(kill sb) in ~ blood; make one's 'blood run ~,* ⮕ blood¹. *pour/throw ~ water on,* ⮕ water¹(1). *'~ chisel,* one for cutting soft metals while they are ~. ˌ~ 'comfort, poor consolation. '~ cream, ointment for cleansing and softening the skin. ˌ~ 'front, ⮕ front(7). ˌ~ 'meat, meat that has been cooked and cooled: ~ *meat for supper.* ˌ~ 'steel, [U] cutting or stabbing weapon (eg a sword or bayonet contrasted with firearms). ˌ~ 'turkey, ⮕ turkey. ˌ~ 'war, struggle for superiority waged by hostile propaganda, economic measures, etc without actual fighting. ˌ~-'blooded /-'blʌdɪd/ adj (a) having blood that varies with the temperature (eg fish, reptiles). (b) (fig, of persons, their actions) without feeling; pitiless. ˌ~-'hearted /-'hɑːtɪd/ adj without sympathy; indifferent. 2 (fig) (a) unkind; unfriendly: *a ~ greeting/welcome, etc.* (b) sexually unresponsive. 3 (of colours) suggesting ~, eg grey and blue. ~-ly adv ~-ness n [U] state of being ~: *Because of the ~ness of the weather, we stayed indoors.*

cold² /kəʊld/ n 1 [U] (the) ~, relative absence of

heat; low temperature (esp in the atmosphere): *He was shivering with ~. He disliked both the heat of summer and the ~ of winter. Don't stay outside in the ~, come indoors by the fire. (be left) out in the ~,* (fig) (be) ignored or neglected. 2 [U] (phys) freezing-point of water at or below: *five degrees of ~.* 3 [C,U] inflammation of the mucous membrane of the nose or throat: *have a ~; catch (a) ~. Half the boys in the school were absent with ~s.*

cole·slaw /'kəʊlslɔː/ n [U] finely shredded dressed raw cabbage (as a salad).

colic /'kɒlɪk/ n [U] severe pain in the stomach and bowels without diarrhoea.

co·li·tis /kə'laɪtɪs/ n [U] (med) inflammation of the mucous membrane of the colon.

col·lab·or·ate /kə'læbəreɪt/ vi 1 [VP2A,3A] ~ *(on sth) (with sb),* work in partnership, esp in literature or art: ~ *on a biography with a friend.* 2 [VP3A] ~ *with,* work treasonably, esp with enemy forces occupying one's country. col·lab·or·ator /kə'læbəreɪtə(r)/ n person who ~s(1,2). col·lab·or·ation /kəˌlæbə'reɪʃn/ n [U] collaborating: *working in collaboration with others.* col·lab·or·ation·ist /kəˌlæbə'reɪʃənɪst/ n person who ~s(2).

col·lage /'kɒlɑːʒ US: kə'lɑːʒ/ n [U,C] (art) (picture made by an) unusual combination of bits of paper, cloth, photographs, metal etc.

col·lapse /kə'læps/ vi [VP2A] 1 fall down or in; come or break to pieces suddenly: *The weight of the snow on the roof caused the shed to ~. The roof ~d under the weight of the snow. If you cut the ropes of a tent, it will ~.* 2 lose physical strength, courage, mental powers, etc; break down: *If you work too hard you/your health may ~. Our plans will ~ unless we get more help. The price of copper ~d,* dropped to a low level. 3 (of apparatus) close or fold up. 4 vt [VP6A] cause to ~: ~ *a canvas chair.* □ n collapsing: *the ~ of a table/tent/tower, etc;* (fig): *the ~ of their plans/hopes; suffer a nervous ~.* col·laps·ible, -able /-səbl/ adj that can be ~d(4) (for packing, etc): *a collapsible boat/chair.*

col·lar /'kɒlə(r)/ n 1 part of a garment that fits round the neck; turned-over neckband of a shirt, dress, etc: *The wind was so cold that he turned his coat ~ up. 'blue/'white ~ workers,* ⮕ blue, white. 2 separate article of clothing (linen, lace, etc) worn round the neck and fastened to a shirt or blouse. '~ stud n small button-like device for fastening a ~ to a shirt. 3 band of leather, etc put round the neck of a dog, horse or other animal. ⮕ the illus at harness. 4 metal band joining two pipes, rods or shafts, eg in a machine. 5 '~-bone n bone joining the shoulder and the breast-bone. ⮕ the illus at skeleton. □ vt [VP6A] 1 seize (sb) by the ~; take hold of roughly: *The policeman ~ed the thief.* 2 (dated colloq) take without permission: *Who's ~ed my pen?*

col·late /kə'leɪt/ vt [VP6A] make a careful comparison between (copies of texts, manuscripts, books, etc) to learn the differences between them: ~ *a new edition with an earlier edition.*

col·lat·eral /kə'lætərəl/ adj 1 secondary or subordinate but from the same source: ~ *evidence; ~ security,* property, eg stocks or bonds, pledged as security for repayment of a loan. 2 descended from a common ancestor but in a different line, ie through different sons or daughters. □ n [U] ~ security.

col·la·tion /kə'leɪʃn/ n [C] (formal) light meal, (usu

cold ~), often one served at a time different from usual meal times.

col·league /'kɒliːg/ *n* one of two or more persons working together and (usu) having similar rank and duties: *the Prime Minister and his* ~*s*, the other members of the Cabinet.

col·lect¹ /kə'lekt/ *vt,vi* 1 [VP6A,15B] ~ *(up/ together)*, bring or gather together; get from a number of persons or places: *The teacher told the boys to* ~ *(up/together) all the waste paper lying about after the picnic and burn it. If he could* ~ *all the money people owe him, he would be a rich man. A man who* ~*s taxes is called a tax-*~*or*. 2 [VP6A] obtain specimens of (books, stamps, etc), eg as a hobby or in order to study sth: ~ *foreign stamps/old china*. 3 [VP2A,C] ~ *(together),* come together: *A crowd soon* ~*s (together) when there's a street accident.* 4 [VP6A] fetch: ~ *a child from school.* 5 [VP6A] gather together, recover control of (one's thoughts, energies, oneself): *Before you begin to make a speech, you should* ~ *your thoughts and ideas.* □ *adj, adv* (US comm) paid for on delivery: *a* ~ *telegram. I'll pay for the goods* ~, when they are delivered. ~**ed** *adj* (esp of a person) calm; not distracted. ~**ed·ly** *adv*

col·lect² /'kɒlekt/ *n* short prayer of the Church of Rome or the Church of England, to be read on certain appointed days.

col·lec·tion /kə'lekʃn/ *n* 1 [U] collecting; [C] instance of this: *How many* ~*s of letters are there every day,* How often does the postman empty the boxes? 2 [C] group of objects that have been collected and that belong together: *a fine* ~ *of old swords/paintings/postage stamps.* 3 heap of materials or objects that have come together: *a* ~ *of dust/rubbish.* 4 [C] money collected at a meeting, a Church service, etc. **take (up)/make a** ~: *The* ~ *will be taken* (up)*/made after the sermon.*

col·lec·tive /kə'lektɪv/ *adj* 1 of a group or society (of persons, nations, etc) as a whole: ~ *leadership,* (emphasis on) government by a group rather than an individual; ~ *ownership of the land/of means of production, etc,* by all citizens for the benefit of all; ~ *security,* security of a State or States against aggression by means of common military, etc preparedness. ~ **farm,** (eg in a Socialist State) one owned by the State and run by the workers for the benefit of all the citizens. 2 ~ **noun,** (gram) one that is singular in form but stands for many individuals, as *cattle, crowd, audience: In 'to catch fish', fish* is a ~ noun. **col·lec·tiv·ize** /kə'lektɪvaɪz/ *vt* [VP6A] change, eg farm lands, from private ownership to a system of State control. **col·lec·tiv·iz·ation** /kəˌlektɪvaɪ'zeɪʃn US: -vɪ'z-/ *n*

col·lec·tor /kə'lektə(r)/ *n* person who collects: *a 'stamp-*~; *a 'tax-*~; *a 'ticket-*~, eg at a railway station. ~*'s* **item/piece,** article sought by ~s, eg a book, a piece of china or furniture, because of its beauty, rarity, etc.

col·leen /'kɒliːn/ *n* (Irish) young girl.

col·lege /'kɒlɪdʒ/ *n* 1 [C,U] school for higher or professional education; body of teachers and students forming part of a university; their building(s): *go to* ~; *be at* ~; *a C*~ *of Agriculture/ Pharmacy, etc; the Oxford and Cambridge* ~*s; Heads of C*~*s,* ⇨ for their titles **Master¹(9), President, Principal, Provost, Rector, Warden.** 2 [C] union of persons with common purposes and privileges: *the C*~ *of Surgeons; the C*~ *of Cardinals,* who elect and advise the Pope. **col·le·giate**

/kə'liːdʒɪət/ *adj* of or like a ~ or ~ student: *collegiate life,* life in ~s and universities.

col·lide /kə'laɪd/ *vi* [VP2A,C,3A] ~ *(with),* 1 come together violently; meet and strike: *As the bus came round the corner, it* ~*d with a van. The bus and the van* ~*d. The ships* ~*d in the fog.* 2 be opposed; be in conflict: *If the aims of two countries* ~, *there may be war.*

col·lie /'kɒli/ *n* Scottish sheepdog with shaggy hair. ⇨ the illus at **dog.**

col·lier /'kɒlɪə(r)/ *n* 1 coal-miner. 2 ship that carries coal as cargo.

col·liery /'kɒlɪərɪ/ *n* (*pl* -ries) coal-mine (and the buildings, etc connected with it).

col·li·sion /kə'lɪʒn/ *n* [U] colliding; [C] instance of this: *a head-on* ~ *between two buses; a railway* ~; *on* (*a*) *'*~ *course,* likely to collide. **be in/come into** ~ *(with),* have collided/collide (with): *The liner is reported to have been in* ~ *with an oil-tanker. The two ships were in/came into* ~. *People with revolutionary ideas may find themselves in* ~ *with the forces of the law,* get into trouble with the police.

col·lo·cate /'kɒləkeɪt/ *vi* [VP2A,3A] ~ *(with),* (of words) combine in a way characteristic of language: *'Weak'* ~*s with 'tea' but 'feeble' does not.* **col·lo·ca·tion** /ˌkɒlə'keɪʃn/ *n* [C,U] coming together; collocating of words: *'Strong tea' and 'heavy drinker' are English* ~*s; so are 'by accident' and 'so as to'.*

col·lo·quial /kə'ləʊkwɪəl/ *adj* (of words, phrases, style) belonging to, suitable for, ordinary conversation; not formal or literary. ~**·ly** *adv* ~**·ism** *n* [C] ~ word or phrase.

col·lo·quy /'kɒləkwɪ/ *n* (*pl* -quies) [C,U] (formal) conversation: *engage in* ~ *with sb.*

col·lu·sion /kə'luːʒn/ *n* [U] secret agreement or understanding for a deceitful or fraudulent purpose: *act in* ~ *with sb;* ~ *between persons who appear to be opposed to each other.* **col·lus·ive** /kə'luːsɪv/ *adj*

colly·wobbles /'kɒlɪwɒblz/ *n* (colloq) stomach-ache; slight feeling of fear (with nausea).

co·lon¹ /'kəʊlən/ *n* lower and greater part of the large intestine. ⇨ the illus at **alimentary.**

co·lon² /'kəʊlən/ *n* punctuation mark (:) used in writing and printing (to direct special attention to what follows). ⇨ **App 9.**

co·lo·nel /'kɜːnl/ *n* army officer above a lieutenant-~ and (in US) commanding a regiment; (abbr for) lieutenant-~.

co·lo·nial /kə'ləʊnɪəl/ *adj* 1 of a colony or colonies(1). '**C**~ **Office,** (GB) former State department in charge of colonies. 2 (esp US) in the style of architecture in the British colonies in N America before and during the Revolution. □ *n* inhabitant of a colony(1), esp a descendant of those who colonized it. ~**·ism** *n* [U] policy of having colonies(1) and keeping them dependent. ~**·ist** *n* supporter of ~ism; one who favours the retention of colonies(1).

col·on·ist /'kɒlənɪst/ *n* pioneer settler in a colony(1).

col·on·ize /'kɒlənaɪz/ *vt* [VP6A] establish a colony in; establish as a colony: *The ancient Greeks* ~*d many parts of the Mediterranean.* **col·on·iz·ation** /ˌkɒlənaɪ'zeɪʃn US: -nɪ'z-/ *n* [U] colonizing: *the colonization of N America by the British, Dutch and French.* **col·on·izer** *n* one who helps to establish a colony(1).

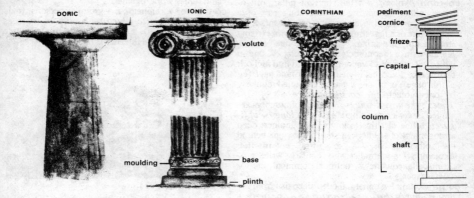

DORIC   IONIC   CORINTHIAN   pediment · cornice · frieze · capital · column · shaft · volute · moulding · base · plinth

col·on·nade /ˌkɒləˈneɪd/ n row of columns(1) set (usu) at equal distances. ⇨ the illus at column.
col·on·naded /ˌkɒləˈneɪdɪd/ adj having a ∿.
col·ony /ˈkɒlənɪ/ n (pl -nies) 1 country or territory settled by migrants from another country, and controlled by it. 2 group of people from another country, or of people with the same trade, profession or occupation, living together: the American ∿ in Paris; a ∿ of artists, eg one living in a place famous for its scenic beauty. 3 (biol) number of animals or plants, living or growing together: a ∿ of ants.
color (US) = colour.
col·ora·tura /ˌkɒlərəˈtʊərə/ n [U] flowery or ornamental passages in vocal music; (attrib): a ∿ soprano.
co·los·sal /kəˈlɒsl/ adj immense.
co·los·sus /kəˈlɒsəs/ n (pl -lossi /-ˈlɒsaɪ/, ∿es /-ˈlɒsəsɪz/) immense statue (esp of a man, much greater than life-size); immense person or personification of sth.
col·our[1] (US = color) /ˈkʌlə(r)/ n 1 [U] sensation produced in the eye by rays of decomposed light; [C] effect produced by a ray of light of a particular wavelength, or by a mixture of these: ∿ films; ∿ TV; Red, blue and yellow are ∿s. There isn't enough ∿ in the picture. '∿-blind adj unable to distinguish between certain ∿s, or to see certain ∿s. '∿ scheme n scheme for combination of ∿s in a design (eg for the furnishing and decoration of a room, the planting of a flower garden). '∿-wash n coloured distemper. 2 [U] redness of the face: She has very little ∿, has a pale face. change ∿, grow paler or redder than usual. have a high ∿, have a red complexion. lose ∿, become pale. be/ feel/look off ∿, (colloq) be/seem unwell, in low spirits. 3 (pl) materials used by artists; paint: 'water-∿s; 'oil-∿s; ⇨ oil, water; appearance produced by their use: paint sth in bright/dark ∿s, (fig) make it appear favourable/unfavourable. (see sth/appear) in its true ∿s, as it really is. 4 [U] (of events, descriptions) appearance of reality or truth; pretext. give/lend ∿ to, give an appearance of probability to: His torn clothing gave ∿ to his story that he had been attacked and robbed. give false ∿ to, give a wrong character or tone to: Newspapers often give false ∿ to the news they report, twist the meaning to suit their aims. 5 local ∿, (in literature) use of details to make a description of a place, scene or time realistic. 6 [U] (in music) timbre, quality; variety of expression. 7 (pl) ribbon, dress, cap, etc, worn as a symbol of a party, a club, a school, etc, or to show ownership of a race-horse, etc: The owner of a horse is always glad to see his ∿s get to the winning-post first, to see his horse win a race. get/win one's ∿s, (at college, etc) be awarded a place in a sports team. 8 (pl) flag (of a ship); ensign or standard of a regiment: salute the ∿s; serve with/join the ∿s, the Navy, Army or Air Force. come through/off with flying ∿s, make a great success of sth. lower one's ∿s, give up one's demands or position; surrender. nail one's ∿s to the mast, make a decision, announce it, and show strong determination not to change it. sail under false ∿s, be a hypocrite or impostor. show one's true ∿s, show what one really is. stick to one's ∿s, refuse to change one's opinion or party. 9 [U] racial characteristic of skin ∿. '∿-bar, legal and/or social distinction between different races. ∿-ful /-fl/ adj full of ∿; bright; gay; exciting; vivid, etc: a ∿ful scene; a ∿ful style of writing; lead a ∿ful life. ∿-less adj without ∿; pale; (fig) lacking in interest, character, vividness: a ∿less style; leading a ∿less existence.
col·our[2] (US = color) /ˈkʌlə(r)/ vt,vi 1 [VP6A,22] give colour to; put colour on: ∿ a wall green. 2 [VP2A,C] ∿ (up), take on colour; blush: The leaves have begun to ∿, to take on their autumn colours of yellow, brown, etc. The girl is so shy that she ∿s (up) whenever a man speaks to her. 3 [VP6A] change or misrepresent in some way: News is often ∿ed, changed to suit the views of those who supply it or those who will read it. Travellers' tales are often highly ∿ed, exaggerated. ∿ed adj 1 (in compounds) having the colour specified: 'cream-∿ed; 'flesh-∿ed. 2 (of persons) partly of European descent; (esp) of the Negro race. (Cape) C∿ed n South African person of mixed race. ∿-ing n [U] sth that produces colour; face colour; style in which sth is ∿ed; style in which an artist uses colour.
colt[1] /kəʊlt/ n young horse (male) up to the age of 4 or 5, ⇨ filly; (fig) young man with little experience. ∿-ish /ˈkəʊltɪʃ/ adj like a ∿; frisky.
colt[2] /kəʊlt/ n (P) (US) early type of revolver or pistol.
col·ter /ˈkəʊltə(r)/ (US) = coulter.
col·um·bine /ˈkɒləmbaɪn/ n garden plant with spur-shaped flowers and petals.

col·umn /'kɒləm/ n 1 tall, upright pillar, usu of stone, either supporting or decorating part of a building, or standing alone as a monument. 2 sth shaped like or suggesting a ∼: a ∼ of smoke (rising straight up); the spinal ∼, the backbone; a ∼ of mercury (in a thermometer); a refining ∼, one in which oil, heated to vapour, is refined into fuel oil, petrol, etc. 3 vertical division of a printed page (eg of this page); or of a newspaper, occupied regularly by one subject: the correspondence ∼s of 'The Times'; the advertising ∼s. 4 series of numbers arranged under one another: add up a long ∼ of figures. 5 line of ships following one another; deep arrangement of soldiers in short ranks, one behind the other. **fifth ∼,** ⇨ fifth. **col·um·nist** /'kɒləmnɪst/ n journalist who regularly writes a ∼ of miscellaneous news, political comment, etc for a newspaper.

coma /'kəʊmə/ n unnatural deep sleep usu from injury or illness. **be in a ∼; go into a ∼,** be in, pass into such a sleep. **∼·tose** /'kəʊmətəʊs/ adj in a ∼; unconscious.

comb /kəʊm/ n 1 piece of metal, rubber, plastic, etc with teeth for cleaning the hair, making it tidy, keeping it in place, etc or as an ornament. 2 part of a machine with a ∼-like look or purpose, esp for tidying and straightening wool, cotton, etc for manufacture. 3 wax structure made by bees for honey. ⇨ honey∼. 4 red fleshy crest of fowl. ⇨ cocks∼. 5 crest of a large wave. □ vt,vi [VP6A,15B] 1 use a ∼ on (the hair). 2 prepare (wool, flax, etc) with ∼s for manufacture. 3 search thoroughly: The police ∼ed the whole city in their efforts to find the murderer. 4 ∼ out, (fig) take out (unwanted things, persons) from a group: ∼ out a government department, get rid of officials who are not really needed, who are inefficient, etc. Hence, '∼-out n act of getting rid of (unnecessary officials, etc). 5 [VP2C,3A] ∼ over, (of a wave) break, curl: waves ∼ing over the ship.

com·bat /'kɒmbæt/ n fight; struggle. **single ∼,** fight between two persons only: (attrib) a ∼ mission. □ vt,vi [VP6A,3A] ∼ (against/with), fight; struggle: ∼ the enemy; ∼ error; a ship ∼ing with the wind and waves. **∼·ant** /'kɒmbətənt/ adj fighting. □ n one who fights: In modern wars both ∼ants and non-∼ants are killed in air attacks. **∼·ive** /'kɒmbətɪv/ adj fond of fighting; ready to fight. **∼·ive·ly** adv

com·bi·na·tion /ˌkɒmbɪ'neɪʃn/ n 1 [U] joining or putting together; state of being joined: in ∼ with; enter into ∼ with; every possible ∼ and permutation, every possible arrangement. 2 [C] number of persons or things that are joined: The college is supported by a ∼ of income from endowments and fees from students. ∼ **room,** (at Cambridge) common-room. ⇨ common¹(1). 3 [C] motor-bike with sidecar attached. 4 (pl) one-piece undergarment covering body and legs. 5 [C] formula, complicated arrangement, for the lock (= '∼-lock) of a safe, strong-room, etc: How did the thieves learn the ∼ used to open the safe?

com·bine¹ /kəm'baɪn/ vt,vi [VP6A,14,2A,3A,4A] ∼ (with), (cause to) join together; possess at the same time: We can't always ∼ work with pleasure. Hydrogen and oxygen ∼/Hydrogen ∼s with oxygen to form water. Some films ∼ education with recreation. Everything ∼d against him, Circumstances, etc made his task difficult or impossible. ∼d operations/exercises, in which air, sea and land forces work together.

com·bine² /'kɒmbaɪn/ n 1 group of persons, trading companies, etc joined for a purpose (such as controlling prices). 2 (also ∼ **'harvester**) machine that both reaps and threshes (grain).

a combine harvester

com·bust·ible /kəm'bʌstəbl/ adj catching fire and burning easily; (fig, of people) excitable. □ n (usu pl) ∼ material.

com·bus·tion /kəm'bʌstʃən/ n [U] process of burning; destruction by fire. ⇨ spontaneous.

come /kʌm/ vi (pt came /keɪm/, pp come) (For uses with adverbial particles and preps, ⇨ 16 below). 1 [VP2A,B,C,3A] ∼ (to/from) (with), (a) move to be with sb, or to be at a place specified: C∼ here! Are you coming to my party? May I come to your party? Who are you coming with? I'll be coming with Keith. I've only ∼ for an hour. (b) arrive: Help has ∼. They came to a river. He's just ∼ from Leeds. (c) [VP4A with infinitive of purpose, 3A] ∼ (for), move, travel, arrive: He has ∼ here to work. They've ∼ all the way from London to look for jobs. He's ∼ to get/∼ for his book. They've ∼ for (= to get) me! C∼ to see what I've done (colloq C∼ and see what I've done, ⇨ and(5)). (d) [VP2E] (with a pres p to indicate two activities or states that occur together): The children came running (= ran) to meet us. He came hurrying (= hurried) to her bedside as soon as he heard she was ill. She came smiling/crying up to me. 2 [VP2C,E] ∼ (into/onto/in/on, etc), move into, etc the place where the speaker is: C∼ into the hallway out of the rain. The train came puffing into the station. Can you ∼ out with me for a walk? He came back to have a word with me. The sunshine came streaming through the windows. 3 [VP3A] (a) ∼ to sth, reach; rise to; fall to (a particular level, figure, point): Your bill ∼s to £20. My earnings ∼ to more than £5000 a year. ∼ to much/little/nothing, amount to much, etc: All his plans came to nothing, had no result, no success. He will never ∼ to much, will never be successful, etc. ∼ to this/that, etc, reach the state of affairs indicated, or a particular state of affairs: What you say ∼s to this, means this. When it ∼s to helping his wife with the housework, John never grumbles. If it ∼s to that..., If that is the state of affairs.... (b) (in fixed phrases) reach the state or condition indicated by the nouns for which there is often an equivalent verb. ⇨ the noun entries. ∼ to an agreement, agree. ∼ to blows (with), start fighting. ∼ to a decision, decide. ∼ to an end, end, finish. ∼ to fruition, ripen, mature. ∼ to a halt/standstill, stop. ∼ to light, become known; be revealed or discovered. ∼ to one's notice/attention, be noticed. ∼ to one's senses/

oneself, (a) become conscious after fainting. (b) become sensible or normal after behaving foolishly. ~ **to terms (with sb),** reach an agreement. **4** (used with *into* in numerous phrases) reach the state or condition indicated by the *nouns.* ⇨ the *nouns* in the phrases. ~ ***into blossom/bud/flower/leaf,*** begin to have blossom, buds, etc. ~ ***into contact (with sb/sth),*** meet sb, touch sth. ~ ***into focus,*** be sharply defined; become prominent. ~ ***into money/a fortune/a legacy etc,*** receive, inherit it. ~ ***into operation,*** start to operate. ~ ***into one's own,*** receive the credit, fame, etc that one deserves, what rightly belongs to one, etc. ~ ***into power,*** (of a political party, etc) form the Government. Cf *go into Opposition.* **come into sight/ view,** appear. ⇨ also collision, effect(1), *existence* at exist, fashion(2), force¹(5), line¹(11), open(*n*), play¹(8), possession(1), *prominence* at prominent, question¹(2), use¹(1). **5** ~ **to sb (from sb),** be left, willed, to sb (by Will and Testament, on death): *He has a lot of money coming to him,* will receive it, eg when sb dies. *The farm came to him on his father's death.* **6** ~ **to sb,** occur to, strike (sb); befall (sb): *The idea came* (= occurred) *to him in his bath. No harm will* ~ *to you if you're careful. He had it coming to him,* (sl, used only of unpleasant events) what happened was fated, and probably deserved. **7** [VP4A] reach a point where one sees, understands, etc: *He came to realize that he was mistaken. He had* ~ *to see the problem in a new light. I have* ~ *to believe that…,* I now believe that…. *When we* ~ *to know them better….* **8** [VP4A] (usu with *how*) asking for an explanation or reason: *How did you* ~ (archaic *How came you*) *to find out where she's living? How did you* ~ *to be so foolish?* (*Now that I*) ~ (= happen) *to think of it….* **How** ~ **(that),** (sl) How does/did sth happen: *How* ~ (*that*) *you just sat there doing nothing?* **9** [VP2C] occur; be found; have as its place: *May* ~s *between April and June. On what page does it* ~? *His resignation came as a surprise/It came as a surprise when he resigned.* **10** [VP2C,D] be; become; prove to be: *Your dream will one day* ~ *true,* be realized. *It* ~s *easily with practice. The handle has* ~ *loose. It* ~s *cheaper if you buy things in bulk. Everything will* ~ (*all*) *right in the end. That sort of thing* ~s *naturally to her,* she does it without having to learn or make an effort. *be as clever/stupid etc as they* ~, be very clever/stupid etc. **11** [VP2D] (with *part adjj* prefixed with *un-*, denoting undesirable conditions, etc) become: *My shoe laces have* ~ *undone. The seam came unstitched. The flap of the envelope has* ~ *unstuck.* ⇨ unstuck for a colloq use. **12** [VP2E] (with a *n* or *adj,* usu with the *def art,* used adverbially as the nominal part of the predicate) (colloq) play the part of; behave, talk, etc as if one were (often with the suggestion of overdoing sth): *Don't* ~ *the bully/the high and mighty over me,* don't (try to) bully me. *He tried to* ~ *the artful/virtuous over me,* impress me by being artful/virtuous. *That's coming it a bit strong,* is making an extravagant claim or assertion. ⇨ also the *noun* entries for *the old soldier, the heavy swell.* **13** (as a *to*-inf, used as a *pred adj*) future: *in years to* ~; *books to* ~, forthcoming books; *the life to* ~, life in the next world; *for some time to* ~, for a period of time in the future. **14** (colloq uses): *two years* ~ *Christmas,* two years including the time from now to Christmas. *She will be 21* ~

May, when May comes, ie next May. *Mary is coming ten,* is in her tenth year, will be ten on her next birthday. **15** [VP2A] (colloq) reach orgasm.
16 [VP2C,3A] (special uses with *adverbial particles* and *preps*):
come about, happen: *It came about in this way. How does it* ~ *about that…?* ⇨ **8** above.
come across sb/sth, (a) find or meet by chance: *I came across this old brooch in a curio shop.* (b) occur to: *The thought came across my mind that…,* occurred to me…. Cf *It crossed my mind that….* ~ **across (with),** (sl) pay (money owing); agree to give information.
come after sb, follow in pursuit of: *The farmer came after the intruders with a big stick.*
come along, (a) (imper) try harder; make more effort: *C~ along, now—someone must know the answer!* (b) progress: *The garden is coming along quite nicely.* (c) appear; arrive: *When the right opportunity* ~s *along, he'll take it.* (d) (imper) hurry up; make haste: *C~ along—we'll be late for the theatre!*
come apart, ~, fall, to pieces: *The teapot just came apart in my hands.*
come at sb/sth, (a) reach; get access to: *The truth is often difficult to* ~ *at* (*get at* is more usu). (b) attack: *The man came at me with a big stick.* Hence, ~**-at-able** /ˌkʌm ˈætəbl/ *adj* (colloq) accessible (*get-at-able* is more usu).
come away (from), become detached: *The light switch came away from the wall.*
come back, return; (of fashions) become popular again: *Will ruffs* ~ *back?* ~ **back at,** retort; retaliate: *He came back at the speaker with some sharp questions.* ~ **back (to one),** return to the memory: *Their names are all coming back to me now,* I'm beginning to remember them. Hence, '~**-back** *n* (a) (eg of actors, politicians, sportsmen etc) successful return to, reinstatement in, a former position: *Can he stage a* ~*-back?* (b) retort; repartee. (c) redress; recompense (for a loss, etc): *If you're uninsured and you're burgled, you'll have no* ~*-back.*
come before sb/sth, (a) be dealt with by: *The complaint will* ~ *before the United Nations Assembly next week.* (b) have precedence over: *Baronets* ~ *before knights.*
come between, (a) interfere with a relationship: *It is not advisable to* ~ *between a man and his wife.* (b) prevent sb from having sth: *He never lets anything* ~ *between him and his evening paper.*
come by sth, (a) obtain by effort; become possessed of: *Was the money honestly* ~ *by? Jobs were hard to* ~ *by.* (b) receive by accident or chance: *How did you* ~ *by that cut on your wrist?*
come down, (a) collapse: *The ceiling came down on our heads.* (b) (of rain, snow, hail) fall: *The rain came down in bucketfuls.* (c) (of prices, temperature, etc) fall. (d) ~ *from a city or large town* to a smaller locality: *She came down from Glasgow last year and settled in the village.* (e) (colloq) pay money: *My rich uncle came down generously,* made a generous gift of money. ~ **down (from),** leave university (esp Oxford or Cambridge): *His son has just* ~ *down from Oxford.* ~ '**down in the world,** lose social position; become poor. Hence, '~**-down** *n* fall in social position; humiliation: *He has had to sell his house and furniture—what a* ~*-down for him!* ~ **down in favour of sb/sth;** ~ **down on the side of sb/sth,** decide to support:

He came down on the side of a more flexible trade policy. ~ **down on sb,** (colloq) rebuke severely: *The headmaster came down on the boy like a ton of bricks.* ~ **down on sb for sth,** demand payment of money owing: *Tradesmen came down on him for prompt settlement of his accounts.* ~ **down to,** (a) reach to: *Her hair ~s down to her waist.* (b) reduce to: *Your choices in the matter ~ down to these.* ~ **down to it,** examine the meaning, the essentials. (c) (of traditions, etc) be handed down: *legends that have ~ down to us,* ie from our ancestors. ~ **down to earth,** return to reality: *Now that his money has all been spent, he's had to ~ down to earth.* ~ **down to doing sth,** be forced, eg by poverty, to do sth humiliating: *He had ~ down to begging.* ~ **down with,** (colloq) contribute: *I had to ~ down with £10 to her favourite charity.*

come forward, (a) offer or present oneself: *Will no one ~ forward as a candidate? No witness of the accident has ~ forward.* (b) (comm) become available: *the number of cattle coming forward for slaughter,* brought to market to be sold.

come from, (a) (not with progressive tenses) have as a birthplace, place of origin, etc: *He ~s from Kent. Much of the butter eaten in England ~s from New Zealand.* (b) = ~ of (b).

come home to, ⇨ home²(2).

come in, (a) (of the tide) rise: *The tide is coming in.* (b) become seasonable: *When do oysters ~ in?* (c) become fashionable: *When did women's trousers ~ in?* (d) (of a batsman in cricket) take his stand at the wicket: *When the next man came in,....* (e) take a place in the result of a race: *Which horse came in first?* (f) be elected; ~ into power: *If the Democrats ~ in,....* (g) be received as income, etc: *There's not much money coming in at present.* (h) have a part to play: *Here is the plan of attack, and this is where you ~ in. Where do I ~ in,* (according to context) What is my share, How do I benefit, etc? ~ **in handy/useful (for sth),** happen to be useful, serve a purpose: *Don't throw it away—it may ~ in handy one day.* ~ **'in for,** (a) receive (as an inheritance, a share, etc): *She has ~ in for a fortune.* (b) attract; be the object of: *Their handling of the case has ~ in for a great deal of criticism.* ~ **in on,** join; take part in: *If you want to ~ in on the scheme, you must decide now.*

come into sth, ⇨ 4 above.

come of, (a) be descended from: *She ~s of an interesting family.* (b) be the result of: *He promised his help, but I don't think anything will ~ of it. No harm can ~ of trying.* ~ **of age,** ⇨ age¹(1).

come off, (a) take place: *The match didn't ~ off. Did the proposed visit to Rome ever ~ off?* (b) (of plans, plans, attempts) succeed: *The experiment didn't ~ off. The film doesn't quite ~ off.* (c) (of persons) fare; prosper; acquit oneself: *They came off well/badly. Who came off best,* who won?

come off (sth), (a) become detached or separated (from): *A button has ~ off my coat. Please use lipstick that doesn't ~ off on the wine glasses. When we came off the gold standard...,* abandoned it.... (b) fall (from): ~ *off a horse/bicycle. Don't ~ off!* (c) get down (from): *C~ off that wall before you fall off (it).* ⇨ also perch²(2). (d) ~ **off it,** (colloq, imper) stop pretending, or talking nonsense: *Oh, ~ off it! What do you know about horseracing?*

come on, (a) follow: *You go first, I'll ~ on later. Hence,* '~**-on** *n* (sl) lure; seductive action. (b) (as a challenge): *C~ on! Let's race to the bottom of*

the hill. (c) make progress; develop: *How's your garden coming on? The baby is coming on well.* (d) (of rain, the seasons, night, illness, etc) start; arrive: *Night/Darkness came on. The rain came on again worse than ever. He said he felt a cold coming on,* was beginning to suffer from a cold. (e) (of questions, lawsuits) arise for discussion: *When does the case ~ on for trial,* When will the court deal with it? (f) (cricket, of a bowler) begin to bowl. (g) (of an actor) appear on the stage; (of a play) be performed: *'Macbeth' is coming on again next month.* ~ **on to** + *inf,* begin to: *It came on to rain.*

come out, (a) appear; become visible: *The sun/stars came out. The buds/flowers are coming out,* are opening. (b) become known: *When the news came out.... If the truth ever ~s out....* (c) be published: *When will his new book ~ out?* (d) (of workmen) strike: *The car workers have all ~ out again.* (e) (of details, etc in a photograph; of qualities) appear: *You have ~ out well in that photograph,* It is a good likeness. *His arrogance ~s out in every speech he makes.* (f) (of stains, etc) be removed: *These ink stains won't ~ out.* (g) (of dyes, etc) fade; disappear: *Will the colour ~ out if the material is washed?* (h) (of problems) be solved: *I can't make this sum/equation ~ out,* can't solve it. (i) make a debut; (colloq) begin to live publicly as sth. (j) (of meaning, sense) become clear: *The meaning of the passage ~s out clearly in his interpretation.* ~ **out at,** (of totals, averages, etc) amount to: *The total ~s out at 756,* is 756. ~ **out first/last, etc,** (in examinations) have a certain position: *Tom came out first.* ~ **out in,** be partially covered in (pimples, a rash, etc): *She's ~ out in spots!* ~ **out with,** utter; say: *He came out with a most extraordinary story/a string of oaths.*

come over, (a) ~ from a distance: *Won't you ~ over to England for a holiday?* (b) change sides or opinions: *He will never ~ over to our side.* ~ **over sb,** (of feelings, influences) take possession of: *What has ~ over you,* Why have you changed in this way? *A fit of dizziness came over her,* She suddenly felt dizzy. ~ **over queer/funny/dizzy,** (colloq) suffer a feeling of faintness/sickness/dizziness.

come round, (a) ~ by a circuitous route: *The road was blocked so we had to ~ round by the fields.* (b) pay an informal visit to: *Won't you ~ round and see me some time?* (c) recur: *Christmas will soon ~ round,* be here again. (d) change views, etc: *He will never ~ round to our way of thinking,* change his views and adopt ours. *He has ~ round,* has accepted/agreed. (e) regain consciousness: *Pour a jug of water on his face—he'll soon ~ round.* (f) recover from ill temper, etc: *Don't scold the boy; he'll ~ round in time.*

come through, (a) recover from a serious illness, from risk of injury: *With such a weak heart, he was lucky to ~ through. How did you manage to ~ through without even a scratch,* to escape even a slight injury? (b) arrive (by telephone, radio, etc): *Listen—a message is just coming through.* (c) pass through official channels: *Your posting has just ~ through: it's Hong Kong!* ~ **through sth,** survive: *He has ~ through two world wars,* has lived safely through them.

come 'to, (a) recover consciousness; ⇨ come round (e). (b) ~ **to sth,** ⇨ 3 above.

come under sth, (a) be classed among; be in (a

certain category, etc): *What heading does this ~ under?* (b) be subjected to: *~ under sb's notice/ influence.*

come up, (a) (of seeds, herbaceous plants, etc) show above the ground: *The seeds/snowdrops haven't ~ up yet.* (b) arise; be put forward: *The question hasn't ~ up yet*, has not been raised or discussed. *Her divorce case ~s up next month*, will be dealt with then. (c) (colloq) be drawn (in a lottery): *My sweepstake ticket came up; I won £100.* (d) occur; arise: *We shall write to you if a vacancy ~s up.* (e) rise in social position: *He came up the hard way*, succeeded through his own, un-aided efforts. *~ up against*, meet (difficulties, opposition). *~ up to, (a)* reach: *The water came up to my waist.* (b) equal: *Your work has not ~ up to my expectations/to the required standards. ~ up with, (a)* draw level with: *We came up with a party of hikers.* (b) produce; find (a solution, an answer).

come upon sb/sth, (a) attack by surprise; strike: *the disaster that came upon them. Fear came upon us.* (b) = come across (a).

com·edian /kə'miːdɪən/ *n* actor who plays comic parts in plays, broadcasts and TV; person who be-haves in a comic way and who cannot be taken seriously. **com·edienne** /kə,miːdɪ'en/ *n* female ~.

com·edy /'kɒmədɪ/ *n* **1** [U] branch of drama that deals with everyday life and humorous events: *He prefers ~ to tragedy;* [C] (*pl* -dies) play for the theatre, of a light, amusing kind. **,musical '~**, such a play, with music, songs and dancing. **2** [C,U] amusing activity or incident in real life: *There's not much ~ in modern war.*

come·ly /'kʌmlɪ/ *adj* (-ier, -iest) (old use, usu of a person) pleasant to look at. **come·li·ness** *n*

comer /'kʌmə(r)/ *n* (chiefly in compounds) one who comes: *the first ~; the late–~s; all ~s.*

com·est·ible /kə'mestəbl/ *n* (formal, usu *pl*) thing to eat.

comet /'kɒmɪt/ *n* heavenly body (looking like a star with a bright centre and a less bright tail) that moves round the sun in an eccentric orbit.

a comet

come-up·pance /kʌm'ʌpəns/ *n* deserved punish-ment or misfortune: *The tyrant President got his ~ when his country was invaded and conquered.*

com·fit /'kʌmfɪt/ *n* (old use) sweetmeat; fruit (eg a plum) preserved in sugar.

com·fort /'kʌmfət/ *n* **1** [U] state of being free from suffering, anxiety, pain, etc; contentment; physical well-being: *become fond of ~ as one grows old; living in great ~.* **2** [U] help or kindness to sb who is suffering: *a few words of ~; news that brought ~ to all of us.* **cold ~**, not much consolation. **3** [C] person or thing that brings relief or help: *Your let-ters have been a great ~ to me. It's a ~ to know that she is safe. The hotel has every modern ~/all modern ~s.* **'~ station**, (US) public lavatory. □ *vt* [VP6A] give ~ to: *~ those who are in trouble. The child ran to its mother to be ~ed.* **~·less** *adj* without ~: *a ~less room.*

com·fort·able /'kʌmftəbl *US:* -fərt-/ *adj* **1** giving comfort to the body: *a ~ chair/bed.* **2** having or providing comfort: *a ~ life/income.* **3** at ease; free from (excessive) pain, anxiety, etc: *to be/feel ~. Make yourself ~!* **com·fort·ably** /-təblɪ/ *adv* in a ~ manner: *a car that holds six people comfortably.* **be comfortably off**, have enough money to live in comfort.

com·forter /'kʌmfətə(r)/ *n* **1** person who comforts. **the C~**, (= *strengthener*) the Holy Spirit. **2** (GB) warm woollen scarf, worn round the neck. **3** (GB) teat of a baby's dummy (US = *pacifier*). **4** (US) quilt.

com·frey /'kʌmfrɪ/ *n* [U] tall wild plant with rough leaves and purple or white flowers.

comfy /'kʌmfɪ/ *adj* (-ier, -iest) (colloq) comfort-able.

comic /'kɒmɪk/ *adj* **1** causing people to laugh: *a ~ song;* intended to amuse: *~ strips,* strips of hu-morous drawings, as printed in newspapers, etc. **2** of comedy: *~ opera.* □ *n* **1** music-hall comedian. **2** (US = '~ **book**) book or magazine containing stories etc in the form of drawings.

comi·cal /'kɒmɪkl/ *adj* amusing; odd: *a ~ old hat.* **~ly** /-klɪ/ *adv*

coming /'kʌmɪŋ/ *n* arrival: *He believes in the Sec-ond C~,* the return of Jesus Christ when the world ends. □ *adj* which will come: *in the ~ years; the ~ generation.* **a ~ man,** a man who is likely to be important, famous, etc.

com·ity /'kɒmɪtɪ/ *n* [U] (formal) harmonious frien-dliness; courtesy. **~ of nations,** friendly recogni-tion, shown by one nation, of the laws, customs, etc of other nations.

comma /'kɒmə/ *n* punctuation mark (,) to indicate a slight pause or break between parts of a sentence. **in,verted '~s,** the marks (" ") or (' '). ⇨ App 9.

com·mand¹ /kə'mɑːnd *US:* -'mænd/ *vt, vi* **1** [VP6A,17,9,2A] order (usu with the right to be obeyed): *Do as I ~ (you). The officer ~ed his men to fire. The pirate chief ~ed that the prisoners should be shot. God ~s and man obeys.* **2** [VP6A,2A] have authority over; be in control of: *The captain of a ship ~s all the officers and men. Who ~s the army? Who ~s here?* **3** [VP6A] res-train; hold back; control (the more usu word): *~ oneself/one's temper/one's passions.* **4** [VP6A] be in a position to use; have at one's service: *He ~s great sums of money,* is able to use them if he so wishes. *A Minister of State ~s the services of many officials.* **5** [VP6A] deserve and get: *Great men ~ our respect. He ~s the sympathy of all who have heard the story of his sufferings.* **6** [VP6A] (of a place) be in a position that overlooks (and may control): *The fort ~ed the entrance to the valley. The hill ~s a fine view,* a fine view can be obtained from the top. **~·ing** *adj* that ~s: *the ~ing officer; in a ~ing tone; in a ~ing position.*

com·mand² /kə'mɑːnd *US:* -'mænd/ *n* **1** [C] order: *His ~s were quickly obeyed. Give your ~s in a loud, confident voice.* **at the word of ~,** (mil) when the ~ is given. **2** [U] authority; power (to control): *General X is in ~ of the army. The army is under the ~ of General X. He has twenty men under his ~.* **have/take ~ of,** have/take author-ity: *When the major was killed, the senior captain took ~ of the company.* **do sth at/by sb's ~,** on his authority: *It was done by the Queen's ~.* **be at sb's ~,** ready to obey: *I am at your ~,* ready to obey you. **'~ module,** part of a spacecraft carrying the crew and control equipment. ～ **performance,** (at a theatre) one given at the request of a head of State. **3** [C] part of an army, air force, etc under separate ～: *Western C～; Bomber C～.* **4** [U] possession and mastery: *He has* (*a*) *good ～ of the English language,* is able to use it well. *He has no ～ over himself,* cannot control his feelings, temper, etc. *He offered me all the money at his ～,* all the money he controlled.

com·man·dant /ˌkɒmən'dænt/ *n* commanding officer.

com·man·deer /ˌkɒmən'dɪə(r)/ *vt* [VP6A] seize (horses, stores, buildings, etc) for military purposes under martial law.

com·mander /kə'mɑːndə(r) *US:* -'mæn-/ *n* person in command: *the ～ of the expedition; C～, Lieu₂tenant-'C～,* naval officers (above lieutenant and below captain); *Wing-C～,* rank in the RAF; ,～-in-'chief, ～ of all the military forces of a State. **com·mand·ment** /kə'mɑːndmənt *US:* -'mænd-/ *n* divine command. **the Ten C～s,** the ten laws given by God to Moses. ⇨ Exod 20: 1-17.

com·mando /kə'mɑːndəʊ *US:* -'mæn-/ *n* (*pl* ～s or ～es) (member of a) body of men specially picked and trained for carrying out raids and making assaults.

com·mem·or·ate /kə'meməreɪt/ *vt* [VP6A] keep or honour the memory of (a person or event); (of things) be in memory of: *Christmas ～s the birth of Christ. A monument was built to ～ the victory.* **com·mem·or·ative** /kə'memərətɪv *US:* -'meməreɪt-/ *adj* serving to ～: *commemorative stamps/medals.*

com·mem·or·ation /kəˌmemə'reɪʃn/ *n* [U] act of commemorating: *in ～ of;* [C] (part of a) service in memory of a person or event.

com·mence /kə'mens/ *vt, vi* [VP6A,C,2A,3A] (formal) begin; start (the more usu words). ～**ment** *n* **1** beginning. **2** (in US universities, and at Cambridge and Dublin) ceremony at which degrees are conferred.

com·mend /kə'mend/ *vt* **1** [VP6A,14] ～ *sb (on/ upon sth);* ～ *sb/sth (to sb),* praise; speak favourably of: ～ *someone upon his good manners;* ～ *a man to his employers. His work was highly ～ed.* **2** [VP14] ～ *sth to,* entrust for safekeeping to: ～ *one's soul to God.* **3** [VP14] ～ *oneself/itself to,* be to the liking of; be acceptable to: *This book does not ～ itself to me. Will the proposal ～ itself to the public?* ～**·able** *adj* worthy of praise. **com·men·da·tion** /ˌkɒmen'deɪʃn/ *n* [U] praise; approval.

com·men·sur·able /kə'menʃərəbl/ *adj* ～ *(to/ with),* that can be measured by the same standard (as): *Their achievements are not ～.*

com·men·sur·ate /kə'menʃərət/ *adj* ～ *(to/with),* in the right proportion (to): *Was the pay you received ～ with the work you did?*

com·ment /'kɒment/ *n* [C,U] opinion given briefly in speech or writing about an event, or in explanation or criticism of sth: *Have you any ～(s) to make upon my story? Her strange behaviour caused a good deal of ～,* of talk, gossip, etc. *No ～!* I've nothing to say on this subject. □ *vi* [VP2A,3A] ～ *(on/upon),* make ～s (on); give opinions.

com·men·tary /'kɒməntrɪ *US:* -terɪ/ *n* (*pl*-ries) **1** collection of comments, eg on a book: *a Bible ～.* **2** series of continuous comments (on an event): *a broadcast ～ on a football match. A running ～,* number of remarks following one another continuously while an event is taking place: *He kept up a*

running ～ on the race. **com·men·tate** /'kɒmənteɪt/ *vi* [VP3A] ～ *on,* give a ～ on. **com·men·ta·tor** /'kɒmənteɪtə(r)/ *n* eye-witness who gives a broadcast ～ on an event, eg a horse-race or football match; writer of a ～(1).

com·merce /'kɒmɜːs/ *n* [U] trade (esp between countries); the exchange and distribution of goods: *a Chamber of C～.*

com·mer·cial /kə'mɜːʃl/ *adj* of or for commerce: ～ *education; a ～ attitude.* ～ **traveller,** person who travels with samples of goods to obtain orders. ～ **TV/radio,** financed by charges made for ～ advertising in programmes. ～ **vehicles,** vans, lorries, etc, for the transport of goods. □ *n* [C] advertisement inserted in a TV or radio programme. ～**·ly** /-ʃəlɪ/ *adv* ～**·ize** /kə'mɜːʃəlaɪz/ *vt* [VP6A] (try to) make money out of: *Is it wise to ～ize sport?*

com·mi·na·tion /ˌkɒmɪ'neɪʃn/ *n* [C,U] (formal) threatening of divine vengeance. **com·mina·tory** /'kɒmɪnətrɪ *US:* -tɔːrɪ/ *adj* threatening.

com·mingle /kə'mɪŋgl/ *vt, vi* [VP6A,2A] mingle together.

com·miser·ate /kə'mɪzəreɪt/ *vi* [VP3A] ～ *with,* feel, say that one feels, pity for: ～ *with a friend on his misfortunes.* **com·miser·ation** /kəˌmɪzə'reɪʃn/ *n* [C,U] (expression of) pity or sympathy (*for* sb).

com·mis·sar /'kɒmɪsɑː(r)/ *n* **1** (formerly) head of a major Government Department of the USSR. **2** (formerly) political officer in the army of the USSR.

com·mis·sar·iat /ˌkɒmɪ'seərɪət/ *n* **1** (formerly) major Government Department of the USSR. **2** (formerly) department that supplied food and other stores to troops. **3** food supply.

com·mis·sary /'kɒmɪsərɪ *US:* -serɪ/ *n* (*pl*-ries) **1** (formal) deputy, delegate. **2** (formerly) officer responsible for supplying food to troops. ,～ **'general,** head of a commissariat(2).

com·mis·sion /kə'mɪʃn/ *n* **1** [U] the giving of authority to sb to act for another; [C] instance of this; [C] action or piece of business that is done: *He has secured two ～s to design buildings for a local authority.* **2** [U] performance or committing (*of* crime). **3** [C,U] payment to sb for selling goods, etc, rising in proportion to the results gained: *He receives a ～ of 10 per cent on sales, as well as a salary. on ～,* drawing a percentage of the receipts: *to sell goods on ～.* **4** [C] official paper (called a *warrant*) giving authority; (esp) (in GB) warrant signed by the Sovereign appointing an officer in the armed services: *get/resign one's ～.* **5** [C] body of persons given the duty of making an inquiry and writing a report: *a Royal C～ to report on betting and gambling.* **6** group of people legally authorized to discharge a task. ,**C～ of the 'Peace,** Justices of the Peace collectively. **7** *in ～,* (eg of a ship) with crew and supplies complete; ready for sea. *out of ～,* kept in reserve; not in working order; (fig) not working, not available. □ *vt* [VP6A,17] give a ～(1) to: ～ *an artist to paint a portrait; be ～ed to buy books for a friend.* **com·mis·sioned** *adj* (of officers) holding rank by ～(4). ⇨ non-～ed.

com·mis·sion·aire /kəˌmɪʃə'neə(r)/ *n* uniformed porter at the entrance to a cinema, theatre, hotel, large shop, etc.

com·mis·sioner /kə'mɪʃənə(r)/ *n* **1** member of a commission(5,6), esp one with particular duties: *the C～s of Inland Revenue,* who control Income Tax; *the Civil Service C～s,* who conduct the Civil Service examinations. **2** person who has been given a commission(1): *a C~ for Oaths*, solicitor (given commission by the Lord Chancellor) before whom documents are sworn on oath. **3** representative of high rank: *the High C~ for Canada*, eg representing the Canadian Government in London; *the British High C~ in Accra*.

com·mit /kə'mɪt/ *vt* (-tt-) **1** [VP6A] perform (a crime, foolish act, etc): ~ *murder/suicide/an offence*. **2** [VP14] ~ *sb/sth to*, entrust, give up, hand over to, for safe keeping or treatment: ~ *a man to prison;* ~ *a patient to a mental hospital;* ~ *sth to paper/to writing*, write it down. *The body was ~ted to the flames*, was cremated. ~ *to memory*, learn by heart. ~ *a prisoner for trial,* ~ him to prison for trial later. **3** [VP6A,14,16A] ~ *oneself (to...)*, make oneself responsible; undertake: *He has ~ted himself to support his brother's children. He refused to ~ himself by talking about the crime*, refused to say anything because it might get him into trouble. **4** [VP6A,14] (often reflex) pledge; bind (oneself): *I won't ~ myself to that course of action.* ⇨ uncommitted. ~**·ment** *n* [U] being ~ted(2,3,4); [C] sth to which one has ~ted(3) oneself; promise; pledge; undertaking: *If you have agreed to give a number of lectures, help to pay your brother's school expenses and give your sister £100 a year for clothes, you have quite a lot of ~ments.*

com·mit·tee /kə'mɪtɪ/ *n* group of persons appointed (usu by a larger group) to attend to special business: *to attend a '~ meeting; to be/sit on the ~; a Parliamentary C~*, one appointed by the House of Commons (or Lords) to examine a Bill. *in ~*, functioning as (a member of) a ~.

com·mode /kə'məʊd/ *n* **1** chest of drawers. **2** piece of bedroom furniture to hold a chamber-pot.

com·modi·ous /kə'məʊdɪəs/ *adj* having plenty of space for what is needed: *a ~ house/cupboard.*

com·mod·ity /kə'mɒdətɪ/ *n* (*pl* -ties) [C] useful thing, esp an article of trade: *household commodities*, eg pots and pans.

com·mo·dore /'kɒmədɔː(r)/ *n* naval officer having rank above a captain and below a rear-admiral; president of a yacht club; senior captain of a shipping line: *the ~ of the Cunard Line; Air C~*, officer in the Air Force.

com·mon[1] /'kɒmən/ *adj* **1** belonging to, used by, coming from, done by, affecting, all or nearly all members of a group or society: *The husband is French, the wife German, and the lodger Italian, but they have English as a ~ language*, they can all use English. *It is to the ~ advantage* (= to everyone's advantage) *that street traffic should be well controlled*. ~ *ground*, (fig) basis for argument accepted by persons in a dispute, etc. ~ *knowledge*, what is known to most persons, esp in a group: *It was ~ knowledge among bankers that....* Cf *general knowledge*. '~ *land*, land that belongs to, or may be used by, the community, esp in a village. ⇨ common[2](1). ~ *factor/multiple*, (maths) belonging to two or more quantities. ~ *law*, (in England) unwritten law developed from old customs, eg in Saxon and Danish times, and decisions made by judges. ⇨ *statute law* at statute, and *case-law* at case[1](2). ~**·law wife**, woman with whom a man lives, as if she were his wife, but without marrying her. **the C~ Market** *n* (officially *the European Economic Community*), economic, social and political association, established in 1958, of Belgium, France, Italy, Luxem-bourg, the Netherlands and West Germany, since enlarged in 1973 by the inclusion of Britain, Ireland and Denmark, with associate membership (for economic preferences) by other countries. ~ *noun*, (gram) name that can be used for any member of a class, eg *book* or *knife*. **a ~ nuisance**, an offence that is harmful to the community and for which there is legal remedy. ⇨ also **cause** and **prayer**. '~**-room**, room for use of the teachers or students at a school, college, etc. **2** usual and ordinary; happening or found often and in many places: *a ~ flower; a ~ experience. Pine-trees are ~ in many parts of the world. Is this word in ~ use?* **the ~ man/people**, the ordinary or average citizen(s): *The ~ man in every country wants peace.* ~ *metre*, hymn stanza of 4 lines, with 8, 6, 8, 6 syllables. ~ *sense*, practical good sense gained by experience of life, not by special study. ~ *time/measure*, two or four beats in a bar. **3** (colloq) (of persons, their behaviour and possessions) vulgar; of inferior quality or taste: ~ *manners; speak with a ~ accent; a girl who looks ~/who wears ~ clothes.* ~**·ly** *adv* **1** usually: *That very ~ly happens. Thomas, ~ly called Tom.* **2** in a ~(3) way: ~*ly dressed.*

com·mon[2] /'kɒmən/ *n* **1** [C] area (usu in or near a village) of unfenced grassland for all to use: *Saturday afternoon cricket on the village ~.* **2** *in ~*, for or by all (of a group). **have in ~ (with)**, share (with): *They have nothing in ~ with one another*, have no similar interests, etc. *in ~ with*, together with: *In ~ with* (= like) *many people he prefers meat to fish. out of the ~*, unusual.

com·mon·alty /'kɒmənəltɪ/ *n* **the ~**, the common people (contrasted with the upper classes).

com·moner /'kɒmənə(r)/ *n* one of the common people, not a member of the nobility.

com·mon·place /'kɒmənpleɪs/ *adj* ordinary or usual: *a ~ kind of man.* □ *n* remark, event, etc that is ordinary or usual: *conversation full of mere ~s. Travel by air is now a ~.*

com·mons /'kɒmənz/ *n pl* **1 the ~**, (old use) the common people. ⇨ **aristocracy**, **nobility**. **the House of 'C~**, assembly of those elected by the common people; lower house of the British parliament. **2** provisions shared in common. **be on short ~**, not have enough to eat.

com·mon·wealth /'kɒmənwelθ/ *n* **1** State; group of States (eg the C~ *of Australia*) associating politically for their common good. **2 the C~**, a free association of sovereign independent states (formerly colonies and dominions of GB) with their dependencies.

com·mo·tion /kə'məʊʃn/ *n* [U] noisy confusion; excitement; [C] instance of this; violent uprising or disturbance: *You're making a great ~ about nothing.*

com·mu·nal /'kɒmjʊnl/ *adj* **1** of or for a community: ~ *disturbances*, eg in countries where there are antagonisms between people of different races and religions. **2** for common use; shared: ~ *land/kitchens.*

com·mune[1] /kə'mjuːn/ *vi* [VP2C,3A] ~ *(together)*; ~ *(with)*, feel at one with; feel, be, in close touch with; talk with in an intimate way: ~ *with nature/one's friends/God in prayer; friends communing together.*

com·mune[2] /'kɒmjuːn/ *n* **1** (in France, Belgium, Italy, Spain) smallest territorial district for purposes of administration, with a mayor and council.

2 organized group of people promoting local interests. **3** group of people living together and sharing property and responsibilities.

com·muni·cable /kə'mju:nɪkəbl/ *adj* (of ideas, illness, etc) that can be communicated or imparted.

com·muni·cant /kə'mju:nɪkənt/ *n* **1** one who (regularly) receives Holy Communion. **2** informer (the more usu word).

com·muni·cate /kə'mju:nɪkeɪt/ *vt,vi* **1** [VP6A,14] ~ *sth (to)*, pass on (news, information, feelings, heat, motion, an illness, etc). **2** [VP3A] ~ *with*, share or exchange (news, etc): *We can ~ with people in most parts of the world by telephone. Young people sometimes complain of not being able to ~ with their parents.* **3** [VP2A,3A] ~ *(with)*, (of rooms, gardens, roads, etc) be connected: *My garden ~s with the garden next door by means of a gate. We asked the hotel to let us have communicating rooms,* rooms with a connecting door.

com·muni·ca·tion /kə,mju:nɪ'keɪʃn/ *n* **1** [U] the act of communicating: *Among the deaf and dumb ~ may be carried on by means of the finger alphabet. Spitting in public places may lead to the ~ of disease. I'm in/I must get into ~ with him on this subject.* **2** [C] that which is communicated (eg news): *This ~ is confidential.* **3** [C,U] means of communicating; roads, railways, telephone or telegraph lines connecting places, radio and TV: *a world ~s network; ~ satellites; mass ~s media. Telegraphic ~/~s between Amman and Baghdad has/have been restored. All ~ with the north has been stopped by snowstorms.* '~ cord, cord that passes along the length of a train inside the coaches, to be pulled (to stop the train) in an emergency.

com·muni·cat·ive /kə'mju:nɪkətɪv *US:* -keɪtɪv/ *adj* ready and willing to talk and give information. ⇨ *reserved* at reserve².

com·mu·nion /kə'mju:nɪən/ *n* **1** [U] sharing in common; participation (*with*). **2** [U] exchange of thought and feelings; intercourse. **hold '~ with oneself**, think deeply (esp about moral or religious problems). **self-~**, thinking about oneself. **3** [C] group of persons with the same religious beliefs: *We belong to the same ~.* **4** (Holy) **C~**, (in the Christian Church) celebration of the Lord's Supper. **go to C~**, (a) attend church for this celebration. (b) receive the Eucharist.

com·mu·niqué /kə'mju:nɪkeɪ/ *n* official announcement, eg as issued to the press.

com·mu·nism /'kɒmjʊnɪzəm/ *n* [U] **1** ideology that proclaims the abolition of class oppression and exploitation, and the foundation of a society based on the common possession of the means of production and the equal distribution of goods. **2** (usu **C~**) (colloq) political system in which the power is held by the Communist or Workers' Party, and the land and its resources, the means of production etc are under State control. **com·mu·nist** /'kɒmjʊnɪst/ *n* believer in, supporter of, ~. □ *adj* of ~.

com·mu·nity /kə'mju:nətɪ/ *n* (*pl* -ties) **1** the ~, the people living in one place, district or country, considered as a whole: *work for the good of the ~.* '~ **centre**, building(s), etc where people meet for adult education classes, amateur dramatics, informal social intercourse, etc. ~ **chest**, (US) welfare fund for helping people in distress. **2** [C] group of persons having the same religion, race, occupation, etc or with common interests: *a ~ of monks; the Jewish ~ in London; the European ~ in Karachi.*

3 [U] condition of sharing, having things in common, being alike in some way: ~ *of race/religion/interests; a ~ spirit,* shared feeling of membership. **in ~, together.** '~ **singing**, organized singing in which all present take part.

com·mut·able /kə'mju:təbl/ *adj* that can be exchanged or converted (*into/for*).

com·mu·ta·tion /,kɒmju'teɪʃn/ *n* **1** [U] commuting; making one kind of payment instead of another, eg money instead of service. **2** [C] payment made in this way. **3** [C] reduced punishment: *a ~ of the death sentence to life imprisonment.* **4** ~ **ticket**, (US) season ticket.

com·mu·ta·tor /'kɒmju:teɪtə(r)/ *n* device for altering the direction of an electric current.

com·mute /kə'mju:t/ *vt,vi* **1** [VP6A,14] ~ *(into/for)*, exchange one thing (esp one kind of payment) for another: ~ *one's pension;* ~ *an annuity into/for a lump sum.* **2** [VP6A,14] ~ *(to)*, reduce the severity of a punishment: ~ *a death sentence (to one of life imprisonment).* **3** [VP2A] travel regularly, eg by train or car, between one's work in a town and one's home in the country or suburbs. **com·muter** *n* person who ~s(3).

com·pact¹ /'kɒmpækt/ *n* agreement between parties; contract; covenant.

com·pact² /kəm'pækt/ *adj* closely packed together; neatly fitted; (of literary style) condensed. □ *vt* (usu passive) join firmly together. ~**·ly** *adv* ~**·ness** *n*

com·pact³ /'kɒmpækt/ *n* small, flat container for face-powder (and often with a mirror), made for carrying in a woman's handbag.

com·pan·ion¹ /kəm'pænɪən/ *n* **1** person who goes with, or is often or always with, another: *my ~s on the journey.* **2** person who shares in the work, pleasures, misfortunes, etc of another: ~*s in arms,* fellow soldiers; ~*s in misfortune,* associated in it; *a faithful ~ of 50 years,* eg said by a man speaking of his wife. **3** person with similar tastes, interests, etc: *He's an excellent ~. His brother is not much of a ~ for him.* **4** one of two or more things that go together; thing that matches another or is one of a pair: *Here's the glove for my left hand, but where's the ~?* (also attrib): *the ~ volume(s).* **5** person paid to keep another (usu old or ill) person company. **6** handbook or reference book: *the Gardener's C~.* **7** **C~**, member of some Orders: *C~ of the Bath.* ⇨ order¹(10). ~**·able** *adj* friendly; sociable. ~**·ship** /-ʃɪp/ *n* [U] state of being ~s: *enjoy sb's ~ship; a ~ship of many years.*

com·pan·ion² /kəm'pænɪən/ *n* (usu '~-**way**) staircase from the deck of a ship to the saloon or cabins.

com·pany /'kʌmpənɪ/ *n* **1** [U] being together with another or others: *I shall be glad of your ~ (= to have you with me) on the journey.* **be good/poor/bad/excellent, etc ~,** be a good, etc, companion(3). **for ~,** to provide companionship: *I'll go with you as far as the station for ~.* **in ~ (with),** together (with): *He came in ~ with a group of boys. We went in ~.* **keep sb ~; keep ~ with sb,** be or go with him: *He stayed at home to keep his wife ~.* **part ~ (with sb),** ⇨ part²(1). **2** [U] group of persons; number of guests: *We're expecting ~ (= guests, visitors) next week. He's not well enough to receive a great deal of ~,* many visitors. **sin in good ~,** better men have done the same. **3** [U] persons with whom one spends one's time: *You may know a man by the ~ he keeps,* judge his character by his friends. *Don't get into/keep bad*

~, Don't become friendly with/mix with bad persons. **4** (often **C~**, abbr **Co**) [C] (*pl* -nies) number of persons united for business or commerce: *a steamship* ~. **a** ,Limited ,Lia'bility **C~**, **C~** whose partners are not named in the title: ,*T* ,*S* '*Smith & Co.* **5** number of persons working together: *a* ~ *of players,* actors who perform plays together; *a theatrical* ~; *the ship's* ~, the crew. **6** subdivision of an infantry battalion, commanded by a captain or major.

com·par·able /'kɒmpərəbl/ *adj* ~ *(to/with),* that can be compared: *The sets of figures are not* ~. *His achievements are* ~ *with the best.*

com·para·tive /kəm'pærətɪv/ *adj* **1** having to do with comparison or comparing: *the* ~ *method of studying,* ie by finding out what is similar and different in two or more branches of knowledge; ~ *religion;* ~ *linguistics.* **2** measured or judged by comparing: *living in* ~ *comfort,* eg comfortably compared with others, or with one's own life at an earlier period. **3** (gram) form of adjectives and adverbs expressing 'more', as in *worse, harder, more difficult, more prettily.* □ *n* ~ degree: '*Better*' is *the* ~ *of* '*good*'. ~·**ly** *adv*

com·pare /kəm'peə(r)/ *vt,vi* **1** [VP6A,14] ~ *(with),* examine, judge to what extent persons or things are similar or not similar: ~ *two translations;* ~ *your translation with the model translation on the blackboard.* ~ *notes,* exchange observations, ideas or opinions. **2** [VP14] ~ *to,* point out the likeness or relation between: *Poets have* ~*d sleep to death. Mine cannot be* ~*d to yours,* is quite different. **3** [VP3A] ~ *with,* be ~ed with; bear comparison with: *He cannot* ~ *with Shakespeare as a writer of tragedies,* is not nearly so great. *This cannot* ~ *with that,* no comparison is possible because they are so different. **4** (gram) form the comparative and superlative degrees (of adjectives and adverbs). □ *n* (poet) comparison (but only in) *beyond/past/without* ~: *She is lovely beyond* ~, so lovely that none can be ~d to her.

com·pari·son /kəm'pærɪsn/ *n* **1** [U] *by/in* ~ *(with),* when compared (with): *This one costs more but is cheaper by/in* ~, is plainly better value when you compare them and examine the quality, etc. *The tallest buildings in London are small in* ~ *with those of New York. the* ~ *of X and/with Y,* the act of comparing X with Y. **2** [C] *(make) a* ~ *between X and Y/of X to Y,* (perform) an act of comparing; an instance of this: *It is often useful to make a* ~ *between two things. The* ~ *of the heart to a pump/between the heart and a pump has often been made. There's no* ~ *between them,* They cannot be compared, one being clearly much better than the other. ~*s are odious,* in this case it is unfair to make any ~. **3** *bear/stand* ~ *with,* be able to be compared favourably with: *That's a good dictionary, but it won't/can't stand* ~ *with this.* **4** *degrees of* ~, (gram) positive, comparative and superlative (of adjectives and adverbs), eg *good, better, best.*

com·part·ment /kəm'pɑːtmənt/ *n* one of several separate divisions of a structure, esp of a railway carriage or coach: *The first-class* ~*s are in front. The ship's hold is built in watertight* ~*s.* **com·part·men·tal·ize** /ˌkɒmpɑːt'mentəlaɪz/ *vt* divide into ~s or categories.

com·pass[1] /'kʌmpəs/ *n* **1** (mag'netic) ~, device with a needle that points to the magnetic north: *the points of the* ~ (N, NE, E, SE, S, SW, W, NW,

etc); similar device, eg *a radio* ~, for determining direction. **2** (old use **pair of** ~**es**) ~(**es**) V-shaped instrument with two arms joined by a hinge, used for drawing circles, measuring distances on a map or chart, etc. ⇨ the illus at dividers. **3** extent; range: *beyond the* ~ *of the human mind; outside the* ~ (= range) *of her voice.*

the points of the compass

com·pass[2] /'kʌmpəs/ *vt* encompass (the more usu word).

com·pas·sion /kəm'pæʃn/ *n* [U] pity; feeling for the sufferings of others, prompting one to give help: *have/take* ~ *on sufferers; be filled with* ~ *for the refugees; look at someone in/with* ~; *give a man money out of* ~. ~·**ate** /kəm'pæʃənət/ *adj* showing or feeling ~: *The soldier was granted* ~*ate leave,* given leave[2](2), eg because personal affairs made necessary his presence at home.

com·pat·ible /kəm'pætəbl/ *adj* ~ *(with),* (of ideas, arguments, principles, etc) suited (to), in accord (with), able to exist together (with): *pleasure* ~ *with duty; driving a car at a speed* ~ *with safety.* **com·pat·ibly** /-əblɪ/ *adv* **com·pati·bil·ity** /kəmˌpætə'bɪlətɪ/ *n* [U] the state of being ~.

com·patriot /kəm'pætrɪət US: -'peɪt-/ *n* person born in, or citizen of, the same country as another; fellow-countryman.

com·peer /'kɒmpɪə(r)/ *n* person equal in rank or capacity.

com·pel /kəm'pel/ *vt* (-ll-) **1** [VP17] ~ *sb/sth to do sth,* force (sb or sth to do sth); get, bring about, by force: *His conscience* ~*led him to confess. He was* ~*led by illness to resign.* **2** [VP14,6A] ~ *(from),* obtain by pressure: *Can they* ~ *obedience from us,* force us to obey?

com·pen·di·ous /kəm'pendɪəs/ *adj* (of authors, books, etc) giving much information briefly.

com·pen·dium /kəm'pendɪəm/ *n* concise and comprehensive account; summary.

com·pen·sate /'kɒmpenseɪt/ *vt,vi* [VP6A,14,3A] ~ *(sb) (for sth),* make a suitable payment, give something to make up (*for* loss, injury, etc): *Do employers in your country* ~ *workers for injuries suffered at their work? Nothing can* ~ *for the loss of one's health.* **com·pen·sa·tory** /kəm'pensətərɪ US: -tɔːrɪ/ *adj* compensating.

com·pen·sa·tion /ˌkɒmpen'seɪʃn/ *n* [U] compensating; [C] sth given to compensate: *He received £5000 in* ~/*by way of* ~/*as a* ~ *for the loss of his right hand.*

com·père /'kɒmpeə(r)/ *n* (F) organizer of a cabaret

or broadcast entertainment who introduces the performers, speakers, etc. □ *vt* act as ~ for.

com·pete /kəm'piːt/ *vi* [VP2A,3A] take part in a race, contest, examination, etc: *to* ~ *in a race (against/with others, for a prize, for the first place,* etc); *to* ~ *against/with other countries in trade.*

com·pet·ence /'kɒmpɪtəns/ *n* **1** [U] being competent; ability: *his* ~ *in handling money/to handle money.* **2** (usu **a** ~) income large enough for a person to live on in comfort: *have/enjoy a small* ~. **3** [U] (of a court, a magistrate) legal capacity: *business that is within/beyond the* ~ *of the court.*

com·pet·ent /'kɒmpɪtənt/ *adj* **1** (of persons) having ability, power, authority, skill, knowledge, etc (to do what is needed): *Is Miss X* ~ *in her work/*~ *as a teacher/*~ *to teach French?* **2** (of qualities) sufficient, adequate: *Has she a* ~ *knowledge of French?* ~·ly *adv*

com·pe·ti·tion /ˌkɒmpə'tɪʃn/ *n* **1** [U] competing; activity in which persons compete: *trade* ~ *between countries; keen* ~ *for a job. At the Olympic Games our representatives were in* ~ (= were competing) *with the best swimmers from all parts of the world.* **2** [C] instance of competing; contest; meeting(s) at which skill, strength, knowledge, etc is tested: *boxing/chess* ~*s.*

com·peti·tive /kəm'petətɪv/ *adj* in or for which there is competition: ~ *examinations for government posts. Our firm offers you* ~ *prices,* prices that compare favourably with those of other firms.

com·peti·tor /kəm'petɪtə(r)/ *n* person who competes.

com·pile /kəm'paɪl/ *vt* [VP6A] collect (information) and arrange (in a book, list, report, etc): ~ *a dictionary/a guide-book/an index.* **com·piler** *n* person who ~s. **com·pi·la·tion** /ˌkɒmpɪ'leɪʃn/ *n* [U] compiling; [C] thing that is ~d.

com·pla·cence /kəm'pleɪsns/ *n* [U] self-satisfaction; quiet contentment. **com·pla·cency** /-'pleɪsnsɪ/ *n*

com·pla·cent /kəm'pleɪsnt/ *adj* self-satisfied: *with a* ~ *smile/air.* ~·ly *adv*

com·plain /kəm'pleɪn/ *vi* [VP2A,3A,B] ~ *(to sb) (about/of sth),* say that one is not satisfied, that sth is wrong, that one is suffering: *She* ~*ed to me of his rudeness/that he had been rude to her. We have nothing to* ~ *of/about. He never* ~*s about the pain/about being in pain.* ~·ing·ly *adv*

com·plain·ant /kəm'pleɪnənt/ *n* (legal) plaintiff.

com·plaint /kəm'pleɪnt/ *n* **1** [U] complaining; [C] statement of, grounds for, dissatisfaction: *You have no cause/grounds of/for* ~. *Have you any* ~*s to make? Some children are full of* ~*s about their food. Why don't you lodge a* ~ *against your noisy neighbours?* **2** [C] illness; disease: *a heart/liver* ~*; childish* ~*s,* illnesses common among children.

com·plais·ance /kəm'pleɪzəns/ *n* [U] easy-going habit of mind; readiness and willingness to do what pleases others: *do sth out of* ~. **com·plais·ant** /-zənt/ *adj* obliging; disposed to please: *a complaisant husband.*

com·ple·ment /'kɒmplɪmənt/ *n* **1** that which makes sth complete; the full number or quantity needed: *the ship's* ~, the full number of officers and men. **2** (gram) word(s) esp *adjj* and *nn,* used after *vv* such as *be* and *become* and qualifying the subject: *In the sentence 'I'm tired' tired is the* ~. ~·ary /ˌkɒmplɪ'mentrɪ/ *adj* forming a ~. □ *vt* [VP6A] complete; form the ~ to.

com·plete¹ /kəm'pliːt/ *adj* **1** having all its parts; whole: *a* ~ *edition of Shakespeare's plays.* **2** finished; ended: *When will the work be* ~? **3** thorough; in every way: *He's a* ~ *stranger to me. It was a* ~ *surprise to me,* I wasn't expecting it and hadn't even thought of it. ~·ly *adv* wholly; in every way: ~*ly successful.* ~·ness *n*

com·plete² /kəm'pliːt/ *vt* [VP6A] finish; bring to an end; make perfect: *The railway is not* ~*d yet. I need one volume to* ~ *my set of Dickens.*

com·ple·tion /kəm'pliːʃn/ *n* [U] act of completing; state of being complete: *You may occupy the house on* ~ *of contract,* when the contract of sale has been completed.

com·plex¹ /'kɒmpleks *US:* kɒm'pleks/ *adj* made up of closely connected parts; difficult to understand or explain: *a* ~ *argument/proposal/situation; a* ~ *system of government; a* ~ *sentence,* (gram) one containing subordinate clauses. ~·ity /kɒm'pleksətɪ/ *n* [U] state of being ~; [C] (*pl* -ties) sth that is ~.

com·plex² /'kɒmpleks/ *n* [C] **1** complex whole; number of dissimilar parts intricately related: *a building* ~. **2** (psych) (abnormal) mental state which is the result of past experiences or suppressed tendencies; (colloq) obsessive concern or fear: *He has a* ~ *about his weight.* ⇨ *inferiority* at **inferior,** *superiority* at **superior.**

com·plexion /kəm'plekʃn/ *n* [C] **1** natural colour, appearance, etc of the skin, esp of the face: *a good/dark/fair* ~. **2** general character or aspect (of conduct, affairs, etc): *This victory changed the* ~ *of the war,* made the probable outcome different, gave hope of an early end, etc.

com·pli·ance /kəm'plaɪəns/ *n* [U] **1** action of complying: *in* ~ *with your wishes,* as you wish(ed) us (to do). **2** tendency to give way to others; unworthy submission.

com·pliant /kəm'plaɪənt/ *adj* ready or disposed to comply.

com·pli·cate /'kɒmplɪkeɪt/ *vt* [VP6A] make complex; make (sth) difficult to do or understand: *This* ~*s matters.* **com·pli·cated** *adj* made up of many parts; difficult to do or understand: *a* ~*d machine;* ~*d business deals.*

com·pli·ca·tion /ˌkɒmplɪ'keɪʃn/ *n* [C] **1** state of being complex, confused, difficult; sth that adds new difficulties: *Here are further* ~*s to worry us.* **2** (med) new illness, or new development of an illness, that makes treatment more difficult: *influenza with* ~*s; if no* ~*s set in.*

com·plic·ity /kəm'plɪsətɪ/ *n* [U] ~ *(in),* taking part with another person (in crime).

com·pli·ment /'kɒmplɪmənt/ *n* [C] **1** expression of admiration, approval, etc, either in words or by action, eg by asking sb for his advice or opinions, or by imitating him. *pay sb a* ~*/pay a* ~ *to sb (on sth): They paid me a well-deserved* ~. **2** (*pl*) (formal) greetings: *My* ~*s to your wife,* Please give her a greeting from me. *With the* ~*s of the season,* phrase used at Christmas and the New Year. *With the author's/publisher's* ~*s,* phrase used when an author/publisher sends a gift of a book newly issued. □ *vt* /'kɒmplɪment/ [VP6A,14] ~ *sb (on sth),* pay a ~ to: *I* ~*ed him on his skill.*

com·pli·men·tary /ˌkɒmplɪ'mentrɪ/ *adj* **1** expressing admiration, praise, etc. **2** given free, out of courtesy or kindness: *a* ~ *ticket/copy of a book,* etc.

com·plin, com·pline /'kɒmplɪn/ *n* (in RC and

Anglo-Catholic ritual) last (church) service of the day.

com·ply /kəm'plaɪ/ vt [VP2A,3A] ~ **(with)**, act in accordance (with a request, command, sb's wishes, etc): *You must* ~ *with* (= obey) *the rules. He refused to* ~.

com·po·nent /kəm'pəʊnənt/ adj helping to form (a complete thing): ~ *parts.* □ *n* ~ part: *the* ~*s of a camera lens.*

com·port /kəm'pɔːt/ vt, vi (formal) **1** [VP15A] (usu reflex) behave; conduct: ~ *oneself with dignity.* **2** [VP3A] ~ **with**, suit, be in harmony with: *His conduct did not* ~ *with his position.* ~**-ment** *n*

com·pose /kəm'pəʊz/ vt, vi **1** [VP6A] (of elements) make up, form: *the parts that* ~ *the whole;* (usu in the passive): *be* ~*d of,* be made up of: *Water* (H_2O) *is* ~*d of hydrogen and oxygen. Our party was* ~*d of teachers, pupils and their parents.* **2** [VP6A,2A] put together (words, ideas, musical notes, etc) in literary, musical, etc, form: ~ *a poem/a song/an opera/a speech. He teaches music and also* ~*s,* writes music. **3** [VP6A] (printing) set up (type) to form words, paragraphs, pages, etc. ⇨ compositor. **4** [VP6A,16A] get under control; calm: ~ *one's thoughts/passions. She* ~*d herself to answer the letter. Try to* ~ *your features,* make yourself look calm. **com·posed** adj calm; with feelings under control. **com·posed·ly** /kəm'pəʊzɪdlɪ/ adv in a ~d manner.

com·poser /kəm'pəʊzə(r)/ *n* (esp) person who composes music.

com·pos·ite /'kɒmpəzɪt/ adj made up of different parts or materials: *a* ~ *illustration,* made by putting together two or more drawings, etc.

com·po·si·tion /ˌkɒmpə'zɪʃn/ *n* **1** [U] act or art of composing, eg a piece of writing or music, type for printing, objects that will be included in a painting: *He played a piano sonata of his own* ~, that he himself had composed. **2** [C] that which is composed, eg a poem, a book, a piece of music, an arrangement of objects to be painted or photographed; (esp) exercise in writing by one who is learning a language. **3** [U] the parts of which sth is made up: *Scientists study the* ~ *of the soil. He has a touch of madness in his* ~, There is an element of madness in him. **4** [C] substance composed of more than one material, esp an artificial substance: ~ *floors.*

com·po·si·tor /kəm'pɒzɪtə(r)/ *n* skilled person who composes type for printing.

compos mentis /ˌkɒmpəs 'mentɪs/ adj (Lat) (colloq) sane: *He's not quite* ~, is a little mad.

com·post /'kɒmpɒst/ *n* [U] prepared mixture, esp of rotted organic matter, manure, etc, for use in horticulture. □ vt [VP6A] make into ~; treat with ~

com·po·sure /kəm'pəʊʒə(r)/ *n* [U] condition of being composed in mind; calmness (of mind or behaviour): *behave with great* ~.

com·pote /'kɒmpɒt/ *n* [C,U] (dish of) fruit cooked with sugar and water.

com·pound¹ /'kɒmpaʊnd/ *n, adj* **1** (sth) made up of two or more combined parts: *Common salt is a* ~ *of sodium and chlorine.* **2** (gram) item composed of two or more parts, (written as one or two words, or joined by a hyphen), themselves usu words, eg '*bus conductor.* ~ '**sentence**, one containing two or more co-ordinate clauses (linked by *and, but,* etc). **3** ~ '**interest**, interest on capital and on accumulated interest. ~ '**fracture**, breaking of a bone complicated by an open wound in the

skin.

com·pound² /kəm'paʊnd/ vt, vi **1** [VP6A] mix together (to make sth new or different): ~ *a medicine; a cake* ~*ed of the best ingredients.* **2** [VP6A,2A,3A] ~ **(with sb) (for sth)**, settle (a quarrel, a debt) by mutual concession; come to terms: *He* ~*ed with his creditors for a remission of what he owed.* **3** [VP6A] add to, increase (an offence or injury) by causing another: *That simply* ~*s the offence.*

com·pound³ /'kɒmpaʊnd/ *n* enclosed area with buildings, etc, eg a number of houses, a commercial or trading centre.

com·pre·hend /ˌkɒmprɪ'hend/ vt [VP6A] **1** understand fully. **2** include.

com·pre·hen·sible /ˌkɒmprɪ'hensəbl/ adj that can be understood fully: *a book that is* ~ *only to specialists.* **com·pre·hen·si·bil·ity** /ˌkɒmprɪˌhensə-'bɪlətɪ/ *n*

com·pre·hen·sion /ˌkɒmprɪ'henʃn/ *n* [U,C] **1** the mind's act or power of understanding: *The problem is above/beyond my* ~. **2** exercise aimed at improving or testing one's understanding of a language (written or spoken). **3** power of including: *a term of wide* ~, eg a word that includes many meanings, uses, etc.

com·pre·hen·sive /ˌkɒmprɪ'hensɪv/ adj that comprehends(2) much: *a* ~ *description/review of the term's work; a man with a* ~ *mind/grasp of ideas.* '~ **(school)**, large school that combines all types of secondary education, ie academic and technical. ~**·ly** adv ~**·ness** *n*

com·press¹ /kəm'pres/ vt [VP6A,14] **1** press together; get into a small(er) space: ~*ed air;* ~ *cotton into bales.* **2** put (ideas, etc) into fewer words; condense.

com·press² /'kɒmpres/ *n* pad or cloth pressed on to a part of the body (to stop bleeding, reduce fever, etc): *a cold/hot* ~.

com·pres·sion /kəm'preʃn/ *n* [U] compressing; being compressed: ~ *of ideas.*

com·prise /kəm'praɪz/ vt [VP6A] be composed of; have as parts or members: *The committee* ~*s men of widely different views. The force* ~*d two battalions and a battery.*

com·pro·mise /'kɒmprəmaɪz/ *n* [U] settlement of a dispute by which each side gives up sth it has asked for and neither side gets all it has asked for; [C] instance of this; settlement reached in this way: *The strike was not ended until they resorted to* ~. *A* ~ *agreement was at last arrived at. Can we effect a* ~? □ vt, vi **1** [VP6A,2A] settle a dispute, etc, by making a ~: *if they agree to* ~. **2** bring (sb, sth, oneself) under suspicion by unwise behaviour, etc: *You will* ~ *yourself/your reputation if you spend all your time gambling.* **3** imperil the safety of (by folly or rashness, etc): *The position of the army was* ~*d by the general's poor judgement.*

comp·trol·ler /kən'trəʊlə(r)/ *n* (in some titles) controller: ~ *of accounts.*

com·pul·sion /kəm'pʌlʃn/ *n* [U] compelling or being compelled. **under** ~, because one must: *A defeated country usually signs a treaty of peace under* ~.

com·pul·sive /kəm'pʌlsɪv/ adj having a tendency or the power to compel; caused by an obsession: *a* ~ *eater/TV viewer,* one who feels compelled to eat/watch TV; *a* ~ *liar,* one who lies repeatedly. ~**·ly** adv

com·pul·sory /kəm'pʌlsərɪ/ adj that must be done;

required: *Is military service* ~ *in your country? Is English a* ~ *subject?* **com·pul·sor·ily** /kəm'pʌlsərəlɪ/ *adv*

com·punc·tion /kəm'pʌŋkʃn/ *n* [U] uneasiness of conscience; feeling of regret for one's action: *She kept me waiting without the slightest* ~.

com·pu·ta·tion /ˌkɒmpjʊ'teɪʃn/ *n* [U] computing; [C] result of computing; calculation: *It will cost £5000 at the lowest* ~. *He has wealth beyond* ~. *Addition and division are forms of* ~.

com·pute /kəm'pju:t/ *vt,vi* [VP6A,14,2A] ~ *(at)*, reckon; calculate: *He* ~*d his losses at £50. What is the* ~*d horse-power of the engine?*

com·puter /kəm'pju:tə(r)/ *n* electronic device which stores information on eg magnetic tape, analyses it and produces information as required from the data on the tapes. ~**·ize** *vt* [VP6A] store (information) with or in a ~ or system of ~s; supply with a ~ or ~s.

com·rade /'kɒmreɪd *US:* -ræd/ *n* **1** trusted companion; loyal friend: ~*s in arms*, fellow soldiers; ~*s in exile*, those who are exiled together. **2** fellow member of a trade union, a (left-wing) political party, etc. ~**·ly** /'kɒmreɪdlɪ/ *adv* ~**·ship** /'kɒmreɪdʃɪp/ *n*

con[1] /kɒn/ *adv* **pro and con**, for and against: *argue pro and con for hours*. □ *n* **the pros and cons**, the arguments for and against.

con[2] /kɒn/ (sl) short for *confidence*, in attrib uses: *a con man; the con game*. ⇨ confidence(1). □ *vt* (-nn-) [VP6A,14] **con** *sb* **(into doing sth)**, (colloq) swindle him after winning his confidence; persuade him to do sth in this way.

con·cat·ena·tion /kɒnˌkætɪ'neɪʃn/ *n* [U] linking together; [C] series of things or events linked together.

con·cave /'kɒŋkeɪv/ *adj* (of an outline or surface) curved inwards like the inner surface of a sphere or ball. ⇨ the illus at convex. **con·cav·ity** /ˌkɒn'kævətɪ/ *n* [U] ~ condition; [C] (*pl* -ties) ~ surface.

con·ceal /kən'si:l/ *vt* [VP6A,14] ~ *(from)*, hide; keep secret: ~ *sth from sb.* He tried to ~ *the fact that*.... *C*~*ed turning*, (as a road sign) warning that a turning into a road is hidden from view, eg by bushes or trees. ~**·ment** *n* [U] of ~ing; state of being ~ed: *stay in* ~*ment until the danger has passed.*

con·cede /kən'si:d/ *vt* [VP6A,9,13A,12A] admit; grant; allow: ~ *a point in an argument. He* ~*d ten points to his opponent/*~*d him ten points*, ie in a game. *They have* ~*d us the right to cross their land. You must* ~ *that I have tried hard. We cannot* ~ *any of our territory*, allow another country to have it.

con·ceit /kən'si:t/ *n* **1** [U] over-high opinion of, too much pride in, oneself or one's powers, abilities, etc: *He's full of* ~. **in one's own** ~, (old use) in one's own judgement. **out of** ~ **with**, (old use) no longer pleased with. **2** [C] humorous or witty thought or expression. ~**ed** *adj* full of ~. ~**ed·ly** /-ɪdlɪ/ *adv*

con·ceive /kən'si:v/ *vt,vi* **1** [VP6A,10,3A,9,14] ~ *(of)*, form (an idea, plan, etc) in the mind: *Who first* ~*d the idea of filling bags with gas to make balloons? I can't* ~ *why you allowed/can't* ~ *of your allowing the child to travel alone. I* ~*d that there must be some difficulties. Why have you* ~*d such a dislike for me?* **2** [VP2A,6A] (of a woman) become pregnant: ~ *a child.* **con·ceiv·able** *adj*

that can be ~d or believed: *It is hardly conceivable (to me) that....* **con·ceiv·ably** /-əblɪ/ *adv*

con·cen·trate /'kɒnsntreɪt/ *vt,vi* **1** [VP6A,14,2A] bring or come together at one point: *to* ~ *soldiers in a town. The troops were ordered to scatter and then* ~ *twenty miles to the south.* **2** [VP14,3A,2A] ~ **(on/upon)**, focus one's attention on: *You should* ~ *(your attention) on your work. You'll solve* ~ *the problem if you* ~ *upon it*, give all your attention to it. *I can't* ~! **3** [VP6A] increase the strength of (a solution) by reducing its volume (eg by boiling it). □ *n* product made by concentrating(3). **con·cen·trated** *adj* **1** intense: ~*d hate;* ~*d fire*, the firing of guns all aimed at one point. **2** increased in strength or value by evaporation of liquid: *a* ~*d solution;* ~*d food.*

con·cen·tra·tion /ˌkɒnsn'treɪʃn/ *n* **1** [C] that which is concentrated: ~*s of enemy troops.* **2** [U] concentrating or being concentrated on: *a book that requires great* ~; *a child with little power of* ~. '~ **camp**, place where civilian political prisoners or internees are brought together and confined.

con·cen·tric /kən'sentrɪk/ *adj* ~ **(with)**, (of circles) having a common centre.

concentric circles   circles not concentric

con·cept /'kɒnsept/ *n* [C] idea underlying a class of things; general notion.

con·cep·tion /kən'sepʃn/ *n* **1** [U] conceiving of an idea or plan; [C] idea or plan that takes shape in the mind: *A good novelist needs great powers of* ~. *I have no* ~ *of what you mean. An actor must have a clear* ~ *of the part he is to play.* **2** [U,C] conceiving(2); becoming pregnant. '~ **control**, more precise, but less common, term for *birth-control*.

con·cern[1] /kən'sɜ:n/ *vt* **1** [VP6A] have relation to; affect; be of importance to: *Does this* ~ *me? Don't trouble about things that don't* ~ *you. He is said to have been* ~*ed in the crime*, to have had some connection with it. *So/As far as I'm* ~*ed...*, so far as the matter is important to me, or affects me.... *Where the children are* ~*ed...*, in matters where it is necessary to think of them.... **as** ~**s**, regarding. **2** [VP14] ~ **oneself with/in/about**, be busy with, interest oneself in. **3** [VP6A] (esp in the passive **be** ~*ed* **about/for sb/sth**) worry; trouble; bother: *Don't let my illness* ~ *you. Please don't be* ~*ed about me. We are all* ~*ed for/about her safety.* ~**·ing** *prep* about.

con·cern[2] /kən'sɜ:n/ *n* **1** [C] relation or connection; sth in which one is interested or which is important to one: *It's no* ~ *of mine*, I have nothing to do with it. *Mind your own* ~*s (business* is more usu), Don't interfere in other people's affairs. *What* ~ *is it of yours*, Why do you take an interest in it? **2** [C] business or undertaking: *The shop has now become a paying* ~, is making profits. **a going** ~, one that is active and in operation, not merely planned. **3** [C] share: *He has a* ~ *in the business*, is a part-owner. **4** [U] anxiety: *filled with* ~; *look at sb in* ~. *There is some cause for* ~ *but no need for alarm.* ~**ed** /-'sɜ:nd/ *adj* anxious: *with a* ~*ed look.* ~**·edly** /-'sɜ:nɪdlɪ/ *adv*

con·cert[1] /'kɒnsət/ *n* **1** [C] musical entertainment,

esp one given in a public hall by players or singers.
~ **grand**, grand piano of the largest size, for ~s.
'~-**hall**, hall for ~s. ⇨ music-hall. *at* ~ '*pitch*,
(fig) in a state of full efficiency or readiness. ⇨
keyed up at key². 2 [U] *in* ~, combination of
voices or sounds: *voices raised in* ~. 3 [U] agreement; harmony. *in* ~ *(with)*, together (with):
working in ~ *with his colleagues.*
con·cert² /kən'sɜːt/ *vt* arrange with others. Chiefly
in ~**ed** *adj* planned, performed, designed (by two
or more together): *to take* ~*ed action; to make a*
~*ed attack.*
con·cer·tina /ˌkɒnsə'tiːnə/ *n* musical wind instrument consisting of a pair of bellows, held in the
hands and played by pressing keys at each end.

a concertina

con·certo /kən'tʃeətəʊ/ *n* (*pl* ~s) musical composition for one or more solo instruments supported
by an orchestra: *a 'piano* ~*; a* ~ *for two violins.*
con·ces·sion /kən'seʃn/ *n* 1 [U] conceding; [C] that
which is conceded, esp after discussion, a difference of opinion, an argument, etc: *As a* ~ *to the
public outcry, the Government reduced the tax on
petrol.* 2 [C] (esp) right given by owner(s) of land,
or by a Government, to do sth (eg take minerals
from land): *oil/mining* ~*s.* **con·ces·sive**
/kən'sesɪv/ *adj* (gram) expressing ~: *a concessive
clause,* eg introduced by *as* or *although,* implying
a contrast between circumstances, etc. ~**·aire**
/kənˌsefə'neə(r)/ *n* holder of a ~(2).
conch /kɒntʃ/ *n* shellfish with a large spiral shell.
⇨ the illus at mollusc. **con·chol·ogy**
/kɒŋ'kɒlədʒɪ/ *n* [U] study of shells and shellfish.
con·ci·erge /ˌkɒnsɪ'eəʒ US: ˌkɒnsɪ'eərʒ/ *n* (F) (in
France, etc) door-keeper, porter (of a block of
flats, etc).
con·cili·ate /kən'sɪlɪeɪt/ *vt* [VP6A] win the support,
goodwill or friendly feelings of; calm the anger of;
soothe. **con·cili·atory** /kən'sɪlɪətərɪ US: -tɔːrɪ/ *adj*
intending to or likely to ~: *a conciliatory act/
gesture/spirit.*
con·cili·ation /kənˌsɪlɪ'eɪʃn/ *n* [U] conciliating or
being conciliated: *The dispute in the engineering
industry is being dealt with by a* ~ *board,* a group
of persons who arbitrate, etc.
con·cise /kən'saɪs/ *adj* (of a person's speech or style
of writing, etc) brief; giving much information
in few words. ~**·ly** *adv* ~**·ness** *n*
con·clave /'kɒŋkleɪv/ *n* [C] private or secret meeting (eg of cardinals to elect a Pope). *sit in* ~, hold
a secret meeting.
con·clude /kən'kluːd/ *vt,vi* 1 [VP6A,14,2A,3A]
come or bring to an end: *to* ~ *a speech/a lecture.
He* ~*d by saying that.... The meeting* ~*d at 8
o'clock. The concert* ~*d with the National Anthem.* 2 [VP6A,14] ~ *sth (with sb),* arrange; bring
about: *Wales* ~*ed a* ~ *with Scotland.* 3 [VP9] ar-

rive at a belief or opinion: *The jury* ~*d, from the
evidence, that the accused man was not guilty.* 4
[VP7A] (esp US) decide, resolve (after discussion):
We ~*d not to go.*
con·clu·sion /kən'kluːʒn/ *n* [C] 1 end: *at the* ~ *of
his speech; bring a matter to a speedy* ~. *in* ~,
lastly. 2 arranging; deciding; settling (*of*): *the* ~ *of
a peace treaty.* 3 belief or opinion which is the result of reasoning: *come to/reach the* ~ *that...; to
draw a* ~ *(from evidence, etc). a foregone* ~,
something settled or decided in advance, not to be
doubted. 4 *try* ~*s with,* have a trial of skill with.
con·clus·ive /kən'kluːsɪv/ *adj* (of facts, evidence,
etc) convincing; ending doubt: ~ *evidence/proof
of his guilt.* ~**·ly** *adv*
con·coct /kən'kɒkt/ *vt* [VP6A] 1 prepare by mixing
together: *to* ~ *a new kind of soup.* 2 invent (a
story, an excuse, a plot for a novel, etc). **con·coc-
tion** /kən'kɒkʃn/ *n* [U] ~ing; [C] sth that is ~ed.
con·comi·tant /kən'kɒmɪtənt/ *adj* (formal) accompanying: ~ *circumstances.* □ *n* [C] (usu *pl*) accompanying thing: *the infirmities that are the* ~*s of old
age.*
con·cord /'kɒŋkɔːd/ *n* 1 [U] agreement or harmony
(between persons or things): *live in* ~ *(with...);*
[C] instance of this. 2 (gram) [U] agreement between words in number, etc, eg between a *verb* and
its subject in the present tense.
con·cord·ance /kən'kɔːdəns/ *n* 1 [U] agreement. 2
[C] arrangement in ABC order of the important
words used by an author or in a book: *a 'Bible* ~*; a
'Shakespeare* ~.
con·cord·ant /kən'kɔːdənt/ *adj* ~ *(with),* agreeing, harmonious.
con·cordat /kən'kɔːdæt/ *n* agreement, eg between
a State and the Church, for settlement of ecclesiastical affairs.
con·course /'kɒŋkɔːs/ *n* 1 coming or moving
together of things, persons, etc: *an unforeseen* ~
of circumstances. 2 place (usu not enclosed) where
crowds come together; (esp US) large hall of a railway station.
con·crete¹ /'kɒŋkriːt/ *adj* 1 of material things; existing in material form; that can be touched, felt,
etc: *A lamp is* ~ *but its brightness is abstract.* ~
music, composed of re-arranged recorded natural
sounds. ~ **noun,** name of a thing, not of a quality.
2 definite; positive: ~ *proposals/evidence/proof.*
□ *n* [U] building material made by mixing cement
with sand, gravel, etc: *roads surfaced with* ~*; a* ~
wall; a '~ *mixer* (usu a revolving drum). □ *vt*
[VP6A] cover with ~: *a road.* ~**·ly** *adv*
con·crete² /'kɒŋkriːt/ *vi* [VP2A] form into a mass;
solidify. **con·cretion** /kən'kriːʃn/ *n* [U] process of
forming into a mass; [C] mass formed in this way.
con·cu·bine /'kɒŋkjʊbaɪn/ *n* 1 (old use) woman
who lives with a man as if she were his wife, without being lawfully married to him. 2 (in some
countries, where polygamy is legal) lesser wife.
con·cu·pis·cence /kən'kjuːpɪsns/ *n* [U] (formal)
sexual desire; lust.
con·cur /kən'kɜː(r)/ *vi* (-rr-) 1 [VP2A,3A] ~ *(with
sb) (in sth),* agree in opinion: *I* ~ *with the speaker
in condemning what has been done.* 2 [VP4A] (of
circumstances, etc) happen together: *Everything*
~*red to produce a successful result.* ~**·rence**
/kən'kʌrəns/ *n* [U,C] agreement; coming
together: *a* ~*rence of ideas;* ~*rence in helping
to find homes for refugees.*
con·cur·rent /kən'kʌrənt/ *adj* concurring; existing

together; co-operating. ~·ly adv

con·cuss /kən'kʌs/ vt [VP6A] injure (the brain) by concussion.

con·cus·sion /kən'kʌʃn/ n [C,U] (an) injury (to the brain); (a) violent shaking or shock (as caused by a blow, knock or fall).

con·demn /kən'dem/ vt 1 [VP6A,14,16B] ~ (for), say that sb is, or has done, wrong or that sth is wrong, faulty or unfit for use: *We all ~ cruelty to children. Everyone ~ed his foolish behaviour. The newspapers ~ed the Prime Minister for.... The meat was ~ed as unfit for human consumption. This old bridge is unsafe; it should be ~ed.* 2 [VP6A,14] ~ **sb (to)**, (legal) give judgement against: ~ *a murderer to life imprisonment.* ~**ed cell**, cell where a person ~ed to death is kept. 3 [VP6A,14,17] ~ **sb (to sth/to do sth)**, doom, send, appoint (to sth unwelcome or painful): *an unhappy housewife, ~ed to spend hours at the kitchen sink. He got well again, although the doctors had ~ed him,* said that he would not recover. 4 [VP6A] declare (smuggled goods, property, etc) to be forfeited: *Merchant ships captured in war were often ~ed,* taken from the owners without compensation. 5 [VP6A] show conviction of guilt: *His looks ~ed him.* **con·dem·na·tion** /ˌkɒndem'neɪʃn/ n [U] ~ing or being ~ed.

con·den·sa·tion /ˌkɒnden'seɪʃn/ n [U] condensing or being condensed: *the ~ of milk,* by taking out most of the water; *the ~ of steam to water;* [C,U] (mass of) drops of liquid formed when vapour condenses: *A cloud is a ~ of vapour.*

con·dense /kən'dens/ vt,vi 1 [VP6A,14,2A,3A] (of a liquid) (cause to) increase in density or strength, to become thicker: *to ~ milk; ~ed milk;* (of a gas or vapour) (cause to) change to a liquid: *Steam ~s/is ~d to water when it touches a cold surface;* (of light) focus, concentrate (by passing through a lens). 2 [VP6A,14] put into fewer words: *a ~d account of an event.*

con·den·ser /kən'densə(r)/ n apparatus for cooling vapour and condensing it to liquid; apparatus for receiving and accumulating static electricity; mirror or lens that concentrates light, eg in a film projector.

con·de·scend /ˌkɒndɪ'send/ vi [VP2A,3A,4A] ~ **to sb/sth;** ~ **to do sth** 1 (in a good sense) do sth, accept a position, etc that one's rank, merits, abilities, etc do not require one to do. 2 (in a bad sense) stoop, lower oneself: *He occasionally ~ed to trickery/to take bribes.* 3 behave graciously, but in a way that shows one's feeling of superiority: *Mr Pigge sometimes ~s to help his wife with the housework. Mrs Drudge doesn't like being ~ed to.* ~**ing** adj ~**ing·ly** adv **con·de·scen·sion** /ˌkɒndɪ'senʃn/ n [U] ~ing (all senses); [C] instance of this.

con·dign /kən'daɪn/ adj (formal) (of punishment, vengeance) severe and well deserved.

con·di·ment /'kɒndɪmənt/ n [C,U] sth used to give flavour and relish to food, eg pepper, salt, spices.

con·di·tion¹ /kən'dɪʃn/ n 1 sth needed before sth else is possible; sth on which another thing depends: *Ability is one of the ~s of success in life. Her parents allowed her to go, but made it a ~ that she should get home before midnight.* **on** ~ **(that)**, only if; provided (that): *You can go swimming on ~ (that) you don't go too far from the river bank.* **on 'this/'that/'no/'what** ~: *You must on no ~ tell him what has happened,* whatever he may say,

do, ask, etc. *On what ~ will you agree,* What is necessary before you agree? 2 the present state of things; nature, quality, character of sth or sb: *The ~ of my health prevents me from working. The ship is not in a ~ to make a long voyage.* **in good, etc** ~, unspoiled, undamaged, etc: *Everything arrived in good ~,* undamaged, fit for use. **in no** ~ **(to)**, unable to because ill, old, etc: *He's in no ~ to travel,* is not well or strong enough. **in/out of** ~, in good/poor health; physically (un)fit: *I can't go climbing this summer: I'm out of ~.* 3 (pl) circumstances: *under existing/favourable ~s.* 4 position in society: *persons of every ~/of all ~s.* 5 state of ill-health: *a heart/liver ~.*

con·di·tion² /kən'dɪʃn/ vt [VP6A] 1 determine; govern; regulate: *My expenditure is ~ed by my income.* 2 bring into a desired state or condition: *We'll never ~ the workers to a willing acceptance of a wage freeze. ˌill-/ˌwell-J~ed;* bring (dogs, horses, etc) into good physical condition: ~*ing powders,* for this purpose. **con·di·tioned** part adj subject to certain provisions or conditions; having a specified condition: *air-~ed cinemas.* ~**ed reflex**, reflex action (one done normally in answer to a stimulus) that is a response, through practice or training, to a different stimulus not naturally connected with it.

con·di·tional /kən'dɪʃənl/ adj ~ **(on/upon)**, depending upon, containing, a condition: *a ~ clause,* beginning with 'if' or 'unless'. *My promise to help is ~ on your good behaviour.* ~**·ly** /-ʃənəlɪ/ adv

con·dole /kən'dəʊl/ vi [VP3A] ~ **with sb (on/ upon sth),** express sympathy, regret, at a loss, misfortune, etc. **con·dol·ence** /kən'dəʊləns/ n (often pl) expression of sympathy: *Please accept my condolences.*

con·dom /'kɒndəm/ n protective sheath, ⇨ sheath(2).

con·do·min·ium /ˌkɒndə'mɪnɪəm/ n joint control of a State's affairs by two or more other States.

con·done /kən'dəʊn/ vt [VP6A,C] (of a person) overlook or forgive (an offence): ~ *a husband's infidelity;* (of an act) atone for; make up for: *good qualities that ~ his many shortcomings.* **con·do·na·tion** /ˌkɒndəʊ'neɪʃn/ n

con·dor /'kɒndɔ:(r)/ n large kind of vulture (in S America).

con·duce /kən'dju:s US: -'du:s/ vi [VP3A] ~ **to/ towards,** (formal) contribute to; help to produce: *Does temperance ~ to good health?* **con·duc·ive** /kən'dju:sɪv US: -'du:s-/ adj **conducive to,** helping to produce: *Good health is conducive to happiness.*

con·duct¹ /'kɒndʌkt/ n [U] 1 behaviour (esp moral): *good or bad ~; the rules of ~.* 2 manner of directing or managing affairs: *People were not at all satisfied with the ~ of the war,* the way in which the leaders were directing it.

con·duct² /kən'dʌkt/ vt,vi 1 [VP6A,14,15A,B] lead or guide: *The Curator ~ed the visitors round the museum. Do you prefer ~ed tours or independent travel? The secretary ~ed me in/out. C~ her to the door!* 2 [VP6A,2A] control; direct; manage: *to ~ a meeting/negotiations; If he ~s his business affairs in the careless way he ~s his private affairs, they must be in confusion. Who is ~ing (the orchestra) this evening?* 3 [VP6A,15A,16A] (reflex, with adv) behave: *He ~s himself well.* 4 [VP6A,2A] (of substances) transmit; allow (heat, electric current) to pass along or through: *Copper ~s electricity better than other materials.* **con-**

duc·tion /kənˈdʌkʃn/ n [U] transmission or ~ing, eg of electric current along wires, of liquids through pipes, of heat by contact. **con·duc·tive** /kənˈdʌktɪv/ adj able to ~ (heat, electric current, etc). **con·duc·tiv·ity** /ˌkɒndʌkˈtɪvətɪ/ n (pl -ties) property or power of ~ing.

con·duc·tor /kənˈdʌktə(r)/ n 1 person who conducts, esp one who conducts a group of singers, a band, an orchestra. 2 person who collects fares on a bus or tram; (US) person in charge of passengers on a train. ⇨ guard (GB). 3 substance that conducts heat or electric current: ~ rail, rail (laid parallel to tracks) from which a locomotive picks up electric current. **con·duc·tress** /kənˈdʌktrɪs/ n woman ~ (on a bus, etc).

con·duit /'kɒndɪt US: -duːɪt/ n large pipe or waterway; tube enclosing insulated electric wires.

cone /kəʊn/ n 1 solid body which narrows to a point from a round, flat base. 2 sth of this shape whether solid or hollow, eg a ~-shaped basket hoisted as a storm signal, as an indication of road repairs, or an edible container for ice-cream. 3 fruit of certain evergreen trees (fir, pine, cedar) ⇨ the illus at tree. □ vt [VP15B] ~ off, mark off with ~s: ~ off a section of the motorway during repairs.

cones

co·ney n = cony.

con·fab /'kɒnfæb/ n, vi (-bb-) (colloq abbr of confabulation or confabulate).

con·fabu·late /ˌkənˈfæbjʊleɪt/ vi [VP2A,3A] ~ (with), have a confabulation. **con·fabu·la·tion** /kənˌfæbjuˈleɪʃn/ n [C] friendly and private conversation.

con·fec·tion /kənˈfekʃn/ n 1 [C] mixture of sweet things; sweet cake. 2 [U] mixing; compounding. 3 [C] (dress-making trade) stylish or fancy ready-made article of dress (usu for a woman). ~er n person who makes and sells pastry, pies, cakes, etc. ~·ery /kənˈfekʃənərɪ US: -ʃənerɪ/ n [U] sweets, chocolates, cakes, pies, pastry, etc; [C] (pl -ries) (place of) business of a ~er.

con·fed·er·acy /kənˈfedərəsɪ/ n (pl -cies) union of states, parties or persons: the Southern C~, the eleven States that separated from the Union (US, 1860—61) and brought about the Civil War.

con·fed·er·ate¹ /kənˈfedərət/ adj joined together by an agreement or treaty: the C~ States of America. ⇨ above. □ n [C] 1 person or State joined with another or others. 2 accomplice (in a plot, etc).

con·fed·er·ate² /kənˈfedəreɪt/ vt,vi [VP6A,14, 2A,3A] ~ (with), bring or come into alliance. **con·fed·er·ation** /kənˌfedəˈreɪʃn/ n [U] confederating or being confederated; [C] alliance; league.

con·fer /kənˈfɜː(r)/ vt,vi (-rr-) 1 [VP14] ~ sth on/ upon, give or grant (a degree, title, favour): The Queen ~red knighthoods on several distinguished men. 2 [VP2A,3A] ~ (with sb) (on/about sth), consult or discuss: ~ with one's lawyer. ~·ment n

con·fer·ence /'kɒnfərəns/ n [C,U] (meeting for) discussion; exchange of views: The Director is in ~ now. Many international ~s have been held in Geneva.

con·fess /kənˈfes/ vt,vi 1 [VP6A,9,14,2A, 3A,3B,25] ~ (to), say or admit (that one has done wrong); acknowledge: He ~ed that he had stolen the money. The prisoner refused to ~ (his crime/to his crime). She ~ed herself (to be) guilty. She ~ed to (having) a dread of spiders, admitted that she was afraid of them. 2 [VP6A,2A,3A] ~ (to), (esp in the RC Church) make known one's sins to a priest; (of a priest) listen to sb doing this: ~ one's sins. The criminal ~ed to the priest. The priest ~ed the criminal. ~·ed·ly /-ɪdlɪ/ adv as ~ed; by one's own confession.

con·fes·sion /kənˈfeʃn/ n 1 [U] confessing; [C] instance of this: The accused man made a full ~. On his own ~ he has taken part in the robbery. She is a Catholic and goes to ~ regularly. The priest is ready to hear ~s in Italian, French or English. ⇨ absolution, penance. 2 [C] declaration (of religious beliefs, or of principles of conduct, etc): a ~ of faith.

con·fes·sional /kənˈfeʃənl/ n private place (stall(4)) in a church where a priest sits to hear confessions: the secrets of the ~.

con·fes·sor /kənˈfesə(r)/ n priest who has authority to hear confessions.

con·fetti /kənˈfetɪ/ n (pl; sing v) small bits of coloured paper showered on people at weddings and carnivals.

con·fi·dant /ˌkɒnfɪˈdænt/ n person who is trusted with private affairs or secrets (esp about love affairs).

con·fide /kənˈfaɪd/ vt,vi 1 [VP14] ~ to, tell (a secret to sb); give to be looked after; give (a task or duty to sb): He ~d his troubles to a friend. The children were ~d to the care of the ship's captain. She ~d to me that... 2 [VP3A] ~ in, have trust or faith in: Can I ~ in his honesty? There's no one here I can ~ in. **con·fid·ing** adj truthful; trusting: The girl is of a confiding nature, ready to trust others, unsuspicious. **con·fid·ing·ly** adv

con·fi·dence /'kɒnfɪdəns/ n 1 [U] (act of) confiding in or to. in strict ~, expecting sth to be kept secret: I'm telling you this in strict ~. take sb into one's ~, tell him one's secrets, etc. 2 [C] secret which is confided to sb: The two girls sat in a corner exchanging ~s about the young men they knew. 3 [U] belief in oneself or others or in what is said, reported, etc; belief that one is right or that one is able to do sth: to have/lose ~ in sb; to put little/complete/no ~ in sb/sth. Don't put too much ~ in what the newspapers say. There is a lack of ~ in the Government, People do not feel that its policies are wise. I hope he will justify my ~ in him/my ~ that he will do well. The prisoner answered the questions with ~. '~ trick, persuasion of a foolish person to entrust valuables to sb as a sign of ~ (3). '~ man/trickster (also 'con-man), one who swindles people in this way.

con·fi·dent /'kɒnfɪdənt/ adj ~ (of/that), feeling or showing confidence; certain: He feels ~ of passing/that he will pass the examination. The little girl gave her mother a ~ smile. We are ~ of success. ~·ly adv

con·fi·den·tial /ˌkɒnfɪˈdenʃl/ adj 1 (to be kept) secret; given in confidence: ~ information. 2 having the confidence of another or others: a ~ clerk/ secretary. 3 (of persons) inclined to give confidences: Don't become too ~ with strangers. ~-

ity /kɒnfɪˌdenʃrˈælətɪ/ n ~·**ly** /-ʃəlɪ/ adv

con·fig·ur·ation /kənˌfɪgjʊˈreɪʃn/ n [C] shape or outline; method of arrangement: *the ~ of the earth's surface.*

con·fine /kənˈfaɪn/ vt 1 [VP14] ~ **to,** keep or hold, restrict, within limits: *I wish the speaker would ~ himself to the subject. Please ~ your remarks to the subject we are debating.* 2 [VP6A,14] keep shut up: *Is it cruel to ~ a lark in a cage? He is ~d to the house by illness. I should hate to be ~d within the four walls of an office all day.* 3 *be ~d,* (passive only) (old use) be in bed to give birth to a child: *She expects to be ~d next month.* **con·fined** adj (of space) limited; narrow; restricted. ~·**ment** n 1 [U] being ~d; imprisonment: *He was placed in ~ment,* in prison, in a mental hospital, etc. *The prisoner was sentenced to three months' solitary ~ment.* 2 [U] giving birth to a child; [C] instance of this: *Dr Spock has attended six ~ments this week. When does she expect her ~ment?*

con·fines /ˈkɒnfaɪnz/ n pl limits; borders; boundaries: *beyond the ~ of human knowledge; within the ~ of this valley.*

con·firm /kənˈfɜːm/ vt [VP6A,9] 1 make (power, ownership, opinions, rights, feelings, etc) firmer or stronger: *Please ~ your telephone message by letter,* send a letter repeating the message. *The report of an earthquake in Greece has now been ~ed,* We now know that the report was true. *What you tell me ~s my suspicions.* 2 ratify; agree definitely to (a treaty, an appointment, etc). 3 admit to full membership of the Christian Church: *She was baptized when she was a month old and ~ed when she was thirteen.* **con·firmed** part adj (esp) unlikely to change or be changed: *a ~ed invalid,* one who is unlikely to be well again; *a ~ed drunkard,* one who cannot be cured of drunken habits; *a ~ed report,* one that can be trusted.

con·fir·ma·tion /ˌkɒnfəˈmeɪʃn/ n [C,U] ~ *(of),* confirming or being confirmed (all senses): *We are waiting for ~ of the news. Evidence in ~ of his statements is lacking. C~ admits persons to full membership of the Church.*

con·fis·cate /ˈkɒnfɪskeɪt/ vt [VP6A] (as punishment or in enforcing authority) take possession of (private property) without compensation or payment: *If you try to smuggle goods into the country, they may be ~d by the Customs authorities.* **con·fis·ca·tion** /ˌkɒnfɪˈskeɪʃn/ n [U] confiscating or being ~d; [C] instance of this: *numerous confiscations of obscene books.*

con·fla·gra·tion /ˌkɒnfləˈgreɪʃn/ n [C] great and destructive fire, esp one that destroys buildings or forests.

con·flict[1] /ˈkɒnflɪkt/ n 1 [C] fight; struggle; quarrel: *a wordy ~,* a bitter argument; *a long-drawn-out ~ between employers and workers.* 2 [C,U] (of opinions, desires, etc) opposition; difference: *the ~ between duty and desire; a ~ of evidence.* **be in ~ (with),** not agree (with): *a statement that is in ~ with other evidence.*

con·flict[2] /kənˈflɪkt/ vi [VP2A,3A] ~ *(with),* be in opposition or disagreement (with): *Our accounts ~. Their account of the causes of the war ~s with ours.* ~·**ing** adj: *~ing views/passions/evidence.*

con·flu·ence /ˈkɒnflʊəns/ n flowing together, esp a place where two rivers unite. **con·flu·ent** /ˈkɒnflʊənt/ adj flowing together; uniting.

con·form /kənˈfɔːm/ vi,vt 1 [VP2A,3A] ~ *(to),* be in agreement (with), comply (with) (generally accepted rules, standards, etc): *You should ~ to the rules/to the wishes of others/to the usages of society/to the usages of the Established Church.* 2 [VP14] ~ *to,* make similar to; adapt oneself to: *~ one's life to certain principles.* ~·**able** adj obedient; submissive; in agreement.

con·for·ma·tion /ˌkɒnfɔːˈmeɪʃn/ n way in which sth is formed; structure.

con·form·ist /kənˈfɔːmɪst/ n person who conforms; conventional person; (hist) person who followed the practices of the Church of England. ⇨ *dissenter* at *dissent*[2]*, nonconformist* at non-.

con·form·ity /kənˈfɔːmətɪ/ n [U] 1 ~ *(to),* action, behaviour, in agreement with what is usual, accepted or required by custom, etc: *C~ to fashion* (= Having things of the latest fashion) *is not essential to the happiness of all women.* 2 *in ~ with,* in agreement with: *in ~ with your request. Was his action in ~ with the law?*

con·found /kənˈfaʊnd/ vt 1 [VP6A] fill with, throw into, perplexity or confusion: *His behaviour amazed and ~ed her. I was ~ed to hear that....* 2 [VP6A,14] ~ *(with),* mix up, confuse (ideas, etc): *Don't ~ the means with the ends.* 3 [VP6A] (liter) defeat; overthrow (enemies, plans, etc). 4 [VP6A] (dated) used to express annoyance or anger: *C~ it! C~ you!* ~**ed** part adj (from 4 above; dated): *You're a ~ed nuisance!* ~·**ed·ly** /-ɪdlɪ/ adv very: *~edly hot.*

con·frère /ˈkɒnfreə(r)/ n (F) fellow member of a profession, learned society, etc.

con·front /kənˈfrʌnt/ vt 1 [VP14] ~ *sb with,* bring face to face with: *The prisoner was ~ed with his accusers. When ~ed with the evidence of his guilt, he confessed at once.* 2 [VP6A] be or come face to face with: *The difficulties that ~ us seem insuperable. A soldier has to ~ danger.* 3 [VP6A] be opposite to: *My house ~s his.*

con·fron·ta·tion /ˌkɒnfrʌnˈteɪʃn/ n [C,U] (instance of) defiant opposition, of being face to face: *the ~ between Israel and the Arab world.*

Con·fu·cian /kənˈfjuːʃn/ adj, n (follower) of Confucius /kənˈfjuːʃəs/, the Chinese philosopher and teacher (551-479 BC).

con·fuse /kənˈfjuːz/ vt [VP6A,14] ~ *(with),* 1 put into disorder; mix up in the mind: *They asked so many questions that they ~d me/I got ~d.* 2 mistake one thing for another: *Don't ~ Austria with/ and Australia.* **con·fus·ed·ly** /-ɪdlɪ/ adv in a ~d manner.

con·fusion /kənˈfjuːʒn/ n [U] being confused; disorder: *He remained calm in the ~ of battle. His unexpected arrival threw me into ~. Everything was in ~. There has been some ~ of names.*

con·fute /kənˈfjuːt/ vt [VP6A] prove (a person) to be wrong; show (an argument) to be false. **con·fu·ta·tion** /ˌkɒnfjuːˈteɪʃn/ n

congé /ˈkɒnʒeɪ/ n 1 formal permission to depart: *give sb his ~.* 2 abrupt and unceremonious dismissal.

con·geal /kənˈdʒiːl/ vt,vi [VP6A,2A] make or become stiff or solid (esp as the effect of cold, or of the air on blood); thicken as if frozen: *His blood was ~ed,* (fig) eg through fear.

con·gen·ial /kənˈdʒiːnɪəl/ adj 1 (of persons) having the same or a similar nature, common interests, etc: *In this small village he found few persons ~ to him.* 2 (of things, occupations, etc) in agreement with one's tastes, nature: *a ~ climate; ~ work.* ~·**ly** /-ɪəlɪ/ adv

con·geni·tal /kən'dʒenɪtl/ adj (of diseases, etc) present, belonging to one, from or before birth: ∼ idiocy.

con·ger /'kɒŋgə(r)/ n (also ∼-'eel) ocean eel of large size. ⇨ the illus at **sea**.

con·gested /kən'dʒestɪd/ part adj **1** too full; over-crowded: streets ∼ with traffic; ∼ areas of a large town. **2** (of parts of the body, eg the brain, the lungs) having an abnormal accumulation of blood.

con·ges·tion /kən'dʒestʃən/ n [U] being congested: ∼ of the lungs; delayed by the ∼ of traffic in town.

con·glom·er·ate¹ /kən'glɒmərət/ adj, n (made up of a) number of things or parts come together in a mass (eg rock made up of small stones held together); (fig; comm) large corporation made up of many different firms.

con·glom·er·ate² /kən'glɒməreɪt/ vt, vi [VP6A,2A] collect into a mass.

con·glom·er·ation /kən,glɒmə'reɪʃn/ n [U] conglomerating or being conglomerated; [C] mass of conglomerated things.

con·gratu·late /kən'grætʃʊleɪt/ vt [VP6A,14] ∼ sb (on/upon sth) **1** tell sb that one is pleased about sth happy or fortunate that has come to him: ∼ sb on his marriage. **2** (reflex) consider oneself fortunate: I ∼d myself on my escape/on having escaped unhurt. **con·gratu·la·tory** /kən'grætʃʊlətərɪ US: -tɔːrɪ/ adj that ∼s: a congratulatory letter/telegram.

con·gratu·la·tion /kən,grætʃʊ'leɪʃn/ n (often pl) words that congratulate: offer a friend one's ∼s on/upon his success.

con·gre·gate /'kɒŋgrɪgeɪt/ vi, vt [VP6A,2A,C] come or bring together: People quickly ∼d round the speaker.

con·gre·ga·tion /,kɒŋgrɪ'geɪʃn/ n [U] congregating; [C] gathering of people; (esp) body of people (usu except the minister and choir) taking part in religious worship. ∼al adj of a ∼. C∼al adj of the Union of Free Churches in which individual churches manage their own affairs.

con·gress /'kɒŋgres US: -grəs/ n **1** [C] meeting, series of meetings, of representatives (of societies, etc) for discussion: a medical ∼; the Church C∼. **2** C∼, law-making body eg of US; political party in India. '∼-man /-mən/ n (pl-men) '∼-woman n (pl-women) member of US C∼. Cf senator. **con·gres·sional** /kən'greʃənl/ adj of a ∼: ∼ional debates.

con·gru·ent /'kɒŋgrʊənt/ adj **1** ∼ (with), suitable; agreeing (with). **2** (geom) having the same size and shape: ∼ triangles.

con·gru·ous /'kɒŋgrʊəs/ adj ∼ (with), (formal) fitting; proper; harmonious.

conic /'kɒnɪk/ adj of a cone: ∼ sections. **coni·cal** /'kɒnɪkl/ adj cone-shaped. ⇨ the illus at projection.

coni·fer /'kɒnɪfə(r)/ n tree of the kind (eg pine, fir) that bears cones. **co·nif·er·ous** /kə'nɪfərəs/ adj (of kinds of trees) that bear cones.

con·jec·ture /kən'dʒektʃə(r)/ vi, vt [VP6A,9,2A,25] guess; put forward an opinion formed without facts as proof: It was just as I ∼d. May we ∼ that…? □ n [C,U] guess; guessing: I was right in my ∼s. We had no facts, so were reduced to ∼. **con·jec·tural** /kən'dʒektʃərəl/ adj involving ∼; inclined to ∼.

con·join /kən'dʒɔɪn/ vt, vi [VP6A,2A] (formal) join together; unite. ∼t /kən'dʒɔɪnt/ adj united; associated. ∼t·ly adv

con·ju·gal /'kɒndʒʊgl/ adj of marriage and wedded life; of husband and wife: ∼ happiness/affection/infidelity. ∼·ly /-gəlɪ/ adv

con·ju·gate /'kɒndʒʊgeɪt/ vt, vi **1** [VP6A] give the forms of a verb (for number, tense, etc). **2** [VP2A] (of a verb) have these forms. **con·ju·ga·tion** /,kɒndʒʊ'geɪʃn/ n [C,U] scheme or system of verb forms; [C] class of verbs ∼d alike.

con·junc·tion /kən'dʒʌŋkʃn/ n **1** [C] (gram) word that joins other words, clauses, etc, eg and, but, or. **2** [U] joining; state of being joined; the ∼ of skill and imagination in planning a garden. **in ∼ with**, together with. **3** [C] combination (of events, etc): an unusual ∼ of circumstances.

con·junc·tiva /,kɒndʒʌŋk'taɪvə/ n (anat) thin transparent membrane connecting the upper and lower inner eyelids, covering the cornea. ⇨ the illus at eye. **con·junc·ti·vitis** /kɒn,dʒʌŋktɪ'vaɪtɪs/ n [U] inflammation of the ∼.

con·junc·tive /kən'dʒʌŋktɪv/ adj serving to join; connective. □ n ∼ word.

con·junc·ture /kən'dʒʌŋktʃə(r)/ n [C] combination of events or circumstances.

con·jur·ation /,kɒndʒʊ'reɪʃn/ n [C] (formal) solemn appeal, incantation.

con·jure /'kʌndʒə(r)/ vt, vi **1** [VP2A,15A] do clever tricks which appear magical, esp by quick movements of the hands: a conjuring trick; ∼ a rabbit out of a hat. **a name to ∼ with**, sb of great importance/influence. **2** [VP15B] ∼ up, cause to appear as if from nothing, or as a picture in the mind: ∼ up visions of the past; compel (a spirit) to appear by invocation: ∼ up the spirits of the dead; ∼ up a meal, produce it quickly. **3** /kən'dʒʊə(r)/ [VP17] (formal) appeal solemnly to: I ∼ you not to betray me. **con·jurer**, **con·juror** /'kʌndʒərə(r)/ n person who performs conjuring tricks. ⇨ **1** above.

conk¹ /kɒŋk/ n (GB sl) nose.

conk² /kɒŋk/ vi ∼ out, (colloq) (of a machine) fail or give signs of failing: The engine's ∼ing out.

conker /'kɒŋkə(r)/ n (colloq) horse chestnut.

con-man /'kɒn mæn/ n ⇨ confidence(3).

con·nect /kə'nekt/ vt, vi **1** [VP6A,15A,B,14,2A,2C,3A] ∼ (up) (to/with), join, be joined (materially, by personal relationships, etc): ∼ telephone subscribers; ∼ (up) the cells of a battery (to/with one another). The two towns are ∼ed by a railway. A railway ∼s Oxford and Reading/∼s Oxford to/with Reading. Where does the cooker ∼ with the gas-pipe? Mr Y has been ∼ed with this firm since 1950. He is ∼ed with the Smiths/He and the Smiths are ∼ed by marriage, ie his wife is a member of the Smith family. The 9.00am train from London ∼s with the 12.05pm train at Crewe, ie arrives at Crewe so as to enable passengers to continue their journeys by the 12.05pm train. **well ∼ed**, with relatives who are high in society, or who hold important positions, etc. **2** [VP14] ∼ (with), think of (different things or persons) as being related to each other: to ∼ Malaya with rubber and tin.

con·nec·tion /kə'nekʃn/ n **1** [C,U] connecting or being connected; point where two things are connected; thing which connects: a bicycle pump ∼. How long will the ∼ of the new telephone take, How long will it take to connect the house by telephone to the exchange? What is the ∼ between the two ideas? **in this/that ∼**, with reference to this/that. **in ∼ with**, with reference to: The meeting is in ∼ with a proposal to construct a new swimming-pool. **2** [C] train, boat, etc timed to leave a station, port, etc soon after the arrival of another, enabling passengers to change from one to the other: *The train was late and I missed my* ~. **3** [C] (collective noun) number of customers, clients, etc: *He set up in business and soon had a good* ~. *This dressmaker has good* ~*s among the well-to-do women of the town.* **4** [C] number of people united in a religious organization: *the Methodist* ~.

con·nect·ive /kə'nektɪv/ *adj* serving to connect. □ *n*(esp) word that connects (eg a conjunction).

con·nex·ion /kə'nekʃn/ occasional GB spelling for connection.

con·ning tower /'kɒnɪŋ taʊə(r)/ *n* (on a warship) superstructure from which steering, etc is directed (esp of a submarine on or near the surface).

con·nive /kə'naɪv/ *vi* [VP3A] ~ **at**, take no notice of (what is wrong, what ought to be opposed) (suggesting that tacit consent or approval is given): ~ *at an escape from prison.* **con·niv·ance** /kə'naɪvəns/ *n* [U] conniving (*at/in a crime*): *done with the connivance of/in connivance with....*

con·nois·seur /ˌkɒnə'sɜː(r)/ *n* person with good judgement on matters in which taste(5) is needed: *a* ~ *of painting/old porcelain/antique furniture/wine.*

con·note /kə'nəʊt/ *vt* [VP6A] (of words) suggest in addition to the fundamental meaning: *The word 'Tropics' means the area between about 23°N and 23°S; it* ~*s heat.* **con·no·ta·tion** /ˌkɒnə'teɪʃn/ *n* [C] that which is ~d.

con·nu·bial /kə'njuːbɪəl/ *US*: -'nuː-/ *adj* (formal) of marriage; of husband and wife.

con·quer /'kɒŋkə(r)/ *vt* [VP6A] **1** defeat or overcome enemies/bad habits, etc. **2** take possession of by force: ~ *a country.* ~**or** /'kɒŋkərə(r)/ *n* one who ~s: *William the C*~*or,* King William I of England.

con·quest /'kɒŋkwest/ *n* **1** [U] conquering (eg a country and its people): *the (Norman) C*~, of England by the Normans in 1066. **2** [C] sth got by conquering: *the Roman* ~*s in Africa.* **make a** ~ **(of),** win the affections (of).

con·quista·dor /kɒn'kwɪstədɔː(r)/ *n* (16th c) one of the Spanish conquerors of Mexico and Peru.

con·san·guin·ity /ˌkɒnsæŋ'ɡwɪnəti/ *n* [U] (formal) relationship by blood or birth: *united by ties of* ~.

con·science /'kɒnʃəns/ *n* [C,U] the consciousness within oneself of the choice one ought to make between right and wrong: *have a clear/guilty* ~. **have no** ~, be as ready to do wrong as right. **(have sth) on one's** ~, (feel) troubled about sth one has done, or failed to do. **'**~ **money,** money paid to rectify sth and ease one's ~ (esp when no other person knows that it is owing). **'**~**-smitten** /-smɪtn/ *adj* filled with remorse. **for '**~**' sake,** to satisfy one's ~. **in all** ~, (form of emphatic declaration) surely; (colloq) by all that is fair: *I cannot in all* ~ *agree.* **make sth/be a matter of** ~, make sth/be a question which one's ~ must decide.

con·scien·tious /ˌkɒnʃɪ'enʃəs/ *adj* **1** (of persons) guided by one's sense of duty: *a* ~ *worker.* ~ **ob·jector,** person who objects to doing sth (esp serving in the armed forces) because he thinks it is morally wrong. **2** (of actions) done carefully and honestly: ~ *work.* ~**·ly** *adv* ~**·ness** *n*

con·scious /'kɒnʃəs/ *adj* **1** ~ **(of/that),** (pred use) awake; aware; knowing things because one is using the bodily senses and mental powers: *They were* ~

of being/that they were being watched. He was ~ *of his guilt. Are you* ~ *(of) how people will regard such behaviour? A healthy man is not* ~ *of his breathing. The old man was* ~ *to the last,* aware of what was happening round him until the moment he died. **2** (of actions, feelings, etc) realized by oneself: *He spoke/acted with* ~ *superiority.* ~**·ly** *adv*

con·scious·ness /'kɒnʃəsnɪs/ *n* [U] **1** being conscious: *We have no* ~ *during sleep. The blow caused him to lose* ~. *He did not recover/regain* ~ *until two hours after the accident.* **2** all the ideas, thoughts, feelings, wishes, intentions, recollections, of a person or persons: *the moral* ~ *of a political party.*

con·script /kən'skrɪpt/ *vt* [VP6A,14] ~ **(into),** compel (sb) by law to serve in the armed forces; summon for such service: ~*ed into the army.* ⇨ draft[1](3). □ *n* /'kɒnskrɪpt/ person who is ~ed; (attrib) ~ *soldiers.* **con·scrip·tion** /kən'skrɪpʃn/ *n* [U] ~ing (of men into the armed forces); taxation or confiscation of property (as a penalty or for war needs).

con·se·crate /'kɒnsɪkreɪt/ *vt* [VP6A,14,23] ~ **(to),** set apart as sacred or for a special purpose; make sacred: *to* ~ *one's life to the service of God/to the relief of suffering. The new church was* ~*d by the Bishop of Chester. He was* ~*d Archbishop last year.*

con·se·cra·tion /ˌkɒnsɪ'kreɪʃn/ *n* [U] consecrating or being consecrated; [C] instance of this: *the* ~ *of a church; the* ~ *of a bishop,* the ceremony at which a priest is made a bishop.

con·secu·tive /kən'sekjʊtɪv/ *adj* following continuously; coming one after the other in regular order: *on five* ~ *days.* ~**·ly** *adv*

con·sen·sus /kən'sensəs/ *n* [C,U] general agreement (*of* opinion, etc); collective opinion. ~ **polit·ics,** the practice of basing policies on what will gain wide support.

con·sent /kən'sent/ *vi* [VP2A,3A,7A] ~ **(to),** give agreement or permission: *He* ~*ed to the proposal. Anne's father would not* ~ *to her marrying a foreigner.* □ *n* [U] ~ **(to),** agreement; permission: *He was chosen leader by general* ~, when everyone agreed. *Her parents refused their* ~ *to the marriage. Silence gives* ~, If no one objects, it seems that ~ is given. **with one** ~, unanimously. **age of '**~, age at which the law recognizes a person's responsibility for agreeing to sexual intercourse, a person's right to ~ to marry, etc.

con·se·quence /'kɒnsɪkwəns *US*: -kwens/ *n* **1** [C] that which follows or is brought about as the result or effect of sth: *If you behave so foolishly you must be ready to take the* ~*s,* accept what happens as a result. **in** ~ **(of),** as a result (of). **2** [U] importance: *It's of no* ~. *Is it of any/much* ~? *He may be a man of* ~ (= an important man, or a man of high rank) *in his own village, but he's nobody here.*

con·se·quent /'kɒnsɪkwənt/ *adj* ~ **on/upon,** (formal) following as a consequence: *the rise in prices* ~ *upon the failure of the crops.* ~**·ly** *adv*

conse·quen·tial /ˌkɒnsɪ'kwenʃl/ *adj* **1** = consequent. **2** (of a person) self-important. ~**·ly** /-ʃəli/ *adv*

con·ser·vancy /kən'sɜːvənsi/ *n* (*pl* -cies) **1** [C] commission controlling a port, river, etc: *the Thames C*~; *the Nature C*~. **2** [U] official conservation (of forests, etc).

con·ser·va·tion /ˌkɒnsə'veɪʃn/ *n* [U] preservation;

prevention of loss, waste, damage, etc: *the ~ of forests/waterpower etc; the ~ of energy,* the principle that the total quantity of energy in the universe never varies.

con·ser·va·tism /kən'sɜːvətɪzəm/ *n* [U] tendency to maintain a state of affairs (esp in politics) without great or sudden change; the principles of the Conservative Party in British politics.

con·ser·va·tive /kən'sɜːvətɪv/ *adj* **1** opposed to (great or sudden) change: *Old people are usually more ~ than young people.* **2 the 'C~ Party,** one of the main political parties in Great Britain. ⇨ *Labour* at labour(3), *Liberal* at liberal(4), *Socialist* at socialism. **3** cautious; moderate: *a ~ estimate of one's future income.* □ *n ~* person; member of the C~ Party. **~·ly** *adv*

con·ser·va·toire /kən'sɜːvətwɑː(r)/ *n* (F) (esp in Europe) public school of music, drama etc.

con·ser·va·tory /kən'sɜːvətrɪ US: -tɔːrɪ/ *n* (*pl -ries*) **1** building, or part of a building, with glass walls and roof in which plants are protected from cold. **2** = conservatoire.

con·serve /kən'sɜːv/ *vt* [VP6A] keep from change, loss or destruction: *~ one's strength/energies/health; ~ fruit,* eg by making it into jam. □ *n* (usu *pl*) fruit preserved in sugar; jam.

con·sider /kən'sɪdə(r)/ *vt* **1** [VP6A,C,8,10] think about: *Please ~ my suggestion. We are ~ing going to Canada. Have you ~ed how to get/how you could get there? Have you ever ~ed the fact that your pension will be inadequate? **one's ~d opin-ion,** one's opinion arrived at after some thought: It's my ~d opinion that you should resign.* **2** [VP6A] take into account; make allowances for: *We must ~ the feelings of other people. You should ~ his youth. **all things ~ed,** taking into account, thinking of, all the events, possibilities, etc.* **3** [VP25,9] be of the opinion; regard as: *They ~ed themselves very important. Do you ~ it wise to interfere? He will be ~ed a weak leader. C~ yourself* (= You are) *under arrest. We ~ that you are not to blame.*

con·sider·able /kən'sɪdərəbl/ *adj* great; much; important: *a ~ income/distance; bought at a ~ expense; a ~ man in local affairs.* **~·ably** /-əblɪ/ *adv* much; a great deal: *It's considerably colder this morning.*

con·sider·ate /kən'sɪdərət/ *adj ~ (of),* thoughtful (of the needs, etc, of others): *It was ~ of you not to play the piano while I was having a sleep.* **~·ly** *adv* **~·ness** *n*

con·sider·ation /kən‚sɪdə'reɪʃn/ *n* **1** [U] act of considering, thinking about: *Please give the matter your careful ~. The proposals are still under ~. **leave sth out of ~,** neglect or fail to consider it: There is one important fact that has been left out of ~. **take sth into ~,** (esp) make allowances for: When marking Tom's examination papers, the teacher took Tom's long illness into ~.* **2** [U] *~ (for),* quality of being considerate; thoughtful attention to the wishes, feelings, etc, of others: *He has never shown much ~ for his wife's feelings. **in ~ of; out of ~ for,** considering(2).* **3** [C] sth which must be thought about; fact, thing, etc thought of as a reason: *Time is an important ~ in this case. Several ~s have influenced me in coming to a decision. **on no ~,** in no circumstances; in no case.* **4** [C] reward; payment: *He's the sort of man who would do anything for a ~,* if he were paid to do it. **5** [U] (rare use) importance: *It's of no

~ at all.*

con·sider·ing /kən'sɪdərɪŋ/ *prep* in view of; having regard to: *She's very active, ~ her age. You've done very well, ~,* ie in view of the circumstances, etc.

con·sign /kən'saɪn/ *vt ~ (to),* **1** [VP6A,14] send (goods, etc) for delivery: *The goods have been ~ed by rail.* **2** [VP14] hand over, give up: *~ a child to its uncle's care; ~ one's soul to God.* **~·ee** /‚kɒnsaɪ'niː/ *n* person to whom sth is ~ed. **~·er, ~or** /-nər/ *nn* person who ~s goods. **~·ment** *n* [U] ~ing; [C] goods ~ed. **on ~ment,** with payment for goods to be made after they have been sold by the receiver: *take/send/ship goods on ~ment.* **'~·ment note,** one sent with a ~ment of goods.

con·sist /kən'sɪst/ *vi* [VP3A] **1** *~ of,* (not in the progressive tenses) be made up of: *The committee ~s of ten members.* **2** *~ in,* have as the chief or only element: *The happiness of a country ~s in the freedom of its citizens.*

con·sist·ence /kən'sɪstəns/ *n* = consistency.

con·sist·ency /kən'sɪstənsɪ/ *n* **1** [U] the state of always being the same in thought, behaviour, etc; keeping to the same principles: *His actions lack ~.* **2** [C,U] (*pl -cies*) degree of thickness, firmness or solidity (esp of a thick liquid, or of sth made by mixing with a liquid): *mix flour and milk to the right ~; mixtures of various consistencies.*

con·sist·ent /kən'sɪstənt/ *adj* **1** (of a person, his behaviour, principles, etc) conforming to a regular pattern or style; regular: *He's been a ~ friend to me. The ideas in his various speeches are not ~.* **2** *~ (with),* in agreement: *What you say now is not ~ with what you said last week.* **~·ly** *adv*

con·sis·tory /kən'sɪstərɪ/ *n* (*pl -ries*) **C~ (Court),** court of clergymen to deal with church business.

con·so·la·tion /‚kɒnsə'leɪʃn/ *n* **1** [U] consoling or being consoled; sth that consoles: *a few words of ~; a letter of ~.* **'~ prize,** one given to a competitor who has just misssed success or come last. **2** [C] circumstances or person that consoles: *That's one ~. Your company has been a great ~ to me.*

con·sola·tory /kən'sɒlətərɪ US: -tɔːrɪ/ *adj* comforting; intended to console: *a ~ letter.*

con·sole¹ /kən'səʊl/ *vt* [VP6A,14] give comfort or sympathy to (sb who is unhappy, disappointed, etc): *~ sb for a loss; ~ oneself with the thought that it might have been worse.* **con·sol·able** *adj* that can be ~d.

con·sole² /'kɒnsəʊl/ *n* **1** bracket to support a shelf. **'~ table,** narrow table held up by a bracket or brackets fixed to a wall. **2** frame containing the keyboards, stops, etc of an organ. **3** radio or TV cabinet made to stand on the floor (not a table model). **4** panel for the controls of electronic or mechanical equipment.

con·soli·date /kən'sɒlɪdeɪt/ *vt,vi* **1** [VP6A,2A] make or become solid or strong: *~ one's position/influence.* **2** [VP6A] unite or combine into one: *~ debts/business companies/banks.* **~d an-nuities,** (also **consols** /'kɒnsɒlz/) Government securities of Great Britain, ~d in 1751 into a single stock. **C~d Fund** *n* fund from taxation, used for payment of interest on the national debt.

con·soli·da·tion /kən‚sɒlɪ'deɪʃn/ *n* [U] consolidating or being consolidated; [C] instance of this: *successive ~s of the national debt.*

con·sols /'kɒnsɒlz/ *n pl* consolidated annuities. ⇨ consolidate(2).

con·som·mé /kən'sɒmeɪ US: ˌkɒnsə'meɪ/ n (F) clear, meat soup.

con·son·ance /'kɒnsənəns/ n [U] 1 agreement. 2 harmony.

con·son·ant¹ /'kɒnsənənt/ n [C] speech sound produced by a complete or partial stoppage of the breath; letter of the alphabet or symbol (eg phonetic) for such a sound: *b, c, d, f,* etc.

con·son·ant² /'kɒnsənənt/ adj (formal) ~ **with,** harmonious: *actions* ~ *with his beliefs; a position in the service* ~ *with your rank.* ~ **to,** agreeable: ~ *to reason.*

con·sort¹ /'kɒnsɔːt/ n 1 husband or wife, esp of a ruler: *the queen* ~, the king's wife; *the prince* ~, the reigning queen's husband. 2 ship sailing with another (esp for safety during a war).

con·sort² /kən'sɔːt/ vi [VP3A,2C] ~ **with,** 1 pass time in the company of: ~ *with criminals/one's equals.* 2 be in harmony, go well: *His practice does not* ~ *with his preaching,* He behaves in one way, but talks in another way.

con·sor·tium /kən'sɔːtɪəm US: -'sɔːrʃɪəm/ n (pl -tia /-tɪə US: -ʃə/) temporary co-operation of a number of powers, companies, banks, etc for a common purpose: *the* ~ *of Upper Clyde shipbuilders.*

con·spec·tus /kən'spektəs/ n (pl ~es /-ɪz/) general view of a subject, scene, etc; synopsis (eg in the form of tables).

con·spic·u·ous /kən'spɪkjʊəs/ adj easily seen; attracting attention; remarkable: ~ *for his bravery. Traffic signs should be* ~. **make oneself** ~, attract attention by unusual behaviour, wearing unusual clothes, etc. ~·**ly** adv ~·**ness** n

con·spir·acy /kən'spɪrəsɪ/ n [U] act of conspiring; [C] (pl -cies) plan made by conspiring: *a* ~ *to overthrow the Government; a* ~ *of silence,* an agreement not to talk publicly about sth.

con·spire /kən'spaɪə(r)/ vi,vt 1 [VP2A,3A,4A] ~ **(with) (against),** make secret plans (with others, esp to do sth wrong): ~ *against the Government. His enemies* ~d *to ruin him.* 2 [VP6A] plot: ~ *sb's ruin.* 3 [VP4A] (of events) act together; combine: *events that* ~d *to bring about his downfall.* **con·spira·tor** /kən'spɪrətə(r)/ n person who ~s. **con·spira·tor·ial** /kənˌspɪrə'tɔːrɪəl/ adj of conspirators or a conspiracy: *with a conspiratorial air.*

con·stable /'kʌnstəbl US: 'kɒn-/ n 1 (GB) (**po·lice**) ~, policeman or policewoman of basic grade. **Chief C**~, head of the police force of a county, etc. **special** ~, person who acts as a ~ on special occasions or for special duty. 2 (hist) principal officer in a royal household; governor of a royal castle, etc. **con·sta·bu·lary** /kən'stæbjʊlərɪ US: -lerɪ/ n (pl -ries) organized body of police ~s; police force.

con·stancy /'kɒnstənsɪ/ n [U] quality of being firm, unchanging: ~ *of purpose.*

con·stant /'kɒnstənt/ adj 1 going on all the time; frequently recurring: ~ *complaints.* 2 firm; faithful; unchanging: *a* ~ *friend. He has been* ~ *in his devotion to scientific studies.* □ n (maths, phys) number or quantity that does not vary. ~·**ly** adv continuously; frequently.

con·stel·la·tion /ˌkɒnstə'leɪʃn/ n named group of fixed stars (eg *the Great Bear*); (fig) group.

con·ster·na·tion /ˌkɒnstə'neɪʃn/ n [U] surprise and fear; dismay: *filled with* ~; *looking back in* ~.

con·sti·pate /'kɒnstɪpeɪt/ vt [VP6A] cause constipation: *to find some kinds of food constipating.*

con·sti·pated /'kɒnstɪpeɪtɪd/ part adj having bowels that can be emptied infrequently or only with difficulty.

con·sti·pa·tion /ˌkɒnstɪ'peɪʃn/ n [U] difficult or infrequent emptying of the bowels.

con·sti·tu·ency /kən'stɪtjʊənsɪ/ n (pl -cies) [C] (body of voters living in a) town or district that sends a representative to Parliament.

con·sti·tu·ent /kən'stɪtjʊənt/ adj 1 having the power or right to make or alter a political constitution: *a* ~ *assembly.* 2 forming or helping to make a whole: *a* ~ *part.* □ n 1 member of a constituency. 2 component part: *the* ~s *of happiness.*

con·sti·tute /'kɒnstɪtjuːt US: -tuːt/ vt 1 [VP23] give (sb) authority to hold (a position, etc): *They* ~d *him chief adviser. What right have you to* ~ *yourself a judge of my conduct?* 2 [VP6A] establish; give legal authority to (a committee, etc). 3 [VP6A] make up (a whole); amount to; be the components of: *Twelve months* ~ *a year. He is so* ~d (= His nature is such) *that he can accept unjust criticism without getting angry.*

con·sti·tu·tion /ˌkɒnstɪ'tjuːʃn US: -'tuːʃn/ n 1 [C] system of government; laws and principles according to which a state is governed: *Great Britain has an unwritten* ~; *the United States has a written* ~. 2 [C] general physical structure and condition of a person's body: *Only people with strong* ~s *should climb in the Himalayas.* 3 [C,U] general structure of a thing; act or manner of constituting: *the* ~ *of the solar spectrum; the* ~ *of one's mind and character.*

con·sti·tu·tional /ˌkɒnstɪ'tjuːʃənl US: -'tuː-/ adj 1 of a constitution(1): ~ *government; a* ~ *ruler,* controlled or limited by a constitution; ~ *reform.* ⇨ **absolute, autocratic** at autocrat. 2 of a person's constitution(2): *a* ~ *weakness.* □ n (dated colloq) short walk for the health's sake: *go for/take a* ~. ~·**ly** /-ʃənəlɪ/ adv ~·**ism** n [U] (belief in) ~ government or ~ principles. ~·**ist** n supporter of ~ principles. ~·**ize** /-ʃənəlaɪz/ vt make ~.

con·sti·tut·ive /kən'stɪtjʊtɪv/ adj constructive; formative; essential.

con·strain /kən'streɪn/ vt [VP6A,17] make (sb) do sth by using force or strong persuasion; (of conscience, inner forces) compel: *I feel* ~ed *to write and ask for your forgiveness.* ~ed *part adj* (of voice, manner, etc) forced; uneasy; unnatural. ~·**ed·ly** /-ɪdlɪ/ adv

con·straint /kən'streɪnt/ n [U] constraining or being constrained: *to act under* ~, because one is forced to do so; *to feel/show* ~ *in a person's presence,* to hold back one's natural feelings.

con·strict /kən'strɪkt/ vt [VP6A] make tight or smaller; cause (a vein or muscle) to become tight or narrow: (fig) *a* ~ed *outlook,* one that is narrow or limited. **con·stric·tion** /kən'strɪkʃn/ n [U] ~ing; [C] feeling of being ~ed: *a* ~ion *in the chest;* [C] sth that ~s.

con·struct /kən'strʌkt/ vt [VP6A] build; put or fit together: *to* ~ *a factory/an aircraft/a sentence/a theory; a well-*~ed *novel.* ~**or** /-tə(r)/ n person who ~s things: *motor-car body*~ors.

con·struc·tion /kən'strʌkʃn/ n 1 [U] act or manner of constructing; being constructed: *the* ~ *of new roads. The new railway is still under* ~/*in the course of* ~. *The new factory is of very solid* ~. 2 [C] sth constructed; structure; building. 3 [C] meaning; sense in which words, statements, acts, etc are taken: *Please do not put a wrong* ~ *on his* *action*, misunderstand its purpose. *The sentence does not bear such a* ~, cannot be understood in that way. ⇨ **construe. 4** [C] arrangement and relationships of words in a sentence: *This dictionary gives the meanings of words and also illustrates their* ~s.

con·struc·tive /kən'strʌktɪv/ *adj* helping to construct; giving helpful suggestions: ~ *criticism/ proposals.* ~**·ly** *adv*

con·strue /kən'struː/ *vt, vi* **1** [VP6A,2A] translate or explain the meaning of words, sentences, acts: ~ *a passage from Homer. His remarks were wrongly* ~*d*, were misunderstood. **2** [VP6A] analyse (a sentence); combine (words with words) grammatically. **3** [VP2A] be capable of being analysed: *This sentence won't* ~.

con·sub·stan·ti·ation /ˌkɒnsəb̩stænʃɪ'eɪʃn/ *n* [U] doctrine that the body and blood of Christ co-exist with the bread and wine in the Eucharist.

con·sul /'kɒnsl/ *n* **1** State's agent living in a foreign town to help and protect his countrymen there. **2** (in ancient Rome) either of the two Heads of the State before Rome became an Empire. **3** any one of the three chief magistrates of the French Republic, 1799—1804. ~**·ship** /-ʃɪp/ *n* position of a ~; period of time during which a ~ holds his position.

con·su·lar /'kɒnsjʊlə(r) *US:* -səl-/ *adj* of a consul or his work.

con·su·late /'kɒnsjʊlət *US:* -səl-/ *n* consul's position; offices of a consul(1); period of consular government in France.

con·sult /kən'sʌlt/ *vt, vi* **1** [VP6A,14] go to a person, a book, etc for information, advice, opinion, etc: *to* ~ *one's lawyer/a map/the dictionary; a* ~*ing engineer*, one with special knowledge of one or more branches of engineering. **2** [VP6A] (old use; *consider* is now preferred) take into consideration or account: *We must* ~ *his convenience*, cause him as little inconvenience as possible. **3** [VP3A] ~ *with*, discuss with: ~ *with one's partners.*

con·sul·tant /kən'sʌltənt/ *n* person who gives expert advice (eg in medicine, surgery, business): (attrib) *a* ~ *surgeon; a firm of* ~s.

con·sul·ta·tion /ˌkɒnsl'teɪʃn/ *n* **1** [U] consulting or being consulted: *in* ~ *with the director.* **2** [C] meeting for consulting: *The doctors held a* ~ *to decide whether an operation was necessary.*

con·sul·ta·tive /kən'sʌltətɪv/ *adj* of, for the purpose of, consulting: *a* ~ *committee.*

con·sume /kən'sjuːm *US:* -'suːm/ *vt, vi* **1** [VP6A] eat or drink. **2** [VP6A] use up; get to the end of; destroy by fire or wastefulness: ~ *all one's energies. The flames quickly* ~*d the wooden huts. He soon* ~*d his fortune*, spent the money wastefully. *He was* ~*d* (= filled) *with envy/hatred/greed. This is time-consuming work*, work that takes up a lot of time. **3** ~ *away*, waste away. **con·sum·ing** *part adj* possessing or dominating: *consuming ambition.*

con·sumer /kən'sjuːmə(r) *US:* -'suː-/ *n* (opp to *producer*) person who uses goods. ~ **goods**, those which directly satisfy human needs and desires (eg food and clothing) (opp to *capital goods*, eg factory equipment). ~ **research**, market research, ⇨ **market¹**(4). ~ **sales resistance**, unwillingness of people to buy a product. ~**·ism** /-ɪzəm/ *n* [U] protection of ~s' interests.

con·sum·mate¹ /kən'sʌmət/ *adj* supremely skilled; perfect: ~ *skill/taste.*

con·sum·mate² /'kɒnsəmeɪt/ *vt* [VP6A] **1** accom-

plish; make perfect: *Her happiness was* ~*d when her father took her to Paris.* **2** make complete (esp marriage, by sexual intercourse).

con·sum·ma·tion /ˌkɒnsə'meɪʃn/ *n* [C,U] action or point of completing, perfecting, or fulfilling: *the* ~ *of a life's work/one's ambitions/a marriage.*

con·sump·tion /kən'sʌmpʃn/ *n* [U] **1** using up, consuming (of food, energy, materials, etc); the quantity consumed: *The* ~ *of beer did not go down when the tax was raised.* **2** (popular name for) pulmonary tuberculosis.

con·sump·tive /kən'sʌmptɪv/ *adj* suffering from, having a tendency to, consumption(2). □ *n* ~ person.

con·tact /'kɒntækt/ *n* **1** [U] (state of) touching or communication; (process of) coming together, esp in: *be in/out of* ~ *(with); come/bring into* ~ *(with)*: *Our troops are in* ~ *with the enemy. The opposing forces are now in/out of* ~ (*with each other*). *A steel cable came into* ~ *with an electric power line. We can learn much by being brought into* ~ *with other minds/opposing opinions, etc.* **make** ~ **(with)**, come into ~ (with), esp after searching, striving, etc: *I finally made* ~ *with him in Paris. We never really succeeded in making* ~. *They made* ~ *by radio/made radio* ~ *with headquarters.* **make/break** ~, complete/interrupt an electric circuit. **'**~ **lens**, one of thin plastic material made to fit closely over and in ~ with the eyeball to improve vision. **2** [C] meeting with a person; person one has met or will meet: *He made many useful social* ~*s while he was in Canada*, met people who could be useful to him. *Do you have any* ~*s in Rangoon?* **3** [C] connection (for electric current); device for effecting this. **4** [C] (med) person recently exposed to a contagious disease. □ *vt* [VP6A] get in ~ with (sb); reach (sb) (by message, telephone, etc): *Where can I* ~ *Jeff's wife?*

con·tagion /kən'teɪdʒən/ *n* [U] the spreading of disease by contact or close association; [C] disease that can be spread by contact; (fig) the spreading of ideas, false rumours, feelings, etc; [C] influence, etc that spreads: *A* ~ *of fear swept through the crowd.*

con·tagious /kən'teɪdʒəs/ *adj* **1** (of disease) spreading by contact: *Scarlet fever is* ~. **2** (of a person) in such a condition that he may spread disease. **3** (fig) spreading easily by example: ~ *laughter/enthusiasm. Yawning is* ~. ~**·ly** *adv*

con·tain /kən'teɪn/ *vt* [VP6A] (not in the progressive tenses) **1** have or hold within itself: *The atlas* ~*s forty maps, including three of Great Britain. Whisky* ~*s a large percentage of alcohol.* **2** be equal to: *A gallon* ~*s eight pints.* **3** be capable of holding: *How much does this bottle* ~? **4** keep feelings, enemy forces, etc under control, within limits: *Can't you* ~ *your enthusiasm? He couldn't* ~ *himself for joy*, was so happy that his feelings burst out. *He couldn't* ~ *his wine*, was sick, became drunk, etc. *Has the cholera outbreak been* ~*ed*, prevented from spreading? **5** (geom) form the boundary of: *The angle* ~*ed by the lines AB*

and AC in the triangle ABC is a right angle. **6** (maths) be divisible by, without a remainder: *12* ~*s 2, 3, 4 and 6.* ~**er** *n* **1** box, bottle, etc designed to ~ sth. **2** large metal box or other sealed ~er for transport of goods by road, rail, sea or air: '~er crane, large crane mounted on a gantry, used on quays, etc to move ~ers(2). '~er train/liner, one designed for such ~ers; '~er traffic; '~er depot, eg where ~ers are loaded and unloaded. ~·ment n [U] policy of preventing a State from extending its sphere of influence.

con·tami·nate /kən'tæmɪneɪt/ vt [VP6A] make dirty, impure or diseased (by touching, or adding sth impure): ~d clothing, eg by poison-gas or radioactive materials. Flies ~ food. His morals have been ~d by bad companions.

con·tami·na·tion /kən,tæmɪ'neɪʃn/ n 1 [U] contaminating or being contaminated: ~ of the water supply. 2 [C] that which contaminates.

con·temn /kən'tem/ vt [VP6A] (liter) despise; disregard.

con·tem·plate /'kɒntempleɪt/ vt,vi 1 [VP6A] look at (with the eyes, or in the mind): She stood contemplating her figure/herself in the mirror. 2 [VP6A,C,19C] have in view as a purpose, intention or possibility: She was contemplating a visit to London. I hope your mother does not ~ coming to stay with us. I do not ~ any opposition from him, do not think this is likely or possible. 3 [VP2A,6A] meditate (esp as a religious practice).

con·tem·pla·tion /,kɒntem'pleɪʃn/ n [U] contemplating; deep thought; intention; expectation: He sat there deep in ~.

con·tem·pla·tive /kən'templətɪv/ adj thoughtful; fond of contemplation; given up to religious contemplation.

con·tem·por·aneous /kən,tempə'reɪnɪəs/ adj ~ (with), originating, existing, happening, during the same period of time: ~ events. ~·ly adv

con·tem·por·ary /kən'tempərərɪ US: -əreri/ adj of the time or period to which reference is being made; belonging to the same time: a ~ record of events, one made by persons living at that time; furniture in ~ style, of the present time (contrasted with period(2) furniture). Dickens was ~ with Thackeray. □ n (pl -ries) person ~ with another: Jack and I were contemporaries at college.

con·tempt /kən'tempt/ n [U] 1 condition of being looked down upon or despised: to fall into ~ by foolish or bad behaviour. Such behaviour will bring you into ~. A man who is cruel to his children should be held in ~. 2 mental attitude of despising: We feel ~ for liars. beneath ~: Such an accusation is beneath ~, not worth despising (because it is so ridiculous, etc). 3 disregard or disrespect; total disregard: in ~ of all rules and regulations. He rushed forward in ~ of danger. He showed his ~ of death by rushing at the enemy. Familiarity breeds ~, (prov) ⇨ familiarity(1). ~ of 'court, disobedience to an order made by a court; disrespect shown to a judge.

con·tempt·ible /kən'temptəbl/ adj deserving or provoking contempt.

con·temptu·ous /kən'temptʃʊəs/ adj showing contempt: ~ of public opinion. ~·ly adv

con·tend /kən'tend/ vi,vt 1 [VP3A] ~ with/ against/for, struggle, be in rivalry or competition: ~ing with difficulties; ~ing for a prize; ~ing passions, strong feelings of different kinds (eg pity, a sense of justice) that make decision difficult. 2 [VP9] argue, assert: ~ that the universe is expanding. ~er n competitor, rival, eg one who challenges the holder of a boxing title.

con·tent¹ /kən'tent/ adj (not used attrib; ⇨ contented below) 1 ~ (with), not wanting more; satisfied with what one has: Are you ~ with your present salary? She is ~ with very little. 2 ~ to do sth, willing or ready (to do sth): I am ~ to remain where I am now. I should be well ~ (= quite pleased) to do so. □ n [U] condition of being satisfied: living in peace and ~. to one's heart's ~, to the extent that brings satisfaction. □ vt [VP6A,14] ~ sb/oneself (with), make ~; satisfy: There's no ~ing some people, It's impossible to please or satisfy them. As there's no butter we must ~ ourselves (= be satisfied) with dry bread. ~ed adj satisfied; showing or feeling ~: with a ~ed look/smile. ~·ed·ly adv ~·ment n [U] state of being ~.

con·tent² /'kɒntent/ n 1 (pl) that which is contained in sth: the ~s of a room/a book/a schoolboy's pockets, etc. table of ~s, list of the matter in a book, periodical, etc. 2 (sing or pl; with sing v) the amount which a vessel will hold; capacity: the ~(s) of a barrel or cask. 3 (sing) substance; essential meaning (of a book, speech, etc as opposed to its form): Do you approve of the ~ of the article/speech? 4 ~ (of sth), (sing; preceded by a n) part (of it): a high fat ~; the silver ~ of a coin; the sugar ~ of milk.

con·ten·tion /kən'tenʃn/ n 1 [U] contending(2); quarrelling or disputing: This is not a time for ~. ⇨ bone. 2 [C] argument used in contending: My ~ is that....

con·ten·tious /kən'tenʃəs/ adj quarrelsome; likely to cause contention: a ~ clause in a treaty.

con·termi·nous /kɒn'tɜːmɪnəs/ adj = coterminous.

con·test /kən'test/ vt,vi 1 [VP6A,9] argue; debate; dispute: ~ a statement/point, try to show that it is wrong; ~ sb's right/that sb has a right to do sth. 2 [VP3A] contend(1). 3 [VP6A] fight or compete for; try to win: ~ a seat in Parliament. The enemy ~ed every inch of the ground, fought with determination not to retreat. □ n /'kɒntest/ [C] struggle; fight; competition: a keen ~ for the prize; a ~ of skill; a 'speed ~; (boxing) a three-round featherweight ~. ~·ant /kən'testənt/ n one who ~s.

con·text /'kɒntekst/ n [C,U] 1 what comes before and after a word, phrase, statement, etc helping to fix the meaning: Can't you guess the meaning of the word from the ~? Don't quote my words out of ~, eg so as to give a false impression of what I mean. 2 circumstances in which an event occurs. con·tex·tual /kən'tekstʃʊəl/ adj according to the ~.

con·ti·guity /,kɒntɪ'gjuːətɪ/ n [U] the state of being contiguous.

con·tigu·ous /kən'tɪgjʊəs/ adj ~ to, (formal) touching; neighbouring; near. ~·ly adv

con·ti·nence /'kɒntɪnəns/ n [U] self-control; self-restraint (esp of passions and desires).

con·ti·nent¹ /'kɒntɪnənt/ n one of the main land masses (Europe, Asia, Africa, etc). the C~, (as used by people in GB) the mainland of Europe. con·ti·nen·tal /,kɒntɪ'nentl/ adj 1 belonging to, typical of, a ~: a ~al climate. 2 of the mainland of Europe: ~al wars/alliances. ~al breakfast, one of coffee and bread only. the ~al Sunday, as in Europe (with wider freedom for theatrical and other entertainments, sport, etc than formerly in GB). □ n inhabitant of the mainland of Europe.

con·ti·nent² /'kɒntɪnənt/ adj (formal) self-controlled; having control of one's feelings and (esp sexual) desires; (med) able to retain excretion voluntarily.

con·tin·gency /kən'tındʒənsı/ *n* [U] uncertainty of occurrence; [C] (*pl* -cies) uncertain event; event that happens by chance; sth that may happen if sth else happens: *to be prepared for all contingencies; a result that depends upon contingencies;* (attrib) ~ *arrangements/plans.*

con·tin·gent¹ /kən'tındʒənt/ *adj* **1** uncertain; accidental: *a ~ advantage.* **2** ~ **upon,** dependent upon (sth that may or may not happen).

con·tin·gent² /kən'tındʒənt/ *n* [C] body of troops, number of ships, lent or supplied to form part of a larger force; group of persons forming part of a larger group.

con·tin·ual /kən'tınjʊəl/ *adj* going on all the time without stopping, or with only short breaks: *Aren't you tired of this ~ rain?* ~·**ly** *adv* again and again; without stopping.

con·tin·uance /kən'tınjʊəns/ *n* (*sing* only) **1** time for which sth continues; duration (the more usu word): *during the ~ of the war.* **2** remaining; staying: *a ~ of prosperity.*

con·tinu·ation /kən,tınjʊ'eıʃn/ *n* ~ **(of), 1** [U] continuing; starting again after a stop: *C~ of study after the holidays was difficult at first.* **2** [C] part, etc by which sth is continued: *The May number of the magazine will contain a ~ of the story.*

con·tinue /kən'tınju:/ *vi,vt* **1** [VP2A,B,D,E,6A,D,7A] go further; go on (being); go on (doing); stay at/in; remain at/in: *The desert ~d as far as the eye could reach. How far does this road ~? I hope this wet weather will not ~. He hopes to ~ at school for another year. The weather ~d calm. He ~d to live with his parents after his marriage. How long will you ~ working? You must ~ your study of French.* **2** [VP6A,2A] start again after stopping: *The story will be ~d in next month's issue. 'Well,' he ~d, 'when we arrived...'* **3** [VP14] retain (sb in office, etc): *The Colonial Secretary was ~d in office.*

con·ti·nu·ity /,kɒntı'nju:ətı US: -'nu:-/ *n* [U] **1** the state of being continuous: *There is no ~ of subject in a dictionary.* **2** (cinema, TV) scenario; arrangement of the parts of a story: *Films and TV programmes are often made out of ~,* eg a scene in the middle may be filmed before a scene near the beginning. **3** connecting comments, announcements, etc, made between the parts of a broadcast programme.

con·tinu·ous /kən'tınjʊəs/ *adj* going on without a break: ~ *performance, 1.00pm to 11.30pm,* eg at a cinema. ~ **tense,** ⇨ progressive(1). ~·**ly** *adv*

con·tinu·um /kən'tınjʊəm/ *n* (pl -uums or -ua /-ʊə/) **1** sth that is continuous. **2** graded sequence of differences. ⇨ cline.

con·tort /kən'tɔ:t/ *vt* [VP6A,14] force or twist out of the usual shape or appearance: *a face ~ed with pain;* (fig) ~ *a word out of its ordinary meaning.*

con·tor·tion /kən'tɔ:ʃn/ *n* [U] contorting or being contorted (esp of the face or body); [C] instance of this; contorted condition: *the ~s of an acrobat.* ~·**ist** /-ʃənɪst/ *n* acrobat clever at contorting his body.

con·tour /'kɒntʊə(r)/ *n* [C] outline (of a coast, mountain range, etc); (on a map, design, etc) line separating differently coloured parts. '~ **line,** line (on a map) showing all points at the same height above sea-level. '~ **map,** one with ~ lines at fixed intervals (eg of 25 metres). '~ **ploughing,**

ploughing in which furrows follow ~ lines (on a hillside, etc) to prevent soil erosion. □ *vt* [VP6A] mark with ~ lines; make (a road) round the ~ of a hill.

contra- /,kɒntrə/ *pref* against.

contra·band /'kɒntrəbænd/ *n* [U] bringing into, taking out of, a country goods contrary to the law; (trade in) goods so brought in or taken out. ~ **of war,** goods (eg ammunition) supplied by neutral countries to countries that are at war, which can be seized by any of the countries at war: (attrib) ~ *goods;* ~ *trade.*

contra·cep·tion /,kɒntrə'sepʃn/ *n* [U] practice, method, of preventing or planning conception(2).

contra·cep·tive /,kɒntrə'septıv/ *n* [C] device or drug intended to prevent conception(2). □ *adj* preventing conception: ~ *pills/devices.*

con·tract¹ /'kɒntrækt/ *n* **1** [C] binding agreement (between persons, groups, states); agreement to supply goods, do work, etc at a fixed price. **enter into/make a ~ (with sb) (for sth),** make such an agreement. **exchange ~s,** eg for the purchase of a house. **sign a ~,** eg for the sale of land or buildings. [U] (phrases in which no article is used): *bind oneself by ~; work to be done by private ~; work on ~; breach of ~; conditions of ~;* (attrib use) ~ *price/date,* price, date, agreed to. **2** '~ '**bridge,** kind of bridge² in which only tricks bid¹(5) and won count towards game¹(4).

con·tract² /kən'trækt/ *vt,vi* **1** [VP6A,14,4A] ~ **(with) (for),** make a contract or agreement: ~ *a marriage;* ~ *to build a bridge;* ~ *with a firm for 1000 tons of cement;* ~ *an alliance with another country.* [VP2C] ~ **out (of),** /,kɒntrækt 'aʊt/, reject, abandon, the terms of a contract: ~ *out of an agreement/alliance.* **2** [VP6A] ~ **debts,** become liable for them. **3** [VP6A] catch (an illness); form; acquire (eg bad habits). ~**or** /-tə(r)/ *n* person, business firm, that enters into ~s: *engineering ~ors; army ~ors.* **con·trac·tual** /kən'træktʃʊəl/ *adj* of (the nature of) a ~.

con·tract³ /kən'trækt/ *vt,vi* [VP6A,14,2A,C] **1** make or become smaller or shorter: *Metals ~ as they become cool. 'I will' is ~ed to 'I'll'.* **2** make or become tighter or narrower: *to ~ a muscle; to ~ the brows/forehead. The valley ~s as one goes up it.* ~·**ible** *adj* that can be ~ed. **con·trac·tile** /kən'træktaıl US: -tl/ *adj* that can ~ or be ~ed: ~*ile wings,* eg of an insect, that can be folded over the body.

con·trac·tion /kən'trækʃn/ *n* **1** [U] contracting or being contracted: *the ~ of a muscle; the ~ of the mercury in a thermometer.* **2** [C] sth contracted; shortened form, as *can't* for *cannot.*

con·tra·dict /,kɒntrə'dıkt/ *vt* [VP6A] **1** deny the truth of (sth said or written); deny (the words of a person): *to ~ a statement. Don't ~ me.* **2** (of facts, statements, etc) be contrary to: *The reports ~ each other.* **con·tra·dic·tion** /,kɒntrə'dıkʃn/ *n* **1** [U] ~ing; [C] instance of this. **2** [U] absence of agreement. **be in ~ion with,** = ~: *Your statements today are in ~ion with (ie they ~) what you said yesterday.* [C] instance of this. **a ~ion in terms,** statement that includes words that ~ each other (eg *a generous miser).* **con·tra·dic·tory** /,kɒntrə-'dıktərı/ *adj* ~ing: ~*ory statements/ reports.*

contra·dis·tinc·tion /,kɒntrədı'stıŋkʃn/ *n* (formal) distinction by contrast: *the crossing of the Atlantic by air in a few hours, in ~ to the longer journey by sea.*

contra·dis·tin·guish /ˌkɒntrədɪ'stɪŋgwɪʃ/ vt [VP14] ∼ **from,** distinguish by contrast.

con·tralto /kən'træltəʊ/ (pl ∼s /-təʊz/) n lowest female voice; woman with, musical part to be sung by, such a voice.

con·trap·tion /kən'træpʃn/ n (colloq) strange-looking apparatus or device.

contra·pun·tal /ˌkɒntrə'pʌntl/ adj of or in counter-point.

contra·riety /ˌkɒntrə'raɪətɪ/ n (formal) [U] opposition or antagonism (in nature, quality or action); [C] (pl -ties) sth that is inconsistent or contrary: contrarieties in nature.

con·trari·wise /'kɒntrərɪwaɪz/ adv 1 on the contrary. 2 in the opposite way. 3 /kɒn'treərɪwaɪz/ perversely; in a manner showing opposition.

con·trary[1] /'kɒntrərɪ US: -trerɪ/ adj 1 opposite (in nature or tendency): 'Hot' and 'cold' are ∼ terms. 2 (of the wind and weather) unfavourable (for sailing): The ship was delayed by ∼ winds. 3 (/kən'treərɪ/) obstinate; self-willed. 4 ∼ to, (compound prep) in opposition to; against: to act ∼ to the rules; events that went ∼ to my interests. What you have done is ∼ to the doctor's orders. The result was ∼ to expectation. **con·trar·ily** /'kɒntrərəlɪ US: -trerəlɪ/ adv in a ∼ manner. **con·trari·ness** /-nɪs/ n being ∼.

con·trary[2] /'kɒntrərɪ US: -trerɪ/ n (pl -ries) 1 [U] **the** ∼, opposite: The ∼ of 'wet' is 'dry'. **on the** ∼, phrase used to make a denial or contradiction more emphatic: 'You've nothing to do now, I suppose.'—'On the ∼, I have piles of work.' **to the** ∼, to the opposite effect: I will come on Monday unless you write to the ∼, telling me not to come. I shall continue to believe it until I get proof to the ∼, proof that it is not true. 2 [C] **by contraries, (a)** ∼ to expectation: Many things in our lives go by contraries. **(b)** by way of opposition: She said that dreams go by contraries, eg that a dream about bad fortune may foretell good fortune.

con·trast[1] /kən'trɑːst US: -'træst/ vt, vi 1 [VP6A,14] ∼ **(with/and),** compare so that differences are made clear: C∼ these imported goods with/and the domestic product. It is interesting to ∼ the two speakers. 2 [VP2C,3A] ∼ **(with),** show a difference when compared: His actions ∼ sharply with his promises. His actions and his promises ∼ sharply.

con·trast[2] /'kɒntrɑːst US: -træst/ n 1 [U] the act of contrasting: C∼ may make something appear more beautiful than it is when seen alone. 2 ∼ **(to/ with);** ∼ **(between/of),** [C,U] difference which is clearly seen when unlike things are put together; sth showing such a difference: There is a remarkable ∼ between the two brothers. The white walls make a ∼ to/with the black carpet. The ∼ of light and shade is important in photography. **by/in** ∼ **(with); in** ∼ **(to),** when a ∼ is made (to/with): His white hair was in sharp ∼ to his dark skin. Tom's marks (eg 90 per cent) by ∼ with Harry's marks (eg 35 per cent) were excellent.

con·tra·vene /ˌkɒntrə'viːn/ vt [VP6A] 1 act in opposition to; go against (a law, a custom). 2 dispute, attack (a statement, a principle). 3 (of things) conflict with; be out of harmony with.

con·tra·ven·tion /ˌkɒntrə'venʃn/ n [C,U] act of contravening (a law, etc). **in** ∼ **of sth,** so as to break or violate it.

contre·temps /'kɒntrətɒm/ n (pl unchanged) (F) unfortunate happening; unexpected hitch; setback.

con·trib·ute /kən'trɪbjuːt/ vt, vi ∼ **(to),** 1 [VP6A,14,2A,3A] join with others in giving help, money, etc (to a common cause, for a purpose); give ideas, suggestions, etc: ∼ food and clothing for the refugees; ∼ to the Red Cross; ∼ new information on a scientific problem. 2 [VP3A] have a share in; help to bring about: Drink ∼d to his ruin. 3 [VP14,3A] write (articles, etc) and send in: Mr Green has ∼d (poems) to the 'London Magazine' for several years. **con·tribu·tor** /-tə(r)/ n person who ∼s (money to a fund, articles to a periodical, etc).

con·tri·bu·tion /ˌkɒntrɪ'bjuːʃn/ n 1 [U] act of contributing; [C] sth contributed: ∼s to the relief fund. Do you consider ∼s to the village funds a duty or a pleasure? The editor is short of ∼s for the May issue. 2 [C,U] compulsory payment. **lay under** ∼, require ∼s from.

con·tribu·tory /kən'trɪbjʊtrɪ US: -tɔːrɪ/ adj 1 helping to bring about: ∼ negligence, eg that helped to cause an accident. 2 for which contributions are to be made: a ∼'pension scheme.

con·trite /'kɒntraɪt/ adj filled with, showing, deep sorrow for wrongdoing: a ∼ heart. ∼·ly adv

con·trition /kən'trɪʃn/ n [U] deep sorrow (for sins, wrongdoing); repentance.

con·triv·ance /kən'traɪvəns/ n 1 [U] act or manner of contriving: the ∼ by which botanists fertilize flowers to obtain hybrids. 2 [U] capacity to invent: Some things are beyond human ∼. 3 [C] sth contrived; deceitful practice; invention or mechanical device: a ∼ to record both sides of a telephone conversation on magnetic tape.

con·trive /kən'traɪv/ vt, vi 1 [VP6A,7A] invent; design; find a way of doing (sth), of causing (sth to happen): to ∼ a means of escape from prison; to ∼ to live on a small income. He ∼d to make matters worse, made them worse by his efforts, even though this was not his intention. Can you ∼ (= manage) to be here early? 2 [VP2A] (liter) manage successfully: She finds it difficult to ∼ (= manage her housekeeping economically) now that prices are rising every month. **con·triver** /kən'traɪvə(r)/ n (liter) one who ∼s, esp one who manages household affairs: His wife is a good ∼r.

con·trol[1] /kən'trəʊl/ n 1 [U] power or authority to direct, order, or restrain: children who lack parental ∼, who are not kept in order by parents. **be in** ∼ **(of),** be in command, in charge. **be/come/ bring/get under** ∼, be, become, cause to be, under authority, under restraint, in order, working properly: get flood waters under ∼. **be/get out of** ∼, in a state where authority, etc is lost: The children are/have got out of ∼. **have/get/keep** ∼ **(over/of),** have, get, keep authority, power, etc: a teacher who has no ∼ over his class; get ∼ over a horse, make it obey. **lose** ∼ **(of),** be unable to manage or contain: lose ∼ of one's temper. **take** ∼ **(of),** take authority: We must find someone to take overall ∼ of this project. 2 [U] management; guidance: ∼ of traffic/traffic ∼; ∼ of foreign exchange. **'birth-**∼, n planning of the number of births, eg by the use of contraceptives. 3 [C] means of regulating, restraining, keeping in order; check: Government ∼s on trade and industry. The chairman's power to veto a proposal is a ∼ over what the committee may do. 4 [C] standard of comparison for results of an experiment: The tests were given to three groups, Group Two being used as a ∼. We must make more ∼ experiments. 5 (usu pl) means by which a machine, etc is operated or regulated: *the ~s of an aircraft*, for direction, altitude, etc; *a car with dual ~s/a dual-~ car; the ~s of a transistor radio*, eg *the volume ~*, regulating the volume of sound; *the '~ tower of an airport*, for regulating air traffic. **6** [C] station at which cars taking part in a race may stop for overhaul, etc. **7** [C] (spiritualism) spirit actuating a medium(4).

con·trol² /kən'trəʊl/ *vt* -ll-) [VP6A] **1** have control, authority, power over: *to ~ one's temper/ expenditure/a horse/oneself*. **~ling interest** *n* (fin) holding of enough stock(5) of a company to ~ policy. **2** regulate (prices, etc). **3** check; verify: *to ~ the accounts*. **~·lable** *adj* that can be ~led.

con·trol·ler /kən'trəʊlə(r)/ *n* **1** (also **comptroller**) person who controls expenditure and accounts. **2** person who controls or directs a department or division of a large organization: *~ of BBC Radio*.

con·tro·ver·sial /ˌkɒntrə'vɜːʃl/ *adj* likely to cause controversy: *a ~ speech;* (of persons) fond of controversy. **~·ly** /-ʃəlɪ/ *adv* **~·ist** *n* person who is fond of or good at controversy.

con·tro·versy /'kɒntrəvɜːsɪ/ *n* (*pl* -sies) [C,U] prolonged argument, esp over social, moral or political matters: *engage in (a) ~ with/against sb (on or about sth); a question that has given rise to much ~; facts that are beyond ~*, that cannot be argued about.

con·tro·vert /ˌkɒntrə'vɜːt/ *vt* [VP6A] (formal) dispute about; deny; oppose.

con·tu·ma·cious /ˌkɒntjuː'meɪʃəs/ *adj* (formal) stubborn and rebellious; obstinate and disobedient. **~·ly** *adv*

con·tu·macy /'kɒntjʊməsɪ *US:* kən'tuːməsɪ/ *n* [U] (formal) obstinate resistance; stubborn disobedience; [C] (*pl* -cies) instance of this.

con·tu·melious /ˌkɒntjuː'miːlɪəs *US:* -tə'm-/ *adj* (formal) insolent; opprobrious. **~·ly** *adv*

con·tu·mely /'kɒntjuːmlɪ *US:* kən'tuːməlɪ/ *n* [U] (formal) abusive language or treatment; [C] instance of this; humiliating insult.

con·tuse /kən'tjuːz *US:* -'tuːz/ *vt* [VP6A] (med) bruise; injure (part of the body) by a blow, without breaking the skin. **con·tusion** /kən'tjuːʒn *US:* -'tuː-/ *n* [C] bruise.

co·nun·drum /kə'nʌndrəm/ *n* [C] puzzling question, esp one asked for fun; riddle.

con·ur·ba·tion /ˌkɒnɜː'beɪʃn/ *n* [C] area of large urban communities where towns, etc have spread and become joined beyond their administrative boundaries.

con·va·lesce /ˌkɒnvə'les/ *vi* [VP2A] regain health and strength after an illness: *She is convalescing after a long illness*. **con·va·les·cent** /ˌkɒnvə'lesnt/ *n, adj* (person who is) recovering from illness: *a ~nt hospital*, one for ~nts. **con·va·les·cence** /ˌkɒnvə'lesns/ *n* [U] gradual recovery of health and strength.

con·vec·tion /kən'vekʃn/ *n* [U] the conveying of heat from one part of a liquid or gas to another by the movement of heated substances.

con·vec·tor /kən'vektə(r)/ *n* apparatus (for heating a room, etc) by which air is warmed as it passes over hot surfaces.

con·vene /kən'viːn/ *vt, vi* **1** [VP6A] summon (persons) to come together; form (a meeting, etc): *~ the people/the meeting*. **2** [VP2A] come together (for a meeting, council, etc). **con·vener** *n* member (of a society, etc) whose duty it is to ~ meetings.

con·veni·ence /kən'viːnɪəns/ *n* **1** [U] the quality of

being convenient or suitable; freedom from difficulty or worry: *I keep my reference books near my desk for ~. The house was planned for ~, not for display*, ie planned so as to be easy to live and work in. *Please send the goods at your earliest ~*, at the earliest time that does not give you trouble. *Please do the work at your own ~*, how and when it best suits you. *It was a marriage of ~*, one in which material advantage was the chief consideration. **2** [C] appliance, device, arrangement, etc that is useful, helpful or convenient: *It was a great ~ to have the doctor living near us. The house has all modern ~s*, eg central heating, hot water supply, points for electric current. *The nearest public ~s* (= WC's, lavatories) *are in West Street*. **make a ~ of sb**, use his services unreasonably; take too much advantage of his good nature. **flag of ~,** ⇨ flag¹. **'~ food** *n* [U,C] food (e g sold in a tin, packet etc) that needs very little preparation.

con·veni·ent /kən'viːnɪənt/ *adj ~ (for)*, suitable; handy; serving to avoid trouble or difficulty; easy to get to or at: *Will it be ~ for you to start work tomorrow? This is a ~ tool for the job. Will the 3.50 train be ~ for you? We must arrange a ~ time and place for the meeting*. **~·ly** *adv* in a ~ manner: *My house is ~ly near the bus stop*.

con·vent /'kɒnvənt *US:* -vent/ *n* **1** society of women (called *nuns*) living apart from others in the service of God. ⇨ monastery. **~ (school)** *n* one run by nuns. **2** building(s) in which nuns live and work: *enter a ~*, become a nun.

con·ven·ticle /kən'ventɪkl/ *n* (building used for) secret religious meetings.

con·ven·tion /kən'venʃn/ *n* **1** [C] conference of members of a society, political party, etc devoted to a particular purpose (eg election of candidates); conference of persons in business, commerce, etc: *the Democratic Party C~*. Cf *conference* in GB. **2** [C] agreement between States, rulers, etc (less formal than a treaty): *the Geneva C~s*, about the treatment of prisoners of war, etc. **3** [U] general (usu tacit) consent (esp about forms of behaviour); [C] practice or custom based on general consent: *When men wore hats, ~ required them to raise them when they met a woman they knew. It is silly to be a slave to ~/to social ~s*. **4** [C] (in various card and board games, esp bridge) practice that is generally followed in bidding, leading cards, making an opening move in chess, etc.

con·ven·tional /kən'venʃənl/ *adj* **1** based on convention(3,4): *~ greetings; a few ~ remarks*. **2** following what has been customary; traditional: *a ~ design for a carpet; ~ art; ~ weapons*, ie excluding atomic bombs, etc; *a ~ power station*, using coal or oil as fuel (contrasted with heat from a nuclear reactor). **~·ly** /-ʃənlɪ/ *adv*

con·ven·tion·al·ity /kənˌvenʃə'nælətɪ/ *n* **1** [U] conventional quality or character: *the ~ of the paintings at the Academy Exhibition*. **2** [C,U] (*pl* -ties) convention(3).

con·verge /kən'vɜːdʒ/ *vi* [VP2A,2C,3A] *~ (at/ on/upon)* (of lines, moving objects, opinions) come towards each other and meet at a point; tend to do this: *armies converging on the capital. Parallel lines ~ at infinity*. **con·ver·gence** /kən'vɜːdʒəns/ *n* **con·ver·gent** *adj*

con·ver·sant /kən'vɜːsnt/ *adj ~ with*, having a knowledge of: *~ with all the rules*.

con·ver·sa·tion /ˌkɒnvə'seɪʃn/ *n* [U] talking; [C] talk: *I saw him in ~ with a friend. No ~ while I'm* *playing the piano, please. I've had several ~s with him.* **~al** /-ʃənl/ *adj* (of words, etc) used in, characteristic of, ~; colloquial.

con·verse¹ /kən'vɜːs/ *vi* [VP2A,C,3A] ~ **(with sb)** *(about/on sth),* (formal) talk.

con·verse² /'kɒnvɜːs/ *n, adj* **1** (idea, statement which is) opposite (to another). **2** (logic) form of words produced by transposing some of the words of another: *'He is happy but not rich' is the ~ of 'He is rich but not happy'.* **~·ly** *adv*

con·verse³ /'kɒnvɜːs/ *n* [U] (old use) conversation.

con·ver·sion /kən'vɜːʃn *US:* -ʒn/ *n* [U] converting or being converted: *the ~ of cream into butter/of forest land into arable land/of pagans to Christianity; the improper ~ of public funds to one's own use,* eg by a government official; [C] instance of ~: *many ~s to Buddhism; building firms which specialize in house ~s,* eg of large houses into flats.

con·vert¹ /kən'vɜːt/ *vt* [VP6A,14] **1** ~ *sth (from sth) (to/into sth),* change (from one form, use, etc into another): *to ~ rags into paper/securities into cash/pounds into francs;* ~ *club funds to one's own use,* use them unlawfully. **2** ~ *sb (from sth) (to sth),* cause him to change his beliefs, etc: *to ~ a man from atheism to Christianity.* **3** (Rugby football) complete (a try) by kicking a goal. **~ed** *part adj* that has been ~ed: *a ~ed mews,* stable(s) rebuilt, decorated, etc for use as a residence.

con·vert² /'kɒnvɜːt/ *n* person converted, esp to a different religion (or from no religion), or to different principles: *a ~ to socialism.*

con·vert·ible /kən'vɜːtəbl/ *adj* that can be converted: *Banknotes are not usually ~ into gold nowadays.* □ *n* (esp US) touring car with a folding or detachable roof. **con·verti·bil·ity** /kənˌvɜːtə'bɪlətɪ/ *n*

con·vex /'kɒnveks/ *adj* with the surface curved like the outside of a ball: *a ~ lens.* ⇨ concave. **~·ly** *adv* **~·ity** /kɒn'veksətɪ/ *n* state of being ~.

convex

concave

con·vey /kən'veɪ/ *vt* [VP6A,14] **1** ~ *(from) (to),* take, carry: *Pipes ~ hot water from this boiler to every part of the building. This train ~s both passengers and goods.* **2** ~ *(to sb),* make known ideas, feelings, etc to another person: *Words fail to ~ my meaning. This picture will ~ to you some idea of the beauty of the scenery.* **3** ~ *to,* (legal) give full legal rights (in land or property): *The land was ~ed to his brother.* **~er,** **-or** /-veɪə(r)/ *n* person or thing that ~s: *a 'coal ~er.* '**~er-belt,** (eg in a factory) flexible band or chain moving over wheels for ~ing packages, etc.

con·vey·ance /kən'veɪəns/ *n* **1** [U] conveying. **2** [C] sth which conveys; carriage or other vehicle. **3** [C,U] (legal) (document) conveying property. **con·vey·ancer** *n* lawyer who prepares ~s.

con·vict¹ /kən'vɪkt/ *vt* [VP6A,14] ~ *sb (of sth)* **1** cause (sb) to be certain that he has done wrong, made a mistake: *to ~ sb of his errors; to be ~ed of sin.* ⇨ convince. **2** (of a jury or a judge) declare in a law court that (sb) is guilty (*of* crime): *He was ~ed of murder.*

con·vict² /'kɒnvɪkt/ *n* person convicted of crime and undergoing punishment.

con·vic·tion /kən'vɪkʃn/ *n* **1** [U] the convicting of a

person for a crime; [C] instance of this: *The ~ of the accused man surprised us. There were five acquittals and six ~s.* **2** [U] the act of convincing, of bringing certainty to the mind. *(not) carry ~,* (not) be convincing. *be open to ~,* be ready to listen to evidence, etc that may convince one. **3** [C,U] firm or assured belief: *I speak in the full ~ that...,* firmly convinced that.... *Do you always act up to your ~s,* do what you are convinced is right, just, etc?

con·vince /kən'vɪns/ *vt* [VP6A,11,14] ~ *sb (of sth/that...)* make (sb) feel certain; cause (sb) to realize: *I am ~d of his honesty/that he is honest. We couldn't ~ him of his mistake.* **con·vinc·ing** *adj* that ~s: *a convincing speaker/argument.* **con·vinc·ing·ly** *adv.* to speak convincingly. **con·vinc·ible** /kən'vɪnsəbl/ *adj* willing, ready, to be ~d.

con·viv·ial /kən'vɪvɪəl/ *adj* **1** gay; fond of chatting, merry-making, drinking, etc:~ *companions.* **2** marked by merry-making, etc: *a ~ evening.* **~·ly** /-ɪəlɪ/ *adv* **~·ity** /kənˌvɪvɪ'ælətɪ/ *n* (*pl* -ties) [C,U] merry-making; being ~.

con·vo·ca·tion /ˌkɒnvə'keɪʃn/ *n* **1** [U] convoking; calling together. **2** [C] legislative assembly of the Church of England, of graduates of some universities.

con·voke /kən'vəʊk/ *vt* [VP6A] (formal) call together, summon (a meeting): *to ~ Parliament.*

con·vol·uted /'kɒnvəluːtɪd/ *part adj* (zool, biol) coiled; twisted (eg a ram's horn); (fig) complicated and difficult: *a ~ argument.*

con·vol·ution /ˌkɒnvə'luːʃn/ *n* [C] coil; twist: *the ~s of a snake.*

con·vol·vu·lus /kən'vɒlvjʊləs/ *n* (*pl* ~es /-ləsɪz/) kinds of twining plant including bindweed and morning-glory (with white, pink or blue flowers).

con·voy¹ /'kɒnvɔɪ/ *vt* [VP6A] (esp of a warship) go with, escort (other ships) to protect (them): *The troopships were ~ed across the Atlantic.*

con·voy² /'kɒnvɔɪ/ *n* **1** [U] convoying or being convoyed; protection: *The supply ships sailed under ~.* **2** [C] protecting force (of warships, troops, etc). **3** [C] ship, number of ships, under escort; supplies, etc under escort: *The ~ was attacked by submarines.*

con·vulse /kən'vʌls/ *vt* [VP6A] (usu in passive) cause violent movements or disturbances: *~d with laughter/anger/toothache; a country that has often been ~d by earthquakes/civil war.*

con·vul·sion /kən'vʌlʃn/ *n* [C] **1** violent disturbance: *a ~ of nature,* eg an earthquake; *civil ~s,* riots, etc; *a political ~,* eg an attempt at revolution. **2** (usu *pl*) violent irregular movement of a limb or limbs, or of the body, caused by contraction of muscles: *The child's ~s filled us with fear.* **3** (*pl*) violent fit of laughter: *The story was so funny that we were all in ~s.*

con·vul·sive /kən'vʌlsɪv/ *adj* violently disturbing; having or producing convulsions: *~ movements.*

cony, coney /'kəʊnɪ/ *n* (*pl* conies, coneys) **1** (US) rabbit. **2** rabbit-skin, esp when dyed and prepared so as to resemble the fur of some other animal.

coo /kuː/ *vi,vt, n* (*pt,pp* cooed /kuːd/, *pres p* cooing) [VP2A] (make a) soft, murmuring sound (as of doves); [VP6A] say in a soft murmur: *to coo one's words.* ⇨ bill².

cook /kʊk/ *vt,vi* **1** [VP6A,2A,12B,13B] prepare (food) by heating (eg boiling, baking, roasting, frying). ~ *sb's goose,* ⇨ goose. **2** [VP2A] undergo ~ing: *These apples ~ well.* '**~ing apple,**

pear, etc, suitable for ~ing. Cf *dessert/eating apples*. **3** [VP15B] ~ **up,** concoct, invent (a story, tale, etc): *Don't give me some ~ed-up yarn!* **4** [VP6A] tamper with; prepare fraudulently: ~ *the books/the accounts,* falsify them. □ *n* person who ~s food. **'~·book** *n* = cookery-book. **'~-house** *n* detached or outdoor kitchen (eg in a camp); ship's galley. **~·ing** *n* [U] **'~ing lessons.**

cooker /'kʊkə(r)/ *n* **1** (esp in compounds, as '*oil-~, 'gas-~*) apparatus, stove, for cooking food. **2** kind of fruit, etc (esp apples, pears, plums) grown for cooking: *These apples are good ~s.* Cf *dessert apples,* to be eaten uncooked.

cook·ery /'kʊkərı/ *n* [U] art and practice of cooking. **'~-book,** one that deals with ~; book of cooking recipes.

cooky, cookie /'kʊkı/ *n* (*pl* -kies) (Scot) small, flat, thin, sweet cake (esp home-made); (US) biscuit.

cool¹ /ku:l/ *adj* **1** between warm and cold: ~ *autumn weather. Let's sit in the shade and keep ~. The coffee's not ~ enough to drink.* **2** providing or allowing a feeling between warm and cold: *a ~ room/dress.* **3** calm; unexcited: *Keep ~! He was always ~ in the face of danger. He has a ~ head,* doesn't get agitated. Hence, **,~-'headed** *adj* **4** impudent in a calm way; without shame: *What ~ behaviour—taking my lawn-mower without asking my permission!* **5** (of behaviour) not showing interest or enthusiasm: *They gave the prime minister a ~ reception.* **play it ~,** (colloq) deal calmly with a situation; be relaxed. **6** (of sums of money, distances, etc) putting emphasis on the figure, and perhaps suggesting complacency: *My new car cost me a ~ thousand. He suggested that we should walk a ~ twenty miles farther.* **7** (US sl) pleasant; fine. □ *n* **1** (usu **the ~**) ~ air or place; **~ness:** *in the ~ of the evening; the ~ of the forest.* **2** [U] (colloq) composure. **keep one's ~,** remain calm, unworried. **~·ly** /'ku:llı/ *adv* **~·ness** *n*

cool² /ku:l/ *vt,vi* [VP6A,2A] make or become cool: *The rain has ~ed the air. Has his anger ~ed yet?* [VP3C] ~ **down/off,** (esp fig) become calm, less excited or enthusiastic: *Her passion for me has ~ed down.* **a ,~ing 'off period,** (in industrial disputes, etc) a compulsory delay (to ~ tempers) before a threatened strike. **~ one's heels,** be kept waiting: *Let him ~ his heels in the outer office—that will teach him to be more polite.* **'~ing-tower** *n* large container used in industry to ~ hot water before re-using it.

cool·ant /'ku:lənt/ *n* [C,U] (kind of) fluid used for cooling (eg in nuclear reactors).

cooler /'ku:lə(r)/ *n* container in which things are cooled: *a wine/butter ~*; (sl) prison cell.

coolie /'ku:lı/ *n* ⚠ (sl, derog) unskilled Asian labourer.

coon /ku:n/ *n* **1** raccoon. **2** ⚠ (sl, derog) Negro.

coop /ku:p/ *n* cage, esp for hens with small chickens. □ *vt* [VP6A,15B] ~ **up,** put in a ~; confine (a person): *How long are we going to stay ~ed up in here?*

co-op /'kəʊ ɒp/ *n* **the ~,** (colloq) the co-operative society (shop, store): *She does all her shopping at the ~.*

cooper /'ku:pə(r)/ *n* maker of tubs, barrels, casks, etc.

co·op·er·ate /kəʊ'ɒpəreıt/ *vi* [VP2A,3A,4A] ~ **(with sb) (in doing/to do sth),** work or act together in order to bring about a result: ~ *with*

friends in starting a social club. *Everything ~d to make our holiday a success.* **co-op·er·ator** /-tə(r)/ *n*

co-op·er·ation /kəʊˌɒpə'reıʃn/ *n* [U] working or acting together for a common purpose. **in ~ with; with the ~ of,** together with: *The workers, in ~ with the management, have increased output by 10 per cent.*

co-op·er·ative /kəʊ'ɒpərətıv/ *adj* of co-operation; willing to co-operate. **a ~ society** *n* group of persons who co-operate, eg to buy machines and services for all to share, or to produce, buy and sell goods among themselves for mutual benefit, or to save and lend money. □ *n* (shop of a) ~ society; ~ group: *agricultural ~s in India and China.*

co-opt /kəʊ 'ɒpt/ *vt* [VP6A,14] (of a committee) add (a person) as a member by the votes of those who are already members: ~ *a new member on to the committee.*

co-or·di·nate¹ /ˌkəʊ 'ɔ:dənət/ *adj* equal in importance. ~ **clause,** (gram) clause in a compound sentence, equal in rank to, and often joined by a conjunction to, the other clause(s) in that sentence. ⇨ **subordinate.** □ *n* ~ thing or person. **~·ly** *adv*

co-or·di·nate² /ˌkəʊ 'ɔ:dıneıt/ *vt* [VP6A] make co-ordinate; bring or put into proper relation: *to ~ ideas; to ~ one's movements when swimming/~ the movements of the arms and legs.* **co-or·di·na-tor** /-neıtə(r)/ *n* person who ~s.

co-or·di·na·tion /ˌkəʊ ˌɔ:dı'neıʃn/ *n* the act of co-ordinating; the state of being co-ordinate.

coot /ku:t/ *n* name of several kinds of swimming and diving birds. **'bald ~,** *n* one with a white spot on the forehead. Hence, **as bald as a ~,** very bald.

cop¹ /kɒp/ *n* (sl) policeman.

cop² /kɒp/ *vt,vi* (-pp-) (sl) **1** *cop it,* be punished. **2** [VP2C] *cop out (of),* abandon (an attempt, responsibility, etc). Hence, **'cop-out** *n* act of or excuse for copping out. □ *n* (sl) **1** capture. *It's a fair cop,* I have/He has, etc been caught and arrested in the act of committing the offence. **2** *not much cop,* nothing to value highly.

co-part·ner /ˌkəʊ 'pɑːtnə(r)/ *n* partner, eg an employee, who has a share in the profits of a business, etc in addition to his salary or wages. **~·ship** /-ʃıp/ *n* system, practice, of having ~s in business or industry.

cope¹ /kəʊp/ *n* long, loose cloak worn by clergy on some special occasions. ⇨ the illus at **vestment.**

cope² /kəʊp/ *vi* [VP2A,3A] ~ **(with),** manage successfully; be equal to: ~ *with difficulties.*

co·peck /'kəʊpek/ *n* (Russian coin worth) one-hundredth part of a rouble.

Co·per·ni·can /kə'pɜːnıkən/ *adj* **the ~ system/theory,** of Copernicus /kə'pɜːnıkəs/ (1473–1543), a Polish astronomer, that the planets including the earth, move round the sun.

cop·ing /'kəʊpıŋ/ *n* (archit) line of (sometimes overhanging) stonework or brickwork on top of a wall. **'~-stone** *n* (fig) final act, crowning, of a piece of work.

copi·ous /'kəʊpıəs/ *adj* plentiful: *a ~ supply; ~ tears;* (of a writer) writing much. **~·ly** *adv*

cop·per¹ /'kɒpə(r)/ *n* **1** [U] common reddish-brown metal (symbol Cu): (attrib) ~ *wire/cable/alloy.* **2** [C] coin made of ~ or a ~ alloy. **3** [C] large vessel made of metal, esp one in which clothes are boiled. ⇨ **boiler(1). 4** ~ **beech** *n* kind of beech-tree with ~-coloured leaves. **,~-'bottomed** *adj* **(a)** (of a ship) having the bottom plated with copper (and therefore seaworthy). **(b)** (fig) safe in every way: ~-**bottomed guarantees**. '~-**head** *n* poisonous snake of the US. ~-'**plate** *n* polished ~ plate on which designs, etc, are engraved. ~-**plate (hand)-writing** *n* ie cursive, neat and clear. '~-**smith** *n* one who works in ~. □ *vt* (also ,~- '**bottom**) sheathe (a ship's bottom, etc) with ~.

cop·per² /'kɒpə(r)/ *n* (sl) policeman.

cop·pice /'kɒpɪs/ *n* [C] small woodland area of undergrowth and small trees (grown for periodical cutting, eg for bean and pea sticks).

copra /'kɒprə/ *n* [U] dried kernels of coconuts, from which oil is extracted for making soap, etc.

copse /kɒps/ *n* = coppice.

Copt /kɒpt/ *n* one of the direct descendants of the ancient Egyptians (about one-tenth of the population of modern Egypt). **Cop·tic** /'kɒptɪk/ *n* language used in the liturgy of the ~ic Church of Egypt and Ethiopia. □ *adj* of the ~s.

cop·ula /'kɒpjʊlə/ *n* (gram) verb form (eg the finites of *be* and *become*) that connects a subject and the complement.

copu·late /'kɒpjʊleɪt/ *vi* [VP2A,3A] ~ *(with)*, (esp of animals) unite in sexual intercourse. **copu·la·tion** /ˌkɒpjʊ'leɪʃn/ *n* act or process of copulating. **copu·lat·ive** /'kɒpjʊlətɪv/ *adj* (formal) serving to connect. □ *n* (gram) word that connects (and which implies combination).

copy¹ /'kɒpɪ/ *n* (*pl* -pies) **1** thing made to be like another; reproduction of a letter, picture, etc: *Make three carbon copies of the letter*. **rough** ~, the first (often imperfect) outline or draft of sth written or drawn. **fair** ~, the final form of sth written or drawn. '~-**book** *n* exercise book containing models of handwriting for learners to imitate: ~*book maxims*, commonplace maxims (as formerly found in ~books). ⇒ also **blot**. '~-**cat** *n* (colloq) slavish imitator. **2** one example of a book, newspaper, etc of which many have been made: *If you can't afford a new* ~ *of the book, perhaps you can find a secondhand* ~. **3** [U] material to be sent to a printer: *The printers are waiting for more* ~. *The fall of the Cabinet will make good* ~, will make exciting news for the journalists to write ·about. '~ **desk** *n* (US) desk in a newspaper office where ~ is edited and prepared for printing. '~-**writer** *n* person who writes advertising or publicity ~.

copy² /'kɒpɪ/ *vt,vi* **1** [VP6A,15A,B] make a copy of: ~ *notes* (*out of a book, etc*) *into a notebook;* ~ *out a letter*, make a complete copy of it; ~ *sth down* (*from the blackboard*). **2** [VP6A] do, try to do, the same as; imitate: *You should* ~ *his good points, not his bad points*. **3** [VP2A] cheat by looking at a neighbour's paper, etc: *He was punished for* ~*ing during the examination*. ~-**ist** /'kɒpɪɪst/ *n* person who copies or transcribes (eg old documents); imitator.

copy·hold /'kɒpɪhəʊld/ *n* [U] (GB) the holding of land on conditions that were laid down in records of the manor; land held in this way. ~**er** *n* person holding land in this way.

copy·right /'kɒpɪraɪt/ *n* [U] sole legal right, held for a certain number of years, by the author or composer of a work, or by someone delegated by him, to print, publish, sell, broadcast, perform, film or record his work or any part of it; (attrib) protected by ~. □ *vt* secure ~ for (a book, etc).

co·quetry /'kɒkɪtrɪ/ *n* [U] flirting; [C] (*pl* -ries) in-

stance of this; flirtatious act.

co·quette /kɒ'ket/ *n* girl or woman who flirts. **co·quet·tish** /kəʊ'ketɪʃ/ *adj* of or like a ~: *coquettish smiles*. **co·quet·tish·ly** *adv*

cor an·glais /ˌkɔːr 'ɒŋgleɪ US: ɔːŋ'gleɪ/ *n* (music) woodwind instrument (tenor oboe). ⇒ the illus at **brass**.

cor·acle /'kɒrəkl/ *n* small, light boat made of wicker, covered with watertight materials, used by fishermen on Welsh and Irish rivers and lakes.

coral /'kɒrəl US: 'kɔːrəl/ *n* **1** [U] hard, red, pink or white substance built on the sea bed by small creatures (*polyps*). ~ '**island**, one formed by the growth of ~. '~-**reef**, accumulation of ~. ⇒ the illus at **atoll**. [C] sea organism that makes this substance. □ *adj* like ~ in colour; red or pink: ~ *lips*.

coral

cor·bel /'kɔːbl/ *n* (archit) stone or timber projection from a wall to support sth (eg a cornice, an arch). ⇒ the illus at **window**.

cord /kɔːd/ *n* **1** [C,U] (length of) twisted strands, thicker than string, thinner than rope. **2** [C] part of the body like a ~: *the spinal* ~; *the vocal* ~*s*. ⇒ **chord(3)**. **3** [C] measure of wood cut for fuel (usu 128 cubic ft). □ *vt* put a ~ or ~s(1) round.

cord·age /'kɔːdɪdʒ/ *n* [U] cords, ropes, etc, esp the rigging of a ship.

cor·dial /'kɔːdɪəl US: 'kɔːrdʒəl/ *adj* warm and sincere (in feeling, behaviour): *a* ~ *smile/welcome/ handshake;* strongly felt: ~ *dislike*. □ *n* sweetened, invigorating liquor: *lime juice* ~. ~·**ly** /-dɪəlɪ US: -dʒəlɪ/ *adv* ~·**ity** /ˌkɔːdɪ'ælətɪ US: ˌkɔːrdʒɪ-/ *n* [U] quality of being ~; [C] (*pl* -ties) expression of ~ feeling.

cor·dite /'kɔːdaɪt/ *n* [U] smokeless explosive substance.

cor·don /'kɔːdn/ *n* [C] **1** line, ring, of police, soldiers, military posts, etc acting as guards: *a sanitary* ~, a guarded line separating infected and uninfected districts. **2** fruit-tree with all its branches pruned back so that it grows as a single stem (usu against a wall or along wires). **3** ornamental ribbon of an Order¹(10) (usu worn across the shoulder). ~ **bleu** /ˌkɔːdɒn 'blɜː/, (F) award to a cook or restaurant for high quality cooking. □ *vt* [VP15B] ~ **off**, separate, keep at a distance, by means of a ~(1): *The crowds were* ~*ed off by the police*.

cor·du·roy /'kɔːdərɔɪ/ *n* **1** [U] thick, coarse, strong cotton cloth with raised lines on it. **2** (*pl*) trousers made of this cloth. **3** ~ **road**, one made of tree trunks laid across swampy land.

cords /kɔːdz/ *n pl* (colloq abbr) corduroy trousers.

core /kɔː(r)/ *n* **1** (usu hard) centre, with seeds, of such fruits as the apple and pear. ⇒ the illus at **fruit**. **2** central or most important part of anything: *the* ~ *of an electro-magnet* (a bar of soft iron); *to get to the* ~ *of a subject*. **to the** ~, right to the centre: *rotten to the* ~, (lit or fig) completely bad. *He is English to the* ~, completely English in manner, speech, dress, etc. □ *vt* [VP6A] take out the ~

of: *to ～ an apple.*

co-re·ligion·ist /ˌkəʊ rɪ'lɪdʒənɪst/ n one of two or more persons who adhere to the same religion.

co-re·spon·dent /ˌkəʊ rɪ'spɒndənt/ n (legal) person charged with adultery with the spouse (husband or wife) of the *respondent* (petitioner or plaintiff) in a divorce suit.

corgi /'kɔːgɪ/ n breed of small Welsh dog.

Co·rin·thian /kə'rɪnθɪən/ n, adj **1** (native) of Corinth /'kɒrɪnθ/. **2** (archit) of the most ornate of the three types of column(1) in ancient Greek architecture, with a decoration of leaves on the capital(4). ⇨ the illus at column.

cork /kɔːk/ n **1** [U] light, elastic, tough substance, the thick outer bark of the tree called the ～*-oak*; (attrib) made of this material: *a ～ jacket.* **2** [C] round piece of this material used as a stopper for a bottle: *to draw/pull out the ～.* '～*-screw* n tool for drawing ～s from bottles. □ vt [VP6A,15A] ～ *(up)*, stop with, or as with, a ～: *to ～ a bottle;* (fig): *to ～ up one's feelings.* **corked** adj (of wine) contaminated by decayed ～ or a bad ～: ～*ed port.*

cork·age /'kɔːkɪdʒ/ n [U] charge made by a restaurant for serving wine not supplied by itself.

corker /'kɔːkə(r)/ n (dated sl) **1** sth remarkable or astonishing. **2** unanswerable argument.

corm /kɔːm/ n (bot) bulb-like swelling on the underground stem of a plant (eg a crocus or a gladiolus), from the top of which buds sprout. Cf *bulb* which has scales.

cor·mor·ant /'kɔːmərənt/ n large, long-necked seabird with a pouch under its beak for holding the fish it catches. ⇨ the illus at water.

corn[1] /kɔːn/ n **1** [U] (collective) (seed of) any of various grain plants, chiefly wheat, oats, rye and (esp US) maize; such plants while growing: *a field of ～; a '～-field; a sheaf of ～.* ⇨ the illus at cereal. '～*-cob*, thick, cylindrical part of an ear of maize, on which the grains grow. ～ *on the cob,* maize cooked and eaten in this form. '～*-crake* /-kreɪk/, common European bird, the male of which has a loud, harsh cry. '～*-exchange*, place where dealers in ～ do business. '～*-flakes* n pl cereal of toasted maize flakes. '～*-flour* (US '～*-starch*), flour made from maize, rice or other grains. '～*-flower*, name of various flowers growing wild in ～-fields, esp a blue-flowered kind (also grown in gardens). 'C～ Laws, (esp) laws in GB, repealed in 1846, regulating trade in ～. '～*pone* /-pəʊn/, (US) baked or fried maize bread. '～*-starch*, (US) ～flour. **2** [C] single grain (of wheat, pepper, etc).

corn[2] /kɔːn/ n small area of hardened skin on the foot, esp on a toe, often with a painful centre and root. *tread on sb's ～s,* (fig) hurt his feelings.

corn[3] /kɔːn/ vt preserve (meat) in salt: ～*ed beef.*

cor·nea /'kɔːnɪə/ n (anat) tough transparent part of the eyeball, covering the pupil and iris. ⇨ the illus at eye. ～l adj of the ～: *a ～l graft.*

cor·nel·ian /kɔː'niːlɪən/ n semi-precious stone, reddish, reddish-brown or white.

cor·ner /'kɔːnə(r)/ n **1** position (exterior or interior) of the angle where two lines, sides, edges or surfaces meet; angle enclosed by two walls, sides, etc that meet: *standing at a street ～; a shop situated on/at the corner; just round the ～,* (colloq) very near; *sitting in the ～ of the room. cut off a ～,* go across, not round, it; take a short cut. *cut ～s,* (of the driver of a motor vehicle) go across, not round them when travelling fast; (fig) simplify proceed-

ings, ignore regulations, etc to get work done quickly: *We've had to cut a few ～s to get your visa ready in time. drive sb into a ～,* (fig) put him in a difficult situation from which escape is difficult. *turn the ～,* (fig) pass a critical point in an illness, a period of difficulty, etc. *be in a tight ～,* in an awkward or difficult situation. '～*-stone* n (a) stone that forms a ～ of the foundation of a building (often laid in position at a ceremony). (b) (fig) foundation: *Hard work was the ～stone of his success.* **2** hidden, secret, or out-of-the-way place: *money hidden in odd ～s; hole-and-～ methods/ transactions,* secret and underhand. **3** region; quarter: *to the four ～s of the earth.* **4** (comm) the buying up of all or as much as possible of the supply of an article of trade, a commodity, a stock, etc in order to secure a monopoly and control the price. *make a ～ in sth,* (eg the buying of wheat). **5** (Assoc football) (also '～*-kick*) kick from the ～ of the field, allowed when the ball has been kicked by an opponent over his own goal-line. □ vt,vi **1** [VP6A] force into a ～; put into a difficult position: *The escaped prisoner was ～ed at last. That question ～ed me.* **2** [VP6A] make a ～(4) in (wheat, etc): ～ *the market.* **3** [VP2A] (of a vehicle, its driver) turn a ～ (on a road, etc): *My new car ～s well,* remains stable when going round ～s. ～*ed adj* (in compounds) having ～s: *a three-～ed hat.*

cor·net[1] /'kɔːnɪt/ n **1** small musical instrument of brass, like a trumpet. **2** piece of paper twisted into the shape of a cone, to hold sweets; cone-shaped container for ice-cream.

cor·net[2] /'kɔːnɪt/ n (in former times) officer in a troop of cavalry who carried the colours[1](8).

cor·nice /'kɔːnɪs/ n (archit) projecting part, above the frieze, above a column, ⇨ the illus at column; ornamental moulding (eg in plaster) round the walls of a room, just below the ceiling; horizontal strip of carved wood or stone along an outside wall; overhanging mass of snow above a precipice.

cor·nu·co·pia /ˌkɔːnjʊ'kəʊpɪə/ n ornamental horn shown in art as overflowing with flowers, fruit and corn; (myth) horn of plenty; (fig) abundant supply.

corny /'kɔːnɪ/ adj (-ier, -iest) (sl) hackneyed; often heard or repeated: ～ *jokes/music.*

co·rolla /kə'rɒlə/ n (bot) ring of petals forming the cup of a flower. ⇨ the illus at flower.

co·rol·lary /kə'rɒlərɪ US: 'kɒrələrɪ/ n (pl -ries) [C] natural sequence or outcome of sth; sth self-evident after sth else has been proved.

co·rona /kə'rəʊnə/ n (pl ～s /-nəz/, ～e /-niː/) ring of light seen round the sun or moon, eg during an eclipse. ⇨ the illus at eclipse.

cor·on·ary /'kɒrənrɪ US: 'kɔːrənerɪ/ adj (anat) of arteries supplying blood to the heart: ～ *thrombosis,* formation of a clot in a ～ artery. □ n (pl -ries) (colloq) attack of ～ thrombosis.

cor·on·ation /ˌkɒrə'neɪʃn US: ˌkɔːr-/ n ceremony of crowning a king, queen or other sovereign ruler: (attrib) *the queen's ～ robes.*

cor·oner /'kɒrənə(r) US: 'kɔːr-/ n official who inquires into the cause of any death thought to be from violent or unnatural causes: ～*'s inquest,* such an inquiry (held with a jury).

cor·onet /'kɒrənɪt US: 'kɔːr-/ n small crown worn by a peer or peeress; band of precious materials worn as (part of) a woman's head-dress; garland of flowers.

cor·poral[1] /'kɔːpərəl/ adj (formal) of the human body. ～ *punishment,* eg whipping, beating.

cor·poral² /'kɔ:pərəl/ n (army) non-commissioned officer (below a sergeant); (navy): *ship's* ~, one with police duties.

cor·por·ate /'kɔ:pərət/ adj **1** of or belonging to a corporation: ~ *property;* ~ *bonds,* (Stock Exchange term for) bonds held by a group or company. **2** of, shared by, members of a group of persons: ~ *responsibility/action.* **3** united in one group: *a* ~ *body.*

cor·por·ation /ˌkɔ:pə'reɪʃn/ n **1** group of persons elected to govern a town: *the Mayor and* ~; *the municipal* ~; (attrib) *the* ~ *tramways.* **2** group of persons authorized to act as an individual, eg for business purposes: *In Great Britain the Electricity Authority and the National Coal Board are public* ~s. **3** (US) limited liability company. **4** (colloq) large belly.

cor·por·eal /kɔ:'pɔ:rɪəl/ adj (formal) **1** of or for the body: ~ *needs,* eg food and drink. **2** physical (contrasted with *spiritual*).

corps /kɔ:(r)/ n (pl corps /kɔ:z/) **1** one of the technical branches of an army: *the ˌRoyal ˌArmy ˈMedical C*~. **2** military force made up of two or more divisions. **3** ~ **de ballet** /kɔ: də 'bæleɪ/ (F) company of dancers in a ballet. **the Diplo'matic C**~; **the C**~ **Diplomatique** /kɔ: ˌdɪpləmæ'ti:k/ (F) all the ambassadors, ministers and attachés of foreign states at a capital or Court.

corpse /kɔ:ps/ n dead body (esp of a human being). ⇨ **carcass**.

cor·pu·lent /'kɔ:pjʊlənt/ adj (of a person or his body) fat and heavy. **cor·pu·lence** /'kɔ:pjʊləns/ n

cor·pus /'kɔ:pəs/ n (pl corpora /'kɔ:pərə/) body, collection, esp of writings on a specified subject or of material for study (eg for linguists, a collection of examples of spoken and written usages).

cor·puscle /'kɔ:pʌsl/ n one of the red or white cells in the blood.

cor·ral /kə'rɑ:l US: -'ræl/ n **1** enclosure for horses and cattle or the capture of wild animals. **2** = **laager**. □ vt (-ll-) [VP6A] drive (cattle, etc) into, shut up in, a ~; form (wagons) into a ~.

cor·rect¹ /kə'rekt/ adj **1** true; right: *a* ~ *answer; the* ~ *time;* ~ *in every particular.* **2** (of conduct, manners, dress, etc) proper; in accord with good taste or convention: *the* ~ *dress for a ceremony; a very* ~ *young lady.* ~·**ly** adv ~·**ness** n

cor·rect² /kə'rekt/ vt [VP6A,14] **1** make right; take out mistakes from: *I* ~ed *my watch by the time signal. Please* ~ *my pronunciation.* **2** point out the faults of; punish: ~ *a child for disobedience.*

cor·rec·tion /kə'rekʃn/ n **1** [U] correcting: *the* ~ *of schoolchildren's work.* **speak under** ~, speak while knowing that one may need to be corrected. **house of** ~, (old name for a) prison. **2** [C] sth put in place of what is wrong: *a written exercise with* ~s *in red ink.*

cor·rec·ti·tude /kə'rektɪtju:d US: -tu:d/ n [U] (formal) correctness (esp of conduct, eg in diplomacy).

cor·rec·tive /kə'rektɪv/ n, adj (sth) serving to correct: ~ *training,* eg for juvenile delinquents.

cor·re·late /'kɒrəleɪt US: 'kɔ:r-/ vt,vi [VP6A,14,2A,3A] ~ **(with),** have a mutual relation, bring (one thing) into such a relation (with another): *Results in the natural sciences seldom* ~ *with those in history or art. Research workers find it hard to* ~ *the two sets of figures/to* ~ *one set with the other.*

cor·re·la·tion /ˌkɒrə'leɪʃn US: ˌkɔ:r-/ n mutual relationship: *the* ~ *between climate and vegetation.*

cor·rela·tive /kɒ'relətɪv/ n, adj (word or thing) having a mutual relation: *'Either' and 'or' are* ~ *conjunctions.*

cor·re·spond /ˌkɒrɪ'spɒnd US: ˌkɔ:r-/ vi [VP2A,3A] **1** ~ **(with),** be in harmony: *The house exactly* ~s *with my needs. His actions do not* ~ *with his words.* **2** ~ **(to),** be equal; be similar (in position, etc): *His expenses do not* ~ *to his income. The American Congress* ~s *to the British Parliament.* **3** ~ **(with),** exchange letters. ~·**ing** adj that ~(s): *Imports for 1—10 July this year are larger by 10 per cent than for the* ~ing *period last year.* ~·**ing·ly** adv

cor·re·spon·dence /ˌkɒrɪ'spɒndəns US: ˌkɔ:r-/ n **1** [C,U] agreement; similarity: *There is not much* ~ *between their ideals and ours.* **2** [U] letter-writing; letters: *I have been in* ~ *with him about the problem. Is commercial* ~ *taught in the school? He has a great deal of* ~ *to deal with.* '~ **course,** course of academic study by posting essays, etc to one's tutor.

cor·re·spon·dent /ˌkɒrɪ'spɒndənt US: ˌkɔ:r-/ n **1** person with whom one exchanges letters: *He's a good/bad* ~, writes regularly/seldom. **2** person regularly contributing local news or special articles to a newspaper: *our Hong Kong* ~; *a foreign/war* ~, person writing reports from a foreign country/a war. **3** (comm) person, firm, bank, etc which has regular business relations with another (esp in a foreign country).

cor·ri·dor /'kɒrɪdɔ:(r) US: 'kɔ:r-/ n long narrow passage from which doors open into rooms or compartments. ~s **of power,** places where influence is unofficially exerted. '~ **train,** one with coaches having ~s which open into compartments.

cor·rie /'kɒrɪ US: 'kɔ:rɪ/ n [C] (Scot) round hollow in a hillside.

corri·gen·dum /ˌkɒrɪ'dʒendəm US: ˌkɔ:r-/ n (pl -da /-də/) thing to be corrected (esp in a printed book).

cor·ri·gible /'kɒrɪdʒəbl US: 'kɔ:r-/ adj (formal) capable of being corrected; (of persons) submitting to correction.

cor·rob·or·ate /kə'rɒbəreɪt/ vt [VP6A] give support or certainty to (a statement, belief, theory, etc). **cor·rob·or·at·ive** /kə'rɒbərətɪv US: -reɪtɪv/ adj tending to ~.

cor·rob·or·ation /kəˌrɒbə'reɪʃn/ n [U] support or strengthening by further evidence; additional evidence: *in* ~ *(of),* giving further support (of).

cor·rode /kə'rəʊd/ vt,vi [VP6A,2A] wear away, destroy slowly by chemical action or disease; be worn away thus: *Rust* ~s *iron. Iron* ~s *easily.* **cor·rosion** /kə'rəʊʒn/ n [U] corroding or being ~d.

cor·ros·ive /kə'rəʊsɪv/ n, adj (substance) that corrodes: *Rust and acids are* ~.

cor·ru·gate /'kɒrəgeɪt US: 'kɔ:r-/ vt,vi [VP6A,2A] make into folds, wrinkles or furrows: ~ *the forehead;* ~d *cardboard,* used for packing fragile goods; ~d *roads in tropical countries,* with a furrowed surface caused by weather and use. ~d '**iron,** sheet iron made into folds, used for roofs, fences, etc. **cor·ru·ga·tion** /ˌkɒrə'geɪʃn US: ˌkɔ:r-/ n [C,U] fold(s); wrinkle(s).

cor·rupt¹ /kə'rʌpt/ adj **1** (of persons, their actions) immoral; depraved; dishonest (esp through taking bribes): ~ *practices,* (esp) the offering and accepting of bribes. **2** impure: ~ *air/blood.* **3** (of languages, texts, etc) debased by errors or alterations:

a ~ *form of Latin.* ~·ly *adv* ~·ness *n*
cor·rupt² /kə'rʌpt/ *vt,vi* [VP6A,2A] make or become corrupt: *young persons whose morals have been* ~*ed; to* ~ *the electorate,* eg try to win their votes by bribing them. *Does pornography* ~*?* ~·ible *adj* that can be ~ed: ~*ible government officials.* ~·i·bil·ity /kəˌrʌptə'bɪlətɪ/ *n*
cor·rup·tion /kə'rʌpʃn/ [U] corrupting or being corrupt; decay: *the* ~ *of the body after death; the* ~ *of a language; officials who are proof against* ~, who cannot be bribed.
cor·sage /kɔː'sɑːʒ/ *n* upper part of a woman's dress (round the bust); (US) small bouquet of flowers to be worn on this part of the dress or at the waist.
cor·sair /'kɔːseə(r)/ *n* (hist) pirate or pirate ship, esp of N Africa, attacking ships of European countries.
corse /kɔːs/ *n* (archaic or poet) corpse.
corse·let, cors·let /'kɔːslɪt/ *n* coat of armour, esp one covering the trunk only.
cor·set /'kɔːsɪt/ *n* close-fitting reinforced undergarment confining the waist and hips, to shape the body to the current style (often named, in trade, a *foundation,* or *foundation garment).*
cor·tege, cor·tège /kɔː'teɪʒ/ *n* (F) train of attendants; procession, eg at the funeral of a king or president.
cor·tex /'kɔːteks/ *n* (*pl* cortices /'kɔːtɪsiːz/) outer shell or covering (eg the bark of a tree); outer layer of grey matter of the brain. **cor·ti·cal** /'kɔːtɪkl/ *adj* of the ~.
cor·ti·sone /'kɔːtɪzəʊn/ *n* (P) [U] substance (a hormone from the adrenal gland) used medically in the treatment of arthritis and some allergies.
co·run·dum /kə'rʌndəm/ *n* hard crystallized mineral used chiefly in abrasives, in powder form (for polishing).
cor·us·cate /'kɒrəskeɪt US: 'kɔːr-/ *vi* [VP2A] flash, sparkle: *coruscating wit.* **cor·us·ca·tion** /ˌkɒrə'skeɪʃn US: ˌkɔːr-/ *n*
cor·vée /'kɔːveɪ/ *n* [C] (F) (in feudal times) day's unpaid work which had to be done by French peasants; (modern use) hard task or duty unwillingly performed.
cor·vette /kɔː'vet/ *n* (old use) warship with sails and one tier of guns; (modern use) small fast warship designed for escorting merchant ships.
cos¹ /kɒs/ *n* (kind of) long-leaved lettuce.
cos² /kɒs/ *n* (abbr of) cosine.
cos³ /kəz/ *conj* (colloq abbr of) because.
cosh /kɒʃ/ *vt, n* (GB sl) (strike with a) length of lead pipe, rubber tubing filled with metal, etc
cosher /'kəʊʃə(r)/ *adj, n* = kosher.
co·sig·na·tory /ˌkəʊ'sɪgnətərɪ US: -tɔːrɪ/ *adj, n* (*pl* -ries) (person) signing jointly with others.
co·sine /'kəʊsaɪn/ *n* (trig; abbr cos) sine of the complement of a given angle.
cos·metic /kɒz'metɪk/ *adj, n* [C] (preparation, substance, esp one that adds colour) designed to make the skin or hair beautiful, eg *face-cream, lipstick.* ~ **surgery,** to restore or correct outward appearance. **cos·me·tician** /ˌkɒzmə'tɪʃn/ *n* person employed in the preparation or sale of ~s.
cos·mic /'kɒzmɪk/ *adj* of the whole universe or cosmos. ~ **rays,** radiations that reach the earth from outer space.
cos·mog·ony /kɒz'mɒgənɪ/ *n* (*pl* -nies) (theory of) the origin, creation and evolution of the universe.
cos·mo·naut /'kɒzmənɔːt/ *n* = astronaut.
cos·mo·poli·tan /ˌkɒzmə'pɒlɪtən/ *adj* **1** of or from all, or many different parts of, the world: *the* ~ *gatherings at the United Nations Assembly.* **2** free from national prejudices because of wide experience of the world: *a statesman with a* ~ *outlook.* ▢ *n* ~(2) person.
cos·mos¹ /'kɒzmɒs/ *n* the universe, all space, considered as a well-ordered system (contrasted with *chaos).*
cos·mos² /'kɒzmɒs/ *n* garden plant with white, pink or purple flowers.
cos·set /'kɒsɪt/ *vt* pamper.
cost¹ /kɒst US: kɔːst/ *vi* (*pt,pp* cost) [VP2B] (the adverbial adjunct indicating price, etc may be preceded by an indirect object; not used in the passive voice). **1** be obtainable at the price of; require the payment of: *The house* ~ *him £15000. It* ~s *them £500 a year to run a car. It* ~s *too much. Compiling a dictionary* ~s *much time and patience.* **2** result in the loss of: *Careless driving may* ~ *you your life.* **3** bring (injury or disadvantage): *The boy's bad behaviour* ~ *his mother many sleepless nights.* **4** *vt* [VP6A] (*pt,pp* ~ed) (industry and comm) estimate the price to be charged for an article based on the expense of producing it. ~·ing *n* [U] (industry) fixing of prices: *the* ~ing *department.*
cost² /kɒst US: kɔːst/ *n* **1** [C,U] price (to be) paid for a thing: *the* ~ *of living; living* ~s, the general level of prices; *the* ~-*of-living index,* ▷ index(3); *the* ~ *price of an article,* the ~ of producing it or the price at which it may be bought wholesale, ▷ retail; *to sell sth at* ~, ie at ~ price. *He built his house without regard to* ~, without considering how much money would be needed. '~ **accountant/clerk,** one who keeps a record of every item of expense in a business, etc. ,**cost-ef'fective** *adj* economical compared with money spent; hence ,**cost-ef'fectiveness** *n* [U]. **2** [C,U *sing* only] that which is used, needed or given to obtain sth: *The battle was won at (a) great* ~ *in human lives,* only after many soldiers had been killed. *at 'all* ~s, whatever the ~ may be. *at the* ~ *of,* at the loss or expense of: *He saved his son from drowning, but only at the* ~ *of his own life.* *count the* ~, consider the risks, possible losses, etc before doing sth. *to one's* ~, to one's loss or disadvantage: *Wasps' stings are serious, as I know to my* ~, as I know because of personal suffering from them. **3** (*pl*) (legal) expense of having sth settled in a law court: *pay a £25 fine and £7* ~s.
co-star /ˌkəʊ 'stɑː(r)/ *vi,vt* (-rr-) (journalism) **1** [VP6A] present (one star(4)) as having equal status with another or others: *The film* ~*red Robert Redford.* **2** [VP14] ~ **with,** (of an actor or actress) appear as a star(4) with: *Laurence Olivier* ~s *with Maggie Smith in this production.* ▢ *n* /'kəʊstɑː(r)/ person who ~s.
cos·ter·monger /'kɒstəmʌŋgə(r)/ *n* person who sells fruit, vegetables, etc from a barrow in the street.
cos·tive /'kɒstɪv/ *adj* (liter) constipated.
costly /'kɒstlɪ US: 'kɔːst-/ *adj* (-ier, -iest) of great value; costing much: *a* ~ *mistake,* one involving great loss or sacrifice. **cost·li·ness** *n*
cos·tume /'kɒstjuːm US: -tuːm/ *n* **1** [U,C] style of dress: *actors wearing historical* ~, clothes in the style of a period in the past; *Scotsmen in Highland* ~, wearing the kilt, etc; *a* '~ *piece/play,* one in which the actors wear historical ~. '~ **jewellery,** artificial jewellery. **2** [C] (dated) woman's suit

(short coat and skirt of the same material). ⇨ bathing. **cos·tumier** /kɒˈstjuːmɪə(r) *US:* -ˈstuː-/ *n* maker of, dealer in, ~s.

cosy[1] /ˈkəʊzɪ/ *adj* (-ier, -iest) warm and comfortable: *a ~ little room.* **cosi·ly** *adv* **cosi·ness** *n*

cosy[2] /ˈkəʊzɪ/ *n* covering for a teapot, or an egg in an egg-cup.

cot[1] /kɒt/ *n* **1** small, narrow, easily moved bed; bed for a young child (usu with sides to prevent the child from falling out) (*US* = *crib*). **2** (US) camp bed; bunk bed on board ship.

cot[2] /kɒt/ *n* **1** small building for sheltering animals: *a sheep-cot.* **2** (poet) cottage.

cote /kəʊt/ *n* shed or shelter for domestic animals or birds: *aˈdove-~; aˈsheep-~.*

co·ten·ant /ˌkəʊ ˈtenənt/ *n* joint tenant.

co·terie /ˈkəʊtərɪ/ *n* group of persons associated by common interests, tastes, etc, esp one that tends to be exclusive: *a literary ~.*

co·termi·nous /ˌkəʊˈtɜːmɪnəs/ *adj* having a common terminus or boundary.

co·til·lion, co·til·ion /kəˈtɪljən/ *n* name of several kinds of lively French dance originated in the 18th c; music for these.

cot·tage /ˈkɒtɪdʒ/ *n* small house, esp in the country: *farm labourers' ~s;* house at a summer resort. **~ cheese,** soft, white kind, made from curds. **~ industry,** one that can be carried on in ~s, eg knitting, pottery, some kinds of weaving.

cot·tar, cot·ter /ˈkɒtə(r)/ *n* (Scot) man living in a cottage on a farm and working on the farm.

cot·ton /ˈkɒtn/ *n* [U] **1** soft, white fibrous substance round the seeds of the 'ᴧ-plant, used for making thread, cloth, etc: (attrib) ~ *yarn;* ~ *cloth;* ~ *goods.* **2** thread spun from ~ yarn: *a ˌneedle and* 'ᴧ. 'ᴧ **batting** *n* (US) cotton-wool. 'ᴧ-**cake,** cattle food made by pressing out oil from seeds of the ~-plant. 'ᴧ **seed 'oil,** oil obtained from ~ seed. ˌᴧ-'**wool,** (GB) cleaned raw ~ or natural ~; absorbent ~ as used for padding, bandaging, etc. 'ᴧ-**tail** *n* (US) rabbit. □ *vi* ~ **up (to),** (dated sl) make friendly advances (to). ~ **on (to),** (sl) understand.

boll

a cotton-plant

coty·ledon /ˌkɒtɪˈliːdn/ *n* (bot) first leaf growing from a seed.

couch[1] /kaʊtʃ/ *n* **1** (liter) bed: *retire to one's ~.* **2** long bed-like seat for sitting on or lying on during the day: *studio-~.*

couch[2] /kaʊtʃ/ *vt, vi* **1** [VP6A,14] ~ **(in),** (formal) put (a thought, etc, in words): *The reply was ~ed in insolent terms.* **2** [VP2A] (of animals) lie flat (either in hiding, or ready for a jump forward): *a deer ~ed on a grassy bank.* **3** [VP6A] lower (a spear or lance) to the position for attack. **4** (*pp* only; liter or poet) reclining (as if) on a couch[1]: *~ed in slumber.*

couch[3], **couch-grass** /ˈkaʊtʃ (grɑːs *US:* græs)/ *n*

[U] kind of grass with long creeping roots.

couch·ant /ˈkaʊtʃənt/ *adj* (heraldry, of animals in a coat of arms, etc) lying with the body resting on the legs and the head raised.

cou·chette /kuːˈʃet/ *n* (F) sleeping berth (in a railway compartment).

cou·gar /ˈkuːɡə(r)/ *n* large wild cat, also called a *puma.* ⇨ the illus at cat.

cough[1] /kɒf *US:* kɔːf/ *vi,vt* [VP2A,15B] send out air from the lungs violently and noisily. ~ *sb* **down,** (of an audience) prevent him, by ~ing, from being heard. ~ *sth up,* get it out of the throat by ~ing; (fig, sl) say, produce (it) reluctantly.

cough[2] /kɒf *US:* kɔːf/ *n* **1** act or sound of coughing: *He gave me a warning ~.* **2** condition, illness, that causes a person to cough often: *to have a bad ~;* '~-*drop,* '~-*lozenge,* taken to relieve a ~.

could /kʊd/, *weak form* /kəd/ (neg **couldn't** /ˈkʊdnt/) *anom fin pt* of **can,** used in indirect speech in place of *can* if the main verb is *pt,* to express conditions, and to express occasional occurrence and inclination. ⇨ can.

couldst /kʊdst/ old form of *could,* used with *thou.*

coul·ter (US = **col·ter**) /ˈkəʊltə(r)/ *n* iron blade fixed vertically in front of a plough share (to cut the soil before it is lifted and turned by the share).

coun·cil /ˈkaʊnsl/ *n* group of persons appointed, elected or chosen to give advice, make rules, and carry out plans, manage affairs, etc, esp of government: *a city/county ~; the municipal ~; to be/to meet in ~; the C~ of the Republic,* upper house in the French legislature; *a ~ of war,* assembly of officers called by the Commander-in-Chief, etc; *the Privy C~.* '~-**board,** table at which members of a ~ sit. '~-**chamber,** in which a ~ meets. '~ **es·tate,** housing estate built by a city, county, etc ~. ⇨ housing. '~ **flat/house,** flat/house in a ~ estate.

coun·cil·lor (US also **coun·cil·or**) /ˈkaʊnsələ(r)/ *n* member of a council.

coun·sel[1] /ˈkaʊnsl/ *n* **1** [U] (formal) advice; consultation; opinions; suggestions. *keep one's own ~,* keep one's views, plans, etc secret. *hold/take ~ with sb,* consult him. *take ~ together,* consult together. **2** (with *indef art* or in *pl* but not with numerals): *a ~/~s of perfection,* excellent advice that cannot be followed. **3** (*pl* unchanged) barrister, or group of barristers, giving advice in a law case: *when the jury had heard ~ on both sides,* the barristers for the prosecution and the defence. ˌ**Queen's/ˌKing's 'C~,** (abbr to **QC/KC**) barrister appointed to act for the State, higher in authority than other barristers.

coun·sel[2] /ˈkaʊnsl/ *vt* (-ll-, US also -l-) [VP6A,B,17] advise; give counsel to: *to ~ an early start; to ~ patience. Would you ~ our giving up/ ~ us to give up the plan?*

coun·sel·lor (US also **coun·sel·or**) /ˈkaʊnsələ(r)/ *n* adviser; (in Ireland and US) lawyer.

count[1] /kaʊnt/ *vt,vi* **1** [VP2A,C,3A] ~ **(from) (to),** say or name (eg the numerals) in order: *to ~ from 1 to 20. He can't ~ yet.* ~·**able** *adj* that can be ~ed. **2** [VP6A] find the total of: *Don't forget to ~ your change. Have the votes been ~ed yet?* '~·**ing-house** *n* building or room where accounts are kept (eg in a bank). **3** [VP6A,14,2A,C] include, be included, in the reckoning: *fifty people, not ~ing the children. That doesn't ~,* need not be considered or reckoned. **4** [VP25,16B] consider (sth or sb) to be: *I ~ myself fortunate in being here. I ~ it* *a great honour to serve you. I'm afraid we must* ~ *him as dead.* **5** [VP14,3A,2C] (special uses with *adverbial particles* and *prepositions*):

~ **against sb;** ~ **sth against sb,** be considered, consider, to the disadvantage of: *His past record* ~*s against him. He is young and inexperienced, but please do not* ~ *that against him.*

~ **among sb/sth;** ~ **sb/sth among sb/sth,** be regarded, regard, as one of: *You* ~*/You are* ~*ed among my best friends. I no longer* ~ *him among my friends.*

~ **down,** ~ seconds backwards (eg 10, 9, 8, 7...) as when launching a rocket, etc into space. Hence, **'~-down** *n*

(not) ~ **for anything/nothing/much/little,** (not) be of any/no etc worth or importance: *Knowledge without common sense* ~*s for little. Such men do not* ~ *for anything.*

~ **sb/sth in,** include: *Go and see how many plates we have—but don't* ~ *in the cracked ones. If you're all going to the pub for a drink, you can* ~ *me in,* I will certainly be one of the party.

~ **on/upon sb/sth,** expect with confidence; rely upon: *We* ~ *on your help/* ~ *on you to help. You had better not* ~ *on an increase in your salary this year.*

~ **sb/sth out, (a)** ~ things (slowly), one by one: *The old lady* ~*ed out fifteen pence and passed it to the salesgirl.* **(b)** ~ up to ten over a boxer who has been knocked out: *The referee* ~*ed him out in the first round.* **(c)** not include: *If it's going to be a rowdy party,* ~ *me out,* I shall certainly not be there. ~ **the House out,** (GB, House of Commons) ~ the members present and declare that, because enough members are not present, there must be an adjournment.

~ **sth up,** find the total of: *Just you* ~ *up the number of times he has failed to keep a promise!*

count² /kaʊnt/ *n* **1** [C] act of counting; number got by counting: *Four* ~*s were necessary before we were certain of the total.* **keep/lose** ~ **(of),** be aware/fail to know how many there are (of): *I've bought so many new books this year that I've lost* ~ *of them.* **take the** ~; **be out for the** ~, (boxing) be counted out. ⇨ count¹(5). **2** [U] account (7); notice (the more usu words): *to take no/some/any/not much, etc* ~ *of what people say.* **3** [C] (legal) one of a number of things of which a person has been accused: *He was found guilty on all* ~*s.*

count³ /kaʊnt/ *n* title of nobility in France, Italy, etc (but not in GB). ⇨ countess, earl.

coun·ten·ance¹ /'kaʊntɪnəns/ *n* (formal) **1** face, including its appearance and expression: *a woman with a fierce* ~; *to change* ~, change one's expression because of emotion. **keep one's** ~, maintain one's composure (esp by not laughing). **put/stare sb out of** ~, disconcert him, cause him to feel troubled or at fault (by looking at him steadily). **2** [U] support; approval: *to give* ~ *to a person/a plan.*

coun·ten·ance² /'kaʊntɪnəns/ *vt* [VP6A] give support or approval to: *to* ~ *a fraud. We can never* ~ *a war of aggression.*

counter¹ /'kaʊntə(r)/ *n* table or flat surface on which goods are shown, customers served, in a shop or bank. **under the** ~, (of goods in shops) bought or sold surreptitiously, eg when they are scarce and difficult to obtain.

counter² /'kaʊntə(r)/ *n* **1** small (usu round) flat piece of metal, plastic, etc used for keeping count in games, etc; piece used in draughts(7), etc. **2** (in compounds) device for keeping count (in machinery, etc): *'speed-*~; *,revo'lution-*~.

counter³ /'kaʊntə(r)/ *adv* ~ **to,** contrary; in the opposite direction; in opposition; *to act* ~ *to a person's wishes; requirements that run/go* ~ *to one's inclinations.*

counter⁴ /'kaʊntə(r)/ *vt,vi* [VP6A,14,2A,3A] ~ **(with),** oppose; meet an attack (with a return attack): *They* ~*ed our proposal with one of their own. The champion* ~*ed with the right,* (boxing) parried a blow and returned it with a right-handed blow.

counter- /ˌkaʊntə(r)/ *pref* **1** opposite in direction: ~*-attraction;* ~*-productive.* **2** made in answer to: '~*-attack;* ˌ~*-'espionage/-in'telligence.* **3** corresponding: '~*part.*

counter·act /ˌkaʊntər'ækt/ *vt* [VP6A] act against and make (action, force) of less or no effect: ~ *(the effects of) a poison/sb's bad influence.* **counter·action** /ˌkaʊntər'ækʃn/ *n* ~ing.

counter·at·tack /'kaʊntər ətæk/ *n* attack made in reply to an attack by the enemy. □ *vt,vi* make a ~ (*on*).

counter·at·trac·tion /ˌkaʊntər ə'trækʃn/ *n* [C] rival attraction.

counter·bal·ance /'kaʊntəbæləns/ *n* [C] weight, force, equal to another and balancing it. □ *vt* /ˌkaʊntə'bæləns/ [VP6A] act as a ~ to.

counter·blast /'kaʊntəblɑːst *US:* -blæst/ *n* [C] violent reply.

counter·claim /'kaʊntəkleɪm/ *n* claim made in opposition to another claim: *a* ~ *for damages,* by a defendant in a lawsuit.

counter-clock·wise /ˌkaʊntə 'klɒkwaɪz/ *adv* = anti-clockwise (the more usu word).

counter-espion·age /ˌkaʊntər 'espɪɑːʒ/ *n* [U] spying directed against the enemy's spying.

counter·feit /'kaʊntəfɪt/ *n, adj* (sth) made or done in imitation of another thing in order to deceive: ~ *money/jewels/grief. This ten-dollar bill is a* ~. □ *vt* [VP6A] copy, imitate (coins, handwriting, etc) in order to deceive. ~**er** *n* person who ~s.

counter·foil /'kaʊntəfɔɪl/ *n* section of a cheque, receipt, etc kept by the sender as a record. ⇨ stub(2).

counter-in·tel·li·gence /ˌkaʊntər ɪn'telɪdʒəns/ *n* [U] = counter-espionage.

counter-ir·ri·tant /ˌkaʊntər 'ɪrɪtənt/ *n* sth used to produce a surface irritation and in this way relieve a more deeply seated pain, eg rheumatism.

counter·mand /ˌkaʊntə'mɑːnd *US:* -'mænd/ *vt* [VP6A] take back, cancel, a command already given.

counter·mine /'kaʊntəmaɪn/ *n* (in war) mine (on land or sea) to counteract one of the enemy's; (fig) counter-plot. □ *vt,vi* oppose by ~s; make a ~.

counter·offer /'kaʊntərɒfə(r)/ *n* offer made in reply to an offer made by sb else.

counter·pane /'kaʊntəpeɪn/ *n* covering for a bed; bedspread.

counter·part /'kaʊntəpɑːt/ *n* person or thing exactly like, or closely corresponding to, another.

counter·plot /'kaʊntəplɒt/ *n* plot made to defeat another plot. □ *vt,vi* (-tt-) make a ~ (against).

counter·point /'kaʊntəpɔɪnt/ *n* (music) **1** [C] melody added as an accompaniment to another melody. **2** [U] art or method of adding melodies as accompaniment according to fixed rules.

counter·poise /'kaʊntəpɔɪz/ n **1** [C] weight used to balance another weight; force, power or influence that counterbalances another. **2** [U] the condition of being in balance; equilibrium. □ vt bring into, keep in, equilibrium.

counter–rev·ol·ution /ˌkaʊntə ˌrevə'lu:ʃn/ n [U,C] political movement directed against a revolution. ~·**ary** /-'lu:ʃənərɪ US: -nerɪ/ adj characteristic of a ~. □ n (pl -ries) person engaged in ~(s).

counter·sign /'kaʊntəsaɪn/ n [C] password; secret word(s) to be given, on demand, to a sentry before he allows sb to pass: 'Advance and give the ~'. □ vt [VP6A] add another signature to (a document) to give it authority.

counter·sink /'kaʊntəsɪŋk/ vt (pt -sank /-sæŋk/, pp -sunk /-sʌŋk/) **1** enlarge the top of (a hole) so that the head of a screw or bolt fits in level with or below the surface. **2** sink (the head of a screw or bolt) in such an enlarged hole.

counter·tenor /'kaʊntətenə(r)/ n (music) (part for an) (adult person with a) male voice higher than tenor; male alto.

counter·vail /'kaʊntəveɪl/ vt,vi **1** [VP6A] counterbalance. **2** [VP2A] have equal or compensating power against: ~ing duties(3), to be paid (as part of a tariff) on imports on which a subsidy is paid in the exporting country.

count·ess /'kaʊntɪs/ n wife or widow of a count or earl; woman to whom an earldom has descended.

count·less /'kaʊntlɪs/ adj that cannot be counted (because too numerous).

coun·tri·fied /'kʌntrɪfaɪd/ adj rural; rustic; having the unsophisticated ways, habits, outlook, etc, of those who live in the country(4), not of towns.

coun·try /'kʌntrɪ/ n (pl -ries) **1** [C] land occupied by a nation: European countries. **2** [C] land of a person's birth or citizenship: to return to one's own ~. **3 the** ~, the people of a ~(1); the nation as a whole: Does the ~ want war? **go to the** ~, (GB) appeal to the public by a general election for the right to form a government(3). **4 the** ~, land used for farming, land consisting of open spaces, etc; the contrary of town and suburb: to live in the ~; to spend a day in the ~. **5** (used attrib) of or in the ~(4): ~ life; ~ roads. ~ **club**, club in the ~ or suburbs, where members may enjoy outdoor sports, etc. ~ **cousin**, (colloq) person who is unaccustomed to town life and ways. ~ **dance**, (esp GB) one in which couples are face to face in two long lines or face inwards from four sides. ~ **gentleman**, man who owns land in the ~ and has a house there. ~**-house**, ~**-seat**, house of a ~ gentleman. '~ **party**, political party supporting agricultural interests (against manufacturing interests). **6** [U] (with attrib adj) area of land (esp considered with reference to its physical or geographical features): We passed through miles of densely wooded ~. This is unknown ~ to me, I have not been through it before (or, fig, This is a branch of learning, etc with which I am unfamiliar).

coun·try·man /'kʌntrɪmən/, **coun·try·woman** /'kʌntrɪwʊmən/ n (pl -men, -women) **1** person living in the country(4). **2** person of one's own (or a specified) country(1).

coun·try·side /'kʌntrɪsaɪd/ n, [U] rural area(s) (contrasted with urban areas): The English ~ looks its best in May and June. The preservation of the ~ is important.

county /'kaʊntɪ/ n **1** [C] division of GB, the largest

unit of local government: the ~ of Kent. ~ **borough**, town having the right to send one or more representatives to Parliament and administrative powers similar to those of a ~ council. ~ **council**, body of persons elected to govern a ~. ~ **court**, local court for certain legal matters, eg recovery of debt. ~ **family**, family that has lived in a ~ for many generations and has an ancestral home in it. ~ **town**, (US = ~ seat) chief town of a ~, where administration is carried on. **the home counties**, those round London. **the** ~, (with sing or pl v) all the ~ families. **2** (in US and other countries) subdivision of a State. **3** (GB; pred use) of a ~ family: Are you ~?

coup /ku:/ n (pl ~s /ku:z/) (F) sudden action taken to get power, obtain a desired result, etc: He pulled off/made a great ~, succeeded in what he attempted. ~ **d'état** /ˌku: deɪ'tɑ:/, violent or unconstitutional change in government. ~ **de grâce** /ˌku: də 'grɑ:s US: 'græs/, finishing stroke.

coupé /'ku:peɪ US: ku:'peɪ/ n (pl ~s /-peɪz/) **1** closed horse-drawn carriage with one inside seat for two people and an outside seat for the driver. **2** (US **coupe** /ku:p/ two-door motor-car for two people.

couple[1] /'kʌpl/ n two persons or things, seen together or associated: married ~s; courting ~s; Ten ~s took the floor, went out into the middle of the room to dance. He went out shooting and came back with a ~ of rabbits.

couple[2] /'kʌpl/ vt,vi **1** [VP6A,14] fasten, join (two things) together: to ~ two railway coaches. The dining-car was ~d on at Crewe. We ~ the name of Oxford with the idea of learning. **2** [VP6A,2A] marry; [VP2A] (of animals) unite sexually; [VP2A] (of things) come together; unite.

coup·let /'kʌplɪt/ n two successive lines of verse, equal in length and with rhyme: a heroic ~, with lines of five feet[1](6) and ten syllables.

coup·ling /'kʌplɪŋ/ n [U] act of joining; [C] link, etc that joins two parts, esp two railway coaches or other vehicles.

cou·pon /'ku:pɒn/ n ticket, part of a document, paper, bond, etc, which gives the holder the right to receive sth or do sth, eg a voucher given with a purchase to be exchanged for goods; entry form for a competition: fill in the football ~s, by forecasting results of matches.

cour·age /'kʌrɪdʒ/ n [U] bravery; quality that enables a person to control fear in the face of danger, pain, misfortune, etc. **have the** ~ **of one's convictions**, be brave enough to do what one feels to be right. **not have the** ~ **(to do sth)**, not be brave enough. **lose** ~, become less brave. **take/pluck up/muster up/summon up** ~, be brave. **take one's** ~ **in both hands**, summon up one's ~ for sth needing to be done.

cou·rageous /kə'reɪdʒəs/ adj brave; fearless: It was ~ of him to oppose his chief. ~**·ly** adv

cour·gette /kʊə'ʒet/ n (US = zucchini) small green marrow(3) eaten as a vegetable. ➪ the illus at vegetable.

cour·ier /'kʊrɪə(r)/ n **1** person who is paid to attend to details of travel (eg buying tickets, arranging for hotels, etc) and (sometimes) accompanying travellers. **2** messenger carrying news or important government papers.

course[1] /kɔ:s/ n **1** [U] forward movement in space or time: the ~ of life from the cradle to the grave; a river in its ~ to the sea; the ~ of events. **in** ~ **of,**

in process of: *The railway is in ~ of construction,* being built. **in due ~,** in the natural order; at the normal time: *Sow the seed now and in due ~ you will have the flowers.* **in the ~ of,** during: *in the ~ of the discussion; in the ~ of conversation,* while we were talking; *in the ~ of centuries,* as the centuries pass. **in the (ordinary) ~ of nature/ events/things,** normally; as part of the normal or expected sequence of events. **in (the) ~ of time,** at length; finally; when (enough) time has passed. **2** [C] direction taken by sth; line along which sth moves; line of action: *a map that shows the ~s of the chief rivers;* (liter) *the stars in their ~s. Our ~ was due north. The ~ of the argument suddenly changed,* went in a different direction. *What are the ~s open to us,* the ways in which we may proceed to act? *He took to evil ~s,* formed bad ways of living. **run/take its ~,** develop as is normal; proceed to the usual end: *The disease must run its ~. The law must take its ~,* the lawyers cannot save you from punishment. *We can do nothing except let matters run/take their ~.* **(as) a matter of ~,** (in) a way that one would expect to be or happen, for which no effort is needed: *You needn't ask him to come; he'll come as a matter of ~. Some people take my help as a matter of ~,* expect to get it without asking for it (or even thanking me for it). **of ~,** naturally; certainly: *'Do you study hard?' 'Of ~ I do'.* **on/off ~,** in the right/wrong direction: *Our ship was blown off ~.* **3** [C] ground for golf: *a 'golf–~;* place for horse-races: *a 'race–~.* **stay the ~,** (lit, fig) continue going until the end; not give up. **4** [C] series of talks, treatments, etc: *a ~ of lectures/study/instruction; a ~ of X-ray treatment/pills; the high-school ~.* **5** [C] continuous layer of brick, stone, etc in a wall: *a 'damp–~,* layer of slate or other material to prevent damp rising from the ground. **6** [C] one of the several parts of a meal, eg soup, fish, dessert: *a dinner of five ~s/a five–~ dinner; the main ~.* **7** (naut) sail fastened to the lowest yard of a mast.

course² /kɔːs/ *vt,vi* **1** [VP6A,2A] chase (esp hares) with dogs (greyhounds). **2** [VP2C] move quickly; (of liquids) run: *The blood ~d through his veins. Tears ~d down her cheeks.* **cours·ing** /'kɔːsɪŋ/ *n* sport of chasing hares with greyhounds (by sight, not scent).

courser /'kɔːsə(r)/ *n* (poet) swift horse.

court¹ /kɔːt/ *n* **1** [C] place where law-cases are held; the judges, magistrates, and other officers who administer justice: *a ,~ of 'law/a 'law ~; a '~-room; a ~ of justice; a po'lice–~; a (military or naval) ~ of inquiry,* one that deals with cases of indiscipline, etc. *The prisoner was brought to ~ for trial. The judge ordered the ~ to be cleared,* ordered members of the public to leave. *The case was settled out of ~,* a settlement was reached that made it unnecessary for the case to be decided in ~. **be ruled/put out of ~; put oneself out of ~,** do or say sth so that one is not entitled to be heard in ~. **~ of assize; ~ of quarter sessions,** ~s in England and Wales before 1971. **Crown C~,** (since 1971) one that may sit anywhere in England and Wales for all cases above magistrates' ~ level (replacing the former assize and quarter sessions). **2** [U] residence of a sovereign; his family and officials, councillors, etc: *The C~ of St James's,* the ~ of the British sovereign. *The C~ went into mourning when the Queen's uncle died.* **be presented at ~,** make one's first appearance at a

state reception at the sovereign's ~. **hold ~,** ⇨ hold¹(12). **'~-card,** playing card with a king, queen or knave. **3** [C] space marked out for certain games: *a 'tennis–~. Do you prefer grass ~s or hard ~s?* ⇨ the illus at tennis. **4** (also '~-yard) unroofed space with walls or buildings round it, eg in a college at Cambridge, in a castle or an old inn; the buildings round such a space. Cf *quadrangle* at Oxford. ⇨ close². **5** [C] small enclosed yard of a house, usu opening off a street. **6** [U] **pay ~ to (a woman),** (formal) try to win her affections.

court² /kɔːt/ *vt,vi* **1** [VP6A,2A] try to win the affections of, with a view to marriage: *He had been ~ing Jane for six months. There were several ~ing couples in the park.* **2** [VP6A] try to win or obtain: *to ~ sb's approval/support; to ~ applause.* **3** [VP6A] act in such a way that one may meet or receive (sth disagreeable): *to ~ defeat/ danger/disaster.*

cour·teous /'kɜːtɪəs/ *adj* having, showing, good manners; polite and kind (*to*). **~·ly** *adv*

court·esan /ˌkɔːtɪ'zæn *US:* 'kɔːtɪzn/ *n* (in former times, esp in court(2) circles) refined or high-placed prostitute who (because of her beauty, wit, success) could limit the number of men to whom she gave herself.

cour·tesy /'kɜːtəsɪ/ *n* **1** [U] courteous behaviour. **2** [C] (*pl* -sies) courteous act. **3** '~ title, (GB) title of nobility having no legal validity. **by ~ of,** by favour or permission, usu free of charge: *a radio programme presented by ~ of....*

court·ier /'kɔːtɪə(r)/ *n* person in attendance at the court of a sovereign: *the King and his ~s.*

court·ly /'kɔːtlɪ/ *adj* (-ier, -iest) polite and dignified. **court·li·ness** *n*

court-mar·tial /ˌkɔːt 'mɑːʃl/ *n* (*pl* courts-martial) court for trying offences against military law; trial by ~. □ *vt* [VP6A] (-ll-) try (sb) in a court of this kind.

court·ship /'kɔːt-ʃɪp/ *n* [U] courting(1); [C] period during which this lasts: *after a year's ~; after a brief ~.*

court·yard /'kɔːtjɑːd/ *n* = court¹(4).

cousin /'kʌzn/ *n* **first ~,** child of one's uncle or aunt. **second ~,** child of one's parent's first ~. **~·ly** *adj* of, suitable for, ~s; ~ly affection.

cove¹ /kəʊv/ *n* small bay².

a cove

cove² /kəʊv/ *n* (GB, dated sl) person.

coven /'kʌvn/ *n* assembly of witches.

cov·en·ant /'kʌvənənt/ *n* **1** (legal) formal agreement that is legally binding. **,deed of '~,** written, signed and sealed agreement, usu concerning property. **2** undertaking to make regular payments to a charity, trust, etc. □ *vt,vi* [VP6A,7A,9,14,3A] **~ (with sb) (for sth)** make a ~.

Cov·en·try /'kɒvntrɪ/ *n* town in Warwickshire, GB. **send a person to** ∼, refuse to associate with him (esp by not speaking to him).

cover[1] /'kʌvə(r)/ *vt* [VP6A,15A,B] **1** place (one substance or thing) over or in front of (another); hide or protect (sth) in this way; lie or extend over; occupy the surface of: *C*∼ *the table with a cloth. Pull your skirt down and* ∼ *your knees. We shall* ∼ *the seat of this old chair with chintz. Snow* ∼ed *the ground. The floods* ∼ed *large areas on both banks of the river. She* ∼ed *her face in/with her hands. He laughed to* ∼ (= hide) *his nervousness.* ∼ **in,** complete the ∼ing of: *The grave was quickly* ∼ed *in,* filled with earth. ∼ **over,** spread sth over: *to* ∼ *over a hole in a roof.* ∼ **up,** wrap up, hide: *C*∼ *yourself up well,* Put on warm clothes, etc. *How can we* ∼ *up our tracks/our mistakes?* Hence, ∼-**up** *n* (fig, colloq) way of hiding: *a* ∼-*up for her shyness.* ∼ed **wagon** *n* (US) large wagon with an arched canvas roof, used by pioneers for travel across the prairies. **2 be** ∼ed **with, (a)** have a great number or amount of: *trees* ∼ed *with blossom/fruit; roses* ∼ed *with greenfly.* **(b)** have as a natural coat: *Cats are* ∼ed *with fur and dogs are* ∼ed *with hair.* **(c)** (of non-material things) be overcome by: ∼ed *with shame/confusion.* **3** sprinkle or strew with: *A taxi went by and* ∼ed *us with mud. The wind blew from the desert and* ∼ed *everything with sand.* **4** (reflex) bring upon oneself: ∼ *oneself with glory/honour/disgrace.* **5** protect: *He* ∼ed *his wife from the man's blows with his own body. Warships* ∼ed *the landing of the invading army,* fired their guns to keep the enemy at a distance, etc. *Are you* ∼ed (= insured) *against fire and theft?* **6** travel (a certain distance): *By sunset we had* ∼ed *thirty miles.* **7** (of guns, fortresses, etc) command(6); dominate: *Our heavy artillery* ∼ed *every possible approach to the town.* **8** keep a gun aimed at sb (so that he cannot shoot or escape): *C*∼ *your man! Keep them* ∼ed! **9** (of money) be enough for: *£10 will* ∼ *my needs for the journey. We have only just* ∼ed *our expenses,* made enough for our expenses, but no profit. **10** include; comprise; extend over; be adequate for: *Professor A's lectures* ∼ed *the subject thoroughly. His researches* ∼ed *a wide field. This book does not fully* ∼ *the subject,* does not deal with all aspects of it. *Do the rules* ∼ (= Are they adequate for) *all possible cases?* **11** (in games such as cricket and baseball) stand behind (a player) to stop balls that he may miss: *The short-stop* ∼ed *second base.* **12** (of a journalist) report (what is said and done at meetings, on public occasions, etc): ∼ *the Labour Party's annual conference.* ∼-**ing** *n* sth that ∼s: *a leafy* ∼ing, the trees. □ *part adj* ∼ing **letter,** one sent with a document, or with goods, etc.

cover[2] /'kʌvə(r)/ *n* **1** thing that covers: *When the water boils, take the* ∼ (= lid) *from the pan. Some chairs are fitted with loose* ∼s. **2** binding of a book, magazine, etc; either half of this: *The book needs a new* ∼. **from** ∼ **to** ∼, from beginning to end: *The child read the book from* ∼ *to* ∼. '∼ **girl,** girl who poses for photographs to be used on the cover of a magazine. **3** wrapper or envelope. **under plain** ∼, in a parcel or envelope which has no indication of the firm, the contents, etc: *The book of photographs of girls in the nude is being sent under plain* ∼. **under separate** ∼, (comm) in a separate parcel or envelope: *We are sending the goods under separate* ∼. **4** [U] place or area giving shelter or protection: *The land was flat and treeless and provided no* ∼ *for the troops.* **take** ∼, place oneself where one is protected or concealed: *There was nowhere where we could take* ∼, eg from rain. **under** ∼, sheltered. **5** [U] woods or undergrowth protecting animals, etc. **break** ∼, (eg of a fox) come out of the undergrowth, etc. **6** [U] **under** ∼ **of,** with a pretence of: *under* ∼ *of friendship/ religion; murders committed under* ∼ *of patriotism.* **7** [U] protection from attack: *give* ∼. **8** place laid at table for a meal: *C*∼s *were laid for six.* '∼ **charge** *n* (in a restaurant) charge in addition to the cost of the food and drink. **9** [U] (comm) money deposited to meet a liability or possible loss. **10** [U] insurance against loss, damage, etc: *Does your policy provide adequate* ∼ *against fire?* '∼ **note,** document from an insurance company to provide temporary ∼ between the acceptance and issue of a policy.

cover·age /'kʌvərɪdʒ/ *n* [U] covering of events, etc: *TV* ∼ *of the election campaign,* eg by televising political meetings, interviews with candidates and voters. ⇨ cover[1](12).

cover·let /'kʌvəlɪt/ *n* bedspread.

cov·ert[1] /'kʌvət/ *adj* (half-) hidden; disguised: ∼ *glances/threats.* ∼·**ly** *adv* ⇨ overt.

cov·ert[2] /'kʌvət/ *n* area of thick undergrowth in which animals hide. **draw a** ∼, search it (for foxes, etc). ⇨ cover[2](5).

covet /'kʌvɪt/ *vt* [VP6A] desire eagerly (esp sth that belongs to sb else).

covet·ous /'kʌvɪtəs/ *adj* ∼ **(of),** eagerly desirous (esp of things belonging to sb else). ∼·**ly** *adv* ∼·**ness** *n*

covey /'kʌvɪ/ *n* (*pl* ∼s) brood, small flock of partridges.

cow[1] /kaʊ/ *n* fully grown female of any animal of the ox family, esp the domestic kind kept by farmers for producing milk, ⇨ the illus at domestic; also female elephant, rhinoceros, whale, etc. ⇨ bull[1](1), calf[1](1), heifer, steer[1]. '**cow·bell,** bell hung round a cow's neck to indicate her whereabouts. '**cow·boy,** man (usu on horseback) who looks after cattle in the western parts of the US. '**cow-catcher,** metal frame fastened to the front of a railway engine to push obstacles off the track. '**cow·hand, 'cow·herd,** person who looks after cattle at pasture. '**cow·hide,** leather (or a strip of leather as a whip) made from a cow's hide. '**cowhouse, 'cow·shed,** building in which cows are kept when not at pasture, or to which they are taken to be milked. '**cow·man** /-mən/ (*pl* -men), man responsible for milking cows. '**cow·skin,** (leather from the) skin of a cow.

cow[2] /kaʊ/ *vt* [VP6A] frighten (sb) into submission: *The child had a cowed look,* looked frightened because of threats of violence, etc.

cow·ard /'kaʊəd/ *n* person unable to control his fear; person who runs away from danger. **turn** ∼, become a ∼. ∼·**ly** *adj* **1** not brave. **2** contemptible; of or like a ∼: *a* ∼ly *lie;* ∼ly *behaviour.*

cow·ard·ice /'kaʊədɪs/ *n* [U] feeling, way of behaviour, of a coward; faint-heartedness.

cower /'kaʊə(r)/ *vi* [VP2A,C] lower the body; crouch; shrink back from cold, misery, fear, shame: *The dog* ∼ed *under the table when its master raised the whip.*

cowl /kaʊl/ *n* **1** long, loose gown (as worn by monks) with a hood that can be pulled over the head; the hood itself. **2** metal cap for a chimney, ventilating pipe, etc, often made so as to revolve with the wind and improve the draught(1). ∼-ing *n* removable metal covering for an (aircraft) engine.

cow·pox /'kaʊpɒks/ *n* contagious disease of cattle, caused by a virus which, when isolated, is the source of vaccine for smallpox.

cow·rie /'kaʊrɪ/ *n* (*pl* ∼s) small shell formerly used as money in parts of Africa and Asia.

cow·slip /'kaʊslɪp/ *n* small plant with yellow flowers, growing wild in temperate countries.

cox /kɒks/ *n* (colloq abbr of) coxswain. □ *vt,vi* [VP6A,2A] act as coxswain (of a rowing-boat): *The Oxford boat was coxed by...*

cox·comb /'kɒkskəʊm/ *n* vain, foolish person, esp one who pays too much attention to his clothes.

cox·swain /'kɒksn/ *n* person who steers a rowing-boat, esp in races; person in charge of a ship's boat and crew. ⇨ the illus at **eight**.

coy /kɔɪ/ *adj* (-er, -est) (esp of a girl) shy, modest; pretending to be shy; seeming more modest than one really is. **coy·ly** *adv* **coy·ness** *n*

coy·ote /kɔɪˈəʊt US:* 'kaɪəʊt/ *n* prairie wolf of western N America.

coypu /'kɔɪpuː/ *n* S American rodent with webbed hind feet, bred for its fur (*nutria fur*). ⇨ nutria.

cozen /'kʌzn/ *vt* [VP6A,14] ∼ *sb (out) of sth,* (liter) defraud him of sth. ∼ *sb into doing sth,* (liter) beguile him into it.

cozy /'kəʊzɪ/ *adj* US = cosy.

crab¹ /kræb/ *n* [C] ten-legged shellfish; [U] its meat as food. ⇨ the illus at **crustacean**. *catch a* ∼, (rowing) make a faulty stroke with one's oar.

crab² /kræb/ *n* (also '∼-apple) wild apple-tree; its hard, sour fruit.

crab³ /kræb/ *vi,vt* (-bb-) (colloq) complain; grumble; criticize.

crab·bed /'kræbɪd/ *adj* **1** bad-tempered; easily irritated. **2** (of handwriting) difficult to read; (of writings, authors) difficult to understand.

crack¹ /kræk/ *n* **1(a)** line of division where sth is broken, but not into separate parts: *a cup with bad* ∼*s in it. Don't go skating today—there are dangerous* ∼*s in the ice.* **(b)** narrow opening. *open sth a* ∼, open it very slightly. *the* ∼ *of dawn,* (colloq) day-break. **2** sudden, sharp noise (as of a rifle or whip, or sth breaking): *the* ∼ *of a pistol shot; a* ∼ *of thunder. the* ∼ *of doom,* the peal of thunder on the Day of Judgement. **3** sharp blow which can be heard: *give sb/get a* ∼ *on the head.* **4** (sl) (= *wise*∼) lively, forceful, or cutting comment or retort, esp one that causes laughter. **5** (sl) attempt. *have a* ∼ *at sth,* try to do sth which is difficult. **6** (attrib use) first-rate; very clever or expert: *a* ∼ *polo-player; a* ∼ *regiment. He's a* ∼ *shot,* expert at using a rifle. **7** '∼-brained *adj* crazy; foolish: *a* ∼*-brained scheme.*

crack² /kræk/ *vt,vi* **1** [VP6A,14,2A,C] get or make a crack or cracks(1) in: *I can* ∼ *it, but I can't break it. You've* ∼*ed the window. The glass will* ∼ *if you pour boiling water into it. He fell out of the window and* ∼*ed his skull.* **2** [VP6A,2A] make, cause to make, a crack or cracks(2): *to* ∼ *a whip/the joints of the fingers. The hunter's rifle* ∼*ed and the deer fell dead. We heard a* ∼*ing noise among the trees.* ∼ *open,* open with a ∼ing sound: ∼ *open a safe.* **3** [VP2A] (of the voice) become harsh; (of a boy's voice when he is reaching puberty) undergo a change and become dissonant (*break* is more usu). **4** [VP6A] decompose (petroleum) by using heat and pressure so as to change thick oils into thinner oils.

Hence, '∼-ing *plant.* **5** (colloq and sl uses) ∼ *down on sb/sth,* take disciplinary action against: ∼ *down on gambling.* Hence, '∼-down *n.* ∼ *sb/ sth up (to be sth),* [VP15B] praise highly, or in an exaggerated way: *He's not so clever as he's* ∼*ed up to be.* ∼ *up,* **(a)** [VP2C] lose strength (in old age); suffer a mental collapse. Hence, '∼-up *n* failure; breakdown. **(b)** [VP2C,15B] (of a vehicle) (cause to) suffer damage, crash. ∼ *a bottle,* open one and drink the contents. ∼ *a joke,* make one. ⇨ crack¹(4). *get* ∼*ing,* get busy (with work waiting to be done).

cracker /'krækə(r)/ *n* **1** thin, flaky, dry biscuit (as eaten with cheese). **2** firework that makes cracking noises when set off: *The Chinese use* ∼*s to frighten away evil spirits.* '**Christmas** ∼, one made of brightly coloured paper, which explodes harmlessly when the ends are pulled. **3** (*pl,* also '**nut-**∼s) instrument for cracking nuts.

crackers /'krækəz/ *pred adj* (GB sl) *mad; crazy.*

crackle /'krækl/ *vi* [VP2A,C] make a series of small cracking sounds, as when one treads on dry twigs, or when dry sticks burn: *a crackling camp-fire. A cheerful wood fire was crackling in the sitting-room.* □ *n* [U] **1** small cracking sounds, as described above: *the distant* ∼ *of machine-gun fire.* **2** (also '∼-china/∼-ware) china, etc covered with a network of what appear to be tiny cracks.

crack·ling /'kræklɪŋ/ *n* [U] **1** ⇨ crackle(1). **2** crisp, well-cooked skin of roast pork.

crack·pot /'krækpɒt/ *n* eccentric person with strange ideas: (attrib) ∼ *ideas.*

cracks·man /'kræksmən/ *n* (*pl*-men) burglar.

cradle /'kreɪdl/ *n* **1** small, low bed sometimes mounted on rockers, for a newborn baby: *from/in the* ∼, from/during infancy; *from the* ∼ *to the grave,* from birth to death. **2** (fig) place where sth is born or begins: *Greece, the* ∼ *of Western culture.* **3** framework resembling a ∼ or which is used like a ∼, eg a structure on which a ship is supported while being built or repaired; platform that can be moved up and down an outside wall by means of ropes and pulleys, used by workmen; part of a telephone apparatus on which the receiver rests. □ *vt* [VP6A,14] place, hold, in or as in a ∼: ∼ *a child in one's arms;* ∼ *the telephone receiver,* put it down.

craft /krɑːft US:* kræft/ *n* **1** [C] occupation, esp one in which skill in the use of the hands is needed; such a skill or technique: *the potter's* ∼; *to learn the* ∼ *of the woodcarver; a school for arts and* ∼*s.* Used in many compounds, as '**needle-**∼, '**wood-**∼, '**handi-**∼, '**stage-**∼. **2** (collective) those engaged in such an occupation, organized in a guild or union: *the* ∼ *of masons; the C*∼, brotherhood of Freemasons. **3** (*pl* unchanged) boat(s), ship(s): *a handy and useful little* ∼. *The harbour was full of all kinds of* ∼/∼ *of all kinds.* ⇨ *air*∼ at air¹(7), *space*∼ at space. **4** [U] cunning; trickery; skill in deceiving: *Be careful when you do business with that man: he's full of* ∼. *He got it from me by* ∼. ∼**y** *adj* (-ier, -iest) full of ∼(4): *a* ∼y *politician; as* ∼y *as a fox.* ∼**·ily** *adv* ∼**·i·ness** *n*

crafts·man /'krɑːftsmən US:* 'kræfts-/ *n* (*pl*-men) skilled workman who practises a craft. ∼**·ship** /-ʃɪp/ *n* skilled workmanship.

crag /kræg/ *n* [C] high, steep, sharp or rugged mass of rock. ∼**·ged** /'krægɪd/ (poet), ∼**·gy** (-ier, -iest) *adjj* having many ∼s. '**crags·man** /-mən/ *n* (*pl*-men) one who is clever at climbing ∼s.

crake /kreɪk/ *n* kinds of bird. ⇨ *corncrake* at

corn¹(1).

cram /kræm/ vt,vi (-mm-) [VP6A,14,15B,2A] **1** ~ *(into)*; ~ *(up)* *(with)*, make too full; put, push, very much or too much into: *to* ~ *food into one's mouth/* ~ *up one's mouth with food; to* ~ *papers into a drawer; an essay* ~*med with quotations.* **2** fill the head with facts (for an examination): *to* ~ *pupils; to* ~ *up a subject*, commit facts to memory (without serious study). ~-'**full** *adj,adv* as full as ~ming can make it. ~-**mer** *n* special school where students are ~med; teacher paid to ~ students for examinations; textbook designed for ~ming; student who ~s for examinations.

cramp¹ /kræmp/ *n* [U] sudden and painful tightening of the muscles, usu caused by cold or overwork, making movement difficult: *writer's* ~, of the finger muscles. *The swimmer was seized with* ~ *and had to be helped out of the water.*

cramp² /kræmp/ *vt* [VP6A] **1** keep in a narrow space; hinder or prevent the movement or growth of: *All these difficulties* ~*ed his progress.* **be** ~**ed for room/space etc,** be without enough room etc. ~ *one's style,* (colloq) prevent one from doing sth as well as one could do it in more favourable circumstances. **2** cause to have, affect with, cramp¹. **3** fasten with a cramp³: ~ *a beam.* **cramped** *part adj* (of handwriting) with small letters close together and for this reason difficult to read.

cramp³ /kræmp/ *n* **1** (also '~-**iron**) metal bar with the ends bent, used for holding together masonry or timbers. **2** = clamp¹.

cram·pon /'kræmpɒn/ *n* (usu *pl*) iron plate with spikes, worn on shoes for walking or climbing on ice, rock etc.

cran·berry /'krænbəri US: -berɪ/ *n* (*pl* -ries) small, red, tart berry of a dwarf shrub, used for making jelly and sauce.

crane¹ /kreɪn/ *n* **1** large wading bird with long legs and neck. ⇨ the illus at **water**. **2** machine with a long arm that can be swung round, used for lifting and moving heavy weights.

jib

cranes

crane² /kreɪn/ *vt,vi* [VP6A,16A,2A,C] stretch (the neck); stretch the neck (like a crane¹(1): *to* ~ *forward; to* ~ *one's neck to see sth.*

crane-fly /'kreɪn flaɪ/ *n* (*pl* -flies) kind of fly with very long legs; daddy-long-legs.

cran·ial /'kreɪnɪəl/ *adj* (anat) of the skull.

cran·ium /'kreɪnɪəm/ *n* (anat) bony part of the head enclosing the brain; skull. ⇨ the illus at **head**.

crank¹ /kræŋk/ *n* L-shaped arm and handle for transmitting rotary motion. '~-**shaft** *n* shaft that turns or is turned by a ~. □ *vt* [VP6A,15B] ~ *(up)*, (of an engine) start, cause to start, by turning a ~.

crank² /kræŋk/ *n* person with fixed (and often strange) ideas, esp on one matter: *a fresh air* ~, one who insists on having windows open, however

cold, stormy, etc, it may be. ~**y** *adj* (-ier, -iest) (of people) odd; eccentric; (of machines, etc) unsteady; unreliable.

cranny /'krænɪ/ *n* (*pl* -nnies) small crack or opening, eg in a wall. **cran·nied** *adj* full of crannies.

crap /kræp/ *vi* (-pp-) ⚠ defecate. □ *n* ⚠ **1** [U] excrement. **2** [C] act of defecating: *have a* ~. **3** [U] (sl) nonsense; sth unpleasant or unwanted. ~**py** *adj* (sl) bad; worthless; unpleasant.

crape /kreɪp/ *n* [U] black silk or cotton material with a wrinkled surface (formerly used for mourning). ⇨ **crêpe**.

craps /kræps/ *n* (also '**crap-shooting**) [U] (US) gambling game played with two dice. **shoot** ~, play this game.

crash¹ /kræʃ/ *n* **1** (noise made by a) violent fall, blow or breaking: *The tree fell with a great* ~. *His words were drowned in a* ~ *of thunder. He was killed in an 'air* ~. '~ **barrier**, fence, rail, wall, etc designed to keep people, vehicles, etc apart where there is danger (eg one in the centre of a motorway). '~-**dive**, sudden dive made by a submarine, eg to escape attack. □ *vi* dive in this way. ,~-'**land** *vi,vt* (of aircraft) land, be landed, partly or wholly out of control, with a ~. Hence, ,**crash-'landing** *n* '~-**helmet**, padded helmet worn to protect the head in case of a ~, eg by a motor-cyclist. '~ **pad,** (sl) place to sleep in an emergency. '~ **programme,** one made with intensive efforts to achieve quick results. **2** ruin; collapse (eg in trade, finance): *The great* ~ *on Wall Street in 1929 ruined international trade.* □ *adv* with a ~.

crash² /kræʃ/ *vt,vi* **1** [VP2A,C,6A] fall or strike suddenly, violently and noisily (esp of things that break): *The bus* ~*ed into a tree. The tree* ~*ed through the window. The dishes* ~*ed to the floor. The aircraft* ~*ed.* **2** [VP2A,C] force or break through violently: ~ *through a barrier;* [VP6A] (sl) = gatecrash. ⇨ **gate. 3** [VP2A] (of a business company, government, etc) come to ruin; meet disaster: *His great financial scheme* ~*ed.* **4** [VP6A] cause to ~: *to* ~ *a plane.*

crash³ /kræʃ/ *n* [U] coarse linen cloth (as used for towels, etc).

crass /kræs/ *adj* (of such qualities as ignorance, stupidity, etc) complete; very great.

crate /kreɪt/ *n* **1** large framework of light boards or basketwork for goods in transport. **2** (sl) old, worn-out motor-car or aircraft. □ *vt* put in a ~.

cra·ter /'kreɪtə(r)/ *n* mouth of a volcano; hole in the ground made by the explosion of a bomb, shell, etc. ~ **lake**, lake in the ~ of an extinct volcano.

cra·vat /krə'væt/ *n* piece of linen, lace, etc loosely folded and worn as a necktie.

crave /kreɪv/ *vt,vi* [VP2A,3A] ~ *(for),* ask earnestly for, have a strong desire for: *to* ~ *(for) mercy/ forgiveness; to* ~ *for a drink.* **crav·ing** /'kreɪvɪŋ/ *n* [C] strong desire: *a craving for strong drink.*

cra·ven /'kreɪvn/ *n, adj* (person who is) cowardly.

craw·fish /'krɔːfɪʃ/ *n* = crayfish.

crawl /krɔːl/ *vi* [VP2A,C] **1** move slowly, pulling the body along the ground or other surface (as worms and snakes do); (of human beings) move in this way, or on the hands and knees: *The wounded soldier* ~*ed into a shell-hole.* ~ *to sb,* (colloq) try to bring oneself into his favour. **2** go very slowly: *Our train* ~*ed over the damaged bridge.* **3** be full of, covered with, things that ~: *The ground was* ~*ing with ants. The child's hair was* ~*ing with vermin.* **4** (of the flesh) feel as if covered with

~ing things: *She says that the sight of snakes makes her flesh ~.* □ *n* **1 a** ~, ~ing movement: *Traffic in Oxford St was reduced to a ~ during the rush hours.* **'pub-~** *vi, n* visit(ing) and drink(ing) at several pubs in succession: *go pub-~ing; go on a pub-~.* **2 (the)** ~, high-speed swimming stroke with alternate circular arm movements and rapid leg kicks. ~**er** *n* person or thing that ~s; (*pl*) overall garment made for a baby to ~ about in.

cray·fish /'kreɪfɪʃ/ *n* freshwater lobster-like shellfish.

crayon /'kreɪən/ *n* stick or pencil of soft coloured chalk, wax or charcoal. □ *vt* draw with ~s.

craze /kreɪz/ *n* enthusiastic interest that may last for a comparatively short time; the object of such interest: *schoolboy ~s,* eg the making of paper darts as weapons; *the modern ~ for bingo.*

crazed /kreɪzd/ *adj* (also **half-~**) wildly excited; mad: *a ~ look/expression; a half-~ prophet.*

crazy /'kreɪzɪ/ *adj* (-ier, -iest) **1** ~ (about), (colloq) wildly excited or enthusiastic: *He is ~ about skiing. I'm ~ about you, darling.* **2** suffering from mental disorder; foolish: *You were ~ to lend that man your money. It was ~ of you to let such a young girl drive your car.* **3** (of buildings, etc) unsafe; likely to collapse. **4** (of quilts, pavements, etc) made up of irregularly shaped pieces fitted together: ~ *paving.* **craz·ily** *adv* **crazi·ness** *n*

creak /kri:k/ *n, vi* [VP2A] (make a) sound like that of an unoiled door-hinge, or badly-fitting floorboards when trodden on. ~**y** *adj* (-ier, -iest) making ~ing sounds: ~*y stairs.* ~**·ily** *adv*

cream /kri:m/ *n* [U] **1** fatty or oily part of milk which rises to the surface and can be made into butter. **2** kind of food containing or resembling ~: ~ *cheese; ice-~; ~ ices; chocolate ~; ~ buns.* **3** substance like ~ in appearance or consistency, used for polishing, as a cosmetic, etc: *'furniture ~; 'shoe-~; 'face-~; 'cold-~.* **4** part of a liquid that gathers at the top: ~ *of tartar/lime.* **5** best part of anything: *the ~ of the crop; the ~ of the story,* the most amusing part, the point of it. **6** (attrib) yellowish-white: ~*-laid/-wove paper,* smooth ~*-coloured writing-paper.* □ *vt* take ~ from (milk); make ~y; add ~ to: ~*ed potatoes,* cooked so that they have the consistency of ~. ~**y** *adj* (-ier, -iest) smooth and rich like ~; containing much ~. ~**·ery** *n* (*pl* -ries) **1** place where milk, ~, butter, cheese, etc are sold. **2** butter and cheese factory.

crease /kri:s/ *n* **1** line made (on cloth, paper, etc) by crushing, folding or pressing: ~*-resistant cloth,* which does not easily form into ~s. **2** (cricket) white line on the ground to mark the positions of certain players (bowlers, batsmen). ⇨ the illus at cricket. □ *vt, vi* [VP6A,2A] make a ~ or ~s in; fall into ~s; get ~s in: *Pack the dresses so that they won't ~. This material ~s easily.*

cre·ate /kri:'eɪt/ *vt* **1** [VP6A] cause sth to exist; make (sth new or original): *God ~d the world. Dickens ~d many wonderful characters in his novels. ~ a part,* (of an actor) be the first to play it. **2** [VP6A] give rise to; produce: *His behaviour ~d a bad impression. Her appearance ~d a sensation.* **3** [VP23,6A] invest (sb) with a rank: *He was ~d Baron of Bunthorp. Eight new peers were ~d.*

cre·ation /kri:'eɪʃn/ *n* **1** [U] the act of creating: *the ~ of great works of art. Economic conditions may be responsible for the ~ of social unrest. Is the ~ of new peers desirable?* **2** [U] all created things:

man, the lord of ~. **(the) C~,** the world or universe as created by God. **3** [C] production of the human intelligence, esp one in which imagination has a part: *the ~s of poets, artists, composers and dramatists. The women were wearing the newest ~s of the Paris dressmakers.*

cre·ative /kri:'eɪtɪv/ *adj* having power to create; of creation: *useful and ~ work,* ie requiring intelligence and imagination, not merely mechanical skill. ~**·ly** *adv* ~**·ness** *n*

cre·ator /kri:'eɪtə(r)/ *n* one who creates. **the C~,** God.

crea·ture /'kri:tʃə(r)/ *n* **1** living animal: *dumb ~s,* animals. **2** (with an *adj*) living person: *a lovely ~,* a beautiful person; *a poor ~,* a contemptible person, or a person who is to be pitied; *a good ~,* a kindhearted person. ~ **comforts,** material needs such as food and drink. **3** person who owes his position to another, esp one who is content to carry out another person's wishes without question: *mere ~s of the dictator.*

crèche /kreʃ US: kreʃ/ *n* **1** (GB) public nursery where babies are looked after while their mothers are at work. **2** (US) crib[1](3).

cre·dence /'kri:dns/ *n* [U] *give/attach ~ to,* (formal) believe (gossip, what is said, etc). *letter of ~,* letter of introduction.

cre·den·tials /krɪ'denʃlz/ *n pl* letters or papers showing that a person is what he claims to be: *His ~ were so satisfactory that he was given the post of manager.*

cred·ible /'kredəbl/ *adj* that can be believed: ~ *witnesses. It hardly seems ~,* seems almost impossible to believe. **cred·ibly** *adv* in a ~ manner: *We are credibly informed that....* **credi·bil·ity** /ˌkredɪ'bɪlətɪ/ *n* [U] the ability to be believed in. **credi'bility gap,** the difference between what sb says and what is considered to be true.

credit[1] /'kredɪt/ *n* **1** [U] belief of others that a person, business company, etc can pay debts, or will keep a promise to pay: *No ~ is given at this shop,* payment must be in cash. *His ~ is good for only £50. If you're very rich, you can probably get unlimited ~. buy/sell on ~,* buy/sell goods, payment being made later. '~ **account,** (US = *charge account*) account with a shop, store, etc under an agreement for payments at a later date (eg monthly or quarterly). '~ **card, (a)** card issued by a business firm enabling the holder to obtain goods and services on ~. **(b)** card issued by a bank, allowing the holder to draw money from its branches and use its cheques in payment for goods and services, with a maximum for each occasion. '~ **note,** (comm) one that gives ~ to a customer for goods returned or for overcharged goods. '~ **sales,** sales for which payment is made, by agreement, later. Cf *cash sales.* **letter of '~,** letter from a bank to its agent(s) giving authority for credit to the holder. '~**-worthy** *adj* accepted by tradesmen, hire-purchase companies, etc as safe for ~. Hence, '~**-worthiness** *n.* **2** [U] money shown as owned by a person, company, etc in a bank account: *How much have I standing to my ~? You have a ~ balance of £250.* **3** [C] sum of money advanced or loaned (by a bank, etc): *The bank refused further ~s to the company.* '~ **squeeze,** (government) policy of making it difficult to borrow money (eg by raising interest rates), as part of a policy against inflation. **4** (bookkeeping) record of a payment received: *Does this item go among the ~s or the debits?* '~**-side,**

right-hand side of an account for recording payment received. ⇨ **debit**. **5** [C] (US) entry on a record to show that a course of study has been completed: ~s *in history and geography; a* '~ *course*, university course depending upon the number of grades and ~s received. **6** [U] honour, approval, good name or reputation: *a man of the highest* ~. **get/take** ~ **(for sth)**, get/take recognition, honour etc: *Candidates will get additional* ~ (ie marks) *for clearly labelled diagrams. It is dishonest to take* ~ *for work done by others.* **give** ~ **(to sb) (for sth)**, give recognition, praise, approval: *He's cleverer than I gave hime* ~ *for*, than I thought. *I gave you* ~ *for being more sensible*, You are less sensible than I thought. *One must give* ~ *where it is due.* **7** *do sb* ~; *do* ~ *to sb*; *be/stand to sb's* ~; *reflect* ~ *on sb*, add to his reputation: *The work does you* ~. *His smart appearance does* ~ *to his tailors. It is/stands greatly to your* ~ *that you have passed such a difficult examination. His fluency in Arabic reflects great* ~ *on/is greatly to the* ~ *of his teacher.* **be a** ~ **to sb/sth**, add to the good name of sb/sth: *The pupils are a* ~ *to their teacher/school.* ~**s**; '~ **titles**, names, shown on a cinema ʋor TV screen, of persons responsible for the acting, direction, production, etc. **8** [U] belief; trust; confidence: *The rumour is gaining* ~. **lend** ~ **to**, strengthen belief in: *The latest news lends* ~ *to the earlier reports.*

credit² /'kredɪt/ *vt* [VP6A,14] ~ *sb/sth* **(with sth)**; ~ *sth* **(to sb/sth)**, **(a)** believe that he/it has sth: *Until now I've always* ~*ed you with more sense. The relics are* ~*ed with miraculous powers. Miraculous powers are* ~*ed to the relics.* **(b)** enter on the ~ side of an account: ~ *a customer with £8;* ~ *£8 to a customer/an account.* ⇨ credit¹(4).

cred·it·able /'kredɪtəbl/ *adj* ~ **(to)**, that brings credit(1,2,3): *a* ~ *attempt; conduct that was very* ~ *to him.* **credi·tably** /'kredɪtəblɪ/ *adv*

credi·tor /'kredɪtə(r)/ *n* person to whom one owes money: *run away from one's* ~*s.*

credo /'kriːdəʊ/ *n* (*pl* ~s /-dəʊz/) creed.

cre·du·lity /krɪ'djuːlətɪ US: -'duː-/ *n* (*pl* -ties) [U,C] too great a readiness to believe things.

credu·lous /'kredjʊləs US: -dʒʊ-/ *adj* (too) ready to believe things: ~ *people who accept all the promises of the politicians.* ~**·ly** *adv*

creed /kriːd/ *n* [C] (system of) beliefs or opinions, esp on religious doctrine. **the C**~, short summary of Christian doctrine.

creek /kriːk/ *n* **1** (GB) narrow inlet of water on the sea-shore or in a river-bank. **2** (N America) small river. **be up the** ~, (sl) be in difficulties.

creel /kriːl/ *n* angler's wicker basket for carrying the fish he catches.

creep /kriːp/ *vi* (*pt,pp* crept /krept/) [VP2A,B,C] **1** move along with the body close to the ground or floor; move slowly, quietly or secretly: *The cat crept silently towards the bird. The thief crept along the corridor.* **2** (of time, age, etc) come on gradually: *Old age* ~*s upon one unawares. A feeling of drowsiness crept over him.* **3** (of plants, etc) grow along the ground, over the surface of a wall, etc: *Ivy had crept over the ruined castle walls.* **4** (of the flesh) have the feeling that things are ~*ing* over it (as the result of fear, repugnance, etc): *The sight of the cold, damp prison cell, with rats running about, made her flesh* ~. ⇨ crawl(4). □ *n* **1** (sl) despicable person who tries to win favour by doing small favours, snooping, etc. **2** *give sb the*

~*s*, (colloq) cause the flesh to ~(4); cause distaste in sb.

creeper /'kriːpə(r)/ *n* insect, bird, etc that creeps; plant that creeps along the ground, over rocks, walls, etc.

creepy /'kriːpɪ/ *adj* (-ier, -iest) (colloq) having or causing a creeping of the flesh, ⇨ creep(4): *a* ~ *story.*

creepy-crawly /ˌkriːpɪ'krɔːlɪ/ *n* (*pl* -ies) (colloq) creeping or crawling insect etc.

cre·mate /krɪ'meɪt/ *vt* [VP6A] burn (a corpse) to ashes: *He says he wants to be* ~*d, not buried.* **cre·ma·tion** /krɪ'meɪʃn/ *n* [U] cremating; [C] instance of this. **cre·ma·tor·ium** /ˌkreməˈtɔːrɪəm/ *n* furnace, building, place, for the cremating of corpses. **cre·ma·tory** /'kremətərɪ US: -tɔːrɪ/ *n* (*pl* -ries) = crematorium.

crème de menthe /ˌkrem də 'mɒnθ/ *n* [U] (F) sweet, thick, green liqueur flavoured with peppermint.

cren·el·lated (US = **-el·ated**) /'krenəleɪtɪd/ *adj* having battlements.

Cre·ole /'kriːəʊl/ *n, adj* **1** (person) of pure European or mixed European and African descent in the West Indies, Spanish America or the old French or Spanish states of the Southern US. **2** (of a) dialect of French, Spanish or English spoken by persons of mixed European and African descent in N and S America and the W Indies.

creo·sote /'krɪəsəʊt/ *n* [U] **1** thick, brown, oily liquid obtained from coal-tar, used to preserve wood. **2** antiseptic obtained from wood-tar.

crêpe, crepe /kreɪp/ *n* [U] **1** any crape that is not black. ⇨ crape. **2** ~ **rubber**, raw rubber pressed into blocks. It has a wrinkled surface and is used for the soles of shoes, etc. **3** ~ **paper**, thin paper with a wavy or wrinkled surface.

crepi·tate /'krepɪteɪt/ *vi* [VP2A] make a series of sharp, crackling sounds. **crepi·ta·tion** /ˌkrepɪ'teɪʃn/ *n* crepitating (sound).

crept ⇨ creep.

cre·pus·cu·lar /krɪ'pʌskjʊlə(r)/ *adj* (formal) of, seen, heard or active during, twilight.

cres·cendo /krɪ'ʃendəʊ/ *n* (*pl* ~s /-dəʊz/), *adv, adj* (passage of music to be played, sth heard) with, of, increasing loudness; (fig) progress towards a climax. ⇨ diminuendo.

cres·cent /'kresnt/ *n* **1** (sth shaped like) the curve of the moon in the first quarter, ⇨ the illus at phase; row of houses in the form of a ~. **2 the C**~, (fig) faith and religion of Islam: *the Cross* (Christianity) *and the C*~. **3** (attrib) ~-shaped; increasing in size: *a* ~ *moon.*

a crescent

cress /kres/ *n* [U] name of various plants, esp the kind with hot-tasting leaves (used in salads and sandwiches).

crest /krest/ *n* **1** tuft of feathers on a bird's head; cock's comb. ⇨ the illus at fowl, water. '~-**fallen**, (fig) dejected, disappointed (at failure, etc). **2** ~-like decoration formerly worn on the top of a helmet; (poet) helmet. **3** design over the shield of a

cricket

PITCH

PLAYERS' POSITIONS

1 third man	14 batsman
2 long stop	15 silly mid-on
3 deep fine leg	16 square leg
4 long leg	17 umpire
5 second slip	18 extra cover
6 first slip	19 mid-off
7 backward point	20 bowler
8 gully	21 umpire
9 wicket keeper	22 batsman
10 leg slip	23 mid-on
11 cover point	24 mid-wicket
12 short extra cover	25 long-off
13 silly mid-off	26 long-on
	... crease

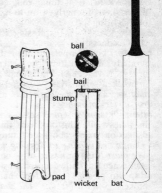

ball

bail

stump

pad wicket bat

Note   Although in fact only eleven men in addition to the
batsmen and umpires are on the field at one time, they can be
placed in any of these positions

coat of arms, or used separately (eg on a seal, or on
notepaper): *the family ~,* one used by a family. **4**
top of a slope or hill; white top of a large wave. **on
the ~ of a wave,** (fig) at the most favourable moment of one's fortunes. **~ed** *adj* having a ~(3):
~ed note-paper; (in compounds, as names of
birds) *the golden-~ed wren.* □ *vt, vi* reach, form
into, a ~ of a hill/wave.
cre·ta·cious /krɪ'teɪʃəs/ *adj* (geol) of (the nature of)
chalk: *the ~ age,* when chalk-rocks were formed.
cre·tin /'kretɪn US:* 'kri:tn/ *n* deformed and mentally
undeveloped person (diseased because of weakness
of the thyroid gland). **~·ous** /'kretɪnəs US:* 'kri:t-/
adj
cre·tonne /'kretɒn/ *n* [U] cotton cloth with printed
designs, used for curtains, furniture covers, etc.
cre·vasse /krɪ'væs/ *n* deep, open crack, esp in ice
on a glacier. ⇨ the illus at **mountain.**
crev·ice /'krevɪs/ *n* narrow opening or crack (in a
rock, wall, etc).
crew[1] /kru:/ *n* **1** (collective noun) all the persons
working on a ship, aircraft, train, etc. **'ground ~,**
mechanics who service an aircraft on the ground. **2**
group of persons working together; gang. **'~-cut** *n*
closely cropped style of hair-cut for men. **'~-neck**
n style of round, close-fitting collar. □ *vi* act as ~
on a boat: *Will you ~ for me in tomorrow's race?*
crew[2] /kru:/ *pt* of **crow**[2].
crib[1] /krɪb/ *n* **1** wooden framework from which
animals can pull out fodder; manger. **2** (US) bin or
box for storing maize, salt, etc. **3** (US = *crèche*)
representation (eg in a church at Christmas) of the
nativity. **4** bed for a newborn baby. □ *vt* (-bb-) shut
up in a small space.
crib[2] /krɪb/ *n* **1** sth copied dishonestly from the
work of another. **2** word-for-word translation of a
foreign text used by students of the language. □
vt, vi (-bb-) use a ~(2); copy (another pupil's written work) dishonestly.
crib·bage /'krɪbɪdʒ/ *n* [U] card-game for two, three
or four persons, who use pegs and a board ('~-
board) with peg-holes in it for keeping the score.
crick /krɪk/ *n* (usu **a ~)** stiff condition of the
muscles of the neck or the back causing sudden,
sharp pain: *to have/get a ~ in the neck.* □ *vt* produce a ~ in: *to ~ one's neck/back.*
cricket[1] /'krɪkɪt/ *n* small, brown jumping insect
which makes a shrill noise by rubbing its front
wings together: *the chirping of ~s.* ⇨ the illus at

insect.
cricket[2] /'krɪkɪt/ *n* [U] ball game played on a grass
field by two teams of eleven players each, with bats
and wickets. **not ~,** (colloq) unfair; unsportsman-
like. **~er** *n* ~ player.
cried /kraɪd/ ⇨ **cry**[1].
crier /'kraɪə(r)/ *n* **1** officer who makes public announcements in a court of law. **,town-'~,** (old use)
man who goes round the streets to make proclamations and announcements. **2** person (esp a young
child) who cries(2) a lot.
cries /kraɪz/ *pres t* of **cry**[1]; *pl* of **cry**[2].
cri·key /'kraɪkɪ/ *int* (colloq) exclamation of surprise.
crime /kraɪm/ *n* **1** [C] offence for which there is
severe punishment by law; [U] such offences collectively; serious law-breaking: *to commit a serious ~; the ~s of which he was proved guilty. It is
the business of the police to prevent and detect ~
and of the law courts to punish ~.* **'~ fiction,**
novels in which the detection of ~ is the chief interest. **2** foolish or wrong act, not necessarily an
offence against the law: *It would be a ~ to send the
boy out on such a cold, wet night.* **3** (in the army)
serious breaking of the regulations (not necessarily
an offence against civil law). **'~ sheet,** record of a
soldier's offences. □ *vt* charge (a man) with, convict (a man) of, a military offence.
crimi·nal /'krɪmɪnl/ *adj* of crime: *a ~ act; a ~ offender; ~ law,* ⇨ *civil law* at civil(1). □ *n* person
who commits a crime or crimes. **~·ly** /-əlɪ/ *adv*
crimi·nol·ogy /ˌkrɪmɪ'nɒlədʒɪ/ *n* [U] the study of
crime.
crimp /krɪmp/ *vt* make (eg hair) wavy or curly (as
with a hot iron).
crim·son /'krɪmzn/ *adj, n* deep red. □ *vt, vi* make or
become ~.
cringe /krɪndʒ/ *vi* [VP2A,C] **1 ~ (at),** move (the
body) back or down in fear: *The dog ~d at the
sight of the whip.* **2** behave (towards a superior) in
a way that shows lack of self-respect; be too humble: *a cringing beggar; to ~ to/before a policeman.*
crinkle /'krɪŋkl/ *n* small, narrow wrinkle (in
material such as foil or paper). □ *vt, vi*
[VP6A,15B,2A,C] **~ (up),** make or get a ~ or ~s
in: *~d paper,* eg crêpe paper. **crin·kly** /'krɪŋklɪ/
adj (-ier, -iest) (of materials) having ~s; (of hair)
curly.

crino·line /'krɪnəlɪn/ n 1 [U] stiff, strong, rough fabric. 2 [C] light framework covered with stiff material, as formerly worn to make a skirt swell out; ⇨ hoop¹(2).

cripes /kraɪps/ int (expressing astonishment, etc) My Goodness!

cripple /'krɪpl/ n person unable to walk or move properly, through injury or weakness in the spine or legs. □ vt [VP6A] (lit, fig) make a ～ of; damage or weaken seriously: ～d soldiers; ～d with rheumatism; a ship that was ～d in a storm; activities ～d by lack of money.

cri·sis /'kraɪsɪs/ n (pl crises /-siːz/) turning-point in illness, life, history, etc; time of difficulty, danger or anxiety about the future: a financial ～. Things are coming to/drawing to/reaching a ～. We must bring things to a ～, do sth to reach the state when a definite decision must be taken.

crisp /krɪsp/ adj 1 (esp of food) hard, dry and easily broken: ～ toast/biscuits. The snow was ～ underfoot. 2 (of the air, the weather) frosty, cold and dry: the ～ air of an autumn morning. 3 (of hair) tightly curled. 4 (of style, manners) quick, precise and decided; showing no doubts or hesitation: a man with a ～ manner of speaking. □ n (US = chip) (also po‚tato '～) thin slice of potato, fried and dried (usu sold in bulk in packets). □ vt,vi make or become ～. ～·ly adv ～·ness n

criss·cross /'krɪskrɒs US: -krɔːs/ adj with crossed lines: a ～ pattern/design. □ adv crosswise. □ vt,vi move crosswise; mark with lines that cross.

cri·terion /kraɪ'tɪərɪən/ n (pl -ria /-rɪə/ or ～s) standard of judgement; principle by which sth is measured for value: Success in money-making is not always a good ～ of real success in life.

critic /'krɪtɪk/ n 1 person who forms and gives judgements, esp about literature, art, music, etc: music(al)/drama(tic)/literary, etc ～s. 2 person who finds fault, points out mistakes, etc: I am my own most severe ～.

criti·cal /'krɪtɪkl/ adj 1 of or at a crisis: We are at a ～ time in our history. The patient's condition is ～, He is dangerously ill. This is a ～ moment, eg one when there will be a change for the better or the worse. 2 of the work of a critic: ～ opinions on art and literature. 3 fault-finding: ～ remarks. She looks on everything with a ～ eye. ～·ly /-ɪklɪ/ adv in a ～ manner: He is ～ly ill.

criti·cism /'krɪtɪsɪzəm/ n 1 [U] the work of a critic; the art of making judgements (concerning art, literature, etc). 2 [C] judgement or opinion on literature, art, etc. 3 [U] fault-finding; [C] remark, etc that finds fault: He hates ～, being criticized. Your frank ～s of his attempts annoyed him.

criti·cize /'krɪtɪsaɪz/ vt,vi [VP6A,14,2A] ～ (for), form and give a judgement of; find fault with: ～ sb's work; ～ sb for doing/not doing sth.

cri·tique /krɪ'tiːk/ n [C] critical essay or review.

croak /krəʊk/ n deep, hoarse sound (as made by frogs or ravens). □ vt,vi [VP2A,6A,15B] ～ (out), make this kind of sound; say (sth) in a ～ing voice; foretell (evil); express dismal views about the future. 3 [VP2A] (sl) die ².

cro·chet /'krəʊʃeɪ US: krəʊ'ʃeɪ/ vt,vi [VP6A,2A] make (needlework, eg a shawl) with a thread looped over others with the help of a small hooked needle (called a '～-hook). □ n [U] material (eg lace) made or being made in this way.

crock¹ /krɒk/ n pot or jar made of baked earth, eg for containing water; broken piece of such a pot:

Fill the bottom of the flower-pot with ～s for drainage.

crock² /krɒk/ n (colloq) horse that has become old, weak and useless; person who cannot work well because of bad health, lameness, etc; very old motor vehicle, etc. □ vi,vt [VP2C,15B] ～ up, become, cause to become, a ～: This attack of influenza has ～ed me up. The poor man is ～ing up.

crock·ery /'krɒkərɪ/ n [U] pots, plates, cups, dishes and other utensils (made of baked clay).

croco·dile /'krɒkədaɪl/ n 1 large river reptile with a long body and tail, covered with a hard skin. ⇨ the illus at reptile. '～ tears n pl insincere sorrow. 2 (GB colloq) school children walking in procession, two by two.

cro·cus /'krəʊkəs/ n (pl ～es /-sɪz/) (kind of) small plant growing from a corm, with coloured flowers early in spring.

Croe·sus /'kriːsəs/ n (6th c BC) wealthy king in Asia Minor. a ～, very wealthy person.

croft /krɒft US: krɔːft/ n (GB) small, enclosed field; small farm. ～er n person who rents or owns a small farm, esp a joint tenant of a divided farm in Scotland.

crom·lech /'krɒmlek/ n prehistoric structure of large flat stones laid horizontally on upright stones.

crone /krəʊn/ n withered old woman.

crony /'krəʊnɪ/ n close friend; companion; close associate.

crook /krʊk/ n 1 stick or staff with a rounded hook at one end, esp such a stick used by a shepherd. ⇨ hook. 2 bend or curve, eg in a river or path. '～-back(ed), hunch-back(ed). 3 (colloq) person who makes a living by dishonest or criminal means. 4 on the ～, (sl) dishonest(ly). □ vt,vi [VP6A,2A] bend into the shape of a ～; to ～ one's finger/arm.

crooked /'krʊkɪd/ adj 1 not straight or level; twisted; bent: a ～ lane. You've got your hat on ～. 2 (of a person or his actions) dishonest; not straightforward. ～·ly adv ～·ness n

croon /kruːn/ vt,vi [VP6A13A,15A,2C] hum or sing gently in a narrow range of notes: ～ to oneself; ～ a lullaby; ～ the baby to sleep. ～er n (1930's and 1940's) person who ～s, esp a public entertainer who sings sentimental songs with a microphone held at the lips.

crop¹ /krɒp/ n [C] 1 yearly (or season's) produce of grain, grass, fruit, etc; (pl) agricultural plants in the fields: the 'potato ～; a good ～ of rice; to get the ～s in; (attrib) ～ failures. The land is in/under ～, being cultivated. The land is out of ～, not being cultivated. '～-dusting, dusting (eg from low-flying aircraft) of growing ～s with insecticide or fertiliser. 2 group of persons or things, amount of anything, appearing or produced together: The Prime Minister's statement produced a ～ of questions.

crop² /krɒp/ n [C] 1 bag-like part of a bird's throat where food is broken up for digestion before passing into the stomach. neck and ～, ⇨ neck. 2 handle of a whip; (also 'hunting-～) whip-handle with a loop instead of a lash. 3 very short hair-cut: You look as if you've had a prison ～, had your hair cut very short, like men in prison.

crop³ /krɒp/ vt,vi (-pp-) 1 [VP6A,22] (of animals) bite off the tops of (grass, plants, etc); graze: The sheep had ～ped the grass short. 2 [VP6A,22] cut short (a person's hair, a horse's tail or ears). 3 [VP6A,14] ～ (with), sow or plant: to ～ ten acres with wheat. 4 [VP2A] bear a crop: The beans ～ped *well this year.* ⇨ crop¹(1). **5** [VP2C] ∼ **up/out,** (of rock, minerals) show up above the earth's surface. ⇨ **outcrop. 6** [VP2C] ∼ **up,** appear or arise (esp unexpectedly): *All sorts of difficulties ∼ped up. The subject ∼ped up in the course of conversation.*

crop·per /'krɒpə(r)/ *n* **1** **good/bad/heavy/light** ∼, plant yielding a good etc crop: *These peas are good ∼s.* **2** person or thing that crops. ⇨ **sharecropper** at **share¹**(1). **3** **come a** ∼, (colloq) have a fall; meet with failure (eg in an examination).

cro·quet /'krəʊkeɪ US: krəʊ'keɪ/ *n* [U] game played on short grass with wooden balls which are knocked with wooden mallets through hoops.

cro·quette /krəʊ'ket/ *n* [C] ball of minced meat, fish, potato etc, coated with bread-crumbs and cooked in fat.

crore /krɔ:(r)/ *n* (India and Pakistan) ten millions; one hundred lakhs (eg of rupees).

cro·sier, cro·zier /'krəʊzɪə(r) US: -ʒər/ *n* bishop's staff, usu shaped like a shepherd's crook. ⇨ the illus at **vestment.**

cross¹ /krɒs US: krɔ:s/ *n* **1** mark made by drawing one line across another, thus: ×, +: *The place is marked on the map with a* ∼. **make one's** ∼, put a ∼ on a document instead of one's signature (as in former times by illiterate persons). **2** line or stroke forming part of a letter (eg the horizontal stroke on a 't'). **3** stake or post with another piece of wood across it like T, † or X, as used in ancient times for crucifixion, esp **the C**∼, that on which Christ died; model of this as a religious emblem; sth (esp a monument) in the form of a ∼ (eg one in stone set up in the market-place of a village or town, called a **'market**∼); sign of a ∼ made with the right hand as a religious act. **4** (fig) suffering; affliction; burden of sorrow: *to bear one's* ∼; *to take up one's* ∼, be ready to bear affliction or suffering. **5** emblem, in the form of a ∼ or a star, (to be) worn by an order of knighthood; decoration for personal valour: *the Victoria C*∼; *the Distinguished Service C*∼. **6** (place of) crossing. **cut on the** ∼, (dressmaking) cut diagonally: *This skirt material was cut on the* ∼, *on the bias.* **7** offspring of animals or plants of different sorts or breeds: *A mule is a* ∼ *between a horse and an ass.*

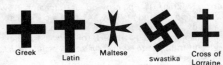

| Greek | Latin | Maltese | swastika | Cross of Lorraine |

crosses

cross² /krɒs US: krɔ:s/ *vt, vi* **1** [VP6A,2A,C] ∼ **(from) (to),** go across; pass from one side to the other side of: *to* ∼ *a road/river/bridge/the sea/the Sahara, etc; to* ∼ *from Dover to Calais.* ∼ **a person's path,** meet him: *I hope I shall never* ∼ *that man's path again.* ∼ **one's mind,** (of ideas, etc) occur to one: *The idea has just* ∼*ed my mind that….* **2** [VP6A,15A,B] ∼ **(off/out/through),** draw a line or lines across or through (to cancel): *Two of the words had been* ∼*ed out. I* ∼*ed his name off the list.* ∼ **a cheque,** draw two lines across it so that payment can be made only through a bank. Hence, ∼**ed 'cheque** *n* one that must be paid into a bank account, and cannot be cashed unless made out to 'self' or 'cash'. ∼ **one's t's and dot one's i's,** (fig) be careful and exact. **3**

[VP6A,14] put or place across or over: *to* ∼ *one's legs; to* ∼ *one's arms on one's chest.* ∼ **sb's palm with silver,** give a coin to him (esp to a fortuneteller). ∼ **swords with sb,** fight or argue with him. **keep one's fingers** ∼**ed,** (fig) hope for the best, that nothing will happen to upset one's plans, etc. **4** ∼ **oneself,** make the sign of the cross on or over oneself as a religious act, to invoke God's protection, or as a sign of awe. **5** [VP6A,2A] (of persons travelling, letters in the post) meet and pass: *We* ∼*ed each other on the way. Our letters* ∼*ed in the post. Your letter* ∼*ed mine in the post.* ∼**ed line,** interruption by mistake into a telephone connection. **6** [VP6A] oppose or obstruct (sb, his plans, wishes, etc): *He was angry at having his plans* ∼*ed. He* ∼*es me in everything. He has been* ∼*ed in love,* has failed to win the love of the woman he was in love with. **7** [VP6A,14] ∼ **(with),** produce a cross(7) by mixing breeds; (cause to) interbreed; cross-fertilize (plants, etc). ⇨ **crossbreed.**

cross³ /krɒs US: krɔ:s/ *adj* **1** (colloq) bad-tempered; easily or quickly showing anger: *Don't be* ∼ *with the child for being late. I've never heard a* ∼ *word from her lips. Don't pull the dog's tail, you'll make him* ∼. **as** ∼ **as two sticks,** (colloq) very bad-tempered. **2** (of winds) contrary; opposed: *Strong* ∼ *winds made it difficult for the yachts to leave harbour.* ∼**·ly** *adv* ∼**·ness** *n*

cross-bar /'krɒsbɑ:(r) US: 'krɔ:s-/ *n* bar going across, eg the bar joining the two upright posts of the goal (in football, etc) or the front and rear ends of a bicycle frame. ⇨ the illus at **bicycle.**

cross-beam /'krɒsbi:m US: 'krɔ:s-/ *n* beam placed across, esp one that supports parts of a structure; girder.

cross-benches /'krɒsbentʃɪz US: 'krɔ:s-/ *n pl* those benches in the House of Commons used by members who do not vote regularly with either the Government or the Opposition. Hence, **cross-bencher** *n* ⇨ **bench.**

cross-bones /'krɒsbəʊnz US: 'krɔ:s-/ *n pl* (design of) two thigh bones laid across each other, usu under a skull, as an emblem of death (used as a warning of danger, and on the black flag once used by pirates).

cross-bow /'krɒsbəʊ US: 'krɔ:s-/ *n* old kind of bow placed across a grooved wooden support, used for shooting arrows, bolts, stones, etc.

cross-bred /'krɒsbred US: 'krɔ:s-/ *adj* produced by crossing breeds: ∼ *sheep.*

cross-breed /'krɒsbri:d US: 'krɔ:s-/ *n* (in farming, etc) animal, plant, etc, produced by crossing different kinds. □ *vt* [VP2A,6A] produce in this way.

cross-check /ˌkrɒs 'tʃek US: ˌkrɔ:s/ *vt, vi* [VP6A,2A] verify, eg a method, calculation, by using a different method, etc: *We* ∼*ed the results twice.* □ *n* verification of this sort: *We'd better do a* ∼ *on these figures.*

cross-country /ˌkrɒs'kʌntrɪ US: ˌkrɔ:s-/ *adj, adv* across the country or fields, not along roads: *a* ∼ *race.*

cross-cur·rent /'krɒs kʌrənt US: 'krɔ:s -/ *n* current flowing across another; (fig) body of opinion contrary to that of the majority (on sth of public interest).

cross-cut /'krɒskʌt US: 'krɔ:s-/ *adj* (of a saw) with teeth designed for cutting across the grain of wood. □ *n* diagonal cut or path; short cut.

cross-division /ˌkrɒs dɪ'vɪʒn US: ˌkrɔ:s/ *n* [U] division of a group according to more than one factor at the same time so that sub-divisions interrelate; [C] instance of this.

crosse /krɒs *US:* krɔːs/ *n* kind of long-handled racquet used in lacrosse.

cross-exam·ine /ˌkrɒs ɪgˈzæmɪn *US:* ˌkrɔːs/ *vt* [VP6A] question closely, esp to test answers already given to someone else, as in a law court, by counsel, etc. **cross-examiner** /-mɪnə(r)/ *n* **cross-exam·in·ation** /ˌkrɒs ɪgˌzæmɪˈneɪʃn *US:* ˌkrɔːs/ *n*

cross·eyed /ˈkrɒsaɪd *US:* ˈkrɔːs-/ *adj* with one or both eyeballs turned towards the nose.

cross-fer·ti·lize /ˌkrɒs ˈfɜːtəlaɪz *US:* ˌkrɔːs/ *vt* (bot) carry pollen from the stamens of one plant to the pistil of another plant to produce hybrids. **cross-fer·ti·li·za·tion** /ˌkrɒs ˌfɜːtəlaɪˈzeɪʃn *US:* ˌkrɔːs/ *n*

cross·fire /ˈkrɒsfaɪə(r) *US:* ˈkrɔːs-/ *n* [U,C] (mil) firing of guns from two or more points so that the lines of fire cross; (fig) situation in which questions are put to sb from different persons.

cross-grained /ˌkrɒs ˈgreɪnd *US:* ˌkrɔːs/ *adj* **1** (of wood) with the grain in crossing directions. **2** (fig) perverse; difficult to please or get on with.

cross-head(·ing) /ˈkrɒs hed(ɪŋ) *US:* ˈkrɔːs/ *n* (in a newspaper, etc) heading within an article, dividing a column.

cross-index /ˌkrɒs ˈɪndeks *US:* ˌkrɔːs/ *n*, *vt* [VP6A] (supply with) cross-reference.

cross·ing /ˈkrɒsɪŋ *US:* ˈkrɔːs-/ *n* **1** [U,C] the act of going across, esp by sea: *We had a rough ~ from Dover to Calais.* **2** [C] place where two roads, two railways, or (esp) a road and a railway cross. **level** '~, one without a bridge (US = *grade* ~). **3** **pe͵destrian/zebra** '~, place on a street where pedestrians are requested to cross (often marked by studs or white lines and sometimes by traffic lights operated by pedestrians) (US = *crosswalk*).

cross·keys /ˌkrɒsˈkiːz *US:* ˌkrɔːs/ *n pl* (design of) crossed keys as Papal arms, and as an inn sign.

cross-legged /ˌkrɒs ˈlegd *US:* ˌkrɔːs/ *adv* (of a person sitting) with one leg placed across the other.

cross·patch /ˈkrɒspætʃ *US:* ˈkrɔːs-/ *n* (colloq) cross, bad-tempered person.

cross-piece /ˈkrɒs piːs *US:* ˈkrɔːs/ *n* piece (of a structure) lying across another piece.

cross-pur·poses /ˌkrɒs ˈpɜːpəsɪz *US:* ˌkrɔːs/ *n pl* *be at ~,* (of two persons or groups) misunderstand one another; have different and conflicting purposes.

cross-question /ˌkrɒs ˈkwestʃən *US:* ˌkrɔːs/ *vt* [VP6A] = cross-examine.

cross-ref·er·ence /ˌkrɒs ˈrefrəns *US:* ˌkrɔːs/ *n* [C] reference from one part of a book, index, file, etc to another, for further information.

cross-road /ˈkrɒsrəʊd *US:* ˈkrɔːs-/ *n* **1** road that crosses another. **2 a/the ~s,** (used with *sing v*) place where two roads meet and cross: *We came to a ~s.* **3 at the ~s,** (fig) at a critical turning-point (in life, etc).

cross-sec·tion /ˌkrɒs ˈsekʃn *US:* ˌkrɔːs/ *n* [C] (drawing of a) piece or slice made by cutting across, eg a tree trunk; (fig) typical or representative sample of the whole: *a ~ of the electors/the middle classes.*

cross-stitch /ˈkrɒs stɪtʃ *US:* ˈkrɔːs/ *n* [C] stitch formed of two stitches that cross; [U] needlework in which this stitch is used.

cross-talk /ˈkrɒs tɔːk *US:* ˈkrɔːs/ *n* [U] (GB, colloq) rapid exchange of remarks, eg by comedians in a

variety entertainment or in a quarrel; talk in which conversation is garbled, eg by crossed telephone lines.

cross·trees /ˈkrɒstriːz *US:* ˈkrɔːs-/ *n pl* two horizontal timbers bolted to a lower mast to support the mast above and to support ropes, etc.

cross·walk /ˈkrɒswɔːk *US* ˈkrɔːs-/ *n* ⇨ crossing(3).

cross·wind /ˈkrɒswɪnd *US:* ˈkrɔːs-/ *n* [C] wind blowing at right angles, eg to an aircraft's line of flight or to traffic on a motorway.

cross-wise /ˈkrɒs waɪz *US:* ˈkrɔːs/ *adv* across; diagonally; in the form of a cross.

cross·word /ˈkrɒswɜːd *US:* ˈkrɔːs-/ *n* (also '~ **puzzle**) puzzle in which words have to be written (from numbered clues) vertically (= clues *down*) and horizontally (= clues *across*) in spaces on a chequered square or oblong.

crotch /krɒtʃ/ *n* **1** place where a branch forks from a tree: *The child was sitting in a ~ of a tree.* **2** place where a pair of trousers or a person's legs fork from the trunk.

crotchet /ˈkrɒtʃɪt/ *n* **1** (music) (US = *quarter note*) black-headed note with stem (♩), half of a minim. ⇨ the illus at notation. **2** strange, unreasonable idea. **~y** *adj* full of ~s(2); bad-tempered.

crouch /kraʊtʃ/ *vi* [VP2A,C,4A] **~ (down),** lower the body with the limbs together (in fear or to hide, or, of animals, ready to spring). □ *n* ~ing position.

croup¹ /kruːp/ *n* [U] children's disease in which there is inflammation of the windpipe, with coughing and difficulty in breathing.

croup² /kruːp/ *n* rump or buttocks of certain animals. ⇨ the illus of *horse* at domestic.

crou·pier /ˈkruːpɪeɪ *US:* -pɪər/ *n* person who rakes in the money at a gaming table and pays out winnings.

crow¹ /krəʊ/ *n* (kinds of) large, black bird with a harsh cry. ⇨ the illus at bird. ⇨ also carrion, jackdaw, raven, rook¹. *as the '~ flies,* in a straight line. '~'s-nest, protected look-out platform fixed at the mast-head of a ship (eg a whaling ship) for the look-out man. '~'s-feet *n pl* network of little lines on the skin near the outer corners of a person's eyes.

crow² /krəʊ/ *vi* (*pt* crowed or (archaic) crew /kruː/, *pp* crowed) [VP6A,3A] **1** (of a cock) make a loud, shrill cry. **2** (of a baby) make sounds showing happiness. **3 ~ (over),** (of persons) express gleeful triumph: *to ~ over an unsuccessful rival.* □ *n* ~ing sound.

crow·bar /ˈkrəʊbɑː(r)/ *n* straight iron bar, often with a forked end, used as a lever for moving heavy objects.

crowd /kraʊd/ *n* [C] **1** large number of people together, but without order or organization: *There were large ~s of people in the streets on New Year's Eve. He pushed his way through the ~. (would) pass in a ~,* is not obviously unsatisfactory or defective. **2 the ~,** the masses; people in general. *follow/move with the ~,* be content to do what most people do. **3** (colloq) company of persons associated in some way; set or clique of persons: *I can't afford to go about with that ~; they're too extravagant.* **4** large number (of things, usu without order): *a desk covered with a ~ of books and papers.* □ *vi, vt* **1** [VP2B,C,6A,14,15A,B] come together in a ~: *~ a beach/square/hall. Now, don't all ~ together!* **~ round,** form a circle (round): *People quickly ~ round when there is a street accident. The pupils ~ed round the teacher to ask questions.* ~ **through/in/into, etc;** ~ **(sth) with,** (cause to) move through, etc in a ~; fill with: *They ~ed through the gates into the stadium. They ~ed the buses with passengers/~ed people into the buses. Let's not ~ the room with furniture. Memories ~ed in upon me,* came thick and fast into my mind. ~ **sb/sth out (of),** keep out by ~ing: *There was an overflow meeting for those who were ~ed out,* unable to obtain admission. *Your contribution to the magazine was ~ed out,* There was no space for it. **2** (naut) ~ **on sail,** hoist many sails (so as to increase speed). **3** [VP6A] (colloq) put pressure on: *Don't ~ me; give me time to think!* ~**ed** *part adj* having large numbers of people: *~ed cities/trains/buses.*

crown¹ /kraʊn/ *n* **1** ornamental headdress of gold, jewels, etc worn by a sovereign ruler; royal power: *to wear the ~,* rule as a sovereign; *succeed to the ~,* become the sovereign ruler; *an officer of the ~,* a State official; *a minister of the ~,* a Cabinet Minister; *a ~ appointment,* one made by the sovereign. **C~ Colony,** one governed completely by Great Britain. ~**-land,** land that belongs to the C~. ~ **prince,** next in succession to the throne. ~ **princess,** wife of a ~ prince. ~ **witness,** witness for the Prosecution in a criminal case. **2** circle or wreath of flowers or leaves worn on the head, esp as a sign of victory, or as a reward: *a martyr's ~.* **3** British coin worth 25p, formerly 5 shillings. **half a ~; a half-~,** (until 1971) British coin worth 12½p. **4** top of the head or of a hat; part of a tooth that shows; (fig) perfection, completion: *the ~ of one's labours; the ~ of the year,* the autumn, season of harvests. **5** ~-shaped ornament (eg a crest or badge).

crown² /kraʊn/ *vt* **1** [VP6A,23] put a crown on (a king or queen): *the ~ed heads* (= kings and queens) *of Europe. They ~ed him king.* **2** [VP6A,14] ~ **(with),** reward with a crown; give honour to; reward: *to be ~ed with victory; efforts that were ~ed with success.* **3** [VP6A,14] ~ **(with),** be or have at the top of: *The hill is ~ed with a wood.* **4** [VP6A] put a happy finishing touch to: *to open a bottle of wine to ~ a feast.* **to ~ (it) all,** to complete good/bad fortune, etc: *It was raining, we had no umbrellas, and, to ~ all, we missed the last bus and had to walk home.* **5** [VP6A] put an artificial cover on a broken tooth. ⇨ crown¹(3). ~**ing** *part adj* (attrib only) completing; making perfect: *the ~ing touch to the evening's entertainment. Her ~ing glory is her hair.*

cro-zier /'krəʊzɪə(r) US: -ʒər/ *n* = crosier.

cru-cial /'kruːʃl/ *adj* decisive; critical: *the ~ test/question; at the ~ moment.* ~**ly** /-ʃəlɪ/ *adv*

cru-cible /'kruːsɪbl/ *n* pot in which metals are melted; (fig) severe test or trial.

cru-ci-fix /'kruːsɪfɪks/ *n* model of the Cross with the figure of Jesus on it.

cru-ci-fixion /ˌkruːsɪ'fɪkʃn/ *n* [U] putting to death, being put to death, on a cross(3); [C] instance of this. **the C~,** that of Jesus.

cru-ci-form /'kruːsɪfɔːm/ *adj* cross-shaped.

cru-cify /'kruːsɪfaɪ/ *vt* put to death by nailing or binding to a cross(3).

crud /krʌd/ *n* (GB sl) unpleasant person. ~**dy** *adj* unpleasant.

crude /kruːd/ *adj* **1** (of materials) in a natural state; not refined or manufactured: ~ *oil,* petroleum; ~ *sugar;* ~ *ore.* **2** not having grace, taste or refinement: ~ *manners.* **3** not finished properly; badly worked out: ~ *schemes/methods/ideas;* ~ *paintings,* showing lack of skill; ~ *facts,* presented in an undisguised way, with no attempt to make them less unpleasant; *a ~ log cabin.* ~**ly** *adv*

crud-ity /'kruːdɪtɪ/ *n* [U] the state or quality of being crude; [C] (*pl* -ties) instance of this; crude act, remark, etc.

cruel /krʊəl/ *adj* (-ller, -llest) **1** (of persons) taking pleasure in the suffering of others; ready to give pain to others: *a ~ master; a man who is ~ to animals. It was ~ of him to make the donkey carry such a heavy load.* **2** causing pain or suffering; showing indifference to the sufferings of others: *a ~ blow/punishment/disease/war; in a ~* (= distressing) *predicament.* ~**ly** /'krʊəlɪ/ *adv*

cruelty /'krʊəltɪ/ *n* **1** [U] readiness to give pain or cause suffering to others; delight in this; cruel nature: *C~ to animals is severely punished in England.* **2** [C] (*pl* -ties) cruel act.

cruet /'kruːɪt/ *n* **1** small glass bottle for vinegar or oil for use at table. **2** (also '~-stand) stand for oil and vinegar ~s, and for mustard, chutney etc

cruise /kruːz/ *vi* [VP2A,C] **1** sail about, either for pleasure, or, in war, looking for enemy ships. **2** (of cars, aircraft) travel at the speed (and of aircraft at the altitude) most economical of fuel, less than the top speed: *The car has a cruising speed of 50 miles an hour.* □ *n* cruising voyage: *to go on/for a ~. The liner is making a round-the-world ~ this year,* a pleasure voyage. **cruiser** /'kruːzə(r)/ *n* **1** fast warship. **2** 'cabin-~r, motor-boat (with sleeping accommodation, etc) designed for pleasure ~s.

crumb /krʌm/ *n* [C] **1** very small piece of dry food, esp a bit of bread or cake rubbed off or dropped from a large piece: *sweep up the ~s;* [U] soft, inner part of a loaf of bread. ⇨ crust(1). **2** (fig) small amount: *a few ~s of information/comfort.*

crumble /'krʌmbl/ *vt,vi* [VP6A,2A,C] break, rub or fall into very small pieces: *to ~ one's bread,* rub it into crumbs; *crumbling walls,* that are falling into ruin; *great empires that have ~d* (= decayed) *and fallen;* (fig) *hopes that ~d to dust,* came to nothing.

crum-bly /'krʌmblɪ/ *adj* easy to crumble.

crummy /'krʌmɪ/ *adj* (sl) bad; worthless; unpleasant: *a ~ party; feel ~,* ill.

crum-pet /'krʌmpɪt/ *n* (GB) **1** flat, round, soft, unsweetened cake, usu toasted and eaten hot with butter spread on it. **2** (sl) head. **3** (sl) sexually attractive girl or woman.

crumple /'krʌmpl/ *vt,vi* [VP6A,15B,2A,C] **1** press or crush into folds or creases: *to ~ one's clothes,* eg by packing them carelessly. **2** become full of folds or creases: *Some kinds of material ~ more easily than others. Do nylon sheets ~?* **3** ~ **up,** (lit, fig) crush; collapse: *to ~ up a sheet of paper into a ball; to ~ up an opposing army. The wings of the aircraft ~d up.*

crunch /krʌntʃ/ *vt,vi* [VP6A,2A,C] **1** crush noisily with the teeth when eating: *The dog was ~ing a bone. People who ~ peanuts in the cinema can be very annoying.* **2** crush, be crushed, noisily under one's feet, under wheels, etc: *The frozen snow ~ed under the wheels of our car. Our feet ~ed the gravel.* □ *n* the act of ~ing; noise made by ~ing. **when it comes to the ~; when the ~ comes,** (colloq) when the moment of crisis or decision is reached.

crup·per /'krʌpə(r)/ n leather strap fastened to the back of a saddle or harness and looped under the horse's tail; hindquarters of a horse. ⇨ the illus at harness.

cru·sade /kru:'seɪd/ n 1 any one of the military expeditions made by the Christian rulers and people of Europe during the Middle Ages to recover the Holy Land from the Muslims. 2 any struggle or movement in support of sth believed to be good or against sth believed to be bad: *a ~ against bribery.* □ *vi* [VP2A,3A] *~ (for/against),* take part in a *~.* **cru·sader** n person taking part in a *~.*

crush[1] /krʌʃ/ *vt,vi* 1 [VP6A,15A,B] press, be pressed, so that there is breaking or injury: *Don't ~ this box; it has flowers in it. Wine is made by ~ing grapes. Several people were ~ed to death as they tried to escape from the burning theatre. We can't ~ any more people into the hall; it's crowded already. ~ up,* make into powder by *~ing. ~ out (of),* force out by *~ing: to ~ out the juice from oranges.* 2 [VP6A,15A,B,2A,C] (cause to) become full of creases or irregular folds; lose shape: *Her dresses were badly ~ed when she took them out of the suitcase. Some of the new synthetic dress materials do not ~.* 3 [VP6A] subdue; overwhelm: *He was not satisfied until he had ~ed his enemies. Our hopes have been ~ed. He smiled at her, but she ~ed him* (= made him feel abashed) *with a haughty look.* 4 [VP2C] (of persons) *~ in/into/through/past, etc,* press or push in, etc: *They all tried to ~ into the front seats.* [VP15A,B] (with cognate object) *We had to ~ our way through the crowd. ~·ing adj* overwhelming: *a ~ing defeat;* in a manner intended to subdue or disconcert: *a ~ing reply. ~·ing·ly adv*

crush[2] /krʌʃ/ n 1 a/the *~,* crowd of people pressed together: *There was a violent ~ at the gate into the stadium. ~ barrier,* one erected to keep back crowds (eg along a pavement when crowds of people are expected). 2 (colloq) crowded social gathering. 3 (sl) *get/have a ~ on sb,* (usu of a young person) be, imagine oneself to be, in love with him. 4 [U] fruit drink made by pressing out juice (eg from oranges).

crust /krʌst/ n 1 [C,U] (piece of the) hard-baked surface of a loaf; outer covering (pastry) of a pie or tart. 2 [C,U] hard surface: *a thin ~ of ice/frozen snow; the earth's ~,* the outer portion. 3 hard deposit on the inside of a bottle of wine. □ *vt,vi* [VP6A,2A,C] *~ (over),* cover, become covered, with a *~;* form into a *~: The snow ~ed over* (= froze hard on top) *during the night.*

crus·ta·cean /krʌ'steɪʃn/ n any of a numerous class of animals, mostly living in water (and popularly called *shellfish*) with a hard shell (eg *crabs, lobsters*).

crusted /'krʌstɪd/ adj 1 having a crust. 2 ancient; venerable. 3 fixed; engrained: *~ prejudices/habits.*

crusty /'krʌstɪ/ adj (-ier, -iest) 1 having a crust; hard like a crust: *~ bread.* 2 (of persons, their behaviour) curt, harsh; quick to show irritation, etc.

crutch /krʌtʃ/ n 1 support used under the arm to help a lame person to walk: *a pair of ~es; to go about on ~es.* 2 support that is like a *~* in shape or use; (fig) any moral support. 3 crotch(2).

crux /krʌks/ n (pl *~es*) part (of a problem) that is the most difficult to solve: *The ~ of the matter is this.*

cry[1] /kraɪ/ *vi,vt* (pt,pp cried) 1 *cry (out),*

[VP2A,B,C,3A,4A] (of persons, animals, birds) make (usu loud) sounds that express feelings (eg pain, fear) but not ideas, thoughts, etc: *A baby can cry as soon as it is born. He cried out with pain when the dentist pulled the tooth out.* 2 [VP2A,B,C,3A,6A,15B] (of persons) weep; shed tears (with or without sounds): *The boy was crying because he had lost his money. She was crying over her misfortunes. The child was crying for* (= because he wanted) *his mother. The boy was crying with pain/hunger. She cried hot tears. cry one's 'eyes/'heart out,* weep very bitterly. *cry oneself to sleep,* cry until one falls asleep. *give sb sth to cry for/about,* punish him for crying without a good or obvious cause. 3 [VP6A,14,9,2C,3A,4A] exclaim; call out loudly in words: *'Help! Help!' he cried. The starving people cried to their chief for bread. He cried for mercy. cry for the moon,* demand sth impossible. ⇨ shame(3). 4 [VP6A,15A,B] announce for sale; make known by calling out: *to cry one's wares; to cry the news all over the town. cry sth down,* suggest that it is worth little. *cry off,* withdraw from sth that one has undertaken: *I had promised to go, but had to cry off at the last moment. cry sth up,* praise it highly.

cry[2] /kraɪ/ n (pl cries) 1 loud sound of fear, pain, grief, etc; loud, excited utterance of words: *a cry for help; the cry of an animal in pain; a cry of triumph; angry cries from the mob. They set up/raised a cry of 'Traitor!' a far/long cry from,* a long way from; very different from: *Being a junior clerk is a far cry from being one of the Directors. in full cry,* (of a pack of hounds) barking together as they pursue or hunt (an animal); (fig) eagerly attacking (sb). *much cry and little wool,* (prov) much fuss with little result. *within cry (of),* within hearing; near enough to hear a call. ⇨ hue[2]. 2 words spoken loudly to give information: *the cry of the night watchman;* call announcing sth for sale (by a person in the street): *the old (street) cries of London, eg 'Fresh Herrings'.* ⇨ crier(1). 3 watchword or phrase, used for a principle or cause: *a 'war-cry; a 'battle-cry. 'Asia for the Asians' was their cry.* 4 fit of weeping: *have a good cry,* find emotional relief by shedding tears. *Let her have her cry out,* let her weep until she becomes calm again. *'cry-baby,* child who cries often or easily without good or apparent cause.

cry·ing /'kraɪɪŋ/ attrib adj (esp of evils) demanding attention: *a ~ shame/evil/need.*

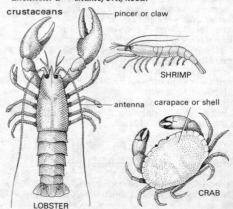

crustaceans — pincer or claw

SHRIMP

antenna — carapace or shell

CRAB

LOBSTER

a church crypt

crypt /krɪpt/ *n* underground room, esp of a church.

cryp·tic /'krɪptɪk/ *adj* secret; with a hidden meaning, or a meaning not easily seen: *a ~ remark.* **cryp·ti·cally** /-klɪ/ *adv*

crypto- /ˌkrɪptəʊ/ (in combination) hidden, secret: *a ˌ~-'fascist,* person who has fascist sympathies but does not make them public.

crypto·gram /'krɪptəgræm/ *n* [C] sth written in a secret code.

crys·tal /'krɪstl/ *n* **1** [U] transparent, natural substance like quartz; [C] piece of this as an ornament: *a necklace of ~s;* (attrib) *~ ornaments; ~ detector,* type used in early radio sets (called a '*~ set*). *~ clear,* entirely clear; (fig) completely understood. '*~-gazing,* looking into a ~ ball in an attempt to see future events pictured there. **2** [U] glassware of best quality, made into bowls, vases, vessels, etc: *The dining-table shone with silver and ~.* **3** [C] (science) definite and regular shape taken naturally by the molecules of certain substances: *sugar and salt ~s; snow and ice ~s.* **4** (US) glass over the face of a watch.

crystals   diamonds

cry·stal·line /'krɪstəlaɪn/ *adj* made of crystal(s); like crystal; very clear.

cry·stal·lize /'krɪstəlaɪz/ *vt,vi* **1** [VP6A,2A] form, cause to form, into crystals. **2** [VP6A] cover (fruit, etc) with sugar-crystals: *~d ginger.* **3** [VP6A,2A] (fig, of ideas, plans) become, cause to be, clear and definite: *His vague ideas ~d into a definite plan.* **crys·tal·li·za·tion** /ˌkrɪstəlaɪ'zeɪʃn US: -lɪ'z-/ *n*

cub /kʌb/ *n* **1** young lion, bear, fox, tiger. **cub re·porter,** young and inexperienced newspaper reporter. **Cub (Scout),** member of the junior branch of the Scout Association. **2** ill-mannered young man.

cubby–hole /'kʌbɪ həʊl/ *n* small enclosed space; snug place.

cube /kju:b/ *n* **1** solid body having six equal square sides; block of something so shaped or similarly shaped. **2** (maths) product of a number multiplied by itself twice: *The ~ of 5 (5^3) is $5 \times 5 \times 5 = 125$. The ~ root of 64 ($\sqrt[3]{64}$) is 4 ($4 \times 4 \times 4 = 64$).* □ *vt* [VP6A] multiply a number by itself twice: *10 ~d is 1000.*

cu·bic /'kju:bɪk/ *adj* having the shape of a cube; of a cube: *one ~ metre,* volume of a cube whose edge is one metre; *~ content,* volume expressed in cubic measurement; *a motor vehicle with a 2000 cc ca-*

pacity, ie 2000 ~ centimetres.

cu·bi·cal /'kju:bɪkl/ *adj* = cubic.

cu·bicle /'kju:bɪkl/ *n* small division of a larger room, walled or curtained to make a separate compartment, eg for sleeping in, or for (un)dressing at a swimming-pool.

cub·ism /'kju:bɪzəm/ *n* [U] style in art in which objects are represented so that they appear to be largely of geometrical shapes. **cub·ist** /'kju:bɪst/ *n* artist who practises ~.

cu·bit /'kju:bɪt/ *n* old measure of length (18 to 22 inches or 45 to 56 centimetres).

cuck·old /'kʌkəʊld/ *n* (archaic) man whose wife has committed adultery. □ *vt* [VP6A] (of a man) make (another man) a ~ by seducing his wife; (of a woman) make (her husband) a ~.

cuckoo /'kʊku:/ *n* bird whose call is like its name, a migratory bird which reaches the British Isles in spring and lays its eggs in the nests of small birds. ⇨ the illus at bird. '*~-clock,* one that strikes the hours with notes like the call of a ~.

cu·cum·ber /'kju:kʌmbə(r)/ *n* [C,U] (creeping plant with) long, green-skinned fleshy fruit, usu sliced and eaten in salads, or made into pickle. ⇨ the illus at vegetable. *as cool as a ~,* unexcited; self-possessed.

cud /kʌd/ *n* [U] food which oxen, etc bring back from the first stomach and chew again. *chew the cud,* (fig) reflect; ponder.

cuddle /'kʌdl/ *vt,vi* [VP6A,15B,2C] **1** hold close and lovingly in one's arms: *The baby doesn't like being ~d herself, but she likes to ~ her doll.* **2** *~ up (to/together),* lie close and comfortably: *They ~d up (together) under the blankets. She ~d up to him to get warm.* □ *n* act of cuddling; hug. *~some* /-səm/, **cud·dly** /'kʌdlɪ/ *adjj* suitable for, inviting, cuddling: *a nice cuddly teddy bear.*

cud·gel /'kʌdʒəl/ *vt, n* (-ll-; US also -l-) [VP6A] (hit with a) short, thick stick or club. *take up the ~s for,* (rhet) fight for; support strongly. *~ one's brains,* think hard on a difficult problem; try to think of sth one has forgotten.

cue¹ /kju:/ *n* [C] **1** sth (eg the last words of an actor's speech) which shows when sb else is to do or say sth. **2** hint about how to behave, what to do, etc. *take one's cue from sb,* observe what he does as a guide to one's own action.

cue² /kju:/ *n* billiard-player's long, tapering, leather-tipped rod, for striking the ball.

cuff¹ /kʌf/ *n* **1** end of a shirt or coat sleeve at the wrist. *play it off the ~,* (colloq) use one's wits in a situation for which one is unprepared. '*~-links,* used for fastening ~s. **2** (US) turned-up fold at the bottom of a leg of a pair of trousers (GB = *turn-up*). **3** (*pl*, colloq) handcuffs.

cuff² /kʌf/ *vt, n* [VP6A] (give sb a) light blow with the open hand.

cuir·ass /kwɪ'ræs/ *n* piece of armour to protect the body; breastplate and plate for the back, fastened together. ⇨ the illus at armour. **cuir·as·sier** /ˌkwɪrə'sɪə(r)/ *n* horse-soldier wearing a ~.

cui·sine /kwɪ'zi:n/ *n* [U] (F) (style of) cooking: *French ~; a hotel where the ~ is excellent.*

cul·de·sac /'kʌl də sæk/ *n* (F) street with an opening at one end only; blind alley.

cu·li·nary /'kʌlɪnərɪ US: -nerɪ/ *adj* of cooking or a kitchen: *a ~ triumph,* a superbly cooked dish or meal; *~ plants,* suitable for cooking.

cull /kʌl/ *vt* [VP6A] pick (a flower); select: *extracts ~ed from the best authors.* □ *n* sth that is ~ed (eg a hen that no longer lays well, picked out and killed for food).

cul·len·der /'kʌləndə(r)/ n = colander.

cul·mi·nate /'kʌlmɪneɪt/ vt [VP3A] ~ in, (of efforts, hopes, careers, etc) reach the highest point: *misfortunes that* ~*d in bankruptcy*. **cul·mi·na·tion** /ˌkʌlmɪ'neɪʃn/ n highest point: *the culmination of his career*.

culp·able /'kʌlpəbl/ adj (legal) blameworthy; deserving punishment: *hold a person* ~; *dismissed for* ~ *negligence*, wrongly neglecting to do sth. **culp·ably** /'kʌlpəblɪ/ adv **cul·pa·bil·ity** /ˌkʌlpə'bɪlətɪ/ n

cul·prit /'kʌlprɪt/ n person who has done wrong; offender.

cult /kʌlt/ n [C] **1** system of religious worship. **2** devotion to a person (esp a single deity) or practice: *the* ~ *of archery; the* ~ *of Browning*. **3** (group of persons devoted to a) popular fashion or craze: (attrib) *a*'~ *word*, one used because it is fashionable among members of such a group.

cul·ti·vable /'kʌltɪvəbl/ adj that can be cultivated.

cul·ti·vate /'kʌltɪveɪt/ vt [VP6A] **1** prepare (land) for crops by ploughing, etc; help (crops) to grow (eg by breaking up the soil around them, destroying weeds, etc). **2** give care, thought, time, etc in order to develop sth: *to* ~ *the mind/sb's friendship*. *He* ~*s* (= tries to win the good will of) *the sort of people who can be useful to him in his business*. **cul·ti·vated** adj (of a person) having good manners and education.

cul·ti·va·tion /ˌkʌltɪ'veɪʃn/ n [U] cultivating or being cultivated: *the* ~ *of the soil; land that is under* ~; *to bring land into* ~; *to allow land to go out of* ~.

cul·ti·va·tor /'kʌltɪveɪtə(r)/ n person who cultivates; machine for breaking up ground, destroying weeds, etc.

cul·tural /'kʌltʃərəl/ adj having to do with culture: ~ *studies*, eg art, literature; *a* ~ *institute*.

cul·ture /'kʌltʃə(r)/ n **1** [U] advanced development of the human powers; development of the body, mind and spirit by training and experience: *Physical* ~ *is important, but we must not neglect the* ~ *of the mind*. **2** [U] evidence of intellectual development (of arts, science, etc) in human society: *He is a man of considerable* ~. *Universities should be centres of* ~. **3** [U] state of intellectual development among a people; [C] particular form of intellectual development: *We owe much to Greek* ~. *He has studied the* ~*s of Oriental countries*. **4** [U] all the arts, beliefs, social institutions, etc characteristic of a community, race, etc: *the* ~ *of the Eskimos*. **5** [U] cultivating; the rearing of bees, silkworms, etc: *He has five acres devoted to bulb* ~, to the growing of such flowers as daffodils and tulips. **6** [C] (biol) growth of bacteria (for medical or scientific study): *a* ~ *of cholera germs*. **cul·tured** adj (of persons) cultivated; having ~ of the mind; (of tastes, interests, etc) refined. '~**d pearl**, pearl produced in an oyster shell into which a piece of grit has been introduced.

cul·vert /'kʌlvət/ n sewer or drain that crosses under a road, railway or embankment; channel for electrical cables under the ground.

cum·ber /'kʌmbə(r)/ vt [VP6A,14] ~ **(with)**, hamper; burden: ~ *oneself with an overcoat on a warm day*; ~*ed with parcels*.

cum·ber·some /'kʌmbəsəm/ adj burdensome; heavy and awkward to carry: *A soldier today*

would find old-fashioned armour very ~.

cum·brous /'kʌmbrəs/ adj = cumbersome.

cum·mer·bund /'kʌməbʌnd/ n sash worn round the waist.

cumu·lat·ive /'kju:mjʊlətɪv US: -leɪtɪv/ adj increasing in amount by one addition after another.

cumu·lus /'kju:mjʊləs/ n (pl -li /-laɪ/), adj (cloud) made up of rounded masses on a flat base.

cunei·form /'kju:nɪfɔ:m US: kju:'nɪəfɔ:rm/ adj wedge-shaped: ~ *characters*, as used in old Persian and Assyrian writing.

cuneiform characters

cun·ning¹ /'kʌnɪŋ/ adj **1** clever at deceiving; showing this kind of cleverness: *a* ~ *old fox; a* ~ *trick*. **2** (old use) skilful: *a* ~ *workman*. **3** (US) attractive; cute: *a* ~ *smile/baby/kitten*. ~·**ly** adv

cun·ning² /'kʌnɪŋ/ n [U] quality of being cunning(1): *The boy showed a great deal of* ~ *in getting what he wanted*. **2** (old use) skill: *My hand has lost its* ~.

cunt /kʌnt/ n △ **1** vagina. **2** female pudenda. **3** (vulg; sl) (by transference) woman or girl, regarded as a sexual object. **4** (vulg; derog sl) despicable person.

cup¹ /kʌp/ n **1** small porcelain bowl, usu with a handle, used with a saucer, for tea, coffee etc; contents of a cup: *a*'*teacup; a ₁cup and*'*saucer; a ₁cup of*'*coffee; two cups of flour* (used as a measure in cooking). **not my cup of tea,** (colloq) not what I like, not what suits me. **2** = chalice. **3** (fig) that which comes to a person; experience: *His cup of happiness was full*. **4** vessel (usu of gold or silver) given as a prize in competitions. ₁**cup-**'**final,** (football) final match to decide a competition. '**cup-tie,** (football) match to eliminate teams competing for a cup. **5** (from '*wine cup*) wine. **in his cups,** partly or wholly intoxicated. '**cup-bearer,** official of a royal or nobleman's household who serves wine at banquets. **6** sth shaped like a cup; *the cup of a flower; an*'*egg-cup;*'*acorn-cups; the cups of a bra*. **7** iced drink of wine, etc, usu flavoured: '*claret-cup;* '*cider-cup*. **cup-ful** /'kʌpfʊl/ n (pl cupfuls) as much as a cup will hold.

cup² /kʌp/ vt (-pp-) [VP6A] **1** put into the shape of a cup: *to cup one's hands*, eg to catch a ball; put round or over like a cup: *with her chin cupped in her hand*. **2** (archaic) perform the operation of cupping on (a person). ⇨ cupping below.

cup·board /'kʌbəd/ n set of shelves with doors, either built into a room as a fixture, or a separate piece of furniture, used for dishes, provisions, clothes, etc: *a ₁kitchen-*'~; *a* '*hanging-*~, one in which dresses, suits, etc may be hung on coathangers. Cf US *china-closet, linen-closet*. '~-**love,** affection that is shown in the hope of getting sth by it (eg a child hoping for cake).

Cu·pid /'kju:pɪd/ n Roman god of love; (picture or statue of a) beautiful boy (with wings and a bow and arrows) as symbol of love.

cu·pid·ity /kju:'pɪdətɪ/ n [U] greed, esp for money or property.

cu·pola /'kju:pələ/ n small dome forming (part of) a roof; ceiling of a dome.

cuppa /'kʌpə/ n (GB sl) cup of tea: *What about a*

∼?

cup·ping /'kʌpɪŋ/ n [U] (archaic) operation of drawing blood to or through the skin by creating a partial vacuum over the area by means of a glass cup (called a ¹∼-*glass*).

cu·pric /'kju:prɪk/ adj containing copper.

cu·pro-nickel /ˌkju:prəʊ 'nɪkl/ n [U] alloy of copper and nickel used for making coins.

cur /kɜː(r)/ n bad-tempered or worthless dog (esp low-bred); cowardly or badly behaved man.

cur·able /'kjʊərəbl/ adj that can be cured. **cura·bil·ity** /ˌkjʊərə'bɪlətɪ/ n

cura·çao, -çoa /ˌkjʊərə'səʊ US: -'saʊ/ n [U] liqueur (sweet and syrupy) flavoured with peel of bitter oranges.

cur·acy /'kjʊərəsɪ/ n (pl -cies) office and work of a curate.

curate /'kjʊərət/ n clergyman who helps a parish priest.

cura·tive /'kjʊərətɪv/ adj helping to, able to, cure (disease or ill health): *the ∼ value of sunshine and sea air.*

cu·ra·tor /kjʊə'reɪtə(r)/ n official in charge (esp of a museum or art gallery).

curb /kɜːb/ n **1** chain or leather strap passing under a horse's jaw, used to control it. ⇨ the illus at har-ness. **2** (fig) sth that holds one back or restrains: *put/keep a ∼ on one's anger/passions.* **3** = kerb. □ vt [VP6A] **1** control (a horse) by means of a ∼. **2** keep (feelings, etc) under control: *to ∼ one's impatience.*

curd /kɜːd/ n **1** (often pl) thick, soft substance, almost solid, formed when milk turns sour, used to make cheese. **2** [U] (in compounds) substance resembling ∼: ˌlemon-¹∼, made from eggs, butter and sugar, flavoured with lemon.

curdle /'kɜːdl/ vi, vt [VP6A,2A] form, cause to form, into curds; become curd-like: *The milk has ∼d;* (fig uses): *What a blood-curdling* (= horrifying) *yell! His blood ∼d at the sight,* He was filled with horror.

cure¹ /kjʊə(r)/ n [C] **1** curing or being ∼d(1): *The doctor cannot guarantee a ∼. His ∼ took six weeks.* **2** substance or treatment which ∼s(1): *Is there a certain ∼ for cancer yet? He has tried all sorts of ∼s, but is still ill. You need a ¹rest-∼,* a holiday from your work. **3** spiritual charge(5): *to obtain/resign a ∼,* a position as a priest.

cure² /kjʊə(r)/ vt, vi [VP6A,14] **1** ∼ *sb (of sth); ∼ sth,* bring (a person) back to health; provide and use successfully a remedy for a disease, ill health, suffering; get rid of (an evil): *to ∼ a man of a disease; to ∼ an illness; to ∼ poverty/drunkenness; to ∼ a child of bad habits; to try to ∼ social discontent at home by making war abroad.* ¹∼-*all* n sth which, it is claimed, ∼s all ills. **2** treat meat, fish, skin, tobacco, etc in order to keep it in good condition by salting, smoking, drying, etc: *well-∼d bacon.*

curé /'kjʊəreɪ US: kjʊ'reɪ/ n parish priest in France.

cur·few /'kɜːfju:/ n **1** (old use) ringing of a bell as a signal for lights to be put out and fires covered; bell for this; hour at which the bell was rung. **2** (modern use) time or signal (under martial law) for people to remain indoors: *to impose a ∼ on a town; to lift/ end the ∼.*

curio /'kjʊərɪəʊ/ n (pl ∼s) work of art of a strange or unusual character and valued for this reason.

curi·os·ity /ˌkjʊərɪ'ɒsətɪ/ n **1** [U] being curious(1,2): *∼ about/∼ to learn about distant lands; to be dy-*

ing of/burning with ∼ to know what was happening. He yielded to ∼ and opened the letter addressed to his sister. **2** [C] (pl -ties) curious(3) thing; strange or rare object.

curi·ous /'kjʊərɪəs/ adj **1** ∼ *(to do sth); ∼ (about sth),* (in a good sense) eager (to learn/know, etc); interested (in sth): *∼ about the origin of mankind. I'm ∼ to know what he said. If a boy is ∼, he is always asking questions.* **2** ∼ *(about sth),* meddlesome; having or showing too much interest in the affairs of others: *∼ neighbours. Don't ask so many ∼ questions. Hide it where ∼ eyes won't see it. What is he so ∼ about?* **3** strange; unusual; hard to understand: *What a ∼ mistake! There was a ∼ silence. Isn't he a ∼-looking little man!* **4** (rather old use) showing the result of care and attention: *a jewel of ∼ workmanship. ∼·ly* adv

curl¹ /kɜːl/ n **1** [C] sth naturally like or twisted into a shape like a spiral or the thread of a screw, esp a lock of hair of this shape: *∼s (of hair) falling over her shoulders; hair falling in ∼s over her shoulders; a ∼ of smoke rising from a cigarette; the ∼ of a wave; a ∼ of the lips,* expressing scorn. **2** [U] the state of being curly: *How do you keep your hair in ∼?*

curl² /kɜːl/ vt, vi [VP6A,15A,B,2A,C] ∼ *(up),* make into curls; twist; grow or be in curls: *She has ∼ed her hair. Does her hair ∼ naturally? The smoke from the camp fire ∼ed upwards. The frost made the young leaves ∼ (up)/∼ed up the young leaves. The dog ∼ed (itself) up on the rug. ∼ (sb) up,* (cause to) collapse: *The cricket ball hit him on the head and he ∼ed up* (= fell to the ground) *at once. She ∼ed up (with laughter) at his joke. The blow ∼ed him up completely.* ¹∼·*er,* small cylindrical object round which warmed or wet hair is wound to create a ∼. ¹∼-*ing-tongs/-irons,* instruments (heated before use) for ∼ing or straightening the hair. ¹∼-*ing-pins,* clips (used cold) for ∼ing the hair.

cur·lew /'kɜːlju:/ n wading bird with a long, slender, down-curved bill. ⇨ the illus at water.

curl·ing /'kɜːlɪŋ/ n [U] Scottish game played on ice with heavy, flat-bottomed stones ('∼-*stones*) with handles, sent along the ice towards a mark.

curly /'kɜːlɪ/ adj (-ier, -iest) having curls; arranged in curls: *∼ hair; a ¹∼-headed girl.*

cur·mudgeon /kɜː'mʌdʒən/ n (colloq) bad-tempered or miserly person.

cur·rant /'kʌrənt/ n **1** small, sweet, dried seedless grape (grown in Greece and neighbouring countries) used in buns, cakes, puddings, etc. **2** (cultivated bush with) small black, red or white juicy fruit growing in clusters.

cur·rency /'kʌrənsɪ/ n **1** [U] the state of being in common or general use: *Many slang words have short ∼,* soon go out of use. *The rumour soon gained ∼,* was repeated until many people were aware of it. *give ∼ to,* make current(1); spread: *Do not give ∼ to idle gossip.* **2** [C,U] (pl -cies) money that is actually in use in a country: *a gold/ paper ∼; foreign currencies; a decimal ∼.*

cur·rent¹ /'kʌrənt/ adj **1** in common or general use; generally accepted: *∼ coin/money; ∼ opinions/ beliefs; words that are no longer ∼.* **2** now passing; of the present time: *∼ expenses/prices; the ∼ issue of a magazine; the ∼ year,* this year; *a newsreel showing ∼ events.* **3** ∼ *account,* (with a bank) one from which money may be drawn without previous notice. ⇨ *deposit account* at deposit¹(1), *savings account* at save¹. ～ **assets,** (comm) assets which are not fixed but which change in the course of business (eg amounts owing). ～**·ly** *adv* in a ～(1,2) manner: *It is* ～*ly reported that....*

cur·rent² /'kʌrənt/ *n* **1** stream of water, air, gas, esp one flowing through slower moving or still water, etc: *A cold* ～ *of air came in when the door was opened. Although he was a strong swimmer he was swept away by the* ～ *and was drowned. The warm* ～*s in the Atlantic influence the climate of Great Britain.* **2** flow of electricity through sth or along a wire or cable. ⇨ alternate²(2), direct¹(5). **3** course or movement (of events, opinions, thoughts, etc): *Nothing disturbs the peaceful* ～ *of her life. The government used the radio to influence the* ～ *of thought.*

cur·ricu·lum /kə'rɪkjʊləm/ *n* (*pl* ～s or -la /-lə/) course of study in a school, college, etc. ～ **vitae** /'viːtaɪ/ (Lat) brief written account of one's past history (eg education. employment), used when applying for a job, etc (US = *résumé*).

cur·rish /'kɜːrɪʃ/ *adj* like a cur. ～**·ly** *adv*

curry¹ /'kʌrɪ/ *n* (*pl* -ries) [C,U] (dish of) meat, fish, eggs, etc cooked with hot-tasting spices: *a chicken* ～; *Madras curries; to eat too much* ～. '～**-powder,** mixture of spices for a ～ ground or beaten to a powder. □ *vt* prepare (food) with hot-tasting spices; flavour (food) with ～-powder: *curried chicken.*

curry² /'kʌrɪ/ *vt* [VP6A] rub down and clean (a horse); prepare (tanned leather) by soaking, scraping, etc. ～ **favour (with sb),** try to win favour or approval (by using flattery, etc).

curse¹ /kɜːs/ *n* **1** word, phrase or sentence calling for the punishment, injury or destruction of sth or sb. *be under a* ～, suffer as the result of a ～. *call down* ～s *(from Heaven) upon sb,* ask God or Heaven to punish him. *lay sb under a* ～, make him suffer as the result of a ～. **2** cause of misfortune or ruin: *Gambling is often a* ～. *The rabbits are a* ～ (ie do a lot of damage to crops, etc) *in this part of the country. His wealth proved a* ～ *to him.* **3** word or words used in violent language expressing anger. *the* ～, (colloq) menses.

curse² /kɜːs/ *vt,vi* **1** [VP6A] use a curse against; use violent language against. **2** [VP2A,3A] ～ *(at),* utter curses: *to* ～ *and swear; to* ～ *at fate.* **3** *be* ～*d with,* suffer misfortune, trouble, etc because of: *to be* ～*d with idle daughters/a violent temper.*

cursed /'kɜːsɪd/ *adj* damnable; hateful (often used colloq merely to show annoyance): *This work is a* ～ *nuisance.* ～**·ly** *adv*

cur·sive /'kɜːsɪv/ *adj* (of handwriting) with the letters rounded and joined together. ⇨ script.

cur·sory /'kɜːsərɪ/ *adj* (of work, reading, etc) quick; hurried; done without attention to details: *a* ～ *glance/inspection.* **cur·sor·ily** /'kɜːsərəlɪ/ *adv*

curst /kɜːst/ *adj* = cursed.

curt /kɜːt/ *adj* (of a speaker, his manner, what he says) short-spoken; hardly polite: *to give sb a* ～ *answer; a* ～ *way of speaking.* ～**·ly** *adv* ～**·ness** *n*

cur·tail /kɜː'teɪl/ *vt* [VP6A] make shorter than was at first planned; cut off a part of: *to* ～ *a speech/one's holidays; to* ～ *the allowance one has been making to sb,* give him less money. ～**·ment** *n* [U,C] act or result of ～ing.

cur·tain /'kɜːtn/ *n* **1** piece of cloth or lace hung up at a window or door or (in former times) round a bed: *Please draw the* ～s, pull them across the window(s). *draw a* ～ *over sth,* (fig) say no more about it. '～**-lecture,** (old use) wife's scolding of her husband in private (originally in bed after the bed-～s were drawn). **2** sheet of heavy material to draw or lower across the front of the stage in a theatre before and after each scene of a play: *The* ～ *rises/is raised,* The play/act begins. *The* ～ *falls,* The play/act ends. '～**-call,** call (given by the audience) to an actor or actress to appear before the ～ for applause. '～**-raiser,** short piece performed before the chief play. '**safety-**～, one that is fireproof. **3** (various senses indicating cover or protection): *A* ～ *of mist hid the view. The troops went forward behind a* ～ *of fire* (gun-fire from their artillery). □ *vt* **1** [VP6A] furnish or cover with ～s: ～*ed windows; enough material to* ～ *all the windows.* **2** [VP15B] ～ *off,* separate or divide with a ～ or ～s: *to* ～ *off part of a room.*

curt·sey, curtsy /'kɜːtsɪ/ *n* (*pl* ～s, -sies) gesture of respect (bending the knees) made by women and girls (eg to a queen): *to make/drop/bob a* ～ (*to sb*). □ *vi* (*pt,pp* ～ed, curtsied) make a ～ (*to*).

cur·va·ture /'kɜːvətʃə(r)/ *US:* -tʃʊər/ *n* [U] curving; the state of being curved: *to suffer from* ～ *of the spine; the* ～ *of the earth's surface.*

curve /kɜːv/ *n* line of which no part is straight and which changes direction without angles: *a* ～ *in the road. The driver of a car should not go round/take* ～s *at high speed.* □ *vt,vi* [VP6A,2A] have, cause to have, the form of a ～: *The river* ～s *round the town.*

cushion /'kʊʃn/ *n* **1** small bag filled with feathers or other soft material (eg foam rubber), to make a seat more comfortable, or to kneel on, etc; sth soft and like a ～ in shape or function: *a* ～ *of moss; a* '*pin-*～; *a* ～ *of air,* as for a hovercraft. **2** soft, resilient lining on the inner sides of a billiard-table where the balls hit. □ *vt* [VP6A,14] supply with ～s; protect from shock with ～s: ～*ed seats;* (fig) protect from harmful changes: *farmers who are* ～*ed against falls in prices,* eg by subsidies.

cushy /'kʊʃɪ/ *adj* (-ier, -iest) (sl) (of a job, etc) not requiring much effort: *get a* ～ *job in the Civil Service.*

cusp /kʌsp/ *n* pointed end (esp of a leaf).

cus·pi·dor /'kʌspɪdɔ:(r)/ *n* (US) spittoon.

cuss /kʌs/ *n* (sl) **1** curse. *not give/care a* ～, be quite unworried. *not worth a tinker's* ～, quite worthless. **2** person: *a queer old* ～.

cussed /'kʌsɪd/ *adj* (colloq) perverse; obstinate. ～**·ly** *adv* ～**·ness** *n*

cus·tard /'kʌstəd/ *n* [C,U] (egg-)～, (dish of) mixture of eggs and milk, sweetened and flavoured, baked or boiled; mixture of powdered eggs, etc ('～**-powder**) prepared by adding sugar and milk to flavoured cornflour, eaten with fruit, pastry, etc.

cus·tod·ian /kʌ'stəʊdɪən/ *n* person who has custody of sth or sb; caretaker of a public building.

cus·tody /'kʌstədɪ/ *n* [U] **1** (duty of) caring for, guarding: *A father has the* ～ *of his children while they are young. When Mary's parents died, she was placed in the* ～ *of her aunt. If you are going away for a long time you should leave your jewellery in safe* ～, eg with your bank. **2** imprisonment. *(be) in* ～, in prison (eg awaiting trial). *give sb into* ～, hand him over to the police. *take sb into* ～, arrest him.

cus·tom /'kʌstəm/ *n* **1** [U] usual and generally accepted behaviour among members of a social group: *Don't be a slave to* ～, Do not do things merely because most people do them and have always done them. *It has become the* ~ (= has become usual) *for our family to go to the seaside in summer.* 2 [C] particular way of behaving which, because it has been long established, is observed by individuals and social groups: *Social* ~s *vary in different countries. It was Tom's* ~ *to get up early and go for a walk before breakfast.* (Cf *habit*, a word that means sth that a person does regularly, and that he cannot easily give up.) 3 [U] regular support given to a tradesman by those who buy his goods: *We should very much like to have your* ~, would like you to buy our goods. *I shall withdraw my* ~ *from that shop*, not buy goods there in future. 4 (*pl*) taxes due to the government on goods imported into a country; import duties; department of government (*the C*~*s*) that collects such duties: *How long will it take us to pass* (= get through) *the C*~*s? The C*~*s formalities are simple.* '~ **house**, office (esp at a port) where ~s are collected. '~**s union**, agreement by States on a common policy on tariffs. 5 (attrib use only) made to order. ~-'**built**, as specified by the buyer. ~-'**made** *adj* (of clothes) made-to-measure, making things to order: ~ *tailors/shoemakers.* ⇨ *bespoke* at bespeak; *tailor-made* at tailor.

cus·tom·ary /ˈkʌstəmərɪ *US:* -merɪ/ *adj* in agreement with, according to, custom(**1,2**): *Is it* ~ *for guests at hotels in your country to tip the waiters? There was the* ~ *vote of thanks to the chairman.* **cus·tom·ar·ily** /ˈkʌstəmərəlɪ *US:* ˌkʌstəˈmerəlɪ/ *adv*

cus·tomer /ˈkʌstəmə(r)/ *n* 1 person who buys things, esp one who gives his custom(**3**) to a shop: *Mr X has lost some of his best* ~*s.* 2 (colloq) person or fellow, esp in: *a queer* ~; *an awkward* ~, person who is difficult to deal with.

cut¹ /kʌt/ *vt,vi* (-tt-) (*pt,pp* cut) (For uses with *adverbial particles* and *preps* ⇨ 10 below; for uses with *adjj* ⇨ 7 below; for uses with *nouns* or *pronouns* ⇨ 6 below.) 1 [VP6A,12B,13B,15A,2A] make an opening, incision (with a sharp-edged instrument, eg a knife, a pair of scissors, or other edged tool); (**a**) make a mark, wound, in sth: *He cut his face/himself while shaving.* ⇨ *cut into* sth in 10 below. (**b**) sever; reap: *Don't pluck the flowers; it's better to cut them. Has the wheat been cut* (= harvested, reaped) *yet?* (**c**) shorten: *to cut one's nails; to cut a hedge; to have one's hair cut.* Hence, '**hair-cut** *n* ⇨ also *cut* sth *short* in 7 below. (**d**) separate; remove from sth larger: *Please cut a slice of cake for me/cut me a slice of cake. Cut yourself some pineapple. Cut some pineapple for your sister. Two scenes/episodes were cut by the censor.* ⇨ also *cut off* and *cut out* in 10 below. (**e**) reduce sth by removing part: *Was your salary cut? The new jet service cuts the travelling time by half.* ⇨ *cut down* in 10 below. (**f**) divide into smaller pieces: *Will you cut the cake?* ie into pieces. *If you'll cut the bread* (ie into slices), *we'll make toast.* ⇨ *cut up* in 10 below. (**g**) divide, separate into two: *Don't cut the string, untie the knots. The Minister cut the tape to open a new section of motorway.* (**h**) make, fashion, by removing material with tools, machines, etc that cut: *to cut steps in the ice; to cut a tunnel through a hill; to cut a road up a hillside; to cut an inscription/one's initials.* ⇨ *cut out* in 10 below. 2 [VP2A,C] (**a**) (of a sharp tool, instrument, etc) be suitable for use: *This knife does not cut well.* (**b**) (of a material) be capable of being cut: *Sandstone cuts easily. This cloth is too narrow to cut well*, is narrow and difficult to cut into the shapes needed. 3 [VP6A] (colloq) stay away from, be absent from (sth one ought to attend): *to cut a class/a lecture.* 4 [VP6A] (of lines) cross: *Let the point where AB cuts CD be called E.* 5 [VP6A] (sport, esp cricket, tennis, billiards) strike (a ball) so that it spins or is deflected; hit the edge of (a ball). 6 [VP6A] (used with *nouns* or *pronouns*) **cut the cards/pack,** lift part of a pack of playing-cards lying face downwards and turn it up to decide sth (eg who is to deal, who are to be partners). **cut one's coat according to one's cloth,** suit one's expenditure to one's income; not be too ambitious in one's plans. **cut (off) a corner,** go across, not round it. **cut corners,** (fig) take a short-cut. **cut a disc/record,** record music, etc on to a gramophone record. **cut the ground from under sb/from under sb's feet,** leave him in a weak or illogical position; destroy the foundation of his plan, argument, etc. **cut no/not much ice (with sb),** have little or no effect or influence (on him). **cut one's losses,** abandon a scheme that has caused financial losses before one loses too much. **cut a tooth,** have a new tooth just begin to show itself above the gum. **cut one's teeth on sth,** learn, gain experience, from: *There's a job for you to cut your teeth on.* **cut both ways,** (of an action or argument) have an effect both for and against. ⇨ also caper¹, dash¹(6), figure(6), Gordian. 7 [VP22] (with an *adj* as complement) **cut sb dead,** pretend not to have seen; treat as a complete stranger: *She cut me dead in the street*, ignored me completely. **cut it fine,** (colloq) leave oneself only the minimum of what is needed (esp time): *He cut it rather fine*, eg by reaching the station half a minute before his train was due to leave. **cut sb/sth free (from),** make or get free by cutting: *He cut himself free from the ropes with which they had bound him.* **cut sth/sb loose (from),** make loose or separate by cutting: *cut loose a boat/cut a boat loose; cut oneself loose from one's family*, live an independent life. **cut sth open,** make an opening or split in: *He fell and cut his head open.* **cut sth short,** make shorter: *to cut a long story short; to cut short a person's remarks; a career cut short by illness.* 8 *C*~*!* (cinema; imper) Stop (shooting a scene)! 9 (uses with the *pp*) **cut and dried,** (of opinions, etc) already formed and unlikely to be changed. ˌcut '**flowers,** flowers cut for decoration (contrasted with flowers growing in the garden, in pots, etc). ˌcut '**glass,** glass with patterns and designs cut on it. ˌcut-'**price,** *attrib adj* at a reduced price, and below those of rivals or those recommended by the manufacturers; etc. ˌcut-'**rate,** *attrib adj* = cut-price. ˌcut to'**bacco,** shredded (contrasted with *cake* tobacco). **cut·ting** *part adj* (**a**) sharp; piercing: *a cutting wind.* (**b**) sarcastic; wounding: *cutting remarks.* 10 [VP3A,15B,A,2C] (uses with *adverbial particles* and *preps*):
cut across sth, (**a**) take a shorter route across (a field, etc). (**b**) be contrary to: *Opinion on preserving the environment cut clean across normal political loyalties.*
cut at sb/sth, aim a sharp blow at (eg with a sword or whip): *cut at a hedge/a group of nettles with a stick.*
cut sth away, remove by cutting: *We cut away all the dead wood from the tree. The yacht was in danger of sinking until they cut away the broken*

mast and rigging.
cut sth back, (a) (of shrubs, bushes, etc) prune close to the stem. **(b)** reduce: *cut back production.* Hence, **'cut-back** *n* **(a)** reduction: *a cutback in expenditure.* **(b)** flashback.
cut sth/sb down, (a) cause to fall by cutting: *to cut down a tree.* **(b)** kill or injure by striking with a sword or other edged weapon: *He cut down his enemy.* **(c)** deprive of life or health (by disease, etc): *He was cut down in the prime of manhood.* **(d)** reduce in quantity, amount, etc: *cut down expenses. I won't have a cigarette, thanks—I'm trying to cut down,* reduce the number of cigarettes I smoke. **(e)** persuade (sb) to reduce a price, charge, etc: *We managed to cut him down by £30.* **(f)** reduce the length of: *cut down a pair of trousers,* eg for sb who is shorter; *cut down an article to make it fit the space available,* in a periodical, etc. **cut 'down on,** reduce one's consumption of: *He's trying to cut down on cigarettes and beer.* **cut sb down to size,** (colloq) show him that he is not so important as he thinks he is: *Some of these so-called experts really need cutting down to size.*
cut in (on), (of the driver of a motor vehicle, etc, who has overtaken another vehicle) return too soon to his own side of the road (with possibility of collision, etc): *Accidents are often caused by drivers who cut in (on other cars).* **cut sb in,** (colloq) include sb in a (profitable) venture: *If you'll contribute £500 we'll cut you in.* **cut in (on)/into,** interrupt (a conversation, etc): *Don't cut into the story/in on the conversation/in so rudely—let her finish.* **cut in half/two/three, etc; cut into halves/quarters/thirds, etc,** divide: *The submarine was cut in half by a destroyer. Cut the cable in two. Cut the apples into halves.*
cut into sth, (a) make a cut in: *Mary cut into her birthday cake and everybody clapped.* **(b)** interfere with: *All this extra homework cuts into his weekends,* leaves him less free time.
cut sb/sth off (from), (a) remove (esp sth at an extremity) by cutting: *Don't cut your fingers off! Cut the chicken's head off. He cut off a metre of cloth from the roll.* **(b)** stop; interrupt; isolate: *be cut off while talking by telephone; cut off the gas/ electricity supply,* eg because of unpaid accounts; *cut off an army from its base,* by getting in between; *cut off stragglers,* separate them from the main body and so capture them; *be cut off from all possibility of help; towns cut off* (= isolated) *by floods; cut off by the tide,* isolated on a rock, sandbank, etc by the incoming tide; *cut off sb's supplies/a son's allowance,* no longer allow him to receive them; *cut off sb with a shilling,* disinherit him (eg a son who has behaved badly) except for a small sum (to show that the act is deliberate). **cut (off) a corner,** ⇨ 6 above.
cut out, stop functioning: *One of the aircraft's engines cut out.* **cut sth out, (a)** remove by cutting (eg from a periodical): *That's an interesting article—I'll cut it out.* **(b)** make by cutting: *cut out a path through the jungle.* **(c)** shape (a garment) by cutting the outlines of the parts on cloth: *cut out a dress.* **(d)** (colloq) leave out; omit: *Let's cut out unimportant details.* **(e)** (colloq) stop doing or using (sth): *My doctor told me I must cut out tobacco,* stop smoking. **cut sb out,** defeat, eliminate (a rival, esp in competition for sth): *cut out all rivals for a girl's affections.* **cut it/that out,** (colloq, imper) stop fighting, squabbling, etc: *Now just cut*

it out, you two! **cut out (the) dead wood,** (colloq) remove unnecessary or unproductive parts: *There's a lot of dead wood to be cut out if the industry is to be efficient.* **(not) be cut out for,** (not) have the qualities and abilities needed for: *He's not cut out for that sort of work.* **have one's work cut out (for one),** be faced with as much work as one can manage: *It's a big job; he'll have his work cut out for him to meet the dead-line.* **'cut-out** *n* **(a)** design, figure, etc (to be) cut out from paper, cardboard, etc. **(b)** (electr) device that interrupts or disconnects a circuit (eg to avoid too heavy a load).
cut sb to the heart/quick, cause him pain or suffering: *His ingratitude cut her to the heart.* **cut sb/sth to pieces,** destroy by cutting, by gunfire, etc: *The enemy were cut to pieces.*
cut sth/sb up, (a) cut into pieces: *cut up one's meat.* **(b)** destroy: *cut up the enemy's forces.* **(c)** (colloq, usu passive) cause mental suffering to: *He was badly cut up by the news of his son's death. Don't be so cut up about it.* **(d)** criticize adversely; point out the faults of: *His latest novel has been cut up by the reviewers.* **cut up (into),** be capable of being cut up (into): *This piece of cloth will cut up into* (= has enough material in it for) *three suits.* **cut up (for),** (colloq) be worth: *The old man cut up for ten thousand,* left £10000 to be divided among his heirs. **cut up rough,** (sl) behave aggressively; be violent and aggressive: *He'll cut up rough if you don't give him what he asked for.*
cut² /kʌt/ *n* **1** act of cutting; stroke with a sword, whip, etc; result of such a stroke; opening made by a knife or other sharp-edged tool, etc: *give a horse a cut across the flanks; a deep cut in the leg; cuts on the face,* eg after shaving. **cut and thrust,** (usu fig) vigorous argument, etc: *The cut and thrust of debate.* **2** reduction in size, amount, length, etc: *a cut in prices/salaries; a cut in expenditure/ production; a power cut,* a reduction in the strength of electrical current, or a period for which current is cut off. **3** a cutting out; part that is cut out: *There were several cuts in the film,* Parts of it had been cut out (eg by the film censors). *Where can we make a cut in this long article?* **4** sth obtained by cutting: *a nice cut of beef; a cut off the joint,* a slice from a cooked joint of meat; *this year's cut of wool,* the wool sheared from the sheep. **5** style in which clothes, etc are made by cutting: *I don't like the cut of his trousers.* ⇨ jib¹(1). **6** (cricket, tennis) quick, sharp stroke: *a cut to the boundary.* **7** remark, etc that wounds a person's feelings: *That remark was a cut at me,* was directed at me. **8** refusal to recognize a person: *give sb a cut.* ⇨ **cut sb dead** at cut¹(7). **9 short cut,** way across (from one place to another) that shortens the distance. **10 a cut above,** (colloq) rather superior to: *She's a cut above the other girls in the office,* is better educated, has wider interests, etc. *That's a cut above me,* above my range of interests, my abilities, etc. **11** railway cutting; canal. ⇨ cutting(1). **12** block or plate on which a design, illustration, etc has been cut; picture, etc, made from such a block. ⇨ woodcut at woodcut(4).
cute /kjuːt/ *adj* (-r, -st) **1** sharp-witted; quick-thinking. **2** (US colloq) attractive; pretty and charming. **~·ly** *adv* **~·ness** *n*
cu·ticle /'kjuːtɪkl/ *n* outer layer of hardened skin (esp at the base of a finger-nail or toe-nail).
cut·lass /'kʌtləs/ *n* **1** (hist) sailor's short, one-edged sword with a slightly curved blade. **2** cutting

tool (= *machete*) used by cacao-growers and copra-growers.

cut·ler /'kʌtlə(r)/ *n* man who makes and repairs knives and other cutting tools and instruments. ～**y** *n* [U] trade of a ～; implements used at table (knives, forks, spoons, esp if made of stainless steel); things made or sold by ～s.

cut·let /'kʌtlɪt/ *n* slice of meat or fish for one person: *a veal* ～.

cut·purse /'kʌtpɜːs/ *n* (hist) pickpocket.

cut·ter /'kʌtə(r)/ *n* **1** person or thing that cuts: *a tailor's* ～, who cuts out cloth; *a 'wire-*～. **2** sailing-vessel with one mast; ship's boat, for use between ship and shore.

cut-throat /'kʌtθrəʊt/ *n* **1** murderer. **2** (attrib uses) ruthless, cruel: ～ *competition*, likely to ruin the weaker competitors. ～ **razor**, one with no guard on the long blade. ⇨ the illus at razor.

cut·ting /'kʌtɪŋ/ *n* **1** unroofed passage dug through the ground for a road, railway, canal, etc. **2** sth cut from a newspaper, etc and kept for reference: '*press* ～*s*. Cf US *clipping*. **3** short piece of a plant, to be used for growing a new plant: *chrysanthemum* ～*s; to take a* ～. **4** [U] process of editing films, tape recordings, etc, by cutting out unwanted parts. Hence, '～-**room**, room where this is done. □ *part adj* (of words, etc) wounding the feelings, etc: ～ *remarks*.

cut·tle·fish /'kʌtlfɪʃ/ *n* sea-water animal with long arms (tentacles), which sends out a black liquid when attacked. ⇨ the illus at mollusc.

cut·worm /'kʌtwɜːm/ *n* caterpillar that eats through the stems of young plants level with the ground.

cy·an·ide /'saɪənaɪd/ *n* [U] poisonous compound substance: *potassium* ～; *sodium* ～.

cy·ber·net·ics /ˌsaɪbə'netɪks/ *n* (*sing v*) the science of communication and control in machines and animals (including man). **cy·ber·netic** *adj*

cyc·la·men /'sɪkləmən *US:* 'saɪk-/ *n* kinds of plant, wild and cultivated, of the primrose family, with delicate, small flowers.

cycle /'saɪkl/ *n* **1** series of events taking place in a regularly repeated order: *the* ～ *of the seasons.* **2** complete set or series: *a song* ～, eg by Schubert; *the Arthurian* /ɑː'θjʊərɪən *US:* -'θʊər-/ ～, the stories of King Arthur and his knights. **3** (short for) bicycle or motor-cycle. □ *vi* [VP2A,B,C] ride a bicycle.

cyc·lic /'saɪklɪk/ *adj* recurring in cycles.

cyc·li·cal /'saɪklɪkl/ *adj* = cyclic.

cyc·list /'saɪklɪst/ *n* person who rides a cycle.

cyc·lone /'saɪkləʊn/ *n* violent wind rotating round a calm central area; violent windstorm. **cyc·lonic** /saɪ'klɒnɪk/ *adj* of or like a ～.

cyclo·pae·dia /ˌsaɪklə'piːdɪə/ *n* = encyclopaedia.

Cyclo·pean /saɪ'kləʊpɪən/ *adj* of or like a Cyclops /'saɪklɒps/ (a one-eyed giant in Greek myth); huge; immense.

cyclo·style /'saɪkləstaɪl/ *n* apparatus for printing copies from a stencil. □ *vt* reproduce (copies) with this.

cyclo·tron /'saɪklətrɒn/ *n* apparatus used for producing heavy electric particles moving at high speed, used experimentally in nuclear research work.

cyder /'saɪdə(r)/ *n* = cider.

cyg·net /'sɪgnɪt/ *n* young swan.

cyl·in·der /'sɪlɪndə(r)/ *n* **1** solid or hollow body with equal, circular ends and regular, curving sides. ⇨ the illus here and at projection. **2** ～-shaped chamber (in an engine) in which gas or steam works a piston: *a six-*～ *engine/motor-car; (working) on all* ～*s*, (colloq) with the maximum power or effort. **cy·lin·dri·cal** /sɪ'lɪndrɪkl/ *adj* ～-shaped.

cylinders

cym·bal /'sɪmbl/ *n* one of a pair of round brass plates struck together to make clanging sounds. ⇨ the illus at percussion.

cynic /'sɪnɪk/ *n* person who sees little or no good in anything and who has no belief in human progress; person who shows this by sneering and being sarcastic. **cyni·cism** /'sɪnɪsɪzəm/ *n* [U] ～'s opinions or attitude of mind; [C] expression of this attitude.

cyni·cal /'sɪnɪkl/ *adj* of or like a cynic; sneering or contemptuous: *a* ～ *smile/remark.* ～·**ly** /-klɪ/ *adv*

cyno·sure /ˌsɪnə'zjʊə(r) *US:* 'saɪnəʃʊər/ *n* sth or sb that draws everyone's attention; centre of attraction.

cy·pher /'saɪfə(r)/ *n* = cipher.

cy·press /'saɪprəs/ *n* (kinds of) tall, thin, cone-bearing evergreen tree with dark leaves and hard wood.

Cyril·lic /sɪ'rɪlɪk/ *adj* **the** ～ **alphabet**, that used for Slavonic languages (eg Russian).

cyst /sɪst/ *n* enclosed hollow organ in the body containing liquid matter.

czar /zɑː(r)/ *n* (also **tsar**) emperor of Russia (before 1917). **czar·ina** /zɑː'riːnə/ *n* Russian empress.

Czech /tʃek/ *n* member of a branch of the Slavs; their language.

Dd

D, d /diː/ (*pl* D's, d's /diːz/) the fourth letter of the English alphabet; Roman numeral for 500. '**d**, used for *had* or *would* (esp after *I, we, you, he, she, they, who*).

dab[1] /dæb/ *vt,vi* (-bb-) [VP6A,14,15A,B,2C,3A] ～ (*at*), touch, put on, lightly and gently: *dab one's eyes with a handkerchief; dab paint on a picture,* suggesting light, quick strokes of the brush. *She was dabbing (at) her cheeks with a powder-puff.* □ *n* [C] **1** small quantity (of paint, etc) dabbed on. **2**

slight tap; brief application of sth to a surface (without rubbing): *A dab with a sponge won't remove the dirt, you'll have to rub it.*

dab[2] /dæb/ *n* kind of flat-fish.

dab[3] /dæb/ *n* ～ (**hand**), (colloq) expert (at games, etc, at doing things): *She's a dab (hand) at tennis.*

dabble /'dæbl/ *vt,vi* **1** [VP6A,15A,B,2C] splash (the hands, feet, etc) about in water; put in and out of water. **2** [VP3A] ～ *at/in*, (art, politics, etc) engage in, study, as a hobby, not professionally.

dab·bler /'dæblə(r)/ n

da capo /,dɑː 'kɑːpəʊ/ (I, music) (as a direction) repeat from the beginning.

dace /deɪs/ n (pl unchanged) small fresh-water fish.

dacha /'dætʃə/ n Russian country house or villa.

dachs·hund /'dækshʊnd/ n small short-legged breed of dog. ⇨ the illus at dog.

da·coit /də'kɔɪt/ n member of a band of armed robbers (formerly, in India, Burma). ~**y** n (pl -ies) robbery by ~s.

dac·tyl /'dæktɪl/ n (prosody) metrical foot of one accented syllable followed by two unaccented syllables (—ᴗᴗ eg 'tenderly), as in: 'under the /'blossom that /'hangs on the /'bough. ~**ic** /dæk'tɪlɪk/ adj

dad /dæd/ n (colloq) father.

daddy /'dædɪ/ n (pl -dies) child's word for 'father'. ~**-long-legs** n (popular name for the) crane-fly (a long-legged flying insect).

dado /'deɪdəʊ/ n (pl ~s, US ~es /-dəʊz/) lower part of a wall in a room, when this is different from the upper part in colour or material.

dae·mon /'diːmən/ n = demon.

daf·fo·dil /'dæfədɪl/ n yellow flower with long narrow leaves growing from a bulb. ⇨ the illus at flower.

daft /dɑːft US: dæft/ adj (-er, -est) (colloq) silly; foolish; reckless. ~**·ly** adv

dag·ger /'dægə(r)/ n 1 short, pointed, two-edged knife used as a weapon. **at ~s drawn (with sb)**, about to fight. **look ~s at sb**, look with an expression of hatred and enmity. 2 (printing) mark of reference (†).

dago /'deɪgəʊ/ n (pl ~s /-gəʊz/) ⚠ (sl, term of contempt for an) Italian, Spaniard or Portuguese.

da·guerreo·type /də'gerətaɪp/ n photograph taken by an early photographic process.

dah·lia /'deɪlɪə US: 'dælɪə/ n garden plant with brightly coloured flowers, growing from tuberous roots.

Dail Eire·ann /,dɔɪl 'eərən/ n legislative assembly of the Republic of Ireland.

daily /'deɪlɪ/ adj, adv happening, done, appearing, every day (or every weekday): Most newspapers appear ~. Thousands of people cross this bridge ~. ~ **dozen**, one's usual physical exercises. **one's ~ bread**, one's necessary food, etc. □ n 1 newspaper published every weekday. 2 (colloq) person who is paid to do housework every weekday.

dainty¹ /'deɪntɪ/ adj (-ier, -iest) 1 (of persons) pretty, neat and delicate(1,3) in appearance and tastes: a ~ little lady. 2 (of persons and animals) rather difficult to please because of delicate tastes: She's ~ about her food. My cat is a ~ feeder. 3 (of things) pretty; delicate(3), easily injured or broken: ~ cups and saucers; ~ spring flowers. 4 (of food) delicate(8) and delicious. **dain·tily** adv in a ~ manner: a daintily dressed young lady. **dain·ti·ness** n

dainty² /'deɪntɪ/ n (pl -ties) (usu pl) dainty morsel or dish of food: There were dainties of every kind in the picnic basket.

dairy /'deərɪ/ n (pl -ries) 1 (part of a) building where milk is kept and milk products are made. '~-**farm**, one that produces milk and butter. '~-**ing**, '~-**farming**, the business of a ~-farm. '~-**cattle**, cows raised to produce milk, not meat. '~-**maid**, woman who works in a ~. 2 shop where

milk, butter, eggs, etc, are sold. '~-**man** /-mən/ (pl-men) dealer in milk, etc.

dais /'deɪɪs/ n (pl ~es /-sɪz/) platform (esp at the end of a hall) for a table, lectern etc.

daisy /'deɪzɪ/ n (pl -sies) small white flower with a yellow centre, commonly growing wild; similar garden flower; other plants of various sorts (Michaelmas ~, etc) resembling it or of the same species. **push up the daisies**, ⇨ push¹(8).

dale /deɪl/ n (esp in N England and in poetry) valley. **dales·man** /'deɪlzmən/ n (pl -men) person who lives in the ~s (in N England).

dal·li·ance /'dælɪəns/ n [U] trifling behaviour; flirting for amusement.

dally /'dælɪ/ vi 1 [VP2A,3A] ~ **(with)**, trifle; think idly about: ~ with an idea or proposal; ~ with a woman's affections, flirt with her. 2 [VP2A,3A] ~ **(over)**, waste time: Don't ~ over your work.

dal·ma·tion /dæl'meɪʃn/ n large, short-haired dog, white with dark spots.

dam¹ /dæm/ n 1 barrier built to keep back water and raise its level (eg to form a reservoir, or for hydro-electric power). (Cf **barrage**, a barrier across a river, usu for irrigation purposes.) 2 reservoir formed by such a barrier. □ vt (-mm-) [VP6A,15B] ~ **(up)**, make a dam across (a narrow valley, etc); hold back by means of a dam; (fig) hold back: to dam up one's feelings/sb's eloquence.

a dam

dam² /dæm/ n mother (of four-footed animals). ⇨ sire(3).

dam·age /'dæmɪdʒ/ n 1 [U] ~ **(to)**, harm or injury that causes loss of value: The storm did great ~ to the crops. The insurance company will pay for the ~ to my car. 2 (pl) (legal) money claimed from or paid by a person causing loss or injury: He claimed £5000 ~s from his employers for the loss of his right arm while at work. 3 **What's the ~?**(colloq) What's the cost? □ vt [VP6A] cause ~(1) to: furniture ~d by fire.

dam·as·cene /'dæməsiːn/ adj of damask. □ vt work into damask steel.

dam·ask /'dæməsk/ n [U] 1 silk or linen material with designs shown up by reflection of light: (attrib) ~ table-cloths; ~ silk. 2 steel with a pattern of wavy lines or with inlaid gold or silver: (attrib) ~ (or damascene) steel. 3 '~ **rose**, variety originally brought from Damascus /də'mæskəs/; colour (bright pink).

dame /deɪm/ n 1 (old use) woman, esp a married woman. 2 (title of a) woman who has been awarded the highest grade of an order¹(10): D~ Ellen Terry.(Cf the title Lady.)3 title as used eg in D~ **Nature, D~ Fortune**, nature, fortune, personified. 4 (US, sl) woman.

damn /dæm/ vt [VP6A] 1 (of God) condemn to everlasting torment. 2 condemn; say that sth or sb is worthless, bad, etc: *The book was ~ed by the critics.* **3** (colloq) (esp as *int*) used to express anger, annoyance, impatience, etc: *D~! I'll be ~ed if I'll go,* I refuse to go. *D~ it all! D~ you/your impudence!* □ *n* (colloq) **not give/care a ~,** not care at all. **not (be) worth a ~,** (be) worthless. □ *adj, adv* (colloq) (intensive): *Don't be ~ silly/a ~ fool.* **~ well,** certainly.

dam·na·ble /'dæmnəbl/ *adj* hateful; deserving to be damned; (colloq) very bad: *~ weather.* **dam·nab·ly** /'dæmnəblɪ/ *adv*

dam·na·tion /dæm'neɪʃn/ *n* [U] being damned; ruin: *to suffer eternal ~.*

damned /dæmd/ *adj* **1** **the ~,** souls in hell. **2** (colloq) damnable: *You ~ fool!* □ *adv* (colloq) extremely: *~ hot/funny.*

Damocles /'dæməkliːz/ *n* **sword of ~,** threatened danger in the midst of prosperity (from the old Greek story of a man who feasted while a sword hung by a thread over him).

damp¹ /dæmp/ *adj* (-er, -est) not thoroughly dry; having some moisture (in or on): *~ clothes; to wipe a window with a ~ cloth. Don't sleep between ~ sheets.* ⇨ squib, ⇨ squib. □ *n* [U] **1** state of being ~; ~ atmosphere; moisture on the surface of, or existing throughout, sth: *The ~ rising from the ground caused the walls to stain badly. Don't stay outside in the ~.* ⇨ *~-course* at course¹(5). **2** *cast/strike a ~ over,* (fig) cause dejection or unhappiness: *Their mother's illness cast a ~ over the celebrations.* **3** (also **'fire-~**) dangerous gas which may collect in coal-mines. **~·ish** *adj* rather ~. **~·ly** *adv* **~·ness** *n*

damp² /dæmp/ *vt, vi* **1** [VP6A] make damp(1): *to ~ clothes before ironing them.* **2** [VP6A] (also **'dampen**) make sad or dull: *Nothing could ~ his spirits.* **3** [VP15B] **~ down,** make (a fire) burn more slowly (eg by heaping ashes on it, or by controlling the draught of air entering a stove, etc). **4** [VP2C] **~ off,** (of young plants) rot and die because of excessive damp(1).

dampen /'dæmpən/ *vt, vi* = damp²(2).

damper /'dæmpə(r)/ *n* **1** movable metal plate that regulates the flow of air into a fire in a stove or furnace. **2** person or thing that checks or discourages. ⇨ damp¹(2).

dam·sel /'dæmzl/ *n* (old use) girl; young unmarried woman.

dam·son /'dæmzn/ *n* (tree producing) small dark-purple plum; dark-purple.

dance¹ /dɑːns US: dæns/ *n* [C] **1** (series of) movements and steps in time with music; special form (eg a *waltz*), tune, piece of music, for such movements and steps: *May I have the next ~,* Will you be my partner in the next ~? *Shall we join the ~,* go out among the dancers? **lead sb a (pretty) ~,** cause him a lot of trouble, make him follow from place to place. **2** social gathering for dancing: *to give a ~,* arrange for and invite persons to such a gathering. **3** (attrib): *'~-rhythm. '~-band/* **orchestra** *nn* providing music for dancing. *'~-hall n* hall for public ~s, with a charge for admission. ⇨ ballroom at ball². **dance²** /dɑːns US: dæns/ *vi, vt* **1** [VP2A,C] move along in rhythmical steps, usu with music, (either alone, or with a partner, or in a group): *Will you ~ with me? They went on dancing until after midnight.* **2** [VP6A] perform (a named kind of such movements or the named (style of) music for it): *to ~ a waltz/a ballet/Swan Lake. Is the polka often*

~d nowadays? ~ attendance upon sb, follow him about, pay great attention to his wishes, etc. *~ to sb's tune,* obey him. **3** [VP2A,C] move in a lively way, quickly, up and down, etc: *The leaves were dancing in the wind. She ~d for joy. The sudden pain made him ~ up and down. Look at that boat dancing on the waves.* **4** [VP6A,15A] cause to ~(3): *to ~ a baby on one's knee.* **dancer** *n* person who ~s: *a clever ~r;* person who ~s in public for pay. ⇨ ballerina, ballet-~r. **danc·ing** *part adj* who or that ~s: *a ,dancing 'dervish.* □ *n* (gerund) [U] **1** (attrib) (stress on the gerund): *'dancing-master,* professional teacher of dancing; *'dancing-partner,* person with whom one (usu) ~s; *'dancing-shoes,* light shoes for dancing. **2** (stress on the first element): *'ballet-dancing; 'tap-dancing.*

dan·de·lion /'dændɪlaɪən/ *n* small wild plant with bright yellow flowers and deeply notched leaves.

dan·der /'dændə(r)/ *n* (colloq, only in) **get sb's ~ up,** make him angry. **get one's ~ up,** become angry.

dandle /'dændl/ *vt* [VP6A,15A,B] move (eg a child) up and down on one's knee(s) or in the arms.

dan·druff /'dændrʌf/ *n* [U] dead skin in small scales among the hair of the scalp; scurf.

dandy¹ /'dændɪ/ *n* man who pays too much care to his clothes and personal appearance. **dan·di·fied** /'dændɪfaɪd/ *adj* dressed up, etc like a ~: *a dandified appearance.*

dandy² /'dændɪ/ *adj* (sl) excellent; first-rate: *fine and ~.*

Dane /deɪn/ *n* native of Denmark.

dan·ger /'deɪndʒə(r)/ *n* **1** [U] chance of suffering, liability to suffer, injury or loss of life: *D~ —thin ice! Is there any ~ of fire? In war a soldier's life is full of ~. at ~:* The signal (on a railway line) was *at ~,* in the position giving a warning of ~. **in ~ (of):** His life was in ~. He was in ~ of losing his life. **out of ~:** He has been very ill, but the doctors say that he is now out of ~, not likely to die. **'~ money,** extra pay for dangerous work. **2** [C] sth or sb that may cause ~: *He looked round carefully for hidden ~s. The wreck is a ~ to shipping. That man is a ~ to society.*

dan·ger·ous /'deɪndʒərəs/ *adj* ~ **(to/for),** likely to cause danger or be a danger: *a ~ bridge/journey/illness. The river is ~ for bathers. That dog looks ~,* looks as though it might attack people. **~·ly** *adv*

dangle /'dæŋgl/ *vi, vt* **1** [VP2A,C,6A,15A] hang or swing loosely; carry (sth) so that it hangs or swings loosely: *a bunch of keys dangling at the end of a chain; to ~ a toy in front of a baby;* (fig) *to ~ bright prospects* (eg of wealth, a well-paid position) *before a man.* **2** [VP2C] **~ round/about,** remain near (sb or sth) (as an admirer) hoping to obtain sth: *She always has half a dozen men dangling round her.*

Dan·iel /'dænɪəl/ *n* upright judge; ⇨ Dan 1 to 6; person of great wisdom; ⇨ Mer of Ven, 4: 1.

Dan·ish /'deɪnɪʃ/ *n, adj* (language) of Denmark or the Danes.

dank /dæŋk/ *adj* (-er, -est) damp in an unpleasant or unhealthy way: *the ~ undergrowth of a forest; a ~ and chilly cave.*

daphne /'dæfnɪ/ *n* kinds of flowering shrub.

dap·per /'dæpə(r)/ *adj* (usu of a small person) neat and smart in appearance; active in movement: *Isn't he a ~ little man!*

dapple/data

218

dapple /ˈdæpl/ vt [VP6A] (usu in pp) mark, become marked, with rounded patches of different colour or shades of colour, esp of an animal, or of sunlight and shadow: ∼d deer; a ∼d horse; ∼d shade, as when sunlight comes through the leaves of trees. ∼-ˈgrey adj, n (horse) of grey with darker patches.

Darby and Joan /ˌdɑːbɪ ən ˈdʒəʊn/ n old and loving married couple: a ∼ club, one for old couples.

dare¹ /deə(r)/ anom fin (pt dared /deəd/ or, less often, durst /dɜːst/) (dare not is abbr to daren't /deənt/, 3rd pers sing is dare, not dares) (Used with an inf without to, chiefly in neg sentences, including those with hardly, never and no one, nobody, and in interr and conditional sentences, and in sentences to indicate doubt) [VP5] have the courage, impudence or effrontery to: Don't (you) ∼ do that again! I ∼n't/don't ∼ speak to him. I wonder whether he ∼ try. No one/Nobody ∼d ask him about his intentions. He will hardly/never ∼ go there again. How ∼ he say such rude things about me! I ∼ say, It seems to me likely or possible: I ∼ say he'll come later.

dare² /deə(r)/ vt,vi 1 [VP5,4A] (with or without to) be brave enough to: He didn't ∼ (to) go. I wonder how he ∼s (to) say such things. I've never ∼d (to) ask him. They wouldn't ∼ (to be so rude)! 2 [VP6A] take the risk of; face: He will ∼ any danger. 3 [VP6A,17] ∼ sb (to do sth), challenge; suggest that sb has not the courage or ability to do sth: I ∼ you to say that again! He ∼d me to jump from the bridge into the river. Go on, insult me! I ∼ you! '∼-devil n (often attrib) person who is foolishly bold or reckless: You ∼-devil! What a ∼-devil fellow he is! □ n challenge. do sth for a ∼, do sth because one is ∼d(3) to do it.

dar·ing /ˈdeərɪŋ/ n [U] adventurous courage; audacity: the ∼ of the paratroops; lose one's ∼. □ adj brave; audacious: a ∼ robbery. What a ∼ thing to do! ∼·ly adv

dark¹ /dɑːk/ n [U] 1 absence of light: All the lights went out and we were left in the ∼. Some children are afraid of the ∼. Don't leave me alone in the ∼. before/after ∼, before/after the sun goes down: Try to get home before ∼. The place is so dangerous that we don't often go out after ∼. 2 (fig) ignorance. keep sb/be in the ∼ (about sth), keep sb/be in ignorance: We were completely in the ∼ about his movements.

dark² /dɑːk/ adj (-er, -est) 1 with no or very little light: a ∼, moonless night; a ∼ corner of the room. It's getting too ∼ to take photographs. '∼-lantern, one that can have its light covered. '∼-room, one that can be made ∼ for photographic work. 2 (of colour) not reflecting much light; nearer black than white: a ∼ dress/suit; ∼ blue/green/brown; ∼-brown eyes. 3 (of the skin) not fair: a ∼ complexion. 4 (fig) hidden, mysterious: a ∼ secret, one that is closely guarded. keep it ∼, keep a secret. the D∼ Continent, Africa (used of the time when most of it was unexplored and mysterious). a ∼ horse, race-horse with unexpected or unknown capabilities; (fig) person whose capabilities may be greater than they are known to be. 5 hopeless; sad; cheerless: Don't look on the ∼ side of things. 6 unenlightened (morally or intellectually). the D∼ Ages, (in European history), from the 6th to the 12th cc; (also) between the end of the Roman Empire (AD 395) and the close of the 10th c. 7 not clear to or in the mind: a ∼ saying,

one that is obscure. ∼·ly adv ∼·ness n [U] the state of being ∼: The room was in complete ∼ness.

darken /ˈdɑːkən/ vt, vi [VP6A,2A] make or become dark. ∼ sb's door, (facet) visit him.

Darkey, Darkie, Darky /ˈdɑːkɪ/ n ⚠ (colloq) (offensive term for a) Negro or Negress.

dar·ling /ˈdɑːlɪŋ/ n 1 person or object very much loved: She's a little ∼. My ∼! 2 (attrib, colloq) charming; delightful: What a ∼ little cottage!

darn¹ /dɑːn/ vt,vi [VP6A,2A] mend (esp sth knitted, eg a sock) by passing thread in and out and in two directions: My socks have been ∼ed again and again. □ n place mended by ∼ing. ∼-ing n (esp) things needing to be ∼ed. '∼ing-needle, large sewing needle used for ∼ing.

darn² /dɑːn/ vt [VP6A] (sl) damn(3): Well, I'll be ∼ed.

dart¹ /dɑːt/ n [C] 1 quick, sudden, forward movement: The child made a sudden ∼ across the road. 2 small, sharp missile (feathered and pointed), to be thrown at a target (marked with numbers for scoring) in the game called ∼s.

dart² /dɑːt/ vi,vt [VP2A,C,6A,15A,B] (cause to) move forward suddenly and quickly; send suddenly and quickly: The deer ∼ed away when it saw us. The snake ∼ed out its tongue. She ∼ed an angry look at him. Swallows were ∼ing through the air. She ∼ed into the shop.

dash¹ /dæʃ/ n 1 [C] sudden rush; violent movement: to make a ∼ for shelter/freedom; to make a ∼ at the enemy. at a ∼, quickly and smartly: The cavalry rode off at a ∼. 2 (usu a/the ∼ of) (sound of) liquid striking sth or being thrown or struck: the ∼ of the waves on the rocks; the ∼ of oars striking the water. A ∼ of cold water will revive a person who has fainted. 3 [C] small amount of sth added or mixed: a ∼ of pepper in the soup; water with a ∼ of whisky in it; red with a ∼ of blue. 4 [C] stroke of the pen or a mark (—) used in printing. ⇨ App 9. 5 the ∼, short race, sprint: the 100-metres ∼. 6 [U] (capacity for) vigorous action; energy: an officer famous for his skill and ∼. cut a ∼, make a brilliant show (in appearance and behaviour). '∼-board, (a) screen on the front part of a horse-drawn cart, wagon, etc to protect from mud splashed up from the road. (b) panel beneath the windscreen of a motor-car, with speedometer, various controls, etc. ⇨ the illus at motor.

dash² /dæʃ/ vt,vi 1 [VP6A,15A,B,2C] send or throw violently; move or be moved violently: The boat was ∼ed against the rocks. The huge waves ∼ed over the rocks. The elephants ∼ed through the undergrowth. D∼ a bucketful of water over this muddy floor. A motor-car ∼ed past us/∼ed mud all over us as it passed. ∼ sth off, write or draw sth quickly: I must ∼ off a few letters before I go out. 2 [VP6A] ∼ sb's hopes, destroy, discourage, them. 3 [VP6A] (colloq, used as a mild substitute for) Damn!: D∼ it! ∼-ing adj impetuous; lively; full of, showing, energy: a ∼ing cavalry charge; a ∼ing rider, eg one who rides a horse boldly. ∼-ing·ly adv

das·tard /ˈdæstəd/ n (old use) bully; coward who is brutal when there is no risk to himself. ∼-ly adj of or like a ∼.

data /ˈdeɪtə/ n pl (pl of Lat datum) 1 facts; things certainly known (and from which conclusions may be drawn): unless sufficient ∼ are available. 2 (usu with sing v) information prepared for and operated on a computer programme: *The ~ is ready for processing.* '~ **bank,** centre with a comprehensive file of computer ~. ~ **'processing,** the performing of operations on ~ to obtain information, solutions to problems, etc.

date¹ /deɪt/ *n* **1** statement of the time, day, month, year, one or all three of these, when sth happened or is to happen: *D~ of birth, 20 April 1974; the ~ of the discovery of America by Columbus (1492). What's the ~ today? Has the ~ for the meeting been fixed?* '~-**line, (a)** (*International* ~-*line*) meridian 180° from Greenwich, east and west of which at any given time the calendar ~s differ by one day. **(b)** phrase giving the ~ and place of origin of an article in a periodical. **2** [U] period of time, eg one to which antiquities belong: *Many ruins of Roman ~* (= of the time of ancient Rome) *are to be seen in the south of France.* **3** (phrases) **be/go ,out of '~,** be/become not modern: *Will denim jeans ever go out of ~?* Hence, **'out-of-~** *adj: out-of-~ clothes/ideas/slang.* **be/bring sth ,up to '~, (a)** be/make it modern. **(b)** be/bring it up to the present time: *bring a catalogue up to ~.* ⇨ update. Hence, **'up-to-~** *adj: up-to-~ styles/methods/books.* **to ~,** so far; until now: *There's no news to ~.* **4** (colloq) social meeting arranged with sb at a certain time and place; appointment: *I've got a ~ with her tonight.* ,**blind '~,** arrangement to meet sb socially, having not met before. **5** (by extension; colloq) companion of the other sex with whom ~s(4) are arranged. **~-less** *adj* endless; immemorial.

date² /deɪt/ *vt,vi* **1** [VP6A] have or put a date(1) on: *Don't forget to ~ your letters. The letter is ~d from London, 24 May.* **2** [VP6A] give a date(2) to: *to ~ old coins/sth found in an excavation. That suit ~s you,* shows your age (because it is old-fashioned). ⇨ **4** below. **3** [VP2C,3A] ~ **from/back to,** have existed since: *The castle ~s back to the 14th century,* was built then. *The prosperity of the family ~s from the war,* They became rich (eg by making munitions) during the war. **4** [VP2A] show signs of becoming out-of-date: *Isn't this textbook beginning to ~?* **5** [VP6A] make a date(4) with. **dated** *adj* out of fashion; (of words and phrases) used in the past but not now current. **datable** *adj* that can be dated(2).

date³ /deɪt/ *n* small, brown, sweet, edible fruit of the date-palm, common in N Africa and SW Asia. ⇨ the illus at palm.

dat·ive /'deɪtɪv/ *n, adj* (gram) (in Latin and other inflected languages) (of the) form of a word showing that it is an indirect object of the verb; (in English, loosely used for) indirect object (eg *me* in 'Tell me your name'). ⇨ case¹(3).

datum /'deɪtəm/ *n* fact. ⇨ data.

daub /dɔːb/ *vt,vi* **1** [VP6A,14,15A,B] put paint, clay, plaster, etc roughly on a surface: *to ~ plaster on a wall; to ~ a wall with paint. Don't ~ the paint on too thickly.* **2** [VP6A,2A] paint (pictures) without skill or artistry. **3** [VP6A,14] make dirty: *trousers ~ed with paint.* □ *n* **1** [C,U] (covering of) soft, sticky material, eg clay. **2** [C] badly painted picture. **~er** *n* person who paints unskilfully.

daugh·ter /'dɔːtə(r)/ *n* one's female child. **~-in-law** /'dɔːtər ɪn lɔː/ (*pl* ~s-in-law /'dɔːtəz ɪn lɔː/) wife of one's son. **~·ly** *adj* befitting a ~: ~*ly affection.*

daunt /dɔːnt/ *vt* [VP6A] discourage: *nothing ~ed,* not at all discouraged.

daunt·less /'dɔːntlɪs/ *adj* not daunted; persevering. **~·ly** *adv*

dau·phin /'dɔːfɪn/ *n* title of the King of France's eldest son (from 1349 to 1830).

dav·en·port /'dævnpɔːt/ *n* **1** (GB) piece of furniture with drawers and a hinged flap that opens so that it can be used as a writing-desk. **2** (US) long seat for two or three persons, with arms and a back. ⇨ settee.

davit /'dævɪt/ *n* one of a pair of small cranes(2), curved at the top, for supporting, lowering and raising a ship's boat.

daw /dɔː/ *n* = jackdaw.

dawdle /'dɔːdl/ *vi,vt* [VP2A,C,15B] ~ **(away),** be slow; waste time: *Stop dawdling and do something useful! Don't ~ away your time! He's always dawdling.* **daw·dler** /'dɔːdlə(r)/ *n* person who ~s.

dawn¹ /dɔːn/ *n* **1** [U,C] first light of day; daybreak: *We must start at ~. He works from ~ till dark. It's almost ~.* **2** [U,C] (fig) beginning; birth: *the ~ of intelligence/love/civilization. The war ended and we looked forward to the ~ of happier days.*

dawn² /dɔːn/ *vi* **1** [VP2A] begin to grow light: *The day was just ~ing.* **2** [VP2A,3A] ~ **(on/upon sb),** begin to appear; grow clear (to the mind): *The truth began to ~ upon him. It has just ~ed on me that...,* I have just begun to realize that....

day /deɪ/ *n* **1** [U] time between sunrise and sunset: *He has been working all day. We travelled day and night/night and day without stopping.* **before day,** before daylight comes. **by day,** during daylight: *We travelled by day and stayed at hotels every night.* **pass the time of day (with sb),** exchange greetings (eg by saying 'Good morning'). **2** [C] period of twenty-four hours (from midnight): *There are seven days in a week. I saw Tom three days ago. I shall see Mary in a few days' time,* a few days from now. *What day of the week is it? It's Monday.* **the day after tomorrow**: *If today is Wednesday, the day after tomorrow will be Friday.* **the day before yesterday**: *If today is Wednesday, the day before yesterday was Monday.* **this day week**: *If today is 1 May, this day week will be 8 May.* **this day fortnight**: *If today is 1 May, this day fortnight will be 15 May.* **day after day**; **every day,** for many days together. **day in, day out,** continuously. **from day to day; from one day to the next:** *No one can be certain about what will happen from day to day.* **one day,** on a day (past or future). **the other day,** a few days ago. **some day,** on some day in the future. **one of these days,** (used in making a promise or a prophecy) before long. **one of those days,** day of much misfortune. **that'll be the day,** (ironic) that will never happen. **if he's a day,** (of age) at least: *He's eighty if he's a day!* **not be one's day,** day when things go badly for one. **to a/the day,** exactly: *three years ago to the/a day.* Note the omission of relatives after *day: the day* (*on which*) *I met you. We shall have many days* (*on which*) *to talk things over.* **3** the hours of the day given to work: *I've done a good day's work. His working day is eight hours. They want a six-hour day and a five-day week. Most workers are paid weekly, but some are paid by the day.* **call it a day,** decide that we have done enough (work) for one day: *Let's call it a day,* stop. **all in a/the day's work,** all part of the normal routine. **at the end of the day,** when the work, etc is completed. **early/late in the day,** (too) early/late. **day 'off,** holiday. **day release,**

permission for a worker to attend a college during a working day. **4** (often *pl*) time; period: *in my school-days; in his boyhood days; in the days of Queen Victoria; in days of old/in olden days,* in former times; *in days to come,* in future times; *the men of other days,* of past times. **better days,** times when one was, or will be, richer, more prosperous, etc: *Let's hope we'll soon see better days.* **fall on evil days,** suffer misfortune. **the present day,** the time we are now living in. Hence **'present-day** *attrib adj: present-day* (= modern) *writers.* **(in) these days,** nowadays. **in those days,** then. **in this day and age,** (cliché) in this present period. **5** (*sing* preceded by *his, her, their,* etc) lifetime; period of success, prosperity, power, etc: *Colonialism has had its day. She was a beauty in her day,* before she grew old. **Every dog has its day,** (prov) We all have good luck or a period of success at some time or other. **Those were the days,** (cliché) ie better times. **6 the day,** contest: *We've won/carried the day. The day is ours. We've lost the day.* **7** (used attrib, and in compounds) **'day bed,** bed or couch for daytime sleep or rest. **'day-book,** (comm) book for record of sales as they take place, for transfer to a ledger. **'day-boy/girl,** one who attends school daily but sleeps at home. **'day-break** *n* [U] dawn. **,day 'care** *n* [U] care for small children, away from home, during the day: *a 'day-care centre.* **'day-dream** *n, vi* [VP2A] (think) pleasant thoughts. **'day-labourer,** one who is hired by the day. **'day-long** *adj, adv* (lasting) for the whole day. **'day nursery,** place where small children may be left during the day. **,day re'lease** *n* [U] system of allowing employees off work (eg for one day per week) for educational purposes. **,day re'turn** *n* [C] return ticket (often at a reduced rate) available both ways on one day only. **'day-school,** used as the opp of *boarding-school, evening school,* and *Sunday school.* **'day shift,** (workers working a) period during the day, esp in a mine. **'day-spring,** (poet) dawn. **'day-time,** day(1), esp: *in the day-time.*

day·light /'deɪlaɪt/ *n* [U] **1** light of day: *Can we reach our destination in ~,* before it gets dark? **~ robbery** *n* [U] **(a)** open cheating. **(b)** high, unfair price(s). **~ saving** *n* [U] putting the hands of the clock forward so that darkness falls later. ⇨ *summertime* at summer. **2** dawn: *leave/arrive before ~.*

daze /deɪz/ *vt* [VP6A] make (sb) feel stupid or unable to think clearly: *If someone gave you a heavy blow on the head, you would probably feel ~d. He looked ~d with drugs/was in a ~d state.* □ *n in a ~,* in a bewildered condition. **dazed·ly** /'deɪzɪdlɪ/ *adv* in a ~d manner.

dazzle /'dæzl/ *vt* [VP6A] make (sb) unable to see clearly or act normally because of too much light, brilliance, splendour, etc: *~d by bright lights; dazzling sunshine/diamonds.* □ *n* [U] glitter.

D-day /'di: deɪ/ *n* (code name for the) day (6 June 1944) on which British and American forces landed in N France, during the Second World War; unnamed day on which important work is to start.

dea·con /'di:kən/ *n* minister or officer who has various duties in certain Christian churches (eg in the Church of England, below a bishop or priest; in nonconformist churches, a layman attending to secular affairs). **~·ess** /'di:kənɪs/ *n* woman with duties similar to a ~'s.

dead /ded/ *adj* **1** (of plants, animals, persons) no longer living: *~ flowers/leaves. The hunter fired*

and *the tiger fell ~.* **D~ men tell no tales,** (prov, used as an argument for killing sb whose knowledge of a secret may cause one loss or trouble). **wait for a ~ man's shoes,** wait for sb to die in order to step into his position. **the ~,** all those who have died or been killed: *to rise from the ~; the ~ and the wounded.* **~ march,** piece of slow, solemn music for a funeral. **2** never having had life: *~ matter,* eg rock. **3** without movement or activity: *in the ~ hours of the night,* when everything is quiet; (as *n*) *in the ~ of winter,* when there is no growth of vegetation, when the weather makes outdoor activity difficult, etc. **~ end,** cul-de-sac. **be at/come to/reach a ~ end,** (fig) the stage from which further progress appears impossible. ⇨ 9 below. **4** (of languages, customs, etc) no longer used or observed. **~ language,** eg ancient Greek. **~ letter, (a)** regulation to which attention is no longer paid. **(b)** letter kept by the post-office because the person to whom it is addressed has not claimed it and neither he nor the sender can be found. **5** (of the hands, etc) numbed, eg by cold; unable to feel anything: *~ fingers.* **~ to,** unconscious of, hardened against: *~ to all feelings of shame; ~ to the world,* (fig) fast asleep. **6** complete; abrupt; exact: *to come to a ~ stop; runners on a ~ level,* running side by side; *a ~ calm,* not even a breath of wind. **go into/be in a ~ faint,** complete unconsciousness. **~ heat,** a race in which two or more runners reach the winning-post together. **~ loss,** a complete loss, with no compensation; (sl, of a person) one who is of no help or use to anyone. **the ~ centre,** the exact centre. **~ shot,** person who hits the target without fail; shot that goes to the exact point aimed at. **~ silence,** complete silence. **~ sleep,** a deep sleep (as if *~*). **7** that can no longer be used: *a ~ match,* one that has been struck; *a ~ wire,* one through which electric current no longer passes. *The telephone went ~,* did not transmit sounds. **8** (of sound) dull, heavy; (of colours) lacking brilliance; (cricket, tennis, etc) (of the surface of the ground) such that balls move slowly: *a ~ pitch;* (of the ball, in various games) out of play. **9** (various uses) **'~-line** *n* fixed limit of time for finishing a piece of work: *meet a ~line,* do, finish sth by the time assigned for it. **~·pan** *adj* (colloq) (of a person's face, looks) showing no emotion. **~ weight** *n* **1** (with *indef art*) heavy inert mass. **2** (comm) ship's loaded weight, including fuel and cargo. □ *adv* completely; absolutely; thoroughly: *~ 'beat/'tired; ~ 'certain/'sure; ~ 'drunk,* so drunk as to be incapable; *~ slow,* as slowly as possible; *~ ahead,* directly ahead. *The wind was ~ against us. You're ~ right! cut sb ~,* ⇨ cut¹(7).

deaden /'dedn/ *vt* [VP6A] take away, deprive of, force, feeling, brightness: *drugs to ~ the pain; thick walls that ~ street noises; thick clothing that ~ed the force of the blow.*

dead·lock /'dedlɒk/ *n* [C,U] complete failure to reach agreement, to settle a quarrel or grievance: *to reach ~; to be at/come to a total ~.* **break the ~,** cause change in the blocked state.

deadly /'dedlɪ/ *adj* (-ier, -iest) **1** causing, likely to cause, death: *~ weapons/poison. Fog is one of the sailor's deadliest enemies.* **2** filled with hate: *~ enemies.* **3** that may result in damnation: *the seven ~ sins.* **4** like that of death: *a ~ paleness.* **5** (colloq) excessive: *~ determination.* □ *adv* like that of death: *~ pale;* (colloq) excessively: *~ seri-*

ous.

deaf /def/ *adj* **1** unable to hear at all; unable to hear well: *to become* ∼; *the* ∼ *and dumb alphabet*, one in which signs made with the hands are used for letters or words; *to be* ∼ *in one ear.* '∼**-aid** *n* hearing aid; small device, usu electronic, that helps a ∼ person to hear. ∼ '**mute** *n* person who is ∼ and dumb. **2** unwilling to listen: ∼ *to all advice/ entreaty. He turned a* ∼ *ear to* (= refused to listen to) *our requests for help.* ∼·**ness** *n*

deafen /'defn/ *vt* [VP6A] make so much noise that hearing is difficult or impossible: *We were almost* ∼*ed by the uproar. There were* ∼*ing cheers when the speaker finished.*

deal¹ /di:l/ *n* (board of) fir or pine wood: (chiefly attrib) ∼ *furniture; a* ∼ *table; made of white* ∼.

deal² /di:l/ *n* **a** (*good/great*) ∼ (*of sth*), much; many: *spend a good* ∼ *of money; take a great* ∼ *of trouble; cause sb a* ∼ *of anxiety; have a great* ∼ *of friends; be a good* ∼ *better; see sb a great* ∼, often.

deal³ /di:l/ *vt,vi* (*pt,pp* dealt /delt/) **1** [VP6A,15B,2A,12A,13A] ∼ (*out*), give out to a number of persons: *The money must be* ∼*t out fairly. Who* ∼*t the cards? He had been* ∼*t four aces. It is the duty of a judge to* ∼ *out justice.* ∼ *sb a blow;* ∼ *a blow at/to sb,* (a) hit or strike him: *He* ∼*t me a hard blow on the chin.* (b) (fig) hurt; upset: *The news* ∼*t me a severe blow.* **2** [VP3A] ∼ *in sth*, stock, sell: *a shop that* ∼*s in goods of all sorts;* spend time on: *to* ∼ *in gossip and slander.* **3** [VP3A] ∼ *with sb/at a place*, do business: *Do you* ∼ *with Smith, the butcher? I've stopped* ∼*ing at that shop—their prices are too high.* **4** [VP3A] ∼ *with*, (a) have relations with: *That man is easy/difficult/impossible to* ∼ *with.* (b) behave towards; treat: *How would you* ∼ *with an armed burglar? What is the best way of* ∼*ing with young criminals,* How can we make them into good citizens? (c) (of affairs) manage; attend to: *How shall we* ∼ *with this problem?* (d) be about; be concerned with: *a book* ∼*ing with West Africa.* **5** ∼ *well/badly by sb*, treat him well/badly (usu in passive): *He has always* ∼*t well by me. You've been badly* ∼*t by.*

deal⁴ /di:l/ *n* [C] **1** (in games) distribution of playing cards: *It's your* ∼, your turn to deal out the cards. **a new** ∼, (originally **the New D**∼) programme of social and economic reform (in US); any new plan that is thought to be just or fair. **2** business transaction or agreement; (colloq) bargain: *Well, it's a* ∼, I agree to do business with you on those terms. *I'll do a* ∼ *with you*, make a bargain. **a fair/square** ∼, fair treatment. **a raw/rough** ∼, harsh or unjust treatment.

dealer /'di:lə(r)/ *n* **1** person who deals out playing-cards. **2** trader: *a* '*horse-*∼; *a* ∼ *in* (= person who buys and sells) *stolen goods; a* '*car* ∼. Cf *a coal merchant.*

deal·ing /'di:lɪŋ/ *n* **1** [U] dealing out or distributing; behaviour towards others: *He is well known for fair* ∼. **2** (*pl*) business relations: *I've always found him honest in his* ∼*s with me. I advise you to have no* ∼*s with that fellow.*

dealt /delt/ *pt,pp* of deal³.

dean /di:n/ *n* **1** clergyman at the head of a cathedral chapter. **2 rural** ∼, clergyman who, under an archdeacon, is responsible for a number of parishes. **3** (in some universities) person with authority to maintain discipline; head of a department of studies. **4** = doyen. ∼·**ery** /'di:nərɪ/ *n* (*pl*-ries) of-

fice, house, of a ∼; group of parishes under a rural ∼.

dear /dɪə(r)/ *adj* (-er, -est) **1** ∼ (*to*), loved (by); lovable: *Your mother is* ∼ *to you. What a* ∼ *little child! hold sth/sb* ∼, (formal) love very much. **2** used as a form of address (polite or ironical) in speech, and at the beginning of letters: *My* ∼ *Jones; D*∼ *Madam/Sir; D*∼ *Mr Green.* **3** high in price; (of a shop) asking high prices: *Everything is getting* ∼*er. That's a* ∼ *shop.* '∼ **money**, (when loans are difficult to obtain) on which a high rate of interest must be paid. **4** ∼ (*to*), precious (to); greatly valued: *He lost everything that was* ∼ *to him.* □ *adv* at a high cost: *If you want to make money, you must buy cheap and sell* ∼. □ *n* **1** lovable person: *Isn't she a* ∼*! Aren't they* ∼*s!* **2** (also ∼·**est**) (used to address a person): '*Come, my* ∼*est*'. '*Yes,* ∼'; (used with *indef art*, esp when coaxing sb): '*Drink your milk up, Anne, there's a* ∼'. □ *int* used to express surprise, impatience, wonder, dismay, etc: *Oh* ∼*! D*∼ *me!* ∼·**ly** *adv* **1** very much: *He would* ∼*ly* (= earnestly) *love to see his mother again. He loves his mother* ∼*ly.* **2** at great cost: *Victory was* ∼*ly bought*, eg when hundreds of soldiers were killed. ∼·**ness** *n* being ∼; great cost.

dearth /dɜ:θ/ *n* ∼ (*of*), (*sing* only) scarcity; too small a supply: *in time of* ∼; *a* ∼ *of food.* ⇨ shortage, a much commoner word.

deary, dearie /'dɪərɪ/ *n* (colloq) dear one; darling (used esp by an older to a younger person, eg by a mother to address her child).

death /deθ/ *n* [C,U] (as shown in the examples) **1** dying; ending of life: *There have been several* ∼*s from drowning here this summer. His mother's* ∼ *was a great blow to him. at* ∼'*s door*, dying; in danger of ∼. *to* ∼, so that dying occurs: *Two children were burnt to* ∼ *in the fire. Don't work yourself to* ∼, work so hard that you become ill and die. *bore sb to* ∼, bore him extremely. *sick to* ∼ *of sb/sth*, extremely tired, bored, etc. '∼**-bed**, bed on which one dies; *The criminal made a* ∼*-bed confession*, confessed his crimes while dying. '∼**-duties**, taxes (to be) paid on a person's property before it passes to his heir(s). '∼'*s head*, human skull (as an emblem of ∼). '∼**-rate**, yearly number of ∼s per 1000 of population. '∼ **rattle** *n* unusual rattling sound in the throat of a dying person. **2** killing or being killed: *The murderer was sentenced to* ∼, to be executed. *be in at the* ∼, (fox-hunting) see the fox killed; (fig) see the end of an enterprise, etc. *put sb to* ∼, kill him; execute him. *stone sb to* ∼, kill him by throwing stones at him. '∼**-roll**, list of persons killed (in war, in an earthquake, etc). '∼**-trap**, place where persons are likely to be killed (eg one where many fatal traffic accidents occur); place, set of circumstances, where people lose their lives (eg a burning building with no means of escape). '∼**-warrant**, official paper giving authority for the execution of a criminal, traitor, etc; (fig) sth which destroys prospects of life or happiness, ends an old custom, etc. **3** [U] state of being dead: *eyes closed in* ∼; *united in* ∼, eg of husband and wife in the same grave. *D*∼ *comes to all men.* (**a fate**) *worse than* ∼, to be greatly dreaded. '∼**-mask**, cast taken of a dead person's face. ⇨ the illus at mask. **4** *be the* ∼ *of sb*, be the cause of sb's ∼: *That old motor-bike will be the* ∼ *of you one of these days*, you will have a fatal accident. *Don't make me laugh so* *much; you'll be the* ~ *of me,* make me die of laughing. **catch one's** ~ **(of cold),** (colloq) catch a cold that will be fatal. '~**-blow,** blow that causes ~; (fig) shock from which recovery is impossible: *a* ~*-blow to his hopes of success.* **the Black 'D**~, pestilence in Europe in the 14th c. **5** (fig) destruction; end: *the* ~ *of one's hopes/plans.*

death-less /'deθlɪs/ *adj* never dying or forgotten; immortal: ~ *fame/glory.*

death-like /'deθlaɪk/ *adj* like that of death: *a* ~ *silence.*

deathly /'deθlɪ/ *adj* like death: *a* ~ *stillness.* □ *adv* like death: ~ *pale.*

deb /deb/ *n* (abbr of) débutante.

dé-bâcle /deɪ'bɑːkl/ *n* (F) confused rush or stampede; sudden and great disaster; downfall.

de-bag /diː'bæg/ *vt* (-gg-) [VP6A] forcibly take off the trousers from.

de-bar /dɪ'bɑː(r)/ *vt* (-rr-) [VP14] ~ **sb from,** shut out; prevent (sb) by a regulation (from doing or having sth): ~ *persons who have been convicted of crime from voting at elections.*

de-bark /dɪ'bɑːk/ *vt, vi* **de-bark-ation** /ˌdiːbɑː'keɪʃn/ *n* = disembark.

de-base /dɪ'beɪs/ *vt* [VP6A] make lower in value, poorer in quality, character, etc: *to* ~ *the coinage,* eg by reducing the percentage of silver. ~**-ment** *n*

de-bat-able /dɪ'beɪtəbl/ *adj* that can be debated or disputed; open to question: ~ *ground.*

de-bate /dɪ'beɪt/ *n* [C,U] formal discussion, eg at a public meeting or in Parliament; contest between two speakers, or two groups of speakers, to show skill and ability in arguing: *After a long* ~ *the bill was passed by the House of Commons and sent to the House of Lords. After much* ~ *Harry was chosen captain of the football team. Who opened the* ~, *was the first to speak? The question under* ~ *was....* □ *vt, vi* [VP6A,8,10,2A,C] have a ~ about; take part in a ~; think over in order to decide: *to* ~ (*upon*) *a question with sb; to* ~ *about sth; a debating society. We were debating whether to go to the mountains or to the seaside.* **de-bater** *n* one who ~s.

de-bauch /dɪ'bɔːtʃ/ *vt* [VP6A] cause (sb) to lose virtue, to act immorally; turn (sb) away from good taste or judgement. □ *n* [C] occasion of excessive drinking, immoral behaviour, usu in company: *a drunken* ~. ~**-ery** /dɪ'bɔːtʃərɪ/ *n* [U] intemperance and indulgence in sensual pleasures: *a life of* ~*ery;* (*pl;* -ries) instances or periods of this. ~**ee** /ˌdɪbɔː'tʃiː/ *n* ~ed person.

de-ben-ture /dɪ'bentʃə(r)/ *n* [C] (fin) certificate given by a business corporation, etc as a receipt for money lent at a fixed rate of interest until the principal(4) is repaid.

de-bili-tate /dɪ'bɪlɪteɪt/ *vt* [VP6A] make (a person, his constitution) weak: *a debilitating climate.*

de-bil-ity /dɪ'bɪlətɪ/ *n* [U] weakness (of health, purpose): *After her long illness she is suffering from general* ~.

debit /'debɪt/ *n* (book-keeping) entry (in an account) of a sum owing. '~**-side** left-hand side of an account, on which such entries are made. ⇨ credit[1](4). □ *vt* [VP6A,14] ~ *sth* (*against/to sb*), put money on the ~ side (of sb's account): ~ *£5 against my account;* ~ *£5 to me.* ~ *sb* (*with sth*), give him a ~ (of money): ~ *sb/sb's account with £5.*

deb-on-air /ˌdebə'neə(r)/ *adj* cheerful; bright and light-hearted.

dé-bouch /dɪ'baʊtʃ/ *vt, vi* [VP6A,2A] (cause to)

emerge or issue.

de-brief /ˌdiː'briːf/ *vt* [VP6A] question, examine, eg persons who have returned from a mission, etc, to obtain information. ⇨ brief[2].

de-bris, dé-bris /'deɪbriː: *US:* də'briː/ *n* [U] scattered broken pieces; wreckage: *searching among the* ~ *after the explosion.*

debt /det/ *n* [C,U] payment which must be, but has not yet been, paid to sb; obligation: *If I pay all my* ~*s I shall have no money left. I owe him a* ~ *of gratitude for all he has done for me.* **be in/out of** ~, owe/not owe money. **get into/out of** ~, reach a point where one owes/does not owe money: *It's much easier to get into* ~ *than to get out of* ~. **National D**~ *n* money owed by the State to those who have lent it money. ⇨ bad[1](4), honour[2](2). ~**or** /-tə(r)/ *n* person who is in ~ to another.

de-bug /ˌdiː'bʌg/ *vt* (-gg-) [VP6A] (colloq) search for and remove (possible causes of trouble, faults, errors, eg from a computer programme, engines on a production line).

de-bunk /diː'bʌŋk/ *vt* [VP6A] reveal the truth about (a person, idea, institution) by stripping away false sentiments, traditions, etc.

debut, début /'deɪbjuː: *US:* dɪ'bjuː/ *n* (esp of a young woman) first appearance at adult parties and other social events; (of an actor, musician, etc) first appearance on a public stage: *to make one's* ~.

debu-tante, déb- /'debjuːtɑːnt/ *n* young woman making her debut into high society.

deca- /'dekə/ *pref* ten (in the metric system).

dec-ade /'dekeɪd/ *n* period of ten years: *the first* ~ *of the 20th century,* ie 1900—1909.

deca-dence /'dekədəns/ *n* [U] falling to a lower level (in morals, art, literature, etc esp after a period at a high level).

deca-dent /'dekədənt/ *adj* in a state of decadence. □ *n* person in this state.

Deca-logue /'dekəlɒg *US:* -lɔːg/ *n* **the** ~, the Ten Commandments of Moses. ⇨ commandment; ⇨ Exod 20: 1-17.

de-camp /dɪ'kæmp/ *vi* [VP2A,3A] ~ (*with*), go away suddenly (and often secretly).

de-cant /dɪ'kænt/ *vt* [VP6A] pour (wine, etc) from a bottle into another vessel slowly so as not to disturb the sediment. ~**er** *n* vessel, usu of decorated glass with a stopper, into which liquor is ~ed.

decanters

de-capi-tate /dɪ'kæpɪteɪt/ *vt* [VP6A] behead (esp as a legal punishment). **de-capi-ta-tion** /dɪˌkæpɪ'teɪʃn/ *n*

de-car-bon-ize /ˌdiː'kɑːbənaɪz/ *vt* remove carbon from, esp an internal combustion engine.

deca-syl-lable /'dekəsɪləbl/ *n* **deca-syl-labic** /ˌdekəsɪ'læbɪk/ *adj* (line) of ten syllables.

de-cay /dɪ'keɪ/ *vi* [VP2A] go bad; lose power, health: ~*ing teeth/vegetables. Our powers* ~ *in old age. What caused the Roman Empire to* ~? □ *n* [U] decaying: *the* ~ *of the teeth. The house is in* ~. *Old civilizations may fall into* ~, lose strength.

de·cease /dɪˈsiːs/ n [U] (formal, legal) (a person's) death. □ *vi* die. **the ~d,** (formal, legal) person who has, persons who have, recently died.

de·ceit /dɪˈsiːt/ n 1 [U] deceiving; causing a person to accept as true or genuine sth that is false: *She is incapable of ~,* would never tell lies, etc. **2** [C] lie; dishonest trick.

de·ceit·ful /dɪˈsiːtfl/ adj 1 in the habit of deceiving: *No one can admire a ~ boy.* **2** intended to deceive; misleading in appearance, etc: ~ *words/ behaviour.* **~ly** /-fʊlɪ/ adv **~·ness** n

de·ceive /dɪˈsiːv/ vt [VP6A,14] ~ *(in/into),* cause (sb) to believe sth that is false; play a trick on; mislead (on purpose): *You can't pass the examination without working hard, so don't ~ yourself. I've been ~d in you,* have found that you were not what I thought you were. *We were ~d into the belief/ ~d into believing that....* **de·ceiver** /-və(r)/ n person who ~s. **de·ceiv·ing·ly** adv

de·celer·ate /ˌdiːˈseləreɪt/ vt,vi (cause to) diminish speed. ⇨ accelerate.

De·cem·ber /dɪˈsembə(r)/ n twelfth month of the year.

de·cency /ˈdiːsnsɪ/ n 1 [U] (the quality of) being decent; (regard for the) general opinion as to what is decent: *an offence against ~,* eg appearing naked in public. **2** (pl) **the decencies,** requirements of respectable behaviour in society: *We must observe the decencies.*

de·cent /ˈdiːsnt/ adj 1 right and suitable; respectful: *Put on some ~ clothes before you call on the Smiths. Poor people cannot always live in ~ conditions.* **2** modest; not likely to shock or embarrass others (the only sense for which *indecent* is the opposite): ~ *language and behaviour. Never tell stories that are not ~.* **3** (colloq) likeable; satisfactory: *He's a very ~ fellow. He gave us quite a ~ dinner.* **~·ly** adv in a ~(1,2) manner: *~ly dressed; behave ~ly;* (colloq): *He's doing very ~ly,* eg making a good income.

de·cen·tra·lize /ˌdiːˈsentrəlaɪz/ vt [VP6A] give greater powers (for self-government, etc) to (places, branches, etc away from the centre). **de·cen·tra·liz·ation** /ˌdiːˌsentrəlaɪˈzeɪʃn US: -lɪˈz-/ n

de·cep·tion /dɪˈsepʃn/ n 1 [U] deceiving; being deceived: *to practise ~ on the public.* **2** [C] trick intended to deceive: *a gross ~.*

de·cep·tive /dɪˈseptɪv/ adj deceiving: *Appearances are often ~,* Things are not always what they seem to be. **~·ly** adv

deci– /ˈdesɪ/ pref one-tenth (in the metric system).

deci·bel /ˈdesɪbel/ n unit for measuring the relative loudness of sounds.

de·cide /dɪˈsaɪd/ vt,vi 1 [VP6A,14,2A,3A] settle (a question or a doubt); give a judgement (*between, for, in favour of, against*): *We ~d the question by experiment. The judge ~d the case. It's difficult to ~ between the two. The judge ~d for/in favour of/against the plaintiff.* **2** [VP6A,7A,8,9,10,3A] ~ *(on/against),* think about and come to a conclusion; make up one's mind; resolve: *The boy ~d not to/~d that he would not become a sailor. It has been ~d that the exhibition shall not be open on Sundays. He could not ~ what to do/what he should do next. In the end she ~d on (buying)/~d to buy the green hat. We ~d against (going for)/ ~d not to go for a holiday in Wales.* **3** [VP17] cause to ~(2): *What ~d you to give up your job?* **de·cided** part adj 1 clear; definite: *There is a ~d difference between them. He's a man of ~d opin-*

ions. **2** (of persons) having firm opinions; determined: *He's quite ~d about it.* **de·cid·ed·ly** adv definitely; undoubtedly: *answer ~dly; ~dly better.*

de·cidu·ous /dɪˈsɪdjʊəs/ adj (of trees) losing their leaves annually (esp in autumn).

deci·mal /ˈdesɪml/ adj of tens or one-tenths: *the'~ system,* for money, weights, etc; *a ~ fraction,* eg 0·091; *the ~ point,* the point in eg 15·61. **~·ize** vt [VP6A] express as a ~ fraction: 1½ ~*ed* is 1·5; change to a ~ system: ~*ize the currency.* **~·iz·ation** /ˌdesɪmələɪˈzeɪʃn US: -lɪˈz-/ n

deci·mate /ˈdesɪmeɪt/ vt [VP6A] kill or destroy a large part of: *a population ~d by disease.*

de·cipher /dɪˈsaɪfə(r)/ vt [VP6A] find the meaning of (sth written in cipher, bad handwriting, sth puzzling or difficult to understand). **~·able** /dɪˈsaɪfrəbl/ adj that can be ~ed.

de·ci·sion /dɪˈsɪʒn/ n 1 [U] deciding; judging; [C] result of this; settlement of a question: *give a ~ on a case. Have they reached/come to/arrived at/ taken/made a ~ yet? His ~ to retire surprised all of us.* **2** [U] ability to decide and act accordingly; the quality of being decided(2): *A man who lacks ~* (= who hesitates, cannot decide questions) *cannot hold a position of responsibility.*

de·ci·sive /dɪˈsaɪsɪv/ adj 1 having a decided or definite outcome or result: *a ~ battle,* deciding which side wins the war. **2** showing decision(2); definite: *He gave a ~ answer.* **~·ly** adv

deck [1] /dek/ n 1 any of the floors of a ship, usu of wooden planks, in or above the hull: *My cabin is on E ~. Shall we go up on ~,* up (from a cabin, saloon, etc) on to the main (or promenade) ~? ⇨ the illus at ship. **clear the ~s,** ⇨ clear[3](1). **'~ cabin,** one on an open ~, not one that is below the main ~. **'~ chair,** collapsible chair of canvas, on a wooden or metal frame, used out of doors, eg in parks, the sea front, and on the ~s of ships. **'~ hand,** member of a ship's crew who works on ~. **'~ officers,** the captain and mates (contrasted with the engineers). **'~ passenger,** one who does not use a cabin or the public rooms, but eats and sleeps on ~. **'~ quoits** /kɔɪts/, game played on a ~(1) in which a ring (*quoit*) is thrown. **2** any similar surface, eg the floor of a bus: *the top ~ of a London bus.* **3** (chiefly US) pack of playing-cards; (comm) collection of punched cards from a particular file. **~er** n (in compounds) having a specified number of ~s: *a three-~er ship; a single-/double-~er bus; a double-/triple-~er sandwich,* one with three/four layers of bread.

deck [2] /dek/ vt [VP6A,14,15A] 1 ~ *(with/out in),* decorate: *streets ~ed with flags. She was ~ed out in her finest clothes.* **2** cover, provide (a boat, ship) with a deck.

deckle–edged /ˌdekl ˈedʒd/ adj (of some kinds of paper, eg hand-made notepaper) having untrimmed edges.

de·claim /dɪˈkleɪm/ vi,vt 1 [VP2A,3A] ~ *(against),* speak with strong feeling; attack in words. **2** [VP6A,2A] speak in the manner of addressing an audience or reciting poetry; recite, eg a poem, rhetorically.

dec·la·ma·tion /ˌdekləˈmeɪʃn/ n [U] declaiming; [C] speech full of strong feeling; formal speech. **de·clama·tory** /dɪˈklæmətərɪ US: -tɔːrɪ/ adj of ~.

dec·lar·ation /ˌdekləˈreɪʃn/ n [U] declaring; [C] that which is declared: *a ~ of war; the D~ of Independence,* that made by the N American colonies of Great Britain, on 4 July 1776, that they were politically independent; *a ~ of income,* one (to be) made to the Inspector of Taxes.

de·clare /dɪ'kleə(r)/ *vt, vi* **1** [VP6A,14,25] make known clearly or formally; announce: *to ~ the results of an election. I ~ this meeting closed. ~ (an innings closed),* (cricket) (of the captain of the team) announce that the team will not continue batting although the innings is not finished: *Australia ~d when the score reached 500. ~ trumps,* (in bridge²) say which suit(5) will be played as trumps. *~ war (on/against),* announce that a state of war exists. **2** [VP9,25] say solemnly; say in order to show that one has no doubt: *The accused man ~d that he was not guilty/~d himself innocent.* **3** [VP3A] *~ for/against,* say that one is/is not in favour of. **4** [VP6A] make a statement (to customs officials) of dutiable goods brought into a country, or (to a Tax Inspector) of one's income: *Have you anything to ~?* **5** (*int*) expressing surprise: *Well, I ~! de·clar·able* /dɪ'kleərəbl/ *adj* that must be ~d(4).

de·class·ify /ˌdiː'klæsɪfaɪ/ *vt* [VP6A] remove from a special class (esp sth hitherto secret): *~ information concerning nuclear fission.* **de·class·ifi·ca·tion** /ˌdiːˌklæsɪfɪ'keɪʃn/ *n*

de·clen·sion /dɪ'klenʃn/ *n* (gram) [U] varying the endings of *nouns, pronouns,* and *adjectives* according to their use in a sentence (eg in Latin), ⇨ case¹(3), decline¹(4); [C] class of words whose endings for different cases are alike.

de·cli·na·tion /ˌdeklɪ'neɪʃn/ *n* deviation of the needle of a compass, E or W from the true north.

de·cline¹ /dɪ'klaɪn/ *vt, vi* **1** [VP6A,7A,2A] say 'No' (to); refuse (sth offered): *to ~ an invitation to dinner. He ~d to discuss his plans with the newspaper men.* **2** [VP2A,C] continue to become smaller, weaker, lower: *a declining birthrate; declining sales. His strength slowly ~d. He spent his declining years* (= the years when, in old age, he was losing strength) *in the country.* **3** [VP2A] (of the sun) go down. **4** [VP6A] (gram) give the cases (ie the *declension*) of a word. ⇨ case¹(3), inflect(1).

de·cline² /dɪ'klaɪn/ *n* declining; gradual and continued loss of strength: *the ~ of the Roman Empire; a ~ in prices/prosperity. fall into a ~,* lose strength. **on the ~,** declining.

de·cliv·ity /dɪ'klɪvətɪ/ *n* [C] (*pl* -ties) downward slope. ⇨ acclivity.

de·clutch /ˌdiː'klʌtʃ/ *vi* [VP2A] disconnect the clutch (of a motor vehicle) in readiness for changing gear.

de·code /ˌdiː'kəʊd/ *vt* [VP6A] decipher (sth written in code). ⇨ encode. **de·coder** *n* (esp) device for translating data from one code to another.

de·coke /ˌdiː'kəʊk/ *vt* (colloq) = decarbonize.

dé·colleté /deɪ'kɒlteɪ *US:* -kɒl'teɪ/ *adj* (F) (of a gown, etc) leaving the neck and shoulders uncovered; (of a woman) wearing such a gown.

de·col·on·ize /ˌdiː'kɒlənaɪz/ *vt* [VP6A] change from colonial to independent status. **de·col·on·iz·ation** /ˌdiːˌkɒlənaɪ'zeɪʃn *US:* -nɪ'z-/ *n*

de·com·pose /ˌdiːkəm'pəʊz/ *vt, vi* **1** [VP6A] separate (a substance, light, etc) into its parts: *A prism ~s light.* **2** [VP6A,2A] (cause to) become bad or rotten; decay. **de·com·po·si·tion** /ˌdiːkɒmpə'zɪʃn/ *n*

de·com·press /ˌdiːkəm'pres/ *vt* [VP6A] bring back (sb in compressed air, eg in a diving suit) to normal pressure; reduce compression in (sth). **de·com-**

pression /ˌdiːkəm'preʃn/ *n: a ~ion chamber.*

de·con·tami·nate /ˌdiːkən'tæmɪneɪt/ *vt* [VP6A] remove contamination from (eg what has been affected by poison-gas or radio-activity). **de·con·tami·na·tion** /ˌdiːkənˌtæmɪ'neɪʃn/ *n*

de·con·trol /ˌdiːkən'trəʊl/ *vt* (-ll-) [VP6A] release from control (eg of trade by the Government during a war).

dé·cor /'deɪkɔː(r) *US:* deɪ'kɔːr/ *n* all that makes up the general appearance, eg of a room or the stage of a theatre.

dec·or·ate /'dekəreɪt/ *vt* [VP6A,14] **1** *~ (with),* put ornaments on; make (more) beautiful by placing adornments on or in: *to ~ a street with flags/the house with holly at Christmas.* **2** paint, plaster, etc the outside of (a building); put paint, wallpaper, etc on the inside rooms of (a building). **3** *~ (for),* give (sb) a mark of distinction (eg a medal, an order): *Several soldiers were ~d for bravery.* **dec·or·ator** /-tə(r)/ *n* workman who ~s(2): *interior decorators.*

dec·ora·tion /ˌdekə'reɪʃn/ *n* **1** [U] decorating or being decorated. **2** [C] sth used for decorating: *Christmas ~s.* **3** [C] medal, ribbon, etc given and worn as an honour or award.

dec·or·ative /'dekərətɪv *US:* 'dekəreɪtɪv/ *adj* suitable for decorating(1): *Holly, with its bright red berries, is very ~.*

dec·or·ous /'dekərəs/ *adj* polite; decent. **~·ly** *adv*

de·corum /dɪ'kɔːrəm/ *n* **1** [U] right and proper behaviour, as required by social custom. **2** (*pl*) requirements of polite society.

de·coy /'diːkɔɪ/ *n* **1** (real or imitation) bird (eg a duck) or animal used to attract others so that they may be shot or caught; place designed for this purpose (eg a sheet of water with nets in which birds are trapped). **2** (fig) person or thing used to tempt sb into a position of danger. □ *vt* /dɪ'kɔɪ/ [VP6A,14] trick (sb or sth) into a place of danger by means of a ~: *He had been ~ed across the frontier and arrested as a spy.*

de·crease /dɪ'kriːs/ *vt, vi* [VP6A,2A] (cause to) become shorter, smaller, less: *Your hunger ~s as you eat. The population of the village has ~d by 150 to 500.* □ *n* /'diːkriːs/ [U] decreasing; [C] amount by which sth ~s: *There has been a ~ in our imports this year.* **on the ~,** decreasing: *Is crime on the ~?*

de·cree /dɪ'kriː/ *n* [C] **1** order given by a ruler or authority and having the force of a law: *issue a ~; rule by ~.* **2** judgement or decision of some law courts: *a ~ of divorce. ~ nisi* /dɪˌnaɪsaɪ/ *n* order for a divorce unless cause to the contrary is shown within a fixed period. □ *vt* /VP6A,9] issue a ~; order by ~: *It had been ~d that.... Fate ~d a surprise.*

de·crepit /dɪ'krepɪt/ *adj* made weak by old age or hard use: *a ~ horse.* **de·crepi·tude** /dɪ'krepɪtjuːd *US:* -tuːd/ *n* [U] the state of being ~.

de·cry /dɪ'kraɪ/ *vt* [VP6A] try, by speaking against sth, to make it seem less valuable, useful, etc; disapprove of.

dedi·cate /'dedɪkeɪt/ *vt* [VP6A,14] *~ (to),* give up, devote (one's time, energy, etc, to a noble cause or purpose): *He ~d his life to the service of his country.* **2** devote with solemn ceremonies (to God, to a sacred use). **3** (of an author) write (or print) a person's name at the beginning of a book (to show gratitude or friendship to). **dedi·ca·tion** /ˌdedɪ'keɪʃn/ *n* [U] dedicating: *the dedication of a* *church;* [C] words used in dedicating a book.

de·duce /dɪ'djuːs US: dɪ'duːs/ *vt* [VP6A,14,9] ~ **(from)**, arrive at (knowledge, a theory, etc) by reasoning; reach a conclusion: *If you saw a doctor leaving a house, you might* ~ *the fact that someone in the house was ill.*

de·duct /dɪ'dʌkt/ *vt* [VP6A,14] take away (an amount or part). ⇨ subtract for numbers. ~**·ible** /dɪ'dʌktəbl/ *adj* that may be ~ed.

de·duc·tion /dɪ'dʌkʃn/ *n* **1** [U] deducting; [C] amount deducted: ~*s from pay for insurance and pension.* **2** [U] deducing; [C] conclusion reached by reasoning from general laws to a particular case. **de·duct·ive** /dɪ'dʌktɪv/ *adj* of, using, reasoning by, ~(2).

deed /diːd/ *n* **1** sth done; act: *to be rewarded for one's good* ~*s. D*~*s are better than words when people are in need of help.* **2** (legal) written or printed signed agreement, esp about ownership or rights. ~ **of 'covenant,** ⇨ covenant(1). '~**-box** *n* one in which legal ~s are stored. '~·**poll** *n* legal ~ made by one person only.

deem /diːm/ *vt* [VP9,25] (formal) believe; consider: *He* ~*ed that it was/*~*ed it his duty to help.*

deep¹ /diːp/ *adj* **1** going a long way down from the top: *a* ~ *well/river.* ⇨ shallow. ~**·,sea,** ~**·,water,** *attrib adjj,* of the deeper parts of the sea, away from the coastal water: ~*-sea fishing.* **go (in) off the** '~ **end,** ⇨ end¹(1). **in** ~ **water(s),** (fig) in great difficulties, etc. **2** going a long way from the surface or edge: *a* ~ *shelf; a* ~ *wound; a huge,* ~*-chested wrestler.* **3** placed or extending down, back or in (with words to indicate extent): *a hole two feet* ~*; with his hands* ~ *in his pockets; water six feet* ~*; ankle-*~ *in mud; to be* ~ *in debt; a plot of land 100 feet* ~, ie going back this distance from a street, road or other frontage. *The people were standing twenty* ~ *to see the Queen go past.* **4** (of sounds) low: *in a* ~ *voice; the* ~ *notes of a cello.* **5** (of sleep) profound: *in a* ~ *sleep,* from which one is not easily awakened. **6** (of colours) strong; intense: *a* ~ *red.* **7** brought from far down: *a* ~ *sigh;* strongly felt; coming from the heart: ~ *sorrow/feelings/sympathy.* **8** ~ **in,** absorbed in; having all one's attention centred on: ~ *in thought/study/a book.* **9** (fig) difficult to understand or learn about: *a* ~ *mystery; a* ~ *secret;* (of a person) artful; concealing his real feelings, motives, etc: *He's a* ~ *one.* **10** (fig) going far; not superficial: ~ *learning; a man with* ~ *insight; a* ~ *thinker.* ~**·en** /'diːpən/ *vt,vi* make or become ~. ~**·ly** *adv* far; profoundly; intensely: *to bite* ~*ly; He is* ~*ly interested in the subject. She felt her mother's death* ~*ly.* ~**·ness** *n*

deep² /diːp/ *adv* far down or in: *We had to dig* ~ *to find water. He went on studying* ~ *into the night.* ***Still waters run* ~,** (prov) said of a person whose real feelings, ideas, etc are not openly displayed. ~**·'freeze** *vt* freeze (food) quickly in order to preserve it for long periods: ~*-frozen fish.* □ *n* special type of refrigerator (or a special part of an ordinary refrigerator) used for this purpose: *put surplus fruit and vegetables in the* ~*-freeze.* ~**·'laid,** (of schemes, etc) secretly and carefully planned. ~**·'mined,** (of coal) from ordinary coal-mines (contrasted with *open-cast;* ⇨ open¹(11)). ~**·'rooted,** not easily removed: *his* ~*-rooted dislike of hard work.* ~**·'seated,** firmly established: *The causes of the trouble are* ~*-seated.*

deep³ /diːp/ *n* (poet) **the** ~, the sea.

deer /dɪə(r)/ *n* (*pl* unchanged) (kinds of) graceful, quick-running animal, the male of which has horns. ⇨ illus at large. '~**·skin,** (leather made of) ~'s skin. '~**·stalker, (a)** sportsman who stalks ~. **(b)** cloth cap with two peaks, one in front and the other behind. '~**·stalking,** sport of hunting ~ by approaching them stealthily or from concealment.

de·esca·late /ˌdiː'eskəleɪt/ *vt* [VP6A] decrease the area or intensity of, eg a war. **de·esca·la·tion** /ˌdiː-ˌeskə'leɪʃn/ *n*

de·face /dɪ'feɪs/ *vt* [VP6A] spoil the appearance of (by marking or damaging the surface of); make engraved lettering (eg on a tombstone) illegible. ~**·ment** *n* [U] defacing or being ~d; [C] sth that ~s.

de facto /ˌdeɪ 'fæktəʊ/ *adj, adv* (Lat) in fact, whether by right (*de jure*) or not: *the* ~ *king.*

de·fal·ca·tion /ˌdiːfæl'keɪʃn/ *n* [U] (legal) misappropriation of money entrusted to one; [C] instance of this; amount of money misappropriated.

de·fame /dɪ'feɪm/ *vt* [VP6A] attack the good reputation of; say evil things about. **defa·ma·tion** /ˌdefə'meɪʃn/ *n* [U] defaming or being ~d; harm done to sb's reputation. **de·fama·tory** /dɪ'fæmətrɪ US: -tɔːrɪ/ *adj* intended to ~: *defamatory statements.*

de·fault¹ /dɪ'fɔːlt/ *n* [U] failure to act: *to win a case/a game by* ~, because the other party/team/ player does not appear. **in** ~ **of,** in the absence of; if (sth) is not to be obtained, does not take place, etc.

de·fault² /dɪ'fɔːlt/ *vi* [VP2A] fail to perform a duty, or to appear (eg in a law court) when required to do so, or to pay a debt. ~**·er** *n* **1** person who ~s. **2** soldier guilty of a military offence.

de·feat /dɪ'fiːt/ *vt* [VP6A] **1** overcome; win a victory over: *They were* ~*ed in their attempt to reach the top of the mountain.* **2** bring to nothing; make useless; cause to fail: *Our hopes were* ~*ed.* □ *n* [U] ~ing or being ~ed: *a baseball team that has not yet suffered* ~; [C] instance of this: *six victories and two* ~*s.* ~**·ism** /-ɪzəm/ *n* [U] attitude, conduct, use of arguments, based on expectations of ~. ~**·ist** /-ɪst/ *n* person with such an attitude, etc.

de·fe·cate /'defəkeɪt/ *vi* [VP2A] (med) empty the bowels. **def·eca·tion** /ˌdefə'keɪʃn/ *n*

de·fect¹ /'diːfekt/ *n* [C] fault; imperfection; shortcoming; sth lacking in completeness or perfection: ~*s in a system of education.*

de·fect² /dɪ'fekt/ *vi* [VP2A,C,3A] ~ **(from) (to),** desert one's country, one's allegiance, etc: *the soldier who* ~*ed from Ruritania to Lilliput,* eg by asking for political asylum. **de·fec·tor** /-tə(r)/ *n* person who ~s: ~*ors from the Republican Party.*

de·fec·tion /dɪ'fekʃn/ *n* [U] falling away from loyalty to a political party (or its leader), religion or duty; [C] instance of this: ~*s from the Socialist Party.*

de·fec·tive /dɪ'fektɪv/ *adj* having a defect or defects; imperfect: ~ *in workmanship/moral sense; mentally* ~, mentally subnormal; *a* ~ *verb,* eg *must.* ~**·ly** *adv* ~**·ness** *n*

de·fence (US = **de·fense**) /dɪ'fens/ **1** [U] defending from attack; fighting against attack: *money needed for national* ~*; to fight in* ~ *of one's country; weapons of offence and* ~. *I never fight except in self-*~. **2** [C] sth used for defending or protecting; means of defending: *coastal* ~*s,* against attacks from the sea. *People used to build strong walls round their towns as a* ~ *against ene-*

mies. A thick overcoat is a good ~ *against the cold.* **3** [C,U] (legal) argument(s) used to contest an accusation; the lawyer(s) acting for an accused person: *The accused man made no* ~. *Counsel for the* ~ *put in a plea for mercy. Counsel worked out a very convincing* ~. ~**·less** *adj* having no ~; unable to defend oneself. ~**·less·ly** *adv* ~**·less·ness** *n*

de·fend /dɪ'fend/ *vt* [VP6A,14] **1** ~ *(against/ from)*, guard; protect; make safe: *to* ~ *one's country against enemies; to* ~ *sb from harm. When the dog attacked me, I* ~*ed myself with a stick.* **2** speak or write in support of: ~ (= uphold) *a claim;* ~ (= contest) *a lawsuit. He made a long speech* ~*ing his ideas. You will need lawyers to* ~ *you.* ~**·er** *n* **1** person who ~s. Note legal term at defence(3). **2** (in sport, eg football) player who guards his goal area against attacks from the other side.

de·fend·ant /dɪ'fendənt/ *n* person against whom a legal action is brought. ⇨ **plaintiff.**

de·fense /dɪ'fens/ (US) ⇨ **defence.**

de·fens·ible /dɪ'fensəbl/ *adj* able to be defended.

de·fens·ive /dɪ'fensɪv/ *adj* used for, intended for, defending: ~ *warfare/measures. Whether a gun is a* ~ *or an offensive weapon may depend upon whether you're behind it or in front of it.* □ *n* (usu) *be/act on the* ~, be in a state/act from a position of defence. ~**·ly** *adv*

de·fer¹ /dɪ'fɜ:(r)/ *vt* (-rr-) [VP6A,C] put off to a later time; postpone: *a* ~*red telegram*, one sent later at a cheaper rate; *a* ~*red annuity; to* ~ *one's departure for a week; to* ~ *making a decision; payment on* ~*red terms,* ie by instalments after purchase. ⇨ **hire-purchase** at hire. ~**·ment** *n*

de·fer² /dɪ'fɜ:(r)/ *vi* (-rr-) [VP3A] ~ *to,* give way; yield (often to show respect): *to* ~ *to one's elders/to sb's opinions.*

de·fer·ence /'defərəns/ *n* [U] giving way to the wishes, accepting the opinions or judgements, of another or others; respect: *to treat one's elders with* ~; *to show* ~ *to a judge. in* ~ *to,* out of respect for. **de·fer·en·tial** /ˌdefə'renʃl/ *adj* showing ~. **de·fer·en·tially** /-ʃəlɪ/ *adv*

de·fiance /dɪ'faɪəns/ *n* [U] open disobedience or resistance; refusal to recognize authority; defying. *in* ~ *of,* showing contempt or indifference of: *to act in* ~ *of orders,* do sth one has been ordered not to do. *He went swimming in the sea in* ~ *of the warning sign telling him not to. bid* ~ *to,* challenge, offer to fight. *set sth at* ~, treat with contempt; challenge: *If you set the law/public opinion at* ~, *you'll get into trouble.*

de·fiant /dɪ'faɪənt/ *adj* showing defiance; openly disobedient. ~**·ly** *adv*

de·fi·ciency /dɪ'fɪʃnsɪ/ *n* (*pl* -cies) **1** [U] the state of being short of, less than, what is correct or needed; [C] instance of this: *suffering from a* ~ *of food;* ~ *diseases,* caused by a ~ of sth, eg vitamins, in diet. **2** [C] amount by which sth is short of what is correct or needed: *a* ~ *of £5.* **3** [C] sth imperfect: *Cosmetics do not always cover up the deficiencies of nature.*

de·fi·cient /dɪ'fɪʃnt/ *adj* not having enough of: ~ *in courage; a mentally* ~ *person,* one who is mentally subnormal.

defi·cit /'defɪsɪt/ *n* [C] amount by which sth, esp a sum of money, is too small; amount by which payments exceed receipts. ⇨ **surplus.**

de·file¹ /dɪ'faɪl/ *vt* [VP6A] make dirty or impure:

rivers ~*d by waste from factories.* ~**·ment** *n* [U] defiling or being ~d; pollution.

de·file² /'di:faɪl/ *n* narrow way, gorge, through mountains. □ *vi* /dɪ'faɪl/ (of troops) march in a single file or a narrow column.

de·fine /dɪ'faɪn/ *vt* [VP6A] **1** state precisely the meaning of (eg words). **2** state or show clearly: *Please listen while I* ~ *your duties. The powers of a judge are* ~*d by law. When boundaries between countries are not clearly* ~*d, there is usually trouble. The mountain was clearly* ~*d against the eastern sky.* **de·fin·able** /-əbl/ *adj* that can be ~d.

defi·nite /'defɪnət/ *adj* clear; not doubtful or uncertain: *I want a* ~ *answer: 'Yes' or 'No'. I want an appointment for a* ~ *time and place.* ~ *'article* in the word 'the'. ~**·ly** /'defɪnətlɪ/ *adv* **1** in a ~ manner. **2** (colloq, in answer to a question) yes, certainly.

defi·ni·tion /ˌdefɪ'nɪʃn/ *n* **1** [U] defining; [C] statement that defines: *To give a* ~ *of a word is more difficult than to give an illustration of its uses.* **2** [U] clearness of outline; making or being distinct in outline; power of a lens (in a camera or telescope) to show clear outlines.

de·fini·tive /dɪ'fɪnətɪv/ *adj* final; to be looked upon as decisive and without the need for, or possibility of, change or addition: *a* ~ *offer/answer/edition of sb's poetry.*

de·flate /dɪ'fleɪt/ *vt* [VP6A] **1** make (a tyre, balloon, etc) smaller by letting out air or gas; (fig) lessen the conceit of: ~ *a pompous politician.* **2** /ˌdi:'fleɪt/ take action to reduce the amount of money in circulation in order to lower or keep steady the prices of salable goods. **de·fla·tion** /-eɪʃn/ *n* [U] the action of deflating. **de·fla·tion·ary** /ˌdi:'fleɪʃnərɪ US: -nerɪ/ *adj* produced, designed or tending to produce monetary deflation: *deflationary measures applied by the Chancellor.* ⇨ inflate.

de·flect /dɪ'flekt/ *vt, vi* [VP6A,14,2A,3A] ~ *(from)*, (cause to) turn aside (from): *The bullet struck a wall and was* ~*ed from its course.* **de·flec·tion** /dɪ'flekʃn/ *n*

de·flower /di:'flaʊə(r)/ *vt* (liter or old use) deprive of virginity; ravage; spoil.

de·foli·ate /ˌdi:'fəʊlɪeɪt/ *vt* [VP6A] destroy the leaves of: *forests* ~*d by chemical means.* **de·foli·ation** /ˌdi:fəʊlɪ'eɪʃn/ *n* **de·foli·ant** /ˌdi:'fəʊlɪənt/ *n* chemical used, eg by spraying, on vegetation to destroy the leaves.

de·for·est /ˌdi:'fɒrɪst US: -'fɔ:r-/ *vt* (esp US) = disafforest.

de·form /dɪ'fɔ:m/ *vt* [VP6A] spoil the form or appearance of; put out of shape. **de·formed** *part adj* (of the body, or a part of it; fig, of the mind) badly shaped; unnaturally shaped: *The boy has a* ~*ed foot and cannot play games.*

de·form·ity /dɪ'fɔ:mətɪ/ *n* [U] being deformed; [C] (*pl* -ties) deformed part (esp of the body).

de·fraud /dɪ'frɔ:d/ *vt* [VP6A,14] ~ *(of)*, trick (sb) out of what is rightly his; get by fraud: ~ *an author of his royalties by ignoring copyright.*

de·fray /dɪ'freɪ/ *vt* [VP6A] supply the money needed for sth; pay (the cost or expenses of sth). ~**·al** /dɪ'freɪəl/ *n* ~**·ment** *n*

de·frock /ˌdi:'frɒk/ *vt* = unfrock.

de·frost /ˌdi:'frɒst US: ˌdi:'frɔ:st/ *vt* [VP6A] remove, get rid of, ice or frost (eg in a refrigerator, on the windscreen of a motor-car). ~**·er** *n* device that ~s.

deft /deft/ *adj* quick and clever (esp with the fingers). ∼·ly adv ∼·ness n

de·funct /dɪ'fʌŋkt/ adj (of persons) dead; (of things, eg laws) extinct. **the** ∼, (legal) the dead person (who is being discussed).

de·fuse /ˌdiː'fjuːz/ vt [VP6A] remove or render useless the fuse of, eg an unexploded bomb or shell; (fig) make calm; reduce the tension in: ∼ a situation/crisis.

defy /dɪ'faɪ/ vt (pt,pp -fied) **1** [VP6A] resist openly; say that one is ready to fight. **2** [VP6A] refuse to obey or show respect to: ∼ing one's superiors. If you ∼ the law, you may find yourself in prison. **3** [VP6A] offer difficulties that cannot be overcome: The problem defied solution, could not be solved. The door defied all attempts to open it. **4** [VP17] ∼ sb to do sth, call on sb to do sth that one believes he cannot or will not do: I ∼ you to prove that I have cheated. ⇨ defiance.

de·gauss /ˌdiː'gaʊs/ vt [VP6A] neutralize the magnetic field of, eg a TV screen.

de·gen·er·ate /dɪ'dʒenəreɪt/ vi [VP2A,3A] ∼ (into), pass from a state of goodness to a lower state by losing qualities which are considered normal and desirable: Thrift is desirable, but do not let it ∼ into avarice. He denied that the young men of today were degenerating, eg that they were becoming less hard-working, less intelligent, less honest, than those of earlier times. ☐ adj /dɪ'dʒenərət/ having lost qualities (physical, moral or mental) that are considered normal and desirable: He didn't let riches and luxury make him ∼. ☐ n /dɪ'dʒenərət/ ∼ person or animal. **de·gen·er·acy** /dɪ'dʒenərəsɪ/ n [U] state or condition of being ∼; process of degenerating. **de·gen·er·ation** /dɪˌdʒenə'reɪʃn/ n [U] degenerating; the state of being ∼d.

de·grade /dɪ'greɪd/ vt [VP6A] **1** reduce in rank or status. **2** cause (sb) to be less moral or less deserving of respect: to ∼ oneself by cheating and telling lies. **degra·da·tion** /ˌdegrə'deɪʃn/ n [U] degrading or being ∼d: a family living in degradation, eg one that lives in slum conditions.

de·gree /dɪ'griː/ n **1** unit of measurement for angles: an angle of ninety ∼s, (90°) a right angle; a ∼ of latitude, about 69 miles. **2** unit of measurement for temperature: Water freezes at 32 ∼s Fahrenheit (32°F) or zero (= nought ∼s) Centigrade (0°C). **3** [C,U] step or stage in a scale or process: The boys show various ∼s of skill in their use of carpentry tools. His work has reached a high ∼ of excellence. He was not in the slightest ∼ interested, was completely uninterested. **by** ∼**s**, step by step; gradually: Their friendship by ∼s grew into love. **to a** ∼, (colloq) = to the highest ∼: He is scrupulous to a ∼. **to a high/the highest** ∼, intensively; exceedingly: He is vain to a high ∼. **to what** ∼, to what extent; how much: To what ∼ are you interested in botany? **first** ∼, stage of seriousness: first ∼ burns; first ∼ murder. **third** ∼, severe and long examination (eg by the police) of an accused man to get information or a confession: Are third-∼ methods used in your country? **4** [U] position in society: persons of high ∼. **5** academic title; rank or grade given by a university to one who has passed an examination: studying for a ∼; the ∼ of Master of Arts (MA). ⇨ graduate, undergraduate. **6** (music) interval from one note to another on a stave. **7** (gram) one of the three forms of comparison of an adj or adv. ∼s of comparison. 'Good', 'better' and 'best' are the positive, comparative and superlative ∼s of 'good'. 'Rich', 'richer' and 'richest' are the positive, comparative and superlative ∼s of 'rich'.

de·hu·man·ize /ˌdiː'hjuːmənaɪz/ vt [VP6A] take away human qualities from.

de·hy·drate /ˌdiː'haɪdreɪt/ vt [VP6A] deprive (a substance) of water or moisture: ∼d vegetables/eggs, often in powdered form.

de·ify /'diːɪfaɪ/ vt (pt,pp -fied) [VP6A] make a god of; worship as a god. **de·ifi·ca·tion** /ˌdiːɪfɪ'keɪʃn/ n [U] ∼ing or being deified: the deification of a Roman emperor.

deign /deɪn/ vi [VP4A] ∼ to do sth, condescend; be kind or gracious enough to: He passed by without ∼ing to look at me.

de·ism /'diːɪzəm/ n belief in the existence of a Divine Being, but without acceptance of revelation or religious dogma. **de·ist** /'diːɪst/ n supporter of ∼. ⇨ theism.

de·ity /'diːɪtɪ/ n **1** [U] divine quality or nature; state of being a god or goddess. **2** [C] (pl -ties) god or goddess: Roman deities, eg Neptune, Minerva. **the D**∼, God.

déjà vu /ˌdeɪʒɑː 'vjuː/ n [U] (F) feeling that one remembers an event or scene that one has not experienced or seen before; (colloq) feeling that one has experienced sth too often.

de·ject /dɪ'dʒekt/ vt (usu in pp) make sad or gloomy: Why is she looking so ∼ed, in such low spirits? **de·ject·ed·ly** adv **de·jec·tion** /dɪ'dʒekʃn/ n [U] ∼ed state; low spirits: He left in ∼.

de jure /ˌdeɪ 'dʒʊərɪ/ adj, adv (Lat) by right; according to law: the ∼ king; king ∼. ⇨ de facto.

dekko /'dekəʊ/ n (sl) **have a** ∼, have a look (at sth).

de·lay /dɪ'leɪ/ vt, vi **1** [VP6A,2A,B] make or be slow or late: Don't ∼. The train was ∼ed (for) two hours. I was ∼ed by the traffic. ∼**ed-action** adj,n operating after a lapse of time: a ∼ed-action bomb, with a device causing it to explode after a pre-determined interval. **2** [VP6A,C] put off until later: We must ∼ our journey until the weather improves. Why have they ∼ed opening the new school? ☐ n **1** [U] ∼ing or being ∼ed: We must leave without ∼. **2** [C] instance of this; time of being ∼ed: after several ∼s; after a ∼ of three hours.

de·lec·table /dɪ'lektəbl/ adj (liter) delightful; pleasant.

de·lec·ta·tion /ˌdiːlek'teɪʃn/ n [U] (liter, ironic) enjoyment; entertainment: TV programmes suitable for the ∼ of half-educated people.

del·egacy /'delɪgəsɪ/ n (pl -cies) system of delegating; body of delegates.

del·egate¹ /'delɪgət/ n person to whom sth is delegated (eg an elected representative sent to a conference or convention).

del·egate² /'delɪgeɪt/ vt [VP17,14] ∼ (to), appoint and send (sb) as a representative to a meeting; entrust (duties, rights, etc to sb): to ∼ sb to perform a task; to ∼ rights to a deputy.

del·ega·tion /ˌdelɪ'geɪʃn/ n **1** [U] delegating or being delegated. **2** [C] group of delegates.

de·lete /dɪ'liːt/ vt [VP6A,14] ∼ (from), strike or take out (sth written or printed): Several words had been ∼d from the letter by the censor. **de·le·tion** /dɪ'liːʃn/ n [U] deleting; [C] sth deleted.

del·eteri·ous /ˌdelɪ'tɪərɪəs/ adj (formal) harmful (to mind or body).

delft /delft/, (also **delf** /delf/, or '∼**-ware**) n [U] kind of glazed earthenware, usu with blue designs or decorations.

de·lib·er·ate¹ /dɪ'lɪbərət/ adj **1** done on purpose; intentional: a ~ lie/insult. **2** slow and cautious (in action, speech, etc): a ~ speech. He entered the room with ~ steps. ~·ly adv

de·lib·er·ate² /dɪ'lɪbəreɪt/ vt,vi [VP6A,8,10,2A,3A] ~ (over/on/upon), consider, talk about, carefully: We were deliberating what to do/how it might be done/whether to buy a new motor-car. They're still deliberating over/upon the question. **de·lib·er·ative** /dɪ'lɪbərətɪv US: -reɪtɪv/ adj for the purpose of deliberating: a deliberative assembly.

de·lib·er·ation /dɪ,lɪbə'reɪʃn/ n **1** [C,U] careful consideration and discussion; debate: After long ~, they decided... What was the result of your ~(s)? **2** [U] being deliberate(2); slowness of movement: to speak/take aim/walk into a room with great ~.

deli·cacy /'delɪkəsɪ/ n (pl -cies) **1** [U] quality of being delicate (all senses): Everyone admired the ~ of her features, their fineness and tenderness. Because of the ~ of her skin (= Because it is easily hurt by the sun), she never sunbathes. The girl's ~ (= The fact that she is delicate in health) has always worried her parents. The political situation is one of great ~, requires careful handling. The violinist played with great ~, with a very fine touch. **2** [C] delicate(8) kind of food: all the delicacies of the season.

deli·cate /'delɪkət/ adj **1** soft; tender; of fine or thin material: as ~ as silk; the ~ skin of a young girl. **2** fine; exquisite: jewellery of ~ workmanship. **3** easily injured; becoming ill easily; needing great care: ~ china/plants; a ~-looking child; in ~ health. **4** requiring careful treatment or skilful handling: a ~ surgical operation, eg on sb's eyes. The international situation is very ~ at present. **5** (of colours) soft; not strong: a ~ shade of pink. **6** (of the senses, of instruments) able to appreciate or indicate very small changes or differences: a ~ sense of smell/touch; the ~ instruments needed by scientists, eg for weighing or measuring. **7** taking great care not to be immodest, not to hurt the feelings of others: a ~ speech. **8** (of food, its flavour) pleasing to the taste and not strongly flavoured: Chicken is more ~ than beef. When people are ill they need ~ food. Some kinds of fish have a more ~ flavour than others. ~·ly adv

deli·ca·tessen /,delɪkə'tesn/ n [C,U] (shop selling) prepared foods ready for serving (esp cooked meat, smoked fish, pickles): The ~ (shop) closes at 5.30.

de·li·cious /dɪ'lɪʃəs/ adj giving delight (esp to the senses of taste and smell, and to the sense of humour): a ~ cake. Doesn't it smell ~! What a ~ joke! ~·ly adv

de·light¹ /dɪ'laɪt/ n **1** [U] great pleasure; joy: to give ~ to sb. To his great ~ his novel was accepted for publication. **take ~ in,** find pleasure in: The naughty boy takes great ~ in pulling the cat's tail. **2** [C] cause or source of great pleasure: Dancing is her chief ~. He often thinks of the ~s of life in the country. ~·ful /-fl/ adj giving ~ (to): a ~ful holiday. ~·fully /-fəlɪ/ adv

de·light² /dɪ'laɪt/ vt,vi **1** [VP6A] give great pleasure to; please greatly: Her singing ~ed everyone. **2** (passive): be ~ed, be greatly pleased: I was ~ed to hear the news of your success/~ed at the news.../~ed that you were successful. **3** [VP3A,4]

~ (in), take or find great pleasure: He ~s in teasing his young sister. He ~s to prove his brother wrong.

de·limit /di:'lɪmɪt/, **de·limi·tate** /di:'lɪmɪteɪt/ vt [VP6A] determine the limits or boundaries of. **de·limi·ta·tion** /di:,lɪmɪ'teɪʃn/ n [C,U].

de·lin·eate /dɪ'lɪnɪeɪt/ vt [VP6A] (formal) show by drawing or by describing; portray. **de·lin·ea·tion** /dɪ,lɪnɪ'eɪʃn/ n [C,U].

de·lin·quency /dɪ'lɪŋkwənsɪ/ n **1** [U] wrong-doing; neglect of duty: the problem of juvenile ~, wrong-doing by young persons. **2** [C] (pl -cies) instance of this; misdeed.

de·lin·quent /dɪ'lɪŋkwənt/ n, adj (person) doing wrong, failing to perform a duty.

deli·ques·cent /,delɪ'kwesnt/ adj (chem) becoming liquid in air (by absorbing moisture).

de·liri·ous /dɪ'lɪrɪəs/ adj **1** suffering from delirium; wildly excited: The patient's temperature went up and he became ~. The children were ~ with joy. **2** showing the effects of delirium: ~ speech. ~·ly adv

de·lirium /dɪ'lɪrɪəm/ n [U] violent mental disturbance caused by illness, often accompanied by wild talk, esp during feverish illness; wild excitement. ~ 'tremens /'tri:menz/ (usu d t(s) /,di: 'ti:(z)/), ~ caused by extreme alcoholism.

de·liver /dɪ'lɪvə(r)/ vt **1** [VP6A] take (letters, parcels, goods, etc) to houses, to the person(s) to whom they are addressed, to the buyer(s): A postman is a man employed to ~ letters and parcels. Did you ~ my message to your father? ~ the goods, (fig) do what is wanted. **2** [VP14] ~ from, (old use) rescue, save, set free: May God ~ us from all evil. **3** [VP6A] give forth in words: to ~ a sermon/a course of lectures; to ~ oneself of an opinion. **4** [VP6A] (of a medical attendant, eg a midwife) help (a woman) in childbirth: to be ~ed of a child, give birth to one. **5** [VP6A,15B] ~ (up/over) (to), surrender; give up; hand over: to ~ up stolen goods; to ~ over one's property to one's son; to ~ (up) a fortress to the enemy. **6** [VP6A] launch; aim; send against: (fig) to ~ a blow in the cause of freedom. ~·er n one who ~s; rescuer; saviour.

de·liver·ance /dɪ'lɪvərəns/ n **1** [U] ~ from, delivering(2); rescue; being set free. **2** [C] formal or emphatic statement of opinion.

de·liv·ery /dɪ'lɪvərɪ/ n **1** [U] delivering (of letters, goods, etc); [C] (pl -ries) periodical performance of this: We guarantee prompt ~ of goods. How many deliveries are there in your town (= How often does the postman deliver letters) every week? on ~, at the time of ~. take ~ of, receive: When can you take ~ of the new car? '~ note n note, usu in duplicate, sent with goods, to be signed by the recipient. '~ truck n (US) goods van. **2** (sing only) manner of speaking (in lectures, etc): His speech was good, but his ~ was poor.

dell /del/ n small valley, usu with trees on its sides.

de·louse /,di:'laʊs/ vt rid (sb or sth) of lice.

Del·phic /'delfɪk/ adj of the oracle of Apollo /ə'pɒləʊ/ at Delphi /'delfaɪ/ (in ancient Greece); obscure: ambiguous.

del·phin·ium /del'fɪnɪəm/ n (kinds of) garden plant, usu with tall spikes of usu blue flowers.

delta /'deltə/ n Greek letter d, ⇨ App 4; land (with alluvial deposits) in the shape of a capital ~ (Δ) at the mouth of a river between two or more branches: the Nile D~; ~ winged, (of aircraft) having ~-

shaped wings.

de·lude /dɪˈluːd/ vt [VP6A,14] ∼ **sb with sth/into doing sth,** deceive; mislead (on purpose): to ∼ sb with promises one does not intend to keep; to ∼ oneself with false hopes; to ∼ sb/oneself into believing that....

del·uge /ˈdeljuːdʒ/ n [C] **1** great flood; heavy rush of water; violent rainfall. **the D∼,** the flood at the time of Noah /ˈnəʊə/ ⇨ Gen 7. **2** anything coming in a heavy rush: a ∼ of words/questions/protests. □ vt [VP6A,14] ∼ **(with),** flood; come down on (sb or sth) like a ∼: He was ∼d with questions.

de·lusion /dɪˈluːʒn/ n [U] deluding or being deluded; [C] false opinion or belief, esp one that may be a symptom of madness: to be under a ∼/under the ∼ that...; to suffer from ∼s.

de·lus·ive /dɪˈluːsɪv/ adj not real; deceptive. ∼·ly adv

de luxe /dɪ ˈlʌks/ adj (F) of very high quality, high standards of comfort, etc: a ∼ edition of a book.

delve /delv/ vt,vi **1** [VP6A,2A] (old use) dig. **2** [VP3A] ∼ **into,** make researches into: ∼ for information into old books; to ∼ into sb's past.

de·mag·net·ize /ˌdiːˈmæɡnɪtaɪz/ vt [VP6A] deprive of magnetic properties. **de·mag·net·iz·ation** /ˌdiːˌmæɡnɪtaɪˈzeɪʃn US: -tɪˈz-/ n

dema·gogue /ˈdeməɡɒɡ US: -ɡɔːɡ/ n political leader who tries, by speeches appealing to the feelings instead of to reason, to stir up the people. **dema·gogy** /ˈdeməɡɒɡɪ/ n [U] principles and practices of a ∼. **dema·gogic** /ˌdeməˈɡɒɡɪk/ adj of or like a ∼.

de·mand¹ /dɪˈmɑːnd US: -ˈmænd/ n ∼ **(for)** **1** [C] act of demanding(1); sth demanded(1): The workers' ∼s (eg for higher pay) were refused by the employers. It is impossible to satisfy all ∼s. I have/ People make many ∼s on my time, I am expected to do many things, etc. There have been ∼s for the prime minister to resign/for his resignation/that he should resign. **on** ∼, when demanded: a cheque payable on ∼. '∼ **(note),** note that demands payment, eg of income tax. **2** [U] (or with an indef art and adj) desire, by people ready to buy, employ, etc (for goods, services, etc): There is a great ∼ for typists than a poor ∼/not much ∼ for clerks. There is little ∼ for these goods. The ∼ for fish this month exceeds the supply. **in** ∼, wanted; popular: His records are always in ∼/are in constant ∼.

de·mand² /dɪˈmɑːnd US: -ˈmænd/ vt **1** [VP6A,7A,9] ask for (sth) as if ordering, or as if one has a right to: ∼ an apology from sb. The gatekeeper ∼ed my business, asked what I wanted. The policeman ∼ed his name and address/∼ed to know where he lived. He came to my house and ∼ed help/∼ed that I should help him. He ∼s that I shall tell him everything/∼s to be told everything. **2** [VP6A] need; require: This sort of work ∼s great patience. Does the letter ∼ an immediate answer, Must it be answered at once?

de·mar·cate /ˈdiːmɑːkeɪt/ vt [VP6A] mark or fix the limits of, eg a frontier.

de·mar·ca·tion /ˌdiːmɑːˈkeɪʃn/ n [U] marking of a boundary or limit; separation: a line of ∼; ∼ problems in industry, eg settling the kind of work to be done by workers in different trades.

dé·marche /ˈdeɪmɑːʃ/ n (F) political step or proceeding; diplomatic representation (to a foreign government).

de·mean /dɪˈmiːn/ vt [VP6A] ∼ **oneself,** lower oneself in dignity, social esteem.

de·mean·our (US = -or) /dɪˈmiːnə(r)/ n [U] way of behaving: I dislike his supercilious ∼.

de·mented /dɪˈmentɪd/ adj mad; (colloq) wild with worry: a poor, ∼ creature. She'll become ∼ if you don't stop asking silly questions. ∼·ly adv

deme·rara /ˌdeməˈreərə/ n [U] ∼ **sugar,** light brown raw cane sugar (from Guyana).

de·merit /diːˈmerɪt/ n [C] fault; defect.

de·mesne /dɪˈmeɪn/ n [U] (legal) the holding of land as one's own property: land held in ∼; [C] landed estate held in this way, not let to tenants.

demi·god /ˈdemɪɡɒd/ n one who is partly divine and partly human; (in Gk myth, etc) the son of a god and a mortal woman, eg Hercules /ˈhɜːkjʊliːz/.

demi·john /ˈdemɪdʒɒn/ n large narrow-necked bottle, usu encased in wicker-work.

de·mili·tar·ize /ˌdiːˈmɪlɪtəraɪz/ vt [VP6A] (of a country, or part of it) require, by treaty or agreement, to have no military forces or installations in: a ∼d zone.

demi·monde /ˌdemɪˈmɔːnd/ n the ∼, (F) (class of society made up of) people on the fringe of respectable society. **demi·mon·daine** /ˌdemɪmɔːnˈdeɪn/ woman of this class.

de·mise /dɪˈmaɪz/ n (legal) death.

de·mist /diːˈmɪst/ vt remove the mist from, eg the windscreen of a motor vehicle. ∼**er** /-stə(r)/ n device that ∼s.

demo /ˈdeməʊ/ n [C] (colloq abbr for) demonstration(2).

de·mob /ˌdiːˈmɒb/ vt (-bb-) and n (GB colloq abbr for) demobilize and demobilization: When do you get ∼bed/your ∼?

de·mo·bil·ize /diːˈməʊbəlaɪz/ vt [VP6A] release from military service. **de·mo·bil·iz·ation** /diːˌməʊbəlaɪˈzeɪʃn US: -lɪˈz-/ n

democ·racy /dɪˈmɒkrəsɪ/ n (pl -cies) **1** [C,U] (country with principles of) government in which all adult citizens share through their elected representatives. **2** [C,U] (country with) government which encourages and allows rights of citizenship such as freedom of speech, religion, opinion and association, the assertion of the rule of law, majority rule, accompanied by respect for the rights of minorities. **3** [C,U] (society in which there is) treatment of each other by citizens as equals and with absence of class feeling: Is there more ∼ in Australia than in Great Britain?

demo·crat /ˈdeməkræt/ n **1** person who favours or supports democracy. **2 D∼,** (US) member of the Democratic Party.

demo·cratic /ˌdeməˈkrætɪk/ adj **1** of, like, supporting, democracy(1,2). **2** (esp) of, supporting, democracy(3); paying no or little attention to class divisions based on birth or wealth. **3 the 'D∼ Party,** (US) one of the two main political parties. ⇨ Republican. **demo·crati·cally** /-klɪ/ adv

de·moc·ra·tize /dɪˈmɒkrətaɪz/ vt [VP6A] make democratic. **de·moc·ra·tiz·ation** /dɪˌmɒkrətaɪˈzeɪʃn US: -tɪˈz-/ n

dé·modé /ˌdeɪˈməʊdeɪ US: ˌdeɪməʊˈdeɪ/ adj (F) outmoded; out of fashion.

de·mog·ra·phy /diːˈmɒɡrəfɪ/ n [U] (study of) statistics of births, deaths, diseases, etc to show the condition of a community. **demo·graphic** /ˌdeməˈɡræfɪk/ adj

de·mol·ish /dɪˈmɒlɪʃ/ vt [VP6A] pull or tear down, eg old buildings; destroy, eg sb's argument; make an end of. **demo·li·tion** /ˌdeməˈlɪʃn/ n [U] ∼ing or being ~ed; [C] instance of this.

de·mon /'di:mən/ *n* evil, wicked or cruel supernatural being or spirit; (colloq) fierce or energetic person: *a* ~ *bowler,* (cricket) very fast bowler. *He's a* ~ *for work,* (colloq) works with great energy. ~·ic /di:'mɒnɪk/ *adj*

de·monet·ize /ˌdi:'mʌnɪtaɪz/ *vt* deprive (a metal) of its value as currency; withdraw (a metal) from use as currency. **de·monet·iz·ation** /di:ˌmʌnɪtaɪ'zeɪʃn US: -tɪ'z-/ *n*

de·mon·iac /dɪ'məʊnɪæk/ *n, adj* (person who is) devilish, frenzied, fiercely energetic. ~·al /ˌdi:mə'naɪəkl/ *adj* = ~. ~·ally /ˌdi:mə'naɪəklɪ/ *adv*

de·mon·strable /'demənstrəbl/ *adj* that can be demonstrated or logically proved. **de·mon·strably** /-blɪ/ *adv* **de·mon·stra·bil·ity** /ˌdemənstrə'bɪlɪtɪ/ *n*

dem·on·strate /'demənstreɪt/ *vt, vi* **1** [VP6A,9] show clearly by giving proof(s) or example(s): *How would you* ~ *that the world is round? The salesman* ~*d the new washing-machine,* showed how it was used. **2** [VP2A,3A] take part in a demonstration(2): *The workers marched through the streets with flags and banners to* ~ *against the rising cost of living.*

dem·on·stra·tion /ˌdemən'streɪʃn/ *n* [C,U] **1** demonstrating(1): *to teach sth by* ~; *a* ~ *of affection,* eg when a child puts its arms round its mother's neck; *a* ~ *of a new car,* to show how it works. **2** public and organised display of opinion by a group, eg of workers, students.

de·mon·stra·tive /dɪ'mɒnstrətɪv/ *adj* **1** (of persons) showing the feelings: *Some children are more* ~ *than others,* readier to show affection, etc. **2** marked by open expression of feelings: ~ *behaviour.* **3** serving to point out; esp (gram) ~ '**pronoun,** (*this, these, that, those*). ~·ly *adv*

dem·on·stra·tor /'demənstreɪtə(r)/ *n* **1** person who demonstrates(2): *The* ~*s were dispersed by the police.* **2** person who teaches or explains by demonstrating(1).

de·moral·ize /dɪ'mɒrəlaɪz US: -'mɔ:r-/ *vt* [VP6A] **1** hurt or weaken the morals of: *a boy who was* ~*d by bad companions.* **2** weaken the courage, confidence, self-discipline, etc of, eg an army. ⇨ **morale. de·moral·iz·ation** /dɪˌmɒrəlaɪ'zeɪʃn US: -ˌmɔ:rəlɪ'z-/ *n*

de·mote /ˌdi:'məʊt/ *vt* [VP6A] reduce to a lower rank or grade. ⇨ **promote. de·motion** /ˌdi:'məʊʃn/ *n*

de·motic /dɪ'mɒtɪk/ *adj* of, used by, the common people: ~ *Greek,* the colloquial form of modern Greek.

de·mur /dɪ'mɜ:(r)/ *vi* (-rr-) [VP2A,3A] ~ (*at/to*), (formal) raise a doubt or an objection: *to* ~ *to a demand; to* ~ *at working on Sundays.* □ *n* [U] hesitation or objection: (chiefly in) *without* ~.

de·mure /dɪ'mjʊə(r)/ *adj* quiet and serious: *a* ~ *young lady;* pretending to be, suggesting that one is, ~: *She gave him a* ~ *smile.* ~·ly *adv* ~·ness *n*

den /den/ *n* **1** animal's hidden home, eg a cave. **2** secret resort: *an opium den; a den of thieves.* **3** (colloq) room in which a person works and studies without being disturbed.

den·ary /'di:nərɪ/ *adj* = decimal.

de·nation·al·ize /ˌdi:'næʃənəlaɪz/ *vt* [VP6A] transfer (a nationalized industry, etc) to private ownership again. ⇨ **nationalize. de·nation·al·iz·ation** /ˌdi:ˌnæʃənəlaɪ'zeɪʃn US: -lɪ'z-/ *n*

de·natured /ˌdi:'neɪtʃəd/ *adj* that has been made

unfit for eating and drinking (but may still be used for other purposes): ~ *alcohol;* having lost natural qualities: ~ *rubber,* no longer elastic.

de·ni·able /dɪ'naɪəbl/ *adj* that one can deny.

de·nial /dɪ'naɪəl/ *n* ~ (*of*), **1** [U] denying(2,3); [C] instance of this: *the* ~ *of justice/a request for help.* **2** [C] statement that sth is not true: *the prisoner's repeated* ~*s of the charge brought against him.* ⇨ *self-* ~ at self-.

den·ier /'denɪə(r)/ *n* unit of fineness for rayon, nylon and silk yarns: *30* ~ *stockings.*

deni·grate /'denɪgreɪt/ *vt* [VP6A] defame. **deni·gra·tion** /ˌdenɪ'greɪʃn/ *n*

denim /'denɪm/ *n* **1** [U] twilled cotton cloth (used for jeans, overalls, etc). **2** (*pl*) (colloq) jeans made from ~.

deni·zen /'denɪzn/ *n* person, kind of animal or plant, living or growing permanently in the district, etc mentioned: ~*s of the Arctic.*

de·nomi·nate /dɪ'nɒmɪneɪt/ *vt* [VP23] give a name to; call.

de·nomi·na·tion /dɪˌnɒmɪ'neɪʃn/ *n* [C] **1** name, esp one given to a class or religious group or sect: *The Protestant* ~*s include the Methodists, Presbyterians and Baptists.* **2** class or unit (in weight, length, numbers, money, etc): *The US coin of the lowest* ~ *is the cent. We can reduce fractions to the same* ~, eg ½, ⅝ = ⅞, ⅒. ~·al /-'neɪʃənl/ *adj* of ~s(1): ~*al schools.*

de·nomi·na·tor /dɪ'nɒmɪneɪtə(r)/ *n* number or quantity below the line in a fraction, eg 4 in ¾.

de·note /dɪ'nəʊt/ *vt* **1** [VP6A] be the sign or symbol of; be the name of: *In algebra the sign* x *usually* ~*s an unknown quantity.* **2** [VP6A,9] indicate: *The mark* (ʌ) ~*s a place of omission/*~*s that something has been omitted.*

dé·noue·ment /ˌdeɪ'nu:mɒ:ŋ US: ˌdeɪnu:'mɒ:ŋ/ *n* (F) final stage, where everything is made clear, in the development of the plot of a story, play, etc.

de·nounce /dɪ'naʊns/ *vt* **1** [VP6A,16B] speak publicly against; give information against: *to* ~ *a heresy; to* ~ *sb as a spy.* **2** [VP6A] give notice that one intends to end (a treaty or agreement).

dense /dens/ *adj* (-r, -st) **1** (of liquids, vapour) not easily seen through: *a* ~ *fog;* ~ *smoke.* **2** (of people and things) crowded together in great numbers: *a* ~ *crowd; a* ~ *forest.* **3** (colloq) stupid; having a mind that ideas can penetrate only with difficulty. ~·ly *adv: a* ~*ly populated country;* ~*ly wooded,* covered with trees growing close together. ~·ness *n*

den·sity /'densətɪ/ *n* **1** [U] the quality of being dense: *the* ~ *of a forest/the fog/the population.* **2** [C,U] (*pl* -ties) (phys) relation of weight to volume.

dent /dent/ *n* hollow, depression, in a hard surface made by a blow or by pressure; (fig, colloq): *a* ~ *in one's pride.* □ *vt, vi* **1** [VP6A] make a ~ or ~s in: *a motor-car badly* ~*ed in a collision.* **2** [VP2A] get ~s in: *metal that* ~*s easily.*

den·tal /'dentl/ *adj* **1** of or for the teeth: *a* ~ *plate,* a denture; *a* ~ *surgeon.* **2** (phon) with the tip of the tongue near or touching the upper front teeth: ~ *sounds,* eg /θ, ð/.

den·ti·frice /'dentɪfrɪs/ *n* [U] tooth-powder or toothpaste (the usu words).

den·tist /'dentɪst/ *n* person whose work is filling, cleaning, taking out teeth and fitting artificial teeth. ~·ry /'dentɪstrɪ/ *n* [U] work of a ~.

den·ture /'dentʃə(r)/ *n* [C] plate (fitted on the

gums) of artificial teeth.

de·nude /dɪ'nju:d US: -'nu:d/ vt [VP6A,14] ~ *(of),*
1 make bare; take away covering: *trees ~d of
leaves; hillsides ~d of trees.* **2** deprive: *~d by his
creditors of every penny he had.* **de·nud·ation**
/ˌdi:nju:'deɪʃn US: -nu:-/ n

de·nunci·ation /dɪˌnʌnsɪ'eɪʃn/ n [C,U] denounc-
ing: *the ~ of a traitor.*

deny /dɪ'naɪ/ vt **1** [VP6A,C,9,25] say that (sth) is
not true: *The accused man denied the charge. I ~
that the statement is true. He denied this to be the
case. He denied knowing anything about/denied
any knowledge of their plans. It cannot be denied
that.../There is no ~ing the fact that...,* Everyone
must admit that.... ⇨ affirm. **2** [VP6A] say that
one knows nothing about; disown; refuse to acknowledge: *He denied the signature, said that it
was not his. Peter denied Christ.* **3** [VP12A,13A]
say 'no' to a request; refuse to give (sth asked for
or needed): *He denies himself/his wife nothing. He
gave to his friends what he denied to his family.
She was angry at being denied admittance.*

deo·dar /'dɪədɑ:(r)/ n Himalayan cedar.

de·odor·ize /di:'əʊdəraɪz/ vt [VP6A] remove odour
(esp bad smells) from.

de·odor·ant /di:'əʊdərənt/ n substance that disguises or absorbs (esp body) odours.

de·part /dɪ'pɑ:t/ vi **1** [VP2A,3A] ~ *(from),* go
away; leave (esp in timetables, abbr dep): *dep
Leeds 4.30pm.* ⇨ arrive. **2** [VP3A] ~ *from,* behave in a way that differs from: *~ from routine/the
usual procedure/old customs; ~ from the truth.* **3**
~ *(from) this life,* (archaic) die. *~ed part adj*
bygone: *thinking of ~ed glories.* □ n **the ~ed,**
(*sing*) person who has recently died; (*pl*) those
who have died: *pray for the souls of the ~ed.*

de·part·ment /dɪ'pɑ:tmənt/ n **1** one of several divisions of a government, business, shop, university,
etc: *the Education D~/D~ of Education; the shipping ~ (a business firm); the men's clothing ~ (in
a large shop); a '~ store,* a large shop where many
kinds of goods are sold in different ~s. **2** (F) administrative district. *~al* /ˌdi:pɑ:t'mentl/ adj of a ~
(contrasted with the whole); *~al duties/
administration.*

de·par·ture /dɪ'pɑ:tʃə(r)/ n ~ *(from),* **1** [U] departing; going away; [C] instance of this: *His ~ was
unexpected. There are notices showing arrivals
and ~s of trains near the booking-office. Which is
the ~ platform,* that from which the train leaves? **2**
[C,U] turning away or aside; changing: *a ~ from
old custom; a new ~ in physics,* eg the discovery
of nuclear fission.

de·pend /dɪ'pend/ vi [VP3A] ~ *on/upon,* **1** (not in
the progressive tenses) need, rely on (the support,
etc of) in order to exist or to be true or to succeed:
*Children ~ on their parents for food and clothing.
Good health ~s upon good food, exercise and getting enough sleep. He ~s on his pen for a living,*
makes a living by writing. **that ~s; it (all) ~s,**
(alone, or at the beginning of a sentence) the result
~s on sth else: *It ~s how you tackle the problem.*
2 trust; be certain about: *You can always ~ upon
John to be there when he is needed. You may ~
upon his coming/~ upon it that he will want to
come. Can I ~ upon this railway guide or is it an
old one? ~ upon it,* (at the beginning or end of a
sentence) you can be quite certain: *The strike will
ruin the country, ~ upon it. ~·able adj* that may
be *~ed upon.*

de·pend·ant (also **-ent**) /dɪ'pendənt/ n sb who depends upon another or others for a home, food, etc;
servant. ⇨ dependent adj.

de·pend·ence /dɪ'pendəns/ n ~ *on/upon,* [U] **1**
the state of depending; being supported by others:
*Why don't you find a job and end this ~ upon your
parents?* **2** confident trust; reliance: *He's not a
man you can put much ~ on,* you can't rely on
him. **3** the state of being determined or conditioned
by: *the ~ of the crops upon the weather; drug ~.*

de·pend·ency /dɪ'pendənsɪ/ n (pl -cies) country
governed or controlled by another: *The Hawaiian
Islands are no longer a ~ of the USA.*

de·pend·ent /dɪ'pendənt/ n = dependant. □ adj
~ *on/upon,* depending: *The man was out of work
and ~ on his son's earnings. Promotion is ~ upon
your record of success.*

de·pict /dɪ'pɪkt/ vt [VP6A] show in the form of a
picture; describe in words: *biblical scenes ~ed in
tapestry.* **de·pic·tion** /dɪ'pɪkʃn/ n

de·pila·tory /dɪ'pɪlətrɪ US: -tɔ:rɪ/ adj, n (liquid,
cream, etc) able to remove superfluous hair.

de·plane /ˌdi:'pleɪn/ vi (usu of troops, etc) disembark from an aircraft.

de·plete /dɪ'pli:t/ vt [VP6A,14] ~ *(of),* use up,
empty until little or none remains: *to ~ a lake of
fish; ~d supplies.* **de·pletion** /dɪ'pli:ʃn/ n [U] de-
pleting or being ~d.

de·plore /dɪ'plɔ:(r)/ vt [VP6A] show, say, that one
is filled with sorrow or regret for; condemn. **de·
plor·able** /dɪ'plɔ:rəbl/ adj that is, or should be,
~d: *deplorable conduct; a deplorable accident.*
de·plor·ably /-əblɪ/ adv.

de·ploy /dɪ'plɔɪ/ vt,vi [VP6A,2A] (mil, of troops
etc) (cause to) spread out, eg into line of battle;
(fig) bring into action: ~ *arguments.* **~·ment** n

de·pon·ent /dɪ'pəʊnənt/ n (legal) person who gives
written testimony for use in a law court.

de·popu·late /ˌdi:'pɒpjʊleɪt/ vt [VP6A] lessen the
number of people living in a place: *a country ~d
by war/famine.* **de·popu·la·tion** /ˌdi:ˌpɒpjʊ'leɪʃn/ n

de·port[1] /dɪ'pɔ:t/ vt [VP6A] expel (an unwanted
person) from a country: *The spy was imprisoned
for two years and then ~ed.* **de·port·ation**
/ˌdi:pɔ:'teɪʃn/ n [U] ~ing or being ~ed: *Years ago
criminals in England could be sentenced to ~ation
to Australia. ~ee* /ˌdi:pɔ:'ti:/ n ~ed person.

de·port[2] /dɪ'pɔ:t/ vt [VP6A,16B] (reflex, formal)
behave: *to ~ oneself with dignity. ~·ment* n [U]
behaviour; way of holding oneself in standing and
walking: *Young ladies used to have lessons in
~ment.*

de·pose /dɪ'pəʊz/ vt,vi **1** [VP6A] remove, esp a
ruler such as a king, from a position of authority;
dethrone. **2** [VP3A,9] ~ *(to + gerund),* (legal)
bear witness, give evidence, esp on oath in a law
court: *to ~ that one saw...; to ~ to having seen....*
⇨ deposition.

de·posit[1] /dɪ'pɒzɪt/ vt [VP6A] **1** lay or put down:
*He ~ed the books on the desk. Some insects ~
their eggs in the ground.* **2** put or store for safe-
keeping: *to ~ money in a bank/papers with one's
lawyer.* **3** make part payment of money that is or
will be owed: *We should like you to ~ a quarter of
the price of the house.* **4** (esp of a liquid, a river)
leave (a layer of matter on): *When the Nile rises it
~s a layer of mud on the land.*

de·posit[2] /dɪ'pɒzɪt/ n [C] **1** money that is deposit-
ed(2,3): *The shopkeeper promised to keep the
goods for me if I left/paid/made a ~.* **money on**

~, money deposited in this way. '~ **account,** money deposited in a bank, not to be withdrawn without notice, on which interest is payable. ⇨ *current account* at current¹(3). '~ **safe,** safe in the strong-room of a bank, rented for the custody of valuables. **2** layer of matter deposited(4): *A thick ~ of mud covered the fields after the floods went down.* **3** layer of solid matter left behind (often buried in the earth) after having been naturally accumulated: *Valuable new ~s of tin have been found in Bolivia.*

de·posi·tion /ˌdepəˈzɪʃn/ *n* **1** [U] deposing from office; dethronement. **2** [C] (legal) statement made on oath. **3** [U] depositing, eg of mud.

de·posi·tor /dɪˈpɒzɪtə(r)/ *n* person who deposits, eg money in a bank.

de·posi·tory /dɪˈpɒzɪtrɪ US: -tɔːrɪ/ *n* (*pl* -ries) place where goods are deposited; storehouse.

de·pot /ˈdepəʊ US: ˈdiːpəʊ/ *n* **1** storehouse, esp for military supplies; warehouse; place for storing vehicles (eg buses). **2** (US) railway or bus station.

de·prave /dɪˈpreɪv/ *vt* [VP6A] make morally bad; corrupt (usu in *pp*): *~d persons; ~d* (= vicious or perverted) *tastes.*

de·prav·ity /dɪˈprævətɪ/ *n* [U] depraved state; viciousness: *sunk in ~;* [C] (*pl* -ties) vicious act.

dep·re·cate /ˈdeprəkeɪt/ *vt* [VP6A,C] (formal) feel and express disapproval of: *Hasty action is to be ~d. He ~s changing the rules at present.* **dep·reca·tion** /ˌdeprəˈkeɪʃn/ *n*

de·pre·ci·ate /dɪˈpriːʃɪeɪt/ *vt, vi* [VP6A,2A] make or become less in value; say that (sth) has little value: *Shares in this company have ~d. Don't ~ my efforts to help.* **de·pre·ci·atory** /dɪˈpriːʃətɔrɪ US: -tɔːrɪ/ *adj* tending to ~: *depreciatory remarks about my work.* **de·pre·ci·ation** /dɪˌpriːʃɪˈeɪʃn/ *n* [U] lessening of value or estimation.

dep·re·da·tion /ˌdeprəˈdeɪʃn/ *n* (usu *pl*) (formal) destruction or pillaging of property.

de·press /dɪˈpres/ *vt* [VP6A] **1** press, push or pull down: *to ~ a lever/the keys of a piano.* *~ed* '**classes,** classes of people who are prevented from rising, or unable to rise, socially or economically, eg by a rigid caste system. **2** make sad, low in spirits: *Wet weather always ~es her. The newspapers are full of ~ing news nowadays,* eg of war, crime, natural disasters, rising prices. **3** make less active; cause (prices) to be lower: *When business is ~ed there is usually an increase in unemployment.* *~ed* '**area,** part of a country where industry is ~ed (with consequent poverty and unemployment).

de·press·ion /dɪˈpreʃn/ *n* **1** [U] being depressed(2); low spirits: *He committed suicide during a fit of ~.* **2** [C] hollow, sunk place, in the surface of sth, esp the ground: *It rained heavily and every ~ in the bad road was soon filled with water. The soldiers hid from the enemy in a slight ~.* **3** [C] time when business is depressed(3). **4** [C] lowering of atmospheric pressure; (esp) area of low barometric pressure; the system of winds round it: *a ~ over Iceland.*

de·press·ive /dɪˈpresɪv/ *adj* tending to depress; of depression(1): *~ financial measures; a ~ fit.* □ *n* person tending to suffer from depression(1).

de·prive /dɪˈpraɪv/ *vt* [VP14] *~ of,* take away from; prevent from using or enjoying: *trees that ~ a house of light. What would a student do if he were ~d of his books?* **de·prived** *adj* = underprivileged. **depri·va·tion** /ˌdeprɪˈveɪʃn/ *n* [U] depriv-

ing or being ~d: *deprivation of one's rights as a citizen;* [C] sth of which one is ~d.

depth /depθ/ *n* **1** [C,U] being deep; distance from the top down, from the front to the back, from the surface inwards: *What is the ~ of the well? Water was found at a ~ of 30 feet. At what ~ is the wreck lying? The snow is three feet in ~. in ~,* thoroug(ly): *explore a subject in ~; a study in ~.* *be/go/get out of one's ~,* (a) be in/enter water too deep to stand in: *If you can't swim, don't go out of your ~.* (b) (fig) attempt the study of sth that is too difficult: *When people start talking about nuclear physics I'm out of my ~.* '~-**bomb/ charge,** bomb used against a submarine, for explosion under water. **2** [C,U] deep learning, thought, feeling, etc: *a book that shows scholarship and ~ of thought. She showed a ~ of feeling that surprised us.* **3 the** ~(**s**), or most central part(s): *in the ~ of one's heart; in the ~ of winter; in the ~s of despair; in the ~ of the country,* a long way from any town.

depu·ta·tion /ˌdepjʊˈteɪʃn/ *n* group of representatives; number of persons given the right to act or speak for others.

de·pute /dɪˈpjuːt/ *vt* [VP14,17] *~ sth to sb/sb to do sth,* give (one's work, authority, etc) to a substitute; give (another person) authority to act as one's representative.

depu·tize /ˈdepjʊtaɪz/ *vi* [VP2A,3A] *~ (for sb),* act as deputy.

dep·uty /ˈdepjʊtɪ/ *n* (*pl* -ties) **1** person to whom work, authority, etc is deputed: *I must find someone to act as* (a) *~ for me during my absence.* **2** (in some countries, eg France) member of a legislative assembly.

de·rail /dɪˈreɪl/ *vt* [VP6A] cause (a train, etc) to run off the rails: *The engine was ~ed.* *~·ment n*

de·range /dɪˈreɪndʒ/ *vt* [VP6A] put out of working order; put into confusion; disturb: *He is mentally ~d,* insane. *~·ment n*

de·rate /diːˈreɪt/ *vt* [VP6A] (GB) relieve (industries, etc) from a proportion of the local rates(3): *the Derating Act, 1929.*

derby¹ /ˈdɑːbɪ US: ˈdɜːrbɪ/ *n* **1 The D~,** annual horserace at Epsom, England. '**D~ Day,** day of the race (in June). **2** (US) any of several annual horseraces. **3** sporting contest. **local ~,** one between local teams.

derby² /ˈdɜːrbɪ/ *n* (US) bowler hat.

der·el·ict /ˈderəlɪkt/ *adj* abandoned; deserted and left to fall into ruin: *a ~ house; a ~ ship; ~ areas,* eg those made squalid by open-cast mining, gravel digging. **der·el·ic·tion** /ˌderəˈlɪkʃn/ *n* [U] **1** making ~: *the dereliction caused by the armies of Genghis Khan.* **2** (wilful) neglect of duty.

de·requi·si·tion /ˌdiːˌrekwɪˈzɪʃn/ *vt* [VP6A] free (requisitioned property, etc).

de·re·strict /ˌdiːrɪˈstrɪkt/ *vt* [VP6A] cancel a restriction upon: *~ a road,* remove a speed limit from it.

de·ride /dɪˈraɪd/ *vt* [VP6A,16B] mock; laugh scornfully at: *They ~d his efforts as childish.*

de rigueur /də rɪˈɡɜː(r)/ *pred adj* (F) required by etiquette or custom: *Evening dress is ~ at the Casino.*

de·ri·sion /dɪˈrɪʒn/ *n* [U] deriding or being derided; ridicule, mockery: *hold sb/sth in ~; be/become an object of ~; make sb/sth an object of ~.*

de·ris·ive /dɪˈraɪsɪv/ *adj* showing or deserving derision: *~ laughter; a ~ offer,* eg £100 for a car that is worth £1000.

de·ris·ory /dɪ'raɪsərɪ/ adj = derisive.

deri·va·tion /ˌderɪ'veɪʃn/ n **1** [U] deriving or being derived; origin; descent: the ~ of words from Latin; a word of Latin ~. **2** [C] first form and meaning of a word; statement of how a word was formed and how it changed: to study the ~s of words.

de·riva·tive /dɪ'rɪvətɪv/ adj, n [C] (thing, word, substance) derived from another; not original or primitive: 'Assertion' is a ~ of 'assert'.

de·rive /dɪ'raɪv/ vt,vi **1** [VP14] ~ from, (formal) get: to ~ great pleasure from one's studies; medicine from which she has ~d little benefit. **2** [VP14,3A] ~ from, take/have as a starting-point, source or origin: Thousands of English words ~ from/are ~d from Latin.

der·ma·tol·ogy /ˌdɜːmə'tɒlədʒɪ/ n [U] medical study of the skin, its diseases, etc. **der·ma·tol·ogist** /ˌdɜːmə'tɒlədʒɪst/ n expert in ~.

dero·gate /'derəgeɪt/ vi [VP3A] ~ from, (formal) take away (a merit, good quality, right). **dero·ga·tion** /ˌderə'geɪʃn/ n [U] lessening (of authority, dignity, reputation, etc).

de·roga·tory /dɪ'rɒgətrɪ US: -tɔːrɪ/ adj (abbr derog used in this dictionary) ~ (to), tending to damage or take away from (one's credit, etc); insulting: remarks that are ~ to my reputation. Is the slang word 'cop' as ~ as 'pig' for 'policeman', Are policemen likely to object to it as being insulting?

der·rick /'derɪk/ n **1** ~ crane, large crane for moving or lifting heavy weights, esp on a ship. **2** (also oil-rig) framework over an oil-well or borehole, to hold the drilling machinery, etc.

derrick cranes　　　　　　an oil derrick

der·ring-do /ˌderɪŋ 'duː/ n [U] (old use) desperate courage: deeds of ~.

derv /dɜːv/ n [U] fuel oil for diesel engines (from diesel engined road vehicle).

der·vish /'dɜːvɪʃ/ n member of an order of Muslim religious enthusiasts: dancing ~es, who engage in whirling dances; howling ~es, who shout loudly.

de·sali·nate /ˌdiː'sælɪneɪt/ vt [VP6A] = desalinize. **de·sali·na·tion** /ˌdiːˌsælɪ'neɪʃn/ n

de·sali·nize /ˌdiː'sælɪnaɪz/ vt [VP6A] remove salt from (sea water or saline water). **de·salin·iz·ation** /ˌdiːˌsælɪnaɪ'zeɪʃn US: -nɪ'z-/ n

de·salt /ˌdiː'sɔːlt/ vt = desalinize.

de·scale /ˌdiː'skeɪl/ vt [VP6A] remove the scale from, eg the inside of boiler tubes.

des·cant /'deskænt/ n (music) additional independent accompaniment (often improvised) to a melody. □ vi /dɪ'skænt/ [VP3A] ~ on/upon, (a) (music) sing or play a ~ on. (b) comment on, enlarge upon (a topic).

de·scend /dɪ'send/ vi,vt **1** [VP2A,C,6A] (formal) come or go down: On turning the corner, we saw that the road ~ed steeply. The balloon ~ed in Poland. He ~ed the stairs. **2** be ~ed from, have as ancestors: According to the Bible, we are all ~ed from Adam. **3** [VP2C] (of property, qualities, rights) pass (from father to son) by inheritance; come from earlier times. **4** [VP3A] ~ on/upon, attack suddenly; (colloq) visit unexpectedly: The bandits ~ed upon the defenceless village. **5** [VP3A] ~ to, lower oneself to: You would never ~ to fraud/cheating. **6** ~ to particulars, pass on (in an argument, etc) to details, eg after a general introduction to a subject. ~-ant /-ənt/ n person who is ~ed from (the person or persons named): the ~ants of Queen Victoria.

de·scent /dɪ'sent/ n **1** [C,U] coming or going down: The land slopes to the sea by a gradual ~, slopes gradually. The ~ of the mountain took two hours. **2** [U] ancestry: of French ~, having French ancestors; Darwin's 'D~ of Man', ie his theory of evolution. He traces his ~ from the Queen of Sheba. **3** [C] ~ on/upon, sudden attack on; (colloq) unexpected visit to: The Danes made numerous ~s upon the English coast during the 10th century. **4** [U] handing down, eg of property, titles, qualities, etc by inheritance.

de·scribe /dɪ'skraɪb/ vt **1** [VP6,14,10,16B] ~ (to/for), say what (sb or sth) is like; give a picture of in words: Words cannot ~ the beauty of the scene. Can you ~ it to/for me? Please ~ what you saw. **2** [VP16B] ~ as, qualify; say that (sb or sth) has certain qualities: I hesitate to ~ him as really clever. He ~s himself as a doctor. **3** [VP6A] mark out, draw (esp a geometrical figure): It is easy to ~ a circle if you have a pair of compasses.

de·scrip·tion /dɪ'skrɪpʃn/ n **1** [U] describing; [C] picture in words: He's not very good at ~. The scenery was beautiful beyond ~. Can you give me a ~ of the thief? ⇨ answer²(4). **2** [C] (colloq) sort: The harbour was crowded with vessels of every ~.

de·scrip·tive /dɪ'skrɪptɪv/ adj serving to describe; fond of describing: There is some excellent ~ writing (eg descriptions of scenery) in Hardy's novels.

des·cry /dɪ'skraɪ/ vt [VP6A] (formal) catch sight of; see (esp sth a long way off).

des·ecrate /'desɪkreɪt/ vt [VP6A] use (a sacred thing or place) in an unworthy or wicked way. **des·ecra·tion** /ˌdesɪ'kreɪʃn/ n [U] desecrating or being ~d.

de·seg·re·gate /ˌdiː'segrɪgeɪt/ vt [VP6A] abolish (esp racial) segregation in: ~ schools in Alabama. **de·seg·re·ga·tion** /ˌdiːˌsegrɪ'geɪʃn/ n

de·sen·si·tize /ˌdiː'sensɪtaɪz/ vt [VP6A] render insensitive or less sensitive, eg to light or pain. **de·sen·si·tiz·ation** /ˌdiːˌsensɪtaɪ'zeɪʃn US: -tɪ'z-/ n

de·sert¹ /dɪ'zɜːt/ vt,vi **1** [VP6A] leave; go away from: The village had been hurriedly ~ed, perhaps because bandits were in the district. The streets were ~ed, no people were to be seen. We sheltered from the storm in a ~ed hut, one that had been abandoned. **2** [VP6A] leave without help or support, esp in a wrong or cruel way: He ~ed his wife and children and went abroad. He has become so rude that his friends are ~ing him. **3** [VP6A,2A] run away from; leave (esp service in a ship, the armed forces) without authority or permission: A soldier who ~s his post in time of war is punished severely. **4** [VP6A] fail: His courage/presence of mind ~ed him. ~er n person who ~s(3). **de·ser·tion** /dɪ'zɜːʃn/ n [C,U] (instance of) ~ing or being ~ed.

des·ert² /'dezət/ *n* [C,U] (large area of) barren land, waterless and treeless, often sand-covered: *the Sahara D~.* □ *adj* **1** barren; uncultivated: *the ~ areas of N Africa.* **2** uninhabited: *wrecked on a ~ island.*

de·serts /dɪ'zɜːts/ *n* (*pl*) what sb deserves: *to be rewarded/punished according to one's ~; to get/ meet with one's ~.*

de·serve /dɪ'zɜːv/ *vt,vi* (not used in the progressive tenses; ⇨ deserving.) **1** [VP6A,7A] be entitled to (because of actions, conduct, qualities); merit: *Good work ~s good pay. He certainly ~s to be sent to prison. These people ~ our help.* **2 to ~ well/ill of,** to ~ to be well/badly treated by: *He ~s well of his country...ought to be given; just...* **de·served** *adj* that ought to be; just: *~ed punishment/reward/praise. His promotion wasn't ~d.* **de·serv·ed·ly** /dɪ'zɜːvɪdlɪ/ *adv* according to what is ~d; justly; rightly: *to be ~dly punished.*

de·serv·ing /dɪ'zɜːvɪŋ/ *adj* ~ (*of*), having merit; worthy: *to give money to a ~ cause; to be ~ of sympathy; a ~ case,* a person who, because of his circumstances, etc, deserves interest, sympathy, help, etc.

dés·habillé /ˌdeɪzæ'biːeɪ/ (F) = dishabille.

des·ic·cant /'desɪkənt/ *n* (US) substance used to absorb moisture.

des·ic·cate /'desɪkeɪt/ *vt* [VP6A] dry out all the moisture from, esp solid food, to preserve it: *~d fruit/coconut.*

de·sid·er·atum /dɪˌzɪdə'rɑːtəm/ *n* (*pl* -rata /-'rɑːtə/) sth felt to be lacking and needed.

de·sign /dɪ'zaɪn/ *n* **1** [C] drawing or outline from which sth may be made: *~s for a dress/garden;* [U] art of making such drawings, etc: *a school of ~.* **2** [U] general arrangement or planning (of a picture, book, building, machine, etc): *The building seats 2000 people, but is poor in ~. A machine of faulty ~ will not sell well.* **3** [C] pattern; arrangement of lines, shapes, details, as ornament, eg on a bowl or carpet: *a vase with a ~ of flowers on it.* **4** [C,U] purpose; intention; mental plan: *Whether by accident or ~, he arrived too late to help us. Was the world made by ~ or did it come into existence by chance?* **have ~s on/against,** intend (selfishly or evilly) to get possession of: *That man has ~s on your money/your life;* (colloq) *He has ~s on that young girl,* wants to be intimate with her. □ *vt,vi* **1** [VP6A] prepare a plan, sketch, etc (of sth to be made): *~ a dress/garden.* **2** [VP2A,C] make *~s*(1) from which sth will be made: *He ~s for a large firm of carpet manufacturers.* **3** [VP14,16A,B] ~ **for,** set apart, intend, plan: *This course of study is ~ed to help those wishing to teach abroad. This room was ~ed for the children/~ed as a children's playroom.* **~·ed·ly** /-ɪdlɪ/ *adv* by ~(4); on purpose.

des·ig·nate¹ /'dezɪgneɪt/ *adj* (placed after the *n*) appointed to an office (but not yet installed): *the bishop ~.*

des·ig·nate² /'dezɪgneɪt/ *vt* **1** [VP6A] mark or point out clearly; give a name or title to: *to ~ boundaries.* **2** [VP6A,17,16B] appoint to a position or office: *He ~d Smith as his successor.*

des·ig·na·tion /ˌdezɪg'neɪʃn/ *n* [U] appointing to an office; [C] name, title or description.

de·sign·er /dɪ'zaɪnə(r)/ *n* person who designs, machinery, dresses.

de·sign·ing /dɪ'zaɪnɪŋ/ *adj* artful and cunning; fond of intrigue. □ *n* [U] art of making designs (for ma-

chinery, etc).

de·sir·able /dɪ'zaɪərəbl/ *adj* to be desired; causing desire; worth having: *This ~ property to be sold or let,* as in a house-agent's advertisement. *It is most ~ that he should attend the conference.* **de·sir·abil·ity** /dɪˌzaɪərə'bɪlətɪ/ *n*

de·sire¹ /dɪ'zaɪə(r)/ *n* **1** [U] strong longing; strong sexual attraction; [C] instance of this; earnest wish: *He has no/not much ~ for wealth. He works hard from a ~ to become rich. He spoke about his country's ~ for friendly relations/that friendly relations should be established. It is impossible to satisfy all their ~s.* **2** (*sing*) request: *at the ~ of Her Majesty.* **3** [C] thing that is wished for: *I hope you will get all your heart's ~s,* all you wish for.

de·sire² /dɪ'zaɪə(r)/ *vt* [VP6A,7A,17,9] **1** (formal) long for; wish; have a desire(1) for: *We all ~ happiness and health. Our rooms at the hotel were all that could be ~d,* were quite satisfactory. *What do you ~ me to do?* **2** (official style) request: *It is ~d that this rule shall be brought to the attention of the staff.*

de·sir·ous /dɪ'zaɪərəs/ *adj* ~ (*of*), (formal, official) feeling desire: *~ of peace; ~ to do sth; ~ that....*

de·sist /dɪ'zɪst/ *vi* [VP2A,3A] ~ (*from*), (formal) cease: *~ from gossiping.*

desk /desk/ *n* **1** piece of furniture (not a table) with a flat or sloping top and drawers at which to read, write or do business, eg one for office or school use. **2** reception desk, ⇨ reception(1): *leave a message at the ~ (of the hotel).* '*~ clerk* *n* (US) reception clerk.

deso·late /'desələt/ *adj* **1** (of a place) in a ruined, neglected state; (of land or a country) unlived in; unfit to live in; barren: *a ~, wind-swept moorland area.* **2** friendless; wretched; lonely and sad: *a ~-looking child; a ~ life.* **~·ly** *adv* □ *vt* /'desəleɪt/ [VP6A] make ~. **deso·la·tion** /ˌdesə'leɪʃn/ *n* [U] making or being ~: *the desolation caused by war.*

des·pair¹ /dɪ'speə(r)/ *n* [U] **1** the state of having lost all hope: *Your stupidity will drive me to ~. He gave up the attempt in ~. He was filled with ~ when he read the examination questions. The refugee's ~ of ever seeing his family again filled us with pity.* **2 be the ~ of,** be sb or sth that causes loss of hope to: *This boy is the ~ of all his teachers,* They no longer hope to teach him anything. *He is the ~ of all other pianists,* plays so well that they cannot hope to rival him.

des·pair² /dɪ'speə(r)/ *vi* [VP2A,3A] ~ (*of*), be in ~ about: *to ~ of success/of ever succeeding. His life was ~ed of,* All hope that he would live was lost. **~·ing·ly** *adv*

des·patch /dɪ'spætʃ/ *n, vt* = dispatch.

des·per·ado /ˌdespə'rɑːdəʊ/ *n* (*pl* ~es; US also ~s /-dəʊz/) person ready to do any reckless or criminal act.

des·per·ate /'despərət/ *adj* **1** (of a person) filled with despair and ready to do anything, regardless of danger: *The prisoners became ~ in their attempts to escape.* **2** lawless; violent: *~ criminals.* **3** extremely serious or dangerous: *The state of the country is ~.* **4** giving little hope of success; tried when all else has failed: *~ remedies.* **~·ly** *adv* **des·per·ation** /ˌdespə'reɪʃn/ *n* [U] the state of being ~(1): *The wretched people rose in desperation against their rulers. You'll drive me to desperation,* (colloq) fill me with despair, make me ready to do sth ~.

des·pic·able /dɪ'spɪkəbl/ *adj* deserving to be despised; contemptible. **des·pic·ably** /-əblɪ/ adv

des·pise /dɪ'spaɪz/ vt [VP6A] feel contempt for; consider worthless: *Strike-breakers are ~d by their workmates. A dish of strawberries and cream is not to be ~d*, is very good and should not be refused.

des·pite /dɪ'spaɪt/ prep in spite of: ~ *what she says....* □ n (obsolescent) ~ *of; in ~ of*, in spite of (which is now the usu phrase). **~·ful** /-fʊl/ adj (archaic) spiteful. **~·fully** /-fəlɪ/ adv

de·spoil /dɪ'spɔɪl/ vt [VP6A,14] ~ *sb (of)*, (liter) rob, plunder.

de·spon·dency /dɪ'spɒndənsɪ/ n [U] loss of hope; melancholy: *to fall into ~*. **de·spon·dent** /dɪ'spɒndənt/ adj having or showing loss of hope: *Don't become despondent.* **de·spon·dent·ly** adv

des·pot /'despɒt/ n ruler with unlimited powers, esp one who uses these powers wrongly or cruelly; tyrant. **~·ic** /dɪ'spɒtɪk/ adj of or like a ~ or tyrant. **~·ism** /'despətɪzəm/ n [U] the rule of a ~; tyranny; [C] country ruled by a ~.

des·sert /dɪ'zɜːt/ n 1 course of fruit, etc, at the end of a meal: (attrib) *a '~ apple.* **'~·spoon**, medium-sized spoon. **'~·spoon·ful** /-fʊl/ n as much as a ~spoon will hold. ⇨ *teaspoon* at tea, tablespoon at table. 2 (US) any sweet dish, eg pie, pudding, ice-cream, served at the end of a meal (GB = *sweet, pudding*).

des·ti·na·tion /ˌdestɪ'neɪʃn/ n place to which sb or sth is going or is being sent.

des·tine /'destɪn/ vt [VP17,14] (usu passive) ~ *(for)*, set apart, decide or ordain in advance: *He was a soldier's son and was ~d from birth for the army*, His father had decided, when the boy was born, that he should become a soldier. *They were ~d never to meet again*, Fate had determined that they should never meet again. *His hopes were ~d to be realized*, His hopes came true.

des·tiny /'destɪnɪ/ n 1 [U] power believed to control events: *the tricks played on human beings by ~*. 2 [C] (pl -nies) that which happens to sb, thought of as determined in advance by fate: *It was his ~ to die in a foreign country, far from his family.*

des·ti·tute /'destɪtjuː US: -tuːt/ adj 1 without food, clothes and other things necessary for life: *When Mr Hill died, his wife and children were left ~.* 2 ~ *of*, not having: *officials who are ~ of ordinary human feelings.* **des·ti·tu·tion** /ˌdestɪ'tjuːʃn US: -'tuːʃn/ n [U] being ~(1): *a war that brought desolation and destitution; reduced to destitution*, to complete poverty.

de·stroy /dɪ'strɔɪ/ vt [VP6A] break to pieces; make useless; put an end to: *Don't ~ that box*—it may be useful. *The forest was ~ed by fire. All his hopes were ~ed.* **~·er** n 1 person or thing that ~s. 2 small, fast warship for protecting larger warships or convoys of merchant-ships.

de·struc·tible /dɪ'strʌktəbl/ adj that can be destroyed. **de·struc·ti·bil·ity** /dɪˌstrʌktə'bɪlətɪ/ n

de·struc·tion /dɪ'strʌkʃn/ n [U] destroying or being destroyed: *the ~ of a town by an earthquake*; that which ruins or destroys: *Gambling was his ~.*

de·struc·tive /dɪ'strʌktɪv/ adj causing destruction; fond of, in the habit of, destroying: *a ~ storm; ~ criticism. Are all small children ~?* **~·ly** adv **~·ness** n

desue·tude /dɪ'sjuːɪtjuːd US: -tuːd/ n [U] (formal, esp in) *fall into ~*, pass out of use: *customs/fashions/words that have fallen into ~.*

des·ul·tory /'desəltrɪ US: -tɔːrɪ/ adj without

system, purpose; not continuous: ~ *reading.*

de·tach /dɪ'tætʃ/ vt 1 [VP6A,14] ~ *(from)*, unfasten and take apart; separate: *to ~ a link from a chain/a coach from a train.* ⇨ attach. 2 [VP6A,16A] (armed forces) send (a party of men, ships, etc) away from the main body: *A number of men were ~ed to guard the right flank.* **de·tached** part adj 1 (of the mind, opinions, etc) impartial; not influenced by others; (colloq) unemotional: *to take a ~ed view of an event.* 2 (of a house) not joined to another on either side. ⇨ *semi-~ed* at semi-. **~·able** /-əbl/ adj that can be ~ed: *a ~able lining in a coat.*

de·tach·ment /dɪ'tætʃmənt/ n 1 [U] detaching or being detached: *the ~ of a key from a key-ring.* 2 [U] the state of being detached; being uninfluenced by surroundings, the opinions of others, etc; being indifferent and uninterested: *He answered with an air of ~.* 3 [C] group of men, ships, etc, detached(2) from a larger number (for a special duty, etc).

de·tail [1] /'diːteɪl US: dɪ'teɪl/ n 1 [C] small, particular fact or item. *Please give me all the ~s. Don't omit a single ~. Every ~ of her dress was perfect.* 2 [U] collection of such small facts or items. **go/enter into ~s; explain sth in ~**, to give the facts, item by item. 3 [U] (in art) the smaller or less important parts considered as a whole: *The composition of the picture is good but there is too much ~.* 4 [C] = detachment(3).

de·tail [2] /'diːteɪl US: dɪ'teɪl/ vt 1 [VP6A,14] ~ *(to/for)*, describe fully; give full ~s of: *a ~ed description*, given with every detail; *The characteristics of the machine are fully ~ed in our brochure.* 2 [VP6A,16A] appoint for special duty: *Three soldiers were ~ed to guard the bridge.* ⇨ detail[1](4).

de·tain /dɪ'teɪn/ vt [VP6A,16A] keep waiting; keep back; prevent from leaving or going forward: *He told his wife that he had been ~ed in the office by unexpected callers. This question need not ~ us long*, can be settled quickly. *The police ~ed the man to make further inquiries.* **~·ee** /ˌdiːteɪ'niː/ n person who is ~ed (esp by the authorities, as one who is suspected of wrong-doing, political agitation, etc).

de·tect /dɪ'tekt/ vt [VP6A] discover (the existence or presence of sb or sth, the identity of sb guilty of wrong-doing): *The dentist could ~ no sign of decay in her teeth. Can you ~ an escape of gas in this corner of the room?* **~·able** /-əbl/ adj that can be ~ed. **~·or** /-tə(r)/ n device for ~ing, eg changes of pressure, temperature or a radio signal. **'lie-~·or**, ⇨ lie[1].

de·tec·tion /dɪ'tekʃn/ n [U] detecting; discovering: *the ~ of crime. He tried to escape ~ by disguising himself as an old man.*

de·tec·tive /dɪ'tektɪv/ n person whose business it is to detect criminals. **'~ story/novel**, one in which the main interest is a puzzling crime and the process of solving it.

dé·tente /deɪ'tɑːnt/ n [U] (F) easing of strained relations, esp between countries.

de·ten·tion /dɪ'tenʃn/ n [U] detaining or being detained, (eg a pupil in school after ordinary hours, as a punishment; a prisoner without a trial).

de·ter /dɪ'tɜː(r)/ vt (-rr-) [VP6A,14] ~ *(from)*, discourage, hinder (sb from doing sth): *Failure did not ~ him from trying again.* **~·rent** /dɪ'terənt US: -'tɜː-/ adj, n (thing) tending to, intended to, ~: *Do you believe that the hydrogen bomb is a*

~*rent*, that it will ~ countries from making war?

de·ter·gent /dɪ'tɜːdʒənt/ *adj*, *n* (substance) that removes dirt, esp from the surface of things: *Most synthetic ~s are in the form of powder or liquid.*

de·terio·rate /dɪ'tɪərɪəreɪt/ *vt*, *vi* [VP6A,2A] make or become of less value, or worse in quality: *Leather quickly ~s in a hot, damp climate.* **de·terio·ra·tion** /dɪ,tɪərɪə'reɪʃn/ *n*

de·ter·mi·nant /dɪ'tɜːmɪnənt/ *adj*, *n* determining or deciding (agent, factor, element, etc).

de·ter·mi·nate /dɪ'tɜːmɪnət/ *adj* limited; definite; fixed.

de·ter·mi·na·tion /dɪ,tɜːmɪ'neɪʃn/ *n* [U] **1** ~ *of*, determining or being determined; deciding: *The ~ of the meaning of a word is often difficult without a context.* **2** ~ *of*, calculation or finding out (of an amount, etc): *the ~ of the amount of metal in a specimen of ore.* **3** ~ *(to do sth)*, firmness of purpose; resolution: *his ~ to learn English; to carry out a plan with ~; with an air of ~*, with a purposeful look.

de·ter·mi·nat·ive /dɪ'tɜːmɪnətɪv US: -neɪtɪv/ *n*, *adj* (thing) having the power to direct, determine, limit; (gram) determiner.

de·ter·mine /dɪ'tɜːmɪn/ *vt*, *vi* **1** [VP6A,10] decide; fix precisely: *to ~ the meaning of a word; to ~ a date for a meeting.* **2** [VP6A] calculate; find out precisely: *to ~ the speed of light/the height of a mountain by trigonometry.* **3** [VP6A,7A,9,8,10,3A] ~ *to do sth;* ~ *on/upon sth,* decide firmly, resolve, make up one's mind: *He ~d to learn Greek. We ~d to start early/~d on an early start. He has ~d on proving/~d to prove his friend's innocence. Have they ~d where the new school will be built? He has ~d that nothing shall/will prevent him. His future has not yet been ~d, but he may study medicine.* **4** [VP17,14] ~ *sb to do sth/against sth,* cause to decide: *What ~d you to accept the offer? The news ~d him against further delay.* **5** [VP6A] be the fact that ~s: *The size of your feet ~s the size of your shoes. Do heredity and environment ~ a man's character?* **de·ter·min·able** /-əbl/ *adj* that can be ~d.

de·ter·miner /dɪ'tɜːmɪnə(r)/ [C] (gram) word that determines or limits the noun that follows.

de·ter·rent ⇨ deter.

de·test /dɪ'test/ *vt* [VP6A,C] hate strongly: *to ~ dogs; to ~ having to get up early.* ~·**able** *adj* hateful; deserving to be hated. ~·**ably** /-əblɪ/ *adv* **de·tes·ta·tion** /,diː'te'steɪʃn/ *n* [U] strong hatred; [C] sth that is strongly hated.

de·throne /,diː'θrəʊn/ *vt* [VP6A] remove (a ruler) from the throne, or (fig, a person) from a position of authority or influence. ~·**ment** *n*

det·on·ate /'detəneɪt/ *vt*, *vi* [VP6A,2A] (cause to) explode with a loud noise. **det·on·ator** /'detəneɪtə(r)/ *n* part of a bomb or shell that explodes first, causing the substance in the bomb, etc to explode. **det·on·ation** /,detə'neɪʃn/ *n* explosion; noise of an explosion.

de·tour /'diːtʊə(r) US: dɪ'tʊər/ *n* roundabout way, eg a way used when the main road is blocked; diversion: *to make a ~.* □ *vt* [VP6A] make a ~.

de·tract /dɪ'trækt/ *vi* [VP3A] ~ *from*, take away (from the credit, value, etc, of): *to ~ from sb's merit,* make it less. **de·trac·tor** /-tə(r)/ *n* person who ~s; person who tries to make sb's reputation, etc, smaller. **de·trac·tion** /dɪ'trækʃn/ *n* ~ing; disparagement.

de·train /,diː'treɪn/ *vt*, *vi* [VP6A,2A] (of troops, etc)

(cause to) get out of a train.

de·tribal·ize /,diː'traɪbəlaɪz/ *vt* [VP6A] render (a person) no longer a member of a tribe; destroy the tribal customs of. **de·tribal·iz·ation** /,diː:,traɪbəlaɪ'zeɪʃn US: -lɪ'z-/ *n*

det·ri·ment /'detrɪmənt/ *n* [U] damage; harm: *I know nothing to his ~,* nothing against him. **to the ~ of,** harming: *He works long hours to the ~ of his health.* **det·ri·men·tal** /,detrɪ'mentl/ *adj* ~ *(to),* harmful: *activities that would be ~al to our interests.* **det·ri·men·tally** /-təlɪ/ *adv*

de·tri·tus /dɪ'traɪtəs/ *n* [U] matter, eg sand, silt, gravel, produced by wearing away (from rock, etc).

de trop /də 'trəʊ/ *pred adj* (F) in the way; not wanted; unwelcome.

deuce[1] /djuːs US: duːs/ *n* **1** the two on playing-cards or dice. **2** (tennis) the score of 40 all, or five games each, after which either side must gain two successive points (or games) to win the match (or set).

deuce[2] /djuːs US: duːs/ *n* (**the**) ~, (dated colloq, in exclamations of annoyance) the devil; bad luck. **deuced** /'djuːst US: 'duːst/ *adj* very great. **deuced·ly** /'djuːsɪdlɪ US: 'duː-/ *adv* very.

de·value /,diː'væljuː/ (US also **de·val·u·ate** /,diː'væljʊeɪt/) *vt* [VP6A] make (the value of a currency) less (esp in terms of gold): *to ~ the dollar/pound.* **de·valu·ation** /,diː:,vælju'eɪʃn/ *n* [U,C] (of currency) change to a new, lower fixed value.

dev·as·tate /'devəsteɪt/ *vt* [VP6A] ruin; make desolate: *towns ~d by fire/floods/war.* **dev·as·ta·tion** /,devə'steɪʃn/ *n* devastating or being ~d.

de·vel·op /dɪ'veləp/ *vt*, *vi* **1** [VP6A,2A,3A] ~ *(from) (into),* (cause to) grow larger, fuller or more mature, organized; (cause to) unfold: *Plants ~ from seeds. A chicken ~s in the egg. We must ~ the natural resources of our country,* make the minerals, forests, etc available for use. *The plot of the new novel gradually ~ed in the author's mind.* ~**ing 'country,** one which is advancing to a higher (economic) state. **2** [VP6A,2A,C] (of sth not at first active or visible) come or bring into a state in which it is active or visible: *Symptoms of malaria ~ed,* appeared. *He ~ed a cough.* **3** [VP6A,2A] (photo) treat (an exposed film or plate) with chemicals so that the picture can be seen. **4** use (an area of land) for the building of houses (or shops, factories, etc) and so increase its value. ~**er** *n* person who, authority which, ~s land, etc; substance used to ~ films and plates.

de·vel·op·ment /dɪ'veləpmənt/ *n* **1** [U] developing or being developed (all senses): *He is engaged in the ~ of his business. Which is more important, moral ~ or physical ~? The ~ of photographic films requires a dark-room. This land is ripe for ~,* for being developed(4). '~ **area,** one to which new industries are directed as a means of increasing employment. **2** [C] new stage which is the result of developing: *the latest ~s in foreign affairs. We must await further ~s.*

de·vi·ant /'diːvɪənt/ *n*, *adv* (person who is) different in moral and social standards from what is normal or customary.

de·vi·ate /'diːvɪeɪt/ *vi* [VP3A] ~ *from*, turn away, leave (what is usual, customary, right, etc): *to ~ from the truth/a rule/one's custom.*

de·vi·ation /,diːvɪ'eɪʃn/ *n* [U] ~ *(from)*, turning aside or away; difference: ~ *from the rules;* [C] instance or amount or degree of this: *slight ~s of the* *magnetic needle*, in a compass; ∼*s from the rules of syntax*. ∼·**ist** *n* person who deviates, esp from the principles of a social or political system. ∼·**ism** /-ɪzəm/ *n*

de·vice /dɪ'vaɪs/ *n* [C] **1** plan; scheme; trick: *a* ∼ *to put the police off the scent*. *leave sb to his own* ∼*s*, let him do as he wishes, without help or advice. **2** sth thought out, invented or adapted, for a special purpose: *a* ∼ *for catching flies; a nuclear* ∼, eg an atomic or hydrogen bomb. **3** sign, symbol or figure used in a decoration, eg a crest on a shield.

devil[1] /'devl/ *n* **1** the spirit of evil; wicked spirit; cruel or mischievous person. *between the* ∼ *and the deep (blue) sea*, in a dilemma. *give the* ∼ *his due*, be just, even to one who does not deserve much or who is unfriendly. *go to the* ∼*!* go away! *play the* ∼ *with*, harm, ruin. *the* **D**∼, the supreme spirit of evil, Satan. ∼*'s advocate*, sb who points out the faults of sb or sth so that there can be a full discussion. **2** (usu *poor* ∼) wretched or unfortunate person. *printer's* ∼, (old use) errandboy in a printing-office. **3** (colloq) used to give emphasis: *what/who/why/ where the* ∼...? *He has the* ∼ *of a time*, ie according to context, a difficult, exciting, amusing, etc time. *He was working/ running like the* ∼, very hard. *There will be the* ∼ *to pay*, trouble to be faced (as the result of sth done or said). ∼·*may*-'*care adj* reckless.

devil[2] /'devl/ *vt, vi* (-ll-, US -l-) **1** [VP6A] grill with hot condiments: ∼*led kidneys/ham*. **2** [VP2A, 3A] ∼ *for*, work (for a barrister).

devil·ish /'devəlɪʃ/ *adj* wicked; cruel: *a* ∼ *plot*. □ *adv* (colloq) very: ∼ *hot*.

devil·ment /'devlmənt/, **dev·ilry** /'devlrɪ/ *nn* **1** [C] mischief: *She's up to some* ∼ *or other*. **2** [U] high spirits: *full of* ∼.

de·vi·ous /'diːvɪəs/ *adj* winding; roundabout; not straightforward: *to take a* ∼ *route to avoid busy streets; to get rich by* ∼ (= cunning, underhand) *ways*. ∼·*ly adv* ∼·*ness n*

de·vise /dɪ'vaɪz/ *vt* **1** [VP6A,8] think out; plan: *to* ∼ *a scheme for making money; to* ∼ *how to do sth*. ⇨ device. **2** [VP14] ∼ *to*, (legal) leave (property) by will.

de·vital·ize /ˌdiː'vaɪtəlaɪz/ *vt* [VP6A] take away strength and vigour from. **de·vital·iz·ation** /ˌdiːˌvaɪtəlar'zeɪʃn US: -lɪ'z-/ *n*

de·void /dɪ'vɔɪd/ *adj* ∼ *of*, without; empty of: ∼ *of shame/sense*.

de·vo·lu·tion /ˌdiːvə'luːʃn US: ˌdev-/ *n* [U] deputing or delegating (of power or authority); decentralization.

de·volve /dɪ'vɒlv/ *vi, vt* **1** [VP3A] ∼ *on/upon*, (of work, duties) be transferred or passed to: *When the President is ill, his duties* ∼ *upon the Vice-President*. **2** [VP6A,14] ∼ *(to/upon)*, pass, transfer (work, duties, to sb).

de·vote /dɪ'vəʊt/ *vt* [VP14] ∼ *oneself/sth to*, give up (oneself, one's time, energy, etc) to: *to* ∼ *oneself to the cure of cancer/one's spare time to sport*. **de·vot·ed** *adj* very loving or loyal: *a* ∼*d friend. She is* ∼*d to her children*. **de·vot·ed·ly** *adv*

devo·tee /ˌdevə'tiː/ *n* ∼ *(of)*, person who is devoted to sth: *a* ∼ *of sport/music;* zealous supporter (of a sect, etc). ⇨ votary.

de·vo·tion /dɪ'vəʊʃn/ *n* **1** [U] ∼ *(for)*, deep, strong love: *the* ∼ *of a mother for her children*. **2** [U] ∼ *(to)*, devoting or being devoted: ∼ *to duty; a teacher's* ∼ *to the cause of education*. **3** (*pl*) pray-

ers: *The priest was at his* ∼*s*. ∼·*al* /-'vəʊʃənl/ *adj* of ∼; used in ∼*s*(3): ∼*al literature*, for use in worship.

de·vour /dɪ'vaʊə(r)/ *vt* [VP6A] **1** eat hungrily or greedily: *The hungry boy* ∼*ed his dinner*. (fig) *She* ∼*ed the new detective story. The fire* ∼*ed twenty square miles of forest*. **2** *be* ∼*ed by* (curiosity, anxiety, etc), be filled with, have all one's attention taken up by.

de·vout /dɪ'vaʊt/ *adj* **1** paying serious attention to religious duties: *a* ∼ *old lady*. **2** (of prayers, wishes, etc) deepfelt; sincere: *a* ∼ *supporter;* ∼ *wishes for your success*. ∼·*ly adv* eagerly; sincerely. ∼·*ness n*

dew /djuː US: duː/ *n* [U] tiny drops of moisture condensed on cool surfaces between evening and morning from water vapour in the air: *The grass was wet with dew*. '**dew drop** *n* small drop of dew. **dewy** *adj* wet with dew.

dew·lap /'djuːlæp US: 'duː-/ *n* fold of loose skin hanging down from the neck of an animal such as a cow or ox.

dex·ter·ity /dek'sterətɪ/ *n* [U] skill, esp in handling things.

dex·ter·ous, dex·trous /'dekstrəs/ *adj* clever, skilful with the hands. ∼·*ly adv*

dex·trose /'dekstrəʊz US: -əʊs/ *n* [U] form of glucose.

dho·ti /'dəʊtɪ/ *n* loin-cloth as customarily worn by male Hindus.

dhow /daʊ/ *n* single-masted ship, esp as used by Arab sailors for coastal voyages.

dia·betes /ˌdaɪə'biːtiːz/ *n* [U] disease of the pancreas in which sugar and starchy foods cannot be properly absorbed.

dia·betic /ˌdaɪə'betɪk/ *adj* of diabetes. □ *n* person suffering from diabetes.

dia·bolic /ˌdaɪə'bɒlɪk/ *adj* of or like a devil; very cruel or wicked. ∼*al* /-kl/ *adj* **dia·boli·cally** /-klɪ/ *adv*

dia·critic /ˌdaɪə'krɪtɪk/ *adj, n* (of a) mark (eg ´ ` ^ ¨), used in writing and printing to indicate different sounds of a letter. ∼*al* /-kl/ *adj* = ∼.

dia·dem /'daɪədem/ *n* crown, worn as a sign of royal power; wreath of flowers or leaves worn round the head.

di·aer·esis, di·er·esis /daɪ'erəsɪs/ *n* (*pl* -eses /-əsiːz/) mark (as in *naïve*) placed over a vowel to show that it is sounded separately from a preceding vowel.

di·ag·nose /'daɪəgnəʊz US: -əʊs/ *vt* [VP6A,16B] determine the nature of (esp a disease) from observation of symptoms: *The doctor* ∼*d the illness as diphtheria*.

di·ag·nosis /ˌdaɪəg'nəʊsɪs/ *n* (*pl* -noses /-'nəʊsiːz/) [U] diagnosing; [C] (statement of the) result of this.

di·ag·nos·tic /ˌdaɪəg'nɒstɪk/ *adj* of diagnosis: *symptoms that were of little* ∼ *value*, that were not very useful in determining the disease.

di·ag·onal /daɪ'ægənl/ *n, adj* (straight line) going across a straight-sided figure, eg an oblong, from corner to corner; slanting; crossed by slanting lines. ⇨ the illus at **quadrilateral**. ∼·*ly* /-nəlɪ/ *adv*

dia·gram /'daɪəgræm/ *n* drawing, design or plan to explain or illustrate something: *a* ∼ *of a gear-box*. ∼·**matic** /ˌdaɪəgrə'mætɪk/, ∼·**mati·cal** /-kl/ *adjj* ∼**mati·cally** /-klɪ/ *adv*

dial /'daɪəl/ *n* **1** face (of a clock or watch). **2** marked face or flat plate with a pointer for measuring (weight, volume, pressure, consumption of gas, etc). **3** plate, disc, etc on a radio set with names or numbers, showing wavelengths of broadcasting stations. **4** part of an automatic telephone, with numbers and/or letters, used to make a connection. □ *vt* (-ll-; US -l-) [VP6A] call by means of a telephone ∼: *to* ∼ *01—230 1212*. '∼**ling code**, code of numbers for a telephone exchange to be ∼led before the number of the person to whom the call is to be made: *The ∼ling code for the London area is 01*. '∼**ling tone**, the sound showing that one may proceed to ∼ the number wanted.

A TELEPHONE DIAL

dials

A CLOCK DIAL

dia·lect /'daɪəlekt/ *n* [C,U] form of a language (grammar, vocabulary and pronunciation) used in a part of a country or by a class of people: *the Yorkshire* ∼; *a play written in* ∼; *(attrib)* ∼ *words/ pronunciations*. ∼**al** /ˌdaɪə'lektl/ *adj* of a ∼ or ∼s: ∼*al differences between two counties.*
dia·lec·tic /ˌdaɪə'lektɪk/ *n* (also *pl* with *sing v*) critical analysis of mental processes; art of logical disputation. **dia·lec·ti·cal** /-kl/ *adj* of ∼: *the ∼al conflict* (= the logical dispute) *between innovators and conservatives*. **∼al ma'terialism**, theory developed principally by Marx combining traditional *materialism*(1) with a critical analysis of *development* by the conflict between an original direction, its direct opposite and their unification. ⇨ Marxist. **dia·lec·tician** /ˌdaɪəlek'tɪʃn/ *n* person skilled in ∼.
dia·logue (US also **dia·log**) /'daɪəlɒg US: -lɔːg/ *n* **1** [U] (writing in the form of a) conversation or talk: *Plays are written in* ∼. *There is some good descriptive writing in the novel, but the* ∼ *is poor*. **2** [C] exchange of views (between leaders, etc): *a* ∼ *between the two Prime Ministers*. **3** [C] talk: *long* ∼*s between two comedians*.
di·am·eter /daɪ'æmɪtə(r)/ *n* measurement acr^ ss any geometrical figure or body; (length of a) straight line drawn from side to side through the centre, esp of a circular, spherical or cylindrical form: *the* ∼ *of a tree-trunk; a lens that magnifies 20* ∼*s*, that makes an object look 20 times longer, wider, etc than it is, ⇨ the illus at circle.
dia·metri·cally /ˌdaɪə'metrɪklɪ/ *adv* completely; entirely: ∼ *opposed views.*
dia·mond /'daɪəmənd/ *n* **1** brilliant precious stone of pure carbon in crystallized form, the hardest substance known: *a ring with a* ∼ *in it*; (attrib) *a* ∼ *ring/necklace*. ⇨ the illus at crystal. ∼ **wedding** *n* sixtieth anniversary of a wedding. **rough** ∼, person with rough manners but a kind heart. **2** piece of this substance (often artificially made) as used in industry, or as a stylus for playing gramophone records. **3** figure with four equal sides whose angles are not right angles; this shape (as printed in red on playing-cards): *the ten of* ∼*s*. ⇨ the illus at card. **4** (baseball) the space inside the lines that connect the bases. ⇨ the illus at baseball.

dia·per /'daɪəpə(r)/ *n* **1** (linen fabric with) geometric pattern of lines crossing to make diamond shapes which are shown up by reflection of light. **2** (US) napkin(2) for a baby.
di·apha·nous /daɪ'æfənəs/ *adj* (of material for veils, dresses, etc) transparent; translucent.
dia·phragm /'daɪəfræm/ *n* **1** internal wall of muscle between the chest and the abdomen. ⇨ the illus at respiratory. **2** arrangement of thin plates that control the inlet of light, eg through a camera lens. **3** vibrating disc or cone in some instruments, eg a telephone receiver, a loudspeaker, producing sound-waves.
di·ar·chy /'daɪɑːkɪ/ *n* (*pl* -chies) government shared by two joint authorities or rulers.
di·ar·rhoea (also **di·ar·rhea**) /ˌdaɪə'rɪə/ *n* [U] too frequent and too watery emptying of the bowels.
diary /'daɪərɪ/ *n* (*pl* -ries) (book for) daily record of events, thoughts, etc: *keep a* ∼. **dia·rist** /'daɪərɪst/ *n* person who keeps a diary.
Di·as·pora /daɪ'æspərə/ *n* **the D∼**, the dispersion of the Jews among the Gentiles after their period of exile (538 BC): *People from every country of the* ∼ *now live in Israel.*
dia·tonic /ˌdaɪə'tɒnɪk/ *adj* (mus) of a key [1](9). ∼ **scale** *n* = key [1](9).
dia·tribe /'daɪətraɪb/ *n* [C] ∼ **(against)**, bitter and violent attack in words.
dibble /'dɪbl/ *n* (also **dib·ber** /'dɪbə(r)/) short wooden tool with a pointed end for making holes in the ground (for tubers, young plants, etc). □ *vt* [VP15B] put (plants, etc, in) with a ∼.
dice /daɪs/ *n pl* (*sing* (formal) **die** or (colloq) **dice**) small cubes of wood, bone, etc marked with 1—6 spots, used in games of chance: *to play* ∼. **The die is cast**, (prov) One's course is determined and cannot now be changed. (Note: except in this prov, *die* is rarely used. 'One of the dice' is preferred to 'a die'.) '∼**-box** *n* deep, narrow box in which ∼ are shaken and from which they are thrown. □ *vi,vt* **1** [VP2A] play ∼. ∼ **with death**, (colloq) act dangerously and at the risk of death. **2** [VP6A] cut (food, eg carrots) into small cubes like ∼.
dicey /'daɪsɪ/ *adj*(colloq) risky; uncertain.
di·chot·omy /daɪ'kɒtəmɪ/ *n* (*pl* -mies) division into two (usu contradictory classes or mutually exclusive pairs): *the* ∼ *of truth and falsehood.*
dick·ens /'dɪkɪnz/ *n* (colloq) used like devil and deuce: *'Who/What/Where the* ∼...?'
dicker /'dɪkə(r)/ *vi* (colloq) [VP2A,3A] bargain or haggle (*with* sb, *for* sth).
dicky[1], **dickey** /'dɪkɪ/ *n* (colloq) **1** (also '∼**-seat**) small, extra folding seat at the back of a two-seater motor-car. **2** false shirt-front. **3** '∼**-bird**, child's word for a bird.
dicky[2] /'dɪkɪ/ *adj* (sl) unsound; weak: *a* ∼ *heart;* liable to break or fall.
Dic·ta·phone /'dɪktəfəʊn/ *n* (P) office machine that records words spoken into it and then reproduces them (for transcription, etc).
dic·tate /dɪk'teɪt US: 'dɪkteɪt/ *vt,vi* **1** [VP6A,2A,14] ∼ **(to)**, say or read aloud (words to be written down by another or others): *to* ∼ *a letter to a secretary. The teacher* ∼*d a passage to the class*. **2** [VP6A,14] ∼ **(to)**, state with the force of authority: *to* ∼ *terms to a defeated enemy*. **3** [VP3A] ∼ **to**, order: *I won't be* ∼*d to*, I refuse to accept orders from you. □ *n* /'dɪkteɪt/ (usu *pl*) direction or order (esp given by reason, conscience, etc): *the* ∼*s of common sense. Follow the* ∼*s of your conscience,*

Do what your conscience tells you to do.

dic·ta·tion /dɪk'teɪʃn/ n 1 [U] dictating; being dictated to: *The pupils wrote at their teacher's ~*. 2 [C] passage, etc that is dictated.

dic·ta·tor /dɪk'teɪtə(r) US: 'dɪkteɪtər/ n ruler who has absolute authority, esp one who has obtained such power by force or in an irregular way. **~·ship** /-ʃɪp/ n [C,U] (country with) government by a ~. **dic·ta·torial** /ˌdɪktə'tɔːrɪəl/ adj of or like a ~: **~ial** government; overbearing; fond of giving orders: *his ~ial manner*. **dic·ta·tori·ally** /-əlɪ/ adv

dic·tion /'dɪkʃn/ n [U] choice and use of words; style or manner of speaking and writing.

dic·tion·ary /'dɪkʃənrɪ US: -nerɪ/ n (pl -ries) book listing and explaining the words of a language, or the words or topics of a special subject, eg the Bible, architecture, and arranged in ABC order.

dic·tum /'dɪktəm/ n (pl ~s, -ta /-tə/) formal expression of opinion; saying.

did /dɪd/ ⇨ do.

di·dac·tic /dɪ'dæktɪk US: daɪ-/ adj 1 intended to teach: ~ poetry. 2 having the manner of a teacher: *A teacher should not be ~ outside the classroom*. **di·dac·ti·cally** /-klɪ/ adv

diddle /'dɪdl/ vt [VP6A,14] ~ sb (out of sth), (colloq) cheat.

die¹ /daɪ/ n 1 (pl dice) ⇨ dice. 2 (pl dies /daɪz/) block of hard metal with a design, etc cut in it, used for shaping coins, type¹(3), medals, etc or stamping paper, leather, etc so that designs stand out from the surface. **'die-cast** adj made by casting metal in a mould: *die-cast toys*, eg small models of cars.

dice   printer's dies

die² /daɪ/ vi (pt,pp died, pres part dying) 1 [VP2A,C,D] come to the end of life; cease to live: *Flowers soon die if they are left without water*. (Note the preps): *to die of an illness/a disease/hunger/grief; to die by violence; to die by one's own hand*, ie commit suicide; *to die from a wound; to die for one's country; to die through neglect; to die in battle; to die happy/poor; to die a beggar/a martyr*. 2 (various phrases) **die in one's bed**, of old age or illness. **die with one's boots on**, while still vigorous, while fighting. **die in the last ditch**, fighting desperately to defend sth. **die game**, facing death bravely. **die hard**, only after a struggle. ⇨ 5 below. **die in harness**, while still at one's usual occupation, still working. 3 [VP3A,4C] **be dying for sth/to do sth**, have a strong wish: *We're all dying for a drink. She's dying to know where you've been*. 4 [VP2A,C] pass from human knowledge; be lost: *His fame will never die. His secret died with him*, He died without telling it to anyone. 5 **'die-hard**, (often attrib) person who obstinately resists being compelled to do anything; politician who obstinately opposes new policies and fights hard in defence of old policies. 6 [VP2C]

(with various *adverbial particles*):

die away, lose strength, become faint or weak: *The breeze died away. The noise died away*.

die back, (of plants) die down to the roots, which remain alive and send up shoots the next growing season: *The dahlias died back when the frosts came*.

die down, (of a fire in a fireplace, etc) burn with less heat; (of excitement, etc) become less violent; (of noise, etc) become less loud.

die off, die one by one: *The leaves of this plant are dying off*.

die out, become extinct; come to a complete end: *With the death of the fifth earl, this old family had died out. Many old customs are gradually dying out*.

di·er·esis /daɪ'erəsɪs/ ⇨ diaeresis.

die·sel /'diːzl/ n (attrib) **~-electric locomotive**, one that generates its own electric current from a ~ engine. **'~ engine**, oil-burning engine (as used for buses, locomotives) in which ignition is produced by the heat of suddenly compressed gas. **'~ oil**, heavy fuel oil.

diet¹ /'daɪət/ n [C] 1 sort of food usually eaten (by a person, community, etc): *the Japanese ~ of rice, vegetables and fish. Too rich a ~* (= Too much rich food) *is not good for you*. 2 sort of food to which a person is limited, eg for medical reasons: *The doctor put her on a ~. No potatoes for me—I'm on a ~*. □ vt,vi [VP6A,2A] restrict (oneself, sb), be restricted, to a ~(2): *She became so fat that she had to ~ herself. My doctor is ~ing me very strictly. Is he still ~ing?* **die·tary** /'daɪətərɪ US: -terɪ/ adj of ~: ~ary rules; ~ary taboos, eg pork for Muslims. **die·tet·ics** /ˌdaɪə'tetɪks/ n (sing v) science of ~. **die·tician, die·titian** /ˌdaɪə'tɪʃn/ n expert in dietetics.

diet² /'daɪət/ n series of meetings for discussion of national, international or church affairs.

dif·fer /'dɪfə(r)/ vi [VP2A,C,3A] 1 ~ (from), be unlike; be distinguishable: *The two brothers are like each other in appearance, but ~ widely in their tastes. French ~s from English in having gender for all nouns. Tastes ~*, Different people have different interests. 2 ~ from sb (about/on sth), disagree; have another opinion: *I'm sorry to ~ from you about/on that question*. **agree to ~**, give up the attempt to convince each other.

dif·fer·ence /'dɪfrəns/ n [C,U] 1 ~ (between) 1 the state of being unlike: *the ~ between summer and winter*. 2 amount, degree, manner, in which things are unlike: *The ~ between 7 and 18 is 11. What a great ~ there is in the temperature today! There are many ~s between the two languages*. **split the ~**, ⇨ split. 3 **make a/some/no/any/not much/a great deal of ~**, be of some/no, etc importance: *It won't make much ~ whether you go today or tomorrow. Does that make any ~*, Is it important, need we consider it? **make a ~ between**, treat differently. 4 disagreement: *Why can't you settle your ~s and be friends again?*

dif·fer·ent /'dɪfrənt/ adj 1 not the same: *They are ~ people with the same name. The two boys are ~ in their tastes. She is wearing a ~ dress every time I see her*. **~ from/to/(US)than**, *Your method is ~ from/to mine*. (Note: ~ **than** may be used when ~ is not immediately followed by its prep: *How ~ life today is than what it was fifty years ago*. Cf *life today is ~ from life fifty years ago*, where ~ is followed immediately by *from*.) 2 separate; distinct: *I*

called three ~ times, but he was out. They are sold in ~ colours, a variety of colours. ~·ly adv
dif·fer·en·tial /ˌdɪfəˈrenʃl/ adj **1** of, showing, depending on, a difference: ~ tariffs, that differ according to circumstances. ⇨ **calculus. ~ (gear),** arrangement of gears (in a motor-car, etc) that allows the rear wheels to turn at different speeds on curves. □ n **(wage)** ~, difference (expressed in a percentage) in wages between skilled and unskilled workers in the same industry: They opposed a flat increase for all workers because that would upset the wage ~.
dif·fer·en·ti·ate /ˌdɪfəˈrenʃɪeɪt/ vt **1** [VP6A,14] ~ **(from),** see as different; show to be different: to ~ varieties of plants; to ~ one variety from another. The report does not ~ the two aspects of the problem. One aspect is not ~ed from the other. **2** [VP3A] ~ **between,** treat as different: It is wrong to ~ between pupils according to their family background. **dif·fer·en·ti·ation** /ˌdɪfərenʃɪˈeɪʃn/ n
dif·fi·cult /ˈdɪfɪkəlt/ adj **1** not easy; requiring effort, strength, skill or ability: a ~ problem/language. He finds it ~ to stop smoking. The sound is ~ to pronounce. It is a ~ sound to pronounce. The place is ~ to reach/~ of access. He was placed in ~ circumstances. **2** (of persons) not easily pleased or satisfied; easily offended: He's a ~ man to get on with. The famous actress was being rather ~, was causing trouble, eg to the other members of the cast, the producer. Please don't be so ~.
dif·fi·culty /ˈdɪfɪkəltɪ/ n **1** [U] the state or quality of being difficult: Do you have any ~ in understanding spoken English? There was some ~ in getting everybody here in time. He did the work without ~/without any/much ~. He did it, but with ~. **2** [C] (pl -ties) sth difficult, hard to do or understand: the difficulties of Greek syntax; to be working under difficulties, in difficult circumstances; to be in financial difficulties, short of money, in debt, etc. If you knew the difficulties I am in! Mary's father raised/made difficulties when she said she wanted to marry a poor school-teacher, He objected to, opposed, the proposal.
dif·fi·dent /ˈdɪfɪdənt/ adj not having, not showing, much belief in one's own abilities; lacking in self-confidence: to be ~ about doing sth; to speak in a ~ manner. ~·ly adv **dif·fi·dence** /-dəns/ n [U] being ~; shyness.
dif·fract /dɪˈfrækt/ vt [VP6A] break up (a beam of light) into a series of dark and light bands or the coloured bands of the spectrum. ⇨ the illus at spectrum. **dif·frac·tion** /dɪˈfrækʃn/ n
dif·fuse[1] /dɪˈfjuːz/ vt,vi **1** [VP6A] send out, spread, in every direction: to ~ learning/knowledge/good humour/light/heat/a scent/an odour; ~d lighting, contrasted with direct lighting. **2** [VP6A,2A] (of gases and liquids) (cause to) mix slowly. **dif·fu·sion** /dɪˈfjuːʒn/ n [U] diffusing or being ~d: the diffusion of knowledge through books and lectures; the diffusion of gases and liquids, their mixing without external force.
dif·fuse[2] /dɪˈfjuːs/ adj **1** using too many words: a ~ writer/style. **2** spread out; scattered: ~ light. ~·ly adv ~·ness n
dig[1] /dɪg/ vt,vi (pt,pp dug /dʌg/) (-gg-) **1** [VP6A,15B,2C] use a tool (eg a spade), a machine, claws, etc to break up and move earth, etc; make a way (through, into, etc) by doing this; make (a hole, etc) by doing this; get (sth) by doing this: It is difficult to dig the ground when it is frozen hard.

They are digging through the hill to make a tunnel/digging a tunnel through the hill. He dug a deep hole. The soldiers were digging trenches. **2** [VP6A] (sl) enjoy; appreciate; understand; follow: I don't dig modern jazz. **3** [VP15B,3A,2C] (uses with adverbial particles and preps):
dig in; dig into sth, serve oneself with food, begin eating, with appetite: dig into a pie. The food's here, so dig in! **dig sth in,** mix with the soil by digging: The manure should be well dug in. **dig sth in; dig sth into sth,** push, thrust, poke: to dig a fork into a pie/a potato. The rider dug his spurs into the horse's flank/dug his spurs in. **dig oneself in,** (a) protect oneself by digging a trench, etc. (b) (fig, colloq) establish oneself securely (in a position, etc). **dig sb in the ribs,** poke one's elbow in his ribs, eg to call attention to sth funny.
dig sb/sth out (of sth), (a) get out by digging: They dug out the fox/dug the fox out of its hole. He was buried by the avalanche and had to be dug out. (b) get by searching: to dig information out of books and reports; to dig out the truth.
dig sth up, (a) break up (land) by digging: to dig up land for a new garden. (b) remove from the ground by digging: We dug the tree up by the roots. (c) bring to light (what has been buried or hidden) by digging: An old Greek statue was dug up here last month. (d) (fig): The newspapers love to dig up scandals.
dig[2] /dɪg/ n **1** push or thrust: give sb a dig in the ribs. That was a dig at me, a remark directed against me. **2** site being excavated by archaeologists. **3** (pl) (GB, colloq) lodgings: Are you living at home or in digs?
di·gest[1] /ˈdaɪdʒest/ n [C] short, condensed account; summary: a ~ of the week's news.
di·gest[2] /dɪˈdʒest/ vt,vi [VP6A,2A] **1** (of food) change, be changed, in the stomach and bowels, so that it can be used in the body: Some foods ~/are ~ed more easily than others. **2** take into the mind; make part of one's knowledge; reduce (a mass of facts, etc) to order: Have you ~ed everything that is important in the book? ~·ible /dɪˈdʒestəbl/ adj that can be ~ed. ~·i·bil·ity /dɪˌdʒestəˈbɪlɪtɪ/ n
di·ges·tion /dɪˈdʒestʃən/ n [U] digesting: food that is easy/difficult of ~; [C] power of digesting food: to have a poor/good ~.
di·ges·tive /dɪˈdʒestɪv/ adj of digestion (of food): suffer from ~ trouble. **the '~ system,** the alimentary canal.
dig·ger /ˈdɪgə(r)/ n **1** (usu in compounds) person who digs: 'gold-~, one who tries to find gold in a gold-field. **2** mechanical excavator. **3** (sl) Australian.
dig·ging /ˈdɪgɪŋ/ n [U] action of digging; [C] (often pl) place where men dig or search for metal, esp gold.
digit /ˈdɪdʒɪt/ n **1** any one of the ten Arabic numerals 0 to 9: The number 57306 contains five ~s. **2** finger or toe. **digi·tal** /ˈdɪdʒɪtl/ adj of ~s. ~**al clock/watch,** one without hands, showing the time by ~s (eg 07.45) only. ~**al computer,** one showing its calculations by ~s (binary or decimal).
dig·nify /ˈdɪgnɪfaɪ/ vt [VP6A,14] ~ **(with),** cause to appear worthy or honourable; give dignity to: to ~ a small collection of books by calling it a library/~ it with the name library. **dig·ni·fied** part adj having or showing dignity: a dignified old lady.
dig·ni·tary /ˈdɪgnɪtərɪ US: -terɪ/ n (pl -ries) person holding a high office.

dig·nity /'dɪgnətɪ/ n 1 [U] true worth; the quality that earns or deserves respect: the ~ of labour. A man's ~ depends not upon his wealth or rank but upon his character. 2 [U] calm and serious manner or style: If you're afraid of losing your ~ (eg of being made to look foolish), you can't expect to learn to speak a foreign language. **beneath one's ~**, below one's moral, social, etc standards: It is beneath your ~ to answer such a rude remark. **stand on/upon one's ~**, insist upon being treated with proper respect; refuse to do what one considers to be below one's moral, social, etc standards. 3 [C] (pl -ties) high or honourable rank, post or title: The Queen conferred the ~ of a peerage on him.

di·graph /'daɪgrɑːf US: -græf/ n two letters that represent a single sound (eg sh /ʃ/, ea /iː/ in sheaf).

di·gress /daɪ'gres/ vi [VP2A,3A] ~ (from), (esp in speaking or writing) turn or wander away (from the main subject). **di·gression** /daɪ'greʃn/ n [U] ~ing; [C] instance of this.

digs /dɪgz/ n pl (GB, colloq) lodgings.

dike, dyke /daɪk/ n 1 ditch (for carrying away water from land). 2 long wall of earth, etc (to keep back water and prevent flooding). 3 ⚠ (derog sl) (masculine) lesbian. □ vi,vt [VP2A,6A] make or provide with a ~ or ~s.

a dike

dil·api·dated /dɪ'læpɪdeɪtɪd/ adj (of buildings, furniture, etc) falling to pieces; in a state of disrepair: a ~-looking car; a ~ old house. **dil·api·da·tion** /dɪˌlæpɪ'deɪʃn/ n [U] being or becoming ~.

di·late /daɪ'leɪt/ vi,vt 1 [VP6A,2A] (cause to) become wider, larger, further open: The pupils of your eyes ~ when you enter a dark room. The horse ~d its nostrils. 2 [VP3A] ~ upon, (formal) speak or write comprehensively about: If there were time, I could ~ upon this subject. **di·la·tion** /daɪ'leɪʃn/ n [U] dilating or being ~d.

dila·tory /'dɪlətərɪ US: -tɔːrɪ/ adj slow in acting; causing delay.

di·lemma /dɪ'lemə/ n situation in which one has to choose between two things, two courses of action, etc both unfavourable or undesirable. **be in/place sb in a ~**: You place me in something of a ~.

dil·et·tante /ˌdɪlɪ'tæntɪ/ n (pl ~s /-tiːz/ or -ti /-tiː/) one who studies sth, but not seriously and not with real understanding.

dili·gence /'dɪlɪdʒəns/ n [U] ~ (in), 1 steady effort; showing care and effort (in what one does).

dili·gent /'dɪlɪdʒənt/ adj ~ (in), hard-working; showing care and effort (in what one does). **~·ly** adv

dill /dɪl/ n herb with spicy seeds, eg as used for flavouring pickles.

dilly-dally /'dɪlɪ dælɪ/ vi [VP2A] dawdle; waste time (by not making up one's mind).

di·lute /daɪ'ljuːt US: -'luːt/ vt [VP6A,14] ~ (with), make (a liquid or colour) weaker or thinner (by adding water or other liquid): to ~ wine with water; (fig) weaken the force of (by mixing): to ~ skilled labour, eg by employing a proportion of unskilled workers. □ adj (of acids, etc) weakened by diluting. **di·lu·tion** /daɪ'ljuːʃn US: -'luː-/ n [U] diluting or being ~d; [C] sth that is ~d.

dim /dɪm/ adj (-mmer, -mmest) 1 not bright; not clearly to be seen: the dim light of a candle; the dim outline of buildings on a dark night; dim memories/recollections of my childhood. 2 (of the eyes, eyesight) not able to see clearly: eyes dim with tears. His eyesight is getting dim. **take a dim view of**, (colloq) regard with disapproval or pessimism. 3 (colloq, of persons) lacking intelligence. □ vt,vi (-mm-) [VP6A,2A] make or become dim: The light of a candle is dimmed by sunlight. **dim·ly** adv in a dim manner: a dimly lit room. **dim·ness** n

dime /daɪm/ n coin of US and Canada worth ten cents.

di·men·sion /dɪ'menʃn/ n 1 [U,C] measurement of any sort (breadth, length, thickness, height, etc): What are the ~s of the room? 2 (pl) size; extent: a building of great ~s; the ~s of the problem. 3 (algebra) number of unknown quantities contained as factors in a product: x^3, x^2y and xyz are all of three ~s. **~·al** /-ʃənl/ adj having a (certain number of) ~s: two-/three-~al figures. **3D** /ˌθriː 'diː/ (abbr of three-~al) stereoscopic, giving the illusion of depth in perspective (as well as height and breadth).

dim·in·ish /dɪ'mɪnɪʃ/ vt,vi [VP6A,2A] make or become less: ~ing food supplies; a war that seriously ~ed the country's wealth; a currency that has ~ed in value.

dim·inu·endo /dɪˌmɪnjʊ'endəʊ/ n (pl ~s /-dəʊz/) [C] (music) gradual decrease in loudness: a sudden ~.

dim·in·ution /ˌdɪmɪ'njuːʃn US: -'nuːʃn/ n [U] diminishing or being diminished; [C] amount of this: to hope for a small ~ in taxes.

dim·inu·tive /dɪ'mɪnjʊtɪv/ adj 1 unusually or remarkably small. 2 (gram, of a suff) indicating smallness. □ n word formed by the use of a suff of this kind, eg streamlet, a small stream, lambkin, a small lamb.

dim·ity /'dɪmɪtɪ/ n [U] (kinds of) cotton cloth woven with raised strips or designs, used for bedroom hangings, etc.

dimple /'dɪmpl/ n small natural hollow in the chin or cheek (either permanent, or which appears eg when a person smiles); slight hollow on water (made eg by a breeze). □ vt,vi [VP6A,2A] make ~s on; form ~s.

din /dɪn/ n [U] (or **a din**) loud, confused noise that continues: The children were making so much din/such a din that I couldn't study. They made/kicked up such a din at the party. □ vi,vt (-nn-) 1 [VP2C] make a din: The cries of his tormentors were still dinning in his ears. 2 **din sth into sb**, tell him again and again, in a forcible manner.

dine /daɪn/ vi,vt 1 [VP2A] (formal) have dinner. **~ out**, dine outside one's home (eg at the house of friends, or at a restaurant). 2 [VP6A] give a dinner for: The great man was wined and ~d wherever he went, People gave dinner-parties for him. **'dining-car**, railway coach in which meals are served. **'dining-room**, room in which meals are eaten. **'dining-table**, table used for eating on.

diner /'daɪnə(r)/ n 1 person who dines. 2 dining-car

on a train. **3** (US) restaurant shaped like a ～(2).

ding-dong /ˌdɪŋ 'dɒŋ/ *n, adv* (with the) sound of bells striking repeatedly. **a ～ struggle/battle,** one in which each of two contestants has the advantage alternately.

din-ghy /'dɪŋgɪ/ *n* (*pl* **-ghies**) (kinds of) small open boat; inflatable rubber boat (eg carried by an aircraft for use if forced down on water).

dingle /'dɪŋgl/ *n* deep dell, usu with trees.

dingy /'dɪndʒɪ/ *adj* (**-ier, -iest**) dirty-looking; not fresh or cheerful: *a ～ manufacturing town; a ～ room in a ～ boarding-house.* **ding·ily** *adv* **dingi-ness** *n*

dining /'daɪnɪŋ/ ⇨ **dine.**

dinky /'dɪŋkɪ/ *adj* (**-ier, -iest**) (GB, colloq) pretty; neat: *What a ～ little hat!*

din-ner /'dɪnə(r)/ *n* main meal of the day, whether eaten at midday or in the evening (note the *preps* and the use and omission of the articles): *It's time for ～/～-time. Have you had* (US = *eaten*) *～ yet? They were at ～/having ～ when I called. He ate too much ～. The ～ was badly served. Shall we give a ～* (= *'～-party*) *for her? Four ～s at £5 a head. Shall we ask him to ～?* **'～-jacket,** black jacket worn by men in the evening for formal occasions. (Cf *dress coat,* with tails, and US *tuxedo.*) **'～-service, '～-set,** set of plates, dishes, etc for ～.

dino·saur /'daɪnəsɔː(r)/ *n* large extinct reptile

a dinosaur

dint /dɪnt/ *n* **1** [C] = **dent. 2 by ～ of,** by means of: *He succeeded by ～ of hard work.*

dio·cese /'daɪəsɪs/ *n* bishop's district. **di·ocesan** /daɪ'ɒsɪsn/ *adj, n* (of a) ～.

di·ox·ide /daɪ'ɒksaɪd/ *n* (chem) oxide formed by combination of two atoms of oxygen and one atom of a metal or other element: *carbon ～,* (CO_2).

dip¹ /dɪp/ *vt,vi* (**-pp-**) **1** [VP6A,14] *dip in/into,* put, lower, (sth) into a liquid: *to dip one's pen into the ink; to dip sheep,* immerse them in a liquid that disinfects them, kills vermin; *to dip candles,* make them by dipping wick into melted fat; *dip a garment,* put it in a liquid dye to change its colour. **'～-stick,** stick or rod (to be) dipped into a tank or other container to measure the depth of liquid in it (eg oil in the sump of an engine). **2** [VP3A] *dip into,* (fig): *to dip into one's purse,* spend money; *to dip into the future,* try to imagine what it will be like; *to dip into a book/an author, etc,* make a cursory study. **3** [VP2A,C] go below a surface or level: *The sun dipped below the horizon. The birds rose and dipped in their flight.* **4** [VP6A,2A] (cause to) go down and then up again: *to dip a flag,* as a salute, eg to another ship; *to dip the headlights of a car,* lower their beams (in order not to dazzle the driver of another car). *The land dips gently to the south.*

dip² /dɪp/ *n* **1** [C] act of dipping, esp (colloq) quick bathe or swim: *to have/take/go for a dip.* **2** [U] cleansing liquid in which sheep are dipped. **3** [C] downward slope: *a dip in the road; a dip among*

the hills. **4** [U] position of a flag when it is dipped(4): *at the dip.*

diph·theria /dɪf'θɪərɪə/ *n* [U] serious contagious disease of the throat causing difficulty in breathing.

diph·thong /'dɪfθɒŋ US: -θɔːŋ/ *n* union of two vowel sounds or (more usu *digraph*) vowel letters, eg the sounds /aɪ/ in *pipe* /paɪp/, the letters *ou* in *doubt.*

di·ploma /dɪ'pləʊmə/ *n* [C] educational certificate of proficiency: *a ～ in architecture.*

di·plo·macy /dɪ'pləʊməsɪ/ *n* [U] **1** management of a country's affairs by its agents abroad (ambassadors and ministers), and their direction by the Ministry of Foreign Affairs at home; skill in this. **2** art of, skill in, dealing with people so that business is done smoothly.

diplo·mat /'dɪpləmæt/ *n* **1** person engaged in diplomacy for his country (eg an ambassador). **2** person clever at dealing with people.

diplo·matic /ˌdɪplə'mætɪk/ *adj* **1** of diplomacy: *the '～ service(2); the '～ corps/body,* all the ambassadors, ministers and their officers in the capital of a country. **2** tactful; having diplomacy(2): *a ～ answer; to be ～ in dealing with people.* **diplo-mati·cally** /-klɪ/ *adv*

di·ploma·tist /dɪ'pləʊmətɪst/ *n* = **diplomat.**

dip·per /'dɪpə(r)/ *n* **1** cup-shaped vessel with a long handle, for ladling out liquids. **2** (US) **the Big D～, the Little D～,** groups of stars in the northern sky. ⇨ **bear¹(3), plough(4).**

dip·so·mania /ˌdɪpsə'meɪnɪə/ *n* [U] insatiable craving for alcoholic drink. **dip·so·maniac** /ˌdɪpsə'meɪnɪæk/ *n* person suffering from ～.

dip·tych /'dɪptɪk/ *n* painting or carving, esp an altarpiece, on two hinged panels that can be closed like a book.

dire /'daɪə(r)/ *adj* dreadful; terrible: *～ news;* extreme: *to be in ～ need of help.*

di·rect¹ /dɪ'rekt/ *adj* **1** (going) straight; not curved or crooked; not turned aside: *in a ～ line; a ～ hit/ shot,* not turned aside by hitting sth else first; *the ～ rays of the sun,* not reflected from sth. **2** with nothing or no one in between; in an unbroken line: *to be in ～ contact with sb; as a ～ result of this decision. He's a ～ descendant of the Duke of Bumford.* **3** straightforward; going straight to the point; frank; unhesitating: *He has a ～ way of speaking/ acting. He made a ～ answer to the charges brought against him.* **4** exact, diametrical: *a ～ contradiction; the ～ opposite/contrary.* **5** (various uses): *～ action,* use of strikes by workmen to get their demands. *～ current,* electric current flowing in one direction. ⇨ **alternate. ～ speech,** speaker's actual words. ⇨ **indirect. '～ tax,** one levied on the person who pays it (eg income tax), not (eg purchase tax) on goods, etc. □ *adv* without interrupting a journey; without going by a roundabout way: *The train goes there ～. He came ～ to London.* ⇨ **directly. ～·ness** *n*

di·rect² /dɪ'rekt/ *vt,vi* **1** [VP6A,14] *～ sb (to),* tell or show (sb) how to do sth, how to get somewhere: *Can you ～ me to the post office? They ～ed me wrongly.* **2** [VP6A,14] *～ sth (to),* address (a letter, parcel, etc): *Shall I ～ the letter to his business address or to his home address?* **3** [VP14] *～ sth to sb,* speak or write to: *My remarks were not ～ed to all of you.* **4** [VP6A,2A] manage; control: *Who is ～ing the workmen? Who ～ed the film?* ⇨ director. **5** [VP14] *～ to/towards,* turn: *We ～ed our steps towards home. Our energies must be ～ed to-*

wards higher productivity. **6** [VP17,9] order: *The officer ~ed his men to advance/that his men should advance.*

di·rec·tion /dɪ'rekʃn/ n **1** [C] course taken by a moving person or thing; point towards which a person or thing looks or faces: *Tom went off in one ~ and Harry in another ~. The aircraft was flying in a northerly ~. When the police arrived, the crowd scattered in all ~s.* (fig) *Reforms are needed in numerous ~s.* '~-**finder,** radio device that shows the ~ from which wireless signals are coming. **2** [U] **have a good/poor sense of ~,** be able/unable to determine well one's position with regard to one's surroundings when there are no known or visible landmarks. **3** (often *pl*) information or instructions about what to do, where to go, how to do sth, etc: *D~s about putting the parts together are printed on the card. He gave me full ~s to enable me to find his house.* **4** (*pl*) address on or for a letter, parcel, etc: *The parcel was returned to the sender because the ~s were insufficient.* **5** [U] management; control; guidance: *~ of labour,* movement of workers from one area, or one kind of work, to another. *He did the work under my ~. She feels the need of ~,* wants sb to guide and advise her. ~**al** /-ʃənl/ *adj* of ~ in space (esp of radio signals transmitted over a narrow angle): *a ~al aerial.*

di·rec·tive /dɪ'rektɪv/ n [C] general or detailed instruction.

di·rect·ly /dɪ'rektlɪ/ *adv* **1** in a direct manner: *He was looking ~ at us.* **2** at once; without delay: *Come in ~.* **3** in a short time: *I'll be there ~.* □ *conj* (colloq) as soon as: *D~ I had done it, I knew I had made a mistake.*

di·rec·tor /dɪ'rektə(r)/ n person who directs, esp one of a group (called **the Board of D~s**) who manage the affairs of a business company; (theatre, cinema, TV) person who supervises and instructs the actors and actresses, the camera crew, etc. ~**ship** /-ʃɪp/ n position of a company ~; time during which he holds his position.

di·rec·tor·ate /dɪ'rektərət/ n **1** office or position of a director. **2** board of directors.

di·rec·tory /dɪ'rektərɪ/ n (*pl* -ries) (book with a) list of persons, business firms, etc in a district; list of telephone subscribers (and usu addresses) in ABC order.

dire·ful /'daɪəfl/ *adj* (liter) dire; terrible. ~**ly** /'daɪəfəlɪ/ *adv*

dirge /dɜːdʒ/ n song sung at a burial or for a dead person.

diri·gible /'dɪrɪdʒəbl/ n [C] balloon (used as an airship) that can be steered; zeppelin.

dirk /dɜːk/ n kind of dagger.

dirndl /'dɜːndl/ n full-skirted dress with a close-fitting bodice.

dirt /dɜːt/ n [U] **1** unclean matter (eg dust, soil, mud) esp when it is where it is not wanted (eg on the skin, clothes, in buildings): *His clothes were covered with ~. How can I get the ~ off the walls?* **2** loose earth or soil: *a ~ road,* (US) unpaved, not macadamized. **as cheap/common as ~,** vulgar; low-class. **fling/throw ~ at sb,** say slanderous things about him. **treat sb like ~,** treat him as if he were worthless. '~ **farmer,** (US) one who does all his own work. ~-'**cheap,** very cheap, almost valueless. '~-**track,** one made of cinders, etc, (for eg motor-cycle races). **3** unclean thought or talk.

dirty¹ /'dɜːtɪ/ *adj* (-ier, -iest) **1** not clean; covered

with dirt: ~ *hands/clothes;* causing one to be ~: ~ *work.* **2** (of the weather) rough; stormy: *I'm glad I haven't to go out on such a ~ night.* **3** unclean in thought or talk; obscene: *scribble ~ words on lavatory walls.* **4** (colloq) mean, dishonourable, underhand: *play a ~ trick on sb,* play a mean trick on him; *get/give sb a ~ look,* one of severe disapproval or disgust. **dirt·ily** *adv*

dirty² /'dɜːtɪ/ *vt,vi* [VP6A,2A] make or become dirty: *Don't ~ your new dress. White gloves ~ easily.*

dis·abil·ity /ˌdɪsə'bɪlətɪ/ n (*pl* -ties) **1** [U] state of being disabled; incapacity. **2** [C] sth that disables or disqualifies one: *Mr Hill has a ~ and a pension from the government,* eg because he lost a leg while he was in the army.

dis·able /dɪs'eɪbl/ *vt* [VP6A] make unable to do sth, esp take away the power of using the limbs: ~*d ex-service men,* former soldiers, crippled in war. ~·**ment** n

dis·abuse /ˌdɪsə'bjuːz/ *vt* [VP6A,14] ~ **(of),** (formal) free (sb, his mind) from false ideas; put (a person) right (in his ideas): *to ~ a man of silly prejudices.*

dis·ad·van·tage /ˌdɪsəd'vɑːntɪdʒ US: -'væn-/ n **1** [C] unfavourable condition, sth that stands in the way of progress, success, etc: *It is a ~ to be small when you're standing in a crowd to look at a football game. His inability to speak English puts him at a ~ when he attends international conferences.* **2** [U] loss; injury: *rumours to his ~,* that hurt his reputation, etc. ~·**ous** /ˌdɪsˌædvən'teɪdʒəs/ *adj* ~**ous (to),** causing a ~: *in a ~ous position.* ~·**ous·ly** *adv*

dis·af·fected /ˌdɪsə'fektɪd/ *adj* discontented; rebellious; disloyal. **dis·af·fec·tion** /ˌdɪsə'fekʃn/ n [U] political discontent; disloyalty.

dis·af·for·est /ˌdɪsə'fɒrɪst US: -'fɔːr-/ *vt* = disforest.

dis·agree /ˌdɪsə'griː/ *vt* **1** [VP2A,3A] ~ **(with),** take a different view; have different opinions; not agree: *Even friends sometimes ~. I'm sorry to ~ with you/with your statement/with what you say. The reports from Rome ~ with those from Milan.* **2** [VP3A] ~ **with sb,** (of food, climate) have bad effects on; prove unsuitable for: *The climate ~s with me.* ~·**able** /-əbl/ *adj* unpleasant: ~*able weather;* bad-tempered: *a ~able fellow.* ~·**able·ness** n ~·**ably** /-əblɪ/ *adv*

dis·agree·ment /ˌdɪsə'griːmənt/ n **1** [U] disagreeing; absence of agreement: *to be in ~ with sb or sth.* **2** [C] instance of this; difference of opinion; slight quarrel: ~*s between husbands and wives.*

dis·al·low /ˌdɪsə'laʊ/ *vt* [VP6A] refuse to allow or accept as correct: *The judge ~ed the claim.*

dis·ap·pear /ˌdɪsə'pɪə(r)/ *vi* [VP2A] go out of sight; be seen no more: *Let's hope our difficulties will soon ~,* vanish. *The snow soon ~ed,* melted. ~·**ance** /-rəns/ n ~ing.

dis·ap·point /ˌdɪsə'pɔɪnt/ *vt* [VP6A] **1** fail to do or be equal to what is hoped for or expected: *The book/match/meeting ~ed me. Please don't ~ me,* don't fail to do what you have promised. **2** prevent a hope, plan, etc from being realized: *I'm sorry to ~ your expectations.* ~**ed** *part adj* ~**ed (in/at sth) (with sb),** sad at not getting what was hoped for, etc: *We were ~ed/~ed to hear/~ed when we heard that you could not come. I was ~ed at not finding/~ed not to find her at home. We were ~ed in our hopes. What are you looking so ~ed about?*

I'm ~*ed with you.* ~*·ed·ly* adv ~*·ing* adj causing sb to be ~ed: *The weather this summer has been* ~*ing.*

dis·ap·point·ment /ˌdɪsə'pɔɪntmənt/ n 1 [U] being disappointed: *To her great* ~, *it rained on the day of the picnic.* 2 [C] sb or sth that disappoints: *He had suffered many* ~*s in love,* Many women had not returned his love.

dis·ap·pro·ba·tion /ˌdɪsˌæprə'beɪʃn/ n (formal) [U] disapproval.

dis·ap·prove /ˌdɪsə'pruːv/ vi,vt [VP2A,3A,6A] ~ *(of),* have, express, an unfavourable opinion: *She wants to train for the theatre but her parents* ~*/*~ *of her intentions.* **dis·ap·proval** /-'pruːvl/ n [U] disapproving: *He shook his head in disapproval,* to show that he ~ed. **dis·ap·prov·ing·ly** /-ɪŋlɪ/ adv in a way that shows disapproval: *When Mary lit a cigarette, her father looked at her disapprovingly.*

dis·arm /dɪs'ɑːm/ vi,vt 1 [VP6A] take away weapons and other means of attack from: *Five hundred rebels were captured and* ~*ed.* 2 [VP2A] (of nations) reduce the size of, give up the use of, armed forces: *It is difficult to persuade the Great Powers to* ~. 3 [VP6A] make it difficult for sb to feel anger, suspicion, doubt: *By frankly admitting that he was not a scholar, he* ~*ed criticism. I felt angry, but her smiles* ~*ed me.* **dis·arma·ment** /dɪs'ɑːməmənt/ n [U] ~ing or being ~ed(2): ~*ament conferences; new proposals for* ~*ament.*

dis·ar·range /ˌdɪsə'reɪndʒ/ vt [VP6A] disturb; upset; put into disorder: *to* ~ *sb's plans/hair.* ~*·ment n*

dis·ar·ray /ˌdɪsə'reɪ/ n, vt [VP6A] (put into) disorder: *The troops were in* ~.

dis·as·so·ci·ate /ˌdɪsə'səʊʃɪeɪt/ vt [VP14] ~ *from* = dissociate.

dis·as·ter /dɪ'zɑːstə(r) US: -'zæs-/ n 1 [C] great or sudden misfortune; terrible accident (eg a great flood or fire, an earthquake, a serious defeat in war, the loss of a large sum of money). 2 [U] great misfortune or suffering: *a record of* ~. **dis·as·trous** /dɪ'zɑːstrəs US: -'zæs-/ adj causing ~: *disastrous floods; a defeat that was disastrous to the country.* **dis·as·trous·ly** adv

dis·avow /ˌdɪsə'vaʊ/ vt [VP6A] (formal) deny belief in, approval or knowledge of: *He* ~*ed my share in the plot.* ~*al* /-'vaʊəl/ n

dis·band /dɪs'bænd/ vt,vi [VP6A,2A] (of organized groups) break up: *The army (was)* ~*ed when the war ended.* ~*·ment n*

dis·be·lieve /ˌdɪsbɪ'liːv/ vt,vi [VP6A,2A,3A] ~ *in,* refuse to believe (sb or sth); be unable or unwilling to believe in. **dis·be·lief** /ˌdɪsbɪ'liːf/ n [U] lack of belief; refusal to believe.

dis·bud /dɪs'bʌd/ vt (-dd-) [VP6A] remove buds from (a plant, etc) (eg to get stronger or better shoots from those that are left).

dis·bur·den /dɪs'bɜːdn/ vt [VP6A,14] ~ *(of),* (formal) relieve of a burden; unburden (the more usu word).

dis·burse /dɪs'bɜːs/ vt,vi [VP6A,2A] pay out (money). ~*·ment n* [U] paying out (of money); [C] sum of money paid out.

disc, disk /dɪsk/ n 1 [C] thin, flat, round plate, eg a coin, a gramophone record; round surface that appears to be flat: *the sun's* ~. '~ **brake,** brake which operates when a flat plate is brought into contact with another (rotating) plate at the centre of a (car) wheel. '~ **harrow,** one with ~s instead of teeth. '~ **jockey,** radio or TV broadcaster who

introduces performers and comments on records and tapes of (esp) light and popular music. 2 (anat) layer of cartilage between vertebrae. **a slipped** ~, one that is slightly dislocated.

dis·card /dɪ'skɑːd/ vt [VP6A] throw out or away; put aside, give up (sth useless or unwanted): *to* ~ *one's winter underclothing when the weather gets warm; to* ~ *old beliefs.* □ /'dɪskɑːd/ n card or cards ~ed in a card game.

dis·cern /dɪ'sɜːn/ vt [VP6A] see clearly (with the eyes or with the mind); (esp) see with an effort: *We* ~*ed the figure of a man clinging to the mast of the wrecked ship. It is often difficult to* ~ *the truth of an event from a newspaper report.* ~*·ing* adj able to see and understand well. ~*·ible* /-əbl/ adj that can be ~ed. ~*·ment n* [U] ~ing; ability to ~; keenness in judging, forming opinions.

dis·charge[1] /'dɪstʃɑːdʒ/ n 1 [U] discharging or being discharged (all senses, the numbers refer to *discharge*[2]): *How long will the* ~(1) *of the cargo take? The* ~(2) *of water from the reservoir is carefully controlled. After his* ~(4) *from the army, he emigrated to Canada. The prisoners were glad to get their* ~(4)*. He is faithful in the* ~(5) *of his duties. Will £50 be enough for the* ~(5) *of your liabilities?* 2 [U,C] that which is discharged: *The wound hasn't healed—there's still some/a* ~.

dis·charge[2] /dɪs'tʃɑːdʒ/ vt,vi [VP6A,14] 1 unload (cargo from) a ship. 2 give or send out (liquid, gas, electric current, etc): *Where do the sewers* ~ *their contents? The Nile* ~*s itself* (= flows) *into the Mediterranean. Lightning is caused by clouds discharging electricity. The wound is still discharging pus.* 3 fire (a gun, etc); let fly (an arrow or other missile). 4 send (sb) away; allow (sb) to leave: *to* ~ *a patient from hospital. The accused man was found not guilty and was* ~*d. The members of the jury were* ~*d,* set free from their duties. 5 pay (a debt); perform (a duty): *a* ~*d bankrupt,* man who, after being made bankrupt, has done what the court requires and is now free to act as he wishes.

dis·ciple /dɪ'saɪpl/ n follower of any leader of religious thought, art, learning, etc. **the Twelve D**~**s,** the twelve personal followers of Jesus Christ.

dis·ci·pli·nar·ian /ˌdɪsəplɪ'neərɪən/ n person able to maintain discipline(5): *a good/strict/poor* ~. *He's no* ~, does not or cannot maintain discipline.

dis·ci·pline[1] /'dɪsɪplɪn/ n 1 [U] training, esp of the mind and character, to produce self-control, habits of obedience, etc: *school* ~; *military* ~. 2 [U] the result of such training; order kept (eg among schoolchildren, soldiers): *The soldiers showed perfect* ~ *under the fire of the enemy. The children were clever, but there was not much* ~ *in the school.* 3 [C] set rules for conduct; method by which training may be given: *Pronunciation drill and question and answer work are good* ~*s for learning a foreign language.* 4 [U] punishment. 5 [C] branch of knowledge; subject of instruction. **dis·ci·plin·ary** /'dɪsɪplɪnərɪ US: -nerɪ/ adj of or for ~: *to take disciplinary measures; disciplinary punishment.*

dis·ci·pline[2] /'dɪsɪplɪn/ vt [VP6A] apply discipline(1) to; train and control the mind and character of; punish: *to* ~ *badly behaved children.*

dis·claim /dɪs'kleɪm/ vt [VP6A,C] say that one does not own, that one has no connection with: *to* ~ *responsibility for sth; to* ~ *all knowledge of an incident.* ~*er n* statement that ~s: *to issue/send sb a*

~*er.*

dis·close /dɪs'kləʊz/ vt [VP6A,14] ~ *(to),* uncover; allow to be seen; make known: *to refuse to ~ one's name and address; to ~ a secret.* **dis·clos·ure** /dɪs'kləʊʒə(r)/ n [U] disclosing or being ~d; [C] that which is ~d (esp what has been kept secret)

disco /'dɪskəʊ/ n (colloq) = discotheque.

dis·col·our (US = -**lor**) /dɪs'kʌlə(r)/ vt,vi 1 [VP6A] change, spoil, the colour of: *walls ~ed by damp.* 2 [VP2A] become changed in colour: *materials that ~ in strong sunlight.* **dis·col·our·ation** (US = -**lor**-) /dɪsˌkʌlə'reɪʃn/ n [U] ~ing or being ~ed; [C] ~ed place; stain.

dis·com·fit /dɪs'kʌmfɪt/ vt [VP6A] baffle; confuse; embarrass. **dis·com·fi·ture** /dɪs'kʌmfɪtʃə(r)/ n [U] ~ing or being ~ed.

dis·com·fort /dɪs'kʌmfət/ n 1 [U] absence of comfort; uneasiness of mind or body. 2 [C] sth that causes uneasiness; hardship: *the ~s endured by explorers in the Antarctic.*

dis·com·mode /ˌdɪskə'məʊd/ vt [VP6A] (formal) put (sb) to inconvenience.

dis·com·pose /ˌdɪskəm'pəʊz/ vt [VP6A] disturb the composure of: *Don't let their objections ~ you.* **dis·com·posure** /-əʊʒə(r)/ n [U] state of being ~d.

dis·con·cert /ˌdɪskən'sɜːt/ vt [VP6A] upset the calmness or self-possession of: *The Manager was ~ed to discover that he had gone to the office without putting in his false teeth.*

dis·con·nect /ˌdɪskə'nekt/ vt [VP6A,14] ~ *(from),* detach from; take (two things) apart: *You should ~ the TV set* (eg by pulling out the plug) *before you make adjustments inside it.* ~ed adj (of speech or writing) having the ideas, etc badly connected.

dis·con·so·late /dɪs'kɒnsələt/ adj unhappy at the loss of sth; without hope or comfort; inconsolable. ~·ly adv

dis·con·tent /ˌdɪskən'tent/ n [U] dissatisfaction; absence of contentment; [C] cause of this; grievance. □ vt [VP6A] (usu in the pp) make dissatisfied: *to be ~ed with one's job.* ~·ed·ly /-ɪdlɪ/ adv

dis·con·tinue /ˌdɪskən'tɪnjuː/ vt,vi [VP6A,C,2A] cease; give up; put an end to; come to an end: *I'm so busy that I shall have to ~ (paying) these weekly visits.* **dis·con·tinu·ance** /-'tɪnjʊəns/ n

dis·con·tinu·ous /ˌdɪskən'tɪnjʊəs/ adj not continuous.

dis·cord /'dɪskɔːd/ n 1 [U] disagreement; quarrelling: *What has brought ~ into the family,* caused its members to be quarrelsome? 2 [C] difference of opinion; dispute. 3 [U] (music) lack of harmony between sounds, notes, etc sounded together; [C] instance of this, offending the ear; clashing sound that lacks harmony. **dis·cor·dance** /dɪ'skɔːdəns/ n [U] want of harmony; disagreement. **dis·cor·dant** /dɪ'skɔːdənt/ adj 1 not in agreement: *~ant opinions.* 2 (of sounds) not harmonious; harsh: *the ~ant noises of motor-car horns.* **dis·cor·dant·ly** adv

dis·co·theque /'dɪskətek/ n (colloq abbr **disco** /'dɪskəʊ/) club or party where people dance to amplified recorded music played by a *disc jockey.*

dis·count[1] /'dɪskaʊnt/ n [C,U] amount of money which may be taken off the full price, eg of goods bought by shopkeepers for resale, of an account if paid promptly, of a bill of exchange not yet due for payment: *We give (a) 10 per cent ~ for cash,* for prompt payment instead of payment at a later date. '~ **broker** n (comm) broker who gets a fee for act-

ing as an intermediary between buyers and sellers. '~ **house** (comm) establishment which specialises in the ~ing of bills of exchange. ⇨ discount[2](1). *at a ~,* (of goods) not in demand; easily obtained; (fig) not in high esteem: *Is honesty at a ~ today?*

dis·count[2] /dɪs'kaʊnt US: 'dɪskaʊnt/ vt [VP6A] 1 (comm) give or receive the present value of a bill of exchange not yet due. 2 refuse complete belief to a piece of news, a story, etc; allow for exaggeration: *You should ~ a great deal of what appears in the newspapers.*

dis·coun·ten·ance /dɪs'kaʊntɪnəns/ vt [VP6A] (formal) refuse to approve of; discourage.

dis·cour·age /dɪ'skʌrɪdʒ/ vt 1 [VP6A] lessen, take away, the courage or confidence of: *Don't let one failure ~ you: try again.* 2 [VP14] ~ *sb from doing sth,* put difficulties in his way; make it seem not worth while; try to persuade him not to do it: *We tried to ~ him from climbing the mountain without a guide.* ~·**ment** n [U] discouraging or being ~d; [C] sth that ~s.

dis·course /'dɪskɔːs/ n [C] speech; lecture; sermon; treatise. □ vi /dɪ'skɔːs/ ~ *upon,* (formal) talk, preach or lecture upon (usu at length).

dis·cour·teous /dɪs'kɜːtɪəs/ adj not courteous; impolite: *It was ~ of you to arrive late.* ~·**ly** adv **dis·cour·tesy** /dɪs'kɜːtəsɪ/ n [U] impoliteness; [C] (pl -sies) impolite act.

dis·cover /dɪ'skʌvə(r)/ vt [VP6A,9,8,10,25] find out; get knowledge of, bring to view (sth existing but not yet known); realize (sth new or unexpected): *Columbus ~ed America, but did not explore the new continent. Harvey ~ed the circulation of the blood. It was never ~ed how he died. I never ~ed how to start the engine. We suddenly ~ed that it was too late to catch the train. We have ~ed him to be* (more usu *that he is*) *quite untrustworthy.* ~·**er** n person who has made a ~y.

dis·covery /dɪ'skʌvərɪ/ n 1 [U] discovering or being discovered: *a voyage of ~; the ~ of new chemical elements; the ~ by Franklin that lightning is electricity.* 2 [C] (pl -ries) sth that is discovered: *He made wonderful scientific discoveries.*

dis·credit[1] /dɪs'kredɪt/ vt [VP6A] refuse to believe or have confidence in; cause the truth, value or credit of sth or sb to seem doubtful: *His theories were ~ed by scientists. The judge advised the jury to ~ the evidence of one of the witnesses.*

dis·credit[2] /dɪs'kredɪt/ n 1 [U] loss of credit or reputation: *If you continue to behave in this way, you will bring ~ upon yourself.* 2 a ~ *to,* person, thing, causing such loss to: *a ~ to the school/to your family.* 3 [U] doubt; disbelief. ~·**able** /-əbl/ adj bringing ~: *~able conduct.* ~·**ably** /-əblɪ/ adv

dis·creet /dɪ'skriːt/ adj careful, tactful, in what one says and does; prudent: *to maintain a ~ silence.* ~·**ly** adv

dis·crep·ancy /dɪ'skrepənsɪ/ n (pl -cies) [C,U] (of statements and accounts) difference; absence of agreement: *There was (a) considerable ~/There were numerous discrepancies between the two accounts of the fighting.*

dis·crete /dɪ'skriːt/ adj discontinuous; individually distinct. ~·**ness** n

dis·cre·tion /dɪ'skreʃn/ n [U] 1 being discreet; prudence: *You must show more ~ in choosing your friends. years/age of ~,* the age at which one is fit to judge and decide for oneself. *D~ is the better part of valour,* (prov) used jokingly to excuse oneself for not taking unnecessary risks. **2** freedom to act according to one's own judgement, to do what seems right or best: *Use your ~. It is within your own ~,* You are free to decide. *You have full ~ to act.* **~·ary** /dɪ'skreʃənərɪ US:-nerɪ/ *adj* having ~(2): *an official with ~ary powers.*

dis·cri·mi·nate /dɪ'skrɪmɪneɪt/ *vt,vi* **1** [VP14,3A] ~ **one thing from another;** ~ **between two things,** be, make, see, a difference between: *Can you ~ good books from bad/~ between good and bad books?* **2** [VP2A,3A] ~ **(against),** treat differently; make distinctions: *laws which do not ~ against anyone,* that treat all people in the same way. **dis·cri·mi·nat·ing** *adj* **1** able to see or make small differences: *a discriminating taste in literature.* **2** giving special or different treatment to certain people, countries, etc; differential(1): *discriminating tariffs/rates/duties.*

dis·cri·mi·na·tion /dɪˌskrɪmɪ'neɪʃn/ *n* [U] discriminating; ability to discriminate: *Some people do not show much ~ in their choice of books. D~ against goods from foreign countries is usually done by means of tariffs. Is there racial ~ in your country?* **dis·crim·i·na·tory** /dɪ'skrɪmɪnətərɪ US: -tɔːrɪ/ *adj* discriminating(2): *discriminatory legislation.*

dis·cur·sive /dɪ'skɜːsɪv/ *adj* (of a person, what he says or does, his style) wandering from one point or subject to another. **~·ly** *adv* **~·ness** *n*

dis·cus /'dɪskəs/ *n* heavy, round plate of stone, metal or wood, thrown in ancient Roman and Greek athletic contests and in modern contests (eg the Olympic Games): *the ~ throw,* name used for this contest.

throwing the discus

dis·cuss /dɪ'skʌs/ *vt* [VP6A,8,10,14] ~ **(with),** examine and argue about (a subject): *to ~ a question with sb; to ~ (with one's friends) what to do/how to do it/how something should be done.*

dis·cus·sion /dɪ'skʌʃn/ *n* [U,C] discussing or being discussed; talk for the purpose of discussing: *after much ~; after several long ~s. We had a long ~ about the question. When will the matter come up for ~? under ~,* being discussed: *The question is still under ~.*

dis·dain /dɪs'deɪn/ *vt* [VP6A,C,7A] look on with contempt; think (it) dishonourable (to do sth); be too proud (to do sth): *A good man should ~ flattery. He ~ed to notice the insult. He ~ed my offer of help.* □ *n* [U] contempt; scorn: *No one likes to be treated with ~.* **~·ful** /-fʊl/ *adj* showing ~: *~ful looks.* **~·fully** /-fəlɪ/ *adv*

dis·ease /dɪ'ziːz/ *n* [U] illness; disorder of body or mind or of plants; [C] particular kind of illness or disorder: *The business of doctors is to prevent and cure ~. Measles, mumps and influenza are common ~s.* **dis·eased** /dɪ'ziːzd/ *part adj* suffering from, injured by, ~: *~d vines; ~d in body and mind.*

dis·em·bark /ˌdɪsɪm'bɑːk/ *vt,vi* [VP6A,14,2A,C] ~ **(from),** put, go, on shore (from a ship). **dis·em-**

bar·ka·tion /ˌdɪsembɑː'keɪʃn/ *n*

dis·em·barrass /ˌdɪsɪm'bærəs/ *vt* [VP14] ~ **of,** (formal) rid (sb, oneself) from embarrassment; rid (sb, oneself) of a burden: *to ~ oneself of a burden/charge/responsibility.* **~·ment** *n*

dis·em·body /ˌdɪsɪm'bɒdɪ/ *vt* [VP6A] (chiefly in *pp*) separate, set free (the soul or spirit) from the body: *a building haunted by a disembodied spirit.*

dis·em·bowel /ˌdɪsɪm'baʊəl/ *vt* (-ll-) (US also -l-) [VP6A] cut out the bowels of.

dis·en·chant /ˌdɪsɪn'tʃɑːnt US: -'tʃænt/ *vt* [VP6A] free from enchantment or illusion: *He is quite ~ed with the Tory Government.* **~·ment** *n*

dis·en·cum·ber /ˌdɪsɪn'kʌmbə(r)/ *vt* [VP6A,14] ~ **(from),** (formal) free from encumbrance: *~ed of his heavy responsibilities.*

dis·en·franchise /ˌdɪsɪn'fræntʃaɪz/ *vt* = disfranchise.

dis·en·gage /ˌdɪsɪn'geɪdʒ/ *vt,vi* [VP6A,14,2A,C] ~ **(from),** separate, detach (oneself or sth): *Two enemy battalions (were) ~d from the battle after suffering heavy casualties.* **dis·en·gaged** *pp* (of a person) free from engagements: *If the Manager is ~d..., If he is free.... ~·ment* *n* (condition of) being ~d: *the military and economic ~ment of the USA from SE Asia.*

dis·en·tangle /ˌdɪsɪn'tæŋgl/ *vt,vi* **1** [VP6A,14] ~ **(from),** free, from complications, tangles or confusion: *to ~ truth from falsehood.* **2** [VP2A] unravel; become clear of tangles: *This skein of wool won't ~,* cannot be ~d. **~·ment** *n*

dis·equi·lib·rium /ˌdɪsiːkwɪ'lɪbrɪəm/ *n* [U] absence, loss, of equilibrium; instability.

dis·es·tab·lish /ˌdɪsɪ'stæblɪʃ/ *vt* [VP6A] end, break up, an established state of affairs, esp the constitutional connection between a national Church (eg the Church of England) and the State. **~·ment** *n*

dis·favour (US = -**favor**) /ˌdɪs'feɪvə(r)/ *n* [U] state of being out of favour; disapproval: *to regard sth with ~; to be in ~; to fall into ~; to incur sb's ~.* □ [VP6A] regard with ~; disapprove of.

dis·figure /dɪs'fɪgə(r) US: -gjər/ *vt* [VP6A] spoil the appearance or shape of: *beautiful scenery ~d by ugly advertising signs; a face ~d by a broken nose/an ugly scar.* **~·ment** *n* [U] disfiguring or being ~d; [C] sth that ~s.

dis·for·est /dɪs'fɒrɪst US: -'fɔːr-/ *vt* [VP6A] clear (land) of forests.

dis·fran·chise /dɪs'fræntʃaɪz/ *vt* [VP6A] deprive of rights of citizenship; (esp) deprive (a place) of the right to send a representative to parliament or (a citizen) of the right to vote for a parliamentary representative. **~·ment** /-'fræntʃɪzmənt/ *n*

dis·gorge /dɪs'gɔːdʒ/ *vt* [VP6A] throw up or out from, or as from, the throat; (fig) give up (esp sth taken wrongfully).

dis·grace[1] /dɪs'greɪs/ *n* **1** [U] loss of respect, favour, reputation: *A man who commits a crime and is sent to prison brings ~ on himself and his family. There need be no ~ in being poor. be in ~,* be in a state of having lost respect, etc: *He told a lie and is in ~.* **2 a** ~, thing, state of affairs, person, that is a cause of shame or discredit: *These slums are a ~ to the city authorities. The continued use of armed forces to settle disputes is a ~ to the rulers of all countries.* **~·ful** /-fl/ *adj* bringing or causing ~: *~ful behaviour.* **~·fully** /-fəlɪ/ *adv.* *to behave ~fully.*

dis·grace[2] /dɪs'greɪs/ *vt* [VP6A] **1** bring disgrace on; be a disgrace to: *Don't ~ the family name.* **2**

put (sb) out of favour.

dis·grun·tled /dɪsˈgrʌntld/ adj ∼ (at sth/with sb), discontented; in a bad mood.

dis·guise[1] /dɪsˈgaɪz/ vt [VP6A,16B] **1** change the appearance, etc of, in order to deceive or to hide the identity of: He ∼d his looks but he could not ∼ his voice. He ∼d himself as a woman/∼d himself by wearing a wig. **2** conceal; cover up: He ∼d his sorrow beneath a cheerful appearance/by appearing cheerful. There is no disguising the fact that..., The fact that... cannot be concealed.

dis·guise[2] /dɪsˈgaɪz/ n **1** [U] disguising; disguised condition: He went among the enemy in ∼. He went to the ball in the ∼ of a clown. **2** [C,U] dress, actions, manner, etc used for disguising: a clever ∼. He had tried all sorts of ∼s. She made no ∼ of her feelings, did not hide them.

dis·gust[1] /dɪsˈgʌst/ n [U] ∼ (at sth/with sb), strong feeling of dislike or distaste (eg caused by a bad smell or taste, a horrible sight, evil conduct): He turned away in ∼. His ∼ at the government's policy caused him to resign.

dis·gust[2] /dɪsˈgʌst/ vt [VP6A] cause disgust in: His behaviour ∼ed everybody. We were ∼ed at/by/ with what we saw. ∼·ing adj: ∼ing political opinions. ∼·ing·ly adv: He is ∼ingly (colloq = extremely) mean with his money. ∼·ed·ly /-ɪdlɪ/ adv with ∼: He looked ∼edly at the dirty room.

dish[1] /dɪʃ/ n **1** shallow, flat-bottomed (often oval or oblong) vessel, of earthenware, glass, metal, etc from which food is served at table: a 'meat-∼. ∼·ful /-fʊl/ n as much as a ∼ will contain. **2** the ∼es, all the crockery (plates, bowls, cups and saucers, etc) used for a meal: to wash up the ∼es. '∼·cloth, cloth for washing ∼es, etc. '∼·washer, power-operated machine for washing dishes, cutlery, etc. '∼·water, water in which ∼es have been washed. **3** food brought to table on or in a ∼: His favourite ∼ is steak and kidney pie. **4** ∼-shaped object, esp a large concave reflector for the reception of radio-waves from outer space, or in radiotelescopes, etc. ⇨ the illus at radio telescope. **5** (sl) attractive person: She's quite a ∼. ∼y adj (ier, -iest) (sl) (of a person) attractive.

dish[2] /dɪʃ/ vt **1** [15B] ∼ sth up, put on or into a ∼ or ∼es: to ∼ (up) the dinner, get it ready for serving; (fig) prepare, serve up facts, arguments, etc: to ∼ up the usual arguments in a new form. ∼ sth out, distribute it. **2** [VP6A] (colloq) upset; thwart: to ∼ one's opponents. The scandal ∼ed his hopes of being elected.

dis·ha·bille /ˌdɪsæˈbiːl/ n [U] (usu in ∼) (usu of a woman) the state of being negligently or partly dressed.

dis·har·mony /dɪsˈhɑːmənɪ/ n [U] lack of harmony; discord. **dis·har·mo·ni·ous** /ˌdɪshɑːˈməʊnɪəs/ adj

dis·hearten /dɪsˈhɑːtn/ vt [VP6A] cause to lose courage or confidence: Don't be ∼ed by a single failure.

di·shev·elled (US = -eled) /dɪˈʃevld/ adj with the hair uncombed; (of the hair and clothes) in disorder; untidy.

dis·hon·est /dɪsˈɒnɪst/ adj not honest; intended to cheat, deceive or mislead. ∼·ly adv **dis·hon·esty** /dɪsˈɒnɪstɪ/ n [U] being ∼; [C] ∼ act, etc.

dis·hon·our (US = -honor) /dɪsˈɒnə(r)/ n [U] **1** disgrace or shame; loss, absence, of honour and self-respect: to bring ∼ on one's family. **2** a ∼ to, person or thing that brings ∼ to: He was a ∼ to his regiment. □ vt [VP6A] **1** bring shame, discredit,

loss of honour on (sb or sth). **2** (of a bank) ∼ a cheque/bill of exchange, refuse to pay money on it (because the bank's customer has not enough credit). ∼·able /-əbl/ adj without honour; shameful. ∼·ably /-əblɪ/ adv

dis·il·lusion /ˌdɪsɪˈluːʒn/ vt [VP6A] set free from mistaken beliefs: They had thought that the new colony would be a paradise, but they were soon ∼ed. □ n [U] the state of being ∼ed. ∼·ment n [U] freedom from illusions: in a state of complete ∼(ment).

dis·in·cen·tive /ˌdɪsɪnˈsentɪv/ n [C] act, measure, etc that tends to discourage efforts, production, etc: Is high taxation a ∼ to members of the managerial class?

dis·in·cli·na·tion /ˌdɪsɪnklɪˈneɪʃn/ n [U,C] ∼ (for sth/to do sth) (usu with indef art) unwillingness: Some schoolboys have a strong ∼ for work. His ∼ to meet people worries his wife, who is very sociable.

dis·in·cline /ˌdɪsɪnˈklaɪn/ vt [VP17,14] (usu passive) be ∼d for sth; be ∼d to do sth, be reluctant or unwilling: He was ∼d to help me. The hot weather made him feel ∼d for work.

dis·in·fect /ˌdɪsɪnˈfekt/ vt [VP6A] make free from bacterial infection: The house was ∼ed after Tom had had scarlet fever. **dis·in·fec·tant** /ˌdɪsɪnˈfektənt/ adj, n ∼ing (chemical). **dis·in·fection** /ˌdɪsɪnˈfekʃn/ n [U] (act of) ∼ing.

dis·in·fest /ˌdɪsɪnˈfest/ vt [VP6A] get rid of vermin. **dis·in·fes·ta·tion** /ˌdɪsɪnfeˈsteɪʃn/ n [U]: ∼ation officer, person employed to get rid of vermin (eg a rat-catcher).

dis·in·fla·tion /ˌdɪsɪnˈfleɪʃn/ n (process of) returning from a state of inflation to a stable or more normal level (in which prices, wages, etc do not vary much).

dis·in·genu·ous /ˌdɪsɪnˈdʒenjʊəs/ adj (formal) insincere; not straightforward. ∼·ly adv ∼·ness n

dis·in·herit /ˌdɪsɪnˈherɪt/ vt [VP6A] take away the right (of sb) to inherit. **dis·in·heri·tance** /ˌdɪsɪnˈherɪtəns/ n [U] (act of) ∼ing.

dis·in·te·grate /dɪsˈɪntɪgreɪt/ vt,vi [VP6A,2A] (cause to) break up into small parts or pieces: rocks ∼d by frost and rain. **dis·in·te·gra·tion** /dɪsˌɪntɪˈgreɪʃn/ n

dis·inter /ˌdɪsɪnˈtɜː(r)/ vt (-rr-) [VP6A] (formal) dig up from the earth (eg from a grave). ∼·ment n

dis·in·ter·ested /dɪsˈɪntrəstɪd/ adj not influenced by personal feelings or interests: His action was not altogether ∼. ⇨ uninterested. ∼·ly adv ∼·ness n

dis·joint /dɪsˈdʒɔɪnt/ vt [VP6A] separate at the joints; take to pieces: to ∼ a chicken.

dis·jointed /dɪsˈdʒɔɪntɪd/ adj (eg of speech and writing) not connected; incoherent. ∼·ly adv ∼·ness n

dis·junc·tive /dɪsˈdʒʌŋktɪv/ adj ∼ conjunction, (gram) one expressing opposition of or contrast between ideas (eg either... or).

disk n ⇨ disc.

dis·like /dɪsˈlaɪk/ vt [VP6A,C] not like: to ∼ getting up early/being disturbed. If you behave like that, you'll get yourself ∼d, become unpopular. □ n [U,C] feeling of not liking; feeling against: to have a ∼ of/for cats; to feel ∼ for sb. take a ∼ to sb, begin to ∼ him. **likes and ∼s** /ˈdɪslaɪks/, preferences and aversions: He has so many likes and ∼s that he is difficult to please.

dis·lo·cate /ˈdɪsləkeɪt US: -ləʊk-/ vt [VP6A] **1** put

(esp a bone in the body) out of position: *He fell from his horse and ~d his collarbone.* **2** put traffic, machinery, business, etc out of order: *Traffic was badly ~d by the heavy fall of snow.* **dis·lo·ca·tion** /ˌdɪslə'keɪʃn US: -ləʊ'k-/ *n* [U,C] dislocating or being ~d: *the dislocation of trade caused by the blocking of the canal.*

dis·lodge /dɪs'lɒdʒ/ *vt* [VP6A,14] ~ *(from),* move, force (sb or sth) from the place occupied: *to ~ a stone from a building/the enemy from their positions.* ~·**ment** *n*

dis·loyal /dɪs'lɔɪəl/ *adj* ~ *to,* not loyal to. ~·**ly** /-'lɔɪəlɪ/ *adv* ~·**ty** /-'lɔɪəltɪ/ *n* [U] ~ *(to),* being ~ (to); [C] (*pl* -ties) ~ act, etc.

dis·mal /'dɪzməl/ *adj* sad, gloomy; miserable; comfortless: ~ *weather; in a ~ voice.* ~·**ly** /'dɪzməlɪ/ *adv*

dis·mantle /dɪs'mæntl/ *vt* [VP6A] **1** take away fittings, furnishings, etc from: *The old warship was ~d,* Its guns, armour, engines, etc were taken out. **2** take to pieces: *to ~ an engine.* ~·**ment** *n* [U] dismantling (now the usu word).

dis·may /dɪs'meɪ/ *n* [U] feeling of fear and discouragement: *The news that the enemy were near filled/struck them with ~. He looked at me in (blank) ~.* □ *vt* [VP6A] fill with ~: *We were ~ed at the news.*

dis·mem·ber /dɪs'membə(r)/ *vt* [VP6A] **1** tear or cut the limbs from: *Poor fellow! He was ~ed by a pack of wolves.* **2** (fig) divide up (a country, etc). ~·**ment** *n*

dis·miss /dɪs'mɪs/ *vt* [VP6A,14] ~ *(from),* **1** send away (from one's employment, from service): *The servant was ~ed for being lazy and dishonest. The officer was ~ed from the service for neglect of duty.* **2** allow to go: *The teacher ~ed his class when the bell rang.* **3** put away from the mind; stop thinking or talking about: *to ~ all thoughts of revenge.* **4** (cricket) of the team that is fielding) put a batsman/a team out: *The fast bowler ~ed Smith for ten runs.* ~·**al** /-'mɪsl/ *n* [U,C] ~ing or being ~ed: ~*al from the Navy.*

dis·mount /ˌdɪs'maʊnt/ *vi,vt* **1** [VP2A,3A] ~ *(from),* get down (from sth on which one is riding): *to ~ from one's horse/bicycle.* (Cf *alight* from a bus, taxi, tram or train.) **2** [VP6A] remove (sth) from its mount: *to ~ a gun* (from the gun-carriage). **3** [VP6A] cause to fall (from a horse, etc). ⇨ *joust.* ~*ed part adj* (of cavalry) fighting as infantry.

dis·obedi·ence /ˌdɪsə'biːdɪəns/ *n* [U] ~ *(to),* failure or refusal to obey: *acts of ~; ~ to orders.* **dis·obedi·ent** *adj* ~ *(to),* not obedient. **dis·obe·di·ent·ly** *adv*

dis·obey /ˌdɪsə'beɪ/ *vt* [VP6A,2A] pay no attention to orders; not obey a person, a law, etc.

dis·oblige /ˌdɪsə'blaɪdʒ/ *vt* [VP6A] (formal) refuse to be helpful or to think about another person's wishes or needs: *I'm sorry to ~ you, but last time I lent you money you did not repay me.*

dis·order /dɪs'ɔːdə(r)/ *n* **1** [U] absence of order; confusion: *The burglars left the room in great ~. The enemy retreated in ~.* **2** [U] absence of order caused by political troubles; [C] angry outburst of rioting caused by political troubles, etc: *Troops were called out to deal with the ~s in the capital.* **3** [C,U] disturbance of the normal working of the body or mind: *a ~ of the digestive system; suffering from mental ~; ~s of the mind.* □ *vt* [VP6A] put into ~: *a ~ed imagination/mind.*

dis·order·ly /dɪs'ɔːdəlɪ/ *adj* **1** in disorder: *a ~ room/desk.* **2** causing disturbance; unruly; lawless: ~ *crowds; a ~ mob; ~ behaviour.* **a ~ house,** a brothel or a place where illegal gambling is carried on.

dis·or·gan·ize /ˌdɪs'ɔːgənaɪz/ *vt* [VP6A] throw into confusion; upset the working or system of: *The train service was ~d by fog.* **dis·or·gan·iz·ation** /dɪsˌɔːgənaɪ'zeɪʃn US: -nɪ'z-/ *n* [U].

dis·orien·tate /dɪs'ɔːrɪənteɪt/ (also, esp US) **dis·orient** /dɪs'ɔːrɪənt/ *vt* [VP6A] (lit, fig) confuse (sb) as to his bearings(4).

dis·own /dɪs'əʊn/ *vt* [VP6A] say that one does not know (sb or sth), that one has not, or no longer wishes to have, any connection with (sb or sth): *The boy was so wicked that his father ~ed him.*

dis·par·age /dɪ'spærɪdʒ/ *vt* [VP6A] say things to suggest that (sb or sth) is of small value or importance. ~·**ment** *n* **dis·par·ag·ing·ly** *adv* in a disparaging manner.

dis·par·ate /'dɪspərət/ *adj* that cannot be compared in quality, amount, kind, etc; essentially different. □ *n pl* things so unlike that comparison is impossible.

dis·par·ity /dɪ'spærətɪ/ *n* [U] inequality; difference; [C] (*pl* -ties) instance or degree of this: ~ *in age/ rank/position; the disparities in the newspaper accounts of the accident.*

dis·pas·sion·ate /dɪs'pæʃənət/ *adj* free from passion; not taking sides, not showing favour (in a quarrel, etc between others). ~·**ly** *adv* ~·**ness** *n*

dis·patch¹, des·patch /dɪ'spætʃ/ *n* **1** [U] dispatching or being dispatched (all senses): *Please hurry up the ~ of these telegrams.* **2** [C] sth dispatched(1), esp, a government, military or newspaper report: *London newspapers receive ~es from all parts of the world. The soldier was mentioned in ~es,* had his name recorded in accounts of fighting, etc because of his bravery, etc. ⇨ *cita·tion* at cite. '~-**box,** one for official ~es. '~-**rider,** man who carries military ~es (usu on a motor-bike). **3** [U] promptness; speed: *to act with ~.*

dis·patch², des·patch /dɪ'spætʃ/ *vt* **1** [VP6A,14] ~ *(to),* send off, to a destination, on a journey, for a special purpose: *to ~ letters/telegrams; to ~ a cruiser to the island to restore order.* **2** [VP6A] finish, get through, business, a meal quickly. **3** [VP6A] kill; give the death blow to: *The executioner quickly ~ed the condemned man.*

dis·pel /dɪ'spel/ *vt* (-ll-) [VP6A] drive away; scatter: *The wind soon ~led the fog. How can we ~ their doubts and fears?*

dis·pens·able /dɪ'spensəbl/ *adj* that can be done without; not necessary.

dis·pens·ary /dɪ'spensərɪ/ *n* (*pl* -ries) place where medicines are dispensed (eg in a hospital).

dis·pen·sa·tion /ˌdɪspen'seɪʃn/ *n* **1** [U] the act of dispensing(1) or distributing: *the ~ of justice/ charity/food.* **2** [U] ordering or management, esp of the world by Providence; [C] sth arranged by Nature or Providence: *A bereavement* (eg the death of a very old person) *is sometimes called a ~ of Providence.* **3** [C,U] permission to do sth that is usually forbidden, or not to do sth that is usually required, esp by ecclesiastical law: *to be granted ~ from fasting during a journey.* **4** [C] religious system prevalent at a period: *the Mosaic ~,* that of the time of Moses.

dis·pense /dɪ'spens/ *vt,vi* **1** [VP6A,14] ~ *(to),* deal out; distribute; administer: *to ∼ charity/alms/ one's favours to people;* (legal) *to ∼ justice* (in law courts). **2** [VP6A] mix; prepare, give out (medicines): *to ∼ a prescription; a dispensing chemist,* one qualified to do this. **3** [VP3A] ∼ **with,** (**a**) do without: *He is not yet well enough to ∼ with the doctor's services.* (**b**) render unnecessary: *The new machinery ∼s with hand-labour.* **dis·penser** *n* **1** person who ∼s, esp medicines. **2** container from which sth can be withdrawn, ejected or otherwise obtained without removing a cover, lid, etc: *a ∼r for liquid soap/toilet powder/paper cups.*

dis·perse /dɪ'spɜːs/ *vt,vi* [VP6A,2A] (cause to) go in different directions; scatter: *The police ∼d the crowd. The crowd ∼d when the police arrived. The soldiers were ∼d* (= stationed at different points) *along a wide front. A prism ∼s light,* breaks it up into its coloured rays. **dis·per·sal** /dɪ'spɜːsl/ *n* [U,C] dispersing or being ∼d. **dis·per·sion** /dɪ'spɜːʃn US: -ʒn/ *n* = dispersal, esp of light. **the Dispersion,** the Jews ∼d among the Gentiles. ➪ Diaspora.

dis·pirit /dɪ'spɪrɪt/ *vt* [VP6A] discourage; dishearten (chiefly in *pp*): *to look ∼ed. ∼·ed·ly adv*

dis·place /dɪs'pleɪs/ *vt* [VP6A] **1** put out of the right or usual position. *∼d 'person,* refugee left homeless, unable or unwilling to return to his own country. **2** take the place of; put sth or sb else in the place of: *The volunteers were ∼d by a professional army.* Tom has ∼d Harry in Mary's affections. **dis·place·ment** /dɪs'pleɪsmənt/ *n* **1** [U] displacing or being displaced: *the ∼ of human labour by machines.* **2** [C] amount of water displaced by a solid body in it, or floating in it: *a ship with a ∼ of 10000 tons.*

dis·play¹ /dɪ'spleɪ/ *vt* [VP6A] **1** show; place or spread out so that there is no difficulty in seeing: *Department stores ∼ their goods in the windows. The peacock ∼ed its fine tail feathers.* **2** allow to be seen; show signs of having: *to ∼ one's ignorance. She ∼ed no sign of emotion when she was told of her son's death.*

dis·play² /dɪ'spleɪ/ *n* [C,U] displaying; show or exhibition: *a fashion ∼,* a showing of new styles in clothes, etc; *a fine ∼ of courage; a ∼ of bad temper; to make a ∼ of one's knowledge,* show what a lot one knows; *to make a ∼ of one's affection,* show great affection (whether genuine or not).

dis·please /dɪs'pliːz/ *vt* [VP6A] not please; offend; annoy; make indignant or angry: *to ∼ one's wife; to be ∼d with sb (for doing sth); to be ∼d at sb's conduct.* **dis·pleas·ing** *adj ∼ (to),* not pleasing. **dis·pleas·ing·ly** *adv*

dis·pleasure /dɪs'pleʒə(r)/ *n* [U] displeased feeling; dissatisfaction: *He incurred his father's ∼. He looked with ∼ at the meal that was set before him.*

dis·port /dɪ'spɔːt/ *vt* [VP6A] ∼ **oneself,** (formal) play; amuse oneself, eg in the sea or in the sunshine.

dis·pos·able /dɪ'spəʊzəbl/ *adj* made so that it may be (easily) disposed of after use: *∼ nappies/ panties,* made of soft paper which disintegrates quickly in water.

dis·posal /dɪ'spəʊzl/ *n* [U] ∼ **(of), 1** the act of disposing(1,2): *the ∼ of property,* eg by selling it, leaving it to sb in one's will; *the ∼ of rubbish,* getting rid of it; *a waste-∼ unit,* kind of machine that shreds waste products so that they can be washed away down the drains; *a bomb ∼ squad,* group of men who, when unexploded bombs are found, try

to make them harmless and remove them; *the ∼ of troops,* the method of using them, placing them in position, etc; *the ∼ of business affairs,* settling them. **2** control; management: *In time of war the government must have entire ∼ of all material resources.* **at one's ∼,** to be used as one wishes: *He placed £50 at my ∼. My car is at your ∼.*

dis·pose /dɪ'spəʊz/ *vi,vt* **1** [VP3A] ∼ **of,** finish with; get rid of; deal with: *to ∼ of rubbish. He doesn't want to ∼ of* (eg sell) *the land. I think we have ∼d of all his arguments,* answered them, proved them unsound. *The dictator soon ∼d of his opponents,* eg by putting them in prison. **2** [VP6A,2A] place (persons, objects) in good order or in suitable positions: *The cruisers were ∼d in line abreast.* **Man proposes, God ∼s,** (prov) Men may propose things, but God determines what shall happen. **3** [VP17] ∼ **sb to do sth,** (formal) make willing or ready: *Your news ∼s me to believe that.... The low salary did not ∼ him to accept the position. I'm not ∼d/don't feel ∼d to help that lazy fellow.* **be well/ill ∼d (towards),** be/not be friendly and helpful: *Most of the newspapers seem to be well ∼d towards the new government.*

dis·po·si·tion /ˌdɪspə'zɪʃn/ *n* [C] **1** arrangement; placing in order: *the ∼ of furniture in a room; a clever ∼ of troops.* **2** person's natural qualities of mind and character: *a man with a cheerful ∼; a ∼ to jealousy/to take offence easily.* **3** inclination: *There was a general ∼ to leave early,* Most people seemed to wish to leave early. **4** power of ordering and disposing: *Who has the ∼ of this property,* the power or authority to dispose of it?

dis·pos·sess /ˌdɪspə'zes/ *vt* [VP14] ∼ **sb of sth,** take away (property, esp land) from; compel (sb) to give up (the house he occupies): *The nobles were ∼ed of their property after the Revolution.* **dis·pos·session** /ˌdɪspə'zeʃn/ *n*

dis·proof /dɪs'pruːf/ *n* [U] disproving; [C] that which disproves; proof to the contrary.

dis·pro·por·tion /ˌdɪsprə'pɔːʃn/ *n* [U] the state of being out of proportion: *∼ in age. ∼·ate* /-'pɔːʃənət/ *adj ∼ (to),* out of porportion; relatively too large or small, etc: *to give a ∼ate amount of one's time to games; pay that is ∼ate to the work done. ∼·ate·ly adv*

dis·prove /ˌdɪs'pruːv/ *vt* [VP6A] prove to be wrong or false.

dis·put·able /dɪ'spjuːtəbl/ *adj* that may be disputed; questionable.

dis·pu·tant /dɪ'spjuːtənt/ *n* person who disputes.

dis·pu·ta·tion /ˌdɪspjuː'teɪʃn/ *n* [U] disputing; [C] debate, controversy.

dis·pu·ta·tious /ˌdɪspjuː'teɪʃəs/ *adj* fond of disputing; inclined to dispute. *∼·ly adv*

dis·pute¹ /dɪ'spjuːt/ *n* **1** [U] debate, argument. *in ∼: The matter in ∼* (= being disputed) *is the ownership of a house. beyond/past (all) ∼,* unquestionably; undoubtedly: *This is beyond ∼ the best book on the subject. in ∼ with,* engaged in a ∼ with: *The workers' union is in ∼ with the management. without ∼,* without fear of contradiction. **2** [C] quarrel; argument; controversy: *There were many religious ∼s in England during the 17th century.*

dis·pute² /dɪ'spjuːt/ *vi,vt* **1** [VP2A,3A] ∼ **(with/ against sb),** argue, debate, quarrel in words: *Some people are always disputing.* **2** [VP6A,8,10] discuss, question the truth or validity of: *to ∼ a statement/a claim/a decision. The election result* *was* ~*d*, eg it was said that the votes had been counted wrongly. *The will was* ~*d*, eg it was said that it had not been made in correct legal form. *They were disputing whether to start at once or wait. They* ~*d (about) how to get the best results.* **3** [VP6A] fight for, try to win: *Our team* ~*d the victory until the last minute of the game.*

dis·qual·ify /dɪs'kwɒlɪfaɪ/ *vt* [VP6A,14] ~ *sb (for sth/from doing sth),* make unfit or unable: *His weak eyesight disqualified him for military service. As he was a professional, he was disqualified from taking part in the Olympic Games.* **dis·quali·fi·ca·tion** /dɪsˌkwɒlɪfɪ'keɪʃn/ *n* [U] ~ing or being disqualified; [C] that which disqualifies.

dis·quiet /dɪs'kwaɪət/ *vt* [VP6A] make troubled, anxious, uneasy: ~*ed by rumours of war.* □ *n* [U] anxiety; troubled condition: *The President's speech caused considerable* ~ *in some European capitals.* ~*ing adj* causing ~: ~*ing news.* ~**ing·ly** *adv* in a way that causes ~: *a* ~*ingly high percentage of errors in the examination papers.* ~·**ude** /dɪs'kwaɪətjuːd *US:* -tuːd/ *n* [U] state of ~; uneasiness.

dis·qui·si·tion /ˌdɪskwɪ'zɪʃn/ *n* [C] ~ *on sth,* long, elaborate speech or piece of writing.

dis·re·gard /ˌdɪsrɪ'gɑːd/ *vt* [VP6A] pay no attention to; show no respect for: ~ *a warning/sb's objections to a proposal.* □ *n* [U] inattention; indifference; neglect: ~ *of a rule;* ~ *for one's teachers.*

dis·re·pair /ˌdɪsrɪ'peə(r)/ *n* [U] the state of needing repair: *The building was in bad* ~, in great need of being repaired.

dis·repu·table /dɪs'repjʊtəbl/ *adj* having a bad reputation: ~ *bars and clubs;* not respectable in appearance: *a* ~*-looking fellow.* ~ *to,* reflecting badly on: *incidents* ~ *to his character as a priest.* **dis·repu·tably** /-təblɪ/ *adv*

dis·re·pute /ˌdɪsrɪ'pjuːt/ *n* [U] condition of being disreputable; discredit: *The hotel has fallen into* ~, no longer has a good reputation.

dis·re·spect /ˌdɪsrɪ'spekt/ *n* [U] rudeness; want of respect: *He meant no* ~ *by that remark,* did not intend to be impolite. ~·**ful** /-fʊl/ *adj* showing ~: *to be* ~*ful to sb.* ~·**fully** /-fʊlɪ/ *adv: to speak* ~*fully of/about sb.*

dis·robe /dɪs'rəʊb/ *vi, vt* [VP6A,2A] undress; take off (esp official or ceremonial robes): *The Queen* ~*d after the coronation ceremony.*

dis·rupt /dɪs'rʌpt/ *vt* [VP6A] break up, split, separate by force a State, an empire, communications, other non-physical things: *Their quarrels seem likely to* ~ *the Coalition.* **dis·rup·tion** /dɪs'rʌpʃn/ *n* [U] ~ing or being ~ed: *the* ~*ion of the Roman Empire.* **dis·rup·tive** /dɪs'rʌptɪv/ *adj* causing ~ion: ~*ive forces.*

dis·sat·is·fac·tion /ˌdɪsˌsætɪs'fækʃn/ *n* [U] ~ *(with sb/sth) (at doing sth),* the state of being dissatisfied.

dis·sat·isfy /dɪ'sætɪsfaɪ/ *vt* [VP6A] (usu passive) fail to satisfy; make discontented. *be dissatisfied (with sb/sth)/(at doing sth): to be dissatisfied with one's salary/at not getting a better salary.*

dis·sect /dɪ'sekt/ *vt* [VP6A] **1** cut up (parts of an animal body, plant, etc) in order to study its structure. **2** (fig) examine (a theory, argument, etc) part by part, to judge its value. **dis·sec·tion** /dɪ'sekʃn/ *n* [U] ~ing or being ~ed; [C] (part of) sth that has been ~ed.

dis·semble /dɪ'sembl/ *vt, vi* [VP6A,2A] (formal) speak, behave, so as to hide one's real feelings,

thoughts, plans, etc, or give a wrong idea of them: *to* ~ *one's emotions.* **dis·sem·bler** /-blə(r)/ *n* person who ~s; deceiver.

dis·semi·nate /dɪ'semɪneɪt/ *vt* [VP6A] distribute or spread widely ideas, doctrines, etc. **dis·semi·na·tion** /dɪˌsemɪ'neɪʃn/ *n*

dis·sen·sion /dɪ'senʃn/ *n* [U] angry quarrelling; [C] angry quarrel: ~*(s) between rival groups in politics.*

dis·sent[1] /dɪ'sent/ *n* [U] dissenting; (expression of) disagreement: *to express strong* ~.

dis·sent[2] /dɪ'sent/ *vi* **1** [VP3A] ~ *from,* have a different opinion from; refuse to assent to: *I strongly* ~ *from what the last speaker has said.* **2** [VP2A,3A] ~ *(from),* (esp) refuse to accept the religious doctrine of the Church of England. ~*er* *n* (often *D*~) one who ~s (esp as in **2** above).

dis·ser·ta·tion /ˌdɪsə'teɪʃn/ *n* [C] long written or spoken account (eg as submitted for a higher university degree): *a* ~ *on/upon/concerning sth.*

dis·ser·vice /dɪs'sɜːvɪs/ *n* [U,C] *(a)* ~ *(to),* harmful or unhelpful action: *to do sb a* ~. *The spreading of such ideas is of great* ~ (= is very harmful) *to the State.*

dis·sever /dɪ'sevə(r)/ *vt* [VP6A] Sever.

dis·si·dent /'dɪsɪdənt/ *adj* disagreeing. □ *n* person who disagrees; dissenter. **dis·si·dence** /-dəns/ *n* [U] disagreement.

dis·simi·lar /dɪ'sɪmɪlə(r)/ *adj* ~ *(from/to),* not the same; not similar: *people with* ~ *tastes.* ~·**ity** /ˌdɪsɪmɪ'lærətɪ/ *n* [U] lack of similarity; [C] (*pl* -ties) point of difference. **dis·sim·ili·tude** /ˌdɪsɪ'mɪlɪtjuːd *US:* -tuːd/ *n* ~ity; unlikeness.

dis·simu·late /dɪ'sɪmjʊleɪt/ *vt, vi* [VP6A,2A] (formal) dissemble. **dis·simu·la·tion** /dɪˌsɪmjʊ'leɪʃn/ *n*

dis·si·pate /'dɪsɪpeɪt/ *vt, vi* **1** [VP6A,2A] (cause to) disperse, go away: *to* ~ *fear/doubt/ignorance.* **2** [VP6A] waste (time, money) foolishly: *He* ~*d his fortune. Don't* ~ *your efforts.* **dis·si·pated** *part adj* given up to foolish and often harmful pleasures: *to lead a* ~*d life; to fall into* ~*d ways.*

dis·si·pa·tion /ˌdɪsɪ'peɪʃn/ *n* [U] dissipating or being dissipated: *a life of* ~; *unwise* ~ *of one's energy.*

dis·so·ci·ate /dɪ'səʊʃɪeɪt/ *vt* [VP6A,14] ~ *(from),* separate (in thought, feeling); not associate with: *It is difficult to* ~ *the man from his position,* to think of the man without also thinking of his work and duties. *A politician's public and private life should be* ~*d. I wish to* ~ *myself from what has just been said.* **dis·so·cia·tion** /dɪˌsəʊsɪ'eɪʃn/ *n* [U] dissociating or being ~d: *dissociation of ideas,* keeping them distinct.

dis·sol·uble /dɪ'sɒljʊbl/ *adj* that can be dissolved or disintegrated; (of non-material things) that can be annulled: *Is marriage* ~? **dis·solu·bil·ity** /dɪˌsɒljʊ'bɪlətɪ/ *n*

dis·so·lute /'dɪsəljuːt *US:* -luːt/ *adj* (of persons) given up to immoral conduct; (of behaviour, etc), evil; vicious: *to lead a* ~ *life;* ~ *conduct.* ~·**ly** *adv*

dis·sol·ution /ˌdɪsə'luːʃn/ *n* [C,U] ~ *(of),* breaking up; undoing or ending (of a marriage, partnership, etc); (esp) ending of Parliament before a general election.

dis·solve /dɪ'zɒlv/ *vt, vi* **1** [VP6A] (of a liquid) soak into a solid so that the solid itself becomes liquid: *Water* ~*s salt.* **2** [VP2A,3A] ~ *(in),* (of a solid) become liquid as the result of being taken into a liquid: *Salt* ~*s in water.* **3** [VP6A,14] ~ *(in),* cause (a solid) to ~: *He* ~*d the salt in water.* **4** [VP2A,C] disappear; fade away: *The view* ~*d in mist.* **5** [VP6A,2A] bring to, come to, an end: *to* ~ *a business partnership/a marriage/Parliament. Parliament* ~*d.*

dis·son·ance /'dɪsənəns/ *n* [U] discord; [C] combination of notes that is discordant.

dis·son·ant /'dɪsənənt/ *adj* not harmonious; harsh in tone.

dis·suade /dɪ'sweɪd/ *vt* [VP6A,14] ~ *sb (from sth/from doing sth)*, advise against; (try to) turn (sb) away: *to* ~ *a friend from marrying.*

dis·sua·sion /dɪ'sweɪʒn/ *n* [U].

dis·taff /'dɪstɑːf *US:* -tæf/ *n* stick round which wool, flax, etc, is wound for spinning by hand. **on the '**~ **side,** on the mother's side of the family.

dis·tance /'dɪstəns/ *n* [C,U] **1** measure of space, between two points, places, etc; being far off: *In the USA* ~ *is measured in miles, not in kilometres. The house stands on a hill and can be seen from a* ~ *of two miles,* from two miles away. *The town is a great* ~ *off,* a long way off. *My house is within easy walking* ~ *of the shops,* near enough for me to walk to them easily. *sb at a* ~, not too near. *in the* ~, far away. *keep sb at a* ~, refuse to let him become familiar; treat him with reserve. *keep one's* ~, (fig) not be too friendly or familiar. *no* ~, near. *some* ~, fairly far away. *long*~ *adj* (a) (of races, journeys, etc) covering an extensive length, area, etc: *long-*~ *runners.* (b) (of telephone calls) to/from a distant place. *middle-*~ *adj* (of races, etc) covering a medium-size length or area. **the middle-**~ *n* that part of a view between the foreground and the background. **2** space of time: *to look back over a* ~ *of fifty years; at this* ~ *of time.* □ *vt* [VP6A,14] ~ *(from),* place or keep at a ~.

dis·tant /'dɪstənt/ *adj* **1** ~ *(from),* far away in space or time: *The school is three miles* ~ *from the station. We had a* ~ *view of Mt Everest.* **2** far off in family relationship: *She is a* ~ *cousin of mine.* **3** (of degree of similarity) not easily seen: *There is a* ~ *resemblance between the cousins.* **4** reserved; not showing familiarity: *Instead of stopping to speak, she passed by with only a* ~ *nod.* ~*·ly adv* in a ~ manner: *He is* ~*ly related to me.*

dis·taste /dɪs'teɪst/ *n* [U,C] *(a)* ~ *(for),* dislike; aversion: *a* ~ *for hard work. He turned away in* ~. ~*·ful* /-fl/ *adj* ~ *(to),* disagreeable; unpleasant: *It is* ~*ful to me to have to say this, but....* ~*·fully* /-fəlɪ/ *adv* ~*·ful·ness* /-fəlnɪs/ *n*

dis·temper¹ /dɪ'stempə(r)/ *n* [U] (method of painting with) colouring matter (to be) mixed with water and brushed on walls and ceilings. □ *vt* [VP6A,22] colour with ~: *We* ~*ed the walls green.*

dis·temper² /dɪ'stempə(r)/ *n* [U] disease of dogs and some other animals, with coughing and weakness.

dis·tend /dɪ'stend/ *vt,vi* [VP6A,2A] (cause to) swell out (by pressure from within): *a* ~*ed stomach/vein.* **dis·ten·sion** (US = -tion) /dɪ'stenʃn/ *n* ~ing or being ~ed.

dis·til (US = -till) /dɪ'stɪl/ *vt,vi* (-ll-) **1** [VP6A,15B,14] ~ *sth (from sth);* ~ *sth off/out,* change (a liquid) to vapour by heating; cool the vapour and collect the drops of liquid that condense from the vapour; purify (a liquid) thus; drive *out* or *off* impurities thus; make (whisky, essences) thus: *Salt water can be* ~*led and made into drinking water.* **2** [VP6A,2A] fall, let fall, in drops: *flowers that* ~ *nectar.* **dis·til·la·tion** /ˌdɪstɪ'leɪʃn/ *n* **1** [U] ~ing or being ~led: *the* ~*lation of malted barley*

(to make whisky). **2** [C,U] substance obtained by ~ling.

dis·til·ler /dɪ'stɪlə(r)/ *n* person who distils (esp whisky). **dis·til·lery** /-lərɪ/ *n* (*pl* -ries) place where liquids (eg gin, whisky) are distilled.

dis·tinct /dɪ'stɪŋkt/ *adj* **1** easily heard, seen, understood; plain; clearly marked: *a* ~ *pronunciation. The earth's shadow on the moon was quite* ~. *There is a* ~ *improvement in her typing.* **2** ~ *(from),* different in kind; separate: *Keep the two ideas* ~, *the one from the other. Hares and rabbits are* ~ *animals.* ~*·ly adv* in a ~ manner: *to speak/remember* ~*ly.* ~*·ness n*

dis·tinc·tion /dɪ'stɪŋkʃn/ *n* **1** [U] being, keeping things, different or distinct(2); distinguishing, being distinguished, as different; [C] instance of this: *The President shook hands with everyone, without* ~ *of rank. The* ~*s of birth* (= The different classes of society into which people are born) *are less important than they used to be. It is difficult to make exact* ~*s between all the meanings of a word. a* ~ *without a difference,* no real difference at all. **2** [C] point of difference; that which makes one thing different from another: *the* ~ *between poetry and prose.* **3** [U] quality of being superior, excellent, distinguished: *a writer/novel of* ~. **4** [C] mark of honour; title; decoration; reward: *academic* ~*s,* eg a doctor's degree; *to win* ~*s for bravery.*

dis·tinc·tive /dɪ'stɪŋktɪv/ *adj* serving to mark a difference or make distinct: *Soldiers wear a* ~ *uniform.* ~*·ly adv*

dis·tin·guish /dɪ'stɪŋgwɪʃ/ *vt,vi* **1** [VP14,3A] ~ *one thing from another;* ~ *between two things,* see, hear, recognize, understand well, the difference: *People who cannot* ~ *between colours are said to be colour-blind. The twins were so much alike that it was impossible to* ~ *(the) one from the other. It is not easy to* ~ *cultured pearls from genuine pearls.* **2** [VP6A] make out by looking, listening, etc: *A person with good eyesight can* ~ *distant objects.* **3** [VP14] ~ *from,* be a mark of character, difference: *Speech* ~*es man from the animals. What* ~*es the hare from the rabbit?* **4** [VP6A] ~ *oneself,* behave so as to bring credit to oneself: *to* ~ *oneself in an examination. He* ~*ed himself by his courage.* ~*·able* /-əbl/ *adj* ~*able (from),* able to be ~ed from sb/sth else: *Tom is hardly* ~*able from his twin brother. The coast was hardly* ~*able* (= could hardly be seen) *through the haze.* ~*ed adj* famous; well known; remarkable; showing distinction(3): *He is* ~*ed for his knowledge of economics/*~*ed as an economist. He has had a* ~*ed career in the diplomatic service.*

dis·tort /dɪ'stɔːt/ *vt* [VP6A] **1** pull, twist, out of the usual shape: *a face* ~*ed by pain. A curved mirror* ~*s the features.* **2** give a false account of; twist out of the truth: *Newspaper accounts of international affairs are sometimes* ~*ed. You have* ~*ed my motives.* **dis·tor·tion** /dɪ'stɔːʃn/ *n* [U] ~ing or being ~ed; [C] instance of this; sth that is ~ed.

dis·tract /dɪ'strækt/ *vt* [VP6A,14] ~ *from,* draw away sb's attention from sth: *The noise in the street* ~*ed me from my reading. What can we do to* ~ *her mind from the sorrow caused by her child's death?* ~*ed adj* ~*ed (with/by),* with the mind confused or bewildered: *to be* ~*ed with/by anxiety/grief.* ~*·ed·ly adv* in a ~ed manner.

dis·trac·tion /dɪ'strækʃn/ *n* **1** [U] distracting or being distracted. **2** [C] sth that distracts, sth annoying and unwelcome: *Noise is a* ~ *when you are trying* *to study.* **3** [C] sth that holds the attention and gives pleasure: *He complained that there were not enough ~s in the small village. There are plenty of ~s* (= interesting and amusing things to see and do) *in a large city.* **4** [U] wildness or confusion of mind. **to ~**: *He loves her to ~,* loves her wildly, passionately. *You will drive me to ~ with your silly questions.*

dis·train /dɪ'streɪn/ *vi* [VP2A,3A] ~ *(upon),* (legal) seize goods to compel a person to pay money due (esp rent): *to ~ upon a person's furniture for rent.* **dis·traint** *n*~ing.

dis·trait /dɪ'streɪ/ *adj* (F) absent-minded; not paying attention.

dis·traught /dɪ'strɔːt/ *adj* distracted; violently upset in mind: ~ *with grief.*

dis·tress¹ /dɪ'stres/ *n* [U] **1** (cause of) great pain, discomfort or sorrow; (suffering caused by) want of money or other necessary things: *At the end of the Marathon race several runners showed signs of ~. His wild behaviour was a great ~ to his mother. He spent his fortune in relieving ~ among the poor.* **2** serious danger or difficulty: *The lifeboat went out to a ship in ~. The ship was flying a ~ signal.*

dis·tress² /dɪ'stres/ *vt* [VP6A] cause distress(1) to: *I am much ~ed to hear the news of your wife's death. What are you looking so ~ed about? Don't ~ yourself,* Don't get worried. ,~**ed 'area,** part of a country where there is serious and continued unemployment. ~**·ful** /-fʊl/, ~**·ing** *adjj* causing or experiencing ~. ~**·fully** /fəlɪ/, ~**·ing·ly** *advv* in a manner that causes distress.

dis·trib·ute /dɪ'strɪbjuːt/ *vt* [VP6A,14] ~ *(to/ among),* **1** put (parts of a set of things) in different places; give or send out: *The firm ~d its profits among its workers. The man had thirty parcels to be ~d to houses all over the town.* **2** spread out (over a larger area): *to ~ manure over a field.* **3** put into groups or classes. **dis·tribu·tor** /-tə(r)/ *n* person or thing that ~s.

dis·tribu·tion /,dɪstrɪ'bjuːʃn/ *n* [U] distributing or being distributed; manner of being distributed; [C] instance or occasion of distributing: *They could not agree about the ~ of the profits. Is the ~ of wealth uneven in your country? The pine-tree has a very wide ~, is found in many parts of the world.*

dis·tribu·tive /dɪ'strɪbjʊtɪv/ *adj* **1** of distribution: *the ~ trades,* eg railways, shop-keeping. **2** (gram) referring to each individual, each member of a class: *'Each', 'every', 'either' and 'neither' are ~ pronouns.* ~**·ly** *adv*

dis·trict /'dɪstrɪkt/ *n* **1** part of a country: *a mountainous ~; purely agricultural ~s.* **the Lake D~,** in north-west England. **2** part of a town or country marked out for a special purpose: *the London postal ~s,* eg NW5, EC4. ⇨ **postcode** at post¹(3); *rural and urban ~s,* for purposes of local government. ~ **nurse,** one who visits people in their homes. **the D~ of Columbia,** the city of Washington, the Federal government area of the US.

dis·trust /dɪs'trʌst/ *n* [U,C] **(a)** ~ *(of),* doubt or suspicion; want of trust or confidence: *The child looked at the big stranger with ~. He has a ~ of foreigners.* □ *vt* [VP6A] have no trust in; be doubtful about: *He would ~ his own friends. He ~ed his own eyes.* ~**·ful** /-fʊl/ *adj* unwilling to trust; suspicious: *I was ~ful of his motives.* ~**·fully** /-fəlɪ/ *adv* ~**·ful·ness** *n*

dis·turb /dɪ'stɜːb/ *vt* [VP6A] break the quiet, calm,

peace or order of; put out of the right or usual position; upset: *He put his oars in the water and ~ed the smooth surface of the lake. She opened the door quietly so as not to ~ the sleeping child. Don't ~ the papers on my desk. He was ~ed to hear of your illness/was ~ed by the news of your illness.* ~ **the peace,** (legal) cause disorder, rioting, etc.

dis·turb·ance /dɪ'stɜːbəns/ *n* [U] disturbing or being disturbed; [C] instance of this; sth that disturbs; disorder (esp social or political): *Were there many political ~s in the country last year?*

dis·union /dɪs'juːnɪən/ *n* [U] breaking of what unites; lack of union; dissension.

dis·unite /,dɪsjuː'naɪt/ *vt,vi* [VP6A,2A] (cause to) become separate.

dis·unity /dɪs'juːnətɪ/ *n* [U] lack of unity; dissension.

dis·use /dɪs'juːs/ *n* [U] state of no longer being used: *rusty from ~; words that have fallen into ~.* ~**d** /dɪs'juːzd/ *part adj* no longer used: *a ~d well.*

di·syl·labic (US = **dis·syl·labic**) /,dɪsɪ'læbɪk/ *adj* of two syllables. **di·syl·lable** (US = **dis·syl·lable**), /dɪ'sɪləbl/ *n* ~ word or metrical foot.

ditch /dɪtʃ/ *n* narrow channel dug in or between fields, or at the sides of a road, etc to hold or carry off water. **dull as '~ water,** very dull(3) indeed. ⇨ die²(2). □ *vt,vi* **1** [VP6A,2A] make, clean, repair or provide with ~es. **2** [VP6A] send or throw into a ~ (or, sl, the sea); (fig, sl) abandon: *The drunken man ~ed his car,* drove it into a ~. *The pilot had to ~ his plane,* make a forced landing on the sea. *He's ~ed his girlfriend,* (sl) suddenly stopped seeing her.

dither /'dɪðə(r)/ *vi* [VP2A,C] (old use) tremble; (colloq) hesitate about what to do; be unable to decide. □ *n* trembling; (colloq) nervous, uncertain, indecisive state: *be all of/in a ~; have the ~s.* (*colloq*) *be all of a ~; have the ~s.*

ditto /'dɪtəʊ/ *n* (abbr **d°, do**) the same thing (used in lists to avoid writing a word or words again): *One hat at £2.25; ~ at £4.50.* **say ~ to,** (colloq) say the same thing as; agree with.

ditty /'dɪtɪ/ *n* (*pl* -ties) short, simple song.

di·ur·nal /daɪ'ɜːnl/ *adj* (formal) of the daytime; (astron) occupying one day.

di·va·gate /'daɪvəgeɪt/ *vi* [VP2A,3A] ~ *(from),* (formal) stray; wander from the point. **di·va·gation** /,daɪvə'geɪʃn/ *n*

di·van /dɪ'væn US: 'daɪvæn/ *n* **1** long, low, soft, backless seat. **'~-bed** such a seat that can be converted into a bed. **2** (in Muslim countries) public audience room; State council or council room.

dive¹ /daɪv/ *n* **1** the act of diving: *a graceful ~.* **2** (colloq) disreputable place for the sale of drink, or for gambling.

dive² /daɪv/ *vi* (US alternative *pt* **dove** /dəʊv/) [VP2A,C] ~ *(off/from/into),* **1** go head first into water: *He ~d from the bridge and rescued the drowning child.* **2** (of a submarine) go under water; (of divers) go under water in a special dress: *to ~ for pearls.* **'diving-bell,** open-bottomed apparatus which can be lowered into water, supplied with air pumped through pipes, and used by underwater workers. **'diving-board** flexible board from which to ~ (eg into a swimming pool). **'diving-dress/ suit,** suit with weighted boots and an air-tight helmet into which air is pumped through tubes, used by divers. **3** go quickly to a lower level; move sth (eg the hand) quickly and suddenly downwards (into sth): *The aircraft ~d steeply. The rabbit ~d* *into its hole. He* ∼*d into his pocket and pulled out a handful of coins.* '∼**-bomb** *vt,vi* (of an aircraft, a '∼**-bomber**) drop bombs at the end of a steep dive. **diver** *n* person who ∼s, esp a person who works under water in a diving-suit.

di·verge /daɪ'vɜːdʒ/ *vi* [VP2A,3A] ∼ *(from),* (of lines, paths, opinions, etc) get farther apart from a point or from each other as they progress; turn or branch away from. **di·ver·gence** /-dʒəns/, **-gency** /-dʒənsɪ/ *n* [U] diverging; [C] (*pl* -ces, -cies) instance of this: *divergencies from the normal.* **di·ver·gent** /-dʒənt/ *adj*

di·vers /'daɪvɜːz/ *adj* (old use) several; more than one.

di·verse /daɪ'vɜːs/ *adj* of different kinds: *The wild life in Africa is extremely* ∼. ∼**·ly** *adv*

di·ver·sify /daɪ'vɜːsɪfaɪ/ *vt* [VP6A] make diverse; give variety to: *a landscape diversified by hills and woods.* **di·ver·si·fi·ca·tion** /daɪ,vɜːsɪfɪ'keɪʃn/ *n*

di·ver·sion /daɪ'vɜːʃn US:* -ʒn/ *n* **1** [U] diverting; the act of turning sth aside or giving it a different direction: *the* ∼ *of a stream;* [C] instance of this: *traffic* ∼*s,* eg when traffic is directed by different routes because of road repairs. **2** [C] sth which turns the attention from serious things; sth giving rest or amusement: *Chess and billiards are his favourite* ∼*s.* **3** [C] method used to turn the attention from sth that one does not wish to be noticed, as when, in war, the enemy's attention is drawn from one place by an unexpected attack at another place: *to create/make a* ∼. ∼**ary** /daɪ'vɜːʃənərɪ *US:* -'ʒənerɪ/ *adj: a* ∼*ary raid.* ∼**·ist** *n* person who engages in disruptive or subversive activities.

di·ver·sity /daɪ'vɜːsətɪ/ *n* [U] the state of being diverse; variety.

di·vert /daɪ'vɜːt/ *vt* [VP6A,14] ∼ *(from),* **1** turn in another direction: *to* ∼ *the course of a river; to* ∼ *a river from its course; to* ∼ *water from a river into the fields.* **2** amuse; entertain; turn the attention away: *Some people are easily* ∼*ed. How can we* ∼ *her thoughts from her sad loss?* ∼**·ing** *adj* amusing. ∼**·ing·ly** *adv*

Dives /'daɪviːz/ *n* (typical name for a) rich man. ⇨ Luke 16: 19.

di·vest /daɪ'vest/ *vt* [VP14] ∼ *sb of,* **1** (formal) take off (clothes): *to* ∼ *a king of his robes.* **2** take away from: *to* ∼ *an official of power and authority.* **3** (reflex) get rid of; give up: *I cannot* ∼ *myself of the idea,* It comes back to my mind.

di·vide[1] /dɪ'vaɪd/ *vt,vi* **1** [VP6A,15B,14,2A,C] ∼ *sth (up/out);* ∼ *sth between/among sb; sth from sth;* separate; split or break up: *We* ∼*d (up/out) the money equally. They* ∼*d the money between/among themselves. The river* ∼*s my land from his. The Nile* ∼*s near its mouth and forms a delta. He* ∼*s his time between London and Cairo. How shall we* ∼ *the work up/*∼ *up the work?* **2** [VP14] ∼ *into;* ∼ *by,* find out how often one number is contained in another: *If you* ∼ *6 into 30/*∼ *30 by 6, the answer is 5.* (With passive force): *12* ∼*s by 3,* can be ∼*d by 3.* **3** [VP14] ∼ *into,* form into smaller parts: *The house was divided into flats.* **4** [VP6A] cause disagreement; cause to disagree: *Please don't let such a small matter* ∼ *us. Opinions are* ∼*d on the question,* There are opposed opinions. **5** [VP2A,6A] (in Parliament, at debates, etc) part in order to vote; cause to part for this purpose: *After a long debate, the House* ∼*d,* voted on the question. *The Opposition does not propose to* ∼ *the House on this question,* does not

insist upon the taking of a vote.

di·vide[2] /dɪ'vaɪd/ *n* sth that divides, esp a watershed (a line of high land that separates two different river systems).

divi·dend /'dɪvɪdend/ *n* **1** (maths) number to be divided by another. ⇨ **divisor.** **2** (comm) (usu periodical) payment of a share of profit, to shareholders in a business company, or of assets to creditors (eg of an insolvent company), or to a policy holder in a mutual insurance company: *to pay a* ∼ *of 10 per cent.* '∼**-warrant,** order on a bank to pay a ∼.

di·vid·ers /dɪ'vaɪdəz/ *n pl (pair of)* ∼, pair of measuring-compasses, used for dividing lines or angles, measuring or marking distances, etc

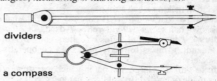

dividers

a compass

div·i·na·tion /,dɪvɪ'neɪʃn/ *n* [U] divining, ⇨ divine[3]; discovery of the unknown or the future by supernatural means; [C] clever guess or forecast.

di·vine[1] /dɪ'vaɪn/ *adj* **1** of, from, or like God or a god: *King Charles I claimed to rule by* ∼ *right,* right given to him by God. **D**∼ **Service,** the public worship of God. **2** (colloq) excellent; very beautiful: ∼ *weather; a* ∼ *hat. She looks* ∼ *in that new dress.* ∼**·ly** *adv*

di·vine[2] /dɪ'vaɪn/ *n* person (usu a priest) learned in theology.

di·vine[3] /dɪ'vaɪn/ *vt,vi* [VP6A,10,2A] discover or learn (sth) about future events, hidden things, etc by means not based on reason: *to* ∼ *sb's intentions; to* ∼ *what the future has in store.*

di·viner /dɪ'vaɪnə(r)/ *n* person who divines, esp one who claims to have the power of learning the presence of subterranean water, metal, etc by using a Y-shaped stick or rod (called a *di‑vining-rod*). ⇨ dowsing.

di·vin·ity /dɪ'vɪnətɪ/ *n* **1** [U] the quality of being divine, ⇨ divine[1]: *the* ∼ *of Christ;* [C] (*pl* -ties) divine being. **2** [U] the study of theology: *the* ∼ *school at Oxford; a doctor of* ∼ (abbr **DD**).

di·vis·ible /dɪ'vɪzəbl/ *adj* (maths) that can be divided without remainder: *8 is* ∼ *by 2.*

di·vi·sion /dɪ'vɪʒn/ *n* **1** [U] dividing or being divided: *the* ∼ *of time into months, weeks and days; a simple problem in* ∼ (eg 50 ÷ 5); *the* ∼ *of labour,* sharing work, giving different kinds of work to different people, according to their capabilities. **2** [C] the effect of dividing; one of the parts into which sth is divided: *the export* ∼ *of a business company. Is that a fair* ∼ *of the money?* **3** [C] line that divides: *A hedge forms the* ∼ *between his land and mine. The* ∼*s between the various classes of society are not so sharply marked as they used to be.* **4** [C,U] disagreement; separation in thought, feeling, etc: *a nation in* ∼. **6** [C] (Parliament, etc) separation into two groups for the counting of votes: *The Bill was read for the second time without a* ∼. '∼ **bell,** bell rung to warn members (who are outside the House) that there is to be a ∼.

di·vi·sive /dɪ'vaɪsɪv/ *adj* creating divisions or differences between people: ∼ *actions/ideas/policies.* ∼**·ly** *adv* ∼**·ness** *n.*

div·isor /dɪ'vaɪzə(r)/ *n* (maths) number by which

another number is divided. ⇨ dividend(1).

di·vorce[1] /dɪˈvɔːs/ n ~ **(from)** 1 [U] legal ending of a marriage so that husband and wife are free to marry again; [C] instance of this: *to sue for a ~; to take/start ~ proceedings; to obtain a ~ (from...)*. 2 [C] ending of a connection or relationship: *the ~ between religion and science*, as when science claims or seems to show that religious beliefs have no foundation.

di·vorce[2] /dɪˈvɔːs/ vt [VP6A,14] ~ **(from)** 1 put an end to a marriage by law: *Did Mr Hill ~ his wife or did she ~ him?* 2 (fig) separate (things usually together): *What happens to the soul when it is ~d from the body?* **di·vor·cee** /dɪˌvɔːˈsiː/ n ~d person.

divot /ˈdɪvət/ n piece of turf sliced off by a golf club in making a bad stroke.

di·vulge /daɪˈvʌldʒ/ vt [VP6A,14] ~ **(to)**, make known (sth secret). **di·vul·gence** /-dʒəns/ n

divvy /ˈdɪvɪ/ n (pl -vies) (colloq abbr of) dividend(2), eg as formerly paid by a co-operative society.

dixie /ˈdɪksɪ/ n large iron pot in which tea, stew, etc is made or carried (by soldiers, campers, etc).

dizzy /ˈdɪzɪ/ adj (-ier, -iest) 1 (of a person) feeling as if everything were turning round, as if unable to balance; mentally confused. 2 (of places, conditions) causing such a feeling: *a ~ height*. □ vt make ~. **diz·zily** adv **diz·zi·ness** n

djinn /dʒɪn/ n = genie.

do[1] /də; *strong form* duː/ *anom fin* (1st and 2nd person sing pres t* neg don't /dəʊnt/, 3rd person sing pres t* does /dəz; *strong form* dʌz/, neg doesn't /ˈdʌznt/, pt did /dɪd/, neg didn't /ˈdɪdnt/, pp done /dʌn/) 1 used with the *main verb* (**a**) for neg sentences with *not*: *He didn't go. Don't go yet.* (**b**) for interr sentences: *Does/Did he want it?* (**c**) after a front-shifted *adverbial*, etc: *So hard did they work that...; Not only did they promise to help, but....* (**d**) to emphasize the positive or negative nature of a sentence (declarative, interr or imper), always stressed: *That's exactly what he 'did say. I tell you I 'don't like him. 'Do stop that noise!* 2 used alone, to refer to a *main verb* or *verb phrase*: (**a**) in comparisons: *She plays the piano better now than she did* (ie played) *last year.* (**b**) in question phrases: *He lives in London, doesn't he? So you want to be a doctor, do you?* (**c**) in answers, comments, etc: *'They work hard'—'Oh, do they?' 'Who broke the window?'—'I did!'*

do[2] /duː/ vt,vi (For uses with *adverbial particles* and *preps* ⇨ 15 below.) 1 (**a**) [VP2A,6A] perform, carry out (an action); busy oneself with: *What are you doing now? What shall I do next? I will do what I can. What does he do for a living*, What is his occupation? *I have nothing to do. Are you doing anything tomorrow? There's nothing to do here*, is no means of passing the time. *What's done cannot be undone. See what kindness will do*, Try the effect of kindness. **do it yourself** (abbr **DIY**), (esp) do house decorating, furnishing, upkeep, etc oneself (instead of employing professional workers): (attrib) *do-it-yourself kits*, materials, etc for doing work of this kind. **easier said than done**, easier to talk about than to do. **No sooner said than done**, done at once. **Well begun is half done**, A good start makes it easy to finish sth. (**b**) [VP2C] act; behave: *When in Rome do as the Romans do. You would do well* (ie be wise) *to take your doctor's advice.* 2 [VP6A,12B,13B] (combined with *nouns* in many senses) (**a**) produce;

make: *Patience and perseverance will do wonders*, produce remarkable results. *I have done* (ie made) *six copies. I will do* (ie make) *a translation for you/do you a translation.* (**b**) work at; be busy with: *She's doing her lessons/homework*, etc. (**c**) perform: *Do your duty. He still has to do his military service.* **do the** + *gerund*: *Who'll do the cooking*, Who'll cook, who'll undertake the task of cooking? also ⇨ **get sth done** at get(2). (**d**) study; learn: *Are you doing science at school? He has been doing engineering at Sheffield University.* (**e**) solve; find the answer to: *I can't do this sum/this problem in algebra.* (**f**) put in order; arrange: *Please do the flowers*, arrange them in vases, etc. (**g**) make tidy: *Go and do your hair.* (**h**) clean, sweep, brush, etc: *Have you done* (ie brushed) *your teeth?* (**i**) deal with, attend to: *I will do you next, sir*, (eg at the barber's) I will attend to you next. *I have a lot of correspondence to do.* (**j**) use, exert: *do one's best/utmost; do all one can; do everything in one's power. He did his best to help us.* ⇨ also credit[1](7), favour[1](4), good[2], harm, homage, honour[1](1), injury, justice, kindness at kind[2], mischief, service, *a good/bad turn* at turn, wrong. **do-gooder** /ˌduː ˈɡʊdə(r)/ n (colloq; often pej) person who is (over-)zealous to improve people, conditions, etc. 3 (the *pp* and perfect tenses) bring to an end; finish: [VP6A] *It's done. I've done it. Will he ever have/be done?* [VP3A] *Have you done* (ie finished) *with my pen yet?* [VP6C] *I've done talking—I'm going to act.* 4 [VP3A,6A] **do (for)**, be good, satisfactory or convenient, enough (for a purpose, for sb): *These shoes won't do* (ie are not strong enough) *for mountain-climbing. This log will do for a seat/do for us to sit on. This room will do me quite well*, will serve my needs. **make sth do/make do (with sth)**, make sth suffice, provide for a need: *Can you make £5 do*, make this sum cover your expenses? *Can't you make that shirt do* (ie wear it) *for another day? It isn't much but I will make it do/make do with it*, manage with it. ⇨ make[1](4). 5 [VP2A] be fitting, suitable, tolerable: *This will never do*, cannot be accepted or allowed! *That will do!* You've said or done enough! **be done**, be considered polite; be the usual custom: *It's not done to talk with your mouth full.* 6 [VP2A] (with passive force; colloq) happen: *He came to ask what was doing*, = being done, happening. *'Can you lend me 50p?'—'Nothing doing!'* (sl) No! 7 [VP2A] (**a**) fare; get on well, badly, etc: *Everything in the garden is doing* (= growing) *well. Roses do well in a clay soil. He's doing well at school.* (**b**) (esp of health) make progress: *The patient is doing quite well.* **How do you do?** (formula used when people are formally introduced) 8 [VP2B,15A] complete (a journey); travel (a distance); go (at a certain speed): *How many miles a day did you do during your tour? We've done eighty miles since lunch. We did the journey in six hours. The car was doing sixty miles an hour.* 9 [VP6A] play the part of: *He does Hamlet well. He does the host admirably*, is an admirable host. *I suppose we must do the polite thing*, (colloq) be sociable, chat, etc. 10 [VP6A,15B] **do sb (out of sth)**, (colloq) cheat, swindle, get the better of: *Please don't think I'm trying to do you. I'm afraid you've been done. She was done out of her money. He once tried to do me out of my job*, supplant me. 11 **do sb/oneself well**, (colloq) provide food, comforts, etc for:

They do you very well at the Bristol Hotel. He does himself well, provides well for his own comfort. **12** [VP6A] (colloq) visit as a sightseer; see the sights of: *Have you done the British Museum yet?* **13** [VP15A] cook in the right degree: *Mind you do the beef well. How would you like your mutton chop done?* ⇨ **underdone, overdone** at **overdo**. **¸done to a ˈturn**, extremely well cooked: *The steak was done to a turn*, cooked perfectly. **14** [VP7B] (with *have*) **have to do with**, be connected with; result from: *I know he behaves badly—It all has to do with the way he was brought up.* **have sth/ nothing/not much/a great deal, etc to do with**, be/not be connected or concerned with; contribute to: *He had something to do with* (= was in some way connected with, perhaps was responsible for) *my decision to teach English. Hard work had a great deal to do with* (= contributed greatly to) *his success.* **15** [VP2C,3A,15B] (uses with *adverbial particles* and *preps*):
do aˈway with, abolish, get rid of: *That department was done away with two years ago. That's a practice that should be done away with. Our dog is getting so old and blind that we shall have to do away with him*, have him put to death.
do well/badly by sb, treat, deal with, well/badly: *A good employer always does well by good work-men.* **(be) hard ˈdone by**, (be) treated unfairly: *He complains that he has been hard done by.* **¸Do as you would be ˈdone by**, (prov) Treat others as you would like to be treated.
do sb down, (colloq) **(a)** get the better of sb (by outwitting or cheating him). **(b)** speak ill of. ⇨ *run sb down* at *run* ¹(28).
do for sb/sth, (colloq) **(a)** act as housekeeper for; perform, esp domestic services, for: *Old Mrs Green has been doing for me since my wife died. He won't employ a housekeeper; he prefers to do for himself.* **(b)** manage: *What/How will you do for water* (= manage to have supplies of water) *while you're crossing the desert?* **(c)** (usu passive) ruin; destroy; kill: *These shoes are done for*, worn out, useless. *Poor fellow, I'm afraid he's done for*, (according to context) ruined in his career, likely to die, etc. *The country's done for*, ruined.
do sb in, (sl) kill him. **be done in**, exhausted: *The horse was done in after the race.*
do sth out, sweep or clean out; put in order: *Tell Tom to do out the stables. This room needs doing out.* **do sb out of sth**, ⇨ 10 above.
do sth over, redecorate: *The dining-room needs doing over.* **do sb over**, (sl) assault sb.
do sth up, **(a)** restore, repair, renovate: *The house needs to be done up/needs doing up*, repainted, restored, etc. **(b)** change the shape of, put new trimmings, etc on: *She has been doing up her last summer's hat.* **(c)** tie or wrap up; make into a bundle or parcel: *Please do up these books and post them to Mr Smith.* **(d)** fasten (a dress or other garment) with buttons, hooks and eyes, etc: *She asked me to do up her dress for her at the back.* **(e)** (of a dress, etc) fasten with buttons, etc: *This dress does up at the back.* **(f)** (usu passive) tire out: *He/His horse was done up (done in* is more usu) *after the long ride.*
do with sb/sth, **(a)** (meanings as in the examples): *What did you do with my umbrella*, Where did you put it, leave it, etc? *What are we to do with* (= How shall we deal with) *this naughty boy? She didn't know what to do with herself*, how to occupy

her time. *Tell me what you did with yourselves* (= how you passed the time) *on Sunday. The children didn't know what to do with themselves for joy/ excitement/impatience*, were so happy, excited, etc that they could not control their feelings. **(b)** tolerate: *I can't do with him and his insolence.* **(c)** (with *can, could*) expressing a need or wish: *You look as if you could do with* (= as if you need) *a good night's sleep. That man could do with* (= would look better if he had) *a shave. I think we can do with* (= will need) *two extra loaves today. I could do with a cup of tea.*
do without sb/sth, dispense with; manage without: *He can't do without the services of a secretary. We shall have to do without a holiday this summer. The hens haven't laid any eggs; we shall have to do without.*

do³ /duː/ *n* (*pl* dos or do's /duːz/) **1** (sl) swindle: *The scheme was a do from the start.* **2** (colloq) entertainment; party: *We're going to a big do at the Fotherington's this evening.* **3** customs, rules: *Some teachers have too many do's and don'ts.* **4** **fair dos/do's** (GB, sl) (as an exclamation) fair shares; let's be fair (eg in sharing something).
do⁴ /ˈdɪtəʊ/ (abbr of) ditto.
do⁵, **doh** /dəʊ/ *n* (music) first and eighth of the notes in the musical octave.
dob·bin /ˈdɒbɪn/ *n* (pet name for a) farm horse.
doc·ile /ˈdəʊsaɪl US: ˈdɒsl/ *adj* easily trained or controlled: *a ~ child/horse.* **do·cil·ity** /dəʊˈsɪlətɪ/ *n* [U] the quality of being ~.
dock¹ /dɒk/ *n* **1** place in a harbour, river, etc with gates through which water may be let in and out, where ships may be (un)loaded or repaired: *to go into/ enter/leave ~; to be in ~.* **ˈdry/graving ~**, one from which water may be pumped out. **ˈfloating ~**, floating structure that may be used as a dry ~. **ˈwet ~**, one in which the water may be kept at high-tide level. **ˈ~-dues**, money paid for the use of a ~. **2** (*pl*) number or row of ~s with the wharves, sheds, offices, etc round them. **ˈ~-yard**, enclosure with ~s and facilities for building and repairing ships: *the naval ~yard at Chatham.* **3** (US) wharf; ship's berth. **~er** *n* ~yard labourer.
dock² /dɒk/ *vi,vt* **1** [VP2A] (of a ship) come or go into a dock. **2** [VP6A] bring, take, (a ship) into a dock. **3** [VP6A] couple (two or more spacecraft) in space; [VP2A] perform this manoeuvre.
dock³ /dɒk/ *n* enclosure in a criminal court for the prisoner: *to be in the ~.*
dock⁴ /dɒk/ *vt* [VP6A,14] *~ (off)*, **1** cut short (an animal's tail). **2** make wages, allowances, supplies, less: *to ~ a workman's wages; to have one's salary ~ed; to ~ the soldiers of part of their rations.*
dock⁵ /dɒk/ *n* common weed with large leaves and small green flowers.
docket /ˈdɒkɪt/ *n* **1** summary of the contents of a letter, document, etc. **2** (comm) list of goods delivered, jobs done, etc; label on a package listing the contents, or giving information about use, method of assembly, etc. □ *vt* [VP6A] enter in or write on a ~; label.
doc·tor /ˈdɒktə(r)/ *n* **1** person who has been trained in medical science. ⇨ **physician, surgeon. 2** person who has received the highest university degree: *D~ of Philosophy.* □ *vt* [VP6A] **1** (colloq) give medical treatment to: *~ a cold/a child; a ~ed tomcat*, one that has been neutered, ⇨ **neuter(v). 2** make (esp food, drink) inferior by adding sth; add

COLLIE

PEKINESE

BULLDOG

BLOODHOUND

ear
withers
loins saddle
croup
stern

forehead
muzzle

brisket

knee

DACHSHUND

tail
hock

paw

dogs

ALSATIAN

drugs to. **3** (fig) falsify accounts, evidence. ∼·**ate** /'dɒktərət/ *n* ∼'s degree.

doc·tri·naire /ˌdɒktrɪ'neə(r)/ *n* person who wants his doctrines to be put into practice without allowing for circumstances, considering their suitability for particular cases, etc. □ *adj* theoretical; unpractical; dogmatic: ∼ *socialism*.

doc·trinal /dɒk'traɪnl US: 'dɒktrɪnl/ *adj* of doctrine(s).

doc·trine /'dɒktrɪn/ *n* [C,U] body of teaching; beliefs and teachings of a church, political party, school of scientists, etc: *a matter of* ∼; *the* ∼ *that the Pope is infallible*.

docu·ment /'dɒkjʊmənt/ *n* sth written or printed, to be used as a record or in evidence (eg birth, marriage and death certificates): ∼ *of title*, providing evidence of rights, ownership, etc; *a human* ∼, number of facts or incidents that illustrate human nature. □ /'dɒkjʊment/ *vt* [VP6A] prove by, supply with, ∼s: *to be well* ∼*ed*. **docu·men·ta·tion** /ˌdɒkjʊmen'teɪʃn/ *n* [U].

docu·men·tary /ˌdɒkjʊ'mentrɪ/ *adj* consisting of documents: ∼ *proof/evidence*. ∼ (**'film**) *n* cinema or TV film showing some aspect of human or social activity (eg the work of the post-office, the lives of fishermen).

dod·der /'dɒdə(r)/ *vi* [VP2A,C] (colloq) walk, move, in a shaky way, as from weakness or old age: *to* ∼ *along*. ∼**er** *n* person who ∼s. ∼**·ing**, ∼**y** *adjj* trembling; weak and uncertain in movement.

dodge¹ /dɒdʒ/ *n* **1** quick movement to evade sth. **2** (colloq) trick; piece of deception: *He's up to all the* ∼*s*, knows them all. **3** (colloq) plan; method; ingenious way of doing sth.

dodge² /dɒdʒ/ *vt,vi* [VP2A,3A,6A] **1** move quickly to one side, change position or direction, in order to escape or avoid sth: *He* ∼*d cleverly when I threw my shoe at him. I* ∼*d behind a tree so that he should not see me. You need to be quick in order to* ∼ *the traffic in London nowadays.* **2** get round (difficulties), avoid (duties, etc) by cunning or trickery: *to* ∼ *military service.* **dodger** *n* person who ∼s, esp an artful or cunning person.

dod·gem /'dɒdʒəm/ *n* (colloq) (at fun fairs, etc)

small car, electrically propelled, (to be) driven on a special platform where there are many others which have to be avoided or dodged.

dodgy /'dɒdʒɪ/ *adj* (colloq) **1** artful. **2** involving risk or loss.

dodo /'dəʊdəʊ/ *n* (*pl* ∼es, ∼s /-dəʊz/) extinct, large, flightless bird of Mauritius.

doe /dəʊ/ *n* female fallow-deer, rabbit or hare. '∼**·skin** *n* skin of a ∼; [U] soft leather made from this skin.

doer /'du:ə(r)/ *n* person who does things (contrasted with persons who merely talk, etc): *He's a* ∼, *not a talker.* (Also in compounds, as *evil-doer*).

does /dʌz/, **doesn't** /'dʌznt/ ⇨ do¹.

doff /dɒf US: dɔːf/ *vt* [VP6A] (old use) take off one's hat, coat, etc.

dog¹ /dɒg US: dɔːg/ *n* **1** common domestic animal, a friend of man, of which there are many breeds; male of this animal and of the wolf and the fox. ⇨ bitch. **2** (phrases): *a case of dog eat dog*, situation, eg in business, where ruthless methods are used. *die like a dog; die a 'dog's death,* die in shame or misery. *a dog in the manger,* person who prevents others from enjoying sth that is useless to himself. *dressed like a dog's dinner,* (colloq) in the height of fashion. *give/throw sth to the dogs,* throw it away as worthless, or as a sacrifice to save oneself. *give a dog a bad name (and hang him),* (prov) give a person a bad reputation, slander him, and the bad reputation will remain. *go to the dogs,* be ruined. *help a lame dog over a stile,* help a person in trouble. *lead a 'dog's life,* be troubled all the time. *lead sb a 'dog's life,* give him no peace; worry him all the time. *let sleeping dogs lie,* (prov) let well alone; not look for trouble. *look like a dog's breakfast/dinner,* (colloq) very untidy; messy. *love me, love my dog,* (prov) if you want me as a friend, you must accept my friends as yours. *not stand (even) a 'dog's chance,* have no chance at all of beating a stronger enemy, surviving a disaster, etc. *be top dog,* be in a position where one rules. *be (the) 'underdog,* be in a position where one must always submit. **3** (colloq) **the dogs,** greyhound race-meetings. **4** (old use; of a man) worthless, wicked or surly person. **5** (with *adjj*, colloq) person: *He's a dirty/sly/lucky/gay dog.* **6** (kinds of) mechanical device for gripping, etc. **7** (*pl*, also **'fire-dogs**) metal supports for logs in a fireplace. **8** (compounds): **'dog-biscuit**, hard, thick biscuit for feeding dogs. **'dog-cart**, high, two-wheeled cart, pulled by a horse, with two seats back to back. **'dog-collar**, (colloq) clerical collar. **'dog-days**, period of very hot weather (July and August). **'dog-eared**, (of a book) having the corners of the leaves turned down with use. **'dog-fish**, small kind of shark. ⇨ the illus at sea. **'dog-house**, (US) kennel. *in the doghouse,* (colloq) in disgrace or disfavour. **'dog paddle**, simple swimming stroke in which the arms and legs are moved in short, quick splashing movements. **'dogs-body**, drudge. **,dog 'tired**, tired out, exhausted. **'dog-tooth**, small pyramid-shaped ornament (in stonework, Norman and Early English architecture). **'dog's-tooth**, checked pattern (in cloth for men's suits, overcoats, etc). **'dog-trot**, gentle, easy trot. **'dog-watch**, (on ships) one of the two-hour watches (4 to 6pm, 6 to 8pm). **'dog-wood**, tree with large white or pinkish flowers in spring. **'dog-like** *adj* like or as of a dog, esp *dog-like devotion*, the kind of devotion given by a dog to its master. **doggy, doggie** /'dɒgɪ US: 'dɔ:gɪ/ *n* (child's word for a) dog.

dog² /dɒg US: dɔ:g/ *vt* (-gg-) [VP6A] keep close behind, in the footsteps of: *dog a suspected thief;* (fig) *dogged by misfortune.*

doge /dəʊdʒ/ *n* elected chief magistrate in the former republics of Venice and Genoa.

dog-ged /'dɒgɪd US: 'dɔ:g-/ *adj* obstinate; stubborn. **~·ly** *adv* **~·ness** *n*

dog-gerel /'dɒgərəl US: 'dɔ:g-/ *n* [U] irregular, inexpert verse.

doggo /'dɒgəʊ US: 'dɔ:g-/ *adv* **lie~**, (sl) lie without making a movement or sound.

dogma /'dɒgmə US: 'dɔ:g-/ *n* **1** [C] belief, system of beliefs, put forward by some authority (esp the Church) to be accepted as true without question. **2** [U] such beliefs collectively.

dog-matic /dɒg'mætɪk US: dɔ:g-/ *adj* **1** put forward as dogmas: **~** *theology.* **2** (of a person) making purely personal statements as if they were dogmas; (of statements) put forward in this way without proof. **dog-mati-cally** /-klɪ/ *adv*

dog-ma-tism /'dɒgmətɪzəm US: 'dɔ:g-/ *n* [U] the quality of being dogmatic; being dogmatic: *His* **~** *aroused their opposition.*

dog-ma-tize /'dɒgmətaɪz US: 'dɔ:g-/ *vi,vt* [VP2A] make dogmatic statements; [VP6A] express (a principle, etc) as a dogma.

doh ⇨ do⁵.

doily /'dɔɪlɪ/ *n* (*pl* -lies) small, round piece of linen, lace, etc placed under a dish on a table or under an ornament on a shelf.

do-ings /'du:ɪŋz/ *n pl* (colloq) things done or being done: *Tell me about all your* **~** *in London.*

dol-drums /'dɒldrəmz/ *n pl in the* **~**, (colloq) in low spirits.

dole¹ /dəʊl/ *vt* [VP15B] **~** *out,* distribute food, money, etc in small amounts. □ *n* **1** [C] sth **~**d out. **2** [U] **the ~**, (colloq term for) weekly payment made under various Insurance Acts in GB (from contributions made by workers, employers and the State) to an unemployed worker. *be/go on the* **~**, receive/begin to receive such payments.

dole-ful /'dəʊlfl/ *adj* mournful; dismal **~·ly**

/-fəlɪ/ *adv*

doll¹ /dɒl/ *n* **1** model of a baby or person, usu for a child to play with. **2** (sl) (pretty but silly) girl or woman.

doll² /dɒl/ *vt,vi* [VP15B,2C] **~** *up,* (colloq) dress (oneself) up smartly: *She was all* **~**ed up for the party.*

dol-lar /'dɒlə(r)/ *n* unit of money (symbol $) in the US, Canada, Australia and other countries.

dol-lop /'dɒləp/ *n* (colloq) shapeless quantity of food, etc: *a* **~** *of cold rice pudding.*

dolly /'dɒlɪ/ *n* (*pl* -lies) **1** (child's word for a) doll. **2** small wheeled frame or platform for moving heavy objects; mobile platform for a heavy camera. **3** (sl) attractive, fashionably dressed but silly girl or young woman.

dol-men /'dɒlmen/ *n* = cromlech.

dol-our (US = **-lor**) /'dɒlə(r) US: 'dəʊl-/ *n* (poet) grief; sorrow. **~·ous** /-rəs/ *adj* sorrowful; distressed; distressing.

dol-phin /'dɒlfɪn/ *n* sea animal like a porpoise. ⇨ the illus at sea.

dolt /dəʊlt/ *n* stupid fellow; blockhead. **~·ish** *adj* stupid.

do-main /dəʊ'meɪn/ *n* lands under the rule of a government, ruler, etc; (fig) field or province of thought, knowledge, activity: *in the* **~** *of science.*

dome /dəʊm/ *n* rounded roof with a circular base; sth shaped like a **~**: *the rounded* **~** (= summit) *of a hill.* **domed** *adj* rounded: *a man with a* **~**d *forehead.*

domes

Domes-day Book /'du:mzdeɪ bʊk/ *n* record of the inquiry, made by King William I in 1086, into the ownership of all the lands in England.

do-mes-tic /də'mestɪk/ *adj* **1** of the home, family, household: *He has had a good many* **~** *troubles. What a charming* **~** *scene!* eg of members of a family happy together at home. *She's a very* **~** *sort of woman,* prefers home life to social activities outside the home. **2** not foreign; native; of one's own country: *The government could get neither foreign nor* **~** *loans,* could not borrow money either abroad or at home. *This newspaper provides more foreign news than* **~** *news.* **3** (of animals, etc) kept by, living with, man: *Horses, cows and sheep are* **~** *animals.* ⇨ wild. **do-mes-ti-cally** /-klɪ/ *adv*

do-mes-ti-cate /də'mestɪkeɪt/ *vt* [VP6A] **1** (chiefly in *pp*) make fond of, interested in, household work and duties: *She's not at all* **~**d, is not fond of, skilled in, cooking, housekeeping, etc. **2** tame (animals). **do-mes-ti-ca-tion** /də,mestɪ'keɪʃn/ *n*

do-mes-tic-ity /,dɒme'stɪsətɪ/ *n* [U] home or family life.

domi-cile /'dɒmɪsaɪl/ *n* (formal) dwelling-place; (legal) place where a person lives permanently.

dom-i-cili-ary /,dɒmɪ'sɪlɪərɪ US: -lɪerɪ/ *adj* (formal) of or to a dwelling-place: *a* **~** *visit,* one made to a house, etc (eg by officials to search or inspect it, or by a doctor to a patient).

domi·nant /'dɒmɪnənt/ *adj* **1** having control or authority; dominating; most important or influential: *the ~ partner in a business.* **2** (of heights) overlooking others: *a ~ cliff.* **3** (music) fifth note of a scale. **~·ly** *adv* **domi·nance** /-nəns/ *n* being ~.

domi·nate /'dɒmɪneɪt/ *vt,vi* [VP6A,2A,3A] ~ *(over),* **1** have control, authority or influence: *A great man can ~ (over) others by force of character. The strong usually ~ (over) the weak.* **2** (of a place, esp a height) overlook: *The whole valley is ~d by this mountain.* **domi·na·tion** /ˌdɒmɪ'neɪʃn/ *n* [U] dominating or being ~.

domi·neer /ˌdɒmɪ'nɪə(r)/ *vi* [VP2A,3A] ~ *(over),* act, speak, in a dominating manner; behave like a tyrant; be overbearing: *Big boys sometimes ~ (over) their small sisters.* **~·ing** *adj: He's a very ~ing sort of fellow,* likes to ~ over others. **~·ing·ly** *adv*

Dom·ini·can /dɒ'mɪnɪkən/ *n, adj* (friar or nun) of the religious order founded in 1212 by St Dominic /'dɒmɪnɪk/.

domi·nie /'dɒmɪnɪ/ *n* (Scot) schoolteacher.

do·min·ion /də'mɪnɪən/ *n* **1** [U] ~ *(over),* authority to rule; control (over). **2** [C] territory of a sovereign government. **3** [C] (old use) one of the self-governing territories of the British Commonwealth of Nations.

dom·ino /'dɒmɪnəʊ/ *n* (*pl* ~es or ~s /-nəʊz/) **1** small, flat, oblong piece of wood or bone, marked with spots. **2** (*pl* with *sing v*) table game played with 28 of these. **3** loose cloak with a mask for the upper part of the face, worn at parties, fancy-dress balls, etc.

don¹ /dɒn/ *n* **1** (GB) teaching member of a university staff. **2** Spanish gentleman; Spanish title (used before a man's name): *Don Juan.* **don·nish**

don² /dɒn/ *vt* (-nn-) [VP6A] (old use) put on clothing, etc. ⟹ doff.

do·nate /dəʊ'neɪt US: 'dəʊneɪt/ *vt* [VP6A,14] ~ *(to),* give (eg money, to a charity, etc); contribute. **do·na·tion** /dəʊ'neɪʃn/ *n* [U] giving; [C] sth given: *donations to the Red Cross/the refugee fund.*

done /dʌn/ ⟹ do¹.

don·jon /'dɒndʒən/ *n* large, strongly fortified main tower of a castle.

don·key /'dɒŋkɪ/ *n* (*pl* ~s /-kɪz/) (the common and usu word for an) ass. ⟹ the illus at domestic. **'~ engine,** small auxiliary steam-engine, esp one on a ship's deck. **'~-jacket,** workman's thick, short coat. **'~-work** *n* drudgery.

do·nor /'dəʊnə(r)/ *n* person who gives sth, eg property or money: *blood ~,* person who gives his own blood for transfusion.

don't /dəʊnt/ **1** = *do not;* ⟹ do¹. **2** *do's and ~s,* ⟹ do³(3).

doodle /'duːdl/ *vi* [VP2A], *n* (colloq) (make) meaningless scrawls or scribbles (while one is or ought to be paying attention to sth else).

doodle·bug /'duːdlbʌg/ *n* (colloq) flying bomb (a pilotless guided missile) used by the Nazis against London in 1944.

doom¹ /duːm/ *n* **1** (usu *sing*) ruin; death; sth evil that is to come: *to go to one's ~; to send a man to his ~.* **2** (also **Doomsday** /'duːmzdeɪ/) the Day of Judgement; the end of the world. *till D~sday,* for ever.

doom² /duːm/ *vt* [VP6A,14,17] ~ *(to),* (usu passive) condemn (sb to some fate/to do sth): (esp in *pp*) *~ed to disappointment; ~ed to die; poems ~ed to oblivion,* certain to be forgotten.

door /dɔː(r)/ *n* **1** that which closes the entrance to a building, room, cupboard, safe, etc: *to open/close/lock, etc the ~; hinged/sliding/revolving ~s. The ~ opened/was opened and a man came*

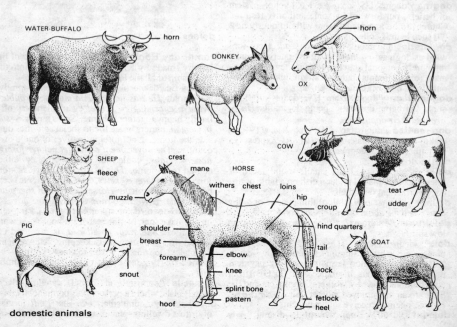

domestic animals

out. **back** ~, ~ at the back of the house (to the yard, garden, etc). **front** ~, chief ~ from a house to the street or road. **next** ~, (in/to) the next house: *Who lives next* ~ *(to you)? I'm just going next* ~ *to see Mrs Jones*. **next** ~ **to**, (fig) nearly, almost. **two/three, etc** ~**s away/down/off**, in the next house but one/two, etc: *My brother lives three* ~*s away*. **from** ~ **to** ~, (a) from the ~ of one building to the ~ of another: *It was raining heavily, but the taxi took us from* ~ *to* ~. (b) from house to house: *He went from* ~ *to* ~ *delivering the milk/selling encyclopaedias.* Hence, ~**-to-**~ *adj: a* ~*-to-*~ *salesman.* **out of** ~**s**, in the open air: *It's cold out of* ~*s; put an overcoat on.* **within** ~**s**, inside; in the house. **at death's** ~, near death. **lay sth at sb's** ~, say that he is responsible for it. **show sb the** ~, lead him out to it (esp when he is unwelcome). **2** (fig) means of obtaining or approaching sth: *a* ~ *to success; to close the* ~ *against an agreement upon disarmament*, make it impossible. **3** (compounds) '~**-bell**, bell inside a building, operated by a button, etc outside. '~**-case/-frame**, framework into which a ~ fits. '~**-handle**, one which releases the latch to open a ~. '~**-keeper**, person on duty or on guard at a ~ or other entrance. '~**-knob**, round knob turned to release the lock on a ~. '~**-knocker**, ⇨ **knocker**. '~**-man** /-mən/ (*pl* -men) uniformed attendant at the entrance to a hotel, cinema, etc. '~**-mat**, rough mat on which shoes may be wiped. '~**-nail**, large-headed nail formerly used to decorate some ~s. **dead as a** ~*-nail*, certainly dead. '~**-plate**, plate (usu brass) fastened to a ~ and with the name of the person living or working in the building or room. '~**-post**, upright post, part of a frame. *deaf as a* ~*-post*, completely deaf. '~**-step**, step up to (usu) an outer ~. '~**-stopper**, heavy object placed in a ~way to prevent the ~ from closing. '~**-way**, opening into which a ~ fits: *standing in the* ~*way*.
dope /dəʊp/ *n* [U] **1** thick, heavy liquid used as varnish. **2** (colloq) harmful drug (eg opium); narcotic. **3** (sl) information. □ *vt* [VP6A] give ~(2) to; make unconscious with a drug or narcotic; stimulate (eg a race-horse) with a drug. ~**y** /'dəʊpɪ/ *adj* (sl) half asleep; (as if) drugged; stupid.
Doric /'dɒrɪk *US:* 'dɔ:r-/ *adj* (archit) of the oldest and simplest of the three types of column(1) in ancient Greek architecture. ⇨ the illus at **column**.
dor·mant /'dɔ:mənt/ *adj* in a state of inactivity but awaiting development or activity: *a* ~ *volcano;* ~ *faculties*, mental powers capable of being developed; *plants which are* ~*/lie* ~ *during the winter*, alive but not growing.
dor·mer /'dɔ:mə(r)/ *n* (usu '~**-window**) upright window built in a sloping roof. ⇨ the illus at window.
dor·mi·tory /'dɔ:mɪtrɪ *US:* -tɔ:rɪ/ *n* (*pl* -ries) sleeping-room with several or many beds, esp in a school or institution.
dor·mouse /'dɔ:maʊs/ *n* (*pl* dormice /'dɔ:maɪs/) small animal (like a mouse or squirrel) that sleeps during cold weather in winter.
dor·sal /'dɔ:sl/ *adj* (anat) of, on, near, the back: *the* ~ *fin*, eg of a shark. ⇨ the illus at sea.
dory[1] /'dɔ:rɪ/ *n* (*pl* -ries) ship's light, flat-bottomed rowing-boat (eg as used by cod-fishers in N America).
dory[2] /'dɔ:rɪ/ *n* (also **,John 'D**~) edible seafish.
dos·age /'dəʊsɪdʒ/ *n* [U] giving of medicines in doses; quantity of a single dose.

dose /dəʊs/ *n* [C] **1** amount (of a medicine/drug) taken at one time: *The bottle contains six* ~*s*. ⇨ salt(4). **2** (fig, colloq) sth given or taken: *give sb a* ~ *of flattery*. **3** (sl) venereal disease: *give sb a* ~. □ *vt* [VP6A,15B,14] give ~(s) to: *to* ~ *oneself with quinine*.
doss /dɒs/ *vi* (GB sl) [VP2C] ~ **down**, go to bed. '~**-house** *n* cheap lodging-house. **dos·ser** /-sə(r)/ *n* tramp (*n*,3).
dos·sier /'dɒsɪeɪ *US:* 'dɔ:s-/ *n* set of papers giving information about a person or event, esp a person's record.
dost /dʌst/ *v* old form, used in *Thou* ~, You do.
dot[1] /dɒt/ *n* **1** small round mark (as over the letters i and j); decimal points: *dots and dashes*, the marks (eg · — · · · — · · — · ·) used for morse signals. **on the dot**, (colloq) at the precise moment. **2** sth like a dot in appearance: *We watched the ship until it was a mere dot on the horizon*. □ *vt* (-tt-) **1** mark with a dot. **dot one's/the i's and cross one's/the t's**, (fig) make (sth) clear and definite. **2** make with, cover with, dots: *dotted about*, scattered here and there; *a field dotted with sheep*, with sheep here and there; *a dotted line*, eg on a document, for a signature. **sign on the dotted line**, (fig) agree without hesitation or protest.
do·tage /'dəʊtɪdʒ/ *n* [U] weakness of mind caused by old age: *He is in his* ~, is growing foolish, is unable to remember things, fails to notice things, etc. **do·tard** /'dəʊtəd/ *n* person in his ~.
dote /dəʊt/ *vi* [VP3A] ~ **on/upon**, show much, or too much, fondness; centre one's affections (on): *She* ~*s on her grandson. He's a doting* (= very loving) *husband*.
doth /dʌθ/ old form used for *does*.
dottle /'dɒtl/ *n* small quantity of tobacco left unsmoked in a pipe.
dotty /'dɒtɪ/ *adj* (-ier, -iest) (colloq) feeble-minded; idiotic; eccentric.
double[1] /'dʌbl/ *adj* **1** twice as (much, large, etc): *His partner is ill and he has to do* ~ *work. His income is* ~ *what it was five years ago. There was a* ~ *knock at the door*, two knocks in quick succession. *Two* ~ *whiskies, please*, two glasses of whisky, each with twice the usual portion. **2** having two of the same things or parts: *a gun with a* ~ *barrel; a railway with a* ~ *track;* ~ *doors;* ~*glazing/*~ *windows* (used in cold countries); *a man with a* ~ *chin*, with a fold of loose flesh below the chin; *a ship/box/trunk with a* ~ *bottom; a sword with a* ~ *edge; a* ~ *exposure*, (photo) two exposures on the same plate or section of film. ⇨ single. **3** made for two persons or things: *a* ~ *bed; a* ~ *harness*, for two horses. **4** combining two things, qualities, etc: *a* ~ *advantage; a piece of furniture that serves a* ~ *purpose*, eg one that is a settee and can be opened out to make a bed; *a man with a* ~ *character*, eg Jekyll and Hyde; *to engage in* ~ *dealing*, be dishonest and deceitful. **5** (of flowers) having more than one set or circle of petals: ~ *daffodils*.
double[2] /'dʌbl/ *adv* **1** twice (as much): *Many things now cost* ~ *what they did a few years ago.* **2** in twos; in a pair; in pairs or couples: *to see* ~, to see two things when there is only one; *to sleep* ~, two to a bed.
double[3] /'dʌbl/ *n* **1** twice the quantity: *Ten is the* ~ *of five.* ~ **or quits,** the decision by chance (eg by throwing dice) whether a person shall pay twice what he owes, or nothing at all. **2** person or thing

that looks exactly, or almost exactly, like another· *She is the ~ of her sister.* **3** (*pl*) (tennis) game with two pairs. **mixed ~s,** a man and woman against another man and woman. **4** *at the ~,* (colloq) quickly. **5** [C] (bridge) act of doubling. ⇨ **double⁴(6).**

dou·ble⁴ /'dʌbl/ *vt, vi* **1** [VP6A,2A] make or become twice as great: *to ~ one's income. Money earning good interest will ~ itself in time.* **2** [VP6A,15B] ~ **(up/over/across),** bend or fold in two: *Let me ~ (over) the shawl and put it round you. He ~d his fists,* clenched them as if ready to fight. **3** [VP2A,C] ~ **(back),** turn sharply back in flight (when running to escape pursuit): *The fox ~d (back) on its tracks.* **~ back,** turn or fold (sth) back. **~ up, (a)** fold (sth) up: *He ~d up his legs and kicked out,* eg when swimming. **(b)** be capable of folding up or rolling up: *This carpet is too thick to ~ up.* **(c)** (of persons) (cause to) bend the body with pain or in helpless laughter: *The stone struck him in the stomach and ~d him up. He ~d up with the pain of the blow.* **5** [VP2C,6A] do two jobs at the same time; (of an actor) act two parts in the same play: *doubling as/doubling the parts of king and slave.* **6** (bridge) bid to cause the points, lost or won by the opponents on the hand(13c), to be twice as much as they would normally have been.

dou·ble⁵ /'dʌbl/ *adj, adv* (in compounds) ,~- '**barrelled** *adj* (of a gun) having two barrels; (fig, of a compliment, etc) ambiguous; (of a surname) compound, hyphenated (as *Smith-Jones*). ,~-'**bass** *n* largest and lowest-pitched instrument in the violin family. ⇨ the illus at string. ,~-'**bedded** *adj* (of a room) with two beds or a ~ bed. (Cf *single-/ twin-bedded.*) ,~ '**bind** *n* dilemma. ,~-'**breasted** *adj* (of a coat or waistcoat) made so as to overlap across the front of the body. ,~-'**check** *vt* check¹(1), twice in order to be certain. ,~-'**cross** *vt* [VP6A] (colloq) cheat or betray. □ *n* act of this kind. ,~-'**dealer** *n* person who says one thing and means another; deceiver. ,~-'**dealing** *n, adj* deceit(ful) (esp in business). ,~-'**decker** *n* ship, tram, bus with two decks. ⇨ deck¹(2). ,~-'**dutch** *n* (colloq) gibberish. ,~-'**dyed** *adj* (chiefly fig) having certain qualities to a very high degree: *a ~-dyed scoundrel,* deeply stained with guilt. ,~- '**edged** *adj* with two cutting edges; (fig, of an argument, compliment) that can be understood as being either for or against. ,~-'**entry** *n* system of book-keeping in which each transaction is entered (written) on the debit side of one account and the credit side of another. ,~-'**faced** *adj* (= *two-faced*) insincere. ,~-'**first** *n* a first-class honours degree in two principal subjects gained at the same time. ,~-'**jointed** *adj* having joints that allow the fingers (or arms, legs) to move or bend in unusual ways. ,~-'**park** *vt, vi* park a car at the side of a car already parked at the side of a street. ,~-'**quick** *adj, adv* very quick(ly): *in ~-quick time.* ,~ '**take** *n* delayed reaction to a situation. '~-**talk** *n* kind of talk that really means the opposite of, or sth quite different from, what it seems to mean. '~-**think** *n* ability to believe two contradictory things.

doub·let /'dʌblɪt/ *n* **1** close-fitting garment for the upper part of the body, worn by men (about 1400—1600). **2** one of a pair, esp one of two words with the same origin but which have become different in form or meaning, eg *hospital/hostel.*

doub·loon /dʌb'lu:n/ *n* (hist) Spanish gold coin.

doubly /'dʌblɪ/ *adv* (used before *adjj*) to twice the extent or amount: *to be ~ careful/sure.*

doubt¹ /daʊt/ *n* [U] uncertainty of mind; [C] feeling of uncertainty: *I have no ~ that you will succeed/no ~ of your ability. There is not much ~ about his guilt,* He is almost certainly guilty. *She had her ~s whether he would come. I have my ~s as to/about this being true. There is no room for ~,* We can be quite certain about it. *There is no ~ about it,* It is certain. *It became a matter of ~ (= became uncertain) whether…. in ~,* uncertain: *When in ~ about the meaning of a word, consult a dictionary. He is in ~ (about) what to do.* **beyond/past (all) ~; without (a) ~,** certainly: *Don't worry; he'll come back without ~.* **no ~,** very probably: *He meant to help, no ~, but in fact he has been a hindrance.* **throw ~ upon sth,** suggest that it is not to be regarded as certain or reliable. ⇨ benefit.

doubt² /daʊt/ *vt* [VP6A,9,10] ~ **(if/whether),** feel doubt about; hesitate to believe; question the truth of: *You cannot ~ your own existence. I ~ the truth of this report. Do you ~ my word,* think I am not telling the truth? *I don't ~ that he will come. Can you ~ that he will win? I ~ whether he will come. I ~ if that was what he wanted.*

doubt·ful /'daʊtfl/ *adj* ~ **(about/of),** feeling doubt; causing doubt; unreliable: *I am/feel ~ (about) what I ought to do. The future looks very ~. The weather looks very ~. It's a ~ blessing,* may or may not be one. *Are you ~ of success? He's a ~ character,* perhaps dishonest. *It is a ~ neighbourhood,* one with a bad reputation, one where ~ characters live. ~**ly** /-fəlɪ/ *adv*

doubt·less /'daʊtlɪs/ *adv* very probably.

douche /du:ʃ/ *n* stream of water applied to a part of the body (outside or inside) for cleaning it or for medicinal purposes; instrument for forcing out such a stream of water.

dough /dəʊ/ *n* [U] mixture of flour, water, etc in a paste (for making bread, pastry, etc); (sl) money. '~-**nut,** sweetened ~ cooked in deep fat, usu in the shape of a ring or a ball. ~**y** /'dəʊɪ/ *adj* of or like ~; soft; flabby.

doughty /'daʊtɪ/ *adj* (old use, or joc) brave and strong; bold: *a ~ warrior; ~ deeds.*

dour /dʊə(r)/ *adj* severe; stern; obstinate: *~ looks; ~ silence.* ~**ly** *adv*

douse, dowse /daʊs/ *vt* [VP6A] put into water; throw water over; (colloq) extinguish (a light).

dove¹ /dʌv/ *n* **1** kind of pigeon; symbol of peace. '~-**cote** /'dʌvkəʊt/ *n* small shelter or house with nesting-boxes for ~s. **flutter the ~-cotes,** alarm quiet people. **2** (colloq) member of a group promoting peace. ⇨ hawk¹(2).

dove² /dəʊv/ (US) alternative *pt* form of dive².

dove·tail /'dʌvteɪl/ *n* joint for two pieces of wood. □ *vt, vi* [VP6A,2A,3A] ~ **(with/into),** join together

ruff

a doublet and hose   a jerkin

a dove   dove-tailing

by means of ~s; (fig) fit (together): *My plans ~ed with his.*

dowa·ger /'daʊədʒə(r)/ *n* **1** woman with property or a title from her dead husband: *the ~ duchess.* **2** (colloq) dignified elderly lady.

dowdy /'daʊdɪ/ *adj* (-ier, -iest) (of clothes, etc) shabby or unfashionable; (of a person) dressed in ~ clothes. **dow·di·ly** *adv* **dow·di·ness** *n*

dowel /'daʊəl/ *n* headless pin or peg for keeping two pieces of wood, metal, stone, etc together.

dower /'daʊə(r)/ *n* **1** widow's share of her husband's property. **2** dowry. **3** gift of nature (eg beauty, intelligence). □ *vt* provide with a ~.

down[1] /daʊn/ *n* [U] first, soft feathers of young birds; soft under-feathers of birds (as used for pillows and cushions); fine soft hair, eg the first hair that comes on a boy's face; the soft hair on some plants and seeds (eg the thistle).

down[2] /daʊn/ *adv part* **1** (with *vv* of motion) from a high(er) level to a low(er) level: *The sun went ~. The flag was hauled ~ at sunset. If you can't jump ~, climb ~. Some kinds of food go ~* (= can be swallowed) *more easily than others.* **2** (with *vv* of motion) from an upright position to a horizontal position: *He was knocked ~ by a bus. If you're tired, go and lie ~. He's ~* (= ill in bed) *with flu. Don't hit a man when he's ~,* (fig) attack him when he has suffered misfortune, etc. **3** (with *vv* indicating change of stance but not of position in space) to or in a lower position or direction: *Sit ~, please. The tall man bent ~ to speak to me.* **4** (with *vv* indicating position or state): *Mary isn't ~ yet,* is not yet dressed and downstairs. *We can't use the telephone—the lines are all ~,* on the ground, eg after a storm. *The river is ~,* back to its normal height, eg after a flood. **5** from a more important place (eg the capital) to a less important place; from an inland place to the coast; from the university: *We went ~ to Brighton* (eg from London) *for the weekend. The Bill was sent ~* (from the House of Lords) *to the House of Commons.* **6** (used with *vv* to indicate reduction to a smaller volume, a lower degree, a state of less activity, etc): *The heels of my shoes have worn ~. Boil the fat ~. The wind died ~. The sea is ~/has calmed ~,* is, has become, calm. *The fire is burning ~,* getting low. *One of the back tyres is ~,* is flat or getting flat. *The clock has run ~,* needs to be wound up. *The temperature has gone ~. The price of fruit is ~.* **7** (used with reference to writing) on paper: *to write sth ~; to get sth ~,* write it. *Please take ~ this letter,* write it (eg in shorthand) as I dictate it. *Put me ~/Put my name ~ for 50p,* as willing to give this sum. *I see you're ~* (= your name appears in the programme) *for a speech at the next meeting.* **8** from an earlier time (to a later time): *the history of Europe ~ to 1914; looking ~ through the ages; coming ~ to modern times.* **9** including the lower limit in a series: *from ocean liners ~ to rowing-boats.* **10** (in various phrases) *D~ with,* let us be rid of: *D~ with the grammarians! ~ under,* (colloq) on the other side of the world from Europe (eg Australia). *up and ~,* to and fro: *walking up and ~. money/cash '~,* payment at the time of purchase (contrasted with credit): *You must pay £10 ~.* Hence '*~ payment. be ~ and out,* (colloq) (**a**) (boxing) be knocked out, unable to resume the fight. (**b**) (fig) be beaten in the struggle of life; be unemployed and without money. Hence, *~-and-'out n* [C]. *get ~ to work/business,* start work in real earnest. *be ~ on sb,* feel ill-will towards him. *~ in the dumps,* (colloq) dejected; in low spirits. *~ in the mouth,* (colloq) sad-looking. *~ on one's luck,* (colloq) having suffered misfortune. *come '~ in the world,* fall to a lower social position. *come ~ on sb,* scold or rebuke him sharply. *~-to-'earth adj* concerned with realities; practical (contrasted with *impractical, vague, idealistic*): *He's a ~-to-earth sort of fellow.*

down[3] /daʊn/ *prep* **1** from a high(er) to a low(er) level: *to run ~ a hill. The tears ran ~ her face. Her hair was hanging ~ her back.* **2** at a lower part of: *Oxford is farther ~ the river.* **3** along (not necessarily with reference to a lower level): *I was walking ~ the street. He has gone ~ town,* from one of the outlying parts, eg a suburb, to the business or shopping quarters of the town. ⇨ down-town. *~ (the) wind,* (of a boat) with the wind behind. **4** (of time) from a farther to a nearer period: *~ the ages.*

down[4] /daʊn/ *vt* [VP6A] (colloq) bring, put, knock, down: *to ~ a player with a tackle; to ~ a glass of beer,* empty the glass. *~ tools,* (of workers) refuse to work, go on strike.

down[5] /daʊn/ *n* **ups and ~s,** changes in fortune, prosperity, etc: *have one's ups and ~s; the ups and ~s of life. have a ~ on sb,* feel ill-will towards him.

down·beat /'daʊnbiːt/ *n* (music) first beat of a bar (when the conductor's hand moves down).

down·cast /'daʊnkɑːst *US*: -kæst/ *adj* (of a person) depressed; discouraged; sad; (of eyes) looking downwards.

down·fall /'daʊnfɔːl/ *n* (usu *sing*) **1** heavy fall (of rain, etc). **2** (fig) ruin; fall from fortune or power: *His ~ was caused by gambling and drink.*

down·grade /ˌdaʊn'greɪd/ *vt* [VP6A] reduce to a lower grade or rank.

down·hearted /ˌdaʊn'hɑːtɪd/ *adj* in low spirits; depressed.

down·hill /ˌdaʊn'hɪl/ *adv* in a downward sloping direction. *go ~,* (fig) get worse (in health, fortune, etc).

Down·ing Street /'daʊnɪŋ striːt/ *n* street in London with official residence of the Prime Minister; (hence) the British Government: *What does ~ think of the matter?*

down·pour /'daʊnpɔː(r)/ *n* (usu *sing*) heavy fall (esp of rain): *to be caught in a ~.*

down·right /'daʊnraɪt/ *adj* **1** forthright; honest; frank: *He has a ~ manner. He is a ~ sort of person.* **2** thorough; complete: *It's a ~ lie. It's ~ nonsense.* □ *adv* thoroughly: *He was ~ rude.* *~-ness n*

downs /daʊnz/ *n* **1** expanse of open high land. **the North/South D~s,** the chalk uplands of S England. **2** the D~s, the sea off the coast of Kent

(SE England): *anchor in the D~s.*

down-stairs /ˌdaʊnˈsteəz/ *adv* to, at, on, of, a lower floor; down the stairs: *He went ~ to breakfast. Our neighbours ~* (= on the lower floor) *are very noisy. Your brother is waiting ~.* □ **down-stair(s)** *adj: the ~(s) rooms.*

down-town /ˈdaʊntaʊn/ *adv* (esp US) to or in the lower part of a town; to or in the main or business part of a town: (attrib) *~ New York; a ~ movie theatre.*

down-trod-den /ˈdaʊntrɒdn/ *adj* oppressed; kept down and treated badly.

down-ward /ˈdaʊnwəd/ *adj* moving, leading, going, pointing, to what is lower: *a ~ slope; on the ~ path; prices with a ~ tendency.* **down-ward(s)** *adv* towards what is lower: *He laid the picture face ~s on the table. The monkey was hanging head ~s from the branch.*

downy /ˈdaʊnɪ/ *adj* of, like, covered with, down. ⇨ **down** [1].

dowry /ˈdaʊərɪ/ *n* (*pl* -ries) [C] property, money, brought by a bride to her husband.

dowse /daʊs/ *vt* ⇨ **douse.**

dows-ing /ˈdaʊzɪŋ/ *n* [U] searching for underground water or metals by using a Y-shaped stick or rod. ⇨ **diviner. dows-er** *n* person who does this.

dox-ol-ogy /dɒkˈsɒlədʒɪ/ *n* (*pl* -gies) words of praise to God, used in church services (eg 'Glory be to God...').

doyen /ˈdɔɪən/ *n* senior member of the diplomatic corps in a capital city, or a society, profession, etc.

doy-ley, doyly *n* = doily.

doze /dəʊz/ *vi* [VP2A,C] sleep lightly; be half asleep. *~ off,* fall lightly asleep: *He ~d off during the sermon.* □ *n* [C] short, light sleep.

dozen /ˈdʌzn/ *n* (also used attrib, *pl* unchanged) **1** twelve: *Eggs are 35p a ~. I want three ~ of these. Pack them in ~s,* in sets or groups of twelve. **talk nineteen to the ~,** talk incessantly. **2** *~s of,* a large number of: *I've been there ~s of times.*

drab /dræb/ *adj* **1** (also as *n*) dull muddy brown. **2** (fig) dull; uninteresting; monotonous: *a ~ existence. ~-ly adv ~-ness n*

drachm /dræm/ *n* **1** = dram(1). **2** (archaic) small quantity.

drachma /ˈdrækmə/ *n* ancient Greek silver coin; modern Greek unit of currency.

dra-co-nian /drəˈkəʊnɪən/ *adj* of a rigorous law or code of laws; harsh: *~ measures.*

draft [1] /drɑːft *US:* dræft/ *n* [C] **1** outline (usu in the form of rough notes) of sth to be done: *a ~ for a speech/letter;* preliminary version: *a ~ for a Parliamentary Bill;* rough sketch: *a ~ for a machine.* **2** written order for payment of money by a bank; drawing of money by means of such an order: *a ~ for £500 upon London,* eg one written by a Paris bank upon its London branch. Hence, **'bank-~. 3** group of men chosen from a larger group for a special purpose; (US) group of men conscripted for the armed forces. **the ~,** conscription. **'~ card,** card summoning a man to serve in the armed forces. **4** (US)draught.

draft [2] /drɑːft *US:* dræft/ *vt* [VP6A] **1** make a draft(1) of: *to ~ a speech.* **2** choose men for a draft(3); (US) conscript (a man) for the armed forces: *to be ~ed into the Army. ~·ee* /ˌdrɑːfˈtiː: *US:* ˌdræfˈtiː/ *n* (US) man *~ed* for military service. *~·ing n* the act of *~ing*; way in which sth is *~ed*(1): *a ~ing committee,* eg of a Parliamentary

Bill. *The ~ing of this section of the Bill is obscure.*

drafts-man /ˈdrɑːftsmən *US:* ˈdræfts-/ *n* (*pl* - men) man who prepares drafts(1), esp in engineering and architecture; person responsible for the careful and exact wording of a legal document, or a (clause in a) parliamentary bill.

drafty /ˈdrɑːftɪ *US:* ˈdræftɪ/ *adj* (-ier, -iest) (US) = draughty.

drag [1] /dræg/ *n* **1** sth that is dragged, eg a net ('~-net) pulled over the bottom of a river (eg to catch fish); a heavy harrow pulled over the ground to break up the soil. **2** (colloq) sth or sb that slows down progress because heavy, dull, etc: *His wife has been a ~ on him all his life,* has hindered him in his career. *Do we have to take your sister with us? She's such a ~.* ⇨ drag [2] (3). **3** [U] (sl) woman's clothes worn by a man: *'As you Like It' performed in ~,* with the women's parts acted by men dressed as women. **4** (sl) puff at a cigarette or cigar.

drag [2] /dræg/ *vt, vi* (-gg-) **1** [VP6A,15B,14] pull along (esp with effort and difficulty): *to ~ a heavy box out of a cupboard. The escaped prisoner was ~ged from his hiding-place. ~ sb into doing sth,* involve him unwillingly in an undertaking: *He hates parties; we had to ~ him into going.* **2** [VP6A,15B,2A,C] (allow to) move slowly and with effort; (allow to) trail: *to walk with ~ging feet. He could scarcely ~ himself along. The ship ~ged its anchor/The ship's anchor ~ged during the night,* it failed to hold, was drawn along the sea bottom. *~ one's feet,* go forward slowly, unwillingly (often fig): *We suspect the Government of ~ging their feet. ~ up (a child),* (colloq) (contrasted with bring up) educate, train, etc it badly. **3** [VP2A,C] *~ (on),* (of time, work, an entertainment) go on slowly in a dull manner: *Classwork often ~s towards the end of term,* pupils lose interest. *The performance ~ged on. Time seemed to ~. ~ out,* make longer (in time): *~ out a meeting/an argument/a performance.* **4** [VP6A,2A] use nets, tools, etc to search the bottom of a river, lake, etc (usu for sth lost or missing): *They ~ged the river for the missing child.*

drag-gled /ˈdrægld/ *adj* (often **be-~**) wet, dirty or muddy (as if dragged through mud, etc).

drago-man /ˈdrægəʊmən/ *n* (*pl* ~s) guide and interpreter (esp in Arabic-speaking countries).

dragon /ˈdrægən/ *n* fabulous creature like a crocodile or snake, often with wings and claws, able to breathe out fire, often guarding a treasure; (colloq) fierce person.

a dragon

drag-on-fly /ˈdrægənflaɪ/ *n* (*pl* -flies) insect with a stick-like body and two pairs of large wings. ⇨ the illus at insect.

dra-goon /drəˈguːn/ *n* horse-soldier; cavalryman. □ *vt* [VP6A,14] *~ sb (into doing sth),* force him (to do sth), harass him.

drain [1] /dreɪn/ *n* **1** pipe, channel, trench, etc for carrying away water, sewage and other unwanted liquids; (*pl*) system of pipes and sewers for carrying away waste liquid, etc from buildings; (US) plug-hole: *There's a bad smell; something wrong with the* ~*s, I suppose.* **go down the** ~, (fig) be wasted. '~·**pipe**, pipe used in a system of ~s. **2** (fig) sth that continually uses up force, time, wealth, etc; cause of weakening or loss: *Military expenditure has been a great* ~ *on the country's resources. All this extra work was a* ~ *on his strength.* '**brain** ~, movement of trained technical and scientific personnel from one country to another (because of better opportunities, etc). **3** (colloq) small drink; mouthful: *Don't drink it all; leave me a* ~*!*

drain² /dreɪn/ *vt, vi* **1** [VP15B,2C] ~ **away/off,** (of liquid) (cause to) run or flow away: *Dig trenches to* ~ *the water away/off. The water will soon* ~ *away/off.* **2** [VP2A,6A] (of land, etc) make, become, dry as water flows away: *to* ~ *swamps/ marshes. Land must be well* ~*ed for some crops. These fields* ~ *into the river. Leave the dishes on the board to* ~. '~·**ing-board,** board at the side of a sink, on which washed dishes, etc are placed to ~. **3** [VP6A,15B,14,2C] ~ **(away/off);** ~ **(of),** (fig) (cause to) lose (strength, wealth, etc) by degrees: *The country was* ~*ed of its manpower and wealth by war. His life was slowly* ~*ing away,* eg of a man bleeding to death. **4** [VP6A,22] drink; empty: *to* ~ *a glass dry.*

drain·age /'dreɪnɪdʒ/ *n* [U] **1** draining or being drained. '~·**basin,** area drained by a river. **2** system of drains(1). **3** that which is drained away or off; sewage.

drake /dreɪk/ *n* male duck.

dram /dræm/ *n* **1** unit of weight: (apothecaries' weight) 60 grains (8 drams = 1 oz or 31·1 grams); (avoirdupois weight) 27⅓ grains (16 drams = 1 oz or 28·35 grams). ⇨ App **5**. **2** small drink of alcoholic spirits: *He's fond of a* ~, eg of whisky.

drama /'drɑːmə/ *n* **1** [C] play for the theatre, radio or TV; [U] **(the)** ~, composition, presentation and performance of such plays: *a student of (the)* ~*; to be interested in (the)* ~. **2** [C,U] series of exciting events.

dra·matic /drə'mætɪk/ *adj* **1** of drama(1): ~ *performances;* ~ *criticism.* **2** sudden or exciting, like an event in a stage play: ~ *changes in the international situation.* **3** (of a person, his speech, behaviour) showing the feelings or character in a lively or exaggerated way. **dra·mati·cally** /-klɪ/ *adv* in a ~ manner. **dra·mat·ics** *n* (usu with *sing v*) **1** ~(1) works or performances by amateurs: *Are you interested in amateur* ~*s?* **2** ~(3) speech, behaviour, etc.

drama·tis per·sonae /ˌdræmətɪs pɜː'səʊnaɪ/ *n pl* (Lat) (list of the) characters in a play.

drama·tist /'dræmətɪst/ *n* writer of plays.

drama·tize /'dræmətaɪz/ *vt* [VP6A] **1** put a story, novel, etc into the form of a drama. **2** treat (a situation, etc) as if it were a drama. **drama·tiz·ation** /ˌdræmətaɪ'zeɪʃn US: -tɪ'z-/ *n* [C,U].

drank /dræŋk/ *pt* of drink.

drape /dreɪp/ *vt* [VP6A,14] **1** ~ **(round/over),** hang curtains, cloth, a cloak or other garment in folds round or over sth: *to* ~ *curtains over a window; to* ~ *a cloak over one's shoulders/a flag over the coffin.* **2** ~ **(with),** cover or decorate: *walls* ~*d with flags; a doorway* ~*d with a heavy curtain.* **3** ~ **(round/over),** allow to rest loosely: *He* ~*d his*

legs over the arms of his chair. □ *n* [C] (chiefly US) cloth hung in folds; curtain.

dra·per /'dreɪpə(r)/ *n* (GB) shopkeeper who sells cloth, linen, clothing, etc. ~**y** *n* **1** [U] ~'s trade; goods sold by a ~: (attrib) *a* ~*y business/store.* **2** [C,U] (*pl* -ries) materials used for garments, hangings, curtains, etc; such materials arranged in folds.

dras·tic /'dræstɪk/ *adj* (of actions, methods, medicines) having a strong or violent effect: ~ *measures to cure inflation,* eg a steep increase in the bank rate; ~ *remedies to cure an illness.* **dras·ti·cally** /-klɪ/ *adv*

drat /dræt/ *vt* (-tt-) (used chiefly in exclamations; dated, colloq) curse: *D*~ *that child! That* ~*ted* (= cursed) *boy!*

draught (US = **draft**) /drɑːft US: dræft/ *n* **1** [C,U] current of air in a room, chimney or other enclosed place: *You'll catch cold if you sit in a* ~. *Turn the electric fan on and make a* ~. *There's not enough* ~ *up the chimney; that's why the fire doesn't burn well.* **2** [C] the pulling in of a net of fish(es). **3** [U] depth of water needed to float a ship: *vessels of shallow* ~*; a ship with a* ~ *of ten feet.* ⇨ draw²(13). **4** [U] drawing of liquid from a container (eg a barrel): *beer on* ~; ~ *beer.* Cf *bottled beer.* **5** [C] (amount drunk during) one continuous process of swallowing: *a* ~ *of water; to drink half a pint of beer at a* ~. **6** (*pl*, with *sing v*) (US = **checkers**) table game for two players using 24 round pieces (called '~**s(men)** on a board with 32 black and 32 white squares. □ *vt* ⇨ draft². '~**horse,** one that pulls heavy loads. ⇨ *pack-horse* at pack¹(1). **draughts·man** /'drɑːftsmən US: 'dræ-/ *n* (*pl* -men) **1** = draftsman. **2** piece used in ~s, ⇨ **6** above.

draughty (US = **drafty**) /'drɑːftɪ US: 'dræftɪ/ *adj* (-ier, -iest) with draughts(1) blowing through: *a* ~ *room.*

draw¹ /drɔː/ *n* **1** the act of drawing (in various senses): *the* ~ *for the fourth round of the tennis tournament. When does the* ~ *take place,* When will the winning numbers for the lottery, etc, be drawn? *The game ended in a* ~, neither side won. *Our team has had five wins and two* ~*s this season.* **2** sb or sth that attracts attention, ⇨ draw²(5): *Mr A is always a great* ~ *at political meetings,* is a popular speaker. *The new play is a great* ~, many people are going to the theatre to see it. **3** **be quick/slow on the** ~, quick/slow at pulling out a sword, revolver, etc; (fig) quick/slow to understand.

draw² /drɔː/ *vt, vi* (*pt* drew /druː/, *pp* drawn /drɔːn/) **1** [VP6A,15B,14] move by pulling: *to* ~ *a boat* (*up*) *out of the water/on to the beach; to* ~ *one's chair up to the table; to* ~ *sb aside,* eg to speak to him quietly; *to* ~ *on/off one's socks/ gloves/tights; to* ~ *a curtain across a window; to* ~ *down the blinds* (of windows); *to* ~ *one's belt tighter; to* ~ *one's pen through a word,* cross it out. *The fisherman drew in his net.* **2** [VP6A,15B] (esp) move by pulling after or behind: *a train* ~*n by two locomotives; tractor-*~*n ploughs. The wagon was being* ~*n by two horses.* **3** [VP6A,15B,14] ~ **(out);** ~ **(from/out of),** take or get out by pulling; extract: *to* ~ *a cork,* out of a bottle; *to* ~ *nails from a plank; to have a tooth* ~*n; to* ~ *stumps,* (cricket) pull them out at the end of play; *to* ~ *trumps,* (in card games such as bridge) cause them to be played; *to* ~ *cards from a pack;*

to ~ for partners, eg when about to play a card game, allow this to decide the question; *to ~ lots,* ⇨ lot²(1); *to ~ the winner,* get a ticket, etc at a lottery, on which there is a payment, prize, etc; *to ~ a gun (on sb),* take it from its holster, ready for use. *~ a blank,* find nothing. *~ sb's teeth,* make him harmless. 4 [VP6A,14] *~ (from/out of),* obtain from a source: *to ~ water from a well; to ~ cider/beer from a cask/barrel; to ~ one's salary; to ~ money from the bank/from one's account; to ~ rations,* get, receive, supplies (of food, etc) from a store; *to ~ inspiration from nature. What moral are we to ~ from this story? ~ it mild,* (originally of beer; fig) be moderate; not exaggerate. *~ tears/applause, etc,* be the cause of: *Her singing drew long applause.* 5 [VP6A,14,15B,2A] *~ (to),* attract: *Street accidents always ~ crowds. The film drew large audiences. He drew (= called) my attention to a point I had overlooked. She didn't feel ~n towards him,* There was nothing in his character, behaviour, etc that attracted her. 6 [VP6A,15B] take in: *to ~ a deep breath; stop to ~ breath,* to rest after exertion. *~ one's first/last breath,* be born/die. 7 [VP2A] (of a chimney, etc) allow a current of air to flow through; be built so that air and smoke pass up or through. *This chimney ~s badly. This cigar does not ~ well.* 8 [VP6A,15B] *~ sb (out),* cause, persuade, (a person) to talk, show his feelings, etc: *He was not to be ~n,* He refused to say anything about the matter. *He has many interesting stories of his travels if you can ~ him out.* 9 [VP2C,D] move; come (in the direction indicated by the *adv,* etc): *Christmas is ~ing near. The day drew to its close. The two ships drew level. The favourite began to ~ (= gain) on the other runners. The Queen's horse quickly drew away from the others,* went ahead of them. *Everyone drew back in alarm. When the enemy saw how strong our forces were, they drew off,* went back. 10 [VP6A,15B] cause to move or come (in the direction indicated by the *adv,* etc): *He drew himself up to his full height,* stood in an erect, stiff attitude. 11 [VP6A,2A] make with a pen, pencil, chalk, etc: *to ~ a straight line/a circle; to ~ a picture/plan/diagram; to ~ a horse. She ~s well,* (fig) describe in words: *The characters in Jane Austen's novels are well ~n. ~ a distinction (between),* point out differences; show the dividing line. *~ a parallel/comparison/ analogy (between),* show how two things are alike. *~ the line (at),* set limits; declare what cannot be allowed; refuse to go as far as or beyond: *I don't mind lending him my razor, but I ~ the line at lending him my toothbrush.* 12 [VP6A,15B] write out: *to ~ a bill/cheque/order (on a banker, etc, for a sum of money).* 13 [VP6A] (of a ship) require (a certain depth of water) in order to float, ⇨ draught(3): *The ship ~s 20 feet of water.* 14 [VP6A,2A] end (a game, etc) without either winning or losing: *to ~ a football or cricket match; a ~n game; to ~ 2—2. The teams drew.* 15 [VP6A,2A,B] extract the essence of: *to let the tea ~ for three minutes.* 16 (usu in *pp*) (of the features) pull out of shape: *a face ~n with pain/anxiety; with ~n features.* 17 [VP2C,3A,14,15B] (special uses with *preps* and *adverbial particles*).
draw back, (fig) show unwillingness: *~ back from a proposal.* ⇨ drawback(1).
draw in, (of a day) (a) reach its end. (b) become shorter: *The days begin to ~ in after midsummer.*

draw on, (of a period of time) approach: *Night drew on. ~ on sth/sb,* take or use as a source: *If newspaper-men cannot get facts for their stories, they sometimes ~ on their imaginations. We mustn't ~ on our savings. You may ~ on me for any sum up to £500,* get sums up to this maximum from me or my agents. *~ sb on,* attract, entice him.
draw out, (of a day) become longer: *Christmas passed and the days began to ~ out. ~ sth out,* stretch; cause to become longer: *He heated the metal and drew it out into a long wire. There was a long-~n-out discussion. He has ~n out the subject into three volumes. ~ sb out,* ⇨ 8 above.
draw (sth/sb) up, (a) (of a vehicle) (cause to) come to a stop: *The taxi drew up in front of the station.* (b) prepare; compose: *to ~ up a contract.* (c) (usu passive) (of troops, etc) bring into regular order: *The troops were ~n up ready for the inspection.*

draw·back /'drɔːbæk/ *n* 1 [C] sth which lessens one's satisfaction, or makes progress less easy; disadvantage *(to).* 2 [U] amount of import duty paid back when goods are exported again.

draw·bridge /'drɔːbrɪdʒ/ *n* bridge that can be pulled up at the end(s) by chains (eg across the moat of a castle in ancient times to prevent passage, or across a river or canal to allow ships to pass)

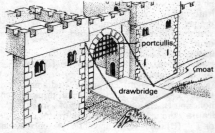

a drawbridge

drawer /drɔː(r)/ *n* 1 box-like container (with a handle or handles) which slides in and out of a piece of furniture, etc. ,chest of '~s, piece of furniture consisting of a set of ~s. 2 *(pl)* old-fashioned two-legged undergarment for the lower part of the body; knickers. 3 /'drɔːə(r)/ person who draws pictures; person who draws a cheque, etc.

draw·ing /'drɔːɪŋ/ *n* [U] the art of representing objects, scenes, etc by lines, with a pencil, chalk, etc; [C] sth made in this way; a sketch, plan, etc. *out of ~,* incorrectly drawn. '~-board, flat board on which to fasten paper for ~, used eg by a draftsman; (fig) planning stage. '~-pin, (US = thumbtack) flat-headed pin for fastening paper to a ~board, notice-board, etc.

draw·ing-room /'drɔːɪŋ rʊm US: ruːm/ *n* room in which guests are received.

drawl /drɔːl/ *vi,vt* [VP2A,C,6A,15B] speak so that the sounds of the vowels are longer than usual: *The speaker ~ed on. Don't ~ (out) your words.* □ *n* slow way of speaking.

drawn /drɔːn/ *pp* of draw²; ⇨ esp 2, 14, 16.

dray /dreɪ/ *n* low, flat, four-wheeled cart, without sides, for heavy loads, eg barrels from a brewery.

dread /dred/ *n* [U] (also *a ~ of*) great fear and anxiety: *to be in ~ of sb or sth; to live in constant ~*

of poverty. Cats have a ~ of water. □ *vt,vi* [VP6A,C,7A] fear greatly: *to ~ a visit to/~ having to visit the dentist. I ~ to think of what may happen.* ~ed *part adj* greatly feared. ~-ful /-f1/ *adj* **1** causing ~: *a ~ful disaster. What a ~ful story!* **2** (colloq) unpleasant: *What ~ful weather!* ~-fully /-fəlı/ *adv* ~-ful-ness *n*

dread·nought /'drednɔːt/ *n* type of battleship in the early years of the 20th century.

dream¹ /driːm/ *n* [C] **1** sth which one seems to see or experience during sleep: *to have a ~ (about sth); to awake from a ~.* '~-land; '~ world, region outside the laws of nature, as experienced in sleep or in the imagination. **2** state of mind in which things going on around one seem unreal: *to live/go about in a ~.* **3** mental picture(s) of the future: *to have ~s of wealth and happiness.* **4** (colloq) beautiful or pleasing person, thing, experience, etc: *His holiday by the sea was a ~.* ~-less *adj* without ~s. ~-like /'driːmlaɪk/ *adj* like a ~.

dream² /driːm/ *vi,vt* (*pt,pp* ~ed /driːmd/ or dreamt /dremt/) **1** [VP2A,3A,6A,15B,9,8,10] ~ (*about/of*), have ~s; see, experience, in a dream; imagine; suppose: *He often ~s. The soldier often ~t of/about home. He ~t that he was at sea. I certainly didn't promise you £100; you must have ~t it. I wouldn't ~ of doing such a thing,* The idea would never occur to me. *He little ~ed that...,* did not imagine or suppose that.... **2** [VP15B] ~ away, spend idly: *~ away one's time/the hours.* **3** [VP15B] ~ up, (colloq) imagine, conceive (a plan, etc). ~er *n* person who ~s; person with impractical ideas, plans, etc.

dreamy /'driːmı/ *adj* (-ier, -iest) **1** (of a person) with thoughts far away from his surroundings or work. **2** (of things, experiences) vague; unreal: *~ recollection of what happened;* (colloq) pleasing; soothing: *~ music.* **dream·ily** /-ılı/ *adv*

dreary /'drɪərı/ *adj* (-ier, -iest) (poet **drear** /drɪə(r)/) dull; gloomy; causing low spirits: *~ work/weather/people.* **drear·ily** /-əlı/ *adv*

dredge¹ /dredʒ/ *n* apparatus for bringing up mud, oysters, specimens, etc from the bed of the sea, rivers, etc. □ *vt,vi* [VP6A,15B,2A,3A] ~ (*up*), bring up with a ~; clean with a ~: *to ~ (up) mud; to ~ (for) oysters; to ~ a channel/harbour.* **dredger** *n* boat carrying a ~.

dredge² /dredʒ/ *vt* [VP6A,14] sprinkle or scatter: *to ~ meat with flour; to ~ sugar over a cake.* **dredger** *n* box with holes in the lid for sprinkling flour, sugar, etc on food.

dregs /dregz/ *n pl* **1** bits of worthless matter which sink to the bottom of a glass, bottle, barrel, etc of liquid. **drink/drain to the ~,** drink and leave only the ~. **2** (fig) worst and useless part: *the ~ of society/humanity.*

drench /drentʃ/ *vt* [VP6A] make wet all over, right through: *to be ~ed with rain/~ed to the skin. They were caught in a downpour and came back ~ed.* ~-ing *n* thorough wetting: *We got a ~ing.*

dress¹ /dres/ *n* **1** [C] one-piece outer garment with a bodice and skirt worn by a woman or girl; gown or frock. **2** [U] clothing in general (for both men and women), esp outer garments: *She doesn't care much about ~,* is not much interested in clothes. '~ circle, lowest gallery in a theatre, in which evening ~ was formerly required. '~ coat, black, swallow-tailed coat worn by men for evening ~. '~-maker, woman who makes women's ~es. '~

rehearsal, final rehearsal of a play, at which actors wear the costumes to be worn at actual performances. '**evening ~,** clothing worn at formal social occasions (eg dinners, evening parties). **,full** '~, kind of clothes worn on special occasions: *ambassadors, naval and military officers, all in full ~.*

dress² /dres/ *vt,vi* **1** [VP6A,2A] put on clothes: *Mary was ~ing her doll. Jim isn't old enough to ~ himself. Have you finished ~ing? How long does it take you to ~ (yourself)?* [VP15B,2C] ~ up, put on special clothes, as for a play, a fancy dress ball, etc: *The children ~ed (themselves) up as pirates.* **2** [VP2A,C] put on evening dress: *We don't ~ for dinner nowadays. You've just time to ~ (=* change into evening dress) *before we leave for the theatre.* **3** [VP2C] (of what is habitual) wear clothes: *He has to ~ well in his position.* **4** be ~ed in, be wearing: *She was ~ed in white. They were ~ed in the height of fashion,* wearing the most fashionable clothes. **5** [VP6A] provide clothes for: *How much does it cost them a year to ~ their children?* **6** [VP6A] make ready to use; prepare: *to ~ leather,* make it soft and smooth; *to ~ a salad,* ⇨ dressing(3); *to ~ a chicken,* clean it ready for cooking. **7** [VP6A,15B] brush and comb, arrange (one's hair); *to ~ down a horse,* brush its coat well. *~ sb down,* (fig) scold him severely; thrash him. Hence, ,~ing-'down *n* severe scolding. **8** [VP6A] clean and bandage (a wound, etc). **9** [VP6A] make cheerful and attractive: *to ~ a shop-window,* eg with attractive goods; *to ~ the streets,* eg with flags; *to ~ a Christmas-tree.* **10** [VP6A,2A] (mil) get or bring (soldiers) into a straight line: *~ the ranks.*

dress·age /'dresɑːʒ/ *n* [U] (F) training of horses (for show-jumping, etc).

dresser¹ /'dresə(r)/ *n* person who dresses, esp (a) one who helps a surgeon to dress wounds in a hospital; (b) person who helps actors and actresses to dress ready for the stage.

dresser² /'dresə(r)/ *n* **1** piece of kitchen furniture with shelves for dishes, and cupboards below, often with drawers for cutlery, etc. **2** (US) dressing-table.

dress·ing /'dresıŋ/ *n* **1** [U] process of dressing (putting on clothes, cleaning and bandaging a wound, etc). '~-case, one for brushes, bottles and other articles of toilet, when travelling. '~-gown, (US = *bath-robe*) loose gown worn over pyjamas, etc before dressing, etc. '~-table, one with a mirror, used in a bedroom. **2** [C,U] sth used for dressing wounds, eg an ointment, bandage, etc. **3** [C,U] mixture of oil, vinegar, condiments, etc used as a sauce for salads and other dishes. **4** [U] substance used to stiffen silk, cotton, etc during manufacture.

dressy /'dresı/ *adj* (-ier, -iest) (colloq) (of persons) fond of, looking smart in, fine clothes; (of clothes) stylish.

drew /druː/ *pt* of draw².

dribble /'drıbl/ *vt,vi* [VP6A,2A] **1** (of liquids) flow, allow to flow, drop by drop or in a slow trickle (esp from the side of the mouth): *Babies often ~ on their bibs.* **2** (football) take (the ball) forward by means of quick, short kicks, either between the feet of one player, or by short passes from one player to another. **drib·bler** *n* person who ~s.

drib·let /'drıblıt/ *n* falling drop; small amount: *in/by ~s,* a little at a time.

dribs and drabs /ˌdrıbz n 'dræbz/ *n pl* (colloq)

small amounts.

dried /draɪd/ *pt,pp* of dry².

drier /'draɪə(r)/ *comp adj*⇨ dry¹; *n*⇨ dry².

drift¹ /drɪft/ *n* **1** [U] drifting movement; being carried along by currents: *the* ~ *of the tide. The general* ~ *of the current was northerly.* '**~-age** /-ɪdʒ/ *n* (of a ship) general movement off course due to currents, winds, tides, etc. '**~-net,** large net into which fish ~ with the tide. **2** [C] sth caused by drifting: *Big* ~s *of snow/Big snow* ~s *made progress slow and difficult. It was buried in a* ~ *of dead leaves.* '**~-ice,** broken ice carried along on the surface of the sea, a river, etc in masses by currents of water or air. '**~-wood,** wood carried along by currents and washed up on beaches. **3** [U] general tendency or meaning: *I caught the* ~ *of what he said. Did you get the* ~ *of the argument?* **4** [U] the way in which events, etc tend to move: *The general* ~ *of affairs was towards war.* **5** [U] the state of being inactive and waiting for things to happen: *Is the government's policy one of* ~?

drift² /drɪft/ *vi,vt* **1** [VP2A,C] be carried along by, or as by, a current of air or water; (fig, of persons) go through life without aim, purpose or self-control: *The boat* ~*ed out to sea. We* ~*ed down the stream. The snow had* ~*ed everywhere. Is the government/the country* ~*ing towards bankruptcy? She* ~s *from one job to another.* **2** [VP6A,15B,14] cause to ~: *The logs were* ~*ed down the stream to the saw-mills. The wind had* ~*ed the snow into high banks.* ~**er** *n* **1** boat used in ~-net fishing and, during war, for mine-sweeping. ⇨ drift¹(1). **2** person who ~s(1).

drill¹ /drɪl/ *n* instrument with a pointed end or cutting edges for making holes in hard substances: *a dentist's* ~. □ *vt,vi* [VP6A] make a hole with a ~: ~ *a hole in a stone wall;* [VP2A] use a ~. '**~-ing rig,** ⇨ rig¹(2).

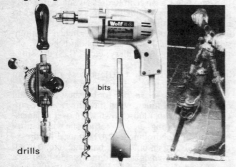

bits

drills

drill² /drɪl/ *n* [C,U] **1** army training in the handling of weapons; formal movements, eg marching, turning, to develop alertness: '*bayonet* ~; '*gun*~. *The soldiers were at* ~ *in the barrack square.* **2** thorough training by practical experiences, usu with much repetition: ~s *in the English vowel sounds.* **3** routine procedure to be followed, eg in an emergency: '*fire*~; '*lifeboat* ~. □ *vt,vi* [VP6A,14,2A] train, be trained, by means of ~s: *to* ~ *troops on a parade ground; a well-*~*ed crew.*

drill³ /drɪl/ *n* furrow; machine for making furrows, sowing seeds in them, and covering the seeds; row of seeds sown in this way. □ *vt* [VP6A] sow (seeds) in ~s.

drill⁴ /drɪl/ *n* [U] heavy, strong linen or cotton cloth.

drill⁵ /drɪl/ *n* kind of West African baboon.

drily /'draɪlɪ/ *adv*⇨ dry¹.

drink¹ /drɪŋk/ *n* [C,U] **1** liquid for drinking: *We should die without food and* ~. *We have plenty of bottled* ~s, beer, lemonade, etc in bottles. **2** alcoholic liquor: *What about a* ~? *I'll bring in the* ~s, eg the gin, whisky, sherry. *He's too fond of* ~. **be in** ~**/the worse for** ~**/under the influence of** ~, intoxicated: *He's a good husband except when he's in* ~. **drive sb to** ~, cause him to take to ~: *Mrs Bell's bad temper drove her husband to* ~. **take to** ~, acquire the habit of drinking regularly and too much. **3 the** ~, (sl) the sea.

drink² /drɪŋk/ *vt,vi* (*pt* drank /dræŋk/, *pp* drunk /drʌŋk/) **1** [VP6A,15B,2A] take (liquid) into the mouth and swallow: *to* ~ *a pint of milk.* ~ **sth down/off/up,** ~ the whole of it (esp at once). **2** [VP6A,15B] ~ **(in/up),** (of plants, the soil, etc) take in, absorb (liquid): *The thirsty plants drank* (*up*) *the water I gave them. The parched soil drank* (*in*) *the rain.* **3** [VP15B] ~ **sth in,** (fig) take into the mind eagerly or with pleasure: *The boy drank in every word of the sailor's story of his adventures.* **4** [VP6A,15B,2A] take alcoholic liquors, beer, wine, etc, esp in excess: *He* ~s *far too much. He* ~s *half his earnings,* spends it on alcoholic liquors. *He will* ~ *himself to death.* **5** [VP6A,3A] ~ **(to),** wish good (to sb) while raising one's glass: *to* ~ *a person's health; to* ~ *a toast to sb; to* ~ *to sb's success; to* ~ *to sb's health.* ~**able** /-əbl/ *adj* suitable or fit for ~ing. ~**er** *n* (esp) person who ~s alcoholic liquor too often or too much: *He's a heavy* ~*er.* ~**ing** *n* process or habit of taking liquid(s), esp alcoholic liquor: *He's fond of* ~*ing.* '**~-ing-bout,** long spell of ~ing. '**~-ing-fountain,** device for providing a supply of ~ing-water in a public place. '**~-ing-song,** one to be sung at a ~ing party; one celebrating the joys of ~ing. '**~-ing-water,** water fit for ~ing.

drip /drɪp/ *vi,vt* (-pp-) [VP2A,C,6A] (of a liquid) fall, allow to fall, in drops: *The rain was* ~*ping from the trees. The tap was* ~*ping. Sweat was* ~*ping from his face. He was* ~*ping sweat. Blood was* ~*ping from his hand. His hand was* ~*ping blood.* ~**ping wet,** very wet. ~-'**dry** *adj* (of a fabric) able to dry quickly, without previous squeezing or wringing out, when hung up to ~: ~-*dry shirts.* □ *vt* dry in this way. □ *n* **1** the drop-by-drop falling of a liquid: *the* ~s *from the trees/of the rain.* **2** (sl) a dull, insipid person.

drip·ping /'drɪpɪŋ/ *n* **1** [U] fat melted out of roasted meat, used for frying, or spread on bread: *a slice of bread and* ~. '**~-pan,** pan in which ~ collects when meat is roasted. **2** (*pl*) liquid that drips or has dripped from sth: *the* ~s *from the roof.*

drive¹ /draɪv/ *n* **1** driving or being driven (in a car, etc, not in a public vehicle): *to go for a* ~; *to take sb for a* ~. *The station is an hour's* ~ *away.* **2** (in US also '**~-way**) private road through a garden or park to a house. **3** (in games played with a ball, eg golf) [U] force given to a ball when it is struck; [C] stroke or hit: *a* ~ *to the boundary.* **4** [U] energy; capacity to get things done: *young men with brains,* ~ *and initiative. The new headmaster lacks* ~/*is lacking in* ~. **5** organized effort or campaign: *a* '*sales* ~, one made to increase sales, eg by reducing prices; *the* '*export* ~, to increase exports; *The school made a great* ~ *to raise £5000 for a new sports ground.* **6** tournament: *a* '*bridge-*~. **7** (mech) apparatus for driving: *front/rear* ~, with power that operates the front/rear wheel(s); *a four-wheel* ∼, with four wheels connected to the source of power; *right-/left-hand* ∼, (of a motor vehicle) having the steering and other controls on the right/left side.

drive² /draɪv/ *vt,vi* (*pt* drove /drəʊv/, *pp* driven /'drɪvn/) **1** [VP6A,15B,14] cause animals, people to move in some direction by using cries, blows, threats or other means: *to* ∼ *cattle to market; to* ∼ *the enemy out of their positions.* ∼ *sb into a corner,* (fig) force him (eg during an argument) into a position from which escape will be difficult. **2** [VP6A,2A] operate, direct the course of a railway engine, bus, motor-car or other vehicle; control, direct the course of an animal or animals drawing a cart, plough, etc: *to* ∼ *a taxi/cart; to take driving lessons. D*∼ *with caution.* '**driving licence,** licence to ∼ a motor vehicle. '**driving school,** one for teaching persons to ∼ a motor vehicle. '**driving test,** test which must be passed to obtain a driving licence. **3** [VP2A,C] travel in a car, etc which is at one's disposal (Cf *ride* in a bus, train or other public vehicle): *We drove right up to the front door. Shall we* ∼ *home or walk? We are merely driving through,* travelling through (the place) without intending to stay. '∼**-in** *n* (and attrib) restaurant, cinema, etc at which persons get service while in their cars: *a* ∼*-in cinema/bank.* **4** [VP15B,14] carry, convey, (sb) in a car, etc (not a public vehicle): *He drove me to the station.* **5** [VP6A] (usu passive) (of steam, electricity or other kind of power) set or keep going; be the power to operate: *The machinery is* ∼*n by steam/water-power, etc.* '**driving-belt,** belt that carries motion from an engine, motor, etc to machinery. '**driving-wheel,** one that communicates power to other parts of a machine. **6** [VP15B,14] (of wind, water) send, throw, (lifeless things) in some direction: *The gale drove the ship on to the rocks. The ship was* ∼*n out of its course. The wind was driving the rain against the window-panes.* **7** [VP2C] go or move along fast or violently: *The ship drove on the rocks/was driving along before the wind. The clouds drove across the sky. The rain was driving in our faces.* **8** [VP15B,14] ∼ **sth in;** ∼ **sth into sth,** force a nail, screw, stake, etc into sth: *With one blow he drove the nail into the plank.* **9** [VP6A,15B,14,2A] hit or strike with force: (cricket) *to* ∼ *a ball to the boundary;* (tennis) *to* ∼ *a ball out of the court.* (golf) *He* ∼*s well.* ∼ **sth home,** (fig) impress deeply on the mind. *let* ∼ *at,* aim a blow at; send a missile at: *He let* ∼ *at me with his left,* aimed a blow at me with his left fist. **10** [VP15B,17A,22B] cause or compel (sb) to be (in a certain state); cause or compel (sb to do sth): *Failure drove him to despair/ desperation. You'll* ∼ *me mad/to my wits' end. He was* ∼*n by hunger to steal.* **11** [VP15,2C] (cause to) work very hard: *He was hard* ∼*n. He* ∼*s himself very hard. Don't* ∼ *the workers too hard.* ∼ *away at* (one's work), work very hard at it. **12** [VP6A,15B,14] bore (a tunnel); make (a horizontal excavation): *to* ∼ *a tunnel/gallery through a hill; to* ∼ *a railway across a hilly district.* **13** [VP6A] manage; bring about: *to* ∼ *a roaring trade,* sell a lot of things very fast. ∼ *a hard bargain,* not give way easily to another person in a business deal. **14** [VP3A] ∼ *at,* (in the progressive tenses only) mean, intend: *What's he driving at,* What's he trying to do, explain, etc? **15** [VP14] postpone; defer: *Don't* ∼ *it to the last minute.*

drivel /'drɪvl/ *vi* (-ll-, US -l-) [VP2A,C] talk nonsense; talk childishly: *What's he* ∼*ling about? He's still* ∼*ling on.* □ *n* [U] silly nonsense; foolish talk. ∼**-ler,** US ∼**er** /'drɪvələ(r)/ *n* person who ∼s.

driven /'drɪvn/ *pp* of **drive²**.

driver /'draɪvə(r)/ *n* **1** person who drives (vehicles): *a* '*taxi*-∼; *a* '*bus*-∼. ⇨ **chauffeur.** *in the* ∼'s *seat,* in control. **2** person who drives animals. ⇨ *drover* at **drove²,** *slave*-∼ at **slave. 3** (mech) part of a machine, etc that receives power directly, eg the driving-wheel of a locomotive. **4** (golf) wooden club for driving the ball long distances from the tee.

drizzle /'drɪzl/ *vi* [VP2A] rain (in many small fine drops): *It* ∼*d all day.* □ *n* [U] fine rain. **driz·zly** /'drɪzlɪ/ *adj* drizzling: *drizzly weather.*

drogue /drəʊg/ *n* **1** sea anchor (sth like a bag, dragged in the sea to steady a boat's movement). **2** wind-sock, ⇨ **wind¹(8). 3** cone towed by one aircraft as a target for use by others in firing practice. **4** '∼ **parachute,** small parachute used to pull a large parachute from its pack.

droll /drəʊl/ *adj* causing amusement (because strange or peculiar). ∼**·ery** /-ərɪ/ *n* [U] jesting; [C] (*pl* -ries) sth peculiar and amusing; amusing trick.

drom·edary /'drɒmədərɪ US: -ədərɪ/ *n* (*pl* -ries) fast, one-humped riding-camel.

drone /drəʊn/ *n* **1** male bee; person who does no work and lives on others. **2** [U] low humming sound (as) made by bees: *the* ∼ *of an aeroplane high in the sky/of distant motorway traffic.* **3** [C] monotonous speech, sermon, speaker: *He's a boring old* ∼. □ *vi,vt* [VP15B,2C] **1** make a ∼(2). **2** talk or sing, say (sth) in a low, monotonous way: *children droning through their lessons. The parson* ∼*d out the psalm.*

drool /druːl/ *vi* ∼ *(over),* drivel; slobber.

droop /druːp/ *vi,vt* **1** [VP2A,C] bend or hang downwards (through tiredness or weakness): *The flowers were* ∼*ing for want of water. Her head* ∼*ed sadly. His spirits* ∼*ed,* He became sad, low-spirited. **2** [VP6A] let (the head, face, eyes) move forward or down. □ *n* ∼*ing* attitude or position. ∼**·ing·ly** *adv*

drop¹ /drɒp/ *n* **1** (a) very small quantity of liquid, usu round- or pear-shaped: '*rain*∼*s. He emptied the glass to the last* ∼. (b) (*pl*) liquid medicine taken in ∼s: *ear/eye/nose* ∼*s. in* ∼*s; by* ∼, slowly, one ∼ at a time. **2** very small quantity. *only a* ∼ *in the bucket/ocean,* a negligible quantity. **3** (glass of) intoxicating liquor: *He has had a* ∼ *too much,* is drunk. **4** sth like a ∼ in shape or appearance: '*acid* ∼*s,* of boiled sugar; '*ear*∼, ⇨ ear¹(1). **5** movement from a higher to a lower level, esp distance of a fall: *a sudden* ∼ *in temperature,* eg from 30°C to 20°C; *a* ∼ *in the price of wheat. There was a* ∼ *of 10 metres from the window to the ground. at the* ∼ *of a hat,* at once; readily or willingly. **6** thing that drops or is dropped(1): *a* ∼ *in a gallows,* platform or trapdoor which falls from under the feet of a person executed by hanging. '∼**-curtain,** curtain lowered between the acts of a play in a theatre. '∼**-kick,** (Rugby football) one in which the ball is dropped and kicked as it rises. '∼**-hammer;** '∼**-press,** machine for shaping or stamping, eg metal sheets for motor-car bodies, using the power of a dropped weight.

drop² /drɒp/ *vt,vi* (-pp-) (For uses with *adverbial particles* and *preps,* ⇨ **13** below.) **1** [VP2A,C,6A] (of liquids), fall, cause to fall, in drops. ⇨ **drip. 2**

[VP6A,2A,C,14,15B] fall (by the force of gravity, by not being held, etc); allow to fall: *It was so quiet you could hear a pin* ~. *The apple blossom is beginning to* ~. *The teapot* ~*ped out of her hand. She* ~*ped the teapot.* ~ **anchor,** lower the anchor; come to anchor. ~ *a brick,* ⇨ brick. ~ *a stitch,* (knitting) let it slip off the needle. **3** [VP2A,C,6A,15A,B] (allow to) become weaker or lower; (allow to) fall in amount, degree, pitch, condition, etc: *The wind/temperature has* ~*ped. His voice* ~*ped/He* ~*ped his voice to a whisper. Don't* ~ *your voice at the end of a sentence. Our boat gently* ~*ped* (= moved with the current) *downstream.* ⇨ drift²(1). **4** [VP2A,C,6A,15A] (cause to) fall or sink to the ground, etc: *They were ready to* ~ *with fatigue,* were so tired that they could scarcely stand. *She* ~*ped into a chair, utterly worn out. He* ~*ped* (*on*) *to his knees,* knelt down. *Supplies were* ~*ped by parachute.* Hence '~**ping-zone,** area where men, supplies, etc are ~*ped by parachute. The enemy were still* ~*ping* (= firing) *shells into the town. He* ~*ped a bird* (= hit one and caused it to fall) *with every shot. He* ~*ped* (= hit) *the ball to the back of the court.* **5** [VP6A,12A,13A] utter or send casually: *to* ~ *sb a hint,* give him one; *to* ~ *a word in sb's ear; to* ~ *sb a postcard/a few lines,* a note. ⇨ let²(4) for *let* ~. **6** [VP6A] omit; fail to pronounce, write or insert: *He* ~*s his h's,* eg by saying 'at for hat. *The relative pronoun is often* ~*ped if it is the object,* eg in 'the man (*whom*) he met yesterday'. **7** [VP15A] set down; stop (a car, etc) to allow sb to get out: *Where shall I* ~ *you? Please* ~ *me at the Post Office.* **8** [VP6A] cease to associate with (sb): *He seems to have* ~*ped most of his friends,* no longer meets them. **9** [VP6A] give up: *to* ~ *a bad habit.* **10** [VP6A,2A] (cause to) come to an end; no longer deal with or discuss: *The correspondence* ~*ped. We* ~*ped the subject. The subject* (*was*) ~*ped. We couldn't agree about the matter, so we decided to let it* ~. *Let's* ~ *it,* stop talking about it. **11** [VP6A] (colloq) lose (money, esp in gambling or a risky enterprise): *He* ~*ped 1000 francs at the Casino last night.* **12** (Rugby football) ~ *a goal,* score one by a ~-kick, ⇨ drop¹(6). **13** [VP2C,3B,15B] (special uses with *adverbial particles* and *preps*):
drop across sb/sth, (= *run across,* which is more usu) meet or find by chance.
drop away, = ~ off(a).
drop back; drop behind, come to a position behind: *The two lovers* ~*ped back. They* ~*ped behind the rest of the party.*
drop in on sb; drop by/in/over/round, pay a casual visit (to): *I wish he wouldn't* ~ *in on me so often. Some friends* ~*ped in to tea/*~*ped by to see me.*
drop off, (**a**) become fewer or less: *His friends* ~*ped off one by one. The doctor's practice has* ~*ped off,* he now has fewer patients. (**b**) fall asleep; doze: *He* ~*ped off during the sermon.* **drop sth/sb off (at sth),** deliver (to): *The bus will* ~ *you off at the station.* ⇨ drop(7) above.
drop out, (**a**) (of persons taking part in a contest, etc) cease to compete: *Three of the runners* ~*ped out.* (**b**) (of persons engaged, or about to engage, in an activity, etc) not take part; give up the idea: *Smith has* ~*ped out of the team.* (**c**) (colloq) withdraw from conventional social activities. Hence, '~-**out** *n* (**a**) person who ~s out, eg one who withdraws from a course of instruction: *University*

~-*outs,* who do not finish their courses. (**b**) person who withdraws from conventional society.
drop through, (colloq) come to nothing; be no longer discussed: *The big scheme he was busy with seems to have* ~*ped through.*
dropsy /'drɒpsɪ/ *n* [U] disease in which watery fluid collects in some part of the body, eg the legs. **drop·si·cal** /'drɒpsɪkl/ *adj* suffering from ~; of or like ~.
droshky /'drɒʃkɪ/ *n* (*pl* -kies) light, four-wheeled, open horse-carriage, as formerly common in Russia.
dross /drɒs *US*: drɔːs/ *n* [U] waste material rising to the surface of melted metals; (fig) anything considered to be worthless, mixed with sth else.
drought /draʊt/ *n* [C,U] continuous (period of) dry weather causing distress; want of rain.
drove¹ /drəʊv/ *pt* of drive².
drove² /drəʊv/ *n* large number of animals (a flock of sheep, a herd of cattle) being driven together; crowd of people moving together: ~*s of sightseers; visitors in* ~*s.* **drover** *n* man who drives cattle, sheep, etc to market; cattle-dealer.
drown /draʊn/ *vt, vi* **1** [VP6A,2A] (cause sb to) die in water because unable to breathe: *a* ~*ing man. He* ~*ed the kittens. Do cats* ~ *easily? He fell overboard and was* ~*ed.* **2** [VP6A,15B] ~ (*out*), (of sound) be strong enough to prevent another sound from being heard: *The noises in the street* ~*ed out the teacher's voice.* **3** (fig): *a face* ~*ed in tears,* wet with tears; ~*ed in sleep,* in a deep sleep (eg caused by exhaustion); *to* ~ *one's sorrows in drink,* to deaden them by getting drunk.
drowse /draʊz/ *vi, vt* [VP15B,2A,C] ~ (*away*), be half asleep; pass (time) half asleep: *to* ~ *away a hot afternoon.* □ *n* half-asleep condition: *in a* ~.
drowsy /'draʊzɪ/ *adj* (-ier, -iest) feeling sleepy; half asleep; making one feel sleepy. **drows·ily** /-əlɪ/ *adv* **drow·si·ness** *n*
drub /drʌb/ *vt* (-bb-) [VP6A,14] give repeated blows to; hit with a stick; (fig) beat an idea, a notion *into* or *out of* sb. ~**bing** *n* beating: *give sb a good/sound* ~*bing,* beat him well.
drudge /drʌdʒ/ *n* person who must work hard and long at unpleasant tasks. □ *vi* [VP2A,C,3A] ~ (*at*), work as a ~ does: *to* ~ *at dictionary-making.* **drudg·ery** /-ərɪ/ *n* [U] hard, unpleasant, uninteresting work.
drug /drʌg/ *n* [C] **1** substance used for medical purposes, either alone or in a mixture; substance that changes the state or function of cells, organs or organisms. '~-**store** *n* (US) place where a wide variety of articles is sold, where prescriptions can be made up, and where food and drink may be bought and eaten. **2** substance (often habit-forming) inducing sleep or producing stupor or insensibility, eg opium, cocaine: *the* ~ *habit,* the habit of taking harmful ~s: *a*'~ *addict;* '~ *addiction; a*'~ *pedlar.* **3** *a* ~ *on the market,* an article that cannot be sold because there is no demand. □ *vt* [VP6A] (-gg-) **1** add harmful ~s to (food and drink): *His wine had been* ~*ged, and they stole his money while he was sleeping heavily.* **2** give ~s to, esp in order to make unconscious: *They* ~*ged the caretaker and then robbed the bank.*
drug·get /'drʌgɪt/ *n* [C,U] (floor covering of) heavy coarse woollen material.
drug·gist /'drʌgɪst/ *n* **1** (GB) tradesman who sells drugs; pharmacist. **2** (US) person who sells medicines, toilet articles and other goods, and usually

food and drinks. ⇨ *drug-store* at drug(1).

Druid, druid /'druːɪd/ *n* member of the priesthood among the Celts of ancient Gaul, Britain and Ireland.

drum¹ /drʌm/ *n* **1** (music) percussion instrument made of a hollow cylinder or hemisphere with parchment stretched over the open side(s), ⇨ the illus at percussion; sound of a ∼ or ∼s, or sound as of ∼s. '∼-**fire**, heavy continuous rapid fire from big guns. ∼-**head court-martial**, one held while military operations are in progress, in order to try an offender without delay. ∼-**head service**, open-air military chuch service in which ∼s form an altar. ˌ∼-'**major**, sergeant in charge of drummers, and leader of a regimental band on the march; (US) (also ˌ∼-**majo'rette** /ˌmeɪdʒə'ret/) leader of any marching band. '∼-**stick**, **(a)** stick for beating a ∼. **(b)** lower part of the leg of a cooked chicken, turkey, etc. **2** sth like a ∼ in shape, eg a cylindrical container for oil, a cylinder or barrel on which thick wire or cable is wound. ⇨ ear¹(1).

drum² /drʌm/ *vt,vi* (-mm-) **1** [VP2A,C] play the drum. **2** [VP6A,14,2C,3A] ∼ **(on)**, make drum-like sounds; beat or tap continuously: *to* ∼ *on the table with one's fingers; to* ∼ *the floor with one's feet;* ∼*ming on the piano/at the door.* **3** [VP15B] ∼ **up**, summon by ∼ming: (fig) ∼ *up* (= get, find) *support for a cause.* **4** [VP14] ∼ *sth into sb/into sb's head,* cause him to remember it by repeating it often. ∼-**mer** *n* person who plays a drum; (colloq, esp US) commercial traveller.

drunk /drʌŋk/ *adj* (usu pred) (*pp* of drink²) intoxicated; overcome by drinking alcoholic liquor: *He was dead/blind/half* ∼. *I've never seen anyone so* ∼. *get* ∼, become intoxicated: *It's easy to get* ∼ *on brandy.* ∼ *with sth,* (fig) elated: *He was* ∼ *with joy/success.* □ *n* person who is ∼; man charged (at a police-station) with drunkenness. ∼-**ard** /-əd/ *n* man who is ∼, or who often gets ∼.

drunken /'drʌŋkən/ *adj* (usu attrib) **1** intoxicated; in the habit of drinking; often drunk: *a* ∼ *and dissolute man.* **2** caused by drinking; showing the effects of drinking: *a* ∼ *frolic.* ∼-**ly** *adv* ∼-**ness** *n*

drupe /druːp/ *n* (bot) fruit with juicy flesh, usu with a hard stone enclosing a seed, eg an olive, a plum, a peach.

dry¹ /draɪ/ *adj* (drier, driest) **1** not wet; free from moisture: *Is this wood dry enough to burn?* ˌ**dry as a 'bone**, ˌbone-'**dry**, quite dry. **2** not rainy: *dry weather;* having a low annual rainfall: *a dry climate.* **3** not supplying water: *a dry well;* not supplying milk: *The cows are dry.* **4** solid, not liquid: *dry goods,* ⇨ 12 below. **5** without butter: *dry bread/toast.* **6** (of wine, etc) not sweet, not fruity in flavour: *dry wines; a dry martini,* a kind of cocktail. **7** (colloq) thirsty; causing thirst: *to feel dry; dry work.* **8** uninteresting; dull: *a dry lecture/book/subject.* ˌ**dry as 'dust**, very dull. **9** unemotional; undemonstrative: *dry humour/sarcasm; a dry fellow.* **10** plain; undisguised: *dry facts.* **11** not connected with liquid: *a dry cough,* without phlegm; *a dry death,* not by drowning; *a dry shampoo,* one in which water is not used. **12** (compounds) ˌ**dry 'battery**, electric battery with two or more dry cells. ˌ**dry-bulb ther'mometer**, one of two thermometers, one dry and the other kept wet, used for measuring the humidity of the atmosphere. ˌ**dry 'cell**, cell in which the chemicals are in a firm paste which does not spill. ˌ**dry-'clean** *v* clean (clothes, etc) by using spirits (eg petrol) instead of

water. Hence ˌ**dry-'cleaner**; ˌ**dry-'cleaning** *nn.* ˌ**dry 'dock**, ⇨ dock¹(1). ˌ**dry 'goods** (also called *soft goods*), (contrasted with *meat, groceries,* etc) corn; (esp US) textiles, drapery. ˌ**dry 'ice**, solid carbon dioxide (used for refrigerating). ˌ**dry 'measure**, measure of capacity for dry goods such a corn. '**dry nurse**, not suckling the baby she is caring for. ˌ**dry 'rot** *n* decay of wood (causing it to crumble to powder), occurring when there is no movement of air over its surface; (fig) hidden or unsuspected moral or social decay. '**dry-shod** *adj, adv* without wetting the feet; with dry feet or shoes. ˌ**dry-'walling**, building of stone walls (eg for a field) without mortar. **drily** /'draɪlɪ/ *adv* **dry-ness** *n*

dry² /draɪ/ *vt,vi* (*pt,pp* dried) **1** [VP6A,15B,2A,C] *dry (out),* make or become dry: *Dry your hands on this towel. We were drying our clothes in front of the fire. Our clothes soon dried out. dry up,* make or become completely dry: *The long drought dried up all the wells. The stream dries up during the hot summer. His imagination seems to have dried up. Dry up!* (sl) Stop talking! Be quiet! **2** [VP6A] (usu the *pp*) preserve by extracting moisture: *dried eggs/milk.* **dryer, drier** /'draɪə(r)/ *n* **1** substance mixed with oil-paints and varnish to quicken drying. **2** (in compounds) thing that dries: *an electric 'hair-dryer;* thing on or in which clothes, etc are placed to dry: *a 'clothes-drier; a 'spin-drier.*

dryad /'draɪəd/ *n* (Gk myth) tree nymph.

dual /'djuːəl/ *adj* of two; double; divided in two: ∼ *control,* for or by two persons; ∼ *ownership;* ∼ *'carriageway* (US = *divided highway);* ∼*'purpose,* adapted so as to, intended to, serve two purposes.

dub /dʌb/ *vt* (-bb-) **1** [VP22,23] make (sb) a knight by touching him on the shoulder with a sword; give (sb) a nickname: *They dubbed him 'Shorty' because he was so tall.* **2** [VP6A] replace or add to the sound-track of a film or magnetic tape, esp in a different language.

dub-bin /'dʌbɪn/ *n* [U] kind of thick grease used to make leather soft and waterproof.

du-biety /djuː'baɪətɪ US: duː-/ *n* [U] (formal) feeling of doubt; [C] (*pl* -ties) doubtful affair.

du-bious /'djuːbɪəs US: 'duː-/ *adj* **1** ∼ *(of/about),* (of persons) feeling doubt: *I feel* ∼ *of his honesty. I feel* ∼ *about/as to what to do next.* **2** (of persons) causing doubt (because probably not very good or reliable): *He's a* ∼ *character.* **3** (of things, actions, etc) causing doubt; of which the value, truth, etc is doubtful: *a* ∼ *compliment; a* ∼ *blessing. The result is still* ∼. ∼-**ly** *adv* ∼-**ness** *n*

du-cal /'djuːkl US: 'duːkl/ *adj* of or like a duke.

ducat /'dʌkət/ *n* gold coin formerly used in many European countries.

Duce /'duːtʃeɪ/ *n* (I) leader (esp as used of Mussolini /ˌmʊsə'liːnɪ/ (1883—1945) Italian Fascist leader).

duch-ess /'dʌtʃɪs/ *n* wife or widow of a duke; woman whose rank is equal to that of a duke.

duchy /'dʌtʃɪ/ *n* (*pl* -chies) (also *dukedom*) land ruled by a duke or duchess.

duck¹ /dʌk/ *n* (*pl* ∼s, but often unchanged when collective) **1** [C] common water-bird, both wild and domestic; female of this, ⇨ drake; ⇨ the illus at fowl; [U] its flesh as food. ˌ**lame '**∼, disabled person or ship; business or commercial organization in financial difficulties. *(take to sth) like a* ∼ *to water,* (begin doing, being etc it) naturally, without fear, hesitation or difficulty. *like water*

off a ~'s back, without producing any effect. **~s and drakes,** game in which flat stones are made to skip along water. **play ~s and drakes with** (eg one's money), squander, waste. **2** (colloq, also **~y**) (GB) darling; delightful person. **3** vehicle (also **DUKW** /dʌk/) able to travel on land and water, used as a landing-craft by troops. **4** (cricket, also sometimes **'~'s egg**) batsman's score of nought, 0: *to make a ~; be out for a ~.* **5** (compounds) **'~·bill; ~·billed 'platypus** ⇨ platypus. **'~·boards,** boards with narrow slats fixed across, for use on soft or muddy ground. **'~·weed,** small flowering plant growing on the surface of shallow water (eg on ponds). **'~·ling** /-lɪŋ/ *n* young ~. **ugly '~·ling,** plain or stupid child who grows up to be attractive or brilliant.

duck² /dʌk/ *vt,vi* [VP6A,2A] **1** move quickly down (to avoid being seen or hit): *to ~ one's head.* **2** go, push (sb), quickly under water for a short time: *The big boy ~ed all the small boys in the swimming-pool.* □ *n* quick downward or sideways movement of the head or body; quick dip below water (when bathing in the sea, etc). **~·ing** *n* thorough wetting: *to give sb a ~ing,* eg by pushing him into or under the water. *It rained heavily and we all got a ~ing.* **'~·ing-stool,** (hist) one (attached to a pole) on which a person was tied and ~ed into a pond, river, etc, as a punishment.

duck³ /dʌk/ *n* [U] strong linen or cotton cloth used for outer clothing of sailors; (*pl*) trousers made of this.

duct /dʌkt/ *n* **1** tube or canal through which liquid is conveyed, esp in the body: *'tear~s.* **2** metal tube and outlet for air (to ventilate, eg an aircraft): *The air ~s above your seat may be adjusted to your convenience.*

duc·tile /'dʌktaɪl US: -tl/ *adj* **1** (of metals) that can be pressed, beaten or drawn into shape while cold, eg copper. **2** (fig, of a person, his character) easily influenced, managed or directed; docile. **duc·til·ity** /dʌk'tɪlɪtɪ/ *n* [U] the quality of being ~(1).

dud /dʌd/ *n, adj* (sl) (thing or person) of no use, eg a shell or bomb that fails to explode or a banknote or cheque of no value.

dude /djuːd US: duːd/ *n* (US) dandy. **'~ ranch,** ranch organized for tourists.

dudg·eon /'dʌdʒən/ *n in high ~,** offended and feeling indignation, or sullen anger: *He went off in high ~.*

duds /dʌdz/ *n pl* (sl) clothes, esp old or ragged clothes.

due¹ /djuː US: duː/ *adj* **1 due (to),** to be paid: *When is the rent due? The wages due to him will be paid tomorrow.* **2** (attrib only) suitable; right; proper: *after due consideration; in due course,* at the right and proper time. **3** (to be) expected; appointed or agreed (for a certain time or date): *When is the steamer due? The train is due (in) at 1.30. Mr Hill is due to speak/lecture twice tomorrow.* **4 due to,** that may be ascribed or attributed to: *The accident was due to careless driving.* (Cf owing to: *Owing to* (= Because of) *his careless driving, we had a bad accident.*) □ *adv* (of points of the compass) exactly, directly: *due east/north.*

due² /djuː US: duː/ *n* **1** (*sing* only) that which must be given to sb because it is right or owing: *give the man his due.* **give the devil his due,** (prov) be fair to a person even though he is not a friend, or does not deserve much. **2** (*pl*) sums of money to be paid, eg for membership of a club, legal charges paid.

duel /'djuːəl US: 'duːəl/ *n* (hist) fight (usu with swords or pistols) agreed between two persons, esp to decide a point of honour, at a meeting arranged and conducted according to rules, in the presence of two other persons called *seconds*; any two-sided contest: *a ~ of wits.* □ *vi* (-ll-, US also -l-) fight a ~ or ~s. **~·list, ~·ist** /'djuːəlɪst US: 'duː-/ *n* person who fights ~s.

du·enna /dju:'enə US: duː-/ *n* (esp in a Spanish or Portuguese family) elderly woman acting as governess and companion in charge of girls; chaperon.

duet /dju:'et US: duː-/ *n* piece of music for two voices or for two players.

duf·fer /'dʌfə(r)/ *n* (colloq) slow-witted, unintelligent or incompetent person.

duffle (also **duf·fel**) /'dʌfl/ *n* [U] coarse woollen cloth with a thick nap. **'~ bag,** a cylindrical kitbag (of cloth or canvas). **'~ coat,** one of this material, usu with toggles instead of buttons, and a hood.

dug¹ /dʌg/ *pt,pp* of dig.

dug² /dʌg/ *n* udder or teat of a female mammal.

du·gong /'duːgɒŋ/ *n* large sea mammal with flippers and a forked tail. ⇨ manatee.

dug-out /'dʌg aʊt/ *n* **1** rough covered shelter made by digging, esp by soldiers for protection in war. **2** canoe made by hollowing a tree trunk.

duke /djuːk US: duːk/ *n* nobleman of high rank (next below a prince); (in some parts of Europe) independent sovereign ruler of a small State. **~·dom** /-dəm/ *n* **1** position and duties, rank of a ~. **2** (= *duchy*) land ruled by a ~ who is a sovereign ruler.

dul·cet /'dʌlsɪt/ *adj* (usu of sounds) sweet; pleasing.

dul·ci·mer /'dʌlsɪmə(r)/ *n* (often portable) musical instrument like a zither with strings struck with two hammers.

dull /dʌl/ *adj* (-er, -est) **1** not clear or bright: *a ~ colour/sound/mirror/day/sky; ~ weather; ~ of hearing,* unable to hear well. **2** slow in understanding: *~ pupils; a ~ mind.* **3** monotonous; uninteresting; not exciting or appealing to the imagination: *a ~ book/speech/sermon/play.* **4** not sharp: *a ~ knife; a knife with a ~ edge;* (of pain) not felt distinctly: *a ~ ache.* **5** (of trade) not active; (of goods) not in demand. □ *vt,vi* [VP6A,2A] make or become ~: *to ~ the edge of a razor; drugs that ~ pain.* **~·y** /'dʌl-lɪ/ *adv* **~·ness** *n*

dull·ard /'dʌləd/ *n* mentally dull person.

duly /'djuːlɪ US: 'duː-/ *adv* in a right or suitable manner; at the right time.

dumb /dʌm/ *adj* (-er, -est) **1** unable to speak: *~ from birth. We must be kind to ~ animals,* ie also to animals other than human beings. **2** temporarily silent: *The class remained ~ when the teacher asked a difficult question.* **strike ~,** make speechless, unable to talk because of surprise, fear, etc: *He was struck ~ with horror.* **'~ show** *n* the communication of ideas by means of acting, etc but without words. **3** (US colloq) stupid; dull. **~·ly** *adv* **~·ness** *n*

dumb-bell /'dʌmbel/ *n* short bar of wood or iron with a metal ball at each end, used in pairs (one in each hand) for exercising the muscles of the arms and shoulders.

dumb·found (US also **dum·found**) /dʌm'faʊnd/ *vt* [VP6A] astonish; strike dumb with surprise.

dumb·waiter /ˌdʌm'weɪtə(r)/ *n* **1** stand with (usu revolving) shelves for food, dishes, etc used at a dining-table. **2** (US; in GB *food-lift*) box with shelves, pulled up and down a shaft, to carry food, etc from one floor to another, eg in a restaurant.

dum·dum /'dʌmdʌm/ n '∼ **bullet,** soft-nosed bullet which expands on contact, causing a gaping wound.

dummy /'dʌmɪ/ n **1** object made to look like and serve the purpose of the real person or thing: *a tailor's* ∼, for fitting clothes; *a baby's* ∼, sucked like the nipple of a mother's breast. **2** (attrib) sham, imitation: *a* ∼ *gun.* **3** (in card games, esp bridge) player whose cards are placed upwards on the table and played by his partner; the cards so placed. **4** person who is present at an event, etc, but who takes no real part, eg because he is a substitute for sb else. **4** (attrib) ∼ **'run,** a trial or practice attack, shoot, performance, etc.

dump /dʌmp/ n **1** place where rubbish, etc may be unloaded and left; heap of rubbish, etc. **2** (place where there is a) temporary store of military supplies: *an ,ammu'nition* ∼. **3** (sl; pej) poorly cared for, dirty or ugly place (eg a village or town): *I should hate to live in a* ∼ *like this.* □ vt [VP6A,15A] **1** put on or into a ∼(1); put or throw down carelessly; let fall with a bump or thud: *Where can I* ∼ *this rubbish? They* ∼*ed the coal outside the shed instead of putting it inside.* **2** (comm) sell abroad at low prices goods which are unwanted in the home market. ∼**er** n (also '∼ **truck**) vehicle with a bin that can be tilted, for carrying and emptying soil, rubble, etc (eg for road building).

dump·ling /'dʌmplɪŋ/ n **1** small round mass of dough steamed or boiled with meat and vegetables. **2** baked pudding made of dough with an apple or other fruit inside it.

dumps /dʌmps/ n pl **(down) in the** ∼, (colloq) in low spirits; feeling gloomy.

dumpy /'dʌmpɪ/ adj (-ier, -iest) short and fat.

dun¹ /dʌn/ adj, n dull greyish-brown.

dun² /dʌn/ vt (-nn-) (continue to) demand payment of a debt or debts: *a dunning letter.* □ n person who duns; debt-collector; importunate demand for payment.

dunce /dʌns/ n slow learner (esp a child at school); stupid person. '∼'**s cap,** pointed paper cap which a ∼ was formerly given to wear in class as a punishment.

dun·der·head /'dʌndəhed/ n blockhead; stupid person.

dune /dju:n US: du:n/ n mound of loose, dry sand formed by the wind, esp near the sea-shore.

dung /dʌŋ/ n [U] excrement dropped by animals (esp cattle), used on fields as manure: *to cart and spread* ∼. '∼**·hill,** heap of ∼ in a farmyard.

dunga·rees /,dʌŋgə'ri:z/ n pl overalls of (usu) coarse calico.

dun·geon /'dʌndʒən/ n (hist) dark underground cell used as a prison.

dunk /dʌŋk/ vt [VP6A,14] dip (a piece of food) into a liquid: ∼ *a doughnut in one's coffee.*

duo·deci·mal /,dju:əʊ'desɪml US: ,du:ə'd-/ adj of twelve or twelfths; proceeding by twelves: *a* ∼ *notation.*

duo·denum /,dju:ə'di:nəm US: ,du:ə-/ n (anat) first part of the small intestine immediately below the stomach. ⇨ the illus at alimentary. **duo·denal** /,dju:ə'di:nl US: ,du:ə-/ adj of the ∼: *a duodenal ulcer.*

duo·logue /'dju:əlɒg US: 'du:əlɔ:g/ n conversation between two persons.

dupe /dju:p US: du:p/ vt [VP6A] cheat; make a fool of; deceive. □ n person who is ∼d.

du·plex /'dju:pleks US: 'du:-/ adj double; twofold: *a* ∼ *(oil-) lamp,* one with two wicks; *a* ∼ *apartment,* (US) one with rooms on two floors with an inner staircase.

du·pli·cate¹ /'dju:plɪkət US: 'du:-/ adj **1** identical: ∼ *keys for the front door of a house.* **2** with two corresponding parts; doubled; twofold. □ n [C] thing that is exactly like another. *in* ∼, (of documents, etc) with a ∼ copy.

du·pli·cate² /'dju:plɪkeɪt US: 'du:-/ vt [VP6A] **1** make an exact copy of (a letter, etc); produce copies of. **2** double. **du·pli·ca·tor** /-tə(r)/ n machine, etc that ∼s sth written or typed. **du·pli·ca·tion** /,dju:plɪ'keɪʃn US: ,du:-/ n [U] duplicating or being ∼d; [C] copy.

du·plic·ity /dju:'plɪsətɪ US: du:-/ n [U] deliberate deception.

dur·able /'djʊərəbl US: 'dʊə-/ adj likely to last for a long time: *a* ∼ *pair of shoes,* not soon worn out or needing repair. □ n (usu pl) (often **consumer** ∼**s**) goods bought and expected to last a long time (eg vacuum cleaners). **dura·bil·ity** /,djʊərə'bɪlətɪ US: 'dʊə-/ n [U].

du·rance /'djʊərəns US: 'dʊə-/ n (old use) imprisonment.

dur·ation /djʊ'reɪʃn US: dʊ-/ n [U] time during which sth lasts or exists: *for the* ∼ *of the war; of short* ∼.

dur·bar /'dɜ:bɑ:(r)/ n (hist) Indian ruler's court; reception given by a ruler in India.

dur·ess /djʊ'res US: dʊ-/ n threats, imprisonment, or violence, used to compel sb to do sth: *under* ∼, compelled by such means.

dur·ing /'djʊərɪŋ US: 'dʊər-/ prep **1** throughout the duration of: *The sun gives us light* ∼ *the day.* **2** at some point of time in the duration of: *He called to see me* ∼ *my absence.*

durst /dɜ:st/ old pt form of dare.

dusk /dʌsk/ n [U] time just before it gets quite dark: *scarcely visible in the* ∼.

dusky /'dʌskɪ/ adj (-ier, -iest) rather dark; dark-coloured; dim.

dust¹ /dʌst/ n **1** [U] dry earth or other matter in the form of fine powder, lying on the ground or the surface of objects, or blown about by the wind: *The* ∼ *was blowing in the streets. When it rains* ∼ *turns into mud.* **bite the** ∼, (sl) fall wounded or killed. **(humbled) in(to) the** ∼, humiliated (as if lying at the feet of an enemy). **shake the** ∼ **off one's feet,** leave in anger or scorn. **throw** '∼ **in a person's eyes,** mislead him; prevent him from seeing the truth. '∼**-bowl,** area that is denuded of vegetation by drought, unwise farming methods, etc. '∼**-coat,** coat worn to keep ∼ off or out. '∼**-jacket/-wrapper,** removable paper cover to protect the binding of a book. '∼**-pan,** pan into which ∼ is swept from the floor. '∼**-sheet** n one for covering furniture not in use. **2** *a* ∼, cloud of ∼: *What a* ∼*!* (fig) commotion. **kick up/make/ raise a** ∼, (sl, fig) cause a commotion. **3** (in compounds) (GB; Cf US *refuse, trash, garbage*) household refuse: '∼**-bin,** rigid receptacle for this (Cf US *ash-can, garbage-box*). '∼**-cart,** vehicle into which ∼bins are emptied. '∼**-man** /-mən/ (pl -men) man employed (by municipal authorities, etc) to empty ∼bins and cart away refuse. **4** (old use, poet or liter) remains of a dead human body: *buried with the* ∼ *of* (= in the same grave as) *one's ancestors.*

dust² /dʌst/ vt **1** [VP6A,15B] *dust sth (down/off),* remove dust from, by wiping, brushing, flicking: ∼ *the furniture;* ∼ *down/off the seat of a car.* ∼ *sb's jacket,* (colloq) beat him. '∼**-up** n (colloq) fight; quarrel. **2** [VP15A] sprinkle with powder: *to* ∼ *a cake with sugar;* sprinkle (powder, etc): *to* ∼ *sugar on to a cake.* ∼**er** n cloth for removing dust from furniture, etc.

dusty /'dʌstɪ/ adj (-ier, -iest) covered with dust; full of dust; like dust; dry as dust. ∼ **answer,** answer that is not pleasing or satisfactory (to the receiver).

Dutch /dʌtʃ/ adj **1** of or from the Netherlands (Holland), its people, their language: ∼ *cheese.* **2** (colloq uses) ∼ **auction,** sale at which the price is reduced by the auctioneer until a buyer is found. ∼ **courage,** that obtained by drinking (spirits, etc): ∼ **treat,** meal, entertainment, etc at which each person pays for himself. **go** ∼ **(with sb),** share expenses. **talk to sb like a** ∼ **uncle,** lecture him candidly but severely. □ n **1 the** ∼, the people of Holland. **2** their language. **double** ∼, unintelligible language. ∼**man** /-mən/ n (pl -men) native of Holland.

du·teous /'djuːtɪəs US: 'duː-/ adj (formal) dutiful (the more usu word); obedient.

duti·able /'djuːtɪəbl US: 'duː-/ adj on which customs duties must be paid: ∼ *goods. Tobacco is* ∼ *in most countries.* ⇨ duty(3).

duti·ful /'djuːtɪfl US: 'duː-/ adj ∼ **(to),** doing one's duty well; showing respect and obedience: *a* ∼ *son.* ∼**ly** /-fəlɪ/ adv

duty /'djuːtɪ US: 'duːtɪ/ n (pl -ties) **1** [C,U] what one is obliged to do by morality, law, a trade, a calling, conscience, etc; inner voice urging one to behave in a certain way: *When* ∼ *calls, no man should disobey. Do not forget your* ∼ *to your parents. His sense of* ∼ *is strong. What are the duties of this post? The* ∼ *of a postman is to deliver letters and parcels.* **on/off** ∼, actually engaged/not engaged in one's regular work: *He goes on* ∼ *at 9am and comes off* ∼ *at 5pm.* **(as) in** ∼ **bound,** as required by ∼. **do** ∼ **for,** be used instead of; serve for: *An old wooden box did* ∼ *for a table.* **2** (attrib) moral obligation. '∼ **call,** visit one makes from a sense of ∼, not because one expects to enjoy it. **3** [C,U] ∼ **(on),** payment demanded by the government on certain goods exported or imported ('*customs duties*'), or manufactured in the country ('*excise duties*'), or when property, etc is transferred to a new owner by sale ('*stamp duties*') or death (*estate* ∼). ∼**-'free,** (of goods) allowed to enter a country without the payment of customs duties: ∼**-free shops,** (eg at airports) selling ∼-free goods.

duvet /'djuːveɪ US: duː'veɪ/ n bed quilt (filled with feathers, eg swan's-down, or an artificial substitute) used in place of blankets.

dwarf /dwɔːf/ n (pl ∼s) person, animal or plant much below the usual size; (in fairy tales) small being with magic powers; (attrib) undersized. ∼**ish** adj like a ∼; undersized: ∼*ish trees/fingers.* □ vt [VP6A] **1** prevent from growing to full size. **2** cause to appear small by contrast or distance: *The big yacht* ∼*ed our little launch.*

dwell /dwel/ vi (pt dwelt /dwelt/) [VP3A] (liter) **1** ∼ **in/at,** reside. **2** ∼ **on/upon,** think, speak or write at length about: *She* ∼*s too much upon her past.* ∼**er** n (in compounds) inhabitant: '*town-*∼*ers;* '*cliff-*∼*ers;* '*cave-*∼*ers.* ∼**·ing** n place of residence (a house, flat, etc). '∼**·ing-house,** one used for living in, not as an office, workshop, etc.

dwindle /'dwɪndl/ vi [VP2A] become less or smaller by degrees.

dy·archy n = diarchy.

dye¹ /daɪ/ vt,vi(3rd pers sing pres t, dyes, pt,pp dyed, pres part dyeing) **1** [VP6A,22] colour, usu by dipping in a liquid: *to dye a white dress blue; to have a dress dyed.* **dye in the wool/in grain,** dye while the material is in the raw state, so that the process is thorough; complete. **2** [VP6A] give colour to: *Deep blushes dyed her cheeks.* **3** [VP2A] take colour from dyeing: *This material does not dye well.*

dye² /daɪ/ n [C,U] substance used for dyeing cloth; colour given by dyeing. **a villain/scoundrel of the blackest/deepest dye,** of the worst kind. '**dye-stuff,** substance yielding a dye or used as a dye. '**dye-works,** one where dyeing is done. **dyer** n one who dyes cloth.

dy·ing ⇨ die².

dyke n = dike.

dy·namic /daɪ'næmɪk/ adj **1** of physical power and forces producing motion. ⇨ static. **2** (of a person) having energy, force of character: *a* ∼ *personality.* □ n **1** (pl with *sing v*) branch of physics dealing with matter in motion. **2** moral force that produces activity or change: *driven by an inner* ∼. **dy·nami·cally** /-klɪ/ adv **dy·na·mism** /'daɪnəmɪzəm/ [U] (of a person or thing) power, energy.

dyna·mite /'daɪnəmaɪt/ n [U] powerful explosive (used in mining and quarrying). □ vt [VP6A] blow up with ∼.

dy·namo /'daɪnəməʊ/ n (pl ∼s /-məʊz/) machine for changing steam-power, water-power, etc into electrical energy.

dyn·ast /'dɪnəst US: 'daɪnæst/ n lord; hereditary ruler. ∼**y** /'dɪnəstɪ US: 'daɪ-/ n (pl -ties) succession of rulers belonging to one family: *the Tudor* ∼*y* (in England). ∼**tic** /dɪ'næstɪk US: daɪ-/ adj of a ∼y.

dyne /daɪn/ n unit of force in the metric system.

dys·en·tery /'dɪsəntrɪ US: -terɪ/ n [U] painful disease of the bowels, with discharge of mucus and blood.

dys·lexia /dɪs'leksɪə/ n [U] disturbance in the ability to read. **dys·lexic** /-'leksɪk/ adj

dys·pep·sia /dɪs'pepsɪə/ n [U] indigestion. **dys·pep·tic** /dɪs'peptɪk/ adj of ∼. □ n person suffering from ∼

Ee

Eifersucht - jealousy
eifersüchtig - jealous

E, e /iː/ (pl E's, e's /iːz/), fifth letter of the English alphabet.

each /iːtʃ/ adj (of two or more) every one, (thing, group, person, etc) taken separately or individually: *He was sitting with a child on* ∼ *side of him. On* ∼ *occasion I just missed the target. He had words of encouragement for* ∼ *one of us.* □ pron **1** ∼ thing, person, group, etc: *E*∼ *of them wants to try. E*∼ *of the boys had a try. He had good advice for* ∼ *of us.* **2** used in apposition, like *all* and *both: We*

~ *took a big risk. Tom, Dick and Harry* ~ *put forward a different scheme.* **3** used *adverbially* meaning 'apiece': *He gave the boys 50p* ~. *The oranges are 6p* ~. **4** ~ *other*, used as the object of a *v* or *prep*; both words usu unstressed; often replaced by *one another* when the reference is to a number more than two: *We see* ~ *other* (= ~ of us sees the other) *at the office every day. They are afraid of* ~ *other*.

eager /'iːgə(r)/ *adj* ~ *(for sth/to do sth)*, full of, showing, strong desire: ~ *for success*; ~ *to succeed*. ,~ 'beaver, (colloq) hardworking and (over) enthusiastic person. ~·ly *adv* ~·ness *n*

eagle /'iːgl/ *n* large, strong bird of prey of the falcon family with keen sight. ⇨ the illus at prey. ,~-'eyed *adj* keen-sighted. **eag·let** /'iːglɪt/ *n* young ~(1).

ear[1] /ɪə(r)/ *n* **1** organ of hearing. ⇨ illus here and the illus at head. **be all ears**, be listening eagerly. **fall on deaf ears**, pass unnoticed. **feel one's ears burning**, imagine that one is being talked about. **give one's ears (for sth/to do sth)**, make any sacrifice, pay any price. **go in (at) one ear and out (at) the 'other**, said of sth that, although heard, makes no impression. **have an ear to the ground**, be alert for what may be happening in secret. **(have) a word in sb's ear**, (say) sth in confidence: *May I have a word in your ear?* **have/win sb's ear(s)**, his favourable attention. **over head and ears**, deeply (in debt, etc). **prick up one's ears**, become suddenly attentive. **set (persons) by the ears**, set them quarrelling. **turn a deaf ear (to)**, refuse to help. **up to the/one's 'ears in (work, etc)**, overwhelmed by it. **wet behind the ears**, naïve. 'ear·ache, pain in the inner ear. 'ear·drop, earring with a hanging ornament. 'ear·drum, thin membrane (in the inner ear) which vibrates when sound-waves strike it. ⇨ the illus here. 'ear·ful /-fʊl/, as much (usu abusive or unsolicited) talk as one can endure. 'ear·mark *n* mark on the ear of a sheep, etc, to mark ownership; (fig) special characteristic. □ *vt* [VP6A,14] **earmark sb/sth (for sth)**, put an earmark on (an animal); (fig) keep sb in mind for a special purpose, work, etc; set sth aside for a special purpose: *earmark sb for an important post; earmark a sum of money for research.* 'ear·piece, earphone of a telephone receiver. 'ear·phone, head-phone. 'ear·ring, ring worn in or on the lobe of the ear as an ornament.

'ear·shot, hearing distance: *out of/within earshot.* 'ear-trumpet, trumpet-shaped tube formerly used by partly deaf people. ⇨ **hearing-aid** at hearing. 'ear·wax, waxy substance secreted in the ear. **2** sense of hearing. **have a good ear for music**, be able to discriminate sound. **(play sth) by ear**, (play) without printed music, or without having memorized it; (fig) (do it) unprepared. **3** ear-shaped thing, esp the handle of a pitcher. **(-)eared** used in compounds: ,long-'eared, having long ears.

ear[2] /ɪə(r)/ *n* seed-bearing part of a cereal (corn, barley, etc): *corn in the ear*, with ears developed. ⇨ the illus at cereal.

earl /ɜːl/ *n* (fem *countess*) title of a British nobleman. ~·dom /-dəm/ *n* rank of an ~.

early /'ɜːlɪ/ (-ier, -iest) *adj*, *adv* near to the beginning of a period of time, sooner than usual or than others: *in the* ~ *part of this century*; *in* ~ *spring*; *an* ~ *breakfast*, eg 5am; ~ *peaches*, ripening ~ in the season; ,~-'closing day, (GB) on which shops, etc are closed during the afternoon. *He's an* ~ *riser*, gets up at an ~ hour. *Please come at your earliest convenience*, as soon as it is convenient for you to do so. *He keeps* ~ *hours*, gets up, goes to bed, ~. *It's better to be too* ~ *than too late. Come as* ~ *as possible. The* ~ *bird gets/catches the worm*, (prov) The person who arrives, etc ~ will (probably) succeed. **early days (yet)**, too soon to tell how sth will develop. **earlier on**, at an earlier stage. Cf *later on* at late[2](1). ,~-'warning *adj* (of radar) giving early indication of the approach of enemy aircraft, missiles, etc: *an* ~-*warning system*.

earn /ɜːn/ *vt* [VP6A,12B,13B] get in return for work, as a reward for one's qualities or in payment for a loan: *to* ~ *£10000 a year*; *to* ~ *one's living/ one's livelihood/one's daily bread. The money* ~s 7% *interest. His achievements* ~ed *him respect and admiration. His eccentricities had* ~ed *for him the nickname 'The Madman'. I had a well-*~ed *rest.* ~·ings *n pl* money ~ed: *He has spent all his* ~*ings*. '~ings yield, (comm) ratio between annual profit and capital.

ear·nest[1] /'ɜːnɪst/ *adj* serious; determined: *an* ~ *worker/pupil; a terribly* ~ *young man*, perhaps over-serious, over-conscientious. □ *n in* ~, in a determined manner; serious(ly): *If you work in* ~, *you will succeed. I'm perfectly in* ~, am not joking. *It is raining in real* ~, heavily, and likely to

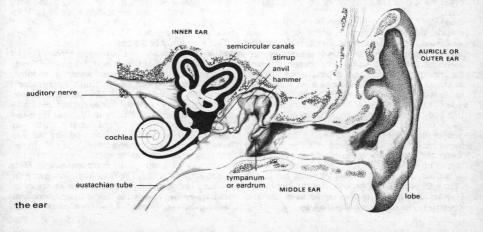

INNER EAR

semicircular canals
stirrup
anvil
hammer

AURICLE OR OUTER EAR

auditory nerve

cochlea

eustachian tube

tympanum or eardrum

MIDDLE EAR

lobe

the ear

continue. **~·ly** *adv* in an ~ manner: *We ~ly hope that…*. **~·ness** *n*

ear·nest² /'ɜːnɪst/ *n* **1** (also '**~-money**) part payment made as a pledge that full payment will follow. **2** sth coming in advance as a sign of what is to come after: *As an ~ of my good intentions I will work overtime this week.*

earth /ɜːθ/ *n* **1** (**the**) **~**, this world; the planet on which we live: *The moon goes round the ~ and the ~ goes round the sun. Who do you think was the greatest man on ~? ⇨ the illus at planet. **2** [U] land surface of the world; contrasted with the sky: *The balloon burst and fell to ~*. **come down/back to ~,** stop day dreaming; return to practical realities. **move heaven and ~ (to do sth),** make every possible effort. **how/why/where/who, etc on ~,** how/why, etc ever…. (used for emphasis; ⇨ ever). **3** [U] soil: *to fill a pit with ~; to cover the roots of a plant with ~.* '**~-closet,** latrine; substitute for a lavatory in places where there is no supply of water from mains, etc. '**~-nut,** groundnut. '**~-work,** embankment of ~ used in fortifications as a defence. '**~-worm,** common kind of worm that lives in the soil. **4** [C] hole of a fox, badger or other wild animal: *to stop an ~,* block it up so that the animal cannot return to it. **run/go to ~,** (of a fox) go into its hole. **run sth/sb to ~,** hunt (a fox) to its burrow; (fig) discover (sth/sb) by searching. **5** [C,U] (electr) (means of) contact with the ground as the completion of a circuit. **6** [C] (chem) one of several metallic oxides. □ *vt* **1** [VP15B] **~ up,** cover with ~: *to ~ up the roots of a newly-planted shrub.* **2** [VP6A] (electr) connect (an apparatus, etc) with the ~. ⇨ **5** above. **~y** *adj* **1** of or like ~ or soil: *an ~y smell.* **2** (fig) grossly material; unaffected, unrefined: *the ~y and robust men and women in the paintings of Rubens.*

earthen /'ɜːθn/ *adj* made of earth: ~ *floors;* made of baked clay: *an ~ jar.* '**~-ware** /-weə(r)/ *n* [U] dishes, etc made of baked clay; (attrib) *an ~ware casserole.*

earthly /'ɜːθlɪ/ *adj* **1** of this world, not of heaven: ~ *joys/possessions.* **2** (colloq) possible; conceivable: *You haven't an ~ (chance),* no chance at all. **no ~ use,** quite useless.

earth·quake /'ɜːθkweɪk/ *n* [C] sudden, violent movement of the earth's surface.

ear·wig /'ɪəwɪg/ *n* small harmless insect with pincers at the rear end of its abdomen. ⇨ the illus at insect.

ease¹ /iːz/ *n* [U] freedom from work, discomfort, trouble, difficulty, anxiety: *a life of ~; ~ of body and mind.* **at ~,** confortable; comfortably: *a mind at ~; sitting at ~.* **ill at ~,** anxious or embarrassed. **stand at ~,** (as a mil command) with the legs apart and the hands behind the back (Cf *at attention, stand easy*). **take one's ~,** stop working or worrying. **with ~,** without difficulty.

ease² /iːz/ *vt,vi* **1** [VP6A,14] **~ (of),** give relief to (the body or mind) from pain, discomfort, anxiety: ~ *sb's anxiety; ~ sb of his pain/trouble. Can I ~ you of your burden?* **2** [VP6A,15A,B,2C] make looser, less tight; lessen speed, efforts: ~ *a coat under the armpits; ~ a drawer,* eg one that sticks fast or opens with difficulty: ~ *(down) the speed of a boat. E~ off a bit, we're going too fast.* **3** [VP2A,C] **~ (off/up),** become less tense or troublesome: *the easing of tension between the two countries. The situation has ~d off/up.*

easel /'iːzl/ *n* wooden frame to support a blackboard or a picture (while the artist is working at it).

east /iːst/ *n* **1** the ~, point of the horizon where the sun rises. ⇨ the illus at compass. **the ,Far 'E~,** China, Japan, etc. **the ,Middle 'E~,** countries from Egypt to Iran. **the ,Near 'E~,** Turkey, etc. **the E~,** (a) the Orient. (b) the eastern side of the USA ~ of the Allegheny /,ælə'geɪnɪ/ Mountains and north of the Mason-Dixon /,meɪsn 'dɪksn/ line (the boundary between the states of Pennsylvania and Maryland). **2** (attrib): *an ~ wind,* one blowing from the ~; towards, at, in the direction of the ~: *on the ~ coast.* **the ,E~ 'End,** the eastern part of London. □ *adv* towards the ~: *to travel ~; to face ~; to sail due ~; a town that lies ~ of the Rhine.* **~·ward** /'iːstwəd/ *adj* towards the ~: *in an ~ward direction.* **~·ward(s)** *adv* towards the ~: *to travel ~wards.*

Easter /'iːstə(r)/ *n* anniversary of the Resurrection of Christ, observed on the first Sunday (~ *Day,* ~ *Sunday*) after a full moon on or after 21 Mar. Used attrib in '**~-week** (beginning on ~ Sunday); *the ~ holidays.* '**~ egg,** egg with a painted or dyed shell, or an egg made of chocolate.

east·er·ly /'iːstəlɪ/ *adj, adv* in an eastern direction or position; (of the wind) coming from the east.

east·ern /'iːstən/ *adj* (attrib) of, from, living in, the east part of the world: ~ *religions.* **the E~ Church,** the Greek Orthodox Church. **the E~ Hemisphere,** Africa, Asia and Europe. **~·most** /-məʊst/ *adj* farthest east.

easy /'iːzɪ/ (-ier, -iest) *adj* **1** not difficult: *an ~ book. The place is ~ to reach. It is an ~ place to reach.* **2** free from pain, discomfort, anxiety, trouble, etc: *to lead an ~ life; in ~ circumstances,* having enough money to live comfortably; *an '~ chair,* one that is soft and restful; ~ *manners,* not showing stiffness or embarrassment; (*to buy furniture*) *on ~ terms,* trade term for hire-purchase; *persons who are ~ to get on with,* people who are informal, not stiff. **,~'going,** (of persons) placid and tolerant; casual; lazy and careless; lax. **3** (comm) (of goods and money on loan) not much in demand. ⇨ tight. □ *adv* in an ~ manner: *E~!* (as a command) Move (it) gently. **take it/things ~,** don't work too hard or too energetically. **go ~ on/with,** (colloq) be careful or moderate with: *Go ~ on the brandy—it's the last bottle! Easier said than done,* It is easier to say one will do it than to do it. **Stand ~!** (as a mil command) Stand with more freedom of movement than when *at ease,* ⇨ ease¹. **eas·ily** /'iːzəlɪ/ *adv* **1** with ease. **2** without doubt: *easily the best TV programme.* **3** possibly: *That may easily be the case.*

eat /iːt/ *vt,vi* (*pt* ate /et US: eɪt/, *pp* eaten /'iːtn/) **1** [VP6A,15B,2A,C,4A] **eat (up),** take (solid food, also soup) into the mouth and swallow it: *to eat one's dinner; to eat up* (= finish eating) *one's food. Where shall we eat? He was too ill to eat. We should eat to live, not live to eat,* not make eating the most important thing in life. **eat its head off,** (a horse) cost more to feed than it is worth. **eat one's heart out,** suffer in silence; be very sad. **eat one's words,** take a statement back, say in a humble way that one was wrong. **2** [VP6A,3A,15B] destroy as if by eating: *Acids eat into metals. He is eaten up with pride. The river had eaten away the banks. The moths have eaten holes in my coat.* '**eating-apple** *n* suitable for eating uncooked. '**eating-house,** restaurant. **eats** *n pl* (sl) food:

etw erfahren - to get to know

There were plenty of eats, but not enough drinks.
eat·able /-əbl/ *adj* fit to be eaten; good to eat: *The prison food was scarcely eatable.* □ *n* (usu *pl*) food.
~er *n* **1** one that eats: *He's a big eater,* eats large quantities. **2** apple, pear, etc for dessert, good when eaten uncooked.
eau /əʊ/ *n* **eau de Cologne** /ˌəʊ də kə'ləʊn/ *n* (F) perfume made at Cologne. **eau-de-vie** /ˌəʊ də 'viː/ *n* (F) brandy.
eaves /iːvz/ *n pl* overhanging edges of a roof: *icicles hanging from the ~.*
eaves·drop /'iːvzdrɒp/ *vi* (-pp-) [VP2A,3A] **~ (on),** listen secretly to private conversation: *~ on a discussion.* **~·per** /-drɒpə(r)/ *n* person who does this.
ebb /eb/ *vi* [VP2A,C] **1** (of the tide) flow back from the land to the sea. **2** (fig) grow less; become weak or faint: *His fortune's beginning to ebb. Daylight was ebbing away.* □ *n* **1** the flowing out of the tide: *the ebb and flow of the sea/the tide. The tide is on the ebb,* is going out. **2** (fig) low state; decline or decay: *His health is at a low ebb.* **ˌebb-'tide** *n* = ebb.
eb·on·ite /'ebənaɪt/ *n* [U] (comm) hard black insulating material made by vulcanising rubber.
eb·ony /'ebənɪ/ *n* [U] hard, black wood. □ *adj* made of, black as, ~: *the ~ keys on a piano.*
ebul·lient /ɪ'bʌlɪənt/ *adj* exuberant. **ebul·lience** /-əns/ *n* exuberance; outburst (of feeling).
ec·cen·tric /ɪk'sentrɪk/ *adj* **1** (of a person, his behaviour) peculiar; not normal or conventional. **2** (of circles) not having the same centre, ➪ the illus at concentric; (of orbits) not circular; (of planets, etc) moving in an ~ orbit. □ *n* **1** ~ person. **2** (mech) device for changing circular motion into backward-and-forward motion.
ec·cen·tric·ity /ˌeksen'trɪsətɪ/ *n* **1** [U] quality of being eccentric; strangeness of behaviour, etc: ~ *in dress.* **2** [C] (*pl* -ties) instance of this; strange or unusual act or habit: *One of his eccentricities is sleeping under the bed instead of in it.*
ec·clesi·as·tic /ɪˌkliːzɪ'æstɪk/ *n* clergyman. **ec·clesi·as·ti·cal** /-kl/ *adj* of the Christian Church; of clergymen. **ec·clesi·as·ti·cally** /-klɪ/ *adv*
eche·lon /'eʃəlɒn/ *n* step-like formation of troops, aircraft, ships, etc as shown in illus: *flying in ~.*

flying in echelon

echo[1] /'ekəʊ/ *n* (*pl* ~es /-əʊz/) **1** [C,U] sound reflected or sent back (eg from a wall of rock): *The speaker was cheered/applauded to the ~,* long and loudly. '**~ chamber,** natural or artifical space for producing ~es. '**~-sounding,** method of ascertaining distances (eg of the ocean bed or underwater objects) by measuring the time taken for waves of sound, etc to be echoed back. Hence, '**~-sounder** *n* instrument used for this. **2** [C] person

who, statement etc which, is a copy or repetition of another.
echo[2] /'ekəʊ/ *vi, vt* [VP6A,15B,2A,C] **~ (back) 1** (of places) send back an echo: *The valley ~ed as he sang. The hills ~ed back the noise of the shot.* **2** (of sounds) be sent back as an echo: *The shot ~ed through the woods.* **3** be an echo of; repeat the words, etc of another: *They ~ed every word of their leader.*
éclair /ɪ'kleə(r)/ *n* (F) small cylindrical pastry iced on top and filled with cream.
éclat /'eɪklɑː US:* eɪ'klɑː/ *n* [U] (F) brilliant, conspicuous success; applause from everyone: *with great ~.*
ec·lec·tic /ɪ'klektɪk/ *adj* (of persons, methods, etc) choosing, accepting, freely from various sources. **ec·lec·ti·cism** /-tɪsɪzəm/ *n*

corona

a total eclipse of the sun

eclipse /ɪ'klɪps/ *n* [C] **1** total or partial cutting off of the light of the sun (when the moon is between it and the earth), or of the reflected light of the moon (when the earth's shadow falls on it). **2** (fig) loss of brilliance, power, reputation, etc: *After suffering an ~ he is now again famous. An author's reputation is often in ~ for some years after his death.* □ *vt* [VP6A] **1** (of the moon, a planet, etc) cause an ~; cut off the light from. **2** (fig) make (sb or sth) appear dull by comparison; outshine: *She was so beautiful that she ~d every other woman at the ball.*
eclip·tic /ɪ'klɪptɪk/ *n* the path of the sun in the sky.
ecol·ogy /iː'kɒlədʒɪ/ *n* [U] branch of biology that deals with the habits of living things, esp their relation to their environment. **eco·logi·cal** /ˌiːkə'lɒdʒɪkl/ *adj* of ~: *the ecological effects of industry,* eg the pollution of the atmosphere, of rivers, etc. **eco·logi·cally** /-klɪ/ *adv.* **ecol·ogist** /iː'kɒlədʒɪst/ *n* student of, expert in, ~. **eco·system** /'iːkəʊ-/ = ecological system.
econ·omic /ˌiːkə'nɒmɪk US:* ˌek-/ *adj* **1** of economics (➪ below): *the government's ~ policy.* **2** designed to give a profit: *an ~ rent,* one that compensates the owner for the cost of the land, building, etc. **3** connected with commerce and industry: *~ geography,* studied chiefly in connection with industry.
econ·omi·cal /ˌiːkə'nɒmɪkl US:* ˌek-/ *adj* careful in the spending of money, time, etc and in the use of goods; not wasteful: *to be ~ of time and energy; an ~ fire,* one that does not waste fuel. **~ly** /-klɪ/ *adv*
econ·omics /ˌiːkə'nɒmɪks US:* ˌek-/ *n* (with *sing v*) [U] science of the production, distribution and consumption of goods; condition of a country as to material prosperity. **econ·om·ist** /ɪ'kɒnəmɪst/ *n* **1** expert in ~; person who writes or lectures on ~ or

political economy. **2** person who is economical or thrifty.

econ·om·ize /ɪˈkɒnəmaɪz/ vt,vi [VP6A,2A,3A] ~ **(on sth)**, be economical; use or spend less than before; cut down expenses: *He ~d by using buses instead of taking taxis. We must ~ on light and fuel.*

econ·omy /ɪˈkɒnəmɪ/ n (pl -mies) **1** [C,U] (instance of) avoidance of waste of money, strength or anything else of value: *to practise ~. In the long run, it is an ~ to buy good quality goods, even though they cost more. By various little economies, she managed to save enough money for a holiday.* '~ **class,** cheapest class of travel (esp by air). **2** [U] control and management of the money, goods and other resources of a community, society or household: *political ~; domestic ~.* **3** [C] system for the management and use of resources: *the totalitarian economies of Germany and Italy before the Second World War.*

ec·stasy /ˈekstəsɪ/ n (pl -sies) [U,C] (feeling of) great joy and spiritual uplift: *in an ~ of delight; to be in/go into/be thrown into ~/ecstasies (over sth).* **ec·static** /ɪkˈstætɪk/ adj of, in, causing, ~. **ec·stati·cally** /-klɪ/ adv

ec·to·plasm /ˈektəplæzəm/ n [U] substance supposed to flow from a spiritualistic medium during a trance.

ecu·meni·cal /ˌiːkjuːˈmenɪkl/ adj **1** of or representing the whole Christian world or universal Church: *an E~ Council,* eg of all the RC church as summoned by the Pope. **2** seeking to restore the unity of the Christian churches: *the ~ movement.*

ec·zema /ˈeksɪmə/ n [U] itching skin disease.

eddy /ˈedɪ/ n (pl -dies) (of wind, smoke, fog, mist, dust, water) circular or spiral movement: *Eddies of mist rose from the valleys. The car went past in an ~ of dust.* □ vi [VP2A,C] move in small circles; move in or like eddies; whirl.

edel·weiss /ˈeɪdlvaɪs/ n small Alpine plant with white leaves and flowers, growing among rocks.

Eden /ˈiːdn/ n (Bible) garden where Adam and Eve lived; place of delight.

edge¹ /edʒ/ n **1** sharp, cutting part of a knife, sword or other tool or weapon: *a knife with a sharp ~; to put an ~ on a knife,* sharpen it. **be on ~,** be excited or irritable. **give sb the ~ of one's tongue,** rebuke him sharply. **have the ~ on sb,** (colloq) have an advantage over him. **set sb's 'teeth on ~,** upset his nerves (as when a scraping sound or a sharp, acid taste causes physical revulsion). **take the ~ off sth,** dull or soften; reduce, eg one's appetite. **2** (line marking the) outer limit or boundary of a (flat) surface: *a cottage on the ~ of a forest; the ~ of a lake; trim the ~s of a lawn,* cut the grass there. *Don't put the glass on the ~ of the table; it may get knocked off. He fell off the ~ of the cliff.* **edgy** /ˈedʒɪ/ adj having one's nerves on ~.

edge² /edʒ/ vt,vi **1** [VP6A,14] ~ **(with),** supply with a border: *to ~ a handkerchief with lace/a garden path with plants;* form a border to: *a road ~d with grass.* **2** [VP6A] sharpen (a tool, etc). **3** [VP15A,B,2C] (cause to) move slowly forward or along: *~ oneself/~ one's way through a crowd; ~ along a narrow ledge of rock; ~ a piano through a door; ~ one's chair nearer to the fireplace.*

edge·ways, edge·wise /ˈedʒweɪz, -waɪz/ adv with the edge outwards or forwards. **not get a word in ~,** be unable to say anything when a very talkative person is speaking.

edg·ing /ˈedʒɪŋ/ n narrow border: *an ~ of lace on a dress.* '~**-shears,** tool for trimming grass on the edges of a lawn.

ed·ible /ˈedɪbl/ adj fit to be eaten; not poisonous. □ n (usu pl) thing fit to be eaten. **edi·bil·ity** /ˌedɪˈbɪlətɪ/ n

edict /ˈiːdɪkt/ n order or proclamation issued by authority; decree.

edi·fi·ca·tion /ˌedɪfɪˈkeɪʃn/ n [U] mental or moral improvement.

edi·fice /ˈedɪfɪs/ n [C] building (esp a large or imposing one); (fig) sth built up in the mind: *The whole ~ of his hopes was destroyed.*

edify /ˈedɪfaɪ/ vt (pt,pp -fied) [VP6A] improve in morals or mind: *~ing books.*

edit /ˈedɪt/ vt [VP6A] **1** prepare (another person's writing) for publication (as a book, or in a newspaper or other periodical): *~ a newspaper; ~ a Shakespeare play for use in schools.* **2** do the work of planning and directing the publication of a newspaper, magazine, book, encyclopaedia, etc. **3** prepare a cinema film, tape recording by putting together parts in a suitable sequence. **4** arrange data for computer processing.

edi·tion /ɪˈdɪʃn/ n **1** form in which a book is published: *a cheap ~; a 'pocket ~.* **2** total number of copies (of a book, newspaper, etc) issued from the same types: *the first ~; a revised ~.* ⇨ impression(3).

edi·tor /ˈedɪtə(r)/ n person who edits (esp a book, newspaper, periodical, radio news programme) or who is in charge of part of a newspaper: *the 'sports/fi'nancial ~.*

edi·tor·ial /ˌedɪˈtɔːrɪəl/ adj of an editor: *the ~ office; ~ work.* □ n [C] special article or discussion of news in a newspaper, etc usu written by the editor.

edu·cate /ˈedʒʊkeɪt/ vt [VP6A,15A,16A] give intellectual and moral training to; train: *The boy had to ~ himself in the evening after finishing his work. I was ~d for the law. You should ~ your children to behave well.* **edu·ca·tor** /-tə(r)/ n person who ~s.

edu·ca·tion /ˌedʒʊˈkeɪʃn/ n [U] **1** systematic training and instruction (esp of the young, in school, college, etc): *No country can afford to neglect ~. Is ~ free and compulsory in your country?* **2** knowledge and abilities, development of character and mental powers, resulting from such training. *~al* /-ʃənl/ adj of, connected with, ~: *~al work; an ~al magazine.* *~·ist* /-ʃənɪst/, *~·al·ist* /-ʃənəlɪst/ n expert in ~.

educe /ɪˈdjuːs US: ɪˈduːs/ vt [VP6A] (formal) bring out, develop (from what is latent or potential).

eel /iːl/ n long, snake-like fish. ⇨ the illus at sea. **as slippery as an eel,** very difficult to hold; (fig) (of a person) untrustworthy; difficult to manage.

e'en /iːn/ adv (poet) even.

e'er /eə(r)/ adv (poet) ever.

eerie, eery /ˈɪərɪ/ adj (-ier, -iest) causing a feeling of mystery and fear: *an ~ shriek.* **eer·ily** /ˈɪərəlɪ/ adv **eeri·ness** n

eff /ef/ vi (sl, euphem for ⚠ fuck): *I told him to eff off. What an effing nuisance!*

ef·face /ɪˈfeɪs/ vt [VP6A] **1** rub or wipe out; make indistinct; (fig) obliterate: *~ an inscription; ~ unpleasant memories of the past.* **2** *~ oneself,* keep in the background in order to escape being noticed; make oneself appear to be unimportant. *~·ment* n

ef·fect /ɪˈfekt/ n **1** [C,U] ([U] in phrases of degree or extent) result; outcome: *the ~ of heat upon metals;*

the ∼s of the hot weather. Did the medicine have any ∼/a good ∼? Punishment had very little ∼ on him, did not reform him, frighten him, etc. Our arguments had no ∼ on them, did not influence them. of no ∼, useless, not doing what was intended or hoped for. in ∼, (a) in fact, really; for practical purposes. (b) (of a rule, law, etc) in operation: The rule is still in ∼. bring/carry/put sth into ∼, cause it to operate: The plans will soon be carried into ∼. come into ∼, reach the stage of being operative: The new tax regulations came into ∼ last week. give ∼ to, cause to become active or have a result. take ∼, (a) produce the result intended or required. (b) come into force; operate; become active. 2 [C,U] impression produced on the mind of a spectator, hearer, reader, etc: wonderful 'cloud ∼s, impressions produced by light on clouds, eg at sunset; 'sound ∼s, (in broadcasting, etc) sounds characteristic of a scene, or incidental to an event, eg the noise of a train. Everything he says and does is calculated for ∼, designed to impress spectators or hearers. 3 to this/that ∼, with this/that meaning: That is what he said, or words to that ∼, words with the same general meaning. to the ∼ that..., stating: I have received a cable to the ∼ that..., with the information that.... to the same ∼, giving the same information: I sent a telegram and wrote a letter to the same ∼. 4 (pl) goods; property: The hotel-keeper seized her personal ∼s because she could not pay her bill. no ∼s, written (often N/E) by bankers on a cheque which is dishonoured. □ vt [VP6A] bring about; accomplish: ∼ one's purpose; ∼ a cure; ∼ (= take out) an insurance policy.

ef·fec·tive /ɪ'fektɪv/ adj 1 having an effect; able to bring about the result intended: ∼ measures to cure unemployment. 2 making a striking impression: an ∼ scheme of decoration. 3 actual or existing: the ∼ membership of the society; (of a military force, soldiers, sailors, etc) fit for service: the ∼ strength of the army. ∼·ly adv ∼·ness n

ef·fec·tual /ɪ'fektʃʊəl/ adj (not used of persons) bringing about the result required; answering its purpose: an ∼ remedy/punishment; to take ∼ steps. ∼·ly /-lɪ/ adv ∼·ness n

ef·femi·nate /ɪ'femɪnət/ adj (of a man, derog) feminine. **ef·femi·nacy** /ɪ'femɪnəsɪ/ n [U].

ef·fendi /e'fendɪ/ n (old use, in Turkey) sir; (in Arab countries) educated or powerful person.

ef·fer·vesce /ˌefə'ves/ vi [VP2A] give off bubbles of gas; (of gas) issue in bubbles; (fig, of persons) be gay and excited. **ef·fer·ves·cence** /ˌefə'vesns/ n [U] **ef·fer·ves·cent** /-snt/ adj

ef·fete /ɪ'fiːt/ adj exhausted; weak and worn out: ∼ civilizations/empires. ∼·ness n

ef·fi·ca·cious /ˌefɪ'keɪʃəs/ adj (not used of persons) producing the desired result: an ∼ cure for a disease. ∼·ly adv **ef·fi·cacy** /'efɪkəsɪ/ n [U] state or quality of being ∼.

ef·fi·cient /ɪ'fɪʃnt/ adj 1 (of persons) capable; able to perform duties well: an ∼ secretary/staff of teachers. 2 producing a desired or satisfactory result: ∼ methods of teaching. ∼·ly adv **ef·fi·ciency** /ɪ'fɪʃnsɪ/ n [U] state or quality of being ∼.

ef·figy /'efɪdʒɪ/ n (pl -gies) [C] representation of a person (in wood, stone, etc). in ∼, as an ∼: hang/burn a person in ∼, make an ∼ of him and hang/burn it (as a sign of hatred, etc).

ef·flor·es·cence /ˌeflə'resns/ n [U] (formal) flowering; bursting out into flower. **ef·flor·es·cent** /-snt/

adj
ef·flu·ent /'efluənt/ n 1 [C] stream flowing from a larger stream or from a lake. 2 [U] discharge of waste liquid matter, sewage, etc, eg from a factory.

ef·flux /'eflʌks/ n [U] flowing out of liquid, gas, etc; [C] that which flows out.

ef·fort /'efət/ n 1 [U] trying hard; use of strength and energy (to do sth); [C] vigorous attempt: He lifted the big rock without ∼. It doesn't need much ∼. Please make an ∼ to arrive early. Does it require a great ∼ of will to give up smoking? I will make every ∼ (= do all I can) to help you. His ∼s at clearing up the mystery failed. 2 [C] (colloq) result of ∼; sth done with ∼: That's a pretty good ∼, ie you have done well. ∼·less adj making no ∼; without ∼; easy: done with ∼·less skill.

ef·front·ery /ɪ'frʌntərɪ/ n [U] shameless boldness; impudence; [C] (pl -ries) instance of this: How can you have the ∼ to ask for another loan?

ef·ful·gent /ɪ'fʌldʒənt/ adj (liter) radiant; resplendent. **ef·ful·gence** /-dʒəns/ n radiance.

ef·fu·sion /ɪ'fjuːʒn/ n 1 [U] sending or pouring out (of liquid, eg blood); [C] quantity poured out. 2 [C] (esp unrestrained) outpouring of thought or feeling: poetical ∼s; ∼s in love letters.

ef·fu·sive /ɪ'fjuːsɪv/ adj (of the feelings, signs of pleasure, gratitude, etc) pouring out too freely: ∼ thanks; ∼ in one's gratitude. ∼·ly adv ∼·ness n

eft /eft/ n newt.

egali·tar·ian /ɪˌgælɪ'teərɪən/ n, adj (person) favouring the doctrine of equal rights, benefits and opportunities for all citizens. Cf elitist. ∼·ism /-ɪzəm/ n

egg¹ /eg/ n 1 female reproducing cell; ovum, (esp an embryo enclosed in a shell, eg of a hen, used as food): Birds, reptiles and insects come from eggs. Chickens are hatched from eggs. The hen laid an egg. Will you have your eggs boiled or fried? [U] You've got some egg (ie a bit of a cooked egg) on your chin. ⇨ the illus at amphibian, prey. **a bad egg,** (colloq) a worthless or dishonest person. **as sure as eggs is eggs,** (colloq) undoubtedly. **in the egg,** at an early stage; undeveloped. **put all one's eggs in one basket,** risk everything one has in a single venture, eg by investing all one's money in one business. **teach one's grandmother to suck eggs,** give advice to sb who has much more experience than oneself. '**egg-cup,** small cup for holding a boiled egg. '**egg-head** n (colloq) intellectual person; theorist. '**egg·plant,** plant with large, purple (rather egg-shaped) fruit (= aubergine), used as a vegetable. ⇨ the illus at vegetable. '**egg-shell,** shell of an egg: egg-shell china, very thin kind; egg-shell paint, kind that gives a finish that is neither glossy nor matt. '**egg-whisk,** utensil for beating eggs.

egg² /eg/ vt [VP15B] ∼ sb on, urge him (to do sth).

eg·lan·tine /'eglən taɪn/ n [U] kind of rose; sweetbriar.

ego /'egəʊ US: 'iːɡəʊ/ n (the) ∼, (psych) individual's perception or experience of himself; individual's capacity to think, feel and act; self-esteem. '**ego-trip** n (colloq) self-centred or self-seeking act. □ vi act in this way.

ego-cen·tric /ˌegəʊ'sentrɪk US: ˌiːɡ-/ adj self-centred; egoistic.

ego·ism /'egəʊɪzəm US: 'iːɡ-/ n [U] 1 (phil) theory that our actions are always caused by the desire to benefit ourselves. 2 systematic selfishness; state of mind in which one is always thinking of oneself. ⇨ altruism. **ego·ist** /-ɪst/ n believer in ∿. **ego·istic** /ˌegəʊˈɪstɪk US: ˌiːg-/, **ego·isti·cal** /-kl/ adj of ∿; of an egoist.

ego·tism /ˈegəʊtɪzəm US: ˈiːg-/ n [U] practice of talking too often or too much about oneself; self-conceit; selfishness. **ego·tist** /-tɪst/ n person who practises ∿; selfish person. **ego·tis·tic** /ˌegəˈtɪstɪk US: ˌiːg-/ adj of ∿; of or like an egotist. **ego·tis·ti·cally** /-klɪ/ adv

egre·gi·ous /ɪˈgriːdʒɪəs/ adj (formal) outstanding, exceptional (used of sb or sth bad): ∿ folly; an ∿ blunder.

egress /ˈiːgres/ n (formal) [U] (right of) going out; [C] way out; exit.

egret /ˈiːgret/ n kind of heron with beautiful long feathers in the tail and on the back; bunch of these feathers as an ornament.

Egyp·tian /ɪˈdʒɪpʃn/ adj, n (native) of Egypt.

eh /eɪ/ int used to express surprise or doubt, or to invite agreement.

eider·down /ˈaɪdədaʊn/ n (bed-covering filled with) soft breast feathers of large, wild duck (called ¹eider).

eight /eɪt/ adj, n 1 the number 8. ⇨ App 4. **have one over the** ∿, drink too much. 2 crew of ∿ in a rowing-boat. ⇨ bow³(2), stroke¹(3). **eighth** /eɪtθ/ adj, n. **eighth·ly** adv. ∿·pence /ˈeɪtpəns US: -pens/ n. ∿·penny /ˈeɪtpənɪ US: -penɪ/ adj. ∿·een /ˌeɪˈtiːn/ adj, n the number 18. ∿·eenth /ˌeɪˈtiːnθ/ adj, n. ∿y /ˈeɪtɪ/ adj, n the number 80. **the** ∿·ies, 80–89. ∿·ieth /ˈeɪtɪəθ/ adj, n

a rowing eight

eight·some /ˈeɪtsəm/ n lively Scottish dance (a reel) for eight dancers.

eis·tedd·fod /ˌaɪˈstɛðvɒd/ n (in Wales) annual gathering of poets and musicians for competitions.

either /ˈaɪðə(r) US: ˈiːðər/ adj, pron 1 ∿ (of), (Cf the use of any, or any one of, when the number is greater than two) one or the other (of two): Take ∿ half; they're exactly the same. E∿ of them/E∿ one will be satisfactory. You must not favour ∿ side in the dispute. In ∿ event/∿ of these events you will benefit. 2 ∿ (of), (Cf the use of both and each, which are more usu) one and the other (of two): There was an armchair at ∿ end of the long table. □ adv, conj 1 used in statements after not; (Cf the use of neither): I don't like the red one, and I don't like the pink one, ∿, ie I dislike both of them. A: 'I haven't been to Paris yet.' B: 'I haven't been there yet, ∿.' (= Neither have I). 2 (used after a negative phrase) moreover; furthermore: There was a time, and not so long ago ∿, when she could walk twenty miles a day. 3 ∿ ... or, (used to introduce the first of two or more alternatives): He must be ∿ mad or drunk. Please ∿ come in or go out: don't stand there in the doorway. E∿ the dog or the cat has eaten it.

ejacu·late /ɪˈdʒækjʊleɪt/ vt [VP6A] 1 say suddenly and briefly. 2 eject (fluid, eg semen) from the body. **ejacu·la·tion** /ɪˌdʒækjʊˈleɪʃn/ n 1 [C] exclamation; sth said suddenly. 2 discharge or ejection of fluid (eg semen) (from the body).

eject /ɪˈdʒekt/ vt, vi [VP6A,14] ∿ (from), 1 compel (sb) to leave (a place); expel: They were ∿ed because they had not paid their rent for a year. 2 send out (liquid, etc): lava ∿ed from a volcano. 3 [VP2A] make an emergency exit, with a parachute, from an aircraft. **ejec·tion** /ɪˈdʒekʃn/ n **ejec·tor** /-tə(r)/ n sth that ∿s. **e'jector-seat**, one in an aircraft for ∿ing the pilot so that he may descend by parachute.

eke /iːk/ vt [VP15B] **eke sth out,** make (small supplies of sth) enough for one's needs by adding sth; make (a living) by doing this: eke out one's coal by saving the cinders for further use; eke out one's livelihood.

elab·or·ate /ɪˈlæbərət/ adj worked out with much care and in great detail; carefully prepared and finished; complicated: ∿ plans; an ∿ design; an ∿ dinner, eg with many courses. □ vt /ɪˈlæbəreɪt/ [VP6A] work out, describe, in detail: Please ∿ your proposals a little. ∿·ly adv ∿·ness n elab·or·ation /ɪˌlæbəˈreɪʃn/ n [U] elaborating or being ∿d; [C] that which is added; detail that ∿s.

élan /eɪˈlɑːn/ n [U] (F) vivacity; impetuosity; enthusiasm.

eland /ˈiːlənd/ n kind of S African antelope.

elapse /ɪˈlæps/ vi [VP2A] (of time) pass.

elas·tic /ɪˈlæstɪk/ adj 1 having the tendency to go back to the normal or previous size or shape after being pulled or pressed: ∿ bands. Rubber is ∿. Sponges are ∿. 2 (fig) not firm, fixed or unalterable; able to be adapted: ∿ rules; an ∿ temperament, eg of a person who soon becomes cheerful again after being sad. □ n [U] cord or material made ∿ by weaving rubber into it: a piece of ∿; (attrib) ∿ braces, made of this material. ∿·ity /ˌelæˈstɪsətɪ US: ɪˌlæ-/ n [U] the quality of being ∿: elasticity of demand, (comm) change in demand because of price changes.

elate /ɪˈleɪt/ vt [VP6A] (usu passive) stimulate; make high-spirited: He was ∿d at the news/by his success. **ela·tion** /ɪˈleɪʃn/ n [U] high spirits: filled with elation.

el·bow /ˈelbəʊ/ n 1 (outer part of) joint between the two parts of the arm, ⇨ the illus at arm; corresponding part of a sleeve (in a jacket, etc). **at one's** ∿, close to; near by. **out at** ∿s, (a) (of a garment) worn-out. (b) (of a person) in worn-out clothes. '∿ **grease** n [U] vigorous polishing; hard work. '∿ **room** n [U] room to move freely. 2 ∿-shaped bend, corner or joint (eg in a pipe or chimney). □ vt [VP6A,15B,14] push or force (one's way through, forward, etc): to ∿ (also shoulder) one's way through a crowd.

el·der¹ /ˈeldə(r)/ adj (attrib only; cf older) (of members of a family, esp closely related members, or of two indicated members) older; senior: My ∿ brother is in India. The ∿ sister is called Mary. **the** ∿, (before or after a person's name to distinguish that person from another of the same name): Pliny the ∿; the ∿ Pitt. ∿ **'statesman** /-mən/ (pl -men), person (usu retired from office) whose unofficial advice is sought and valued because of his long experience. □ n 1 (pl) persons of greater age: Should we always follow the advice of our ∿s and betters? 2 official in some Christian churches, member of a governing body (session) in Presbyterian churches. **3 the/sb's** ~, older of two persons: *He is my* ~ *by several years*.

el·der² /'eldə(r)/ *n* (kinds of) bush or small tree with clusters of white flowers and red or black berries. ~**·berry 'wine**, wine made from these berries.

el·der·ly /'eldəlɪ/ *adj* getting old; rather old.

el·dest /'eldɪst/ *adj* (attrib only; cf *oldest*) firstborn or oldest surviving (member of a family): *my* ~ *son/brother*.

El Dorado /ˌel də'rɑːdəʊ/ *n* (*pl* ~s /-dəʊz/) fictitious country or city rich in precious metals.

elect¹ /ɪ'lekt/ *adj* **1** (after the *n*) chosen, selected: *the bishop* ~, not yet in office. **2 the** ~, those persons specially chosen, or considered to be the best.

elect² /ɪ'lekt/ *vt* **1** [VP6A,25,23,14] ~ *(to)*, choose (sb) by vote: *to* ~ *a president; to* ~ *Smith* (*to be*) *chairman; to* ~ *Green to the Academy*. **2** [VP7] choose; decide: *He had* ~*ed to become a lawyer*.

elec·tion /ɪ'lekʃn/ *n* [U] choosing or selection (of candidates for an office, etc) by vote; [C] instance of this: (attrib) ~ *results*. ˌgeneral '~, of representatives, (GB members of the House of Commons), for the whole country. ˌlocal '~, of representatives, (GB councillors), for a town/borough/district council. **'by-**~, of one member, to fill a vacancy. ~**·eer·ing** /ɪˌlekʃə'nɪərɪŋ/ *n* [U] working in ~s, eg by canvassing, making speeches.

elec·tive /ɪ'lektɪv/ *adj* **1** having the power to elect: *an* ~ *assembly*. **2** chosen or filled by election: *an* ~ *office*. **3** (US) not compulsory; that may be chosen: ~ *subjects in college*. ⟹ *optional* at option.

elec·tor /ɪ'lektə(r)/ *n* person having the right to elect (esp by voting at a parliamentary election). ~**al** /ɪ'lektərəl/ *adj* of an election; of ~s: *the* ~*al roll/register*, the list of ~s. *The E*~*al College in the USA elects the President*. ~**·ate** /ɪ'lektərət/ *n* whole body of qualified ~s.

elec·tric /ɪ'lektrɪk/ *adj* of, worked by, charged with, capable of developing, electricity: *an* ~ *current/torch/iron/shock;* ~ *light;* ~ *flex/cord; the* ~ *chair*, used for electrocuting criminals; ~ *blue*, steely blue; *an* ~ *guitar*, one that has amplifiers for the sound; *an* ~ *eye*, a photo–electric cell. **elec·tri·cal** /ɪ'lektrɪkl/ *adj* **1** relating to electricity: ~ *engineering*. **2** (fig) (eg of news) causing strong and sudden emotion. ~**·ly** /-klɪ/ *adv*

elec·tri·cian /ɪˌlek'trɪʃn/ *n* expert in setting up, repairing and operating electrical apparatus.

elec·tric·ity /ɪˌlek'trɪsətɪ/ *n* [U] **1** all the phenomena associated with electrons (negative charge) and protons (positive charge); the study of these phenomena. **2** supply of electric current: *When did* ~ *come to the village?*

elec·trify /ɪ'lektrɪfaɪ/ *vt* (*pt,pp* -fied) [VP6A] **1** charge (sth) with electricity. **2** equip (a railway, etc) for the use of electric power. **3** (fig) excite, shock, as if by electricity: *to* ~ *an audience by an unexpected announcement*. **elec·tri·fi·ca·tion** /ɪˌlektrɪfɪ'keɪʃn/ *n* ~ing, eg the conversion of a steam railway to an electric railway.

elec·tro- /ɪ'lektrəʊ/ *pref* (in compounds) involving electricity: ~**·'cardio·gram** /-'kɑːdɪəʊɡræm/ curve traced by an ~cardiograph, used in the diagnosis of heart disease. ~**·'cardio·graph** /-'kɑːdɪəʊɡrɑːf US: -ɡræf/ apparatus which detects and records electric activity in the muscles of the

heart. ~**·'chem·is·try**, electricity as applied to chemistry. ~**·'mag·net**, piece of soft iron that becomes magnetic when an electric current is passed through wire coiled round it. ~**·mag·'netic** *adj* having both electric and magnetic character. Hence, ~**·'mag·net·ism** *n* '~**·plate** *vt* coat with a thin layer of metal (eg silver) by electrolysis. □ *n* [U] articles plated with silver in this way.

elec·tro·cute /ɪ'lektrəkjuːt/ *vt* [VP6A] kill accidentally, put to death, by means of an electrical current. **elec·tro·cu·tion** /ɪˌlektrə'kjuːʃn/ *n*

elec·trode /ɪ'lektrəʊd/ *n* solid conductor by which an electric current enters or leaves a vacuum tube, etc. ⟹ anode, cathode.

elec·tro·ly·sis /ɪˌlek'trɒləsɪs/ *n* [U] separation of a substance into its chemical parts by electric current.

elec·tron /ɪ'lektrɒn/ *n* [C] (phys) subatomic particle of matter having a negative electric charge. ~ **microscope**, using ~s instead of visible light. ~**ic** /ɪˌlek'trɒnɪk/ *adj* of ~s; operated by, based on, ~s. ~**ic music**, produced by manipulating natural or artificial sounds by means of electric or ~ic equipment. ~**ic ˌdata 'processing**, (abbr EDP) use of ~ic computers to derive information or to achieve a required order of data. ~**ics** *n* (with *sing v*) the science and technology of ~ic phenomena, devices and systems, as in radio, TV, tape recorders, computers, etc.

elee·mosy·nary /ˌelɪiː'mɒsɪnərɪ US: -nerɪ/ *adj* (formal) of, dependent upon, alms; charitable.

el·egant /'elɪɡənt/ *adj* showing, having, good taste; graceful; done with care, skill and taste: *an* ~ *young man;* ~ *manners; leading a life of* ~ *ease*. ~**·ly** *adv* **el·egance** /-əns/ *n* [U].

el·egiac /ˌelɪ'dʒaɪək/ *adj* **1** (of metre) suited to elegies: ~ *couplets*. **2** mournful. □ *n pl* ~ verses.

el·egy /'elədʒɪ/ *n* (*pl* -gies) poem or song of sorrow, esp for the dead.

el·ement /'elɪmənt/ *n* **1** (science) substance which cannot be split up into a simpler form by ordinary chemical methods: *Water is a compound containing the* ~s *hydrogen and oxygen*. **2** (according to the ancient philosophers): *the four* ~s, earth, air, fire and water (out of which the material universe was thought to be composed). *in/out of one's* ~, in/not in suitable or satisfying surroundings: *He's in his* ~ *when taking part in a political debate*, is doing sth that pleases and satisfies him. *I'm out of my* ~ *when people start talking about economics*. **3** (*pl*) **the** ~s, the forces of nature, the weather, etc: *exposed to the fury of the* ~s, to the winds, storms, etc. **4** (*pl*) beginnings or outlines of a subject of study; parts that must be learnt first: *the* ~s *of geometry*. **5** necessary or characteristic feature: *Justice is an important* ~ *in good government*. **6** suggestion, indication, trace: *There's an* ~ *of truth in his account of what happened*. ⟹ atom(2). **7** resistance wire in an electrical appliance (eg a heater). **el·emen·tal** /ˌelɪ'mentl/ *adj* of the four ~s(2); of the ~s(3): *the* ~*al fury of the storm*.

ele·men·tary /ˌelɪ'mentrɪ/ *adj* of or in the beginning stage(s); not developed; simple: *the* ~ *rules of social conduct;* ~ *arithmetic*. **ele·men·tar·ily** /ˌelɪ'mentərəlɪ US: ˌelɪmən'terəlɪ/ *adv*

el·eph·ant /'elɪfənt/ *n* largest four-footed animal now living, with curved ivory tusks and a long trunk (proboscis). ⟹ the illus at large. ˌwhite '~, costly or troublesome possession useless to its owner. **el·ephan·ti·asis** /ˌelɪfən'taɪəsɪs/ *n* [U] skin disease causing great enlargement of limbs. **ele-phan·tine** /ˌelɪ'fæntaɪn/ adj of or like ~s; heavy; clumsy: an ~ine task; ~ine humour; an ~ine memory, extremely reliable one.

el·ev·ate /'elɪveɪt/ vt [VP6A, 14] ~ (to), (formal) lift up; raise; (fig) make (the mind, morals) higher and better: ~ the voice, speak louder; ~ a man to the peerage, make him a peer; an elevating book/ sermon; an ~d railway/railroad, one built on piers (usu in a town) to run overhead.

el·ev·ation /ˌelɪ'veɪʃn/ n 1 [U] elevating or being elevated: ~ to the peerage; [C] instance of this. 2 [U] grandeur or dignity: ~ of thought/style/ language. 3 [C] height (esp above sea-level); hill or high place: an ~ of 2000 metres. 4 [C] angle (eg of a gun) with the horizon. 5 [C] plan (drawn to scale) of one side of a building. ⇨ plan. ⇨ the illus at perspective.

el·ev·ator /'elɪveɪtə(r)/ n 1 machine like a continuous belt with buckets at intervals, used for raising grain, etc. 2 store-house for grain. 3 thing that elevates, eg part of an aircraft that is used to gain or lose altitude. 4 (US) lift n (2).

eleven /ɪ'levn/ adj, n the number 11, ⇨ App 4; a team of eleven players for football, hockey or cricket. **elev·enth** /ɪ'levnθ/ adj, n at the ~th hour, at the latest possible time. **elev·enses** /ɪ'levnzɪz/ n pl (GB) snack and drink taken during the morning.

elf /elf/ n (pl elves /elvz/) small fairy; mischievous little creature. **elfin** /'elfɪn/ adj of elves: elfin dances/laughter. **elf·ish** /'elfɪʃ/ adj mischievous.

eli·cit /ɪ'lɪsɪt/ vt [VP6A, 14] ~ sth (from sb), draw out; cause to come out: to ~ the truth/a reply. **eli·ci·ta·tion** /ɪˌlɪsɪ'teɪʃn/ n

elide /ɪ'laɪd/ vt [VP6A] leave out a vowel or syllable in pronunciation. ⇨ elision.

eli·gible /'elɪdʒəbl/ adj ~ (for), fit, suitable, to be chosen; having the right qualifications: ~ for promotion/a position/a pension/membership in a society; an ~ young man, eg one who would be a satisfactory choice as a husband. **el·igi·bil·ity** /ˌelɪdʒə'bɪlətɪ/ n [U] the state of being ~.

elim·in·ate /ɪ'lɪmɪneɪt/ vt [VP6A, 14] ~ (from), remove; take or put away, get rid of (because unnecessary or unwanted): ~ slang words from an essay; ~ a possibility, set it aside and pay no consideration to it; ~ waste products from the body, excrete them. **elim·in·ation** /ɪˌlɪmɪ'neɪʃn/ n

eli·sion /ɪ'lɪʒn/ n (from elide) [U] leaving out of a vowel or syllable in pronunciation (as in let's); [C] instance of this.

élite /eɪ'liːt/ n group in society considered to be superior because of the power, talent, privileges, etc of its members: an educated ~. ⇨ egalitarian. **élitism** /-tɪzəm/ n [U] belief that the education system, etc should aim at developing ~s. **élitist** /-tɪst/ n

elixir /ɪ'lɪksə(r)/ n [C] 1 preparation by which medieval scientists hoped to change metals into gold or (~ of life) to prolong life indefinitely. 2 remedy that cures all ills.

Eliza·bethan /ɪˌlɪzə'biːθn/ adj of the time of Queen Elizabeth I of England: the '~ age; ~ drama. □ n person who lived during her reign, eg Shakespeare.

elk /elk/ n one of the largest kinds of living deer, found in N Europe, N Asia, and (called a moose) N America.

el·lipse /ɪ'lɪps/ n regular oval. **el·lip·tic** /ɪ'lɪptɪk/, **el·lip·ti·cal** /-kl/ adj shaped like an ~.

el·lip·sis /ɪ'lɪpsɪs/ n (pl -pses /-psiːz/) [U] omission from a sentence of words needed to complete the construction or meaning; [C] instance of this. **el·lip·ti·cal** /ɪ'lɪptɪkl/ adj containing ~: an elliptical sentence.

elm /elm/ n [C] common deciduous tree that grows to a great size and height ⇨ the illus at tree; [U] its hard, heavy wood.

elo·cu·tion /ˌelə'kjuːʃn/ n [U] art or style of speaking well, esp in public. ~·ary /-ənərɪ US: -ənerɪ/ adj of ~. ~·ist /-ʃənɪst/ n expert in ~.

elon·gate /'iːlɒŋgeɪt US: ɪ'lɔːŋ-/ vt, vi [VP6A, 2A] make or become long(er) in space. **elon·ga·tion** /ˌiːlɒŋ'geɪʃn US: -lɔːŋ-/ n [U] making longer; [C] the part (of a line, etc) produced this way.

elope /ɪ'ləʊp/ vi [VP2A, C, 3A] ~ (with), (of a woman) run away from home or a husband (with a lover). ~·ment n

elo·quence /'eləkwəns/ n [U] skilful use of language to persuade or to appeal to the feelings; fluent speaking. **elo·quent** /-ənt/ adj having or showing ~. **elo·quent·ly** adv

else /els/ adv 1 (with indef or interr pron) besides; in addition: Did you see anybody ~, any other person(s)? Have you anything ~ to do? Ask somebody ~ to help you. That must be somebody ~'s (= some other person's) hat; it isn't mine. Nothing ~ (= Nothing more), thank you. We went nowhere ~, to no other place. What ~ should I do? Who ~ was there? How ~ (= In what other way) would you do it? little ~, not much more. 2 otherwise; if not: Run (or) ~ you'll be late. He must be joking, or ~ he's mad.

else·where /ˌels'weə(r) US: -'hweər/ adv somewhere else; in, at or to some other place.

elu·ci·date /ɪ'luːsɪdeɪt/ vt [VP6A] (formal) make clear; explain; throw light on (a problem, difficulty). **elu·ci·da·tion** /ɪˌluːsɪ'deɪʃn/ n

elude /ɪ'luːd/ vt [VP6A] escape capture by (esp by means of a trick); avoid: ~ one's enemies; ~ observation.

elu·sive /ɪ'luːsɪv/ adj tending to elude or escape: an ~ criminal; tending to escape from the memory; not easy to recall: an ~ word.

el·ver /'elvə(r)/ n young eel.

elves /elvz/ pl of elf.

elv·ish /'elvɪʃ/ adj = elfish.

Ely·sium /ɪ'lɪzɪəm/ n (Gk myth) home of the blessed after death; place or state of perfect happiness. **Ely·sian** /ɪ'lɪzɪən/ adj of ~; heavenly; blissful.

'em /əm/ pron (colloq) = them.

em·aci·ate /ɪ'meɪʃɪeɪt/ vt [VP6A] make thin and weak (usu passive): ~d by long illness. **emaciation** /ɪˌmeɪsɪ'eɪʃn/ n [U].

ema·nate /'eməneɪt/ vi [VP3A] ~ from, (formal) come, flow, proceed from. **ema·na·tion** /ˌemə'neɪʃn/ n [U] emanating; [C] sth that ~s.

eman·ci·pate /ɪ'mænsɪpeɪt/ vt [VP6A, 14] ~ (from), set free (esp from legal, political or moral restraint): ~ slaves; an ~d young woman, one who has freed herself from the conventions or restrictions of the community to which she belongs. **eman·ci·pa·tion** /ɪˌmænsɪ'peɪʃn/ n [U] emancipating or being emancipated: the ~ of women, giving or obtaining all or some of the rights, opportunities, etc that men have: ~ from the authority of one's parents.

emas·cu·late /ɪ'mæskjʊleɪt/ vt [VP6A] deprive of (masculine) vigour; weaken; impoverish **emas-**

cu·la·tion /ˌɪˌmæskjʊˈleɪʃn/ n

em·balm /ɪmˈbɑːm/ vt [VP6A] preserve (a dead body) from decay by using spices or chemicals; preserve from oblivion; fill with fragrance. ~·ment n

em·bank·ment /ɪmˈbæŋkmənt/ n [C] wall or mound of earth, stone, etc to hold back water or support a raised road or railway; roadway supported by such a wall: the Thames E~.

em·bargo /ɪmˈbɑːɡəʊ/ n (pl ~es /-ɡəʊz/) order that forbids trade, movement of ships, etc; stoppage of commerce, or of a branch of commerce: a gold ~, one that forbids or restricts the buying and selling of gold; (fig) blocking; prohibition. lift/raise/remove an ~ (from sb), start trading (with him) again. place/lay sb under (an) ~; put an ~ on sb, do no trade with him. □ vt (pt,pp ~ed /-ɡəʊd/) [VP6A] lay under an ~; seize (ships or goods) by government authority, for the service of the State.

em·bark /ɪmˈbɑːk/ vi,vt 1 [VP2A,C,6A] go, put or take on board a ship: The soldiers ~ed for Malta. The ship ~ed passengers and cargo. 2 ~ on/upon [VP3A] start, take part in: ~ upon a new business undertaking. **em·bar·ka·tion** /ˌembɑːˈkeɪʃn/ n [U] ~ing; [C] instance of this; that which is ~ed.

em·bar·rass /ɪmˈbærəs/ vt [VP6A] 1 make to feel awkward or ashamed; cause mental discomfort or anxiety to: ~ing questions; ~ed by lack of money. 2 (old use) hinder the movement of: He fell into the river and, because he was ~ed by his heavy overcoat, only just managed to swim to the bank. ~·ing adj ~·ing·ly adv ~·ment n [U] ~ing or being ~ed; [C] sth that ~es: financial ~ments; an ~ment (= an over-abundance) of riches.

em·bassy /ˈembəsɪ/ n (pl -ssies) duty and mission of an ambassador; his official residence; ambassador and his staff: to go/come/send sb on an ~ (to sb); the French ~ in London; (attrib) ~ officials.

em·battled /ɪmˈbætld/ adj (of an army, etc) drawn up ready for battle; (fig) in a condition of defence; (of a tower or building) having battlements.

em·bed /ɪmˈbed/ vt (-dd-) [VP6A,14] (usu passive) ~ (in), fix firmly (in a surrounding mass): stones ~ded in rock; (fig) facts ~ded in one's memory.

em·bel·lish /ɪmˈbelɪʃ/ vt [VP6A,14] ~ (with), make beautiful; add ornaments or details to: ~ a dress with lace and ribbons: ~ a story, eg by adding amusing but perhaps untrue details. ~·ment n [U] ~ing or being ~ed; [C] that which ~es: artistic addition.

em·ber /ˈembə(r)/ n (usu pl) small piece of burning wood or coal in a dying fire; (pl) ashes of a dying fire.

em·bezzle /ɪmˈbezl/ vt [VP6A] use (money placed in one's care) in a wrong way for one's own benefit. ~·ment n [U] embezzling; [C] instance of this.

em·bit·ter /ɪmˈbɪtə(r)/ vt [VP6A] arouse bitter feelings in: ~ed by repeated failures. ~·ment n

em·blazon /ɪmˈbleɪzn/ vt [VP6A,14] ~ (with), 1 adorn (eg a shield or banner) with heraldic devices: ~ed with the coat of arms of the family. 2 extol; exalt.

em·blem /ˈembləm/ n symbol; device that represents sth: an ~ of peace, eg a dove; an ~ of love, eg a heart. ~·atic /ˌembləˈmætɪk/ adj ~ (of), serving as an ~.

em·body /ɪmˈbɒdɪ/ vt (pt,pp -died) [VP6A,14] ~ (in), 1 give form to ideas/feelings, etc: ~ one's ideas in a speech. 2 include; comprise: The latest locomotives ~ many new features. 3 clothe (a spirit) with a body: an embodied spirit. **em·bodi·ment** /ɪmˈbɒdɪmənt/ n [C] that which embodies sth or is embodied: She is the embodiment of kindness.

em·bolden /ɪmˈbəʊldən/ vt [VP6A,17] give courage or confidence to: Their sympathy ~ed me to ask them for help.

em·bon·point /ˌɒmbɒnˈpwɑːŋ/ n (F) plumpness (used as a polite way of saying that sb, usu a woman, is very fat).

em·boss /ɪmˈbɒs US: -ˈbɔːs/ vt [VP6A,14] ~ (with), cause a pattern, figure, etc to stand out on (the surface of sth); raise the surface of sth into a pattern: ~ed notepaper, with the address ~ed on it; a silver vase ~ed with a design of flowers.

em·brace /ɪmˈbreɪs/ vt,vi 1 [VP6A,2A] take (a person, etc) into one's arms, as a sign of affection: ~ a child. They ~d. 2 [VP6A] accept; make use of: ~ an offer/opportunity. 3 [VP6A] (of things) include: ~ many examples in a single formula. □ n [C] act of embracing: He held her to him in a warm ~.

em·brasure /ɪmˈbreɪʒə(r)/ n [C] 1 bevelled opening in a parapet for a gun. 2 bevelled opening (esp interior side of a doorway or window), eg in an old stone castle.

em·bro·ca·tion /ˌembrəˈkeɪʃn/ n [U] liquid (a linament) for rubbing a bruised or aching part of the body.

em·broider /ɪmˈbrɔɪdə(r)/ vt,vi 1 [VP6A,2A] ornament (cloth) with needlework: ~ one's initials on a handkerchief; a design ~ed in gold thread. 2 [VP6A] (fig) add fanciful details to a story. ~y /-dərɪ/ n [U] ~ed needlework.

em·broil /ɪmˈbrɔɪl/ vt [VP6A,14] ~ sb/oneself (in), cause (sb, oneself) to be mixed up in a quarrel: I don't want to become ~ed in their quarrels.

em·bryo /ˈembrɪəʊ/ n (pl ~s /-əʊz/) [C] offspring of an animal in the early stage of its development before birth (or before coming out of an egg); (fig) sth in its rudimentary stage. in ~, (lit, fig) still undeveloped. **em·bry·onic** /ˌembrɪˈɒnɪk/ adj in ~: an ~nic plan.

emeer /eˈmɪə(r)/ n = emir.

emend /ɪˈmend/ vt [VP6A] take out errors from: ~ a passage in a book. **emen·da·tion** /ˌiːmenˈdeɪʃn/ n [U] ~ing; [C] sth that is ~ed.

em·er·ald /ˈemərəld/ n bright green precious stone; colour of this.

emerge /ɪˈmɜːdʒ/ vi [VP2A,3A] ~ (from), 1 come into view; (esp) come out (from water, etc): The moon ~d from behind the clouds. 2 (of facts, ideas) appear; become known: No new ideas ~d during the talks. **emerg·ence** /-dʒəns/ n [U] emerging. **emerg·ent** /-dʒənt/ adj emerging: (the recently ~d and) emergent countries of Africa, those changing from dependence to independence, becoming modernized, etc.

emerg·ency /ɪˈmɜːdʒənsɪ/ n (pl -cies) 1 [U,C] serious happening or situation needing prompt action: This fire extinguisher is to be used only in (an) ~. 2 (attrib use): an '~ exit; an '~ fund, one to be used in an ~.

emeri·tus /ɪˈmerɪtəs/ adj (Lat) retired from service but retaining an honorary title: ~ professor.

em·ery /ˈemərɪ/ n [U] hard metal used (esp in powdered form) for grinding and polishing: '~-cloth/-paper/-wheel, with ~ on the surface.

em·etic /ɪˈmetɪk/ n medicine causing a person to vomit, eg when suffering from food-poisoning.

emi·grate /'emɪgreɪt/ vi [VP2A,3A] ~ (to) (from), go away (from one's own country to another to settle there). ⇨ **immigrate**. **emi·grant** /'emɪgrənt/ n person who ~s: emigrants to Canada; (attrib) emigrant labourers. **emi·gra·tion** /,emɪ'greɪʃn/ n [U] emigrating; [C] instance of this.

émi·gré /'emɪgreɪ US: ,emɪ'greɪ/ n (F) person who has left his own country, usu for political reasons.

emi·nence /'emɪnəns/ n 1 [U] state of being famous or distinguished; superiority of position: reach ~ as a doctor; win ~ as a scientist. 2 [C] area of high or rising ground. 3 His/Your E~, title used of/to a cardinal.

emi·nent /'emɪnənt/ adj 1 (of a person) distinguished: ~ for her virtues; ~ as a sculptor. 2 (of qualities) remarkable in degree: a man of ~ goodness. ~·ly adv

emir /e'mɪə(r)/ n (title of a) Muslim ruler. ~·ate /e'mɪəreɪt/ n rank, lands, etc of an ~: the great ~ates of Northern Nigeria.

em·iss·ary /'emɪsərɪ/ n (pl -ries) person sent to deliver a message (often of an unpleasant and secret kind).

emission /ɪ'mɪʃn/ n ~ (of), [U] sending out or giving off (of light, heat, smell, etc); [C] that which is sent out or given off.

emit /ɪ'mɪt/ vt (-tt-) [VP6A] give or send out: A volcano ~s smoke and ashes.

emolu·ment /ɪ'mɒljʊmənt/ n [C] (usu pl) (formal) profit from official employment; fee; salary.

emo·tion /ɪ'məʊʃn/ n 1 [U] stirring up, excitement, of the mind or (more usu) the feelings; excited state of the mind or feelings: He thought of his dead child with deep ~. He spoke in a voice touched with ~. 2 [C] strong feeling of any kind: Love, joy, hate, fear and grief are ~s. He appealed to our ~s rather than to our reason. ~·less adj without ~. ~al /-ʃənl/ adj 1 of, directed to, the ~: an ~al appeal; ~al music. 2 having ~s that are easily excited; capable of expressing ~s: an ~al woman/ actor/nature. ~·ally /-ʃənəlɪ/ adv **emot·ive** /ɪ'məʊtɪv/ adj of, tending to excite, the ~s.

em·pale /ɪm'peɪl/ vt = impale.

em·panel /ɪm'pænl/ vt (-ll-, US also -l-) [VP6A] enter (a person's name) on a panel; enrol (a jury).

em·pa·thy /'empəθɪ/ n [U] (psych) (power of) projecting oneself into (and so fully understanding, and losing one's identity in) a work of art or other object of contemplation; (power of) sharing another person's feelings.

em·peror /'empərə(r)/ n ruler of an empire. ⇨ **empress**.

em·pha·sis /'emfəsɪs/ n (pl -ases /-əsiːz/) n [C,U] force or stress laid on a word or words to make the significance clear, or to show importance; (the placing of) special value or importance: Some schools lay/put special ~ on language study. I insist, with all the ~ at my command, that.... **em·pha·size** /'emfəsaɪz/ vt [VP6A] put ~ on; give ~ to: He emphasized the importance of careful driving. **em·phatic** /ɪm'fætɪk/ adj having, showing, using, ~: an emphatic gesture/opinion; an emphatic person. **em·phati·cally** /-klɪ/ adv

em·pire /'empaɪə(r)/ n 1 [C] group of countries under a single supreme authority: the Roman E~. 2 [U] supreme political power: the responsibilities of ~. the First E~, (in France) period of the reign of Napoleon I (1804—15); (E~, attrib) of the style of furniture or dress fashionable in this period. the Second E~, the period of the reign of Napoleon

III (1852—70).

em·piric, em·piri·cal /ɪm'pɪrɪk, -kl/ adj relying on observation and experiment, not on theory. **em·piri·cally** /-klɪ/ adv **em·piri·cism** /ɪm'pɪrɪsɪzəm/ n ~ practice. **em·pir·i·cist** /-sɪst/ n ~ person.

em·place·ment /ɪm'pleɪsmənt/ n prepared position for a heavy gun or guns.

em·plane /ɪm'pleɪn/ vi,vt [VP2A,6A] go, put, on board an aircraft.

em·ploy /ɪm'plɔɪ/ vt [VP6A,16B,14] 1 give work to, usu for payment: They ~ five waiters. He is ~ed in a bank. 2 make use of: How do you ~ your spare time? □ n in the ~ of, ~ed by, working for. ~·able /-əbl/ adj that can be ~ed. ~·er /-ə(r)/ n person who ~s others. ~·ee /,emplɔɪ'iː/ n person ~ed for wages.

em·ploy·ment /ɪm'plɔɪmənt/ n [U] employing or being employed; one's regular work or occupation: to find ~; to give ~ to sb; the men in my ~; to be thrown out of ~. be in/out of ~, have/not have a job. '~ agency, business establishment which helps persons (for a fee) to find ~. '~ exchange, Government office which puts employers and unemployed persons in touch and where unemployment benefits are paid.

em·por·ium /ɪm'pɔːrɪəm/ n centre of commerce; market; large retail store.

em·power /ɪm'paʊə(r)/ vt [VP17] ~ sb to do sth, give power or authority to act.

em·press /'emprɪs/ n woman governing an empire; wife of or widow of an emperor.

empty¹ /'emptɪ/ adj having nothing inside; containing nothing: an ~ box; ~ promises, not meaning anything, not giving satisfaction; feeling ~, (colloq) hungry; words ~ of meaning, meaningless words. The house was ~, unoccupied. ,~-'handed adj bringing back nothing; carrying nothing away. ~-'headed adj witless; lacking in common sense. □ n (usu pl) box, bottle, crate, etc that has been emptied: Empties (eg ~ beer bottles) are not taken back, the brewery will not accept them and allow credit for them. **emp·ti·ness** /'emptɪnɪs/ n

empty² /'emptɪ/ vt,vi (pt,pp -tied) [VP6A,15B,2A,C,3A] ~ (out), make or become empty, remove what is inside (sth): ~ one's glass, drink everything in it; ~ (out) a drawer; ~ a box of rubbish into a rubbish-cart; ~ one's pockets of their contents. The streets soon emptied/were soon emptied when the rain started. The Rhone empties (= flows) into the Mediterranean. The water empties (= flows out) slowly. The cistern empties (= becomes empty) in five minutes.

em·purpled /ɪm'pɜːpld/ adj made purple.

em·py·rean /,empaɪ'riːən/ n the highest heaven; the visible heavens. □ adj heavenly; celestial.

emu /'iːmjuː/ n large flightless Australian bird that runs well. ⇨ the illus at rare.

emu·late /'emjʊleɪt/ vt [VP6A] try to do as well as or better than.

emu·la·tion /,emjʊ'leɪʃn/ n [U] emulating: in a spirit of ~; in ~ of each other.

emu·lous /'emjʊləs/ adj ~ (of), (formal) wishing or anxious to do as well as or better than: ~ of all rivals; imitating (others) in a jealous spirit, desiring to obtain: ~ of fame/honours. ~·ly adv

emul·sion /ɪ'mʌlʃn/ n [C,U] (kinds of) creamy liquid in which particles of oil or fat are suspended: ~ paint, in which the colour is in an ~-like liquid. **emul·sify** /ɪ'mʌlsɪfaɪ/ vt (pt,pp -fied) [VP6A] make an ∼ of.

en·able /ɪ'neɪbl/ vt [VP17] make able, give authority or means (to do sth): The collapse of the strike ∼d the company to resume normal bus services. **en·abling** /ɪ'neɪblɪŋ/ part adj making possible: enabling legislation.

en·act /ɪ'nækt/ vt 1 [VP6A,9] make (a law); decree; ordain: as by law ∼ed. Be it further ∼ed that.... (legal style). 2 [VP6A] perform on, or as though on, the stage of a theatre. ∼·ment n [U] ∼ing or being ∼ed; [C] law.

en·amel /ɪ'næml/ n [U] 1 glass-like substance used for coating metal, porcelain, etc, for decoration or as a protection: '∼ ware, manufactured goods with ∼ surfaces; '∼ paint, paint which dries to make a hard, glossy surface. 2 hard outer covering of teeth. □ vt (-ll-, US also -l-) cover, decorate, with ∼ (esp with designs or decorations).

en·amour (US = -amor) /ɪ'næmə(r)/ vt [VP6A] (usu in passive) be ∼ed of, fond of, delighted with and inclined to use: ∼ed of one's own voice.

en·camp /ɪn'kæmp/ vt,vi [VP6A,2A] settle in a camp; lodge in tents. ∼·ment n place where troops, etc are ∼ed.

en·case /ɪn'keɪs/ vt [VP6A,14] ∼ (in), put into a case; surround or cover as with a case: a knight ∼d in armour.

en·caus·tic /en'kɔːstɪk/ adj prepared by using heat: ∼ bricks/tiles, inlaid with coloured clays that are burnt in.

en·cepha·li·tis /ˌenkefə'laɪtɪs/ n [U] inflammation of the brain.

en·chain /ɪn'tʃeɪn/ vt [VP6A] fasten with chain(s); (fig) hold fast (the attention, etc).

en·chant /ɪn'tʃɑːnt US: -'tʃænt/ vt [VP6A] 1 charm; delight: She was ∼ed with/by the flowers you sent her. 2 use magic on; put under a magic spell: the ∼ed palace, eg in a fairy tale. ∼·er /-ə(r)/ n man who ∼s. ∼·ress /-trɪs/ n woman who ∼s. ∼·ing·ly adv∼·ment n 1 [U] being ∼ed. 2 [C] sth which ∼s; magic spell. 3 [U] charm; delight: the ∼ment of moonlight.

en·circle /ɪn'sɜːkl/ vt [VP6A] surround; form a circle round: a lake ∼d by trees; ∼d by enemy forces. ∼·ment n

en clair /ˌɒn 'kleə(r)/ adv phrase (F) (used in telegrams, official dispatches, etc) (= in clear) in ordinary language, not in code or cipher.

en·clave /'enkleɪv/ n [C] territory wholly within the boundaries of another.

en·close /ɪn'kləʊz/ vt [VP6A,14] ∼ (with), 1 put a wall, fence, etc round; shut in on all sides: ∼ a garden with a wall; ∼ common land, put fences, etc round land which has been used by everyone. 2 put (sth) in an envelope, parcel, etc: I'll ∼ your letter with mine. A cheque for £5 is ∼d. E∼d, please find..., (comm style) You will find, ∼d with this....

en·clos·ure /ɪn'kləʊʒə(r)/ n 1 [U] enclosing: ∼ of common land; [C] instance of this. 2 [C] sth that is enclosed (esp with a letter).

en·code /ɪn'kəʊd/ vt [VP6A] put in a code. ⇨ code v.

en·co·mium /ɪn'kəʊmɪəm/ n (usu pl) (formal) very high praise.

en·compass /ɪn'kʌmpəs/ vt [VP6A] encircle, surround; envelop; comprise.

en·core /'ɒŋkɔː(r)/ int Repeat! Again! □ vt, n [VP6A] (call for a) repetition (of a song, etc) or further performance by the same person(s): The

violinist got an ∼. The singer gave three ∼s. The audience ∼d the pianist.

en·coun·ter /ɪn'kaʊntə(r)/ vt [VP6A] find oneself faced by (danger, difficulties, etc); meet (an enemy or enemies); meet (a friend, etc) unexpectedly. □ n [C] ∼ (with), sudden or unexpected (esp hostile) meeting.

en·cour·age /ɪn'kʌrɪdʒ/ vt [VP6A,14,17] ∼ sb in sth/to do sth, give hope, courage or confidence to; support: ∼ a man to work harder; ∼ a boy in his studies; feel ∼d by the progress one has made. Don't ∼ him in his idle ways. ∼·ment n [U] encouraging: cries of ∼ment; [C] sth that ∼s: Praise acts as an ∼ment to the young.

en·croach /ɪn'krəʊtʃ/ vi [VP3A] ∼ on/upon, go beyond what is right or natural or desirable: ∼ (up)on sb's rights (time, land). The sea is ∼ing (up)on the land, washing it away. ∼·ment n [U] ∼ing; [C] sth gained by ∼ing; advance beyond the original limits: ∼ments made by the sea upon the land.

en·crust /ɪn'krʌst/ vt,vi 1 [VP6A,14] ∼ (with), cover with a crust; overlay (a surface) with a crust of ornamental or costly material: a gold vase ∼ed with precious stones. 2 [VP2A] form into a crust.

en·cum·ber /ɪn'kʌmbə(r)/ vt [VP6A,14] ∼ (with), 1 get in the way of, hamper, be a burden to: be ∼ed with a large family; an estate ∼ed with mortgages; ∼ oneself with unnecessary luggage. 2 crowd; fill up: a room ∼ed with old and useless furniture. **en·cum·brance** /ɪn'kʌmbrəns/ n [C] thing that ∼s; burden.

en·cyc·li·cal /ɪn'sɪklɪkl/ adj, n (letter written by the Pope) for wide circulation.

en·cy·clo·pedia (also -paedia) /ɪnˌsaɪklə'piːdɪə/ n book, or set of books, giving information about every branch of knowledge, or on one subject, with articles in ABC order. **en·cy·clo·pedic, -paedic** /ɪnˌsaɪklə'piːdɪk/ adj dealing with, having knowledge of, a wide variety of subjects.

end¹ /end/ n 1 farthest or last part: the end of a road/stick/line, etc; the house at the end of the street; (attrib) the end house; the end carriage, the last carriage in a train; the west/east end of a town, the parts in the west/east; the ends of the earth, most remote parts, parts difficult of access. **begin/start at the wrong end**, in the wrong way, at a wrong point. **get hold of the wrong end of the stick**, have a completely mistaken idea of what is intended or meant. **keep one's 'end up**, (GB) continue cheerful, full of fighting spirit, in the face of difficulties, etc. **at a loose end**, unoccupied, having nothing important or interesting to do. **on end**, (a) upright: Place the barrel/box on (its) end. The ghost story set their hair on end. (b) continuously: two hours on end. **end on**, with the ends meeting: The two ships collided end on, the stern (or bows) of one struck the stern (or bows) of the other. **end to end**, in a line with the ends touching: Arrange the tables end to end. **go (in) off the 'deep end**, express strong feeling without trying to control it. **make (both) ends meet**, live within one's income; balance one's income with one's expenditure. **(reach) the end of the line/road**, (fig) (reach) the point at which no more of what has happened before is possible or desirable. 2 small piece that remains; remnant: candle ends; a cigarette end. '**end-papers**, (usu) blank pages pasted to the inside covers of a book. ⇨ odds (5). 3 finish; conclusion: at the end of the day/the century; the end *of a story/adventure. We shall never hear the end of the matter,* It will be talked about for a long time to come. *(be) at an end; at the end (of): The war was at an end,* finished. *She was at the end of her patience/tether,* had no patience left. *He was at the end of his resources.* **come to an end,** finish: *The meeting came to an end at last.* **come to a bad end,** be led by one's actions to ruin, disgrace, punishment, etc: *If you don't give up crime, you'll come to a bad end,* eg be sent to prison for life as a murderer. **draw to an end:** *As the year drew to its end....* **make an end of sth; put an end to sth,** finish it, get rid of it (according to context): *We must put an end to these abuses. Death put an end to his wicked career.* **in the end,** finally, at last: *He tried many ways of earning a living; in the end he became a farm labourer.* **no end of,** (colloq) very many or much, very great, etc: *We met no end of interesting people. He thinks no end of himself,* has a high opinion of his abilities, etc. **without end,** never reaching an end: *We had trouble without end.* **4** death: *He's nearing his end,* is dying. *She came to an untimely end,* died young. **5** purpose, aim: *gain/win/achieve one's end(s); with this end in view; for/to this end; to the end that,* in order that; *to no end,* in vain. **The end justifies the means,** (prov) for a good purpose even wrong or unfair methods may be allowed.

end² /end/ *vi,vt* [VP2A,C,3A,6A,15B] (cause to) come to an end; reach an end: *The road ends here,* goes no farther. *How does the story end? Let's end our quarrel.* **end in sth,** have as a result: *The scheme ended in failure. He ended his days in peace,* the last period of his life was peaceful. **end (sth) off,** finish: *He ended off his speech with some amusing stories.* **end (sth) up,** finish: *If you continue to steal, you'll end up in prison,* will one day be sent to prison. *We started with soup, and had fruit to end up with.* **end-all** ⇨ be³(4). **end·ing** *n* [C] end, esp of a word or a story.

en·dan·ger /ɪn'deɪndʒə(r)/ *vt* [VP6A] put in danger; cause danger to: *~ one's chances of success.*

en·dear /ɪn'dɪə(r)/ *vt* [VP14] *~ sb/oneself to,* make dear or liked: *~ oneself to everyone; an ~ing smile.* *~·ing·ly adv ~·ment n* [C,U] act, word, expression, of affection: *a term of ~ment,* eg *darling; the ~ments that a wife expects from her husband.*

en·deav·our (US = **-vor**) /ɪn'devə(r)/ *n* [C] (formal) effort, attempt: *Please make every ~ to be early. His ~s to persuade her to go with him failed.* □ *vi* [VP4A] (formal) try: *~ to please one's wife.*

en·demic /en'demɪk/ *n, adj* (disease) prevalent or often recurring in a country or area, or among a particular class of people, eg miners. ⇨ epidemic.

en·dive /'endɪv US: -daɪv/ *n* [C] kind of curly-leaved chicory, used as salad.

end·less /'endlɪs/ *adj* having no end; never stopping: *a woman with ~ patience; an ~ belt/chain/cable,* one with the ends joined, to pass continuously over wheels, etc to transmit power in a machine. *~·ly adv*

en·dorse /ɪn'dɔːs/ *vt* [VP6A] **1** write one's name on the back of (a cheque); write comments, etc in, on the back of (a document): *His driving licence has been ~d,* a record of a motoring offence has been entered in it. **2** approve, support a claim, statement, etc. *~·ment n* [U] endorsing; [C] instance of this; statement, etc that *~s.*

en·dow /ɪn'daʊ/ *vt* [VP6A,14] *~ (with),* **1** give money, property, etc to provide a regular income for (eg a college): *~ a bed in a hospital; ~ a school.* **2** (usu passive) *be ~ed with,* possess naturally, be born with (qualities, etc): *be ~ed by nature with great talents.* *~·ment n* **1** [U] *~ing.* **2** [C] money, property, etc given to provide an income: *The Oxford and Cambridge colleges have numerous ~ments.* **3** [C] talent: *natural ~ments,* eg a good ear for music.

en·due /ɪn'dju US: -'duː/ *vt* [VP14] (usu passive) *be ~d with,* be furnished, supplied, with.

en·dur·ance /ɪn'djʊərəns US: -'dʊə-/ *n* [U] ability to endure: *He showed remarkable powers of ~. He came to the end of his ~. past/beyond ~,* to an extent that can no longer be endured. *'~ test,* test of how long sb or sth can endure sth.

en·dure /ɪn'djʊə(r) US: -'dʊər/ *vt,vi* **1** [VP6A,2A,C] suffer, undergo pain, hardship, etc: *~ toothache. If help does not come, we must ~ to the end,* suffer until death comes. **2** [VP6A,D,17 esp in neg] bear; put up with: *I can't ~ that woman. She can't ~ seeing/~ to see animals cruelly treated.* **3** [VP2A] last; continue in existence: *as long as life ~s; fame that will ~ for ever.* **en·dur·able** /-rəbl/ *adj* that can be *~d;* bearable. **en·dur·ing** *adj* lasting: *an enduring peace.* **en·dur·ingly** *adv*

end·ways /'endweɪz/, **end·wise** /-waɪz/ *adv* with the end towards the spectator; end forward; end to end.

en·ema /'enɪmə/ *n* (syringe used for an) injection of liquid into the rectum.

en·emy /'enəmɪ/ *n* (*pl -mies*) *~ (of/to),* **1** one who tries or wishes to harm or attack; one who has ill feeling or hatred towards sb or sth: *A successful man often has many enemies. Don't make an ~ of him,* Do nothing that will cause him to be your *~. He's an ~ of/to reform.* **2** the *~,* armed forces of a nation with which one's country is at war: *~-occupied territory. The ~ were forced to retreat,* (attrib) of the *~: ~ aircraft/ships.* **3** member of such a hostile force. **4** anything that harms or injures: *Laziness is his chief ~. Idleness is an ~ to discipline,* weakens discipline.

en·ergy /'enədʒɪ/ *n* **1** [U] force, vigour; capacity to do things and get things done: *He had so much ~ that he did the work of three men. He's full of ~.* **2** (in *pl, -gies*) (person's) powers available for working, or as used in working: *apply/devote all one's energies to a task.* **3** [U] (science) capacity for, power of, doing work: *electrical ~; kinetic ~; potential ~.* **en·er·getic** /ˌenə'dʒetɪk/ *adj* full of, done with, *~(1).* **en·er·geti·cally** /-klɪ/ *adv*

en·er·vate /'enəveɪt/ *vt* [VP6A] cause to lose physical (sometimes moral) strength: *a country with an enervating climate.*

en famille /ˌɒn fæ'miː/ *adv* (F) at home; among one's family.

en·fant ter·rible /ˌɒnfɒn te'riːbl/ *n* (F) young or new person whose behaviour, ideas, etc cause annoyance or embarrassment to those who hold conventional opinions.

en·feeble /ɪn'fiːbl/ *vt* [VP6A] make feeble.

en·fold /ɪn'fəʊld/ *vt* [VP6A,14] *~ sb (in),* enclose (esp in one's arms).

en·force /ɪn'fɔːs/ *vt* [VP6A,14] **1** *~ (on/upon),* compel obedience to; make effective; impose: *~ a law; ~ discipline/silence; ~ a course of action upon sb.* **2** give force or strength to: *Have you any*

statistics that would ~ *your argument?* ~**·able**
/-əbl/ *adj* that can be ~d. ~**·ment** *n* [U] enforcing
or being ~d: *strict* ~*ment of a new law.*

en·fran·chise /ɪn'fræntʃaɪz/ *vt* [VP6A] **1** give political rights to (esp, the right to vote at parliamentary elections): *In Great Britain women were* ~*d in*
1918. **2** set free (slaves). ~**·ment**
/ɪn'fræntʃɪzmənt/ *n*

en·gage /ɪn'geɪdʒ/ *vt,vi* **1** [VP6A,16B] obtain the
right to employ: ~ *a servant;* ~ *sb as a guide/as*
an interpreter; get the right to use or occupy: ~ *a*
taxi (*hire* is the preferred word). **2** [VP7,17,9,3A]
promise; undertake; bind (oneself); guarantee: *I*
will ~ (*myself*) *to manage the business if you will*
~ (*yourself*) *to provide the capital. Can you* ~
that all his statements are trustworthy? That is
more than I can ~ *for,* guarantee, take responsibility for. **3** [VP3A] ~ *in,* take part in; busy oneself
with: ~ *in politics.* **4** *be* ~*d to/to marry,* be
bound by a promise to marry: *Tom and Anne are*
~*d. Tom is* ~*d to Anne.* **5** *be* ~*d (in),* be busy, be
occupied (with): take part in: *be* ~*d in business/in*
writing a novel. My time is fully ~*d. The line/*
number is ~*d,* (telephoning) Someone else is using
the line. **6** [VP6A] (usu passive) attract: *Nothing*
~*s his attention for long. Her attention was* ~*d by*
the display of new sweaters in the shop window. **7**
[VP6A,2A] attack; begin fighting with: *The gener-*
al did not ~ *the enemy. Our orders are to* ~ *at*
once. **8** [VP2A,3A,6A,14] ~ (*with*), (of parts of a
machine) lock together; (cause to) fit into: *The two*
cog-wheels ~. *The teeth of one wheel* ~ *with*
those of the other. (motoring) *E*~ *the clutch/the*
first gear. **en·gag·ing** *adj* likely to ~ the attention;
charming: *an engaging smile/manner.* **en·gag-**
ingly *adv*

en·gage·ment /ɪn'geɪdʒmənt/ *n* [C] **1** (formal)
promise or undertaking, esp one that is formal or
made in writing: *He has only enough money to*
meet his ~*s,* to make the payments he has undertaken to make. **2** agreement to marry: *Their* ~ *was*
announced in the papers. '~ **ring,** one given by a
man to a woman when they agree to marry. **3** arrangement to go somewhere, meet someone or do
sth, at a fixed time: *I have numerous* ~*s for next*
week. **4** battle: *The admiral tried to bring about an*
~, to make the enemy fight. **5** [C,U] engaging (of
part of a machine, etc): ~ *of first gear.*

en·gen·der /ɪn'dʒendə(r)/ *vt* [VP6A] be the cause
of (a situation or condition): *Crime is often* ~*ed by*
poverty.

en·gine /'endʒɪn/ *n* **1** machine that converts energy
into power or motion: *a* '*steam-/'oil-*~; *a new* ~
(petrol or diesel) *for a motor vehicle.* ⇨ the illus at
motor. '~**-driver** *n* (esp) man who drives a railway ~. **2** (old use) machine or instrument: ~*s of*
war, eg cannons.

en·gin·eer /ˌendʒɪ'nɪə(r)/ *n* **1** person who works in
a branch of engineering; person who designs engines, machines, bridges, railways, docks, etc: *a*
civil/mining/electrical ~. **2** skilled and trained
person in control of an engine or engines: *the chief*
~ *of a ship;* (US) man who drives a locomotive. **3**
member of the branch of an army (called the **E**~**s**)
that builds roads and bridges, controls communications, etc. □ *vt,vi* [VP6A,2A] **1** act as an ~; construct or control as an ~. **2** (colloq) arrange or
bring about skilfully: ~ *a scheme/plot;* ~ *that...*

en·gin·eer·ing /ˌendʒɪ'nɪərɪŋ/ *n* [U] the application
of science for the control and use of power, esp by

the use of machines; the technology, work or
profession of an engineer: *chemical/mechanical/*
electrical ~; *a triumph of* ~, eg a magnificent
bridge; *an* ~ *works.*

Eng·lish /'ɪŋglɪʃ/ *n* [U] the ~ language. *in plain* ~,
in language so simple that the meaning is quite
clear. **the ,Queen's/,King's '**~, standard, educated English. □ *adj* **1** of England. **the** ~, (*pl*) ~
people. **2** of, written in, spoken in, the ~ language. ~**·man** /-mən/ (*pl* -men) *n* ~**·woman**
/-wʊmən/ (*pl*-women) *n*

en·graft /ɪn'grɑːft US: -'græft/ *vt* [VP6A,14] ~
(*into/on/upon*), insert (a shoot of one tree into another). ~ (*in*), (fig) implant (principles in the mind
or character).

en·grave /ɪn'greɪv/ *vt* **1** [VP6A,14] ~ *on/upon,*
cut or carve (lines, words, designs, on) a hard surface: ~ *a design on a metal plate* (for printing); *a*
name ~*d on a tombstone.* **2** [VP14] ~ *with,* mark
such surfaces with (an inscription, etc). **3** [VP14]
~ *on/upon,* (fig) impress deeply (on the memory
or mind). **en·graver** *n* person who ~s designs, etc
on stone, metal, etc. **en·grav·ing** /ɪn'greɪvɪŋ/ *n* [U]
art of cutting or carving designs on metal, stone,
etc; [C] copy of a picture, design, etc printed from
an ~d plate.

en·gross /ɪn'grəʊs/ *vt* **1** [VP6A] (usu passive) take
up all the time or attention of: ~*ed in his work; an*
~*ing story.* **2** (legal) write (eg a legal document) in
large letters or in formal legal style.

en·gulf /ɪn'gʌlf/ *vt* [VP6A] swallow up (as in a
gulf): *a boat* ~*ed in/by the sea/waves.*

en·hance /ɪn'hɑːns US: -'hæns/ *vt* [VP6A] add to
(the value, attraction, powers, price, etc).

enigma /ɪ'nɪgmə/ *n* [C] question, person, thing,
circumstance, that is puzzling. **enig·matic**
/ˌenɪg'mætɪk/ *adj* puzzling; mysterious. **enig-**
mati·cally /-klɪ/ *adv*

en·join /ɪn'dʒɔɪn/ *vt* [VP6A,17,9,14] ~ (*on sb*),
give an order for; urge; prescribe; command: ~
silence/obedience; ~ *on sb the necessity for eco-*
nomy; ~ *a duty on sb;* ~ *sb to obey the rules;* ~
that sth should be done.

en·joy /ɪn'dʒɔɪ/ *vt* [VP6A,C] **1** get pleasure from;
take delight in: ~ *one's dinner. I've* ~*ed talking to*
you about old times. **2** have as an advantage or
benefit: ~ *good health/a good income.* **3** ~
oneself, experience pleasure; be happy. ~**·able**
/-əbl/ *adj* giving joy; pleasant. ~**·ably** /-əblɪ/ *adv*
en·joy·ment /ɪn'dʒɔɪmənt/ *n* **1** [U] pleasure; joy;
satisfaction: *to think only of/live for* ~. **2** [U] possession and use: *be in the* ~ *of the full possession*
of one's faculties, be physically and mentally well.
3 [C] sth that gives joy and pleasure.

en·kindle /ɪn'kɪndl/ *vt* [VP6A] cause (flame, passion, etc) to flare up; inflame (with passion, etc).

en·large /ɪn'lɑːdʒ/ *vt,vi* **1** [VP6A,2A] make or become larger: ~ *a photograph/one's house. Will*
this print ~ *well,* will it be good if it is reproduced
on a larger scale? **2** [VP3A] ~ *on/upon,* say or
write more about: *I need not* ~ *upon this matter;*
you all know my views. ~**·ment** *n* [U] enlarging or
being ~d; [C] result of this, esp a photograph.

en·lighten /ɪn'laɪtn/ *vt* [VP6A,14] ~ (*on*), give
more knowledge to; free from ignorance, misunderstanding or false beliefs: *Can you* ~ *me on this*
subject, help me to understand it better? ~*ed part*
adj free from ignorance, prejudice, superstition,
etc: *in these* ~*ed days.* ~**·ment** *n* [U] ~ing or being ~ed: *living in an age of* ~*ment; work for the*

~ment of mankind. the E~ment, the period (esp 18th c) when men believed that reason and science (and not religion) would advance human progress.

en-list /ɪn'lɪst/ vt,vi 1 [VP6A,14,16B,2A,C] ~ (in), take into, enter, the armed forces: ~ a recruit; ~ as a volunteer; ~ed men, soldiers, etc; ~ in the army. 2 [VP6A,14] ~ (in/for), obtain; get the support of: ~ sb's sympathy and help in a charitable cause/for the Red Cross. ~·ment n [U] ~ing or being ~ed; [C] instance of this.

en·liven /ɪn'laɪvn/ vt [VP6A] make lively: How can we ~ the party?

en masse /ˌɒn 'mæs/ adv (F) in a mass; all together.

en·mesh /ɪn'meʃ/ vt [VP6A,14] ~ (in), take (as) in a net; entangle.

en·mity /'enmətɪ/ n [U] condition of being an enemy; hatred: be at ~ with one's neighbours; [C] (pl-ties) particular feeling of hostility or hatred.

en·noble /ɪ'nəʊbl/ vt [VP6A] 1 make (sb) a member of the nobility. 2 (fig) make morally noble; make dignified. ~·ment n

en·nui /ɒn'wi:/ n [U] (F) weariness of mind caused by lack of any interesting occupation; [C] instance of this.

enor·mity /ɪ'nɔ:mətɪ/ n 1 [U] great wickedness: Does he realize the ~ of his offence? 2 [C] (pl-ties) serious crime. 3 [U] immense size: the ~ of the problem of feeding the world's population in AD 2000.

enor·mous /ɪ'nɔ:məs/ adj very great; immense: an ~ sum of money. ~·ly adv to an ~ extent: The town has changed ~ly during recent years. ~·ness n

enough /ɪ'nʌf/ adj, n (of a quantity) as great as is needed; as much or as many as necessary (as an adj ~ occurs in the pattern ~ + noun or noun + ~): There's ~ food/food enough for everybody. Have you had ~ peanuts? (as a noun ~ occurs in the pattern ~ (of the/this/that/his etc + noun) (for sb/to do sth): Will £5 be ~ for you/~ to cover the journey? Have you had ~ of this TV programme yet? I've had ~ of your grumbling and groaning. ~ is as good as a feast, be glad that you have had as much as you needed. more than ~, too much. □ adv of degree (placed after adjj, advv and pp; also after a noun used as an adj, as when fool means foolish; used in the pattern adj + ~ (for sb/to do sth)) 1 to the right or necessary degree; sufficiently: The meat is not cooked ~. Are you warm ~? You know well ~ (= quite well) what I mean. I was fool (= foolish) ~ to believe her. He wasn't man (= manly) ~ to admit his mistake. You're old ~ to know better. This book is easy ~ for a six-year-old child to read. 2 sometimes used in a disparaging way, suggesting that sth could be better, etc: It's interesting ~ in its way, moderately interesting. She sings well ~, indicating faint praise. 3 oddly/curiously/strangely etc ~, in a way that is odd, etc. sure ~, in a degree that satisfies doubt; as one expected.

en·plane /en'pleɪn/ vi, vt ⇨ emplane.

en·quire, en·quiry /ɪn'kwaɪə(r), ɪn'kwaɪərɪ/ v,n = inquire, inquiry.

en·rage /ɪn'reɪdʒ/ vt [VP6A] fill with rage: ~d at/ by sb's stupidity.

en·rap·ture /ɪn'ræptʃə(r)/ vt [VP6A] fill with great delight or joy.

en·rich /ɪn'rɪtʃ/ vt [VP6A,14] ~ (with), make rich;

improve in quality, flavour, etc: ~ the mind (with knowledge); soil ~ed with manure. ~·ment n

en·roll, en·rol /ɪn'rəʊl/ vt,vi [VP6A,14,16B,2A,C] ~ (in), (cause to) become a member (of): to ~ in evening classes; to ~ (sb) as a member of a society/club; to be ~ed in a register of electors; to ~ new students. ~·ment n [U] ~ing or being ~ed; [C] number ~ed: a school with an ~ment of 800 pupils.

en route /ˌɒn 'ru:t/ adv ~ (from/to), on the way (from/to): We stopped at Paris ~ from Rome to London.

en·sconce /ɪn'skɒns/ vt [VP14] ~ oneself in, establish oneself in (a safe, secret, comfortable, etc place).

en·semble /ɒn'sɒmbl/ n [C] (F) 1 sth viewed as a whole; general effect. 2 (music) passage of music in which all the performers unite; group of musicians who play together regularly (smaller than an orchestra). 3 (trade use) woman's matched clothing outfit (dress, coat, etc designed to be worn together).

en·shrine /ɪn'ʃraɪn/ vt [VP6A,14] ~ (in), (formal) place or keep in, or as in, a shrine; serve as a shrine for: the casket that ~s the relics; memories ~d in her heart; basic human rights ~d in the constitution.

en·shroud /ɪn'ʃraʊd/ vt [VP6A] cover completely: hills ~ed in mist.

en·sign /'ensən/ n 1 (esp naval) flag or banner: white ~, used by the Royal Navy; red ~, used by British merchant ships; blue ~, used by the Royal Naval Reserve. 2 (US) lowest commissioned officer in the navy. 3 /'ensaɪn/ (old uses) badge or symbol (showing office, authority, etc); infantry officer who carried the regimental colours.

en·si·lage /'ensɪlɪdʒ/ n = silage.

en·slave /ɪn'sleɪv/ vt [VP6A] make a slave of. ~·ment n

en·snare /ɪn'sneə(r)/ vt [VP6A,14] ~ (in), catch in, or as in, a snare or trap.

en·sue /ɪn'sju: US: -'su:/ vi [VP2A,3A] ~ (from), happen later; follow, happen as a result: the trouble that ~d from this misunderstanding; in the ensuing (= next) year.

en·sure (US = in·sure) /ɪn'ʃʊə(r)/ vt,vi 1 [VP9] make sure; guarantee: I can't ~ that he will be there in time. 2 [VP14,3A] ~ (sb) against sth, make safe: We ~d (ourselves) against possible disappointment. You should ~ (yourself) against loss of heat by having double glazing. 3 [VP12A,13A] secure; assure: These documents ~ to you the authority you need. I cannot ~ you a good post. 4 (formerly) = insure.

en·tail /ɪn'teɪl/ vt [VP6A,14] ~ (on), 1 make necessary; impose (expense, etc on sb): That will ~ an early start. These plans ~ great expense on us. 2 (legal) leave, settle, (land) to a line of heirs so that none of them can give it away or sell it: ~ an estate on sb. □ n [U] settlement of landed property in this way; [C] the property so settled.

en·tangle /ɪn'tæŋgl/ vt [VP6A,15A,14] ~ (in), 1 catch in a snare or among obstacles: My fishing line got ~d in weeds. The duck flew into the nets and the more it struggled the more it ~d itself. 2 (fig) put or get into difficulties, in unfavourable circumstances: ~ oneself with money-lenders. ~·ment n 1 [U] entangling or being ~d; [C] situation that ~s: ~ments with rogues; emotional ~ments. 2 (pl) barrier of stakes and barbed wire to impede the enemy's advance.

en·tente /ɒn'tɒnt/ n [C] (F) (group of States with a) friendly understanding. ~ **cordi·ale** /ˌkɔːdɪ'ɑːl/ n ~, esp between two governments.

en·ter /'entə(r)/ vt,vi **1** [VP6A,2A] come or go into: ~ a room. The train ~ed a tunnel. Where did the bullet ~ the body? (Stage direction in a printed play) E~ Hamlet, Hamlet comes on to the stage. **2** [VP6A] become a member of; join: ~ a school/college; ~ the Army/Navy; ~ the Church, become a priest; ~ a profession. **3** [VP3A] ~ **into sth (with sb),** begin, open: ~ into conversation with sb; ~ into negotiations with a business firm. ~ **into sth, (a)** begin to deal with: ~ into details/particulars. **(b)** sympathize with; be able to understand and appreciate: ~ into sb's feelings; ~ into the spirit of the occasion. **(c)** form a part of: a possibility that had not ~ed into our calculations. **4** [VP3A] ~ **on/upon, (a)** make a start on: ~ upon a new career/one's duties/another term of office. **(b)** take possession of; begin to enjoy: ~ upon one's inheritance. **5** [VP6A,14,15B] ~ **(in/up);** ~ **(in),** unite, record names, details, etc in a book, etc: ~ (in/up) an item in an account-book. **6** [VP3A,14] ~ **for;** ~ **sb for,** give the name of sb for a competition, race, etc: ~ oneself for an examination; ~ for the high jump; ~ a horse for the Derby.

en·teric /en'terɪk/ adj of the intestines: ~ fever, typhoid. **en·ter·itis** /ˌentə'raɪtɪs/ n [U] inflammation of the intestines.

en·ter·prise /'entəpraɪz/ n **1** [C] undertaking, esp one that needs courage or that offers difficulty. **2** [U] courage and willingness to engage in ~s(1): We need a spirit of ~ if we are to overcome our difficulties. He is a man of great ~. **3** [U] carrying on of ~s(1): private ~ versus government control of commerce and industry. ⇨ free¹(3); private(1). **en·ter·pris·ing** adj having, showing, ~(2). **en·ter·pris·ing·ly** adv

en·ter·tain /ˌentə'teɪn/ vt [VP6A,14,2A] **1** ~ **(to),** receive (people) as guests; give food and drink to: ~ friends to dinner. The Smiths ~ a great deal/do a great deal of ~ing, often give dinner parties, etc. **2** ~ **(with),** amuse, interest: ~ the children with tricks. We were all ~ed by his tricks. **3** be ready to consider: ~ a proposal; have in the mind: ~ ideas/doubts, etc. ~·ing adj pleasing; amusing. ~·ing·ly adv ~·ment n **1** [U] ~ing or being ~ed(2): He fell into the water, much to the ~ment of the onlookers. **2** [C] public performance (at a theatre, circus, etc). ~er n person who ~s(2), esp professionally.

en·thral (also, esp US **en·thrall**) /ɪn'θrɔːl/ vt (-ll-) [VP6A] **1** take the whole attention of; please greatly: ~ed by an exciting story. **2** enslave (usu fig): ~ed by a woman's beauty.

en·throne /ɪn'θrəʊn/ vt [VP6A] place a king, bishop on a throne; (fig) give a high place to, in one's judgement or affection: a ruler ~d in the hearts of his subjects. ~·ment n

en·thuse /ɪn'θjuːz/ US: -'θuːz/ vi [VP3A] ~ **over,** (colloq) show enthusiasm for.

en·thusi·asm /ɪn'θjuːzɪæzəm/ US: -'θuː-/ n [U] ~ **(for/about),** strong feeling of admiration or interest: arouse ~ in sb; a play that moved the audience to ~; feel no ~ for/about sth; an outburst of ~.

en·thusi·ast /ɪn'θjuːzɪæst/ US: -'θuː-/ n ~ **(for/about),** person filled with enthusiasm: a sports ~; an ~ for/about politics.

en·thusi·astic /ɪnˌθjuːzɪ'æstɪk US: -ˌθuː-/ adj ~ **(about/over),** full of enthusiasm: ~ admirers of a film star; become ~ over sth. **en·thusi·asti·cally** /-klɪ/ adv

en·tice /ɪn'taɪs/ vt [VP6A,15A,17] tempt or persuade: ~ a young girl away from home; ~ sb into doing sth/to do sth wrong; ~ a man from his duty. ~·ment n [U] enticing or being ~d; [C] sth that ~s.

en·tire /ɪn'taɪə(r)/ adj whole, complete; in one piece, unbroken: The ~ village was destroyed. Is your stamp collection still ~? ~·ly adv completely: ~ly unnecessary/different. My life is ~ly given up to work. ~·ty /ɪn'taɪərətɪ/ n [U] the state of being ~; completeness: We must examine the question in its ~ty, as a whole, not in parts only.

en·title /ɪn'taɪtl/ vt **1** be ~d, have as a title: a book ~d 'Adam Bede'. **2** [VP14,17] ~ **sb to sth/to do sth,** (usu in passive) (of conditions, circumstances, qualities, etc) give a right (to): If you fail three times, you are not ~d to try any more. ~·ment n that which ~s(2).

en·tity /'entətɪ/ n (pl -ties) **1** [C] sth that has real existence; a thing's existence (contrasted with its qualities, relations, etc). **2** [U] being; existence.

en·tomb /ɪn'tuːm/ vt [VP6A] place in a tomb; serve as a tomb for.

ento·mol·ogy /ˌentə'mɒlədʒɪ/ n [U] the study of insects. **en·to·mol·ogist** /-dʒɪst/ n student of, expert in, ~. **en·to·mo·logi·cal** /ˌentəmə'lɒdʒɪkl/ adj

en·tour·age /ˌɒntʊ'rɑːʒ/ n all those accompanying and attending on an important or high-ranking person: the President and his ~.

en·tr'acte /'ɒntrækt/ n [C] (F) (performance in an) interval between acts in a play.

en·trails /'entreɪlz/ n pl bowels; intestines.

en·train /en'treɪn/ vt,vi [VP6A,2A] get, put troops, etc into a train.

en·trance¹ /'entrəns/ n **1** [C] opening, gate, door, passage, etc by which one enters: The ~ to the cave had been blocked up. **2** [C,U] coming or going in; coming of an actor upon the stage; entering: the university ~ examination. E~ into/upon ministerial office requires a visit to the Queen. Actors must learn their ~s and exits, when to come upon and leave the stage. **3** [C,U] right of entering: to be refused ~. '~-fee; '~-money, charge for admission.

en·trance² /ɪn'trɑːns US: -'træns/ vt [VP6A] ~ **(at/with),** (usu in passive) fill with emotion and delight: ~d with the music. She stood ~d at the sight.

en·trant /'entrənt/ n person who enters to a profession, for a competition, race, etc.

en·trap /ɪn'træp/ vt (-pp-) [VP6A] = trap (the usu word).

en·treat /ɪn'triːt/ vt [VP6A,17,14] ~ **(of),** (formal) ask (sb) earnestly: ~ sb to show mercy; ~ a favour of sb. ~·ing·ly adv

en·treaty /ɪn'triːtɪ/ n (pl -ies) [C,U] earnest request(ing): deaf to all entreaties; with a look of ~.

en·trée /'ɒntreɪ/ n (F) **1** [U] right or privilege of admission. **2** [C] dish served between the fish and the meat course.

en·trench /ɪn'trentʃ/ vt [VP6A] **1** surround or protect with a trench or trenches: The enemy were strongly ~ed on the other side of the river. **2** establish firmly: customs ~ed by tradition; ~ed clauses/provisions, those (in a constitution(1)) which can be changed only by a special procedure.

~·ment *n*

entre·pot /'ɒntrəpəʊ/ *n* (F) storehouse; commercial centre for the import, export, collection and distribution of goods.

entre·pre·neur /ˌɒntrəprə'nɜː(r)/ *n* person who organizes and manages a commercial undertaking. ~·ial /-'nɜːrɪəl/ *adj*

en·trust /ɪn'trʌst/ *vt* [VP14] ~ *sth to sb;* ~ *sb with sth,* trust sb to complete or safeguard sth: *Can I* ~ *the task to you/* ~ *you with the task? Ought I to* ~ *to them/* ~ *them with such confidential and important plans?*

en·try /'entrɪ/ *n* [C] (*pl* -tries) **1** coming or going in: *the* ~ *of the USA into world politics. The army made a triumphal* ~ *into the town. Thieves had forced an* ~ *into the building.* '~ **visa,** ⇨ visa. **2** [C,U] (place of) entrance; right of entering: *The sign* ● *means 'No* ~'. **3** item in a list; item noted in an account book: *dictionary entries; make an* ~ *of a transaction; book-keeping by double/single* ~, in which each item is entered twice/once in a ledger. **bill of** ~, ⇨ bill³(6). **4** list, number, of persons, etc entering for a competition: *a large* ~ *for the 5000 metres race;* person or thing that is entered for a competition: *nearly fifty entries for the Marathon race.*

en·twine /ɪn'twaɪn/ *vt* [VP6A,14] ~ *(with/round),* make by twining; curl (one thing) (*with* or *round* another).

enu·mer·ate /ɪ'njuːməreɪt *US:* ɪ'nuː-/ *vt* [VP6A] count, go through (a list of articles) naming them one by one. **enu·mer·ation** /ɪˌnjuːmə'reɪʃn *US:* ɪˌnuː-/ *n* [U] enumerating; [C] list.

enun·ci·ate /ɪ'nʌnsɪeɪt/ *vt,vi* **1** [VP6A,2A] say, pronounce (words): *He* ~s (*his words*) *clearly.* **2** express a theory, etc clearly or definitely. **enun·ci·ation** /ɪˌnʌnsɪ'eɪʃn/ *n*

en·velop /ɪn'veləp/ *vt* [VP6A,14] ~ *(in),* wrap up, cover, on all sides: *hills* ~ed *in mist; a baby* ~ed *in a shawl;* ~ *a subject in mystery.* ~·ment *n*

en·vel·ope /'envələʊp/ *n* wrapper or covering, esp one made of paper for a letter; covering of a balloon or airship.

en·venom /ɪn'venəm/ *vt* [VP6A] put poison on or in, eg a weapon; (fig) fill with bitter hate: ~ed *quarrels/tempers.*

en·vi·able /'envɪəbl/ *adj* causing envy; likely to excite envy (used both of the object and the person, etc, possessing it): *an* ~ *school record,* one of great success, etc; *an* ~ *woman,* eg one who has a kind, handsome and rich husband.

en·vi·ous /'envɪəs/ *adj* ~ *(of),* full of envy; feeling envy; showing or expressing envy: ~ *of sb's success;* ~ *looks; looking at sth with* ~ *eyes.* ~·ly *adv*

en·viron /ɪn'vaɪərən/ *vt* [VP6A] be in a position round; surround: *a town* ~ed *by/with forests.*

en·vi·ron·ment /ɪn'vaɪərənmənt/ *n* [U,C] surroundings, circumstances, influences: *a healthy* ~. *Students of social problems investigate the home, social and moral* ~(s) *of different classes of people.* **Department of the E**~, (GB) Government Department responsible for land planning, construction industries, transport, preservation of public amenities, control of air and water pollution, the protection of the coast and the countryside. ~·al /ɪnˌvaɪərən'mentl/ *adj* ~·ally /-təlɪ/ *adv*

en·virons /ɪn'vaɪərənz/ *n pl* districts surrounding a town, etc: *Berlin and its* ~.

en·vis·age /ɪn'vɪzɪdʒ/ *vt* [VP6A] picture in the mind (esp in a particular way): *He had not* ~d *the matter*

in that light.

en·voy¹ /'envɔɪ/ *n* messenger, esp one sent on a special mission; diplomatic agent next in rank below an ambassador.

en·voy² (also **en·voi**) /'envɔɪ/ *n* [C] concluding part of a poem, esp a short stanza at the end of some archaic forms of poetry.

envy¹ /'envɪ/ *n* [U] **1** ~ *at sth/of sb,* feeling of disappointment and resentment (at another's better fortune): *He was filled with* ~ *of me/at my success. My success excited his* ~. *They say such scandalous things about you out of* ~. **2** object of such feeling: *His splendid new car was the* ~ *of all his friends/an object of* ~ *to all his friends.*

envy² /'envɪ/ *vt* (*pt,pp* -vied) [VP6A,12C] feel envy of: *I* ~ *you. I* ~ *your good fortune. I don't* ~ *him his bad-tempered wife,* am glad I am not married to her.

en·wrap /ɪn'ræp/ *vt* (-pp-) = wrap (the more usu word).

en·zyme /'enzaɪm/ *n* [C] organic chemical substance (a catalyst) formed in living cells, able to cause changes in other substances without being changed itself.

eon /'iːən/ *n* = aeon.

ep·aulet (also **ep·aul·ette**) /'epəlet/ *n* shoulder ornament on a naval or military officer's uniform.

épée /'eɪpeɪ/ *n* (F) sharp-pointed slender sword used in fencing.

ephem·er·al /ɪ'femərəl/ *adj* living, lasting, for a very short time.

epic /'epɪk/ *n, adj* (poetic account) of the deeds of one or more great heroes, or of a nation's past history, eg Homer's *Iliad;* (colloq) (subject) fit to be celebrated as heroic: *an* ~ *achievement.*

epi·centre (US = **-center**) /'epɪsentə(r)/ *n* point at which an earthquake reaches the earth's surface.

epi·cure /'epɪkjʊə(r)/ *n* person who understands the pleasures to be had from delicate eating and drinking.

epi·cur·ean /ˌepɪkjʊ'riːən/ *n, adj* (person) devoted to pleasure (esp refined sensuous enjoyment): *an* ~ *feast.*

epi·demic /ˌepɪ'demɪk/ *n, adj* (disease) spreading rapidly among many people in the same place for a time: *an influenza* ~. ⇨ endemic.

epi·der·mis /ˌepɪ'dɜːmɪs/ *n* [U] outer layer of the skin.

epi·dia·scope /ˌepɪ'daɪəskəʊp/ *n* optical lantern which projects on a screen transparent objects (eg film-strip) and opaque objects (eg coins, pictures).

epi·glot·tis /ˌepɪ'glɒtɪs/ *n* structure of tissue at the root of the tongue, lowered during swallowing to prevent food, etc from entering the windpipe. ⇨ the illus at head.

epi·gram /'epɪgræm/ *n* short poem or saying expressing an idea in a clever and amusing way. ~·matic /ˌepɪgrə'mætɪk/ *adj* short and witty in expression; (of a person) fond of making ~s.

epi·lepsy /'epɪlepsɪ/ *n* [U] nervous disease causing a person to fall unconscious (often with violent involuntary movements). **epi·lep·tic** /ˌepɪ'leptɪk/ *adj* of ~: *an epileptic fit.* □ *n* person suffering from ~.

epi·logue (US = **-log**) /'epɪlɒg *US:* -lɔːg/ *n* last part of a literary work, esp a poem spoken by an actor at the end of a play; (radio, TV) religious programme at the end of the day's transmission.

Epiph·any /ɪ'pɪfənɪ/ *n* commemoration (6 Jan) of the coming of the Magi /'meɪdʒaɪ/ (the *Three Wise Men*) to Jesus at Bethlehem. Cf *Twelfth Night.*

epis·co·pal /ɪˈpɪskəpl/ adj of, governed by, bishops: *the E~ Church*, (esp) the Anglican Church in the US and Scotland. **epis·co·pa·lian** /ɪˌpɪskəˈpeɪlɪən/ n, adj (member) of an ~ church.

epi·sode /ˈepɪsəʊd/ n [C] (description of) one event in a chain of events. **epi·sodic** /ˌepɪˈsɒdɪk/ adj sporadic.

epistle /ɪˈpɪsl/ n (old use, or joc) letter. **the E~s**, letters included in the New Testament, written by the Apostles. **epis·tol·ary** /ɪˈpɪstələrɪ US: -lerɪ/ adj of, carried on by, letters.

epi·taph /ˈepɪtɑːf US: -tæf/ n [C] words commemorating a dead person (eg as cut on his tombstone).

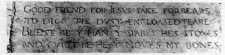

the epitaph on Shakespeare's tombstone

epi·thet /ˈepɪθet/ n adjective or descriptive phrase used to indicate the character of sb or sth, as in 'Alfred *the Great*'.

epit·ome /ɪˈpɪtəmɪ/ n short summary of a book, speech, etc; sth which shows, on a small scale, the characteristics of sth much larger; sth or sb that perfectly displays a quality, type, etc: *the ~ of a loving mother*. **epit·om·ize** /ɪˈpɪtəmaɪz/ vt [VP6A] make/be an ~ of: *She epitomizes a loving mother*.

ep·och /ˈiːpɒk US: ˈepək/ n (beginning of a) period of time in history, life, etc marked by special events or characteristics: *Einstein's theory marked a new ~ in mathematics*. **'~-making**, beginning a new ~: *an ~-making discovery*, eg of America by Columbus.

Ep·som salts /ˌepsəm ˈsɔːlts/ n pl hydrated magnesium sulphate **(MgSO₄)**, used medically to empty the bowels.

equable /ˈekwəbl/ adj steady; regular; not changing much: *an ~ climate/temper*. **equably** /ˈekwəblɪ/ adv

equal /ˈiːkwəl/ adj **1** the same in size, amount, number, degree, value, etc: *~ pay for ~ work; ~ opportunity; ~ in ability; divide sth into two ~ parts; two boys of ~ height. He speaks English and Arabic with ~ ease. Things which are ~ to the same thing are ~ to one another.* **2** ~ **to sth/to doing sth**, having strength, courage, ability, etc for: *He was ~ to the occasion*, was able to deal with it. *She did not feel ~ to receiving visitors.* □ n person or thing ~ to another: *Is he your ~ in ·strength? Let x be the ~ of y.* □ vt (-ll-, US also -l-) [VP6A,15A] be ~ to: *He ~s me in strength but not in intelligence. He is ~led by no one in strength.* **~·ly** /ˈiːkwəlɪ/ adv in an ~ manner; in ~ shares: *~ly clever. Divide it ~ly.* **~·ity** /ɪˈkwɒlətɪ/ n [U] the state of being ~: *on terms of ~ (with)*, on ~ terms (with). **~i·tarian** /ɪˌkwɒlɪˈteərɪən/ n = egalitarian. **~·ize** /ˈiːkwəlaɪz/ vt [VP6A] make ~: *~ize incomes.* **~·iz·ation** /ˌiːkwəlaɪˈzeɪʃn US: -lɪˈz-/ n

equa·nim·ity /ˌekwəˈnɪmətɪ/ n [U] calmness of mind or temper: *bear misfortune with ~; disturb sb's ~.*

equate /ɪˈkweɪt/ vt [VP6A,14] ~ **(with)**, consider, treat (one thing as being equal): (maths) *~ two quantities.*

equa·tion /ɪˈkweɪʒn/ n **1** (maths) [C] statement of equality between two expressions by the sign = as in: $2x + 5 = 11$. **2** [U] ~ **(with)**, making equal, balancing, eg of demand and supply.

equa·tor /ɪˈkweɪtə(r)/ n imaginary line round the earth; line drawn on maps to represent points at an equal distance from the north and south poles. ⇨ the illus at projection. **~·ial** /ˌekwəˈtɔːrɪəl/ adj of or near the ~: *~ial Africa.*

equerry /ɪˈkwerɪ/ n (pl -rries) officer in the court of a ruler; officer in attendance on a member of the royal family.

eques·trian /ɪˈkwestrɪən/ adj of horse-riding: *~ skill; an ~ statue*, of a person on horseback. □ n person clever at horse-riding.

equi·dis·tant /ˌiːkwɪˈdɪstənt/ adj ~ **(from)**, separated by equal distances.

equi·lat·eral /ˌiːkwɪˈlætərəl/ adj having all sides equal: *an ~ triangle.*

equi·lib·rium /ˌiːkwɪˈlɪbrɪəm/ n [U] state of being balanced: *maintain/lose one's ~; scales (on a balance) in ~.*

equine /ˈekwaɪn/ adj (formal) of, like, a horse; of horses.

equi·noc·tial /ˌiːkwɪˈnɒkʃl/ adj of, at or near, the equinox: *~ gales/tides.*

equi·nox /ˈiːkwɪnɒks/ n time of the year at which the sun crosses the equator and when day and night are of equal length: *the spring (= vernal) ~*, around 20 Mar; *the autumnal ~*, around 22 Sept.

equip /ɪˈkwɪp/ vt (-pp-) [VP6A,14] ~ **(with)**, supply (a person, oneself, a ship, etc) (with what is needed, for a purpose): *~ oneself for a task; ~ a ship for a voyage; ~ soldiers with uniforms and weapons.* **~·ment** n [U] **1** ~ping or being ~ped: *The ~ment of his laboratory took time and money.* **2** (collective *noun*) things needed for a purpose: *a factory with modern ~ment;* '*radar ~ment.*

equi·page /ˈekwɪpɪdʒ/ n [C] equipment, outfit; carriage, horses and attendants (of a rich person in former times).

equi·poise /ˈekwɪpɔɪz/ n [U] equilibrium; [C] thing that counterbalances.

equi·table /ˈekwɪtəbl/ adj fair; just; reasonable. **equi·tably** /-blɪ/ adv

equity /ˈekwɪtɪ/ n **1** [U] fairness; right judgement; (esp, ' English law) principles of justice outside common law or Statute law, used to correct laws when these would apply unfairly in special circumstances. **2** (often pl) (-ties) ordinary stocks and shares not bearing fixed interest.

equiv·al·ent /ɪˈkwɪvələnt/ adj ~ **(to)**, equal in value, amount, meaning: *What is £5 ~ to in French francs?* □ n sth that is ~: *Is there a French word that is the exact ~ of the English word 'home'?* **equiv·al·ence** /-əns/ n [U] being ~; [C] sth that is ~.

equivo·cal /ɪˈkwɪvəkl/ adj **1** having a double or doubtful meaning; open to doubt: *an ~ reply.* **2** questionable; suspicious: *an ~ success.* **equivo·ca·tion** /ɪˌkwɪvəˈkeɪʃn/ n **1** [U] the use of ~ statements to mislead people. **2** [C] ~ expression.

era /ˈɪərə/ n [C] period in history, starting from a particular time or event: *the Christian era.*

eradi·cate /ɪˈrædɪkeɪt/ vt [VP6A] pull up by the roots; put an end to, get rid of: *~ crime/typhoid fever.* **eradi·ca·tion** /ɪˌrædɪˈkeɪʃn/ n

erase /ɪˈreɪz US: ɪˈreɪs/ vt [VP6A] rub or scrape out; remove all traces of: *~ pencil marks.* **~r** /ɪˈreɪzə(r) US: -sər/ n thing used to ~: *a pencil ~r* (usu =

rubber¹(2)). **eras·ure** /ɪ'reɪʒə(r)/ n [U] erasing; [C] sth ~d; place where sth has been ~d.

ere /eə(r)/ adv, prep (old use, or poet) before.

erect¹ /ɪ'rekt/ adj upright; standing on end: *stand* ~; *hold a banner* ~. ~·**ly** adv ~·**ness** n

erect² /ɪ'rekt/ vt [VP6A] **1** build, set up, establish: ~ *a monument;* ~ *a statue* (*to sb*)*;* ~ *a tent.* **2** set upright: ~ *a flagstaff.* **erec·tile** /ɪ'rektaɪl US: -tl/ adj (physiol) (capable of) becoming rigid from dilation of the blood-vessels: ~ *tissue.* **erec·tion** /ɪ'rekʃn/ n **1** [U] act of ~ing; state of being ~ed; (physiol) hardening and swelling of the penis or clitoris. **2** [C] sth ~ed; building or structure.

ere·mite /'erɪmaɪt/ n = hermit.

erg /ɜːg/ n unit of energy in the metric system.

ergo /'ɜːgəʊ/ adv (Lat) (usu hum) therefore.

ergo·nom·ics /ˌɜːgə'nɒmɪks/ n pl (with *sing vb*) study of the environment, conditions and efficiency of workers.

Erin /'erɪn/ n (old name for) Ireland.

er·mine /'ɜːmɪn/ n **1** small animal whose fur is brown in summer and white (except for its black-pointed tail) in winter. **2** [U] its fur; garment made of this fur: *dressed in* ~*; a gown trimmed with* ~.

erode /ɪ'rəʊd/ vt [VP6A] (of acids, rain, etc) wear away; eat into: *Metals are* ~*d by acids.* **ero·sion** /ɪ'rəʊʒn/ n [U] eroding or being ~d: *soil erosion,* by wind and rain; *coast erosion,* by the sea. **ero·sive** /ɪ'rəʊsɪv/ adj

erogen·ous /ɪ'rɒdʒənəs/ adj (esp in): ~ '**zone,** area of the body particularly sensitive to sexual stimulation.

erotic /ɪ'rɒtɪk/ adj of sexual desire. **erot·ica** /ɪ'rɒtɪkə/ n pl books, pictures, etc intended to arouse sexual desire. **eroti·cism** /ɪ'rɒtɪsɪzəm/ n [U] sexual desire.

err /ɜː(r) US: eər/ vi (formal) make mistakes; do or be wrong: *It is better to err on the side of mercy,* be too merciful than too severe.

er·rand /'erənd/ n **1** short journey to take or get sth, eg a message, goods from a shop: *to go on* ~*s for sb; to run* ~*s.* **2** object or purpose of such a journey. **fool's** ~, one with no real or useful purpose.

er·rant /'erənt/ adj erring; mistaken: *an* ~ *husband,* one who is unfaithful to his wife.

er·ratic /ɪ'rætɪk/ adj **1** (of a person or his behaviour) irregular in behaviour or opinion; likely to do unusual or unexpected things. **2** (of things, eg a clock) uncertain in movement; irregular. **er·ratically** /-klɪ/ adv

er·ratum /e'rɑːtəm/ n (pl -ta /-tə/) (Lat) error in printing or writing: *an errata slip,* list of errors, misprints, etc in a printed book.

er·ron·eous /ɪ'rəʊnɪəs/ adj incorrect; mistaken. ~·**ly** adv

er·ror /'erə(r)/ n **1** [C] sth done wrong; mistake: *spelling* ~*s; printer's* ~*s,* misprints; *an* ~ *of judgement; a clerical* ~, made in writing. **2** [U] condition of being wrong in belief or conduct: *fall/lead sb into* ~; *do sth in* ~, by mistake.

er·satz /'eəzæts US: 'eərzɑːts/ adj (G) imitation, substitute (esp inferior): ~ *coffee/whisky/silk.*

Erse /ɜːs/ n Scottish Gaelic or Irish Gaelic.

eruc·ta·tion /ˌiːrʌk'teɪʃn/ n [U,C] (formal) belching, esp of a volcano.

eru·dite /'eruːdaɪt/ adj (formal) having, showing, great learning; scholarly. ~·**ly** adv **eru·di·tion** /ˌeruː'dɪʃn/ n [U] learning.

erupt /ɪ'rʌpt/ vi [VP2A] (esp of a volcano) break out. **erup·tion** /ɪ'rʌpʃn/ n [C,U] outbreak of a vol-

cano; (fig) outbreak of war, disease, etc: ~*ions of ashes and lava; in a state of* ~*ion.*

ery·sip·elas /ˌerɪ'sɪpɪləs/ n [U] skin disease that causes fever and produces deep red inflammation.

es·ca·late /'eskəleɪt/ vt, vi [VP2A,6A] increase, develop, intensify by successive stages. **es·ca·la·tion** /ˌeskə'leɪʃn/ n

es·ca·la·tor /'eskəleɪtə(r)/ n moving stairway carrying people up or down between floors or different levels.

es·ca·lope /'eskələʊp/ n slice of boneless meat, esp veal.

es·ca·pade /ˌeskə'peɪd/ n [C] daring, mischievous or adventurous act, often causing gossip or trouble.

es·cape¹ /ɪ'skeɪp/ n **1** [C,U] (act of) escaping; fact of having escaped: *E*~ *from Dartmoor prison is difficult. There have been very few successful* ~*s from this prison. I congratulate you on your* ~ *from the shipwreck. Don't look for an* ~ *of gas with a lighted match.* '~ **velocity,** the speed at which a projectile or spacecraft must travel in order to leave a (eg the earth's) gravitational field. **2** [C] means of escape: *a* '*fire*~*; an* '~*-pipe/-valve,* for carrying off steam or water. **3** (sth that provides) temporary distraction from reality or dull routine (eg through music, reading). **es·capee** /ˌɪskeɪ'piː/ n (esp) prisoner who has ~d. **es·cap·ism** /-ɪzəm/ n [U] habit of escaping from unpleasant realities into a world of fancy. **es·cap·ist** /-ɪst/ n person whose conduct is characterized by escapism: (attrib) *escapist literature.*

es·cape² /ɪ'skeɪp/ vi, vt **1** [VP2A,3A] ~ (*from*), get free; get away; (of steam, fluids, etc) find a way out: *Two of the prisoners have* ~*d. The canary has* ~*d from its cage. Is the gas escaping somewhere? Make a hole and let the water* ~. **2** [VP6A,C,2A] avoid; keep free or safe from: *You were lucky to* ~ *punishment/being punished. Where can we go to* ~ *the crowds? How can we* ~ *observation/being seen?* **3** [VP6A] be forgotten or unnoticed by: *His name* ~*s me for the moment,* I cannot recall it.

es·cape·ment /ɪ'skeɪpmənt/ n [C] device in a clock or watch to regulate the movement.

es·carp·ment /ɪ'skɑːpmənt/ n long steep slope or cliff separating two areas of different levels.

es·cha·tol·ogy /ˌeskə'tɒlədʒi/ n [U] branch of theology concerned with death, judgement, heaven and hell.

es·chew /ɪs'tʃuː/ vt [VP6A] (formal) avoid (the more usu word); keep oneself away from, abstain from: ~ *political debate.*

es·cort¹ /'eskɔːt/ n [C] **1** one or more persons going with another or others, or with valuable goods, to protect them, or as an honour: *an* ~ *of soldiers; under police* ~. **2** one or more ships, aircraft, etc giving protection or honour: *When the Queen sailed, her yacht had an* ~ *of ten destroyers and fifty aircraft.* **3** person or persons accompanying sb for courtesy's sake: *Mary's* ~ *to the ball.*

es·cort² /ɪ'skɔːt/ vt [VP6A,15B] go with as an escort: *a convoy of merchant ships* ~*ed by destroyers. Who will* ~ *this young lady home?*

es·cri·toire /ˌeskrɪ'twɑː(r)/ n writing-desk with drawers for stationery.

es·cutcheon /ɪ'skʌtʃən/ n shield with a coat of arms on it. ⇨ the illus at armour. *a blot on one's* ~, a stain on one's reputation.

Es·kimo /'eskɪməʊ/ n (pl ~s or ~es /-məʊz/), member of a people living in the Arctic regions of N America and E Siberia.

esopha·gus (also **oesopha·gus**) /i:'sɒfəgəs/ n passage from the pharynx to the stomach; gullet. ⇨ the illus at **alimentary, head**.

eso·teric /ˌesəʊ'terɪk/ adj intended only for those who are initiated, for a small circle of disciples or followers; abstruse.

es·palier /ɪ'spælɪeɪ/ n (tree or shrub trained on a) trellis or a wire framework.

es·pecial /ɪ'speʃl/ adj particular; exceptional: *a question of ~ importance; for your ~ benefit. in ~, above all.* **~·ly** /-ʃəlɪ/ adv to an exceptional degree; in particular: *She likes the country, ~ly in spring.*

Es·per·anto /ˌespə'ræntəʊ/ n [U] an artificial language designed for world use.

espion·age /'espɪənɑ:ʒ/ n [U] practice of spying or using spies.

es·pla·nade /ˌesplə'neɪd/ n [C] level area of ground where people may walk or ride for pleasure, often by the sea.

es·pouse /ɪ'spaʊz/ vt [VP6A] **1** give one's support to (a cause, theory, etc). **2** (old use; of a man) marry. **es·pousal** /ɪ'spaʊzl/ n **1** espousing (of a cause, etc). **2** (old use; usu pl) marriage or betrothal.

es·presso /e'spresəʊ/ n ~ **'coffee**, coffee made by forcing boiling water under pressure through ground coffee.

esprit /e'spri:/ n [U] (F) lively wit. **~ de corps** /eˌspri: də 'kɔ:(r)/ n spirit of loyalty and devotion which unites the members of a group or society.

espy /ɪ'spaɪ/ vt (pt,pp -pied) [VP6A] (usu joc) catch sight of.

Es·quire /ɪ'skwaɪə(r)/ US: 'es-/ n title of courtesy (used in GB and written **Esq**, esp in the address of a letter after a man's family name instead of *Mr* before it): *Edgar Broughton, Esq.*

es·say[1] /'eseɪ/ n piece of writing, usu short and in prose, on any one subject. **~·ist** /-ɪst/ n writer of ~s.

es·say[2] /e'seɪ/ vt,vi [VP6A,4A] try; attempt: *~ a task; ~ to do sth.* □ n /'eseɪ/ **1** testing or trial of the value or nature of sth. **2** attempt.

es·sence /'esns/ n **1** [U] that which makes a thing what it is; the inner nature or most important quality of a thing: *Is the ~ of morality right intention? Caution is the ~ of that man's character. The two things are the same in outward form but different in ~.* **2** [C,U] extract obtained from a substance by taking out as much of the mass as possible, leaving all its important qualities in concentrated form: *meat ~s; ~ of peppermint.*

es·sen·tial /ɪ'senʃl/ adj **1** necessary; indispensable; most important: *Is wealth ~ to happiness? Exercise, fresh air and sleep are ~ for the preservation of health. 'Wanted, a good secretary: experience ~.'* **2** of an essence(2): *~ oils.* **3** fundamental: *Love of fair play is said to be an ~ part of the English character.* □ n [C] (usu pl) fundamental element: *the ~s of English grammar. We've time to pack only the basic ~s,* the minimum amount (of clothes, etc) that is necessary. **~·ly** /ɪ'senʃəlɪ/ adv in an ~(3) manner: *We are an ~ly peace-loving people.*

es·tab·lish /ɪ'stæblɪʃ/ vt [VP6A,14,16B] **1** set up, put on a firm foundation: *~ a new state/ government/business.* **2** settle, place a person, oneself in a position, office, place, etc: *We are now comfortably ~ed in our new house. Mr X was ~ed as governor of the province.* **3** cause people to accept a belief, claim, custom, etc: *He succeeded in ~ing a claim to the title. Newton conclusively ~ed the law of gravity. E~ed customs are difficult to change. His honesty is well ~ed.* **4** make (a church) national by law.

es·tab·lish·ment /ɪ'stæblɪʃmənt/ n **1** [U] establishing or being established: *the ~ of a new state.* **2** [C] that which is established, eg a large organized body of persons (eg the army or navy; a civil service; a business firm, with many employees; a hotel and the staff in it). **3 the E~**, (GB) those persons in positions of power and authority, exercising influence in the background of public life or other field of activity.

es·tami·net /e'stæmɪneɪ US: eˌstæmɪ'neɪ/ n (F) small French café selling beer, wine, coffee, etc.

es·tate /ɪ'steɪt/ n **1** [C] piece of property in the form of land, esp in the country: *He owns large ~s in Scotland.* **'~ agent,** (US = Realtor) person who buys and sells buildings and land for others. **'hous·ing ~,** area of land on which many houses are built, either by private enterprise or (**'council ~**) by a public authority. **in'dustrial ~,** area of land development for industrial use (factories, etc). **2** [U] (legal) a person's whole property. **'real ~,** land and buildings. **'personal ~,** money and other kinds of property. **3** [C] political or social group or class: *the three ~s of the realm,* the Lords Spiritual (Bishops in the House of Lords), the Lords Temporal (other lords) and the House of Commons; *the fourth ~,* the press(3). **4** (old use) condition; stage in life: *reach man's ~; the holy ~ of matrimony.* **5** **'~ car,** (US = station-wagon) saloon-type motor vehicle with removable or collapsible rear seats and door(s) at the back, for easy loading of luggage, etc.

es·teem /ɪ'sti:m/ vt **1** [VP6A] (formal) have a high opinion of; respect greatly: *No one can ~ your father more than I do.* **2** [VP25] (formal) consider; regard: *I shall ~ it a favour if.... I ~ it a privilege to address this audience.* □ n [U] high regard: *He lowered himself in our ~ by this foolish behaviour. We all hold him in great ~.*

es·thetic /i:s'θetɪk/ = aesthetic.

es·ti·mable /'estɪməbl/ adj worthy of esteem.

es·ti·mate[1] /'estɪmət/ n [C] judgement; approximate calculation (of size, cost, etc): *I hope the builders don't exceed their ~. I do not know enough about him to form an ~ of his abilities. Can you give me a rough ~ of the cost?* ⇨ **rough**[1](3); outside adj (2). **the E~s,** figures supplied each year by the Chancellor of the Exchequer showing the probable national expenditure, etc.

es·ti·mate[2] /'estɪmeɪt/ vt,vi [VP9,14,3A] **~ (at),** form a judgement about; calculate the cost, value, size, etc of sth: *The firm ~d the cost of the work at £8000. We ~ that it would take three months to finish the work. I ~ his income at/to be about £5000. Ask a contractor to ~ for the repair of the building.*

es·ti·ma·tion /ˌestɪ'meɪʃn/ n [U] judgement; regard: *in my ~; in the ~ of most people.*

es·trange /ɪ'streɪndʒ/ vt [VP6A,14] **~ (from),** bring about a separation in feeling and sympathy: *foolish behaviour that ~d all his friends; ~ sb from his friends. He is ~d from his wife,* living apart from her. **~·ment** n [U] being ~d; [C] instance of this: *cause an ~ment between two old friends.*

es·tu·ary /'estʃʊərɪ US: -ʊerɪ/ n (pl -ries) [C] river

mouth into which the tide flows: *the Thames* ~.

et cet·era /ɪt 'setərə *US:* et/ (Lat, usu shortened to **etc**) and other things; and so on.

etch /etʃ/ *vt,vi* [VP6A,2A] use a needle and acid to make a picture, etc on a metal plate from which copies may be printed; make (pictures, etc) in this way. ~**er** *n* person who ~es. ~**ing** *n* [U] the art of the ~er; [C] copy printed from an ~ed plate.

eter·nal /ɪ'tɜːnl/ *adj* **1** without beginning or end; lasting for ever: *the E~ God; the E~ City*, Rome. *Does the Christian religion promise ~ life?* **2** (colloq) unceasing; too frequent: *Stop this ~ chatter.* **the ~ triangle,** situation of conflict in which two men want the same woman or two women the same man. ~**ly** /ɪ'tɜːnəlɪ/ *adv* throughout all time; for ever; (colloq) (too) frequently.

eter·nity /ɪ'tɜːnətɪ/ *n* (*pl* -ties) **1** [U] time without end; the future life: *send a man to* ~, to his death. **2 an** ~, period of time that seems endless: *It seemed an* ~ *before news of his safety reached her.* **3** (*pl*) eternal truths.

ether /'iːθə(r)/ *n* [U] **1** liquid made from alcohol, used in industry, and medically as an anaesthetic. **2** medium(3) through which, it was once believed, light waves were transmitted through all space. **3** (poet) the pure, upper air above the clouds.

eth·ereal /ɪ'θɪərɪəl/ *adj* **1** of unearthly delicacy; seeming too light or spiritual for this world: ~ *beauty/music; the* ~ *figure of an angel.* **2** (poet) of the pure, upper air above the clouds.

ethic /'eθɪk/ *n* **an** ~, system of moral principles, rules of conduct: *Was Islam in Turkey a traditional social code or an* ~ *for living?* **eth·ics** *n pl* (**a**) (with *sing v*) science of morals. (**b**) (with *pl v*) moral soundness: *E~s is a branch of philosophy. The* ~*s of his decision are doubtful.* **ethi·cal** /-kl/ *adj* of morals or moral questions: *an* ~ *basis for education.* **ethi·cally** /-klɪ/ *adv*

eth·nic /'eθnɪk/ *adj* of race or the races of mankind; (colloq) of a particular cultural group: ~ *clothes/ food/music; an* ~ *restaurant.* **eth·ni·cally** /klɪ/ *adv*

eth·no·gra·phy /eθ'nɒɡrəfɪ/ *n* [U] scientific description of the races of mankind. **eth·no·gra·pher** /eθ'nɒɡrəfə(r)/ *n* **eth·no·graphic** /ˌeθnə'ɡræfɪk/ *adj*

eth·nol·ogy /eθ'nɒlədʒɪ/ *n* [U] science of the races of mankind, their relations to one another, etc. **eth·nol·o·gist** /-dʒɪst/ *n* student of, expert in, ~. **eth·no·logi·cal** /ˌeθnə'lɒdʒɪkl/ *adj* of ~.

ethos /'iːθɒs/ *n* characteristics of a community or of a culture; code of values by which a group or society lives.

ethyl /'eθɪl/ *n* ~ **alcohol,** the base of alcoholic drinks, also used as a fuel or solvent.

eti·ology /ˌiːtɪ'ɒlədʒɪ/ *n* assignment of a cause; (med) study of the causes of disease.

eti·quette /'etɪket/ *n* [U] rules for formal relations or polite social behaviour among people, in a class of society or a profession: *medical/legal* ~.

ety·mol·ogy /ˌetɪ'mɒlədʒɪ/ *n* **1** [U] science of the origin and history of words. **2** [C] account of the origin and history of a word. **ety·mol·ogist** /-dʒɪst/ *n* student of ~. **ety·mo·logi·cal** /ˌetɪmə'lɒdʒɪkl/ *adj* of ~.

euca·lyptus /ˌjuːkə'lɪptəs/ *n* sorts of tall evergreen tree (including the Australian gum tree) from which an oil is obtained.

Eu·char·ist /'juːkərɪst/ *n* **the E~,** the Lord's Supper; the bread and wine taken at this. ⇨ lord(2).

Eu·clid·ean /juː'klɪdɪən/ *adj* of the geometric prin-

ciples of Euclid /'juːklɪd/ (about 300 BC) the Greek mathematician.

eu·gen·ics /juː'dʒenɪks/ *n pl* (with *sing v*) science of the production of healthy offspring with the aim of improving the human genetic stock.

eu·logize /'juːlədʒaɪz/ *vt* [VP6A] (formal) praise highly in speech or writing. **eu·logist** /'juːlədʒɪst/ *n* person who does this. **eu·logis·tic** /ˌjuːlə'dʒɪstɪk/ *adj* giving or containing high praise. **eu·logy** /'juːlədʒɪ/ *n* (*pl* -gies) [C,U] (speech or writing full of) high praise.

eu·nuch /'juːnək/ *n* castrated man, esp one formerly employed in some Oriental courts.

eu·phem·ism /'juːfəmɪzəm/ *n* [C,U] (example of the) use of other (mild, vague and indirect) words or phrases in place of what is required by truth or accuracy: *'Pass away' is a* ~ *for 'die'. 'Pass water' is a* ~ *for 'urinate'.* **eu·phem·is·tic** /ˌjuːfə'mɪstɪk/ *adj* of the nature of ~: *euphemistic language/expressions.* **eu·phe·mis·ti·cally** /-klɪ/ *adv*

eu·phony /'juːfənɪ/ *n* [U] pleasantness of sound; [C,U] (*pl* -nies) pleasant sound.

eu·phoria /juː'fɔːrɪə/ *n* [U] state of well-being and pleasant excitement; elation. **eu·phoric** /juː'fɒrɪk *US:* -'fɔːr-/ *adj*

eu·phu·ism /'juːfjuːɪzəm/ *n* [C] (instance of) elaborately artificial style of writing and speaking (as fashionable in England in the late 16th and early 17th cc).

Eur·asia /juə'reɪʒə/ *n* Europe and Asia. **Eur·asian** /juə'reɪʒn/ *n, adj* (person) of mixed European and Asian parentage; of Europe and Asia.

eu·reka /juə'riːkə/ *int* (Gk = 'I have found it!') cry of triumph at a discovery.

eu·rhyth·mics (also **eu·ryth-**) /juː'rɪðmɪks/ *n pl* (with *sing v*) harmony of bodily movement, esp as a system of physical training with music.

Euro·dollar /'juərəudɒlə(r)/ *n* US dollar put in European bank to act as an international currency and help the financing of trade and commerce.

Euro·pean /ˌjuərə'pɪən/ *n, adj* (native) of Europe /'juərəp/; happening in, extending over, Europe: ~ *countries; a* ~ *reputation.*

Euro·vision /'juərəvɪʒn/ *n* European TV network.

Eu·sta·chian tube /juːˌsteɪʃn 'tjuːb *US:* 'tuːb/ *n* (anat) duct extending from the middle ear to the pharynx. ⇨ the illus at ear.

eu·tha·nasia /ˌjuːθə'neɪzɪə *US:* -'neɪʒə/ *n* [U] (bringing about of a) mercifully easy and painless death (for persons suffering from an incurable and painful disease).

evacu·ate /ɪ'vækjʊeɪt/ *vt* **1** [VP6A] (esp of soldiers) withdraw from; leave empty: ~ *a fort/town.* **2** [VP6A,14] ~ *sb (from) (to),* remove him from a place or district, eg one considered to be dangerous in time of war: *The children were* ~*d to the country.* **3** [VP6A] empty (*of* its contents, esp defecate). **evacu·ation** /ɪˌvækjʊ'eɪʃn/ *n* [U] evacuating or being ~d; [C] instance of this. **evacuee** /ɪˌvækjuː'iː/ *n* person who is ~d(2).

evade /ɪ'veɪd/ *vt* [VP6A,C] **1** get, keep, out of the way of; ~ *a blow/one's enemies/an attack.* **2** find a way of not doing sth: ~ *paying income tax;* ~ *military service;* avoid answering (fully or honestly): ~ *a question.*

evalu·ate /ɪ'væljʊeɪt/ *vt* [VP6A] find out, decide, the amount or value of. **evalu·ation** /ɪˌvæljʊ'eɪʃn/ *n*

evan·escent /ˌiːvə'nesnt *US:* ˌev-/ *adj* quickly fading; soon going from the memory: ~ *political triumphs*. **evan·escence** /-sns/ *n*

evan·geli·cal /ˌiːvænˈdʒelɪkl/ *adj* **1** of, according to, the teachings of the Gospel: ~ *preaching*. **2** of the beliefs and teachings of those Protestants who maintain that the soul can be saved only by faith in Jesus Christ. ~·**ism** /-ɪzəm/ *n* [U] ~(**2**) beliefs or teachings.

evan·gel·ist /ɪˈvændʒəlɪst/ *n* **1** one of the writers (Matthew, Mark, Luke or John) of the Gospels. **2** preacher of the Gospel, esp one who travels and holds religious meetings wherever he goes, preaching to any who are willing to listen. **evan·gel·is·tic** /ɪˌvændʒəˈlɪstɪk/ *adj*

evap·or·ate /ɪˈvæpəreɪt/ *vt, vi* **1** [VP6A,2A] (cause to) change into vapour: *Heat* ~*s water. The water soon* ~*d*. **2** [VP6A] remove liquid from a substance, eg by heating: ~*d milk*. **3** [VP2A] disappear; die: *His hopes* ~*d*, He no longer felt any hope. **evap·or·ation** /ɪˌvæpəˈreɪʃn/ *n*

evas·ion /ɪˈveɪʒn/ *n* **1** [U] evading: ~ *of responsibility*. **2** [C] statement, excuse, etc made to evade sth; act of evading: *His answers to my questions were all* ~*s*.

evas·ive /ɪˈveɪsɪv/ *adj* tending, trying, to evade: *an* ~ *answer; take* ~ *action*, do sth in order to evade danger, etc. ~·**ly** *adv* ~·**ness** *n*

Eve /iːv/ *n* (in the Bible story of the Creation) the first woman.

eve /iːv/ *n* day or evening before a Church festival or any day or event; time just before anything: *Christmas Eve*, 24 Dec; *New Year's Eve*, 31 Dec; *on the eve of great events*.

even¹ /ˈiːvn/ *adj* **1** level; smooth: *A billiard-table must be perfectly* ~. **2** regular; steady; of unchanging quality: *His* ~ *breathing showed that he had got over his excitement. His work is not very* ~, it is a mixture of good and bad. **3** (of amounts, distances, values) equal: *Our scores are now* ~. *The two horses were* ~ *in the race*. **be/get** ~ **with sb**, have/get one's revenge on him. ~ **odds**, chances which are the same for£or against. **break** ~, (colloq) make neither a profit nor a loss. **4** (of numbers) that can be divided by two with no remainder: *The pages on the left side of a book have* ~ *numbers*. ⇨ odd. **5** equally balanced: *an* ~ *chance;* ~ *money*, (in betting). ~-**handed** *adj* fair: ~-*handed justice*. **6** (of temper, etc) calm; not easily disturbed: *an* ~-*tempered baby*. □ *vt* [VP6A,15B] ~ **(up)**, make ~ or equal: *That will* ~ *things up*, make them equal. ~·**ly** *adv* ~-**ness** *n*

even² /ˈiːvn/ *adv* **1** (used to invite a comparison between what happened and what might have happened. *He never* ~ '*opened the letter* (so he certainly did not read it). *He didn't answer* ~ '*my letter* (not to mention letters from others). *It was cold there* ~ *in Ju'ly* (so you may imagine how cold it was in winter). *E*~ *a* '*child can understand the book* (so adults can certainly do so). **2** ~ **if/ though,** (used to call attention to the extreme nature of what follows): *I'll get there* ~ *if I have to pawn my watch to get the railway fare. She won't leave the TV set,* ~ *though her supper's on the table.* **3** (with comparatives) still, yet: *You know* ~ *less about it than I do. You seem* ~ *more stupid than usual today.* **4** ~ **as,** just at the time when: *E*~ *as I gave the warning the car skidded.* ~ **now/then,** in spite of these or those circumstances, etc: *E*~ *now he won't believe me. E*~ *then he would not admit his mistake.* ~ **so,** though

that is the case: *It has many omissions;* ~ *so, it is quite a useful reference book.*

even³ /ˈiːvn/ *n* (poet) evening. '~-**song** *n* Evening Prayer in the Church of England. '~-**tide** *n* (poet) evening.

even·ing /ˈiːvnɪŋ/ *n* **1** [C,U] that part of the day between sunset and bedtime: *a cool* ~; *musical* ~*s*, evenings given to playing or listening to music; *two* ~*s ago;* (no *prep*) *this/tomorrow/yesterday* ~; *in the* ~; *on Sunday* ~; *on the* ~ *of the 8th; one warm summer* ~. **2** (attrib): '~ **dress**, dress as worn for formal occasions in the ~. ~ '**paper**, newspaper published after midday. ~ '**prayer**, church service; vespers. **the** ~ '**star**, planet, (Venus or Mercury), seen in the western sky after sunset.

even·song /ˈiːvnsɒŋ *US:* -sɔːŋ/ ⇨ even³.

event /ɪˈvent/ *n* **1** happening, usu sth important: *the chief* ~*s of 1789. It was quite an* ~ (often used to suggest that what happened was on an unusual scale, memorable, etc). **in the natural/normal/ usual course of** ~*s*, in the order in which things naturally happen. **2** fact of a thing happening: *in the* ~ *of his death*, if he dies. **3** outcome; result. **at** '**all** ~*s*, whatever is so. **in** '**any** ~, whatever is so. **in** '**either** ~, whichever is so. **in** '**that** ~, if that is so. **in the** ~, as it in fact happens. **4** one of the races, competitions, etc in a sports programme: *Which* ~*s have you entered for?* ~-**ful** /-fl/ *adj* full of notable ~*s: He had had an* ~*ful life. The past year has been* ~*ful*.

even·tide /ˈiːvntaɪd/ *n* ⇨ even³.

event·ual /ɪˈventʃʊəl/ *adj* coming at last as a result; ultimate: *his foolish behaviour and* ~ *failure*. ~·**ly** /-tʃʊəlɪ/ *adv* in the end: *He fell ill and* ~*ly died.* ~·**ity** /ɪˌventʃʊˈælətɪ/ *n* (*pl* -ties) [C] possible event.

ever /ˈevə(r)/ *adv* **1** (usu in neg and interr sentences, and in sentences expressing doubt or conditions; usu placed with the *v*) at any time: *Nothing* ~ *happens in this village. Do you* ~ *wish you were rich? She seldom, if* ~, *goes to the cinema. If you* ~ *visit London....* **2** (with the present perfect tense, in questions) at any time up to the present: *Have you* ~ *been up in a balloon?* (Note that *ever* is not used in the answer: either 'Yes, I have' or 'No, never', etc.) **3** (after a comparative or superlative): *It is raining harder than* ~, than it has been doing so far. *It is more necessary than* ~ (= than it has been so far) *for all of us to win. This is the best work you have* ~ *done.* **4** (chiefly in phrases) at all times; continuously: ~ *afterwards: for* ~ (*and* ~); ~ *since I was a boy.* **5** (colloq) (used as an intensifier): *Work as hard as* ~ *you can. I'll tell her as soon as* ~ *she arrives.* '~ **so;** '~ **such (a),** (colloq) very: ~ *so rich;* ~ *such a rich man.* **6** (used after interrogatives as an intensifier): *When/ Where/How* ~ *did you lose it? What* ~ *do you mean?* **7 did you** ~ ...! used to express surprise, incredulity, etc: *Well, did you* ~ *hear such nonsense!* **As if** ... ~, used in a similar way: *As if he would* ~ *do such a thing!* He would certainly not do it! **8** (old use) always: *You will find me* ~ *at your service.* **9 Yours** ~, used at the end of a letter, informal or familiar style.

ever·green /ˈevəɡriːn/ *n, adj* (tree, shrub) having green leaves throughout the year: *The pine, cedar and spruce are* ~*s*. ⇨ deciduous.

ever·last·ing /ˌevəˈlɑːstɪŋ *US:* -ˈlæst-/ *adj* **1** going on for ever: ~ *fame/glory*. **the E**~, God. **2** repeat-

ed too often: *I'm tired of his ~ complaints.*
ever·more /ˌevəˈmɔː(r)/ *adv* for ever.
every /ˈevrɪ/ *adj* (used attrib with *sing* [C] *nouns*; cf the use of *all* with *pl nouns* and [U] *nouns*) **1** (Cf *every* and *each.* When *every* is used, attention is directed to units comprising a whole; when *each* is used, attention is directed simply to the unit) all or each one of a whole: *E~ boy in the class* (= All the boys, The whole class) *passed the examination.* (Cf: *Each boy may have three tries*). *I have read ~ book* (= all the books) *on that shelf. Not ~ horse* (= Not all horses) *can run fast.* **2** (not replaceable by *all* and the *plural noun*) each one of an indefinite number (the emphasis being on the unit, not on the total or whole): *He enjoyed ~ minute of his holiday. Such things go ~ day. He spends ~ penny he earns.* **3** (used with abstract *nouns*) all possible; complete: *You have ~ reason to be satisfied. I have ~ reason/There is ~ reason to believe that.... There is ~ prospect of success.* **4** (used with cardinal and ordinal numbers, and with *other* and *few*, to indicate recurrence, or intervals in time or space): *Write on ~ other line, on alternate lines. There are buses to the station ~ ten minutes. I go there ~ other day/~ three days/~ third day/~ few days, etc. He was stopped ~ dozen yards by friends who wanted to congratulate him.* **~ now and then/again,** from time to time. **5** (used with, and placed after, possessives; replaceable by *all* + *pl*): *His ~ movement was watched,* All his movements.... *He tries to meet her ~ wish,* all her wishes. **6** (in phrases) **~ bit,** quite: *This is ~ bit as good as that.* **~ time, (a)** always: *Our football team wins ~ time.* **(b)** whenever: *E~ time I meet him, he tries to borrow money from me.* **~ 'one of them/us/you,** (placed at the end) without exception: *You deserve to be hanged, ~ one of you. in ~ way,* in all respects: *This is in ~ way better than that.* **~·body** /ˈevrɪbɒdɪ/, **~·one** /ˈevrɪwʌn/ *pron ~* person: *In a small village ~ one knows ~ one else.* **~·day** /ˈevrɪdeɪ/ *adj* (attrib only) happening or used daily; common and familiar: *an ~ day occurrence; in his ~ day clothes.* **'~·place** (US colloq) *~* where. **~·thing** /ˈevrɪθɪŋ/ *pron* **(a)** all things: *This shop sells ~ thing needed for camping. Tell me ~ thing about it.* **(b)** (pred) thing of the greatest importance: *Money is ~ thing to him. She's beautiful, I agree, but beauty is not ~ thing.* **~·where** /ˈevrɪweə(r)/ *US:* -hweər/ *adv* in, at, to, ~ place: *I've looked ~ where for it. E~ where seemed to be quiet.*
evict /ɪˈvɪkt/ *vt* [VP14] **~ (from),** expel (a tenant) (from a house or land) by authority of the law: *They were ~ ed for not paying the rent.* **evic·tion** /ɪˈvɪkʃn/ *n* [U] ~ ing or being ~ ed; [C] instance of this.
evi·dence /ˈevɪdəns/ *n* **1** [U] anything that gives reason for believing sth, that makes clear or proves sth: *There wasn't enough ~ to prove him guilty. Have you any ~ for this statement? We cannot condemn him on such slight ~. The scientist must produce ~ in support of his theories.* **(be) in ~,** (be) clearly or easily seen: *She's the sort of woman who likes to be very much in ~,* who likes to be seen and noticed. *Smith was nowhere in ~,* could not be seen anywhere. **bear/give/show ~ of,** show signs of: *When the ship reached port, it bore abundant ~ of the severity of the storm,* ie signs of damage. **turn Queen's/King's/**(US)**State's ~,** (of a criminal) give ~ in court against accom-

plices. **2** (used in *pl*) indication, mark, trace: *There were ~ s of glacial action on the rocks.* □ *vt* [VP6A] (rare) prove by ~; be ~ of. *His answer ~ d a guilty conscience.*
evi·dent /ˈevɪdənt/ *adj* plain and clear (to the eyes or mind): *It must be ~ to all of you that.... He looked at his twelve children with ~ pride.* **~·ly** *adv*
evil /ˈiːvl/ *adj* **1** wicked, sinful, bad, harmful: ~ *men/thoughts; live an ~ life; the 'E~ One,* the Devil. **,~·'minded** *adj* having ~ thoughts and desires. **2** likely to cause trouble; bringing trouble or misfortune: *in an ~ hour; fall on ~ days; an ~* (= slanderous) *tongue.* **~ eye,** malicious look; supposed power to cause harm by a look or glance. □ *n* **1** [U] sin; wrong-doing: *return good for ~; the spirit of ~.* **'~·doer** *n* person who does ~. **2** [C] ~ thing; disaster: *War, famine and flood are terrible ~ s.* **be/choose the lesser of two ~ s,** the less harmful of two bad choices. **~·ly** /ˈiːvəlɪ/ *adv* in an ~ manner: *He eyed her ~ ly.*
evince /ɪˈvɪns/ *vt* [VP6A,9] (formal) show that one has (a feeling, quality, etc:) *a child who ~ s great intelligence.*
evis·cer·ate /ɪˈvɪsəreɪt/ *vt* [VP6A] disembowel.
evoca·tive /ɪˈvɒkətɪv/ *adj* that evokes, or is able to evoke: ~ *words,* that call up memories, emotions, in addition to their ordinary meanings.
evoke /ɪˈvəʊk/ *vt* [VP6A] call up, bring out: ~ *a spirit from the other world;* ~ *admiration/ surprise/a smile/memories of the past.* **evo·ca·tion** /ˌiːvəʊˈkeɪʃn/ *n*
evol·ution /ˌiːvəˈluːʃn US:* ˌev-/ *n* **1** [U] evolving; process of opening out or developing: *the ~ of a plant from a seed. In politics England has preferred ~* (= gradual development) *to revolution* (= sudden or violent change). **2** [U] (theory of the) development of more complicated forms of life (plants, animals) from earlier and simpler forms. **3** [C] movement according to plan (of troops, warships, dancers, etc). **~·ary** /ˌiːvəˈluːʃənrɪ *US:* ˌevəˈluːʃənerɪ/ *adj* of, being produced by, ~; developing.
evolve /ɪˈvɒlv/ *vi,vt* [VP2A,6A] (cause to) unfold; develop; be developed, naturally and (usu) gradually: *The American constitution was planned; the British constitution ~ d. He has ~ d a new plan/ theory.*
ewe /juː/ *n* female sheep. ⇨ ram.
ewer /ˈjuːə(r)/ *n* large wide-mouthed pitcher for holding water, eg as used with a basin on a washstand in a bedroom without a piped supply of water.
ex- /eks/ *pref* ⇨ App 3.
ex·acer·bate /ɪgˈzæsəbeɪt/ *vt* [VP6A] (formal) irritate (a person); aggravate (= make worse) (pain, disease, a situation). **ex·acer·ba·tion** /ɪgˌzæsəˈbeɪʃn/ *n*
exact[1] /ɪgˈzækt/ *adj* **1** correct in every detail; free from error: *Give me his ~ words. What is the ~ size of the room? I want ~ directions for finding your house.* **2** capable of being precise: ~ *sciences; an ~ memory; an ~ scholar.* **~·ly** *adv* **1** correctly; quite: *Your answer is ~ ly right. That's ~ ly* (= just) *what I expected.* **2** (as an answer or confirmation) quite so; just as you say. **~·ness, ~·i·tude** /ɪgˈzæktɪtjuːd *US:* -tuːd/ *nn.*
exact[2] /ɪgˈzækt/ *vt* [VP6A,14] **~ (from), 1** demand and enforce payment of: ~ *taxes (from people);* ~ *payment (from a debtor).* **2** insist on: ~ *obe-*

dience. **3** (of circumstances) require urgently; make necessary: *work that ~s care and attention.* **~·ing** *adj* making great demands; severe; strict: *an ~ing piece of work; an ~ing master.* **ex·action** /ɪgˈzækʃn/ *n* **1** [U] ~ing of money, etc. **2** [C] that which is ~ed, esp a tax which is considered to be too high; a great demand (on one's time, strength, etc).

exag·ger·ate /ɪgˈzædʒəreɪt/ *vt,vi* [VP6A,2A] stretch (a description) beyond the truth; make sth seem larger, better, worse, etc than it really is: *You ~ the difficulties. If you always ~, people will no longer believe you. He has an ~d sense of his own importance,* thinks he is far more important than he really is. **exag·ger·ation** /ɪgˌzædʒəˈreɪʃn/ *n* [U] exaggerating or being ~d; [C] ~d statement: *a story full of exaggerations.*

exalt /ɪgˈzɔːlt/ *vt* [VP6A] **1** make high(er) in rank, great(er) in power or dignity. **2** praise highly. **~ed** *adj* dignified; ennobled: *a person of ~ed rank.* **exal·ta·tion** /ˌegzɔːlˈteɪʃn/ *n* [U] (fig) elation; state of spiritual delight

exam /ɪgˈzæm/ *n* (colloq abbr of) examination.

exam·in·ation /ɪgˌzæmɪˈneɪʃn/ *n* **1** [U] examining or being examined: *On ~, it was found that the signature was not genuine. The prisoner is still under ~,* being examined. **2** [C] instance of this, esp **(a)** a testing of knowledge or ability: *an ~ in mathematics; ~ questions/papers; an oral ~.* **(b)** an inquiry into or inspection of sth: *an ~ of a botanical specimen; an ~ of business accounts; an ~ of one's eyes.* **(c)** questioning by a lawyer in a law court: *an ~ of a witness.*

exam·ine /ɪgˈzæmɪn/ *vt* [VP6A,14] **1** ~ *(for),* look at carefully in order to learn about or from: *~ old records; have one's teeth/eyes ~d for decay/ weakening; ~ a new theory. She needs to have her head ~d,* (colloq) is foolish or impudent. **2** ~ *(in),* put questions to in order to test knowledge or get information: *~ pupils in Latin/on their knowledge of Latin; ~ a witness in a court of law.* **exam·iner·** *n* person who ~s.

example /ɪgˈzɑːmpl US: -ˈzæmpl/ *n* **1** fact, thing, etc which illustrates or represents a general rule: *This dictionary has many ~s of how verbs are used.* **for ~,** (abbr **eg**) by way of illustration: *Many great men have risen from poverty—Lincoln and Edison, for ~.* **2** specimen showing the quality of others in the same group or of the same kind: *This is a good ~ of Shelley's lyric poetry.* **3** [C,U] thing or person, person's conduct, to be copied or imitated: *follow sb's ~; set an ~ to sb; set sb a good ~; learn by ~.* **4** warning: *Let this be an ~ to you.* **make an ~ of sb,** punish him as a warning to others.

exas·per·ate /ɪgˈzæspəreɪt/ *vt* [VP6A] irritate; produce ill feeling in; make ill feeling, anger, etc worse: *~d by/at sb's stupidity. It is exasperating to lose a train by half a minute.* **exas·per·ation** /ɪgˌzæspəˈreɪʃn/ *n* state of being ~d: *'Stop that noise', he cried out in exasperation.*

ex·ca·vate /ˈekskəveɪt/ *vt* [VP6A] make, uncover, by digging: *~ a trench/a buried city.* **ex·ca·vator** /-tə(r)/ *n* person engaged in, machine used for, excavating. **ex·ca·va·tion** /ˌekskəˈveɪʃn/ *n* [U] excavating or being ~d; [C] place that is being or has been ~d.

ex·ceed /ɪkˈsiːd/ *vt* [VP6A] **1** be greater than: *Their success ~ed all expectations. London ~s Glasgow in size and population.* **2** go beyond what is al-

lowed, necessary or advisable: *~ the speed limit,* drive faster than is allowed; *~ one's instructions,* do more than one has authority to do. **~·ing·ly** *adv* extremely; to an unusual degree: *an ~ingly difficult problem.*

ex·cel /ɪkˈsel/ *vi,vt* (-ll-) ~ *(in/at),* **1** [VP2C,3A] do better than others, be very good: *He ~s in courage/as an orator. The firm ~s in/at producing cheap transistor radios.* **2** [VP6A,15A] do better than; surpass (the more usu word): *He ~s all of us in/at tennis.*

ex·cel·lence /ˈeksələns/ *n* **1** [U] ~ *(in/at),* the quality of being excellent; great merit: *a prize for ~ in furniture design; his ~ in/at all forms of sport.* **2** [C] thing or quality in which a person excels: *They do not recognize her many ~s.*

Ex·cel·lency /ˈeksələnsɪ/ *n* (*pl* -cies) title of ambassadors, governors and their wives, and some other officers and officials: *Your/His/Her ~.*

ex·cel·lent /ˈeksələnt/ *adj* very good; of high quality. **~·ly** *adv*

ex·cel·sior /ekˈselsɪɔː(r)/ *n* [U] (US) soft, fine wood shavings used for packing easily damaged goods, eg glassware.

ex·cept¹ /ɪkˈsept/ *prep* not including; but not: *He gets up early every day ~ Sunday. Nobody was late ~ me.* Cf: Five others were late *besides* me. *My papers seem to be everywhere ~ where they ought to be.* ~ **for,** (used when what is excluded is different from what is included): *Your essay is good ~ for the spelling.* (The comparison is between the spelling, which is not good, and other things, eg ideas, grammar, which are satisfactory). Cf *All the essays are good ~ John's.* ~ **that,** apart from the fact that: *She knew nothing about his journey ~ that he was likely to be away for three months.* □ *conj* (old or liter use) unless: (biblical style) *E~ ye be born again.*

ex·cept² /ɪkˈsept/ *vt* [VP6A,14] ~ *(from),* exclude (from); set apart (from a list, statement, etc): *I discovered that I had been ~ed from the list of those who were being sent to India. All those who took part in the plot, nobody ~ed, were punished.* **present company ~ed,** not including those here present. **~·ing** *prep* (used after *not, always* and *without)* leaving out; excluding: *the whole staff, not ~ing the heads of departments.*

ex·cep·tion /ɪkˈsepʃn/ *n* **1** [U,C] excepting; sb or sth that is excepted (not included). **make an ~ (of sb/sth),** treat (sb/sth) as an ~, a special case: *You must all be here at 8am; I can make no ~s,* cannot excuse any of you. **with the ~ of,** except: *I enjoyed all his novels with the ~ of his last.* **without ~,** excepting nobody/nothing: *All men between 18 and 45 without ~ are expected to serve in the army during a war.* **2** [C] sth that does not follow the rule: *~s to a rule of grammar.* ⇨ prove(1). **3** [U] objection. **take ~ (to sth),** object to; protest against; be offended by: *He took great ~ to what I said.* **~·able** /-əbl/ *adj* objectionable. **~·al** /-ʃənl/ *adj* unusual; out of the ordinary: *weather that is ~al for June; ~al advantages.* **~·ally** /-ʃənəlɪ/ *adv* unusually: *an ~ally beautiful boy.*

ex·cerpt /ˈeksɜːpt/ *n* [C] passage, extract, from a book etc, eg one printed separately.

ex·cess¹ /ɪkˈses/ *n* **1 an ~ of,** fact of being, amount by which sth is, more than sth else, or more than is expected or proper: *an ~ of enthusiasm; an ~ of imports over exports.* **in ~ of,** more than: *luggage in ~ of 100kg will be charged extra.* **to**

~, to an extreme degree: *Don't carry your grief to ~. She is generous to ~.* 2 [U] immoderation; intemperance. 3 (*pl*) personal acts which go beyond the limits of good behaviour, morality or humanity: *The ~es* (= acts of cruelty, etc) *committed by the troops when they occupied the capital will never be forgotten.* ~·ive /ɪk'sesɪv/ *adj* too much; too great; extreme: ~*ive charges.* ~·ive·ly *adv*

ex·cess² /'ekses/ *adj* extra; additional: ~ *fare,* eg for travelling farther than is allowed by one's ticket: ~ *luggage,* weight above what may be carried free; ~ *postage,* charged when a letter, etc is understamped: ~ *profits duty,* extra tax on profits increased by, eg, war conditions.

ex·change¹ /ɪk'stʃeɪndʒ/ *n* 1 [C,U] (act of) exchanging: *Is five apples for five eggs a fair ~? There have been numerous ~s of views between the two governments. E~ of prisoners during a war is unusual. He is giving her French lessons in ~ for English lessons.* 2 [U] the giving and receiving of the money of one country for that of another; relation in value between kinds of money used in different countries: *the rate of ~* (between the dollar and the pound, etc). '*E~ Control,* system of protecting gold and reserves of foreign currency. 3 [C] place where merchants or financiers meet for business: *the 'Cotton E~; the 'Stock E~,* for the buying and selling of stocks, shares, bonds. 4 '*lab-our ~,* (GB) Government offices where unemployed workmen may be put in touch with prospective employers. '*telephone ~,* control office where lines are connected.

ex·change² /ɪk'stʃeɪndʒ/ *vt* [VP6A,14] ~ *sth (for sth) (with sb),* give, receive (one thing) in place of another: ~ *greetings/glances;* ~ *five apples for five eggs. Mary ~d seats with Anne.* ~ *blows/words (with),* fight/quarrel. ~·able /-əbl/ *adj* that may be ~d.

ex·chequer /ɪks'tʃekə(r)/ *n* 1 the E~, (GB) government department in charge of public money. '*Chancellor of the 'E~,* minister at the head of this department (= Minister of Finance in other countries). 2 supply of money (public or private); treasury.

ex·cise¹ /'eksaɪz/ *n* [U] government tax on certain goods manufactured, sold or used within a country: *the ~ on beer/tobacco;* '~ *duties; the Commissioners of Customs and E~.* '~·man /-mən/ (*pl* -men), '*E~ Officer,* officer collecting ~ and preventing breaking of ~ laws.

ex·cise² /ɪk'saɪz/ *vt* [VP6A] (formal) remove by, or as if by, cutting (a part of the body, a passage from a book, etc). ex·cision /ɪk'sɪʒn/ *n* [U] excising or being ~d; [C] sth ~d.

ex·cite /ɪk'saɪt/ *vt* [VP6A,14,17] 1 ~ (to), stir up the feelings of; cause (sb) to feel strongly: *Don't ~ yourself!* Keep calm! *Everybody was ~d by the news of the victory. It's nothing to get ~d about. Agitators were exciting the people to rebellion/to rebel against their rulers.* 2 ~ (in sb), get (a feeling) in motion; rouse; bring about: ~ *admiration/ envy/affection in an audience;* ~ *a riot.* 3 cause (a bodily organ) to be active: *drugs that ~ the nerves.* ex·cit·able /ɪk'saɪtəbl/ *adj* easily ~d. ex·cit·abil-ity /ɪk,saɪtə'bɪlətɪ/ *n* quality of being excitable. ex-cit·ed·ly *adv* in an ~d manner.

ex·cite·ment /ɪk'saɪtmənt/ *n* 1 [U] state of being excited: *news that caused great ~; jumping about in ~.* 2 [C] that excites; exciting incident, etc· *He kept calm amid all these ~s.*

ex·claim /ɪk'skleɪm/ *vt,vi* [VP9,2A] cry out suddenly and loudly from pain, anger, surprise, etc: '*What!' he ~ed, 'Are you leaving without me?'*

ex·cla·mation /,eksklə'meɪʃn/ *n* 1 [U] exclaiming: '~ *mark,* the mark (!). ⇨ App 9. 2 [C] sudden short cry, expressing surprise, pain, etc. '*Oh!' 'Look out!', and 'Hurrah!' are ~s.*

ex·clama·tory /ɪk'sklæmətrɪ US: -tɔːrɪ/ *adj* using, containing, in the nature of, an exclamation: *an ~ sentence.*

ex·clude /ɪk'skluːd/ *vt* [VP6A,14] ~ (from), 1 prevent (sb from getting in somewhere): ~ *a person from membership of a society/immigrants from a country.* 2 prevent (the chance of sth arising): ~ *all possibility of doubt;* leave out of account, ignore as irrelevant: *We can ~ (from the reckoning) the possibility that the money won't arrive.* ex·clu·sion /ɪk'skluːʒn/ *n* [U] ~ (from), excluding or being ~d. *to the exclusion of,* so as to ~.

ex·clus·ive /ɪk'skluːsɪv/ *adj* 1 (of a person) not willing to mix with others (esp those considered to be inferior in social position, education, etc). 2 (of a group or society) not readily admitting new members: *He moves in ~ social circles and belongs to the most ~ clubs.* 3 (of a shop, goods sold in it, etc) of the sort not to be found elsewhere; uncommon. 4 reserved to the person(s) concerned; ~ *privileges; have ~ rights/an ~ agency for the sale of Ford cars in a town; an ~ story/interview,* eg given to only one newspaper. 5 ~ of, not including: *The ship had a crew of 57 ~ of officers.* 6 excluding all but what is mentioned: *Dictionary-making has not been his ~ employment.* ~·ly *adv*

ex·cogi·tate /eks'kɒdʒɪteɪt/ *vt* [VP6A] (formal or hum) think out (a plan). ex·cogi·ta·tion /,eks,kɒdʒɪ'teɪʃn/ *n*

ex·com·muni·cate /,ekskə'mjuːnɪkeɪt/ *vt* [VP6A] exclude (as a punishment) from the privileges of a member of the Christian Church, eg marriage or burial in church, Holy Communion. ex·com·muni·ca·tion /,ekskə,mjuː·nɪ'keɪʃn/ *n* [U] excommunicating or being ~d; [C] instance of this; official statement announcing this.

ex·cori·ate /ɪk'skɔːrɪeɪt/ *vt* [VP6A] (formal) strip, peel off (skin); (fig) criticize severely. ex·cori-ation /ɪk,skɔːrɪ'eɪʃn/ *n*

excre·ment /'ekskrəmənt/ *n* [U] solid waste matter discharged from the bowels.

ex·cres·cence /ɪk'skresns/ *n* [C] abnormal (usu ugly and useless) outgrowth on an animal or vegetable body.

ex·creta /ɪk'skriːtə/ *n pl* waste (excrement, urine, sweat) expelled from the body.

ex·crete /ɪk'skriːt/ *vt* [VP6A] (of an animal or plant) discharge from the system, eg waste matter, sweat. ex·cre·tion /ɪk'skriːʃn/ *n* [U] excreting; [C,U] that which is ~d.

ex·cru·ciat·ing /ɪk'skruːʃɪeɪtɪŋ/ *adj* (of pain, bodily or mental) acute. ~·ly *adv*

ex·cul·pate /'ekskʌlpeɪt/ *vt* [VP6A,14] ~ (from), (formal) free from blame; say that (sb) is not guilty of wrongdoing: ~ *a person from a charge.*

ex·cur·sion /ɪk'skɜːʃn US: -ʒn/ *n* [C] short journey, esp one made by a number of people together for pleasure: *go on/make an ~ to the mountains; an* '~ *train; an* '~ *ticket,* one issued at a reduced fare. ~·ist *n* person who makes an ~.

ex·cuse¹ /ɪk'skjuːs/ *n* [C] reason given (true or invented) to explain or defend one's conduct; apology: *He's always making ~s for being late. He had numerous ~s to offer for being late. Please give them my ~s.* **2 in ~ of**: *Where the law is concerned, you cannot plead ignorance in ~ of your conduct.* **without ~**: *Those who are absent without (good) ~ will be dismissed.*

ex·cuse² /ɪk'skjuːz/ *vt* **1** [VP6A,C,14,19C] **~ (for)**, give reasons showing, or intended to show, that a person or his action is not to be blamed; overlook a fault, etc: *~ sb's conduct. Nothing can ~ such rudeness. Please ~ my coming late/~ me for being late/~ my late arrival. E~ my interrupting you.* **2** [VP14,6A] **~ (from)**, set (sb) free from a duty, requirement, punishment, etc: *He was ~d (from) attendance at the lecture. They may be ~d from complying with this regulation.* **3** E~ *me*, used as an apology when one interrupts, disagrees, has to behave impolitely or disapprove: *E~ me, but I don't think that statement is quite true.* ⇨ pardon(2); sorry(2). **ex·cus·able** /ɪk'skjuːzəbl/ *adj* that may be ~d: *an excusable mistake.* **ex·cus·ably** /-əblɪ/ *adv*

ex·di·rec·tory /ˌeks dɪ'rektərɪ/ *adj* (of a telephone number) not listed in the telephone directory (for reasons of security, privacy, etc).

ex·ecrable /'eksɪkrəbl/ *adj* very bad; deserving hate: *~ manners/weather.*

ex·ecrate /'eksɪkreɪt/ *vt* [VP6A] express or feel hatred of. **ex·ecra·tion** /ˌeksɪ'kreɪʃn/ *n*

ex·ecute /'eksɪkjuːt/ [VP6A] *vt* **1** carry out (what one is asked or told to do): *~ sb's commands; ~ a plan/a piece of work/a purpose.* **2** (legal) give effect to: *~ a will.* **3** (legal) make legally binding: *~ a legal document*, by having it signed, witnessed, sealed and delivered. **4** carry out punishment by death on (sb): *~ a murderer.* **5** perform on the stage, at a concert, etc: *The piano sonata was badly ~d.* **execu·tant** /ɪg'zekjʊtənt/ *n* person who ~s a design, etc; person who performs music, etc.

ex·ecu·tion /ˌeksɪ'kjuːʃn/ *n* **1** [U] the carrying out or performance of a piece of work, design, etc: *His intention was good, but his ~ of the plan was unsatisfactory.* **put/carry sth into ~**, complete it, do what was planned. **2** [U] skill in performing, eg music: *a pianist with marvellous ~.* **3** [U] (of weapons) destructive effect: *The artillery did great ~*, killed and wounded many. **4** [U] infliction of punishment by death; [C] instance of this: *~ by hanging; five ~s last year.* **~er** *n* public official who ~s criminals.

execu·tive /ɪg'zekjʊtɪv/ *adj* **1** having to do with managing or executing(1): *~ duties; ~ ability.* **2** having authority to carry out decisions, laws, decrees, etc: *the ~ branch of the government; the ~ head of the State*, eg the President of the US. □ *n* **1** **the ~**, the ~ branch of a government. ⇨ administration, judiciary, legislature. **2** (in the Civil Service) person who carries out what has been planned or decided. **3** person or group in a business or commercial organization with administrative or managerial powers.

execu·tor /ɪg'zekjʊtə(r)/ *n* person who is appointed by the maker of a will to carry out the terms of the will. **execu·trix** /ɪg'zekjʊtrɪks/ *n* woman ~.

exe·gesis /ˌeksɪ'dʒiːsɪs/ *n* [U] explanation and interpretation (of a written work).

exemp·lary /ɪg'zemplərɪ/ *adj* serving as an example or a warning: *~ conduct/punishment.*

exemp·lify /ɪg'zemplɪfaɪ/ *vt* (*pt,pp* -fied) [VP6A] illustrate by example; be an example of. **exemp·lifi·ca·tion** /ˌɪgˌzemplɪfɪ'keɪʃn/ *n* [U] ~ing; [C] example.

exempt /ɪg'zempt/ *vt* [VP6A,14] **~ (from)**, free (from an obligation): *Poor eyesight will ~ you from military service.* □ *adj* **~ (from)**,not liable; free: *~ from tax.* **exemp·tion** /ɪg'zempʃn/ *n* [U] **~ (from)**, ~ing or being ~ed; [C] instance of this.

ex·er·cise¹ /'eksəsaɪz/ *n* **1** [U] employment or practice (of mental or physical powers, of rights): *Walking, running, rowing and horse-riding are all healthy forms of ~. The doctor advised her to take more ~. E~ of the mental faculties is as important as bodily ~. The ~ of patience is essential in diplomatic negotiations. His tales showed considerable ~ of the imagination.* **2** [C] activity, drill, etc designed for bodily, mental or spiritual training: *vocal/gymnastic/deep-breathing, etc ~s; ~s for the harp/flute, etc; five-finger ~s for the piano; ~s in logic/English composition; spiritual ~s*, eg prayer. *An ~ in clear thinking would benefit many public speakers.* **3** (*pl*) series of movements for training troops, crews of warships, etc: *military ~s; The third cruiser squadron has left for ~s in the North Sea.* **4** (*pl*, US) ceremonies: *graduation ~s; opening ~s*, eg speeches at the start of a conference.

ex·er·cise² /'eksəsaɪz/ *vt,vi* **1** [VP6A,15A,2A] take exercise; give exercise to, ⇨ exercise¹(1): *Horses get fat and lazy if they are not ~d. He ~s himself in fencing. You don't ~ enough.* **2** [VP6A] employ; make use of: *~ patience; ~ authority over sb; ~ one's rights.* **3** [VP6A] (usu passive) perplex; trouble; worry the mind of: *The problem that is exercising our minds.... I am very much ~d about the future/about the education of my son.*

exert /ɪg'zɜːt/ *vt* [VP6A,14,16A] **1** **~ (on/upon)**, put forth; bring into use: *~ all one's strength/influence, etc (to do sth); ~ pressure on sb.* **2** **~ oneself**, make an effort: *~ oneself to arrive early; ~ yourself on my behalf.*

exer·tion /ɪg'zɜːʃn US: -ʒn/ *n* [U] exerting; [C] instance of this: *E~ of authority is not always wise; persuasion may be better. He failed to lift the rock in spite of all his ~s. Now that I am 90, I am unequal to the ~s of travelling.*

ex·eunt /'eksɪənt/ *vi* (Lat) (as a stage direction) *~ Antony and Cleopatra*, they leave the stage. ⇨ exit.

ex gratia /ˌeks 'greɪʃə/ *n* (Lat) **~ payment**, payment not legally binding but for which some moral obligation is felt.

ex·hale /eks'heɪl/ *vt,vi* [VP6A,2A] breathe out; give off gas, vapour; be given off (as gas or vapour): *~ air from the lungs.* **ex·ha·la·tion** /ˌekshə'leɪʃn/ *n* **1** [C] act of exhaling. **2** [U,C] sth ~d.

ex·haust¹ /ɪg'zɔːst/ *n* [C,U] (outlet, in an engine or machine, for) steam, vapour, etc that has done its work. **'~-pipe** *n* pipe for this. ⇨ the illus at motor.

ex·haust² /ɪg'zɔːst/ *vt* [VP6A] **1** use up completely: *~ one's patience/strength; ~ oneself by hard work; feeling ~ed*, tired out. **2** make empty: *~ a well; ~ a tube of air.* **3** say, find out, all there is to say about (sth): *~ a subject.*

ex·haus·tion /ɪg'zɔːstʃən/ *n* [U] exhausting or being exhausted; total loss of strength: *They were in a state of ~ after climbing the mountain.*

ex·haus·tive /ɪg'zɔːstɪv/ *adj* thorough; complete: *an ~ inquiry.* **~·ly** *adv*

ex·hibit¹ /ɪg'zɪbɪt/ *n* [C] **1** object or collection of objects, shown publicly, eg in a museum: *Do not* *touch the* ~*s.* **2** document, object, etc produced in a law court and referred to in evidence, eg a weapon said to have been used by the accused person. **3** (US) exhibition(1).

ex·hibit² /ɪgˈzɪbɪt/ *vt* [VP6A] **1** show publicly (for pleasure, for sale, in a competition, etc): ~ *paintings in an art gallery/flowers at a flower show;* [VP2A]: *Mr X* ~*s in several galleries.* **2** give clear evidence of (a quality): *The girls* ~*ed great powers of endurance during the climb.* **ex·hibi·tor** /-tə(r)/ *n* person who ~s at a show of pictures, a flower show, etc.

ex·hi·bi·tion /ˌeksɪˈbɪʃn/ *n* **1** [C] collection of things shown publicly (eg of works of art); display of commercial or industrial goods for advertisement; public display of animals, plants, flowers, etc (often shown in competition, for prizes, and colloq called a *show*). **2** (*sing* only) act of showing: *an* ~ *of bad manners; an opportunity for the* ~ *of one's knowledge.* **make an** ~ **of oneself,** behave in public so that one receives contempt. **3** (GB) money allowance to a student from school or college funds for a number of years. ~**er** *n* student to whom an ~(3) is granted. ~**ism** /-ɪzəm/ *n* [U] tendency towards extravagant behaviour designed to attract attention to oneself. ~**ist** /-ɪst/ *n* person given to ~ism.

ex·hil·ar·ate /ɪgˈzɪləreɪt/ *vt* [VP6A] (usu passive) fill with high spirits; make lively or glad: *exhilarating news.* **ex·hil·ar·ation** /ɪgˌzɪləˈreɪʃn/ *n*

exhort /ɪgˈzɔːt/ *vt* [VP6A,14,17] ~ *sb to sth/to do sth,* (formal) urge, advise earnestly: ~ *sb to do good/to work harder;* ~ *one's listeners to action.* **ex·hor·ta·tion** /ˌeksɔːˈteɪʃn/ *n* [U] ~ing; [C] earnest request, speech etc that ~s sb.

exhume /eksˈhjuːm *US:* ɪgˈzuːm/ *vt* [VP6A] take out (a dead body) from the earth (for examination). **exhum·ation** /ˌekshjuːˈmeɪʃn/ *n* [U] exhuming or being ~d; [C] instance of this.

exi·gency /ˈeksɪdʒənsɪ/ *n* (*pl* -cies) [C] condition of great need; emergency: *measures to meet the exigencies of this difficult period.* **exi·gent** /-dʒənt/ *adj* **1** urgent; pressing. **2** exacting.

exigu·ous /egˈzɪgjʊəs/ *adj* (formal) scanty: *an* ~ *diet.*

exile /ˈeksaɪl/ *n* **1** [U] being sent away from one's country or home, esp as a punishment: *be/live in* ~; *go/be sent into* ~; *a place of* ~; [C] instance of this: *after an* ~ *of ten years.* **2** [C] person who is sent away in this way. □ *vt* [VP6A,15A] send (sb) into ~: ~ *sb from his country;* ~*d for life.*

exist /ɪgˈzɪst/ *vi* **1** [VP2A,C] be; have being; be real: *The idea* ~*s only in the minds of poets. Do you believe that fairies* ~, *that there really are fairies? Does life* ~ *on Mars?* **2** [VP2A,C,3A] continue living: *We cannot* ~ *without food and water. She* ~*s on very little. How do they* ~ *in such wretched conditions?* ~**ence** /-əns/ *n* **1** [U] the state of ~ing: *When did this world come into* ~*ence? Do you believe in the* ~*ence of ghosts? This is the oldest Hebrew manuscript in* ~*ence.* **2 an** ~*ence,* manner of living: *lead a happy* ~*ence.* ~**ent** /-ənt/ *adj* ~ing; actual.

exis·ten·tial·ism /ˌegzɪˈstenʃəlɪzəm/ *n* doctrine (deriving from Kierkegaard /ˈkɪəkəgɑːd/ (1813—55), the Danish philosopher, and popularized by Sartre /ˈsɑːtrə/ (born 1905), the French writer and philosopher) that man is a unique and isolated individual in an indifferent or hostile universe, responsible for his own actions and free to choose his destiny.

exit /ˈeksɪt/ *n* **1** departure of an actor from the stage: *make one's* ~, go out or away. **2** way out, eg from a theatre or cinema. □ (as a stage direction) *E*~ *Macbeth,* Macbeth goes off the stage. ⇨ exeunt.

ex·odus /ˈeksədəs/ *n* [C] (*sing* only) going out or away of many people: *the* ~ *of people to the sea and the mountains for the summer holidays.* **the E**~, the ~ of the Israelites from Egypt, in about 1300BC.

ex officio /ˌeks əˈfɪʃɪəʊ/ *adv, adj* (Lat) because of one's office or position: *an* ~ *member of the committee; present at the meeting* ~.

exon·er·ate /ɪgˈzɒnəreɪt/ *vt* [VP6A,14] ~ *sb (from),* free, clear: ~ *sb from blame/ responsibility.* **exon·er·ation** /ɪgˌzɒnəˈreɪʃn/ *n*

exor·bi·tant /ɪgˈzɔːbɪtənt/ *adj* (of a price, charge or demand) much too high or great. ~**·ly** *adv* **exor·bi·tance** /-təns/ *n*

ex·or·cize /ˈeksɔːsaɪz/ *vt* [VP6A,14] ~ *(sth from)/(sb of),* drive out (an evil spirit) by prayers or magic.

exotic /ɪgˈzɒtɪk/ *adj* **1** (of plants, fashions, words, ideas) introduced from another country. **2** foreign or unusual in style; striking or pleasing because colourful, unusual: ~ *birds.*

ex·pand /ɪkˈspænd/ *vt,vi* [VP6A,14,2A,C] ~ *(in/ into),* **1** make or become larger: *Metals* ~ *when they are heated.* ⇨ contract³(1). *A tyre* ~*s when you pump air into it.* ⇨ shrink. *The river* ~*s* (= broadens) *and forms a lake. The small pocket dictionary was* ~*ed into a larger volume. Our foreign trade has* ~*ed during recent years.* **2** unfold or spread out: *His face* ~*ed in a smile of welcome. The petals of many flowers* ~ *in the sunshine.* **3** (of a person) become good-humoured or genial.

ex·panse /ɪkˈspæns/ *n* [C] wide and open area: *the broad* ~ *of the Pacific; the blue* ~ *of the sky; a broad* ~ *of brow,* eg of a man with a high forehead and bald head.

ex·pan·sion /ɪkˈspænʃn/ *n* [U] expanding or being expanded(1): ~ *of the currency,* by putting more banknotes into circulation; ~ *of territory,* eg by winning new territory; *the* ~ *of gases when heated.*

ex·pan·sive /ɪkˈspænsɪv/ *adj* **1** able, tending, to expand. **2** (of persons, speech) unreserved, effusive. ~**·ly** *adv* ~**·ness** *n*

ex·patiate /ɪkˈspeɪʃɪeɪt/ *vi* [VP3A] ~ *upon,* (formal) write or speak at great length, in detail, about.

ex·patri·ate /eksˈpætrɪət *US:* -ˈpeɪt-/ *n* person living outside his own country: *American* ~*s in Paris;* (attrib) ~ *Americans.* □ *vt* /-rɪeɪt/ [VP6A] ~ *oneself,* leave one's own country to live abroad; renounce one's citizenship.

ex·pect /ɪkˈspekt/ *vt* [VP6A,17,7,9,14] think or believe that sth will happen or come, that sb will come; wish for and feel confident that one will receive: *We* ~*ed you yesterday. We were* ~*ing a letter from her. I* ~ *to be/*~ *that I shall be back on Sunday. You would* ~ *there to be/that there would be strong disagreement about this. You can't learn a foreign language in a week; it's not to be* ~*ed. You are* ~*ing too much of her. 'Will he be late?'—'I* ~ *so.' 'Will he need help?'—'No, I don't* ~ *so'* (or) *'No, I* ~ *not.' They* ~ (= require) *me to work on Saturdays. I* ~ (= require) *you to be punctual. 'Who has eaten all the cake?'—'Oh, I* ~ (colloq = suppose) *it was Tom.* ~**·ancy** /-ənsɪ/ *n* the state of ~ing: *with a look/an* *air of* ~*ancy; life* ~*ancy.* ~**·ant** /-ənt/ *adj* ~ing: *an* ~**ant** *mother,* woman who is pregnant. ~**·ant·ly** *adv* ~**ed** *adj* that is ~ed: *an* ~*ed reply;* ~*ed objections.*

ex·pec·ta·tion /ˌekspek'teɪʃn/ *n* **1** [U] expecting; awaiting: *He ate a light lunch in* ~ *of a good dinner.* **2** (often *pl*) thing that is expected. **beyond** ~, in a way greater or better than was expected. **contrary to** ~**(s)**, in a way different from what was expected. **fall short of/not come up to one's** ~**s**, be less good than what was expected. **3** (*pl*) future prospects, esp sth to be inherited: *a young man with great* ~*s,* eg one who has a millionaire uncle who has promised to leave him his wealth. **4** ~ **of life,** years a person is expected to live: *A life assurance company can tell you the* ~ *of life of a man who is 40 years old.*

ex·pec·tor·ate /ɪk'spektəreɪt/ *vt, vi* [VP6A,2A] (formal) spit; send out (phlegm from the throat, blood from the lungs) by coughing. **ex·pec·tor·ant** /-rənt/ *n* medicine promoting expectorating.

ex·pedi·ent /ɪk'spiːdɪənt/ *adj* (usu pred) likely to be useful or helpful for a purpose; advantageous though contrary to principle: *In times of war governments do things because they are* ~. *Do what you think* ~. □ *n* [C] ~ plan, action, device, etc. ~**ly** *adv* **ex·pedi·ence** /-əns/, **ex·pedi·ency** /-ənsɪ/ *n* [U] suitability for a purpose; being ~; self-interest: *act from expediency, not from principle.*

ex·pedite /'ekspɪdaɪt/ *vt* [VP6A] (formal) help the progress of; speed up (business, etc).

ex·pedi·tion /ˌekspɪ'dɪʃn/ *n* **1** [C] (men, ships, etc making a) journey or voyage for a definite purpose: *a hunting* ~; *go/send a party of men on an* ~ *to the Antarctic; members of the Mount Everest* ~. **2** [U] (formal) promptness; speed. ~**·ary** /-ʃənərɪ US: -nerɪ/ *adj* of, making up, an ~: *an* ~*ary force,* eg an army sent to take part in a war abroad. **ex·pedi·tious** /ˌekspɪ'dɪʃəs/ *adj* (formal) acting quickly; prompt and efficient. ~**·ly** *adv*

ex·pel /ɪk'spel/ *vt* (-ll-) [VP6A,14] ~ **(from),** send out or away by force: ~ *the enemy from a town;* ~ *a boy from school,* as a punishment.

ex·pend /ɪk'spend/ *vt* [VP6A,14] ~ *sth* **(on/upon** *sth/in doing sth),* **1** spend: ~ *all one's capital on equipment;* ~ *time and care in doing sth.* **2** use up: *They had* ~*ed all their ammunition.* ~**·able** /-əbl/ *adj* that may be ~ed, esp that may be sacrificed to achieve a purpose: *The general considered that these troops were* ~*able.*

ex·pen·di·ture /ɪk'spendɪtʃə(r)/ *n* **1** [U] spending or using: *the* ~ *of money on armaments.* **2** [C,U] amount expended: *an* ~ *of £500 on new furniture. Limit your* ~*(s) to what is essential.*

ex·pense /ɪk'spens/ *n* **1** [U] spending of money; cost: *Most children in Great Britain are educated at the public* ~. *I want the best you can supply; you need spare no* ~, you need not try to economize. **at the** ~ **of,** with the sacrifice of: *He became a brilliant scholar, but only at the* ~ *of his health.* **at his/her/my, etc** ~, (a) with him, her, me, etc paying: *We were all entertained at the director's* ~. (b) (fig) bringing discredit, ridicule or contempt on him, her, me, etc: *We had a good laugh at his* ~, We laughed at him because he had done sth ridiculous, been deceived, etc. **go to/put sb to the** ~ **of,** spend/cause him to spend money on: *It's foolish to go to the* ~ *of taking music lessons if you never practise. I don't want to put you to the* ~ *of*

providing my meals. '~ **account,** record of expenses incurred and either paid out of money supplied by, or to be refunded by, the employer, eg of a business man for travel, entertainment, etc. **2** (usu *pl*) money used or needed for sth: *travelling* ~*s. Illness, holidays and other* ~*s reduced his bank balance to almost nothing.*

ex·pens·ive /ɪk'spensɪv/ *adj* causing expense; high priced: *an* ~ *education; too* ~ *for me to buy.* ~**·ly** *adv*

ex·peri·ence /ɪk'spɪərɪəns/ *n* **1** [U] process of gaining knowledge or skill by doing and seeing things; knowledge or skill so gained: *We all learn by* ~. *Has he had much* ~ *in/of work of this sort? He hasn't had enough* ~ *for the job.* **2** [C] event, activity, which has given one ~(1); event that affects one in some way: *an unpleasant/trying/unusual* ~. □ *vt* [VP6A] have ~ of; feel; meet with: ~ *pleasure/pain/difficulty/great hardships.* **ex·peri·enced** *adj* having ~; having knowledge or skill as the result of ~: *an* ~*d nurse/lover.*

ex·peri·ment /ɪk'sperɪmənt/ *n* [C] test or trial carried out carefully in order to study what happens and gain new knowledge: *perform/carry out an* ~ *in chemistry;* [U] *learn sth by* ~. □ *vi* [VP2A,C,3A] make ~s: ~ *with new methods;* ~ *upon dogs.* **ex·peri·men·ta·tion** /ɪkˌsperɪmen'teɪʃn/ *n* [U] ~ing. **ex·peri·men·tal** /ɪkˌsperɪ'mentl/ *adj* of, used for, based on, experiments: ~ *methods; an* ~ *farm.* ~**ly** /-təlɪ/ *adv*

ex·pert /'ekspɜːt/ *n* person with special knowledge, skill or training: *an agricultural* ~; *an* ~ *in economics; get the advice of the* ~*s.* □ *adj* trained by practice; skilful: *according to* ~ *advice/opinions; men who are* ~ *at driving racing cars.* ~**·ly** *adv* ~**·ness** *n*

ex·pert·ise /ˌekspɜː'tiːz/ *n* [U] **1** (comm) expert appraisal; valuation. **2** expert's report. **3** expert knowledge and skill. ⇨ *know-how* at *know.*

ex·pi·ate /'ekspɪeɪt/ *vt* [VP6A] make amends for, submit to punishment for (wrongdoing): ~ *sin/a crime.* **ex·pi·ation** /ˌekspɪ'eɪʃn/ *n* [U].

ex·pir·ation /ˌekspɪ'reɪʃn/ *n* [U] **1** ~ **(of),** expiring, ending, esp of a period of time: *at the* ~ *of the lease.* **2** (formal) breathing out (of air).

ex·pire /ɪk'spaɪə(r)/ *vi* [VP2A] **1** (of a period of time) come to an end: *His term of office as President* ~*s next year. When does your driving licence* ~? **2** (liter) die.

ex·piry /ɪk'spaɪərɪ/ *n* (*pl* -ries) ~ **(of),** expiring, ending, esp of a period of time of a contract or agreement: *the* ~ *of a driving licence.*

ex·plain /ɪk'spleɪn/ *vt* **1** [VP6A,9,8,10,14] ~ *sth* **(to sb),** make plain or clear; show the meaning of: *A dictionary tries to* ~ *the meanings of words. Please* ~ *this problem to me. Please* ~ *to me what this means. He* ~*ed that he had been delayed by the weather. Please* ~ *yourself,* make your meaning clear. ⇨ **2** below. **2** [VP6A,15B] account for: *Can you* ~ *his behaviour? That* ~*s his absence. Please* ~ *yourself,* give reasons for your conduct. ~ *sth away,* show why one should not be blamed for a fault, mistake, etc: *You will find it difficult to* ~ *away your use of such offensive language.*

ex·pla·na·tion /ˌeksplə'neɪʃn/ *n* **1** [U] (process of) explaining: *Not much* ~ *will be needed. I had better say a few words by way of* ~. *Had he anything to say in* ~ *of his conduct?* **2** [C] statement, fact, circumstances, etc that explains: *an* ~ *of his conduct/of a mystery; after repeated* ~*s.*

ex·plana·tory /ɪkˈsplænətrɪ US: -tɔːrɪ/ adj serving or intended to explain.

ex·ple·tive /ɪkˈspliːtɪv US: ˈeksplətɪv/ n [C] violent (often meaningless) exclamation, eg 'My goodness', or an oath such as 'Damn'.

ex·plic·able /ekˈsplɪkəbl/ adj (formal) that can be explained.

ex·pli·cate /ˈeksplɪkeɪt/ vt [VP6A] (formal) explain and analyse in detail.

ex·plicit /ɪkˈsplɪsɪt/ adj (of a statement, etc) clearly and fully expressed; definite: He was quite ∼ about the matter, left no doubt about what he meant. ∼·ly adv ∼·ness n

ex·plode /ɪkˈspləʊd/ vt,vi 1 [VP6A,2A] (cause to) burst with a loud noise: ∼ a charge of gunpowder/a bomb. When the boiler ∼d many people were hurt by the steam. The shell ∼d in the barrel of the gun. 2 [VP2A,C] (of feelings) burst out; (of persons) show violent emotion: At last his anger ∼d. He ∼d with rage/jealousy. 3 [VP6A] destroy, expose (an idea, a theory, etc); show the falsity of: ∼ a superstition: an ∼d idea.

ex·ploit¹ /ˈeksplɔɪt/ n [C] bold or adventurous act; brilliant achievement.

ex·ploit² /ɪkˈsplɔɪt/ vt [VP6A] 1 use, work or develop (eg mines, waterpower, other natural resources of a country). 2 use selfishly, or for one's own profit: ∼ child labour. **ex·ploi·ta·tion** /ˌeksplɔɪˈteɪʃn/ n [U] ∼ing or being ∼ed (both senses): the ∼ation of a new country.

ex·plore /ɪkˈsplɔː(r)/ vt [VP6A] 1 travel into or through (a country, etc) for the purpose of learning about it: ∼ the Arctic regions. Columbus discovered America but did not ∼ the new continent. 2 examine thoroughly in order to test, learn about: ∼ possibilities/problems. **ex·plorer** /-rə(r)/ n person who ∼s. **ex·plo·ra·tion** /ˌekspləˈreɪʃn/ n [U] exploring: the exploration of the ocean depths; [C] instance of this. **ex·plora·tory** /ɪkˈsplɒrətrɪ US: -tɔːrɪ/ adj for the purpose of exploring.

ex·plosion /ɪkˈspləʊʒn/ n [C] 1 exploding; (loud noise caused by) sudden and violent bursting: a bomb ∼. The ∼ was heard a mile away. 2 ∼ (of), outburst or outbreak (of anger, laughter, etc). 3 great and sudden increase: the population ∼ after the war.

ex·plos·ive /ɪkˈspləʊsɪv/ n, adj (substance) tending to or likely to explode: a shell filled with high ∼. Dynamite and gun-cotton are ∼s. The old man has an ∼ temper, often explodes with anger, etc. That's an ∼ issue, one likely to inflame feeling. ∼·ly adv

expo /ˈekspəʊ/ n international exposition(2).

ex·po·nent /ɪkˈspəʊnənt/ n ∼ (of), 1 person or thing that explains or interprets, or is a representative or example: Huxley was an ∼ of Darwin's theory of evolution. 2 (alg) symbol that indicates what power of a factor is to be taken: In a³, the figure 3 is the ∼; in xⁿ, the symbol ⁿ is the ∼.

ex·port¹ /ˈekspɔːt/ n 1 [U] (business of) exporting: a ban on the ∼ of gold; (attrib) the '∼ trade; '∼ duties. 2 [C] sth exported: Last year ∼s exceeded imports in value. What are the chief ∼s of your country?

ex·port² /ɪkˈspɔːt/ vt [VP6A] send (goods) to another country for purposes of trade: ∼ cotton goods. ∼er n trader who ∼s goods. ∼·able /-əbl/ adj that can be ∼ed. **ex·por·ta·tion** /ˌekspɔːˈteɪʃn/ n [U] the ∼ing of goods; goods ∼ed.

ex·pose /ɪkˈspəʊz/ vt [VP6A,14,15A] ∼ (to), 1 un-

cover; leave uncovered or unprotected: ∼ soldiers to unnecessary risks/to the enemy's gunfire; ∼d to the wind and rain; be ∼d to ridicule. 2 display: ∼ goods in a shop window. 3 disclose, make known: ∼ a plot/project/plan; reveal the guilt or wrongdoing of; unmask: ∼ a crime/criminal. 4 (photo) allow light to reach (camera film, etc): ∼ 30 metres of cinema film.

ex·posé /ekˈspəʊzeɪ US: ˌekspəˈzeɪ/ n 1 orderly setting out or précis of a body of facts or beliefs. 2 making public of discreditable fact(s).

ex·po·si·tion /ˌekspəˈzɪʃn/ n 1 [U] expounding or explaining; [C] instance of this; explanation or interpretation of a theory, plan, etc. 2 [C] (abbr **expo** /ˈekspəʊ/) exhibition of goods, etc: an industrial ∼.

ex·postu·late /ɪkˈspɒstjʊleɪt/ vi [VP2A,3A] ∼ (with sb) (on/about sth), make a friendly protest; reason or argue. **ex·postu·la·tion** /ɪkˌspɒstjʊˈleɪʃn/ n [C,U] friendly protest(ing): My expostulation(s) had no results.

ex·po·sure /ɪkˈspəʊʒə(r)/ n 1 [U] exposing or being exposed (all senses): The climbers lost their way on the mountain and died of ∼. E∼ of the body to strong sunlight may be harmful. The ∼ of the plot against the President probably saved his life. 2 [C] instance of exposing or being exposed (all senses): As a result of these ∼s the government took strong measures against bribery and corruption. How many ∼s have you got left? How many pictures remain on the (camera) film? An ∼ of one-hundredth of a second will be enough. '∼ meter n (photo) device to measure illumination and to indicate correct duration of ∼. ⇨ illus at camera.

ex·pound /ɪkˈspaʊnd/ vt [VP6A,14] ∼ (to), explain, make clear, by giving details: ∼ a theory/ one's views (to sb).

ex·press¹ /ɪkˈspres/ adj 1 clearly and definitely stated, not suggested or implied: You cannot ignore such an ∼ command. It was his ∼ wish that you should not wait for him. 2 going, sent, quickly; designed for high speed: an '∼ train; ∼ delivery, by special postal messenger; an ∼ letter/ messenger. '∼way n (US) major road for fast travel. ⇨ (GB) motorway. □ adv by ∼ delivery; by ∼ train: send a parcel ∼; travel ∼. ∼·ly adv 1 plainly; definitely: You were ∼ly forbidden to touch my papers. 2 specially; on purpose: a dictionary ∼ly compiled for foreign students of English.

ex·press² /ɪkˈspres/ n 1 very fast train: the 8.00am ∼ to Edinburgh. 2 (US) company that undertakes to deliver goods fast and safely. 3 [U] service rendered by the post office, railways, road services, etc for carrying goods quickly: send goods by ∼.

ex·press³ /ɪkˈspres/ vt 1 [VP6A,10,15A] make known, show by words, looks, actions: I find it difficult to ∼ my meaning. A smile ∼ed her joy at the good news. I cannot easily ∼ (to you) how grateful I am for your help. ∼ oneself, communicate one's thoughts or feelings through words, gestures, etc: He is still unable to ∼ himself in English. He ∼ed himself strongly (= spoke in a forceful way) on the subject. 2 [VP6A] send a letter, goods, etc fast by special delivery. 3 [VP6A,14] ∼ (from/out of), (formal) press or squeeze out juices/oil: juice ∼ed (pressed is more usu) from grapes.

ex·press·ion /ɪkˈspreʃn/ n 1 [U] process of expressing(1): give ∼ to one's gratitude, say or show how grateful one is; read (aloud) with ∼, in a way that shows feeling for the meaning; [C] instance of this (esp a look on sb's face): *There was an ~ of discontent on her face*, a discontented look. **beyond/past** ~, in a manner that cannot be expressed: *The scenery was beautiful beyond ~*, indescribably beautiful. **find ~ in**, be expressed by means of: *Her feelings at last found ~ in tears.* 2 [C] word or phrase: *'Shut up'* (= Stop talking) *is not a polite ~*. **Slang** ~s should be avoided in an *essay.* 3 [C] (maths) group of symbols expressing a quantity, eg $3xy^2$. **~·less** *adj* without ~(1): *in an ~less voice; an ~less face.*

ex·press·ion·ism /ɪkˈspreʃənɪzəm/ n [U] (in painting, music, etc) the symbolic or stylised expression of emotional experience. **ex·press·ion·ist** /-ɪst/ n

ex·press·ive /ɪkˈspresɪv/ adj ~ (of), serving to express: *looks ~ of despair; a cry ~ of pain; an ~ smile.* **~·ly** adv

ex·pro·pri·ate /eksˈprəʊprɪeɪt/ vt [VP6A,14] ~ (from), take away (property); dispossess (sb of an estate, etc). **ex·pro·pri·ation** /ˌeksˌprəʊprɪˈeɪʃn/ n [U].

ex·pul·sion /ɪkˈspʌlʃn/ n [U] ~ (from), expelling or being expelled; [C] instance of this: *the ~ of a student from college; an '~ order*, official order expelling a person from a country.

ex·punge /ɪkˈspʌndʒ/ vt [VP6A,14] ~ (from), (formal) wipe or rub out words, names, etc from a book, etc.

ex·pur·gate /ˈekspəgeɪt/ vt [VP6A] take out from (a book, etc what are considered to be) improper or objectionable parts: *an ~d edition of a novel.* **ex·pur·ga·tion** /ˌekspəˈgeɪʃn/ n

ex·quis·ite /ˈekskwɪzɪt US: ekˈskwɪzɪt/ adj 1 of great excellence; brought to a high state of perfection: ~ *workmanship;* ~ *designs; a piece of ~ lace.* 2 (of pain, pleasure, etc) keenly felt. 3 (of power to feel) keen, delicate: ~ *sensibility.* **~·ly** adv ~·ness n

ex–ser·vice /ˌeks ˈsɜːvɪs/ adj having formerly served in the armed forces. **~·man** /-mən/ n (pl -men) (GB): an ~men's organization.

ex·tant /ekˈstænt US: ˈekstənt/ adj still in existence (esp of documents, etc): *the earliest ~ manuscript of this poem.*

ex·tem·por·ary /ɪkˈstempərərɪ US: -pəreɪrɪ/ adj = extempore. **ex·tem·por·ar·ily** /-rərəlɪ US: ˈrerəlɪ/ adv

ex·tem·pore /ekˈstempərɪ/ adv, adj (spoken or done) without previous thought or preparation: *speak ~*, without notes; *an ~ address.* **ex·tem·por·aneous·(ly)** /ˌekˌstempəˈreɪnɪəs(lɪ)/ adj, adv = ~.

ex·tend /ɪkˈstend/ vt,vi 1 [VP6A] make longer (in space or time); enlarge: ~ *a railway/a fence/a wall/the city boundaries. Can't you ~ your visit for a few days*, stay a few days longer? ~ *credit*, (fin) prolong the time for which credit is given. 2 [VP6A,15A] lay or stretch out the body, a limb or limbs, at full length: ~ *one's arm horizontally;* ~ *one's hand to sb*, shake hands with him. 3 [VP6A,14] ~ *sth (to sb)*, offer, grant, accord: ~ *hospitality/an invitation/a greeting/a warm welcome to sb;* ~ *help.* 4 [VP2B,C] (of space, land, etc) reach, stretch: *a road that ~s for miles and miles. My garden ~s as far as the river.* 5 [VP6A,15A] cause to reach or stretch: ~ *a cable between two posts.* 6 [VP6A] (usu passive) tax or use the powers of a person, horse, etc to the utmost: *The horse was fully ~ed.* ⇨ **flat out** at flat²

adv(3).

ex·ten·sion /ɪkˈstenʃn/ n 1 [U] extending or being extended: *the ~ of useful knowledge; University E~*, teaching for, examination of, part-time or extramural students; *the ~ of socialist influence in Africa.* 2 [C] additional part; addition or continuance; enlargement: *an ~ of one's summer holidays; build an ~ to a hospital; get an ~ of time*, eg for paying a debt; *an ~ to a sentence*, (gram) word or words amplifying the subject or predicate; *telephone No 01—629—8494, ~ 15*, ie a line extending from the switchboard to another room or office.

ex·ten·sive /ɪkˈstensɪv/ adj extending far; far-reaching: *an ~ view; ~ repairs/inquiries; a scholar with an ~ knowledge of his subject.* **~·ly** adv

ex·tent /ɪkˈstent/ n [U] 1 ~ (of), length; area; range: *From the roof we were able to see the full ~ of the park. I was amazed at the ~ of his knowledge. They are building a new racing track, six miles in ~.* 2 degree: *to a certain/to some ~*, partly, somewhat; *to such an ~ that...; to what ~; in debt to the ~ of £100.*

ex·tenu·ate /ɪkˈstenjʊeɪt/ vt [VP6A] make (wrongdoing) less serious (by finding an excuse): *Nothing can ~ his base conduct. There are extenuating circumstances in this case.* **ex·tenu·ation** /ɪkˌstenjʊˈeɪʃn/ n 1 [U] extenuating or being ~d: *He pleaded poverty in extenuation of the theft.* 2 [C] sth that ~s; partial excuse.

ex·terior /ɪkˈstɪərɪə(r)/ adj outer; situated on or coming from outside: *the ~ surface of a hollow ball; the ~ features of a building.* ⇨ interior. □ n outside; outward aspect or appearance: *a gentle man with a rough ~.* **~·ize** vt /-raɪz/ = externalize.

ex·ter·mi·nate /ɪkˈstɜːmɪneɪt/ vt [VP6A] make an end of (disease, ideas, people's beliefs); destroy completely. **ex·ter·mi·na·tion** /ɪkˌstɜːmɪˈneɪʃn/ n

ex·ter·nal /ɪkˈstɜːnl/ adj outside; situated on the outside; of or for the outside: ~ *evidence*, obtained from independent sources, not from what is being examined; *alcohol for ~ use*, for use on the skin, not to be drunk; ~ *examination*, one conducted by authorities outside the school, college, etc of the person(s) examined; ~ *examiner*, person (not on the staff of those setting the examination) conducting such an examination. ⇨ internal. □ n (usu pl) ~ circumstances; outward features: *the ~s of religion*, acts and ceremonies (contrasted with inner and spiritual aspects); *judge people by ~s.* **~·ize** /-aɪz/ vt [VP6A] make ~. **~·ly** /ekˈstɜːnəlɪ/ adv

ex·ter·ri·tor·ial /ˌeksˌterɪˈtɔːrɪəl/ adj (eg of ambassadors, etc) free from the jurisdiction of the State in which one resides: ~ *privileges and rights.*

ex·tinct /ɪkˈstɪŋkt/ adj 1 no longer burning; no longer active: *an ~ volcano.* 2 (of feelings, passions) dead. 3 no longer in existence; having died out: *an ~ species; become ~.*

ex·tinc·tion /ɪkˈstɪŋkʃn/ n [U] 1 making, being, becoming, extinct: *a tribe threatened by ~; research that may lead to the ~ of a disease.* 2 act of extinguishing: *the ~ of a fire/of sb's hopes.*

ex·tin·guish /ɪkˈstɪŋgwɪʃ/ vt [VP6A] 1 put out (eg a light, fire). 2 end the existence of (eg hope, love, passion, etc). 3 wipe out (a debt). **~er** n (kinds of) apparatus for discharging a jet of liquid chemicals for ~ing a fire.

ex·tir·pate /ˈekstəpeɪt/ vt [VP6A] (formal) pull up by the roots; destroy utterly: ~ *social evils.* **ex·tir·pa·tion** /ˌekstəˈpeɪʃn/ n [U].

ex·tol /ɪk'stəʊl/ vt (-ll-) [VP6A,15A] praise highly; ~ sb to the skies, greatly; ~ sb's merits; ~ sb as a hero.

ex·tort /ɪk'stɔːt/ vt [VP6A,14] ~ (from), obtain by violence, threats, etc: ~ money from sb. The police used torture to ~ a confession from him. **ex·tor·tion** /ɪk'stɔːʃn/ n [U] ~ing; [C] instance of this. **ex·tor·tion·ate** /ɪk'stɔːʃənət/ adj (of demands, prices) much too great or high. ~·ly adv

extra /'ekstrə/ adj additional; beyond what is usual, expected or arranged for: ~ pay for ~ work; without ~ charge. There were so many people that the company put on ~ buses. □ adv 1 more than usually: an ~ strong box; ~ fine quality. 2 in addition: price £1.30, packing and postage ~. □ n 1 ~ thing; sth for which an ~ charge is made: Her regular school fees are £50 a term; music and dancing are ~s. 2 (cricket) run not scored off the bat. 3 (cinema, TV, etc) person employed and paid (usu by the day) for a minor part, eg in a crowd scene.

ex·tract /ɪk'strækt/ vt [VP6A,14] ~ (from), 1 take or get out (usu with effort or by force): ~ a cork from a bottle; have a tooth ~ed; ~ a bullet from a wound; (fig) ~ money/information from sb, who is unwilling to give it. 2 obtain (juices, etc) by pressing, crushing, boiling, etc: ~ oil from cotton-seed/olives. 3 select and present words, examples, passages, etc (from a book, speech, etc). □ n /'ekstrækt/ 1 [U,C] that which has been ~ed(2) and concentrated: vanilla ~; beef ~; ~ of malt. 2 [C] passage ~ed(3): ~s from a long poem. **ex·trac·tion** /ɪk'strækʃn/ n [U] 1 ~ing or being ~ed(1): the ~ion of a tooth. 2 descent; lineage: Is Mr Mansion of French ~ion?

extra·cur·ric·u·lar /ˌekstrəkə'rɪkjʊlə(r)/ adj outside the regular course of academic work or studies: ~ activities, eg belonging to a dramatic society.

ex·tra·dite /'ekstrədaɪt/ vt [VP6A] 1 give up, hand over (a person) from the State where he is a fugitive to the State where he is alleged to have committed, or has been convicted of, a crime. 2 obtain (such a person) for trial. **ex·tra·di·tion** /ˌekstrə'dɪʃn/ n

extra·ju·dicial /ˌekstrədʒuː'dɪʃl/ adj beyond the authority of a court; outside the (normal) authority of the law.

extra·mari·tal /ˌekstrə'mærɪtl/ adj outside marriage: ~ relations, adultery.

extra·mural /ˌekstrə'mjʊərəl/ adj 1 outside the boundaries (eg of a town). 2 additional to the full-time activities of a university, etc: ~ lectures/ studies/students.

ex·traneous /ɪk'streɪnɪəs/ adj not related (to the object to which it is attached); not belonging (to what is being dealt with); coming from outside: ~ interference.

extra·ordi·nary /ɪk'strɔːdnrɪ US: -dənerɪ/ adj 1 beyond what is usual or ordinary; remarkable: a man of ~ talents; ~ weather. 2 (of officials) additional, specially employed: envoy ~. **ex·tra·ordi·nar·ily** /ɪk'strɔːdnrəlɪ US: -dənerəlɪ/ adv

extra·sen·sory /ˌekstrə'sensərɪ/ adj (esp) ~ perception (abbr **ESP**), perception of external events without the use of any of the known senses.

extra·terri·tor·ial /ˌekstrəˌterɪ'tɔːrɪəl/ adj = exterritorial.

ex·trava·gant /ɪk'strævəgənt/ adj 1 wasteful; (in the habit of) wasting (money, etc): an ~ man; ~ tastes and habits. 2 (of ideas, speech, behaviour) going beyond what is reasonable usual or conventional; not properly controlled: ~ praise/ behaviour. ~·ly adv **ex·trava·gance** /-gəns/ n 1 [U] being ~: His extravagance explains why he is always in debt. 2 [C] ~ statement, act, etc.

ex·trava·gan·za /ɪkˌstrævə'gænzə/ n [C] 1 (music, theatre, literature) irregular and fanciful composition; burlesque; spectacular entertainment.

ex·treme /ɪk'striːm/ n 1 either end of anything; (fig) highest degree: annoying in the ~, most annoying. 2 (pl) qualities, etc as wide apart, as widely different, as possible: the ~s of heat and cold. Love and hate are ~s. **go to/be driven to ~s**, to ~ measures, to do more than is usu considered right or desirable. □ adj 1 at the end(s); farthest possible: the ~ edge of a field; in ~ old age; the ~ penalty of the law (in some countries) is the death penalty. 2 reaching the highest degree: ~ patience/kindness; in ~ pain. 3 (of persons, their ideas) far from moderate; going to great lengths in views or actions: hold ~ opinions; the ~ left/ right, (in politics) those who support communism/fascism. ~·ly adv (used intensively with adjj and advv) to a very high degree. **ex·trem·ist** /-ɪst/ n person who holds ~ views (esp in politics). **ex·trem·ity** /ɪk'stremətɪ/ n (pl -ties) [C] 1 ~ point, end or limit; (pl) hands and feet. 2 (sing only) ~ degree (of joy, misery, esp of misfortune): an extremity of pain. How can we help them in their extremity? 3 (usu pl) ~ measures, eg for punishing wrongdoers, taking revenge: Both armies were guilty of extremities.

ex·tri·cate /'ekstrɪkeɪt/ vt [VP6A,14] ~ (from), free; disentangle: ~ oneself from a difficulty. **ex·tri·cable** /ek'strɪkəbl/ adj that can be ~d. **ex·tri·ca·tion** /ˌekstrɪ'keɪʃn/ n [U].

ex·trin·sic /ek'strɪnsɪk/ adj ~ (to), (of qualities, values, etc) not a part of the real character; operating or originating from the outside; not essential.

ex·tro·vert /'ekstrəvɜːt/ n person more interested in what goes on around him than in his own thoughts and feelings; (colloq) lively, cheerful person; (attrib): ~ behaviour. ⇨ introvert. **ex·tro·ver·sion** /ˌekstrə'vɜːʃn US: -ʒn/ n [U] state of being ~ed.

ex·trude /ɪk'struːd/ vt [VP6A,14] ~ (from), force sb or sth out; shape (eg plastic or metal) by forcing through a die. **ex·tru·sion** /ɪk'struːʒn/ n

ex·uber·ant /ɪg'zjuːbərənt US: -'zuː-/ adj 1 growing vigorously; luxuriant: plants with ~ foliage. 2 full of life and vigour; high-spirited; overflowing: children in ~ spirits; an ~ imagination. ~·ly adv **ex·uber·ance** /-rəns/ n [U] state or quality of being ~: The speaker's exuberance won over an apathetic audience.

ex·ude /ɪg'zjuːd US: -'zuːd/ vt,vi [VP2A,C,6A] (of drops of liquid) come or pass out slowly; ooze out: Sweat ~s through the pores.

ex·ult /ɪg'zʌlt/ vi [VP2A,3A,4C] rejoice greatly: ~ at/in a success; ~ to find that one has succeeded; ~ (= triumph) over a defeated rival. ~·ant /-ənt/ adj ~ing; triumphant. ~·ant·ly adv **ex·ul·ta·tion** /ˌegzʌl'teɪʃn/ n [U] great joy (at); triumph (over).

eye[1] /aɪ/ n 1 organ of sight: We see with our eyes. He opened/closed his eyes. He is blind in one eye. He lost an eye in the war. ⇨ the illus here and at head. **an eye for an eye**, punishment as severe as the injury suffered; retaliation. **eyes right/left/ front**, (mil command) Turn the head and look to the right, etc. **if you had half an eye**, if you were not so dull, unobservant. **in the eyes of the law, etc**, from the point of view of the law, etc; as the law, etc sees it. *in the eyes of sb; in my/his, etc eyes,* in the judgement of: *You're only a child in his eyes. under/before one's very eyes,* (a) in one's presence, in front of one. (b) with no attempt at concealment. *up to the eyes in* (work, etc), deeply engaged in. *with an eye to,* with a view to, hoping for. *be all eyes,* be watching intently. *be in the public eye,* be often seen in public; be well known. *close one's eyes to,* refuse to see or take notice of. *get one's eye in,* (cricket and other ball games) become able, through practice, to follow with one's eyes the movement of the ball. *give sb a black eye; black sb's eye,* give him a blow so that there is a discoloured bruise round the eye. *have an eye for,* be a good judge of, have a proper sense of: *He has a good eye for beauty/the picturesque. have an eye to,* have as one's object: *He always has an eye to business,* looks for possibilities of doing business. *keep an eye on,* (lit, fig) keep a watch on. *make eyes at,* look amorously at. *make sb open his eyes,* make him take notice. *Mind your eye,* (colloq) Take care, Look out. *open sb's eyes to,* cause him to realize. *see eye to eye (with),* agree entirely, have identical views. *see sth with half an eye,* see it at a glance. *set/ clap eyes on,* see: *I hope I shall never set eyes on her again.* never take one's eyes off, never stop watching. ⇨ catch¹(7), dust¹(1). **2** thing like an eye: *the eye of a needle,* the hole for the thread; *a hook and eye,* fastening with a hook and loop for a dress; *the eye of a potato,* point from which a leaf-bud will grow. **3** (compounds, etc) **'eye-ball** *n* the eye within the lids and socket. *eyeball to eyeball,* (colloq) face to face. **'eye-bath**; **'eye-cup** *nn* small glass for holding lotion, etc, in which to bathe the eye. **'eye-brow** *n* arch of hair above the eye. *raise one's eyebrows,* express surprise, doubt, etc. **'eye-catching** *adj* easy to see and pleasant to look at; attractive. **'eye-ful** /-fʊl/ *n* as much as one is capable of viewing; as much as one can see at a glance. *have/get an eyeful (of),* have a good long look (at sth that has strongly attracted the attention because one is curious about it). **'eye-glass** *n* lens (for one eye) to help defective sight. **'eye-glasses** *n pl* pair of lenses in a frame; spectacles or glasses (the usu words). **'eye-lash** *n* hair, row of hairs, on the edge of the eyelid. **eye-less** *adj* without eyes. **'eye-lid** *n* upper or lower covering of the eye. *hang on by the eyelids,* have a very slight, insecure hold. **'eye-opener** *n* cir-

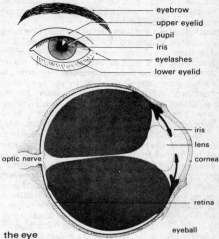

eyebrow
upper eyelid
pupil
iris
eyelashes
lower eyelid

optic nerve

iris
lens
cornea

retina

eyeball

the eye

cumstance, etc that brings enlightenment and surprise. **'eye-piece** *n* lens at the end of a telescope or microscope, to which the eye is applied. **'eye-shadow** *n* [U] cosmetic applied to the eyelids. **'eye-shot** *n* [U] seeing distance: *beyond/out of/ in/within eyeshot.* **'eye-sight** *n* [U] power, faculty, of seeing: *to have good/poor eyesight.* **'eye-sore** *n* ugly object; sth unpleasing to look at. **'eye-strain** *n* [U] tired condition of the eyes (as caused, for example, by reading very small print). **'eye-tooth** *n* canine tooth. ⇨ the illus at mouth. **'eye-wash** *n* [U] (a) liquid for bathing the eyes. (b) (colloq) sth said or done to deceive; nonsense. **'eye-witness** *n* person who can bear witness from what he has himself seen: *an eye-witness account of a crime.* **-eyed** *suff* (in compounds): *a blue-eyed girl,* girl having blue eyes; *a one-eyed man,* man having only one eye; *starry-eyed,* (colloq) idealistic.

eye² /aɪ/ *vt* [VP6A,15A] observe, watch: *He eyed me with suspicion. They were ey(e)ing us jealously.*

eye-let /'aɪlɪt/ *n* [C] small hole in cloth, in a sail, etc for a rope, etc to go through; metal ring round such a hole, to strengthen it.

eyrie, eyry /'eərɪ/ *n* ⇨ aerie.

Ff

F, f /ef/ (*pl* F's, f's /efs/) the sixth letter of the English alphabet.

fa /fɑː/ *n* fourth note in the musical octave.

fab /fæb/ *adj* (dated sl) fabulous(3).

Fabian /'feɪbɪən/ *n, adj* **1** (person) using cautious and slow strategy to wear out opposition: *a ~ policy.* **2** (GB) (person) aiming at gradual socialist change.

fable /'feɪbl/ *n* **1** [C] short tale, not based on fact, esp one with animals in it (eg **Aesop's** /'iːsɒps/ ~s, and intended to give moral teaching. **2** [U] (collective *sing*) myths; legends: *sort out fact from ~.* **3** [C] false statement or account. **fabled** /'feɪbld/ *adj* celebrated in ~; legendary.

fab-ric /'fæbrɪk/ *n* [C,U] **1** (kind of) textile material; *woollen/silk ~s; ~ gloves,* made of woven material, not of leather. **2** structure; sth put together: *the ~ of society; funds for the upkeep of the ~,* eg an ancient building.

fab-ri-cate /'fæbrɪkeɪt/ *vt* [VP6A] construct; put together; make up (sth false); forge (a document): *~ an accusation/a will: a ~d account of adventures.* **fab-ri-ca-tion** /ˌfæbrɪ'keɪʃn/ *n* [U] fabricating; [C] sth ~d, eg a forged document, a false story of events.

fabu-lous /'fæbjʊləs/ *adj* **1** celebrated in fable(2): *~ heroes.* **2** incredible or absurd: *~ wealth.* **3** (colloq) wonderful; marvellous. *~-ly adv* incre-

flirter – to make a fuss over s.b.

dibly: ∼ly *rich.*

fa·çade /fə'sɑːd/ *n* [C] front or face of a building (towards a street or open place); (fig) false appearance: *a ∼ of indifference.*

face[1] /feɪs/ *n* **1** the front part of the head (forehead, eyes, nose, mouth, cheeks, chin): *He fell on his ∼. The stone struck him on the ∼. Her ∼ is her fortune,* (said of a woman who has beauty, but no dowry or talents. **bring two persons/parties ∼ to ∼; bring sb ∼ to ∼ with sb,** bring them together so that they confront one another: *The two politicians were brought ∼ to ∼ in a TV interview.* **come ∼ to ∼ with sb; meet sb ∼ to ∼,** come into his presence, meet or confront him. **look sb in the ∼,** look at him steadily. **be unable to look sb in the ∼,** be unable to look at sb because of feeling ashamed, bashful, etc. **set one's ∼ against sb,** oppose him. **show one's ∼,** appear, let oneself be seen: *How can you show your ∼ here after the way you behaved last night? in (the) ∼ of,* (a) confronted with: *What could he do in the ∼ of all these difficulties?* (b) in spite of: *He succeeded in ∼ of great danger.* **fly in the ∼ of sth,** openly defy, disregard (eg Providence/public disapproval/the facts): *Your claim flies in the ∼ of all the evidence.* **in one's ∼; in the ∼,** (a) straight against/at: *The sun was shining in our ∼s.* (b) with no attempt at concealment: *Death stared him in the ∼. She'll only laugh in your ∼.* (Cf *laugh up one's sleeve* at laugh[2](1)). **to one's ∼,** openly, in one's hearing. *I'll tell him so to his ∼,* ie I'm not afraid to tell him. Cf *behind one's back* at back[1](1). **2** (compounds) '∼-ache *n* neuralgia. '∼-card *n* (playing-card) king, queen, or knave. '∼-cloth, (esp) small square towel for washing the ∼. '∼-cream, cosmetic cream for the skin on the ∼. '∼-lift(ing) *n* operation of tightening the skin to smooth out wrinkles and make the ∼ look younger. '∼-pack *n* paste applied to clean and freshen the skin of the ∼. '∼-powder *n* cosmetic powder for the ∼. **3** look; expression: *a sad ∼; smiling ∼s. She is a good judge of ∼s,* judges the character well from the expression of the ∼. **keep a straight ∼,** hide one's amusement (by not smiling or laughing). **make/pull a ∼/∼s (at sb),** pull the ∼ out of shape; make grimaces (at him). **put on/wear a long ∼,** look serious or dismal. **4** (in various senses) **have the ∼ (to do sth),** (more usu the *cheek*) be bold or impudent enough. **lose ∼,** be humiliated, suffer loss of credit or reputation. **put a good/bold/brave ∼ on sth,** make it look well; show courage in dealing with it. **put a new ∼ on sth,** alter its aspect, make it look different. **save (one's) ∼,** refrain from, evade, shaming oneself openly; avoid losing one's dignity or suffering loss of credit or reputation. Hence, '∼-saver *n* act or event that allows this. '∼-saving *n, part adj:* ∼-*saving moves.* **on the ∼ of it,** judging by appearances, when first seen or heard: *On the ∼ of it, his story seems unconvincing.* **5** surface; façade (of a building); front: *the ∼ of a clock. He laid the cards ∼ down on the table. A dice has six ∼s. A diamond crystal has many ∼s. The team climbed the north ∼ of the mountain. They disappeared from/ off the ∼ of the earth. The miner worked at the coal∼ for six hours. The value of a coin or banknote is shown on its ∼.* Hence, ∼ **value,** the nominal value of a coin or banknote; (fig) what sth or sb seems to be from appearances. **take sth at its ∼ value,** accept that it is what it seems to be. ⇨ the

illus at **crystal; mountain. 6** size or style of the surface of a piece of type cast for printing: *bold-∼ type.* ∼**·less** *adj* (fig) anonymous; unknown to the general public: *the ∼less men who have power in commerce and industry.*

face[2] /feɪs/ *vt,vi* **1** [VP6A,C] have or turn the ∼ to, or in a certain direction; be opposite to: *Turn round and ∼ me. Who's the man facing us? The window ∼s the street. The picture ∼s page 10. 'Which way does your house ∼?'—'It ∼s south.'* **About/ Left/Right ∼!** (US mil commands) Turn right round/to the left/right. Cf (GB) *About/Left/Right turn!* **2** [VP6A,15B,2C] meet confidently or defiantly: *∼ the enemy; ∼ dangers.* ∼ **sth/it out,** refuse to give way, carry it through with courage. ∼ **the music,** show no fear at a time of trial, danger, difficulty. ∼ **up to (sth),** recognize and deal with, honestly and bravely: *∼ up to the fact that one is no longer young.* **let's ∼ it,** (colloq) it must be acknowledged. **3** [VP6A] recognize the existence of: *∼ facts/altered circumstances.* **4** [VP6A] present itself to: *the problem that ∼s us.* **5** [VP6A,14] ∼ **(with),** cover with a layer of different material: *∼ a wall with concrete; a coat ∼d with silk,* eg with silk on the lapels. **facer** *n* (GB dated colloq) serious difficulty by which one is suddenly or unexpectedly ∼d.

facet /'fæsɪt/ *n* one of the many sides of a cut stone or jewel; (fig) aspect, eg of a problem.

fa·cetious /fə'siːʃəs/ *adj* humorously teasing or mocking; fond of, marked by, inappropriate or bitter joking: *a ∼ remark/young man.* ∼**·ly** *adv* ∼**·ness** *n*

facia /'feɪʃə/ *n* = fascia.

fa·cial /'feɪʃl/ *adj* of or for the face: *a ∼ massage.* □ *n* ∼ massage.

facile /'fæsaɪl US: -sl/ *adj* **1** easily done or obtained: *a ∼ victory.* **2** (of a person) able to do things easily; (of speech or writing) done easily but without attention to quality: *a ∼ liar/remark; a man with a ∼ pen/tongue.*

fa·cili·tate /fə'sɪlɪteɪt/ *vt* [VP6A] (of an object, process) make easy; lessen the difficulty of: *Modern inventions have ∼d housework.* (Note: ∼ is never used when the subject is a person).

fa·cil·ity /fə'sɪlətɪ/ *n* (*pl* -ties) **1** [U] quality which makes learning or doing things easy or simple: *have great ∼ in learning languages; show ∼ in performing a task; play the piano with ∼.* **2** (*pl*) aids, circumstances, which make it easy to do things: *facilities for travel,* eg buses, trains, air services; *facilities for study,* eg libraries, laboratories; '*sports facilities,* eg running tracks, swimming pools.

facing /'feɪsɪŋ/ *n* **1** coating of different material, eg on a wall. **2** (*pl*) material of a different colour on a garment, eg on the cuffs, collar: *a purple jacket with green ∼s.* ⇨ face[2](5).

fac·sim·ile /fæk'sɪməlɪ/ *n* [C] exact copy or reproduction of writing, printing, a picture, etc: *reproduced in ∼,* exactly.

fact /fækt/ *n* **1** [C] sth that has happened or been done. **accessary before the ∼,** (legal) accessary who is not present when a crime is committed. **accessary after the ∼,** (legal) who knowingly helps another who has committed a crime. **2** [C] sth known to be true or accepted as true: *No one can deny the ∼ that fire burns. Poverty and crime are ∼s. I know it for a ∼,* I know that it is really true. **a ∼ of life,** sth that cannot be ignored, however unpleasant. *the ~s of life,* (colloq, euphem) details of human sexual reproduction (eg as told to children). '*~-finding* adj: A *~-finding commission has been appointed,* one to inquire into ~s, to find out what is true and what is not true. **3** [U] reality; what is true; what exists: *The story is founded on ~. It is important to distinguish ~ from fiction. The ~ of the matter is...,* The truth is.... *in ~; as a matter of ~; in point of ~,* really: *I think so; in ~, I'm quite sure.*

fac-tion /'fækʃn/ n **1** [C] discontented, often unscrupulous and self-interested group of persons within a party (esp political): *The party split into petty ~s.* **2** [U] quarrelling among such groups; party strife. **fac-tious** /'fækʃəs/ adj of, caused by, ~; fond of ~: *a factious spirit.*

fac-ti-tious /fæk'tɪʃəs/ adj (formal) unnatural; artificial; created or developed by design: *~ enthusiasm; a ~ demand for goods,* eg as the result of extensive advertising.

fac-tor /'fæktə(r)/ n **1** (arith) whole number (except 1) by which a larger number can be divided exactly: *2, 3, 4 and 6 are ~s of 12.* **2** fact, circumstance, etc helping to bring about a result: *evolutionary ~s,* environmental influences, etc that have caused sth to evolve or develop; *~s in the making of a nation; an unknown ~,* sth unknown, likely to influence a result; *the ~ of safety,* eg in engineering. Hence, '**safety-~** n. **3** agent; person who buys and sells on commission; (in Scotland) land-agent, steward. *~-ize* /'fæktəraɪz/ vt [VP6A] find the ~s of (a number).

fac-tory /'fæktərɪ/ n (pl -ries) **1** building(s) where goods are made (esp by machinery); workshop: (attrib) *~ workers.* **F~ Acts,** (in GB) laws dealing with safety regulations, working conditions of employees, etc. **2** (hist) merchant company's trading station abroad.

fac-to-tum /fæk'təʊtəm/ n (**general**) *~,* (often hum) servant doing all kinds of work.

fac-tual /'fæktʃʊəl/ adj concerned with, full of, fact(s). *~-ly* adv

fac-ulty /'fækltɪ/ n (pl -ties) [C] **1** power (of mind); ability (to do sth): *the mental faculties,* the reason; *the ~ of making friends easily; have a great ~ for learning languages; the ~ of speech; be in possession of all one's faculties,* be able to see, hear, speak, understand, etc. **2** (in a university) department or grouping of related departments: *the F~ of Law/Science;* all the teachers, lecturers, professors, etc in one of these: *a member of (the) ~; a ~ meeting;* (US) the whole teaching staff of a university.

fad /fæd/ n [C] fanciful fashion, interest, preference, enthusiasm, unlikely to last: *Will Tom continue to collect foreign stamps or is it only a passing fad? She is full of fads and fancies,* has rather silly likes and dislikes. **faddy** /'fædɪ/ adj having fads; having silly likes and dislikes, eg about food. **fad-dily** /'fædɪlɪ/ adv

fade /feɪd/ vt,vi *~ (away),* **1** [VP6A,2A,C] (cause to) lose colour, freshness or vigour: *The strong sunlight had ~d the curtains. Flowers soon ~ when cut. Will the colour in this material ~? She is fading away,* losing strength. **2** [VP2A,C] go slowly out of view, hearing or the memory: *Daylight ~d away. As evening came the coastline ~d into darkness. The sound of the cheering ~d away in the distance. His hopes ~d. All memory of her childhood ~d from her mind.* **3** [VP15B,2C,3A]

(cinema, broadcasting) (cause to) decrease or increase in strength: *~ one scene into another* (on a cinema screen); *~ a conversation out/in,* (in broadcasting) gradually reduce/increase the volume of sound to inaudibility/audibility.

faeces (US = **feces**) /'fiːsiːz/ n pl (med) waste matter excreted from the bowels.

faerie, faery /'feərɪ/ n (old use) fairyland; (attrib) visionary; fancied.

fag¹ /fæg/ n **1** [C,U] (sing only) (colloq) tiring job: *What a fag! It's too much (of a) fag.* **2** (formerly at public schools in England) junior pupil who performs certain duties for a senior pupil. **3** (GB sl) cigarette. **4** = faggot(3).

fag² /fæg/ vi,vt (-gg-) **1** [VP2C,3A] *~ (at),* (colloq) do very tiring work: *fag (away) at sth/at doing sth.* **2** [VP6A,15B] *~ (out),* (colloq) (of work) make very tired: *Doesn't that sort of work fag you (out)? He was almost fagged out,* exhausted. *Your horse looks fagged.* **3** [VP2A,3A] *~ (for),* act as a fag(2).

fag-end /'fæg end/ n (colloq) inferior or useless remnant; worthless part of anything; cigarette butt.

fag-got (US also **fagot**) /'fægət/ n **1** bundle of sticks or twigs tied together for burning as fuel. **2** meat ball for frying. **3** ⚠ (US sl, derog) male homosexual.

Fahr-en-heit /'færənhaɪt/ n name of a thermometer scale with freezing-point at 32° and boiling-point at 212°. ⇨ App 5.

fa-ience /feɪ'ɑːns/ n [U] (F) decorated and glazed earthenware or porcelain.

fail¹ /feɪl/ n (only in) **without ~,** for certain, no matter what difficulties, etc there may be: *I'll be there at two o'clock without ~.*

fail² /feɪl/ vi,vt **1** [VP2A,3A,4A,6A] *~ (in),* be unsuccessful: *~ (in) an examination; ~ to pass an examination. All our plans/attempts ~ed.* **2** [VP6A] (of examiners) reject (a candidate); decide that (a candidate) has *~ed: The examiners ~ed half the candidates.* **3** [VP2A,C] (often with an *indirect object*) be not enough; come to an end while still needed or expected: *The crops ~ed because of drought. Our water supply has ~ed. The wind ~ed (us),* There was not enough wind for our sails. *Words ~ me,* I cannot find words (to describe my feelings, etc). *His heart (= courage) ~ed him.* '*~-safe* (attrib adj), (of a mechanical device, etc) designed to compensate automatically for a failure (thus eliminating danger, etc). **4** [VP2A,C] (of health, eyesight, etc) become weak: *His eyesight is ~ing. He has suffered from ~ing health/has been ~ing in health for the last two years.* **5** [VP4A] omit; neglect; (or, in many cases, simply making, with the inf, a neg of an affirm): *He never ~s to write (= always writes) to his mother every week. His promises ~ed to (= did not) materialize. He did not ~ to keep (= he did keep) his word.* **6** [VP2A] become bankrupt: *Several of the biggest banks ~ed during the depression.* **7** [VP3A] *~ in,* be insufficiently equipped with; be lacking in: *He's a clever man, but ~s in perseverance.*

fail-ing¹ /'feɪlɪŋ/ n [C] weakness or fault (of character); shortcoming: *We all have our little ~s.*

fail-ing² /'feɪlɪŋ/ prep in default of; in the absence of: *~ this,* if this does not happen; *~ an answer,* if no answer is received; *~ Smith,* if Smith is not available.

fail-ure /'feɪljə(r)/ n **1** [U] failing; lack of success:

F∼ in an examination should not deter you from trying again. All his efforts ended in ∼, were unsuccessful. **2** [C] instance of failing; person, attempt, or thing that fails: Success came after many ∼s. He was a ∼ as a teacher. **3** [U] state of not being adequate; non-performance of what is normal, expected or required; [C] instance of this: 'heart ∼; 'engine ∼s. F∼ of crops often results in famine. Crop ∼s caused great hardship for the people. **4** [C] bankruptcy: numerous bank ∼s. **5** [C,U] neglect, omission, inability (to do sth): His ∼ to help us was disappointing. His ∼ to answer questions made the police suspicious.

fain /feɪn/ adv (poet, or old use after would) willingly; with pleasure: I would ∼ have stayed at home.

faint¹ /feɪnt/ adj (-er, -est) **1** (of things perceived through the senses) weak; indistinct; not clear: The sounds of the music grew ∼er in the distance. She called for help in a ∼ voice. Only ∼ traces of the tiger's tracks could be seen. **2** (of things in the mind) weak; vague: There is a ∼ hope that she may be cured. I haven't the ∼est idea (of) what you mean. **3** (of the body's movements and functions) weak; failing: His breathing became ∼. His strength grew ∼. **4** (pred only) (of persons) likely to lose consciousness; giddy: She looks/feels ∼. **5** (pred only) (of persons) weak, exhausted: ∼ with hunger and cold. **6** (of actions, etc) weak; unlikely to have much effect: a ∼ show of resistance; make a ∼ attempt to do sth. **7** ∼ heart, timid spirit: (prov) F∼ heart never won fair lady. ,∼-'hearted adj lacking in courage. ∼·ly adv ∼·ness n

faint² /feɪnt/ vi [VP2A,C] **1** lose consciousness (because of loss of blood, the heat, shock, etc): He ∼ed from hunger. **2** become weak: He was ∼ing with hunger. **3** (= fade) become weak: The sounds ∼ed away. □ n act, state, of ∼ing(1). in a (dead) ∼, (completely) unconscious.

fair¹ /feə(r)/ adj **1** not showing favour to either person, side, etc; acting in an honest and honourable manner; in accordance with what is deserved or with the rules (of a game, etc): Everyone must have a ∼ share. It was a ∼ fight, eg the rules of boxing were observed. We charge ∼ prices and are content with ∼ (= reasonable) profits. **give sb/get a ∼ hearing**, an opportunity to defend his conduct, etc, eg in a law court. ∼ **play**, ➪ play¹(2). ,∼-'minded, not prejudiced. **2** average; quite good: a ∼ chance of success. His knowledge of French is ∼, but ought to be better. The goods arrived in ∼ condition. She has a ∼ amount of sense. **3** (of the weather) good; dry and fine; (of winds) favourable: hoping for ∼ weather. They set sail with the first ∼ wind. The glass is at set ∼, The needle of the barometer is stationary (= set) at ∼ (indicating a likelihood of good weather). ,∼-'weather 'friend, person who ceases to be a friend when one is in trouble. **4** satisfactory; abundant: a ∼ heritage; promising: be in a ∼ way to succeed, be at the stage where success seems assured; in a ∼ way of business, quite prosperous. **5** (of the skin, hair) pale; light in colour; blond: a '∼-haired girl; a ∼ complexion. **6** (of speeches, promises, etc) carefully chosen to seem polite and gentle in order to please and persuade: put sb off with ∼ words/ promises; the ∼ speeches of the politicians, eg before an election. **7** clean; clear; without blemish: Please make a ∼ copy of this letter, a new one without the errors, corrections, etc. Such behavi-

our will spoil your ∼ name, good reputation. **8** (old use) beautiful: a ∼ maiden. **the '∼ sex**, women. ∼·ish /'feərɪʃ/ adj of ∼(2) size or quality.

fair² /feə(r)/ adv **1** in a fair¹(1) manner: play ∼. ∼ **enough**, (colloq) used to indicate agreement or reasonable disagreement. **2** in a fair¹(7) manner: write/copy sth out ∼. **3** (old use) politely, courteously: speak sb ∼.

fair³ /feə(r)/ n **1** market (esp for cattle, sheep, farm products, etc) held periodically in a particular place, often with entertainments. **a day before/ after the ∼**, too early/late. **'∼-ground**, open space for ∼s. **2** large-scale exhibition of commercial and industrial goods: a world ∼. **3** bazaar(3).

fair·ly¹ /'feəlɪ/ adv **1** in a fair¹(1) manner; honestly: treat sb ∼; come by (= obtain) sth ∼, by honest means. **2** (colloq) utterly; completely: We were ∼ caught in the trap, had no chance of escape. He was ∼ beside himself with rage, as angry as he could possibly be. His suggestion ∼ took my breath away, left me quite breathless (with surprise, etc).

fair·ly² /'feəlɪ/ adv of degree (Cf rather, which may be used with too and comparatives; fairly cannot be used in this way) moderately: This is a ∼ easy book (and is, therefore, perhaps suitable). (Cf This is a rather easy book, suggesting 'rather too easy', and, therefore, perhaps unsuitable.) He wants a ∼ large car, not small, but not very large. (Cf That car is rather larger than he wants.)

fair·way /'feəweɪ/ n **1** navigable channel for ships. **2** (golf) part of a golf-links, between a tee and a green, free from hazards.

fairy /'feərɪ/ n (pl -ries) **1** small imaginary being with supernatural powers, able to help or harm human beings; (attrib) of or like fairies: a ∼ shape, beautiful, small, delicate; ∼ voices/footsteps. **'∼ lamps/lights**, small lamps of coloured glass used for decoration. **'∼-land** n (a) home of fairies(1). (b) enchanted region; beautiful place. **'∼-tale** n (a) tale about fairies. (b) untrue account, esp by a child. **2** ⚠ (sl, derog) male homosexual.

fait accompli /,feɪt ə'kɒmpli: US: əkʌm'pli:/ n (F, = accomplished fact) sth done and, for this reason, not reversible.

faith /feɪθ/ n **1** [U] ∼ (in sb/sth), trust; strong belief; unquestioning confidence: have/put one's ∼ in God. Have you any ∼ in what he says? I haven't much ∼ in this medicine. I've lost ∼ in that fellow, can no longer trust him. **'∼ cure**, one (alleged to be) made through religious ∼. **'∼-healing**, (belief in) healing (of disease, etc) by prayer, appealing to and strengthening a person's religious ∼, apart from the use of medicines, etc. **2** [C] belief in divine truth without proof; religion: the Christian, Jewish and Muslim ∼s. **3** [U] promise; engagement. **give/pledge one's ∼ to sb**, promise solemnly to support him. **keep/break ∼ with sb**, be loyal/disloyal to sb. **4** [U] loyalty; sincerity. **in bad ∼**, with the intention of deceiving. **in good ∼**, honestly; sincerely.

faith·ful /'feɪθfl/ adj ∼ (to), **1** keeping faith; loyal and true (to sb, to a cause, to a promise, etc): a ∼ friend; ∼ to one's promise; ∼ in (= in respect of) word and deed. **2** true to the facts; accurate: a ∼ copy/description/account. **3** the ∼ n pl the true believers, esp of Islam and Christianity. ∼·ly /-fəlɪ/ adv in a ∼ manner. **Yours ∼ly**, formula for closing a letter in formal or business style. ∼·ness n

faith·less /'feɪθlɪs/ adj not trustworthy. ～·ly adv
～·ness n

fake /feɪk/ n [C] story, work of art, etc that seems
genuine but is not; person who tries to deceive by
claiming falsely to be or have sth: (attrib) a ～ picture. □ vt [VP6A,15B] ～ (up), make (eg a work of
art, a story) in order to deceive: ～ an oil-painting.
There wasn't a word of truth in what he said; the
whole story had been ～d (up), invented.

fakir /'feɪkɪə(r) US: fə'kɪə-/ n Muslim or Hindu religious mendicant who is regarded as a holy man, a
prophet, or a wonder-worker.

fal·con /'fɔːlkən US: 'fælkən/ n small bird of prey
trained to hunt and kill other birds and small animals. ▷ the illus at prey. ～·ry /-rɪ/ n [U] sport of
hunting with ～s; art of training ～s.

fall¹ /fɔːl/ n [C] **1** act of falling: a ～ from a horse;
the ～ of an apple from a tree; a ～ in price/
temperature; the ～ (= collapse) of the Roman
Empire. **the F～** (of man), Adam's sin and its results. '～ **guy** n (colloq) (a) dupe; easy victim. (b)
scapegoat. **2** amount of rain that falls; distance by
which sth falls or comes down: The ～ of the river
here is six feet. **3** (often pl) place where a river falls
over cliffs, etc: Niagara F～s. **4** (US) autumn: in
the ～ of 1970; (attrib) ～ fashions.

fall² /fɔːl/ vi (pt fell /fel/, pp ～en /'fɔːlən/) (For
special uses with adverbial particles and preps, ▷
14 below.) **1** [VP2A,B,C,3A] ～ (**down/over**),
come or go down freely (by force of weight, loss of
balance, etc): The book fell from the table to the
floor. He fell over into the water. The rain was
～ing steadily. The leaves ～ in autumn. He slipped
and fell ten feet. This basket is full of eggs—don't
let it ～ down. The lambs are beginning to ～, be
born. ▷ drop²(2). ～ **on one's feet,** (fig) be fortunate; get out of a difficulty successfully: Some
people always seem to ～ on their feet, be lucky
and successful. ～ **short,** (of a missile) not go far
enough: The arrow fell short. ～ **short of,** fail to
equal; be inferior to: Your work ～s short of my expectations. ,～ing 'star, object (eg a meteor) seen
as a bright streak in the sky as it burns up. **2**
[VP2A,C,3A] ～ (**down/over**), no longer stand;
come to the ground; collapse; be overthrown:
Many trees fell in the storm. Babies often ～ down
when they are learning to walk. He fell over and
broke his left leg. He fell full length. He fell on/to
his knees (= knelt down) and begged for mercy.
He fell in battle, was killed. Six tigers fell to his
rifle, He shot six tigers. Six wickets fell before
lunch, (cricket) Six batsmen were out. ～ **flat,** (fig)
fail to have the intended effect: His best jokes all
fell flat, did not amuse his listeners. The scheme
fell flat, was unsuccessful. ～ **flat on one's face,**
～ face down to the ground. ～ **to the ground,** ▷
ground¹(1). ～ **'over oneself,** (a) ～ because one
is awkward, clumsy, or in too much of a hurry. (b)
(fig) be very eager: The big firms were ～ing over
themselves/each other for the services of this brilliant young scientist. **the ～en,** those killed in war.
3 [VP2C] ～ (**down**), hang down: His beard fell to
his chest. Her hair/cloak fell over her shoulders. **4**
[VP2A,B,C,3A] come or go to a lower level or
point; become lower or less: The temperature fell
rapidly. His voice fell to a whisper. Her spirits fell
at the bad news, She became low-spirited, sad. His
face/jaw fell, He showed dismay (Cf put on a long
face at face¹(3)). The wind fell during the night,
became less strong. **5** [VP2C,D,3A] ～ (**into**), be-

come; pass into (the state indicated by the adj or
phrase): His horse fell lame. He fell silent. The old
man fell asleep. He has ～en ill. When does the
rent ～ due, When must it be paid? He fell into a
doze, began to doze. Don't fall into bad habits!
Don't acquire or adopt them. They have ～en into
poverty, become poor. She fell an easy prey to him.
～ **in love (with)**, become filled with love (for):
He fell in love with an actress. I've ～en in love
with your beautiful house. ～ **out of love (with)**,
cease to feel love (for). ▷ foul¹(6). **6** [VP2A,C,3A]
～ **upon**, descend upon: Darkness fell upon the
scene, It became dark. A great stillness had ～en
upon everything, Everything had become quiet and
motionless. Fear fell upon them, They became
frightened. **7** [VP2A,C] (old use) sin; give way to
wrongdoing: Eve tempted Adam and he fell. ,～en
'woman, (old use) one who has lost her virginity
before marriage. **8** [VP2A] (of a city, fort, etc) be
captured: Rome has ～en! be overcome or defeated: The Government has ～en again. **9** [VP3A] ～
on, take the direction or position (indicated by the
adv or phrase): A shadow fell on the wall. His eye
fell on (= He suddenly saw) a curious object.
Strange sounds fell on our ears, We heard strange
sounds. The lamplight fell on her face. In 'formidable' the stress may ～ on either the first or the second syllable. **10** [VP3A] ～ **on/upon/to,** come by
chance, design, or right: All the expenses fell on
me, I had to pay them. The responsibility/blame,
etc fell upon me. It fell to my lot/to me to open the
discussion, I had to speak first. He has fallen on
evil days, is suffering misfortune. **11** [VP2C] (of
land) slope: The ground ～s towards the river. **12**
[VP2C] occur, have as date: Easter ～s early next
year. Christmas Day ～s on a Monday this year.
13 [VP2A,C] be spoken: Not a word fell from his
lips. I guessed what she was going to do from the
few words that she let fall, from what she said. **14**
[VP2C,3A] (special uses with adverbial particles
and preps):

fall about (laughing/with laughter), (colloq)
laugh uncontrollably: They fell about when Sir
Harold slipped on the banana skin.

fall among sb, get mixed up with, come by chance
among: ～ among thieves, evil companions.

fall away, (a) desert: His supporters began to ～
away. (b) disappear, vanish: In this crisis, prejudices fell away and all classes co-operated well.

fall back, retreat; move or turn back: Our attack
was so vigorous that the enemy had to ～ back. ～
'back on sth, have recourse to; turn to for support:
If you don't need the money now, bank it—it's always useful to have something to ～ back on.

fall behind (with sth), fail to keep level (with);
lag: He always ～s behind when we're going uphill. I've ～ behind with my correspondence, have
many unanswered letters. Don't ～ behind with
your rent, or you'll be evicted.

fall down (on sth), (colloq) fail (in a task, in expectation): ～ down on one's promises/obligations
(to sb).

fall for sth/sb, (colloq) yield to the charms, attractions or merits of (esp when deceived): He ～s for
every pretty face he sees. Did he ～ for your suggestion, Did he decide that it was good, and agree
to it?

fall in, (a) collapse; give way: The roof fell in. The
(sides of the) trench fell in. (b) (mil) (cause to) go
on parade: The sergeant ordered the men to ～ in.

(c) (of a lease) expire. (d) (of a debt) become due. ~ **in with sb/sth,** (a) happen to meet. (b) agree to: *He fell in with my views at once.*

fall into sth, be naturally divisible into: *The subject ~s into four divisions.* ~ **into line (with sth/sb),** agree(to what others are doing or wish to do); accept (a course of conduct, procedure, etc.)

fall off, become smaller, fewer or less: *The takings at the football stadium have ~en off,* Less money has been paid for admission. *The daily number of passengers by this line shows a slight ~ing off.*

fall on sth/sb, attack; assault (the enemy).

fall out, (a) (mil) (cause to) go off parade. (b) happen: *It (so) fell out that I could not get there in time. Everything fell out as we had hoped.* (c) discontinue; give up: *the '~-out rate,* eg of pupils who give up a course of study. ⟹ *drop-out* at drop²(13). ~ **out (with sb),** quarrel (with): *The two men fell out. He has fallen out with the girl he was going to marry.* '~-out *n* [U] radio-active dust in the atmosphere, after a nuclear explosion.

fall through, fail; miscarry; come to nothing: *His scheme fell through.*

fall 'to, begin to do sth: *They fell to with a good appetite.* ~ **to 'doing sth:** *I fell to wondering where to go for my holidays.*

fall under sth, be classifiable under: *The results ~ under three heads.*

fal·lacy /'fæləsɪ/ *n (pl -cies)* **1** [C] false or mistaken belief. **2** [U] false reasoning or argument: *a statement based on ~.* **fal·lacious** /fə'leɪʃəs/ *adj* misleading; based on error.

fallen *pp* of fall².

fal·lible /'fæləbl/ *adj* liable to error. **fal·li·bil·ity** /ˌfælə'bɪlətɪ/ *n* (state of) being ~.

Fallopian tube /fə'ləʊpɪən 'tjuːb *US:* 'tuːb/ *n* (anat) = oviduct. ⟹ the illus at reproduce.

fal·low /'fæləʊ/ *adj, n* [U] (land) ploughed but not sown or planted: *allow land to lie ~; plough (up) ~ land.*

fal·low-deer /'fæləʊ dɪə(r)/ *n (pl* unchanged) small Eurasian deer with a reddish-yellow coat with, in the summer, white spots.

false /fɔːls/ *adj* **1** not right, true or real: *a ~ alarm; ~ ideas; ~ weights,* eg one of 90 grammes marked as 100 grammes; *take a ,~ 'step,* stumble; (fig) act wrongly; *sing a ~ note; ~ shame/pride,* based on wrong ideas, etc; *make a ~ start,* (athletics) start before the signal has been given; (fig) start wrongly. **2** deceiving; lying: *give a ~ impression; bear/ give ~ witness,* tell lies or deceive (eg in a law court); *be ~ to one's word,* fail to keep a promise. **act under ~ pretences,** ⟹ pretence. **put sb/be in a ~ position,** in circumstances that cause misunderstanding or make it necessary for sb to act contrary to principles. **sail under ~ colours,** (a) (of a ship) with a flag which it has no right to use. (b) (fig) pretend or appear to be different from what one really is. **a ~ bottom,** a secret compartment in a container such as a suitcase. **3** not genuine; sham; artificial: *~ hair/teeth; ~ coins.* **4** improperly so called: *the ~ acacia* (not really an acacia tree). □ *adv* (only in) **play sb ~,** cheat or betray him. **~·ly** *adv* in a ~ manner; *~ly accused.* **~·ness** *n*

false·hood /'fɔːlshʊd/ *n* **1** [C] lie; untrue statement: *How can you utter such ~s?* **2** [U] telling lies; lying: *guilty of ~. Truth, if exaggerated, may become ~.*

fal·setto /fɔːl'setəʊ/ *n (pl ~s /-təʊz/)* high voice in

men; counter-tenor: *to sing ~;* (attrib) of or in such a voice: *in a ~ tone.*

fal·sies /'fɔːlsɪz/ *n pl* (colloq) brassieres filled with soft material to exaggerate the size of the breasts.

fals·ify /'fɔːlsɪfaɪ/ *vt (pt,pp -fied)* [VP6A] **1** make false: *~ records/accounts;* tell falsely: *~ a story.* **2** misrepresent: *~ an issue.* **falsi·fi·ca·tion** /ˌfɔːlsɪfɪ'keɪʃn/ *n* [U] *~ing* or being falsified; [C] change made in order to deceive.

fals·ity /'fɔːlsətɪ/ *n.* **1** [U] falsehood; incorrectness; error. **2** [C] *(pl -ties)* false or treacherous act, statement, etc.

fal·ter /'fɔːltə(r)/ *vi,vt* **1** [VP2A,C] move, walk or act in an uncertain or hesitating manner, from either weakness or fear. **2** [VP2A] (of the voice) waver: *His voice ~ed as he tried to speak.* [VP15B] ~ *(out),* (of a person) speak in a hesitating way or with a broken voice: *He ~ed out a few words.* ~·**ing·ly** /'fɔːltərɪŋlɪ/ *adv*

fame /feɪm/ *n* [U] (condition of) being known or talked about by all; what people say (esp good) about sb: *He was not anxious for ~. His ~ as a poet did not come until after his death.* **famed** *adj* famous: *~d for their courage.*

fam·il·iar /fə'mɪlɪə(r)/ *adj* **1** ~ **with,** having a good knowledge of: *facts with which every schoolboy is ~. I am not very ~ with botanical names.* **2** ~ **to,** well known to: *facts that are ~ to every schoolboy; subjects that are ~ to you.* **3** common; usual; often seen or heard: *the ~ scenes of one's childhood; the ~ voices of one's friends.* **4** close; intimate; personal: *Are you on ~ terms with Mr Green?* eg Do you address him as 'Tom'? *Don't be too ~ with him; he's a dishonest man.* **5** claiming a greater degree of amorous friendship than is proper: *He made himself much too ~ with my wife.* □ *n* intimate friend. **~·ly** *adv* in a ~ manner; without ceremony.

fam·ili·ar·ity /fəˌmɪlɪ'ærətɪ/ *n (pl -ties)* **1** [U] ~ **(with/to),** (the state of) being familiar: *His ~ with the languages used in Nigeria surprised me. You should not treat her with such ~.* **F~ breeds contempt,** (prov) When we know sth or sb very well, we may lose respect, fear, etc. **2** *(pl)* acts that lack ceremony; instances of familiar behaviour: *She dislikes such familiarities as the use of her first name by men she has only just met.*

fam·ili·ar·ize /fə'mɪliəraɪz/ *vt* **1** [VP14] ~ **sb/ oneself with,** make well acquainted with: *~ oneself with a foreign language/the use of a new tool/the rules of a game.* **2** [VP6A] make well known: *The newspapers and radio have ~d the word 'automation'.*

fam·ily /'fæməlɪ/ *n (pl -lies)* **1** [C] (collective *n*) group of parents and children: *Almost every ~ in the village has a man in the army*(Note here *sing v* after collective *n*). *My ~ are early risers* (Note here *pl v* after *family* = members of my family.) **2** (collective *n*) person's children: *He has a large ~. Has he any ~? Tom is the eldest of the ~,* the eldest child. **3** [C] all those persons descended from a common ancestor: *families that have been in Surrey for hundreds of years.* **4** [U] ancestry: *a man of distinguished ~.* **5** [C] group of living things (plants, animals, etc) or of languages, with common characteristics and a common source: *animals of the cat ~,* eg lions and tigers; *the Germanic ~ of languages* (including German, Dutch, English). **6** (attrib) of or for a ~: *the ~ estate/jewels, etc.* **in the ~ way,** (sl; of a woman) pregnant. ~ **doctor,**

a general practitioner. ~ **hotel**, one with lower rates for families. ~ **likeness**, resemblance between members of a ~. '~ **man**, one who is fond of home life with his ~. ~ **name**, surname. ~ **planning**, (use of birth control, contraceptives, for) planning the number of children, intervals between births, etc in a ~. ~ **tree**, a genealogical tree or chart.

fam·ine /'fæmɪn/ n **1** [U] extreme scarcity of food in a region: *Parts of India have often suffered from* ~. **2** [C] particular occasion when there is such scarcity: *a* ~ *in Ethiopia*. **3** (attrib) caused by ~: ~ *prices*, high prices.

fam·ish /'fæmɪ/ vi,vt **1** [VP2A,3A] suffer from extreme hunger: *They were ~ing for food. I'm ~ing!* (colloq) very hungry. **2** [VP6A] (usu passive) cause (sb) to suffer from hunger: *The child looked half ~ed. I'm ~ed!* (colloq) very hungry.

fa·mous /'feɪməs/ adj **1** known widely; having fame; celebrated: *a* ~ *scientist. The town is* ~ *for its gambling casino/as a gambling resort*. **2** (dated colloq) excellent. ~·**ly** adv in a ~(2) manner: *get on* ~*ly with sb; do* ~*ly in/at sth*.

fan¹ /fæn/ n (flat, semi-circular, usu folding) object waved in the hand, or (with rotating blades) operated mechanically, for making a current of air (eg to cool a room, oneself or to blow dust, etc away); sth that is like a hand fan in shape, eg the tail of a peacock. '**fan belt** n rubber belt transferring circular motion to the cooling fan of an engine. '**fan-light** n fan-shaped window over a door. ,**fan 'vaulting** n (archit) style of vaulting in which ribs, like those of a folding fan, rise and spread from a single point.

fans

fan² /fæn/ vt,vi (-nn-) **1** [VP6A] send a current of air on to: *fan oneself; fan a fire*, to make it burn up; *fan the flame*, (fig) increase excitement or emotion. **2** [VP6A] (of a breeze) blow gently on: *The breeze fanned our faces*. **3** [VP2C] ~ **out**, open in fan-shaped formation: *The troops stormed the enemy's trenches and fanned out across the fields*. **4** [VP6A] spread out (eg playing cards) like a fan.

fan³ /fæn/ n (colloq) keen supporter of sth: '*baseball fans;* '*fan mail*, letters from fans, eg to a popular singer.

fa·natic /fə'nætɪk/ n person filled with excessive (and often mistaken) enthusiasm, eg in religion: *food* ~*s*, willing to eat only certain kinds of food. □ adj (also **fa·nati·cal** /-kl/) excessively enthusiastic; of or like a ~: ~*(al) beliefs*. **fa·nati·cally** /-klɪ/ adv **fa·nati·cism** /-sɪzəm/ n [U] violent, un-

reasoning enthusiasm; [C] instance of this.

fan·cier /'fænsɪə(r)/ n person with special knowledge of and love for some article, animal, etc (the name being prefixed): *a'dog* ~; *a'rose* ~.

fan·ci·ful /'fænsɪfl/ adj **1** (of persons) full of fancies(2); led by imagination instead of reason and experience: *a* ~ *writer*. **2** unreal; curiously designed: ~ *drawings*. ~·**ly** /-fəlɪ/ adv

fancy¹ /'fænsɪ/ n (pl -cies) **1** [U] power of creating mental pictures (often a passive process), (⇨ imagination, in which the mind is more active): *a world of mere* ~. **2** [C] sth imagined; unfounded opinion or belief: *the fancies of a poet. Did I really hear someone come in or was it only a* ~? *I have a* ~ (= a vague idea) *that she will be late*. **3** [C] **a** ~ **(for)**, fondness, liking, desire: *I have a* ~ *for some wine with my dinner*. **take a** ~ **to**, become fond of: *The children have taken quite a* ~ *to their cousin*. **take/catch the** ~ **of**, please or attract: *She saw the dress in a shop window and it caught her* ~. **a passing** ~, sth that attracts one's attention and liking for a short period of time only. ,~-'**free** adj not in love; not committed to anything; not taking things seriously. ⇨ foot¹(8).

fancy² /'fænsɪ/ adj (usu attrib; not in the comp or superl) **1** (esp of small things) brightly coloured; made to please the eye: ~ *cakes;* ~ *goods*. **2** not plain or ordinary: ~ *bread*. ~ **dress**, unusual costume, often historical or exotic, as worn at balls, called ~-'**dress balls**. '~ **work**, ornamental sewing. **3** bred for particular points of beauty: ~ *dogs/pigeons;* ~ *pansies*, having two or more colours. **4** extravagant: ~ *ideas/prices*. **5** (US, of goods) superior in quality: '*F~ Crab*' (on a label, etc). **6** imagined: *a* ~ *portrait*.

fancy³ /'fænsɪ/ vt (pt,pp -cied) **1** [VP6A,16B,19C] picture in the mind; imagine: *Can you* ~ *me as a pirate? I can't* ~ *his doing such a thing*. **2** [VP25,9] be under the impression that (without being certain, or without enough reason): *I rather* ~ *(that) he won't come. He fancied he heard footsteps behind him. Don't* ~ *that you can succeed without hard work. When she saw Tom, whom she had fancied (to be) dead,....* **3** [VP6A] (colloq) have a fancy(3) for: *What do you* ~ *for your dinner? I don't* ~ *this place at all. Do you* ~ *that girl*, find her attractive, likeable? **4** ~ **oneself**, have an excessively high opinion of oneself; be rather conceited: *He fancies himself as an orator*. **5** [VP6A,C] exclamatory style, expressing surprise: *F~ her saying such unkind things about you! F~ that, now! Just* ~! How strange! How surprising!

fan·dango /fæn'dæŋgəʊ/ n (pl ~es /-gəʊz/) (music for a) lively Spanish or S American dance.

fan·fare /'fænfeə(r)/ n [C] (music) flourish of trumpets or bugles.

fan-light ⇨ fan¹.

fang /fæŋ/ n long, sharp tooth (esp of dogs and wolves); snake's poison-tooth.

fan·ny /'fænɪ/ n (pl -nies) (US sl) buttocks.

fan-tan /fæn'tæn US: 'fæntæn/ n Chinese gambling game.

fan·tasia /fæn'teɪzɪə US: -'teɪʒə/ n artistic composition in which a fanciful style is more important than structure.

fan·ta·size /'fæntəsaɪz/ vi,vt [VP2A,3A,6A] ~ **(about)**, have a fantasy(2) (of); imagine. **fan·ta·sist** n person who ~s.

fan·tas·tic /fæn'tæstɪk/ adj **1** wild and strange; grotesque: ~ *dreams/shapes/fashions*. **2** (of ideas, plans) impossible to carry out; absurd. **3** (sl) marvellous; wonderful: *Christina's a really ~ girl!* **fan·tas·ti·cally** /-klɪ/ *adv*

fan·tasy /ˈfæntəsɪ/ *n* (*pl* -sies) **1** [U] fancy(1); imagination, esp when extravagant: *live in a world of ~;* (attrib) *one's ~ life,* that part devoted to ~. **2** [C] product of the imagination: *sexual fantasies.* **3** [C] = **fantasia.**

far¹ /fɑː(r)/ *adj* (⇨ farther, farthest, further, furthest) **1** (usu in liter style) distant: *a far country.* **a far cry from,** a long way from; (fig) a very different thing from. **2 the Far East,** China, Korea, Japan, etc. **the Far West,** the Pacific coast area of the US. **3** (= *farther*) more remote: *at the far end of the street; on the far bank of the river.*

far² /fɑː(r)/ *adv* (⇨ farther, farthest, further, furthest) **1** (indicating a great distance, commonly used in the interr and neg, but not usually, except as shown in **2** below, in the affirm): *How far did you go? We didn't go far.* Cf (in the affirm): *We went a long way. We went only a short way.* **2** (with other *advv* and *preps*) (*indicating a great distance*): *far away/off/out/back/in; far beyond the bridge; far above the clouds; not far from here; far into the night; far back in history; as far back as 1902.* **far from,** not at all: *Your work is far from* (*being*) (= is not at all) *satisfactory. The newspaper accounts are far from* (*being*) *true,* are in many points false. *Far from* (= Instead of) *admiring his paintings, I dislike them intensely.* **by far,** (with *comp* or *superl*) by a large amount or degree: *by far the smallest/heaviest; better by far.* **from far,** from a great distance. **go far,** (a) (of persons) be successful; do much: *He's clever and intelligent, and will go far.* (b) (of money) buy goods, services, etc: *A pound does not go so far today as it did five years ago.* **go/carry sth too far,** go beyond the limits of what is considered reasonable: *Don't carry the joke too far.* (Cf *It's beyond a joke.*) *Don't carry your modesty too far,* Don't be unnecessarily modest. **go far towards/to doing sth,** help or contribute greatly to: *The loan will go far towards clearing my debt.* **far and near/wide,** everywhere: *They searched far and wide for the missing child. People come from far and near to hear the famous violinist.* **far be it from me to do sth,** I would/should/could never do it. **'so far,** until now: *So far the work has been easy.* **,So far, so 'good,** Up to now everything has gone well. **as/so far as,** (a) to the place mentioned: *He walked as far as the post office.* (b) the same distance: *We didn't go so far as the others* (*did*). (c) to the extent that (to indicate a limit of advance or progress): *So far as I know he will be away for three months. He will help you as far as he can/as far as* (*is*) *possible/as far as lies in his power. We have gone so far as to collect some useful statistics.* **3** (with qualifying *adjj* and *advv*) (by) much; considerably; to a great extent: *This is far better. It fell far short of our expectations.* **far and away,** (with *comp* or *superl*) by a large amount or degree: *He's far and away the best actor I've seen.* **'far-away** *adj* (a) distant, remote: *far-away places/times.* (b) (of a look in a person's eyes) dreamy; as if fixed on sth far away in space or time. **,far-'famed** *adj* (rhet) widely known. **,far-'fetched** *adj* (of a comparison) forced; unnatural. **,far-'flung** *adj* (rhet) widely extended. **,far 'gone,** deeply advanced (into eg illness, madness, drunkenness, debt). **,far-'off** *adj* = *far-away.* **,far-'reaching** *adj* likely to have many con-

sequences; having a wide application: *far-reaching proposals.* **,far-'seeing** *adj* seeing far into the future. **,far-'sighted** *adj* (a) able to see distant objects more clearly than near objects. (b) (fig) having a good judgement of future needs, etc.

farce /fɑːs/ *n* **1** [C] play for the theatre, full of ridiculous situations intended to make people laugh; [U] this style of drama. **2** [C] series of actual events like a ~; absurd and useless proceedings: *The prisoner's trial was a ~.* **far·ci·cal** /ˈfɑːsɪkl/ *adj* of or like a ~; absurd. **far·ci·cally** /-klɪ/ *adv*

fare¹ /feə(r)/ *n* [C] **1** money charged for a journey by bus, ship, taxi, etc: *All ~s, please!* (cried by the conductor of a bus, etc). **2** passenger in a hired vehicle: *The taxi-driver had only six ~s all day.*

fare² /feə(r)/ *n* [U] food provided at table: *fine/simple/homely ~.* **,bill of '~,** list of dishes; menu.

fare³ /feə(r)/ *vi* [VP2C] **1** progress; get on: *How did you ~ during your journey,* What were your experiences? *It has ~d well with him,* He has done well, been fortunate. **You may go farther and ~ worse,** (prov, used to suggest that one should be content with one's present conditions). **2** (old use) go, journey. **~ forth,** start out.

fare·well /ˌfeəˈwel/ *int* goodbye. **(bid/say) ~ to,** (have) no more of. □ *n* leave-taking: *make one's ~s.* say goodbye; (attrib) *a ~ speech.*

fari·na·ceous /ˌfærɪˈneɪʃəs/ *adj* starchy; of flour or meal: *~ foods,* eg bread, potatoes.

farm¹ /fɑːm/ *n* **1** area of land (usu divided into fields) and buildings (eg barns), under one management (either owned or rented) for growing crops, raising animals, etc: *working on the ~.* Cf *in* the fields. **'~-hand** *n* (US) ~ worker; agricultural labourer. **'~-yard** *n* space enclosed by ~ buildings (sheds, barns, etc). **2** (also '~-house, '~-stead /-sted/) farmer's house on a ~.

farm² /fɑːm/ *vt, vi* **1** [VP6A,2A] use (land) for growing crops, raising animals, etc: *He ~s 200 acres. He is ~ing in Africa. He is engaged in* **'sheep-~ing.** **2** [VP15B] **~ out (to),** (a) send (work) out to be done by others. (b) arrange for (a child) to be cared for by others. **~er** *n* man who owns or manages a ~. (Cf *peasant,* a word not used of a ~er or farm worker in GB or US.)

far·rago /fəˈrɑːgəʊ/ *n* (*pl* ~s, ~es /-gəʊz/) medley, mixture: *a ~ of nonsense/useless knowledge.*

far·rier /ˈfærɪə(r)/ *n* smith who shoes horses.

far·row /ˈfærəʊ/ *vi* give birth to pigs: *When will the sow ~?* □ *n* litter of pigs; giving birth to pigs: *15 at one ~.*

fart /fɑːt/ *vi,* *n* ⚠ (not in polite use) (send out, sending out of) wind through the anus.

far·ther /ˈfɑːðə(r)/ *adv* (comp of *far*) to/at a greater distance/depth: *We can't go any ~ without a rest. They went ~ into the forest.* □ *adj* more distant: *on the ~ bank of the river; at the ~ end of the street.*

far·thest /ˈfɑːðɪst/ *adv, adj* (superl of *far*) to/at the greatest distance/depth: *Which village in England is ~ from London? at (the) ~,* (a) at the greatest distance: *It's five miles away at the ~,* is not more than five miles away. (b) (of time) at the latest.

far·thing /ˈfɑːðɪŋ/ *n* (formerly) coin worth one-quarter of a penny. **It doesn't matter/He doesn't care a ~,** not in the least.

fas·cia (also **facia**) /ˈfeɪʃə/ *n* dashboard or panel on a motor vehicle, etc (with gauges, dials, etc). ⇨ the illus at motor.

fas·ci·nate /ˈfæsɪneɪt/ *vt* [VP6A] **1** charm, attract or interest greatly: *The children were ~d by all the* *toys in the shop windows.* **2** take away power of movement by a fixed look, as a snake does. **fas·ci-nat·ing** *adj* having strong charm or attraction: *a fascinating voice/story/glimpse.* **fas·ci·nat·ing·ly** *adv* **fas·ci·na·tion** /ˌfæsɪ'neɪʃn/ *n* [U] fascinating or being ~d; power to ~; [C] thing that ~s: *Girls have a fascination for Brian,* ie they ~ him. *Brian has a fascination for girls,* ie he ~s them.

fas·cism /'fæʃɪzəm/ *n* F~, philosophy, principles and organization of the aggressive nationalist and anti-communist dictatorship started in Italy in 1922 and dissolved in 1943; similar movement in other countries. **fas·cist** /'fæʃɪst/ *n* supporter of ~. □ *adj* of ~; extreme right-wing; reactionary.

fashion /'fæʃn/ *n* **1 a/the** ~, manner of doing or making sth: *He walks in a peculiar* ~. **after/in a** ~, somehow or other, but not satisfactorily: *He can speak and write English, after a* ~. **after the** ~ **of,** like, in imitation of: *a novel after the* ~ *of Graham Greene.* **2** [C,U] (as shown in the examples) (of clothes, behaviour, thought, custom, etc) prevailing custom; that which is considered most to be admired and imitated during a period or at a place: *dressed in the latest* ~. *F~s for men's clothes change less frequently than* ~*s for women's clothes.* **be all the** ~, (of dress, behaviour, etc) be very popular. **come into/go out of** ~, become/no longer be popular: *When did that style of dress come into/go out of* ~? **follow/be in the** ~, do what others do in matters of dress, behaviour, etc. **set the** ~, give the example by adopting new ~s. **a man/woman of** ~, one belonging to fashionable society and conforming to its usages. **'~ plate** *n* picture showing a style of dress. □ *vt* [VP6A,15A] give form or shape to; mould: ~ *a canoe out of a tree-trunk/a whistle from a piece of wood/a lump of clay into a bowl.*

fashion·able /'fæʃnəbl/ *adj* following the fashion(2); used by, visited by, many people, esp the rich: ~ *clothes; a* ~ *dressmaker/hotel/summer resort.* **fashion·ably** /-əblɪ/ *adv* in a ~ manner: *fashionably dressed.*

fast¹ /fɑːst *US:* fæst/ *adj* **1** firmly fixed; not easily moved: *The post is* ~ *in the ground. Make the boat* ~, Make it secure. *Take* (*a*) ~ *hold of the rope,* hold it tightly. **hard and** ~ **rules,** rigid rules. **2** steady; steadfast; loyal; close: *a* ~ *friend/friendship.* **3** (of colours) unfading. □ *adv* firmly, securely, tightly: *hold* ~ *to sth. The ship was* ~ *aground,* could not be refloated. *She was* ~ *asleep,* in a deep sleep. **stand** ~, not move or retreat; refuse to give way. **stick** ~, (a) = stand ~. (b) be unable to make progress. *F~ **bind,** ~ **find,*** (prov) If you make things secure, eg by locking them up, you will not lose them. **play** ~ **and loose with,** repeatedly change one's attitude towards; trifle with: *play* ~ *and loose with a girl's affections.*

fast² /fɑːst *US:* fæst/ *adj* (-er, -est) **1** quick; rapid: *a* ~ *train/horse; a* ~ *trip; a* ~ *draw,* of a gun from a holster. **2** (dated) (of a person, his way of living) spending too much time and energy on pleasure and excitement; dissipated: *lead a* ~ *life; a* ~ *woman;* ~ *society.* **3** (of a watch or clock) showing time later than the true time: *My watch is five minutes* ~, eg showing 2.05 at 2.00. **4** (of a surface) promoting quick motion: *a* ~ *cricket pitch/billiard-table.* **5** (of photographic film) suitable for very brief exposures.

fast³ /fɑːst *US:* fæst/ *adv* **1** quickly: *Don't speak so*

~. *It was raining* ~, heavily. *Her tears fell* ~. **2 live** ~, live in a dissipated way; use much energy in a short time. **3** (old use) close: ~ *by/behind the church.*

fast⁴ /fɑːst *US:* fæst/ *vi* [VP2A,B] go without food, or without certain kinds of food, esp as a religious duty: *days devoted to* ~*ing and penitence,* eg in Lent. □ *n* **1** (period of) going without food: *a* ~ *of three days; break one's* ~. **2** day ('~**-day)** or season of ~ing.

fas·ten /'fɑːsn *US:* 'fæsn/ *vt,vi* **1** [VP6A,15A,B] ~ (*up/down*), make fast¹; fix firmly; tie or join together: *Have you* ~*ed all the doors and windows? He* ~*ed the two sheets of paper together. He* ~*ed up/down the box,* closed it and made it secure. **2** [VP14] ~ **on/upon,** fix (a nickname, accusation, etc) upon sb; direct (one's looks, thoughts, attention, etc) upon sb: *He* ~*ed his eyes on me.* **3** [VP2A,C] become fast¹ or secured: *The door won't* ~. *This dress* ~*s down the back,* has buttons, etc down the back. **4** [VP3A] ~ **on/upon,** lay hold of, seize upon; single (a person) out for attack: *He* ~*ed on the idea.* ~**er** *n* thing that ~s things together: *a paper* ~*er; a zip-*~*er.* ~**·ing** *n* thing that ~s, esp a slide or a bolt.

fas·tid·ious /fə'stɪdɪəs *US:* fæ-/ *adj* hard to please; quick to find fault: *He is* ~ *about his food/clothes, etc.* ~**·ly** *adv* ~**·ness** *n*

fast·ness /'fɑːstnɪs *US:* 'fæs-/ *n* **1** [C] stronghold; fortress: *a mountain* ~, eg of bandits. **2** [U] the quality of being fast¹(3): *We guarantee the* ~ *of these dyes.*

fat¹ /fæt/ *adj* (fatter, fattest) **1** covered with, having much, fat: *fat meat; a fat man; fat cheeks; fat cattle,* made fat ready for slaughter. **'~fat-head** *n* dull, stupid person. **2** thick; well filled: *a fat wallet,* one stuffed with banknotes. **a 'fat lot,** (sl) a great deal (ironic, = very little): *A fat lot you care,* ie you don't care at all. **3** rich, fertile: *fat lands.* **fat·tish** *adj* rather fat. **fat·ness** *n*

fat² /fæt/ *n* [C,U] (kinds of) white or yellow substance, oily or greasy, found in animal bodies; this substance purified for cooking purposes; oily substance obtained from certain seeds: *Give me red meat, please; I don't like fat. Fried potatoes are cooked in deep fat. Vegetable cooking fats are sold in tins.* **chew the fat,** continue to grumble about sth. **live off the fat of the land,** have the best of everything. **The fat's in the fire,** What has been done (usu irrevocably) will cause a lot of trouble. **fat·less** *adj*⇔ fatty.

fat³ /fæt/ *vt* (-tt-) fatten: *fatted cattle.* **kill the fat-ted calf,** (fig) welcome sb back with joy.

fatal /'feɪtl/ *adj* **1** ~ (*to*), causing, ending in, death or disaster: *a* ~ *accident. The cyclist was knocked down by a lorry and received* ~ *injuries. His illness was* ~ *to our plans,* caused them to fail. **2** like fate; of, appointed by, destiny: *the* ~ *day.* /'feɪtəlɪ/ *adv* in a ~ manner: ~*ly injured/wounded.*

fatal·ism /'feɪtəlɪzəm/ *n* [U] belief that events are decided by fate(1); submission to all that happens as inevitable. **fatal·ist** /'feɪtəlɪst/ *n* believer in ~. **fatal·is·tic** /ˌfeɪtə'lɪstɪk/ *adj* of ~: *a fatalistic attitude.*

fatal·ity /fə'tælətɪ/ *n* (*pl* -ties) **1** [C] misfortune, calamity, esp one that causes death and destruction: *floods, earthquakes and other fatalities.* **2** [C] death by accident, in war, etc: *There have been numerous bathing fatalities this summer,* Many people have lost their lives while bathing. **3** [U] state of being subject to fate(1) or destiny. 4 [U] fatal infuence; deadliness: *the ~ of certain diseases*, eg cancer.

fate /feɪt/ n 1 [U] power looked upon as controlling all events in a way that cannot be resisted; destiny: *He had hoped to become President, but ~ decided otherwise*. **as sure as ~**, quite certain(ly). **the F~s**, the three Greek goddesses of destiny. 2 [C] the future as decided by ~ for sth or sb; what is destined to happen: *They met their various ~s. They left/abandoned the men to their ~*. 3 (*sing*) death; destruction; person's ultimate condition: *go to one's ~; decide a person's ~*, eg whether he shall be killed or allowed to live; *meet one's ~*, be killed, die. □ vt [VP17] (usu passive) destine: *He was ~d to be hanged. It was ~ed that...*, F~ decided that...: *It was ~d that we should fail*.

fate·ful /'feɪtfl/ adj 1 controlled by, showing the power of, fate(1); important and decisive: *a ~ decision; on this ~ day; these ~ events. When the judge pronounced the ~ words...*, eg sentence of death. 2 prophetic. **~ly** /-fəlɪ/ adv

fa·ther¹ /'fɑːðə(r)/ n 1 male parent: *You have been like a ~ to me. The property had been handed down from ~ to son for many generations. The child is ~ to the man*, (prov) One's childhood decides the way in which one will develop in later years. *The wish is ~ to the thought*, (prov) We are likely to believe what we wish to be true. '**~-in-law** /'fɑːðər ɪn lɔː/ n (pl ~s-in-law) ~ of one's wife or husband. '**~ figure**, older man respected because of eg his concern for one's welfare. 2 (usu pl) ancestor(s): *sleep with one's ~s*, be buried in the ancestral tomb or grave. 3 founder or first leader: *the F~s of the Church*, Christian writers of the first five centuries; *the Pilgrim F~s*, English Puritans who founded the colony of Plymouth, Massachusetts, USA in 1620; *the F~ of English poetry*, Chaucer. 4 *Our* (*Heavenly*) *F~*, God. 5 priest, esp one belonging to a religious order; head of a monastic house (⇨ brother for a monk): *the Holy F~*, the Pope. 6 title used in personifications: *F~ Christmas; F~ Time*. '**~-hood** /-hʊd/ n [U] state of being a ~. '**~-land** /-lænd/ n one's native country (*mother country* is the normal English usage). **~-less** adj without a living ~ or a known ~. **~-ly** adj of or like a ~: *~ly love/smiles*.

fa·ther² /'fɑːðə(r)/ vt 1 [VP6A] be the originator of an idea, plan, etc. 2 [VP6A] admit oneself to be the father or author of a child, book, etc. 3 [VP14] ~ **on/upon**, fix the paternity of (a child), the authorship of or responsibility for (sth): *Please don't ~ this magazine article on me*, don't lead people to think that I wrote it.

fathom /'fæðəm/ n measure (six feet or 1·8 metres) of depth of water: *The ship sank in six ~s. The harbour is four ~(s) deep*. □ vt [VP6A] find the depth of; get to the bottom of; comprehend: *I cannot ~ his meaning*. **~-less** adj too deep to ~.

fa·tigue /fə'tiːg/ n 1 [U] condition of being very tired: *Several men dropped with ~ during the long march*. 2 [U] weakness in metals caused by prolonged stress. 3 [C] tiring task; non-military duty of soldiers, such as cleaning, cooking, etc. '**~-party** n group of soldiers given such duties. □ vt [VP6A] cause ~ to: *feeling ~d; fatiguing work*.

fat·ten /'fætn/ vt,vi [VP6A,15B,2A,C] ~ **(up)**, make or become fat: ~ *cattle*.

fatty /'fætɪ/ adj (-ier, -iest) like fat; consisting of fat: ~ *bacon*.

fatu·ous /'fætʃʊəs/ adj without purpose or sense; showing foolish self-satisfaction: *a ~ smile; a ~ young man*. **~-ly** adv **fa·tu·ity** /fə'tjuːətɪ US: -'tuː-/ n [U] state of being ~; [C] (pl -ties) ~ remark, act, etc. **~-ness** n

fau·cet /'fɔːsɪt/ n (esp US) device (*tap* in GB) for controlling the outflow of liquid from a pipe or container.

faugh /fɔː/ (*spontaneously, as an explosive puffing sound*)/ int expression of disgust.

fault /fɔːlt/ n 1 [C] sth that makes a person, thing, etc imperfect; defect; blemish; flaw: *She loves me in spite of all my ~s. Her only ~ is excessive shyness. There is a ~ in the electrical system. at ~*, in the wrong, at a loss; in a puzzled or ignorant state: *My memory was at ~. to a ~*, excessively: *She is generous to a ~*. **find ~ (with)**, complain (about): *I have no ~ to find with your work. He's always finding ~*. Hence, '**~-finder**; '**~-finding**. 2 [U] responsibility for being wrong: *Whose ~ is it that we are late? It's your own ~. The ~ lies with you, not with me*, You are to blame. 3 [C] thing wrongly done; (tennis, etc) ball wrongly served. 4 [C] place where there is a break in the continuity of layers of rock, etc. □ vt [VP6A] find ~ with: *No one could ~ his performance*. **~-less** adj **~-less·ly** adv **~y** adj having a ~ or ~s. **~-ily** /-ɪlɪ/ adv in a ~y manner.

a fault·in rock   a faun

faun /fɔːn/ n (Roman myth) one of a class of gods of the woods and fields, with a goat's horns and legs.

fauna /'fɔːnə/ n pl all the animals of an area or an epoch: *the ~ of E Africa*.

faux pas /ˌfəʊ 'pɑː/ n (F) (pl unchanged) indiscreet action, remark, etc esp a social blunder.

fa·vour¹ (US = **fa·vor**) /'feɪvə(r)/ n 1 [U] friendly regard; willingness to help, protect, be kind to: *win a person's ~; look on a plan with ~*, approve of it. **be/stand high in sb's ~**, be well regarded by him. **be in/out of ~ (with sb)**, have/not have his friendly regard, etc. **find/lose ~ with sb/in sb's eyes**, win/lose sb's ~. 2 [U] aid; support. **in ~ of**, (a) in sympathy with; on the side of: *Was he in ~ of votes for women?* (b) on behalf of; to the advantage or account of: *Cheques should be drawn in ~ of the Society, not in ~ of the Treasurer*. **in sb's ~**, to the advantage of: *The exchange rate is in our ~*, will benefit us when we change money. 3 [U] treatment that is generous, lenient; partiality: *He obtained his position more by ~ than by merit or ability*. **without fear or ~**, with impartial justice. 4 [C] act of kindness: *May I ask a ~ of you*, ask you to do sth for me? *I would consider it a ~ if you would answer promptly*. **do sb a ~; do a ~ for sb**, do sth to help sb: *Do me a ~——turn the radio down while I'm on the phone, will you?* 5 [C] ornament or decoration, eg a badge, knot of ribbon, given or worn as a sign of favour.

fa·vour² (US = **fa·vor**) /'feɪvə(r)/ vt 1 [VP6A] show favour to; support: *Fortune ~s the brave.* **2** [VP6A] treat with partiality; show more favour to one person, group, etc than to another: *A teacher should not ~ any of his pupils.* **most ~ed nation clause,** clause (in a commercial treaty) agreeing that a nation shall be accorded the lowest scale of import duties. **3** [VP14] ~ **sb with sth,** (old use, or formal) oblige; do something for: *Will you ~ me with an interview? Miss Sharp will now ~ us with a song,* will sing for us. **4** [VP6A] (of circumstances) make possible or easy: *The weather ~ed our voyage.* **5** [VP6A] (old use) resemble in features: *The child ~s its father,* looks more like its father than its mother. ¡ill/¡well-'~ed adj having an unpleasing/pleasing appearance.

fa·vour·able (US = **-vor-**) /'feɪvərəbl/ adj giving or showing approval; helpful: *a ~ report on one's work; ~ winds. Is he ~ to the proposal?* **fa·vour·ably** /-əblɪ/ adv in a ~ manner: *speak favourably of a plan; look favourably on sb.*

fa·vour·ite (US = **-vor-**) /'feɪvərɪt/ n **1** person or thing preferred above all others: *He is a ~ with his uncle/a ~ of his uncle's/his uncle's ~. This book is a great ~ of mine.* **2 the ~,** (racing) the horse, etc generally expected to win: *back the ~,* bet money on it. *The ~ came in third.* **3** person who receives too much favour, is given unfair advantages. □ *attrib adj* best liked: *He is his uncle's ~ nephew. What is your ~ colour?* **fa·vour·it·ism** (US = **-vor-**) /-ɪzəm/ n [U] (practice of) having ~s(3).

fawn¹ /fɔːn/ n **1** young fallow deer less than one year old. **2** light yellowish brown.

fawn² /fɔːn/ vi [VP2A,3A] ~ **(on), 1** (of dogs) show pleasure and affection by jumping about, tail-wagging, etc. **2** (of persons) try to win sb's favour by servile behaviour, flattery, etc: *~ on a rich relative.*

fe·alty /'fiːəltɪ/ n (pl -ties) (in feudal times) tenant's or vassal's (acknowledgement of) fidelity to his lord: *do/make/swear ~ (to one's lord, for one's land); take an oath of ~.*

fear¹ /fɪə(r)/ n **1** [C,U] feeling caused by the nearness or possibility of danger or evil: *They stood there in ~ and trembling,* frightened and shaking. *He was overcome with/by ~. The thief passed the day in ~ of discovery. Grave ~s are felt for the safety of the missing climbers. A sudden ~ came over him. He obeyed from ~. He was unable to speak for ~.* **for ~ of,** because of anxiety about: *She asked us not to be noisy, for ~ of waking the baby.* **for ~ (that/lest)...,** in order that... should not occur: *I daren't tell you what he did, for ~ (that/lest) he should be angry with me.* **2** [U] ~ **of,** anxiety for the safety of: *He is in ~ of his life.* **3** [U] likelihood: *There's not much ~ of my losing the money. No ~!* (colloq) Certainly not! **4** [U] dread and reverence: *the ~ of God.* **~·ful** /-fl/ adj **1** causing ~; terrible: *a ~ful railway accident;* (colloq) annoying; very great: *What a ~ful mess!* **2** frightened; apprehensive: *~ful of wakening sb; ~ful that/lest the baby should wake up.* **~·fully** /-fəlɪ/ adv **~·ful·ness** n **~·less** adj without ~: *~less of the consequences.* **~·less·ly** adv **~·less·ness** n **~·some** /'fɪəsəm/ adj (usu jokingly) frightening in appearance: *a ~some apparition.*

fear² /fɪə(r)/ vt,vi **1** [VP6A,C] feel fear of, be afraid of: *~ death. These men are not to be ~ed.* **2**

[VP2A,4] feel fear; be afraid; hesitate: *Never ~! Don't be afraid/Don't worry! She ~ed to speak in his presence. He did not ~ to die.* **3** [VP3A] ~ **for,** feel anxiety about: *We ~ed for his life/safety.* **4** [VP6A,9] have an uneasy feeling or anticipation of: *~ the worst,* be afraid that the worst has happened or will happen. *I ~ (that) he has failed. 'Will he get well?'—'I ~ not.' 'Is he going to die?'—'I ~ so.'* **5** [VP6A] regard with awe and reverence: *F~ God and honour the Queen.*

feas·ible /'fiːzəbl/ adj **1** that can be done: *The reconstruction of the destroyed town is ~,* We can, if we choose, do it. **2** (colloq) that is convenient or plausible; that can be believed: *His story sounds ~,* may be true. **feasi·bil·ity** /ˌfiːzə'bɪlətɪ/ n

feast /fiːst/ n **1** '~(-day),** religious anniversary or festival, eg Christmas or Easter. ⇨ also **movable**. **2** splendid meal with many good things to eat and drink; (fig) sth that pleases the mind or senses: *a ~ of colours and sounds.* □ vt,vi **1** [VP6A,2A,B] take part in a ~; give a ~ to; pass (time) in ~ing: *~ one's friends; ~ all evening. He sat there ~ing (himself).* **2** [VP14] ~ **on,** give sensuous pleasure to: *~ one's eyes on beauty.*

feat /fiːt/ n sth difficult well done, esp sth showing skill, strength or daring: *brilliant ~s of engineering; perform ~s of valour.*

feather¹ /'feðə(r)/ n one of the light coverings that grow from a bird's skin. ⇨ the illus at **bird, prey, rare, water**. **a '~ in one's cap,** sth one may justly be proud of. **as light as a ~,** very light indeed. **in full/high ~,** in high spirits. **birds of a ~ (flock together),** people of the same sort (will be found together). **show the white ~,** show fear. **~-'bed** n mattress stuffed with ~s. □ vt (-dd-) pamper by giving generous help; make things easy for: *~-bed the farmers,* eg by subsidizing them. **'~-brained** adj empty-headed; flighty. **'~-weight** n (esp) boxer weighing between 118 and 126 lb (or 53·5 to 57 kg). **~·y** adj light and soft like ~s: *~y snow.*

feather² /'feðə(r)/ vt [VP6A] **1** supply with feathers: *~ an arrow.* **~ one's nest,** make things comfortable for oneself; enrich oneself. **2** ~ **one's oar,** (rowing) turn it so as to pass flat along the surface of the water.

fea·ture /'fiːtʃə(r)/ n [C] **1** one of the named parts of the face: *Her eyes are her best ~.* **2** (pl) the face as a whole: *a man of handsome ~s.* **3** characteristic or striking part: *the geographical ~s of a district,* eg mountains, lakes; *unusual ~s in a political programme.* **4** (often attrib) prominent article or subject in a newspaper; full-length film in a cinema programme, etc: *a newspaper that makes a ~ of (= gives special prominence to) sport; a two-~ programme,* ie with two long films. □ vt [VP6A] be a ~(3) of; make (sb or sth) a ~(3,4) of; have a prominent part for: *a film that ~s a new French actress. ~·less adj* uninteresting; with no obvious ~s(3).

feb·rile /'fiːbraɪl/ adj of fever; feverish.

Feb·ru·ary /'febrʊərɪ US: -ʊerɪ/ n the second month of the year.

feces ⇨ **faeces**.

feck·less /'feklɪs/ adj futile; inefficient; irresponsible. **~·ly** adv **~·ness** n

fec·und /'fiːkənd US 'fek-/ adj prolific, fertile. **~·ity** /fɪ'kʌndətɪ/ n [U] fertility; productiveness.

fed pt,pp of **feed**.

fed·er·al /'fedərəl/ adj **1** of, based upon, federation: *In the USA foreign policy is decided by the ~*

(ie central) *government, and* ~ *laws are made by Congress.* F~ **Bureau of Investigation** (abbr **FBI**), (US) department which is responsible for investigating violations of ~ law and safeguarding national security. ⇨ state¹(2). **2** relating to, supporting, central (as distinct from individual State) government. ~·**ist** /'fedərəlɪst/ *n* supporter of ~ union or power. ~·**ism** /-ɪzəm/ *n*

fed·er·ate /'fedəreɪt/ *vt,vi* [VP6A,2A] (of States, societies, organizations) combine, unite, into a federation.

fed·er·ation /ˌfedə'reɪʃn/ *n* **1** [C] political system in which a union of States leave foreign affairs, defence, etc to the central (Federal) government but retain powers of government over some internal affairs. **2** [C] such a union of States, eg the US; similar union of societies, trade unions, etc. **3** [U] act of federating.

fee /fiː/ *n* **1** [C] charge or payment for professional advice or services, eg private teachers, doctors, lawyers, surveyors; entrance money for an examination, club, etc. **2** [U] (legal) inherited estate: *land held in fee simple/fee tail,* with the right to pass it to any class of heirs/one particular class of heirs. ⇨ entail. □ *vt* [VP6A] pay a fee to, engage for a fee: *fee a barrister.*

feeble /'fiːbl/ *adj* weak; faint; without energy: *a* ~ *old man; a* ~ *cry/argument. His pulse was very* ~. ~·**minded** /-'maɪndɪd/ *adj* subnormal in intelligence. **feebly** /'fiːblɪ/ *adv* ~·**ness** *n*

feed¹ /fiːd/ *n* **1** [C] (chiefly of animals and babies; jokingly of persons) meal: *We stopped to let the horses have a* ~. **2** [U] food for animals: *There isn't enough* ~ *left for the hens.* **3** [C] pipe, channel, etc through which material is carried to a machine; [U] material supplied. '~·**back** *n* [U] **1** return of part of the output of a system to its source (so as to modify it). **2** (colloq) information, etc (about a product) given by the user to the supplier, maker, etc; response: *interesting* ~*back via the market research department.*

feed² /fiːd/ *vt,vi* (*pt,pp* fed /fed/) **1** [VP6A,14] ~ (**on**), give food to: *Have the pigs been fed yet? Have you fed the chickens? What do you* ~ *your dog on,* What kind of food do you give it? ~ **oneself,** put food into the mouth: *The baby can't* ~ *itself yet.* [VP15B] ~ **up,** give extra food to, give nourishing food to: *There are hundreds of poor children there who need* ~*ing up.* **be fed up (with),** (fig, sl) have had too much (of); be discontented (with): *I'm fed up with your grumbling.* '~·**ing-bottle** *n* bottle from which hand-fed infants are given milk, etc. **2** [VP14] ~ **to,** give to as food: ~ *oats to horses. I wouldn't* ~ *that stinking meat to my dog.* **3** [VP2A,C] (chiefly of animals, colloq or hum of persons) eat: *The cows were* ~*ing in the meadows. Have you fed yet?* **4** [VP3A] ~ **on,** take as food: *Cattle* ~ *chiefly on grass.* **5** [VP6A,15A] supply with material; supply (material) to: *This moving belt* ~*s the machine with raw material/*~*s raw material into the machine. The lake is fed by two rivers.*

feeder /'fiːdə(r)/ *n* [C] **1** (of plants and animals, with *adjj*) one that feeds: *This plant is a gross* ~, needs much manure. **2** child's feeding-bottle or bib. **3** (often attrib) branch railway line, airline, canal, etc linking outlying areas with the main line, etc.

feel¹ /fiːl/ *n* (*sing* only) **1** the ~, the sense of touch: *rough/smooth, etc to the* ~, when touched

or felt. **2** the ~, the sensation characteristic of sth when touching or being touched: *You can tell it's silk by the* ~. *The monk didn't like the* ~ *of the hair shirt they gave him.* **3** act of feeling: *Let me have a* ~.

feel² /fiːl/ *vt,vi* (*pt,pp* felt /felt/) **1** [VP6A,10] (try to) learn about, explore, by touching, holding in the hands, etc: *Blind persons can often recognize objects by* ~*ing them. The doctor felt my pulse. Just* ~ *the weight of this box! F*~ *whether there are any bones broken.* ~ **one's way,** (a) go forward carefully, as in the dark, or as a blind man does. (b) be cautious in dealing with sth: *They were* ~*ing their way towards an agreement.* **2** [VP2C,3A] ~ (**about**) (**for**), search with the hand(s) (or the feet, a stick, etc): *He was* ~*ing about in the dark for the electric-light switch. He felt in his pocket for a penny. He felt along the wall for the door.* **3** [VP6A,18A,19A] be aware of (through contact): *I can* ~ *a nail in my shoe. I felt something crawl(ing) up my arm.* **4** [VP6A,18A,19A] be aware of, perceive (not through contact): *Did you* ~ *the earthquake? He felt his heart beating wildly. She felt apprehension stealing over her.* [VP15B] ~ **sb out,** try cautiously to learn the opinion of him: *I'll* ~ *out the members of the committee.* **5** [VP2D,C] be consciously; be in a certain physical, moral or emotional state: ~ *cold/hungry/comfortable/sad/happy, etc. How are you* ~*ing today? You will* ~ *better after a night's sleep. She doesn't* ~ (*quite*) *herself today,* is not as well, calm, self-possessed, etc as usual. *He* ~*s confident of success. He felt cheated. We don't* ~ *bound* (= obliged) *to accept this offer. Please* ~ *free* (= consider yourself welcome) *to call on us whenever you like.* **6** [VP2A] be capable of sensation: *The dead cannot* ~. **7** [VP3A] ~ **for/with,** have sympathy (*with*), compassion (*for*): *I* ~ *with you in your sorrow. I* ~ *for you.* **8** ~ **as if/though,** have, give, the impression that: *She felt as if her head were splitting. Her head felt as if it were splitting.* **9** [VP2D] give or produce the impression of being: *Your hands* ~ *cold. How does it* ~ *to be home again after twenty years abroad? This new shirt doesn't* ~ *right.* **10** '~ **like,** (of persons) be in the mood for: *I don't* ~ *like* (*eating*) *a big meal now. We'll go for a walk if you* ~ *like it.* ~ **equal to;** (colloq) ~ **up to,** be well enough to, be capable of: *I don't* ~ *equal to the task. He doesn't* ~ *up to a long walk.* **11** [VP6A,C] be sensitive to: suffer because of: *He doesn't* ~ *the heat at all,* is not troubled by it. *He felt the insult keenly. She will* ~ (= be saddened by) *having to sell up her old home.* **12** [VP9,25] have the idea; be of the opinion: *He felt the plan to be unwise/felt that the plan was unwise. We all felt that our luck was about to turn. He felt in his bones that he would succeed.* **13** [VP6A] appreciate; understand properly: *We all felt the force of his arguments. Don't you* ~ *the beauty of this landscape?*

feeler /'fiːlə(r)/ *n* [C] **1** organ, eg an antenna, in certain animals for testing things by touch. ⇨ the illus at insect. **2** proposal, suggestion, made to test the opinions or feelings of others, before one states one's own views. **put out** ~**s/a** ~, test the views of others, by discreet inquiries.

feel·ing /'fiːlɪŋ/ *n* **1** [U] power and capacity to feel: *He had lost all* ~ *in his legs.* **2** [C] physical or mental awareness; emotion: *a* ~ *of hunger/well-being/discomfort/gratitude/joy;* idea or belief not based wholly on reason: *a ~ of danger/that something dreadful was about to happen;* (usu *sing*) general opinion: *The ~ of the meeting* (= The opinion of the majority) *was against the proposal.* **3** (*pl*) emotional side of a person's nature (contrasted with the intellect): *Have I hurt your ~s*, offended you? *The speaker appealed to the ~s of his audience rather than to their reason. No hard ~s, I hope!* ie no bitterness, no ill will. **4** [U] sympathy; understanding: *He doesn't show much ~ for the sufferings of others. She's a woman of ~.* **good ~,** friendliness. **ill/bad ~,** bitterness. **5** [C,U] excitement of mind, esp of enmity and resentment: *His speech aroused strong ~(s) on all sides. F~ over the dismissal ran high,* There was much bitterness. **6** [U] taste and understanding; sensibility: *He hasn't much ~ for natural beauty. She plays the piano with ~.* □ *adj* sympathetic; showing emotion: *a ~ remark.* **~·ly** *adv* so as to express ~: *speak ~ly on a subject.*

feet /fi:t/ *n pl* of foot.

feign /feɪn/ *vt* **1** [VP6A,9] pretend: *~ illness/indifference/death; ~ that one is mad; ~ed modesty.* **2** [VP6A] invent: *~ an excuse.*

feint /feɪnt/ *n* **1** pretence (the more usu word): *make a ~ of doing sth.* **2** sham attack (in war and boxing) in one place to draw attention away from the place where the real attack is made. □ *vi* [VP2A,3A] make a ~ *at/upon/against.*

feld·spar, fel·spar /'feldspɑː(r), 'felspɑː(r)/ *n* [U] (kinds of) crystalline mineral rock.

fel·ici·tate /fə'lɪsɪteɪt/ *vt* [VP6A,14] *~ sb (on/upon sth),* (formal) congratulate. **fel·ici·ta·tion** /fə‚lɪsɪ'teɪʃn/ *n*

fel·ici·tous /fə'lɪsɪtəs/ *adj* (formal) (of words, remarks) well chosen. **~·ly** *adv*

fel·ic·ity /fə'lɪsətɪ/ *n* (formal) **1** [U] great happiness or contentment. **2** [U] pleasing manner of speaking or writing: *express oneself with ~;* [C] (*pl* -ties) well-chosen expression or phrase.

fe·line /'fiːlaɪn/ *adj* of or like a cat: *walk with ~ grace.*

fell[1] *pt* of fall[2].

fell[2] /fel/ *adj* (poet) fierce, ruthless, terrible: *a ~ disease; with one ~ blow.*

fell[3] /fel/ *n* animal's hide or skin with the hair.

fell[4] /fel/ *n* stretch of rocky, bare moorland or bare hilly land (esp in N England): *the Derbyshire F~s.*

fell[5] /fel/ *vt* [VP6A] cause to fall; strike down; cut down (a tree): *He ~ed his enemy with a single blow.*

fel·lah /'felə/ *n* (*pl ~in,* *~een* /‚felə'hiːn/) peasant (in Arab countries).

fel·low /'feləʊ/ *n* **1** (colloq) man or boy: *He's a pleasant ~. Poor ~! A ~ must have a holiday occasionally* (used here for 'one' or 'I'). **2** (usu *pl*) comrade, companion: *'school ~s; 'bed~s; ~s in good fortune/misery.* **be ‚hail-~-well-'met with sb,** be (superficially or falsely) on friendly terms with him. **‚~-'feeling** *n* [U] sympathy. **3** (attrib) of the same class, kind, etc: *~ 'creatures; ‚~-'citizen;* **‚~-'countryman,** person from the same country or nation. **‚~-'traveller** *n* **(a)** person travelling with one. **(b)** one who sympathizes with the aims of a political party (esp the Communist Party) but is not a member. **4** member of a learned society: *F~ of the British Academy;* member of the governing body of some university colleges; incorporated graduate member of a college. **5** one of a pair: *Here's one of my shoes, but where's its ~?*

fel·low·ship /'feləʊʃɪp/ *n* **1** [U] friendly association; companionship: *offer sb the hand of ~; enjoy ~ with people; ~ in misfortune.* **2** [C] number of persons associated together; group or society; [U] membership in such a group: *admitted to ~.* **3** [C] position of a college fellow(4).

fel·ony /'felənɪ/ *n* (*pl* -nies) [C,U] major serious crime, eg murder, armed robbery, arson. ⇨ misdemeanour. **felon** /'felən/ *n* person guilty of ~. **fel·oni·ous** /fɪ'ləʊnɪəs/ *adj* criminal.

fel·spar ⇨ feldspar.

felt[1] *pt,pp* of feel[2].

felt[2] /felt/ *n* [U] wool, hair or fur, compressed and rolled flat into a kind of cloth: (attrib) *~ hats/slippers.*

fe·lucca /fe'lʌkə/ *n* narrow Mediterranean coasting vessel with oars or sails or both.

fe·male /'fiːmeɪl/ *adj* **1** of the sex that produces offspring: *a ~ child/dog;* (of plants or their parts) fruit-bearing. **2** of women: *~ suffrage; ~ workers.* **3** (mech) having a hollow part designed to receive an inserted part, eg a plug. □ *n ~* animal; (derog) *~ person.* ⇨ male.

femi·nine /'femənɪn/ *adj* **1** of, like, suitable for, women: *a ~ voice.* **2** (gram) of the gender proper to the names of females: *~ nouns and pronouns,* eg actress, lioness, she, her. **fem·i·nin·ity** /‚femə'nɪnətɪ/ *n* [U] quality of being ~. ⇨ masculine.

fem·in·ism /'femɪnɪzəm/ *n* [U] movement for recognition of the claims of women for rights (legal, political, etc) equal to those possessed by men ⇨ lib. **fem·in·ist** /-ɪst/ *n* supporter of ~.

fe·mur /'fiːmə(r)/ *n* (anat) thigh-bone. ⇨ the illus at skeleton.

fen /fen/ *n* area of low marshy land. **the Fens,** low-lying districts in Cambridgeshire and Lincolnshire.

fence[1] /fens/ *n* [C] barrier made of wooden or metal stakes or rails, or wire, esp one put round a field, garden, etc to keep animals from straying or to keep out intruders. **come down on one side or the other of the ~,** give one's support to one side or the other. **come down on the right side of the ~,** join the winner. **mend one's ~s,** make peace. **sit/be on the ~,** not commit oneself; wait to see where one can win most advantage. Hence, **(a)** **'~-sit·ter** *n* person who does this. **(b)** **'~-sit·ting** *n* □ *vt* [VP6A,15B] surround, divide, provide with a ~ or ~s: *Farmers ~ their fields. His land is ~d with barbed wire. The land is ~d in/round.* **fenc·ing** /'fensɪŋ/ *n* [U] material for making ~s.

fence[2] /fens/ *vt* [VP2A,C,3A] practise the art of fighting with long slender swords or foils; (fig) avoid giving a direct answer to a question(er): *~ with a question.* **fencer** *n* person who ~s. **fenc·ing** /'fensɪŋ/ *n* [U] art of fighting with swords.

fencing

fence³ /fens/ n (sl) receiver of stolen goods; his place of business.
fend /fend/ vt,vi 1 [VP15B] ~ off, defend oneself from: ~ off a blow. 2 ~ for oneself, look after oneself: When his father died, Tom had to ~ for himself. Most animals let their young ~ for themselves from an early age.
fend·er /'fendə(r)/ n 1 metal frame bordering an open fireplace (to prevent burning coal, etc from rolling on to the floor). 2 (on the front of a vehicle, car, etc) strong bar, etc, used to lessen shock or damage in a collision. 3 log of wood, heavy mass of rope, old rubber tyre etc hung on the side of a boat to prevent damage, eg when the boat comes alongside a wharf or another ship. 4 (US) = mudguard, ⇨ mud.
fen·nel /'fenl/ n [U] yellow-flowered herb, used as a flavouring.
feoff /fi:f/ n = fief.
fe·ral /'fɪərəl/ adj wild; untamed; brutal.
fer·ment¹ /'fɜ:ment/ n 1 [C] substance, eg yeast, that causes other substances to ferment. 2 in a ~, (fig) in a state of, eg social, political, excitement.
fer·ment² /fə'ment/ vt,vi [VP6A,2A] 1 (cause to) undergo chemical changes through the action of organic bodies (esp yeast): Fruit juices ~ if they are kept a long time. When wine is ~ed, it gives off bubbles of gas. 2 (fig) (cause to) become excited. **fer·men·ta·tion** /ˌfɜ:men'teɪʃn/ n [U] ~ing or being ~ed: the ~ation of milk (when cheese is being made); (fig) excitement and unrest.
fern /fɜ:n/ n [C] sorts of feathery, green-leaved flowerless plant: hillsides covered with ~ (collective sing); ~s growing in pots. ~y adj
fer·ocious /fə'rəʊʃəs/ adj fierce, cruel, savage. ~·ly adv
fer·oc·ity /fə'rɒsəti/ n [U] fierceness; savage cruelty; [C] (pl -ties) fierce, savage or cruel act.
fer·ret /'ferɪt/ n small animal of the weasel family, used for driving rabbits from their burrows, killing rats, etc. □ vt,vi 1 [VP2A] hunt with ~s: go ~ing. 2 [VP15B,2C] ~ sth out; ~ about (for sth), discover by searching; search: ~ out a secret; ~ about among old papers and books for sth lost.
fer·ro·con·crete /ˌferəʊ'kɒŋkri:t/ n [U] reinforced concrete.
fer·rous /'ferəs/ adj containing or relating to iron: ~ chloride (FeCl₂).
fer·rule /'feru:l/ US: 'ferəl/ n metal ring or cap placed on the end of a stick (eg of an umbrella) or tube, to prevent splitting; band strengthening or forming a joint.
ferry /'ferɪ/ n (pl -ries) [C] (place where there is a) boat, hovercraft or aircraft that carries people and goods across a river, channel, etc. □ vt,vi [VP6A,15A,B,2A,C] take, go, across in a ~: ~ people/a boat across a river; aircraft ~ing motor-cars between England and France. '~boat n '~-man /-mən/ (pl -men) n
fer·tile /'fɜ:taɪl US: -tl/ adj 1 (of land, plants, etc) producing much; (of a person, his mind, etc) full of ideas, plans, etc: ~ fields/soil; a ~ imagination. 2 able to produce fruit, young; capable of developing: ~ seeds/eggs. ⇨ sterile. **fer·til·ity** /fə'tɪlətɪ/ n [U] state of being ~.
fer·til·ize /'fɜ:təlaɪz/ vt [VP6A] make fertile or productive: ~ the soil (by using manure); ~ flowers (as bees do when they collect nectar). **fer·ti·lizer** /-zə(r)/ n [U] chemical plant food; artificial manure; [C] substance of this kind: Bonemeal and nit-

rates are common fertilizers. **fer·ti·liz·ation** /ˌfɜ:təlaɪ'zeɪʃn US: -lɪ'z-/ n [U] fertilizing or being ~d.
fer·ule /'feru:l US: 'ferəl/ n flat ruler for punishing children by striking them on the hand.
fer·vent /'fɜ:vənt/ adj 1 hot, glowing. 2 showing warmth of feeling; passionate: ~ love/hatred; a ~ lover/admirer. ~·ly adv **fer·vency** /'fɜ:vənsɪ/ n
fer·vid /'fɜ:vɪd/ adj fervent(2); spirited; showing earnest feeling: a ~ orator. ~·ly adv
fer·vour (US = -vor) /'fɜ:və(r)/ n [U] strength or warmth of feeling; earnestness.
fes·tal /'festl/ adj of a feast or festival; festive (the more usu word): a ~ occasion, eg a wedding, a birthday party; ~ music.
fes·ter /'festə(r)/ vi [VP2A] 1 (of a cut or wound) (cause to) fill with poisonous matter (pus): If the cut gets dirty, it will probably ~. 2 (fig) act like poison in the mind; become resentful, embittered: The insult ~ed in his mind.
fes·ti·val /'festɪvl/ n 1 (day or season for) rejoicing; public celebrations: Christmas and Easter are Church ~s. 2 series of performances (of music, ballet, drama, etc) given periodically (usu once a year): the Edinburgh F~; a jazz ~. 3 (attrib) festive; of a feast or feast-day.
fes·tive /'festɪv/ adj of a feast or festival; joyous: a '~ season, eg Christmas; the ~ board, a table on which a feast is spread.
fes·tiv·ity /fe'stɪvətɪ/ n (pl -ties) 1 [U] rejoicing; merry-making. 2 (pl) festive, joyful events: wedding festivities.
fes·toon /fe'stu:n/ n [C] chain of flowers, leaves, ribbons, etc hanging in a curve or loop between two points, as a decoration. □ vt [VP6A] make into, decorate with, ~s: a room ~ed with Christmas decorations.
fetch /fetʃ/ vt,vi 1 [VP6A,15A,15B,13B,12B] go for and bring back (sb or sth): F~ a doctor at once. Please ~ the children from school. The chair is in the garden; please ~ it in. Shall I ~ your coat for you/~ you your coat from the next room? ~ and carry (for), be busy with small duties for; be a servant for: He expects his daughter to ~ and carry for him all day. 2 [VP6A,15A] cause to come out; draw forth: ~ a deep sigh/a dreadful groan; ~ tears to the eyes. 3 [VP6A,12B] (of goods) bring in; sell for (a price): These old books won't ~ (you) much. 4 [VP12C] (colloq) deal, give (a blow) to: She ~ed me a slap across the face/a box on the ears. ~·ing adj (colloq) attractive, delightful: What a ~ing little hat! What a ~ing smile!
fête /feɪt/ n (usu outdoor) festival or entertainment: the village ~, often one at which funds are raised. '~-day n saint's-day. ⇨ saint(5). □ vt [VP6A] honour by entertaining; make a fuss of: The hero was ~d wherever he went.
fetid /'fetɪd/ adj stinking.
fet·ish /'fetɪʃ/ n 1 object worshipped by pagan people because they believe a spirit lives in it. 2 anything to which abnormal, excessive respect or attention is given; (colloq) obsession: Some women make a ~ of clothes.
fet·lock /'fetlɒk/ n (tuft of hair on a) horse's leg above and behind the hoof. ⇨ the illus at domestic.
fet·ter /'fetə(r)/ n chain for the ankles of a prisoner or the leg of a horse; (fig, usu pl) sth that hinders progress. □ vt [VP6A] put in ~s or chains; (fig) restrain.

fettle /'fetl/ *n in fine/good ~*, in good (physical) condition; in high spirits.

fe·tus ⇨ foetus.

feud /fju:d/ *n* [C] bitter quarrel between two persons, families or groups, over a long period of time.

feu·dal /'fju:dl/ *adj* of the method (**the '~ system**) of holding land (by giving services to the owner) during the Middle Ages in Europe: *~ law; the ~ barons.* ⇨ vassal. *~ism* /-izəm/ *n* [U] the *~* system.

feuda·tory /'fju:dətərɪ US: -tɔ:rɪ/ *adj* owing service to a lord: *~ obligations.* □ *n* vassal.

fe·ver /'fi:və(r)/ *n* **1** [U,C] condition of the human body with temperature higher than usual, esp as a sign of illness: *She hasn't much ~. He has a high ~.* '*~ heat*, high temperature of the human body in *~*. **2** [U] one of a number of diseases in which there is high *~*: *yellow/typhoid/rheumatic ~.* **3** (usu *a ~*) excited state; nervous agitation: *in a ~ of impatience.* **at/to** '*~ pitch*, at/to a high level of excitement: *The crowd was at ~ pitch.* *~ed adj* affected by a *~*: *a ~ed imagination*, highly excited. *~ish* /-rɪʃ/ *adj* having symptoms of *~*; caused by *~*; causing *~*: *in a ~ish condition; ~ish dreams; ~ish swamps.* *~ish·ly adv*

few /fju:/ *adj* (-er, -est), *pron* (contrasted with *many*; ⇨ little, less, much) **1** (attrib, with a *pl n*) not many: *Few people live to be 100 and fewer still live to be 110. Which of you made the fewest mistakes*, the smallest number of mistakes? *He is a man of few words*, He says very little. **no fewer than**, as many as: *No fewer than twenty workers were absent through illness.* **2** (pred, rare in colloq style): *Such occasions are few. We are very few, fewer than at the last meeting of the society.* **3** *a few*, a small number (Note that *few* is neg and *a few* is positive: *We are going away for a few days. I'd like a few more red roses.* **some few; a good few; quite a few; not a few**, a considerable number, a fair number. **4** *every few minutes/days, etc.* ⇨ every(5). **5 the few**, the minority. □ *pron few of*, (neg) not many of: *Few of those roses are worth buying.* **a few of**, (positive) a small number of: *I know a few of these people.* **few·ness** *n*

fey /feɪ/ *adj* **1** (Scot) having a feeling of approaching death. **2** clairvoyant. **3** otherworldly.

fez /fez/ *n* red felt hat with a flat top and no brim, worn by some Muslim men.

fi·ancé (fem **fi·ancée**) /fɪ'ɒnseɪ US: ˌfi:ɑ:n'seɪ/ *n* (F) man (woman) to whom one is engaged to be married.

fi·asco /fɪ'æskəʊ/ *n* (*pl ~s*, US also *~es* /-kəʊz/) complete failure, breakdown, in sth attempted: *The new play at the Ritz Theatre was a ~.*

fi·at /'faɪæt US: 'fi:ət/ *n* [C] order or decree made by a ruler.

fib /fɪb/ *n* (colloq) untrue statement (esp about sth unimportant). □ *vi* (-bb-) [VP2A] tell a fib. **fib·ber** *n* person who tells fibs. **fib·bing** *n* [U] telling fibs.

fibre (US = **fiber**) /'faɪbə(r)/ *n* **1** [C] one of the slender threads of which many animal and vegetable growths are formed, eg cotton, wood, nerves, muscles. **2** [U] substance formed of a mass of *~s*, for manufacture into various materials: *hemp ~*, for making rope; *cotton ~*, for spinning. '*~·board* *n* [U] board made of compressed *~*. '*~·glass* *n* [U] material of glass *~s* in resin, used as an insulating material, and made into structural materials, eg for boat-building. **3** [U] structure; texture: *material of*

coarse *~*; (fig) character: *a person of strong moral ~*. **fi·brous** /'faɪbrəs/ *adj* made of, like, *~s*.

fib·ula /'fɪbjʊlə(r)/ *n* (anat) outer of the two bones between the knee and the foot. ⇨ the illus at skeleton.

fickle /'fɪkl/ *adj* (of moods, the weather, etc) often changing; not constant: *~ fortune; a ~ lover.* *~ness* *n*

fic·tion /'fɪkʃn/ *n* **1** [C] sth invented or imagined (contrasted with truth). *a legal/polite ~*, sth assumed to be true, although it may be false, for legal/social convenience. **2** [U] (branch of literature concerned with) stories, novels and romances: *works of ~; prefer history to ~. Truth is often stranger than ~.*

fic·ti·tious /fɪk'tɪʃəs/ *adj* not real; imagined or invented: *The account he gives of his movements is quite ~.*

fiddle /'fɪdl/ *n* **1** (colloq) violin; any instrument of the violin family, eg a cello or viola. **have a face as long as a ~**, look dismal. **fit as a ~**, very well; in good health. **play second ~ (to)**, take a less important part (than). '*~·stick* *n* bow¹(2). '*~·sticks* *int* Nonsense! **2** instance of fiddling; ⇨ 3 below. □ *vt* **1** [VP6A,2A] (colloq) play the *~*; play a tune, etc on the *~*. **2** [VP2A,C] *~ (about) (with)*, make aimless movements; play aimlessly (*with* sth in one's fingers): *Stop fiddling! He was fiddling (about) with a piece of string.* **3** [VP6A] (sl) make or keep dishonestly inaccurate records of figures (in business accounts, etc): *~ an income-tax return*, prepare it so as to try to escape correct tax payments. **fid·dler** *n* person who plays the *~*; person who *~s*(3). **fid·dling** *adj* (colloq) trivial; futile: *fiddling little jobs.*

fi·del·ity /fɪ'delətɪ/ *n* [U] *~ (to)*, **1** loyalty, faithfulness: *~ to one's principles/religion/leader/wife.* **2** accuracy; exactness: *translate sth with the greatest ~; high ~ equipment*, with high quality sound reproduction. ⇨ hi-fi.

fidget /'fɪdʒɪt/ *vi,vt* [VP2A,C,6A] *~ (about) (with)*, (cause sb to) move the body (or part of it) about restlessly; make (sb) nervous: *Stop ~ing! The boy was ~ing (about) with his knife and fork. What's ~ing you*, making you nervous or uneasy? *Hurry up, your father's beginning to ~*, show signs of impatience. □ *n* **1** (usu **the ~s**) *~ing* movements: *Having to sit still for a long time often gives small children the ~s.* **2** person who *~s*: *What a ~ you are!* *~y adj* having the *~s*; restless: *a ~y child.*

fie /faɪ/ *int* (usu hum) for shame: *Fie upon you*, You ought to be ashamed!

fief /fi:f/ *n* [C] land held from a feudal lord.

field¹ /fi:ld/ *n* [C] **1** area of land, either grassland for cattle, etc or arable land for crops, usu enclosed by means of hedges, fences, etc (not normally used of unenclosed land or uncultivated land): *working in the ~s* (Cf *on the farm*). *What a fine ~ of wheat!* **2** (usu in compounds) wide area or expanse; open space: *an 'ice~*, eg round the North Pole; *a 'flying-~; a 'landing ~* (for aircraft); *a 'baseball/ 'cricket/'football ~.* '*~ events* *n pl* athletic contests such as jumping and discus-throwing, but not races or other contests that take place on a track. '*~ glasses* *n pl* long-distance binoculars for outdoor use. '*~ sports* *n pl* hunting, shooting and fishing. **3** (usu in compounds) area of land from which minerals, etc are obtained: '*gold-~s; a new 'oil-~;* '*'coal-~s.* **4** province or department of study or activity: *the* ∼ *of politics/art/science/ medicine. That is outside my* ∼, is not in the departments of knowledge that I have studied. '∼ **work** *n* [U] scientific, technical or social investigation made outside laboratories, etc eg by surveyors, geologists or by students of social science who visit and talk to people. **5** range (of operation, activity, use); area or space in which forces can be felt: *a magnetic* ∼, round a magnet: *a wide* ∼ *of vision; an object that fills the* ∼ *of a telescope; the earth's gravitational* ∼, the space in which the earth's gravity is exerted. **6** place, area, where a battle or war is or was fought: *the* ∼ *of battle* ('*battle-*∼); *take the* ∼, go to war. '∼ **artillery;** '∼ **gun** *nn* light and mobile, for use in battle. '∼ **day** *n* day on which military operations are practised; (fig) great or special occasion. **have a** ∼ **day,** (fig) have a celebration or triumph. '∼-**hospital** *n* temporary hospital near the scene of fighting. ⸲F∼ '**Marshal** *n* army officer of highest rank. '∼-**officer** *n* major or colonel. '∼-**work** *n* temporary fortification made by troops in the ∼. **7** (sports and athletics) (in foxhunting) all those taking part in the hunt; (in a contest, esp a horse-race) all the competitors; (in cricket and baseball) team that is not batting; (cricket) the fielding side.

field² /fi:ld/ *vt,vi* **1** [VP6A,2A] (cricket and baseball) (stand ready to) catch or stop (the ball): *He* ∼*ed the ball smartly. He* ∼*s well. Well* ∼*ed, sir!* **2** [VP6A] (of football teams, etc) put into the ∼: *Brazil are* ∼*ing a strong team for the World Cup.* ∼**er; fields·man** /-mən/ *n* (*pl* -men) (cricket, etc) person who ∼s: *He doesn't bat well, but he's an excellent* ∼*er.* ⇨ the illus at baseball.

fiend /fi:nd/ *n* devil; very wicked or cruel person; (colloq) person devoted to or addicted to sth (indicated by the word prefixed: *a drug* ∼; *a ⸲fresh-'air* ∼. ∼**-ish** /-ɪʃ/ *adj* savage and cruel. ∼**-ish·ly** *adv*

fierce /fɪəs/ *adj* (-r, -st) **1** violent and angry: ∼ *dogs/winds; look* ∼; *have a* ∼ *look on one's face.* **2** (of heat, desire, etc) intense: ∼ *hatred.* ∼**·ly** *adv* ∼**·ness** *n*

fiery /'faɪərɪ/ *adj* **1** flaming; looking like, hot as, fire: *a* ∼ *sky;* ∼ *eyes,* angry and glaring. **2** (of a person, his actions, etc) quickly or easily made angry; passionate: *a* ∼ *temper/speech.* **fier·ily** /-əlɪ/ *adv* **fieri·ness** *n*

fi·esta /fɪ'estə/ *n* (Sp) religious festival; saint's day; holiday, festival.

fife /faɪf/ *n* small musical wind instrument like a flute, used with drums in military music: *a drum and* ∼ *band.*

fif·teen /ˌfɪf'ti:n/ *n, adj* the number 15, ⇨ App **4;** team of Rugby players. ∼**th** /ˌfɪf'ti:nθ/ *n, adj*

fifth /fɪfθ/ *n, adj* ⇨ App **4.** ∼ '**column,** organized body of persons sympathizing with and working for the enemy within a country at war. ∼**·ly** *adv* in the ∼ place.

fifty /'fɪftɪ/ *n* (*pl* -ties), *adj* the number 50. ⇨ App **4. the fifties,** 50-59. **go** ⸲∼-'∼ **(with); be on a** ∼**-**∼ **basis (with),** have equal shares (with). *a* ∼**-**∼ **chance,** equal chance. **fif·ti·eth** /'fɪftɪəθ/ *n, adj* ⇨ App 4.

fig /fɪg/ *n* (broad-leaved tree having a) soft, sweet, pear-shaped fruit full of small seeds. ⇨ the illus at fruit. **not care/give a fig (for),** not care in the least; consider as valueless or unimportant. '∼-**leaf,** (with reference to the story of Adam and Eve) conventional device for concealing genital organs in old drawings, statues, etc.

fight¹ /faɪt/ *n* **1** [C] act of fighting: *a* ∼ *between two dogs; the* ∼ *against poverty; a prize-*∼ (boxing). **put up a good/poor** ∼, fight with/without courage and determination. **a free** ∼, ⇨ free¹(3). **a stand-up** ∼, ⇨ stand²(11). **2** [U] fighting spirit; desire or ability for fighting: *In spite of numerous defeats, they still had plenty of* ∼ *left in them. The news that their leader had surrendered took all the* ∼ *out of them.* **show** ∼, show readiness to fight.

fight² /faɪt/ *vi, vt* (*pt,pp* fought /fɔ:t/) **1** [VP2A,B,C,3A,4A,6A] use the force of the body or of weapons (against); use physical force (as in war); use all resources available (against) to defeat: *to* ∼ *poverty/oppression. When dogs* ∼, *they use their teeth. The dogs were* ∼*ing over a bone/*∼*ing for the possession of a bone. Great Britain has often fought with* (= against) *her enemies. Great Britain fought with* (= on the side of) *France. They were* ∼*ing for* (= in order to secure or maintain) *their independence. They were* ∼*ing to preserve their freedom.* ∼ *to a finish,* until there is a decision. ∼ *shy of,* keep away from, not get mixed up with. **2** [VP6A] ∼(1) in: ∼ *a battle/a duel/an election.* **3** [VP15A,B] ∼ *sth down,* repress; overcome: ∼ *down a feeling of repugnance.* ∼ *sb/sth off,* drive away; struggle against: ∼ *off a cold,* eg by taking aspirin. ∼ *one's way forward/out (of),* advance, go forward, by ∼ing. ∼ *it out,* ∼ until a dispute is settled. **4** [VP6A] manoeuvre (ships, etc) in battle: *The captain fought his ship well.* ∼*er n* person or thing that ∼s, esp a fast aircraft designed for attacking bombers: *a ⸲jet-'*∼*er;* (attrib) *a* '∼*er pilot/squadron.* ∼*·ing n* [U]: '*street* ∼*ing. a* ∼*ing chance,* a possibility of success if great efforts are made.

fig·ment /'fɪgmənt/ *n* [C] sth invented or imagined: ∼*s of the imagination.*

figu·ra·tive /'fɪgjərətɪv/ *adj* (of words and language) used not in the literal sense but in an imaginative way (as when *fiery* is used of a man who is easily made angry). ∼**·ly** *adv*

fig·ure /'fɪgə(r) US: 'fɪgjər/ *n* **1** symbol for a number, esp 0 to 9: *He has an income of six figures,* £100000 or more. *We bought the house at a high/ low* ∼, for a high/low price. **double** ∼**s,** any number from 10 to 99 inclusive. **2** (*pl*) arithmetic: *Are you good at* ∼*s?* **3** diagram; drawing to illustrate sth: *The blackboard was covered with geometrical* ∼*s,* ie squares, triangles, etc. **4** person's ∼ drawn or painted, or cut in stone, etc; drawing, painting, image, of the body of a bird, animal, etc. '∼-**head** *n* (a) carved image (either bust or full-length) placed for ornament at the prow of a ship. **(b)** person in high position but with no real authority. **5** human form, esp the appearance and what it suggests: *I saw a* ∼ *approaching in the darkness. He has a good/poor/handsome, etc* ∼. *She's a fine* ∼ *of a̅ woman,* is well-shaped. *I'm dieting to keep my* ∼, in order not to grow stout. *She was a* ∼ *of distress,* Her attitude and appearance suggested distress. **cut a fine/poor/sorry, etc** ∼, make a fine, etc, appearance. **6** person, esp his characer or influence: *dominating* ∼*s like Napoleon.* **7** ∼ *of speech,* expression, eg a simile or metaphor, that gives variety or force, using words out of their literal meaning. □ *vt,vi* **1** [VP15A] imagine; picture mentally: ∼ *sth to oneself.* **2** [VP2C] ∼ *(in),* appear; have a part; be prominent: ∼ *in history/in a play. He* ∼*s in all the books on the subject.* **3**

[VP15B] ~ **sth/sb out,** calculate; think about until one understands: *I can't ~ that man out,* He puzzles me. **4** [VP3A,9,25] ~ **(on),** (US) reckon; estimate; conclude: *They ~d on your arriving early. I ~ed (that) he was honest. I ~ him (to be) honest.*

fig·ured adj ornamented; decorated: *a ~d glass window,* with designs, eg in stained glass; *~d silk,* with patterns or designs on it.

fila·ment /'fɪləmənt/ n [C] slender thread, eg of wire in an electric light bulb.

fila·ture /'fɪlətʃə(r)/ n workshop in which raw silk is reeled from cocoons.

fil·bert /'fɪlbət/ n (nut of a) cultivated hazel.

filch /fɪltʃ/ vt [VP6A] pilfer; steal (sth of small value).

file¹ /faɪl/ n metal tool with rough surface(s) for cutting or smoothing hard substances. ⇨ the illus at tool. □ vt [VP6A,22,15A] use a ~ on; make smooth with a ~; remove, cut through, with a ~: *~ one's fingernails; ~ sth smooth; ~ an iron rod in two.*

fil·ings /'faɪlɪŋz/ n pl bits ~d off or removed by a ~.

file² /faɪl/ n [C] holder, cover, case, box, drawer etc for keeping papers, etc together and in order for reference purposes, usu with wires, metal rods or other devices on which the papers, etc may be threaded: *Where's the ~ of 'The Times'? We have placed the correspondence on our ~s. on ~,* on or in a ~. □ vt [VP6A,15B] place on or in a ~; place on record: *~ an application; ~ (away) letters; a 'filing clerk,* one who ~s correspondence, etc.

file³ /faɪl/ n line of persons or things one behind the other; (mil) man in the front rank and the man or men straight behind him. **(in) single ~; (in) In·dian ~,** (in) one line, one behind the other. **the rank and ~,** soldiers who are not officers; (fig) ordinary, undistinguished persons. □ vi [VP2C] march in ~: *The men ~d in/out,* came or went in/out.

fil·ial /'fɪlɪəl/ adj of a son or daughter: *~ duty/piety.*

fili·bus·ter /'fɪlɪbʌstə(r)/ n **1** person who obstructs the making of decisions in meetings, parliament, etc by eg making long speeches. **2** such a speech. □ vi act as a ~(1).

fili·gree /'fɪlɪgriː/ n [U] ornamental lace-like work of gold, silver or copper ware: (attrib) *a ~ brooch; ~ ear-rings.*

fil·ings /'faɪlɪŋz/ n pl⇨ file¹.

fill¹ /fɪl/ n **1** [U] full supply; as much as is wanted: *eat/drink one's ~.* **have one's ~ (of sth),** (colloq) have as much as one can bear. **2** [C] enough to fill sth: *a ~ of tobacco,* enough to fill a pipe. *~-ing* n [C] sth put in to ~ sth: *a ~ing in a tooth.*

fill² /fɪl/ vt,vi **1** [VP6A,14,15B,12B,13B,2A,C] ~ **(with),** make or become full; occupy all the space in: *~ a hole with sand/a tank with petrol. Tears ~ed her eyes. I was ~ed with admiration. The smoke ~ed the room. Go and ~ this bucket with water for me/~ me* (less usu) *this bucket with water. The hall soon ~ed. The wind ~ed the sails. The sails ~ed* (= swelled out) *with wind. ~ in,* add what is necessary to make complete: *~ in an application form,* write one's name, and other particulars required; *~ in an outline,* add details, etc. *~ out,* **(a)** make or become larger, rounded or fatter: *Her cheeks began to ~ out.* **(b)** (esp US) = *~ in. ~ up,* make or become quite full: *~ up with petrol; ~ up a tank. The channel of the river ~ed up with mud.* '*~-ing station,* place where petrol,

oil, etc is sold to motorists. Cf *service station,* where motor repairs may be done. **2** [VP6A] hold a position and do the necessary work; put (sb) in a position: *The vacancy has already been ~ed. He ~s the post satisfactorily,* performs the duties well. **~ the bill,** (colloq) meet one's needs: *These new machines really ~ the bill.* **3** [VP6A] execute, carry out an order, etc: *~ a doctor's prescription.*

fil·let /'fɪlɪt/ n **1** band (often ornamental) worn to keep the hair in place. **2** slice of fish or meat without bones. □ vt [VP6A] cut (fish) into ~s: *~ed plaice.*

fil·lip /'fɪlɪp/ n [C] quick, smart blow or stroke given with a finger; (fig) incentive or stimulus: *an advertising campaign that gave a ~ to sales.*

filly /'fɪlɪ/ n (-lies) female foal. ⇨ colt¹.

film¹ /fɪlm/ n **1** [C] thin coating or covering: *a ~ of dust; a ~ of oil on water; a ~ of mist.* **2** [C,U] roll or sheet of thin flexible material for use in photography: *a roll* (US = *spool*) *of ~; expose 50 feet of ~; ~ stock,* cinema ~ not yet exposed; '*~-strip,* length of ~ with a number of photographs (of scenes, diagrams, etc) to be shown on a screen separately (not as a motion picture). **3** [C] motion picture. **the ~s,** the cinema. '**~ test,** photographic test of sb who wishes to act for the ~s. '**~-star,** well-known cinema actor or actress. **filmy** adj (-ier, -iest) like a ~(1): *~y clouds.*

film² /fɪlm/ vt,vi **1** [VP2A,6A] make a motion picture (of): *~ a play. They've been filming for six months.* **2** [VP6A,2A,C] ~ **(over),** cover, become covered, with a film(1): *The mirror ~ed over.* **3** [VP2A,C] be well, badly suited for reproduction in a motion picture: *She ~s well. ~·able* /-əbl/ adj (of a novel, etc) suitable for ~ing.

fil·ter /'fɪltə(r)/ n apparatus (containing, eg sand, charcoal, paper, cloth) for holding back solid substances in an impure liquid passed through it; coloured glass (as used on a camera lens) which allows light only of certain wave-lengths to pass through; (radio) device which suppresses signals from unwanted frequencies. '**~ tip,** cigarette end containing material that acts as a ~ for smoke. Hence, '**~-tipped** adj □ vt,vi [VP6A,14,15B,2A,C] **1** (cause to) flow through a ~; purify (a liquid) by using a ~. **2** (fig, of a crowd, road traffic, news, ideas, etc) make a way; pass or flow: *new ideas ~ing into people's minds. The news of the defeat ~ed through.* **3** (of traffic in GB) be allowed to pass or turn to the left when traffic going straight ahead or to the right is held up by a red light.

filth /fɪlθ/ n [U] disgusting dirt; obscenity. *~y* adj (-ier, -iest) disgustingly dirty; vile; obscene; (colloq) very dirty. *~y rich,* (colloq) very rich. *~·ily* /-ɪlɪ/ adv *~i-ness* n

fil·trate /fɪl'treɪt/ vt,vi = filter v(1). **fil·tra·tion** /-'treɪʃn/ n [U] process of filtrating. □ n /'fɪltreɪt/ ~d liquid.

fin /fɪn/ n projecting part of a fish used in swimming; thing shaped like or used in the same way as a fin, eg the '*tail-fin* of an aircraft. ⇨ the illus at fish, sea.

fi·nal /'faɪnl/ adj **1** coming at the end: *the ~ chapter of a book.* **2** putting an end to doubt or argument: *a ~ decision/judgement.* □ n **1** (often pl) last of a series of examinations or contests: *the law ~(s); take one's ~s; the tennis ~s,* at the end of a tournament; *the Cup F~,* last football match in a series. **2** (colloq) edition of a newspaper published latest in the day: *'Late night ~'. ~·ist* /-nəlɪst/ n **1**

player who takes part in the last of a series of contests. **2** undergraduate in his ～ year. ～·ly /-nəlɪ/ *adv* **1** lastly; in conclusion. **2** once and for all: *settle a matter* ～*ly*.

fi·nale /fɪˈnɑːlɪ *US:* -ˈnælɪ/ *n* (music) last movement of an instrumental composition, eg a symphony; closing scene of an opera; end.

fi·nal·ity /faɪˈnælətɪ/ *n* [U] state or quality of being final: *speak with an air of* ～, giving the impression that there is nothing more to be said or done.

fi·nal·ize /ˈfaɪnəlaɪz/ *vt* [VP6A] give a final form to.

fi·nance /ˈfaɪnæns *US:* fɪˈnæns/ *n* **1** [U] (science of) the management of (esp public) money: *an expert in* ～; *the Minister of F*～ (in GB called *the Chancellor of the Exchequer*). '～ **house/company,** one that provides ～ for hire-purchase sales. **2** (*pl*) money (esp of a government or a business company): *Are the country's* ～*s sound?* □ *vt* [VP6A] provide money for (a scheme, etc).

fi·nan·cial /faɪˈnænʃl *US:* fɪˈnæn-/ *adj* of finance: *in* ～ *difficulties*, short of money; *a* ～ *centre*, eg London or New York. **the** ～ **year**, the annual period for which accounts are made up. **fi·nan·cial·ly** /-ʃəlɪ/ *adv*

fin·an·cier /faɪˈnænsɪə(r) *US:* ˌfɪnənˈsɪər/ *n* person skilled in finance; capitalist.

finch /fɪntʃ/ *n* kinds of small bird (usu with a distinctive epithet or prefix, as 'chaf～, 'green～, 'bull-～).

find¹ /faɪnd/ *n* [C] finding; sth found, esp sth valuable or pleasing: *I made a great* ～ *in a secondhand bookshop yesterday*, found a rare or valuable old book.

find² /faɪnd/ *vt* (*pt,pp* found /faʊnd/) **1** [VP6A,12B,13B] get back, after a search, (sth/sb lost, left behind, forgotten, etc): *Did you ever* ～ *that pen you lost? Please help Mary to* ～ *her bag. Please* ～ *Mary her bag/* ～ *Mary's bag for her. The missing child has not been found yet.* ～ **one's place** (in a book, etc), turn to the page where one wishes to continue reading etc. ～ **one's voice/ tongue,** be able to speak (after being silent because of shyness, etc). **2** [VP6A,12A,B,13A,B,15A,B] get or discover (sth/ sb not lost, forgotten, etc) after search, experience or effort: ～ *a cure/remedy* (*for sth*); ～ *a solution/an answer* (*to a problem*); ～ (*the*) *time to do sth. They dug five metres and then found water. I can* ～ *nothing new to say on this subject. Did you* ～ *him what he wanted? They couldn't* ～ *the way in/out/back. Where will they* ～ *money for the journey?* ～ **favour with sb,** ⇨ favour¹(1). ～ **fault (with),** ⇨ fault. ～ **one's feet,** (a) be able to stand and walk, eg as a baby does: *How old was the baby when it began to* ～ *its feet?* (b) become able to act independently, without the help and guidance of others. ～ **oneself,** discover one's vocation; learn one's powers and abilities and how to use them. ⇨ also 5 below. ～ **it in one's heart/ oneself to do sth,** (chiefly neg and interr with *can/could*) be so unkind or callous as to: *How can you* ～ *it in your heart to drown these little kittens?* **3** [VP6A,15A,B] arrive at naturally: *Rivers* ～ *their way to the sea. Water always* ～*s its own level.* **4** [VP6A,19B,22,15A] discover by chance; come across: *He was found dying/dead/injured at the foot of a cliff. I found him in the cellar drinking my best brandy.* **5** [VP9,15A,22,25] become informed or aware of, by experience or trial: *We found the beds quite comfortable. We found him* (*to be*)

dishonest/found he was dishonest. They found him (*to be*) *the right man for the job. Do you* ～ *that honesty pays/that it pays to be honest? I never* ～ *the best too good for me. You must take us as you* ～ *us,* accept us as we are, not expect special treatment or ceremony. *I* ～ *it difficult to understand him/* ～ *him difficult to understand. I called at Smith's this morning and found him still in bed. I was disappointed to* ～ *her out* (ie not at home) *when I called.* ～ **oneself** + *adj/adv,* discover, realize, that one is: *When he regained consciousness, he found himself in hospital,* eg after a motor accident. *How do you* ～ *yourself this morning,* How are you feeling? *He found himself alone with a strange woman.* **6** [VP6A,15B,8,10] ～ (**out),** learn by study, calculation, inquiry: *What do you* ～ *the total? Please* ～ *out when the train starts/ whether there is an express train/how to get there.* ～ **sb out,** detect sb in wrongdoing or error: *Do you think the police will* ～ *us out?* **7** [VP15A] (equivalent to a construction with *there is/are,* etc with no suggestion of discovery or inquiry, the subject being *one* or *you*): *One doesn't/You don't find* (= There isn't) *much vegetation in this area. Pine-trees are found* (= There are pine-trees) *in most European countries.* **8** [VP6A,15A] supply; furnish; provide: *Who will* ～ *the money for the expedition?* ～ **sb/oneself in,** provide with: *He pays his housekeeper £25 a week and she* ～*s herself in clothes,* buys them herself, from her wages. **all found,** everything provided: *Wanted, a good cook, £100 a month and all found,* board, lodging, etc provided free in addition to wages. **9** [VP22,25,9] (legal) determine and declare; give as a verdict: *How do you* ～ *the accused? The jury found the accused man guilty. They found* (= brought in) *a verdict of guilty. They found it* (= the offence) *manslaughter.* ～ **for,** (elliptical use) decide in favour of: ～ *for the defendant/plaintiff.* ～**er** *n* **1** person who ～*s* sth: *Lost, a diamond ring:* ～*er will be rewarded.* **2** device in a camera ('*view-*～*er*) or telescope used to ～ the object to be photographed, examined, etc. ～**·ing** *n* (usu *pl*) **1** what has been learnt as the result of inquiry: *the* ～*ings of the Commission.* **2** what is determined by a jury, etc.

fine¹ /faɪn/ *n* [C] sum of money (to be) paid as a penalty for breaking a law or rule. □ *vt* [VP6A,14] ～ (**for),** punish by a ～: ～ *sb for an offence;* ～ *sb £5.* ～**·able** (also **finable**) /ˈfaɪnəbl/ *adj* liable to a ～.

fine² /faɪn/ *n* (only in) **in** ～, (old use) in short, finally, to sum up.

fine³ /faɪn/ *adj* (-r, -st) **1** (of weather) bright; clear; not raining: *It rained all morning, but turned* ～ *later.* **one** ～ **day,** (in story-telling) one day past or future. **one of these** ～ **days,** at some (vague) time in the future. **2** enjoyable; pleasing; splendid: *a* ～ *view; have a* ～ *time;* ～ *clothes. She has grown up to be a* ～ *young lady. That's a* ～ *excuse,* (ironic) a very poor excuse. *She thinks herself a* ～ *lady,* considers herself a lady of fashion, too superior to do housework, etc. **3** delicate; carefully made and easily injured: ～ *workmanship;* ～ *silk.* **4** of very small particles: ～ *dust. Sand is* ～*r than gravel.* **5** slender; thin; sharp: ～ *thread; a pencil with a* ～ *point.* **not to put too** ～ **a point on it,** to express it plainly. ～**-tooth comb** ⇨ tooth(2). **6** (of metals) refined; pure: ～ *gold; gold 18 carats* ～, with 18 parts of pure gold and 6 of alloy. **7** (to be) seen only with difficulty or effort: *a*

~ *distinction;* capable of delicate perception, able to make delicate distinctions: *a ~ sense of humour; a ~ taste in art.* **the ~ arts; ~ art,** the visual arts that appeal to the sense of beauty, esp painting and sculpture. **8** (of speech or writing) too ornate; insincerely complimentary. *call sth/sb by ~ names,* (a) (of sth) use euphemisms about it. (b) (of sb) flatter him. **9** in good health: *I'm feeling ~.* **~·ly** *adv* **1** splendidly: *~ly dressed.* **2** into small particles or pieces: *carrots ~ly chopped up.* **~ness** *n*

fine⁴ /faɪn/ *adv* **1** (colloq) very well: *That will suit me ~.* **2** (in compounds) *,~-'drawn,* subtle; *,~-'spoken,* insincerely complimentary; *,~-'spun,* delicate. **3** *cut it ~,* ⇨ cut¹(7).

fin·ery /'faɪnərɪ/ *n* [U] gay and elegant dress or appearance: *young men in their Saturday night ~,* smart clothes; *the garden in its summer ~,* with its brightly coloured flowers, green lawns, etc.

fi·nesse /fɪ'nes/ *n* [U] artful or delicate way of dealing with a situation: *show ~ in dealing with people;* [C] (cards) attempt to win using *~.*

fin·ger /'fɪŋgə(r)/ *n* one of the five members (*'little ~, 'ring ~, 'middle ~, 'index* or *'fore~, thumb*) at the end of the hand. ⇨ the illus at arm. *There are five ~s* (or *four ~s and one thumb) on each hand. sb's ~s are all thumbs,* he is very clumsy. ⇨ thumb. *burn one's ~s,* suffer because of incautious or meddlesome behaviour, etc. *have a ~ in every/the pie,* ⇨ pie. *keep one's ~s crossed,* ⇨ cross²(3). *lay a ~ on,* touch (however slightly): *I forbid you to lay a ~ on the boy,* to punish him by hitting him, etc. *lay/put one's ~ on,* point out precisely (where sth is wrong, the cause of a problem). *not lift a ~ (to help sb),* do nothing to help when help is needed. *put the ~ on sb,* (sl) inform against (a criminal). *slip through one's ~s,* ⇨ slip¹(3). *twist sb round one's (little) ~,* cajole him; dominate him. *'~-alphabet n* method (using the ~s in various ways) for talking with the deaf. *'~-board,* wood (on a guitar, violin, etc) where the strings are held against the neck with the ~s. *'~-bowl n* one for rinsing the ~s at meals. *'~-mark n* mark, eg on a wall, made by a dirty *~.* *'~-nail n* nail at the tip of the *~.* *'~-plate n* one fastened on a door near the handle or key-hole to prevent *~-marks.* *'~-post n* signpost giving directions with boards shaped like *~s.* *'~-print n* mark made by *~s* when pressed on a surface, used for identifying criminals. ⇨ the illus at whorl. *'~-stall n* protective cover (worn over an injured *~*). *'~-tip,* top of a *~.* *have sth at one's ~tips,* be thoroughly familiar with it. □ *vt* [VP6A] touch with the *~s: ~ a piece of cloth,* touch, feel, it (to test its quality).

fini·cal /'fɪnɪkl/ *adj* too fussy or fastidious about food, clothing, etc.

fin·icky /'fɪnɪkɪ/ *adj* = finical.

fi·nis /'fɪnɪs/ *n* (*sing* only) (Lat) (at the end of a book) the end.

fin·ish /'fɪnɪʃ/ *vt,vi* **1** [VP6A,C,2A,C,15B,24] bring or come to an end; complete: *~ one's work; ~ reading a book. Have you ~ed that book yet,* read it to the end? *Term ~es next week. We have ~ed the pie,* eaten all of it. *That long climb almost ~ed me,* (colloq) almost caused my death. *~ sb off,* (sl) kill, destroy, him. *That fever nearly ~ed him off. ~ sth off/up,* eat up completely: *We ~ed up everything on the table. ~ ('up) with sth* have at the end: *We had an excellent dinner, and ~ed up*

with a glass of brandy. *~ with sb/sth,* no longer be engaged with sb or busy with sth: *I haven't ~ed with you yet,* still have sth to say. *Have you ~ed with that dictionary?* **2** [VP6A] make complete or perfect; polish: *The woodwork is beautifully ~ed,* smoothed and polished. *They gave a ~ed performance of the quartet. He gave the picture a few ~ing touches.* *'~ing school,* private school preparing girls for social life. □ *n* (*sing* only) **1** [C] last part: *the ~ of a race. It was a close ~,* The competitors were close together at the *~.* *be in at the ~,* be present when the fox is killed at the end of the hunt; (fig) be present during the last stage (of a struggle, etc). *a fight to the ~,* until one side is defeated or exhausted. **2** [C,U] the state of being *~ed* or perfect; the manner in which sth is *~ed: woodwork with a smooth ~. His manners lack ~.*

fi·nite /'faɪnaɪt/ *adj* **1** limited; having bounds: *Human understanding is ~,* There are things that man cannot understand. **2** (gram) agreeing with a subject in number and person: *'Am', 'is', 'are', 'was', and 'were' are the ~ forms of 'be'; and 'be', 'being' and 'been' are the non-~ forms.*

Finn /fɪn/ *n* native of Finland. *~·ish adj, n* (language) of the *~s.*

finnan /'fɪnən/ *n* (also *~* **'haddock/haddie** /'hædɪ/) (kind of) smoked haddock.

fiord, fjord /fɪ'ɔːd/ *n* long, narrow arm of the sea, between high cliffs (as in Norway).

fir /fɜː(r)/ *n* conifer with needle-like leaves; ⇨ the illus at tree. [U] wood of this tree. *'fir-cone n*

fire¹ /'faɪə(r)/ *n* **1** [U] condition of burning: *F~ burns. There is no smoke without ~,* (prov) There is always some reason for a rumour. *on ~,* burning: *The house was on ~. play with ~,* take foolish risks. *set sth on ~; set ~ to sth,* cause it to begin burning: *He set the haystack on ~. not (ever)/never set the 'Thames on ~,* not do anything remarkable: *Tom's not the sort of boy who will ever set the Thames on ~,* distinguish himself. *take/catch ~,* begin to burn: *Paper catches ~ easily. strike ~ from,* get sparks from (by striking or rubbing): *strike ~ from flint.* **2** [U] destructive burning: *Have you insured your house against ~? ~ and sword,* burning and killing (in war). *~ risk(s),* possible or likely cause(s) of *~.* **3** [C] instance of destructive burning: *forest ~s; a ~ in a coal-mine.* **4** [C] burning fuel in a grate, furnace, etc to heat a room, building, for cooking, etc: *The weather is too warm for ~s. There's a ~ in the next room. lay a ~,* put paper, wood, coal, etc together ready for use. *make a ~,* lay a *~* and light it. *make up a ~,* add fuel as it burns low. *e,lectric '~,* heater using an incandescent element(7). *'gas ~,* heater using lighted gas(2). **5** [U] shooting (from guns). *between two ~s,* shot at from two directions. *hang ~,* ⇨ hang²(4). *open/cease ~,* start/stop shooting. *under ~,* being shot at. *running ~,* (a) a succession of shots from a line of troops. (b) (fig) succession of criticisms, hostile questions, etc. **6** [U] strong emotion; angry or excited feeling; enthusiasm: *a speech that lacks ~,* is uninspiring; *eyes full of ~.* **7** (compounds) *'~-alarm n* apparatus (bell, etc) for making known the outbreak of a *~.* *'~-arm n* (usu *pl*) rifle, gun, pistol or revolver. *'~-ball n* (esp) centre of an exploding atomic bomb. *'~-bird n* N American bird with orange and black plumage. *'~-bomb n* one that burns fiercely and causes destruction by *~.* ⇨ napalm. *'~-box n* fuel-chamber of a steam-engine. '~-brand n piece of burning wood; (fig) person who stirs up social or political strife. '~-break n (a) (in a forest) wide strip of land without trees (to lessen the risk of a forest ~ spreading). (b) wall or barrier of incombustible material in a warehouse, factory, etc. '~-brick n kind of brick, proof against ~, used in grates, furnaces, chimneys, etc. '~-brigade n organized team of men who put out ~s. '~-bug n (sl) person who commits arson. '~-clay n [U] kind used for ~-bricks. '~-control n [U] system of regulating the firing of guns. '~-cracker n small ~work that explodes with a cracking noise. '~-damp n [U] gas in coal-mines, explosive when mixed in certain proportions with air. '~-dog n andiron. '~ drill n practice of routine to be followed when ~ breaks out, eg on a ship. '~-eater n person who quickly gets angry and ready to fight. '~-engine n machine, manned by ~men, for throwing water on to a ~. '~-escape n outside staircase by means of which people may leave a burning building; apparatus, kind of extending ladder, used by ~men to save people from a burning building. '~-extinguisher n portable metal cylinder with chemical substance, etc, inside, for putting out a small ~. '~-fighter n = ~man(b); (esp) man who fights forest ~s. '~-fly n (pl -flies) winged beetle that sends out phosphorescent light. '~-guard n protective metal framework or grating round a ~ in a room. '~-hose n hose-pipe used for extinguishing ~s. '~-irons n pl poker, tongs, shovel, etc (kept near a ~place). '~-light n light from the ~ in a ~place: sitting in the ~light. '~-lighter n piece or bundle of fuel for kindling a ~(4). '~-man /-mən/ n (pl -men) (a) man who looks after the ~ in a furnace or steam-engine. (b) member of a ~-brigade. '~-place n grate or hearth for a ~ in a room, usu of brick or stone in the wall. '~ plug n connection in a water-main for a ~-hose. '~-power n [U] capacity to fire(6), expressed as the total number and weight of shells fired per minute: the ~-power of a cruiser. '~-proof adj that does not burn; that does not crack or break when heated. '~-raising n [U] arson. 'F~ Service, (now the official term for) ~-brigade(s). '~-side n the ~side, part of a room round the ~place: sitting at the ~side; (fig) home life; (attrib) a ~side chair; a homely ~side scene. '~ station n building for a ~-brigade and its equipment. '~-stone n ~proof stone (in a ~place, etc). '~-walking n [U] ceremony of walking barefoot over stones heated by ~, or over white-hot wood-ash, etc. Hence, '~-walker n'~-watcher n (in World War II) person whose duty was to watch for ~s started by bombs dropped from the air. Hence, '~-watching n [U] '~-water n (colloq) spirits such as whisky, gin and rum. '~-wood n wood prepared for lighting ~s or as fuel. '~-work n [C] device containing gunpowder and chemicals, used for making a display at night, or as a signal; (pl) (fig) display of wit, anger, etc.

fire² /'faɪə(r)/ vt, vi 1 [VP6A] set fire to with the intention of destroying; cause to begin burning: ~ a haystack. 2 [VP6A] use artificial heat on sth in order to change it in some way: ~ (= bake) bricks/pottery in a kiln; ~ tea, cure it, make green leaves dry and dark. 3 [VP6A] supply (a furnace) with fuel: an oil-~d furnace. 4 ~ up, (of a person) (more usu flare up) become excited or angry: She ~s up at the least thing. 5 [VP6A] excite or stimu-

late. ~ sb with sth, fill with enthusiasm, zeal. 6 [VP6A] discharge (a gun, etc); send (a shell, etc) from a gun; explode (a charge of explosive): ~ a gun. They ~d a salute, discharged guns as a salute. [VP2A] shoot: The officer ordered his men to ~. ~ at/into/on/upon, [VP3A] direct fire towards: ~ at a target; ~ upon a fort/ship. The police ~d into the crowd. ~ away, [VP2C] (a) continue firing: They were firing away at the enemy. (b) (fig) go ahead; begin: I'm ready to answer questions; ~ away. [VP15B] They ~d away all their ammunition, expended it all. 'firing-line n front line (of trenches) where soldiers ~ at the enemy. 'firing-party/-squad n number of soldiers ordered to ~ volleys at a military funeral or to carry out a military execution. 7 [VP6A] (colloq) dismiss (an employee): ~ the manager for being incompetent.

fir·kin /'fɜ:kɪn/ n small cask.

firm¹ /fɜ:m/ adj (-er, -est) 1 solid; hard; not yielding when pressed: ~ flesh/muscles; ~ ground; as ~ as a rock. be on ~ ground, be sure of one's facts. 2 not easily changed or influenced; showing strength of character and purpose: a ~ faith; take ~ measures; be ~ with children, insist upon obedience and discipline; ~ in/of purpose; be ~ in one's beliefs. 3 (of a person, his body, its movements, characteristics, etc) steady, stable: walk with ~ steps. The baby is not very ~ on its feet yet, does not stand or walk confidently. He spoke in a ~ voice. He gave me a ~ glance. □ vt, vi make or become ~. □ adv in a ~ way: stand ~ (lit or fig); hold ~ to one's beliefs. ~·ly adv in a ~ way. ~·ness n

firm² /fɜ:m/ n [C] (two or more) persons carrying on a business.

fir·ma·ment /'fɜ:məmənt/ n the ~, the sky, thought of as containing the stars, planets, moon and sun.

first¹ /fɜ:st/ adj 1 (abbr 1st) coming before all others in time or order: January, the ~ month of the year; the ~ chapter (or Chapter One); King Edward the F~ (King Edward I); a ~ edition copy of a book; the ~ man who arrived/the ~ man to arrive; at the ~ (= earliest) opportunity; ~ (= basic) principles. at ~ sight, when seen or examined for the ~ time: fall in love at ~ sight. At ~ sight the problem seemed easy. in the '~ place, (in making a list) as a beginning; ~ly. ~ thing, as a ~ action; before doing anything else: ~ thing tomorrow morning. ~ things ~, the most important things before the others. not to know the ~ thing about sth, to know nothing whatsoever about it. 2 (special uses, compounds): ~ 'aid n [U] treatment given at once to a sick or injured person before a doctor comes. ~ 'base n (baseball) ~ base¹(6) on the field. get to ~ base, (fig) make a successful start. ~ 'class n [U] best accommoda-

a firework display

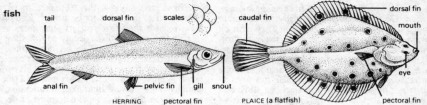

fish

tail · dorsal fin · scales · caudal fin · dorsal fin · mouth

anal fin · pelvic fin · gill · snout · eye

HERRING · pectoral fin · PLAICE (a flatfish) · pectoral fin

tion in a train, ship, aircraft, etc. ⇨ class(7). ~-
'class adj of the ~ class; excellent: ~-class
hotels/cabins/passengers; a ~-class (university)
degree; ~-class food/entertainment. □ adv by the
~ class: travel ,~-'class. ~ 'cost n (comm) cost
not including profit. ,~ de'gree, ⇨ degree. ~-
'floor n (GB) floor immediately above the ground
floor; (US) ground floor. '~ form n (GB) lowest
class in secondary schools. '~-fruits n pl earliest
produce (crops, etc) of the season; (fig) ~ results
of one's work. ,~ 'gear, lowest gear(1). ,~-'hand
adj, adv (obtained) directly from the source: ~-
hand information; learn something ,~-'hand. at ~
hand, directly. ,~ 'lady n (US) wife of a President
or a Governor of a State. '~ name n given name
(contrasted with family name): be on ~ name
terms with the boss (suggesting informality). ,~
'night n evening on which a play or opera is
presented for the ~ time. Hence, ,~-'nighter,
person who regularly attends ~ nights. ,~ 'mate n
⇨ mate¹(2). ,~ of'fender, one against whom no
previous conviction has been recorded. ,~ 'person
(gram) the pronouns I, me, we, us (and the verb
forms used with them). ,~-'rate adj of the best
class; excellent: ~-rate acting. □ adv (colloq) very
well: getting on ,~-'rate. ~-ly adv (in making a
list) as a beginning; in the ~ place.
first² /fɜ:st/ adv 1 before anyone or anything else
(often, for emphasis, ~ of all; ~ and foremost):
Which horse came in ~, won the race? Women
and children ~, ie before men. F~ come, ~
served, Those who come ~ will be served ~. last
in, ~ out, (esp) the last to be employed are the ~
to be dismissed when dismissals are necessary. ~
and last, taking one thing with another; on the
whole. '~-born n, adj eldest (child). 2 for the ~
time: When did you ~ see him/see him ~? 3 before some other (specified or implied) time: I must
finish this work ~, ie before starting sth else. 4 in
preference: He said he would resign ~, eg resign
rather than do sth dishonest for his employers.
first³ /fɜ:st/ n 1 at ~, at the beginning. from the
~, from the start. from ~ to last, from beginning
to end; throughout. 2 (in examinations, competitions) place in the first class; person who takes this:
He got a ~ in Modern Languages.
firth /fɜ:θ/ n narrow arm of the sea; (esp in Scotland) river estuary.
fis·cal /'fɪskl/ adj of public revenue. ⇨ year(4).
fish¹ /fɪʃ/ n (pl ~ or ~es) 1 [C] cold-blooded animal living wholly in water and breathing through
gills, with fins for swimming: catch a ~/two
~es/a lot of ~. ⇨ the illus here and at sea. a
'pretty kettle of ~, a state of confusion. have
'other ~ to fry, more important business to attend
to. There's as good ~ in the sea as ever came
out of it, (prov) Even if one chance, etc has not
been seized, there will be plenty of others. 2 [U] ~
as food: boiled/fried/grilled ~; a ~ course
(as part of a meal). 3 (compounds) '~-bone,

bone of a ~. '~-cake, ~ rissole. ,~ and
'chips, fried fish with fried chips of potato. ,~
'finger (US ,~ 'stick), small, long piece
of ~, covered with breadcrumbs, eaten fried
or grilled. '~-hook, metal hook used for catching ~. '~-knife, knife with which ~ is eaten. '~-
monger, tradesman who sells ~. '~-paste, paste
of ~ or shellfish (spread on sandwiches, etc). '~-
slice, knife for carving and serving ~ at table. '~-
wife, (colloq) crude, abusive woman. ~y adj 1
smelling or tasting like ~: a ~y smell. 2 (colloq)
causing a feeling of doubt: a ~y story.
fish² /fɪʃ/ vi, vt 1 [VP2A,C] try to catch fish: go
~ing; ~ in the sea; (fig) try to get, by indirect
methods: ~ for information/compliments. ~ in
troubled waters, try to win advantages for
oneself from a disturbed state of affairs. 2 [VP6A]
try to catch ~ in: ~ a river/a pool; try to catch by
~ing: ~ trout. 3 [VP15A,B] ~ up (out of)/
(from); ~ out (of/from), draw or pull (from): ~
out a coin from/~ a coin out of one's pocket; ~ up
a dead cat out of a canal. ~-ing n [U] catching fish
for a living or for pleasure. '~-ing-line n line¹(1)
with a ~-hook attached for ~ing. '~-ing-rod n
long tapered rod (often jointed) to which a ~ing-
line is fastened. '~-ing-tackle n [U] equipment
needed for ~ing.
fisher /'fɪʃə(r)/ n (old use) fisherman. ~-man
/-mən/ n (pl -men) man who earns a living by
fishing. ⇨ angler at angle².
fish·ery /'fɪʃərɪ/ n (pl -ries) part of the sea where
fishing is carried on: in-shore fisheries, near the
coast; deep-sea fisheries.
fish-plate /'fɪʃpleɪt/ n one of two iron plates used to
fasten rails to a sleeper (on a railway track).
fis·sile /'fɪsaɪl US: 'fɪsl/ adj that tends to split: ~
material, eg that can be split up in a nuclear reactor.
fis·sion /'fɪʃn/ n [U] splitting or division, eg of one
cell into new cells, or of the nucleus of certain atoms, eg uranium, when an atomic bomb is exploded. ~-able /-əbl/ adj that can be split by ~; capable of atomic ~.
fis·sip·ar·ous /fɪ'sɪpərəs/ adj (of cells) reproducing
by fission.
fis·sure /'fɪʃə(r)/ n [C] cleft made by splitting or
separation of parts.
fist /fɪst/ n hand when tightly closed (as in boxing):
He struck me with his ~. He shook his ~ at me. ⇨
the illus at arm. ~i-cuffs /'fɪstɪkʌfs/ n pl (usu
hum) fighting with the ~s.
fis·tula /'fɪstjʊlə/ n long pipe-like ulcer with a narrow mouth.
fit¹ /fɪt/ adj (fitter, fittest) 1 fit (for), suitable or
suited; well adapted; good enough: The food was
not fit to eat, was too bad to be eaten. It was a dinner fit for a king. That man is not fit for the position. We must decide on a fit time and place for the
meeting. 2 right and proper: It is not fit that you
should mock your mother so. think/see fit (to do

sth), decide to: *He didn't see fit to adopt my suggestion. Do as you think fit.* **3** ready; in a suitable condition; (also colloq, as an *adv*): *They went on working till they were fit to drop,* ready to drop from exhaustion. *He was laughing fit to burst himself,* so violently that he seemed ready to burst. **4** in good athletic condition; in good health: *I hope you're keeping fit.* ⇨ **keep¹**(14). *He has been ill and is not fit for work/fit to travel yet.* **fit·ly** *adv* **fit·ness** *n* [U] **1** suitability (*for*): *the fitness of things,* what is right or suitable. **2** the state of being physically fit: *a national fitness campaign,* one for improving the nation's health.

fit² /fɪt/ *vt,vi* (-tt-) **1** [VP6A,2A] be the right measure, shape and size for: *shoes that fit well; a badly fitting door. This coat doesn't fit me. The key doesn't fit the lock.* **2** [VP15A,B] **fit (on),** put on (esp clothing) to see that it is the right size, shape, etc: *have a new coat fitted.* **3** [VP15A,B] **fit (on),** put into place: *fit a new lock on a door.* **4** [VP6A,14,16A] **fit (for),** make (sb, oneself) suitable or competent: *fit oneself for one's new duties. Military training fits men for long marches/to make long marches. Can we make the punishment fit the crime?* **5** [VP15B,2C] **fit in (with),** (cause to) be in a suitable or harmonious relation (with); find, be in, the right or a suitable time or place for: *I must fit my holidays in with yours. My holiday arrangements must fit in with yours.* **fit sb/sth out/ up,** supply with what is needed; equip: *fit out a ship for a long voyage/a party for a polar expedition; a hotel fitted up with modern comforts and conveniences.* □ *n* (usu **a** + *adj* + ∼) style, manner, in which sth, eg a garment, fits: *The coat is a tight/good/excellent fit.*

fit³ /fɪt/ *n* **1** sudden (usu short) attack of illness: *a fit of coughing; a 'fainting fit.* **2** sudden attack of hysteria, apoplexy, paralysis, with loss of consciousness and violent movements: *fall down in a fit.* **give sb a fit,** (colloq) do sth that greatly shocks or outrages him. **have a fit,** (colloq) be greatly surprised or outraged: *She almost had a fit when she saw the bill.* **3** sudden onset lasting for a short time; outburst: *a fit of energy/enthusiasm/anger.* **by/in fits and starts,** in short periods, from time to time, not regularly. **4** mood: *when the fit was on him,* when he felt in the right mood (*for* sth). **fit·ful** /-fl/ *adj* occurring, coming and going, in short periods; irregular: *a fitful breeze; fitful bursts of energy.* **fit·fully** /-fəlɪ/ *adv*

fit·ment /'fɪtmənt/ *n* piece of furniture or equipment: *kitchen* ∼*s,* eg sinks, cupboards, working tables, esp when made as units in a series.

fit·ter /'fɪtə(r)/ *n* **1** (tailoring and dressmaking) person who cuts out, fits and alters garments. **2** (eng) workman who fits together and adjusts the finished parts of an engine, machine, etc.

fit·ting /'fɪtɪŋ/ *adj* proper; right; suitable. □ *n* **1** act of fitting: *go to the tailor's for a* ∼. **2** fixture in a building, esp (*pl*) things permanently fixed: *gas and electric light* ∼*s.* **3** (*pl*) furnishings: *office* ∼*s,* eg desks, chairs, filing cabinets.

five /faɪv/ *n, adj* the number 5, ⇨ App 4,5: *a* ∼*-day week,* one of ∼ working days. **'**∼**·fold** *adj* with ∼ parts; ∼ times as much. ∼**·pence** /'faɪfpəns/ *n* ∼ pence. ∼**·penny** /'faɪfpənɪ/ *adj* costing ∼pence. **fiver** /'faɪvə(r)/ *n* (colloq) (GB) £5 note; (US) $5 bill.

fives /faɪvz/ *n* (GB) ball game played with the hands or a bat in a walled court.

fix¹ /fɪks/ *vt,vi* **1** [VP6A,15A,B] make firm or fast; fasten (sth) so that it cannot be moved: *fix a post in the ground/a shelf to a wall; fix facts/dates, etc in one's mind,* implant them deeply so that they will not be forgotten. **2** [VP14] **fix on,** direct (the eyes, one's attention, etc) steadily on or to: *fix one's attention on what one is doing. He fixed his eyes on me.* **3** [VP6A] (of objects) attract and hold (the attention): *This unusual sight fixed his attention/kept his attention fixed.* **4** [VP6A] determine or decide: *fix the rent; fix a date for a meeting; sell goods only at fixed prices,* prices with no discount, with no possibility of bargaining; *a man with fixed* (= definite and decided) *principles.* **fixed odds,** ⇨ odds(3). **5** [VP6A] treat (photographic films, colours used in dyeing, etc) so that light does not affect them. **6** [VP15A] single out (sb) by looking steadily (at him): *fix a man with an angry stare.* **7** [VP15B] **fix sb up (with sth); fix sth up (with sb),** arrange; organize; provide for; put in order: *fix sb up with a job; fix up a friend for the night,* give him a bed; *fix up a meeting with sb; fix one's room/drawers/shelves up.* **8** [VP3A] **fix on/upon,** settle one's choice, decide to have: *They've fixed upon a little bungalow near Rye.* **9** [VP6A] (sl) **(a)** use bribery or deception, improper influence: *You can't fix a judge in Britain.* **(b)** get even with sb: *I'll fix him.* **10** [VP6A] (colloq) put in order; prepare: *fix one's hair,* brush and comb it; *fix a watch,* repair it; *fix a salad,* mix and dress it. **fixed** /fɪkst/ *adj* unchanging: *fixed costs,* overhead expenses. ⇨ overhead; *a fixed idea,* one in which a person persists and which tends to occupy his thoughts too much; *a fixed star,* one that seems to keep the same position relative to others, not changing it as planets do. **fix·ed·ly** /'fɪksɪdlɪ/ *adv* in a fixed manner (esp of looking): *look/gaze fixedly at sb.*

fix² /fɪks/ *n* **1** **be in/get oneself into a fix,** a dilemma, an awkward situation. **2** finding of a position, position found, by taking bearings, observing the stars, etc. **3** (sl) hypodermic injection of a drug, eg heroin.

fix·ate /fɪk'seɪt/ *vt* [VP6A] **1** stare at. **2** (usu passive) cause a fixation(2). ∼*ed (on),* (colloq) obsessed (with).

fix·ation /fɪk'seɪʃn/ *n* **1** [U] fixing or being fixed: *the* ∼ *of a photographic film.* **2** [C] ∼ *(on),* (psych) immature and abnormal emotional attachment to another person, with difficulty in forming other, normal, attachments; (colloq) obsession.

fixa·tive /'fɪksətɪv/ *n* substance that fixes(5) eg photographs, paintings; substance that preserves animal tissue for study under a microscope; substance for keeping hair or dentures in position.

fix·ture /'fɪkstʃə(r)/ *n* [C] **1** sth fixed in place, esp (*pl*) built-in cupboards, electric-light fittings, etc which are bought with a building: *The owner of the house charged us for* ∼*s and fittings.* **2** (day fixed or decided for a) sporting event: *football and racing* ∼*s.* **3** (colloq) person or thing that appears unlikely to move from or leave a place: *Professor Gravity seems to be a* ∼ *in the college.*

fizz /fɪz/ *vi* [VP2A,C] make a hissing sound (as when gas escapes from a liquid). □ *n* [U] this sound; aeration by carbon dioxide: *This soda-water has lost its* ∼, has gone flat²(10). ∼**y** *adj* (-ier, -iest).

fizzle /'fɪzl/ *vi* [VP2A,C] hiss or splutter feebly. ∼ **out,** end feebly; come to a weak, unsatisfactory end.

fjord /fɪ'ɔːd/ = fiord.

flab·ber·gast /'flæbəɡɑːst US: -ɡæst/ vt [VP6A] (colloq) overwhelm with amazement.

flabby /'flæbɪ/ adj (-ier, -iest) **1** (of the muscles, flesh) soft; not firm: A man who never takes exercise is likely to have ~ muscles. **2** (fig) weak; without moral force: a ~ will/character. **flab·bily** /-ɪlɪ/ adv **flab·bi·ness** n

flac·cid /'flæksɪd/ adj hanging loose and limp; flabby. ~·ity /flæk'sɪdətɪ/ n

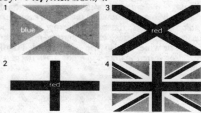

1 St Andrew's   3 St Patrick's
flags 2 St George's   4 the Union Jack

flag¹ /flæɡ/ n (usu square or oblong) piece of cloth, attached by one edge to a rope, used as the distinctive symbol of a country, or as a signal: the national ~ of Great Britain, the Union Jack, ⇨ illus here; the Red Cross ~; streets decorated with ~s. ~ **of convenience**, ~, eg of Panama, Liberia, used to obscure actual ownership of ships and so evade taxation. **lower/strike one's** ~, take it down as a sign of surrender. '~**-captain** n captain of a ~ship. '~**-day** (a) day on which money is raised for a charitable cause by persons in public places, a small paper ~ being given to those who contribute. (b) (US) 14 June, anniversary of the day in 1777 when the Stars and Stripes became the national ~. '~ **officer**, admiral. '~**-pole**, pole on which a ~ is flown. '~**-ship**, warship having an admiral on board '~**-staff**, pole on which a ~ is flown. ⇨ also black, white² and yellow. □ vt (-gg-) **1** [VP6A] place a ~ or ~s on; decorate with ~s: streets ~ged to celebrate a victory. **2** [VP6A,15B] ~ (down), signal to (sb); stop a train, car, etc by moving one's outstretched arm up and down or waving a ~. ⇨ semaphore.

flag² /flæɡ/ vi (-gg-) [VP2A] (of plants, etc) droop, hang down, become limp; (fig) become tired or weak: My strength/interest/enthusiasm is ~ging.

flag³ /flæɡ/ n (also '~**-stone**) flat, square or oblong piece of stone for a floor, path or pavement.

flag⁴ /flæɡ/ n kinds of plant with blade-like leaves, growing in moist land, esp kinds of iris.

flagel·lant /'flædʒələnt/ n person who whips himself or another, eg as a religious penance. **flagel·late** /'flædʒəleɪt/ vt [VP6A] whip. **flagel·la·tion** /ˌflædʒə'leɪʃn/ n

flageo·let /ˌflædʒəʊ'let/ n small flute, like a whistle, with six stops.

flagon /'flæɡən/ n **1** large, rounded bottle in which wine, cider, etc is sold, usu holding about twice as much as an ordinary bottle. **2** vessel with a handle, lip and lid for serving wine at table.

fla·grant /'fleɪɡrənt/ adj (of crime or a criminal, etc) openly and obviously wicked; glaring; scandalous: ~ offences/sinners. ~·ly adv

flail /fleɪl/ n old-fashioned tool for threshing grain, consisting of a strong stick hinged on a long handle. □ vt [VP6A] beat with (or as with) a ~.

flair /fleə(r)/ n [U,C] natural or instinctive ability

(to do sth well, to select or recognize what is best, most useful, etc): have a ~ for languages, be quick at learning them; have a ~ for bargains, be good at recognizing them.

flak /flæk/ n [U] anti-aircraft guns or gunfire; (fig) criticism: get/take a lot of ~. '~ **jacket**, protective jacket of heavy material, reinforced with metal.

flake /fleɪk/ n [C] small, light, leaf-like piece: 'snow-~s; ~s of rust falling from old iron; 'soap-~s. □ vi [VP2A,C] ~ (off), fall off in ~s. **flaky** adj (-ier, -iest) made up of ~s: flaky pastry. **flaki·ness** n

flam·beau /'flæmbəʊ/ n (pl ~x or ~s /-bəʊz/) flaming torch.

flam·boy·ant /flæm'bɔɪənt/ adj brightly coloured and decorated; (of a person, his character) florid, showy. ~·ly adv **flam·boy·ance** /-əns/ n

flame¹ /fleɪm/ n **1** [C,U] (portion of) burning gas; visible part of a fire: The house was in ~s, was on fire, burning. He put a match to the papers and they burst into ~(s). '~**-thrower** n weapon which projects a steady stream of burning fuel. **2** [C] blaze of light; brilliant colour: the ~s of sunset. **3** [C] passion: a ~ of anger/indignation/enthusiasm. **4** [C] (colloq) sweetheart: She's an old ~ of his, a woman with whom he was once in love.

flame² /fleɪm/ vi [VP2A,C] burn with, send out, flames; be or become like flames in colour: make the fire ~ up; hillsides flaming with the colours of autumn, eg of maple-trees. His face ~d with anger. His anger ~d out. The boy's face ~d still redder, became redder, with anger, embarrassment, etc. **flam·ing** adj burning; very hot: a flaming sun; (colloq, vulg) bloody(3): You flaming idiot!

fla·mingo /flə'mɪŋɡəʊ/ n (pl ~s, ~es /-ɡəʊz/) large, long-legged, long-necked wading bird with pink feathers. ⇨ the illus at water.

flam·mable /'flæməbl/ adj (= inflammable, but preferred in US and in technical contexts) having a tendency to burst into flames and to burn rapidly.

flan /flæn/ n [C] tart containing fruit, etc, not covered with pastry.

flange /flændʒ/ n projecting or outside rim or collar, eg of a wheel, to keep sth in position. ⇨ the illus at flagon.

flank /flæŋk/ n **1** fleshy part of the side of a human being or animal between the last rib and the hip. ⇨ the illus at trunk. **2** side of a building or mountain. **3** right or left side of an army or body of troops: attack the left ~; make a ~ attack. □ vt [VP6A] **1** be situated at or on the ~ of. **2** go round the ~ of (the enemy).

flan·nel /'flænl/ n **1** [U] loosely woven woollen cloth: a yard of ~; ~ trousers/shirts. **2** (pl) ~ trousers used for summer sports and games, eg cricket. **3** [C] piece of ~ for cleaning, rubbing, etc: a 'face-~. **4** [U] (sl) nonsense. ~**-ette** /ˌflænə'let/ n [U] cotton material made to look like ~.

flap¹ /flæp/ n [C] **1** (sound of a) flapping blow or

a flagon   a flange

movement: *A ~ from the tail of the whale upset the boat.* **2** piece of material that hangs down or covers an opening: *the ~ of a pocket; the gummed ~ of an envelope; the ~ of a table,* a hinged section that can hang down when not being used, as on a gate-legged table, ⇨ gate(2). **3** part of the wing of an aircraft that can be lifted in flight to alter its upward direction and speed. ⇨ the illus at aircraft. **4 be in/get into a ~,** (sl) a state of nervous excitement or confusion (caused by fear of making errors, being incompetent, etc, eg while awaiting a visit from one's superiors).

flap² /flæp/ *vt, vi* (-pp-) **1** [VP2A,C,6A] (cause to) move up and down or from side to side: *The sails were ~ping against the mast. The wind ~ped the sails. The curtains were ~ping at the open window. The bird was ~ping its wings. The heron came ~ping over the water.* **2** [VP6A,15B] give a light blow to with sth soft and flat: *~ the flies off/away.* **3** [VP2A] (sl) get into a ~¹(4).

flap-jack /'flæpdʒæk/ *n* [C] sweet oatcake; (US) pancake.

flap-per /'flæpə(r)/ *n* **1** sth broad and flat (used to swat flies, etc). **2** (fish's) broad fin. **3** (sl use in the 1920's) fashionable young woman.

flare¹ /fleə(r)/ *vi* **1** [VP2A] burn with a bright, unsteady flame: *flaring gas-jets. The candle began to ~.* **2** [VP2C] **~ up,** burst into bright flame; (fig) into rage; (of violence) suddenly break out: *When he was accused of lying, he ~d up. She ~s up at the least thing. Rioting ~d up again later.* Hence, **'~-up** *n* sudden breaking into flame; short sudden outburst (of anger, etc). □ *n* **1** [U] flaring flame: *the ~ of torches; the sudden ~ of a match in the darkness.* **2** [C] device for producing a flaring light, used as a signal, etc: *The wrecked ship was using ~s to attract the attention of the coastguards.* **'~-path** *n* lit-up landing strip for aircraft.

flare² /fleə(r)/ *vi, vt* [VP2A,6A] (of a skirt, a trouser-leg, the sides of a ship, etc) (cause to) spread gradually outwards; become, make, wider at the bottom. □ *n* gradual widening (eg of a skirt); upward bulge (eg in a ship's sides).

flash¹ /flæʃ/ *n* **1** sudden burst of flame or light: *a ~ of lightning; ~es of light from a moving mirror; ~es from the guns during a battle;* (fig) *a ~ of wit/merriment/inspiration.* **in a ~,** instantly, at once. *a ~ in the pan,* an effort that at once ends in failure, or is quickly over and cannot be repeated or developed. **'~-back** *n* (also *cutback*) (cinema) part of a film that shows a scene earlier in time than the rest of the film (eg the childhood days of the hero). **'~-bulb** *n* (photo) bulb giving a momentary bright light. **'~-gun** *n* (photo) device to synchronize the release of a ~bulb or electronic light source and a shutter in a camera. **'~-light** *n* (a) light used for signals, in lighthouses, etc. (b) (also ~ or **'photo-~**) any device for producing a brilliant ~ of light for taking a photograph indoors or when natural light is too weak. ⇨ the illus at camera. (c) (US) electric hand-light (GB = *torch*). **'~-point** *n* temperature at which vapour from oil may be ignited. **2** coloured stripe worn as a distinguishing emblem on a military uniform, eg on the shoulder. Cf *a badge of rank.* **3** (also **'news·~**) brief item of news received by telephone, cable, teleprinter, etc. **4** (attrib use; colloq) showy; smart: *a ~ sports car.*

flash² /flæʃ/ *vi, vt* **1** [VP2A,C] send, give out, a sudden bright light: *The lightning ~ed across the sky. A lighthouse was ~ing in the distance.* **2**

[VP2C] come suddenly (into view, into the mind): *The idea ~ed into/through his mind. The express train ~ed past.* **3** [VP6A,15A,12C] send suddenly or instantly: *~ a light in sb's eyes; ~ a signal,* eg using a heliograph or torch; *~ news across the world* (by radio or TV). *She ~ed him a despairing glance.* **4** [VP6A] send or reflect like a ~ or ~es: *Her eyes ~ed fire/defiance.*

flashy /'flæʃi/ *adj* (-ier, -iest) brilliant and attractive but not in good taste; given to (rather vulgar) display: *~ clothes/jewellery; ~ men.* **flash·ily** /-ɪli/ *adv* in a ~ manner: *a flashily-dressed girl.*

flask /flɑ:sk *US:* flæsk/ *n* **1** narrow-necked bottle used in laboratories, etc. **2** narrow-necked bottle for oil or wine. **3** (also **'hip-~**) flat-sided bottle of metal or (often leather-covered) glass for carrying spirits in the pocket.

flasks

flat¹ /flæt/ *n* (US = *apartment*) suite of rooms (living-room, bedroom, kitchen, etc) on one floor of a building as a residence: *an old house divided into ~s; a new block of ~s;* **'~-dwellers,** people who live in ~s. **~·let** /-lɪt/ *n* tiny ~.

flat² /flæt/ *adj* (-ter, -test) **1** smooth and level; even; having an unbroken surface: *A floor must be ~. The top of a table is ~. People used to think that the world was ~; now we know that it is round. One of the tyres is ~,* has no or not enough air in it. **~-'bottomed** *adj* (of a boat) having a ~ bottom (for use in shallow water). **'~-car** *n* (US) railway carriage without a roof or sides, for carrying freight. **'~-fish** *n* kinds of fish (including sole, plaice, turbot) having a ~ body and swimming on one side. ⇨ the illus at fish. **~-'footed** *adj* (a) having feet with flat soles. (b) (colloq) downright; resolute. **'~-iron** *n* ⇨ iron¹(2). **~ racing; the F~,** (horse-racing) over level ground with no obstacles. ⇨ *steeplechase* at steeple. **'~-top** *n* (US colloq) aircraft-carrier. **2** with a broad level surface and little depth: *~ plates/dishes/pans. The cake was ~,* had failed to rise while cooking. **3** dull; uninteresting; monotonous: *Life seemed ~ to him. The party/conversation was rather ~. The soup is ~,* lacks flavour. *fall ~,* fail to win applause or appreciation: *His best jokes fell ~.* **4** (music) below the true pitch: *sing ~; a ~ note; A ~ (= A♭),* note half a tone lower than A. ⇨ sharp(10). **5** absolute; downright; unqualified: *give sb a ~ denial/refusal,* deny or refuse sth absolutely. And that's ~! Let there be no doubt about that! **6** (comm) **'~ rate,** common price paid for each of different things or services bought in quantity. **7** (of colours, coloured surfaces) uniform, without relief: *a ~ tint; ~ paint,* without a gloss. *His paintings all seem rather ~,* lack relief, shading, etc. **8** (of a battery) run down; needing to be recharged. **9** (of gaseous or aerated liquids) no longer containing gas: *This beer tastes/has gone ~.* ⇨ fizz. **10 ~ 'spin, (a)** (often uncontrollable) fast descent of a horizontal, spinning aircraft. **(b)**

(colloq) (mental) state of great confusion: *in a ~ spin.* □ *adv* **1** in a ~ manner: *sing ~.* **2** (lying) spread out; (lying) at full length: *He fell ~ on his back. He knocked his opponent ~. The earthquake laid the city ~,* caused all the buildings to fall. **3** positively: *He told me ~ that.... He went ~ against orders.* ~ **broke,** (colloq) with no money at all. **4** ~ **out, (a)** (colloq) with all one's strength and resources: *He was working/running ~ out.* **(b)** exhausted. ~**·ly** *adv* in a ~(6) manner: *The suggestions were ~ly opposed. He ~ly refused to join us.* ~**·ness** *n*

flat³ /flæt/ *n* **1** the ~ (of), flat part of anything: *the ~ of the hand; with the ~ of his sword.* **2** (usu *pl*) stretch of low flat land, esp near water: *'mud ~s; 'salt ~s,* near the sea. **3** (music) flat note; the sign ♭: *sharps and ~s,* the black notes on a piano keyboard. ⇨ the illus at notation. **4** (esp US) deflated tyre, eg after a puncture. **5** piece of stage scenery on a movable frame.

flat·ten /'flætn/ *vt,vi* [VP6A,15A,B,2A,C] ~ **(out),** make or become flat: *a field of wheat ~ed by storms;* ~ **(out)** *a piece of metal by hammering it;* ~ *oneself against a wall,* eg to avoid being struck by a lorry in a narrow street; (fig) humiliate. ~ **out,** (of an aircraft) fly horizontally again.

flat·ter /'flætə(r)/ *vt* **1** [VP6A] praise too much; praise insincerely (in order to please). **2** [VP6A] give a feeling of pleasure to: *I feel greatly ~ed by your invitation to address the meeting.* **3** [VP6A] (of a picture, artist, etc) show (sb) as better looking than he is: *This photograph ~s you.* **4** ~ **oneself that...,** be pleased with one's belief that...: *He ~ed himself that he spoke French with a perfect accent.* ~**er** *n* person who ~s. ~**y** *n* [U] ~ing; insincere praise; [C] (*pl* -ries) instance of this; ~ing remark: *Don't be deceived by her flatteries.*

flatu·lence /'flætjʊləns/ *n* [U] gas in the alimentary canal; feeling of discomfort caused by an accumulation of this. ~**·lent** /-lənt/ *adj*

flaunt /flɔːnt/ *vt,vi* **1** [VP6A] show off complacently; ostentatiously attract attention to: ~ *oneself;* ~ *one's new clothes/riches, etc.* **2** [VP2A,C] wave proudly: *flags and banners ~ing in the breeze.*

flau·tist /'flɔːtɪst/ *n* flute-player.

fla·vour (US = -**vor**) /'fleɪvə(r)/ *n* **1** [U] sensation, when eating, of taste and smell: *When you have a cold, your food sometimes has very little ~.* **2** [C] distinctive taste; special quality or characteristic: *a ~ of garlic; various ~s in ice-cream; a newspaper story with a ~ of romance.* □ *vt* [VP6A] give a ~ to: ~ *a sauce with onions.* ~**·ing** *n* [C,U] sth used to give ~ to (food, etc): *too much vanilla ~ing in the cake. Many ~ings have little or no food value.* ~**·less** *adj* having no ~.

flaw /flɔː/ *n* [C] crack (in an object); sth that lessens the value, beauty or perfection of sth: ~*s in a jewel/an argument/a person's character.* ~**·less** *adj* perfect. ~**·less·ly** *adv*

flax /flæks/ *n* [U] plant cultivated for the fibre obtained from its stem; this fibre (for making linen). ~**en** /'flæksn/ *adj* (of hair) pale yellow.

flay /fleɪ/ *vt* [VP6A] take the skin or hide off (an animal); (fig) criticize severely or pitilessly: *The tutor ~ed the idle students.*

flea /fliː/ *n* small wingless jumping insect that feeds on the blood of human beings and some animals. ⇨ the illus at insect. **(go off/send sb off with a)** ~ **in his ear,** (with a) stinging rebuke. '~**-bite** *n* (fig) small inconvenience, sth not very troublesome.

'~**-bitten** *adj* (fig) (of an animal's colouring) speckled. '~ **market,** open-air market selling cheap and second-hand goods. '~**-pit** *n* (colloq) old and dirty place of entertainment, eg a cinema, theatre.

fleck /flek/ *n* [C] **1** small spot or patch: ~*s of colour on a bird's breast;* ~*s of sunlight on the ground under a tree.* **2** small particles (of dust, etc). □ *vt* [VP6A] mark with ~s: *a sky ~ed with clouds.*

fled *pt,pp* of flee.

fledged /fledʒd/ *adj* (of birds) with fully grown wing feathers; able to fly. ,**fully-**'~ (fig) *adj* trained and experienced: *a fully-~ engineer.*

fledg(e)·ling /'fledʒlɪŋ/ *n* young bird just able to fly; (fig) young inexperienced person.

flee /fliː/ *vi,vt* (*pt,pp* fled /fled/) [VP2A,C,6A] run or hurry away (from): *The enemy fled in disorder. The clouds fled before the wind. He killed his enemy and fled the country.*

fleece /fliːs/ *n* [C,U] **1** woolly covering of a sheep or similar animal; quantity of wool cut from a sheep in one operation: *a coat lined with ~.* ⇨ the illus at domestic. **2** ~-like head of hair. □ *vt* [VP6A,14] ~ **sb (of sth),** (fig) rob (sb) by trickery: *He was ~d of his money.* **fleecy** *adj* (-ier, -iest) like ~: *fleecy clouds/hair/falls of snow.*

fleet¹ /fliːt/ *n* [C] **1** number of warships under one commander; all the warships of a country. **2** number of ships, aircraft, buses, etc moving or working under one command or ownership.

fleet² /fliːt/ *adj* (poet, liter) quick-moving: ~ *of foot,* ~**-footed.** ~**·ly** *adv* ~**·ness** *n*

Fleet Street /'fliːt striːt/ *n* (street in central London where there are many newspaper offices, hence) the press; London journalism.

fleet·ing /'fliːtɪŋ/ *adj* passing quickly: *pay sb a ~ visit,* a short visit before one goes on to another place; ~ *happiness,* lasting for a short time.

flesh /fleʃ/ *n* [U] **1** soft substance, esp muscle, between the skin and bones of animal bodies: *Tigers are ~-eating animals.* ~ **and blood,** human nature with its emotions, weaknesses, etc: *more than ~ and blood can stand,* more than human nature can bear. *one's own ~ and blood,* one's near relatives. *in the ~,* in life, in bodily form. *go the way of all ~,* die. *have/demand one's pound of ~,* insist cruelly on the exact repayment of what was borrowed. ⇨ Shakespeare's Mer of Ven IV, Sc 1. *make a person's '~ creep,* frighten or horrify him (esp with dread of sth supernatural). *put on/lose ~* (more usu *weight*), become fat/thin. '~**-pots** *n pl* (places supplying) good food and material comforts. '~**-wound** *n* one that does not reach the bone or vital organs. **2 the ~,** physical or bodily desires; sensual appetites: *the sins of the ~.* **3** the body (contrasted with the *mind* and *soul*): *The spirit is willing but the ~ is weak,* (of a person who is willing to do sth, but is physically or morally weak or lazy). **4** pulpy part of fruits and vegetables. ~**·ly** *adj* of the body; sensual. ~**y** *adj* fat; of ~.

flesh·ings /'fleʃɪŋz/ *n pl* flesh-coloured tights, eg as worn by ballet dancers.

fleur-de-lis, -lys /,flɜː də 'liː/ *n* (*pl* fleurs-de-lis, -lys pronunciation unchanged) heraldic lily; royal arms of France. ⇨ the illus at armour.

flew /fluː/ *pt* of fly¹.

flex¹ /fleks/ *n* [C,U] (length of) flexible insulated cord for electric current.

flex² /fleks/ vt [VP6A] bend, eg a limb, one's muscles.

flex·ible /'fleksəbl/ adj easily bent without breaking; (fig) easily changed to suit new conditions; (of persons) adaptable. **flexi·bil·ity** /ˌfleksə'bɪlətɪ/ n [U].

flib·ber·ti·gib·bet /ˌflɪbətɪ'dʒɪbɪt/ n frivolous person too fond of gossip.

flick /flɪk/ n [C] **1** quick light blow, eg with a whip or the tip of a finger. **2** short sudden movement; jerk. '∼-knife n knife with a blade (inside the handle) which can be brought into position with a ∼ for use. **3** (sl) cinema film. **the ∼s**, the cinema. □ vt **1** [VP6A,15A,22] strike with a ∼, give a ∼ with (a whip, etc); touch lightly: He ∼ed the horse with his whip/∼ed his whip at the horse. He ∼ed the switch, eg for electric light. He ∼ed the knife open. **2** [VP15B] ∼ sth **away/off**, remove with a ∼: She ∼ed the crumbs off the table-cloth.

flicker /'flɪkə(r)/ vi [VP2A,C] **1** (of a light; fig of hopes, etc) burn or shine unsteadily; flash and die away by turns: The candle ∼ed and then went out. A faint hope still ∼ed in her breast. **2** move back and forth, wave to and fro: leaves ∼ing in the wind; ∼ing shadows; the ∼ing tongue of a snake. □ n (usu sing) ∼ing movement: a weak ∼ of hope.

flier /'flaɪə(r)/ = flyer.

flight¹ /flaɪt/ n **1** [U] flying through the air: the art of ∼; study the ∼ of birds, how they fly. **in ∼**, while flying. **2** [C] journey made by air; distance covered: a non-stop ∼ from Paris to New York; ∼s in a balloon; the spring and autumn ∼s (= seasonal migrations) of birds. '∼ **deck** n (on an aircraft-carrier) deck for taking off from and landing on; (in an airliner) compartment used by the pilot, navigator, engineer, etc. **3** [U] movement (and path) through the air: the ∼ of an arrow; (attrib) the ∼ path of an airliner. **4** [C] number of birds or objects moving together through the air: a ∼ of arrows/swallows. **in the first ∼**, taking or occupying a leading place. **5** [U] swift passing: the ∼ of time. **6** [C] soaring; going up above the ordinary: a ∼ of wit/fancy/ambition/the imagination. **7** [C] series (of stairs, etc without change of direction); stairs between two landings: My bedroom is two ∼s up. There was no lift and we had to climb six ∼s of stairs. **8** [C] group of aircraft in a country's Air Force. **F∼ Lieutenant**, rank in the Royal Air Force below Squadron Leader. **F∼ Sergeant**, rank in the Royal Air Force below Warrant Officer. □ vt [VP6A] (cricket) move (the ball) sideways when bowling it, so as to deceive the batsman: a well-∼ed delivery. ∼-**less** adj (of birds) unable to fly.

flight² /flaɪt/ n **1** [U] (act of) fleeing or running away (from danger, etc): seek safety in ∼; put the enemy to ∼, defeat them and cause them to flee. **take ∼; take to ∼**, run away. **2** [C] instance of this: the ∼ into Egypt (of Mary with the infant Jesus); a ∼ of capital, eg when capital is sent abroad during a financial crisis.

flighty /'flaɪtɪ/ adj (of behaviour, character) influenced by whims; unsteady; fickle.

flimsy /'flɪmzɪ/ adj (-ier, -iest) (of material) light and thin; (of objects) easily injured and destroyed: a ∼ cardboard box; (fig) a ∼ excuse/argument, one that is not convincing. □ n [U] thin paper, eg as used when several carbon copies are made on a typewriter. **flims·ily** /-ɪlɪ/ adv **flim·si·ness** n

flinch /flɪntʃ/ vi [VP2A,3A] ∼ **(from)**, draw or move back; wince: have a tooth pulled out without

∼ing. You mustn't ∼ from an unpleasant duty.

fling /flɪŋ/ vt,vi (pt,pp flung /flʌŋ/) **1** [VP6A,15A,B,22,12A,13A] throw violently: ∼ one's hat up (in the air); ∼ a stone at sb or sth; ∼ one's clothes on, dress hurriedly; ∼ the doors and windows open, open them quickly and forcibly; be flung into prison; ∼ caution to the winds, act recklessly; ∼ off one's pursuers, escape from them. She flung him a scornful look. **2** [VP6A,15A,B] move oneself, one's arms, etc violently, hurriedly, impulsively or angrily: ∼ one's arms up/about; ∼ oneself into a chair. **3** [VP2C] go angrily or violently; rush: She flung out of the room. He flung off without saying goodbye. □ n [C] **1** act of ∼ing; ∼ing movement. **have a ∼ at**, (shot or go are the more usu words) make an attempt at. **2** kind of energetic dance: the Highland ∼, as danced in Scotland. **have one's ∼**, have a time of unrestricted pleasure.

flint /flɪnt/ n [U] hard kind of stone found in lumps like pebbles, steel-grey inside and white outside; [C] piece of this used with steel to produce sparks; [C] piece of hard alloy used in a cigarette-lighter to produce sparks. '∼-**stone** n [U] ∼ pebbles used for building walls, etc. ∼**y** adj (-ier, -iest) very hard, like ∼.

flip /flɪp/ vt,vi (-pp-) [VP6A,15A,B] put (sth) into motion by a snap of the finger and thumb; throw with a jerk: ∼ a coin (down) on the counter. □ n **1** quick, light blow. **2** (colloq) short flight in an aeroplane for pleasure. □ adj (colloq) flippant; glib. **the'∼ side**, (colloq) the reverse side (of a gramophone record).

flip·pant /'flɪpənt/ adj not showing deserved respect or seriousness: a ∼ answer/remark. ∼·**ly** adv **flip·pancy** /-ənsɪ/ n [U] being ∼; [C] ∼ remark, etc.

flip·per /'flɪpə(r)/ n **1** limb of certain sea animals (not fish) used in swimming: Seals, turtles and penguins have ∼s. ⇨ the illus at sea. **2** device worn on the feet to increase the thrust of leg movements in swimming. ⇨ the illus at frogman.

flirt /flɜːt/ vi [VP2A,3A] ∼ **(with)**, **1** show affection for amusement, without serious intentions: She ∼s with every handsome man she meets. **2** pretend to be interested in; think about, but not seriously: He's been ∼ing with the idea of going to Moscow. □ n sb who ∼s with many people. **flir·ta·tion** /flɜː'teɪʃn/ n [U] ∼ing; [C] instance of this: carry on a ∼ation. **flir·ta·tious** /flɜː'teɪʃəs/ adj fond of ∼ing; of ∼ing.

flit /flɪt/ vi (-tt-) **1** [VP2C] fly or move lightly and quickly: bees ∼ting from flower to flower; bats ∼ting about in the dusk; (fig) fancies that ∼ through one's mind. **2** (colloq) remove from one house to another; change one's abode, eg secretly, to avoid paying debts. □ n (colloq) act of ∼ting(2): do a (moonlight) ∼.

float¹ /fləʊt/ n [C] **1** piece of cork or other light material used on a fishing-line (to indicate when the bait has been taken) or to support the edge of a fishing-net. **2** hollow ball or other air-filled container, eg to regulate the level of water in a cistern, or to support an aircraft on water. **3** low platform on wheels, used for showing things in a procession; kind of wagon or cart with a low floor.

float² /fləʊt/ vi,vt **1** [VP2A,C] be held up in air, gas or (esp) on the surface of liquid; move with moving liquid or air: dust ∼ing in the air. Wood ∼s on water. A balloon ∼ed across the sky. The boat

~ed down the river. 2 [VP6A,15A,B] cause to ~;
keep ~ing: ~ a raft of logs down a river. The ship
was ~ed by the tide, eg after sticking fast on a
sand-bank. There wasn't enough water to ~ the
ship. 3 [VP6A] (comm) get (esp financial) support
for in order to start; launch: ~ a new business
company. 4 [VP6A] (finance) allow the foreign exchange value (of a currency) to vary (usu within
narrow limits): ~ the pound/dollar. 5 circulate: ~
a rumour/an idea. ~-ing adj 1 fluctuating; variable: the ~ing population, that part which varies
very much, eg sailors in a seaport; the ~ing vote,
the votes of those persons who are not committed
to a political party. 2 ~ing debt, one of which part
must be paid on demand, or at a stated time. '~ing
rib, (anat) one of the two lower pairs of ribs not attached to the breastbone.

floa·ta·tion, flo·ta·tion /fləʊˈteɪʃn/ n [C,U] float-
ing(3) of a business company or enterprise.

flock¹ /flɒk/ n 1 number of birds or animals (usu
sheep, goats) of one kind, either kept together or
feeding and travelling together: a ~ of wild geese;
~s and herds, sheep and cattle. 2 crowd of people:
Visitors came in ~s to see the new bridge. 3
Christian congregation; number of people together
in sb's charge: a priest and his ~. □ vi [VP2C,4A]
gather, come or go together in great numbers: The
children ~ed round their teacher. People ~ed to
hear the new prophet.

flock² /flɒk/ n [C] tuft of wool or hair; (pl) wool or
cotton waste for stuffing mattresses, etc.

floe /fləʊ/ n [C] sheet of floating ice.

flog /flɒg/ vt (-gg-) [VP6A] 1 beat severely with a
rod or whip. ~ a dead horse, waste one's efforts.
~ sth to death, be so persistent or repetitive
about it (eg a joke, an idea) that people lose interest
in it. 2 (sl) sell or exchange (esp sth illicitly obtained, or sth secondhand): ~ stolen goods/one's
old car. ~-ging n [U] beating or whipping; [C] instance of this.

flood¹ /flʌd/ n [C] 1 (coming of a) great quantity of
water in a place that is usually dry: The rainstorms
caused ~s in the low-lying parts of the town. in ~,
(of a river) overflowing its banks. the F~; Noah's
F~, (biblical) that described in Genesis. 2 great
outpouring or outburst: ~s of rain/tears; a ~ of
light/anger/words/letters. 3 (also '~-tide) the
flowing in of the tide (from the sea to the land):
The tide is at the ~. ⇔ ebb. '~-gate n gate
opened and closed to admit or keep out water, esp
the lower gate of a lock. '~-lights n pl artificial
lighting thrown in a bright and broad beam. '~-
light vt (pt,pp -lighted, -lit /-lɪt/) light up by this
method: The cathedral was ~lit.

flood² /flʌd/ vt,vi 1 [VP6A,14,16A] ~ (with),
cover or fill with a flood (liter, fig): The meadows
were ~ed. The soldiers broke the dikes and ~ed
the countryside to keep back the enemy. We have
been ~ed with requests for help. The stage of the
theatre was ~ed with light. 2 (of rain) fill (a river)
to overflowing: rivers ~ed by heavy rainstorms. 3
[VP15B] ~ out, compel to leave because of a ~;
(fig) inundate: Thousands of people were ~ed out,
forced to leave their homes. 4 [VP3A] ~ in, come
in in great quantities or numbers: Applications
~ed in.

floor¹ /flɔː(r)/ n [C] 1 lower surface of a room; part
on which one walks: sitting on the ~; a bare ~,
one with no carpet, rugs or other covering. wipe
the ~ with sb, utterly defeat him, eg in a fight or

argument. '~-board n plank of a wooden floor. '~
show, cabaret entertainment. 2 number of rooms,
etc on the same level in a building. 'ground ~,
(GB) ~ level with the street. 'first ~, (GB) ~
above the ground ~; (US) ground ~. 'second/
'third etc ~, (GB) ~s above the first ~; (US) ~s
above the ground ~. get in on the ground ~, ⇔
ground¹(10). '~-walker n (US) = shop-walker.
3 bottom of the sea, of a cave, etc. 4 part of an assembly hall, eg the Houses of Parliament, Congress, where members sit. take the ~, speak in a
debate. 5 (opp of ceiling) lower limit (of prices).
~-ing n [U] material, eg boards, used for making
~s.

floor² /flɔː(r)/ vt [VP6A] 1 put (a floor) in a building. 2 knock down: ~ a man in a boxing match. 3
(of a problem, argument, etc) puzzle, defeat: Tom
was ~ed by two of the questions in the examination
paper.

floozy, floo·zie /ˈfluːzɪ/ n (sl) slovenly woman, esp
a prostitute.

flop /flɒp/ vi,vt (-pp-) 1 [VP2A,C] move, fall,
clumsily or helplessly: The fish we had caught
were ~ping about in the bottom of the boat. He
~ped down on his knees and begged for mercy. 2
[VP15A,B] ~ down, put down or drop clumsily or
roughly: ~ down a heavy bag. 3 [VP2A] (sl) (of a
book, a play for the theatre, etc) fail. □ n act or
sound of ~ping; (sl) failure of a book, play, etc. □
adv with a ~: fall ~ into the water. ~-py adj (-ier,
-iest) inclined to ~; hanging down loosely: a ~py
hat.

flora /ˈflɔːrə/ n pl all the plants of a particular area
or period.

floral /ˈflɔːrəl/ adj of flowers: ~ designs.

flori·cul·ture /ˈflɔːrɪkʌltʃə(r)/ n [U] the cultivation
of flowering plants.

florid /ˈflɒrɪd US: ˈflɔːr-/ adj 1 very much ornamented; (too) rich in ornament and colour: ~
carving; a ~ style, eg of writing. 2 (of a person's
face) naturally red: a ~ complexion. ~·ly adv

florin /ˈflɒrɪn US: ˈflɔːr-/ n former name of a British
coin worth one tenth of £1 (until 1971, two shillings; now ten pence).

flor·ist /ˈflɒrɪst US: ˈflɔːr-/ n person who grows or
sells flowers.

floss /flɒs US: flɔːs/ n [U] rough silk threads on the
outside of a silkworm's cocoon; (also '~ silk) silk
spun from these for needlework. 'candy-~, soft,
coloured mass of spun sugar, eaten off a stick.

flo·ta·tion /fləʊˈteɪʃn/ = floatation.

flo·tilla /fləˈtɪlə/ n fleet of small warships, eg destroyers.

flot·sam /ˈflɒtsəm/ n [U] (legal) parts of a wrecked
ship or its cargo floating on the sea. ⇔ jetsam.

flounce¹ /flaʊns/ vi [VP2C] move with exaggerated
or impatient movements: ~ out of/about the room.
□ n [C] fling; jerk; sudden impatient movement of
the body.

flounce² /flaʊns/ n [C] (often ornamental) strip of
cloth or lace sewn by the upper edge to a woman's
skirt. □ vt [VP6A] trim with a ~ or ~s.

floun·der¹ /ˈflaʊndə(r)/ vi [VP2A,C] make violent
and usu vain efforts (as when trying to get out of
deep snow, or when one is in deep water and unable to swim); (fig) hesitate, make mistakes, when
trying to do sth: ~ through a speech, eg in a
foreign language.

floun·der² /ˈflaʊndə(r)/ n small flatfish, used as
food.

flour /'flaʊə(r)/ n [U] fine meal, powder, made from grain, used for making bread, cakes, pastry, etc. □ vt [VP6A] cover or sprinkle with ~. ~y adj of, like, covered with, ~.

flour·ish /'flʌrɪʃ/ vi,vt 1 [VP2A] grow in a healthy manner; be well and active; prosper: *His business is ~ing. I hope you are all ~ing*, keeping well. 2 [VP6A] wave about and show: ~ *a sword.* 3 [VP2A] (of a famous person) be alive and active (at the time indicated): *When did the troubadours ~?* □ n [C] ~ing movement; curve or decoration, ornament in handwriting, eg to a signature; loud, exciting passage of music; fanfare: *a ~ of trumpets,* eg to welcome a distinguished visitor.

flout /flaʊt/ vt [VP6A] oppose; treat with contempt: ~ *sb's wishes/advice.*

flow /fləʊ/ vi (pt, pp ~ed) [VP2A,C] 1 move along or over as a river does; move smoothly: *Rivers ~ into the sea. The tears ~ed from her eyes. The river ~ed over* (= overflowed) *its banks. Gold ~ed* (= was sent) *out of the country.* 2 (of hair, articles of dress, etc) hang down loosely: *~ing robes; a ~ing tie; hair ~ing down her back.* 3 come from; be the result of: *Wealth ~s from industry and economy.* 4 (of the tide) come in; rise: *The tide began to ~.* ⇨ ebb. □ n (*sing* only) ~ing movement; quantity that ~s: *a good ~ of water; a ~ of angry words; the ebb and ~ of the sea. The tide is on the ~,* coming in.

flower /'flaʊə(r)/ n 1 that part of a plant that produces seeds. *in ~,* with the ~s out. '~-bed n plot of land in which ~s are grown. '~ garden, one with ~ing plants, not vegetables, etc. '~-girl n girl who sells ~s, eg in a market. '~ children/

people, (colloq, in the 1960's) hippies favouring universal love and peace. '~ power, the ideals of these people. '~-pot n pot, eg of red earthenware or plastic, in which a plant may be grown. '~ show n exhibition at which ~s are shown (often in competition for prizes). 2 the ~ of, the finest part of: *in the ~ of one's strength; the ~ of the nation's manhood,* the finest men. 3 ~ of speech, ornamental phrase. □ vi [VP2A,C] produce ~s: *~ing bushes; late-~ing chrysanthemums.* **flow·ered** adj decorated with floral patterns: *~ed chintz.* ~y adj (-ier, -iest) having many ~s: *~y fields;* (fig) full of ~s of speech: *~y language.* ~·less adj not having, not producing, ~s: *~less plants.*

flown /fləʊn/ pp of fly.

flu /fluː/ n (colloq abbr of) influenza.

fluc·tu·ate /'flʌktʃʊeɪt/ vi [VP2A,C] (of levels, prices, etc) move up and down; be irregular: *fluctuating prices; ~ between hope and despair.* **fluc·tu·ation** /ˌflʌktʃʊ'eɪʃn/ n [U] fluctuating; [C] fluctuating movement: *fluctuations of temperature; fluctuations in the exchange rates.*

flue /fluː/ n [C] channel, pipe or tube for carrying heat, hot air or smoke to, from or through a boiler, oven, etc: *clean the ~s of soot.*

flu·ent /'fluːənt/ adj (of a person) able to speak smoothly and readily: *a ~ speaker;* (of speech) coming smoothly and readily: *speak ~ French.* ~·ly adv **flu·ency** /'fluːənsɪ/ n [U] the quality of being ~.

fluff /flʌf/ n 1 [U] soft, feathery stuff given off by blankets or other soft woolly material; soft fur or down[1]. 2 bungled attempt. ⇨ 2 below. □ vt 1 [VP6A,15B] ~ (out), shake, puff or spread out: ~

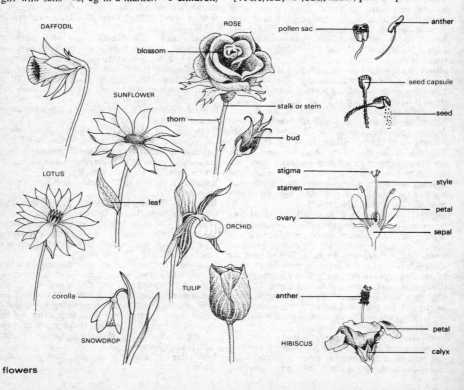

DAFFODIL

ROSE — blossom

SUNFLOWER

LOTUS — leaf

corolla

SNOWDROP

thorn

stalk or stem

bud

ORCHID

TULIP

anther

HIBISCUS

pollen sac — anther

seed capsule

seed

stigma

stamen

ovary

style

petal

sepal

petal

calyx

flowers

out a pillow. The bird ~ed (out) its feathers. **2**
[VP6A] bungle (sth in games, in speaking one's
lines in a play, etc): *~ a stroke,* eg in golf; *~ a
catch,* eg fail to catch the ball in cricket. **~y** *adj*
(-ier, -iest) of or like ~; covered with ~: *Newly
hatched chickens are like ~y balls.*
fluid /'flu:ɪd/ *adj* able to flow (as gases and liquids
do); (of ideas, etc) not fixed; capable of being
changed: *~ opinions/plans.* □ *n* [C,U] (chem) *~*
substance, eg water, air, mercury; (colloq) liquid
substance. *~ ounce,* ⇨ App 5. **~·ity** /flu:'ɪdətɪ/ *n*
quality of being ~.
fluke¹ /flu:k/ *n* [C] sth resulting from a fortunate
accident; lucky stroke: *win* (eg a game of billiards)
by a ~.
fluke² /flu:k/ *n* **1** broad, triangular flat end of each
arm of an anchor. **2** either lobe of a whale's tail. ⇨
the illus at sea.
fluke³ /flu:k/ *n* parasite flat worm, found in a
sheep's liver.
flume /flu:m/ *n* [C] artificial channel for carrying
water for industrial use, eg to a water-wheel in a
mill, or for carrying logs.
flum·mox /'flʌməks/ *vt* [VP6A] (colloq) disconcert; confound.
flung /flʌŋ/ *pt,pp* of fling.
flunk /flʌŋk/ *vi,vt* ~ *(out),* [VP2A,2C,6A,15B]
(US colloq) fail (an examination); fail (a candidate): *to ~ Biology/to be ~ed (out) in Biology.*
flun·key, flunky /'flʌŋkɪ/ *n* (*pl* -keys, -kies
/-kɪz/) (derog) servant in uniform.
flu·or·escent /fluə'resnt/ *adj* (of substances) taking
in radiations and sending them out in the form of
light: *~ lamps/lighting.* **flu·or·escence** /-sns/ *n*
flu·or·ine /'fluərɪ:n/ *n* (chem) (symbol **F**) pale-
yellow gas resembling chlorine. **flu·or·ide**
/'fluəraɪd/ *n* (chem) any compound of ~. **flu·ori-
date** /'fluərɪdeɪt/ *vt* [VP6A] add a fluoride to (a
water supply) to prevent dental decay. **flu·ori·da-
tion** /ˌfluərɪ'deɪʃn/ *n* **flu·ori·dize** /'fluərɪdaɪz/ *vt* =
fluoridate. **flu·ori·diz·ation** /ˌfluərɪdaɪ'zeɪʃn US:
-dɪ'z-/ *n* = fluoridation.
flurry /'flʌrɪ/ *n* (*pl* -ries) [C] short, sudden rush of
wind or fall of rain or snow; (fig) nervous hurry: *in
a ~ of excitement/alarm.* □ *vt* [VP6A] cause (sb) to
be confused, in a nervous hurry, etc: *Keep calm!
Don't get flurried.*
flush¹ /flʌʃ/ *adj* ~ *(with),* **1** even; in the same
plane; level: *doors ~ with the walls.* **2** (pred) having plenty; well supplied: *~ with money.*
flush² /flʌʃ/ *n* **1** rush of water; rush of blood to the
face; reddening caused by this; rush of emotion,
excitement caused by this: *in the first ~ of victory.*
2 [U] *(first)* ~, fresh growth of vegetation, etc;
high point or new access of strength: *the first ~ of
spring,* the time when trees and plants send out new
leaves; *in the first ~ of youth.*
flush³ /flʌʃ/ *n* (in card games) hand in which all the
cards are of the same suit. **'royal ~,** (poker) hand
with the five highest cards of one suit.
flush⁴ /flʌʃ/ *vi,vt* **1** [VP2A,C,D] (of a person, his
face) become red because of a rush of blood to the
skin: *The girl ~ed (up) when the man spoke to
her. He ~ed crimson with indignation.* **2** [VP6A]
(of health, heat, emotions, etc) cause (the face) to
become red in this way; (fig) fill with pride; encourage: *Shame ~ed his cheeks. She was ~ed
with exercise. The men were ~ed with success/
joy/insolence.* **3** [VP6A] clean or wash with a ~ of
water: *~ the drains; ~ the pan,* eg in a lavatory,

by emptying the cistern. **4** [VP2A,C] (of water)
rush out in a flood.
flush⁵ /flʌʃ/ *vt,vi* **1** [VP6A,2A] (of birds) (cause to)
rise suddenly and fly away: *~ a pheasant.* **2**
[VP14] *~ from/out of,* chase, drive from a
hiding-place: *snipers ~ed from fox-holes.*
flus·ter /'flʌstə(r)/ *vt* [VP6A] make nervous or confused. □ *n* nervous state: *all in a ~.*
flute¹ /flu:t/ *n* musical woodwind instrument in the
form of a pipe, blown at the side, with holes
stopped by keys. ⇨ the illus at brass. □ *vi* play the
~. **flut·ist** /'flu:tɪst/ *n* (chiefly US) flautist.
flute² /flu:t/ *vt* [VP6A] make vertical grooves in (a
pillar etc): *~d columns.* **flut·ing** *n* [U] grooves cut
on a surface as a decoration.
flut·ter /'flʌtə(r)/ *vi,vi* **1** [VP2A,C,6A,15A,B] (of
birds) move the wings hurriedly or irregularly
without flying, or in short flights only; cause (the
wings) to move in this way: *The wings of the bird
still ~ed after it had been shot down. The bird
~ed its wings in the cage. The wounded bird ~ed
to the ground.* **2** [VP2A,C,6A] (cause to) move
about in a quick, irregular way; (of the heart) beat
irregularly: *curtains ~ing in the breeze; apple-
blossom petals ~ing to the ground. She ~ed nervously about the room.* □ *n* **1** (usu *sing*) ~ing
movement: *the ~ of wings.* **2** *a ~,* state of nervous
excitement: *in a ~; cause/make a ~.* **3** [U] vibration: *wing ~,* as a defect of an aircraft in flight;
distortion in sound reproduced from a disc or tape
caused by faulty recording or reproduction. **4** [C]
(colloq) gambling venture; spree: *go to the races
and have a ~,* make a bet or bets.
flu·vial /'flu:vɪəl/ *adj* of, found in, rivers.
flux /flʌks/ *n* **1** [U] continuous succession of
changes: *in a state of ~.* **2** [C] (*sing* only) flowing;
flowing out. **3** [C] substance mixed with metal to
promote fusion.
fly¹ /flaɪ/ *n* (*pl* flies) **1** two-winged insect, esp the
common *'housefly;* ⇨ the illus at insect. *a fly in
the ointment,* (fig) a small circumstance that
prevents pleasure from being perfect. *There are
no flies on him,* (fig; sl) He is no fool, cannot be
tricked, etc. **'fly-blown** *adj* (of meat) (going bad
because) containing flies' eggs; (fig) in bad condition; stale. **'fly-catcher** *n* kind of bird; trap for
catching flies. **'fly-paper** *n* strip of sticky paper
used for catching flies. **'fly-fish** *vi* [VP2A] fish with
artificial flies as bait. Hence, **'fly-fishing** *n* [U].
'fly-trap *n* trap for catching flies. **'fly-weight** *n*
boxer weighing 112 lb (50·8 kg) or less.
fly² /flaɪ/ *vi,vt* (*pt* flew /flu:/, *pp* flown /fləʊn/) **1**
[VP2A,B,C,D,4A] move through the air as a bird
does, or in an aircraft: *birds flying in the air; fly
from London to Paris; fly (across) the Atlantic. fly
high,* be ambitious. *The bird is/has flown,* The
person wanted has escaped. **2** [VP6A,15A,B] direct
or control the flight of (aircraft); transport goods/
passengers in aircraft: *Five thousand passengers
were flown to Paris during Easter weekend.* **3**
[VP2A,C,D,4A] go or move quickly; rush along;
pass quickly: *He flew down the road. The children
flew to meet their mother. It's getting late; we must
fly. The door flew open. He paid us a flying visit, a
very short, fleeting visit. fly at sb,* rush angrily at
sb. *let fly (at),* ⇨ let¹(4). *fly off the handle,* ⇨
handle. *fly in the face of,* (a) defy openly: *You're
flying in the face of the law.* (b) be quite contrary
to: *This version of what happened flies in the face
of all the evidence. fly into a rage/passion/*

temper, become suddenly angry. **fly to arms,** take up arms eagerly. **fly to bits/into pieces,** break to bits and scatter. **make the'feathers/'fur fly,** cause quarrelling or fighting. **make the money fly,** spend it quickly, recklessly. **send sb flying,** strike him so that he falls over or backwards. **send things flying,** send or throw them violently in all directions. **4** [VP6A] cause (a *kite*) to rise and stay high in the air; raise (a *flag*) so that it waves in the air. **5** flee from: *fly the country.*

fly³ /flaɪ/ *n* (*pl* flies) **1** (also, colloq, *pl* used with *sing* meaning) flap of cloth on a garment to contain or cover a zip fastener or buttonholes, eg down the front of a pair of trousers: *John, your fly is/flies are undone!* **2** flap of canvas at the entrance to a tent or covered wagon. **3** (old use) one-horse hackney carriage. **4** outer edge of a flag farthest from the flagpole.

fly⁴ /flaɪ/ *adj* (sl) cunning; alert; not to be deceived or hoodwinked.

flyer, flier /'flaɪə(r)/ *n* **1** animal, vehicle, etc going with exceptional speed. **2** airman.

fly·ing /'flaɪɪŋ/ *part adj, gerund* (in compounds): '**~ boat** *n* form of seaplane without floats and with a fuselage that floats on water. **,~-'bomb** *n* rocket filled with explosives that can be fired to a great distance. **,~ 'buttress** *n* (archit) one arching from a column up to a wall, ⇨ the illus at church. '**~ club,** club for those interested in **~** as a sport. **,~ 'colours,** flags on display (as during a ceremony). **come through/off with ~ colours,** ⇨ colour¹(8). **,~ 'column,** (mil) body of troops able to move rapidly and act independently. '**~ field,** airfield. '**~-fish,** (kind of) tropical fish able to rise out of the water and move forward. **,~-'fox,** (kind of) large fruit-eating bat. '**F~ Officer,** rank in the Royal Air Force below Flight Lieutenant. **,~ 'jump,** one made with a running start. **,~ 'saucer,** unidentified flying object seen, or thought to have been seen, moving across the sky, eg one said to have come from another planet. '**~-squad,** part of a police force organized (with fast cars) for pursuit of (suspected) criminals. **,~ 'visit,** hasty visit made while passing.

fly·leaf /'flaɪliːf/ *n* blank leaf at the beginning or end of a book.

fly·over /'flaɪəʊvə(r)/ *n* **1** (US = *overpass*) roadway, bridge, etc which crosses above another roadway, etc (as on a motorway). **2** (GB) flypast.

flyovers

fly·past /'flaɪpɑːst *US:* -pæst/ *n* flight of aircraft in formation, usu at a low altitude, as part of a military display.

fly·post /'flaɪpəʊst/ *vt* [VP6A] post⁵(1) up rapidly (and often illegally). **~er** *n* sth **~ed**; sb who **~s**.

fly·wheel /'flaɪwiːl *US:* -hwiːl/ *n* heavy wheel revolving on a shaft to regulate machinery.

foal /fəʊl/ *n* young horse (colt or filly). ⇨ the illus

at domestic. *in/with* **~,** (of a mare) pregnant. □ *vi* [VP2A] give birth to a **~.**

foam /fəʊm/ *n* [U] **1** white mass of small air bubbles formed in or on a liquid by motion, or on an animal's lips, eg after exertion. **2** (also **,~-'rubber**) spongy rubber used in upholstery (eg in seats, mattresses). □ *vi* [VP2A,C] form **~**; break into **~**; send out **~** (at the mouth): *waves ~ing along the beach; a glass of ~ing beer,* beer with froth on it; (fig) *~ing with rage,* looking angry. **~y** *adj*

fob¹ /fɒb/ *vt* (-bb-) [VP15B] **~ sth off on sb; ~ sb off with sth,** get a person to accept sth of little or no value by deceit or trickery. **fo·cal** /'fəʊkl/ *adj* of or at a focus: *the ~ length/distance of a lens,* from the surface of a lens to its focus.

fo'c'sle /'fəʊksl/ *n* = forecastle.

fo·cus /'fəʊkəs/ *n* (*pl* **~es** or foci /'fəʊsaɪ/) **1** meeting-point of rays of light, heat, etc; point, distance, at which the sharpest outline is given (to the eye, through a telescope, through a lens on a camera plate, etc): *The image is in/out of ~. Bring the object into ~ if you want a good photograph.* **2** point at which interests, tendencies, etc meet: *the ~ of attention; the ~ of an earthquake/storm/ disease, etc.* □ *vt,vi* (-s- or -ss-) **1** [VP2A,C,6A,14] **~ (on),** (cause to) come together at a **~**; adjust (an instrument, etc) so that it is in **~**: *~ the sun's rays on sth with a burning-glass; ~ the lens of a microscope.* **2** [VP14] **~ on,** concentrate: *~ one's attention/thoughts/efforts on a problem.*

fod·der /'fɒdə(r)/ *n* [U] dried food, hay, etc for farm animals, horses, etc.

foe /fəʊ/ *n* (poet) enemy.

foe·tus (US = **fe·tus**) /'fiːtəs/ *n* fully developed embryo in the womb or in an egg. ⇨ the illus at reproduce. **foe·tal** (US = **fe·tal**) /'fiːtl/ *adj* of, like, a **~**: *the foetal position* (in the womb).

fog /fɒg *US:* fɔːg/ *n* **1** [U] vapour suspended in the atmosphere at or near the earth's surface, thicker than mist and difficult to see through: *Fog is the sailor's worst enemy. in a fog,* (fig) puzzled; at a loss. '**fog-bank** *n* dense mass of fog on the sea. '**fog-bound** *adj* unable to proceed safely because of fog. '**fog-horn** *n* instrument used for warning ships in fog. '**fog-lamp,** headlamp (on a motor vehicle) providing a strong beam of light for use in foggy weather. '**fog-signal,** device placed on railway lines in fog to explode when a train passes over it and so warn drivers. **2** [C] period of fog; abnormal darkened state of the atmosphere: *London used to have bad fogs in winter.* **3** [C,U] (area of) cloudiness on a developed photographic plate or film. □ *vt* (-gg-) cover with, as with, fog; bewilder: *I'm a bit fogged,* puzzled. **foggy** *adj* (-ier, -iest) **1** dense, not clear, because of fog: *a foggy evening; foggy weather.* **2** obscure, confused: *have only a foggy idea of what something means. I haven't the foggiest idea,* I don't know.

fogey (US = **fogy**) /'fəʊgɪ/ *n* (*pl ~s*, US fogies) **(old) ~,** person with old-fashioned ideas which he is unwilling to change.

foible /'fɔɪbl/ *n* [C] slight peculiarity or defect of character, often one of which a person is wrongly proud.

foil¹ /fɔɪl/ *n* **1** [U] metal rolled or hammered into a thin, flexible sheet: *lead/tin/aluminium ~,* eg as wrapped round chocolate or cigarettes. **2** [C] person or thing that contrasts with, and thus sets off, the qualities of another: *A plain old woman serves* *as a* ∼ *to a beautiful young woman.*

foil² /fɔɪl/ *n* light sword without a sharp edge and with a button on the point, for fencing.

foil³ /fɔɪl/ *vt* [VP6A] baffle; prevent (sb) from carrying out his plans; make plans/designs ineffective: *We* ∼*ed him/his plans. He was* ∼*ed in his attempt to deceive the girl.*

foist /fɔɪst/ *vt* [VP14,15A] ∼ **sth (off) on sb,** trick him into accepting (a useless article, etc).

fold¹ /fəʊld/ *vt,vi* **1** [VP6A,15B] bend one part of a thing back over on itself: ∼ *a letter,* before putting it in an envelope; ∼ *up a newspaper;* ∼ *back the bedclothes.* **2** [VP2A,C] become ∼ed; be able to be ∼ed: ∼*ing doors,* having hinged parts; *a* ∼*ing boat/bed/chair,* made so as to occupy a smaller space when not in use. *The window shutters* ∼ *back.* ∼ **(up),** (fig; colloq) collapse; come to an end: *The business finally* ∼*ed up last week.* **3** ∼ **one's arms,** cross them over the chest. ∼ **sb/sth in one's arms,** hold him/it to the breast. **4** [VP15A,B] cover, wrap up: ∼ *sth (up) in paper;* ∼ *sth round; hills* ∼*ed in mist.* **5** (cooking) mix an ingredient (eg beaten eggs) into another (eg flour) by turning them with a wooden spoon. □ *n* **1** part that is ∼ed: *a dress hanging in loose* ∼*s;* line made by ∼ing. **2** hollow in mountain. ∼**er** *n* **1** holder (made of ∼ed cardboard or other stiff material) for loose papers. **2** ∼ing card or paper with advertisements, railway timetables, etc printed on it, or (US) as a container, eg for matches.

fold² /fəʊld/ *n* [C] enclosure for sheep; (fig) body of religious believers; members of a Church. **return to the** ∼, come or go back home (esp rejoin a body of believers). □ *vt* [VP6A] enclose (sheep) in a

fo·li·age /ˈfəʊlɪdʒ/ *n* [U] all the leaves of a tree or plant.

fo·lio /ˈfəʊlɪəʊ/ *n* (*pl* ∼s) **1** sheet of paper numbered on one side only; page number of a printed book; (bookkeeping) two opposite pages of a ledger, used for both sides of an account. **2** large sheet of paper folded once to make two leaves or four pages (of a book); volume made of such sheets: ∼ *volumes; in six volumes* ∼.

folk /fəʊk/ *n* **1** (collective *n*, used with *pl v*) people in general: *Some* ∼ *are never satisfied. Is there more honesty among country* ∼ *than among towns*∼*?* **2** (in compounds) of the common people of a country. '∼**-dance** *n* (music for a) traditional popular dance. '∼**-lore** *n* [U] (study of the) traditional beliefs, tales, etc of a community. '∼**-music/song** *nn* popular music/song handed down from the past. '∼**-tale** *n* popular story handed down orally from past generations. **3** (*pl*) (colloq) relatives: *the old* ∼*s at home.*

folksy /ˈfəʊksɪ/ *adj* (colloq) unpretentious in manners; simple; friendly and sociable.

fol·low /ˈfɒləʊ/ *vt,vi* **1** [VP2A,B,C,6A] come, go, have a place, after (in space, time or order): *You go first and I will* ∼ *(you). Monday* ∼*s Sunday. They* ∼*ed us for miles. One misfortune* ∼*ed (upon) another. His arguments were as* ∼*s,* as now to be given. ∼ **on,** (a) ∼ after a period of time. (b) (cricket, of a side) bat again after failing to get the necessary number of runs. Hence, ∼**-'on** *n* second innings following the first at once. ∼ **through,** (a) (tennis, golf, etc) complete a stroke by moving the racket, club, etc after hitting the ball. Hence, '∼**-through** *n* [C] such a stroke. (b) complete a task, carry out a promise. **2** [VP6A] go

along, keep to (a road, etc): *F*∼ *this road until you get to the church; then turn left.* **3** [VP6A,2A] understand (an argument, sth said, etc): *Do you* ∼ *my argument? He spoke so fast that I couldn't* ∼ *him/* ∼ *what he said.* **4** [VP6A] engage in as a business, trade, etc: ∼ *the law;* ∼ *the trade of a builder.* **5** [VP6A] take or accept as a guide, an example, etc: ∼ *sb's advice;* ∼ *the fashion.* ∼ **suit,** do what has just been done by sb else. **6** [VP2A] be necessarily true: *Because he is good, it does not* ∼ *that he is wise. It* ∼*s from what you say that....* **7** [VP15B] ∼ **sth out,** keep to, carry out, to the end: ∼ *out an enterprise.* ∼ **sth up,** pursue, work at further: ∼ *up an advantage/a victory.* Hence, '∼**-up** *n* (esp) second letter, circular, visit, referring to an earlier one. ∼**er** *n* **1** supporter; disciple: *Mahatma Ghandi and his* ∼*ers.* **2** pursuer. ∼**-ing** *adj* **the** ∼**ing,** the one or ones about to be mentioned. □ *n* body of supporters: *a political leader with a large* ∼*ing.*

folly /ˈfɒlɪ/ *n* (*pl* -lies) [U] foolishness; [C] foolish act, idea or practice; ridiculous thing.

fo·ment /fəʊˈment/ *vt* [VP6A] **1** put warm water, clothes, lotions, etc on (a part of the body, to lessen pain, etc). **2** (fig) cause or increase (disorder, discontent, ill feeling, etc). **fo·men·ta·tion** /ˌfəʊmenˈteɪʃn/ *n* [U] ∼ing; [C] that which is used for ∼ing.

fond /fɒnd/ *adj* (-er, -est) **1** (pred only) **be** ∼ **of,** like, be full of love for, take pleasure in: ∼ *of music.* **2** loving and kind: *a* ∼ *mother;* ∼ *looks.* **3** foolishly loving; doting: *a young wife with a* ∼ *husband.* **4** (of hopes, ambitions) held, but unlikely to be realized. ∼**·ly** *adv* **1** lovingly: *look* ∼*ly at sb.* **2** in a foolishly optimistic manner: *He* ∼*ly imagined that he could learn French in six weeks.* ∼**-ness** *n*

fon·dant /ˈfɒndənt/ *n* [C] kind of soft sweet that melts in the mouth.

fondle /ˈfɒndl/ *vt* [VP6A] touch or stroke lovingly: ∼ *a baby/a doll/a kitten.*

fon·due /ˈfɒndjuː/ *n* dish of melted cheese, into which pieces of bread are dipped; dish of hot fat, into which pieces of raw meat are dipped; dish of hot chocolate, into which pieces of fruit are dipped.

font /fɒnt/ *n* **1** basin or vessel (often in carved stone) to hold water for baptism; basin for holy water. **2** = fount(2).

food /fuːd/ *n* **1** [U] that which can be eaten by people or animals, or used by plants, to keep them living and for growth: ∼ *and water;* (attrib) ∼ *rationing;* (fig) ∼ *for thought/reflection,* sth to think/reflect about. **2** [C] kind of ∼: *breakfast/ frozen/packaged* ∼*s.* '∼**-stuff** *n* material used as ∼. ∼**-less** *adj* without ∼.

fool¹ /fuːl/ *n* **1** person without much sense; stupid or rash person; person whose conduct one considers silly: *What* ∼*s we were not to see the trap! She was* ∼ *enough* (= enough of a fool) *to believe him.* **be a** ∼ **for one's pains,** do sth for which one gets neither reward nor thanks. **be/live in a** ∼**'s paradise,** be/live in a state of carefree happiness that cannot last. **be sent/go on a** ∼**'s errand,** on an errand that is seen in the end to be useless. **make a** ∼ **of sb,** trick him; cause him to seem like a ∼. **play the** ∼, behave stupidly. **no** ∼ **like an old** ∼, (prov) said of an aged lover. **2** (in the Middle Ages) man employed by a ruler or noble as a clown or jester. **3** ,**April** '∼, person deceived, or sent on a ∼'s errand, on ,**All 'F**∼**s' Day,** 1st April. **4** (used attrib, colloq) foolish; silly: *a scheme devised by* *some* ∼ *politician.* □ *vi,vt* **1** [VP2A,C] ∼ *(about/around)*, behave like a ∼; trifle; be idle and silly: *If you go on ∼ing with that gun, there'll be an accident. Stop ∼ing (about)!* **2** [VP6A,14,15B] ∼ *sb (out of sth)*, cheat; deceive: *He ∼led her out of her money. You can't/don't ∼ me!*

fool² /fuːl/ *n* creamy liquid of stewed fruit (esp gooseberries), crushed and mixed with cream or custard.

fool·ery /'fuːlərɪ/ *n* [U] foolish behaviour; *(pl; -ries)* foolish acts, ideas or utterances.

fool·hardy /'fuːlhɑːdɪ/ *adj* foolishly bold; taking unnecessary risks. **fool·hardi·ness** *n*

fool·ish /'fuːlɪʃ/ *adj* without reason, sense or good judgement; silly: *How ∼ of you to consent! It would be ∼ for us to quarrel.* ∼**·ly** *adv* ∼**·ness** *n*

fool·proof /'fuːlpruːf/ *adj* incapable of failure, error or misinterpretation: *a ∼ scheme/design/gadget.*

fools·cap /'fuːlskæp/ *n* [U] size (17x13½ inches) of writing or printing paper.

foot¹ /fʊt/ *n* (*pl* feet /fiːt/) **1** part forming the lower end of the leg, beginning at the ankle; part of a sock, etc covering the ∼: *A dog has four feet. A dog's feet are called paws. He rose to his feet*, stood up. ⇨ the illus at leg. **on ∼**, (a) walking, not riding. Cf *by bus/car/tram etc.* (b) (fig) started: *A project is on ∼ to build a new tunnel here.* **be on one's feet**, (a) be standing: *I've been on my feet all day.* (b) rise (to speak): *The Minister was on his feet at once to answer the charge.* (c) (fig) be in good health after an illness: *It's nice to see you on your feet again.* **fall on one's feet**, (colloq) be fortunate, have good luck. **find one's feet**, ⇨ find²(2). **have feet of clay**, be weak or cowardly. **have one ∼ in the grave**, be near death, eg because of old age. **keep one's feet**, not fall, eg when walking on ice. **put one's ∼ down**, (colloq) object; protest; be firm. **put one's ∼ in it**, (colloq) say or do sth wrong or stupid; blunder. **put one's feet up**, (colloq) rest with the legs in a horizontal position. **put one's best ∼ forward**, walk (fig, get on with one's work) as fast as one can. **set sth/sb on its/his feet**, make him/it self-supporting, no longer in need of help. **set sth on ∼**, start it; get it going. **sweep sb off his feet**, fill him with strong enthusiasm. **under ∼**, on the ground: *wet under ∼.* **wait on/bind sb hand and ∼**, ⇨ hand¹(1). **2** step, pace, tread: *light/swift/fleet of ∼*, stepping or walking lightly, swiftly, etc. **3** lowest part; bottom: *at the ∼ of the page/ladder/wall/mountain.* **4** lower end of a bed or grave. ⇨ head¹(10). **5** measure of length, = 12 inches: (with *pl* unchanged) *George is very tall —he's six ∼ two* (six feet two inches). **6** division or unit of verse, each with one strong stress and one or more weak stresses, as in: *for 'men/may 'come/ and 'men/may 'go.* **7** [U] (mil, old use) infantry: *the Fourth Regiment of F∼;* ∼ *and horse*, infantry and cavalry. **8** (compounds) *∼-and-'mouth disease*, disease of cattle and other cloven-hoofed animals. '**∼·ball** *n* [C] inflated leather ball used in games; [U] the game played with it. ⇨ the illus below and at Rugby. '**∼·bath** *n* (small bath used for a) washing of the feet. '**∼·board** *n* sloping board for the feet of the driver (in a carriage, etc). '**∼·bridge** *n* one for the use of persons on ∼, not vehicles. '**∼·fall** *n* sound of a ∼step. '**∼·fault** *n* (tennis) service not allowed because the server's feet are wrongly placed. '**∼·hills** *n pl* hills lying at the ∼ of a mountain or a range of mountains. '**∼·hold**

n support for the ∼, eg when climbing on rocks or ice; (fig) secure position. '**∼·lights** *n pl* row of screened lights at the front of the stage of a theatre. *the ∼ lights*, (fig) the profession of an actor. '**∼·loose** *adj* (also *∼loose and fancy free*) independent and without cares or responsibilities. '**∼·man** /-mən/ *n* (*pl* -men) manservant who admits visitors, waits at table, etc. '**∼·mark** *n* = ∼print. '**∼·note** *n* note at the ∼ of a page. '**∼·path** *n* path for the use of persons on ∼, esp one across fields or open country, or at the side of a country road. Cf US *trail*. ⇨ pavement, *sidewalk* at side¹(14). '**∼·plate** *n* platform in a locomotive for the driver and fireman: *∼plate workers*, drivers and firemen. '**∼·pound** *n* unit of work (done in lifting 1lb through 1ft). '**∼·print** *n* impression left on a soft surface by a ∼. '**∼·race** *n* running race between persons. '**∼ rule** *n* ruler (strip of wood or metal) 12 inches long. '**∼·slog** *vi* (colloq) walk, tramp, march far and with effort. Hence, '**∼·slogger** *n* (colloq) person who walks or marches long distances. '**∼·sore** *adj* having sore feet, esp from walking. '**∼·step** *n* (sound of a) step of sb walking; ∼print. **follow in one's father's ∼steps**, do as he did. '**∼·stool** *n* low stool for resting the feet on. '**∼·sure** *adj* not stumbling; not making false steps. '**∼·wear** *n* [U] (tradesmen's term for) boots, shoes, etc. '**∼·work** *n* [U] manner of using the feet, eg in boxing, dancing.

foot² /fʊt/ *vt,vi* **1** [VP6A] knit the ∼ of, eg a stocking. **2** ∼ *it*, (colloq) go on ∼; walk: *We've missed the last bus, so we'll have to ∼ it.* ∼ *the bill*, (colloq) (agree to) pay it. ∼**ed** (in compounds) having the number of feet indicated: *,wet-'∼ed; ,sure-'∼ed; ,flat-'∼ed.*

foot·age /'fʊtɪdʒ/ *n* [U] length measured in feet, esp length of exposed cinema film.

footer /'fʊtə(r)/ *n* **1** (colloq) the game of football. **2** (compounds) *a ,six-'footer*, a person six feet tall.

foot·ing /'fʊtɪŋ/ *n* [C] (*sing* only) **1** placing of the feet; surface for standing on: *He lost his ∼* (= stumbled, slipped) *and fell.* **2** position (in society, a group): *get a footing in musical circles*; relationship (with sb); condition(s). *be/get on a ... ∼ (with)*, be/get in a ... relationship/state (with): *be on a friendly ∼ with Julie's family.* **3** conditions; state of the army, etc: *on a peace/war ∼*, in the state usual for peace/war.

footle /'fuːtl/ *vi,vt* (colloq) trifle; play the fool: ∼ *about;* ∼ *away one's time.* **foot·ling** /'fuːtlɪŋ/ *adj* insignificant, trifling: *footling little jobs.*

fop /fɒp/ *n* man who pays too much attention to his clothes and personal appearance. **fop·pish** /-ɪʃ/ *adj* of or like a ∼.

for¹ /fə(r); *strong form:* fɔː(r)/ *prep* **1** (indicating

American football

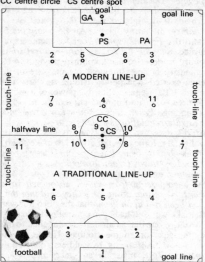

GA goal area   PA penalty area   PS penalty spot
CC centre circle   CS centre spot

A MODERN LINE-UP

A TRADITIONAL LINE-UP

halfway line

football

A TRADITIONAL LINE-UP 1 goalkeeper 2 right back
3 left back 4 right half (back) 5 centre half (back)
6 left half (back) 7 outside right or right winger
8 inside right 9 centre forward 10 inside left
11 outside left or left winger

A MODERN LINE-UP 1 goalkeeper 2 5 6 3 defenders
or backs 7 4 11 midfield link men 8 9 10 strikers
or forwards

Association football (soccer)

destination, or progress or endeavours towards) **(a)**
(after *vv*): *set out for home; make for home,* turn
one's steps towards home; *a ship bound for the
Baltic. The ship was making for* (= sailing towards) *the open sea. The swimmers struck out for
the shore.* **(b)** (after *nn*): *the train for Glasgow; letters for the provinces; passengers for Cairo.* **2** (indicating what is aimed at, or the attaining of sth,
shown by the *noun* after *for*): *He was educated for
the law/trained for the priesthood. He felt that he
was destined for something great.* **3** (indicating
eventual possession): *Here's a letter for you. Are
all these for me? Save it for me. She made some
coffee for us.* **be 'for it,** (colloq) be likely to be
punished, get into trouble, etc. **4** (indicating preparation to deal with a situation): *prepare/
preparations for an examination; lay in supplies of
coal for the winter; dress for dinner; get ready for
school.* **5** (indicating purpose) **(a)** (used in place of
an *inf*) in order to be, have, obtain, etc; with a view
to: *go for a walk/ride/swim, etc; run for one's life;
work for one's living; read for pleasure.* **what...
for,** for what purpose: *What's this tool for? What's
this hole in the door for? It's for the cat to come in
and out by.* ⇨ **24 (g)** below. *What did you do that
for? Why did you do that?* **(b)** (followed by a gerund): *a mill for* (= for the purpose of) *grinding
coffee; a room for sleeping in.* **6** (introducing a
complement): *They were sold for slaves. They left
him on the battlefield for dead. They chose him for*
(= as, to be) *their leader.* **take sb/sth for sb/sth,**
mistakenly conclude that he/it is sb/sth else: *He
took me for my brother. What do you take me for?
You seem to have a mistaken or poor idea of my*

character, judging from what you say, etc. **for certain,** as being certain: *I cannot say for certain
that....* **7** (followed by an object of hope, wish,
search, inquiry, etc): *hope for the best; pray for
peace; fish for trout; ask for* (= to see) *the manager; go to sb for help; a cry for help; fifty applicants
for a post.* **8** (indicating liking, affection, etc):
*have a liking for sb or sth; a taste for art; no regret
for the truth; a weakness for fine clothes.* **9** (indicating aptitude): *an aptitude for foreign languages;
a good ear for music; an eye for the picturesque.*
10 (indicating suitability, fitness): *bad/good for
your health; fit/unfit for food; clothes proper for
the occasion. This is no place for a young, innocent girl. You are the very man for the job.* **11**
(with *adj* not otherwise followed by *for,* in the patterns *too + adj + for,* or *adj + enough + for*):
too beautiful for words; quite risky enough for me.
12 considering (the circumstances, etc); in view
of: *It's quite warm for January. Not bad for a beginner! She is tall for her age. For all the good
you're doing, you may as well stop trying to help.*
for 'all that, in spite of all that has been said, done,
etc. **13** representing; instead of; in place of: *B for
Benjamin; the member for Coventry,* the person
representing Coventry in the House of Commons;
*substitute one thing for another. Will you please
act for me in the matter?* **stand for,** represent: *The
letters MP stand for Member of Parliament and the
letters PM stand for Prime Minister.* **14** in defence
or support of; in favour of: *Are you for or against
the proposal? The rate of exchange is for us,* in our
favour. *Three cheers for the President! I'm all for
an early start/for starting early.* **15** with regard to;
so far as concerns: *hard up for money; anxious for
sb's safety; for my part,* so far as it concerns me;
speaking for myself, and in the name of all my colleagues. *You may take my word for it,* believe me
so far as this is concerned. **16** because of; on account of: *for this reason; for my sake; for the sake
of peace; for fear of discovery; noted/famous for its
scenery; dance/cry for joy; suffer for one's sins;
sent to prison for stealing; win a medal for
bravery. She couldn't speak for laughing,* because
she was laughing so much. *We trembled for their
safety.* **17** (after a comparative) as the result of; because of: *My shoes are the worse for wear. Are
you any the better for your long sleep?* **18** in spite
of; notwithstanding: *For* (= In spite of) *all you
say, I still like her. For all his wealth, he is unhappy.* **19** to the amount or extent of: *Put my name
down for £5. He drew on his bank for £40.* (cricket)
*The score is 157 for 8 wickets. They were all out
for 80.* **20** in exchange for: *I paid 60p for the book.
He did the job for nothing. Don't translate word
for word. Plant a new tree for every tree you cut
down.* **21** in contrast with: *For one enemy he has
fifty friends.* **22** (indicating extent in time): *I'm going away for a few days. He will be a cripple for
life. That's enough for the present.* **for good,** ⇨
good²(2). **23** (indicating extent in space; for may
be omitted if it occurs directly after the *v*): *We
walked (for) three miles. For miles and miles
there's not a house to be seen. The road is lined
with trees for ten miles.* **24** (in the pattern *for +
noun/pronoun + to-*inf) **(a)** (as the subject of a
sentence, usu with preparatory *it*): *For a woman to
divorce her husband is impossible in some countries. It's impossible for there to be a quarrel between us. It seemed useless for them to go on.* **(b)**

(as a complement): *Their hope was for David to marry a wealthy girl.* (c) (after *adjj*, esp with *too* and *enough*, usu replaceable by a clause): *I am anxious for you and my sister to* (= anxious that you and my sister should) *become acquainted. This box is too heavy for her to lift.* (d) (after *nn*): *There's no need for anyone to know* (= that anyone should know). *It's time for little girls to be in bed. I'm in no hurry for them to do anything about it yet.* (e) (after *vv*, including some that normally take *for* and others that do not normally take *for*): *We didn't wait for the others to join us. She couldn't bear for Tom and Mary not to be friends.* (f) (after *than* and as (*if*)): *Is there anything more ridiculous than for a man of 80 to marry a girl of 18? She had her arms wide apart, as if for the child to run into them.* (g) indicating purpose, design, determination, etc: *I have brought the books for you to examine. The crowd made way for the procession to pass. I'd have given anything for this not to have happened. It's for you to decide. For production to be increased we must have efficient organization.*

for² /fə(r)/ *conj* (rare in spoken English; not used at the beginning of a sentence) seeing that; since; the reason, proof, explanation, being that: *I asked her to stay to tea, for I had something to tell her.*

for·age /ˈfɒrɪdʒ US: ˈfɔːr-/ *n* [U] food for horses and cattle. □ *vi* [VP2A,3A] ∼ *(for)*, search (*for* food, etc).

for·as·much as /ˌfɔːrəzˈmʌtʃ əz/ *conj* (legal) seeing that; since.

foray /ˈfɒreɪ US: ˈfɔːreɪ/ *n* [C] raid; sudden attack (esp to get food, animals, etc): *go on/make a* ∼. □ *vi* [VP2A] make a ∼.

for·bad, for·bade /fəˈbæd US: -ˈbeɪd/ *pt* of forbid.

for·bear¹ /fɔːˈbeə(r)/ *vt,vi* (*pt* forbore /fɔːˈbɔː(r)/, *pp* forborne /fɔːˈbɔːn/) [VP6C,7A,2A,3A] ∼ *(from)*, (formal) refrain (from); not use or mention; be patient: *I ∼ to go into details. I cannot ∼ from going into details. We begged him to ∼.* ∼**ance** /fɔːˈbeərəns/ *n* [U] patience; self-control: *show ∼ance towards sb; show ∼ance in dealing with people.*

for·bear² (US = **fore·bear**) /ˈfɔːbeə(r)/ *n* (usu *pl*) ancestor.

for·bid /fəˈbɪd/ *vt* (*pt* forbade or forbad /fəˈbæd US:* -ˈbeɪd/, *pp* forbidden /fəˈbɪdn/) [VP6A,17,12C] order (sb) not to do sth; order that sth shall not be done; not allow: ∼ *a girl to marry;* ∼ *a marriage;* ∼ *sb to leave;* ∼ *his departure. Students are* ∼*den the use of the office duplicator. I* ∼ *you to use that word. God* ∼ *that...,* used to express a wish that something may not happen. ∼**den ˈfruit**, sth desired because it is not allowed (with reference to Eve and the apple). ∼**ding** *adj* stern; repellent; threatening: *a* ∼*ding appearance/look; a* ∼*ding coast,* one that looks dangerous. ∼**ding·ly** *adv*

for·bore, for·borne ⇨ forbear¹.

force¹ /fɔːs/ *n* **1** [U] strength; power of body or mind; physical power: *the* ∼ *of a blow/an explosion/argument;* ∼ *of character;* overcome by the ∼ *of her emotion; by* ∼ *of contrast. The enemy attacked in (great)* ∼. *He overcame his bad habits by sheer* ∼ *of will. Owing to* ∼ *of circumstances the plans had to be postponed.* **in** ∼, (usu of people) in large numbers. **2** [C] person or thing that makes great changes: *the* ∼*s of nature,* eg storms,

earthquakes. *Is religion a* ∼ *for good in the lives of people? The Left and the Right have always been the principle political* ∼*s.* **3** [C] organized body of armed or disciplined men: *the armed* ∼*s of a country,* the Army, Navy, Air F∼; *join the F∼s;* (attrib) *a F∼s newspaper,* one for members of the armed ∼s; *the poˈlice* ∼. **join** ∼**s (with)**, unite (with) in order to use combined strength. **4** [C,U] (intensity of, measurement of) pressure or influence exerted at a point, tending to cause movement. **5** [U] (legal) authority; power of binding(6). **in/into** ∼, in/into power: *put a law into* ∼, make it binding. *When does the new law come into* ∼? *The rule/regulation is no longer in* ∼.

force² /fɔːs/ *vt* **1** [VP6A,15A,B,17A,22] compel, oblige; use force to get or do sth, to make sb do sth; break open by using force: ∼ *one's way through a crowd;* ∼ *a way in/out/through;* ∼ *an entry into a building,* eg by breaking a door; ∼ *(open) a door;* ∼ *a confession from sb;* ∼ *sb/oneself to work hard;* ∼ *sb into doing sth. They said that the war had been* ∼*d upon them,* that they had not wanted to make war, but had been compelled to do so. ∼**d ˈlanding,** one that an aircraft is compelled to make, eg because of engine trouble. Hence, ∼**-ˈland** *vt,vi* ∼**d ˈmarch,** eg by soldiers, one requiring special effort, made in an emergency. ∼ **sb's hand,** make him do sth unwillingly, or earlier than he wished or intended to do it. **2** [VP6A] cause plants, etc to mature earlier than is normal, eg by giving them extra warmth: (fig) ∼ *a pupil,* hurry on his education by making him do extra study. **3** [VP6A] produce under stress: ∼ *a smile,* eg when one is unhappy; *a* ∼*d laugh,* one that is not the result of real amusement. *The singer had to* ∼ *her top notes.*

force-feed /ˈfɔːsfiːd/ *vt* (*pt,pp* force-fed /ˈfɔːsfed/) [VP6A] compel (an animal, a prisoner or a patient) to take food and drink.

force·ful /ˈfɔːsfl/ *adj* (of a person, his character, of an argument, etc) full of force: *a* ∼ *speaker/style of writing.* ∼**ly** /-fəlɪ/ *adv* ∼**·ness** *n*

force majeure /ˌfɔːs mæˈʒɜː(r)/ *n* [U] (F) (legal) compulsion; superior force.

force-meat /ˈfɔːsmiːt/ *n* [U] meat chopped up finely, mixed with herbs, etc used as stuffing, eg in a roast chicken.

for·ceps /ˈfɔːseps/ *n* (*sing* or *pl*) small pincers or tongs used by dentists (when pulling out teeth) and by doctors for gripping things: *a* ∼ *delivery* (of a baby).

forc·ible /ˈfɔːsəbl/ *adj* **1** done by, involving the use of, physical force: *a* ∼ *entry into a building;* ∼ *expulsion.* **2** (of a person, his acts, words, etc) convincing; persuasive. **forc·ibly** /-əblɪ/ *adj*

ford /fɔːd/ *n* [C] shallow place in a river where it is possible to walk or drive across. □ *vt* [VP6A] cross (a river) by walking or driving through the water. ∼**·able** /-əbl/ *adj* that can be ∼ed.

fore /fɔː(r)/ *adj* (attrib only) situated in the front (opp of *back, aft*): *in the* ∼ *part of the train; the* ∼ *hatch,* (in a ship). □ *n* [U] ∼ part (of a ship). **to the** ∼, ready to hand; on the spot; prominent: *He has come to the* ∼ *recently,* has become prominent. □ *adv* (naut) in front. ∼ **and aft,** at the bow and stern of a ship; lengthwise in a ship: ∼ *and aft sails/ rigged,* with sails set lengthwise. ⇨ square-rigged. □ *int* (golf) warning (to people in front) that the player is about to drive the ball.

fore·arm¹ /ˈfɔːrɑːm/ *n* arm from the elbow to the

wrist or finger-tips. ⇨ the illus at arm.

fore·arm² /ˌfɔːrˈɑːm/ vt [VP6A] (usu in passive) arm beforehand; prepare for trouble in advance: To be forewarned is to be ∼ed.

fore·bear n = forbear².

fore·bode /fɔːˈbəʊd/ vt (formal) **1** [VP6A] be a sign or warning of: These black clouds ∼ a storm. **2** [VP6A,9] have a feeling of (usu sth evil); have a feeling (that): ∼ disaster. **fore·bod·ing** n [C,U] feeling that trouble is coming.

fore·cast /ˈfɔːkɑːst US: -kæst/ vt (pt,pp ∼ or ∼ed) [VP6A] say in advance what is likely to happen. □ n statement that ∼s sth: inaccurate weather ∼s.

fore·castle, fo'c's'le /ˈfəʊksl/ n (in some merchant ships) part under the bows where the seamen have their living and sleeping accommodation.

fore·close /fɔːˈkləʊz/ vt,vi [VP2A,3A,6A] ∼ (on), (legal) use the right (given by a mortgage) to take possession of property (when interest or capital has not been paid at the required time): The Bank ∼d (on) (the mortgage). **fore·clos·ure** /fɔːˈkləʊʒə(r)/ n [C,U] (act of) foreclosing a mortgage.

fore·court /ˈfɔːkɔːt/ n enclosed space in front of a building.

fore·doom /fɔːˈduːm/ vt [VP6A,14] (usu passive) ∼ (to), destine (to): an attempt that was ∼ed to failure.

fore·father /ˈfɔːfɑːðə(r)/ n (usu pl) ancestor.

fore·fin·ger /ˈfɔːfɪŋɡə(r)/ n first finger, next to the thumb; index finger. ⇨ the illus at arm.

fore·foot /ˈfɔːfʊt/ n (pl forefeet /ˈfɔːfiːt/) one of the front feet of a four-legged animal.

fore·front /ˈfɔːfrʌnt/ n the ∼, most forward part: in the ∼ of the battle; in the ∼ of my mind.

fore·gather ⇨ forgather.

forego¹ /fɔːˈɡəʊ/ vt,vi (pt forewent /fɔːˈwent/, pp foregone /fɔːˈɡɒn US: -ˈɡɔːn/) precede (but rarely used except in) **fore·going** adj preceding, already mentioned. **fore·gone** /ˈfɔːɡɒn US: -ɡɔːn/ adj a foregone conclusion, ending that can be seen or could have been seen from the start.

forego² ⇨ forgo.

fore·ground /ˈfɔːɡraʊnd/ n **1** part of a view (esp in a picture) nearest to the observer. **2** (fig) most conspicuous position: keep oneself in the ∼, where one is most easily seen or noticed.

fore·hand /ˈfɔːhænd/ adj (of a stroke at tennis, etc) made with the palm turned forward. (Cf backhand = stroke made with the back of the hand turned forward and from the left side of the body, by a right-handed player).

fore·head /ˈfɒrɪd US: ˈfɔːrɪd/ n part of the face above the eyes. ⇨ the illus at head.

foreign /ˈfɒrən US: ˈfɔːr-/ adj **1** of, in, from, another country, not one's own: ∼ languages/countries; ∼ trade. the 'F∼ Office, the department of state dealing with ∼ affairs; its building in London. ,F∼ 'Secretary, head of the F∼ Office. **2** ∼ to, not natural to, unconnected with: Lying is ∼ to his nature. **3** coming or introduced from outside: a ∼ body in the eye, eg a bit of dirt blown into it by the wind. ∼er n person from, living in, or born in a ∼ country.

fore·knowl·edge /ˌfɔːˈnɒlɪdʒ/ n [U] knowledge of sth before its occurrence or existence.

fore·land /ˈfɔːlənd/ n cape; promontory.

fore·leg /ˈfɔːleɡ/ n one of the front legs of a four-footed animal.

fore·lock /ˈfɔːlɒk/ n lock of hair growing just above the forehead. take time by the ∼, not let an op-

portunity slip by; use an opportunity promptly.

fore·man /ˈfɔːmən/ n (pl -men /-mən/) **1** workman in authority over others. **2** chief member and spokesman of a jury.

fore·mast /ˈfɔːmɑːst US: -mæst/ n mast nearest the bow of a ship. ⇨ the illus at barque.

fore·most /ˈfɔːməʊst/ adj first; most notable; chief: the ∼ painter of his period. □ adv first in position. first and ∼, before all else; in the first place.

fore·name /ˈfɔːneɪm/ n (as used in official style, eg on forms) name preceding the family name.

fore·noon /ˈfɔːnuːn/ n (old use) part of the day between sunrise and noon.

for·en·sic /fəˈrensɪk/ adj of, used in, courts of law: ∼ skill, skill as needed by barristers, etc; ∼ medicine, medical knowledge as needed in legal matters, eg a poisoning trial.

fore·or·dain /ˌfɔːrɔːˈdeɪn/ vt [VP6A,14,17] determine or appoint beforehand: what God has ∼ed.

fore·run·ner /ˈfɔːrʌnə(r)/ n **1** sign of what is to follow: swallows, the ∼s of spring. **2** person who prepares for the coming of another.

fore·sail /ˈfɔːseɪl/ n principal sail on the foremast. ⇨ the illus at barque.

fore·see /fɔːˈsiː/ vt (pt foresaw /fɔːˈsɔː/, pp foreseen /fɔːˈsiːn/) [VP6A,9,10] know beforehand or in advance: ∼ trouble; ∼ what will happen/how things will turn out/that things will go well. ∼able /-əbl/ adj that can be known beforehand. the ∼able future, period from the present for which events can reasonably be predicted.

fore·shadow /fɔːˈʃædəʊ/ vt [VP6A] be a sign or warning of (sth to come).

fore·shore /ˈfɔːʃɔː(r)/ n part of the shore between the sea and land that is cultivated, built on, etc.

fore·shorten /fɔːˈʃɔːtn/ vt [VP6A] (in drawing pictures) show (an object) by the use of perspective(1).

fore·sight /ˈfɔːsaɪt/ n [U] ability to see future needs; care in preparing for these: If you had had more ∼, you would have saved yourself a lot of trouble.

fore·skin /ˈfɔːskɪn/ n fold of skin covering the end of the penis.

for·est /ˈfɒrɪst US: ˈfɔːr-/ n **1** [C,U] (large area of) land covered with trees (and often undergrowth); the trees growing there: ∼s stretching for miles and miles; (attrib): ∼ animals/fires. **2** (GB) area where game (eg deer) is or was hunted (and preserved), not necessarily wooded; (with proper name prefixed, as Sherwood F∼) district that was formerly ∼ but is now partly under cultivation: the deer ∼s in Scotland. **3** (fig) sth that suggests ∼ trees: a ∼ of masts, eg in a harbour. ∼er n officer in charge of a ∼ (protecting wild animals, watching for fires, etc); man who works in a ∼. ∼ry n [U] (science of) planting and caring for ∼s.

fore·stall /fɔːˈstɔːl/ vt [VP6A] do sth first and so prevent another from doing it; upset (sb, his plans) by doing sth unexpectedly early: ∼ a competitor.

fore·swear /fɔːˈsweə(r)/ v = forswear.

fore·taste /ˈfɔːteɪst/ n ∼ (of), partial experience (of sth) in advance: a ∼ of suffering/pleasure.

fore·tell /fɔːˈtel/ vt (pt,pp foretold /fɔːˈtəʊld/) [VP6A,9,10,12A,13A] tell beforehand; predict: ∼ sb's future. Is this the prophet whose coming was foretold (to) us?

fore·thought /ˈfɔːθɔːt/ n [U] careful thought or planning for the future.

fore·told pt,pp of foretell.

fore·top /'fɔːtɒp/ n (naut) platform at the head of a foremast; ⇨ the illus at barque.

for·ever /fə'revə(r)/ adv always; at all times; endlessly.

fore·warn /fɔː'wɔːn/ vt [VP6A] warn beforehand.

fore·woman /'fɔːwʊmən/ n (pl -women /-wimin/) woman in authority over other women workers.

fore·word /'fɔːwɜːd/ n [C] introductory remarks to a book, printed in it, esp by someone not the author of the book.

for·feit /'fɔːfɪt/ vt [VP6A] (have to) suffer the loss of sth as a punishment or consequence, or because of rules: ~ the good opinion of one's friends; ~ one's health. □ n [C] 1 sth (to be) ~ed: His health was the ~ he paid for overworking. 2 (pl) game in which a player gives up various articles if he makes an error and can redeem them by doing sth ludicrous: Let's play ~s. ~·ure /'fɔːfɪtʃə(r)/ n [U] ~ing: (the) ~ure of one's property.

for·gather, fore·gather /fɔː'gæðə(r)/ vi [VP2A,C] come together.

for·gave /fə'geɪv/ pt of forgive.

forge¹ /fɔːdʒ/ n [C] 1 workshop with fire and anvil where metals are heated and shaped, esp one used by a smith for making shoes for horses, repairing agricultural machinery, etc. 2 (workshop with) furnace or hearth for melting or refining metal.

forge² /fɔːdʒ/ vt [VP6A] 1 shape by heating and hammering: ~ an anchor; (fig) Their friendship was ~d by shared adversity. 2 make a copy of sth, eg a signature, a banknote, a will, in order to deceive. **forger** n person who ~s(2). **forg·ery** /'fɔːdʒərɪ/ n 1 [U] forging(2) of a document, signature, etc. 2 [C] (pl -ries) ~d document, signature, etc. **forg·ing** n [C] piece of metal that has been ~d(1) or shaped under a press.

forge³ /fɔːdʒ/ vi [VP2C] ~ ahead, make steady progress; take the lead (in a race, etc).

for·get /fə'get/ vt,vi (pt forgot /fə'gɒt/, pp forgotten /fə'gɒtn/) 1 [VP6A,C,D,8,9,10,2A,3A] ~ (about), lose remembrance of; fail to keep in the memory; fail to recall: I ~/I've forgotten her name. I shall never ~ your kindness to me. Did you ~ (that) I was coming? I have forgotten how to do it/where he lives/whether he wants it. I forgot all about it. I shall never ~ hearing Chaliapin singing the part of Boris Godunov. **forget-me-not** /fə'get mi nɒt/ n small plant with blue flowers. 2 [VP7A] neglect or fail (to do sth): Don't ~ to post the letters. He has forgotten to pay me. 3 [VP6A,2A] put out of the mind; stop thinking about: Let's ~ our quarrels. Forgive and ~. 4 [VP6A] omit to pay attention to: Don't ~ the waiter, Give him a tip. 5 ~ oneself, (a) behave thoughtlessly in a way not suited to one's dignity, to the circumstances. (b) act unselfishly, thinking only of the interests of others. ~·ful /-fl/ adj in the habit of ~ting: He's very ~ful of things. Old people are sometimes ~ful. ~·fully /-fəlɪ/ adv ~·ful·ness n

for·give /fə'gɪv/ vt,vi (pt forgave /fə'geɪv/, pp forgiven /fə'gɪvn/) [VP6A,14,12C,2A] 1 ~ sb (sth/ for doing sth), say that one no longer has the wish to punish sb; no longer have the wish to punish sb for an offence, a sin; pardon or show mercy to (sb); no longer have hard feelings towards (sb): ~ sb for being rude/~ his rudeness. Am I ~n? F~ us our trespasses. Your sins will be ~n you. 2 not de-

mand repayment of (a debt); not demand repayment of a debt from (sb): He forgave the debt. Will you ~ me the debt? **for·giv·able** /-əbl/ adj that can be ~n. **for·giv·ing** adj ready or willing to ~: a forgiving nature. **for·giv·ing·ly** adv ~·ness n [U] forgiving or being ~n; willingness to ~: ask for/ receive ~ness; full of ~ness.

forgo /fɔː'gəʊ/ vt (pt forwent /fɔː'went/, pp forgone /fɔː'gɒn US: -'gɔːn/) do without; give up: ~ pleasures in order to study hard.

for·got, for·got·ten ⇨ forget.

fork /fɔːk/ n [C] 1 implement with two or more points (prongs), used for lifting food to the mouth, carving, etc. '~ lunch/supper, one (for more persons than can be seated at table) at which food is served as a buffet where guests serve themselves. 2 farm or gardening tool for breaking up the ground, lifting hay, straw, etc. ⇨ the illus at tool. 3 place where a road, tree-trunk, etc divides or branches; part of a bicycle to which a wheel is fixed. ⇨ also tuning-~ at tune. 4 ,~-lift 'truck, powered truck or trolley with mechanical means of lifting and lowering goods (to or from storage space, or for loading and unloading). □ vt,vi 1 [VP6A,15A,B] lift, move, carry, with a ~: ~ hay/straw; ~ in manure, dig it into the ground with a ~; ~ the ground over, turn the soil over with a ~. 2 [VP2A,C] (of a road, river, etc) divide into branches; (of persons) turn (left or right): We ~ed right at the church. 3 [VP15B,2C] ~ sth out, ~ up/ out, (colloq) hand over, pay: I've got to ~ out a lot of money to the Collector of Taxes this year. ~ed adj branching; dividing into two or more parts: a ~ed road; the ~ed tongue of a snake; a bird with a ~ed tail; ~ed lightning.

a fork-lift truck

for·lorn /fə'lɔːn/ adj (poet or liter) unhappy; uncared for; forsaken. ~ hope, desperate enterprise; plan or enterprise which has very little likelihood of success. ~·ly adv ~·ness n

form¹ /fɔːm/ n 1 [U] shape; outward or visible appearance: without shape or ~; take ~, begin to have a (recognizable) shape; [C] person or animal as it can be seen or touched: A dark ~ could be seen in the distance. Proteus was a Greek sea-god who could appear in the ~ of any creature he wished. He has a well-proportioned ~, a well-shaped body. 2 [U] general arrangement or structure; way in which parts are put together to make a whole or a group; style or manner of presentation: a piece of music in sonata ~; have a sense of ~ in painting (~ being contrasted with colouring); literary ~ (~ being contrasted with subject-matter). 3 [C] particular kind of arrangement or structure; manner in which a thing exists; species, kind or variety: ~s of government; ~s of animal and vegetable life. Ice, snow and steam are ~s of water. 4 [U] (gram) shape taken by a word (in sound or spelling): change ~; different in ~ but identical in *meaning;* [C] one of the shapes taken by a word (in sound or spelling): *The word 'brother' has two plural ~s, 'brothers' and 'brethren'. The past tense ~ of 'run' is 'ran'.* 5 [U] manner of behaving or speaking fixed, required or expected by custom or etiquette: *do sth for ~'s sake,* ie because it is usual, not because one wishes to do it or likes doing it; *say 'Good morning' as a mere matter of ~,* ie not because one is really pleased to see the person to whom the words are spoken. **good/bad** '~, behaviour according to/not according to custom or etiquette. 6 [C] particular way of behaving, etc; greeting, utterance, act, as required by custom or etiquette; established practice or ritual: *the ancient ~s observed at the coronation of a sovereign; pay too much attention to ~s;* a ~ *of prayer used at sea; ~s of worship.* 7 [C] printed paper with space to be filled in: *'telegraph ~s; appli' cation ~s;* printed or typewritten letter sent out in great numbers (also called a ~ **letter**). 8 [C] condition of health and training (esp of horses and athletes): *If a horse is not in good ~ it is unlikely to win a race. On ~* (= Judging from recent performances as evidence of condition and training), *the Aga Khan's horse is likely to win the race.* **in /out of ~; on/off ~,** in good/bad condition: *Smith is out of ~/is not on ~/is off ~ and is unlikely to run in the 100 metres race tomorrow.* 9 [U] spirits: *Jack was in great ~ at the dinner party,* in high spirits, lively. 10 [C] long wooden bench, usu without a back, for several persons to sit on. 11 [C] class in GB schools, the youngest boys and girls being in the first ~ and the oldest in the sixth ~. **~·less** *adj* without shape. **~·less·ly** *adv*

form² /fɔːm/ *vt, vi* 1 [VP6A, 15A] give shape or form to; make, produce: *~ words and sentences; ~ the plural of a noun by adding -s or -es; ~ one's style* (in writing) *on good models.* 2 [VP6A] develop, build up, conceive: *~ good habits; ~ a child's character/mind,* by training, discipline, etc; *~ ideas/plans/judgements/opinions/conclusions.* 3 [VP6A,15A] organize: *~ a class for beginners in French. They ~ed themselves into a committee.* 4 [VP6A] be (the material of), be (one or part of): *What ~s the basis of this compound? This series of lectures ~s part of a complete course on French history.* 5 [VP14,2C] *~ into,* (mil) (cause to) move into a particular order: *~ a regiment into columns; ~ into line. The company was ~ed into three ranks.* 6 [VP2A,C] come into existence; become solid; take shape: *The idea ~ed in his mind. The words would not ~ on her lips,* She could not bring herself to speak them. *Ice ~s at the temperature of 0°C.*

for·mal /'fɔːml/ *adj* 1 in accordance with rules, customs and convention: *pay a ~ call on the Ambassador; ~ dress,* as required by custom for certain occasions; *make a ~* (= ceremonious) *bow to sb; a ~ receipt,* according to commercial custom, regular and in good order. 2 regular or geometric in design; symmetrical: *~ gardens,* eg with flower beds, hedges, etc in geometrical patterns. 3 of the outward shape or appearance (not the reality or substance): *a ~ resemblance between two things.* 4 ,~ '**grammar**, of the forms of words, of rules (of syntax, etc). **~·ly** /-məlɪ/ *adv* **~·ism** /-ɪzəm/ *n* [U] exact observance of forms and ceremonies, eg in religious duties, in behaviour.

for·mal·de·hyde /fɔː'mældɪhaɪd/ *n* [U] (chem) colourless gas (**HCHO**) used, dissolved in water, as a

preservative and disinfectant. **for·malin** /'fɔːməlɪn/ *n* [U] (chem) solution of ~ used as a disinfectant.

for·mal·ity /fɔː'mælətɪ/ *n (pl* -ties) 1 [U] strict attention to rules, forms and convention: *There was too much ~ in the Duke's household.* 2 [C] formal act; sth required by custom or rules: *legal formalities; comply with all the necessary formalities.* **a mere ~,** sth one is required or expected to do, but which has little meaning or importance.

for·mat /'fɔːmæt/ *n* 1 shape and size of a book, including the type, paper and binding: *reissue a book in a new ~.* 2 arrangement; procedure; style: *the ~ of a meeting/conference/interview.*

for·ma·tion /fɔː'meɪʃn/ *n* 1 [U] forming or shaping: *the ~ of character/of ideas in the mind;* [C] that which is formed: *Clouds are ~s of condensed water vapour.* 2 [U] structure or arrangement: *troops/warships in 'battle ~; military aircraft flying in ~;* (attrib) '~ *flying/dancing;* [C] particular arrangement or order: *rock ~s;* [C] the arrangement of the players at the start of a (football, Rugby) match.

for·ma·tive /'fɔːmətɪv/ *adj* 1 giving, or tending to give, shape to: *~ influences,* eg on a child's character. 2 pliable: *the ~ years of a child's life,* the years during which its character is formed.

for·mer /'fɔːmə(r)/ *adj* 1 of an earlier period: *in ~ times; my ~ students; customs of ~ days. She looks more like her ~ self,* eg looks well again after her illness. 2 (also as *pron*) **the ~** (contrasted with **the latter**), the first-mentioned of two: *I prefer the ~ alternative to the latter. Of these alternatives I prefer the ~.* **~·ly** *adv* in ~ times.

for·mic /'fɔːmɪk/ *adj* ,~ '**acid,** the acid (used to make insecticides, fumigants, etc) contained in the fluid emitted by ants but now usu produced synthetically.

For·mica /fɔː'maɪkə/ *n* [U] (P) heat-resistant plastic made in sheets (for covering surfaces).

for·mi·dable /'fɔːmɪdəbl/ *adj* 1 causing fear or dread: *a man with a ~ appearance.* 2 requiring great effort to deal with or overcome: *~ obstacles/opposition/enemies/debts.* **for·mi·dably** /-əblɪ/ *adv*

for·mula /'fɔːmjʊlə/ *n (pl ~s,* or, in scientific usage, *~e /-liː/)* 1 form of words used regularly (as 'How d'you do?', 'Excuse me', 'Thank you'); phrase or sentence regularly used in legal documents, church services, etc: *the ~ used in baptism.* 2 statement of a rule, fact, etc esp one in signs or numbers, as in mathematics; (chem) expression in symbols of the constituent parts of a substance, eg H_2O (water).3 set of directions, usu in symbols, for a medical preparation: *a ~ for a cough mixture.*

for·mu·late /'fɔːmjʊleɪt/ *vt* [VP6A] express clearly and exactly: *~ one's thoughts/a doctrine.* **for·mu·la·tion** /ˌfɔːmjʊ'leɪʃn/ *n* [U] formulating; [C] exact and clear statement.

for·ni·ca·tion /ˌfɔːnɪ'keɪʃn/ *n* [U] voluntary sexual intercourse between persons not married to one another, esp when both are unmarried. ⇨ **adultery.** **for·ni·cate** /'fɔːnɪkeɪt/ *vi* [VP21] commit ~.

for·ra·der /'fɒrədə(r)/ *adv* (colloq) more forward: *can't get any ~,* can't make any progress.

for·sake /fə'seɪk/ *vt* (pt forsook /fə'sʊk/, pp forsaken /fə'seɪkən/) [VP6A] give up; break away from; desert: *~ one's wife and children; ~ bad habits. His friends forsook him when he became poor.*

for·sooth /fɔː'suːθ/ *adv* (used in irony) no doubt; in truth.

for·swear /fɔː'sweə(r)/ vt (pt forswore /fɔː'swɔː(r)/, pp forsworn /fɔː'swɔːn/) [VP6A] **1** give up doing or using (sth): ~ bad habits/ smoking. **2** ~ oneself, perjure oneself.

for·sythia /fɔː'saɪθɪə US: fər'sɪθɪə/ n [U] shrub with bright yellow flowers in spring.

fort /fɔːt/ n building or group of buildings specially erected or strengthened for military defence.

forte¹ /'fɔːteɪ US: fɔːrt/ n person's special talent; sth a person does particularly well: Singing is not my ~, I do not sing well.

forte² /'fɔːteɪ/ adj, adv (I; music) (abbr f) loud(ly).

forth /fɔːθ/ adv **1** (archaic) out. **2** (formal) onwards; forwards: from this day ~. and so ~, and so on. **back and** ~, to and fro (which is more usu). **3 hold** ~, ⇨ hold¹(14).

forth·com·ing /ˌfɔːθ'kʌmɪŋ/ adj **1** about to come out: a list of ~ books, books about to be published. **2** (pred) ready for use when needed: The money/ help we hoped for was not ~, We did not receive it. **3** ready to be helpful, give information, etc: The girl at the reception desk was not very ~.

forth·right /'fɔːθraɪt/ adj outspoken; straightforward.

forth·with /ˌfɔːθ'wɪθ US: -'wɪð/ adv at once; without losing time.

for·ti·eth /'fɔːtɪəθ/ ⇨ forty.

for·tify /'fɔːtɪfaɪ/ vt (pt,pp -fied) [VP6A,14] ~ (against), strengthen (a place) against attack (with walls, trenches, guns, etc); support or strengthen oneself, one's courage, etc: ~ a town against the enemy; a fortified city/zone; ~ oneself against the cold, eg by wearing a fur coat; fortified with the rites of the Church, prepared, by having received the Sacraments, for death. **fortified wine**, wine, eg sherry, strengthened by the addition of grape brandy. **for·ti·fi·ca·tion** /ˌfɔːtɪfɪ'keɪʃn/ n [U] ~ing; [C] (often pl) defensive wall(s), tower(s), earthwork(s), etc.

for·tis·simo /fɔː'tɪsɪməʊ/ adj, adv (I; music) (abbr ff) very loud(ly).

for·ti·tude /'fɔːtɪtjuːd US: -tuːd/ n [U] calm courage, self-control, in the face of pain, danger or difficulty.

fort·night /'fɔːtnaɪt/ n period of two weeks: a ~'s holiday; go away for a ~; a ~ (=a ~ from) today/tomorrow/next Monday; a ~ ago yesterday. ~·ly adj, adv happening or occurring every ~: ~ly sailings to Bombay; go ~ly.

for·tress /'fɔːtrɪs/ n fortified building or town.

for·tu·itous /fɔː'tjuːɪtəs US: -'tuː-/ adj (formal) happening by chance: a ~ meeting. ~·ly adv

for·tu·nate /'fɔːtʃənət/ adj favoured by fortune; lucky; prosperous; having, bringing, brought by, good fortune: be ~ in life. You were ~ to escape being injured. He was ~ enough to have a good income. That was ~ for you. You were ~ in your choice/in winning his sympathy. ~·ly adv in a ~ manner: ~ly for everybody.

for·tune /'fɔːtʃuːn/ n **1** [C,U] chance; chance looked upon as a power deciding or influencing sb or sth; fate; good or bad luck coming to a person or undertaking: have ~ on one's side, be lucky. **the ~(s) of war**, what may happen in war. **try one's** ~, take a risky step. **tell sb his** ~, say, eg as gypsies do, from a reading of playing cards, or the lines on his palm, what will happen to him. '~ **teller** n person who claims to be able to do this. **2** [C,U] prosperity; success; great sum of money: a man of ~; seek one's ~ in a new country. **come into a** ~,

inherit a lot of money. **make a** ~, make a lot of money. **marry a** ~, marry sb who is or will be rich, eg an heiress. **a small** ~, a lot of money: spend a small ~ on clothes. '~ **hunter** n man seeking a rich woman to marry.

forty /'fɔːtɪ/ adj, n the number 40: a man of ~, aged 40; under/over ~. ⇨ App 4. **the forties**, 40–49. **have** ~ **winks**, ⇨ wink. **for·ti·eth** /'fɔːtɪəθ/ adj, n ⇨ App 4.

fo·rum /'fɔːrəm/ n (in ancient Rome) public place for meetings; any place for public discussion: TV is an accepted ~ for the discussion of public affairs.

for·ward¹ /'fɔːwəd/ adj (⇨ backward) **1** directed towards the front; situated in front; moving on, advancing: a ~ march/movement; the ~ ranks of a column of troops; ~ planning, for future needs, etc; be well ~ with one's work. **2** (of plants, crops, seasons, children) well advanced; making progress towards maturity: a ~ spring. **3** eager or impatient; ready and willing: ~ to help others; too eager; rather presumptuous: a ~ young girl. **4** advanced or extreme: ~ opinions. **5** (comm) relating to future produce: ~ prices, for goods to be delivered later; a ~ contract. □ n one of the first–line players in football (now often called a striker), hockey, etc. ⇨ illus at football. ~·**ness** n [U] the state of being ~(2): the ~ness of the season.

for·ward² /'fɔːwəd/ vt [VP6A,12A,13A,15A] **1** help or send forward; help to advance: ~ sb's plans. **2** send, dispatch: ~ goods to sb. We have today ~ed you our new catalogue. '~**ing agent** n person or business company that ~s goods. '~**ing instructions**, instructions concerning the destination, etc of goods. **3** send a letter, parcel, etc after a person to a new address: Please ~ my letters to this address.

for·ward(s) /'fɔːwəd(z)/ adv (Note: ~s is not much used except as in 4 below.) **1** onward so as to make progress: rush/step ~; go ~. ⇨ carriage(3); forrader. **2** towards the future; onwards in time: from this time ~; look ~, think ahead, think about the future. **look ~ to sth**, ⇨ look¹(7). **3** to the front; into prominence: bring ~ (= call attention to) new evidence; come ~, offer oneself for a task, a post, etc. **4 backward(s) and ~(s)**, to and fro.

fosse /fɒs/ n [C] long, narrow ditch or trench, eg a moat, or as a fortification.

fos·sil /'fɒsl/ n [C] **1** recognizable (part, trace or imprint of a) prehistoric animal or plant once buried in earth, now hardened like rock: hunt for ~s; (attrib) ~ bones/shells; ~ ferns in coal. **2** (collog) person who is out of date and unable to accept new ideas: Isn't Professor Baboon an old ~! ~·**ize** /'fɒsəlaɪz/ vt, vi [VP6A,2A] change or turn into stone; (fig) make or become out of date or antiquated. ~·**iz·ation** /ˌfɒsəlaɪ'zeɪʃn US: -əlɪ'z-/ n

a fossil

fos·ter /'fɒstə(r) US: 'fɔː-/ vt [VP6A] care for; help the growth and development of; nurture: ~ a child, bring it up as one's own without legally adopting it; ~ *the sick;* ~ *musical ability;* ~ *evil thoughts/a desire for revenge.* '~**-brother/-sister** *nn* one ~ed by one's parent(s). '~**-child** *n* one brought up by ~-parents. '~**-parent/-mother/-father** *nn* one who acts as a parent in place of a natural parent, but without legal guardianship. ⇨ **adopt.**

fought /fɔːt/ *pt,pp* of fight.

foul[1] /faʊl/ *adj* **1** causing disgust; having a bad smell or taste; filthy: *a* ~ *prison cell; medicine with a* ~ *taste;* ~*-smelling drains; a* ~ *meal*, (sl) a poor meal. **2** wicked, evil; (of language) full of oaths, obscene; (of the weather) stormy, rough. ,~**-'spoken/-'mouthed** *adj* using ~ language. **by** ,*fair means or* '~, somehow or other, whether by good or evil methods. **3** ,~ **'play, (a)** (in sport) sth contrary to the rules. **(b)** violent crime, esp murder: *Is* ~ *play suspected,* Do the police think this is a case of murder? **4** entangled: *a* ~ *rope.* **5** (of a flue, pipe, gun-barrel, etc) clogged up, not clear: *The fire won't burn; perhaps the chimney is* ~, needs sweeping. **6** *fall* ~ *of,* (a) (of a ship) run against, collide with, become entangled with. **(b)** (fig) get into trouble with: *fall* ~ *of the law.* □ *n* **1** [C] (sport) sth contrary to the rules; irregular stroke or piece of play. **2** [U] *through fair and* ~, through good and bad fortune; through everything. ~**.ly** /'faʊlɪ/ *adv* in a ~ manner: *He was* ~*ly murdered.* ~**-ness** *n*

foul[2] /faʊl/ *vt,vi* [VP6A,2A,2C] ~ *(up),* **1** make or become foul: *factory chimneys that* ~ *up the air with smoke;* ~ *one's name/reputation;* ~ *a drain/gun-barrel.* **2** collide; collide with; make or become entangled: *The rope* ~*ed the anchor chain. His fishing-line got* ~*ed up in the weeds.* **3** (sport) commit a ~(1) against: ~ *an opponent.*

found[1] /faʊnd/ *pt,pp* of find.

found[2] /faʊnd/ *vt* **1** [VP6A] start the building of; lay the base of; establish: ~ *a new city/a colony in a new country.* **2** [VP6A] get sth started by providing money (esp endowments): ~ *a new school.* **3** [VP14] ~ *sth on/upon,* base on: *a novel* ~*ed on fact; arguments* ~*ed on facts.*

foun·da·tion /faʊn'deɪʃn/ *n* **1** [U] founding or establishing (of a town, school, church or other institution). **2** [C] sth that is founded, eg a college, monastery, hospital; fund of money for charity, research, etc: *the Ford F*~. **3** [C] (often *pl*) strong base of a building, usu below ground-level, on which it is built up: *the* ~(*s*) *of a block of flats. The huge lorries shook the house to its* ~*s.* '~**-stone** *n* stone laid at a ceremony to celebrate the founding of a building. **4** [C,U] that on which an idea, belief, etc rests; underlying principle; basis; starting-point: *the* ~*s of religious beliefs; lay the* ~(*s*) *of one's career; a story that has no* ~ *in fact/is without* ~. **5** ~ **garment,** (trade use) woman's corset or other garment to shape and support the body (often with a bra attached). '~ **cream,** (cosmetics) cream used on the skin before other cosmetics are applied.

foun·der[1] /'faʊndə(r)/ *n* person who founds or establishes a school, etc. **found·ress** /'faʊndrɪs/ *n* woman ~.

foun·der[2] /'faʊndə(r)/ *vi,vt* [VP2A,6A] **1** (of a ship) (cause to) fill with water and sink. **2** (of a horse) fall or stumble (esp in mud) or from overwork; cause (a horse) to break down from overwork. **3** (of a plan, etc) fail.

found·ling /'faʊndlɪŋ/ *n* deserted or abandoned

child of unknown parents. '~ **hospital,** (formerly) institution where ~s are taken in and cared for.

foun·dry /'faʊndrɪ/ *n* (*pl* -dries) place where metal or glass is melted and moulded: *a* '*type* ~, where type for printing is made.

fount /faʊnt/ *n* **1** (poet) spring of water. **2** (also *font*) set of printer's type of the same size and face. **3** (poet or rhet) source.

foun·tain /'faʊntɪn US: -tn/ *n* **1** spring of water, esp one made artificially with water forced through holes in a pipe or pipes for ornamental purposes. '**drinking-**~ *n* one that supplies drinking-water in a public place. '~**-pen** *n* pen with a supply of ink inside the holder. '**soda-**~, ⇨ soda. **2** (fig) source or origin: *the* ~ *of justice.* '~**-head** *n* original source.

four /fɔː(r)/ *n, adj* the number 4: *a child of* ~, ~ *years old; a coach and* ~, *with* ~ *horses; the* ~ *corners of the earth,* the farthest parts; *scatter sth to the* ~ *winds,* in all directions. ⇨ App 4. ,~**-letter 'word,** word of ~ letters, eg *shit,* which is regarded as obscene. *on all* ~*s,* (crawling) on the hands and knees. *be on all* ~*s (with),* be quite the same (as). *a* ~, a rowing-boat with a crew of ~; (cricket) hit for ~ runs. ,~**-in-'hand** *n* vehicle (coach or carriage) pulled by ~ horses and with no outrider. '~**-part** *adj* (music) arranged for ~ voices to sing. ~**-pence** /'fɔːpəns/ *n* the sum of 4p: *apples,* ~*pence each.* ~**-penny** /'fɔːpnɪ US:* -penɪ/ *adj* costing 4p: *a* ~*penny loaf.* '~**-ply** *adj* (of wool, wood, etc) having ~ strands or thicknesses. ,~**-'poster** *n* bed with ~ posts to support a canopy or curtains. ,~**-'pounder** *n* gun throwing a 4lb shot. '~**-score** *adj, n* 80. '~**-square** *adj* square-shaped; (fig) steady; solidly based. ,~**-'wheeler** *n* hackney carriage with ~ wheels (not a hansom cab). ~**-fold** /'fɔːfəʊld/ *adj,adv* repeated ~ times; having ~ parts; ~ times as much or as many. ~**-some** /'fɔːsəm/ *n* game (esp of golf) between two pairs: *a mixed* ~*some,* with one man and one woman in each pair. ~**-teen** /ˌfɔː'tiːn/ *n, adj* the number 14; ⇨ App 4. ~**-teenth** /ˌfɔː'tiːnθ/ *n, adj* ⇨ App 4. **fourth** /fɔːθ/ *n, adj* ⇨ App 4. **Fourth of July,** (US) anniversary of the Declaration of Independence (1776). **fourth·ly** *adv*

fowl /faʊl/ *n* **1** (old use) any bird: *the* ~*s of the air.* **2** (with a *pref*) one of the larger birds: '*wild*~, '*water*~. **3** domestic cock or hen: *keep* ~*s.* '~**-pest** *n* infectious disease of ~s. '~**-run** *n* piece of (usu enclosed) land where ~s are kept. **4** [U] flesh of ~s as food: *roast* ~ *for dinner.* □ *vi* (usu as gerund) catch, hunt, snare, wild~: *go* ~*ing.* '~**-ing-piece** *n* light shot-gun used in ~ing. ~**er** *n* person who shoots or traps wild birds for food.

fox[1] /fɒks/ *n* (fem **vixen** /'vɪksn/) wild animal of the dog family, with (usu) red fur and a bushy tail, preserved in Britain for hunting, and proverbial for its cunning. ⇨ the illus at small. '**fox-glove** *n* plant with tall-growing spikes of purple or white flowers. '**fox-hole** *n* (mil) hole in the ground used as a shelter against enemy fire and as a firing-point. '**fox·hound** *n* kind of hound bred and trained to hunt foxes. '**fox·hunt** *n, vi* chasing of, chase, foxes with hounds. ,**fox-'terrier** *n* small and lively short-haired dog used for driving foxes from earths, or kept as a pet. '**fox·trot** *n* (music for a) ballroom dance with slow and quick steps. **foxy** *adj* crafty; crafty-looking.

fox[2] /fɒks/ *vt* [VP6A] (colloq) deceive by cunning; confuse; puzzle: *He was completely foxed.*

PHEASANT · crest · wattle · PARTRIDGE · DUCK · GROUSE · QUAIL · COCK · HEN · TURKEY · GOOSE · webbed foot · fowl

foyer /'fɔɪeɪ *US:* 'fɔɪər/ *n* large space in a theatre for the use of the audience during intervals; entrance hall of a cinema or hotel.

fra·cas /'fræka: *US:* 'freɪkəs/ *n* (*pl* GB ~ /-ka:z/; *US* ~es /-kəsəz/) noisy quarrel.

frac·tion /'frækʃn/ *n* **1** small part or bit. **2** number that is not a whole number (eg ⅓, 5/8, 0·76). ~**al** /-ʃənl/ *adj* of or in ~s. ~**al distillation**, partial separation of liquids, eg petroleum, having different boiling-points by gradual heating.

frac·tious /'frækʃəs/ *adj* irritable; peevish; bad-tempered. ~**·ly** *adv* ~**·ness** *n*

frac·ture /'fræktʃə(r)/ *n* [U] breaking or being broken, eg of a bone, a pipe-line; [C] instance of this: *compound/simple* ~*s*, with/without skin wounds. □ *vt, vi* [VP6A,2A] break; crack: ~ *one's leg; bones that* ~ *easily.*

frag·ile /'frædʒaɪl *US:* -dʒəl/ *adj* easily injured, broken or destroyed: *china/health/happiness.* **fra·gil·ity** /frə'dʒɪlətɪ/ *n* [U].

frag·ment /'frægmənt/ *n* [C] part broken off; separate or incomplete part: *try to put the* ~*s of a broken vase together; overhear* ~*s of conversation.* □ /fræg'ment/ *vi* [VP2A] break into ~s: *The shell* ~*s on impact.* **frag·men·tary** /'frægməntrɪ *US:* -terɪ/ *adj* incomplete: *a* ~*ary report of an event.* **frag·men·ta·tion** /ˌfrægmen'teɪʃn/, '~**ation bomb**, one that breaks up into small ~s.

fra·grant /'freɪɡrənt/ *adj* sweet-smelling: ~ *flowers;* (fig) pleasant: ~ *memories.* **fra·grance** /-əns/ *n* [U,C] sweet or pleasing smell.

frail /freɪl/ *adj* weak; fragile: *a* ~ *child,* one with a weak constitution; *a* ~ *support;* ~ *happiness.* ~**ty** /'freɪltɪ/ *n* [U] the quality of being ~: *the* ~*ty of human life;* [C] (*pl* -ties) fault; moral weakness: *He loved her in spite of her little frailties.*

frame¹ /freɪm/ *n* [C] **1** skeleton or main structure, eg steel girders, brick walls, wooden struts, of a ship, building, aircraft, etc which makes its shape, esp in the process of building. '~ **aerial** *n* one in which the wire is round a ~ (instead of being stretched out between two poles, etc). '~ **house** *n* one with a wooden skeleton covered with wooden boards or shingles. **2** border of wood or other

material in which a picture, photograph, window or door is enclosed or set; structure that holds the lenses of a pair of spectacles. ⇨ the illus at window. **3** human or animal body: *a girl of slender* ~. *Sobs shook her* ~. **4** box-like structure of wood and glass for protecting plants from the cold: *a cold/heated* ~. **5** ~ *of mind,* temporary condition of mind; temper: *in a cheerful* ~ *of mind; in the* ~ *of mind to welcome any diversion.* **6** (more usu '~work) established order or system: *the* ~ *of society.* **7** single exposure on a roll of photographic film. '~**·work** *n* that part of a structure that gives shape and support: *a bridge with a steel* ~*work; the* ~*work of a policy.*

frame² /freɪm/ *vt, vi* **1** [VP6A] put together; shape; build up: ~ *a plan/theory/sentence; a man not* ~*d for severe hardships,* unable to endure them well. **2** [VP6A] put a frame(2) round; enclose in a frame: ~ *a photograph; have an oil-painting* ~*d;* serve as a frame: *a landscape* ~*d in an archway.* **3** [VP2A,C] develop; give promise of developing: *plans that* ~ *well/badly.* **4** [VP6A] (sl) form a plan to make (sb) appear guilty of sth; put together a false charge against (sb): *The accused man said he had been* ~*d.* '~**-up** *n* (sl) scheme or conspiracy to make an innocent person appear guilty.

franc /fræŋk/ *n* standard unit of a decimal currency in eg Belgium, France, Switzerland.

fran·chise /'fræntʃaɪz/ *n* **1** [U] the ~, full rights of citizenship given by a country or town, esp the right to vote at elections. **2** [C] (chiefly US) special right given by public authorities to a person or company: *a* ~ *for a bus service.* □ *vt* [VP6A] (US) grant a ~(2) to.

Fran·cis·can /fræn'sɪskən/ *n, adj* (friar or nun) of the religious order founded in 1209 by St Francis /'frɑ:nsɪs/ of Assisi /ə'si:sɪ/.

Franco- /'fræŋkəʊ/ *pref* (used in compounds) French: *the* ˌ~*-German 'War of 1870—71;* '~**phile,** (one who is) friendly towards France; '~**phobe,** (one who is) hostile towards France.

Frank /fræŋk/ *n* member of the Germanic tribes that conquered Gaul (= France) in the 6th c AD.

frank¹ /fræŋk/ *adj* showing clearly the thoughts

and feelings; open: *a* ~ *look/smile/face; make a* ~ *confession of one's guilt; be quite* ~ *with sb* (*about sth*). ~·ly *adv* ~·ness *n*

frank² /fræŋk/ *vt* [VP6A] put a stamp or a mark on (a letter, etc) to show that postage has been paid. '~·ing-machine *n* machine that automatically stamps letters etc passed through it, with a counting mechanism to show the total charge.

frank·furter /'fræŋkfɜːtə(r)/ *n* seasoned and smoked sausage made of beef and pork.

frank·in·cense /'fræŋkɪnsens/ *n* [U] kind of resin from trees, giving a sweet smell when burnt.

frank·lin /'fræŋklɪn/ *n* (in GB, 14th and 15th cc) landowner not of noble birth, higher in rank than a yeoman.

fran·tic /'fræntɪk/ *adj* wildly excited with joy, pain, anxiety, etc: ~ *cries for help; drive sb* ~. **fran·ti·cally** /-klɪ/ *adv*

fra·ter·nal /frə'tɜːnl/ *adj* brotherly: ~ *love*. ~ly /-nəlɪ/ *adv*

fra·ter·nity /frə'tɜːnətɪ/ *n* (*pl* -ties) **1** [U] brotherly feeling. **2** [C] society of men, eg monks, who treat each other as equals; men who are joined together by common interests: *the* ~ *of the Press*, newspaper writers. **3** [C] (US) society of students, with branches in various colleges, usu with names made up of Greek letters. ⇨ sorority.

frat·er·nize /'frætənaɪz/ *vi* [VP2A,C,3A] ~ (*with*), become friendly (with): *Men from the two armies stopped fighting and* ~*d on Christmas Day*. **frat·er·niz·ation** /ˌfrætənaɪ'zeɪʃn US: -nɪ'z-/ *n*

frat·ri·cide /'frætrɪsaɪd/ *n* [C,U] (person guilty of) wilful killing of one's brother or sister.

Frau /frau/ *n* (*pl* Frauen /'frauən/) (G) (of a German wife or widow) Mrs; German woman.

fraud /frɔːd/ *n* **1** [U] criminal deception; [C] act of this kind: *get money by* ~. **2** [C] person or thing that deceives: *This hair-restorer is a* ~; *I'm as bald as ever*. ~u·lent /'frɔːdjʊlənt US: -dʒʊ-/ *adj* acting with ~; deceitful; obtained by ~: ~ulent gains. ~u·lent·ly *adv*

fraught /frɔːt/ *pred adj* **1** involving; attended by; threatening (unpleasant consequences): *an expedition* ~ *with danger*. **2** filled with: ~ *with meaning*.

Fräu·lein /'frɔɪlaɪn/ *n* (G) (of an unmarried German woman) Miss; German spinster.

fray¹ /freɪ/ *n* (lit, fig) fight; contest: *eager for the* ~.

fray² /freɪ/ *vt,vi* [VP6A,2A,C] (of cloth, rope, etc) become worn, make worn, by rubbing so that there are loose threads: ~*ed cuffs*, eg on a coat sleeve; (fig) strained; exasperated: ~*ed nerves/tempers*.

frazzle /'fræzl/ *n* exhausted state: *worn to a* ~.

freak /friːk/ *n* **1** abnormal or unusual idea, act or occurrence: (attrib) *a* ~ *storm*. **2** (also ~ of '**nature**) person, animal or plant that is abnormal in form, eg a five-legged sheep. □ *vi,vt* [VP2C,15B] ~ *out*, (sl) (cause to) have an intense emotional experience as from hallucinatory drugs. Hence, '~-out *n* ~·ish /-ɪʃ/ *adj* abnormal: ~*ish behaviour*. ~·ish·ly *adv* ~·ish·ness *n* ~y *adj* = ~ish.

freckle /'frekl/ *n* one of the small light-brown spots on the human skin; (*pl*) such spots on the face and hands caused by sunburn. □ *vt,vi* [VP6A,2A] (cause to) become covered with ~s: *a* ~*d forehead*. *Some people* ~ *more easily than others*.

free¹ /friː/ *adj* (freer /'friːə(r)/, freest /'friːɪst/) **1** (of a person) not a slave; not in the power of another person or other persons; not in prison; having personal rights and social and political liberty: *The prisoners were pardoned and set* ~. *Were the*

Pyramids built by slave labour or by ~ *labour?* ⇨ also ~ labour below. '~-born *adj* inheriting liberty and rights of citizenship. '~·man /-mən/ *n* (*pl* -men) person who is not a slave or a serf. ⇨ also ~man at (9) below. **2** (of a State, its citizens, and institutions) not controlled by a foreign government; having representative government in which private rights are respected: ~ *democracies; Ruritania, the land of the* ~. **3** not fixed or held back; able to move about without hindrance; unrestricted; not controlled by rules, regulations or conventions: *leave one end of the rope* ~, loose; ~ *hydrogen*, not combined with another element. *You are* ~ *to go or stay as you please. Please feel* ~ *to ask questions. She is not* ~ *to marry*, cannot do so, eg because she has to look after her parents. *One of the parts has worked* ~, become loose, out of position. **allow sb/give sb/have a** ~ **hand,** permission or discretion to do what seems best without consulting others. ~ '**agent** *n* person who is ~ to act without restrictions. ,F~ 'Church *n* (a) nonconformist Church. (b) Church not under State control. ~ '**enterprise** the conduct of trade and industry with the minimum of State control. ,~-**and-**'**easy** *adj* unceremonious. ~ '**fall** *n* fall from an aircraft at a great height without use of a parachute (until this is needed): *a* ~*-fall parachutist.* ~ '**fight**, one in which anyone present may join; one without rules. '~-**for-all** *n* dispute, quarrel, etc in which all are allowed to express their views, fight for their own points of view, etc. '~-**hand** *adj* (of drawings) done by hand with easy movements, no rules, compasses or other instrument being used: *a* ~*hand sketch*. ,~-'**handed** *adj* generous; giving and spending money generously. '~-**hold** *n* (legal) (holding of) land in absolute ownership. ⇨ *leasehold* at lease. '~-**holder** *n* person who possesses ~hold estate. '~ **house** *n* (GB) publichouse not controlled by a brewery, and able, for this reason, to stock and sell all brands of beer, etc. ⇨ *tied house* at tie². '~ '**labour** *n* workers not belonging to trade unions. ⇨ **1** above. '~-**lance** /-lɑːns US: -læns/ *n* (a) (in the Middle Ages) soldier ready to serve anyone for pay. (b) independent journalist, writer, etc earning his living by selling his services, wherever he can. □ *vi* work in this way: *He gave up his regular job in order to* ~*lance*. ~-'**liver** *n* person who indulges ~ly in (esp) food and drink; hence ,~-'**living** *adj, n* [U]. ~-'**load** *vi* [VP2A] (sl) = sponge (3); hence ~-'**loader** *n*. ~ '**love** *n* [U] (old use) agreed sexual relations without marriage. ~ '**kick** *n* (football) kick allowed for a penalty without opposition from any other player. '~ **port** *n* port open to all traders alike, with no trade restrictions, taxes, import duties, etc. ~-'**range** *adj* (of poultry) allowed to range freely (contrasted with *battery* birds). ~ '**speech** *n* [U] right to speak in public without interference from the authorities. ,~-'**spoken** *adj* not concealing one's opinions; speaking or spoken frankly. ~-'**standing** *adj* not supported; standing independently so that it may be viewed from all sides. '~-**stone** *n* [U] easily sawn sandstone and limestone. '~-**style** *n* [U] (swimming) race where the competitors choose their own stroke, usually the crawl. ~-'**thinker** *n* person not accepting traditional religious teaching, but basing his ideas on reason. Hence, ~-'**thinking** *adj*, ~-'**thought** *n* [U]. ~ '**trade** *n* [U] trade not hindered by customs duties to restrict imports or protect home industries; hence, ~-'**trader** *n* supporter of this principle. ~ **trans'lation** *n* not word for word, but giving the general meaning. ~ '**verse** *n* [U] without regular metre and rhyme. '~-**way** *n* (US) highway with several lanes; expressway. ~-'**wheel** *vi* [VP2A,C] move along on a bicycle with the pedals at rest (as when going downhill); (fig) act or live without effort or constraint. ~ '**will** *n* [U] individual's power of guiding and choosing his actions (subject to limitations of the physical world, social environment, and inherited characteristics): *do sth of one's own ~ will,* without being required or compelled. '~-**will** *adj* voluntary: *a ~will offering.* **4** ~ **from,** without: ~ *from blame/error/anxiety;* released or exempt from: ~ *from the ordinary regulations.* ~ *of,* (a) outside: *as soon as the ship was ~ of the harbour.* (**b**) without: *a harbour ~ of ice. At last I am ~ of her,* have got away from her. **5** without payment; costing nothing: ~ *tickets for the theatre; give sth away ~; 50p post ~,* 50p including cost of postage; *admission ~; ~ of income tax,* on which income tax need not be paid, or has been paid in advance (eg dividends on shares). (*get sth) for ~,* (colloq) without charge or payment. '~-**list** *n* (a) list of persons (to be) admitted ~, eg to a theatre or concert-hall. (**b**) list of goods (to be) admitted ~ of customs duties. ~ '**pass** *n* authority to travel etc without paying. ~ **on 'board,** (abbr **fob**) (comm) where the exporter pays all the charges for putting the goods onto the ship. **6** (of place or time) not occupied or engaged; not being used; (of persons) not having time occupied; not doing anything: *There will be no rooms ~ in the hotel until after the holidays. Her afternoons are usually ~. She is usually ~ in the afternoon(s).* **have one's hands ~,** (a) have them empty, not being used. (**b**) be in a position to do as one likes; have no work or duties that demand attention. ⇨ *be tied up* at tie². **7** coming or given readily; lavish; profuse: *a ~ flow of water; ~ with his money; ~ bloomers,* plants that have a large number of blooms. *He is very ~ with his advice,* willingly gives plenty of advice. **8** without restraint: *He is somewhat ~ in his conversation,* not quite as proper or decent as he ought to be. *make ~ with sth/sb,* use property, persons as if they were one's own: *He seems to have made ~ with my whisky while I was away. He is/makes rather too ~ with the waitresses/the wives of his friends,* is too familiar or impudent in his behaviour. **9** *make sb ~ of,* give him the right to share in the privileges *of* a company, citizenship *of* a city; give him the unrestricted use *of* one's library, etc. ~-**man** /-mən/ *n* (*pl* -men) one who has been given the privileges of a city, usu a distinguished person. ⇨ **1** above. ~-**ly** *adv* in a ~ manner; readily.

free² /friː/ *vt* (*pt,pp* freed /friːd/) [VP6A,14] ~ *(from/of)* make free (*from*); rid (*of*); set at liberty: ~ *an animal from a trap; ~ a country of cholera; ~ oneself from debt.* **freed-man** /'friːdmən/ *n* (*pl* -men) slave set free.

free-dom /'friːdəm/ *n* [U] condition of being free (all senses); [C] particular kind of ~: *the four ~s,* ~ of speech, ~ of religion, ~ from fear, ~ from want; *give slaves their ~; give sb ~ to do what he thinks best; speak with ~,* without constraint, fearing nothing; *the ~ of the seas,* (in international law) the right of ships of neutral countries to sail the seas without interference from warships of

countries at war; *give a friend the ~ of one's house/library,* allow him to use it freely. *give sb/ receive the ~ of a town/city,* full rights of citizenship (as an honour for distinguished services).

Free-mason /'friːmeɪsn/ *n* member of a secret society (with branches in many parts of Europe and America) for mutual help and fellowship. ~**ry** *n* [U] system and institutions of the ~s; (f~**ry**) instinctive sympathy between people of similar interests, the same sex: *the f~ry of the Press.*

free-sia /'friːzɪə US: 'friːʒə/ *n* kinds of flowering bulbous plant.

freeze /friːz/ *vt,vi* (*pt* froze /frəʊz/, *pp* frozen /'frəʊzn/) **1** [VP2A,C] (impers) be so cold that water turns into ice: *It was freezing last night. What freezing weather! It froze hard yesterday.* '~-**ing-point** *n* temperature at which a liquid (esp water) turns solid. **2** [VP2A,C] ~ *(over/up),* (of water) become ice; (of other liquids) become solid; (of other substances) become hard or stiff from cold: *Water ~s when the temperature falls below 0°C (32°F). The lake froze over,* became covered with ice. *make one's 'blood ~,* fill one with terror. **3** [VP2A,C] be or feel very cold: *I'm freezing. Two of the men froze to death,* died of cold. **4** [VP6A,15B] ~ *(over/up),* make cold; make hard; cover with ice: *frozen food,* preserved by being kept very cold, ⇨ *refrigeration* at refrigerate; *frozen roads,* with the surface of mud, snow, etc hardened by frost. *The lake was frozen over. If this frost lasts the ships in the harbour will be frozen in,* be fast in the ice. ~ *one's blood,* fill one with terror. '**freezing-mixture** *n* one of salt, snow, etc used to ~ liquids. **5** [VP6A] (fin) make assets, credits, etc temporarily or permanently unable to be exchanged for money; stabilize prices, wages: '*price-,freezing* and '*wage-,freezing* (as methods to cure inflation). **6** [VP15B] ~ *sb out,* (colloq) exclude him from business, society, etc by competition, cold behaviour, etc. **7** [VP3A] ~ *on to sth,* (colloq) take or keep a very tight hold of it. **8** [VP2A,C] become motionless, eg of an animal that stands quite still to avoid attracting attention. [VP2C] ~ *up,* (of an actor) be unable to speak, move etc on the stage. □ *n* **1** period of freezing weather. **2** (fin) severe control, stabilization, of incomes, wages, dividends, etc: *a '*wage-~. **3** ,**deep-**'~, (part of a) refrigerator where a very low temperature is used. ⇨ also *deep-freeze* at deep².

freezer /'friːzə(r)/ *n* (part of a) refrigerator or room for storing food etc at a very low temperature for a long time.

freight /freɪt/ *n* [U] (money charged for) the carriage of goods from place to place by water (in US also by land); the goods carried. '~-**liner** *n* liner-train, ⇨ liner(2). '~-**train** *n* (US) goods train, ⇨ goods (2). □ *vt* [VP6A,14] ~ *(with),* load (a ship) with cargo; send or carry (goods): *a ship ~ed with wheat; ~ a boat with fruit.* ~**er** *n* ship or aircraft that carries mainly ~ (cargo).

French /frentʃ/ *adj* of France or the people of France. *take ~ leave,* do sth, go away, without asking permission or giving notice. ~ '**bread**/'**loaf** *n* long, thin, crisp, light, white bread/loaf. ~ '**dressing** *n* [U,C] salad dressing of oil and vinegar. ~ '**fries** *n pl* (US) potato chips. ~ '**horn** *n* brass wind instrument. ⇨ the illus at brass. ~ '**letter** *n* (GB colloq) protective sheath. ⇨ sheath(2). ~ '**window** *n* one that is both a window and a door, opening on to a garden or balcony. ⇨ the illus at

window. □ *n* the ~ language. '~·man /-mən/ '~·
woman *nn* man/woman of ~ birth or nationality.
fren·etic /frə'netɪk/ *adj* frenzied; frantic.
frenzy /'frenzɪ/ *n* [U] violent excitement: *in a ~ of
despair/enthusiasm; rouse an audience to absolute
~.* **fren·zied** /'frenzɪd/ *adj* driven to ~; wildly excited. **fren·zied·ly** *adv*
fre·quency /'fri:kwənsɪ/ *n* **1** [U] frequent occurrence: *the ~ of earthquakes in Japan.* **2** [C] (*pl*
cies) rate of occurrence; number of repetitions (in
a given time): *a ~ of 25 per second,* eg of an alternating electric current.
fre·quent[1] /frɪ'kwent/ *vt* [VP6A] go often to (a
place); be often found in or at: *Frogs ~ wet places.
He no longer ~s bars.*
fre·quent[2] /'fri:kwənt/ *adj* often happening; habitual: *Hurricanes are ~ here in autumn. He's a ~
visitor.* **~·ly** *adv* often: *~ly occurring hurricanes.*
fresco /'freskəʊ/ *n* (*pl* ~s, ~es /-kəʊz/) **1** [U] pigment applied to moist plaster surfaces and allowed
to dry; method of painting with this pigment:
painting in ~. **2** [C] picture painted in this way: *the
~(e)s in the Sistine Chapel, Rome.* □ *vt* paint (a
wall, etc) in ~.
fresh /freʃ/ *adj* (-er, -est) **1** newly made, produced, gathered, grown, arrived, etc: *~ flowers/
fruit/eggs/milk; ~ paint* (= still wet); *a man ~
from the country; a boy ~ from school,* who has
only recently finished his school course. ⇨ stale;
⇨ *faded* at fade. '~·man /-mən/ *n* (*pl* -men)
student in his first year at a college or university. **2**
(of food) not salted, tinned or frozen; *~ butter/
meat;* (of water) not salt; not sea-water. '~·water
adj of ~ water, not of the sea: *~water fish; ~wat-
er fishermen.* **3** new or different: *Is there any ~
news? Take a ~ sheet of paper and start again. He
didn't throw much ~ light* (= give much new information) *on the subject.* **break ~ ground,** (fig)
start sth new, find new facts. **4** (of the air, wind,
weather) cool; refreshing: *go out for some ~ air;
in the ~ air,* out of doors. **~ breeze/wind,** blowing rather strongly. **5** bright and pure: *~ colours;*
bright and pure in colour: *a ~ complexion.* **6** (US
colloq) presumptuous, impudent (esp towards sb of
the opposite sex): *Tell that young man not to get/be
so ~ with your sister.* □ *adv* (in hyphened compounds) *~ly,* newly: *~-caught fish; ~-killed
meat; ~-painted doors.* **~·ly** *adv* (only with *pp,*
without hyphen) recently: *~ly picked peaches.*
~·er *n* = ~man. **~·ness** *n*
freshen /'freʃn/ *vi,vt* [VP2A,C,6A,15B] ~ (*up*),
become or make fresh; revive: *feel ~ed up after a
shower; ~en a drink,* add more to it; *the breeze
~ed,* grew stronger.
fret[1] /fret/ *vi,vt* (-tt-) **1** [VP2A,C,3A,15A] worry;
(cause to) be discontented or bad-tempered: *What
are you ~ting about? Don't ~ over trifles. She ~s
at even the slightest delays. Small babies often ~
in hot weather. She'll ~ herself to death one of
these days.* **2** [VP6A] wear away by rubbing or biting at: *a horse ~ting its bit; ~ted rope; a channel
~ted through the rock by a stream.* □ *n* state of irritation or querulousness: *in a ~.* **~·ful** /-fl/ *adj*
discontented; irritable; *a ~ful baby.* **~·fully**
/-fəlɪ/ *adv*
fret[2] /fret/ *vt* (-tt-) [VP6A] decorate (wood) with
patterns made by cutting or sawing. '~·saw *n* very
narrow saw, fixed in a frame, for cutting designs in
thin sheets of wood. '~·work *n* [U] work in decorative patterns; wood cut with such patterns by us-

ing a ~saw.
fret[3] /fret/ *n* one of the metal ridges set at intervals
across the fingerboard of a guitar, banjo, etc to act
as a guide for the fingers to press the strings at the
correct place.
Freud·ian /'frɔɪdɪən/ *adj* of the psychoanalytic
theories of Sigmund Freud /frɔɪd/ (1856—1939),
the Austrian psychoanalyst. **,~ 'slip,** (colloq) instance when a speaker accidentally says something
contrary to what was intended and which seems to
reveal his true thoughts.
fri·able /'fraɪəbl/ *adj* easily crumbled. **fria·bil·ity**
/ˌfraɪə'bɪlətɪ/ *n*
friar /'fraɪə(r)/ *n* man who is a member of one of
certain religious orders.
fric·assee /'frɪkəsɪ/ *n* [C,U] (dish of) meat or
poultry cut up, fried or stewed, and served with
sauce. □ *vt* /ˌfrɪkə'si:/ make a ~ of.
frica·tive /'frɪkətɪv/ *adj, n* (phon) (consonant) produced with audible friction when the air is expelled
through a narrowing of the air passage: *The sounds
/f, v, θ/ are ~s.*
fric·tion /'frɪkʃn/ *n* **1** [U] the rubbing of one thing
against another, esp when this wastes energy. **2**
[C,U] (instance of a) difference of opinion leading
to argument and quarrelling: *political ~ between
two countries; ~(s) between parents and children.*
Fri·day /'fraɪdɪ/ *n* sixth day of the week. **,Good '~,**
the ~ before Easter; the anniversary of the crucifixion of Jesus. **,man '~,** (from the story of Robinson Crusoe) faithful servant.
fridge /frɪdʒ/ *n* (abbr of) refrigerator.
fried /fraɪd/ *pt,pp* of fry.
friend /frend/ *n* **1** person, not a relation, whom one
knows and likes well: *We are great/good ~s. He
has been a good ~ to me.* **be ~s with,** be a ~ of.
make ~s, become mutual ~s. *make '~s again,*
become ~s again after a disagreement, etc. **make
'~s with; make a '~ of,** become the ~ of. **2**
helpful thing or quality: *Among these wild young
people, her shyness was her best ~.* **3** helper or
sympathizer: *a good ~ of the poor.* **4 F~,** member
of the Society of F~s; Quaker. **~·less** *adj* having
no ~s. **~·less·ness** *n*
friend·ly /'frendlɪ/ *adj* (-ier, -iest) acting, or ready
to act, as a friend; showing or expressing kindness:
*be ~ with sb; be ~ to a cause; a ~ smile; be on ~
terms with sb; a ~ match/game,* one not played in
competition for a prize, etc. **'F~ Society,** one for
the mutual benefit of its members, eg during illness, unemployment, old age. **friend·li·ness** *n* [U]
~ feeling and behaviour.
friend·ship /'frendʃɪp/ *n* **1** [U] being friends; the
feeling or relationship that exists between friends:
live together in ~; my ~ for her. **2** [C] instance or
period of this feeling: *a ~ of twenty years; never to
forget old ~s.*
frieze /fri:z/ *n* [C] ornamental band or strip along a
wall (usu at the top), eg a horizontal band of sculpture on the outside of a building, or a strip of wallpaper with a special design just below the ceiling of
a room. ⇨ the illus at column.
frig·ate /'frɪɡət/ *n* fast sailing-ship formerly used in
war; (modern use) (GB) fast escort vessel; (US)
medium speed naval warship.
fright /fraɪt/ *n* **1** [U] great and sudden fear: *die of
~; take ~* (*at sth*); [C] instance of this. *give sb/
get/have a ~.* **2** [C] (colloq) ridiculous-looking
person or thing: *What a ~ you look in that old hat!*
□ *vt* (poet) frighten.

frighten /'fraɪtn/ vt [VP6A,15B,14] fill with fright or terror; alarm suddenly: *Did the noise ~ you? The barking of the dog ~ed the burglar away. She was nearly ~ed out of her life.* **~ sb into/out of doing sth,** cause him to do/not do sth by ~ing him. **fright·ened** adj (colloq) afraid: *be ~ed of sb or sth;* alarmed: *~ed at the idea of sth happening.* **~·ing** adj causing fright or terror: *a ~ing experience.*

fright·ful /'fraɪtfl/ adj **1** causing fear; dreadful: *a ~ accident.* **2** (colloq) very great; unpleasant: *a ~ mess; a ~ journey,* a very uncomfortable one. **~ly** /-fəlɪ/ adv **1** in a ~ way. **2** (colloq) very. **~·ness** n.

frigid /'frɪdʒɪd/ adj **1** cold: *a ~ climate; the ~ zones,* those within the polar circles. **2** unfriendly; without ardour or sympathy; apathetic: *a ~ welcome; a ~ manner; ~ conversation; a ~ woman,* lacking in sexual desire. **~·ly** adv **frigid·ity** /frɪ'dʒɪdətɪ/ n [U].

frill /frɪl/ n **1** ornamental border on a dress, etc. **2** (pl) unnecessary adornments, eg to speech or writing; airs¹(6b), affectations. **fril·led** adj having ~s(1): *a ~ed skirt.* **frilly** adj having ~s; (colloq) too much ornamented.

fringe /frɪndʒ/ n **1** ornamental border of loose threads, eg on a rug or shawl. **2** edge (of a crowd, forest, etc): *on the ~(s) of the forest.* '**~ area,** area on the border of a district etc; (fig) less important area. '**~ benefits,** eg a rent-free house, the use of a car, additional to wages or salary. '**~ group,** group of persons loosely attached to a larger group or party (but who may be rebellious or nonconformist in some respects); hence ,~ '*medicine/'theatre,* etc. **3** part of hair cut short and allowed to hang over the forehead. □ vt[VP6A] put a ~ on; be a ~ to: *a roadside ~d with trees.*

frip·pery /'frɪpərɪ/ n [U] needless ornament, esp on dress; [C] (pl -ries) cheap ornament or useless trifle.

Fris·bee /'frɪzbɪ:/ n (P) piece of light plastic, shaped like a plate, thrown between players in a game.

frisk /frɪsk/ vi,vt **1** [VP2A,C] jump and run about playfully. **2** [VP6A] pass the hands over (sb) to search for concealed weapons. **~y** adj lively; ready to ~: *as ~y as a kitten.* **~·ily** /-ɪlɪ/ adv

fris·son /'fri:sɒn US: fri:'sɒn/ n (F) emotional thrill: *a ~ of delight/horror.*

frit·ter¹ /'frɪtə(r)/ vt [VP15B] **~ sth away,** waste it on divided aims: *~ away one's time/energy/ money.*

frit·ter² /'frɪtə(r)/ n [C] piece of fried batter, usu with sliced fruit in it.

frivol /'frɪvl/ vi,vt (-ll-) **1** [VP2A] behave in a silly, time-wasting way. **2** [VP15B] **~ away,** waste time, money, etc, foolishly.

friv·ol·ous /'frɪvələs/ adj **1** not serious or important: *~ remarks/behaviour.* **2** (of persons) not serious; pleasure-loving. **~·ly** adv **friv·ol·ity** /frɪ'vɒlətɪ/ n **1** [U] ~ behaviour; lightness of character. **2**[C] (pl -ties) ~ act or utterance.

frizz /frɪz/ vt [VP6A] (of hair) form into masses of small curls. **~y** adj (of hair) ~ed.

frizzle¹ /'frɪzl/ vt,vi [VP6A,2A] cook, be cooked, with a spluttering noise: *bacon frizzling in the pan.*

frizzle² /'frɪzl/ vt,vi [VP2C,15B] **~ up,** (of hair) twist in small, crisp curls.

fro /frəʊ/ adv **to and fro,** backwards and forwards: *walking to and fro; journeys to and fro between London and Paris.*

frock /frɒk/ n **1** woman's or girl's dress. **2** monk's long gown with loose sleeves. **3** ,~-'**coat** n long coat, usu with square corners, formerly worn by men in the 19th c (now replaced by the *morning-coat*).

frog /frɒg US: frɔ:g/ n **1** small, cold-blooded, tailless jumping animal living in water and on land. ⇨ the illus at amphibian. '**~-man** /-mən/ n (pl -men) person skilled in swimming under water with the aid of flippers on the feet and breathing apparatus. '**~-march** vt [VP6A] carry (a prisoner) away, face downwards, by four men holding his arms and legs. **2** long button and loop for fastening to it, used to fasten cloaks, etc.

a frogman

frolic /'frɒlɪk/ vi (pt,pp ~ked) [VP2A,C] play about in a gay, lively way. □ n [C] outburst of gaiety or merrymaking; wild or merry prank. **~·some** /-səm/ adj inclined to ~; playful and merry.

from /frəm; *strong form:* frɒm/ prep **1** (used to introduce the place, point, person, etc that is the starting-point): *jump (down) ~ a wall; travel ~ London to Rome; bees going ~ flower to flower.* **2** (used to indicate the starting of a period of time): *~ the first of May; ~ childhood; ~ day to day; ~ beginning to end.* **3** (used to indicate the place, object, etc whose distance, absence, etc is stated): *ten miles ~ the coast; stay away ~ school; be/go away ~ home; far ~ blaming you,* not in any way doing so. **4** (showing the giver, sender, etc): *a letter ~ my brother; a present ~ his father. Tell him ~ me that....* **5** (art, showing the model, etc): *painted ~ nature/life,* with the actual scene, object, etc in front of the artist. **6** (showing the lower limit): *We have good Italian wine ~ £1·50 a bottle,* at this price and at higher prices. *There were ~ ten to fifteen boys absent.* **7** (used to indicate the source from which sth is taken): *quotations ~ Shakespeare; draw water ~ a well; draw conclusions ~ the evidence; judge ~ appearances; ~ this point of view.* **8** (showing the material, etc used in a process, the material being changed as a result): *Wine is made ~ grapes. Steel is made ~ iron.* Cf *That bridge is made of steel.* **9** (used to indicate separation, removal, prevention, escape, avoidance, deprivation, etc. ⇨ v/n + ~, in v and n entries): *Take that knife (away) ~ the baby. When were you released ~ prison? What prevented/stopped/hindered you ~ coming?* **10** (used to indicate change): *Things are going ~ bad to worse. The price has been increased ~ 20p to 25p.* **11** showing reason, cause or motive: *collapse ~ fatigue; suffer ~ starvation and disease; do sth ~ necessity, not ~ a sense of duty. F~ his looks you might think him stupid. F~ what I heard, the driver was to blame.* **12** (showing distinction or difference): *distinct/different ~ others; to differ ~ others. How would you know an Englishman ~ an American?* **13** (governing advv and prep phrases):

seen ~ above/below; looking at me ~ above/under her spectacles.

frond /frɒnd/ n leaf-like part of a fern or palm-tree.

front /frʌnt/ n **1** the ~, foremost or most important side: *the ~ of a building*, that with the main entrance; *the east/west ~ of the Palace; sitting in the ~ of the class*, in one of the foremost rows facing the teacher (cf *standing in ~ of the class*, facing the pupils); (attrib): *a ~ seat; the ~ garden; a ~ room*, one in the ~ of a house; *the ~ page of a newspaper*, page 1; *~-page news*, news important enough for the ~ page; *a seat in the ~ part of the train.* **(be) in the ~ rank**, (fig) (be) well known or important. **come to the ~,** (fig) become conspicuous, well known, etc. **in ~** (*adv*), **in ~ of** (*prep*): *Please go in ~. There are some trees in ~ of the house.* ⌐ **'runner** (in an election, etc) person likely to win. ⇨ also **bench, door. 2** [C] (war) part where the fighting is taking place: *go/be sent to the ~; a ~ of 500 miles;* (fig) organized body or department of activity: *How are things on the domestic ~,* (colloq) at home? **3** road, promenade bordering the part of a town facing the sea; road or path bordering a lake: *have a walk along the ('sea)~; drive along the lake ~; a house on the ~,* facing the sea. **4** [U] **have the ~ (to do sth),** be impudent enough. **put on/show/present a bold ~,** face a situation with (apparent) boldness. **5** ('shirt) ~, breast of a shirt (esp the starched ~ part of a man's (dress) shirt). **6** (theatre) auditorium; part where the audience sits. **7** (met) boundary between masses of cold and warm air: *a cold/warm ~.* **8** (poet, rhet) forehead; face. **9** apparent leader ('~ **man**) or group of persons ('~ **organization**) serving as a cover for the secret or illegal activities of an anonymous person or group. ⌐ *vt, vi* **1** [VP6A,2A,C] face: *hotels that ~ the sea; windows ~ing the street; a house ~ing north, ~ing upon/towards the lake.* **2** [VP6A] (old use) confront; oppose: *~ danger.*

front·age /'frʌntɪdʒ/ n [C] extent of a piece of land or a building along its front, esp bordering a road or river: *For sale, office buildings with ~s on two streets; factory premises with a good river ~; a building site with a road ~ of 500 metres.*

frontal /'frʌntl/ adj of, on or to, the front: *a ~ attack; full ~ nudity*, of the whole of the front of the body. ⇨ flank; rear.

fron·tier /'frʌntɪə(r) US: frʌn'tɪər/ n [C] **1** part of a country bordering on another country; (land on each side of a) boundary: *a town on the ~;* (attrib) *~ disputes/incidents;* (esp US, in the past) farthest part of a country to which settlement has spread, beyond which there is wild or unsettled land. '~s-**man** /-zmən/ n (pl -men) man who lives on a ~; pioneer in a newly settled district near the ~. **2** (fig) extreme limit: *the ~s of knowledge;* underdeveloped area (eg of scientific research).

front·is·piece /'frʌntɪspiːs/ n illustration placed opposite the title-page of a book.

frost /frɒst US: frɔːst/ n **1** [U] weather condition with temperature below the freezing-point of water; [C] occasion or period of such weather: *plants killed by ~; ten degrees of ~; early ~s,* ie in autumn; *late ~s,* ie in spring. **Jack 'F~,** ~ personified. '~-**bite** n [U] injury to tissue in the body from freezing. '~-**bitten** adj having, suffering from, ~-bite. '~-**bound** adj (of the ground) made hard by ~. **2** [U] white powder-like coating of frozen vapour on the ground, roofs, plants, etc:

'white/'hoar ~, with this coating; 'black ~, without it. **3** [C] (colloq) event which fails to come up to expectations or to arouse interest: *The party was a ~,* no one enjoyed it. ⌐ *vt, vi* **1** [VP6A] cover with ~(2): *~ed window-panes;* cover (a cake, etc) with finely powdered sugar. **2** [VP6A] injure or kill (plants, etc) with ~(1). **3** [VP6A] give a roughened surface to (glass) to make it opaque: *~ed glass.* **4** [VP2A,C] ~ **(over/up),** become covered with ~(2): *The windscreen of my car ~ed over during the night.* ~-**ing** n [U] icing(1).

frosty /'frɒstɪ US: 'frɔːstɪ/ adj **1** cold with frost: ~ *weather; a ~ morning.* **2** (fig) unfriendly; without warmth of feeling: ~ *smiles/looks; a ~ welcome.* **frost·ily** adv **frosti·ness** n

froth /frɒθ/ n [U] **1** creamy mass of small bubbles; foam: *a glass of beer with a lot of ~ on it.* **2** light, worthless talk or ideas. ⌐ *vi* [VP2A,C] have, give off, ~: *A rabid dog may ~ at the mouth.* ~**y** adj (-ier, -iest) of, like, covered with, ~: ~*y beer/conversation.* ~**·ily** /-ɪlɪ/ adv ~**i·ness** n

fro·ward /'frəʊəd/ adj (old use) perverse; not easily controlled.

frown /fraʊn/ vi [VP2A,3A] draw the eyebrows together, causing lines on the forehead (to express displeasure, puzzlement, deep thought, etc): ~ *at sb.* ~ **on/upon,** disapprove of: *Gambling is very much ~ed upon here.* ⌐ n [C] ~ing look; drawing together of the eyebrows: *a ~ of disapproval. There was a deep ~ on his forehead.* ~**·ing·ly** adv

frowsty /'fraʊstɪ/ adj (of the atmosphere of a room) warm and musty; fuggy.

frowzy /'fraʊzɪ/ adj **1** ill-smelling; stuffy (like an overheated room). **2** untidy; uncared for.

froze, frozen ⇨ freeze.

fruc·tify /'frʌktɪfaɪ/ vt, vi (pt, pp -fied) [VP6A,2A] (formal) make or become fruitful or fertile. **fruc·ti·fi·ca·tion** /ˌfrʌktɪfɪ'keɪʃn/ n

fru·gal /'fruːgl/ adj ~ **(of),** careful, economical (esp of food, expenditure); costing little: *a ~ meal; a ~ housekeeper; be ~ of one's time and money.* ~**·ly** /-gəlɪ/ adv ~**·ity** /fruː'gælətɪ/ n [U] being ~; [C] (pl -ties) instance of this.

fruit /fruːt/ n **1** [U] (collective n) that part of a plant or tree that contains the seeds and is used as food, eg apples, bananas; [C] kind of ~: *People are eating more ~ than they used to. F~ is expensive these days. Is a tomato a ~?* '~-**cake** n rich cake containing dried currants, peel, etc. '~-**fly** n (pl-flies) small fly that feeds on decaying ~. '~ **knife** n one with an acid-proof blade, for cutting ~ at meals. ,~ '**salad** n [U,C] (GB) various kinds of ~, cut up and mixed in a bowl, often served with cream; (US) jelly(2) prepared with pieces of fruit in it. **2** [C] (bot) that part of any plant in which the seed is formed. **3** *the ~s of the earth,* those plant or vegetable products that may be used for food, including grain, etc. **4** (fig, often pl) profit, result or reward (of labour, industry, study, etc): *the ~s of industry. I hope your hard work will bear ~. His knowledge is the ~ of long study.* **5** '~-**machine** n (GB colloq) coin-operated gambling machine. ⌐ *vi* (of trees, bushes, etc) bear ~: *These trees ~ well.* ~**·erer** /'fruːtərə(r)/ n person who sells ~. ~**·ful** /-fl/ adj producing ~ or (fig) good results; productive: *a ~ful career. The last session of Parliament was particularly ~ful,* much useful work was accomplished. ~**·fully** /-fəlɪ/ adv ~**·ful·ness** n ~**·less** adj without ~ or (fig) results or success; profitless: ~*less efforts.*

~·**less·ly** *adv* ~·**less·ness** *n* ~y *adj* **1** of or like ~ in smell or taste. **2** (colloq) full of rough (often suggestive) humour: *a* ~y *novel*. **3** (colloq) rich; mellow; florid: *a* ~y *voice*.

fru·ition /fruːˈɪʃn/ *n* [U] realization of hopes; getting what was wanted: *aims brought to* ~; *plans that come to* ~.

frump /frʌmp/ *n* person dressed in old-fashioned and dowdy clothes. ~·**ish** /-ɪʃ/, ~y *adjj*

frus·trate /frʌˈstreɪt *US:* ˈfrʌstreɪt/ *vt* [VP6A,15A] prevent (sb) from doing sth; prevent (sb's plans) from being carried out: ~ *an enemy in his plans/ the plans of an enemy; be* ~d *in an attempt to do sth*. **frus·tra·tion** /frʌˈstreɪʃn/ *n* [U] frustrating or being ~d; [C] instance of this; defeat or disappointment: *embittered by numerous frustrations*.

fry¹ /fraɪ/ *vt,vi* (*pt,pp* fried /fraɪd/) [VP6A,2A] cook, be cooked, in boiling fat: *fried chicken. The sausages are frying/being fried*. ˈ**fry·ing-pan** (US also ˈ**fry-pan**) *n* shallow pan with a long handle used for frying. *out of the frying-pan into the fire*, from a bad situation to one that is worse. **fry·er; frier** /ˈfraɪə(r)/ *n* small young chicken for frying.

fry² /fraɪ/ *n pl* newly hatched fishes. ˈ**small fry**, young or insignificant creatures; persons of no importance.

fuchsia /ˈfjuːʃə/ *n* shrub with bell-like drooping flowers, pink, red or purple.

fuck /fʌk/ *vt,vi* ⚠ (sl) [VP6A,2A] have sexual intercourse (with). ~ (*it*)**!** (int, used to express irritation, anger, etc.) ~ *off*, (esp imper) go away. ~ *sth up*, spoil, ruin it. Hence, ~*ed* (*up*), spoilt, ruined. ˈ~-**all** *n* nothing. ~**er** *n* fool. ~·**ing** *adj* (used to express irritation, etc, but often meaningless.) ~**ing well**, surely(1).

fuddle /ˈfʌdl/ *vt* [VP6A,15A] confuse, stupefy, (esp with alcoholic drink): ~ *oneself/one's brain with gin; in a* ~d *state*.

fuddy-duddy /ˈfʌdɪ dʌdɪ/ *n* (*pl* -duddies)

fruit

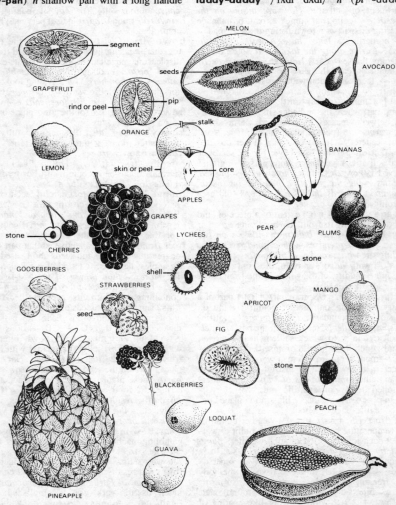

GRAPEFRUIT — segment

ORANGE — rind or peel — pip

LEMON

MELON — seeds

AVOCADO

stalk

APPLES — skin or peel — core

BANANAS

GRAPES

CHERRIES — stone

LYCHEES

PEAR

PLUMS

GOOSEBERRIES

STRAWBERRIES — shell — seed

PEAR — stone

MANGO

APRICOT

FIG

BLACKBERRIES

PEACH — stone

LOQUAT

GUAVA

PINEAPPLE

PA(W)PAW

(colloq) fussy and old-fashioned person.

fudge /fʌdʒ/ n [U] sort of soft sweet made with milk, sugar, chocolate, etc. □ int (dated) Nonsense!

fuel /'fjuːəl/ n [U] material for producing heat or other forms of energy, eg wood, coal, oil, uranium; [C] kind of ∼; (fig) sth that inflames the passions. **add ∼ to the flames,** make passions stronger. □ vt,vi (-ll-, US also -l-) [VP6A,2A] supply with or obtain ∼: a power station ∼led by uranium; a ∼ ship; a '∼ling station, one where oil, coal, etc may be obtained.

fug /fʌg/ n (colloq) stuffy atmosphere (as in an overcrowded or badly ventilated room, etc): What a fug! **fuggy** adj

fugi·tive /'fjuːdʒɪtɪv/ n ∼ **(from),** person running away from justice, danger, etc: ∼s from an invaded country; ∼s from justice; (attrib) a ∼ prisoner. □ adj (attrib) of temporary interest or value; lasting a short time only: ∼ verses.

fugue /fjuːg/ n [C] musical composition in which one or more themes are introduced by the different parts or voices in turn and then repeated in a complex design.

ful·crum /'fʊlkrəm/ n (pl ∼s or fulcra /'fʊlkrə/) point on which a lever turns. ⇨ illus at lever.

ful·fil (US also **ful·fill**) /fʊl'fɪl/ vt (-ll-) [VP6A] perform or complete a task, duty, etc; do what is required (by conditions, etc): ∼ one's duties/a command/an obligation/sb's expectations or hopes. ∼·ment n ∼ling or being ∼led.

full /fʊl/ adj (-er, -est) **1** ∼ (of), holding or having plenty (of), holding or having as much or as many (of) as possible; completely filled: pockets ∼ of money; a lake ∼ of fish; a girl ∼ of vitality. The box is ∼. The room was ∼ of people. ∼ **up,** (colloq) completely ∼: The greedy girl ate and ate until she was ∼ up. The drawers were ∼ to overflowing. **2** ∼ **of,** completely occupied with thinking of: She was ∼ of the news, could not refrain from talking about it. He was ∼ of himself/his own importance, could talk of nothing else. **3** plump; rounded: a ∼ figure; rather ∼ in the face. **4** (of clothes) **(a)** having material arranged in wide folds: a ∼ skirt. **(b)** easy fitting: Please make this coat a little ∼er across the back. **5** reaching the usual or the specified extent, limit, length, etc: apple-trees in ∼ blossom; wait a ∼ hour, not less than an hour. He fell ∼ length, so that he was lying stretched out on the floor/ground. Her dress was a ∼ three inches below the knee. **6** (esp in comp and superl) complete: A ∼/∼er account will be given later. This is the ∼est account yet received. **7** (phrases and compounds) **at ∼ speed,** at the highest possible speed. **in ∼,** without omitting or shortening anything: write one's name in ∼, eg John Henry Smith, not J H Smith; pay a debt in ∼, pay the whole of what is owed. **in ∼ career,** while at the maximum rate of progress. **to the ∼,** to the utmost extent: enjoy oneself to the ∼. '∼-**back** n player (defender) placed farthest from the centre line, behind the half-backs (in football, etc). ⇨ the illus at football. ∼-'**blooded** adj **(a)** vigorous; hearty. **(b)** of unmixed ancestry or race. ∼-'**blown** adj (of flowers) completely open. ∼ '**dress** n [U] dress as worn on ceremonial occasions. ∼-**dress** adj formally complete: a ∼-dress rehearsal, (theatre) with the costumes, etc that are to be worn at public performances; a ∼-dress debate (in Parliament) on an important question. ∼ '**face** n with the face turned to the viewer(s): a ∼-

face portrait. ⇨ profile. ∼-'**fashioned** adj (trade use, of garments) made to fit the shape of the body: ∼-fashioned stockings/sweaters. ∼-'**fledged** adj (of a bird) having all its flight feathers; able to fly; (fig) having completed training, etc: a ∼-fledged barrister. ∼-'**grown** adj having reached maturity. ∼ '**house** n (theatre) with no unoccupied seats. ∼-'**length** adj **(a)** (of a portrait) showing the whole figure. **(b)** of standard or usual length: a ∼-length novel. ∼ '**marks** n pl highest marks[1](5) possible. ∼ '**moon** n seen as a complete disc. ⇨ the illus at phase. ∼-'**page** adj filling a whole page: a ∼-page advertisement in a newspaper. ∼-'**scale** adj (of drawings, plans, etc) of the same size, area, etc as the object itself; (colloq) complete. ∼ '**stop,** the punctuation mark (.) ⇨ App 9. **come to a ∼ stop,** stop completely. ∼ '**time** n the end of a game of football, etc. ∼-'**time** adj, adv occupying all normal working hours: a ∼-time worker; working ∼-time. It's a ∼-time job, one that leaves no time for leisure or other work. ⇨ part-time at part[1](1). ∼**y** /'fʊlɪ/ adv **1** completely: ∼y satisfied; a ∼y paid up debt. I feel ∼y rewarded. **2** at least: The journey will take ∼y two hours. ∼**y-fashioned/fledged/grown** (7) above. ∼-**ness** n [U] state of being ∼: have a feeling of ∼ness after a meal. **in the ∼ness of time,** at the appointed time; eventually.

fuller /'fʊlə(r)/ n person who cleans and thickens freshly woven cloth. ∼'s '**earth,** kind of clay used for cleaning and thickening textile materials.

ful·mar /'fʊlmə(r)/ n seabird like a petrel, about the size of a seagull.

ful·mi·nate /'fʌlmɪneɪt US: 'fʊl-/ vi [VP2A,3A] ∼ **(against),** protest loudly and bitterly: ∼ against the apparent idleness of the younger generation. **ful·mi·na·tion** /ˌfʌlmɪ'neɪʃn US: ˌfʊl-/ n [U] fulminating; [C] instance of this; bitter denunciation or protest.

ful·some /'fʊlsəm/ adj (of praise, flattery, etc) excessive and insincere. ∼·**ly** adv ∼·**ness** n

fumble /'fʌmbl/ vi,vt **1** [VP2A,C] feel about uncertainly with the hands; use the hands awkwardly: ∼ in one's pockets for a key; ∼ at a lock, eg, as a drunken man might; ∼ in the dark. **2** [VP6A,2A] handle or deal with (sth) nervously or incompetently: ∼ a ball, eg in cricket. **fumbler** /'fʌmblə(r)/ n person who ∼s.

fume /fjuːm/ n **1** (usu pl) strong-smelling smoke, gas or vapour: air thick with the ∼s of cigars; petrol ∼s; ∼s of incense. **2** (liter) excited state of mind: in a ∼ of anxiety. □ vi,vt **1** [VP2A,C,3A] ∼ **(at),** give off ∼s; pass away in ∼s; (fig) betray repressed anger or irritation: ∼ because one is kept waiting; ∼ at sb's incompetence. **2** [VP6A] treat (wood, etc) with ∼s (to darken the surface, etc): ∼d oak.

fu·mi·gate /'fjuːmɪgeɪt/ vt [VP6A] disinfect by means of fumes: ∼ a room used by someone with an infectious disease; ∼ rose-bushes, to kill insect pests. **fu·mi·ga·tion** /ˌfjuːmɪ'geɪʃn/ n

fun /fʌn/ n [U] **1** amusement; enjoyment; playfulness: What fun the children had at the seaside, How they enjoyed themselves! He's full of fun. I don't see the fun of doing that, do not think it is amusing. '**fun·fair** n amusement park. ⇨ amuse. **fun and games,** (colloq) lively merry-making; pranks. **make fun of; poke fun at,** ridicule; cause people to laugh at: It is cruel to make fun of a cripple. **for/in fun,** as a joke, for amusement; not seriously: *He said it only in fun.* **2** that which causes merriment or amusement: *Your new friend is great fun,* is very amusing. **3** (attrib, colloq): *a 'fun car/ hat/fur,* used, worn, for amusement.

func·tion /'fʌŋkʃn/ *n* [C] **1** special activity or purpose of a person or thing: *the ~s of a judge/an officer of state; the ~ of the heart,* ie to pump blood through the body; *the ~s of the nerves; the ~ of education.* **2** public ceremony or event; social gathering of an important and formal kind: *the numerous ~s that the Queen must attend.* **3** (maths) variable quantity, dependent in value on another. □ *vi* [VP2A,C] fulfil a ~(1); operate; act: *The telephone was not ~ing,* was out of order. *Some English adverbs ~ as adjectives.* ~**al** /-ʃənl/ *adj* of a ~; having, designed to have, ~s(1): *a ~al disorder,* an illness caused by the failure of an organ of the body to perform its ~; ~*al architecture,* designed to serve practical purposes, beauty of appearance being secondary; *schools designed according to ~al principles.* ~**al·ism** /-ʃənlɪzəm/ *n* principle that the ~ of objects, etc should determine their design, the materials used, etc. ~**al·ist** /-ʃənlɪst/ *n* adherent of ~alism.

func·tion·ary /'fʌŋkʃənərɪ US: -nerɪ/ *n* (*pl* -ries) (often derog) person with official functions.

fund /fʌnd/ *n* [C] **1** store or supply (of non-material things): *a ~ of common sense/humour/amusing stories.* **2** (often *pl*) sum of money available for a purpose: *a re lief ~,* eg to help sufferers from a flood or other disaster; *'school ~s,* to finance schools. **the (public)** ~**s,** the stock of the national debt as a form of investment: *have £5000 in the ~s. no ~s,* notice (given by a bank) that the person who has drawn a cheque on it has no money in his account. □ *vt* [VP6A] **1** provide with money: *a project ~ed by the government.* **2** (fin) convert (a short-term debt) into a long-term debt at fixed interest.

fun·da·men·tal /ˌfʌndə'mentl/ *adj* ~ (*to*), of or forming a foundation; of great importance; serving as a starting-point: *the ~ rules of arithmetic,* those which must be learnt first and on which everything that follows depends. □ *n* essential part. **the ~s,** ~ rules or principles: *the ~s of mathematics.* ~**·ly** /-təlɪ/ *adv* ~**·ism** /-ɪzəm/ *n* [U] maintenance of the literal interpretation of the traditional beliefs of the Christian religion (such as the accuracy of everything in the Bible), in opposition to more modern teachings. ~**·ist** /-ɪst/ *n* supporter of ~ism.

fu·neral /'fju:nərəl/ *n* [C] **1** burial or cremation of a dead person with the usual ceremonies. **2** (attrib use) of or for a ~: *a '~ procession; a '~ march,* sad and solemn piece of music; *a '~ pile/pyre,* pile of wood, etc on which a corpse is burnt; *a '~ parlor,* (US) undertaker's offices. *it's/that's 'my/ 'your etc ~,* (colloq) it's/that's my/your etc concern, worry etc. **fu·ner·eal** /fju:'nɪərɪəl/ *adj* of or like a ~; gloomy; dismal; dark: *a funereal expression.*

fun·gus /'fʌŋgəs/ *n* (*pl* -gi /-gaɪ/ or ~es /-gəsɪz/) plant without leaves, flowers or green colouring matter, growing on other plants or on decaying matter, eg old wood: *Mushrooms, toadstools and mildew are all fungi.* **fun·gi·cide** /'fʌndʒɪsaɪd/ *n* [U,C] substance that destroys fungi. **fun·goid** /'fʌŋgɔɪd/ *adj* of or like fungi. **fun·gous** /'fʌŋgəs/ *adj* of or like, caused by, fungi.

fu·nicu·lar /fju:'nɪkjʊlə(r)/ *n* ~ (**railway**), railway

on a slope, worked by a cable and a stationary engine.

funk /fʌŋk/ *n* (colloq) **1** great fear: *be in a ~.* **2** coward. □ *vi,vt* [VP6A,2A] show fear; (try to) escape (doing sth) because of fear. ~**y** *adj* (US sl) (of music) emotional and rhythmic.

funnel /'fʌnl/ *n* **1** tube or pipe wide at the top and narrowing at the bottom, for pouring liquids or powders into a small opening. **2** outlet for smoke (ie smoke-stack, metal chimney) of a steam ship, locomotive etc. ⇨ the illus at ship. ,**two-/,three-'~led** *adj* having two/three ~s. □ *vt,vi* (-ll-, US -l-) [VP6A,2A] (cause to) move through, or as if through, a ~.

funny /'fʌnɪ/ *adj* (-ier, -iest) **1** causing fun or amusement: *~ stories.* **2** strange; queer; causing surprise: *There's something ~ about the affair,* sth strange, perhaps not quite honest or straightforward. '~**-bone** *n* part of the elbow over which a very sensitive nerve passes. **the funnies** *n pl* (colloq) comic strips. **fun·nily** /-ɪlɪ/ *adv* in a ~ way: *funnily* (= strangely) *enough.* **fun·ni·ness** *n*

fur /fɜ:(r)/ *n* **1** [U] soft thick hair covering certain animals, eg cats, rabbits. *make the 'fur fly,* cause a disturbance. *fur and feather,* furred animals and birds. **2** [C] animal skin with the fur on it, esp when made into garments: *a fine fox fur; wearing expensive furs;* (attrib) *a fur coat,* one made of furs. **3** [U] rough coating on a person's tongue when ill; crust forming on the inside of a kettle, boiler, etc when the water heated in it contains lime. □ *vt,vi* (-rr-) [VP6A,2A,C] ~ (*up*), cover, be or become covered, with fur: *a furred tongue/kettle.* **furry** /'fɜ:rɪ/ *adj* (-ier, -iest) of or like fur; covered with fur.

fur·be·low /'fɜ:bɪləʊ/ *n* (often used in *frills and* ~s) (old-fashioned) piece of elaborate or unnecessary trimming (on a dress, etc).

fur·bish /'fɜ:bɪʃ/ *vt* [VP6A] polish, eg by removing rust from; make like new (esp sth that has not been used for a long time): *~ a sword; newly ~ed skills.*

furi·ous /'fjʊərɪəs/ *adj* violent; uncontrolled; full of fury: *a ~ struggle/storm/quarrel; running at a ~ pace; be ~ with sb/at what sb has done.* *fast and ~,* uproarious, wild: *The fun was fast and ~.* ~**·ly** *adv*

furl /fɜ:l/ *vt,vi* [VP6A,2A] (of sails, flags, umbrellas, etc) roll up: *~ the sails of a yacht. This fan/ umbrella doesn't ~ neatly.*

fur·long /'fɜ:lɒŋ US: -lɔ:ŋ/ *n* 220 yards (= 201 metres); eighth of a mile.

fur·lough /'fɜ:ləʊ/ *n* [C,U] (permission for) absence from duty (esp civil officials, members of the armed forces, working abroad): *going home on ~; six months' ~; have a ~ every three years.* ⇨ leave².

fur·nace /'fɜ:nɪs/ *n* **1** enclosed fireplace for heating buildings with hot water or steam in pipes. **2** enclosed space for heating metals, making glass, etc.

fur·nish /'fɜ:nɪʃ/ *vt* [VP6A,14] ~ *sth* (*to sb*); ~ *sb/sth with sth,* supply or provide; put furniture

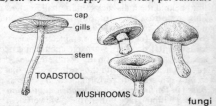

TOADSTOOL

MUSHROOMS

fungi

in: ~ *a library with books;* ~ *an army with supplies/*~ *supplies to an army;* ~ *a room/an office; a* ~*ed house/flat,* one rented with the furniture. ~**ings** *n pl* furniture and equipment.

fur·ni·ture /'fɜːnɪtʃə(r)/ *n* [U] all those (usu) movable things such as chairs, beds, desks, etc needed in a house, room, office, etc.

fu·rore (US = **fu·ror**) /fjʊ'rɔːrɪ *US:* 'fjuːrɔːr/ *n* general uproar: *The new play at the National Theatre created a* ~, was received with general excitement.

fur·rier /'fʌrɪə(r)/ *n* person who prepares, or who deals in, furs.

fur·row /'fʌrəʊ/ *n* [C] **1** long cut in the ground made by a plough: *newly turned* ~*s*. **2** wrinkle; line in the skin of the face, esp the forehead. □ *vt* [VP6A] make ~s in: *a forehead* ~*ed by old age/anxiety, etc.*

furry /'fɜːrɪ/ ⇨ **fur**.

fur·ther /'fɜːðə(r)/ *adv,adj* **1** (often used for *farther*) more far: *It's not safe to go any* ~. **2** (not interchangeable in this sense with *farther*) more; in addition; additional: *We must get* ~ *information. The Museum will be closed until* ~ *notice. We need go no* ~ *into the matter,* need make no more inquiries. *I'll offer you £50 but I can't go any* ~, offer more. **3** (also ~*more*, ⇨ below) moreover; also; besides: *He said that the key was lost and,* ~, *that there was no hope of its being found.* □ *vt* [VP6A] help forward; promote: ~ *sb's interests;* ~ *the cause of peace.* ~**ance** /-rəns/ *n* [U] ~ing; advancement: *for the* ~*ance of public welfare; in* ~*ance of your aims.* ~**more** /ˌfɜːðə'mɔː(r)/ *adv* moreover; in addition. '~**most** /-məʊst/ *adj* most distant; furthest.

fur·thest /'fɜːðɪst/ *adj, adv* = farthest.

fur·tive /'fɜːtɪv/ *adj* done secretly so as not to attract attention; having or suggesting a wish to escape notice: *a* ~ *glance/manner;* ~ *behaviour; be* ~ *in one's movements.* ~**ly** *adv* ~**ness** *n*

fury /'fjʊərɪ/ *n* (*pl* -ies) **1** [U] violent excitement, esp anger: *filled with* ~; *the* ~ *of the elements,* wild storms, winds; *in the* ~ *of battle.* **2** [C] outburst of wild feelings: *She was in one of her furies. He flew into a* ~ *when I refused to lend him the money.* **3** [C] violently furious woman or girl: *What a little* ~ *she is!* **4 the Furies,** snake-haired goddesses in Greek mythology sent from the underworld to punish crime.

furze /fɜːz/ *n* [U] = gorse.

fuse[1] /fjuːz/ *n* [C] tube, cord, etc for carrying a spark to explode powder, etc, eg in a firecracker, bomb or blasting charge; (US = *fuze*) part of a shell or mine that detonates the explosive charge. '~**time**-~ *n* one that does this after a pre-arranged interval of time.

fuse[2] /fjuːz/ *vt,vi* [VP6A,15A,B,2A] make or become liquid as the result of great heat; join, become joined, as the result of melting: ~ *two pieces of wire together.* **2** [VP2A] (of an electric circuit, or part of it) be broken through melting of the fuse[1]: *The light has* ~*d.* **3** [VP6A,15A,B] (fig) make into one whole. □ *n* [C] (in an electric circuit) short piece of wire which melts and breaks the circuit if the circuit is overloaded. '~ **wire** *n* [U] kinds of wire used for this purpose.

fu·sel·age /'fjuːzəlɑːʒ/ *n* body of an aircraft (to which the engine(s), wings and tail are fitted). ⇨ the illus at air.

fu·sil·ier /ˌfjuːzə'lɪə(r)/ *n* soldier (of certain British regiments) formerly armed with a light musket.

fus·il·lade /ˌfjuːzɪ'leɪd *US:* -sə-/ *n* [C] continuous discharge of firearms.

fusion /'fjuːʒn/ *n* [C,U] mixing or uniting of different things into one: *the* ~ *of copper and tin; a* ~ *of races/political parties.* '~ **bomb** *n* hydrogen bomb; ⇨ atomic.

fuss /fʌs/ *n* [U] unnecessary nervous agitation, esp about unimportant things; [C] nervous state: *Don't make so much* ~/*get into such a* ~ *about trifles.* **make a** ~, **(a)** be nervously agitated. **(b)** be ostentatiously active. **(c)** complain vigorously. **make a** ~ **of,** pay ostentatious attention to: *Don't make so much* ~ *of the children.* '~**pot** *n* (colloq) very ~y person. □ *vt,vi* [VP6A,2A,C] get into a ~; cause (sb) to be in a ~: *Stop* ~*ing. She* ~*ed about, unable to hide her impatience. Don't* ~ *over the children so much. Don't* ~ *me,* make me nervous. ~**y** *adj* (-ier, -iest) **1** nervously active or agitated. **2** full of, showing, close attention to detail: *be too* ~*y about one's clothes/food.* **3** (of dress, style, etc) over-ornamented; having too many unimportant details, etc. ~**ily** /-ɪlɪ/ *adv* ~**i·ness** *n*

fus·tian /'fʌstɪən *US:* -tʃən/ *n* [U] **1** thick, strong, coarse cotton cloth; (attrib) made of this cloth. **2** (fig) high-sounding but empty talk; (attrib) worthless; bombastic.

fusty /'fʌstɪ/ *adj* stale-smelling; smelling of mould and damp; (fig) old-fashioned in ideas, etc: *a* ~ *old professor,* eg one who has much book knowledge, but is out of touch with modern ideas, real life.

fu·tile /'fjuːtaɪl *US:* -tl/ *adj* **1** (of actions) of no use; without result: *a* ~ *attempt.* **2** (of persons) unlikely to accomplish much; vain or frivolous. **fu·til·ity** /fjuː'tɪlətɪ/ *n* (*pl* -ties) [U] the state of being ~; [C] ~ action or utterance.

fu·ture /'fjuːtʃə(r)/ *n, adj* **1** [U,C] (time, events) coming after the present: *The* ~ *must always be uncertain. I hope you have a happy* ~ *before you. I've given up my job; there was no* ~ *in it/it didn't have a* ~, no prospects of higher salary, advancement, etc. **for the** ~, with ~ time in mind: *Have you provided for the* ~, saved money, taken out an insurance policy, etc? **in** ~, from this time onwards: *Try to live a better life in* ~. **2** (*adj,* or attrib use of the *n*) of or in the ~: *the* ~ *life,* after death of the body; *his* ~ *wife,* the woman he will marry. **3** (*pl*) (comm) (orders for) goods and stocks bought at prices agreed upon at the time of purchase, but to be paid for and delivered later. ~**less** *adj* having no (successful) ~.

fu·tur·ism /'fjuːtʃərɪzəm/ *n* [U] (early 20th c) movement in art and literature marked by a complete abandonment of tradition in favour of expressing the energy of contemporary life as influenced by modern machinery. **fu·tur·ist** /-ɪst/ *n* supporter of ~.

fu·tur·ity /fjuː'tjʊərətɪ *US:* -'tʊər-/ *n* (*pl* -ties) [U] future; [U,C] future events.

fuze /fjuːz/ *n* (US) = fuse[1].

fuzz /fʌz/ *n* [U] fluff; fluffy or frizzed hair. **the** ~, (US sl) the police.

fuzzy /'fʌzɪ/ *adj* (-ier, -iest) like fuzz; blurred, indistinct (in shape or outline); frayed or fluffy

Gg

G, g /dʒi:/ (*pl* G's, g's /dʒi:z/) the seventh letter of the English alphabet; (US sl) one thousand dollars.
gab /gæb/ *n* [U] (colloq) talk(ing): *Stop your gab,* (sl) be quiet. *have the gift of the gab,* be good at speaking eloquently.
gab·ar·dine, gab·er·dine /ˌgæbəˈdi:n/ *n* [U] strong, smooth twill-woven cloth.
gabble /ˈgæbl/ *vt,vi* [VP6A,15B,2A,C] speak, say things, quickly and indistinctly: *The little girl ∼d her prayers and jumped into bed. Listen to those children gabbling away.* □ *n* [U] fast, confused, unintelligible talk.
gable /ˈgeɪbl/ *n* [C] three-cornered part of an outside wall, under sloping roofs. **gabled** /ˈgeɪbld/ *adj* having a ∼ or ∼s: *a ∼d house.* ⇨ the illus at window.
gad¹ /gæd/ *vi* (-dd-) [VP2C] *gad about,* (colloq) go from place to place for excitement or pleasure. *'gad·about n* person who does this.
gad² /gæd/ *int* (also *By 'gad!*) (old-fashioned) used to express surprise, etc.
gad-fly /ˈgædflaɪ/ *n* (*pl*-flies) fly that stings horses and cattle.
gadget /ˈgædʒɪt/ *n* (colloq) small (usu mechanical) contrivance or device: *a new ∼ for opening tin cans.* ∼ry *n* [U] ∼s collectively.
Gael /geɪl/ *n* Scottish or Irish Celt. ∼ic /ˈgeɪlɪk/ *adj, n* (language) of the Scottish or Irish Celts.
gaff¹ /gæf/ *n* stick with an iron hook for landing fish caught with rod and line.
gaff² /gæf/ *n blow the ∼,* (sl) let out a secret; disclose the plot.
gaffe /gæf/ *n* [C] blunder; indiscreet act or remark.
gaffer /ˈgæfə(r)/ *n* (colloq) elderly man, esp a countryman; foreman (of a gang of workmen). ⇨ boss¹, guvnor.
gag /gæg/ *n* [C] **1** sth put in a person's mouth to keep it open (eg by a dentist), or into or over it to prevent him from speaking or crying out. **2** words or action added to his part by an actor in a play. **3** joke, funny story, esp as part of a comedian's act (in the theatre, on radio or TV). □ *vt,vi* (-gg-) **1** [VP6A] put a gag(1) into or over the mouth of; silence; (fig) deprive (sb) of free speech. **2** [VP2A] (of an actor, etc) use gags(2,3). **3** [VP2A] (colloq) retch.
gaga /ˈgɑːgɑː/ *adj* (sl) in senile dotage; crazy.
gage¹ /ˈgeɪdʒ/ *n* **1** (old use) sth given as security or a guarantee; pledge. **2** (= *gauntlet*) glove thrown down (by knights in the Middle Ages) as a challenge to a fight. □ *vt* [VP6A] (old use) give or offer as a ∼; pledge as a guarantee.
gage² /ˈgeɪdʒ/ ⇨ gauge.
gaggle /ˈgægl/ *n* flock (of geese); (hum) group (of talkative girls or women).
gai·ety /ˈgeɪətɪ/ *n* **1** [U] being gay; cheerfulness; bright appearance: *flags and bunting that added to the ∼ of the scene.* **2** (*pl*-ties) merrymaking; joyful, festive occasion: *the gaieties of the Christmas season.*
gaily /ˈgeɪlɪ/ *adv* ⇨ gay.
gain¹ /geɪn/ *n* **1** [U] increase of possessions; acquiring of wealth: *the love of ∼; interested only in ∼.* **2** (*pl*) **capital ∼s,** ⇨ capital. **ill-gotten ∼s,**

dishonestly obtained profits, etc. **3** [C] increase in amount or power: *a ∼ in weight/health; a ∼ to knowledge.* ∼·ful /-fl/ *adj* yielding money: *∼ful occupations.* ∼·fully /-fəlɪ/ *adv* in a ∼ful manner: *∼fully employed.*
gain² /geɪn/ *vt,vi* **1** [VP6A,14,12B,13B] obtain (sth wanted or needed); increase, add: *∼ experience/momentum/weight; ∼ an advantage over a competitor; ∼ strength,* eg become strong again after an illness. *∼ ground,* make progress. *∼ time,* improve one's chances by delaying sth, making pretexts, etc. *∼ the upper hand,* be victorious. **2** [VP2A,B,C] *∼ (from),* make progress; be improved; benefit: *∼ from an experience. She is ∼ing in* (more usu *putting on*) *weight.* **3** [VP2A,B] (of a watch or clock) become fast, ahead of the correct time: *This watch neither ∼s nor loses. The clock ∼s three minutes a day.* **4** [VP3A] *∼ on/upon,* **(a)** get closer to (the person or thing pursued): *∼ on the other runners in a race.* **(b)** go faster than, get farther in advance of: *∼ on one's pursuers.* **(c)** (of the sea) advance gradually and eat away (the land). **5** [VP6A] reach, arrive at (a desired place, esp with effort): *∼ the top of a mountain. The swimmer ∼ed the shore.* ∼·ings *n pl* earnings; profits; winnings.
gain·say /ˌgeɪnˈseɪ/ *vt* (*pt,pp* -said /-ˈsed/) [VP6A] (liter) chiefly in neg and interr) deny; contradict: *There is no ∼ing his honesty,* We cannot deny that he is honest.
gait /geɪt/ *n* manner of walking or running: *an awkward/slouching ∼.*
gai·ter /ˈgeɪtə(r)/ *n* cloth or leather covering for the leg from knee to ankle, or for the ankle: *a pair of ∼s.*
gal /gæl/ *n* (dated colloq) girl.
gala /ˈgɑːlə US: ˈgeɪlə/ *n* festive occasion; (attrib): *a ∼ night,* eg at a theatre, with special features.
ga·lac·tic /gəˈlæktɪk/ *adj* of a galaxy or the Galaxy: *extra-∼ systems,* systems outside the Galaxy.
gal·an·tine /ˈgælənti:n/ *n* white meat, boned, spiced, cooked in the form of a roll, and served cold.
gal·axy /ˈgæləksɪ/ *n* (*pl* -xies) **1** any of the large-scale clusters of stars in outer space. **the G∼,** that which includes our solar system, visible as a luminous band known as 'the Milky Way'. **2** brilliant company of persons: *a ∼ of talent/beautiful women.*
gale /geɪl/ *n* **1** strong and violent wind: *The ship lost her masts in the ∼. It was blowing a ∼.* **2** noisy outburst: *∼s of laughter.*
gall¹ /gɔːl/ *n* [U] **1** bitter liquid (bile) secreted by the liver. *'∼ bladder n* (anat) vessel attached to the liver containing and discharging ∼. ⇨ the illus at alimentary. *'∼-stone n* hard mass that forms in the ∼ bladder. **2** bitter feeling: *with a pen dipped in ∼,* used of a writer who makes bitter attacks. **3** (colloq) impudence: *Of all the ∼!*
gall² /gɔːl/ *n* [C] painful swelling on an animal, esp a horse, caused by rubbing (of harness, etc); place rubbed bare. □ *vt* **1** [VP6A] rub sore. **2** (fig) hurt the feelings of; humiliate: *∼ sb with one's remarks. It was ∼ing to him to have to ask for a loan.*

gall³ /gɔːl/ *n* unnatural growth produced on a tree by insects, eg on the oak.

gal-lant /ˈgælənt/ *adj* **1** (archaic) brave: *a ~ knight; ~ deeds.* **2** fine; grand; stately: *a ~-looking ship; a ~ display.* **3** (also /gəˈlænt/) showing special respect and courtesy to women: *He was very ~ at the ball.* □ (also /gəˈlænt/) *n* young man of fashion, esp one who is fond of and attentive to women. **~·ly** *adv* **~·ry** *n* **1** [U] bravery. **2** [U] devotion, chivalrous attention, to women. **3** [C] (*pl-ries*) elaborately polite or amorous act or speech to a woman.

gal-leon /ˈgælɪən/ *n* Spanish sailing-ship (15th to 17th cc) with a high stern.

galleons

gal-lery /ˈgælərɪ/ *n* (*pl -ries*) **1** room or building for the display of works of art. **2** (people in the) highest and cheapest seats in a theatre. **play to the ~,** try to win approval or popularity by appealing to the taste of the masses. **3** raised floor or platform extending from an inner wall of a hall, church, etc: *the 'press ~ of the House of Commons,* used by newspaper reporters. **4** covered walk or corridor, partly open at one side; colonnade. **5** long, narrow room: *a 'shooting-~,* for indoor target practice. **6** horizontal underground passage in a mine. ⇨ shaft.

gal-ley /ˈgælɪ/ *n* (*pl ~s*) **1** (hist) low, flat single-decked ship, using sails and oars, rowed by slaves or criminals; ancient Greek or Roman warship. '**~-slave** *n* person condemned to row in a ~. **2** ship's kitchen. **3** oblong metal tray in which type is assembled by compositors. '**~-proof** *n* proof(4) on a long slip of paper, before division into pages.

Gal-lic /ˈgælɪk/ *adj* of Gaul or the Gauls; (often hum) French. **gal-li-cism** /ˈgælɪsɪzəm/ *n* [C] French way of saying sth, used in another language.

gal-li-vant /ˈgælɪˈvænt/ *vi* [VP2C] **~ about/off,** (not used in the simple tenses) = gad about, ⇨ gad¹: *Where are you ~ing off to now?*

gal-lon /ˈgælən/ *n* measure for liquids, four quarts (4·5 litres). ⇨ App 5.

gal-lop /ˈgæləp/ *n* (of a horse, etc) fastest pace with all four feet off the ground at each stride; period of riding at such a pace: *He rode away at a ~/at full ~. Shall we go for a ~?* □ *vi, vt* **1** [VP2A,B,C,6A] (cause to) go at a ~: *He ~ed across the field.* **2** [VP2A,B,C] hurry: *~ through one's work/lecture;* progress rapidly: *in a ~ing consumption,* ill with tuberculosis which is rapidly getting worse.

gal-lows /ˈgæləʊz/ *n pl* (usu with *sing v*) wooden framework on which to put criminals to death by hanging: *send a man to the ~,* condemn him to be hanged. *He'll end up on the ~,* will end by being hanged. '**~-bird** *n* person who is thought by some to deserve hanging.

Gallup poll /ˈgæləp pəʊl/ *n* questioning of a representative sample of people to assess general public opinion about sth, eg how they will vote at a general election, esp as a means of making a forecast.

ga-lore /gəˈlɔː(r)/ *adv* in plenty: *a meal with beef and beer ~.*

ga-loshes /gəˈlɒʃɪz/ *n pl* (**pair of**) ~, rubber overshoes worn in wet weather.

ga-lumph /gəˈlʌmf/ *vi* (made from *gallop* and *triumph*) prance clumsily or noisily in triumph.

gal-van-ism /ˈgælvənɪzəm/ *n* [U] (science of, medical use of) electricity produced by chemical action from a battery. **gal-vanic** /gælˈvænɪk/ *adj* **1** of ~. **2** (fig) (of smiles, movements, etc) sudden and forced (as if produced by an electric shock).

gal-van-ize /ˈgælvənaɪz/ *vt* **1** [VP6A] coat (sheet iron, etc) with metal, eg zinc: *~d iron.* **2** [VP6A,14] **~ sb (into doing sth),** shock or rouse.

gam-bit /ˈgæmbɪt/ *n* kinds of opening move in chess (in which a player sacrifices a pawn or other piece to secure certain ends); (fig) any initial move: *His opening ~ at the debate was a direct attack on Government policy.*

gamble /ˈgæmbl/ *vi, vt* **1** [VP2A,B,C] play games of chance for money; take great risks for the chance of winning sth or making a profit: *He lost his money gambling at cards/gambling on the Stock Exchange/gambling in oil shares, etc.* **2** [VP15B] **~ sth away,** lose by gambling: *He has ~d away half his fortune.* □ *n* [C] undertaking or attempt with risk of loss and chance of profit or advantage. **take a ~ (on sth),** risk (it). **gam-bler** *n* person who ~s. **gamb-ling** *n* [U] playing games for money; taking risks for possible advantage: *fond of gambling.* '**gambling-den/house** *n* (old use) place where gambling is carried on. ⇨ game³.

gam-boge /gæmˈbuːʒ US: -ˈbəʊʒ/ *n* [U] deep yellow colouring matter used by artists.

gam-bol /ˈgæmbl/ *n* (usu *pl*) quick, playful, jumping or skipping movement, eg of lambs, children. □ *vi* (-ll-, US also -l-) [VP2A,C] make such movements.

game¹ /geɪm/ *n* **1** [C] form of play, esp with rules, eg tennis, football, cards: *play ~s; have a ~ of whist. He plays a good ~ of snooker,* is a good player. **be off one's ~,** be out of form, not playing well. **have the ~ in one's hands,** be sure to win it, be able to direct it. **play the ~,** keep the rules; (fig) be straightforward and honest. '**~s-master/ -mistress,** teacher in charge of ~s at a school. **~s-man-ship** /ˈgeɪmzmənʃɪp/ *n* (colloq) the art of winning ~s by upsetting the confidence of one's opponents. **2** [C] apparatus, etc needed for a ~, eg one played by children with a board and dice and counters, such as ludo and draughts. **3** (*pl*) (international) athletic contests: *the Olympic/ Commonwealth/Highland G~s;* (in Greece and Rome, ancient times) athletic and dramatic contests. **4** [C] single round in some contests, eg tennis: *win four ~s in the first set;* score needed to win; state of the ~: *the ~ is four all; ~ all,* equal score; *~, set and match.* **5** [C] scheme, plan or undertaking; dodge or trick: *He was playing a deep ~,* engaged in a secret scheme of some sort. *I wish I knew what his ~ is,* what he is trying to do. *That's a ~ two people can play,* said when two people use the same scheme against each other. *So that's your little ~,* said when one discovers what sb is scheming to do. *The ~ is up,* The scheme is discovered and thwarted. *You're playing Smith's ~,* You are, unintentionally, helping to advance Smith's scheme. *None of your little ~s!* Don't try to play tricks on me! *You're having a ~ with me,*

trying to trick me, deceive me, etc. ,**give the** '~
away, reveal a secret trick, scheme, etc. **make** ~
of sb, ridicule him. **6** [U] (collective) (flesh of)
wild animals and birds hunted for sport or food.
big ~ *n* [U] the larger animals (elephants, lions,
tigers). **fair** ~ *n* [U] what may be lawfully hunted
or shot; (fig) person or institution that may with
reason be attacked or criticized. '**~-bag,** bag for
holding ~ killed by sportsmen. '**~-bird,** wild bird
(eg grouse, pheasant) hunted for sport or food. ⇨
illus at fowl. '**~-cock,** of the kind bred for cock-
fighting. '**~-keeper,** man employed to breed and
protect ~, eg pheasants, grouse, on a country estate. '**~ laws,** laws regulating the killing and
preservation of ~. '**~-licence,** one to kill and deal
in ~. **gamy** /'geɪmɪ/ *adj* having the flavour and
odour of ~(6), esp when high¹(8).
game² /geɪm/ *adj* **1** brave; ready to go on fighting;
spirited. **2** ~ **for/to do sth,** spirited enough, willing: *Are you* ~ *for a 10-mile walk? He's* ~ *to do*
anything you may suggest. ~**ly** *adv*
game³ /geɪm/ *vi,vt* [VP2A,C,15B] gamble.
'**gaming-house/rooms/table,** house etc (usu
licensed) for gambling.
game⁴ /geɪm/ *adj* (of a leg, arm, etc) lame; crippled.
gamma /'gæmə/ *n* third letter of the Greek alphabet. ⇨ App 4. '**~-rays** *n pl* rays of very short
wave-length emitted by radio-active substances.
gam·mon /'gæmən/ *n* [C] piece of bacon from the
side of a pig, including the hind leg; [U] smoked or
cured ham.
gammy /'gæmɪ/ *adj* (colloq) = game⁴: *a* ~ *leg.*
gamp /gæmp/ *n* (hum; dated) umbrella (esp a
large, untidy one).
gamut /'gæmət/ *n* **the** ~, complete extent or scope
of sth: *the whole* ~ *of feeling,* eg from the greatest
joy to the depths of despair or misery. **run the** ~
(of sth), experience the whole range (of it).
gan·der /'gændə(r)/ *n* male goose.
gang /gæŋ/ *n* **1** group of persons going about or
working together, esp for criminal purposes. ⇨
gangster. **2** (colloq) group of persons going about
together, disapproved of by the speaker: *Don't get*
mixed up with that ~; *they spend too much time*
drinking and gambling. ~ **up** [VP2C] ~ **up,** act
together as a ~: *They* ~*ed up on/against me.* ~**er**
/'gæŋə(r)/ *n* foreman of a ~(1).
gan·gling /'gæŋglɪŋ/ *adj* (of a person) lanky; tall,
thin and awkward-looking.
gan·glion /'gæŋglɪən/ *n* (*pl* ~s or -lia /-lɪə/)
group of nerve-cells from which nerve-fibres radiate; (fig) centre of force, activity or interest.
gang·plank /'gæŋplæŋk/ *n* movable plank placed
between a ship or boat and the land, or between
two boats or ships.
gan·grene /'gæŋgriːn/ *n* [U] death and decay of a
part of the body, eg because the supply of blood to
it has been stopped: *G*~ *set in and his leg had to be*
amputated. □ *vt,vi* [VP6A,2A] affect, become affected, with ~. **gan·gren·ous** /'gæŋgrɪnəs/ *adj*
gang·ster /'gæŋstə(r)/ *n* member of a gang of armed criminals: (attrib) '~ *films.*
gang·way /'gæŋweɪ/ *n* **1** opening in a ship's side;
movable bridge from this to the land. **2** (US =
aisle) passage between rows of seats, eg in the
House of Commons, in a theatre or concert-hall, or
between rows of people. □ *int* Make way, please!
gan·net /'gænɪt/ *n* kind of large sea-bird.
gan·try /'gæntrɪ/ *n* (*pl* -ries) structure of steel bars

to support a travelling crane, railway signals over
several tracks, etc.
gaol, jail /dʒeɪl/ *n* (usu *jail* in US) [C] public prison; [U] confinement in prison: *three years in* ~;
be sent to ~. '**~-bird** *n* prisoner, esp one who has
often been in prison; rogue. '**~-break** *n* [C] escape
from ~. □ *vt* [VP6A] put in ~. **gaoler, jailer, jail-**
or /'dʒeɪlə(r)/ *nn* man in charge of a ~ or the prisoners in it.
gap /gæp/ *n* **1** break or opening in a wall, hedge,
etc: *The sheep got out of the field through a gap in*
the hedge. We must see that there is no gap in our
defences. **2** unfilled space; interval; wide separation (of ideas, etc): *a gap in a conversation,* interval of silence; *fill in the gaps in one's education,*
study what one failed to learn while at school, etc;
a wide gap between the views of the two statesmen.
bridge/fill/stop a gap, supply sth lacking. ⇨
stopgap at stop¹(8). **credi'bility gap,** failure of
one person, group, etc to convince another that he
or it is telling the truth. **gene'ration gap,** failure or
inability of the younger and older generations to
communicate, understand one another. ,**gap-**
'**toothed** /'tuː.θt/ *adj* having teeth which are wide
apart. **3** gorge or pass between mountains.
gape /geɪp/ *vi* [VP2A,C] ~ (**at sb/sth**) **1** open the
mouth wide; yawn; stare open-mouthed and in surprise: *country visitors gaping at the neon lights.* **2**
be or become open wide: *a gaping chasm.* □ *n*
yawn; open-mouthed stare. **the** ~**s,** (a) disease of
poultry causing them to gape until they die (with
the beak wide open). (b) (joc) fit of yawning.
gar·age /'gærɑːʒ US: gə'rɑːʒ/ *n* **1** building in which
to keep a car or cars. **2** (US = *service station*)
roadside petrol and service station. □ *vt* [VP6A] put
(a motor-vehicle) in a ~.
garb /gɑːb/ *n* [U] (style of) dress (esp as worn by a
particular kind of person): *a man in clerical* ~. □ *vt*
[VP6A] (usu passive) dress: ~*ed in motley.*
gar·bage /'gɑːbɪdʒ/ *n* [U] **1** waste food put out as
worthless, or for pigs, etc; (US) rubbish, refuse (of
any kind). '~**-can** *n* (US) dustbin. **2** (colloq)
worthless material; meaningless or irrelevant data
in a storage device of a computer.
garble /'gɑːbl/ *vt* [VP6A] make an incomplete or
unfair selection from statements, facts, etc, esp in
order to give false ideas: *a* ~*d report of a speech.*
gar·den /'gɑːdn/ *n* **1** [C,U] (piece of) ground used
for growing flowers, fruit, vegetables, etc: *a kit-*
chen ~, for vegetables; *a market* ~, for vegetables, fruit and flowers for sale in public markets;
(attrib) *a* ~ *wall;* ~ *flowers/plants. We have not*
much ~/*only a small* ~. **lead sb up the** ~ **path,**
(colloq) mislead him. ,~ '**city/'suburb** *n* one laid
out with many open spaces, and planted with
numerous trees. '~ **party** *n* social gathering held
out of doors on a lawn, in a ~ or park, etc. **2** (usu
pl) public park: *Kensington G*~*s,* in London;
botanical/zoological ~*s.* □ *vi* [VP2A] cultivate a
~: *He's been* ~*ing all day.* ~**er** *n* person who
works in a ~, either for pay or as a hobby. ~**ing** *n*
[U] cultivating of ~s: *fond of* ~*ing;* (attrib) ~*ing*
gloves/tools.
gar·denia /gɑː'diːnɪə/ *n* (kind of) tree or shrub with
large white or yellow flowers, usu sweet-smelling.
gar·gan·tuan /gɑː'gæntjʊən/ *adj* enormous; gigantic.
gargle /'gɑːgl/ *vt,vi* [VP6A,2A] wash the throat with
liquid kept in motion by a stream of breath. □ *n*
liquid used for this purpose; act of gargling.

gar·goyle /'gɑːgɔɪl/ n stone or metal spout, usu in the form of a grotesque human or animal creature, to carry off rain-water from the roof of a building (esp Gothic-style churches) ⇨ the illus at **church**.

gar·ish /'geərɪʃ/ adj unpleasantly bright; over-coloured or over-decorated: ~ clothes. ~·ly adv

gar·land /'gɑːlənd/ n circle of flowers or leaves as an ornament or decoration; this as a prize for victory, etc. □ vt [VP6A] decorate, crown, with a ~ or ~s.

gar·lic /'gɑːlɪk/ n [U] onion-like plant with strong taste and smell, used in cooking: a clove of ~, one of the small bulbs making up the compound bulb of a ~ plant; too much ~ in the food; smelling of ~.

gar·ment /'gɑːmənt/ n [C] article of clothing: (US, attrib) the ~ industry; ~ workers.

gar·ner /'gɑːnə(r)/ n (poet, rhet) storehouse for grain, etc (also fig). □ vt [VP6A,15B] ~ (in/up), store, gather.

gar·net /'gɑːnɪt/ n semi-precious gem of deep transparent red.

gar·nish /'gɑːnɪʃ/ vt [VP6A,14] ~ (with), decorate, esp food for the table: fish ~ed with slices of lemon. □ n sth used to decorate a dish of food for the table.

gar·ret /'gærət/ n room (often small, dark, etc) on the top floor of a house, esp in the roof.

gar·ri·son /'gærɪsn/ n [C] military force stationed in a town or fort: (attrib) a ~ town, one in which a ~ is permanently stationed. □ vt [VP6A] supply a town, etc with a ~; place troops, etc on ~ duty.

gar·rotte, ga·rotte /gə'rɒt/ vt [VP6A] execute (a person condemned to death) by strangling or throttling (a stick being twisted to tighten a cord over the windpipe); murder (sb) in this way. □ n this method of capital punishment; apparatus used for it.

gar·ru·lous /'gærələs/ adj talkative; talking too much about unimportant things. **gar·ru·lity** /gə'ruːlətɪ/ n [U].

gar·ter /'gɑːtə(r)/ n (elastic) band worn round the leg to keep a stocking in place. **the G~**, (badge of) the highest order of English knighthood.

gas /gæs/ n (pl gases /'gæsɪz/) **1** [C] kind of air-like substance, (used chiefly of those that do not become liquid or solid at ordinary temperatures): Air is a mixture of gases. Hydrogen and oxygen are gases. **2** [U] pure gas or mixture of gases used for lighting and heating, eg natural gas or the kind manufactured from coal; gas manufactured for use in war (poison gas), or occurring naturally, eg in a coal mine: put the kettle on the gas, ie on the gas-ring or cooker. **'gas-bag** n **(a)** bag for holding gas, eg in an airship. **(b)** (colloq) person who talks too much without saying anything useful or interesting. **'gas-bracket** n pipe with one or more burners projecting from a wall. **'gas chamber** n room filled with gas for lethal purposes. **'gas-cooker** n stove (with gas-rings and an oven) for cooking by gas. **'gas fire** n one for heating a room by gas. **'gas-fitter** n workman who provides a building with **'gas-fittings** n pl apparatus, eg pipes, burners, etc for heating or lighting with gas. **'gas-helmet** n = gas-mask. **'gas-holder** n = gas-ometer. **'gas-light** n [U] light produced by burning coal-gas. **'gas-mask** n breathing apparatus to protect the wearer against harmful gases. **'gas-meter** n meter for registering the amount of gas that passes through it. **'gas-oven** n **(a)** one heated by gas. **(b)** = gas chamber. **'gas poker** n metal

rod with holes in one end, connected to a supply of gas, used to light fires in a fireplace. **'gas-ring** n metal ring with numerous small holes and supplied with gas for cooking, etc. **'gas-stove** = gas-cooker. **'gas tar** n [U] coal-tar produced during the manufacture of coal-gas. **'gas-works** n pl (sing v) place where coal-gas is manufactured. **3** (also '**laughing-gas**) nitrous oxide (**N₂O**), used by dentists as an anaesthetic. **4** (US colloq) (abbr of gas-oline) petrol. **step on the gas**, press down the accelerator pedal; increase speed. **'gas-engine** n one from which power is obtained by the regular explosion of gas in a closed cylinder. **'gas-station**, (US) petrol station. **5** (fig, colloq) empty talk; boasting. □ vt,vi (-ss-) **1** [VP6A] poison or overcome by gas. **2** [VP2A,C] (colloq) talk for a long time without saying much that is useful.

gas·eous /'gæsɪəs/ adj of or like gas: a ~ mixture.

gash /gæʃ/ n [C] long deep cut or wound. □ vt [VP6A] make a ~ in.

gas·ify /'gæsɪfaɪ/ vt,vi [VP6A,2A] (cause to) change into gas. **gasi·fi·ca·tion** /ˌgæsɪfɪ'keɪʃn/ n

gas·ket /'gæskɪt/ n **1** strip or soft, flat piece of material used for packing a joint, piston, etc to prevent steam, gas, etc from escaping. **2** (usu pl) (naut) small cords used for tying a furled sail to a yard.

gaso·line (also **-lene**) /'gæsəliːn/ n [U] (US) petrol; motor spirit.

gas·ometer /gə'sɒmɪtə(r)/ n large round tank in which gas is stored and measured (usu at a gas-works) and from which it is distributed through pipes.

gasp /gɑːsp US: gæsp/ vi,vt **1** [VP2A,C] struggle for breath; take short, quick breaths as a fish does out of water: ~ing for breath; ~ing (= breathless) with rage/surprise. **2** [VP6A,15B] ~ (out), utter in a breathless way: He ~ed out a few words. □ n [C] catching of the breath through pain, surprise, etc: at one's last ~, exhausted; at the point of death.

gassy /'gæsɪ/ adj of or like gas; full of gas; (of talk, etc) empty; vain and boastful.

gas·tric /'gæstrɪk/ adj of the stomach: a ~ ulcer; ~ fever; ~ juices. **gas·tri·tis** /gæ'straɪtɪs/ n [U] inflammation of the stomach.

gas·tron·omy /gæ'strɒnəmɪ/ n [U] art and science of choosing, preparing and eating good food. **gas·tron·omic** /ˌgæstrə'nɒmɪk/ adj of ~.

gate /geɪt/ n opening in the wall of a city, hedge, fence or other enclosure, capable of being closed by means of a barrier; barrier that closes such an opening, either of solid wood or of iron gratings or bars, usu on hinges; barrier used to control the passage of water, eg into or out of a lock on a canal: He opened the garden ~ and went into the street. He jumped over the ~ into the field. **'~-crash** vt [VP6A] enter (a building at which there is a private social occasion of some sort) without invitation or payment. Hence, **'~-crasher** n. **'~-house** n house built at the side of, or over, a ~, eg at the entrance to a park, the house being used by a '~-keeper. **~-legged 'table**, table with legs that can be moved out to support a folding top. **'~ money** n total sum paid for admission to a public spectacle in a stadium, etc. **'~-post** n post on which a ~ is hung or against which it is closed. **between you (and) me and the ~-post**, in strict confidence. **'~-way** n way in or out that can be closed by a ~ or ~s; (fig) means of approach: a ~way to fame/knowledge. **2** = ~ money, ⇨ **1** above. **3 'start-**

ing ～, barrier (either of horizontal ropes that are lifted or of rows of stalls with barriers) at the start of a horse or greyhound race. □ *vt* [VP6A] confine (a student) to college or school (as a penalty).

a gate-legged table

gâ·teau /'gætəʊ US: gæ'təʊ/ *n* (*pl* ～x /-təʊz/ or ～s) (F) rich fancy cake, often served in slices.
gather /'gæðə(r)/ *vt, vi* **1** [VP6A,15A,B,2A,C] get, come or bring together: *He soon ～ed a crowd round him. A crowd soon ～ed round him. The clouds are ～ing; it's going to rain.* **be ～ed to one's fathers,** (liter or rhet) die. **2** [VP6A,12B,13B] pick (flowers, etc); collect: ～ *one's papers and books together. Please ～ me some flowers/～ some flowers for me.* **3** [VP6A] obtain gradually; gain little by little: ～ *information/impressions/experience. The train ～ed speed as it left the station.* **4** [VP6A,9] understand; conclude: *What did you ～ from his statement? I ～, from what you say, that....* **5** [VP6A,15A,B] (in sewing) pull together into small folds by putting a thread through; draw parts of material, a garment closer together: *a skirt ～ed at the waist.* **6** [VP2A] (of an abscess or boil) form pus and swell up; come to a head. **～·ing** *n* [C] **1** coming together of people; meeting. **2** swelling with pus in it.
gauche /gəʊʃ/ *adj* socially awkward; tactless. **gauch·erie** /'gəʊʃəri US: ˌgəʊʃə'ri:/ *n* [U] ～ behaviour; [C] ～ act, movement, etc.
gaucho /'gaʊtʃəʊ/ *n* (*pl* ～s) cowboy of mixed European and American Indian descent.
gaud /gɔːd/ *n* [C] showy ornament.
gaudy[1] /'gɔːdɪ/ *adj* (-ier, -iest) too bright and showy; gay or bright in a tasteless way: ～ *decorations; cheap and ～ jewels.* **gaud·ily** /-ɪlɪ/ *adv*
gaudy[2] /'gɔːdɪ/ *n* annual college dinner, given to former members.
gauge (US also **gage**) /geɪdʒ/ *n* **1** [U] standard measure; extent: *take the ～ of (eg sb's character),* estimate, judge. **2** [U,C] distance between rails (or between opposite wheels on a vehicle that runs on rails): *standard ～; broad ～,* more than 4 ft 8½ in; *narrow ～,* less than 3 ft 8½ in. **3** [U] thickness of wire, sheet-metal, etc; diameter of a bullet, etc. **4** [C] instrument for measuring, eg rainfall, strength of wind, size, diameter, etc of tools, wire, etc. □ *vt* [VP6A] measure accurately: *～ the diameter of wire/the contents of a barrel/the rainfall/the strength of the wind;* (fig) make an estimate, form a judgement, of: ～ *a person's character.*
Gaul /gɔːl/ *n* Celt of ancient ～ (the area now known as France and Belgium).
gaunt /gɔːnt/ *adj* (of a person) lean, haggard, as from hunger, ill-health or suffering; (of a place) grim or desolate: *a ～ hillside.* **～·ness** *n*
gaunt·let[1] /'gɔːntlɪt/ *n* **1** glove with metal plates

worn by soldiers in the Middle Ages. ⇨ the illus at armour. **throw down/pick up/take up the ～,** give/accept a challenge to a fight. **2** strong glove with a wide cuff covering the wrist, used for driving, fencing, etc.
gaunt·let[2] /'gɔːntlɪt/ *n* (only in) **run the ～,** run between two rows of men who strike the victim as he passes; (fig) be exposed to continuous severe criticism, risk, danger: *He ran the ～ of their criticism/scorn.*
gauze /gɔːz/ *n* [U] thin, transparent net-like material of silk, cotton, etc (for medical use) or of wire (for screening windows against insects, etc). **gauzy** *adj*
gave /geɪv/ *pt* of give.
gavel /'gævl/ *n* hammer used by an auctioneer or a chairman as a signal for order or attention.
ga·votte /gə'vɒt/ *n* [C] (music for an) old French dance like the minuet but more lively.
gawk /gɔːk/ *n* awkward or bashful person. **～y** *adj* (-ier, -iest) (of persons) awkward, bashful, ungainly. **～·i·ness** *n*
gawp /gɔːp/ *vi* [VP2A,3A] ～ *(at),* look at in an intense, foolish way: *What are they all ～ing at?*
gay /geɪ/ *adj* (-er, -est) **1** light-hearted; cheerful; happy and full of fun: *the gay voices of young children; gay looks/laughter.* **2** suggesting happiness and joy: *gay music; gay colours; streets that were gay with flags.* **3** (colloq) homosexual. □ *n* [C] (colloq) homosexual. **gaily** /'geɪlɪ/ *adv* in a gay manner. **gay·ness** *n*
gaze /geɪz/ *n* (*sing* only) long, steady look: *with a bewildered ～.* □ *vi* [VP2A,C,3A] ～ *(at),* look long and steadily: *What are you gazing at? Stop gazing round.* ～ *on/upon,* (formal) set eyes on: *She was the most beautiful woman he had ever ～d upon.*
ga·zelle /gə'zel/ *n* small, graceful kind of antelope.
ga·zette /gə'zet/ *n* **1** official periodical with legal notices, news of appointments, promotions, etc of officers and officials. **2** (as part of a title) newspaper: *the Marlowe G～.* □ *vt* (usu passive) **be ～d,** be published in the official ～: (of an army officer) *be ～d to a regiment.*
ga·zet·teer /ˌgæzə'tɪə(r)/ *n* index of geographical names, eg at the end of an atlas.
ga·zump /gə'zʌmp/ *vi, vt* [VP2A,6A] (colloq) cheat by increasing the price demanded for property between the date of acceptance of an offer and the date for signing the contract.
gear /gɪə(r)/ *n* **1** [C] set of toothed wheels working together in a machine, esp such a set to connect the engine of a motor-vehicle with the road wheels: *change ～;* particular state of adjustment of such a set: *a car with five ～s, first, second, third, fourth and reverse.* ⇨ the illus at bicycle, motor. **high/ low ～,** mechanism causing the driven part to move relatively fast/slowly, low ～ being used when starting, or when driving on a steep hill. **in/ out of ～,** engaged/disengaged from the mechanism. **top/bottom ～,** highest/lowest ～. **'～-box/ -case,** case that encloses the ～ mechanism. **'～ shift/lever/stick,** device for engaging or disengaging ～s. **2** [C] apparatus, appliance, mechanism, arrangement, of wheels, levers, etc for a special purpose: *the 'steering～ of a ship; the 'landing～ of an aircraft.* **3** [U] equipment in general: *'hunting-～;* (modern colloq) clothes: *party ～.* □ *vt, vi* [VP15A,14,2A,C,3A] ～ **up/ down,** (= change up/down) put into a higher/ lower ～. ～ **to,** adjust one thing to the working of

another, make dependent on: *The country's eco-nomics must be ~ed to wartime requirements.*

gecko /'gekəʊ/ *n* (*pl* ~s, ~es /-kəʊz/) kind of small house lizard, found in warm countries.

gee¹ (also **gee-up**) /dʒi: ('ʌp)/ *int* (command to a horse) go on; go faster. **gee-gee** /'dʒi: dʒi:/ *n* (child's word for a) horse.

gee² (also **gee whiz**) /dʒi: ('wɪz)/ *int* (US) mild exclamation indicating surprise, admiration, etc: *Gee, I like your new hat!*

geese /gi:s/ *n pl* of **goose**.

geezer /'gi:zə(r)/ *n* (sl) (old) person, esp if eccentric.

Geiger /'gaɪgə(r)/ *n* (esp '~ **counter**) metal tube containing an electrode, used for detecting and measuring radio-activity.

geisha /'geɪʃə/ *n* Japanese girl or woman trained to entertain men by singing and dancing at parties, etc.

gel /dʒel/ *n* semisolid like a jelly. □ *vi* (-ll-) **1** set into a jelly. **2** = **jell**.

gela·tine /dʒelə'ti:n US: 'dʒelətɪn/ (also **gela·tin** /'dʒelətɪn/) *n* [U] clear, tasteless substance, made by boiling bones and waste parts of animals, dissolved in water to make jelly. **gel·ati·nous** /dʒɪ'lætɪnəs/ *adj* of or like ~; jelly-like in consistency, etc.

geld /geld/ *vt* [VP6A] castrate. **~·ing** *n* ~ed animal, esp a horse.

gel·ig·nite /'dʒelɪgnaɪt/ *n* [U] explosive made from nitric acid and glycerine.

gem /dʒem/ *n* **1** precious stone or jewel, esp cut or polished. **2** sth valued because of great beauty; sth much prized: *the gem of the collection*, the most valued item in it. **gem·med** *part adj* adorned with, or as with, gems: *the night sky, gemmed with stars.*

Gem·ini /'dʒemɪnɪ/ *n* third sign of the zodiac. ⇨ the illus at **zodiac**.

gen /dʒen/ *n* (sl) (**the**) **gen**, information. □ *vt* [VP15B] **gen up**, provide with information.

gen·darme /'ʒɒndɑ:m/ *n* (in France and some other countries, but not GB or US) member of a military force employed in police duties. **~·rie** /ʒɒn'dɑ:mərɪ/ *n* (collective sing) force of ~s.

gen·der /'dʒendə(r)/ *n* **1** grammatical grouping of words (nouns and pronouns) into classes (masculine, feminine and neuter). **2** sex(1).

gene /dʒi:n/ *n* [C] (biol) unit in chromosome controlling heredity.

gen·eal·ogy /dʒi:nɪ'ælədʒɪ/ *n* **1** [U] science of the development of plants and animals from earlier forms. **2** [C] (*pl* -gies) (diagram illustrating the) descent or line of development of a plant or animal from earlier forms; person's pedigree. **gen·eal·ogist** /dʒi:nɪ'ælədʒɪst/ *n* student of ~. **genea·logi·cal** /dʒi:nɪə'lɒdʒɪkl/ *adj* of ~: *a genealogical tree*, a diagram (a table like a tree with branches) showing the descent of a family or species.

genea·logi·cal·ly /-klɪ/ *adv*

gen·era /'dʒenərə/ *n pl* of **genus**.

gen·eral /'dʒenrəl/ *adj* **1** of, affecting, all or nearly all; not special, local or particular: *a matter of ~ interest*, one in which all or most people are likely to be interested; *a ~ meeting*, one to which all members (of a society, etc) are invited; *a ~ strike*, one by workmen of all, or nearly all, the trade unions; *a good ~ education*, in all the chief subjects; *a word that is in ~ use*, used by all people; *the ~ opinion on this subject*, what most people think about it. *The cold weather has been ~*, has been experienced in all or most parts of the country. *as a ~ rule; in ~*, in most cases; usually. '~ **degree**, non-specialist university degree involving a course in two or more subjects. **~ e'lec·tion**, one for representatives in Parliament from the whole country. Cf *by-election, local election*. ~ '**knowledge**, of a wide variety of subjects. Cf *common knowledge*, knowledge (of a particular fact, etc) possessed by every member of a class or community of people. ~ '**practice**, work of a ~ **prac'titioner** (abbr **GP**), (GB) doctor who is not a specialist or consultant. **2** not in detail; not definite: *a ~ outline of a scheme*; *have a ~ idea of what a book is about*; *explain something in ~ terms*. **3** (after an official title) chief: *postmaster-'~*; *in,spector-'~*. □ *n* army officer with the highest rank below Field Marshal (and also, by courtesy, of *Lieu,tenant-'~* and *,Major-'~*).

gen·er·al·is·simo /dʒenərə'lɪsɪməʊ/ *n* (*pl* ~s) commander of combined military and naval and air forces, or of combined armies.

gen·er·al·ity /dʒenə'rælətɪ/ *n* (*pl* -ties) **1** [C] general rule or statement; vague or indefinite remark, etc: *I wish you would come down from generalities to particularities*. **2** [U] **the ~ (of)**, majority or greater part: *The ~ of Swedes are blonde*. **3** [U] quality of being general: *a rule of great ~*, one with few exceptions.

gen·er·al·iz·ation /dʒenrəlaɪ'zeɪʃn US: -lɪ'z-/ *n* **1** [U] generalizing: *it is unwise to be hasty in ~*. **2** [C] statement or proposition obtained by generalizing, esp one based on too few examples.

gen·er·al·ize /'dʒenrəlaɪz/ *vi,vt* **1** [VP2A,3A] **~ (from)**, draw a general conclusion; make a general statement. **2** [VP6A,14] **~ (from)**, state (sth) in general terms or principles: *~ a conclusion from a collection of instances or facts*. **3** [VP6A] bring into general use: *~ the use of a new invention*.

gen·erally /'dʒenrəlɪ/ *adv* (usu with the finite *v*) **1** usually; as a general rule: *I ~ get up at six o'clock*. **2** widely; for the most part: *The new plan was ~ welcomed*, was welcomed by most people. **3** in a general sense; without paying attention to details: *~ speaking*.

gen·er·ate /'dʒenəreɪt/ *vt* [VP6A] cause to exist or occur; produce: *~ heat/electricity; hatred ~d by racial prejudices.*

gen·er·ation /dʒenə'reɪʃn/ *n* **1** [U] generating; bringing into existence: *the ~ of electricity by steam or water-power; the ~ of heat by friction.* **2** [C] single stage or step in family descent: *three ~s, children, parents, grandparents.* **3** [C] average period (regarded as 30 years) in which children grow up, marry, and have children: *a ~ ago.* '~ **gap**, ⇨ gap(2). **4** [C] all persons born about the same time, and, therefore, of about the same age: *the present/past/coming ~; the rising ~*, the young ~.

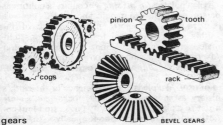

gears   BEVEL GEARS

gen·er·at·ive /'dʒenərətɪv/ adj able to produce;
productive.

gen·er·ator /'dʒenəreɪtə(r)/ n [C] machine or apparatus that generates (electricity, steam, gas, vapour, etc) (US = dynamo).

gen·eric /dʒɪ'nerɪk/ adj of a genus; common to a
whole group or class, not special. **gen·eri·cally**
/-klɪ/ adv

gen·er·os·ity /ˌdʒenə'rɒsətɪ/ n 1 [U] the quality of
being generous; nobility of mind; greatness of
heart: show ∼ in dealing with a defeated enemy. 2
[C] (pl -ties) generous act, etc.

gen·er·ous /'dʒenərəs/ adj 1 giving, ready to give,
freely; given freely; noble-minded. He is ∼ with
his money/∼ in giving help. It was ∼ of them to
share their house with the refugees. What a ∼ gift!
He has a ∼ nature. 2 plentiful: a ∼ helping of
meat and vegetables; a ∼ harvest. ∼·ly adv

gen·esis /'dʒenəsɪs/ n 1 beginning; starting-point:
the ∼ of civilization. 2 G∼, the first book of the
Old Testament.

gen·etic /dʒɪ'netɪk/ adj of genes; of ∼s. **gen·etics**
n pl (with sing v) science (branch of biology) dealing with heredity, the ways in which characteristics
are passed on from parents to offspring. **gen·eti·**
cist /dʒɪ'netɪsɪst/ n specialist in ∼s.

ge·nial /'dʒiːnɪəl/ adj 1 kindly, sympathetic; sociable: a ∼ old man; ∼ smiles; under the ∼ influence of good wine. 2 favourable to growth; mild;
warm: a ∼ climate; ∼ sunshine. ∼·ly adv ∼·ity
/ˌdʒiːnɪ'ælətɪ/ n [U] quality of being ∼; [C] (pl -
ties) ∼ look, act, utterance, etc.

ge·nie /'dʒiːnɪ/ n (pl ∼s or genii /'dʒiːnɪaɪ/) (in
Arabic stories) spirit or goblin with strange powers.

geni·tal /'dʒenɪtl/ adj of generation(1) or of animal
reproductive organs. ∼s n pl external sex organs.

geni·tive /'dʒenətɪv/ adj ∼ (case), (gram) showing
source or possession.

gen·ius /'dʒiːnɪəs/ n (pl ∼es, but ⇨ 5 below) 1 [U]
great and exceptional capacity of the mind or imagination; creative or inventive capacity: men of ∼. 2
[C] person having this capacity: Einstein was a
mathematical ∼. 3 a ∼ for, natural ability for:
have a ∼ for languages/acting/making friends. 4
the ∼ (of), guardian spirit of a person, place or institution, (hence, by extension) special and inborn
character, spirit or principles of a language, a
period of time, an institution, etc; prevalent feeling, opinions, taste, etc of a race of people: the
French ∼; the ∼ of the British Constitution/the
Renaissance period in Italy. ∼ 'loci /'ləʊsaɪ/ n
(sing only) (Lat) associations, atmosphere, etc of a
place. 5 (pl genii /'dʒiːnɪaɪ/) supernatural being.
one's good/evil ∼, spirit or angel working for
one's salvation/damnation; person who has a strong
influence upon one for good/ill.

geno·cide /'dʒenəsaɪd/ n [U] extermination of a
race or community by mass murder, or by imposing conditions that make survival impossible.

genre /'ʒɑːnrə/ n 1 (F) kind; style; category (esp of
literary form, eg poetry, drama, the novel). 2 (also
'∼-painting) portrayal of scenes, etc, from ordinary life.

gent /dʒent/ n (colloq abbr of) gentleman. **the/a**
G∼s n (GB colloq) public toilet for men.

gen·teel /dʒen'tiːl/ adj (usu ironic in modern use,
but serious in former use) polite and well-bred;
elegant; characteristic of, suitable for, the upper
classes of society: living in ∼ poverty, trying to
maintain the style of the upper classes, although

too poor to do so. ∼·ly adv

gen·tian /'dʒenʃn/ n (kind of usu) blue-flowered
plant growing in mountainous districts.

gen·tile /'dʒentaɪl/ n, adj (person) not Jewish.

gen·til·ity /dʒen'tɪlətɪ/ n [U] state of being genteel:
living in shabby ∼, trying, without real success, to
keep up an appearance of being genteel.

gentle /'dʒentl/ adj (-r, -st) 1 mild, quiet, careful;
not rough, violent, severe: a ∼ nature/heart/
look/voice/call/touch; ∼ manners; a ∼ breeze; a
∼ heat, ie not too hot; a ∼ slope, ie not steep. 2
(of a family) with good social position: a person of
∼ birth. '∼-folk n pl persons of ∼ birth. ∼·ness n

gentle·man /'dʒentlmən/ n (pl -men /-mən/) 1
man who shows consideration for the feelings of
others, who is honourable and courteous. ∼'s agreement, one that is binding in honour, but cannot
be enforced at law. 2 (hist) man of good family attached to a court or the household of a great noble:
one of the king's gentlemen. ∼-at-'arms, one of
the sovereign's bodyguard. 3 (hist) man entitled to
bear arms but not a member of the nobility. 4 (dated use) man of wealth and social position, esp one
who does not work for a living: 'What does he do
for a living?'—'Nothing; he's a ∼.'∼ 'farmer, ∼
who has a farm, but does no manual work himself. 5
polite form of address to men (eg in an audience):
Gentlemen! Ladies and Gentlemen! Also used instead of Sirs or Dear Sirs when writing to a business firm, etc. ∼·ly adj feeling, behaving, or looking like a ∼(1) ; suitable or right for a ∼(1): a ∼ly
apology.

gentle·woman /'dʒentlwʊmən/ n (pl -women
/-wɪmɪn/) lady.

gen·tly /'dʒentlɪ/ adv in a gentle manner: Hold it
∼, carefully. Speak ∼ (= softly, kindly) to the
child. The road slopes ∼ (= gradually) to the sea.

gen·try /'dʒentrɪ/ n pl (the) ∼, people of good social position next below the nobility. **gen·tri·fy**
/'dʒentrɪfaɪ/ vt [VP6A] (colloq) modernize, smarten,
restore (a house, area, etc) to make suitable for
middle-class occupiers: the gentrifying of inner city
working-class districts.

genu·flect /'dʒenjʊflekt/ vi [VP2A] bend the knee,
esp in worship. **genu·flec·tion, genu·flex·ion**
/ˌdʒenjʊ'flekʃn/ nn

genu·ine /'dʒenjʊɪn/ adj true; really what it is said
to be: a ∼ picture by Rubens; ∼ pearls; ∼ sorrow;
a ∼ signature. ∼·ly adv ∼·ness n

ge·nus /'dʒiːnəs/ n (pl genera /'dʒenərə/) 1 (biol)
division of animals or plants within a family: ∼
'Homo /'həʊməʊ/, mankind. 2 sort; kind; class.

geo- /ˌdʒiːəʊ/ pref (form of Greek word for 'earth',
used in combinations): **geo·cen·tric**
/ˌdʒiːəʊ'sentrɪk/ adj having or representing the earth
as centre. **geo·phys·ics** /ˌdʒiːəʊ'fɪzɪks/ n pl (sing
v) study of the earth's magnetism, meteorology,
etc. **geo·physi·cal** /-'fɪzɪkl/ adj **geo·poli·tics**
/ˌdʒiːəʊ'pɒlətɪks/ n pl (sing v) country's politics as
determined by its geographical position.

ge·ogra·phy /dʒɪ'ɒgrəfɪ/ n [U] science of the
earth's surface, physical features, divisions, climate, products, population, etc. **ge·ogra·pher**
/dʒɪ'ɒgrəfə(r)/ n authority on ∼. **geo·graphi·cal**
/ˌdʒɪə'græfɪkl/ adj of ∼. **geo·graphi·cally** /-klɪ/
adv

ge·ol·ogy /dʒɪ'ɒlədʒɪ/ n [U] science of the earth's
history as shown by its crust, rocks, etc. **ge·ol·**
ogist /dʒɪ'ɒlədʒɪst/ n authority on ∼. **geo·logi·cal**
/ˌdʒɪə'lɒdʒɪkl/ adj of ∼. **geo·logi·cally** /-klɪ/ adv

ge·ometry /dʒɪ'ɒmətrɪ/ n [U] science of the properties and relations of lines, angles, surfaces and solids. **geo·met·ric, –metri·cal** /ˌdʒɪə'metrɪk(l)/ adj of ∼; of or like the lines, figures, etc used in ∼: *geometrical patterns.* **geo,metrical pro'gression,** series of numbers with a constant ratio between successive quantities, the numbers either increasing by a common multiplier, or decreasing by a common divisor, as 1 : 3 : 9 : 27 : 81. **geo·met·ri·cally** /-klɪ/ adv

George /dʒɔːdʒ/ n 1 St ∼, patron saint of England; St '∼'s day, 23 Apr; St ,∼'s 'Cross, vertical and horizontal red bars crossing in the centre. ⇨ illus at flag. 2 (sl) automatic pilot of aircraft. □ int by ∼! (dated) exclamation of surprise, determination, etc.

geor·gette /dʒɔː'dʒet/ n [U] thin silk dress material.

Geor·gian /'dʒɔːdʒən/ adj 1 of the time (1714-1811) of any of the Kings George I, II and III of Britain: (esp) ∼ architecture. 2 of **Geor·gia** /'dʒɔːdʒə/ (republic in USSR, or state in US).

ger·anium /dʒə'reɪnɪəm/ n kind of garden plant with red, pink or white flowers.

geri·atrics /ˌdʒerɪ'ætrɪks/ n pl (sing v) medical care of old people. **geri·atric** adj of ∼: *the geriatric ward,* of a hospital. **geria·tri·cian** /ˌdʒerɪə'trɪʃn/ n expert in ∼.

germ /dʒɜːm/ n [C] 1 portion of a living organism capable of becoming a new organism; (fig) beginning or starting-point (of an idea, etc). 2 microbe or bacillus, esp one causing disease: ∼ warfare, use of bacteria as a weapon in war.

Ger·man /'dʒɜːmən/ adj of Germany and its people. ,∼ 'shepherd n (US) = Alsatian (dog). □ n native of Germany; language of the ∼ people ∼ic /dʒə'mænɪk/ adj of the group of languages now including German, English and Dutch.

ger·mane /dʒə'meɪn/ adj ∼ (to), relevant, pertinent (to).

ger·mi·cide /'dʒɜːmɪsaɪd/ n substance used to destroy germs (esp bacteria).

ger·mi·nate /'dʒɜːmɪneɪt/ vi,vt [VP2A,6A] (of seeds) (cause to) start growth. **ger·mi·na·tion** /ˌdʒɜːmɪ'neɪʃn/ n [U] germinating; sprouting.

ger·on·tol·ogy /ˌdʒerɒn'tɒlədʒɪ/ n [U] branch of science concerned with the processes of growing old, esp in human beings.

gerry·man·der /ˌdʒerɪ'mændə(r)/ vt [VP6A] manipulate (a constituency, etc by division into voting areas) so as to give unfair advantages to one party or class in elections; practise trickery □ n such a falsification.

ger·und /'dʒerənd/ n 1 form of a verb when used as a noun. 2 the *-ing* form of an English verb when used as a noun (as in 'fond of *swimming*').

Ges·tapo /ge'stɑːpəʊ/ n German secret State police of the Nazi regime.

ges·ta·tion /dʒe'steɪʃn/ n carrying or being carried in the womb between conception and birth; this period.

ges·ticu·late /dʒe'stɪkjʊleɪt/ vi [VP2A] use movements of the hands, arms or head instead of, or to accompany, speaking. **ges·ticu·la·tion** /dʒeˌstɪkjʊ'leɪʃn/ n [U] gesticulating; [C] movement used in this.

ges·ture /'dʒestʃə(r)/ n 1 [C] movement of the hand or head to indicate or illustrate an idea, feeling, etc; sth done to convey a friendly intention: a ∼ of refusal; make a friendly ∼ to sb. 2 [U] use of expressive movements: *an actor who is a master of*

the art of ∼. □ vi [VP2A] gesticulate.

get /get/ vt,vi (pt got /gɒt/, pp got, (US) gotten /'gɒtn/) (For uses with *adverbial particles* and *preps* ⇨ 15, 16, 17, below.) 1 [VP2D] (cause oneself to) become; pass from one state to another: *get dressed/excited/lost/married/tired/wet. He went out and got drunk. She'll soon get well/better again. You'll soon get used to the climate here. Get lost!* (sl) Go away! **get even with sb,** ⇨ even² ⇨ also wise². 2 [VP22,24C] bring to a certain condition; cause to be or become: *She soon got the children ready for school. I must get the breakfast ready/cooked. Did you get the sum right,* produce the correct answer? *He got his wrist broken,* broke it by accident. **get sth done,** complete it: *The farmer got his planting done before the rains came.* 3 [VP2E] reach the stage where one is doing something: *Get going! Start! It's time we got going,* made a start. *Things haven't really got going yet,* are not yet at the stage of full activity. *When does women get talking, they go on for hours.* 4 [VP19B] bring sb/sth to the point where he/it is doing sth: *Can you really get that old car going again,* restart or repair it? *It's not hard to get the children talking; the problem is to stop them. We'll soon get things going.* 5 [VP4A] reach the stage where one knows, feels, etc sth: *When you get to know him you'll like him. They soon got to be (= became) friends. After a time you get to realize that.... One soon gets to like it here. How did you get to know* (= learn) *that I was here?* 6 [VP17,24C] bring, persuade, cause (sb/sth) to do sth or act in a certain way: *You'll never get him to understand. I can't get this old radio to work. I can't get her to talk. I can't get anyone to do the work/can't get the work done by anybody.* Cf (*I must get my hair cut/get somebody to cut my hair*). 7 [VP6A,14] **get sth (of),** receive; have; obtain; procure; acquire: *get news/knowledge/possession of sth. I've got* (= now have) *your telegram. This room gets* (= receives, admits) *very little sunshine. I'll come as soon as I get time. The soldier got leave* (= permission) *to go home. He got* (= received) *a nasty blow on the head. The bullet got him/The soldier got it in the leg,* He was injured there. *Where did you get that hat? How does he get* (= earn) *his living? If we divide 12 by 4, we get 3. Can you get* (= receive) *distant stations on your transistor? Go and get* (= take, eat) *your breakfast.* [VP12B,13B] *Get me a ticket, please. Get yourself a haircut/Get some more food for the guests.* **'get one,** = get one's goat, ⇨ goat. **get the better/best of,** ⇨ better³ and best³. **get the boot,** ⇨ boot¹(1). **get a glimpse of,** ⇨ glimpse. **get hold of sth,** ⇨ hold²(1). **get the sack,** ⇨ sack². **get (a) sight of,** ⇨ sight¹(2). **get the upper hand (of),** ⇨ upper. **get one's own way,** ⇨ way. **get wind of,** ⇨ wind¹(4). **get the wind up,** ⇨ wind¹(1). **get the worst of,** ⇨ worst. 8 [VP6A] catch (an illness): *get the measles; get religion,* (colloq) be converted (from disbelief or indifference). 9 [VP6A] receive as a penalty: *get six months,* be sentenced to six months' imprisonment. **get told off,** (colloq) be admonished: *I daren't be late home again or I'll get told off.* 10 [VP6A] (colloq) understand: *I don't get you/your meaning. She didn't get the joke. Get it?* Do you understand? *You've got it wrong,* have misunderstood it. *I didn't get* (= hear) *your name.* 11 [VP6A] (esp in the perfect tenses) puzzle; catch in an argument; bring an accusation against sb to which he cannot supply a good answer: *Ah! I've got you there! That's got him!* **12** [VP6A] **have got,** have, eg as a possession or characteristic: *We've got a new car. What ugly teeth he's got!* **13** [VP7B] **have got to,** must, be compelled or obliged to: *It has got to* (= must) *be done today. She's got to work hard for her living. You haven't got to* (= needn't) *go to the office today, have you?* ⟹ have³(1). **14** [VP7A] (US) succeed: *Do you ever get to see him,* have opportunities of seeing him? **15** [VP2C,3A] (non-idiomatic intransitive uses with *adverbial particles* and *preps;* for idiomatic uses, ⟹ **17** below) move to or from a specified point or in a particular direction: *He gets about a good deal. A car makes it easier to get about. The bridge was destroyed so we couldn't get across,* couldn't cross the river. *Did you manage to get away* (= have a holiday) *this Easter? Get back!* (imper) Move backwards, eg away from danger. *When did you get back* (= return) *from the country? She got back into bed. Please let me get by,* pass. *He got down from the bus. I can't get in/out,* I can't enter/leave. *I'm getting off* (= leaving the train) *at the next station. When did you get here/there,* arrive here/there? *Dust got into his eyes. Get off the grass/my toes! Get a move on!* Hurry up! *Can you get over that wall? We didn't get to bed until 2am. Where have they got to? Where can it have got to?* Where can it be? **get (sb) under one's skin,** ⟹ skin(1). **get somewhere/anywhere/nowhere,** obtain some/any/no result; make some/any/no progress. **'get there,** (colloq) succeed; accomplish sth. **16** [VP15A,B] (non-idiomatic transitive uses with *adverbial particles* and *preps;* for idiomatic uses, ⟹ **17** below) cause to move to or from a point, or in a particular direction: *The general had to get his troops across the river. He never lends books; he says it's too difficult to get them back. If you'll come and help me, I promise to get you back* (= see that you reach home again) *before dark. He's drunk again—we'd better call a taxi and get him home. It was nailed to the wall and I couldn't get it off. Get* (= Put) *your hat and coat on. I can't get the lid on/off. We couldn't get the piano through the door.* **17** [VP2C,15B,3A,14] (idiomatic uses with *adverbial particles* and *preps*):

get about, (a) (of sb who has been ill) be no longer confined to bed, to the house: *He's getting about again after his accident.* (b) (of news, rumours, stories) spread from person to person, usu by gossip: *The news of his resignation soon got about.*
get a'bove oneself, have a feeling of self-satisfaction not in strict proportion to one's merits; have too high an opinion of oneself. ⟹ swollen-headed at swell.
get sth across (to sb), (cause sth to) be understood: *I spoke slowly, but my meaning didn't get across. I failed to get my joke across to the crowd.*
get ahead (of sb), go forward and pass sb; make progress: *get ahead of one's class-mates.*
get along, (a) manage: *We can't get along without money.* (b) make progress: *How are you getting along? How is he getting along with his French?* **get along (with sb),** be friendly and in harmony: *He gets along well with his boss. He and his boss get along well.* **Get a'long with you!** (colloq imper) Go away! (or) Don't expect me to believe that!
get at sb/sth, reach; gain access to: *The books are*

locked up and I can't get at them. Hence, **get-'at-able** /ˌgetˈætəbl/ *adj* accessible. **get at sb,** (a) bribe; corrupt: *One of the witnesses had been got at.* (b) taunt: *He's always getting at his wife.* **get at sth,** discover; lay bare: *get at the truth/the facts.* **be getting at,** (colloq) be implying; be trying to say or suggest: *What are you getting at?*
get away, manage to leave; escape: *Two of the prisoners got away.* Hence, **'get-away** *n*: *make one's get-away,* escape; (attrib) *The get-away car had been stolen.* **get away with sth,** pursue successfully a course of action which might usually be expected to result in blame, punishment or misfortune: *The thieves got away with the contents of the safe. If I cheat in the examination, do you think I might get away with it? Get a'way with you!* Get along with you. ⟹ get along above.
get back, return to power or prominence after losing it for a time: *The Democrats hope to get back at the next election.* **get 'back at sb/get one's 'own back (on sb),** have one's revenge: *He tricked me this time but I'll get my own back one day.*
get by, (a) pass; be accepted, without comment or criticism: *I have no formal clothes for this occasion; perhaps I can get by in a dark suit.* (b) manage; survive: *How can he get by on such low wages? She can't get by without him.*
get down, leave the table, after a meal. **get sb down,** (colloq) depress: *Don't let this cold weather get you down.* **get sth down,** (a) swallow: *The medicine was bitter, and she couldn't get it down.* (b) write down: *Did you get that telephone message down?* **get down to sth,** deal seriously with; tackle: *get down to one's work after the holidays; get down to the facts,* deal with them, ignoring speculations, etc. **get down to brass tacks,** ⟹ brass.
get home (to) sb, be fully understood (by): *That remark of yours about Sally got home,* She understood (and reacted).
get in, (a) arrive: *The train got in five minutes early.* (b) be elected: *He got in* (= was elected MP) *for Islington.* **get sb in,** call sb to one's house, etc to perform a service: *We must get someone in to repair the TV.* **get sth in,** (a) collect; gather: *get in the crops/the harvest; get in debts/taxes.* (b) obtain a supply of sth: *get coal in for the winter; get in more wine for Christmas.* **get one's hand/eye in, not get a word in edgeways, get a blow in,** ⟹ hand¹(1), eye¹(1), edgeways, and blow³(1).
get into sth, (a) put on: *I can't get into these shoes—they're two sizes too small!* (b) pass into a particular condition: *get into trouble/a rage/a temper; get into debt.* **get a girl into trouble,** (colloq) make her pregnant. ⟹ also get with below. (c) acquire: *get into bad habits.* (d) associate with: *get into undesirable company.* (e) learn by experience or experiment: *get into the way/habit/routine of doing something.* **get it into one's head that...; get 'this into your head that...,** become convinced, understand, that...
get off, start: *We got off immediately after breakfast.* **get off lightly/cheaply,** escape severe punishment or suffering. **tell sb where to get off/where he gets off,** (colloq) tell him how far his misbehaviour, impudence, etc will be tolerated, or that it will no longer be tolerated (= put sb in his place). **get sb/sth off,** send: *get letters/parcels off in good time; get the children off to school.* **get sth off one's chest/hands,** ⟹ chest(2), hand¹(1). **get sb off,** save from punishment or a penalty: *His*

youth and inexperience got him off. A clever bar-rister may be able to get you off. **get sb off to sleep,** help him to fall asleep: *She got the baby off to sleep,* eg by rocking it. **get sth off,** remove: *get a ring off one's finger; get off one's gloves.* **get sth off (by heart),** learn it until the words can be repeated mechanically. **get off with sb,** (colloq) have a romantic or sexual encounter with him: *The nurse got off with a young doctor at the dance.* **get off with sth,** escape more severe punishment or misfortune: *He got off with only a fine,* eg instead of possible imprisonment.

get on, (a) become older. **(b)** make progress; advance: *How's Jim getting on at school? He's getting on well. Time is getting on,* is passing. **get on sth,** mount: *He got on his bike/horse/the train.* **get on one's feet,** stand; (fig) recover after a set-back: *The industry will need time to get on its feet again.* **get on one's nerves,** ⇨ nerve(2). **be get-ting 'on for,** (of age or time) be approaching: *He's getting on for seventy,* will soon be 70 years old. *It's getting on for midnight.* **get 'on to sb, (a)** get in touch with, eg by telephone; make contact with: *If you're not satisfied with the firm's service, get on to the manager.* **(b)** (colloq) succeed in recogniz-ing, eg dishonesty, deceit: *He has tricked many of us but people are beginning to get on to him at last.* **get on (with sb),** work or live in a sociable way: *The new manager is easy to get on with. They don't get on at all well (together).* **get on (with sth),** continue: *Please get on with your work.*

get out, become known: *The secret got out. If the news gets out there'll be trouble.* **get sth out, (a)** utter: *He managed to get out a few words of thanks.* **(b)** produce; publish; distribute: *Will we get the new dictionary out by the end of the year?* **get out of (doing) sth, (a)** (fig) avoid; escape (from): *I wish I could get out of (going to) that wedding.* **(b)** (fig) abandon gradually: *get out of bad habits.* **get sth out of sb,** extract: *The police have got a con-fession out of him,* have made him confess. *Just try getting money out of him!*

get over sb, (colloq) forget: *He never got over Jane, you know,* She stayed in his memory. **get over sth, (a)** recover from, eg illness, surprise, a loss: *I can't get over his rudeness. Fred didn't re-marry; he never got over the shock of losing Jane.* **(b)** overcome: *She can't get over her shyness.* **get sth over (with),** reach the end of sth unpleasant or troublesome: *I have to see my dentist today; I'll be glad to get it over with.* **get sth over (to sb),** cause (him) to understand it.

get round sb, persuade sb into some action to which he was at first opposed or indifferent; influ-ence sb in one's favour; coax: *Alice knows how to get round her father.* **get round sth,** evade, eg a law or regulation, but without committing a legal offence; circumvent: *A clever lawyer might find ways of getting round that clause.* **get round to (doing) sth,** deal with it (when more important matters have been dealt with): *I'm very busy this week but I hope to get round to (answering) your request next week.*

get through (to sb), arrive; reach (sb); make con-tact (with sb): *I left as soon as your message got through (to me). I rang you several times yester-day but couldn't get through.* **get through (sth),** pass, eg an examination: *Tom failed but his sister got through.* **get through (with) sth,** reach the end of: *I've got through a lot of correspondence to-*

day. He has got through (= spent) all his money. As soon as I get through (with) my work, I'll join you. **get through to sb that** ..., communicate to him that ...: *Try to get through to him that he's ruining his own life.* **get sb through (sth),** help to pass an examination: *get pupils through (an exam-ination).* **get sth through,** ensure that it is done; make it law: *get the proposal through the commit-tee,* have it discussed and accepted; *get a Bill through Parliament.*

get to sth/sb, reach (a place, state, person, etc): *When she got to the station, the train had already left. He got to thinking (= began to think) that she wouldn't come after all.* **get to work,** ⇨ work[1](1).

get together (with sb), come or meet together, e g for discussion or for social purposes: *get together for a friendly chat; get together with sb to discuss a problem.* Hence, **'get-together** *n* [C]. **get it/sth together,** (colloq) organise or manage it; put it in order. **get oneself together,** (colloq) get control of oneself, one's feelings, etc. **get people/things together,** collect them: *The rebel leader couldn't get an army together.*

get sth under control, ⇨ control. **get sth under way,** ⇨ way(8).

get up, (a) rise: *When do you get up,* ie from bed? *He got up (= stood up) to sing.* Hence, **get-up-and-'go** *n* [U] (colloq) energy. **(b)** mount (a horse). **(c)** begin to be violent: *The wind/sea is getting up.* **get sb/sth up, (a)** cause to rise, to be out of bed: *Get me up at seven o'clock.* **(b)** arrange sb's/sth's appearance: *got up to look like an Arab princess. The book is well got up,* well printed and bound. Hence, **'get-up** *n* (colloq) **(a)** style or ar-rangement, eg of a book, periodical. **(b)** style of dress, esp if unusual: *I wouldn't be seen dead with you in that get-up!* **get sth up,** organize: *We're getting up a party for his birthday.* **get up steam,** ⇨ steam. **get up to sth, (a)** reach: *We got up to page seventy-two last lesson. We soon got up to the others,* caught up with them. **(b)** become in-volved in (sth unusual): *What will they get up to next?*

get sb with child, (archaic) make her pregnant. **get with it,** (colloq) ⇨ with(12).

geum /'dʒiːəm/ *n* [C] kind of small garden plant.

gey·ser /'giːzə(r) *US:* 'gaɪzər/ *n* **1** natural spring sending up at intervals a column of hot water or steam. **2** (GB) apparatus for heating water, eg by gas, in a kitchen, bathroom, etc.

a geyser

gharry /'gæri/ *n* (*pl* -ries) (in India, etc) (horse-drawn) carriage.

ghast·ly /'gɑːstlɪ *US:* 'gæs-/ *adj* (-ier, -iest) **1** death-like; pale and ill: *looking* ∼; (also as *adv*): ∼ *pale.* **2** causing horror or fear: *a* ∼ *accident.* **3** (colloq) very unsatisfactory or unpleasant: *a* ∼ *dinner.*

ghat /gɑːt/ *n* [C] (in India) flight of steps leading to a landing-place on a river bank. '**burning** ∼, level area at the top of a ∼ on which Hindus cremate their dead.

ghee /giː/ n [U] clarified Indian buffalo-milk butter.

gher·kin /'gɜːkɪn/ n small, green cucumber for pickling.

ghetto /'getəʊ/ n (pl ∼s /-təʊz/) 1 (formerly, in some countries) Jewish quarter of a town. 2 section of a town, lived in by underprivileged classes, or people who are discriminated against, eg because of race or religion.

ghost /gəʊst/ n 1 spirit of a dead person appearing to sb still living: He looked as if he had seen a ∼, looked frightened. I don't believe in ∼s. 2 (old use) spirit of life. **give up the** ∼, die. 3 Spirit of God: (only in) **the Holy G**∼, the Third Person of the Trinity. 4 sth shadowy or without substance: '∼ **town,** one now deserted, eg an area where gold was once mined, but is now abandoned. **not have the** '∼ **of a chance,** no chance at all. 5 (also '∼-**writer**), person who does literary or artistic work for which his employer takes the credit. 6 duplicated image on a television screen. □ vt, vi act as a ∼-writer (for): ∼ed memoirs, compiled by a ∼-writer.

ghost·ly /'gəʊstlɪ/ adj 1 of, like, suggesting, a ghost: vague shapes, looking ∼ in the darkness. 2 (archaic) spiritual; from a priest: ∼ comfort/counsel. **ghost·li·ness** n

ghoul /guːl/ n (in stories) spirit that robs graves and feeds on the corpses in them. 2 person with gruesome and unnatural tastes and habits. ∼·**ish** /-ɪʃ/ adj gruesome; revolting.

GI /dʒiː 'aɪ/ n enlisted soldier of the US army: a GI bride, bride (in or from a country other than the US) of such a soldier.

gi·ant /'dʒaɪənt/ n 1 (in fairy tales) man of very great height and size. 2 man, animal or plant much larger than normal; (fig) person of extraordinary ability or genius. 3 (attrib) of great size or force: ∼ strength; a ∼ cabbage. ∼·**ess** /'dʒaɪəntes/ n female ∼.

gib·ber /'dʒɪbə(r)/ vi [VP2A,C] talk fast or make meaningless sounds (like an ape, or as when the teeth knock together through cold or fear). ∼·**ish** /'dʒɪbərɪʃ/ n [U] meaningless sounds; unintelligible talk.

gib·bet /'dʒɪbɪt/ n 1 (hist) gallows. 2 wooden post with an arm, on which corpses of executed criminals were formerly exposed as a warning. 3 death by hanging. □ vt put to death by hanging; expose on a gibbet; (fig) hold up to contempt or ridicule.

gib·bon /'gɪbən/ n kinds of long-armed ape. ⇨ the illus at ape.

gib·bous /'dʒɪbəs/ adj 1 (of the moon) having the bright part greater than a semicircle and less than a circle. ⇨ the illus at phase. 2 humped; hunchbacked.

gibe, jibe /dʒaɪb/ vi [VP2A,3A] ∼ (at), jeer or mock; make fun of: ∼ at a boy's mistakes. □ n taunt; cruel joke: cheap ∼s, easy but unnecessary mockery. **gib·ing·ly** /'dʒaɪbɪŋlɪ/ adv

gib·lets /'dʒɪblɪts/ n pl heart, liver, gizzard, etc of a goose, hen, etc taken out before the bird is cooked: giblet soup, soup made from these parts.

giddy /'gɪdɪ/ adj (-ier, -iest) 1 causing, having, the feeling that everything is turning round; feeling that one cannot stand firm: look down from a ∼ height. If you turn round quickly fifty times, you

will feel ∼. 2 too fond of pleasure; not serious; without steady principles: a ∼ young girl; a ∼ life of pleasure. **play the** ∼ **goat,** ⇨ goat. **gid·dily** adv **gid·di·ness** n

gift /gɪft/ n 1 [C] sth given: ∼s to charities; ½ ∼ vouchers/coupons. Cf birthday and Christmas presents. 2 [C] natural ability or talent: have a ∼ for art/languages; a woman of many ∼s, talented by nature. **look a** ∼-**horse in the mouth,** ⇨ mouth¹(1). 3 [U] right or power to give: The post is in the ∼ of the Prime Minister, He has the right to bestow it. □ vt [VP6A] bestow, eg land, as a ∼ to sb. ∼ed adj having great natural ability: ∼ed with rare talents; a ∼ed pianist.

gig /gɪg/ n 1 (hist) small, light two-wheeled carriage pulled by one horse. 2 (naut) ship's small boat for oars or sails, eg for the captain's use. 3 (colloq) (pop or jazz music) engagement to play.

gi·gan·tic /dʒaɪˈgæntɪk/ adj of immense size: He has a ∼ appetite, and eats ∼ meals.

giggle /'gɪgl/ vi [VP2A] laugh lightly in a nervous or silly way; [VP6A] express by giggling: She ∼d her appreciation of my silly joke. □ n laugh of this kind.

gig·olo /'ʒɪgələʊ/ n (pl ∼s /-ləʊz/) professional male dancing-partner who may be hired by wealthy women; paid male companion of a wealthy older woman.

gild¹ /gɪld/ vt (pp usu ∼ed, sometimes gilt /gɪlt/, ⇨ gilt below) [VP6A] cover with gold leaf or gold-coloured paint; make bright as if with gold: ∼ a picture-frame. ∼ **the lily,** spoil the beauty of sth by unnecessary embellishment. ∼ **the pill,** make an unpleasant necessity seem attractive. ∼ed **youth,** young people of fashion and wealth. ∼er n person who ∼s (picture-frames, etc). ∼·**ing** n [U] material with which things are ∼ed.

gild² ⇨ guild.

gill¹ /gɪl/ n (usu pl) 1 organ (one on each side) with which a fish breathes. ⇨ the illus at fish. 2 one of the many thin vertical sheets on the under side of a mushroom. ⇨ the illus at fungus. 3 (pl) person's flesh under the ears and jaw. **be green/white about the** ∼**s,** be sick/afraid.

gill² /dʒɪl/ n one-quarter of a pint liquid measure. ⇨ App 5.

gil·lie /'gɪlɪ/ n man or boy attending a sportsman in Scotland while fishing or shooting.

gilt /gɪlt/ n [U] gilding. ⇨ gild. **take the** ∼ **off the gingerbread,** (prov) take away the most attractive feature. ∼-**edged 'stocks/se'curities,** investments that are considered safe.

gim·bals /'dʒɪmblz/ n (usu pl) contrivance (of rings and pivots) for keeping instruments, eg a compass, horizontal on a ship at sea.

gim·crack /'gɪmkræk/ adj worthless, flimsy and badly made: ∼ ornaments.

gim·let /'gɪmlɪt/ n small tool, with a handle usu fixed crosswise, used for boring holes in wood, etc. ⇨ the illus at tool. ∼ **eye,** searching glance.

gim·mick /'gɪmɪk/ n [C] (colloq) trick, device, catchword, mannerism, article of wear, etc used for publicity purposes, to identify sth or sb.

gin¹ /dʒɪn/ n 1 trap or snare for catching animals, etc. 2 (**cotton**) ∼, machine for separating raw cotton from its seeds. □ vt (-nn-) [VP6A] 1 catch (animals, etc) in a trap or snare. 2 treat (cotton) in a gin.

gin² /dʒɪn/ n [U] colourless alcoholic drink distilled from grain or malt and flavoured with juniper berries, often drunk with tonic water, and used in many kinds of cocktail.

gin·ger /'dʒɪndʒə(r)/ *n* [U] **1** (plant with) hot-tasting root used in cooking, as a flavouring and for making a kind of wine. **2** liveliness; spirit; energy: *a '~ group*, (in Parliament) group of MP's that urges the Government to be more active. **3** (also as *adj*) light reddish-yellow colour: ~ *hair*. **4** ,~ **'beer/'ale**, kinds of non-alcoholic aerated drink flavoured with ~. '~**·bread** *n* dark-coloured cake or biscuit flavoured with ~. ⟹ **gilt**. '~ **nut**, biscuit flavoured with ~. □ *vt* [VP6A,15B] ~ *(up)*, make more vigorous or lively.

gin·ger·ly /'dʒɪndʒəlɪ/ *adv* with great care and caution to avoid harming, making a noise, etc: *set about sth* ~. □ *adj* cautious: *in a ~ fashion*.

ging·ham /'gɪŋəm/ *n* [U] printed cotton or linen cloth, usu with designs in stripes or checks.

gingko /'gɪŋkəʊ/ *n* (*pl* ~s, ~es /-kəʊz/) tree native to China and Japan with fan-shaped leaves.

gin·seng /'dʒɪnseŋ/ *n* [U] plant of which the aromatic root is used in medicine.

gipsy, Gypsy /'dʒɪpsɪ/ *n* (*pl*-sies) **1 gipsy**, (playfully) attractive or mischievous person, esp one with black, sparkling eyes. **2 Gypsy**, member of a wandering, originally Asiatic people, who move about in caravans and make camps from time to time, and earn a living by collecting scrap material, horse-dealing, fortune-telling, basket-making, etc: (attrib) *a ~ girl/camp/orchestra*.

gi·raffe /dʒɪ'rɑːf US: -'ræf/ *n* African animal with a very long neck and legs and dark patches on its coat. ⟹ the illus at **large**.

gird /gɜːd/ *vt* (*pt,pp* girded or girt /gɜːt/) (poet or rhet) **1** [VP15B] ~ *on*, fasten, attach: ~ *on a sword*. **2** [VP15B] ~ *up*, raise and fasten, eg with a belt or sash: ~ *up one's clothes*. ~ *up one's loins*, prepare for action. **3** encircle: *a sea-girt isle*, surrounded by the sea.

girder /'gɜːdə(r)/ *n* wood, iron or steel beam to support the joists of a floor; compound structure of steel forming the span of a bridge, roof, etc.

girdle¹ /'gɜːdl/ *n* **1** cord or belt fastened round the waist to keep clothes in position. **2** corset. **3** sth that encircles like a ~: *a ~ of green fields round a town*. □ *vt* [VP15A,B] ~ *about/around/with*, encircle: *a lake ~d with trees*.

girdle² /'gɜːdl/ *n* (Scot) = **griddle**.

girl /gɜːl/ *n* female child; daughter; young woman; woman working in a shop, office, etc. '~**·(friend)** regular companion with whom one may or may not be in love. (GB) **,G~ 'Guide**, (US) **,G~ 'Scout**, member of an organization for ~s, with principles and aims similar to those of the Scout Association. '~**·hood** /-hʊd/ *n* [U] state or time of being a ~. ~**·ish** /-ɪʃ/ *adj* of, for, like a ~: ~*ish games/ behaviour/laughter*. ~**·ish·ly** *adv* ~**·ish·ness** *n*

giro /'dʒaɪərəʊ/ *n* [U](comm)system of credit transfer between banks. **National G~**, (GB) similar system operated by the Post Office.

girt /gɜːt/ ⟹ **gird**.

girth /gɜːθ/ *n* **1** leather or cloth band tightened round the body of a horse to keep the saddle in place. ⟹ the illus at **harness**. **2** measurement round anything that is roughly like a cylinder in shape: *a tree 10 metres in* ~, in circumference; *my* ~, my waist measurement.

gist /dʒɪst/ *n* **the** ~, main points or substance; general sense: *Tell me the* ~ *of what he said*.

give¹ /gɪv/ *vt,vi* (*pt* gave /geɪv/, *pp* given /'gɪvn/)

(For uses with *adverbial particles* and *preps*, ⟹ **13** below.) **1** [VP12A,13A,2A] ~ *(to)*, hand over (to sb) without payment or exchange, eg as a present or gift: *I gave David a book. I gave a book to each of the boys. Each of the boys was ~n a book. A book was ~n to each of them. I gave it him* (= to him). *G~ me one. G~ one to me. He* ~*s generously*, is generous in giving money, etc. **2** [VP12B,16A] ~ *for sth*; ~ *to do sth*, cause (sb) to have (sth) in exchange for sth else, for payment, as compensation, etc: *How much will you* ~ *me for my old car? I would* ~ *anything to know what happened*. **3** [VP12A,13A] ~ *(to)*, allow (sb or sth) to pass into the care or safekeeping or custody of; entrust (to): *G~ the porter your bags. G~ your money to the hotel manager to be looked after*. **4** [VP12A] allow (sb) to have, eg time; cause (sb) to have, eg trouble; concede; grant: *You'd better* ~ *yourself half an hour for the journey. G~ me five minutes and I'll change the wheel. They gave me a week to make up my mind. 'The car has a good engine' 'OK, I'll* ~ *you that* (= concede that you're right on that point) *but the body's very rusty'*. ~ *sb (some/no/any, etc) trouble*, cause or make trouble to: *Did you* ~ *your parents much trouble when you were young?* **5** [VP6A,12A,13A] furnish; supply; provide: *The sun* ~*s us warmth and light. You should* ~ (more usu *set*) *them a good example. You should* ~ *a good example to your young brothers and sisters*. **6** [VP12A,13A] be the source or origin of: *You've* ~*n me your cold*, I've caught a cold from you. **7** [VP6A,13A Note that 12A is not used] devote; dedicate: *He gave his life to the cause of peace*. **8** [VP12A] (used in the *imper* to show preference): *G~ me liberty or* ~ *me death*, if I cannot have liberty, I prefer to die. *G~ me Bach and Beethoven, not these modern crash-bang-tinkle composers*. **9** [VP6A,12A,13A] (used with a *n* in a pattern that may be replaced by one in which the *n* is used as a *v*): ~ *a groan/laugh/sigh/yell*, groan, laugh, sigh, yell; ~ *a shrug of the shoulders*, shrug the shoulders; ~ *three cheers*, cheer three times; ~ *sb a kick/push/shove*, kick/push/shove him; ~ *sb a ring*, phone him. **10** (in fixed phrases) ~ *birth (to)*, ⟹ birth. ~ *chase (to)*, ⟹ chase¹. ~ *currency (to)*, ⟹ currency. ~ *one's ears*, ⟹ ear¹(1). ~ *evidence of*, ⟹ evidence. ~ *ground*, ⟹ ground¹(2). ~ *place to*, ⟹ place¹(10). ~ *rise to*, ⟹ rise¹(5). ~ *or take...*, plus or minus: *She'll be here at 4 o'clock*, ~ *or take a few minutes. He's six feet tall*, ~ *or take an inch or two*. Cf *give and take* at give². ~ *sb best*, (old use) admit his superiority. ~ *sb to understand that...*, inform, assure him, that...: *I was* ~*n to understand that you might help me to find employment*. ~ *it to sb*, (colloq) punish or reprimand him. ~ *sb sth to cry for*, ⟹ cry¹(2). ~ *sb what for/a piece of one's mind*, (colloq) punish or scold him. ~ *way*, (a) retire, retreat: *Our troops had to* ~ *way*. (b) fail to support: *The ice gave way and we all went through into the water. I felt the foundations giving way. The rope gave way, broke, snapped*. ~ *way (to sth/sb)*, (a) yield; allow priority to: *G~ way to traffic coming in from the right*. (b) be replaced by: *Tears gave way to smiles*. (c) abandon oneself to: *Don't* ~ *way to despair/grief/tears*. (d) make concessions (to): *We mustn't* ~ *way to these unreasonable demands*. **11** [VP2A] lose firmness; bend; yield to pressure: *The branch gave* (eg swung downwards) *but did not*

break. His knees seemed to ∿, to feel weak (so that he fell down). *This chair* ∿*s comfortably*, is soft and springy. *The frost is beginning to* ∿, is less severe. **12 g∿n** *pp* **(a)** (in formal documents) delivered: ∿*n under my hand and seal in this fifth day of May, 1705.* **(b)** granting or assuming that one has, eg as a basis for reasoning: *G∿n good health, I hope to finish the work this year.* **(c)** agreed upon; assigned: *under the* ∿*n conditions. They were to meet at a* ∿*n time and place.* **(d)** '∿**n name,** name ∿n to a child in addition to its family name, eg *David in David Hume.* **(e) be** ∿**n to sth/doing sth,** have as a habit: *He's* ∿*n to boasting. I'm not much* ∿*n to wild forecasts.* **13** [VP2C,15B,3A] (uses with *adverbial particles* and *preps*):
give sb away, (esp) hand over (the bride) to the bridegroom at a wedding: *The bride was* ∿*n away by her father.* ∿ **sth away, (a)** allow sb else to have; sacrifice: *You've* ∿*n away a good chance of winning the match.* **(b)** distribute: *The Mayor gave away the prizes at the sports meeting.* **(c)** ∿ freely, not expecting anything in return: *He gave away all his money.* **(d)** reveal, intentionally or unintentionally: *Don't* ∿ *away my secret. His accent gave him away,* made known who or what he was. Hence, '∿**-away** *n* (colloq) **(a)** sth given without charge: *airlines which present* ∿*-aways* (= gifts) *to their passengers. The last question on the exam paper was a* ∿*-away,* so easy that it needed no effort, etc. **(b)** sth revealed, intentionally or unintentionally: *The expression on the thief's face was a* ∿*-away,* showed his guilt. ∿ *the* '**game away,** ⇨ game¹(5).
give sth back (to sb); ∿ **sb back sth,** restore; return: ∿ *a thing back to its rightful owner;* ∿ *a man back his liberty; a wall of rock that* ∿*s back loud echoes.*
give sth forth, (old use or liter) give sth off.
give in (to sb), surrender; yield; submit: *The rebels were forced to* ∿ *in. He has* ∿*n in to my views,* has accepted them. *Mary usually has to* ∿ *in to her big brother,* accept his plans, etc and abandon her own. ∿ **sth in,** hand over (papers, etc) to the proper authorities: *Please* ∿ *in your examination papers now.* ∿ **one's name in (to sb),** make known one's willingness or readiness for sth; eg a duty, as a candidate, etc.
give sth off, emit, send out, eg smoke, smell, etc.
give on to, look out on; overlook: *The bedroom windows* ∿ *on to a courtyard.*
give out, come to an end; be exhausted: *Our food supplies began to* ∿ *out. Her patience/strength gave out.* ∿ **sb out/not out,** (cricket, of the umpire) say that the batsman has been/has not been defeated. ∿ **sth out,** distribute; send out: ∿ *out books/handbills.* ∿ **sb out to be;** ∿ **it out that sb is,** announce: *It was* ∿*n out that Mr Hall would be the chief speaker.*
give upon, = ∿ on to.
give over, (sl) stop: *Please* ∿ *over crying. Do* ∿ *over!* ∿ **sb/sth over (to sb),** hand (the usu word) over; deliver: ∿ *sb over to the police.* **be** ∿**n over to sth, (a)** be abandoned to (an undesirable state): *be* ∿*n over to despair.* **(b)** be devoted to: *The period after supper was* ∿*n over to games.*
give up, abandon the attempt (to do sth, to find the answer to sth): *I can do nothing more; I* ∿ *up. I can't answer that puzzle; I* ∿ *up.* ∿ **sb up, (a)** say that one regards sb, or his state, as hopeless: *Even*

his teachers have ∿*n him up,* have decided that he cannot be reformed. *The doctors have* ∿*n him up,* say that they cannot cure him. **(b)** (colloq) stop keeping company with him: *She was tired of Tom's nagging so she gave him up.* **(c)** no longer expect sb: *She was so late that we had* ∿*n her up.* ∿ **sb up for lost,** no longer expect him to be found or saved. ∿ **sb/oneself/sth up (to sb),** surrender; part with: ∿ *up a fortress;* ∿ *one's seat to sb,* eg in a crowded bus. *Shall we let the thief go or* ∿ *him up* (= deliver him) *to the police? The escaped prisoner gave himself up.* ∿ **sth up,** stop (doing) it: *I wish I could* ∿ *up smoking.* **give up the ghost,** die.
give² /gɪv/ *n* [U] quality of being elastic, of yielding to pressure: *A good dance floor should have a certain amount of* ∿ *in it. A stone floor has no* ∿ *in it;* (fig) (of a person) quality of yielding: *There's no* ∿ *in him,* He does not concede anything, eg in negotiations, argument. ⇨ give¹(11). ∿ **and take,** compromise; mutual concession; willingness on both sides to give way: *There must be* ∿ *and take if the negotiations to settle an industrial dispute are to succeed.* (attrib) *Is marriage a* ∿*-and-take affair?*
given /'gɪvn/ *pp* of give¹.
giver /'gɪvə(r)/ *n* one who gives: *a generous/ cheerful* ∿.
giz·zard /'gɪzəd/ *n* bird's second stomach for grinding food; (fig, colloq) throat: *It sticks in my* ∿, is a proposal, etc that I dislike intensely.
glacé /'glæseɪ US: glæ'seɪ/ *adj* (of fruits) iced, sugared; (of leather, cloth) smooth, polished.
gla·cial /'gleɪsɪəl US: 'gleɪʃl/ *adj* of ice or the ice age: *the* ∿ *era/epoch,* the time when large areas of the northern hemisphere were covered with ice; (fig) *a* ∿ (= icy) *manner/smile.*
gla·cier /'glæsɪə(r) US: 'gleɪʃər/ *n* [C] mass of ice, formed by snow on mountains, moving slowly along a valley. ⇨ the illus at mountain.
glad /glæd/ *adj* (-der, -dest) **1** (*pred* only) pleased: *be/look/feel* ∿ *about something;* ∿ *to see someone. I am* ∿ *of your success/that you have succeeded.* **2** causing or bringing joy; joyful: *Have you heard the* ∿ *news/tidings? All nature seemed* ∿, was bright and beautiful, as if rejoicing. **give sb the** '∿ **eye,** (sl) give an amorous, inviting look. **give sb the** ∿ **hand,** (sl) offer the hand of welcome. '∿ **rags,** (sl) clothes for a festive occasion. ∿·**den** /'glædn/ *vt* [VP6A] make ∿. ∿·**ly** *adv* ∿·**ness** *n* ∿·**some** /-səm/ *adj* (liter) cheerful; joyful.
glade /gleɪd/ *n* clear, open space in a forest.
gladi·ator /'glædɪeɪtə(r)/ *n* (in ancient Rome) man trained to fight with weapons at public shows in an arena. **gladia·tor·ial** /ˌglædɪə'tɔːrɪəl/ *adj* of ∿s: ∿*ial combats.*
gladi·olus /ˌglædɪ'əʊləs/ *n* (*pl* -li /-laɪ/ or ∿es) plant with sword-shaped leaves and spikes of brightly coloured flowers.
glam·our (US also **glamor**) /'glæmə(r)/ *n* [U] **1** charm or enchantment; power of beauty or romance to move the feelings: *the* ∿ *of moonlight on the sea.* **2** alluring beauty or charm, often with sex-appeal. **glamor·ous** /-əs/ *adj* full of ∿: *glamorous film stars.* **glamor·ize** /-aɪz/ *vt* [VP6A] make glamorous: *newspapers that glamorize the lives of film stars.* **glamor·iz·ation** /ˌglæməraɪ'zeɪʃn US: -rɪ'z-/ *n*
glance /glɑːns US: glæns/ *vi,vt* **1** [VP2C,3A] ∿ **at/over/through/round,** take a quick look: ∿ *at*

the clock; ∼ *over/through a letter;* ∼ *round a room. She* ∼*d shyly at him from behind her fan.* [VP15A] *He* ∼*d his eye down the classified advertisements.* 2 [VP3A] ∼ *off,* (of a weapon or a blow) quickly slip or slide: *The arrow* ∼*d off his armour.* 3 [VP2C] (of bright objects, light) flash: *Their helmets* ∼*d in the sunlight.* □ *n* 1 quick look: *take a* ∼ *at the newspaper headlines; loving* ∼*s.* **at a** ∼, immediately on looking. **at first** ∼, = at first sight, ⇨ sight¹(2). 2 (sudden movement producing a) flash of light: *a* ∼ *of spears in the sunlight.*

gland /glænd/ *n* simple or complex organ that separates from the blood those substances that are to be used by or expelled from the body: *a snake's poison* ∼*s; milk-producing* ∼*s in a female; sweat* ∼*s.* ∼**u·lar** /'glændjʊlə(r) *US:* -dʒʊ-/ *adj* of, like, or involving a gland.

glan·ders /'glændəz/ *n* [U] contagious disease of horses with swellings below the jaw, and sores in the nose and throat.

glare¹ /gleə(r)/ *n* 1 [U] strong, fierce, unpleasant light: *the* ∼ *of the sun on the water;* (fig) *in the full* ∼ *of publicity,* with public attention directed towards one. 2 [C] angry or fierce look; fixed look: *look at someone with a* ∼.

glare² /gleə(r)/ *vi,vt* 1 [VP2A,C] shine in a dazzling or disagreeable way: *The tropical sun* ∼*d down on us all the day.* 2 [VP2A,C,3A] ∼ *(at),* stare angrily or fiercely: *They stood glaring at each other.* [VP6A,14] ∼ *(at), They* ∼*d defiance/hate at me.* **glar·ing** *adj* 1 dazzling: *a car with glaring headlights; glaring neon signs.* 2 angry; fierce: *glaring eyes.* 3 gross; conspicuous: *a glaring error/ blunder; glaring injustice.* 4 (of colours) crude; gaudy.

glass /glɑːs *US:* glæs/ *n* 1 [U] hard, brittle substance (as used in windows), usu transparent: *bottles made of* ∼; *a man with a* ∼ *eye.* 2 [C] article made of this substance. (a) ∼ drinking vessel or its contents: *drink a* ∼ *of milk; have a* ∼ *too much,* drink too much alcoholic liquor, be rather drunk. (b) (also '**looking‑**∼) mirror made of ∼. (c) telescope: *The sailor looked through his* ∼. (d) barometer: *The* ∼ *is falling.* (e) (*pl*) (rarely '**eye‑**∼**es**) spectacles: *She can't read without* ∼*es.* (f) (*pl*) binoculars. (g) '**magnifying** ∼, ∼ lens on a handle for making writing, etc appear larger. ⇨ the illus at **magnet.** 3 [U] vessels and articles made of ∼: *There's plenty of* ∼ *in the house,* plenty of drinking ∼es, wine ∼es, ∼ bowls and dishes, etc. *There are many acres of* ∼ *in Jersey,* acres covered with ∼houses (for growing plants). 4 (compounds) '∼**-blower** *n* workman who blows molten ∼ to shape it into bottles, etc. '∼**-cutter** *n* workman who cuts designs on ∼; tool for cutting ∼. '∼**-house** *n* building with ∼ sides and roof (for growing plants); (sl) military prison. *People who live in* ∼*houses shouldn't throw stones,* (prov) People with faults shouldn't criticize those of others. '∼**·ware** /-weə(r)/ *n* [U] articles made of ∼. ,∼**-'wool** *n* [U] fine ∼ fibres used for filtering and in man-made fibres. '∼**-works** *n pl* (with *sing v*) factory where ∼ is manufactured. □ *vt* [VP6A,15B] ∼ *(in),* fit with ∼; glaze: *a* ∼*ed-in veranda.* ∼**-ful** /-fʊl/ *n* as much as a drinking ∼ will hold. ∼**y** *adj* (-ier, -iest) like ∼ in appearance: *a* ∼*y calm;* (of the sea, etc) smooth and shiny; *a* ∼*y stare/look/eye,* lifeless, expressionless, fixed.

glau·coma /glɔː'kəʊmə/ *n* [U] eye disease invol-

ving gradual loss of sight.

glau·cous /'glɔːkəs/ *adj* 1 dull greyish green or blue. 2 (of leaves, grapes, etc) covered with bloom(3).

glaze /gleɪz/ *vt,vi* 1 [VP6A,15B] ∼ *(in),* fit glass into: ∼ *a window/house;* ∼ *in a porch/veranda,* enclose it with glass. 2 [VP6A,15B] ∼ *(over),* cover with a glass-like surface: ∼ *pottery/ porcelain/bricks.* 3 [VP2A,C] ∼ *(over),* (of the eyes) become glassy: *His eyes* ∼*d over. His eyes were* ∼*d in death.* □ *n* [C,U] (substance used for, surface obtained by giving, a) thin glassy coating: *a Satsuma vase with a fine crackle* ∼.

glaz·ier /'gleɪzɪə(r) *US:* -ʒə(r)/ *n* workman who fits glass into the frames of windows, etc.

gleam /gliːm/ *n* [C] 1 beam or ray of soft light, esp one that comes and goes: *the* ∼ *of a distant lighthouse; the first* ∼*s of the morning sun.* 2 (fig) brief show of some quality or emotion: *a novel with an occasional* ∼ *of humour/intelligence; a* ∼ *of hope; a man with a dangerous* ∼ *in his eye,* with a threatening look. □ *vi* [VP2A,C] send out ∼s: *a cat's eyes* ∼*ing in the darkness; glass reflector studs* ∼*ing in the roadway.*

glean /gliːn/ *vi,vt* [VP2A,6A] pick up grain left in a harvest field by the workers; (fig) gather news, facts in small quantities: ∼ *a field;* ∼ *corn.* ∼**er** *n* person who ∼s. ∼**·ings** *n pl* (usu fig) small items of knowledge ∼ed from various sources.

glebe /gliːb/ *n* 1 (poet) earth; field. 2 portion of land that forms part of a clergyman's benefice.

glee /gliː/ *n* 1 [U] feeling of joy caused by success or triumph: *shout with* ∼. *She was in high* ∼ *when she learnt the news.* 2 [C] song for three or four voices singing different parts in harmony. ∼**·ful** /-fl/ *adj* full of ∼; joyous. ∼**·fully** /-fəlɪ/ *adv*

glen /glen/ *n* narrow valley.

Glen·garry /ˌglen'gærɪ/ *n* (*pl* -ries) kind of cap worn in the Highlands of Scotland.

glib /glɪb/ *adj* (-bber, -bbest) (of a person, what he says or how he says it) ready and smooth, but not sincere: *a* ∼ *talker;* ∼ *excuses;* ∼ *in finding excuses; have a* ∼ *tongue.* ∼**·ly** *adv* ∼**-ness** *n*

glide /glaɪd/ *vi* [VP2A,C] move along smoothly and continuously: *The skier* ∼*d skilfully down the snow-covered slope. The skaters* ∼*d across the ice. A boat* ∼*d past.* □ *n* gliding movement or sound. ∼**r** /'glaɪdə(r)/ *n* aircraft without an engine. **glid·ing** *n* sport of flying in ∼rs.

glim·mer /'glɪmə(r)/ *vi* [VP2A,C] send out a weak, uncertain light: *lights* ∼*ing in the distance.* □ *n* weak, faint, unsteady light: *a* ∼ *of light through the curtains;* (fig) *a* ∼ *of hope; not the least* ∼ *of intelligence.*

glimpse /glɪmps/ *n* short look (*at* sth or sb). **get/ catch a** ∼ **of sb/sth,** have a quick, imperfect view: *get/catch a* ∼ *of something from the window of a train.* □ *vt* [VP6A,19A] catch a ∼ of.

glint /glɪnt/ *vi* gleam. □ *n* gleam or flash: ∼*s of gold in her hair.*

glis·sade /glɪ'seɪd *US:* -'sɑːd/ *vi* (mountaineering) slide on the feet down a steep slope of ice or snow (usu with the support of an ice-axe); (ballet) make a sliding step. □ *n* such a slide or step.

glissando /glɪ'sændəʊ/ *adv, adj* (music) passing quickly up or down the scale.

glis·ten /'glɪsn/ *vi* [VP2A,C] (esp of wet or polished surfaces, tear-filled eyes) shine brightly; sparkle: ∼*ing dew-drops; eyes* ∼*ing with tears.*

glis·ter /'glɪstə(r)/ *vi, n* (poet) glitter.

glit·ter /'glɪtə(r)/ vi [VP2A,C] shine brightly with flashes of light; sparkle: *stars ~ing in the frosty sky; ~ing with jewels.* □ n [U] brilliant, sparkling light: *the ~ of the Christmas tree decorations. ~ing adj* brilliant; attractive: *~ing prizes.*

gloam·ing /'gləʊmɪŋ/ n **the ~,** (poet) evening twilight.

gloat /gləʊt/ vi [VP2A,3A] ~ *(over sth),* look at with selfish delight: *~ over one's wealth/the ruin of a rival; a miser ~ing over his gold.* **~·ing·ly** adv

glo·bal /'gləʊbl/ adj world-wide; embracing the whole of a group of items, etc.

globe /gləʊb/ n **1** object shaped like a ball; model of the earth; spherical chart of the earth or the constellations. **the ~,** the earth. **2** spherical glass vessel, esp a lampshade or a fishbowl. **3** '~ **fish** n fish able to inflate itself into the shape of a ~. '~**-trot** vi [VP2A] travel hurriedly through many foreign countries. '**trotter** n person who does this.

glob·ule /'glɒbjuːl/ n tiny drop, esp of liquid. **glo·bu·lar** /'glɒbjʊlə(r)/ adj globe-shaped; made of ~s.

glock·en·spiel /'glɒkənspiːl/ n musical instrument consisting of metal bars which are struck with two light hammers. ⇨ the illus at percussion.

gloom /gluːm/ n [C,U] **1** semi-darkness; obscurity. **2** feeling of sadness and hopelessness: *The future seems to be filled with ~. The news cast a ~ over the village.*

gloomy /'gluːmɪ/ adj (-ier, -iest) **1** dark, unlighted. **2** depressed; depressing: *a ~ outlook over roofs and chimneys; feeling ~ about the future.* **gloom·ily** /-ɪlɪ/ adv

glor·ify /'glɔːrɪfaɪ/ vt (pt,pp -fied) [VP6A] **1** give adoration and thanksgiving to (God); worship; give honour and glory to (a hero). **2** invest (sth common or simple) with splendour; make (sth or sb) seem more imposing: *His weekend cottage is only a glorified barn.* **glori·fi·ca·tion** /ˌglɔːrɪfɪ'keɪʃn/ n [U] ~ing or being glorified.

glori·ous /'glɔːrɪəs/ adj **1** splendid; magnificent: *a ~ sunset/view.* **2** illustrious; honourable; possessing or conferring glory: *a ~ victory; the ~ reign of Queen Elizabeth I.* **3** (colloq) enjoyable: *have a ~ time; ~ fun.* **4** (ironic) dreadful: *What a ~ mess!* **~·ly** adv

glory /'glɔːrɪ/ n [U] **1** high fame and honour won by great achievements. **2** adoration and thanksgiving offered to God: *'G~ to God in the highest.'* **3** quality of being beautiful or magnificent: *the ~ of a sunset.* **4** (sometimes [C] pl -ries) reason for pride; subject for boasting; sth deserving respect and honour: *the glories of ancient Rome.* **5** heavenly splendour: *the saints in ~.* **6** (colloq uses) *go to ~,* die; *send sb to ~,* kill him. '~**-hole** n room, drawer, filled untidily with miscellaneous articles. □ vi [VP3A] ~ **in,** rejoice in, take great pride in: *~ in one's strength/in working for a good cause.*

gloss¹ /glɒs/ n **1** smooth, bright surface: *the ~ of silk and satin; material with a good ~.* ~ '**paint** n paint which, when dry, leaves a ~ (usu washable) surface. **2** (usu **a ~**) deceptive appearance: *a ~ of respectability,* eg over a life of secret wrongdoing. □ vt [VP15A] ~ **over,** give a ~(2) to; cover up or explain away (an error, etc): *~ over sb's faults.* ~**y** adj (-ier, -iest) smooth and shiny: *a ~y photographic print; ~y hair; ~y periodicals,* those printed on high quality ~y paper, with photo-

graphs, coloured illustrations, etc, esp those periodicals dealing with clothes, fashions, etc. ~**ily** /-ɪlɪ/ adv ~**i-ness** n

gloss² /glɒs/ n [C] explanation (in a footnote, or in a list at the end of an article, a book, etc) of a word in the text; comment; interpretation. □ vt [VP6A] add a ~ or ~es to (a text); write ~es on; make comments on.

gloss·ary /'glɒsərɪ/ n (pl -ries) [C] collection of glosses; list and explanations of special, eg technical, obsolete, words.

glot·tis /'glɒtɪs/ n opening between the vocal cords at the upper part of the windpipe. ⇨ the illus at head. **glot·tal** /'glɒtl/ adj of the ~. **glottal stop,** speech sound produced by a complete closure of the ~, followed by an explosive release of breath.

glove /glʌv/ n covering of leather, knitted wool, etc for the hand, usu with separated fingers. ⇨ the illus at base. **fit like a ~,** fit perfectly. **be hand in ~ (with),** be in close relations (with). **take off the ~s to sb; handle sb without ~s,** argue or contend in earnest, without mercy. '~**-compartment** n compartment in the dashboard of a car, for small articles.

glow /gləʊ/ vi [VP2A,C] **1** send out brightness or warmth without flame: *~ing embers/charcoal; ~ing metal from the furnace.* **2** (fig) be, look, feel, warm or flushed (as after exercise or when excited): *~ing with enthusiasm/health/pride.* **3** show strong or warm colours: *woods and forests ~ing with autumn tints.* □ n (sing only, with def or indef art) ~ing state; warm or flushed look; warm feeling: *in a ~ of enthusiasm; cheeks with the ~ of health on them; (all) in a ~ after a hot bath; the ~ of the sky at sunset.* '~**-worm** n insect of which the wingless female gives out a green light at its tail. ~**ing** adj showing warm colour or (fig) enthusiasm: *give a ~ing account of what happened; describe an event in ~ing colours.* ~**ing·ly** adv

glower /'glaʊə(r)/ vi [VP2A,3A] ~ *(at),* look in an angry or threatening way. ~**ing·ly** adv

glu·cose /'gluːkəʊs/ n [U] grape sugar.

glue /gluː/ n [U] thick, sticky liquid used for joining things, eg broken wood, crockery. □ vt (pt,pp glued; pres p gluing) [VP6A,15A,B] ~ *(to),* **1** stick, make fast, with ~: *~ two pieces of wood together; ~ a piece of wood on to something.* **2** put tightly or closely: *His eyes were/His ear was ~d to the keyhole. Why must you always remain ~d to your mother?* Why can you never be separated from your mother? ~**y** /'gluːɪ/ adj sticky, like ~.

glum /glʌm/ adj (-mmer, -mmest) gloomy; sad. ~**·ly** adv ~**·ness** n

glut /glʌt/ vt (-tt-) [VP6A,14] ~ *(with),* **1** supply too much to: *~ the market (with fruit, etc).* **2** overeat; satisfy to the full; fill to excess: *~ one's appetite; ~ oneself with rich food; ~ted with pleasure.* □ n [C] supply in excess of demand: *a ~ of pears in the market.*

glu·ten /'gluːtən/ n [U] sticky substance (protein) that is left when starch is washed out of flour. **glu·ti·nous** /'gluːtɪnəs US: -tənəs/ adj of or like ~; sticky.

glut·ton /'glʌtn/ n person who eats too much: *You've eaten the whole pie, you ~! He's a ~ for work,* (fig) is always willing and ready to work. ~**·ous** /'glʌtənəs/ adj very greedy (for food). ~**·ous·ly** adv ~**y** /-tənɪ/ n [U] habit or practice of eating too much.

gly·cer·ine (US = **gly·cer·in**) /'glɪsəriːn US: -rɪn/

n [U] thick, sweet, colourless liquid made from fats and oils, used in medical and toilet preparations and explosives.

G-man /ˈdʒiː mæn/ *n* (US colloq) federal criminal investigation officer.

gnarled /nɑːld/ *adj* (of tree trunks) twisted and rough; covered with knobs: *a* ~ *old oak;* ~ (= knotty, deformed) *hands/fingers.*

gnash /næʃ/ *vi,vt* **1** [VP2A] (of the teeth) strike together, eg in rage. **2** [VP6A] (of a person) cause (the teeth) to do this: *wailing and* ~*ing of teeth.*

gnat /næt/ *n* small two-winged fly that stings; (fig) insignificant annoyance. **strain at a** ~, hesitate over a trifle.

gnaw /nɔː/ *vt,vi* **1** [VP6A,15B,3A] ~ *(at),* bite steadily at (sth hard): *The dog was* ~*ing (at) a bone. The rats had* ~*ed away some of the wood- work. He was* ~*ing his finger-nails with impat- ience.* **2** [VP6A,3A] ~ *(at),* torment; waste away: *fear and anxiety* ~*ing (at) the heart; the* ~*ing pains of hunger.*

gnome /nəʊm/ *n* (in tales) small goblin living un- der the ground (often guarding treasures of gold and silver).

gnu /nuː/ *n* wildebeest. ⇨ the illus at large.

go[1] /gəʊ/ *vi* (*3rd pers pres t* goes /gəʊz/, *pt* went /went/, *pp* gone /gɒn US:* gɔːn/) (For idiomatic uses with *adverbial particles and preps,* ⇨ **29** be- low.) **1** [VP2A,C,3A,4A] (with a *prep* or *adv* of place or direction, present or implied; ⇨ come) **go (from/to),** move, pass, *from* one point *to* another and away from the speaker, etc (cf *come from/to*): *Shall we go (there) by train or by plane? He has gone to China,* is now in, or on his way to, China. *He has gone to see his sister. Go and get your hat. Let's go to the cinema. Let's go,* Let's leave. *They came at six and went* (= left) *at nine. I must be go- ing now,* must leave now. *I wish this pain would go (away). All hope is gone* (more usu today, *has gone). Be gone! Go away!* (the more usu expres- sion today). *Who goes there?* (challenge from a sentry = Say who you are). **2** [VP2C] **(a)** be placed; have as a usual or proper position: *Where do you want your piano to go?* Where shall we put it? *'Where does this teapot go?' 'In that cup- board.'* This dictionary *goes on the top shelf.* **(b)** be fitted or contained in: *My clothes won't go into this small suitcase. 7 into 15 won't go,* 15 does not contain exact multiples of 7. **3** [VP2A,B,C,3A] **go (from/to),** reach, extend; last; (of a person's be- haviour, remarks, achievements, etc) reach certain limits: *This road goes to London. I want a rope that will go from the top window to the ground. Differences between employers and workers go deep,* Their views are far apart. **go a long way,** **(a)** last: *She makes a little money go a long way,* buys many things, etc by careful spending. *A little of this paint goes a long way,* covers a large area. **(b)** (colloq) be as much as one can bear: *A little of his company goes a long way,* One can endure his company for a short time only. **go a long way/go far towards doing sth,** make a considerable con- tribution towards: *The Prime Minister's statement went a long way towards reassuring the nation.* **go (very) far, (a)** last: *A pound doesn't go far nowa- days,* doesn't last, doesn't buy much. **(b)** (of a per- son, future tense) succeed: *He will go far in the di- plomatic service,* will win promotion, etc. **go too far,** go beyond acceptable limits: *That's going too far,* saying or doing more than is right. *You must*

apologize at once—you've gone too far, exceeded the limits of accepted behaviour, etc. **go (any) further,** go beyond a certain point: *I'll give you £50, but I can't go any further. Need I go any further,* do or say anything more? **go as/so far as to do sth,** do or say sth to a certain limit: *I won't go as far as to say he's dishonest,* won't accuse him of this, even though I may suspect him of it. *I would go so far as to suggest that the House of Lords should be abolished.* **as far as it goes,** to a limited extent: *That's all very well as far as it goes,* The limitations of the statement, explanation, etc must be realised. *What he says is true as far as it goes,* suggesting that further information, knowl- edge, etc is needed or desirable. **go to great lengths/trouble/pains (to do sth),** take care to do sth well: *He went to great trouble to make his guests comfortable.* **go to one's head,** ⇨ head[1](19). **go as low/high as,** (of a price) reach a certain level: *I'll go as high as £250,* will offer this sum, eg at an auction. **go one better (than sb),** improve on what he has done: *I hit the target 17 times out of 20, but Tom went one better and scored 18. It all/just goes to show/prove that,* tends or helps to show/prove that. **4 go on a journey/trip/outing,** make a journey, take a trip, have an outing, etc. **go for a walk/swim, etc,** go out in order to walk, swim, etc. **go walking/ swimming, etc,** take part in the activity of walk- ing, swimming, etc: *Do they often go sailing?* Is sailing sth they often do? (Cf *Let's go for a walk,* referring to a specified occasion.) *Bill has gone (out) shopping,* has gone to buy things in the shops. **5** (in the pattern **go** + *prep* + *n*) **(a)** pass into/from the state indicated by the *n.* **go into abeyance,** ⇨ abeyance. **go from bad to worse,** ⇨ bad[1](4). **go into a coma/trance,** ⇨ coma, trance. **go out of fashion,** ⇨ fashion. **go into li- quidation,** ⇨ liquidation at liquidate. **go to pieces,** ⇨ piece[1](1). **go to pot,** ⇨ pot[1](2). **go to rack and ruin,** ⇨ rack[4]. **go into retirement,** ⇨ retirement at retire. **go to seed,** ⇨ seed. **go to sleep,** ⇨ sleep[1](3). **go out of use,** ⇨ use[1](1). **go to war,** ⇨ war. **(b)** go to the place, etc indicated for the purpose associated with it. **go to the block/stake,** ⇨ block[1](3), stake. **go to church,** attend a church service. **go to hospital,** ⇨ hospi- tal. **go to market,** ⇨ market. **go to school/ college/university,** attend school, etc in order to learn or study. **go to sea,** become a sailor. **go on the stage,** ⇨ stage. **go on the streets,** ⇨ street. **(c)** have recourse to. **go to the country,** ⇨ country. **go to law,** ⇨ law(6). **6** [VP3A] **go to sb,** pass into sb's possession; be allotted to: *Who did the property go to when the old man died,* Who in- herited it? *Honours do not always go to those who merit them. The first prize went to Mr Hill.* **7** [VP2D] become; pass into a specific condition: *go blind/mad, etc. He went purple with anger/grey with worry. Fish soon goes bad* (= rotten) *in hot weather. The children went wild with excitement. This material has gone a nasty colour. Kensington went Labour at the by-election,* changed politically by returning the Labour candidate to Parliament. *Will the country go Democrat next year?* **go ber- serk,** ⇨ berserk. **go broke,** become penniless. **go dry,** ⇨ dry[1](12). **go flat,** (of liquid) lose its gas content: *This beer has gone flat.* **go haywire,** ⇨ hay. **go native,** adopt the mode of life of the na- tives of the country in which one is living. **go**

phut, (colloq) (of machines) collapse: *The old car went phut half way up the hill;* (fig): *His plan/ scheme/project has gone phut.* **go scot-free/ unchallenged/unpunished,** be free from penalty or punishment; escape being challenged. **8** [VP2A,C] be moving, working, etc: *This clock doesn't go. Is your watch going? Her tongue was going nineteen to the dozen,* ⇨ dozen. *The play went (down) like a bomb,* (colloq) was very favourably received. ⇨ go down in 28 below. *a go- ing concern,* a business in working order, operating well. **9** [VP2C,D] be or live habitually in a specific state or manner: *Refugees often go hungry. The men of this tribe used to go naked. He went in fear of his life. You'd better go armed* (= carry a weapon) *while in the jungle. She is six months gone,* six months pregnant. **10** [VP2C,D,E] (after *How*) progress: *How's everything going? How's work going? How goes work? How goes it?* (colloq) How are you? (with an *adv* or *adv* equivalent, eg *adjj* such as *slow, easy,* indicating manner of progress): **go badly/well,** (of work, events) proceed (un)satisfactorily: *All has gone well with our plans,* they've succeeded. *Things went better than had been expected.* **go easy (on/with sb/ sth),** be less strenuous, less severe; handle gently or carefully: *Go easy with/on the butter, that's all we have,* don't be wasteful. *Go easy with her, she's too young to realise her mistake.* **go slow, (a)** (of traffic) move forward slowly. **(b)** (of workers in factories, etc) work slowly, esp to reduce output, as a protest against sth or to draw attention to demands. Hence, **'go-slow** *n* [C] such slow work. *be going strong,* be proceeding vigorously; be still flourishing: *He's ninety and/but still going strong.* **11** [VP2A,C] work; operate: *This machine goes by electricity. I've been going hard (at it) all day and I'm exhausted.* **12** [VP2A,C] (in progressive tenses only) be available, be offered: *Are there any jobs going?* **13** [VP2C,3A] **go (to sb) for,** be sold (to sb) for: *The house went cheap. I shan't let mine go* (= sell it) *for less than £8000.* **go for a song,** ⇨ song. *Going! Going! Gone!* (used at an auction to announce the closing of the bidding). **14** [VP3A] **go on/in,** (of money) be spent on: *How much of your money goes on food and clothes/in rent? Half the money he inherited went in gambling debts.* **15** [VP2A,C] be given up, abandoned, lost: *I'm afraid the car must go, We can no longer afford to run it,* so must sell it. *My sight is going,* I'm losing my ability to see. **16** [VP2A,C] be current or accepted; be commonly thought of or believed: *The story goes that....* It is said that.... **17** [VP2A] *as people/things go,* considering the average person/thing: *They're good cars as cars go nowadays,* judging them from the average or usual type today. *Five pounds for a pair of shoes is not bad as things go today,* in view of how much things cost today. **18** [VP2A] fail; collapse; give way; break off: *First the sails and then the mast went in the storm. The bank may go* (= fail) *any day. He's far gone,* is critically ill or (colloq) is mad. *let oneself go,* relax, enjoy oneself, etc. **19** die: *He is going/ has gone, poor fellow! dead and gone,* dead and buried. **20** [VP2A,C] be decided: *The case* (ie in a law court) *went against him,* he lost. *The case went in his favour,* he won. *How did the election go at Hull,* Who was elected? *Does promotion go by favour in your firm?* **21** (various phrases) **go bail (for sb),** ⇨ bail[1]. **go Dutch (with sb),** ⇨ Dutch. **go**

shares/halves (in sth with sb), ⇨ share[1](1), half. **go sick,** ⇨ sick[1](2). **'go it,** (colloq) act vigorously, indulge in wild spending, etc. **go it alone,** act by oneself, without support. **22** [VP2A,C] **(a)** have a certain wording or tune: *I'm not quite sure how the words go/tune goes.* **(b)** (of a verse or song) be adaptable (to a certain tune): *It goes to the tune of 'Three Blind Mice'.* **23** (colloq) (followed by *and* and another *v*) proceed to do sth: *Go and shut the door, would you?* (as an informal request). *Go and ask that policeman the way. Now you've gone and done it,* (sl) have made a mistake, blundered. **24** [VP2A,C] make a specific sound: *The clock goes 'tick-tock, tick-tock'. 'Bang!' went the gun.* **25** (in bridge[2]) [VP6A] bid; declare: *go two spades/three no trumps.* **26** [VP2A] begin an activity: *One, two, three, go!* or *Ready, steady, go!* (eg as a signal for competitors in a race to start). *Well, here goes!* (used to call attention to the fact that one is about to start to do sth). **27** (used to express the future) *be going to do sth,* **(a)** indicating what is intended, determined or planned: *We're going to spend our holidays in Wales this year. I'm going to have my own way. We're going to buy a house when we've saved enough money.* **(b)** indicating what is considered likely or probable: *Look at those black clouds—we're going to have/there's going to be a storm.* **(c)** expressing the immediate or near future (= *about to*): *I'm going to tell you a story. I'm going to be twenty next month.* **28** (compounds) **'go-ahead** *n* ⇨ go ahead in 29 below. **,go-as-you-'please** *attrib adj* untroubled by regulations. **'go-by,** ⇨ go by in 29 below. **go- 'slow,** ⇨ 10 above. **,go-to-'meeting** *attrib adj* (dated colloq of hats, clothes, etc) worn on special occasions, eg for church: *wearing their Sunday go-to-meeting clothes.* **29** [VP2C,15B,3A] (idiomatic uses with *adverbial particles* and *preps*): **go about, (a)** move from place to place; pay visits: *I don't go about much anymore.* **(b)** (of rumours, stories, etc) pass from person to person, usu verbally; be current: *A story/rumour is going about that....* **(c)** (of a ship) change course or tack(3). **go about sth,** set to work at: *You're not going about that job in the right way. We'll have to go about it more carefully.* **go about one's business,** deal with one's own affairs (rather than with sb else's). **go about with sb,** spend time (in public) regularly with him: *go about with a bunch of thugs.* **go after sb/sth,** try to win or obtain: *He's going after that pretty Swedish girl,* is trying to win her interest or affection. *He's gone after a job in the City.* **go against sb, (a)** oppose: *Don't go against your father.* **(b)** have an unsatisfactory outcome: *The war is going against them,* They seem likely to be defeated. ⇨ also 20 above. **go against sth,** be contrary to: *It goes against my principles/interests.* **go against the grain,** ⇨ grain. **go ahead, (a)** make progress: *He's going ahead fast. The Joneses are very go-ahead* (= progressive) *people; it's difficult to keep up with them.* **(b)** proceed without hesitation: *'May I start now?' 'Yes, go ahead'.* Hence, **'go-ahead** *n* permission to proceed: *give them the go-ahead.* **go along,** proceed: *You may have some difficulty first but you'll find it easier as you go along.* **go along with sb, (a)** accompany: *I'll go along with you as far as the main road.* **(b)** agree with: *I can't go along with you on that point.*

go at sb/sth, (a) rush at; attack: *They went at each other furiously. They went at it tooth and nail/ hammer and tongs,* fought furiously. **(b)** take sth in hand, deal with it energetically: *They were going at the job for all they were worth,* making the utmost possible effort to do the work. **go away,** leave. **go away with sb/sth,** take with, abscond with: *He has gone away with my razor,* has taken it with him. **go back, (a)** return. **(b)** extend backwards in space or time: *His family goes back to the time of the Norman Conquest,* can be traced back to then. **go back on/upon,** fail to keep; break or withdraw from, eg a promise: *He's not the sort of man who would go/to go back on his word.* **go before (sth),** precede: *Pride goes before a fall.* **go behind sth,** search for sth: *go behind a person's words,* look for a hidden meaning in what he says. **go behind sb's back,** do or say sth without his knowledge. **go beyond sth,** exceed: *You've gone beyond your instructions. That's going beyond a joke,* is too serious to be amusing. **go by,** pass: *Time went by slowly. We waited for the procession to go by.* '**go by sth, (a)** be guided or directed by: *I shall go entirely by what my solicitor says,* shall follow his advice. *That's a good rule to go by,* to be guided by. **(b)** form an opinion or judgement from: *Have we enough evidence to go by? It's not always wise to go by appearances. I go by what I hear.* ˌ**go by the 'book,** follow the rules closely. **go by/under the name of,** use the name of; be called, '**go-by** n. **give sb/sth the go-by,** (colloq) ignore; disregard; slight or snub: *He gave me the go-by in the street yesterday,* ignored me completely. **go down, (a)** (of a ship, etc) sink. **(b)** (of the sun, moon, etc) set. **(c)** (of food and drink) be swallowed: *This pill won't go down,* I can't swallow it. **(d)** leave a university for the vacation, having graduated, etc. **(e)** (of the sea, wind, etc) become calm: *The wind has gone down a little,* is less strong. **(f)** (of prices) go lower: *The price of eggs/The cost of living has gone down.* **(g) go down to the sea/ country, etc,** pay a visit to the seaside, countryside, etc. **go down before sb,** be defeated or overthrown: *Rome went down before the barbarians.* **go down (in sth),** be written in; be recorded or remembered in: *It all goes down in his notebook. He'll go down in history as a great statesman.* **go down to,** be continued or extended as far as: *This 'History of Europe' goes down to 1970.* **go down (with sb),** (of an explanation or excuse; of a story, play, etc) be accepted or approved (by the listener, reader, audience, etc): *The new play went down well/like a bomb* (= extremely well) *with provincial audiences. That explanation won't go down well with me. The new teacher doesn't go down well with his pupils.* **go down (with sth),** fall ill (with an illness): *Poor Peter —he's gone down with 'flu.* **go for sb, (a)** go to fetch: *Shall I go for a doctor?* **(b)** attack: *The dog went for the postman as soon as he opened the garden gate. Go for him!* (said to a dog to urge him to attack): *They went for me in the correspondence columns of the papers.* **(c)** be applicable to: *What I have said about Smith goes for you, too.* **go for nothing/little,** be considered of no/little value: *All his work went for nothing.* **go forth,** (formal) be published or issued: *The or-*

der went forth that....
go forward, (a) advance: *A patrol went forward to investigate.* **(b)** make progress: *The work is going forward well.* **go in, (a)** enter: *The key won't go in (the lock). This cork's too big; it won't go in. She went in to cook the dinner.* **(b)** (of the sun, moon, etc) be obscured by clouds: *The sun went in and it grew rather cold.* **(c)** (cricket, etc) begin an innings: *Who goes in next?* **(d)** enter as a competitor: *Go in and win!* (used as a form of encouragement). **go in for sth,** (a) take, enter (an examination or competition). **(b)** have an interest in, have as a hobby, etc: *go in for golf/stamp-collecting/growing orchids.* **go into sth, (a)** enter: *go into business; go into the Army/the Church/Parliament.* *go into Europe,* join the EEC? **go into details,** ⇨ detail¹(2). **(b)** investigate; examine carefully: *go into the evidence; go deeply into a question. This problem will need a lot of going into,* will need thorough investigation. **(c)** (allow oneself to) pass into (a certain state): *go into fits of laughter/ hysterical fits.* **go into mourning,** wear black clothes as a symbol of mourning. **go off, (a)** explode; be fired: *The gun went off by accident.* **(b)** lose good quality; deteriorate: *The cooking in the hotel has started to go off. This milk has gone off,* turned sour. *Meat and fish go off quickly in hot weather.* **(c)** become unconscious, either in sleep or in a faint: *Hasn't the baby gone off yet? She went off into a faint.* **(d)** (of goods) be got rid of by sale: *The goods went off quickly.* **(e)** (of events) proceed well, etc: *The performance/ concert went off well. How did the sports meeting go off?* **(f)** (as a stage direction in a printed play) leave the stage; exit/exeunt: *Hamlet goes off.* **go off sb/sth,** lose interest in or one's taste for: *Jane seems to have gone off Peter. I've gone off beer.* **go off the beaten track,** ⇨ beaten. **go off the deep end,** ⇨ end¹(1). **go off one's head,** ⇨ head¹(19). **go off with sb/sth,** go away with, esp abscond with or steal: *He's gone off to Edinburgh with his neighbour's wife. The butler went off with some of the duke's treasured possessions.* **go on, (a)** (of time) pass: *As the months went on, he became impatient.* **(b)** conduct oneself; behave, esp in a wrong, shameful or excited way: *If you go on like this you'll be thrown out.* **(c)** happen; take place; be in progress: *What's going on there? There's nothing interesting going on here at present. Harvesting was going on in the south. Things are going on much as usual.* **(d)** (theatre) appear on the stage: *She doesn't go on until Act Two.* **(e)** take one's turn at doing sth; (eg cricket) begin bowling: *The captain told Snow to go on next.* '**go on sth,** take or accept, eg as evidence: *What evidence have we got to go on,* to be guided by in reaching a decision, etc? **go on the dole/ social security/(US) welfare,** obtain, eg when unemployed, payments under various government schemes. **go on the pill,** start using contraceptive pills. **go on about sth,** talk persistently and often irritatingly about: *I wish you'd stop going on about my smoking.* **go on (at sb),** rail; nag; scold: *She goes on at her husband continually. Oh, you do go on! be going on (for),** (of age or time) be approaching: *He's going on (for) seventy.* **be gone on,** (sl) be infatuated with: *It's a pity Peter's so gone on Jane.* **go on to sth/to do sth,** do or say it next; proceed to it: *Let's now go on to the next item*

on the agenda. He went on to say that..., He next said that.... *I shall now go on to deal with our finances.* **go on (with sth/doing sth),** continue, persevere, with: *Go on with your work. How much longer will this hot weather go on? That's enough to go on with/to be going on with,* enough for our immediate needs. *Go on trying. I hope it won't go on raining all day.* **Go on (with you)!** (colloq) Don't expect me to believe that! Don't be so silly! etc, according to context. **,goings-'on** *n pl* (colloq) (often with *such strange/queer* happenings; behaviour: *I've never seen such queer goings-on!* **'on-going** *adj* continuing; progressing; evolving.

go out, (a) leave the room, building, etc: *She was (all) dressed to go out,* wearing outdoor clothes. *Out you go! Do you often go out riding* (ie on a horse)? **(b)** attend social functions, go to parties, dances, etc: *She still goes out a great deal, even at seventy-five.* **go out on a spree/on the town,** ⇨ spree, town. **(c)** be extinguished: *The fire* (eg the fire burning in the grate) *has gone out. There was a power cut and all the lights went out.* **(d)** become unfashionable: *Has the fashion for boots/Have boots gone out?* **(e)** (of a government) retire from power. **(f)** (as used by workers of themselves) strike: *Are we likely to gain anything by going out?* ⇨ **come out** in **come(15) (d).** **(g)** (of a year, etc) end: *The year went out gloomily.* **go out on a limb,** ⇨ limb(2). **go out to,** leave, eg one's own country, and go to: *He couldn't get work at home* (eg in England) *so went out to Australia.* **go out to sb,** (of the heart, feelings) be extended to: *Our hearts/sympathies go out to those poor children orphaned by war.* **go out with sb,** (colloq) be regularly in sb's company: *How long has Jane been going out with David? How long have Jane and David been going out together?*

go over, (colloq) make an impression: *I wonder whether this new play will go over,* whether it will impress the public, be favourably received. *David didn't go over well with Jane's parents at the weekend.* **go over sth, (a)** examine the details of: *We must go over the accounts carefully before we settle them.* **(b)** look at; inspect: *We should like to go over the house before deciding whether we want to buy it.* **(c)** rehearse; study or review carefully: *Let's go over this chapter/lesson/the main facts/ Scene 2 again.* Hence, **,going-'over** *n* (*pl* goings-over) **(a)** (colloq) process of examining or putting in good working order: *The document will need a careful going-over before we can make a decision. The patient was given a thorough going-over by/from the doctor.* **(b)** (sl) beating: *The thugs gave him a thorough going-over,* beat him repeatedly. **go over to sb/sth,** change one's political party, side, a preference, etc: *He has gone over to the Democrats. I'm going over to a milder brand of cigarettes.*

go round, (a) be enough, in number or amount, for everyone to have a share: *There aren't enough apples/isn't enough whisky to go round.* **(b)** reach one's destination by using a route other than the usual or nearest way: *The main road to Worcester was flooded and we had to go* (*a/the long way*) *round.* **go round (to a place/to do sth),** visit: *We're going round to my mother's/to see my mother at the weekend.* **go round the bend,** (colloq) become hysterical, enraged, mad, etc.

go through, (a) (= get through) be passed or approved: *The Bill* (ie in Parliament) *did not go through.* **(b)** be concluded: *The deal did not go through.* **go through sth, (a)** discuss in detail: *Let's go through the arguments again.* **(b)** search: *The police went through the pockets of the suspected thief.* **(c)** perform; take part in: *She made him go through both a civil and religious wedding. How long will it take to go through* (= complete) *the programme?* **(d)** undergo; suffer: *go through hardships. If you only knew what she has to go through with that husband of hers!* **(e)** (of a book) be sold: *The book went through ten editions,* Ten editions were sold out. **(f)** reach the end of; spend: *go through a fortune/all one's money.* **go through with sth,** complete; not leave unfinished: *He's determined to go through with the marriage in spite of his parents' opposition.*

go to/towards sth, contribute to, be contributed to: *What qualities go to the making of a statesman? This money can go towards the motor-bike you're saving up for.*

go together, (a) (of two or more things) be a normal accompaniment (of one another): *Crime and poverty often go together.* **(b)** match; be suitable together: *Do my green shirt and my blue jeans go together?* ⇨ go with **(c)** below.

go under, (a) sink. **(b)** (fig) fail; succumb; become bankrupt: *The firm will go under unless business improves.*

go up, (a) rise: *The barometer/temperature/ thermometer is going up. Everything went up* (ie in price) *in the budget except pensions.* **(b)** be erected: *New office blocks are going up everywhere.* **(c)** be blown up; be destroyed by explosion or fire: *The bridge went up with a roar when the mine exploded. The whole building went up in flames.* **(d)** enter a university or travel to a town, esp the capital: *go up to London/to town. When will you go up* (eg to Cambridge)? **go up sth,** climb: *go up a tree/ladder/wall/hill.* **go up the wall,** ⇨ wall.

go with sb/sth, (a) accompany: *I'll go with you. We must go with the times/tide,* do as others do nowadays. *He always goes with his party,* votes, etc as the party does. **(b)** take the same view as: *I can't go with you on that,* can't agree with you. **(c)** be a normal accompaniment of: *Five acres of land go with the house,* become the property of the buyers or are for the use of the tenant. *Disease often goes with squalor, but it is wrong to say that crime always goes with poverty.* **(d)** match; be fitting and suitable with: *These new curtains don't go well with your carpet,* don't suit them. *I want some shoes to go with these trousers.* **(e)** (colloq) (of a young man or girl) be often in the company of a person of the opposite sex possibly with a view to marriage: *go with a girl,* ⇨ go out with sb above.

go without (sth), endure the lack of: *The poor boy often has to go without supper. There's no money for a holiday this year; we'll just have to go without.* **go without saying,** be understood without actually being stated: *It goes without saying that she's a good cook.*

go² /gəʊ/ *n* (*pl* goes /gəʊz/) (all uses colloq) **all systems go,** (of launching or operating eg a spacecraft) all is ready to proceed. **all the go,** very popular, fashionable: *Leather pyjamas were all the go last year.* **at one go,** at one attempt: *He blew out all the candles on his birthday cake at one go.* **be full of go; have plenty of go,** be full of energy, enthusiasm. **be on the go,** be busy, active: *She's been on the go all day,* has had no rest.

have a go (at sth), make an attempt: *He had several goes at the high jump before he succeeded in clearing it. The police warned the public not to have a go because the bank raiders were armed,* not to try to intercept, catch them. *near go,* narrow escape. *no go,* **(a)** false start. **(b)** impossible or hopeless situation: *It'll be no go to ask/asking for a rise when you arrive so late.* ,*no-'go area,* one to which access is prohibited to those who do not live there.

go-between /'gəʊ bɪtwiːn/ *n* messenger or negotiator for two persons or groups who do not or can not meet: *In some countries marriages are arranged by* ~*s.*

go-cart /'gəʊ kɑːt/ *n* light handcart.

go-kart /'gəʊ kɑːt/ *n* small low racing car with open framework.

goad /gəʊd/ *n* pointed stick for urging cattle on; (fig) sth urging a person to action. □ *vt* [VP6A,15B,14,17] ~ *sb on;* ~ *sb into doing sth,* urge, drive forward: ~ *sb into a fury; be* ~*ed by hunger into stealing.*

goal /gəʊl/ *n* **1** point marking the end of a race; (football) posts between which the ball is to be driven in order to score; point(s) made by doing this: *score/kick a* ~*; win by three* ~*s to one; keep* ~, protect the ~. '~*-keeper,* ~*ie* /'gəʊli/ *n* (colloq) player whose duty is to keep the ball out of the ~. '~*-kick n* (Association football) kick by the defending side after the attacking side sends the ball over the ~-line; (Rugby football) attempt to kick a ~. '~*-line n* (football) line behind the ~ posts, reaching to the touch-lines. ⇨ *touch-line* at touch ¹(7); ⇨ the illus at football, Rugby. **2** (fig) object of efforts or ambition: *one's* ~ *in life; the* ~ *of his desires.*

goat /gəʊt/ *n* small, active horned animal, ⇨ the illus at domestic. '*she-*~ (or '*nanny-*~), female goat, kept for its milk. '*he-*~ (or '*billy-*~), male goat. ⇨ kid ¹(1). *get one's* ~, (sl) irritate or annoy one. *play/act the giddy* ~, play the fool; behave in a foolish and excited way. *separate the sheep from the* ~*s,* the good from the bad. '~*-herd n* person who looks after a flock of ~s. '~*-skin n* [C,U] (garment made of) skin of a goat. ~*-ee* /gəʊ'tiː/ *n* small tuft of hair on the chin like a ~'s beard.

gob¹ /gɒb/ *n* (vulg) clot or lump of slimy substance.

gob² /gɒb/ *n* (derog sl) mouth.

gob³ /gɒb/ *n* (US sl) sailor.

gob-bet /'gɒbɪt/ *n* [C] lump or chunk, esp of meat.

gobble¹ /'gɒbl/ *vt,vi* [VP6A,15B,2A] ~ *(up),* eat fast, noisily and greedily.

gobble² /'gɒbl/ *vi* [VP2A,C] (of a turkeycock) make the characteristic sound in the throat; (of a person) make such a sound when speaking, because of rage, etc. □ *n* characteristic sound made by a turkeycock.

gobble·dy·gook /'gɒbldɪguːk/ *n* [U] incomprehensible or pompous specialist's jargon.

gob-bler /'gɒblə(r)/ *n* (US) male turkey.

gob-let /'gɒblɪt/ *n* glass or pottery drinking-vessel with a stem and base and no handle.

gob-lin /'gɒblɪn/ *n* mischievous demon; ugly-looking evil spirit.

god /gɒd/ *n* **1** being regarded or worshipped as having power over nature and control over human affairs; image in wood, stone, etc to represent such a being: *the blind god* (or *god of love*), Cupid

/'kjuːpɪd/; *the god of the sea,* Neptune /'neptjuːn US:* -tuːn/; *a feast/sight for the gods,* something extraordinary, exquisite, etc. **2 God,** the Supreme Being, creator and ruler of the universe. *God (almighty)! Good God! int* (colloq) exclamations of surprise, shock etc. *God willing,* if circumstances permit. *God knows,* = *goodness knows,* ⇨ goodness(3). **3** person greatly adored or admired; very influential person; sth to which excessive attention is paid: *make a god of one's belly,* think excessively about food and drink. *He thinks he's a (little) tin god,* used eg of an official who expects undeserved and excessive respect. **4** (theatre) **the gods,** (persons in the) gallery seats. **5** (compounds) '*god-child,* '*god-daughter,* '*god-son nn* person for whom a godparent acts as sponsor at baptism. '*god-father,* '*god-mother,* '*god-parent nn* person who undertakes, when a child is baptized, to take an active interest in its welfare. '*god-damn(ed);* (US) '*god-dam* /'gɒdæm/ *adj, adv* ⚠ (sl; intensive) very; very great. '*god-fearing adj* reverent; living a good life and sincerely religious. '*god-for-saken adj* (of places) dismal; wretched. *God's 'acre n* (old use) churchyard. '*god-send* /-send/ *n* piece of good fortune coming unexpectedly; sth welcome because it is a great help in time of need. ,*god-'speed n bid/wish sb godspeed,* wish him success on a journey etc.

god-dess /'gɒdɪs/ *n* female god, esp in Greek and Latin mythology: *Diana, the* ~ *of hunting.*

god-head /'gɒdhed/ *n* [U] being God or a god; divine nature. *the G*~, God.

god-less /'gɒdlɪs/ *adj* wicked; not having belief in God; not recognizing God. ~*-ness n*

god-like /'gɒdlaɪk/ *adj* like God or a god in some quality.

god-ly /'gɒdlɪ/ *adj* (-ier, -iest) loving and obeying God; deeply religious. **god-li-ness** *n*

go-down /'gəʊdaʊn/ *n* (in the East) warehouse.

go-get-ter /,gəʊ 'getə(r)/ *n* (colloq) pushing, enterprising person.

goggle /'gɒgl/ *vi* [VP2A,3A] ~ *(at),* roll the eyes about (or *at* sth); stare at with bulging eyes: *He* ~*d at her in surprise. The frog's eyes seemed to be goggling out of its head.* '~*-box n* (sl) TV set. '~*-eyed adj* having staring, prominent, or rolling eyes.

goggles /'gɒglz/ *n pl* large round spectacles with hoods to protect the eyes from the wind, dust, water etc (worn by racing motorists, frogmen etc). ⇨ the illus at frog.

go-ing /'gəʊɪŋ/ *n* (⇨ also go ¹) **1** [U] condition of the ground, a road, a race-course, etc, for walking, riding, etc: *The* ~ *is hard over this mountain road.* **2** [U] method or speed of working or travelling: *For a steam train, 70 miles an hour is good* ~. **3** (usu *pl*) *comings and* ~*s,* (lit or fig) arrivals and departures: *the comings and* ~*s in the corridors of power.* □ *adj* a ~ *concern,* ⇨ go ¹(8).

goitre (US = **goi-ter**) /'gɔɪtə(r)/ *n* morbid swelling of the thyroid gland (in the neck).

gold /gəʊld/ *n* [U] **1** precious yellow metal used for making coins, ornaments, jewellery, etc: *currencies backed by* ~*; £500 in* ~, in ~ coins; (attrib) *a* ~ *watch/bracelet. worth one's weight in* ~, invaluable; indispensable. **2** money in large sums; wealth. **3** (fig) brilliant or precious things or qualities: *a heart of* ~*; a voice of* ~. **4** colour of the metal: *the red and* ~ *of the woods in autumn; old* ~, a dull, brownish-golden yellow. **5** (compounds) '~-**beater** *n* person whose trade is to beat ~ into ~-leaf. '~-**digger** *n* person who digs for ~; (sl) girl or woman who uses her attractions to extract money from men. '~-**dust** *n* ~ in the form of dust, as often found in ~fields. '~·**field** *n* district in which ~ is found. '~·**finch** *n* bright-coloured song-bird with yellow feathers in the wings. '~·**fish** *n* small red carp kept in bowls or ponds. ,~-'**foil**, ,~-'**leaf** *n* [U] ~ beaten into thin sheets. '~·**mine** *n* place where ~ is mined; (fig) source of wealth, eg a shop that is very successful in making money. ,~-'**plate** *n* [U] articles (spoons, dishes and other vessels) made of ~. '~-**rush** *n* rush to a newly discovered ~field. '~·**smith** *n* smith who makes articles of ~. '~ **standard**, ⇨ standard(4).

golden /'gəʊldən/ *adj* **1** of gold or like gold in value or colour: ~ *hair*. **2** precious; excellent; important: *a* ~ *opportunity*. **the** ,~ '**age**, (in Gk stories) the earliest and happiest period in history; period in a nation's history when art or literature was most flourishing. ,~ '**handshake**, (usu large) sum of money given to a high-ranking member of a company when he retires (in recognition of good work and loss of continuation of salary). **the** ,~ '**mean**, the principle of moderation. **the** ,~ '**rule**, any important rule of conduct (esp Matt 7:12, *Treat others as you would like them to treat you*). ,~ '**wedding**, fiifieth wedding anniversary.

golf /gɒlf/ *n* [U] game played by two or four persons, each with a small, hard '~-**ball**, driven with a '~-**club**, into a series of 9 or 18 holes on smooth greens(4) over a stretch of land (a '~-**course**/ **links**). □ *vi* play ~. ~**er** *n* person who plays ~.

Gol·iath /gə'laɪəθ/ *n* giant. ⇨ 1 Sam 17.

gol·li·wog /'gɒlɪwɒg/ *n* black-faced doll with thick stiff hair.

golly /'gɒlɪ/ *int* (sl) used to express surprise.

go·losh *n* ⇨ galosh.

gon·dola /'gɒndələ/ *n* long, flat-bottomed boat with high peaks at each end, used on canals in Venice. **gon·do·lier** /,gɒndə'lɪə(r)/ *n* man who propels a ~.

a gondola

gone /gɒn US: gɔːn/ *pp* of go.

goner /'gɒnə(r) US: 'gɔːn-/ *n* (sl) person or thing in desperate straits, ruined or doomed.

gong /gɒŋ/ *n* metal disc with a turned rim giving a resonant note when struck with a stick, esp as a signal, eg for meals. □ *vt* (of traffic police) direct (a motorist) to stop by striking a ~.

gonna /'gɒnə/ (US sl) = *going to*. ⇨ go¹(27).

gon·or·rhea (also **-rhoea**) /,gɒnə'rɪə/ *n* [U] contagious venereal disease which causes an inflammatory discharge from the genital organs.

goo /guː/ *n* [U] (sl) sticky wet material; sentimentality. **gooey** /'guːɪ/ *adj* sticky.

good¹ /gʊd/ *adj* (better, best) **1** having the right or desired qualities; giving satisfaction: *a* ~ (eg sharp) *knife; a* ~ *fire*, one that is bright and cheerful, giving warmth; ~ (= fertile) *soil. Is raw herring* ~ *eating*, Is it enjoyable to eat it? **2** beneficial; wholesome: *Is this water* ~ *to drink*, Is it

clean and pure? *Milk is* ~ *for children. Exercise is* ~ *for the health.* **3** efficient; competent; able to do satisfactorily what is required: *a* ~ *teacher/ driver/worker; a* ~ *man for the position;* ~ *at mathematics/languages/describing scenery. She has been a* ~ *wife to him.* **4** pleasing; agreeable; advantageous: ~ *news. It's* ~ *to be home again.* **have a** ~ **time**, enjoy oneself. Hence, '~-**time** **girl**, (colloq) one whose chief aim is enjoyment. **(all) in** ~ **time**, at a suitable or advantageous time. **be a** ~ **thing**, be sth that one approves of: *Do you think lower taxes are a* ~ *thing?* **be a** ~ **thing that ...**, be fortunate that ...: *have a good/bad night*, sleep well/badly. **put in/say a** ~ **word for sb**, say sth in his favour. **start/arrive/leave in** ~ **time**, early. **5** kind; benevolent; willing to help others: *It was* ~ *of you to help them. Will you be* ~ *enough to/be so* ~ *as to come early? How* ~ *of you!* Cf *do sb a* ~ *turn*, ⇨ turn¹(5); (in exclamations of surprise, shock, etc.) ,G~ 'God! ,G~ 'Gracious! ,G~ 'Heavens! **6** thorough; sound; complete: *give sb a* ~ *beating/scolding; have a* ~ *drink; find a* ~ *excuse; go for a* ~ *long walk.* **have a** ~ **mind (to do sth)**, feel a strong desire to: *I've a* ~ *mind to report you to the police.* **7** strong; vigorous: *His eyesight is still* ~. *The children were in* ~ *spirits.* ⇨ *low spirits* at low²(6). **8** amusing: *a* ~ *story/joke; as* ~ *as a play.* **9** fresh; eatable; untainted: *Fish does not keep* ~ *in hot weather. This meat doesn't smell quite* ~. **10** reliable; safe; sure: *a car with* ~ *brakes;* ~ *debts*, debts that will certainly be paid. ⇨ *bad debts* at bad¹(4). *He's a* ~ *life*, is healthy and is, therefore, likely to be acceptable for life assurance. ~ **for**, (a) safely to be trusted for (the amount stated): *His credit is* ~ *for £5000.* (b) (of a draft, etc) drawn for (the amount stated): ~ *for £5.* (c) having the necessary energy, inclination, etc: *He's* ~ *for several years' more service. My car is* ~ *for another five years. Are you* ~ *for a five-mile walk?* (d) valid: *The return half of the ticket is* ~ *for three months.* '~-**for-nothing**, '~-**for-naught** *adjj, nn* worthless (person). **11** (esp of a child) well behaved; not giving trouble: *Try to be a* ~ *boy.* **as** ~ **as gold**, giving no trouble. **12** morally excellent; virtuous: *a* ~ *and holy man; live a* ~ *life.* ,~ '**works**, charitable deeds, helping the poor, the sick, etc. **13** right; proper; expedient: *He thought it* ~ *to offer his help.* (As an *int*, expressing approval): 'You will come with us?' 'G~!' **14** in forms of greeting and farewell: *G~ morning/afternoon/evening/night*. **15** as a polite (but often ironical, patronizing or indignant) form of address: *my* ~ *sir/man/friend*; or as a polite (but often condescending) description: *How's your* ~ *man* (ie your husband)? *How's the* ~ *lady* (ie your wife)? **the** '~ **people**, the fairies. **16** as a form of commendation: ~ *men and true. G~ old Smith! That's a* ~ *'un!* /'gʊdn/ (colloq) an amusing lie or story. **17** considerable in number, quantity, etc: *a* ~ *deal of money; a* ~ *many people; a* ~ *few*, a considerable number. *We've come a* ~ *way*, quite a long way. **18** not less than; rather more than: *We waited for a* ~ *hour. It's a* ~ *three miles to the station. He ate a* ~ *half of the duck.* **19** *as* ~ *as*, practically; almost: *He as* ~ *as said I was a liar*, suggested that I was a liar without actually using the word 'liar'. *My car is as* ~ *as new*, even though I've had it a year. *The matter is as* ~ *as settled*, We may look upon it as being settled. **20** *make* ~, accomplish what one attempts; prosper: *He went to Canada, where he soon made* ~. [VP22] **make sth** ~, (a) compensate for; pay for (sth lost or damaged): *make* ~ *a loss or theft*. (b) effect (a purpose): *make* ~ *one's escape*. (c) prove the truth of an accusation, a statement, etc. (d) restore to sound condition: *The plaster will have to be made* ~ *before you paint it.* 21 (phrases and compounds) ~-'**fellowship** *n* sociability. ~ '**humour** *n* cheerful mood; happy state of mind. ~-'**humoured** *adj* cheerful, amiable. ~ '**looks** *n pl* personal beauty. ~-'**looking** *adj* (usu of persons) handsome. ~ '**money**, (a) genuine money. (b) (colloq) high wages. **throw** ~ **money after bad,** lose money in trying to regain money lost. ~-'**natured** *adj* kind; ready and willing to help others, even by sacrificing one's own interests. ~-'**neighbourliness** *n* friendly conduct and relations. ~ '**sense** *n* [U] soundness of judgement; practical wisdom. ~-'**tempered** *adj* not easily irritated or made angry.

good[2] /gʊd/ *n* [U] 1 that which is ~; what is morally right, beneficial, advantageous, profitable, etc; what has use, worth, value. **do** ~, help: *Social workers do a lot of* ~. ⇨ do-gooder at do[2](2). **(do sth) for the** ~ **of,** in order to benefit: *He works for the* ~ *of the country. I'm giving you this advice for your* ~. *Is it right to deceive people, even if it's for their own* ~? **do sb** ~, benefit him: *Eat more fruit: it will do you* ~. *Smoking does you more harm than* ~. *Much* ~ *may it do you,* (usu ironic, meaning) You won't get much benefit from it. **be up to no** ~, be engaged in sth wrong, mischievous, etc. **be no/not much/any/some** ~ **(doing sth),** be no, not much, etc use, of no, little, etc value: *It's no* ~ *(my) talking to him. Was his advice ever any* ~? *What* ~ *was it? This gadget isn't much* ~. **2 for** ~ **(and all),** permanently; finally: *He says that he's leaving the country for* ~, intending never to return to it. **3 to the** ~, as balance on the right side, as net profit: *We were £5 to the* ~. **4** (*adj* as *pl n*) good or virtuous persons: *G*~ *and bad alike respected him.*

good·bye /ˌgʊd'baɪ/ *int, n* *fast or informal:* gʊ'baɪ/ (saying of) farewell: *'I must say* ~ *now',* It is time for me to leave. *Have you said all your* ~s?

good·ish /'gʊdɪʃ/ *attrib adj* rather large, extensive, etc: *It's a* ~ *step from here,* quite a long way.

good·ly /'gʊdlɪ/ *adj* (-ier, -iest) (liter) 1 handsome; pleasant-looking. 2 of considerable size: *a* ~ *sum of money; a* ~ *heritage.*

good·ness /'gʊdnɪs/ *n* [U] 1 quality of being good; virtue: ~ *of heart.* **have the** ~ **to,** be kind enough to: *Have the* ~ *to come this way, please.* 2 strength or essence: *meat with the* ~ *boiled out.* 3 (in exclamations) used instead of *God!: G*~ *Gracious! G*~ *me! For* ~' *sake! Thank* ~*! I wish to* ~ *that...,* wish very strongly that.... *G*~ *knows,* (a) I do not know. (b) I appeal to Heaven to witness: *G*~ *knows I've tried hard.*

goods /gʊdz/ *n pl* 1 movable property; merchandise: *He buys and sells leather* ~s. *Half his* ~s *were stolen.* ~s **and** '**chattels,** (legal) personal belongings. 2 things carried by rail, etc (contrasted with passengers): *a* '~s *agent/station.* '~ **train,** ie not a passenger train (US = *freight train*). **piece of** ~s, (colloq) person: *She's a sexy little piece of* ~s, a sexy young girl.

good·will /ˌgʊd'wɪl/ *n* [U] 1 friendly feeling: *a policy of* ~ *in international relations.* 2 privilege of trading as the successor to a well-established busi-

ness: *The* ~ *is to be sold with the business.*

goody /'gʊdɪ/ *n* (colloq) sweetmeat; desirable thing.,

goody-goody /'gʊdɪ gʊdɪ/ *adj, n* (person who is) primly or pretentiously virtuous.

gooey /'guːɪ/ *adj* ⇨ goo.

goof /guːf/ (sl) *n* silly or stupid person. □ *vi,vt* [VP2A,6A] make a mess (of). ~y *adj* silly, stupid, crazy.

goog·ly /'guːglɪ/ *n* (*pl* -lies) (cricket) ball bowled as if to break in one way that actually breaks in the opposite way.

goon /guːn/ *n* (sl) stupid or awkward person.

goose /guːs/ *n* (*pl* geese /giːs/) 1 water bird larger than a duck; female of this, ⇨ gander; ⇨ the illus at fowl. [U] its flesh as food. **cook sb's** ~, put an end to his hopes; prevent him from being a nuisance, etc. **kill the** ~ **that lays the golden eggs,** (prov) sacrifice future gains to satisfy present needs. **be unable to say 'boo' to a** ~, be very timid. **All one's geese are swans,** One overestimates or exaggerates the good qualities of persons and things. '~-**flesh** *n* [U] rough bristling skin caused by cold or fear. '~-**step** *n* way of marching without bending the knees. 2 simpleton: *You silly* ~!

goose·berry /'gʊzbərɪ *US:* 'guːsberɪ/ *n* (*pl* -ries) [C] (bush with) green, smooth berry (used for jam, tarts, etc). ⇨ the illus at fruit. **play** ~, be present with two persons, eg lovers, who prefer to be alone.

go·pher /'gəʊfə(r)/ *n* burrowing rat-like animal in N America.

Gor·dian /'gɔːdɪən/ *adj* (only in) ~ **knot,** knot difficult or impossible to untie; difficult problem or task. **cut the** ~ **knot,** solve a problem by force or by disregarding the conditions.

gore[1] /gɔː(r)/ *n* [U] (liter, chiefly in descriptions of fighting) thickened blood from a cut or wound.

gore[2] /gɔː(r)/ *vt* [VP6A] pierce, wound, with the horns or tusks: ~*d to death by an infuriated bull.*

gorge[1] /gɔːdʒ/ *n* 1 narrow opening, usu with a stream, between hills or mountains. 2 gullet; contents of the stomach: *His* ~ *rose at the sight/It made his* ~ *rise,* He was sickened or disgusted.

gorge[2] /gɔːdʒ/ *vi,vt* [VP6A,14,2A,C] ~ **(oneself) (on/with sth),** eat greedily; fill oneself: ~ *on rich food;* ~ *oneself with meat.* □ *n* act of gorging; surfeit.

gorg·eous /'gɔːdʒəs/ *adj* 1 richly coloured; magnificent: *a* ~ *sunset.* 2 (colloq) giving pleasure and satisfaction: ~ *weather; a* ~ *dinner.* ~-**ly** *adv*

Gor·gon /'gɔːgən/ *n* (Gk myth) one of three snake-haired sisters whose looks turned to stone anyone who saw them.

Gor·gon·zola /ˌgɔːgən'zəʊlə/ *n* [U] rich creamy blue-veined cheese (from ~ in Italy).

gor·illa /gə'rɪlə/ *n* man-sized, tree-climbing African ape. ⇨ the illus at ape.

gor·man·dize /'gɔːməndaɪz/ *vi* eat, devour, greedily for pleasure.

gorse /gɔːs/ *n* [U] yellow-flowered evergreen shrub with sharp thorns, growing on waste land (also called *furze* or whin).

gory /'gɔːrɪ/ *adj* (-ier, -iest) covered with blood; of bloody physical violence: ~ *details/incidents.*

gosh /gɒʃ/ *int* (sl) (also **by** ~) by God.

gos·ling /'gɒzlɪŋ/ *n* young goose.

gos·pel /'gɒspl/ *n* **the G**~ [U] (the life and teachings of Jesus as recorded in the) first four books of the New Testament; [C] any one of these; set of principles that one acts upon or believes in: *the ~ of health; the ~ of soap and water,* (hum for) firm belief in the value of cleanliness.

gos·sa·mer /'gɒsəmə(r)/ *n* **1** [C,U] (thread of the) fine silky substance of webs made by small spiders, floating in calm air or spread on grass, etc. **2** [U] soft, light, delicate material: *as light as ~*; (attrib) *a ~ veil.*

gos·sip /'gɒsɪp/ *n* **1** [U] idle, often ill-natured, talk about the affairs of other people: *Don't believe all the ~ you hear. She's too fond of ~.* **2** [U] informal writing about persons and social happenings, eg in letters or in newspapers: (attrib) *the '~ column,* of a newspaper; *a '~ writer/columnist.* **3** [C] instance of this; friendly chat: *have a good ~ with a neighbour over the garden fence.* **4** [C] person who is fond of ~: *She's an old ~.* □ *vi* (-p- or -pp-; US -p-) [VP2A,C] talk or write ~.

got *pt,pp* of **get.**

Goth /gɒθ/ *n* member of a Germanic tribe that invaded the Roman Empire in the 3rd and 4th cc; rough, uncivilized person. ⇨ **vandal.**

Gothic /'gɒθɪk/ *adj* **1** of the Goths or their language. **2** of the style of architecture common in Western Europe in the 12th to 16th cc, characterized by pointed arches, clusters of columns, etc. ⇨ the illus at **church.** **3** of an 18th c style of fantastic, romantic literature: *~ novels.* **4** (of printing type) thick or heavy, as formerly used for German. □ *n* ~ language; ~ architecture; ~ type.

gotta /'gɒtə/ (US sl) = *have got to.* ⇨ **get(13).**

got·ten *pp* (in US) of **get.**

gouache /gʊ'ɑːʃ/ *n* [U] opaque watercolour paint; method of painting using this material.

gouge /gaʊdʒ/ *n* tool with a sharp semicircular edge for cutting grooves in wood. □ *vt* [VP6A,15B] ~ *(out),* cut with a ~; shape with a ~; force out with, or as with, a ~: *~ out the stone from a horseshoe.*

gou·lash /'guːlæʃ/ *n* [C,U] (dish of) stew of steak and vegetables, seasoned with paprika.

gourd /gʊəd/ *n* (large, hard-skinned fleshy fruit of) kind of climbing or trailing plant; bottle or bowl consisting of the dried skin of this fruit.

decorated gourds

gour·mand /'gʊəmənd/ *n* lover of food.

gour·met /'gʊəmeɪ/ *n* person who enjoys, and is expert in the choice of, delicate food, wines, etc.

gout /gaʊt/ *n* [U] disease causing painful swellings in joints, esp toes, knees and fingers. ~**y** *adj* suffering from ~.

gov·ern /'gʌvn/ *vt,vi* **1** [VP6A,2A] rule (a country, etc); control or direct the public affairs of (a city, country, etc): *In Great Britain the sovereign reigns but does not ~.* **2** [VP6A] control: *~ one's temper.*

3 [VP6A] (usu passive) determine; influence: *be ~ed by the opinions of others. Don't be ~ed by what other people say.* **4** (gram, esp of a *v* or *prep*) require, make necessary (a certain case or form of another word). ~**·ing** *adj* having the power or right to ~: *the ~ing body of a school/college, etc.*

gov·ern·ance /'gʌvənəns/ *n* [U] (formal) act, fact, manner, of governing; sway, control.

gov·ern·ess /'gʌvənɪs/ *n* woman who is employed to teach young children in a private family.

gov·ern·ment /'gʌvənmənt/ *n* **1** [U] governing; power to govern: *What the country needs is strong ~.* **2** [U] method or system of governing: *We prefer democratic ~.* **3** [C] body of persons governing a State: *The Prime Minister has formed a G~,* has chosen his colleagues, selected Ministers for the Cabinet. *The G~* (collectively) *has welcomed the proposal. The G~* (its members) *are discussing the proposal.* **G~ House,** official residence of the Governor (of a province, etc). **G~ securities,** bonds, exchequer bills, etc, issued by the state. ~**al** /ˌgʌvn'mentl/ *adj* connected with ~.

gov·ernor /'gʌvənə(r)/ *n* **1** G~, person who governs a province or colony or (US) a State: *the G~ of New York State.* Cf *the Mayor of New York City.* ˌG~-'General *n* (in the British Commonwealth) representative of the Crown, having no special powers: *the G~-General of Canada.* **2** member of the governing body of an institution (eg a school in England, a college, a hospital). **3** (colloq) chief; employer; father. **4** regulator in a machine, automatically controlling speed or the intake of gas, steam, etc.

gown /gaʊn/ *n* **1** woman's dress, esp one for special occasions: *a 'ball-/'night-~.* **2** loose, flowing robe worn by members of a university, judges, etc. ⇨ the illus at **judge.** □ *vt* (chiefly *pp*) dress in a ~: *beautifully ~ed women.*

grab /græb/ *vt,vi* (-bb-) [VP6A,3A] ~ *(at),* take roughly; selfishly or eagerly snatch: *The dog ~bed the bone and ran off with it. Don't ~! He ~bed at the opportunity of going abroad.* □ *n* [C] **1** sudden snatch: *make a ~ at something.* **2** mechanical device for taking up and holding sth to be lifted or moved. ~**·ber** *n* person who ~s; greedy person whose chief aim in life appears to be making money.

grace /greɪs/ *n* **1** [U,C] quality of being pleasing, attractive or beautiful, esp in structure or movement: *She danced with ~/with a ~ that surprised us.* **2** [C] (usu *pl*) pleasing accomplishment; elegance of manner. **airs and ~s,** ways of speaking and behaving that are intended to impress and attract people. **3** [U] favour; goodwill. **an act of ~,** sth freely given, not taken as a right. **days of ~,** time allowed by the law or custom after the day on which a payment, eg of a bill of exchange, or an insurance premium, is due. **give sb a day's/week's, etc ~,** allow him an extra day, etc before requiring him to fulfil an obligation. **be in sb's good ~s,** enjoy his favour and approval. **4** [U] **have the ~ to do sth,** realize that it is right and proper, and do it: *He had the ~ to say that he was sorry.* **do sth with a good/bad ~,** do it willingly/reluctantly. **5** [U,C] short prayer of thanks before or after a meal: *say (a) ~.* **6** [U] God's mercy and favour towards mankind; influence and result of this. **in the year of ~,** in the 19..., in the 19...th year after the birth of Jesus. **in a state of ~,** being influenced by the strength and inspiring power of God; having been

pardoned; having received the Sacraments. **fall from ~,** fall to a lower moral state after being in a state of ~. **7** as a title, used when speaking of or to an archbishop, duke or duchess: *His/Her/Your G~.* **8 the G~s,** (Gk myth) three beautiful sister goddesses who gave beauty, charm and happiness. □ *vt* [VP6A] add ~ to; confer honour or dignity on; be an ornament to: *The occasion was ~d by the presence of the Queen. Her character is ~d with every virtue.*
grace·ful /'greɪsfl/ *adj* having or showing grace(1,4): *a ~ dancer; a ~ letter of thanks.* **~ly** /-fəlɪ/ *adv*
grace·less /'greɪslɪs/ *adj* without grace(4); without a sense of what is right and proper: *~ behaviour.* **~·ly** *adv*
gra·cious /'greɪʃəs/ *adj* **1** (of persons and their behaviour) kind; generous; courteous: *her ~ Majesty the Queen. It was ~ of her to come.* **2** (of God) merciful. **3** (in exclamations) expressing surprise: *Good(ness) G~! G~ me!* **~·ly** *adv* **~·ness** *n*
gra·da·tion /grə'deɪʃn *US:* greɪ-/ *n* [C,U] step, stage, degree in development; gradual change from one thing to another or from one state to another: *the ~s of colour in the rainbow.*
grade¹ /greɪd/ *n* [C] **1** step, stage or degree in rank, quality, value, etc; number or class of things of the same kind: *The rank of major is one ~ higher than that of captain. Potatoes are sold in ~s, and G~ A potatoes are of the best quality. This pupil has a high ~ of intelligence.* **2** (US) division of the school course; one year's work; pupils in such a division: *An elementary school in the US has eight ~s and is called a '~ school'. Its teachers are called '~ teachers'.* **3** the mark, eg 80%, or rating, eg 'Excellent' or 'Fair', given to a pupil for his work in school. **make the ~,** (colloq) reach a good standard; do as well as is required. **4** (US) slope of a road, railway, etc (GB = *gradient*). **on the 'up/'down ~,** rising/falling: *Business is on the up ~,* is improving. **~ crossing,** (US) level crossing.
grade² /greɪd/ *vt* [VP6A] **1** arrange in order in grades or classes: *~ potatoes; ~d by size.* **2** make land (esp for roads) more nearly level by reducing the slope. **3** [VP6A,15B] **~ (up),** cross (cattle) with a better breed.
gra·di·ent /'greɪdɪənt/ *n* degree of slope: *a ~ of one in nine; a steep ~.*
grad·ual /'grædʒʊəl/ *adj* taking place by degrees; (of a slope) not steep: *a ~ increase in the cost of living.* **~·ly** /-dʒʊlɪ/ *adv* by degrees. **~·ness** *n*
grad·uate¹ /'grædʒʊət/ *n* **1** (GB) person who holds a university degree, esp the first, or Bachelor's, degree: *Oxbridge ~s; a ~ student; post-~ studies.* **2** (US) one who has completed a course at an educational institution: *high school ~s; a ~ nurse,* one from a College or School of Nursing. (Cf *trained nurse* in GB).
grad·uate² /'grædʒʊeɪt/ *vt,vi* **1** [VP6A] mark with degrees for measuring: *a ruler ~d in both inches and centimetres; a ~d glass,* for measuring quantities of liquid. **2** [VP6A] arrange according to grade. **3** [VP2A,C] take an academic degree: *He ~d from Oxford/~d in law.* (US, of other institutions): *a ~ from the Boston School of Cookery.* **4** [VP6A] (chiefly US) give a degree or diploma to: *The university ~d 350 students last year. He had been ~d from Maryland College in the Class of 1868.*
gradu·ation /ˌgrædʒʊ'eɪʃn/ *n* graduating or being

~d; (US) ceremony at which degrees are conferred.
graf·fito /grə'fi:təʊ/ *n* (*pl* -ti /-ti:/) (usu *pl*) (I) drawing, words, scratched on a hard surface, esp a wall.
graft¹ /grɑ:ft *US:* græft/ *n* **1** shoot from a branch or twig of a living tree, fixed in a cut made in another tree, to form a new growth. **2** (surgery) piece of skin, bone, etc from a living person or animal, transplanted on another body or another part of the same body. □ *vt,vi* [VP6A,15A,B,2A] put a ~ in or on: *~ one variety on/upon/in/into another; ~ on briar roots; ~ new skin.*

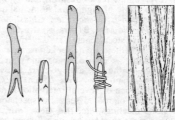

grafting   wood grain

graft² /grɑ:ft *US:* græft/ *n* [C,U] (instance of) getting business advantages, profit-making, etc through illegal or unethical means, eg by taking wrong advantage of connections in politics, by bribery etc. □ *vi* practise ~.
grail /greɪl/ *n* (usu **the Holy G~**) platter or cup used by Jesus at the Last Supper and in which one of his followers is said to have received drops of his blood at the Crucifixion.
grain /greɪn/ *n* **1** [U] (collective *sing*) small, hard seed of food plants such as wheat and rice: *~ imports; a cargo of ~.* '~ *elevator,* storehouse for ~, with devices for lifting ~. ⇨ the illus at cereal. **2** [C] single seed of such a plant: *give a beggar a few ~s of rice; eat up every ~ of rice in one's bowl.* **3** [C] tiny, hard bit: *~s of sand/salt/gold;* (fig) small amount: *a boy without a ~ of sense; receive a few ~s of comfort.* **4** smallest unit of weight, 1/7000 lb or 0·065 gm. ⇨ App 5. **5** [U] natural arrangement or pattern of the lines of fibre in wood, etc as seen on a surface that has been sawn or cut: *woods of fine/coarse ~.* **be/go against the ~,** (fig) contrary to one's nature or inclination.
gram /græm/ *n* metric unit of weight. ⇨ App 5.
gram·mar /'græmə(r)/ *n* **1** [U] study or science of, rules for, the combination of words into sentences (*syntax*), and the forms of words (*morphology*). **2** [C] book containing the rules of ~ of a language. '~ **school,** (in GB) type of secondary school which provides academic (contrasted with technical) courses. **~·ian** /grə'meərɪən/ *n* expert in ~.
gram·mati·cal /grə'mætɪkl/ *adj* of, conforming to, the rules of grammar: *a ~ error/explanation/sentence.* **~·ly** /-klɪ/ *adv*
gramme /græm/ *n* = gram.
gramo·phone /'græməfəʊn/ *n* (US = *phonograph*) machine for reproducing music and speech recorded on flat discs (*record-player* is now the usu word).
gram·pus /'græmpəs/ *n* large dolphin-like sea animal; person who breathes loudly.
gran·ary /'grænərɪ/ *n* (*pl* -ries) storehouse for

grain.

grand /grænd/ *adj* **1** (in official titles) chief; most important: *G~ Master,* eg of some orders of knighthood; *a ~ master,* chess champion; *G~ Vizier,* (former title of) chief minister of Turkey. **2** of most or greatest importance: *the ~ finale; the ~ question; the ~ staircase/entrance,* of a large building. **3** magnificent; splendid: *a ~ view; living in ~ style; ~ clothes.* **4** self-important; proud: *He puts on a very ~ manner/air.* **5** (colloq) very fine or enjoyable: *We had a ~ time. What ~ weather!* **6** full; complete: *a ~ orchestra,* one with all kinds of instruments (not strings only); *the ~ total,* including everything; *the ~ result of our efforts.* **7** impressive because of high moral or mental qualities: *Lincoln had a ~ character. Gladstone was called the G~ Old Man.* **8** (phrases) **the ,G~ 'National,** annual steeplechase at Liverpool. **,~ 'opera,** in which there are no spoken parts, everything being sung. **,~ pi'ano,** large piano with horizontal strings. ⇨ the illus at keyboard. **,baby '~,** small-size ~ piano. **G~ Prix** /ˌɡrɑːn 'priː/, (F) (motor-racing) one of several international races. **'~-stand,** rows of roofed seats for spectators at races, sports-meetings, etc. **the ,G~ 'Tour,** (formerly) tour of the chief towns, etc of Europe, completing the education of a wealthy young person. **~·ly** *adv*

grand- /grænd/ *pref* **'~-child, '~-daughter, '~-son** *nn* daughter or son of one's son or daughter. **'~-parent, '~-father, '~-mother** *nn* father or mother of one's father or mother. **'~-nephew, '~-niece** *nn* son or daughter of one's nephew or niece. **'~-uncle, '~-aunt** *nn* uncle or aunt of either of one's parents. **'~-father clock** *n* clock worked by weights in a tall wooden case.

grand-dad, gran-dad /'grændæd/ *n* (colloq for) grandfather.

gran-dee /græn'diː/ *n* (hist) Spanish or Portuguese nobleman of high rank.

gran-deur /'grændʒə(r)/ *n* [U] greatness; magnificence: *the ~ of the Swiss Alps.*

gran-dilo-quent /græn'dɪləkwənt/ *adj* using, full of, pompous words: *a ~ speaker; written in a ~ style.* **gran-dilo-quence** /-əns/ *n* [U].

gran-di-ose /'grændɪəʊs/ *adj* planned on a large scale; imposing.

grand-ma /'grænmɑː/ *n* (colloq for) grandmother.

grand-pa /'grænpɑː/ *n* (colloq for) grandfather.

grange /greɪndʒ/ *n* country house with farm buildings attached.

gran-ite /'grænɪt/ *n* [U] hard, usu grey, stone used for building.

granny, gran-nie /'grænɪ/ *n* (colloq for) grandmother. **'~ knot,** reef-knot crossed the wrong way and therefore insecure. ⇨ the illus at knot.

grant /grɑːnt/ *US:* grænt/ *vt* **1** [VP6A,12A,13A] consent to give or allow (what is asked for): *~ a favour/request; ~ sb permission/a request to do sth. He was ~ed a pension.* **2** [VP6A,9,25] agree (that sth is true): *~ the truth of what someone says; ~ing this to be true/that this is true. I ~ his honesty/~ that he is honest. He's an honest man, I ~ you.* **take sth for ~ed,** regard it as true or as certain to happen. **take sb for ~ed,** treat his presence and actions as a due rather than a favour. □ *n* sth ~ed, eg money or land from a government: *~s towards the cost of a university education; ~-aided schools/students.*

granu-lar /'grænjʊlə(r)/ *adj* of or like grains.

granu-late /'grænjʊleɪt/ *vt,vi* [VP6A,2A] form into grains; roughen the surface of: *~d sugar,* sugar in the form of small crystals.

gran-ule /'grænjuːl/ *n* [C] small grain.

grape /greɪp/ *n* green or purple berry growing in clusters on vines, used for making wine: *a bunch of ~s.* ⇨ the illus at fruit. **sour ~s; the ~s are sour,** said when sb says that sth he wants but cannot get has little or no value. **'~-shot** *n* [U] (hist) cluster of small iron balls fired together from a cannon to make a hail of shot. ⇨ shrapnel. **'~-sugar** *n* dextrose or glucose, a kind of sugar found in ripe ~s and other kinds of fruit. **'~-vine** *n* (a) kind of vine on which ~s grow. **(b)** (fig) means by which news gets about, eg in an office, school or a group of friends: *I heard on the ~-vine that Jill is to be promoted.*

grape-fruit /'greɪpfruːt/ *n* (*pl* ~ or ~s) [C] fruit like a large orange but with an acid taste. ⇨ the illus at fruit.

graph /grɑːf *US:* græf/ *n* [C] diagram consisting of a line or lines (often curved) showing the variation of two quantities, eg the temperature at each hour. **'~ paper,** paper with small squares of equal size.

graphic /'græfɪk/ *adj* **1** of visual symbols (eg lettering, diagrams, drawings): *a ~ artist; ~ displays; the ~ arts.* **2** (of descriptions) causing one to have a clear picture in the mind: *a ~ account of the battle.* □ *n pl* ~s, lettering, drawings, etc. **graphi-cally** /-klɪ/ *adv* by writing or diagrams; (fig) vividly.

graph-ite /'græfaɪt/ *n* [U] soft, black substance (a form of carbon) used in lubrication, as a moderator in atomic piles, and in making lead pencils.

grap-nel /'græpnəl/ *n* **1** anchor with many flukes[2]; instrument as used for dragging along the bed of a river, lake, etc when searching for sth. **2** instrument like this formerly used in sea battles for holding enemy ships.

grapple /'græpl/ *vi* [VP2A,C,3A] ~ **(with),** seize firmly; struggle with sb/sth at close quarters; (fig) try to deal with (a problem, etc): *~ with an enemy. The wrestlers ~d together.* **'grappling-iron** *n* grapnel.

grasp /grɑːsp *US:* græsp/ *vt,vi* **1** [VP6A] seize firmly with the hand(s) or arm(s); understand with the mind: *~ sb's hand/a rope; ~ an argument/sb's meaning.* **2** [VP3A] ~ **at,** try to seize; accept eagerly: *~ at an opportunity. A man who ~s at too much may lose everything.* □ *n* (usu *sing*) firm hold or grip; (power of) grasping: *in the ~ of a wicked enemy; have a thorough ~ of the problem; a problem within/beyond my ~,* that I can/cannot understand. **~·ing** *adj* eager to ~; greedy (for money, etc): *a ~ing rascal.*

grass[1] /grɑːs *US:* græs/ *n* **1** [U] kinds of common, wild, low-growing plant of which the green blades and stalks are eaten by cattle, horses, sheep, etc. **not let the ~ grow under one's feet,** (fig) waste no time in doing sth. **2** [C] (*pl* ~es) any species of this plant (including, in botanical use, cereals, reeds and bamboos). **3** [U] grazing land; pasture: (of animals) *at ~,* grazing. **put/send/turn animals out to ~,** put them to graze. **~-land** /-lænd/ *n* area of land covered with ~ where there are few trees. **~·'roots** *n pl* (often attrib) ordinary people remote from political decisions, but who are affected by these decisions: *a ~roots movement/ rebellion. We must not neglect the ~roots.* **~ 'widow** *n* wife whose husband is temporarily not living with her. ~y adj (-ier, -iest) covered with ~.

grass² /grɑːs US græs/ vt,vi **1** [VP6A,15B] ~ (over), cover with turf; [VP6A] (US) feed with grass. **2** [VP2A,3A] ~ (on sb), (GB sl) inform (on); betray.

grass-hopper /'grɑːshɒpə(r) US: 'græs-/ n jumping insect which makes a shrill, chirping noise. ⇨ the illus at insect.

grate¹ /greɪt/ n (metal frame for holding coal, etc, in a) fireplace.

grate² /greɪt/ vt,vi **1** [VP6A,15A] rub into small pieces, usu against a rough surface; rub small bits off: ~ cheese into beaten eggs, eg when making a cheese omelette. **2** [VP6A,2A,3A] ~ (on), make a harsh noise by rubbing; (fig) have an irritating effect (on a person, his nerves): His bad manners ~d on everyone. Out-of-date slang ~s. The gate ~s on its hinges. **grat·ing·ly** adv. ~r n device with a rough surface for grating food, etc: a 'nutmeg ~r.

grate·ful /'greɪtfl/ adj **1** ~ (to sb) (for sth), feeling or showing thanks: We are ~ to you for your help. **2** (liter) pleasant; agreeable; comforting: trees that afford a ~ shade. ~ly /-fəlɪ/ adv

grat·ify /'grætɪfaɪ/ vt (pt,pp -fied) [VP6A] **1** give pleasure or satisfaction to: We were all gratified with/at the result. It gratified me to learn that you had been successful. **2** indulge; give what is desired to: ~ a person's whims/his fancies for something; ~ a child's thirst for knowledge. ~·ing adj: It is always ~ing to have one's efforts rewarded. **grati·fi·ca·tion** /ˌgrætɪfɪ'keɪʃn/ n **1** [U] ~ing or being gratified; state of being pleased or satisfied: I have the gratification of knowing that I have done my duty. **2** [C] that which causes one to feel gratified.

grat·ing /'greɪtɪŋ/ n [C] framework of wooden or metal bars, either parallel or crossing one another, placed across an opening, eg a window, to keep out burglars or to allow air to flow through.

gra·tis /'greɪtɪs/ adv, adj free of charge: be admitted ~.

grati·tude /'grætɪtjuːd US: -tuːd/ n [U] ~ (to sb) (for sth), thankfulness, being grateful.

gra·tu·itous /grə'tjuːɪtəs US: -'tuː-/ adj **1** given, obtained or done, without payment: ~ service/ information/help/advice. **2** done or given, acting, without good reason: a ~ insult; a ~ lie/liar. ~·ly adv

gra·tu·ity /grə'tjuːətɪ US: -'tuː-/ n (pl -ties) **1** gift (of money in addition to pay) to a retiring employee for services. **2** tip (for service).

grave¹ /greɪv/ adj (-r, -st) serious; requiring careful consideration: ~ news; make a ~ mistake; as ~ as a judge. The situation is more ~/is ~r than it has been since the end of the war. ~·ly adv

grave² /greɪv/ n hole dug in the ground for a corpse; the mound of earth or the monument over it. have one foot in the ~, be nearing death, be very old. '~-clothes n pl wrappings in which a corpse is buried. '~-stone n stone over a ~, with the name, etc of the person buried there. ⇨ the illus at church. '~-yard n burial ground.

grave³ /grɑːv/ n (also ~ accent) mark ` placed over a vowel to indicate how it is to be sounded (as in French mère).

grave⁴ /greɪv/ vt (pp graven /'greɪvn/) (archaic or liter) carve: ~n on my memory, indelibly fixed. ~n 'image, an idol.

gravel /'grævl/ n [U] small stones with coarse sand, as used for roads and paths: a load of ~; (attrib) a

~ path/pit. **grav·elly** /'grævəlɪ/ adj (of a voice) deep and rough. □ vt (-ll-, US also -l-) [VP6A] **1** cover with ~: ~ a road; ~led paths. **2** (colloq) perplex; puzzle.

grav·ing dock /'greɪvɪŋ dɒk/ n dry dock in which the outside of a ship's hull may be cleaned.

gravi·tate /'grævɪteɪt/ vi [VP3A] ~ to/towards, move or be attracted: Young people in the country districts seem to ~ towards the cities. **gravi·ta·tion** /ˌgrævɪ'teɪʃn/ n [U] process of gravitating; gravity(1).

grav·ity /'grævətɪ/ n [U] **1** (phys) force of attraction between any two objects, esp that force which attracts objects towards the centre of the earth. **2** (phys) weight: centre of ~. spe,cific '~, relation between the weight of a substance and that of the same volume of a standard substance (usu water for liquids and solids, and air for gases). **3** quality of being serious or solemn: the ~ of the international situation; the ~ of his appearance. He could hardly keep his ~, could with difficulty refrain from smiling or laughing.

gra·vure /grə'vjʊə(r)/ n = photogravure.

gravy /'greɪvɪ/ n [U] **1** juice which comes from meat while it is cooking; sauce made from this. '~-boat n vessel in which ~ is served at table. **2** (sl) money or profit easily or unexpectedly acquired. '~ train n source of much and easy money, etc: get on the ~ train, get a job where such money, etc is easily acquired.

gray /greɪ/ adj, n = grey.

graze¹ /greɪz/ vi,vt **1** [VP2A,C] (of cattle, sheep, etc) eat growing grass: cattle grazing in the fields. **2** [VP6A] put (cattle, etc) in fields to ~: ~ sheep; use grassland for cattle: ~ a field. 'grazing-land n land used for grazing cattle. **graz·ier** /'greɪzɪə(r) US: 'greɪʒə(r)/ n person who feeds cattle for market.

graze² /greɪz/ vt,vi **1** [VP6A] touch or scrape lightly in passing; rub the skin from: The bullet ~d his cheek. **2** [VP2C] pass and touch while going against/along/by/past. □ n place where the skin is ~d.

grease /griːs/ n [U] **1** animal fat melted soft. **2** any thick, semi-solid oily substance: 'axle ~, used to lubricate axles. '~-gun n device for forcing ~ into the parts of an engine, machine, etc. '~-paint n [U] mixture of ~ and paint used by actors to make up their faces. □ vt put or rub ~ on or in (esp parts of a machine). ~ sb's palm, bribe him. ~r n man who ~s machinery, eg a ship's engines.

greasy /'griːsɪ/ adj (-ier, -iest) covered with grease; slippery: ~ fingers; a ~ road. **greas·ily** /-ɪlɪ/ adv **greasi·ness** n

great /greɪt/ adj (-er, -est) **1** well above the average in size, quantity or degree: take ~ care of sth; an essay that shows ~ ignorance of grammar; a ~ friend of mine, one for whom I feel more than ordinary friendship. ~ with child, (old use) pregnant. '~-coat n heavy overcoat. **2** of remarkable ability or quality: ~ men; a ~ painter/painting/musician. **3** important; noted; of high rank or position: a ~ occasion; the G~ Powers of Europe; a ~ lady; Alexander the G~. **4** (colloq, preceding another adj which is often weakly stressed; implying surprise, indignation, contempt, etc according to context): See what a ~ big fish I've caught! Take your ~ big head out of my light! What a ~ thick stick! **5** (also G~er) used as a distinctive epithet of the larger of two. the G~ Bear, ⇨ bear¹(3). G~ Bri-

tain, (abbr **GB**) England, Wales and Scotland, excluding Northern Ireland. **the G~ Lakes,** series of five large lakes in N America along the boundary between Canada and the US. **G~er London,** an administrative area of local government that includes inner London and the outer suburbs. **the G~ War,** that of 1914—18. **6** (attrib only) fully deserving the name of: *He's a ~ liar. They are ~ friends.* **7** (with agent *nouns;* attrib only) doing or being sth to a high degree: *He's a ~ reader/eater,* reads/eats very much. *He's a ~ landowner,* owns a large area of land. **8** combined with words indicating quantity, etc: *a ~ deal,* very much; *a ~ number; a ~ while ago; the ~ majority,* much the larger part. **9** (colloq) splendid; satisfactory: *We had a ~ time in Paris. Wouldn't it be ~ if we could go there again!* **10** (colloq; pred only) **~ at,** clever or skilful at. **~ on,** having a good knowledge of. **11** prefixed to a kinship words in *grand-* to show a further stage in relationship: *,~-'grandfather,* one's father's or mother's grandfather; *,~-'grandson,* grandson of one's son or daughter. **~·ly** *adv* much; by much: *~ly amused.* **~·ness** *n*

greaves /griːvz/ *n pl* pieces of armour to protect the shins. ⇨ the illus at armour.

grebe /griːb/ *n* kind of short-bodied diving bird. ⇨ the illus at water.

Gre·cian /'griːʃn/ *adj* (eg of architecture, pottery, culture and features of the face) Greek.

greed /griːd/ *n* [U] strong desire for more food, wealth, etc, esp for more than is right or reasonable.

greedy /'griːdɪ/ *adj* (-ier, -iest) **1 ~ (for sth/to have sth),** filled with greed: *not hungry, just ~; looking at the cakes with ~ eyes; ~ for gain/honours.* **2 ~ (to do sth),** intensely desirous. **greed·ily** /-ɪlɪ/ *adv* **greedi·ness** *n*

Greek /griːk/ *n* [C] member of the Greek people, either of ancient Greece or modern Greece; [U] the Greek language. **be ~ to one,** be beyond one's understanding. □ *adj* of Greece, its people, or the Greek language.

green¹ /griːn/ *adj* (-er, -est) **1** of the colour between blue and yellow in the spectrum, the colour of growing grass, and the leaves of most plants and trees: *a ~ Christmas,* Christmas season when the weather is mild and there is no snow. **~ 'belt,** wide area of land round a town, where building is controlled (by town-planning) so that there are ~ fields, woods, etc. **give sb/get the ~ light,** (colloq, from the ~ of traffic lights) permission to go ahead with a project, etc. **2** (of fruit) not yet ripe: *~ apples; ~ figs,* young and tender figs; (of wood) not yet dry enough for use: *G~ wood does not burn well.* **3** inexperienced; undeveloped; gullible; untrained: *a boy who is still ~ at his job. I'm not so ~ as to believe that.* **4** (fig) flourishing; full of vigour: *live to a ~ old age; keep a person's memory ~,* not allow it to fade. **5** (of the complexion) pale; sickly looking. *,~-'eyed adj* jealous. **the ,~-eyed 'monster,** jealousy. **~ with envy,** very envious. **6** (special uses and compounds): **'~·back** *n* US banknote, the back printed in ~. **'~ 'fingers** *n* (colloq) skill in gardening. **'~·fly** *n* (collective *pl;* [U]) kinds of aphis. **'~·gage** /-ɡeɪdʒ/ *n* kind of plum with greenish-yellow skin and flesh and fine flavour. **'~·grocer** *n* shopkeeper selling vegetables and fruit. **'~·grocery** *n* (*pl* -ries) business of, things sold by, a ~grocer. **'~·horn** *n* inexperienc-

ed and easily deceived person. **'~·house** *n* building with sides and roof of glass, used for growing plants that need protection from the weather. **'~ room** *n* room in a theatre for actors and actresses when they are not on the stage. **'~-stuffs,** **~s** *n pl* ~ vegetables. **'~·sward** *n* [U] turf. **~ 'tea** *n* tea made from steam-dried leaves. **'~·wood** *n* woodlands, esp in summer; forest in full leaf, esp as the home of outlaws in olden times.

green² /griːn/ *n* **1** [U,C] green colour; what is green: *a girl dressed in ~; a picture in ~s and blues,* with various shades of ~ and blue. **2** (*pl*) green leaf vegetables, eg cabbage, spinach, before or after cooking; vegetation: (US) *Christmas ~s,* eg branches of fir and holly for decoration. **3** [C] area of land with growing grass. (a) public or common land: *the village ~.* (b) for the game of bowls: *a 'bowling-~.* (c) surrounding a hole on a golf course: *a 'putting ~.*

greenery /'griːnərɪ/ *n* [U] green foliage; verdure: *the ~ of the woods in spring.*

greenish /'griːnɪʃ/ *adj* somewhat green: (in compounds) *~-'yellow; ~-'brown.* **~·ness** *n*

Greenwich /'grenɪtʃ/ *n* suburb of London, east and west of whose meridian longitude is measured. **~ 'mean time** (abbr **GMT**), mean² time for the meridian of ~, used as a basis for calculating time in most parts of the world (now called *Universal time*).

greet /griːt/ *vt* [VP6A,14] **~ (with),** **1** say words of welcome to; express one's feelings on receiving (news, etc); write (in a letter) words expressing respect, friendship, etc: *~ a friend by saying 'Good morning!'; ~ someone with a smile. The news was ~ed with dismay. They ~ed me with a shower of stones.* **2** (of sights and sounds) meet the eyes and ears: *the view that ~ed us at the hill-top.* **~·ing** *n* first words used on seeing sb or in writing to sb; expression or act with which sb or sth is ~ed: *'Good morning' and 'Dear Sir' are ~ings; a '~ings telegram,* one sent with, eg birthday, ~ings.

greg·ari·ous /ɡrɪ'ɡeərɪəs/ *adj* living in groups or societies; liking the company of others. **~·ly** *adv* **~·ness** *n*

Greg·or·ian /ɡrɪ'ɡɔːrɪən/ *adj* **1 ~ chant,** the kind of church music (*plainsong*) named after Pope Gregory I (540—604). **2 ~ calendar,** the calendar introduced by Pope Gregory XIII (1502—85), with the days and months arranged as now. ⇨ Julian.

grem·lin /'ɡremlɪn/ *n* goblin said to cause mechanical trouble.

gre·nade /ɡrɪ'neɪd/ *n* small bomb thrown by hand ('*hand-~*) or fired from a rifle ('*rifle-~*).

grena·dier /,ɡrenə'dɪə(r)/ *n* (formerly) soldier who threw grenades; (now) soldier in *the G~s, the G~ Guards,* British infantry regiment.

grew /ɡruː/ *pt* of grow.

grey, gray /ɡreɪ/ *adj* between black and white, coloured like ashes, or the sky on a dull, cloudy day: *His hair has turned ~.* '~·beard *n* old man. *,~-'headed adj* old; of long service. '~ matter, material of the brain: *a boy without much ~ matter,* a not very intelligent boy. □ *n* [U,C] ~ colour; ~ clothes: *dressed in ~.* □ *vt,vi* [VP6A,2A] make or become ~.

grey·hound /'ɡreɪhaʊnd/ *n* slender, long-legged, keen-sighted dog, able to run fast, used in chasing live hares and, as a modern sport (*~ racing*), mechanical hares moved along a rail.

grey·ish /'greɪɪʃ/ adj somewhat grey.

grid /grɪd/ n [C] **1** system of overhead cables carried on pylons, for distributing electric current over a large area. **2** network of squares on maps, numbered for reference. **3** grating: a 'cattle ~, one placed at a gate, etc designed to prevent cattle from straying on to a road, etc. **4** frame of spaced parallel spirals or networks of wires in a radio valve. **5** gridiron.

griddle /'grɪdl/ n circular iron plate used for baking cakes.

grid·iron /'grɪdaɪən/ n **1** framework of metal bars used for cooking meat or fish over a clear fire. **2** field for American football (marked with numerous parallel lines).

grief /griːf/ n **1** [U] deep or violent sorrow: driven almost insane by ~; die of ~. **2** [C] sth causing ~: His taking to drugs was a great ~ to his parents. **3** **bring sb/come to ~,** (cause sb to) meet with misfortune, injury or ruin.

griev·ance /'griːvns/ n [C] ~ (against), real or imagined cause for complaint or protest: The trade union leader spoke about the ~s of the workers.

grieve /griːv/ vt, vi **1** [VP6A] cause grief to: ~ one's parents. **2** [VP2A,C] feel grief: ~ for the dead/ over sb's death; ~ about one's misfortunes/at bad news.

griev·ous /'griːvəs/ adj **1** causing grief or suffering: a ~ railway accident; ~ wrongs. **2** severe: ~ pain; ~ bodily harm. ~·ly adv

grif·fin /'grɪfɪn/ (also **grif·fon, gry·phon** /'grɪfən/) n (Gk myth) fabulous creature with the head and wings of an eagle and a lion's body. ⇨ the illus at armour.

grill /grɪl/ n [C] **1** grating; grille; gridiron. **2** dish of meat, etc cooked directly over or under great heat: a mixed ~, steak, liver, bacon, etc. **3** (also '~-room) room (in a hotel or restaurant) where ~s are cooked and served. □ vt, vi **1** [VP6A,2A,C] cook, be cooked, on a gridiron, or over great heat; expose oneself to great heat: lie ~ing in the hot sun. **2** [VP6A] eg of the police, question closely and severely.

grille /grɪl/ n screen of parallel bars used to close an open space, eg in a convent; similar screen over a counter, eg in a post office or bank as a protection.

grim /grɪm/ adj (-mmer, -mmest) stern; severe; forbidding; without mercy: a ~ struggle; a ~ smile/expression; looking ~; a ~ joke/story, one with an element of cruelty in it. **hold on like ~ death,** very firmly. ~·ly adv ~·ness n

gri·mace /grɪ'meɪs US: 'grɪmɪs/ n [C] ugly, twisted expression (on the face), expressing pain, disgust, etc or intended to cause laughter. □ vi [VP2A] make ~s.

grime /graɪm/ n [U] dirt, esp a coating on the surface of sth or on the body: the soot and ~ of a big manufacturing town; a face covered with ~ and sweat. □ vt [VP6A] make dirty with ~: ~d with dust. **grimy** /'graɪmɪ/ adj (-ier, -est) covered with ~: grimy faces/roofs/windows.

grin /grɪn/ vi, vt (-nn-) **1** [VP2A,C] smile broadly so as to show the teeth, expressing amusement, foolish satisfaction, contempt, etc: ~ning with delight; ~ from ear to ear. ~ **and bear it,** endure pain, disappointment, etc, uncomplainingly. **2** [VP6A] express by ~ning: He ~ned his approval. □ n [C] act of ~ning: the tigerish ~ on the murderer's face; ~s of derision.

grind /graɪnd/ vt, vi (pt, pp ground /graʊnd/) **1** [VP6A,15A,B] ~ (down) (to/into), crush to grains or powder between millstones, the teeth, etc: ~ sth to pieces; ~ sth down; ~ coffee beans; ~ wheat in a mill; ~ corn into flour. **2** [VP2A,C] be capable of ~ing: This wheat ~s well. This wheat will not ~ fine, cannot be ground fine. **3** [VP6A] produce in this way: ~ flour. **4** [VP6A,15A,B] ~ (down), (usu passive) (fig) oppress or crush: people who were ground (down) by poverty/taxation/tyranny; tyrants who grind down the poor. **5** [VP6A] polish or sharpen by rubbing on or with a rough, hard surface: ~ a knife/lens. **have an axe to** ~, ⇨ axe. **6** [VP6A,15A,B] rub harshly together, esp with a circular motion: ~ one's teeth (together); a ship ~ing on the rocks; ~ one's heel into the ground. ~ **to a halt,** (of a vehicle) stop noisily (with brakes that ~); (fig) (of a process) stop slowly: The strikes brought industry ~ing to a halt. **7** [VP6A,15A] work by turning; produce by turning: ~ a hand-mill/coffee-mill/barrel-organ; ~ out a tune on an organ; (fig) ~ out some verses, produce them slowly and with effort. **8** [VP2C,15B] ~ **(away) (at),** (cause to) work or study hard and long: ~ away at one's studies; ~ for an exam. □ n (colloq) long, monotonous task: the examination ~, the task of preparing for an examination. Do you find learning English a ~?

grinder /'graɪndə(r)/ n **1** thing that grinds, eg a molar tooth, apparatus for grinding coffee: a 'coffee-~. **2** (in compounds) person who grinds: a 'knife-~; an 'organ-~, person who produces tunes by turning the handle of a barrel-organ.

grind·stone /'graɪndstəʊn/ n stone shaped like a wheel, turned on an axle, used for sharpening tools. **keep sb's nose to the** ~, force him to work hard without rest.

grip /grɪp/ vt, vi (-pp-) [VP6A,2A] take and keep a firm hold of; seize firmly: The frightened child ~ped its mother's hand. The brakes failed to ~ and the car ran into a wall. The speaker ~ped the attention of his audience. The film is a ~ping story of love and hate. □ n **1** (sing only except as shown) act, manner, or power of ~ping: let go one's ~ of sth; take a ~ on a rope; have a good ~ (fig, = understanding) of a problem; have a good ~ on an audience, hold their attention and interest. **be at** ~s **with; come/get to** ~s **with,** be attacking, begin to attack, in earnest; be in close combat: get to ~s with a problem. **take a '~ on oneself,** (colloq) stop being idle and inattentive. **2** [C] (in a machine, etc) part that ~s or clips; clutch; part that is to be ~ped. **3** [C] (also '~·sack) (US) traveller's handbag: a leather ~.

gripes /graɪps/ n pl (the) ~, (colloq) violent pains in the abdomen.

grippe /griːp/ n the ~, influenza.

gris·ly /'grɪzlɪ/ adj causing horror or terror; ghastly.

grist /grɪst/ n [U] grain to be ground (chiefly in fig phrases). **It's all** ~ **to the mill; All is** ~ **that comes to his mill,** (prov) He makes use of everything.

gristle /'grɪsl/ n [U] tough, elastic tissue in animal bodies, esp in meat: I can't eat this meat—it's all ~.

grit /grɪt/ n [U] **1** (collective sing) tiny, hard bits of stone, sand, etc: spread ~ on icy roads. I've got some ~ in my shoe. **2** quality of courage and endurance: The soldiers showed that they had plenty of ~. □ vt (-tt-) ~ **one's teeth,** keep one's jaws tight together; (fig) show courage and endurance.

~ty adj (-ier, -iest) of or like ~(1): *The sand-storm made the food ~ty.*

grits /grɪts/ n pl husked but unground oats; coarse oatmeal.

grizzle /'grɪzl/ vi (colloq) (esp of children) cry fret-fully.

griz·zled /'grɪzld/ adj grey; grey-haired.

griz·zly /'grɪzlɪ/ n (also ~ **bear**) large, fierce grey bear of N America. ⇨ the illus at bear.

groan /grəʊn/ vi, vt **1** [VP2A,C] make a deep sound forced out by pain, or expressing despair or dis-tress: *The wounded men lay there ~ing, with no one to help them. The teacher ~ed with dismay. The people ~ed under injustice.* **2** [VP2A,C] (of things) make a noise like that of ~ing: *The ship's timbers ~ed during the storm. The table ~ed with food,* (fig) was weighed down with large quantities of food. **3** [VP6A,15B] ~ *(out)*, express with ~ing: *He ~ed out a sad story.* **4** [VP15B] ~ *down*, silence in ~ing: *The speaker was ~ed down by his audience,* They prevented him from being heard. □ n [C] deep sound made in ~ing: *the ~s of the injured men; give a ~ of dismay; a speech interrupted by ~s of disapproval.*

groat /grəʊt/ n (hist) (14th to 17th cc) English sil-ver coin worth fourpence.

groats /grəʊts/ n pl (crushed) grain, esp oats, that has been hulled.

grocer /'grəʊsə(r)/ n shopkeeper who sells food in packets, tins, or bottles, and general small house-hold requirements. ~y n **1** [U] ~'s trade: *a '~y business.* **2** (pl) ~ies, things sold by a ~.

grog /grɒg/ n [U] (a word used by sailors) drink of spirits mixed with water.

groggy /'grɒgɪ/ adj (-ier, -iest) **1** unsteady; likely to collapse or fall: *The legs of that chair look rath-er ~.* **2** weak and unsteady as the result of illness, shock, lack of sleep, etc: *That last attack of flu left me rather ~.*

groin /grɔɪn/ n **1** depression between the stomach and the thigh. ⇨ the illus at trunk. **2** (archit) curved edge where two vaults meet (in a roof). ⇨ the illus at church. **3** (US) = groyne. □ vt build with ~s.

groom /gru:m/ n **1** person in charge of horses. **2** bridegroom. □ vt [VP6A] **1** feed, brush and in other ways look after (horses); clean the fur and skin of: *a female ape ~ing her mate.* **2** (usu in the pp, of persons): *well/badly ~ed,* well/badly dressed (esp of the hair, beard and clothes). **3** (colloq) prepare (sb for a career, etc).

groove /gru:v/ n **1** long, hollow channel in the sur-face of hard material, esp one made to guide the motion of sth that slides along it, eg a sliding door or window; spiral cut on a gramophone disc (in which the needle or stylus moves). **2** way of living that has become a habit. *get into/be stuck in a ~,* become set in one's ways, one's style of living. *in the ~,* (dated sl) in the right mood (for sth); exhi-larated. □ vt make ~s in: *a ~d shelf.* ~r n (sl) up-to-date person. **groovy** adj (sl) up-to-date; in the latest fashion (esp of young people): *a groovy restaurant; groovy clothes/people.*

grope /grəʊp/ vi, vt [VP2A,C,3A,15A] ~ *(about) (for/after),* (lit or fig) feel or search about as one does in the dark: *grope for the door-handle/the light switch/an answer. We ~d our way along the dark corridor.* **grop·ing·ly** adv in the manner of one who ~s.

gross¹ /grəʊs/ n (pl unchanged) twelve dozen; 144. ⇨ App 4.

gross² /grəʊs/ adj **1** vulgar; not refined; coarse in mind or morals: ~ *language/jokes/morals.* **2** (of food) coarse, greasy; liking such food: *a ~ eater.* **3** (of the senses) heavy and dull. **4** flagrant; glar-ing; clearly seen: ~ *injustice/negligence; a ~ error/overcharge.* **5** (of vegetation) luxuriant: *the ~ vegetation of the tropical rain-forest.* **6** (of per-sons) repulsively fat. **7** (opposite of *net*) total, whole: *the ~ amount; his ~ income.* ~ **national product** (abbr **GNP**), annual total value of goods produced, and services provided, in a country. **8** *in (the)* ~, wholesale; in bulk; in a general way. □ vt [VP6A] make as a total amount: *His last film ~ed five million pounds.* ~·ly adv extremely: ~ly *unfair/fat.* ~·ness n

grot /grɒt/ n (poet) grotto.

gro·tesque /grəʊ'tesk/ adj **1** absurd; fantastic; laughable because strange and incongruous: *a ~ appearance;* ~ *manners.* **2** (in art) combining hu-man, animal and plant forms in a fantastic way; made up of comically distorted figures and designs. □ n **1** ~ person, animal, figure or design. **2** *the* ~, painting, carving, etc in which the ~ style appears. ~·ly adv ~·ness n

grotto /'grɒtəʊ/ n (pl ~es, ~s /-təʊz/) cave, esp one made artificially as a garden shelter.

grotty /'grɒtɪ/ adj (sl) unpleasant; ugly.

grouch /graʊtʃ/ vi (colloq) complain. □ n fit of ill temper; sulky, discontented person. ~y adj sullen-ly discontented.

ground¹ /graʊnd/ n **1** *the* ~, solid surface of the earth: *lie on/sit on/fall to the* ~; (in compounds): ~-*to-air missiles,* fired from the ~ (at aircraft). *The airliner made a* ~-*controlled approach,* approached the runway directed by the control tower. *above* ~, alive. *below* ~, dead and buried. *fall/be dashed to the* ~, (cause to) fail, be disappointed: *The scheme/Our plans fell to the* ~. *Our hopes were dashed to the* ~. *get off the* ~, (of an aircraft) rise into the air; (fig, of an un-dertaking or scheme) pass from the planning stage and make a start. **2** [U] position, area or distance on the earth's surface. *cut the* ~ *from under sb's feet,* anticipate his plans, arguments, defences, etc and in this way embarrass him. *cover (much, etc)* ~, *(a)* travel: *We've covered a great deal of* ~ *to-day,* have come a long way. *(b)* (fig, of a lecture, report, inquiry, etc) deal with a variety of subjects; be far-reaching: *The committee's report covers much new* ~, deals with many new matters. *gain* ~, make progress; win a success or an advantage. *give/lose* ~, retreat; fail to keep one's position or advantage. *hold/stand/keep one's* ~, stand firm; not yield; maintain one's claim, intention, ar-gument, etc. *shift one's* ~, change one's argu-ment, etc. *suit sb down to the* ~, suit him thor-oughly: *Her new hairstyle/job suits her down to the* ~. *common* ~, subject on which two or more persons or parties are in agreement or on which they have similar views. *forbidden* ~, subject that must be avoided. **3** [U] soil; earth: *till the* ~. *The*

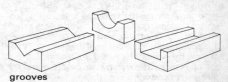

grooves

frost has made the ∼ *hard.* **break fresh/new** ∼, (a) cultivate land that has not been cultivated before. (b) (fig) do sth new; deal with a subject for the first time. **4** [C] area or piece of land for a special purpose or a particular use: *a 'football/ 'cricket/'sports* ∼; *a 'parade/,recre'ation* ∼; *a 'play*∼; *'hunting/'fishing*–∼*s*, areas used for hunting/fishing. **5** (always *pl*) land, gardens, round a building, often enclosed with walls, hedges or fences: *the* ∼*s of Buckingham Palace. The mansion has extensive* ∼*s.* **6** [U] bottom of the sea or of any other body of water: (chiefly in) **touch** ∼, (of a ship) strike the bottom. ⇨ aground. **7** (*pl*) particles of solid matter that sink to the bottom of a liquid: (esp) *'coffee*–∼*s*. **8** (*pl* or [U]) reason(s) for saying, doing or believing sth. **be/give/have** ∼*s* **for**, be/give/have a cause or reason for: *There are no* ∼*s for anxiety. I have good* ∼*s for believing his version of events. They don't give me much* ∼/ *many* ∼*s for complaint. What are the* ∼*s for divorce in this country*, What is recognized as a basis for an action of divorce? **on the** ∼*s* **of**, because of: *excused on the* ∼*s of youth; reject a man on' medical* ∼*s. On what* ∼*s do you suspect him?* **9** [C] surface on which a design is painted, printed, cut, etc; undecorated part: *a design of pink roses on a white* ∼. **10** (compounds) '∼**-bait** *n* [U] food thrown to the bottom of a fishing–∼ to attract fish. '∼**-fish** *n* fish living at or near the bottom. ∼ **'floor** *n* the floor of a building level with the ∼. **be/get in on the** ∼ **floor,** (colloq) join an enterprise at its beginning. '∼**-nut** *n* kind of pea with pods ripening under the ∼ (also called *earthnut* and *peanut*). '∼**-plan** *n* plan of a building at ∼ level. '∼**-rent** *n* rent paid for the use of land leased for building. ∼**s·man** /-mən/ *n* (*pl* -men) man employed to look after a cricket ∼. '∼**-sheet** *n* waterproof sheet spread on the ∼, eg under bedding in a tent. '∼ **speed** *n* aircraft's speed on the ∼ (contrasted with *air speed*). '∼ **staff/crew** *n* mechanics who service aircraft on the ∼; non-flying members of the staff of an airfield, etc. '∼ **swell** *n* [U] heavy, slow-moving waves caused by a distant or recent storm. '∼**·work** *n* [U] (usu fig) foundation; basis.

ground² /graʊnd/ *vt,vi* **1** [VP6A,2A] (of a ship) (cause to) touch the sea bottom; (of aircraft, airmen) compel to stay on the ground: *Our ship* ∼*ed in shallow water. All aircraft at London Airport were* ∼*ed by fog yesterday.* **2** [VP6A] ∼ **arms**, (mil) lay (esp rifles) on the ground. **3** [VP14] ∼ **sth on sth**, base (the more usu word) (a belief, etc) on: ∼ *one's arguments on facts; a well*–∼*ed theory.* **4** [VP14] ∼ **sb in sth**, give (sb) good teaching or basic training in: *The teacher* ∼*ed his pupils in arithmetic.* **5** [VP6A] connect (a piece of electrical apparatus) with the ∼ as conductor, as a safety precaution (*earth* is the usu word). ∼**·ing** *n* thorough teaching of the elements of a subject: *a good* ∼*ing in grammar.*

ground³ /graʊnd/ *pt,pp* of grind: ∼ *rice*, reduced to fine powder. ∼ **glass**, made non-transparent by grinding.

ground·less /'graʊndlɪs/ *adj* without foundation or good reason: ∼ *fears/anxieties/rumours.* ⇨ ground¹(8).

ground·sel /'graʊnsl/ *n* [U] kinds of weed, the commonest kind of which is used as food for some cage-birds.

group /gru:p/ *n* [C] number of persons or things gathered or placed together, or naturally associated; number of jointly-controlled business companies, eg as the result of a merger: *a* ∼ *of girls/ trees/houses; people standing about in small* ∼*s; the Germanic* ∼ *of languages.* '**G**∼ **captain,** Air Force officer. □ *vt,vi* [VP6A,15A,B,2C] form into, gather in, a ∼ or ∼s: *The police* ∼*ed (themselves) round the demonstrators. G*∼ *the roses together.*

grouse¹ /graʊs/ *n* (*pl* unchanged) bird with feathered feet, shot for sport and food: '∼ *shooting*, the shooting of red ∼ on the moors of Scotland and northern England. ⇨ the illus at fowl.

grouse² /graʊs/ *vi* [VP2A,C] (colloq) grumble; complain. □ *n* complaint.

grove /graʊv/ *n* group of trees; small wood.

grovel /'grɒvl/ *vi* (-ll-; US also -l-) [VP2A,C] lie down on one's face, crawl, in front of sb whom one fears, (as if) begging for mercy; (fig) humble oneself; behave in a way that shows one has no self-respect: ∼ *at the feet of a conqueror.* ∼**-ler** *n* person who ∼*s*.

grow /graʊ/ *vi,vt* (*pt* grew /gru:/, *pp* grown /graʊn/) **1** [VP2A,C,D] develop; increase in size, height, length, etc: *Rice* ∼*s in warm climates. How quickly you are* ∼*ing! How tall you've* ∼*n! She has decided to let her hair* ∼, not have it cut short. *A full*–∼*n elephant is very large. He has* ∼*n into a fine young man. Plants* ∼ *from seeds. She has* ∼*n in stature but not in wisdom.* ∼ **out of**, (a) become too big for: ∼ *out of one's clothes.* (b) become too old for; cease to practise; abandon: *He has* ∼*n out of the bad habits of his boyhood days.* (c) have as a source: *His troubles grew out of his bad temper.* ∼ **up**, (a) (of persons, animals) reach the stage of full development; become adult or mature: *When the boys* ∼ *up,... He has a* ∼*n-up son.* (b) develop: *A warm friendship grew up between the two men.* '∼**-ing-pains** *n pl* (a) pains in the limbs of young children, popularly believed to be caused by rapid growth. (b) (fig) problems arising while a new enterprise is developing: *The business is still suffering from* ∼*ing pains.* '∼**n-up** /'graʊnʌp/ *n* [C] adult person (contrasted with a child). □ *adj* adult; mature. **2** [VP2D] become: ∼ *older;* ∼ *smaller. It began to* ∼ *dark.* **3** [VP4A] ∼ *to be/like, etc,* reach the point or stage where one is/likes, etc: *One* ∼*s to like what one is accustomed to. My friendship with them grew to be* (= by degrees became) *considerable.* **4** [VP6A,12B,13B] cause or allow to ∼: ∼ *roses. He's* ∼*ing a beard. Will you* ∼ *some herbs for me/*∼ *me some herbs this year?* **5** [VP3A] ∼ **on/ upon,** (a) become more deeply rooted: *a habit that* ∼*s on you.* (b) come to have a greater attraction for; win the liking of: *a book/a piece of music that* ∼*s on you.* ∼**er** *n* **1** person who ∼*s* things: *a 'fruit*–∼*er;* '*rose*–∼*ers.* **2** plant, etc that ∼*s* in a certain way: *a free/rapid* ∼*er.*

growl /graʊl/ *vi,vt* **1** [VP2A,C] (of animals, men, thunder) make a low, threatening sound: *The dog* ∼*ed at me. We heard thunder* ∼*ing in the distance.* **2** [VP6A,15B] ∼ **(out)**, say in a ∼ing manner: *He* ∼*ed (out) his answer.* □ *n* [C] low threatening sound; angry complaint. ∼**·ing·ly** *adv*

growler /'graʊlə(r)/ *n* (old colloq use) four-wheeled horse-drawn cab.

grown /graʊn/ *pp* of grow: *a* ∼ *man*, a mature man.

growth /graʊθ/ *n* **1** [U] growing; development; process of growing: *the rapid* ∼ *of our economy.*

At what age does an elephant reach full ~, its greatest size? **2** [U] increase: '*~ shares,* thought likely to increase in value. **3** [U] cultivation: *apples of foreign ~,* grown abroad. **4** [C] sth that grows or has grown: *a thick ~ of weeds; a three-days' ~ of beard.* **5** [C] diseased formation in the body, eg a cancer.

groyne (US = **groin**) /grɔɪn/ *n* [C] structure of wood, etc, or a low, broad wall of stone, concrete, etc built to prevent sand and pebbles from being washed away by the sea, the current of a river, etc.

grub[1] /grʌb/ *n* **1** [C] larva of insect. **2** [U] (sl) food.

grub[2] /grʌb/ *vt, vi* (-bb-) [VP6A, 15B, 2C] turn over the soil, esp in order to get sth up or out: *~bing up weeds. The pigs were ~bing about among the bushes.*

grubby /'grʌbɪ/ *adj* (-ier, -iest) **1** dirty; unwashed. **2** having grubs in it.

grudge /grʌdʒ/ *vt* [VP12A, 13A, 6C] be unwilling to give or allow: *I don't ~ him his success,* I admit that he deserves it. *His cruel master ~d him even the food he ate,* gave him his food unwillingly. *I ~ paying £2 for a bottle of wine that is not worth 50p.* □ *n* [C] feeling of ill-will, resentment, envy or spite: *I bear him no ~. He has a ~ against me. I owe that man a ~,* think I have good reason to feel ill-will towards him. **grudg·ing·ly** *adv* in a grudging manner: *His employer grudgingly raised his salary.*

gruel /'gruːəl/ *n* [U] liquid food of oatmeal, etc boiled in milk or water.

gruel·ling (US =**grue·ling**) /'gruːəlɪŋ/ severe; exhausting: *a ~ling race.*

grue·some /'gruːsəm/ *adj* filling one with horror or disgust; frightful. *~·ly adv ~·ness n*

gruff /grʌf/ *adj* (of a person, his voice, behaviour) rough; surly. *~·ly adv ~·ness n*

grumble /'grʌmbl/ *vi, vt* **1** [VP2A, C, 3A] *~ (at/ about/over sth),* complain or protest in a bad-tempered way: *He's always grumbling. He ~d at the low pay offered to him.* **2** [VP6A, 15B] *~ (out),* say in a sullen, dissatisfied way: *~ (out) a reply.* **3** [VP2A, C] make a low, growling sound: *thunder grumbling in the distance.* □ *n* [C] (usu bad-tempered) complaint or protest: *That fellow is full of ~s.* **grum·bler** /'grʌmblə(r)/ *n* person who *~s.*

grumpy /'grʌmpɪ/ *adj* (-ier, -iest) bad-tempered; surly. **grump·i·ly** /-ɪlɪ/ *adv* **grumpi·ness** *n*

Grundy·ism /'grʌndɪzəm/ *n* [U] conventional propriety; prudery.

grunt /grʌnt/ *vi, vt* **1** [VP2A] (of animals, esp pigs) make a low, rough sound; (of persons) make a similar sound expressing disagreement, boredom, irritation, etc. **2** [VP6A, 15B] *~ (out),* utter in a ~ing way: *~ (out) an answer.* □ *n* [C] low, rough sound.

gry·phon /'grɪfən/ *n* = griffin.

guano /'gwɑːnəʊ/ *n* (*pl* -nos /-nəʊz/) [C] dung dropped by sea-birds, used as fertilizer.

guar·an·tee[1] /ˌgærən'tiː/ *n* [C] **1** (in law, **gua·ranty**) promise or undertaking (usu in writing or print) that certain conditions agreed to in a transaction will be fulfilled: *a year's ~ with a watch,* a promise to keep it in good repair, etc. **2** (in law, **guaranty**) undertaking given by one person to another that he will be responsible for sth to be done, eg payment of a debt, by a third person. **3** (in law, **guarantor**) person who gives such an undertaking: *be ~ for a friend's good behaviour. If I try to borrow £1000 from the bank, will you be my ~?* **4** (in

law, **guaranty**) sth offered, eg the deeds of a house or other document of ownership of property, as security for the fulfilling of conditions in a ~(1,2): *'What ~ can you offer?' 'I can offer my house and land as a ~.'* **5** (colloq) sth that seems to make an occurrence likely: *Blue skies are not always a ~ of fine weather.*

guar·an·tee[2] /ˌgærən'tiː/ *vt* [VP6A, 7A, 25, 9, 12A, 13A] **1** give a guarantee(1,2,3) for (sth or sb): *~ a man's debts; ~ to pay a man's debts; ~ that the debts will be paid; ~ the payment of the debts. We cannot ~ the punctual arrival of trains in foggy weather. This clock is ~d for one year. We can't ~ our workers regular employment.* **2** (colloq) promise (without legal obligation): *Many shopkeepers ~ satisfaction to customers.*

guar·an·tor /ˌgærən'tɔː(r)/ *n* (legal word for) guarantee(3).

guar·an·ty /'gærəntɪ/ *n* (legal word for) guarantee(1,2,4).

guard[1] /gɑːd/ *n* **1** [U] state of watchfulness against attack, danger or surprise: *The sentry/soldier is on ~,* at his post, on duty. *The soldier was ordered to keep ~.* **2** [U] attitude of readiness to defend oneself, eg in fencing, boxing, bayonet-drill. *be on/off one's ~,* be prepared/unprepared against an attack or surprise: *Be on your ~ against pickpockets. He struck me while I was off my ~.* **3** [C] soldier or party of soldiers keeping ~; sentry. *change ~,* (mil) replace one ~ by another. Hence, *the changing of the ~,* eg at Buckingham Palace. *mount ~,* take up one's post as a sentry. *relieve ~,* take the place of a sentry who has finished his period of duty. *stand ~,* act as a sentry. **4** man (also called *warder*) or group of men in charge of a prison. **5** (GB) official in charge of a railway train. (US = *brakeman*). **6** (*pl*) **G~s,** (in GB and some other countries) troops employed originally to protect the sovereign: *the G~s; the Royal Horse G~s; a G~s officer.* '*~s·man* /-mən/ *n* (*pl* -men) soldier of the G~s. **7** [C] body of soldiers with the duty of protecting, honouring or escorting a person: *The Duke, on his arrival, inspected the ~ of honour at the station.* ⇨ also *rear~* at rear[1](4), *Home G~* at home[1](7). **8** (esp in compounds) (part of) an article or apparatus designed to prevent injury or loss: *a 'fire-~,* in front of a fireplace; *a 'mud~* (over the wheel of a bicycle, etc); *the ~ of a sword,* the part of the hilt that protects the hand. **9** (compounds) '*~-boat n* one sent round a fleet of warships in harbour. '*~-house n* (mil) building for a military ~ or one in which prisoners are kept. '*~-rail n* rail, eg on a staircase, to prevent falling or (elsewhere) to prevent persons from danger, eg from traffic. '*~-room n* room for soldiers on ~ or for soldiers under ~. '*~-ship n* ship protecting a harbour.

guard[2] /gɑːd/ *vt, vi* **1** [VP6A, 15A] protect; keep from danger: *~ a camp; ~ one's life/one's reputation; ~ prisoners,* prevent them from escaping. **2** [VP3A] *~ against,* use care and caution to prevent: *~ against disease/bad habits/suspicion. ~ed adj* (of statements, etc) cautious: *a ~ed answer: be ~ed in what one says. ~·ed·ly adv* cautiously.

guard·ian /'gɑːdɪən/ *n* (offical or private) person who guards, esp (legal use) one who is responsible for the care of a young or incapable person and his property. *~ 'angel,* spirit watching over a person or place. **'⁓-ship** /-ʃɪp/ *n* position or office of a ⁓.

guava /'gwɑːvə/ *n* (topical tree with) pink edible fruit surrounded by a light yellow outer skin. ⇨ the illus at fruit.

gu·ber·na·torial /ˌguːbənə'tɔːrɪəl/ *adj* (US, Nigeria, etc) of a (state) Governor.

gudg·eon /'ɡʌdʒən/ *n* small freshwater fish used as bait.

guel·der rose /'ɡeldə rəʊz/ *n* plant with round bunches of white flowers; snowball tree.

guer·rilla, guer·illa /ɡə'rɪlə/ *n* person, not a member of a regular army, engaged in fighting in small, secret groups. ⁓ **warfare** *n* [U] such fighting. ⁓ **war** *n* [C] war fought by ⁓s on one side or both sides. **urban** ⁓ *n* ⁓ who operates in towns only.

guess /ɡes/ *vt, vi* [VP6A,25,9,8,10,2A,C,3A] ⁓ **(at)**, form an opinion, give an answer, make a statement, based on supposition, not on careful thought, calculation or definite knowledge: *Can you ⁓ my weight/what my weight is/how much I weigh? I should ⁓ his age at 50/⁓ him to be 50/⁓ that he is 50. Can't you even ⁓ at her age? G⁓ what I'm thinking. You've ⁓ed right/wrong. I ⁓* (US colloq, = *suppose*) *you're right.* □ *n* [C] opinion formed by ⁓ing: *make/have a ⁓* (*at sth*). *One man's ⁓ is as good as another's. it's anybody's ⁓,* no one can be sure about it. *at a ⁓,* making a ⁓: *At a ⁓ I should say there were 50 people present. by ⁓,* by the use of ⁓ing: *Don't answer by ⁓; work the problem out.* **'⁓-timate** /'ɡestɪmət/ *n* (modern colloq) estimate made by combining ⁓ing with reasoning. **'⁓-work** *n* [U] ⁓ing; result of ⁓ing.

guest /ɡest/ *n* person staying at or paying a visit to another's house or being entertained at a meal· *We're expecting ⁓s to dinner.* **'⁓-room** *n* bedroom kept for the use of ⁓s. **'⁓-house** *n* boarding-house. **'⁓-night** *n* evening on which members of a club, college, mess², etc may bring in and entertain their friends as ⁓s. **,paying '⁓** *n* boarder in sb's house. ⇨ **board¹**(8), **board²**(2).

guf·faw /ɡə'fɔː/ *vi, n* (give a) noisy laugh.

guid·ance /'ɡaɪdns/ *n* [U] guiding or being guided; leadership.

guide /ɡaɪd/ *n* **1** person who shows others the way, esp a person employed to point out interesting sights on a journey or visit. **,Girl 'G⁓,** ⇨ girl. **2** sth that directs or influences (conduct, etc): *Instinct is not always a good ⁓.* **'⁓-line** *n* (usu *pl*) advice (usu from sb in authority) on policy, etc: *⁓-lines on prices and incomes.* **3** (also **'⁓-book**) book for travellers, tourists, etc with information about a place: *a ⁓ to the British Museum; a ⁓ to Italy.* **4** book of information; manual: *a G⁓ to Poultry Keeping.* **5** bar, rod or part of a machine or apparatus that keeps other parts, etc, moving as desired. □ *vt* [VP6A,15A,B] act as ⁓ to: *⁓ sb to a place; ⁓ sb in/out/up, etc. You must be ⁓d by your sense of what is right and just. ,⁓d 'missile,* rocket (for use in war) which can be ⁓d to its destination while in flight by electronic devices.

guild /ɡɪld/ *n* (older spelling **gild**) society of persons for helping one another, forwarding common interests, eg trade, social welfare. **,G⁓-'hall** *n* hall in which members of a ⁓ met in the Middle Ages. **the 'G⁓-hall,** hall of the Corporation of the City of London, used for banquets, receptions, etc. ⁓ **socialism,** system by which an industry is to be controlled by a council of its members.

guilder /'ɡɪldə(r)/ *n* unit of currency of the Nether-

lands.

guile /ɡaɪl/ *n* [U] deceit; cunning: *a man full of ⁓; get sth by ⁓.* **⁓·less** *adj* ⁓·**ful** /-fl/ *adj*

guille·mot /'ɡɪlɪmɒt/ *n* kinds of arctic sea-bird. ⇨ the illus at water.

guillo·tine /'ɡɪlətiːn/ *n* **1** machine for beheading (criminals in France) with a heavy blade sliding in grooves dropped from a height. **2** kind of machine for cutting the edges of books during manufacture, trimming sheets of paper, etc. **3** (in Parliament) method of stopping obstruction of a bill (by excessive debate) by fixing times for taking votes. □ *vt* [VP6A] use the ⁓ on.

guilt /ɡɪlt/ *n* [U] condition of having done wrong; responsibility for wrong-doing: *The ⁓ of the accused man was in doubt. innocent; without ⁓: ⁓less of the offence;* not having knowledge or possession. ⁓**y** *adj* (-ier, -iest) ⁓**y (of), 1** having done wrong: *plead ⁓y to a crime; be ⁓y of a crime.* **2** showing or feeling guilt: *look ⁓y; ⁓y looks; a ⁓y conscience.* ⁓·**ily** /-ɪlɪ/ *adv* ⁓·**iness** *n*

guinea /'ɡɪnɪ/ *n* (*pl* ⁓s abbr **gns**) (called *money of account,* ⇨ account ¹(2)) formerly the sum of twenty-one shillings (now £1.05, or 105p), for which there was neither coin nor banknote, used in stating prices of goods, professional fees, charges, subscriptions, etc: *the 2000 Gns race,* horse-race with a prize of 2000 ⁓s.

guinea-fowl /'ɡɪnɪ faʊl/ *n* (*pl* unchanged) domestic fowl of the pheasant family, with dark grey feathers spotted with white.

guinea-pig /'ɡɪnɪ pɪɡ/ *n* short-eared animal like a big rat, often used in scientific experiments; sb allowing himself to be used in medical or other experiments. ⇨ the illus at small.

Guin·ness /'ɡɪnɪs/ *n* (P) kind of bitter stout; bottle or glass of this: *A pint of draught ⁓, please.*

guise /ɡaɪz/ *n* [C] **1** (old use) style of dress: *in the ⁓ of a monk.* **2** *in/under the ⁓ of,* assuming a particular manner or appearance: *under the ⁓ of friendship.*

guitar /ɡɪ'tɑː(r)/ *n* (usu) six-stringed musical instrument, plucked with the fingers or a plectrum. ⇨ the illus at string.

gulch /ɡʌltʃ/ *n* (US) deep, narrow, rocky valley.

gul·den /'ɡʊldən/ *n* = guilder.

gulf /ɡʌlf/ *n* **1** part of the sea almost surrounded by land: *the G⁓ of Mexico.* **the 'G⁓ Stream,** warm ocean current flowing north from the G⁓ of Mexico to Europe. **2** deep hollow; chasm; abyss; (fig) dividing line, division (*between* opinions, etc).

gull¹ /ɡʌl/ *n* large, long-winged sea-bird. ⇨ the illus at water.

gull² /ɡʌl/ *vt* [VP6A,15A] cheat; deceive: *⁓ a fool out of his money.* □ *n* person who is easily ⁓ed. ⁓·**ible** /-əbl/ *adj* easily ⁓ed. ⁓·**i-bil·ity** /ˌɡʌlə'bɪlətɪ/ *n*

gul·let /'ɡʌlɪt/ *n* food passage from the mouth to the stomach; throat. ⇨ the illus at head.

gully /'ɡʌlɪ/ *n* (*pl* -lies) narrow channel cut or formed by rainwater, eg on a hillside, or made for carrying water away from a building.

gulp /ɡʌlp/ *vt, vi* [VP2A,6A,15B] ⁓ **(down),** swallow (food or drink) quickly or greedily: *⁓ down a cup of tea;* hold back or suppress (as if swallowing sth); make a ⁓ing motion. □ *n* [C] act of ⁓ing: *empty a glass at one ⁓;* amount that is ⁓ed; mouthful, esp of sth liquid: *a ⁓ of cold tea.*

gum¹ /ɡʌm/ *n* (usu *pl*) firm, pink flesh round the

teeth: *The dog bared its gums at me.* ⇨ the illus at mouth. **gum·boil** /'gʌmbɔɪl/ *n* boil or abscess on the gums.

gum² /gʌm/ *n* **1** [U] sticky substance exuded from some trees, used for sticking things together. **2** [U] gum that has been specially prepared in some way: *chewing-gum;* [C] (also '*gum-drop*) hard, transparent sweet made of gelatine, etc. **3** (also '*gum-tree*) eucalyptus tree. **up a gum-tree,** (sl) in difficulties. '**gum·boot,** high rubber boot. '**gum·shoe,** (US) **(a)** rubber shoe or overshoe. **(b)** (sl) detective. □ *vt* (-mm-) [VP6A,15A,B] stick together with gum; spread gum on the surface of: *gum sth down; gum two things together.* **gummy** *adj* (-ier, -iest) sticky.

gum³ /gʌm/ *n* (esp N England) (in oaths, etc) God: *By gum!*

gum·bo /'gʌmbəʊ/ *n* (US) thick okra soup.

gump·tion /'gʌmpʃn/ *n* [U] (colloq) common sense and initiative; qualities likely to bring success: *The lad lacks* ～.

gun /gʌn/ *n* **1** general name for any kind of firearm that sends shells or bullets from a metal tube: *a warship with 16-inch guns; machine-guns.* ⇨ cannon, carbine, musket, pistol, revolver, rifle¹. **be going great guns,** be proceeding vigorously and successfully. **blow great guns,** (of the wind) blow violently. **stick to one's guns,** maintain one's position against attack or argument. '**gun·boat** *n* small warship carrying heavy guns, or long-range missiles. **gun-boat diplomacy,** (fig) diplomacy backed by the threat of force. '**gun·carriage** *n* wheeled support of a big gun, or part on which a gun slides when it recoils. '**gun·cotton** *n* [U] explosive of acid-soaked cotton. '**gun·fire** *n* [U] firing of gun(s). **gun·man** /-mən/ *n* (*pl*-men) man who uses a gun to rob or kill people. '**gun·metal** *n* alloy of copper and tin or zinc; dull blue-grey colour. '**gun·powder** *n* explosive powder used in guns, fireworks, blasting, etc. **the 'Gunpowder Plot,** plot to blow up the Houses of Parliament, 5 Nov 1605. '**gun·room** *n* (in a warship) room for junior officers. '**gun·running** *n* [U] introduction of firearms, secretly and illegally, into a country, eg to help a revolt. '**gun·runner** *n* person engaged in this. '**gun·shot** *n* **(a)** [C] shot fired by a gun. **(b)** [U] range of a gun: *be out of/within gunshot.* '**gun·smith** *n* person who makes and repairs small firearms. **2** person using a sporting gun, as a member of a shooting party. **3 big gun,** (colloq) important or powerful person. □ *vt* [VP6A,15B] *gun sb (down),* shoot with a gun.

gun·ner /'gʌnə(r)/ *n* (in the army) soldier in the artillery; (in the navy) warrant officer in charge of a battery of guns. ～**y** *n* [U] construction and management of large guns.

gunny /'gʌni/ *n* [U] strong, coarse material used for making sacks, bales, bags, etc.

gun·wale /'gʌnl/ *n* (naut) upper edge of the side of a boat or a small ship. ⇨ the illus at row.

gurgle /'gɜːgl/ *n* [C,U] bubbling sound as of water flowing from a narrow-necked bottle: ～*s of delight.* □ *vi* make this sound: *The baby was gurgling happily.*

Gur·kha /'gɜːkə/ *n* member of a ruling group in Nepal who became famous as soldiers in the British Indian army.

guru /'gʊruː/ *n* Hindu spiritual teacher; (colloq) respected and influential teacher or authority.

gush /gʌʃ/ *vi* [VP2A,C,3A] **1** burst, flow, out suddenly: *oil* ～*ing from a new well; blood* ～*ing from a wound.* **2** talk with excessive enthusiasm: *young mothers* ～*ing over their babies; girls who* ～ *over handsome film stars.* □ *n* sudden outburst or outflow: *a* ～ *of oil/anger/enthusiasm.* ～**er** *n* oil-well with a strong natural flow (so that pumping is not needed). ～**ing** *adj;* ～*ing compliments.* ⇨ **2** above. ～**ing·ly** *adv*

gus·set /'gʌsɪt/ *n* [C] (usu triangular or diamond-shaped) piece of cloth inserted in a garment to strengthen or enlarge it.

gust /gʌst/ *n* [C] sudden, violent rush of wind; burst of rain, hail, fire or smoke; (fig) outburst of feeling: *The wind was blowing in* ～*s.* ～**y** *adj* (-ier, -iest) stormy; with wind blowing in ～*s.*

gus·ta·tion /gʌ'steɪʃn/ *n* [U] (formal) tasting.

gusto /'gʌstəʊ/ *n* [U] enjoyment in doing sth.

gut /gʌt/ *n* **1** (*pl*) (colloq) intestines; bowels: *stick a bayonet into a man's guts.* **hate sb's guts,** hate him intensely. **2** (*pl*) (colloq) contents of anything: *His speech had no guts in it,* no real arguments, force, etc. **The real guts** (= The essence) *of his speech is....* **3** (*pl*) (colloq) courage and determination: *a man with plenty of guts.* **4** [U] strong cord made from the intestines of animals, used for the strings of violins, etc. ⇨ catgut. □ *vt* (-tt-) [VP6A] **1** take the guts(1) out of (a fish, etc). **2** destroy the inside of or the contents of: *a building gutted by fire.* **gut·less** *adj* lacking in guts(3).

gutta-per·cha /,gʌtə 'pɜːtʃə/ *n* [U] rubber-like substance made from the juice of various Malayan trees.

gut·ter¹ /'gʌtə(r)/ *n* [C] **1** channel or trough (usu metal) fixed under the edge of a roof to carry away rainwater; channel at the side of a road for the same purpose. **2 the** ～, (fig) poor or debased state of life: *the language of the* ～, low and vulgar language. **take a child out of the** ～, remove it from poor and wretched conditions. **the 'gutter press,** newspapers giving much space to salacious stories, scandals, etc. '～**·snipe** /-snaɪp/ *n* poor, badly-dressed child who plays in slum streets.

gut·ter /'gʌtə(r)/ *vi* [VP2A] (of a candle) burn unsteadily so that the melted wax flows down the sides.

gut·tural /'gʌtərəl/ *n, adj* (sound that seems to be) produced in the throat: ～ *consonants.* ～**·ly** *adv*

guv·nor /'gʌvnə(r)/ *n* (GB sl) boss.

guy¹ /gaɪ/ *n* [C] rope or chain used to keep sth steady or secured, eg to hold a tent in place.

guy² /gaɪ/ *n* **1** figure in the form of a man, dressed in old clothes (eg as burned on 5 Nov in memory of Guy Fawkes's Gunpowder Plot). **2** person dressed in a strange or queer-looking way. **3** (sl) man. ⇨ *fall-guy* at fall¹(1). □ *vt* (*pt,pp* guyed) [VP6A] ridicule; exhibit (sb) in effigy.

Guy's /gaɪz/ *n* (used for) Guy's Hospital (in London).

guzzle /'gʌzl/ *vi,vt* [VP2A,6A,15B] (colloq) eat or drink greedily: *be always guzzling;* ～ *beer.* **guz·zler** /-zlə(r)/ *n* person who ～*s.*

gybe (US **jibe**) /dʒaɪb/ *vi,vt* [VP2A,6A] (naut) (of a sail or boom) swing from one side of the ship to the other; (of a ship or a ship's crew) cause this to happen. ⇨ the illus at barque.

gym /dʒɪm/ *n* (sl) (short for) gymnasium, gymnastics: '*gym-shoes; the 'gym mistress.* '**gym-slip** *n* sleeveless tunic worn in GB by some girls as part of school uniform.

gym·khana /dʒɪm'kɑːnə/ *n* public display of athletics, horse-riding or vehicle-driving competitions.

gym·nasium /dʒɪm'neɪzɪəm/ n (pl ~s) room or hall with apparatus for physical training.

gym·nas·tic /dʒɪm'næstɪk/ adj of physical training. ~s n pl (forms of) exercises for physical training. **gym·nast** /'dʒɪmnæst/ n expert in ~s.

gynae·col·ogy (US = **gyne-**) /ˌgaɪnɪ'kɒlədʒɪ/ n [U] science of the diseases of women and pregnancies. **gynae·colo·gist** (US = **gyne-**) expert in ~. **gynae·co·logi·cal** (US = **gyne-**) /ˌgaɪnɪkə'lɒdʒɪkl/ adj

gyp¹ /dʒɪp/ vt [VP6A] (sl) cheat.

gyp² /dʒɪp/ n **give sb gyp,** (sl) scold or punish him without mercy.

gyp·sum /'dʒɪpsəm/ n [U] mineral (calcium sulphate, $CaSO_4$) from which plaster of Paris is made; also used as a fertilizer.

Gypsy /'dʒɪpsɪ/ n ⇨ gipsy.

gy·rate /ˌdʒaɪ'reɪt US: 'dʒaɪreɪt/ vi move round in circles or spirals; revolve. **gy·ra·tion** /ˌdʒaɪ'reɪʃn/ n [C,U] revolving; revolution.

gyro /'dʒaɪərəʊ/ n (colloq abbr of) gyroscope.

a gyroscope

gyro·scope /'dʒaɪrəskəʊp/ n wheel which, when spinning fast, keeps steady the object in which it is fixed. **gyro·scopic** /ˌdʒaɪrə'skɒpɪk/ adj

Hh

H, h /eɪtʃ/ (pl H's, h's /'eɪtʃɪz/), the eighth letter of the English alphabet. **drop one's h's,** omit the sound /h/, eg by saying *'ot* for *hot.*

ha /hɑ:/ int used to express surprise, joy, triumph, suspicion, etc. When repeated in print ('*Ha! Ha! Ha!*') it indicates laughter.

ha·beas cor·pus /ˌheɪbɪəs 'kɔ:pəs/ n (Lat; legal) *(writ of)* ~, order requiring a person to be brought before a judge or into court, esp to investigate the right of the law to keep him in prison.

hab·er·dasher /'hæbədæʃə(r)/ n shopkeeper who sells clothing, small articles of dress, pins, cotton, etc. **~y** n [U] ~'s goods or business.

ha·bili·ments /hə'bɪlɪmənts/ n pl (liter or hum) clothing.

habit /'hæbɪt/ n **1** [C] sb's settled practice, esp sth that cannot easily be given up: *the* ~ *of smoking;* ~*-forming drugs.* **be in/fall into/get into the** ~ **of,** have, acquire, the ~ of. **fall/get into bad** ~**s,** acquire them: *Don't let yourself get into bad* ~**s.** **get sb into the** ~ **of/into bad** ~**s,** cause him to have the ~ of/bad ~s: *Don't let him get you into the* ~ *of taking drugs.* **fall/get out of the** ~ **of,** abandon the ~ of. **make a** ~ **of sth,** do it regularly. **2** [U] usual behaviour: *H*~ *is second nature.* **creature of** ~, sb whose life is marked by many ~s(1). **do sth/act from force of** ~, because it is one's ~. **do sth out of** ~, because it is one's ~. **3** [C] (old use) condition, general quality (of mind or body): *a cheerful* ~ *of mind.* **4** [C] dress worn by members of a religious order: *a monk's* ~. **'riding** ~, woman's coat and skirt for horse-riding.

hab·it·able /'hæbɪtəbl/ adj fit to be lived in: *The old house is no longer* ~.

habi·tat /'hæbɪtæt/ n (of plants, animals) usual natural place and conditions of growth; home.

habi·ta·tion /ˌhæbɪ'teɪʃn/ n **1** [U] living in: *houses that were not fit for* ~. **2** [C] (liter) place to live in: *On these plains there was not a single human* ~.

ha·bit·ual /hə'bɪtʃʊəl/ adj **1** regular, usual: *He took his* ~ *seat at the dining-table.* **2** acting by habit; having a regular habit: *a* ~ *liar/drunkard/ cinema-goer.* **~ly** /-tʃʊəlɪ/ adv as a habit: *Tom is* ~*ly late for school.*

ha·bitu·ate /hə'bɪtʃʊeɪt/ vt [VP14] ~ **sb/oneself**

to sth, (formal) accustom; get (sb/oneself) used to (sth): ~ *oneself to hard work/getting up early/a cold climate;* ~ *a horse to the sound of gunfire.*

habi·tude /'hæbɪtju:d US: -tu:d/ n [U] (formal) custom; tendency; habitual way of acting or doing things.

ha·bitué /hə'bɪtʃʊeɪ/ n person who regularly goes to a place: *a* ~ *of the orchestral concerts/of the Café Royal.*

haci·enda /ˌhæsɪ'endə/ n (pl ~s) (in Latin American countries) large landed estate with a house.

hack¹ /hæk/ vt,vi [VP6A,15A,B,2A,C,3A] ~ *(at),* cut roughly or clumsily; chop: *After the murderer had killed his victim, he* ~*ed the body to pieces. He* ~*ed at the branch* (ie struck heavy blows at it) *until it fell to the ground.* ~**ing cough,** short, dry cough. '~**saw** n one with a replaceable blade in a frame, for cutting through metal. ⇨ the illus at tool.

hack² /hæk/ n **1** horse that may be hired. **2** person paid to do hard and uninteresting work as a writer: *publisher's* ~**s.** □ vi ride on horseback on roads, at an ordinary pace: *go* ~*ing.*

hackles /'hæklz/ n pl long feathers on the neck of the domestic cock: *with his* ~ *up,* (of a cock, dog or man) angry; ready to fight. **have one's/get sb's** ~ **up,** be, make sb angry, ready to fight.

hack·ney /'hæknɪ/ n ordinary kind of horse for riding or driving. '~ **carriage,** one that may be hired. ~**ed** /'hæknɪd/ adj (esp of sayings) too common; repeated too often.

had /hæd/ ⇨ have¹.

had·dock /'hædək/ n (pl unchanged) sea-fish much used for food, esp *smoked* ~.

Hades /'heɪdi:z/ n (Gk myth) the underworld; place where the spirits of the dead go.

Hadji /'hædʒɪ/ n (title of a) Muslim pilgrim who has been to Mecca.

haem- ⇨ hem-.

haft /hɑ:ft US: hæft/ n handle of an axe, knife, dagger, etc.

hag /hæg/ n witch; ugly old woman, esp one who does, or is thought to do, evil. '**hag-ridden,** afflicted by nightmares; harassed.

hag·gard /'hægəd/ adj (of a person, his face) looking tired and lined, esp from worry, lack of sleep

hag·gis /'hægɪs/ n Scottish dish of various parts of a sheep, cut up, mixed with oatmeal, and cooked in a sheep's stomach.

haggle /'hægl/ vi [VP2A,3A] ~ **(with sb) (about/over sth),** argue, dispute, esp the price of sth or the terms of a bargain.

hagi·ol·ogy /ˌhægɪ'ɒlədʒɪ/ n literature of the lives and legends of saints.

haha /'hɑːhɑː/ n wall or fence bounding a park or garden, sunk in a hollow so as not to interfere with the view.

hail¹ /heɪl/ n 1 [U] frozen rain-drops falling from the sky. '~-**stone** n [C] small ball of ~: ~stones as big as peas. '~-**storm** n storm with fall of ~. 2 (usu **a** ~ **of**) sth coming in great numbers and force: a ~ of blows/curses. □ vi,vt 1 (impers) (of ~) come down: It ~ed in the late afternoon. 2 [VP2C,15B] ~ **(sth) down (on sb),** (of blows, etc) come, send down, hard and fast (on): Blows ~ed down on his back. They ~ed curses down on us.

hail² /heɪl/ vt,vi 1 [VP6A,16B,23] greet; give a welcoming cry to; call out to (so as to attract attention): Cheerful voices ~ed us as we entered the hall. They ~ed him (as) king. He was ~ed as a hero. Let's ~ a taxi, shall we? 2 [VP3A] ~ **from,** come from: Where does the ship ~ from, Which is her home port? (colloq, of persons) They ~ from all parts of the country. □ n greeting; ~ing cry. **within** ~, (esp of ships) near enough to be ~ed. **be** ~-**fellow-well-'met (with sb),** be very familiar and friendly.

hair /heə(r)/ n 1 [U] (collective sing) all the thread-like growths on the skin of animals, esp on the human head, ⇨ the illus at **head**; thread-like growth on the stems and leaves of some plants; ~-like thing: brush one's ~; have one's '~ cut; a cat with a fine coat of ~; [C] single thread of ~: find a ~ in the soup; two blonde ~s on his coat collar; (archaic) (pl, in collective sense): It will bring down my grey ~s in sorrow to the grave, cause me, who am old, to die of sorrow. **get sb by the 'short ~s,** (sl) have him at one's mercy; get complete control of him. **keep your '~ on,** (sl) keep cool; don't lose your temper. **let one's '~ down,** (of a woman) remove the pins and allow the ~ to fall over the shoulders; (fig) relax after a period of being formal. **lose one's ~,** (a) become bald. (b) lose one's temper. **make one's'~ stand on end,** fill one with fright or horror. **put one's '~ up,** arrange it so that it is rolled up on one's head. **split ~s,** make or pretend to see differences of meaning, distinctions, etc, so small as to be unimportant. Hence, '~-**splitting** n [U] acting in this way. **tear one's ~,** show great sorrow or vexation. **not turn a ~,** give no sign of being troubled. **to a ~,** (of describing sth) exactly. 2 (compounds) '~('s)-**breadth** n very small distance: escape by a ~'s-breadth; have a ~-breadth escape, a very narrow one. '~-**brush** n toilet brush for the ~. ⇨ the illus at **brush.** '~-**cloth** n cloth made of a mixture of fabric and animal's ~ for various purposes. '~-**cut** n act or style of cutting the ~ (by a barber or ~dresser). '~-**do** n (colloq) haircut. '~-**dresser** n person who dresses and cuts ~. ⇨ barber. '~-**dye** n dye for the ~. '~-**line** n area where the roots of ~ join the forehead; width of a ~; (attrib) very narrow: a ~line space/fracture. '~-**net** n net for keeping the ~ in place. '~-**oil** n oil for dressing the ~. '~-**piece** n tress of false ~. '~-**pin** n

hairpin bends

(woman's) pin for keeping the ~ in place. '~-**pin 'bend** n sharp bend on a road, esp on a steep road, so that the road doubles back. '~-**raising** adj terrifying. ~-'**shirt** n shirt made of ~cloth, uncomfortable to wear, for ascetics. '~-**slide** n metal clip for keeping ~ tidily in place. '~-**spring** n very delicate spring in a watch, controlling the balance-wheel. '~-**style** n style of haircut. '~-**stylist** n ~dresser. '~-**trigger,** one that fires a gun, etc at the slightest pressure. ~-**less** adj without ~; bald. '~-**like** adj ~y adj (-ier, -iest) of or like ~; covered with ~: a ~y chest. ~**i-ness** n

hake /heɪk/ n (pl unchanged) fish of the cod family, used as food.

hal·berd /'hælbəd/ n weapon used in the Middle Ages, a combined spear and battle-axe on a long handle. **hal·ber·dier** /ˌhælbə'dɪə(r)/ n soldier armed with a ~.

hal·cyon /'hælsɪən/ adj calm and peaceful: ~ days/weather.

hale /heɪl/ adj (usu of old persons) (rare except in) ~ **and hearty,** strong and healthy.

half /hɑːf US: hæf/ n (pl halves /hɑːvz US: hævz/) adj, adv 1 one of two equal or corresponding parts into which a thing is divided: The ~ of 6 is 3/H~ of 6 is 3. Two halves make a whole. Two pounds and a ~/Two and a ~ pounds. H~ of the fruit is bad. H~ (of) the plums are bad. I want ~ as much again, one and a ~ the amount. Cut it in ~/into halves. **(do sth) by halves,** incompletely, imperfectly. **go halves (with sb) (in sth),** share equally. **too clever, etc by ~,** far too clever, etc. **one's better** ~, (colloq) one's wife, husband, etc. **2** (as adv) to the extent of a ~; to a considerable degree; nearly: meat that is only ~ cooked; ~-cooked cabbage; not ~ (= not nearly) long enough; ~ dead, (colloq) tired out, exhausted; not ~ bad, (sl) not at all bad; quite good. **not ~,** (sl) to the greatest possible extent: He didn't ~ swear, He swore very violently. 'Was she annoyed?' 'Not ~!' (ie she was intensely annoyed). **3** (in compounds) ˌ~ a '**crown,** a ˌ~-'**crown** nn (before 1971) coin or amount of 2½ shillings (12½p). ˌ~ a '**dozen** n six. ˌ~ **and** '~ n what is ~ one thing and ~ the other, eg a mixture of beer and lemonade. '~-**back** n (in football/hockey, etc) (position of) player (defender) between the forwards and the backs. ˌ~-'**baked** adj (colloq) dull-witted; crude and inexperienced: a ~-baked young man; foolish; of poor quality: ~-baked ideas. '~-**blood** n (relationship of a) person having one parent in common with another. '~-**breed** n (a) person with parents of different races. (b) offspring of two animals or plants of different species. '~-**brother** n brother by one parent only. '~-**caste** n ~-breed person. ~ '**cock** n position of the hammer of a gun when pulled ~-way back. **go off at** ~ **cock,** (fig) act too soon and fail. ˌ~-'**hardy** adj (of plants) requiring protection from frost but otherwise suitable for growing in the open. ˌ~-'**hearted** adj done with, showing, little interest or enthusiasm: a ~-hearted *attempt.* Hence, ,~-'heartedly *adv* ,~-'holiday *n* day of which ~ (usu the afternoon) is free from work or duty. , ~ an 'hour, a ,~-'hour *nn* period of 30 minutes. ,~-'hourly *adj, adv* done, occurring every 30 minutes: *a ~-hourly bus service.* ,~-'length *adj* (of a portrait) of the upper ~ of a person. *at ,~-mast,* (of a flag) at the position, near the middle of a mast, to indicate mourning: *Flags were at ~-mast everywhere on the day of the President's funeral.* ,~-'pay *n* [U] reduced pay given to sb when not fully employed but not yet retired: *placed on ~-pay.* ~penny /'heɪpnɪ *US:* 'hæfpenɪ/ *n* British coin worth ~ a penny (½d before 1971, ½p now). ~penny·worth /'heɪpnɪwɜ:θ *US:* hæf'penɪwɜ:θ/, ha'p'orth /'heɪpəθ/ *n* as much as ½d would buy before 1971; now chiefly fig. ⇨ App 5. ,~-'price *adv* at ~ the usual price: *Children admitted ~-price.* ,~-seas-'over *pred adj* (colloq) ~ drunk. '~-sister *n* sister by one parent only. ,~-'size *adj* ~ the usual or regular size. ,~-'timbered *adj* (of a building) having walls of a wooden framework filled in with brick, stone or plaster. ,~-'time *n* [U] (a) work and pay for ~ the usual time: *Owing to the business depression the workers are on ~-time this month.* (b) the interval between the two halves of a game of football, etc: *The score at ~-time was 2—2.* '~-tone *n* black and white photograph reproduced on paper, eg as an illustration in a book. '~-track *n* troop-carrying vehicle with tracks(5) on both sides at the rear and wheels at the front. Hence, ,~-tracked *adj* '~-truth *n* statement that conveys only a part of the truth. ,~-'way *adj* (a) situated at an equal distance from two places. (b) going ~ the way; not thorough: *In an emergency ~-way measures are usually unsatisfactory.* □ *adv* to or at ~ the distance: *meet a person ~-way,* be ready to make a compromise. ,~-'witted *adj* weak-minded. Hence, '~-wit *n* ~-witted person. ,~-'yearly *adj, adv* (done, occurring) every ~ year.

hali·but /'hælɪbət/ *n* (*pl* unchanged) large, flat sea-fish used as food.

hali·tosis /ˌhælɪ'təʊsɪs/ *n* [U] bad-smelling breath.

hall /hɔ:l/ *n* 1 (building with) large room for meetings, concerts, public business, etc: *the Town/City H~; the County H~; the H~ of Justice; the Festival H~,* for concerts, in London; '*dance-~s.* 2 [U] (in colleges at English universities) large room for meals: *dine in ~.* 3 building for university students: *a ~ of residence.* 4 (in England) large country house, usu one that belongs to the chief landowner in the district. 5 passage, space, into which the main entrance or front door of a building opens: *Leave your hat and coat in the ~.* '~-stand *n* piece of furniture for hats, coats, umbrellas, etc. 6 building of a guild: *Saddlers' H~.*

hall·mark /'hɔ:lmɑ:k/ *n* mark used for marking the standard of gold and silver in articles (as a guarantee of quality); (fig) distinguishing characteristic (usu of excellence). □ *vt* stamp a ~ on.

hal·le·lu·jah /ˌhælɪ'lu:jə/ *n, int* praise to God.

hal·liard /'hæljəd/ *n* = halyard.

hallo /hə'ləʊ/ *int* = hullo.

hal·loo /hə'lu:/ *int, n* cry to urge on hounds; shout to attract attention. □ *vi* shout 'H~!', esp to hounds.

hal·low[1] /'hæləʊ/ *vt* [VP6A] (usu passive) make holy; regard as holy: *ground ~ed by sacred memories.*

hal·low[2] /'hæləʊ/ *n* (only in) **All H~'s Day,** ⇨

all[1](6).

Hal·low·e·en /ˌhæləʊ'i:n/ *n* 31 Oct, eve of All Saints' Day or All Hallows' Day.

hal·luci·na·tion /həˌlu:sɪ'neɪʃn/ *n* [C,U] (instance of) seeming to see sth not present, sth imagined: *Drunken men are sometimes subject to ~s.* **hal·luci·na·tory** /hə'lu:sɪnətrɪ *US:* -tɔ:rɪ/, **hal·luci·no·genic** /həˌlu:sɪnə'dʒenɪk/ *adjj* (of drugs) inducing ~.

halma /'hælmə/ *n* [U] game played on a board of 256 squares where pieces are moved from one corner to the other.

halo /'heɪləʊ/ *n* (*pl* ~es, ~s /-ləʊz/) circle of light round the sun or moon or (in paintings) round or above the heads of Christ or sacred figures.

halt[1] /hɔ:lt/ *n* 1 (chiefly mil, of soldiers) *call a ~ (to),* make a short stop on a march or journey: *The officer called a ~. It's time to call a ~ to vandalism,* (fig) end it. 2 (more general use) *come to a ~,* make a stop or pause: *The train came to a ~.* ⇨ grind(6). 3 stopping-place (smaller than a station) on a railway-line, where trains stop for a short time only. □ *vi, vt* 1 [VP2A] (as a mil command) stop marching; come to a ~. 2 [VP6A] bring to a ~: *The officer ~ed his troops for a rest.*

halt[2] /hɔ:lt/ *vi* [VP2A,C] hesitate; walk in a hesitating way: *~ between two opinions; in a ~ing voice.* □ *adj* (archaic) lame: *the ~ and the blind.* ~ing·ly *adv* in a ~ing way.

hal·ter /'hɔ:ltə(r)/ *n* 1 rope or leather strap put round a horse's head (for leading or fastening the horse). 2 rope used for hanging a person.

halve /hɑ:v *US:* hæv/ *vt* [VP6A] 1 divide into two equal parts: *~ an apple.* 2 lessen by one half: *The newest planes have ~d the time needed for crossing the Atlantic.*

halves /hɑ:vz *US:* hævz/ *pl* of half.

hal·yard /'hæljəd/ *n* rope for raising or lowering a sail or flag.

ham /hæm/ *n* 1 [C] upper part of a pig's leg, salted and dried or smoked: *hams hanging on hooks;* [U] this as meat: *a slice of ham; a ham sandwich.* 2 [C] (chiefly used of animals) back of the thigh, thigh and buttock. 3 (sl) poor actor or performer; amateur who sends and receives radio messages: *a radio ham;* (attrib) *ham actors/acting/radio.* ,ham-'handed/-'fisted *adj* clumsy in using the hands. □ *vt, vi* (-mm-) [VP2A,6A,15B] *ham (up),* (colloq) act in a deliberately artificial, exaggerated way.

hama·dryad /ˌhæmə'draɪəd/ *n* nymph living and dying with the tree she inhabited; poisonous Indian snake.

ham·burger /'hæmbɜ:gə(r)/ *n* 1 ground or chopped beef made into round flat cakes and fried. 2 sandwich or bread roll filled with this.

ham·let /'hæmlɪt/ *n* group of houses in the country; small village, esp one without a church.

ham·mer /'hæmə(r)/ *n* 1 tool with a heavy metal head used for breaking things, driving in nails, etc. ⇨ the illus at tool. *be/go at it ~ and tongs,* fight, argue, with great energy and noise. *throwing the ~,* athletic competition in which a heavy long-handled ~ is thrown as far as possible. 2 (in a piano, etc) one of the ~-like parts that strike the strings. 3 part of the firing device of a gun that strikes and explodes the charge. 4 wooden mallet used by an auctioneer. *be/come under the ~,* be sold by auction. 5 (anat) bone in the ear. ⇨ the illus at ear. □ *vt, vi* [VP6A,22,15B,2A,C,3A] *~ (in/*

out/down); ~ *(at),* **1** strike or beat with a ~, or as if with a ~: ~ *nails into wood;* ~ *down the lid of a box,* fasten it down by ~ing; ~ *in a nail/*~ *a nail in;* ~ *a piece of metal flat;* ~ *sth out,* make it flat or smooth by ~ing; ~ *at the door,* eg with a stick, one's fists; ~ *at the keys,* play the piano loudly, without feeling. **2** (fig) [VP15B] ~ *out,* produce by hard work: ~ *out a scheme;* [VP3A] ~ *at,* work hard at: ~ *away at a problem/a solution/a compromise;* [VP6A] force: ~ *an idea into sb's head.* **3** (colloq) inflict heavy defeats on (sb) in war or in games.

ham·mock /'hæmək/ *n* hanging bed of canvas or rope network, eg as used by sailors, or in gardens.

ham·per[1] /'hæmpə(r)/ *n* packing-case or basket with a lid, esp one used for sending food: *a Christmas* ~, one sent as a present, with food, wine, etc.

ham·per[2] /'hæmpə(r)/ *vt* [VP6A] hinder; prevent free movement or activity: ~*ed by a heavy overcoat.*

ham·ster /'hæmstə(r)/ *n* rodent like a large rat, kept by children as a pet.

ham·string /'hæmstrɪŋ/ *vt* (*pt,pp* ~ed or hamstrung /'hæmstrʌŋ/) [VP6A] cripple (a person or animal) by cutting the tendon(s) at the back of the knee(s); (fig) destroy the power or efficiency of.

hand[1] /hænd/ *n* **1** part of the human arm beyond the wrist: *with his* ~*s in his pockets.* ⇨ the illus at **arm. at** ~, near; within reach: *He lives close at* ~, quite near. *The examinations are at* ~. **at sb's** ~*s,* from sb: *I did not expect such unkind treatment at your* ~*s.* **bind sb** ~ **and foot,** (lit, fig) make him completely helpless. **serve/wait on sb** ~ **and foot,** attend to his every wish; perform every sort of service for him. **by** ~, (a) without the use of machinery: *Are your socks knitted by* ~*/* ~*-knitted or machine-made?* (b) without the use of the post office: *The note was delivered by* ~, by a messenger. **bring up a baby/a calf, etc by** ~, rear it by feeding from a bottle: *The lamb had to be brought up by* ~. **eat/feed out of one's** ~, (a) (eg of a bird) be quite tame. (b) (fig) be ready to obey without question. **from** ~ **to** ~, directly, from one person to another: *Buckets of water were passed from* ~ *to* ~ *to put the fire out.* **fight** ~ **to** ~, at close quarters. Hence, ~*-to-*~ *fighting.* **give/lend (sb) a** ~ **(with sth),** help with, take a part in, doing sth: *Give (me) a* ~ *with the washing-up, please.* **give one's** ~ **on a bargain,** take sb's ~ and clasp it to seal the bargain. **be** ~ **in glove (with sb),** ⇨ glove. **have one's**[1] ~*s full,* have all the work one can do; be fully occupied. **have/get the upper** ~ **(of sb),** ⇨ upper. **have a free** ~; **give/allow sb a free** ~, ⇨ free[1](3). ~ **in** ~, holding ~s; together: *They walked away* ~ *in* ~. (fig) *War and misery go* ~ *in* ~. **H**~**s off!** Don't touch or interfere! **H**~**s up!** Put your ~s up! Surrender! ~ **over** ~, with each ~ used alternately (as when climbing, etc); (fig) rapidly and steadily. **in** ~, (a) in reserve, available for use: *I still have some money in* ~. *Cash in* ~, £27.25. (b) receiving attention; in course of completion: *The work is in* ~ *and will be finished by the end of the month. We have the situation well in* ~, are dealing with it satisfactorily. **in the** ~*s of,* being looked after or managed by. **in good** ~*s,* being well cared for. **lay (one's)** ~*s on sth/sb,* ⇨ lay[1](2). **lend a** ~, ⇨ *give a* ~, above. **not lift a** ~; **not do a** ~'s **turn,** make not the least attempt to help. **lift/raise a** ~*/one's* ~ *against sb,*

threaten, attack him. **live from** ~ **to mouth,** precariously, spending money as soon as it is received. Hence, *a* ~*-to-mouth existence.* **(get sth) off one's** ~*s,* taken from one's responsibility: *I'd be glad to get it off my* ~*s,* to rid myself of responsibility for it. **on** ~, available: *We have some new woollen goods on* ~, in our shop, warehouse, etc. **on one's** ~*s,* resting on one ~ as a responsibility: *I have an empty house on my* ~*s,* one for which I want to find a buyer or tenant. *Time hangs heavy on his* ~*s,* seems burdensome, passes slowly. **out of** ~, (a) out of control; undisciplined: *The football fans have got quite out of* ~. (b) at once, without hesitation: *The situation needs to be dealt with out of* ~. **shake** ~*s* **with sb; shake sb's** ~, grasp his ~ as a greeting, or to express agreement, etc. **take a** ~ **(in),** help; play a part (in sth). **take sth/sb in** ~, take charge of; undertake to control or manage. **be to** ~, (comm style for) be received: *Your letter is to* ~, has reached me and is receiving attention. **wash one's** ~*s of,* say that one will no longer be responsible for. **win** ~*s down,* win easily. **(rule) with a heavy** ~, oppressively; severely. **win a lady's** ~, win her consent to marriage. **2** (*pl*) power; possession; responsibility. **in sb's hands:** *The property is no longer in my* ~*s,* It is no longer mine, or my responsibility. *The matter is in your* ~*s,* You must decide how to deal with it. *He's still in the* ~*s of the moneylenders.* **change** ~*s,* pass to another owner: *The property has changed* ~*s recently,* has been sold. **3** (*sing* only) influence or agency: *The* ~ *of an enemy has been at work here.* **4** (*sing* only) person from whom news, etc comes: (only in) **at first** ~, directly, without an intermediary: *I heard/learnt the news at first* ~. **at second** ~, indirectly. **5** (*sing* only) skill in using one's ~s: *She has a light* ~ *at pastry,* makes it with skill. *Why don't you try your* ~ *at editing the staff magazine,* see whether you have the skill needed? **get one's** ~ **in,** acquire or return to one's usual degree of skill by practice. **keep one's**[1] ~ **in,** practise a skill, in order to retain it: *practise the piano every day to keep one's* ~ *in.* **6** [C] person who does what is indicated by the context; performer: *a good* ~ *at fencing,* a good fencer. *He's an old* ~ *at this sort of work,* has long experience of it. *He's an old parliamentary* ~, a person with long experience of parliamentary duties. **7** workman, eg in a factory or dockyard; member of a ship's crew: *The factory has taken on 200 extra* ~*s. All* ~*s on deck!* All seamen are needed on deck! **8** turn; share in an activity. **have a** ~ **(in sth),** have a share: *Let me have a* ~ *now. Do you think he had a* ~ *in it,* was involved? **9** [C] pointer or indicator on the dial of a watch, clock or other instrument: *the 'hour/ 'minute/'second* ~ *of a watch.* **10** position or direction (to right or left). **on every/either** ~; **on all** ~*s,* to or from all quarters. **on the one** ~ ... **on the other** ~, used to indicate contrasted points of view, arguments, etc. **11** (*sing* only) handwriting: *He writes a good/legible* ~. **12** (formal) signature: *set one's* ~ *to a document. Given under my* ~ *and seal,* authenticated by my signature and seal. **13** (card games, eg bridge) (a) (number of) cards dealt to, held by, a player at one time. **have a good/ bad/poor** ~, good/bad etc cards. **play a good/ bad** ~, play well/badly. **take a** ~ **at sth,** join in and play it. **play into sb's** ~*s,* do sth that is to his advantage. (b) player at cards: *We have only three* *players—we need a fourth* ~. **(c)** one round in a game of cards: *Let's play one more* ~, *shall we?* **14** [C] unit of measurement, about four inches (10·16 cm), the breadth of the ~, used for the height of a horse (from the ground to the top of the shoulder). **15** (colloq) applause by clapping. *give sb/get a good* ~, a lot of applause. **16** (compounds) '~-bag *n* woman's bag for money, keys, handkerchief, etc. (US = *purse*.) '~-barrow *n* light two-wheeled barrow. '~-bill *n* printed advertisement or announcement distributed by ~. '~-book *n* small book giving useful facts; guidebook. '~-brake *n* auxiliary brake in a motorvehicle, used when the vehicle is stationary. '~-cart *n* small cart pushed or pulled by ~. '~-clap *n* clapping: *a slow* ~*clap*, slow rhythmical clapping to show impatience. '~-cuff *n* (usu *pl*) one of a pair of metal rings joined by a chain, fastened round a prisoner's wrists. □ *vt* put ~cuffs on. ~-ful /-fʊl/ *n* (*pl* ~fuls) **(a)** as much or as many as can be held in one ~. **(b)** small number: *Only a* ~*ful of people came to the meeting.* **(c)** (colloq) person or animal difficult to control: *That young boy of hers is quite a* ~*ful*, is lively and unruly. '~-grenade *n* grenade thrown by hand. '~-hold *n* (esp) anything a climber may grip, eg on a rock face. '~-luggage *n* luggage light enough to be carried by hand. ,~-'made *adj* made by ~ (contrasted with *machine-made*). '~-maid *n* (archaic) woman servant or attendant. '~-me-down *n* sth passed on (esp sth used and discarded, eg clothes) to another. '~-organ *n* portable barrel-organ with a crank turned by ~. ,~-'picked *adj* carefully selected. '~-rail *n* railing along the edge of a staircase, etc. '~-saw *n* saw used with one hand only. '~-shake *n* greeting given by grasping a person's ~ with one's own. '~-stand *n* acrobatic feat of supporting oneself in an upright position on the ~s: *do a* ~*stand*. '~-work *n* [U] work done by ~, not by machinery. '~-writing *n* [U] (person's style of) writing by ~: *Whose* ~*writing is this?* ,off-'~ *adj* ⇨ off-hand.

hand² /hænd/ *vt* [VP12A,13A,15A,B] give or pass (to sb); help with the ~(s): *Please* ~ *me that book. He* ~*ed the book to the man at his side. He* ~*ed* (= helped) *his wife out of the railway carriage.* ~ *sth down* **(to sb)**, pass by tradition, inheritance, etc: *We cannot always observe the traditions* ~*ed down to us from the past.* ~ *sth on* **(to sb)**, send, give, to another: *Please* ~ *on the magazine to your friends.* ~ *sth out* **(to sb)**, distribute; (colloq) give as alms. Hence, '~-out *n* **(a)** prepared statement given, eg by a politician, to newspaper men; leaflet, etc, distributed free of charge. **(b)** sth given as alms, eg food or money to a beggar at the door. ~ *sb over* **(to sb)**, deliver a person to authority: ~ *sb over to the police.* ~ *sth over* **(to sb)**, transfer: *You can't play with my gun—hand it over at once. I've* ~*ed over my place on the committee.* ~ *it to sb*, (colloq) give him the credit that is his due: *He's done well! You've got to* ~ *it to him.*

handi-cap /'hændɪkæp/ *n* [C] **1** (competition, race, in which there is a) disadvantage imposed on a competitor to make the chances of success more nearly equal for all, eg a weight to be carried by a horse. **2** anything likely to lessen one's chance of success: *Poor eyesight is a* ~ *to a student.* □ *vt* (-pp-) [VP6A] give or be a ~ to: ~*ped by ill health;* ~*ped children*, suffering from some disability.

handi-craft /'hændɪkrɑːft *US:* -kræft/ *n* [C] art or craft needing skill with the hands, eg needlework,

pottery, woodwork, weaving.

handi-work /'hændɪwɜːk/ *n* [U] work done, [C] thing made, by the hands; sth done by a named person: *That's some of Smith's* ~.

hand-ker-chief /'hæŋkətʃɪf/ *n* square piece of cotton, silk, linen, etc carried in the pocket or handbag, for blowing the nose into or wiping the face; similar square worn for ornament, eg round the neck.

handle /'hændl/ *n* **1** part of a tool, cup, bucket, door, drawer, etc by which it may be held in the hand. '~-bar *n* (usu *pl*) bar with a ~ at each end, for steering a bicycle, etc. ⇨ the illus at bicycle. *fly off the* ~, (colloq) get into a rage and lose self-control. *give a* ~ *(to sb) (against sb)*, provide an excuse or pretext that may be taken advantage of and used: *Your indiscreet behaviour may give your enemies a* ~ *against you.* **2** (sl) title: *have a* ~ *to one's name*, have, eg 'Sir' or 'Lord' as part of it. □ *vt* [VP6A] **1** touch with, take up in, the hands: *Gelignite is dangerous stuff to* ~. *Wash your hands before you* ~ *my books, please.* **2** manage; deal with; control (men): *An officer must know how to* ~ *men. Can you* ~ *the situation*, deal with it? **3** treat; behave towards: *The speaker was roughly* ~*d by the crowd.* **4** (comm) buy and sell: *This shop does not* ~ *imported goods.* **han-dler** /'hændlə(r)/ *n* person who trains and controls an animal, eg a police dog.

hand-some /'hænsəm/ *adj* **1** of fine appearance; (of men) good-looking, having virile beauty; (of women) having a fine figure, vigour and dignity: *What a* ~ *horse you have! What a* ~ *old building it is! Would you describe that woman as* ~ *or beautiful?* **2** (of gifts, behaviour) generous: *He said some very* ~ *things about you. £500 is quite a* ~ *birthday present. H*~ *is as/that* ~ *does*, (prov) A fine person is one who acts generously. ~**ly** *adv* in a ~(2) manner: *He came down* ~*ly*, made a generous gift.

handy /'hændɪ/ *adj* (-ier, -iest) **1** (of persons) clever with the hands. ~**-man** /-mæn/ *n* (*pl* -men) person clever at doing odd jobs of various kinds. **2** (of things, places) convenient; useful: *A good toolbox is a* ~ *thing to have in the house. come in* ~, be useful some time or other: *Don't throw that plastic bag away; it may come in* ~. **3** not far away; available for use: *Always keep a first-aid kit* ~. **hand-ily** /-ɪlɪ/ *adv* **handi-ness** *n*

hang¹ /hæŋ/ *n* (*sing* only) **1** way in which a thing hangs: *the* ~ *of a coat/skirt.* **2** *get the* ~ *of sth*, (colloq) **(a)** see how sth, eg a machine, works or is managed: *I've been trying to get the* ~ *of this new electric typewriter.* **(b)** see the meaning or significance of sth said or written: *I don't quite get the* ~ *of your argument.* **3** *not give/care a* ~, (colloq) (euphem for *damn*) not care at all.

hang² /hæŋ/ *vt,vi* (*pt,pp* hung /hʌŋ/ or, for **2** and **3** below, ~ed) (For uses with *adverbial particles* and *preps*, ⇨ **7** below.) **1** [VP6A,15A,B,2A,C] support, be supported, from above so that the lower end is free: ~ *a lamp from the ceiling; curtains* ~*ing over the window; windows hung with curtains; pictures* ~*ing on the wall. She hung the washing out in the garden. H*~ *your coat on that hook. A dog's tongue* ~*s out when it runs fast.* **2** (*pt,pp* ~ed) put, be put, to death by ~ing with a rope around the neck: *He was* ~*ed for murder. He said he would* ~ *himself*, commit suicide by ~ing. **3** (dated sl; mild equivalent of *damn*.) **4** (various

uses) ∼ *wallpaper*, attach it to a wall with paste; ∼ *bells*, fit them (eg in a belfry); ∼ *a door*, fasten it on hinges so that it swings freely to and fro. ∼ *by a hair/a single thread*, (of a persons's fate etc) be in a delicate state, depend upon sth small. ∼ *one's head*, let it fall forward (eg when ashamed). ∼ *fire*, (a) (of a gun) be slow in going off. (b) (of events) be slow in developing. *let things go* ∼, (colloq) be indifferent to them; take no interest in or care of them. ∼ *in the balance*, (of a result, decision, etc) not be certain. **5** [VP6A,2B] leave, eg meat, ∼ing until in the right condition for eating: *Hares and pheasants need to be well hung. How long has this meat hung for?* **6** (compounds) ∼-man /-mən/ n (pl-men) executioner who ∼s criminals. **'∼-dog** *attrib adj* (of sb's look) sly and ashamed. **'∼-over** n (a) unpleasant after-effects of excessive drinking. (b) (fig) survival of out-of-date news, rules, etc. **7** [VP2C,15A,B,3A] (with *adverbial particles* and *preps*):
hang about/(a)round, be standing or loitering about, doing nothing definite: *men ∼ing about at street corners, waiting for the pubs to open. There's thunder ∼ing about,* Thunder seems likely at any time.
hang back, hesitate; show unwillingness to act or advance: *When volunteers were asked for, not one man hung back.*
hang on, (a) hold tight: *He hung on until the rope broke.* (b) persevere: *It's hard work, but if you ∼ on long enough you'll succeed. H∼ on (a minute)!* (colloq) Wait (a minute)! ∼ *on/upon sb's words*, listen attentively to them. ∼ *on to sth*, hold it tightly.
hang out, (sl) live; lodge: *Where are you ∼ing out now?* ∼ *sth out*, (a) hang (wet clothes, etc) out to dry: *She's in the yard, ∼ing out the washing.* (b) display: ∼ *out flags for the Queen's visit.*
hang together, (a) (of persons) support one another; act in unison: *If we all ∼ together, our plan will succeed.* (b) fit well together: *Their accounts of what happened don't ∼ together,* are inconsistent, contradictory.
hang up, replace the receiver at the end of a telephone conversation: *She hung up on me,* (colloq) hung up the receiver before I had said all I wanted to say. *be hung up,* (colloq) (a) be delayed or frustrated. (b) be emotionally inhibited or disturbed. Hence, **'∼-up** n (a) difficulty. (b) inhibition; obsession; neurosis.
hang·ar /'hæŋə(r)/ n building in which aircraft are housed.
hang·er /'hæŋə(r)/ n device, loop, etc to, on or by which sth is hung; (in compounds): **'dress-/ 'clothes-/'coat-∼**, device on which dresses, etc are hung. **∼-on** /ˌhæŋər 'ɒn/ (pl ∼s-on) n person who forces his company upon another or others in the hope of profit or advantage. **'paper-∼**, person who hangs (= pastes) wallpaper on to walls.
hang·ing /'hæŋɪŋ/ n **1** [U,C] death by hanging: *There were three ∼s here last month.* **2** (usu˜ pl) curtains, drapery, etc with which walls are hung.
hang·nail /'hæŋneɪl/ n loose skin near the root of a finger-nail.
hank /hæŋk/ n (twisted) coil of wool, silk, etc thread: *wind a ∼ of wool into balls.*
han·ker /'hæŋkə(r)/ vi [VP3A] ∼ *after/for sth*, have a strong desire: ∼ *for sympathy;* ∼ *after wealth.* **∼ing** n strong desire: *have a ∼ing for/ after fame.*

hanky /'hæŋkɪ/ n (pl -kies) (child's word for) handkerchief.
hanky-panky /ˌhæŋkɪ 'pæŋkɪ/ n [U] (colloq) underhand dealing; trickery.
Han·sard /'hænsɑːd/ n official report of proceedings in Parliament.
han·som /'hænsəm/ n (also ˌ∼ **'cab**) (hist) two-wheeled horse-drawn cab for two passengers, with the driver's seat high at the back and reins going over the roof.

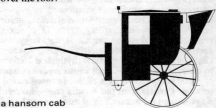

a hansom cab

hap /hæp/ n (archaic) chance; luck. □ vi (-pp-) come about by chance; happen.
hap·haz·ard /hæp'hæzəd/ adj, adv without order or plan; (at) random. **∼·ly** adv
hap·less /'hæplɪs/ adj (archaic) unlucky.
hap·ly /'hæplɪ/ adv (archaic) by chance; perhaps.
ha'p'orth /'heɪpəθ/ n (colloq) halfpennyworth. ⇨ half(3).
hap·pen /'hæpən/ vi **1** [VP2A,3A] ∼ *(to)*, take place; come about: *How did the accident ∼? What ∼ed next? Accidents will ∼,* They are to be expected. *If anything ∼s to him* (= If he meets with an accident), *let me know.* **2** [VP2A,4E] chance; have the fortune: *I ∼ed to be out when he called. It so ∼ed that I had no money with me. as it ∼s,* by chance: *As it ∼s, I have my cheque-book with me.* **3** [VP3A] ∼ *on/upon,* find by chance: *I ∼ed on just the thing I'd been looking for.* **∼·ing** /'hæpənɪŋ/ n (often pl) event: *There have been strange ∼ings here lately.*
happy /'hæpɪ/ adj (-ier, -iest) **1** fortunate; lucky; feeling or expressing pleasure, contentment, satisfaction, etc: *Their marriage has been a ∼ one. He is ∼ in having congenial work. as ∼ as the day is long,* very ∼. **2** (in polite formulas) pleased: *We shall be ∼ to accept your kind invitation.* **3** (of language, conduct, suggestions) well suited to the situation: *a ∼ thought/idea, etc.* **∼-go-lucky** /ˌhæpɪ gəʊ 'lʌkɪ/ adj taking what fortune brings; carefree: *She goes through life in a ∼-go-lucky fashion.* **hap·pily** /-ɪlɪ/ adv **hap·pi·ness** n
hara-kiri /ˌhærə 'kɪrɪ/ n [U] suicide by disembowelment as practised in the past by Japanese samurai when they believed they had failed in their duty.
har·angue /hə'ræŋ/ n long, loud (often scolding) talk or speech. □ vt, vi [VP6A,2A] make a ∼ (to).
har·ass /'hærəs US: hə'ræs/ vt [VP6A] **1** trouble; worry: *∼ed by the cares of a large family; ∼ed-looking housewives.* **2** make repeated attacks on: *In olden days the coasts of England were ∼ed by the Vikings.* **∼·ment** n [U] ∼ing or being ∼ed.
har·bin·ger /'hɑːbɪndʒə(r)/ n sb or sth that foretells the coming of sb or sth: *The crowing of the cock is a ∼ of dawn. The cuckoo is a ∼ of spring.*
har·bour (US = **-bor**) /'hɑːbə(r)/ n **1** place of shelter for ships: *a natural ∼,* eg an inlet of the sea: *an artificial ∼,* one made with sea-walls, breakwaters. **'∼ dues** n pl money (to be) paid for

anchoring or mooring a ship in a ~. **2** (fig) any place of safety or shelter. □ *vt,vi* **1** [VP6A] give lodging or shelter to; protect; conceal: ~ *an escaped criminal. My dog has long, thick hair that* ~*s fleas.* **2** [VP6A] hold in the mind: ~ *thoughts of revenge.* **3** [VP2A] come to anchor (in a ~). ~**age** /'hɑ:bərɪdʒ/ *n* (place of) shelter.

hard¹ /hɑ:d/ *adj* (-er, -est) **1** (contrasted with *soft*) firm; not yielding to the touch; not easily cut; solid: *as* ~ *as rock; ground made* ~ *by frost. Teak is a* ~ *kind of wood. a* ~ *nut to crack,* (fig) a difficult problem; person difficult to deal with or influence. **2** (contrasted with *easy*) difficult (to understand or explain); needing mental or moral effort: ~ *words,* difficult for learners, (also ⇨ **4** below) *a* ~ *problem/book/language; a subject that is* ~ *to understand. She found it* ~ *to make up her mind. That man is* ~ *to please/He is a* ~ *man to please. It's* ~ *to say which is better. It's* ~ *for an old man to change his way of living.* **3** causing unhappiness, discomfort, or pain; difficult to endure: *have/be given a* ~ *time,* experience difficulties, misfortunes, etc; *in these* ~ *times,* in these times of money shortage, unemployment, etc when life is difficult. *(find sth)* ~ *going,* (find progress) difficult. *(find sb)* ~ *going,* (find him) difficult (to understand), or boring (to listen to). *learn (sth) the* ~ *way,* with perseverance and hardship. **4** severe; harsh: *a* ~ *father,* one who treats his children severely; ~ *words,* harsh, showing lack of sympathy. *be* ~ *on sb,* treat him severely. *drive a* ~ *bargain,* ⇨ bargain. *take a* ~ *line,* be uncompromising. Hence, ~**'liner** *n* person who is uncompromising. ⇨ line¹(11). **5** (of the body) having ~ muscles and not much fat: *Regular physical exercises soon made the boys* ~. *as* ~ *as nails,* **(a)** strong and muscular. **(b)** (fig) without sentiment, or sympathy; ~**-hearted. 6** done, doing (sth), with much effort or force; strenuous: *a* ~ *blow; go for a* ~ *gallop; a* ~ *worker.* **7** (of the weather) severe: *a* ~ *winter/frost.* **8** (of sounds) The letter 'c' is hard in 'cat' and soft in 'city'. The letter 'g' is ~ in 'gun' and soft in 'gin'. **9** (various uses) ~ *and fast (rules, etc),* that cannot be altered to fit special cases. ~ *of hearing,* rather deaf. '~**back**/**-cover** *n* book bound in a ~ (= stiff) cover (contrasted with paper-backed books): *The book has just appeared in* ~*back.* Hence, '~**backed**/**-covered**/**-bound** *adj.* '~**board** /-bɔ:d/ *n* [U] kind of material like plywood in appearance and use, made by compressing waste wood that has been ground up finely. ,~ '**cash** *n* [U] coins and notes, not a cheque or a promise to pay. '~ **core** *n* **(a)** broken brick, rubble, etc (as used for foundations, roadmaking). **(b)** solid, central, basic or underlying part; nucleus: *the* ~ *core of the opposition/rebellion.* '~ **court** *n* (tennis) court with a ~ surface, not of grass. ,~ '**currency** *n*one that is reliable and stable. ,~ '**drug** *n*one likely to lead to addiction, eg *heroin.* ,~**-'headed** /'hedɪd/ *adj* practical; not sentimental; business-like. ,~**-'hearted** /'hɑ:tɪd/ *adj* unfeeling; lacking in sympathy or the gentler emotions. ,~ '**labour** *n* [U] imprisonment with ~ physical labour as a punishment. ,~ '**liquor**/**drink** *n* [U] with high alcoholic content eg whisky. ,~ '**luck**/'**lines** *n* [U] worse fortune than is deserved. Hence, ,~**-'luck story,** one seeking pity, sympathy (for oneself). ,~ '**shoulder** *n* ~ surface at the side of a motorway, to be used in an emergency: *The lorry driver pulled over to the*

~ *shoulder when one of the tyres burst.* ,~ '**standing** *n* [U] area of ~ surface, eg, concrete, for the parking of vehicles. '~**-top** *n* car with a steel top and no sliding roof. '~**-ware** *n* [U] **(a)** ironmongery; metal goods for domestic use, eg *pans, nails, locks.* **(b)** *military* ~*ware,* weapons and equipment, eg armoured vehicles. **(c)** *computer* ~*ware,* mechanical equipment (contrasted with information and programmes, called *software*). ,~ '**water** *n* [U] containing mineral salts that interfere with the lathering of soap. '~**-wood** *n* [U] ~ heavy wood, eg *oak, ebony, teak,* contrasted with soft wood, eg *pine, fir:* (attrib) ~*wood floors.* ~**-ness** *n*

hard² /hɑ:d/ *adv* **1** with great energy; strenuously; with all one's force: *work/study/think/pull/push* ~; *try* ~ *to succeed; drink/swear* ~. ,~**-'hitting** *adj* vigorous, direct: *a* ~*-hitting speech.* ,~**-'working** *adj* working with care and energy. **2** severely; heavily: *freezing/raining* ~. **3** with difficulty; with a struggle; painfully: *my* ~*-earned money*⇨ hardly(5). *be* ~ *hit,* be suffering severely, eg by financial losses, the death of sb much loved. *be* ~ *pressed (for sth),* be under pressure, strained. *be* ~ '*put to it (to do sth),* find it difficult: *He was* ~ *put to it to explain what had happened. be* ~ '*up,* be short of money. *be* ~ '*up for (sth),* in want of; at a loss for: *He's* ~ *up for ideas/something to do.* **4** so as to be ~(1), solid: *boil eggs* ~. ,~**-'baked** *adj* baked until ~. ,~**-'boiled** *adj* (eg of eggs) boiled ~; (fig) callous. ,~**-'bitten** *adj* (of a person) stubborn in fighting; tough because of a difficult life, etc. **5** closely; immediately: *follow* ~ *after/upon/behind someone.* ~ *by,* close by; not far away. *run sb* ~, pursue him closely.

harden /'hɑ:dn/ *vt,vi* [VP6A,2A] make or become hard, strong, hardy, etc: ~ *steel;* ~ *the heart; a* ~*ed criminal,* one who is callous, who shows no signs of shame or repentance; ~ *the body,* eg by taking exercise. *be* ~*ed to,* made insensitive to. [VP15B,2C] ~ *off,* (of young plants, esp seedlings) make or become hardy, ready for planting outside.

hardi·hood /'hɑ:dɪhʊd/ *n* [U] boldness; audacity.

hard·ly /'hɑ:dlɪ/ *adv* **1** only just; not quite; scarcely: *I* ~ *know her,* have only a very slight acquaintance with her. *We had* ~ *got/H*~ *had we got into the country when it began to rain.* (Cf No sooner... than.) *I'm so tired I can* ~ *walk.* **2** (used to suggest that sth is improbable, unlikely or unreasonable): *He can* ~ *have arrived yet. You can* ~ *expect me to lend you money again.* **3** (neg in meaning) almost no; almost not: *He* ~ *ever* (= very seldom) *goes to bed before midnight.* Cf His wife *almost always* goes to bed before midnight. *I need* ~ *say* (= It is almost unnecessary for me to say) *that I am innocent. There's* ~ *any coal left. H*~ *anybody* (= Very few people) *came to the meeting.* **4** (from hard¹(4)) severely: ~ *treated.* **5** (from hard¹(6)) with effort or difficulty. For this sense the *adv* 'hard' is usu preferred. (Cf *hard-earned money* and *salary that was* ~ (ie only just, barely) *earned*).

hard·ship /'hɑ:dʃɪp/ *n* **1** [C] circumstance that causes discomfort or suffering: *the* ~*s borne by soldiers during a war.* **2** [U] severe suffering: *bear* ~ *without complaining.*

hardy /'hɑ:dɪ/ *adj* (-ier, -iest) **1** strong; able to endure suffering or hardship: *A few* ~ *men broke the ice on the lake and had a swim.* **2** (of plants) able to endure frost without being injured: ~ *annuals.* **3** bold; ready to face danger. **hardi·ness** *n*

hare /heə(r)/ n fast-running field animal with long ears and a divided upper lip, like but larger than a rabbit. ~ **and hounds,** paper-chase, a game in which two persons called 'hares' run across country dropping torn-up bits of paper and are followed by others, called 'hounds', who try to catch them. **run with the ~ and hunt with the hounds,** try to keep the favour of both sides in a dispute; play a double game. **mad as a March ~,** very mad or wild. **start a ~,** raise a topic, argument, etc unrelated to the main issue. '~**bell** n round-leaved plant with blue bell-like flowers (in Scotland called *bluebell*). '~**brained** adj rash; foolish: ~*-brained schemes.* ,~**'lip** n person's upper lip divided (from birth) like that of a ~. □ vi [VP2C] run fast or away: *They ~d off.*

harem /'hɑːriːm/ n women's part of a traditional Muslim household; women living in it.

hari·cot /'hærɪkəʊ/ n (also ~ **bean**) kidney bean; French bean.

hark /hɑːk/ vi 1 (chiefly imper) ~ **at,** (colloq, teasing) listen to: *Just ~ at him!* 2 ~ **back (to),** refer back to sth done or said earlier.

har·le·quin /'hɑːlɪkwɪn/ n character in Italian comedy; mute character in English pantomime, full of tricks and very lively, wearing a mask and multi-coloured costume; (hence) person fond of practical jokes; buffoon. ~**ade** /ˌhɑːlɪkwɪ'neɪd/ n part of a pantomime in which a ~ plays the chief part.

Har·ley Street /'hɑːlɪ striːt/ n London street where many fashionable doctors and surgeons live.

har·lot /'hɑːlət/ n (archaic, or as a term of abuse) prostitute.

harm /hɑːm/ n [U] damage; injury: *He probably meant no ~,* did not intend to hurt anyone or anyone's feelings. *There's no ~ in your staying up late occasionally,* no reason why you should not do so. **do sb ~,** cause injury to him: *A few drinks will do you no ~.* **out of ~'s way,** in a place of safety. □ vt [VP6A] cause ~ to: *It hasn't ~ed you, has it?* ~**ful** /-fl/ adj causing ~ (to). ~**fully** /-fəlɪ/ adv ~**less** adj 1 not doing ~ (to): ~*less snakes.* 2 innocent; inoffensive: *Several ~less spectators were wounded during the rioting.* ~**less·ly** adv

har·mat·tan /ˌhɑːmə'tæn/ n cold, dry wind from the north that blows in W Africa from December to March.

har·monic /hɑː'mɒnɪk/ n (music) higher note produced (by vibration of strings) with a note that is played, and having a fixed relation to it.

har·mon·ica /hɑː'mɒnɪkə/ n mouth-organ.

har·moni·ous /hɑː'məʊnɪəs/ adj 1 pleasingly or satisfactorily arranged: *a ~ group of buildings.* 2 in agreement; free from ill feeling: ~ *families/*

neighbours. 3 sweet-sounding; tuneful. ~**ly** adv

har·mo·nium /hɑː'məʊnɪəm/ n small musical keyboard instrument (like an organ), with the notes produced by air blown through metal reeds.

har·mon·ize /'hɑːmənaɪz/ vt,vi 1 [VP6A,14] ~ **(with),** bring (one thing) into harmony (with another); (music) add notes (to a melody) to make chords. 2 [VP2A,C] ~ **(with),** be in harmony or agreement: *colours that ~ well (with the decorations/with each other.)* **har·mon·iz·ation** /ˌhɑːmənaɪ'zeɪʃn US: -nɪ'z-/ n

har·mony /'hɑːmənɪ/ n (pl -nies) 1 [U] agreement (of feeling, interests, opinions, etc): *There was not much ~ in international affairs during those years.* **be in ~ (with),** match; agree (with): *His tastes are in ~ with mine.* 2 [C,U] (instance or example of) pleasing combination of related things: *the ~ of colour in nature,* eg the greens, browns, etc of trees in autumn. 3 [C,U] (music) pleasing combination of notes sounded together to make chords.

har·ness /'hɑːnɪs/ n (collective sing) all the leather-work and metal-work by which a horse is controlled and fastened to the cart, waggon, plough, etc, that it pulls. ⇨ **yoke.** *in ~,* (fig) doing one's regular work. **die in ~,** die while engaged in one's regular work, not after retiring. **work/run in double ~,** work with a partner, or with a husband or wife. □ vt [VP6A] 1 put a ~ on (a horse). 2 use (eg a river, waterfall, etc) to produce (esp electric) power.

harp /hɑːp/ n freestanding musical instrument with vertical strings played with the fingers. ⇨ the illus at string. □ vi 1 play the ~. 2 ~ **on sth,** (fig) talk repeatedly or tiresomely about: *She is always ~ing on my faults.* ~**er; ~·ist** /-ɪst/ nn player on the ~.

har·poon /hɑː'puːn/ n spear on a rope, thrown by hand or fired from a gun, for catching whales and other large sea animals. □ vt strike with a ~.

harp·si·chord /'hɑːpsɪkɔːd/ n piano-like instrument used from the 16th to the 18th cc (and today for music of these centuries). ⇨ the illus at keyboard.

harpy /'hɑːpɪ/ n (pl -pies) 1 (Gk myth) cruel creature with a woman's face and a bird's wings and claws. 2 cruel, greedy, hard-hearted woman.

har·ri·dan /'hærɪdən/ n worn-out, bad-tempered old woman.

har·rier /'hærɪə(r)/ n 1 hound used for hunting hares; (pl) pack of these with huntsmen. 2 cross-country runner.

har·row /'hærəʊ/ n heavy frame with metal teeth or discs for breaking up ground after ploughing. □ vt [VP6A] pull a ~ over (a field, etc); (fig) distress (the feelings): *a ~ing tale of misfortunes.*

harry /'hærɪ/ vt (pt,pp -ried) [VP6A] 1 lay waste and plunder; attack frequently: *The Vikings used to*

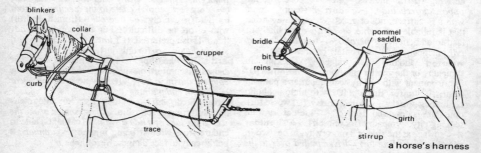

a horse's harness

~ *the English coast.* **2** annoy or worry: *money-lenders ~ing their debtors.*

harsh /hɑːʃ/ *adj* (-er, -est) **1** rough and disagreeable, esp to the senses: *a ~ texture/voice/contrast; ~ to the ear.* **2** stern, cruel, severe: *a ~ judge/ judgement/punishment.* **~·ly** *adv* **~·ness** *n*

hart /hɑːt/ *n* adult male of (esp red) deer; stag.

harum-scarum /ˌheərəm ˈskeərəm/ *adj, n* (colloq) reckless, impulsive (person).

har·vest /ˈhɑːvɪst/ *n* **1** (season for) cutting and gathering in of grain and other food crops; quantity obtained: *this year's wheat ~; a succession of good ~s.* ~ **'festival** *n* service of thanksgiving in Christian churches after the ~ has been gathered. ~**'home** *n* festival given by farmers to their workers when the ~ is gathered in. ~ **'moon** *n* full moon nearest to the autumn equinox. **2** (fig) consequences of action or behaviour: *reap the ~ of one's hard work,* be rewarded for it. □ *vt* [VP6A] reap, gather, dig up, a crop: ~ *rice/potatoes.* ~**er** *n* **1** person who ~s; reaper. **2** machine for cutting and gathering grain, esp the kind that also binds the grain into sheaves or (ˌcombine-ˈ~er) threshes the grain.

has ⇨ have[1].

has-been /ˈhæz biːn/ *n* (colloq) person who, or thing which, has lost a quality, skill, etc formerly possessed; sb or sth now out of date.

hash /hæʃ/ *vt* [VP6A,15B] ~ **(up),** chop or cut up (meat) into small pieces. □ *n* **1** [U] (dish of) cooked meat, ~ed and re-cooked. **2 make a ~ of sth,** (fig) do it very badly, make a mess of it. **settle sb's ~,** deal with him in such a way that he gives no more trouble. **3** (colloq) hashish.

hash·ish /ˈhæʃiːʃ/ *n* [U] dried hemp leaves made into a drug for smoking or chewing; cannabis.

hasn't /ˈhæznt/ = has not. ⇨ have[1].

hasp /hɑːsp US: hæsp/ *n* metal fastening for a door, window, etc used with a staple. ⇨ the illus at padlock.

has·sle /ˈhæsl/ *n* (colloq) **1** difficulty; struggle: *a real ~ to get on the train.* **2** argument; quarrel. □ *vi, vt* **1** [VP2A,3A] ~ **(with sb),** argue; quarrel. **2** [VP6A] bother; annoy: *Don't keep hassling me!*

has·sock /ˈhæsək/ *n* cushion for kneeling on, eg in church.

hast /hæst/ (archaic): *thou ~,* you have.

haste /heɪst/ *n* [U] quickness of movement; hurry: *Why all this ~?* Why are you in such a hurry? He went off in great ~. **Make ~!** Hurry! **More ~, less speed,** (prov) The more you hurry, the less real progress you will make.

hasten /ˈheɪsn/ *vi, vt* **1** [VP2A,C,4A] move or act with speed: ~ *away/home/to the office;* ~ *to tell sb the good news.* **2** [VP6A] cause (sb) to hurry; cause (sth) to be done or to happen quickly or earlier: *Artificial heating ~s the growth of plants.*

hasty /ˈheɪstɪ/ *adj* (-ier, -iest) said, made or done (too) quickly: ~ *preparations for flight; a ~ departure;* ~ *words that are regretted afterwards.* **hast·ily** /-ɪlɪ/ *adv* **hasti·ness** *n*

hat /hæt/ *n* covering for the head, usu with a brim, worn out of doors. (Cf *cap* and *bonnet* without a brim). **go/come hat/cap in hand,** obsequiously, apologetically. **send/pass round the hat,** ask for, collect, contributions of money (usu for sb who has suffered a loss). **take one's hat off to,** (fig) express admiration for. Hence, **Hats off to…!** Let us congratulate…! **talk through one's hat,** (sl) talk foolishly. **a bad hat,** (sl) bad person. **'hat-band** *n*

band round the crown of a hat, above the brim. **'hat-pin** *n* long pin used (formerly) by women to fasten a hat to the hair. **'hat trick** *n* (cricket) taking of three wickets with successive balls; similar success in other sports or activities. **hat·ful** /-fʊl/ *n* as much as a hat holds. **hat·less** *adj* not wearing a hat. **hat·ter** *n* man who makes or sells hats. **as mad as a hatter,** very mad.

hatch[1] /hætʃ/ *n* **1** (movable covering over an) opening in a door or floor, esp (ˈ~-way) one in a ship's deck through which cargo is lowered and raised; opening in a wall between two rooms, esp a kitchen and a dining room, through which dishes, etc, are passed. **under ~es,** below deck. **2** lower half of a divided door.

hatch[2] /hætʃ/ *vt, vi* **1** [VP6A,2A] (cause to) break out (of an egg): ~ *an egg;* ~ *chickens. When will the eggs ~? Three chickens ~ed today.* **Don't count one's chickens before they're ~ed,** (prov) Don't rely too much upon sth which is uncertain. **2** [VP6A] think out and produce (a plot, etc). ~**·ery** /ˈhætʃərɪ/ *n* (*pl* -ries) place for ~ing (esp fish): *a* ˈ*trout—~ery.* Cf incubator, for chicks.

hatch[3] /hætʃ/ *vt* [VP6A] draw on or engrave (a surface) with parallel lines. ~**·ing** *n* [U] such lines.

hatchet /ˈhætʃɪt/ *n* light, short-handled axe. ⇨ the illus at tool. **bury the ~,** stop quarrelling or fighting and be friendly.

hatch·way /ˈhætʃweɪ/ *n* ⇨ hatch[1].

hate /heɪt/ *vt* [VP6A,D,7A,17,19] have a strong dislike of or for; (colloq) regret: *My cat ~s dogs. I ~ to trouble you. I ~ you to be troubled. She ~s getting to the theatre late. She ~s anyone listening while she's telephoning.* □ *n* [U] strong dislike or ill-will: *He was filled with ~ for his opponent.*

hate·ful /ˈheɪtfl/ *adj* exciting hatred or strong dislike: *The sight of food was ~ to the seasick girl.* ~**·ly** /-fəlɪ/ *adv*

hath /hæθ/ (archaic) *3rd pers sing pres t* of have.

hatred /ˈheɪtrɪd/ *n* ~ **of/for,** hate; strong dislike: *He looked at me with ~.*

hat·ter /ˈhætə(r)/ *n* ⇨ hat.

hau·berk /ˈhɔːbɜːk/ *n* coat of chain mail (as worn by soldiers in the Middle Ages); ⇨ the illus at armour.

haughty /ˈhɔːtɪ/ *adj* (-ier, -iest) arrogant; having or showing a high opinion of oneself: *The nobles used to treat the common people with ~ contempt.* **haught·ily** /-ɪlɪ/ *adv* **haugh·ti·ness** *n*

haul /hɔːl/ *vt, vi* [VP6A,15A,B,2C,3A] pull (with effort or force): *elephants ~ing logs;* ~ *timber to a saw-mill;* ~ *at/upon a rope. They ~ed the boat up the beach.* ~ **down one's flag/colours,** surrender. ~ **sb over the coals,** scold him severely (for wrongdoing). □ *n* [C] **1** act of ~ing; distance along which sth is ~ed: *long ~s on the railways.* **2** amount gained as the result of effort, esp of fish ~ed up in a net: *a good ~ of fish. The thief made a good ~,* What he stole was valuable.

haul·age /ˈhɔːlɪdʒ/ *n* [U] transport (of goods): *the road ~ industry,* concerned with carriage of goods by road in lorries, etc; *a ~ contractor.*

haul·ier /ˈhɔːlɪə(r)/ *n* person or firm that owns lorries, and contracts to carry goods by road; haulage contractor.

haulm /hɔːm/ *n* (collective *sing*) stems and stalks of peas, beans, potatoes, etc, esp after the crop is gathered.

haunch /hɔːntʃ/ *n* (in man and animals) part of the body round the hips, or between the ribs and the thighs: *a ~ of venison. The dog was sitting on its ~es.*

haunt /hɔːnt/ *vt* [VP6A] **1** visit, be with, habitually or repeatedly; (esp of ghosts and spirits) appear repeatedly in: *The old castle is said to be ~ed.* **2** return to the mind repeatedly: *a ~ing melody/face. A wrongdoer is constantly ~ed by fear of discovery.* □ *n* place frequently visited by the person(s) named: *a ~ of criminals; revisit the ~s of one's schooldays,* the places where one spent one's time then.

haut·boy /'həʊbɔɪ/ *n* = oboe.

hau·teur /əʊ'tɜː(r)/ *n* [U] hautiness of manner.

Ha·vana /hə'vænə/ *n* cigar made at ~ or elsewhere in Cuba.

have¹ */usu form after 'I, we, you, they*: v; *usu form after a pause*: həv; *usu form elsewhere*: əv; *strong form*: hæv/ *aux v* (*3rd pers sing* has */usu form*: z; *after* p,t,k,f,θ *only*: s; *after* s,z,ʃ,ʒ, tʃ, dʒ *only*: əz; *after a pause*: həz; *strong form*: hæz/, *pt* had */usu form after 'I, we, you, they'*: d; *usu form after a pause*: həd; *usu form elsewhere*: əd; *strong form*: hæd/; *neg forms*: haven't /'hævnt/, hasn't /'hæznt/, hadn't /'hædnt/) **1** used in forming the perfect tenses and the perfect inf: *I ~/I've finished. He has/He's gone. H~ you done it? Yes, I ~. No, I ~n't. I shall ~ done it by next week. You ought to ~ done it.* **2** (By inverting the finite *had* with the subject, the equivalent of an *if*-clause is obtained): *Had I* (= If I had) *known,....* ⇨ if(1).

have² /hæv/ *anom v* (*3rd pers sing* has /hæz/; *pt,pp* had /hæd/; *neg forms* haven't /'hævnt/, hasn't /'hæznt/, hadn't /'hædnt/) (conjugated (for the neg and interr forms) without the *aux v* 'do' in GB usage, but not always in US usage; in GB colloq style often replaced by have¹ got, eg *I've got for I ~*) **1** (in sentences that can be recomposed with the *v* 'be'): [VP6B] *I ~ no doubt* (= There is no doubt in my mind) *that.... Has the house* (= Is there with the house) *a good garden?* **2** [VP6B] possess; own (sth concrete): *He's* (*got*) *a house in the country. How many books ~ you/do you ~?* **3** [VP6B] possess or show as a mental or physical characteristic (often equivalent to a construction with *be*): *Has she blue eyes or brown eyes?* Are her eyes blue or brown? *He hasn't a good memory.* His memory isn't good. (Notes: In US usage aux *do* is common: *Does she ~ blue eyes? Do you ~ a good memory?* In GB colloq styles, the *pp* got is common: *Has she got blue eyes?*) **4** [VP6B] used to indicate various connections: *How many children ~ they? He hasn't many friends here.* (The notes above on GB and US usage apply here, too.) **5** (followed by an abstract *n* + *to*-inf, in a construction equivalent to *be* + *adj* + *to*-inf): *Will you ~ the kindness/goodness, etc* (= Please be kind or good enough) *to hand me that book? How dare you ~ the impudence* (= be so impudent as) *to say that! Had she/Did she ~ the cheek* (= Was she cheeky enough) *to ask for more money?* **6** (in colloq style usu with *got*) hold or keep in the mind; exercise some quality of the mind; experience (some emotion): *H~ you* (*got*)/*Do you ~ any idea where he lives? What reason ~ you* (*got*) *for thinking that he's dishonest? What kind of holiday ~ you in mind?* **7** [VP6A,18C,19B] (in the inf only and always stressed) allow; endure: *I won't '~ such conduct. I won't '~ you saying such things.*

have³ (for pronunciations ⇨ have²) *vt* (Used in the neg and interr with or without the *aux v* 'do'. The

distinction is not always clear and there can be recommendations only, not rules. When the reference is to sth regular or habitual, the use of *do* for neg and interr is to be preferred. When the reference is to a particular occasion, constructions without *do*, and, in colloq style, with *got*, are to be preferred.) **1** [VP7B] *~ to do sth,* (*have to* = /'hæf tə/; *has to* = /'hæs tə/; *had to* = /'hæt tə/) expressing obligation or necessity: *Do you often ~ to go to the dentist's? H~ you* (*got*) *to go to the dentist's today? The children don't ~ to go to school on Sundays, do they? You ~n't* (*got*) *to go to school today, ~ you? I ~ to be getting along* (= must leave) *now. He's so rich that he doesn't ~ to work. We had to leave early. Had you/Did you ~ to leave early? These shoes will ~ to be repaired.* ⇨ must², need². **2** [VP6A] (in various senses as shown in these examples): *Do you often ~* (= suffer from) *colds? H~ you* (*got*) (= Are you suffering from) *a cold now? Do you ~* (ie as a rule, generally) *much time for reading? H~ you* (*got*) (ie now, or on the occasion specified) *time to come with me? Has your dog* (*got*) *any puppies now? How often does your dog ~* (ie give birth to) *puppies? Can you ~* (= take and look after) *the children for a few days?*

have⁴ (for pronunciations ⇨ have²) *non-anom v* (neg and interr always with the *aux v* 'do') **1** [VP6A] take; receive; accept; obtain: *There was nothing to be had,* obtained. *Do you ~ tea or coffee for breakfast? What shall we ~ for dinner?* **2** [VP6A] (with a *n*, so that *have* and the *n* are equivalent to a *v* identical with the *n*): *~ a swim/walk/wash/rest. Let me ~ a try/look. Go and ~ a lie down. Do you ever ~ dreams?* **3** [VP6A] experience; undergo: *We didn't ~ much difficulty. Did you ~ a good holiday? You've never had it so good,* never had so much, or such good quality, of it before. *let him/them ~ it,* (sl) shoot, punish sb, etc according to the situation. *~ had it,* (sl) not be going to receive or enjoy sth: *Here come the police—I'm afraid we've had it!* **4** [VP24C] *~ sth done,* cause (sb to do sth): *You'd better ~ that bad tooth pulled out. I must ~ these shoes repaired. When did you last ~ your hair cut?* ⇨ get(2). ⇨ also 6 below. **5** [VP18C] *~ sb do sth,* want him to do it: *I would ~ you know that...,* I want you to know that.... *What would you ~ me do? I wouldn't ~ you do that,* should prefer you not to do it. *~ to do with,* ⇨ do²(14). **6** [VP24B] *~ sth done,* experience or suffer it: *He had his pocket picked,* sth stolen from his pocket. *Charles I had his head cut off.* **7** [VP6A] (colloq) (**a**) trick; deceive: *I'm afraid you've been had. Mind he doesn't ~ you.* (**b**) beat; win an advantage over: *He had me in that argument. You had me there!* **8** (with *it* and a clause) express; maintain: *Rumour has it* (= There is a rumour) *that the Prime Minister is going to resign. He will ~ it* (= He insists) *that our plan is impracticable. ... as Plato has it* (used when giving a quotation, etc). **9** [VP15B] (uses with *adverbial particles* and *preps*):

have sth back: *You shall ~ it back* (= It will be returned to you) *next month. Let me ~ it back soon.*

have sb down, entertain sb as a visitor or guest: *We're having the Greens down* (eg from London) *for a few days.*

have sb in, receive him in the room, house, etc: *We shall be having the decorators in next month,*

The men will be decorating the house. ∼ **sth in,** possess in the house, etc: *Do we* ∼ *enough coal in for winter?*
have it off/away (with sb), ⚠ (sl) ∼ sexual intercourse (with).
have sb on, (colloq) play a trick on him, deceive him. ⇨ 7 above. ∼ **sth on, (a)** be wearing: *He had nothing on,* was naked. **(b)** ∼ an engagement: *I* ∼ *nothing on tomorrow evening,* I am free.
have sth out, cause sth to be taken out: ∼ *a tooth out.* ∼ **one's sleep out,** continue sleeping until one wakes naturally: *Let her* ∼ *her sleep out.* ∼ **it out with sb,** reach an understanding about sth by frank discussion.
have sb over/round, be visited at home by him: *We had Sue and Steve round for dinner last night.*
have sb up, (a) receive sb as a visitor (up to one's room, up from the country, etc). **(b)** (usu passive) (colloq) cause sb to appear before a magistrate, in a court of law, etc: *He was had up* (= was prosecuted) *for exceeding the speed limit.*
have⁵ /hæv/ *n pl the* ,∼**s and the** '∼**-nots,** the rich and the poor (of people and countries).
ha·ven /'heɪvn/ *n* harbour; (fig) place of safety or rest.
hav·er·sack /'hævəsæk/ *n* canvas bag, esp as used by soldiers, hikers and others, for carrying food, etc.
havoc /'hævək/ *n* [U] widespread damage; destruction: *The floods caused terrible* ∼. **play** ∼ **with/ among; make** ∼ **of,** destroy or injure.
haw¹ /hɔː/ *n* fruit (a red berry) of the hawthorn bush.
haw² /hɔː/ *vi, n*⇨ hum(4).
haw-haw /'hɔː hɔː/ *n, int* boisterous laugh.
hawk¹ /hɔːk/ *n* **1** strong, swift, keen-sighted bird of prey. ⇨ the illus at prey. ,∼-'**eyed** *adj* having keen sight. **2** person who favours the use of military force in foreign policy. ⇨ dove.
hawk² /hɔːk/ *vt* [VP6A,15B] ∼ **(about/around),** offer (goods) for sale, by going from house to house, street to street, etc; (fig) spread: ∼ *news/ gossip about.* ∼**er** *n* person who ∼s goods (usu from a barrow or cart). ⇨ pedlar.
haw·ser /'hɔːzə(r)/ *n* thick, heavy rope; thin steel cable (used on ships).
haw·thorn /'hɔːθɔːn/ *n* thorny shrub or tree with white, red or pink blossom and small red berries (called *haws*), often used for hedges in GB.
hay /heɪ/ *n* [U] grass cut and dried for use as animal food. **make hay,** turn it over for exposure to the sun; (hence) '**hay-maker,** '**hay-making** *nn* **make hay of,** throw into confusion. **make ,hay while the** '**sun shines,** (prov) make the earliest use of one's opportunities. '**hay·cock** *n* cone-shaped pile of hay in a field, to be carted away when dry. '**hay fever** *n* [U] disease affecting the nose and throat, caused by pollen or dust. '**hay-fork** *n* long-handled two-pronged fork for turning and lifting hay. '**hay·rick,** '**hay·stack** *nn* large pile of hay firmly packed for storing, with a pointed or ridged top. '**hay·wire** *n* [U] wire for tying up bales of hay. □ *pred adj* (colloq) out of order; excited or distracted. **go haywire,** (of persons) become distraught; (of sth, eg a plan) become badly disorganised.
haz·ard /'hæzəd/ *n* **1** [C] risk; danger: '*health* ∼s, eg smoking cigarettes; *a life full of* ∼s. **at all** ∼s, whatever the risks may be. **2** [U] game at dice, with complicated chances. □ *vt* [VP6A] **1** take the risk of; expose to danger: *Rock-climbers sometimes* ∼

their lives. **2** venture to make: ∼ *a guess/remark.* ∼·**ous** /-əs/ *adj* risky: *a* ∼*ous climb.*
haze¹ /heɪz/ *n* [C,U] thin mist; (fig) mental confusion or uncertainty.
haze² /heɪz/ *vt* (US) harass (sb) by making him perform humiliating jobs; bully or persecute.
hazel /'heɪzl/ *n* [C] bush with edible nuts; [U] (esp of eyes) colour of the shell of the nut, reddish brown.
hazy /'heɪzɪ/ *adj* (-ier, -iest) misty: ∼ *weather;* (fig) vague; slightly confused; uncertain: ∼ *about what to do next.* **haz·ily** /-ɪlɪ/ *adv* **hazi·ness** *n*
H-bomb /'eɪtʃ bɒm/ *n* hydrogen bomb.
he /*strong or initial form:* hiː; *medial weak form:* iː/ *pron* **1** male person or animal previously referred to: *Where's your brother? He's in Paris.* ∼ (as *pref*) male: '*he-goat.* '**he-man** /-mæn/ *n* (*pl -* men) (facet) strong man. **3** (liter style) *he who,* the one who, anyone who.
head¹ /hed/ *n* **1** that part of the body which contains the eyes, nose, mouth and brain: *They cut his* ∼ *off. Hit him on the* ∼ (note: *the* ∼, not *his* ∼). *It cost him his* ∼, his life. *Many nobles lost their* ∼s *during the French Revolution.* ⇨ the illus here and at insect. **2** (as a measure) ∼'s length: *The Queen's horse won by a* ∼. *Tom is taller than Harry by a* ∼. **be** ∼ **and** '**shoulders above sb,** (fig) be considerably superior in intelligence or ability. **3** ∼(s), that side of a coin on which the ∼ of a person appears, the other side being *tails* or *the tail. H*∼**s or tails?** (said when spinning a coin to decide sth by chance): *H*∼*s—I win!* **be unable to make** ∼ **or tail of sth,** be unable to understand it in the least. **4** person: *50 dinners at £1.50 a* ∼. **5** (*pl* unchanged) unit of a flock or herd: *50* ∼ *of cattle; a large* ∼ (= number) *of game.* **6** intellect; imagination; power to reason: *He made the story up out of his own* ∼, It was an original story, not one that he had heard or read. **7** natural aptitude or talent: *He has a good* ∼ *for business.* **8** sth like a ∼ in form or position, eg the part that is pressed (*the* ∼ *of a pin*), struck (*the* ∼ *of a nail*), used for striking (*the* ∼ *of a hammer*) or for cutting (*the* ∼ *of an axe*); *a tape-recorder* ∼, attachment that holds or contains an electronic device to record, read or erase material on magnetic tape, disc, etc. **9** top: *at the* ∼ *of the page; standing at the* ∼ *of the staircase; at the* ∼ *of the poll,* having received most votes at an election. **10** upper end: *the* ∼ *of a lake,* the end at which a river enters it; *the* ∼*- waters of the Nile,* its sources and upper streams; *the* ∼ *of a bed,* where a person's ∼ rests. **11** (of plants) mass of leaves or flowers at the top of a stem or stalk: *a fine* ∼ *of cabbage; a* ∼ *of lettuce; a* '*clover* ∼; *a* '*flower* ∼. **12** (often attrib) ruler; chief; position of command: ∼s *of government,* eg the President of the US, the Prime Minister of GB; *the crowned* ∼s *of Europe,* the kings and queens; *the* ∼ *of the family; the* ∼ *office,* the chief or most important office (contrasted with *branch* offices); *the* ∼ *waiter. H*∼ *of* '**State** *n* (*pl* H∼s of State) the chief public representative of a country, who may also be the head of government. **13** front; front part: *at the* ∼ *of the procession; marching at the* ∼ *of the regiment. The ship was down by the* ∼, with the bows deeper in the water than the stern. **14** (chiefly in proper names) cape or promontory: *Beachy H*∼. ⇨ *headland* in 20 below. **15** body of water kept at a certain height (eg for a water-mill or a hydro-electric power station); pres-

the head and the neck

1 hair
2 forehead
3 eyebrow
4 bridge
5 temple
6 eye
7 ear
8 cheek
9 nose
10 nostril
11 mouth
12 jaw
13 chin
14 nape
15 neck
16 throat

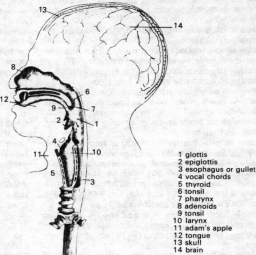

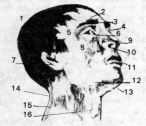

1 glottis
2 epiglottis
3 esophagus or gullet
4 vocal chords
5 thyroid
6 tonsil
7 pharynx
8 adenoids
9 tonsil
10 larynx
11 adam's apple
12 tongue
13 skull
14 brain

sure or force (per unit of area) of a confined body of steam, etc: *They kept up a good ~ of steam.* **16** main division in a discourse, essay, etc: *a speech arranged under five ~s; treat a question under several ~s.* ⇨ heading. **17** foam of liquid (esp liquor) that has been poured out: *the ~ on a glass of beer.* **18** point rising from a boil or other swelling on the flesh, esp when the boil is ripening and about to burst: *The boil came to a ~.* **come to a ~,** (fig) reach a crisis, culminate: *Discontent has come to a ~.* **19** (various phrases) *above/over one's ~,* (in a way that is) too difficult for one to understand: *be/talk above one's ~; go above one's head,* be too difficult for one. **an old ~ on young shoulders,** wisdom in a young person. **bite sb's '~ off,** scold them angrily. **eat one's '~ off,** (of a horse) eat a great deal and do little work. **give sb his ~,** allow him to act freely, unchecked. **go to one's ~,** **(a)** (of liquor) intoxicate: *The whisky went to his ~.* **(b)** excite: *His successes have gone to his ~,* made him over-confident, conceited, etc. **have a ,good '~ on one's shoulders,** have practical ability, common sense, etc. **~ over heels,** topsy-turvy; (fig) deeply or completely: *~ over heels in debt/in love.* **keep one's ~,** keep calm. **keep one's ~ above water,** (fig) stay out of debt, difficulty, etc. **keep one's '~ down,** avoid danger or distraction. **laugh/scream one's '~ off,** laugh/scream loudly, with great energy. **lose one's ~,** become confused or over-excited. **(go) off one's ~,** (become) crazy. **(stand, etc) on one's ~,** with feet in the air: *I could do it (standing) on my ~,* (colloq) It is very easy. **on one's own ~ be it,** the consequences will rest on one. **over one's ~,** = *above one's ~.* **(be promoted) over another's ~/over the ~s of others,** before another or others with prior or stronger claims. **,put our/your/their '~s together,** consult together. **put sth into a person's ~,** suggest it to him. **put sth out of one's ~,** stop thinking about it; give up the idea: *You'd better put the idea of marriage out of your ~.* **put sth out of sb's ~,** make him forget it: *An interruption put it out of my ~.* **take sth into one's ~,** come to believe it: *He took it

into his ~ that I was secretly opposing him.* **talk one's '~ off,** talk too much. **talk sb's '~ off,** weary him with talk. **Two ~s are better than one,** (prov) The opinions, advice, etc of a second person are valuable. **turn sb's ~,** make them conceited. **(be) weak in the ~,** (be) not very intelligent. **20** (compounds) '**~ache** *n* [C,U] **(a)** continuous pain in the ~: *suffer from ~ache(s); have a bad ~ache.* **(b)** (sl) troublesome problem: *more ~aches for the Department of the Environment.* '**~band** *n* band worn round the ~. '**~dress** *n* covering for the ~, esp woman's ornamental kind. '**~gear** *n* hat, cap, ~dress. '**~hunter** *n* savage who cuts off and keeps as trophies the ~s of his enemies; (fig) ruthless recruiter. '**~lamp** *n* = headlight. '**~land** /-lənd/ *n* promontory, cape. '**~light** *n* large lamp on the front of a locomotive, motor-car, etc. ⇨ the illus at bicycle, motor. '**~line** *n* newspaper heading; line at the top of a page containing title, etc; (*pl*) summary of broadcast news: *'Here are the news ~lines.'* '**~man** /-mæn/ *n* (*pl*-men) chief man of a village, tribe, etc. ,**~'master/·'mistress** *nn* principal master/ mistress of a school. **~-'on** *adj, adv* (of collisions) with the front parts (of vehicles) meeting: *a ~-on collision; meet/strike ~-on.* '**~phones** *n pl* receivers fitting over the ~ (for radio, etc); earphones. '**~piece** *n* **(a)** helmet. **(b)** (colloq) intelligence; brains. ,**~'quarters** *n* (*sing* or *pl*) place from which (eg police, army) operations are controlled. '**~-rest** *n* sth that supports the ~. '**~room** *n* = clearance(2). '**~set** *n* ~phones. '**~ship** /-ʃɪp/ *n* position of a ~master or ~mistress: *apply for a ~ship.* '**~stall** *n* part of a bridle or halter that fits round the ~. '**~stone** *n* stone set up at the ~ of a grave. '**~waters** *n pl* ⇨ (10) above. '**~way** *n* [U] progress. **make some/no ~way,** (not) make progress. '**~wind** *n* one that blows directly into one's face, or against the course of a ship, etc. '**~word** *n* word used as a heading, eg the first word, in heavy type, of a dictionary entry. **~ed** *adj* (in compounds) ,**three-'~ed,** having three ~s; ,**long-'~ed,** having a long skull. **~less** *adj* having no ~.

head² /hed/ *vt, vi* **1** [VP 6A] be at the head or top of: ～ *a procession;* ～ *a revolt/rebellion,* act as the leader. *Smith's name ～ed the list.* **2** [VP6A] strike, touch, with the head (eg the ball in football). **3** [VP15B] ～ *sth/sb off,* get in front of, so as to turn back or aside: ～ *off a flock of sheep* (to prevent them from going the wrong way); (fig) prevent: ～ *off a quarrel.* **4** [VP2C] move in the direction indicated: ～ *south;* ～ *straight for home;* (fig) *be ～ing for disaster. Where are you ～ed (for)?*

header /'hedə(r)/ *n* **1** fall, dive or jump with the head first: *take a ～ into a swimming pool.* **2** (football) act of striking the ball with the head.

head·ing /'hedɪŋ/ *n* word or words at the top of a section of printed matter (to show the subject of what follows).

head·long /'hedlɒŋ US: -lɔːŋ/ *adv, adj* **1** with the head first: *fall ～.* **2** thoughtless(ly) and hurried-(ly): *rush ～ into danger; a ～ decision.*

head·strong /'hedstrɒŋ US: -strɔːŋ/ *adj* self-willed; obstinate.

heady /'hedɪ/ *adj* (-ier, -iest) **1** acting, done, on impulse; headstrong. **2** (of alcoholic drink) having a quick effect on the senses; quickly causing intox-ication: *a ～ wine;* (fig) (eg of sudden success) having an exciting effect.

heal /hiːl/ *vt, vi* **1** [VP6A, 2A, C] (esp of wounds) (cause to) become healthy and sound: *The wound is not yet ～ed,* the new skin has not yet covered it. *The wound ～ed slowly. It soon ～ed up/over.* **2** [VP6A] (archaic or biblical) restore (a person) to health; cure (a disease): ～ *sb of a disease* (*cure* is now the usu word). ⇨ also *faith-～ing* at faith. **3** [VP6A] end: ～ *a quarrel. Time ～s all sorrows.* ～**er** *n* person or thing that ～s: *Time is a great ～er.* ～**ing** *adj* having the power to ～: *～ing ointments.*

health /helθ/ *n* **1** [U] condition of the body or the mind: *be in/enjoy/have good/poor ～. Fresh air and exercise are good for the ～* (more colloq *good for you*). '**～ food** *n* [U] food that is nutritious and free of artificial substances: (attrib) *a ～ food restaurant/shop.* **2** (in names of organizations, etc): *the ,World 'H～ Organisation* (abbr **WHO**); *the Department of H～ and Social Security* (in GB, abbr **DHSS**); *the ,National 'H～ Service* (in GB, abbr **NHS**). **3** [U] state of being well and free from illness: *restored to ～.* **4 drink sb's ～; drink a ～ (to sb),** (as a social custom) raise one's glass and wish good ～ to him. ～**·ful** /-fl/ *adj* ～-giving; good for the ～.

healthy /'helθɪ/ *adj* (-ier, -iest) **1** having good health; well, strong and able to resist disease: *The children look very ～. The children are quite ～, although they have slight colds at present.* (Note that *well* is the usu word when the reference is to a specific occasion: eg *I hope you're quite well*). **2** likely to produce good health: *a ～ climate; a ～ way of living.* **3** showing good health: *a ～ appe-tite.* **health·ily** /-ɪlɪ/ *adv* in a ～ way.

heap /hiːp/ *n* [C] **1** number of things, mass of material, piled up: *a big ～ of books; a ～ of sand; building material lying about in ～s.* **be struck/ knocked all of a ～,** (colloq) be overwhelmed; be thrown into a state of bewilderment or confusion. **2** ～**s (of),** (colloq) large number; plenty: *We have ～s of books/time. She has been there ～s of times,* very often. *There is ～s more I could say on this question.* **3** ～**s,** (as *adv;* colloq) much: *feeling ～s better.* □ *vt* **1** [VP6A, 15A, B] ～ **(up),** put in a ～: ～

(up) stones; ～ *up riches.* **2** [VP14] ～ *sth on/ upon sb/sth;* ～ *sb/sth with sth,* fill; load: ～ *a plate with food;* ～ *favours upon a person;* ～ *a person with favours; a ～ed spoonful.*

hear /hɪə(r)/ *vt, vi* (*pt, pp* heard /hɜːd/) **1** [VP2A, 6A, 18A, 19A, 24A] perceive (sound, etc) with the ears: *Deaf people cannot ～. I ～d someone laughing. He was ～d to groan. Did you ～ him go out? Have you ever ～d that song sung in Italian? We listened but could ～ nothing. She doesn't/can't ～ very well.* (Note the frequent use of *can-could* when an effort of perception is implied.) **2** [VP6A, 9, 3A] be told or informed: *Have you ～d the news? I ～d that he was ill. I've ～d (say) that your country is beautiful.* ～ *about sth,* be given information about; learn about: *I've just ～d about his dismissal/illness. You will ～ about this later,* sometimes implying that there will be a rebuke, etc. ～ *from sb,* receive a letter, news, etc: *How often do you ～ from your sister?* ～ *of sb/ sth,* have knowledge of: *I've never ～d of her/the place,* know nothing of her/the place. ～ *tell of,* ～ people talking about: *I've often ～d tell of such happenings.* **3** [VP6A, 10, 15A, 3A] listen to; pay at-tention to; (of a judge in a law court) try (a case): *You'd better ～ what they have to say. The court ～d the evidence. Which judge will ～ the case?* ～ *sb out,* listen to the end: *Don't judge me before I've finished my explanation:* ～ *me out, please.* **not ～ of,** (usu with *will, would*) refuse to consider or allow: *I won't ～ of such a thing! She wouldn't ～ of it.* **4 ,H～!'H～!** used as a form of cheering to express approval or agreement, but also ironically. ～**er** *n* person who ～s, esp a member of an audi-ence.

hear·ing /'hɪərɪŋ/ *n* **1** [U] perception by sound: *Her ～ is poor,* she is rather deaf. **hard of ～,** rather deaf. '**～-aid** *n* electronic device for helping deaf people to hear. **2** [U] distance within which one can hear: *In some countries it is unwise to talk about politics in the ～ of strangers,* where strangers may hear. **within/out of ～,** near enough/not near enough to hear or be heard: *Please keep within ～.* **3** [C] opportunity of being heard (esp in self-defence). **gain a ～,** an opportunity to be heard. **give sb/get a fair ～,** an opportunity of being lis-tened to impartially. **4** (legal) trial of a case at law, esp before a judge without a jury.

hearken /'hɑːkən/ *vi* (archaic) listen (*to*).

hear·say /'hɪəseɪ/ *n* [U] common talk; rumour; what one has heard another person or other persons say: *I don't believe it; it's merely ～. H～ evidence is not accepted in law courts.*

hearse /hɜːs/ *n* carriage, car, for carrying a coffin at a funeral.

heart /hɑːt/ *n* **1** that part of the body which pumps blood through the system: *When a man's ～ stops beating, he dies. He had a '～ attack,* a sudden ill-ness with irregular and violent beating of the ～. ⇨ the illus at respiratory. **2** centre of the emotions, esp love; deepest part of one's nature: *a man with a kind ～; a kind-～ed man.* **sb after one's own ～,** of the sort one very much likes or approves of. **at ～,** deep down; basically. **have sth at ～,** be deeply interested in it, anxious to support or en-courage it. **from (the bottom of) one's ～,** sin-cerely. **in one's ～ of ～s,** in one's inmost feel-ings. **to one's ～'s content,** as much as, for as long as, etc one wishes. **with all one's ～,** com-pletely and willingly: *I love you with all my ～.* ～

and soul, completely: *I'm yours ~ and soul.* **break a person's ~,** make him very sad. Hence, ,**broken-**'~**ed,** '~**-broken** adjj. **cry one's** '~ **out,** pine or brood over sth, esp in secret. **do one's** '~ **good,** cause one to feel encouraged, cheerful, etc. **(get/learn/know sth) by ~,** from memory. **have a ~,** show sympathy, understanding. **(have) a change of ~,** (experience) a change of opinion. **have the ~ to,** (usu neg, or interr with *can–could)* be hard-~ed or unsympathetic enough to: *How can you have the ~ to drown the kittens?* **have one's ~ in sth,** be interested in it and fond of it. **have one's ~ in one's boots,** be greatly discouraged, feel hopeless. **have one's ~ in one's mouth,** be badly frightened. **have one's ~ in the right place,** have true or kind feelings. **have one's ~ set on sth,** desire greatly. **lose ~,** be discouraged. **lose one's ~ to sb/sth,** become very fond of; fall in love with. **set one's ~ on sth/having sth/doing sth, etc,** be. very anxious (to have, to do, etc). **take (fresh) ~ (at sth),** be confident. **take sth to ~,** be much affected by it; grieve over it. **wear one's ~ on/upon one's sleeve,** show one's feelings quite openly. **3** central part: *in the ~ of the forest; the ~ of the matter,* the essence; *get to the ~ of a subject/mystery; a cabbage with a good solid ~.* **4** [U] (of land) fertility: *in good ~,* in good condition; *out of ~,* in poor condition. **5** ~-shaped thing, esp the design used on playing-cards: *the ten/queen/etc of ~s. H~s are trumps.* ⇨ the illus at card. **6** (as a term of endearment to a person) *dear ~;* '*sweet~.* **7** (compounds) '~**-ache** n [U] deep sorrow. '~**-beat** n [C] movement of the ~ (about 70 beats a minute). '~**-break** n [U] overwhelming sorrow. '~**-breaking** adj causing ~break. '~**-broken** adj crushed by ~break. '~**-burn** n [U] burning sensation in the lower part of the chest, caused by indigestion. '~**-burning** n [U] (and also in pl) envious, discontented feeling(s), usu caused by disappointment. '~**-disease** n [U] disease of the ~. '~**-failure** n [U] failure of the ~ to function. '~**-felt** adj sincere: ~*felt emotion/thanks.* '~**-rending** adj causing deep grief. '~**'s-ease** n [U] (old name for) pansy. '~**-sick** adj low-spirited. '~**-strings** n pl deepest feelings of love: *play upon sb's ~strings,* touch his feelings. ~**ed** adj in compounds: *hard-~ed; sad-~ed; faint-~ed,* lacking in courage. ~**less** adj unkind; without pity. ~**-less-ly** adv ~**-lessness** n

hearten /'hɑ:tn/ vt [VP6A] give courage to; cheer: ~*ing news.*

hearth /hɑ:θ/ n floor of a fireplace; (fig) fireside as representing the home: *fight for ~ and altar,* (rhet) in defence of one's home and religion. '~**-rug** n rug spread out in front of the ~.

heart-i-ly /'hɑ:tɪlɪ/ adv **1** with goodwill, courage or appetite: *set to work ~; eat ~.* **2** very: ~ *glad that...;* ~ *sick of this wet weather.*

hearty /'hɑ:tɪ/ adj (-ier, -iest) **1** (of feelings) sincere: *give sb a ~ welcome; give one's ~ approval/support to a plan.* **2** strong; in good health: *still hale and ~ at eighty-five.* **3** big: *a ~ meal/appetite.*

heat¹ /hi:t/ n **1** [U] **(the)** ~, high temperature: *the ~ of the sun's rays. Cold is the absence of ~. She's suffering from the ~,* from the hot weather. ,**prickly** '~, ⇨ prickle. **2** [U] **(the)** ~, (fig) intense feeling: *speak with considerable ~; in the ~ of the debate/argument.* **3** [C] competition the winners of

which take part in (the further competitions leading to) the finals: *trial/preliminary ~s.* ⇨ also **dead** ~, at dead(6). **4** [U] (of female mammals) period or condition of sexual excitement. **be in/on/at ~. 5** (compounds) ~ **barrier** n = thermal barrier, ⇨ thermal. '~**-flash** n intense ~, eg as released from the explosion of an atomic bomb. '~ **pump** n machine that transfers ~ from a substance at a relatively low temperature to one at a higher temperature, eg for ~ing a building. '~ **shield** n device (esp on the nose-cone of a spacecraft) that gives protection against excessive ~. '~**-spot** n mark or point on the skin caused by or sensitive to ~. '~**-stroke** n sudden illness, prostration, caused by excessive ~. '~**-wave** n unbroken period of unusually hot weather.

heat² /hi:t/ vt,vi [VP6A,15B,2C] ~ **(up),** make or become hot: ~ *(up) some water;* ~ *up the cold meat for supper.* ~**ed** adj excited; passionate: *a* ~*ed discussion,* one during which feelings are roused; *get ~ed with wine.* ~**-ed-ly** adv in a ~ed manner. ~**er** n device for supplying warmth to a room, or for ~ing water, etc: *a 'gas-~er; an 'oil-~er.* ~**-ing** n [U] means of creating ~: *electric/ gas/oil ~ing.* ⇨ central.

heath /hi:θ/ n **1** [C] area of flat unused land, esp if covered with ~. **2** [C,U] (kind of) low evergreen shrub with small purple, pink or white bell-shaped flowers, eg *ling* and *heather.*

hea·then /'hi:ðn/ n **1** [C] (pl ~s or, collectively, **the** ~) believer in a religion other than the chief world religions: *The Saxons who invaded England were ~s. He went abroad to preach Christianity to the ~.* **2** [C] (colloq) person whose morals, etc are disapproved of: *They've allowed their daughter to grow up as a young ~,* wild, ill-mannered, without moral training. **3** (attrib): *a ~ land;* ~ *customs.* ~**-ish** /-ɪʃ/ adj of or like ~s; barbarous.

heather /'heðə(r)/ n [U] variety of heath(2), with small light-purple or white flowers, common in Scotland. **take to the ~,** (in olden times) become an outlaw. '~**-mixture** n (of cloth) of mixed colours supposed to be like ~.

heave /hi:v/ vt,vi (pt,pp ~d or (6 and 7 below), nautical use, hove /həʊv/) **1** [VP6A] raise, lift up (sth heavy): ~ *the anchor.* **2** [VP6A] utter: ~ *a sigh/groan.* **3** [VP6A,15A,B] (colloq) lift and throw: ~ *sth overboard;* ~ *a brick through a window.* **4** [VP2A,C,3A] ~ **(at/on sth),** pull (at a rope, etc): ~ *(away) at the capstan. H~ away! H~ ho!* (sailors' cries when pulling at ropes or cables). **5** [VP2A] rise ·and fall vigorously and regularly: *a heaving chest; the heaving billows,* ie waves. **6** [VP2C,15B] ~ **to,** (of a sailing-ship) (cause to) come to a standstill (without anchoring or mooring). **7** ~ **in sight,** become visible. □ n act of heaving: *with a mighty ~,* a strong pull or throw.

heaven /'hevn/ n **1** home of God and the saints: *die and go to ~.* **2** H~, God, Providence: *It was the will of H~. H~ forbid! Thank H~ you were not killed.* Also in exclamations: *For H~'s sake! Good H~s! ~'sent* adj providential: *a ~sent opportunity.* **3** place, state, of supreme happiness. **4** (often the ~s) the firmament: *the broad expanse of ~/the ~s.* **move ~ and earth,** do one's utmost. ~**-ward(s)** /-wəd(z)/ adj,adv towards ~.

heav-en-ly /'hevnlɪ/ adj **1** of, from, like, heaven: *a ~ angel/vision.* **the** ~ **bodies,** ie the sun, moon, planets, etc. **the** ~ **city,** Paradise. **2** of more than earthly excellence. **3** (colloq) very pleasing: *What ~ peaches!*

heavy /'hevɪ/ adj (-ier, -iest) **1** having weight (esp great weight); difficult to lift, carry or move: *It's too ~ for me to lift. Lead is a ~ metal.* **'~-weight** n boxer weighing 175 lb (79·3 kg) or more. **2** of more than usual size, amount, force, etc: *~ guns/ artillery*, of the largest class; *~* (= abundant) *crops; ~ rain; ~ work; a ~ blow*, one with great force behind it; *a ~ fall*, one likely to cause shock; *a ~ heart*, made sad; *~ tidings*, bad news; *~ soil*, difficult to cultivate; *~ roads*, muddy and sticky, difficult to travel over; *a ~ sky*, dark with clouds; *a ~ sea*, rough, with big waves; *~ food*, rich, difficult to digest; *~ bread*, dense, sticky, like dough: *a ~ day*, full of difficult work; *a ~ sleep/sleeper*, a deep sleep/a person who is difficult to wake up; *a ~ drinker/smoker*, sb who drinks (alcoholic drink)/smokes much; *~ reading*, difficult to read. *~* **'hydrogen**, isotope of hydrogen with atoms twice the normal weight. *~* **'water**, water whose molecules consist of two *~* hydrogen atoms and one ordinary oxygen atom. **3** (of persons) slow in speech or thought; (of writing or painting) dull, tedious; (of parts in a play for the theatre) serious or solemn; *play the part of the ~ father*; (of bodily states) inactive: *~ with sleep/ wine.* **(find sth) ~ going,** (find progress) difficult. **(find sb) ~ going,** (find him) difficult (to understand), or boring (to listen to). **make~ weather of sth,** ⇨ weather (1). **4** (US sl) dangerous; troublesome. **5** (compounds) *~*-**'handed** adj awkward, clumsy. *~*-**'hearted** adj melancholy. □ adv heavily: *The crime lies ~ on his conscience. Do you ever find time hangs ~ on your hands*, Does it ever pass too slowly? *~*-**'laden** adj carrying a *~* load; (fig) having a *~* (= sad) heart. **heav·i·ly** /'hevɪlɪ/ adv in a *~* manner: *a heavily loaded lorry.* **heavi·ness** n

Heavi·side layer /'hevɪsaɪd leɪə(r)/ ⇨ iono-sphere.

heb·doma·dal /heb'domədl/ adj weekly: *H~ Council*, one that meets weekly.

He·braic /hiː'breɪk/ adj Hebrew.

He·brew /'hiːbruː/ n **1** [C] Jew; Israeli. **2** [U] language used by the ancient *~*s (as in the Old Testament); language now spoken by the people of Israel. □ adj of the *~* language or people.

heca·tomb /'hekətuːm/ n (in ancient Greece) great public sacrifice; blood-offering (esp of 100 oxen).

heck /hek/ n (sl, euphem) hell (used in exclamations): *Oh! What the ~!*

heckle /'hekl/ vt [VP6A] interrupt and ask many troublesome questions at a public meeting: *~ the Socialist candidate.* **heck·ler** /'heklə(r)/ n

hec·tare /'hekteə(r)/ n measure of area in the metric system, 10000 sq metres (= 2·471 acres). ⇨ App 5.

hec·tic /'hektɪk/ adj **1** unnaturally red; feverish; consumptive: *~ cheeks; a ~ colouring.* **2** (colloq) full of excitement and without rest: *have a ~ time; lead a ~ life; for one ~* (= exciting) *moment.*

hecto- /'hektəʊ/ pref (in comb) hundred: *'~gram(me)*, 100 grammes. ⇨ App 5.

hec·tor /'hektə(r)/ vt, vi bully; bluster.

he'd /strong or initial form: hiːd; medial weak form: iːd/ = he had; he would.

hedge /hedʒ/ n **1** row of bushes, shrubs or tall plants, etc usu cut level at the top, forming a boundary for a field, garden, etc: *a ' beech-~. Will this ~ keep the sheep in the field?* **'~-hop** vi fly (an aircraft) not much above ground level, eg when spraying crops. **'~-row** n row of bushes forming a *~.* **'~-sparrow** n common GB and US bird. **2** (fig) means of defence against possible loss: *buy gold/diamonds as a ~ against inflation.* □ vt, vi **1** [VP6A,15A,B] put a *~* or (fig) barrier round: *~ a field; ~ a person in/round with rules and regulations*, restrict his freedom of action. **2** [VP2A] refuse to commit oneself; avoid giving a direct answer to a question: *Answer 'yes' or 'no'—don't ~!* **3** [VP2A,6A] (colloq) secure oneself against loss, esp when betting, by compensating transactions: *~ one's bets.* **4** [VP2A] make or trim *~*s.

hedge·hog /'hedʒhɒg US: -hɔːg/ n insect-eating animal covered with spines, that rolls itself up into a ball to defend itself. ⇨ the illus at small.

he·don·ism /'hiːdənɪzəm/ n [U] belief that pleasure is the chief good. **he·don·ist** /-ɪst/ n believer in *~.* **he·don·is·tic** /ˌhiːdə'nɪstɪk/ adj

heed /hiːd/ vt [VP6A] (formal) pay attention to: *~ a warning; ~ what a person says.* □ n [U] **pay/ give ~ (to); take ~ (of)**, give attention, notice: *pay no ~ to a warning.* **~·ful** /-fl/ adj **~ful (of)** attentive: *be more ~ful of advice.* **~·less** adj **~ (of)**, inattentive: *~less of danger.*

hee-haw /'hiːhɔː/ n ass's bray; loud laugh.

heel¹ /hiːl/ n **1** back part of the human foot; part of a sock, stocking, etc covering this; part of a shoe, boot, etc supporting this. ⇨ the illus at leg. **at/on the ~s of sth; at/on sb's ~s**, close behind it/ him: *Famine often follows on the ~s of war. The thief ran off with an angry crowd at his ~s.* **bring/come to ~**, (of a dog) bring/come close behind its master, under control; (fig) submit to discipline and control. **down at ~**, (of shoes) with the *~*s badly worn down; (of a person) wearing such shoes, or untidy and slovenly in appearance. **head over ~s**, upside down, in a somersault; (fig) completely. **kick/cool one's ~s**, be kept waiting. **kick up one's ~s**, behave excitedly (esp to show joy at freedom). **lay sb by the ~s**, confine or imprison him. **show a clean pair of ~s**, escape in a great hurry. **take to one's ~s**, run away. **turn on one's ~**, turn sharply round. **under the ~ of**, (fig) dominated by. **2** (US sl) cad; low-down person. □ vt [VP6A] put a *~* on: *sole and ~ a pair of shoes.* **well-'~ed** adj (sl) very rich.

heel² /hiːl/ vi, vt [VP2A,C,15B] **~ (over)**, (of a ship) (cause to) lean over to one side.

hef·ty /'heftɪ/ adj (-ier, -iest) (colloq) big and strong: *a ~ farm worker.*

he·gem·ony /hɪ'gemənɪ US: 'hedʒəməʊnɪ/ n (pl -nies) [U,C] (formal) leadership, authority, influence, esp of one state in a group of states.

He·gira, He·jira /'hedʒɪrə US: hɪ'dʒaɪərə/ n **the ~**, Muhammad's flight from Mecca to Medina; Muslim era reckoned from this (AD 622).

heifer /'hefə(r)/ n young cow that has not yet had a calf.

heigh-ho /ˌheɪ'həʊ/ int used to express disappointment, boredom, etc.

height /haɪt/ n **1** [U,C] measurement from bottom to top; distance to the top of sth from a level, esp sea-level: *the ~ of a mountain. What is your ~, How tall are you? He is six feet in ~.* **2** [C] high place: *on the mountain ~s.* **3** [U] utmost degree: *the ~ of his ambition; dressed in the ~ of fashion. The storm was at its ~.*

heighten /'haɪtn/ vt, vi [VP6A,2A] make or become

high(er); make greater in degree: ~ *a person's anger;* ~ *an effect; her* ~*ed colour,* the increased colour in her face, eg caused by emotion.

hei·nous /'heɪnəs/ *adj* (of crime) odious; atrocious. ~·**ly** *adv* ~·**ness** *n*

heir /eə(r)/ *n* person with the legal right to receive a title, property, etc when the owner dies: *The eldest son is usually the* ~. *He is* ~ *to a large fortune. Who is* ~ *to the throne?* ~ **ap'parent** *n* (*pl* ~s apparent) ~ whose right cannot be superseded by the birth of a nearer ~. ~ **pre'sumptive** *n* whose right of inheritance may be lost by the birth of a nearer ~. ~·**ess** /'eərɪs/ *n* female ~.

heir·loom /'eəluːm/ *n* sth handed down in a family for several generations.

He·jira /'hedʒɪrə *US:* /hɪ'dʒaɪərə/ *n* = Hegira.

held /held/ *pt,pp* of hold.

heli·cop·ter /'helɪkɒptə(r)/ *n* kind of aircraft with horizontal revolving blades or rotors, able to take off and land in a very small space and remain stationary in the air.

a helicopter

he·lio·trope /'hiːlɪətrəʊp/ *n* plant with small, sweet-smelling purple flowers; colour of these.

heli·port /'helɪpɔːt/ *n* airport for helicopters.

he·lium /'hiːlɪəm/ *n* [U] light, colourless gas (symbol He) that does not burn, used in balloons and airships.

hell /hel/ *n* **1** (in some religions) home of devils and of damned souls after death. **2** place, condition, of great suffering or misery: *suffer* ~ *on earth; make sb's life a* ~. *We gave the enemy* ~. **3** (colloq, in exclamations, to express anger, or to intensify a meaning) *H*~*! What the* ~ *do you want? He ran like* ~, very fast. *I like him a* ~ *of a lot. What a* ~ *of a noise!* **for the** ~ **of it,** for no particular reason. **ride** ~ **for leather,** as quickly as possible. '~·**cat** *n* spiteful or furious person. ~·**ish** /-ɪʃ/ *adj* horrible; devilish. **be** ,~·'**bent on sth,** (sl) be recklessly determined to do it.

he'll /*strong or initial form:* hiːl; *medial weak form often:* iːl/ = he will, he shall.

Hel·lene /'heliːn/ *n* subject of modern Greece; person of genuine Greek race in ancient times. **Hellenic** /he'liːnɪk *US:* he'lenɪk/ *adj* of the Greeks, their arts, culture, etc.

hello /hə'ləʊ/ *int* = hullo.

helm [1] /helm/ *n* handle (also called *tiller)* or wheel for moving the rudder of a boat or ship: *the man at the* ~, the steersman, (fig) leader. *the* ~ *of state,* (fig) the government of the nation. '~s·**man** /-mən/ *n* (*pl*-men) man at the ~.

helm [2] /helm/ *n* (archaic) helmet.

hel·met /'helmɪt/ *n* protective head-covering worn by soldiers, firemen, miners, motorbike riders, divers (as part of a diving-suit), and some policemen. ⇨ the illus at armour. ⇨ also *sun-*~ at sun. ~**ed** *adj* wearing, provided with, a ~.

helot /'helət/ *n* one of a class of slaves in ancient Sparta; (fig) member of any social class that is despised and kept in subjection.

help [1] /help/ *n* **1** [U] act of ~ing: *Thank you for your kind* ~. **be of** ~ **(to sb); be (of) any/ much/no/some** ~ **(to sb),** be ~ful: *Can I be of* any ~ *to you? It wasn't much* ~, didn't ~ much. **2** a ~, sb or sth that ~s: *Your advice was a great* ~. *Far from being a* ~ *to me, you're a hindrance.* **3** [U] remedy: *There's no* ~ *for it,* It can't be ~ed. ⇨ help [2](3). **4** [C] (usu non-resident) person who ~s with the housework: *a home* ~, ⇨ home [1](3). *The* ~ *hasn't come this morning.* ~·**ful** /-fl/ *adj* giving ~: *be* ~*ful to one's friends.* ~·**fully** /-fəlɪ/ *adv* ~·**ful·ness** *n* ~·**less** *adj* **1** without ~; not receiving ~. **2** unable to act; dependent upon others: *a* ~*less invalid; as* ~*less as a baby.* ~·**less·ly** *adv* ~·**less·ness** *n* ~·**er** *n* person who ~s. ~·**ing** *n* (esp) portion of food served at a meal: *three* ~*ings of pie; a generous* ~*ing of pudding.*

help [2] /help/ *vt,vi* **1** [VP6A,17,18B,15A,B,2A,C] do part of the work of another person; make it easier for (sb) to do sth or for (sth) to happen; do sth for the benefit of (sb in need): *I can't lift this box alone, please* ~ *me. I* ~*ed him* (*to*) *find his things.* (The omission of *to* is more usual in US than in GB usage.) *Please* ~ *me up/down/out, etc with this heavy trunk,* ~ me to carry it up, etc. *Will you* ~ *me on with my overcoat, please,* ~ me to put it on? *We* ~*ed the injured man off with his clothes,* ~ed him to get them off. *Tom has to* ~ *his father, who is too old to work. Would it* ~ *you to know that...,* if I told you that.... ~ **out,** give ~ (esp in a crisis). **2** [VP6A,14] ~ **sb/oneself (to sth),** serve with food, drink, etc: *May I* ~ *you to some more meat? H*~ *yourself to the fruit/cigarettes.* **3** [VP6A,C] **can** ~ **sth/doing sth,** avoid; refrain; prevent: *Don't tell him more than you can* ~, more than you must. *I can't* ~ *thinking he's still alive. She burst out crying; she couldn't* ~ *it. I can't* ~ *my husband having so many dull relations. It can't be* ~*ed,* is inevitable. **4** *So* ~ *me God,* (in an oath) (as I speak the truth, etc) may God ~ me.

help·mate /'helpmeɪt/, **help·meet** /'helpmiːt/ *nn* helpful partner, esp a wife or husband.

hel·ter-skel·ter /,heltə 'skeltə(r)/ *adv* in disorderly haste. □ *n* tall spiral slide [1](2) in a fairground, etc.

helve /helv/ *n* handle of a tool, esp an axe.

hem [1] /hem/ *n* border or edge of cloth, esp one on an article of clothing, when turned and sewn down. '**hemming-stitch** *n* style of sewing hems on dresses, skirts, etc by joining the turned edge to the length of material using diagonal stitches. '**hem·line** *n* (esp) lower edge of a skirt or dress: *lower/ raise the hemline,* make a skirt, etc longer/shorter. □ *vt* (-mm-) **1** [VP6A] make a hem on: *hem a handkerchief.* **2** [VP15B] ~ **about/around/in,** enclose; confine; surround: *hemmed in by the enemy.*

hem [2] (also **h'm**) /hem, hm/ *int* sound used to indicate doubt or sarcasm, or to call attention. □ *vi* (-mm-) make this sound; hesitate in speech. *hem and haw/ha,* = hum and haw/ha, ⇨ hum.

he·ma·tite (also **hae-**) /'hemətaɪt/ *n* iron oxide (Fe_2O_3) the main ore of iron.

hemi·sphere /'hemɪsfɪə(r)/ *n* half a sphere; half the earth. **the Northern/Southern** ~, north/south of the equator. **the Eastern** ~, Europe, Asia, Africa and Australia. **the Western** ~, N and S America.

hem·lock /'hemlɒk/ *n* plant with finely divided leaves and small, white flowers, from which a poison is made. '~ **spruce** *n* evergreen tree, common in America and Asia, valuable for its timber.

he·mo·glo·bin (also **hae-**) /,hiːmə'gləʊbɪn/ *n* [U] substance present in the red corpuscles of the blood.

he·mo·philia (also **hae-**) /ˌhiːməˈfɪlɪə/ n [U] (usu hereditary) tendency of blood (from a wound, etc) not to clot, so that bleeding continues. **he·mo·phil·iac** (also **hae-**) /ˌhiːməˈfɪlɪæk/ n person having ~.

hem·or·rhage (also **hae-**) /ˈhemərɪdʒ/ n [U] bleeding; [C] escape of blood.

hem·or·rhoids (also **hae-**) /ˈhemərɔɪdz/ n pl swelling of a vein or veins, esp at or near the anus; piles.

hemp /hemp/ n [U] (kinds of) plant from which coarse fibres are obtained for the manufacture of rope and cloth. **(Indian)** ~, narcotic from the flowering tops, seed and resin of such plants, also called *bhang, cannabis, hashish, marijuana.* ~**en** /ˈhempən/ adj made of ~; like ~: a ~en rope.

hem·stitch /ˈhemstɪtʃ/ vt, n (ornament the hem of a handkerchief, dress, skirt, towel, etc with a) decorative stitch made by pulling out some of the threads and tying the cross-threads in groups.

hen /hen/ n **1** female of the common domestic fowl. ⇨ **cock**[1](1). ⇨ the illus at fowl. **'hen·bane** n (narcotic obtained from a) poisonous plant. **'hen·coop** n coop for keeping poultry in. **'hen·house** n (usu wooden) building for poultry. **'hen·party** n (colloq) party for women only. ⇨ *stag party* at stag. **'hen·pecked** adj (of a man) ruled by his wife. **'hen·roost** n place where fowls roost at night. **2** female (of the bird named): *'guinea-hen, 'pea-hen.*

hence /hens/ adv (formal) **1** from here; from now: *a week* ~, in a week's time. **2** for this reason. ~-**'forth,** ~-**'forward** advv from this time on; in future.

hench·man /ˈhentʃmən/ n (pl -men /-mən/) faithful supporter, esp a political supporter who obeys without question the orders of his leader: *the Dictator and his henchmen.*

henna /ˈhenə/ n [U] (plant, kind of Egyptian privet, producing) reddish-brown dye stuff for colouring leather, the finger-nails, the hair, etc. **hen·naed** /ˈhenəd/ adj dyed with ~.

hep /hep/ n ⇨ hip[4].

hepa·ti·tis /ˌhepəˈtaɪtɪs/ n [U] inflammation of the liver.

hep·ta·gon /ˈheptəgən US: -gɒn/ n plane figure with 7 (esp equal) sides.

her /strong or initial form: hɜː(r); medial weak form: ɜ(r)/ pers pron (as an object, corresponding to she): *She's in the garden; I can see her. Give her the book.* □ poss adj belonging to her: *Mary's mother is dead but her father is alive. That's her hat, not yours.* **hers** /hɜːz/ poss pron belonging to her: *Is that his or hers? I've borrowed a book of hers,* one of her books.

her·ald /ˈherəld/ n **1** (hist) person making public announcements for, and carrying messages from, a ruler. **2** person or thing foretelling the coming of sb or sth: *In England the cuckoo is a* ~ *of spring.* **3** official who keeps records of families that have coats of arms. **H**~**s' College,** corporation that records pedigrees and grants coats of arms. □ vt [VP6A] proclaim the approach of. **her·al·dic** /heˈrældɪk/ adj of ~s or ~ry. ~**ry** n [U] science dealing with the coats of arms, descent, and history of old families.

herb /hɜːb US: ɜːrb/ n low-growing, soft-stemmed plant which dies down at the end of the growing season; plant of this kind whose leaves or seeds, because of their scent or flavour, are used in medi-

cine or for flavouring food, eg sage, mint, dill. ~ **beer** n drink made from ~s. ~**age** /-ɪdʒ/ n [U] ~s collectively; grass and other field plants. ~**al** /ˈhɜːbl US: ˈɜːrbl/ adj of (esp) medicinal ~s: ~al *remedies.* ~**al·ist** /ˈhɜːbəlɪst US: ˈɜːrb-/ n person who grows or sells ~s for medical use. **her·bivor·ous** /hɜːˈbɪvərəs US: ɜː-/ adj (of animals) feeding on ~age. ⇨ *carnivorous* at carnivore.

her·ba·ceous /hɜːˈbeɪʃəs US: ɜː-/ adj (of plants) having stems that are not woody: *a* ~ *border,* (in a garden) border with plants which come up and flower year after year (not shrubs, annuals, etc).

her·cu·lean /ˌhɜːkjʊˈliːən/ adj having, needing, great powers of body or mind: *a* ~ *task.*

herd /hɜːd/ n **1** number or company of animals, esp cattle, feeding or going about together: *a* ~ *of cattle/deer/elephants.* **2** (chiefly in compounds) keeper of a ~: '*cow*~; '*goat*~. **3** (derog) *the common/vulgar* ~, the mass of common people; *the* ~ *instinct,* the instinct to act, feel, think, etc like the mass of people, and to be with the mass. □ vi, vt [VP2C,15A,B] (cause to) gather into a ~ or as in a ~; look after a ~: *people who* ~*ed/were* ~*ed together like cattle.* '~**s·man** /-mən/ n (pl -men) keeper of a ~.

here /hɪə(r)/ adv **1** in, at, to this point or place: *Come* ~. *I live* ~. *Put the box* ~. *Look* ~. **2** (with front position, and inversion of the subject and finite v if the subject is a n, but not if the subject is a pers pron): *H*~ *comes the bus! H*~ *it comes! H*~ *are the others! H*~ *they/we are! H*~'*s something interesting. H*~ *you are/it is!* H~ is what you asked for, are looking for, etc according to context. **3** at this point (in a series of events, in a process, etc): *H*~ *he stopped reading and looked up. H*~ *the speaker paused to have a drink. H*~ *goes!* Now I'm going to make a start, have a go. **4** (after preps): *Come over* ~, near to where I am. *Do you live near* ~, near this place? **5** ~ *and there,* in various places. ~, *there and everywhere,* in all parts; all round. *neither* ~ *nor there,* (colloq) irrelevant. **6** (used after a n to call attention, or for emphasis): *My friend* ~ *was a witness of the accident.* **7** (used when drinking to sb's health, wishing success to an enterprise, etc): *H*~'*s to the bride and bridegroom!* ~**·abouts** /ˌhɪərəˈbaʊts/ adv near or about ~. ~**·after** /hɪərˈɑːftə(r) US: -ˈæf-/ adv, n (in the) future; the life to come. ~**·by** /hɪəˈbaɪ/ adv (legal) by means or by reason of this. ~**·in** /ˌhɪərˈɪn/ adv (legal) in this. ~**·of** /hɪərˈɒv/ adv (legal) of or about this. ~**·to** /hɪəˈtuː/ adv (legal) to this. ~**·to·fore** /ˌhɪətuːˈfɔː(r)/ adv (legal) until now; formerly. ~**·upon** /ˌhɪərəˈpɒn/ adv (formal) at this point; in consequence of this. ~**·with** /hɪəˈwɪð US: -ˈwɪθ/ adv (comm) with this.

her·edita·ment /ˌherɪˈdɪtəmənt/ n (legal) property that can be inherited.

her·ed·itary /hɪˈredɪtrɪ US: -terɪ/ adj passed on from parent to child, from one generation to following generations: ~ *rulers/beliefs/diseases.*

her·ed·ity /hɪˈredətɪ/ n [U] tendency of living things to pass their characteristics on to offspring, etc; characteristics, qualities, etc so passed on: ~ *factors/genes.*

her·esy /ˈherəsɪ/ n (pl -sies) [C,U] (holding of a) belief or opinion contrary to what is generally accepted, esp in religion: *fall into* ~; *be guilty of* ~; *the heresies of the Protestants.* **her·etic** /ˈherətɪk/ n person guilty of ~ or supporting a ~; person who holds an unorthodox opinion. **her·eti·cal** /hɪˈretɪkl/

adj of ∿ or heretics: *heretical beliefs.*

heri·table /'herɪtəbl/ *adj* (legal) capable of inheriting or being inherited.

heri·tage /'herɪtɪdʒ/ *n* that which has been or may be inherited.

her·maph·ro·dite /hɜː'mæfrədaɪt/ *n* [C] animal or other creature, eg an earthworm, which has both male and female sexual organs or characteristics.

her·metic /hɜː'metɪk/ *adj* completely air-tight: *a* ∿ *seal.* **her·meti·cally** /-klɪ/ *adv.* ∿*ally sealed,* sealed so as to keep all the air in or out.

her·mit /'hɜːmɪt/ *n* person (esp man in early Christian times) living alone. ∿*age* /-ɪdʒ/ *n* cell or living-place of a ∿ or groups of ∿s.

her·nia /'hɜːnɪə/ *n* [U,C] rupture, esp one caused by a part of the bowel being pushed through a weak point of the muscle wall of the abdomen.

hero /'hɪərəʊ/ *n* (*pl* ∿es /-rəʊz/) **1** person respected for bravery or noble qualities. **2** chief person in a poem, story, play, etc. ∿*ine* /'herəʊɪn/ *n* female ∿. ∿*ism* /'herəʊɪzəm/ *n* [U] quality of being a ∿; courage.

her·oic /hɪ'rəʊɪk/ *adj* **1** of, like, fit for, a hero: ∿ *deeds/tasks; use* ∿ *remedies,* hazardous remedies but worth trying. **2** of a size larger than life: *a statue of* ∿ *size/on a* ∿ *scale.* **3** of poetry dealing with heroes. ∿ **'verse,** lines of ten syllables and five stresses, rhyming in pairs. **4** (of language) grand; attempting great things; (hence) ∿s *n pl* high-flown or high-sounding talk or sentiments. **he·roi·cally** /-klɪ/ *adv*

her·oin /'herəʊɪn/ *n* [U] narcotic drug prepared from morphine, used medically to cause sleep or relieve pain, or used by drug addicts.

heron /'herən/ *n* long-legged water-bird living in marshy places. ⇨ the illus at water. ∿**ry** *n* (*pl*-ries) place where ∿s breed.

Herr /heə(r)/ *n* (*pl* Herren /'herən/) German equivalent of *Mr;* German gentleman.

her·ring /'herɪŋ/ *n* (*pl* often unchanged) sea-fish, usu swimming in immense shoals, valued as food (fresh, salted, or dried). ⇨ the illus at fish. '∿**-bone** *n* [U] pattern (like the spine and bones of a ∿) used for stitching, designs on cloth, etc. ,**red** '∿, ⇨ red(3).

hers /hɜːz/ ⇨ her.

her·self /hɜː'self; *weak form:* ɜː's-/ reflex, emph *pron* **1** (reflex) *She hurt* ∿. *She ought to be ashamed of* ∿. **(all) by** ∿, **(a)** alone. **(b)** without help: *Can she do it by* ∿ *or does she need help?* **2** (emph) *She* ∿ *told me the news. She told me the news* ∿. *I saw Mrs Smith* ∿, ie not one of her family, one of her staff, etc. **3** *She's not quite* ∿ *today,* not in her normal state of health or mind. *She has come to* ∿, is now in her normal mental state. (Cf *She has come to,* has regained consciousness.)

hertz /hɜːts/ *n* (symbol **Hz**) unit of frequency equal to one cycle per second.

Hertz·ian /'hɜːtsɪən/ *adj* ∿ **waves,** electromagnetic waves as used in radio.

he's /*strong or initial form:* hiːz; *medial weak form:* iːz/ = he is, he has.

hesi·tant /'hezɪtənt/ *adj* tending or inclined to hesitate. ∿·**ly** *adv* **hesi·tance** /-əns/, **hesi·tancy** /-ənsɪ/ *nn* [U] (formal) state or quality of being ∿.

hesi·tate /'hezɪteɪt/ *vi* [VP2A,3A,B,4C] show signs of uncertainty or unwillingness in speech or action: *He's still hesitating about joining/over whether to join the expedition. He* ∿s *at nothing. I* ∿ *to spend*

so much money on clothes. He ∿d (*about*) *what to do next.* **hesi·tat·ing·ly** *adv*

hesi·ta·tion /,hezɪ'teɪʃn/ *n* [U] state of hesitating; [C] instance of hesitating: *She agreed without the slightest* ∿. *I have no* ∿ *in stating that...; There's no room for* ∿. *His doubts and* ∿s *were tiresome.*

hes·sian /'hesɪən US: 'heʃn/ *n* [U] strong, coarse cloth of hemp or jute; sack-cloth.

het·ero·dox /'hetərədɒks/ *adj* not orthodox. ∿**y** /-sɪ/ *n* [U] opposite of orthodoxy.

het·ero·gen·eous /,hetərə'dʒiːnɪəs/ *adj* made up of different kinds: *the* ∿ *population of the USA,* of many different races. ⇨ homogeneous.

het·ero·sex·ual /,hetərə'sekʃuəl/ *adj* sexually attracted to persons of the opposite sex. □ *n* ∿ person. ∿**ity** /,hetərə,sekʃu'ælətɪ/ *n* [U] the condition of being ∿.

het-up /,het 'ʌp/ *adj* excited; over-wrought.

heu·ris·tic /hjʊə'rɪstɪk/ *adj* of the theory in education that a learner should discover things for himself. ∿s *n* method of solving problems by inductive reasoning, by evaluating past experience and moving by trial and error to a solution.

hew /hjuː/ *vt,vi* (*pt* hewed, *pp* hewed or hewn /hjuːn/) [VP6A,15A,B,2A,C] **1** cut (by striking or chopping); aim cutting blows (*at, among*): *hew down a branch. He hewed his enemy to pieces,* eg with his sword. **2** shape by chopping: *hewn timber,* roughly shaped by hewing. **3** make by hard work: *hew one's way through dense jungle,* cut out and beat a path; *hew out a career for oneself.* **hewer** *n* person who hews, esp a man who cuts out coal in a mine: *hewers of wood and drawers of water,* persons doing hard menial work. (⇨ Josh 9: 21.)

hexa·gon /'heksəgən US: -gɒn/ *n* plane figure with 6 (esp equal) sides. **hex·ag·on·al** /heks'ægənl/ *adj* six-sided.

hex·am·eter /heks'æmɪtə(r)/ *n* (kind of) line of verse (esp Gk or Lat) with six feet.

hey /heɪ/ *int* used to call attention, or to express surprise or interrogation. ,**Hey 'presto!** conjuror's phrase used to announce the completion of a trick.

hey–day /'heɪ deɪ/ *n* (*sing* only) time of greatest prosperity or power: *in the* ∿ *of youth. The 19th century was the* ∿ *of steam railways.*

hi /haɪ/ *int* **1** = hey. **2** (esp US) = hullo.

hi·atus /haɪ'eɪtəs/ *n* (*pl*-es /-sɪz/) gap in a series, making it incomplete; break in continuity.

hi·ber·nate /'haɪbəneɪt/ *vi* [VP2A] (of some animals) pass the whole of the winter in a torpid state. **hi·ber·na·tion** /,haɪbə'neɪʃn/ *n* [U]

hi·bis·cus /hɪ'bɪskəs US: haɪ-/ *n* [U] cultivated plant or shrub with brightly coloured flowers (chiefly in the tropics). ⇨ the illus at flower.

hic·cup, hic·cough /'hɪkʌp/ *vi, n* (have a) sudden stopping of the breath with a cough-like sound. **(the)** ∿s, an attack of ∿s: *have the* ∿s.

hick /hɪk/ *n, adj* (sl; derog) (of a) countryman, yokel.

hick·ory /'hɪkərɪ/ *n* (*pl*-ries) (hard wood of a) N American tree with edible nuts.

hid, hidden ⇨ hide¹.

hide¹ /haɪd/ *vt,vi* (*pt* hid /hɪd/, *pp* hidden /'hɪdn/ or (archaic) hid) [VP6A,14] **1** ∿ *(from),* put or keep (sb, sth, oneself) out of sight; prevent from being seen, found or known: *Quick,* ∿ *yourself! The sun was hidden by the clouds. The future is hidden from us. She tried to* ∿ *her feelings. His words had a hidden meaning.* **2** [VP2A] be or become hidden: *You had better* ∿. *Where is he hid-*

ing? ~**-and-seek** /ˌhaɪdnˈsiːk/ *n* [U] children's game in which one child ~s and others try to find him. □ *n* (US = *blind*) place where wild animals, birds, etc may be observed, eg by photographers, without alarming them. '~**-out/-away** *nn* (colloq) hiding-place: *a guerrilla ~-out in the mountains.* **hid·ing** *n* [U] (used of persons) *be in/go into hiding,* be hidden/~ oneself. *come out of hiding,* show oneself. '**hiding-place** *n* place where sb or sth is or could be hidden.

hide² /haɪd/ *n* **1** [C] animal's skin, esp as an article of commerce and manufacture. **2** [U] (colloq) human skin. *save one's* ~, save oneself from a beating, from punishment. *tan sb's* ~, give him a beating.

hide·bound /ˈhaɪdbaʊnd/ *adj* narrow-minded; having, showing, too much respect for rules and traditions.

hid·eous /ˈhɪdɪəs/ *adj* very ugly; filling the mind with horror; frightful: *a ~ face/crime/noise.* ~**·ly** *adv*

hid·ing /ˈhaɪdɪŋ/ *n* [C] beating; thrashing: *give sb/ get a good hiding.*

hie /haɪ/ *vi* (archaic, or joc) go quickly (*to*).

hi·er·archy /ˈhaɪərɑːkɪ/ *n* (*pl* -chies) [C] organization with grades of authority from lowest to highest: *the ~ of the Civil Service;* group of persons in authority; group of bishops of a country. **hi·er·archi·c(al)** /ˌhaɪəˈrɑːkɪk(l)/ *adj* organized priesthood.

hi·ero·glyph /ˈhaɪərəglɪf/ *n* picture or figure of an object, representing a word, syllable or sound, as used in the writing of the ancient Egyptians and Mexicans; other secret or unintelligible written symbol. ~**ic** /ˌhaɪərəˈglɪfɪk/ *adj* of, written in, ~s. ~**·ics** *n pl* = ~s.

hieroglyphics

hi-fi /ˌhaɪ ˈfaɪ/ *n, adj* (colloq abbr of) high-fidelity; apparatus producing this: *a ~* (*set*). ⇨ high(12).

hig·gledy-pig·gledy /ˌhɪgldɪ ˈpɪgldɪ/ *adj, adv* (colloq) mixed up; without order.

high¹ /haɪ/ *adj* (-er, -est) (For combinations of ~ and *nn, participles,* etc with meanings not at once to be identified from the meanings in the definitions, ⇨ 12 below.) **1** extending far upwards; measuring (the distance given) from the base to the top. (Note that *tall* is used for human beings and for a few things which have great height in relation to breadth, eg *a tall building/tower*): *There was an aeroplane ~ in the sky. How ~ is Mt Everest? ~ and dry,* (**a**) (of a ship) stranded; aground; out of the water. (**b**) (fig) abandoned; isolated; out of the current of events. *be/get on one's ~ horse,* ⇨ horse(1). *(do sth) with a ~ hand,* arrogantly (*~-handed(ly*) is preferred). **2** chief; important: *a ~ official; a ~ caste; the ~ altar,* in a church; *the Most H~,* (in the Bible) God; *~ society,* the upper classes. *~ and low,* all classes of society. **3** (of sounds) at or near the top of the scale; shrill; sharp: *speak in a ~ tone/key.* **4** extreme; intense; great: *~ prices/temperatures; bought at a ~ cost; a ~ wind; in ~ favour; have a ~ opinion of sb; in ~ spirits; ~* (= angry) *words; in ~ latitudes,* near the Poles; *have a ~* (= enjoyable) *time; ~* (=

luxurious) *living; ~ noon/summer,* at or near its peak. **5** ~ **time,** time when sth should be done at once: *It's ~ time you started,* You should start at once. *It's ~ time to go,* We must go at once. **6** noble; virtuous: *a woman of ~ character; ~ aims/ideals; a ~ calling,* eg that of a priest, doctor or nurse. **7** H~ **Church,** that section of the C of E that gives an important place to the authority of bishops and priests, to ritual and the sacraments. Hence, **H~ Churchman.** **8** (of food, esp meat and game) slightly tainted. **9** (colloq) drunk. **10** (colloq) under the influence of hallucinatory drugs: *~ on marijuana.* **11** (as *n*) ~ level: *from* (*on*) *~,* from Heaven. *Shares* (ie on the Stock Exchange) *reached a new ~* (= the ~est recorded level) *last month.* **12** (compounds) '~**-ball** *n* (US) spirits with soda water, ginger ale, etc, served with ice in a tall glass. '~**-born** *adj* of noble birth. '~**-boy** *n* (US) tallboy. '~**-brow** *n, adj* (person) with tastes and interests considered to be superior (often used contemptuously for *intellectual*): *~ drama/music.* ,~ '**chair** *n* one on ~ legs for an infant at table, or a baby's chair with a hinged tray attached to it. ,H~ '**Church** *n* ⇨ 7 above. ,~'**class** *adj* first-class. ,~ '**colour** *n* reddish complexion. ,H~ **Com'missioner** *n* representative of one Commonwealth country in another, equivalent to an ambassador. '**H~ Court** *n* supreme court of justice. '~ **day** *n* festival (only in): *~ days and holidays.* '~**er-ups** *n pl* (colloq) persons ~er in rank or status. ,~ **ex-'plosive** *n* very powerful explosive, eg TNT. ,~**fa'lutin** /fəˈluːtɪn/ *adj* (colloq) ridiculously pompous, bombastic or pretentious: *~ falutin ideas/ language.* ,~**-fi'delity** *n, adj* (abbr **hi-fi**) (of radios, records, tapes and equipment for reproducing sound) (quality of) giving faithful reproduction by the use of a wide range of sound waves. ,~**flier/'flyer** *n* ambitious person who goes to great extremes to get what he aims at. ,~'**flown** *adj* exalted; bombastic and pretentious: *a ~flown style,* eg of writing. ,~'**flying** *adj* (fig) (of persons) ambitious. ,~'**frequency** *n* (abbr **hf**) radio frequency between 3 and 30 megacycles per second. **H~ German** *n* literary German; standard spoken German. ,~'**grade** *adj* of ~ or superior quality. ,~'**handed** *adj* domineering; using power or authority without consideration for the feelings of others. ,~'**handed·ly** *adv* ~ '**hat** *adj, n* snobbish (person). □ *vt* treat (sb) in a snobbish or condescending way. '~**-jack** *vt* (variant spelling of) hijack. ,~ '**jinks,** ⇨ jinks. **the '~ jump** *n* athletic contest for jumping over an adjustable horizontal bar: *enter for/win the ~ jump. be for the ~ jump,* (sl) due for severe punishment. ,~'**keyed** *adj* (⇨ 3 above) having a ~ pitch; (fig) easily excited or made nervous. '~**land** /-lənd/ *n* mountainous region; (*pl*) mountainous parts of a country (esp **The H~lands,** those of NW Scotland). ,H~**land 'fling** *n* Scottish reel³. '**H~lander** *n* one who lives in The H~lands; soldier in a (Scottish) H~land regiment. ,~'**level** *adj* (attrib only) (of conferences, etc) conducted by persons in ~ position, eg in government, commerce. '~ **life** *n* [U] (**a**) fashionable and luxurious style of living. (**b**) (in W Africa) popular kind of music and dance. '~**light** *n* (usu *pl*) luminous area on a photograph, picture, etc which shows reflected light; reflection of light on a shiny object; (fig) most conspicuous or prominent part: *the ~lights of the week's events.* □ *vt* give prominence or emphasis to. ,H~ '**Mass** *n* (RC

Church) ⇨ Mass². ‚~-'minded /'maɪndɪd/ adj of morally ~ character; having ~ ideals or principles. Hence, ‚~-'minded‧ly adv ‚~-'minded‧ness n ‚~-'necked adj (of a dress) with the neckline cut ~. ‚~-'octane adj having a ~ octane number. ⇨ octane. ‚~-'pitched adj (a) (of sounds) shrill. (b) (of roofs) having a steep slope. ‚~-'powered adj having, using, great power: a ~-powered salesman, aggressive in selling his goods. ‚~-'pressure n [U] pressure ~er than normal, esp ~er than atmospheric pressure; (fig) aggressive and persistent: ~-pressure salesmanship. ‚~-'priced adj expensive. ‚~ 'priest n chief priest. ‚~-'principled adj honourable. '~-ranking adj (of officers, etc) having ~ rank. ‚~ re'lief n ⇨ relief²(1). '~-rise adj (attrib only) used of tall buildings with many storeys or levels, reached by lifts (elevators): ~-rise flats. ⇨ tower-block at tower. '~-road n main road; (fig) most direct way: Is there a ~road to happiness? 'H~ School n secondary school giving more advanced education than primary or elementary schools. the ‚~ 'seas n pl all parts of the seas and oceans beyond territorial waters. '~-sounding adj (of style) impressively pretentious. ‚~-'speed adj (able to be) operated at very fast speeds. ‚~-'spirited adj lively; (of a horse) frisky. '~ spot n outstanding feature, memory, event, etc. '~ street n (esp in proper names) main street of a town: There are three banks in the ~ street. ‚~ 'table n table (on a dais) where senior members of a college dine. ‚~ 'tea n (GB) early evening meal (or late tea) in homes where dinner is not eaten in the evening, usu with meat or fish. ‚~-'tension adj (electr) (of wires) having a ~ voltage. ‚~ 'tide n (time at which the) tide is at its ~est level. ‚~ 'time n ⇨ 5 above. ‚~-'toned adj socially or intellectually superior: a ~-toned finishing school for girls. ‚~ 'treason n [U] treason against the State or a sovereign. '~-up n (colloq) person of ~ rank or great importance. ‚~ 'water n [U] ~ tide. ‚~ 'water mark n mark showing the ~est point reached by the tide (or any body of water); (fig) ~est point of achievement. '~-way n main public road; main route (by air, sea or land); (fig) easiest or most direct way. ‚H~-way 'Code n official guide-book for users of public roads. '~-way‧man /-mən/ n (pl -men) (formerly) man (usu on horseback) who robbed travellers on ~ways by using, or threatening to use, violence.

high² /haɪ/ adv in or to a ~ degree: climb ~; aim ~; (lit, fig) pay ~, pay a ~ price; play ~, play a card of ~ value, eg an ace; live ~, on rich, luxurious food and drink. fly ~, (fig) have great ambitions. hold one's head ~, be proud. run ~, (a) (of the sea) have a strong current with a ~ tide. (b) (of the feelings) be excited: Popular feelings/passions ran ~, were strong. search/hunt/look ~ and low (for sth), look everywhere (for it).

high‧ly /'haɪlɪ/ adv in or to a high degree: a ~ paid official; a ~ amusing film; think ~ of sb, have a high opinion of him; speak ~ of sb, praise him.

high‧ness /'haɪnɪs/ n 1 [U] (opposite of lowness) state or quality of being high: the ~ of his character/aims. 2 title used of and to British and various foreign princes: His/Her/Your Royal/Imperial H~.

hi‧jack (also **high‧jack**) /'haɪdʒæk/ vt [VP6A] 1 steal goods from (an aircraft or vehicle) by stopping it in transit. 2 use force, or the threat of force,

against those in control of an aircraft or vehicle, in order to achieve certain aims or to reach a desired destination. □ n [C] instance of ~ing. ~er n person taking part in a ~.

hike /haɪk/ vi, n (colloq) (go for a) long walk in the country, taken for pleasure or exercise. ~r n person who ~s. ⇨ hitch hike.

hil‧ari‧ous /hɪ'leərɪəs/ adj noisily merry. ~ly adv **hil‧ar‧ity** /hɪ'lærətɪ/ n [U] noisy merriment; loud laughter.

hill /hɪl/ n 1 natural elevation on the earth's surface, lower than a mountain. '~-side n side of a ~. '~-top n top of a ~. 2 slope, eg on a road: push a bicycle up a steep ~. 3 heap of earth: 'ant-hills; 'mole-~s. ~y adj (-ier, -iest) having many ~s: ~y country; a ~y road.

hill-billy /'hɪl bɪlɪ/ n (pl -lies) (colloq, often used derog) farmer, farm-worker, etc from the mountains in the SE of the US; (attrib) of these people: ~ music.

hill‧ock /'hɪlək/ n small hill(1).

hilt /hɪlt/ n handle of a sword or dagger. ⇨ the illus at sword. (up) to the ~, completely: His guilt was proved to the ~.

him /strong form: hɪm; medial weak form: ɪm/ pers pron used as object form of he: Mr Smith is in town; I saw him yesterday. Give him the money. That's him, (colloq) That's he.

him‧self /hɪm'self; weak form: ɪm's-/ reflex, emph pron 1 (reflex) He cut ~. He ought to be ashamed of ~. (all) by ~, (a) alone. (b) without help. 2 (emph) He ~ says so. He says so ~. Did you see the manager ~? 3 He's not quite ~ today, not in his normal state of health or mind.

hind¹ /haɪnd/ adj (of things in pairs, front and back; cf fore) at the back: the ~ legs of a horse. ‚~ 'quarters n pl ~ legs and loin of the carcass of lamb, mutton, beef, etc. '~-most /-məʊst/ adj farthest behind or back. '~-sight /-saɪt/ n [U] perception of an event after its occurrence.

hind² /haɪnd/ n female of (esp the red) deer.

hin‧der /'hɪndə(r)/ vt [VP6A,C,15A] obstruct; delay; get in the way of: Don't ~ me in my work. I was ~ed from getting here earlier. I have much business that has ~ed my answering your letter.

Hindi /'hɪndi:/ n, adj (of) one of the official languages of N India.

hin‧drance /'hɪndrəns/ n [C] sth or sb that hinders: You are more of a ~ than a help.

Hin‧du /‚hɪn'du:; US: 'hɪndu:/ n person, esp of N India, whose religion is ~ism. □ adj of the ~s. ~ism /'hɪndu:ɪzəm/ n religion of most of the ~s.

Hin‧du‧stani /‚hɪndʊ'stɑːnɪ/ n, adj (of) a form of Hindi.

hinge /hɪndʒ/ n joint on which a lid, door or gate turns or swings; (fig) central principle on which sth depends: Take the door off its ~s and rehang it. □ vt, vi 1 [VP6A] support, attach with, a ~ or ~s. 2 [VP3A] ~ on/upon, turn or depend on: Everything ~s upon what happens next.

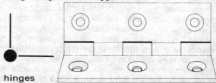

hinges

hint /hɪnt/ n [C] slight or indirect indication or suggestion: She gave him a ~ that she would like him *to leave.* **drop (sb) a** ~, indicate or suggest sth indirectly (to sb). **take a** ~, realise and do what is suggested. □ *vt, vi* **1** [VP9,6A] ~ **(to sb)**, suggest indirectly; give a ~: *I* ~*ed that he ought to work harder. He* ~*ed to me nothing of his intentions.* **2** [VP3A] ~ **at**, refer indirectly to: *He* ~*ed at my extravagance.*

hin·ter·land /'hɪntəlænd/ *n* parts of a country behind the coast or a river's banks.

hip[1] /hɪp/ *n* part on either side of the body where the bone of a person's leg is joined to the trunk: *He stood there with his hands on his hips.* ⇨ the illus at trunk. **'hip-bath** *n* small tub in which one can sit immersed up to the hips. **'hip-flask** *n* small flask (for brandy, etc) to be carried in the hip-pocket. **ˌhip-'pocket** *n* pocket (in a pair of trousers) on the hip.

hip[2] /hɪp/ *n* fruit (red when ripe) of the wild rose.

hip[3] /hɪp/ *int* (only in) **ˌHip, hip, hur'rah!** cry, cheer, of satisfaction or approval.

hip[4] /hɪp/ *adj* (also *hep*) (sl) aware of, in keeping with, advanced trends.

hip-pie /'hɪpɪ/ *n* ⇨ hippy.

hippo /'hɪpəʊ/ *n* (*pl* ~s /-pəʊz/) (colloq abbr of) hippopotamus.

Hip·po·cratic /ˌhɪpə'krætɪk/ *adj* ~ **'oath**, oath to observe the medical code of ethical and professional behaviour, sworn by entrants to the profession.

hip·po·drome /'hɪpədrəʊm/ *n* place for horse- or chariot-races in ancient Greece and Rome.

hip·po·pota·mus /ˌhɪpə'pɒtəməs/ *n* (*pl* ~es /-sɪz/ or -mi /-maɪ/) large, thick-skinned African river animal. ⇨ the illus at large.

hippy, hip·pie /'hɪpɪ/ *n* (*pl* -pies) (late 1960's) person who rejects established social conventions and institutions and expresses his personality by unusual styles of dress, living habits, etc.

hire /'haɪə(r)/ *vt* [VP6A,15B] ~ **(out)**, obtain or allow the use or services of in return for fixed payment: ~ *a horse/a concert-hall;* ~ *out boats.* (CF *rent a house.*) □ *n* [U] (money paid for) hiring: *bicycles on* ~, *50p an hour; pay for the* ~ *of a hall; work for* ~. **(pay for/buy sth) on** ~ **pur-chase,** (abbr **HP**) (buy by a) contract to pay by instalments, and the right to use it after the first payment. ~**ling** /'haɪəlɪŋ/ *n* (derog) person whose services may be ~d.

hir·sute /'hɜːsjuːt *US:* -suːt/ *adj* (formal) hairy; rough; shaggy (eg of a man with untidy long hair and beard).

his /*strong or initial form:* hɪz; *medial weak form:* ɪz/ *adj, pron* belonging to him: *He hurt his hand. That book is his, not yours. I'm a friend of his.*

hiss /hɪs/ *vi, vt* **1** [VP2A] make the sound /s/, or the noise heard when water falls on a very hot surface: *The snake raised its head and* ~*ed. The steam escaped with a* ~*ing sound.* **2** [VP6A,15A,3A] ~ **(off);** ~ **(at),** show disapproval by making this sound: ~ *an actor off the stage;* ~ *(at) a new play.* □ *n* [C] ~*ing* sound: *The speaker was received with a mixture of applause and* ~*es.*

his·tor·ian /hɪ'stɔːrɪən/ *n* writer of history.

his·toric /hɪ'stɒrɪk *US:* -'stɔːr-/ *adj* **1** notable or memorable in history; associated with past times: *a* ~ *spot/event/speech.* ~ **times,** of which the history is known and recorded (contrasted with *pre-historic times*). **2** *the* ~ **present,** (gram) simple present tense used for events in the past (to make the description more vivid).

his·tori·cal /hɪ'stɒrɪkl *US:* -'stɔːr-/ *adj* **1** belonging

or pertaining to history (as contrasted with legend and fiction): ~ *events and people,* real, not imaginary; *a* ~ *novel/play/film/painting, etc,* one dealing with real events in history. **2** having to do with history: ~ *studies; the* ~ *method of investigation.* ~**ly** /-klɪ/ *adv*

his·tory /'hɪstrɪ/ *n* (*pl* -ries) **1** [U] branch of knowledge dealing with past events, political, social, economic, of a country, continent or the world: *a student of* ~. **make** ~, do sth which will be recorded in ~. **ancient** ~, to AD 476, when the Western Roman Empire was destroyed. **medieval** ~, to 1453, when Constantinople was taken by the Turks. **modern** ~, since 1453. **2** [C] orderly description of past events: *a new* ~ *of Europe.* **3** [C] train of events connected with a person or thing; interesting or eventful past career: *a house with a strange* ~; *the inner* ~ *of the papal conclave.* **4 natural** '~, systematic account of natural phenomena.

his·tri·onic /ˌhɪstrɪ'ɒnɪk/ *adj* **1** of drama, the theatre, acting: ~ *ability.* **2** theatrical; insincere.

his·tri·on·ics *n pl* **1** theatrical performances. **2** dramatic or theatrical manners, behaviour, etc, esp when exaggerated to create an effect.

hit /hɪt/ *vt, vi* (-tt-; *pt, pp* hit) **1** [VP6A,15A,12C] give a blow or stroke to; strike (a target, an object aimed at); come against (sth) with force: *hit a man on the head; be hit by a falling stone; hit sb a hard blow; hit the mark/target; hit a ball over the fence. He hit his forehead against the kerb when he fell.* **hit a man when he's down; hit a man below the belt,** act contrary to the rules of boxing; (fig) take an unfair advantage. **hit it; hit the nail on the head,** guess right; say or do exactly the right thing. **hit it off (with sb/together),** agree, get on well: *They hit it off well.* **ˌhit-and-'run** *attrib adj* (of a road accident) in which a pedestrian or vehicle is hit by a vehicle which does not stop. **2 hit sb hard,** cause him to suffer: *The slump hit his business hard. He was hard hit by his financial losses. He has fallen in love and is hard hit.* **3** [VP6A] go to; find; reach: *hit the right path,* find it during a journey. **hit the headlines,** (colloq, of news) be printed prominently in the headlines (because sensational, etc). **hit the road,** (colloq) set out on the road. **4** [VP2C] strike: *Hit hard!* **hit out (against),** strike vigorously; (fig) attack strongly: *The Minister hit out against trade union leaders.* **5** [VP3A] **hit on/upon sth,** find by chance or unexpectedly: *hit upon an idea/the right answer/a plan for making money.* **6** [VP15B] **hit sth/sb off,** (colloq) describe briefly and accurately (in words); make a quick sketch of. **7** [VP6A] (cricket) score: *He quickly hit 60 runs.* □ *n* **1** blow; stroke: *three hits and five misses; a clever hit.* **'hit man** *n* (sl) person who is paid to kill sb. **2** successful attempt or performance: *hit songs,* **'song hits,** songs that win wide popularity; *a lucky hit. The new play is quite a hit,* has been welcomed by the public. **make a hit (with sb),** (colloq) make a very favourable impression (with him). **'hit parade** *n* list of top selling popular records. **3** stroke of sarcasm, etc: *That was a hit at me,* the words were directed against me.

hitch /hɪtʃ/ *vt, vi* **1** [VP6A,15B] ~ **sth up,** pull up with a quick movement: ~ *up one's trousers.* **2** [VP15A,2C] fasten, become fastened, on or to a hook, etc, or with a loop of rope, etc: ~ *a horse to a fence;* ~ *a rope round a bough of a tree. Her* *dress* ~*ed on a nail.* **3** [VP2A,6A] ~ *(a ride/lift),* (colloq) ask the driver of a vehicle for a ride. ⇨ hitchhike. □ *n* **1** sudden pull or push. **2** kind of noose or knot used by sailors. ⇨ the illus at knot. **3** temporary stoppage or impediment: *Everything went off without a* ~, *quite smoothly, without difficulty: The blast-off was delayed by a technical* ~.

hitch·hike /'hɪtʃhaɪk/ *vi* [VP2A] (colloq abbr *hitch*) get a free ride by signalling for one (from a passing car, lorry, etc). **hitch·hiker** *n*

hither /'hɪðə(r)/ *adv* (old use) to this place. ~·**to** /ˌhɪðə'tuː/ *adv* until now.

hive /haɪv/ *n* **1** (also '**bee·**~) box (of wood, straw, etc) for bees to live in; the bees living in a ~. **2** place full of busy people: *What a* ~ *of industry!* □ *vt,vi* **1** [VP6A] cause (bees) to go into a ~: ~ *a swarm;* (of bees) store (honey) in a ~. **2** [VP2C] enter a ~; live close together as bees do. ~ *off (from),* (fig) become a separate (and perhaps self-governing) body (as when a colony of bees leaves a ~ and forms a new ~); separate and make independent (a part of an organization): ~ *off parts of the nationalized steel industry.*

hives /haɪvz/ *n pl* skin disease with red patches and itching.

h'm /hm/ ⇨ hem².

ho /həʊ/ *int* expressing surprise, admiration, etc.

hoar /hɔː(r)/ *adj* (liter) (of hair) grey or white with age; (of a person) having such hair. '~·**frost** *n* [U] white frost; frozen dew on grass, the surface of leaves, roofs, etc.

hoard /hɔːd/ *n* carefully saved and guarded store of money, food or other treasured objects; collection of coins, valuable objects, etc dug up, eg one dating from Saxon times in GB: *a miser's* ~; *a squirrel's* ~ *of nuts.* □ *vt,vi* [VP6A,15B] ~ *(up),* save and store: ~ *gold;* ~ *up treasure.* ~**er** *n* person who ~s.

hoard·ing /'hɔːdɪŋ/ *n* (US = *billboard*) (often temporary) fence of boards round waste land, building work, etc, frequently used for posting advertisements.

hoarse /hɔːs/ *adj* (of the voice) rough and harsh; (of a person) having a ~ voice: *He shouted himself* ~. ~·**ly** *adv* ~·**ness** *n*

hoary /'hɔːrɪ/ *adj* (-ier, -iest) grey or white with age; very old: *the* ~ *ruins of English abbeys.* **hoari·ness** *n*

hoax /həʊks/ *n* [C] mischievous trick played on sb for a joke. □ *vt* [VP6A,14] deceive (sb) in this way: ~ *sb into believing or doing sth foolish.* ~**er** *n*

hob /hɒb/ *n* flat metal shelf at the side of a fireplace (with a surface level with the top of the grate) where pots and pans can be kept warm or a kettle boiled.

hobble /'hɒbl/ *vi,vt* **1** [VP2A,C] walk as when lame, or as when the feet or legs are impeded: *The old man* ~*d along with the aid of his stick.* **2** [VP6A] tie two legs of a horse or donkey to prevent it from going far away. □ *n* stumbling or limping way of walking. '~·**skirt** *n* very narrow skirt which caused the wearer to walk with short steps.

hobble·de·hoy /'hɒbldɪhɔɪ/ *n* awkward overgrown youth.

hobby /'hɒbɪ/ *n* (*pl* -bies) [C] occupation, not one's regular business, for one's leisure time, eg stamp-collecting, growing roses.

hobby·horse /'hɒbɪhɔːs/ *n* [C] wooden horse on rockers as a child's toy, or on a merry-go-round; long stick with a horse's head; figure of a horse (in wickerwork) fastened to a dancer (in the morris-dance); (fig) favourite topic (of conversation, etc): *Now he's started on his* ~, begun to talk on his favourite subject.

hob·gob·lin /ˌhɒb'gɒblɪn/ *n* [C] mischievous imp; ugly and evil spirit.

hob·nail /'hɒbneɪl/ *n* short nail with a heavy head used for the soles of heavy shoes and boots, eg for mountain-climbing. ~**ed** *adj* (of boots, etc) set with ~s.

hob·nob /'hɒbnɒb/ *vi* (-bb-) [VP2A,C,3A] ~ *(together)/(with sb),* have friendly social relations: *I used to* ~ *with the rich and famous.*

hobo /'həʊbəʊ/ *n* (*pl* ~s, ~es /-bəʊz/) (US, sl) unemployed worker who wanders from place to place; vagrant.

Hob·son's choice /ˌhɒbsnz 'tʃɔɪs/ *n* ⇨ choice.

hock¹ /hɒk/ *n* middle joint of an animal's hind leg. ⇨ the illus at dog, domestic.

hock² /hɒk/ *n* [U] (kind of) German white wine.

hock³ /hɒk/ *vt* (sl) [VP6A] pawn²(1). □ *n in* ~, pawned.

hockey /'hɒkɪ/ *n* [U] '**field** ~, game played with sticks on a field by two teams of eleven players each and a ball. '**ice** ~, game played on ice by two teams of six players each wearing skates and with sticks and a rubber disc (a *puck*). '~ **stick,** long curved or angled stick used to hit the ball or puck.

ho·cus·po·cus /ˌhəʊkəs 'pəʊkəs/ *n* [U] talk, behaviour, designed to draw one's attention away from sth; deception.

hod /hɒd/ *n* light open box with a long handle used by workmen for carrying bricks, etc on the shoulder.

hodge·podge /'hɒdʒpɒdʒ/ *n* [U] = hotch-potch.

hoe /həʊ/ *n* tool for loosening the soil, uprooting weeds among growing crops, etc. ⇨ the illus at tool. **Dutch hoe,** the kind pushed forward by the user. □ *vt,vi* (*pt,pp* hoed) [VP6A,15B,2A] work with a hoe: *hoeing up weeds.*

hog /hɒg US: hɔːg/ *n* castrated male pig reared for

field hockey

ice hockey

meat. ⇨ boar(2), sow¹; (fig) greedy, dirty, selfish person. **go the whole hog,** do sth thoroughly.
'hog·wash *n* swill(2); (fig) nonsense; rubbish (esp of sth said or written). □ *vt* [VP6A] take more than one's fair share of; take greedily and selfishly.
hog·gish /-ɪʃ/ *adj* greedy and selfish.
Hog·ma·nay /'hɒgmənei/ *n* (Scotland) New Year's Eve (and its festivities).
hogs·head /'hɒgzhed US: 'hɔːg-/ *n* large barrel for beer; liquid measure (52½ gallons in GB or about 238·5 litres, 62 gallons in US or about 234·5 litres).
hoi pol·loi /ˌhɔɪ pəˈlɔɪ/ *n* the ~, (pej) the masses; the rabble.
hoist /hɔɪst/ *vt* [VP6A,15B] lift with an apparatus of ropes and pulleys or a kind of elevator: ~ *a flag/ sail;* ~ *casks and crates aboard;* ~ *in the boats,* raise them from the water up to the deck. □ *n* apparatus for ~ing: *an ammunition* ~ (on a warship); (colloq) pull or push: *give sb a* ~, eg when he is climbing a wall.
hoity-toity /ˌhɔɪtɪ 'tɔɪtɪ/ *adj* (colloq) supercilious and haughty. □ *int* used to a ~ person to express disapproval of him or her.
hold¹ /həʊld/ *vt,vi* (*pt,pp* held /held/) (For uses with *adverbial particles* and *preps,* ⇨ 14 below.) **1** [VP6A,15A,B] have or keep in one's possession, keep fast or steady, in or with the hand(s), arm(s) or other part of the body, eg the teeth, or with a tool: *The girl was* ~*ing her father's hand. They held hands/held each other's hands. She held me by the sleeve. She was* ~*ing up an umbrella. He held the knife in his teeth as he climbed the tree.* ~ *the line,* keep a telephone connection (eg while the person at the other end goes away to find sth or sb). ⇨ also baby, brief²(1), pistol. **2** [VP6A,15A,B] restrain; keep back; control: *The police held back the crowd. It took three of us to* ~ *the madman. Try to* ~ *the thief until the police arrive. He held his attacker at arm's length. The dam gave way; it was not strong enough to* ~ *the flood waters.* ~ *one's breath,* eg from excitement or fear: *The watchers held their breath as the acrobat crossed the tightrope.* ~ *(one's) fire,* stop shooting for a time. ~ *one's tongue/peace,* be quiet. **There is no** ~*ing sb/sth,* It is impossible to restrain or control him/it: *There was no* ~*ing her,* eg because she was so determined or high-spirited. **3** [VP15A,B,2C] keep or maintain sb/sth in a specified position, manner, attitude or relationship: *H*~ *your head up. H*~ *your arms up/out. H*~ *yourself still for a moment while I take your photograph.* ~ *oneself in readiness (for),* be prepared (for sth, an emergency). ~ *one's sides with laughter,* laugh heartily. **4** [VP6A] maintain a grip of: *This new car* ~*s the road well/has good road-*~*ing qualities,* is stable, eg when cornering at speed. **5** [VP6A] support; bear the weight of: *This nail won't* ~ *such a heavy mirror. Come down—that branch won't* ~ *you!* **6** [VP6A] be filled by; have the capacity to contain or accommodate: *Will this suitcase* ~ *all your clothes? This barrel* ~*s 25 litres. What does the future* ~ *for us? He* ~*s* (= has) *strange views on religion.* ~ *sth in one's head,* retain, not forget, eg a mass of details, statistics. **(not)** ~ *water,* (not) be sound, valid, logical: *Your argument doesn't* ~ *water.* **7** [VP6A,22] keep the interest or attention of: *The speaker held his audience spellbound.* **8** [VP9,15A,B,22,25] consider; regard; believe; affirm: ~ *a man to be a fool/*~ *that he is foolish;* ~ *the view that a plan is/*~ *a*

plan to be impracticable. The President is not held in great respect. He does not ~ *himself responsible for his wife's debts.* ~ *sb in high/low esteem,* have a high/low regard for him. ~ *sth dear/ cheap,* place a high/low value on it: *He* ~*s his reputation dear.* **9** [VP6A] defend; keep possession of: *They held the fort against all attacks.* ~ *the fort,* (fig) be in charge during sb's absence: *Jane had to* ~ *the fort* (be in charge of the house) *while her mother was in hospital.* ~ *one's ground,* stand firm, not retreat: *Our soldiers held their ground bravely.* ~ *one's own,* not give way: *The patient is still* ~*ing his own,* maintaining his strength. *Mr Green held his own,* eg in a debate, maintained his position (by arguing well). **10** [VP6A] be the legal owner or possessor of: ~ *shares/stock.* ⇨ *land*~*er* at land1(6), *share*~*er* at share¹(3), *stock*~*er* at stock¹(5). **11** [VP6A] occupy; have the position of: *The Social Democrats held office then,* were the government. Hence, 'office-~er. **12** [VP6A] have; conduct; cause to take place: ~ *a meeting/debate/examination. We* ~ *a General Election every four or five years. The Motor Show is usually held in October.* ~ *court,* (fig) entertain, welcome, admirers: *a film-star* ~*ing court at London Airport.* ⇨ court¹(2). **13** [VP2A,D] remain unbroken, unchanged, secure, under strain, pressure, etc. ⇨ 5 above: *How long will the anchor* ~, stay fast in the sea bed? *How long will this fine weather* ~, continue? ⇨ break¹(5). *The argument still* ~*s (good/true),* is still valid. **14** [VP15B,3A,2C,14] (uses with *adverbial particles* and *preps;* for non-idiomatic uses ⇨ 1,2,3 above):
hold sth against sb, allow sth to influence one's opinions adversely: *Don't* ~ *his criminal convictions against him.*
hold (oneself) aloof, ⇨ aloof.
hold back, hesitate; show unwillingness: *Buyers are* ~*ing back,* making few or no offers. *When danger came, no one held back.* ~ *sb/sth back,* **(a)** ⇨ 2 above. **(b)** hinder the progress of: *His poor education is* ~*ing him back.* **(c)** keep secret or to oneself: ~ *back information.*
hold sb/sth down, (a) ⇨ 3 above. **(b)** oppress; keep down or under: *rulers who* ~ *the people down,* oppress them. *We must* ~ (= keep) *prices down.* ~ *a job down,* (colloq) keep it by proving one's capabilities.
hold forth, speak rather pompously, as if in public. ~ *sth forth,* (~ *sth out,* below is preferred) offer; propose.
hold sth in, check; restrain: ~ *in one's temper;* ~ *oneself in,* control one's feelings, eg of indignation.
hold off, (a) remain at a distance: *The storm held off. Will the rain* ~ *off until after the picnic?* **(b)** delay action: *H*~ *off for a minute.* ~ *sb/sth off,* keep at a distance: *H*~ *your dog off! His cold manner* ~*s* (better *keeps*) *people off,* deters them from trying to be friendly.
hold on, (a) stand firm when there is danger, difficulty, etc: *How much longer do they think we can* ~ *on?* **(b)** (usu imper) stop: *H*~ *on a minute!* Not so fast! Don't go further in what you're doing. ~ *on to,* **(a)** keep one's grip on; not let go of: ~ *on to one's hat on a windy day. The boy held on to the bush until someone climbed down the cliff to rescue him.* **(b)** not give up the ownership of: *You should* ~ *on to your oil shares.* ~ *sth on,* keep in posi-

tion: *These bolts and nuts ~ the wheels on.*
hold out, (a) maintain resistance; not give way: *How long can we ~ out against these attacks?* **(b)** last: *How long will our food supplies ~ out? I can't ~ out (= retain my urine) much longer—I must find a toilet. ~ out for,* continue to demand: *The workers are still ~ing out for higher wages,* insisting on being granted their demands. **~ out on,** refuse to deal with: *He's still ~ing out on me,* still opposing my wishes, refusing my request. **~ sb/sth out, (a)** ⇨ 3 above. **(b)** offer: *The doctors ~ out little hope of recovery.*
hold sth over, defer; postpone; adjourn: *The matter was held over until the next meeting. ~ sth over sb,* use it as a threat: *He's ~ing my past record over me.*
hold to sth, (a) remain loyal or steadfast to: *He held to his convictions/choice/course of action.* **(b)** keep to: *The ship held to a Southerly course. ~ sb to sth,* make sb keep, eg a promise: *We must ~ the contractors to their estimates,* not allow them to exceed them. **~ sb (up) to ransom,** demand money by threatening penalties, etc; blackmail: *Those strikers were not ~ing the country (up) to ransom.* ⇨ ransom.
hold together, (a) be and continue whole: *The bodywork of this old car hardly ~s together,* is falling apart, eg from rust. **(b)** remain united: *We Tories always ~ together in times of crisis. ~ sb/ sth together,* cause to remain together; unite: *The country needs a leader who will ~ the nation together.*
hold sb/sth up, (a) ⇨ 1,2 above. **(b)** delay: *They were held up by fog/the immigration authorities.* **(c)** stop by the use or threat of force, for the purpose of robbery: *The travellers were held up by bandits.* Hence, **'~-up** *n*: *a ~-up on the Underground,* eg by a power failure; *a bank ~-up,* eg one by armed robbers. **(d)** put forward as an example: *Don't ~ me up as a model husband. ~ sb up to derision/scorn/ridicule,* expose him to derision, etc.
hold with sth, approve of: *Do you ~ with nudity on the stage?*
hold² /həʊld/ *n* **1** [C,U] act, manner, power of holding: *catch/get/take/lay/seize ~ of sth; let go/ lose (one's) ~ of sth. He has a great ~ (= influence) over his younger brother. How long can the Government keep its ~ over the district,* keep the district under control? **2** [C] sth that may be used for holding on to: *The rock face afforded few ~s to climbers.* ⇨ *foothold* at foot¹(8). **3** (boxing and wrestling) (kinds of) grip: *all-in wrestling, with no ~s barred.*
hold³ /həʊld/ *n* part of a ship below deck, where cargo is stored.
hold-all /'həʊld ɔːl/ *n* portable bag or case large enough to hold clothes, etc when travelling. ⇨ hold¹¹(6).
holder /'həʊldə(r)/ *n* person or thing that holds: *a 'share ~; a ciga'rette-~; an 'office-~; a 'kettle-~,* cloth for handling a hot kettle.
hold-ing /'həʊldɪŋ/ *n* sth (esp land) held or owned; tenure or ownership (esp of land). **'small-~** *n* small area of land farmed by the tenant himself. **a '~ company,** one formed to hold the shares of subsidiary companies.
hold-up /'həʊld ʌp/ *n* ⇨ hold¹(14).
hole /həʊl/ *n* **1** opening or hollow place in a solid body: *a ~ in a tooth; roads full of ~s; ~s in the*

walls and roof of a building, caused by shell fire; *wear one's socks into ~s,* wear them until there are *~s.* **make a ~ in,** use a large amount of: *The hospital bills made a large ~ in his savings.* **pick ~s in,** find fault with, eg an argument. **a square peg in a round ~,** person not fitted for the position he occupies. **2** (colloq) awkward situation: *You've put me in a bad ~.* **3** animal's burrow: *a mouse's ~/ 'mouse-~; the ~ of a fox;* (fig) small, dark, wretched place; den; hiding-place: *What a wretched little ~ he lives in!* **~-and-'corner** *adj* (colloq, attrib) secret; underhand: *We don't like these ~- and-corner methods.* **4** (golf) hollow into which the ball must be hit; point scored by a player who gets his ball from one ~ to another with the fewest strokes: *a 'nine-~ golf course; win the first ~.* □ *vt,vi* **1** [VP6A] make a ~ or ~s in or through: *~ a ship,* eg by striking a rock. **2** [VP6A,15B,2C] **(out),** get (a ball) into a ~ (in golf, etc): *~ out in one,* get the ball from the tee into the ~ with only one stroke. **3** [VP2C] **~ up,** (sl) hide.
holi·day /'hɒlədeɪ/ *n* **1** day of rest from work: *Sunday is a ~ in Christian countries; Friday is a ~ in Muslim countries.* ⇨ also bank ~ at bank³(1). **2** (often *pl*) (US = *vacation*) period of rest from work: *the school ~s; the Christmas ~s; take a month's ~ in summer;* (attrib) *'~ camps. on ~,* having a ~: *Our typist is away on ~ this week.* **'~-maker** *n* person on ~.
holi·ness /'həʊlɪnɪs/ *n* **1** [U] being holy or sacred. **2 His/Your H~,** title used of/to the Pope.
hol·ler /'hɒlə(r)/ *vi,vt* (sl) yell (to indicate excitement, etc): *Stop ~ing—nobody's going to hurt you!*
hol·loa /'hɒləʊ/ *n,vi,int* shout, esp to hounds (during a fox-hunt).
hol·low /'hɒləʊ/ *adj* **1** not solid; with a hole or empty space inside: *a ~ tree; a ~ ball.* **2** (of sounds) as if coming from sth ~: *a ~ voice/groan.* **3** (fig) unreal; false; insincere: *~ sympathy/ words/promises; a ~ laugh; ~ joys and pleasures,* not giving true happiness; *a ~ victory,* one without real value. **4** sunken: *~ cheeks; ~-eyed.* **5** (colloq, as *adv*) **beat sb ~,** completely. □ *n* hole; *~ place: a ~ in the ground;* small valley: *a wooded ~,* small valley with trees. □ *vt* [VP6A,15A,B] *~ (out),* make a ~ or ~s'in; bend into a ~ shape: *river banks ~ed out by rushing water.*
holly /'hɒlɪ/ *n* [U] evergreen shrub with hard, shiny, dark-green sharp-pointed leaves and, in winter, red berries.

berries

holly

holly·hock /'hɒlɪhɒk/ *n* [C] tall garden plant with brightly coloured flowers.
Holly·wood /'hɒlɪwʊd/ *n* centre of the US film industry: *~ films/stars.*
holm-oak /'həʊm əʊk/ *n* [C] evergreen oak, ilex.
holo·caust /'hɒləkɔːst/ *n* [C] large-scale destruction, esp of human lives by fire, etc: *a nuclear ~.*
holo·graph /'hɒləgrɑːf *US:* -græf/ *n* document written wholly by the person in whose name it appears.
hol·ster /'həʊlstə(r)/ *n* leather case for a pistol or revolver.

holy /'həʊlɪ/ *adj* (-ier, -iest) **1** of God; associated with God or with religion: *the H~ Bible; H~ Writ,* the Bible; *the 'H~ Land,* where Jesus lived; *the H~ City,* Jerusalem; *'H~ Week,* the week before Easter Sunday; *'H~ Communion; the H~ Father,* the Pope; *the H~ Office,* the Inquisition; *The H~ Ghost/Spirit,* the Third Person of the Trinity; *~ ground,* land held in religious awe; *~ water,* water blessed by a priest; *a ~ war,* one fought in defence of sth sacred. **2** devoted to religion: *a ~ man; live a ~ life.* **3** *a ~ terror,* (sl) formidable person; mischievous, embarrassing child. □ *n* **the ,H~ of 'Holies, (a)** most sacred inner chamber in a Jewish temple, entered by the High Priest once a year. **(b)** (fig) any sacred place.

holy·stone /'həʊlɪstəʊn/ *n* [U] soft sandstone used for scrubbing the wooden deck of a ship.

hom·age /'hɒmɪdʒ/ *n* [U] **1** expression of respect; tribute paid (*to* sb, his merits). *do/pay ~ (to sb),* express respect for: *Many came to do the dead man ~. We pay ~ to the genius of Shakespeare.* **2** (in feudal times) formal and public acknowledgement of loyalty to a lord or ruler.

home[1] /həʊm/ *n* **1** place where one lives, esp with one's family: *He left ~ at the age of 16,* left his parents and began an independent life. *He looks forward to seeing the old ~ again,* eg his birthplace. *He was born in England, but he now looks on Paris as his ~. When I retire I shall make my ~ in the country. He left India for ~,* for his own country. *at ~,* **(a)** in the house: *I've left my books at ~. Is there anybody at ~?* **(b)** (football, etc) in the town, etc to which the team belongs: *Is our next match at ~ or away?* Hence **the '~ team,** the team playing at *~.* **(c)** expecting and ready to receive visitors at an appointed time: *'Mrs Carr will be at ~, Monday, 1 May, 5pm.'* **at-'~** *n* social function at which guests are expected at a time announced. *not at ~ (to),* not receiving visitors: *Mrs Hill is not at ~ to anyone except relatives.* *make oneself/be/feel/ at ~,* as if in one's own house; at one's ease: *The boy did not feel at ~ in such a splendid house. at ~ in,* familiar with, accustomed to: *Is it difficult to feel at ~ in a foreign language,* to feel easy and confident while using one? *be ~ and dry,* (colloq) succeed. *a ~ from ~,* a place where one is as happy, comfortable, etc as in one's own *~: Prison is not usually a ~ from ~. nothing to write ~ about,* (colloq) nothing remarkable. **2** institution or place (for the care of children, old or sick people, etc): *an 'orphans' ~; a 'nursing ~; ma'ternity ~s.* **3** (often attrib) family or domestic life: *the pleasures of ~; ~ comforts/ joys; ~ life. ~* **eco'nomics** = housecraft. *,~* **'help** *n* (GB) person employed to help the elderly, infirm or ill (and who are without the help of relatives or friends). **4** (= habitat) place where an animal or plant is native or most common: *the ~ of the tiger and the elephant,* eg the jungle; *the ~ of the fur-seal.* **5** (in sport and in various games) goal; place where a player is safe and cannot be caught, put out, etc. **the '~ plate,** (baseball) base at which the batsman stands to bat. *,~* **'run,** (baseball) one made after a hit which enables the batsman to go round all the bases without stopping. **the ,~ 'straight/'stretch,** last part of a track, near the winning-post. **6** (attrib) of the *~;* of one's own country (= domestic, inland, contrasted with *foreign*): *~ industries/products; the ~ trade/ market.* **one's ,~ 'town,** town (not necessarily

one's birthplace) in which one lives permanently. **the ,H~ 'Counties,** those round London. **the 'H~ Office,** department controlling local government, police, etc in England and Wales, under the minister called the *H~ Secretary,* or *Secretary of State for H~ Affairs* (US = *Department of the Interior*). **7** (compounds) *,~-'baked adj* (of bread, etc) baked at *~,* not bought from a shop. *,~-'brewed adj* beer, etc brewed at *~* (contrasted with beer from a brewery). *'~-coming n* arrival at *~,* coming to one's *~; ~coming weekend,* (US) when alumni or alumnæ return to their school, etc. *,~-'cured adj* (of food, esp bacon) treated (by smoking, salting, etc) at *~* (contrasted with food cured in factories). *'~-farm n* farm that supplies the needs of a large estate or establishment (contrasted with farmland that is rented out). **the ,~ 'front,** the civilians (in a country at war). *,~-'grown adj* (of food, etc) produced in the country (contrasted with what is imported). *,H~ 'Guard n* (member of the) British citizen army (1940-57). *'~-land /-lænd/ n* native land; country from which one's ancestors came. *,~-'made adj* (of bread, cakes, etc) made at *~* (contrasted with what is bought from shops). *,H~ 'Rule,* government of a country by its own citizens. *'~-sick adj* sad because away from *~;* Hence, *'~-sick·ness n* '~-spun adj, *n* (cloth made of yarn) spun at *~;* (fig) (anything) plain and homely. *'~-stead /-sted/ n* house with the land and outbuildings round it; farmhouse; (US) land given to sb by the state on condition that he lives on it and cultivates it. *'~ thrust n* attack (with a weapon or in words) that is effective. *,~ 'truth n* unpleasant fact that one is made aware of. *'~-work n* [U] work which a pupil is required to do **(a)** at *~* in the evening and take to his teacher(s) at school. **(b)** (colloq) preparatory work, eg for a report or discussion. ⇨ *housework* at house[1](7). *'~-less adj* having no *~. '~-like adj* like *~. '~-ward /-wəd/ adj* going towards *~. '~-ward(s) /-wəd(z)/ adv* towards *~.*

home[2] /həʊm/ *adv* **1** at, in or to one's *~* or country: *Is he ~ yet? I saw him on his way ~. He went ~. Send the children ~. We ought to turn back and get ~,* ie to the starting-point, whether this is or is not one's usual place of residence. **2** to the point aimed at; so as to be in the right place: *drive a nail ~,* strike it so that it is completely in. *bring sth/come ~ to sb,* (cause sb to) realize fully: *The stupidity of his behaviour was brought/ came ~ to him. drive a point/an argument ~,* cause its full force to be understood.

home·ly /'həʊmlɪ/ *adj* (-ier, -iest) **1** simple and plain; of the sort used every day: *a ~-looking old lady,* not trying to seem important or dignified; *a ~ meal.* **2** causing one to think of home or feel at home: *a ~ atmosphere.* **3** (US) (of people, their features) not attractive or good-looking. **home·li·ness** *n*

ho·meo·path *n* = homoeopath.

Ho·meric /həʊ'merɪk/ *adj* of, in the style of, Homer /'həʊmə(r)/ (about 10th c BC; Greek poet) or his epics. *~ laughter,* loud, boisterous laughter like that of the gods in Homer's epics.

homey /'həʊmɪ/ *adj* (US colloq) like home; cosy.

homi·cide /'hɒmɪsaɪd/ *n* [U] killing of a human being; [C] person who kills a human being: *H~ is not criminal when committed in self-defence. '~ squad,* (US) group of police officers who investigate *~s.* ⇨ murder. **homi·cidal** /,hɒmɪ'saɪdl/ *adj* of ～: *a homicidal lunatic; homicidal tendencies.*

hom·ily /'hɒmɪlɪ/ *n* (*pl* -lies) [C] sermon; long and tedious moralizing talk. **homi·letic** /ˌhɒmɪ'letɪk/ *adj* of homilies. **homi·let·ics** *n pl* art of preaching.

hom·ing /'həʊmɪŋ/ *adj* (of pigeons) having the instinct to fly home (when released a long way from home); (of torpedoes, missiles) fitted with electronic devices that enable them to reach a predetermined target: '～ *devices; a* ,～ '*guidance system.*

hom·iny /'hɒmɪnɪ/ *n* [U] ground maize boiled in water or milk: ～ *grits,* biscuits made from ground maize.

homo /'həʊməʊ/ *n* (Lat) man. ,～ '**sapiens** /'sæpɪenz/, modern man regarded as a species.

ho·moe·opathy (US = **ho·me·o-**) /ˌhəʊmɪ'ɒpəθɪ/ *n* [U] treatment of disease by drugs (usu in small doses) that, if given to a healthy person, would produce symptoms like those of the disease. **ho·moeo·path** (US = **ho·meo-**) /'həʊmɪəpæθ/ *n* person who practises ～.

ho·mo·gene·ous /ˌhɒmə'dʒiːnɪəs/ *adj* (formed of parts) of the same kind. ⇨ heterogeneous. **ho·mo·gene·ity** /ˌhɒmədʒɪ'niːətɪ/ *n* quality of being ～. **hom·ogen·ize** /hə'mɒdʒɪnaɪz/ *vt* [VP6A] make ～; (esp) make milk more uniform in consistency by breaking down and blending the particles of fat.

homo·graph /'hɒməgrɑːf US: -græf/ *n* word spelt like another but with a different meaning or pronunciation, eg *bow*[1] /bəʊ/; *bow*[2] /baʊ/.

homo·nym /'hɒmənɪm/ *n* homograph or homophone; word that is the same in form and sound as another but different in meaning, eg *see*[1]; *see*[2].

homo·phone /'hɒməfəʊn/ *n* word pronounced like another but different in meaning, spelling or origin, eg *some/sum* /sʌm/; *knew/new* /njuː/.

homo·sex·ual /ˌhɒmə'seksjʊəl/ *adj* sexually attracted to persons of one's own sex. □ *n* ～ person. ～·**ity** /ˌhɒməseksjʊ'ælətɪ/ *n* [U] the condition of being ～.

hone /həʊn/ *n* [C] stone used for sharpening tools (eg old-style razors). □ *vt* [VP6A] sharpen on a ～.

hon·est /'ɒnɪst/ *adj* 1 not telling lies; not cheating or stealing; straightforward: *an* ～ *man;* ～ *in business; give an* ～ *opinion.* **to be quite** ～ **about it,** phrase used before a statement that one wishes to be believed. **earn an** ～ **penny,** earn money fairly. 2 showing, resulting from, an ～ mind: *an* ～ *face; look* ～; *an* ～ *piece of work,* done conscientiously; ～ *weight,* not short weight. **make an** ～ **woman of sb,** (dated use) marry her after seducing her. ～·**ly** *adv* in an ～ manner; really: *Honestly, that's all the money I have.* **hon·esty** *n* [U] the quality of being ～; freedom from deceit, cheating, etc.

honey /'hʌnɪ/ *n* 1 [U] sweet, sticky yellowish substance made by bees from nectar; (fig) sweetness. '～·**bee** *n* ordinary kind of bee that lives in hives. '～·**dew** *n* [U] (a) sweet, sticky substance found on the leaves and stems of plants in hot weather. (b) tobacco sweetened with molasses. ～·**suckle** /'hʌnɪsʌkl/ *n* [U] climbing shrub with sweet-smelling tube-shaped yellow or reddish flowers. 2 [C] (*pl* ～s) (colloq) sweetheart; darling: *Come here, my* ～s, eg a mother to her children. ～**ed** /'hʌnɪd/ *adj* sweet as ～: ～*ed words.*

honey·comb /'hʌnɪkəʊm/ *n* [C,U] wax structure of six-sided cells made by bees for honey and eggs; (piece of) ornamental work in a ～ pattern. □ *vt* [VP6A] fill with holes, tunnels, etc: *The rock at Gibraltar is* ～*ed with galleries.*

honey·moon /'hʌnɪmuːn/ *n* holiday taken by a newly married couple; (fig) period of harmony at the start of an undertaking, etc. □ *vi* spend a ～: *They will* ～ *in Paris.*

honk /hɒŋk/ *n* cry of the wild goose; sound made by (the old style of) motor horn. □ *vi* make a ～.

hon·or·ar·ium /ˌɒnə'reərɪəm/ *n* fee offered (but not claimed) for professional services.

hon·or·ary /'ɒnərərɪ US: 'ɒnərerɪ/ *adj* 1 (shortened in writing to **Hon**) (of a position) unpaid: *the* ～ *secretary.* 2 (of a degree, rank) conferred as an honour, without the usual requirements: *an* ～ *degree/doctorate;* holding an ～ title or position: *an* ～ *vice-president.*

ho·nor·ific /ˌɒnə'rɪfɪk/ *n, adj* (expression) implying respect: *the* ～*s so frequently used in oriental languages.*

hon·our[1] (US = **honor**) /'ɒnə(r)/ *n* 1 [U] great respect; high public regard: *win* ～ *in war; a ceremony in* ～ *of those killed in battle; show* ～ *to one's parents.* **do sb** ～; **do** ～ **to sb,** show courtesy to, esteem of: *Twenty heads of state attended the Queen's coronation to do her* ～. ,**maid of** '～, lady in attendance upon a queen, princess, etc. ,**guard of** '～, number of soldiers chosen to escort or welcome a distinguished person as a mark of respect. 2 [U] good personal character; reputation for good behaviour, loyalty, truthfulness, etc. **on one's** ～, on one's reputation for telling the truth. **an affair of** ～, (hist) duel fought to settle a question of ～. **be/feel in** ～ **bound to do sth,** required to do it as a moral duty, but not by law. **one's word of** ～, guarantee to fulfil an obligation, keep a promise, etc. **pay/incur a debt of** ～, one that need not be paid legally, but which one's good name requires one to pay. **put sb on his** ～, trust him, his ～ being lost if he fails to do what is required, breaks a promise, etc. 3 (in polite formulas) giving of ～. **do sb the** ～ **of; have the** ～ **of/to:** *May I have the* ～ *of your company at dinner? Will you do me the* ～ *of dining with me this evening?* (formal style) *I have the* ～ *to inform you that....* 4 **Your/His H**～, title of respect used to/of some judges. 5 **an** ～, person or thing bringing credit: *He is an* ～ *to his school/family.* 6 (*pl*) marks of respect, distinction, etc; titles; civilities. **birthday** ～s, (in GB) list of titles, decorations, etc conferred by the Sovereign on her or his birthday. **New Year H**～s, similar list awarded on 1 Jan. **full military** ～s, ceremonies, marks of respect, paid by soldiers at the burial of a soldier, to distinguished visitors, eg Presidents. **do the** ～s, (colloq) (of the table, house, etc) act as host(ess), guide, etc and do what politeness requires; perform some small ceremony, eg propose a toast. 7 (*pl*) (in universities) (place in) top division of marks in degree examinations; special distinction for extra proficiency. ～s **degree,** one requiring some specialization. ⇨ general, pass[1](1). 8 (in card games, whist and bridge) card of highest value, eg 10,

honeycomb

hon·our² (US = honor) /'ɒnə(r)/ vt [VP6A] **1** respect highly, feel honour for; confer honour on: *Fear God and ~ the Queen. I feel highly ~ed by the kind things you say about me. Will you ~ me with a visit?* **2** (comm) accept and pay when due: *~ a bill/cheque/draft, etc; ~ one's signature*, agree that one has signed a bill, note, etc and pay the money.

hon·our·able (US = hon·or-) /'ɒnərəbl/ adj **1** possessing or showing the principles of honour; consistent with honour(1,2): *~ conduct; conclude an ~ peace; ~ burial.* **2** H~ (abbr **Hon**) title given eg to judges, to the children of peers below the rank of Marquis, and, (during debates) to members of the House of Commons: *my H~ friend the member for Chester.* **Right H~,** (abbr **Rt Hon**) title given eg to cabinet ministers, privy councillors and peers below the rank of Marquis. **hon·our·ably** /-əblɪ/ adv

hooch /hu:tʃ/ n [U] (US sl) alcoholic liquor.

hood¹ /hʊd/ n **1** bag-like covering for the head and neck, often fastened to a cloak so that it can hang down at the back when not in use; (in universities) fold of cloth worn over an academic gown showing by its colour the degree gained by the wearer and the university by which it was conferred. **2** anything like a ~ in shape or use; folding roof over a carriage (for protection against rain or sun), or over an open motor-car; (US) hinged cover over the engine of a motor-car (GB = *bonnet*). ⇨ the illus at motor. □ vt (chiefly in pp) cover with, or as with, a ~: *a ~ed falcon.*

hood² /hʊd/ n (US sl) (abbr of) hoodlum.

hood·lum /'hu:dləm/ n (sl) gangster; dangerous criminal.

hoo·doo /'hu:du:/ n (chiefly US) (person or thing regarded as bringing) bad luck. □ vt render unlucky.

hood·wink /'hʊdwɪŋk/ vt [VP6A,14] ~ sb (into), deceive; trick; mislead.

hooey /'hu:ɪ/ n [U] (sl) humbug; nonsense.

hoof /hu:f/ n (pl ~s or hooves /hu:vz/) horny part of the foot of a horse, ox or deer: *buy cattle on the ~, alive* ⇨ the illus at domestic.

hook¹ /hʊk/ n **1** curved or bent piece of metal or other material, for catching hold of sth, or for hanging sth on: *a 'fish-~; a 'crochet ~; a 'clothes-~; ~s and eyes,* for fastening a dress. *~, line and sinker,* (from fishing) (fig) entirely; completely. *be on the ~,* (colloq) in a position where one has problems, difficult or distressing decisions to make. *be/get off the ~,* no longer in such a position. *sling one's ~,* ⇨ sling¹¹. **'~-nosed** adj having a nose shaped like a ~ (or like the nose of an eagle). **'~-worm** n worm that infests the intestines of men and animals, the male of which has ~-like spines. **2** curved tool for cutting (grain, etc) or for chopping (branches, etc): *a 'reaping-~; a 'bill-~. by ~ or by crook,* by one means or another. **3** (cricket, golf) kind of stroke; (boxing) short blow with the elbow bent: *a left ~.*

hook² /hʊk/ vt,vi **1** [VP6A,15A,B,2C] fasten, be fastened, catch, with a ~ or ~s: *the dress ~s/is ~ed at the back; ~ something on/up; ~ a fish; ~ a husband,* (fig) catch a man and marry him. **2** make into the form of a ~: *~ one's finger.* **3** ~ it, (sl) run away. **4** **'~-up** n network of broadcasting stations connected to transmit the same programme: *speak over an international ~-up.* ~ed

adj **1** ~-shaped: *a ~ed nose;* furnished with hooks. **2** ~ed (on), (sl) addicted to; completely committed to: *be/get ~ed on heroin. My aunt is ~ed on package holidays in Spain.*

hookah /'hʊkə/ n tobacco pipe (also called a *hubble-bubble*) with a long flexible tube through which smoke is drawn through water in a vase and so cooled.

a hookah

hooky /'hʊkɪ/ n play ~, (US sl) play truant.

hoo·li·gan /'hu:lɪgən/ n one of a gang of disorderly persons making disturbances in the streets or other public places. **~·ism** /-ɪzəm/ n

hoop¹ /hu:p/ n **1** circular band of wood, metal etc. **2** small iron arch fixed in the ground, through which balls are hit in the game of croquet. **3** large ring with paper stretched over it through which circus riders and animals jump. *put sb/go through the ~(s),* (fig) undergo an ordeal. □ vt bind (a cask, etc) with ~s.

hoop² /hu:p/ vt = whoop.

hoop-la /'hu:p lɑ:/ n [U] game in which rings are thrown at small objects which are won if the rings encircle them.

hoo·ray /hu:'reɪ/ int = hurrah.

hoot /hu:t/ n **1** cry of an owl. **2** sound made by a motor-car horn, steam-whistle, foghorn, etc. **3** shout or cry expressing disapproval or scorn. *not care a ~/two ~s,* (sl) not care at all. □ vi,vt **1** [VP2A,C] make a ~ or ~s: *an owl ~ing in the garden. The crowd ~ed and jeered at the speaker.* **2** [VP6A,15A,B] make ~s at, drive away by doing this: *~ an actor; ~ a speaker down/off/away.* **~·er** n siren or steam-whistle, esp as a signal for work to start or stop; similar device in a motor-vehicle to attract attention from other motorists, pedestrians, etc.

Hoov·er /'hu:və(r)/ n (P) kind of vacuum cleaner. □ vt [VP6A] (colloq) clean (carpets, etc) with a vacuum cleaner.

hooves /hu:vz/ pl of hoof.

hop¹ /hɒp/ n [C] tall climbing plant with flowers growing in clusters; (pl) ripe cones (seed-vessels) of this plant, dried and used for giving a bitter flavour to beer, etc. **'hop-garden/-field** nn field for the cultivation of hops. **'hop-pole** n tall pole to support wires on which hop plant is trained. **'hop-picker, hop-per** nn worker, machine, employed to pick hops. □ vi (-pp-) gather hops: *go hopping in Kent.*

hop² /hɒp/ vi,vt (-pp-) **1** [VP2A,C] (of persons) jump on one foot; (of other living creatures, eg birds, frogs, grasshoppers) jump with both or all feet together: *Sparrows were hopping about on the lawn. He had hurt his left foot and had to hop along. hop off; hop it,* (sl) go away. *hopping mad,* (colloq) very angry. **2** [VP6A] cross (a ditch, etc) by hopping. □ n **1** the action of hopping. *on the hop,* active, restless. *catch sb on the hop,* when he is unprepared, off guard. *keep sb on the hop,* keep him active, alert. **2** short jump. *hop, skip/step and jump,* athletic exercise consisting of these three movements one after the other. **3** (colloq) informal party and dance, with popular music. **4** (flying) one stage in a long-distance flight: *from Berlin to Tokyo in three hops.* **hop-scotch** /'hɒpskɒtʃ/ *n* [U] children's game of throwing a stone into numbered squares, etc marked on the ground, and hopping from square to square to collect it.

hope[1] /həʊp/ *n* **1** [C,U] feeling of expectation and desire; feeling of trust and confidence: *There is not much ∼ that they are/of their being still alive.* **hold out some/no/little/not much ∼ (of sth),** give some, etc encouragement or expectation: *The doctors could hold out no ∼ of recovery.* **be past/beyond ∼;** **not have a ∼,** be without possibility of success, recovery, etc. **in the ∼ of doing sth,** hoping to do it: *I called in the ∼ of finding her at home.* **live in ∼(s) of sth,** have ∼(s) of: *I haven't much money now but live in ∼. We live in ∼s of better times.* **raise sb's ∼s,** give him encouragement of better fortune, etc: *Don't raise his ∼s too much.* **2** [C] person, thing, circumstance, etc on which ∼ is based: *He was the ∼ of the school. You are my last ∼; if you can't help, I'm ruined.* '∼ **chest** *n* (US) chest or drawer used by a young woman for storing linen, articles for household use, etc in anticipation of marriage (GB = *bottom drawer*).

hope[2] /həʊp/ *vt,vi* [VP7A,9,2A,3A] expect and desire: *We ∼ to see you soon. I ∼ you haven't hurt yourself. 'Will it be fine tomorrow?'—'I ∼ so.' 'Will it rain tomorrow?'—'I ∼ not.' Let us ∼ for the best. We've had no news from him but we're still hoping.* ∼ **against** ∼, ∼ even though there is only a mere possibility.

hope-ful /'həʊpfl/ *adj* **1** having hope: *be/feel ∼ about the future; feel ∼ of success/that he will succeed.* **2** giving hope; promising: *The future does not seem very ∼. He seems quite a ∼ pupil,* likely to do well. **3** (as *n*) **(young)** ∼, boy or girl who seems likely to succeed. ∼**ly** /-fəlɪ/ *adv* **1** in a ∼ way. **2** = 'I hope' or 'it is to be hoped'. ∼**ness** *n*

hope-less /'həʊplɪs/ *adj* **1** feeling no hope; giving or promising no hope: *give way to ∼ grief; a ∼ case; a ∼ illness.* **2** incurable: *a ∼ idiot.* ∼**ly** *adv* ∼**ness** *n*

hopped-up /hɒpt 'ʌp/ *adj* (US sl) souped up, supercharged: *a ∼ engine.*

hop-per[1] /'hɒpə(r)/ *n* hop-picker. ⇨ hop[1].

hop-per[2] /'hɒpə(r)/ *n* **1** structure like an inverted cone or pyramid through which grain passes to a mill, coal or coke to a furnace, etc; any similar contrivance for feeding materials into a machine, etc. **2** any hopping insect, eg a flea, a young locust; (in Australia) kangaroo.

horde /hɔːd/ *n* **1** wandering tribe (of nomads): *a Gypsy ∼; ∼s of Tartars.* **2** (usu contemptuous) crowd; great number: *∼s of people.* **3** multitude: *a ∼ of locusts.*

hor-izon /hə'raɪzn/ *n* **1** the ∼, line at which the earth or sea and sky seem to meet: *The sun sank below the ∼.* **2** (fig) limit of one's knowledge, experience, thinking, etc. **hori-zon-tal** /ˌhɒrɪ'zɒntl US:* ˌhɔːr-/ *adj* parallel to the ∼; flat or level: *a ∼tal line; ∼tal bars above the floor for gymnastic exercises.* ⇨ vertical. □ *n* ∼tal line, bar, etc. ∼**tally** /-təlɪ/ *adv*

hor-mone /'hɔːməʊn/ *n* (kinds of) internal secretion that passes into the blood and stimulates the bodily organs; medical preparation made from a secretion of this kind.

horn /hɔːn/ *n* **1** one of the hard, pointed, usu curved, outgrowths on the heads of cattle, deer, and some other animals. ⇨ the illus at **domestic, large.** ⇨ bull[1](1). **2** [U] substance of these outgrowths: *a knife with a handle of ∼/a ∼ handle; a ∼ spoon.* '∼**-rimmed** *adj* (of spectacles) with the frame made of material that resembles ∼. **3** article made from this substance (or a modern substitute): *a 'shoe-∼.* **a ∼ of plenty,** = cornucopia. **4** (music) wind instrument: *a 'hunting ∼.* **(French)** ∼, brass orchestral instrument. ⇨ the illus at **brass. English** ∼, (also, esp GB **cor anglais** /ˌkɔːr 'ɒŋgleɪ US:* ɒŋ'gleɪ/) woodwind instrument like, but larger than, an oboe, and lower in pitch. **5** device for making warning sounds: *a 'fog-∼; a 'motor-∼.* **6** ∼-like part, eg on the head of a snail. '∼**-bill** *n* bird with a ∼like growth on its beak. **draw in one's ∼s,** (fig) draw back, show less zeal for an undertaking. **7** either of the ends of the crescent moon. ⇨ the illus at **phase. on the ∼s of a dilemma,** faced with a choice between things that are equally undesirable, etc. □ *vi* (sl, only in) ∼ **in (on),** intrude; join in without being invited. ∼**ed** *adj* having ∼s(3): *∼ed cattle; the ∼ed owl,* with tufts like ∼s. ∼**less** *adj* without ∼s: *∼less cattle.* ∼**like** *adj* ∼y *adj* (-ier, -iest) made of ∼; hard like ∼: *hands ∼y from hard work.*

horn-beam /'hɔːnbiːm/ *n* small tree with hard wood.

hor-net /'hɔːnɪt/ *n* large insect of the wasp family, able to inflict a severe sting. **stir up a '∼s' nest; bring a '∼s' nest about one's ears,** stir up enemies; cause an outburst of angry feeling.

horn-pipe /'hɔːnpaɪp/ *n* [C] (music for a) lively dance (usu for one person, esp a sailor).

hor-ol-ogy /hɒ'rɒlədʒɪ/ *n* [U] art of designing and constructing clocks.

horo-scope /'hɒrəskəʊp US:* 'hɔːr-/ *n* diagram of, observation of, positions of planets at a certain time, eg a person's birth, for the purpose of forecasting future events; such a forecast.

hor-rible /'hɒrəbl US:* 'hɔːr-/ *adj* **1** exciting horror: *∼ cruelty/crimes.* **2** (colloq) unpleasant: *∼ weather.* **hor-ribly** /-əblɪ/ *adv*

hor-rid /'hɒrɪd US:* 'hɔːrɪd/ *adj* **1** frightful; terrible. **2** (colloq) disagreeable: *∼ weather.* ∼**ly** *adv* ∼**ness** *n*

hor-rific /hə'rɪfɪk/ *adj* (colloq) horrifying.

hor-rify /'hɒrɪfaɪ US:* 'hɔːr-/ *vt* (*pt,pp* -fied) [VP6A] fill with horror; shock: *We were horrified by what we saw. Don't let the children see such ∼ing scenes.*

hor-ror /'hɒrə(r) US:* 'hɔːr-/ *n* [C,U] (sth that causes a) feeling of extreme fear or dislike: *She recoiled in ∼ from the snake. She expressed her ∼ of cruelty. To her ∼ she saw her husband knocked down by a bus. We have all read about the ∼s of modern warfare.* ˌ**chamber of '∼s,** collection of objects, representations, etc, connected with crime, cruelty, etc. '∼ **fiction/comics/films,** in which the subject matter and treatment are intended to arouse feelings of ∼. '∼**-struck/-stricken** *adj* overcome with ∼.

hors de com-bat /ˌɔː də 'kɒmbɑː/ *pred adj* (F) unable to take further part in fighting because wounded or disabled.

hors d'oeuvres /ˌɔː 'dɜːvrə US:* 'dɜːv/ *n pl* dishes of food served at the beginning of a meal as a relish.

horse /hɔːs/ *n* **1** four-legged solid-hoofed animal with flowing mane and tail, used from early times to carry loads, for riding, etc. ⇨ the illus at domestic. ⇨ colt¹, filly, foal, mare, stallion. *a* **dark** ∿, person whose chances of success are not yet known, or have been overlooked. *a* ∿ *of another colour,* quite a different matter. *back the* **wrong** ∿, support the loser in a contest. *be/get on one's high* ∿, insist on being treated with proper respect. *eat/work like a* ∿, eat a lot/work hard. *flog a dead* ∿, ⇨ flog. *hold one's* ∿*s,* hesitate; show restraint. *look a gift* ∿ *in the mouth,* accept sth ungratefully esp by examining it critically for faults (because a ∿'s teeth indicate its age). *put the cart before the* ∿, ⇨ cart. *(straight) from the* ∿*'s mouth,* (of tips, advice, information) from a first-hand source. 2 (collective *sing*) cavalry: ∿ *and foot,* cavalry and infantry; *light* ∿, lightly armed mounted soldiers; ∿ *artillery,* light artillery with mounted gunners; *the* '*H*∿ *Guards,* ⇨ guard¹(6). 3 framework, often with legs, on which sth is supported: *a* '*clothes-*∿, on which clothes may be dried in front of a fire; *a* '*vaulting-*∿, block used in a gymnasium for vaulting over. 4 (compounds) '∿-**back** *n* (only in) *on* ∿*back,* on a ∿. '∿-**box** *n* closed vehicle for taking a ∿ by rail, or towing behind a car, etc. ,∿-'**chestnut** *n* large tree with spreading branches and clusters of white or pink blossom; shiny reddish-brown nut of this tree. '∿-**flesh** *n* [U] (a) flesh of ∿s as food. (b) ∿s collectively: *He's a good judge of* ∿*flesh.* '∿-**fly** *n* (*pl* -flies) large insect troublesome to ∿s and cattle. '∿-**hair** *n* [U] hair from the mane or tail of ∿s, formerly used for stuffing sofas, etc. '∿-**laugh** *n* loud, coarse laugh. '∿-**man** /-mən/ *n* (*pl* -men) rider on ∿back, esp one who is skilled. '∿-**man·ship** /-ʃɪp/ *n* [U] art of riding, skill in riding, on ∿back. '∿-**meat** *n* = ∿flesh. '∿-**play** *n* [U] rough, noisy fun or play. '∿-**pond** *n* pond for watering and washing ∿s. '∿-**power** *n* [U] unit for measuring the power of an engine, etc (550 foot-pounds per second). '∿-**race** *n* race between ∿s with riders. '∿-**racing** *n* [U]. '∿-**radish** *n* [U] (plant with a) hot-tasting root which is ground or scraped to make a sauce (eaten with beef). '∿-**sense** *n* ordinary wisdom. '∿-**shoe** /'hɔːʃuː/ *n* U-shaped metal shoe for a ∿; sth of this shape, eg *a* ∿*shoe table.* '∿-**whip** *n, vt* (-pp-) (thrash with a) whip for ∿s. '∿-**woman** *n* woman who rides on ∿back.

horsy /'hɔːsɪ/ *adj* concerned with, fond of, horses or horse-racing; showing by dress, conversation, manners, etc familiarity with horses, horse-racing, grooms, jockeys, etc.

hor·ta·tive /'hɔːtətɪv/ *adj* (formal) exhorting; serving to encourage.

hor·ti·cul·ture /'hɔːtɪkʌltʃə(r)/ *n* [U] (art of) growing flowers, fruit and vegetables. **hor·ti·cul·tural** /ˌhɔːtɪ'kʌltʃərəl/ *adj* of ∿: *a horticultural show/society.* **hor·ti·cul·tur·ist** /ˌhɔːtɪ'kʌltʃərɪst/ *n* person who practises ∿.

ho·sanna /həʊ'zænə/ *n, int* cry of praise and adoration (to God).

hose¹ /həʊz/ *n* [C,U] (length of) flexible tubing (of rubber, canvas or plastic) for directing water on to fires, watering gardens, cleaning streets, etc: *60 feet of plastic* ∿; *plenty of fire* ∿*s in the building.* '∿-**pipe** *n* length of ∿. □ *vt* [VP6A,15B] ∿ *(down),* water (a garden, etc) with a ∿; wash (a motor-car, etc) by using a ∿: ∿ *(down) the car.*

hose² /həʊz/ *n* 1 (collective, as *pl*) (trade name for) stockings and socks: *six pair of* ∿. 2 (hist)

garment from the waist to the knees or feet worn by men in former times; tights: *dressed in doublet and* ∿. ⇨ the illus at doublet.

ho·sier /'həʊzɪə(r) *US:* -ʒə(r)/ *n* tradesman who sells ∿²(1) and knitted underwear. **ho·siery** /'həʊzɪərɪ *US:* 'həʊʒərɪ/ *n* [U] goods sold by a ∿.

hos·pice /'hɒspɪs/ *n* 1 house of rest for travellers. 2 hospital for dying people.

hos·pit·able /hɒ'spɪtəbl/ *adj* giving, liking to give, hospitality: *a* ∿ *man/household.* **hos·pit·ably** /-əblɪ/ *adv*

hos·pi·tal /'hɒspɪtl/ *n* place where people are treated for, nursed through, their illness or injuries: *He's still in* ∿. *I'm going to the* ∿ *to see my brother. His sister is a* ∿ *nurse. go to* ∿, enter a ∿ as a patient. ∿-**ize** *vt* send to, admit into, ∿. ∿-**iz·ation** /ˌhɒspɪtəlaɪ'zeɪʃn *US:* -lɪ'z-/ *n* state of being ∿ized.

hos·pi·tal·ity /ˌhɒspɪ'tælətɪ/ *n* [U] friendly and generous reception and entertainment of guests, esp in one's own home.

host¹ /həʊst/ *n* 1 great number (*of*): *He has* ∿*s of friends. We are faced with a* ∿ *of difficulties.* 2 (archaic) army: *Lord of H*∿*s,* Jehovah, God of the Hebrews.

host² /həʊst/ *n* 1 person who entertains guests: *As Mr Hill was away, Tom, the eldest son, acted as* ∿ *at the dinner party,* welcomed the guests, etc. (In the *pl* this word may be common gender.) *The Parnwells are such good* ∿*s.* 2 inn-keeper; hotel-keeper. *reckon without one's* ∿, make calculations, plans, etc without consulting the chief person(s) concerned; overlook possible opposition. 3 (biol) organism which harbours a parasite. □ *vt* [VP6A] (US colloq) act as ∿ to or at.

Host /həʊst/ *n* the ∿, bread eaten at Holy Communion.

hos·tage /'hɒstɪdʒ/ *n* person (less often, a thing) given or left as a pledge that demands will be satisfied: *take sb* ∿. *The bandits demanded that one of the travellers should stay with them as a* ∿. *give* ∿*s to fortune,* by an unwise step, take the risk of being harmed in future.

hos·tel /'hɒstl/ *n* 1 building in which board and lodging are provided (with the support of the authorities concerned) for students, workmen in training, etc: *a YMCA* ∿. '**youth** ∿, one for young people walking, riding or cycling on holiday tours, used by members of the International Youth H∿ Association. 2 (archaic) inn. ∿-**ry** *n* (archaic) inn. ∿-**ler** /'hɒstələ(r)/ *n* person travelling from ∿ to ∿, esp youth ∿lers.

host·ess /'həʊstɪs/ *n* 1 woman who entertains guests; wife of one's host. 2 woman inn-keeper. 3 '**air** ∿, ⇨ air¹(7).

hos·tile /'hɒstaɪl *US:* -tl/ *adj* 1 of an enemy: *a* ∿ *army.* 2 feeling or showing enmity (*to*); unfriendly: *a* ∿ *crowd;* ∿ *looks;* ∿ *to reform.* ∿-**ly** /-llɪ/ *adv*

hos·til·ity /hɒ'stɪlətɪ/ *n* 1 [U] enmity; ill will: *feelings of* ∿; *feel no* ∿ *towards anyone: show* ∿ *to sb.* 2 (*pl* -ties) (acts of) war: *at the outbreak of*

nozzle

a hosepipe

hostilities; open/suspend hostilities, begin/stop fighting.

hot /hɒt/ *adj* (-ter, -test) **1** having a high temperature: *hot weather; a hot day; feel hot. I like my food hot. This coffee is too hot to drink.* **be in/get into hot water,** in trouble or disgrace (because of foolish behaviour, etc). **be/get hot under the collar,** angry, excited, indignant. **make a place/make it too hot for sb,** (fig) compel him to leave by rousing hostility against him. **2** producing a burning sensation to the taste: *This curry is too hot. Pepper and mustard are hot.* **3** fiery; eager; intense; violent; impetuous: *get hot over an argument; a man with a hot temper; in the hottest part of the election campaign.* **be hot on the trail of sb/on sb's tracks,** near to what is being pursued; close behind. **4** (in hunting, of the scent) fresh and strong. **5** (of music, esp jazz) strongly rhythmical and emotional. **6** (sl) (of stolen goods) difficult to dispose of (because of determined efforts made by the police to trace them): *These articles are too hot to handle/hold.* **7** (as *adv*) (a) recently: *hot off the press.* ⇨ hot news below. (b) **blow hot and cold,** (fig) be by turns favourable and unfavourable. (c) **give it sb hot,** punish or scold severely. **8** (special uses with *nn* and *participles*) **hot 'air** *n* [U] meaningless talk, promises, etc. **hot-air balloon** *n* ⇨ balloon. **'hot-bed** *n* bed of earth heated by rotting manure to promote growth of plants; (fig) place favourable to growth, esp of sth evil: *a hotbed of vice/crime.* **hot-'blooded** *adj* passionate. **hot cross 'bun** *n* one with a cross marked on it, eaten on Good Friday. **hot 'dog** *n* hot sausage served with onions and mustard in a sandwich or bread roll. **hot-'foot** *adv* eagerly; in great haste: *run ~ after the pickpocket.* □ *vi* go hastily: *hotfoot it down to the swimming-pool.* **hot 'gospeller** *n* (colloq) fervent evangelist preacher. **'hot-head** *n* impetuous person. **hot-'headed** *adj* impetuous. **'hot-house** *n* heated building, usu made of glass, for growing delicate plants. **'hot line** *n* direct line of communication (telephone or teleprinter) between heads of governments, eg between Moscow and Washington. **hot 'money** *n* [U] short-term funds moved from one financial centre to another by speculators seeking high interest rates and security. ⇨ also 6 above. **hot 'news** *n* [U] recent (esp sensational) news. **'hot-plate** *n* flat surface of a cooking-stove; similar surface (not part of a stove) that can be heated, eg electrically, for cooking, boiling water, etc. **hot po'tato** *n* (fig, colloq) sth difficult or unpleasant to deal with: *The issue is a political hot potato.* **'hot rod** *n* (US sl) supercharged car. **the 'hot seat** *n* electric chair (for the electrocution of murderers); (fig) position of sb who has to make difficult, often agonizing, decisions, eg of a head of state. **hot 'spring** *n* naturally heated spring¹(2). **hot 'stuff** *n* [U] (sl) sb/sth of first-rate quality. **hot-'tempered** *adj* easily angered. **hot-'water-bottle** *n* container (often of rubber) to be filled with hot water for warmth in bed. □ *vt,vi* (-tt-) [VP2C,15B] **hot (sth) up,** (colloq) make or become hotter or (fig) more exciting: *Things are hotting up.* **hot-ly** *adv* passionately; excitedly: *He replied hotly that...; It was a hotly contested match.*

hotch-potch /'hɒtʃpɒtʃ/ *n* jumble; number of things mixed together without order: *His essay was a ~ of other people's ideas.*

ho-tel /həʊ'tel/ *n* (either *a ~* or *an ~*) building where meals and rooms are provided for travellers. **~-ier** /həʊ'telɪeɪ *US*: ˌhəʊtel'jer/ *n a* ~-keeper.

hound /haʊnd/ *n* **1** (kinds of) dog used for hunting and racing: *'fox~; 'blood~; 'grey~.* (When not in a compound, ~ usu means *fox~.*) **follow the ~s; ride to ~s,** hunt with a pack of ~s. **Master of H~s,** the master of a hunt(2). **2** (dated colloq) mean, wretched, contemptible fellow. □ *vt* [VP6A] chase or hunt with, or as with, ~s; harass: *be ~ed by one's creditors,* worried by requests for payment of money owing.

hour /'aʊə(r)/ *n* **1** twenty-fourth part of a day; 60 minutes: *hire a horse by the ~; walk for ~s (and ~s); a three ~s' journey; the happiest ~s (= period) of my life; work a forty-~ week; 1800 ~s,* time calculated on a 24-~ basis, = 6.00pm, ⇨ App 4. **at the eleventh ~,** when almost too late. **the 'small ~s,** the three or four ~s after midnight. **'~-glass** *n* sand-glass which runs out in one ~. **'~ hand** *n* small hand on a clock or watch, pointing to the ~. **2** time of day; point or period of time: *The church clock was striking the ~ as we got home. This clock strikes the ~s and the half-~s, but not the quarters. Please come at an early ~. They disturb me at all ~s of the day and night,* constantly. **3** (*pl*) fixed periods of time, esp for work: *'school ~s. 'Office ~s, 9am to 5pm. after ~s,* after the period of regular business, etc. **out of ~s,** outside (before or after) regular ~s (of duty, etc). **keep good/bad/early/late/regular, etc ~s,** get up, go to bed, start/stop work, leave/arrive home, etc, early/late, etc. **4** a particular, or the present, point in time: *questions of the ~,* now being discussed; *in the ~ of danger/temptation; in a good/evil ~,* at a lucky/unlucky time.

houri /'hʊərɪ/ *n* young and beautiful woman of the Muslim Paradise.

hour-ly /'aʊəlɪ/ *adv* **1** every hour; once every hour: *This medicine is to be taken ~.* **2** at any hour: *We're expecting news ~.* □ *adj* **1** done or occurring every hour: *an ~ service of trains; an ~ bus service.* **2** continual: *live in ~ dread of discovery.*

house¹ /haʊs/ (*pl* ~s /'haʊzɪz/) **1** building made for people to live in, usu for one family (or a family and lodgers, etc): *New ~s are going up everywhere. I've bought a ~.* ⇨ home¹(1). **get on like a '~ on fire,** (of people) quickly become friendly and jolly together. **under ~ arrest,** forbidden by law to leave one's ~ or receive visitors. **2** (usu with a *pref*) building made or used for some particular purpose or occupation: *'hen~; 'cow~; 'store~; 'ware~; 'alms-~; 'bake~; 'custom-~,* etc, ⇨ these entries. **the H~ of God,** church or chapel. **~ of cards,** one built by a child out of playing cards; (fig) scheme likely to collapse. **~ of ill fame,** (old use) brothel. **on the ~,** at the expense of the inn, firm, etc. **3** (building used by an) assembly: *the H~ of Commons/Lords; the H~s of Parliament.* **the H~,** (colloq, GB) (a) the Stock Exchange. (b) the H~ of Commons or Lords: *enter the H~,* become an MP. (c) (US) the H~ of Representatives. (d) business firm. **4** [U] **keep ~,** manage the affairs of a ~hold. **keep a good ~,** provide good food and plenty of comfort. **keep open ~,** be ready to welcome guests at any time. **set/put one's '~ in order,** put one's affairs straight. **5** household; family line; dynasty: *the H~ of Windsor,* the British Royal family; *an ancient ~; an old trading ~,* business firm. **6** spectators, audience, in a theatre: *make oneself heard in* *every part of the* ~; *a full* ~, every seat occupied. *The second* ~ (= performance) *starts at 9 o'clock. Is there a doctor in the* ~? **bring down the** ~; **bring the** '~ **down**, win very great applause and approval. **7** (compounds) '~ **agent** *n* (GB) person who sells or lets ~s for others. ⇨ (US) realtor. '~-**boat** *n* boat fitted up as a place to live in, eg on a river or estuary. '~-**bound** *adj* confined to the ~, eg through ill-health: *Should wives with children be* ~*bound?* '~-**breaker** *n* (a) person who enters another's ~ by day to steal. ⇨ burglar. (b) (US = '~-**wrecker**) workman employed to pull down old buildings. '~-**coat** *n* usu cotton or silk coat worn by women in the house during the day. '~-**craft** *n* [U] theory and practice of running a home[1](1). '~-**dog** *n* dog trained to guard a ~. '~-**father** *n* man in charge of children in an institution. '~ **flag** *n* flag flown by a firm's ships. ⇨ **5** above. '~-**fly** *n* (*pl*-flies) ⇨ fly[1]. ~-**ful** /-fʊl/ *n* as much as a ~ can contain or accommodate. '~-**hold** *n* all persons (family, lodgers, etc) living in a ~: ~*hold cavalry/troops*, employed to guard the Sovereign; ~*hold duties/expenses.* ~-**'word**, commonly used word or name. '~-**holder** *n* person leasing or owning and occupying a ~, not sb living in a hotel, lodgings, etc. '~-**keeper** *n* person employed to manage the affairs of a ~hold. '~-**lights** *n pl* lights in the auditorium of a theatre, cinema, etc. '~-**maid** *n* female servant in a ~, esp one who cleans rooms, etc. ~**maid's 'knee**, inflammation of the kneecap due to kneeling. '~-**man** /-mən/ *n* (*pl*-men) (GB) doctor who is an assistant to a physician or surgeon in a hospital (US = **intern**). '~ **martin** *n* common bird which nests in the walls of ~s and cliffs. '~-**master** *n* teacher in charge of a school boarding-~. '~-**mother** *n* woman in charge of children in an institution. '~-**party** *n* party of guests being entertained for several days at a country ~, etc. '~ **physician** *n* one who resides in a hospital. '~-**proud** *adj* very much concerned with the care of the ~, with the appearance of the furnishings, etc. '~-**room** *n* space: *I wouldn't give that table* ~*room*, would not have it in my ~, would not accept it even as a gift. '~-**sparrow** *n* common grey and brown bird. '~-**surgeon** *n* one who resides in a hospital. '~-**top** *n* (chiefly US) *cry/publish/proclaim sth from the* ~*tops*, make known to all; declare publicly. '~-**trained** *adj* (of domestic pets) trained not to defecate and urinate inside buildings. '~-**warming** *n* party given to friends by a person who moves into a new ~. '~-**wife** *n* (a) woman head of a family, who runs the home, brings up the family, etc. (b) /ˈhʌzɪf/ (dated) case for needles and thread. '~-**wife·ly** *adj* of a ~wife(1). '~-**wifery** /-wɪfərɪ/ *n* [U] work of a ~wife. '~-**work** *n* [U] work done in a ~, cleaning, cooking, etc. ⇨ **homework** at home[1](7).

house² /haʊz/ *vt* [VP6A] **1** provide a house or shelter for; find room for: *We can* ~ *you and your friends if the hotels are full.* **2** store (goods, etc): ~ *one's old books in the attic.*

hous·ing /ˈhaʊzɪŋ/ *n* [U] accommodation in houses, etc: *More* ~ *is needed for old people. The* ~ *in this part of the town is sub-standard.* '~ **as·sociation** *n* non-profitmaking society for the construction and provision of ~ing. '~ **estate** *n* area of houses planned and built either by a local authority or other organization, to be let or sold.

hove /həʊv/ *pt,pp* of heave.

hovel /ˈhɒvl *US:* ˈhʌvl/ *n* small house or cottage that is unfit to live in; open-sided shed or outhouse.

hover /ˈhɒvə(r) *US:* ˈhʌvər/ *vi* [VP2A,C] **1** (of birds) remain in the air at one place: *a hawk* ~*ing overhead/*~*ing over its prey; a helicopter* ~*ing over the house.* '~-**craft** *n* craft capable of moving over land or water while supported on a cushion of air made by jet engines. **2** (of persons) wait about; remain at or near: (fig) ~ *between life and death.*

a hovercraft

how /haʊ/ *adv* **1** in what way or manner; by what means: *How is the word spelt? Tell me how to spell the word. How did you escape? Tell me how you escaped.* **2** (in questions and exclamations) to what extent; in what degree: *How old is he? How often do you go there? How many are there? How much do you want? How dirty the house is! How kind you are! How he snores!* ie he snores very loudly. *How well you look!* **And how!** (emphatic) Yes! **3** in what state of health: *How are you? How's your father? How do you do?* (formula used as a conventional greeting, esp when persons are formally introduced; used only with the *pron* 'you'.) **how-d'ye-do** /ˈhaʊ djə duː/ *n* (colloq) awkward state of affairs: *Well, here's a pretty how-d'ye-do!* **4** (introducing an indirect statement) that: *He told me how* (= that) *he had read about it in the newspapers.* **5** used in asking for an opinion, decision, explanation, etc: *How about going* (= What do you think about going) *for a walk? How do you find your new job,* Do you like it, etc. **How come...,** (colloq) Why is it that...: *How come we don't see you more often?* **How's that?** (a) What's the explanation of that? (b) What's your opinion of that? eg an object pointed to. (c) (in cricket, to the umpire) Is the batsman out or not out? **How so?** Can you prove that it is so? **how-beit** /haʊˈbiːɪt/ *conj* (archaic) nevertheless. **how-ever** /haʊˈevə(r)/ *adv* **1** in whatever way or degree: *He will never succeed, however hard he tries. We must do something, on however humble a scale.* **2** (also *conj*) although that is/may be/was, etc so: *Later, however, he decided to go. He was mistaken, however.*

how-dah /ˈhaʊdə/ *n* seat (usu with a canopy) on an elephant's back.

how·it·zer /ˈhaʊɪtsə(r)/ *n* short gun for firing shells at a high angle at short range.

howl /haʊl/ *n* [C] long, loud cry, eg of a wolf; long cry of a person in pain, or of sb expressing scorn, amusement, etc: ~*s of derision.* □ *vi,vt* **1** [VP2A,C] utter such cries: *wolves* ~*ing in the forest. The wind* ~*ed through the trees. The boys* ~*ed with laughter.* **2** [VP6A,15A,B] ~ (*down*), utter ~s at; utter with ~s: ~ *defiance at the enemy;* ~ *down a speaker,* prevent him from being heard. ~*er n* (colloq) foolish and laughable mistake. ~**ing** *adj* (sl) extreme; glaring: *a* ~*ing shame.*

hoy·den /ˈhɔɪdn/ *n* boisterous girl. ~**·ish** /-ɪʃ/ *adj* of or like a ~.

hub /hʌb/ *n* central part of a wheel from which the

spokes radiate, ⇨ the illus at bicycle; (fig) central point of activity or importance: *a hub of industry/commerce. He thinks that Boston is the hub of the universe.*

hubble-bubble /'hʌbl bʌbl/ *n* = hookah.

hub·bub /'hʌbʌb/ *n* [U] confused noise, eg of many voices; uproar.

hubby /'hʌbɪ/ *n* (GB) (colloq) husband.

hu·bris /'hju:brɪs/ *n* [U] (Gk) arrogant pride.

hucka·back /'hʌkəbæk/ *n* strong, rough, cotton or linen material used for towels, etc.

huckle·berry *US:* -berɪ/ *n* (*pl* -ries) (small, dark-blue berry of a) low shrub common in N America.

huck·ster /'hʌkstə(r)/ *n* hawker.

huddle /'hʌdl/ *vt, vi* 1 [VP2C] crowd together: *sheep huddling together for warmth.* 2 [VP2C] ∼ **up (against),** curl or coil up against: *Tom was cold, so he* ∼*d up against his brother in bed.* 3 [VP15A,B] heap up in a confused mass: ∼ *things together/up/into sth.* □ *n* number of things or persons close together without order or arrangement. **be in/go into a** ∼, (colloq, of persons) be/get together to confer.

hue¹ /hju:/ *n* [C] (shade of) colour: *the hues of the rainbow; the dark hue of the ocean.* **hued** /hju:d/ (in compounds) having the hue(s) indicated: '*dark-hued;* '*many-hued.*

hue² /hju:/ *n* (only in) **hue and cry,** /ˌhju: ən 'kraɪ/, general outcry of alarm (as when a criminal is being pursued, or when there is opposition to sth): *raise a hue and cry against new tax proposals.*

huff¹ /hʌf/ *n* fit of ill temper. **be in/get into a** ∼. ∼**ish** /-ɪʃ/, ∼**y** *adjj* in a ∼; taking offence easily. ∼**ily** /-ɪlɪ/ *adv*

huff² /hʌf/ *vi* puff; blow.

hug /hʌg/ *vt* (-gg-) [VP6A] 1 put the arms round tightly, esp to show love: *The child was hugging her doll.* 2 cling to love: *hug cherished beliefs.* 3 **hug the shore,** (of a ship) keep close to it. 4 **hug oneself (with pleasure/delight) over sth,** be very pleased with oneself, congratulate oneself. □ *n* [C] tight embrace: *She gave her mother a big hug.*

huge /hju:dʒ/ *adj* very great. ∼**ly** *adv* enormously; very much.

hug·ger-mug·ger /'hʌgə mʌgə(r)/ *n, adj, adv* secrecy; secret(ly); confusion; confused(ly).

Hu·gue·not /'hju:gənəʊ/ *n* (16th and 17th cc) French Protestant.

hula /'hu:lə/ *n* native Hawaiian dance.

hulk /hʌlk/ *n* 1 old ship no longer in use or used only as a storehouse; (formerly) old ship used as a prison. 2 big, clumsy ship, thing or person. ∼**ing** *adj* clumsy; awkward: *Get out of my way, you* ∼*ing great idiot!*

hull¹ /hʌl/ *n* outer covering of some fruits and seeds, esp the pods of peas and beans. □ *vt* remove the ∼s of.

hull² /hʌl/ *n* body or frame of a ship. ⇨ the illus at barque. ∼ **down** (a) (of a ship almost below the horizon) with only the mast(s), funnel(s), etc, visible. (b) (of a tank) with only the turret showing.

hul·la·ba·loo /ˌhʌləbə'lu:/ *n* uproar; disturbance: *What a* ∼*! What's all this* ∼ *about?*

hullo (also **hallo, hello**) /hə'ləʊ/ *int* used as a greeting, to call attention, to express surprise, and to answer a call, eg on the telephone.

hum /hʌm/ *vi, vt* (-mm-) [VP6A,2A,C] 1 make a continuous sound like that made by bees; sing with closed lips: *She was humming a song to herself.*

The bees were humming in the garden. '**hum·ming-bird** *n* name used of several species, usu small and brightly coloured, that make a humming sound by vibration of the wings. '**humming-top** *n* top that hums when it spins. 2 be in a state of activity: *make things hum; a factory humming with activity.* 3 (sl) smell unpleasantly: *This ham is beginning to hum.* 4 usu **hum and haw/ha,** (colloq) make sounds expressing hesitation or doubt. □ *n* humming noise: *the hum of bees/of distant traffic; a hum of voices/conversation from the next room.*

hu·man /'hju:mən/ *adj* 1 of man or mankind (contrasted with animals, God): *a* ∼ *being;* ∼ *nature;* ∼ *affairs. 'To err is* ∼, *to forgive divine.'* 2 having, showing, the qualities that distinguish man: *His cruelty suggests that he is less than* ∼. ∼**ly** *adv* (esp) by ∼ means; without divine help: *The doctors have done all that is* ∼*ly possible.* ∼'**kind** *n* [U] mankind.

hu·mane /hju:'meɪn/ *adj* 1 tender; kind-hearted: *a man of* ∼ *character; a* ∼ *officer.* ∼ **killer,** instrument for the painless killing of animals. 2 (of branches of study) tending to refinement; polished. ⇨ humanity(4). ∼**ly** *adv.*

hu·man·ism /'hju:mənɪzəm/ *n* [U] 1 devotion to human interests; system that is concerned with ethical standards (but not with theology), and with the study of mankind. 2 literary culture (of about the 14th to 16th cc) based on Greek and Roman learning.

hu·man·ist /'hju:mənɪst/ *n* 1 student of human nature or human affairs (as opposed to theological subjects). 2 supporter of humanism. 3 (esp in the 14th to 16th cc) student of Greek and Roman literature and antiquities.

hu·mani·tar·ian /hju:ˌmænɪ'teərɪən/ *adj, n* (of, holding the views of, a) person who works for the welfare of all human beings by reducing suffering, reforming laws about punishment, etc. ∼**ism** /-ɪzəm/ *n*

hu·man·ity /hju:'mænətɪ/ *n* [U] 1 the human race; mankind: *crimes against* ∼. 2 human nature. 3 quality of being humane(1): *treat people and animals with* ∼. 4 (*pl*) **the humanities,** the branches of learning concerned with ancient Greek and Latin culture; the Arts subjects, esp literature, history and philosophy.

hu·man·ize /'hju:mənaɪz/ *vt, vi* [VP6A,2A] make or become human or humane.

humble /'hʌmbl/ *adj* (-r, -st) 1 having or showing a modest opinion of oneself, one's position, etc: *He is very* ∼ *in the company of his superiors.* **eat** ∼ **pie,** make an abject apology, humiliate oneself. 2 (of persons) low in rank or position; obscure and unimportant; (of things) poor; mean: *men of* ∼ *birth; a* ∼ *home; a* ∼ *occupation.* □ *vt* [VP6A] make ∼; make lower in rank or self-opinion: ∼ *one's enemies;* ∼ *sb's pride;* ∼ *oneself before God.* **hum·bly** *adv* in a ∼ way: *beg most humbly for forgiveness; humbly born,* of ∼ parents.

hum·bug /'hʌmbʌg/ *n* 1 [C,U] (instance of) dishonest and deceiving behaviour or talk; [C] dishonest, deceitful person. 2 (GB) hard boiled sweet flavoured with peppermint. □ *vt* (-gg-) [VP6A,14] deceive or trick (sb *into* or *out of* sth): *Don't try to* ∼ *me!* □ *int* Nonsense!

hum·dinger /ˌhʌm'dɪŋə(r)/ *n* (US sl) sth marvellous or extraordinary.

hum·drum /'hʌmdrʌm/ *adj* dull; commonplace; monotonous: *live a* ∼ *life; engaged in* ∼ *tasks.*

hu·merus /'hju:mərəs/ *n* (anat) bone of the upper arm in man. ⇨ the illus at skeleton.

hu·mid /'hju:mɪd/ *adj* (esp of air, climate) damp. **~·ify** /hju:'mɪdɪfaɪ/ *vt* (*pt,pp* -fied) make ~. **~·ity** /hju:'mɪdətɪ/ *n* [U] (degree of) moisture (in the air).

hu·mili·ate /hju:'mɪlɪeɪt/ *vt* [VP6A] cause to feel ashamed; put to shame; lower the dignity or self-respect of: *a country that was ~d by defeat; humiliating peace terms.* **hu·mili·ation** /hju:ˌmɪlɪ'eɪʃn/ *n* [U] humiliating or being ~d; [C] instance of this: *the humiliation of having to surrender.*

hu·mil·ity /hju:'mɪlətɪ/ *n* [U] humble condition or state of mind.

hum·ming·bird /'hʌmɪŋbɜ:d/ *n* ⇨ hum(1).

hum·mock /'hʌmək/ *n* hillock; rising ground in a marsh; hump in an ice-field.

hu·mor·ist /'hju:mərɪst/ *n* humorous talker or writer; facetious person.

hu·mor·ous /'hju:mərəs/ *adj* having or showing a sense of humour; funny: *a ~ writer,* eg Mark Twain; *~ remarks.* **~·ly** *adv*

hu·mour (US = **hu·mor**) /'hju:mə(r)/ *n* 1 [U] (capacity to cause or feel) amusement: *a story full of ~; have no/not much/a good sense of ~.* 2 [U] person's state of mind (esp at a particular time); temper: *in a good/bad ~; not in the ~ for work,* not feeling inclined to work; *in no ~ to trifle; when the ~ takes him,* when he feels so inclined. *out of ~,* displeased; in a bad mood. 3 [C] (old use) one of four liquids (blood, phlegm, choler, melancholy) in the body, said to determine a person's mental and physical qualities. □ *vt* [VP6A] give way to, gratify: *When a person is ill he may have to be ~ed,* his wishes may have to be granted, even if they are senseless. *Is it wise to always ~ a child,* give it everything it wants?

hump /hʌmp/ *n* 1 round lump, eg on a camel's back or (as a deformity) on a person's back. ⇨ the illus at large. '**~-back** *n* (person having a) back with a ~. '**~-backed** *adj* having such a back. 2 *have/give sb the ~,* (sl) fit of depression or irritation. □ *vt* [VP6A,15B] ~ (*up*), make ~-shaped; gather the shoulders into a ~: *The cat ~ed (up) her back when she saw the dog.*

humph /hʌmf or spontaneously as a grunt with lips closed and then puffed open/ *int* used to show doubt or dissatisfaction.

hu·mus /'hju:məs/ *n* [U] earth formed by the decay of vegetable matter (dead leaves, plants).

Hun /hʌn/ *n* member of an Asiatic race which ravaged Europe in the 4th and 5th cc.

hunch /hʌntʃ/ *n* 1 thick piece; hunk; hump. '**~-back(ed),** = humpback(ed). 2 *have a ~ that...,* (colloq) think it likely that.... □ *vt* [VP6A,15B] ~ (*up*), arch to form a hump: *sitting at the table with his shoulders ~ed up.*

hun·dred /'hʌndrəd/ *n, adj* the number 100: *two ~ and five,* 205; *a few ~ people; ~s of people.* ⇨ App 4. '**~-weight** *n* (often written **cwt**) 1/20 of one ton, 112 lb (in US 100 lb). ⇨ App 5. '**~-fold,** (US) **~·'fold** *adv* one ~ times as much or as many. **~th** /'hʌndrədθ/ *n, adj* next after the 99th; one of a ~ equal parts.

hung /hʌŋ/ *pt,pp* of hang.

hun·ger /'hʌŋgə(r)/ *n* 1 [U] need, desire for food: *die of ~; satisfy one's ~. be/go on (a) '~-strike,* (eg of a prisoner) refuse to take food as a protest, in order to win release, etc. '**~-march** *n* one undertaken, eg by unemployed workers, to call attention

to sufferings, etc. Hence, '**~-marcher** *n.* 2 (fig) any strong desire: *a ~ for excitement/adventure.* □ *vi* [VP2A,3A,4C] ~ *for/to do sth,* feel, suffer from, ~; have a strong desire: *~ for news.*

hun·gry /'hʌŋgrɪ/ *adj* (-ier, -iest) feeling, showing signs of, causing, hunger: *be/go ~. The boy had a ~ look. Hay-making is ~ work. The orphan child was ~ for affection.* **hun·grily** /'hʌŋgrəlɪ/ *adv*

hunk /hʌŋk/ *n* thick piece cut off: *a ~ of bread/ cheese/meat.*

hun·kers /'hʌŋkəz/ *n pl* (colloq) haunches, esp *on one's ~,* in a squatting position.

hunt¹ /hʌnt/ *n a/the ~,* 1 act of ~ing: *have a good ~; find sth after a long ~,* search. 2 (esp in GB) group of persons who regularly ~ foxes and stags with horses and hounds; the area in which they do this: *The Quorn H~; a member of the ~.* **,~ 'ball,** ball organized by members of a ~. **~·er** *n* (a) person who ~s: *~ers of big game in Africa.* (Note that in GB a person who ~s foxes, etc on horseback or shoots grouse, pheasants, etc is not called a ~er. 'Do you hunt/shoot?' is preferred to 'Are you a ~er?') **(b)** horse used in fox-hunting. 3 pocket watch with a metal cover protecting the glass face. **~·ing** *n* [U] (a) the act of ~ing; (esp in GB) fox-~ing: *He's fond of ~ing.* **(b)** (attrib) *a '~ing-man; a '~ing-horn.* '**~ing ground,** (fig) place where one may search for sth with hope of success. **,~ing 'pink,** shade of red worn by huntsmen. **~·ress** /'hʌntrɪs/ *n* (liter) woman who ~s, eg the goddess Diana.

hunt² /hʌnt/ *vi,vt* 1 [VP6A,2A,C] go after (wild animals) for food or sport: *~ big game; go out ~ing. Wolves ~ in packs.* ⇨ *shooting* at shoot. 2 [VP2A,3A,15B] search for. ~ *down,* pursue and find; bring to bay: *~ down a criminal/an escaped prisoner. ~ for,* search for; try to find: *~ for a lost book. ~ out,* (try to) find by searching (sth that has been put away and forgotten): *~ out an old diary/a black tie that hasn't been needed for years. ~ up,* search for (sth hidden or difficult to find): *~ up old records/references/quotations.* 3 [VP6A,15A] drive or chase away: *~ the neighbour's cats out of the garden.* 4 [VP6A] (special uses in GB; foxhunting) follow the hounds through or in (a district): *~ the county;* employ (a horse) in ~ing: *~ one's horse all winter;* act as master or huntsman of (a pack of hounds): *~ the hounds.*

hunts·man /'hʌntsmən/ *n* (*pl* -men) 1 hunter(1). 2 man in charge of the hounds during a hunt(2).

hurdle /'hɜ:dl/ *n* 1 (GB) movable upright oblong frame of wood, etc used for making temporary fences, eg for sheep pens. 2 light upright frame to be jumped over in a '**~-race.** 3 (fig) difficulty to be overcome. □ *vt,vi* 1 [VP15B] ~ *off,* fence with ~s. 2 [VP2A] jump over a ~; run in a ~-race. **hur·dler** *n* person who makes ~s(1); person who runs in

hurdling

~-races.

hurdy-gurdy /'hɜːdɪ gɜːdɪ/ n street piano or barrel organ, usu mounted on wheels, played by turning a handle.

hurl /hɜːl/ vt [VP6A,15A,B] throw violently: ~ a spear at a tiger. They ~ed themselves at/upon the enemy and attacked them violently. □ n violent throw.

hurl·ing /'hɜːlɪŋ/ n [U] Irish ball game resembling hockey.

hurly-burly /'hɜːlɪ bɜːlɪ/ n [U] noisy commotion; uproar.

hur·rah /hʊ'rɑː/ (also **hur·ray** /hʊ'reɪ/) int expressing joy, welcome, approval, etc: H~ for the Queen! Hip, hip, ~!□ vi shout ~; cheer.

hur·ri·cane /'hʌrɪkən US: -keɪn/ n [C] violent windstorm (esp a W Indian cyclone. '~ lamp/ lantern nn kind with the light protected from the wind.

hurry /'hʌrɪ/ n [U,C] eager haste; wish to get sth done quickly; (with neg, or in the interr) need for haste: Everything was ~ and excitement. Why all this ~? Is there any/a ~, need for ~? Don't start yet—there's no ~, there's plenty of time. in a ~, (a) impatient; acting, anxious to act, quickly: He was in a ~ to leave. In his ~ to catch the train, he left his luggage in the taxi. (b) (colloq) soon, willingly: I shan't ask that rude man to dinner again in a ~. (c) (colloq) easily: You won't find a better specimen than that in a ~. □ vt,vi (pt,pp -ried) [VP6A,15A,B,2A,C] (cause to) move or do sth quickly or too quickly: Don't ~; there's plenty of time. It's no use ~ing her/trying to make her ~. If we ~ the work, it may be spoiled. He picked up his bag and hurried off. More soldiers were hurried to the front line. H~ up! Make haste. H~ him up! Make him ~. **hur·ried** adj done, etc in a ~; showing haste: a hurried meal; write a few hurried lines. **hur·ried·ly** adv

hurt /hɜːt/ vt,vi (pt,pp hurt) 1 [VP6A,B,2A] cause bodily injury or pain to; damage: He ~ his back when he fell. He was more frightened than ~. Did you ~ yourself? These shoes are too tight; they ~ (me). 2 [VP6A] pain a person, his feelings: Their criticisms have ~ him deeply. She was ~ to find that no one admired her performance. 3 [VP2A] suffer injury; come to harm; have a bad effect: It won't ~ to postpone the matter for a few days. □ n [U] (or with indef art) harm; injury: I intended no ~ to his feelings. It was a severe ~ to his pride. ~·ful /-fl/ adj causing ~: ~ful to the health.

hurtle /'hɜːtl/ vi [VP2C] rush or fly violently: During the gale chimney-pots and roof-tiles came hurtling down.

hus·band /'hʌzbənd/ n man to whom a woman is married. □ vt [VP1,6A] use sparingly: ~ one's resources/strength.

hus·band·man /'hʌzbəndmən/ n (pl -men /-mən/) (old use) farmer. **hus·bandry** /'hʌzbəndrɪ/ n [U] farming; management: animal husbandry; good/bad husbandry.

hush /hʌʃ/ vt,vi [VP2A,15A,B] make or become silent or quiet: H~! Be silent! She ~ed the baby to sleep. ~ sth up, prevent it from becoming public knowledge: She tried unsuccessfully to ~ up the fact that her husband was an ex-convict. □ n a/the ~, silence; stillness: in the ~ of night; there was a sudden ~. '~-money n money paid to ~ sth up (usu sth scandalous or discreditable). ~·'~ adj (colloq) (to be) kept very secret: a ~-~ affair.

husk /hʌsk/ n (usu pl) dry outer covering of seeds, esp of grain: rice in the ~, with the ~s not removed; (fig) worthless outside part of anything. ⇨ the illus at cereal. □ vt remove ~s from.

husky /'hʌskɪ/ adj (-ier, -iest) 1 (dry) like husks. 2 (of a person, his voice) hoarse; with a dry and almost whispering voice: a ~ voice/cough. You sound ~ this morning. 3 (colloq) big and strong: a fine ~ woman, excellent as a farmer's wife. □ n 1 thick-coated dog of N American Eskimos. 2 ~ (3) person. **husk·ily** /-ɪlɪ/ adv **huski·ness** n

hus·sar /hʊ'zɑː(r)/ n soldier of a light cavalry regiment.

hussy /'hʌsɪ/ n (pl -sies) worthless woman; ill-mannered girl.

hus·tings /'hʌstɪŋz/ n pl the ~, proceedings (canvassing, speech-making, etc) leading up to a parliamentary election.

hustle /'hʌsl/ vt,vi [VP6A,15A,B,2A,C] 1 push or jostle roughly; (force sb to) hurry: The police ~d the thief into their van. I don't want to ~ you into a decision. 2 (esp US) (colloq) sell or obtain sth by energetic (esp deceitful) activity. 3 (US sl) engage in prostitution. □ n (sing only) quick and energetic activity: The railway station was a scene of ~ and bustle. **hus·tler** n person who ~s; (US sl) prostitute.

hut /hʌt/ n 1 small, roughly made house or shelter: Alpine huts, for the use of mountain climbers. 2 temporary wooden building for soldiers. '**hut·ment** n encampment of huts. **hut·ted** adj: hutted camps, with huts, not tents (for troops, etc)

hutch /hʌtʃ/ n box or cage with a front of wire netting, esp one used for rabbits.

hya·cinth /'haɪəsɪnθ/ n plant growing from a bulb; its sweet-smelling flowers. '**water·~**, wild plant that grows in floating masses on rivers, lakes, etc and may hinder navigation.

hy·aena /haɪ'iːnə/ ⇨ hyena.

hy·brid /'haɪbrɪd/ n, adj (animal, plant, etc) from parents of different species or varieties: A mule is a ~ animal. 'Cablegram' is a ~; half the word is Latin and half is Greek. ~·ize /-aɪz/ vt,vi [VP6A,2A] (cause to) produce ~s; interbreed.

hy·dra /'haɪdrə/ n (Gk myth) great sea serpent with many heads that grew again if cut off.

hy·drangea /haɪ'dreɪndʒə/ n shrub with large round heads of white, blue or pink flowers.

hy·drant /'haɪdrənt/ n pipe from a water-main (esp in a street) with a nozzle to which a hose can be attached for street-cleaning, putting out fires, etc.

hy·drate /'haɪdreɪt/ n chemical compound of water with another substance. □ vt,vi combine with water to make a ~; become a ~.

hy·drau·lic /haɪ'drɔːlɪk/ adj of water moving through pipes; worked by the pressure of a fluid, esp water: a ~ lift; ~ brakes, in which the braking force is transmitted by compressed fluid; hardening under water: ~ cement. **hy·drau·lics** n pl science of using water to produce power.

hy·dro·car·bon /ˌhaɪdrə'kɑːbən/ n [C] substance formed of hydrogen and carbon, eg benzene, paraffin, coal-gas.

hy·dro·chloric /ˌhaɪdrə'klɒrɪk US: -'klɔːr-/ adj: ~ acid, acid (HCl) containing hydrogen and chlorine.

hy·dro·elec·tric /ˌhaɪdrəʊɪ'lektrɪk/ adj of electricity produced by water-power.

hy·dro·foil /'haɪdrəfɔɪl/ n boat equipped with plates or fins which, when the boat is in motion, raise the hull out of the water.

hy·dro·gen /'haɪdrədʒən/ *n* gas (symbol **H**) without colour, taste or smell, that combines with oxygen to form water. '∼ **bomb** (also *fusion bomb*) variety of *atomic bomb*, ➪ atomic. ∼ **pe'roxide** *n* solution of peroxide of ∼, (H_2O_2), used as an antiseptic and bleaching agent.

hy·drop·athy /haɪ'drɒpəθɪ/ *n* [U] use of water (internally and externally) in the treatment of disease. **hy·dro·pathic** /ˌhaɪdrə'pæθɪk/ *adj* of ∼.

hy·dro·pho·bia /ˌhaɪdrə'fəʊbɪə/ *n* [U] rabies; disease marked by strong contractions of the muscles of the throat and consequent inability to drink water.

hy·dro·plane /'haɪdrəpleɪn/ *n* hydrofoil; motorboat with a flat bottom, able to skim very fast over the surface; (old name for) seaplane.

hy·dro·pon·ics /ˌhaɪdrə'pɒnɪks/ *n pl* art of growing plants without soil, in water to which necessary chemical food is supplied.

hy·ena, hy·aena /haɪ'iːnə/ *n* flesh-eating wild animal, like a wolf, with a laughing cry. ➪ the illus at large.

hy·giene /'haɪdʒiːn/ *n* [U] science of, rules for, healthy living; cleanliness. **hy·gienic** /haɪ'dʒiːnɪk US: ˌhaɪdʒɪ'enɪk/ *adj* of ∼; likely to promote health; free from disease germs: *hygienic conditions.* **hy·gieni·cally** /-klɪ/ *adv*

hy·men /'haɪmən/ *n* **1** **H∼**, Greek god of marriage. **2** (anat) fold of tissue partly closing the vagina of a virgin girl or woman.

hymn /hɪm/ *n* song of praise to God, esp one for use in a religious service. □ *vt* praise (God) in ∼s; express (praise) in ∼s. **hym·nal** /'hɪmnəl/ *n* book of ∼s.

hy·per·bola /haɪ'pɜːbələ/ *n* curve produced when a cone is cut by a plane passing anywhere except through its point.

hy·per·bole /haɪ'pɜːbəlɪ/ *n* [U] (use of) exaggerated statement(s) made for effect and not intended to be taken literally; [C] instance of this, eg *waves as high as Everest.*

hy·per·criti·cal /ˌhaɪpə'krɪtɪkl/ *adj* too critical, esp of small faults.

hy·per·market /'haɪpəmɑːkɪt/ *n* immense supermarket occupying an extensive area, outside a town, with a large car park, selling all varieties of goods.

hy·phen /'haɪfn/ *n* the mark (-) used to join two words together (as in *Anglo-French*), or to show

that a word has been divided between the end of one line and the beginning of another. ➪ App 9. □ *vt* join (words) with a ∼; write (a compound word) with a ∼. ∼**·ate** /-eɪt/ *vt* = ∼.

hyp·no·sis /hɪp'nəʊsɪs/ *n* (*pl* -ses /-siːz/) [U,C] state like deep sleep in which a person's acts may be controlled by another person. **hyp·notic** /hɪp'nɒtɪk/ *adj* of ∼: *in a hypnotic state.* **hyp·not·ism** /'hɪpnətɪzəm/ *n* [U] artificial production of ∼. **hyp·not·ize** /'hɪpnətaɪz/ *vt* [VP6A] produce ∼ in (sb). **hyp·not·ist** /'hɪpnətɪst/ *n* person able to produce ∼.

hypo /'haɪpəʊ/ *n* (colloq abbr of) sodium thiosulphate ($Na_2S_2O_2$), used in photography as a fixing agent.

hy·po·chon·dria /ˌhaɪpə'kɒndrɪə/ *n* [U] state of mental depression either without apparent cause or due to unnecessary anxiety about one's health. **hy·po·chon·driac** /ˌhaɪpə'kɒndrɪæk/ *adj* of, affected by, ∼. □ *n* person who suffers from ∼.

hy·poc·risy /hɪ'pɒkrəsɪ/ *n* (*pl* -sies) [C,U] (instance of) falsely making oneself appear to be virtuous or good. **hyp·ocrite** /'hɪpəkrɪt/ *n* person guilty of ∼. **hy·po·criti·cal** /ˌhɪpə'krɪtɪkl/ *adj* of ∼ or a hypocrite. **hy·po·criti·cally** /-klɪ/ *adv*

hy·po·der·mic /ˌhaɪpə'dɜːmɪk/ *adj* (of drugs, etc) injected beneath the skin: ∼ *injections; a* ∼ *needle/syringe,* used for giving such injections. ➪ the illus at syringe. □ *n* ∼ injection or syringe.

hy·pot·en·use /haɪ'pɒtənjuːz US: -tnuːs/ *n* side of a right-angled triangle opposite the right angle.

hy·poth·ecate /haɪ'pɒθɪkeɪt/ *vt* (legal) pledge; mortgage.

hy·poth·esis /haɪ'pɒθɪsɪs/ *n* (*pl* -ses /-siːz/) idea, suggestion, put forward as a starting-point for reasoning or explanation. **hy·po·theti·cal** /ˌhaɪpə'θetɪkl/ *adj* of, based on, a ∼; not based on certain knowledge.

hys·sop /'hɪsəp/ *n* strong-smelling plant formerly used in medicine.

hys·teria /hɪ'stɪərɪə/ *n* [U] **1** disturbance of the nervous system, with outbursts of emotion, often uncontrollable. **2** senseless, uncontrolled excitement, eg in a crowd at a football match. **hys·teri·cal** /hɪ'sterɪkl/ *adj* caused by, suffering from, ∼: *hysterical laughter; an hysterical outburst of fury.* **hys·teri·cally** /-klɪ/ *adv.* **hys·ter·ics** /hɪ'sterɪks/ *n pl* attack of ∼: *go into hysterics,* become hysterical.

Ii

I¹ i /aɪ/ (*pl* I's i's /aɪz/), the ninth letter of the English alphabet; symbol for Roman numeral 1, ➪ App 4.

I² /aɪ/ *pers pron* used by a speaker or writer to refer to himself. Cf *me,* object form, and *we, us,* plural forms.

iamb /'aɪæm/ *n* = iambus.

iam·bus /aɪ'æmbəs/ *n* (*pl* ∼es or -bi /-baɪ/) (prosody) metrical foot of one unaccented and one accented syllable eg *a'lone.* **iam·bic** /aɪ'æmbɪk/ *adj* of, containing, ∼es: *iambic feet,* eg I 'come / from 'haunts / of 'coot / and 'fern. □ *n pl* **iam·bics** iambic verse.

ibex /'aɪbeks/ *n* wild goat (of the Alps and Pyrenees) with large curved horns.

ibi·dem /'ɪbɪdem/ *adv* (Lat) in the same book,

chapter, etc (previously quoted).

ibis /'aɪbɪs/ *n* large wading bird (like a stork or heron) found in lakes and swamps in warm climates.

ice¹ /aɪs/ *n* **1** [U] frozen water; water made solid by cold: *Is the ice thick enough for skating?* **break the ice,** (fig) get people on friendly terms; overcome formality or reserve; take the first steps in a delicate matter. **cut no ice (with sb),** have little or no effect or influence (on him). **keep sth on ice,** in a refrigerator; (fig) reserve for later use. **be skating on thin ice,** (fig) in a dangerous or delicate situation. **dry ice,** ➪ dry¹(13). **2** [C] frozen sweet of various kinds: *water-ice; cream ices; two strawberry ices.* ➪ ice-cream below. **3** (compounds) **'Ice Age** *n* time when much of the N hemisphere was covered with glaciers; glacial period. **'ice-axe**

an iceberg

icicles

n axe used by mountain climbers for cutting steps in ice. **'ice-berg** *n* mass of ice (broken off a glacier) moving in the sea; (fig) unemotional person: *his iceberg of a wife.* **'ice-boat** *n* boat fitted with runners and sails for travelling on a frozen lake or sea. **'ice-bound** *adj* (of harbours, etc) obstructed by ice. **'ice-box** *n* box in which ice is used to keep food cool; (US) refrigerator. **'ice-breaker** *n* ship with strong curved bows used for breaking a passage through ice. **'ice-cap** *n* permanent covering of ice sloping down on all sides from a high centre. **,ice-'cream** *n* [C,U] (portion of) cream or custard (or various modern substitutes), sweetened, and flavoured and frozen. **'ice-cube** *n* cube of ice made in an icetray in a refrigerator. **'ice-fall** *n* steep part of a glacier, like a frozen waterfall. **'ice-field** *n* large expanse of (esp marine) ice in the Polar regions. **'ice-floe** /-fləʊ/ *n* large sheet of floating ice. **'ice-free** *adj* (of a port or harbour) free from ice. ⇨ ice-bound above. **'ice hockey,** ⇨ hockey. **'ice-house** *n* building often partly or wholly underground for storing ice in winter for use in summer. **,ice-'lolly** *n* flavoured ice on a stick. **'ice-man** /-mæn/ *n* (*pl* -men) (US) man who retails and delivers ice (for use in ice-boxes, etc). **'ice-pack** *n* (a) stretch of sea covered with broken ice that has drifted into masses. (b) bag of broken ice used as an application, eg to the head, for fever. **'ice-show** *n* variety entertainment in which the performers are on ice-skates (on a floor of artificial ice). **'ice-pick** *n* tool for breaking ice. **'ice-rink** *n* indoor skating-rink with a floor of artificial ice. **'ice-skate** *n* thin metal runner or blade on a boot for skating on ice. □ *vi* skate on ice. ⇨ the illus at skate. **'ice-tray** *n* one kept in the deep-freeze compartment of a refrigerator, for making cubes of ice.

ice² /aɪs/ *vt, vi* **1** [VP6A] make very cold: *ice a bottle of beer; iced water.* **2** [VP2C,15B] ~ *over/ up,* cover, become covered, with a coating of ice: *The pond (was) iced over. The wings of the aircraft had iced up.* **3** [VP6A] cover (a cake) with sugar icing. ⇨ icing.

ich-neu-mon /ɪk'njuːmən *US:* -'nuː-/ *n* **1** small brown weasel-like animal noted for destroying crocodiles' eggs. **2** (also '~-fly) insect which lays its eggs in or on the larva of another insect.

icicle /'aɪsɪkl/ *n* pointed piece of ice formed by the freezing of dripping water.

icing /'aɪsɪŋ/ *n* [U] **1** mixture of sugar, white of egg, flavouring, etc for covering cake(s). **2** formation of ice on the wings of aircraft.

icon /'aɪkɒn/ *n* (in the Eastern Church) painting, carving or mosaic of a sacred person, itself regarded as sacred.

icono-clast /aɪ'kɒnəklæst/ *n* person who took part in the movement against the use of images in reli-

gious worship in the churches of Eastern Europe in the 8th and 9th cc (also applied to Puritans in England, 17th c); (fig) person who attacks popular beliefs or established customs which he thinks mistaken or unwise.

icy /'aɪsɪ/ *adj* (-ier, -iest) very cold, like ice: *icy winds;* covered with ice: *icy roads;* (fig) *an icy welcome/manner.* **icily** /'aɪsɪlɪ/ *adv* (lit, fig) in an icy manner.

id /ɪd/ *n* (psych) (**the**) ~, person's unconscious instincts and impulses.

I'd /aɪd/ = *I had* or *I would.*

idea /aɪ'dɪə/ *n* **1** thought; picture in the mind: *This book gives you a good ~ of life in ancient Greece.* **2** plan; scheme; design; purpose: *That man is full of new ~s.* **3** opinion: *You shouldn't force your ~s on other people.* **4** vague belief; fancy; feeling that sth is probable: *I have an ~ that she will be late.* **5** conception: *What ~ can a man who is blind from birth have of colour? Picnicking is not my ~ of pleasure. You can have no ~ (of) how anxious we have been.* **put '~s into sb's head,** give him expectations that are not likely to be realized. **6** (in exclamations): *The ~ of such a thing! What an ~!* (used to suggest that what has been suggested is unrealistic, outrageous, etc). **7** way of thinking: *the young ~,* the child's mind.

ideal /aɪ'dɪəl/ *adj* **1** satisfying one's idea of what is perfect: ~ *weather for a holiday.* **2** (contrasted with *real*) existing only in the imagination or as an idea; not likely to be achieved: ~ *happiness;* ~ *plans for reforming the world.* □ *n* [C] idea, example, looked upon as perfect: *the high ~s of the Christian religion. She's looking for a husband but hasn't found her ~ yet.* ~**ly** /aɪ'dɪəlɪ/ *adv*

ideal-ism /aɪ'dɪəlɪzəm/ *n* [U] **1** living according to, being guided by, one's ideals. **2** (in art) (opposite of *realism*) imaginative treatment, showing beauty and perfection even if this means being untrue to facts. **3** (in philosophy) system of thought in which ideas are believed to be the only real things or the only things of which we can know anything. **ideal-ist** /-ɪst/ *n* person who believes in ~. **ideal-istic** /aɪ,dɪə'lɪstɪk/ *adj* of idealists and ~.

ideal-ize /aɪ'dɪəlaɪz/ *vt* [VP6A] see, think of, as perfect: *Some biographers ~ their subjects.* **ideal-iz-ation** /aɪ,dɪəlaɪ'zeɪʃn *US:* -lɪ'z-/ *n*

idem /'aɪdem/ *n, adj* (Lat) (by) the same author, etc; the same word, book, authority, etc (already mentioned).

ident-ical /aɪ'dentɪkl/ *adj* ~ (**to/with**), **1** the same: *This knife is ~ to the one with which the murder was committed.* **2** exactly alike; agreeing in every way: *The fingerprints of no two persons are ~. Our views of what should be done are ~. 40 inches is ~ with 3 feet 4 inches.* **3** ~ **'twins,** twins from one single fertilized ovum. ~**ly** /-klɪ/ *adv*

ident-ify /aɪ'dentɪfaɪ/ *vt* (*pt, pp* -fied)

icons

[VP6A,14,3A] **1** say, show, prove, who or what sb or sth. is; establish the identity of: *Could you ~ your umbrella among a hundred others? His accent was difficult to ~*. **2** *~ sth with sth*, treat (sth) as identical (with); equate (one thing with another). **3** *~ (oneself) with sb/sth*, give support to, be associated with; feel close to: *He refused to ~ himself/become identified with the new political party*. **identi·fi·ca·tion** /aɪˌdentɪfɪˈkeɪʃn/ n [U] ~ing or being identified: *the identification of persons killed in a road accident*, finding out who they are.

iden·ti·kit /aɪˈdentɪkɪt/ n composite drawing of the face of an unidentified person (esp a suspected criminal), from features recalled by those who saw him.

ident·ity /aɪˈdentətɪ/ n (pl -ties) **1** [U] state of being identical; absolute sameness; exact likeness. **2** [C,U] who sb is; what sth is: *There is no clue to the ~ of the thief*, nothing to show who he is. *The cheque will be cashed upon proof of ~. He was arrested because of mistaken ~.* '~ **card/disc/ certificate**, card, etc that gives proof of one's ~.

ideo·gram /ˈɪdɪəɡræm/, **ideo·graph** /ˈɪdɪəɡrɑːf US: -ɡræf/ nn written or printed character, used in making up words, that symbolizes the idea of a thing without indicating the sounds that make up the word, eg as used in Chinese writing. **ideo·graphic** /ˌɪdɪəˈɡræfɪk/ adj

爐 遙 人 似 月
皓 腕 凝 霜 雪
未 老 莫 還 鄉
還 鄉 須 斷 腸

東

ideograms

ideol·ogy /ˌaɪdɪˈɒlədʒɪ/ n (pl -gies) **1** [C] manner of thinking, ideas, characteristic of a person, group, etc, esp as forming the basis of an economic or political system: *bourgeois, Marxist and totalitarian ideologies*. **2** [U] unproductive thought. **ideo·logi·cal** /ˌaɪdɪəˈlɒdʒɪkl/ adj **ideo·logi·cally** /-klɪ/ adv

ides /aɪdz/ n pl (in the calendar of ancient Rome) the 15th of March, May, July, Oct or the 13th of other months.

id est /ˌɪd ˈest/ (abbr **i e**) (Lat) that is to say.

idi·ocy /ˈɪdɪəsɪ/ n **1** [U] state of being an idiot; extreme stupidity. **2** [C] (pl -cies) extremely stupid act, remark, etc.

idio·lect /ˈɪdɪəlekt/ n the total of a person's language that he knows and uses at any stage of his language development: *Is the word 'psychosis' part of your ~?*

id·iom /ˈɪdɪəm/ n **1** [U] language of a people or country; specific character of this, eg one peculiar to a country, district, group of people, or to one individual: *the French ~; the ~ of the New England countryside*, ie the kind of English used by country people there; *Shakespeare's ~*, the method of expression peculiar to him. **2** [C] phrase or sentence whose meaning is not obvious through knowledge of the individual meanings of the constituent words but must be learnt as a whole, eg *give way, in order to, be hard put to it*. **idio·matic** /ˌɪdɪəˈmætɪk/ adj **1** in accordance with the ~s(2) of a language, dialect, etc: *speak ~atic English*. **2** full of ~s(2): *an ~atic language*. **idi·om·ati·cally** /ˌɪdɪəˈmætɪklɪ/ adv

idio·syn·crasy /ˌɪdɪəˈsɪŋkrəsɪ/ n (pl -sies) [C] way

of thinking or behaving that is peculiar to a person; personal mannerism. **idio·syn·cratic** /ˌɪdɪəsɪŋˈkrætɪk/ adj

id·iot /ˈɪdɪət/ n **1** person so weak-minded that he is incapable of rational conduct. **2** (colloq) fool: *'I've left my suitcase in the train. What an ~ I am!'* **idiotic** /ˌɪdɪˈɒtɪk/ adj stupid. **~i·cally** /-klɪ/ adv

idle /ˈaɪdl/ adj (-r, -st) **1** doing no work; not employed; not active or in use; (of time) not spent in doing something: *When men cannot find employment they are ~* (though not necessarily lazy). *During the business depression half the machines in the factory were ~. We spent many ~ hours during the holidays*. **2** (of persons) not willing to work; lazy (which is the commoner word for this sense); *~, worthless girl*. **3** useless; worthless: *Don't listen to ~ gossip/tales. It's ~ to expect help from that man.* □ vi,vt **1** [VP2A,C] be ~; *Don't ~ (about)*. **2** [VP15B] *~ away*, spend in an ~ manner: *Don't ~ away your time*. **3** (of a car engine) run slowly in neutral gear. **idler** /ˈaɪdlə(r)/ n person who ~s. **idly** /ˈaɪdlɪ/ adv **~·ess** n state of being ~: *live in ~ness*.

idol /ˈaɪdl/ n **1** image in wood, stone, etc of a god; such an image used as an object of worship; false god. **2** sb or sth greatly loved or admired: *He was an only child, and the ~ of his parents. Don't make an ~ of wealth*. **~·ater** /aɪˈdɒlətə(r)/ n **1** worshipper of ~s. **2** devoted admirer (of...). **~·atress** /aɪˈdɒlətrɪs/ n woman ~ater. **~·atrous** /aɪˈdɒlətrəs/ adj (of a person) worshipping ~s; of the worship of ~s. **~·atrous·ly** adv **~·atry** /aɪˈdɒlətrɪ/ n **1** [U] the worship of ~s; excessive devotion to or admiration of (sb or sth). **2** [C] (pl -ries) instance of this. **~·ize** /ˈaɪdəlaɪz/ vt [VP6A] make an ~ of; love or admire to excess. **~·ization** /ˌaɪdəlaɪˈzeɪʃn US: -lɪˈz-/ n ~izing or being ~ized.

idyll /ˈɪdɪl US: ˈaɪdl/ n short description, usu in verse, of a simple scene or event, esp of country life; period of great peace and happiness. **idyl·lic** /ɪˈdɪlɪk US: aɪˈd-/ adj suitable for, like, an ~; simple, peaceful and pleasant.

if /ɪf/ conj **1** on the condition that; supposing that: **(a)** (Present or Present Perfect Tense in the *if*-clause, indicating that sth is possible, probable, or likely): *If you ask him, he will help you. If (it is) necessary, I can come at six. If you have finished with that book, take it back to the library.* **(b)** (with *should* in the *if*-clause, to indicate that an event is unlikely or improbable): *If anyone should call, please let me know. If it should be necessary, I could come at six.* **(c)** (with *will* in the *if*-clause, not to show future time, but as part of the polite formula 'Will you, please'): *If you will wait a moment* (= Please wait a moment) *and I'll go and tell the manager that you are here.* **(d)** (Past Tense in the *if*-clause, indicating a condition that cannot be, or is unlikely to be realized, or is one put forward for consideration): *If you were a bird, you could fly. If I asked him/If I were to ask him for a loan, would he agree? If you would lend me £5 until Monday, I should be grateful.* **(e)** (Past Perfect Tense in the *if*-clause, indicating that the condition was not fulfilled, eg because it was an impossible one, or through sb's failure to act): *If they'd started earlier, they would have arrived in time. If they had not started when they did, they wouldn't be here now.* (After some vv, eg *think, remember, ask*, the main clause depending upon the condition is usu omitted): *If you think about it,* (you realize that) *there were many bright boys in that class. If you ask me,* (I will tell you) *he's a fool.* **2** (In literary style *if* may be omitted, and an inversion of subject and *aux v,* esp *were/had/should,* used instead): *Should it* (= If it should) *be necessary...; Were I* (= If I were) *in your place...; Had I* (= If I had) *known earlier....* **3** (When *if* is used meaning 'when' or 'whenever', so that there is no condition, tenses in the main clause and the *if*-clause may be the same): *If you mix yellow and blue you get green. If she wants the steward she rings the bell.* **4** *(even) if,* granting or admitting that: *If I'm mistaken, you're mistaken, too. Even if he did say that, I'm sure he didn't intend to hurt your feelings.* **5** *(even) if,* although: *If I'm taken ill, even if it takes me all the afternoon.* **6** (colloq) (*if* replacing *whether,* to introduce an interrogative clause): *Do you know if Mr Smith is at home? She asked if that was enough.* (Note: *if* should not replace *whether* in cases where there may be ambiguity: cf *Let me know whether you are coming,* (information wanted in either case). *Let me know if* (= only if) *you are coming,* (information wanted only in the one case). **7** *as if,* as it would be if (*it isn't as if...* suggests that the contrary of what follows is true): *It isn't as if we were rich,* ie We are *not* rich. *It isn't as if he doesn't know the rules,* ie He *does* know the rules. (*As if* often introduces an exclamation): *As if I would allow it!* ie I would certainly *not* allow it! ⇨ as²(11). **8** *if only,* (often introduces a wish, or indicates an unfulfilled condition, esp in exclamations): *If only he arrives in time! If only she would marry me! If only she had known about it* (but she did not know)*! If only you could/If you could only have seen it.* **9** (*if,* followed by a *v* in the neg, is used in exclamations to indicate dismay, surprise, etc): *Well, if I haven't left my umbrella in the train! And if he didn't try to knock me down! What do you think he did? He tried to knock me down!*

ig·loo /'ɪglu:/ *n* (*pl* ~s) dome-shaped hut made of blocks of hard snow, used by the Eskimos.

ig·neous /'ɪgnɪəs/ *adj* (of rocks) formed by volcanic action.

ig·nis fatuus /ˌɪgnɪs 'fætjʊəs/ *n* (*pl* ignes fatui /ˌɪgni:z 'fætjʊaɪ/) **1** = will-o'-the-wisp. **2** (colloq) sth misleading.

ig·nite /ɪg'naɪt/ *vt, vi* [VP6A, 2A] set on fire; take fire. **ig·ni·tion** /ɪg'nɪʃn/ *n* [U] igniting or being ~d; (in a petrol engine) electrical mechanism for igniting the mixture of explosive gases: *switch on the ignition.* ⇨ the illus at motor.

ig·noble /ɪg'nəʊbl/ *adj* **1** dishonourable; shameful: *an ~ man/action; an ~ peace.* **2** (old use) of low birth. **ig·nobly** /-'nəʊblɪ/ *adv*

ig·nom·ini·ous /ˌɪgnə'mɪnɪəs/ *adj* bringing contempt, disgrace, shame; dishonourable: *~ behaviour; an ~ defeat.* ~·ly *adv*

ig·nom·iny /'ɪgnəmɪnɪ/ *n* **1** [U] public dishonour or shame. **2** [C] (*pl* -nies) dishonourable or disgraceful act; [U] dishonourable behaviour.

ig·nor·amus /ˌɪgnə'reɪməs/ *n* (*pl* ~es /-sɪz/) ignorant person.

ig·nor·ance /'ɪgnərəns/ *n* [U] ~ (of), the state of being ignorant; want of knowledge: *We are in complete ~ of his plans. If he did wrong, it was from/through ~.*

ig·nor·ant /'ɪgnərənt/ *adj* **1** ~ (of), (of persons) knowing little or nothing; not aware: *He's not stu-*

pid, merely ~. *You are not ~ of the reasons for her behaviour. What his plans are I am quite ~ of.* **2** showing ignorance; resulting from ignorance: *an ~ reply; ~ conduct.* ~·ly *adv*

ig·nore /ɪg'nɔ:(r)/ *vt* [VP6A] take no notice of; refuse to take notice of: *~ rude remarks; be ~d by one's superiors.*

iguana /ɪ'gwɑ:nə/ *n* large tree-climbing lizard of tropical America.

ikon /'aɪkɒn/ *n* = icon.

ilex /'aɪleks/ *n* holm-oak; (bot) genus of trees including the common holly.

ilk /ɪlk/ *n of that/his etc ilk,* (colloq, hum) of that/his etc family, set, type.

I'll /aɪl/ = I will or I shall.

ill /ɪl/ *adj* **1** (usu pred) in bad health; sick: *She was ill with anxiety. fall/be taken ill,* become ill. ⇨ worse, worst. **2** (attrib) bad: *ill health; in an ill temper/humour; ill repute; do sb an ill turn; have ill luck; a bird of ill omen. It's an ill wind that blows 'nobody any good,* (prov) An affair must be very bad indeed if it does not benefit somebody. *Ill weeds grow apace,* (prov) Harmful things grow or spread rapidly. ,ill-'breeding *n* bad manners. ,ill-'favoured *adj* (of a person) unpleasant to look at; ugly. ,ill-'mannered *adj* having bad manners; rude. ,ill-'natured *adj* bad-tempered. ,ill-'omened *adj* destined to misfortune. ,ill-'starred *adj* born under an evil star; unlucky. ,ill-'treatment/-'usage *n* [U] cruelty; harsh treatment. ,ill 'will *n* enmity; unkind feeling. □ *n* **1** [U] evil; injury: *do ill.* **2** [C] misfortune; trouble: *the various ills of life.* □ *adv* badly; imperfectly; unfavourably: *They were ill* (= insufficiently) *provided with ammunition. We could ill* (= not well, not easily) *afford the time and money. It ill becomes you to criticize him,* It is not right or proper for you to do so. *be/feel ill at ease,* uncomfortable, embarrassed. *speak ill of sb,* in an unkind or unfavourable way. ,ill-ad'vised *adj* unwise; imprudent. ,ill-af'fected (towards) *adj* not well-disposed; not feeling favour. ,ill-'bred *adj* badly brought up; rude. ,ill-dis'posed (towards) *adj* (a) wishing to do harm (to). (b) unfavourable (towards a plan, etc). ,ill-'fated *adj* destined to misfortune; bringing misfortune. ,ill-gotten 'gains *n* pl money gained by evil or unlawful methods. ,ill-'judged *adj* done at an unsuitable time; showing poor judgement: *an ill-judged attempt.* ,ill-'timed *adj* badly timed; done at a wrong or unsuitable time. ,ill-'treat/-'use *vt* treat badly or cruelly.

il·legal /ɪ'li:gl/ *adj* not legal; contrary to law. ~·ly /-gəlɪ/ *adv* ~·ity /ˌɪlɪ'gælətɪ/ *n* [U] being ~; [C] (*pl* -ties) ~ act.

il·leg·ible /ɪ'ledʒəbl/ *adj* difficult or impossible to read. **il·leg·ibly** /-əblɪ/ *adv* **il·leg·ibil·ity** /ɪˌledʒə'bɪlətɪ/ *n* [U].

il·legit·imate /ˌɪlɪ'dʒɪtɪmət/ *adj* **1** not authorized by law; contrary to law. **2** born of parents who were not married to each other: *an ~ child; of ~ descent.* **3** (of a conclusion in an argument, etc) not logical; wrongly inferred. □ *n* an ~ person. ~·ly *adv* **il·legit·imacy** /ˌɪlɪ'dʒɪtɪməsɪ/ *n* [U].

il·lib·eral /ɪ'lɪbərəl/ *adj* not befitting a free man; narrow-minded; intolerant; ungenerous; mean. ~·ly /-rəlɪ/ *adv* ~·ity /ɪˌlɪbə'rælətɪ/ *n*

il·licit /ɪ'lɪsɪt/ *adj* unlawful; forbidden: *the ~ sale of opium.* ~·ly *adv*

il·limit·able /ɪ'lɪmɪtəbl/ *adj* boundless; without limits: *~ space/ambition.*

il·lit·er·ate /ɪ'lɪtərət/ *adj* with little or no education; unable to read or write; showing such ignorance: *an ~ letter*, one full of spelling and grammatical errors. □ *n ~* person. **il·lit·er·acy** /ɪ'lɪtərəsɪ/ *n* [U,C] (instance of) being ~.

ill·ness /'ɪlnɪs/ *n* 1 [U] state of being ill (contrasted with *health*): *There has been no/not much/a great deal of ~ in the village this winter.* 2 [C] specific kind of, occasion of, ~: *~es of children; a serious ~; one ~ after another.*

il·logi·cal /ɪ'lɒdʒɪkl/ *adj* without logic; contrary to logic. *~ly* /-klɪ/ *adv* *~·ity* /ɪˌlɒdʒɪ'kælətɪ/, *~·ness* *nn* [U,C] (instance of) being ~.

il·lume /ɪ'lu:m/ *vt* (poet) illuminate.

il·lumi·nate /ɪ'lu:mɪneɪt/ *vt* [VP6A] 1 give light to; throw light on: *a street ~d by oil lamps; poorly ~d rooms.* 2 decorate (streets, etc) with bright lights as a sign of rejoicing. 3 decorate (initial letters in a manuscript) with gold, silver and bright colours (as was the custom in the Middle Ages). 4 make clear, help to explain: *~ a difficult passage in a book.* **il·lumi·na·tion** /ɪˌlu:mɪ'neɪʃn/ *n* 1 [U] illuminating or being ~d. 2 (usu *pl*) lights, etc, used to ~(2) a town for a special occasion. 3 (*pl*) decorations on a manuscript. **il·lu·mine** /ɪ'lu:mɪn/ *vt* [VP6A] (liter) enlighten spiritually; make bright.

il·lu·sion /ɪ'lu:ʒn/ *n* 1 [C] (the seeing of) sth that does not really exist, or of sth as different from the reality; false idea or belief: *an optical ~.* *be un·der an ~*, be deceived by one. *cherish an ~/the ~ that...*, like to believe.... *have no ~s about sb/sth*, have no false beliefs about him/it. 2 [U] state of mind in which one is deceived in this way. *~·ist* /-ɪst/ *n* person who produces optical ~s on the stage; conjurer.

il·lu·sive /ɪ'lu:sɪv/, **il·lu·sory** /ɪ'lu:sərɪ/ *adjj* deceptive; based on illusion.

il·lus·trate /'ɪləstreɪt/ *vt* [VP6A] 1 explain by examples, pictures, etc. 2 supply a book, article, lecture, etc with pictures, diagrams, etc: *a well-~d textbook.* **il·lus·tra·tor** /-tə(r)/ *n* person who ~s books, etc. **il·lus·tra·tion** /ˌɪlə'streɪʃn/ *n* 1 [U] illustrating or being ~d: *cite instances in illustration of a theory. Illustration is often more useful than definition for giving the meanings of words.* 2 [C] sth that ~s; picture, diagram, etc. **il·lus·tra·tive** /'ɪləstrətɪv US: ɪ'lʌs-/ *adj* serving to ~, as an explanation or example (*of* sth).

il·lus·tri·ous /ɪ'lʌstrɪəs/ *adj* greatly distinguished; celebrated. *~·ly adv*

I'm /aɪm/ = *I am.* ⇨ **be**¹.

im·age /'ɪmɪdʒ/ *n* [C] 1 likeness or copy of the shape of sb or sth, esp one made in wood, stone, etc: *an ~ of the Virgin Mary; graven ~s,* ~s carved in wood, etc and regarded as gods. 2 close likeness; counterpart: *Did man create God in his own ~? be the (very/spitting) ~ (of sth/sb),* be exactly like it/him. 3 mental picture or idea; concept of sth or sb, eg a politician, political party, commercial firm, product, held by the public: *How can we improve our ~?* 4 simile; metaphor: *speak in ~s,* use figures of speech that bring pictures to the mind. 5 reflection seen in a mirror or through the lens of a camera. ⇨ the illus at **camera**. □ *vt* [VP6A] 1 make an ~ of, portray. 2 reflect; mirror. *~ry* /'ɪmɪdʒərɪ/ *n* [U] the use of ~s(4), or figures of speech, in writing; ~s(1) collectively.

im·agin·able /ɪ'mædʒɪnəbl/ *adj* that can be imagined: *We had the greatest difficulty ~ getting here in time.*

im·agin·ary /ɪ'mædʒɪnərɪ US: -ənerɪ/ *adj* existing only in the mind; unreal.

im·agin·ation /ɪˌmædʒɪ'neɪʃn/ *n* 1 [C,U] power of the mind to imagine: *He hasn't much ~. Novelists use their ~. Children are encouraged to use their ~s.* 2 what is imagined: *You didn't really see a ghost—it was only ~.* **im·agin·ative** /ɪ'mædʒɪnətɪv US: -əneɪtɪv/ *adj* of, having, using, ~: *imaginative writers.*

im·ag·ine /ɪ'mædʒɪn/ *vt* [VP6A,C,9,10,16B,19A,C,25] form a picture of in the mind; think of (sth) as probable: *wild imaginings. Can you ~ life without electricity and other modern conveniences? I~ yourself (to be) on a desert island. I~ you've been ship-wrecked. I ~ him as a big, tall man. Can you ~ him/yourself becoming famous as an actor? I can't ~ (my) marrying a girl of that sort. Don't ~ (= get the idea) that I can lend you money every time you need it!*

imam /ɪ'mɑ:m/ *n* prayer leader in a mosque. *I~,* title of various Muslim leaders.

im·bal·ance /ˌɪm'bæləns/ *n* absence of balance between two totals, eg payments; lack of proportion: *the country's ~ in world payments,* the state that exists when the total sum paid for imports, etc, is unequal to the total received for exports, services, etc; *the increasing ~ between rich and poor countries,* the increasing wealth of some and the increasing poverty of others.

im·be·cile /'ɪmbəsi:l US: -sl/ *adj* weak-minded; stupid: *~ remarks/conduct.* □ *n ~* person; fool. **im·be·cil·ity** /ˌɪmbə'sɪlətɪ/ *n* [U] stupidity; [C] (*pl* -ties) stupid act, remark, etc.

im·bed /ɪm'bed/ *vt* (-dd-) = embed.

im·bibe /ɪm'baɪb/ *vt* (formal) drink; take in: *~ ideas/knowledge.*

im·bro·glio /ɪm'brəʊlɪəʊ/ *n* (*pl* ~s /-z/) complicated, confused or embarrassing (esp political or emotional) situation.

im·bue /ɪm'bju:/ *vt* (*pt,pp* -bued) [VP14] *~ with,* (formal) fill, inspire: *~d with patriotism/hatred, etc; politicians ~d with a sense of their own importance.*

imi·tate /'ɪmɪteɪt/ *vt* [VP6A] 1 copy the behaviour of; take as an example: *You should ~ great and good men.* 2 mimic (consciously or not): *Parrots ~ human speech.* 3 be like; make a likeness of: *wood painted to ~ marble.* **imi·ta·tor** /-tə(r)/ *n*

imi·ta·tion /ˌɪmɪ'teɪʃn/ *n* 1 [U] imitating: *I~ is the sincerest form of flattery. He sets us a good example for ~. She was pirouetting in ~ of her teacher.* 2 (attrib) not real: *~ leather/jewellery.* 3 [C] sth made or done in ~: *~s of the cries of birds and animals. Beware of ~s.*

imi·tat·ive /'ɪmɪtətɪv US: -teɪtɪv/ *adj* following the model or example of: *the ~ arts,* painting and sculpture; *~ words,* eg *buzz, plop,* the sound of the word being considered similar to the sound it represents; *as ~ as a monkey.*

im·macu·late /ɪ'mækjʊlət/ *adj* 1 pure; faultless: *~ conduct.* *the I~ Conception,* (RC church) teaching that the Virgin Mary was free of Original Sin. 2 perfectly clean; without a flaw; right in every detail: *an ~ suit/record. ~·ly adv: ~ly dressed.*

im·ma·nent /'ɪmənənt/ *adj* *~ (in),* (of qualities) present; inherent; (of God) permanently pervading the universe. **im·ma·nence** /-əns/ *n*

im·ma·terial /ˌɪmə'tɪərɪəl/ *adj* 1 *~ (to),* unimportant: *~ objections. That's quite ~ to me.* 2 not having physical substance: *as ~ as a ghost.*

im·ma·ture /,ımə'tjʊə(r) *US:* -'tʊər/ *adj* not yet fully developed: *an ~ girl; the ~ minds of young children.* **im·ma·tur·ity** /,ımə'tjʊərətɪ *US:* -'tʊər-/ *n* [U].

im·measur·able /ı'meʒərəbl/ *adj* that cannot be measured.

im·medi·ate /ı'miːdıət/ *adj* **1** (of time or space) without anything coming between; nearest: *two objects in ~ contact; the ~ heir to the throne,* the next in succession, not a remote heir; *my ~ neighbours; ~ information,* first-hand or direct, not second-hand. **2** occurring, done, at once: *an ~ answer; take ~ action.* **im·medi·acy** /-əsɪ/ *n* [U] being ~. **~·ly** *adv* **1** at once; without delay. **2** directly or closely. □ *conj* as soon as: *You may leave ~ly he comes.*

im·mem·or·ial /,ımə'mɔːrɪəl/ *adj* going back beyond the reach of memory: *the ~ privileges of the House of Commons. from time ~,* for a very long time back.

im·mense /ı'mens/ *adj* very large. **~·ly** *adv* in an ~ degree; (colloq) very much: *They enjoyed themselves ~ly.* **im·men·sity** /ı'mensətɪ/ *n* [U] great size; (*pl;* -ties) things that are ~.

im·merse /ı'mɜːs/ *vt* [VP6A,14] ~ *(in),* **1** put under the surface of (water or other liquid): *~ one's head in the water.* **2** absorb, involve deeply: *be ~d in a book/thought/work/one's business.* **im·mer·sion** /ı'mɜːʃn *US:* -ʒn/ *n* immersing or being ~d; (esp) baptism by putting the whole body into water. **im-'mersion heater,** electric water-heater (usu one that is fixed in a hot-water tank).

im·mi·grate /'ımıgreıt/ *vi* [VP2A,3A] ~ *(to/into),* come as a settler (to/into another country), not as a tourist or visitor. **im·mi·grant** /'ımıgrənt/ *n* person who ~s: *European immigrants in Australia.* **im·mi·gra·tion** /,ımı'greıʃn/ *n* [U] immigrating; [C] instance of this: *the numerous immigrations into the US.*

im·mi·nent /'ımınənt/ *adj* (of events, esp dangers) likely to come or happen soon: *A storm is ~. He was faced with ~ death.* **~·ly** *adv* **im·mi·nence** /-əns/ *n* [U] being ~.

im·mo·bile /ı'məʊbaıl *US:* -bl/ *adj* not able to move or be moved; motionless. **im·mo·bi·lize** /ı'məʊbəlaız/ *vt* [VP6A] make ~; render armed forces, vehicles, etc incapable of being moved; take capital, specie out of circulation. **im·mo·bil·iz·ation** /ı,məʊbəlaı'zeıʃn *US:* -lı'z-/ *n* **im·mo·bil·ity** /,ımə'bılətɪ/ *n* [U] being ~.

im·mod·er·ate /ı'mɒdərət/ *adj* excessive; extreme: *~ eating and drinking.* **~·ly** *adv*

im·mod·est /ı'mɒdıst/ *adj* **1** lacking in modesty; indecent or indelicate: *an ~ dress; ~ behaviour.* **2** impudent: *~ boasts.* **~·ly** *adv* **~y** *n* [U] ~ behaviour; boldness; [C] (*pl* -ties) ~ act or remark.

im·mo·late /'ıməleıt/ *vt* [VP6A,14] ~ *(to),* (formal) kill as an offering; sacrifice (one thing *to* another). **im·mo·la·tion** /,ımə'leıʃn/ *n* [U] immolating or being ~d; [C] instance of this.

im·moral /ı'mɒrəl *US:* ı'mɔːrəl/ *adj* contrary to morality; wicked and evil: *~ conduct. You ~ swindler!* **~·ly** /-rəlı/ *adv* **~·ity** /,ımə'rælətɪ/ *n* [U] ~ conduct: *a life of ~ity;* [C] (*pl* -ties) ~ act.

im·mor·tal /ı'mɔːtl/ *adj* living for ever: *the ~ gods/soul;* never forgotten: *~ poetry/music; ~ fame.* □ *n* ~ being. **the ~s,** the gods of ancient Greece and Rome. **~·ity** /,ımɔː'tælətɪ/ *n* [U] endless life or fame. **~·ize** /ı'mɔːtəlaız/ *vt* [VP6A] give

endless life or fame to.

im·mov·able /ı'muːvəbl/ *adj* **1** that cannot be moved: *~ property,* eg buildings, land. **2** steadfast: *~ in purpose.* **im·mov·ably** /-əblı/ *adv*

im·mune /ı'mjuːn/ *adj* ~ *(from/against/to),* free, secure: *~ from smallpox as the result of vaccination; ~ to/against poison/disease/infection/ criticism/attack.* **im·mun·ity** /ı'mjuːnətɪ/ *n* [U] safety, security (*from* disease, etc); exemption (*from* taxation, etc): *diplomatic immunity.* **im·mu·nize** /'ımjʊnaız/ *vt* [VP6A,14] ~ *(against),* make ~ *(against).* **im·mu·niz·ation** /,ımjʊnaı'zeıʃn *US:* -nı'z-/ *n* [U]. **im·mu·nology** /,ımjʊ'nɒlədʒɪ/ *n* [U] study of resistance to infection.

im·mure /ı'mjʊə(r)/ *vt* [VP6A] (formal) imprison; shut (oneself) up: *~d in a windowless prison cell; ~ oneself in one's study to work undisturbed.*

im·mut·able /ı'mjuːtəbl/ *adj* (formal) that cannot be changed. **im·mut·ably** /-əblı/ *adv* **im·muta·bil·ity** /ı,mjuːtə'bılətɪ/ *n*

imp /ımp/ *n* child of the devil; little devil; (playfully) mischievous child.

im·pact /'ımpækt/ *n* ~ *(on),* **1** [C] collision. **2** [U] force exerted by one object when striking against another: *The car body collapses on ~,* when it collides with sth. **3** strong impression or effect: *the ~ of new ideas on discontented students.* □ *vt* /ım'pækt/ pack, drive or wedge firmly together: *an ~ed tooth,* not able to grow out of the jawbone.

im·pair /ım'peə(r)/ *vt* [VP6A] weaken; damage: *~ one's health by overwork.* **~·ment** *n*

im·pala /ım'pɑːlə/ *n* (kind of) African antelope.

im·pale /ım'peıl/ *vt* [VP6A,15A] pierce through, pin down, with a sharp-pointed stake, spear, etc. **~·ment** *n*

im·pal·pable /ım'pælpəbl/ *adj* that cannot be touched or felt; not easily grasped by the mind.

im·panel /ım'pænl/ = empanel.

im·part /ım'pɑːt/ *vt* [VP6A,14] ~ *(to),* (formal) give, pass on, a share of sth, a quality, a secret, news, etc: *I have nothing of interest to ~ to you.*

im·par·tial /ım'pɑːʃl/ *adj* fair (in giving judgements, etc); not favouring one more than another. **~·ly** *adv* **im·par·tial·ity** /,ım,pɑːʃɪ'ælətɪ/ *n* [U] the quality of being ~.

im·pass·able /ım'pɑːsəbl *US:* -'pæs-/ *adj* impossible to travel through or on: *Country roads/Alpine passes ~ in winter.*

im·passe /'æmpɑːs *US:* 'ımpæs/ *n* blind alley; place, position, from which there is no way out; deadlock.

im·pas·sioned /ım'pæʃnd/ *adj* full of, showing, deep feeling: *an ~ speech.*

im·pass·ive /ım'pæsɪv/ *adj* showing no sign of feeling; unmoved. **~·ly** *adv* **~·ness, im·pass·iv·ity** /,ımpæ'sıvətɪ/ *nn*

im·pa·tient /ım'peıʃnt/ *adj* **1** ~ *(at sth/with sb),* not patient: *~ at the delay; ~ with a tired child. ~ of sth,* (formal) intolerant of it. **2** ~ *(for sth/to do sth),* eager: *~ for a journey to start; ~ to start a journey. The audience are growing ~.* **~·ly** *adv.* **im·pa·tience** /ım'peıʃns/ *n* [U].

im·peach /ım'piːtʃ/ *vt* **1** [VP6A] (formal) question, raise doubts about (sb's character, etc): *Do you ~ my motives,* suggest that they are dishonourable? **2** [VP14] ~ *sb for/of/with sth; ~ sb for doing sth,* (legal) accuse sb of wrongdoing; (esp) accuse (sb) of a crime against the State: *~ a judge for taking bribes; ~ sb of a crime.* **~·ment** *n* [U] ~ing or being ~ed; [C] instance of this.

im·pec·cable /ɪmˈpekəbl/ adj (formal) faultless; incapable of doing wrong: an ~ character/record.

im·pe·cuni·ous /ˌɪmpɪˈkjuːnɪəs/ adj (formal) having little or no money.

im·pede /ɪmˈpiːd/ vt [VP6A] get in the way of; hinder: What ~s your making an early start?

im·pedi·ment /ɪmˈpedɪmənt/ n [C] sth that hinders, esp a defect in speech, eg a stammer. **im·pedi·menta** /ɪmˌpedɪˈmentə/ n pl baggage (esp of an army).

im·pel /ɪmˈpel/ vt (-ll-) [VP17,14] ~ (to), drive, force, urge: He said he had been ~led to crime by poverty. The President's speech ~led the nation to greater efforts. ~·ler n rotor or rotor blade (of a jet engine).

im·pend /ɪmˈpend/ vi (chiefly in pres part) (formal) be imminent; be about to come or happen: her ~ing arrival; the ~ing storm; the danger ~ing over us.

im·pen·etrable /ɪmˈpenɪtrəbl/ adj ~ (to), that cannot be penetrated: ~ forests and swamps; dig down to ~ rock; ~ darkness; men who are ~ to reason.

im·peni·tent /ɪmˈpenɪtənt/ adj (formal) not penitent. ~·ly adv im·peni·tence /-əns/ n

im·pera·tive /ɪmˈperətɪv/ adj **1** urgent; essential; needing immediate attention: Is it really ~ for them to have such a large army? Is it ~ that they should have/for them to have six cars? **2** not to be disobeyed; done, given with, authority: The duke's orders were ~. 'Go at once!', he said, with an ~ gesture. **3** (gram) (also n) (of the) form of a verb or a sentence expressing a command: the ~ mood. ~·ly adv

im·per·cep·tible /ˌɪmpəˈseptəbl/ adj that cannot be perceived; very slight or gradual. **im·per·cep·tibly** /-əblɪ/ adv

im·per·fect /ɪmˈpɜːfɪkt/ adj **1** not perfect or complete. **2** ~ tense, (gram) that denotes action in progress but not completed (also called progressive or continuous tense), as in eg 'I am/was/have been/will be speaking.' □ n ~ tense. ~·ly adv **im·per·fec·tion** /ˌɪmpəˈfekʃn/ n [U] state of being ~; [C] fault.

im·perial /ɪmˈpɪərɪəl/ adj **1** of an empire or its ruler(s): ~ trade; His I~ Majesty. **2** majestic; august; magnificent: with ~ generosity. **3** (of weights and measures) used by law in the United Kingdom: an ~ pint/gallon. □ n small, pointed beard grown beneath the lower lip. ~·ly /-rɪəlɪ/ adv **im·peri·al·ism** /ɪmˈpɪərɪəlɪzəm/ n belief in the value of colonies; policy of extending a country's empire and influence. **im·per·ial·ist** /-ɪst/ n supporter of, believer in, ~. **im·per·ial·is·tic** /ɪmˌpɪərɪəˈlɪstɪk/ adj of ~: imperialistic views.

im·peril /ɪmˈperəl/ vt (-ll-, US also -l-) [VP6A] (liter) put or bring into danger.

im·peri·ous /ɪmˈpɪərɪəs/ adj (formal) **1** commanding; haughty; arrogant: ~ gestures/looks. **2** urgent; imperative. ~·ly adv ~·ness n

im·per·ish·able /ɪmˈperɪʃəbl/ adj (formal) that cannot perish; that will never pass away: ~ fame/glory.

im·per·ma·nent /ɪmˈpɜːmənənt/ adj (formal) not permanent. **im·per·ma·nence** /-əns/ n

im·per·me·able /ɪmˈpɜːmɪəbl/ adj ~ (to), (formal) that cannot be permeated (esp by fluids); impervious.

im·per·sonal /ˌɪmˈpɜːsənl/ adj **1** not influenced by personal feeling; not referring to any particular person: ~ remarks; an ~ discussion. ~ pronoun, the pronouns one[4] and you(2). **2** having no existence as a person: ~ forces, eg those of nature. **3** (of verbs) used after 'it' to make general statements such as 'It is raining/freezing'. ~·ly /-ənəlɪ/ adv

im·per·son·ate /ɪmˈpɜːsəneɪt/ vt [VP6A] **1** act the part of (in a play, etc); pretend to be (another person). **2** personify. **im·per·son·ation** /ɪmˌpɜːsəˈneɪʃn/ n **1** [U] impersonating or being ~d. **2** [C] instance of this: He gave some clever impersonations of well-known men. **im·per·son·ator** /-neɪtə(r)/ n person who ~s.

im·per·ti·nent /ɪmˈpɜːtɪnənt/ adj **1** not showing proper respect; impudent; saucy: ~ remarks; an ~ boy. **2** not pertinent; not pertaining to the matter in hand. ~·ly adv **im·per·ti·nence** /-əns/ n [U] being ~; [C] ~ act or remark.

im·per·turb·able /ˌɪmpəˈtɜːbəbl/ adj (formal) not capable of being excited; calm. **im·per·turb·abil·ity** /ˌɪmpəˌtɜːbəˈbɪlətɪ/ n [U].

im·per·vi·ous /ɪmˈpɜːvɪəs/ adj ~ (to), **1** (of materials) not allowing (water, etc) to pass through: Rubber boots are ~ to water. **2** (fig) not moved or influenced by: ~ to criticism/argument.

im·pe·tigo /ˌɪmpɪˈtaɪgəʊ/ n [U] contagious skin disease.

im·petu·ous /ɪmˈpetʃʊəs/ adj moving quickly or violently; acting, inclined to act, on impulse, energetically but with insufficient thought or care; done or said hastily: Children are usually more ~ than old people. Your ~ remarks will get you into trouble. ~·ly adv **im·petu·os·ity** /ɪmˌpetʃʊˈɒsətɪ/ n [U] quality of being ~; [C] (pl -ties) ~ act, remark, etc.

im·pe·tus /ˈɪmpɪtəs/ n (pl ~es /-sɪz/) **1** [U] force with which a body moves. **2** [C] impulse; driving force: The treaty will give an ~ to trade between the two countries.

im·pi·ety /ɪmˈpaɪətɪ/ n (formal) **1** [U] lack of reverence or dutifulness. **2** [C] (pl -ties) act, remark, etc that shows lack of reverence or dutifulness.

im·pinge /ɪmˈpɪndʒ/ vi [VP3A] ~ on/upon, (formal) make an impact. ~·ment n

im·pi·ous /ˈɪmpɪəs/ adj (formal) not pious. ~·ly adv

imp·ish /ˈɪmpɪʃ/ adj of or like an imp; mischievous. ~·ly adv ~·ness n

im·plac·able /ɪmˈplækəbl/ adj (formal) that cannot be appeased; relentless: an ~ enemy; ~ hatred/love.

im·plant /ɪmˈplɑːnt US: -ˈplænt/ vt [VP6A,14] ~ in, fix or put ideas, feelings, etc in: deeply ~ed hatred; ~ sound principles in the minds of children.

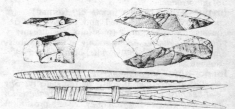

primitive stone implements

im·ple·ment[1] /ˈɪmplɪmənt/ n tool or instrument for working with: farm ~s; stone and bronze ~s made by primitive man. ⇨ the illus at tool.

im·ple·ment² /'ɪmplɪment/ vt [VP6A] carry an undertaking, agreement, promise into effect: ~ a scheme. **im·ple·men·ta·tion** /ˌɪmplɪmen'teɪʃn/ n

im·pli·cate /'ɪmplɪkeɪt/ vt [VP6A,14] ~ (in), (formal) show that (sb) has a share (in a crime, etc): ~ officials in a bribery scandal. ⇨ involve.

im·pli·ca·tion /ˌɪmplɪ'keɪʃn/ n (formal) 1 [U] implicating or being implicated (in a crime, etc). 2 [C] what is implied; sth hinted at or suggested, but not expressed: What are the ~s of this statement? What is implied by it?

im·pli·cit /ɪm'plɪsɪt/ adj (formal) 1 ~ (in), implied though not plainly expressed: an ~ threat; ~ in the contract. ⇨ explicit. 2 unquestioning: ~ belief. ~·ly adv

im·plore /ɪm'plɔː(r)/ vt [VP6A,17,14] ~ (for), request earnestly: ~ a judge for mercy; ~ a friend to help one; an imploring glance. **im·plor·ing·ly** adv

im·plo·sion /ɪm'pləʊʒn/ n [U,C] bursting inward, collapse, of a vessel, eg an electric light bulb, from external pressure. ⇨ explosion.

im·ply /ɪm'plaɪ/ vt (pt,pp -plied) [VP6A,9] give or make a suggestion (that); involve the truth (of sth not definitely stated): an implied rebuke. Silence sometimes implies consent, failure to say 'No' may be taken to mean 'Yes'. Are you ~ing that I am not telling the truth?

im·po·lite /ˌɪmpə'laɪt/ adj not polite. ~·ly adv ~·ness n

im·poli·tic /ɪm'pɒlətɪk/ adj (formal) not politic; not expedient.

im·pon·der·able /ɪm'pɒndərəbl/ adj 1 (phys) that cannot be weighed or measured. 2 of which the effect cannot be estimated. □ n ~ thing; (esp pl) qualities, emotions, etc of which the effect cannot be estimated.

im·port /ɪm'pɔːt/ vt 1 [VP6A,14] ~ (from) (into), bring in, introduce, esp goods from a foreign country: ~ wool from Australia. 2 [VP6A,9] (formal) mean; signify; make known (that): What does this ~? What is its significance? □ n /'ɪmpɔːt/ 1 (usu pl) goods ~ed: ~s of raw cotton; food ~s. 2 [U] act of ~ing goods. 3 [U] what is implied; meaning: What is the ~ of his statement? 4 [U] (formal) importance: questions of great ~. ~·er n person (usu a merchant) who ~s goods. **im·port·ation** /ˌɪmpɔː'teɪʃn/ n [U] act of ~ing (goods); [C] sth ~ed.

im·port·ant /ɪm'pɔːtnt/ adj 1 of great influence; to be treated seriously; having a great effect: ~ decisions/statements, etc. 2 (of a person) having a position of authority. ~·ly adv **im·port·ance** /-tns/ n [U] being ~: The matter is of great/no/not much/little importance to us. He spoke with an air of importance.

im·por·tu·nate /ɪm'pɔːtʃʊnət/ adj (formal) 1 (of persons) making repeated and inconvenient requests: an ~ beggar. 2 (of affairs, etc) urgent: ~ demands/claims. ~·ly adv **im·por·tun·ity** /ˌɪmpə'tjuːnətɪ US: -'tuː-/ n [U] being ~(1); (pl; -ties) instance of this.

im·por·tune /ˌɪmpə'tjuːn/ vt [VP6A,9,14,17] ~ (for), (formal) 1 beg urgently and repeatedly: She ~d her husband for more money/with requests for money/to give her more money. 2 (of a prostitute) solicit(3).

im·pose /ɪm'pəʊz/ vt,vi 1 [VP14] ~ on, lay or place a tax, duty, etc on: New taxes were ~d on wines and spirits. I must perform the task that has been ~d upon me. 2 [VP14] ~ on sb, force (sth,

oneself, one's company) on sb: Don't ~ yourself/your company on people who don't want you. 3 [VP3A] ~ upon sth, take advantage of: ~ upon sb's good nature. **im·pos·ing** adj making a strong impression because of size, character, appearance: an imposing old lady; an imposing display of knowledge. **im·pos·ing·ly** adv

im·po·si·tion /ˌɪmpə'zɪʃn/ n 1 [U] the act of imposing(1): Everyone grumbled at the ~ of new taxes. 2 [C] sth imposed, eg a tax, burden, punishment, unwanted guest.

im·poss·ible /ɪm'pɒsəbl/ adj 1 not possible: an ~ scheme/story. the ~, that which is ~: Don't ask me to do the ~. 2 that cannot be endured: It's an ~ situation! He's an ~ person. **im·poss·ibly** /-əblɪ/ adv **im·possi·bil·ity** /ɪmˌpɒsə'bɪlətɪ/ n [U] state of being ~; [C] (pl -ties) sth that is ~.

im·pos·tor /ɪm'pɒstə(r)/ n person pretending to be sb he is not.

im·pos·ture /ɪm'pɒstʃə(r)/ n [C] act of deception by an impostor; [U] fraudulent deception: make a living by lying and ~.

im·po·tent /'ɪmpətənt/ adj lacking sufficient strength (to do sth); unable to act; (of males) wholly lacking in sexual power. ~·ly adv **im·po·tence** /-əns/ n [U] state of being ~: We have reduced the enemy to impotence, made them quite powerless.

im·pound /ɪm'paʊnd/ vt [VP6A] 1 take possession of by law or by authority. 2 (in former times) shut up (cattle that had strayed) in a pound. ⇨ pound².

im·pov·er·ish /ɪm'pɒvərɪʃ/ vt [VP6A] (formal) cause to become poor; take away good qualities: ~ed by doctors' bills; ~ed soil, eg when crops are grown year after year without the use of fertilizers; ~ed rubber, rubber that has lost its elasticity. ~·ment n

im·prac·ti·cable /ɪm'præktɪkəbl/ adj 1 that cannot be put into practice: an ~ scheme. 2 (of routes) impassable; that cannot be used. **im·prac·ti·cably** /-əblɪ/ adv **im·prac·ti·ca·bil·ity** /ɪmˌpræktɪkə-'bɪlətɪ/, ~·ness nn

im·prac·ti·cal /ɪm'præktɪkl/ adj not practical.

im·pre·cate /'ɪmprɪkeɪt/ vt [VP14] ~ on/upon sb, (formal) invoke, call down (evil on sb). **im·pre·ca·tion** /ˌɪmprɪ'keɪʃn/ n [C] curse.

im·preg·nable /ɪm'pregnəbl/ adj that cannot be overcome or taken by force; able to resist all attacks: an ~ fortress; ~ defences/arguments. **im·preg·nably** /-əblɪ/ adv **im·preg·na·bil·ity** /ɪmˌpregnə'bɪlətɪ/ n

im·preg·nate /'ɪmpregneɪt US: ɪm'preg-/ vt [VP6A,14] ~ (with), 1 make pregnant; fertilize, eg an ovum. 2 fill, saturate: water ~d with salt. 3 imbue, fill with feelings, moral qualities, etc.

im·pre·sario /ˌɪmprɪ'sɑːrɪəʊ/ n (pl ~s /-z/) manager of an operatic or concert company; sponsor of commercial public entertainment.

im·press /ɪm'pres/ vt [VP6A,14] ~ (on/upon)/(with), 1 press (one thing on or with another); make (a mark, etc) by doing this: ~ wax with a seal; ~ a seal on wax; ~ a figure/design on sth. 2 have a strong influence on; fix deeply (on the mind, memory): His words are strongly ~ed on my memory. The book did not ~ me at all, I did not think it good, useful, etc. I ~ed on him the importance of his work. He ~ed me unfavourably, I formed an unfavourable opinion of him. □ n /'ɪmpres/ mark made by stamping a seal, etc on sth.

im·pres·sion /ɪm'preʃn/ n [C] 1 mark made by

pressing: *the ~ of a seal on wax.* **2** print (of an engraving, etc). **3** (product of) any one printing operation: *a first ~ of 5000 copies. Forty ~s* (= reprints without resetting; ⇨ **edition**) *of this book have been sold so far.* **4** effect produced on the mind or feelings: *It's my ~ that...; The speech made a strong ~ on the House. I'm surprised you got an unfavourable ~ of him. What were your first ~s of London? First ~s are often misleading.* **5** (vague or uncertain) idea, belief: *It's my ~ that he doesn't want to come.* **be under the ~ that...,** have a vague idea, think, that... **~·ism** /-ɪzəm/ *n* [U] method of painting or writing so as to give the general effect without elaborate detail. **~·ist** /-ɪst/ *n* person who uses this method. **~·is·tic** /ɪmˌpreʃə'nɪstɪk/ *adj* **1** of, characteristic of, ~ism or ~ists. **2** giving only a general ~.

im·pres·sion·able /ɪm'preʃənəbl/ *adj* easily influenced: *children who are at the ~ age,* adolescent; *an ~ young lady,* eg one who easily falls in love.

im·pres·sive /ɪm'presɪv/ *adj* making a deep impression on the mind and feelings: *an ~ ceremony.* **~·ly** *adv* **~·ness** *n*

im·pri·ma·tur /ˌɪmprɪ'meɪtə(r)/ *n* (RC Church) official permission to print; (fig) sanction, approval.

im·print /ɪm'prɪnt/ *vt* [VP14] **~ with/on,** print; stamp: *~ a letter with a postmark/a postmark on a letter; ideas ~ed on the mind.* □ *n* /'ɪmprɪnt/ [C] that which is ~ed: *the ~ of a foot* (= footprint); *the ~ of suffering on a person's face; a publisher's/printer's ~,* his name, address, etc on the title-page or at the end of the book.

im·prison /ɪm'prɪzn/ *vt* [VP6A] put or keep in prison. **~·ment** *n* [U] ~ing or being ~ed: *sentenced to one year's ~ment.*

im·prob·able /ɪm'prɒbəbl/ *adj* not likely to be true or to happen: *an ~ story/result. Rain is ~.* **im·prob·ably** /-əblɪ/ *adv* **im·prob·abil·ity** /ɪmˌprɒbə'bɪlətɪ/ *n* [U] being ~; [C] (*pl* -ties) sth which is or seems ~: *Don't worry about such improbabilities as floods and earthquakes.*

im·promptu /ɪm'prɒmptjuː US: -tuː/ *adj, adv* without preparation: *an ~ speech; speak ~.* □ *n* musical composition that seems to have been improvised.

im·proper /ɪm'prɒpə(r)/ *adj* **1** not suited for the purpose, situation, circumstances, etc: *Laughing and joking are ~ at a funeral.* **2** incorrect: *~ diagnosis of disease.* **3** indecent: *~ stories.* **~·ly** *adv*

im·pro·pri·ety /ˌɪmprə'praɪətɪ/ *n* (formal) [U] incorrectness; unsuitability; [C] (*pl* -ties) improper act, remark, etc.

im·prove /ɪm'pruːv/ *vt, vi* **1** [VP6A,2A] make or become better: *This is not good enough; I want to ~ it. He came back from his holiday with greatly ~d health. He is improving in health. His health is improving.* [VP3A] **~ on/upon,** produce sth better than: *Your complexion is wonderful; don't try to ~ upon nature.* **2** [VP6A] make good use of; turn to account: *~ the occasion.* **~·ment** *n* **1** [U] improving or being ~d: *There is need for ~ment in your handwriting. Little/no/not much ~ment seemed possible.* **2** [C] sth which ~s, which adds to beauty, usefulness, value, etc: *I have noticed a number of ~ments in the town since I was here six years ago. We all hope for an ~ment in the weather. This is an ~ment upon your first attempt.*

im·provi·dent /ɪm'prɒvɪdənt/ *adj* (formal) wasteful; not looking to future needs. **~·ly** *adv* **im·pro·vi·dence** /-əns/ *n* [U].

im·pro·vise /'ɪmprəvaɪz/ *vt, vi* [VP6A,2A] **1** compose music while playing, compose verse while reciting, etc: *If an actor forgets his words, he has to ~. The pianist ~d an accompaniment to the song.* **2** provide, make or do sth quickly, in time of need, using whatever happens to be available: *an ~d meal for unexpected guests; an ~d bed,* eg one made up on a couch. **im·pro·vis·ation** /ˌɪmprəvaɪ'zeɪʃn US: -vɪ'z-/ *n* [U,C].

im·prud·ent /ɪm'pruːdnt/ *adj* rash; indiscreet: *Isn't it ~ of you to marry while your salary is so low?* **~·ly** *adv* **im·prud·ence** /-ns/ *n* [U] being ~; [C] ~ act, remark, etc.

im·pu·dent /'ɪmpjʊdənt/ *adj* shamelessly rude; rudely disrespectful: *He was ~ enough to call me a fool.* **~·ly** *adv* **im·pu·dence** /-əns/ *n* [U] being ~; ~ words and actions: *None of your impudence! He had the impudence to thumb his nose at me.*

im·pugn /ɪm'pjuːn/ *vt* [VP6A] (formal) challenge, express doubt about (a statement, act, quality, etc).

im·pulse /'ɪmpʌls/ *n* **1** [C] push or thrust; impetus: *give an ~ to trade/education.* **2** [C] sudden inclination to act without thought about the consequences: *seized with an ~ to do sth; feel an irresistible ~ to jump out of a window,* eg during a fit of insanity. **3** [U] state of mind in which such inclinations occur; tendency to act without reflection: *a man of ~. on (an) ~,* without reflection or planning: *phone sb on ~.* **'~-buy** *vt, vi* buy on ~. **4** (science) sudden, brief force.

im·pul·sion /ɪm'pʌlʃn/ *n* [U] impelling; driving or being driven forward; [C] impetus; mental impulse.

im·pul·sive /ɪm'pʌlsɪv/ *adj* **1** (of persons, their conduct) acting on impulse; resulting from impulse: *a girl with an ~ nature.* **2** (of a force) tending to impel. **~·ly** *adv* **~·ness** *n*

im·pun·ity /ɪm'pjuːnətɪ/ *n* [U] freedom from punishment. **with ~,** without risk of injury or punishment.

im·pure /ɪm'pjʊə(r)/ *adj* not pure: *the ~ air of towns; ~ milk; ~ motives.* **im·pur·ity** /-ətɪ/ *n* [U] state of being ~; [C] (*pl* -ties) ~ thing: *impurities in food.*

im·pute /ɪm'pjuːt/ *vt* [VP14] **~ to,** (formal) consider as the act, quality, or outcome of: *They ~d the accident to the driver's carelessness. He was innocent of the crime ~d to him.* **im·pu·ta·tion** /ˌɪmpjʊ'teɪʃn/ *n* [U] act of imputing; [C] accusation or suggestion of wrong-doing, etc: *imputations on a person's character.*

in¹ /ɪn/ *adv part* (contrasted with *out*) **1** (used with many *vv*, in obvious meanings, as *come in* (= enter) and meanings that are not obvious, as *give in* (= surrender); ⇨ the *v* entries for these) **2** *be in,* **(a)** at home: *Is there anyone in? My husband won't be in until six o'clock.* **(b)** arrive: *Is the train in yet, Has it arrived?* **(c)** (of crops) harvested; brought in from the fields: *The wheat crop/the harvest is safely in.* **(d)** in season; obtainable: *Strawberries are in now. When will oysters be in?* **(e)** in fashion: *Long skirts are in again.* **(f)** elected; in power; in office: *The Democrats are in. The Liberal candidate is in,* has been elected. **(g)** burning: *Is the fire still in?* **(h)** (cricket, baseball) batting: *Which side is in? He was bowled before he had been in* (= at the wicket) *five minutes.* **3** *be in for sth,* **(a)** likely to have or experience (esp sth unpleasant): *I'm afraid we're in for a storm. You're in for an unpleasant surprise.* **(b)** committed to; having agreed to take part in: *I'm in for the competition*, shall be a competitor. *Are you in for the 1000 metres race?* **have it in for sb,** be wanting to take revenge on him. **be in on sth,** (colloq) participate in; have a share in: *I'd like to be in on this scheme.* **day in, day out; week in, week out; year in, year out,** day after day, week after week, etc in a monotonous way. *in and out,* now in and now out: *He's always in and out of hospital,* is frequently ill and in hospital. **be (well) in with sb,** be on good terms with him (and likely to benefit from his friendship). **4** (preceding a *n*): *an 'in-patient,* one who lives in a hospital while receiving treatment (contrasted with '*out-patient*).

in² /ɪn/ *prep* (For the use of *in* with many *nn* and *vv*, ⇨ the *n* and *v* entries, eg *in print, in memory of, fail in an examination*). **1** (of place; ⇨ at): *the highest mountain in the world; in Africa; in the east of Asia; in Denmark; in the provinces; in Kent; in London; the village in which he was born; the only shop in the village; islands in the Pacific Ocean; sailing in British waters,* ie on the seas round Britain; *in every quarter of the town; children playing in the street; not a cloud in the sky; swimming in the lake; standing in the corner of the room.* Cf *the house at the corner; working in the fields/in coal-mines; a picnic in the woods; a holiday in the country/in the mountains.* Cf *at the seaside; a light in the distance; in the background/ foreground; lying in bed.* Cf *sitting on the bed; sitting in an armchair.* Cf *on a chair without arms; in school/church/prison; a ride in a motor-car. He was wounded in the leg. The key is in the lock. There were plants in the window,* ie *on the window-sill,* framed by the window. *What would you do in my place,* if you were situated as I am situated? *I read about it in the newspapers. He had a stick in his hand and a cigar in his mouth. You will find the verse in the second chapter of Genesis.* **2** (of direction): *in this/that direction; in all directions.* **3** (indicating direction of motion or activity) into: *He dipped his pen in the ink. He put his hands in his pockets. Cut the apple in two,* into halves. *Cut/break it in two. Throw it in the fire. They fell in love.* **4** (of time when): *in the 20th c; in 1970; in the reign of Queen Anne; in spring/summer, etc; in my absence; in his youth; in old age; still in her teens; in these/those days; in the morning/ afternoon/evening.* Cf *on Monday morning; in the daytime; at ten o'clock in the night.* Cf *at night; in (the) future; in the past; in the end,* finally; *in time of war; in the hour of victory/death, etc. He has met many famous men in his time,* during his lifetime. *She was a famous beauty in her day,* during her best years. *The school was quite small in my time,* when I was there. **5** (of time) in the course of; within the space of: *I shall be back in a short time/in a few days/in a week's time, etc. Can you finish the work in an hour? I'll be ready in a moment.* Cf also *in time.* **6** (indicating inclusion) *seven days in a week; four quarts in a gallon; a man in his thirties,* ie between 30 and 39 years of age; *in the early thirties of this century,* ie between 1930 and 1934 or 1935. *There is 10 per cent for service in the (hotel) bill. He has nothing of the hero in him,* Heroism is not among his characteristics. *He has in him the makings of a good soldier,* has qualities, abilities, etc that will help him to become a good soldier. **7** (indicating ratio): *a slope/ gradient of one in five. He paid his creditors 25p in* the pound. *Not one in ten of the boys could spell well.* **8** (of dress, etc): *dressed/clothed in rags; the man in the top hat; a prince in disguise; the woman in white,* wearing white clothes; *in uniform; in mourning; in brown shoes; in his shirt sleeves,* not wearing a jacket or coat; *a prisoner in irons.* **9** (indicating physical surroundings, circumstances, etc): *go out in the rain; sitting in the sun(shine); standing outside in the cold; sleep in the open; a temperature of 95°F in the shade; lose one's way in the dark; unable to work in this heat; go for a walk in the moonlight.* **10** (indicating state or condition): *in a troubled state; in good order; in poor health; in good repair; in a good humour; in a fever of excitement; in despair; in a rage; in tears; in a hurry; living in luxury; in poverty; in ruins; not in the mood for work; in debt; in love; in doubt; in wonder; in public; in secret; in fun/jest/joke; in earnest.* **11** (indicating form, shape, arrangement): *a novel in three parts; books packed in bundles of ten; men standing about in groups; children sitting in rows; wolves hunting in packs; words in alphabetical order; with her hair in curls/in ringlets; dancing in a ring; cloth hanging in folds.* **12** (indicating the method of expression, the medium, means, material, etc): *speaking/writing in English; a message in code; written in ink/pencil; (printed) in italic type; in two colours; in writing; in a few words; in round numbers,* eg 200000 for 197563; *talking in a loud voice; bound in leather; painted in oils; carved in oak; cast in bronze; a statue in marble; payment in cash/in kind.* **13** (indicating degree or extent): *in large/small quantities; in great numbers; in some measure; in part. The enemy appeared in great strength. in all,* as the total: *We were fifteen in all.* **14** (indicating identity): *You will always have a good friend in me,* I shall always befriend you. *We have lost a first-rate teacher in Jim,* Jim, who has left us, was a first-rate teacher. *The enemy lost 200 in killed and wounded,* 200 of them were killed or wounded. **15** (indicating relation, reference, respect): *in some/all respects; in every way; inferior in physique but superior in intellect; young in years but old in wisdom; weak in the head,* not intelligent; *deficient in courage; a country rich/poor in minerals; blind in the left eye; my equal in strength; ten feet in length/depth/ diameter, etc; wanting/lacking in judgement.* **16** (indicating occupation, activity, etc): *He's in the army/in insurance/in the motor business/in the Cabinet/in the Air Ministry. He's in politics,* is a politician. *He was killed in action,* while fighting in war. *How much time do you spend in reading?* **17** (used in numerous prepositional phrases of the pattern *in* + *n* + *prep,* ⇨ the *n* entries, eg): *in defence of; in exchange for; in justice to; in memory of; in touch with.* **18 in camera,** (legal) in private, in the judge's private room, not in open court; (colloq) secretly. *in that,* since, because: *The higher income tax is harmful in that it may discourage people from trying to earn more. in as/so far as,* in such measure as; to the extent that: *He is a Russian in so far as he was born in Russia, but he became a French citizen in 1920. in itself,* in its own nature; absolutely; considered apart from other things: *Card playing is not harmful in itself; it is only when combined with wild gambling that it may be harmful.*

in³ /ɪn/ *n* (only in) **the ins and (the) outs,** (a) political party in office and political party out of office. **(b)** the different parts; the details and complexities: *know all the ins and outs of a problem.*

-in /ɪn/ *suff* added to another word (usu a *v*) to indicate participation in a group activity, etc. ⇨ the *v* entries, eg *sit-in, teach-in.*

in·abil·ity /ˌɪnəˈbɪlətɪ/ *n* [U] ∼ *(to do sth),* being unable; lack of power or means.

in·ac·cess·ible /ˌɪnækˈsesəbl/ *adj* ∼ *(to),* (formal) not accessible. **in·ac·cessi·bil·ity** /ˌɪnækˌsesəˈbɪlətɪ/ *n* [U].

in·ac·cur·ate /ɪnˈækjərət/ *adj* not accurate. ∼**·ly** *adv* **in·ac·cur·acy** /-əsɪ/ *n* [U] being ∼; [C] (*pl*-cies) ∼ statement, etc.

in·ac·tion /ɪnˈækʃn/ *n* [U] doing nothing; lack of activity.

in·ac·tive /ɪnˈæktɪv/ *adj* not active. **in·ac·ti·vate** /ˌɪnˈæktɪveɪt/ *vt* make ∼: *inactivate a virus.* **in·ac·tiv·ity** /ˌɪnækˈtɪvətɪ/ *n* [U].

in·ad·equate /ɪnˈædɪkwət/ *adj* ∼ *(for sth/to do sth),* not adequate; insufficient. ∼**·ly** *adv* **in·ad·equacy** /ɪnˈædɪkwəsɪ/ *n* [U].

in·ad·miss·ible /ˌɪnədˈmɪsəbl/ *adj* that cannot be admitted or allowed: ∼ *evidence;* ∼ *in evidence.*

in·ad·ver·tent /ˌɪnədˈvɜːtənt/ *adj* (formal) not paying or showing proper attention; (of actions) done thoughtlessly or not on purpose. ∼**·ly** *adv* **in·ad·ver·tence** /-təns/ *n* [U] the quality of being ∼; [C] oversight or error which is the result of being ∼.

in·alien·able /ɪnˈeɪlɪənəbl/ *adj* (formal) (of rights, etc) that cannot be given away or taken away.

in·ane /ɪˈneɪn/ *adj* silly; senseless: *an ∼ remark.* ∼**·ly** *adv* **in·an·ity** /ɪˈnænətɪ/ *n* [U] being ∼; [C] (*pl*-ties) ∼ remark, act, etc.

in·ani·mate /ɪnˈænɪmət/ *adj* **1** lifeless: ∼ *rocks and stones.* **2** without animal life: ∼ *nature,* outside the animal world. **3** spiritless; dull: ∼ *conversation.*

in·ani·tion /ˌɪnəˈnɪʃn/ *n* [U] (formal) **1** emptiness. **2** extreme weakness from lack of food.

in·ap·pli·cable /ɪnˈæplɪkəbl/ *adj* ∼ *(to),* not applicable.

in·ap·preci·able /ˌɪnəˈpriːʃəbl/ *adj* not worth reckoning; too small or slight to be perceived: *an ∼ difference.*

in·ap·pro·pri·ate /ˌɪnəˈprəʊprɪət/ *adj* ∼ *to,* not appropriate or suitable.

in·apt /ɪnˈæpt/ *adj* unskilful; not bearing on the subject: ∼ *remarks.* **in·ap·ti·tude** /ɪnˈæptɪtjuːd *US:* -tuːd/ *n* [U] being ∼.

in·ar·ticu·late /ˌɪnɑːˈtɪkjʊlət/ *adj* **1** (of speech) not clear or distinct; not well joined together; (of a person) not speaking distinctly; not able to express himself clearly and fluently; not of the nature of speech: ∼ *rage/sounds/letters.* **2** not jointed: *an ∼ body,* eg a jelly-fish.

in·as·much as /ˌɪnəzˈmʌtʃ əz/ *adv* since; because.

in·at·ten·tion /ˌɪnəˈtenʃn/ *n* [U] lack of, failure to pay, attention. **in·at·ten·tive** /ˌɪnəˈtentɪv/ *adj* not attentive.

in·aud·ible /ɪnˈɔːdəbl/ *adj* that cannot be heard. **in·audi·bil·ity** /ɪnˌɔːdəˈbɪlətɪ/ *n* [U].

in·aug·ural /ɪˈnɔːgjʊrəl/ *adj* of or for an inauguration: *an ∼ lecture.* □ *n* ∼ address.

in·au·gur·ate /ɪˈnɔːgjʊreɪt/ *vt* [VP6A] **1** introduce a new official, professor, etc at a special ceremony: ∼ *a president.* **2** enter, with public formalities, upon (an undertaking); open an exhibition/a new public building with formalities. **3** be the beginning of: *The invention of the internal combustion engine ∼d a new era in travel.* **in·aug·ur·ation**

/ɪˌnɔːgjʊˈreɪʃn/ *n* [U,C] inaugurating or being ∼d: *the inauguration of the President of the US* (20 Jan).

in·aus·picious /ˌɪnɔːˈspɪʃəs/ *adj* not auspicious; not of good omen. ∼**·ly** *adv*

in·board /ˈɪnbɔːd/ *adj* within the hull of a ship: *an ∼ motor.* ⇨ outboard.

in·born /ˌɪnˈbɔːn/ *adj* (of a quality) possessed (by a person or animal) at birth; implanted by nature: *a boy with an ∼ love of mischief; an ∼ talent for art.*

in·bound /ˈɪnbaʊnd/ *adj* (of a ship) inward or homeward bound.

in·bred /ˌɪnˈbred/ *adj* **1** inborn; innate: ∼ *courtesy.* **2** bred for several or many generations from ancestors closely related. **in·breed·ing** /ˌɪnˈbriːdɪŋ/ *n* [U] breeding from closely related ancestors, stocks, etc.

in·built /ˌɪnˈbɪlt/ *adj* = built-in, ⇨ build¹(3).

in·cal·cu·lable /ɪnˈkælkjʊləbl/ *adj* **1** too great to be calculated: *This has done ∼ harm to our reputation.* **2** that cannot be reckoned beforehand. **3** (of a person, his character, etc) uncertain: *a lady of ∼ moods.*

in·can·descent /ˌɪnkænˈdesnt/ *adj* giving out, able to give out, light when heated: *an ∼ filament,* eg in an electric-light bulb. **in·can·descence** /-sns/ *n* [U] being or becoming ∼.

in·can·ta·tion /ˌɪnkænˈteɪʃn/ *n* [C,U] (the use of) (a form of) words used in magic; charm or spell.

in·capable /ɪnˈkeɪpəbl/ *adj* ∼ *(of),* not capable: ∼ *of telling a lie,* too honest to do so. **drunk and ∼,** helplessly drunk. **in·capa·bil·ity** /ɪnˌkeɪpəˈbɪlətɪ/ *n* [U].

in·ca·paci·tate /ˌɪnkəˈpæsɪteɪt/ *vt* [VP6A,14] ∼ *sb (for/from),* **1** make incapable or unfit: *His poor health ∼d him for work/from working.* **2** disqualify.

in·ca·pac·ity /ˌɪnkəˈpæsətɪ/ *n* [U] ∼ *(for sth/for doing sth/to do sth),* inability; powerlessness.

in·car·cer·ate /ɪnˈkɑːsəreɪt/ *vt* [VP6A] (formal) imprison. **in·car·cer·ation** /ɪnˌkɑːsəˈreɪʃn/ *n*

in·car·nate /ɪnˈkɑːneɪt/ *adj* **1** having a body; (esp) in human form: *That prison officer is a devil ∼/an ∼ fiend.* **2** (of an idea, ideal, etc) appearing in human form: *Liberty ∼.* □ *vt* /ˈɪnkɑːneɪt/ [VP6A] **1** make ∼. **2** put (an idea, etc) into a real or material form. **3** (of a person) be a living form of (a quality): *a wife who ∼s all the virtues.*

in·car·na·tion /ˌɪnkɑːˈneɪʃn/ *n* **1 the I∼,** the taking of bodily form by God in Jesus. **2** [C] person looked upon as a type of a quality: *She looked the ∼ of every desirable quality.*

in·cau·tious /ɪnˈkɔːʃəs/ *adj* not cautious; rash. ∼**·ly** *adv*

in·cen·di·ary /ɪnˈsendɪərɪ *US:* -dɪerɪ/ *n* (*pl*-ries), *adj* **1** (person) setting fire to property unlawfully and with an evil purpose; (person) tending to stir up violence: *an ∼ speech/newspaper article.* **2** (bomb) causing fire. **in·cen·di·ar·ism** /ɪnˈsendɪərɪzəm/ *n* [U].

in·cense¹ /ˈɪnsens/ *n* [U] (smoke of a) substance producing a sweet smell when burning.

in·cense² /ɪnˈsens/ *vt* [VP6A] make angry: ∼*d by sb's conduct;* ∼*d at sb's remarks.*

in·cen·tive /ɪnˈsentɪv/ *n* ∼ *(to sth/to do sth/to doing sth),* [C,U] that which incites, rouses or encourages a person: *He hasn't much ∼/many ∼s to work hard/to hard work.*

in·cep·tion /ɪnˈsepʃn/ *n* (formal) start.

in·cer·ti·tude /ɪnˈsɜːtɪtjuːd *US:* -tuːd/ *n* [U] (formal) uncertainty.

in·cess·ant /ɪnˈsesnt/ *adj* continual; often repeated: *a week of ~ rain.* **~·ly** *adv*

in·cest /ˈɪnsest/ *n* [U] sexual intercourse between near relations, eg brother and sister. **in·ces·tuous** /ɪnˈsestjʊəs/ *adj* of ~; guilty of, involving, ~.

inch /ɪntʃ/ *n* **1** measure of length, one-twelfth of a foot: *six ~es of rain in one day.* ⇨ App 5. **2** small amount. **~ by ~,** by degrees. **by ~es, (a)** only just: *The car missed me by ~es.* **(b)** bit by bit; gradually. **every ~,** entirely, completely: *He's every ~ a soldier.* **within an ~ of,** very near, almost: *He came within an ~ of being struck by a falling tile.* **not yield an ~,** not give way at all. □ *vt, vi* [VP15A, B, 2C] move by ~es; edge one's way: *~ one's way forward; ~ along a ledge on a cliff.*

in·cho·ate /ɪnˈkəʊeɪt/ *adj* (formal) just begun; in an underdeveloped, half-formed state. **in·choa·tive** /ɪnˈkəʊətɪv/ *adj* expressing the beginning of an action or state: (gram) *inchoative verbs,* eg *get* in *get dark, fall* in *fall ill.*

in·ci·dence /ˈɪnsɪdəns/ *n* way in which sth affects things: *the ~ of a disease,* the range or extent of its effect, the number and kind of people who catch it; *the ~ of a tax,* the way it falls to certain people to pay it.

in·ci·dent[1] /ˈɪnsɪdənt/ *adj ~ to,* (formal) forming a natural or expected part of; naturally connected with: *the risks ~ to the life of a test pilot; the social obligations ~ to life in the diplomatic service.*

in·ci·dent[2] /ˈɪnsɪdənt/ *n* **1** event, esp one of less importance than others: *frontier ~s,* eg disputes between forces on a frontier. **2** happening which attracts general attention. **3** (modern use) happening, eg rebellion, bomb explosion, war, which for various reasons persons in authority do not wish to describe precisely. **4** separate piece of action in a play or poem.

in·ci·den·tal /ˌɪnsɪˈdentl/ *adj ~ (to),* **1** accompanying but not forming a necessary part: *~ music to a play.* **2** small and comparatively unimportant: *~ expenses,* additional to the main expenses. **3** liable to happen or occur: *discomforts ~ to exploration in a wild country.* **~·ly** /-tlɪ/ *adv* in an ~ manner; by chance.

in·cin·er·ate /ɪnˈsɪnəreɪt/ *vt* [VP6A] burn to ashes. **in·cin·er·ator** /-tə(r)/ *n* furnace, enclosed fireplace, for burning rubbish, etc. **in·cin·er·ation** /ɪnˌsɪnəˈreɪʃn/ *n* [U] burning up: *Household and industrial waste disposal—the choice is between tipping and incineration.*

in·cipi·ent /ɪnˈsɪpɪənt/ *adj* beginning; in an early stage: *~ decay of the teeth.*

in·cise /ɪnˈsaɪz/ *vt* [VP6A] make a cut in; engrave. **in·ci·sion** /ɪnˈsɪʒn/ *n* [U] cutting (into sth); [C] cut, eg one made in a surgical operation.

in·cis·ive /ɪnˈsaɪsɪv/ *adj* sharp and cutting; (of a person's mind, remarks) acute; clear-cut: *~ criticism.* **~·ly** *adv*

in·cisor /ɪnˈsaɪzə(r)/ *n* (in human beings) any one of the eight sharp-edged front cutting teeth, four in the upper and four in the lower jaw. ⇨ the illus at mouth.

in·cite /ɪnˈsaɪt/ *vt* [VP6A, 14, 17] *~ sb (to sth/to do sth),* stir up, rouse: *Insults ~ resentment. The soldier was shot for inciting his comrades to rise against their officers.* **~·ment** *n* [U] inciting or being ~d; [C] instance of this; sth that ~s.

in·civ·il·ity /ˌɪnsɪˈvɪlətɪ/ *n* (formal) [U] impoliteness; [C] (*pl* -ties) impolite act, remark, etc.

in·clem·ent /ɪnˈklemənt/ *adj* (formal) (of weather or climate) severe; cold and stormy. **in·clem·ency** /-ənsɪ/ *n* [U] being ~.

in·cli·na·tion /ˌɪnklɪˈneɪʃn/ *n* **1** [C] bending; bowing; slope; slant: *an ~ of the head,* a nod; *an ~ of the body,* a bow; *the ~ of a roof,* its degree of slope. **2** [C, U] *~ (to sth/to do sth),* mental leaning; liking or desire; disposition: *Are you usually ready to sacrifice ~ to duty,* put on one side what you like doing in order to do your duty? *He showed no ~ to leave. She is not free to follow her own ~s, even in the matter of marriage. He has an ~* (= tendency) *to stoutness/to grow fat.*

in·cline[1] /ɪnˈklaɪn/ *vt, vi* **1** [VP6A, 15A, 2A] (cause to) lean, slope or slant; bend (the head, body, oneself) forward or downward: *~ the head in prayer.* **2** [VP17] (liter) dispose; direct: *'I~ our hearts to keep this law.'* **3** [VP17] (usu passive) direct the mind in a certain direction; cause (sb) to have a tendency or wish (*to do* sth): *The news ~s me/I am ~d to start at once. His letter ~s me to believe that he doesn't want to come. I am ~d to think* (= I have a feeling or idea) *that he is opposed to the plan. He's ~d to be lazy. We can go for a walk if you feel so ~d.* **4** [VP4C] tend; be disposed: *I ~ to believe in his innocence.* **5** [VP3A] *~ to/ towards sth,* have a physical or mental tendency: *He ~s to leanness. She ~s towards melancholia.*

in·cline[2] /ˈɪnklaɪn/ *n* slope; sloping surface: *run down a steep ~; an ~ of 1 in 5.* ⇨ gradient.

in·close, in·clos·ure /ɪnˈkləʊz, ɪnˈkləʊʒə(r)/ = enclose, enclosure.

in·clude /ɪnˈkluːd/ *vt* [VP6A, C] bring in, reckon, as part of the whole: *This atlas contains fifty maps, including six of North America. Price £2.75, postage ~d. Your duties will ~ putting the children to bed.* **in·clu·sion** /ɪnˈkluːʒn/ *n* [U] including or being ~d.

in·clus·ive /ɪnˈkluːsɪv/ *adj ~ (of),* **1** including: *£10, ~ of interest; from 1 May to 3 June ~,* 1 May and 3 June being included. ⇨ (US) **through**[2](4). **2** including much or all: *~ terms,* (at a hotel, etc) without any extra charges. **~·ly** *adv*

in·cog·nito /ˌɪnkɒgˈniːtəʊ/ *adj* concealed under a disguised identity; with an assumed name: *a king ~.* □ *adv* with one's name, identity, etc concealed: *The millionaire called himself Dick Brown and travelled ~.*

in·co·her·ent /ˌɪnkəʊˈhɪərənt/ *adj* not coherent: *so drunk as to be quite ~.* **~·ly** *adv* **in·co·her·ence** /-əns/ *n*

in·com·bus·tible /ˌɪnkəmˈbʌstəbl/ *adj* (formal) that cannot be consumed by fire.

in·come /ˈɪŋkʌm/ *n* money received during a given period (as salary, receipts from trade, interest from investments, etc): *live within one's ~,* spend less than one receives. *Tax was payable on ~ over £2000.* **~·tax** /ˈɪŋkəm tæks/ *n* tax levied on ~ above a certain level.

in·com·ing /ˌɪnˈkʌmɪŋ/ *adj* coming in: *the ~ tide/ tenant.*

in·com·men·sur·ate /ˌɪnkəˈmenʃərət/ *adj ~ (to/ with),* **1** not comparable (*to*) in respect of size; not worthy to be measured (*with*): *His abilities are ~ to the task he has been given.* **2** that cannot be compared; having no common measure.

in·com·mode /ˌɪnkəˈməʊd/ *vt* [VP6A] (formal) cause trouble or inconvenience to: *Will it ~ you if I don't pay what I owe you until next year?*

in·com·muni·cado /ˌɪnkəˌmjuːnɪˈkɑːdəʊ/ *adj* (of sb

in confinement) not permitted to communicate with persons outside.

in·com·par·able /ɪn'kɒmprəbl/ *adj* ~ *(to/with)*, not to be compared; without equal: *her* ~ *beauty*. **in·com·par·ably** /-əblɪ/ *adv*

in·com·pat·ible /ˌɪnkəm'pætəbl/ *adj* ~ *(with)*, opposed in character; unable to exist in harmony; inconsistent: *Excessive drinking is* ~ *with good health. They are sexually* ~. **in·com·pati·bil·ity** /ˌɪnkəmˌpætə'bɪlətɪ/ *n* [U] being ~: *Incompatibility of temper may cause friction between husband and wife.*

in·com·pe·tent /ɪn'kɒmpɪtənt/ *adj* not qualified or able: ~ *to teach science/for teaching science/as a teacher of science*. ~·**ly** *adv* **in·com·pe·tence** /-əns/, **in·com·pe·tency** /-ənsɪ/ *nn* [U] being ~.

in·com·plete /ˌɪnkəm'pliːt/ *adj* not complete. ~·**ly** *adv*

in·com·pre·hen·sible /ɪnˌkɒmprɪ'hensəbl/ *adj* (formal) that cannot be understood. **in·com·pre·hen·si·bil·ity** /ɪnˌkɒmprɪˌhensə'bɪlətɪ/ *n* [U].

in·com·pre·hen·sion /ɪnˌkɒmprɪ'henʃn/ *n* [U] failure to understand.

in·com·press·ible /ˌɪnkəm'presəbl/ *adj* (formal) that cannot be compressed; hard and unyielding.

in·con·ceiv·able /ˌɪnkən'siːvəbl/ *adj* that cannot be imagined; (colloq) hard to believe; very remarkable.

in·con·clus·ive /ˌɪnkən'kluːsɪv/ *adj* (of evidence, arguments, discussions, actions) not decisive or convincing; not bringing a definite result. ~·**ly** *adv*

in·con·gru·ous /ɪn'kɒŋgrʊəs/ *adj* ~ *(with)*, not in harmony or agreement; out of place. ~·**ly** *adv* **in·con·gru·ity** /ˌɪnkɒŋ'gruːətɪ/ *n* [U] the quality of being ~; [C] (*pl* -ties) sth ~.

in·con·sequent /ɪn'kɒnsɪkwənt/ *adj* not following naturally what has been said or done before: *an* ~ *remark;* (of a person) saying or doing ~ things. ~·**ly** *adv* **in·con·sequen·tial** /ɪnˌkɒnsɪ'kwenʃl/ *adj* = ~; unimportant.

in·con·sid·er·able /ˌɪnkən'sɪdrəbl/ *adj* not worth considering; of small size, value, etc.

in·con·sid·er·ate /ˌɪnkən'sɪdərət/ *adj* (of a person, his actions) thoughtless; lacking in regard for the feelings of others; ~ *children;* ~ *remarks*. ~·**ly** *adv*

in·con·sist·ent /ˌɪnkən'sɪstənt/ *adj* ~ *(with)*, **1** not in harmony: *actions that are* ~ *with one's principles*. **2** contradictory; having parts that do not agree: *His account of what happened was* ~. ~·**ly** *adv* **in·con·sist·ency** /-ənsɪ/ *n* [U] the quality of being ~; [C] (*pl* -cies) instance of this.

in·con·sol·able /ˌɪnkən'səʊləbl/ *adj* that cannot be consoled: ~ *grief. The widow was* ~.

in·con·spic·u·ous /ˌɪnkən'spɪkjʊəs/ *adj* not conspicuous: *The shy girl tried to make herself as* ~ *as possible*, tried to avoid attention. *She always dresses in* ~ *colours*, colours that are not striking or obvious. ~·**ly** *adv*

in·con·stant /ɪn'kɒnstənt/ *adj* (formal) (of persons) changeable in feelings, intentions, purpose, etc: *an* ~ *lover*. **in·con·stancy** /-ənsɪ/ *n* [U] being ~; [C] instance of this.

in·con·test·able /ˌɪnkən'testəbl/ *adj* that cannot be disputed.

in·con·ti·nent /ɪn'kɒntɪnənt US: -tənənt/ *adj* lacking in self-control or self-restraint; (med) unable to control excretion or urination. **in·con·ti·nence** /-əns/ *n* [U].

in·con·tro·vert·ible /ɪnˌkɒntrə'vɜːtəbl/ *adj* (formal)

that cannot be disputed.

in·con·ven·ience /ˌɪnkən'viːnɪəns/ *n* [C,U] (cause or instance of) discomfort or trouble: *I was put to/I suffered great* ~. *They have been at great* ~ *in order to help us. Think of the* ~*s of living in such a small house with a large family*. □ *vt* [VP6A] cause ~ to.

in·con·ven·ient /ˌɪnkən'viːnɪənt/ *adj* causing discomfort, trouble or annoyance. ~·**ly** *adv*

in·con·vert·ible /ˌɪnkən'vɜːtəbl/ *adj* that cannot be converted, eg paper money that cannot be exchanged for gold. **in·con·ver·ti·bil·ity** /ˌɪnkənˌvɜːtə'bɪlətɪ/ *n*

in·cor·por·ate¹ /ɪn'kɔːpərət/ *adj* incorporated; formed into, united in, a corporation.

in·cor·por·ate² /ɪn'kɔːpəreɪt/ *vt,vi* [VP6A,14,23,2A,3A] ~ *(in/into/with)*, make, become, united in one body or group; (legal) form into, become, a corporation(2): *Hanover was* ~*d into Prussia in 1886. He was* ~*d a member of the college. Your suggestions will be* ~*d in the plan. The firm* ~*d with others*. **in·cor·por·ation** /ɪnˌkɔːpə'reɪʃn/ *n* incorporating or being ~*d*.

in·cor·por·eal /ˌɪnkɔː'pɔːrɪəl/ *adj* (formal) not composed of matter; having no bodily form.

in·cor·rect /ˌɪnkə'rekt/ *adj* not correct. ~·**ly** *adv* ~·**ness** *n*

in·cor·ri·gible /ɪn'kɒrɪdʒəbl US: -'kɔːr-/ *adj* (of a person, his faults, etc) that cannot be cured or corrected: *an* ~ *liar;* ~ *bad habits*.

in·cor·rupt·ible /ˌɪnkə'rʌptəbl/ *adj* that cannot decay or be destroyed; that cannot be corrupted, esp by being bribed: *as* ~ *as an English judge*. **in·cor·rupti·bil·ity** /ˌɪnkəˌrʌptə'bɪlətɪ/ *n*

in·crease¹ /'ɪŋkriːs/ *n* [U] ~ *(in)*, increasing; growth; [C] amount by which sth ~*s*: *I* ~ *in population made emigration necessary. There was a steady* ~ *in population*. **on the** ~, growing: *Is the consumption of beer still on the* ~?

in·crease² /ɪn'kriːs/ *vt,vi* [VP6A,2A] make or become greater in size, number, degree, etc: *The population has* ~*d by 200000 to 50000000. The driver* ~*d speed. Our difficulties are increasing*. **in·creas·ing·ly** /ɪn'kriːsɪŋlɪ/ *adv* more and more.

in·cred·ible /ɪn'kredəbl/ *adj* that cannot be believed; (colloq) difficult to believe; surprising. **in·cred·ibly** /-əblɪ/ *adv* **in·credi·bil·ity** /ɪnˌkredə'bɪlətɪ/ *n*

in·credu·lous /ɪn'kredjʊləs US: -dʒʊ-/ *adj* unbelieving; showing disbelief: ~ *looks/smiles*. ~·**ly** *adv* **in·credul·ity** /ˌɪnkrɪ'djuːlətɪ US: -'duː-/ *n*

in·crement /'ɪŋkrəmənt/ *n* **1** [U] profits; increase: *unearned* ~, increased value of sth, eg land, due not to the owner's labour but to other causes, eg a big demand for land. **2** [C] amount of increase: *'Salary £4000 per annum, with yearly* ~*s of £250 to a maximum of £5500.'*

in·crimi·nate /ɪn'krɪmɪneɪt/ *vt* [VP6A] say, be a sign, that (sb) is guilty of wrongdoing: *Don't say anything that may* ~ *your friends*.

in·crus·ta·tion /ˌɪnkrʌ'steɪʃn/ *n* [U] encrusting; [C] crust; hard coating.

in·cu·bate /'ɪŋkjʊbeɪt/ *vt,vi* [VP6A,2A] **1** hatch (eggs) by sitting on them or by artificial warmth; sit on eggs. **2** (of bacteria, etc) develop under favourable conditions. **in·cu·ba·tion** /ˌɪŋkjʊ'beɪʃn/ *n* **1** hatching (of eggs): *artificial incubation*, hatching by artificial warmth. **2** ~ **(period)**, (path) (of a disease) period between infection and the appearance of the first symptoms. **in·cu·ba·tor** /-tə(r)/ *n* apparatus for hatching eggs by artificial warmth or for rearing small, weak babies (esp those born prematurely).

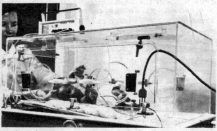

an incubator

in·cu·bus /'ɪŋkjʊbəs/ n (pl ~es /-sɪz/, or -bi /-baɪ/) nightmare; evil spirit supposed to lie on a sleeping person and weigh him down; sb or sth, eg a debt, an approaching examination, that oppresses one like a nightmare.
in·cul·cate /'ɪnkʌlkeɪt US: ɪn'kʌl-/ vt [VP6A, 14] ~ **sth (in sb)** (formal) fix (ideas, etc) firmly by repetition: ~ *in young people the duty of loyalty.*
in·cul·pate /'ɪnkʌlpeɪt US: ɪn'kʌl-/ vt [VP6A] (formal) involve (sb) in a charge or wrongdoing; blame.
in·cum·bent /ɪn'kʌmbənt/ adj **be ~ on/upon sb (to do sth)**, (formal) be his duty: *It is ~ upon you to warn the boy of the danger of smoking.* □ n person holding an official position. **in·cum·bency** /-ənsɪ/ n (pl -cies) position of an ~.
in·cur /ɪn'kɜ:(r)/ vt (-rr-) [VP6A] bring upon oneself: ~ *debts;* ~ *hatred;* ~ *great expense.*
in·cur·able /ɪn'kjʊərəbl/ adj that cannot be cured: ~ *diseases/habits.* □ n person who is ~: *a home for ~s.* **in·cur·ably** /-əblɪ/ adv
in·curi·ous /ɪn'kjʊərɪəs/ adj (formal) having no curiosity; not inquisitive; inattentive.
in·cur·sion /ɪn'kɜ:ʃn US: -ʒn/ n ~ **on/upon**, sudden attack or invasion (not usu made for the purpose of permanent occupation): *the Danish ~s on our coasts in early times;* (fig) ~s *upon my leisure time.*
in·curved /ˌɪn'kɜ:vd/ adj curved inwards; bent into a curve.
in·debted /ɪn'detɪd/ adj ~ **to sb**, owing money or gratitude: *I am greatly ~ to you for your help.* ~**ness** n
in·de·cent /ɪn'di:snt/ adj 1 (of behaviour, talk, etc) not decent(2); obscene. 2 (colloq) improper: *leave a party in ~ haste,* eg as if to suggest that one is glad to escape from boredom. ~**·ly** adv **in·de·cency** /-nsɪ/ n [U] being ~; [C] (pl -cies) act, gesture, expression, etc that is ~.
in·de·cipher·able /ˌɪndɪ'saɪfrəbl/ adj that cannot be deciphered.
in·de·cision /ˌɪndɪ'sɪʒn/ n the state of being unable to decide; hesitation.
in·de·cis·ive /ˌɪndɪ'saɪsɪv/ adj not decisive: *an ~ battle/answer;* ~ *evidence;* hesitating; uncertain: *a man with an ~ manner.* ~**·ly** adv
in·dec·or·ous /ɪn'dekərəs/ adj (formal) in bad taste; not in accordance with good manners. ~**·ly** adv
in·de·cor·um /ˌɪndɪ'kɔ:rəm/ n [U] lack of decorum; improper behaviour.
in·deed /ɪn'di:d/ adv 1 really; as you say; as you

may imagine: *I was ~ very glad to hear the news.* '*Are you pleased at your son's success?*'—'*Yes, ~*' (or) '*I~, yes.*' 2 (to intensify) *Thank you very much ~. It was very kind ~ of you to help.* 3 used as a comment to show interest, surprise, irony, etc: '*He spoke to me about you.*'—'*Oh, ~!*' '*Oh, did he?*' '*Who is this woman?*'—'*Who is she, ~?*' 'That's what we all want to know!'
in·de·fati·gable /ˌɪndɪ'fætɪgəbl/ adj (formal) untiring; that cannot be tired out: ~ *workers.*
in·de·feas·ible /ˌɪndɪ'fi:zəbl/ adj (formal) that cannot be forfeited or done away with: ~ *rights/ claims.*
in·de·fens·ible /ˌɪndɪ'fensəbl/ adj that cannot be defended, justified or excused.
in·defin·able /ˌɪndɪ'faɪnəbl/ adj that cannot be defined.
in·defi·nite /ɪn'defɪnət/ adj vague; not clearly defined or stated: *He has rather ~ views on the question. He gave me an ~ answer,* neither 'Yes' nor 'No'. **the ~ 'article**, *a* or *an*. ~**·ly** adv
in·del·ible /ɪn'deləbl/ adj (of marks, stains, ink or (fig) of disgrace) that cannot be rubbed out or removed: *an ~ pencil;* ~ *shame.* **in·del·ibly** /-əblɪ/ adv
in·deli·cate /ɪn'delɪkət/ adj (of a person, his speech, behaviour, etc) lacking in refinement; immodest: ~ *remarks.* **in·deli·cacy** /-kəsɪ/ n [U] being ~; [C] (pl -cies) ~ act, utterance, etc.
in·dem·nify /ɪn'demnɪfaɪ/ vt (pt,pp -fied) 1 [VP6A,14] ~ **sb (from/against)**, (legal, comm) make (sb, oneself) safe: ~ *a person against harm/loss.* 2 [VP6A,14] ~ **sb (for sth)**, pay sb back: *I will ~ you for any expenses you may incur on my behalf.* **in·dem·ni·fi·ca·tion** /ɪnˌdemnɪfɪ'keɪʃn/ n [U] ~ing or being indemnified; [C] sth given or received as compensation or repayment.
in·dem·nity /ɪn'demnətɪ/ n (pl -ties) 1 [U] security against damage or loss; compensation for loss. 2 [C] sth that gives security against damage or loss; sth given or received as compensation, esp a sum of money, or goods, demanded from a country defeated in war.
in·dent /ɪn'dent/ vt,vi 1 [VP6A] break into the edge or surface of (as if with teeth): *an ~ed* (= very irregular) *coastline.* 2 [VP6A] start (a line of print or writing) farther from the margin than the others: *You must ~ the first line of each paragraph.* 3 [VP3A] ~ **(on sb) for sth,** (comm) order goods by means of an ~. *The firm ~ed for new machinery.* □ n /'ɪndent/ (comm) trade order placed in the United Kingdom for goods to be exported; official requisition for stores. **in·den·ta·tion** /ˌɪnden'teɪʃn/ n 1 [U] ~ing or being ~ed. 2 [C] deep recess in a coastline; notch; space left at the beginning of a line of print or writing.
in·den·ture /ɪn'dentʃə(r)/ n agreement of which two copies are made, esp one binding an apprentice to his master. **take up one's ~s**, receive them back at the end of the period of training. □ vt [VP6A] bind (a person) by ~s (as an apprentice).
in·de·pen·dence /ˌɪndɪ'pendəns/ n [U] ~ **(from)**, the state of being independent: *When a boy leaves college and begins to earn money he can live a life of ~. Several of these colonies have claimed and have been given ~ from the mother country.* '**I~ Day**, 4 July, celebrated in the US as the anniversary of the day, in 1776, on which the Declaration of I~ (that the American colonies were free and in-

dependent of GB) was made.

in·de·pen·dent /ˌɪndɪˈpendənt/ adj **1** ~ (of), not dependent on or controlled by (other persons or things); not relying on others; not needing to work for a living: *If you have a car you are* ~ *of trains and buses. They went camping, so as to be* ~ *of hotels.* ~ **means,** private means. **2** self-governing: *when the colony became* ~. **3** acting or thinking upon one's own lines; free from control; not influenced by others: *an* ~ *thinker; an* ~ *witness;* ~ *proof/research*, resulting from ~ work, not related to the work of others. □ *n* (esp) MP, candidate, etc who does not belong to a political party: *Vote for the* ~*s!*/~·**ly** adv

in·de·scrib·able /ˌɪndɪˈskraɪbəbl/ adj that cannot be described. **in·de·scrib·ably** /-əblɪ/ adv

in·de·struct·ible /ˌɪndɪˈstrʌktəbl/ adj that cannot be destroyed: ~ *plastics.* **in·de·struct·ibil·ity** /ˌɪndɪˌstrʌktəˈbɪlətɪ/ n [U].

in·de·ter·mi·nate /ˌɪndɪˈtɜːmɪnət/ adj not fixed; vague or indefinite: (maths) *an* ~ *quantity*, with no fixed value. **in·de·ter·min·able** /ˌɪndɪˈtɜːmɪnəbl/ adj that cannot be determined, decided or (esp of an industrial dispute) be settled. **in·de·ter·min·ably** /-əblɪ/ adv **in·de·ter·min·acy** /-əsɪ/ n the state or quality of being ~: *the indeterminacy of small-scale physical events*, the impossibility of determining them in advance.

in·dex /ˈɪndeks/ n (pl ~es or, in science, **indices** /ˈɪndɪsiːz/) **1** sth that points to or indicates; pointer (on an instrument) showing measurements: *The increasing sale of luxuries was an* ~ *of the country's prosperity.* **the** '~ **finger,** the finger next to the thumb, used for pointing. ⇨ the illus at arm. **2** list of names, subjects, references, etc in ABC order, at the end of a book, or on cards (a **'card** ~) in a library, etc. **the I**~, (hist) list of books not to be read by members of the RC Church without permission. **3** '~ **number/figure,** one that indicates the relative level of prices or wages at a particular date compared with the figure 100 (for an earlier period) as a standard: *the cost of living* ~; (of wages, pensions) ~ *linked/related*, adjusted accordingly. **4** (alg) exponent: *In* $b^3 + x^n$, 3 *and* n *are indices.* □ *vt* [VP6A] make an ~ for a book, collection of books, etc; put a word, reference, etc in an ~: *The book is not well* ~ed. ~**er** n person who prepares an ~ (2).

In·dia /ˈɪndɪə/ n '~ **paper** n very thin paper, eg for airmail editions of newspapers. '~·**man** /-mən/ n (pl -**men**) (formerly) sailing-ship engaged in the trade with India. ,~-'**rubber** n [C] piece of rubber for rubbing out pencil or ink marks.

In·dian /ˈɪndɪən/ adj, n **1** (native) of the Republic of India. **2** A,**merican** '~, (one) of the original inhabitants of America. ,**West** '~, (native) of the West Indies. **3** (various uses) '~ **club,** bottle-shaped club, for use in gymnastic exercises. '~ **corn,** [U] maize. **in** ~ **file,** in single file, one behind the other. ~ '**hemp,** ⇨ hemp. ,~ '**ink,** black ink made in China and Japan (used when writing ideographs with a brush). ~ '**red,** (soil of a) yellowish-red colour. ,~ '**summer,** period of calm, dry hazy weather in late autumn, esp in the northern part of the US; (fig) revival of the feelings of youth in old age.

in·di·cate /ˈɪndɪkeɪt/ vt [VP6A,9,14] point to; point out; make known; be a sign of; show the need of; state briefly: *A sign-post* ~d *the right road for us to follow. He* ~d *that the interview was over. The*

sudden rise in temperature was indicating the use of penicillin. A fresh approach to industrial relations is ~d, is necessary or advisable. **in·di·ca·tion** /ˌɪndɪˈkeɪʃn/ n **1** [U] indicating or being ~d. **2** [C,U] sign or suggestion; that which ~s: *Did he give you any indication of his feelings? There was not much indication/were not many indications that the next few years would be peaceful.*

in·dica·tive /ɪnˈdɪkətɪv/ adj **1** (gram) stating a fact or asking questions of fact: *the* ~ *mood.* **2** ~ *of/ that*, giving indications (of): *Is a high forehead* ~ *of great mental power?*

in·di·cator /ˈɪndɪkeɪtə(r)/ n person, thing, that points out or gives information, eg a pointer, needle, recording apparatus, on a machine, etc showing speed, pressure, etc: *Litmus paper can be used as an* ~ *of the presence or not of acid in a solution;* ('traffic-~) (on a motor vehicle) flashing light or other device to indicate a change of direction; ('train ~) one in a railway station showing times of arrivals and departures of trains, their platform numbers, etc.

in·di·ces /ˈɪndɪsiːz/ pl of **index**.

in·dict /ɪnˈdaɪt/ vt [VP6A,14,16B] (legal) accuse (sb): ~ *sb for riot/as a rioter/on a charge of rioting.* **in·dict·able** /-əbl/ adj liable to be ~ed; for which one may be ~ed: ~**able offences,** that may be tried by jury. ~·**ment** n [C] written statement that ~s sb: *bring in an* ~**ment against sb. This is a clear** ~**ment of government mismanagement.** [U] ~ing or being ~ed.

in·dif·fer·ence /ɪnˈdɪfrəns/ n [U] ~ (to), the state of being indifferent; absence of interest or feeling: *He treated my request with* ~. *Success or failure cannot be a matter of* ~ *to you. His* ~ *to future needs is unfortunate.*

in·dif·fer·ent /ɪnˈdɪfrənt/ adj **1** ~ (to), having no interest in; neither for nor against; not caring for: *How can you be so* ~ *to the sufferings of these children? The explorers were* ~ *to the discomforts and dangers of the expedition. We cannot remain* ~ (= neutral) *in this dispute. It is quite* ~ *to me whether you go or stay*, I don't care which you do. **2** commonplace; not of good quality or ability: *an* ~ *book; a very* ~ *footballer.* ~·**ly** adv

in·dig·en·ous /ɪnˈdɪdʒɪnəs/ adj ~ (to), native, belonging naturally (to): *Kangaroos are* ~ *to Australia;* ~ *language*, that of the people regarded as the original inhabitants of an area.

in·di·gent /ˈɪndɪdʒənt/ adj (formal) poor. **in·di·gence** /-əns/ n [U] poverty.

in·di·gest·ible /ˌɪndɪˈdʒestəbl/ adj difficult or impossible to digest.

in·di·ges·tion /ˌɪndɪˈdʒestʃən/ n [U] (pain from) difficulty in digesting food: *suffer from* ~; *have an attack of* ~.

indig·nant /ɪnˈdɪgnənt/ adj angry and scornful, esp at injustice or because of undeserved blame, etc: ~ *at a false accusation;* ~ *with a cruel man.* ~·**ly** adv

in·dig·na·tion /ˌɪndɪgˈneɪʃn/ n [U] anger caused by injustice, misconduct, etc: *arouse the* ~ *of the people; to the* ~ *of all decent people. They felt strong* ~ *against their teachers.*

in·dig·nity /ɪnˈdɪgnətɪ/ n [U] rude or unworthy treatment causing shame or loss of respect; [C] (pl -ties) sth said or done that humiliates a person: *The hijackers subjected us to all sorts of indignities.*

in·digo /ˈɪndɪgəʊ/ n [U] deep blue dye (obtained

from plants). ∼ **(blue)**, blue-violet. ⇨ the illus at spectrum.

in·direct /ˌɪndɪˈrekt/ adj **1** not straight or direct; not going straight to the point: an ∼ road; make an ∼ reference to sb, not mentioning his name although making clear who is referred to; an ∼ answer to a question; ∼ lighting, by reflected light. **2** (of taxes) not paid direct to a tax-collector, but in the form of higher prices for taxed goods: the ∼ taxes on tobacco, wines, etc. **3** ,∼ **'object**, person etc secondarily affected by the v, and replaceable by to/for + object, eg him (= to him) in Give him the money. ∼ **'question**, question in ∼ speech. ,∼ **'speech**, speech as it is reported with the necessary changes of pronouns, tenses, etc, eg He said he would come for He said 'I will come'. **4** not directly aimed at: an ∼ result. ∼·**ly** adv ∼·**ness** n

in·dis·cern·ible /ˌɪndɪˈsɜ:nəbl/ adj that cannot be discerned.

in·dis·ci·pline /ɪnˈdɪsɪplɪn/ n [U] absence of discipline.

in·dis·creet /ˌɪndɪˈskri:t/ adj not wary, cautious or careful. ∼·**ly** adv **in·dis·cre·tion** /ˌɪndɪˈskreʃn/ n [U] ∼ conduct; lack of discretion; [C] ∼ remark or act; offence against social conventions.

in·dis·crete /ˌɪndɪˈskri:t/ adj not formed of distinct or separate parts.

in·dis·crimi·nate /ˌɪndɪˈskrɪmɪnət/ adj acting, given, without care or taste: ∼ in making friends; give ∼ praise; deal out ∼ blows, hit out at anyone, whether an enemy or not. ∼·**ly** adv

in·dis·pens·able /ˌɪndɪˈspensəbl/ adj ∼ **to**, that cannot be dispensed with; absolutely essential: Air, food and water are ∼ to life. **in·dis·pen·sa·bil·ity** /ˌɪndɪˌspensəˈbɪlətɪ/ n [U].

in·dis·posed /ˌɪndɪˈspəʊzd/ adj **1** unwell: She has a headache and is ∼. **2** ∼ **for/to do sth**, not inclined: He seems ∼ to help us.

in·dis·po·si·tion /ˌɪndɪspəˈzɪʃn/ n [C,U] **1** ill health; slight illness. **2** ∼ **for/to do sth**, feeling of unwillingness or disinclination; feeling of aversion.

in·dis·put·able /ˌɪndɪˈspju:təbl/ adj that cannot be disputed.

in·dis·sol·uble /ˌɪndɪˈsɒljʊbl/ adj (formal) that cannot be dissolved or broken up; firm and lasting: the ∼ bonds of friendship between my country and yours. The Roman Catholic Church regards marriage as ∼.

in·dis·tinct /ˌɪndɪˈstɪŋkt/ adj not distinct: ∼ speech; ∼ sounds/memories. ∼·**ly** adv ∼·**ness** n

in·dis·tin·guish·able /ˌɪndɪˈstɪŋgwɪʃəbl/ adj that cannot be distinguished.

in·dite /ɪnˈdaɪt/ vt [VP6A] (archaic) put into words; compose.

in·di·vid·ual /ˌɪndɪˈvɪdʒʊəl/ adj **1** (opp of general) specially for one person or thing: A teacher cannot give ∼ attention to his pupils if his class is very large. **2** characteristic of a single person, animal, plant or thing: an ∼ style of speaking/dressing. □ n **1** any one human being (contrasted with society): Are the rights of the/an ∼ more important or less important than the rights of society as a whole? **2** (colloq) person: What a scruffy ∼ he is! ∼**ly** /-dʒʊəlɪ/ adv (opp of collectively) separately; one by one: speak to each member of a group ∼ly.

in·di·vid·ual·ism /ˌɪndɪˈvɪdʒʊəlɪzəm/ n [U] **1** social theory that favours the free action and complete liberty of belief of individuals (contrasted with the theory favouring the supremacy of the state). **2** feeling or behaviour of a person who puts his own private interests first; egoism. **in·di·vid·ual·ist** /-ɪst/ n supporter of ∼. **in·di·vid·ual·is·tic** /ˌɪndɪˌvɪdʒʊəˈlɪstɪk/ adj of ∼ or its principles.

in·di·vidu·al·ity /ˌɪndɪˌvɪdʒʊˈælətɪ/ n (pl -ties) **1** [U] all the characteristics that belong to an individual and that mark him out from others: a man of marked ∼. **2** state of separate existence. **3** (usu pl) individual tastes, etc.

in·di·vid·ual·ize /ˌɪndɪˈvɪdʒʊəlaɪz/ vt [VP6A] **1** give an individual or distinct character to: Does your style of writing ∼ your work? **2** specify; treat separately and in detail.

in·di·vis·ible /ˌɪndɪˈvɪzəbl/ adj that cannot be divided.

Indo- /ˌɪndəʊ/ pref (in compounds) = Indian. ,∼·,**Euro'pean**, of the family of languages spoken in Europe and parts of western Asia, esp Iran, Pakistan and India.

in·doc·tri·nate /ɪnˈdɒktrɪneɪt/ vt [VP6A,14] ∼ **with**, fill the mind of (sb) (with particular ideas or beliefs). **in·doc·tri·na·tion** /ɪnˌdɒktrɪˈneɪʃn/ n [U].

in·do·lent /ˈɪndələnt/ adj lazy; inactive. ∼·**ly** adv **in·dol·ence** /-əns/ n [U].

in·domi·table /ɪnˈdɒmɪtəbl/ adj that cannot be subdued or conquered; unyielding: ∼ courage; an ∼ will.

in·door /ˈɪndɔ:(r)/ adj (attrib only) belonging to, carried on, situated, inside a building: ∼ games/photography; an ∼ swimming-bath.

in·doors /ˌɪnˈdɔ:z/ adv in or into a building: go/stay ∼; kept ∼ all week by bad weather.

in·dorse /ɪnˈdɔ:s/ = endorse.

in·drawn /ˌɪnˈdrɔ:n/ adj drawn in: an ∼ breath.

in·dubi·table /ɪnˈdju:bɪtəbl/ US: -'du:-/ adj (formal) that cannot be doubted.

in·duce /ɪnˈdju:s/ US: -'du:s/ vt **1** [VP17] ∼ **sb to do sth**, persuade or influence; lead or cause: What ∼d you to do such a thing? We couldn't ∼ the old lady to travel by air. **2** [VP6A,14] bring about: ill-ness ∼d by overwork; ∼ labour, (in childbirth) by artificial means; ∼ magnetism in a piece of iron, by holding it near a magnet. ∼·**ment** n [C,U] that which ∼s; incentive: He hasn't much ∼ment/many ∼ments to study English.

in·duct /ɪnˈdʌkt/ vt [VP6A,14,16B] ∼ **sb (to/into/as)**, install formerly or with ceremony in position or office; admit as a member of.

in·duc·tion /ɪnˈdʌkʃn/ n **1** inducting or being inducted: an ∼ course, one designed to provide general knowledge of future activities, requirements, etc. **2** method of reasoning which obtains or discovers general laws from particular facts or examples; production of facts to prove a general statement. ⇨ deduction. **3** the bringing about of an electric or magnetic state in a body by proximity (without actual contact) of an electrified or magnetized body: ∼ coils/motors. ⇨ induce(2).

in·duc·tive /ɪnˈdʌktɪv/ adj **1** (of reasoning) based on induction(2). **2** of magnetic or electrical induction.

in·due /ɪnˈdju:/ US: -'du:/ = endue.

in·dulge /ɪnˈdʌldʒ/ vt,vi **1** [VP6A] gratify; give way to and satisfy (desires, etc); overlook the faults of: It is sometimes necessary to ∼ a sick child/the fancies of a sick child. **2** [VP3A] ∼ **in**, allow oneself the pleasure of: He occasionally ∼s in the luxury of a good cigar. **in·dul·gent** /-ənt/ adj inclined to ∼; indulgent parents, parents who ∼ their children. **in·dul·gent·ly** adv

in·dul·gence /ɪnˈdʌldʒəns/ n **1** [U] indulging(1);

the state of being indulged(1). **2** [U] ∿ *(in)*, (the habit of) gratifying one's own desires, etc: *Constant* ∿ *in bad habits brought about his ruin.* **3** [C] sth in which a person indulges(2): *One pint of beer a day and an occasional game of billiards are his only* ∿*s.* **4** [U] (in the RC Church) granting of freedom from punishment still due for sin after sacramental absolution; [C] instance of this.

in·dus·trial /ɪn'dʌstrɪəl/ *adj* of industries: *the* ∿ *areas of England* (contrasted with *agricultural*, etc). ∿ **action**, striking²(5). **take** ∿ **action**, strike²(5). ∿ **alcohol**, for ∿ use (unfit for drinking). ∿ **dispute**, one between workers and management. ∿ **estate**, area of land planned and used for the building of factories (to be rented to manufacturers). **the** ∿ **revolution**, the changes brought about by mechanical inventions in the 18th and early 19th cc. ∿**·ism** /-ɪzəm/ *n* social system in which large-scale industries have an important part. ∿**·ist** /-ɪst/ *n* owner of a large-scale ∿ undertaking; supporter of ∿ism.

in·dus·tri·ous /ɪn'dʌstrɪəs/ *adj* hard-working; diligent. ⇨ industry(1). ∿**·ly** *adv*

in·dus·try /'ɪndəstrɪ/ *n* (*pl* -tries) **1** [U] quality of being hard-working; being always employed usefully: *His success was due to* ∿ *and thrift.* **2** [C,U] (branch of) trade or manufacture (contrasted with distribution and commerce): *the cotton and woollen industries.*

in·dwell·ing /ˌɪn'dwelɪŋ/ *adj* (formal) living, always present, in the mind or soul.

in·ebri·ate /ɪ'niːbrɪeɪt/ *vt* [VP6A] (formal or joc) make drunk; intoxicate. □ *n, adj* /ɪ'niːbrɪət/ (person who is habitually) drunk: *an institution for* ∿*s.* **in·ebri·ation** /ɪˌniːbrɪ'eɪʃn/, **in·ebri·ety** /ˌɪnɪ'braɪətɪ/ *nn* [U] drunkenness.

in·ed·ible /ɪn'edɪbl/ *adj* (formal) (of a kind) not suitable to be eaten.

in·ef·fable /ɪn'efəbl/ *adj* (formal) too great to be described in words: ∿ *joy/beauty.* **in·ef·fably** /-əblɪ/ *adv*

in·ef·fec·tive /ˌɪnɪ'fektɪv/ *adj* not producing the effect(s) desired; (of a person) inefficient. ∿**·ly** *adv* ∿**·ness** *n*

in·ef·fec·tual /ˌɪnɪ'fektʃʊəl/ *adj* without effect; unsuccessful; lacking resolution and unable to get things done: *an* ∿ *teacher/leader.* ∿**·ly** /-tʃʊəlɪ/ *adv*

in·ef·fic·ient /ˌɪnɪ'fɪʃnt/ *adj* (of persons) wasting time, energy, etc in their work or duties: *an* ∿ *management/administration;* (of machines, processes, etc) wasteful; not producing adequate results. ∿**·ly** *adv* **in·ef·fic·iency** /-nsɪ/ *n* [U].

in·elas·tic /ˌɪnɪ'læstɪk/ *adj* not flexible or adaptable; unyielding: *an* ∿ *programme/timetable.*

in·el·egant /ɪn'elɪgənt/ *adj* not graceful or refined. ∿**·ly** *adv* **in·el·egance** /-əns/ *n*

in·eli·gible /ɪn'elɪdʒəbl/ *adj* ∿ *(for)*, not eligible; not suitable or qualified: ∿ *for the position.* **in·eli·gi·bil·ity** /ɪnˌelɪdʒə'bɪlətɪ/ *n* [U].

in·eluc·table /ˌɪnɪ'lʌktəbl/ *adj* (formal) that cannot be escaped from: *the victim of* ∿ *fate.*

in·ept /ɪ'nept/ *adj* unskilful; said or done at the wrong time: ∿ *remarks.* ∿**·ly** *adv* **in·ep·ti·tude** /ɪ'neptɪtjuːd/ *US:* -tuːd/ *n* [U] quality of being ∿; [C] ∿ action, remark, etc.

in·equal·ity /ˌɪnɪ'kwɒlətɪ/ *n* (*pl* -ties) **1** [U] want, absence of, equality in size, degree, circumstances, etc; difference in size, rank, wealth, etc; [C] instance of this: *Great inequalities in wealth*

cause social unrest. **2** (*pl*) (of a surface) irregularity: *the inequalities of the landscape,* the rise and fall of the ground, etc.

in·equi·table /ɪn'ekwɪtəbl/ *adj* (formal) unjust; unfair: *an* ∿ *division of the profits.*

in·equity /ɪn'ekwətɪ/ *n* (*pl* -ties) [C,U] (instance of) injustice or unfairness.

in·eradi·cable /ˌɪnɪ'rædɪkəbl/ *adj* that cannot be rooted out; firmly and deeply rooted: *an* ∿ *fault/failing.*

in·ert /ɪ'nɜːt/ *adj* **1** without power to move or act: ∿ *matter.* **2** without active chemical properties: ∿ *gases.* **3** heavy and slow in (mind or body). **in·er·tia** /ɪ'nɜːʃə/ *n* [U] **1** state of being ∿(3). **2** property of matter by which it remains in a state of rest or, if it is in motion, continues in the same direction and in a straight line unless it is acted upon by an external force.

in·es·cap·able /ˌɪnɪ'skeɪpəbl/ *adj* not to be escaped from: *we were forced to the* ∿ *conclusion that he was an embezzler.*

in·es·ti·mable /ɪn'estɪməbl/ *adj* too great, precious, etc to be estimated.

in·evi·table /ɪn'evɪtəbl/ *adj* **1** that cannot be avoided, that is sure to happen. **2** (colloq) so frequently seen, heard, etc that it is familiar and expected: *a tourist with his* ∿ *camera.* **in·evi·ta·bil·ity** /ɪnˌevɪtə'bɪlətɪ/ *n* [U].

in·ex·act /ˌɪnɪg'zækt/ *adj* not exact. **in·ex·acti·tude** /ˌɪnɪg'zæktɪtjuːd *US:* -tuːd/ *n* [U] being ∿; [C] instance of this: *terminological* ∿*itudes,* (joc euphem for) lies.

in·ex·cus·able /ˌɪnɪk'skjuːzəbl/ *adj* that cannot be excused: ∿ *conduct/delays.*

in·ex·haust·ible /ˌɪnɪg'zɔːstəbl/ *adj* that cannot be exhausted: *My patience is not* ∿.

in·exor·able /ɪn'eksərəbl/ *adj* relentless; unyielding: ∿ *demands/pressures.* **in·exor·ably** /-əblɪ/ *adv*

in·ex·pedi·ent /ˌɪnɪk'spiːdɪənt/ *adj* not expedient. **in·ex·pedi·en·cy** /-ənsɪ/ *n* [U] quality of being ∿.

in·ex·pen·sive /ˌɪnɪk'spensɪv/ *adj* not expensive; low priced. ∿**·ly** *adv*

in·ex·pe·ri·ence /ˌɪnɪk'spɪərɪəns/ *n* [U] lack of experience: *He didn't get the job because of his* ∿. **in·ex·pe·ri·enced** *adj* lacking experience.

in·ex·pert /ɪn'ekspɜːt/ *adj* unskilled: ∿ *advice/guidance.* ∿**·ly** *adv*

in·ex·pi·able /ɪn'ekspɪəbl/ *adj* (formal) (of an offence) that cannot be expiated; (of resentment, hatred, etc) that cannot be appeased.

in·ex·plic·able /ˌɪnɪk'splɪkəbl/ *adj* that cannot be explained.

in·ex·press·ible /ˌɪnɪk'spresəbl/ *adj* that cannot be expressed in words: ∿ *sorrow/anguish.*

in·ex·tin·guish·able /ˌɪnɪk'stɪŋgwɪʃəbl/ *adj* that cannot be extinguished or quenched: ∿ *hatred.*

in·ex·tri·cable /ˌɪnɪk'strɪkəbl/ *adj* that cannot be reduced to order, solved, untied, or escaped from: ∿ *confusion/difficulties.*

in·fal·lible /ɪn'fæləbl/ *adj* **1** incapable of making mistakes or doing wrong: *None of us is* ∿. **2** never failing: ∿ *remedies/cures/methods/tests.* **in·fal·li·bil·ity** /ɪnˌfælə'bɪlətɪ/ *n* complete freedom from the possibility of being in error: *the infallibility of the Pope.*

in·fa·mous /'ɪnfəməs/ *adj* wicked; shameful; disgraceful: ∿ *behaviour; an* ∿ *plot/traitor.* **in·famy** /'ɪnfəmɪ/ *n* **1** [U] being ∿; public dishonour: *hold a person up to infamy.* **2** [U] ∿ behaviour; [C] (*pl* -

mies) ~ act.

in·fancy /'ɪnfənsɪ/ n [U] **1** state of being, period when one is, an infant; early childhood; (legal, in GB) minority(1), period before one reaches 18. ⇨ minority. **2** early stage of development or growth: *the ~ of a nation; when aviation was still in its ~.*

in·fant /'ɪnfənt/ n **1** child during the first few years of its life; (legal) minor. **2** (attrib) ~ *voices;* ~ *food; an '~-school,* part of a primary school for children under 7; ~ *industries,* new, in an early stage.

in·fan·ti·cide /ɪn'fæntɪsaɪd/ n [U] crime of killing an infant; the custom, among some peoples in the past, of killing unwanted new-born children.

in·fan·tile /'ɪnfəntaɪl/ adj characteristic of infants: ~ *diseases/pastimes;* ~ *paralysis,* name formerly used for poliomyelitis. **in·fan·til·ism** /ɪn'fæntɪlɪzəm/ n [U] mentally and physically under-developed or arrested state.

in·fan·try /'ɪnfəntrɪ/ n (collective *sing*) [U] soldiers who fight on foot: *two regiments of ~; an ~ regiment.* '~·man /-mən/ n (pl -men) soldier in an ~ regiment. ⇨ cavalry.

in·fatu·ate /ɪn'fætʃʊeɪt/ vt be ~d with/by sb, be filled with a wild and foolish love for: *He's ~d with that girl.* **in·fatu·ation** /ɪn,fætʃʊ'eɪʃn/ n [U] infatuating or being ~d; [C] ~ (for), instance of this; unreasoning love or passion.

in·fect /ɪn'fekt/ vt [VP6A,14] ~ (with), contaminate; give disease, (fig) feelings, ideas, to a person, his body or mind: ~ *a wound; ~ed with cholera. Mary's high spirits ~ed all the girls in the class.*

in·fec·tion /ɪn'fekʃn/ n **1** [U] infecting or being infected; communication of disease, esp by agency of the atmosphere or water, ⇨ contagion. **2** [C] disease, (fig) influence, that infects.

in·fec·tious /ɪn'fekʃəs/ adj **1** infecting with disease; (of disease) that can be spread by means of bacteria carried in the atmosphere or in water. ⇨ contagious. **2** (fig) quickly influencing others; likely to spread to others: ~ *humour.*

in·fer /ɪn'fɜ:(r)/ vt (-rr-) [VP6A,9,14] ~ (from sth) (that...), conclude; reach an opinion (from facts or reasoning): *Am I to ~ from your remarks that you think I am a liar?* ~·ence /'ɪnfərəns/ n **1** [U] process of ~ring: *by ~ence,* as the result of drawing a conclusion. **2** [C] that which is ~red; conclusion: *Is that a fair ~ence from his statement?* ~·en·tial /,ɪnfə'renʃl/ adj that may be ~red.

in·ferior /ɪn'fɪərɪə(r)/ adj low(er) in rank, social position, importance, quality, etc: ~ *goods/ workmanship; an ~ officer/court of law; make sb feel ~.* □ n person who is ~ (in rank, ability, etc). ~·ity /ɪn,fɪərɪ'ɒrətɪ US: -'ɔ:r-/ n [U] state of being ~. '~·ity complex, state of mind in which a person who has a morbid feeling of being ~ to others may try to win recognition for himself by boasting and being aggressive.

in·fer·nal /ɪn'fɜ:nl/ adj of hell; devilish; abominable: *the ~ regions; ~ cruelty.* ~·ly /-nəlɪ/ adv

in·ferno /ɪn'fɜ:nəʊ/ n (pl ~s /-nəʊz/) hell; scene of horror, eg a blazing building in which people are trapped.

in·fer·tile /ɪn'fɜ:taɪl US: -tl/ adj not fertile; barren. **in·fer·til·ity** /,ɪnfə'tɪlətɪ/ n [U].

in·fest /ɪn'fest/ vt [VP6A] (of rats, insects, etc) be present in large numbers: *warehouses ~ed with rats; clothes ~ed with vermin/lice.* **in·fes·ta·tion** /,ɪnfe'steɪʃn/ n [U,C] (instance of) ~ing or being

~ed.

in·fi·del /'ɪnfɪdəl/ n **1** (hist) person with no belief in a religion, esp in what is considered to be the true religion. **2** (attrib) unbelieving; of unbelievers: *He showed an ~ contempt for sacred places.*

in·fi·del·ity /,ɪnfɪ'delətɪ/ n (pl -ties) [C,U] (formal) (act of) disloyalty or unfaithfulness; adultery: *conjugal ~, ~ to one's husband or wife.*

in·field /'ɪnfi:ld/ n (cricket) (opp of *outfield*) part of the ground near the wicket; fieldsmen stationed there; baseball diamond.

in·fight·ing /'ɪn faɪtɪŋ/ n [U] boxing at rather close quarters; (colloq) often ruthless competition between colleagues or rivals (esp in commerce and industry).

in·fil·trate /'ɪnfɪltreɪt/ vt,vi [VP6A,14,2A,3A] ~ sth (into sth); ~ (into/through), (cause to) pass through or into by filtering; (of troops) pass through defences without attracting notice; (of ideas) pass into people's minds. **in·fil·tra·tion** /,ɪnfɪl'treɪʃn/ n [U] infiltrating or being ~d; (esp) gradual and unnoticed occupation of land by small groups, eg of soldiers or settlers.

in·fi·nite /'ɪnfɪnət/ adj endless; without limits; that cannot be measured, calculated, or imagined: ~ *space; the ~ goodness of God. Such ideas may do ~ harm.* **the ~,** God. ~·ly adv in an ~ degree: *Atoms and molecules are ~ly small.* **in·fi·nitesi·mal** /,ɪnfɪnɪ'tesɪml/ adj ~ly small.

in·fini·tive /ɪn'fɪnɪtɪv/ adj, n (gram) (in English) non-finite form of a *v* used with or without *to,* eg let him *go;* allow him *to go.*

in·fini·tude /ɪn'fɪnɪtju:d US: -tu:d/ n [U] (formal) the state of being endless or boundless; boundless number or extent (*of*): *the ~ of God's mercy;* [C] infinite number, quantity, or extent: *an ~ of small particles.*

in·fin·ity /ɪn'fɪnətɪ/ n [U] the state of being endless or boundless; (maths) infinite quantity (expressed by the symbol ∞).

in·firm /ɪn'fɜ:m/ adj **1** physically weak (esp through age): *walk with ~ steps.* **2** mentally or morally weak. ~ **of purpose,** not purposeful; undecided. **in·firm·ity** /ɪn'fɜ:mətɪ/ n (pl -ties) [C,U] (particular form of) weakness: *I~ity often comes with old age. Deafness and failing eyesight are among the ~ities of old age.*

in·firm·ary /ɪn'fɜ:mərɪ/ n (pl -ries) **1** hospital. **2** (in a school, institution, etc) room used for people who are ill or injured.

in·flame /ɪn'fleɪm/ vt,vi [VP2A,6A] (cause to) become red, angry, overheated: ~d *eyes; an ~d boil,* red and angry looking; *speeches that ~d popular feeling,* roused people to anger, indignation, etc; ~d *with passion.*

in·flam·mable /ɪn'flæməbl/ adj easily set on fire or (fig) excited: *Petroleum—Highly I~!* ⇨ flammable.

in·flam·ma·tion /,ɪnflə'meɪʃn/ n [U] inflamed condition (esp of some part of the body): ~ *of the lungs/liver;* [C] instance of this; place on or in the body where there is redness, swelling and pain.

in·flam·ma·tory /ɪn'flæmətrɪ US: -tɔ:rɪ/ adj **1** tending to inflame: ~ *speeches.* **2** of, tending to produce, inflammation: *an ~ condition of the lungs,* eg as a symptom of pneumonia.

in·flate /ɪn'fleɪt/ vt [VP6A,14] ~ sth (with), **1** fill a tyre, balloon, etc with air or gas; (cause to) swell: (fig) ~d *with pride;* ~d *language,* full of high-sounding words but containing little substance. **2**

take action to increase the amount of money in circulation so that prices rise. ⇨ **deflate. in-flat-able** /-əbl/ *adj* that can be ~d: *an inflatable rubber dinghy.* **in-fla-tion** /ɪnˈfleɪʃn/ *n* [U] act of inflating; state of being ~d; (esp) (rise in prices brought about by the) expansion of the supply of bank money, credit, etc. **in-fla-tion-ary** /ɪnˈfleɪʃnrɪ US: -nerɪ/ *adj* of, caused by, inflation: *the inflationary spiral,* economic situation in which prices and wages rise in turn as the supply of money is increased.

in-flect /ɪnˈflekt/ *vt* [VP6A] **1** (gram) change the ending or form of (a word) to show its relationship to other words in a sentence. **2** modulate (the voice); bend inwards; curve.

in-flec-tion /ɪnˈflekʃn/ *n* **1** [U] inflecting. **2** [C] inflected form of a word, eg *am, are, is;* suffix used to inflect, eg *-ed, -ing.* **3** [U] rise and fall of the voice in speaking. ~**al** /-ʃənl/ *adj* of ~: ~*al endings/forms,* eg *-ed.*

in-flex-ible /ɪnˈfleksəbl/ *adj* that cannot be bent or turned; (fig) rigid; unbending; not to be turned aside: ~ *courage; an* ~ *will.* **in-flex-ibly** -əblɪ/ *adv* **in-flexi-bil-ity** /ɪnˌfleksəˈbɪlətɪ/ *n* [U].

in-flex-ion /ɪnˈflekʃn/ *n* = inflection.

in-flict /ɪnˈflɪkt/ *vt* [VP6A,14] ~ *sth (on/upon),* give (a blow, etc); cause to suffer; impose: ~ *a blow/a severe wound upon sb. The judge* ~*ed the death penalty upon the murderer. I'm sorry to have to* ~ *myself/my company upon you,* force my company upon you. **in-flic-tion** /ɪnˈflɪkʃn/ *n* [U] ~ing or being ~ed: *the unnecessary* ~*ion of pain and suffering;* [C] sth ~ed; painful or troublesome experience.

in-flor-escence /ˌɪnflɔːˈresns/ *n* [U] arrangement of a plant's flowers on the stem; collective flower of a plant; (lit or fig) flowering. ⇨ the illus at flower.

in-flow /ˈɪnfləʊ/ *n* [U] flowing in; [C,U] that which flows in: *an* ~ *of capital/investment; an* ~ *of 25 litres an hour;* (attrib) *an* ~ *pipe.*

in-flu-ence /ˈɪnflʊəns/ *n* ~ *on/upon,* **1** [U] power to affect sb's character, beliefs or actions through example, fear, admiration, etc; [C] person, fact, etc that exercises such power; [U] the exercise of such power: *Many a woman has had a civilizing* ~ *upon her husband. He's an* ~ *for good in the town. Heredity and environment are* ~*s on character. He was under the* ~ *of alcohol,* had had too much to drink. **2** [U] action of natural forces: *the* ~ *of the moon (on the tides); the* ~ *of climate (on vegetation).* **3** [U] power due to wealth, position, etc: *Will you please use your* ~ *with the manager on my behalf? Will you use your* ~ *to get me a job?* □ *vt* [VP6A] exert an ~ on; have an effect on: *Can the planets* ~ *human character, as astrologers claim? Don't be* ~*d by bad examples.*

in-flu-en-tial /ˌɪnflʊˈenʃl/ *adj* having influence: ~ *politicians; considerations which are* ~ *in reaching a decision.* ~**ly** /-ʃəlɪ/ *adv*

in-flu-enza /ˌɪnflʊˈenzə/ *n* [U] (colloq abbr flu)infectious disease with fever, muscular pain and catarrh.

in-flux /ˈɪnflʌks/ *n* [U] flowing in; [C] (*pl* ~es) constant inflow of large numbers or quantities: *repeated* ~*es of visitors; an* ~ *of wealth.*

in-form /ɪnˈfɔːm/ *vt,vi* **1** [VP6A,11,14,21] ~ *sb (of sth)/(that...),* give knowledge to: *We were* ~*ed that two prisoners had escaped. Keep me* ~*ed of fresh developments. He's a well-*~*ed man. Have you* ~*ed them of your intended departure?* **2**

[VP3A] ~ *against/on sb,* (legal) bring evidence or an accusation against him (to the police). ~**ant** /-ənt/ *n* person who gives information; (ling) native speaker of a language who helps a foreign scholar who is making an analysis of it. ~**er** *n* person who ~s(2), esp against a criminal or fugitive.

in-for-mal /ɪnˈfɔːml/ *adj* not formal(1,2); irregular; without ceremony or formality: *an* ~ *visit;* ~ *dress;* ~ *conversations between the statesmen of two countries,* no official records being kept. ~**ly** /-məlɪ/ *adv* ~**ity** /ˌɪnfɔːˈmælətɪ/ *n* [U] being ~; [C] (*pl* -ties) ~ act, etc.

in-for-ma-tion /ˌɪnfəˈmeɪʃn/ *n* [U] ~ *on/about,* **1** informing or being informed. **2** sth told; news or knowledge given: *That's a useful piece/bit of* ~*. Can you give me any* ~ *on/about this matter? The '*~ *bureau may be able to help you.*

in-forma-tive /ɪnˈfɔːmətɪv/ *adj* giving information; instructive: ~ *books; an* ~ *talk.* ~**ly** *adv*

in-fra /ˈɪnfrə/ *adv* (Lat, formal) below; farther or later on (in a book, etc): *See* ~ *p21,* see p21 farther on in this book. ~ '**dig** /dɪg/ *pred adj* beneath one's dignity. □ *pref,* ~-'**red** *adj* of those invisible rays below the red in the spectrum. '~-**structure** *n* the parts of a system that compose the whole; (esp) permanent military installations forming a basis for defence. ⇨ supra.

in-frac-tion /ɪnˈfrækʃn/ *n* [U] breaking of a rule, law, etc; [C] instance of this.

in-fre-quent /ɪnˈfriːkwənt/ *adj* not frequent; rare. ~**ly** *adv* **in-fre-quency** /-kwənsɪ/ *n* [U].

in-fringe /ɪnˈfrɪndʒ/ *vt,vi* **1** [VP6A] break (a rule, etc); transgress; violate: ~ *a rule/an oath/ copyright/a patent.* **2** [VP3A] ~ *upon,* encroach: *Be careful not to* ~ *upon the rights of other people.* ~**ment** *n* [U] infringing; [C] ~**ment of,** instance of this, eg the unlawful use of a trade name or of copyright material.

in-furi-ate /ɪnˈfjʊərɪeɪt/ *vt* [VP6A] fill with fury or rage: *infuriating delays.*

in-fuse /ɪnˈfjuːz/ *vt,vi* (formal) **1** [VP14] ~ *into/ with,* put, pour (a quality, etc *into*); fill (sb with): ~ *fresh courage/new life into soldiers;* ~ *soldiers with fresh courage.* **2** [VP6A] pour (hot) liquid on (leaves, herbs, etc) to flavour it or to extract its constituents: ~ *herbs.* **3** [VP2A] undergo infusion: *Let the herbs* ~ *for three minutes.*

in-fu-sion /ɪnˈfjuːʒn/ *n* **1** [U] infusing or being infused. **2** [C] liquid made by infusing. **3** [U] pouring in; mixing: *the* ~ *of new blood into old stock,* the use of new breeds to improve old breeds.

in-gath-er-ing /ˈɪngæðərɪŋ/ *n* [C] (formal) gathering in; harvest.

in-geni-ous /ɪnˈdʒiːnɪəs/ *adj* **1** (of a person) clever and skilful (at making or inventing); showing skill, etc: *an* ~ *mind.* **2** (of things) skilfully made: *an* ~ *toy/tool.* ~**ly** *adv* **in-ge-nuity** /ˌɪndʒɪˈnjuːətɪ US: -'njuː-/ *n* [U] cleverness and skill; originality in design.

in-gé-nue /ˈænʒeɪnju: US: 'ændʒənu:/ *n* (F) (formal) simple, innocent girl, esp as a type in dramas; actress playing such a part.

in-genu-ous /ɪnˈdʒenjʊəs/ *adj* (formal) frank; open; innocent; natural: *an* ~ *smile.* ~**ly** *adv* ~**ness** *n*

in-gest /ɪnˈdʒest/ *vt* [VP6A] (formal) (lit or fig) take in (food, etc) by, or as if by, swallowing.

ingle-nook /ˈɪŋgl nʊk/ *n* chimney-corner (in a wide old-fashioned fireplace) where the fire burns on an open hearth.

in·glori·ous /ɪn'glɔːrɪəs/ adj **1** shameful; ignomini-
ous. **2** obscure. ~·ly adv
in·going /'ɪngəʊɪŋ/ adj going in: the ~ (= new)
tenant of a house/flat.
in·got /'ɪŋgət/ n [C] (usu brick-shaped) lump of
metal (esp gold and silver), cast in a mould.
in·graft /ɪn'grɑːft US: -'græft/ v = engraft.
ingrained /ˌɪn'greɪnd/ adj **1** (of habits, tendencies,
etc) deeply fixed; thorough: ~ prejudices/honesty.
2 going deep: ~ dirt.
in·grati·ate /ɪn'greɪʃɪeɪt/ vt [VP14] ~ oneself
with sb, bring oneself into favour, esp in order to
gain an advantage: with an ingratiating smile. **in-
grati·at·ing·ly** adv
in·grati·tude /ɪn'grætɪtjuːd US: -tuːd/ n [U] want of
gratitude.
in·gredi·ent /ɪn'griːdɪənt/ n [C] one of the parts of a
mixture: the ~s of a cake; the ~s of a man's character, all those qualities, etc that together form it.
in·gress /'ɪngres/ n [U] (formal) going in; (right of)
entrance: a means of ~. ⇨ egress.
in·grow·ing /'ɪngrəʊɪŋ/ adj growing inwards: an ~
toe-nail, one growing into the flesh.
in·habit /ɪn'hæbɪt/ vt [VP6A] live in; occupy. **in-
hab·it·able** /-əbl/ adj that can be lived in. **in·hab-
it·ant** /-ənt/ n person living in a place.
in·hale /ɪn'heɪl/ vt,vi [VP6A,2A] draw into the
lungs: ~ air/gas/tobacco smoke. I~! Exhale!
Breathe in! Breathe out! **in·haler** n device for producing a chemical vapour to make breathing easier.
in·har·moni·ous /ˌɪnhɑː'məʊnɪəs/ adj not harmonious.
in·herent /ɪn'hɪərənt/ adj ~ (in), existing as a natural and permanent part or quality of: Weight is an
~ quality of matter. He has an ~ love of beauty.
The power ~ in the office of President must not be
abused.
in·herit /ɪn'herɪt/ vt,vi [VP6A,2A] **1** receive
property, a title, etc as heir: The eldest son will ~
the title. **2** derive (qualities, etc) from ancestors:
She ~ed her mother's good looks and her father's
bad temper. **in·herit·ance** /-əns/ n [U] ~ing:
receive sth by ~ance; [C] (liter, fig) what is ~ed:
an ~ance of ill-feeling.
in·hibit /ɪn'hɪbɪt/ vt [VP6A,14] ~ sb (from sth/
doing sth), hinder, restrain: ~ wrong desires and
impulses; an ~ed person, one who is unable or unwilling to express his feelings. **in·hi·bi·tion**
/ˌɪnɪ'bɪʃn/ n [U] (psych) restraint on, habitual
shrinking from, an action for which there is an impulse or desire; [C] instance of this: Wine weakens
a person's ~ions. **in·hibi·tory** /ɪn'hɪbɪtrɪ US: -
tɔːrɪ/ adj tending to ~; of an inhibition.
in·hos·pi·table /ˌɪnhɒ'spɪtəbl/ adj not hospitable;
(of a place, coast, etc) not affording shelter: an ~
coast.
in·hu·man /ɪn'hjuːmən/ adj cruel; unfeeling: ~
treatment. ~·ity /ˌɪnhjuː'mænətɪ/ n [U] ~ conduct
or behaviour: man's ~ity to man; [C] (pl -ties) ~
act.
in·hu·mane /ˌɪnhjuː'meɪn/ adj not humane; cruel;
without pity. ~·ly adv
in·imi·cal /ɪ'nɪmɪkl/ adj ~ (to), (formal) unfriendly
or harmful: actions ~ to friendly relations between
countries.
in·imi·table /ɪ'nɪmɪtəbl/ adj (formal) too good,
clever, etc to be imitated. **in·imi·tably** /-əblɪ/ adv
in·iqui·tous /ɪ'nɪkwɪtəs/ adj (formal) very wicked
or unjust: an ~ system/regime. ~·ly adv **in·iquity**
/ɪ'nɪkwətɪ/ n [U] being ~; [C] (pl -ties) ~ act.

in·itial /ɪ'nɪʃl/ adj of or at the beginning: the ~ letter of a word; the ~ stages of an undertaking. □ n
~ letter, esp (pl) first letters of a person's names,
as GBS (for George Bernard Shaw). □ vt (-ll-, US
also -l-) [VP6A] mark, sign, with one's ~s: ~ a
note or document. ~·ly /-ʃəlɪ/ adv at the beginning.
in·iti·ate /ɪ'nɪʃɪeɪt/ vt **1** [VP6A] set (a scheme, etc)
working: ~ a plan. **2** [VP14] ~ sb into sth, admit
or introduce sb to membership of (a group, etc). **3**
[VP14] ~ sb into sth, give sb elementary instruction, or secret knowledge of: ~ students into the
mysteries of interstellar communication. □ n, adj
/ɪ'nɪʃɪət/ n (person) who has been ~d(2,3): an ~
member of a secret society. **in·iti·ation** /ɪˌnɪʃɪ'eɪʃn/
n [U] initiating or being ~d; being made acquainted with the rules of a society, etc: (attrib) initiation
ceremonies.
in·iti·at·ive /ɪ'nɪʃətɪv/ n **1** [U,C] first or introductory step or move: peace ~s. act/do sth on one's
own ~, without an order or suggestion from
others. have the ~, be in the position to make the
first move, eg in war. take the ~ (in doing sth),
make the first move towards it. **2** [U] capacity to
see what needs to be done and enterprise enough to
do it: A statesman must have/show/display ~. **3**
[C] power or right of citizens outside the legislature
to put forward proposals for legislation (as in Switzerland).
in·ject /ɪn'dʒekt/ vt [VP6A,14] ~ sth (into sb/
sth); ~ sb/sth (with sth), drive or force a liquid,
drug, etc into sth with, or as with, a syringe; fill
(sth with a liquid, etc) by ~ing: ~ penicillin into
the blood-stream; ~ sb's arm with morphia; (fig,
colloq) His appointment may ~ some new life into
the committee. **in·jec·tion** /ɪn'dʒekʃn/ n [U] ~ing;
[C] instance of this: five ~ions of glucose; an ~ion
in the left buttock; [C] liquid, etc that is ~ed. **'fuel
injection**, method by which liquid fuel is converted to vapour and sprayed into the cylinders of an
internal combustion engine.
in·ju·di·cious /ˌɪndʒuː'dɪʃəs/ adj (formal) not
well-judged: ~ remarks. ~·ly adv
in·junc·tion /ɪn'dʒʌŋkʃn/ n [C] authoritative order,
esp a written order from a law court, demanding
that sth shall or shall not be done (called an inter-
dict in Scotland).
in·jure /'ɪndʒə(r)/ vt [VP6A] hurt; damage. **in·jured**
adj wounded; hurt; wronged; offended: ~d looks;
in an ~d voice; the dead and the ~d, those people
killed and hurt (in an accident, etc).
in·juri·ous /ɪn'dʒʊərɪəs/ adj ~ (to), (formal) causing, likely to cause, injury; hurtful: behaviour that
is ~ to social order; habits that are ~ to health.
in·jury /'ɪndʒərɪ/ n (pl -ries) **1** [U] harm; damage;
wrongful treatment: If you knock a man down with
your car, and then call him a fool, you are adding
insult to ~. do sb an ~, cause sb harm. **2** [C]
place (in the body) that is hurt or wounded; act that
hurts; insult: The cyclist suffered severe injuries.
This insult was a severe ~ to his reputation.
in·jus·tice /ɪn'dʒʌstɪs/ n [U] lack of justice; [C] unjust act, etc. do sb an ~, judge him unfairly.
ink /ɪŋk/ n [U] (kinds of) coloured liquid used for
writing and printing; black liquid ejected by cuttle-
fish, etc: written in ink; a pen and ink drawing.
'ink-bottle/-pot nn for holding ink. **'ink-pad** n
pad for ink used on rubber stamps. **'ink-stand** n
stand for one or more ink-bottles, with grooves or
a tray for pens, etc. **'ink-well** n ink-pot that fits

into a hole in a desk. □ *vt* [VP6A, 15B] ∼ *(in),* mark with ink: *ink one's fingers; ink in a drawing,* mark with ink lines previously drawn in pencil. **inky** (-ier, -iest) marked with ink: *inky fingers;* black like ink: *inky darkness.*

ink·ling /'ɪŋklɪŋ/ *n* [C] *give sb/have/get an/ some/no* ∼ *(of sth),* give sb/have/get a hint, slight understanding of it.

in·laid /ˌɪn'leɪd/ *pt,pp* of inlay.

in·land /'ɪnlənd/ *adj* **1** situated in the interior of a country, far from the sea or border: ∼ *towns; the* I∼ *Sea of Japan,* area of sea almost enclosed by large islands. **2** carried on, obtained, within the limits of a country: ∼ (= domestic) *trade.* **the** ˌI∼ **'Revenue,** (GB) money obtained by taxation within the country (excluding taxes on imported goods); (colloq) department responsible for collecting these taxes. □ *adv* /ɪn'lænd/ in or towards the interior.

in·laws /'ɪn lɔːz/ *n pl* (colloq) relatives by marriage: *All my* ∼ *will be visiting us this summer.*

in·lay /ˌɪn'leɪ/ *vt* (*pt,pp* inlaid /-leɪd/) [VP6A,14] ∼ *(in/into/with),* set pieces of (designs in) wood, metal, etc in the surface of another kind of wood, metal, etc so that the resulting surface is smooth and even: *gold inlaid into ivory; ivory inlaid with gold.* □ *n* /'ɪnleɪ/ **1** [U] inlaid work; materials used for this; [C] design, pattern, made by ∼ing. **2** [C,U] (dentistry) (method of making a) solid filling of gold, plastic, etc for a cavity in a tooth.

in·let /'ɪnlet/ *n* **1** strip of water extending into the land from a larger body of water (the sea, a lake), or between islands. **2** sth let in or inserted, eg a piece of material inserted into a garment. **3** (attrib) way in: ∼ *and outlet channels,* eg in a reservoir.

in loco par·en·tis /ɪn ˌləʊkəʊ pə'rentɪs/ (Lat) in the place or position of a parent: *I stood towards him* ∼.

in·mate /'ɪnmeɪt/ *n* one of a number of persons living together, esp in a hospital, prison or other institution.

in mem·oriam /ˌɪn mə'mɔːrɪəm/ (Lat) (used in epitaphs, on gravestones) in memory of; as a memorial to.

in·most /'ɪnməʊst/ *adj* most inward; farthest from the surface; (fig) most private or secret: *my* ∼ *feelings.*

inn /ɪn/ *n* **1** public house where lodgings, drink and meals may be had, usu (today) in the country. ⇨ hotel. **'inn-keeper** *n* person who keeps an inn. **2** ˌInn of 'Court,** (building of) one of four law societies in London having the exclusive right of admitting persons to the bar. ⇨ bar¹(12).

in·nards /'ɪnədz/ *n pl* (colloq) **1** stomach and bowels; entrails. **2** any inner parts.

in·nate /ɪ'neɪt/ *adj* (of a quality, etc) in one's nature; possessed from birth: ∼ *aggression.* ∼·ly *adv*

in·ner /'ɪnə(r)/ *adj* (of the) inside: *an* ∼ *room.* ∼ 'city, the oldest parts of a city, at or near its centre: ∼ *city decay.* '∼ **tube,** circular tube, filled with air, in a pneumatic tyre. **the** ∼ **man, (a)** sb's soul or mind (contrasted with *body*). **(b)** (joc) the stomach: *satisfy the* ∼ *man.* ∼·most /-məʊst/ *adj* = inmost.

in·ning /'ɪnɪŋ/ *n* **1** (baseball) division of a game in which each team bats. **2** ∼s, (with *sing v*) (cricket) time during which a player or team is batting: *Our team made 307 runs in its first* ∼s. *The first batsman had a short* ∼s. (fig) period of power, eg of a political party, or of opportunity to show one's ab-

ility, period of active life: *have a good* ∼s, (colloq) have a long and happy life.

in·no·cent /'ɪnəsnt/ *adj* **1** ∼ *(of),* not guilty: ∼ *of the charge/accusation.* **2** harmless: ∼ *amusements.* **3** knowing nothing of evil or wrong: *as* ∼ *as a new-born babe.* **4** foolishly simple: *Don't be so* ∼ *as to believe everything the politicians say.* □ *n* ∼ person, esp a young child. ∼·ly *adv* **in·no·cence** /-sns/ *n* [U] quality or state of being ∼.

in·noc·u·ous /ɪ'nɒkjʊəs/ *adj* causing no harm: ∼ *snakes/drugs.*

in·no·vate /'ɪnəveɪt/ *vi* [VP2A] make changes; introduce new things. **in·no·va·tor** /-tə(r)/ *n* person who ∼s. **in·no·va·tion** /ˌɪnə'veɪʃn/ *n* [U] innovating; [C] instance of this; sth new that is introduced: *technical innovations in industry.*

in·nu·endo /ˌɪnju:'endəʊ/ *n* (*pl* ∼es /-dəʊz/) indirect reference (usu sth unfavourable to a person's reputation): *If you throw out such* ∼es *against the Minister, you'll be sued for libel.*

in·numer·able /ɪ'nju:mərəbl US: ɪ'nu:-/ *adj* too many to be counted.

in·ocu·late /ɪ'nɒkjʊleɪt/ *vt* [VP6A,14] ∼ *sb (with sth) (against sth),* inject a serum or vaccine into him to give him a mild form of the disease to safeguard him against it: ∼ *sb against cholera;* (fig) fill the mind with opinions, etc: ∼*d with evil doctrines.* **in·ocu·la·tion** /ɪˌnɒkjʊ'leɪʃn/ *n* [U] inoculating or being ∼d; [C] instance of this: *have inoculations against cholera and yellow fever.* ⇨ vaccinate.

in·of·fen·sive /ˌɪnə'fensɪv/ *adj* not giving offence; not objectionable: *an* ∼ *remark/person.*

in·op·er·able /ˌɪn'ɒpərəbl/ *adj* (of tumours, etc) that cannot be cured by a surgical operation.

in·op·er·at·ive /ˌɪn'ɒpərətɪv/ *adj* (of laws, rules, etc) not working or taking effect; invalid.

in·op·por·tune /ˌɪn'ɒpətju:n US: -tu:n/ *adj* (esp of time) not appropriate: *at an* ∼ *moment.* ∼·ly *adv*

in·or·di·nate /ɪ'nɔːdɪnət/ *adj* (formal) not properly restrained or controlled; excessive: ∼ *passions; the* ∼ *demands of the Tax Collector.* ∼·ly *adv*

in·or·ganic /ˌɪnɔː'gænɪk/ *adj* **1** not having an organized physical structure, esp as plants and animals have; not forming part of the substance of living bodies: ∼ *chemistry. Rocks and metals are* ∼ *substances.* **2** not the result of natural growth: *an* ∼ *form of society.* **in·or·gani·cally** /-klɪ/ *adv*

in·pa·tient /'ɪn peɪʃnt/ *n* person who lives in hospital while receiving treatment. ⇨ out-patient.

in·pour·ing /'ɪnpɔːrɪŋ/ *n, adj* (formal) pouring in: *an* ∼ *of spiritual comfort.*

in·put /'ɪnpʊt/ *n* [U] ∼ *(to),* what is put in or supplied, eg data for processing in a computer, power supplied to a machine.

in·quest /'ɪnkwest/ *n* ∼ *(on),* official inquiry to learn facts, esp concerning a death which may not be the result of natural causes.

in·quie·tude /ɪn'kwaɪətjuːd US: -tuːd/ *n* [U] (formal) uneasiness of mind; anxiety.

in·quire /ɪn'kwaɪə(r)/ *vt, vi* [VP6A,8,10,14,2A] ∼ *sth (of sb),* ask to be told: ∼ *a person's name;* ∼ *what a person wants/where to stay/how to do sth/ at the railway station;* ∼ *of sb the reason for sth.* **2** [VP3A] ∼ *about/concerning/upon,* ask for information about: ∼ *about trains to London. I* ∼ *within upon everything,* eg as the title of a small encyclopaedia. ∼ *after,* ask about (sb's health, welfare). ∼ *for,* ask for (goods in a shop), ask to see (sb): ∼ *for a book in a shop;* ∼ *for the manag-*

er. ~ *into,* try to learn the facts about; investigate: *We must* ~ *into the matter.* **in·quirer** *n* person who ~s. **in·quir·ing** *adj* in the habit of asking for information: *an inquiring mind,* showing a desire to learn; *inquiring looks.* **in·quir·ing·ly** *adv*

in·quiry /ɪn'kwaɪərɪ US: 'ɪnkwərɪ/ *n* (*pl* -ries) **1** [U] asking; inquiring: *learn sth by* ~. *on* ~, when one has asked. **court of** ~, (mil) one to investigate charges brought against sb. **2** [C] question; investigation: *make inquiries about sb or sth; hold an official* ~ *into sth.*

in·qui·si·tion /ˌɪnkwɪ'zɪʃn/ *n* **1** [U] thorough search or investigation; [C] instance of this, esp a judicial or official inquiry. **2 the I**~, (also called *the Holy Office*) court appointed by the Church of Rome to suppress heresy (esp active in 15th and 16th cc) and to compile the Index(2).

in·quisi·tive /ɪn'kwɪzətɪv/ *adj* fond of, showing a fondness for, inquiring into other people's affairs. ~·ly *adv* ~·ness *n*

in·quisi·tor /ɪn'kwɪzɪtə(r)/ *n* investigator, esp an officer of the Inquisition(2); person appointed by law to make an inquiry. **in·quisi·tor·ial** /ɪnˌkwɪzɪ'tɔːrɪəl/ *adj* of or like an ~.

in·road /'ɪnrəʊd/ *n* sudden attack (into a country, etc), esp one made for the purpose of plunder. *make* ~s *on/upon,* encroach: *make* ~s *upon one's leisure time/one's savings.*

in·rush /'ɪnrʌʃ/ *n* rushing in: *an* ~ *of water/ tourists.*

in·sane /ɪn'seɪn/ *adj* mad; senseless: *an* ~ *person; an* ~ *asylum,* place where ~ people are cared for, now called a mental hospital or home. ~·ly *adv* **in·san·ity** /ɪn'sænətɪ/ *n* [U] madness.

in·sani·tary /ɪn'sænɪtrɪ US: -terɪ/ *adj* not sanitary: *living under* ~ *conditions.*

in·sa·tiable /ɪn'seɪʃəbl/ *adj* ~ *(of/for),* (formal) that cannot be satisfied; very greedy: ~ *appetites; politicians who are* ~ *of power.* **in·sa·tiably** /-ʃəblɪ/ *adv*

in·sa·tiate /ɪn'seɪʃɪət/ *adj* (formal) never satisfied.

in·scribe /ɪn'skraɪb/ *vt* [VP6A,15A] ~ *(on/in/ with),* write (words, one's name, etc in or on); mark (sth with words, etc): ~ *names on a war memorial/one's name in a book;* ~ *a tomb with a name.* ~**d stock,** (comm) stock of which the names of the holders are recorded in lists or registers. **in·scrip·tion** /ɪn'skrɪpʃn/ *n* [C] sth ~d, esp words cut on a stone, eg a monument, or stamped on a coin or medal. ⊏> the illus at epitaph.

in·scru·table /ɪn'skruːtəbl/ *adj* that cannot be understood or known; mysterious: *the* ~ *ways of Providence; the* ~ *face of the Sphinx.*

in·sect /'ɪnsekt/ *n* sort of small animal, eg ant, fly, wasp, having six legs and no backbone and a body divided into three parts (head, thorax, abdomen); (incorrect but pop usage) similar tiny, crawling creature, eg spider. '~**-powder** *n* powder for killing or driving away ~s. **in·sec·ti·cide** /ɪn'sektɪsaɪd/ *n* preparation used for killing ~s, eg DDT. **in·sec·tivor·ous** /ˌɪnsek'tɪvərəs/ *adj* eating ~s as food: *Swallows are* ~*ivorous.*

in·secure /ˌɪnsɪ'kjʊə(r)/ *adj* **1** not safe; not providing good support; not to be relied on: *have an* ~ *hold on sth,* eg when rock-climbing. **2** feeling unsafe; without protection; lacking confidence. ~·ly *adv* **in·se·cur·ity** /ˌɪnsɪ'kjʊərətɪ/ *n* [U] *suffer from feelings of insecurity.*

in·semi·nate /ɪn'semɪneɪt/ *vt* [VP6A] sow seed into; introduce semen into. **in·semi·na·tion**

/ɪnˌsemɪ'neɪʃn/ *n* [U] inseminating. **,artificial in,semi'nation,** the introduction of semen taken, eg from a pedigree animal, into the generative organs of a female animal so that offspring may be produced without sexual union.

in·sen·sate /ɪn'senseɪt/ *adj* (formal) **1** without the power to feel or experience: ~ *rocks.* **2** unfeeling; without sensibility; foolish: ~ *rage/cruelty.*

in·sen·si·bil·ity /ɪnˌsensə'bɪlətɪ/ *n* [U] (formal) lack of mental feeling or emotion; state of being unable to know, recognize, understand or appreciate: ~ *to pain/beauty/art; in a state of* ~, unconscious.

in·sen·sible /ɪn'sensəbl/ *adj* **1** unconscious as the result of injury, illness, etc: *The rock struck her on the head and she was* ~ *for nearly an hour.* **2** ~ *(of),* unaware (of): *He seemed to be* ~ *of his danger. I'm not* ~ *how much I owe to your help.* **3** ~ *(to),* without feeling: *When your hands are frozen they become* ~, numb. **4** unsympathetic; emotionless; callous. **5** (of changes) too small or gradual to be perceived: *by* ~ *degrees.* **in·sen·sibly** /-əblɪ/ *adv*

in·sen·si·tive /ɪn'sensətɪv/ *adj* ~ *(to),* not sensitive (to touch, light, the feelings of other people). ~·ly *adv* **in·sen·si·tiv·ity** /ɪnˌsensə'tɪvətɪ/ *n* [U].

in·sen·tient /ɪn'senʃnt/ *adj* (formal) inanimate; without feeling or awareness.

in·sep·ar·able /ɪn'seprəbl/ *adj* ~ *(from),* that cannot be separated: ~ *friends.*

in·sert /ɪn's3ːt/ *vt* [VP6A,15A] put, fit, place (sth *in, into, between,* etc): ~ *a key in a lock/an advertisement in a newspaper/a new paragraph in an essay.* □ *n* /'ɪns3ːt/ sth ~ed, eg in a book. **in·ser·tion** /ɪn's3ːʃn/ *n* [U] ~ing or being ~ed; [C] sth ~ed, eg an announcement or advertisement in a newspaper, a piece of lace, etc ~ed in a dress.

in·ser·vice /'ɪn s3ːvɪs/ *attrib adj,* while in service (contrasted with *pre*-service training, etc): *the* ~ *training of teachers.* Cf *refresher course.*

in·set /'ɪnset/ *n* [C] extra page(s) inserted in a book, etc; small map, diagram, etc within the border of a printed page or of a larger map; piece of material, eg lace, let into a dress. □ *vt* /ˌɪn'set/ (*pt,pp* inset) put in; insert.

in·shore /ˌɪn'ʃɔː(r)/ *adj, adv* close to the shore: *an* ~ *current;* ~ *fisheries.*

in·side /ɪn'saɪd/ *n* **1** inner side or surface; part(s) within: *the* ~ *of a box; a door bolted on the* ~. ~ /'ɪnsaɪd/ *out,* with the inner side out: *He put his socks on* ~ *out. The wind blew her umbrella* ~ *out. The burglars turned everything* ~ *out,* put drawers, boxes, etc and their contents into great disorder. *He knows the subject* ~ *out,* knows it thoroughly. **2** part of a road, track, etc on the inner edge of a curve; part of a pavement or footpath farthest from the road. **3** (colloq) stomach and bowels: *a pain in his* ~. □ *adj* (or *n* used attrib) /'ɪnsaɪd/ situated on or in, coming from the ~: *the* ~ *pages of a newspaper.* ,~ **'left/'right,** (football, etc) player in the forward (attacking) line immediately to the left/right of the centre-forward. ⊏> the illus at football. **the** '~ **track,** (in racing) track nearest to the inner edge of a curve, giving an advantage to those using it; (fig) a position of advantage. **an** '~ **job,** (sl) theft committed by, or with the help of, sb employed in a building. □ *adv* **1** on or in or to the ~: *Is this coat worn with the fur* ~ *or outside? Look* ~. *Go* ~. *There's nothing* ~. ~ *of,* (colloq) in less than: *We can't finish the work* ~ *of a week.* **2** (GB sl) in prison: *Jones is* ~ *for*

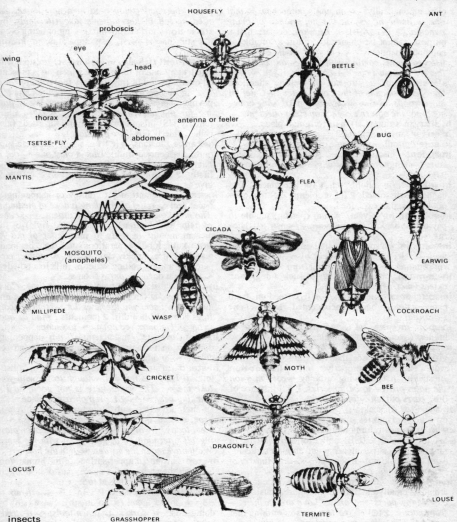

insects

three years. □ prep on the inner side of: *Don't let the dog come ~ the house. She was standing just ~ the gate.* **in·sider** n /ɪnˈsaɪdə(r) person who, because he is a member of some society, organization, etc is in a position to obtain facts and information, or win advantages, that others cannot get for themselves. ⇨ **outsider.**

in·sidi·ous /ɪnˈsɪdɪəs/ adj doing harm secretly, unseen: *an ~ enemy/disease.* ~·ly adv ~·ness n

in·sight /ˈɪnsaɪt/ n 1 [U] ~ (into sth), understanding; power of seeing into sth with the mind; [C] instance of this: *a man of ~; show ~ into human character; a book full of remarkable ~s.* 2 [C] (often sudden) perception, glimpse, or understanding: *When he spoke, she had an unpleasant ~ into what life would be like as his wife.*

in·sig·nia /ɪnˈsɪɡnɪə/ n pl symbols of authority, dignity, or honour, eg the crown and sceptre of a king; (mil) identifying badge of a regiment, etc.

in·sig·nifi·cant /ˌɪnsɪɡˈnɪfɪkənt/ adj having little or no value, use, meaning or importance: *~ talk; an ~-looking little man.* ~·ly adv **in·sig·nifi·cance** /-əns/ n [U].

in·sin·cere /ˌɪnsɪnˈsɪə(r)/ adj not sincere. ~·ly adv **in·sin·cer·ity** /ˌɪnsɪnˈserətɪ/ n [U].

in·sinu·ate /ɪnˈsɪnjʊeɪt/ vt 1 [VP6A,14] ~ sth/ oneself (into), make a way for (oneself/sth) gently and craftily: *~ oneself into a person's favour.* ⇨ worm. 2 [VP9] ~ (to sb) that, suggest unpleasantly and indirectly: *~ (to sb) that a man is a liar.* **in·sinu·ation** /ɪnˌsɪnjʊˈeɪʃn/ n [U] insinuating; [C] sth ~d; indirect suggestion.

in·sipid /ɪnˈsɪpɪd/ adj without taste or flavour: *~ food;* (fig) *~ conversation; a pretty but ~ young lady,* one who is lacking in interest or spirit. ~·ly adv ~·ness n **in·si·pid·ity** /ˌɪnsɪˈpɪdətɪ/ n [U].

in·sist /ɪnˈsɪst/ vi,vt [VP3A,B] 1 ~ on/that, urge with emphasis, against opposition or disbelief; declare emphatically: ~ *on one's innocence;* ~ *that one is innocent;* ~ *on the importance of being punctual.* 2 [VP3A,B] ~ *on/that,* declare that a purpose cannot be changed; urge in a forcible or emphatic manner: *I* ~*ed that he should come with us/*~*ed on his coming with us. I* ~ *on your being there. 'You must come'*—*'All right, if you* ~.' **in-sist-ent** /-ənt/ *adj* urgent; compelling attention: *the* ~*ent demands of the Commander-in-Chief for more troops.* **in-sist-ence** /-əns/ *n* [U] ~ing or being ~ed: *the officer's* ~*ence on strict obedience.*

in situ /ˌɪn ˈsɪtjuː/ (Lat) in its (original) place.

in-so-far /ˌɪnsəˈfɑː(r)/ (US) = in so far. ⇨ in ¹(18).

in-sole /ˈɪnsəʊl/ *n* inner sole of a shoe.

in-so-lent /ˈɪnsələnt/ *adj* ~ *(to),* insulting; offensive; contemptuous. ~·**ly** *adv* **in-so-lence** /-əns/ *n* [U] being ~.

in-sol-uble /ɪnˈsɒljʊbl/ *adj* 1 (of substances) that cannot be dissolved. 2 (of problems, etc) that cannot be solved or explained.

in-sol-vent /ɪnˈsɒlvənt/ *n, adj* (person) unable to pay debts; bankrupt. **in-sol-vency** /-ənsɪ/ *n* [U] being ~.

in-som-nia /ɪnˈsɒmnɪə/ *n* [U] inability to sleep; want of sleep: *ill after weeks of* ~. **in-som-niac** /ɪnˈsɒmnɪæk/ *n* person suffering from ~.

in-so-much /ˌɪnsəʊˈmʌtʃ/ *adv* to such a degree or extent *(that/as).*

in-souci-ance /ɪnˈsuːsɪəns/ *n* [U] freedom from care; state of being unconcerned. **in-souci-ant** /-ənt/ *adj*

in-span /ɪnˈspæn/ *vt* (S African) (-nn-) yoke or harness (oxen, etc) to a vehicle.

in-spect /ɪnˈspekt/ *vt* [VP6A] examine carefully; visit officially to see that rules are obeyed, that work is done properly, etc. **in-spec-tion** /ɪnˈspekʃn/ *n* 1 [U] ~ing or being ~ed: *On* ~*ion the notes proved to be forgeries.* 2 [C] instance of this: *carry out ten* ~*ions a week.*

in-spec-tor /ɪnˈspektə(r)/ *n* 1 official who inspects, eg schools, factories, mines: ˌ*I*~ *of¹ Taxes,* offical who examines returns of income and assesses the tax to be paid. 2 (GB) police officer who is, in rank, below a superintendent and above a sergeant. ~·**ate** /ɪnˈspektərət/ *n* body of ~s: *the Ministry of Education* ~*ate.*

in-spi-ra-tion /ˌɪnspəˈreɪʃn/ *n* 1 [U] influence(s) arousing creative activity in literature, music, art, etc: *Many poets and artists have drawn their* ~ *from nature.* 2 [C] ~ *(to/for),* person or thing that inspires: *His wife was a constant* ~ *to him.* 3 [C] (colloq) good thought or idea that comes to the mind: *have a sudden* ~. 4 [U] divine guidance held to have been given to those who wrote the Bible.

in-spire /ɪnˈspaɪə(r)/ *vt* [VP6A,14,17] ~ *sth (in sb);* ~ *sb (with sth/to do sth),* 1 put uplifting thoughts, feelings or aims into: ~ *sb with hope/ enthusiasm/confidence;* ~ *confidence in sb. What* ~*d him to give such a brilliant performance?* 2 fill with creative power: ~*d poets/artists; in an* ~*d moment.* 3 (pp) ~*d,* (of sth written or spoken) one secretly suggested by an influential person who has special information.

in-sta-bil-ity /ˌɪnstəˈbɪlətɪ/ *n* [U] lack of stability (usu of character, moral qualities).

in-stall (US also **in-stal**) /ɪnˈstɔːl/ *vt* [VP6A,14] ~ *sb/sth (in sth),* 1 place (sb) in a new position of authority with the usual ceremony: ~ *a priest.* 2 place, fix (apparatus) in position for use: ~ *a heating or lighting system.* 3 settle (sb/oneself) in a

place: *be comfortably* ~*ed in a new home. She* ~*ed herself in her father's favourite chair.* **in-stal-la-tion** /ˌɪnstəˈleɪʃn/ *n* [U] ~ing or being ~ed; [C] sth that is ~ed, esp apparatus: *a heating* ~*ation.*

in-stal-ment (US also **in-stall-ment**) /ɪnˈstɔːlmənt/ *n* [C] 1 any one of the parts in which sth is presented over a period of time: *a story that will appear in* ~s, eg in a periodical. 2 any one of the parts of a payment spread over a period of time: *We're paying for the television by monthly* ~*s.* '~ **plan,** (chiefly US) this method of paying for goods (also called, chiefly GB, *hire purchase*).

in-stance /ˈɪnstəns/ *n* [C] 1 example; fact, etc supporting a general truth: *This is only one* ~ *out of many.* **for** ~, by way of example. **in the first** ~, firstly. 2 **at the** ~ **of,** at the request of. □ *vt* [VP6A] give as an example.

in-stant¹ /ˈɪnstənt/ *adj* 1 coming or happening at once: *feel* ~ *relief after taking a dose of medicine. The novel was an* ~ *success.* 2 urgent: *in* ~ *need of help.* 3 (abbr **inst**) (comm; dated style) of the present month: *in reply to your letter of the 9th inst.* 4 (of food preparations) that can be made ready for use quickly and easily: ~ *coffee,* prepared by adding boiling water or milk to a powder. ~·**ly** *adv* at once. □ *conj* as soon as.

in-stant² /ˈɪnstənt/ *n* 1 precise point of time: *Come here this* ~! at once! *He left that* ~*/on the* ~, immediately. *I sent you the news the* ~ *(that) I heard it,* as soon as I heard it. 2 moment: *I shall be back in an* ~. *Help arrived not an* ~ *too soon.*

in-stan-taneous /ˌɪnstənˈteɪnɪəs/ *adj* happening, done, in an instant: *Death was* ~, eg in an accident. ~·**ly** *adv*

in-stead /ɪnˈsted/ *adv* as an alternative or substitute: *If Harry is not well enough to go with you, take me* ~. *The water here is not good, so I'm drinking beer* ~. ~ **of,** *prep phrase* in place of; as an alternative to or substitute for (followed by a *n, pron, gerund,* or *prep phr*): *Shall we have fish* ~ *of meat today? I will go* ~ *of you. He has been playing all afternoon* ~ *of getting on with his work. We'll have tea in the garden* ~ *of in the house.*

in-step /ˈɪnstep/ *n* upper surface of the human foot between the toes and the ankle; part of a shoe, etc covering this. ⇨ the illus at leg.

in-sti-gate /ˈɪnstɪgeɪt/ *vt* [VP6A,17] ~ *sth/sb to do sth,* incite; goad (sb to do sth); cause (sth) by doing this: ~ *workers to down tools;* ~ *a strike.* **in-sti-ga-tor** /-tə(r)/ *n* **in-sti-ga-tion** /ˌɪnstɪˈgeɪʃn/ *n* instigating or being ~d.

in-stil (US = **in-still**) /ɪnˈstɪl/ *vt* (-ll-) [VP6A,14] ~ *sth into sb,* introduce (ideas, etc) gradually. **in-stil-la-tion** /ˌɪnstɪˈleɪʃn/ *n*

in-stinct /ˈɪnstɪŋkt/ *n* 1 [U] natural tendency to behave in a certain way without reasoning or training: *Birds learn to fly by* ~. 2 [C] innate impulse or intuition; instance of ~(1): *He seems to have an* ~ *for always doing and saying the right thing.* □ *pred adj* /ɪnˈstɪŋkt/ ~ **with,** filled with, animated by: *a picture* ~ *with life; a poem* ~ *with passion.* **in-stinc-tive** /ɪnˈstɪŋktɪv/ *adj* based on ~, not coming from training or teaching: *Animals have an* ~*ive dread of fire.* **in-stinc-tive-ly** *adv*

in-sti-tute¹ /ˈɪnstɪtjuː/ *US:* -tuːt/ *n* [C] society or organization for a special (usu a social or educational) purpose; its office(s) or building(s).

in-sti-tute² /ˈɪnstɪtjuː/ *US:* -tuːt/ *vt* 1 [VP6A] establish, start, an inquiry, custom, rule, etc: ~ *legal* *proceedings against sb;* ∼ *an action at law;* ∼ *restrictions on the use of pesticides.* **2** [VP6A,14] ∼ *sb (to),* appoint him (to an official position).

in·sti·tu·tion /ˌɪnstɪ'tjuːʃn US: -'tuːʃn/ *n* **1** [U] instituting or being instituted: *the* ∼ *of customs/rules, etc;* ∼ *as a bishop.* **2** [C] long-established law, custom, or group (eg a club or society); familiar object or person. **3** (building of) organization for social welfare, eg an orphanage, a home for old people. ∼**al** /-ʃənl/ *adj* of or connected with an ∼(3): *old people in need of* ∼*al care.* ∼**al·ize** /-ʃənəlaɪz/ *vt* [VP6A] make into an ∼(2).

in·struct /ɪn'strʌkt/ *vt* **1** [VP6A,15A] teach a school subject, a skill: ∼ *a class in history;* ∼ *recruits/a class of apprentices.* **2** [VP17,20,21] give orders or directions to: ∼ *sb to start early;* ∼ *sb how to do his work.* **3** [VP11,20,21] inform: *I have been* ∼*ed by my agent that you still owe me £50.* **in·struc·tor** /-tə(r)/ *n* person who ∼s; trainer. **in·struc·tress** /-trɪs/ *n* woman who ∼s.

in·struc·tion /ɪn'strʌkʃn/ *n* **1** [U] instructing or being instructed: ∼ *in chemistry; give/receive* ∼. **2** (*pl*) directions; orders: *give sb* ∼*s to arrive early;* ∼*s* (= coded commands) *to a computer.* ∼**al** /-ʃənl/ *adj* educational: ∼*al films,* eg of industrial processes.

in·struc·tive /ɪn'strʌktɪv/ *adj* giving or containing instruction: ∼ *books.* ∼**·ly** *adv*

in·stru·ment /'ɪnstrʊmənt/ *n* [C] **1** implement, apparatus, used in performing an action, esp for delicate or scientific work: *optical* ∼*s,* eg a microscope; *surgical* ∼*s,* eg a scalpel. Cf *tools* used by labourers and craftsmen. **2** apparatus for producing musical sounds, eg a piano, violin, flute or drum. ⇨ the illus at brass, percussion, string. **3** person used by another for his own purposes: *be made the* ∼ *of another's crime.* **4** formal (esp legal) document: *The King signed the* ∼ *of abdication.* **in·stru·men·ta·tion** /ˌɪnstrʊmen'teɪʃn/ *n* [U] arrangement of music for ∼s; the development and manufacture of ∼s for scientific use.

in·stru·men·tal /ˌɪnstrʊ'mentl/ *adj* **1** serving as an instrument or means: *be* ∼ *in finding well-paid work for a friend.* **2** of or for musical instruments: ∼ *music.* ∼**·ist** /-təlɪst/ *n* player of a musical instrument. ∼**·ity** /ˌɪnstrʊmen'tælətɪ/ *n* [U] agency: *by the* ∼*ity of,* by means of.

in·sub·or·di·nate /ˌɪnsə'bɔːdɪnət/ *adj* disobedient; rebellious. **in·sub·or·di·na·tion** /ˌɪnsəˌbɔːdɪ'neɪʃn/ *n* [U] being ∼; [C] instance of this.

in·sub·stan·tial /ˌɪnsəb'stænʃl/ *adj* **1** not solid or real; lacking substance: *an* ∼ *vision.* **2** without good foundation: *an* ∼ *accusation.*

in·suf·fer·able /ɪn'sʌfrəbl/ *adj* over-proud; unbearably conceited; unbearable: ∼ *insolence.*

in·suf·fi·cient /ˌɪnsə'fɪʃnt/ *adj* not sufficient: ∼ *evidence/grounds.* ∼**·ly** *adv* **in·suf·fi·ciency** /-ʃnsɪ/ *n*

in·su·lar /'ɪnsjʊlə(r) US: -sələr/ *adj* **1** of an island: *an* ∼ *climate.* **2** of or like islanders; (esp) narrowminded: ∼ *habits and prejudices.* ∼**·ism** /-ɪzəm/, **in·su·lar·ity** /ˌɪnsjʊ'lærətɪ US: -sə'l-/ *nn* state of being ∼ (esp 2).

in·su·late /'ɪnsjʊleɪt US: -səl-/ *vt* [VP6A,14] ∼ **(from),** **1** cover or separate (sth) with nonconducting materials to prevent loss of heat, prevent passage of electricity, etc: ∼ *a cookingstove with asbestos;* '*insulating tape,* as used for covering joins in flex for electric current. **2** separate (sb or sth) (from): *children carefully* ∼*d from*

harmful experiences; isolate. **in·su·la·tor** /-tə(r)/ *n* [C] substance, device, for insulating, esp a device of porcelain used for supporting bare electric wires and cables. **in·su·la·tion** /ˌɪnsjʊ'leɪʃn US: -sə'l-/ *n* [U] insulating or being ∼d; materials used for this.

in·su·lin /'ɪnsjʊlɪn US: -səl-/ *n* [U] substance (a hormone) prepared from the pancreas of sheep, used in the medical treatment of sufferers from diabetes.

in·sult /ɪn'sʌlt/ *vt* [VP6A] speak or act in a way that hurts or is intended to hurt a person's feelings or dignity. ☐ *n* /'ɪnsʌlt/ [C,U] remark or action that ∼s. ∼**·ing** *adj* ∼**·ing·ly** *adv*

in·sup·er·able /ɪn'sjuːprəbl US: -'suː-/ *adj* (of difficulties, etc) that cannot be overcome: ∼ *barriers.*

in·sup·port·able /ˌɪnsə'pɔːtəbl/ *adj* unbearable; that cannot be endured.

in·sur·ance /ɪn'ʃʊərəns/ *n* **1** [U] (undertaking, by a company, society, or the State, to provide) safeguard against loss, provision against sickness, death, etc in return for regular payments. **2** [U] payment made to or by such a company, etc: *When her husband died, she received £20000* ∼. *He pays out £110 in* ∼/in ∼ *premiums every year.* '∼ **pol-icy** *n* contract made about ∼. **3** [C] ∼ policy: *How many* ∼*s have you?* **4** any measure taken as a safeguard against loss, failure, etc: *He's sitting an entrance exam at Leeds University as an* ∼ *against failure at York.*

in·sure /ɪn'ʃʊə(r)/ *vt* [VP6A,14] ∼ **(against),** make a contract that promises to pay, secures payment of, a sum of money in case of accident, damage, loss, injury, death, etc: ∼ *one's house against fire;* ∼ *oneself/one's life for £50000. Insurance companies will* ∼ *ships and their cargoes against loss at sea.* **the** ∼**d,** the person to whom payment will be made. **the** ∼**r,** the person or company undertaking to make payment in case of loss, etc. **the in·surant** /ɪn'ʃʊərənt/, (legal) the person who pays the premiums.

in·sur·gent /ɪn'sɜːdʒənt/ *adj* (rarely *pred*) rebellious; in revolt. ☐ *n* rebel soldier.

in·sur·mount·able /ˌɪnsə'maʊntəbl/ *adj* (of obstacles, etc) that cannot be surmounted or overcome.

in·sur·rec·tion /ˌɪnsə'rekʃn/ *n* [U] rising of people in open resistance to the government; [C] instance of this.

in·tact /ɪn'tækt/ *adj* untouched; undamaged; complete: *He lived on the interest and kept his capital* ∼.

in·taglio /ɪn'tɑːlɪəʊ/ *n* (*pl* ∼s /-z/) [U] (I) (process of) carving in depth; [C] (gem with) figure or design made by cutting into the surface of metal or stone. ⇨ cameo.

in·take /'ɪnteɪk/ *n* **1** [C] place where water, gas, etc is taken into a pipe, channel, etc. **2** [C,U] quantity, number, etc entering or taken in (during a given period): *an annual* ∼ *of 100000 men,* eg for military service. **3** (area of) land reclaimed from a moor, marsh or the sea.

in·tan·gible /ɪn'tændʒəbl/ *adj* that cannot be touched or grasped; (esp) that cannot be grasped by the mind: ∼ *ideas;* ∼ *assets,* assets (of a business) which cannot be measured, eg a good reputation. **in·tan·gi·bil·ity** /ɪnˌtændʒə'bɪlətɪ/ *n*

in·te·ger /'ɪntɪdʒə(r)/ *n* whole number (contrasted with *fraction*): *1, 3 and − 3 are* ∼*s,* ¾ *is not an* ∼.

in·te·gral /'ɪntɪɡrəl/ *adj* **1** necessary for completeness: *The arms and legs are* ∼ *parts of a human* *being*. **2** whole; having or containing all parts that are necessary for completeness. ⇨ **calculus**. **3** (maths) of, denoted by, an integer; made up of integers. **~·ly** /-grəlɪ/ *adv*

in·te·grate /ˈɪntɪgreɪt/ *vt* [VP6A,2A] **1** combine (parts) into a whole; complete (sth that is imperfect or incomplete) by adding parts: *an ~d personality*, person whose physical, mental and emotional components fit together well. **~d 'circuit** *n* very small circuit (**4**) made of a single chip of eg silicon. **2** bring or come into equality by the mixing of groups or races. **in·te·gra·tion** /ˌɪntɪˈgreɪʃn/ *n* [U] integrating or being ~d: *the integration of black children into the school system in the Southern States of America.*

in·teg·rity /ɪnˈtegrətɪ/ *n* [U] **1** quality of being honest and upright in character: *a man of ~; commercial ~.* **2** state or condition of being complete: *The old Roman walls may still be seen, but not in their ~. Wasn't this Treaty supposed to guarantee our territorial ~?*

in·tegu·ment /ɪnˈtegjʊmənt/ *n* (formal) (usu natural) outer covering, eg skin, a husk, rind or shell.

in·tel·lect /ˈɪntəlekt/ *n* **1** [U] power of the mind to reason (contrasted with feeling and instinct): *I~ distinguishes man from the animals. He's a man of ~.* **2** (collective *sing*, or in *pl*) person(s) of good understanding, reasoning power, etc: *the ~(s) of the age.*

in·tel·lec·tual /ˌɪntəˈlektʃʊəl/ *adj* **1** of the intellect: *the ~ faculties.* **2** having or showing good reasoning power; interested in things of the mind (the arts, ideas for their own sake): *~ people; ~ interests/pursuits.* □ *n* [C] ~ person: *a play/book for the ~s.* **~·ly** /-tʃʊəlɪ/ *adv*

in·tel·li·gence /ɪnˈtelɪdʒəns/ *n* [U] **1** the power of perceiving, learning, understanding and knowing; mental ability: *a boy who shows little ~. The children were given an ~ test. When the water-pipe burst, she had the ~ to turn the water off at the main.* **2** news; information, esp with reference to important events: *have secret ~ of the enemy's plans; the I~ Department/Service*, eg of an army or navy, collecting and studying information useful in war. **in·tel·li·gent** /-ənt/ *adj* having, showing, ~: *intelligent questions/answers; an intelligent child; an intelligent expression on sb's face.* **in·tel·li·gent·ly** *adv*

in·tel·li·gent·sia /ɪnˌtelɪˈdʒentsɪə/ *n* (usu collective *sing* **the ~**) that part of a community which can be regarded (or which regards itself) as intellectual and capable of serious independent thinking.

in·tel·li·gible /ɪnˈtelɪdʒəbl/ *adj* that can be easily understood; clear to the mind: *~ speech; an ~ explanation.* **in·tel·li·gibly** /-əblɪ/ *adv* **in·tel·li·gi·bil·ity** /ɪnˌtelɪdʒəˈbɪlətɪ/ *n* the quality of being ~.

in·tem·per·ate /ɪnˈtempərət/ *adj* (formal) (of a person or his behaviour) not moderate; showing lack of self-control: *~ habits*, (esp) habits of excessive drinking. **~·ly** *adv* **in·tem·per·ance** /-pərəns/ *n* [U].

in·tend /ɪnˈtend/ *vt* [VP6A,D,7A,9,14,17] **1** *(for)*, have in mind as a purpose or plan: *What do you ~ to do/~ doing today? They ~ that this reform shall be carried through this year. We ~ them to do it/that they shall do it. His son is ~ed for the medical profession. This book is ~ed for you*, is to be given to you. *Is this sketch ~ed to be me*, Is it a sketch of me? *Does he ~ marriage or is he only flirting with her? Let me introduce you to*

my ~ed, (sl for 'my future wife'). **2** ~ *(by)*, (old use) mean: *What do you ~ by this word?*

in·tense /ɪnˈtens/ *adj* **1** (of qualities) high in degree: *~ heat.* **2** (of feelings, etc) ardent; violent; (of persons) highly emotional: *~ political convictions.* **~·ly** *adv*

in·ten·sify /ɪnˈtensɪfaɪ/ *vt,vi* (*pt,pp* –fied) [VP6A,2A] make or become more intense. **in·ten·si·fi·ca·tion** /ɪnˌtensɪfɪˈkeɪʃn/ *n* [U,C].

in·ten·sity /ɪnˈtensətɪ/ *n* [U] state or quality of being intense; strength or depth (of feeling, etc); [C] instance of these.

in·ten·sive /ɪnˈtensɪv/ *adj* **1** characterized by, relating to, intensity (as opposed to extent); deep and thorough: *make an ~ study of a subject; ~ methods of horticulture*, producing large quantities by concentrating labour and care on small areas of land; *an ~ bombardment.* **~ care** *n* medical treatment with constant observation etc of the patient. *~ 'care unit* part of a hospital where this is given. **2** (gram) giving force and emphasis: *In 'a bloody difficult book' and 'a terribly hot day', 'bloody' and 'terribly' are used colloquially as ~ words.* **~·ly** *adv*

in·tent¹ /ɪnˈtent/ *adj* **1** (of looks) eager; earnest: *There was an ~ look on her face as she watched the game.* **2** ~ *on/upon sth/doing sth*, (of persons) with the desires or attentions directed towards: *He was ~ on his work/on getting to the office in time.* **~·ly** *adv* **~·ness** *n*

intent² /ɪnˈtent/ *n* **1** [U] (chiefly legal) purpose; intention: *shoot with ~ to kill; with good/evil/malicious ~.* **2** (*pl*) **to all ~s and purposes**, in all essential points.

in·ten·tion /ɪnˈtenʃn/ *n* [C,U] intending; thing intended; aim; purpose: *If I've hurt your feelings, it was quite without ~. He went to Paris with the ~ of learning French. His ~s are good, but he seldom carries them out. Has he made known his ~s*, said what he intends to do? (-)**in·ten·tioned** *adj: ,well-¹~ed*, having good ~s; *,ill-¹~ed*, having bad, wrong, etc ~s.

in·ten·tional /ɪnˈtenʃənl/ *adj* intended; done with purpose: *If I hurt your feelings, it was not ~.* **~·ly** /-ʃənəlɪ/ *adv* with purpose.

in·ter /ɪnˈtɜː(r)/ *vt* (-rr-) (formal) place (a corpse) in a grave or tomb; bury.

in·ter·act /ˌɪntərˈækt/ *vi* act on each other. **in·ter·ac·tion** /-ˈækʃn/ *n* **in·ter·ac·tive** /-ˈæktɪv/ *adj*

in·ter alia /ˌɪntər ˈeɪlɪə/ (Lat) among other things.

in·ter·breed /ˌɪntəˈbriːd/ *vt,vi* (*pt,pp* –bred /-ˈbred/) [VP6A,2A] crossbreed; produce hybrids.

in·ter·ca·lary /ɪnˈtɜːkələrɪ US: -lerɪ/ *adj* (of a day or month) added to make the calendar year correspond to the solar year; (of a year) having such an addition.

in·ter·cede /ˌɪntəˈsiːd/ *vi* [VP3A] ~ *(with sb) (for sb)*, plead (as a peacemaker, or to obtain a favour): *~ with the father for/on behalf of the daughter.* **in·ter·ces·sion** /ˌɪntəˈseʃn/ *n* [U] interceding; [C] prayer or entreaty for another.

in·ter·cept /ˌɪntəˈsept/ *vt* [VP6A] stop, catch (sb or sth) between starting-point and destination: *~ a letter/a messenger. Can our fighter-planes ~ the enemy's bombers?* **in·ter·cep·tion** /ˌɪntəˈsepʃn/ *n* [U,C]. **in·ter·cep·tor** /-tə(r)/ *n* sb or sth that ~s, eg a fast fighter-plane.

in·ter·change /ˌɪntəˈtʃeɪndʒ/ *vt* **1** [VP6A] (of two persons, etc) give and receive; make an exchange of: *~ views/gifts/letters.* **2** [VP6A,2A] put (each of

two things) in the other's place. ~·able /-əbl/ adj
that can be ~d: True synonyms are ~able. This
machine has ~able parts. □ n /'ɪntətʃeɪndʒ/ [U,C]
interchanging: an ~ of views.

in·ter·col·legi·ate /ˌɪntəkə'liːdʒɪət/ adj carried on,
etc between colleges: ~ games/debates.

in·ter·com /'ɪntəkɒm/ n (colloq) system of (inter-)
communication, eg in aircraft: receive a message
on/over the ~.

in·ter·com·mu·ni·cate /ˌɪntəkə'mjuːnɪkeɪt/ vi communicate with one another: The prisoners ~ by using the Morse code. in·ter·com·mu·ni·ca·tion
/ˌɪntəkəˌmjuːnɪ'keɪʃn/ n [U].

in·ter·com·mu·nion /ˌɪntəkə'mjuːnɪən/ n mutual
communion, esp between different Churches, eg
Catholic and Orthodox.

in·ter·con·ti·nen·tal /ˌɪntəkɒntɪ'nentl/ adj between
continents: ~ ballistic missiles, that can be fired
from one continent to another.

in·ter·course /'ɪntəkɔːs/ n [U] 1 social dealings between individuals; exchanges of trade, ideas, etc
between persons, societies, nations, etc: our commercial ~ with S America. 2 (sexual) ~, = coitus.

in·ter·de·nomi·na·tional /ˌɪntədɪˌnɒmɪ'neɪʃənl/
adj common to, shared by, different religious denominations, eg Methodist, Baptist, Catholic.

in·ter·de·pen·dent /ˌɪntədɪ'pendənt/ adj depending
on each other. in·ter·de·pen·dence /-əns/ n

in·ter·dict /ˌɪntə'dɪkt/ vt [VP6A] (formal) prohibit
(an action); forbid (the use of sth); (RC Church)
exclude from sacraments and church services. □ n
/'ɪntədɪkt/ [C] formal or authoritative prohibition,
esp (RC Church) an order debarring a person or
place from sacraments and church services: lay a
priest/a town under an ~. in·ter·dic·tion
/ˌɪntə'dɪkʃn/ n [U,C] ~ing; ~(n).

in·ter·dis·ci·plin·ary /ˌɪntəˌdɪsɪ'plɪnərɪ/ adj of more
than one branch of learning: ~ studies/degrees.

in·ter·est¹ /'ɪntrəst/ n 1 [U] condition of wanting to
know or learn about sth or sb: feel/take no/not
much/a great ~ in politics; events that arouse
great ~. ⇨ lose. 2 [U] quality that arouses concern
or curiosity, that holds one's attention: a matter of
considerable/not much ~. Suspense adds ~ to a
story. 3 [C] sth with which one concerns oneself:
Her chief ~ seems to be horse-racing. His two
great ~s in life are music and painting. 4 [C] (often pl) advantage; profit; well-being: look after
one's own ~s; work in the ~(s) of humanity;
travel in Asia in the ~s of a business firm. It is to
your ~ to go. 5 [C] legal right to a share in sth, esp
in its profits: have an ~ in a brewery, eg by owning shares; have an ~ in an estate, a legal claim to
part of it; American ~s in the Caribbean, eg capital invested in the countries of that area; He has
sold his ~ in the company. 6 [U] money charged or
paid for the use of money: rate of ~/4 ~ rate, payment made by a borrower for a loan, expressed as a
percentage, eg 5%; pay 6 per cent ~ on a loan.
with ~, (fig) with increased force: return a blow/
sb's kindness with ~, give back more than one
received. 7 (often pl) group of persons engaged in
the same trade, etc or having sth in common: the
landed ~, landowners collectively; the business
~s, large business firms collectively; the brewing
~, brewers collectively.

in·ter·est² /'ɪntrəst/ vt [VP6A,14] ~ sb (in sth),
cause (sb) to give his attention to: Can I ~ you in
this question? He is ~ed in shipping, (a) likes to

know and learn about ships. (b) has money invested in the shipping industry. ~ed adj ~ed (in) 1
having an interest(1) in; not impartial: When manufacturers demand higher tariffs, we may suspect
them of having ~ed motives. 2 showing interest(1):
an ~ed look. 3 taking an interest(1) in: ~ed spectators; not ~ed in botany/his work. I shall be ~ed
to know what happens. ~·ing adj holding the attention; arousing interest(1): ~ing men/books/
conversation. ~·ing·ly adv

in·ter·face /'ɪntəfeɪs/ n 1 surface common to two
areas. 2 (fig) area common to two or more systems,
processes, etc: at the ~ of creative art and experimental science.

in·ter·fere /ˌɪntə'fɪə(r)/ vi 1 [VP2A,3A] ~ (in sth),
(of persons) break in upon (other person's affairs)
without right or invitation; Please don't ~ in my
business. Isn't she an interfering old lady! It's unwise to ~ between husband and wife. 2 [VP2A,3A]
~ (with), (of persons) meddle; tamper (with): Do
not ~ with this machine. 3 [VP3A] ~ with, (of
events, circumstances, etc) come into opposition;
hinder or prevent: Do you ever allow pleasure to ~
with duty? in·ter·fer·ence /ˌɪntə'fɪərəns/ n [U] interfering: interference from foreign broadcasting
stations, eg when these have a wave-length close
to that of the station one wishes to receive; (computers) existence of unwanted signals in a communications circuit.

in·terim /'ɪntərɪm/ n 1 in the ~, meanwhile; during the time that comes between. 2 (attrib) as an instalment: ~ dividends, paid between annual dividends as advance payments; provisional or temporary: an ~ report, one that precedes the final report.

in·terior /ɪn'tɪərɪə(r)/ adj 1 situated inside; of the
inside. 2 inland; away from the coast. 3 home or
domestic (contrasted with foreign). □ n the ~, 1
the inside: (used attrib) ~ decorators, those who
decorate the inside of a building (with paint, wallpaper, etc). 2 inland areas. 3 (department dealing
with the) domestic affairs of a country: (US) the
Department of the I~. (Cf Home Office in GB.)

in·ter·ject /ˌɪntə'dʒekt/ vt [VP6A] put in suddenly (a
remark, etc) between statements, etc made by another. in·ter·jec·tion /ˌɪntə'dʒekʃn/ n word or
phrase used as an exclamation, eg Oh! For goodness sake!

in·ter·lace /ˌɪntə'leɪs/ vt,vi [VP6A,2A,14] ~
(with), join, be joined, by weaving or lacing
together, one with another; cross as if woven: in-
terlacing branches.

in·ter·lard /ˌɪntə'lɑːd/ vt [VP14] ~ with, (formal)
mix writing, speech, etc with foreign phrases, etc:
essays ~ed with quotations from the poets.

in·ter·leave /ˌɪntə'liːv/ vt [VP6A,14] ~ (with), insert (usu blank leaves) between the leaves of (a
book, etc): a diary ~ed with blotting-paper.

in·ter·link /ˌɪntə'lɪŋk/ vt,vi [VP6A,2A] link together.

in·ter·lock /ˌɪntə'lɒk/ vt,vi [VP6A,2A] lock or join
together; clasp firmly together.

in·ter·locu·tor /ˌɪntə'lɒkjʊtə(r)/ n person taking
part in a discussion or dialogue.

in·ter·lo·per /'ɪntələʊpə(r)/ n person who, esp for
profit or personal advantage, pushes himself in
where he has no right.

in·ter·lude /'ɪntəluːd/ n 1 interval of different character between two events or two periods of time:
~s of bright weather. 2 interval between two acts

of a play, two scenes of an opera or between parts of a psalm, hymn etc; music played during such an interval.

in·ter·marry /ˌɪntə'mærɪ/ vi (pt,pp -married) [VP2A,3A] ~ (with), (of tribes, races, etc) become connected by marriage with other tribes, etc. **in·ter·mar·riage** /ˌɪntə'mærɪdʒ/ n [U] marriage between members of different families, tribes, castes, etc.

in·ter·medi·ary /ˌɪntə'miːdɪərɪ US: -dɪerɪ/ n (pl -ries), adj 1 ~ (between), (sb or sth) acting as a link between (persons and groups); go-between; mediator. 2 (sth) intermediate.

in·ter·medi·ate /ˌɪntə'miːdɪət/ adj situated or coming between in time, space, degree, etc: at an ~ stage, eg the cocoon stage of development of a butterfly; ~ courses, between elementary and advanced; ~-range ballistic missiles. □ n sth that is ~. ~·ly adv

in·ter·ment /ɪn'tɜːmənt/ n [U] being buried; [C] instance of this; burial.

in·ter·mezzo /ˌɪntə'metsəʊ/ n (pl ~s /-tsəʊz/ or -zzi /-tsɪ/) short musical composition to be played between the acts of a drama or an opera, or one that connects the main divisions of a large musical work such as a symphony.

in·ter·mi·nable /ɪn'tɜːmɪnəbl/ adj endless; tedious because too long: an ~ debate/sermon. **in·ter·mi·nably** /-əblɪ/ adv

in·ter·mingle /ˌɪntə'mɪŋgl/ vt,vi [VP6A,14] ~ (with), mix together (two things, one with the other); mingle: The conference delegates ~d over coffee.

in·ter·mis·sion /ˌɪntə'mɪʃn/ n pause; interval: The film lasted for three hours without ~/with a short ~ half-way through.

in·ter·mit·tent /ˌɪntə'mɪtnt/ adj pausing or stopping at intervals; stopping and starting again: ~ fever. ~·ly adv

in·ter·mix /ˌɪntə'mɪks/ vt,vi = mix (the usu word). ~·ture /-tʃə(r)/ n

in·tern [1] /ɪn'tɜːn/ vt [VP6A] compel (a person, esp an enemy alien during a war) to live within certain limits or in a special building, camp, etc. ~·ment n [U] ~ing or being ~ed: '~ment camp. ~ee /ˌɪntɜː'niː/ n person who is ~ed.

in·tern [2] (US also **in·terne**) /'ɪntɜːn/ n (US) young doctor who is completing his training by residing in a hospital and acting as an assistant physician or surgeon there. (GB = houseman.)

in·ter·nal /ɪn'tɜːnl/ adj 1 of or in the inside: suffer ~ injuries in an accident; ~ bleeding, eg in the bowels. ~ combustion, the process by which power is produced by the explosion of gases or vapours inside a cylinder (as in the engine of a car). 2 domestic; of the home affairs of a country: ~ trade/revenue, (also Inland Revenue). 3 derived from within the thing itself: ~ evidence, eg of when an old book was written, or of the date of an old manuscript. ~·ly /-nəlɪ/ adv

in·ter·na·tional /ˌɪntə'næʃnəl/ adj existing, carried on, between nations: ~ trade/law/agreements/conferences. ~ 'money order, one which may be cashed in a country other than the country of origin. □ n the 1st/2nd/3rd I~, three socialist or communist associations for workers of all countries, formed in 1864, 1889 and 1919. ~·ism /-nəlɪzəm/ n the doctrine that the common interests of nations are greater and more important than their differences. ~·ist /-ɪst/ n person who

supports and advocates ~ism. ~·ize /-ʃnəlaɪz/ vt [VP6A] make ~; bring under the combined control or protection of all or many nations: Should the Suez and Panama Canals be ~ized? ~·iz·ation /ˌɪntəˌnæʃnəlaɪ'zeɪʃn US:-lɪ'z-/ n [U]. ~·ly adv

in·ter·na·tio·nale /ˌɪntənæʃə'nɑːl/ n The I~, (revolutionary) socialist song.

in·terne /'ɪntɜːn/ n ⇨ intern [2].

in·ter·necine /ˌɪntə'niːsaɪn/ adj (usu of war) causing destruction to both sides.

in·ternee /ˌɪntɜː'niː/ n ⇨ intern [1].

in·ter·pel·late /ɪn'tɜːpəleɪt US: ˌɪntər'peleɪt/ vt [VP6A] (in some Parliaments, eg the French and Japanese) interrupt the proceedings and demand a statement or explanation from (a Minister). **in·ter·pel·la·tion** /ɪnˌtɜːpə'leɪʃn US: ˌɪntər-/ n [U] interpellating or being ~d; [C] instance of this.

in·ter·phone /'ɪntəfəʊn/ n (US) = intercom.

in·ter·plan·etary /ˌɪntə'plænɪtrɪ US: -terɪ/ adj between planets: an ~ journey in a spacecraft.

in·ter·play /'ɪntəpleɪ/ n [U] operation of two or more things on each other: the ~ of colours, their combined effect.

In·ter·pol /'ɪntəpɒl/ n International Police Commission.

in·ter·po·late /ɪn'tɜːpəleɪt/ vt [VP6A] make (sometimes misleading) additions to a book, etc. **in·ter·po·la·tion** /ɪnˌtɜːpə'leɪʃn/ n [U] interpolating; [C] sth ~d.

in·ter·pose /ˌɪntə'pəʊz/ vt,vi 1 [VP6A] put forward an objection, a veto, etc as an interference: Will they ~ their veto yet again? 2 [VP6A,2A] say (sth) as an interruption; make an interruption. 3 [VP2A,3A,14] ~ (oneself) between; ~ in, place oneself, be, between others: ~ between two persons who are quarrelling; mediate (in a dispute). **in·ter·po·si·tion** /ˌɪntəpə'zɪʃn/ n [U] interposing; [C] sth ~d.

in·ter·pret /ɪn'tɜːprɪt/ vt,vi 1 [VP6A] show, make clear, the meaning of (either in words or by artistic performance): ~ a difficult passage in a book; (of an actor) ~ a role; (of a conductor) ~ a symphony. Poetry helps to ~ life. 2 [VP6A,16B] consider to be the meaning of: We ~ed his silence as a refusal. 3 [VP2A] act as ~er: Will you please ~ for me, translate what is (to be) said? ~·er n person who gives an immediate oral translation of words spoken in another language. **in·ter·pre·ta·tion** /ɪnˌtɜːprɪ'teɪʃn/ n [U] interpreting; [C] result of this; explanation or meaning: The announcement may be given several ~ations.

in·ter·racial /ˌɪntə'reɪʃl/ adj between, involving, different races.

in·ter·reg·num /ˌɪntə'regnəm/ n (pl ~s, -na /-nə/) period during which a State has no normal or legitimate ruler, esp between the end of a Sovereign's reign and the beginning of his successor's reign; pause or interval.

in·ter·re·late /ˌɪntərɪ'leɪt/ vt,vi [VP6A,2A] come or bring together in reciprocal relationship: ~d studies, of separate but related subjects as a united group, eg politics, philosophy and economics.

in·ter·re·lation /ˌɪntərɪ'leɪʃn/ n ~ of/between, mutual relation. ~·ship /-ʃɪp/ n mutual relationship.

in·ter·ro·gate /ɪn'terəgeɪt/ vt [VP6A] put questions to, esp closely or formally: ~ a prisoner. **in·ter·ro·ga·tor** /-tə(r)/ n person who ~s. **in·ter·ro·ga·tion** /ɪnˌterə'geɪʃn/ n 1 [U] asking questions. **in·ter·ro·ga·tion point**, question mark; the mark (?).

2 [C,U] oral examination; inquiry: *long and tiring interrogations by police officers.*

in·ter·roga·tive /ˌɪntəˈrɒgətɪv/ *adj* **1** showing or having the form of a question; of inquiry: *an ~ look/glance; in an ~ tone.* **2** (gram) used in questions: *~ pronouns/adverbs,* eg who, why. □ *n ~* word, esp a pronoun. *~·ly adv*

in·ter·roga·tory /ˌɪntəˈrɒgətrɪ *US:* -tɔːrɪ/ *adj* of inquiry: *in an ~ tone.*

in·ter·rupt /ˌɪntəˈrʌpt/ *vt,vi* [VP6A,2A] **1** break the continuity of: *The war ~ed the flow of commerce between the two countries. Traffic was ~ed by floods. Those trees are growing so high that they ~* (= obstruct) *the view.* **2** break in upon (a person's action, speech, etc): *Don't ~ (me) while I'm busy. Don't ~ the speaker; ask your questions afterwards. ~er n* person or thing that *~s.* **in·ter·rup·tion** /ˌɪntəˈrʌpʃn/ *n* [U] *~ing* or being *~ed;* [C] instance of this; sth that *~s: Numerous ~ions have prevented me from finishing the work.*

in·ter·sect /ˌɪntəˈsekt/ *vt,vi* **1** [VP6A] divide by cutting, passing or lying across. **2** [VP6A,2A] (of lines) cut or cross each other: *The lines AB and*

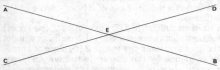

intersecting lines

CD ~ at E. The line AB ~s the line CD at E. **in·ter·sec·tion** /ˌɪntəˈsekʃn/ *n* [U] *~ing* or being *~ed;* [C] point where two lines, etc *~.*

in·ter·sperse /ˌɪntəˈspɜːs/ *vt* [VP14] *~ among/ between,* place here and there. *~ with,* diversify: *a speech ~d with witty remarks.*

in·ter·state /ˌɪntəˈsteɪt/ *adj* (US) between States: *~ commerce.*

in·ter·stel·lar /ˌɪntəˈstelə(r)/ *adj* between the stars: *~ matter,* eg the masses of gas between stars; *~ communications.*

in·ter·stice /ɪnˈtɜːstɪs/ *n* crack; chink; crevice: *~s* (= very small spaces) *between stones in a heap.*

in·ter·tribal /ˌɪntəˈtraɪbl/ *adj* between tribes: *~ wars.*

in·ter·twine /ˌɪntəˈtwaɪn/ *vt,vi* [VP6A,2A] twine or twist together; become twined or twisted together: *a lattice ~d with vines.*

in·ter·val /ˈɪntəvl/ *n* **1** time (between two events or two parts of an action); (esp) time between two acts of a play, two parts of a concert, etc: *buses leaving at short ~s,* ie very frequently. **2** space between (two objects or points): *arranged at ~s of ten feet.* **3** (music) difference of pitch between two notes on a given scale.

in·ter·vene /ˌɪntəˈviːn/ *vi* **1** [VP2A] (of events, circumstances) come between (others) in time: *I shall leave on Sunday if nothing ~s.* **2** [VP2A,3A] *~ (in),* (of persons) interfere so as to prevent sth or change the result: *~ in a dispute; ~ between people who are disputing.* **3** [VP2A] (of time) come or be between: *during the years that ~d.* **in·ter·ven·tion** /ˌɪntəˈvenʃn/ *n* [U] intervening (esp **2** above): *armed intervention by one country in the affairs of other countries;* [C] instance of this.

in·ter·view /ˈɪntəvjuː/ *n* [C] meeting with sb for formal consultation or examination, eg between employers and applicants for posts; meeting (of a

reporter, etc) with sb whose views are requested: *The Ambassador refused to give any ~s to journalists or TV men.* □ *vt* [VP6A] (of a reporter, etc) have or obtain an *~* with.

in·ter·weave /ˌɪntəˈwiːv/ *vt* (*pt* -wove /-ˈwəʊv/, *pp* -woven /-ˈwəʊvn/) [VP6A,14] *~ (with),* weave together (one with another).

in·tes·tate /ɪnˈtesteɪt/ *adj* not having made a will before death occurs: *die ~.*

in·tes·tine /ɪnˈtestɪn/ *n* (usu *pl*) lower part of the food canal from below the stomach to the anus: *small/large ~,* parts of this. **in·tes·ti·nal** /ɪnˈtestɪnl/ *adj* of the *~s: intestinal disorders.* ⇨ abdominal; ⇨ the illus at alimentary.

in·ti·mate¹ /ˈɪntɪmət/ *adj* **1** close and familiar: *~ friends.* **be/get on ~ terms (with),** eg when one calls a man 'Jack' instead of 'Mr Hill'. **2** innermost; private and personal: *tell a friend the ~ details of one's life; an ~ diary,* one in which one records experiences, thoughts, emotions, etc usu kept secret. **3** resulting from close study or great familiarity: *an ~ knowledge of Greek philosophy.* □ *n ~* friend. *~·ly adv* **in·ti·macy** /ˈɪntɪməsɪ/ *n* (*pl* -cies) **1** [U] the state of being *~;* close friendship or relationship; (euphem) sexual relations. **2** (*pl*) *~ actions,* eg caresses or kisses.

in·ti·mate² /ˈɪntɪmeɪt/ *vt* [VP6A,9,14] *~ sth (to sb); ~ (to sb) that...,* make known; show clearly: *~ one's approval of a plan/that one approves of a plan. He ~d to me his intention of leaving early/ that he intended to leave early.* **in·ti·ma·tion** /ˌɪntɪˈmeɪʃn/ *n* [U] intimating; [C] sth *~d;* notification; suggestion.

in·timi·date /ɪnˈtɪmɪdeɪt/ *vt* [VP6A,14] *~ (into),* frighten, esp in order to force (sb into doing sth): *~ a witness,* eg by threatening him. **in·timi·da·tion** /ɪnˌtɪmɪˈdeɪʃn/ *n* [U] intimidating or being *~d:* surrender to intimidation.

into /ˈɪntə; *strong form:* ˈɪntuː/ *prep* **1** (indicating motion or direction to a point within): *Come ~ the house/garden. Throw it ~ the fire. He worked late ~ the night.* **2** (indicating change of condition, result): *She burst ~ tears. Don't get ~ trouble. The rain changed ~ snow. He poked the fire ~ a blaze,* poked it so that it blazed up. *Collect them ~ heaps. He frightened her ~ submission.* **be ~ sth,** (mod use, colloq) be involved in, concerned with, it: *She's heavily ~ vegetarianism.* **3** (maths): *5 ~ 25* (= 25 divided by 5) *goes 5.*

in·tol·er·able /ɪnˈtɒlərəbl/ *adj* that cannot be tolerated or endured: *~ heat/insolence. Is the world becoming an ~ place to live in?* **in·tol·er·ably** /-əblɪ/ *adv*

in·tol·er·ant /ɪnˈtɒlərənt/ *adj ~ (of),* not tolerant: *a man who is ~ of opposition. ~·ly adv* **in·tol·er·ance** /-əns/ *n*

in·ton·ation /ˌɪntəˈneɪʃn/ *n* [U] the rise and fall of the pitch of the voice in speaking; this as an element of meaning in language.

in·tone /ɪnˈtəʊn/ *vt,vi* [VP6A,2A] recite a prayer, psalm, etc in a singing tone; speak with a particular tone.

in toto /ɪn ˈtəʊtəʊ/ (Lat) totally; altogether.

in·toxi·cant /ɪnˈtɒksɪkənt/ *adj, n* intoxicating (liquor).

in·toxi·cate /ɪnˈtɒksɪkeɪt/ *vt* [VP6A] **1** make stupid with, cause to lose self-control as the result of taking, alcoholic drink: *If a man drinks too much whisky, he becomes ~d.* **2** excite greatly, beyond self-control: *be ~d by success; ~d with joy.* **in-**

toxi·ca·tion /ɪnˌtɒksɪˈkeɪʃn/ n [U] being ∼d; alcoholic poisoning.

in·trac·table /ɪnˈtræktəbl/ adj not easily controlled or dealt with; hard to manage: ∼ children; an ∼ temper. **in·trac·ta·bil·ity** /ɪnˌtræktəˈbɪlətɪ/ n

in·tra·mural /ˌɪntrəˈmjʊərəl/ adj 1 existing, done, within the walls of a town, building, etc: ∼ burial, inside a church instead of in the churchyard. 2 intended for full-time, residential students. ⇨ extramural.

in·tran·si·gent /ɪnˈtrænsɪdʒənt/ adj (formal) uncompromising, esp in politics. **in·tran·si·gence** /-əns/ n

in·tran·si·tive /ɪnˈtrænsətɪv/ adj (of verbs) used without a direct object. ∼·ly adv ⇨ transitive.

in·tra·uter·ine /ˌɪntrə ˈjuːtəraɪn/ adj (med) within the uterus. ∼ device, (abbr **IUD**), loop or spiral inserted in the uterus as a contraceptive.

in·tra·venous /ˌɪntrəˈviːnəs/ adj within a vein or veins: ∼ injections, and so into the blood stream.

in·trench /ɪnˈtrentʃ/ = entrench.

in·trepid /ɪnˈtrepɪd/ adj fearless. ∼·ly adv **in·trep·id·ity** /ˌɪntrɪˈpɪdətɪ/ n [U] fearlessness; [C] (pl -ties) fearless act.

in·tri·cate /ˈɪntrɪkət/ adj complicated; puzzling; difficult to follow or understand: a novel with an ∼ plot; an ∼ piece of machinery. ∼·ly adv **in·tri·cacy** /ˈɪntrɪkəsɪ/ n (pl -cies) [U] the quality of being ∼; (pl) ∼ things, events, etc.

in·trigue /ɪnˈtriːg/ vi, vt 1 [VP2A,3A] ∼ (with sb) (against sb), make and carry out secret plans or plots: ∼ with Smith against Robinson. 2 [VP6A] arouse the interest or curiosity of: The news ∼d all of us. □ n 1 [U] secret plotting. 2 [C] plot; secret plan; secret love affair.

in·trin·sic /ɪnˈtrɪnsɪk US: -zɪk/ adj (of value, quality) belonging naturally; existing within, not coming from outside: a man's ∼ worth, eg such qualities as honour and courage, contrasted with extrinsic qualities, eg family connections; the ∼ value of a coin, the value of the metal in it, usu less than its face value. **in·trin·si·cally** /-klɪ/ adv

in·tro·duce /ˌɪntrəˈdjuːs US: -ˈduːs/ vt [VP6A,15A] 1 bring in; bring forward: ∼ a Bill before Parliament. 2 [VP14] ∼ into/to, bring (sth) into use or into operation for the first time; cause (sb) to be acquainted with (sth): ∼ new ideas into a business. Tobacco was ∼d into Europe from America. The teacher ∼d his young pupils to the intricacies of geometry. 3 [VP6A,14] ∼ sb (to sb), make (persons) known by name (to one another), esp in the usual formal way: ∼ two friends. He ∼d me to his parents. The chairman ∼d the lecturer to the audience. 4 [VP6A,14] ∼ (into), insert: ∼ a tube into a wound; ∼ a subject into a conversation.

in·tro·duc·tion /ˌɪntrəˈdʌkʃn/ n 1 [U] introducing or being introduced: a letter of ∼, one that introduces the bearer to friends of the writer; foreign words of recent ∼, recently introduced into the language. 2 [C] introducing of persons to one another: It was necessary to make ∼s all round, to introduce many people to one another. 3 [C] sth that leads up to sth else; the opening paragraph of a letter, essay, speech, etc; explanatory article at or before the beginning of a book. 4 [C] elementary textbook: 'An I∼ to Greek Grammar.'

in·tro·duc·tory /ˌɪntrəˈdʌktərɪ/ adj serving to introduce: an ∼ chapter; a few ∼ remarks by the chairman.

in·tro·spect /ˌɪntrəˈspekt/ vi [VP2A] (formal) ex-

amine one's own thoughts and feelings. **in·tro·spec·tion** /ˌɪntrəˈspekʃn/ n [U] ∼ing. **in·tro·spec·tive** /-tɪv/ adj inclined towards, based on, ∼ion.

in·tro·vert /ˌɪntrəˈvɜːt/ vt [VP6A] turn (the mind, thought) inward upon itself. □ n /ˈɪntrəvɜːt/ person who habitually does this; one who is more interested in his own thoughts and feelings than in things outside himself. **in·tro·ver·sion** n [U] state of being ∼ed. ⇨ extrovert.

in·trude /ɪnˈtruːd/ vt, vi [VP14,2A,3A] ∼ (oneself) on/upon sb; ∼ (oneself/sth) into sth, force (sth, oneself, upon sb, into a place); enter without invitation: the thought/suspicion that ∼d itself into my mind; ∼ oneself into a meeting; ∼ upon a person's time/privacy. I hope I'm not intruding. **in·truder** n person or thing that ∼s: (attrib) ∼r aircraft; ∼r patrols, ie intruding into the enemy's country.

in·tru·sion /ɪnˈtruːʒn/ n ∼ (on/upon/into), [U] intruding: guilty of unpardonable ∼ upon sb's privacy; [C] instance of this: angry at numerous ∼s on one's privacy by rude journalists. **in·tru·sive** /ɪnˈtruːsɪv/ adj intruding: the intrusive 'r', eg the r-sound often heard in eg 'awe and wonder'.

in·trust /ɪnˈtrʌst/ = entrust.

in·tuit /ɪnˈtjuːɪt US: -ˈtuː-/ vt, vi [VP2A,6A] sense by intuition.

in·tu·ition /ˌɪntjuːˈɪʃn US: -tuː-/ n 1 [U] (power of) the immediate understanding of something without conscious reasoning or study. 2 [C] piece of knowledge gained by this power. **in·tu·itive** /ɪnˈtjuːɪtɪv US: -ˈtuː-/ adj of ∼: intuitive knowledge; possessing ∼: Are women more intuitive than men? **in·tu·itive·ly** adv

in·tu·mes·cence /ˌɪntjuːˈmesns US: -tuː-/ n (med) process or condition of swelling or expanding.

in·un·date /ˈɪnʌndeɪt/ vt [VP6A,14] ∼ (with), flood; cover (with water) by overflowing; (fig, esp passive) overwhelm: be ∼d with requests for help/applications for a post. **in·un·da·tion** /ˌɪnʌnˈdeɪʃn/ n [U] flooding; [C] instance of this; flood.

in·ure /ɪˈnjʊə(r)/ vt [VP14] ∼ oneself/sb to, (usu passive) accustom: Living in the far North had ∼d him to cold. He had become ∼d to ridicule.

in·vade /ɪnˈveɪd/ vt [VP6A] 1 enter (a country) with armed forces in order to attack; (fig) crowd into; enter: a city ∼d by tourists; a mind ∼d by worry and anxiety. 2 violate; interfere with: ∼ sb's rights. **in·vader** n person or thing that ∼s.

in·valid[1] /ɪnˈvælɪd/ adj not valid: ∼ excuses/ claims/arguments; an ∼ will/cheque, eg one without a signature; declare a marriage ∼. **in·vali·date** /ɪnˈvælɪdeɪt/ vt [VP6A] make ∼. **in·vali·da·tion** /ɪnˌvælɪˈdeɪʃn/ n [U] state of being ∼; [C,U] (act of) rendering sth ∼: the invalidation of a passport. **in·val·id·ity** /ˌɪnvəˈlɪdətɪ/ n [U] state of being ∼.

in·va·lid[2] /ˈɪnvəlɪd/ adj 1 weak or disabled through illness or injury: a home of rest for ∼ soldiers. 2 suitable for ∼ persons: an ∼ chair, one with wheels; an ∼ diet. □ n ∼ person. □ vt [VP15A] (esp of members of the armed forces) remove from active service as an ∼; send (home) as an ∼: be ∼ed home; ∼ed out of the army. ∼·ism /-ɪzəm/ n chronic ill health.

in·valu·able /ɪnˈvæljʊəbl/ adj ∼ (to), of value too high to be measured: Her services are ∼ to me.

in·vari·able /ɪnˈveərɪəbl/ adj never changing; unchangeable; constant: an ∼ pressure/temperature. **in·vari·ably** /-əblɪ/ adv

in·vasion /ɪnˈveɪʒn/ n [U] invading or being invaded; [C] instance of this: *an ~ of privacy.*

in·vas·ive /ɪn'veɪsɪv/ *adj* making invasion; tending to spread.

in·vec·tive /ɪn'vektɪv/ *n* [U] abusive language: *speeches filled with ~;* (*pl*) curses; violent expressions: *a stream of coarse ~s.*

in·veigh /ɪn'veɪ/ *vi* [VP3A] *~ against sb/sth,* speak bitterly; attack violently in words.

in·veigle /ɪn'veɪgl/ *vt* [VP14] *~ sb into (doing) sth,* trick by using flattery, deception, etc: *~ sb into investing his money unwisely.*

in·vent /ɪn'vent/ *vt* [VP6A] **1** create or design (sth not existing before): *When was the steam engine ~ed?* Cf *discover,* find sth existing before, but unknown. **2** make up, think of: *~ a story/an excuse.* **in·ven·tive** /ɪn'ventɪv/ *adj* able to *~: an ~ive mind; ~ive powers.* **in·ven·tor** /-tə(r)/ *n* person who *~s* things.

in·ven·tion /ɪn'venʃn/ *n* **1** [U] inventing: *the ~ of the telephone;* capacity for inventing: *Necessity is the mother of ~.* **2** [C] sth invented: *the numerous ~s of Edison; newspapers that are full of ~s,* invented, untrue stories.

in·ven·tory /'ɪnvəntrɪ *US:* -tɔːrɪ/ *n* (*pl* -ries) detailed list, eg of household goods, furniture, etc.

in·verse /ɪn'vɜːs/ *adj* inverted; reversed in position, direction or relations: *~ ratio/proportion,* that between two quantities one of which increases proportionally as the other decreases. □ *n* /'ɪnvɜːs/ [U] inverted state. *~·ly adv*

in·vert /ɪn'vɜːt/ *vt* [VP6A] put upside down or in the opposite order, position or arrangement: *~ a glass,* so that it is bottom upwards. *,~ed 'commas,* quotation marks ("" or ''). ⇨ App 9. **in·ver·sion** /ɪn'vɜːʃn *US:* -ʒn/ *n* [U] *~*ing or being *~*ed; [C] instance of this; sth *~*ed.

in·vert·ebrate /ɪn'vɜːtɪbreɪt/ *adj* not having a backbone or spinal column, eg molluses, insects, worms; (fig) weak-willed. □ *n~* animal.

in·vest /ɪn'vest/ *vt,vi* **1** [VP6A,14] *~ (in),* put (money in): *~ £1000 in government stock; ~ one's savings in a business enterprise.* **2** [VP3A] *~ in,* (colloq) buy (sth considered useful): *~ in a new kettle.* **3** [VP14] *~ with,* clothe; endow; decorate; surround (with qualities): *The military governor has been ~ed with full authority. The old ruins were ~ed with romance.* **4** [VP6A] surround a fort, town, etc with armed forces; lay siege to. *~or /-tə(r)/* *n* person who *~s* money. *~·ment n* **1** [U] *~*ing money: *By careful ~ment of his capital, he obtained a good income.* **2** [C] sum of money that is *~*ed; that in which money is *~*ed: *an ~ment of £500 in oil shares; wise and profitable ~ments.* **3** [U] act of *~*ing a town, fort, etc; blockade. **4** = investiture.

in·ves·ti·gate /ɪn'vestɪgeɪt/ *vt* [VP6A] examine, inquire into; make a careful study of: *~ a crime/the causes of a railway accident; ~ the market for sales of a product.* **in·ves·ti·ga·tor** /-tə(r)/ *n* person who *~s.* **in·ves·ti·ga·tion** /ɪn,vestɪ'geɪʃn/ *n* [U] careful and thorough inquiry; [C] instance of this: *The matter is under investigation.*

in·ves·ti·ture /ɪn'vestɪtʃə(r) *US:* -tʃʊər/ *n* (from invest(3)) ceremony of investing sb *with* an office, rank, power or dignity.

in·vest·ment ⇨ invest.

in·vet·er·ate /ɪn'vetərət/ *adj* (esp of habits, feelings) deep-rooted; long-established: *an ~ smoker; ~ prejudices.*

in·vidi·ous /ɪn'vɪdɪəs/ *adj* likely to cause ill-feeling

(because of real or apparent injustice): *make ~ distinctions. ~·ly adv*

in·vigi·late /ɪn'vɪdʒɪleɪt/ *vi* [VP2A,6A] watch over (eg students during examinations). **in·vigi·la·tor** /-tə(r)/ *n* person who *~s.* **in·vigi·la·tion** /ɪn,vɪdʒɪ'leɪʃn/ *n* [U,C].

in·vig·or·ate /ɪn'vɪgəreɪt/ *vt* [VP6A] make vigorous; give strength or courage to: *an invigorating climate/speech.*

in·vin·cible /ɪn'vɪnsəbl/ *adj* too strong to be overcome or defeated: *an ~ will.* **in·vin·cibly** /-əblɪ/ *adv* **in·vin·ci·bil·ity** /ɪn,vɪnsə'bɪlətɪ/ *n* [U].

in·viol·able /ɪn'vaɪələbl/ *adj* (formal) not to be violated, dishonoured or profaned: *an ~ oath/law.*

in·viol·ate /ˌɪn'vaɪələt/ *adj* (formal) kept sacred; held in respect; not violated: *keep an oath/a promise/rule ~; remain ~.*

in·vis·ible /ɪn'vɪzəbl/ *adj* that cannot be seen: *stars that are ~ to the naked eye. ~ exports/imports,* money that goes out of/comes into a country as interest on capital, payments for shipping services, tourist expenditure, etc. *~ ink,* ink which, when used for writing, can be seen only after treatment by heat, etc. *~ mending,* repair of woven materials, silk stockings, etc by interweaving threads so that the repair is hardly noticeable. **in·vis·ibly** /-əblɪ/ *adv* **in·visi·bil·ity** /ɪn,vɪzə'bɪlətɪ/ *n* [U].

in·vite /ɪn'vaɪt/ *vt* **1** [VP15A,B,17] ask (sb to do sth, come somewhere, etc): *~ a friend to dinner/to one's house. He didn't ~ me in. We are old now, and seldom get ~d out.* **2** [VP6A] ask for: *~ questions/opinions/confidences.* **3** [VP6A,17] encourage: *The cool water of the lake ~d us to swim. Don't leave the windows open—it's inviting thieves to enter.* □ *n* /'ɪnvaɪt/ (sl) = invitation(2). **in·vit·ing** *adj* tempting; attractive: *The doors were invitingly open,* open in a way that *~d* people to enter. **in·vi·ta·tion** /ˌɪnvɪ'teɪʃn/ *n* **1** [U] inviting or being *~d: a letter of invitation; admission by invitation only.* **2** [C] request to come or go somewhere, or do sth: *send out invitations to a party.*

in·vo·ca·tion /ˌɪnvə'keɪʃn/ *n* ⇨ invoke.

in·voice /'ɪnvɔɪs/ *vt, n* [VP6A] (make a) list of goods sold with the price(s) charged: *~ sb for goods.*

in·voke /ɪn'vəʊk/ *vt* **1** [VP6A] call upon God, the power of the law, etc for help or protection. **2** [VP6A,14] *~ sth on/upon,* request earnestly; call down from heaven: *~ vengeance on one's enemies.* **3** [VP6A] summon up (by magic): *~ evil spirits.* **in·vo·ca·tion** /ˌɪnvə'keɪʃn/ *n* [U] invoking or being *~d;* [C] prayer or appeal that *~s.*

in·vol·un·tary /ɪn'vɒləntrɪ *US:* -terɪ/ *adj* done without intention; done unconsciously: *an ~ movement of fear.* **in·vol·un·tar·ily** /ɪn'vɒləntrəlɪ *US:* ɪn,vɒlən'terəlɪ/ *adv*

in·vo·lute /'ɪnvəluːt/ *adj* complex; intricate; (bot) curled spirally. **in·vo·lu·tion** /ˌɪnvə'luːʃn/ *n* anything internally complex or intricate.

in·volve /ɪn'vɒlv/ *vt* **1** [VP6A,14] *~ (in),* cause (sb or sth) to be caught or mixed up (in trouble, etc); get (sb or sth) into a complicated or difficult condition: *They are deeply ~d in debt. Don't ~ yourself in unnecessary expense.* **2** [VP6A,19C] have as a necessary consequence: *To accept the position you offer would ~ my living in London. The war ~d a great increase in the national debt. ~d adj* **(a)** complex: *an ~d sentence/explanation; Henry*

James's ~*d style of writing.* (b) *be/become/get* ~*d in sth/with sb*, be, etc concerned with sth/connected with sb: *become* ~*d in criminal activities; get emotionally* ~*d with sb.* ~**·ment** *n*

in·vul·ner·able /ɪn'vʌlnərəbl/ *adj* that cannot be wounded or hurt: (fig) *in an* ~ *position.*

in·ward /'ɪnwəd/ *adj* **1** situated within; inner: ~ *happiness*, ie of the spirit; *one's* ~ (ie mental or spiritual) *nature.* **2** turned towards the inside: *an* ~ *curve.* ~**·ly** *adv* in mind or spirit: *grieve* ~*ly*, ie so as not to show one's grief. ~**·ness** *n* (person's) inner nature; spiritual quality: *the true* ~*ness of Christ's teaching.* ~**(s)** *adv* towards the inside; into or towards the mind or soul.

in·wrought /ˌɪn'rɔːt/ *adj* (of a fabric) decorated (*with* a pattern, etc); (of a pattern or design) worked or woven (*in* or *on*).

iod·ine /'aɪədiːn *US*: -daɪn/ *n* [U] non-metallic element (symbol **I**) found in seawater and seaweed, used as an antiseptic (in the form *tincture of* ~) and in photography.

ion /'aɪən/ *n* electrically charged particle formed by losing or gaining electrons. Such particles make a solution of certain chemicals a conductor of electricity. **ion·ize** /'aɪənaɪz/ *vi, vt* [VP2A,6A] be converted or convert into ions. **ion·iz·ation** /ˌaɪənaɪ'zeɪʃn *US*: -nɪ'z-/ *n* [U]. **iono·sphere** /aɪ'ɒnəsfɪə(r)/ *n* (also known as the *Heaviside Layer*) set of layers of the earth's atmosphere, which reflect radio waves and cause them to follow the earth's contour.

Ionic /aɪ'ɒnɪk/ *adj* (archit) of the type of column(1) in ancient Greek architecture having scrolls on the capital(4). ⇨ the illus at column.

iota /aɪ'əʊtə/ *n* the Greek letter ɪ; (fig) smallest amount: *not an* ~ *of truth in the story*, no truth at all.

IOU /ˌaɪ əʊ 'juː/ *n* (= *I owe you*) signed paper acknowledging that one owes the sum of money stated.

ipse dixit /ˌɪpsɪ 'dɪksɪt/ (Lat) (= *he himself said it*) dogmatic statement made on sb's unsupported word.

ipso facto /ˌɪpsəʊ 'fæktəʊ/ *adv phrase* (Lat) by that very fact.

iras·cible /ɪ'ræsəbl/ *adj* (formal) easily made angry. **iras·ci·bil·ity** /ɪˌræsə'bɪlətɪ/ *n* tendency to anger; angry behaviour.

irate /aɪ'reɪt/ *adj* (formal) angry. ~**·ly** *adv*

ire /'aɪə(r)/ *n* (poet or formal) anger. **ire·ful** /-fl/ *adj* angry.

iri·des·cent /ˌɪrɪ'desnt/ *adj* (formal) showing colours like those of the rainbow; changing colour as light falls from different directions. **iri·des·cence** /-'desns/ *n* [U].

irid·ium /ɪ'rɪdɪəm/ *n* [U] hard white metal (symbol **Ir**).

iris /'aɪərɪs/ *n* **1** coloured part round the pupil of the eye. ⇨ the illus at eye. **2** kinds of flowering plant with sword-shaped leaves.

Irish /'aɪərɪʃ/ *adj* of Ireland: *the* ~ *Free State/the* ~ *Republic* (also *Eire* /'eərə/), part of Ireland that became independent in 1922. ~ **stew**, one of mutton, boiled with onions and other vegetables. □ *n* *the* ~ *language* (= ~ *Gaelic*, ⇨ Gael). **the** ~, ~ people. ~**·man** /-mən/ *n* (*pl* -men) ~**·woman** /-wʊmən/ *n* (*pl* -women) native of Ireland.

irk /ɜːk/ *vt* trouble; annoy (chiefly in): *It irks me to* (*do sth*). **irk·some** /-səm/ *adj* tiresome.

iron¹ /'aɪən *US*: 'aɪərn/ *n* **1** [U] commonest of all metallic elements (symbol **Fe**), used in various

forms (⇨ *cast* ~ at cast¹(3), *wrought* ~ at wrought): ~ *ore; as hard as* ~; (fig) *an* ~ *will.* **rule with a rod of** ~/**with an** ~ **hand**, with extreme severity. *a man of* ~, a hard, unyielding or merciless man. **an** ~ **fist in a velvet glove**, an appearance of gentleness concealing severity, determination. **strike while the** ~ **is hot**, act while the opportunity is good. **the 'I~ Age**, prehistoric period, following the Bronze Age, when ~ came into use for tools and weapons. ~ **curtain**, (fig) frontier between countries, considered as a barrier to information and trade. ~ **lung**, apparatus fitted over the whole body, except the head, to provide a person with artificial respiration by the use of mechanical pumps. ~ **rations**, store of food for use in an emergency as for troops/explorers. **2** [C] (esp in compounds) tool, etc made of ~: ('*flat-*)~, flat-bottomed household implement, heated (usu electrically) and used for smoothing clothes, etc; '*fire*-~*s*, poker, tongs, etc used at a fireplace or stove; golf-club with an ~ head; branding tool; (*pl*) fetters: *put sb in* ~*s*, fasten his wrists and ankles in chains. **have too many** ~*s* **in the fire**, too many undertakings needing attention at the same time. **3** (compounds) '~**·clad** *adj* protected by ~. '~**foundry** *n* foundry where cast-~ is produced. ,~'**grey** *adj, n* (of) the colour of freshly broken cast-~. '~**·monger** /-mʌŋgə(r)/ *n* dealer in metal goods. '~**·mongery** /-mʌŋgərɪ/ *n* business of an ~monger. '~**·mould** *n* discolouration caused by ~ rust or ink. '~**·side** *n* one of Oliver Cromwell's cavalry troopers (17th c); (fig) tough, obstinate man. '~**·ware** /-weə(r)/ *n* [U] goods made of ~; hardware. '~**·work** *n* anything made of ~, eg gratings, rails, railings. '~**·works** *n* (usu with *sing* *v*) place where ~ is smelted or where heavy ~ goods are made.

iron² /'aɪən *US*: 'aɪərn/ *vt, vi* [VP6A,15A,B,2A,C] smooth cloth/clothes with an ~ (a flat-~): ~ *a shirt. Do clothes* ~ *more easily when they are damp? She's been* ~*ing all afternoon.* ~ *out*, remove by ~ing: ~ *out wrinkles;* (fig) remove: ~ *out misunderstandings/points of disagreement.* '~**ing-board** *n* padded board on which to ~ clothes, etc.

ironic /aɪ'rɒnɪk/, **ironi·cal** /aɪ'rɒnɪkl/ *adjj* of, using, expressing, irony: *an* ~ *smile/remark/person.* **ironi·cally** /-klɪ/ *adv*

irony /'aɪərənɪ/ *n* **1** [U] the expression of one's meaning by saying sth which is the direct opposite of one's thoughts, in order to make one's remarks forceful. **2** [C] (*pl* -nies) event, situation, etc which is itself desirable, but which, because of the circumstances, is of little or no value, thus appearing to be directed by evil fate: *the* ~ *of fate/ circumstances. If a poor man inherits a large fortune and dies a month later, one might call it one of life's ironies.*

ir·ra·di·ate /ɪ'reɪdɪeɪt/ *vt* [VP6A] (formal) **1** send rays of light upon; subject to sunlight, ultra-violet rays, or radioactivity; (fig) throw light on (a subject). **2** light up: *faces* ~*d with joy.*

ir·ration·al /ɪ'ræʃənl/ *adj* **1** not endowed with reason: *behave like an* ~ *animal.* **2** not guided by reason: ~ *fears/behaviour.* ~**·ly** /-ʃnəlɪ/ *adv*

ir·rec·on·cil·able /ɪˌrekən'saɪləbl/ *adj* (formal) (of persons) that cannot be reconciled; (of ideas, actions) that cannot be brought into harmony.

ir·re·cover·able /ˌɪrɪ'kʌvərəbl/ *adj* (formal) that cannot be recovered or remedied: ~ *losses.*

ir·re·deem·able /ˌɪrɪ'di:məbl/ adj 1 (of paper currency) that cannot be exchanged for coin; (of government annuities) that cannot be terminated by repayment. 2 that cannot be restored, reclaimed, saved: *an ~ loss/misfortune*.

ir·re·den·tist /ˌɪrɪ'dentɪst/ n person who advocates the reunion to his own country of territory which has been lost to a foreign government, or which is culturally related to his own country, eg to Italy of Italian-speaking districts. **ir·ri·den·tism** /-ɪzəm/ n

ir·re·duc·ible /ˌɪrɪ'dju:səbl US: -'du:s-/ adj ~ *(to)*, (formal) 1 that cannot be reduced or made smaller: *£250 is the ~ minimum for repairs to the house*. 2 that cannot be brought (*to* a desired condition).

ir·re·fut·able /ˌɪrɪ'fju:təbl/ adj that cannot be proved false: *an ~ argument/case*.

ir·regu·lar /ɪ'regjʊlə(r)/ adj 1 contrary to rules, to what is normal and established: *an ~ proceeding/ marriage; be ~ in church attendance*, be absent frequently; *~ troops*, not trained for, or not forming part of, the regular army. 2 uneven; not regular in shape, arrangement, etc: *~ lines and figures; a coast with an ~ outline*, with many bays, inlets, etc. 3 (gram) not inflected in the usual way: *'Child' has an ~ plural*. □ n (usu *pl*) member of an ~ military force. **~·ly** adv **~·ity** /ɪˌregjʊ'lærətɪ/ n (*pl*-ties*) [U] state or quality of being ~; [C] sth ~: *~ities in behaviour; the ~ities of the earth's surface*.

ir·rel·evant /ɪ'reləvənt/ adj ~ *(to)*, not relevant (to); not connected (with): *~ remarks/evidence. What you say is ~ to the subject*. **ir·rel·evance** /-əns/, **ir·rel·evancy** /-ənsɪ/ nn (*pl ~*s, -cies) [U] state of being ~; [C] ~ remark, question, etc: *Let us ignore these irrelevancies*.

ir·re·li·gious /ˌɪrɪ'lɪdʒəs/ adj opposed to, showing no interest in, religion: *~ acts/persons*.

ir·re·medi·able /ˌɪrɪ'mi:dɪəbl/ adj that cannot be remedied: *~ acts/faults*.

ir·re·mov·able /ˌɪrɪ'mu:vəbl/ adj that cannot be removed (esp from office).

ir·rep·ar·able /ɪ'repərəbl/ adj (of a loss, injury, etc) that cannot be put right or restored: *~ harm*.

ir·re·place·able /ˌɪrɪ'pleɪsəbl/ adj of which the loss cannot be supplied.

ir·re·press·ible /ˌɪrɪ'presəbl/ adj that cannot be held back or controlled: *a girl with ~ high spirits*.

ir·re·proach·able /ˌɪrɪ'prəʊtʃəbl/ adj free from blame or fault: *~ conduct*.

ir·re·sist·ible /ˌɪrɪ'zɪstəbl/ adj too strong, convincing, delightful, etc to be resisted: *~ desires/ temptations. On this hot day the sea was ~*, We couldn't resist the desire to go to or into the sea.

ir·res·ol·ute /ɪ'rezəlu:t/ adj undecided; hesitating. **ir·res·ol·ution** /ɪˌrezə'lu:ʃn/ n [U].

ir·re·spec·tive /ˌɪrɪ'spektɪv/ adj ~ *of*, not paying consideration to; not taking into account: *He rushed forward to help, ~ of the consequences*.   ·

ir·re·spon·sible /ˌɪrɪ'spɒnsəbl/ adj 1 not responsible for conduct, etc; not to be blamed or punished: *an ~ child*. 2 (doing things, done) without a proper sense of responsibility; not trustworthy: *~ teenagers; ~ behaviour*. **ir·re·spon·si·bil·ity** /ˌɪrɪˌspɒnsə'bɪlətɪ/ n [U].

ir·re·triev·able /ˌɪrɪ'tri:vəbl/ adj that cannot be retrieved or remedied: *an ~ loss*.

ir·rev·er·ent /ɪ'revərənt/ adj feeling or showing no respect for sacred things. **~·ly** adv **ir·rev·er·ence** /-əns/ n [U].

ir·re·vers·ible /ˌɪrɪ'vɜ:səbl/ adj that cannot be

reversed or revoked: *an ~ decision*.

ir·revo·cable /ɪ'revəkəbl/ adj final and unalterable; that cannot be revoked: *an ~ decision/judgement; an ~ letter of credit*.

ir·ri·gate /'ɪrɪgeɪt/ vt [VP6A] 1 supply (land, crops) with water (by means of rivers, water-channels, overhead pipes, etc): *~ desert areas and make them fertile*. 2 construct reservoirs, canals, etc for the distribution of water (to fields). 3 wash out (a wound, etc) with a constant flow of liquid. **ir·ri·ga·tion** /ˌɪrɪ'geɪʃn/ [U] irrigating: (attrib) *an irrigation project; irrigation canals*.

ir·ri·table /'ɪrɪtəbl/ adj easily annoyed or made angry. **ir·ri·tably** /-əblɪ/ adv **ir·ri·ta·bil·ity** /ˌɪrɪtə'bɪlətɪ/ n [U].

ir·ri·tant /'ɪrɪtənt/ adj causing irritation. □ n ~ substance, eg dust or pepper in the nose; sth that irritates the mind.

ir·ri·tate /'ɪrɪteɪt/ vt [VP6A] 1 make angry or annoyed; excite the temper of: *~d by the delay*. 2 cause discomfort to (part of the body); make sore or inflamed: *The smoke ~d her eyes*. **ir·ri·ta·tion** /ˌɪrɪ'teɪʃn/ n [U] irritating or being ~d; [C] instance of this.

ir·rup·tion /ɪ'rʌpʃn/ n sudden and violent entry; bursting in.

is ⇨ be[1].

isin·glass /'aɪzɪŋglɑ:s US: -glæs/ n [U] clear white jelly made from the air bladders of some freshwater fish, used for making glue.

Is·lam /ɪz'lɑ:m US: 'ɪslɑ:m/ n faith, religion, proclaimed by the Prophet Muhammad; all Muslims; all the Muslim world. **~·ic** /ɪz'læmɪk US: ɪs'lɑ:mɪk/ adj

is·land /'aɪlənd/ n piece of land surrounded by water; sth resembling an ~ because it is detached or isolated: *a 'traffic ~*, a raised place in a busy street where people may be safe from traffic. **~·er** n person born on or living on an ~.

isle /aɪl/ n island (not much used in prose, except in proper names): *the I~ of Wight; the British I~s*. **is·let** /'aɪlɪt/ n small island.

ism /'ɪzəm/ n distinctive doctrine or practice: *behaviourism and all the other isms of the twentieth century*.

isn't ⇨ be[1].

iso·bar /'aɪsəbɑ:(r)/ n line on a map, esp a weather chart, joining places with the same atmospheric pressure at a particular time.

iso·late /'aɪsəleɪt/ vt [VP6A, 14] ~ *(from)*, 1 separate, put or keep apart from others: *feel ~d from one's fellows. When a person has an infectious disease, he is usually ~d. Several villages in the north have been ~d by heavy snowfalls*. 2 (chem) separate a substance, germ, etc from its combinations.

iso·la·tion /ˌaɪsə'leɪʃn/ n [U] ~ *(from)*, isolating or being isolated. *in ~*, alone; separated: *consider facts in ~ from others*. '*~ hospital/ward*, one for persons with infectious diseases. **~·ism** /-ɪzəm/ n (in international affairs) policy of non-participation in the affairs of other countries. **~·ist** /-ɪst/ n supporter of ~ism.

isos·celes /aɪ'sɒsəli:z/ adj (of a triangle) having two sides equal.

iso·therm /'aɪsəθɜ:m/ n line on a map joining places having the same mean temperature.

iso·tope /'aɪsətəʊp/ n atom of an element, eg heavy hydrogen, having a nuclear mass different from that of other atoms of the same element although chemically identical: *radio-active* ∼*s*, unstable forms used in medicine and industry.

issue /'ɪʃuː/ *vi,vt* **1** [VP2A,3A] ∼ *(out/forth) (from)*, come, go, flow, out: *smoke issuing from chimneys; blood issuing from a wound.* **2** [VP6A,14] ∼ *(sth to sb)*; ∼ *(sb with sth)*, distribute for use or consumption: ∼ *warm clothing to the troops;* ∼ *them with warm clothing.* **3** [VP6A,14] ∼ *(to)*, publish (books, etc); put stamps, banknotes, shares¹(3), etc into circulation. □ *n* **1** [U] outgoing; outflowing: *the point or place of* ∼; [C] the act of flowing out; that which flows out: *an* ∼ *of blood from the nose.* **2** [U] putting forth; sending out; publication: *the* ∼ *of a newspaper/a new coinage; buy new stamps on the day of* ∼; [C] that which is sent out, etc: *new* ∼*s of banknotes; the most recent* ∼*s of a periodical; an* ∼ *of winter clothing to the troops.* **3** [C] question that arises for discussion: *debate an* ∼; *raise a new* ∼; *argue political* ∼*s.* **join/take** ∼ **with sb (on/ about sth)**, proceed to argue with him (about it). **the point/matter at** ∼, the point being discussed. **4** [C] result; outcome; consequence: *bring a campaign to a successful* ∼; *await the* ∼. **5** [U] (legal) offspring: *die without* ∼, ie childless.

isth·mus /'ɪsməs/ *n* (*pl* ∼es /-sɪz/) neck of land joining two larger bodies of land: *the I*∼ *of Panama.*

it /ɪt/ *pron* (*pl* they /ðeɪ/, them /ðəm; strong form: ðem/) **1** (used of lifeless things, of animals (when sex is unknown or unimportant), and of a baby or small child when the sex is unknown or a matter of indifference): *This is my watch; it's a Swiss one. Where's my book?—Have you seen it? 'Where's the cat?'—'It's in the garden.' She's expecting another baby and hopes it will be a boy.* **2** (used to refer to a group of words which follows, this being the grammatical subject. This may be) **(a)** an infinitive phrase: *Is it difficult to learn written Chinese?* **(b)** a construction with *for*, a *noun/pronoun*, and a *to*-infinitive: *It was hard for him to live on his small pension.* **(c)** a gerundial phrase: *It doesn't seem much use going on. It's no use your trying to do that.* **(d)** a clause: *It seems unlikely that he will catch the train.* I think *it a pity that you didn't try harder. It doesn't matter whether we start now or later. Does it matter what you do next?* **3** (used to refer backwards or forwards to identify sb or sth. Note that if the identity of a person is already known, *it* is not used): *'Who's that at the door?'—'It's the postman.'* (Cf *Mr Smith is at the door. He wants to see you.*) *'What was that noise?'—'It was a mouse.'* **4** (used as a formal or meaningless word to supply a subject) **(a)** dealing with the weather, atmospheric conditions, etc: *It is raining/snowing, etc. It's warm/cold/windy, etc. Isn't it a nice day! How dark it is! It's* **(b)** for time: *It's six o'clock. It is past midnight. It's Monday, the 1st of May. It is three years since I last met you. It's a month to Christmas.* **(c)** for distance: *It's ten miles to Oxford. It's only a short way now.* **(d)** vaguely for the general situation, or for sth that is to be understood from the context: *So it seems. It can't be helped. Whose turn is it next? That's the best/worst of it! Keep at it,* ie at whatever you are doing. *You've got what it takes,* have the qualities, etc needed for this job, situation, etc. *You've had it,* there's nothing more to be had from this situa-

tion, experience, etc. *Go it!* Go on with your efforts, etc. *Now you've done it!* ie You've done sth wrong or foolish! *Now you'll catch it!* You'll be reprimanded, punished, etc! *As it happened,…; If it hadn't been for your help,….* **5** (used to bring into prominence one part of a sentence) **(a)** the subject: *It was his work during the weekend that exhausted him.* **(b)** the object of a *v*: *It's the red book that I want, not the green one.* **(c)** the object of a *prep*: *It was John I gave the book to, not Harry.* **(d)** an adverbial adjunct: *It was on Sunday that I saw him, not on Saturday.* **its** /ɪts/ *poss adj* of it: *The dog wagged its tail. The child fell and hurt its knee. I don't like this hat—its shape is wrong.* **itself** /ɪt'self/ *reflex pron*: *The dog got up and stretched itself.* □ *emph pron*: *The thing itself is not valuable, but I want it as a keepsake.* **by itself, (a)** automatically: *The machine works by itself.* **(b)** alone: *The farmhouse stands by itself in the fields.*

italic /ɪ'tælɪk/ *adj* (of printed letters) sloping: *This is* ∼ *type.* □ *n pl* ∼ letters: *in* ∼*s.* **itali·cize** /ɪ'tælɪsaɪz/ *vt* print in ∼s. ⇨ Roman(2).

itch /ɪtʃ/ *n* **1** (with *def* or *indef art*, but rarely *pl*) feeling of irritation on the skin, causing a desire to scratch: *have/suffer from the* ∼*/an* ∼. **2** (usu with the *indef art* or a *poss adj*) restless desire or longing: *have an* ∼ *for money; his* ∼ *to go to the South Seas.* □ *vi* **1** [VP2A,4A] have an ∼: *scratch where it* ∼*es. Scratch yourself if you* ∼. *Are your mosquito bites still* ∼*ing?* **2** [VP3A] ∼ **for**, (colloq) long for: *The boys were* ∼*ing for the lesson to end.* **have an** ∼**ing palm,** be ∼ing for money. ∼**y** *adj* (-ier, -iest): *an* ∼*y scalp.*

item /'aɪtəm/ *n* **1** single article or unit in a list, etc: *the first* ∼ *on the programme; number the* ∼*s in a catalogue.* **2** detail or paragraph (of news): *Are there any interesting 'news* ∼*s/*∼*s of news in the paper this morning?* □ *adv* also (used to introduce successive articles in a list): *I*∼, *one chair;* ∼, *two carpets.* ∼**·ize** /-aɪz/ *vt* [VP6A] give, write, every ∼ of: *an* ∼*ized account;* ∼*ize a bill.*

it·er·ate /'ɪtəreɪt/ *vt* [VP6A] say again and again; make (an accusation, etc) repeatedly. **it·er·ation** /ˌɪtə'reɪʃn/ *n* [U] iterating; [C] sth ∼d.

i·tin·er·ant /aɪ'tɪnərənt/ *adj* travelling from place to place: ∼ *musicians.*

i·tin·er·ary /aɪ'tɪnərərɪ *US:* -rerɪ/ *n* (*pl* -ries) [C] plan for, details or records of, a journey; route.

it'll /'ɪtl/ = *it will.*

it's /ɪts/ = *it is* or *it has.*

its, it·self /ɪts, ɪt'self/ ⇨ it.

I've /aɪv/ = *I have.*

ivory /'aɪvərɪ/ *n* [U] white, bone-like substance forming the tusks of elephants, used for ornaments, piano-keys, etc; (attrib) the colour of ∼: *an* ∼ *skin/complexion.* ∼ **tower,** place of seclusion or retreat from the realities of life.

ivy /'aɪvɪ/ *n* [U] climbing, clinging, evergreen plant with dark, shiny (often five-pointed) leaves. **ivied** /'aɪvɪd/ *adj* covered with ivy: *ivied walls.*

ivy

Jj

J, j /dʒeɪ/ (*pl* J's, j's /dʒeɪz/) the tenth letter of the English alphabet.

jab /dʒæb/ *vt,vi* (-bb-) **1** [VP3A] **jab at**, poke or push at sb/sth with force: *jab at sb/sth with a knife*. *He jabbed at his opponent*, (boxing) aimed a quick blow at him. **2** [VP14] **jab sth into sth/sb**, force sth into sth/sb: *He jabbed his elbow into my side*. **3** [VP15B] **jab sth out**, force or push out by jabbing: *Be careful! Don't jab my eye out with your umbrella!* □ *n* sudden, rough blow or thrust: *a jab in the arm*, (colloq) an injection or inoculation: *Have you had your cholera jabs yet?*

jabber /'dʒæbə(r)/ *vi,vt* **1** [VP2A,C] talk excitedly; talk in what seems to be a rapid and confused manner: *Listen to those children ~ing away!* **2** [VP6A,15B] utter (words, etc) rapidly and indistinctly: *~ (out) one's prayers*. □ *n* [U] *~ing*; chatter: *Listen to the ~ of those monkeys. ~er n* person who *~s*.

jabot /'ʒæbəʊ/ *n* [C] ornamental frill on the front of a woman's blouse or a man's shirt.

jack¹ /dʒæk/ *n* **1** J*~*, familiar form of the name *John*. **J*~* Frost**, frost personified. **'J*~* in office**, self-important official who fusses over details. **,J*~* of 'all trades**, person who can turn his hand to anything; workman knowing something of many trades. **before one can say J*~* Robinson**, very quickly or suddenly. **J*~* is as good as his master**, the workman is the equal of his employer. **2** (colloq) man. **every man *~***, everybody. **3** (usu portable) device for raising heavy weights off the ground, esp one for raising the axle of a car so that a wheel may be changed. **4** (in the game of bowls) small white ball towards which bowls are rolled. **5** ship's flag to show nationality. **the Union J*~***, flag of the United Kingdom. ⇨ the illus at flag. **'*~* staff** *n* staff on which a ship's flag is flown to show nationality. **6** (in a pack of playing-cards) knave. **7** (compounds) **'*~*-in-the-box** *n* toy in the form of a box with sth inside which springs up when the lid is opened. **,*~*-o'-'lantern** *n* will-o'-the-wisp; pumpkin cut to look like a face and used as a lantern (by placing a candle inside) in fun. **'*~* rabbit** *n* large hare of Western N America. **~ tar** *n* (old name for a) naval rating; ordinary seaman in the Navy, wearing a jumper and wide-bottomed trousers.

jack² /dʒæk/ *vt* [VP15B] **~ sth in**, (sl) abandon (the work, attempt, etc. **~ sth up**, lift with a jack(2): *J~ up the car and change the wheel with the punctured tyre*.

jackal /'dʒækɔːl US: -kl/ *n* wild dog-like animal.

jack·a·napes /'dʒækəneɪps/ *n* **1** conceited person. **2** (often playfully of a child) impudent or mischievous person.

jack·ass /'dʒækæs/ *n* male ass; foolish person. **laughing *~***, (in Australia) Giant Kingfisher.

jack-boot /'dʒæk buːt/ *n* large boot coming above the knee (as formerly worn by cavalrymen).

jack·daw /'dʒækdɔː/ *n* bird of the crow family (noted for flying off with small bright objects).

jacket /'dʒækɪt/ *n* **1** short, sleeved coat. **dust a person's *~***, beat him. **2** outer covering round a boiler, tank, pipe, etc to lessen loss of heat, or (*a*

water ~) to cool an engine. **3** skin (of a potato): *baked in their ~s*. **4** (also '*dust-~*) loose paper cover in which a hardback book is issued.

jack-knife /'dʒæk naɪf/ *n* large pocket-knife with a folding blade. □ *vi* [VP2A] (esp of an articulated truck) fold and double back like the blade and handle of a *~*.

jack-plane /'dʒæk pleɪn/ *n* plane² for rough smoothing of wood.

jack·pot /'dʒækpɒt/ *n* accumulated stakes in various games (esp poker), increasing in value until won. **hit the *~***, have great success or good fortune.

Jaco·bean /,dʒækə'bɪən/ *adj* of the reign of James I (1603—25) of England: *~ literature/ architecture/furniture*.

Jac·obin /'dʒækəbɪn/ *n* member of a group of revolutionaries organized in 1789 during the French Revolution. □ *adj* violent; extremely radical. **~ism** /-ɪzəm/ *n* (politics) extreme radicalism.

Jac·obite /'dʒækəbaɪt/ *n* supporter of James II (reigned 1685—1688) of England after his overthrow or of his descendants who claimed the English throne.

jade¹ /dʒeɪd/ *n* [U] hard, usu green stone, carved into ornaments, etc.

jade² /dʒeɪd/ *n* **1** tired out or worn-out horse. **2** (either contemptuous or playful) woman: *You saucy little ~!* **~d** /'dʒeɪdɪd/ *adj* worn out; overworked; dulled: *He looks ~d. He has a ~d appetite*.

jag¹ /dʒæg/ *n* sharp projection, eg of rock. **jaggy** *adj* having *~s*.

jag² /dʒæg/ *vt* (-gg-) [VP6A] cut or tear in an uneven manner; give an edge like that of a saw to. **jag·ged** /'dʒægɪd/ *adj* notched; with rough, uneven edges: *jagged rocks*.

jag·uar /'dʒægjʊə(r)/ *n* large, fierce, cat-like meat-eating animal of Central and South America. ⇨ the illus at cat.

jail /dʒeɪl/ *n* ⇨ gaol.

jakes /dʒeɪks/ *n* (sl) water-closet.

ja·lopy /dʒə'lɒpɪ/ *n* (*pl* -pies) (colloq) old, rickety or battered automobile or aircraft.

jam¹ /dʒæm/ *n* [U] fruit boiled with sugar until it is thick, and preserved in jars, pots, tins, etc. **money for jam**, (sl) something for nothing; something coming by good luck. **'jam-jar/-pot** *nn* one for containing jam. **'jam session** *n* impromptu performance by jazz musicians.

jam² /dʒæm/ *vt,vi* (-mm-) **1** [VP6A,15A,B,14,2A,C] **~ (in/under/between etc)**, crush, be crushed, between two surfaces or masses; squeeze, be squeezed: *a ship jammed in the ice*. *The logs jammed in the river*, became tightly packed. **2** [VP15B,2A,C] **~ (on)**, (of parts of a machine, etc) (cause to) become fixed so that movement or action is prevented: *jam the brakes on/jam on the brakes*. *The brakes jammed and the car skidded badly*. **3** [VP6A,15A,B] push (things) together tightly: *jam one's clothes into a small suitcase*. *The corridors were jammed by/with hordes of schoolchildren*. **4** [VP6A] make the reception of a broadcast programme impossible or difficult by broadcasting a signal that deliberately interferes: *jam the enemy's stations during a war.* □ *n* [C] **1** number of things or people crowded together so that movement is difficult or impossible: '*traffic-jams in our big towns; a*'*log-jam,* on a river, etc. **2** stoppage of a machine due to jamming(2). **3** (sl) awkward position; difficult situation: *be in/get into a jam.*

jamb /dʒæm/ *n* vertical side post of a doorway, window frame, etc; (*pl*) stone sides of a fireplace.

jam·boree /ˌdʒæmbəˈriː/ *n* **1** merry meeting. **2** large rally or gathering, esp of Scouts or Guides.

jam·pack /ˌdʒæmˈpæk/ *vt* [VP6A] (colloq) crowd to capacity: *a stadium ~ed with spectators.*

jangle /ˈdʒæŋgl/ *vt,vi* [VP6A,2A] (cause to) give out a harsh metallic noise; argue noisily. □ *n* [U] harsh noise.

jani·tor /ˈdʒænɪtə(r)/ *n* **1** doorkeeper. **2** (US) person hired to take care of a building, offices, etc, eg by cleaning, stoking the furnaces.

Jan·uary /ˈdʒænjʊərɪ US: -jʊerɪ/ *n* the first month of the year.

Ja·nus /ˈdʒeɪnəs/ *n* ancient Roman god, guardian of gates and doors, beginnings and ends, represented with two faces, one on the front and the other on the back of his head.

ja·pan /dʒəˈpæn/ *vt* (-nn-), *n* (cover with) hard, shiny black enamel.

jape /dʒeɪp/ *n* (old use) joke.

ja·pon·ica /dʒəˈpɒnɪkə/ *n* [U] (sorts of) ornamental variety of pear or quince.

jar¹ /dʒɑː(r)/ *n* [C] **1** (usu harsh) sound or vibration: *We felt a jar when the engine was coupled to the train.* **2** shock; thrill of the nerves; discord: *The fall from his horse gave him a nasty jar. It was an unpleasant jar to my nerves.*

jar² /dʒɑː(r)/ *n* tall vessel, usu round, with a wide mouth, with or without handle(s), of glass, stone or earthenware; its contents: *a jar of strawberry jam.* **jar·ful** /-fʊl/ *n*

jar³ /dʒɑː(r)/ *vi,vt* (-rr-) **1** [VP3A] *jar against/on,* strike with a harsh unpleasant sound. **2** [VP3A] *jar on,* have an unpleasant effect (on): *The way he laughs jars on me/on my ears/on my nerves.* **3** [VP6A] send a shock through (the nerves): *He was badly jarred by the blow. She was jarred by this sad news.* **4** [VP2A,3A] *jar (with),* be out of harmony: *His opinions jar with mine. Try to avoid colours that jar when choosing curtains and rugs.* **jar·ring** *adj* causing disharmony; harsh: *a jarring note.* **jar·ring·ly** *adv*

jar·gon /ˈdʒɑːgən/ *n* [U] **1** language difficult to understand, because it is badly formed or spoken badly: *Only a mother can understand her baby's ~.* **2** language full of technical or special words: *the ~ of radio technicians/linguists.*

jas·mine /ˈdʒæsmɪn/ *n* [U] shrub with white or yellow sweet-smelling flowers.

jas·per /ˈdʒæspə(r)/ *n* [U] semi-precious stone, red, yellow or brown.

jaun·dice /ˈdʒɔːndɪs/ *n* [U] disease, caused by stoppage of the flow of bile, marked by yellowness of the skin and the whites of the eyes; (fig) state of mind in which one is jealous, spiteful, envious and suspicious. □ *vt* (usu passive) affect with ~: *take a ~d view,* one influenced by jealousy, spite, etc.

jaunt /dʒɔːnt/ *n* short journey for pleasure. □ *vi* [VP2A,C] make such a journey. '*~ing-car* *n* light, two-wheeled horse-drawn vehicle with seats back to back, used in Ireland.

jaunty /ˈdʒɔːntɪ/ *adj* (-ier, iest) feeling or showing self-confidence and self-satisfaction: *He wore his hat at a ~ angle,* tipped to one side as a sign of high spirits, etc. **jaunt·ily** /-ɪlɪ/ *adv* **jaunti·ness** *n* [U].

javelin /ˈdʒævlɪn/ *n* light spear for throwing (usu in sport).

throwing the javelin

jaw /dʒɔː/ *n* **1** (**lower/upper**) **jaw**, either of the bone structures containing the teeth: *Which jaw moves up and down when you talk?* ⇨ the illus at head. '**jaw-bone** *n* one of the bones in which the teeth are set. '**jaw-breaker** *n* (colloq) word hard to pronounce. **2** (*pl*) framework of the mouth, including the teeth; (*sing*) lower part of the face: *a man with a strong jaw.* **3** (*pl*) narrow mouth of a valley, channel, etc: (fig) *into/out of the jaws of death,* into/out of great danger. **4** (*pl*) parts of a tool, machine, etc, eg a vice, between which things are gripped or crushed. **5** (colloq) talkativeness: *None of your jaw!* **6** (colloq) long, dull talk giving moral advice. □ *vi* [VP2A,C,3A] *jaw (at),* (colloq) talk, esp at tedious length; give a moral talk to: *Stop jawing at me!*

jay /dʒeɪ/ *n* noisy European bird with brightly coloured feathers; (fig) impertinent person who chatters too much. '**jay-walker** *n* person who walks erratically across or along streets without paying attention to traffic. '**jay-walk** *vi* walk in this way.

jazz /dʒæz/ *n* [U] popular music first played by Negro groups in Southern USA in the early 20th c, characterized by improvisation and strong rhythms, called *traditional* ~; similar music played by large bands for dancing; a later variation much influenced by the *blues* to produce an unhurried unemotive style, called *modern* ~: *the* '~ *age;* (attrib) ~ *music; a* '~ *band.* □ *vt* **1** [VP6A] play or arrange in the style of ~: ~ *a song/tune;* dance to ~ music. **2** [VP15B] ~ *sth up,* (fig, colloq) liven up; put more energy into: ~ *up a party;* ~ *things up a bit.* **jazzy** *adj* (-ier, -iest) (colloq) of or like ~; flashy, showy: ~*y cushions; a* ~*y sports car.*

jeal·ous /ˈdʒeləs/ *adj* **1** feeling or showing fear or ill will because of possible or actual loss of rights or love: *a* ~ *husband;* ~ *looks.* **2** ~ (*of sb/sth*), feeling or showing unhappiness because of the better fortune, etc of others: ~ *of sb else's success.* **3** ~ (*of sb/sth*), taking watchful care (*of*): ~ *of one's rights; keep a* ~ *eye on sb.* **4** (in the Bible, of God) requiring exclusive loyalty and wholehearted worship and service. ~**·ly** *adv* **jeal·ousy** /ˈdʒeləsɪ/ *n* (*pl* -sies) **1** [U] being ~: *a lover's* ~*y.* **2** [C] instance of this; act or utterance that shows ~*y*: *I'm tired of all these jealousies and quarrels.*

jean /dʒiːn/ *n* **1** [U] heavy, strong cotton cloth: (attrib) ~ *overalls.* **2** ~**s**, tough (usu denim) trousers worn informally by men, women and children.

jeep /dʒiːp/ *n* small, light utility motor vehicle with great freedom of movement, useful on rough ground.

jeer /dʒɪə(r)/ *vi,vt* [VP2A,3A,6A] ~ *(at sb)*, mock, laugh rudely: ~ *at a defeated enemy;* ~ *(at) the speaker; a* ~*ing crowd.* □ *n* [C] ~ing remark; taunt. ~**·ing·ly** *adv*

Je·ho·vah /dʒɪˈhəʊvə/ *n* name of God used in the Old Testament.

je·june /dʒɪˈdʒuːn/ *adj* (formal) (of writings) dry; uninteresting; unsatisfying to the mind. ~**·ly** *adv* ~**·ness** *n* [U].

Jekyll and Hyde /ˌdʒekl ən ˈhaɪd/ *n* single person with two personalities, one good (*Jekyll*) and one bad (*Hyde*).

jell /dʒel/ *vi,vt* [VP2A,6A] (colloq) (cause to) become like jelly; take shape: *My ideas are beginning to* ~.

jel·laba /ˈdʒeləbə/ *n* loose hooded cloak worn by Arab men.

jelly /ˈdʒelɪ/ *n* (*pl* -lies) **1** [U] soft, semi-solid food substance made from gelatin; similar substance made of fruit juice and sugar. **2** [C,U] (portion of) this substance prepared in a mould, flavoured and coloured, as a sweet dish. **3** [C,U] ~-like substance. '~**-fish** *n* ~-like sea animal. ⇨ the illus at sea. □ *vt,vi* [VP6A,2A] (cause to) become like ~. **jel·lied** *adj* set in ~; prepared in ~; like ~: *jellied eels.*

jemmy /ˈdʒemɪ/ *n* (*pl* -mies) (US = *jimmy*) crowbar, esp as used by burglars for forcing open doors, windows and drawers.

jenny /ˈdʒenɪ/ *n* ⇨ *spinning* ~ at spin.

jeop·ard·ize /ˈdʒepədaɪz/ *vt* [VP6A] put in danger.

jeop·ardy /ˈdʒepədɪ/ *n* [U] danger of harm or loss, usu in the phrase: *be/place/put in jeopardy.*

jer·boa /dʒɜːˈbəʊə/ *n* small rat-like animal of Asia and the N African deserts with long hind legs and the ability to jump well.

jere·miad /ˌdʒerɪˈmaɪæd/ *n* long, sad and complaining story of troubles, misfortunes, etc.

jerk¹ /dʒɜːk/ *n* [C] **1** sudden push, pull, start, stop, twist, lift or throw: *The train stopped with a* ~/*a series of* ~*s.* **2** sudden involuntary twitch of a muscle or muscles. **3 physical** ~**s**, (colloq) gymnastic exercises. **4** (sl) foolish person. □ *vt,vi* [VP6A,15A,B,2C] give a ~ to; move with a ~ or ~s: *He* ~*ed the fish out of the water. The train* ~*ed along/*~*ed to a stop. Don't* ~ *out your words; try to recite more smoothly.* ~**y** *adj* (-ier, -iest) with ~s; not smooth: *a* ~*y ride in an old bus.* ~**·ily** /-ɪlɪ/ *adv* ~**·i·ness** *n* [U].

jerk² /dʒɜːk/ *vt* [VP6A] cure (esp beef) by cutting it into long slices and drying it in the sun.

jer·kin /ˈdʒɜːkɪn/ *n* short, close-fitting jacket, usu of leather (as worn by men in olden times). ⇨ the illus at doublet.

jerry /ˈdʒerɪ/ *n* (*pl* -ries) **1** '~**-builder/-building**, builder/building of houses of poor quality with bad materials. Hence, '~**-built** *adj.* **2** '~**-can**, army-style metal container used for carrying extra supplies of water or petrol on long journeys. **3 J**~, (army sl) German soldier. **4** (sl) chamber-pot.

jer·sey /ˈdʒɜːzɪ/ *n* (*pl* -seys) **1** [U] ('~**-wool**) soft, fine knitted fabric used for clothes; [C] close-fitting knitted woollen garment with sleeves. ⇨ jumper, pullover, sweater. **2 J**~, cow of the breed that originally came from J~, one of the Channel Islands (near the French coast).

jest /dʒest/ *n* [C] **1** joke; sth said or done to cause amusement. *in* ~, as a joke, not in earnest. **2** ob-

ject of ridicule: *a standing* ~, sth or sb always laughed at. □ *vi* [VP2A,3A] ~ *(with)*, make ~s; act or speak lightly: *Don't* ~ *about serious things. He's not a man to* ~ *with.* ~**·ing** *adj* spoken in ~: ~*ing remarks;* fond of ~s: *a* ~*ing fellow.* ~**·ing·ly** *adv*

jest·er /ˈdʒestə(r)/ *n* person who jests, esp (in olden times) a man whose duty it was to make jokes to amuse the court or noble household in which he was employed.

Jesuit /ˈdʒezjʊɪt *US:* ˈdʒeʒʊɪt/ *n* member of the Society of Jesus, a RC order founded in 1534 by Ignatius Loyola /ɪɡˌneɪʃəs lɔɪˈəʊlə/ (1491—1556), Spanish priest, taking vows of obedience, poverty and chastity; (as used by opponents of the Society) person who thinks that it may be right to dissemble or prevaricate if this helps to obtain good results. ~**·i·cal** /ˌdʒezjʊˈɪtɪkl *US:* ˌdʒeʒʊ-/ *adj* of or like the ~s.

Jesus /ˈdʒiːzəs/ *n* the founder of the Christian religion.

jet¹ /dʒet/ *n* [C] **1** fast, strong stream of gas, liquid, steam or flame, forced out of a small opening: *The pipe burst and a jet of water shot across the kitchen.* ˌ**jet-pro·pulsion (engine)**, propulsion of aircraft and spacecraft by engines that suck in air at the front, mix the air with gases, and send out the hot, burnt gases in jets at the back. Hence, ˌ**jet** ('**aircraft**/'**airliner**/'**fighter**) *nn* ˌ**jet-pro·pelled** *adj.* ⇨ the illus at air. **the** '**jet set**, wealthy persons who often travel by jet aircraft for holidays. **2** (*pl*) (often a brief but repeated) stream of liquid, gas, etc: *He cut his wrist so badly that jets of blood spurted out.* **3** narrow opening from which a jet comes out: *a* ˈ*gas-jet.* □ *vi,vt* (-tt-) **1** come, send out, in a jet or jets. **2** (colloq) travel by jet airliner.

jet² /dʒet/ *n* [U] hard, black mineral that takes a brilliant polish, used for buttons, ornaments, etc; the colour of this mineral; (attrib) made of jet; (also ˌ**jet-'black**) deep, glossy black.

jet·sam /ˈdʒetsəm/ *n* [U] goods thrown overboard from a ship at sea to lighten it, eg in a storm; such goods washed up on the seashore. **flotsam and** ~, (fig use) persons whose lives have been wrecked: *Sick and starving refugees are the flotsam and* ~ *of war.*

jet·ti·son /ˈdʒetɪsn/ *vt* [VP6A] throw (goods) overboard in order to lighten a ship, eg during a storm; abandon, discard (what is unwanted): ~ *an unpleasant passenger/an unworkable plan.*

jetty /ˈdʒetɪ/ *n* (*pl* -ties) structure built out into a body of water as a breakwater or as a landing-place for ships and boats.

Jew /dʒuː/ *n* person of the Hebrew people or religion. **Jew·ess** /ˈdʒuːɪs/ *n* female Jew. **Jew·ish** /ˈdʒuːɪʃ/ *adj* of the Jews.

jewel /ˈdʒuːəl/ *n* **1** precious stone, eg a diamond or a ruby; ornament with a ~ or ~s set in it. **2** artificial diamond: *This watch has 15* ~*s.* **3** (fig) sth or sb highly valued: *His wife is a* ~. □ *vt* (-ll-, US -l-) adorn with ~s: (usu in *pp*) *a* ~*led ring; a* ~*led watch,* with industrial, not gem diamonds, in the movement. ~**·ler,** (US = ~**er**) /ˈdʒuːələ(r)/ *n* trader in ~s; person who sells ~s. ~**ry,** ~**·lery** /ˈdʒuːəlrɪ/ *n* [U] ~s collectively, ie precious stones, ornaments set with ~s, etc.

Jeze·bel /ˈdʒezəbl *US:* -bel/ *n* (as a term of abuse) shameless, immoral woman. ⇨ **Kings 1 : 18.**

jib¹ /dʒɪb/ *n* **1** small triangular sail (in front of the mainsail). ˌ**jib-'boom** *n* spar to which the lower part of a jib is fastened. ⇨ the illus at barque, sail. **the cut of his jib,** his personal appearance. **2** projecting arm of a crane or derrick. ⇨ the illus at crane.

jib² /dʒɪb/ *vi* (-bb-) [VP2A] (of a horse, etc) stop suddenly; refuse to go forwards; (fig) refuse to proceed: *On seeing the gate the horse jibbed.* [VP3A] **jib at,** (fig) show unwillingness or dislike: *He jibbed at working overtime every day. My small car sometimes jibs at a steep hill.*

jibe /dʒaɪb/ *vi* (US) **1** = gibe. **2** = gybe.

jiffy /'dʒɪfɪ/ *n* (colloq) moment. **in a ~,** very soon.

jig /dʒɪg/ *n* [C] **1** (music for a) quick, lively dance. **2** appliance that holds a piece of work and guides the tools that are used on it. □ *vi, vt* (-gg-) **1** [VP2A,C] dance a jig. **2** [VP15B,2C] move up and down in a quick, jerky way: *jigging up and down in excitement; jig a baby (up and down) on one's knees.*

jig·ger /'dʒɪgə(r)/ *n* **1** flea or other parasite that burrows under the skin; (in England) harvest mite. **2** small measure for liquor (esp spirits), as fitted to bottles in bars.

jig·gered /'dʒɪgəd/ *adj* (*pred* only, colloq) **1** amazed: *Well, I'm ~!* **2** exhausted.

jig·gery-po·kery /ˌdʒɪgərɪ 'pəʊkərɪ/ *n* [U] (colloq) hocus-pocus; humbug.

jig·gle /'dʒɪgl/ *vt, vi, n* joggle.

jig·saw /'dʒɪgsɔː/ *n* **1** machine fretsaw. **2** '**~ (puzzle),** picture, map, etc pasted on thin board or wood and cut in irregularly shaped pieces which are to be fitted together again.

ji·had /dʒɪ'hɑːd/ *n* religious war by Muslims against unbelievers; (fig) campaign for or against a teaching, practice, etc.

jilt /dʒɪlt/ *vt* [VP6A] give up, send away, (sb) after giving him encouragement or a promise to marry: *When he lost his job, she ~ed him.* □ *n* person who jilts sb.

Jim Crow /ˌdʒɪm 'krəʊ/ *n* ⚠ (US) contemptuous name for a Negro.

ji·miny /'dʒɪmənɪ/ *int* (colloq) exclamation of surprise.

jim–jams /'dʒɪm dʒæmz/ *n pl* (sl) **the ~,** the jitters.

jimmy /'dʒɪmɪ/ *n* (US) = jemmy.

jingle /'dʒɪŋgl/ *n* [C] **1** metallic clinking or ringing sound (as of coins, keys or small bells). **2** series of the same or similar sounds in words, esp when designed to attract the attention; jingling verse. □ *vt, vi* **1** [VP6A,15B,2A,C] (cause to) make a light, ringing sound: *He ~d his keys. The money in his pocket ~d.* **2** [VP2A] (of verse) be full of alliterations and rhymes that make it easy to learn and remember.

jingo /'dʒɪŋgəʊ/ *n* (*pl* ~es /-gəʊz/) person who combines excessive patriotism with contempt for other countries, esp one who supports a warlike policy. **By ~!** (dated sl) exclamation expressing surprise, pleasure, etc or giving emphasis to a statement. **~·ism** /-ɪzəm/ *n* attitude of mind, principles, of ~es. **~·ist** /-ɪst/ *n* **~·is·tic** /ˌdʒɪŋgəʊ'ɪstɪk/ *adj* characteristic of ~es.

jinks /dʒɪŋks/ *n* [U] (only in) **high ~,** noisy merry-making; uncontrolled fun.

jinn /dʒɪn/ *n* = genie.

jinx /dʒɪŋks/ *n* (colloq) person or thing that brings bad luck. **put a ~ on sb,** do sth to bring him bad luck.

jit·ney /'dʒɪtnɪ/ *n* (US colloq) **1** (old use) nickel. **2** small motor-bus.

jit·ters /'dʒɪtəz/ *n pl* **the ~,** (sl) extreme nervousness: *have/get/give sb the ~.* **jit·ter-bug** /'dʒɪtəbʌg/ *n* **1** (person who participated in a) lively, popular dance of the 1940's to swing music. **2** (old use) flustered person. **jit·tery** /'dʒɪtərɪ/ *adj* nervous; frightened.

jive /dʒaɪv/ *n* style of popular music with a strong beat; dancing to this. □ *vi* dance to ~ music.

job¹ /dʒɒb/ *n* **1** piece of work, either to be done, or completed: *Your new Bentley car is a lovely job,* is magnificent. **on the job,** (colloq) at work; busy. **be paid by the job,** separately for each job. **make a good/fine job of sth,** do it well. **odd jobs,** bits of work not connected with one another. **,odd-'job man,** one who makes a living by doing any bits of work he is asked to do. **2** *a good job,* (colloq) a fortunate state of affairs: *He lost his seat in Parliament, and a good job, too!* **give sb/sth up as a bad job,** (colloq) decide that sb/sth is hopeless. **make the best of a bad job,** do what one can to remedy an unfortunate state of affairs. **3** *be/have a (hard) job doing/to do sth,* be/have a difficult task: *It's a (hard) job for a poor man to keep his wife and children clothed and fed. You'll have a job convincing your wife that you were really detained at the office.* **4** employment: *to have/lose a job;* (attrib) *job safety/satisfaction. He lost his job.* **out of a job,** unemployed. **jobs for the boys,** (colloq) positions for one's supporters, friends, etc. '**job centre,** employment exchange, ⇨ employment. **5 job lot,** mixed collection of articles, bought together. **6 just the job,** (colloq) exactly what is wanted. **7** (sl) sth done by intrigue or dishonesty for private profit or advantage: *a put-up job.* ⇨ *put up* at put¹(11). **8** (sl) criminal act, esp theft: *He got three years for a job he did in Leeds.*

job² /dʒɒb/ *vt, vi* **1** [VP2A] ⇨ **1** above; do odd jobs: *a jobbing gardener,* one who works for several employers and is paid by the hour/day; *a jobbing printer,* one who prints leaflets, posters, etc. **2** [VP6A] (on the Stock Exchange) act as a broker; buy, sell (stocks and shares) for others. **3** [VP2A,14] (colloq) use a position of trust for private advantage or for the benefit of one's friends: *He jobbed his brother into a well-paid post.* **jobber** *n* **1** dealer in Stock Exchange securities. ⇨ broker. **2** person who jobs(1). **3** person who jobs(3). **job·bery** /'dʒɒbərɪ/ *n* [U] jobbing; (esp) use of unfair means to gain private advantage.

Job /dʒəʊb/ *n* (from Job in the Book of Job in the Old Testament) person of great patience. **try the patience of Job,** be very difficult to endure, very vexatious. **a Job's comforter,** one who aggravates the distress of the person he is supposed to be comforting.

jockey /'dʒɒkɪ/ *n* (*pl* ~s) professional rider in horse-races. ⇨ also disc. '**J~ Club,** club that controls horse-racing in England. □ *vt, vi* [VP15A,3A] trick; cheat: *He ~ed Green out of his job.* **~ for position,** (a) (in racing) jostle other riders in order to get a more favourable position. (b) (fig) try by skilful management, by tricky manoeuvring, to gain an advantage.

jo·cose /dʒəʊ'kəʊs/ *adj* (formal) humorous; playful. **~·ly** *adv* **~·ness, jo·cos·ity** /dʒəʊ'kɒsətɪ/ *nn*

jocu·lar /'dʒɒkjʊlə(r)/ *adj* meant as a joke; given to joking. **~·ly** *adv* **~·ity** /ˌdʒɒkjʊ'lærətɪ/ *n* (*pl* -ties) [U] being ~; [C] ~ act or utterance.

joc·und /'dʒɒkənd/ *adj* (liter) merry; cheerful. **~·ity** /dʒəʊ'kʌndətɪ/ *n* (*pl* -ties) [U] being ~; [C] ~

act or utterance.

jodh·purs /'dʒɒdpəz/ n pl long breeches for horse-riding, close-fitting from knee to ankle.

jog /dʒɒg/ vt,vi (-gg-) **1** [VP6A,15B] give a slight knock or push to; shake with a push or jerk: *The horse jogged its rider up and down. He jogged my elbow,* touched it, eg to attract my attention, to warn me, etc. *jog sb's memory,* try to make him remember or recall sth. **2** [VP15B] cause to move unsteadily, in a shaking manner: *The old bus jogged us up and down on the rough mountain road.* **3** [VP2C] *jog along/on,* make slow, patient progress: *We jogged along the bad roads. Matters jog along. We must jog on somehow until business conditions improve.* **4** [VP2A] (mod colloq) run slowly and steadily for a time, for physical exercise. **jog·ger** /'dʒɒgə(r)/ n person who jogs(4). **jog·ging** /'dʒɒgɪŋ/ n [U] the physical exercise of jogging(4). □ n [C] **1** slight push, shake or nudge. **2** (also **'jog-trot**) slow walk or trot.

joggle /'dʒɒgl/ vt,vi [VP6A,2A] shake, move, by or as if by repeated jerks. □ n slight shake.

john /dʒɒn/ n (sl) water-closet.

John Bull /ˌdʒɒn 'bʊl/ n the English nation; typical Englishman.

John Doe /ˌdʒɒn 'dəʊ/ n (esp US) **1** (legal) invented name for an unknown person. **2** ordinary, typical man.

joie de vivre /ˌʒwɑː də 'viːvrə/ n (F) carefree enjoyment of life.

join /dʒɔɪn/ vt,vi **1** [VP6A,14,15A,B] ~ *sth to sth;* ~ *things together/up,* put together; unite; connect (two points, things) with a line, rope, bridge, etc: ~ *one thing to another;* ~ *two things together;* ~ *the pieces together;* ~ *an island to the mainland* (*with a bridge*); ~ *two persons in marriage,* make them man and wife. *Where does this stream* ~ *the Danube?* ~ *battle,* begin fighting. ~ *hands,* clasp each other's hands; (fig) combine in an enterprise, etc. ~ *forces (with...),* unite in action; work together. **2** [VP2A,C] come together; unite: *Parallel lines are, by definition, lines that never* ~. *Which two rivers* ~ *at Lyons?* **3** [VP6A] become a member of: ~ *the army/a club.* [VP2C] *join up,* (colloq) join the army. **4** [VP6A,15A,3A] ~ *(sb) in sth,* come into the company of; associate with (sb in sth): *I'll* ~ *you in a few minutes. Will you* ~ *us in a walk,* come with us? *Why doesn't Tom* ~ *in the conversation,* Why is he silent? *May I* ~ *in* (*the game*)? □ n place or line where two things are ~ed: *The two pieces were put together so cleverly that the* ~ *could not be seen.*

joiner /'dʒɔɪnə(r)/ n skilled workman who makes the inside woodwork of buildings, etc. ⇨ carpenter, *cabinet-maker* at cabinet. **join·ery** n [U] work of a ~: *learn* ~*y; lessons in* ~*y.*

joint¹ /dʒɔɪnt/ adj (attrib only) held or done by, belonging to, two or more persons together: ~ *efforts/ownership/responsibility;* ~ *heirs to a legacy; a* ~ *account,* bank account in the name of more than one person, eg a husband and wife; *a* ~*-stock company,* a number of persons who carry on a business with capital contributed by all; *during their* ~ *lives,* (legal) while they are both (or all) living; *settle a trade dispute by* ~ *consultation,* eg workers and management. ~*·ly adv*

joint² /dʒɔɪnt/ n **1** place, line or surface at which two or more things are joined: *the* ~*s in a jigsaw puzzle.* **2** device or structure by which things, eg lengths of pipe, bones, are joined together: '*finger*

~*s. out of* ~, (of bones) dislocated; pushed out of position: *He fell and put his knee out of* ~. *put sb's 'nose out of* ~, (fig) take his place in another's affections or favour; upset or humble sb who is a nuisance. **3** limb (shoulder, leg) or other division of an ox, a sheep, etc which a butcher supplies to customers: *a slice off the* ~, eg of roast beef. **4** (sl) place visited by people for gambling, drinking or drug-taking. '*clip* ~, bar, night-club, etc at which extortionate charges are made (often for services not rendered). **5** (sl) cigarette containing a drug.

joint³ /dʒɔɪnt/ vt [VP6A] **1** provide with a joint or joints(2): *a* ~*ed fishing-rod/doll.* **2** divide at a ~ or into ~s(3).

join·ture /'dʒɔɪntʃə(r)/ n [C] (legal) property settled on a woman during her marriage, to be used by her after her husband's death.

joist /dʒɔɪst/ n one of the parallel pieces of timber (from wall to wall) to which floorboards are fastened; steel beam supporting a floor or ceiling.

joke /dʒəʊk/ n sth said (eg a story with a funny ending) or done to cause amusement, laughter, etc: *tell/make a* ~; sth that causes amusement. *have a* ~ *with sb,* share one with him. *make a* ~ *about sb or sth,* speak lightly or amusingly about. *play a* ~ *on sb,* cause him to be the victim of a practical ~. *a practical* ~, a trick played on sb in order to make him appear ridiculous. *It's no* ~, It's a serious matter. *the* ~ *of the village/town, etc,* the laughing-stock; person, event, etc which causes great amusement. □ vi [VP2A,C] make ~s: *He's always joking. I was only joking.* **jok·ing·ly** adv in a joking manner.

joker /'dʒəʊkə(r)/ n **1** person who is fond of making jokes. **2** (sl) fellow. **3** extra playing card (the 53rd) which is used in some games as the highest trump or as a wild(10) card.

jolly /'dʒɒlɪ/ adj (-ier, -iest) joyful; gay; merry; slightly drunk. J~ *Roger,* pirate's black flag (with skull and crossbones). □ adv (GB colloq) very: *I'll take* ~ *good care not to lend him money again.* □ vt [VP6A,15A,B] (colloq) keep (sb) in a good humour (esp in order to win his co-operation): *They jollied me along until I agreed to help them.* **jol·li·fi·ca·tion** /ˌdʒɒlɪfɪ'keɪʃn/ n [U] merry-making; festivity; [C] instance of this. **jol·lity** /'dʒɒlətɪ/ n [U] state of being ~.

jolly-boat /'dʒɒlɪbəʊt/ n kind of ship's boat.

jolt /dʒəʊlt/ vt,vi [VP6A,15A,B,2A,C] give a jerk or jerks to; shake up; (of a vehicle) move along by jerks: *The old bus* ~*ed us as it went over the stony road. The bus* ~*ed along.* □ n jerk; sudden bump or shake; (fig) surprise, shock. ~*y adj* ~*ing.*

Jo·nah /'dʒəʊnə/ n person whose presence seems to bring ill luck; person who is sacrificed lest he should bring ill luck.

jon·quil /'dʒɒŋkwɪl/ n kind of narcissus.

joss /dʒɒs/ n (in China) carving in stone, etc, of a god. '~*-house* n temple. '~*-stick* n stick of incense.

jostle /'dʒɒsl/ vt,vi [VP6A,2C] push roughly (against); push: *We were* ~*d by the crowd. The pickpocket* ~*d against me in the crowd.*

jot¹ /dʒɒt/ n a jot, (usu with neg) small amount: *not a jot of truth in a story,* no truth at all.

jot² /dʒɒt/ vt (-tt-) [VP15B] *jot sth down,* make a quick written note of: *The policeman jotted down my name and address.* **jot·ter** n notebook or pad for rough notes. **jot·tings** n pl notes jotted down.

joule /dʒuːl/ n (electr) (abbr **J**) unit of energy or work.

jour·nal /'dʒɜːnl/ n **1** daily newspaper; other periodical: *the Ladies' Home J~; the Economic J~.* **2** daily record of news, events, business accounts, etc. **~·ese** /ˌdʒɜːnə'liːz/ n [U] style of language full of clichés, common in some ~s, eg the use of 'prior to interment' for 'before burial'. **~·ism** /-ɪzəm/ n [U] work of writing for, editing, or publishing ~s. **~·ist** /-ɪst/ n person engaged in ~ism. **~·is·tic** /ˌdʒɜːnə'lɪstɪk/ adj of ~ism; characteristic of ~ism.

jour·ney /'dʒɜːnɪ/ n (pl ~s) (distance travelled (esp on land) in) going to a place, esp a distant place: *reach one's ~'s end; go/come/send sb on a ~; make a ~ half-way round the world.* ⇨ flight¹(2), voyage. □ vi [VP2A,C] travel; make a ~.

jour·ney·man /'dʒɜːnɪmən/ n (pl -men /-mən/) skilled workman who works for a master (contrasted with an *apprentice*).

joust /dʒaʊst/ vi, n (hist) (engage in a) fight on horseback with lances (as between knights in the Middle Ages).

Jove /dʒəʊv/ n Jupiter, esp *By ~!* (as an exclamation of surprise, etc).

jov·ial /'dʒəʊvɪəl/ adj full of fun and good humour; merry: *a ~ fellow; in a ~ mood.* **~·ly** /-ɪəlɪ/ adv **~·ity** /ˌdʒəʊvɪ'ælətɪ/ n [U] being ~; good humoured behaviour; [C] (pl; -ties) ~ acts or utterances.

jowl /dʒaʊl/ n jaw; lower part of the face: *a man with a heavy ~/a heavy-jowled man,* one with heavy jaws, a fold or folds of flesh hanging from the chin. **cheek by ~,** ⇨ cheek(1). **~·y** adj with a heavy ~.

joy /dʒɔɪ/ n **1** [U] deep pleasure; great gladness: *I wish you joy. We heard with joy that she had escaped injury. He has been a good friend to me, both in joy and in sorrow. They danced/jumped for joy,* because they were full of joy. '**joy-bells** n pl bells rung to celebrate a happy occasion. '**joy-ride** n (sl) ride in a vehicle for fun and thrills. '**joy-stick** n (sl) control lever on an aircraft. **2** [C] sth that gives joy; occasion of great happiness: *the joys and sorrows of life.* □ vi (poet) rejoice: *joy in a friend's success.* **joy·ful** /-fl/ adj filled with, showing, causing, joy. **joy·fully** /-fəlɪ/ adv **joy·less** adj without joy; gloomy; sad. **joy·less·ly** adv **joy·ful·ness, joy·less·ness** nn **joy·ous** /'dʒɔɪəs/ adj full of joy. **joy·ous·ly** adv **joy·ous·ness** n

ju·bi·lant /'dʒuːbɪlənt/ adj (formal) triumphant; showing joy. **~·ly** adv **ju·bi·la·tion** /ˌdʒuːbɪ'leɪʃn/ n [U] rejoicing; [C] occasion of this.

ju·bi·lee /'dʒuːbɪliː/ n [C] (celebration of a special anniversary of some event, eg a wedding. **diamond ~,** 60th anniversary. **golden ~,** 50th anniversary. **silver ~,** 25th anniversary.

Ju·da·ism /'dʒuːdeɪɪzəm US:-dɪɪzəm/ n the religion of the Jewish people; their culture and social way of life. **Ju·daic** /dʒuː'deɪɪk/ adj of Jews and ~.

Judas /'dʒuːdəs/ n (from ~ who betrayed Jesus Christ; ⇨ Mark 3: 19) betrayer; traitor.

jud·der /'dʒʌdə(r)/ vi shudder violently.

judge¹ /dʒʌdʒ/ n **1** (of God) supreme arbiter; public officer with authority to hear and decide cases in a law court: *~-made law,* principles based on ~s' decisions, not statute law; *as grave as a ~.* ⇨ justice(3,4), magistrate. **2** person who decides in a contest, competition, dispute, etc: *the ~s at a flower show.* **3** person qualified and able to give opinions on merits and values: *a good ~ of horses. He says the diamonds are not genuine; but then, he's no ~,* does not know much about diamonds. **4** (in Hebrew history) officer given temporary authority as ruler in the period between Joshua and the Kings. **J~s,** the book of the Old Testament recording this period.

judge² /dʒʌdʒ/ vt, vi (pres p judging) **1** [VP6A,2A] act as a judge(1); hear and try (cases) in a law court: *God will ~ all men.* **2** [VP6A,2A] give a decision (in a competition, etc): *Who is going to ~ the roses at the Flower Show? Will you ~ at the Baby Show next week?* **3** [VP6A,9,10,22,25,2A,3A] estimate; consider; form an opinion about: *I ~d him to be about 50. I can't ~ whether he was right or wrong. I ~d, from his manner, that he was guilty. The committee ~d it better to postpone the meeting. Don't ~ (of) a man by his looks. Judging from what you say, he ought to succeed.*

judge·ment (US, and in GB legal use **judg·ment**) /'dʒʌdʒmənt/ n **1** [U] judging or being judged: *sit in ~ on a case,* (in a law court); *pass ~ on a prisoner,* give a decision after trial. **the Day of J~,** (also '**J~ Day, the Last J~**) the day when God will judge all men. **2** [C] decision of a judge or court: *The ~ was in his favour.* **3** [U] process of judging: *an error of ~. His ~ was at fault.* **4** [U] good sense; ability to judge(2,3): *a man of ~. He showed excellent ~ in choosing the wine.* **5** [C] misfortune considered to be a punishment from God: *Your failure is a ~ on you for being so lazy.* **6** [C,U] opinion: *in my ~; in the ~ of most people.*

ju·di·ca·ture /'dʒuːdɪkətʃə(r)/ n **1** [U] administration of justice: *the Supreme Court of J~,* full title of the English Courts of Justice. **2** [C] body of judges.

ju·di·cial /dʒuː'dɪʃl/ adj **1** of or by a court of justice; of a judge or of judgement: *the ~ bench,* the judges; *take/bring ~ proceedings against sb,* bring a law case against him; *a ~ separation,* the right to separate from a husband or wife, granted by a judge, usu with arrangements favourable to the wronged person concerning money or children; *~ murder,* legal but unjust sentence of death. **2** critical; impartial: *a man with a ~ mind.* **~·ly** /-ʃəlɪ/ adv

ju·dici·ary /dʒuː'dɪʃərɪ US: -ʃɪerɪ/ n (pl -ries) **1** the judges of a country collectively. **2** the system of law courts in a country.

ju·di·cious /dʒuː'dɪʃəs/ adj (formal) showing or having good sense. **~·ly** adv **~·ness** n

judo /'dʒuːdəʊ/ n [U] Japanese art of wrestling and self-defence in which an opponent's own weight and strength are used against him.

jug¹ /dʒʌg/ n **1** deep vessel with a handle and lip; the contents of such a vessel: *a 'milk-jug; drink a jug of milk.* **2** (sl) prison. **jug·ful** /-fʊl/ n (pl jugfuls) amount a jug will hold.

judges

jug² /dʒʌg/ vt (-gg-) [VP6A] **1** (usu in pp) stew or boil (hare, etc) in a jug or jar: *jugged hare.* **2** (colloq) imprison.

jug·ger·naut /'dʒʌgənɔːt/ n **1** cause or belief to which persons are sacrificed or to which they sacrifice themselves: *the ~ of war.* **2** (colloq) huge long-distance transport vehicle.

juggle /'dʒʌgl/ vi,vt **1** [VP2A,3A] ~ **(with),** do tricks, perform (with balls, plates, etc) to amuse people; play tricks (with facts, figures, etc) to deceive people. **2** [VP6A,16A] play tricks with; deceive: *The manager ~d his figures to make it seem that the company was prosperous.* **jug·gler** n person who ~s.

jugu·lar /'dʒʌgjʊlə(r)/ adj of the neck or throat: ~ *veins,* the large veins of the neck, returning blood from the head to the heart.

juice /dʒuːs/ n [C,U] **1** fluid part of fruits, vegetables and meat: *a glass of 'orange ~; a mixture of 'fruit ~s.* **2** fluid in organs of the body: *gastric/ digestive ~s,* those that help to digest food. **3** [U] (colloq) electricity, petrol or other source of power.

juicy /'dʒuːsɪ/ adj (-ier, -iest) **1** containing much juice: ~ *oranges.* **2** (colloq) interesting (esp because scandalous, etc). **juici·ness** n

ju-jitsu /ˌdʒuː'dʒɪtsuː/ n Japanese art of self-defence from which judo was developed.

juju /'dʒuːdʒuː/ n West African charm or fetish; its magic power.

ju·jube /'dʒuːdʒuːb/ n [C] lozenge of gelatin, flavoured and sweetened.

juke-box /'dʒuːk bɒks/ n [C] coin-operated record-player.

ju·lep /'dʒuːlɪp/ n (US) spirit (eg whisky), mint and ice: *mint ~.*

Jul·ian /'dʒuːlɪən/ adj of Julius Caesar. ~ **calend·ar,** the calendar introduced by him in Rome in 46 BC. ⇨ Gregorian.

July /dʒuː'laɪ/ n seventh month of the year.

jumble /'dʒʌmbl/ vi,vt [VP15B,2C] ~ **(up),** mix, be mixed, in a confused way: *The untidy girl's toys, books, shoes and clothes were all ~d up together in the cupboard.* □ n confused mixture; muddle. '~-sale n sale of a mixed collection of old or second-hand articles.

jumbo /'dʒʌmbəʊ/ adj unusually large: ~ *jets; ~-sized.*

jump¹ /dʒʌmp/ n **1** act of jumping; sudden spring from the ground. **the 'long/'high ~,** athletic competitions in which competitors jump a distance/ height. **2** sudden movement caused by fear. **give sb a ~,** frighten him. **the ~s,** (colloq) form of nervous excitement with uncontrollable bodily movements. **3** sudden rise in amount, price, value, etc: *a ~ in car exports.* **jumpy** adj (-ier, -iest) excited and nervous. **~i·ness** n

jump² /dʒʌmp/ vi,vt **1** [VP2A,C] move quickly by the sudden use of the muscles of the legs or (of fish) the tail; rise suddenly (from a seat, etc); move quickly (*into* sth): ~ *to one's feet;* ~ *over a fence;* ~ *up out of one's chair;* ~ *into a taxi,* enter one quickly; (fig) ~ *from one subject to another in a speech.* ~ **down sb's throat,** answer, interrupt, him violently. **'~ing-'off place,** starting point. '~ed-up adj (colloq) upstart. **2** [VP6A] pass over by moving in this way: ~ *a ditch;* cause (a horse, etc) to move in this way: ~ *a horse over a fence.* ~ **the rails/track,** (of a train, tram, etc) leave the rails suddenly. **3** [VP2A,C] move with a jerk or jerks from excitement, joy, etc; start suddenly: ~

for joy; ~ *up and down in excitement. Her heart ~ed when she heard the news.* **4** [VP2A,C] rise suddenly in price: *Gold shares ~ed on the Stock Exchange yesterday.* **5** ~ **at,** accept eagerly: ~ *at an offer.* ~ **to conclusions,** reach them hastily. ,~ 'to it, act quickly or promptly. ~ **on/upon,** attack, reprove severely; scold. **6** ~ **(one's) bail,** fail to appear for trial, ⇨ bail¹. ~ **a claim,** (colloq) take possession of land or mining rights, eg in a new goldfield, to which another person has already established a claim. ~ **the gun,** start too soon (as from the use of a shot to start a race). **(go and)** ~ **in the lake,** (colloq, imper) go away (said dismissively or angrily). ~ **the queue,** (lit or fig) obtain sth without waiting for one's proper turn. ~ **a train,** travel illegally by goods train, eg by riding in or under a closed wagon.

jumper /'dʒʌmpə(r)/ n **1** outer knitted garment, with or without sleeves, pulled on over the head and coming down to the hips, ⇨ jersey, pullover, sweater; (US) pinafore. **2** person, animal or insect, that jumps.

junc·tion /'dʒʌŋkʃn/ n **1** [U] joining or being joined; [C] instance of this: *The allied armies hope to effect a ~,* meet and unite. **2** [C] place where roads, railway lines or sections of an electrical circuit meet or diverge.

junc·ture /'dʒʌŋktʃə(r)/ n [C] (formal) **1** junction(1). **2** state of affairs, esp in the phrase: **at this ~,** at this time, when affairs are/were in this state.

June /dʒuːn/ n sixth month of the year.

jungle /'dʒʌŋgl/ n **1** (usu the ~, sing or pl) (land covered with) thickly growing underwood and tangled vegetation: *cut a path through the ~;* ~ *warfare;* ~ *birds and animals;* '~ *fever,* malarial fever. **the law of the ~,** (fig) ruthless competition or exploitation. **2** (in compounds) '~-cat, '~-fowl.

jun·gly /'dʒʌŋglɪ/ adj of, like, from the ~ or its inhabitants.

jun·ior /'dʒuːnɪə(r)/ n, adj **1** (person) younger, lower in rank, than another: *a ~ high school;* ~ *dress sizes. He is my ~ by two years. He is the ~ partner in the firm. Tom Brown, Junior* (or abbr **Jun, Jnr, Jr**), used of a son having the same first name as his father, or the younger of two boys of the same surname in a school, etc. **2** (US schools and colleges) student in his third year (of four).

ju·ni·per /'dʒuːnɪpə(r)/ n evergreen shrub with dark berries from which an oil (*oil of ~*), is obtained used in medicine, etc.

junk¹ /dʒʌŋk/ n [U] old, discarded things of little or no value: *an attic full of ~; a ~ dealer.* '~-shop, one selling cheap second-hand goods.

junk² /dʒʌŋk/ n [C] flat-bottomed Chinese sailing-vessel.

a junk

junket /'dʒʌŋkɪt/ n **1** [C,U] (dish of) milk curdled by the addition of acid, often sweetened and flavoured. **2** social gathering for a feast; picnic. □ vi take part in a ~(2). Hence, **~·ing** n [U] feasting;

merrymaking.

junkie, junky /'dʒʌŋkɪ/ n (sl) drug (esp heroin) addict.

Juno-esque /ˌdʒuːnəʊ'esk/ adj (of a woman) having a stately beauty (like the goddess Juno).

junta /'dʒʌntə US: 'hʊntə/ n (in Spain and Italy) deliberative or administrative council; group of army officers who have seized power by a coup d'état.

Jupi-ter /'dʒuːpɪtə(r)/ n (ancient Rome) ruler of gods and men; largest planet of the solar system. ⇨ the illus at planet.

ju-ri-di-cal /dʒʊə'rɪdɪkl/ adj of law or legal proceedings.

ju-ris-dic-tion /ˌdʒʊərɪs'dɪkʃn/ n [U] administration of justice; legal authority; right to exercise this; extent of this: *The courts have ~ not only over our own citizens but over foreigners living here. This matter does not come/fall within our ~,* We have no authority to deal with it.

ju-ris-pru-dence /ˌdʒʊərɪs'pruːdns/ n [U] science and philosophy of human law.

jur-ist /'dʒʊərɪst/ n expert in law.

juror /'dʒʊərə(r)/ n member of a jury.

jury /'dʒʊərɪ/ n (pl -ries) [C] **1** body of persons (in US and GB twelve) who swear to give a decision (*verdict*) on issues of fact in a case in a court of justice: *trial by ~. The ~ found the prisoner not guilty.* '~-box n enclosure for a ~ in court. **2** grand ~, specially chosen body of 12 to 23 persons who (GB until 1933) inquire into a charge in order to decide whether there is enough evidence to justify a trial or whether the case should be abandoned. coroner's ~, one that decides the cause of a death (if unnatural death, eg suicide or murder, is suspected). **3** body of persons chosen to give a decision or make an award in a competition; (fig) *the ~ of public opinion,* the public, thought of as a ~, deciding a question. '~-man /-mən/ (pl -men) n member of a jury; juror.

jury-mast /'dʒʊərɪ mɑːst US: mæst/ n temporary mast put up in place of one that is broken or lost overboard.

just¹ /dʒʌst/ adj **1** in accordance with what is right: *a ~ man; a ~ sentence; be ~ to a person.* **2** well deserved; fairly earned: *get/receive one's ~ deserts,* be rewarded or punished as one deserves. **3** reasonable; based on reasonable grounds: *a ~ opinion; ~ suspicions.* ~-ly adv: *to feel ~ly ashamed.* ~-ness n

just² /dʒʌst/ adv **1** used (GB) in the perfect tenses and (US often) with the simple past tense, placed with the v, to indicate an immediate past: (GB) *I've ~ had dinner.* (US) *I ~ had dinner. Cf I had dinner an hour ago. My son had ~ left school.* **2** (followed by nn, n phrases and clauses) exactly; precisely: *It's ~ two o'clock. This is ~ what I wanted. That's ~ what I was going to say. J~ my luck! J~ the thing!* **3** ~ as (+ adj + as), (a) exactly as: *Leave everything ~ as (tidy as) you find it. Come ~ as you are,* Do not make any special preparations. *This is ~ (= quite) as good as the other.* (b) (introducing adverbials of time) when: *He arrived ~ as I was about to go out/~ as I was shaving.* (c) (introducing clauses of comparison) in the same way as: *J~ as you find it difficult to like Mr Green, so I find it easy to like his wife.* **4** (with advv) exactly: *~ here/there.* **5** (used to indicate approximation) more or less: *I've had ~ about enough of your impudence,* almost more than I can endure.

Put it ~ over there, near that place. *It's ~ about tall enough,* will be satisfactory. **6** at this/that very moment: *We're ~ off/~ about to start. His new book is ~ out/~ published. ~ now,* (a) at this moment: *I'm busy ~ now.* (b) a short time ago: *Tom came in ~ now—he's probably upstairs.* **7** (only) ~, almost not; with a very little time/space/margin etc to spare: *We (only) ~ caught the train,* almost missed it. *Jane ~ managed to pass the exam. Cf She almost failed. I've ~ enough money to last me till pay-day.* **8** (used in familiar, colloquial style, esp with imperatives, to call attention to sth, sometimes to soften what follows): *J~ listen to him!* and note how clever/silly/amusing, etc he is! *J~ taste this!* (so that you may judge its quality, say whether it is right, etc). *J~ feel it!* and note how hard, soft, smooth, etc it is! *J~* (= please) *come here a moment. J~ a moment, please,* Please wait a moment. **9** only; merely: *He's ~ an ordinary man. I've come here ~* (= on purpose) *to see you. Would you walk five miles ~ to see a film?* **10** (colloq) very; very much: *The concert was ~ splendid. 'Did you enjoy yourselves?'—'I should ~ say we did!' or Didn't we ~!'* (emph) We had a most enjoyable time.

jus-tice /'dʒʌstɪs/ n **1** [U] just conduct; the quality of being right and fair: *treat all men with ~. in ~ to,* in order to be just to. *do ~ to,* treat fairly; show that one has a just opinion of, that one realizes the value of: *To do him ~, we must admit that his intentions were good. He did ~ to the dinner,* showed by eating heartily that the food was good. *do oneself ~,* behave in a way that is worthy of one's abilities: *You're not doing yourself ~,* You could do much better if you tried. **2** [U] the law and its administration: *a court of ~. bring sb to ~,* arrest, try and sentence (a criminal). **3** [C] judge of the Supreme Courts: *the Lord Chief J~; the Lords J~s; the Chief J~ of England; Mr J~ Smith.* **4** ,J~ of the 'Peace, (abbr JP) magistrate. **Department of J~,** (US) executive department, headed by the Attorney General, supervising internal security, naturalization, immigration, etc.

jus-tici-ary /dʒʌ'stɪʃərɪ US: -ʃɪerɪ/ n (pl -ries) (jurisdiction of a) judge or chief justice: (in Scotland) *the High Court of J~.*

jus-tify /'dʒʌstɪfaɪ/ vt (pt,pp -fied) [VP6A,19C] **1** show that (a person, statement, act, etc) is right, reasonable or proper: *The Prime Minister justified the action of the Government. You can hardly ~ such conduct. You'd be hard put to it to ~ your behaviour.* **2** be a good reason for: *Your wish to go for a walk does not ~ your leaving the baby alone in the house.* **3** adjust (a line of type) to fill a space neatly. **jus-ti-fi-able** /ˌdʒʌstɪ'faɪəbl/ adj that can be justified: *justifiable homicide.* **jus-ti-fi-ably** /-əblɪ/ adv **jus-ti-fi-ca-tion** /ˌdʒʌstɪfɪ'keɪʃn/ n [U] **1** sth that justifies: *His justification for stealing was that his children were starving.* **in justification (for/of sth/sb),** ~ing it/him: *It can be said in justification for what he had done that....* **2** the act of ~ing sth. **3** the state of being free from blame.

jut /dʒʌt/ vi (-tt-) [VP2C] **jut out,** stand out from; be out of line (from what is around): *The soldier saw a gun jutting out from a bush. The balcony juts out over the garden.*

jute /dʒuːt/ n [U] fibre from the outer skin of certain plants, used for making canvas, rope, etc: *the ~ mills of Bangladesh.*

ju-ven-ile /'dʒuːvənaɪl/ n young person. □ adj of,

characteristic of, suitable for, ~s: ~ *books; a* ~ *appearance; a* ~ *court,* where children are tried; ~ *delinquency,* law-breaking by young people; ~ *delinquent,* young offender; *a* ~ *sense of humour,* eg in an adult.

jux·ta·pose /ˌdʒʌkstəˈpəʊz/ *vt* [VP6A] place side by side. **jux·ta·po·si·tion** /ˌdʒʌkstəpəˈzɪʃn/ *n* [U] placing side by side; state of being placed side by side.

Kk

K, k /keɪ/ (*pl* K's, k's /keɪz/) the 11th letter of the English alphabet.

kaf·fir /ˈkæfə(r)/ *n* ⚠ (offensive word for) black African person.

Kaiser /ˈkaɪzə(r)/ *n* Emperor (esp of Germany before 1918).

kake·mono /ˌkækɪˈməʊnəʊ/ *n* Japanese painting in a hanging scroll of silk or paper.

kale, kail /keɪl/ *n* kind of curly-leaved cabbage.

ka·leido·scope /kəˈlaɪdəskəʊp/ *n* [C] **1** tube containing mirrors and small, loose pieces of coloured glass. When the tube is turned, constantly changing patterns are seen through the eye-piece. **2** (fig) frequently changing pattern of bright scenes: *Sunlight and shadow made the landscape a* ~ *of colour.* **ka·leido·scopic** /kəˌlaɪdəˈskɒpɪk/ *adj* quickly changing.

kal·ends /ˈkælendz/ *n pl* ⇨ calends.

kam·pong /ˈkæmpɒŋ/ *n* (in Malaysia) enclosed space; village.

kan·ga·roo /ˌkæŋɡəˈruː/ *n* Australian marsupial that jumps along on its strong hind legs. The female has a pouch in which its young are carried. ⇨ the illus at large. ~ **court,** one set up without authority by workers, prisoners, etc to try someone whom they consider to have acted against their interests.

kao·lin /ˈkeɪəlɪn/ *n* [U] fine white clay used in making porcelain, etc.

ka·pok /ˈkeɪpɒk/ *n* [U] soft cotton-like material (from seeds of a tropical tree) used for filling cushions, life-belts, mattresses, etc.

ka·put /kəˈpʊt/ *adj* (pred only) (G) (sl) done for; ruined; smashed.

karat /ˈkærət/ *n* (US) = carat(2).

ka·rate /kəˈrɑːtɪ/ *n* [U] Japanese method of unarmed combat using blows made with the hand, foot, head or elbow.

karma /ˈkɑːmə/ *n* (in Buddhism) person's acts in one of his successive existences, looked upon as deciding his fate in his next existence.

kava /ˈkɑːvə/ *n* [U] (intoxicating drink made from the roots of a) Polynesian shrub.

kayak /ˈkaɪæk/ *n* Eskimo canoe of light wood covered with sealskins; any small, covered canoe. ⇨ the illus at canoe.

ke·bab /kəˈbæb/ *n* dish of small pieces of meat, seasoned and roasted on skewers.

ked·ger·ee /ˈkedʒəriː/ *n* [U] rice cooked with fish, eggs, etc.

keel /kiːl/ *n* timber or steel structure on which the framework of a ship is built up: *lay down a* ~, start the building of a ship. *(keep) on an even* ~, **(a)** (of a ship) without movement to one side or the other. **(b)** (fig) steady; steadily; calm(ly). □ *vt, vi* **1** [VP6A] turn a (ship) over on one side to repair it, clean the ~, etc. **2** [VP15B,2C] ~ *over,* capsize; upset.

keen¹ /kiːn/ *adj* (-er, -est) **1** (of points and edges) sharp: *a knife with a* ~ *edge;* (fig) *a* ~ (= cutting) *wind;* ~ *sarcasm.* **2** (of interest, the feelings) strong; deep: *He has a* ~ *interest in his work.* **3** (of the mind, the senses) active; sensitive; sharp: ~

sight; ~-*'sighted; a* ~ *intelligence.* **4** (of persons, their character, etc) eager; anxious to do things: *a* ~ *sportsman. He's very* ~ *to see his birthplace again.* ~ *on,* (colloq) interested in, fond of, eager to/for: ~ *on going abroad. Mrs Hill is* ~ *on Tom('s) marrying Stella/*~ *that Tom should marry Stella. Tom is not very* ~ *on Stella,* does not like her much. *I'm not very* ~ *on jazz.* ~·**ly** *adv* ~·**ness** *n*

keen² /kiːn/ *n* Irish funeral song accompanied by wailing. □ *vi, vt* utter this song; lament (a person) in this way.

keep¹ /kiːp/ *vt, vi* (*pt, pp* kept /kept/) (For idiomatic uses with *adverbial particles* and *preps,* ⇨ **18** below. For *keep* and *nn* not given here, ⇨ the *n* entries, eg ~ *pace/step,* ~ *time,* ~ *watch,* ~ *good/ early hours.*) **1** [VP22,15A] cause sb/sth to remain in a specified state or position: ~ *the children quiet/happy. The cold weather kept us indoors. If your hands are cold,* ~ *them in your pockets. Will they* ~ *me in prison/custody? Extra work kept* (= detained) *me at the office. Will you* ~ *these things safe for me?* ~ *an eye on,* (colloq) watch over closely: *Please* ~ *an eye on the baby while I'm in the garden.* ~ *sth in mind,* remember it: *Do* ~ *it in mind that we expect a report next week.* ~ *track of/tabs on/a tab on,* ⇨ track(1), tab(2). **2** [VP19B] cause a process or state to continue: *Please* ~ *the fire burning. I'm sorry I've kept you waiting.* ~ *sb going,* help him to continue in some way: *Will £10* ~ *you going until pay-day,* cover your expenses? *The doctors manage to* ~ *me going,* help me to remain active. ~ *the ball rolling,* ⇨ ball¹. ~ *the pot boiling,* ⇨ pot¹(2). **3** [VP14] ~ *sb/sth from doing sth,* prevent, hold back, refrain: *What kept you from joining me?* Often shortened to *'What kept you?'. We must* ~ *them from getting to know our plans. We must do something to* ~ *the roof from falling in.* [VP3A] ~ *from doing sth,* refrain: *I couldn't* ~ *from laughing.* **4** [VP15B,14] ~ *sth (back) (from),* **(a)** not let others know about it: *She can* ~ *nothing (back) from her friends.* **(b)** hold back; withhold: *They* ~ *back £20 a month from my salary for National Insurance.* ~ *sth to oneself,* **(a)** (often imper) not express, eg comments, views, etc: *K*~/*You may* ~ *your remarks to yourself,* I don't want to hear them. **(b)** refuse to share: *He kept the good news to himself.* ~ *one's own counsel,* ⇨ counsel¹. ~ *a secret,* ⇨ secret. **5** [VP6A] (with an implied complement, eg *inviolate*) pay proper respect to; be faithful to; observe; fulfil: ~ *a promise/a treaty/an appointment/the law.* ~ *faith with sb,* ⇨ faith. **6** [VP6A] celebrate: ~ *the Sabbath,* ie ~ it sacred; ~ *Christmas/one's birthday.* **7** [VP6A] guard; protect: ~ *goal,* ⇨ goalkeeper; ~ *wicket,* (cricket) stand behind the wicket to stop or catch the ball, ⇨ wicket-keeper. *May God/the Lord bless and* ~ *you,* ie keep you safe. **8** [VP6A] continue to have; have in one's possession and not give away; not lose; preserve, eg for future use or reference: *You may* ~ *this—I don't want it back. K*~ *the change,*

ie from money offered in payment. *Please ~ these things for me while I'm away. We'll ~ these for another day.* ~ **hold of;** ~ **a firm/tight hold on,** not let go: *K~ a tight hold on the horse's reins.* **9** [VP6A,15A,22] support; take care of; provide what is needed for; maintain: *Does he earn enough to ~ himself and his family? He has a wife and ten children to ~, poor fellow! She lives with her parents but earns enough to ~ herself in clothes,* to buy her own clothes. *He ~s sheep in the Highlands. He ~s a mistress in Chelsea* (hence, now dated, **kept woman**, one whose needs are provided by a man whose mistress she is). **10** [VP6A] have habitually on sale or in stock: *'Do you sell batteries for transistor sets?'—'Sorry, but we don't ~ them'.* **11** ~ **house,** be responsible for the housework, cooking, shopping, etc: *His sister ~s house for him.* ⇨ **housekeeper** at house¹. ~ **open house,** be ready to entertain friends, etc at any time. **12** [VP6A] own or manage, esp for profit: *~ hens/bees/pigs; ~ a shop/an inn.* Hence, **'shop~er, 'inn~er.** **13** [VP6A] make entries in, records of: *~ a diary.* ~ **accounts,** records of money paid out and received. ~ **books,** = ~ accounts. Hence, **'book-~er.** **14** [VP2C,D] continue to be, remain, in a specified condition: *If you've got the 'flu, you'd better go to bed and ~ warm. Please ~ quiet! I hope you're ~ing well. K~ cool!* (fig) Don't get excited! ~ **fit,** (do physical exercise to) remain in good health: (attrib) *~-fit classes.* **15** [VP6A,2C,3A] ~ **on/to,** continue in a particular direction; remain in a particular relationship to a place, etc: *We kept (on) our way/course all morning. While that big lorry ~s (to) the middle of the road, we can't possibly overtake it. K~ straight on until you get to the church. Traffic in Britain ~s (to the) left. K~ left,* as a traffic sign. *He was ill and had to ~ to his bed/the house for weeks. She couldn't ~ her seat,* ie on her horse. **16** [VP2E,3A] ~ **(on) doing sth,** continue doing sth; do sth frequently or repeatedly: *K~ smiling! Why does she ~ (on) giggling? My shoe lace ~s (on) coming undone.* ~ **going,** not stop; not give up; continue to function: *This is exhausting work, but I manage to ~ going. I'm not sure that the company can ~ going,* continue in business. **17** [VP2A] (of food) remain in good condition: *Will this meat ~ till tomorrow? Cf ~ fresh,* ⇨ **14** above. *This news will ~,* (fig) need not be told now, can be told later. **18** [VP2C,3A,14,15B] (uses with *adverbial particles* and *preps*):
keep 'at sth, work at it: *K~ at it,* don't give up! ~ **sb 'at sth,** make him work: *K~ them at it!* Don't let them get lazy!
keep away (from sth), avoid coming/going near (to): *K~ away from the water's edge.* ~ **sb/sth away (from),** prevent from going/coming near: *K~ the child away from the water's edge.*
keep back (from sth), remain in the rear, at the back. ~ **sb back,** restrain sb; prevent sb from advancing. ~ **sth back,** ⇨ 4 above.
keep sb down, hold in subjection; oppress: ~ *down subject nations.* ~ **sth down,** (a) control: *He couldn't ~ down his anger. This chemical will ~ the weeds down.* (b) limit: *We must ~ down expenses.* (c) retain: *He couldn't ~ his food down,* had to vomit.
keep in, eg of a coal fire in a grate, continue burning: *Will the fire ~ in until we get back?* (Cf **go out.**) ~ **in with sb,** remain on good terms with,

continue to be friendly with: *You must ~ in with your customers,* retain their goodwill. ~ **sb in,** (esp) detain (a child in school) as a punishment. ~ **sth in,** (a) see that (a fire) continues to burn; ⇨ ~ in, above: *Shall we ~ the fire in or let it out?* (b) restrain. *He couldn't ~ in his indignation.* (Cf **burst out.**)
keep off, remain at a distance; not come: *if the rain ~s off,* if it doesn't start to rain. ~ **off sth,** refrain from: *Please ~ off that subject,* say nothing about it. *Do please ~ off drugs,* Don't use them. ~ **sb/sth off,** hold, cause to remain, at a distance: *They made a big fire to ~ wild animals off. K~ your hands off,* Don't touch it, me, etc.
keep on (doing sth), continue; persist: ~ *on (working) although one is tired. Don't ~ on asking silly questions. Why do the dogs ~ on barking?* ⇨ also **16** above. ~ **sth on,** continue to wear: ~ *one's hat on.* ~ **your hair on,** ⇨ hair. ~ **one's shirt on,** ⇨ shirt(1). ~ **sb on,** continue to employ: ~ *an old employee on,* not dismiss her/him. ~ **on at sb,** worry with repeated complaints, questions, etc.
keep out (of sth), remain outside: *Danger! K~ out! K~ out of their quarrels,* Don't get involved in them. ~ **sb/sth out (of sth),** prevent from entering: *Shut the window and ~ the cold out. K~ that dog out of my study.*
keep to sth, (a) do what one has agreed to do: *He always ~s to his promises/an agreement/his word.* (b) limit oneself to: *keep to the subject/the point at issue.* ~ **(oneself) to oneself,** avoid meeting people.
keep sb/sth under, control; repress: *The firemen managed to ~ the fire under,* prevented it from spreading. *That boy needs ~ing under,* needs discipline. ~ **sb under observation,** ⇨ observation(2).
keep up (with sb/sth), progress at the same rate (as sb/sth): *I can't ~ up with you,* eg walk as fast as you. *Dave couldn't ~ up with the rest of the class,* eg learn as quickly as his fellow pupils. *Is your salary ~ing up with inflation,* growing as fast? **keep up with sb/sth,** stay in contact with: *try to ~ up with old friends far away;* stay informed about: *Alexander is careful to ~ up with the latest fashions in clothes.* **keep up with the Joneses,** compete with one's neighbours, etc (in the purchase of articles, eg clothes, a car, indicating social status). ~ **sb up,** delay sb from going to bed: *It's wrong to ~ the children up so late,* They should go to bed. *I don't want to ~ you up; you look sleepy and ready for bed.* ~ **sth up,** (a) prevent from sinking or getting low: *K~ up your courage/spirits. K~ your chin up!* Cheer up, have courage, etc. (b) observe: ~ *up old customs.* (c) continue: *They kept up the attack all day.* (d) maintain in proper condition: *How much does it cost you to ~ up your large house and garden?* ~ **up appearances,** ⇨ appearance. (e) continue; carry on: ~ *up a correspondence with an old friend.* ~ **one's end up,** ⇨ end¹. *Do you still ~ up your Greek,* still read the Greek classics? ~ **it up,** continue without slackening: *He works far too hard; he'll never be able to ~ it up.* ⇨ upkeep.
keep² /ki:p/ *n* **1** [U] (food needed for) support: *The dog doesn't earn his ~,* is not useful enough to be worth the cost of keeping him. **2** [C] tower of a fortress, etc (in olden times): *the castle ~.* **3 for ~s,** (colloq) permanently: *Is this mine for ~s?*

keeper /'kiːpə(r)/ n 1 guard, eg a person who looks after animals in a zoo. 2 (in compounds) person with special duties: 'park~; 'lighthouse~; game~, ⇨ game¹(6); 'goal~, ⇨ goal; person who manages a shop, inn, etc: 'shop~; 'inn~. ⇨ keep¹(11,12,13).

keeping /'kiːpɪŋ/ n [U] 1 care. in safe ~, being kept carefully: The valuables are in safe ~. 2 (in verbal senses): the ~ of bees; 'bee-~. in/out of ~ (with), in/out of harmony (with): His actions are not in ~ with his promises.

keep·sake /'kiːpseɪk/ n sth kept in memory of the giver: Please have this ring for a ~.

keg /keg/ n small barrel, usu of less than 10 gallons: a ~ of brandy.

kelp /kelp/ n [U] large kinds of seaweed.

Kelt /kelt/ n = Celt.

ken¹ /ken/ n [U] (only in) beyond/outside my ~, (colloq) not wihin one's range of knowledge.

ken² /ken/ vt (-nn-) [VP6A,9] (Scot) know.

ken·nel /'kenl/ n 1 hut to shelter a dog. 2 (establishment for a) pack of hounds; place where dogs are cared for (eg during quarantine). □ vt,vi (-ll-, US also -l-) put, keep, in a ~; live in a ~.

kepi /'keɪpɪ/ n French military cap with a horizontal peak.

kept /kept/ ⇨ keep².

kerb (also **curb**) /kɜːb/ n stone edging to a raised path or pavement. '~·stone n stone forming a part of this.

ker·chief /'kɜːtʃɪf/ n [C] (old use) square piece of cloth or lace used by women as a head covering.

ker·nel /'kɜːnl/ n [C] 1 softer, inner (usu edible) part of a nut or fruit-stone. ⇨ the illus at palm. 2 part of a seed, eg a grain of wheat, within the husk; (fig) central or important part of a subject, problem, etc.

kero·sene /'kerəsiːn/ n [U] paraffin oil: (attrib) a ~ lamp.

kes·trel /'kestrəl/ n kind of small hawk.

ketch /ketʃ/ n small two-masted sailing vessel used in coastal trading.

ketch·up /'ketʃəp/ n [U] highly-flavoured sauce made from tomato juice, vinegar etc.

kettle /'ketl/ n metal vessel with lid, spout and handle, for boiling water. a 'pretty ~ of fish, ⇨ fish¹(1).

kettle·drum /'ketldrʌm/ n drum shaped like a hemisphere, made of brass or copper, with parchment stretched over the edge. ⇨ the illus at percussion. ⇨ timpani.

key¹ /kiː/ n 1 metal instrument for moving the bolt of a lock: put the key in the lock; turn the key. ⇨ the illus at bunch. 'master/'skeleton key, one that will open several locks. 'key·hole n hole in a lock, door, etc, into which a key fits. 'key money n [U] extra payment (requested by some house agents, now illegal in GB) before completion of an agreement about renting a house, flat, etc. 'key·ring n (usu split) ring on which to keep keys. 2 instrument for winding a clock or a watch by tightening the spring. 3 ~ (to), (fig) sth that provides an answer (to a problem or mystery). 4 set of answers to exercises or problems; translation of sth from a foreign language: a key for the use of teachers only, eg to a book of problems in algebra. 5 (also attrib) place which, from its position, gives control of a route or area: a key position. Gibraltar has been called the key to the Mediterranean. 6 (attrib) essential: key industry, one (eg coal-mining) that is essential to the carrying on of others; a key man/a man in a key position, one whose work is essential to the work of others. 'key·stone n (archit) stone at the top of an arch locking the others into position; (fig) central principle on which everything depends. ⇨ the illus at window. 7 operating part (lever or button) of a typewriter, piano, organ, flute, etc pressed down by a finger. ⇨ the illus here

keyboard instruments

HARPSICHORD   GRAND PIANO

music rest
strings
keyboard
stool
pedal
stop
key

UPRIGHT PIANO   SPINET   ELECTRIC ORGAN

and at brass. **'key-board** *n* row of such keys (on a piano, organ, typewriter). **8** (bot) usu one-seeded winged fruit of some trees, eg the ash and elm. **9** (music) scale of notes definitely related to each other and based on a particular note called the **'key-note**: *the key of C major;* (fig) tone or style of thought or expression: *in a minor key,* sadly; *all in the same key,* monotonously, without expression; *speak in a high/low key,* urgently/not urgently. **'key-note** *n* (**a**) (music) note on which a key is based. (**b**) (fig) prevailing tone or idea: *The key-note of the Minister's speech was the need for higher productivity.* **key-less** *adj* not having or needing a key.

key² /kiː/ *vt* [VP6A] tune (the strings of a musical instrument by tightening or loosening). **key sth 'in,** bring it into harmony. **key sth to sth,** bring sth into harmony with sth; make connections between (the two things). **key sb up,** stimulate or raise the standard of (a person, his activity, etc): *The thought of the coming adventure keyed him up to a state of great excitement. The crowd was keyed up for the football match.*

key³ /kiː/ *n* low island or reef, esp off the coasts of Florida, W Indies.

khaki /'kɑːkɪ/ *n, adj* (cloth, military uniform, of a) dull yellowish-brown.

khan¹ /kɑːn/ *n* title used by some rulers and officials in Central Asia, Afghanistan, etc; (in olden times) title used by supreme rulers of Turkish, Tartar and Mongol tribes.

khan² /kɑːn/ *n* (in the East) inn built round a court-yard where caravans may rest.

kib-butz /kɪ'bʊts/ *n* (*pl* ~im /ˌkɪbʊ'tsiːm/) communal farm or settlement in Israel. **~nik** /-nɪk/ *n* member of a ~.

kick¹ /kɪk/ *n* **1** act of kicking: *give a* ~ *at the door; give sb a* ~ *in the arse. The bruise was caused by a* ~. **more** ~**s than halfpence,** more harsh treatment than reward (for what one does). **'~-back** *n* (US sl) percentage payment made to sb who has enabled one to make money. ⇨ *rake-off* at **rake¹**. **,~-'start(er)** *n* lever on a motor cycle or lawn-mower which is ~ed to start the engine. **2** (colloq) thrill; excitement: *He gets a good deal of* ~/*a big* ~ *out of motor-racing. He gets his* ~*s by playing football.* **do sth/live for** ~**s,** for thrills; for excitement: *I don't expect to win when I bet—I do it for* ~*s.* **be on a** ~, (sl) be deeply absorbed in a new activity: *She's on a health-food* ~ *at the moment.* **3** [U] (colloq) resilience; strength: *He has no* ~ *left in him,* is exhausted. *This beer has a lot of* ~ *in it,* is strong.

kick² /kɪk/ *vt, vi* **1** [VP6A,15A,B,2A,C] hit with the foot; move the foot; move sth by doing this; move the foot or feet jerkily: ~ *a ball;* ~ *a man on the shin;* ~ *a hole in sth,* make one by ~ing. *The baby was* ~*ing and screaming. This horse* ~*s,* has the habit of ~ing. ~ **the bucket,** (sl) die. ~ **a goal,** (Rugby football) score a penalty; convert a try. Cf *score a goal* in Association football. ~ **one's heels,** be idle (as when forced to waste time when waiting for sth/sb). ~ **sb upstairs,** (fig) get sb out of the way, eg from the House of Commons, by giving him a higher position, eg a peerage, so that he sits in the House of Lords. **2** [VP2A] (of a gun) recoil when fired: *The old rifle* ~*s badly.* **3** [VP2A,C,3A,15B] (special uses with *adverbial particles* and *preps*): ~ **against/at,** show annoyance; protest: *He* ~*ed at/against the treatment he*

was receiving. ~ **off,** (football) start the game; resume after half-time, by making the first ~. Hence, **'~-off** *n*: ~*-off at 2.30.* ~ **sth off,** remove by ~ing: *He* ~*ed off his slippers.* ~ **sb out,** expel him: *The drunken man was* ~*ed out of the bar.* ~ **over the traces,** ⇨ **trace³.** ~ **sth up,** raise by ~ing: ~ *up the carpet,* turn up the edge by striking it with the foot. ~ **up a fuss/ shindy/row/stink,** (colloq) cause a disturbance, eg by protesting vigorously. ~ **up one's heels,** (of a horse) make lively jumps, showing enjoyment of freedom after a period of work; (fig) enjoy oneself.

kid¹ /kɪd/ *n* **1** [C] young goat. **2** [U] leather made from skin of this: *a book bound in kid.* **kid gloves** *n pl* gloves made of kid. **handle sb with kid gloves,** deal with him gently, avoiding severe methods. Hence, (attrib): *kid-glove methods.* **3** (sl) child; (US sl) young person: *college kids.* **kiddy** *n* (*pl* -dies) (sl) (young) child.

kid² /kɪd/ *vt, vi* (-dd-) (sl) tease by telling a lie; hoax: *You're kidding (me)! Cf You're pulling my leg!*

kid-nap /'kɪdnæp/ *vt* (GB -pp-, US -p-) steal (a child); carry away (sb) by force and unlawfully (esp in order to obtain a ransom). **~-per** *n* person who ~s.

kid-ney /'kɪdnɪ/ *n* (*pl* ~s) one of a pair of organs in the abdomen that separate waste liquid (urine) from the blood; ~ of sheep, cattle, etc as food. **,~-'bean** *n* (plant with pod containing) reddish-brown ~-shaped bean (either the dwarf French bean or the runner bean). **'~ machine** *n* one which does the work of diseased ~s by washing the blood and removing waste materials.

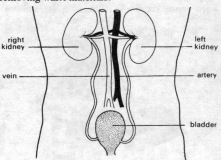

the kidneys and the bladder

kill /kɪl/ *vt, vi* **1** [VP6A,2A] put to death; cause the death of: ~ *animals for food. Thou shalt not* ~, (biblical, one of the Ten Commandments). *The troops were shooting to* ~, eg in a riot, shooting with the intention of ~ing, not merely to warn or wound the rioters. *The frost* ~*ed the flowers.* ~ **sb/sth off,** [VP15B] get rid of: *The frost* ~*ed off most of the insect pests.* ~ **time,** find ways of passing the time without being bored, eg when compelled to wait for sb/sth. ~ **two birds with one stone,** ⇨ **bird.** **2** [VP6A] neutralize, make ineffective by contrast: *The scarlet carpet* ~*s* (= deadens) *your curtains.* **3** [VP6A] cause the failure or defeat of; veto: ~ *a proposal/a Bill in Parliament.* **'~-joy** *n* person who throws gloom over those who are enjoying themselves. **4** [VP6A,2A] overwhelm; impress deeply. ~ *sb with kindness,* harm him by being excessively or mistakenly kind. *(be) dressed/got up to* ~, dressed elaborately, so as to impress people. □ *n* (*sing* only) **1** act of ~ing, esp in hunting. *be in at the* ~, be present when sth, eg a fox, is ~ed. **2** (in hunting) number of animals ~ed: *There was a plentiful* ~, many animals were ~ed. ~·ing *adj* (colloq, dated) amusing: *a* ~ing *joke;* exhausting: *a* ~ing *experience.* □ *n* *make a* ~ing, be extraordinarily successful. ~ing·ly *adv* ~er *n* one who, that which, ~s; (journalese) murderer.

kiln /'kɪln/ *n* furnace or oven for burning, baking or drying, esp 'brick-~, for baking bricks; 'hop-~, for drying hops; 'lime-~, for burning lime.

kilo /'kiːləʊ/ *n* (pl ~s) (abbr of) kilogram.

kilo- /'kɪlə-/ *pref* 1000, esp in **kilo·cycle** /'kɪləsaɪkl/ *n* unit of frequency of vibration, used of wireless waves. **kilo·gram** /'kɪləgræm/ *n* 1000 grams. **kilo·litre** *n* 1000 litres. **kilo·metre** (US = **-meter**) /'kɪləmiːtə(r) US: kɪ'lɒmɪtər/ *n* 1000 metres. **kilo·watt** /'kɪləwɒt/ *n* 1000 watts. ⇨ App **5.**

kilt /kɪlt/ *n* pleated skirt, usu of tartan cloth, from waist to knee, worn as part of male dress in the Scottish Highlands; similar skirt worn by women and children. ~ed *regiment,* regiment of Scottish soldiers wearing ~s.

kilts

bagpipes

tassel

sporran

tartan kilt

kim·ono /kɪ'məʊnəʊ US: -nə/ *n* (pl ~s) **1** wide-sleeved long flowing gown, characteristic of Japanese traditional costume. ⇨ the illus at sarong. **2** style of loose garment worn as a dressing-gown.

kin /kɪn/ *n* (collective pl) family; relations: *We are near kin,* are closely related. *next of kin,* nearest relation(s).

kind¹ /kaɪnd/ *adj* (-er, -est) having, showing, thoughtfulness, sympathy or love for others: *be* ~ *to animals. Will you be* ~ *enough/so* ~ *as to close the door? It was* ~ *of you to help us.* ,~·'hearted *adj* having a ~ nature; sympathetic. ~·ly *adv* **1** in a ~ manner: *speak* ~ly *to sb; treat sb* ~ly. **2** (in polite formulas) *Will you* ~ly *tell me the time?* **3** naturally; easily: *He took* ~ly *to his new duties. He doesn't take* ~ly *to being treated as an inferior.* ~·ness *n* **1** [U] ~ nature; being ~. *out of* ~ness *(to sb),* because of feeling ~ (towards): *He did it all out of* ~ness, not in the hope of reward. **2** [C] *do/show sb a* ~ness, perform a ~ act: *He has done/shown me many* ~nesses.

kind² /kaɪnd/ *n* **1** race, natural group, of animals, plants, etc: ,man'~; ,human'kind. **2** class, sort or variety: *apples of several* ~s/*several* ~s *of apples; people of this* ~. *What* ~ *of tree is this? She's the* ~ *of woman who likes to help other people. She's not the* ~ (*of person) to talk scandal. nothing of the* ~, not at all like it. *something of the* ~, sth like the thing in question. *of a* ~, **(a)** of the same ~: *two of a* ~. **(b)** (implying contempt) scarcely deserving the name: *They gave us coffee of a* ~. *a*

~ *of...,* used when there is uncertainty: *I had a* ~ *of suspicion* (= I vaguely suspected) *that he was cheating.* ~ *of,* (sl, sometimes spelt ~a /'kaɪndə/) *adv* to some extent: *I* ~ *of thought this would happen.* **3** [U] nature; character: *They differ in degree but not in* ~. **4** *in* ~, (of payment) in goods or natural produce, not in money: *benefits in* ~, benefits other than wages or salary received by employees, eg the right to buy articles at cost price; (of repayment, fig) with what was received: *repay insolence in* ~, be insolent in return.

kin·der·gar·ten /'kɪndəgɑːtn/ *n* school for children too young to begin formal education.

kindle /'kɪndl/ *vt, vi* [VP6A,2A] **1** (cause to) catch fire or burst into flames or flaming colour: *The sparks* ~d *the dry wood. This wood is too wet to* ~. *The setting sun* ~d *the sky.* **2** rouse, be roused, to a state of strong feeling, interest, etc: ~ *the interest of an audience. Her eyes* ~d *with excitement.* **kind·ling** /'kɪndlɪŋ/ *n* [U] material for lighting a fire, esp light, dry sticks of wood.

kind·ly¹ /'kaɪndlɪ/ *adj* (-ier, -iest) friendly: *speak in a* ~ *tone; give sb* ~ *advice.*

kind·ly² /'kaɪndlɪ/ *adv* ⇨ kind¹.

kin·dred /'kɪndrɪd/ *n* **1** [U] relationship by birth between persons: *claim* ~ *with sb.* **2** (collective *pl*) family; relations: *Most of his* ~ *are still living in Ireland.* □ *adj* (attrib only) **1** related; having a common source: ~ *languages,* eg English and Dutch; *dew, frost and* ~ *phenomena;* ~ *tribes/races.* **2** similar: ~ *natures; a* ~ *spirit,* sb whom one feels to be congenial, sympathetic.

kine /kaɪn/ *n pl* (old form) cows.

kin·etic /kɪ'netɪk/ *adj* of, relating to, produced by, motion. ~ 'art, sculptural objects parts of which may be in motion, eg from air currents. ,~ 'energy, energy of a moving body because of its motion. ~s *n pl* (with *sing v*) science of the relations between the motions of bodies and the forces acting on them.

king /kɪŋ/ *n* **1** male sovereign ruler (esp one whose position is hereditary) of an independent state: *the K~ of Denmark.* ⇨ queen. **K~'s/Queen's Bench,** ⇨ bench. **K~'s/Queen's Counsel,** ⇨ counsel¹(3). *turn K~'s/Queen's evidence,* (of one who has shared in a crime) give evidence against accomplices (often in order to escape punishment). ~'s *evil,* scrofula, formerly thought to be curable by the touch of a ~. **K~s,** either of two books in the Old Testament, giving the history of the ~s of Israel and Judah. **2** person of great influence: *an* 'oil ~. **3** principal piece in the game of chess, ⇨ the illus at chess; (playing cards) court-card with a picture of a ~: *the* ~ *of spades.* **4** largest variety of a species; most prominent member of a group, category, etc: *the* ~ *of beasts,* the lion; *the* ~ *of the forest,* the oak; *the* ~ *of terrors,* death; ~ *cobra/crab/penguin.* **5** (compounds) '~·cup *n* large variety of buttercup; marsh marigold. '~·fisher *n* small brightly-coloured bird feeding on fish in rivers, etc. ⇨ the illus at bird. '~·pin *n* vertical bolt used as a pivot; (fig) indispensable or essential person or thing. '~·size(d) *adj* (in advertising, etc) larger than normal; very large: ~-*size cigarettes.* '~·like, ~·ly *adj* of, like, suitable for, a ~; majestic; regal. ~·ship /-ʃɪp/ *n* [U] state or office of a ~.

king·dom /'kɪŋdəm/ *n* **1** country ruled by a king or a queen. **the United K~ (the UK),** the Union of Great Britain (ie England, Scotland and Wales) and

Northern Ireland. **2** the spiritual reign of God: *Thy ~ come,* May the rule of God be established. **gone to k~ come,** (colloq) dead, gone to the next world. **3** any one of the three divisions of the natural world: *the animal, vegetable and mineral ~s.* **4** realm or province: *the ~ of thought,* the mind.

kink /kɪŋk/ *n* **1** irregular back-twist in a length of wire, pipe, cord, etc such as may cause a break or obstruction. **2** (fig) mental twist; sth abnormal in a person's way of thinking. □ *vt,vi* make a ~ in; form a ~ or ~s: *This hosepipe ~s easily.* **~y** *adj* (colloq) eccentric; perverted.

kins·folk /'kɪnzfəʊk/ *n pl* relations by blood. **kins·man** /-mən/ *n* (*pl* -men) male relative. **kins·woman** *n* (*pl*-women) female relative.

kin·ship /'kɪnʃɪp/ *n* [U] relationship by blood; similarity in character.

kiosk /'kiːɒsk/ *n* **1** small open-fronted structure, esp a round one, for the sale of newspapers, sweets, cigarettes, etc, eg in a park. **2** small booth for a public telephone.

kip /kɪp/ *n* (GB sl) (room or bed in a) house where beds may be rented; sleep. □ *vi* [VP2A,C] go to bed; sleep: *time to kip down.*

kip·per /'kɪpə(r)/ *n* kind of salted herring, dried or smoked. ➪ **bloater.**

kirk /kɜːk/ *n* (Scot) church.

kirsch /kɪəʃ/ *n* [U] colourless liqueur made from the juice of wild cherries.

kirtle /'kɜːtl/ *n* (archaic) woman's gown or outer petticoat; man's tunic.

kis·met /'kɪzmet/ *n* [U] destiny; the will of Allah.

kiss /kɪs/ *vt,vi* [VP6A,2A,15A,B] touch with the lips to show affection or as a greeting: *~ the children goodnight. He ~ed her (on the) cheek. She ~ed the child goodbye. She ~ed away the child's tears. ~ the book, ~* the Bible on taking an oath. **~ the dust/ground,** (a) give abject submission to a conqueror. (b) be killed. **~ hands/the Queen's hand, ~** the sovereign's hand on being appointed to an office (eg as a member of the Cabinet). **~ the rod,** accept punishment meekly. □ *n* touch, caress, given with the lips. **~ of life,** method of mouth-to-mouth resuscitation, eg for sb rescued from drowning. **~er** *n* (sl) mouth.

kit /kɪt/ *n* **1** (collective *sing*) all the equipment (esp clothing) of a soldier, sailor or traveller: '*kit inspection,* examination of kit by an officer to see that it is complete, etc. '**kit-bag** *n* long canvas bag in which kit is carried. **2** [C] equipment needed by a workman for his trade: *a plumber's kit.* **3** [C,U] outfit or equipment needed for sport or some other special purpose: '*shooting/'golfing/'skiing kit; a sur vival kit,* articles to be used by a person in distress, eg an airman who has come down in a desert or jungle. **4** [C] ,*do-it-your'self kit,* collection of parts, eg for a piece of furniture, or a set, to be assembled by the purchaser. □ *vt* (-tt-) [VP 15B] *kit sb out/up (with sth),* equip.

kit·chen /'kɪtʃɪn/ *n* room in which meals are cooked or prepared, and for other forms of housework; (in many homes in GB) general purpose rooms, eg where meals are eaten. ,~ '**garden** *n* one for fruit and vegetables. **~ sink,** ➪ sink¹ ,**~-sink 'drama,** drama in GB (late 1950's, early 1960's) portraying working-class family life, showing political, social and educational awareness. '**~ unit,** unit combining two or more articles of ~ equipment, eg a sink and a storage cabinet. **~·ette** /,kɪtʃɪ'net/ *n* tiny room or alcove used as a

~ (esp in a small flat).

kite /kaɪt/ *n* **1** bird of prey of the hawk family. **2** framework of wood, etc covered with paper or cloth, made to fly in the wind at the end of a long string or wire. **fly a ~,** (fig) test possible public reactions by means of hints, rumours, etc. Cf *see which way the wind blows.* '**~-balloon,** sausage-shaped captive balloon for military observation.

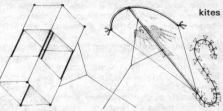

kites

kith /kɪθ/ *n* (only in) **~ and kin,** friends and relations.

kitsch /kɪtʃ/ *adj* (in the arts, design, etc) pretentious; superficial; showy.

kit·ten /'kɪtn/ *n* young cat. **~·ish** /-ɪʃ/ *adj* like a ~; playful.

kitty /'kɪtɪ/ *n* **1** (in some card games) pool of stakes to be played for; (colloq) any joint pool or fund, eg of savings. **2** (bowls) jack¹(4). **3** child's name for a cat.

kiwi /'kiːwiː/ *n* New Zealand bird with undeveloped wings; (sl) New Zealander. ➪ the illus at rare.

klaxon /'klæksn/ *n* (P) powerful electric warning horn(4).

kleenex /'kliːneks/ *n* (P) [U,C] tissue paper. ➪ tissue(3).

klep·to·mania /,kleptə'meɪnɪə/ *n* obsessive wish to steal, not necessarily from poverty. **klep·to·man·iac** /-nɪæk/ *n* person with ~.

knack /næk/ *n* (rarely *pl*) cleverness (intuitive or acquired through practice) enabling one to do sth skilfully: *There's a ~ in it,* You have to learn by doing it. *It's quite easy to drive a car when you have/get the ~ of it.*

knacker /'nækə(r)/ *n* **1** person who buys and slaughters useless horses (to sell the meat and hides). **2** person who buys and breaks up old houses, ships, etc for the materials in them. **~'s yard,** place where old metal goods, etc are broken up for scrap.

knap /næp/ *vt* (-pp-) break (flints for roads) with a hammer.

knap·sack /'næpsæk/ *n* [C] canvas or leather bag, strapped to the back and used (by soldiers, travellers) for carrying clothing, food, etc.

knave /neɪv/ *n* **1** (old use) dishonest man; man without honour. **2** (playing cards) court-card between 10 and Queen in value: *the ~ of hearts.* ➪ jack. **knav·ery** /'neɪvərɪ/ *n* [U] dishonesty; [C] (*pl* -ries) dishonest act. **knav·ish** /'neɪvɪʃ/ *adj* deceitful: *knavish tricks.* **knav·ish·ly** *adv*

knead /niːd/ *vt* [VP6A] **1** make (flour and water) into a firm paste (dough) by working with the hands; do this with wet clay; make (bread, pots) in this way. **2** massage; apply hands to (muscles, etc) as if making dough.

knee /niː/ *n* **1** joint between the thigh and the lower part of the leg in man, ➪ the illus at leg; corresponding part in animals. **be on/go (down) on one's ~s,** be kneeling/kneel down (to pray, or in submission). **bring sb to his ~s,** force him to submit. **2** part of a garment covering the ~s: *the ~s of a pair of trousers.* **3** (compounds) '~-breeches /-brɪtʃɪz/ *n pl* breeches reaching down to or just below the ~s. '~-cap *n* (a) flat, movable bone forming the front part of the ~-joint. ⇨ the illus at skeleton. (b) protective covering for the ~. ,~-'deep *adj, adv* so deep as to reach the ~s: *The water was ~-deep.* ,~-'high *adj, adv* so high as to reach the ~s: *The grass was ~-high.*

kneel /niːl/ *vi* (*pt,pp* knelt /nelt/) [VP2A,C] ~ (*down*), go down on the knees; rest on the knees: *He knelt down to look for a coin he had dropped. Everyone knelt in prayer.*

knell /nel/ *n* (*sing* with *a* or *the*) sound of a bell, esp for a death or at a funeral; (fig) sign of the end or death of sth; *toll the ~; the ~ of her hopes.*

knelt /nelt/ ⇨ kneel.

Knes·set /'kneset/ *n* Israeli parliament.

knew /njuː; *US*: nuː/ ⇨ know.

knicker·bock·ers /'nɪkəbɒkəz/ *n pl* loose wide breeches gathered in below the knees.

knickers /'nɪkəz/ *n pl* **1** (US) knickerbockers. **2** (dated) woman's or girl's drawers from the waist to the thighs. *get one's '~ in a twist,* (GB sl) become confused.

knick-knack /'nɪk næk/ *n* small ornament, piece of jewellery, article of dress, piece of furniture, etc.

knife /naɪf/ *n* (*pl* knives /naɪvz/) sharp blade with a handle, used as a cutting instrument or as a weapon: *a 'table ~,* used for food at table; *a 'pocket ~,* one with hinged blade(s). *get one's ~ into sb,* have the wish to harm him. *war to the ~,* war without mercy; relentless enmity. '~-edge *n* cutting edge of the blade of a ~. *on a ~-edge,* (of (a person awaiting) an important outcome, result, etc) extremely uncertain. □ *vt* [VP6A] cut or stab with a ~.

knight /naɪt/ *n* **1** (in the Middle Ages) man, usu of noble birth, raised to honourable military rank (after serving as a page and squire). ,~-'errant /-'erənt/ *n* (*pl* ~s-errant) ~ who went about in search of adventure. **2** (GB modern use) man on whom a title or honour is conferred (lower than that of baronet) as a reward for services to the State. (The title *Sir* is always used before the man's first name, with or without his surname, as in *Sir Harold; Sir James Hill*). **3** (GB history) ~ (*of the shire*), person who represented a shire or county in Parliament. **4** piece in the game of chess, usu made with a horse's head. ⇨ the illus at chess. □ *vt* [VP6A] make (sb) a ~. ~-hood /-hʊd/ *n* **1** [U] rank, character or dignity of a ~; [C] a particular ~hood: *The Queen conferred ~hoods on two magicians.* **2** [U] ~s collectively: *the ~hood of the Commonwealth.* ~-ly *adj* chivalrous; brave and gentle; like a ~: *~ly qualities.*

knit /nɪt/ *vt,vi* (*pt,pp* ~ted or (old use) knit; -tt-) [VP6A,15A,B,2A,C] ~ *sth (up) (from/into),* **1** make (an article of clothing, etc) by looping wool, silk, etc yarn on long needles: *~ stockings out of wool; ~ wool into stockings; ~ sth up,* repair it by ~ting. *She often ~s while reading.* **2** unite firmly or closely: *~ broken bones; a closely ~ argument. Mortar is used to ~ bricks together. The two families are ~ together by common interests.* **3** draw together. ~ *one's/the brows,* frown. ~-ter *n* person who ~s. ~-ting *n* [U] **1** action of one who ~s. **2** material that is being ~ted: *Her ~ting fell from her lap to the floor.* '~-ting-machine *n* machine that ~s. '~-ting-needle *n* long slender rod

of steel, wood, etc two or more of which are used together in ~ting. ~-wear /-weə(r)/ *n* [U] (trade use) ~ted garments.

knives /naɪvz/ ⇨ knife.

knob /nɒb/ *n* [C] **1** round-shaped handle of a door, drawer, walking-stick, etc; control, eg of a radio or television set: *turn the ~ clockwise to switch the set on.* **2** round-shaped swelling or mass on the surface of sth, eg a tree trunk. **3** small lump (eg of coal). '~-ker·rie /'nɒbkerɪ/ *n* short stick with a ~ at one end of it, formerly used as a weapon (by S African tribes).

knob·ble /'nɒbl/ *n* small knob. **knob·bly** /'nɒblɪ/ *adj* (-ier, -iest) having ~s: *~bly knees.*

knock[1] /nɒk/ *n* [C] **1** (short, sharp sound of a) blow: *He got a nasty ~ on the head when he fell. I heard a ~ at the door. I knew him by his ~,* because of the way he ~ed (at the door). *~ for ~,* situation in a motoring accident when insurance companies agree to pay only for the damage to the vehicle for which they are liable. **2** sound of ~ing in a petrol engine. ⇨ knock[2](3), and anti-~. **3** (cricket) innings: *have a good ~.* **4** (sl) criticism; insult; financial loss: *He's taken a bad ~,* suffered a financial reverse. ~-er *n* person or thing that ~s; (esp) hinged metal device on a door for ~ing on it (now often replaced by an electric bell).

knock[2] /nɒk/ *vt,vi* **1** [VP6A,15A,B,14,2A,C] hit; strike; cause to be (in a certain state) by hitting; make by hitting: *Someone is ~ing at the door/on the window. Come in—don't ~. He ~ed the bottom out of the box. Let's ~ a hole in the wall. He ~ed (= struck by accident) his head on/against the wall. The blow ~ed me flat/senseless. ~ one's head against a brick wall,* (fig) achieve nothing. *~ sb/sth into a cocked hat,* ⇨ cock[3](1). *~ the bottom out of an argument,* ⇨ bottom(7). *~ spots off sth/sb,* ⇨ spot. **2** [VP6A] (sl) surprise; shock: *What ~s me is his impudence.* **3** [VP2A] (of a petrol engine) make a tapping or thumping noise (because of a defect that prevents the engine from running smoothly): *The engine of this old car is ~ing badly.* ⇨ antiknock. **4** [VP6A] (sl) criticize unfavourably: *Why must you always ~ my driving?* **5** (compounds) (also ⇨ (6) below) '~-about *adj* (of a comic performance) = slapstick. ⇨ slap; (of clothes) suitable for rough wear. '~-down *adj* (a) (of prices, eg at an auction) lowest at which goods are to be sold; reserve price. (b) (fig) overwhelming; stunning. ~-'kneed *adj* having legs curved so that the knees touch when walking. '~-out *adj, n* (a) (abbr KO) (blow) that ~s a boxer out. (b) (of a) tournament or competition for eliminating weaker competitors. (c) (colloq) (person, thing) impressive or attractive: *Isn't she a ~-out!* (d) (sl) drug, etc which induces sleep or unconsciousness: *~ out-pills.* **6** [VP2C,15B] (uses with *adverbial particles* and *preps*):

knock about, (colloq) lead an unsettled life, travelling and living in various places: *He has ~ed about all over Asia. ~ about (with sb),* (sl) have a (casual) (sexual) relationship with sb: *She's ~ing about with a married man. ~ sb/sth about,* hit repeatedly, treat roughly: *The ship had been ~ed about by storms.*

knock sth back, (sl) drink: *~ back a pint of beer.*

knock sb down, strike to the ground or floor: *He was ~ed down by a bus. He ~ed his opponent down. You could have ~ed me down with a* *feather*, I was very surprised. ~ *sth down*, (a) demolish: *These old houses are to be ~ed down*. (b) take to pieces to save cost and space in transport: *The machines will be ~ed down before being packed for shipment to Singapore*. Hence, '~-*down furniture, etc*, which can be taken to pieces. ~ *sth down to sb*, (at an auction sale) sell (to a bidder): *The painting was ~ed down to Mr Smith for £50*. ~ *sth/sb down (to sth)*, (compel sb to) lower a price: *He asked £500 for his car but I managed to ~ him down 10 per cent/~ed his price down to £450*. Hence, ~-*down prices*. also ⇨ *knock-down* at (5) above.

knock sth in, strike so that sth goes/stays in: ~ *in a nail*; ~ *in the top of a barrel*.

knock off (work), stop work: *It's time to ~ off for tea*. ~ *sb off*, (sl) quickly seduce and then abandon. ~ *sth off*, (a) deduct: *I'll ~ 50p off the price*. (b) compose or finish rapidly: ~ *off an article/some verses for a magazine*. (c) (cricket) score quickly: ~ *off the runs needed to win a match*. (d) (sl) break into, rob: ~ *off a bank*. **K~ it off!** (sl) Stop it!

knock on, (Rugby) ~ the ball forward when trying to catch it (a foul). Hence, '~-*on* n. '~-*on effect* n (colloq) (usu unpleasant) consequence.

knock sb out, (a) (boxing) strike (an opponent) so that he cannot rise to his feet for the count. (b) (fig) overwhelm; stun: *She was ~ed out by the news*. (c) ~ *sb out (of)*, eliminate him (from a competition) (by defeating him). ~ *sth out*, empty by ~ing: ~ *out one's pipe*, ie of ash, etc.

knock (things) together, make roughly or hastily: ~ *boards together for a camp table*. *The bookshelves had obviously been ~ed together*, not made with care. ~ *your/their heads together*, use force to prevent you/them from quarrelling, being foolish or stubborn.

knock up, (tennis) practise shots before the start of a match. ~ *sb up*, (a) (GB colloq) waken or rouse sb by ~ing at his door, etc: *Please could you ~ me up at seven o'clock*. (b) (GB colloq) make tired; exhaust: *He was ~ed up after the long steep climb*. (c) (US sl) attack; beat up. (d) ⚠ (US vulg sl) (of a man) have sexual intercourse with; make pregnant. ~ *sth up*, (a) drive upwards with a blow: *K~ his arm up!* (b) arrange, put together quickly: ~ *up a meal from whatever there is in the larder*; ~ *up a shelter for mountain-climbers*. (c) score (runs) at cricket. ~ *up copy*, prepare material for printing (in a newspaper, etc).

knoll /nəʊl/ n small hill; mound.

knot /nɒt/ n [C] **1** part of one or more pieces of string, rope, etc, twisted together, usu to make a fastening: *tie a ~ in a rope; tie a rope in a firm ~; make a ~;* (fig) sth that ties together: *the 'marriage-~*. **2** piece of ribbon, etc twisted and tied as an ornament. **3** difficulty; hard problem. *tie oneself in/up in/into ~s*, get badly confused about sth. ⇨ **Gordian**. **4** hard lump in wood where a branch grew out from a bough or trunk; round cross-grained piece caused by this in a board. '~-**hole** n hole (in a board) from which such a piece has come out. **5** group of persons or things: *People were standing about in ~s*, anxiously waiting for news. **6** measure of speed for ships: *a vessel of 20 ~s*, able to sail 20 nautical miles an hour. ⇨ **App 5**. □ *vt,vi* (-tt-) [VP6A, 15B, 2A] make a ~ or ~s in; tie sth with ~s; form ~s: ~ *two ropes together;* ~ *a parcel firmly;* string that ~s easily. ~**ty** adj (-

ier, -iest) full of ~s: *a ~ty board*. ~**ty problem**, one that is difficult to solve.

know /nəʊ/ *vt,vi* (*pt* knew /njuː US: nuː/, *pp* known /nəʊn/) **1** [VP6A,8,9,10,17,25,2A] have in the mind as the result of experience or of being informed, or because one has learned: *Every child ~s that two and two make four. He ~s a lot of English. Do you ~ how to play chess? I don't ~ whether he is here or not. I ~ (that) he's an honest man. I ~ him to be honest. I'm not guessing—I really ~. Oh, yes, I ~ all about that. There's no ~ing* (= It is impossible to ~) *when we shall meet again*. [VP17,18B] (past and perfect tenses only): *I have never ~n a man (to) die of love, but I have ~n a disappointed lover (to) lose weight*. ~ *one's business/what's 'what/the ropes/a 'thing or two*, have common sense, good judgement, practical experience. ~ *better than to do sth*, be wise enough (not to...): *You ought to ~ better than to go swimming on such a cold day*. **2** [VP6A] be acquainted with (a person); be able to distinguish (sb) from others: *Do you ~ Mr Hill? Have you met him, talked with him, etc? (Cf Do you ~(1) who Napoleon was?) I ~ Mr White by sight but have never spoken to him. I've ~n Mrs Grey since I was a child. I was introduced to Miss Wood last week, but I've a bad memory for faces and might not ~* (= recognize) *her again. make oneself ~n to sb*, introduce oneself: *There's your host; you'd better make yourself ~n to him. be ~n to*: *He's ~n to the police*, The police have his name in their records, eg because he has been a criminal. *be ~n as*: *He's ~n as* (= has the reputation of being) *a successful architect*. ~ *sb from sb*, distinguish from: *They're twins and it's almost impossible to ~ one from the other. not ~ sb from Adam/from a bar of soap*, (colloq) have no idea who he is. **3** [VP6A] have personal experience of: *He knew poverty and sorrow in his early life. He's ~n better days*, has not always been so poor, unfortunate, etc, as he is now. **4** [VP6A] be able to recognize: *He ~s a good singing voice when he hears one. She doesn't ~ a swallow from a house-martin*. **5** [VP3A] ~ *about/of*, have information concerning; be aware of: *I knew about that last week. I didn't ~ about that*, was in ignorance. *I ~ of an excellent little restaurant near here. 'Has Smith been ill-?'—'Not that I ~ of.'* I am not aware of his having been ill. *I don't actually ~(2) the man you mention, but of course I ~ 'of him*, I'm aware of his existence. **6** (compounds) ,*don't-'~* n (colloq) person who is unable to give an answer in a *poll¹(2)*. '~-*all* n person who ~s, or claims to ~, everything. '~-*how* n [U] faculty of ~ing how (to do sth); knowledge of methods; ingenuity (contrasted with theoretical knowledge). □ n (only in) *in the ~*, (colloq) having information not shared by all or not available to all.

know·ing /'nəʊɪŋ/ *adj* cunning; wide-awake; hav-

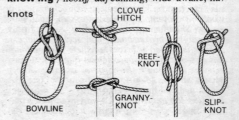

knots

CLOVE HITCH

REEF-KNOT

GRANNY-KNOT

BOWLINE

SLIP-KNOT

ing, showing that one has, intelligence, sharp wits, etc: *a ~ fellow; ~ looks. ~-ly adv* 1 consciously; intentionally: *He would never ~ly do anything to hurt your interests.* 2 in a *~* manner: *look ~ly at someone.*

knowl·edge /'nɒlɪdʒ/ *n* [U] 1 understanding: *A baby has no ~ of good and evil.* 2 familiarity gained by experience; range of information: *My ~ of French is poor. K~ of the defeat soon spread. It has come to my ~* (= I have been informed) *that you have been spreading gossip about me. To the best of my ~* (= As far as I know) *he is honest and reliable. She married without the ~ of her parents. ~·able /-əbl/ adj* well-informed; having much *~*.

knuckle /'nʌkl/ *n* 1 bone at a finger-joint: *give a boy a rap over/on the ~s.* ⇨ the illus at arm.2 (in animals) knee-joint, or part joining leg to foot (esp as food). □ *vi ~ down to,* (of a task, etc) apply oneself earnestly. *~ under,* submit, yield.

ko·ala /kəʊ'ɑːlə/ *n* Australian tree-climbing tailless mammal, like a small bear. ⇨ the illus at small.

kobo /'kɒbəʊ/ *n* (Nigeria) 100th part of a naira; coin of this value.

kohl /kəʊl/ *n* [U] cosmetic preparation used in the East to darken the eyelids.

kohl·rabi /ˌkəʊl'rɑːbɪ/ *n* [C,U] cabbage with turnip-shaped stem.

kola /'kəʊlə/ *n* W African tree. '*~-nut n* the white or pink bitter edible seed of the *~* tree, used in cooking or to chew.

kooka·burra /'kʊkəbʌrə/ *n* large Australian kingfisher (also called *laughing jackass*).

ko·peck /'kəʊpek/ *n* = copeck.

kopje, kop·pie /'kɒpɪ/ *n* (in S Africa) small hill.

Ko·ran /kɔː'rɑːn US: -'ræn/ *n* sacred book containing the Prophet Muhammad's oral revelations, written in Arabic. *~·ic adj*

ko·sher /'kəʊʃə(r)/ *n, adj* (food, foodshop) fulfilling the requirements of Jewish dietary law.

kou·miss /'kuːmɪs/ *n* = kumis.

kow·tow, ko·tow /ˌkaʊ'taʊ/ *n* (former Chinese custom) touching of the ground with the forehead (as a sign of respect, submission, etc). □ *vi ~ (to),* make a *~*; act obsequiously (to).

kraal /krɑːl US: krɔːl/ *n* (in S Africa) fenced-in village of huts; enclosure for domestic animals.

Krem·lin /'kremlɪn/ *n* citadel of a Russian town, esp that of Moscow. **the ~,** the Government of the USSR.

krona /'krəʊnə/ *n* (*pl* -nor /-nə/) unit of currency in Sweden.

krone /'krəʊnə/ *n* (*pl* -ner /-nə/) unit of currency in Denmark and Norway.

ku·dos /'kjuːdɒs/ *n* [U] (colloq) honour and glory; credit.

kumis, kou·miss /'kuːmɪs/ *n* [U] fermented liquor of Central Asia made from mare's milk.

küm·mel /'kʊməl/ *n* [U] herb-flavoured liqueur.

kung fu /ˌkʊŋ 'fuː/ *n* [U] Chinese form of karate.

kvass /kvæs/ *n* [U] kind of Russian beer.

kwela /'kweɪlə/ *n* [U] kind of S African jazz music.

Ll

L, l /el/ (*pl* L's l's /elz/) the 12th letter of the English alphabet; symbol for the Roman numeral 50, ⇨ App 4.

la /lɑː/ *n* sixth note of the musical octave.

laa·ger /'lɑːgə(r)/ *n* camp, defensive encampment, esp inside a circle of carts or wagons; (mil) park for armoured vehicles.

lab /læb/ *n* (colloq abbr of) laboratory.

label /'leɪbl/ *n* piece of paper, cloth, metal, wood or other material used for describing what sth is, where it is to go, etc: *plant ~s; put ~s on one's luggage.* □ *vt* (-ll-, US -l-) [VP6A] put a *~* or *~s* on: *properly ~led luggage;* (fig) *~ sb as a demagogue,* assign him to this class of persons.

la·bial /'leɪbɪəl/ *adj* of the lips; made with the lips: *~ sounds,* eg /m, p, v/.

labor /'leɪbə(r)/ *n* (US) = labour.

lab·ora·tory /lə'bɒrətrɪ US: 'læbrətɔːrɪ/ *n* (*pl* -ries) room or building used for scientific experiments, research, testing, etc esp in chemistry. ⇨ language.

la·bori·ous /lə'bɔːrɪəs/ *adj* 1 (of work, etc) requiring great effort: *a ~ task.* 2 showing signs of great effort; not fluent or easy: *a ~ style of writing. ~·ly adv*

la·bour (US = **la·bor**) /'leɪbə(r)/ *n* 1 [U] bodily or mental work: *The majority of men earn their living by manual ~.* **hard ~** *n* [U] work done by criminals (sentenced to penal servitude) as a punishment. '*~-saving adj* that reduces the amount of *~* needed: *~-saving devices,* eg washing-machines, vacuum cleaners. 2 [C] task; piece of work. *a ~ of love,* task gladly undertaken (eg one for the good of sb one loves). 3 [U] workers as a class (contrasted with the owners of capital, etc): *skilled and unskilled ~; ~ relations,* between workers and employers. '**L~ Exchange,** Government agency used by employers for finding workers and by workers for finding jobs. **the 'L~ Party,** one of the two large political parties in Britain, representing socialist opinion. **L~ leaders,** leaders of this party; trade union officials. **the L~ vote,** of those who support the L~ Party. '**Labor Day,** (US) first Monday in September, a legal holiday in honour of the working class. '**labor union,** (US) = trade union. 4 [U] process of childbirth: *a woman in ~.* □ *vi,vt* 1 [VP2A,C,4A] work; try hard: *~ for the happiness of mankind; ~ at a task; ~ to complete a task; ~ in the cause of peace.* 2 [VP2A,C] move, breathe, slowly and with difficulty: *The ship ~ed through the heavy seas. The old man ~ed up the hillside.* 3 [VP3A] *~ under sb/sth,* be the victim of, suffer because of: *~ under a delusion/difficulty/disadvantage.* 4 [VP6A] work out in detail; treat at great length: *There's no need to ~ the point/argument. ~ed adj* 1 slow and troublesome: *~ed breathing.* 2 not easy or natural; showing too much effort: *a ~ed style of writing. ~er n* man who performs heavy unskilled work: *agricultural* ~*ers*, farm workers. **L~-ite** /-aɪt/ *n* member or supporter of the L~ Party.

la·bur·num /ləˈbɜːnəm/ *n* small tree with yellow flowers that hang down gracefully and with seeds in long pods.

lab·y·rinth /ˈlæbərɪnθ/ *n* network of winding paths, roads, etc through which it is difficult to find one's way without help; (fig) entangled state of affairs. **laby·rin·thine** /ˌlæbəˈrɪnθaɪn US: -θɪn/ *adj*

lace /leɪs/ *n* 1 [U] delicate, ornamental openwork fabric of threads: *a dress trimmed with ~; a ~ collar.* **gold/silver ~,** braid used for trimming uniforms, eg of diplomats, army officers. 2 [C] string or cord put through small holes in shoes, etc to draw edges together: *a pair of 'shoe~s.* □ *vt, vi* [VP6A,15A,B,2A,C] ~ *(up),* 1 fasten or tighten with ~s(2): ~ *(up) one's shoes; a corset that ~s (up) at the side.* 2 [VP3A] ~ *into sb,* lash him, beat him. 3 [VP14] ~ *with,* flavour or strengthen (a liquid) (with some kind of spirit): *a glass of milk ~d with rum.*

lace

lac·er·ate /ˈlæsəreɪt/ *vt* [VP6A] tear (the flesh; (fig) the feelings). **lac·er·ation** /ˌlæsəˈreɪʃn/ *n* [U] tearing; [C] tear or injury.

lach·ry·mal /ˈlækrɪml/ *adj* of tears: (esp) ~ *glands.* **lach·ry·mose** /ˈlækrɪməʊs/ *adj* tearful; in the habit of weeping.

lack /læk/ *vt, vi* 1 [VP6B,3A] ~ *(in),* be without; not have; have less than enough of: ~ *wisdom. I ~ words with which to express my thanks. What I ~ in experience I make up in curiosity.* **be ~ing in** *sth,* not have enough of it: *He's ~ing in* (= He ~s) *courage.* **2 be ~ing,** be in short supply, not be available: *Money was ~ing* (= There was no money) *for the plan.* 3 [VP3A] ~ *for,* (formal) need: *They ~ed for nothing,* had everything they wanted. □ *n* [U] want, need, shortage: *The plants died for ~ of water.* '~**-lustre** *adj* (of eyes) dull.

lacka·daisi·cal /ˌlækəˈdeɪzɪkl/ *adj* appearing tired, uninterested, unenthusiastic. ~**ly** /-klɪ/ *adv*

lackey /ˈlækɪ/ *n* (*pl* ~s) manservant (usu in livery); (fig) person who is too obsequious, who obeys orders without question, etc.

la·conic /ləˈkɒnɪk/ *adj* using, expressed in, few words: *a ~ person/reply.* **la·coni·cally** /-klɪ/ *adv* **la·coni·cism** /-nɪsɪzəm/, **lac·on·ism** /ˈlækənɪzəm/ *nn* [U] being ~; [C] instance of this; short, pithy saying.

lac·quer /ˈlækə(r)/ *n* [U] varnish used to give a hard, bright coating to metal (esp brass); varnish used for wooden articles (esp **Japanese ~**); liquid sprayed on the hair to keep it in place. □ *vt* [VP6A] coat with ~.

la·crosse /ləˈkrɒs US: -ˈkrɔːs/ *n* [U] outdoor game, popular in N America, played with a ball which is caught in, carried in, and thrown from, a racket with a net (called a *crosse*).

lac·tic /ˈlæktɪk/ *adj* of milk. ~ **'acid,** the acid in sour milk.

la·cuna /ləˈkjuːnə/ *n* (*pl* ~s or ~e /-niː/) blank;

empty part; missing portion, esp in writing, or in an argument.

lacy /ˈleɪsɪ/ *adj* (-ier, -iest) of or like lace.

lad /læd/ *n* boy; young man.

lad·der /ˈlædə(r)/ *n* 1 two lengths of wood, metal or rope, with crosspieces (called *rungs*), used in climbing up and down walls, a ship's side, etc. ⇨ *'step - ~* at step ²(5). 2 (US = *run*) fault in a stocking caused by stitches becoming undone, so that there is a vertical ~-like flaw. '~**-proof** *adj* proof against such flaws. □ *vi* (of stockings etc) develop ~s: *Have you any tights that won't ~?*

lad·die /ˈlædɪ/ *n* = lad.

lade /leɪd/ *vt* (*pp* laden /ˈleɪdn/) [VP6A] load (which is the usu word).

laden /ˈleɪdn/ *adj* ~ *with,* weighted or burdened with: *trees ~ with apples; a mind ~ with grief.*

la-di-da /ˌlɑː dɪ ˈdɑː/ *adj* (colloq) pretentious; genteel; affected (esp in pronunciation).

lad·ing /ˈleɪdɪŋ/ *n* [U] (naut) cargo; freight. **bill of '~,** list with details of a ship's cargo.

ladle /ˈleɪdl/ *n* large, deep, cup-shaped spoon for dipping out liquids: *a 'soup ~.* □ *vt* [VP6A,15B] ~ *(out),* serve with or as from a ~: ~ *out soup;* (fig) ~ *out honours.*

lady /ˈleɪdɪ/ *n* (*pl* -dies) 1 (corresponding to *gentleman*) woman belonging to the upper classes; woman who has good manners and some claim to social position. ~**-in-'waiting,** ~ **of the 'bedchamber,** ~ attending upon a queen. 2 (used courteously for any) woman of any kind or class, with or without good manners and refinement. 3 (*pl* only) form of address, esp *'Ladies and Gentlemen'*. 4 (attrib) female: ~ *doctor/clerk,* (*woman* being preferable). 5 **Ladies** (as a *sing n*) women's public lavatory: *Is there a Ladies near here?* 6 **L~,** (title in GB) used of and to the wives of some nobles; (prefixed to Christian names) titles used of and to the daughters of some nobles. 7 **My L~,** formal term of address used to holders of the title *Lady* (as in 6 above). 8 (compounds) '~**-bird** reddish-brown or yellow insect (a small flying beetle) with black spots. **Our 'L~,** the Virgin Mary. '**L~-chapel,** chapel (in a large church) dedicated to the Virgin Mary. '**L~ Day,** the feast of the Annunciation, 25th March. '~**-killer** *n* man with the reputation of being very successful with women. '~**'s-maid** *n* ~'s personal servant, esp in charge of her toilet. '~**'s/'ladies' man,** man fond of the society of women. '~**-like** *adj* behaving as a ~; befitting a ~; genteel. '~**-ship** /-ʃɪp/ *n* **Your/ Her L~ship,** used in speaking to or of a titled ~.

lag¹ /læg/ *vi* (-gg-) [VP2A,C] go too slow, not keep up with: *The lame child lagged behind.* □ *n* ('**time) lag,** period of time by which sth is slower or later.

lag² /læg/ *n* (sl) person convicted of crime; (esp) **old lag,** one who has served several sentences of imprisonment.

lag³ /læg/ *vt* (-gg-) [VP6A,14] *lag (with),* encase (waterpipes, cisterns, etc) with material that will not conduct heat or cold, esp to prevent freezing of water in pipes, waste of heat, etc. **lag·ging** *n* [U] material used for this.

la·ger /ˈlɑːgə(r)/ *n* [U] sort of light beer; [C] bottle or glass of this.

lag·gard /ˈlægəd/ *n* person who lags behind; person who is lacking in energy, etc.

la·goon /ləˈguːn/ *n* (usu shallow) salt-water lake separated from the sea by sandbank(s) or coral reef(s); water enclosed by an atoll. ⇨ the illus at atoll.

laic /'lenk/ adj of the laity; secular. **lai-cize** /'lensaiz/ vt [VP6A] free from ecclesiastic control; make, eg priest, a layman.

laid /leid/ pt,pp of lay¹.

lain /lein/ pp of lie².

lair /leə(r)/ n wild animal's resting-place or den.

laird /leəd/ n (Scot) landowner.

laissez-faire /,lersei 'feə(r)/ n [U] (F) (policy of) allowing individual activities (esp in commerce) to be conducted without government control.

laity /'lerəti/ n (usu **the ~**, and a pl v) **1** all laymen (ie all those persons not in Holy Orders, those who are not clergy). **2** all those persons outside a particular learned profession (thus, used by a doctor, the word may mean all those not trained for the medical profession).

lake¹ /leik/ n large area of water enclosed by land. **the 'L~ District, the L~s,** part of NW England with many ~s. **'L~ Poets,** poets who lived in this area, esp Coleridge and Wordsworth. **the Great L~s,** ⇨ great. **'~ dwelling,** ⇨ pile-dwelling at pile¹.

lake² /leik/ n (often crimson ~) dark red colouring material.

lakh /lɑ:k/ n (India and Pakistan) 100000. ⇨ crore.

lam /læm/ vt,vi (-mm-) (sl) [VP6A] thrash. [VP3A] **lam into sb,** attack him, physically or verbally.

lama /'lɑ:mə/ n Buddhist monk in Tibet or Mongolia. **~-sery** /'lɑ:məsəri US: -seri/ n (pl -ries) monastery of ~s.

lamb /læm/ n **1** [C] young of the sheep, ⇨ the illus at domestic; [U] its flesh as food: a leg of ~; roast ~. **2** innocent, mild-mannered person; dear person. **like a ~,** without resistance or protest. □ vi bring forth ~s: the '~ing season, when ~s are born. **'~-kin** /-kin/ n very young ~. **'~-skin** n [C] skin of a ~ with the wool on it (as used for coats, gloves, etc); [U] leather made from ~skin.

lam-baste /læm'beist/ vt (sl) thrash; beat; scold violently.

lam-bent /'læmbənt/ adj (liter) (of a flame or light) moving over the surface with soft radiance; (of the eyes, sky) shining softly; (of humour, wit) gently brilliant. **lam-bency** /-ənsi/ n

lame /leim/ adj **1** not able to walk normally because of an injury or defect: ~ in the left leg. ~ **duck,** ⇨ duck¹(1). **2** (of an excuse, argument, etc) unconvincing; unsatisfactory. **3** (of metre) halting. □ vt make ~. **~-ly** adv **~-ness** n

lamé /'lɑ:mei US: lɑ:'mei/ n [U] fabric with metal threads interwoven.

la-ment /lə'ment/ vt,vi [VP6A,3A,2A] ~ (for/over), show, feel, express, great sorrow or regret: ~ the death of a friend; ~ for a friend; ~ (over) one's misfortunes. □ n [C] expression of grief; (music) song or poem expressing grief: a funeral ~. **lam-en-table** /'læmantəbl/ adj regrettable; to be deplored: a ~able (= poor, unsatisfying) performance of an opera. **'lam-en-tably** /-əbli/ adv **lam-en-ta-tion** /,læmen'teiʃn/ n [U] ~ing; [C] ~; expression of grief.

lami-nate /'læmineit/ vt,vi [VP6A,2A] beat or roll (metal) into thin plates; split into layers; manufacture by placing layer on layer; cover with metal plates: ~d wood/plastics, of layers one over the other.

Lam-mas /'læmas/ n (hist) 1st August, formerly a harvest festival in England.

lamp /læmp/ n container with oil and wick, used to

give light; (in modern times) any apparatus for giving light (from gas, electricity, etc). **'~-black** n [U] black colouring matter made from the soot of burning oil, formerly used in making paint and printing-ink. **'~-light** n [U] light from a ~: read by ~light. **'~-lighter** n (hist) man who went round the streets to light public ~s (when gas was used). **'~-post** n (usu metal) post for a street ~. **'~-shade** n globe of glass, screen of silk, parchment, etc placed round or over a lamp.

lam-poon /læm'pu:n/ n [C] piece of satirical writing attacking and ridiculing sb. □ vt [VP6A] write a ~ against.

lam-prey /'læmpri/ n (pl ~s) eel-like water animal.

lance¹ /lɑ:ns US: læns/ n (hist) weapon with a long wooden shaft and a pointed steel head used by a horseman; similar instrument used for spearing fish. **,~-'corporal** n grade of non-commissioned officer in the army. **~r** n soldier of a cavalry regiment originally armed with ~s. **~rs** n pl (with sing v) (music for a) dance for four or more couples.

lance² /lɑ:ns US: læns/ vt [VP6A] cut open, prick, with a lancet: ~ an abscess.

lan-cet /'lɑ:nsit US: 'læn-/ n **1** pointed, two-edged knife used by surgeons. **2** (archit) high, narrow, pointed arch or window.

land¹ /lænd/ n **1** [U] solid part of the earth's surface (contrasted with sea, water): travel over ~ and sea; come in sight of ~; glad to be on ~/to reach ~/to come to ~ again. Are you going by ~ or by sea, by train, car, etc, or by boat? a ~ breeze, one blowing from the land towards the sea (after sunset); ~-based aircraft, using bases on ~ (contrasted with aircraft based on carriers). **make ~,** see, reach the shore. **see/find out how the '~ lies,** ⇨ lie²(4). **2** [U] ground, earth, as used for farming, etc: working on the ~; '~-workers; rough and stony ~. **'~ army,** (GB) body of women farm workers in World War II. **3** [U] property in the form of ~: How far does your ~ extend? Do you own much ~ here? '~-agent, (chiefly GB) person employed to manage an estate; person who buys and sells estates (US = real estate agent). **4** (pl) estate; area of ~ with the trees, etc on it: own houses and ~s. **5** country and its people (liter or emotive in this sense, country being the ordinary word): my native ~; visit distant ~s. **the ~ of the living,** this present existence. **the Promised L~, the L~ of Promise,** Canaan /'keinən/, promised by God to the Israelites. **6** (compounds, etc) '~-fall n approach to ~, esp for the first time during a voyage: a good ~fall, one that corresponds well to the calculations made by the ship's officers. '~ forces n pl military forces (not naval). '~-holder n owner or (more usu) tenant of ~. '~-lady n (pl-ladies) woman who owns a house which she leases to a tenant, or who rents a house, rooms of which she sublets to tenants: owe one's ~lady a month's rent. '~-locked adj (of a bay, harbour, etc) almost or entirely surrounded by ~. '~-lord n (a) person from whom another rents ~ or building(s). (b) keeper of an inn, a public house, a boarding-house or lodging-house. '~-lubber /læbə(r)/ n (used by sailors to describe a) person not accustomed to the sea and ships. '~-mark n [C] (a) object that marks the boundary of a piece of ~. (b) object, etc easily seen from a distance and helpful to travellers (eg navigating officers of a ship).

(c) (fig) event, discovery, change, etc that marks a stage or turning-point: ~*marks in the history of mankind.* '~**-mine** *n* [C] explosive charge laid in or on the ground or dropped by parachute and exploded by vehicles passing over it. '~**-owner** *n* owner of ~. '**L**~**-rover** *n* (P) strongly-built motor vehicle for use over rough ground. '~**-slide** *n* [C] (**a**) sliding down of a mass of earth, rock, etc from the side of a cliff, hillside, railway cutting, etc. (**b**) sudden change in political opinion resulting in an overwhelming majority of votes for one side in an election: *a Democratic* ~*slide,* a great victory for the Democratic party. '~**·slip** *n* = ~slide(a). '~**s**-**man** /-mən/ *n* (*pl* -men) person who is not a sailor.

land² /lænd/ *vt,vi* **1** [VP6A,2A,C] go, come, put, on ~ (from a ship, aircraft, etc): *The passengers* ~*ed/were* ~*ed as soon as the ship reached harbour. We* ~*ed at Bombay. The airliner* ~*ed safely. The pilot* ~*ed the airliner safely.* ⇨ also *crash-*~ at crash¹ and *soft*~ at soft. ~ *on one's feet,* (fig) be lucky; escape injury. **2** ~ *sb/oneself in sth,* get into (trouble, difficulties, etc): *What a mess you've* ~*ed us all in!* ~ *up,* (colloq) arrive; find oneself: *If you go on behaving in this way, you'll* ~ *up in prison one day. Tom has been away for months, but he'll* ~ *up one of these days. She* ~*ed up in a strange city without any money or friends.* **3** [VP6A] (colloq) obtain: ~ *a good job/a contract for building a factory.* **4** [VP12C] (sl) strike (a blow): *She* ~*ed him one in the eye.* ~**ed** *adj* **1** consisting of ~: ~*ed property.* **2** owning ~: *the* ~*ed classes/gentry.* ~**·less** *adj* without ~; not owning ~.

lan·dau /'lændɔː/ *n* (hist) four-wheeled horse-carriage with a folding roof in two sections.

land·grave /'lændgreɪv/ *n* (hist) title of some German princes.

land·ing /'lændɪŋ/ *n* **1** act of coming or bringing to land: *the* ~ *of the Pilgrim Fathers in America. The pilot made an emergency* ~. '~**-craft** *n* ship whose bows can be opened up to allow (usu military) vehicles to get ashore without being lifted out. '~**-field/-strip** *n* area of land for aircraft to take off from and land on. '~**-gear** *n* undercarriage and wheels of an aircraft. '~**-net** *n* bag-shaped net on a long handle for landing fish caught with a rod and line. '~**-party** *n* party of armed men who are landed (eg to keep order). **2** (also '~**-place**) place where people and goods may be landed from a boat, etc. '~**-stage** *n* platform (usu floating) on which passengers and goods are landed. **3** area at the top of a flight of stairs on to which doors may open.

land·scape /'lændskeɪp/ *n* [C] (picture of) inland scenery; [U] branch of art dealing with this. ~ '**gardening/**'**architecture** *n* [U] the laying out of grounds and gardens in imitation of natural scenery.

lane /leɪn/ *n* **1** narrow country road, usu between hedges or banks. **2** (usu as part of a proper name) narrow street or alley between buildings: *Drury L*~. **3** passage made or left between lines of persons. **4** route regularly used by ships or aircraft. **5** marked division of a wide road for the guidance of motorists; line of vehicles within such a division: *the inside/nearside* ~; *the outside/offside* ~; *four-*~ *traffic.* **6** marked course for a competitor in a race (eg on a running track or a swimming pool).

lang·syne /ˌlæŋ'saɪn/ *adv, n* (Scot) (in) the old

days; (in) past time.

lan·guage /'læŋgwɪdʒ/ *n* **1** [U] human and non-instinctive method of communicating ideas, feelings and desires by means of a system of sounds and sound symbols. **2** [C] form of ~ used by a group: *the* ~*s of Asia; foreign* ~*s.* **dead** ~, one no longer in spoken use (eg classical Greek). '~ **laboratory,** classroom(s) where ~s are taught using tape-recorders, etc. **3** [U] manner of using words: *a person with a good command of* ~, person who is fluent or eloquent. **4** [U] words, phrases, etc used by a profession or class: *technical/legal* ~; *the* ~ *of diplomacy.* **5** [U] **bad** ~; **strong** ~, language full of oaths, violent words, etc. **6** [U,C] system of signs used as ~: *com'puter* ~, ordered system for giving instructions to a computer; '*finger* ~, as used by deaf and dumb persons; *the* ~ *of flowers; the* ~ *of algebra.*

lan·guid /'læŋgwɪd/ *adj* lacking in energy; slow-moving. ~**·ly** *adv*

lan·guish /'læŋgwɪʃ/ *vi* [VP2A,C] be or become languid; lose health and strength; be unhappy because of a desire (*for* sth): ~ *in prison;* ~ *for love and sympathy. She gave the young man a* ~*ing look,* one that suggested a desire for love or sympathy.

lan·guor /'læŋgə(r)/ *n* **1** [U] weakness of body (as produced by hard work) or of spirit (as produced by sorrow or an unhappy love affair); lack of life or movement; stillness or heaviness: *the* ~ *of a summer day.* **2** (often *pl*) soft or tender mood. ~**·ous** /-əs/ *adj* ~**·ous·ly** *adv*

lan·gur /læŋ'gʊə(r)/ *n* (kind of) long-tailed monkey.

lank /læŋk/ *adj* **1** (of hair) straight and lying limp or flat. **2** tall and lean.

lanky /'læŋkɪ/ *adj* (-ier, -iest) (of a person, his arms or legs) long and lean in an ungraceful way: *a* ~, *overgrown girl.*

lano·lin /'lænəlɪn/ *n* [U] fat extracted from sheep's wool used as the basis of ointments for the skin.

lan·tern /'læntən/ *n* case (usu metal and glass) protecting a light from the wind, etc, outdoors. ⇨ dark²(1), magic. '~**-jawed** *adj* having long and thin jaws so that the face has a hollow look.

lan·yard /'lænjəd/ *n* **1** cord (worn by sailors and soldiers) for a whistle or knife. **2** short rope used on a ship for fastening or moving sth.

lap¹ /læp/ *n* front part of a person's legs from the waist to the knees, when sitting, as the place on which a child is nursed or sth held: *The mother had the baby on her lap. be/live in the lap of luxury,* in fortunate and luxurious circumstances. *in the lap of the gods,* (of future events) uncertain. '**lap-dog** *n* small pet dog.

lap² /læp/ *vt,vi* (-pp-) **1** [VP15B] wrap or fold (cloth, etc) *round* or *in.* **2** [VP6A,2A,C] (cause to) overlap: *Put the slates on the roof so that they lap over.* ⇨ **overlap.** □ *n* **1** amount by which one thing laps over. **2** one circuit round a track or racecourse: *Smith overtook the other runners/riders/drivers on the last lap.*

lap³ /læp/ *vi,vt* (-pp-) **1** [VP15B] *lap up,* drink by taking up with the tongue, as a cat does: *The cat quickly lapped up all the milk.* **2** (colloq) (of human beings) take quickly or eagerly: *lap up compliments.* **3** [VP2A,C] (of water) move with a sound like the lapping up of liquid: *waves lapping on the beach; water lapping against the sides of a canoe.* **4** [VP6A] (in a race) become ahead of by a lap²(2).

□ *n* **1** act of lapping: *The dog emptied the plate with three laps of the tongue.* **2** [U] sound of lapping: *the lap of the waves against the side of the boat.*

la·pel /lə'pel/ *n* part of the breast of a coat or jacket folded back and forming a continuation of the collar.

lapi·dary /'læpɪdərɪ *US:* -derɪ/ *adj* cut on stone; (fig) neat; precise: *a ~ inscription/speech.* □ *n* person who cuts, polishes or engraves, gems.

lap·is la·zuli /ˌlæpɪs 'læzjʊlɪ *US:* 'læʒəlɪ/ *n* [U,C] bright blue semi-precious stone; its colour.

lapse /læps/ *n* [C] **1** slight error in speech or behaviour; slip of the memory, tongue or pen. **2** ~ *(from) (into)*, falling away from what is right: *a ~ from virtue; a ~ from true belief into heresy.* **3** (of time) passing away; interval: *the ~ of time; a long ~ of time.* **4** (legal) ending of a right, etc from failure to use it or ask for its renewal. □ *vi* **1** [VP2A,3A] ~ *(from) (into)*, fail to keep one's position; fall (from good ways into bad ways): ~ *from virtue into vice;* ~ *into bad habits; a ~d Catholic.* **2** [VP2A] (legal) (of rights and privileges) be lost because not used, claimed or renewed.

lap·wing /'læpwɪŋ/ *n* bird of the plover family; pewit.

lar·board /'lɑːbəd/ *n, adj* left side of a ship when looking forward (now always called the *port* side). ⇨ **starboard**.

lar·ceny /'lɑːsənɪ/ *n* (*pl* -nies) [U] (legal) stealing; theft; [C] instance of this.

larch /lɑːtʃ/ *n* [C] deciduous tree with small cones and light-green leaves; [U] its wood.

lard /lɑːd/ *n* [U] fat of pigs prepared for use in cooking. □ *vt* [VP6A] put ~ on; put pieces of bacon into or on (meat, etc) before cooking, in order to add to the flavour. ~ *with*, (fig, often derog) enrich: *a speech ~ed with boring quotations.*

lar·der /'lɑːdə(r)/ *n* room or cupboard where meat and other kinds of food are stored.

large /lɑːdʒ/ *adj* (-r, -st) **1** of considerable size; taking up much space; able to contain much: *A man with a ~ family needs a ~ house. She inherited a ~ fortune. as ~ as life,* ⇨ **life**(10). (Note that *large* is less colloq than *big* and not so emotive as *great.* 'A great city' is large, but the use of 'great' suggests that it is also important or famous. *Large* is seldom used of persons, but note ~ *of limb,* having ~ limbs.) '~-**scale** *adj* (**a**) extensive: ~-*scale operations.* (**b**) made or drawn to a ~ scale: *a ~-scale map.* **2** liberal; generous; unprejudiced (chiefly in the following): *a ~ heart,* (hence) ,~-'hearted; ,~-'minded, hence, ,~-'mindedness.* **3** of wide range; not confined or restricted: *give an official ~ powers/discretion; a man with ~ ideas;* ~ *and small farmers,* men farming on a ~ and a small scale. □ *n* (only in) *at ~,* (**a**) at liberty; free: *The escaped prisoner is still at ~.* (**b**) at full length; with details: *to talk/write at ~.* (**c**) in general: *Did the people at ~ approve of the government's policy?* (**d**) at random; without definite aim: *scatter accusations at ~.* □ *adv* **1** (only in) *bulk/loom/writ ~,* ⇨ **bulk**, **loom**[2], **write**(6). *by and ~,* ⇨ **by**[1](4). **2** boastfully: *talk ~.* ~**ish** /-ɪʃ/ *adj* rather ~. ~**ly** *adv* **1** to a great extent: *His success was ~ly due to luck.* **2** generously; freely: *He gives ~ly to charity.* ~**ness** *n*

lar·gesse (US also **lar·gess**) /lɑː'dʒes/ *n* [U] generous or excessive giving; money or other things given generously or excessively given.

largo /'lɑːgəʊ/ *n* (*pl* ~s /-gəʊz/), *adv* (piece of

music, movement) in very slow and solemn time.

lar·iat /'lærɪət/ *n* rope for tethering a horse; long rope with a noose; lasso.

lark[1] /lɑːk/ *n* small songbird, esp the skylark. ⇨ the illus at bird.

lark[2] /lɑːk/ *n* [C] bit of fun; frolic: *Boys are fond of having a ~. He did it for a ~,* in fun. *What a ~! How amusing!* □ *vi* [VP2A,C] play pranks: *Stop ~ing about and get on with your work.*

lark·spur /'lɑːkspɜː(r)/ *n* tall garden plant with blue, white or pink flowers.

larn /lɑːn/ *vt, vi* (dial) learn.

larva /'lɑːvə/ *n* (*pl* ~e /-viː/) insect in the first stage of its life-history, after coming out of the egg. ⇨ the illus at butterfly. **lar·val** /'lɑːvl/ *adj* of or in the form of a ~.

lar·ynx /'lærɪŋks/ *n* (anat) upper part of the windpipe where the vocal cords are. ⇨ the illus at head. **lar·yn·gi·tis** /ˌlærɪn'dʒaɪtɪs/ *n* [U] inflammation of the ~.

las·car /'læskə(r)/ *n* seaman from the East Indies.

las·civ·ious /lə'sɪvɪəs/ *adj* feeling, causing, expressing, lust. ~**ly** *adv* ~**ness** *n*

laser /'leɪzə(r)/ *n* device for generating, amplifying and concentrating light waves into an intense beam in one specific direction: (attrib) ~ *beams.*

lash[1] /læʃ/ *n* **1** part of a whip with which strokes are given; (usu leather) thong; blow or stroke given with a ~: *He was given twenty ~es.* **the ~,** punishment of flogging: *mutinous sailors sentenced to the ~;* (fig) *the ~ of criticism; the ~ of an angry woman's tongue.* **2** = eyelash.

lash[2] /læʃ/ *vt, vi* **1** [VP6A,14,2C] strike violently; make a sudden movement of (a limb, etc): *The rain was ~ing (against) the windows. The tiger ~ed its tail angrily. He ~ed his faint-hearted men with his whip.* **2** ~ *sb into (a state),* rouse into: *The speaker ~ed his listeners into a fury.* ~ *out (against/at sb/sth),* attack violently (with blows or words): *The horse ~ed out at me,* kicked or tried to kick, me. *The speaker ~ed out against the government.* **3** [VP15A,B] ~ *one thing to another;* ~ *things together,* fasten tightly together (with rope, etc). ~ *sth down,* make it secure with rope, etc. '~-**up** *n* improvised or roughly constructed piece of apparatus.

lash·ing /'læʃɪŋ/ *n* **1** [C] cord or rope used for binding or fastening. **2** [C] whipping or beating. **3** (*pl,* colloq) plenty: *strawberries with ~s of cream; ~s of drink/~s to drink.*

lass /læs/ *n* girl; sweetheart.

las·sie /'læsɪ/ *n* = lass.

lassi·tude /'læsɪtjuːd *US:* -tuːd/ *n* [U] tiredness; state of being uninterested in things.

lasso /læ'suː/ *n* (*pl* ~s, ~es /-'suːz/) long rope with a slip-knot, used for catching horses and cattle, esp in America. □ *vt* catch with a ~.

last[1] /lɑːst *US:* læst/ *adj* **1** (contrasted with *first.* ⇨ **late**[1].) coming after all others in time or order: *the ~ month of the year; the ~ Sunday in June; the ~ time I saw you; the ~ letters of the alphabet,* ie XYZ; *the two ~/the ~ two persons to arrive; a ~-minute appeal,* one made just before sth is to be done, decided, etc. ~ *but not least,* coming at the end, but not least in importance. *be on one's ~ legs,* ⇨ **leg**(2). *the L~ Day,* ⇨ **Doomsday** at **doom**[1]. *the ~ post,* ⇨ **post**[2]. *the ~ straw,* ⇨ **straw**. *have the ~ word,* ⇨ **word**. **2** (contrasted with *next*) coming immediately before the present:

CAMEL
Hc 167cm

hump

BISON
Hc 189cm

LLAMA
Hc 189cm

KANGAROO
Lc 152cm

ELEPHANT
Hc 350cm

HYENA
Hc 67cm

tusk — trunk

WILDEBEEST
or GNU
Hc 152cm

tine

horn

antlers

RHINOCEROS
Hc 167cm

REINDEER
Hc 167cm

GIRAFFE
Hc 548cm

ZEBRA
Hc 152cm

ANTELOPE
Hc 183cm

large wild animals

~ night/week/month/summer/year; on Tuesday ~; ~ May; in May ~; in/for/during the ~ few days/weeks, etc; this day ~ week, a week ago. **3** only remaining: *He had spent his ~ dollar. He would share his ~ crust with a beggar. This is our ~ hope. I wouldn't marry you if you were the ~ person on earth.* **4** least likely, suitable, willing, desirable, etc: *She's the ~ woman I want to sit next to at dinner,* I have no wish whatever to do so. *That's the ~ thing I should expect him to do,* it seems most improbable that he will do it. **5** final; leaving nothing more to be said or done: *I've said my ~ word on this question. This is the ~ thing* (= the newest, the most up-to-date, thing) *in labour-saving devices.* □ *adv* **1** (contrasted with *first*) after all others: *I am to speak ~ at the meeting. The horse I bet on came in ~.* **2** (contrasted with *next*) on the ~ occasion before the present time: *When did you ~ get a letter from her? She was quite well when I saw her ~/when I ~ saw her. When were you ~ in London/in London ~?* □ *n the ~ of,* that which comes at the end of: *These are the ~ of our apples. James* II *was the ~ of the Stuart kings. We shall never hear the ~ of this,* People will always talk about it. *I hope we've seen the ~ of her,* that we shall never see her again. **at** (**long**) ~, in the end; after (much) delay: *At* (*long*) ~ *we reached London. The holidays came at* ~.

to/till the ~, until the end; (liter or rhet) until death: *faithful to the* ~. **breathe one's** ~, (liter) die. ~-**ly** *adv* (in making a list) in the ~ place; finally: *L~ly I must explain that....*
last[2] /lɑːst US: læst/ *vi* [VP2A,B,C] ~ (*out*), **1** continue; endure: *How long will the fine weather ~? Will Jim ~ out in his new job?* **2** be adequate or enough (for): *We have enough food to ~* (*us*) *three days.* ~-**ing** *adj* continuing for a long time: *a ~ing peace.*
last[3] /lɑːst US: læst/ *n* block of wood shaped like a foot for making shoes on. **stick to one's** ~, not try to do things one cannot do well.
latch /lætʃ/ *n* **1** simple fastening for a door or gate, the bar falling into a catch and being lifted by a small lever. **2** small spring lock for a door opened from outside with a ~**key. on the** ~, fastened with a ~, but not locked. '~**key,** key for releasing or turning back a ~. '~**key child,** (colloq) one left

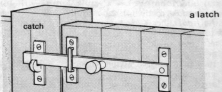

a latch

catch

to look after himself because both parents go out to work. □ *vt,vi* **1** [VP6A,2A] fasten with a ~: *L~ the doors. This door won't ~ properly.* **2** [VP2C,3A] ~ **on (to),** (colloq) cling to; get possession of; understand.

late¹ /leɪt/ (-r, -st. ⇨ last¹, latter.) *adj* **1** (contrasted with *early*) after the right, fixed or usual time: *Am I ~? Don't be ~ for work. The train was ten minutes ~. The crops are ~ this year.* **2** far on in the day or night, in time, in a period or season: *at a ~ hour; in the ~ afternoon; in ~ summer,* eg in Sept; *in the ~ eighties,* eg of the 19th c, in the years just before 1890; ~ *Latin,* between classical Latin and the Latin of the Middle Ages; *keep ~ hours,* ie much after the usual times. *The ~ edition of this paper appears at 3pm; there's a later one at 5pm; the final edition comes out at 7pm.* **3** recent; that recently was: *the ~ political troubles; the ~st news/fashions; the very ~st improvements; Mr Greene's ~st novel,* the most recently published. (Cf *latest* and *last: Mr Greene has said that his ~st novel will be his last,* that he will write no more novels.) **4** former, recent (and still living): *the ~ prime minister.* **5** former, recent (and not now living): *her ~ husband; the ~ King.* **6** *of ~,* recently. *at (the) ~st,* before or not later than: *Be here on Monday at (the) latest.*

late² /leɪt/ *adv* **1** (contrasted with *early*) after the usual, right, fixed or expected time: *get up/go to bed/arrive home ~; marry ~ in life,* eg at the age of 50; *two years ~r; sit/stay up ~,* not go to bed until a ~ hour. *Better ~ than never.* ~ *in the day,* ~er than desired or expected. *~r on,* at a ~r time; afterwards: *a few days ~r on; as we shall see ~r on.* **early and ~,** at all hours: *He's at his desk early and ~.* **sooner or ~r,** some time or other. **2** recently: *I saw him as ~ as/no ~r than yesterday.* **lat·ish** /'leɪtɪʃ/ *adj* rather ~.

la·teen /lə'tiːn/ *adj* (naut) (only in) ~ **sail,** triangular sail on a long yard at an angle of 45° to the mast.

late·ly /'leɪtlɪ/ *adv* (usu in neg and interr sentences, or with *only,* or in *as ~ as*) in recent times; recently: *Have you seen Sam ~? I haven't been home ~.* (Cf in the affirm: *I saw Sam a few days ago. I was home not long ago.*) *I saw her as ~ as last Sunday. It is only ~ that she has been well enough to go out.*

latent /'leɪtnt/ *adj* present but not yet active, developed or visible: ~ *bacteria;* ~ *energy; the ~ image on a photographic film,* not visible until the film is developed; ~ *abilities.*

lat·eral /'lætərəl/ *adj* of, at, from, to, the side(s): *Pinch out the ~ buds to get large chrysanthemum blooms.*

lat·erite /'lætərait/ *n* [U] kind of red soil much used for road-making in the tropics.

latex /'leɪteks/ *n* [U] milk-white liquid of (esp rubber) plants; emulsion of rubber globules used in paints, etc.

lath /lɑːθ *US:* læθ/ *n* (*pl* ~s /lɑːðz *US:* /læðz/) long, thin strip of wood, esp as used in plaster walls and ceilings, and for making trellises, Venetian blinds.

lathe /leɪð/ *n* machine for holding and turning pieces of wood or metal while they are being shaped, etc.

lather /'lɑːðə(r) *US:* 'læð-/ *n* [U] **1** soft mass of white froth from soap and water (as made on a man's face before shaving). **2** frothy sweat on a

horse. □ *vt,vi* **1** [VP6A] make ~ on: ~ *one's chin before shaving. The horse was badly ~ed.* **2** [VP2A] form ~: *Soap does not ~ in sea-water.* **3** [VP6A] (colloq) whip or beat.

lathi /'lɑːtɪ/ *n* long, iron-bound stick used as a weapon (by the police) in India.

Latin /'lætɪn *US:* 'lætn/ *n* language of ancient Rome. □ *adj* of the ~ language; of peoples speaking languages descended from ~ (in Italy, France, Spain, Portugal, etc). ~ **America,** countries of S and Central America in which Spanish and Portuguese are spoken. **the ~ Church,** the RC Church. ~ **cross,** ⇨ the illus at cross. **the '~ Quarter,** (in Paris) area on the south bank of the Seine, a centre for students and artists for many centuries. ~**·ist** /-ɪst/ *n* ~ scholar. ~**·ize** /-aɪz/ *vt* give a ~ form to (a word); put (sth) into ~.

lati·tude /'lætɪtjuːd *US:* -tuːd/ *n* **1** [U] distance north or south of the equator measured in degrees. ⇨ the illus at projection. **2** (*pl*) regions or districts: *high/low ~s,* places a long way from/near to the equator; *warm ~s.* **3** [U] (measure of) freedom in action or opinion: *Does your government allow much ~ in political belief,* allow people to hold widely different political beliefs? **4** (photo) time limits within which a film may safely be under- or over-exposed. **lati·tudi·nal** /ˌlætɪ'tjuːdɪnl *US:* -'tuːdənl/ *adj* **lati·tudi·nar·ian** /ˌlætɪtjuːdɪ'neərɪən *US:* -ˌtuːdn'eər-/ *adj, n* (person who is) tolerant, broad-minded (esp in religious beliefs and dogmas).

la·trine /lə'triːn/ *n* (in places where there are no sewers, eg camps) pit or trench to receive human urine and excrement.

lat·ter /'lætə(r)/ *adj* **1** recent; belonging to the end (of a period): *the ~ half of the year.* ~**-'day** *adj* modern. **2** (also as *pron*) **the ~,** (contrasted with **the former**) the second of two things or persons already mentioned: *Of these two men the former is dead, but the ~ is still alive.* ~**·ly** *adv* of late; nowadays.

lat·tice /'lætɪs/ *n* framework of crossed laths or metal strips as a screen, fence or door, or for climbing plants to grow over: (attrib) *a ~ frame/ girder/pylon,* made with iron or steel ~-work. ~ **window,** one with small square- or diamond-shaped pieces of glass in a framework of lead. ⇨ the illus at window. ~**d** /'lætɪst/ *adj* made in the form of a ~; provided with a ~.

laud /lɔːd/ *vt* [VP6A] (formal) praise; glorify. ~**able** /-əbl/ *adj* deserving praise. ~**·ably** /-əblɪ/ *adv*

lauda·num /'lɔːdənəm/ *n* [U] opium prepared for use as a sedative.

lauda·tory /'lɔːdətərɪ *US:* -tɔːrɪ/ *adj* (formal) expressing or giving praise.

laugh /lɑːf *US:* læf/ *vi,vt* **1** [VP2A,B,C,3A] make sounds and movements of the face and body,

a lathe

showing amusement, joy, contempt, etc: *The jokes made everyone* ~. ~ *at,* (a) be amused by: ~ *at a joke/a funny story.* (b) make fun of; ridicule: *It's unkind to* ~ *at a person who is in trouble.* (c) disregard; treat with indifference: ~ *at difficulties.* ~ **in sb's face,** defy openly, show contempt for. ~ **one's 'head off,** ~ heartily. ~ **on the other side of one's face,** change from joy or triumph to sorrow or regret. ~ **over,** ~ while discussing, examining, etc: ~ *over a letter.* ~ **up one's sleeve,** be secretly amused. *He* ~*s best who* ~*s last; He who* ~*s last* ~*s longest,* (prov) warning against expressing triumph too soon. 2 [VP15B] ~ **away,** dismiss (a subject) by ~ing: ~ *away sb's fears or doubts,* suggest, by ~ing, that they are without real cause. ~ **down,** silence by ~ing scornfully; reject by ~ing: *They* ~*ed the speaker/the proposal down.* ~ **off,** escape from, get rid of, by ~ing: ~ *off an embarrassing situation.* 3 [VP22,15A] arrive at a state, obtain a result, by ~ing: ~ *oneself silly/helpless;* ~ *oneself into convulsions;* ~ *a person out of his depression/out of a foolish belief.* ~ **sb/sth out of court,** dismiss him/it completely by ridicule. 4 [VP6B] express with or by means of a ~: *He* ~*ed his denial.* □ *n* [C] sound made in ~ing; act of ~ing: *We've had a good many* ~*s over his foolishness. They all joined in the* ~. *"Oh, yes", she answered with a* ~. **have/get the** ~ **of sb,** score off him. ⇨ score²(4). **have the last** ~, get one's satisfaction. '**belly-**~, ⇨ belly¹(1). ~-**able** /-əbl/ *adj* amusing; causing persons to ~: *a* ~*able mistake.* ~-**ably** /-əblɪ/ *adv* ~-**ing** *adj* showing happiness, amusement, etc: ~*ing faces.* '~-**ing-gas** *n* nitrous oxide (N₂O) used in dental surgery. '~-**ing-stock** *n* ⇨ stock¹(7). ~-**ing-ly** *adv*

laugh-ter /'lɑːftə(r)/ *US:* 'læf-/ *n* [U] laughing: *burst into* ~; *roar with* ~; *an outburst of* ~.

launch¹ /lɔːntʃ/ *vt,vi* 1 [VP6A] set (a ship, esp one newly built) afloat: ~ *a new passenger liner.* 2 [VP6A,15A] ~ **sth (against/at),** set in motion; send; aim: ~ *an attack;* ~ *threats at an opponent;* ~ *a missile/spacecraft into outer space.* '~-**ing-pad** *n* base or platform from which spacecraft, etc are ~ed. '~-**ing-site** *n* place for ~ing-pads. ⇨ the illus at rocket. 3 [VP6A,15A] (fig) get started; set going: ~ *a new business enterprise;* ~ *a man into business.* 4 [VP2C,3A] ~ **out;** ~ **(out) into,** make or start (on): ~ *out into a new argument/debate;* ~ *into a new subject;* ~ *out into extravagance.* □ *n* act of ~ing (a ship or spacecraft).

launch² /lɔːntʃ/ *n* mechanically propelled passenger-carrying boat (on rivers and lakes, in harbours).

launder /'lɔːndə(r)/ *vt,vi* [VP6A,2A] wash and press (clothes): *Send these sheets to be* ~*ed. Will these shirts* ~ *well?*

laun-der-ette /lɔːn'dret/ *n* laundry at which members of the public may launder their clothes, etc in coin-operated automatic washing-machines and dryers.

laun-dress /'lɔːndrɪs/ *n* woman who earns money by washing and ironing clothes.

laun-dry /'lɔːndrɪ/ *n* (*pl* -dries) 1 [C] laundering business; place where clothes, sheets, etc, are sent to be laundered. 2 the ~, clothes (to be) laundered: *Has the* ~ *come back yet?* '~-**man** /-mæn/ *n* (*pl*-men) man who collects and delivers ~.

laur-eate /'lɔːrɪət *US:* 'lɒːr-/ *adj* crowned with a laurel wreath. *n* the (,Poet) 'L~, poet officially ap-

pointed to the Royal Household in GB. The holder may write poems on great national occasions.

laurel /'lɒrəl *US:* 'lɔːrəl/ *n* evergreen shrub with smooth, shiny leaves, used by ancient Romans and Greeks as an emblem of victory, success and distinction. **look to one's** ~**s,** beware of losing one's reputation; be on the look-out for possible successes among rivals. **rest on one's** ~**s,** be content with one's successes and rest. **win/gain one's** ~**s,** win reputation, honour. ~-**led** *adj* crowned with ~.

lav /læv/ *n* (colloq abbr of) lavatory.

lava /'lɑːvə/ *n* [U] hot liquid material flowing from a volcano: *a stream of* ~; this material when it has cooled and hardened: '~ *beds.* ⇨ pumice.

lava-tory /'lævətrɪ *US:* -tɔːrɪ/ *n* (*pl*-ries) [C] room for washing the hands and face in; water-closet.

lave /leɪv/ *vt* (poet) wash; bathe; (of a stream) flow gently past or against.

lav-en-der /'lævəndə(r)/ *n* [U] plant with pale purple sweet-scented flowers; the dried flowers and stalks (sewn up in bags and placed among linen sheets, etc); the colour of ~. '~ **water** *n* [U] perfume distilled from ~.

lav-ish /'lævɪʃ/ *adj* 1 ~ (**of sth/in doing sth**), giving or producing freely, liberally or generously: *He is never* ~ *of praise/in giving money to charity.* 2 (of what is given) given abundantly; excessive: ~ *praise/expenditure on luxuries.* □ *vt* [VP14] ~ **on,** give abundantly and generously to: ~ *care on an only child.* ~-**ly** *adv*

law /lɔː/ *n* 1 [C] rule made by authority for the proper regulation of a community or society or for correct conduct in life: *When a Bill is passed by Parliament and signed by the Sovereign, it becomes a law.* '**law-giver** *n* man who gives a code of laws (eg Moses in Hebrew history, Solon in Greek history). '**law-officer** *n* (esp) Attorney or Solicitor-General. ⇨ regulation, statute. 2 [U] **the law,** the whole body of laws considered collectively: *If a man fails to observe the law he can be punished. Does the law allow me to do this?* **break the law,** fail to observe it. **lay down the law,** talk authoritatively, as if one were certain of being right. '**law-abiding** *adj* obeying the law. '**law-breaker** *n* person who disobeys the law. 3 [U] controlling influence of the laws: *maintain law and order,* see that the laws are respected. *Necessity knows no law,* When sth cannot be avoided, ordinary laws and rules will be ignored or broken. 4 [U] the laws as a system or science; the legal profession: *study law; law students; read law,* study in order to become a lawyer. ⇨ jurisprudence. 5 [U] (with a defining word) one of the branches of the study of law: *commercial law; the law of nations; international law.* 6 [U] operation of the law (as providing a remedy for wrongs). **go to law (against sb); have the law on sb,** (colloq) appeal to the law courts. **take the law into one's own hands,** use force to redress a wrong. '**law court** *n* court of justice. '**law suit** *n* prosecution of a claim in a law court. 7 [C] rule of action or procedure, esp in the arts or a game: *the laws of perspective/harmony; the laws of cricket.* **be a law unto oneself,** disregard rules and conventions; do what one thinks right. 8 [U,C] (also **law of nature** or **natural law**) factual statement of what always happens in certain circumstances; regularity in nature, eg the order of the seasons: *Newton's law; the laws of motion; the law of* *supply and demand; the law of self-preservation,* the instinct of men and animals to behave in a way that will save them from danger. **law·ful** /-fl/ *adj* **1** allowed by law; according to law: *lawful acts; the lawful ruler.* **2** (of offspring) legitimate: *the lawful heir.* **law·fully** /-fəlɪ/ *adv* **law·less** *adj* **1** not in accordance with the law; not conforming to the law; not restrained by law; unruly: *lawless acts; lawless tribes.* **law·less·ly** *adv* **law·less·ness** *n* [U].

lawn¹ /lɔːn/ *n* [C] area of grass (turf) kept closely cut and smooth, eg in a private garden or a public park; such an area of grass used for a game: *a* '*croquet* ∼; *a* '*tennis* ∼. '∼-**mower** *n* machine for cutting grass on ∼s. ∼ '**tennis** *n* [U] the game of tennis played on an unwalled court, either hard surfaced or turfed. ⇨ the illus at tennis.

lawn² /lɔːn/ *n* [U] kind of fine linen used for dresses, blouses and esp for a bishop's sleeves.

law·yer /'lɔːjə(r)/ *n* person who practises law, esp a barrister or solicitor.

lax /læks/ *adj* **1** negligent; inattentive; not strict or severe: *lax discipline/behaviour; lax in morals.* **2** (of the bowels) free in action. **lax·ity** /'læksətɪ/ *n* [U] being lax; [C] (*pl* -ties) instance of being lax. **lax·ly** *adv*

laxa·tive /'læksətɪv/ *n, adj* (medicine, drug) causing the bowels to empty.

lay¹ /leɪ/ *vt,vi* (*pt,pp* laid /leɪd/) For uses with *adverbial particles* and *preps* ⇨ 12 below. **1** [VP6A,15A] put on a surface; put in a certain position, in the proper place for a purpose: *Who will lay the carpet,* spread it out, fasten it down, etc? *He laid his hand on my shoulder. A new submarine cable was laid between England and Holland. The woodcutter laid his axe to the tree,* began to chop. *A bricklayer is a man who lays bricks.* **lay a snare/trap/an ambush (for sb/sth),** prepare one. **2** [VP6A,15B] (of non-material things, and fig uses) place; put. **lay (one's) hands on sth/sb,** (a) seize; get possession of: *He keeps everything he can lay (his) hands on.* (b) do violence to: *How dare you lay hands on me? He laid violent hands on himself,* (dated) tried to commit suicide. (c) find: *I have the book somewhere, but can't lay my hands on it just now.* (d) (eccles) confirm; ordain; consecrate. Hence, **laying-on of hands,** confirmation; ordination; consecration. **lay the blame (for sth) on sb,** say that he is responsible for what is wrong, etc. **lay a (heavy) burden on sb,** cause sb to be responsible for sth likely to be difficult, to cause suffering, etc. **lay one's hopes on,** = pin (the more usu word) one's hopes on. **lay a strict injunction on sb (to do sth),** give him strict orders (to do it). **lay great/little store by/on sth,** value very much/little. **lay stress/emphasis/ weight on sth,** treat it as important; emphasize it. **lay a tax on sth,** impose one. **3** [VP15A] cause to be in a certain state, condition, or situation. **lay sb to rest,** (esp) bury sb: *He was laid to rest in the churchyard.* **lay sb under a/the necessity/ obligation,** make it necessary or obligatory for him (to do sth): *Your conduct lays me under the necessity of dismissing you. He was laid under an obligation to support the wife he had deserted.* **lay sb under contribution,** compel him to contribute money, etc. **lay sth to sb's charge,** hold him responsible. **lay claim to sth,** ⇨ claim. **lay sth at sb's door,** ⇨ door. **lay one's finger on,** ⇨ finger. **lay siege to,** ⇨ siege. **4** [VP22] (*lay* + *n, adj* or *adv phrases*) cause to be in a specified condi-

tion. **lay sth bare,** show; reveal: *lay bare one's heart,* reveal one's inmost feelings, etc. **lay sth flat,** cause to be flat: *crops laid flat by heavy rainstorms.* **lay sth open,** (a) expose, reveal: *lay open a plot.* (b) cut, gash: *lay open one's cheek,* eg by falling and striking it against a rock. **lay oneself open to sth,** render oneself liable to criticism, calumny, etc. **lay sth waste,** ravage, destroy: *a countryside laid waste by invading armies.* **5** [VP6A] cause to be down, settle: *sprinkle water on the roads to lay the dust.* **lay sb's doubts,** get rid of them, ⇨ allay, the more usu word. **lay a ghost/spirit,** expel or exorcize it; cause it to stop appearing to people. **6** [VP6A,2A] (of birds and insects) produce (eggs): *Are your hens laying yet? How many eggs does this hen lay each week? New laid eggs, 5p each.* **7** [VP15A] (usu passive) set (a story, etc) in time and place: *The scene is laid in Athens, in the third century,* BC. **8** [VP6A] place or arrange by laying (ready for use, etc): *lay the table (for breakfast),* put out plates, knives, etc; *lay the cloth,* spread it on the table ready for a meal; *lay a fire,* put wood, coal, etc in a fireplace, ready for lighting. **9** [VP6A,12C,14] put down (a sum of money) as a wager or stake (on sth of which the result is uncertain); offer as a bet: *They laid a wager on the result of the race. I'll lay you £5 that he won't come. I'll lay (= make) you a bet that....* **10** [VP6A,15A] cover; coat: *Lay carpet on the floor/ lay the floor with carpet; lay straw over the yard/ lay the yard with straw; lay colours on canvas.* ⇨ *lay on* at 12 below. **11** [VP6A] (sl) have sexual intercourse with. **12** [VP2C,B] (uses with *adverbial particles* and *preps*):

lay about one (with sth), hit out in all directions: *When they rushed at him, Harry laid about him with his big stick.*

lay sth aside, (a) save; keep for future use: *lay aside money for one's old age.* (b) put down: *He laid his book aside to listen to me.* (c) abandon; give up: *lay aside bad habits.*

lay sth back, turn back: *The horse laid back its ears.*

lay sth by, = lay sth aside(a).

lay sb/oneself down, place in a lying or recumbent position: *Lay the baby down gently. She laid herself down.* **lay sth down,** (a) pay or wager: *How much are you ready to lay down?* (b) (begin to) build: *lay down a new ship.* (c) convert (land) to pasture: *lay down land in/to/with/under grass.* (d) store (wine) in a cellar: *lay down claret and port.* **lay sth down; lay it down that...,** establish: *You can't lay down hard and fast rules. It was laid down that all applicants should sit a written examination. These prices have been laid down by the manufacturers.* **lay down one's arms,** put one's weapons down as a sign of surrender. **lay down the law,** say with (or as if with) authority what must be done. **lay down one's life,** sacrifice it: *He laid down his life for his country.* **lay down office,** resign a position of authority.

lay sth in, provide oneself with a stock of: *lay in provisions/stores.*

lay off, (colloq) (a) discontinue work or activity; rest: *The doctor told me to lay off for a week.* (b) stop doing sth which irritates or annoys: *I hear you've been pestering my sister again—Well, you can just lay off.* **lay sb off,** dismiss temporarily: *lay off workmen,* eg because of a shortage of materials. Hence, '**lay-off** *n* period during which men are temporarily dismissed.

lay sth on, (a) supply gas, water, electricity to a building: *We can't occupy the new house until gas and water are laid on.* **(b)** (colloq) provide: *Sightseeing tours were laid on for the distinguished visitors from Poland.* **lay it on (thick/with a trowel),** use exaggerated praise, flattery, etc: *To call him a genius is laying it on a bit too thick!*

lay sth out, (a) spread out ready for use or so as to be seen easily: *lay out one's evening clothes; the magnificent scene that was laid out before the climbers when they reached the summit.* **(b)** prepare for burial: *lay out a corpse.* **(c)** spend (money): *lay out one's money carefully.* **(d)** make a plan for; arrange: *well laid-out streets and avenues; lay out a printed page.* Hence, **'lay-out** *n* arrangement, plan, design of a printed page, an advertisement, a book, a group of buildings. **lay oneself out (to do sth),** exert oneself, take pains: *She laid herself out to make her guests comfortable.*

lay over, (US) (GB = stop over) stop at a place during a journey because of a requirement in a schedule. **'lay-over** *n* such a stop.

lay sth up, (a) save; store: *lay up provisions.* **(b)** ensure by what one does or fails to do that one will have trouble, etc in future: *You're only laying up trouble for yourself.* **(c)** put (a ship) out of commission: *lay a ship up for repairs.* **lay sb up,** (usu passive) force sb to stay in bed: *He's laid up with a broken leg. The flu has laid him up for a few days.*

lay² /leɪ/ *n* (chiefly in) **the lay of the land** (*lie* is more usu), the nature or formation of an area of land.

lay³ /leɪ/ *n* (sl) partner in sexual intercourse. ⇨ lay¹(11).

lay⁴ /leɪ/ *n* (liter) minstrel's song; ballad.

lay⁵ /leɪ/ *pt* of lie².

lay⁶ /leɪ/ *adj* (attrib only) **1** of, for, done by, persons who are not priests: *a lay brother/sister,* one who wears the dress and has taken the vows of a religious order, but who does manual work and is excused other duties. ⇨ laity. **2** non-professional; not expert (esp with reference to the law and medicine): *lay opinion,* what non-professional people think. *To the lay mind the language of a lawyer seems to be full of jargon.* **'lay-man** /-mən/ *n* (*pl* -men*) lay(2) person: *Where the law is concerned I am only a layman,* I have no expert knowledge.

lay-about /'leɪəbaʊt/ *n* (GB sl) loafer; person who avoids working for a living.

lay-by /'leɪbaɪ/ *n* (GB) area at the side of a road where vehicles may park without hindering the flow of traffic.

layer /'leɪə(r)/ *n* [C] **1** thickness of material (esp one of several) laid or lying on or spread over a surface, or forming one horizontal division: *a ~ of clay.* **'~-cake,** one with horizontal divisions separated by cream, jam, etc. **2** (gardening) shoot of a plant fastened down to take root while still growing from the parent plant. **3** (of hens) *good/bad ~s,* hens that lay eggs in large/small numbers. □ *vt* [VP6A] fasten down (a shoot of a plant): *~ carnations.*

lay-ette /leɪ'et/ *n* garments, blankets, etc for a new-born baby.

lay fig-ure /ˌleɪ 'fɪgə(r)/ *n* jointed wooden figure of the human body (used by artists for arranging drapery, etc); (fig) dummy.

lay-man ⇨ lay⁶.

lazar /'læzə(r)/ *n* (archaic) poor and diseased person, esp a leper.

laza-retto /ˌlæzə'retəʊ/ (*pl* ~s /-təʊz/) (also **laza-ret, laza-rette** /ˌlæzə'ret/) *n* quarantine station; ship's storeroom.

Laz-arus /'læzərəs/ *n* beggar; (in contrasts) very poor man: *~ and Dives.* ⇨ Luke 16:19.

laze /leɪz/ *vi,vt* [VP2A,C,15B] *~ (away),* be lazy; pass (time) in idleness: *~ all day; lazing away the afternoon.*

lazy /'leɪzɪ/ *adj* (-ier, -iest) unwilling to work; doing little work; suitable for, causing, inducing, inactivity: *a ~ fellow; a ~ afternoon.* ⇨ idle. **'~-bones** *n ~* person. **lazi-ly** *adv* **lazi-ness** *n*

lea /liː/ *n* (poet) stretch of open grass land.

leach /liːtʃ/ *vt* **1** [VP6A] cause (a liquid) to percolate through some material. **2** [VP15B] *~ out/away,* purge (a soluble matter) away or out by the action of a percolating fluid: *the ~ing of the soil,* the washing away, eg by heavy rainfall, of elements in it necessary for plant growth.

lead¹ /led/ *n* **1** [U] soft, heavy, easily melted metal (symbol **Pb**) of a dull bluish-grey colour used for water- and gas-pipes, as a roofing material, and in numerous alloys. **'~-ore** *n* [U] rock containing ~. **~ 'poisoning** *n* diseased condition caused by taking ~ into the system. **~ shot,** ⇨ shot¹(4). **'~ works** *n sing.* place where ~-ore is smelted. **2** [U] (also **'black** ~) graphite; stick of graphite as used in a ~-pencil. **3** [C] lump of ~ fastened to a line marked in fathoms for measuring the depth of the sea from ships. **cast/heave the ~,** take soundings. **swing the ~,** (sl) evade one's proper share of work by pretending to be ill, using tricks, etc. **4** (*pl*) strips of ~ used to cover a roof; area of (esp horizontal) ~-covered roof; ~ frames for glass, eg in a lattice window. **~ed** /'ledɪd/ *adj* secured with strips of ~: *~ed windows.* **~ed light,** ⇨ light³(9). **~en** /'ledn/ *adj* **1** made of ~: *a ~en coffin.* **2** having the colour or appearance of ~: *~en clouds.* **3** dull and heavy like ~: *~en sleep; a ~en heart.* **~-ing** /'ledɪŋ/ *n* [U] space between lines of print.

lead² /liːd/ *n* **1** [U,C] (*sing* only) action of guiding or giving an example; direction given by going in front; sth that helps or hints. **follow sb's ~,** follow his example. **give sb a ~,** encourage him by doing sth first, or by giving a hint towards the solution of a problem. **take the ~,** take the leading place, give an example. **2 the ~,** first place or position: *have/gain the ~ in a race;* (attrib) *the ~ story,* (journalism, news broadcasting) item of news given the greatest prominence. **a ~,** distance by which one leads: *have a ~ of ten feet.* **take over/lose the ~,** move to the front/fall behind in a race, in business, etc. **3** [C] cord, leather strap, for leading a dog: *Keep your dog on the ~ in these busy streets.* **4** [C] principal part in a play; actor or actress who plays such a part: *the juvenile ~,* eg the actor who plays the part of the handsome young hero. **5** [C] artificial watercourse leading to a mill; channel of open water in an ice-field. **6** [C] (electr) conductor conveying current from a source to the place where it is used. **7** [C] (in card games) act or right of playing first: *Whose ~ is it?*

lead³ /liːd/ *vt,vi* (*pt,pp* led /led/) **1** [VP6A,15A,B] guide or take, esp by going in front: *Our guide led us through a series of caves. The secretary led the visitors in/out/back.* **~ the way (to),** go first; show the way. **'~-in** *n* (a) preliminary remarks, introduction (to). **(b)** wire joining an aerial to a wireless receiver or television set. **2** [VP6A,15A,B] conduct (sb) by the hand, by touching him, or by a rope, etc: ~ *a blind man;* ~ *a horse,* by holding the halter and walking at its head. ~ *sb astray,* (fig) tempt him to do sth wrong. ~ *sb by the nose,* control him completely; make him do everything one wishes him to do. ~ *sb on,* (fig) entice sb to do more than he intended. ~ *a woman to the altar,* (joc) marry her. **3** [VP6A,2A] act as chief; direct by example or persuasion; direct the movements of: ~ *an army/an expedition/a mutiny;* ~ *the Conservative Party;* ~ *the fashion;* ~ *the choir/the singing. Who's going to* ~? **4** [VP6A,2A,C] have the first place in; go first: *A brass band led the regiment. Which horse is* ~*ing?* eg in a race. ~ *off,* start. *Who's going to* ~ *off? He led off by saying that....* **5** [VP6A,17,14] ~ *(to),* guide the actions and opinions of; influence; persuade: *What led you to this conclusion? He is easier led than driven. I am led to believe* (= Certain facts, etc cause me to believe) *that he is disloyal to us. What led you to think so?* **6** [VP2C] be a path, way or road to; (fig) have as a result: *Where does this road* ~? *Your work seems to be* ~*ing nowhere,* getting no result. *This led to great confusion.* ~ *up to,* be a preparation for or an introduction to; direct the conversation towards: *That's just what I was* ~*ing up to. Chapter One describes the events that led up to the war.* **All roads** ~ **to Rome,** (fig) There are many ways of reaching the same result. **7** [VP6A,12C] (cause sb to) pass, go through; spend (life, etc): ~ *a miserable existence;* ~ *a double life/a Jekyll and Hyde existence.* ~ *sb a (pretty) dance,* ⇨ dance¹(1). ~ *sb a* '*dog's life,* make his life wretched. **8** [VP6A,2A] (in card games) put down, as first player (a certain card or kind of card): ~ *the two of clubs;* ~ *trumps.* **9** [VP3A] ~ *with,* (journalism) have as the main article or news story: *We'll* ~ *with the dock strike.*

leader /'li:də(r)/ *n* **1** person who leads: *the* ~ *of an army/an expedition/the Labour Party; the* ~ *of the choir; the* ~ *of an orchestra* (usu the first violinist). **2** principal counsel in a law court case: *the* ~ *for the defence.* **3** (GB) leading article (in a newspaper). ⇨ leading below. **4** shoot growing at the end of a stem or principal branch. **5** tendon or sinew. ~·less *adj* '~·ship /-ʃɪp/ *n* [U] being a ~; power of leading; the qualities of a ~.

lead·ing /'li:dɪŋ/ *adj* chief; most important: *the* ~ *men of the day; the* ~ *topics of the hour,* those now being discussed; *the* ~ *lady,* the actress with the chief part in a play; *L*~ *Aircraftman,* non-commissioned rank in the RAF. ~ '*article,* (in a newspaper) one giving editorial opinions on events, policies, etc. ~ '*case,* (legal) one that establishes a precedent. ~ '*light,* (colloq) prominent person. ~ '*question,* one that suggests the answer that is hoped for. ◻ *n* act of leading. '~-rein *n* for ~ a horse. '~-strings *n pl* straps, etc with which babies were formerly taught to walk: *in* ~*-strings,* (fig) guided and controlled like a young child.

leaf /li:f/ *n* (*pl* leaves /li:vz/) **1** one of the parts (usu green and flat) growing from the side of a stem or branch or direct from the root of a tree, bush, plant, etc (collectively called *foliage*): *sweep up dead leaves in autumn;* (colloq) petal (as in *rose-leaves*). ⇨ the illus at **flower, tree.** *in* ~, with the leaves grown: *The trees will soon be in* ~. *come into* ~, grow leaves: *The trees come into* ~ *in spring.* '~-bud *n* one from which leaves, not

flowers, develop. '~-mould *n* [U] soil composed chiefly of decaying leaves. **2** single sheet of paper forming two pages of a book. *take a* ~ *out of sb's book,* take him as a model. *turn over a new* ~, make a new and better start. **3** hinged or loose part of an extending table (used to make the table larger). **4** [U] very thin sheet of metal, esp of gold or silver: *gold* ~. ◻ *vi* ~ *through (a book, etc),* turn over the pages quickly; glance through. ~·less *adj* having no leaves. ~·y *adj* (-ier, -iest) covered with leaves; having leaves; made by leaves: *a* ~*y shade.*

leaf·let /'li:flɪt/ *n* **1** young leaf. **2** printed sheet (unbound but sometimes folded) with announcements, etc esp one for free distribution.

league¹ /li:g/ *n* (old) measure of distance (about three miles or 4·8 kms).

league² /li:g/ *n* [C] **1** agreement made between persons, groups or nations for their common welfare, eg to work for peace; the parties that make such an agreement. **the L**~ **of Nations,** that formed in 1919 after the First World War, with headquarters at Geneva, dissolved in 1946. ⇨ **United Nations.** *in* ~ *with,* allied with; having made an agreement with. **2** group of sports clubs or teams playing matches among themselves: ~ *football matches.* ◻ *vt,vi* [VP6A,15A,B,2C] form into, become, a ~: *countries that are* ~*d together.*

leak /li:k/ *n* **1** hole, crack, etc caused by wear, injury, etc through which a liquid, gas, etc may wrongly get in or out: *a* ~ *in the roof,* allowing rain to enter; *a* ~ *in the gas-pipe,* allowing gas to escape; (fig) *a* ~ *of information; an inspired* ~, of news that is deliberately disclosed. *spring a leak,* ⇨ spring³(6). **2** the liquid, gas, etc that gets out or in. ◻ *vi,vt* **1** [VP2A,C] (allow to) pass out or in through a ~: *The rain is* ~*ing in. The ship was* ~*ing badly.* **2** [VP2A,6A,14] ~ *(out) (to),* (of news, secrets, etc) (cause to) become known by chance or with authority: *The news has* ~*ed out. Who* ~*ed the news to the press?* '~-age /-ɪdʒ/ *n* **1** [U] the process of ~ing: ~*age of military secrets.* **2** [C] instance of this; that which ~s in or out; amount that ~s in or out. ~·y *adj* having a ~: *a* ~*y kettle.*

leal /li:l/ *adj* (Scot or liter) loyal.

lean¹ /li:n/ *adj* (-er, -est) **1** (of persons and animals) having less than the usual proportion of fat; (of meat) containing little or no fat. **2** not productive; of poor quality: *a* ~ *harvest;* ~ *years,* years of scarcity. ◻ *n* [U] meat with little or no fat. ~·ness *n*

lean² /li:n/ *vi,vt* (*pt,pp* ~t /lent/ or leaned /li:nd/) **1** [VP2A,C] be or put in a sloping position; ~ *backwards;* ~ *out of a window; trees that* ~ *over in the wind; the L*~*ing Tower of Pisa.* ~ *over backward(s) (to do sth),* (colloq) make a great effort (to please sb, get a result, etc). **2** [VP2C,3A] ~ *(on/upon),* rest in a sloping position for support: ~ *on a table;* ~ *upon one's elbows;* ~ *on sb's arm.* **3** [VP15A] cause to rest against and be supported by: ~ *a ladder against a wall/one's elbows on a table.* **4** [VP3A] ~ *towards,* have a tendency: *Do some oriental philosophies* ~ *towards fatalism?* **5** [VP3A] ~ *on/upon,* depend: ~ *on a friend's advice;* ~ *upon others for guidance.* ~·ing *n* [C] tendency (of mind *towards* sth): *He has pacifist* ~*ings/*~*ings towards pacificism.* '~-to *n* building with the rafters of its roof resting against the side of another building: (attrib) *a* ~*-to green-*

house.

leap /li:p/ *vi,vt* (*pt,pp* leapt /lept/ or leaped /li:pt/) **1** [VP2A,C,3A] jump (*jump* is the usu word; *leap* is used in liter and rhet style): *He ~t at the opportunity,* seized it eagerly. **Look before you ~,** ⇨ look¹(1). **2** [VP6A,15A] (cause to) jump over: *~ a wall; ~ a horse over a fence.* □ *n* [C] jump; sudden upward or forward movement: *a great ~ forward,* (fig) a great advance. **a ~ in the dark,** an attempt to do sth the result of which cannot be foreseen. **by ~s and bounds,** very rapidly. **'~-frog** *n* [U] game in which players jump with parted legs over others who stand with bent backs. □ *vt* (-gg-) jump over in this way. **'~-year** *n* in which February has 29 days.

learn /lɜ:n/ *vt,vi* (*pt,pp* ~t /lɜ:nt/, ~ed /lɜ:nd/) [VP2A,3A,6A,7A,8,9,10,15A,B] **1** gain knowledge of or skill in, by study, practice or being taught: *~ a foreign language; ~ to swim/how to ride a horse. Has he ~t his lessons? Some boys ~ slowly. ~ sth by heart,* memorize it. **2** be told or informed: *I'm sorry to ~ of his illness/that he's ill. We have not yet ~ed whether he arrived safely.* **3** (vulg or dialect sometimes *larn* /lɑ:n/) teach: *I'll ~ you* (= punish you and so teach you how unwise it is) *to come into my orchard and steal apples.* **~ed** /'lɜ:nɪd/ *adj* having or showing much knowledge, esp of the humanities: *the ~ed professions,* those needing much knowledge; *~ed men; ~ed books/periodicals/societies; to look ~ed.* **~ed·ly** *adv* **~er** *n* person who is ~ing; beginner: *He hasn't passed his driving test yet; he's only a ~er.* **~·ing** *n* [U] wide knowledge gained by careful study: *a man of great ~ing.*

lease /li:s/ *n* [C] contract by which the owner of land or a building (*the lessor*) agrees to let another (*the lessee*) have the use of it for a certain time for a fixed money payment (called *rent*); the rights given under such a contract: *take a farm on a ~ of several years. When does the ~ expire?* **by/on ~:** *We took the land on ~.* **give sb/get a new ~ of life,** a better chance of living longer, or of being happier, more active. □ *vt* [VP6A] give, take possession of (land, etc), by ~. **~-'lend** *n* [U] arrangement (1941) by which the President of the US could supply war materials to countries whose defence he considered important. **'~-hold** *n, adj* (land) (to be) held for a term of years on ~. ⇨ *freehold* at free¹(3). **'~-holder** *n* person who holds a ~; lessee.

leash /li:ʃ/ *n* [C] leather strap or thong for holding or controlling an animal (esp a hound): *hold in ~,* (fig) control. **strain at the ~,** (fig) show eagerness to be free, to have an opportunity to do sth.

least /li:st/ *adj, n* (contrasted with *most*; ⇨ less, little) **1** (the) ~, smallest in size, amount, extent, etc: *A has little, B has less, and C has* (*the*) ~. *There isn't the ~ wind today,* no wind at all. *That's the ~ of my anxieties.* **The ~ said the better,** The best thing is silence. **L~ said soonest mended,** (prov) Talking will only make things worse. **2** (phrases) **at ~:** *It will cost at ~ five pounds,* five pounds and perhaps more. *He is at ~ as tall as you. You should at ~ have warned her. You can at ~ try.* **(not) in the ~:** *It doesn't matter in the ~. I don't understand in the ~ what this author is trying to say. 'Would you mind holding this box?' 'Not in the ~.'* I do not mind at all. **.to say the ~ (of it),** without saying more; without exaggeration: *It wasn't a very good dinner, to say*

the ~ of it. □ *adv* (**the**) ~, to the smallest extent: *He works hardest and is being paid ~. This is the ~ useful of the four books.* **~ of all:** *None of you can complain, Charles ~ of all,* Charles has the ~ reason for complaining. *L~ of all would I want to hurt your feelings,* That is sth I would never do. **'~-wise** /-waɪz/, **'~-ways** /-weɪz/ *advv* or at least, or rather.

leather /'leðə(r)/ *n* [U] material made by curing animal skins, used for making shoes, gloves, bags, etc: *~ upholstery, eg for the seats of a car.* **'~-jacket** *n* grub of the crane-fly. **'~-neck** *n* (US, sl) marine. **~y** *adj* like ~: *~y meat,* hard, tough. **~·'ette** /-'ret/ *n* imitation ~.

leave¹ /li:v/ *vt, vi* (*pt,pp* left /left/) **1** [VP6A,2A,3A] go away from: *When did you ~ London? It's time for us to ~/time we left. ~ for,* go away to: *We're leaving for Rome next week.* **2** [VP6A,15A,2A] go away finally or permanently; no longer live (in a place); cease to belong to a school, society, etc; give up working for (an employer, etc): *When did you ~ school? The secretary has threatened to ~. The boy left home and went to sea. He left medicine for the law,* changed from the medical to the legal profession. *My typist has left me,* has resigned. **be/get nicely left,** (colloq) be tricked, deceived or deserted. **3** [VP15A,B] neglect or fail to take, bring or do sth: *I've left my umbrella in the train. I left my books on the table. He left half his work until the next day.* **~ sb/sth behind,** neglect or forget to bring or take: *The luggage has been left behind! Don't ~ me behind!* **4** [VP15A,B,22,19B,2C,24,25] allow or cause to remain in a certain place or condition: *L~ your hat and coat in the hall. Always ~ things where you can find them again. Did you ~ the doors and windows firmly fastened? Who left that window open? His illness has left him weak. Don't ~ her waiting outside in the rain.* **~ sb/sth alone,** not touch, spoil or interfere with: *L~ the cat alone,* Don't tease it. **~ well alone,** (prov) Don't try to improve what is already satisfactory. **~ off,** stop: *Has the rain left off yet? We left off at the end of Chapter Five.* **~ sth off,** (a) stop: *It's time to ~ off work. Do ~ off biting your nails, Jane!* (b) no longer wear: *They left off their woollen underwear when the weather got warm.* **~ sth/sb out,** omit; fail to consider: *~ out a possibility; ~ out a letter,* eg spell *embarrass* with one r instead of two r's. *Don't ~ me out, please!* Don't forget me—I want a share, a place, etc. **~ sth over,** postpone: *That matter can be left over until the committee meets next week.* **~ it at that,** do or say nothing more: *There's nothing we can do; we must ~ it at that.* **~ sb to himself/to his own devices,** not try to control or direct his activities: *The children were left very much to themselves during the holidays,* were allowed to do what they liked, without guidance or help. **~ sth unsaid,** not say it: *Some things are better left unsaid,* It is better to remain silent about them. **~ much/a lot/sth/nothing to be desired,** be (un)satisfactory: *His behaviour ~s a lot/nothing to be desired,* is very unsatisfactory/is quite satisfactory. **~ go/hold (of sth),** (more usu *let go*) cease holding: *L~ go of my hair, you brute!* **5** [VP6A,12B,13B,14] (cause to) remain; allow to remain: *Three from seven ~s four* (7 − 3 = 4). *When I've paid all my debts, there'll be nothing left/I'll have nothing left. Have you left anything for me/left me anything?* **To be left until called**

for, used as a direction for a letter, package, etc which is to be collected. **6** [VP6A,14,12B,13B] hand over before going away: *Did the postman ~ anything for me?* **~ word (with sb) (for sb),** give a message etc: *Please ~ word (for me) with your secretary if you get news of what happened.* **7** [VP16A,14] entrust; commit; hand over: *I'll ~ the matter in your hands/~ it to you/~ you to attend to the matter. He left his assistant in charge of the shop/left the shop in his assistant's charge.* **8** [VP6A,12B,13B,15A,22] **~ sth (to sb); ~ sb sth,** bequeath by will; have at the time of one's death: *She left all her money to charity. He left me £500. He died leaving nothing but debts. He ~s a widow and two sons. He left her poor.* **9** [VP15A] pass beyond (a place, etc) so that it is in the direction or relation indicated: *L~ the church on your left and go on up the hill.*

leave² /li:v/ *n* **1** [U] permission; consent; authority, esp to be absent from duty or work: *You have my ~ to stay away from the office tomorrow.* **~ of absence,** permission to be absent: *The soldier asked for ~ of absence.* **on ~,** absent with permission: *He went home on ~.* **by/with your ~,** with your permission. **(take) French ~,** absence without permission. **2** [C] period of such absence; occasion of being absent from duty, etc: *have only two ~s in six years; a six months' ~.* **3** [U] departure. **take (one's) ~ (of sb),** say goodbye. Hence, '**~-taking** *n.* **take ~ of one's senses,** behave as if mad.

leaven /'levn/ *n* [U] substance, eg yeast, used to make dough rise before it is baked to make bread; (fig) quality or influence spreading in and changing sth. □ *vt* [VP6A] add ~ to: act like ~ upon.

leaves /li:vz/ *pl* of **leaf.**

leav·ings /'li:vɪŋz/ *n pl* what is left, esp sth unwanted or of little value: *Give the ~,* eg unwanted food, *to the dog.*

lech·er·ous /'letʃərəs/ *adj* lustful; having, giving way to, strong sexual desires. **lecher** /'letʃə(r)/ *n* ~ person. **lech·ery** /'letʃərɪ/ *n* [U] lust; [C] (*pl* -ries) lustful or lascivious act.

lec·tern /'lektən/ *n* sloping reading-desk as for a Bible in church.

lec·ture /'lektʃə(r)/ *n* [C] **1** talk (to an audience or class) for the purpose of teaching: *give/read a ~; a course of ~s on Greek philosophy; go on a ~ tour.* **2** reproof: *give sb a ~,* scold or reprove him. □ *vi,vt* **1** [VP2A,3A] **~ (on),** give a ~ or course of ~s: *~ on modern drama.* **2** [VP6A,14] **~ sb (for),** scold, reprove: *The teacher ~d the boys for being lazy.* **~r** /'lektʃərə(r)/ *n* person, lower in rank than a professor, who gives ~s, esp at a college or university. **~·ship** /-ʃɪp/ *n* post as a ~r at a university, etc.

led /led/ *pt,pp* of **lead³.**

ledge /ledʒ/ *n* **1** narrow horizontal shelf coming out from a wall, cliff or other upright surface: *a 'window ~; a ~ for chalk at the bottom of a blackboard.* **2** ridge of rocks under water, esp near the shore.

ledger /'ledʒə(r)/ *n* **1** book in which a business firm's accounts are kept. **2** (music) '**~ (or 'leger) line,** short line added above or below the stave for outside notes. ⇨ the illus at **notation.**

lee /li:/ *n* [U] (place giving) protection against wind. **lee (side),** the side away from the wind (contrasted with the *windward* or *weather* side): *the lee side of a ship; a 'lee shore,* on the lee side of

one's ship; *a 'lee tide,* one flowing in the same direction as the wind.

leech /li:tʃ/ *n* **1** small blood-sucking worm living in wet places of which one kind was formerly used by doctors for bleeding patients: *stick like a ~,* (fig) be very persistent, be difficult to get rid of. **2** (fig) person who sucks profit out of others. **3** (old use) doctor.

leek /li:k/ *n* onion-like vegetable with a long, slender white bulb. ⇨ the illus at **vegetable.**

leer /lɪə(r)/ *n* [C] sly, unpleasant look that suggests evil desire or ill will. □ *vi* [VP2A,3A] **~ (at sb),** look with a ~: *~ing at his neighbour's pretty young wife.*

lees /li:z/ *n pl* dregs; sediment (of wine, etc); basest part; residue (as at the bottom of a cask, etc). **drink/drain to the ~,** (fig) experience the last extremes of suffering, passion, etc.

lee·ward /'li:wəd/ (among sailors: /'lu:əd/) *adj, adv* on or to the sheltered side (contrasted with *windward*). □ *n* [U] lee side; sheltered side: *on the ~; steer to ~.*

lee·way /'li:weɪ/ *n* [U] sideways drift (of a ship) in the direction towards which the wind is blowing; (fig) freedom to vary (while still being tolerated or safe). **make up ~,** make up for lost time; get back into position.

left¹ *pt,pp* of **leave.**

left² /left/ *adj, n, adv* (opposite of *right*) (of, in, on, the) side of a person's body which is towards the west when he faces north: *Not many people write with the ~ hand. The ~ bank of a river is on your ~ as you face the direction in which it flows. Come and sit on my ~,* ie at my ~ side. *Turn (to the) ~ at the pub.* **the L~ (Wing),** more radical group(s), party or parties, eg socialists, communists: (attrib) *~-wing militants.* '**~-hand** *adj* of, situated on, the ~ side: *a house on the ~-hand side of the street; a ~-hand blow/stroke.* **~·handed** *adj* (of a person) using the ~ hand more easily or with more skill than the right. *a ~-handed compliment,* one that is ambiguous, of doubtful sincerity. '**~·ist** /-ɪst/ *n* supporter of socialism or radicalism.

leg /leg/ *n* **1** one of the parts of an animal's or a person's body used for walking, esp (of a human body) the part above the foot: *have a leg of mutton for dinner. He lost his right leg in the war.* **be all legs,** (of a person) be overgrown, lanky and thin. **be off one's legs,** resting: *Poor woman! She's never off her legs,* is always working. **be on one's legs** (or joc, **on one's hind legs),** (a) be standing, esp to make a speech. (b) (after an illness) be well enough to walk about again. **be on one's last legs,** (a) fatigued, exhausted. (b) near one's death or end. **feel/find one's legs,** (*feet* is more usu) (a) (of a baby) get the power of standing or walking. (b) (fig) begin to realize one's powers, abilities, etc; become self-confident. **find one's 'sea-legs,** ⇨ sea(7). **give sb a leg up,** (lit) help him to mount a horse or to climb up sth; (fig) help him in time of need. **pull sb's leg,** try, for a joke, to make him believe sth that is untrue. Hence, '**leg-pull** [C] and '**leg-pulling** [U] *nn.* **run sb off his legs,** tire him by keeping him constantly busy. **shake a leg,** (colloq) dance; (imper) start. **show a leg,** (colloq) get out of bed; (imper) do sth with more effort. **not have a ,leg to 'stand on,** have nothing to support one's opinion, defence, etc. **stretch one's legs,** go for a walk (esp to take exercise after sitting for a

long time). *take to one's legs,* (*heels* is more usu)
run away. *walk one's 'legs off; walk sb off his
legs,* tire oneself/him out with walking. **2** that part
of a garment that closely covers a leg: *the leg of a
stocking; the legs of a pair of trousers.* **3** support of
a chair, table, etc: *a stool with three legs; the legs
of a bed.* **be on its last legs,** weak and likely to
collapse. **4** [U] (cricket) part of the field to the left
rear of a right-handed batsman in position (or vice
versa): *leg-stump,* stump nearest to this; *hit a ball
to leg.* ⇨ the illus cricket. **5** one section of a journey, esp by air: *the first leg of a round-the-world
flight;* one of a series of games in a competition.
-legged /legd/ *adj* (in compounds) ,*long-' legged,*
having long legs; ,*three-' legged,* having three legs,
eg a stool; ,*bare-' legged,* having bare legs.
,**three-'legged** (/'legɪd/) **race** *n* race for pairs with
one leg of each pair tied together.

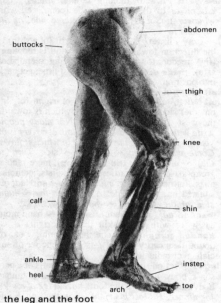

the leg and the foot

labels: abdomen, buttocks, thigh, knee, calf, shin, ankle, heel, arch, instep, toe

leg·acy /'legəsɪ/ *n* (*pl* -cies) [C] **1** money, etc (to
be) received by a person under the will of and at the
death of another person. **2** (fig) sth handed down
from ancestors or predecessors: *a ~ of ill will.*
legal /'li:gl/ *adj* connected with, in accordance
with, authorized or required by, the law: *~ affairs;
my ~ adviser/representative,* eg a solicitor; *take
~ action (against sb); the ~ fare; ~ tender,* form
of money which must be accepted if offered in payment; *a ~ offence,* one against the law, contrasted
with an offence against convention; *free ~ aid,*
help (from lawyers paid by the State) given to persons unable to pay the usual charges. **~·ly** /'li:gəlɪ/
adv '**~·ism** /-ɪzəm/ *n* [U] strict adherence to, un-
due respect for, the law and *~* forms.
legal·ity /li:'gælətɪ/ *n* [U] the state or quality of being legal: *the ~ of an act.*
legal·ize /'li:gəlaɪz/ *vt* [VP6A] make legal: *~ the
sale of alcoholic drinks.* **legal·iz·ation** /ˌli:gə-
laɪ'zeɪʃn *US:* -lɪ'z-/ *n* [U].
leg·ate /'legɪt/ *n* the Pope's ambassador to

a country.
lega·tee /ˌlegə'ti:/ *n* (legal) person who receives
a legacy.
leg·ation /lɪ'geɪʃn/ *n* [C] (house, offices, etc, of a)
diplomatic minister below the rank of ambassador,
with those under him, representing his government
in a foreign country.
le·gato /lɪ'gɑːtəʊ/ *adj, adv* (musical direction) (to
be played) smoothly, without breaks.
leg·end /'ledʒənd/ *n* **1** [C] old story handed down
from the past, esp one of doubtful truth: *the ~s of
King Arthur.* **2** [U] literature of such stories:
heroes who are famous in ~. **3** [C] inscription on a
coin or medal; explanatory words on a map, a picture, etc. *~·ary* /'ledʒəndrɪ *US:* -derɪ/ *adj* famous,
known only, in *~s: ~ary heroes.*
leger /'ledʒə(r)/ ⇨ ledger(2).
leger·de·main /ˌledʒədə'meɪn/ *n* [U] juggling;
quick and clever performance of tricks with the
hands; (fig) deceitful argument.
leg·ging /'legɪŋ/ *n* (usu *pl*) outer covering, of leather or strong cloth, for the leg up to the knee, or (for
small children) for the whole of the leg: *a pair of
~s.*
leggy /'legɪ/ *adj* having long legs (esp of young
children, puppies and colts).
leg·horn /le'gɔːn *US:* 'legən/ *n* **1** kind of domestic
fowl. **2** hat made of the kind of straw imported
from Leghorn (also called Livorno), a town in NW
Italy.
leg·ible /'ledʒəbl/ *adj* (of handwriting, print) that
can be read easily. **leg·ibly** /-əblɪ/ *adv* **legi·bil·ity**
/ˌledʒə'bɪlətɪ/ *n*
legion /'li:dʒən/ *n* **1** division of several thousand
men in the armies of ancient Rome; (fig) great
number: *Their numbers are ~.* **2** British L~, national association of ex-service men formed in
1921. **(French) Foreign L~,** body of non-French
volunteers who serve in the French army, usu overseas. **L~ of Honour,** high French decoration (civilian and military). **3** (in liter or rhet style) vast host
or number. **legion·ary** /'lɪdʒənərɪ *US:* -nerɪ/ *n* (*pl*
-ries) *adj* (member) of a *~,* esp the (French)
Foreign L~.
legis·late /'ledʒɪsleɪt/ *vi* [VP2A,3A] make laws: *~
against gambling.* **legis·la·tion** /ˌledʒɪs'leɪʃn/ *n* [U]
making laws; the laws made.
legis·lat·ive /'ledʒɪslətɪv *US:* -leɪtɪv/ *adj* (of) law-
making: *~ assemblies; ~ reforms.*
legis·la·tor /'ledʒɪsleɪtə(r)/ *n* member of a law-
making body.
legis·la·ture /'ledʒɪsleɪtʃə(r)/ *n* law-making body,
eg Parliament in GB.
le·git·imate /lɪ'dʒɪtɪmət/ *adj* **1** lawful, regular: *the
~ king; use public money only for ~ purposes.* **2**
reasonable; that can be justified: *a ~ reason for
being absent from one's work.* **3** born of persons
married to one another; the result of lawful marriage: *a ~ child; of ~ birth.* **4 the ~ theatre,** drama, not revue or musical comedy etc. *~·ly adv* **le-
git·imacy** /lɪ'dʒɪtɪməsɪ/ *n* [U] being *~.* **le·git-
ima·tize** /lɪ'dʒɪtɪmətaɪz/ *vt* make *~.*
leg·umin·ous /lɪ'gju:mɪnəs/ *adj* of, like, the botanical family that includes peas and beans (and other
seeds in pods).
lei /'leɪɪ:/ *n* garland of flowers worn round the neck
(as in Polynesian islands).
lei·sure /'leʒə(r) *US:* 'li:ʒər/ *n* [U] **1** spare time;
time free from work: *have no ~ for sport.* **at ~,**
(when) not occupied: *I am seldom at ~.* **at one's**

∼, when one has free time: *Please look through these papers at your* ∼. **2** (attrib) ∼ *time/hours/ clothes.* ∼·ly *adv* without haste or hurry: *work* ∼*ly.* □ *adj* unhurried; deliberate: ∼*ly movements.*

∼d /'leʒəd *US:* 'liːʒərd/ *adj* having plenty of ∼: *the* ∼d *classes.*

lem·ming /'lemɪŋ/ *n* small arctic migratory rodent like a field–mouse.

lemon /'lemən/ *n* **1** (tree with) pale yellow fruit with acid juice used for drinks and flavouring. ⇨ the illus at **fruit.** '∼ **drop** *n* piece of boiled sugar flavoured with ∼. ⟋∼ '**squash** *n* drink of ∼–juice and water or soda–water. '∼ **squeezer** *n* device for pressing juice out of a ∼. ⟋∼ '**sole** *n* kind of edible flatfish, like a plaice. **2** (GB *sl*) silly and plain-looking person. ∼·**ade** /ˌlemə'neɪd/ *n* [U] drink made from ∼–juice, sugar and water.

lemur /'liːmə(r)/ *n* nocturnal animal of Madagascar, similar to a monkey but with a foxlike face.

lend /lend/ *vt* (*pt,pp* lent /lent/) [VP6A,12A,13A,14] ∼ *sth to sb;* ∼ *sb sth,* give (sb) the use of (sth) for a period of time on the understanding that it or its equivalent will be returned: *I will* ∼ *you £100, but I can't* ∼ *money to everyone.* ∼ **a hand (with sth),** help. '∼**ing-library,** one from which books may be borrowed. **2** [VP14] ∼ *sth to sth,* contribute: *facts that* ∼ *probability to a theory.* **3** [VP14] ∼ **oneself to sth,** give; accomodate: *Don't* ∼ *yourself to such dishonest schemes. This peaceful garden* ∼*s itself to* (= is favourable for) *meditation.* ∼·**er** *n* person who ∼s.

length /leŋθ/ *n* **1** [U] measurement from end to end (in space or time): *the* ∼ *of a road/field/stick; a river 300 miles in* ∼; *a room 8 metres in* ∼ *and 6 in breadth; a river navigable for most of its* ∼; *make a stay in Rome for some* ∼, *for a considerable period of time; the* ∼ *of time needed for the work. at* ∼, **(a)** at last; finally. **(b)** for a long time: *speak at* (*great*) ∼. **(c)** in detail; thoroughly: *treat a subject at* ∼. **(at) full** ∼, with the body stretched out and flat: *lying at full* ∼ *on the grass.* **keep sb at arm's** ∼, avoid being friendly with him. **2** [C] measurement of a particular thing from end to end: *The car can turn in its own* ∼. *The horse/boat won by a* ∼, by its own ∼, this being used as a unit of measurement. **3** [U,C] extent; extreme. **go to any** ∼(**s**), do anything necessary to get what one wants. **4** [C] piece of cloth, etc, long enough for a purpose: *a* '*dress* ∼; *a* ∼ *of tubing/pipe.* ∼**en** /'leŋθən/ *vt,vi* [VP6A,2A] make or become longer: ∼*en a skirt. The days* ∼*en in March.* '∼·**wise** /-waɪz/, '∼·**ways** /-weɪz/ *adv, adj* in the direction from end to end. ∼**y** *adj* (of speech, writing) very long; too long.

leni·ent /'liːnɪənt/ *adj* not severe (esp in punishing people): ∼ *parents/judges.* **leni·ence** /-əns/, **leni·ency** /-ənsɪ/ *nn* [U] being ∼. ∼·**ly** *adv*

len·ity /'lenətɪ/ *n* [U] (formal) mercifulness; mercy shown.

lens /lenz/ *n* (*pl* lenses) **1** piece of glass or glasslike substance with one or both sides curved, for use in spectacles, cameras, telescopes and other optical instruments. ⇨ the illus at **camera. concave.** **2** (anat) transparent part of the eye, behind the pupil, through which light is refracted. ⇨ the illus at **eye.**

lent /lent/ *pt,pp* of **lend.**

Lent /lent/ *n* (in Christian Churches) period of forty days before Easter, the weekdays of this period being observed by devout persons as a period of fasting and penitence. ∼ **lily,** daffodil. ∼**en** /'lentən/ *adj* of ∼: ∼*en services* (in church); sparse: ∼*en fare.*

len·til /'lentl/ *n* [C] kind of bean plant; edible seed of this: ∼ *soup.*

lento /'lentəʊ/ *adj, adv* (musical direction) slow-(ly).

Leo /'liːəʊ/ *n* the fifth sign of the zodiac. ⇨ the illus at zodiac.

leo·nine /'liːənaɪn/ *adj* of or like a lion.

leop·ard /'lepəd/ *n* large African and South Asian flesh–eating animal with a yellowish coat and dark spots. ⇨ the illus at **cat.** ∼·**ess** /ˌlepə'des/ *n* female ∼.

leper /'lepə(r)/ *n* person suffering from leprosy.

lep·re·chaun /'leprəkɔːn/ *n* (in Irish folklore) fairy or sprite.

lep·rosy /'leprəsɪ/ *n* [U] skin disease that forms silvery scales on the skin, causes local insensibility to pain, etc and the loss of fingers and toes. **lep·rous** /'leprəs/ *adj* of, having, ∼.

les·bian /'lezbɪən/ *n* homosexual woman. ∼·**ism** /-ɪzəm/ *n*

lese maj·esty /ˌleɪz 'mædʒɪstɪ *US:* ˌliːz-/ *n* [U] treason; (joc) presumptuous conduct on the part of inferiors.

lesion /'liːʒn/ *n* [C] harmful change in the tissues of a bodily organ, caused by injury or disease.

less /les/ *adj* (∼ is contrasted with *more.* It is an independent comparative, with no real corresponding positive. ⇨ little, least.) **1** (used with a *n* that stands for what is measured by amount or quality or degree; *fewer* is used before a *pl n*) not so much; a smaller quantity of: ∼ *butter.* Cf *fewer eggs;* ∼ *food.* Cf *fewer meals;* ∼ *manpower.* Cf *fewer workers;* ∼ *shipping.* Cf *fewer ships; pay* ∼ *money for the house.* Cf *pay a lower rent; have* ∼ *difficulty with one's work.* Cf *meet with fewer difficulties;* ∼ *size means* ∼ *weight; of* ∼ *value/ importance.* **2** (followed by *than*): *I have* ∼ *money than you.* □ *adv* **1** (modifying *vv*) to a smaller extent; not so much: *Eat* ∼, *drink* ∼, *and sleep more.* **2** (with *adjj, participles* and *advv*) not so: *Tom is* ∼ *clever than his brother. Please behave* ∼ *foolishly.* Note that *less... than* may be replaced by *not so... as,* eg *He was* ∼ *hurt than frightened.* Cf *He was not so hurt as frightened. Try to be* ∼ *impatient.* Cf *Try not to be so impatient.* **3 the** ∼: *I was the* ∼ *surprised as I had been warned,* My surprise was ∼ *because.... The* ∼ *you worry about it the better it will be.* ⇨ the². **any the** ∼, in a lower degree: *I don't think any the* ∼ *of him* (= My opinion of him is not lower) *because of this one failure.* **even/still** ∼, and certainly not: *I don't suspect him of robbery, still* ∼ *of robbery with violence.* **no less** (...) **than**..., not a smaller amount (of sth) than...: *He won no* ∼ *than £50 in the lottery/He won £50, no* ∼, *in the lottery* (expressing suprise at the amount). *Our soldiers fought with no* ∼ *daring than skill,* Their daring equalled their skill. **none the** ∼, but for all that; all the same: *Though he cannot leave the house, he is none the* ∼ (= he is, in spite of that) *busy and active.* □ *n* [U] smaller amount, quantity, time, etc: *in* ∼ *than an hour. I won't sell it for* ∼ *than £50. I want* ∼ *of this and more of that.* Cf *fewer of these and more of those. I expect to see* ∼ *of her* (= to see her ∼ often) *in future.* □ *prep* minus; with the deduction of: *£30 a week* ∼ *£2 for National Insur-*

ance contribution.

les-see /le'si:/ *n* person who holds land, a building, etc on a lease.

les-sen /'lesn/ *vt,vi* **1** [VP6A,2A] make or become less: *to ~ the impact/effect of sth.* **2** [VP6A] cause (sth) to appear smaller, less important; belittle: *~ a person's importance.*

les-ser /'lesə(r)/ *adj* (attrib only) not so great as the other: *choose the ~ evil. in/to a ~ degree,* not so much as the other.

les-son /'lesn/ *n* **1** sth to be learnt or taught; period of time given to learning or teaching: '*English ~s; a ~ in music.* **2** (*pl*) children's education in general: *Tom is very fond of his ~s.* **3** sth experienced, esp sth serving as an example or a warning: *Let his fate be a ~ to all of you!* **4** passage from the Bible read aloud during a church service.

les-sor /'lesɔ:(r)/ *n* (legal) person who grants a lease.

lest /lest/ *conj* **1** for fear that; in order that... not: *He ran away ~ he should be seen.* **2** (after *fear, be afraid/anxious etc*) that: *We were afraid ~ he should get here too late.*

let[1] /let/ *vt,vi* (*pt,pp* let) (-tt-) (For uses with *adverbial particles* and *preps* ⇨ 8 below.) **1** [VP18B] (followed by a *noun/pronoun* and an *infinitive* without *to;* rarely used in the passive in this sense) allow to: *Her father will not let her go to the dance. She wants to go to the party but her father won't let her* (ie let her *go.* The omission of the *infinitive* is frequent when it may be inferred from the context). *Please let me know* (ie inform me) *what happens. Don't let the fire go out.* **2** [VP18B] (used with first and third person *pronouns* to supply an indirect imperative): *Let's start at once, shall we? Don't let's start yet! Let me see—where did I leave my hat? Let us both have a try! Let her do it at once. Let there be no mistake about it,* Don't make any mistake, don't misunderstand me, etc. *Live and let live,* ⇨ live[2](2). **3** [VP18B] (*let,* in the imperative, may also indicate an assumption. It may also indicate permission, with a suggestion of defiance): *Let AB be equal to CD. Let ABC be an angle of ninety degrees. Let them do their worst!* I defy them to do their worst! *Let them all come!* **4** [VP18B] (The pattern *let + noun + infinitive,* as in *let the waitress go,* is sometimes replaced by the pattern *let + infinitive + noun,* as in *let drop a hint.* In some cases, eg in *let fly,* the object of *let* is omitted). Note the following: *let sb/sth be,* allow to be quiet or unworried: *Let me be,* Don't worry me. *Let the poor dog be,* Don't tease it. *let drive (at sb/sth),* aim a blow (at); throw sth (at): *He let drive with his left fist. He let drive at me with a stone. let sb/sth drop,* allow to drop; (fig) utter (on purpose or by chance). *let sth fall,* allow to fall; (fig) allow to be heard: *He let fall a hint of his intentions. let fly (at sb/sth),* discharge; send out violently; shoot; strike out (at): *He aimed carefully and then let fly* (ie fired) *at the ducks. The angry man let fly a volley of oaths. let sb/sth go; let go of sb/sth,* release one's hold of him/it: *Don't let the rope go/let go of the rope. Let me go!* Take your hands off me; don't hold or keep me. *let oneself go,* give way to, no longer hold back, one's feelings, desires, impulses, etc: *He let himself go on the subject. let it go at that,* say no more about it; dismiss the subject: *I don't agree with all you say but we'll let it go at that. let sth pass,* overlook; disregard: *It's not a serious error;*

we can let it pass, I think. let sth slip, (a) miss (an opportunity, etc). **(b)** = let sth drop/fall, (see above). **5** [VP22] (combined with *adjj*) *let sb/sth alone,* allow (sb) to do sth unaided; not interfere with: *Let it alone! Let well alone,* (prov) Don't try to improve sth that is already satisfactory. *let alone,* (colloq) to say nothing of; not to mention: *There were seven people in the car, let alone a pile of luggage and three dogs. let sb/sth loose (on sb/sth),* allow to be free (somewhere); (fig) release (one's anger, etc, on sb): *Don't let that dog loose.* **6** [VP6A,14,22,24A] *~ sth (to),* give the use of (buildings, land) in return for regular money payments: *This house is to be let. The house would let* (= could be let) *easily. She has let her house furnished. to let,* offered for renting. *let out,* put out to hire: *He used to let out horses by the day.* **7** [VP6A] (surgery) *~ blood,* cause it to flow. Hence, '**blood-letting** *n* [U]. **8** [VP15A,B,2C,14] (uses with *adverbial particles* and *preps*):

let sth down, lower; put or take down: *Please let the window down. This skirt needs letting down,* lengthening by lowering the hem-line. *She let down her hair. That chair has a broken leg, it might let you down,* might not support you. *let sb down,* (fig) disappoint; fail to help: *Harry will never let you down,* You can rely upon him to help you always. *I've been badly let down,* placed in a difficult or awkward situation through the failure of others to support me. Hence, '**let-down** *n* feeling of having been let down; disappointment. *let the side down,* ⇨ side[1](10).

let sb/sth in/into sth, allow to enter: *Windows let in light and air. These shoes let in water. He let himself in/into the flat with a latch-key,* opened the door using the key. *Who let you into the building? let sth in,* make (a garment, etc) narrower: *This skirt needs letting in at the waist. let sb in for sth,* involve in loss, difficulty, hard work, etc: *He didn't know what a lot of unpaid work he was letting himself in for when he agreed to become secretary of the society. let sb into sth,* allow to share (a secret): *She has been let into* (= told) *the secret. let sth into sth,* put into the surface of: *We must let another window into this wall.*

let sb off, excuse; not compel; not punish; not punish severely: *He was let off with a fine instead of being sent to prison. You have let him off lightly,* eg by excusing him from too much work, by punishing him lightly, etc. *let sth off,* fire off: *The boys were letting off fireworks.*

let on (that...), (colloq) reveal a secret: *He knew where the boy was hiding but he didn't let on,* didn't tell anyone.

let sb/sth out, allow to go (flow, etc) out: *He let the air out of the tyres. Let the water out of the bath-tub. let sth out,* make (a garment, etc) looser, larger, etc: *He's getting so fat that his trousers need to be let out round the waist.* ⇨ also 6 above. *let out at sb,* aim a violent blow, kick, etc, at him; (fig) use violent language to him: *Be careful! That mule has a habit of letting out at people.*

let sb/sth through (sth), allow to pass (an examination, etc): *He got only 40%, so the examiners couldn't possibly let him through.*

let up, become less strong, etc: *Will the rain never let up?* '**let-up** *n* (colloq) cessation; diminution: *There has been no let-up in the rain yet. I've been*

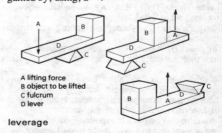

working ten hours without a let-up. **let up on sb,** (colloq) treat more leniently.

let[2] /let/ *n* (from **let**[1](6)) letting; lease: *I can't get a let for my house,* can find no one willing to rent it from me. **let·ting** *n* [C] property that is let: *a furnished letting,* a furnished house or flat that is let.

let[3] /let/ *vt* (archaic) hinder; obstruct. □ *n* **1** hindrance, esp in the legal phrase: *without let or hindrance.* **2** (tennis) ball which when served, strikes the net before dropping into the opponent's court.

lethal /'li:θl/ *adj* causing, designed to cause, death: *a ~ dose of poison; ~ weapons; a ~ chamber,* eg in which sick animals may be put to death painlessly.

leth·argy /'leθədʒɪ/ *n* [U] (state of) being tired, uninterested; want of energy. **leth·ar·gic** /lɪ'θɑːdʒɪk/ *adj* sleepy; lacking in energy; caused by, likely to cause, ~. **leth·ar·gi·cally** /-klɪ/ *adv*

Lethe /'li:θɪ/ *n* (Gk myth) (river in Hades /'heɪdiːz/, the Greek underworld, producing) forgetfulness of the past.

let's /lets/ = let us. ⇨ **let**[1](2).

let·ter /'letə(r)/ *n* **1** character or sign representing a sound, of which words in writing are formed: *the 26 ~s of the English alphabet; capital ~s* (A, B, C, etc) *and small ~s* (a, b, c, etc). Cf phonetic *symbol.* **2** written message, request, account of events, etc sent by one person to another: *I have some ~s to write. Inform me by ~ of your plans. ~ of* **'credit,** ⇨ credit[1](1). **'~-box** *n* (US = *mail box*) **(a)** box (in the street, at a post office) in which ~s are posted; pillar-box. **(b)** box (in a building) for receiving ~s from the post. **'~-card** *n* folded card with a gummed edge for use instead of notepaper and an envelope. **'~-case** *n* pocket-book for holding ~s. **'~-head** *n* (sheet of paper with a) printed name and address, eg of a business firm. **'~-press** *n* [U] contents of an illustrated book other than the pictures; printing from type. **3** (phrases) *keep (to) the ~ of the law/an agreement,* carry out the stated conditions without regard to its spirit or true purpose. *to the ~,* paying strict attention to every detail: *carry out an order to the ~.* **4** (*pl*) literature and learning: *the profession of ~s; a man of ~s.* **~ed** /'letəd/ *adj* having a good knowledge of books: *a ~ed young man.* **~-ing** /'letərɪŋ/ *n* [U] ~s, words, esp with reference to their style and size: *the ~ing on a book cover; poor ~ing on a gravestone.*

let·tuce /'letɪs/ *n* [C] garden plant with crisp green leaves used in salads; [U] these leaves as food. ⇨ the illus at **vegetable.**

leu·co·cyte (US = **leu·ko·cyte**) /'lu:kəsaɪt/ *n* [C] white blood-cell.

leu·kae·mia (US = **leu·ke·mia**) /lu:'ki:mɪə/ *n* [U] disease in which there is an excess of leucocytes, with changes in the lymph glands.

Lev·ant /lɪ'vænt/ *n* **the ~,** Eastern part of the Mediterranean, its countries and islands. **~-ine** /-aɪn/ *n, adj* (native) of the ~.

lev·ant /lɪ'vænt/ *vi* abscond; leave (esp without paying gambling losses).

levee[1] /'levɪ/ *n* (hist) formal reception; (GB) assembly held by a king or his representative at which men only were received.

levee[2] /'levɪ/ *n* (US) embankment built to protect land from a river in flood: *the ~s along the Mississippi.*

level[1] /'levl/ *adj* **1** having a horizontal surface: *~ ground; make a surface ~. ~ crossing,* (US =

grade crossing) place where a road and a railway cross on the same ~. **2** on an equality: *a ~ race,* one in which the competitors keep close together; *draw ~ with the other runners.* **3** *have a ~ head,* be steady and well-balanced, able to judge well. Hence, **~-'headed** *adj. do one's ~ best,* do all that one can do, do everything possible.

level[2] /'levl/ *n* **1** [C] line or surface parallel with the horizon; such a surface with reference to its height: *1000 metres above sea ~. The water rose until it was on a ~ with the river banks. Water always finds its own ~.* **2** natural or right position, stage, social standing, etc: *He has found his own ~,* (fig) has found the kind of people with whom he is morally, socially or intellectually equal. *They'll rise to higher ~s* (= advance in civilization, etc) *very quickly.* **3** [U] (group of persons having) equal position or rank: *consultations at cabinet ~,* among members of the cabinet; *top-level talks,* talks between persons in the highest positions (in government, etc). (Cf *summit* talks.) **'O-/'A-~** **(exami·nation)** *n* [C] ~ of achievement (Ordinary/ Advanced) in the school-leaving examination in England and Wales: *a girl with five O-~s and three A-~s.* **4** *on the ~,* (colloq) honest(ly); straightforward(ly): *Is he on the ~?* ⇨ crooked(2). **5** **'spirit-~,** ⇨ spirit(11).

level[3] /'levl/ *vt,vi* (-ll-, US -l-) **1** [VP6A,15A,B] make or become ~ or flat: *~ a building with the ground. Death ~s all men,* makes them equal by ending social distinctions, etc. *~ sth down/up,* make (incomes, marks, standards, surfaces, etc) equal by lowering the higher or raising the lower. **2** [VP6A,14,2C,3A] bring or come into a horizontal plane: *~ a gun at a tiger,* raise it and aim. *~ sth against sb,* put forward (a charge, an accusation, etc). *~ off/out,* **(a)** cause an aircraft to fly parallel to the earth's surface: *On reaching 1000 metres, the pilot ~led off.* **(b)** (fig) reach a point in one's career etc beyond which no further progress is likely: *You're unlikely to get further promotion—we all have to ~ off some time.* **~-ler,** (US) **~er** /'levələ(r)/ *n* (esp) person who wishes to abolish social distinctions.

lever /'li:və(r)/ *US:* 'levər/ *n* bar or other tool turned on a fulcrum to lift sth or to force sth open, eg a window or drawer; (fig) means by which moral force may be exerted. □ *vt* [VP6A,15B] move (sth up, along, into/out of position, etc) with a ~. **~-age** /-ɪdʒ/ *n* [U] action of, power or advantage gained by, using, a ~.

A lifting force
B object to be lifted
C fulcrum
D lever

leverage

lev·eret /'levərɪt/ *n* young (esp first-year) hare.

lev·ia·than /lɪ'vaɪəθən/ *n* **1** (in the Bible) sea animal of enormous size. **2** anything of very great size and power.

levis /'li:vaɪz/ *n pl* (P) jeans.

levi·tate /'levɪteɪt/ *vt,vi* [VP6A,2A] (with reference

to powers claimed by spiritualists) (cause to) rise and float in the air in defiance of gravity. **levi·ta·tion** /ˌlevɪˈteɪʃn/ n

lev·ity /ˈlevətɪ/ n [U] (formal) tendency to treat serious matters without respect; lack of seriousness; [C] (pl -ties) instance of this.

levy /ˈlevɪ/ vt,vi (pt,pp levied) 1 [VP6A,14] ~ (on), impose; collect by authority or force: ~ a tax/a fine/a ransom on sb; ~ing an army/troops, using compulsion to get men as soldiers. 2 ~ war upon/against, declare, make, war on after ~ing men and supplies. 3 [VP3A] ~ on, seize by law: ~ on a person's property/estate, seize this in order to get money for an unpaid debt. □ n (pl levies) [C] act of ~ing; amount of men, number of men, so obtained. **capital** ~, ⇨ capital².

lewd /ljuːd US: luːd/ adj indecent; lustful. ~·ly adv ~·ness n

lexi·cal /ˈleksɪkl/ adj (contrasted with grammatical) of the vocabulary of a language. ~·ly /-klɪ/ adv **lexis** /ˈleksɪs/ n [U] vocabulary.

lexi·cogra·phy /ˌleksɪˈkɒɡrəfɪ/ n [U] dictionary compiling. **lexi·cogra·pher** /ˌleksɪˈkɒɡrəfə(r)/ n person who compiles a dictionary.

lexi·con /ˈleksɪkən US: -kɒn/ n dictionary (esp of Greek, Latin or Hebrew).

ley /leɪ/ n [C] area of land temporarily under grass: new-sown leys.

lia·bil·ity /ˌlaɪəˈbɪlətɪ/ n (pl -ties) 1 [U] the state of being liable: ~ to pay taxes; ~ for military service, in a country where there is conscription; ~ to disease; Don't admit ~ for the accident, eg because of car insurance claims. ,limited '~ company, ⇨ limit². 2 (pl) debts; sums of money that must be paid (contrasted with assets). 3 (colloq) handicap: His wife is more of a ~ at a party than an asset.

li·able /ˈlaɪəbl/ adj (usu pred) 1 ~ for, responsible according to law: Is a man ~ for his wife's debts in your country? 2 be ~ to sth, be subject to: If you drive a car to the danger of the public, you make yourself ~ to a heavy fine, or even to imprisonment. He is ~ to seasickness. 3 be ~ to do sth, have a tendency to, be likely to: We are all ~ to make mistakes occasionally.

li·aison /lɪˈeɪzn US: ˈlɪəzɒn/ n 1 [U] connection; linkage between two separate groups. '~ officer, one who keeps two such groups in touch with each other; member of a committee, etc acting as a link between the committee and other people. 2 [C] illicit (eg sexual) relationship.

li·aise /lɪˈeɪz/ vi [VP2A,3A] ~ (with/between), (colloq) act as a link.

li·ana /lɪˈɑːnə US: -ˈænə/ n climbing and twining tropical plant.

liar /ˈlaɪə(r)/ n person who tells an untruth or who has told an untruth; person who habitually tells lies.

lib /lɪb/ n (colloq abbr for) liberation. **gay/ women's lib**, movement (early 1970's) for the liberation of homosexuals/women from legal, social, economic and self oppression.

li·ba·tion /laɪˈbeɪʃn/ n [C] (pouring out of an) offering of wine, etc to a god: make a ~ to Jupiter.

li·bel /ˈlaɪbl/ n 1 [U,C] (the publishing of a) written or printed statement that damages sb's reputation: sue a newspaper for ~; utter/publish a ~ against sb. 2 [C] ~ on, (colloq) anything that brings discredit upon or fails to do justice to: The portrait is a ~ on me. □ vt (-ll-, US -l-) [VP6A] publish a ~

against; fail to do full justice to. ~·lous,(US)~·ous/ˈlaɪbələs/ adj containing a ~; in the nature of a ~: ~lous reports; in the habit of uttering ~s: a ~lous person/periodical.

lib·eral /ˈlɪbərəl/ adj 1 giving or given freely; generous: a ~ giver to charities; a ~ supply of food and drink; a ~ table, one with plenty of food and drink. He is ~ of promises but not ~ of money, gives plenty of promises but not much money. 2 open-minded; having, showing, a broad mind, free from prejudice. 3 (of education) directed chiefly towards the broadening of the mind, not specially to professional or technical needs. **the** ~ **arts**, eg philosophy, history, languages. 4 (politics in GB) of the party (dominant until the 1920's), favouring moderate democratic reforms. □ n person in favour of progress and reform and opposed to privilege. **L~**, member of the L~ party in GB. ~·ism /-ɪzəm/ n [U] ~ views, opinions and principles. ~·ize /ˈlɪbrəlaɪz/ vt make ~; free from narrow-mindedness. ~·iz·ation /ˌlɪbrəlaɪˈzeɪʃn US: -lɪˈz-/ n

lib·er·al·ity /ˌlɪbəˈrælətɪ/ n (pl -ties) 1 [U] generosity; free giving; quality of being broad-minded; freedom from prejudice. 2 (pl) instances of generosity.

lib·er·ate /ˈlɪbəreɪt/ vt [VP6A,14] ~ (from), set free: ~ slaves; ~ the mind from prejudice. **lib·er·ator** /-tə(r)/ n **lib·er·ation** /ˌlɪbəˈreɪʃn/ n [U] liberating or being ~d. ⇨ lib.

lib·er·tine /ˈlɪbətiːn/ n licentious person. **chartered** ~, person whose irregularities and eccentricities of behaviour are tolerated.

lib·erty /ˈlɪbətɪ/ n (pl -ties) 1 [U] state of being free (from captivity, slavery, imprisonment, despotic control, government by others); right or power to decide for oneself what to do, how to live, etc: They fought to defend their ~. at ~, (of a person) free; not imprisoned: You are now at ~ to leave any time, may do so. **set sb at** ~, release: set prisoners/slaves at ~. ~ of conscience, freedom to have one's own (esp religious) beliefs without interference. ~ of speech, freedom to say openly, in public, what one thinks, eg on social and political questions. ~ of the press, freedom to write and print in periodicals, books, etc whatever one wishes without interference. 2 [U] ungranted and sometimes improper familiarity; setting aside of convention. **take the** ~ **of doing sth/to do sth**: I took the ~ of borrowing your lawn-mower while you were away on holiday. **take liberties with**: You must stop taking liberties with the young woman, stop treating her with too much familiarity. 3 (pl) privileges or rights granted by authority: the liberties of the City of London.

li·bid·in·ous /lɪˈbɪdɪnəs/ adj lustful.

li·bido /lɪˈbiːdəʊ/ n [U,C] (psych) sexual desire; emotional energy or cravings.

Libra /ˈliːbrə/ n the seventh sign of the zodiac (also called 'the scales' or 'the balance'). ⇨ the illus at zodiac.

li·brary /ˈlaɪbrərɪ US: -brerɪ/ n (pl -ries) 1 room or building for a collection of books kept there for reading; the books in such a room or building: the public ~, maintained by a town or city council, etc; a 'circulating ~, one that lends books for profit, members paying a subscription fee; 'reference ~, one in which books may be consulted but not taken away. 2 (attrib) a '~ book; a '~ edition, book usu of large size and print and with a strong binding. **3** writing and reading room in a private house. **4** series of books issued by a publisher in uniform binding and connected in some way: *the Home University L~*. **li·brar·ian** /laɪˈbreərɪən/ *n* person in charge of a ~. **li·brar·ian·ship** *n* [U] the work of a librarian.

li·bretto /lɪˈbretəʊ/ *n* (*pl* ~s /-təʊz/ or -tti /-tiː/) book of words of an opera or musical play. **li·bret·tist** /lɪˈbretɪst/ *n* writer of a ~.

lice /laɪs/ *n pl* of louse.

li·cence (US = **li·cense**) /ˈlaɪsns/ *n* **1** [C] (written or printed statement giving) permission from someone in authority to do sth; [U] authorization: *a ~ to drive a car/a 'driving ~; a ~ to practise as a doctor; marry by (special) ~* (contrasted with *banns*); *a ~ for the sale of alcoholic drinks.* '**~-plate** *n* (US) *number-plate*, ⇨ number(2). '**on-~** *n* [C] (GB) licence for the sale of alcoholic drinks to be consumed on the premises. '**off-~** *n* [C] (GB) licence for the sale of liquor to be taken away; shop where liquor is sold and taken away. **2** [U] wrong use of freedom; disregard of laws, customs, etc; licentious behaviour: *The ~ shown by the troops when they entered enemy territory disgusted everyone.* **poetic ~**, freedom from the ordinary rules of language, eg of word order, allowed in verse.

li·cense (also **li·cence**) /ˈlaɪsns/ *vt* [VP6A,17A] give a licence to: *shops ~d to sell tobacco; ~ a doctor to practise medicine; a ~d house/~d premises*, where the sale of alcoholic drinks is allowed, eg hotels, restaurants; *a ~d victualler; the ~d quarters*, (in some countries) part of a town where there are ~d brothels. **li·cen·see** /ˌlaɪsənˈsiː/ *n* person holding a licence (esp to sell alcohol).

li·cen·tiate /laɪˈsenʃɪət/ *n* person who has a licence or certificate showing that he is competent to practice a profession.

li·cen·tious /laɪˈsenʃəs/ *adj* immoral (esp in sexual matters); not held back by morality. **~·ly** *adv* **~·ness** *n*

li·chee, li·chi /ˈlaɪtʃiː/ = lychee.

li·chen /ˈlaɪkən/ *n* [U] dry-looking plant that grows on rocks, walls, tree-trunks, etc, usu green, yellow or grey.

lich·gate, lych·gate /ˈlɪtʃgeɪt/ *n* roofed gateway of a churchyard, where, at a funeral, the coffin used to await the arrival of the clergyman.

licit /ˈlɪsɪt/ *adj* lawful; permitted.

lick /lɪk/ *vt,vi* **1** [VP6A,15A,B,22] pass the tongue over or under: *The cat was ~ing its paws. He ~ed the spoon clean.* *~ sb's boots*, cringe before sb; be abject, servile. *~ one's lips*, show eagerness or satisfaction. *~ one's wounds*, try to recover after a defeat. *~ sth off*, remove by ~ing: *The boy ~ed the jam off his lips. ~ sth up*, take it up by ~ing: *The cat ~ed up the milk. ~ into shape*, (fig) make presentable, efficient, properly trained: *The recruits were soon ~ed into shape by the drill sergeants. ~ the dust*, (rhet) fall to the ground, defeated or killed. **2** [VP6A] (esp of waves, flames) touch lightly: *The flames ~ed the sides of the fireplace.* **3** [VP6A] (colloq) overcome; triumph over; give a whipping to: *Well, that ~s everything!* That is more surprising than anything I've ever seen or heard! **4** [VP2A] (sl) go; hurry: *He went off as hard as he could ~.* □ *n* **1** act of ~ing with the tongue. *give sth a ~ and a promise*, a feeble attempt to clean, polish, etc (with a promise of sth more thorough later). **2** (also '*salt-~*) place to which animals go for salt. **3** (sl) *at a great ~; at full ~*, at a

great pace. **~·ing** *n* (colloq) beating; defeat: *Our football team got a ~ing yesterday.*

licor·ice /ˈlɪkərɪs/ *n* ⇨ liquorice.

lid /lɪd/ *n* **1** movable cover (hinged or detachable) for an opening, esp at the top of a container: *the lid of a kettle/box; the 'teapot lid.* **2** eyelid. **~·less** *adj*

lido /ˈliːdəʊ/ *n* (*pl* ~s /-dəʊz/) public open-air swimming pool or bathing beach.

lie¹ /laɪ/ *vi* (*pt,pp* lied, *pres p* lying) [VP2A] make a statement that one knows to be untrue: *He lied to me. He's lying.* □ *n* such a statement: *He's telling lies. What a pack of lies!* What a lot of untrue statements! *He lived a lie*, deceived without using words. **white lie**, ⇨ white¹(3). *give sb the lie*, accuse him of lying. '**lie-detector** *n* device which records physiological changes, eg heart beats, rate of breathing, caused by emotional stresses while a person is being questioned.

lie² /laɪ/ *vi* (*pt* lay /leɪ/, *pp* lain /leɪn/, *pres p* lying) [VP2A,C,D,3A] **1** be, put oneself, flat on a horizontal surface or in a resting position; be at rest: *lie on one's back/side; lie face downwards. Don't lie in bed all morning! His body lies* (= He is buried) *in the churchyard. He lay on the grass enjoying the sunshine.* **lie back**, get into, be in a resting position: *lie back in an armchair.* **take sth lying down**, submit to a challenge, an insult without protest. **lie down under (an insult, etc)**, fail to protest, resist, etc. **lie in**, (a) stay in bed after one's usual time for getting up. Hence, '**lie-in** *n*: *have a nice lie-in on Sunday morning.* (b) remain in bed to give birth to a child: *The time had come for her to lie in.* '**lying-'in** hospital (old use) maternity hospital. **lie in ambush**, ⇨ ambush. **lie low**, (colloq) ⇨ low¹(12). **lie up**, stay in bed or in one's room (from illness, etc). **lie with**, (old use, biblical, now usu *sleep with*) have sexual intercourse with. *Let sleeping dogs lie*, (prov) Avoid discussing problems that are likely to cause trouble. '**lie-abed** /-əbed/ *n* lazy person who lies in bed instead of getting up. **2** (of things) be resting flat on sth: *The book lay open on the table. How long has your bicycle been lying out on the wet grass?* **3** be kept, remain, in a certain state or position: *money lying idle in the bank; towns lying in ruins; men who lay* (= were) *in prison for years. The snow lay thick on the ground. The fields lay thickly covered with snow.* **lie heavy on sth**, cause discomfort, trouble, distress to it: *The lobster lay heavy on his stomach. The theft lay heavy on his conscience.* **lie over**, be left for action at a future time: *Let the matter lie over until the next committee meeting.* **4** be spread out to view; extend: *The valley lay before us. The coast was undefended and lay open to attack. If you are young, life still lies before you.* *find out/see how the 'land lies*, (fig) learn how matters stand, what the state of affairs is. **5** be situated: *ships lying at anchor. The ship is lying at No 5 berth. The fleet lay off the headland.* **lie 'to**, (of a ship) come almost to a stop, facing the wind. **6** (of abstract things) exist; be in a certain position or manner: *The trouble lies* (= is) *in the engine. The answer to this difficulty lies in not putting too much pressure on the engine. He knows where his interest lies*, where he may win an advantage, make a profit. *I will do everything that lies in* (= that is within) *my power.* **lie at sb's door**, be attributable to: *At whose door should the blame/fault/responsibility lie*, Who should we attribute it to? (Cf *lay sth at sb's door*, ⇨ door(1).)

lie with sb, be sb's duty or responsibility: *The solution/The burden of proof lies with you. It lies with you* (= It is your duty) *to accept or reject the proposal. as far as in me lies*, to the best of my power. **7** (legal) be admissible: *The appeal will not lie*, is not according to law, cannot be admitted. □ *n* (*sing* only) the way sth lies; (golf) the position of a ball when it comes to a stop. *the lie of the land*, the natural features (esp the contours) of an area; (fig) the state of affairs.

lied /liːt/ *n* (*pl* ~er /'liːdə(r)/) (G) German song or lyric. '~er-singer, person who sings ~er.

lief /liːf/ *adv* (archaic or liter) willingly: *I would/ had as ~ join the Crusade as anything*, would do this more willingly than anything else.

liege /liːdʒ/ *adj* (legal) (only in) '~ **lord/ sovereign**, (feudal times) ruler, landowner, entitled to receive service and homage. '~-man /-mən/ *n* (*pl*-men) feudal vassal; faithful follower. □ *n*~ lord; ~man.

lien /liːən/ *n* legal claim (*upon* property) until a debt on it is repaid: *A shipping company has a ~ upon cargo until the freight is paid.*

lieu /luː/ *n* (only in) *in ~ (of)*, instead (of).

lieu·ten·ant /lefˈtenənt US: luːˈt-/ *n* **1** army officer below a captain; (/ləˈtenənt/) junior officer in the Navy. **2** (in compounds) officer with the highest rank under: ,~-ˈgeneral; ,~-ˈcolonel; ,~-comˈmander; ,~-ˈgovernor, official under a governor-general. **3** deputy or substitute; one who acts for a superior. **Lord L~ (of the County),** the Queen's representative in a county. **L~ of the Tower,** (ie the Tower of London). **lieu·ten·ancy** /-ənsɪ/ *n* rank, position, of a ~.

life /laɪf/ *n* (*pl* lives /laɪvz/) **1** [U] condition that distinguishes animals and plants from earth, rock, etc: *How did ~ begin? Where did ~ come from?* **life force**, vital energy thought of as working for the survival of the human race and the individual. **2** [U] living things collectively, in general; plants, animals, people: *Is there any ~ on the planet Mars? A naturalist studies animal and plant ~.* **3** [U] state of existence as a human being: *L~ is sweet. The battle was won, but only with great loss of ~*, many were killed. *bring to ~*, cause to live; cause to recover from a faint, an illness thought to be fatal, etc. *come to ~*, recover consciousness, recover from a faint, etc: *We all thought he was drowned, but after an hour's artificial respiration he came* (*back*) *to ~. run for one's ~/for dear ~*, in order to, or as if to, save oneself from death. *a matter of ~ and/or death*, one on which sb's continued existence depends. *kiss of ~*, ⇨ kiss. *this ~, ~ on earth. the 'other ~; future/ eternal/everlasting ~*, conscious existence, the state of existence, after bodily death. *with all the pleasure in ~*, with the greatest possible pleasure. **4** [C] state of existence as an individual living being: *How many lives were lost in the disaster? take sb's ~*, kill him. *take one's own ~*, kill oneself; commit suicide. *a ~ for a ~*, phrase used to express the view that murder must be revenged by the killing or execution of the murderer or (in a vendetta) by the killing of a member of his family. *cannot for the '~ of one*, cannot, however hard one tries: *For the ~ of me I couldn't recall her name. Not on your ~!* (colloq *int*) Quite definitely not. **5** [C] period between birth and death, or between birth and the present, or between the present and death: *He lived all his ~ in London. I have lived*

here all my ~. The murderer received a ~ sentence/was sentenced to imprisonment for ~. The murderer is doing ~/was given ~, (sl) imprisonment for ~. *~ annuity*, one that will be paid for the rest of a person's ~. '~ *cycle*, progression through different stages of development: *the ~ cycle of a frog*, from the egg to the tadpole to the final stage. *~ interest*, (legal) benefit valid (from property, etc) during a person's ~. *~ peer*, member of the House of Lords, whose title is not inherited by his heirs. *early/late in ~*, during the early/late part of one's ~: *marry early/late in ~. have the time of one's ~*, (colloq) enjoy oneself immensely, as never before. **6** [U] human relations; the business, pleasures, social activities, etc, of the world: *Sailors don't earn much money, but they do see ~*, see how people everywhere live. *There is not much ~* (eg social activity) *in our small village. true to ~*, (of a story, drama, etc) giving a true description of how people live. **7** [C,U] (way of) living; career: *Some people have easy lives. Which do you prefer, town ~ or country ~? That's the ~ for me!* That's how I should like to live. '*high ~*, ⇨ high¹(12). **8** [C] written account of sb's ~; biography: *Do you enjoy reading the lives of great men? He has written a new ~ of Newton.* '~ *story*, biography. **9** [U] activity, liveliness, interest: *The children are full of ~*, are active and cheerful. *Put more ~ into your work. the ~ (and soul) of the party*, person who is the most lively and amusing member of a social gathering. **10** [U] living form or model: *a portrait/picture taken from* (*the*) *~; a '~ drawing; a '~ class*, (in an art school) one in which students draw or paint from living models. *to the ~*, with great fidelity or exactness: *draw/portray/imitate sb to the ~.* ⇨ lifelike below. *as large as ~*, (a) of natural or ordinary size: *a statue as large as ~.* (b) (colloq and in joke) in person; without possibility of doubt or error. **11** [C] fresh start or opportunity after a narrow escape from death, disaster, etc: *The batsman was given a ~*, eg when the fielders missed an easy catch. *They say a cat has nine lives.* **12** [C] period during which sth is active or useful: *the ~ of a steamship/a government.* **13** '~ *assurance/ insurance*, ⇨ these words. *expectation of ~;' ~ expectancy*, (insurance) statistically determined number of years that a person at a particular age may expect to live. *a good/bad ~*, person who is likely to pass/not to reach this average. **14** (compounds) '~-*belt* *n* belt of cork or other buoyant material to keep a person afloat in water. '~-*blood* *n* [U] blood necessary to ~; (fig) vitalizing influence; sth that gives strength and energy. '~-*boat* *n* (a) boat specially built for going to the help of persons in danger at sea along the coast. (b) boat carried on a ship for use in case the ship is in danger of sinking, is on fire, etc. '~-*buoy* *n* ~belt in the form of a ring, through which a person puts his head, shoulders and arms. '~ *cycle* *n* ⇨ 5 above. '~ *estate* *n* property that a person enjoys for ~, but cannot dispose of further. '~-*giving* *adj* that strengthens or restores physical or spiritual ~. '~-*guard* *n* (a) expert swimmer on duty at dangerous places where people swim. (b) bodyguard of soldiers. '**L~ Guards** *n pl* cavalry regiment in the British army. ,~ '*history* *n* (biol) record of the ~ cycle of an organism. '~-*jacket* *n* one of cork or other buoyant material or one that can be inflated. '~-*like* *adj* **1** resembling real ~; looking like the person represented: *a ~like portrait*. **2** like a living thing: *a ~like cloud*. '**~·line** *n* rope used for saving ~, eg one attached to a ~buoy, or one fastened along the deck of a ship during a storm, for persons to cling to; diver's line for signalling to the ship from which he is working; (fig) anything on which one's ~ depends; (palmistry) line across the palm of the hand, alleged to show one's length of ~, major events in one's ~, etc. '**~·long** *adj* continuing for a long time; lasting throughout ~. '**~·office** *n* life assurance office or business. **~ peer** *n* ⇨ **5** above. '**~·preserver** *n* (**a**) (GB) short stick with a heavy, weighted end, used as a weapon of defence. (**b**) (US) = ~-jacket. '**~·saver** *n* (esp in Australia) ~guard(a). '**~·size(d)** *adj* (of pictures, statues, etc) having the same size, proportions, etc, as the person represented. '**~·span** *n* (biol) longest period of ~ of an organism known from the study of it. **~·sup'port system,** equipment in a spacecraft which provides an environment in which astronauts may live. '**~·time** *n* duration of a person's ~. **the chance of a ~time,** an opportunity that comes only once. **~·work** *n* task that occupies one's whole ~ or to which one devotes all one's ~. **~·less** *adj* **1** never having had ~: *~less stones*. **2** having lost ~; dead. **3** dull; not lively: *answer in a ~less manner*. **~·less·ly** *adv* **lifer** /'laɪfə(r)/ *n* **1** (with *adj* prefixed) person who lives a certain kind of ~: *a simple-lifer*. **2** (sl) (one who serves a) sentence of ~ imprisonment.

a life-buoy

a life-jacket

lift /lɪft/ *vt, vi* **1** [VP6A,15A,B] raise to a higher level or position: *~ (up) a table*; *~ sth out of a box/a child out of his cot. This box is too heavy for me to ~ (it). This piece of good luck ~ed her spirits.* *~ up one's eyes (to...),* look up (at). *have one's face ~ed,* have a face-lift; ⇨ face¹(2). *not ~ a finger,* ⇨ finger. *~ up one's voice,* raise it, cry out. **2** [VP2C] *~ off,* (of a rocket, spacecraft) rise from the launching site. Hence, '**~-off** *n*: *We have ~-off*. **3** [VP2A] yield to an attempt to ~: *This window won't ~,* won't go up. **4** [VP2A] (of clouds, fog, etc) rise; pass away: *The mist began to ~.* **5** [VP6A] dig up (root crops); remove (plants, shrubs, etc) from the ground: *~ potatoes*. **6** [VP6A] steal: *~ articles in a supermarket.* '**shop·~,** ⇨ shop(1). take without permission or proper acknowledgement: *Long passages in this textbook have been ~ed from other authors.* **7** [VP6A] end a ban, prohibition, blockade, siege. □ *n* [C] **1** act of ~ing. *give sb/get a ~,* (**a**) offer sb/be offered a ride in a car or other vehicle: *Can you give me a ~ to the station?* ⇨ also *air ~* at air¹(7). (**b**) (fig) (of a person's spirits) become/make more cheerful, contented: *The big increase in her salary gave her a tremendous ~.* **2** (US = *elevator*) box-like apparatus in a building for taking people up or down to another floor: *take the ~ to the tenth floor.* '**~-**

man /-mæn/ *n* one who operates a ~.

liga·ment /'lɪɡəmənt/ *n* [C] band of tough, strong tissues that holds two or more bones together in the body.

liga·ture /'lɪɡətʃə(r)/ *n* [C] **1** bandage, piece of thread, etc used in tying, esp cord used to tie up a bleeding artery. **2** (printing) two or more letters jointed, eg *ʃ* and *l* joined as fl.

light¹ /laɪt/ *adj* (-er, -est) (opposite of *dark*) **1** (of a place) well provided with light³(1): *a ~ room. It's beginning to get ~.* **2** pale-coloured: *~ hair; a ~ complexion; ~ blue/green/brown.* '**~-coloured** *adj* having a ~ colour: *a ~-coloured dress.*

light² /laɪt/ *adj* (-er, -est) (opposite of *heavy*) **1** not heavy; not having much weight (for its size): *as ~ as air/as a feather; a ~ fall of snow; a pair of ~ shoes; a ~ cart or van,* one made for ~ loads and quick movement; *~ clothing,* for summer; *a ~ building/bridge; a ~ railway,* for ~ traffic; *a ~ cruiser,* with ~ armour and guns. **~ horse,** light-armed cavalry: *a' ~ (horse) brigade,* with ~ equipment and weapons. Hence, **~-'armed** *adj* **2** gentle; delicate: *give sb a ~ touch on the shoulder; walk with ~ footsteps/movements; have a ~ hand for pastry,* have delicacy of touch that gives good results. Hence, **~-'handed** *adj* having a ~ hand. **~-'handedly** *adv* **~-'fingered** *adj* skilful in using the fingers; clever at stealing, eg as a pickpocket. **3** below the correct weight, amount, etc: *a ~ coin; give ~ weight. We're about 50p ~ on the petty cash,* 50p short. **4** (of beer, wines) not very strong; (of food) easily digested; (of meals) small in quantity: *a ~ supper,* (hence) *a ~ eater;* (of sleep) not deep; easily disturbed; (of sleepers) easily waked; (of books, plays, music) primarily for amusement, not for serious entertainment or study: *~ reading/music/comedy; a ~ comedian;* (of soil) easily broken up; (of work) easily done; (of taxes, punishment) not difficult to bear; (of a syllable) not stressed, unemphatic. *make ~ work of sth,* do it without much effort. **5** not serious or important: *a ~ attack of illness. make ~ of,* treat as of no or little importance: *He makes ~ of his illness.* **6** thoughtless; frivolous; jesting: *~ conduct; a man of ~ character,* not troubling much about moral questions. **~-'minded** *adj* frivolous. Hence, **~-'mindedness** *n* **7** cheerful; free from sorrow: *a ~ heart.* Hence, **~-'hearted** *adj* **~-'heartedly** *adv* **~-'heartedness** *n* **8** without moral discipline; wanton: *a ~ woman.* **9** dizzy, delirious: (chiefly in) **~-'headed** *adj* **~-'headedly** *adv* and **~-'headedness** *n* **10** (compounds) **~-o'-'love** *n* fickle woman; harlot. '**~-weight** *n, adj* (man or animal) below average weight; (esp, boxing) boxer weighing between 126 and 135 lb (or 57 to 61 kg); (fig) (person) not important or serious. **~-'heavyweight** *n* (esp) boxer weighing between 160 and 175 lb (or 72·5 to 79·3 kg). □ *adv* in a ~ manner: *tread/sleep ~; travel ~,* with little luggage; *get off ~(ly),* (colloq) escape without heavy punishment. **~·ly** *adv* **~·ness** *n*

light³ /laɪt/ *n* (opposite of *dark*¹ or *darkness*) **1** [U] (and with *indef art* and *adjj*) that which makes things visible: *the ~ of the sun/a lamp/the fire; read by the ~ of a candle; a bright/dim ~; go for a walk by 'moon~; bathed in 'sun~. We need more ~. The ~ (ie day~) began to fail,* It began to get dark. *in a good/bad ~,* (**a**) so as to be seen well/badly: *The picture has been hung in a bad ~.* (**b**) (fig) so as to make a good/bad impression: *Press* *reports always make him appear in a bad* ~. *see the* ~, (a) (liter or rhet) be born. (b) be made public. (c) realize the truth of sth that one has been obstinate about. (d) undergo religious conversion. *be/stand in sb's* ~, (a) obscure what he is looking at. (b) (fig) hamper, hinder (sb's chances of success, progress). *stand in one's own* ~, (a) so as to obscure one's work, etc. (b) (fig) act against one's own interests. '~ *year,* (astron) unit of measurement for distances between stars; distance travelled by ~ in one year (about 6 million million miles). 2 [C] source of ~; sth that gives ~, eg a candle or lamp: '*traffic* ~s; ,navi'gation ~s. *L*~s *were burning in every room. Turn/Switch the* ~s *on/off. Put that* ~ *out! All the* ~s *went out—there was a power failure.* ~, (bugle call signalling) the time when ~s are to be turned out. *northern/southern* ~s, ⇨ aurora. 3 [C] flame; spark; sth used for producing a spark or flame: *Can you give me a* ~, *please?* eg for a cigarette or pipe. Note that *fire* is not used in this sense. *Strike a* ~, make a ~ by striking a match. 4 [U] expression of brightness or liveliness in a person's face (esp in the eyes), suggesting happiness or other emotion: *The* ~ *died out of her eyes,* Her looks changed from happiness to sadness, from liveliness to lack of interest. *the* ~ *of sb's countenance,* (biblical) his favour, approval. 5 [U] knowledge or information that helps understanding; [C] fact or discovery that explains. *come/bring sth to* ~, become/ cause sth to be visible or known: *Much new evidence has come to* ~/*has been brought to* ~ *in recent years. shed/throw* ~/(a) *new* ~ *on sth,* make sth clearer, provide new information: *These facts shed* (*a*) *new* ~ *on the matter. by the* ~ *of nature,* without the help of revelation or teaching. *in the* ~ *of,* with the help given by or gained from. 6 [U] aspect; way in which sth appears: *I cannot view your conduct in a favourable* ~, cannot approve of it. *I have never looked upon the matter in that* ~. *In the* ~ *of the new evidence, it was decided to take the manufacturers to court.* 7 (*pl*) (natural or acquired) abilities; mental powers. *according to one's* ~s, to the best of one's abilities. 8 [C] famous person; person (to be) regarded as an example or model: *one of the leading/shining* ~s *of our age.* 9 [C] window or opening in a wall or roof for the admission of ~ (esp in a roof): *a* '*sky*~; compartment of glass in the side or roof of a greenhouse or frame (used for ventilation). **leaded** ~, small pane or panel of glass, secured in strips of lead, often coloured, forming part of a larger window. ⇨ also *quarter-*~ at quarter(16). 10 [C] (painting) part of a picture shown as lighted up: '*high* ~s, the brightest parts; ~ *and shade.* 11 (compounds) '~·**house** *n* tower or other tall structure containing beacon ~s for warning or guiding

a lighthouse

ships at sea. '~·**ship** *n* ship moored or anchored and provided with beacon ~s for the same purpose as those in a ~house.

light[4] /laɪt/ *vt,vi* (*pt,pp* lit /lɪt/ or ~ed) (~ed is more usu as a *pred adj,* as in *a* ~ed *candle*). 1 [VP6A] cause to begin burning or to give out ~: ~ *a lamp/candle/cigarette;* ~ *a fire,* put a burning match to the material in a fireplace, etc. 2 [VP6A] provide lights[3](2) to or for: *Is your flat* ~ed/lit *by gas or by electricity? Our streets are* ~ed/lit *by electricity.* 3 [VP15B] ~ *sth up,* cause to become bright: *The shops were brilliantly lit up. The burning building lit up the whole district.* 4 [VP2C] ~ *up,* (a) switch on (electric) ~s; turn on gas-lamps, etc: *It's getting dark—time to* ~ *up.* Hence, ~ing-'**up time** *n* time at which, according to regulations, lamps in the roads and on vehicles must be lit. (b) (colloq) begin to smoke a pipe or cigarette: *He struck a match and lit up.* 5 [VP2C,15B] ~ *up (with),* (of a person's face or expression) (cause to) become bright: *Her face lit up with pleasure. A smile lit up her face.* 6 [VP15A] guide with or by a light: ~ *a person on his way.*

light[5] /laɪt/ *vi* (*pt,pp* lit /lɪt/ or ~ed) [VP3A] ~ *on/upon,* come upon a find by chance: ~ *upon a rare book in a secondhand bookshop.*

lighten[1] /laɪtn/ *vt,vi* [VP6A,2A] make or become less heavy; reduce the weight of: ~ *a ship's cargo;* ~ *a ship of her cargo;* ~ *taxes. Her heart* ~ed *when she heard the news.*

lighten[2] /laɪtn/ *vt,vi* 1 [VP6A] make light or bright: *A solitary candle* ~ed *the darkness of the cellar.* 2 [VP2A] become light or bright: *The eastern sky* ~ed. 3 [VP2A] send out lightning: *It's thundering and* ~ing.

lighter[1] /laɪtə(r)/ *n* [C] 1 device for lighting cigarettes or cigars. 2 (chiefly in compounds) person or thing that lights: '*lamp-*~, man who went round the streets with a ladder to light gas-lamps.

lighter[2] /laɪtə(r)/ *n* boat, usu flat-bottomed, used for loading and unloading ships not brought to a wharf, and for carrying goods in a harbour or river: *a tug with a string of* ~s *behind it.* □ *vt* remove (goods) in a ~. '~·**age** /-ɪdʒ/ *n* fees charged for carrying goods in ~s.

lightning

light·ning /laɪtnɪŋ/ *n* [U] flash of bright light produced by natural electricity between clouds in the sky or clouds and the ground, with thunder: *struck/killed by* ~. *like* ~; *with* ~ *speed,* very fast. ~ *bug, n* (US) firefly. '~-**rod/-conductor** *nn* metal rod fixed on the top of a high building, etc and connected with the earth, to prevent damage by ~. ~ **strike** *n* strike, of workers, started without warning.

lights /laɪts/ *n pl* lungs of sheep, pigs, bullocks, etc used as food.

light·some /laɪtsəm/ *adj* 1 graceful. 2 merry; light-hearted; frivolous. ~·**ly** *adv* ~·**ness** *n*

lig·neous /lɪgnɪəs/ *adj* (of plants) woody. ⇨ herbaceous.

lig·nite /'lɪgnaɪt/ n [U] soft, brownish-black coal.

lik·able, like·able /'laɪkəbl/ adj of a kind that is, or deserves to be, liked; pleasing: a ∼ man/tune.

like¹ /laɪk/ adj ⇨ alike. (used attrib and pred) similar; having the same or similar qualities, etc; having a resemblance: The two girls are very ∼. L∼ (ie similar) causes produce ∼ (ie similar) results. He writes well on this and ∼ subjects. They are as ∼ as two peas. L∼ father, ∼ son; ∼ master, ∼ man (prov) As the one is, so the other will be. ,∼-'minded /'maɪndɪd/ adj having the same tastes, aims, etc. □ adv 1 ∼ as, (archaic) in the same manner as. 2 probably: (only in) ∼ enough/most/very ∼; as ∼ as not, very probably (likely is more usu, ⇨ likely(2)). □ conj 1 as (common use among those who have not been taught to avoid it; considered incorrect, but found in many good writers): She can't cook ∼ her mother does. Don't think you can learn grammatical rules ∼ you learn the multiplication tables. 2 (non-standard use) as if: It rained like the skies were falling. □ n 1 ∼ person or thing; that which is equal or similar to sth else: That was acting, the ∼ of which we shall not see again, We shall not see acting equally good. Music, painting and the ∼, and similar branches of the arts. I never heard the ∼ (of it), anything so strange, etc according to context. 2 the ∼s of, (colloq) person(s) thing(s) similar to: the ∼s of us/them. Have you ever seen the ∼s of this? □ prep 1 (Often governing a pron, n, or gerund; originally like to/unto, this being now archaic or poet) such as; resembling: What is he ∼? What sort of person is he—in looks, behaviour, etc, according to the situation? He was wearing a hat rather ∼ this one. It looks ∼ gold, has the appearance of gold. This is nothing ∼ as good, not nearly so good. **nothing** ∼, nothing to equal; nothing to be compared with: There's nothing ∼ (= nothing as good as) leather. There's nothing ∼ walking as a means of keeping fit. **something** ∼, nearly; about: The cost will be something ∼ five pounds. This is something '∼ a dinner! This is a remarkably good or satisfactory dinner! 2 '**feel** ∼, be in a state or mood right or suitable for: Do you feel ∼ having a rest? She felt ∼ crying. We'll go for a walk if you feel ∼ it. '**look** ∼, look as if sb/it might be (used to show probability or likelihood): He looks ∼ winning, It seems likely that he will win. It looks ∼ being a fine day, Appearances suggest that the day will be fine. It looks ∼ rain. 3 characteristic of: That's just ∼ him! He has behaved, spoken, etc just as one would expect! It's (just) ∼ her to think of others before thinking of herself. 4 in the manner of; to the same degree as: Don't talk ∼ that, in that way. If I were to behave ∼ you..., in the way you behave.... If everyone worked ∼ me,.... It fits him ∼ a glove, closely, tightly. He drinks ∼ a fish. 5 (colloq, sl) ∼ **anything**, as hard, etc as can be expected or imagined: She works ∼ anything when she's interested. ∼ **mad/crazy**, as if crazy: He complains ∼ mad when things go wrong. ∼ **hell/blazes**, (a) furiously; energetically: He moans ∼ hell when he loses a bet. (b) (as an int) of course (not)!: 'But you were there, weren't you?' 'L∼ hell, I was!' I certainly wasn't!

like² /laɪk/ vt 1 [VP6A,D,7A] be fond of; have a taste for; find satisfactory or agreeable: Do you ∼ fish? I ∼ to read in bed but I don't ∼ having meals in bed. She ∼s him but she doesn't love him. I ∼ his impudence! (ironic, meaning that his im-

pudence is preposterous or amusing). Well, I ∼ that! (ironic, meaning that what has been said or done is surprising, unexpected, etc). 2 [VP6D,7A] (in neg sentences) be unwilling or reluctant: I didn't ∼ to disturb you. I don't ∼ troubling her. 3 [VP6A,7A] (with should, would) used to indicate a wish: I should ∼ to go there, if it were possible, if I were invited, etc. I shouldn't ∼ to do that, have no wish to do it. She would ∼ a cup of tea, I think. I should ∼ to know/to see..., often ironic, meaning that it would be difficult to explain, show, etc. They would have ∼ed to come.... 4 [VP6A,7A,17,19B,C,22] prefer; choose; wish: I ∼ people to tell the truth. How do you ∼ your tea? I ∼ (= prefer) it rather weak. I ∼ this more (or, colloq better) than that. You wouldn't ∼ there to be another war, would you? I don't ∼ you to smoke/you smoking/your smoking. **if you** ∼, used to express consent to a request or suggestion: I will come if you ∼. 5 [VP6A] suit the health of: I ∼ lobster but it doesn't ∼ me, ie it gives me indigestion. □ n (pl, only in) ∼s and 'dis∼s, ⇨ dislike.

like·ly /'laɪklɪ/ adj (-ier, -iest) 1 that is expected: the ∼ winner of the contest. Is he ∼ to win? 2 that seems reasonable, suitable, or right for a purpose: That's a ∼ story/excuse (often used ironically). This looks a ∼ field for mushrooms. What do you think is the likeliest/the most ∼ time to find him at home? Which are the most ∼ candidates, those with the best chance of success? 3 ∼ + to-inf; ∼ **that...**, to be expected: He is not ∼ to succeed. It's highly (= very) ∼ that he will succeed. An incident ∼ to lead to war is reported from X. That is not ∼ to happen. □ adv **most/very** ∼, probably. I shall very ∼ be here again next month. **as** ∼ **as not**, with greater probability: He will succeed as ∼ as not. He'll forget all about it as ∼ as not. **like·li·hood** /-hʊd/ n [U] probability: In all likelihood (= Very probable), we shall be away for a week.

liken /'laɪkən/ vt [VP14] ∼ **sth to sth**, point out the likeness of one thing (to another): ∼ the heart to a pump.

like·ness /'laɪknɪs/ n 1 [U] resemblance; being like: I can't see much ∼ between the two boys. **in the** ∼ **of**, in the form, shape or external appearance of. 2 [C] point of resemblance; instance of being like: There's a family ∼ in all of them. 3 [C] representation (in a portrait, picture, photograph etc): The portrait is a good ∼.

like·wise /'laɪkwaɪz/ adv in the same or a similar way: Watch him and do ∼. □ conj also; moreover.

lik·ing /'laɪkɪŋ/ n (a) ∼, fondness. **have a** ∼ **for**, be fond of. **to one's** ∼, as one likes it; satisfactory: Is everything to your ∼?

li·lac /'laɪlək/ n 1 shrub with sweet-smelling pale purple or white blossom: an avenue of ∼s, ∼ shrubs; a bunch of ∼ (sing for the blossom). 2 pale purple or pinkish-purple: a ∼ dress.

Lil·li·pu·tian /,lɪlɪ'pjuːʃn/ n native of Lilliput /'lɪlɪpʌt/ (the country described in Swift's Gulliver's Travels). □ adj very small.

lilt /lɪlt/ n [C] (lively song or tune with a) well-marked rhythm or swing. □ vt, vi go, sing with a ∼: a ∼ing waltz.

lily /'lɪlɪ/ n (pl -lies) (kinds of) plant growing from a bulb, of many sizes, shapes and colours: ,∼ of the 'valley; 'water lilies; 'Easter lilies; 'calla lilies. ∼-**livered** /'lɪlɪ lɪvəd/ adj cowardly. ∼-'**white** adj as white as a ∼; pure white.

limb /lɪm/ n 1 leg, arm or wing (the more usu

words): *rest one's tired ~s; be torn ~ from ~ by wolves; escape with life and ~,* without serious injury. **2** bough (of a tree). **leave sb/be/go out on a ~,** (colloq) leave sb/be/put oneself in a vulnerable position, eg because separated from supporters. **3** (colloq) **~ of the devil/of Satan,** mischievous child. **-limbed** /lımd/ *suff* (in compounds) *,long-/ ,strong-/~ed,* having long/strong ~s.

lim·ber /'lımbə(r)/ *adj* flexible, pliable. □ *vt,vi* [VP15B,2C] **~ (oneself) up,** make oneself (one's muscles) pliant, flexible.

limbo /'lımbəʊ/ *n* (*pl ~s /-bəʊz/*) **1** [U] *in ~,* in a condition of being forgotten and unwanted (colloq) *The idea of forming a staff association is in ~* (= has been put to one side) *until the new Manager is appointed.* **2** [C] place for forgotten and unwanted things. **3** (usu **L~**) region for souls of unbaptized infants and pre-~Christian righteous persons.

lime¹ /laɪm/ *n* [U] **1** white substance (calcium oxide, **CaO**) obtained by burning limestone, used in making cement and mortar. **'quick-~,** ~ before water is added. **,slaked '~,** ~ after being acted upon by water. ⇨ calcium. **'~-kiln** *n* kiln in which ~stone is burnt. **'~-light** *n* [U] intense white light produced by heating ~ in a very hot flame, formerly used for lighting the stage in theatres. *the ~light,* publicity: *fond of the ~light.* **in the ~light,** receiving publicity. **'~-stone** *n* [U] (kinds of) rock containing much ~, quarried for industrial use. **2** [U] **'bird-)~,** sticky substance made from holly bark for catching small birds. □ *vt* [VP6A] put ~ on (fields, etc) (to control acidity).

lime² /laɪm/ *n* (also **'~-tree**) tree with smooth heart-shaped leaves and sweet-smelling yellow blossoms.

lime³ /laɪm/ *n* (tree with) round juicy fruit like, but more acid than, a lemon. **'~-juice** *n* juice of this fruit used for flavouring, as a drink, and medicinally.

lim·er·ick /'lımərık/ *n* humorous or nonsense poem of five lines.

limey /'laɪmɪ/ *n* (*pl ~s*) (US sl) British person.

limit¹ /'lımıt/ *n* [C] line or point that may not or cannot be passed; greatest or smallest amount, degree, etc of what is possible: *within the city ~s, boundaries; within a ~ of five miles/a five-mile ~. We must set a ~ to the expense of the trip,* fix a sum not to be exceeded. *As we grow older we learn the ~s of our abilities,* learn what we can do and what we cannot do. *His greed knows no ~s. There is a ~ to my patience. She reached the ~ of her patience.* **within ~s,** in moderation: *I'm willing to help you, within ~s.* **without ~,** to any extent or degree: *If only the banks would lend money without ~! off ~s,* (US) = out of bounds, ⇨ bound¹. *That's the ~,* (colloq) That is as much as (or more than) can be tolerated. **'age ~** *n* age¹(1) given as a ~ for participation in an activity, etc.

limit² /'lımıt/ *vt* [VP6A,14] **~ sb/sth (to sth),** put a limit or limits to; be the limit of: *We must ~ the expense to what we can afford. I shall ~ myself to three aspects of the subject.* **~ed** *pp* small; restricted; narrow: *a ~ed edition,* one ~ed to a specified number of copies. *Our accommodation is very ~ed. He seems to have only a ~ed intelligence.* **~ed ,lia'bility company,** (abbr **Ltd,** placed after the name) business company whose members are liable for its debts only to the extent of the capital sum they have provided. **~ed 'monarchy,** one

that is restricted by the constitution. ⇨ absolute(2). **~·less** *adj* without ~: *the ~less ocean; a dictator whose ambitions were ~less.*

limi·ta·tion /,lımɪ'teɪʃn/ *n* **1** [U] limiting; condition of being limited. **2** [C] condition, fact or circumstance that limits; disability or inability: *He knows his ~s,* knows well that in some respects his abilities are limited.

limn /lım/ *vt* (old use) paint (a picture); portray (in drawing or in words).

limou·sine /'lıməzi:n/ *n* large, luxurious motor-car with an enclosed body, the front seats being separated by means of a partition (as in a London taxi). (Cf *saloon-car,* with no partition behind the driver.)

limp¹ /lımp/ *adj* not stiff or firm; lacking strength: *The book is bound in ~ cloth; a ~ edition of a book. The flowers looked ~ in the heat.* **~·ly** *adv* **~·ness** *n*

limp² /lımp/ *vi* [VP2A,C] walk lamely or unevenly as when one leg or foot is hurt or stiff: *The wounded soldier ~ed off the battlefield. The damaged ship ~ed* (= managed with difficulty to get) *back to port.* □ *n* (usu **a ~**) lame walk: *walk with/have a bad ~.*

lim·pet /'lımpıt/ *n* small shellfish that fastens itself tightly to rocks, ⇨ the illus at **mollusc**; (fig) person who sticks tightly to an office, a position or another person. **'~ mine,** explosive mine (to be) placed in position against the hull of a ship, eg by frogmen.

lim·pid /'lımpıd/ *adj* (lit, fig, rhet) (of liquids, the atmosphere, the eyes) clear; transparent. **~·ly** *adv* **~·ity** /lım'pıdəti/ *n* [U] quality or state of being ~.

linch·pin /'lıntʃpın/ *n* iron pin passed through the end of an axle to keep the wheel in position; (fig) vital part; person who, because of his work, etc, keeps an organization, etc together.

Lin·coln green /,lıŋkən 'grin/ *n* bright green cloth as made at Lincoln: *Robin Hood and his men, dressed in ~.*

lin·den /'lındən/ *n* (also **'~-tree**) = lime².

line¹ /laɪn/ *n* **1** piece or length of thread, string, rope or wire for various purposes: **'fishing ~s; 'telephone ~s.** *Hang* (out) *the clothes on the ~,* (ie the **'clothes-~**). *L~ fishing is quite different from net-fishing. He's clever with rod and ~,* is a good angler. *The ~s* (ie telephone, etc ~s) *are all down as a result of the blizzard. Give me a ~, please,* (to the operator of a telephone switchboard) Connect me to the Exchange, please (so that I can dial direct). *L~ engaged!* (US *L~ busy*) used of a telephone ~ already in use. **crossed ~,** ⇨ cross²(5). **'hot ~,** ⇨ hot¹(8). **'party/shared ~,** telephone ~ serving two or more subscribers. **2** long, narrow mark made on a surface: *L~s may be straight, crooked or curved. Draw a ~ from A to B. In mathematics a ~ is defined as having length but not breadth or thickness.* **3** [U] the use of ~s(2) in art, etc: *a '~ drawing,* eg with a pen or pencil; **'~-engraving,** done with ~s cut on a surface; *the beauty of ~ in the work of Botticelli; translate life into ~ and colour,* represent living things by means of ~s and colour. **4** (in games) mark made to limit a court or ground, or special parts of them: *Did the ball cross the ~?* ⇨ lineman. **5** mark like a ~ on the skin of the face; furrow or wrinkle; one of the marks on the palm of the hand: *There were deep ~s on her face.* **6** (*pl*) contour; outline: *a ship of fine ~s,* with a graceful outline; *the delicate*

~s of Gothic architecture; (in shipbuilding) plans, esp of horizontal, vertical and oblique sections. **7** row of persons or things: *a ~ of trees/chairs/ people waiting to go into a cinema; manufactured goods on the as'sembly ~; a long ~ of low hills.* **in (a)** ~, forming a ~: *The boys were standing in (a) ~.* **in ~ for,** next in order for: *He's in ~ for promotion.* **on the ~,** (of objects exhibited, esp paintings) with the centre about level with the eyes of the viewer. **8** edge, boundary, that divides: *cross the ~ into Canada* (ie from US); equator: *cross the ~.* **draw the ~ (at),** ⇨ draw²(13). **9** railway; single track of railway ~s: *the 'up/'down ~,* to/ from the chief terminus; *the main ~; a'branch ~. Cross the ~ by the bridge.* **reach the end of the ~,** (fig, eg of a relationship) reach the point where it breaks down, ends. **10** organized system of transport under one management and giving a regular service: *an 'air~; a new 'bus ~; a 'steamship ~.* **11** direction; course; track; way of behaviour, dealing with a situation, etc: *the ~ of march of an army; ,communi'cation ~s. Don't stand in the ~ of fire! You'll get shot! You should keep to your own ~,* be independent of others. **choose/ follow/take the ~ of least resistance,** the easiest way of doing things. **take a strong/firm ~ (over sth),** deal with a problem, etc resolutely: *Should the government take a stronger ~ over inflation? What ~ do you intend to take,* How will you approach the problem? **do sth along/on sound/correct, etc ~s,** use good, etc methods: *He is studying the subject on sound ~s/on the wrong ~s. I shall proceed along/on these ~s until further notice.* **(be) in/out of ~ (with),** in agreement/disagreement (with). **bring sth into ~,** cause sth to conform. **come/fall into ~ (with),** (persuade or cause sb to) accept views, conform, agree. **toe the ~,** (fig) submit to discipline, accept the ideas, programme, etc of a (political, etc) party. **the party ~,** the agreed or established policy of a political party: *follow the party ~,* vote, speak, write, etc in accordance with this policy. **12** connected series of persons following one another in time, esp of the same ancestry: *a long ~ of great kings; the last of his ~; trace back one's family ~,* one's ancestry; *a descendant of King David in a direct ~/in the male ~.* **13** row of words on a page of writing or in print: *page 5, ~ 10. 'L~s to a friend on her birthday',* eg as the title of a poem. **drop sb a ~,** (colloq) write to sb: *Drop me a ~ to say how you're getting on.* **read between the ~s,** (fig) find more meaning than the words appear to express. **'marriage ~s,** (GB colloq) certificate of marriage. **~s,** (a) words of an actor's part: *The leading actor was not sure of his ~s.* **(b)** form of punishment by which a schoolchild is required to write out a specified number of ~s. **14** series of connected military defence posts, trenches, etc: *go into the front ~(s),* the area nearest to the enemy's ~s; *high-ranking officers well behind the ~s.* **all along the ~,** at every point; in every way. **go up the ~,** leave base for the front ~(s). **15** (mil) row of tents, huts, etc in a camp: *inspect the ~s; the 'horse ~s.* **16 the ~,** (GB army) regular infantry regiments (excluding the Guards and Rifles): *regiments of the ~; a ~ regiment; infantry of the ~;* (US army) regular fighting forces of all classes. **17** [U] (mil) double row (front and rear ranks) of men standing side by side (contrasted with *file* and *column*): *The troops attacked in extended ~.* The men

formed into ~. **18** (naval) **~ abreast,** (number of parallel ships) abreast of each other. **~ astern,** (number of ships) in a ~ one behind the other. **ship of the ~; ~-of-battle ship,** (in former times) ship of 74 or more guns; largest type of warship. **19** department of activity; business; occupation: *He's in the 'drapery ~. His ~ is stockbroking/banking. That's not much in my ~,* I don't know much about it, am not much interested in it. **20** (trade use) class of commercial goods: *a cheap ~ in felt hats; the best-selling ~ in woollen underwear.* **21 Hard ~s!** Bad luck! **22** (sl) **shoot a ~,** brag, boast. Hence, **'~-shooting,** '~**-shooter** *nn* **23** (colloq) **give sb/get/have a ~ on sth,** give etc information about it.

line² /laɪn/ *vt,vi* **1** [VP6A,15B] mark (sth) with lines: *~d paper,* with lines printed on it; *~ in a contour,* on a blank map; *~ sth out on paper,* mark it out with ~s. **2** [VP6A] cover with lines: *a ~d face; a face ~d with anxiety. Pain had ~d her forehead.* **3** [VP2C,15B] *~ up,* (cause to) be in a line, get into a line. *The general ~d up his troops. The soldiers quickly ~d up.* ⇨ line-up. *~ up (for sth),* (US) queue (for it). **4** [VP6A] form, be placed, in a line or lines along: *a road ~d with trees; a road ~d with police. Crowds of people ~d the kerb to see the funeral procession.*

line³ /laɪn/ *vt* [VP6A,14] *~ sth (with sth),* **1** provide with an inside covering; add a layer of (usu different) material to the inside of (bags, boxes, articles of clothing): *fur~d gloves; an overcoat ~d with silk.* ⇨ lining. **2** (fig) fill (one's purse, pocket, stomach, etc): *He has ~d his purse well,* made a lot of money.

lin·eage /'lɪnɪɪdʒ/ *n* [U] family line; ancestry; line of descent.

lin·eal /'lɪnɪəl/ *adj* in the direct line of descent (from father to son, etc): *a ~ descendant/heir.* **~·ly** /-ɪəlɪ/ *adv*

lin·ea·ment /'lɪnɪəmənt/ *n* (formal) (usu *pl* except after *each* and *every*) line, detail, distinctive feature or characteristic (of the face): *the ~s of a Mongol face.*

lin·ear /'lɪnɪə(r)/ *adj* **1** of or in lines: *a ~ design.* **2** of length: *~ measure,* eg feet and inches or metres. ⇨ App 5.

line·man /'laɪnmən/ *n* **1** man who puts up and maintains telegraph and telephone lines. **2** (US) = linesman.

linen /'lɪnɪn/ *n* [U] cloth made of flax; articles made from this cloth, esp shirts and collars, bed-sheets, tablecloths and table napkins: (attrib) *~ handkerchiefs.* **'~-draper** *n* person who sells ~ and cotton goods. **wash one's dirty ~ in public,** discuss family quarrels, unpleasant personal affairs, etc in the presence of other people.

liner /'laɪnə(r)/ *n* **1** ship or aircraft of a line(10) of ships or aircraft: *a fast 'air~; a trans-Atlantic ~.* ⇨ the illus at ship. **2** '~(-train) (also 'freight~), long distance express goods train between industrial centres and seaports, with facilities for fast (un)loading of goods.

lines·man /'laɪnzmən/ *n* (sport) person who helps the umpire or referee by saying whether or where the ball touches or crosses one of the lines.

line-up /'laɪn ʌp/ *n* **1** way in which persons, states, etc are arranged or allied; alignment: *a new ~ of Afro-Asian powers; a ~ of men in an identification parade.* **2** formation of players ready for action (in a game such as baseball or football). **3** programme of items (esp for radio or TV): *This evening's* ~ *includes an interview with the Chairman of British Rail.*

ling[1] /lɪŋ/ *n* [U] (kinds of) heather.

ling[2] /lɪŋ/ *n* long, slender N European seafish (usu salted) for food.

lin·gam /'lɪŋgəm/ *n* phallic emblem (as a symbol of the Hindu god Siva /'ʃiːvə/).

lin·ger /'lɪŋgə(r)/ *vi* [VP2A,C] be late or slow in going away; stay at or near a place: ~ *on after everyone else has left;* ~ *about/around. The custom* ~*s on,* is still observed but is now weak. ~**ing** *adj* long; protracted: *a* ~*ing illness; a* ~*ing look,* one showing regret, unwillingness to leave or give up sth; *a few* ~*ing* (remaining) *doubts.* ~**ing·ly** *adv* ~**er** *n* person who ~s.

linge·rie /'lænʒəri: US: ˌlɑːndʒə'reɪ/ *n* [U] (F) (trade name for) women's underclothing.

lingo /'lɪŋgəʊ/ *n* (*pl* ~es /-gəʊz/) (hum or derog) language, esp one that one does not know; way of talking, vocabulary, of a special subject or class of people: *the strange* ~ *used by experts in radio and television.*

lin·gua franca /ˌlɪŋgwə 'fræŋkə/ *n* language adopted for local communication over an area in which several languages are spoken, eg Swahili in E Africa.

lin·gual /'lɪŋgwəl/ *adj* of the tongue, speech or languages, esp in compounds, as ˌaudio-'~, (of methods, devices, etc) requiring one to listen and speak: *audio-*~ *aids,* eg a tape-recorder. ˌbi'~, speaking two languages. ˌmulti-'~, speaking many languages.

lin·guist /'lɪŋgwɪst/ *n* **1** person skilled in foreign languages: *She's a good* ~*. I'm no* ~, am poor at foreign languages. **2** one who makes a scientific study of language(s).

lin·guis·tic /lɪŋ'gwɪstɪk/ *adj* of (the scientific study of) languages: *the* ~ *study of literature,* centred on the language. ~**s** *n pl* (with *sing v*) the science of language, eg of its structure, acquisition, relationship to other forms of communication. **ap,plied** '~**s**, this study put to practical uses, esp in the teaching of languages.

lini·ment /'lɪnɪmənt/ *n* [C,U] (kind of) liquid usu made with oil for rubbing on stiff or aching parts of the body.

lin·ing /'laɪnɪŋ/ *n* **1** [C] layer of material added to the inside of sth: *an overcoat with a fur* ~; *a jewel-box with a velvet* ~. *Every cloud has a silver* ~, (prov) There is sth good in every evil. **2** [U] material used for this purpose.

link[1] /lɪŋk/ *n* **1** one ring or loop of a chain. **2** (usu *pl*) one of a pair of fasteners for the sleeves of a shirt: '*cuff-*~*s*. **3** person or thing that unites or connects two others: *a* ~ *in a chain of evidence; the* ~ *between the past and the future.* **missing** ~, that which is needed to complete a series; animal supposed to have existed, of a type between the apes and man. '~**·man** /-mæn/ *n* (*pl* -men) person who provides the connecting ~ between two groups. **4** measure of length, one hundredth of a chain; 7·92 inches or about 20 centimetres. ⇨ App 5. □ *vt,vi* [VP6A,15A,B,2A,C] ~ *(up),* join, be joined, with, or as with, a ~ or ~s: ~ *things together;* ~ *one's arm in/through another person's arm; two towns* ~*ed by a canal;* ~*ing verbs,* eg *be. How do religion and philosophy* ~ *up?* Hence, '~**-up** *n* act or result of ~ing.

link[2] /lɪŋk/ *n* (hist) torch formerly used for lighting

people along streets. '~**·boy,** '~**·man** /-mæn/ *nn* one formerly employed to carry ~s and guide people through badly lighted streets.

links /lɪŋks/ *n* **1** (with *pl v*) grassy land, esp sandhills, near the sea. **2** (often **a** ~, with *sing v*) golf-course.

lin·net /'lɪnɪt/ *n* small brown songbird, common in Europe.

lino /'laɪnəʊ/ *n* [U] (abbr for) linoleum. '~**-cut** *n* [C] design cut in relief on a block of linoleum; print made from this.

lin·oleum /lɪ'nəʊlɪəm/ *n* [U] strong floor-covering of canvas treated with powdered cork and oil.

lino·type /'laɪnəʊtaɪp/ *n* (P) machine (with a keyboard like that of a typewriter) used for setting type, each line of type being cast in the form of a complete bar of metal.

lin·seed /'lɪnsiːd/ *n* [U] seed of flax. ~ **oil** *n* [U] oil pressed from ~, used in making printing-ink, linoleum, etc.

lin·sey-wool·sey /ˌlɪnzɪ 'wʊlzɪ/ *n* [U] strong, coarse material made from inferior wool woven with cotton.

lint /lɪnt/ *n* [U] linen, with one side scraped so as to be fluffy, used for dressing wounds: (attrib) *a* ~ *bandage.*

lin·tel /'lɪntl/ *n* horizontal piece of wood or stone forming the top of the frame of a door or window. ⇨ the illus at window.

lion /'laɪən/ *n* **1** large, strong, flesh-eating animal found in Africa and S Asia, called 'the King of Beasts' because of its fine appearance and courage. ⇨ the illus at cat. *the* ~*'s share,* the larger or£largest part. '~**-hearted** *adj* brave. **2** person whose company is very much desired at social gatherings, eg a famous author or musician. '~**-hunter** *n* person who tries to get ~s as guests at dinner parties, etc. ~**·ess** /-es/ *n* female ~. ⇨ the illus at cat. '~**·ize** /-aɪz/ *vt* [VP6A] treat as a ~(2): *The famous explorer was* ~*ized when he returned home.*

lip /lɪp/ *n* **1** one or other of the fleshy edges of the opening of the mouth: *the lower/upper lip; a man with a cigar between his lips. She refused to open her lips,* wouldn't say anything. ⇨ the illus at mouth. *bite one's lip,* show vexation. *curl one's lip,* show scorn. *give/pay* '*lip-service to sth,* make promises, express regret, admiration etc about it, not sincerely felt. *hang on/upon sb's lips,* listen eagerly to every word he says. *keep a stiff upper lip,* show no emotion, sign of fear, anxiety, etc. *lick/smack one's lips,* show (anticipation of) enjoyment. '**lip-reading** *n* [U] method (taught to deaf people) of understanding speech from lip movements. Hence, '**lip-read** *vt.* '**lip-stick** *n* [C,U] (stick of) cosmetic material for reddening the lips: *buy three lipsticks; use too much lipstick.* **2** edge of a hollow vessel or opening: *the lip of a saucer/crater.* **3** [U] (sl) impudence: *None of your lip!* Don't be impudent! **-lipped,** in compounds: ,*thick-/,dry-'lipped,* having thick/dry lips.

liquefy /'lɪkwɪfaɪ/ *vt,vi* (*pt,pp* -fied) [VP6A,2A] make or become liquid. **lique·fac·tion** /ˌlɪkwɪ'fækʃn/ *n* [U] making or becoming liquid; being liquified.

li·ques·cent /lɪ'kwesnt/ *adj* becoming, apt to become, liquid.

li·queur /lɪ'kjʊə(r) US: -'kɜːr/ *n* strong usu sweet alcoholic drink for taking in small quantities: ~ *brandy,* of special quality for drinking as a ~; '~ *glass,* very small for ~s.

liquid /'lɪkwɪd/ n **1** [C,U] substance like water or oil that flows freely and is neither a solid nor a gas: *Air is a fluid but not a ~; water is both a fluid and a ~. You have added too much ~ to the mixture.* **2** (phon) the consonant /r/ or /l/. □ *adj* **1** in the form of a ~; not solid or gaseous: *~ food,* soft, easily swallowed, suitable for sick people; *~ mud,* so soft that it can be poured. *~ gas,* gas reduced to a ~ state by intense cold. **2** clear, bright and moist-looking: *~ eyes,* bright and shining; *a ~ sky.* **3** (of sounds) clear; pure; not guttural: *the ~ notes of a blackbird.* **4** not fixed; easily changed: *~ opinions.* **5** (in finance) easily sold or changed into cash: *~ assets.*

liqui·date /'lɪkwɪdeɪt/ vt, vi **1** [VP6A] pay or settle (a debt). **2** [VP6A] bring (an unsuccessful business company) to an end by dividing up its property to pay debts; [VP2A] (of a company) go through this process. **3** [VP6A] (colloq or newspaper style) get rid of, put an end to; kill: *gangsters who ~ their rivals.* **liqui·da·tion** /ˌlɪkwɪ'deɪʃn/ n [U] liquidating or being ~ed. *go into liquidation,* become bankrupt. **liq·ui·da·tor** /-tə(r)/ n official who ~s (2).

liq·uid·ity /lɪ'kwɪdətɪ/ n [U] state of being liquid(5); state of being able to raise funds easily by selling assets.

liquid·ize /'lɪkwɪdaɪz/ vt [VP6A] crush, eg fruit, vegetables, to a liquid pulp. *~r* n device (usu with an electric motor) for liquidizing fruit, etc.

liquor /'lɪkə(r)/ n [C,U] **1** (GB) any alcoholic drink: *under the influence of ~,* partly drunk; *the worse for ~,* drunk; *malt ~,* beer; *brandy and other spirituous ~s.* **2** (US) any distilled alcoholic drink: *~ store.* **3** liquid produced by boiling or fermenting a food substance.

liquor·ice (US = **licor·ice**) /'lɪkərɪs/ n [U] (plant from whose root is obtained a) black substance used in medicine and in sweets.

lira /'lɪərə/ n (pl lire /'lɪəreɪ, 'lɪərə/ or ~s) unit of money in Italy.

lisle /'laɪl/ n [U] fine, hard-twisted cotton fabric, used for stockings, gloves, etc.

lisp /lɪsp/ vi, vt [VP2A,6A,15B] fail to use the sounds /s/ and /z/ correctly, eg by saying /θɪk'θtiːn/ for *sixteen*; say in a ~ing manner: *She ~s. He ~ed (out) his words.* □ n lisping way of speaking: *The child has a bad ~. ~·ing·ly* adv

lis·som, lis·some /'lɪsəm/ adj lithe; quick and graceful in movement. *~·ness* n

list[1] /lɪst/ n number of names (of persons, items, things, etc) written or printed: *a 'shopping ~; make a ~ of things one must do; put sb's name on/take his name off the list. ~ price,* (comm) published or advertised price. *the active ~, ~ of officers in the armed forces who may be called upon for service. the free ~,* (a) those goods admitted into a country free of duty. (b) those persons who are admitted to a cinema, theatre, concert hall, etc without payment. □ vt [VP6A] make a ~ of; put on a ~: *~ all one's engagements; ~ sb's name.*

list[2] /lɪst/ vi [VP2A,C] (esp of a ship) lean over to one side, eg because the cargo has shifted: *The ship ~s to starboard.* □ n ~ing of a ship: *a bad ~ to port.*

list[3] /lɪst/ vt, vi (old use) listen (to).

list[4] /lɪst/ vi (old use) please; choose: *'The wind bloweth where it ~eth.'*

lis·ten /'lɪsn/ vi [VP2A,C,3A] *~ (to),* **1** try to hear; pay attention: *We ~ed but heard nothing. The*

boys heard their father's voice but were not ~ing to what he was saying. Please ~ carefully for the telephone while I'm upstairs. ~ in (to), (a) listen to a broadcast programme: *Did you ~ in to the Prime Minister yesterday evening?* (b) *~ in to a* conversation, eg by tapping telephone lines or using an extension telephone receiver. **2** agree to a suggestion, request, etc: *Don't ~ to him; he wants to get you into trouble. ~·er* n one who ~s.

list·less /'lɪstlɪs/ adj too tired to show interest or do anything. *~·ly* adv *~·ness* n

lists /lɪsts/ n pl (hist) (palisades enclosing an) area of ground for fights between men on horseback wearing armour and using lances. *enter the ~ (against sb),* (fig) challenge (sb) or accept a challenge (from sb) to a contest.

lit /lɪt/ pt, pp of light[4]. *lit up,* (sl) drunk.

lit·any /'lɪtənɪ/ n (pl -nies) form of prayer for use in church services, recited by a priest with responses from the congregation. *the L~,* that in the Book of Common Prayer of the Church of England.

lit·chi /'laɪtʃiː/ = lychee.

liter /'liːtə(r)/ ⇨ litre.

lit·er·acy /'lɪtərəsɪ/ n [U] ability to read and write.

lit·eral /'lɪtərəl/ adj **1** connected with, expressed in, letters of an alphabet: *a ~ error,* a misprint. **2** corresponding exactly to the original: *a ~ transcript/ copy of an old manuscript; a ~ translation.* (Cf *free* translation.) **3** (contrasted with *figurative*) taking words in their usual and obvious sense, without allegory or metaphor: *I hear nothing in the ~ sense of the word,* (ie of the word 'hear') get no news by hearing people speak (though I may get news from letters, etc). **4** (of a person) prosaic; matter of fact; lacking in imagination: *He has a rather ~ mind.* □ *n ~ error;* misprint. *~·ly* /'lɪtərəlɪ/ adv **1** word for word; strictly: *translate ~ly; carry out orders too ~ly.* **2** (informal use, to intensify meaning) without exaggeration: *The children were ~ly starving.*

lit·er·ary /'lɪtərərɪ US: 'lɪtərerɪ/ adj of literature or authors: *the ~ profession; a ~ man,* either an author or a man interested in literature; *~ style,* as used in literature contrasted with *colloquial,* etc. *~ property,* the right of an author to fees, royalties, etc coming from his writings.

lit·er·ate /'lɪtərət/ adj **1** able to read and write. **2** cultured; well-read: *He's a remarkably ~ young man.* □ *n ~* person.

lit·er·ati /ˌlɪtə'rɑːtɪ/ n pl the literary intelligentsia.

lit·era·ture /'lɪtrətʃə(r) US: -tʃʊər/ n [U] **1** (the writing or the study of) books, etc valued as works of art (drama, fiction, essays, poetry, biography, contrasted with technical books and journalism). **2** (also with *indef art*) all the writings of a country (*French ~*) or a period (*18th century English ~*); books dealing with a special subject: *travel ~; the ~ of poultry-farming. There is now an extensive ~ dealing with the First World War.* **3** [U] printed material describing or advertising sth, eg pamphlets: *We shall be glad to send you some ~ about our refrigerators/package holidays.*

lithe /laɪð/ adj (of a person, a body) bending, twisting or turning easily: *~ movements; make one's muscles ~.*

lith·ogra·phy /lɪ'θɒɡrəfɪ/ n [U] process of printing from parts of a flat stone or sheet of zinc or aluminium that are prepared to receive a greasy ink. **li·tho·graph** /'lɪθəɡrɑːf US: -ɡræf/ n sth (esp a picture) printed by this process. □ vt, vi print by this process. **litho·graphic** /ˌlɪθəˈgræfɪk/ *adj* of ∼.

liti·gant /ˈlɪtɪgənt/ *n* person engaged in a lawsuit.

liti·gate /ˈlɪtɪgeɪt/ *vi,vt* **1** [VP2A] go to law; make a claim at a court of law. **2** [VP6A] contest (sth) at a court of law. **liti·ga·tion** /ˌlɪtɪˈgeɪʃn/ *n* [U] litigating; going to law. **lit·igious** /lɪˈtɪdʒəs/ *adj* **1** fond of going to law. **2** that can be disputed at law.

lit·mus /ˈlɪtməs/ *n* blue colouring–matter that is turned red by acid and can then be restored to blue by alkali. '∼-**paper**, paper stained with ∼ and used as a test for acids and alkalis.

li·totes /ˈlaɪtəʊtiːz/ *n* understatement used ironically, esp using a negative to express the contrary, as 'I shan't be sorry when it's over' meaning 'I shall be very glad', or 'It was no easy matter' for 'It was very difficult'.

litre (US = **liter**) /ˈliːtə(r)/ *n* unit of capacity in the metric system. 1 ∼ = about 1¾ pints. ⇨ App 5.

lit·ter[1] /ˈlɪtə(r)/ *n* **1** (hist) couch or bed (often with a covering and curtains) in which a person may be carried about, eg on men's shoulders, and as used in ancient Rome. **2** sort of stretcher for carrying a sick or wounded person.

lit·ter[2] /ˈlɪtə(r)/ *n* **1** [U] odds and ends, bits of paper, discarded wrappings, bottles, etc left lying about in a room or public place: *Pick up your* ∼ *after a picnic.* '∼-**bin/-basket** *n* bin, basket, into which to place ∼. '∼-**lout** *n* (colloq) person who leaves ∼ about in public places. **2 a** ∼, state of untidiness that results when things are left lying about instead of being put away: *Her room was in such a* ∼ *that she was ashamed to ask me in.* **3** [U] straw and dung of a farmyard; straw and similar material, eg dry bracken, used as bedding for animals or for protecting plants from frost. **4** [C] all the newly born young ones of an animal: *a* ∼ *of puppies; ten little pigs at a* ∼. □ *vt,vi* **1** [VP6A,15A,B,14] ∼ **sth (up) with sth,** make untidy with odds and ends; scatter ∼(1): *a* ∼ *desk with papers;* ∼ *up one's room.* **2** [VP6A,15B] ∼ **sth (down),** supply a horse, etc) with straw; make a bed for an animal: ∼ *down a horse/a stable.* **3** [VP2A] (of animals, esp dogs and pigs) bring forth a ∼ of young ones.

little /ˈlɪtl/ *adj* (In senses 1, 2 and 4 ∼ has no real *comp and superl;* ∼r and ∼st are occasionally used but are better avoided; ⇨ less and least for senses 3 and 5.) **1** small, or small in comparison; (as a distinctive epithet) *the* ∼ *finger/toe.* **2** (often preceded by another *adj* with no connotation of smallness, to indicate affection, tenderness, regard, admiration, or the contrary, depending upon the preceding *adj*): *Isn't he a* ∼ *devil!* (indicating affectionate regard). *What a pretty* ∼ *house! That poor* ∼ *girl!* (indicating sympathy). *What horrid* ∼ *children! She's a nice* ∼ *thing* (indicating tenderness or regard, but possibly patronage, or a feeling of superiority). *Such a dear* ∼ *man* (suggesting benign patronage) *came round and fixed my central heating. He's quite the* ∼ *gentleman!* (suggesting patronage). *the* '∼ *people/folk,* (esp in Ireland) fairies; elves. **3** short (in time, distance, stature): *Won't you stay a* ∼ *time with me? Come a* ∼ *way with me.* **4** young: *How are the* ∼ *ones,* the children? *Here come the* ∼ *Smiths,* the Smith children. **5** not much: *He gained* ∼ *advantage from the scheme. I have very* ∼ *time for reading. He knows* ∼ *Latin and less Greek.* **6 a** ∼, some but not much; a small quantity of: *He knows a* ∼ *French. A* ∼ *care would have prevented the accident. Will you have a* ∼ *cake,* a piece or slice of cake? (Cf *Will you have a cake,* one of these cakes?) *not a* ∼, (euphem) much: *It has caused me not a* ∼ *anxiety,* considerable anxiety. □ *adv* **1** not much; hardly at all; only slightly: *He is* ∼ *known. She slept very* ∼ *last night. I see him very* ∼ (ie rarely) *nowadays. He left* ∼ *more than an hour ago. That is* ∼ *short of* (= is almost) *madness! He is* ∼ *better than* (= is almost as bad as) *a thief.* **a** ∼, (used *adverbially* meaning) rather; somewhat: *She seemed to be a* ∼ *afraid. This hat is a* ∼ *too large for me. He was not a* ∼ *annoyed,* was considerably annoyed. **2** (with such *vv* as *know, think, imagine, guess, suspect, realize,* and always placed before the *v*) not at all: *They* ∼ *suspect/L∼ do they suspect that their plot has been discovered. He* ∼ *knows/L∼ does he know that the police are about to arrest him.* ∼-**ness** *n* [U] the quality of being ∼. □ *n* (⇨ less, least). **1** not much; only a small amount: *You have done very* ∼ *for us,* have not helped us much. *I see very* ∼ *of him,* do not see him often or for long. *The* ∼ *of his work that I have seen seems excellent. I got* ∼ *out of it,* not much advantage or profit. *He did what* ∼ *he could. Every* ∼ *helps.* ∼ *by* ∼, gradually; by degrees. ∼ *or nothing,* hardly anything. *in* ∼, on a small scale. **2 a** ∼, a small quantity; something (*a* ∼ is positive; ∼ is negative): *He knows a* ∼ *of everything. A* ∼ *makes some people laugh. Please give me a* ∼. *after/for a* ∼, after/for a short time or distance.

lit·toral /ˈlɪtərəl/ *n, adj* (part of a country which is) along the coast.

lit·urgy /ˈlɪtədʒɪ/ *n* (*pl* -gies) [C,U] fixed form of public worship used in a church. **li·turgi·cal** /lɪˈtɜːdʒɪkl/ *adj*

liv·able, live·able /ˈlɪvəbl/ *adj* (of life) tolerable. ∼ (*in*), (of a house, room, climate, etc) fit to live in. ∼ (*with*), (of persons) easy to live with.

live[1] /laɪv/ *adj* (rarely pred; ⇨ living and alive for pred uses) **1** having life: ∼ *fish;* (joc) actual, not pretended: *There's a real* ∼ *burglar under my bed!* **2** burning or glowing: ∼ *coals/embers;* unexploded: *a* ∼ *shell/cartridge/bomb;* not used: *a* ∼ *match;* charged with electricity: *a* ∼ *rail,* carrying current for trains. *a* '∼ *wire,* (fig) a lively energetic person. **3** (of sth broadcast) not recorded in advance (on tape or records): *It was a* ∼ *broadcast, not a recording.* **4** '∼-**birth** *n* (contrasted with *still-birth*) baby born alive: *the ratio of* ∼-*births to still-births.* **5** full of energy, activity, interest, importance, etc: *a* ∼ *question/issue,* one in which there is great interest. □ *adv* (from **3** above): *The concert will be broadcast* ∼.

live[2] /lɪv/ *vi,vt* **1** [VP2A] have existence as a plant or animal; be alive (the more usu phrase: *He's still alive* is preferable to *He still* ∼*s*). **2** [VP2A,B,C,4A] continue to be alive; remain alive: ∼ *to be old/to a great age;* ∼ *to see all one's grandchildren married. She's very ill—the doctors don't think she will* ∼. *Can he* ∼ *through the night?* ∼ *on,* continue to ∼: *The old people died but the young people* ∼*d on in the village.* ∼ *through,* experience and survive: *He has* ∼*d through two wars and three revolutions. You/We* ∼ *and learn,* phrase used when one hears sth new, esp sth surprising. ∼ *and* '*let* ∼, be tolerant; ignore the failings of others in order that one's failings may be ignored. **3** [VP3A] ∼ *by doing sth,* earn one's livelihood by doing it. ∼ *by one's wits,* get money by ingenious and irregular

methods, not necessarily honest. ~ **off the land,**
use its agricultural products for one's food needs.
~ **on sth,** have it as food or diet: ~ *on fruit/a milk
diet;* depend upon for support, etc: ~ *on one's
salary/on £3000 a year/on one's wife's income.* ~
on one's name/reputation, keep one's position,
continue to earn money, because one has been successful in the past. 4 [VP2C,3A] ~ *(in/at),* make
one's home; reside: ~ *in England;* ~ *at home;* ~
abroad; ~ *in lodgings/an hotel. Where do you* ~?
~ **in/out,** (esp of domestic servants, shop assistants, workers) lodge in/out of the building where
one is employed. ~ **together,** live in the same
house, etc; (of two persons of opposite sex) live as
if married: *I hear that Jane and Bill are living
together.* 5 [VP6B,2D] (with cognate object) spend,
pass, experience: ~ *a happy life/a virtuous life;* ~
a double life, act two different parts in life. *He* ~d
the life of a Christian. He ~d *and died a bachelor.*
6 [VP2C,D] conduct oneself; pass one's life in a
specified way: ~ *honestly/happily;* ~ *like a saint;*
~ *well,* live a life satifying all the appetites. ~ **a
lie,** express a lie by one's manner of living. ~ **to
oneself,** in isolation, without trying to make
friends. 7 [VP15B] ~ **sth down,** live in such a way
that (past guilt, scandal, foolishness, etc) is forgotten: *He hopes to* ~ *down the scandal caused by the
divorce proceedings.* [VP2C] ~ **up to sth,** put
(one's faith, principles, etc) into practice; reach the
standard that may be expected: *It's difficult to* ~ *up
to the principles of the Christian religion. He
didn't* ~ *up to his reputation.* [VP3A] ~ **with sth,**
accept and endure it: *I don't like the noise of these
jet aircraft, but I've learnt to* ~ *with it.* 8 [VP2A]
(of things without life) remain in existence; survive: *His memory will always* ~, He will never be
forgotten. *No ship could* ~ *in such a rough sea.* 9
[VP2A] enjoy life intensely: *'I want to* ~', *she
said, 'I don't want to spend my days cooking and
cleaning and looking after babies.'* ~ **it up,** live a
life of hectic enjoyment.
live·li·hood /'laɪvlɪhʊd/ *n* means of living; way in
which one earns money: *earn/gain one's* ~ *by
teaching; earn an honest* ~; *deprive a man of his*
~.
live·long /'lɪvlɒŋ US: 'laɪvlɔːŋ/ *adj* (only in) **the** ~
day/night, the whole length of the day/night
(implying, according to context, weariness or delight).
live·ly /'laɪvlɪ/ *adj* (-ier, -iest) **1** full of life and
spirit; gay and cheerful: *She's as* ~ *as a kitten.
The patient seems a little livelier/a little more* ~
this morning. He has a ~ *imagination. They had a*
~ *time,* exciting, perhaps with an element of danger. **look** ~, move more quickly, show more
energy. **make things** ~ **for sb,** make it exciting
and perhaps dangerous for him. **2** (of colour)
bright; gay. **3** (of non-living things) moving quickly or causing quick movement: *a* ~ *ball; a* ~
(*cricket*) *pitch.* **4** lifelike; realistic: *a* ~ *description of a football game; give sb a* ~ *idea of what
happened.* **live·li·ness** *n* [U] state of being ~.
liven /'laɪvn/ *vt,vi* [VP15B,2C] ~ **up,** make or become lively: *How can we* ~ *things up? The party
is beginning to* ~ *up.*
liver¹ /'lɪvə(r)/ *n* **1** [C] large, reddish-brown organ
in the body which secretes bile and purifies the
blood. ⇨ the illus at alimentary. **2** [U] animal's ~
as food. ~**·ish** /-ɪʃ/, ~**y** *adjj* (colloq) suffering
from ~ trouble; bilious.

liver² /'lɪvə(r)/ *n* person who lives in a specified
way: *an evil/clean/loose* ~.
liver·wurst /'lɪvəwɜːst/ *n* (US) sausage of chopped
liver, popular in sandwiches.
liv·ery /'lɪvərɪ/ *n* (*pl* -ries) **1** special dress or uniform worn by men servants in a great household
(esp of a king or noble) or by members of one of
the city companies of London (trade or craft
guilds). **in/out of** ~, wearing/not wearing such
dress or uniform. '~ **company,** one of the London
trade guilds that has a distinctive uniform. **2** (fig,
poet) dress; covering: *trees in the* ~ *of spring,* with
new green leaves; *birds in their winter* ~. **3** '~
(stable), stable where horses are kept for their
owners, fed and looked after for payment; stable
from which horses may be hired. **liv·er·ied**
/'lɪvərɪd/ *adj* wearing ~(1). '~**·man** /-mən/ *n* (*pl*
-men) **1** member of a ~ company. **2** keeper of,
worker in, a ~ stable.
lives /laɪvz/ *pl* of life.
live·stock /'laɪvstɒk/ *n* [U] (esp farm) animals kept
for use or profit, eg cattle, sheep, pigs.
livid /'lɪvɪd/ *adj* of the colour of lead, blue-grey; (of
a person or his looks) furiously angry: ~ *marks/
bruises on the body;* ~ *with cold/rage.* ~**·ly** *adv*
liv·ing¹ /'lɪvɪŋ/ *adj* **1** alive, esp now existent: ~
languages. No man ~ (= No man who is now
alive) *could do better.* **within/in** ~ **memory,**
within the memory of people now alive. **2** (of a
likeness) true to life: *He's the* ~ *image of* (= is
exactly like) *his father.* **3** strong; active; lively: *a*
~ *hope/faith.* **the** ~ **theatre,** the ordinary theatre
(contrasted with the cinema, TV, etc). □ *n* **the** ~,
(with *pl v*) those now alive: *He's still in the land of
the* ~.
liv·ing² /'lɪvɪŋ/ *n* **1** means of keeping alive, of earning what is needed for life: *earn/gain/get/make a*
~ *as a car salesman.* **2** [U] manner of life: *good*
~, having good food, etc; *plain* ~ *and high thinking,* having plain, simple food and leading a philo-
sophic life; *the high cost/standard of* ~ *in the US;
the art of* ~. ,~ **'wage,** minimum wage for a
worker and his family to live on. '~**-room** *n* room
for general use during the day (often a general purpose room, used for meals, recreation, etc). '~**-
space** *n* area of land considered by a State as
necessary for further expansion. **3** (Church of England) benefice.
liz·ard /'lɪzəd/ *n* small, creeping, long-tailed,
four-legged reptile. ⇨ the illus at reptile.
llama /'lɑːmə/ *n* S American animal with a thick
woolly coat, used as a beast of burden. ⇨ the illus
at large.
Lloyd's /'lɔɪdz/ *n* society of underwriters in London. **A1 at** ~, (dated sl) excellent.~**'s Register,**
annual list of ships in various classes.
lo /ləʊ/ *int* (old use) Look! See! *Lo and behold!*
This will surprise you.
load¹ /ləʊd/ *n* [C] **1** that which is (to be) carried or
supported, esp if heavy: (fig) weight of care, responsibility, etc: *a heavy* ~ *on one's shoulders; a*
'*coach*-~ *of passengers.* **take a** ~ **off sb's mind,**
relieve him of anxiety, etc. ~**s of,** (colloq) a large
amount of: ~*s of friends/money/time.* '~**-line** *n*
= Plimsoll line. **2** amount which a cart, etc can
take: *a* '*cart*-~ *of hay; two* '*lorry*-~*s of coal.* ⇨
also *pay-load* at pay¹. **3** amount of work that a
dynamo, motor, engine, etc is required to do;
amount of current supplied by a generating station
or carried by an electric circuit. '~**-shedding** *n*

cutting off the supply of current on certain lines when the demand for current is greater than the supply.

load² /ləʊd/ *vt,vi* **1** [VP6A,14,15A,B,2A,C] ~ *sth into/on to sth/sb;* ~ *sth/sb (with sth);* ~ *sb/ sth down (with sth),* put a ~ in or on: ~ *sacks on to a cart/a donkey;* ~ *a cart with coal;* ~ *a lot of work on to one's staff; a poor old woman* ~*ed (down) with her shopping;* (fig) ~ *a man with favours/honours; a heart* ~*ed with sorrow.* ~ *(sth) up,* fill with goods, materials, etc: *Have you finished* ~*ing up (the van) yet?* **2** [VP6A,2A] put a cartridge or shell into (a gun) or a length of film into (a camera): *Are you* ~*ed?* Is there a cartridge in your gun? **3** [VP6A] weight with lead; add extra weight to: *a* ~*ed cane/stick,* one having lead added to make the cane useful as a weapon; ~*ed dice,* so weighted as to fall with a certain face, eg the six, uppermost. ~ *the dice (against sb),* (fig) do sth that gives one an unfair advantage (over him). *a* ~*ed question,* one that is intended to trap a person into making an admission which may be harmful. ~*ed adj* (sl) having much money.
load-star, load-stone ⇨ lode.
loaf¹ /ləʊf/ *n* (*pl* loaves /ləʊvz/) **1** mass of bread cooked as a separate quantity: *a two-pound* ~. *Half a* ~ *is better than none/no bread,* It is better to take what one can get or is offered than to run the risk of having nothing. **2** 'sugar-~ *n* [C] cone-shaped mass of sugar, as formerly made and sold. '~-sugar *n* [U] sugar cut into small lumps. **3** [C,U] (quantity of) food shaped and cooked: (*a*) *meat* ~, made of minced meat, eggs, etc. **4** (sl) *use one's* ~, think intelligently; reflect.
loaf² /ləʊf/ *vi,vt* [VP2A,C,15A,B] (colloq) waste time; spend time idly: *out-of-work men* ~*ing at street corners. Don't* ~ *about while there's so much work to be done. Don't* ~ *away your time.* □ *n* (*sing* only) ~ing. ~er *n* person who ~s.
loam /ləʊm/ *n* [U] rich soil with some sand or a little clay, and with much decayed vegetable matter in it. ~y *adj* of or like ~: ~y *land.*
loan /ləʊn/ *n* **1** [C] sth lent, esp a sum of money: *government* ~s, sum lent to the government; *domestic and foreign* ~s. **2** [U] lending or being lent. *have the* ~ *of sth; have sth on* ~ *(from sb),* have it as a borrower: *May I have the* ~ *of your sewing-machine? I have the book out on* ~ *from the library.* '~-collection *n* number of pictures, etc lent by their owners for exhibition. '~-office *n* one for lending money to private borrowers. '~-word *n* word taken from another language. □ *vt* [VP6A,14] ~ *sth (to sb),* lend (which is the more usu word except in formal style).
loath, loth /ləʊθ/ *adj* (pred only) ~ *to do sth,* unwilling. *nothing* ~, quite willing.
loathe /ləʊð/ *vt* [VP6A,C] **1** feel disgust for; dislike greatly: *She was seasick, and* ~*d the smell of greasy food.* **2** (colloq) dislike: *He* ~*s travelling by air.* **loath-ing** *n* [U] disgust. **loath-ly,** (rare), **loath-some** /-səm/ *adjj* disgusting; causing one to feel shocked: *a loathsome disease.*
loaves /ləʊvz/ *pl* of loaf¹.
lob /lɒb/ *vi,vt* (-bb-) [VP6A,15A,2C] strike or send (a ball) in a high arc (in tennis). □ *n* ball bowled underhand at cricket or hit high up into the air at tennis.
lobby /'lɒbɪ/ *n* (*pl* -bies) **1** porch, entrance-hall, anteroom, corridor: *the* ~ *of a hotel/theatre.* **2** (in the House of Commons, etc) large hall used for in-

terviews between members and the public; group of people who try to influence members, eg of the House of Commons, the Senate in Washington, DC, to support or oppose proposed legislation. **3** (di'vision) ~, (House of Commons) one of two corridors to which members retire when a vote is taken in the House. □ *vt,vi* [VP6A,15A,2A,C] (try to) influence the members of a law-making body; get (a bill) passed or rejected in this way: ~ *a bill through the Senate; the National Union of Farmers* ~*ing in order to maintain subsidies/*~*ing for higher subsidies/*~*ing their MP's.* '~-ist /-ɪst/ *n* person who lobbies.
lobe /ləʊb/ *n* **1** lower rounded part of the external ear. ⇨ the illus at ear. **2** subdivision of the lungs or the brain. ⇨ the illus at respiratory. ~d *adj* having ~s.
lob·ster /'lɒbstə(r)/ *n* **1** [C] shellfish with eight legs and two claws, bluish-black before and scarlet after being boiled. ⇨ the illus at crustacean. '~-pot *n* basket in which ~s are trapped. **2** [U] its flesh as food.
lo·cal /'ləʊkl/ *adj* **1** of, special to, a place or district: *the* ~ *doctor,* living in the district; ~ *customs; a column of* ~ *news;* ~ *government.* ~ *col-our,* details of the scenes and period described in a story, added to make the story more real. ~ *option/veto,* (in some countries) system by which people may decide, by voting, whether they do or do not want sth, eg the sale of alcoholic drink, in their district. ~ *time,* time at any place in the world as calculated from the position of the sun: *L*~ *time changes by one hour for every 15° longitude.* **2** affecting a part, not the whole: *a* ~ *pain/ injury; a* ~ *anaesthetic.* □ *n* **1** (usu *pl*) inhabitant of a particular district. **2** item of ~ news in a newspaper. **3** (colloq) ~ public house: *pop into the* ~ *for a pint.* ~·ly /-kəlɪ/ *adv*
lo·cale /ləʊ'kɑːl US: -'kæl/ *n* [C] scene of an event; scene of a novel, etc.
lo·cal·ism /'ləʊkəlɪzəm/ *n* **1** [U] interest in a district, esp one's own; favouring of what is local; narrowness of ideas that may be the result of this. **2** [C] local idiom, pronunciation, etc.
lo·cal·ity /ləʊ'kælətɪ/ *n* (*pl* -ties) **1** [C] thing's position; place in which an event occurs; place, district, neighbourhood. **2** [U] faculty of remembering and recognizing places, features of the landscape, etc, esp as a help in finding one's way: *She has a good sense of* ~.
lo·cal·ize /'ləʊkəlaɪz/ *vt* [VP6A] **1** make local, not general; confine within a particular part or area: *There is little hope of localizing the disease.* **2** invest with local characteristics. **lo·cal·iz·ation** /ˌləʊkəlar'zeɪʃn US: -lɪ'z-/ *n*
lo·cate /ləʊ'keɪt US: 'ləʊkeɪt/ *vt* [VP6A,15A] **1** discover, show, the locality of: ~ *a town on a map.* **2** establish in a place: *a new school to be* ~*d in the suburbs. Where is the new factory to be* ~*d?* **3** *be* ~*d,* be situated. **lo·ca·tion** /ləʊ'keɪʃn/ *n* **1** [U] locating or being ~. **2** [C] position or place: *suitable locations for new factories.* **3** place, not a film studio, where (part of) a cinema film is photographed. *on location,* shooting film in this way. **4** (in S Africa) suburb where Africans are constrained to live.
loch /lɒk/ *n* (Scot) **1** long, narrow arm of the sea almost enclosed by land. **2** lake.
loci /'ləʊsaɪ/ *pl* of locus.
lock¹ /lɒk/ *n* portion of hair that naturally hangs or

a canal lock

clings together; (*pl*) hair of the head: *my scanty* ~*s*.

lock² /lɒk/ *n* **1** appliance, mechanism, by which a door, gate, lid, etc may be fastened with a bolt that needs a key to work it. *keep sth/put sth/be under ~ and key*, in sth fitted with a ~. '**~-smith** *n* maker and mender of ~s. **2** mechanism by which a gun is fired. ~, *stock and barrel*, the whole of the thing; completely. **3** enclosed section of a canal or river at a point where the water level changes, for raising or lowering boats by the use of gates fitted with sluices. ,~-'**gate**, gate on a lock. '**~-keeper** *n* keeper of a canal or river ~, who opens and shuts the gates to allow boats to pass through. **4** [U] condition of being fixed or jammed so that movement is impossible. '**~-jaw** *n* [U] form of disease (tetanus) that causes the jaws to be firmly locked together. '**~-nut** *n* extra nut screwed over another to prevent its turning. '**~-stitch** *n* sewing-machine stitch by which two threads are firmly joined together. ⇨ also *air* ~ at *air*¹(7). **5** (motoring) extent of the turning arc of a steering wheel: *full* ~, with the steering wheel turned (right or left) as far as it will go.

lock³ /lɒk/ *vt,vi* **1** [VP6A,15A,B] fasten a door, box, etc with a lock. ~ *the stable door after the horse has bolted/has been stolen*, take precautions when it is too late. ~ *sth away*, put it away in a ~ed box, drawer, etc; (fig) keep securely: *have a secret safely* ~*ed* (*away*) *in one's breast.* ~ *sb in*, put sb in a room of which the door is ~ed on the outside. ~ *oneself in*, ~ the door so that no one can enter from outside, or so that one cannot open it again. ~ *sb out*, keep him outside, prevent him from entering, by ~ing the gate or door(s) on the inside: *If you don't get back before midnight, you'll be* ~*ed out.* '**~-out** *n* refusal of employers to allow workmen to enter their place of work until certain conditions are agreed to or demands given up. ⇨ *strike*¹. ~ *sth/sb up*, (a) make safe by placing in sth that ~s: *L~ up your jewellery before you go away.* (b) shut up a house, etc by ~ing all the doors. (c) put (a person) in a ~ed room, a prison, a mental home, etc. (d) invest (money) in such a way that it cannot easily or quickly be exchanged for cash: *All his capital is* ~*ed up in land.* '**~-up** *n* place where prisoners may be kept temporarily; (colloq) any prison. □ *adj* (attrib only) that can be ~ed: *a* ~*-up garage*, one, eg at a hotel, that can be ~ed. **2** [VP2A] become ~ed; be capable of being ~ed: *This trunk doesn't* ~, has no lock or has a lock that does not work. *The door* ~*s easily.* **3** [VP6A,2A,C] (cause to) become fixed, unable to move: *His jaws were tightly* ~*ed. He* ~*ed the wheels of the car to prevent its being*

stolen. *They were* ~*ed together in a fierce struggle. They were* ~*ed in each other's arms. The parts* ~ *into each other*, interlock. **4** [VP2C] ~ *on to*, (of a missile, etc) find and automatically follow (a target) by radar.

locker /'lɒkə(r)/ *n* **1** small cupboard, esp one of a number used for keeping one's clothes, eg at a swimming-pool or golf-club. **2** box or compartment in a ship used for clothes, stores, ammunition, etc. *be in/go to Davy Jones's* ~, be drowned at sea.

locket /'lɒkɪt/ *n* small (often gold or silver) case for a portrait, a lock of hair, etc, usu worn round the neck on a chain.

loco /'ləʊkəʊ/ *adj* (sl) mad.

lo·co·mo·tion /,ləʊkə'məʊʃn/ *n* [U] moving, ability to move, from place to place. **lo·co·mo·tive** /'ləʊkəməʊtɪv/ *adj* of, having, causing, ~. □ *n* self-propelled engine for use on railways: *steam/ Diesel/electric locomotives.*

locum /'ləʊkəm/ (also ~ '**tenens** /'tiːnenz/) *n* doctor or priest performing the duties of another who is away, eg on holiday.

lo·cus /'ləʊkəs/ *n* (*pl* loci /'ləʊsaɪ/) exact place of sth. ~ *classicus* /'klæsɪkəs/, best known or most authoritative passage on a subject.

lo·cust /'ləʊkəst/ *n* **1** (kinds of) migratory African and Asian winged insect which flies in great swarms and destroys crops and vegetables. ⇨ the illus at insect. ⇨ hopper²(2). **2** '~(-tree), (kind of) tree, esp *carob* and a N American tree, *false acacia.*

loc·ution /lə'kjuːʃn/ *n* [U] style of speech; way of using words; [C] phrase or idiom.

lode /ləʊd/ *n* vein of metal ore. '~-star *n* star by which a ship may be steered; the pole-star; (fig) guiding principle. '~-stone *n* magnetized iron ore.

lodge¹ /lɒdʒ/ *n* **1** small house, esp one at the entrance to the grounds of a large house, occupied by a gatekeeper, gardener or other employee of the estate. **2** country house used in the hunting or shooting season: *a 'hunting* ~ *in the Highlands;* (US) hut or cabin for temporary use: *a 'skiing* ~. **3** porter's room(s) in the chief gateway or entrance to a college, factory, block of flats, etc. **4** (GB) residence of the head of a college. **5** (place of meeting for) members of a branch of a society such as the Freemasons. **6** beaver's lair.

lodge² /lɒdʒ/ *vt,vi* **1** [VP6A,15A] supply (sb) with a room or place to sleep in for a time; receive as a guest: *The shipwrecked sailors were* ~*d in the school.* **2** [VP3A] ~ *at/with*, live as a paying guest: *Where are you lodging now? I'm lodging at Mrs P's/with Mr and Mrs X.* **3** [VP3A] ~ *in*, enter and become fixed: *The bullet* ~*d in his jaw.* **4**

[VP6A,15A] ~ *(in)*, cause (sth) to enter and become fixed (*in*); put or place (in a particular place): ~ *a bullet in a man's brain.* 5 [VP6A,15A] put (money, etc) for safety: ~ *one's valuables in the bank while away from home on holiday.* 6 [VP6A,14] ~ *sth (with sb) (against sb)*, place (a statement, etc) with the proper authorities: ~ *a complaint against one's neighbours with the authorities.* ~r *n* person paying for rooms, etc in sb's house: *The widow makes a living by taking in lodgers.*
lodge·ment (also **lodg·ment**) /'lɒdʒmənt/ *n* 1 [U] act or process of lodging: *the ~ of a complaint.* ⇨ **lodge²**(6). 2 [C] sth that has accumulated or been deposited: *a ~ of dirt in a pipe.* 3 [C] (mil) position gained in enemy territory: *gain a ~ on an enemy-held coast.*
lodg·ing /'lɒdʒɪŋ/ *n* (usu *pl*) room or rooms (not in a hotel) rented to live in: *It's cheaper to live in ~s than in a hotel. Where can we find ~s/a ~ for the night?* '~-**house** *n* house in which ~s are let (usu by the week).
lo·ess /'ləʊes/ *n* [U] deposit of fine yellowish-grey soil, found esp in northern China, central USA and central Europe.
loft¹ /lɒft *US*: lɔːft/ *n* 1 room, place, used for storing things, in the highest part of a house, under the roof; space under the roof of a stable or barn, where hay or straw is stored. 2 gallery in a church or hall: *the' organ-~.*
loft² /lɒft *US*: lɔːft/ *vt* [VP6A] (golf, cricket) hit (a ball) high: ~ *a ball over the fielders' heads.*
lofty /'lɒftɪ *US*: 'lɔːftɪ/ *adj* (-ier, -iest) 1 (not used of persons) of great height: *a ~ tower/mountain.* 2 (of thoughts, aims, feelings, etc) distinguished; noble: ~ *sentiments; a ~ style.* 3 haughty; proud; consciously superior: *a ~ appearance; in a ~ manner.* **loft·ily** /-ɪlɪ/ *adv* **lofti·ness** *n*
log¹ /lɒg *US*: lɔːg/ *n* [C] rough length of tree-trunk that has fallen or been cut down; short piece of this for a fire: *a raft of logs,* floating down a river. *like a log,* unconscious; immovable. *sleep like a log,* sleep soundly and with little or no movement. ˌlog-'**cabin** *n* cabin with walls and roof made of logs, not boards. '**log-jam** *n* mass of floating logs tightly mixed together; (US) deadlock. '**log-rolling** *n* practice of giving support to others in return for support from them, eg by author-reviewers who praise each other's books. **log·ging** *n* work of cutting down forest trees for timber: *a logging camp.*
log² /lɒg *US*: lɔːg/ *n* 1 device attached to a knotted line, trailed from a ship, to measure its speed through the water: *sail by the log,* calculate a ship's position by means of information gained from the log. 2 (also '**log-book**) book with a permanent daily record of events during a ship's voyage (esp the weather, ship's position, speed, and distance as recorded by the log); (by extension) any record of performance, eg of a car or aircraft. 3 (colloq) registration book (of a motor-vehicle). □ *vt* (-gg-) [VP6A] enter (facts) in the log-book of a ship or aircraft.
log³ /lɒg *US*: lɔːg/ (colloq abbr for) logarithm.
lo·gan·ber·ry /'ləʊgənberɪ/ *n* (*pl* -ries) large dark-red berry from a plant that is a cross between a blackberry and a raspberry.
log·ar·ithm /'lɒgərɪðəm *US*: 'lɔːg-/ *n* (arith) one of a series of numbers set out in tables which make it possible to work out problems in multiplication and division by adding and subtracting.

log·ger·heads /'lɒgəhedz/ *n* (only in) *at ~ (with)*, disagreeing or disputing: *He's constantly at ~ with his wife.*
log·gia /'lɒdʒɪə/ *n* (I) open-sided gallery or arcade; part of a house with one side open to the garden.
logic /'lɒdʒɪk/ *n* [U] science, method, of reasoning; (person's) ability to argue and convince: *argue with learning and ~.* **logi·cal** /-kl/ *adj* in accordance with the rules of ~; able to reason correctly: *a ~al mind/argument/conclusion; ~al behaviour.* **logi·cally** /-klɪ/ *adv* **logi·cal·ity** /ˌlɒdʒɪ'kælətɪ/ *n* [U] being ~al. **lo·gician** /lə'dʒɪʃn/ *n* person skilled in ~.
lo·gis·tics /lə'dʒɪstɪks/ *n* (with *sing v*) supply, distribution and replacement of materials and personnel, eg for the armed forces.
loin /lɔɪn/ *n* 1 (*pl*) the lower part of the body on both sides of the spine between the ribs and the hip-bones. ⇨ the illus at dog, domestic. *gird (up) one's ~s,* (biblical) prepare for a journey; make ready for action. '~-**cloth** *n* piece of cloth covering the middle of the body, folded between the legs, and fastened round the ~s. 2 joint of meat which includes the ~s: ~ *of mutton.*
loi·ter /'lɔɪtə(r)/ *vi,vt* [VP2A,C,15B] go slowly and stop frequently on the way somewhere; stand about; pass time thus: ~ *on one's way home;* ~ *the hours away;* ~ *over a job.* ~**er** *n* ~ing person.
loll /lɒl/ *vi,vt* [VP2A,C] ~ *(about/around)*, rest, sit or stand (*about*) in a lazy way. 2 [VP2C,15B] ~ *out,* (of the tongue) (allow to) hang: *The dog ~ed its tongue out. The dog's tongue was ~ing out.*
lol·li·pop /'lɒlɪpɒp/ *n* large sweet of boiled sugar on a stick, held in the hand and sucked. '~ **man/woman,** (colloq) one who carries a pole with a disc marked 'Stop! Children crossing', to conduct children across busy roads, eg outside a school.
lolly /'lɒlɪ/ *n* 1 (colloq) lollipop. **ice(d)** ~, quantity of frozen fruit juice on a stick. 2 (sl) money, (esp money easily earned and lavishly spent).
lone /ləʊn/ *adj* (attrib only; ⇨ alone and lonely, which are more usu) solitary; without companions; unfrequented. *play a ~ hand,* (fig) do sth without the help or support of others, esp sth not very popular.
lone·ly /'ləʊnlɪ/ *adj* (-ier, -iest) 1 without companions: *a ~ traveller.* 2 sad or melancholy because one lacks companions, sympathy, friendship: *a ~-looking girl; feel ~.* 3 (of places) not often visited; far from inhabited places or towns: *a ~ house; a ~ mountain village.* **lone·li·ness** *n* [U] state of being ~: *suffer from loneliness.*
lone·some /'ləʊnsəm/ *adj* 1 sad because alone: *feel ~;* causing a feeling of loneliness: *a ~ journey.* 2 solitary, unfrequented: *a ~ valley.*
long¹ /lɒŋ *US*: lɔːŋ/ *adj* (-nger, -ŋgə(r)/, -ngest /-ŋgɪst/) 1 of extent in space; measuring much from end to end: *How ~ is the River Nile? The new road is twenty miles ~. Your car is ~er than mine. What a lot of men have ~ hair nowadays! What a lot of ~-haired men we see today! put on a ~ face,* ⇨ face¹(3). 2 in phrases indicating (great) extent. *have a ~ arm,* be able to make one's power felt far. *the ~ arm of the law,* its far-reaching power. *make a ~ arm for sth,* reach out for sth, eg at table. *It's as broad as it's ~,* ⇨ broad¹(9). 3 expressing duration or extent in time: *the ~ vacation,* the summer vacation of law courts and universities. *He was ill for a ~ time. How ~*

are the holidays? They're six weeks ~. *He won't be* ~ (*in*) *making up his mind,* will soon do so. *Don't be too* ~ *about it,* Do it soon or quickly. ~ **time no see!** (colloq; as greeting) We haven't met for a long time. **4** (of vowel sounds) usually taking more time to utter than others: *'Sit' has a short vowel and 'seed' has a* ~ *vowel. The 'u' in 'rude' is* ~. **5** (in phrases concerned with extent in time) ~ **bond,** (fin) which matures in 20 years or more. **take a** ~ **cool/hard look at sth,** consider facts, problems shrewdly and at length. **take the** ~ **view,** consider events, factors, etc a ~ time ahead, rather than the present situation, etc. **in the** ~ **run,** ⇨ run¹(7). **in the** ~ **term,** looking ahead for a ~ time. Hence, ~**-'term,** *attrib adj* lasting for a ~ time: ~*-term agreements/contracts/investments.* **6** (compounds) '~**·boat** *n* sailing-ship's largest boat. '~**·bow** *n* bow drawn by hand, equal in length to the height of the archer, used with feathered arrows. ⇨ crossbow. **draw the ~bow,** tell exaggerated or invented stories. ~**-'distance** *attrib adj* covering a ~ distance: ~*-distance runners* (in sport); *a* ~*-distance telephone call; a* ~*-distance lorry driver.* ~ **drink** *n* large quantity, eg of beer, served in a tall glass (contrasted with a *short drink,* eg neat whisky). **a** ~ **dozen,** thirteen. '~**-hand** *n* [U] ordinary handwriting (contrasted with *shorthand* and *typing*). ~**-'haired** *adj* (**a**) ⇨ **1** above. (**b**) intellectual; artistic; unconventional. **a** ~ **haul,** ⇨ haul. ~**-'headed** *adj* shrewd; having foresight. **the** ~ **jump,** (athletic contest) measured along the ground for distance. ⇨ **high jump** at high¹(12). ~ **measure,** ⇨ App 5. ~ **metre** *n* [U] stanza of four eight-syllable lines. ~ **odds** *n pl* (in betting) very uneven, eg 50 to 1. ~**-play(ing)** '**disc/'record** *n* (abbr **LP**) playing (at slow speed) for a ~er time than earlier kinds. '~**-range** *attrib adj* of ~ periods of time or ~ distances: *a* ~*-range weather forecast,* eg for one month ahead; ~*-range planning,* for a ~ time ahead, eg ten years; ~*-range missiles.* '~**-shoreman** *n* man who works on shore (on wharves, in dockyards) loading and unloading ships. **a** '~ **shot,** ⇨ shot¹(2). ~**-'sighted** *adj* able to see things a great distance away; (fig) prudent; having foresight. **a** ~ **suit,** ⇨ suit¹(5). '~ **stop** *n* [U] (cricket) player who fields straight behind the wicket-keeper ⇨ the illus at cricket. '~**-time** *attrib adj* that has lasted for a long time: *a* ~*-time acquaintance.* ~ **ton** *n* 2240 lb. ~ **wave** *n* [U] (radio telegraphy) one having a wave-length of 1000 metres or over. ~**-'winded** *adj* tedious and diffuse in speaking or writing: *a* ~*-winded and boring lecturer.* Hence, ~**-'windedness.**
long² /lɒŋ *US:* lɔːŋ/ *n* **1** [U] ~ time or interval: *I shall see you before* ~. *The work won't take* ~. *Will you be away for* ~? **at** (**the**) ~**est,** to give the most distant date, etc: *I can wait only three days at* ~*est,* not after the third day from now. **the** ~ **and the short of it,** all that need be said; the general effect or result. **2** [C] ~ syllable, esp in Latin verse: *four* ~*s and six shorts.*
long³ /lɒŋ *US:* lɔːŋ/ *adv* (-er /-ŋgə(r)/, -est /-ŋgɪst/) **1** (*for*) ~, for a long time: *Stay* (*for*) *as* ~ *as you like. I've* ~ *wanted to meet her.* **as/so** ~ **as,** on condition that, provided that: *You may borrow the book so* ~ *as you don't lend it to anyone else.* **2** (in numerous compounds): ~**-drawn-'out** *adj* extended; unduly prolonged: *a* ~*-drawn-out visit from my mother-in-law.* ~**-'lived** *adj* having

a long life; living for a long time: *a* ~*-lived family.* ~**-'standing** *adj* that has lasted for a long time: *a* ~*-standing invitation to visit the Browns.* ~**-'suffering** *adj* patient and uncomplaining in spite of trouble, provocation, etc: *his* ~*-suffering wife.* **3 at a long time** (from a point of time): ~ *ago/ before/after/since. That happened* ~ *ago.* **4** (with *nn* indicating duration) throughout the specified time: *all day* ~, throughout the whole day; *all my life* ~. **5** *no/any/much* ~*er,* after a certain point of time: *I can't wait any/much* ~*er. He's no* ~*er living here.*
long⁴ /lɒŋ *US:* lɔːŋ/ *vi* [VP3A,4C] ~ **for sth/for sb to do sth,** desire earnestly; wish for very much: *She* ~*ed for him to say something. I'm* ~*ing to see you. The children are* ~*ing for the holidays.* ~**ing** *n* [C,U] (an) earnest desire: *a* ~*ing for home.* □ *adj* having or showing an earnest desire: *a* ~*ing look; with* ~*ing eyes.* ~**·ing·ly** *adv*
lon·gev·ity /lɒn'dʒevətɪ/ *n* [U] long life.
longi·tude /'lɒndʒɪtjuːd *US:* -tuːd/ *n* distance east or west (measured in degrees) from a meridian, esp that of Greenwich, in London. ⇨ the illus at projection. **longi·tudi·nal** /ˌlɒndʒɪ'tjuːdɪnl *US:* -'tuːdnl/ *adj* **1** of ~. **2** of or in length. **3** running lengthwise: *longitudinal stripes,* eg in a flag.
long·ways /'lɒŋweɪz *US:* 'lɔːŋ-/, **long·wise** /'lɒŋwaɪz *US:* 'lɔːŋ-/ *adv* = lengthways.
loo /luː/ *n* (GB colloq) water-closet.
loo·fah, loofa /'luːfə/ *n* [C] dried pod of a plant (kind of gourd or pumpkin) used as a sponge.
look¹ /lʊk/ *vi, vt* (*pt,pp* ~ed) (For uses with *adverbial particles* and *preps* ⇨ **7** below.) **1** [VP2A,C,3A,4A] ~ (*at*), use one's sight; turn the eyes in some direction; try to see: ~ (*up*) *at the ceiling;* ~ (*down*) *at the floor. We* ~*ed but saw nothing. I happened to be* ~*ing another way,* in a different direction. *L*~ *to see whether the road's clear before you cross.* **to** ~ **at him/it, etc,** judging by the outward appearance: *To* ~ *at her you'd never guess that she was a university teacher. L*~ **before you leap,** (prov) Avoid acting hastily, without considering the possible consequences. '~**·ing-glass** *n* mirror made of glass. **2** [VP2D,4D] seem to be; have the appearance of being: ~ *sad/ ill/tired. The town always* ~*s deserted on Sunday mornings. It* ~*s very suspicious to me,* I suspect that it is not strictly honest, straightforward, etc. *The girl* ~*ed puzzled.* (**not**) ~ **oneself,** (not) have one's normal appearance: *You're not* ~*ing yourself today,* You're ~*ing ill,* worried, etc. *He's beginning to* ~ *himself again,* ~ well again, eg after an illness. ~ **one's age,** have an appearance that conforms to one's age: *She* ~*s her age,* seems as old as she in fact is. *You don't* ~ *your age,* You look younger than you are. ~ **one's best,** appear to the greatest advantage: *She* ~*s her best in jeans.* ~ **black** (**at**), ~ angrily (at). ~ **blue,** appear sad or discontented. ~ **good,** (**a**) seem attractive, enticing, etc. (**b**) seem to be making satisfactory progress, doing well, etc: *The horse I put my money on* ~*ed good until the last hundred metres.* Hence, **good-'~·ing** *adj* of fine appearance. ~ **small,** ~ mean or insignificant: *We made him* ~ *small,* exposed him as being insignificant. *L*~ **alive!** Get busy! Make haste! *L*~ **here!** often used to call attention to sth; or demand attention. *L*~ **sharp!** Hurry up! ~ **well,** (**a**) (of persons) be healthy in appearance. (**b**) (of things) be attractive, pleasing, satisfactory: *Does this hat* ~ *well on me?* (**c**) (of a

person wearing sth) ∿ attractive: *He ∿s well in naval uniform.* **3** [VP2C] ∿ **like/as if,** seem (to be): *It ∿s like salt and it is salt. It ∿s like* (= threatens to) *rain. It ∿s like being* (= promises to be) *a fine day. This ∿s to me like a way in. She ∿s as if she were about to faint. You ∿ as if you slept badly. It doesn't ∿ to me as if we shall get there in time.* **4** [VP8] pay attention; learn by seeing: *L∿ where you're going! L∿ who's here! L∿ (and see) whether the postman has been yet.* **5** (= ∿ at) ∿ **sb/sth in the eye(s)/face,** confront calmly and bravely: ∿ *death/one's enemy in the face.* **6** [VP6A] express by one's appearance: ∿ *one's thanks/consent.* **7** [VP2C,3A,15B] (uses with *adverbial particles* and *preps*):

look about (for sth), be on the watch, in search of; examine one's surroundings, the state of affairs, etc: *Are you still ∿ing about for a job?* ∿ **about one,** examine one's surroundings; give oneself time to make plans: *We hardly had time to* ∿ *about us before we had to continue our journey.*

look after sb/sth, (a) take care of; watch over; attend to: *Who will* ∿ *after the children while their mother is in hospital? He needs someone to* ∿ *after him. He's well able to* ∿ *after himself/to* ∿ *after his own interests.* (b) follow with the eyes: *They* ∿*ed after the train as it left the station.*

look at sth, (special uses) (a) **not** ∿ **at sth,** usu with *will, would*) not consider: *They wouldn't* ∿ *at my proposal.* (b) examine: *We must* ∿ *at the question from all sides. Will you please* ∿ *at the battery of my car? Doctor, will you* ∿ *at my ankle?* (c) in polite requests: *Will you please* ∿ *at* (ie read) *this letter?* **good/bad, etc to** ∿ **at,** of good, etc appearance: *The hotel is not much to* ∿ *at,* does not appear to be good from the outside.

look away (from sth), turn the eyes away.

look back (on/to sth), (fig) turn one's thoughts to sth in the past. **never** ∿ **back,** make uninterrupted progress.

look down on sb/sth, despise; consider oneself superior to; show false contempt for: *When she married the boss, she* ∿*ed down on the office girls she had worked with.* ∿ **down one's nose at sb/ sth,** (colloq) regard with displeasure or contempt.

look for sb/sth, (a) search for; try to find: *Are you still* ∿*ing for a job? That foolish fellow is* ∿*ing for trouble,* is behaving in a way that will get him into trouble. (b) expect: *It's too soon yet to* ∿ *for results.*

look forward to sth, anticipate (usu with pleasure): *We're* ∿*ing forward to seeing you again.*

look in (on sb), make a short (usu casual) visit; pay a call: *Why don't you* ∿ *in* (*on me*) *next time you're in town? The doctor will* ∿ *in again this evening.* **give sb/get a '∿-in,** (colloq, sport, etc) chance (of winning, etc): *You won't get a* ∿*-in with such strong competition.*

look into sth, (a) investigate; examine: ∿ *into a question.* (b) dip into (a book, etc). (c) ∿ at the inside of, the depths of: *He* ∿*ed into the box/the mirror/her eyes.*

look on, (a) be a spectator; watch: *Why don't you play football instead of just* ∿*ing on?* Hence, ∿**er-'on** *n* person who ∿s on. ∿ **on/upon sb/ sth as,** regard as: *Do you* ∿ *on him as an authority on the subject?* ∿ **on/upon sb/sth with,** regard in the way specified: *He seems to* ∿ *on me with distrust.* ∿ **on to,** (of a place, room, etc) overlook,

give a view of: *My bedroom ∿s on to the garden.*

look out (of sth) (at sth), *He stood at the window and* ∿*ed out* (*at the view*). *They were* ∿*ing out of the window.* ∿ **out on (to)/over,** supply an outlook or view over: *Our hotel room here* ∿*s out on the sea front.* ∿ **out (for sb/sth),** be prepared (for), be on the watch (for): *L∿ out!* Be on the watch, be careful! *Will you go to the station and* ∿ *out for Mr Hill?* Hence, '∿**-out** *n* (a) **keep a good** ∿**-out (for);** **be on the** ∿**-out (for),** be watchful (for). (b) [C] place from which to watch; person who has the duty of watching: (attrib) *a* ∿*-out post; send* ∿*-outs in advance.* (c) (*sing* only) prospect; what seems likely to come or happen: *It seems a bad* ∿*-out for their children. That's your own* ∿*-out,* sth you yourself must be responsible for. ∿ **sth out (for sb),** select by making an inspection: ∿ *out some books for a friend in hospital.*

look over sth, inspect; examine: *We must* ∿ *over the house before we decide to rent it.* ∿ **sth over,** inspect one by one or part by part: *Here's the correspondence; I've* ∿*ed it over.* Hence, '∿**-over** *n*: *give something a* ∿*-over,* examine it.

look round, (a) (fig) examine possibilities before deciding sth: *Don't make a hurried decision;* ∿ *round well first.* (b) turn the head (to see): *When I* ∿*ed round for her, she was leaving the hall.* ∿ **round (sth),** go sight-seeing, etc: *Have we time to* ∿ *round* (*the town*) *before lunch?*

look through sth, revise (a lesson, etc); study; examine: *L∿ through your notes before the examination. I must* ∿ *through these bills and check them before I pay them.* ∿ **sth through,** inspect carefully or successively: *He* ∿*ed the proposals through before approving them.*

look to sth, be careful of or about: *The country must* ∿ *to its defences. L∿ to your manners, my boy,* Don't be so rude. *L∿ to it* (= Take care) *that this does not happen again.* ∿ **to sb for sth/to do sth,** rely on: *They all* ∿ *to you for help. They're* ∿*ing to you for a solo/to sing to them.* ∿ **to/ towards,** face: *a house* ∿*ing towards the river/to the south.*

look up, (a) raise the eyes: *Don't* ∿ *up.* (b) improve in price or prosperity: *Business is/Oil shares are* ∿*ing up.* ∿ **sth up,** search for (a word in a dictionary, facts in a reference book, etc): *Please* ∿ *up a fast train to Leeds,* in a railway guide. ∿ **sb up,** pay a call on; visit: *Do* ∿ *me up next time you're in London.* ∿ **up to sb (as...),** respect: *They all* ∿ *up to him as their leader.* ∿ **sb up and down,** examine him carefully or contemptuously.

look² /lʊk/ *n* [C] **1** act of looking: *Let me have a* ∿ *at your new car.* **2** facial expression; appearance: *A* ∿ *of pleasure came to her face. There were angry* ∿*s from the neighbours. The town has a European* ∿. **give sth/get a new** ∿, a new and more up-to-date appearance: *The High Street has been given a new* ∿. **3** (*pl*) person's appearance: *She's beginning to lose her* ∿*s,* her beauty. ∿**er** *n*: *a ,good-'*∿*er,* a good-looking person.

loom¹ /luːm/ *n* machine for weaving cloth.

loom² /luːm/ *vi* [VP2C,D] **loom (large),** appear indistinctly and in a threatening way; (fig) appear great and fill the mind: *The dark outline of another ship* ∿*ed* (*up*) *through the fog. The threat of the H-bomb* ∿*ed large in their minds.*

loon¹ /luːn/ *n* large diving-bird that lives on fish and has a loud, wild cry.

loon² /lu:n/ n (Scot and archaic) foolish, idle, good-for-nothing person.

loony /'lu:nɪ/ n, adj (sl) lunatic. '**~·bin** /-bɪn/ n (sl) mental home.

loop /lu:p/ n **1** (shape produced by a) curve crossing itself as in the letters *l* and *h* in ordinary handwriting). **2** part of a length of string, wire, ribbon, etc in such a shape, eg as a knot or fastening; curved piece of metal as a handle; (colloq) ~-shaped intra-uterine contraceptive device. **3** (also '**~-line**) railway or telegraph line that separates from the main line, runs in a curve, and then rejoins the main line farther on. **4** circuit in which an aviator, motor-cyclist, etc is for a time travelling in a ~ or in ~s: *The airman looped the ~ five times,* flew the shape of a ~ five times. □ vt, vi **1** [VP6A,15B] form or bend into a ~ or ~s; supply with a ~ or ~s: ~ *the curtains up/back;* ~ *things together.* **2** [VP6A,2A] perform a ~(4); make a ~ or ~s.

loop·hole /'lu:phəʊl/ n **1** narrow vertical opening in a wall for shooting or looking through, or to admit light and air (as in old forts, stockades, etc). **2** (fig) way of escape from control, esp one provided by careless and inexact wording of a rule: *find a ~ in the law.*

loopy /'lu:pɪ/ adj (sl) crazy.

loose¹ /lu:s/ adj (-r, -st) **1** free; not held, tied up, fastened, packed, or contained in sth: *Many Englishmen carry their small change* (ie coins) ~ *in their trouser pocket, not in a purse. That dog is too dangerous to be left ~.* **break/get ~,** escape confinement: *One of the tigers in the zoo has broken/got ~,* has escaped from its cage. **let sth ~,** allow it to be free from control: *He let ~ his indignation,* did not control it. '**~ box,** separate compartment in a stable or railway van, in which a horse can move about freely. **~-'leaf** attrib adj (of a notebook) with leaves that may be detached separately and replaced. **2** not close-fitting; not tight or tense: *a ~ collar;* ~-*fitting clothes.* **3** moving more freely than is right or usual: *a ~ tooth;* ~ *bowels,* with a tendency to diarrhoea; *a ~ thread; a ~ window,* one that shakes or rattles in the wind. **come ~,** (of a fastening, etc) come unfastened or insecure. **have a 'screw ~,** (colloq) be unsound in one's mind. **have a ~ tongue,** be in the habit of talking too freely. **ride with a ~ rein,** (a) allow the horse freedom. (b) (fig) manage a person indulgently. **work ~,** (of a bolt, etc) become insecure, no longer tight. **4** not firmly or properly tied: *a ~ knot; a ~ end of rope,* one that is not fastened. **at a ~ end,** (fig of a person) having nothing to do. **5** (of talk, behaviour, etc) not sufficiently controlled: ~ *conduct; lead a ~ life; a ~* (= immoral) *woman.*

(be) on the ~, (colloq) free from the restraints of morality or discipline; dissipated. **play fast and ~ (with sb),** behave dishonestly or in a deceitful manner. **6** not strict; inexact; indefinite; (of translations) not close to the original: ~ *thinking; a ~ thinker; a ~* (= badly constructed) *argument.* **7** not compact; not closely packed: ~ *soil; cloth with a ~ weave.* **8** (of the human body) not closely knit: *a ~ frame;* ~ *limbs,* rather awkward, ungainly in appearance; (of bodily actions) careless, bungling or inaccurate: ~ *bowling and fielding* (in cricket). **~·ly** adv in a ~ manner: *words ~ly employed,* ⇨ 6 above; *rules ~ly enforced.*

loose² /lu:s/ vt [VP6A] make free or loose: *Wine ~d his tongue,* made him talk freely (*loosen* is more usu).

loosen /'lu:sn/ vt, vi [VP6A,2A,15B] ~ *(up),* make or become loose or looser: *L~ the screw. The screw has ~ed. This medicine may ~ your cough,* help to get up the phlegm. *I must take some exercise and ~ up my muscles.*

loot /lu:t/ n [U] goods (esp private property) taken away unlawfully and by force, eg by thieves, or by soldiers in time of war. □ vt, vi [VP6A,2A] carry off ~ from: *The brutal soldiers ~ed and massacred for three weeks.* ~**er** n

lop¹ /lɒp/ vt (-pp-) [VP6A,15B] *lop (away/off),* cut off, separate branches, etc from a tree.

lop² /lɒp/ vi (-pp-) hang down loosely; (chiefly in compounds): '**lop-ears** n pl drooping ears. '**lop-eared** adj having lop-ears: *a lop-eared rabbit.* ,**lop-'sided** adj with one side lower than the other.

lope /ləʊp/ vi [VP2A,C] move along with long, easy steps or strides (as a hare does). □ n step or stride of this kind: *The deer went off at an easy ~.*

lo·qua·cious /lə'kweɪʃəs/ adj talkative; fond of talking. ~**·ly** adv ~**·ness,** **lo·quac·ity** /lə'kwæsətɪ/ nn [U] being ~.

lo·quat /'ləʊkwɒt/ n [C] (tree, common in China and Japan, with a) yellow or yellowish-red fruit that grows in clusters and has a sharp taste. ⇨ the illus at fruit.

lor /lɔ:(r)/ int (vulg substitute for) Lord! (= God).

lord /lɔ:d/ n **1** supreme male ruler: *our sovereign ~ the King.* **2** the **L~,** God; Christ. *L~! L~ God! Good L~! L~ knows! L~ bless us/me!* exclamations of surprise, etc. **Our L~,** Christ. **the 'L~'s Day,** Sunday. **the ,L~'s 'Prayer,** that given by Jesus to his followers. **the ,L~'s 'Supper,** the taking of bread and wine to commemorate the last meal taken by Jesus Christ with his twelve disciples before his death. **3** peer; nobleman: *live/treat sb like a ~,* sumptuously. **as drunk as a ~,** excessively drunk. **the House of L~s,** (in GB) the upper division of Parliament, consisting of *the ~s spiritual* (the Archbishops and Bishops) and *the ~s temporal* (hereditary and life peers). **4** (in feudal times) superior. **the ~ of the manor,** man from whom vassals held land and to whom they owed service. **5** (joc, also ~ *and master*) husband; great leader of industry: *the'cotton ~s* (cf '*beer barons*)*; the ~s of creation,* mankind (contrasted with the animals). **6** person in a position of authority: *the L~s of the Admiralty/Treasury,* the chief members of these Boards; *the First L~ of the Admiralty,* the president of this Board. **7** first word in many official titles: *the L~ Mayor of London; the L~ Chamberlain,* etc. **8** title prefixed to names of peers and barons: *L~ Derby.* Cf *the Earl of Derby.* **9** *My ~,* respectful formula for addressing certain

shuttle —

a hand loom

noblemen and judges and bishops. □ *vt* (chiefly in) ~ *it over sb*, rule over like a ~: *'I will not be ~ed over',* she said to her husband. ~**-less** *adj* without a ~.

lord·ly /'lɔːdlɪ/ *adj* (-ier, -iest) **1** haughty; insolent. **2** like, suitable for, a lord; magnificent. **lord·li·ness** *n*

lord·ship /'lɔːdʃɪp/ *n* **1** [U] ~ *over*, rule, authority. **2** [C] *His/Your L~,* used when speaking of/to a lord.

lore /lɔː(r)/ *n* [U] learning or knowledge, esp handed down from past times, or possessed by a class of people: *'Irish ~; 'gypsy ~;* or of a special subject: *'fairy ~/'bird ~/'folk ~.*

lor·gnette /lɔː'njet/ *n* pair of eye-glasses held to the eyes on a long handle.

lorn /lɔːn/ *adj* (poet or hum) forlorn; desolate: *a lone, ~ widow.*

lorry /'lɒrɪ US: 'lɔːrɪ/ *n* (*pl* -ries) (US = *truck*) long, low, open motor-vehicle, for carrying goods by road.

lose /luːz/ *vt,vi* (*pt,pp* lost /lɒst US: lɔːst/) **1** [VP6A] no longer have; have taken away from one by accident, carelessness, misfortune, death, etc: ~ *one's money;* ~ *a leg,* eg in a road accident; ~ *a lot of money at the races* (by betting); ~ *one's balance,* fall over. *He lost two sons in the war,* They were killed. *She lost her husband,* He is dead. *He has lost his job,* has been dismissed. *You're losing your hair,* getting bald. *She has lost her good looks,* is no longer good-looking. *It was so cold that we lost the use of our hands,* could not use them. *He's losing patience,* is becoming impatient. ~ *one's cool,* (colloq) lose one's composure; be no longer calm or composed. ~ *ground,* ⇨ ground¹(2). ~ *one's head,* ⇨ head¹(19). ~ *heart,* ⇨ heart(2). ~ *one's heart to sb,* ⇨ heart(2). ~ *interest (in sb/sth),* cease to be interested in, attracted by. ~ *one's reason/senses,* become insane or wildly excited. ~ *one's temper,* become angry. ~ *A to B,* have A taken away by B: *The little grocery shop is losing all its customers to the new supermarket.* ~ *touch (with),* ⇨ touch²(6). **2** (passive) be lost, disappear; die; be dead: *The ship and all its crew were lost. Is letter-writing a lost art,* Has the art of writing (social) letters died, eg because of the use of the telephone? *be lost to sth,* be no longer affected by, be insensible to, eg all sense of shame, decency, honour, duty. *be lost in sth,* be deeply occupied or filled with, eg thought, wonder, admiration. **3** [VP6A] (contrasted with *find, recover*) be unable to find: *I've lost the keys of my car. The books seem to be lost/to have been lost. She lost her husband in the crowd.* ~ *one's place,* (in a book, etc) be unable to find the page, paragraph, etc where one stopped reading. ~ *oneself/one's way,* get lost, be unable to find the right way, road, etc; not know where one is: *The children lost their way in the forest. We lost our way in the dark. I hope the children haven't got lost/lost themselves.* ~ *sight of sth,* (a) overlook; fail to take account of: *We mustn't ~ sight of the fact that....* (b) no longer be able to see: *The early navigators disliked losing sight of land. We lost sight of him in the crowd.* ~ *the thread of sth,* eg an argument, ⇨ thread. ~ *one's tongue,* ⇨ tongue. ~ *track of sth,* ⇨ track. **4** [VP6A] (contrasted with *catch*) be too late for; fail to hear, see, etc: ~ (more usu *miss*) *one's train/the bus.* ~ *the post,* get to the post office, etc too late for the

collection; ~ (= not hear) *the end of a sentence. What he said was lost in the applause that greeted him.* **5** [VP12C] cause (sb) the loss of: *Such insolence will ~ you your situation. This remark lost him our sympathy.* **6** [VP6A,2A] fail to win, be defeated: ~ *a game/a match/a battle/a war/a lawsuit/a prize;* ~ *a motion,* fail to carry it in a debate. *a lost cause,* one that has already been defeated or is sure to be defeated. *(play) a losing game,* one in which defeat is likely or certain. ~ *out (to),* (colloq) be overcome and replaced (by): *Has the cinema lost out to TV?* **7** [VP6A,15A,3A] ~ *by/in/on sth,* be or become worse: *You will ~ nothing by waiting,* will not suffer any loss. *Will the publisher ~ by it,* be worse off because of publishing the book? *How much did he lose on the transaction? The story does not ~ in the telling,* is not made less interesting, is perhaps exaggerated. **8** [VP2A,B] (of a watch or clock) go too slowly; fail to keep correct time because of this: *Does your watch gain or ~? My watch ~s two minutes a day.* **9** [VP6A] spend time, opportunity, efforts to no purpose; waste: *There's not a moment to ~. I shall ~ no time in doing it,* shall do it at once. *be lost upon sb,* fail to influence or attract the attention of: *My hints were not lost upon him,* They were noted. **10** ~ *oneself in sth,* (reflex) become engrossed in it: *She lost herself in a book,* became so deeply interested in it that she was unaware of other things. ~*r n* person who ~s or is defeated: *He's a good/bad ~r,* is cheerful/discontented when he ~s.

loss /lɒs US: lɔːs/ *n* **1** [U] act or fact or process of losing: ~ *of blood;* ~ *of prestige. L~ of health is more serious than ~ of money. The ~ of his heavyweight title doesn't seem to worry him. The ~ of so many ships worried the Admiral.* **2** [U] (and with *indef art*) failure to keep, maintain or use: *a heavy ~;* ~ *of opportunities; without (any)* ~ *of time. There was a temporary ~ of power.* **3** [U] failure to win or obtain: *the ~ of a contract.* **4** [C] that which is lost: *sell sth at a ~; suffer heavy ~es in war,* men killed, wounded, captured; ships and aircraft lost. ⇨ gain¹, profit¹(2). *a total ~,* sth from which nothing can be saved: *The ship was wrecked and became a total ~.* ~*-'leader n* (comm) article, etc sold at a ~ in order to attract customers to buy other goods. **5** (*sing* only) disadvantage or deprivation: *Such a man is no great ~,* We need not regret losing his services. *be a dead ~,* (colloq, of a person) be quite worthless: *We'd better fire Smith—He's a dead ~.* **6** *(be) at a ~ for sth/to do sth,* be perplexed, uncertain: *He was at a ~ for words/to know what to say,* did not know how to express himself.

lost /lɒst US: lɔːst/ *pt,pp* of lose.

lot¹ /lɒt/ *n* (colloq) **1** *the lot; the whole lot; all the lot,* the whole number or quantity: *That's the lot,* That's all or everything. *Take the (whole) lot. Go away, the whole lot of you/all the lot of you,* (emphat for) 'all of you', 'every one of you'. *She wants a new car, a fridge, and a colour TV—the lot!* **2** *a lot (of); lots (and lots) (of),* a great amount or number (of): *What a lot of time you take to dress! She spends a lot of money on clothes. There were such a lot of people in the shops! I want lots. I saw quite a lot of her* (= saw her often) *when I was in London last month. We don't see a lot of her nowadays.* **3** (used *adverbially*) very much: *He's feeling a lot better today. A lot 'you* *care!* (ironic) You don't care at all! Cf *a good deal, a little.*

lot² /lɒt/ *n* **1** [U] (one of a set of objects used in) the making of a selection or decision by methods depending upon chance: *divide property by lot. draw/cast lots,* eg by taking pieces of paper marked in some way from a box: *They drew lots as to who should begin.* **2 the lot,** decision or choice resulting from this: *The lot came to/fell upon me.* **3** person's fortune or destiny: *His lot has been a hard one. Such good fortune falls to the lot of few men. It has fallen to my lot to oppose the President in the election. cast/throw in one's lot with sb,* decide to share the fortunes of. **4** item, or number of items, (to be) sold at an auction sale: *Lot 46, six chairs.* **5** collection of objects of the same kind: *We have received a new lot of hats from the manufacturers.* **6 a bad lot,** (colloq) a bad person. **7** (cinema) studio and surrounding land. **8** plot of land: (esp US) *a 'parking lot,* for cars; *a vacant lot,* a building site.

loth /ləʊθ/ *adj* ⇨ loath.

lo·tion /'ləʊʃn/ *n* [C,U] (kind of) medicinal liquid for use on the skin: *a bottle of cleansing ~ for the face; soothing ~s for insect bites.*

lot·tery /'lɒtərɪ/ *n* (*pl* -ries) [C] **1** arrangement to give prizes to holders of numbered tickets previously bought by them and drawn by lot: (attrib) *'~ tickets.* **2** (fig) sth considered to be as uncertain as the winning of prizes in a ~: *Is marriage a ~?*

lot·to /'lɒtəʊ/ *n* [U] game of chance; bingo.

lo·tus /'ləʊtəs/ *n* (*pl* ~es /-sɪz/) (not often used in the *pl*; '~ *blooms* is preferred). **1** (kinds of) water-lily, esp Egyptian and Asiatic kinds. ⇨ the illus at flower. **2** (in old Gk legends) plant represented as bringing about a distaste for an active life. '~-**eater** *n* person who gives himself up to indolent enjoyment.

loud /laʊd/ *adj* (-er, -est) **1** not quiet or soft; easily heard: *~ voices/cries/laughs. The bomb exploded with a ~ noise.* ⚡-'**hailer** *n* electronic device that enables a voice to be magnified and so be audible at a great distance: *The naval officer called to the trawler by ~-hailer across the water.* ⚡-'**speaker** *n* (often shortened to *speaker*) part of a radio receiving apparatus that converts electric impulses into audible sounds. **2** (of a person's behaviour; of colours) of the kind that forces itself on the attention. □ *adv* (after *talk, speak, laugh* etc) in a ~ manner: *Don't talk so ~. They laughed ~ and long. Speak ~er! Who laughed ~est?* ~·**ly** *adv* in a ~ manner: *Someone knocked ~ly at the door. What a ~ly dressed girl!* ~·**ness** *n*

lough /lɒk/ *n* (in Ireland) lake; arm of the sea.

lounge /laʊndʒ/ *vi* [VP2A,C] sit, stand about (leaning against sth) in a lazy way: *idlers lounging at street corners; lounging over a café table.* ~r *n* person who ~s. □ *n* **1** act of lounging: *have a ~.* **2** comfortable sitting-room, esp in a club or hotel. '~-**lizard** *n* (dated sl) professional dance-partner for women at dances in which ~s. **3** '~-**bar** *n* smartest bar in a public house. '~-**chair** *n* comfortable easy-chair. '~-**suit** *n* man's ordinary suit of jacket, (waistcoat), and trousers.

lour, lower /'laʊə(r)/ *vi* [VP2A,3A] ~ *at/on/ upon,* frown; look sullen or threatening; (of the sky, clouds) look dark, as if threatening a storm. ~·**ing·ly** *adv*

louse /laʊs/ *n* (*pl* lice /laɪs/) **1** small insect living on the bodies of animals and human beings under

dirty conditions; similar insect living on plants. **2** (sl) contemptible person: *He's an absolute ~.*

lousy /'laʊzɪ/ *adj* (-ier, -iest) infested with lice; (colloq) bad: *a ~ dinner;* (sl) well provided (*with*): *He's ~ with money.*

lout /laʊt/ *n* clumsy, ill-mannered person. '**litter-** ~, ⇨ litter²(1). '~-**ish** /-ɪʃ/ *adj* of or like a ~: *~ish behaviour.*

louvre (also **lou·ver**) /'luːvə(r)/ *n* arrangement of fixed or moveable slats (in a door or window) for ventilation (like the slats in a Venetian blind). **lou·vered** *adj* having ~s: *a ~ed door.*

lov·able /'lʌvəbl/ *adj* deserving or inspiring love; worthy of love: *a ~ child; a child's ~ ways.*

love¹ /lʌv/ *n* **1** [U] warm, kind feeling; fondness; affectionate and tender devotion: *a mother's ~ for her children; a ~ of learning/adventure; ~ of (one's) country,* patriotism; *show ~ towards one's neighbours. give/send sb one's ~,* give or send an affectionate greeting. *play for ~,* for the pleasure of the game, not for stakes. *not to be had for ~ or money,* impossible to get by any means. *There's ,no ~ lost between them,* They dislike each other. *a labour of ~,* (a) sth that one enjoys doing for its own sake. (b) one does for the ~ of sb. *for the ~ of,* (in appeals, etc) for the sake of; in the name of: *Put that gun down, for the ~ of God!* '~-**feast** *n* meal taken by early Christians in token of brotherly ~; religious service imitating this. **2** [U] warm, kind feeling between two persons; sexual passion or desire; this as a literary subject: *a '~-story; marry for ~, not for money. be in ~ (with sb),* have ~ and desire (for): *Hero and Leander were in ~. Leander was in ~ with Hero. fall in ~ (with sb),* come to feel ~ (for); begin to be in ~ (with). *make ~ (to sb),* show that one is in ~ with sb; do the things that lovers do, eg kiss, caress; have sexual intercourse: *Jana thinks it's more fun to make ~ than to make the beds. Make ~, not war!* Hence, '~-**making** *n* '~-**affair** *n* instance of being in ~, often with a physical relationship: *a girl who had numerous ~-affairs before her marriage.* '~-**bird** *n* small brightly coloured parrot said to pine away when it loses its mate; (*pl*) lovers very much in ~. '~-**child** *n* child of unmarried parents. '~-**knot** *n* bow of ribbon, tied in a special way, formerly given or worn as a pledge of ~. '~-**letter** *n* letter between persons in ~ and concerned with their ~. '~-**lorn** /-lɔːn/ *adj* unhappy because one's ~ is not returned; pining with ~. '~-**match** *n* marriage made for love's sake, not an arranged marriage. '~-**philtre/-potion** *nn* magic drink supposed to make the person who drinks it fall in ~ with the person from whom it is received. '~-**seat** *n* S-shaped bench with two seats facing in opposite directions. '~-**sick** *adj* languishing because of ~. '~-**song** *n* song about or expressing ~. '~-**story** *n* novel or story of which the main theme is ~. '~-**token** *n* sth given as a symbol of ~. **3** form of address between lovers, husband and wife, or to a child: *Come here, my ~.* **4** (colloq) delightful or lovable person or thing: *Isn't she a little ~? What a ~ of a cottage!* **5** person who is a sweetheart: *She was an old ~ of mine years ago (flame* is more usu). **6** personification of ~, ie a Cupid. **7** [U] (in games) no score, nothing, nil: *~ all,* no score for either side; *'~ game,* one in which the loser did not score. ~-**less** *adj* unloving; unloved; without ~: *a ~less marriage.*

love² /lʌv/ vt **1** [VP6A] have strong affection or deep tender feelings for: ~ one's parents/one's country/one's husband. **2** [VP6A] worship: ~ God. **3** [VP6A] have kind feelings towards: The Bible tells us to ~ all men. **4** [VP6A,D,7A,17] (colloq) be very fond of; like; find pleasure in: ~ comfort/mountain-climbing. She ~s to have/~s having a lot of dogs and young men round her. 'Will you come with me?'—'I should ~ to'. I'd ~ you to come with me.

love·ly /ˈlʌvlɪ/ adj **1** beautiful; attractive; pleasant: a ~ view; a ~ woman; a ~ hair/weather. **2** (colloq) enjoyable; amusing: We had a ~ holiday. What a ~ joke! It's ~ and warm here, ~ because warm. **love·li·ness** n

lover /ˈlʌvə(r)/ n **1** person who is fond of or devoted to (sth): a ~ of music/horses/good wine. **2** person in love with another; regular sexual partner. '~-like adj in the manner of a ~.

lov·ing /ˈlʌvɪŋ/ adj feeling or showing love: a ~ friend. '~-cup n large wine-cup passed round from person to person so that everyone may drink from it. ~-'kindness n [U] tender consideration; mercy and kindness coming from love.~·ly adv in a ~ way: Yours ~ly, formula at the end of a letter, eg from a child to its parents.

low¹ /ləʊ/ adj (-er, -est) **1** not high; not extending far upwards: a low wall/ceiling/shelf; a low range of hills; low-rise housing, of houses not many storeys high. The moon was low in the sky. The glass is low, the mercury in the barometer is low. He has a low brow, short distance between the hair and the eyebrows. She was wearing a dress low in the neck/a 'low-necked dress, one leaving the neck and (part of) the shoulders and breasts visible. ,low-re'lief, ⇨ bas-relief. **2** below the usual or normal level or intensity: low-lying land; low pressure, eg of the atmosphere, of gas or water from the mains; a low-density housing estate, with comparatively few houses to the acre. The rivers were low during the dry summer. **low gear,** ⇨ gear(1). **low tide/water,** time when the tide is out and far from the shore or river bank. ,low-'water mark, lowest points reached at low tide. **be in low water,** (fig) short of money. **3** (of sounds) not loud; not high in pitch: speak in a low voice; the low notes of a cello. A tenor cannot get so low as a baritone. ,low-'keyed, (fig) restrained in style or quality. ,low-'pitched, (music) low in pitch. **4** of or in inferior rank or social class: all classes of people, high and low; men of low birth; have a low station in life. **be brought low,** be humbled. **5** commonplace; coarse; vulgar; little civilized: low manners; low company; low life, of persons who are vulgar, coarse, etc; low tastes; low cunning, cunning typical of sb who is mean or morally degraded. I never fell as low as that, never let my standard of behaviour fall so low. **6** feeble; lacking in strength of body or mind: in a low state of health; feel low/ in low spirits, unhappy, depressed. Hence, ,low-'spirited adj **7** of small amount as measured by a scale or by degrees: a low temperature; a low pulse; low prices/wages/rates of pay. **low latitudes,** near the equator. **have a low opinion of sb/sth,** think very little of him, his work, etc. **at lowest,** at the least possible figure, quantity, etc. **8** (of a supply of anything) **be/run low,** be/become nearly exhausted: Our stock of coal is running low. Food supplies were running low in the besieged town. **9** (of the position of the tongue when speak-

ing) not raised: a low vowel, one, eg the vowel /ɑː/) made with the tongue low in the mouth. **10** not highly developed: low forms of life. **11 Low Church,** party in the Church of England giving a low place to the authority of bishops and priests, ecclesiastical organization, ritual, etc (contrasted with High Church). Hence, **Low Churchman,** supporter of this. **12** (phrases) **bring/lay sb/sth low,** make low in health, wealth, position, etc; defeat; humble. **lie low,** (fig) keep quiet or hidden; say nothing and wait: The escaped prisoners had to lie low for months. **13** (compounds) ,low-'born adj of humble birth. ,low-'bred adj having vulgar manners. 'low·brow n, adj (person) showing little interest in or taste for intellectual things, esp art, music, literature (contrasted with highbrow). **lower case,** (in printing) small letters, not capitals. **Lower Chamber/House,** lower branch of a legislative assembly, eg the House of Commons in GB, the House of Representatives in US. **low comedian,** person who acts in **low comedy,** kind of drama bordering on farce, with laughable situations, comic dialogue, etc. the **lower deck,** (in the Navy) the ratings; those who are not officers. 'low-down adj (colloq) caddish; dishonourable: ~-down behaviour/tricks. **give sb/get the low-down (on sth/sb),** (colloq) give/get the true facts, inside information which is not generally known. 'low·lander /-ləndə(r)/ n person who lives in lowlands, esp (L~) one who lives in the Scottish Lowlands. 'low·lands /-ləndz/ n pl low level country: the lowlands of Scotland. **Low Latin,** late, popular Latin (contrasted with classical Latin). **Low Mass,** (formerly) celebration of the Eucharist without a choir. **Low Sunday, Low Week,** coming after Easter Day and Easter Week. 'low·er·most adj lowest. **low·ness** n

low² /ləʊ/ adv (-er, -est) in or to a low position; in a low manner; aim/shoot low; bow low to the Queen; buy low (= at low prices) and sell high; play low, (in gambling) for small sums; speak low.

low³ /ləʊ/ n sth low; low level or figure: Several industrial shares reached new lows yesterday, Their prices went down to a new low price (on the stock market).

low⁴ /ləʊ/ n sound made by cattle. □ vi (of cattle) make this characteristic sound.

lower¹ /ˈləʊə(r)/ vt,vi **1** [VP6A] let or bring down; cause to be down: ~ the sails/a flag. ~ (naut) lower a boat, sail, etc. **2** [VP6A,15A,2A] make or become less high: ~ the rent of a house. The stocks ~ed in value. He ~ed his voice to a whisper. We can't ~ the ceiling. **3** [VP15A] ~ oneself, degrade; disgrace: He would never ~ himself by taking bribes. **4** [VP6A] weaken: Poor diet ~s resistance to illness.

lower² /ˈlaʊə(r)/ vi = lour.

low·ly /ˈləʊlɪ/ adj (-ier, -iest) humble; simple; modest. **low·li·ness** n

loyal /ˈlɔɪəl/ adj true and faithful (to): ~ subjects of the Queen; ~ supporters; ~ to one's country. '~-ist /-ɪst/ n person who is ~ to his ruler and government, esp one who supports the head of an established government during a revolt: (attrib) the ~ist army/troops. ~ly /ˈlɔɪəlɪ/ adv ~ty n (pl -ties) **1** [U] being ~; ~ conduct. **2** (pl) kinds of ~ attachment: tribal loyalties.

loz·enge /ˈlɒzɪndʒ/ n **1** four-sided, diamond-shaped figure. **2** small tablet of flavoured sugar, esp one containing medicine: cough ~s.

L-plate /'el pleɪt/ n plate with a large capital L, fixed to a motor vehicle being driven by a learner who has not passed his driving test.

LSD /ˌel es 'di:/ n [U] odourless, colourless and tasteless semi-synthetic substance causing hallucinations (often referred to as 'acid'). ⇨ App 2.

£sd /ˌel es 'di:/ n [U] term used, before British currency was decimalized, for pounds, shillings and pence; (colloq) money: I'm short of £sd just now. ⇨ App 5.

lub·ber /'lʌbə(r)/ n big, clumsy, stupid fellow. ⇨ land-~ at land¹(6). ~·ly adj

lu·bri·cate /'lu:brɪkeɪt/ vt [VP6A] put oil or grease into (machine parts) to make (them) work easily; (fig) do sth that makes action, etc easier. **lu·bri·cant** /'lu:brɪkənt/ n [U,C] substance that ~s. **lu·bri·ca·tion** /ˌlu:brɪ'keɪʃn/ n [U,C] (instance of) lubricating or being ~d.

lu·cent /'lu:snt/ adj (liter) shining; translucent.

lu·cerne /lu:'sɜ:n/ n [U] (GB) clover-like plant used for feeding animals. (US = alfalfa).

lu·cid /'lu:sɪd/ adj 1 clear; easy to understand: a ~ explanation; a ~ literary style; a ~ mind. 2 mentally sound: ~ intervals, periods of sanity between periods of insanity. 3 (poet) bright, clear, transparent. ~·ly adv ~·ity /lu:'sɪdətɪ/ n [U] quality of being ~.

Luci·fer /'lu:sɪfə(r)/ n 1 Satan, the chief rebel angel: as proud as ~. 2 (the planet Venus as) the morning star.

luck /lʌk/ n [U] chance; fortune (good or bad); sth that is considered to come by chance: have good/bad ~ in one's affairs; have hard ~, be unfortunate. As ~ would have it,... Fortunately,... (or Unfortunately,... according to context). It was hard ~ on you that..., used to show sympathy. He tried his ~ at the gaming tables, gambled, hoping for success. What rotten ~! Bad ~! (used to show sympathy). Good ~! (used to encourage, express hopes of good fortune, etc). Just my ~! I am unlucky, as usual. My ~'s in/out, I am/am not fortunate. I never have any ~. I had the ~ (= was fortunate enough) to find him at home. **be down on one's ~**, (colloq) be unfortunate; suffer misfortune. **be in/out of ~**, have/not have good fortune. **for ~**, to bring good fortune: keep sth for ~. **worse ~**, (used parenthetically) more's the pity; unfortunately. ~·less adj unfortunate; turning out badly: a ~less day/attempt.

lucky /'lʌkɪ/ adj (-ier, -iest) having, bringing, resulting from, good luck: a ~ escape/guess/man. It's my ~ day, one on which I am having good fortune. You are ~ to be alive after being in that accident. ~ 'dip n tub, etc containing articles of various values for which a person may dip in (taking the chance of getting sth of value) for a payment: L~ dip, 10p. **luck·ily** /'lʌkɪlɪ/ adv in a ~ manner; fortunately: Luckily for me the train was late, so I just caught it.

lu·cra·tive /'lu:krətɪv/ adj profitable; bringing in money.

lucre /'lu:kə(r)/ n [U] (in a bad sense) profit or money-making (as a motive for action): a man who would do anything for ~.

Lud·dite /'lʌdaɪt/ n member of bands of workers who, in England, 1811—16, destroyed new machinery which, they thought, would cause unemployment.

lu·di·crous /'lu:dɪkrəs/ adj ridiculous; causing laughter. ~·ly adv

ludo /'lu:dəʊ/ n [U] simple game played by moving counters on a special board after throwing dice.

luff /lʌf/ vt,vi (naut) bring the head of a ship in a direction nearer to that of the wind; turn (the helm) so that this happens.

lug¹ /lʌg/ vt (-gg-) [VP6A,15A,B] pull or drag roughly and with much effort: lugging two heavy suitcases up the stairs; lug a handcart along. □ n hard or rough pull.

lug² /lʌg/ n projecting part (of a metal casting) by which it is kept securely in place.

luge /lu:ʒ/ n (F) short toboggan for one person, as used in Switzerland.

lug·gage /'lʌgɪdʒ/ n [U] bags, trunks, etc and their contents taken on a journey: six pieces of ~; get one's ~ through the Customs. (US = baggage.) '~-carrier n metal frame, eg one fixed behind the saddle of a bicycle, for ~. '~-rack n rack (above the seats) in a railway carriage, coach, etc, or on the roof of a motor-car, for ~. '~-van n van for ~ on a railway train.

lug·ger /'lʌgə(r)/ n small ship with one or more four-cornered sails set fore and aft.

lug·sail /'lʌgseɪl/ n (naut) four-cornered sail.

lu·gu·bri·ous /lə'gu:brɪəs/ adj (formal) dismal; mournful. ~·ly adv ~·ness n

luke·warm /ˌlu:k'wɔ:m/ adj 1 (of liquids, etc) neither very warm nor cold. 2 (fig) not eager either in supporting or opposing: give only ~ support to a cause; ~ friendship. ~·ly adv ~·ness n

lull /lʌl/ vt,vi [VP6A,15A,2A] make or become quiet or less active: ~ a baby to sleep, eg by rocking it and singing to it; ~ a person's fears/suspicions. The wind/sea was ~ed. The wind ~ed. □ n [C] interval of quiet; period of lessened activity, etc: a ~ in the storm/in the conversation.

lull·aby /'lʌləbaɪ/ n (pl -bies) song for lulling a baby to sleep; gentle, soft sound, eg made by wind in trees or by the running water of a brook.

lum·bago /lʌm'beɪgəʊ/ n [U] muscular pain in the lumbar regions.

lum·bar /'lʌmbə(r)/ adj of the loins: the ~ regions, the lower part of the back.

lum·ber¹ /'lʌmbə(r)/ n [U] 1 roughly prepared wood; wood that has been sawn into planks, boards, etc. '~-man /-mæn/, '~-jack nn man who fells trees; man who saws or transports ~. '~-mill n saw-mill. '~-yard n place where ~ is stored. 2 (chiefly GB) useless or unwanted articles stored away or taking up space (eg old furniture, pictures). '~-room n one in which ~ is stored. □ vt [VP6A,14,15A,B] ~ sth (up) (with), (often in passive) fill with ~; fill space inconveniently; encumber: a room ~ed up with useless articles; (fig) a mind that is ~ed (up) with useless bits of information.

lum·ber² /'lʌmbə(r)/ vi [VP2C] move in a heavy, clumsy, noisy way: The heavy army tanks ~ed along/by/past. What a big ~ing cart!

lu·min·ary /'lu:mɪnərɪ US: -nerɪ/ n (pl -ries) 1 star; the sun or moon; any light-giving body in the sky. 2 (fig) person who, because of his learning, is like a shining light; great moral or intellectual leader.

lu·mi·nous /'lu:mɪnəs/ adj 1 giving out light; bright: ~ paint, as used on road signs, clocks and watches, visible in the dark. 2 (fig) clear; easily understood: a ~ speaker/explanation. **lu·min·os·ity** /ˌlu:mɪ'nɒsətɪ/ n [U] quality of being ~.

lummy, lumme /'lʌmɪ/ int (dated GB sl) indicating surprise.

lump[1] /lʌmp/ n [C] **1** hard or compact mass, usu without a regular shape: *a ~ of clay; break a piece of coal into small ~s; a ~ of sugar; '~ sugar,* sugar cut into cubes. *in the ~,* added together; taken as a whole. **~ sum,** one payment for a number of separate sums that are owed. **2** swelling or bump; bruise: *He has a bad ~ on the forehead.* **have a ~ in one's/the throat,** a feeling of pressure (as caused by strong emotion). **3** (colloq) heavy, dull person: *Get out of my way, you big fat ~ of a man!* □ *vt* **1** [VP6A,15B] **~ (together),** put together in one ~; include (a number of things) under one heading: *The boys agreed to ~ the expenses of their camping holiday. Can we ~ all these items together under the heading 'incidental expenses'?* **2** [VP2A] form into ~s: *This oatmeal ~s if you don't stir it well.* **~·ish** /-ɪʃ/ adj (of a person) thickset; clumsy; stupid. **~·y** adj (-ier, -iest) full of, covered with ~s: *a ~y sauce;* (of the surface of water) cut up by wind into small waves; choppy.

lump[2] /lʌmp/ vt (only in) **~ it,** (colloq) endure, put up with, sth unpleasant or unwanted: *If you don't like it you can ~ it. Well, you'll just have to ~ it!*

lu·na·cy /'lu:nəsɪ/ n (pl -cies) **1** [U] madness; state of being a lunatic; mad or foolish behaviour: *It's sheer ~.* **2** (pl) mad or very foolish acts.

lu·nar /'lu:nə(r)/ adj of the moon: *a ~ month,* average time between successive new moons, about 29½ days; *a ~ module,* detachable section of a spacecraft that orbits the moon and may descend to its surface; *a ~ orbit* (by a spacecraft); *a ~ year,* period of 12 ~ months.

lu·na·tic /'lu:nətɪk/ n **1** mad person: mental patient (the preferred term). **'~ asylum,** hospital (*mental home* and *mental hospital* are the names in present-day use) for the care and treatment of ~s. **2** (attrib) mad; extremely foolish: *a ~ proposal.* **·~ 'fringe,** minority group with extreme views, or engaged in eccentric activities, eg in politics or literature.

lunch /lʌntʃ/ n meal taken in the middle of the day: *They were at ~ when I called.* □ *vi, vt* eat ~; provide ~ for: *He ~ed me well at the Savoy.* **~eon** /'lʌntʃən/ n (formal word for) ~.

lung /lʌŋ/ n **1** either of the two breathing organs in the chest of man and other animals: *the '~ passages/tissues; ~ cancer. That opera singer has good ~s,* produces a great volume of sound. ⇨ the illus at respiratory. **'~-power** n [U] power of voice. **2** (fig) open space in or close to a large city.

lunge /lʌndʒ/ n sudden forward movement, eg with a sword, or forward movement of the body (eg when aiming a blow). □ *vi* [VP2A,C] make a ~: *He ~d at his opponent/~d out suddenly.*

lu·pin (US = **lu·pine**) /'lu:pɪn/ n garden or fodder plant with tall spikes of flowers of various colours.

lurch[1] /lɜ:tʃ/ n (only in) **leave sb in the ~,** leave him when he is in difficulties and needing help.

lurch[2] /lɜ:tʃ/ n sudden change of weight to one side; sudden roll or pitch: *The ship gave a ~ to starboard.* □ *vi* [VP2C] move along with a ~ or ~es: *The drunken man ~ed across the street.*

lurcher /'lɜ:tʃə(r)/ n dog, a cross between a sheepdog and a greyhound, used for retrieving game (esp by poachers).

lure /lʊə(r)/ n [C] bunch of brightly coloured feathers used to attract and recall a trained hawk; bait or decoy to attract wild animals; (fig) sth that attracts

or invites; the attraction or interest that sth has: *the ~ of the sea; the ~s used by a pretty woman to attract men.* □ *vt* [VP6A,15B] attract, tempt: *~ sb away from his duty; be ~d on to destruction.*

lu·rid /'lʊərɪd/ adj **1** highly coloured, esp suggesting flame and smoke: *a ~ sky/sunset; ~ thunderclouds.* **2** (fig) sensational; violent and shocking: *~ details of a railway accident; a ~ tale.* **~·ly** adv **~·ness** n

lurk /lɜ:k/ vi [VP2C] be, keep, out of view, lying in wait or ready to attack: *a suspicious-looking man ~ing in the shadows. Some suspicion still ~ed in his mind.* **'~·ing-place** n hiding-place.

luscious /'lʌʃəs/ adj **1** rich and sweet in taste and smell, attractive: *~ peaches/lips.* **2** (of art, music, writing) very rich in ornament; suggesting sensual delights. **~·ly** adv **~·ness** n

lush /lʌʃ/ adj (esp of grass and vegetation) growing luxuriantly: *~ meadows; a ~ growth of vegetation after the rains;* (fig) luxuriously comfortable. □ *n* (US sl) drunkard.

lust /lʌst/ n [U] violent desire to possess sth, esp strong sexual desire (*for*); passionate enjoyment (*of*): *filled with ~;* [C] instance of this: *a ~ for power/gold; the ~s of the flesh.* □ *vi* [VP3A] **~ after/for,** have ~ for: *~ for/after gold;* (biblical) *~ after a woman,* have strong sexual desire. **~·ful** /-fl/ adj full of ~. **~·fully** /-fəlɪ/ adv

lustre (US = **lus·ter**) /'lʌstə(r)/ n **1** [U] quality of being bright, esp of a smooth or polished surface; sheen; soft reflected light: *the ~ of pearls.* **2** [U] (fig) glory; distinction: *add ~ to one's name; deeds that shed ~ on an honoured family,* make its reputation more distinguished. **3** (glass pendant of a) chandelier. **lus·trous** /'lʌstrəs/ adj having ~: *lustrous pearls; her lustrous eyes.*

lusty /'lʌstɪ/ adj healthy and strong; vigorous: *a ~ girl from the country; ~ cheers.* **lust·ily** /-ɪlɪ/ adv: *work/fight/shout lustily.*

lute /lu:t/ n stringed musical instrument (14th to 17th cc) associated with poets and poetry. **lu·tan·ist** /'lu:tənɪst/ n player of the ~.

Lu·theran /'lu:θərən/ adj, n (follower) of Martin Luther /'lu:θə(r)/ (1483—1546); (member) of the Protestant Church named after Luther.

luxe /lʌks/ = de luxe.

lux·ur·iant /lʌg'ʒʊərɪənt/ adj **1** strong in growth; abundant: *the ~ vegetation of the tropics;* (fig) *a ~ imagination.* **2** (of liter and artistic style) richly ornamented; very elaborate. **~·ly** adv **lux·ur·iance** /-əns/ n [U] ~ growth.

lux·ur·iate /lʌg'ʒʊərɪeɪt/ vi [VP3A] **~ in,** take great delight in: *~ in the warm spring sunshine.*

lux·ur·ious /lʌg'ʒʊərɪəs/ adj **1** supplied with luxuries; very comfortable: *live in ~ surroundings; a ~ hotel.* **2** choice and costly: *~ food.* **3** fond of luxuries; self-indulgent: *~ habits.* **~·ly** adv

lux·ury /'lʌkʃərɪ/ n (pl -ries) **1** [U] state of life in which, to an excessive degree, one has and uses things that please the senses (good food and drink, clothes, comfort, beautiful surroundings): *live in ~; a life of ~.* **2** (attrib use) enabling people to live this kind of life: *a ~ hotel/ocean liner* (perhaps suggesting ostentation rather than real comfort, etc. ⇨ luxurious). **3** [C] sth not essential but which gives enjoyment and pleasure, esp sth expensive, out of season, etc: *His salary is low and he gets few luxuries.*

lycée /'li:seɪ US: li:'seɪ/ n state secondary school in France.

ly·ceum /laɪˈsiːəm/ n (US) lecture hall; (building of an) association for organizing lectures, concerts, etc.

ly·chee (also **li·chee**, **li·tchee**, **li·tchi**) /ˈlaɪtʃiː/ n fruit-tree, originally from China, widely grown in Bengal; its fruit consisting of a thin brown shell containing a white pulp round a single seed. ⇨ the illus at fruit.

lych·gate n = lichgate.

lye /laɪ/ n alkali obtained by passing water through wood ashes, used in washing; any alkaline solution or detergent.

ly·ing /ˈlaɪɪŋ/ pres p of lie¹, lie².

lymph /lɪmf/ n [U] colourless fluid in animal matter, like blood but without colouring matter. **lym·phatic** /lɪmˈfætɪk/ adj 1 of or carrying ~: the ~atic vessels, carrying ~ from the tissues with any waste matter. 2 (of persons) sluggish; slow in thought and action.

lynch /lɪntʃ/ vt [VP6A] put to death (usu by hanging) without a lawful trial (sb believed to be guilty of crime). □ n '~ law, procedure of persons who executed a (supposed) criminal in this way.

lynch·pin /ˈlɪntʃpɪn/ = linchpin.

lynx /lɪŋks/ n short-tailed wild animal of the cat family, noted for its keen sight. ⇨ the illus at cat. Hence, ~-**eyed** adj keen-sighted.

lyre /ˈlaɪə(r)/ n kind of harp with strings fixed in a U-shaped frame, used by the ancient Greeks. '~-**bird** n Australian bird, the male having a long tail, shaped like a ~ when spread out.

lyric /ˈlɪrɪk/ adj 1 of, composed for, singing. 2 of poetry expressing direct personal feeling. □ n [C] ~ poem; (pl) verses of a song, eg in a musical play.

lyri·cal /ˈlɪrɪkl/ adj 1 = lyric. 2 full of emotion; enthusiastic: She became/waxed quite ~ over the new dresses she had brought back from Paris. ~ly /-klɪ/ adv

ly·sol /ˈlaɪsɒl/ US: -sɔːl/ n [U] (P) dark oily liquid used as an antiseptic and disinfectant.

Mm

mitglieder · members

M, m /em/ (pl M's, m's /emz/) the 13th letter of the English alphabet; symbol for the Roman numeral 1000. ⇨ App 4.

ma /mɑː/ n (colloq, abbr of) mamma.

ma'am /mæm/ n madam, used in addressing a Queen.

mac /mæk/ n (GB colloq, abbr of) mackintosh.

ma·cabre /məˈkɑːbrə/ adj gruesome; suggesting death. **danse** /dɑːns/ ~ n (F) dance of death.

ma·cadam /məˈkædəm/ n [U] ~ **road**, road with a surface of several layers of crushed rock or stone, each rolled hard before the next is put down. ~**ize** /-aɪz/ vt make or cover with such layers: ~ized roads. ⇨ tarmac.

maca·roni /ˌmækəˈrəʊnɪ/ n [U] flour paste made in the form of long tubes (often chopped into short pieces), prepared for eating by being boiled.

maca·roon /ˌmækəˈruːn/ n [C] small, hard, flat, sweet cake or biscuit made of sugar, white of egg, and crushed almonds or coconut.

ma·caw /məˈkɔː/ n large, long-tailed parrot of tropical America.

mace¹ /meɪs/ n 1 large, heavy club, usu with a metal head covered with spikes, used as a weapon in the Middle Ages. 2 ceremonial rod or staff (often very much ornamented) carried or placed before an official, eg a Mayor. '~-**bearer** n person who carries an official ~.

a ceremonial mace

mace² /meɪs/ n [U] dried outer covering of nutmegs, used as spice.

mac·er·ate /ˈmæsəreɪt/ vt, vi [VP6A,2A] make or become soft by soaking in water or caustic potash.

Mach /mɑːk/ n '~ **number**, ratio of the air speed of an aircraft to the speed of sound: ~ two, twice the speed of sound.

ma·chete /məˈtʃetɪ US: -ˈʃetɪ/ n cutlass (2); broad, heavy knife used in Latin America and the W Indies as a cutting tool and weapon.

mach·ia·vel·lian /ˌmækɪəˈvelɪən/ adj showing or having no scruples in gaining what is wanted; of or like the ideas set out by Machiavelli /ˌmækɪəˈvelɪ/ (Italian statesman, 1469—1527), who advocated putting expediency above political morality and the use of deceit in statecraft.

machi·na·tion /ˌmækɪˈneɪʃn/ n [C,U] (esp evil) plot/plotting; scheme/scheming.

ma·chine /məˈʃiːn/ n [C] 1 appliance or mechanical device with parts working together to apply power, often steam or electric power (a 'printing-~), but also human power (a 'sewing-~). We live in the ~ age, the age in which ~s more and more replace hand labour. '~-**gun** n gun that fires continuously while the trigger is pressed. ~-'**made** adj made by ~ (contrasted with hand-made). '~ **tool**, tool, mechanically operated, for cutting or shaping materials. 2 persons organized to control a group: (US) the Democratic ~. □ vt [VP6A] operate on, make (sth) with, a ~ (esp of sewing and printing). **ma·chin·ist** /məˈʃiːnɪst/ n one who makes, repairs or controls ~ tools; one who works a ~, esp a sewing-~.

ma·chin·ery /məˈʃiːnərɪ/ n [U] 1 moving parts of a machine; machines collectively: How much new ~ has been installed? (Cf How many new machines have been installed?) 2 methods, organization (eg of government).

ma·chismo /məˈtʃɪzməʊ/ n [U] exaggerated male pride; man's need to prove his virility.

mack·erel /ˈmækrəl/ n (pl unchanged) striped sea-fish used as food. ~ **sky** n sky with bars of cloud like the stripes on a ~'s back.

mack·in·tosh /ˈmækɪntɒʃ/ n (GB) rainproof coat made of cloth treated with rubber.

mac·ro·bi·otic /ˌmækrəʊbaɪˈɒtɪk/ adj prolonging life. ~ **food**, containing pure vegetable substances grown and prepared without chemical assistance.

mac·ro·cosm /ˈmækrəʊkɒzəm/ n the universe; any great whole. ⇨ microcosm.

mad /mæd/ adj (-dder, -ddest) 1 having, resulting from, a diseased mind; mentally ill. **drive/send sb mad**, cause him to be mad. **as mad as a March**

hare/as a hatter, very mad. **'mad·house** *n* (colloq) mental hospital. **'mad·man** /-mən/, **'mad·woman** *nn* person who is mad. **2** (colloq) much excited; filled with enthusiasm: *mad about pop music;* (esp US) angry: *mad about/at missing the train;* wild: *mad with pain. The dog was mad for water,* behaving wildly because it needed water; foolish: *What a mad thing to do!* **be/go mad,** be/become wildly excited, angry, upset, etc. *like mad,* (colloq) with great energy; much: *work/ run/smoke like mad.* **'mad·cap** /-kæp/ *n* person acting recklessly or on impulse. **3** (of a dog, etc) rabid. **mad·ly** *adv* in a mad manner; (colloq) extremely: *madly excited/jealous.* **mad·ness** *n* [U] the state of being mad; mad behaviour: *It would be madness to try to climb the mountain in such a snowstorm.* **mad·den** /'mædn/ *vt* [VP6A] make mad; irritate; annoy: *maddening delays.*

madam /'mædəm/ *n* **1** respectful form of address to a woman (whether married or unmarried): *Can I help you,* ∼? (eg asked by a shop assistant); used in letters, as *Sir* is used to a man: *Dear M*∼. **2** (colloq) woman or girl who likes to order people about: *She's a bit of a* ∼*. Isn't she a little* ∼*!* **3** (colloq) woman who manages a brothel.

Mad·ame /mə'dɑːm US: mə'dæm/ *n* (abbr **Mme**) (*pl* **Mesdames** /meɪ'dɑːm/) French title before the name of a married woman; also used before names of married women who are not British or American.

mad·der /'mædə(r)/ *n* [U] (red dye obtained from the root of a) herbaceous climbing plant with yellowish flowers.

made /meɪd/ *pt,pp* of **make**[1].

Ma·deira /mə'dɪərə/ *n* white dessert wine from ∼ (an island in the Atlantic Ocean). **'∼ cake** *n* kind of sponge-cake.

Mad·emoi·selle /ˌmædmwə'zel/ *n* (abbr **Mlle**) (*pl* **Mesdemoiselles** /ˌmeɪdmwə'zel/) French title used before the name of a young girl or an unmarried woman.

Ma·donna /mə'dɒnə/ *n* **the** ∼, (picture or statue of) Mary, Mother of Jesus Christ. **'∼ lily,** kind of pure white lily (as often shown in pictures of the ∼).

mad·ri·gal /'mædrɪgl/ *n* part-song for several voices without instrumental accompaniment.

mael·strom /'meɪlstrəm/ *n* great whirlpool: (fig) violent or destructive force; whirl of events: *the* ∼ *of war.*

mae·nad /'miːnæd/ *n* priestess of Bacchus, the Greek god of wine; frenzied woman.

maes·tro /'maɪstrəʊ/ *n* (*pl* ∼**s** or **maestri** /'maɪstriː/) (I) eminent musical composer, teacher, or conductor.

maf·fick /'mæfɪk/ *vi* go in for wild public merry-making and rejoicing (eg in war, when there is news of a victory).

Ma·fia /'mæfɪə US: 'mɑːf-/ *n* **the** ∼, secret organization in Sicily, opposed to legal authority and engaged in crime; similar organization on the mainland of Italy and in US.

mag /mæg/ *n* (colloq abbr of) **magazine(3)**: *the colour mags.*

maga·zine /ˌmægə'ziːn US: 'mægəziːn/ *n* **1** store for arms, ammunition, explosives, etc. **2** chamber for holding cartridges to be fed into the breech of a rifle or gun; place for rolls or cartidges of film in a camera. ⇨ the illus at **rifle**. **3** paper-covered (usu weekly or monthly, and illustrated) periodical,

with stories, articles, etc by various writers.

ma·genta /mə'dʒentə/ *adj, n* bright crimson (substance used as a dye).

mag·got /'mægət/ *n* larva or grub, esp of a kind of fly (the bluebottle) that lays its eggs in meat, and of the cheese-fly. **have a '∼ in one's head,** have a strange whim or fancy. ∼**y** *adj* having ∼**s**: ∼*y cheese.*

a maggot

Magi /'meɪdʒaɪ/ *n pl* **the M**∼, the three wise men from the East who brought offerings to the infant Jesus. ⇨ Matt 2:1.

magic /'mædʒɪk/ *n* [U] **1** art of controlling events by the pretended use of supernatural forces; witchcraft; primitive superstitious practices based on a belief in supernatural agencies. *like* ∼*; as if by* ∼, in a mysterious manner. **black/white** ∼, ∼ done with/without the help of devils. **2** art of obtaining mysterious results by tricks: *The conjurer used* ∼ *to produce a rabbit from his hat.* **3** the identification of a symbol with the thing it stands for, as when the wearing of a lion's skin is thought to give the wearer a lion's courage. **4** (fig) mysterious charm; quality produced as if by ∼: *the* ∼ *of Shakespeare's poetry/of the woods in autumn.* □ *adj* done by, or as if by, ∼; possessing ∼; used in ∼: ∼ *arts/words; a* ∼ *touch.* ∼ **eye,** (colloq) name used for various electronic devices which control or indicate sth, eg the automatic opening and closing of doors, exact tuning of a radio set. ∼ **lantern,** apparatus (now a toy) for throwing a magnified image of a picture, etc from a glass slide on to a white screen (*projector* is the name of the modern apparatus). ⇨ the illus at **lantern.** ∼ **square,** large square divided into smaller squares, each with a number, so that the sum of each row, vertical, horizontal or diagonal is always the same. **magi·cal** /-kl/ *adj* or like ∼; (colloq) charming: *a* ∼*al stage set.* **magi·cally** /-klɪ/ *adv* **ma·gician** /mə'dʒɪʃn/ *n* person skilled in ∼(2); wizard.

magis·terial /ˌmædʒɪ'stɪərɪəl/ *adj* of, conducted by, a magistrate; having or showing authority: ∼ *rank; a* ∼ *manner/opinion.* ∼**ly** /-rəlɪ/ *adv*

magis·trate /'mædʒɪstreɪt/ *n* civil officer acting as a judge in the lowest courts; Justice of the Peace. **magis·tracy** /'mædʒɪstrəsɪ/ *n* (*pl* -cies) position of a ∼. **the magis·tracy,** ∼**s** collectively.

mag·nani·mous /mæg'nænɪməs/ *adj* having, showing, generosity. ∼**ly** *adv* **mag·na·nim·ity** /ˌmægnə'nɪmətɪ/ *n* [U] being ∼; [C] (*pl* -ties) act, etc.

mag·nate /'mægneɪt/ *n* wealthy leading man of business or industry; person who has power through wealth or position: *territorial* ∼*s,* influential landowners.

mag·nesia /mæg'niːʃə/ *n* [U] white, tasteless powder (carbonate of magnesium, **MgO**) used medicinally and in industry.

mag·nesium /mæg'niːzɪəm/ *n* [U] silver-white metal (symbol **Mg**) used in the manufacture of aluminium and other alloys, fireworks and flash photography: ∼ *light,* bright light obtained by burning

~ wire.

mag·net /'mægnɪt/ n [C] **1** piece of iron, often a horseshoe shape, able to attract iron, either natural (as in lodestone) or by means of an electric current. **2** (fig) person or thing that attracts. **~·ic** /mæg'netɪk/ adj **1** having the properties of a ~; able to attract, etc: ~ic field, area in all parts of which a ~ic force may be detected; a ~ic mine, submarine mine that is detonated when a large mass of iron (eg a ship) approaches it; a ~ic needle, one that points north and south; the ~ic north, the point indicated by such a needle; a ~ smile/personality, attracting the attention of people. ~ic tape, kind of tape coated with iron oxide used for recording sound and vision. **2** of magnetism. **mag·neti·cally** /-klɪ/ adv

a magnet

a magnifying glass

mag·net·ism /'mægnɪtɪzəm/ n [U] (the science of) magnetic phenomena and properties; (fig) personal charm and attraction.

mag·net·ize /'mægnɪtaɪz/ vt [VP6A] give magnetic properties to; (fig) attract as a magnet does, eg by personal charm, moral or intellectual power.

mag·neto /mæg'ni:təʊ/ n (pl ~s /-təʊz/) electric apparatus for producing sparks in the ignition system of an internal combustion engine.

Mag·nifi·cat /mæg'nɪfɪkæt/ n song of the Virgin Mary in Luke 1: 46—55.

mag·nifi·cent /mæg'nɪfɪsnt/ adj splendid; remarkable; important-looking: a ~ house; his ~ generosity. **~·ly** adv **mag·nifi·cence** /-sns/ n [U].

mag·nify /'mægnɪfaɪ/ vt (pt,pp -fied) [VP6A] **1** make (sth) appear larger (as with a lens or microscope): a '~ing glass, lens for this purpose. **2** exaggerate: ~ dangers. **3** extol; give praise to (God): ~ the Lord. **mag·ni·fier** /-faɪə(r)/ n instrument, etc, that magnifies. **mag·ni·fi·ca·tion** /ˌmægnɪfɪ'keɪʃn/ n (esp) power of ~ing, eg of a lens, a pair of binoculars.

mag·nil·oquent /mæg'nɪləkwənt/ adj (of words, speech) pompous; (of a person) using pompous or high-sounding words. **~·ly** adv **mag·nil·oquence** /-əns/ n

mag·ni·tude /'mægnɪtju:d US: -tu:d/ n [U] size; (degree of) importance; comparative brightness of stars.

mag·no·lia /mæg'nəʊlɪə/ n tree with large, sweet-smelling wax-like flowers.

mag·num /'mægnəm/ n (bottle containing) two quarts (of wine or spirit).

mag·pie /'mægpaɪ/ n noisy black-and-white bird which is attracted by, and often takes away, small, bright objects; (fig) person who chatters very much; (fig) petty thief.

Mag·yar /'mægjɑː(r)/ n, adj (member, language) of the largest group of people in Hungary.

Ma·ha·ra·ja(h) /ˌmɑːhə'rɑːdʒə/ n title of a prince in India, esp a sovereign ruler of one of the indigenous states. **Ma·ha·ra·nee** /ˌmɑːhə'rɑːni:/ n wife of a ~; queen or princess with a position like that of a ~.

Ma·hatma /mə'hætmə/ n (in India, etc) (title given to) one of a class of persons revered as having great high-mindedness and love of humanity.

mah·jong /ˌmɑː'dʒɒŋ/ n Chinese game for four persons played with 136 (or 144) pieces or tiles of wood, bone or ivory.

ma·hog·any /mə'hɒgənɪ/ n (tropical tree with) dark-brown wood much used for furniture.

maid /meɪd/ n **1** (liter) girl. **2** (old use) young, unmarried woman. **old ~**, elderly woman who is considered unlikely to marry. **~ of 'honour**, **(a)** unmarried woman attending a queen or princess. **(b)** principal bridesmaid. **3** (usu modern sense) woman servant: It's the ~'s day off; (in compounds): '~servant, 'house~, 'nurse~.

maiden /'meɪdn/ n (liter) girl; young unmarried woman. □ adj (attrib only) **1** of a girl or woman. '~ name, family name before marriage. **2** first or earliest: a ship's ~ voyage. ~ speech, first speech in Parliament of a new member. **3** ~ (over), (cricket) one in which no runs are scored. **4** (of a woman) unmarried: my ~ aunt. **5** (compounds) '~-hair n (kinds of) fern with fine stalks and delicate fronds. '~-head /-hed/ n [U] the hymen; virginity. '~-hood /-hʊd/ n state of being a ~, period when one is a ~. '~-like, ~-ly adjj gentle; modest; of or like a ~.

mail¹ /meɪl/ n [U] body armour of metal rings or plates: a coat of ~; 'chain-~. ~ed adj only in the ~ed fist, (threat of) armed force.

mail² /meɪl/ n **1** [U] government system of collecting, carrying and delivering letters and parcels: send a letter by air~; the '~-coach, (formerly) horse-drawn stage-coach for carrying ~. '~-bag n stout bag in which ~ is carried. '~-boat n one that transports ~. '~-box n (US) letter-box. '~-man /-mæn/ n (pl -men) (US) postman. ~ order n order for goods to be delivered by post; a ~-order business, one in which the buying and selling of goods is conducted by correspondence; a ~-order catalogue, one with a price-list of goods. '~-train n train that carries ~. **2** [C,U] letters, parcels, etc, sent or delivered by post; the letters, etc, sent, collected or delivered at one time: Is there any ~ this morning? I had a lot of ~ last week. My secretary usually opens the ~. The ship sank and the ~s were lost. □ vt [VP6A] (chiefly US; in GB post is more usu) send by ~. '~-card, (US) postcard. '~-ing-list n list of names of persons to whom sth, eg announcements of new books from a publisher, is regularly sent: Please add my name to your ~ing-list.

maim /meɪm/ vt [VP6A] wound or injure so that some part of the body is useless: He was seriously ~ed in the war.

main¹ /meɪn/ adj (attrib only; no comp or superl) **1** chief; most important: the ~ thing to remember; the ~ street of a town; the ~ line of a railway; the ~ point of my argument; the ~ current/stream of traffic; the ~ course of a meal. **have an eye to the ~ chance**, ⇨ chance¹(3). **2** exerted to the full. **do sth by ~ force**, using one's strength to the utmost. **3** (compounds) '~ deck n upper deck. '~-land /-lænd/ n country, continent or land mass, without its islands. '~-mast n principal mast of a sailing-ship. '~-spring n (a) principal spring of a clock or watch. (b) (fig) driving force or motive. '~·stay /-steɪ/ n rope from the top of the ~mast to the bottom of the foremast; (fig) chief support. '~·stream n 1 dominant trend, tendency, etc: *the ~stream of political thought*. 2 style of jazz between traditional and modern. ~·ly adv chiefly; for the most part: *The people in the streets were ~ly tourists. You are ~ly to blame*.

main² /meɪn/ n 1 [C] (often the ~s) principal pipe bringing water or gas, principal wire transmitting electric current, from the source of supply into a building (contrasted with pipes from a cistern inside the building, etc); principal sewer to which pipes from a building are connected: *My new house is not yet connected to the ~s. We take our electric current from the ~s. '~s set*, radio set to be connected to the ~s for current, not a battery set. 2 *in the ~*, for the most part; on the whole. 3 *with might and ~*, ⇨ might². 4 (poet) sea, esp a wide expanse of sea. 5 *the Spanish M~*, that part of the NE coast of S America and the adjoining part of the Caribbean Sea, visited by the early Spanish navigators.

main·tain /meɪn'teɪn/ vt 1 [VP6A] keep up; retain; continue: ~ *friendly relations* (*with…*); ~ *prices*, keep them steady; ~ *law and order*; ~ *a speed of 60 miles an hour. The improvement in his health is being ~ed*. ~ *an open mind on sth*, be ready to listen to and consider the views of others on a subject. 2 [VP6A] support: ~ *a son at the university*; *neglect to ~ one's family. Can you ~ my daughter* (ie if you marry her) *in the style she has been accustomed to? It's difficult to ~ a family on £30 a week*. 3 [VP6A,9,25] assert as true: ~ *one's innocence*; ~ *that one is innocent of a charge*. 4 [VP6A] keep in good repair or working order: ~ *the roads*. 5 [VP6A] defend: ~ *one's rights*. ~·able /-əbl/ adj that can be ~ed.

main·ten·ance /'meɪntənəns/ n [U] maintaining or being maintained; (esp) what is needed to support life. '~ order n (legal) order made by a court of law obliging sb to support sb, eg a husband to support his wife from whom he is separated. '~ men/gang n workmen who maintain roads and other public services. ,retail ,price '~, practice of maintaining fixed retail prices. ⇨ *cut price* at cut¹(9).

mai·son·nette /,meɪzə'net/ n flat¹ on two floors¹(2).

maize /meɪz/ n [U] (also called *Indian corn*) sort of grain plant. ⇨ the illus at cereal.

ma·jes·tic /mə'dʒestɪk/ adj having, showing, majesty. **ma·jes·ti·cally** /-klɪ/ adv

maj·esty /'mædʒəstɪ/ n (pl -ties) 1 [U] kingly or queenly appearance, conduct, speech, causing respect; stateliness; royal power. 2 *His/Her/Your M~; Their/Your Majesties*, form used when speaking of or to a sovereign ruler or rulers.

ma·jol·ica /mə'dʒɒlɪkə/ n [U] (kinds of) Italian ornamented pottery; modern imitations of these, with white or coloured glazes.

ma·jor¹ /'meɪdʒə(r)/ adj 1 (contrasted with *minor*) greater or more important: ~ *roads; the ~ portion; a ~ operation*, (surgery) one that may be dangerous to the person's life. ~ *premise* n ⇨ premise. ~ *scale* n (music) scale having two full tones between the key note and the third note. ~ *suit* n (cards, bridge) either spades or hearts. 2 (placed after a name) elder or first of two persons of the same name, eg in a school: *Smith ~*. ⇨ minor,

senior. □ vi [VP3A] ~ *in sth*, specialize in (a certain subject) at college or university: *Christina ~ed in two subjects at Keele University. Brian ~ed in economics*. □ n subject ~ed in.

ma·jor² /'meɪdʒə(r)/ n army officer between a captain and a colonel. ,~-'general n army officer next above a brigadier and under a lieutenant-general.

ma·jor-domo /,meɪdʒə 'dəʊməʊ/ n (pl ~s /-məʊz/) head steward in a great household, esp of a prince in Italy or Spain in former times.

ma·jor·ity /mə'dʒɒrətɪ US: -'dʒɔːr-/ n (pl -ties) 1 (with *sing* or *pl* v) *a/the ~ (of)*, the greater number or part (*of*): *The ~ of people seem to prefer watching games to playing games. The ~ were/was in favour of the proposal*. 2 [C] number by which votes for one side exceed those for the other side: *He was elected by a large ~/by a ~ of 3749. The Government's ~ was a small one. be in the/a ~*, have the ~. *a ~ verdict*, verdict of the ~ (of a jury, etc). 3 *one's ~*, (a) legal age of reaching manhood or womanhood: *He will reach his ~ next month*. (b) army rank of major: *obtain one's ~*.

make¹ /meɪk/ vt, vi (pt,pp made /meɪd/) (For uses with *nn*, ⇨ 25,26 below; for uses with *adjj*, ⇨ 27 below; for uses with *adverbial particles* and *preps*, ⇨ 30 below.) 1 [VP6A,14,12B,13B] ~ *sth from/ (out) of sth*; ~ *sth into sth*, construct or produce by combining parts or putting materials together; form or shape from material; bring into existence (esp by effort): ~ *bricks*; ~ *bread*; ~ *a coat*; ~ (= manufacture) *paper. She made* (= prepared) *coffee for all of us. I made myself a cup of tea. Cloth is made of cotton, wool, silk and other materials. Wine is made from grapes. We ~ bottles (out) of glass. Glass is made into bottles. God made man. show sb/let sb see what one is made of*, show sb one's qualities, powers, abilities, etc. *be as clever etc as they ~ 'em*, be very clever etc. ⇨ come(10). 2 [VP6A] cause to appear by breaking, tearing, removing material: ~ *a hole in the ground/a gap in a hedge*. ~ *a hole/dent in one's savings/reserves/finances etc*, reduce them by a considerable amount. 3 [VP6A,16A] enact; establish: *The regulations were made to protect children. Who made this ridiculous rule?* 4 [VP6A] draft; draw up: *Father is making a fresh will. A treaty has been made with our former enemies. I'll get my solicitor to ~ a deed of transfer*. 5 [VP6A] eat, have (a meal): *We made a good breakfast before leaving. He made a hasty lunch*. 6 [VP6A,13B] cause to be: *Why ~ a disturbance at this time of night? I don't want to ~ any trouble for you*. 7 [VP16A] (passive only) be meant or intended: *John and Mary seem to have been made for each other*, eg because they get on so well together. *In England we think bacon and eggs were made to be eaten together*. 8 [VP22,24A] cause to be or become: *The news made her happy. He made his meaning clear. He made clear his objections/ made it clear that he objected to the proposal. His actions made him universally respected. He soon made himself understood. Can you easily ~ yourself understood in English? The full story was never made known/public. He couldn't ~ himself/his voice heard above the noise of the traffic. ~ oneself useful* (*about the house etc*), do sth to help: *Don't stand about doing nothing—~ yourself useful! ~ it worth sb's while* (*to do sth*), pay or reward him: *If you'll help me with this job, I'll ~ it worth your while. ~ sth good*, ⇨ good¹(20).

9 [VP6A] earn; win; gain; acquire: ~ £5000 a year; ~ a profit/loss of £100. He first made his name/reputation as a junior Minister. He made a name/reputation for himself at the Bar, ie as a barrister. He soon made a fortune on the Stock Exchange. ~ **a pile/packet,** (colloq) acquire a great deal of money. ~ **one's living (as/at/by/from),** have as one's work or livelihood: He ~s his living by giving piano lessons. Can you ~ a living from freelance journalism? Does he ~ a living at it? **10** [VP2A, 6A] (various uses in card games, eg bridge) **(a)** win (a trick); play to advantage: He made his Queen of Hearts. **(b)** (of a card) win a trick: Your ace and king won't ~ until you've drawn trumps. **(c)** win (what one has set out to win): Little slam bid and made. **(d)** shuffle, mix (the cards): Will you ~ the pack? My turn to ~. **11** [VP6A] score (at cricket): ~ a century in a test match. 50 runs were made in the first hour. **12** [VP2A] (of the tide) begin to flow or ebb: The tide is making fast. The ebb was now making, The ebb tide was flowing. **13** ~ **or break/mar,** either be successful or be ruined. **a made man,** one whose success has been assured: Get the Minister's help and you'll be a made man. **14** [VP18B] compel; force; persuade; cause (sb) to do sth; cause (sth) to happen: They made me repeat/I was made to repeat the story. Can you ~ this old engine start? The children never behave well and no one ever tries to ~ them (= ~ them behave well). What ~s the grass grow? I can't ~ anyone hear, eg by ringing the doorbell, knocking, calling. His jokes made us all laugh. ~ **one's 'blood boil;** ~ **one's 'hackles rise,** anger one. ~ **one's 'hair stand on end,** shock or frighten one: His ghost stories made our hair stand on end. ~ **(sth) do;** ~ **do with sth,** manage with it although it may not be really adequate or satisfactory: You'll have to ~ do with cold meat for dinner. There's not much of it but I'll try to ~ (it) do. ~ **do and mend,** manage without buying new articles, eg clothing, bed linen, household articles, esp by repairing and remaking old ones. ~ **sth go round,** make it last or be enough: I don't know how she ~s the money go round. ~ **believe (that…/to be…),** pretend: Let's ~ believe that we're Red Indians. The children made believe that they were/made believe to be shipwrecked on a desert island. Hence, '~-**believe** n [U] pretending; [C] pretence. **15** [VP22,18B,23] represent as; cause to appear as; allege (to be, to do): Olivier, in the film, ~s Hamlet a figure of tragic indecision. Most of the old Chronicles ~ the king die in 1026, give 1026 as the date of his death. In the play the author ~s the villain commit suicide, describes him as doing this. You've made my nose too big, eg in a drawing or painting. **16** [VP6A,25] estimate or reckon (to be); put (a total, etc) at: What time do you ~ it? What do you ~ the time? How large do you ~ the audience? I ~ the total (to be) about £50. I ~ the distance about 70 miles. **17** [VP6A] come to, equal; add up to; constitute; amount to (in significance): Twenty shillings used to ~ one pound. Twelve inches ~ one foot. 5 and 7 is 12, and 3 is 15, and 4 more ~s 19. How many members ~ a quorum? His adventures ~ excellent reading. The play ~s an excellent evening's entertainment. ~ **(good/ not much) sense,** seem to have (plenty of/little) sense: His arguments have never made much sense. One swallow doesn't ~ a summer, ⇨ swallow¹. **18** [VP6A] be (in a series); count as:

This ~s the fifth time you've failed this examination. Will you ~ a fourth at bridge? **19** [VP6A,23] turn into; turn out to be; prove to be: If you train hard, you will ~ a good footballer. He will ~ an excellent husband. She will ~ him a good wife, will be one. This length of cloth will ~ me a suit, can be made up into one. **20** [VP6A] (colloq uses) travel over (a distance); reach, maintain (a speed); be in time to catch or reach; (US) gain the rank or place of: We've made 80 miles since noon. We've made good time, travelled the distance in good time, ie fast. The ship was making only nine knots. The disabled cruiser was only just able to ~ (= reach) port. The train leaves at 7.13; can we ~ it, reach the station in time? He's tired out already —he'll never ~ the summit. His new novel has made the best-seller list, has sold enough copies to be on this list. He'll never ~ (= win a place on) the team. Jones made (= reached the rank of) sergeant in six months. **21** [VP23] elect; appoint; nominate; raise to the dignity of: ~ sb King/an earl/a peer. Newton was made President of the Royal Society. He was made General Manager by the directors. We ~ you our spokesman. He made her his wife, married her. **22** [VP12A,13A] offer, propose, hold out (to sb): M~ me an offer, suggest a price! We made them two or three attractive proposals. The Chairman of British Rail has made a new offer to the men, eg of a rise in wages during a strike. I made him a bid for the antique table. I made her a present of the vase. **23** ~ **sth of sb/ sth;** ~ **sth/sb sth,** cause sb/sth to be or become sth: His parents want to ~ a doctor of him, want him to be educated for the medical profession. We must ~ an example of him, eg by punishing him as a warning to others. Don't ~ a habit of it/Don't ~ it a habit, Don't let it become a habit. Don't ~ a hash/mess/muddle of it, Don't do the job badly. He has made a business of politics, has made politics his chief concern. Don't ~ an ass/fool of yourself, behave foolishly. Don't ~ a practice of cheating at exams. Don't ~ cheating a practice. ⇨ n entries esp in **25** and **26** below for other examples of this pattern. **24** [VP2C] behave as if about to do sth: He made as if to strike me. He made to reply (= seemed to be about to do so) and then became silent. **25** [VP6A,14] (used with many nn where ~ + n have the same meaning as a v related in form to the n). ~ **allowance(s) (for),** ⇨ allowance(3). ~ **(an) application (to sb) (for sth),** apply (to sb) (for sth). ~ **arrangements for,** arrange for. ~ **a decision,** decide. ~ **a guess (at),** guess (at). ~ **an impression (on),** impress. ~ **a request (to sb) (for sth),** request (sth) (from sb). ~ **a success of sth,** succeed with it/in doing it. (For other phrases of this kind, ⇨ the n entries.) **26** [VP6A,14] (used with a large number of nn in special senses; cf do²(2) for nn used with do; examples below are a selection only; ⇨ the n entries): ~ much ado (about); ~ advances (to); ~ amends (to sb/for sth); ~ an appointment; ~ an attempt; ~ a bid (for); ~ the bed(s); ~ a bee-line (for); ~ the best of; ~ no bones about; ~ make a break for it; ~ a clean breast of; ~ capital (out) of sth; ~ a change; ~ one's day; ~ a deal (with sb); ~ demands (of/on); ~ some/ little difference; ~ an effort; ~ an excuse; ~ eyes at; ~ a face/faces (at); ~ fun of; ~ a fuss (of); ~ a game of; ~ a gesture; ~ a go of sth; ~ hay of; ~ head or tail of; ~ a hit (with); ~

inroads *into;* ~ *a good/poor* job *of;* ~ a man *of;* ~ *one's* mark; ~ mincemeat *of;* ~ mischief; ~ a mockery *of;* ~ money; ~ *the* most *of;* ~ *a* mountain *out of a molehill;* ~ much *of;* ~ *a* name *for oneself;* ~ *a* night *of it;* ~ nonsense *of;* ~ *a* pass *at;* ~ *one's* peace (*with*); ~ *great* play (*with*); ~ *a* point (*of*); ~ room (*for*); ~ *a* secret *of;* ~ shift *with;* ~ *a* song *and dance about;* ~ war (*on*); ~ water; ~ *one's* way *in the world;* ~ *heavy* weather *of;* ~ *the* worst *of.* **27** [VP2D] (used with *adjj* in special senses; ⇨ the *adj* entries): ~ *so* bold (*as to*); ~ certain (*of/that*); ~ *sth* fast; ~ free *with;* ~ *sth* good; ~ light *of;* ~ merry; ~ sure. **28** [VP2C,3A] (of arguments, evidence, etc) point; tend: *All the evidence* ~s (*points* is more usu) *in the same direction.* ~ **against,** (rare) be contrary, unfavourable, prejudicial or harmful to: *These dissipations* ~ *against your chance of success.* **29** (compounds) '~-**believe** *n* ⇨ **14** above. '~-**shift** *n* sth used for a time until sth better is obtainable: *use an empty crate as a* ~*shift for a table/as a* ~*shift table.* '~-**up** *n* (⇨ ~ *up* in **30** below) (a) arrangement of type, etc on a printed page. (b) character, temperament: *people of that* ~-*up.* (c) [C,U] cosmetics, etc as used by actors; result of using these: *What a clever* ~-*up!* (d) [U] cosmetics as used on the face: *use too much* ~-*up/the wrong kind of* ~-*up.* '~-**weight** *n* small quantity added to get the weight required; (fig) sth or sb of small value that fills a gap, supplies a deficiency. **30** [VP2C,14,15B,3A] (uses with *adverbial particles* and *preps*):

make after sb, (formal) pursue; chase: *She made after him like a madwoman.*

make at sb, move aggressively towards: *The angry woman made at me with her umbrella.* ⇨ *come at* at come(**15**).

make away with oneself, commit suicide: *Why did he* ~ *away with himself?* ~ **away with sth,** destroy or steal it.

make for sb/sth, (a) move in the direction of; head for: *The frigate made for the open sea. It's late; we'd better turn and* ~ *for home.* (b) charge at, rush towards: *The bull made for me and I had to run. When the interval came everyone made for the bar,* ie to buy drinks. (c) contribute to, tend towards: *Does early rising* ~ *for good health? The improved lid of this jar* ~s *for easier opening.*

make sth/sb into sth, change or convert to: *The huts can be made into temporary houses. He wasn't always a bully—you made him into one.*

make sth of sb/sth, understand, interpret: *What do you* ~ *of it all? What are we to* ~ *of his behaviour? I can* ~ *nothing of all this scribble.*

make off, hurry away (esp in order to escape): *The get-away car made off at top speed.* ~ **off with sth,** steal and hurry away: *The cashier made off with the firm's money.*

make sth out, (a) write out; complete or fill in: ~ *out a cheque for £10;* ~ *out a list for the grocer;* ~ *out a document in duplicate.* (b) manage to see, read (usu implying difficulty): *We made out a figure in the darkness. The outline of the house could just be made out.* ~ **out that…/**~ **sb out to be,** claim; assert; maintain: *He made out that he had been badly treated. He* ~s *himself out to be cleverer than he really is. He's not such a good lawyer as some people* ~ *out,* ie ~ him out to be. ~ **sb out,** understand sb's nature: *What a queer fellow he is! I can't* ~ *him out at all.* ~ **it out;** ~

(*it*) **out if/whether,** understand: *I can't* ~ *out what he wants. I couldn't* ~ *it out—did they want our help or not? How do you/does he, etc* ~ *that out?* How do you/does he reach that conclusion, support that contention? ~ **out (with sb),** progress, get on: *How are things making out? How are you making out with Lucy?* How's your friendship progressing? ~ **out a case for/against/that…,** argue for/against: *He has made out a strong case for prison reform. A case could be made out that Smith should be released/for Smith's release.*

make sth/sb over, (a) change, transform, convert: *The basement has been made over into a workshop. You can't* ~ *over a personality in one day.* (b) transfer the possession or ownership of to: *He has made over the whole of his property to the National Trust. How much did he* ~ *over?*

make sth up, (a) complete: *We still need £5 to* ~ *up the sum we asked for. They need ten more men to* ~ *up their full complement.* (b) supply; ~ good: *Our losses have to be made up with more loans.* (c) invent; compose (esp to deceive): *The whole story is made up. It's all a made-up story. Stop making things up!* (d) arrange type, illustrations, etc in columns or pages for printing: *Who is in charge of making up/the* ~-*up of the financial pages?* (e) form; compose; constitute: *Are all animal bodies made up of cells? What are the qualities that* ~ *up Hamlet's character? I object to the way the committee is made up/to the* ~-*up of the committee.* (f) prepare, eg medicine, a prescription, tonic, by mixing ingredients: *Ask the chemist to* ~ *this up for you.* (g) put together; shape: ~ *up a bundle of old clothes for the church bazaar. The grocer was making up the butter into packages of half a kilo. Have you made up Mrs Smith's order yet,* ie collected the items, articles, etc she ordered? (h) ~ (material, cloth, etc) into a garment: *Customer's own materials made up. Can you* ~ *up this suit length for me? This material will* ~ *up into two dresses.* (i) add fuel to, eg a fire in a fireplace or stove: *The fire needs making up,* needs to have more coal put on it. *If the stove isn't made up, it will go out.* (j) prepare (a bed) not at present in use (as for a new hospital patient); prepare (a new makeshift bed, eg on the floor): *You can't go into the ward yet; your bed's still to be made up. They made up a bed on the sofa for the unexpected visitor.* ~ **sb/oneself up,** prepare (an actor/oneself) for the stage by applying grease-paint, hair, etc to his/one's face or body; apply cosmetics to the face: *It takes him more than an hour to* ~ *up/do his* ~-*up for the part of Othello. Isn't she badly made up!* Hence, '~-**up** *n.* ~ **up one's/sb's mind,** come/cause sb to come to a decision: *I've made up my mind. My mind's made up. He needs someone to* ~ *up his mind for him.* ~ **up for sth,** compensate for; outweigh: *Hard work can often* ~ *up for a lack of intelligence. Do you think her beauty could* ~ *up for her stupidity?* ~ **up for lost time,** hurry, work hard, etc after losing time, starting late, etc. ~ **up to sb for sth,** atone; redress; ~ amends for: *How can we* ~ *it up to them for what they have suffered?* ~ **up to sb,** ~ oneself pleasant to sb, to win favours: *He's always making up to influential people. He doesn't welcome being made up to.* ~ **it up to sb,** compensate sb for sth missed or suffered, or for money etc spent: *Thanks for buying my ticket—I'll* ~ *it up to you later,* by refunding you. ~ **it up (with sb),** end a quarrel, dispute or misunderstanding: *They quarrel every morning and* ~ *it up every evening. Why don't you* ~ *it up with her?*

make² /meɪk/ *n* [C,U] **1** way a thing is made; method or style of manufacture: *cars of all* ~*s; an overcoat of first-class* ~. *Is this your own* ~, made by you? **on the** ~, (sl) concerned with making a profit, gaining sth. **2** (electr) completion of an electric circuit.

maker /'meɪkə(r)/ *n* **1 the/our M**~, the Creator; God. **2** (esp in compounds) person or thing that makes: '*dress*~.

mak·ing /'meɪkɪŋ/ *n* **1 be the** ~ **of,** cause the well-being of; cause to develop well: *The two years he served in the Army were the* ~ *of him,* made him develop well (physically, etc according to context). **2 have the** ~*s of a,* have the necessary qualities for becoming: *He has in him the* ~*s of a great man.*

ma·lac·ca /mə'lækə/ *n* ~ '*cane,* cane walkingstick.

mala·chite /'mæləkaɪt/ *n* [U] green mineral, a kind of stone used for ornaments, decoration, etc.

mal·adjusted /ˌmælə'dʒʌstɪd/ *adj* badly adjusted; (esp of a person) unable to adapt himself properly to his environment, eg social or occupational. **mal·adjust·ment** *n* [U] condition of being ~.

mal·adroit /'mælədrɔɪt/ *adj* not adroit; clumsy; tactless. ~·ly *adv* ~·ness *n*

mal·ady /'mælədɪ/ *n* (*pl* -dies) [C] disease; illness: *a social* ~; *spiritual maladies.*

mal·aise /mæ'leɪz/ *n* [U,C] feeling of bodily discomfort, but without clear signs of a particular illness: (fig) *years of* ~ *in industrial relations.*

mala·prop·ism /'mæləprɒpɪzəm/ *n* [C] misuse of a word, esp in mistake for one that resembles it, causing amusement, eg '*Come girls, this gentleman will exhort* (for *escort*) *us!'*

mal·apro·pos /ˌmælæprə'pəʊ/ *adj, adv* inappropriate(ly); inopportune(ly).

ma·laria /mə'leərɪə/ *n* [U] kinds of fever conveyed by mosquitoes, which introduce the germs into the blood. **ma·lar·ial** /-ɪəl/ *adj* of ~; having ~: *a* ~*l patient; a* ~*l district.*

Ma·lay /mə'leɪ/ *adj, n* (language, member) of the people living in the ~ peninsula and adjacent areas.

mal·con·tent /'mælkəntent/ *adj, n* [C] (person who is) discontented and inclined to rebel.

male /meɪl/ *adj* **1** of the sex that does not give birth to offspring; of or for this sex: *a* ~ *voice* '*choir,* of men and/or boys. **2** (of parts of tools, etc) designed for insertion into a bore or socket, the corresponding female part: *a* ~ *screw.* □ *n* ~ person, animal, etc.

mal·edic·tion /ˌmælɪ'dɪkʃn/ *n* [C] curse; prayer to God that sb or sth may be destroyed, hurt, etc.

mal·efac·tor /'mælɪfæktə(r)/ *n* wrongdoer; criminal.

ma·lefi·cent /mə'lefɪsnt/ *adj* hurtful (*to*).

ma·levo·lent /mə'levəlnt/ *adj* wishing to do evil or cause harm to others; spiteful (*to/towards*). ~·ly *adv* **ma·levo·lence** /-əns/ *n* [U] ill will.

mal·feas·ance /ˌmæl'fiːzns/ *n* (legal) [U] wrongdoing; [C] illegal act, esp an instance of official misconduct.

mal·for·ma·tion /ˌmælfɔː'meɪʃn/ *n* [U] state of being badly formed or shaped; [C] badly formed part: *a* ~ *of the spine.* **mal·formed** /ˌmæl'fɔːmd/ *adj* badly formed or shaped.

mal·func·tion /ˌmæl'fʌŋkʃn/ *vi* [VP2A] fail to

function in a normal or satisfactory manner. □ *n* [U,C] failure of this sort.

mal·ice /'mælɪs/ *n* [U] ~ (*towards*), active ill will; desire to harm others: *bear sb no* ~; *with* ~ *towards none.* **(with)** ~ **aforethought,** (legal) (with) conscious intention to cause harm, do wrong. **ma·licious** /mə'lɪʃəs/ *adj* feeling, showing, caused by, ~: *malicious gossip.* **ma·licious·ly** *adv*

ma·lign /mə'laɪn/ *adj* (of things) injurious: *exercise a* ~ *influence.* □ *vt* [VP6A] speak ill of (sb); tell lies about: ~ *an innocent person.*

ma·lig·nant /mə'lɪgnənt/ *adj* **1** (of persons, their actions) filled with, showing, a desire to hurt (~ is stronger in meaning than *malicious* and *malevolent*): ~ *fairies;* ~ *glances.* **2** (of diseases) harmful to life; violent: ~ *cancer.* ~·ly *adv* **ma·lig·nancy** /-nənsɪ/ *n* [U] the state of being ~.

ma·lig·nity /mə'lɪgnətɪ/ *n* (*pl* -ties) **1** [U] deep-rooted ill will; [C] instance of this; act, remark, etc, caused by such ill will. **2** (of diseases) malignant character.

ma·linger /mə'lɪŋgə(r)/ *vi* [VP2A] pretend to be ill, protract an illness, in order to escape duty or work. ~·er *n* person who ~s.

mal·lard /'mælɑːd/ *US:* 'mælərd/ *n* kind of wild duck.

mal·leable /'mælɪəbl/ *adj* **1** (of metals) that can be hammered or pressed into new shapes. **2** (fig, eg of a person's character) easily trained or adapted. **mal·lea·bil·ity** /ˌmælɪə'bɪlətɪ/ *n*

mal·let /'mælɪt/ *n* **1** hammer with a wooden head, eg for striking the handle of a chisel. ⇨ the illus at tool. **2** long-handled wooden-headed hammer for striking a croquet or polo ball.

mal·low /'mæləʊ/ *n* wild plant with hairy stems and leaves and pink, mauve or white flowers; garden varieties of this.

malm·sey /'mɑːmzɪ/ *n* [U] a sweet wine from Greece, Spain, etc.

mal·nu·tri·tion /ˌmælnjuː'trɪʃn *US:* -nuː-/ *n* [U] condition caused by not getting enough food or (enough of) the right kind(s) of food.

mal·odor·ous /ˌmæl'əʊdərəs/ *adj* (formal) ill-smelling.

mal·practice /ˌmæl'præktɪs/ *n* (legal) [U] wrongdoing; neglect of duty; [C] instance of this, eg the dishonest use of a position of trust for personal gain.

malt /mɔːlt/ *n* [U] grain (usu barley) allowed to germinate, used for brewing or distilling: (attrib) ~ *liquors,* eg beer, stout. □ *vt,vi* **1** [VP6A] make (grain) into ~; [VP2A] (of grain) come to the condition of ~. **2** [VP6A] prepare with ~: ~*ed milk.*

Mal·tese /ˌmɔːl'tiːz/ *adj, n* (*pl* unchanged) (language, native) of Malta: ~ *cross,* ⇨ the illus at cross.

Mal·thu·sian /mæl'θjuːzɪən *US:* -'θuːʒn/ *adj* (supporter) of the principles of T R Malthus /'mælθəs/, 1766—1834, English economist (who declared that the growth of the world's population would, unless checked, lead to a world shortage of food).

mal·treat /ˌmæl'triːt/ *vt* [VP6A] treat roughly or cruelly. ~·ment *n* [U] ~ing or being ~ed.

malt·ster /'mɔːltstə(r)/ *n* person who makes malt.

mal·ver·sa·tion /ˌmælvə'seɪʃn/ *n* [U] (formal) corrupt administration (*of* public money, etc).

mamba /'mæmbə/ *n* black or green poisonous African snake. ⇨ the illus at snake.

mam(m)a /mə'mɑː *US:* 'mɑːmə/ *n* familiar word

for *mother*.
mam·mal /'mæml/ *n* any of the class of animals
which feed their young with milk from the breast.
⇨ the illus at **ape, cat, domestic, large, small**.
mam·mon /'mæmən/ *n* [U] wealth (regarded as an
evil influence). **M~**, the god of greed: *worshippers of M~*.
mam·moth /'mæməθ/ *n* large hairy kind of elephant now extinct; (attrib) immense: ~ *business
enterprises*.

tusk

a mammoth

mammy /'mæmɪ/ *n* (*pl* -mies) **1** (child's word
for) mother. **2** (US) (old use, now derog) ⚠ negro
nursemaid for white children.
man¹ /mæn/ *n* (*pl* men /men/) **1** adult male human being. **one's man of business**, one's agent
or solicitor. **a man of letters**, a writer and scholar.
a man about town, one who spends much time in
society, in clubs, at parties, theatres, etc. **a man of
the world**, one with wide experience of business
and society. **man and boy**, from boyhood onwards: *He has worked for the firm, man and boy,
for thirty years*. **2** human being; person: *All men
must die. Growing old is something a man has to
accept*. **be one's own man**, be free to act or do as
one pleases; be in full possession of one's own
senses. **every man for himself (and devil take
the hindmost)**, all must see to their own safety.
the man in the street, person looked upon as representing the interests and opinions of ordinary
people. **to a man; to the last man**, all without
exception: *They answered 'Yes' to a man. They
were killed to the last man*. **3** (*sing* only, no *article*) the human race; all mankind: *Man is mortal.*
4 husband (usu in *man and wife*). **5** male person
under the authority of another; manservant or valet:
masters and men, employers and workers; *officers
and men*, eg in the army. **6** piece used in such
games as chess. **7** male person having the good
qualities associated with men: *Be a man! Play the
man!* Be brave! *He's only half a man*, is lacking in
spirit, strength, courage. *How can we make a man
of him?* **8** (as a vocative, to call attention; used in a
lively or impatient way): *Hurry up, man! Nonsense, man!* **9** (with *possessive adjj*) the person required: *If you want to sell your car, I'm your man,
I'll make an offer. If you want a good music teacher, here's your man*, here's someone suitable. **10**
(as second element in compounds): '*clergyman;*
'*postman;* '*fisherman*, etc. ⇨ App 3. **11** (compounds) ,**man-at-'arms** *n* soldier, esp (in the Middle Ages) a mounted soldier with heavy armour and
weapons. '**man-eater** *n* cannibal; man-eating tiger
or shark. '**man-handle** *vt* move by physical

strength; handle roughly: *The drunken man was
manhandled by the police*. '**man-hole** *n* opening
(usu with a lid) through which a man may enter (an
underground sewer, boiler, tank, etc) for inspection purposes. '**man-hour** *n* work done by one
man in one hour. ,**man-of-'war** *n* (old use) armed
ship belonging to a country's navy. '**man-power** *n*
number of men available for military service, industrial needs, etc: *a shortage of manpower in the
coal-mines*. '**man-servant** *n* male servant. '**man-sized** *adj* of a size or type right for a man; large-scale: *a man-sized beefsteak*. '**man-slaughter** *n*
[U] act of killing a human being unlawfully but not
wilfully. '**man-trap** *n* trap for catching trespassers,
poachers, etc.
man² /mæn/ *vt* (-nn-) [VP6A] supply with person(s) for service or defence: *man a fort/a ship;
man a telephone switchboard*.
man·acle /'mænəkl/ *n* (usu *pl*) fetter or chain for
the hands or feet. □ *vt* [VP6A] fetter with ~s; (fig)
restrain.
man·age /'mænɪdʒ/ *vt,vi* **1** [VP6A] control: ~ *a
horse;* ~ *a sailing-boat*, handle the sails, etc,
properly; ~ *a business/household;* ~ *a naughty
child/one's wife; the managing director*, who controls the business operations of a company. *Mrs
Hill is a very managing woman*, one who likes to
~ or control other people. **2** [VP2A,C,4A,3A] ~
(to do sth); ~ **(with/without sth/sb)**, succeed;
contrive: *I shan't be able to* ~ *without help. If I
can't borrow the money I shall have to* ~ *without.
We can't* ~ *with these poor tools. In spite of these
insults, she* ~*d to keep her temper*. **3** [VP6A]
(colloq, with *can, could, be able to*) make use of:
eat: *can you* ~ *another slice of cake?* ~**·able**
/-əbl/ *adj* that can be ~d; easily controlled. ~**·abil·ity** /,mænɪdʒə'bɪlətɪ/ *n*
man·age·ment /'mænɪdʒmənt/ *n* **1** [U] managing
or being managed: *The failure was caused by bad
~. The business is under new ~*. **2** [U] skilful
treatment; delicate contrivance (and perhaps trickery): *It needed a good deal of* ~ *to persuade them
to give me the job*. **3** [C,U] (with *sing* or *pl v*) all
those concerned in managing an industry, enterprise, etc: *joint consultation between workers and
~. What this department store needs is a stronger
~*.
man·ager /'mænɪdʒə(r)/ *n* **1** person who controls a
business, a hotel, etc. **2** (usu with an *adj*) one who
conducts business, manages household affairs, etc,
in a certain way: *My wife is an excellent* ~. ~**·ess**
/,mænɪdʒə'res/ *n* woman ~(1).
mana·gerial /,mænɪ'dʒɪərɪəl/ *adj* of managers: *the
'~ class*, people such as managers, directors, etc.
mana·tee /,mænə'ti:/ *n* large sea mammal with
flippers and a broad, flat tail; sea-cow. ⇨ dugong.
man·da·rin /'mændərɪn/ *n* **1** (old use) name for
high Chinese government official. **2** standard
spoken Chinese language. **3** ~ **duck**, small
Chinese duck with brightly coloured feathers. **4** ~
orange, tangerine. **5** person whose behaviour and
language seems deliberately remote and difficult:
(attrib): *the* ~ *prose of some civil servants*.
man·date /'mændeɪt/ *n* [C] **1** order from a superior; command given with authority. **2** (hist) authority to administer a territory authorized by the
League of Nations after the First World War. **3**
authority given to representatives by voters, members of a trade union, etc: *the* ~ *given to us by the*

electors. □ *vt* [VP6A] put (a territory) under a ∼(2): *the* ∼*d territories*. **man·da·tory** /'mændətrɪ *US:* -tɔːrɪ/ *adj* of, conveying, a command; compulsory, obligatory: *the mandatory power*. □ *n* (also **-tary** /-tərɪ *US:* -terɪ/) person or state to whom a ∼ has been given.

man·dible /'mændɪbl/ *n* 1 jaw, esp the lower jaw in mammals and fishes. 2 either part of a bird's beak. 3 (in insects) either half of the upper pair of jaws, used for biting and seizing.

man·do·lin /'mændəlɪn/ *n* musical instrument with 6 or 8 metal strings stretched in pairs on a rounded body.

man·drag·ora /mæn'drægərə/ *n* [U] poisonous plant used in medical preparations (as an emetic and for causing sleep).

man·drake /'mændreɪk/ *n* = mandragora.

man·drill /'mændrɪl/ large baboon of West Africa.

mane /meɪn/ *n* [C] long hair on the neck of a horse, lion, etc; (colloq or hum) thick hair on a man's head. ⇨ the illus at **cat, domestic**.

manes /'mɑːneɪz/ *n pl* (Lat) (among the ancient Romans) spirits of the dead, esp of ancestors worshipped as guardian influences.

ma·neu·ver /mə'nuːvə(r)/ *n, v* (US spelling of) manoeuvre.

man·ful /'mænfl/ *adj* brave; resolute; determined. ∼**ly** /-fəlɪ/ *adv*

man·ga·nese /'mæŋɡəniːz/ *n* [U] hard, brittle, light-grey metal (symbol **Mn**) used in making steel, glass, etc.

mange /meɪndʒ/ *n* [U] contagious skin disease, esp of dogs and cats. **mangy** /'meɪndʒɪ/ *adj* 1 suffering from ∼: *a mangy dog*. 2 squalid; neglected. **mang·ily** /'meɪndʒɪlɪ/ *adv*

man·gel·wur·zel /'mæŋɡl wɜːzl/ *n* [C] large round root, a kind of beet, used as cattle food.

manger /'meɪndʒə(r)/ *n* long open box or trough for horses or cattle to feed from. **dog in the** ∼, ⇨ **dog**[1](2).

mangle[1] /'mæŋɡl/ *n* [C] machine with rollers for pressing out water from and for smoothing clothes, etc, that have been washed. □ *vt* [VP6A] put (clothes, etc) through a ∼.

mangle[2] /'mæŋɡl/ *vt* [VP6A] 1 cut up, tear, damage, badly: *He was knocked down by a lorry and badly* ∼*d*. 2 (fig) spoil by making bad mistakes: ∼ *a piece of music*.

mango /'mæŋɡəʊ/ *n* (*pl* ∼es or ∼s /-ɡəʊz/) (tropical tree bearing) pear-shaped fruit with yellow flesh: ∼ *chutney*, kind made with (green) unripe ∼es. ⇨ the illus at fruit.

man·go·steen /ˌmæŋɡəʊ'stiːn/ *n* (E Indian tree bearing) fruit with thick red rind and white juicy pulp.

man·grove /'mæŋɡrəʊv/ *n* [C] tropical tree growing in swamps and sending down new roots from its branches.

mangy /'meɪndʒɪ/ ⇨ mange.

man·handle ⇨ man[1](11).

man·hat·tan /mæn'hætn/ *n* (US) cocktail of whisky and vermouth.

man·hood /'mænhʊd/ *n* [U] 1 the state of being a man: *reach* ∼; ∼ *suffrage*, giving the vote to male citizens. 2 manly qualities; courage; sexual virility. 3 all the men (collectively, *of* a country): *the* ∼ *of Scotland*.

mania /'meɪnɪə/ *n* 1 [U] violent madness. 2 [C] ∼ **(for)**, extreme enthusiasm (*for* sth): *a* ∼ *for collecting china ornaments*. **maniac** /'meɪnɪæk/ *n*

raving madman; (fig) extreme enthusiast. **ma·nia·cal** /mə'naɪəkl/ *adj* violently mad; (fig) extremely enthusiastic. **ma·niacally** /mə'naɪəklɪ/ *adv*

manic–depressive /ˌmænɪk dɪ'presɪv/ *adj*, *n* (person) suffering from alternating periods of happy excitement and melancholic depression.

mani·cure /'mænɪkjʊə(r)/ *n* [U] care of the hands and finger-nails: *have a course in* ∼; [C] treatment of this kind: *She has a* ∼ *once a week*. □ *vt* [VP6A] give ∼ treatment to; cut, clean and polish the finger-nails. **'mani·cur·ist** /-ɪst/ *n* person who practises ∼ as an occupation.

mani·fest[1] /'mænɪfest/ *n* list of a ship's cargo; list of passengers in an aircraft; list of trucks of a goods train.

mani·fest[2] /'mænɪfest/ *adj* clear and obvious: *a* ∼ *truth; sth that should be* ∼ *to all of you*. □ *vt* [VP6A] 1 show clearly: ∼ *the truth of a statement*. 2 give signs of: *She doesn't* ∼ *much desire to marry him*. 3 (reflex) come to light; appear: *No disease* ∼*ed itself during the long voyage. Has the ghost* ∼*ed itself recently?* **mani·fes·ta·tion** /ˌmænɪfe'steɪʃn/ *n* [U] ∼ing; making clear; [C] act or utterance that ∼s. ∼**·ly** *adv* clearly; obviously.

mani·festo /ˌmænɪ'festəʊ/ *n* (*pl* ∼s or ∼es /-təʊz/) public declaration of principles, policy, purposes, etc by a ruler, political party, etc or of the character, qualifications of a person or group.

mani·fold /'mænɪfəʊld/ *adj* having or providing for many (uses, forms, parts etc); many and various. □ *vt* [VP6A] (now usu **duplicate**) make a number of copies of (a letter, etc) on a machine. □ *n* pipe or chamber with several openings, for connections, eg for leading gases into or out of cylinders.

mani·kin /'mænɪkɪn/ *n* 1 small, undersized man; dwarf. 2 anatomical model of the human body; figure of the human body used by artists, eg for drapery, clothes.

Ma·nilla (US also **Ma·nila**) /mə'nɪlə/ *n* 1 ∼ **(hemp)**, plant fibre used for making ropes, mats, etc. 2 **m**∼ **paper**, strong, brown wrapping paper made from ∼ hemp. **m**∼ **envelopes**, strong variety. 3 cheroot made in ∼, the capital of the Philippine Islands.

ma·nipu·late /mə'nɪpjʊleɪt/ *vt* [VP6A] 1 operate, handle, with skill: ∼ *the gears and levers of a machine*. 2 manage or control (sb or sth) skilfully or craftily, esp by using one's influence or unfair methods: *A clever politician knows how to* ∼ *his supporters/*∼ *public opinion*. **ma·nipu·la·tion** /məˌnɪpjʊ'leɪʃn/ *n* [U] manipulating or being ∼d; [C] instance of this: *make a lot of money by clever manipulation of the Stock Market*.

man·kind *n* [U] 1 /ˌmæn'kaɪnd/ the human species. 2 /'mænkaɪnd/ the male sex (contrasted with 'womankind).

man·like /'mænlaɪk/ *adj* having the qualities (good or bad) of a man.

man·ly /'mænlɪ/ *adj* (-ier, -iest) having the good qualities expected of a man; (of a woman) having a man's qualities; (of things, qualities, etc) right for a man. **man·li·ness** *n*

manna /'mænə/ *n* [U] (in the Bible) food provided by God for the Israelites during their forty years in the desert (⇨ Exod 16); (fig) sth unexpectedly supplied or that gives spiritual refreshment.

man·ne·quin /'mænɪkɪn/ *n* 1 woman employed to display new clothes for sale by wearing them (*model* is the usual word today). 2 life-size dummy of a human body, used by tailors and in shops and shop-windows for the display of clothes.

man·ner /'mænə(r)/ n [C] **1** way in which a thing is done or happens: *Do it in this ~. (as) to the ~ born,* as if knowing how to deal with a situation, practice, custom, etc from birth; naturally fitted for a position, duty, etc. **2** (*sing* only) person's way of behaving towards others: *He has an awkward ~. I don't like his ~.* **3** (*pl*) habits and customs; social behaviour: *good/bad ~s. He has no ~s at all,* is very badly behaved. *It is bad ~s to stare at people. Aren't you forgetting your ~s, Mary?* (eg to a child who forgets to say 'Thank you' for a present). *comedy of ~s,* play which is a satire on the customs of (a certain section of) society. **4** style in literature or art: *a painting in the ~ of Raphael.* **5** kind, sort: *What ~ of man is he? all ~ of,* every kind of. *in a ~,* in a certain degree; to a certain extent. *in a ~ of speaking,* as one might say (used to weaken or qualify what one says). *by 'no ~ of means,* in no circumstances. *~ed adj* **1** (in compounds) *,ill-/,well-/,rough-'~ed,* having bad/good/rough ~s(3). **2** showing mannerisms.

man·ner·ism /'mænərızəm/ n [C] peculiarity of behaviour, speech, etc, esp one that is habitual; excessive use of a distinctive manner in art or literature.

man·ner·ly /'mænəlı/ adj having good manners; polite.

man·nish /'mænıʃ/ adj **1** (of a woman) like a man. **2** more suitable for a man than for a woman: *a ~ style of dress;* characteristic of a man.

ma·noeuvre (US = **ma·neu·ver**) /mə'nuːvə(r)/ n **1** planned movement (of armed forces); (*pl*) series of such movements, eg as training exercises: *army/fleet ~s; troops on ~s.* **2** movement or plan, made to deceive, or to escape from sb, or to win or do sth: *the despicable ~s of some politicians.* □ *vi, vt* [VP2A,C,6A,15A] (cause to) perform ~s: *The fleet is manoeuvring off the east coast. Can we ~ the enemy out of their strong position? She ~d her car into a difficult parking space. Can you ~ me into a good job,* use your influence, etc in order to get a good job for me? *The yachts were manoeuvring for position,* moving about to get advantageous positions (in a race). **ma·noeuvr·able** (US = **ma·neu·ver·able**) /-vrəbl/ adj that can be ~d. **ma·noeuvr·abil·ity** (US = -neu·ver-) /mə,nuːvrə'bılətı/ n ~r (US = **ma·neu·verer**) n

manor /'mænə(r)/ n (in England) **1** unit of land under the feudal system, part of which was used directly by the lord of the ~ (⇨ lord(4)) and the rest occupied and farmed by tenants who paid rent in crops and service. **2** (modern use) area of land with a principal residence (called the '~-**house**). **ma·nor·ial** /mə'nɔːrɪəl/ adj of a ~.

man·sard /'mænsɑːd/ n ~ (**roof**), roof with a double slope, the lower being steeper than the upper.

manse /mæns/ n church minister's house, esp in Scotland.

man·sion /'mænʃn/ n **1** large and stately house. **the 'M~ House,** the official residence of the Lord Mayor of London. **2** (*pl,* in proper names) block of flats: *Victoria M~s.*

man·tel /'mæntl/ n structure of wood, marble, etc above and around a fireplace; (in modern houses, usu '~piece) shelf projecting from the wall above a fireplace.

man·tilla /mæn'tılə/ n large veil or scarf worn by Spanish women to cover the hair and shoulders.

man·tis /'mæntıs/ n (**praying**) ~, (kinds of) long-legged insect. ⇨ the illus at insect.

mantle¹ /'mæntl/ n **1** loose, sleeveless cloak; (fig) covering: *hills with a ~ of snow.* **2** lace-like cover fixed round the flame of a gas lamp and becoming incandescent, to provide bright light.

mantle² /'mæntl/ vt,vi **1** [VP6A] cover in, or as in, a mantle: *an 'ivy-~d wall.* **2** [VP6A,2C] (old use, or liter) (of blood) flow into the blood-vessels of; (of the face) flush: *Blushes/Blood ~d (over) her cheeks. Her face ~d with blushes.* (fig) *Dawn ~d in the sky.*

man·ual /'mænjʊəl/ adj of, done with, the hands: ~ *labour;* ~ *training,* eg in schools, training in carpentry, metal work; ~ *exercises,* eg drill in handling a rifle. □ n **1** handbook or textbook: *a shorthand ~.* **2** keyboard of an organ, played with the hands. ~ly /-jʊəlı/ adv

manu·fac·ture /,mænjʊ'fæktʃə(r)/ vt [VP6A] **1** make, produce (goods, etc) on a large scale by machinery: ~ *shoes/cement; manufacturing industries;* ~d *goods* (contrasted with raw materials, hand-made goods, etc). **2** invent (a story, an excuse, etc). □ n **1** [U] the making or production of goods and materials: *firms engaged in the ~ of plastics; goods of foreign ~.* **2** (*pl*) ~d goods and articles. **manu·fac·turer** n person, firm, etc that ~s things.

manu·mit /,mænjʊ'mıt/ vt (-tt-) (in former times) set (a slave) free. **manu·mission** /,mænjʊ'mıʃn/ n

ma·nure /mə'njʊə(r)/ n [U] animal waste, eg from stables and cow barns, or other material, natural or artificial, spread over or mixed with the soil to make it fertile. ⇨ *fertilizer,* the usu word for chemical or artificial manure, at fertilise. □ vt [VP6A] put ~ in or on land/soil.

manu·script /'mænjʊskrɪpt/ n (shortened to **MS,** *pl* **MSS**) book, etc as first written out or typed: *send a ~ to the printers. in ~,* not yet printed: *poems still in ~.*

Manx /mæŋks/ adj of the Isle of Man. '~ **cat,** tailless kind of cat. □ n~ language.

many /'menı/ adj, n (contrasted with *few;* ⇨ more, most) **1** (used with *pl* nn; ⇨ much; in purely affirm sentences it is often preferable to use *a large number* (*of*), *numerous,* or (colloq) *a lot* (*of*), *lots* (*of*), *plenty* (*of*)): *Were there ~ people at the meeting? I have some, but not ~. M~ people think so. M~ of them were poorly. M~ of us left early. How ~ do you want? How ~ of them were absent? You gave me two too ~. Do you need so ~? He made ten spelling mistakes in as ~ lines,* ie in ten lines. *I have six here and as ~ again* (ie six more) *at home. a great/good ~,* a large number (of): *I have a good ~ things to do today. one too ~,* one more than the correct or needed number: *I wish Jane would go away; she's one too ~ here,* We don't want her company. *He's had one too ~ again,* is slightly drunk. *be one too ~ for,* be more than a match(2) for; get the better of; outwit: *He was one too ~ for you that time. the ~,* the masses; the large numbers of ordinary people: *Is it right that the ~ should starve while the few have plenty?* **2** ~ *a,* (used with a *sing n;* rather liter, usu replaced by ~ and the *pl n* in ordinary style): *M~ a man* (= M~ men) *would welcome the opportunity. I've been here ~ a time. ~'s the sth/sb that/who...,* it/he has often.... *~'s the time (that) sth/sb...,* it/he often... *,~-'sided adj* having ~ sides; (fig) having ~ aspects, capabilities, etc: *a ~-sided problem.*

Mao·ism /'maʊɪzəm/ *n* political theories and practice of Mao Tse-Tung /ˌmaʊ tseɪ 'tʊŋ/ (1893—1976) chairman of the Communist Party in China 1943—1976. **Mao·ist** /'maʊɪst/ *n* supporter of ~.

Maori /'maʊrɪ/ *n* member, language, of the aboriginal race of New Zealand.

map /mæp/ *n* representation on paper, etc of the earth's surface or a part of it, showing countries, oceans, rivers, mountains, etc; representation of the sky showing positions of the stars, etc. ⇨ the illus at projection. ⇨ chart, plan. **on the map,** (fig) important, to be reckoned with. **off the map,** (colloq, of a place) inaccessible; (fig) unimportant. **'map-reader** *n* (with an *adj*) person able to get information from maps: *He's a good/poor map-reader.* □ *vt* (-pp-) [VP6A] make a map of; show on a map; [VP15B] **map out,** plan, arrange: *map out one's time.*

maple /'meɪpl/ *n* **1** [C] (sorts of) tree of the northern hemisphere, grown for timber and ornament. ⇨ the illus at tree. **~ sugar/syrup** *n* sugar/syrup obtained from the sap of one kind of ~. **'~-leaf** *n* emblem of Canada. **2** [U] wood of this tree.

ma·quis /'mæki: *US:* 'mɑːki:/ *n* **the ~,** the secret army of French patriots during World War II, fighting in France against the Germans.

mar /mɑː(r)/ *vt* (-rr-) [VP6A] injure; spoil; damage: *Nothing marred the happiness of our outing.* **make or mar,** make a great success of or ruin completely.

mara·bou /'mærəbuː/ *n* large W African stork; tuft of its soft feathers as trimming, eg for a hat.

mar·as·chino /ˌmærə'skiːnəʊ/ *n* (*pl* ~s /-nəʊz/) sweet liqueur made from a small black kind of cherry.

mara·thon /'mærəθən *US:* -θɒn/ *n* **the M~,** long-distance race on foot (about 26 miles (or 41·8 kilometres) at modern sports meetings); (fig) test of endurance.

ma·raud /mə'rɔːd/ *vi* [VP2A] go about in search of plunder or prey: *The Roman Empire was attacked by ~ing Goths and Huns.* **~er** *n* person or animal that ~s.

marble /'mɑːbl/ *n* **1** [U] (sorts of) hard limestone used, when cut and polished, for building and sculpture: (attrib) *a ~ statue/tomb.* **2** (*pl*) works of art in ~; collection of ~ sculptures. **3** small ball of glass, clay or stone used in games played by children. **~s,** game played with these balls: *Let's have a game of ~s.* **4** (attrib) like ~: *a ~ brow,* smooth and white; *a ~ breast,* hard and unsympathizing personality. **~d** /'mɑːbld/ *adj* stained or printed so as to look like variegated ~: *a book with ~d edges.*

March /mɑːtʃ/ *n* the third month of the year: *M~ hare,* ⇨ hare.

march¹ /mɑːtʃ/ *vi,vt* **1** [VP2A,B,C] walk as soldiers do, with regular and measured steps: *They have ~ed twenty miles today. They ~ed into the town. Quick ~!* (military command to begin ~ing). *The troops ~ed by/past/in/out/off/away. He ~ed impatiently up and down the station platform.* **'~ing orders,** orders for troops to leave for manœuvres, for war, etc; (fig) dismissal. **2** [VP15A,B] cause to ~: *They ~ed the prisoner away. He was ~ed off to prison.*

march² /mɑːtʃ/ *n* **1** [U] act of marching (by soldiers, etc). **on the ~,** marching. **a line of ~,** a

route followed by troops when ~ing: *Scouts were sent out to discover the enemy's line of ~.* **2** [C] instance of marching; distance travelled: *a ~ of ten miles. a ~ past,* ie of troops past a saluting point at a review. *a forced ~,* one made more quickly than usual, or for a greater distance, in an emergency. *steal a '~ on sb,* win a position of advantage by doing sth earlier than expected by him. **3 the ~ of,** progress; onward movement: *the ~ of events/time.* **4** [C] piece of music for marching to: *military ~es; a dead ~,* one in slow time for a funeral. **~er** *n*

march³ /mɑːtʃ/ *n* (usu *pl*) (hist) frontier areas (esp between England and Scotland or Wales), esp land that is in dispute: *riding round the ~es.* □ *vi* [VP3A] **~ upon/with,** (archaic) (of countries, estates, etc) border upon; have a common frontier with: *Our territory ~es with theirs.*

mar·chion·ess /ˌmɑːʃə'nes/ *n* wife or widow of a marquis; woman who holds in her own right a position equal to that of a marquis.

Mardi Gras /ˌmɑːdɪ 'grɑː/ *n* (F) Shrove Tuesday; last day of carnival before Lent, celebrated in some places with parades and merrymaking.

mare /'meə(r)/ *n* female horse or donkey. *a '~'s nest,* a hoax; a discovery that turns out to be false or worthless.

mar·gar·ine /ˌmɑːdʒə'riːn *US:* 'mɑːrdʒərɪn/ *n* [U] food substance, used like butter, made from animal or vegetable fats.

marge /mɑːdʒ/ *n* (colloq abbr for) margarine.

mar·gin /'mɑːdʒɪn/ *n* [C] **1** blank space round the printed or written matter on a page: *wide/narrow ~s; notes written in the ~.* **2** edge or border: *sit on the ~ of a lake/swimming pool; road ~s.* **3** amount of time, money, etc) above what is estimated as necessary. **4** condition near the limit or borderline, below or beyond which sth is impossible: *a safety ~. He escaped defeat by a narrow ~.* **5** (comm) difference between cost price and selling price: *an increase of a penny a gallon in the dealer's ~ on the price of petrol.* **~al** /-nl/ *adj* **1** of or in a ~(1): *~al notes.* **2** of a ~(4): *The differences between the employers and the workers are ~al. ~al land,* land which is not fertile enough for profitable farming except when prices of farm products are high. **~al seat/constituency,** one where the MP has been elected by a small majority. **~·ally** /-nəlɪ/ *adv*

Mar·grave /'mɑːgreɪv/ *n* hereditary title of certain princes in the Holy Roman Empire.

mar·guer·ite /ˌmɑːgə'riːt/ *n* kinds of daisy, esp the ox-eye daisy with white petals round a yellow centre.

mari·gold /'mærɪgəʊld/ *n* (kinds of) plant with orange or yellow flowers.

mari·juana, mari·huana /ˌmærɪ'wɑːnə/ *n* (also called *hashish, cannabis, pot*) dried leaves and flowers of Indian hemp, (esp) smoked in cigarettes (called *reefers* or *joints*) to induce euphoria.

mar·imba /mə'rɪmbə/ *n* musical instrument similar to the xylophone.

ma·rina /mə'riːnə/ *n* harbour designed for pleasure boats (small yachts, cabin cruisers, etc) often with hotels, etc.

mari·nade /ˌmærɪ'neɪd/ *n* [U] pickle of wine, vinegar and spice; fish or meat pickled in this. □ *vt* (also **mari·nate** /'mærɪneɪt/) steep, make tender, in ~.

mar·ine /mə'riːn/ *adj* **1** of, by, found in, produced by, the sea: ∼ products; a '∼ painter, artist who paints seascapes. 2 of ships, sea-trade, the navy, etc: ∼ insurance, of ships and cargo; ∼ stores, materials and supplies for ships. '∼ corps, body of soldiers serving on warships and trained for amphibious warfare. □ n 1 ,merchant/,mercantile '∼, all the merchant ships of a country. 2 [C] soldier of a ∼ corps serving on a warship. the M∼s, country's general body of such soldiers. Tell that to the ∼s, (used to express disbelief in an impossible story).

mari·ner /'mærɪnə(r)/ n sailor, esp one who assists in navigating a ship: a ∼'s compass. **master** ∼, captain of a merchant ship.

mari·on·ette /,mærɪə'net/ n jointed doll or puppet moved by strings on a small stage. ⇨ the illus at puppet.

mari·tal /'mærɪtl/ adj of a husband; of marriage: ∼ obligations, eg providing for one's wife.

mari·time /'mærɪtaɪm/ adj 1 connected with the sea or navigation: ∼ law; the great ∼ powers. 2 situated or found near the sea: the ∼ provinces of the USSR.

mar·joram /'mɑːdʒərəm/ n [U] sweet-smelling herb used as seasoning in cooking and in medicine.

mark[1] /mɑːk/ n 1 line, scratch, cut, stain, etc that spoils the appearance of sth: Who made these dirty ∼s on my new book? 2 noticeable spot on the body by which a person or animal may be recognized: a horse with a white ∼ on its head; a 'birth∼. 3 visible trace; sign or indication (of a quality, etc): ∼s of suffering/old age. Please accept this gift as a ∼ of my esteem. 4 figure, design, line, etc, made as a sign or indication: ,punctu'ation ∼s; 'price-∼s, on goods; 'trade ∼s. 5 numerical or alphabetical symbol, eg β + , to indicate an award in an examination, or for conduct. give sb/get/gain a good/ bad, etc ∼ (for sth): get 72 ∼s out of 100 for geography/full ∼s for science. He got the best ∼s of his year. 6 target; sth aimed at. be/fall wide of the ∼, be inaccurate, imprecise: Your guess/ calculation is wide of the ∼. hit/miss the ∼, (fig) succeed/fail in an attempt. an easy ∼, (colloq) person who is easily cheated, persuaded or ridiculed. beside the ∼, irrelevant. 7 [U] distinction; fame: make one's ∼, become distinguished. 8 the ∼, (a) standard. be up to/below the ∼, equal to/below the required standard. (b) what is normal. not be/feel (quite) up to the ∼, not in one's usual health. 9 cross made on a document by an illiterate person: make one's ∼. John Doe, his ∼, cross made by John Doe instead of a signature. 10 (athletics) line indicating the starting-point of a race: On your ∼s, get set, go! (words used by the starter). 11 (with numbers) model or type: Meteor M∼ 3, eg of an aircraft.

mark[2] /mɑːk/ vt 1 [VP6A,15A,B] ∼ sth on/with sth; ∼ sth down/up, put or leave a ∼ on sth by writing, stamping, etc: ∼ one's name on one's clothes/∼ one's clothes with one's name. All our stock has been ∼ed down for the sales, reduced in prices. The new tax made it necessary to ∼ up all the goods in the shop, put higher price ∼s on them. Hence, '∼-up n amount by which a price is ∼ed up: a 10% ∼-up. '∼-ing-ink n indelible ink for ∼ing linen, etc. 2 (passive) have natural ∼s or visible signs: A zebra is ∼ed with stripes. His face is ∼ed with smallpox, has the scars of smallpox. Her face is ∼ed with grief. 3 [VP6A] give ∼s(5) to: ∼ examination papers; have twenty essays to ∼/to be

∼ed. 4 [VP22] indicate sth by putting a ∼, eg a tick or a cross, on or against: ∼ sth wrong; ∼ a pupil absent. 5 [VP6A,8,10,2A] pay attention (to): M∼ carefully how it is done/how to do it/how he does it. (You) m∼ my words, Note what I say (and you will find, later, that I am right). a ∼ed man, one whose conduct is watched with suspicion or enmity. 6 [VP6A] be a distinguishing feature of: What are the qualities that ∼ a great leader? 7 [VP6A] signal; denote: His death ∼ed the end of an era. There will be ceremonies to ∼ the tenth anniversary of the Queen's accession. 8 ∼ time, stamp the feet as when marching but without moving forward; (fig) wait until further progress becomes possible. 9 [VP15B] (uses with adverbial particles) ∼ sth off, put ∼s on (to show boundary lines, measurements, etc). ∼ sth out, put lines on sth to indicate limits, etc: ∼ out a tennis-court. ∼ sb out for sth, decide in advance that sb will receive sth: ∼ sb out for promotion. Peter was ∼ed out for a special management course. ∼ed /mɑːkt/ adj clear; readily seen: a ∼ed difference/ improvement; a man of ∼ed ability. ∼-ed·ly /'mɑːkɪdlɪ/ adv in a ∼ed manner. ∼·ing n (esp) pattern of different colours of feathers, skin, etc.

mark[3] /mɑːk/ n unit of German currency.

marker /'mɑːkə(r)/ n 1 person or tool that marks, esp a person who marks the score at games, eg billiards. 2 sth that marks or indicates, eg a flag or post on a playing field, a post showing distances.

mar·ket[1] /'mɑːkɪt/ n 1 [C] public place (an open space or a building) where people meet to buy and sell goods; time during which such a meeting takes place: She went to (the) ∼ to buy food for the family. There are numerous small ∼s in the town. The next ∼ is on the 15th. bring one's eggs/hogs to a bad ∼/to the wrong ∼, fail in one's plans, fail because one goes to the wrong people for help. go to ∼, go there for the purpose of shopping. go to a bad/good ∼, be (un)successful. '∼-day n fixed day on which a ∼ is held. ,∼-'garden n one where vegetables are grown for ∼s. Hence, ∼-'gardening n [U] the practice of doing this. '∼-place/-square n square or open place in a town where a ∼ is held. '∼ hall, (usu large) roofed area for a ∼. '∼-town n one where a ∼ (esp one for cattle and sheep) is held. 2 trade in a class of goods: the 'corn ∼; the 'coffee ∼; state of trade as shown by prices: a dull/lively ∼. The ∼ rose/ fell/was steady, Prices rose/fell/did not change much. ∼ price, price for which sth, eg commodities/securities, is sold in the open ∼. 'down-/'up-∼ adjj (trade use) low/high class. 3 demand: There's no/not much/only a poor ∼ for these goods. 4 the ∼, buying and selling. be on/ come on (to) the ∼, be offered for sale: This house will probably come on the market next month. be in the ∼ for sth, be ready to buy or (fig) consider sth. play the ∼, speculate (by buying and selling shares, commodities, etc). put sth on the ∼, offer it for sale. ∼ re'search, study of the reasons why people buy, or do not buy, certain goods, how sales are affected by advertising, etc. 5 [C] area, country, in which goods may be sold: We must find new ∼s for our products. Which countries are Brazil's best ∼s for coffee? ,Common 'M∼, ⇨ common[1](1).

mar·ket[2] /'mɑːkɪt/ vi,vt 1 [VP2A] buy or sell in a ∼: go ∼ing. 2 [VP6A] take or send to ∼; prepare for (a/the) ∼ and offer for sale. ∼·able /-əbl/ adj that can be sold; fit to be sold: ~*able products.* ~-**ing** *n* theory and practice of (large-scale) selling.

marks·man /'mɑːksmən/ *n* (*pl*-men /-mən/) person skilled in aiming at a mark, esp with a rifle. ~-**ship** /-ʃɪp/ *n* skill in shooting.

marl /mɑːl/ *n* [U] soil consisting of clay and carbonate of lime, used as a fertilizer.

mar·line·spike /'mɑːlɪnspaɪk/ *n* pointed iron tool used for separating the strands of a rope which is to be spliced.

mar·ma·lade /'mɑːməleɪd/ *n* [U] (bitter) jam made from citrus fruit (usu oranges).

mar·mor·eal /mɑːˈmɔːrɪəl/ *adj* (poet) white, cold or polished, like marble.

mar·mo·set /'mɑːməzet/ *n* small, tropical American monkey with soft, thick hair and a bushy tail. ⇨ the illus at ape.

mar·mot /'mɑːmət/ *n* small animal of the squirrel family.

ma·ro·cain /'mærəkeɪn/ *n* [U] thin, fine dress material of silk or wool.

ma·roon[1] /məˈruːn/ *adj*, brownish-red (colour).

ma·roon[2] /məˈruːn/ *n* rocket, esp the kind used as a warning signal.

ma·roon[3] /məˈruːn/ *vt* [VP6A] put (sb) on a desert island, uninhabited coast, etc, and abandon him there.

marque /mɑːk/ *n* ,**letters of**'~, authority formerly given to private persons to fit out an armed ship and use it to attack, capture, and plunder.

mar·quee /mɑːˈkiː/ *n* large tent (as used for flower shows, garden parties, or for a circus).

mar·quetry /'mɑːkɪtrɪ/ *n* [U] inlaid work (wood, ivory, etc) used for decorating furniture.

mar·quis, mar·quess /'mɑːkwɪs/ *n* (GB) nobleman next in rank above an earl and below a duke; (in other countries) nobleman next in rank above a count. ⇨ **marchioness**.

mar·riage /'mærɪdʒ/ *n* **1** [C,U] (instance of a) legal union of a man and woman as husband and wife; state of being married: *A* ~ *has been arranged between... and.... She has had an offer of* ~. **give sb** (esp one's daughter) **in** ~ **(to sb)**, offer her as a wife. **take sb in** ~, take as husband or wife. '~ **certificate/licence/settlement**, ⇨ these words. '~ **lines**, (colloq) ~ certificate. **2** (usu *wedding*) ceremony of being married: *Was it a civil or a church* ~? ⇨ civil(1). ~-**able** /-əbl/ *adj* (of a young person) old enough, fit for, ~: *a girl of* ~*able age.* ~-**abil·ity** /ˌmærɪdʒəˈbɪlətɪ/ *n*

mar·ried /'mærɪd/ *adj* united in marriage; of marriage: ~ *couples;* ~ *life.*

mar·row /'mærəʊ/ *n* **1** [U] soft, fatty substance that fills the hollow parts of bones. **chilled to the** ~, cold through and through. '~-**bone** *n* bone containing edible ~. **2** [U] (fig) essence; essential part: *the pith and* ~ *of his statement.* **3** [C] (**vegetable**) ~, vegetable of the gourd family (US = squash, like a large fat cucumber); [U] this as food, eg stuffed with minced meat: *stuffed* ~ *for lunch.* ⇨ the illus at **vegetable**.

marry /'mærɪ/ *vt,vi* (*pt,pp* -ried) **1** [VP6A,2A,D,4A] take as a husband or wife; have a husband or wife: *John is going to* ~ *Jane. Tom and Alice are going to get married. Mary married young. Harry didn't* ~ *until he was over fifty. She married again six months after the death of her first husband. She married to get away from her tyrannical mother.* **2** [VP6A] (of a priest, a civil official)

join as husband or wife: *Which priest is going to* ~ *them?* **3** [VP6A,15B] ~ (*off*), give in marriage: *He married both his daughters to rich directors. She has married off all her daughters, has found husbands for them.* **4** [VP6A] obtain by ~ing: ~ *money/wealth.*

Mars /mɑːz/ *n* **1** (Roman myth) the god of war. **2** (astron) planet fourth in order from the sun. ⇨ the illus at planet.

Mar·sala /mɑːˈsɑːlə/ *n* [U] sweet white wine originally exported from Marsala, Sicily.

Mar·seil·laise /ˌmɑːsəˈleɪz/ *n* French national anthem.

marsh /mɑːʃ/ *n* [C,U] (area of) low-lying, wet land: *miles and miles of* ~; *the Romney* ~*es.* '~ **gas**, fire-damp; methane. ~-'**mallow** *n* (a) shrubby herb that grows near salt ~es. (**b**) soft, spongy sweetmeat. ~**y** *adj* (-ier, -iest) of or like a ~.

mar·shal[1] /'mɑːʃl/ *n* **1** Officer of highest rank: ,Field-'**M**~, (in the Army); ,Air-'**M**~, (in the Air Force). **2** official responsible for important public events or ceremonies, eg one who accompanies a High Court judge; an officer of the royal household. **3** (US) official with the functions of a sheriff; head of a fire or police department.

mar·shal[2] /'mɑːʃl/ *vt* (-ll-, US -l-) [VP6A,15A,B] **1** arrange in proper order: ~ *facts/military forces.* '**marshalling-yard** *n* railway yard in which goods trains, etc are assembled. **2** guide or lead (sb) with ceremony: ~ *persons into the presence of the Queen.*

mar·su·pial /mɑːˈsuːpɪəl/ *adj*, *n* (animal) of the class of mammals the females of which have a pouch in which to carry their young, which are born before developing completely, eg kangaroos.

mart /mɑːt/ *n* **1** (liter) market-place; centre of commerce. **2** auction room.

mar·ten /'mɑːtɪn/ *US:* -tn / *n* [C] small animal of the weasel family; [U] its fur.

mar·tial /'mɑːʃl/ *adj* **1** of, associated with, war: ~ *music;* ~ *bearing.* ~ '**law**, military government, by which ordinary law is suspended, eg during a rebellion; *declare* ~ *law; be under* ~ *law.* **2** brave; fond of fighting: *show a* ~ *spirit*, show eagerness for war. ~**ly** /-ʃəlɪ/ *adv*

Mar·tian /'mɑːʃn/ *n, adj* (hypothetical inhabitant) of the planet Mars.

mar·tin /'mɑːtɪn *US:* -tn/ *n* ('**house-**)~, bird of the swallow family that builds a mud nest on walls, etc.

mar·ti·net /ˌmɑːtɪˈnet *US:* -tnˈet/ *n* person who requires and enforces strict discipline.

mar·tini /mɑːˈtiːnɪ/ *n* cocktail made of gin and dry vermouth.

mar·tyr /'mɑːtə(r)/ *n* person who is put to death or caused to suffer greatly for his religious beliefs or for the sake of a great cause or principle: *the early Christian* ~*s in Rome. He died a* ~ *in the cause of science*, lost his life through his efforts to help forward the cause of science. **make a** ~ **of oneself**, sacrifice one's own wishes or advantage (or pretend to do so) in order to get credit or reputation. **be a** ~ **to sth**, suffer greatly from: *He's a* ~ *to rheumatism.* ▢ *vt* [VP6A] put to death, cause to suffer, as a ~. '~-**dom** /-dəm/ *n* ~'s suffering or death: *His wife's never-ending complaints made his life one long* ~*dom.*

mar·vel /'mɑːvl/ *n* [C] **1** wonderful thing; sth causing great surprise, pleased astonishment: *the* ~*s of*

*modern science. It's a ~ to me that he escaped un-
hurt. The doctor's pills worked ~s*, had wonderful
results. **2 ~ of sth**, wonderful example: *She's a ~
of patience. Your room is a ~ of neatness and or-
der.* □ *vi* (-II-, US -I-) **1** [VP3A] ~ **at sth**, be greatly surprised at: ~ *at sb's boldness*. **2** [VP3B] ~
that/why, etc, wonder: *I ~ that she should agree
to marry that man/~ why she should want to marry
him*. ~**·lous**, (US = ~·ous) /'mɑ:vələs/ *adj* astonishing; wonderful. ~·**lous·ly** (US = ~·ous·ly)
adv

Marx·ist /'mɑ:ksɪst/ *n* follower of Karl Marx
/mɑ:ks/, (1818—83) the German economist and
socialist: (attrib) ~ *criticism; a ~ party*. **Marxism** /'mɑ:ksɪzəm/ *n* (esp) political and economic
theory that class struggle has been the major force
behind historical change, that the dominant class
has exploited the other classes and that capitalism
will inevitably be superseded by socialism and a
classless society.

mar·zi·pan /'mɑ:zɪpæn/ *n* [U] thick paste of ground
almonds, sugar, etc, made up into small cakes; [C]
small cake made of this mixture.

mas·cara /mæ'skɑːrə US: -'skærə/ *n* [U] cosmetic
preparation for darkening the eyelashes.

mas·cot /'mæskət/ *n* person, animal or object considered likely to bring good fortune.

mas·cu·line /'mæskjʊlɪn/ *adj* **1** of, like, the male
sex: *a ~ style; a ~ woman*. **2** of male gender: *'He'
and 'him' are ~ pronouns*. **mas·cu·lin·ity**
/ˌmæskjʊ'lɪnəti/ *n* quality of being ~. ⇨ feminine.

ma·ser /'meɪzə(r)/ *n* device for producing or amplifying microwaves.

mash /mæʃ/ *n* [U] **1** grain, bran, etc cooked in
water for poultry, cattle or pigs. **2** [U,C] any substance softened and crushed, eg boiled potatoes
beaten and crushed: *a plate of sausage and ~*. **3**
mixture of malt and hot water used in brewing. □ *vt*
[VP6A] beat or crush into a ~: *~ed turnips*. **~er** *n*
cooking utensil for ~ing, eg potatoes.

mask¹ /mɑ:sk US: mæsk/ *n* **1** covering for the
face, or part of it, eg a piece of silk or velvet for
hiding the face; replica of the face carved in wood,
ivory, etc; disguise. **do sth under a/the ~ of
friendship**, while pretending to be a friend. **throw
off one's ~**, (fig) show one's true character and
intentions. **2** ('gas)-~, breathing apparatus, in
some cases for the whole of the head, worn as a
protection against poisonous gas, smoke, etc, eg in
coalmines, or by a fireman in a burning building. **3**
pad of sterile gauze worn over the mouth and nose
by eg doctors and nurses, eg for a surgical operation. **4** replica of the face worn by an actor or actress. **5** likeness of a face made by taking a mould
in wax, etc. **'death ~**, one made by taking a mould
of the face of a dead person. **6** face or head of a
fox.

death
mask

masks

mask² /mɑ:sk US: mæsk/ *vt* [VP6A] **1** cover (the
face) with a mask: *a ~ed woman*, one wearing a
mask; *a ~ed ball*, one at which masks are worn. **2**
conceal: *~ one's enmity under an appearance of
friendliness; ~ed guns*, hidden from the enemy.

maso·chism /'mæsəkɪzəm/ *n* [U] getting satisfaction (esp sexual pleasure) from pain or humiliation.
⇨ Sadism. **maso·chist** /-kɪst/ *n* **maso·chis·tic**
/ˌmæsə'kɪstɪk/ *adj*

ma·son /'meɪsn/ *n* **1** stone-cutter; worker who
builds or works with stone. **2** freemason. **~ic**
/mə'sɒnɪk/ *adj* of freemasons. **~ry** /'meɪsnrɪ/ *n* **1**
stonework; that part of a building made of stone
and mortar. **2** freemasonry.

Mason–Dixon line /ˌmeɪsn 'dɪksn laɪn/ *n* (US hist)
boundary between Pennsylvania and Maryland, dividing the free and the slave States before the Civil
War.

masque /mɑːsk US: mæsk/ *n* drama in verse, often
with music, dancing, fine costumes and pageantry,
esp as given in castles and great mansions in England during the 16th and 17th cc.

mas·quer·ade /ˌmɑːskə'reɪd US: ˌmæsk-/ *n* **1** ball
at which masks and other disguises are worn. **2**
(fig) false show or pretence. □ *vi* [VP2A,C] ~ *(as)*,
appear, be, in disguise: *a prince who ~d as a
peasant*.

mass /mæs/ *n* **1** [C] ~ *(of)*, lump, quantity of matter, without regular shape; large number, quantity
or heap: *~es of dark clouds in the sky. The azaleas
made a ~ of colour in the garden. A ~ of snow
and rock broke away and started an avalanche.
The poor fellow was a ~ of bruises*, (colloq) was
covered with bruises. **2 the ~es**, the proletariat;
(manual) workers. **in the ~**, in the main; as a
whole: *The nation in the ~ was not interested in
politics*. **~ meeting**, large meeting, esp of people
wishing, or requested, to express their views
(protesting against sth, urging that sth be done,
etc). **~ communications; ~ media**, means (esp
newspapers, radio, TV) of imparting information
to, influencing the ideas of, enormous numbers of
people. **~ observation**, study of the social customs of ordinary people. **~ production**, manufacture of large numbers of identical articles by standardized processes. Hence, **~-produce** *vt* **3** [U]
(science) quantity of material in a body measured
by its resistance to change of motion. ⇨ size¹(1). □
vt,vi [VP6A,2A] form or collect into a ~: *~ed
bands*, number of bands(5) playing together.
*Troops are ~ing/are being ~ed on the frontier.
The clouds are ~ing*. **~y** *adj* solid; massive.

Mass /mæs/ *n* [C,U] celebration (esp RC church)
of the Eucharist: *solemn ~*, with eg incense, music
and considerable ceremony; *go to ~; hear ~.
M~es were said for peace in the world.*

mass·acre /'mæsəkə(r)/ *n* [C] cruel killing of large
numbers of (esp defenceless) people (occasionally
used of animals). □ *vt* [VP6A] make a ~ of.

mass·age /'mæsɑːʒ US: mə'sɑːʒ/ *n* [C,U] (instance
of) pressing and rubbing the body, usu with the
hands, esp the muscles and joints, in order to lessen
pain, stiffness, etc. □ *vt* [VP6A] apply ~ to.

mass·eur /mæ'sɜː(r)/, **mass·euse** /mæ'sɜːz/ *nn*
man, woman, who practises ~. ⇨ *physiotherapist*
at physiotherapy.

massif /mæ'siːf/ *n* compact group of mountain
heights.

mass·ive /'mæsɪv/ *adj* **1** large, heavy and solid: *a
~ monument*. **2** (of the features) heavy-looking: *a*

~ *forehead.* **3** (fig) substantial; impressive. **~·ly**
adv **~·ness** *n*

mast¹ /mɑːst *US:* mæst/ *n* **1** upright support (of
wood or metal) for a ship's sails. ⇨ the illus at
barque, ship. *sail before the* ~, work as an ordinary seaman (with a berth in the forepart of the
ship). **'~-head** *n* highest part of a ~, used as a
look-out post. **2** tall pole (for a flag). **3** tall steel
structure for aerials of a radio or television transmitter; (also '*mooring-*~) tall tower to which an
airship may be moored.

mast² /mɑːst *US:* mæst/ *n* [U] fruit of beech, oak
and other forest trees (as food for pigs).

mas·ter¹ /'mɑːstə(r) *US:* 'mæs-/ *n* **1** man who has
others working for him or under him: ~ *and man,*
employer and workman (or manservant); (attrib)
skilled workman or one in business on his own account: *a* ~ *carpenter/builder, etc. be one's own*
~, be free and independent. **2** male head of a
household: *the* ~ *of the house.* **be** ~ **in one's**
own house, manage one's affairs without interference from others. **3** captain of a merchant ship:
a ~ *mariner; obtain a* ~'*s certificate,* one that
gives the holder the right to be a ship's captain. **4**
male owner of a dog, horse, etc. **5** male teacher:
the ,*mathe'matics* ~; *'school*~; *'house*~, ⇨
house¹(7); male teacher of subjects taught outside
school: *a* '*dancing/'fencing/'riding-*~. **6** ~ *of,*
person who has control or who has (sth) at his disposal: *He is* ~ *of the situation,* has it under control.
If only I could be ~ *of this subject,* come to know it
thoroughly. *He has made himself* ~ *of the lan-*
guage, has learnt it well, so that he can use it freely. *You cannot be the* ~ *of your fate,* cannot decide
your own destiny. *He is* ~ *of a large fortune,* can
use it as he wishes. **7 the M~,** Jesus Christ. ,**M~**
of 'Arts/'Science, etc, holder of the second university degree. ⇨ bachelor. **8** (with a boy's name)
young Mr: *M~ Charles Smith,* sometimes used
when speaking of or to a boy up to about the age of
14. **9** title of the heads of certain colleges: *the M~*
of Balliol, Oxford. **10** great artists, esp **old ~s,** the
great painters of the 13th to 17th cc; painting by
one of these artists. **11** (attrib) commanding;
superior: *the work of a* ~ *hand,* a superior and
skilful artist, etc. *His* ~ *passion* (= The passion
that dominates his thoughts, etc) *is motor-racing.*
'**~·mind** *n* person with superior brains (esp one
who plans work to be carried out by others).
Hence, '**~-mind** *vt* plan, direct, a scheme: *The*
whole affair was ~-*minded by the publicity de-*
partment. **12** as title of various officials. **M~ of**
the Horse, official in the royal household. **M~ of**
foxhounds, man who controls them. **M~ of**
Ceremonies, (abbr **MC**) person who superintends
the forms to be observed on various social occasions, eg a public banquet. **13** (compounds) ,~-
at-'arms *n* police officer in the Navy and in passenger ships of the merchant service. '**~-key** *n* one
that will open many different locks, each also
opened by a separate key. '**~-piece** *n* sth made or
done with very great skill. '**~-stroke** *n* surpassing-
ly skilful act or piece (of policy, etc). ⇨ (for senses
1–5) mistress.

mas·ter² /'mɑːstə(r) *US:* 'mæs-/ *vt* [VP6A] become
the ~ of; overcome: ~ *one's temper/feelings;* ~ *a*
foreign language/the saxophone. **~·less** *adj* having no ~.

mas·ter·ful /'mɑːstəfl *US:* 'mæs-/ *adj* fond of controlling others; dominating: *speak in a* ~ *manner.*

~·ly /-fəlɪ/ *adv*

mas·ter·ly /'mɑːstəlɪ *US:* 'mæs-/ *adj* worthy of a
great master; very skilful: *with a few* ~ *strokes of*
the brush.

mas·ter·ship /'mɑːstəʃɪp *US:* 'mæs-/ *n* **1** [U] dominion; control. **2** [C] office, duties, of a (esp
school-) master: *He was offered an assistant-*~
(now usu *teaching post*) *in Bolton.*

mas·tery /'mɑːstərɪ *US:* 'mæs-/ *n* [U] **1** ~ *(of),*
complete control or knowledge: *his* ~ *of the violin;*
get ~ *of a wild horse.* **2** ~ *(over),* supremacy:
Which side will get the ~?

mas·ti·cate /'mæstɪkeɪt/ *vt* [VP6A] chew; soften,
grind up (food) with the teeth. **mas·ti·ca·tion**
/,mæstɪ'keɪʃn/ *n*

mas·tiff /'mæstɪf/ *n* large, strong dog with drooping ears, much used as a watchdog. ⇨ the illus at
dog.

mas·to·don /'mæstədɒn/ *n* large extinct
elephant-like animal.

mas·toid /'mæstɔɪd/ *n* bone at the back of the ear.
~·itis /,mæstɔɪ'daɪtɪs/ *n* inflammation of the ~.

mas·tur·bate /'mæstəbeɪt/ *vi,vt* [VP2A,6A] procure or provide sexual excitement by manual or
other stimulation of the genital organs. **mas·tur·**
ba·tion /,mæstə'beɪʃn/ *n*

mat¹ /mæt/ *n* **1** piece of material (woven or plait-
ed, of straw, rope, rushes, rags, fibre, etc) used for
a floor covering, for sleeping on, or (a '*doormat*)
for wiping dirty shoes on. **2** small piece of material
placed under vases, ornaments, etc, or (a '*table-*
mat of cork, asbestos, etc) under hot dishes on a
table (to prevent injury to a varnished surface, etc).
3 anything thickly tangled or twisted together: *a*
mat of weeds; comb the mats out of a dog's thick
hair. □ *vt,vi* (-tt-) [VP6A] cover or supply with
mats; [VP6A,15A,2A,C] (cause to) be or become
tangled or knotted: *matted hair.*

mat², matt (US also **matte**) /mæt/ *adj* (of surfaces, eg paper) dull; not shiny or glossy: *paint*
that dries with a ~ *finish.* ⇨ gloss¹(1).

mata·dor /'mætədɔː(r)/ *n* man whose task is to kill
the bull in the sport of bull-fighting.

match¹ /mætʃ/ *n* short piece of wood, pasteboard,
wax taper, etc, with a head made of material that
bursts into flame when rubbed on a rough or
specially prepared surface (the second kind being
called '*safety* ~*es*): *strike a* ~; *a box of* ~*es.* '**~-**
box *n* box for holding ~es. '**~-wood** *n* **(a)** wood
suitable for making ~es. **(b)** splinters or fragments
of wood: *smashed to* ~*wood,* completely broken
up.

match² /mætʃ/ *n* **1** contest; game: *a* '*football/*
'*wrestling* ~; *a* '*boxing* ~ *of twenty rounds.* ,~-
'**point,** final point needed to win a ~, eg tennis. **2**
person able to meet another as his equal in strength,
skill, etc: *find/meet one's* ~. *He is up against*
more than his ~, has met sb who is his superior (in
skill, etc). *You are no* ~ *for him,* are not strong,
clever, etc enough to compete with him. **3** marriage: *They decided to make a* ~ *of it,* (of two persons) They decided to marry. '**~-maker** *n* (esp)
person who is fond of arranging ~es(3) for others.
4 person considered from the point of view of marriage: *He's a good* ~, is considered satisfactory or
desirable as a possible husband. **5** person or thing
exactly like, or corresponding to, or combining
well with, another: *colours/materials that are a*
good ~. **~·less** *adj* unequalled.

match³ /mætʃ/ *vt,vi* **1** [VP14] ~ *sth/sb against/*

with, put in competition: *I'm ready to ~ my strength with/against yours.* **2** [VP6A] be equal to; be, obtain, a match(2) for: *a well-~ed pair,* eg boxers about equal in skill. *No one can ~ him in archery. Can you ~ that story,* tell one that is equally good, amusing, etc? **3** [VP6A,2A] be equal to or corresponding (with) (in quality, colour, design, etc): *The carpets should ~ the curtains. The curtains and carpets should ~. She was wearing a brown dress with hat and gloves to ~.* ⇨ clash(4). **4** [VP6A,12B,13B] find a material, etc that ~es(3) with (another): *Can you ~ (me) this silk?*

match·et /'mætʃɪt/ *n* = machete.

match·lock /'mætʃlɒk/ *n* old-fashioned style of musket.

mate¹ /meɪt/ *n* **1** (colloq) friend; companion; fellow-worker (often as a form of address): *Where are you going, ~?* ⇨ class-~ at class, play~ at play¹(1). **2** ship's officer (not an engineer) below the rank of captain: *the chief ~,* below the captain; *the first/second/third ~.* **3** helper: (in titles) *the cook's/gunner's/surgeon's ~; a plumber's ~.* **4** one of a pair of birds or animals: *the lioness and her ~.* **5** (colloq) partner in marriage, ie husband or wife: *She has been a faithful ~ to him.*

mate² /meɪt/ *vt,vi* [VP6A,14,2A,3A] ~ *(with),* (of birds or animals) (cause to) unite for the purpose of having sexual intercourse, producing young: *the 'mating season,* spring, when birds make their nests. *The zoo's camels have not ~d this year.*

mate³ /meɪt/ *n, v* (in chess) = checkmate.

maté /'mɑːteɪ/ *n* (tea made from) dried leaves of a S American evergreen holly shrub.

ma·terial /mə'tɪərɪəl/ *adj* **1** (contrasted with *mental* and *spiritual*) made of, connected with, matter or substance: *the ~ world; a '~ noun,* naming a material, eg stone, wood, wool. **2** of the body; of physical needs: *~ needs,* eg food and warmth; *~ comforts and pleasures; a ~ point of view,* worldly, considering only the things of the senses. **3** (legal) important; essential: *~ evidence/testimony. The judge warned the witness not to hold back ~ facts,* facts that might influence a decision. *Is this point ~ to your argument?* ~**ly** /-rəlɪ/ *adv* in a ~(3) manner; essentially.

ma·terial² /mə'tɪərɪəl/ *n* **1** [C,U] that of which sth is or can be made or with which sth is done: *raw ~s,* not yet used in manufacture; *'dress ~s,* cloth; fabrics from which dresses may be made; *too much ~ for one overcoat; not enough ~ for two overcoats.* '**writing ~s,** pen, ink, paper, etc. **2** [U] (fig) facts, happenings, elements: *~ for a newspaper article; the ~ from which history is made.*

ma·teri·al·ism /mə'tɪərɪəlɪzəm/ *n* [U] **1** theory, belief, that only material things exist. **2** tendency to value, valuation of, material things (wealth, bodily comforts, etc) too much and spiritual, artistic and intellectual things too little. **ma·teri·al·ist** /-ɪst/ *n* believer in ~; person who ignores religion, painting, music, etc. **ma·teri·al·is·tic** /mə,tɪərɪə'lɪstɪk/ *adj* of ~ or materialists. **ma·teri·al·is·ti·cally** /-klɪ/ *adv*

ma·teri·al·ize /mə'tɪərɪəlaɪz/ *vi* [VP6A,2A] take material form; (cause to) become fact: *Our plans did not ~,* came to nothing, were not carried out. **ma·teri·al·iz·ation** /mə,tɪərɪəlaɪ'zeɪʃn US: -lɪ'z-/ *n*

ma·ternal /mə'tɜːnl/ *adj* of or like a mother: *~ care/instincts; my ~ grandfather/aunt, etc,* on my mother's side of the family. ~**ly** /-nəlɪ/ *adv*

ma·tern·ity /mə'tɜːnətɪ/ *n* [U] being a mother: (at-

trib) '~ ward/hospital, for women who are about to become mothers.

matey /'meɪtɪ/ *adj* ~ *(with),* (colloq) sociable, familiar, friendly.

mathe·mat·ics /,mæθə'mætɪks/ *n* (with *sing* or *pl v*) science of size and numbers (of which arithmetic, algebra, trigonometry and geometry are branches): *His ~ are weak. M~ is his weak subject.* **math·emat·ical** /,mæθə'mætɪkl/ *adj* of ~. **math·emat·ically** /-klɪ/ *adv* **math·ema·tician** /,mæθəmə'tɪʃn/ *n* expert in ~.

maths (US = **math**) /mæθs US: mæθ/ *n* (colloq abbr of) mathematics.

mati·née /'mætɪneɪ US: ,mætn'eɪ/ *n* [C] afternoon performance at a cinema or theatre: '*~ idol,* much admired actor.

mat·ins /'mætɪnz US: -tnz/ *n pl* service of Morning Prayer in the Church of England; prayers recited at daybreak in the RC Church.

ma·tri·arch /'meɪtrɪɑːk/ *n* woman head of a family or tribe. **ma·tri·archy** /-ɑːkɪ/ *n* social organization in which mothers are the heads of families. **ma·tri·ar·chal** /,meɪtrɪ'ɑːkl/ *adj*

ma·tric /mə'trɪk/ *n* (colloq abbr of) matriculation.

ma·trices /'meɪtrɪsiːz/ *pl* of matrix.

mat·ri·cide /'mætrɪsaɪd/ *n* [U] killing of one's own mother; [C] instance of this; [C] person guilty of this.

ma·tricu·late /mə'trɪkjʊleɪt/ *vt,vi* **1** [VP6A,2A] (allow to) enter a university as a student, usu after passing an examination; admit, be admitted, as a member of a university. **2** [VP2A,C] (formerly) pass the final school examination. **ma·tricu·la·tion** /mə,trɪkjʊ'leɪʃn/ *n* **1** [U] matriculating or being ~d; [C] instance of this. **2** [U] (formerly) final school examination.

mat·ri·mony /'mætrɪmənɪ US: -məʊnɪ/ *n* [U] state of being married: *unite persons in holy ~.* **mat·ri·mo·nial** /,mætrɪ'məʊnɪəl/ *adj* of ~: *solicitors who help people who have matrimonial troubles,* eg persons wanting divorce.

ma·trix /'meɪtrɪks/ *n* (*pl* matrices /'meɪtrɪsiːz/, or ~es) **1** mould into which hot metal, or other material in a soft or liquid condition, is poured to be shaped, eg in the printing trade, or for making gramophone records. **2** substance in which a mineral, etc is found embedded in the ground. **3** place where sth begins or develops.

ma·tron /'meɪtrən/ *n* **1** woman housekeeper in a school or other institution. **2** woman who manages the domestic affairs and nursing staff of a hospital. **3** married woman or widow (often used with a suggestion of dignity and social position): (dressmaking) *styles suitable for ~s,* for middle-aged women. ~**ly** *adj* of, like, suitable for, ~s: ~ly *duties; a ~ly* (ie dignified) *manner.*

matt /mæt/ *adj* = mat².

mat·ted /'mætɪd/ *adj* ⇨ mat¹ *v.*

mat·ter¹ /'mætə(r)/ *n* **1** [U] substance(s) of which a physical thing is made (contrasted with mind, spirit, etc): *organic/inorganic ~.* **2** material for thought or expression; substance of a book, speech, etc contrasted with the form or style: *The ~ in your essay is good but the style is deplorable.* **3** [U] sth printed or written. '**reading ~,** books, periodicals, etc. '**postal ~,** everything sent by post. '**printed ~,** (used on sth sent by post, to show that it goes out at a rate cheaper than for ordinary letters, etc). **4** [C] sth to which attention is given; piece of business; affair: '*money ~s. This is* *a ~ I know little about. There are several ~s to be dealt with at the committee meeting.* **a ~ of course,** sth to be expected in the natural course of events. Hence, **~-of-'course** *adj* to be expected. **a ~ of opinion,** sth about which opinions may differ. **as a ~ of fact,** in reality; although you may not know it or may be surprised. Hence, **~-of-'fact** *adj* (of a person, his manner) unimaginative; ordinary; keeping to the facts. **for'that ~; for the ~ of that,** so far as that is concerned. **in the ~ of,** as regards, in what concerns: *He is strict in the ~ of discipline.* **a'hanging ~,** a crime for which the penalty may be death by hanging. **no'laughing ~,** sth serious, sth not to be joked about. **5** [U] importance. **(make/be) no ~,** (be) of no importance: *If you can't do it, no ~. It's no ~/it makes no ~ whether you arrive early or late.* **no ~ who/ what/where, etc,** whoever (it is), whatever (happens, etc): *Don't trust him, no ~ what* (= whatever) *he says. Don't believe the rumour, no ~ who* (= whoever) *repeats it/no ~ how often you hear it.* **6 be the ~ (with),** be wrong (with): *What's the ~ with it?* (colloq) Surely this is all right, isn't it? *Is there anything the ~ with him,* Is he ill, in trouble, etc (according to context)? **7 a ~ of,** approximately; only: *a ~ of 20 weeks/10 miles/£50; within a ~ of hours.*

mat·ter² /'mætə(r)/ *vi* [VP2A,C] (chiefly in interr, neg and conditional sentences) be of importance: *What does it ~? It doesn't ~ much, does it? It hardly ~s at all. It doesn't ~ to me what you do or where you go.*

mat·ting /'mætɪŋ/ *n* [U] rough woven material used for floor covering and for packing goods: *coconut-~.*

mat·tins /'mætɪnz/ *US:* -tnz/ *n pl* = matins.

mat·tock /'mætək/ *n* heavy tool with a long handle and an iron head, one end of which is pointed and the other blunt, used for breaking up hard ground, etc. ⇨ the illus at **tool.**

mat·tress /'mætrɪs/ *n* [C] long, thick, flat, oblong pad of wool, hair, feathers, foam rubber, etc on which to sleep. **spring ~,** one with coiled wires fitted inside a padded cover of canvas or other frame of strong material.

matu·rate /'mætjʊreɪt/ *vi* [VP2A] become mature. **matu·ra·tion** /,mætjʊ'reɪʃn/ *n* [U] process of becoming mature.

ma·ture /mə'tjʊə(r) *US:* -'tʊər/ *vt,vi* [VP6A,2A] **1** come or bring to full development or to a state ready for use: *His character ~d during these years. These years ~d his character. This wine has not ~d properly.* **2** (of bills) become due. □ *adj* **1** fully grown or developed; ripe with fully developed powers: *persons of ~ years.* **2** careful; perfected: *after ~ deliberation; ~ plans,* based on ~ deliberation. **3** (comm, of bills) due for payment. **~·ly** *adv* **ma·tur·ity** /mə'tjʊərətɪ *US:*-'tʊə-/n [U] the state of being ~.

ma·tuti·nal /mə'tju:tɪnl *US:* -'tu:tnl/ *adj* (formal) of, occurring in, the morning.

maud·lin /'mɔːdlɪn/ *adj* sentimental or self-pitying in a silly or tearful way: *The drunken man began to get ~.*

maul /mɔːl/ *vt* [VP6A,15B] hurt or injure by rough or brutal handling: *~ed by a tiger. Stop ~ing the cat. His latest novel has been ~ed by the critics,* They have written extremely adverse reviews. *Stop ~ing me about!*

maul·stick /'mɔːlstɪk/ *n* light stick held by a paint-

er's (left) hand as a support to the (right) hand that holds the brush.

maun·der /'mɔːndə(r)/ *vi* [VP2A,C] talk in a rambling way; move or act in a listless way.

Maundy Thurs·day /,mɔːndɪ 'θɜːzdɪ/ *n* Thursday before Easter, commemorating the Last Supper. ⇨lord(2); John 13: 14.

mau·so·leum /,mɔːsə'li:əm/ *n* magnificent and monumental tomb.

mauve /məʊv/ *adj, n* bright but delicate pale purple.

mav·er·ick /'mævərɪk/ *n* (US) **1** unbranded calf. **2** unorthodox person; person who dissents from the ideas, etc of an organized group: *~ politicians.*

ma·vis /'meɪvɪs/ *n* (poet) song-thrush.

maw /mɔː/ *n* animal's stomach or throat; (fig) devouring or destructive agency ready to swallow or engulf sth.

mawk·ish /'mɔːkɪʃ/ *adj* foolishly sentimental. **~·ly** *adv* **~·ness** *n*

maxi- /'mæksɪ/ *pref* of a large or long size, length, etc. ⇨ mini-.

maxim /'mæksɪm/ *n* widely accepted rule of conduct or general truth briefly expressed, eg 'Waste not, want not'.

maxi·mize /'mæksɪmaɪz/ *vt* [VP6A] increase to a maximum: *~ educational opportunities.* **maxi·mi·za·tion** /,mæksɪmaɪ'zeɪʃn *US:* -mɪ'z-/ *n*

maxi·mum /'mæksɪməm/ *n, adj* (*pl* ~s or -ma /-mə/) (opposite of *minimum*) (of) greatest possible or recorded degree, quantity, etc: *the ~ temperature recorded in London; a ~ and minimum thermometer,* made so as to register ~ and minimum temperatures; *obtain 81 marks out of a ~ of 100. The ~ load for this lorry is one ton.*

may /meɪ/ *anom fin* (*pt* might /maɪt/) (*neg* may not, shortened to mayn't/'meɪənt/ and might not shortened to mightn't /'maɪtnt/) [VP5] **1** (used to indicate possibility or probability; as *might* is used to indicate a future condition, the perfect infinitive *might have* is used for past time): *That may or may not be true. He may have* (= Perhaps he has) *missed his train. This medicine may/might cure your cough. This might have cured your cough,* if you had taken it. *You may walk* (= It is possible to walk) *for miles and miles among the hills without meeting anyone.* **2** (used to indicate permission or request for permission; *might* suggests greater hesitation or diffidence. ⇨ can²(3)): *May I come in? Might I make a suggestion? Well, if I may say so,.... You may come if you wish.* **3** (used to indicate uncertainty, and asking for information, or expressing wonder): *Well, who may you be? How old may/might she be?* **4** (used with *well* to suggest 'There is good reason'): *You may well say so. Well may/might you be surprised! We may as well stay where we are,* It seems reasonable to do so. *You might just as well go as not,* There is just as much to be said in favour of going as there is against. ⇨ well²(4). **5** (used to express wishes and hopes): *May you both be happy! Long may she live to enjoy her good fortune!* **6** (used to express requests): *You might do me a favour,* Please do sth for me. *I think you might at least offer to help.* **7** (in clauses) (used to express purpose, and after *wish, fear, be afraid,* etc): *He died so that others might live. I'll write to him today so that he may know when to expect us. I'm afraid the news may be true.*

May /meɪ/ *n* **1** the fifth month of the year. **'May Day,** 1st of May, celebrated as a spring festival and also as a day for socialist and labour demonstrations. **'May Queen**, girl crowned with flowers on May Day. **'may-beetle, 'may-bug** nn cockchafer. **'may-fly** n short-lived insect that appears in May. **'may-pole** n flower-decorated pole danced round on May Day. **2 m~**, hawthorn (blossom).

may-be /'meɪbi:/ adv perhaps; possibly. **as soon as ~**, as soon as possible.

may-day /'meɪdeɪ/ n (radio telephony) (from French m'aider, help me) international signal (used by aircraft and ships) of distress: a ~ call from an airliner.

May-fair /'meɪfeə(r)/ n fashionable district in the West End of London.

may-hem /'meɪhem/ n 1 (old use, and US) crime of maiming. 2 state of violent disorder; havoc: cause/create ~.

may-on-naise /ˌmeɪə'neɪz US: 'meɪəneɪz/ n [U] thick dressing of eggs, cream, oil, vinegar, etc used on cold foods, esp salads; dish of food with this dressing: salmon ~.

mayor /meə(r) US: 'meɪər/ n head of a municipal corporation of a city or borough. **~-ess** /meə'res US: 'meɪərəs/ n wife or female relative of a ~, helping in social duties; woman holding the office of ~. **~-alty** /'meərəltɪ US: 'meɪər-/ n ~'s (period of) office.

maze /meɪz/ n 1 network of lines, paths, etc; labyrinth: a ~ of narrow alleys. 2 state of confusion or bewilderment (when faced by a confused mass of facts, etc). **be in a ~**, be puzzled, bewildered. **mazed** adj bewildered.

ma-zurka /mə'zɜ:kə/ n (piece of music for a) lively Polish dance for four or eight couples.

Mc-Carthy-ism /mə'kɑ:θɪzəm/ n (US, 1950's; after J R McCarthy, 1909—1957, US politician) political policy of accusing persons of disloyalty (esp by saying they were pro-Communist); unscrupulous methods of investigation used for this purpose; witchhunt.

me /mi:/ pron object form for the pronoun I: He saw me. Give me one. It's me (now usu for 'It is I').

mead¹ /mi:d/ n [U] alcoholic drink made from fermented honey and water.

mead² /mi:d/ n [C] (poet) meadow.

meadow /'medəʊ/ n [C,U] (area, field, of) grassland, esp kept for hay.

meagre (US = **mea-ger**) /'mi:gə(r)/ adj 1 thin; lacking in flesh: a ~ face. 2 insufficient; poor; scanty: a ~ meal; ~ fare; a ~ attendance at the council meeting. **~-ly** adv **~-ness** n

meal¹ /mi:l/ n [C] 1 occasion of eating: three ~s a day; breakfast, the first ~ of the day. **'~-time** n usual time for taking a ~. 2 food that is eaten: have a good ~.

meal² /mi:l/ n [U] grain coarsely ground: 'oat~; 'corn ~, (US) ~ of maize or other grain. Cf flour for grain finely ground.

mealie /'mi:lɪ/ n (S Africa) (pl) maize; [C] an ear of maize.

mealy /'mi:lɪ/ adj (-ier, -iest) of, like, containing, covered with, meal; (of potatoes when boiled) dry and powdery. **'~-bug** n insect that infests vines, etc. **~-'mouthed** adj too squeamish in the choice of words; tending to avoid plain speaking.

mean¹ /mi:n/ adj (-er, -est) 1 poor in appearance; shabby-looking: a ~ house in a ~ street. 2 (of behaviour) unworthy; discreditable: That was a ~ trick! It was ~ of you to eat all the peaches! He

took a ~ advantage of me. What a ~ revenge! 3 (of persons, their character, etc) having or showing a fondness for ~ behaviour: a ~ rascal. Don't be so ~ to your little brother, Don't tease him, treat him unkindly, etc. He's a ~-minded sort of fellow. 4 of low rank or humble birth. 5 (of the understanding, the natural powers) inferior; poor: This should be clear even to the ~est intelligence. He is no ~ scholar, is a good one. 6 lacking in generosity; selfish: Her husband is rather ~ over money matters. 7 (colloq) secretly ashamed: feel rather ~ for not helping more. 8 (US) nasty; vicious: He's a really ~ fellow—he likes to see people suffer. **~-ly** adv **~-ness** n **~ie, ~y** /'mi:nɪ/ nn (colloq) ~-minded person: What a ~ie you are! ⊏> 6 above.

mean² /mi:n/ adj occupying the middle position between two extremes; average: the ~ annual temperature in Malta. **Greenwich M~ Time**, ⊏> Greenwich. **~ price**, (fin, Stock Exchange) the average between the Stock jobber's buying and selling price; the market price of an investment.

mean³ /mi:n/ n 1 [C] condition, quality, course of action, etc that is halfway between two extremes. **the happy/golden ~**, a moderate course of action. 2 (maths) term between the first and the last of a series: In 1:3 :: 3:9, the ~ is 3. The ~ of 3, 5 and 7 is 5 (because 3 + 5 + 7 = 15 and 15 ÷ 3 = 5).

mean⁴ /mi:n/ vt (pt,pp meant /ment/) 1 [VP6A] (of words, sentences, etc) signify; import: A dictionary tries to tell you what words ~. The Latin word 'amo' ~s 'I love'. 2 [VP6AC,9] be a sign of; be likely to result in; entail: This new frontier incident probably ~s war/that there will be war. These new orders for our manufacturers will ~ working overtime. 3 [VP6A,9,14,16B,17] ~ (by), have as a purpose; contemplate; intend; refer to: What do you ~ by saying that? What have you in mind? (or if the context allows) How dare you say that? I wasn't serious—I ~t it/It was ~t as a joke. Do you ~ (= refer to) Miss Elsie Smith or Miss Dora Smith? I didn't ~ you to read the letter. Is this figure ~t to be a 1 or a 7? I'm sorry if I hurt your feelings—I didn't ~ to. I ~ there to be/that there should be no argument about this, won't allow any argument. Is this valuable painting ~t for me, Is the owner thinking of giving it to me? **~ business**, (colloq) be in earnest, ready to act (not merely talk). **~ mischief**, have in mind sth evil or injurious. 4 [VP7A,12A,13A,14,17] ~ (for), intend; be determined; destine: He ~s to succeed. He ~s his son to succeed. He ~s you no harm, does not intend to hurt you. He ~s no harm to anyone. I ~t this for my son, intended to give it to him. He seems obviously ~t for the army/~t to be a soldier, is the sort of man destined for the army. 5 [VP14] ~ sth to sb, be of importance or value to: Your friendship ~s a great deal to me, I value it highly. £20 ~s a lot to her, is quite a large sum in her view. I can't tell you what Mary has ~t to me, what a difference she has made in my life. The high cost of living ~s nothing to some people, They do not worry about it (eg because they are very rich). 6 ~ well, have good intentions (though perhaps not the will or capacity to carry them out): Of course he ~s well. **~ well by sb**, have kindly intentions towards sb: We all know that he ~s well by you. **~-ing** n [C,U] what is ~t or intended: a word with many distinct ~ings; a passage without much ~ing. He looked at me with ~ing. What's *the* ~*ing of this?* (asked, for example, by sb who thinks he has been badly treated, etc). □ *adj* full of ~ing: *a* ~*ing look; well-*~*ing,* having good intentions. ~·ing·ful /-fl/ *adj* significant; full of ~ing. ~·ing·fully /-fəlɪ/ *adv* ~·ing·less *adj* without ~ing or motive. ~·ing·ly *adv* with ~ing.

me·an·der /mɪˈændə(r)/ *vi* [VP2A,C] wander here and there; (fig) speak in an aimless way; (of a stream) follow a winding course, flowing slowly and gently. ~·ings /mɪˈændrɪŋz/ *n pl* winding path, course, etc. ~·ing·ly /mɪˈændrɪŋlɪ/ *adv*

means¹ /miːnz/ *n pl* (often treated as a *sing,* as in examples) method, process, by which a result may be obtained: *a* ~ *to an end,* a way of achieving sth. *There is/are no* ~ *of learning what is happening. Every* ~ *has/All possible* ~ *have been tried. Does the end always justify the* ~*,* If the aim or purpose is good, may any methods, even if bad, be employed? *by* ~ *of,* through; with the help of: *Thoughts are expressed by* ~ *of words. by* '*all* ~*,* certainly. *by* '*no* ~*,* not at all: *These goods are by no* ~ *satisfactory. by* '*no manner of* ~*,* in no way. *by some* ~ *or other,* somehow or other; if not in one way, then in another. *by fair* ~ *or foul,* by any methods, just or unjust. *ways and* ~*,* methods, esp of providing money by taxation for government needs.

means² /miːnz/ *n pl* money; wealth; resources: *a man of* ~*,* a rich man; *a man of your* ~*,* with the money, etc you have at your disposal; *have private* ~*,* an income from property, investments, etc (not earned as salary, etc). *live beyond/within one's* ~*,* spend more/less than one's income. '~ *test n* inquiry into the ~ of sb seeking help from the State or local authorities (eg if unemployed or too old to work).

meant /ment/ *pt,pp* of mean⁴.

mean·time /ˈmiːntaɪm/ *adv, n (in the)* ~*,* meanwhile.

mean·while /ˈmiːnwaɪl US: -hwaɪl/ *adv* in or during the time between.

measles /ˈmiːzlz/ *n* (with *sing v*) [U] infectious disease, marked by fever and small red spots that cover the whole body.

measly /ˈmiːzlɪ/ *adj* (colloq) of little value; of poor quality; of small size or amount: *What a* ~ *birthday present! What a* ~ *helping of ice-cream!*

measure¹ /ˈmeʒə(r)/ *n* **1** [U] size, quantity, degree, weight, etc as found by a standard or unit. *give full/short* ~*,* give the full/less than the full amount. *made to* ~*,* (of clothes) specially made for sb after taking ~ments. *get/take the* ~ *of sb,* (fig) form an estimate of his character, abilities, etc. **2** [C] unit, standard or system used in stating size, quantity, or degree: *liquid/dry* ~*. An inch is a* ~ *of length. Twenty* ~*s of wheat means twenty bushels.* ⇨ App **5. 3** [C] sth with which to test size, quantity, etc: *a pint* ~*. A yardstick is a* ~*; so is a foot-rule. A chain's weakest link is the* ~ *of its strength. Words cannot always give the* ~ *of one's feelings,* cannot show the depth or strength of one's feelings. '*tape-*~*,* ⇨ tape. *,greatest ,common* '~*,* (abbr GCM) largest number that will divide each of several given numbers exactly. **4** extent. *beyond* ~*,* very great(ly): *Her joy was beyond* ~*. in* '*some/*'*any* ~*,* to some/any extent or degree. *in great/large* ~*,* to a large extent: *Their success was in some* ~*/in great* ~ *the result of thorough preparation. set* ~*s to,* limit: *set* ~*s to one's ambitions.* **5** [C] (proposed) law. **6** [C] proceeding,

step: *What* ~ *(= plan) do you propose? They took strong* ~*s (= acted vigorously) against dangerous drivers.* **7** [U] verse-rhythm; metre; time of a piece of music; [C] (archaic) dance. *tread a* ~ *(with sb),* dance (with him).

measure² /ˈmeʒə(r)/ *vt,vi* **1** [VP6A,2A] find the size, extent, volume, degree, etc of (sth or sb): ~ *a piece of ground/the strength of an electric current/the speed of a car; tested for speed over a* ~*d mile. The tailor* ~*d me for a suit. Can you* ~ *accurately?* **2** [VP2B] be (a certain length, etc): *This room* ~*s 10 metres across.* **3** [VP6A,15A,B] ~ *out/off,* give a ~d quantity of: ~ *out a dose of medicine;* mark out: ~ *off 2 metres of cloth.* **4** ~ *one's length,* fall flat on the ground. ~ *swords against/with sb,* (fig) try out one's strength against him. ~ *one's strength (with sb),* try or test it. meas·ured *adj* **1** (of language) considered and weighed: ~*d words.* **2** in slow and regular rhythm: *with a* ~*d tread.* measur·able /ˈmeʒərəbl/ *adj* that can be ~d: *We came within measurable distance of* (close to) *success.* measur·ably /-əblɪ/ *adv* ~·less *adj* immeasurable; limitless. ~·ment *n* **1** [U] measuring: *the metric system of* ~*ment.* **2** (*pl*) figures about length, breadth, depth, etc: *the* ~*ments of a room.*

meat /miːt/ *n* **1** [U] flesh of animals used as food, excluding fish and birds: ~*-eating animals; cold* ~*,* meat that has been cooked and has then become cold; *chilled/frozen* ~*,* meat chilled/frozen in order to keep it in good condition; *fresh* ~*,* from a recently killed animal. '~*-ball n* small ball of minced meat or sausage-meat. '~*-safe n* cupboard for storing ~*,* usu with sides of wire gauze. ~ *pie n* ~ cooked with a covering of pastry. *a* ~ *tea,* high tea with some kind of ~ dish included. ⇨ high¹(12). **2** (fig) important or substantial part of sth: *There's not much* ~ *in this argument.* **3** (old use) food in general: ~ *and drink. one man's* ~ *is another man's poison,* (prov) What one person likes is not necessarily liked by anyone else. ~·less *adj* without ~: ~*less days during the war.* ~·y *adj* (-ier, -iest) (fig) full of substance; substantial.

Mecca /ˈmekə/ *n* **1** city in Saudi Arabia, birthplace of Muhammad and the spiritual centre of Islam. **2** goal of one's ambitions; place one is anxious to visit: *Stratford-on-Avon, the* ~ *of tourists in Britain.*

mech·anic /mɪˈkænɪk/ *n* skilled workman, esp one who repairs or adjusts machinery and tools: *a* '*motor-*~.

mech·an·ical /mɪˈkænɪkl/ *adj* **1** of, connected with, produced by, machines: ~ *power/ transport/engineering.* **2** (of persons, their actions) like machines; automatic; as if done without thought: ~ *movements.* ~·ly /-klɪ/ *adv* in a ~ way: ~*ly operated.* ⇨ *manually* at manual.

mech·an·ics /mɪˈkænɪks/ *n* **1** (usu with *sing v*) science of motion and force; science of machinery: *M*~ *is taught by Mr MacHine.* **2** (with *pl v*) (method of) construction: *the* ~ *of play-writing.*

mech·an·ism /ˈmekənɪzəm/ *n* [C] **1** working parts of a machine collectively; structure or arrangement of parts that work together as the parts of a machine do: *the* ~ *of the body; the* ~ *of government.* **2** way in which sth works or is constructed.

mech·an·is·tic /ˌmekəˈnɪstɪk/ *adj* the ~ theory, the theory that all changes in the universe and all living creatures are caused by physical and chemical forces only.

mech·an·ize /'mekənaɪz/ vt [VP6A] use machines in or for; give a mechanical character to: ~d forces, eg in the army, using motor transport instead of horses or mules. **mech·ani·z·ation** /ˌmekənaɪ'zeɪʃn US: -nɪ'z-/ n

medal /'medl/ n flat piece of metal, usu shaped like a coin, with words and a design stamped on it, given as an award for bravery, to commemorate sth, or for distinction in scholarship. ~·list (US = ~·ist) /'medəlɪst/ n person who has been awarded a ~, eg for distinction in literature, sport.

me·dal·lion /mɪ'dælɪən/ n large medal; large, flat circular ornamental design, eg on a carpet or on a lace curtain.

meddle /'medl/ vi [VP2A,3A] ~ (in sth), busy oneself in sth without being asked to do so: *Don't ~ in my affairs. Don't ~ in politics.* ~ (with sth), interfere: *Who's been meddling with my papers? You're always meddling.* **meddler** n person who ~s. '~·some /-səm/ adj fond of, in the habit of, meddling.

me·dia /'miːdɪə/ n the ~, (usu with sing v) mass communications, eg television, radio, the press. ⇨ mass(2), medium.

medi·aeval /ˌmedɪ'iːvl US: ˌmiːd-/ = medieval.

me·dial /'miːdɪəl/ adj 1 situated in the middle. 2 of average size. ~·ly /-ɪəlɪ/ adv

me·dian /'miːdɪən/ adj situated in, passing through, the middle. □ n ~ point, line, part, etc.

me·diate /'miːdɪeɪt/ vi,vt 1 [VP2A,3A] ~ (between), act as go-between or peacemaker: ~ between two warring countries/between employers and their workers. 2 [VP6A] bring about by doing this: ~ a settlement/a peace. **me·di·ation** /ˌmiːdɪ'eɪʃn/ n [U] mediating: *All offers of mediation by a third party were rejected.* **me·di·ator** /-tə(r)/ n one who ~s.

medic /'medɪk/ n (colloq abbr for) medical student.

medi·cal /'medɪkl/ adj 1 of the art of medicine (the treatment of disease): *a '~ examination,* to ascertain one's state of health; *a ~ practitioner,* a qualified doctor; *a '~ school;* '~ students/knowledge; ~ jurisprudence, legal knowledge required by a doctor. 2 of the art of medicine (contrasted with surgery): ~, not surgical, treatment. *The hospital has a ~ ward and a surgical ward.* □ n 1 (colloq) ~ student. 2 ~ examination. ~·ly /-klɪ/ adv

medic·ament /mɪ'dɪkəmənt/ n substance used in medical treatment, internally or externally. ⇨ medicine(2).

Medi·care /'medɪkeə(r)/ n [U] (US) government programme providing medical care (esp for old persons).

medi·cate /'medɪkeɪt/ vt [VP6A] treat medically; permeate with a medicinal substance: ~d soap/ gauze. **medi·ca·tion** /ˌmedɪ'keɪʃn/ n [U] process of medicating: *mass medication,* eg, the addition of fluorine to public water supplies; the supply of vitamin tablets through the social services; [C] medicine.

med·ici·nal /mɪ'dɪsɪnl/ adj having healing or curative properties: ~ preparations for both internal and external use.

medi·cine /'medsn US: 'medɪsn/ n 1 [U] the art and science of the prevention and cure of disease: *study ~ and surgery; a ˌDoctor of 'M~.* 2 [C,U] (kind of) substance, esp one taken through the mouth, used in ~: *He's always taking ~s. He takes too much ~. This is a good (kind of) ~ for a cough.*

(Note: for remedies not taken through the mouth, ⇨ injection at inject, lotion, medicinal preparation at medicinal, ointment.) '~·ball n large, heavy ball thrown and caught for physical exercise. '~·chest n chest with a selection of useful medicinal preparations. 3 (fig) deserved punishment. *take one's ~,* (fig) submit to what is unwelcome and unpleasant. *get some/a little of one's own ~,* be given the kind of unwelcome treatment that one has given to others. 4 [U] (among primitive peoples) spell; charm; fetish; magic. '~·man /-mæn/ n (pl -men) witch-doctor.

med·ico /'medɪkəʊ/ n (pl ~s /-kəʊz/) (colloq, hum) doctor or medical student.

medi·eval (also **medi·aeval**) /ˌmedɪ'iːvl US: ˌmiːd-/ adj of the Middle Ages (about AD 1100—1500).

me·di·ocre /ˌmiːdɪ'əʊkə(r)/ adj not very good; neither very good nor very bad; second-rate. **me·di·oc·rity** /ˌmiːdɪ'ɒkrətɪ/ n (pl -ties) [U] quality of being ~; [C] person who is ~ (in qualities, abilities, etc): *a Government of mediocrities.*

medi·tate /'medɪteɪt/ vt,vi 1 [VP6A] think about; consider: ~ revenge/mischief. 2 [VP2A,3A] ~ (up/upon), give oneself up to serious (esp religious) thought: *He sat there meditating upon his misfortunes.* **medi·ta·tion** /ˌmedɪ'teɪʃn/ n 1 [U] meditating: *deep in ~.* 2 [C] instance of this: *a ~ on the causes of aggression in man.* **medi·tat·ive** /'medɪtətɪv US: -teɪt-/ adj of ~; fond of ~. **medi·tat·ive·ly** adv

Medi·ter·ra·nean /ˌmedɪtə'reɪnɪən/ adj of, characteristic of, the M~ Sea or the countries, etc bordering this sea: ~ climate.

me·dium /'miːdɪəm/ n (pl ~s or media /'miːdɪə/) 1 that by which sth is expressed: *Commercial television is a ~ for advertising. Vacant positions can be made known through the ~ of the press,* by putting announcements in newspapers. *Oil paints and water colours are ~s for the creation of works of art.* ⇨ also mass(2). 2 middle quality or degree. *the happy ~,* avoidance of extremes, eg by being neither very lax nor very severe in maintaining discipline. 3 (pl often media) substance, surroundings, in which sth exists or through which sth moves: *Air is the ~ of sound.* 4 person who acts as a go-between, esp in spiritualism; person who claims to be able to receive messages from the spirits of the dead. □ adj coming halfway between; not extreme: *a man of ~ height; a ~-sized firm; ~ bonds,* maturing in a period between 15 and 20 years; *the ~ income group,* those who have incomes between high and low. '~ wave, (radio telegraphy) one having a length of from 100 to 1000 metres.

med·lar /'medlə(r)/ n (tree with) fruit like a small brown apple, eaten when it begins to decay.

med·ley /'medlɪ/ n (pl ~s) [C] mixture of things or persons of different sorts: *the ~ of races in Hawaii.*

meed /miːd/ n (poet) deserved portion (of praise, etc).

meek /miːk/ adj (-er, -est) mild and patient; unprotesting (the contrary of self-assertive): *She's as ~ as a lamb.* ~·ly adv ~·ness n

meer·schaum /'mɪəʃəm/ n [U] white clay-like substance; [C] tobacco pipe with a bowl made of this.

meet[1] /miːt/ vt,vi (pt,pp met /met/) 1 [VP6A,2A,C] come face to face with (sb or sth coming from the opposite or a different direction); come together from different points or directions: ~ *sb in the street. We met (each other) quite by chance. Goodbye till we ~ again. The two trains* ~ (= pass each other) *at Crewe. We write regularly but seldom* ~, see each other. *Can you* ~ (= face) *misfortune with a smile? The Debating Society* ~*s every Friday at 8pm.* ~ **with, (a)** experience: ~ *with misfortune/an accident/great kindness.* **(b)** come upon by chance: ~ *with obstacles;* ~ *with an old friend at a dinner party.* **(c)** (US) have a meeting with. **2** [VP6A,2A] make the acquaintance of; be introduced to: *I know Mrs Hill by sight, but have never met her/we've never met.* (As a form of introduction) *M*~ *my wife. Pleased to* ~ *you.* **3** [VP6A] go to a place and await the arrival of: *Will you* ~ *me at the station? I'll* ~ *your train. The hotel bus* ~*s all the trains.* **4** [VP6A] satisfy (a demand, etc): ~ *sb's wishes,* do what he wants. *Can you* ~ *their objections/criticisms,* answer them in a satisfactory way? ~ *the case,* be adequate, satisfactory: *I'm afraid your proposal hardly* ~*s the case.* ~ *sb halfway,* (fig) compromise; give way to some extent in order to satisfy him. ~ *all expenses/bills, etc,* pay them. **5** [VP6A,2A] come into contact; touch: *Their hands met. His hand met hers. My waistcoat won't* ~, is too small to be buttoned. *make (both) ends* ~, make one's income and one's expenditure equal. **6** ~ *the eye/ear,* be visible/audible. *There is more to/in sth/sb than* ~*s the eye,* it/he has qualities, characteristics, etc that are not immediately seen. ~ *sb's eye,* look in his eyes: *She was afraid to* ~ *my eye.*

meet² /miːt/ *n* **1** (GB) gathering of riders and hounds at a fixed place (for foxhunting). **2** (US) coming together of a number of people for a purpose: *an ath'letic* ~; *a 'track/'swimming* ~ (*meeting* is the usu word in GB).

meet³ /miːt/ *adj* (archaic) right; suitable; proper.

meet·ing /'miːtɪŋ/ *n* **1** coming together of a number of persons at a certain time and place, esp for discussion: *political* ~*s. Mr Smith will now address the* ~. '~*-house* *n* building for ~*s,* esp those held by Quakers. '~*-place* *n* place fixed for a ~. **2** any coming together: *a 'race~; a 'sports~. The* ~ *between the two families was a joyful one. She is shy at a first* ~, when she meets sb for the first time.

mega·cycle /'megəsaɪkl/ *n* [C] one million cycles (of changes of radio current).

mega·death /'megədeθ/ *n* death of one million people (in nuclear war).

mega·lith /'megəlɪθ/ *n* large stone, esp one used as a monument. **mega·lithic** /ˌmegə'lɪθɪk/ *adj* made of ~*s;* marked by the use of ~*s* (esp in very early times).

megaliths

mega·lo·ma·nia /ˌmegələ'meɪnɪə/ *n* [U] form of madness in which a person has exaggerated ideas of his importance, power, wealth, etc: *The dictator was obviously suffering from* ~. **mega·lo·ma·niac** /-nɪæk/ *n* person suffering from ~.

mega·phone /'megəfəʊn/ *n* [C] horn for speaking through, carrying the voice to a distance.

mega·ton /'megətʌn/ *n* explosive force equal to one million tons of TNT.

me·grim /'miːgrɪm/ *n* (archaic) **1** migraine. **2** (*pl*) low spirits.

mei·osis /maɪ'əʊsɪs/ *n* = litotes.

mel·an·cholic /ˌmelən'kɒlɪk/ *adj* melancholy; with a tendency to melancholy.

mel·an·choly /'melənkɒlɪ/ *n* [U] sadness; low spirits. □ *adj* sad; low-spirited; causing sadness or low spirits: ~ *news; a* ~ *occasion,* eg a funeral. **mel·an·cholia** /ˌmelən'kəʊlɪə/ *n* [U] mental illness marked by ~.

mé·lange /'meɪlɑːnʒ US: meɪ'lɑːnʒ/ *n* (F) mixture; medley.

mê·lée /'meleɪ US: meɪ'leɪ/ *n* (F) confused struggle; confused crowd of people.

meli·or·ate /'miːlɪəreɪt/ *vt,vi* [VP6A,2A] make or become better; improve. **melio·ra·tion** /ˌmiːlɪə'reɪʃn/ *n* process of improving. **meli·or·ism** /'miːlɪərɪzəm/ *n* belief that mankind tends to ~, and that conscious human effort may further this tendency.

mel·lif·lu·ous /me'lɪflʊəs/ *adj* (of a person's voice or words, of music, etc) sweet-sounding; smooth-flowing.

mel·low /'meləʊ/ *adj* (-er, -est) **1** soft and sweet in taste; soft, pure and rich in colour or sound: *a* ~ *wine; the* ~ *colours of the roofs in Dubrovnik.* **2** made wise and sympathetic by age or experience: ~ *judgement.* **3** (colloq) genial; slightly intoxicated. □ *vt,vi* [VP6A,2A] make or become ~. ~*·ly adv* ~*·ness n*

mel·odic /mɪ'lɒdɪk/ *adj* of melody; melodious.

mel·odi·ous /mɪ'ləʊdɪəs/ *adj* of, producing, melody; sweet-sounding: *the* ~ *notes of a thrush.* ~*·ly adv* ~*·ness n*

melo·drama /'melədrɑːmə/ *n* **1** [C] exciting and emotional (often sensational, exaggerated) drama, usu with a happy ending; event or series of events, piece of behaviour or writing, which suggests a stage ~. **2** [U] language, behaviour, suggestive of plays of this kind. **melo·dram·atic** /ˌmelədrə'mætɪk/ *adj* of, like, suitable for, ~. **melo·dram·ati·cally** /-klɪ/ *adv*

mel·ody /'melədɪ/ *n* (*pl* -dies) **1** [U] sweet music; tunefulness; arrangement of notes in a musically expressive succession. **2** [C] musical arrangement of words; song or tune: *old Irish melodies.* **3** [C] principal part or thread in harmonized music: *The* ~ *is next taken up by the flutes.*

melon /'melən/ *n* (kinds of) large, juicy, round fruit growing on a plant that trails along the ground: *a slice of* ~. ⇨ the illus at fruit.

melt /melt/ *vt,vi* (*pt,pp* ~ed) *pp* as *adj* (*of metal*) molten /'məʊltən/) **1** [VP6A,15B,2A,C] (cause to) become liquid through heating: *The ice will* ~ *when the sun shines on it. The hot sun soon* ~*ed the ice. It is easy to* ~ *butter.* ~ *away,* become less, disappear, by ~ing: *The snow soon* ~*ed away when the sun came out. Her money seemed to* ~ *away in Paris. The crowd quickly* ~*ed away* (= dispersed) *when the storm broke.* ~ *sth down,* ~ (a metal article) in order to use the metal as raw material. **2** [VP2A,C] (of soft food) dissolve, be softened, easily: *This cake/pear* ~*s in the mouth.* **3** [VP2A,6A] (of a solid in a liquid) dissolve: *Sugar* ~*s in hot tea/Hot tea* ~*s sugar.* **4** [VP6A,2C] (of a person, heart, feelings) soften, be softened: *Her* *heart* ~*ed with pity. Pity* ~*ed her heart. She* ~*ed into tears.* **5** [VP2C] fade; go (slowly) away: *One colour* ~*ed into another,* eg in the sky at sunset. ~**·ing** *adj* (fig) tender; sentimental: *in a* ~*ing voice/mood.* '~**·ing-point** *n* temperature at which a solid ~s: *Lead has a lower* ~*ing-point than iron.* '~**·ing-pot** *n* (a) pot in which metals, etc, are ~ed. **go into the** ~**·ing-pot,** (fig) undergo a radical change. **(b)** place, country, eg US, where immigrants from many different countries are assimilated.

mem·ber /'membə(r)/ *n* **1** person belonging to a group, society, etc: *a* ~ *of a club. Every* ~ *of her family came to her wedding.* ,**M**~ **of 'Parliament,** (abbr **MP**) elected representative in the House of Commons. **2** part of a human or animal body: *The tongue is sometimes called 'the unruly* ~*'.* ~**·ship** /-ʃɪp/ *n* **1** [U] the state of being a ~ (of a society, etc). **2** (no *pl*) number of ~s: *The society has a large* ~*ship/a* ~*ship of 80.*

mem·brane /'membreɪn/ *n* [C] soft, thin, pliable skin-like covering or lining, or connecting part, in an animal or vegetable body; [U] tissue of which such coverings, etc, are made. **mem·bra·nous** /'membrənəs/ *adj* of or like ~.

mem·ento /mɪ'mentəʊ/ *n* (*pl* ~s, ~es /-təʊz/) sth that serves to remind one of a person or event.

memo /'meməʊ/ *n* (*pl* ~s /-məʊz/) short for memorandum.

mem·oir /'memwɑː(r)/ *n* **1** record of events, esp by someone with first-hand knowledge. **2** (*pl*) person's written account of his own life or experiences: *the flood of war* ~*s by generals and politicians.*

mem·or·able /'memərəbl/ *adj* deserving to be remembered. **mem·or·ably** /-əblɪ/ *adv*

mem·or·an·dum /,memə'rændəm/ *n* (*pl*-da /-də/ or ~s) (abbr **memo**) **1** note or record for future use: *make a* ~ *of sth.* **2** informal business communication, usu without a personal signature, on paper headed *M*~ (or *Memo*). **3** (legal) record of an agreement that has been reached but not yet formally drawn up and signed.

mem·or·ial /mɪ'mɔːrɪəl/ *n* **1** sth made or done to remind people of an event, person, etc: *a* ~ *to the dead; a 'war* ~, a monument with the names of men killed in wars. **2** (attrib use) serving to keep in mind: *a* ~ *tablet,* eg in the wall of a church, in memory of someone; *a* ~ *service.* '**M**~ **Day,** (US) day set aside by law for honouring the memory of members of the armed forces killed in war (30 May in most States). **3** (usu *pl*) historical records or chronicles. **4** (more usu **petition**) written statement of facts, views, etc sent to authorities making a request or protest. ~**·ize** /-aɪz/ *vt* [VP6A] **1** (more usu **petition**) present a ~(4) to. **2** commemorate (which is the more usu word).

mem·or·ize /'meməraɪz/ *vt* [VP6A] learn by heart; commit to memory.

mem·ory /'memərɪ/ *n* (*pl* -ries) **1** [U] power of keeping facts in the conscious mind and of being able to call them back at will; preservation of past experience for future use. *commit sth to* ~, learn it by heart. *speak from* ~, ie without referring to notes, etc. *to the best of my* ~, as far as I can remember. *in* ~ *of sb; to the* ~ *of sb,* serving to recall sb, to keep him fresh in people's minds. **2** [C] this power in an individual (also used, by extension, of the unit of a computer which stores data for future use): *Some people have better memories*

than others. He has a bad ~ *for dates.* **3** [U] period over which the ~ can go back: *beyond/within the* ~ *of men.* **within living** ~, within the years that people now alive can remember. **4** [C] sth that is remembered; sth from the past stored in the ~: *memories of childhood.* **5** [U] reputation after death (esp of saints, great rulers): *the late king/pope, of blessed* ~.

mem·sa·hib /'memsɑːb/ *n* (In India) (form of address to a) European woman.

men /men/ *n pl* of **man** ¹(1).

men·ace /'menəs/ *n* [C,U] danger; threat: *a* ~ *to world peace; in a speech filled with* ~. *That woman is a* ~, is a nuisance, is troublesome! □ *vt* [VP6A] threaten: *countries* ~*d by/with war.* **men·ac·ing·ly** *adv* in a threatening manner.

mé·nage /meɪ'nɑːʒ/ *n* (F) household.

men·ag·erie /mɪ'nædʒərɪ/ *n* collection of wild animals in captivity, esp for a travelling circus.

mend /mend/ *vt,vi* **1** [VP6A] remake, repair, set right (sth broken, worn out, or torn); restore to good condition or working order: ~ *shoes/a broken window.* **2** [VP6A,2A] (~ *amend*) free from faults or errors: *That won't* ~ (= improve) *matters.* **It's never too late to** ~, (prov) reform one's way of living. ~ *one's ways,* ➪ way(10). **3** [VP2A] regain health; heal: *The patient is* ~*ing nicely.* **4** [VP6A] increase: ~ *one's pace,* quicken it; walk faster; ~ *the fire,* (regional use) put more coal on it. □ *n* damaged or torn part, that has been ~ed: *The* ~*s were almost invisible.* **on the** ~, improving in health or condition. ~**er** *n* (chiefly in compounds) one who ~s: '*road-*~*er.* '~**·ing** (esp) work of ~ing (clothes, etc): *a basketful of* ~*ing,* of clothes, etc, to be ~ed: *invisible* ~*ing,* ➪ invisible.

men·da·cious /men'deɪʃəs/ *adj* false; untruthful: ~ *newspaper reports.* ~**·ly** *adv* **men·dac·ity** /men'dæsətɪ/ *n* (formal) [U] untruthfulness; [C] (*pl*-ties) untrue statement.

Men·delian /men'diːlɪən/ *adj* of the theory of genetics of Mendel /'mendl/, 1822—1884, the Czechoslovakian biologist.

men·di·cant /'mendɪkənt/ *n, adj* (person) getting a living by asking for alms, or as a beggar; ~ *friars.*

men·folk /'menfəʊk/ *n pl* (colloq) men, esp the men of a family: *The* ~ *have all gone out fishing.*

me·nial /'miːnɪəl/ *adj* suitable for, to be done by, a household servant: *such* ~ *tasks as washing pots and pans.* □ *n* (usu derog) servant. ~**·ly** /-nɪəlɪ/ *adv*

men·in·gi·tis /,menɪn'dʒaɪtɪs/ *n* [U] (serious illness caused by) inflammation of any or all of the membranes enclosing the brain and spinal cord.

meno·pause /'menəpɔːz/ *n* final cessation of the menses at the age of about 50 (colloq called '*change of life*').

men·ses /'mensiːz/ *n pl* monthly bleeding from the uterus.

men·stru·ate /'menstrʊeɪt/ *vi* [VP2A] discharge the menses. **men·stru·ation** /,menstrʊ'eɪʃn/ *n* [U] this process. **men·strual** /'menstrʊəl/ *adj* of the menses or menstruation.

men·sur·ation /,mensjʊ'reɪʃn/ *n* process of, mathematical rules for, finding length, area and volume. **men·sur·able** /'mensjʊrəbl/ *adj* (rare) measurable.

men·tal /'mentl/ *adj* of or in the mind. '~ **age,** person's ~ level measured in terms of the average age of children having the same ~ standard. ~ **a'rith·metic,** done in the mind without using written figures or a mechanical device. ⁓ de'ficiency, subnormal development of intellectual powers, preventing a person from learning normally, looking after himself, etc. '⁓ home/hospital, one for ⁓ patients. ⁓ 'illness, illness of the mind. ⁓ patient, person suffering an illness of the mind. ⁓ reser'vation, one concerning a statement, oath, etc present in the mind but not spoken in words. ⁓ly /'mentəlɪ/ adv: ⁓ly deficient/defective, suffering from ⁓ illness; unable to profit from the ordinary kind of school education; ⁓ly deranged, (colloq = mad).

men·tal·ity /men'tælətɪ/ n 1 [U] general intellectual character; degree of intellectual power: persons of average ⁓. 2 [C] (pl -ties) characteristic attitude of mind: a war ⁓.

men·thol /'menθɒl/ n [U] solid white substance obtained from oil of peppermint, used, eg by being rubbed on the skin, to relieve neuralgia, etc and as a flavouring, eg in ⁓ cigarettes. men·tho·lated /'menθəleɪtɪd/ adj containing ⁓.

men·tion /'menʃn/ vt [VP6A,C,9,13A] speak or write sth about; say the name of; refer to: He ⁓ed to me that he had seen you. I shall ⁓ it to him. Did I hear my name ⁓ed, Was somebody talking about me? not to ⁓; without ⁓ing, phrases used either to excuse ⁓ of sth unimportant or to emphasize sth important: We're too busy to take a long holiday this year, not to ⁓ the fact that we can't afford it. Don't ⁓ it, phrase used to indicate that thanks, an apology, etc are unnecessary. □ n 1 [U] ⁓ing or naming: He made no ⁓ of your request. 2 [C] brief notice or reference: Did the concert get a ⁓ in the paper? -men·tioned adj (with an adv prefixed): a,bove-/be,low-'mentioned, referred to above/below.

men·tor /'mentɔ:(r)/ n wise and trusted adviser and helper (of an inexperienced person).

menu /'menju:/ n list of courses at a meal or of dishes available at a restaurant.

Mephi·stoph·elian /,mefɪstə'fi:lɪən/ adj of or like Mephistopheles /,mefɪ'stɒfəli:z/ (the devil in a German legend); fiendish.

mer·can·tile /'mɜ:kəntaɪl/ adj of trade, commerce and merchants. ⁓ marine, country's merchant ships and seamen.

Mer·ca·tor's pro·jec·tion /mə,keɪtəz prə'dʒekʃn/ n method of making maps of the world in which meridians and parallels of latitude cross at right angles (so that areas far from the equator are exaggerated in size). ⇨ the illus at projection.

mer·cen·ary /'mɜ:sɪnərɪ US: -nerɪ/ adj working only for money or other reward; inspired by love of money: ⁓ politicians; act from ⁓ motives. □ n (pl -ries) soldier hired for pay to serve in a foreign army.

mer·cer /'mɜ:sə(r)/ n (GB) dealer in woven materials, esp silk and other textiles.

mer·cer·ize /'mɜ:səraɪz/ vt [VP6A] treat (cotton threads) so that they are better able to take dyes and become glossy like silk: ⁓d cotton.

mer·chan·dise /'mɜ:tʃəndaɪz/ n [U] goods bought and sold; trade goods.

mer·chant /'mɜ:tʃənt/ n 1 (usu wholesale) trader, esp one doing business with foreign countries. 2 (chiefly attrib) of commercial shipping: (attrib) ⁓ ships. the ⁓ navy/service/marine, the ⁓ ships and seamen of a country collectively. ⁓ seaman, sailor in a ⁓ ship. 3 (as the second half of a compound n) person trading inside a country in the

goods indicated: a 'coal-⁓/'wine-⁓. 4 (GB sl) person who is very fond of (sth) or addicted to (sth): a 'speed ⁓, person who likes to drive at high speeds. ⁓·man /n (pl -men) ⁓ ship.

mer·ci·ful /'mɜ:sɪfl/ adj (to), having, showing, feeling mercy (to). ⁓ly /-fəlɪ/ adv

mer·ci·less /'mɜ:sɪlɪs/ adj ⁓ (to), showing no mercy (to). ⁓ly adv

mer·cur·ial /mɜ:'kjʊərɪəl/ adj 1 of, like, caused by, containing, mercury: ⁓ ointment; ⁓ poisoning. 2 (fig) lively; quickwitted. 3 (of persons) changeable; inconstant.

mer·cury /'mɜ:kjʊrɪ/ n [U] (also called quicksilver) heavy, silver-coloured metal (symbol Hg) usu liquid, as in thermometers and barometers.

Mer·cury /'mɜ:kjʊrɪ/ n (Roman myth) messenger of the gods; (astron) planet nearest the sun. ⇨ the illus at planet.

mercy /'mɜ:sɪ/ n (pl -cies) 1 [U] (capacity for) holding oneself back from punishing, or from causing suffering to, sb whom one has the right or power to punish; They showed little ⁓ to their enemies. We were given no ⁓. He threw himself on my ⁓, begged me to have ⁓ on him, not to punish him, etc. The jury brought in a verdict of guilty, with a recommendation to ⁓, asking that the punishment should not be too severe. at the ⁓ of, in the power of; without defence against: The ship was at the ⁓ of the waves, was out of control, likely to be wrecked, etc. be left to the tender ⁓/ mercies of, be exposed to the probably unkind, rough or cruel treatment of. 2 [C] piece of good fortune; sth to be thankful for; relief: That's a ⁓! We must be thankful for small mercies. His death was a ⁓, eg of sb with a painful and incurable illness. '⁓ killing n (colloq for) euthanasia. 3 M⁓! M⁓ on us! exclamations of surprise or (often pretended) terror.

mere¹ /mɪə(r)/ adj not more than: She's a ⁓ child. It's a ⁓/the ⁓st trifle, nothing at all important, nothing of any value, etc. ⁓ words (= Words without acts) won't help. ⁓·ly adv only; simply: I ⁓ly asked his name. I said it ⁓ly as a joke.

mere² /mɪə(r)/ n pond; small lake.

mere·tri·cious /,merɪ'trɪʃəs/ adj attractive on the surface but of little value: ⁓ jewellery; a ⁓ style, superficially attractive. ⁓·ly adv ⁓·ness n

merge /mɜ:dʒ/ vt,vi 1 [VP2A,3A,6A,14] ⁓ (in/ into/with), (comm) (of business companies) (cause to) become one: We are merging with the company that supplies components for our cars. The small banks ⁓d/were ⁓d into one large organization. 2 [VP3A] ⁓ into, fade or change gradually into: Twilight ⁓d into darkness. His fear gradually ⁓d into curiosity to know what was happening. merger /'mɜ:dʒə(r)/ n [U] merging; [C] instance of this; combining of estates, business companies, etc.

mer·id·ian /mə'rɪdɪən/ n 1 (either half of a) circle round the globe, passing through a given place and the north and south poles: the ⁓ of Greenwich, longitude 0°. 2 highest point reached by the sun or other star as viewed from a point on the earth's surface; 12 noon. 3 (fig) period of greatest splendour, success, power, etc. 4 (attrib) of a ⁓: line/ altitude; (fig) in his ⁓ splendour.

mer·idi·onal /mə'rɪdɪənl/ adj of the south; of the south of Europe, esp the south of France.

me·ringue /mə'ræŋ/ n [U,C] whites of egg and sugar baked and used as a covering over pies, tarts, etc; small cake made of this mixture.

mer·ino /mə'riːnəʊ/ n (pl ~s /-nəʊz/) 1 (also '~- **sheep**) breed of sheep with long, fine wool. 2 [U] yarn or cloth from this wool; soft wool and cotton material.

merit /'merɪt/ n 1 [U] quality or fact of deserving well; worth; excellence: *There isn't much ~ in giving away things you don't value or want. Do men of ~ always win recognition? She was awarded a certificate of ~ for her piano playing.* 2 [C] quality, fact, action, etc, that deserves reward: *We must decide the case on its ~s,* according to the rights and wrongs of the case, without being influenced by personal feelings. **make a ~ of sth,** represent it as deserving reward or praise: *Don't make a ~ of being punctual—it's only what we expect of you.* □ vt [VP6A] deserve; be worthy of: *~ reward/punishment.*

meri·toc·racy /ˌmerɪ'tɒkrəsɪ/ n (pl -cies) (system of government or control by) persons of high practical or intellectual ability.

meri·tori·ous /ˌmerɪ'tɔːrɪəs/ adj praiseworthy; deserving reward: *a prize for ~ conduct.* **~·ly** adv

mer·maid /'mɜːmeɪd/ n (in children's stories, etc) woman with a fish's tail in place of legs. **mer·man** /'mɜːmæn/ n (pl -men) male ~.

merry /'merɪ/ adj (-ier, -iest) 1 happy; cheerful; bright and gay: *a ~ laugh; wish sb a ~ Christmas.* **make ~,** be gay and cheerful; laugh, talk, sing and feast. '**~-maker** n person who does this. '**~-making** n [U] doing this. '**~-go-round** n revolving machine with horses, cars, etc on which children ride at fun fairs, etc. 2 (old use) pleasant: *the ~ month of May; M~ England.* **mer·rily** /'merəlɪ/ adv **mer·ri·ment** /'merɪmənt/ n [U].

mé·sal·liance /ˌmeɪ'zælɪɑːns/ n marriage with a person of lower social position.

mes·cal /'meskl/ n 1 globe-shaped cactus of Mexico. 2 Mexican liquor distilled from the juices of the agave plant. **mes·ca·line** /'meskəlɪn/ n [U] hallucinatory drug extracted from the ~ cactus.

Mes·dames /meɪ'dɑːm/ n pl of madame.

Mes·demoi·selles /ˌmeɪdmwə'zel/ n pl of mademoiselle.

me·seems /mɪ'siːmz/ vi (old use) it seems to me.

mesh /meʃ/ n 1 one of the spaces in a net or wire screen: *a net with half-inch ~es;* spaces in other material. ⇨ micromesh. 2 (pl) network: *the ~es of a spider's web;* (fig) *entangled in the ~es of political intrigue.* 3 (mechanics) *in ~,* (of the geared teeth of wheels) engaged, interlocked. ⇨ also synchromesh. □ vt,vi 1 [VP6A] catch (eg fish) in a net. 2 [VP2A,3A] ~ **(with),** (of toothed wheels) interlock; be engaged (with others); (fig) harmonize: *Our ways of looking at these problems don't ~.*

mes·mer·ism /'mezmərɪzəm/ n [U] (older name for) hypnotism. **mes·meric** /mez'merɪk/ adj hypnotic. **mes·mer·ist** /-ɪst/ n hypnotist. **mes·mer·ize** /-aɪz/ vt [VP6A] hypnotize.

me·son /'miːsɒn/ n (phys) type of subatomic particle with a mass between that of an electron and a proton.

mess¹ /mes/ n (with indef art, but rarely pl) state of confusion, dirt or disorder: *The workmen cleaned up the ~ before they left. Who's going to clear up the ~ made by the cat? You've made a ~ of the job, have done it very badly. He has got into another ~,* is in trouble again. *A nice ~ you've made of it,* You've spoilt it! *I've never seen so much ~ and disorder!* □ vt,vi 1 [VP6A,15B] ~ **sth (up),** make a ~ of; put into disorder or confusion: *The late arrival of the train ~ed up all our plans.* Hence, '**~-up** n (colloq) disorder or confusion: *There's been a bit of a ~-up* (= a misunderstanding, a failure to do what was needed) *about booking seats for that concert.* 2 [VP2C,15B] ~ **sth/sb about, (a)** do things with no very definite plan; behave foolishly. **(b)** make a ~ or muddle (of sth); treat (sb) roughly or inconsiderately: *Stop ~ing me about!* **~y** adj (-ier, -iest) dirty; in a state of disorder: *a ~y job,* eg one that makes the hands and clothes dirty.

mess² /mes/ n [C] company of persons taking meals together (esp in the Armed Forces); these meals; the room, etc in which the meals are eaten. '**~-jacket** n (uniform) jacket worn at ~. '**~-mate** n member of the same ~ (esp a ship's ~ in the Navy). □ vi ~ **with sb;** ~ **together,** eat meals. *The five young men ~ together.* '**~-ing allowance** n money allowed (in the Armed Forces) for cost of meals in a ~.

mess·age /'mesɪdʒ/ n 1 piece of news, or a request, sent to sb: *Radio ~s told us that the ship was sinking. Will you take this ~ to my brother? Got the ~?* (sl) Have you understood? 2 social, moral or religious teaching: *the ~ of Muhammad to his age.*

mess·en·ger /'mesɪndʒə(r)/ n person carrying a message.

Mess·iah /mɪ'saɪə/ n person expected by the Jews to come and set them free; Jesus Christ considered as this.

Mess·ieurs /meɪ'sjɜː(r)/ n pl of monsieur.

Messrs /'mesəz/ n (abbr of *Messieurs*) used as the pl of *Mr* before a list of men's names: ~ *Smith, Brown and Robinson,* and before names of business firms: ~ *T Brown & Co.*

mes·suage /'meswɪdʒ/ n (legal) dwelling-house with the outbuildings and land that go with it.

met /met/ pt, pp of meet.

Met /met/ n (abbr of) Meteorological: *get the latest ~ report,* issued by the '*Met Office* on the weather.

me·tab·olism /mɪ'tæbəlɪzəm/ n [U] process by which food is built up into living matter or by which living matter is broken down into simple substances. **meta·bolic** /ˌmetə'bɒlɪk/ adj of ~.

meta·car·pal /ˌmetə'kɑːpl/ adj, n (anat) (of a) bone in the hand. ⇨ the illus at skeleton.

metal /'metl/ n 1 [C] any of a class of mineral substances such as tin, iron, gold and copper: *a worker in ~s.* '**~-work** n artistic work in ~. '**~-worker** n one who shapes objects in ~. 2 [U] one of these (as a material n): *Is it made of wood or ~?* 3 [U] ('**road-)~,** (GB) broken stone used for making roads or the beds of railways. 4 (pl) railway-lines: *The train left/jumped the ~s.* □ vt (-ll-; US -l-) [VP6A] make or repair a road with ~(3): *~led roads; a ~led road surface.*

me·tal·lic /mɪ'tælɪk/ adj of or like metal: *a ~ currency,* ie with metal coins; ~ *compounds;* ~ *sounds,* eg as made by brass objects struck together.

me·tal·lurgy /mɪ'tælədʒɪ US: 'metələːrdʒɪ/ n [U] science and technology of metals, eg of separating metal from ore, purifying it, and of working in metal. **me·tal·lur·gist** /-dʒɪst/ n expert in ~. **me·tal·lur·gi·cal** /ˌmetə'lɜːdʒɪkl/ adv of ~.

meta·mor·phose /ˌmetə'mɔːfəʊz/ vt,vi [VP6A,14,3A] ~ **(sb/sth) (into),** change in form, change the nature of (as by sorcery): *Circe* ∼*d the companions of Odysseus into swine.*

meta·mor·pho·sis /ˌmetə'mɔːfəsɪs/ *n (pl -oses* /-əsiːz/) change of form or character, eg by natural growth or development: *the* ∼ *in the life of an insect,* from the egg, etc; *the social* ∼ *that has occurred in China.*

meta·phor /'metəfə(r)/ *n* [C,U] (example of) the use of words to indicate sth different from the literal meaning, as in 'I'll make him *eat* his words' or 'He has a heart *of stone'.* Cf *simile:* 'a heart *like stone'.* ∼**i·cal** /ˌmetə'fɒrɪkl *US:* -'fɔːr-/ *adj* of or like a ∼; containing or using ∼s. ∼**i·cally** /-klɪ/ *adv*

meta·phys·ics /ˌmetə'fɪzɪks/ *n* (with *sing v*) **1** branch of philosophy dealing with the nature of existence, truth and knowledge: *M*∼ *deals with abstractions. Do we need a new* ∼? (Note: on the analogy of French and German, *metaphysic* is sometimes used, meaning 'system of ∼'). **2** (pop use) speculative philosophy; abstract talk. **meta·phys·ical** /ˌmetə'fɪzɪkl/ *adj* of ∼; based on abstract reasoning.

meta·tar·sal /ˌmetə'tɑːsl/ *adj, n* (anat) (of a) bone in the foot. ⇨ the illus at **skeleton.**

mete /miːt/ *vt* [VP15B] ∼ *out,* portion or measure: ∼ *out rewards/punishments. Justice was* ∼*d out to them.*

me·teor /'miːtɪə(r)/ *n* [C] small particle of matter that enters the earth's atmosphere from outer space and becomes bright (as a *'shooting star'* or *'falling star'*) in the night sky as it is burnt up.

me·teoric /ˌmiːtɪ'ɒrɪk *US:* -'ɔːr-/ *adj* **1** of the atmosphere or of atmospheric conditions; of meteors. **2** (fig) brilliant but brief: *a* ∼ *career.*

me·teor·ite /'miːtɪəraɪt/ *n* [C] fallen meteor; fragment of rock or metal that has reached the earth's surface from outer space.

me·teor·ol·ogy /ˌmiːtɪə'rɒlədʒɪ/ *n* [U] science of the weather; study of the earth's atmosphere and its changes. **me·teor·ol·ogist** /ˌmiːtɪə'rɒlədʒɪst/ *n* expert in ∼. **me·teoro·logi·cal** /ˌmiːtɪərə'lɒdʒɪkl *US:* ˌmiːtɪɔːr-/ *adj* of ∼: *weather forecasts from the Central Meteorological Office.*

an electricity meter   a metronome

me·ter¹ /'miːtə(r)/ *n* [C] apparatus which measures, esp one that records the amount of whatever passes through it, or the distance travelled, fare payable, etc: *an ˌelec'tricity-*∼; *a 'gas-*∼; *a 'water-*∼; *an ex'posure-*∼, for measuring the time needed for exposure of photographic film, etc; *a 'parking-*∼, one that measures the time during which a car is (for a fee) parked in a public place; *fares mounting up on the* ∼, eg of a taxi-cab.

me·ter² /'miːtə(r)/ *n* (US) = metre.

meth·ane /'miːθeɪn/ *n* [U] odourless, colourless inflammable gas (**CH₄**) that occurs in coalmines (as fire damp, causing explosions) and (as natural gas,

marsh gas) on marshy areas.

me·thinks /mɪ'θɪŋks/ *vi (pt* methought /mɪ'θɔːt/) (old use) it seems to me.

method /'meθəd/ *n* **1** [U] system(2), orderliness: *He's a man of* ∼. *There's* ∼ *in his madness,* His behaviour, etc is not so unreasonable as it seems. **2** [C] way of doing sth: *modern* ∼*s of teaching arithmetic;* ∼*s of payment,* eg cash, cheques, monthly instalments. ∼**i·cal** /mɪ'θɒdɪkl/ *adj* **1** done, carried out, with order or ∼: ∼*ical work.* **2** doing things with ∼; having orderly habits: *a* ∼*ical worker.* ∼**i·cally** /-klɪ/ *adv* ∼·**ol·ogy** /ˌmeθə'dɒlədʒɪ/ *n* [U] science or study of ∼; [C] set of ∼s used in working at sth.

Meth·od·ism /'meθədɪzəm/ *n* teaching, organization and manner of worship in the Christian denomination deriving from John Wesley /'wezlɪ/ 1703—1791. **Meth·od·ist** /-ɪst/ *n, adj* (member) of this denomination. ⇨ **Wesleyan.**

me·thought /mɪ'θɔːt/ *pt* of methinks.

meths /meθs/ *n pl* (colloq abbr for) methylated spirits.

Me·thuse·lah /mɪ'θjuːzələ/ *n* (in the Bible) man stated to have lived 969 years; (hence) man who lives to a great age. ⇨ Gen 5: 27.

methyl /'meθɪl/ *n* ∼ **alcohol,** kind of alcohol (also called *wood spirit*) present in many organic compounds. '∼·**ated** /-eɪtɪd/ *adj* ∼**ated spirit(s),** [U] form of alcohol (made unfit for drinking) used for lighting and heating.

me·ticu·lous /mɪ'tɪkjʊləs/ *adj* ∼ *(in),* giving, showing, great attention to detail; careful and exact. ∼·**ly** *adv*

mé·tier /'metɪeɪ/ *n* one's trade, profession or line of business.

metre¹ (US = **me·ter**) /'miːtə(r)/ *n* unit of length in the metric system. ⇨ App 5.

metre² (US = **me·ter**) /'miːtə(r)/ *n* [U] verse rhythm; [C] particular form of this; fixed arrangement of accented and unaccented syllables.

met·ric /'metrɪk/ *adj* of the metre¹: **the '**∼ **system,** the decimal measuring system based on the metre as the unit of length, the kilogram as the unit of mass and the litre as the unit of capacity. ∼ **ton,** 1000 kilograms. **met·ri·cize** /'metrɪsaɪz/ *vt* convert to the ∼ system.

metri·cal /'metrɪkl/ *adj* **1** of, composed in, metre² (contrasted with ordinary prose): *a* ∼ *translation of the Iliad.* **2** connected with measurement: ∼ *geometry.* ∼·**ly** /-klɪ/ *adv*

metri·ca·tion /ˌmetrɪ'keɪʃn/ *n* conversion to the metric system.

Metro /'metrəʊ/ *n* (**the**) ∼, the underground railway system in Paris. Cf in London, *Underground* or *tube.*

met·ro·nome /'metrənəʊm/ *n* (music) graduated inverted pendulum for sounding an adjustable number of beats per minute. ⇨ the illus at **meter.**

me·trop·olis /mə'trɒpəlɪs/ *n (pl* ∼es) chief city of a country; capital; (in GB) *the* ∼, London.

metro·poli·tan /ˌmetrə'pɒlɪtən/ *adj* **1** of or in a capital city: *the* ∼ *police.* **2** of an ecclesiastical province. ∼ **bishop,** one (usu an archbishop) having authority over the bishops in his province. **3** *M*∼ **France,** France itself as distinct from its dependencies overseas. □ *n* **1** person who lives in a metropolis. **2 M**∼, ∼ bishop.

mettle /'metl/ *n* [U] quality, eg in persons, horses, of endurance and courage: *a man of* ∼; *a horse that is full of* ∼; *try sb's* ∼, test his quality. **be on**

one's ~; *put sb on his* ~, rouse oneself/him to do one's/his best, put oneself/him in a position that tests one's/his ~. '~·**some** /-səm/ *adj* high-spirited.

mew /mju:/ *n* (also *miaow*) sound made by a cat or a sea-bird. □ *vi* [VP2A] make this sound: *We heard the mewing of a cat.*

mews /mju:z/ *n* (with *sing v*) (old use) square or street of stables behind a residential street; (modern use) such stables rebuilt for use as garages or converted into flats, etc: *living in a Chelsea* ~.

mezza·nine /'mezəni:n/ *n, adj* (floor) between ground floor and first floor, often in the form of a balcony.

mezzo /'metsəʊ/ *adv* (musical direction) moderately; half: ~ *forte*, moderately loud. ~-**so·prano** /ˌmetsəʊsə'prɑːnəʊ *US:* -'præn-/ *n* (person with, part for a) voice between soprano and contralto.

mezzo·tint /'metsəʊtɪnt/ *n* [C,U] (print produced by a) method of printing from a metal plate which has a rough surface of small dots scraped and polished to produce areas of light and shade.

mi, me /mi:/ *n* third note in the musical octave.

mi-aou, mi-aow /mi:'aʊ/ *n, vi* = mew.

mi-asma /mɪ'æzmə/ *n* unhealthy mist rising from the ground; (fig) unhealthy environment or influence.

mica /'maɪkə/ *n* [U] transparent mineral substance easily divided into thin layers, used as an electrical insulator, etc.

mice /maɪs/ *n pl* of mouse.

Michael·mas /'mɪklməs/ *n* 29 Sept, the feast of St Michael. ~ '**daisy,** perennial aster flowering in autumn, with blue, white, pink or purple flowers.

mickey /'mɪkɪ/ *n take the* ~ *(out of sb),* (sl) hold (him) up to ridicule; mock or tease (him).

mickle /'mɪkl/ (also **muckle** /'mʌkl/) *n* (Scot) large amount: *Many a little makes a* ~.

microbe /'maɪkrəʊb/ *n* tiny living creature that can be seen only with the help of a microscope, esp kinds of bacteria causing diseases and fermentation.

micro·bi·ol·ogy /ˌmaɪkrəʊbaɪ'ɒlədʒɪ/ *n* [U] study of micro-organisms.

micro·chip /'maɪkrəʊtʃɪp/ *n* chip used in an integrated circuit. ⇨ integrate (1).

micro·cosm /'maɪkrəʊkɒzəm/ *n* [C] sth, (esp man, by the ancient philosophers) considered as representing (on a small scale) mankind or the uni-verse; miniature representation (*of* a system, etc). ⇨ macrocosm.

micro·dot /'maɪkrəʊdɒt/ *n* photograph reduced to the size of a dot.

micro-elec·tron·ics /ˌmaɪkrəʊˌɪlek'trɒnɪks/ *n* (with *sing v*) design, construction and use of devices with extremely small (usu solid state) components.

micro·fiche /'maɪkrəʊfiːʃ/ *n* [C,U] sheet of micro-film.

micro·film /'maɪkrəʊfɪlm/ *n* [C,U] (roll, section, of) photographic film for small-scale reproduction of documentary material, etc. □ *vt* [VP6A] photograph in this way: ~ *old historical records/bank accounts.*

mi·crom·eter /maɪ'krɒmɪtə(r)/ *n* device for measuring very small objects.

mi·cron /'maɪkrɒn/ *n* unit of length (symbol μ) equal to one millionth of a metre.

micro-or·gan·ism /ˌmaɪkrəʊ'ɔːgənɪzəm/ *n* organism so small as to be visible only under a microscope.

a microphone　　　a microscope

micro·phone /'maɪkrəfəʊn/ *n* instrument for changing sound waves into electrical current, as in telephones, radio, etc.

micro-pro·ces·sor /ˌmaɪkrəʊ'prəʊsesə(r)/ *n* (comp) type of integrated circuit used in a computer. ⇨ integrate (1).

micro·scope /'maɪkrəskəʊp/ *n* instrument with lenses for making very small near objects appear larger: *examine sth under the* ~. **micro·scopic** /ˌmaɪkrə'skɒpɪk/, **micro·scopi·cal** /-kl/ *adj* of the ~; too small to be visible except under a ~. **micro·scopi·cally** /-klɪ/ *adv*

micro·wave /'maɪkrəʊweɪv/ *n* very short wave (as used in radio and radar).

mid¹ /mɪd/ *adj* **1** the middle of: *from mid June to mid August; in mid winter; a collision in mid Channel/in mid air.* **2** (in compounds used attrib): *a midwinter day; mid-morning coffee.* **the** ˌ**Mid-'west,** (also known as **the** ˌ**Middle 'West**) that part of the US which is the Mississippi basin as far south as Kansas, Missouri and the Ohio River. **3** (cricket) ˌ**mid-'off,** ˌ**mid-'on,** fielder near the bowler on the off, on, side. ⇨ the illus at cricket. **mid·most** /'mɪdməʊst/ *adj, adv* (*superl* of mid) (that is) in the very middle.

mid² /mɪd/ *prep* (poet) amid; among.

mid·day /ˌmɪd'deɪ/ *n* noon: (attrib) *the* ~ *meal,* ie lunch.

mid·den /'mɪdn/ *n* heap of dung or rubbish.

middle /'mɪdl/ *n* **1** the ~, point, position or part, which is at an equal distance from two or more points, etc or between beginning and end: *the* ~ *of a room; in the* ~ *of the century; in the very* ~ *of the night; standing in the* ~ *of the street; a pain in the* ~ *of the back. They were in the* ~ *of dinner* (= were having dinner) *when I called. I was in the* ~ *of reading* (= was busy reading) *when she telephoned.* ˌ~-of-the-'road, (attrib) (of policies, etc) avoiding extremes. **2** (colloq) waist: *seize sb round the* ~; *fifty inches round the* ~. **3** (attrib use) in the ~: *the* ~ *house in the row.* ˌ~ 'age, the period of life between youth and old age. Hence, ˌ~-'aged /-ˈeɪdʒd/ *adj* of ~ age: *a* ~-*aged woman.* ˌ~-age(d) 'spread, (colloq) corpulence that tends to come with ~ age. **the** ˌ**M**~ '**Ages,** the period (in European history) from about AD 1100 to 1500. ˌ~ 'class, class of society between the lower and upper classes (eg shopkeepers, business men, professional workers). Hence, ˌ~-'class *adj* of this class: *a* ~-*class residential area.* (**take/follow) a** ~ **course,** a compromise between two extreme courses (of action). **the** ˌ~ 'distance, that part of a landscape, scene, painting, etc between the foreground and the background. **the** ˌ~ 'ear, hollow space of the central part of the ear, in front of the ear-drum. ⇨ the illus at ear. **the** ˌ**M**~ '**East,** ⇨ East. ˌ~ '**finger,** the second. **the** ˌ**M**~ '**Kingdom,** (an old name for) China. '~-**man** /-mæn/ *n* (*pl*-men) any trader through whose hands goods pass between the producer and the consumer. ˌ~ '**name,** second of two given names, eg *Bernard* in

George Bernard Shaw. '∼ **school,** (in some countries) type of school between elementary school and high school. **the** ∼ **'watch,** (on ships) between midnight and 4am. '∼**·weight,** (esp) boxer weighing between 147 and 160 lb or (66·6 to 72·5 kg). **the ,M**∼ **'West,** ▷ *Midwest* at mid¹(2).

mid·dling /'mɪdlɪŋ/ *adj* of middle or medium size, quality, grade, etc: *a town of* ∼ *size. He says he's feeling only* ∼ (often *fair to* ∼), (colloq) in fairly good but not very good health. □ *adv* (colloq) moderately: ∼ *tall.* □ *n* (usu *pl*) goods of second or inferior quality, esp coarse-ground wheat flour mixed with bran.

middy /'mɪdɪ/ *n* (*pl* -dies) (colloq abbr of) midshipman. '∼ **blouse,** loose blouse like that worn by naval seamen.

midge /mɪdʒ/ *n* small winged insect like a gnat.

midget /'mɪdʒɪt/ *n* extremely small person, eg one exhibited as a curiosity at a circus; (attrib) very small: *a* ∼ *submarine.*

mid·land /'mɪdlənd/ *n* (often attrib) middle part of a country. **the M**∼**s,** the ∼ counties of England.

mid·night /'mɪdnaɪt/ *n* 1 12 o'clock at night: *at/ before/after* ∼. 2 (attrib) during the middle of the night; at ∼: *the* ∼ *hours.* **burn the** ∼ *oil,* sit up and work late at night. *the* ∼ *sun,* the sun as seen at ∼ in summer within the Arctic or Antarctic Circle.

mid·riff /'mɪdrɪf/ *n* 1 (anat) diaphragm. 2 abdomen, belly: (boxing) *a blow on the* ∼.

mid·ship·man /'mɪdʃɪpmən/ *n* (*pl* -men) non-commissioned officer ranking below a sub-lieutenant in the Royal Navy; student training to be commissioned as an officer in the US Navy.

mid·ships /'mɪdʃɪps/ *adv* = amidships.

midst /mɪdst/ *n* (liter or archaic) middle part: *in/ into/from/out of the* ∼ (*of*). **in our/your/their** ∼, among, with us etc. □ *prep* (liter or archaic) in the middle of; amidst.

mid·stream /ˌmɪd'striːm/ *n* [U] the part of a stream, river, etc away from both its banks. *in* ∼, in the middle of the action, event, etc.

mid·sum·mer /ˌmɪd'sʌmə(r)/ *n* [U] period about 21 June. **,M**∼ **'day,** 24 June. **∼ 'madness,** the height of madness.

mid·way /ˌmɪd'weɪ/ *adj, adv* ∼ *(between),* situated in the middle; halfway.

mid·wife /'mɪdwaɪf/ *n* (*pl* midwives /-waɪvz/) woman trained to help women in childbirth. **mid·wifery** /'mɪdwɪfrɪ/ *n* [U] profession and work of a ∼; obstetrics: *take a course in* ∼*ry.*

mien /miːn/ *n* (liter) person's appearance or bearing (as showing a mood, etc): *with a sorrowful* ∼*; of pleasing* ∼*; the severity of his* ∼.

might¹ /maɪt/ *pt* of may.

might² /maɪt/ *n* [U] great power; strength: *work with all one's* ∼*; 'M*∼ *is right',* he said, ie Having power to enforce one's will gives one the right to do so. *with* ∼ *and main,* using all one's physical force.

mighty /'maɪtɪ/ *adj* (-ier, -iest) 1 (liter, biblical) powerful: *a* ∼ *nation.* 2 great; massive: *the* ∼ *ocean.* **high and** ∼, very proud. □ *adv* (colloq) very: *think oneself* ∼ *clever.* **'might·ily** /-ɪlɪ/ *adv* greatly; (dated colloq) extremely: *mightily indignant.*

mignon·ette /ˌmɪnjə'net/ *n* [U] garden plant with small, sweet-smelling, greenish-white flowers.

mi·graine /'miːɡreɪn/ *n* severe, frequently recurring, headache (usu on one side only of the head or face), often accompanied by nausea.

mi·grant /'maɪɡrənt/ *n* one who migrates, esp a bird: *Swallows are* ∼*s.* ∼ **labour,** that available in a country from (short-term) immigrants.

mi·grate /maɪˈɡreɪt *US:* 'maɪɡreɪt/ *vi* [VP2A,3A] ∼ *(from/to),* 1 move from one place to another (to live there). 2 (of birds and fishes) come and go with the season; travel regularly from one region to another. **mi·gra·tion** /maɪˈɡreɪʃn/ *n* [U] migrating; [C] instance of this; [C] number of persons, animals, etc migrating together. **mi·gra·tory** /'maɪɡrətrɪ *US:* -tɔːrɪ/ *adj* having the habit of migrating: *migratory birds.*

mi·kado /mɪˈkɑːdəʊ/ *n* (name formerly used outside, but not inside, Japan for) Emperor of Japan.

mike /maɪk/ *n* (colloq abbr for) microphone.

mi·lady /mɪˈleɪdɪ/ *n* (*pl* -dies) (dated form of address to a) lady. Cf current use *My Lady.*

mi·lage /'maɪlɪdʒ/ *n* = mileage.

milch /mɪltʃ/ *adj* (of domestic mammals) kept for, giving, milk: '∼ *cows.*

mild /maɪld/ *adj* (-er, -est) 1 soft; gentle; not severe: ∼ *weather;* ∼ *punishments; a* ∼ *answer. I'm the* ∼*est man alive,* No one is gentler, etc than I am. 2 (of food, drink, tobacco) not sharp or strong in taste or flavour: ∼ *cheese; a* ∼ *cigar;* ∼ (*ale) and bitter,* ∼ and bitter beer mixed. **draw it** ∼, ▷ draw²(5). 3 ∼ **steel,** tough and malleable, with a low percentage of carbon. ∼**·ly** *adv* in a ∼ manner. **to put it** ∼**ly,** to say the least of it, to speak without exaggeration. ∼**·ness** *n*

mil·dew /'mɪldjuː *US:* -duː/ *n* [U] (usu destructive) growth of tiny fungi forming on plants, leather, food, etc in warm and damp conditions: *roses ruined by* ∼. □ *vt,vi* [VP6A,2A] affect, become affected, with ∼.

mile /maɪl/ *n* measure of distance, 1760 yards: *For* ∼*s and* ∼*s there's nothing but desert. It's a 30* ∼*/a 30* ∼*s' journey. He ran the* ∼ *in 4 minutes/a 4-minute* ∼. *She's feeling* ∼*s better today,* (colloq) very much better. *There's no one within* ∼*s of him as a tennis player,* no one who can rival him. ▷ nautical;. ▷ App 5. ∼**·om·eter** /maɪˈlɒmɪtə(r)/ *n* device (in a motor-vehicle) recording the number of ∼s travelled. '∼**·stone** *n* (a) stone set up at the side of a road showing distances. (b) (fig) (important) stage or event in history or in human life.

mile·age /'maɪlɪdʒ/ *n* 1 distance travelled, measured in miles: *a used car with a small* ∼, one that has not run many miles. 2 allowance for travelling expenses at so much a mile.

miler /'maɪlə(r)/ *n* (colloq) runner specializing in one mile races: *He's our best* ∼.

mi·lieu /'miːljɜː *US:* ˌmiː'ljɜː/ *the 3: having no r quality/ n* environment; social surroundings.

mili·tant /'mɪlɪtənt/ *adj* ready for fighting; actively engaged in or supporting the use of force or strong pressure: ∼ *students/workers.* □ *n* ∼ person, eg in trade unionism, politics. '**mili·tancy** /-ənsɪ/ *n*

mili·tar·ism /'mɪlɪtərɪzəm/ *n* [U] belief in, reliance upon, military strength and virtues. **mili·tar·ist** /'mɪlɪtərɪst/ *n* supporter of, believer in ∼. **mili·tar·istic** /ˌmɪlɪtə'rɪstɪk/ *adj*

mili·tary /'mɪlɪtrɪ *US:* -terɪ/ *adj* of or for soldiers, an army; of or for all the armed forces: *in* ∼ *uniform;* ∼ *government; called up for* ∼ *service,* eg to train or serve as a soldier. □ *n* [U] (with *sing* or *pl v*) **the** ∼, the soldiers; the army; the armed forces: *The* ∼ *were called in to deal with the rioting.*

mili·tate /'mɪlɪteɪt/ vi [VP3A] ~ **against,** (of evidence, facts) have force, operate: *Several factors combined to ~ against the success of our plan.*

mil·itia /mɪ'lɪʃə/ n (usu **the ~**) force of civilians trained as soldiers but not part of the regular army. '**~·man** /-mən/ n (pl-men) member of the ~.

milk¹ /mɪlk/ n [U] **1** white liquid produced by female mammals as food for their young, esp that of cows, drunk by human beings and made into butter and cheese: ~ *fresh from the cow; tinned ~; ~ puddings,* eg rice, sago or tapioca baked with ~ in a dish. **the ~ of human kindness,** the kindness that should be natural to human beings. *It's no use crying over spilt ~,* over a loss or error for which there is no remedy. ~ *and water,* (fig) feeble discourse or sentiment. **2** (compounds) '**~·bar** n bar for the sale of drinks made from ~, ice-cream and other light refreshments. '**~·churn** n large vessel fitted with a lid for carrying ~. '**~ loaf,** sweet-tasting white bread. '**~·maid** n woman who milks cows and works in a dairy. '**~·man** /-mən/ n (pl -men) man who sells ~; man who goes from house to house delivering ~. '**~·powder** n ~ dehydrated by evaporation. '**~ round** n ~man's route from house to house, street to street. '**~·shake** n beverage of ~ with ice-cream mixed into it and beaten up. '**~·sop** /-sɒp/ n man or youth who is lacking in spirit, who is too soft and gentle. '**~·tooth** n (pl-teeth) one of the first (temporary) teeth in young mammals. ,**~·'white** adj as white as ~. **3** ~-like juice of some plants and trees, eg the juice inside a coconut. '**~·weed** n name used for several kinds of wild plant with a juice like ~. **4** ~-like preparation made from herbs, drugs, etc: ~ *of magnesia.*

milk² /mɪlk/ vt,vi **1** [VP6A] draw milk from a cow/ewe/goat, or juice from a plant, or venom from a snake; extract money, information, etc (by guile or dishonesty) from a person or institution. **2** [VP2A] yield milk: *The cows are ~ing well.* '**~ing-machine** n apparatus for ~ing cows mechanically.

milky /'mɪlkɪ/ adj (-ier, -iest) of or like milk; mixed with milk; (of a liquid) cloudy, not clear. **the ,M~ 'Way,** the broad luminous band of stars encircling the sky; the Galaxy (as seen from earth).

mill¹ /mɪl/ n **1** (building ('*flour-~*) with) machinery or apparatus for grinding grain into flour (old style, '*water~*, '*wind*~). **put sb/go through the ~,** (cause to) undergo hard training or experience. **run-of-the-~,** ⇨ run¹(10). '**~-dam** n dam built across a stream to make water available for a ~. '**~-pond** n water retained by a ~-dam, to flow to the ~: *like a ~-pond,* (of the sea) very calm. '**~-race** n current of water that turns a '**~-wheel.** '**~-stone** n one of a pair of circular stones between which grain is ground. **a ~stone round one's neck,** (fig) heavy burden: *That mortgage has been like a ~stone round my neck.* **be between the upper and nether** (= lower) **~stone,** be subject to irresistible pressure. '**~-wheel** n wheel (esp a water-wheel) that supplies power to drive a ~. '**~-wright** n man who builds and repairs water~s and wind~s. **2** building, factory, workshop, for industry: *a* '*cotton/*'*paper/* '*silk/*'*steel-~.* '**~-hand** n factory worker. '**~-girl** n girl who works in a ~, esp a cotton-~. **3** small machine for grinding: *a*'*coffee-~; a*'*pepper-~.*

mill² /mɪl/ vt,vi **1** [VP6A] put through a machine for grinding; produce by doing this: ~ *grain;* ~ *flour;* ~ *ore,* crush it; ~ *steel,* make it into bars. **2** [VP6A] produce regular markings on the edge of (a coin): *silver coins with a ~ed edge.* **3** [VP2C] ~ *about/around,* (of cattle, crowds of people) move in a confused way; move in a mass.

mill·board /'mɪlbɔ:d/ n [U] stout pasteboard used in binding books.

mil·len·nium /mɪ'lenɪəm/ n (pl -nia /-nɪə/, ~s) **1** period of 1000 years. **2** (fig) future time of great happiness and prosperity for everyone. **mil·lenarian** /,mɪlɪ'neərɪən/ n person who believes that the ~(2) will come.

mil·le·pede /'mɪlɪpi:d/ n small worm-like creature with very many legs, usu in double pairs at each segment. ⇨ the illus at insect.

mil·ler /'mɪlə(r)/ n owner or tenant of a mill, esp the old-fashioned flour-mill worked by wind or water.

mil·let /'mɪlɪt/ n [U] cereal plant growing 3 to 4 feet high and producing a large crop of small seeds; the seeds (as food).

milli- /'mɪlɪ/ pref (in the metric system) one-thousandth part of: '*~gram;*'*~metre.* ⇨ App 5.

mil·liard /'mɪlɪɑ:d/ n (GB) thousand millions (1000000000) (US = *billion*). ⇨ App 4.

mil·li·bar /'mɪlɪbɑ:(r)/ n unit of atmospheric pressure.

mil·liner /'mɪlɪnə(r)/ n person who makes and sells women's hats, and sells lace, trimmings, etc for hats. **~y** /-nərɪ US: -nerɪ/ n [U] (the business of making and selling) women's hats, with lace, ribbons, etc.

mil·lion /'mɪlɪən/ n, adj one thousand thousand (1000000). (Note: the pl is rarely used after a number): ~s *of pounds; six* ~ *people.* **make a ~,** make a ~ pounds/dollars, etc. **~·aire** /,mɪlɪə'neə(r)/ n person who has a ~ dollars, pounds, etc: extremely rich man. '**~·fold** adv a ~ times. **mil·lionth** /-lɪənθ/ n, adj ⇨ App 4.

mil·li·pede /'mɪlɪpi:d/ = millepede.

mil·ometer /maɪ'lɒmɪtə(r)/ n = mileometer. ⇨ mile.

mi·lord /mɪ'lɔ:d/ n (F word formerly used for) English lord; wealthy Englishman.

milt /mɪlt/ n [U] (soft) roe of male fish; fish sperm.

mime /maɪm/ n [U] (in the theatre, etc) use of only facial expressions and gestures to tell a story; [C] such a performance; actor in such drama. □ vi,vt **1** [VP2A] act in a ~. **2** [VP6A] express by ~.

mimeo·graph /'mɪmɪəgrɑ:f US: -græf/ n apparatus for making copies of written or typed material from a stencil. □ vt [VP6A] make (copies) with a ~.

mi·metic /mɪ'metɪk/ adj of, given to, imitation or mimicry.

mimic /'mɪmɪk/ attrib adj imitated or pretended: ~ *warfare,* as in peacetime manoeuvres; ~ *colouring,* eg of animals, birds and insects that have the colours of their natural surroundings. □ n person who is clever at imitating others, esp in order to make fun of their habits, appearance, etc. □ vt (pt,pp ~ked) [VP6A] **1** ridicule by imitating: *He was ~king his uncle's voice and gestures very cleverly.* **2** (of things) resemble closely: *wood painted to ~ marble.* **~ry** n [U] ~king: *protective ~ry,* the resemblance of birds, animals and insects to their natural surroundings, giving some protection from enemies.

mim·osa /mɪ'məʊzə US: -'məʊsə/ n [U,C] shrub with clusters of small, ball-shaped, sweet-smelling yellow flowers.

min·a·ret /ˌmɪnəˈret/ n tall, slender spire, connected with a mosque, from the balconies of which people are called to prayer by a muezzin (or, often today, by loudspeaker). ⇨ the illus at mosque.

mina·tory /ˈmɪnətərɪ/ US: -tɔːrɪ/ adj threatening.

mince /mɪns/ vt,vi 1 [VP6A] cut or chop (meat, etc) into small pieces (with a knife, or a machine with revolving blades, called a 'mincing machine or mincer). not to '∼ matters/∼ one's 'words, to speak plainly or bluntly in condemnation of sth or sb; not to take pains to keep within the bounds of politeness. 2 [VP6A] say (words) with an affectation of delicacy; [VP2A] put on fine airs when speaking or walking, trying to appear delicate or refined. □ n minced meat. '∼-meat n [U] mixture of currants, raisins, sugar, candied peel, apples, suet, etc for a ∼-pie. make ∼meat of, (colloq) defeat a person/an argument, etc. ∼-'pie n small round pie containing ∼meat. mincer n device for mincing food. 'minc·ing adj take mincing steps; an affected, mincing young girl, ⇨ 2 above. 'minc·ing·ly adv

mind¹ /maɪnd/ n 1 [U] memory; remembrance. bear/keep sth in ∼, remember sth. bring/call sth to ∼, recall it to the memory. go/pass from/out of one's ∼, be forgotten. put sb in ∼ of sth, remind sb of, cause sb to think of sth. Out of sight, out of ∼, (prov) What is not seen is soon forgotten. 2 [U] (but with indef art or pl in some phrases, as shown below) what a person thinks or feels; way of thinking; conscious thoughts; feeling, wishing; opinion; intention; purpose: Nothing was further from his ∼, his intentions. absence of ∼, failure to think of what one is doing. ⇨ absent-minded at absent¹. presence of ∼, ability to act or decide quickly when this is needed. be out of one's ∼/not in one's right ∼, mad. be of one ∼ (about sth), be in agreement; have the same opinion. be of the same ∼, (a) (of a number of persons) be in agreement. (b) (of one person) be unchanged in an opinion, decision, etc: Is he still of the same ∼? be in two ∼s about sth, feel doubtful, hesitate, about sth. bend one's ∼, influence the ∼ so that it is permanently affected (by beliefs, etc). Hence, '∼-bending adj blow one's ∼, (colloq) (of drugs, extraordinary or sensational sights, sounds, etc) cause mental excitement, state of ecstasy, etc. Hence, '∼-blowing adj '∼-boggling adj alarming; extraordinary. change one's ∼, change one's purpose or intention. give one's ∼ to sth, direct one's attention to sth. give sb a piece of one's ∼, ⇨ piece¹(2). have a good ∼ to do sth, be strongly disposed to do sth. have half a ∼ to do sth, be rather inclined to do sth. have sth on one's ∼, be troubled about sth which, one feels, one ought to deal with. keep one's ∼ on sth, continue to pay attention to, not be diverted from: Keep your ∼ on what you're doing. know one's own ∼, know what one wants, have no doubts: He never knows his own ∼, often doubts, hesitates, about what to do. make up one's ∼, (a) come to a decision; I've made up my ∼ to be a doctor. Have you made up your ∼ about what you'll do? (b) reconcile oneself to sth that cannot be changed, etc: We're no longer a first-class power; we must make up our ∼s to that. read sb's ∼, know what he is thinking. Hence, '∼-reading, guessing; knowing by intuition what sb is thinking. Hence, '∼-reader n set one's ∼ on sth, want very much; be determined to have:

We've set our ∼s on a holiday in France. speak one's ∼, say plainly what one thinks. take one's/sb's ∼ off sth, turn one's/sb's attention away from sth; distract from. in the ∼'s eye, in imagination; in memory. to 'my ∼, according to my way of thinking: To my ∼, this is just a nonsense. 3 [C,U] (person with) mental ability; intellect: He has a very good ∼. He has one of the great ∼s of the age. No two ∼s think alike.

mind² /maɪnd/ vt,vi 1 [VP6A,9] take care of; attend to: Who is ∼ing the baby? When Mr Green was called to the phone, his wife had to ∼ the shop, to attend to the shop. M∼ the step, Watch out for it. M∼ your head, (as a warning to stoop, eg at a low doorway). M∼ the dog, Beware of it. M∼ that you don't forget. ∼ out (for sth), be careful (of it): M∼ out! (as a warning). Could you ∼ out, please —I want to pass. When you go into the garden, remember to ∼ out for the new seedlings. ∼ one's P's and Q's, be careful and polite about what one says or does. ˌM∼ your ˌown 'business, Do not interfere in the affairs of others. ∼ 'you or ∼, used as an int meaning 'Please note': I have no objection, ∼ (you), but I think it unwise. 2 [VP6A,C,2A,19C] (usu in interr, neg and conditional sentences, and in affirm sentences that answer a question) be troubled by; feel objection to: He doesn't ∼ the cold weather at all. Do you ∼ if I smoke? Do you ∼ my smoking? Would you ∼ opening the window, Will you please do this? Would you ∼ my opening the window, Would you object if I did this? 'Do you ∼ my leaving this payment until next year?'—'Yes, I do ∼', I object to that. I shouldn't ∼ a glass of iced beer, I should like one. Never ∼, (a) It doesn't matter. (b) Don't worry about it. ∼er n person whose duty it is to attend to sth; (in compounds) ma'chine-∼er; 'baby-∼er.

minded /ˈmaɪndɪd/ adj 1 (pred only) ∼ to do sth, disposed or inclined: He could do it if he were so ∼. If she were ∼ to help,.... 2 having the kind of mind indicated (by an adj or adv prefixed): a 'strong-∼ man; 'high-∼ leaders; 'evil-∼ opponents; com'mercially-∼ men. 3 conscious of the value or importance of (what is indicated by a n prefixed): He has become very 'food-∼ since his holiday in France, has become a gourmet.

mind·ful /ˈmaɪndfl/ adj ∼ of, giving thought and attention to: ∼ of one's duties/the nation's welfare. ∼ly /-fəlɪ/ adv ∼·ness n

mind·less /ˈmaɪndlɪs/ adj 1 ∼ of, paying no attention to; forgetful of: ∼ of danger. 2 quite lacking in or not requiring intelligence: ∼ drudgery; ∼ labours. ∼·ly adv ∼·ness n

mine¹ /maɪn/ poss pron of or belonging to me: Is this book yours or ∼? He's an old 'friend of ∼, one of my old friends. □ poss adj (in poet and biblical style only, before a vowel sound or h; sometimes placed after the n) my: ∼ eyes; ∼ heart; O mistress ∼; ∼ enemy.

mine² /maɪn/ n 1 excavation with shafts, galleries, etc made in the earth from which coal, mineral ores, etc, are extracted. ⇨ quarry for stone or slate: 'coal-∼; 'gold-∼; (fig) rich or abundant source: A good encyclopaedia/My grandmother is a ∼ of information. 2 (tunnel for) charge of high explosive (as used to destroy enemy fortifications); charge of high explosive buried and exploded, eg electrically, from a distance or laid on or just below the ground, exploded by contact with a vehicle, or a time fuse, etc: *The lorry was destroyed by a buried* ∼. **3** (in war at sea) charge of high explosives in a metal case, placed in the sea, exploded on contact, or electrically, or magnetically. **4** '∼-**detector** *n* electro-magnetic device for finding ∼s(2,3). '∼-**disposal** *n* the making of ∼s harmless (by defusing them, etc): ∼-*disposal squads*. '∼-**field** *n* (a) area of land or sea where ∼s(2,3) have been laid. (b) area of land where there are many ∼s(1). '∼-**layer** *n* ship or aircraft used for laying ∼s at sea. Hence, '∼-**laying,** as in ∼-*laying vessel*. '∼-**sweeper** *n* naval vessel (usu a trawler) employed for clearing the sea of ∼s. Hence, '∼-**sweeping** *n*

mine³ /main/ *vt,vi* **1** [VP6A,2A,3A] ∼ *(for),* dig (for coal, ores, etc) from the ground; obtain (coal, etc) from mines: ∼ *(for) coal/gold;* ∼ *the earth for coal. Gold is* ∼*d from deep under ground.* **2** [VP6A] (= *undermine*) make tunnels (in the earth) under: ∼ *the enemy's trenches/forts.* **3** [VP6A] lay mines(2,3) in; destroy by means of these: ∼ *the entrance to a harbour. The cruiser was* ∼*d, and sank in five minutes.* **4** [VP6A] (fig) weaken; undermine (which is the more usu word).

miner /'mainə(r)/ *n* **1** man who works in a mine underground: '*coal*∼*s.* **2** soldier trained to dig tunnels and lay mines under enemy trenches, etc.

min·eral /'minərəl/ *n* [C] natural substance (not vegetable or animal) got from the earth by mining, esp one that has a constant chemical composition: *Coal and iron ore are* ∼*s.* □ *adj* of the class of ∼s; containing, mixed with, ∼s: ∼ *ores.* **the** ∼ **kingdom,** natural substances of inorganic matter. ⇨ animal and vegetable. '∼ **oil,** any oil of ∼ origin. '∼ **pitch,** asphalt. '∼ **water,** (a) water that naturally contains a ∼ substance, esp one said to have medicinal value. (b) (GB) non-alcoholic drink (usu bottled, often flavoured) containing soda-water. '∼ **wool,** inorganic fibrous material (used for insulating, etc).

min·er·al·ogy /,minə'rælədʒi/ *n* [U] the study and science of minerals. **min·er·al·ogist** /,minə'rælədʒist/ *n* student of ∼.

min·estrone /,mini'strəuni/ *n* [U] (I) rich soup (of Italian origin) of mixed vegetables, vermicelli and meat broth.

mingle /'miŋgl/ *vt,vi* [VP6A,14,2A,C] ∼ *(with),* mix: *truth* ∼*d with falsehood;* ∼ *with* (= go about among) *the crowds; two rivers that join and* ∼ *their waters.*

mingy /'mindʒi/ *adj* (-ier, -iest) (GB colloq) mean, ungenerous, stingy: *a* ∼ *fellow.*

mini- /'mini/ *pref* of small size, length, etc. ⇨ maxi-: '∼*bus;* '∼*cab;* '∼*skirt;* '∼*tour.*

minia·ture /'minitʃə(r) US: -tʃuər/ *n* **1** [C] very small painting of a person, esp one on ivory or vellum; [U] this branch of painting. *in* ∼, on a small scale. **2** [C] small-scale copy or model of any object. **3** (attrib) on a small scale: *a* ∼ *railway; a* ∼ *camera,* one for 35 mm or sub-standard size of film. **minia·tur·ist** /'minitʃərist/ *n* painter of ∼s.

minim /'minim/ *n* (music) note half the value of a semibreve. ⇨ the illus at notation.

mini·mal /'miniml/ *adj* smallest in amount or degree: *On these cliffs vegetation is* ∼.

mini·mize /'minimaiz/ *vt* [VP6A] reduce to, estimate at, the smallest possible amount or degree: ∼ *an accident,* try to reduce its importance, say that it is not serious.

mini·mum /'miniməm/ *n, adj* (*pl* -ma /-mə/, ∼s)

(opposite of *maximum*) (of) least possible or recorded amount, degree, etc: *reduce sth to a* ∼; *the* ∼ *temperature; a maximum and* ∼ *thermometer; a* ∼ *wage,* lowest wage that regulations allow to be paid.

min·ing /'mainiŋ/ *n* the process of getting minerals, etc from mines: *a* '∼ *engineer; the* '∼ *industry; open-cast* ∼, getting coal, etc that is near the surface, using mechanical shovels, etc.

min·ion /'miniən/ *n* (derog) servant who, in order to win favour, obeys a master slavishly. **the** ∼ **s of the law,** police, jailers.

min·is·ter¹ /'ministə(r)/ *n* **1** person at the head of a Department of State (and often a member of the Cabinet): *the M*∼ *of Employment and Productivity; the Prime M*∼. **2** person representing his Government in a foreign country of lower rank than an ambassador. **3** Christian priest or clergyman, esp one in the Presbyterian and Noncomformist Churches. Cf *priest* for the RC Church, and *vicar, rector, curate* for the Church of England.

min·is·ter² /'ministə(r)/ *vi* [VP3A] ∼ *to,* give help or service: ∼ *to the wants of a sick man;* ∼*ing to her husband's needs,* satisfying them.

min·is·ter·ial /,mini'stiəriəl/ *adj* **1** of a Minister of State, his position, duties, etc: ∼ *functions/duties.* **2** of or for a ministry(1) (or Cabinet): *the* ∼ *benches.* ∼**ly** /-riəli/ *adv*

min·is·trant /'ministrənt/ *attrib adj* (formal) administering. □ *n* attendant; supporter or helper.

min·is·tra·tion /,mini'streiʃn/ *n* [U] ministering or serving, eg in performing a religious service; [C] act of this kind: *Thanks to the* ∼*s* (= nursing, services) *of my devoted wife, I was restored to health.*

min·is·try /'ministri/ *n* (*pl* -ries) **1** Department of State under a Minister: *the* '*Air M*∼; *the* ,*M*∼ *of* '*Finance.* **2** **the** ∼, the ministers of religion as a body: *He was intended for the* ∼, destined to be a minister, eg by his parents. **enter the** ∼, become a minister of religion. **3** [C] office, duties, term of service, of a minister of religion.

mini·ver /'minivə(r)/ *n* [U] ermine fur (as for the ceremonial robes of peers).

mink /miŋk/ *n* [C,U] (valuable brown fur skin of a) small stoat-like animal: (attrib) *a* ∼ *coat.*

min·now /'minəu/ *n* (sorts of) very small freshwater fish.

mi·nor /'mainə(r)/ *adj* **1** smaller, less important: ∼ *repairs/alterations; a broken leg and* ∼ *injuries.* **2** comparatively unimportant: *the* ∼ *planets,* the asteroids; ∼ *poets; play only a* ∼ *part in the play;* (cards) *a* ∼ *suit,* ie diamonds or clubs. **3** (in schools) second or younger of two boys (esp in the same school): *Smith* ∼. **4** (music) *a* ∼ *third,* an interval of three semi-tones; *a* ∼ *key,* in which the scale has a ∼ third. *in a* ∼ *key,* (fig) in a melancholy or depressed mood. ⇨ major. □ *n* (legal) person not yet legally of age.

mi·nor·ity /mai'nɒrəti US: -'nɔːr-/ *n* (*pl* -ties) **1** [U] (legal) the state of being under age (in GB under 18). **2** [C] the smaller number or part, esp of a total of votes; small racial, religious, etc group in a community, nation, etc. **be in a/the** ∼, be in the smaller of two groups: *We're in the* ∼, More people are against us than with us. *I'm in a* ∼ *of one,* have had support from no one. '∼ **government,** one which has a ∼ of the total number of seats in a legislative assembly. '∼ **programme,** (TV, radio) one viewed or listened to by a comparatively small proportion of the total viewers or listeners. '~ **report**, one made (after an official inquiry or investigation) by the ~, giving views, etc, different from those of the majority.

Mino·taur /'maɪnətɔː(r)/ *n* **the ~**, (Gk myth) monster, half man and half bull, fed with human flesh, kept in the labyrinth in Crete.

a centaur

the Minotaur

min·ster /'mɪnstə(r)/ *n* large or important church, esp one that once belonged to a monastery: *York ~.*

min·strel /'mɪnstrəl/ *n* **1** (in the Middle Ages) travelling composer, player and singer of songs and ballads. **2** one of a company of public entertainers. ~**sy** /'mɪnstrəlsɪ/ *n* [U] the art, songs, etc, of ~**s**(1).

mint¹ /mɪnt/ *n* [U] (sorts of) plant whose leaves are used for flavouring (eg in drinks and in chewinggum) and in making a sauce: ~ *sauce*, chopped-up ~ *leaves*, in vinegar and sugar, as eaten with lamb.

mint² /mɪnt/ *n* **1** place where coins are made, usu under State authority: *coins fresh from the ~.* **2** *make/earn a* ~ *(of money)*, (colloq) a large amount. **3** (attrib, of medals, stamps, prints, books, etc) unused. *in ~ condition*, as if new; unsoiled; perfect. □ *vt* [VP6A] **1** make (coin) by stamping metal: ~ *coins of 50p.* **2** (fig) invent a word, phrase, etc.

min·uet /ˌmɪnjʊ'et/ *n* [C] (piece of music for a) slow, graceful dance for groups of two couples (dating from the middle of the 17th c).

minus /'maɪnəs/ *adj* **1 the '~ sign**, the sign −. ⇨ plus. **2** ⇨ positive. negative: *a ~ quantity*, a quantity less than zero (eg −2x²). □ *prep* less; with the deduction of: *7 ~ 3 is 4;* (colloq) without: *He came back from the war ~ a leg.* □ *n* ~ sign or quantity.

min·us·cule /'mɪnəskjuːl/ *adj* tiny; very small.

min·ute¹ /'mɪnɪt/ *n* **1** the sixtieth part of one hour: *seven ~s to six; arrive ten ~s early.* ⇨ App 4. '~**-gun** *n* one fired at intervals of a ~, eg at a grand funeral. '~**-hand** *n* hand indicating the ~s on a watch or clock. '~**-man** /-mən/ *n* (*pl*-men) (US hist) militiaman ready to fight at a minute's notice. *in a ~*, soon: *I'll come downstairs in a ~. to the ~*, exactly: *The train arrived at 5 o'clock to the ~. the ~ (that)*, as soon as: *I'll give him your message the ~ (that) he arrives. up to the ~*, most recent or fashionable. ,**up-to-the-'~** *attrib adj* most recent or fashionable: *up-to-the-~ information/hairstyles.* **2** the sixtieth part of a degree (in an angle): *37° 30′*, 37 degrees 30 ~s. **3** [C] official record giving authority, advice or making comments: *make a ~ of sth.* **4** (*pl*) summary, records, of what is said and decided at a meeting, esp of a society or committee: *read and confirm the ~s of the last meeting.* '~**-book** *n* book in which ~s are written. □ *vt* [VP6A] record (sth) in the ~s(4); make a record of sth in a memorandum.

mi·nute² /maɪ'njuːt *US:* -'nuːt/ *adj* **1** very small: ~ *particles of gold dust.* **2** giving small details; careful and exact: *a ~ description; the ~st details.* ~**·ly** *adv* ~**·ness** *n*

mi·nu·tiae /maɪ'njuːʃiː *US:* mɪ'nuːʃiː/ *n pl* precise or trivial details.

minx /mɪŋks/ *n* sly, impudent girl.

mir·acle /'mɪrəkl/ *n* **1** act or event (sth good or welcome) which does not follow the known laws of nature; remarkable and surprising event: *work/ accomplish ~s. Her life was saved by a ~.* The doctors said that her recovery was a ~. '~ *play*, dramatic representation (in the Middle Ages) based on the life of Jesus or the Christian saints. **2** ~ *of*, remarkable example or specimen: *It's a ~ of ingenuity.* **mir·acu·lous** /mɪ'rækjʊləs/ *adj* like a ~; contrary to the laws of nature; surprising. **mir·acu·lous·ly** *adv*

mi·rage /'mɪrɑːʒ *US:* mɪ'rɑːʒ/ *n* [C] **1** effect, produced by hot air conditions, causing an optical illusion, esp the illusive appearance of a sheet of water eg in the desert. **2** (fig) any illusion or hope that cannot be realized.

mire /'maɪə(r)/ *n* [U] swampy ground; soft, deep mud. *be in the ~*, (fig) be in difficulties. *drag sb/sb's name through the ~*, bring disgrace on him, expose him to contempt. □ *vt,vi* **1** [VP6A] cover with mud; cause to be fast in deep mud. **2** [VP2A] sink in mud. **3** [VP6A] (fig) involve (sb) in difficulties. **miry** /'maɪərɪ/ *adj* muddy: *miry roads.*

mir·ror /'mɪrə(r)/ *n* **1** polished surface that reflects images: *a 'driving ~, ~ in a motor-car to enable the driver to see what is behind him. ~ 'image*, reflection or copy of sth with the right and left sides reversed. **2** (fig) sth that reflects or gives a likeness: *Pepys's 'Diary' is a ~ of the times he lived in.* □ *vt* [VP6A] (lit or fig) reflect as in a ~: *The still water of the lake ~ed the hillside.*

mirth /mɜːθ/ *n* [U] being merry, happy and bright; laughter. ~**·ful** /-fl/ *adj* full of ~; merry. ~**·fully** /-fəlɪ/ *adv* ~**·less** *adj* without ~: *a ~less laugh.*

mis·ad·ven·ture /ˌmɪsəd'ventʃə(r)/ *n* [C,U] (event caused by) bad luck; misfortune. *death by ~*, by accident.

mis·ad·vise /ˌmɪsəd'vaɪz/ *vt* [VP6A] (usu passive) advise wrongly.

mis·al·liance /ˌmɪsə'laɪəns/ *n* unsuitable alliance, esp marriage; mésalliance.

mis·an·thrope /'mɪsənθrəʊp/ *n* person who hates mankind; person who avoids society. **mis·an·thropic** /ˌmɪsn'θrɒpɪk/ *adj* hating or distrusting mankind or human society. **mis·an·thropy** /mɪs'ænθrəpɪ/ *n* [U] hatred of mankind.

mis·apply /ˌmɪsə'plaɪ/ *vt* (*pt,pp* -lied) [VP6A] apply wrongly; use for a wrong purpose, eg public funds. **mis·ap·pli·ca·tion** /ˌmɪsæplɪ'keɪʃn/ *n* wrong or unjust use (*of*).

mis·ap·pre·hend /ˌmɪsæprɪ'hend/ *vt* [VP6A] misunderstand. **mis·ap·pre·hen·sion** /ˌmɪsæprɪ'henʃn/ *n do sth/be under a misapprehension*, do sth because of/have a failure to understand correctly.

mis·ap·pro·pri·ate /ˌmɪsə'prəʊprɪeɪt/ *vt* [VP6A] take and use wrongly; apply (sb else's money) to a wrong (esp one's own) use: *The treasurer ~d the society's funds.* **mis·ap·pro·pri·ation** /ˌmɪsəˌprəʊprɪ'eɪʃn/ *n: misappropriation of public funds.*

mis·be·got·ten /ˌmɪsbɪ'gɒtn/ *adj* illegitimate; bastard; (colloq, as a term of scorn): *Who's the* *author of these* ~ (= ill-advised, worthless) *plans?*

mis·be·have /ˌmɪsbɪ'heɪv/ *vt,vi* [VP6B,2A] behave (oneself) improperly. **mis·be·hav·iour** (US = -**ior**) /ˌmɪsbɪ'heɪvɪə(r)/ *n*

mis·cal·cu·late /ˌmɪs'kælkjʊleɪt/ *vt,vi* calculate (amounts, etc) wrongly. **mis·cal·cu·la·tion** /ˌmɪskælkjʊ'leɪʃn/ *n*

mis·call /ˌmɪs'kɔːl/ *vt* call by a wrong name: *King Robert, ~ed 'the Just'.*

mis·car·riage /ˌmɪs'kærɪdʒ/ *n* 1 [U] ~ *of justice,* failure of a court to administer justice properly; mistake in judgement or in punishment; [C] instance of this. 2 [U] failure to deliver to, or arrive at, the destination: ~ *of goods;* [C] instance of this. 3 [U] premature expulsion of a foetus from the womb; [C] instance of this: *have a ~.*

mis·carry /ˌmɪs'kærɪ/ *vt* (*pt,pp* -ried) [VP2A] 1 (of plans, etc) fail; have a result different from what was hoped for. 2 (of letters, etc) fail to reach the right destination. 3 (of a woman) have a miscarriage(3).

mis·cast /ˌmɪs'kɑːst US:* -'kæst/ *vt* (*pt,pp* miscast) [VP6A] (usu passive) 1 (of an actor) be cast for a role for which he is unfitted: *She was badly ~ as Juliet.* ⇨ cast¹(6). 2 (of a play) have the parts badly allocated to the actors and actresses.

mis·cegen·ation /ˌmɪsɪdʒɪ'neɪʃn/ *n* [U] mixture of races; the production of offspring by the sexual union of two people of different races.

mis·cel·lan·eous /ˌmɪsə'leɪnɪəs/ *adj* of mixed sorts; having various qualities and characteristics: *a ~ collection of goods;* Milton's ~ *prose works.* **mis·cel·lany** /mɪ'selənɪ US:* 'mɪsəleɪnɪ/ *n* (*pl* - nies) collection, eg of writings on various subjects by various authors. **mis·cel·lanea** /ˌmɪsə'leɪnɪə/ *n pl* literary miscellany.

mis·chance /ˌmɪs'tʃɑːns US:* -'tʃæns/ *n* [C,U] (piece of) bad luck: *by ~; through a ~.*

mis·chief /'mɪstʃɪf/ *n* 1 [U] injury or damage done by a person or other agent, esp on purpose: *a storm that did much ~ to shipping.* **do sb a ~,** hurt him. 2 [U] moral harm or injury: *Such wild speeches may work great ~,* eg may rouse evil passions. **make ~ (between...),** cause discord or ill feeling. Hence, '~-maker, '~-making. 3 [U] foolish or thoughtless behaviour likely to cause trouble; not very serious wrongdoing: *Boys are fond of ~,* of playing tricks, etc. *Tell the children to keep out of ~. He's up to ~ again,* planning some piece of ~. *She's always getting into ~.* 4 light-hearted, innocent desire to tease: *Her eyes were full of ~.* 5 [C] person who is fond of ~(3,4): *Those boys are regular ~s. Where have you hidden my book, you little ~?*

mis·chiev·ous /'mɪstʃɪvəs/ *adj* 1 causing mischief (2); harmful: *a ~ letter/rumour.* 2 filled with, fond of, engaged in, mischief(3,4); showing a spirit of mischief (3,4): ~ *looks/tricks; as ~ as a monkey.* ~·ly *adv* ~·ness *n*

mis·con·ceive /ˌmɪskən'siːv/ *vt,vi* 1 [VP6A] understand wrongly. 2 [VP3A] ~ *of,* have a wrong conception of: ~ *of one's duty.* **mis·con·cep·tion** /ˌmɪskən'sepʃn/ *n* [U] misconceiving; [C] instance of this.

mis·con·duct /ˌmɪs'kɒndʌkt/ *n* [U] 1 improper behaviour. 2 bad management. □ *vt* /ˌmɪskən'dʌkt/ 1 [VP6B,14] ~ *oneself (with sb),* behave badly. 2 [VP6A] manage badly: ~ *one's business affairs.*

mis·con·struc·tion /ˌmɪskən'strʌkʃn/ *n* [U] false

or inaccurate interpretation or understanding; [C] instance of this: *Your words were open to ~.*

mis·con·strue /ˌmɪskən'struː/ *vt* [VP6A] get a wrong idea of (sb's words, acts, etc): *You have ~d my words.*

mis·count /ˌmɪs'kaʊnt/ *vt,vi* [VP6A,2A] count wrongly. □ *n* [C] wrong count, esp of votes at an election.

mis·cre·ant /'mɪskrɪənt/ *n* (dated) scoundrel; villain.

mis·date /ˌmɪs'deɪt/ *vt* [VP6A] give a wrong date to an event, etc; put a wrong date on a letter, cheque, etc.

mis·deal /ˌmɪs'diːl/ *vt,vi* (*pt,pp* -dealt /-'delt/) [VP6A,2A] deal (playing-cards) wrongly. □ *n* error in dealing cards: *I've got 14 cards; it's a ~.*

mis·deed /ˌmɪs'diːd/ *n* wicked act; crime: *be punished for one's ~s.*

mis·de·mean·our (US = -**meanor**) /ˌmɪsdɪ'miːnə(r)/ *n* (legal) offence less serious than a felony.

mis·di·rect /ˌmɪsdɪ'rekt/ *vt* [VP6A] direct wrongly: ~ *a letter,* by failing to put the full or correct address on it; ~ *one's energies or abilities,* eg by using them for a bad purpose; ~ *a jury,* (of a judge in a law court) give the jury wrong information on a point of law. **mis·di·rec·tion** /ˌmɪsdɪ'rekʃn/ *n*

mis·doing /ˌmɪs'duːɪŋ/ *n* (usu *pl*) misdeed.

mise en scène /ˌmiːz ɒn 'seɪn/ *n* scenery and properties of an acted play; (fig) general surroundings of an event.

miser /'maɪzə(r)/ *n* person who loves wealth for its own sake and spends as little as possible. ~·ly *adj* like a ~; stingy. ~·li·ness *n*

mis·er·able /'mɪzrəbl/ *adj* 1 wretched; very unhappy: ~ *from cold and hunger; the ~ lives of the refugees in Europe after the war. He makes her life ~.* 2 causing wretchedness and unhappiness: ~ *weather;* ~ *slums.* 3 poor in quality: *What a ~ meal! What a ~ pension after fifty years' hard work!* **mis·er·ably** /-əblɪ/ *adv: die miserably; be miserably poor; miserably underpaid.*

mis·ery /'mɪzərɪ/ *n* (*pl* -ries) 1 [U] state of being miserable; great suffering (of mind or body): *be in a ~/suffer ~ from the toothache; living in ~ and want,* in wretched conditions and poverty. *put the animal out of its ~,* end its sufferings by killing it. 2 (*pl*) painful happenings; great misfortunes: *the miseries of mankind.* 3 (colloq) person who is always miserable and complaining: *I've had enough of your complaints, you little ~!*

mis·fire /ˌmɪs'faɪə(r)/ *vi* [VP2A] (of a gun) fail to go off; (of a motor-engine) fail to ignite in a cylinder; (colloq of a joke, etc) fall flat; fail to have the intended result. □ *n* such a failure.

mis·fit /'mɪsfɪt/ *n* article of clothing which does not fit well the person it is meant for; (fig) person not well suited to his position or his associates.

mis·for·tune /ˌmɪs'fɔːtʃuːn/ *n* 1 [U] bad luck: *suffer* ~; *companions in ~.* 2 [C] instance of bad luck; unfortunate accident or happening: *He bore his ~s bravely.*

mis·give /ˌmɪs'gɪv/ *vt* (*pt* misgave /-'geɪv/, *pp* misgiven /-'gɪvn/) (used impersonally; old use) *My mind/heart ~s me,* I am filled with suspicion or foreboding, I feel doubtful, troubled. **mis·giv·ing** /ˌmɪs'gɪvɪŋ/ *n* [C,U] (feeling of) doubt, suspicion, distrust, etc: *a heart/mind full of misgiving(s).*

mis·gov·ern /ˌmɪs'gʌvn/ *vt* [VP6A] govern (the

State, etc) badly. ~ment n [U].

mis·guide /ˌmɪsˈgaɪd/ vt [VP6A,14] give wrong or misleading information or directions to: *We had been ~d into thinking that....* **mis·guided** adj foolish and wrong (because of bad or wrong guidance or influence): ~d *conduct/zeal;* ~d *boys.*

mis·handle /ˌmɪsˈhændl/ vt deal with roughly, rudely or inefficiently.

mis·hap /ˈmɪshæp/ n [C] unlucky accident: *meet with a slight ~; arrive home after many ~s;* [U] bad luck; accident: *arrive without ~.*

mish·mash /ˈmɪʃmæʃ/ n [U] confused mixture; hotchpotch.

mis·in·form /ˌmɪsɪnˈfɔːm/ vt [VP6A] give wrong information to; mislead: *You've been ~ed.*

mis·in·ter·pret /ˌmɪsɪnˈtɜːprɪt/ vt [VP6A] give a wrong interpretation to; make a wrong inference from: *He ~ed her silence as giving consent.*

mis·judge /ˌmɪsˈdʒʌdʒ/ vt,vi [VP6A,2A] judge or estimate wrongly; form a wrong opinion of: *You have ~d my motives. He ~d the distance and fell into the stream.*

mis·lay /ˌmɪsˈleɪ/ vt (pt,pp mislaid /-ˈleɪd/) [VP6A] put (sth) by an oversight where it cannot easily be found: *I've mislaid my passport.*

mis·lead /ˌmɪsˈliːd/ vt (pt,pp misled /-ˈled/) [VP6A] lead wrongly; cause to be or do wrong; give a wrong idea to: *be misled by a guide,* during a journey; *misled by bad companions,* led into evil ways. *You misled me as to your intentions. This information is rather ~ing,* gives a wrong impression.

mis·man·age /ˌmɪsˈmænɪdʒ/ vt [VP6A] manage badly or wrongly. ~ment n

mis·name /ˌmɪsˈneɪm/ vt [VP6A] (usu passive) call by a wrong or improper name.

mis·nomer /ˌmɪsˈnəʊmə(r)/ n [C] wrong use of a name or word: *It's a ~ to call this place a first-class hotel.*

mis·ogyn·ist /mɪˈsɒdʒɪnɪst/ n hater of women.

mis·place /ˌmɪsˈpleɪs/ vt [VP6A] **1** put in a wrong place. **2** (usu passive) give love, affection wrongly or unwisely: ~d *confidence,* given to sb who does not deserve it or who misuses it.

mis·print /ˌmɪsˈprɪnt/ vt [VP6A] (make an) error in printing, eg *errors and omissions expected* for *errors and omissions excepted.* □ n /ˈmɪsprɪnt/ such an error.

mis·pro·nounce /ˌmɪsprəˈnaʊns/ vt [VP6A] pronounce wrongly. **mis·pro·nun·ci·ation** /ˌmɪsprəˌnʌnsɪˈeɪʃn/ n

mis·quote /ˌmɪsˈkwəʊt/ vt [VP6A] quote wrongly. **mis·quo·ta·tion** /ˌmɪskwəʊˈteɪʃn/ n [C,U].

mis·read /ˌmɪsˈriːd/ vt (pt,pp misread /-ˈred/) [VP6A] read or interpret wrongly: ~ *one's instructions.*

mis·rep·re·sent /ˌmɪsˌreprɪˈzent/ vt represent wrongly; give a false account of: *be grossly ~ed by the press.* **mis·rep·re·sen·ta·tion** /ˌmɪsˌreprɪzenˈteɪʃn/ n [C,U].

mis·rule /ˌmɪsˈruːl/ n [U] bad government; lawlessness; confusion.

miss¹ /mɪs/ n [C] failure to hit, catch, reach, etc: *ten hits and one ~. That was a lucky ~,* a fortunate escape. **give sth a ~,** (colloq) omit it, leave it alone: *I'll give the fish course a ~.* **A ~ is as good as a mile,** (prov) A narrow escape is the same in effect as an escape by a wide margin.

miss² /mɪs/ n **1** M~, title prefixed to the (first name +) surname of an unmarried woman: *M~*

(*Gloria*) *Kelly.* M~ Jamaica, eg as the title of a beauty queen. **2** (small *m,* usu playful or perhaps derog) young girl, schoolgirl: *She's a saucy ~.* **3** (as a vocative, eg by schoolchildren to a woman teacher, also to shopkeepers, etc): *Good morning, ~! Two cups of coffee, ~.* **4** (trade use, pl) young girls: *shoes, coats, etc for Junior M~es,* (today, often replaced by *teenagers*).

miss³ /mɪs/ vt,vi (pt,pp missed) **1** [VP6A,B,C,2A] fail to hit, hold, catch, reach, see, etc what it is desired to hit, hold, etc: *fire at a tiger and ~ (it); ~ one's aim; ~ the target.* He ~ed his footing, slipped, eg while climbing on rocks. *He ~ed the 9.30 train* (= was too late for it, did not catch it), *and therefore ~ed* (ie luckily escaped) *the accident. The house is at the next corner; you can't ~ it,* you'll certainly see it. *He ~ed* (= failed to see) *the point of my joke. I ~ed* (= did not hear) *the first part of the speech. We only just ~ed* (= escaped) *having a nasty accident. We ~ed seeing* (= didn't see, failed to see) *that film when it was at the local cinema.* **2** [VP6A] realize, learn, feel regret at, the absence of: *When did you ~ your purse,* realize that you no longer had it? *He's so rich that he wouldn't ~ £100. She'd ~ her husband if he died. Old Smith won't be ~ed,* Nobody will feel regret in his absence, death, retirement, etc. **3** [VP2C] ~ **out (on sth),** (colloq) lose an opportunity to benefit from sth, enjoy oneself: *If I don't go to the party, I shall feel that I'm ~ing out. I ~ed out on his offer of a free holiday in Spain.* [VP15B] ~ **sth out,** omit; fail to put in or say: *The printers have ~ed out a word/line. I shall ~ out the sweet course,* ie at a meal, not take it. *When we sing this song, ~ out the second and fourth verses,* don't sing them. ~-**ing** adj not to be found; not in the place where it ought to be: *a book with two pages ~ing; the dead, wounded and ~ing,* ie soldiers in war; ~ing *persons,* persons who cannot be traced. **the ~ing link.** ⇨ link¹(1).

mis·sal /ˈmɪsl/ n book containing the order of service for Mass in the RC Church; book of prayers and devotions.

mis·shapen /ˌmɪsˈʃeɪpən/ adj (esp of the body or a limb) deformed; badly shaped.

mis·sile /ˈmɪsaɪl US: ˈmɪsl/ n object or weapon that is thrown (eg a stone), shot (eg an arrow) or projected (eg a rocket): (attrib) ~ *sites/bases,* for ballistic ~s, etc. **guided** ~, eg from ground to air, for destroying aircraft, guided by electronic devices. **inter–continental ballistic** ~ (abbr **ICBM**), long-range rocket with a warhead.

mission /ˈmɪʃn/ n **1** (the sending out of a) number of persons entrusted with special work, usu abroad: *a trade ~ to S America; go/come/send sb on a ~ of inquiry; complete one's ~ successfully.* **2** (the sending out of) religious teachers (~aries) to convert people by preaching, teaching, etc: *Foreign M~s; Home M~s,* ie to preach to people in the home country, esp those not usu interested in religion. **3** place where the work of a ~(2) is carried on; building(s), organization, etc needed for such work; settlement where charitable or medical work is carried on, esp among poor people. **4** ~ **in life,** that work which a person feels called upon to do: *She feels her ~ in life is to reform juvenile delinquents.* **5** (esp US) special task, assigned to an individual or a unit of the armed forces: *The group has flown twenty ~s.*

mission·ary /ˈmɪʃənrɪ US: -nerɪ/ n (pl -ries) person sent to preach his religion, esp among people who are ignorant of it; (attrib) of missions(2) or missionaries: *a ~ meeting*, at which a ~ talks about his work or one held to raise funds; *a ~ box*, in which money is collected for charitable missions.

mis·sis /'mɪsɪz/ *n* ⇨ missus.

mis·sive /'mɪsɪv/ *n* (used hum for) (esp a long, serious-looking) letter.

mis·spell /ˌmɪs'spel/ *vt* (*pt,pp* misspelled or misspelt /-'spelt/) [VP6A] spell wrongly. **~·ing** *n*

mis·spend /ˌmɪs'spend/ *vt* (*pt,pp* misspent /-'spent/) [VP6A] spend or use wrongly or foolishly (esp *pp*): *a misspent youth*, (used of one who spends or has spent his early years only in foolish pleasures).

mis·state /ˌmɪs'steɪt/ *vt* [VP6A] state wrongly: *He was careful not to ~ his case*. **~ment** *n*

mis·sus, mis·sis /'mɪsɪz/ *n* (colloq or sl) (used with *the, my, his, your*) wife: *How's the ~? My ~ won't like that.*

missy /'mɪsɪ/ *n* (*pl* -sies) (colloq, familiar) young girl; Miss: *Well, ~, what do you want?*

mist /mɪst/ *n* **1** [C,U] (occasion when there is, an area with) water vapour in the air, at or near the earth's surface, less thick than fog and not so light as haze: *Hills hidden/shrouded in ~;* (fig) *lost in the ~s of time;* such vapour condensed on a surface, eg glass, clouding its appearance. **2** [C] filmy appearance before the eyes (caused by tears, etc); (fig) sth that darkens the mind, makes understanding difficult, etc: *see things through a ~.* □ *vi,vt* [VP2C,6A] ~ (*over*), cover, be covered, with ~: *The scene ~ed over. The mirror ~ed over. Her eyes (were) ~ed with tears.* **~y** *adj* (-ier, iest) **1** with ~: *a ~y evening; ~y weather; a ~y view.* **2** not clear: *have only a ~y idea.* **~·ily** /-ɪlɪ/ *adv* **~·i·ness** *n*

mis·take¹ /mɪ'steɪk/ *n* [C] wrong opinion, idea or act: *spelling ~s. We all make ~s occasionally. There's some ~! There must be some ~! by ~,* as the result of carelessness, forgetfulness, etc; in error: *I took your umbrella by ~. and no ~,* (colloq) without any doubt: *It's hot today and no ~!*

mis·take² /mɪ'steɪk/ *vt,vi* (*pt* mistook /mɪ'stʊk/, *pp* mistaken /mɪ'steɪkn/) **1** [VP6A,10] be wrong, have a wrong idea, about: ~ *sb's meaning. We've ~n the house*, come to the wrong house. ***There's no mistaking***, no possibility of being wrong about: *There's no mistaking what ought to be done.* **2** [VP14] ~ *sb/sth for*, wrongly suppose that sb or sth is (sb or sth else): *Don Quixote mistook the windmills for giants. She is often ~n for her twin sister.* **3** (older uses) *If I ~ not*, unless I am wrong. *You ~, my dear*, you're wrong. **mis·taken** (*pp* as) *adj* **1** in error; wrong in opinion: *a case of ~n identity; ~n ideas. be ~n (about sth)*, be in error: *If I'm not ~n, there's the man we met on the train. Your're ~n.* **2** ill-judged: *~n kindness/ zeal.* **mis·tak·en·ly** *adv*

mis·ter /'mɪstə(r)/ *n* **1** (always written **Mr**) title prefixed to a man's (first name +) surname when he has no other title: *Mr (Henry) Green*, or to his office: *Mr Secretary.* ⇨ Mrs; Ms. **2** (used without a person's name; sl, or used by children): *Listen to me, ~. Please, ~, can I have my ball back?*

mis·time /ˌmɪs'taɪm/ *vt* (used esp in the *pp*) say or do sth out of season, at an unsuitable time: *a ~d* (= inopportune) *intervention*.

mistle·toe /'mɪsltəʊ/ *n* [U] parasitic evergreen

plant (growing on fruit and other trees) with small white sticky berries (used in making bird-lime and as a Christmas decoration).

mis·took /mɪ'stʊk/ *pt* of mistake.

mis·tral /'mɪstrəl/ *n* cold, dry wind blowing from the north through the Rhone valley in France.

mis·trans·late /ˌmɪstrænz'leɪt/ *vt* [VP6A] translate wrongly. **mis·trans·la·tion** /-'leɪʃn/ *n* [C,U].

mis·tress /'mɪstrɪs/ *n* **1** woman at the head of a household or family; woman in authority who gives orders to servants: *Servants willingly obey a kind ~. Is your ~ at home?* **2** woman school teacher: *the 'French mistress*, teacher of French (but not necessarily a Frenchwoman); *the 'games ~*, in charge of games (hockey, etc). **3** woman with a good knowledge or control of sth: *a ~ of needlework. She is ~ of the situation. Venice used to be called the ~ of the Adriatic.* **4** (in stories, plays, etc dealing with periods before the 18th c, and still in Scotland by some people) title equivalent to the modern *Mrs* or *Miss*. **5** (poet) woman loved and courted by a man: *'O ~ mine!'* **6** woman having regular sexual intercourse with one man to whom she is not married. Cf *paramour* (liter) and *concubine* (dated). ⇨ master.

mis·trial /ˌmɪs'traɪəl/ *n* (legal) trial which is made invalid because of some error in the proceedings.

mis·trust /ˌmɪs'trʌst/ *vt* [VP6A] feel no confidence in: ~ *one's own powers.* □ *n* [U] (also with *indef art*) (a) ~ (*of*), want of confidence or trust (in): *She had a strong ~ of anything new and strange.* **~·ful** /-fl/ *adj* suspicious (*of*). **~·fully** /-fəlɪ/ *adv* ~ mist.

misty /'mɪstɪ/ ⇨ mist.

mis·un·der·stand /ˌmɪsʌndə'stænd/ *vt* (*pt,pp* - stood /-'stʊd/ [VP6A] take a wrong meaning from (instructions, messages, etc); form a wrong opinion of (sb or sth): *His intentions were misunderstood. She had always felt misunderstood.* **~·ing** *n* [C,U] failure to understand rightly, esp when this has led or may lead to ill feelings: *~ings between nations that may lead to war; clear up a ~ing.*

mis·use /ˌmɪs'juːz/ *vt* [VP6A] use wrongly; use for a wrong purpose; treat badly. □ *n* /ˌmɪs'juːs/ [U] using wrongly; [C] instance of this: *the ~ of power.*

mite¹ /maɪt/ *n* **1** very small or modest contribution or offering: *offer a ~ of comfort; give one's ~ to a good cause.* **2** tiny object, esp a small child (usu as an object of sympathy): *Poor little ~! What a ~ of a child!*

mite² /maɪt/ *n* [C] small parasitic arachnid that may be found in food, eg *'cheese ~s*, and may carry disease.

mi·ter /'maɪtə(r)/ *n* (US) = mitre.

miti·gate /'mɪtɪgeɪt/ *vt* [VP6A] make less severe, violent or painful. ***mitigating circumstances***, those that may make a mistake, crime, etc seem less serious. **miti·ga·tion** /ˌmɪtɪ'geɪʃn/ *n* [U].

mitre (US = **mi·ter**)/'maɪtə(r)/ *n* **1** tall head-dress worn by bishops at some ceremonies. ⇨ the illus at vestment. **2** '~(-joint)*, joint whose line of junction bisects the angle between the two bevelled surfaces it joins.

mitt /mɪt/ *n* **1** mitten. **2** baseball glove; (colloq) boxing-glove. **3** (sl) hand; fist.

mit·ten /'mɪtn/ *n* **1** kind of glove covering four fingers together and the thumb separately. **2** covering for the back and palm of the hand only, leaving the thumb and fingers bare.

mix¹ /mɪks/ *vt,vi* **1** [VP6A,12B,13B,14,2A,C] (of different substances, people, etc) put, bring or come together so that the substances, etc are no longer distinct; make or prepare (sth) by doing this: *mix flour and water. The doctor mixed me a bottle of medicine/mixed a bottle of medicine for me. We can sometimes mix business with pleasure. She was mixing* (= preparing) *a salad. Oil and water don't mix. You can't mix oil with water. Many races are mixed in Hawaii.* **2** [VP2A,3A] **mix (with),** (of persons) come or be together in society: *He doesn't mix well,* doesn't get on well with people, esp people of different social classes or different interests. **3** [VP15B] **mix sth/sb up (with sth/sb),** mix thoroughly (with); confuse in the mind (with); be unable to distinguish (from): *Mix up the salt with the pepper. Now you've mixed me up completely!* completely confused me! *You're always mixing me up with my twin brother.* **be/get mixed up in/with sth,** be involved in/with: *Don't get mixed up in politics/mixed up with those politicians,* keep clear of them: *I don't want to be mixed up in the affair,* I don't want to be connected with it in any way. **'mix-up** *n* confused state: *What a mix-up! There's been some mix-up about who should be invited to the party,* some confusion and mistakes. **'mixed-up** *adj* mentally confused; maladjusted: *He feels very mixed-up about life,* cannot see clearly what principles, etc to adopt. *I'm sorry for these mixed-up kids,* children who are confused by social problems.

mix² /mɪks/ *n* (chiefly in trade and comm) ingredients, mixed or to be mixed, for a purpose, eg for plaster, mortar, concrete or kinds of food: *an ice-'cream mix; a 'cake mix,* of flour, egg-powder, sugar, etc to be used in making cakes.

mixed /mɪkst/ *adj* of different sorts: ~ *biscuits/ pickles; a* ~ *school,* for boys and girls; *a* ~ *company,* including people of different classes, tastes, etc. **have** ~ **feelings (about sth),** feel eg both sorrow and pleasure (about it). ~ **'blessing,** sth that has both advantages and disadvantages. ~ **'doubles,** (tennis, etc) with two players, one man and one woman, on each side. ~ **'farming,** eg dairy farming and cereals. ~ **'grill,** eg liver, kidney and bacon. ~ **'marriage,** one between persons of different races or religions. ~ **'metaphor,** two or more metaphors used inconsistently together, producing a ludicrous effect, eg 'The scourge of tyranny had burnt his fingers'.

mixer /'mɪksə(r)/ *n* **1** person or thing that mixes: *a ce'ment* ~; *an electric 'food-*~; (TV, films) person or thing that combines shots on to one length of film or video-tape. **2 be a good** ~, (colloq) one who is at ease with others on social occasions. ⇨ mix¹(2).

mix·ture /'mɪkstʃə(r)/ *n* **1** [U] mixing or being mixed. **2** [C] sth made by mixing: *a 'smoking* ~, made by blending different kinds of tobacco; *a 'cough* ~, ~ of several medicines. *Air is a* ~, not

a compound, of gases. the ~ *as before,* (colloq) the same procedure, treatment, etc as in the past.

miz·zen, mizen /'mɪzn/ *n* **1** '~(-mast), mast nearest the stern on a ship with three masts. **2** '~(-sail),** lowest square sail set on this mast. ⇨ the illus at barque.

mizzle /'mɪzl/ *vi* (dial or colloq) [VP2A] rain in fine drops; drizzle.

mne·monic /nɪ'mɒnɪk/ *adj* of, designed to help, the memory: ~ *verses,* eg for remembering irregular declensions or conjugations. **mne·mon·ics** *n pl* art of, system for, improving the memory.

mo /məʊ/ *n* (sl abbr of) moment: *half a mo.*

moan /məʊn/ *n* [C] low sound of pain or regret, or one suggesting suffering: *the* ~*s of the wounded; the* ~ *of the wind on a winter evening.* □ *vi,vt* [VP2A,C,15B] utter ~s; say with ~s: ~ (*out*) *a plea for help. What's she* ~*ing* (= complaining) *about now?*

moat /məʊt/ *n* deep, wide ditch filled with water, round a castle, etc as a defence. ⇨ the illus at drawbridge. ~**ed** *adj* having a ~: *a* ~*ed manor house.*

mob /mɒb/ *n* [C] **1** disorderly crowd, rabble, esp one that has gathered for mischief or attack: (attrib) *mob law, mob rule,* imposed or enforced by a mob. **2 the mob,** the masses: *mob oratory,* the kind of speech-making that appeals to the emotions of the masses, not to their intellect. **3** gang of criminals. □ *vt* (-bb-) [VP6A] (of people) crowd round in great numbers, either to attack or to admire: *The pickpocket was mobbed by angry women. The pop singer was mobbed by teenagers.* **mob·ster** /'mɒbstə(r)/ *n* member of a gang or mob of rowdy persons.

mob·cap /'mɒbkæp/ *n* (18th c) woman's indoor head-dress covering the whole of the hair.

mo·bile /'məʊbaɪl *US:* -bl/ *adj* **1** moving, able to be moved, easily and quickly from place to place: ~ *troops/artillery.* **2** easily and often changing: ~ *features,* quickly showing changes of thought and emotion. □ *n* ornamental structure with parts that move in currents of air. **mo·bil·ity** /məʊ'bɪlətɪ/ *n* [U] being ~.

mo·bi·lize /'məʊbɪlaɪz/ *vt,vi* [VP6A,2A] collect together for service or use, esp in war. **mo·bi·liz·ation** /,məʊbɪlaɪ'zeɪʃn *US:* -lɪ'z-/ *n* mobilizing or being ~d: (attrib) *mobilization orders.*

mob·ster /'mɒbstə(r)/ *n* ⇨ mob.

moc·ca·sin /'mɒkəsɪn/ *n* [U] soft leather made from deerskin; (*pl*) shoes made from this, as worn by N American Indians, or in similar style. ⇨ the illus at mitten.

mo·cha /'mɒkə *US:* 'məʊkə/ *n* [U] fine quality of coffee, originally shipped from the Arabian port of M~.

mock /mɒk/ *vt,vi* **1** [VP6A,3A] ~ *sb;* ~ *at sb,* make fun of; ridicule (esp by copying in a funny or contemptuous way): *The naughty boys* ~*ed the blind man. They* ~*ed at my fears.* '~**ing bird** *n* American bird of the thrush family that mimics the notes of other birds. **2** [VP6A] defy contemptuously: *The heavy steel doors* ~*ed the attempts of the thieves to open the safe.* '~**-up** *n* (a) full-scale model, eg of an aircraft, made of wood, showing the appearance of a proposed machine (or any part of it). (b) lay-out of sth to be printed. □ *attrib adj* not real or genuine: *a* ~ *battle;* ~*-turtle soup,* made to imitate turtle soup; ~*-'modesty,* pretence of being modest; ~*-he'roic,* making fun of heroic

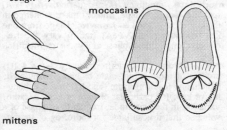

moccasins

mittens

style in literature. □ *n* (archaic) derision. **make a**
~ of, ridicule. **~er** *n* person who **~**s. **~·ing·ly**
adv

mock·ery /'mɒkərɪ/ *n* (*pl* -ries) **1** [U] mocking;
ridicule: *hold a person up to* **~**. **2** [C] sb or sth that
is mocked; occasion when sb or sth is mocked. **3**
[C] bad or contemptible example (of sth): *His trial*
was a **~** *of justice. He received only the* **~** *of a*
trial.

mod /mɒd/ *adj* (sl) up-to-date and smart (esp in
dress). □ *n* **Mod**, (1960's in GB) young person
wearing smart clothes and riding on motor-
scooters: *Mods and Rockers*, ⇨rock².

mo·dal /'məʊdl/ *adj* relating to mode or manner
(contrasted with substance); (gram) the mood of a
verb: **~** *auxiliaries*, eg *can, may*. **mo·dal·ity**
/məʊ'dælɪtɪ/ *n* **1** [U] being **~**. **2** [C] way in which
sth is done.

mode /'məʊd/ *n* [C] **1** way in which sth is done;
way of speaking or behaving: *a* **~** *of life/dressing*
the hair; fashion or style: *the latest* **~**s (of clothes).
2 (music) one of the two chief scale systems in
modern music: *the major and the minor* **~**s.

model¹ /'mɒdl/ *n* [C] **1** small-scale reproduction or
representation of sth; design to be copied: **~** *of an*
ocean liner; a clay or wax **~** *for a statue*, to be copied in stone or metal; (attrib) **~** *aircraft/trains*. **2**
person or thing to be copied: *He's a* **~** *of industry.*
Make yours on the **~** *of your brother's.* **3** (colloq)
person or thing exactly like another: *She's the* **~**/*a*
perfect **~** *of her mother.* **4** person who poses for
sculptors, painters or photographers. **5** person employed to wear clothes, hats, etc so that prospective
buyers may see them; mannequin. **6** article of
clothing, hat, etc shown publicly by **~**s(5): *the*
latest Paris **~**s, clothes, etc from the Paris dressmakers. **7** design or structure of which many copies
or reproductions are (to be) made: *the latest* **~**s *of*
Ford cars; a' sports **~**, a car designed for fast driving. **8** (attrib) perfect; deserving to be imitated: **~**
behaviour; a **~** *wife*.

model² /'mɒdl/ *vt, vi* (-ll-, US -l-) **1**
[VP6A,14,15A] **~** *(in)*, shape (in some soft substance): **~** *sb's head in clay;* (fig): *delicately* **~**led
features. **2** [VP2A,6A] practise as a model(4,5):
She earns a living by **~**ling *clothes/hats.* **3** [VP14]
~ oneself on/upon sb, make from a model; take
as a copy or example: **~** *oneself on one's father.*
~(l)er *n* person who practises **~**ling. **~**(l)ing *n*
[U] art of making **~**s(1); way in which this is done;
working as a **~**(5): *She did some* **~**ling *as a*
student to earn pocket-money.

mod·er·ate¹ /'mɒdərət/ *adj* **1** not extreme; limited;
having reasonable limits: *He has a* **~** *appetite.*
Prices in this hotel are strictly **~**, not at all high.
I'd like a **~**-*price room*, eg in a hotel. *We need a*
~-*sized house*, eg with 3 or 4 bedrooms, not 7 or
8. **2** keeping or kept within reasonable limits: *a*
man of **~** *opinions; a* **~** *political party; a* **~** *drink-*
er; be **~** *in one's demands.* □ *n* person who holds
~ opinions, eg in politics. **~·ly** *adv* to a **~** extent:
a **~**ly *large audience.*

mod·er·ate² /'mɒdəreɪt/ *vt, vi* [VP6A,2A] **1** make
or become less violent or extreme: **~** *one's*
enthusiasm/demands. The wind is moderating. His
wife exercises a moderating influence upon him, is
able to restrain him. **2** act as moderator.

mod·er·ation /ˌmɒdə'reɪʃn/ *n* **1** [U] quality of being moderate; freedom from excess: *My doctor has*
advised **~** *in eating and drinking. in* **~**, in a

moderate manner or degree: *alcoholic drinks are*
not harmful taken in **~**. **2** (*pl*) (shortened to
Mods) first public examination for a degree in
classical studies at Oxford. ⇨ *Greats* at great(12).

mod·er·ator /'mɒdəreɪtə(r)/ *n* **1** Presbyterian minister presiding over a church court. **2** presiding
examiner at some university examinations. **3**
material in which neutrons are slowed down in an
atomic pile.

mod·ern /'mɒdn/ *adj* **1** of the present or recent
times: **~** *history*, eg of Europe, from 1475 onwards; **~** *languages*, those now spoken and written; *M*~ *English*, from the 15th c onwards; **~** *in-*
ventions and discoveries. ,secondary '**~** school,
(GB) 1950's and 1960's) type of non-academic,
semi-technical, secondary school. ⇨ secondary.
2 new and up-to-date: **~** *methods and ideas; a*
house with all **~** *conveniences*. □ *n* person living in
~ times.

mod·ern·ism /'mɒdənɪzəm/ *n* [U] modern views or
methods; (theology) subordination of tradition to
modern thought. **mod·ern·ist** /-ɪst/ *n* believer in,
supporter of, **~**. **mod·ern·is·tic** /ˌmɒdə'nɪstɪk/ *adj*
of **~**.

mo·dern·ity /mə'dɜːnətɪ/ *n* [U] being modern.

mod·ern·ize /'mɒdənaɪz/ *vt* [VP6A] make suitable
for present-day needs; bring up to date: *Ought we*
to **~** *our spelling?* **mod·ern·iz·ation**
/ˌmɒdənaɪ'zeɪʃn US: -nɪ'z-/ *n* [U].

mod·est /'mɒdɪst/ *adj* **1** having, showing, a not too
high opinion of one's merits, abilities, etc: *be* **~**
about one's achievements; a **~** *hero*. **2** moderate;
not large in size or amount: *He lives in a* **~** *little*
house, not showy or splendid. *My demands are*
quite **~**. *He is* **~** *in his requirements*. **3** taking,
showing, care not to do or say anything impure or
improper: **~** *in speech, dress and behaviour*. **~·ly**
adv **mod·esty** /'mɒdɪstɪ/ *n* [U] state of being **~** (all
senses): *Her* **~**y *prevented her from making her*
feelings known to him. in all **~**y, without the least
intention of boasting, etc.

modi·cum /'mɒdɪkəm/ *n* (*sing* only) small or
moderate amount: *achieve success with a* **~** *of ef-*
fort; a simple meal with a **~** *of wine.*

mod·ify /'mɒdɪfaɪ/ *vt* (*pt,pp* -fied) [VP6A] **1** make
changes in; make different: *The industrial revolu-*
tion modified the whole structure of English so-
ciety. **2** make less severe, violent, etc: *You'd bet-*
ter **~** *your tone*, eg be less rude. *He won't* **~** *his*
demands, reduce them. **3** (gram) qualify the sense
of (a word): *Adjectives* **~** *nouns*. **modi·fier**
/-faɪə(r)/ *n* (gram) word that modifies, eg an *adj* or
adv. **modi·fi·ca·tion** /ˌmɒdɪfɪ'keɪʃn/ *n* [U] **~**ing or
being modified; [C] instance of this; change or alteration.

mod·ish /'məʊdɪʃ/ *adj* fashionable. **~·ly** *adv*

mo·diste /məʊ'diːst/ *n* (formal) milliner; dressmaker.

modu·late /'mɒdjʊleɪt US: -dʒʊ-/ *vt, vi* **1** [VP6A]
regulate; adjust; adapt; (music) make a change in
the key of. **2** [VP2C] **~** *from/to*, change from one
key to another. **3** [VP6A] (radio) vary the frequency, amplitude or phase of a wave. ⇨ modulation.

modu·la·tion /ˌmɒdjʊ'leɪʃn US: -dʒʊ'l-/ *n* **1** [U]
process of modulating; state of being modulated;
[C] change resulting from this; [U] (music) changing of key; [C] particular change of key. **2** (radio)
variation in the amplitude, frequency or phase of a
wave so that it is suitable for radio, eg of the hu-

man voice to a wave for radio or the telephone.

mod·ule /'mɒdju:l/ *US:* -dʒu:l/ *n* [C] **1** standard or unit of measurement as used in building. **2** standard uniform component used in the structure of a building or in sectional furniture; unit of electronic components as used in the assembly of a computer: *a* '*memory* ∼, unit of components in a mechanical system. **3** independent and self-contained unit of a spacecraft. **com'mand** ∼, for the astronaut in command. '**lunar** ∼, to be separated for a moon landing. **modu·lar** /'mɒdjʊlə(r)/ *US:* -dʒʊ-/ *adj* based on a ∼ or unit: *modular design/ construction*, based on a ∼ which is repeated throughout the design.

modus op·er·andi /ˌməʊdəs ˌɒpə'rændiː/ *n* (Lat) method of dealing with a piece of work; method of being operated.

modus vi·vendi /ˌməʊdəs vɪ'vendiː/ *n* (Lat) way of living; (way of getting a) temporary agreement (while awaiting the final settlement of a dispute, etc).

mo·gul /'məʊgl/ *n* (colloq) very rich or important person: *Hollywood* ∼*s*.

mo·hair /'məʊheə(r)/ *n* [U] (thread, cloth, made from the) fine, silky hair of the Angora goat.

Mo·ham·medan /məʊ'hæmɪdən/ *n* ⇨ Muham-mad.

moi·ety /'mɔɪətɪ/ *n* (*pl* -ties) (esp in legal sense) one of two parts into which sth is divided.

moil /mɔɪl/ *vi* (only in) **toil and** ∼, work hard.

moist /mɔɪst/ *adj* (esp of surfaces) slightly wet: *eyes* ∼ *with tears; a* ∼ *wind from the sea.* ∼**en** /'mɔɪsn/ *vt, vi* [VP6A,2A] make or become ∼: ∼*en the lips*, eg by licking them; ∼*en a sponge.* ∼**·ure** /'mɔɪstʃə(r)/ *n* [U] condensed vapour on a surface; liquid in the form of vapour.

moke /məʊk/ *n* (GB sl) donkey.

mo·lar /'məʊlə(r)/ *n, adj* (one) of the teeth used for grinding food. ⇨ the illus at mouth.

mo·las·ses /mə'læsɪz/ *n* [U] thick dark syrup drained from raw sugar during the refining process.

mold, molder, mold·ing, moldy, ⇨ mould, etc.

mole[1] /məʊl/ *n* permanent, small, dark spot on the human skin.

mole[2] /məʊl/ *n* small, dark-grey, fur-covered animal with tiny eyes, living in tunnels (or burrows) which it makes in the ground. ⇨ the illus at small. **blind as a** ∼, having bad eye-sight. '∼**-skin** *n* fur of a ∼, used for making garments and hats. '∼**-hill**

n pile of earth thrown up by a ∼ while burrowing. *make a mountain out of a* ∼**-hill**, make a trivial matter seem important.

mole[3] /məʊl/ *n* stone wall built in the sea as a breakwater or causeway. ⇨ the illus at breakwater.

mol·ecule /'mɒlɪkju:l/ *n* smallest unit (one or more atoms) into which a substance can be divided without a change in its chemical nature. **mol·ecu·lar** /mə'lekjʊlə(r)/ *adj* of or related to ∼s: *molecular structure.*

mo·lest /mə'lest/ *vt* [VP6A] trouble or annoy intentionally. **mol·es·ta·tion** /ˌməʊle'steɪʃn/ *n* [U].

moll /mɒl/ *n* (sl) woman companion of a gangster, vagrant, etc; prostitute.

mol·lify /'mɒlɪfaɪ/ *vt* (*pt,pp* -fied) [VP6A] make (a person, his feelings) calmer or quieter: ∼*ing remarks;* ∼ *sb's anger.* **mol·li·fi·ca·tion** /ˌmɒlɪfɪ'keɪʃn/ *n* [U].

mol·lusc (US also **mol·lusk**) /'mɒləsk/ *n* one of a class of animals with soft bodies (and often hard shells), eg oysters, mussels, cuttlefish, snails, slugs.

molly·coddle /'mɒlɪkɒdl/ *n* person who takes too much care of his health, who pampers himself and likes others to pamper him. □ *vt* [VP6A] (often reflex) pamper (sb, oneself).

Mo·loch /'məʊlɒk/ *n* (in the Bible) god to whom children were sacrificed; (fig) dreadful thing, eg war, that requires great sacrifice of human life.

molt /məʊlt/ ⇨ moult.

mol·ten /'məʊltən/ *pp* of melt. **1** (of metals) in a melted (and therefore very hot) state: ∼ *steel.* **2** made of metal that has been melted and cast: *a* ∼ *image*, eg of a god.

molto /'mɒltəʊ *US:* 'məʊltəʊ/ *adv* (musical direction) very: ∼ *espressivo*, with much expression.

mo·lyb·denum /mə'lɪbdənəm/ *n* [U] silvery-white brittle metallic element (symbol **Mo**) used in alloys for making high-speed tools.

mo·ment /'məʊmənt/ *n* **1** [C] point or very brief period of time: *It was all over in a few* ∼*s. Please wait a* ∼*. Just a* ∼*, please. He'll be here (at) any* ∼*, very soon now. It was done in a* ∼*. He arrived at the last* ∼*, almost too late. Study your notes at odd* ∼*s*, whenever you have a few minutes to spare. *I have just this* ∼*/only this* ∼ *heard the news*, heard it only a ∼ ago. *Not for a* ∼, never: '*Have you ever thought of making your own dresses?'—'Not for a* ∼*!'* *man of the* ∼, man who is

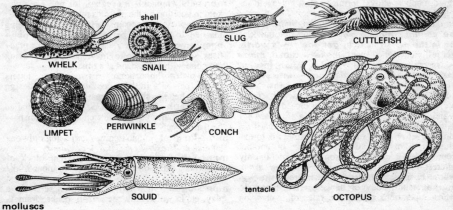

shell

WHELK   SNAIL   SLUG   CUTTLEFISH

LIMPET   PERIWINKLE   CONCH

SQUID   tentacle   OCTOPUS

molluscs

important just now. **2 the ~,** (used as a *conj*) as soon as; at the time when: *I started the ~ your letter arrived. The ~ I saw you I knew you were angry with me.* **3** [U] *of (great, small, little, no, etc)* ~, of (great, small, etc) importance: *an affair of great ~; a matter of ~; men of ~.*

mo·men·tary /ˈməʊməntrɪ US: -terɪ/ *adj* **1** lasting for, done in, a moment. **2** at every moment: *with a learner at the wheel, and in ~ expectation of an accident.* **mo·men·tar·ily** /ˈməʊməntrəlɪ US: ˌməʊmənˈterəlɪ/ *adv*

mo·men·tous /məˈmentəs/ *adj* important; serious. **~·ly** *adv* **~·ness** *n*

mo·men·tum /məˈmentəm/ *n* [U] **1** (science) quantity of motion of a moving body (the product of its mass and velocity): *Do falling objects gain ~?* **2** (fig, of events) impetus gained by movement: *lose/gain ~.*

mon·arch /ˈmɒnək/ *n* supreme ruler (a king, queen, emperor or empress). **mon·ar·chic** /məˈnɑːkɪk/ *adj* of a ~ or a ~y. ⇨ absolute(2), limited². **mon·ar·chism** /-ɪzəm/ *n* [U] system of government by a single ruler or ~. **mon·ar·chist** /-ɪst/ *n* supporter of ~ism. **mon·archy** /ˈmɒnəkɪ/ *n* [U] government by a ~; [C] (*pl* -chies) state ruled by a ~.

mon·as·tery /ˈmɒnəstrɪ US: -sterɪ/ *n* (*pl* -ries) place where monks live as a community under religious vows.

mon·as·tic /məˈnæstɪk/ *adj* of monks or monasteries: ~ *vows,* eg of poverty, chastity, and obedience; ~ *architecture,* of the kind used for monasteries, abbeys, etc. **mon·as·ti·cism** /məˈnæstɪsɪzəm/ *n* [U] system of living as practised by monks in monasteries.

mon·aural /ˌmɒnˈɔːrəl/ *adj* for one ear; (with trade abbr *mono*; of sound-reproducing equipment and recordings) not stereophonic.

Mon·day /ˈmʌndɪ/ *n* second day of the week.

mon·et·ary /ˈmʌnɪtrɪ US: -terɪ/ *adj* of money or a currency: *a ~ policy,* of control over money; ~ *reform,* eg to create a decimal coinage. *The ~ unit of the US is the dollar.* **mon·et·ar·ism** /-tərɪzəm/ *n* [U] policy of control over money as the chief method of managing a country's economy. **mon·et·ar·ist** /-tərɪst/ *n* person favouring monetarism.

mon·et·ize /ˈmʌnətaɪz/ *vt* [VP6A] **1** put (coins, notes) into circulation as money. **2** give (a currency) a fixed value.

money /ˈmʌnɪ/ *n* **1** [U] coins stamped from metal (gold, copper, alloys), printed notes, given and accepted when buying and selling, etc: *I keep my ~ in the bank. I could hear ~ jingling in his pocket.* **be ˈcoining/ˈminting ~,** be getting rich quickly. **be in the ~,** (sl) be rich. **get one's ˈ~ ˈs worth,** get full value for ~ spent. **make ~,** earn it. **marry ~,** marry a rich person. **(pay) ~ down,** (pay) in cash (contrasted with *credit*). **put ~ into sth,** invest ~ in an enterprise, etc. **~ of acˈcount,** ⇨ account¹(2). **ready ~,** cash contrasted with *credit,* etc. **2** (compounds) **ˈ~-box** *n* closed box into which coins are dropped through a slit, used for savings or for collecting contributions (to charities, etc). **ˈ~-changer** *n* one whose business is to exchange ~ of one country for that of another country. **ˈ~-grubber** *n* person whose chief or only interest in life is making ~. **ˈ~-lender** *n* one whose business is to lend ~ at interest. **the ˈ~-market** *n* the body of bankers, financiers, etc whose operations decide the rates of interest on

borrowed capital. **ˈ~ order** *n* order¹(7) bought from a post office for ~ to be paid by another post office to a named person. **ˈ~-spinner** *n* (colloq) book, play, etc that makes a lot of ~. **3** (*pl,* moneys or monies /ˈmʌnɪz/) (legal or archaic) sums of ~: *~s paid in/out; sundry ~s owing to the estate.* **~ed** /ˈmʌnɪd/ *adj* having (much) ~: *a ~ed man: the ~ed classes; the ~ed interest,* the owners of capital. **~·less** *adj* having no ~.

mon·ger /ˈmʌŋɡə(r)/ *n* (chiefly in compounds) trader, dealer: *ˈiron~; ˈfish~; ˈscandal~.*

mon·gol·ism /ˈmɒŋɡəlɪzəm/ *n* [U] congenital condition in which a child is born with mental deficiency and a flattened broad skull and slanting eyes. **mon·gol** /ˈmɒŋɡl/ *n, attrib adj* (person) suffering from ~: *a mongol baby.*

mon·goose /ˈmɒŋɡuːs/ *n* (*pl* ~s /-sɪz/) small Indian animal clever at destroying venomous snakes. ⇨ the illus at small.

mon·grel /ˈmʌŋɡrəl/ *n* **1** dog of mixed breed. **2** any plant or animal of mixed origin. □ *attrib adj* of mixed breed or origin.

mon·ies /ˈmʌnɪz/ *n pl* ⇨ money(3).

moni·tor /ˈmɒnɪtə(r)/ *n* **1** pupil given authority over his fellows. **2** person employed to listen to and report on foreign broadcasts. **3** apparatus for testing transmissions by radio or TV, for detecting radio-activity, for tracing the flight of missiles, etc. **ˈ~ (screen),** television screen used in a studio to check or select transmissions. □ *vt,vi* act as ~(3).

monk /mʌŋk/ *n* member of a community of men living together under religious vows in a monastery. **ˈ~-ish** /-ɪʃ/ *adj* of or like ~s.

mon·key /ˈmʌŋkɪ/ *n* (*pl* ~s) **1** member of the group of animals most closely resembling man. ⇨ the illus at ape. **be/get up to ˈ~ business/tricks,** to mischief. **have aˈ~ on one's back,** (sl) (a) be a drug addict; (b) bear a grudge. **get one's ~ up,** (sl) become angry. **put sb's ~ up,** (sl) make him angry. **ˈ~-jacket** *n* short, close-fitting jacket as worn by some sailors. **ˈ~-nut** *n* groundnut. **ˈ~-puzzle** *n* Chilean pine tree. **ˈ~-wrench** *n* wrench (spanner) with a jaw that can be adjusted to various lengths. ⇨ the illus at tool. **2** (playfully) person, esp a child, who is mischievous. **3** (sl) £500 or $500. □ *vi* [VP2C] ~ *about,* fool about.

mono, mono- ⇨ monaural and App 3.

mono·chrome /ˈmɒnəkrəʊm/ *n* painting in (different tins of) one colour. □ *adj* having one colour.

mon·ocle /ˈmɒnəkl/ *n* eyeglass for one eye only, kept in position by the muscles round the eye.

mon·og·amy /məˈnɒɡəmɪ/ *n* [U] practice of being married to only one person at a time. ⇨ polygamy. **mon·og·amist** /-ɪst/ *n* person who practises ~. **mon·og·amous** /məˈnɒɡəməs/ *adj* having only one wife or husband at a time.

mono·gram /ˈmɒnəɡræm/ *n* two or more letters (esp a person's initials) combined in one design (used on handkerchiefs, notepaper, etc).

mono·graph /ˈmɒnəɡrɑːf US: -ɡræf/ *n* detailed learned account, esp a published report on one particular subject.

mono·lin·gual /ˌmɒnəˈlɪŋɡwəl/ *adj* using only one language: *The OALDCE is a ~ dictionary.*

mono·lith /ˈmɒnəlɪθ/ *n* single upright block of stone (as a pillar or monument). **~ic** /ˌmɒnəˈlɪθɪk/ *adj* of or like a ~.

mono·logue /ˈmɒnəlɒɡ US: -lɔːɡ/ *n* scene in a play, etc in which only one person speaks; dramatic composition for a single performer; soliloquy.

mono·ma·nia /ˌmɒnəʊˈmeɪnɪə/ n [U] state of mind, sometimes amounting to madness, caused by the attention being occupied exclusively by one idea or subject; [C] instance of this. ⇨ **paranoia**. **mono·maniac** /ˌmɒnəʊˈmeɪnɪæk/ n sufferer from ∼.

mono·plane /ˈmɒnəpleɪn/ n aircraft with one wing on each side of the fuselage. ⇨ **biplane**.

mon·op·ol·ize /məˈnɒpəlaɪz/ vt [VP6A] get or keep a monopoly of; control the whole of, so that others cannot share: *Don't let me ∼ the conversation.* **mon·op·ol·iz·ation** /məˌnɒpəlaɪˈzeɪʃn US: -lɪˈz-/ n **mon·op·oly** /məˈnɒpəlɪ/ n (pl -lies) [C] **1** (possession of the) sole right to supply; the supply or service thus controlled. **2** complete possession of trade, talk, etc: *In many countries tobacco is a government* ∼. **3** anything over which one person or group has control and which is not or cannot be shared by others. **mon·op·ol·ist** /-lɪst/ n person who has a ∼. **mon·op·ol·is·tic** /məˌnɒpəˈlɪstɪk/ adj

mono·rail /ˈmɒnəʊreɪl/ n single rail serving as a track for vehicles; railway system for vehicles using such a rail, or for vehicles suspended from one.

mono·syl·lable /ˈmɒnəsɪləbl/ n word of one syllable. **mono·syl·labic** /ˌmɒnəsɪˈlæbɪk/ adj having only one syllable; made up of words of one syllable: *monosyllabic answers*, eg 'Yes' or 'No'.

mono·theism /ˈmɒnəʊθiːɪzəm/ n doctrine that there is only one God (contrasted with *polytheism*). **mono·theist** /ˈmɒnəʊθiːɪst/ n believer in ∼. **mono·the·istic** /ˌmɒnəʊθiːˈɪstɪk/ adj

mono·tone /ˈmɒnətəʊn/ n (keeping a) level tone in talking or singing; utterance without change of pitch: *speak in a* ∼.

mon·ot·onous /məˈnɒtənəs/ adj (uninteresting because) unchanging, without variety: *a ∼ voice*, one with little change of pitch; *∼ work.* **∼·ly** adv **mon·ot·ony** /məˈnɒtənɪ/ n [U] the state of being monotonous; wearisome absence of variety.

mono·type /ˈmɒnətaɪp/ n (P) composing machine that casts, sets and assembles type letter by letter.

mon·ox·ide /məˈnɒksaɪd/ n [C,U] oxide containing one oxygen atom in the molecule: *carbon ∼*, (CO).

Mon·roe /mənˈrəʊ/ n ∼ **doctrine**, (based on statements by James Monroe, US president (1817—1825) in 1823) US policy of opposing any interference by European powers in N and S America.

Mon·sieur /məˈsjɜː(r)/ n (abbr M) (pl Messieurs /meɪˈsjɜː(r)/) French title before the name of a man; Mr, sir, gentleman: *M∼ Hercule Poirot; yes*, ∼.

Mon·si·gnor /mɒnˈsiːnjə(r)/ n (title of honour given to) certain priests in the RC Church.

mon·soon /mɒnˈsuːn/ n seasonal wind blowing in the Indian Ocean from SW from April to October (*wet ∼*) and from NE during the other months (*dry ∼*); the rainy season that comes with the wet ∼.

mon·ster /ˈmɒnstə(r)/ n **1** abnormally misshapen animal or plant; person or thing of extraordinary size, shape or qualities; (in stories) imaginary creature (eg half animal, half bird): *Mermaids, griffins and dragons are ∼s. A five-legged dog is a ∼.* **2** person who is remarkable for some bad or evil quality: *a ∼ of cruelty/ingratitude; the Commissioners of Inland Revenue, those ∼s of greed.* **3** (attrib) huge: *a ∼ ship.*

mon·strance /ˈmɒnstrəns/ n (in RC Church) vessel in which the Host is exposed for veneration.

mon·strous /ˈmɒnstrəs/ adj **1** of or like a monster; of great size. **2** atrocious; causing horror and disgust: *∼ crimes.* **3** (colloq) quite absurd; incredible; scandalous: *It's perfectly ∼ that men should be paid more than women for the same job.* **∼·ly** adv **mon·stros·ity** /mɒnˈstrɒsətɪ/ n (pl -ties) [U] state of being ∼; [C] monster; hideous object, building, etc.

mon·tage /ˈmɒntɑːʒ US: mɒnˈtɑːʒ/ n (F) [U] selection, cutting and arrangement of photographic film, etc to make a consecutive whole; process of using many pictures, designs, etc sometimes superimposed, to make a composite picture.

month /mʌnθ/ n **calendar ∼**, any of the twelve parts into which the year is divided; period of time from a day in one ∼ to the corresponding day in the next ∼ (eg 2 Jan to 2 Feb). **lunar ∼**, period in which the moon makes a complete revolution round the earth; period of 28 days: *a baby of three ∼s: a three-∼ old baby. In which ∼ were you born? I shall be back this day ∼*, four weeks from today. **a ∼ of Sundays**, a very long time: *Never in a ∼ of Sundays!* **∼·ly** adj, adv done, happening, published, etc, once a ∼; valid for one ∼: *a ∼ly season ticket*, eg for railway travel. □ n **1** periodical issued once a ∼. **2** (pl -lies) (colloq, dated use) occurrence of menstruation.

monu·ment /ˈmɒnjʊmənt/ n **1** building, column, statue, etc serving to keep alive the memory of a person or event: *a ∼ to soldiers killed in the war.* **the M∼**, the column in London that commemorates the Great Fire of London in 1666. **2 Ancient M∼s**, objects, of special historic interest, such as prehistoric fortifications and remains, old buildings and bridges (often preserved by offical bodies). **3** piece of scholarship or research that deserves to be remembered; work of literature or science of lasting value: *a ∼ of learning.*

monu·men·tal /ˌmɒnjʊˈmentl/ adj **1** of, serving for, a monument: *a ∼ inscription; ∼ masons*, eg making tombstones. **2** (of books, studies, etc) of lasting value: *a ∼ production*, eg the *Oxford English Dictionary.* **3** (of qualities, buildings, tasks) very great: *∼ ignorance.*

moo /muː/ n sound made by a cow. □ vi (pt mooed) make the sound moo. **'moo-cow** n (child's word for) cow.

mooch /muːtʃ/ vi [VP2C] ∼ **about**, (colloq) loiter about: *out-of-work men ∼ing about* (*the streets*).

mood¹ /muːd/ n [C] state of mind or spirits: *in a merry ∼; in the ∼ for work*, inclined to work; *not in the ∼ for serious music. He's a man of ∼s*, his ∼s change often. **∼y** adj (-ier, -iest) **1** having ∼s that often change. **2** gloomy; bad-tempered. **∼·ily** /-ɪlɪ/ adv **∼·i·ness** n

mood² /muːd/ n (gram) one of the groups of forms that a verb may take to show whether things are regarded as certain, possible, doubtful, etc: *the indicative/imperative/subjunctive ∼.*

moon¹ /muːn/ n **1** the ∼, the body which moves round the earth once in a month and shines at night by light reflected from the sun: *Men have explored*

a monogram

a monolith

the surface of the ~. *The* ~ *shone brightly. a +
adj +* ~, this body regarded as an object distinct
from that seen at other times: *a new/half/full* ~. ⇨
new; ⇨ the illus at phase. *a/no* ~, the ~
visible/invisible: *There was no* ~, It was a night
with no ~ visible in the sky. *Is there a* ~ *tonight?*
cry for the ~, yearn for sth impossible. *promise
sb the* ~, make extravagant promises. **2** (compounds) '~·beam *n* ray of ~light. '~ buggy/
rover *n* vehicle for travelling on the ~. '~·flower
n ox-eye daisy. '~·light *n* light of the ~; (often
attrib) *go swimming in the* ~light/by ~light; a
~light night. '~·lit *adj* lit by the ~: *a* ~lit *scene/
landscape.* '~·shine *n* (a) light of the ~. (b) foolish or idle talk, ideas, etc. (c) (US) whisky or other
spirits illicitly distilled or smuggled. '~·stone *n*
semi-precious felspar. '~·struck *adj* wild and
wandering in the mind (supposedly as the result of
the ~'s influence). **3** [C] satellite of another planet:
How many ~*s has the planet Jupiter?* **4** [C] (poet)
month. *once in a blue* ~, (colloq) rarely or never.
~·less *adj* without a visible ~: *a dark,* ~less
night.
moon² /muːn/ *vi,vt* **1** [VP2C] ~ *about/around,*
move or look listlessly. **2** [VP15B] ~ *away,* pass
(time) listlessly or aimlessly: ~ *away the summer
holidays.* ~·y *adj* (-ier, -iest) given to ~ing away
the time.
moor¹ /mʊə(r)/ *n* [C,U] (area of) open, uncultivated land, esp if covered with heather (and often, in
GB, used for preserving game, esp grouse). '~·
fowl, '~·game *nn* (*pl* unchanged) red grouse.
'~·cock *n* male of this. '~·hen *n* (a) female of
this. ⇨ the illus at water. (b) water-hen. '~·land
/-lənd/ *n* land consisting of open ~ and covered
with heather.
moor² /mʊə(r)/ *vt* [VP6A,15A] make (a boat, ship,
etc) secure (to land or buoys) by means of cables,
etc. '~·ing-mast *n* one for ~ing airships. ~·ings
/'mʊərɪŋz/ *n pl* **1** cables, anchors and chains, etc,
by which a ship or boat is ~ed. **2** place where a
ship is ~ed.
Moor /mʊə(r)/ *n* member of the Muslim peoples of
mixed Arab and Berber blood who now live in NW
Africa; one of the Muslim Arabs who invaded
Spain in the 8th c: *the conquest of Spain by the* ~s.
Moor·ish /'mʊərɪʃ/ *adj* of the Moors and their culture: ~ *palaces in Granada.*
moose /muːs/ *n* (*pl* ~ or ~s /-sɪz/) large sort of
deer with coarse fleece and thick antlers, found in
the forests of N America, and (where it is called an
elk) in northern Europe and Asia.
moot /muːt/ *adj* (only in) *a* ~ *point/question,*
one about which there is uncertainty. □ *vt* [VP6A]
raise or bring forward for discussion: *This question
has been* ~ed *again.*
mop¹ /mɒp/ *n* **1** bundle of coarse strings, cloth, etc
fastened to a long handle for cleaning floors, etc;
similar material on a short handle for cleaning
dishes, etc. **2** mass of thick, untidy hair. □ *vt* (-pp-)
1 [VP6A] clean with a mop: *mop the floor.* **2**
[VP6A,15B] ~ (*up*), wipe (away) with, or as with,
a mop: *mop one's brow,* wipe away sweat, eg with
a handkerchief: *mop up a mess.* *mop up,* (colloq
uses) finish off, make an end of: *mop up arrears of
work; mopping-up operations* (in a military campaign, getting rid of defeated remnants of enemy
troops). *mop the floor with sb,* defeat him completely, eg in a debate.
mop² /mɒp/ *vi* (-pp-) (archaic or liter; only in)

mop and mow, make grimaces.
mope /məʊp/ *vi* [VP2A,C] pity oneself, give
oneself up to sadness or low spirits: ~ (*about*) *in
the house all day.* □ *n* the ~s, low spirits: *suffer
from the* ~s; *have a fit of the* ~s.
mo·ped /'məʊped/ *n* (GB) motor-cycle with pedals
and a petrol engine of low power.
mo·quette /məˈket US: məʊ-/ *n* [U] synthetic fabric used for carpets and soft furnishings.
mo·raine /mɒˈreɪn US: mɔː-/ *n* heap or mass of
earth, gravel, rock, etc carried down and deposited
by a glacier. ⇨ the illus at mountain.
moral¹ /'mɒrəl US: 'mɔːrəl/ *adj* **1** concerning principles of right and wrong: ~ *standards; a* ~ *question; the* ~ *sense,* the power of distinguishing right
and wrong; ~ *law;* ~ *rights/obligations,* based on
~ law; ~ *philosophy,* ethics, the study of right and
wrong in human behaviour. **2** good and virtuous:
live a ~ *life; a* ~ *man.* **3** able to understand the
difference between right and wrong: *At what age
do we become* ~ *beings?* **4** teaching or illustrating
good behaviour: *a* ~ *book/story/talk.* **5** (contrasted with *physical* or *practical*) connected with the
sense of what is right and just: *a* ~ *victory,* outcome of a struggle in which the weaker side is
comforted because it has established the righteous-
ness of its cause. *a* ~ *certainty,* sth so probable
that there is little room for doubt. ~ *courage/
cowardice,* strength/lack of strength to face contempt or ridicule rather than do wrong. *give sb* ~
support, help by saying that he has justice and
right on his side. ~ly /-rəlɪ/ *adv* in a ~ manner:
M~ly he is all that she desired.
moral² /'mɒrəl US: 'mɔːrəl/ *n* **1** that which a story,
event or experience teaches: *And the* ~ *of this
story is that a young girl should not speak to
strange men. You may draw your own* ~ *from this.*
2 (*pl*) moral habits; standards of behaviour; principles of right and wrong: *a man without* ~s; *a
man of loose* ~s; *improve the* ~s *of a country.*
mo·rale /məˈrɑːl US: -ˈræl/ *n* [U] state of discipline
and spirit (in a person, an army, a nation, etc);
temper, state of mind, as expressed in action: *The
army recovered its* ~ *and fighting power. The failing* ~ *of the enemy* (= Their loss of confidence in
themselves) *helped to shorten the war.*
mor·al·ist /'mɒrəlɪst US: 'mɔːr-/ *n* person who
points out morals(1); person who practises or
teaches morality.
mor·al·is·tic /ˌmɒrəˈlɪstɪk US: ˌmɔːr-/ *adj* concerned with morals(2).
mor·al·ity /məˈrælətɪ/ *n* (*pl* -ties) **1** [U] (standards,
principles, of) good behaviour: *Have standards of
political* ~ *improved in recent years? Is commercial* ~ *high in your country?* **2** [C] particular
system of morals: *Muslim* ~. **3** [C] '~ (play), form
of drama, popular in the 16th c, teaching good behaviour, the chief characters being personifications
of virtues and vices.
mor·al·ize /'mɒrəlaɪz US: 'mɔːr-/ *vt,vi* **1**
[VP2A,3A] ~ (*about/on/upon*), deal with moral
questions; talk or write on questions of duty, right
and wrong, etc: ~ *upon the failings of the young
generation. Oh, do stop moralizing! None of your
moralizing!* Stop preaching at me! **2** [VP6A] give a
moral interpretation of.
mo·rass /məˈræs/ *n* [C] stretch of low, soft, wet
land; marsh; (fig) entanglement.
mora·tor·ium /ˌmɒrəˈtɔːrɪəm US: ˌmɔːr-/ *n* (*pl* ~s
or -ria /-rɪə/) [C] legal authorization to delay pay-

ment of debts; agreed deferment or delay.

mor·bid /'mɔːbɪd/ adj **1** diseased: a ~ growth, eg a cancer or tumour; ~ anatomy, the study of diseased organs in the body. **2** (of sb's mind or ideas) unhealthy: a ~ imagination, one that dwells on horrible or nasty things. ~·ly adv ~·ity /mɔː'bɪdəti/, ~·ness nn state of being ~.

mor·dant /'mɔːdnt/ adj biting; sarcastic: ~ criticism; a ~ wit.

more /mɔː(r)/ (contrasted with less and fewer; ⇨ many, most[1], much[1]) adj (independent comp) greater in number, quantity, quality, degree, size, etc; additional: We need ~ men/help, etc. Instead of fewer helpers, we want ~. Have you any ~ paper? Would you like some/a little ~ soup/a little ~ of this soup? □ n a greater amount, number, etc; an additional amount: What ~ do you want? There are still a few ~. There is hardly any ~. That is ~ than enough. May I have one ~? I should like as many ~, the same number again. I hope to see ~ of you, to see you ~ often. □ adv **1** (forming the comparative degree of most adjj and advv of more than two syllables and of some of two syllables, esp if stressed on the first): ~ beautiful/useful/interesting/serious (than...); ~ easily/quietly/foolishly (than...). **and what is** ~, ~ important, serious, etc (according to context). **2** to a greater extent; in a greater degree: You need to sleep ~, ie ~ than you sleep now. You must attend to your work ~. He was ~ frightened than hurt. He likes summer ~ than autumn. **3** again: Once ~, please. I shall not go there any ~, ever again. We saw him no ~, did not see him again. **4** ~ **and** ~, by ~ stages, degrees, etc: The story gets ~ and ~ exciting. Life is becoming ~ and ~ expensive. ~ **or less**, about: It's an hour's journey, ~ or less. **5** (with a n, equivalent to an adj): (The) ~ fool you to believe him, You are, if you believe him, foolish in a higher degree. It had ~ the characteristic (= was ~ characteristic) of a foolish dream than of a nightmare. (The) ~'s the pity, It is, to that extent, a greater pity. ⇨ also the (adv). **no** ~, neither: A: 'I can't understand this at all.' B: 'No ~ can I.' **no** ~... **than**: He's no ~ able to read Chinese than I am, He is as unable to do so as I am.

mo·rello /mə'reləʊ/ n (pl ~s /-ləʊz/) ~ (cherry), bitter kind of cherry (used for jam).

more·over /mɔː'rəʊvə(r)/ adv further; besides; in addition (to this).

mo·res /'mɔːreɪz/ n pl (formal) customs, usages, conventions, regarded as essential to a social group.

Mo·resque /mɔː'resk/ adj (of style, design, decoration, architecture) Moorish.

mor·ga·natic /ˌmɔːgə'nætɪk/ adj ~ **marriage**, one between a man of high rank (eg a prince) and a woman of lower rank, who remains in her lower social station, the children having no claim to succeed to the property, titles, etc, of their father.

morgue /mɔːg/ n **1** building in which bodies of persons found dead are kept until they are identified and claimed by members of their families. ⇨ mortuary. **2** file (in the office of a newspaper or magazine) with obituary notices of famous people still living (ready for use when they die).

mori·bund /'mɒrɪbʌnd US: 'mɔːr-/ adj at the point of death; about to come to an end: ~ civilizations.

Mor·mon /'mɔːmən/ n, adj (member) of a religious organization founded in the US in 1830, officially called 'The Church of Jesus Christ of Latter-day

Saints'. ~·ism /-ɪzəm/ n

morn /mɔːn/ n (poet) morning.

morn·ing /'mɔːnɪŋ/ n **1** [C,U] early part of the day between dawn and noon (or, more generally, before the midday meal): in/during the ~; this ~; yesterday/tomorrow ~; every ~; on Sunday/Monday, etc ~; the ~ of May the 1st; one ~ last week; one summer ~; a few ~s ago; several ~s lately. When he awoke it was ~. **2** (attrib): a ~ walk; an early ~ swim. '~ **coat**, long black coat with the front cut away. '~ **dress**, ~ coat with striped trousers. **M**~ **Prayer**, service used in the Church of England at ~ service. **the** ~ **star**, Venus, or other bright star seen about dawn. **the** ~ **watch**, (at sea) period of duty, 4am to 8am. ~·**'glory** n climbing plant of the convolvulus family, with flowers that fade by midday. '~-**room** n sitting-room for the ~. '~ **sickness** n (feeling of) nausea early in the morning, during the first few months of pregnancy.

mo·rocco /mə'rɒkəʊ/ n [U] soft leather made from goatskins.

mo·ron /'mɔːron/ n feeble-minded person (with a mental level not so low as imbeciles or idiots); (colloq) stupid person. ~·ic /mə'rɒnɪk/ adj

mo·rose /mə'rəʊs/ adj sullen; ill-tempered; unsocial. ~·ly adv ~·ness n

mor·pheme /'mɔːfiːm/ n (ling) smallest meaningful part into which a word can be divided: 'Run-s' contains two ~s and 'un-like-ly' contains three.

Mor·pheus /'mɔːfɪəs/ n (Gk myth) god of dreams and sleep.

mor·phia /'mɔːfɪə/, **mor·phine** /'mɔːfiːn/ nn [U] drug, usu in the form of a white powder, made from opium and used for relieving pain.

mor·phol·ogy /mɔː'fɒlədʒɪ/ n [U] **1** (biol) branch of biology dealing with the form and structure of animals and plants. **2** (ling) study of the morphemes of a language and of how they are combined to make words. ⇨ syntax.

mor·ris dance /'mɒrɪs dɑːns US: 'mɔːrɪs dæns/ n old English folk-dance for men.

mor·row /'mɒrəʊ US: 'mɔːr-/ n **1** (liter) the next day after the present or after any given day: What had the ~ in store for them? **2** (archaic) morning: Good ~!

Morse /mɔːs/ n '~ **(code)**, system of dots and dashes, or short and long sounds or flashes of light, representing letters of the alphabet and numbers, to be signalled by lamp, radio, etc: a message in ~; the ~ alphabet.

mor·sel /'mɔːsl/ n [C] tiny piece (esp of food); mouthful: I haven't had a ~ of food since I left the house. What a dainty/choice ~!

mor·tal /'mɔːtl/ adj **1** (contrasted with immortal) which must die; which cannot live for ever: Man is ~, All men must die. Here lie the ~ remains of..., (eg on a tombstone) Here is buried what now remains of the body of.... **2** causing death: a ~ wound. His injuries proved ~. ~ **sins**, causing spiritual death. **3** lasting until death: ~ hatred. ~ **combat**, only ended by the death of one of the fighters. ~ **enemies**, whose enmity will not end until death. **4** accompanying death: in ~ agony. **5** (colloq) extreme; very great or long: in ~ fear; in a ~ hurry. □ n human being. ~·ly /-təlɪ/ adv **1** so as to cause death: ~·ly wounded. **2** deeply, seriously: ~·ly offended.

mor·tal·ity /mɔː'tælətɪ/ n [U] **1** state of being mortal. **2** number of deaths caused by sth (eg a disaster or disease): *an epidemic with a heavy* ∼, a large number of deaths. **3** death-rate: '∼ **tables,** (insurance) tables showing how long people at various ages may expect to live.

mor·tar[1] /'mɔːtə(r)/ *n* [U] mixture of lime, sand and water used to hold bricks, stones, etc together in building. '∼**-board** *n* (a) small, flat board with a short handle on the underside, used for holding a supply of ∼ (while laying bricks, etc). (b) square cap worn as part of their academic costume by members of a college, etc. □ *vt* [VP6A] join (bricks, etc) with ∼.

mor·tar[2] /'mɔːtə(r)/ *n* **1** bowl of hard material in which substances are crushed with a pestle. ⇨ the illus at pestle. **2** (mil) cannon for firing shells at high angles.

mort·gage /'mɔːgɪdʒ/ *vt* [VP6A,14] ∼ **(to) (for),** give sb a claim on (property) as a security for payment of a debt or loan: ∼ *a house* (*to sb for £20000*); *land that may be* ∼*d.* □ *n* act of mortgaging; agreement about this: *raise a* ∼ (*on one's house*) *from a bank. I can buy the house only if a* ∼ *for £20000 is obtainable. We must pay off the* ∼ *this year.* **be** ∼*d* **up to the hilt,** have the maximum ∼ possible (on property). **mort·gagee** /ˌmɔːgɪ'dʒiː/ *n* person to whom property is ∼d. **mort·gagor** /ˌmɔːgɪ'dʒɔː(r)/ *US:* 'mɔːrgɪdʒər/ *n* person who gives a ∼ on his property.

mor·tice /'mɔːtɪs/ *n* ⇨ mortise.

mor·ti·cian /mɔː'tɪʃn/ *n* (US) funeral director; undertaker.

mor·tify /'mɔːtɪfaɪ/ *vt,vi* (*pt,pp* -fied) **1** [VP6A] cause (sb) to be ashamed, humiliated, or hurt in his feelings: *mortified by sb's rudeness; feel mortified at one's failure to pass an examination; a* ∼*ing defeat.* **2** [VP6A] ∼ **the flesh,** discipline bodily passions, overcome bodily desires. **3** [VP2A] (of flesh, eg round a wound) decay, be affected with gangrene. **mor·ti·fi·ca·tion** /ˌmɔːtɪfɪ'keɪʃn/ *n* [U] ∼ing or being mortified (all senses).

mor·tise, mor·tice /'mɔːtɪs/ *n* hole (usu rectangular) cut in a piece of wood, etc to receive the end of another piece (the *tenon*). '∼ **lock,** secure lock which is fitted inside the woodwork (of a door, etc), not screwed on to the surface. □ *vt* [VP15A,B] join or fasten in this way: ∼ *two beams together;* ∼ *one beam to/into another.*

mor·tu·ary /'mɔːtʃəri *US:* -tʃʊeri/ *n* (*pl* -ries) room or building (eg part of a hospital) to which dead bodies are taken to be kept until burial; (attrib) of death or burial: ∼ *rites.*

mo·saic /məʊ'zeɪɪk/ *n, adj* (form or work of art) in which designs, pictures, etc are made by fitting together differently coloured bits of stone, etc: *a design in* ∼; *a* ∼ *pavement/ceiling.*

Mo·saic /məʊ'zeɪɪk/ *adj* of Moses. **(the)** ∼ **law,** the first five books of the Old Testament.

mo·selle /məʊ'zel/ *n* dry, white wine from the valley of the River M∼ (in W Germany).

mosey /'məʊzɪ/ *vi* [VP2A,C] ∼ **(along),** (sl) amble aimlessly.

Mos·lem /'mɒzləm/ *n, adj* = Muslim.

mosque /mɒsk/ *n* building in which Muslims worship Allah.

mos·quito /mə'skiːtəʊ/ *n* (*pl* ∼es /-təʊz/) small, flying, blood-sucking insect, esp the sort that spreads malaria. ⇨ the illus at insect. '∼**-net** *n* net, hung over a bed, through which ∼es cannot fly. '∼**-craft** *n* (collective *pl*) small, armed ships with high speed and able to manoeuvre easily.

moss /mɒs *US:* mɔːs/ *n* [U] sorts of small green or yellow plant growing in thick masses on wet surfaces: ∼*-covered rocks/roofs/tree-trunks.* **A rolling stone gathers no** ∼, (prov) A person who too frequently changes his occupation or who never settles in one place will not succeed in life. '∼**-grown** *adj* covered with growing ∼. ∼**y** *adj* (-ier, -iest) covered with ∼; like ∼: ∼*y green.*

most[1] /məʊst/ (contrasted with *least* and *fewest;* ⇨ many, more, much[1]) *adj, n* **1** (independent superl) (the) greatest in number, quantity, degree, etc: *Which is* ∼, *3, 13 or 30? Which of you has made (the)* ∼ *mistakes? Those who have (the)* ∼ *money are not always (the) happiest. Do the* ∼ *you can.* **at (the)** ∼; **at the very** ∼, not more than: *I can pay only £10 at the* ∼. *There were only 30 people at the meeting at the very* ∼, There were 30 or fewer. **make the** ∼ **of,** use to the best advantage: *We have only a few hours so we must make the* ∼ *of our time. She's not really beautiful, but she makes the* ∼ *of her looks.* **for the** '∼ **part,** usually; on the whole: *Japanese TV sets are, for the* ∼ *part, of excellent quality.* **2** (not preceded by *def art* in this sense) the majority of; the greater part of: *M*∼ *people fear pain. He was ill* ∼ *of the summer.* ∼ *suff* (with *preps* or *adjj* of position): *top*∼, highest; *in*(*ner*)∼, furthest in.

most[2] /məʊst/ *adv* **1** (forming the superlative degree of nearly all *adjj* and *advv* of more than one syllable): *the* ∼ *beautiful/interesting/useful, etc;* ∼ *carefully/accurately, etc.* **2** (modifying *vv,* but not to be placed between a *v* and its object): *What is troubling you* ∼? *What* ∼ *pleased me/What pleased me* ∼ *was that....* **3** (intensive, modifying an *adj;* may be preceded by *indef art*) very; exceedingly: *This is a* ∼ *useful book. He was* ∼ *polite to me. Your news is* ∼ *interesting.* **4** (modifying an *adv*) quite: *I shall* ∼ *certainly go.* **5** (dial and US colloq) almost: *M*∼ *everybody has gone home.* ∼**·ly** *adv* chiefly; almost all; generally: *The medicine was* ∼*ly sugar and water. The village is* ∼*ly of mud houses. We are* ∼*ly out on Sundays,* are not at home on ∼ Sundays.

mote /məʊt/ *n* particle (of dust, etc): ∼*s dancing in a sunbeam.* **the** ∼ **in sb's eye,** the fault that he has committed (trifling if compared to one's own fault). ⇨ Matt 7: 3.

mo·tel /məʊ'tel/ *n* motorists' hotel (with rooms or cabins, a parking area, service station, etc).

moth /mɒθ *US:* mɔːθ/ *n* sorts of winged insect flying chiefly at night, attracted by lights. ⇨ the illus at insect. '∼**-ball** *n* small ball (of camphor, etc) intended to discourage clothes-∼s. ⇨ *naphthalene* at naphtha. **in** ∼**-balls,** (fig) in storage: *After ten years in* ∼*-balls the ships were sent to be broken*

a mosque

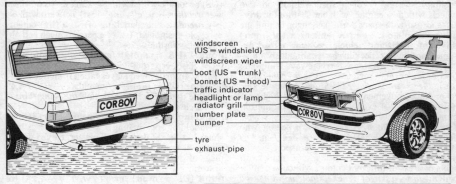

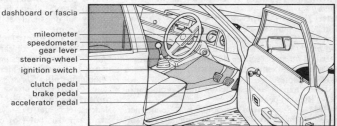

the motor-car

up. '**clothes-~** n kind which breeds in cloth, fur, etc, its grub feeding on the cloth and making holes. '**~-eaten** adj eaten or destroyed by clothes-~s; (fig) antiquated; out-of-date. '**~-proof** adj (of fabrics) treated chemically against damage by clothes-~s. □ vt make ~-proof: ~-proof carpets.
mother /'mʌðə(r)/ n 1 female parent; woman who has adopted a child; woman (often '*housemother*) who is in charge of children in a boarding-school or home¹(2). 2 quality or condition that gives rise to sth: *Misgovernment is often the ~ of revolt. Necessity is the ~ of invention,* (prov). 3 head of a female religious community. **M~ Superior,** head of a convent. 4 (various uses) **the '~ country,** (a) one's native land. (b) a country in relation to colonies, etc. **~-in-law** /'mʌðər ɪn lɔː/ n (pl ~s-in-law) ~ of one's wife or one's husband. **,~-of-'pearl** n [U] hard, smooth, shiny, rainbow-coloured material that forms the lining of some shells, esp the pearl-oyster, used for making buttons, ornaments, etc. **~ ship** n one from which other ships (eg submarines) get supplies. **~ tongue** n one's native language. **~ wit** n common sense; the intelligence with which one is born. '**~-hood** /-hʊd/ n [U] state of being a ~. **~-less** adj having no ~. '**~-like** adj in the manner of a ~. **~-ly** adj having, showing, the tender, kind qualities of a ~. **~-li-ness** n □ vt [VP6A] take care of (as a ~ does); protect or adopt (a child) as one's own.
mo-tif /məʊ'tiːf/ n [C] theme in music for treatment and development, often one which recurs; main feature in a work of art.
mo-tion /'məʊʃn/ n 1 [U] (manner of) moving: *If a thing is in ~, it is not at rest. put/set sth in ~,* cause it to start moving or working. **~ picture** n cinema film. Cf (colloq) *moving pictures; the movies. time-and-~,* ⇨ time¹(6). 2 [C] gesture; particular movement; way of moving the hand, body, etc: *If you watch my ~s carefully you will see how*

the trick is performed. All her ~s were graceful. **go through the ~s,** (colloq) do sth (that one is expected or required to do) in a perfunctory or insincere manner. 3 [C] proposal to be discussed and voted on at a meeting: *On the ~ of Mr X the committee agreed to... The ~ was adopted/carried/ rejected, etc by a majority of six.* 4 [C] = movement(6). □ vt, vi 1 [VP17,15A,B] direct (sb) by a motion or gesture: *~ sb in/away/to a seat. He ~ed me to enter.* 2 [VP3A] **~ to sb (to do sth),** indicate by a gesture: *He ~ed to me to come nearer.* **~-less** adj not moving; still.
mo-ti-vate /'məʊtɪveɪt/ vt [VP6A] be the motive of; give a motive or incentive to; act as an incentive. **mo-ti-va-tion** /ˌməʊtɪ'veɪʃn/ n
mo-tive /'məʊtɪv/ adj (attrib only) causing motion: *~ power/force,* eg steam, electricity. □ n [C] 1 that which causes sb to act: *actuated by low and selfish ~s; do sth from ~s of kindness. Hatred was his ~ for attacking me.* 2 = motif. **~-less** adj without a ~.
mot-ley /'mɒtlɪ/ adj 1 of various colours: *a ~ coat,* eg that worn by a jester or fool in olden times. 2 of varied character or various sorts: *a ~ crowd,* eg people of many different occupations, social classes, etc. □ n [U] jester's dress. **wear the ~,** play the part of a fool or jester.
mo-tor /'məʊtə(r)/ n 1 device which imparts or utilizes power (esp electric power) to produce motion, but not used of a steam engine: *fans driven by electric ~s.* 2 (attrib, and in compounds) having, driven by, an internal combustion engine, a diesel engine, etc which generates mechanical power: '**~-vehicles;** a '**~-boat/-coach/-scooter,** etc. **~-as'sisted** adj (eg of a pedal bicycle) having an engine to help propulsion. '**~-cade** n (US) procession of ~ vehicles. '**~-car** (also **car**) n closed road vehicle on four wheels with a ~ engine, with seats usu both front and back, for 2—6 people. '**~-cycle**

(colloq '∼-**bike**) *n* open road vehicle on two wheels with a ∼ engine, with one seat for the driver, and usu with space for a passenger behind the driver. ⇨ pillion. '∼·**man** /-mæn/ *n* (*pl* -men) driver of an electric vehicle. '∼·**way** *n* road designed and built especially for continuously moving fast traffic, with dual carriageways and going over or under other roads. **3** = ∼-*car* (*car* is more usu): *the* '∼ *trade; the* '*M*∼ *Show*. **4** muscle able to produce movement of a part of the body. ∼ **nerve**, nerve that excites movements of a muscle or muscles. □ *vi* [VP2A,C] travel by ∼-car: ∼ *from London to Brighton*. ∼·**ist** /-ɪst/ *n* person who drives (and usu owns) a ∼-car. ∼·**ize** /-aɪz/ *vt* [VP6A] equip (troops, etc) with ∼ transport.

mottle /'mɒtl/ *vt* [VP6A] (usu in *pp*) mark with spots or areas of different colours without a regular pattern: *the* ∼*d skin of a snake; linoleum with a* ∼*d finish*.

motto /'mɒtəʊ/ *n* (*pl* ∼es or ∼s /-təʊz/) **1** short sentence or phrase used as a guide or rule of behaviour (eg *'Every man for himself', 'Always merry and bright'*). **2** short sentence or phrase written or inscribed on an object (eg a coat of arms) expressing a suitable sentiment; quotation prefixed to a book or chapter.

mou·jik /'muːʒɪk/ *n* (esp before the Revolution of 1917) Russian peasant.

mould¹ (US = **mold**) /məʊld/ *n* [C] container, hollow form, into which molten metal or a soft substance is poured to cool into a desired shape; the shape or form given by this container; jelly, pudding, etc made in such a container. **be cast in one/the same/a different, etc** ∼, (fig) have the same, different, etc (eg heroic, stubborn, rugged) character. □ *vt* [VP6A,14] ∼ *sth* **(in/from/out of sth)**, make sth in, or as in, a ∼, from some material: ∼ *a head out of/in clay*; (fig) guide or control the growth of; influence: ∼ *a person's character*.

mould² (US = **mold**) /məʊld/ *n* woolly or furry growth of fungi appearing upon moist surfaces, eg leather, cheese or on objects left in a moist, warm atmosphere. ⇨ *iron*∼ at iron¹(3). □ *vi* [VP2A]

(US) become covered with ∼: *Cheese* ∼*s in warm, wet weather*. ∼·**y** *adj* (-ier, -iest) **1** coverd with ∼: ∼*y bread*. **2** stale; smelling of ∼. **3** (fig) out-of-date; old-fashioned; (sl, of a person) mean and obstructive; worthless.

mould³ (US = **mold**) /məʊld/ *n* [U] soft, fine, loose earth, esp from decayed vegetable matter, eg '*leaf* ∼, from decayed leaves fallen from trees.

moulder (US = **molder**) /'məʊldə(r)/ *vi* [VP2A,C] crumble to dust by natural decay: *the* ∼*ing ruins of an old castle*.

mould·ing (US = **mold-**) /'məʊldɪŋ/ *n* **1** [U] act of moulding or shaping; way in which sth is shaped. **2** line of ornamental plaster, carved woodwork, etc round a wall or window, or in the cornices of a building, or on a pillar. ⇨ the illus at column.

moult (US = **molt**) /məʊlt/ *vt, vi* [VP6A,2A] (of birds) lose (feathers) before a new growth; (more rarely, of dogs and cats) lose hair. □ *n* process or time of ∼ing.

mound /maʊnd/ *n* [C] mass of piled up earth; small hill: *a* '*burial-*∼, of earth over a grave; ∼*s built for defensive purposes in olden times*.

mount¹ /maʊnt/ *n* (liter except in proper names) mountain, hill: *Christ's sermon on the* ∼; (shortened to *Mt* before proper names): *Mt Etna*.

mount² /maʊnt/ *vt, vi* **1** [VP6A,2A] go up (a hill, a ladder, etc); get on to (a horse, etc); supply (sb) with a horse; put (sb) on a horse: *He* ∼*ed* (*his horse*) *and rode away. The* ∼*ed police were called out to control the crowds*. ∼ **the throne**, become king, etc. **2** [VP2A,C] ∼ **(up)**, become greater in amount: *Our living expenses are* ∼*ing up. Bills soon* ∼ *up at hotels*. **3** (of blood) rise into the cheeks: *A blush* ∼*ed to* (= spread over) *the child's face*. **4** [VP6A] put and fix in position: ∼ *a gun*, on a gun-carriage; ∼ *pictures*, fix them with backings, margins, etc; ∼ *jewels in gold*; ∼ *specimens*, eg on a slide for a microscope; ∼ *insects*, eg for display or preservation in a museum. **5** (mil uses): ∼ *an offensive/attack*, take the offensive, attack. ∼ **guard (at/over)**, act as a guard or sentinel: *The Household Troops* ∼ *guard at Buckingham Pa-*

1 valley
2 peak
3 pass
4 shoulder
5 saddle
6 scree
7 crevasses
8 arête
9 chimney
10 plateau
11 glacier
12 moraine
13 col
14 face

mountain features

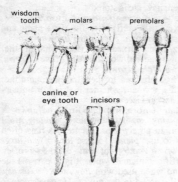

the mouth

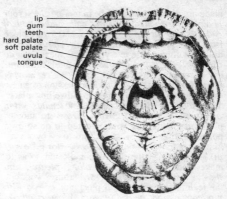

lace. **6** [VP6A] put (a play) on the stage: *The play was well ~ed*, was provided with good scenery, costumes, etc. **7** (esp of large animals, eg a stallion) get up on (a female animal) in order to copulate. □ *n* [C] that on which a person or thing is or may be ~ed (eg a card for a drawing or photograph, a glass slide for specimens, a horse for riding on, a gun-carriage, the ornamental metal part in which a jewel is fixed).

moun·tain /'maʊntɪn US: -ntn/ *n* **1** mass of very high land going up to a peak: *Everest is the highest ~ in the world.* **~ ash**, the rowan tree, with scarlet berries. **~ chain**, series of ~s. **~ dew**, (colloq) Scotch whisky. **~ range**, series of ~s more or less in a line. '**~ sickness**, illness caused by rarefied air on high ~s. **2** (fig uses) sth immense: *a ~ of debts/difficulties. The waves were ~ high*, very high. **~·eer** /ˌmaʊntɪ'nɪə(r) US: -ntn'ɪər/ *n* person who lives among ~s or is skilled at climbing ~s; hence, **~·eer·ing** *n* [U] climbing ~s (as a sport). **~·ous** /'maʊntɪnəs US: -ntənəs/ *adj* having ~s; *~ous country*; huge: *~ous waves.*

moun·te·bank /'maʊntɪbæŋk/ *n* sb who tries to cheat people by clever talk.

Mountie /'maʊntɪ/ *n* (colloq) member of the Royal Canadian Mounted Police.

mourn /mɔːn/ *vi,vt* [VP3A,6A] **~ (for/over)**, feel or show sorrow or regret (for/over); grieve (for/over): *~ for a dead child; ~ over the child's death; ~ the loss of one's mother.* **~er** *n* person who ~s, esp one who attends a funeral as a relative or friend of the dead person. **~·ful** /-fl/ *adj* sad; sorrowful. **~·fully** /-fəlɪ/ *adv*

mourn·ing /'mɔːnɪŋ/ *n* [U] **1** grief. **2** *go into/be in ~*, (start to) wear black clothes as a sign of grief. '**~-band** *n* band of black crepe worn round the sleeve. '**~-ring** *n* (formerly) worn as a memorial of a dead person.

mouse /maʊs/ *n* (*pl* mice /maɪs/) sorts of small rodent ('*house ~, 'field-~, 'harvest-~*); (fig) shy, timid person. '**~-trap** *n* trap for catching mice: *~-trap cheese*, (hum) unpalatable kind of cheese. □ *vi* [VP2A] (of cats) hunt for, catch, mice: *Our cat ~s well.* **mouser** /'maʊzə(r)/ *cat who does this.*

mousy /'maʊsɪ/ *adj* (-ier, -iest) (esp of hair) dull brown; (of a person) timid, shy.

mousse /muːs/ *n* [C,U] (dish of) meat, fish, flavoured cream, etc beaten and served cold: *chocolate ~.*

mous·tache (US = **mus·tache**) /mə'stɑːʃ US: 'mʌstæʃ/ *n* [C] hair allowed to grow on the upper lip.

mouth¹ /maʊθ/ *n* (*pl* ~s /maʊðz/) **1** opening through which animals take in food; space behind this containing the teeth, tongue, etc. ⇨ the illus here. *by word of ~*, (of news, etc) orally (not in writing, etc). *down in the ~*, sad, dejected. *out of the ~s of babes and sucklings*, (prov) innocent young people may speak wisely. *laugh on the wrong side of one's ~*, lament, be disappointed, *look a gift-horse in the ~*, accept sth ungratefully esp by examining it critically for faults. *put words into sb's ~*, (a) tell him what to say. (b) suggest or claim that he has said something. *take the words out of sb's ~*, say what he was about to say; anticipate his words. **~·ful** /-fʊl/ *n* as much as can be put into the ~ comfortably at one time: *swallow sth at a ~ful; have only a ~ful of food.* '**~-organ** *n* small musical wind-instrument with metal reeds, played by passing it along the lips and blowing; harmonica. '**~-piece** *n* (a) that part of a tobacco pipe, a musical instrument, etc placed at or between the lips. (b) person, newspaper, etc, that expresses the opinions of others: *Which newspaper is the ~piece of the Socialists?* '**~-watering** *adj* ⇨ water²(3). **2** opening or outlet (of a bag, bottle, tunnel, cave, river, etc).

mouth² /maʊð/ *vt,vi* [VP6A,2A] **1** speak with movement of the jaw but no sound. **2** utter pompously: *An actor who ~s his words is a poor actor.* **3** take (food) into the ~; touch with the ~.

mov·able /'muːvəbl/ *adj* **1** that can be moved; (of property) that can be taken from place to place (eg furniture, contrasted with land and buildings, called *real* property or estate). ⇨ portable. **2** varying in date: *Christmas is fixed but Easter is a ~ feast.* □ *n pl* personal property; articles that can be removed from the house (contrasted with *fixtures*).

move¹ /muːv/ *n* [C] **1** change of place or position, esp of a piece in chess or other games played on boards; player's turn to do this: *Do you know all the ~s in chess? Whose ~ is it?* **2** sth (to be) done to achieve a purpose: *a ~ towards settling the strike. What's our next ~?* **3** *on the ~*, moving about: *Our planes reported that large enemy forces were on the ~. make a ~*, (a) ~ to a different place: *Shall we make a ~ now?* (b) begin to act: *Unless we make a ~ soon, we shall be in a hopelessly weak position. get a ~ on*, (sl) hurry up.

move² /muːv/ *vt,vi* **1** [VP6A,15A,B,2A,C] (cause to) change position; put, cause to be, in a different place or attitude; (cause to) be in motion: *M~ your chair nearer to the fire. It was calm and not a leaf ~d. It's your turn to ~,* (in chess, etc) to ~ a piece from one square to another. **~ heaven and earth,** do one's utmost, use every possible means (*to do* sth). **2** [VP6A,2C] **~ (house),** take one's furniture, etc to another house, flat, etc: *We're moving (house) next week.* **~ in,** take possession of a new dwelling-place. **~ out,** give up a dwelling-place: *We ~d out on Monday and the new tenants ~d in on Tuesday.* **3** [VP2C,15B] **~ on,** ~ to another place or position (eg when ordered to do so by a policeman). **~ sb on,** cause him to ~ by giving him the order 'M~ on, please'. **~ along/down/ up,** ~ farther in the direction indicated so as to make space for others. *'M~ along, please', said the bus conductor.* **4** [VP6A,15A] arouse, work on, the feelings of; affect with pity, etc: *be ~d with pity/compassion; be ~d to tears. We were all ~d by her entreaties. The story of their sufferings ~d us deeply. It was a moving sight.* **5** [VP17] cause (to do sth): *Nothing I said ~d him to offer his help. The spirit ~d him to get up and address the meeting,* He felt a desire to do this. *Who was the moving spirit in the enterprise,* Who started it and was most active? **6** [VP6A,9] put forward for discussion and decision (at a meeting): *Mr Chairman, I ~ that the money be used for library books.* ⇨ motion(3). **7** [VP3A] **~ for,** make formal application (*for*): *The noble Lord ~d for papers,* ie in a debate in the House of Lords. **8** [VP2A,C] make progress; go forward: *Time ~s on. The work ~s slowly. Things are not moving as rapidly as we had hoped.* **9** [VP2A,C] take action: *Nobody seems willing to ~ in the matter.* **10** [VP2C] live one's life; pass one's time: *They ~ in the highest society.* **11** [VP6A,2A] cause (the bowels) to act, to empty; (of the bowels) be emptied.

move·ment /'mu:vmənt/ *n* **1** [U] moving or being moved; activity (contrasted with quiet and rest): *He lay there without ~. The novel/play lacks ~,* ie there is not enough action in it. **2** [C] act of changing position, esp a military evolution: *By a series of rapid ~s the general placed his forces in an advantageous position.* **3** [C] moving part of a machine or mechanism or a particular group of such parts: *the ~ of a clock or a watch.* **4** [C] united actions and efforts of a group of people for a special purpose: *the ~ to abolish slavery.* **the 'Labour M~,** organized(2) (manual) workers. **5** [C] (music) principal division of a musical work with a distinctive structure of its own: *the final ~ of the Ninth Symphony.* **6** [C] emptying of the bowels. **7** [U] activity (in a stock market, etc) for some commodity: *not much ~ in oil shares.*

mov·er /'mu:və(r)/ *n* (esp) person who moves(6) a proposal. **the prime ~,** the person chiefly responsible for starting sth.

movie /'mu:vɪ/ *n* (colloq) **1** (motion picture. **2 the ~s,** the cinema; the cinema industry: *How often do you go to the ~s?*

mow¹ /məʊ/ *vt* (*pt* mowed, *pp* mown /məʊn/ or mowed) **1** [VP6A,2A] cut (grass, etc) with a scythe or a machine: *mow the lawn; new-mown hay; mow a field.* **2** [VP15B] **mow down,** cut down like grass; destroy as if by sweeping movements: *Our men were mown down by the enemy's machine-gun fire.* **mower** /'məʊə(r)/ *n* person or machine that mows: *a 'lawn-mower.*

mow² /məʊ/ *n* [C] heap of hay, straw, etc; place in

a barn where hay, etc is stored.

mow³ /maʊ/ *vi* **mop and mow,** ⇨ mop².

Mr /'mɪstə(r)/ title prefixed to the (first name and the) surname of a man: *Mr (John) Brown.*

Mrs /'mɪsɪz/ title prefixed to the (first name and the) surname of a married woman: *Mrs (Jane) Brown;* (formal): *Mrs John Brown.*

Ms /mɪz/ title prefixed to the (first name and the) surname of a woman, whether married or unmarried: *Ms (Mary) Green.*

much¹ /mʌtʃ/ (more, most. ⇨ little) *adj, n* (~ is used with *sing nn,* uncountable. Cf *many,* used with *pl nn.* In purely affirm sentences it is often preferable to use *plenty (of), a lot (of), a large quantity (of), a good/great deal (of). M~* is often used in affirm sentences when it is (a part of) the subject, and when used with *how, too, so,* or *as*): *There isn't ~ food in the house. He never eats ~ breakfast. Did you have ~ difficulty in finding the house? M~ of what you say is true. We have ~ to be thankful for. You have given me too ~.* **come to ~,** ⇨ come(3).**how ~,** (a) what quantity: *How ~ flour* (= What weight) *do you want?* (b) what price: *How ~ a kilo is that beef?* **be up to ~,** be worth ~: *I don't think his work is up to ~,* ie it is not good. **not ~ of a,** not a good: *He's not ~ of a linguist/scholar, etc. It wasn't ~ of a dinner. I'm not ~ of a cinema-goer,* I seldom go to the cinema. **this/that ~,** the quantity, extent, etc indicated: *Can you let me have this ~? I will say this ~ in his favour...,* I will admit in his favour that.... *This ~ is certain, that he will never try to play that trick on us again.* **be too ~ for,** be more than a match for, too difficult for; be superior in skill, etc, to: *The school tennis champion was too ~ for me. I couldn't finish that philosophy book, it was too ~ for me.* **make ~ of,** (a) understand: *I didn't make ~ of that lecture.* (b) attach importance to; exaggerate: *We mustn't make too ~ of this incident. He makes (too) ~ of his connections with rich people.* **think ~ of,** have a good opinion of: *I don't think ~ of my English teacher.* **as ~ (as),** the same (as): *Give me as ~ again,* the same quantity again. *I thought as ~,* That is what I thought. *You have always helped me and I will always do as ~ for you,* will always help you. *It is as ~ your responsibility as mine,* You and I are equally responsible. *It was as ~ as he could do to* (= He could do no more than) *pay his way. That is as ~ as to say* (= is the same thing as saying) *that I am a liar.* **(with) not/ without so ~ as,** not even: *He left without so ~ as saying 'Thank you'. He rushed past me with not so ~ as a 'By your leave',* without any apology. *He hadn't so ~ as his fare home.* ⇨ also *so ~ (many), not so ~ as, so ~ so that, so ~ for,* under so¹(6).

much² /mʌtʃ/ *adv* **1** (modifying comparatives and superlatives, preceding the *def art*): *He is ~ better today. You must work ~ harder. This is ~* (= by far) *the best. He's not ~ the worse for his fall into the canal.* **~ more/less,** (used to indicate that what has been stated about sth applies with greater force to the following statement): *It is difficult to understand his books, ~ more his lectures. I didn't even speak to him, ~ less discuss your problems with him.* **2** (modifying passive *participles* and *pred adjj* such as *afraid.* Cf *very,* used to modify passive and *present participles* which are true *adjj* as *very frightened*): *I am very ~ afraid that...; I shall be ~ surprised if he succeeds. I hope you will *not be* ~ *inconvenienced.* **3** (When *much* modifies a *v* phrase, it may occur within the *v* phrase or in end position, but may not occur between this *v* phrase and its object): *It doesn't* ~ *matter. It doesn't matter very* ~. *I very* ~ *enjoyed the concert. I enjoyed it very* ~. *He doesn't like beef* ~. **4** (in phrases) ~ *as*: *M*~ *as I should* (= Although I should ~) *like to go,...*; *M*~ *as she disliked the idea* (= Although she ~ disliked the idea),.... ~ *the same,* about the same: *The patient's condition is* ~ *the same.* ~ *to,* greatly to; to one's great...: *M*~ *to her surprise/regret, etc. how* ~, to what extent: *How* ~ *do you really want to marry the man?* ⇨ *much*¹. *too* ~, too highly: *He thinks too* ~ *of himself. not so much X as Y,* Y rather than X: *Oceans don't so* ~ *divide the world as unite it,* They serve to unite countries rather than to divide them. ~**-ness** *n* (only in the colloq phrase) ~ *of a* ~*ness,* ~ the same; almost alike.

mu·ci·lage /'mju:sɪlɪdʒ/ *n* [U] kinds of vegetable glue (obtained from plants, seaweed, etc), used as an adhesive.

muck /mʌk/ *n* [U] **1** dung; farmyard manure (the droppings of animals). '~**-heap** *n* heap of farmyard ~. '~**-raker** *n* (usu fig) person who is always looking for scandal, corruption, etc. Hence, '~**-raking** *n* **2** dirt; filth; (colloq) anything disgusting or dirty. *make a* ~ *of sth,* (colloq) make a mess of it; make it dirty; spoil it. □ *vt,vi* **1** [VP6A,15B] ~ *sth (up),* (colloq) make a mess of it; spoil it. **2** [VP2C] ~ *about,* (GB sl) do useless or unnecessary things; go about, spend time, aimlessly: *'What's he up to?'—'Oh, just* ~*ing about.'* **3** [VP2C,15B] ~ *out,* clean out (stables, etc) by removing dung: *She* ~*s out (the stables) every morning.* ~**y** *adj* (-ier, -iest) dirty.

muckle /'mʌkl/ *n* ⇨ **mickle.**

mu·cous /'mju:kəs/ *adj* of, like, covered with, mucus. *the* ~ *membrane,* the moist skin that lines the nose, mouth and food canal.

mu·cus /'mju:kəs/ *n* [U] sticky, slimy substance produced by the mucous membrane; similar slimy substance: *Snails and slugs leave a trail of mucus.*

mud /mʌd/ *n* [U] soft, wet earth: *Rain turns dust into mud. throw/fling/sling mud at sb,* speak evil of him, try to damage his reputation. Hence, '**mud-slinger** *n.* *sb's name is mud,* he is in disgrace. '**mud-bath** *n* bath in mud of mineral springs (eg for treating rheumatism). '**mud flat** *n* muddy land covered by the sea at high tide and not covered at low tide. '**mud-guard** *n* curved cover over a wheel (of a bicycle, etc). ⇨ the illus at bicycle. □ *vt* (-dd-) [VP6A] cover with mud: *You've mudded the carpet.* **muddy** *adj* (-ier, -iest) **1** full of, covered with, mud: *muddy roads/shoes.* **2** mud-coloured; like mud because thick: *a muddy stream; a muddy skin; muddy coffee; muddy* (fig, = confused) *ideas.* □ *vt* (*pt,pp* -died) [VP6A] make muddy.

muddle /'mʌdl/ *vt,vi* **1** [VP6A,15B] ~ *(up),* bring into a state of confusion and disorder; make a mess of: *You've* ~*d the scheme completely. A glass of whisky soon* ~*s him. Don't* ~ (= mix) *things up (together).* ~ *sth/sb up with sth/sb,* (colloq) be unable to distinguish sth/sb from sth/sb else. **2** [VP2C] ~ *along/on,* get on in a foolish or helpless way, with no clear purpose or plan: *He's still muddling on/along.* ~ *through,* reach the end of an undertaking in spite of inefficiency, obstacles of one's own making, etc. □ *n* (usu *a* ~) ~*d* state;

confusion of ideas: *Everything was in a* ~ *and I couldn't find what I wanted. You have made a* ~ *of it,* mismanaged it, bungled it. '~**-headed** *adj* confused in mind; stupid.

muesli /'mju:zlɪ/ *n* [U] breakfast food of a mixture of uncooked cereal, nuts, dried fruit, etc.

mu·ez·zin /mu:'ezɪn *US:* mju:-/ *n* man who proclaims the hours of prayers from the minaret of a mosque.

muff¹ /mʌf/ *n* covering, usu a cylindrical padded bag of fur, open at both ends, used to keep the hands warm; similar covering for the foot.

muff² /mʌf/ *n* person who is awkward or clumsy, esp in games (eg by failing to catch the ball at cricket). □ *vt* [VP6A] bungle; fail to catch; miss: ~ *a ball;* ~ *an easy catch.*

muf·fin /'mʌfɪn/ *n* small, light, flat, round cake, usu eaten hot with butter.

muffle /'mʌfl/ *vt* **1** [VP6A,15B] ~ *(up),* wrap or cover for warmth or protection: ~ *oneself up well;* ~ *one's throat,* eg by putting a scarf round it; ~*d up in a heavy overcoat.* **2** [VP6A] make the sound of sth (eg a bell or a drum) dull by wrapping it up in cloth, etc: ~ *the oars of a boat,* to deaden the sound of their touching the water; ~*d voices,* eg from persons whose mouths are covered.

muf·fler /'mʌflə(r)/ *n* **1** cloth, scarf, worn round the neck for warmth. **2** (US) silencer.

mufti /'mʌftɪ/ *n* (usu *in* ~) plain, ordinary clothes worn by someone (eg an official, an army officer) who has the right to wear uniform.

mug¹ /mʌg/ *n* **1** (usu straight-sided) drinking vessel of china or metal with a handle, for use without a saucer; its contents: *a*'*beer-mug; a mug of milk.* **2** (sl) face; mouth.

mug² /mʌg/ *n* (sl) simpleton; easily deceived person. *a*'*mug's game,* sth unlikely to bring profit.

mug³ /mʌg/ *vt* (-gg-) [VP15B] *mug sth up,* (colloq) (try to) become quite familiar with sth on which one is to be tested.

mug⁴ /mʌg/ *vt* (-gg-) [VP6A] (colloq) attack (sb) violently and rob (eg in a dark street, a lift, an empty corridor, etc). **mug·ger** *n* **mug·ging** *n* [U,C].

mug·gins /'mʌgɪnz/ *n* (colloq) fool.

muggy /'mʌgɪ/ *adj* (-ier, -iest) (of the weather, a day, etc) damp and warm; close and sticky: ~ *days during the rainy season.* **muggi·ness** *n*

mug·wump /'mʌgwʌmp/ *n* (US) conceited person; person who has a high opinion of his own importance.

Mu·ham·mad /mə'hæmɪd/ *n* Prophet and Founder of Islam. ~**an** /-ən/ *n, adj* Muslim. **Mu·ham·ma·dan·ism** /mə'hæmɪdənɪzəm/ *n* Islam (the preferred name).

mu·latto /mju:'lætəʊ *US:* mə'l-/ *n* (*pl* ~s, ~es /-təʊz/) person who has one parent of black race and one of white race.

mul·berry /'mʌlbrɪ *US:* 'mʌlberɪ/ *n* (*pl* -ries) [C] tree with broad, dark-green leaves on which silk-worms feed; its fruit (dark purple or white).

mulch /mʌltʃ/ *n* [C] protective covering of peat, spread over the roots of trees and bushes, to retain moisture, smother weeds, etc. □ *vt* cover (ground) with a ~.

mulct /mʌlkt/ *vt* [VP12C,14] ~ *(in/of)* (rare) punish by means of a fine; take (sth) away from: ~ *a man £5;* ~ *a man in £5; be* ~*ed of one's money.*

mule¹ /mju:l/ *n* **1** animal that is the offspring of an ass and a mare. *as obstinate/stubborn as a* ~, very obstinate/stubborn. **2** (colloq) stubborn person. **3** kind of spinning-machine. **mu·le·teer** /ˌmjuːləˈtɪə(r)/ n ~-driver. **mul·ish** /-ɪʃ/ adj stubborn; obstinate. **mu·lish·ly** adv **mu·lish·ness** n

mule² /mjuːl/ n heelless slipper.

mull¹ /mʌl/ vt [VP6A] make (wine, beer) into a hot drink with sugar, spices, etc: ~ed claret.

mull² /mʌl/ n (Scot) (in place-names) promontory: the M~ of Kintyre.

mull³ /mʌl/ vt [VP15A] ~ sth over; ~ over sth, ponder over it.

mul·lah /ˈmʌlə/ n Muslim learned in theology and sacred law.

mul·lein /ˈmʌlɪn/ n kinds of plant with leaves covered with grey hairs, and small yellow flowers.

mul·let /ˈmʌlɪt/ n kinds of seafish used as food, esp red ~ and grey ~.

mul·li·ga·tawny /ˌmʌlɪɡəˈtɔːnɪ/ n ~ (soup), thick, highly seasoned soup with curry powder in it, often with boiled rice added.

mul·lion /ˈmʌlɪən/ n vertical stone division between parts of a window. ⇨ the illus at window. ~ed /ˈmʌlɪənd/ adj having ~s.

multi- /ˈmʌltɪ/ pref having many of (eg ~-coloured, of many colours; a ~-,millioˈnaire, person having 2 or more millions of money); a ~-,stage ˈrocket, with parts that ignite (and then fall away) in stages; a ,~-,racial ˈcountry, with many races of people.

multi·far·ious /ˌmʌltɪˈfeərɪəs/ adj many and various: his ~ duties; having great variety. ~·ly adv

multi·form /ˈmʌltɪfɔːm/ adj having many forms or shapes.

multi·lat·eral /ˌmʌltɪˈlætərəl/ adj involving two or more participants: ~ disarmament, after agreement between two or more countries; ~ trade, carried on between many or all countries without the need for pairs of countries to balance payment between themselves.

multiple /ˈmʌltɪpl/ adj having many parts or elements: a man of ~ interests; a ~ shop/store, one with many branches. Cf chain store, the more usu term; a ~-unit train, made up of several coaches (eg Diesel coaches) each of which can run independently. □ n quantity which contains another quantity a number of times without remainder: 28 is a ~ of 7. 30 is a common ~ of 2, 3, 5, 6, 10 and 15. **least/lowest common ~,** (abbr **LCM**) least quantity that contains two or more given quantities exactly: 12 is the LCM of 3 and 4. ⇨ factor(1).

multi·plex /ˈmʌltɪpleks/ adj having many parts or forms; of many elements.

multi·pli·ca·tion /ˌmʌltɪplɪˈkeɪʃn/ n **1** [U] multiplying or being multiplied: The symbol × stands for ~. ˈ~ table, list of numbers, usu 1 to 12, showing the results of multiplying by the same number successively. **2** [C] instance of this: 3 × 11 is an easy ~.

multi·plic·ity /ˌmʌltɪˈplɪsətɪ/ n [U] being great in number: the ~ of small city states into which ancient Greece was divided; a ~ of duties.

multi·ply /ˈmʌltɪplaɪ/ vt,vi (pt,pp -lied) **1** [VP14] ~ sth by sth, add (a given quantity or number) a given number of times: ~ 3 by 5, to make 15. 6 multiplied by 5 is 30, 6 × 5 = 30. **2** [VP6A] produce a large number of; make greater in number: ~ instances, produce a larger number of examples. **3** [VP2A] increase in number by procreation: Rabbits ~ rapidly.

multi·tude /ˈmʌltɪtjuːd US: -tuːd/ n **1** [C] great

number (esp of people gathered together). **2 the ~,** the common people; the masses: demagogues who appeal to the ~. **3** [U] greatness of number: like the stars in ~. **multi·tud·in·ous** /ˌmʌːˈtjuːdɪnəs US:-ˈtuːdənəs/ adj very numerous; great in number.

mul·tum in parvo /ˌmʌltəm ɪn ˈpɑːvəʊ/ n (Lat) much in a small space.

mum¹ /mʌm/ int, n Silence! **Mum's the word!** Say nothing about this. □ adj **keep mum,** silent.

mum² /mʌm/ n (colloq) mother.

mumble /ˈmʌmbl/ vt,vi [VP6A,2A,C] **1** say sth, speak one's words, indistinctly: The old man was mumbling away to himself. Don't ~ your words. **2** bite or chew as with toothless gums.

mumbo-jumbo /ˌmʌmbəʊ ˈdʒʌmbəʊ/ n meaningless or obscure ritual; gibberish.

mum·mer /ˈmʌmə(r)/ n actor in an old form of drama without words. ~·y n (pl -ries) **1** [C] performance by ~s; dumb show. **2** [U] foolish or unnecessary ceremonial (esp religious); [C] instance of this.

mum·mify /ˈmʌmɪfaɪ/ vt (pt,pp -fied) [VP6A] preserve (a corpse) by embalming; shrivel. **mum·mi·fi·ca·tion** /ˌmʌmɪfɪˈkeɪʃn/ n

mummy¹ /ˈmʌmɪ/ n (pl -mies) body of a human being or animal embalmed for burial; dried-up body preserved from decay (as in early Egypt).

a mummy in a sarcophagus

mummy² /ˈmʌmɪ/ n (pl -mies) (chiefly child's word for) mother.

mumps /mʌmps/ n (with sing v) contagious disease with painful swellings in the neck.

munch /mʌntʃ/ vt,vi [VP6A,2A,C] chew with much movement of the jaw: ~ing away at a hard apple; cattle ~ing their fodder.

mun·dane /mʌnˈdeɪn/ adj **1** worldly (contrasted with spiritual or heavenly): When a man is near death he loses interest in ~ affairs. **2** dull, ordinary: ~ occupations/speeches. ~·ly adv

mu·nici·pal /mjuːˈnɪsɪpl/ adj of a town or city having self-government: ~ buildings, eg the town hall, public library; ~ undertakings, eg the supply of water, tram and bus services; the ~ debt. ~·ly /-pəlɪ/ adv ~·ity /mjuːˌnɪsɪˈpælətɪ/ n (pl -ties) town, city, district, with local self-government; governing body of such a town, etc.

mu·nifi·cent /mjuːˈnɪfɪsnt/ adj (formal) extremely generous; (of sth given) large in amount or splendid in quality. ~·ly adv **mu·nifi·cence** /-sns/ n [U] great generosity.

mu·ni·ments /ˈmjuːnɪmənts/ n (legal) documents kept as evidence of rights or privileges.

mu·ni·tion /mjuːˈnɪʃn/ n (pl except when attrib) military supplies, esp guns, shells, bombs, etc: The war was lost because of a shortage of ~s/a ~ shortage. □ vt [VP6A] provide with ~s: ~ a fort.

mural /ˈmjʊərəl/ adj of, like, on, a wall: a ~ painting. □ n [C] wall-painting; fresco.

mur·der /ˈmɜːdə(r)/ n **1** [U] unlawful killing of a human being on purpose; [C] instance of this: commit ~; be declared guilty of ~; six ~s in one week. **cry blue ~,** (colloq) shout loudly and in alarm. ˌ***M~ will ˈout,*** (prov) cannot be hidden. ⇨ homicide, manslaughter, regicide, etc. **2** [U] unjustifiable sacrifice of life (eg in war): *Nothing could justify the bombing of the town; it was sheer ~.* □ *vt* [VP6A] **1** kill (a human being) unlawfully and on purpose. **2** spoil by lack of skill or knowledge: *~ a piece of music,* play it very badly. *Do you ever ~ the English language?* **~er** *n* person guilty of ~. **~·ess** /-ɪs/ *n* woman ~er. **~·ous** /ˈmɜːdərəs/ *adj* planning, suggesting, designed for, ~: *a ~ous-looking villain; a ~ous burst of fire from the enemy's guns.* **~·ous·ly** *adv*

murk /mɜːk/ *n* [U] darkness; gloom. **~y** *adj* (-ier, -iest) dark; gloomy: *a ~y night;* (of darkness) thick. **~·ily** /-ɪlɪ/ *adv*

mur·mur /ˈmɜːmə(r)/ *n* **1** low, continuous, indistinct sound, rising and falling very little in pitch: *the ~ of bees in the garden; the ~ of a distant brook/of distant traffic.* **2** softly spoken word(s): *a ~ of conversation from the next room.* **3** subdued expression of feeling: *a ~ of delight. They paid the higher taxes without a ~,* ie without complaining. □ *vi,vt* **1** [VP2A,C] make a ~(1): *a ~ing brook.* **2** [VP2A,C,3A] ***~ (at/against),*** complain in a ~(3): *~ at injustice; ~ against new taxes.* **3** [VP6A] utter in a low voice: *~ a prayer.*

murphy /ˈmɜːfɪ/ *n* (*pl* -phies) (sl) potato.

mur·rain /ˈmʌrɪn/ *n* **1** [U] infectious disease of cattle. **2** (old use): *A ~ on you!* A plague on you! Curse you!

mus·ca·tel /ˌmʌskəˈtel/ *n* [U] rich, sweet wine made from musk-flavoured kinds of grape.

muscle /ˈmʌsl/ *n* [C,U] (band or bundle of) elastic substance in an animal body that can be tightened or loosened to produce movement: *When you walk you exercise your leg ~s. Physical exercises develop ~. Don't move a ~,* stay perfectly still. **ˈ~-man** /-mæn/ *n* (*pl* -men) man of great muscular development. **ˈ~-ˌbound** *adj* having stiff ~s as the result of over-training or excessive exercise. □ *vi* [VP2C] ***~ ˈin (on sth),*** (colloq) use force to get a share (of sth considered advantageous).

Mus·covy /ˈmʌskəvɪ/ *n* (old name for) Russia. **Mus·co·vite** /ˈmʌskəvaɪt/ *n, adj* (citizen) of Moscow.

mus·cu·lar /ˈmʌskjʊlə(r)/ *adj* **1** of the muscles: *~ tissue/rheumatism.* **2** having strong muscles.

muse¹ /mjuːz/ *n* **1 the M~s,** (Gk myth) the nine goddesses, daughters of Zeus, who protected and encouraged poetry, music, dancing, history and other branches of art and learning. **2 (the) M~,** poet's genius; spirit that inspires a poet.

muse² /mjuːz/ *vi* [VP2A,3A] ***~ (over/on/upon),*** think deeply or dreamily, ignoring what is happening around one: *musing over memories of the past.* **mus·ing·ly** *adv*

mu·seum /mjuːˈzɪəm/ *n* building in which objects illustrating art, history, science, etc are displayed. ***a ˈ~ piece,*** fine specimen suitable for a ~; (fig) sth or sb antiquated.

mush /mʌʃ/ *n* [U] soft, thick mixture or mass; (US) boiled corn meal. **~y** *adj* like ~; (colloq) weakly sentimental.

mush·room /ˈmʌʃrʊm *US:* -ruːm/ *n* [C] fast-growing fungus of which some kinds can be eaten: (attrib) *the ~* (= rapid) *growth of London suburbs. The ~ cloud* (because of its ~ shape) *of a nuclear explosion.* ⇨ the illus at fungus. □ *vi* **1** ***go ~ing,*** go out into the fields to gather ~s. **2** [VP2C] spread or grow rapidly: *English language schools are ~ing in Bournemouth.*

mu·sic /ˈmjuːzɪk/ *n* [U] art of making pleasing combinations of sounds in rhythm, harmony and counterpoint; the sounds and composition so made; written or printed signs representing these sounds: (attrib) *a ~ lesson/teacher.* ***face the ~,*** face one's critics; face difficulties boldly. ***set/put sth to ~,*** provide words, eg of a poem, with ~. **ˈ~-box** *n* (US) musical-box, ⇨ musical. **ˈ~-hall** *n* (GB) hall or theatre used for variety entertainment (eg songs, acrobatic performances, juggling). ⇨ *concert-hall* at concert¹(1). **ˈ~-stand** *n* light (usu folding) framework for holding sheets of printed music. **ˈ~-stool** *n* seat without a back (usu adjustable in height) used when playing a piano. ⇨ the illus at brass, keyboard, notation, percussion, string.

mu·si·cal /ˈmjuːzɪkl/ *adj* of, fond of, skilled in, music: *~ instruments,* eg the violin, piano, harp; *She's not at all ~,* does not enjoy or understand music. **ˈ~-box** *n* box with a mechanical device that produces a tune when the box is opened. **ˌ~ ˈchairs,** game in which players go round a row of chairs one fewer than the number of players. Each time the music stops, the players sit down and the one left without a chair is eliminated. **ˌ~ ˈcomedy,** a light, amusing play with songs and dancing. □ *n* [C] **1** musical comedy. **2** cinema film in which songs have an essential part. **~ly** /-klɪ/ *adv*

mu·si·cian /mjuːˈzɪʃn/ *n* person skilled in music; composer of music. **~·ship** *n* [U] art and skill in (performing) music.

musk /mʌsk/ *n* [U] **1** strong-smelling substance produced in glands by male deer, used in the manufacture of perfumes. **ˈ~-deer** *n* small hornless deer of central Asia. **ˈ~-rat** (or *musquash*) *n* large rat-like water animal of N America, valuable for its fur. **2** kinds of plant with musky smell. **ˈ~ melon** *n* sweet juicy kind of melon. **ˈ~-rose** *n* rambling rose with large, sweet-smelling flowers. **~y** *adj* (-ier, -iest) having the smell of ~.

mus·ket /ˈmʌskɪt/ *n* firearm used by foot-soldiers (16th to 19th cc) now replaced by the rifle. **~·eer** /ˌmʌskɪˈtɪə(r)/ *n* foot-soldier armed with a ~. **~ry** /ˈmʌskɪtrɪ/ *n* [U] **1** (science of, instruction in) shooting with rifles. **2** (old use) troops armed with ~s.

Mus·lim /ˈmʊzlɪm *US:* ˈmʌzləm/ *n* one who professes Islam; follower of Muhammad; (attrib) of ~s and Islam: *~ historians/holidays.*

mus·lin /ˈmʌzlɪn/ *n* [U] thin, fine, cotton cloth, used for dresses, curtains, etc.

mus·quash /ˈmʌskwɒʃ/ *n* (fur of the) musk-rat. ⇨ musk(1).

muss /mʌs/ *n* (US) [U] disorder; [C] muddle. □ *vt* [VP6A,15B] ***~ (up),*** put into disorder: *Don't ~ up my hair!*

mus·sel /ˈmʌsl/ *n* (sorts of) mollusc with a black shell in two parts. ⇨ the illus at bivalve.

must¹ /mʌst/ *n* [U] grape-juice before fermentation has changed it into wine.

must² /*weak form:* məst; *strong form:* mʌst/ *aux v, anom fin* (No infinitive, no participles, no inflected forms; *~ not* may be contracted to ~n't /ˈmʌsnt/.) [VP5] **1** (expressing an immediate or future obligation or necessity; *~ not* expresses a prohibition. Cf the use of *may* to express permission and of *need not* to express non-obligation. Cf the use of *had to* for a past obligation and *shall/will have to* for a future obligation): *You ~ do as you're told. Soldiers*

~ *obey orders. Cars* ~ *not be parked in front of the entrance. You* ~*n't do that. We* ~*n't be late,* ~ *we? A: 'M~ you go so soon?' B: 'Yes, I* ~' (or) *'No, I needn't.'* **2** (= *had to* , used to indicate what was necessary or obligatory at a time in the past): *She said she* ~ *have a new hat for Easter. As he had broken it, he agreed that he* ~ *buy a new one. On the other side of the wood was a field that he* ~ *cross.* **3** (with less emphasis on necessity; stressing what is desirable or advisable): *We* ~ *see what can be done. I* ~ *ask you not to do that again.* **4** (expressing certainty): *Don't bet on horse-races, you* ~ *lose* (= will certainly lose) *in the long run.* **5** (expressing strong probability): *You* ~ *be hungry after your long walk. This* ~ *be* (= very probably is) *the book you want. You* ~ *have known* (= Surely you knew) *what she wanted. You* ~ *be joking!* You can't be serious! **6** (indicating the occurrence of sth unwelcome, sth contrary to what was wanted): *He* ~ *come and worry her with questions, just when she was busy cooking the dinner!* □ *n* (colloq) sth that ~ be done, seen, heard, etc: *Green's new novel is a* ~ *for all lovers of crime fiction.*

mus·tache /'mʌstæʃ/ *n* (US) = **moustache**.

mus·tachio /məˈstɑːʃɪəʊ *US:* -ˈstæʃ-/ *n* (*pl* ~s /-ɪəʊz/) a large (usu long-haired) moustache.

mus·tang /'mʌstæŋ/ *n* small wild or half-wild horse of the American plains.

mus·tard /'mʌstəd/ *n* [U] **1** plant with yellow flowers and seeds (black or white) in long, slender pods. **2** fine, yellow powder made from the seeds of this plant; this powder made into hot-tasting sauce. **'~ gas** *n* kind of liquid poison with vapour that burns the skin (used in World War I). **'~ plaster** *n* poultice made with ~. **as keen as** ~, very keen. **grain of** ~ **seed,** sth very small capable of developing into sth very large. ⇨ Matt 13: 31.

mus·ter /'mʌstə(r)/ *n* assembly or gathering of persons, esp for review or inspection. **pass** ~, be considered satisfactory; be good enough for the purpose or occasion. □ *vt,vi* [VP6A,15B,2A] ~ **(up),** call, collect or gather together: *Go and* ~ *all the men you can find. They* ~*ed* (*up*) *all their courage.*

musty /'mʌstɪ/ *adj* (-ier, -iest) **1** stale; smelling or tasting mouldy: ~ *books; a* ~ *room.* **2** (fig) stale; out-of-date: *a professor with* ~ *ideas.* **musti·ness** /'mʌstɪnɪs/ *n*

mu·table /'mjuːtəbl/ *adj* liable to change; likely to change. **mu·ta·bil·ity** /ˌmjuːtəˈbɪlətɪ/ *n* [U].

mu·ta·tion /mjuːˈteɪʃn/ *n* [U] change; alteration; [C] instance of this: *Are* ~*s in plants caused by cosmic rays?*

mu·ta·tis mu·tan·dis /muːˌtɑːtɪs muːˈtændɪs/ *adv* (Lat) with necessary alterations or changes (when comparing cases).

mute /mjuːt/ *adj* **1** silent; making no sound: *staring at me in* ~ *amazement.* **2** (of a person) dumb; unable to speak. **3** (of a letter in a word) not sounded: *The 'b' in 'dumb' is* ~. □ *n* **1** dumb person. **2** piece of bone or metal used to soften the sounds produced from a stringed instrument; pad placed in the mouth of a wind instrument for the same purpose. □ *vt* [VP6A] deaden or muffle the sound of (esp a musical instrument). ~·**ly** *adv*

mu·ti·late /'mjuːtɪleɪt/ *vt* [VP6A] damage by breaking, tearing or cutting off a necessary part; destroy the use of (a limb, etc). **mu·ti·la·tion** /ˌmjuːtɪˈleɪʃn/ *n* [U] mutilating or being ~d; [C] injury or loss

caused by this.

mu·ti·nous /'mjuːtɪnəs/ *adj* guilty of mutiny; rebellious: ~ *sailors;* ~ *behaviour.*

mu·tiny /'mjuːtɪnɪ/ *n* (*pl* -nies) [U] (esp of soldiers and sailors) open rebellion against lawful authority; [C] instance of this. □ *vi* [VP2A,3A] ~ **(against),** be guilty of ~; revolt. **mu·tin·eer** /ˌmjuːtɪˈnɪə(r)/ *n* person guilty of ~.

mutt /mʌt/ *n* (sl) **1** ignorant blunderer: *You silly big* ~! **2** mongrel dog.

mut·ter /'mʌtə(r)/ *vt,vi* [VP6A,14,2A,C] speak, say (sth), in a low voice not meant to be heard; grumble in an indistinct voice: *He was* ~*ing away to himself. Are you* ~*ing threats at me? We heard thunder* ~*ing in the distance.* □ *n* ~ed utterance or sound. ~**er** *n* person who ~s.

mut·ton /'mʌtn/ *n* [U] flesh of fully grown sheep: *a leg/shoulder of* ~; *roast* ~; *a* ~ *chop,* piece of ~ rib. **as dead as** ~, quite dead. ~ **dressed as lamb,** used of an elderly person dressed in a style suitable for a young person. '~-**head** *n* (colloq) dull, stupid person.

mu·tual /'mjuːtʃʊəl/ *adj* **1** (of love, friendship, respect, etc) shared; exchanged equally; (of feelings, opinions, etc) held in common with others: ~ *suspicion/affection.* **2** each to the other(s): ~ *enemies/well-wishers;* ~ *aid.* ~ **funds,** (US) = unit trusts. **a** ~ **in'surance company,** one in which some or all of the profits are divided among the policy-holders. **3** common to two or more persons: *our* ~ *friend Smith,* ie Smith, a friend of both of us. ~·**ly** /-ʊəlɪ/ *adv*

muzzle /'mʌzl/ *n* **1** nose and mouth of an animal (eg dog or fox); guard of straps or wires placed over this part of an animal's head to prevent it biting, etc. ⇨ the illus at dog. **2** ⇨ the illus at cannon. open end or mouth of a fire-arm: *a* ~-*loading gun.* '~-**velocity,** speed of a projectile as it leaves the ~. ⇨ breech. □ *vt* [VP6A] put a ~ on (a dog, etc); (fig) prevent (a person, society, newspaper, etc) from expressing opinions freely.

muzzy /'mʌzɪ/ *adj* (-ier, -iest) **1** confused in mind; spiritless; stupid from drinking. **2** blurred.

my /maɪ/ *poss adj* **1** belonging to me: *Where's my hat? This car is my own.* **2** as a part of a form of address: *Yes, my dear. My dear fellow!* **3** in exclamations: *My goodness! Oh, my!*

my·col·ogy /maɪˈkɒlədʒɪ/ *n* [U] science or study of fungi.

my·na(h) /'maɪnə/ *n* '~ **(bird),** (kinds of) starling of SE Asia, known for their ability to mimic human speech. ⇨ the illus at rare.

my·el·itis /maɪəˈlaɪtɪs/ *n* (path) inflammation of the spinal cord.

my·opia /maɪˈəʊpɪə/ *n* [U] short-sightedness. **my·opic** /maɪˈɒpɪk/ *adj* short-sighted.

myr·iad /'mɪrɪəd/ *n* [C] ~ **(of),** very great number.

myr·mi·don /'mɜːmɪdən *US:* -dɒn/ *n* (contemptuous or humorous term for a) person who carries out any kind of order without questions: ~*s of the law,* eg bailiffs.

myrrh /mɜː(r)/ *n* [U] sweet-smelling, bitter-tasting kind of gum or resin obtained from shrubs, used for making incense and perfumes.

myrtle /'mɜːtl/ *n* (kinds of) evergreen shrub with shiny leaves and sweet-smelling white flowers.

my·self /maɪˈself/ *pron* (reflex and emphat): *I hurt* ~. *I can do it* (*all*) *by* ~, ie without help. *I tired* ~ *out. I* ~ *said so. I said so* ~. *I'm not* ~ *today,* am not feeling so well as I usually do.

mys·teri·ous /mɪˈstɪərɪəs/ *adj* full of, suggesting, covered in, mystery: *a ~ crime; a ~-looking parcel.* **~·ly** *adv*

mys·tery /ˈmɪstərɪ/ *n* (*pl* -ries) **1** [C] sth of which the cause or origin is hidden or impossible to understand: *The murder remained an unsolved ~.* **2** [U] condition of being secret or obscure: *The origin of this tribe is lost in ~, It has been impossible to learn anything about it.* **3** (*pl*) secret religious rites and ceremonies (of ancient Greeks, Romans, etc). **4** [C] '*~* (**play**), medieval drama based on episodes in the life of Jesus.

mys·tic /ˈmɪstɪk/ *adj* of hidden meaning or spiritual power; causing feelings of awe and wonder: *~ rites and ceremonies; ~ teachings.* □ *n* person who seeks union with God and, through that, realization of truth beyond men's understanding. **mys·ti·cal** /ˈmɪstɪkl/ *adj* = mystic.

mys·ti·cism /ˈmɪstɪsɪzəm/ *n* [U] beliefs, experiences, of a mystic; teaching and belief that knowledge of God and of real truth may be obtained through meditation or spiritual insight, independently of the mind and the senses.

mys·tify /ˈmɪstɪfaɪ/ *vt* (*pt,pp* -fied) [VP6A] puzzle; bewilder. **mys·ti·fi·ca·tion** /ˌmɪstɪfɪˈkeɪʃn/ *n* [U]

~ing or being mystified; [C] sth that mystifies.

mys·tique /mɪˈstiːk/ *n* **1** esoteric character of a person, institution, etc caused by mystical devotion and veneration: *the ~ of the monarchy in Great Britain.* **2** incommunicable quality; skill known only to a few practitioners.

myth /mɪθ/ *n* **1** [C] story, handed down from olden times, esp concepts or beliefs about the early history of a race, explanations of natural events, such as the seasons: *ancient Greek ~s.* **2** [U] such stories collectively: *famous in ~ and legend.* **3** [C] person, thing, etc, that is imaginary, fictitious, or invented: *That rich uncle of whom he boasts is only a ~.* **~·i·cal** /ˈmɪθɪkl/ *adj* **1** of ~; existing only in ~: *~ical heroes; ~ical literature.* **2** imaginary; fictitious: *~ical wealth.*

myth·ol·ogy /mɪˈθɒlədʒɪ/ *n* (*pl* -gies) **1** [U] study or science of myths. **2** [U] myths collectively: *Greek ~;* [C] body or collection of myths: *the mythologies of primitive races.* **myth·ol·ogist** /mɪˈθɒlədʒɪst/ *n* student of ~. **mytho·logi·cal** /ˌmɪθəˈlɒdʒɪkl/ *adj* of ~ or myths; unreal.

myxo·ma·to·sis /ˌmɪksəməˈtəʊsɪs/ *n* [U] infectious fatal disease of rabbits.

Nn

N, n /en/ (*pl* N's, n's /enz/) the 14th letter of the English alphabet.

nab /næb/ *vt* (-bb-) (colloq) catch in wrongdoing; seize: *The thief was nabbed by the police.*

na·bob /ˈneɪbɒb/ *n* (18th c use) wealthy, luxury-loving person.

na·celle /næˈsel/ *n* outer casing for an engine of an aircraft or airship. ⇨ the illus at air.

nacre /ˈneɪkə(r)/ *n* [U] mother-of-pearl. ⇨ mother(4).

na·dir /ˈneɪdɪə(r)/ *n* point of the heavens directly beneath an observer. (fig) lowest, weakest, point: *at the ~ of one's hopes.* ⇨ zenith.

nag¹ /næg/ *n* (colloq) (usu old) horse.

nag² /næg/ *vt, vi* (-gg-) [VP6A,2A,C,3A] **nag (at)** (*sb*), find fault with continuously; worry or annoy by scolding: *She nagged (at) him all day long.* **nag·ger** *n*

naiad /ˈnaɪæd/ *n* (*pl* ~s, ~es /-diːz/) (Gk myth) water-nymph.

nail /neɪl/ *n* **1** layer of hard substance over the outer tip of a finger ('**finger-~**) or toe ('**toe-~**). ⇨ the illus at arm, leg. **fight tooth and ~**, with all one's strength, making every possible effort to win. '**~-brush** *n* for cleaning the ~s. ⇨ the illus at brush. '**~-file**, small, flat file for shaping the ~s. '**~-scissors** *n* for trimming the ~s. '**~-varnish/-polish** *n* for giving a shiny tint to the ~s. **2** piece of metal, pointed at one end and with a head at the other, (to be) hammered into articles to hold things together, or into a wall, etc to hang sth on. **drive a ~ into sb's coffin,** ⇨ coffin. **as hard as ~s,** (of a person) (a) in first rate physical condition. (b) pitiless; unsympathetic. **hit the ~ on the head,** pick out the real point at issue; give the true explanation. **right as ~s,** quite right. (**right**) **on the ~,** at once. □ *vt* [VP15A,B] **1** make fast with a ~ or ~s: *~ a lid on a box.* **~ sb down (to sth),** make him say clearly what he intends to do (about sth). **~ sth**

down, make (eg a carpet, a cover) secure by using nails. **~ sth up,** make (a door, window, etc) secure with ~s. **~ one's colours to the mast,** ⇨ colour¹(8). **~ a lie (to the counter),** prove that a statement is false. **2** hold fast, keep fixed (a person, sb's attention, etc): *He ~ed me in the corridor.*

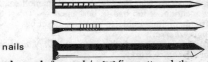

nails

nain·sook /ˈneɪnsʊk/ *n* [U] fine cotton cloth.

naira /ˈnaɪrə/ *n* [C] unit of Nigerian currency, = 100 kobos.

naïve, naive /naɪˈiːv/ *adj* natural and innocent in speech and behaviour (eg because young or inexperienced); amusingly simple: *~ remarks/tourists.* **~·ly** *adv* **~té** /-teɪ/, **~ty** /-tɪ/ *n* [U] artlessness; being ~; [C] ~ remark, etc.

naked /ˈneɪkɪd/ *adj* **1** without clothes on: *as ~ as the day he was born.* **2** without the usual covering: *a ~ sword,* without its sheath; *fight with ~ fists,* without boxing-gloves; *~ trees,* without leaves; *a ~ light,* not protected from the wind by glass, without a lampshade. **see sth with the ~ eye,** without using a microscope, telescope or other aid to seeing. **the ~ truth,** not disguised, softened, ornamented. **~·ly** *adv* **~·ness** *n*

namby-pamby /ˌnæmbɪ ˈpæmbɪ/ *adj* (of persons, talk) foolishly sentimental. □ *n* person of this sort.

name¹ /neɪm/ *n* **1** word(s) by which a person, animal, place, thing, etc is known and spoken to or of: *A person of the ~ of Smith* (= Someone who is called Smith) *wants to see you. He writes under the ~ of Nimrod,* uses Nimrod instead of his real name. *I know the man by ~,* only by hearsay, not by personal acquaintance. *The teacher knows all the pupils in his class by ~,* knows them individ-

Nützen ziehen aus - to profit hann/to take advantage of sth

ually. *in the ~ of,* (a) with the authority of: *Stop! in the Queen's ~. In the ~ of the law....* (b) in the cause of (used when making an appeal): *In the ~ of common sense, what are you doing? call sb ~s,* call him insulting ~s (eg liar, coward). *enter/put down one's ~ for,* (a school, college, etc), apply for entry (at a future date). *not have a penny to one's ~,* be without money. *lend one's ~ to,* (an enterprise, etc), allow it to be quoted in support or in favour of (the enterprise, etc). *take sb's ~ in vain,* use a ~ (esp God's) disrespectfully. **'~-day** *n* feast day of the Saint whose ~ one was given at christening. **'~-dropping** *n* the practice of casually mentioning the ~s of important people to impress. Hence, **'~-drop** *vi* [VP2A] talk in this way. **'~-part** *n* title-role of a play: *Who will play the ~-part in 'Hamlet'?* **'~-plate** *n* plaque (on the door of a building, room, etc) with the ~ of the occupant. **'~-sake** *n* person or thing with the same ~ as another. **2** (*sing* only) reputation; fame. *make/ win a ~ for oneself,* become well-known. *The firm has a ~ for good workmanship.* **3** famous person: *the great ~s of history.*

name² /neɪm/ *vt* **1** [VP6A,14,23] ~ *(after/* (US)*for),* give a ~ to: *They ~d the child John. The child was ~d after its father,* given its father's first ~. *Tasmania was ~d after its discoverer, A J Tasman.* **2** [VP6A] say the ~(s) of: *Can you ~ all the plants and trees in this garden?* **3** make an offer of (price, etc): *N~ your price,* Say what price you want. **4** state (what is desired, etc): *Please ~ the day,* say on what date you will be willing to (eg marry). **5** [VP6A,14] ~ *(for),* nominate for, appoint to, a position: *Mr X has been ~d for the directorship.*

name·less /'neɪmlɪs/ *adj* **1** not having a name; having an unknown name: *a ~ grave; a well-known person who shall be ~,* whose name I shall not mention. **2** too bad to be named: ~ *vices.* **3** difficult or impossible to name or describe: *a ~ longing/horror.*

name·ly /'neɪmlɪ/ *adv* that is to say: *Only one boy was absent, ~ Harry.*

nan·keen /næn'kiːn/ *n* [U] kind of cotton cloth, originally made of naturally yellow cotton.

nanny /'nænɪ/ *n* (*pl* -nies) = nurse¹(1).

nanny-goat /'nænɪ gəʊt/ *n* female goat. ⇨ billy-goat.

nap¹ /næp/ *n* [C] short sleep (esp during the day, not necessarily in bed): *have/take a nap after lunch on a hot day.* □ *vi* (-pp-) (rare, except in) *catch sb napping,* find him asleep; catch him unawares (in error, etc).

nap² /næp/ *n* [U] surface of cloth, felt, etc, made of soft, short hairs or fibres, smoothed and brushed up.

nap³ /næp/ *n* (GB) name of a card-game.

na·palm /'neɪpɑːm/ *n* [U] jellied petroleum used in making fire-bombs.

nape /neɪp/ *n* back (of the neck). ⇨ the illus at head.

na·pery /'neɪpərɪ/ *n* [U] (old use) household linen, esp table linen (tablecloths and napkins).

naph·tha /'næfθə/ *n* [U] kinds of inflammable oil obtained from coaltar and petroleum. **~·lene** /-liːn/ *n* [U] strong-smelling substance made from coaltar and petroleum, used in the manufacture of dyes and (in the form of white 'moth balls') to put among clothes.

nap·kin /'næpkɪn/ *n* [C] **1** ('table) ~, piece of cloth used at meals for protecting clothing, for wiping the lips, etc. **'~-ring** *n* ring to hold and distinguish a person's ~. ⇨ serviette. **2** (US = *diaper*) (*nappy* is more usu) towel folded round a baby's bottom and between its legs, to absorb excreta.

Na·po·leon·ic /nəˌpəʊlɪ'ɒnɪk/ *adj* of or like Napoleon Bonaparte /nəˌpəʊlɪən 'bəʊnəpɑːt/ (1769—1821), ruler of France.

nappy /'næpɪ/ *n* (*pl* -pies) (GB colloq) = napkin(2).

nar·ciss·ism /'nɑːsɪsɪzəm/ *n* [U] (psych) obsessive and exclusive interest in one's own self.

nar·cissus /nɑː'sɪsəs/ *n* (*pl* ~es /-səsɪz/ or -cissi /-sɪsaɪ/) sorts of bulb plant (daffodil, jonquil, etc), esp the kind having heavily scented white or yellow flowers in the spring.

nar·cotic /nɑː'kɒtɪk/ *n, adj* (kinds of drug) producing sleep, often blunting the senses and, in large doses, producing complete insensibility: *Opium is a ~ drug. The use of ~s by teenagers is a problem in many countries;* (*person*) addicted to ~s.

nark¹ /nɑːk/ *n* (GB sl) police decoy or spy.

nark² /nɑːk/ *vt* (GB sl) annoy: *feel ~ed at unjust criticism.*

nar·rate /nə'reɪt/ *vt* [VP6A] tell (a story); give an account of: ~ *one's adventures.* **nar·rator** /-tə(r)/ *n* person who ~s. **nar·ra·tion** /nə'reɪʃn/ *n* [U] telling of a story, etc; [C] story; account of events.

nar·ra·tive /'nærətɪv/ *n* **1** [C] story or tale; orderly account of events; [U] (composition that consists of) story-telling. **2** (attrib) in the form of, concerned with, story-telling: ~ *literature,* stories and novels; ~ *poems; a writer of great ~ power,* able to describe events well.

nar·row /'nærəʊ/ *adj* (-er, -est) (opposite of *wide*) **1** measuring little across in comparison with length: *a ~ bridge. The road was too ~ for cars to pass. A ~-gauge railway is one with rails less than 4 ft 8 in apart.* **2** small, limited: *a ~ circle of friends; living in ~ circumstances,* in poverty. **3** with a small margin: *a ~ escape from death. a ~ squeak,* (colloq) sth barely avoided or escaped from; *elected by a ~ majority,* eg when voting is 67 to 64. **4** strict; exact: *a ~ search. What does the word mean in the ~est sense?* **5** limited in outlook; having little sympathy for the ideas, etc, of others. ,~-'minded /'maɪndɪd/ *adj* not easily seeing or sympathizing with the ideas of others. ,~-'minded·ly *adv* ,~-'mindedness *n* □ *vt, vi* [VP6A,2A] (cause to) become ~. □ *n* (usu *pl*) ~ strait or channel between two larger bodies of water; ~ place in a river or pass. **~·ly** *adv* **1** only just; with little to spare: *He ~ly escaped drowning.* **2** closely; carefully: *Watch that fellow ~ly.* **~·ness** *n*

nar·whal /'nɑːwəl/ *n* Arctic whale with (in the male) a long spiral tusk.

na·sal /'neɪzl/ *adj* of, for, in, the nose: ~ *sounds,* eg /m, n, ŋ/; ~ *catarrh; a ~ douche.* □ *n* [C] nasal sound. **~·ize** /'neɪzəlaɪz/ *vt* [VP6A] make (a sound) with the air stream, or part of it, passing through the nose.

nascent /'næsnt/ *adj* (formal) coming into existence; beginning to exist.

nas·tur·tium /nə'stɜːʃəm US: næ-/ *n* [C] garden plant with red, orange or yellow flowers, round-shaped leaves, and seeds that may be pickled and eaten.

nasty /'nɑːstɪ US: 'næ-/ *adj* (-ier, -iest) **1** dirty; disgusting; unpleasant: *medicine with a ~ smell* *and a nastier taste.* **2** morally dirty and unpleasant: *a man with a ~ mind; ~ stories.* **3** showing ill will and spite: *a ~ temper.* **4** dangerous; threatening: *There was a ~ sea when we got out of the harbour. There was a ~ look in his eye.* **5** causing difficulty or danger; awkward: *That's a ~ corner for a car that's travelling fast.* **nas·ti·ly** /-ɪlɪ/ *adv* **nas·ti·ness** *n*

na·tal /'neɪtl/ *adj* of, from, one's birth.

na·tion /'neɪʃn/ *n* [C] large community of people associated with a particular territory usu speaking a single language and usu having a political character or political aspirations: *the ~s of Western Europe; the United N~s Organization,* UNO. ⇨ **state**[1](2). ˌ~·'wide *adj, adv* throughout a ~; concerning, expressed by, all citizens.

na·tion·al /'næʃnəl/ *adj* of a/the nation; common to a/the whole nation; characteristic of a/the nation: *a ~ theatre, one supported by the State; ~ opposition to a government policy,* expressed by all citizens. ˌ~ **'anthem,** song or hymn of a nation (eg 'God Save the Queen' in GB). **the** ˌN~ **'Debt,** total money owed by the State to those who have lent it money. ˌ~ **'monument,** structure, landmark, site of historic interest (often one maintained by the government). ˌ~ **'park,** area of land declared to be public property, for the use and enjoyment of the people. ˌ~ **'service,** period of compulsory service in the armed forces. ˌN~ **'Trust,** (in GB) society founded in 1895 to preserve places of natural beauty or historic interest for the nation. **the** ˌ**Grand 'N~,** the chief steeplechase in GB, run in March. □ *n* citizen of a particular nation: *One of a consul's duties is to help his own ~s,* his fellow countrymen. ~**·ly** /'næʃnəlɪ/ *adv*

na·tion·al·ism /'næʃnəlɪzəm/ *n* [U] **1** strong devotion to one's own nation; patriotic feelings, efforts, principles. **2** movement for political/economic, etc independence (in a country controlled by another).

na·tion·al·ist /'næʃnəlɪst/ *n* supporter of nationalism(2): *Scottish ~s,* those who want Scotland to have more self-government. □ *adj* (also ~**ic** /ˌnæʃnə'lɪstɪk/) favouring, supporting, nationalism: *~ movements in Zimbabwe.*

na·tion·al·ity /ˌnæʃə'nælətɪ/ *n* (*pl* -ties) [C,U] being a member of a nation: *What is your ~? There were men of all nationalities in Geneva.*

na·tion·al·ize /'næʃnəlaɪz/ *vt* [VP6A] **1** transfer from private to State ownership: *~ the railways/ the coal-mines/the steel industry.* **2** make (a person) a national: *~d Poles and Greeks in the US.* **3** make into a nation: *The Poles were ~d after the war of 1914—18,* They became an independent nation. **na·tion·ali·zation** /ˌnæʃnəlaɪ'zeɪʃn* US: -lɪ'z/ *n* nationalizing or being ~d: *the nationalization of the railways.*

na·tive /'neɪtɪv/ *n* **1** person born in a place, country, etc and associated with it by birth: *a ~ of London/Wales/India/Kenya.* **2** such a person as distinguished from immigrants, residents, visitors, tourists, etc from other countries, usu when the race to which he belongs is different in culture: *the first meetings between Captain Cook and the ~s* (= the aboriginal inhabitants) *of Australia.* **3** animal or plant natural to and having its origin in a certain area: *The kangaroo is a ~ of Australia.* **4** (GB) oyster reared wholly or partly in British waters, esp in artificial beds: *Whitstable ~s.* □ *adj* **1** associated with the place and circumstances of one's birth: *your ~ land/place.* **2** of ~s(2 above):

~ customs. **3** (of qualities) belonging to a person by nature, not acquired through training, by education, etc: *~ ability/charm.* **4** ~ **to,** (of plants, animals, etc) having their origin in: *plants ~ to America,* eg tobacco, potatoes. *One of the animals ~ to India is the tiger.* **5** (of metals) found in a pure state, uncombined with other substances: *~ gold.*

na·tiv·ity /nə'tɪvətɪ/ *n* (*pl* -ties) birth, esp (**the** **N~**) of Jesus Christ; picture of the N~ of Christ. **a 'N~ Play,** one about the N~.

nat·ter /'nætə(r)/ *vi* [VP2A,C] (GB colloq) chatter, grumble (esp to oneself): *What's she ~ing (on) about now?*

natty /'nætɪ/ *adj* (-ier, -iest) (colloq) **1** neat; smart and tidy: *new and ~ uniforms for bus conductresses.* **2** quick and skilful. **nat·ti·ly** /-ɪlɪ/ *adv*

natu·ral /'nætʃrəl/ *adj* **1** of, concerned with, produced by, nature: *animals living in their ~ state,* wild, not domesticated; *a country's ~ resources,* its minerals, forests, etc; *land in its ~ state,* not used for industry, farming, etc. ˌ~ **'forces/ phe'nomena,** the forces of nature, such as storms, thunder and lightning. ˌ~ **'gas,** gas occurring with petroleum deposits, eg North Sea gas. ˌ~ **'history,** botany and zoology; (formerly) scientific study of all nature. ˌ~ **'law,** rules for behaviour considered as innate and universal. ˌ~ **phi'losophy,** (name formerly used for) the science of physics, or physics and dynamics. ˌ~ **re'ligion,** religion and ethics based on reason (contrasted with religion from divine revelation). ˌ~ **se'lection,** evolutionary theory that animals and plants survive or become extinct in accordance with their ability to adapt themselves to their environment. **2** of, in agreement with, the nature(4) of a living thing: *~ gifts/abilities.* **3** (of persons) possessing qualities by nature(4); born with qualities or powers: *He's a ~ orator,* makes speeches easily. *She's a ~ linguist,* learns languages easily. *It comes ~ to her.* ⇨ **come**(9). **4** ordinary; normal; to be expected: *die a ~ death,* not as the result of an accident, violence, etc. *It is ~ for a bird to fly. He was sentenced to prison for the term of his ~ life,* ie until he died. **5** simple; not cultivated or self-conscious: *~ behaviour; speak in a ~ voice,* not affected. *It was a ~ piece of acting,* with no exaggeration. **6** (music) neither sharp nor flat: *B ~* (cf *B* sharp, *B* flat).⇨ the illus at notation. **7** (of a son or daughter) illegitimate. □ *n* **1** (music) ~ note; musical note that is not a sharp or a flat; the sign (♮) placed before a note (in printed music) to make it a ~. **2** person born without ordinary intelligence; person feeble-minded from birth. **3** (colloq) **a ~ for sth,** person naturally fitted or qualified: *He's a ~ for the job/the part.*

natu·ral·ism /'nætʃrəlɪzəm/ *n* [U] **1** adherence to nature in literature and art; drawing and painting things in a way true to nature. **2** (phil) system of thought which rejects the supernatural and divine revelation and holds that natural causes and laws explain all phenomena.

natu·ral·ist /'nætʃrəlɪst/ *n* person who makes a special study of animals or plants.

natu·ral·is·tic /ˌnætʃrə'lɪstɪk/ *adj* of naturalism: *a ~ painter.* ⇨ abstract[1](1), cubism, surrealism.

natu·ral·ize /'nætʃrəlaɪz/ *vt,vi* **1** [VP6A] give (sb from another country) rights of citizenship: *She was ~d in Japan,* was made a Japanese subject. **2** [VP6A] take (a word) from one language into another: *English sporting terms have been ~d in* *many languages.* **3** [VP6A] introduce and acclimatize (an animal or plant) into another country. **4** [VP6A] plant (bulbs, etc) in woodland areas so that the flowers appear to be growing wild or naturally. **5** [VP2A] become ~d. **natu·rali·zation** /ˌnætʃrəlaɪˈzeɪʃn *US:* -lɪˈz-/ *n* [U] naturalizing or being ~d: *Naturalization papers,* the documents that prove that a person has been admitted to citizenship of another country.

nat·urally /ˈnætʃrəlɪ/ *adv* **1** by nature(4): *She's ~ musical.* **2** of course; as might be expected: *'Did you answer her letter?'—'N~!'* **3** without artificial help, special cultivation, etc: *Her hair curls ~. Plants grow ~ in such a good climate.* **4** without artifice: *She speaks and behaves ~.*

na·ture /ˈneɪtʃə(r)/ *n* **1** [U] the whole universe and every created thing. *Is ~ at its best in spring?* '~ **study,** the study of animals, plants, insects, etc. '~ **worship,** the worship of trees, oceans, the winds, etc. **2** [U] force(s) controlling the phenomena of the physical world: *Man is engaged in a constant struggle with ~. Miracles are contrary to ~.* '~ **cure,** form of therapy relying upon natural remedies (eg sunlight, diet, exercise). **pay the debt of ~; pay one's debt to ~,** die. **in the course of ~,** according to the ordinary course of things. **3** [U] simple life without civilization; outdoor, animal-like existence: *Some 18th-century writers were in favour of a return to ~,* to the simple and primitive life that people were thought to have led before mankind became civilized. **be in a state of ~,** be completely naked (as in a nudist camp). **4** [C,U] qualities and characteristics, physical, mental and spiritual, which belong to a person or thing: *It is the ~ of a dog to bark. Cats and dogs have quite different ~s. That man is proud by ~.* Chemists study the ~ of gases. ˌhuman '~, the qualities possessed by man (in contrast with animals). **good ~,** unselfishness; willingness and readiness to help; kind-heartedness. Hence, ˌgood-/ˌill-'~ed, having a good/ill ~. **5** qualities of non-material things (eg art, knowledge, language) **6** sort; kind: *Things of this ~ do not interest me. His request was in the ~ of a command,* could not be ignored.

na·tur·ism /ˈneɪtʃərɪzəm/ *n* nudism. **na·tur·ist** /-ɪst/ *n* nudist.

naught /nɔːt/ *n* = nought(1).

naughty /ˈnɔːtɪ/ *adj* (-ier, -iest) **1** (of children, their behaviour, etc) bad; wrong; disobedient; causing trouble: *a ~ child. It was ~ of you to pull the cat's tail.* **2** taking pleasure in shocking, intended to shock, people: *a ~ novel(ist); ~ stories.* **naught·ily** /-ɪlɪ/ *adv* **naughti·ness** *n*

nausea /ˈnɔːsɪə *US:* ˈnɔːz-/ *n* [U] feeling of sickness (eg as caused by bad food) or disgust; seasickness: *overcome by ~ after eating octopus; filled with ~ at the sight of cruelty to animals.* **naus·eate** /ˈnɔːsɪeɪt *US:* ˈnɔːz-/ *vt* [VP6A] cause ~: *nauseating food; a nauseating sight.* **nauseous** /ˈnɔːsɪəs *US:* ˈnɔːʃəs/ *adj* disgusting; causing ~.

nautch /nɔːtʃ/ *n* performance by a professional dancing-girl ('~-girl) in India, etc.

nauti·cal /ˈnɔːtɪkl/ *adj* of ships, sailors or navigation: ~ *terms,* used by sailors: *a ~ almanac,* with information about the sun, moon, tides, etc: *a ~ mile,* 1/60 of a degree, 6080 ft (= 1852 metres).

nauti·lus /ˈnɔːtɪləs *US:* ˈnɔːtələs/ *n* (*pl* ~es /-ləsɪz/) small sea animal of which the female has

a very thin shell.

na·val /ˈneɪvl/ *adj* of a navy; of warships: ~ *officers/battles.*

nave /neɪv/ *n* central part of a church where the people sit. ⇨ the illus at church.

na·vel /ˈneɪvl/ *n* small depression in the middle of the surface of the belly (left by the severance of the umbilical cord). ⇨ the illus at trunk. ~ **orange,** large orange with a ~-like formation in the top.

navi·gable /ˈnævɪgəbl/ *adj* **1** (of rivers, seas, etc) that can be navigated; suitable for ships: *The Rhine is ~ from Strasbourg to the sea.* **2** (of ships, etc) that can be steered and sailed: *not in a ~ condition.* **navi·ga·bil·ity** /ˌnævɪgəˈbɪlətɪ/ *n*

navi·gate /ˈnævɪgeɪt/ *vt,vi* [VP6A,2A] **1** plot the course, find the position, etc of a ship, aircraft, etc, using maps and instruments. **2** steer (a ship); pilot (an aircraft); (fig) direct: ~ *a Bill through the House of Commons.* **3** sail over (a sea); sail up or down (a river). **navi·gator** /-tə(r)/ *n* **1** person who ~s(1). **2** sailor with skill and experience who has taken part in many voyages; (esp) early explorer: *the 16th c Spanish and Portuguese navigators.* **navi·ga·tion** /ˌnævɪˈgeɪʃn/ *n* [U] **1** the act of navigating. **2** the art or science of navigating. **3** the making of voyages on water or of journeys through the air: *inland ~,* by river and canal. *There has been an increase in ~ through the Panama Canal,* more ships use it.

navvy /ˈnævɪ/ *n* (*pl* -vies) (GB) unskilled workman.

navy /ˈneɪvɪ/ *n* (*pl* -vies) **1 (a/the) ~,** (with *sing* or *pl v*) that part of a country's military forces that is organized for fighting at sea: *join the ~; an officer/sailor in the Royal N~.* ~ **'blue,** dark blue as used for naval uniforms. **2** a country's warships collectively: *a small ~.*

nay /neɪ/ *adv* (old use) no; (rhet) not only that, but also: *I suspect, nay, I am certain, that he is wrong.*

Nazi /ˈnɑːtsɪ/ *n, adj* (member) of the German National Socialist Party founded by Hitler. **Nazism** /ˈnɑːtsɪzəm/ *n* the ideology of the ~s.

Ne·an·der·thal /niːˈændətɑːl/ *adj* ~ **man,** extinct type of man of the stone age.

neap /niːp/ *n* '~(-tide),** tide when high water is at its lowest level of the year. ⇨ *spring tide* at spring¹(3).

Nea·poli·tan /nɪəˈpɒlɪtən/ *n, adj* **1** (inhabitant) of Naples (ˈneɪplz/. **2** (small *n*) with many flavours and colours: ~ *ice-cream.*

near¹ /nɪə(r)/ *adj* (-er, -est) **1** not far from; close in space or time: *The post office is quite ~. Christmas is ~. Come ~er. Can you tell me the ~est (= shortest) way to the station? She was ~ to tears,* was almost crying. **the ~ distance,** that part of a scene between the foreground and the background. **a ~ miss,** eg of a bomb or shell, not a direct hit, but close enough to the target to cause damage. **a ~ thing,** a narrow escape. ˌ~-'sighted *adj* short-sighted; seeing well only when sth, eg a book, is held close to the eyes. **2** close in relation or affection: *a ~ relation,* eg a mother, a son or daughter; *friends who are ~ and dear to us.* **3** (contrasted with *off*) (of parts of animals and vehicles, or of horses in a team, when on a road, etc) the left side: *the ~ foreleg; the ~ front wheel of a car.* '~-**side** *n* side ~est the kerb: *the ~side lane of traffic.* **4** niggardly (contrasted with *generous*): *He's very ~ with his money.* □ *vt,vi* [VP6A,2A] come or draw ~ (to); approach: *The ship was*

~ing land. He's ~ing his end, is dying. The road is ~ing completion. ~·ness n

near² /nɪə(r)/ adv not far; to or at a short distance in space or time: We searched far and ~ (= everywhere) for the missing child. **as ~ as**, nearly: As ~ as I can guess (= My ~est or best guess is that) there were forty people present. He was as ~ as could be to (= only just escaped, narrowly escaped) being knocked down by the bus. **as ~** (= nearly) **as makes no difference**, with no difference worth considering: They're the same height, or as ~ as makes no difference. **~ at hand**, (**a**) within easy reach: Always have your reference books ~ at hand. (**b**) not far distant in the future: The examinations are ~ at hand. **~ on/upon**, not far in time from; almost: It was near upon midnight. **nowhere**/(colloq)**not ~**, far from: The concert hall was nowhere ~ full. She's nowhere ~ as old as her husband. **~ by**, not far off. Hence, '**~·by** adj

near³ /nɪə(r)/ prep (equivalent to near¹ with to) close to (in space, time, relationship, etc): Come and sit ~ me. It's convenient living so ~ the station.

near·ly /'nɪəlɪ/ adv **1** almost: It's ~ one o'clock/~ time to start. I'm ~ ready. ⇨ hardly, scarcely. **2** closely: We're ~ related, are near relations. **3 not ~**, far from: I have £20, but that isn't ~ enough for my journey, I shall need much more.

neat /niːt/ adj (-er, -est except 5 below) **1** (liking to have everything) tidy; in good order with nothing out of place; done carefully: ~ work; a ~ worker; a ~ desk; ~ writing. **2** simple and pleasant; in good taste: a ~ dress. **3** pleasing in shape and appearance: a ~ figure. **4** cleverly said or done: a ~ answer/conjuring trick. **5** (of wines and spirits) unmixed with water; undiluted: drink one's whisky ~. **~·ly** adv **~·ness** n

'**neath** /niːθ/ prep (poet) beneath.

neb·ula /'nebjʊlə/ n (pl ~e /-liː/ or ~s) [C] cluster of very distant stars, diffuse mass of gas, seen in the night sky as an indistinct patch of light. **nebu·lar** /-lə(r)/ adj of ~s.

nebu·lous /'nebjʊləs/ adj cloud-like; hazy; indistinct; vague.

necess·ar·ily /ˌnesə'serəlɪ/ adv as a necessary result; inevitably: Big men are not ~ strong men.

necess·ary /'nesəsərɪ US: -serɪ/ adj which has to be done; which must be; which cannot be done without or escaped from: Sleep is ~ to health. Is war a ~ evil in this world? Is it ~ for you to be/Is it ~ that you should be so economical? □ n [C] (usu pl) things ~ (for living).

necessi·tate /nɪ'sesɪteɪt/ vt [VP6A,C] make necessary: Your proposal ~s borrowing money. The increase in population ~s a greater food supply.

necessi·tous /nɪ'sesɪtəs/ adj (formal) poor; needy: in ~ circumstances, in poverty.

necess·ity /nɪ'sesətɪ/ n (pl -ties) **1** [U] urgent need; circumstances that compel sb to do sth; natural laws that direct human life and action: He was driven by ~ to steal food for his starving children. The doctor asked us not to call him during the night except in case of ~, eg unless the patient's condition changed very much for the worse. **be under the ~ of...**, be compelled by.... **bow to ~**, do what one is compelled to do. **make a virtue of ~**, accept credit without protest; claim credit for doing sth that one cannot help doing. **of ~**, as a matter of ~. **2** [C] sth that is necessary: The necessities of

life, food, clothing and shelter. **3** [C] sth of which the absence or non-occurrence cannot be imagined: Is it a logical ~ that the cost of living will go up if wages go up? Can the one be considered possible without the other?

neck /nek/ n **1** part of the body that connects the head and the shoulders: wrap a scarf round one's ~. ⇨ the illus at head. **break one's ~**, work extremely hard to achieve sth. ⇨ breakneck. **breathe down sb's ~**, (colloq) be close behind, almost touching, eg in a race; be watching closely. **get it in the ~**, (sl) suffer a severe or a fatal blow; have a painful experience. **have the ~** (more usu **nerve**) **to do sth**, (sl) be impudent, cheeky enough to do it. **save one's ~**, escape hanging; (fig) escape the results of being foolish, etc. **stick one's '~ out**, (sl) do or say sth that may bring severe criticism, or result in a painful experience. **win/ lose by a ~**, (horse-racing) by the length of a horse's ~; (fig) by a narrow margin. **~ and crop**, headlong; altogether; bag and baggage: throw him out ~ and crop. **~ and ~**, (of horse-racing, and fig) side by side, with no advantage over the other in a race or struggle. **~ or nothing**, taking desperate risks; venturing everything. **2** flesh of an animal's ~ as used for food, esp ~ of mutton. **3** sth like a ~ in shape or position: the ~ of a bottle; a narrow ~ of land, eg an isthmus. **4** (compounds) '**~·band** n part of a shirt, etc that goes round the ~. '**~·cloth** n cravat. **~·er·chief** /'nekətʃɪf/ n (old use) cloth or scarf worn round the ~. '**~·lace** /-lɪs/ n string of beads, pearls, etc worn round the ~ as an ornament. '**~·let** /-lɪt/ n ornament (eg of beads) for the ~. '**~·line** n (of fashions for women's clothes) line of a garment at or near the ~: This year the ~line is up and the hemline is down. '**~· tie** n (now usu **tie**) band of material worn round the ~ and knotted in front. '**~·wear** /-weə(r)/ n [U] (term used by shopkeepers for) collars and ties. □ vi (sl) (of couples) exchange kisses, caresses and hugs: sitting on park benches petting and ~ing in the dark.

nec·ro·mancy /'nekrəmænsɪ/ n [U] art or practice of communicating by magic with the dead in order to learn about the future. **nec·ro·man·cer** /-sə(r)/ n person who practises ~.

ne·crop·olis /nɪ'krɒpəlɪs/ n (pl ~es /-lɪsɪz/) cemetery, esp a large one in an ancient town.

nec·tar /'nektə(r)/ n [U] **1** (in old Gk stories) the drink of the gods. ⇨ ambrosia. **2** sweet liquid in flowers, collected by bees; any delicious drink.

nec·tar·ine /'nektərɪn/ n kind of peach with thin, smooth skin and firm flesh.

née /neɪ/ adj (F) born (put after the name of a married woman and before her father's family name): Mrs J Smith, née Brown.

need¹ /niːd/ anom fin (no inf, no participles, 3rd p sing present tense is need, not needs; int and interr followed by inf without to; need not contracted to needn't /'niːdnt/) [VP5] **1** be obliged; be necessary: N~ you go yet? No, I ~n't. Yes, I must. You ~n't go yet, ~ you? I ~ hardly tell you (= You must already know or guess) that.... **2** (followed by a perfect infinitive, ~ indicates that although sth may have occurred or been done in the past, it was or may have been unnecessary): N~ it have happened? We ~n't have hurried, We hurried but now we see that this was unnecessary. Cf We didn't ~ to hurry, We didn't hurry because it was unnecessary. ⇨ need³(2). **~·ful** /-fl/ adj ~ed; necessary:

do what is ~*ful. do the* ~*ful,* (colloq) provide the money, perform the action, that is required. ~·**ful-ly** /-fəlɪ/ *adv* ~·**less** *adj* not ~ed; unnecessary: ~*less work/trouble. N*~*less to say, he kept his promise.* ~·**less·ly** *adv*

need² /niːd/ *n* **1** [U] ~ *(for),* circumstances in which sth is lacking, or necessary, or requiring some course of action: *There's no* ~ *(for you) to start yet. There's no/not much* ~ *for anxiety. There's a great* ~ *for a book on this subject. if* ~ *be,* if necessary. **2** (used in *pl*) requirement; sth felt to be necessary: *He earns enough to satisfy his* ~*s,* ie to buy food, clothing, etc. *My* ~*s are few. £10 will meet my immediate* ~*s.* **3** [U] poverty; misfortune; adversity: *He helped me in my hour of* ~*. A friend in* ~ *is a friend indeed,* (prov) A friend who helps when one is in trouble is a real friend. ~·**y** *adj* (-ier, -iest) very poor; lacking the necessities of life: *a* ~*y family; help the poor and* ~*y.*

need³ /niːd/ *vt* **1** [VP6A,E] want; require: *The garden* ~*s rain. Does he* ~ *any help? It only* ~*s good will from both sides. This chapter* ~*s rewriting/*~*s to be rewritten.* **2** [VP7A] be under a necessity or obligation: *He didn't* ~ *to be reminded about it. Does he* ~ *to know? It* ~*s to be done carefully. He* ~*s to be kept informed about developments.* **3** [VP6A] deserve; ought to have: *What he* ~*s is a good whipping!*

needle /'niːdl/ *n* **1** small, thin piece of polished steel, pointed at one end and with a small hole at the other end for thread, used in sewing and darning: *look for a* ~ *in a haystack,* (prov) engage in a hopeless search. *as sharp as a* ~, quick-witted; observant. '~·**woman** *n* (*pl* -women) woman who sews. '~·**craft,** '~·**work** *nn* [U] sewing; embroidery. ,**pins** and '~·**s,** ⇨ pin¹(1). **2** long, thin piece of polished wood, bone or metal (without an eye), with a pointed end (for knitting) or a hook (for crocheting). **3** thin steel pointer in a compass, showing the magnetic north; similar pointer in a telegraphic instrument. **4** sth like a ~(1) in shape, appearance or use (eg the thin, pointed leaves of pine-trees; a sharp, pointed peak or rocky summit; the sharp, hollow end of a syringe used for giving injections). ⇨ the illus at tree; syringe. **5** stylus used in recording and playing gramophone records. Cf *sapphire* and *diamond styluses.* **6 the** ~, (sl) nervous excitement: *give sb the* ~, provoke or excite him; *get the* ~, be provoked. **7** obelisk: *Cleopatra's* ~, in London. □ *vt* **1** [VP6A,15A] sew, pierce, operate on, with a ~; thread (one's way) between or through things. **2** (colloq) goad, provoke (sb, esp by making cruel comments, etc).

needs /niːdz/ *adv* (now used only with *must*) of necessity. *N*~ *must when the devil drives,* (prov) Circumstances may compel us to act in a certain way. (When the *adv* follows *must,* as in 'He must ~', the sense is usu sarcastic, as here): *He must* ~ *go away just when I want his help,* He foolishly or stupidly insisted on going away....

ne'er /neə(r)/ *adv* (poet) never. ~·**do-well** /'neə du: wel/ *n* useless or good-for-nothing person.

nefarious /nɪ'feərɪəs/ *adj* (formal) wicked; unlawful. ~·**ly** *adv* ~·**ness** *n*

ne·gate /nɪ'ɡeɪt/ *vt* [VP6A] (formal) deny; nullify.

ne·ga·tion /nɪ'ɡeɪʃn/ *n* [U] **1** (opp of *affirmation*) act of denying: *Shaking the head is a sign of* ~. **2** absence of any positive or real quality or meaning: *The life of an evil man is a moral* ~.

nega·tive /'neɡətɪv/ *adj* **1** (opp of *affirmative*) (of

words and answers) indicating *no* or *not: give sb a* ~ *answer.* **2** (opp of *positive*) expressing the absence of any positive character; that stops, hinders or makes powerless: ~ *criticism,* that does not help by building up, making suggestions; ~ *praise,* not finding fault; ~ *virtue,* doing nothing wrong, but doing nothing good or right, either. **3** (maths) of a number or quantity that has to be subtracted (eg — x^2y). **4** of that kind of electricity produced by rubbing wax, vulcanite, etc; of or from the cathode: *the* ~ *plate in a battery,* from which electrons will flow to the positive plate. **the** ~ **pole,** (made of zinc) in a cell. **5** (photo) having lights and shades reversed. □ *n* [C] **1** word or statement that denies: *'No', 'not' and 'neither' are* ~*s. The answer is in the* ~, is 'No'. **2** (maths) a minus quantity (eg — 5*x*). **3** (photo) developed plate or film on which lights and shades are reversed. □ *vt* [VP6A] **1** prove (a theory, etc) to be untrue: *Experiments* ~*d his theory.* **2** reject; refuse to accept; neutralize (an effect). ~·**ly** *adv*

the negative of the photograph at *ski*

ne·glect /nɪ'ɡlekt/ *vt* **1** [VP6A] pay no attention to; give no or not enough care to: ~ *one's studies/children/health.* **2** [VP7A,6C] omit or fail (*to* do sth); leave undone (what one ought to do): *He* ~*ed to write and say 'Thank you'. Don't* ~ *writing to your mother.* □ *n* [U] ~*ing* or being ~*ed: He lost his job because of* ~ *of duty. The garden was in a state of* ~. ~·**ful** /-fl/ *adj* in the habit of ~*ing* things: *boys who are* ~*ful of their appearance.* ~·**fully** /-fəlɪ/ *adv* ~·**ful·ness** *n: He has a tendency to* ~*fulness.*

nég·li·gé, neg·li·gee /'neɡlɪʒeɪ US: ,neɡlɪ'ʒeɪ/ *n* [C,U] (condition of being in a) loose, free style of informal dress.

neg·li·gence /'neɡlɪdʒəns/ *n* [U] **1** carelessness; failure to take proper care or precautions: *The accident was due to* ~. **2** neglected condition or appearance: ~ *of dress.*

neg·li·gent /'neɡlɪdʒənt/ *adj* taking too little care, guilty of neglect: *He was* ~ *in* (= in respect of) *his work. He was* ~ *of his duties.* ~·**ly** *adv*

neg·li·gible /'neɡlɪdʒəbl/ *adj* that need not be considered; of little or no importance or size: *a* ~ *quantity.*

ne·go·ti·able /nɪ'ɡəʊʃɪəbl/ *adj* **1** that can be negotiated(2): *Is the dispute* ~*?* **2** that can be changed into cash, or passed from person to person instead of cash: ~ *securities/instruments,* eg cheques, promissory notes. **3** (of roads, rivers, etc) that can be passed over or along.

ne·go·ti·ate /nɪ'ɡəʊʃɪeɪt/ *vi,vt* **1** [VP2A,3A] ~ *(with sb),* discuss, confer, in order to come to an agreement: *We've decided to* ~ *with the employers about our wage claims.* **2** [VP6A,14] ~ *sth (with sb),* arrange by discussion: ~ *a sale/a loan/a* *treaty/peace.* **3** [VP6A] get or give money for (cheques, bonds, etc). **4** [VP6A] get past or over: *This is a difficult corner for a large car to* ~. *My horse* ~d (ie jumped over) *the fence very well.* **ne·go·ti·ator** /-tə(r)/ *n* one who ~s.

ne·go·ti·ation /nɪˌgəʊsɪˈeɪʃn/ *n* [C,U] negotiating: *enter into/open/start/carry on/resume* ~s *with sb; be in* ~ *with sb. The price is a matter of* ~.

Ne·gress /ˈniːgres/ *n* Negro woman or girl.

Ne·gro /ˈniːgrəʊ/ *n* (*pl* ~es /-rəʊz/) member (or, outside Africa, descendant) of one of the black-skinned African peoples south of the Sahara.

Ne·groid /ˈniːgrɔɪd/ *adj* of or akin to Negroes or the Negro race. □ *n* person of the ~ race.

ne·gus /ˈniːgəs/ *n* hot, sweetened wine, lemon juice, nutmeg and water.

Ne·gus /ˈniːgəs/ *n* (title of the) ruler of Ethiopia.

neigh /neɪ/ *vi, n* (make the) cry of a horse.

neigh·bour (US = **-bor**) /ˈneɪbə(r)/ *n* person living in a house, street, etc near another; person, thing or country that is near(est) another: *We're nextdoor* ~s, Our houses are side by side. *We were* ~s *at dinner,* We sat together at table. *When the big tree fell, it brought down two of its smaller* ~s, two smaller trees near it. *Britain's nearest* ~ *is France.* □ *vt, vi* [VP6A,3A] ~ *(on/upon),* (chiefly in the form ~*ing*) be near to: ~*ing countries; in the* ~*ing village.* '~·**hood** /-hʊd/ *n* **1** (people living in a) district; area near the place, etc referred to: *There's some beautiful scenery in our* ~*hood. He was liked by the whole* ~*hood. He wants to live in the* ~*hood of London.* **2** condition of being near: *The* ~*hood of this noisy airport is a serious disadvantage. He lost a sum in the* ~*hood of £500.* ~·**ly** *adj* kind; friendly. ~·**li·ness** *n* [U] friendly feeling, help, that is expected from ~s.

nei·ther /ˈnaɪðə(r)/ *US:* ˈniːð-/ *adj, pron* (used with a *sing n* or *pron*; cf *either*) not one nor the other (of two): *N*~ *statement is true. N*~ (*one*) *is satisfactory. I like* ~ *of them. I can agree in* ~ *case. In* ~ *case can I agree.* □ *adv, conj* **1** ~... **nor**..., not... and not...: *He* ~ *knows nor cares what happened. It's* ~ *pleasant to eat nor good for you. N*~ *you nor I could do it. The cat has not been fed:* ~ *has the dog* (or) *N*~ *the cat nor the dog has been fed.* **2** (after a negative *if*-clause, etc) and not: *If you don't go,* ~ *shall I. As he won't help you,* ~ *will I. I haven't been to the Exhibition;* ~ *do I* (= and I do not) *either*. A: *'I don't like it'*—B: *'N*~ *do I'* Cf *Nor do I. No more do I.*

Nelly /ˈnelɪ/ *n* (only in) **not on your** ~, (GB *sl*) certainly not!

nem con /ˌnem ˈkɒn/ *adv* (abbr Lat) unanimously; without any objection being raised: *The resolution was carried* ~.

nem·esis /ˈneməsɪs/ *n* (*pl* -eses /-əsiːz/) (formal) **1** deserved fate; just punishment for wrong-doing. **2** N~, goddess of vengeance.

neo- /ˈniːəʊ/ *pref* new; modern. ▷ App 3.

neo·col·onial·ism /ˌniːəʊ kəˈləʊnɪəlɪzəm/ *n* control by powerful countries of former colonies, or less developed countries by economic pressure.

neo·lithic /ˌniːəˈlɪθɪk/ *adj* of the new or later stone age: ~ *man.*

neol·ogism /niːˈɒlədʒɪzəm/ *n* [U] coining or using of new words; [C] newly coined word.

neon /ˈniːɒn/ *n* [U] colourless gas forming a very small proportion of the earth's atmosphere. ~ **light** *n* coloured light produced when an electric current passes through this gas in a low-pressure

bulb or tube. ~ **sign** *n* advertisement, etc in which ~ light is used.

neo·phyte /ˈniːəfaɪt/ *n* person who has newly been converted to some belief or religion.

nephew /ˈnevjuː/ *US:* ˈnefjuː/ *n* son of one's brother or sister.

neph·ri·tis /nɪˈfraɪtɪs/ *n* [U] inflammation of the kidneys.

neo·plasm /ˈniːəʊplæzəm/ *n* (path) tumor.

ne plus ultra /ˌniː plʌs ˈʌltrə/ *n* (Lat) farthest point attained or attainable; highest point, culmination (*of*).

nep·ot·ism /ˈnepətɪzəm/ *n* [U] the giving of special favour (esp employment) by a person in high position to his relatives.

Nep·tune /ˈneptjuːn/ *US:* -tuːn/ *n* **1** (Roman god of) the sea. **2** one of the farthest planets of the solar system. ▷ the illus at **planet**.

ne·reid /ˈnɪərɪɪd/ *n* (Gk myth) sea-nymph.

nerve /nɜːv/ *n* **1** [C] fibre or bundle of fibres carrying feelings and impulses between the brain and all parts of the body. '~**-cell** *n* cell that conducts impulses. '~**-centre** *n* group of closely connected ~-cells; (fig) centre of control. **2** (*pl*) condition of being easily excited, worried, irritated: *He is suffering from* ~s, quickly and easily becomes excited, frightened, etc. *That man doesn't know what* ~s *are,* is never worried, upset, etc by events. *He has* ~s *of iron,* is never upset, etc. **get on one's** ~s, worry or annoy: *That noise gets on my* ~s. **war of** ~s, campaign in which an attempt is made to weaken an opponent by destroying his morale. '~**-racking** *adj* inflicting strain on the ~s. **3** [U] quality of being bold, self-reliant, etc: *A test pilot needs plenty of* ~. *What a* ~! *What cheek!* **have the** ~ **to do sth,** (a) have the necessary courage, self-reliance: *have the* ~ *to drive a racing car.* (b) (colloq) be impudent enough: *He had the* ~ *to suggest that I was cheating.* **have a** ~, (colloq) be self-assured or audacious: *He's got a* ~, *going to work dressed like that!* **lose/regain one's** ~, lose/recover one's courage and self-assurance. **4** [C] (old use) sinew, tendon. **strain every** ~ **to do sth,** make great efforts. **5** (bot) rib, esp mid-rib, of a leaf. □ *vt* [VP6A,14,16A] ~ **oneself for sth/to do sth,** summon up one's strength (physical or moral): ~ *oneself for a task;* ~ *oneself ready to face troubles.* ~·**less** *adj* from ~(4) lacking in vigour or spirit; without energy: *The knife fell from his* ~*less hand.* ~·**less·ly** *adv*

nerv·ous /ˈnɜːvəs/ *adj* **1** of the nerves(1): *the* ~ *system of the human body.* **a** ~ **'breakdown,** neurasthenia. **2** having or showing nerves(2): *Are you* ~ *in the dark? What's she so* ~ *about?* **3** tense; excited: *full of* ~ *energy; a* ~ *style of writing.* ~·**ly** *adv* ~·**ness** *n*

nervy /ˈnɜːvɪ/ *adj* **1** (GB colloq) suffering from nervous strain. **2** (sl) impudent.

nes·cience /ˈnesɪəns/ *n* [U] (formal) absence of knowledge. **nes·cient** /-ənt/ *adj* without knowledge.

ness /nes/ *n* (usu in place names) promontory; headland.

nest /nest/ *n* **1** place made or chosen by a bird for its eggs. ▷ the illus at **prey**. **feather one's** ~, ▷ feather[2](1). **foul one's own** ~, abuse(2) one's own family, home, etc. '~**-egg** *n* (fig) sum of money saved for future use. **2** place in which certain living things have and keep their young: *a* '*wasps'* ~; *a* '*turtle's* ~. **3** comfortable place:

make oneself a ~ *of cushions.* 4 number of like things (esp boxes, tables) fitting one inside another. 5 (fig) shelter; hiding-place; secluded retreat: *a* ~ *of crime/vice/pirates; machine-gun* ~*s,* where they are hidden from direct view. □ *vi* [VP2A,C] 1 make and use a ~: *The swallows are* ~*ing in the woodshed.* 2 *go* ~*ing,* search for the ~s of wild birds and take the eggs.

nestle /'nesl/ *vt,vi* 1 [VP2C] ~ *(down),* settle comfortably and warmly: ~ *down among the cushions;* ~ *down in bed.* 2 [VP2C] ~ *up (against/ to),* press oneself lovingly (to): *The child was nestling closely up to her mother.* 3 [VP15A] cradle: *She* ~*d the baby in her arms.*

nest·ling /'nestlɪŋ/ *n* [C] bird too young to leave the nest.

Nes·tor /'nestə(r)/ *n* wise, old counsellor (the name of one of the Greeks in Homer's *Iliad*).

net¹ /net/ *n* [U] 1 open-work material of knotted string, hair, wire, etc; [C] such material made up for a special purpose: *a mosquito-net,* for use over a bed; '*fishing-nets;* '*tennis nets;* '*hair-nets* (used by women to keep the hair in place). ⇨ the illus at tennis. 2 (fig) moral or mental snare. 3 '**net·ball** *n* girls' game in which a ball has to be thrown so that it falls through a net fastened to a ring on the top of a post. **the nets,** (cricket) wickets set up inside a net for practice: *have an hour at the nets.* '**net·work** *n* (a) complex system of lines that cross: *a network of railways/canals.* (b) connected system: *An intelligence/spy network. A world communications network,* eg for radio and TV, using satellites. □ *vt* (-tt-) [VP6A] 1 catch (fish, animals, etc) with or in a net. 2 cover (eg fruit trees) with a net or nets: *net strawberries/currant bushes,* against birds. 3 put nets in place in: *net a river.*

net², **nett** /net/ *adj* remaining when nothing more is to be taken away: *net price,* off which discount is not to be allowed; *net profit,* when working expenses have been deducted; *net weight,* of the contents only, excluding the weight of packing, the container, etc. □ *vt* (-tt-) [VP6A] gain as a net profit: *He netted £5 from the deal.*

nether /'neðə(r)/ *adj* 1 (archaic) lower: *the* ~ *regions/world,* the world of the dead; hell. 2 (joking style) ~ *garments,* trousers. ~·**most** /-məʊst/ *adj*

Neth·er·lander /'neðələndə(r)/ *n* native of the Netherlands (Holland). ⇨ App 6.

nett ⇨ net².

net·ting /'netɪŋ/ *n* [U] 1 making or using nets. 2 netted string, thread or wire: *five yards of wire* ~; *windows screened with* ~.

nettle /'netl/ *n* [C] common wild plant which has on its leaves hairs that sting and redden the skin when touched. '~·**rash** *n* eruption on the skin with red patches like those caused by ~s. □ *vt* [VP6A] sting (oneself) with ~s; (fig) make rather angry; annoy: *She looked* ~*d by my remarks.*

net·work ⇨ net¹.

neu·ral /'njʊərəl US: 'nʊərəl/ *adj* of the nerves.

neu·ral·gia /njʊə'rældʒə US: nʊ-/ *n* [U] sharp, jumping pain in the nerves, esp of the face and head. **neu·ral·gic** /nju:'rældʒɪk/ *adj* of ~.

neur·as·thenia /ˌnjʊərəs'θi:nɪə US: ˌnʊr-/ *n* [U] exhausted condition of the nervous system; low state of health, general weakness, accompanying this condition. **neur·as·thenic** /-'θenɪk/ *adj* suffering from, related to, ~. □ *n* person suffering from ~.

neur·itis /njʊə'raɪtɪs US: nʊ-/ *n* [U] inflammation

of a nerve or nerves.

neur·ol·ogy /njʊə'rɒlədʒɪ US: nʊ-/ *n* [U] branch of medical science that is concerned with nerves. **neur·ol·ogist** /njʊə'rɒlədʒɪst US: nʊ-/ *n* expert in ~.

neur·osis /njʊə'rəʊsɪs US: nʊ-/ *n* (*pl* -oses /-əʊsi:z/) functional derangement or something due to disorder of the nervous system or by something in the subconscious mind. **neur·otic** /njʊə'rɒtɪk US: nʊ-/ *adj* (of a person) suffering from a ~; of abnormal sensitivity; obsessed. □ *n* neurotic person.

neu·ter /'nju:tə(r) US: 'nu:-/ *adj* 1 (gram; of gender) neither feminine nor masculine. 2 (of plants) without male or female parts. 3 (of insects, eg worker ants) sexually undeveloped; sterile. □ *n* 1 ~ noun or gender. 2 sexually undeveloped insect; castrated animal: *My cat is an enormous ginger* ~. □ *vt* castrate: *a* ~*ed tomcat.*

neu·tral /'nju:trəl US: 'nu:-/ *adj* 1 helping neither side in a war or quarrel: ~ *nations; be/remain* ~. 2 of a country that remains ~ in war: ~ *territory/ ships.* 3 having no definite characteristics; not clearly one (colour, etc) or another: ~ *tints.* 4 (chem) neither acid nor alkaline. 5 (of gear mechanism) of the position in which no power is transmitted: *leave a car in* ~ *gear.* □ *n* ~ person, country, etc; ~ position of gears: *slip the gears into* ~. ~·**ity** /nju:'trælətɪ US: nu:-/ *n* [U] state of being ~, esp in war: *armed* ~*ity,* readiness to fight if attacked, but remaining ~ unless or until this happens. ~·**ize** /-aɪz/ *vt* [VP6A] 1 make ~; declare by agreement that (a place) shall be treated as ~ in war; exempt or exclude from hostilities. 2 take away the effect or special quality of, by means of sth with an opposite effect or quality: ~*ize a poison.* ~·**iz·ation** /ˌnju:trəlaɪ'zeɪʃn US: -lɪ'z-/ *n*

neu·tron /'nju:trɒn US: 'nu:-/ *n* particle carrying no electric charge, of about the same mass as a proton, and forming part of the nucleus of an atom.

never /'nevə(r)/ *adv* 1 at no time; on no occasion: *She* ~ *goes to the cinema. He has* ~ *been abroad. They say that he* ~ *told a lie. I'm tired of listening to your* ~*-ending complaints.* (Front position for emphasis): *N*~ *in all my life have I heard such nonsense!* (modifying *again* and *before*): *I shall* ~ *again stay at that hotel. Such a display has* ~ *before been seen/has* ~ *been seen before.* 2 (used as an emphatic substitute for *not*): *That will* ~ *do,* won't do at all. *I* ~ *slept a wink all night. He* ~ *so much as smiled,* didn't smile even once. 3 (phrases) *Well, I* '~ *(did)!* expressing surprise. *N*~ *mind!* Don't worry! Don't trouble about it. **the ˌN**~ **'N**~ **Land,** imaginary land. **on the ˌ**~-'~, (sl) on the hire-purchase system: *buy sth on the* ~-~. ~·**more** /ˌnevə'mɔ:(r)/ *adv* ~ again.

never·the·less /ˌnevəðə'les/ *adv, conj* however; in spite of that; still: *There was no news;* ~, *she went on hoping.*

new /nju: US: nu:/ *adj* (-er, -est) 1 not existing before; seen, heard of, introduced, for the first time; of recent origin, growth, manufacture, etc: *a new school/idea/film/novel/invention; new potatoes,* lifted from the soil early in the season; *new clothes/furniture; new* (= freshly baked) *bread; the newest* (= latest) *fashions; new members of Parliament,* elected to Parliament for the first time. **new look,** ⇨ look²(2). **the New Testament,** (abbr NT) the second part of the Bible. 2 already in existence, but only now seen, discovered, etc: *learn new words in a foreign language; discover a* *new star.* **the New World,** N and S America. **3** *new to,* unfamiliar with; not yet accustomed to: *I am new to this town. They are still new to the work/trade.* **new from,** freshly or recently arrived from: *an office boy new from school; a person new from the provinces.* **4** (with *def art*) later, modern, having a different character. **the new poor/rich,** those people recently made poor/rich by social changes, etc. **the new woman,** (as used in the first half of the 20th c) woman having or claiming independence, social freedom, etc. *a new deal,*⟶ deal⁴(1). **5** beginning again. **lead a new life,** give up old habits, etc. *a/the new moon,* seen as a thin crescent. **wish sb a Happy New Year,** ie on **New Year's Day,** 1 Jan, or on **New Year's Eve,** 31 Dec. □ *adv* (preceding, joined or hyphened to, the word it qualifies) recently: *a newborn baby; new-laid eggs; new-fallen snow; new-made graves.* **'new-comer** *n* person who has recently arrived in a place. **,new-'fangled** /-'fæŋgld/ *adj* newly come into use or fashion (and, for this reason, disliked by some): *new-fangled ideas about education.* **new·ly** *adv* **1** recently: *a newly married couple; her newly awakened curiosity.* **'newly-wed** *n* newly married person. **2** in a new, different way: *newly arranged furniture.* **new·ness** *n*

newel /'nju:əl *US:* 'nu:əl/ *n* centre pillar of a winding stair; post supporting a hand-rail at the top, bottom or turn of a staircase.

new-fangled /,nju:'fæŋgld *US:* ,nu:/ *adj*⟶ new.

New·found·land /'nju:fəndlənd *US:* 'nu:-/ *n* large breed of spaniel, originally from ~, a large island in Canada, noted for its intelligence and swimming powers.

New·mar·ket /'nju:mɑːkɪt *US:* 'nu:-/ *n* English town noted for horse-races; kind of card-game.

news /nju:z *US:* nu:z/ *n sing* [U] new or fresh information; report(s) of what has most recently happened: *What's the latest ~?* (TV and radio): *Here is the ~. Here are the ~ headlines. Here is a ~ summary/a summary of the ~. Here are some interesting items/pieces/bits of ~. That's no ~ to me,* I already know that. *Sandra is in the ~,* is being written about in the papers. *The ~ that the enemy were near alarmed the citizens. Have you any ~ of* (= concerning) *where your brother is staying?*,*No ~ is'good ~,* (prov) If there were bad ~ we should hear it. **'~·agent** *n* shopkeeper who sells ~papers, periodicals, etc. **'~ agency** *n* agency that collects ~ and sells it to the press. **'~-boy** *n* boy who sells ~papers in the streets. **'~-cast** *n* broadcast of ~. **'~·caster** *n* person who does this. **'~ cinema/theatre,** cinema showing ~reels, cartoons, and other short films. **'~·dealer,** (US) = ~agent. **'~·letter** *n* letter or circular sent out to members of a society, etc. **'~·monger** *n* person who gossips. **'~·paper** /'nju:speɪpə(r) *US:* 'nu:z-/ *n* printed publication, usu issued every day, with ~, advertisements, etc. **'~·paper-man** /-mæn/ *n* (*pl* -men) journalist. **'~·print** *n* [U] paper for printing ~papers on. **'~·reel** *n* cinema film of recent events. **'~·room** *n* room (in a library, etc) where ~papers and other periodicals may be read. **'~·sheet** *n* simple form of ~paper. **'~·stand** *n* stall for the sale of ~papers, etc. **'~·vendor** *n* seller of ~papers. **'~·worthy** *adj* sufficiently interesting for reporting, eg in a newspaper. **~·less** *adj* without ~. **~·y** *adj* (colloq) full of ~ or gossip: *a ~y letter.*

newt /nju:t *US:* nu:t/ *n* (kinds of) small lizard-like animal which spends most of its time in the water. ⟶ the illus at amphibian.

New·to·nian /nju:'təʊnɪən *US:* nu:-/ *adj* related to Sir Isaac Newton /'nju:tn *US:* 'nu:-/, 1642—1727, English scientist and philosopher, and his theories, esp his law of gravity. □ *n* follower of Newton and his system.

next /nekst/ *adj,* n **1** ~ *(to sth/sb),* coming immediately after, in order or space: *What's the ~ thing to do? Take the ~ turning to the right. Miss Green was the ~* (*person*) *to arrive. Come and sit down ~ to me. Which is the town ~ to London in size?* **the ~ best (thing),** that which is chosen or accepted if the first choice fails: *There are no tickets left for the Circus: the ~ best thing is the Zoo. ~ to nothing,* scarcely anything; almost nothing: *No wonder she's ill! She eats ~ to nothing. ~ door,* in the ~ house: *He lives ~ door (to me). The people ~ door are very noisy. We are ~-door neighbours. ~ door to,* (fig) almost; not far from: *Such ideas are ~ door to madness. next of kin,* ⟶ kin. **2** (of time; *def art* needed if the reference is to a time that is future in relation to a time already mentioned): *I shall go there ~ Friday/week/year. We shall be in France by this time ~ week. He will spend the first week of his holiday in France and the ~ (week) in Italy. We arrived in Turin on a Monday; the ~ day we left for Rome. That summer was very wet; the ~ summer was even wetter. Is he coming this weekend* (ie the coming weekend) *or ~ weekend* (ie the following weekend)? □ *adv* **1** after this/that; then: *What are you going to do ~? When I ~ saw her she was dressed in green. come ~,* follow: *What comes ~,* what's the ~ thing (to do, etc). **2** used to express surprise or wonder: *What will he be saying ~? A new motor-car! What ~?* □ *prep* (archaic) = next to.

nexus /'neksəs/ *n* (*pl* ~es /-səsɪz/) connection; bond; connected series.

nib /nɪb/ *n* split pen-point (to be) inserted in a pen-holder.

nibble /'nɪbl/ *vt,vi* [VP6A,2A,3A] ~ *(at),* **1** take tiny bites: *fish nibbling (at) the bait.* **2** (fig) show some inclination to accept (an offer), agree to (a suggestion, etc), but without being definite. □ *n* [C] act of nibbling: *I felt a ~ at the bait.*

nice /naɪs/ *adj* (-r, -st) **1** (contrary to *nasty*) pleasant; agreeable; kind; friendly; fine: *a ~ day; ~ weather; a ~ little girl; ~ to the taste/the feel, etc; medicine that is not ~ to take. ~ and + adj, ~ because...: ~ and warm by the fire; ~ and cool in the woods.* **2** needing care and exactness; sensitive; subtle: *a ~ point of law,* one that may be difficult to decide; *~(= delicate) shades of meaning.* **3** (ironic) difficult; bad: *You've got us into a ~ mess.* **4** hard to please; having or showing delicate tastes: *too ~ in one's dress.* **5** punctilious; scrupulous: *He's not too ~ in his business methods.* **~·ly** *adv* **1** in a ~ manner. **2** (colloq) very well; all right: *That will suit me ~ly. The patient is doing ~ly,* is making good progress. **~·ness** *n*

nicety /'naɪsətɪ/ *n* (*pl* -ties) **1** [U] accuracy; exactness: *~ of judgement; a point of great ~,* one needing most careful and exact consideration. **2** [C] delicate distinction: *the niceties of criticism. to a ~,* exactly right: *He judged the distance to a ~.*

niche /nɪtʃ/ *n* [C] **1** (usu shallow) recess (often with a shelf) in a wall, eg for a statue or ornament. **have a ~ in the temple of fame,** have achievements that will not be forgotten. **2** (fig) suitable or fitting position: *He found the right* ~ *for himself,* a place where he could do what he wanted to do, comfortably and happily.

nick¹ /nɪk/ *n* **1** small V-shaped cut (made in sth), eg as a record. **2** *in the* ~ *of time,* only just in time; at the critical or opportune time. **3** *in the* ~, (sl) in prison. □ *vt* make a ~ in: ~ *one's chin,* while shaving; cut a notch in.

nick² /nɪk/ *n* (sl) (only in) *in good/poor* ~, in good health or condition: *feeling in very good* ~. *The house is in pretty poor* ~.

Nick /nɪk/ *n* short for *Nicholas.* **Old N~,** the devil.

nickel /'nɪkl/ *n* **1** [U] hard, silver-white metal (symbol **Ni**) used in the form of ~-plating and in alloys (,~-'steel, ,~-'silver). **2** US coin, value 5 cents. □ *vt* (-ll-, US = -l-) coat with ~.

nick-nack /'nɪknæk/ *n* = knick-knack.

nick-name /'nɪkneɪm/ *n* name given in addition to or altered from or used instead of the real name (eg *Fatty* for a fat person; *Shorty* humorously for a very tall person). □ *vt* [VP6A,23] give a ~ to: *They* ~*d him Hurry.*

nic-otine /'nɪkəti:n/ *n* [U] poisonous, oily substance in tobacco-leaves: ~-*stained fingers; cigarettes with a low* ~ *content.*

niece /ni:s/ *n* daughter of one's brother(-in-law) or sister(-in-law).

niff /nɪf/ *n* (GB sl, dial) (unpleasant) smell. ~y *adj* (sl) having a bad smell.

nifty /'nɪftɪ/ *adj* (sl) **1** smart; stylish. **2** having an unpleasant smell. **3** quick, efficient: *Look* ~! (more usu *Look nippy!*)

nig-gard /'nɪgəd/ *n* mean, stingy person. ~-**ly** *adj* giving, given, unwillingly, in small amounts; miserly: ~*ly contributions.* ~-**li-ness** *n*

nig-ger /'nɪgə(r)/ *n* ⚠ (impolite and offensive word for) Negro.

niggle /'nɪgl/ *vi* give too much time or attention to unimportant details; complain about trivial matters. **nig-gling** *adj* trifling; lacking in boldness of effect.

nigh /naɪ/ *adv, prep* (-er, -est) (archaic and poet) near (to).

night /naɪt/ *n* [C,U] **1** dark hours between sunset and sunrise or twilight and dawn: *in/during the* ~; *on Sunday* ~; *on the* ~ *of Friday, the 13th of June; a late-*~ *show at the cinema,* one given much later than the usual shows. *He stayed three* ~*s with us,* slept at our house three ~*s. Can you stay over* ~, spend the ~ with us? *What a dirty* ~ *it has been,* how stormy, rainy, etc the ~ has been! ~ *after* ~, for many ~*s* in succession. *all* ~ *(long),* throughout the whole ~. ~ *and day,* continuously: *travel* ~ *and day for a week. at* ~, when ~ comes; during the ~: *6 o'clock at* ~, 6pm. *by* ~, during the ~: *travel by* ~. *get/have/take a* ~ *off,* a ~ free from work usually done at ~. *have a good/bad* ~, sleep well/badly. *have a* ~ *out,* spend an evening and ~ in pleasure, eg by having dinner out, followed by a visit to the cinema. *make a* ~ *of it,* spend all ~ in pleasure-making, esp at a party. *turn* ~ *into day,* do at ~ what is usu done during the day. *work* ~*s,* work on ~ shift: *My husband's working* ~*s this week.* ⇨ shift¹(2). **2** (compounds) '~-**bell** *n* bell (eg on the street door, at a doctor's house) to be used at ~. '~-**bird** *n* (a) bird (eg an owl) which is active at ~. (b) person (usu disreputable) who goes about at ~. '~-**cap** *n* (a) cap (formerly) worn in bed. (b) (usu alcoholic) drink taken before going to bed. '~-**club** *n* club open until the early hours of the morning to mem-

bers for dancing, supper, entertainment, etc. '~-**dress** *n* long, loose garment worn by a woman or child in bed. '~-**fall** *n* [U] the coming of ~; evening. '~-**gown** *n* = ~dress. ~**ie,** ~y *n* (colloq) = ~dress. '~-**jar** *n* ~-flying bird that resembles a swift. '~ **life** *n* [U] entertainment, eg cabaret, ~clubs, available in a town late at ~. '~-**light** *n* light (eg a short, thick candle, or a small electric bulb) kept burning in a bedroom at ~ (esp for a small child or an invalid). '~-**line** *n* line left in a river, lake, etc with baited hooks, to catch fish by ~. '~-**long** *adj* lasting the whole ~. '~-**mare** /-meə(r)/ *n* [C] (a) terrible, frightening dream. (b) haunting fear; sth dreaded; (memory of a) horrible experience: *Travelling on those bad mountain roads was a* ~*mare.* '~-**porter** *n* hotel porter on duty during the ~. '~ **safe** *n* facility or opening like a letter-box in a wall of a bank, so that valuables, money, etc may be deposited after banking hours. '~ **school** *n* one that gives lessons to persons who are unable to attend classes during the day. '~-**shade** *n* [U] name of various wild plants with poisonous berries. '~ **shift** *n* ⇨ shift¹(2). '~-**shirt** *n* boy's or man's long shirt for sleeping in. '~-**soil** *n* contents of earth-closets and cesspools, removed during the ~. '~ **stop** *n,* '~-**stop** *n* break in a journey for a night. '~-**time** *n* time of darkness: *in the* ~-*time,* by ~. ,~-'**watch** *n* (person or group of persons keeping) watch by ~. *in the* ~-*watches,* during the wakeful, restless, or anxious periods of ~. ,~-'**watchman** /-mən/ *n* (*pl* -men) man employed to keep watch (eg in a factory) at ~. '~-**work** *n* work that is done, or must be done, by ~. ~-**ly** *adj, adv* (taking place, happening, existing) in the ~ or every ~: ~*ly performances; a film show twice* ~*ly; do something* ~*ly.*

night-in-gale /'naɪtɪŋgeɪl US: -tɪŋ-/ *n* small, reddish-brown migratory bird that sings sweetly by night as well as by day. ⇨ the illus at bird.

ni-hil-ism /'naɪɪlɪzəm/ *n* [U] total rejection of current political institutions and religious and moral beliefs. **ni-hil-ist** /-ɪst/ *n* believer in ~. **ni-hil-is-tic** /,naɪɪ'lɪstɪk/ *adj* relating to ~.

nil /nɪl/ *n* nothing: *The result of the game was three nil/three goals to nil,* ie 3—0.

Ni-lotic /naɪ'lɒtɪk/ *adj* of the Nile, the Nile region, or its inhabitants.

nimble /'nɪmbl/ *adj* **1** quick-moving: *as* ~ *as a goat.* **2** (of the mind) sharp; quick to understand. **nim-bly** /'nɪmblɪ/ *adv* ~-**ness** *n*

nim-bus /'nɪmbəs/ *n* (*pl* ~es /-bəsɪz/, -bi /-baɪ/) **1** bright disc round or over the head of a saint (in a painting, etc). ⇨ halo. **2** rain-cloud.

nim-iny-pim-iny /,nɪmɪnɪ 'pɪmɪnɪ/ *adj* affected; mincing; prim.

Nim-rod /'nɪmrɒd/ *n* great hunter. ⇨ Gen 10: 8,9.

nin-com-poop /'nɪŋkəmpu:p/ *n* foolish, weakminded person.

nine /naɪn/ *n, adj* the number 9, ⇨ App 4. *a* ~-*days' wonder,* sth that attracts attention for a few days and is then forgotten. *dressed up to the* ~*s,* (colloq) dressed very elaborately or extravagantly. ~ *times out of ten,* very often. **nine-pence** /'naɪnpəns US: -npens/ *n* **nine-penny** /'naɪnpənɪ US: -npenɪ/ *adj* ~-**teen** /,naɪn'ti:n/ *n, adj* the number 19. *(talk)* ~*teen to the dozen,* (talk) continually. ~-**teenth** /,naɪn'ti:nθ/ *n, adj* the next after the 18th; one of 19 equal parts. ~-**ti-eth** /'naɪntɪəθ/ *n, adj* the next after the 89th; one of 90 equal parts.

~ty /'naɪntɪ/ n, adj the number 90. ~ty-~ **times out of a hundred,** almost always. **the ~ties,** 90-99. '~-fold /-fəʊld/ adj, adv ~ times as many or much. **ninth** /naɪnθ/ n, adj the next after the 8th; one of 9 equal parts. **ninth-ly** adv

nine-pins /'naɪnpɪnz/ n pl (with sing v) **1** game in which a ball is rolled along the floor at nine bottle-shaped pieces of wood. ⇨ tenpins. **2** (sing) one of these pieces. **go down like a ninepin,** fall heavily.

ninny /'nɪnɪ/ n (pl -nies) fool; simpleton.

Niobe /'naɪəbɪ/ n (Gk myth) woman who was changed into a stone fountain while weeping for her children who had been killed; woman who weeps and cannot be comforted.

nip /nɪp/ vt, vi (-pp-) **1** [VP6A,15A,B] pinch; press hard (eg between finger and thumb, or with the claws, as a crab does, or with the teeth, as a dog or horse might do): A crab nipped my toe while I was swimming. He nipped his finger in the door, ie between the door and the door-post. The gardener was nipping off (= pinching out) the side shoots from his chrysanthemums; (sewing) alter the size slightly: The dress fits me now that I've nipped in the sides a little, reduced the width by altering the seams. **2** [VP6A,15A] (of frost, wind, etc) stop the growth of; damage. **nip sth in the bud,** stop its development. **3** [VP2A] perform the action of biting or pinching. **4** (colloq) [VP2C] hurry: nip along. He nipped in (= got in quickly) just in front of me. I'll nip on ahead and open the door. □ n [C] **1** sharp pinch or bite: a cold nip in the air, a feeling of frost. **2** small drink (esp of) (spirits): a nip of brandy. **'nip-ping** adj (of the air or wind) sharp; biting cold. ⇨ nippy(1).

nip-per /'nɪpə(r)/ n **1** (pl; colloq) pincers, forceps or other tool for gripping. **2** crustacean's claw. **3** (GB colloq) small child.

nipple /'nɪpl/ n **1** part of the breast through which a baby gets its mother's milk; similar small projection on the breast of a human male. Cf teat for other mammals. **2** (more usu teat) rubber mouthpiece of a baby's feeding bottle. **3** sth shaped like a ~: 'greasing ~s, through which grease is injected.

Nip-pon-ese /ˌnɪpə'niːz/ adj of Nippon /'nɪpɒn/ (= Japan).

nippy /'nɪpɪ/ adj (-ier, -iest) (colloq) **1** (GB) biting cold. **2** nimble. **look ~,** be quick.

nir-vana /nɪə'vɑːnə/ n (in Buddhism) state in which individuality becomes extinct by being absorbed into the supreme spirit.

nisi /'naɪsaɪ/ conj (Lat, legal) unless: **decree ~,** decree (of divorce, etc) valid unless cause is shown for rescinding it before the time when it is made absolute.

Nis-sen hut /'nɪsn hʌt/ n prefabricated semicircular hut of sheets of corrugated iron, erected over a concrete floor.

nit[1] /nɪt/ n egg of a louse or other parasitic insect.

nit[2] /nɪt/ n = nitwit.

ni-ter /'naɪtə(r)/ ⇨ nitre.

ni-trate /'naɪtreɪt/ n salt formed by the chemical reaction of nitric acid with an alkali, esp potassium ~ and sodium ~, used as fertilizers. (Used in pl for 'kinds of ~').

nitre (US = **niter**) /'naɪtə(r)/ n [U] potassium or sodium nitrate (also called saltpetre).

ni-tric /'naɪtrɪk/ adj of, containing, nitrogen. ~ **acid, (HNO₃),** clear, colourless, powerful acid that eats into and destroys most substances.

ni-tro-chalk /ˌnaɪtrəʊ'tʃɔːk/ n [U] fertilizer used in spring to encourage growth of grass.

ni-tro-gen /'naɪtrədʒən/ n [U] gas (symbol **N**) without colour, taste or smell, forming about four-fifths of the atmosphere.

ni-tro-glycer-ine, -glycerin /ˌnaɪtrəʊ'ɡlɪsəriːn US: -rɪn/ n [U] powerful explosive made by adding glycerine to a mixture of nitric and sulphuric acids.

ni-trous /'naɪtrəs/ adj of, like, nitre. ~ **oxide,** gas **(N₂O)** (also called laughing-gas) sometimes used by dental surgeons to make a person unconscious while having a tooth or teeth pulled out.

nitty-gritty /ˌnɪtɪ 'ɡrɪtɪ/ n [U] **the ~,** (colloq) the basic fact(s) of a matter.

nit-wit /'nɪtwɪt/ n (colloq) person with very little intelligence. Hence, ~**-ted** /ˌnɪt'wɪtɪd/ adj unintelligent.

nix /nɪks/ n (sl) nothing.

no /nəʊ/ adj **1** not one; not any: She had no friends. The poor boy had no money. No words can describe the scene. There was no end to our troubles, They were endless. **no end of,** (colloq) a large number or quantity of; very great: He spends no end of money on clothes. We had no end of a good time, a very enjoyable time. (Note that no precedes numerals and other): No one man could have done it, No man could have done it by himself. No two men think alike. No other man could do the work. **2** (implying the opposite of the following word): He's no friend of mine. The task is no easy one. This nightclub is no place for a young and innocent girl. Matilda is no beauty, is not at all beautiful. **3** (in the pattern: there + be + no + gerund): There's no saying (= It is impossible to say) what he'll be doing next. There's no denying (= We cannot deny) that.... **4** (in elliptical constructions): No smoking (= Smoking is not allowed). No surrender! It's raining hard and no mistake, and there can be no doubt about it. **5** (phrases) **It's no go,** (colloq) can't be done, won't succeed. **be no good/use,** useless: It's no good crying over spilt milk. ⇨ milk¹(1). **be no wonder (that),** not surprising (that). **by 'no means,** ⇨ means¹. **in 'no time,** very soon, very quickly. **,no-'ball,** unlawfully delivered ball in cricket. **,no-'go area,** (colloq) (usu urban) area barricaded to prevent the police or security force from entering. **'no-man's-land,** (in war) ground between the fronts of two opposing armies. **'no one, 'no-one,** pron = nobody. □ adv **1** (used with comparatives): We went no farther than (= only as far as) the bridge. I hope you're feeling no worse this morning. I have no more money. **2** (phrases) **no more... than,** ⇨ more(5). **no such,** ⇨ such. **3 whether or no,** = whether or not: Whether or no you like it, you've got to do it. □ particle **1** (opposite of 'Yes'): Is it Monday today?—No, it isn't. Isn't it Monday today?—No, it isn't. Aren't you busy?—No, I'm not. **2** (used with not or nor to emphasize a negative): One man couldn't lift it; no, nor half a dozen. □ n [C] refusal; denial: The noes /nəʊz/ have it, Those voting 'no' are in the majority.

Noah's ark /ˌnəʊəz 'ɑːk/ n model of the ark in which Noah and his family were saved from the Flood, with small animal and human figures. ⇨ Gen, chap 59.

nob[1] /nɒb/ n (sl) head.

nob[2] /nɒb/ n (sl) member of the upper classes; person of high rank.

nobble /'nɒbl/ *vt* (GB sl) [VP6A] **1** tamper with (a race-horse) to lessen its chance of winning. **2** (colloq) get the attention of (in order to gain an advantage, etc); get sth dishonestly or by devious means.

Nobel Prize /nəʊˌbel 'praɪz/ *n* any of the prizes awarded each year by the Nobel Foundation for outstanding achievements in literature, science and the promotion of world peace (after A B Nobel /nəʊ'bel/, 1833—1896, Swedish inventor of dynamite who established the awards).

no·bil·ity /nəʊ'bɪlətɪ/ *n* [U] **1** quality of being noble; noble character, mind, birth, rank. **2** (usu with *def art*) the nobles as a class: *a member of the* ~; *marry into the* ~.

noble /'nəʊbl/ *adj* **1** having, showing, high character and qualities: *a* ~ *leader;* ~ *sentiments; a* ~ *mind.* Hence, ~ '**minded** /'maɪndɪd/ *adj* ~-'**minded·ness** *n* **2** of high rank, title or birth: *a man of* ~ *rank/birth.* **3** splendid; that excites admiration: *a building planned on a* ~ *scale; a* ~ *horse;* ~ *metals,* eg gold, silver, platinum, that do not easily tarnish in air or water. □ *n* person of ~ birth. '~·**man** /-mən/ *n* (*pl* -men) (GB) peer; person of parallel rank in other countries. **nobly** /'nəʊblɪ/ *adv* in a ~ manner; splendidly.

no·blesse /nəʊ'bles/ *n* (F) class of nobles. ~ **o'b-lige** /ə'bliːʒ/ (prov) privilege entails responsibility.

no·body /'nəʊbədɪ/ *pron* (*pl* -dies) **1** not anybody; no person: *We saw* ~ *we knew. He said he would marry me or* ~. *N*~ *could find their luggage* (colloq for *his or her luggage*). *N*~ *else* (= No other person) *offered to help.* **2** (used in the *sing* with the *indef art*, and in the *pl*) unimportant or unimpressive person: *Don't marry a* ~ *like James.*

noc·tam·bu·list /nɒk'tæmbjʊlɪst/ *n* sleepwalker.

noc·tur·nal /nɒk'tɜːnl/ *adj* of or in the night; done, active, or happening in, the night: *a man of* ~ *habits;* ~ *birds,* eg owls.

noc·turne /'nɒktɜːn/ *n* [C] **1** painting of a scene at night. **2** soft, dreamy piece of music.

nod /nɒd/ *vi,vt* (-dd-) **1** [VP2A,3A,4A] *nod (to/at),* bow the head slightly and quickly as a sign of agreement or as a familiar greeting: *He nodded to me as he passed. He nodded to show that he understood.* **have a nodding acquaintance with,** ⇨ acquaintance. **2** [VP2A,2C] *nod (off),* let the head fall forward when sleepy or falling asleep; make a mistake as if asleep or half asleep: *She sat nodding by the fire. She often nods off* (= falls asleep) *during the afternoon. The teacher caught one of her pupils nodding,* falling asleep, or so sleepy as to make mistakes. *Homer sometimes nods,* (prov) Even the greatest may make a small mistake. **3** [VP2C,6A,12A,13A] indicate by nodding: *He nodded approval/in approval/approvingly. He nodded me a welcome/nodded a welcome to Mary.* □ *n* **1** nodding of the head: *He gave me a nod as he passed.* **2** *the Land of Nod,* sleep. **3** *on the* ~, (US sl) on credit.

noddle /'nɒdl/ *n* (colloq) head.

node /nəʊd/ *n* [C] **1** (bot) point on the stem of a plant where a leaf or bud grows out. **2** (phys) point or line of rest in a vibrating body. **3** (fig) point at which the parts of sth begin or meet.

nod·ule /'nɒdjuːl *US:* 'nɒdʒuːl/ *n* small rounded lump; small knob or swelling. **nod·u·lar** /-lə(r)/, **nod·u·lat·ed** /-leɪtɪd/ *adj* having ~s.

Noel /nəʊ'el/ *n* Christmas.

nog·gin /'nɒgɪn/ *n* small measure, usu ¼ pint, of li-

quor; (sl) head.

no·how /'nəʊhaʊ/ *adv* (colloq) in no way; not at all.

noise /nɔɪz/ *n* [C,U] loud and unpleasant sound, esp when confused and undesired: *the* ~ *of jet aircraft. Don't make so much* ~/*such a loud* ~! *What's that* ~? *What are those strange* ~s? *make a* ~ *(about sth),* talk or complain in order to get attention. *make a '*~ *in the world,* become famous, be much talked about. *a '***big** ~, (sl) important person. □ *vt* ~ *sth abroad,* make public: *It was* ~*d abroad that he had been arrested.* ~·**less** *adj* making little or no ~: *with* ~*less footsteps.* ~·**less·ly** *adv* ~·**less·ness** *n*

noi·some /'nɔɪsəm/ *adj* offensive; (esp, of smell) disgusting.

noisy /'nɔɪzɪ/ *adj* (-ier, -iest) **1** making, accompanied by, much noise: ~ *children;* ~ *games.* **2** full of noise: *a* ~ *classroom.* **nois·ily** /-ɪlɪ/ *adv* **noisi·ness** *n*

no·mad /'nəʊmæd/ *n* member of a tribe that wanders from place to place, with no fixed home. ~**ic** /nəʊ'mædɪk/ *adj* of ~s: *a* ~*ic society.*

nom de plume /ˌnɒm də 'pluːm/ *n* (*pl* noms /nɒm/ de plume) (F) pen-name.

no·men·cla·ture /nə'menklətʃə(r)   *US:* 'nəʊmənkleɪtʃər/ *n* [C] (formal) system of naming: *botanical* ~; *the* ~ *of chemistry.*

nom·inal /'nɒmɪnl/ *adj* **1** existing, etc, in name or word only, not in fact: *the* ~ *ruler of the country; the* ~ *value of the shares.* **2** of little importance or value: *a* ~ *sum; a* ~ *rent,* one very much below the actual value of the property. **3** (gram) of a noun or nouns. **4** of, bearing, a name: *a* ~ *roll.* ~·**ly** /-nəlɪ/ *adv*

nomi·nate /'nɒmɪneɪt/ *vt* [VP6A,14,23] **1** ~ *sb (for),* put forward for election to a position: ~ *a man for the Presidency;* ~ *Mr X for Mayor.* **2** ~ *sb (to),* appoint to office: *a committee of five* ~*d members and eight elected members.* **nomi·nee** /ˌnɒmɪ'niː/ *n* person who is ~d for an office or appointment.

nomi·na·tion /ˌnɒmɪ'neɪʃn/ *n* **1** [U] nominating; [C] instance of this: *How many* ~*s have there been* (= How many persons have been nominated) *so far?* **2** [U] right of nominating sb for an office or position.

nomi·na·tive /'nɒmɪnətɪv/ *adj, n* (of the) form of a word (eg the pronoun *we*) when it is the grammatical subject: *the* ~ *case.* ⇨ case¹(3).

nomi·nee /ˌnɒmɪ'niː/ *n* ⇨ nominate.

non- /ˌnɒn/ *pref* who or which is not, does not, etc: ˌnon-a'**lignment** *n* principle or practice of not joining either of the great power blocs.

ˌnon-ag'**gression** *n* not attacking; not starting hostilities: *a ˌnon-ag'gression pact.*

ˌnon-'**combatant** *n* person (esp in the armed forces, eg a surgeon or chaplain) who does not take part in the fighting.

ˌnon-com'**missioned** *adj* (esp of army officers such as sergeants and corporals) not holding commissions(4).

ˌnon-com'**mittal** *adj* not committing oneself to a definite course of action to either side (in a dispute, etc): *give a non-committal answer.*

ˌnon-com'**pliance** *n* refusal to comply (with an order, etc).

ˌnon-con'**ductor** *n* substance that does not conduct heat or electric current.

ˌnoncon'**formist** *n* **1** person who does not conform

to society's standards. **2** (in England) member of a sect that has separated from the Church of England.

‚noncon'formity *n* **1** failure to conform. **2** (beliefs and practices of) nonconformists as a body.

‚non-con'tentious *adj* not likely to cause contention.

‚non-e'vent *n* (colloq) planned event which turns out to be unworthy of what it was expected or hoped to be.

‚non-'fiction *n* [U] prose books other than writings (eg novels, stories, plays) which deal with fictitious events and persons.

‚non-'flammable *adj* (in official use, contrary to *inflammable*) having no tendency to burst into flames.

‚non-‚inter'ference, ‚non-‚inter'vention *nn* principle or practice, esp in international affairs, of keeping out of other people's disputes.

‚non-'moral *adj* that cannot be considered or judged as either moral or immoral.

‚non-ob'servance *n* failure to observe (a rule, etc).

‚non-'payment *n* failure or neglect to pay (a debt, etc).

‚non-'resident *adj* who does not reside in: *a nonresident priest*, not living where he performs his duties. □ *n* person not staying at a hotel, etc: *Meals served to non-residents.*

‚non-'skid *adj* (of tyres) designed to prevent or reduce the risk of skidding.

‚non-'smoker *n* person who does not smoke tobacco; place, eg a train compartment, where smoking is forbidden.

‚non-'starter *n* horse which, although entered for a race, does not run; (fig) person who has no chance of success in sth he undertakes to do.

‚non-'stick *adj* (eg of a pan) made so that food, etc will not stick to its surface.

‚non-'stop *adj, adv* without a stop: *a non-stop train from London to Brighton; fly non-stop from New York to Paris.*

‚non-'U *adj* ⇨ App 2.

‚non-'union *adj* not belonging to a trade union; not observing trade union rules: *non-union labour.*

‚non-'violence *n* policy of rejecting violent means (but using peaceful protest, etc) to gain a political or social objective.

non·age /'nəʊnɪdʒ/ *n* [U] = minority(1); immaturity.

nona·gen·ar·ian /‚nɒnədʒɪ'neərɪən/ *n, adj* (person who is) between 89 and 100 years old.

nonce /nɒns/ *n* (old use, or liter; only in) **for the ~,** for the present time only. **'~-word** *n* word coined for one occasion.

non·cha·lant /'nɒnʃələnt/ *adj* not having, not showing, interest or enthusiasm; deliberately casual. **~·ly** *adv* **non·cha·lance** /-ləns/ *n* [U]

non com·pos men·tis /‚nɒn ‚kɒmpəs 'mentɪs/ (Lat) (legal) not legally responsible because not of sound mind; (colloq) confused in one's mind.

non·de·script /'nɒndɪskrɪpt/ *n, adj* (person or thing) not easily classed; not having a definite character; uninteresting.

none /nʌn/ *pron* **1** not any, not one: *I wanted some string but there was ~ in the house. N~ of this money is mine. 'Is there any coal left?' 'No, ~ at all.' There are faults from which ~ of us* (= not one of us, or not any of us) *is/are free. N~ of them has/have come back yet. He is aware, ~ better than he* (ie no one is better aware than he), *that....*

~ the less, nevertheless. **~ but,** only: *They chose none but the best.* **~ other than**: *The new arrival was ~ other than the President* (emph for *the President himself*). **2** (in constructions equal to an imperative): *N~ of that!* Stop that! *N~ of your impudence!* Don't be impudent! **3** (separated from its *n,* in liter or rhet style): *They looked down on the plain, but village there was ~. Sounds there were ~* (= There were no sounds) *except the murmur of the bees.* □ *adv* by no means; in no degree; not at all: *I hope you're ~ the worse for that fall from your horse. I'm afraid I'm ~ the wiser for your explanation. The salary they pay me is ~ too high. There are ‚~ so ‚deaf as those who will not 'hear,* (prov) who refuse to hear.

non·en·tity /nɒ'nentətɪ/ *n* (*pl* -ties) [C] **1** unimportant person. **2** thing that does not really exist or that exists only in the imagination.

none·such, non·such /'nʌnsʌtʃ/ *n* person or thing without equal; paragon.

non·pareil /‚nɒn pə'reɪl US: -'rel/ *adj, n* (formal) unique or unrivalled (person or thing).

non·plus /nɒn'plʌs/ *vt* (-ss-, US -s-) [VP6A] (usu passive) surprise or puzzle (sb) so much that he does not know what to do or say: *I was completely ~sed when she said 'No' to my proposal of marriage.*

non·sense /'nɒnsns US: -sens/ *n* (usu [U]) meaningless words; foolish talk, ideas, behaviour: *You're talking ~! I want no more of your ~. What (a) ~!* **non·sen·si·cal** /nɒn'sensɪkl/ *adj* not making sense: *nonsensical remarks.*

non·such ⇨ nonesuch.

non se·qui·tur /‚nɒn 'sekwɪtə(r)/ *n* (Lat) (logic) conclusion which does not follow from the premises; illogical step.

noodle [1] /'nuːdl/ *n* fool.

noodle [2] /'nuːdl/ *n* (usu *pl*) type of paste of flour and water or flour and eggs prepared in long, narrow strips and used in soups, with a sauce, etc.

nook /nʊk/ *n* out-of-the-way place; inside corner: *search every ~ and cranny,* everywhere.

noon /nuːn/ *n* midday; 12 o'clock in the middle of the day; *at ~; the ~ gun.* **'~·day** /-deɪ/, **'~·tide** /-taɪd/ *nn* = ~.

no-one, no one /'nəʊ wʌn/ *pron* = nobody(1).

noose /nuːs/ *n* ⇨ the illus at knot. loop of rope (with a running knot) that becomes tighter when the rope is pulled: *the hangman's ~.* **put one's head in the ~,** (fig) allow oneself to be caught. □ *vt* catch with a ~; make a ~ on a cord, rope, etc.

nope /nəʊp/ *int* (sl) No!

nor /nɔː(r)/ *conj* **1** (after *neither* or *not*) and not: *I have neither time nor money for skiing. Not a flower nor even a blade of grass will grow in this desert.* **2** and... not: *He can't do it; nor can I, nor can you, nor can anybody. Nor was this all, And this was not all. Nor will I* (= And I will not) *deny that....*

nor'- /‚nɔː(r)/ *pref* ⇨ north.

Nor·dic /'nɔːdɪk/ *n, adj* (member) of the European type marked by tall stature, blond hair, and blue eyes, esp in Scandinavia.

Nor·folk /'nɔːfək/ *n* English county. **~ jacket,** man's loose-fitting jacket with a waistband.

norm /nɔːm/ *n* **1** standard; pattern; type (as representative of a group when judging other examples). **2** (in some industries, etc) amount of work required or expected in a working day: *set the workers a ~; fulfil one's ~.*

nor·mal /'nɔːml/ *adj* in agreement with what is representative, usual, or regular: *the ~ temperature of the human body.* '~ **school**, (in some countries, not in GB) one for the training of teachers (usu in elementary grades). □ *n* [U] usual state, level, standard, etc: *above/below ~.* ~**ly** /'nɔːməlɪ/ *adv* ~**ity** /nɔː'mælətɪ/, ~**cy** /'nɔːmlsɪ/ *nn* [U] the state of being ~. ~**ize** /'nɔːməlaɪz/ *vt* make ~. ~**iz-ation** /ˌnɔːməlaɪ'zeɪʃn *US:* -lɪ'z-/ *n* [U].

Nor·man /'nɔːmən/ *n* inhabitant or native of Normandy /'nɔːməndɪ/; descendant of the mixed Scandinavian and Frankish race established there in the 9th c. □ *adj* of the ~s, esp those who conquered England in the 11th c: *the ~ Conquest; ~ architecture.*

nor·ma·tive /'nɔːmətɪv/ *adj* setting a standard: *a ~, prescriptive grammar of the English language.*

Norse /nɔːs/ *n* the Norwegian language. □ *adj* of Norway.

north /nɔːθ/ *n* **1** one of the four cardinal points of the compass, lying to the left of a person facing the sunrise; part of any country lying farther in this direction than other parts: *the ~ of England; cold winds from the ~.* ⇨ the illus at compass. **2** (attrib) situated in, living in, pertaining to, coming from, the ~: *the N~ Star,* the pole-star; *the ~ pole; a ~ wind; a ~ light,* from the ~, as usu desired by artists in studios; *the 'N~ Country,* ~ part of England; *a ˌN~ 'countryman* /-mən/ a native of the ~ of England. □ *adv* to or towards the ~: *sailing ~.* ˌ~·'**east**, ˌ~·'**west** (abbr NE, NW) *nn, advv* (sometimes, esp naut, **nor'-east** /ˌnɔːr 'iːst/, **nor'-west** /ˌnɔː 'west/) (regions) midway between ~ and east, ~ and west. **the ˌN~-west 'Passage**, the sea route from the Atlantic to the Pacific along the ~ coast of Canada and Alaska. ˌ~-~·'**east**, ˌ~-~·'**west** (abbr NNE, NNW) *nn, adjj, advv* (sometimes, esp naut, **nor'-nor'-east** /ˌnɔː nɔːr 'iːst/, **nor'-nor'-west** /ˌnɔː nɔː 'west/) (regions) midway between ~ and east, west. ˌ~·'**easter** *n* strong wind, storm, or gale, from the ~east. ˌ~·'**easter·ly** *adj* (of wind) blowing from the ~east; (of direction) towards the ~east. ˌ~·'**wester** *n* strong wind from the ~west. ˌ~·'**wester·ly** *adj* (of wind) from the ~west; (of direction) towards the ~west. ˌ~·'**eastern** /-'iːstən/ *adj* of, from, situated in, the ~east. ˌ~·'**western** /-'westən/ *adj* of, from, situated in the ~west. '**N~·man** /-mən/ *n* (*pl* -men) (hist) Viking; native of Scandinavia. ~·**wards** /'nɔːθwədz/ *adv* towards the ~.

north·er·ly /'nɔːðəlɪ/ *adj, adv* (of winds) from the north; towards the north; in or to the north.

north·ern /'nɔːðən/ *adj* in or of the north: *the ~ hemisphere.* **the ~ lights**, streamers and bands of light appearing in the ~ sky; the aurora borealis. ~**er** /'nɔːðənə(r)/ *n* person born in or living in the ~ regions of a country. '~·**most** /-məʊst/ *adj* lying farthest north.

Nor·we·gian /nɔː'wiːdʒən/ *n, adj* (native, language) of Norway.

nose¹ /nəʊz/ *n* **1** part of the face above the mouth, through which breath passes, and serving as the organ of smell: *hit a man on the ~* (note *def art*). ⇨ the illus at head. *bite/snap sb's ~* (*head* is more usu) *off,* answer him sharply and angrily. *count/tell ~s,* (*heads* is more usu) count the number of persons (esp supporters, when voting to decide sth). *cut off one's ~ to spite one's face,* damage one's own interests in an attempt at revenge on sb. *follow one's ~,* go straight forward; be guided by

instinct. *keep a person's ~ to the grindstone,* make him work hard without rest. *lead sb by the ~,* ⇨ lead³(2). *look down one's ~ at sb,* treat haughtily. *pay through the ~,* pay an excessive price. *poke/stick one's ~ into,* (sb else's business), intrude; ask questions without being asked to do so. *put sb's '~ out of joint,* ⇨ joint²(2). *turn one's '~ up at,* show disdain for. *as plain as the ~ on one's face,* obvious; easily seen. *(right) under one's very ~,* (a) directly in front of one. (b) in one's presence, and regardless of one's disapproval. **2** sense of smell: *a dog with a good ~*; (fig) *a reporter with a ~ for news/scandal/a story.* **3** sth like a ~ in shape or position, eg the open end of a pipe, bellows or retort; the most forward part of the fuselage of an aircraft. **4** (compounds) '~**bag** *n* bag for food (oats, etc) fastened on a horse's head. '~·**bleed** *n* bleeding from the ~. '~·**cone** *n* most forward section of a rocket or guided missile, usu separable. ⇨ the illus at capsule. '~·**dive** *n* sharp vertical descent made by an aircraft. □ *vi* (of an aircraft) come down steeply with the ~ pointing to earth. '~·**flute** *n* musical instrument blown with the ~, as used in some Asian countries. '~·**gay** *n* bunch of cut (esp sweet-scented) flowers. '~·**ring** *n* ring fixed in the ~ of a bull, etc, for leading it. '~·**wheel** *n* the front landing-wheel under the fuselage of an aircraft. -**nosed** *suff* (in compounds) having the kind of ~ indicated: *red-~d; long-~d.*

nose² /nəʊz/ *vt, vi* **1** [VP15A] go forward carefully, push (one's way): *The ship ~d its way slowly through the ice.* **2** [VP15B] *~ sth out,* discover by smelling: *The dog ~d out a rat. That man will ~ out a scandal anywhere.* **3** [VP2C,3A] *~ about (for sth),* smell for; (fig) pry or search for. *~ into sth,* pry into: *a man who is always nosing into other people's affairs.*

nosey, nosy /'nəʊzɪ/ *adj* (-ier, -iest), *n* (sl) inquisitive (person). ˌ~ '**parker** *n* (colloq) inquisitive person.

nosh /nɒʃ/ *n* [U] (GB sl) food. '~-**up** *n* a good meal. □ *vi* (colloq) eat.

nos·tal·gia /nɒ'stældʒə/ *n* [U] home-sickness; wistful longing for sth one has known in the past. **nos·tal·gic** /nɒ'stældʒɪk/ *adj* of, feeling or causing, ~. **nos·tal·gi·cally** /-klɪ/ *adv*

nos·tril /'nɒstrəl/ *n* either of the two external openings into the nose. ⇨ the illus at head.

nos·trum /'nɒstrəm/ *n* [C] (usu contemptuous) medicine, etc, prepared by the person who recommends it; quack remedy; scheme for political or social reform (called a ~ by its opponents).

not /nɒt/ *adv* **1** (used to make negative one of the 24 *anom fin vv* listed in the Introduction under 'Anomalous Verbs'): *is not; must not; could not;* often contracted to -n't /-nt/: *hasn't* /'hæznt/, *needn't* /'niːdnt/.) **2** (used with non-finite *vv*): *He warned me not to be late. You were wrong in not making a protest.* **3** (used after certain *vv*, esp *think, suppose, believe, expect, fear, fancy, trust, hope, seem, appear, be afraid,* as equivalent to a *that-*clause): *'Can you come next week?'—'I'm afraid not.'* I'm afraid that I cannot come. *'Will it rain this afternoon?'—'I hope not.'* **4** (used elliptically, in phrases.) *as likely as not,* probably: *He'll be at home now, as likely as not. as soon as not,* ⇨ soon(5). *not at all,* /ˌnɒt ə'tɔːl/ used as a polite response to thanks, enquiries after sb's health, etc: *'Thank you very much.'—'Not at all',* No need to mention it. *'Are you tired?'—'Not at all',* Not in the least. **'not that**, it is not suggested that: *If he ever said so—not that I ever heard him say so—he told a lie*. **'not but what**, nevertheless; although: *I can't do it; not but what a younger man might be able to do it*. **5** (in understatements): *not a few*, = many; *not seldom*, = often; *not without reason*, = with good reason; *not half*, (sl) exceedingly; *in the not-so-distant* (= recent) *past*. **6** (used to indicate the absence, opposite, or negative of sth: *not here; not anything; not clean/hot/good; not he/John/my son*.

nota bene /ˌnəʊtə 'beneɪ/ *v imper* (Lat) (abbr **NB**, **nb** /ˌen 'biː/) observe carefully.

no‧table /'nəʊtəbl/ *adj* deserving to be noticed; remarkable: ~ *events/speakers/artists*. □ *n* eminent person. **no‧tably** /'nəʊtəblɪ/ *adv* **nota‧bil‧ity** /ˌnəʊtə'bɪlətɪ/ *n* (*pl*-ties) **1** [U] the condition of being ~. **2** [C] ~ person.

no‧tary /'nəʊtərɪ/ *n* (*pl*-ries) (often ˌ~ 'public) official with authority to perform certain kinds of legal transactions, esp to record that he has witnessed the signing of legal documents.

no‧ta‧tion /nəʊ'teɪʃn/ *n* **1** [C] system of signs or symbols representing numbers, amounts, musical notes, etc. **2** [U] representing of numbers, etc by such signs or symbols.

notch /nɒtʃ/ *n* V-shaped cut (*in* or *on* sth); (US) narrow pass through mountains; defile². □ *vt* **1** [VP6A] make or cut a ~ or ~es in or on, eg a stick, as a way of keeping count. **2** [VP15B] ~ **up**, (colloq) achieve; score: ~ *up a new record*.

note¹ /nəʊt/ *n* **1** short record (of facts, etc) made to help the memory: *He spoke for an hour without a* ~/*without* ~s. '~·**book** *n* book in which to write ~s. **2** short letter: *a* ~ *of thanks; an exchange of* ~s *between two governments*. '~·**paper** *n* [U] paper for (esp private) correspondence. **3** short comment on or explanation of a word or passage in a book, etc: *a new edition of 'Hamlet', with copious* ~s. ⇨ *footnote* at foot¹(8). **4** observation (not necessarily written): *He was comparing* ~s *with a friend*, exchanging views, comparing experiences, etc. **5** (US = *bill*) piece of paper money; bank~: *a £5* ~. '~·**case** *n* wallet(1). **6** single sound of a certain pitch and duration: *the blackbird's merry* ~; sign used to represent such a sound in manuscript or printed music ⇨ the illus at notation; any one of the keys of a piano, organ, etc. **sound a** ~ **of warning (against sth)**, warn against sth. **strike**

the right ~, (fig) speak in such a way that one wins the approval or sympathy of one's listeners. **strike/sound a false** ~, (fig) do or say sth that causes one to lose sympathy or approval. **7** quality (esp of voice) indicating the nature of sth (usu *sing* with the *indef art*): *There was a* ~ *of self-satisfaction in his speech*. **8** [U] distinction; importance: *a singer of* ~. **9** [U] notice; attention: *worthy of* ~. **Take** ~ *of what he says*, pay attention to it.

note² /nəʊt/ *vt* **1** [VP6A,8,9,10] notice; pay attention to: *Please* ~ *my words. N~ how to do it/how I did it. She* ~d *that his hands were dirty*. **2** [VP6A,15B] ~ **sth** (**down**), make a ~ of; write down in order to remember: *The policeman* ~d *down every word I said*. **noted** *adj* celebrated (*for*, *as*): *a town* ~d *for its pottery/*~d *as a health resort*. '~·**worthy** *adj* deserving to be ~d; remarkable.

no‧thing /'nʌθɪŋ/ *n* **1** (with *adj, inf*, etc, following) not anything: *There's* ~ *interesting in the newspaper. He's had* ~ *to eat yet. N~ (that) I could say had any influence on her. N~ ever pleases her. He's five foot* ~, exactly five foot tall. *There's little or* ~ *wrong with him*, very little wrong. *There's* ~ *like leather* (= is so good as leather) *for shoes*. **2** (phrases) **be** ~ **to**, (a) be a matter of indifference to: *She's* ~ *to him*, He is indifferent to, uninterested in, her. (b) be as ~ if compared: *My losses are* ~ *to yours*. **come to** ~, fail; be without result. **go for** ~, be without reward, result, value: *Six months' hard work all gone for* ~. **have** ~ **to do with**, (a) avoid; have no dealings with: *I advise you to have* ~ *to do with that man*. (b) not to be the business or concern of: *This has* ~ *to do with you*. **make** ~ **of**, be unable to understand. **mean** ~ **to**, (a) have no meaning for: *These technical words mean* ~ *to me*. (b) be sth or sb that sb has no concern or interest in: *He used to like Jane but she means* ~ *to him now*. **to say** ~ **of**, not to mention: *He had his wife and seven children with him in the car, to say* ~ *of* (= as well as) *two dogs, a cat and a parrot*. **think** ~ **of**, consider as ordinary, usual or unremarkable: *He thinks* ~ *of a twenty-mile walk/of asking me to lend him £20*. **think** ~ **'of it**, friendly reply to sb who offers thanks, an apology, etc: *'You didn't mind my using your typewriter?'—'Of course not! Think* ~ *of it!'* **for** ~, (a) free; without payment. (b) without a re-

NOTES						
RESTS	semibreve (US=whole note)	minim ($\frac{1}{2}$ note)	crotchet ($\frac{1}{4}$ note)	quaver ($\frac{1}{8}$ note)	semi-quaver ($\frac{1}{16}$ note)	demisemi-quaver ($\frac{1}{32}$ note)

treble clef   bass clef   C clef

1 staff or stave	4 flat	7 bar	10 leger lines (added above or below the staff for notes too high or too low for the staff)
2 bar-line	5 natural	8 slur	
3 sharp	6 time signature	9 tie	

musical notation

ward or result; to no purpose: *It was not for ~ that he spent three years studying the subject.* **next to ~**, ⇨ next. **~ but**, merely: *N~ but doubts can prevent you from succeeding;* only: *N~ but a miracle can save him.* **There's ~ 'for it but to...**, The only thing we can do is to.... **N~ doing!** (colloq) expression used to indicate refusal of a request, etc. □ *adv* not at all; in no way: *The house is ~ near as large as I expected. His new book is ~ like as good as his earlier books.* **~·ness** *n* [U] being ~; the state of non-existence: *pass into ~ness.*

no·tice /'nəʊtɪs/ *n* 1 [C] (written or printed) news of sth about to happen or sth that has happened: *put up a ~; ~s of births, deaths and marriages in the newspapers.* **'~-board** *n* one provided for ~s to be affixed to. 2 [U] warning (of what will happen): *give a member of staff a month's ~*, tell him that he must leave one's employment at the end of one month; (of a tenant) *receive two months' ~ to quit*, to vacate a house, etc; (of an employee) *give one's employer ~ that one intends to leave; leave without ~*, without giving any warning. **(do sth) at short ~**, with little warning, little time for preparation, etc. 3 [U] attention. **be beneath one's ~**, be sth one should ignore: *Their insults should be beneath your ~.* **bring sth to sb's ~**, call sb's attention to sth. **come to sb's ~**, have one's attention called to sth: *It has come to my ~ that...*, I have learnt that.... **sit up and take ~**, (of sb who is ill, etc) show signs of recovery from illness. **make sb sit up and take ~**, make sb keenly aware of events: *This new process should make our competitors sit up and take ~.* **take no ~ (of sth)**, pay no attention to sth: *Take no ~ of what they're saying about you.* 4 [C] short review of a new book, play, etc in a periodical. □ *vt, vi* 1 [VP6A,8,9,10,18A,19A,2A] take ~ (of); observe: *I didn't ~ you. I ~d that he left early. I wasn't noticing. Did you ~ him pause? Did you ~ his hand shaking? He was too proud to ~ me.* 2 [VP6A] say or write sth about (a book, play, etc). **~·able** /-əbl/ *adj* easily seen or ~d. **~·ably** /-əbli/ *adv*

no·ti·fi·able /'nəʊtɪfaɪəbl/ *adj* that must be notified (esp of certain diseases that must be notified to public health authorities).

no·tify /'nəʊtɪfaɪ/ *vt* (*pt, pp* -fied) [VP6A,14,11] **~ sb of sth; ~ sth to sb**, give notice of; report: *~ the police of a loss; ~ a loss to the police; ~ a birth; ~ the authorities that....* **no·ti·fi·ca·tion** /ˌnəʊtɪfɪ'keɪʃn/ *n* [U] ~ing; [C] instance of this (eg to the authorities, of births, deaths, cases of infectious disease).

no·tion /'nəʊʃn/ *n* [C] **1** idea; opinion: *I have no ~ of what he means. Your head is full of silly ~s. He has a ~ that I'm cheating him.* **2** (*pl*) (US) small miscellaneous goods. ⇨ novelty(3). **~·al** /-ʃənl/ *adj* **1** (of knowledge, etc) speculative; not based on experiment or demonstration. **2** nominal; token.

no·tori·ous /nəʊ'tɔːrɪəs/ *adj* widely known (esp for sth bad): *a ~ criminal; ~ for his goings-on; ~ as a rake.* **~·ly** *adv* **no·tor·iety** /ˌnəʊtə'raɪəti/ *n* [U] state of being ~.

not·with·stand·ing /ˌnɒtwɪθ'stændɪŋ/ *prep* in spite of. □ *adv* nevertheless; all the same. □ *conj* although.

nou·gat /'nuːgɑː/ *US:* 'nuːgət/ *n* sort of hard sweet made of sugar, nuts, etc.

nought /nɔːt/ *n* **1** nothing. **bring sb/sth to ~**, ruin; baffle. **come to ~**, be ruined; fail. **set sb/ sth at ~**, disregard; defy; despise. **2** the figure 0;

zero: *point ~ one*, ie ·01. **~s and crosses**, game played by writing ~s (zero signs) and crosses on lines of vertical and horizontal squares.

noun /naʊn/ *n* (gram) word (not a *pron*) which can function as the subject or object of a *v*, or the object of a *prep*; word which is marked *n* in this dictionary.

nour·ish /'nʌrɪʃ/ *vt* [VP6A] **1** keep (sb) alive and well with food; make well and strong; improve (land) with manure, etc: *~ing food; ~ the soil.* **2** have or encourage (feelings): *~ feelings of hatred; ~ hope in one's heart.* **~·ment** *n* [U] food.

nous /naʊs/ *n* [U] (Gk) **1** (phil) intellect; (divine) reason. **2** (GB colloq) common sense; gumption.

nou·veau riche /ˌnuːvəʊ 'riːʃ/ *n* (usu in *pl* nouveaux riches, pronunciation unchanged) (F) person who has recently become rich, esp one who is ostentatious.

nova /'nəʊvə/ *n* (*pl* ~s, -vae /-viː/) (astron) star that suddenly increases its brilliance for a period.

novel[1] /'nɒvl/ *adj* strange; of a kind not previously known: *~ ideas.*

novel[2] /nɒvl/ *n* story in prose, long enough to fill one or more volumes, about either imaginary or historical people: *the ~s of Dickens.* **~·'ette** /-'et/ *n* short ~. **'~·ist** /-ɪst/ *n* writer of ~s.

nov·elty /'nɒvltɪ/ *n* (*pl* -ties) **1** [U] newness; strangeness; quality of being novel: *The ~ of his surroundings soon wore off*, He became accustomed to them. **2** [C] previously unknown thing, idea, etc; sth strange or unfamiliar. **3** (*pl*) miscellaneous manufactured goods of low cost, eg toys, small ornaments.

No·vem·ber /nəʊ'vembə(r)/ *n* the eleventh month of the year, with thirty days.

nov·ice /'nɒvɪs/ *n* person who is still learning and who is without experience, esp a person who is to become a monk or a nun. **no·vi·ci·ate, no·vi·ti·ate** /nə'vɪʃɪət/ *nn* period or state of being a ~.

now /naʊ/ *adv* **1** at the present time; in the present circumstances: *Where are you now living/living now? Now is the best time to visit Devon. I cannot now* (ie in the circumstances, after what has happened, etc) *ever believe you again.* **2** (used after a *prep*): *He will be in London by now.* **Up to/till/ until now** we have been lucky. *From now onwards I shall be stricter.* **3** (phrases) **(every) now and then/again**, occasionally; from time to time: *We go to the opera now and then.* **now... now/ then...**, at one time..., at another time...: *What mixed weather, now fine, now/then showery!* **4** at once; immediately: *Do it now. Now or never!* **just now**, ⇨ just[2](6). **5** (used without reference to time, to indicate the mood of the speaker, to explain, warn, comfort, etc): *Now what happened was this* (explanatory). *Now stop quarrelling and listen to me* (entreaty or reproof). *No 'nonsense, now* (warning). **,now, 'now; 'now then**, (used at the beginning of a sentence, often as a protest or warning, or simply to call attention): *Now then, what's troubling you?* □ *conj* as a consequence of the fact (that): *Now* (*that*) *you mention it, I do remember. Now* (*that*) *you're grown up, you must stop this childish behaviour.*

now·adays /'naʊədeɪz/ *adv* at the present time (and often used in contrasts between present day manners, customs, etc, and those of past times): *N~ children prefer TV to reading.*

no·where /'nəʊweə(r) *US:* -hweər/ *adv* not anywhere: *The boy was ~ to be found. Such methods* *will get you* ~, will not produce results. *£50 is* ~ *near enough*, not nearly enough. *come (in)/be* ~, fail to win or get a place (in a competition).

no·wise /'nəʊwaɪz/ *adv* (old use) not at all; in no way.

noxious /'nɒkʃəs/ *adj* harmful: ~ *gases.* ~·**ly** *adv* ~·**ness** *n*

nozzle /'nɒzl/ *n* metal end of a hose or bellows, through which a stream of liquid or air is directed. ⇨ the illus at hose-pipe.

nuance /'njuːɑːns *US:* 'nuː-/ *n* [C] delicate difference in, or shade of, meaning, opinion, colour, etc.

nub /nʌb/ *n* **1** small lump or knob (eg of coal). **2** (colloq, fig) gist or point (of a story, affair).

nu·bile /'njuːbaɪl *US:* 'nuːbl/ *adj* (of girls) marriageable; old enough to marry.

nu·clear /'njuːklɪə(r) *US:* 'nuː-/ *adj* of a nucleus, esp of a heavy atom, with release of energy: ~ *energy*, obtained by ~ fission; *a* ~ *power station;* ~*-powered submarines;* ~ *bombs/missiles;* ~ *disarmament*, the renunciation of ~ weapons.

nu·cleic /njuː'kleɪɪk *US:* nuː-/ *adj* ~ **acid**, one of two complex compounds occurring in all living cells.

nu·cleus /'njuːklɪəs *US:* 'nuː-/ *n* (*pl* nuclei /-klɪaɪ/) central part, round which other parts are grouped or round which other things collect; (esp) central part of an atom, consisting of protons and neutrons. ⇨ the illus at cell.

nude /njuːd *US:* nuːd/ *adj* naked. □ *n* [C] ~ human figure (esp in art). *in the* ~, unclothed: *pose in the* ~ *for an artist.* **nu·dist** /-ɪst/ *n* person who believes that exposure of the naked body to sun and air is good for the health. **'nudist camp/colony**, place where nudists practise their beliefs. **nu·dism** /-ɪzəm/ *n* the practice of going ~. **nu·dity** /'njuːdətɪ *US:* 'nuː-/ *n* nakedness.

nudge /nʌdʒ/ *vt* [VP6A] touch or push slightly with the elbow in order to draw sb's attention privately. □ *n* push given in this way.

nu·ga·tory /'njuːgətərɪ *US:* 'nuːgətɔːrɪ/ *adj* (formal) trifling; worthless; not valid.

nug·get /'nʌgɪt/ *n* lump of metal, esp gold, as found in the earth.

nui·sance /'njuːsns *US:* 'nuː-/ *n* [C] thing, person, act, that causes trouble or offence: *The mosquitoes are a* ~. *What a* ~ *that child is!*

null /nʌl/ *adj* of no effect or force. ~ *and void*, (legal) without legal effect; invalid. ~**ify** /'nʌlɪfaɪ/ *vt* (*pt,pp* -fied) [VP6A] make ~ and void. **nul·li·fi·ca·tion** /ˌnʌlɪfɪ'keɪʃn/ *n* [U] making ~. **nul·lity** /'nʌlətɪ/ *n* [U] being ~; invalidity: *nullity of marriage; a* '*nullity suit*, one that asks for ~ity of marriage.

numb /nʌm/ *adj* without ability to feel or move: *fingers* ~ *with cold.* □ *vt* [VP6A] make ~; deaden: ~*ed with grief.* ~·**ly** *adv* ~·**ness** *n*

num·ber /'nʌmbə(r)/ *n* **1** *3, 13, 33* and *103* are ~s. ⇨ App 4. **2** quantity or amount: *a large* ~ *of people. N* ~*s of people* (= Very many people) *came from all parts of the country to see the exhibition. The* ~ *of books missing from the library is large. A* ~ *of books* (= Some books) *are missing from the library.* *any* ~, ⇨ any[1](6). *His/Your, etc* ~ *is up*, (colloq) He is/You are, etc ruined; going to die, to pay a penalty, etc. *in* ~: *They were fifteen in* ~, There were fifteen of them. *to the* ~ *of,* mounting to. *without* ~, too many to be counted. *times without* ~, very often; so often that counting is impossible. '~*-plate* *n* plate

showing the licence number of a motor vehicle, the ~ of a house, etc. ⇨ the illus at motor. **3** (attrib use before a definite ~(1), usu shortened to **No**, *pl* **Nos**): *Room No 145*, eg in a hotel; *living at No 4*, house number four. **No 10 (Downing Street)**, official residence of the British Prime Minister. *look after/take care of* ~ *one,* (colloq) look after oneself and one's own interests. **4** one issue of a periodical, esp for one day, week, etc: *the current* ~ *of 'Punch'; back* ~s (= earlier issues) *of 'Nature'. a back* ~, (fig) out of date or old-fashioned. **5** part of an opera indicated by a ~; dance, song, etc for the stage. **6** (gram) variations in the forms of *nn, vv,* etc according to whether only one or more than one is to be indicated: *Man/men, does/do and I/we illustrate grammatical* ~ *in English.* **7** (*pl*) numerical superiority: *The enemy won by* ~*s/by force of* ~*s.* **8** (*pl*) arithmetic: *He's not good at* ~*s.* □ *vt* [VP6A,14] **1** give a ~ to: *Let's* ~ *them from 1 to 10.* **2** amount to; add up to: *We* ~*ed 20 in all.* **3** [VP14] ~ *sb/sth among,* include; place: ~ *sb among one's friends.* **4** (passive) be restricted in ~: *His days are* ~*ed,* He has not long to live. **5** [VP2C] ~ *off*, (mil) call out one's ~ in a rank of soldiers: *The company* ~*ed off from the right.*

num·er·able /'njuːmərəbl *US:* 'nuː-/ *adj* that can be numbered or counted.

nu·meral /'njuːmərəl *US:* 'nuː-/ *n, adj* (word, figure or sign) standing for a number; of number. **Arabic** ~s, *1, 2, 3,* etc. **roman** ~s, I, II, III, etc. ⇨ App 4.

nu·mer·ate /'njuːmərət *US:* 'nuː-/ *adj* (of a person) having a good basic competence in mathematics and science. ⇨ literate. **nu·mer·acy** /'njuːmərəsɪ *US:* 'nuː-/ *n*

nu·mer·ation /ˌnjuːmə'reɪʃn *US:* ˌnuː-/ *n* method or process of numbering or calculating; expression in words of numbers written in figures.

nu·mer·ator /'njuːməreɪtə(r) *US:* 'nuː-/ *n* number above the line in a vulgar fraction, eg 3 in ¾. ⇨ denominator.

nu·meri·cal /njuː'merɪkl *US:* nuː-/ *adj* of, in, denoting, numbers: ~ *symbols.* ~**ly** /-klɪ/ *adv: The enemy were* ~*ly superior.*

nu·mer·ous /'njuːmərəs *US:* 'nuː-/ *adj* great in number; very many: *her* ~ *friends.*

nu·min·ous /'njuːmɪnəs *US:* 'nuː-/ *adj* awe-inspiring; divine.

nu·mis·mat·ics /ˌnjuːmɪz'mætɪks *US:* ˌnuː-/ *n* (with *sing v*) the study of coins, coinage and medals. **nu·mis·ma·tist** /njuː'mɪzmətɪst *US:* nuː-/ *n* expert in ~; collector of coins and medals.

num·skull /'nʌmskʌl/ *n* stupid person.

nun /nʌn/ *n* woman who, after taking religious vows, lives with other women, in a convent, a life in the service of God. **nun·nery** /'nʌnərɪ/ *n* (*pl* -ries) house of nuns; convent. ⇨ monk, monastery.

nun·cio /'nʌnsɪəʊ/ *n* (*pl* ~s) ambassador or representative of the Pope in a foreign country.

nup·tial /'nʌpʃl/ *adj* of marriage or weddings: ~ *happiness; the* ~ *day.* **nup·tials** *n pl* wedding.

nurse[1] /nɜːs/ *n* **1** ('~)**maid**, woman or girl employed to look after babies and small children. ~ nanny. **2** ('wet-)~, woman employed to suckle the infant of another. ~ **3** [U] nursing or being nursed: *put a child to* ~. **4** person who, usu trained, who cares for people who are ill or injured: *hospital* ~s; *Red Cross* ~s; *male* ~s, eg in a mental home for men. **5** country, college, institution, etc which protects or encourages a certain quality: *Iceland, the ~ of liberty.*

nurse² /nɜːs/ *vt* [VP6A] **1** take charge of and look after (persons who are ill, injured, etc) (but not used as in the sense of nurse¹(1)): (gerund) *the nursing profession; take up nursing as a career. Careful nursing will be needed.* '**nursing-home** *n* building, usu privately owned and smaller than a hospital, where persons who are ill may be cared for, operated on, etc. **2** feed (a baby) at the breast; suckle. **3** hold (a baby, a child, a pet dog) on the knees; clasp caressingly. **4** give special care to: *~ young plants.* ⇨ nursery(2); *~ a constituency,* keep in touch with the voters (to obtain or retain their support). *~ a cold,* stay at home, keep warm, in order to cure it. **5** have in the mind, think about a great deal: *~ feelings of revenge.*

nurs·ery /'nɜːsərɪ/ *n* (*pl* -ries) **1** room for the special use of small children. '**day ~,** building where mothers who go out to work may leave babies and young children. '**~ rhyme,** poem or song (usu traditional) for young children. '**~ school,** for children of 2 to 5; pre-primary school. *~ slope,* (skiing) slope suitable for learners. **2** place where young plants and trees are raised (for transplanting later, and usu for sale). '**~·man** /-mən/ *n* (*pl* -men) man who works in a ~(2).

nurse·ling, nurs·ling /'nɜːslɪŋ/ *n* infant, esp in relation to its nurse.

nur·ture /'nɜːtʃə(r)/ *n* [U] (formal) care, training; education (of children). □ *vt* bring up; give ~ to: *a delicately ~d girl.*

nut /nʌt/ *n* **1** fruit consisting of a hard shell enclosing a kernel that can be eaten. *a hard nut to crack,* a problem difficult to solve. '**nut-brown** *adj* (eg of ale) coloured like ripe hazel-nuts. ,**nut-'butter** *n* butter substitute made from nuts (eg *peanut butter*). '**nut-crackers** *n pl* device for cracking nuts open. '**nut·shell** *n* hard outside covering of a nut. *(put sth) in a nutshell,* (fig) in the fewest possible words. **2** small piece of metal with a threaded hole for screwing on to a bolt. ⇨ the illus at bolt. **3** (sl) head (of a human being). *off one's nut,* (sl) insane. '**nut-house** *n* (sl) mental hospital. **4** (*pl*)

small lumps of coal. □ *vi go nutting,* look for, gather nuts (eg hazel-nuts in the woods and hedges).

nut·meg /'nʌtmeg/ *n* **1** [C] hard, small, round, sweet-smelling seed of an E Indian evergreen. **2** [U] this seed grated to powder, used as a flavouring.

nu·tria /'njuːtrɪə US: 'nuː-/ *n* skin or fur of the small S American rodent called coypu.

nu·tri·ent /'njuːtrɪənt US: 'nuː-/ *adj* (formal) serving as or providing nourishment.

nu·tri·ment /'njuːtrɪmənt US: 'nuː-/ *n* (formal) nourishing food.

nu·tri·tion /njuːˈtrɪʃn US: nuː-/ *n* (formal) [U] the process of supplying and receiving nourishment; the science of food values: *the care and ~ of children.*

nu·tri·tious /njuːˈtrɪʃəs US: nuː-/ *adj* (formal) nourishing; having high value as food.

nu·tri·tive /'njuːtrɪtɪv US: 'nuː-/ *adj* (formal) serving as food; of nutrition.

nuts /nʌts/ *adj* (sl) crazy; insane. *be ~ about-/over sb/sth,* be in love with, infatuated with.

nutty /'nʌtɪ/ *adj* (-ier, -iest) **1** tasting like nuts. **2** (sl) mad; crazy. **3** containing, made up of, nuts(4): *~ slack coal.*

nuzzle /'nʌzl/ *vt,vi* **1** [VP6A] press the nose against: *The horse ~d my shoulder.* **2** [VP2C] *~ up (against/to),* rub or push with the nose: *The horse ~d up against my shoulder.*

ny·lon /'naɪlɒn/ *n* **1** [U] synthetic fibre used for hosiery, rope, brushes, etc: *~ stockings/blouses, etc.* **2** (*pl*) *~* stockings.

nymph /nɪmf/ *n* **1** (in old Gk and Roman stories) one of the lesser goddesses, living in rivers, trees, hills, etc; (liter) beautiful young woman. **2** pupa; chrysalis.

nym·phet /nɪmˈfet/ *n* (colloq) young girl looked upon as sexually desirable.

nym·pho /'nɪmfəʊ/ *n* (*pl* ~s /-fəʊz/) (colloq abbr of) nymphomaniac.

nym·pho·mania /ˌnɪmfəˈmeɪnɪə/ *n* [U] abnormal sexual desire in women. **nym·pho·maniac** /-ˈmeɪnɪæk/ *n, adj* (woman) suffering from ~.

Oo

O, o /əʊ/ (*pl* O's, o's /əʊz/) the 15th letter of the English alphabet; O-shaped sign or mark; (in quoting telephone numbers) 6033, 'six O double three'. ⇨ App 4.

O, oh /əʊ/ *int* cry of surprise, fear, pain, sudden pleasure, etc.

o' /ə/ (abbr of) *of,* as in *o'clock, man-o'-war.*

oaf /əʊf/ *n* (*pl* ~s or, rarely oaves /əʊvz/) awkward lout. '**oaf·ish** /-ɪʃ/ *adj* roughly behaved; loutish.

oak /əʊk/ *n* [C] sorts of large tree with tough, hard wood, common in many parts of the world. ⇨ the illus at tree; [U] the wood of this tree: *a forest of oak(s)/oak-trees; an oak door; oak panels.* '**oak-apple** *n* growth on an oak leaf or stem caused by an insect. **the Oaks,** name of a classic horse-race, run at Epsom, near London. **oaken** /'əʊkən/ *adj* made of oak.

oa·kum /'əʊkəm/ *n* [U] loose fibre or threads obtained by picking old ropes, used for filling up

spaces between the boards of a ship.

oar /ɔː(r)/ *n* pole with a flat blade, pulled by hand against a pin, rowlock or other support on the side of a boat, in order to propel the boat through the water. ⇨ the illus at eight, row. *pull a good oar,* be a good oarsman. *put/shove one's oar in,* (colloq) interfere. *rest on one's oars,* stop working for a time. **oars·man** /'ɔːzmən/ *n* (*pl* -men), '**oars·woman** *n* (*pl* -women) rower. Hence, '**oars·man·ship** *n*.

oasis /əʊˈeɪsɪs/ *n* (*pl* oases /-siːz/) fertile place, with water and trees, in a desert; (fig) experience, place, etc which is pleasant in the midst of what is dull, unpleasant, etc.

oast /əʊst/ *n* kiln for drying hops. '**~·house** *n* building containing an ~.

oat /əʊt/ *n* (usu *pl*) (grain from a) hardy cereal plant grown in cool climates as food (*oats* for horses, *oatmeal* for human beings). ⇨ the illus at cereal. *feel one's oats,* (colloq) feel gay, lively, ready for activity, active. **sow one's wild oats,** lead a life of pleasure and gaiety while young before settling down seriously. **'oat-cake** *n* (esp in Scot and N England) thin, unleavened cake made of oatmeal. **'oat-meal** *n* meal made from oats, used in porridge and oatcakes. **2** (*pl* with *sing v*) oatmeal porridge: *Is Scotch ~s on the breakfast menu?*

oath /əʊθ/ *n* (*pl* ~s /əʊðz/) **1** solemn undertaking with God's help to do sth; solemn declaration that sth is true. **be on ~,** (legal) having sworn to tell the truth: *The judge reminded the witness that he was still under ~.* **put sb under ~,** (legal) require sb to swear an ~. **swear/take an ~,** promise solemnly to give (one's loyalty, allegiance, etc). **on one's ~,** (non-legal) used to emphasize that one is telling the truth: *I didn't say anything to him about you, on my ~.* **2** wrongful use of God's name or of sacred words to express strong feeling; swear-word; piece of profanity.

ob-bli-ga-to /ˌɒblɪˈɡɑːtəʊ/ *n* (*pl* ~s /-təʊz/), *adj* (music) **1** (to be) performed without any omissions (opp to *ad libitum*). **2** (accompanying part) forming an integral part of a composition.

ob-du-rate /ˈɒbdjʊərət US: -dər-/ *adj* (formal) stubborn; impenitent. **~-ly** *adv* **ob-du-racy** /ˈɒbdjʊərəsɪ US: -dər-/ *n* [U].

obedi-ent /əˈbiːdɪənt/ *adj* doing, willing to do, what one is told to do: *~ children.* **your ~ ser-vant,** formula used at the end of letters of an official or public nature. **~-ly** *adv* **obedi-ence** /-əns/ *n* [U] being ~: *Soldiers act in obedience to the orders of their superior officers.*

obeis-ance /əʊˈbeɪsns/ *n* [C] (formal) deep bow (of respect or homage): *do/pay ~ to a ruler,* show respectful homage or submission.

ob-elisk /ˈɒbəlɪsk/ *n* tall, pointed, tapering, four-sided stone pillar, set up as a monument or landmark.

obese /əʊˈbiːs/ *adj* (of persons) very fat. **obes-ity** /əʊˈbiːsətɪ/ *n* [U] being ~.

obey /əˈbeɪ/ *vt, vi* [VP6A,2A] do what one is told to do; carry out (a command): *~ an officer; ~ or-ders.*

ob-fus-cate /ˈɒbfəskeɪt/ *vt* [VP6A] (formal) darken or obscure (the mind); bewilder.

obi /ˈəʊbɪ/ *n* (*pl* obis) (Japanese) broad sash (often ornamental) fastened round the waist so that there is a large bow.

obiter dic-tum /ˌɒbɪtə ˈdɪktəm/ *n* (*pl* dicta /ˈdɪktə/) (Lat) incidental remark or statement.

obitu-ary /əˈbɪtʃʊərɪ US: -tʃʊerɪ/ *n* (*pl* -ries) printed notice of sb's death, often with a short account of his life; (attrib) *~ notices,* eg in a newspaper.

ob-ject¹ /ˈɒbdʒɪkt/ *n* **1** sth that can be seen or touched; material thing: *Tell me the names of the ~s in this room.* '**~ lesson,** (a) one (to be) taught or learnt from an example, or from specimens, etc placed before or shown to the learner. (b) practical illustration of some principle, often given or used as a warning. '**~ glass/lens** *n* = objective *n*(2). **2** person or thing to which action or feeling or thought is directed; thing aimed at; end; purpose: *an ~ of pity/admiration,* sb or sth pitied/admired; *with no ~ in life; work with the ~ of earning fame; fail/succeed in one's ~.* **no ~,** no hindrance; not important: *money/time/distance, etc no ~,* (in advertisements, eg for jobs) the person answering may make his own terms about money, time, etc. **3**

person or thing of strange appearance, esp if ridiculous, pitiful or contemptible: *What an ~ you look in that old hat!* **4** (gram) *n* or *n* equivalent (eg a clause) towards which the action of the *v* is directed, or to which a preposition indicates some relation, as in (direct object) 'He took *the money*' or 'He took *what he wanted*' or (indirect ~) 'I gave *him* the money' or (prepositional ~) 'I gave the money to *the treasurer*'.

ob-ject² /əbˈdʒekt/ *vi, vt* **1** [VP2A,3A] **~ (to),** say that one is not in favour of sth; be opposed (to); make a protest against: *I ~ to all this noise/to being treated like a child. He stood up and ~ed in strong language.* **2** [VP9] **~ (against sb) that,** give as a reason against: *I ~ (against him) that he is too young for the position.* **ob-jec-tor** /-tə(r)/ *n* person who ~s. **conscientious ~or,** ⇨ concientious.

ob-jec-tion /əbˈdʒekʃn/ *n* **1** [C,U] statement or feeling of dislike, disapproval or opposition: *He has a strong ~ to getting up early. O~s to the plan will be listened to sympathetically.* **take ~ to,** object to. **2** [C] that which is objected to; drawback; defect. **~-able** /-əbl/ *adj* likely to be objected to; unpleasant: *an ~able smell; ~able remarks.* **~-ably** /-əblɪ/ *adv*

ob-jec-tive /əbˈdʒektɪv/ *adj* **1** (in philosophy) having existence outside the mind; real. ⇨ subjective. **2** (of persons, writings, pictures) uninfluenced by thought or feeling; dealing with outward things, actual facts, etc uninfluenced by personal feelings or opinions. **3** (gram) of the object(4): *the ~ case,* in Latin and other inflected languages. ▢ *n* **1** object aimed at; purpose; (esp mil) point to which armed forces are moving to capture it: *All our ~s were won.* **2** lens of a microscope or telescope closest to the object being looked at. **~-ly** *adv* in an ~(2) manner. **ob-jec-tiv-ity** /ˌɒbdʒekˈtɪvɪtɪ/ *n* state of being ~; impartial judgement; ability to free oneself from personal prejudice.

ob-jur-gate /ˈɒbdʒəgeɪt/ *vt* [VP6A] (liter) scold; rebuke. **ob-jur-ga-tion** /ˌɒbdʒəˈgeɪʃn/ *n* [C,U] scolding; rebuke.

ob-late /ˈɒbleɪt/ *adj* (geom) flattened at the poles: *The earth is an ~ sphere.*

ob-la-tion /əˈbleɪʃn/ *n* [C] offering made to God or a god.

ob-li-gate /ˈɒblɪgeɪt/ *vt* [VP17] **~ sb to do sth,** (formal) bind (a person, esp legally) (usu passive): *He felt ~d to help.*

ob-li-ga-tion /ˌɒblɪˈgeɪʃn/ *n* [C] promise, duty or condition that indicates what action ought to be taken (eg the power of the law, duty, a sense of what is right): *the ~s of good citizenship/of conscience; fulfil/repay an ~,* eg by returning hospitality that one has received. **be/place sb under an ~,** be/make sb indebted to another.

ob-li-ga-tory /əˈblɪgətrɪ US: -tɔːrɪ/ *adj* that is required by law, rule or custom: *Is attendance at school ~ or optional in that country? It is ~ on café owners to take precautions against fire.*

ob-lige /əˈblaɪdʒ/ *vt* **1** [VP17] **~ sb to do sth,** require, bind (sb) by a promise, oath, etc: *The law ~s parents to send their children to school.* **2** [VP17] (esp in passive) **be ~d to do sth,** compel: *They were ~d to sell their house in order to pay their debts.* ⇨ have³(1). **3** [VP6A,14] do sth for sb as a favour or in answer to a request: *Please ~ me by closing the door. Can you ~ me with...,* lend or give me...? *I'm much ~d to you,* I'm grateful for what you've done. **oblig·ing** adj willing to help: obliging neighbours. **oblig·ing·ly** adv

ob·lique /ə'bliːk/ adj **1** sloping; slanting: an ~ angle, any angle that is not a right angle (ie not 90°). **2** indirect: an ~ reference to sth. **~·ly** adv

ob·li·quity /ə'blɪkwətɪ/ n (pl -ties) **1** [U] state of being ~. **2** [C,U] (instance of) moral perversity.

ob·lit·er·ate /ə'blɪtəreɪt/ vt [VP6A] rub or blot out; remove all signs of; destroy. **ob·lit·er·ation** /ə,blɪtə'reɪʃn/ n [U].

ob·liv·ion /ə'blɪvɪən/ n [U] state of forgetting or being quite forgotten: sink/fall into ~; (colloq) unconsciousness.

ob·livi·ous /ə'blɪvɪəs/ adj ~ of, unaware, having no memory: ~ of one's surroundings/of what was taking place.

ob·long /'ɒblɒŋ US: -lɔːŋ/ n, adj (figure) having four straight sides and angles at 90°, longer than it is wide.

ob·loquy /'ɒbləkwɪ/ n [U] public shame or reproach; abuse; discredit.

ob·nox·ious /əb'nɒkʃəs/ adj nasty; very disagreeable (to). **~·ly** adv **~·ness** n

oboe /'əʊbəʊ/ n woodwind instrument of treble pitch with a double-reed mouthpiece. ⇨ the illus at brass. **'obo·ist** /-ɪst/ n player of the ~.

ob·scene /əb'siːn/ adj (of words, thoughts, books, pictures, etc) morally disgusting; offensive; likely to corrupt and deprave (esp by regarding or describing sex indecently). **~·ly** adv **ob·scen·ity** /əb'senətɪ/ n (pl -ties) [U] being ~; ~ language, etc; [C] instance of this.

ob·scure /əb'skjʊə(r)/ adj **1** dark; hidden; not clearly seen or understood: an ~ view/corner. Is the meaning still ~ to you? **2** not well known: an ~ village/poet. □ vt [VP6A] make ~: The moon was ~d by clouds. Mist ~d the view. **~·ly** adv **ob·scur·ity** /əb'skjʊərətɪ/ n (pl -ties) **1** [U] state of being ~: content to live in obscurity. **2** [C] sth that is ~ or indistinct: a philosophical essay full of obscurities. **ob·scur·ant·ism** /,ɒbskjʊ'ræntɪzəm/ n [U] **1** opposition to enlightenment. **2** deliberate vagueness. **ob·scur·ant·ist** /-ɪst/ n person who practises obscurantism.

ob·sequies /'ɒbsɪkwɪz/ n pl funeral ceremonies.

ob·sequi·ous /əb'siːkwɪəs/ adj ~ (to/towards), too eager to obey or serve; showing excessive respect (esp from hope of reward or advantage): ~ to the Manager. **~·ly** adv **~·ness** n

ob·serv·able /əb'zɜːvəbl/ adj that can be seen or noticed; deserving to be observed. **ob·serv·ably** /-əblɪ/ adv

ob·serv·ance /əb'zɜːvəns/ n **1** [U] the keeping or observing(2) of a law, custom, festival, etc: the ,Lord's ,Day Ob'servance Society, ie for seeing that proper respect is paid to Sunday; the ~ of the Queen's birthday. **2** [C] act performed as part of a ceremony, or as a sign of respect or worship.

ob·serv·ant /əb'zɜːvənt/ adj **1** quick at noticing things: an ~ boy. **2** careful to observe(2) laws, customs, etc: ~ of the rules. **~·ly** adv

ob·ser·va·tion /,ɒbzə'veɪʃn/ n **1** [U] observing or being observed: ~ of natural phenomena; escape ~. be/come under ~, be observed. keep sb under ~, watch him carefully (eg a suspected criminal by the police; a hospital patient by the medical staff). **'~ car,** (in a railway train) one with wide windows through which to watch the scenery, etc. **'~ post,** (mil) post as near to the enemy's lines as possible, from which reports of the enemy's move-

ments may be obtained. **2** [U] power of taking notice: a man of little ~. **3** [U] (usu pl) collected and recorded information: Has he published his ~s on bird life in the Antarctic yet? **4 take an ~,** take the altitude of the sun or other heavenly body in order to find the latitude and longitude of one's position.

ob·serv·atory /əb'zɜːvətrɪ US: -tɔːrɪ/ n (pl -ries) building from which natural phenomena (eg the sun and the stars, volcanic activity, marine life) may be observed.

an astronomical observatory

ob·serve /əb'zɜːv/ vt, vi **1** [VP6A,8,9,10,25,2A, and 18A,19A, in passive] see and notice; watch carefully: ~ the behaviour of birds. The accused man was ~d to enter the bank/trying to force the lock of the door. I have never ~d him do otherwise. He ~d that it had turned cloudy. He ~s keenly but says little. **2** [VP6A] pay attention to (rules, etc); celebrate (festivals, birthdays, anniversaries, etc): Do they ~ Christmas Day in that country? **3** [VP6A,9] say by way of comment: He ~d that we should probably have rain. **~r** n **1** one who ~s(1): an ~r of nature. **2** one who observes(2): an ~r of the Sabbath. **3** person who attends a conference, etc to listen but who does not otherwise take part. **ob·serv·ing** adj quick to notice. **ob·serv·ing·ly** adv

ob·sess /əb'ses/ vt [VP6A] (usu passive, ~ed by/ with) (of a fear, a fixed or false idea) occupy the mind of; continually distress: ~ed by/with fear of unemployment. **~·ion** /əb'seʃn/ n **1** [U] state of being ~ed. **2** [C] ~ion (about/with sth/sb), sth that ~es; fixed idea that occupies one's mind. **~·ive** /əb'sesɪv/ adj of or like an obsession.

ob·sid·ian /əb'sɪdɪən/ n dark volcanic rock like the glass of which some bottles are made.

ob·sol·escent /,ɒbsə'lesnt/ adj becoming out of date; passing out of use. **ob·sol·escence** /-'lesns/ n [U] being ~.

ob·sol·ete /'ɒbsəliːt/ adj no longer used; out of date.

ob·stacle /'ɒbstəkl/ n sth in the way that stops progress or makes it difficult: ~s to world peace. **'~ race,** one in which ~s, natural or artificial, eg ditches, hedges, have to be crossed.

ob·stet·ric /əb'stetrɪk/ (also **ob·stet·ri·cal** /-kl/) adj of obstetrics: the ~ ward (in a hospital). **ob·stet·rics** n pl (with sing v) branch of medicine and surgery connected with childbirth, its antecedents and sequels. **ob·ste·tri·cian** /,ɒbstɪ'trɪʃn/ n expert in obstetrics.

ob·sti·nate /'ɒbstɪnət/ adj **1** not easily giving way to argument or persuasion: an ~ character/streak. **2** not easily overcome: ~ resistance; an ~ disease. **~·ly** adv **ob·sti·nacy** /-nəsɪ/ n [U] being ~; stubbornness.

ob·strep·er·ous /əb'strepərəs/ adj unruly; noisily resisting control: ~ behaviour/children. ~·ly adv ~·ness n

ob·struct /əb'strʌkt/ vt [VP6A] 1 be, get, put, sth in the way of; block up (a road, passage, etc): The mountain roads were ~ed by falls of rock. Trees ~ed the view. 2 make (the development, etc of sth) difficult: ~ the progress of a Bill through the House of Commons.

ob·struc·tion /əb'strʌkʃn/ n 1 [U] obstructing or being obstructed: The Opposition adopted a policy of ~. 2 sth that obstructs: ~s on the road, eg trees blown down in a gale. ~·ism /-ɪzəm/ n systematic ~ of plans, legislation, etc. ~·ist /-ɪst/ n

ob·struc·tive /əb'strʌktɪv/ adj causing, likely or intended to cause, obstruction: a policy ~ to our plans. ~·ly adv

ob·tain /əb'teɪn/ vt,vi 1 [VP6A] get; secure for oneself; buy; have lent or granted to oneself: ~ what one wants. Where can I ~ the book? 2 [VP2A] (of rules, customs) be established or in use: The custom still ~s in districts. ~·able /-əbl/ adj that can be ~ed.

ob·trude /əb'truːd/ vt,vi [VP14,2A] ~ (upon), push (oneself, one's opinions, etc) forward, esp when unwanted. **ob·tru·sive** /əb'truːsɪv/ adj inclined to ~. **ob·tru·sive·ly** adv

ob·tuse /əb'tjuːs US: -'tuːs/ adj 1 blunt. 2 (of an angle) between 90° and 180°. ⇨ the illus at angle. 3 slow in understanding; stupid. ~·ly adv ~·ness n

ob·verse /'ɒbvɜːs/ n side of a coin or medal having on it the head or principal design. ⇨ reverse; face of anything intended to be presented; counterpart; (attrib) the ~ side.

ob·vi·ate /'ɒbvɪeɪt/ vt [VP6A] get rid of; clear away; anticipate: ~ dangers/difficulties.

ob·vi·ous /'ɒbvɪəs/ adj easily seen or understood; clear; plain. ~·ly adv ~·ness n

oca·rina /ˌɒkə'riːnə/ n small, egg-shaped musical wind-instrument (with holes for the finger-tips) made of porcelain, plastic or metal.

oc·ca·sion /ə'keɪʒn/ n 1 [C] time at which a particular event takes place; right time (for sth): on this/that ~...; on the present/last ~...; on one ~, once; on rare ~s. I have met Mr White on several ~s. This is not an ~ (= a suitable time) for laughter. He has had few ~s to speak French. **on ~**, now and then; whenever the need arises. **rise for the ~**, show that one is equal to what needs to be done. **take this/that ~ to say sth**, avail oneself of the opportunity. 2 [U] reason; cause; need: I've had no ~ to visit him recently. You have no ~ to be angry. 3 [C] immediate, subsidiary or incidental cause of sth: The real causes of the strike are not clear, but the ~ was the dismissal of two workmen. □ vt [VP6A,12A,13A] be the cause of: The boy's behaviour ~ed his parents much anxiety.

oc·ca·sional /ə'keɪʒənl/ adj 1 happening, coming, seen, etc from time to time, but not regularly: He pays me ~ visits. There will be ~ showers during the day. **the ~ + n**, = an ~ + n: He pays me the ~ visit, an ~ visit. 2 used or meant for a special event, time, purpose, etc: ~ verses, eg written to celebrate an anniversary. ~·ly /-nəlɪ/ adv now and then; at times: He visits me ~ly.

Oc·ci·dent /'ɒksɪdənt/ n **the ~**, (liter) the countries of the West, ie Europe and America, contrasted with the Orient. **Oc·ci·den·tal** /ˌɒksɪ'dentl/ n, adj (native) of the ~ or a country in the ~.

oc·cult /ɒ'kʌlt US: ə'kʌlt/ adj 1 hidden; secret; only for those with special knowledge. 2 supernatural, magical: ~ sciences, eg astrology. **the ~**, that which is ~.

oc·cu·pant /'ɒkjʊpənt/ n person who occupies a house, room or position; person in actual possession of land, etc. **oc·cu·pancy** /-pənsɪ/ n act, fact, period of occupying a house, land, etc by being in possession.

oc·cu·pa·tion /ˌɒkjʊ'peɪʃn/ n 1 [U] act of occupying(1); taking and holding possession of: the ~ of a house by a family; an army of ~, one that occupies conquered territory until peace is made. 2 [U] period during which land, a building, etc is occupied. 3 [C] business, trade, etc; that which occupies one's time, either permanently or as a hobby, etc: useful ~s for long winter evenings. ~al /-ʃnl/ adj arising from, connected with, a person's ~. ~al 'hazards, risks that arise from a person's ~ (eg explosions in coalmines). ~al 'therapy, treatment of illness, etc by activity in creative or productive employment.

oc·cu·pier /'ɒkjʊpaɪə(r)/ n occupant; person in (esp temporary or subordinate) possession of land or a building (contrasted with the owner or tenant).

oc·cupy /'ɒkjʊpaɪ/ vt (pt,pp -pied) [VP6A] 1 live in, be in possession of (a house, farm, etc). 2 take and keep possession of (towns, countries, etc, in war): ~ the enemy's capital. 3 take up, fill (space, time, attention, the mind): The dinner and speeches occupied three hours. Many anxieties ~ my mind. He is occupied in translating/occupied with a translation of a French novel. 4 hold, fill: My sister occupies an important position in the Department of the Environment.

oc·cur /ə'kɜː(r)/ vi (-rr-) 1 [VP2A] take place; happen: Don't let this ~ again. When did the accident ~? 2 [VP3A] ~ to, come into (sb's mind): An idea has ~red to me. Did it ever ~ to you that..., Did you ever have the idea that...? 3 [VP2C] exist; be found: Misprints ~ on every page.

oc·cur·rence /ə'kʌrəns/ n 1 [C] happening; event: an everyday ~; an unfortunate ~. 2 [U] fact or process of occurring: of frequent/rare ~, happening frequently/rarely.

ocean /'əʊʃn/ n 1 the great body of water that surrounds the land masses of the earth: an ~ voyage. ~-going ships, (contrasted with coastal ships). 2 one of the main divisions of this: the Atlantic/ Pacific/Indian O~. **the ~ lanes**, the routes regularly used by ships. 3 (colloq) great number or quantity: ~s of time/money. ~ic /ˌəʊʃɪ'ænɪk/ adj of, like, living in, the ~.

ochre (US also **ocher**) /'əʊkə(r)/ n [U] sorts of earth used for making pigments varying from light yellow to brown; pale yellowish-brown colour.

o'clock /ə'klɒk/ particle (= of the clock) used in asking and telling the time (to specify an hour): He left at five ~/between five and six ~. ⇨ App 4.

oc·ta·gon /'ɒktəgən US: -gɒn/ n plane figure with eight sides and angles. **oc·tag·onal** /ɒk'tægənl/ adj eight-sided.

oc·tane /'ɒkteɪn/ n paraffin hydro-carbon: high ~, (of fuels used in internal-combustion engines) having good anti-knock properties; '~ rating, measure of these properties, esp of petrol. ⇨ knock²(3).

oc·tave /'ɒktɪv/ n 1 (music) the note that is six whole tones above or below a given note; the interval of five whole tones and two semi-tones (do, re, mi, fa, so, la, ti, do); note and its ~ sounded together. ⇨ scale²(7). **2** (poetry) first eight lines of a sonnet; stanza of eight lines.

oc·tavo /ɒk'teɪvəʊ/ *n* (abbr **8vo**, or **oct**; *pl* ~s /-vəʊz/) (size of a) book or page produced by folding sheets of paper three times or into eight leaves.

oc·tet, oc·tette /ɒk'tet/ *n* **1** (piece of music for) eight singers or players. **2** = octave(2).

Oc·to·ber /ɒk'təʊbə(r)/ *n* the tenth month of the year, with 31 days.

oc·to·gen·arian /ˌɒktədʒɪ'neərɪən/ *n, adj* (person) of an age from 80 to 89.

oc·to·pus /'ɒktəpəs/ *n* (*pl* ~es /-pəsɪz/) sea animal with a soft body and eight arms (*tentacles*) provided with suckers. ⇨ the illus at mollusc.

oc·troi /'ɒktrwɑː US: ɒk'trwɑː/ *n* [C] duty levied (in some European countries) on goods brought into a town; place where, officials by whom, the levy is collected.

ocu·lar /'ɒkjʊlə(r)/ *adj* of, for, by, the eyes; of seeing: ~ *proof/demonstration*.

ocu·list /'ɒkjʊlɪst/ *n* specialist in diseases of the eye.

oda·lisque /'əʊdəlɪsk/ *n* Eastern female slave or concubine, eg in a seraglio in olden times.

odd /ɒd/ *adj* **1** (of numbers) not even; not exactly divisible by two: *1, 3, 5 and 7 are odd numbers.* **2** of one of a pair when the other is missing: *an odd shoe/boot/glove.* **3** of one or more of a set or series when not with the rest: *two odd volumes of an encyclopaedia; an odd player,* (in a game) an extra player above the number actually needed. **,odd man 'out,** (**a**) person or thing left when the others have been arranged in pairs. (**b**) (colloq) person who stands aloof from, or cannot fit himself into, the society, community, etc, of which he is a member. **4** with a little extra: *five'hundred odd,* a number greater than 500; *'thirty-odd years,* between 30 and 40; *twelve 'pounds odd,* £12 and some pence extra. **5** not regular, habitual, or fixed; occasional: *make a living by doing odd jobs; weed the garden at odd times/moments,* at various and irregular times. **the odd** + **n,** = an odd + *n: The landscape was bare except for the odd cactus.* **6** (-er, -est) strange; peculiar: *He's an odd/odd-looking old man. How odd!* **odd·ly** *adv* in an odd manner: *oddly enough,* strange to say.

odd·ity /'ɒdɪtɪ/ *n* (*pl* -ties) **1** [U] quality of being odd(6); strangeness: ~ *of behaviour/dress.* **2** [C] queer act, thing or person: *He's something of an* ~, is unusual in some ways.

odd·ment /'ɒdmənt/ *n* [C] **1** remnant; sth left over; old piece: *The chair was sold as an* ~ *at the end of the auction.* **2** (*pl*) odd pieces. ⇨ *odds and ends* at odds(5).

odds /ɒdz/ *n pl* **1** the chances in favour of or against sth happening: *The* ~ *are against us,* We are unlikely to succeed. *The* ~ *are in your favour,* You are likely to succeed. *The* ~ *are that...,* It is probable that...; *They were fighting against heavy* ~. *It makes no* ~, makes no difference, will not influence the outcome. *What's the* ~*?* (colloq) What does it matter? *give/receive* ~, give/receive an equalizing allowance (eg a number of strokes in golf, when a player is known to be stronger or weaker than another). **2** things that are not even; inequalities: *make* ~ *even.* **3** (betting) difference in amount between the money staked on a chance and the money that will be paid if the chance is successful: ~ *of ten to one.* **fixed** ~, (eg football pools) with a promise to pay agreed odds, eg

100—1, regardless of the number of punters, gamblers. **lay** ~ **of,** offer ~ of: *I'll lay* ~ *of three to one that....* **long** ~, eg 20 to 1. **short** ~, eg 3 to 1. ~-'**on,** better than even (chance). **4 be at** ~ **(with sb) (over/on sth),** be quarrelling or disagreeing. **5** ~ **and ends,** small articles, bits and pieces, of various sorts and usu of small value.

ode /əʊd/ *n* poem, usu in irregular metre and expressing noble feelings, often in celebration of some special event.

odi·ous /'əʊdɪəs/ *adj* hateful; repulsive. ~·**ly** *adv*

odium /'əʊdɪəm/ *n* [U] general or widespread hatred; strong feeling against sth: *behaviour that exposed him to* ~.

odor·ifer·ous /ˌəʊdə'rɪfərəs/ *adj* (formal) fragrant.

odor·ous /'əʊdərəs/ *adj* (chiefly poet) fragrant.

odour (US = **odor**) /'əʊdə(r)/ *n* **1** [C] smell (pleasant or unpleasant). **2** [U] reputation; approval; favour. *be in good/bad* ~ *(with sb),* enjoy/ not enjoy his favour or approval. ~·**less** *adj*

od·ys·sey /'ɒdɪsɪ/ *n* long, adventurous journey or series of adventures (from the voyage of Odysseus /ə'dɪsɪəs/ after the siege of Troy, in Homer's epic).

oecu·meni·cal /ˌiːkjuː'menɪkl/ *adj* = ecumenical.

Oedi·pus com·plex /'iːdɪpəs kɒmpleks US: 'ed-/ *n* (psych) sexual love of an infant for the parent of the opposite sex, with jealousy of the other parent.

o'er /ɔː(r)/ *adv, prep* (poet) over.

oesoph·agus /iː'sɒfəgəs/ *n* = esophagus.

of /usual form: əv; strong form: ɒv/ *prep* **1** (indicating separation in space or time): *five miles south of Leeds; within a hundred yards of the station; within a year of his death;* (US) *five minutes/a quarter of* (= before) *two,* (GB = 'five minutes/a quarter *to* two'). **2** (indicating origin, authorship): *a man of humble origin; of royal descent; the works of Shakespeare; the Iliad of Homer.* **3** (indicating cause): *die of grief/hunger, etc; do sth of necessity/of one's own choice/of one's own accord; sick/proud/ashamed/afraid/glad/tired, etc of sth or sb; taste/smell, etc of sth; because of; for fear of. The explosion couldn't have happened of itself,* ie without an external cause. **4** (indicating relief, deprivation, riddance): *cure sb of a disease/a bad habit, etc; rid a warehouse of rats; be/get rid of sth or sb; rob sb of his money; relieve sb of anxiety; clear oneself of an accusation; destitute of sense; trees bare of leaves; free of customs duty; independent of help; short of money.* **5** (indicating material or substance): *a table of wood; a house of stone; a dress of silk; made of steel and concrete; built of brick.* **6** (forming *adj* phrases; descriptive genitive): *goods of our own manufacture; tomatoes of my own growing,* that I have grown myself; *a girl of ten years,* a girl ten years old, a ten-year-old girl; *a man of foreign appearance; a man of genius; a man of ability,* an able man; *a woman of no importance,* an unimportant woman; *the vice of drunkenness,* the vice that is drunkenness; *a coat of many colours,* a many-coloured coat; *the city of Dublin; the Isle of Wight.* **7** (in the pattern 'noun¹ *of* noun²' = noun² that is noun¹): *They live in a palace of a house,* a house that is a palace, a palatial house. *He has the devil of a temper,* a devilish temper. *Where's that fool of an assistant,* that foolish assistant? *What a mountain of a wave,* a mountainous wave! *She's a fine figure of a woman,* a woman with a fine figure. *Where's your rascal of a husband,* your rascally husband? **8** (objective genitive): *a maker of pots,* a man who makes pots; *the love of study; the writing of a letter; loss of power/appetite; great eaters of fish,* people who eat much fish; *the fear of God,* ie felt by men towards God. **9** (subjective genitive): *the love of God,* God's love for mankind. (⇨ **8** above, *the fear of God*); *the love of a mother,* a mother's love, the love that a mother has for her children. Cf *his love of* (ie for) *his mother.* **10** (indicating connection, reference or relation): *the cause of the accident; the result of the debate; a topic of conversation; the first day of June; the manners of the present day; those of the middle classes; the master of the house; the wall of the garden,* the garden wall; *the leg of the table,* the table leg; *the opposite of what I intended; Doctor of Medicine; Master of Arts; think well of sb; admitting/allowing of no doubt; accused/suspected/convicted of a crime; speaking/talking/dreaming of sth; sure/certain/confident/fond/guilty/innocent, etc of sth; hard of hearing,* deaf; *blind of* (= in respect of) *one eye; at thirty years of age. What of* (= about) *the risk? Well, what of it?* **11** (indicating partition, inclusion, measure): (a) *a sheet of paper; a roll of cloth; a pint of milk; a ton of coal; 3 acres of land; 2 yards of cloth; some of that cake; one/a few/all of us; a lot/a great deal/not much of this stuff; no more of that. The car won't hold the six of us.* (b) (after superlatives): *He is the most dangerous of enemies. You have had the best of teachers,* the best of those teachers who were available. (c) (= out of): *It surprises me that you, of all men, should be so foolish. On this day of all days.* (d) (intensive): *the song of songs; the Holy of Holies,* best deserving the name. **12** (in the pattern *n + of + possessive*) (a) from among the number of: *a friend of mine; no business of yours; reading a volume of Ruskin's,* a book, one of a number of which Ruskin was the author; *a painting of the king's,* one of a number belonging to, or painted by, the king. Cf *a portrait of the king,* a painting to show the king's appearance. (b) (used when the *n* is modified by a demonstrative or other word that cannot be combined with a possessive): *that long nose of his; this essay of Green's; that foolish young wife of yours; that queer-looking hat of hers.* **13** (in the pattern *adj + of + n/pron*): *How kind of you to help! It was good of your brother to come.* **14** (indicating time): *What do you do of a Sunday,* on Sundays? *He sometimes comes in of an evening,* in the evenings. *In days of old/of yore,* in the past; *of late,* recently; *of late years,* during recent years. **15** by: *beloved of all.*

off¹ /ɒf *US:* ɔːf/ *adj* **1** (contrasted with *near*) (of horses, vehicles) on the right-hand side: *the off front wheel; the off hind leg of a horse; the off horse* (of a pair). **2** (remotely) possible or likely. **on the off chance,** ⇨ chance¹(2). **3** inactive; dull: *the 'off season,* ⇨ season.

off² /ɒf *US:* ɔːf/ *adverbial particle* (For special uses with *off* as an *adverbial particle* such as *go off; turn sth off* ⇨ the *v* entries.) **1** indicating distance in space or time, departure, removal, separation at or to a distance; away: *The town is five miles off. We're still some way off,* from our destination. *The holidays are not far off. Why don't you have that long beard off,* cut off, shaved off? *He's off to London. It's time I was off/I must be off now,* I must leave now. *We're off/Off we go!* We've started/We're starting! *They're off!* (in racing) The race has started! *Off with him!* Take him away! *Off*

with his head! Cut his head off! **2** (contrasted with *on*) indicating the ending of sth arranged, planned, etc: *Their engagement* (ie to marry) *is off/broken off,* ended. *The miners' strike is off,* will not now take place. **3** (contrasted with *on*) disconnected; no longer available: *The water/gas/electricity is off. Are the brakes off? The central heating is off. That dish is off,* (in a restaurant) no more of that dish is available (even though it is on the menu). **4** indicating absence or freedom from work or duty: *I think I'll take the afternoon off,* not do my usual work, etc. *The manager gave the staff a day off,* a day's holiday. *You mustn't take time off* (= stay away from work) *just because you want to see a football match.* **5** (of food) no longer fresh: *This fish has gone slightly off,* is beginning to smell or taste rather bad. **6** (in a theatre) behind or at the side(s) of the stage: *Noises off,* eg as a stage direction in a printed play. **7** (phrases) **off of,** (US) = off (*prep*). **on and off; off and on,** from time to time; now and again; irregularly: *It rained on and off all day.* **badly/comfortably/well off,** ⇨ these adverbs. **better/worse off,** ⇨ better²(1), worse *adv*(1). **right/straight off,** at once; immediately.

off³ /ɒf *US:* ɔːf/ *prep* **1** not on; down from; away from: *fall off a ladder/a tree/a horse. The rain ran off the roof. The ball rolled off the table. Keep off the grass. Cut another slice off the loaf. Can you take something off* (ie reduce) *the price?* **2** (of a road or street) extending or branching from: *a narrow lane off the main road; a street off the Strand,* branching from the street called the Strand. **3** at some distance from: *a house off the main road; a short distance seaward of: an island off the Cornish coast; a ship anchored off the harbour entrance. The battle was fought off Cape Trafalgar.* **4** (colloq) feeling averse to; not taking or indulging in: *I'm off my food,* have little or no appetite, don't enjoy it. *She's off smoking/drugs,* does not smoke/take drugs any more.

off⁴ /ɒf *US:* ɔːf/ *pref* (used in numerous compounds) ⇨ the entries below.

of·fal /'ɒfl *US:* 'ɔːfl/ *n* [U] those parts, eg heart, head, kidneys, which are considered less valuable than the flesh when an animal is cut up for food.

off-beat /ˌɒf 'biːt *US:* ˌɔːf-/ *adj* (colloq) unusual; unconventional: *an ∼ TV comedy.*

off-day /'ɒf deɪ *US:* 'ɔːf-/ *n* (colloq) day when one is unlucky, when one does things badly, clumsily, etc: *I'm afraid this is one of my ∼s.*

of·fence (US = **of·fense**) /ə'fens/ *n* **1** [C] *an ∼ against,* crime, sin, breaking of a rule: *an ∼ against the law/against good manners; be charged with a serious ∼.* **2** [U] the hurting of sb's feelings; condition of being hurt in one's feelings. **give/cause ∼ (to sb); take ∼ (at sth)**: *He is quick to take ∼,* is easily offended. **No ∼!** (phrase used to say) I did not intend to hurt your feelings. **3** [U] attack: *weapons of ∼. They say that the most effective defence is ∼.* **4** [C] that which annoys the senses or makes sb angry: *That cess-pool is an ∼ to the neighbourhood.* **∼·less** *adj* without ∼; not giving ∼.

of·fend /ə'fend/ *vi,vt* **1** [VP3A] *∼ against,* do wrong; commit an offence: *∼ against good manners/the law/traditions, etc.* **2** [VP6A] hurt the feelings of; give offence to: *I'm sorry if I've ∼ed you. He was ∼ed at/by my remarks. She was ∼ed by/with her husband.* **3** [VP6A] displease; annoy: *sounds that ∼ the ear; ugly buildings that ∼ the* *eye.* **~·er** *n* person who ~s, esp by breaking a law; *first* ~ers, found guilty for the first time and not usu treated severely; *an old* ~er, one who has often been found guilty.

of·fense /ə'fens/ ⇨ offence.

of·fen·sive /ə'fensɪv/ *adj* **1** causing offence to the mind or senses; disagreeable: *fish with an* ~ *smell;* ~ *language.* **2** used for, connected with, attack: ~ *weapons/wars.* ⇨ defensive. □ *n* attack; an attitude of attack. **go into/take the** ~, go into attack. **a peace** ~, (modern jargon) sustained effort the declared aim of which is to lessen the risk of war. ~·ly *adv* ~·ness *n*

of·fer /'ɒfə(r) *US:* 'ɔːf-/ *vt,vi* **1** [VP6A,7A,12A,13A,14] ~ *sth to sb;* ~ *sb sth;* ~ *sth for sth,* hold out, put forward, to be accepted or refused; say what one is willing to pay, give or exchange: *They* ~ed *a reward for the return of the jewels that had been lost. I have been* ~ed *a job in Japan. He* ~ed *to help me. He* ~ed *me his help. We* ~ed *him the house for £20000/*~ed *him £20000 for the house.* ~ *battle,* give the enemy an opportunity of fighting. ~ *one's hand,* hold it out (to shake hands). ~ *one's hand (in marriage),* make a proposal of marriage to a woman. **2** [VP6A,12A,13A,15B] ~ *sth (up) (to God),* present (to God): ~ *prayers to God;* ~ *up a sacrifice.* **3** [VP6A,7A,14] ~ *(to),* attempt; give signs of: ~ *no resistance to the enemy.* **4** [VP2A] occur; arise: *Take the first opportunity that* ~s, that there is. **as occasion** ~s, when there is an opportunity. □ *n* [C] statement ~ing to do sth or give sth; that which is ~ed: *an* ~ *of help; your kind* ~ *to help; an* ~ *of marriage,* a proposal. *I've had an* ~ *of £20000 for the house. Make me an* ~. **be open to an** ~, be willing to consider a price to be named by a buyer. **(goods) on** ~, for sale at a certain price. ~·ing /'ɒfərɪŋ *US:* 'ɔːf-/ *n* **1** [U] act of ~ing: *the* ~ing *of bribes.* **2** [C] sth ~ed or presented: *a* '*peace* ~ing, sth ~ed in the hope of restoring friendship after a quarrel, etc.

of·fer·tory /'ɒfətrɪ *US:* -tɔːrɪ/ *n* (*pl* -ries) [C] gifts collected in church during, or at the end of, a service.

off-hand /ˌɒf 'hænd *US:* ˌɔːf/ *adj* **1** without previous thought or preparation; extempore: ~ *remarks.* **2** (of behaviour, etc) casual; curt: *in an* ~ *way.* □ *adv* without previous thought: *I can't say* ~. ˌoff-'handed(ly) *adj, adv* = ~.

of·fice /'ɒfɪs *US:* 'ɔːf-/ *n* [C] **1** (often *pl*) room(s) used as a place of business: *a lawyer's* ~; *working in an* ~, in business, eg as a clerk or typist; *our London* ~, our branch in London; (US) surgery. '**booking** ~, ⇨ book²(2). '**box-**~, ⇨ box¹(2). '~**-block,** (usu large) building containing ~s (often of more than one company or firm). '~**-boy** *n* boy employed to do less important duties in an ~. **2** (buildings of a) government department, including the staff, their work and duties: *the* '*Foreign O*~. **3** the work which it is sb's duty to do, esp in a public position of trust and authority: *enter upon/ leave/accept/resign* ~, esp of positions in the government service. *Which party will be in* ~ *after the next general election? The Liberals have been out of* ~ *for a long time now.* '~**-bearer** *n* person who holds an ~. **4** duty: *the* ~ *of host/chairman.* **5** (*pl*) attentions, services, help: *through the good* ~s (= kind help) *of a friend; perform the last* ~s *for...,* conduct the burial service of.... **Divine O**~, certain forms of worship in the Roman Catholic

and Episcopal Churches.

of·fi·cer /'ɒfɪsə(r) *US:* 'ɔːf-/ *n* **1** person appointed to command others in the armed forces, in merchant ships, aircraft, the police force, etc usu wearing special uniform with indications of rank: *commissioned and non-commissioned* ~s; ~s and crew. **2** person with a position of authority or trust, engaged in active duties, eg in the government: *executive/clerical* ~s, in the civil service; *a customs* ~; ~s of state, ministers in the government; *the* ~s of the Debating Society, ie the President, Secretary, Treasurer; *the Medical O*~ *of Health;* '*Welfare O*~s. **3** form of address to a policeman.

of·fi·cial /ə'fɪʃl/ *adj* **1** of a position of trust or authority; said, done, etc with authority: ~ *responsibilities/records; in his* ~ *uniform;* ~ *statements. The news is not* ~. **2** characteristic of, suitable for, persons holding office: *written in* ~ *style.* □ *n* person holding public office (eg in national or local government): *government* ~s. ~**ly** /-ʃəlɪ/ *adv* in an ~ manner; with ~ authority. ~**·dom** /-dəm/ *n* ~s collectively; the ways of doing the business of (government) ~s. ~**ese** /əˌfɪʃə'liːz/ *n* [U] language characteristic of the writing of some government ~s (considered to be too formal or obscure). ⇨ *journalese* at journal.

of·fici·ate /ə'fɪʃɪeɪt/ *vi* [VP2A,C,3A] ~ *(as) (at),* perform the duties of an office or position: ~ *as chairman;* ~ *as host at a dinner party;* ~ *at a marriage ceremony,* (of a priest) perform the ceremony.

of·fi·cious /ə'fɪʃəs/ *adj* too eager or ready to help, offer advice, use authority. ~**·ly** *adv* ~**·ness** *n*

off·ing /'ɒfɪŋ *US:* 'ɔːf-/ *n* part of the sea distant from the point of observation but visible: *a ship in the* ~; (fig) *a quarrel in the* ~, one that appears likely to break out.

off·ish /'ɒfɪʃ *US:* 'ɔːf-/ *adj* (colloq) inclined to aloofness; distant in manner. ⇨ *stand-offish* at stand²(11).

off-licence /'ɒf laɪsns *US:* 'ɔːf/ *n* licence to sell beer and other alcoholic drinks for consumption off the premises; shop, part of a public house, where such drinks may be bought and taken away.

off-peak /'ɒf piːk *US:* 'ɔːf/ *attrib adj* ⇨ peak¹(4).

off-print /'ɒf prɪnt *US:* 'ɔːf/ *n* [C] separate printed copy of an article in part of a larger publication.

off-putting /ˌɒf 'pʊtɪŋ *US:* ˌɔːf/ *adj* (colloq) disconcerting. ⇨ *put off* at put¹(11).

off-scour·ings /'ɒf skaʊərɪŋz *US:* 'ɔːf/ *n pl* (usu fig) refuse; dregs.

off·set /'ɒfset *US:* 'ɔːf-/ *vt* (-tt-) [VP6A,14] balance, compensate for: *He has to* ~ *his small salary by living economically.* □ *n* **1** ~ **(process),** method of printing in which the ink is transferred from a plate to a rubber surface and then on to paper. **2** = offshoot.

off·shoot /'ɒfʃuːt *US:* 'ɔːf-/ *n* [C] stem or branch growing from a main stem (liter or fig): *an* ~ *of a plant/a mountain range/a family.*

off-shore /ˌɒf 'ʃɔː(r) *US:* ˌɔːf/ *adj* **1** in a direction away from the shore or land: ~ *breezes.* **2** at a short way out to sea: ~ *islands/fisheries.* **3** ~ **purchases,** (US) goods purchased by the US for countries in receipt of economic or military aid, but which do not come from the US directly, eg aluminium shipped from Canada to Europe.

off·side /ɒf 'saɪd *US:* ɔːf/ *attrib adj, adv* (football, hockey) (of a player) in a position on the field in relation to the ball which is debarred by the rules:

~ *play; the* ~ *rule.*

off-spring /'ɒfsprɪŋ *US:* 'ɔːf-/ *n* (*pl* unchanged) child; children; young of animals: *He is the* ~ *of a scientific genius and a ballet dancer. Their* ~ *are all slightly mad.*

off-street /'ɒf striːt *US:* 'ɔːf/ *attrib adj* not on the main streets: ~ *parking,* of motor vehicles; ~ (*un*)*loading,* eg of lorries at the rear entrances of buildings.

off-white /ˌɒf 'waɪt *US:* ˌɔːf 'hwaɪt/ *adj* not pure white, but with a pale greyish or yellowish tinge.

oft /ɒft *US:* ɔːft/ *adv* (in poetry) often: *an oft-told tale; many a time and oft,* very often. **'oft-times** *adv* (archaic) often.

of-ten /'ɒfn *US:* 'ɔːfn/ *adv of frequency* (usu occupying mid-position (ie with the *v*); may occupy front-position or end-position for emphasis (esp when modified by *very* or *quite*), or for contrast; comp and sup either ~*er,* ~*est,* or *more* ~, *most* ~.) **1** many times; in a large proportion of the instances: *We* ~ *go there. We have* ~ *been there. We've been there quite* ~. *It very* ~ *rains here in April.* **2** (in phrases) **how** ~: *How* ~ *do the buses run?* **as** ~ **as,** each time that: *As* ~ *as I tried to ring him the line was engaged.* **as** ~ **as not; more** ~ **than not,** very frequently: *During foggy weather the trains are late more* ~ *than not.* **every so** ~, from time to time. **once too** ~, once more than is wise, safe, etc: *He exceeded the speed limit once too* ~ *and was fined £50.*

ogle /'əʊgl/ *vi,vt* [VP3A,6A] ~ (*at*), look at (suggesting lust or longing): *ogling all the pretty girls.*

ogre /'əʊgə(r)/ *n* [C] (in fables) cruel man-eating giant. **ogress** /'əʊgres/ *n* female ~. **'**~**-ish** /-ɪʃ/ *adj* like an ~.

oh /əʊ/ *int* exclamation of surprise, fear, etc.

ohm /əʊm/ *n* [C] unit of electrical resistance (symbol Ω).

oho /əʊ'həʊ/ *int* exclamation of surprise or triumph.

oil /ɔɪl/ *n* [C,U] **1** (sorts of) (usu easily burning) liquid which does not mix with water, obtained from animals (eg *whale-oil*), plants (*coconut oil, olive-oil, oil of peppermint, essential oils*), or found in rock underground (*mineral oil, petroleum*): *cod-liver oil; salad oil; hair oil.* **2** (phrases) **burn the midnight oil,** sit up late at night to study, etc. **paint in oils,** paint with oil-colours (⇨ below). **pour oil on the flame(s),** make anger more intense, make a quarrel more bitter, etc. **pour oil on troubled waters,** act or speak in such a way as to end quarrelling, bitterness, etc. **smell of the midnight oil,** bear marks of study (as if done late at night by the light of an oil-lamp). **strike oil,** find petroleum in the ground by sinking a shaft, etc; (fig) become very prosperous or successful. **3** (compounds) **'oil-bearing** *adj* (eg rock strata) containing mineral oil. **'oil-burner** *n* engine, ship, heater, etc that uses oil as fuel. **'oil-cake** *n* [U] cattle food made from seeds after the oil has been pressed out. **'oil-can** *n* can with a long nozzle, used for oiling machinery. **'oil-cloth** *n* [U] cotton material waterproofed and used as a covering for shelves, etc. **'oil-colours, oils** *n pl* paints made by mixing colouring matter in oil. **'oil-field** *n* area where petroleum is found. **'oil-fired** *adj* (eg of a furnace) burning oil as fuel: *oil-fired central heating.* **'oil-painting** *n* [U] art of painting in oil-colours; [C] picture painted in oil-colours. **'oil-palm** *n* tropical palm tree yielding oil. **'oil-paper** *n*

paper made transparent and waterproof by being treated with oil. **'oil-rig** *n* structure and machinery for drilling (eg in the sea-bed) for oil. ⇨ derrick(2). **'oil-silk** *n* silk cloth treated with oil to make it air-tight and water-tight, used for making raincoats, etc. **'oil-skin** *n* [C,U] (coat etc, made of) cloth treated with oil to make it waterproof; (*pl*) suit of clothes made of this material, as worn by sailors, etc. **'oil-slick,** ⇨ slick. **'oil-tanker** *n* ship, large vehicle, for carrying oil (esp petroleum). **'oil-well** *n* well from which petroleum is obtained. □ *vt* [VP6A] put oil on or into (eg to make a machine run smoothly): *oil a lock/bicycle; oil the wheels/works,* (fig) make things go smoothly by being tactful; *oil* (more usu *grease*) *sb's palm,* give him a bribe. **oiled** *adj* (usu *well-oiled*) (sl) rather drunk.

an oil-tanker

oiler /'ɔɪlə(r)/ *n* **1** ship built for carrying oil; oil-tanker. **2** oil-can for oiling machinery. **3** person who oils machinery, eg in the engine-room of a ship.

oily /'ɔɪlɪ/ *adj* (-ier, -iest) **1** of or like oil: *an* ~ *liquid.* **2** covered or soaked with oil: ~ *fingers.* **3** (of speech or manner) too smooth; fawning; trying by fawning to win favour. **oili-ness** *n.* also ⇨ oleaginous.

oint-ment /'ɔɪntmənt/ *n* [C,U] (sorts of) medicinal paste made from oil or fat and used on the skin (to heal injuries or roughness, or as a cosmetic).

okapi /əʊ'kɑːpɪ/ *n* rare forest ruminant animal of Central Africa.

okay /ˌəʊ'keɪ/ (abbr **OK**) *adj, adv* (colloq) all right; correct; approved. □ *vt* [VP6A] agree to; approve of. □ *n* agreement; sanction: *Have they given you their OK?*

okra /'əʊkrə/ *n* (tropical and semi-tropical plant with) edible green seed pods used as a vegetable.

old /əʊld/ *adj* (-er, -est) ⇨ also elder[1], eldest. **1** (with a period of time, and with *how*) of age: *He's forty years old. At fifteen years old he left home to become a sailor. How old are you? He is old enough to know better. Ought a seven-year-old child to be able to read?* **2** (contrasted with *young*) having lived a long time; no longer young or middle-aged: *Old people cannot be so active as young people. He's far too old for a young girl like you to marry. What will he do when he grows/is/gets old?* **the old,** old people. **young and old,** everyone. **old age,** the latter part of life. **old age pension** (abbr **OAP**), (or *retirement pension*) pension paid by the State to old persons. Hence, **old age pensioner** *n* (or *senior citizen*). **the old man,** (colloq) (**a**) one's husband or father. (**b**) (among sailors) the captain of a ship. **the old woman,** (colloq) one's wife. **ˌold-'womanish** *adj* fussy and timid. **an old maid,** ⇨ maid. **ˌold-'maidish** *adj* precise, tidy, fidgety. **3** (contrasted with *new, modern, up-to-date*) belonging to past times; having been in existence or use for a long time: *old customs/families/civilizations; old houses/clothes.* **one of the 'old school,** conservative; old-

-fashioned. **the Old World,** Europe, Asia and Africa. **,old-'fashioned** adj (a) out of date: *old-fashioned styles/clothes.* (b) keeping to old ways, ideas, customs, etc: *an old-fashioned aunt; an old-fashioned child,* one who behaves like a much older person. (c) (of glances) reproving: *She gave him an old-fashioned look.* □ n (US) kind of cocktail made with whiskey. **old fogey** n⇨ fogey. **old hat,** (colloq) out of date. **'old-time** adj belonging to, typical of, past times: *old-time dances.* **'old-world** adj belonging to, typical of, past times; not modern: *an old-world cottage/garden.* **4** long known or familiar: *an old friend of mine,* one who has been a friend for a long time (but not necessarily old in years). **Old Glory,** used by Americans of the flag of the US. **5** former; previous (but not necessarily old in years). **'old boy/girl,** former member of the school in question. **the 'old country,** one's mother country (used esp when one has left it to settle elsewhere). **the/one's old school,** the school one attended as a boy/girl. **the/one's old school tie, (a)** tie worn by former pupils. **(b)** feeling of solidarity, wish to give mutual help, among former pupils of the same school or similar types of school. **6** having much experience or practice: *a man who is old in diplomacy.* **the old guard,** long-standing, faithful supporters. **old offender,** person who has often been convicted of crime. **an old hand (at sth),** person with long experience. **old-'timer** n person who has for many years lived in a place, been associated with (a club, occupation, etc). **come the old soldier (over sb),** (colloq) claim, because of long experience, to have superior knowledge or ability. **7** (colloq) used in addressing persons, and with names (and nicknames) giving intimacy, or in joking style: *'Good old John!' 'Listen, old man.' 'Hullo, old thing!'* **the 'old one; the old gentleman; old Harry/Nick/Scratch,** the devil. **8** (sl) used as an intensive: *We're having a high old time,* a very good time. *Any old thing* (= Anything whatever) *will do.* □ n the past: *in days of old; the men of old.* **old·ish** /-ɪʃ/ adj rather old.

olden /'əʊldən/ adj (archaic, liter) of former age: *in ~ times/days.*

old·ster /'əʊldstə(r)/ n (colloq) (opposite to *youngster*) old person: *Some of us ~s have more energy than the youngsters.*

ole·agi·nous /,əʊlɪ'ædʒɪnəs/ adj having properties of oil; producing oil; fatty; greasy.

ole·an·der /,əʊlɪ'ændə(r)/ n [C] evergreen shrub with tough leaves and red, pink or white flowers growing in clusters.

ol·fac·tory /ɒl'fæktərɪ/ adj concerned with smelling: *the ~ nerves.*

oli·garchy /'ɒlɪɡɑːkɪ/ n (pl -chies) [C,U] (country with) government by a small group of all-powerful persons; such a group. **oli·garch** /'ɒlɪɡɑːk/ n member of an ~.

ol·ive /'ɒlɪv/ n 1 ⇨ the illus at tree. **'~(-tree),** (evergreen tree common in S Europe bearing a) small oval fruit with a hard stone-like seed and a bitter taste, yellowish-green when unripe and bluish-black when ripe; used for pickling, to be eaten as a relish, and for oil, (**,~-'oil),** which is used for cooking, dressing salads, etc. **2** leaf, branch or wreath of ~ as an emblem of peace. **,hold out the '~-branch,** show that one is ready to discuss peace-making. □ adj the colour of the unripe fruit, yellowish-green or yellowish-brown.

Olym·piad /ə'lɪmpɪæd/ n period of four years between celebrations of the Olympic Games.

Olym·pian /ə'lɪmpɪən/ adj (of manners, etc) magnificent; god-like: *~ calm.* □ n one of the greater gods of ancient Greece; person with god-like qualities.

Olym·pic /ə'lɪmpɪk/ adj **the ~ Games, (a)** the contests held at Olympia in Greece in ancient times. **(b)** the international athletic competitions held in modern times every four years in a different country.

om·buds·man /'ɒmbʊdzmæn/ n **the O~,** (in GB officially called *Parliamentary Commissioner*) experienced person having authority to inquire into and pronounce upon grievances of citizens against public authorities.

omega /'əʊmɪɡə US: əʊ'meɡə/ n the last letter (Ω) of the Greek alphabet, ⇨ App 4; final development. *Alpha and O~,* the beginning and the end.

om·elette, om·elet /'ɒmlɪt/ n [C] eggs beaten together and fried, often flavoured with cheese or containing herbs, etc or (*sweet ~*) jam, sugar.

omen /'əʊmen/ n [C,U] (thing, happening, regarded as a) sign of sth good or warning of evil fortune: *an ~ of success; an event of good/bad ~.* □ vt [VP6A] be an ~ of.

om·in·ous /'ɒmɪnəs/ adj of bad omen; threatening: *an ~ silence; ~ of disaster. ~·ly* adv

omission /ə'mɪʃn/ n 1 [U] act of omitting, leaving out or undone: *sins of ~,* leaving undone those things that ought to be done. **2** [C] sth that is omitted.

omit /ə'mɪt/ vt (-tt-) 1 [VP7A,6C] *~ to do/doing sth,* fail: *~ to do/~ doing a piece of work.* **2** [VP6A] fail to include; leave out: *This chapter may be ~ted.*

om·ni·bus /'ɒmnɪbəs/ n (pl ~es /-bəsɪz/) **1** (former name for a) bus; (in names): *The ,Midland 'O~ Co.* **2** (attrib) for, including, many purposes: *an ~ volume,* a large book in which a number of books, eg by the same author, are reprinted.

om·nip·otence /ɒm'nɪpətəns/ n [U] infinite power: *the ~ of God.* **om·nip·otent** /-ənt/ adj having infinite power: *the O~,* God.

om·nis·cience /ɒm'nɪsɪəns/ n [U] (formal) infinite knowledge. **om·nis·cient** /-sɪənt/ adj having infinite knowledge.

om·niv·or·ous /ɒm'nɪvərəs/ adj (formal) eating all kinds of food; (fig) reading all kinds of books, etc: *an ~ reader.*

on¹ /ɒn/ adverbial particle (For special uses with *on* as an *adverbial particle* such as *go on, go on sth,* ⇨ the v entries.) **1** (expressing the idea of progress, advance, continued activity; ⇨ v entries for special uses): *Come on! They hurried on. He'll follow on,* come after you. *He's getting on in years,* growing old. *The war still went on,* did not end. *How can you work on* (= continue working) *so long without a rest? On with the show!* Let the show begin! Let the show continue! *and 'so on,* and other things of the same kind; et cetera. *later on,* at, during, a later time. *on and on,* without stopping: *We walked on and on.* **2** (corresponding in meaning to *on²(1): On with your coat,* Put it on. *Your hat is not on straight. He had nothing on,* was naked. *Has he got his spectacles on?* Is he wearing them? **on to, onto** prep to a position on: *She fainted and fell on to the floor. The actor stepped onto the stage. We ran out of the sea and on to the beach.* **3** (contrasted with off²(3)) **(a)** in action; in use; functioning; flowing, running, etc: *The lights were all full on,* giving their maximum light. *Someone has left the bathroom tap on,* running. *I can smell gas—is one of the taps on,* is gas escaping from one of them? *Be sure the handbrake is on before you leave the car. The performance is on,* has begun. **(b)** available or procurable when or if needed: *Is the water on yet?* Is a supply available from the mains? *The strike of postal workers is still on,* has not ended yet. **4** (combined with *be* and *have* in various meanings): *What's on?* What's the programme? What's happening? *What's on* (= What films are being shown) *at the local cinema this week? There's nothing on tomorrow, is there,* eg no meeting I ought to attend, no engagement I ought to carry out? *Have you anything on this evening,* any engagements, plans, etc? **be 'on about sth,** (colloq) talk or grumble about it: *what's he on about now?* **be'on at sb,** (colloq) nag or pester him (*about* or *to do* sth). **be 'on to sb/ sth, (a)** be in contact with: *I've been on to the President, and he told me that...* **(b)** be aware of the plans, actions, importance etc of; be in pursuit of: *be on to a conspiracy/scandal/murderer.* **be ,on to a good 'thing,** be lucky or successful. **5** towards: *a ship broadside on to the dock gates,* with its side facing towards the gates; *end on,* ie with the end forward.

on² /ɒn/ *prep* **1** supported by; fastened or attached to; covering or forming part of (a surface); lying against; in contact with: *a carpet on the floor; the jug on the table; pictures on the wall; the words* (written) *on the blackboard; flies on the ceiling; a blister on the sole of my foot; put a roof on the shed; sit on the grass; floating on the water; write on paper; hang sth on a peg/a nail; stick a stamp on the envelope; live on the Continent.* Cf live *in* Europe; *have a hat on one's head/a ring on one's finger; carry a coat on/over one's arm; be/go on board a ship; have lunch on the train; continued on page five.* Cf in *a book, magazine,* etc. *Have you a match/any money on you,* ie in your pockets, etc? **2** (indicating time) **(a)** *on Sunday(s); on the 1st of May; on the evening of May the first.* Cf in *the evening; on New Year's Day/Eve; on a sunny day in July.* ⇨ one ¹(4); *on that day; on this occasion.* **(b)** at the time of: *on the death of his parents,* when they died; *on my arrival home; payable on demand; on* (my) *asking for information.* **(c)** *on time, on the minute,* ie punctually. **3** about; concerning: *speak/lecture/write on international affairs; a lecture on Shakespeare; be keen/bent/determined/set on sth/on doing sth.* **4** (indicating membership): *He is on the committee/the jury/the staff. He's on 'The Daily Telegraph',* is a member of the staff of this newspaper. **5** (indicating direction) towards: *marching on the enemy's capital; turn one's back on sb; smile/frown on sb; draw a knife on sb,* ie to attack him; *a ship drifting on* (to) *the rocks; hit sb on the head,* (note: not *his* head); *give sb a box/ blow on the ear.* **6** (expressing the basis, ground or reason for sth): *on this/that/no account; a story based on fact; have sth on good authority; act on your lawyer's advice; arrested on a charge of theft; retire on a pension; on penalty of death; on an average; swear sth on the Bible; be on one's oath/ one's honour.* **7** (indicating a charge or imposition): *put a tax on tobacco; charge interest on money; place a strain on the economy.* **8** (indicating proximity) close to; against: *Henley-on-*

Thames; a town on the coast; a house on the main road; a village on the frontier; on both sides of the river; on my right/left; just on (= almost) *2 o'clock; just on a year ago; just on £10.* **9** (followed by a *n,* or *adj*) (indicating an activity, action, manner, state): *on business,* engaged in business; *on holiday; on tour,* touring; *go on an errand; on the way; on the sly,* in a sly manner; *buy sth on the cheap,* (colloq) at a low price; *on his best behaviour,* behaving very well; *be on the look-out for sb,* watching for him; *on fire,* burning; *on sale; on loan.* **10** added to: *suffer disaster on disaster/insult on insult.*

once /wʌns/ *adv* **1** (usu end position) for one time, on one occasion, only: *I have been there ~. This clock needs winding ~ a week. He goes to see his parents in Wales ~* (in) *every six months. We go to the cinema ~ a week/a fortnight,* every week/ every two weeks. *~ more,* again; another time. *~ or twice; ~ and again; ~ in a while,* now and again; occasionally; a few times. *(for) this ~; (just) for ~,* on this one occasion only, as an exception. *~ (and) for all,* ⇨ all ⁵(5). *~ in a blue moon,* ⇨ blue¹. **2** (often mid position) at some indefinite time in the past; formerly: *He ~ lived in Persia. This novel was ~ very popular but nobody reads it today. ,~ upon a 'time,* (in story-telling style): *O~ upon a time there was a giant with two heads.* **3** (in negative, conditional or indefinite clauses) ever; at all; even for one time: *He didn't ~/He never ~ offered to help. O~* (= If you ~, As soon as) *you understand this rule, you will have no further difficulty.* **4 at ~, (a)** without delay; immediately: *I'm leaving for Rome at ~. Come here at ~!* **(b)** at the same time: *Don't all speak at ~! I can't do two things at ~. The book is at ~ interesting and instructive. all at ~,* suddenly: *All at ~ I saw a rabbit dart across the road. get/give sb/sth the ~-over,* (colloq) get/give sb/sth a rapid inspection or examination.

on·com·ing /'ɒnkʌmɪŋ/ *adj* advancing; approaching: *the ~ shift,* the shift (of workers) coming on duty (in a factory); *~ traffic.* □ *n* approach: *the ~ of winter.*

one¹ /wʌn/ *numeral adj, pron* **1** the number 1, ⇨ App 4. **(a)** as in the series: *one pen, two pencils and three books;* as in: *one from twenty leaves nineteen; one is enough; one o'clock;* as in: *,twenty-'one, ,thirty-'one,* etc. **(b)** as in: *one hundred, one thousand, one million; one half, one third,* etc. (Except in formal, precise or legal style, *a year and a half* or *eighteen months* is preferred to *one and a half years; a million and a half* to *one and a half millions; a pound of tea* to *one pound of tea.*) **(c)** as in: *one pound ten,* one pound and ten pence. **2** (as a *n,* with *pl* ones) the symbol or figure 1: *a row of ones,* ie 1 1 1 1. **3** as in: *Book One, Chapter One,* the first book, the first chapter. **4** as in: *one day/morning/afternoon/evening/night,* (similar in function to the *indef art,* but with the difference that the *prep 'on'* is used before the *indef art.* ⇨ on²(2a). Cf *one summer evening* and *on a summer evening; one morning in June* and *on a June morning).* **5** (*One* is used to indicate a contrast (expressed or implied) with *the other,* or *another,* or *other(s)*): *The two girls are so much alike that it is difficult for strangers to tell* (the) *one from the other. He did not know which to admire more, the one's courage or the other's determination. Well, that's one way of doing it, but there are other* *and better ways. I, for one, don't like the idea,* suggesting 'and there may also be others who do not like it'. **for 'one thing,** for one reason (out of several or many): *I can't help you. For one thing, I've no money.* **6** (always stressed; used for emphasis): *There's only 'one way to do it. That's the 'one thing needed. No 'one of you could lift it,* ie two or more of you would be needed. *They went forward as one man,* ie all together, in a body. **7** (before a family name, with or without a title; ⇨ a²(9); a certain: *I heard the news from one (Mr) Smith,* (dated formal) from a certain person named Smith. (Note that if *one* is replaced by the *indef art* a title must be used: *A Mr Smith has called to see you).* **8** (as *adj*) the same: *They all went off in one direction.* **be at 'one (with sb),** be in agreement. *I'm at one with you on this subject/We are at one on this subject,* Our opinions are the same. **It's all one (to sb),** It's all the same, it makes no difference: *It's all one to me whether you go or don't go.* **one and the same,** (emph for) the same: *One and the same idea occurred to each of them.* **become one; be made one,** be united; be married. **9** (phrases) **one and all,** everyone. **(all) in one,** combined: *He is President, Chairman and Secretary in one.* **one or two,** a few: *I shall be away only one or two days.* **by ones and twos,** one or two at a time: *People began to leave the meeting by ones and twos.* **be one 'up (on sb),** have an advantage over him, be one step ahead of him. Hence, ,one-'up-man-ship /-mənʃɪp/ *n* technique of being one up. ,number 'one, (colloq) oneself; one's own interests: *He's always thinking of 'number one',* of himself, his own welfare. **10** (with an *of*-adjunct) a single person or thing of the sort indicated or supplied (with *some, any, several,* etc for the *pl;* ⇨ a²(3) and one²(1)): *One of my friends (pl some* of my friends) *arrived late. One of them (pl any* of them) *should need help...; I borrowed one of your books* (= a book of yours; *pl some* of your books) *last week.* (Note the use of *his, her, herself* and *himself* in these examples): *One of the boys/girls lost his/her shoe. One of the girls/boys has hurt herself/himself.* **11** (compounds) ,one-'armed *adj* having only one arm. ,one-armed 'bandit *n* (colloq) coin-operated gambling machine (also called a *fruit-machine).* ,one-'eyed *adj* having only one eye. ,one-'horse *adj* (a) drawn or worked by a single horse. (b) (fig, sl) poorly equipped: *a one-horse town,* a small provincial town with few attractions, etc. ,one-i'dea'd *adj* possessed by a single idea. ,one-'sided *adj* having one side only; occurring on one side only; partial; unfair; prejudiced: *a one-sided argument; a one-sided account of a quarrel.* 'one-time *adj* former: *a one-time politician.* ,one-track 'mind *n* one dominated by one interest, subject, etc. ,one-way 'street *n* street in which traffic may proceed in one direction only.

one² /wʌn/ *indef pron* (used in place of a preceding or following *n* standing for a member of a class) **1** (with an *of*-adjunct, indicating inclusion; equivalent to *among;* ⇨ a²(3); no corresponding *pl* word): *Mr Smith is not one of* (= not numbered or included among) *my customers.* Cf for *pl: Mr Green and Mr Smith are not customers of mine. This problem is one of great difficulty (pl: These problems are of great difficulty). We have always treated her as one* (= as a member) *of the family (pl: We have always treated them as members of the family). One of my friends was ill (pl: Some of*

my friends were ill). ⇨ one¹(10). **2** (Cf *one* and *it. One* replaces a *n* modified by the *indef art* or a *pl n* modified by *some* or *any. It* replaces a *n* made definite in some way, eg a *n* modified by *the, this, that): I haven't a pen. Can you lend me one? I haven't any stamps. Will you please give me one?* Cf *I'd like to look at that atlas. May I borrow it? Where's the railway timetable? Have you seen it?* **3** (the *pron* 'one', *pl* 'ones', is used, in colloq style, equivalent to *that, those): I drew my chair nearer to the one* (= to that) *on which Mary was sitting. It's in that drawer—the one* (= that) *with the key in the lock. The students who do best in examinations are not always the ones* (= those) *with the best brains.* **4** (when the *pron* 'one' is used after the *def art,* or after an *adj* (or a *n* used as an *adj),* it may be called a 'prop-word'. As an *adj* cannot stand alone for one or more members of a class, *one* is used to support or 'prop up' the *adj,* as in): *a better one; that one; my old ones. Your plan is a good one on paper. There's a right answer and a wrong one. Yours may be the right answer and mine the wrong one. The chance was too good a one to let pass. He keeps his postage-stamps—he has some very rare ones—in a fire-proof safe.* **5** (The 'prop-word' *one* is not used, except in colloquial style, after a possessive (eg *your, Mary's)* unless there is also an *adj.* It is not used after *own): This is my hat and that is my brother's.* Not: *my brother's one. Tom's exercise book is neater than John's.* Not: *John's one. Do you rent the house or is it your own?* Not: *your own one.* (With an *adj): My cheap camera seems to be just as good as John's expensive one. Your old suit looks as smart as your brother's new one.* **6** (In formal or written style it is preferable to avoid the use of the 'prop-word' *one,* esp when there are two *adjj* indicating a contrast. The *n* is placed after only one of the *adjj): If we compare British with American universities* (better than: *If we compare British universities with American ones)....* Cf *Don't praise the younger child in the presence of the elder. I put my right arm through Mary's left. At home Hanako prefers Japanese to European-style clothes. What the teacher said seemed to go in at one ear and out at the other.* **7** (*One* is used after *this* and *that,* but is better avoided, in formal or written style, after *these* and *those): Will you have this (one) or that (one)? Will you have these or those?* (With an *adj,* 'one' is necessary): *Will you have this green one/ these green ones or that blue one/those blue ones?* **8** (The 'prop-word' *one* is used with *which,* esp to distinguish *sing* from *pl): Here are some books on European history. Which one(s) do you want?*

one³ /wʌn/ *pers pron* **1** (used, always with a qualifying word or phrase, for a particular person or creature): *the 'Holy One,* God; *the 'Evil One,* Satan, the Devil; *the absent one,* eg the absent member of the family; *the little ones,* the children; *a nest with five young ones,* young birds; *my sweet one,* as a term of endearment. **2** (used, in liter style, with a following *adj,* phrase or clause): *He lay there like one dead,* as if he were dead. *He worked like one possessed,* like a man possessed by a spirit. *He was one* (= the sort of person) *who never troubled about his personal comfort. He's not one to be* (= not a man who is) *easily frightened.* **3** *one another,* (used like *each other,* to indicate mutual action or relation; may be the object of a *v* or a *prep;* possessive form is *one another's;*

both words usu unstressed): *They don't like one another. They have quarrelled and no longer speak to one another. They were fighting with cudgels, trying to break one another's heads.*

one⁴ /wʌn/ *impers pron* (standing for any person, including the speaker or writer. Cf French *on*, German *man*. Possessive: *one's*; reflexive: *oneself.* ⇨ one¹(10)): *One cannot always find time for reading. If one wants a thing done well, one had best do it oneself. One doesn't like to have one's word doubted.* (In colloq style it is more usual to employ *you, we, people*) Cf *We live and learn. You never can tell. What's a chap/a fellow to do in such a situation?* (In American usage, *one* may be followed by *he, him, his, himself* instead of by *one, one's, oneself*): *One does not like to have his word doubted.*

on·er·ous /'ɒnərəs/ *adj* needing effort; burdensome (*to*): ～ *duties.* ～·**ly** *adv*

one·self /wʌn'self/ *reflex, emphat pron* one's own self: *wash/dress oneself. One should not live for oneself alone.*

on·go·ing /'ɒn gəʊɪŋ/ *adj* ⇨ go on at go¹(29).

onion /'ʌnɪən/ *n* [C] **1** vegetable plant with a round bulb of many concentric coats, a strong smell and flavour, used in cooking and pickled: *spring-～s; Spanish ～s;* [U] this plant as food: *too much ～ in the salad; the ～-domed churches of Austria,* having ～-shaped domes. ⇨ the illus at **vegetable**. **know one's ～s**, (sl) be clever (because experienced). **2** (sl) head. **off his ～,** (sl) mentally unbalanced.

on·looker /'ɒnlʊkə(r)/ *n* person who looks on at sth happening. **The ～ sees most of the game,** (prov) The spectator is in a better position to judge than those who are taking part.

only¹ /'əʊnlɪ/ *adj* **1** (with a *sing n*) that is the one specimen of its class; single: *Smith was the ～ person able to do it. Harry is an ～ child,* has no brothers or sisters. *Her ～ answer was a shrug.* **2** (with a *pl n*) that are all the specimens or examples: *We were the ～ people there.* **3** best; most or best worth consideration: *He's the ～ man for the position. She says holidays in Ireland are the ～ thing these days.*

only² /'əʊnlɪ/ *adv* solely; and no one, nothing, more. **1** (modifying a single word, and placed, in written or formal style, close to the word it modifies; in speech the stress-pattern may indicate this, so that *only* may have various positions): *I ～ saw 'Mary,* I saw Mary and no one else (= written style, *I saw ～ Mary*). Cf *I ～ 'saw Mary,* I saw her but didn't speak to her. *O～ the teachers are allowed to use this room. O～ five men were seriously hurt in the accident. We've ～ half an hour to wait now. Ladies ～,* eg on a compartment in a railway carriage. *We can ～ guess* (= We cannot be certain about) *what happened.* **2** ～ **too,** (with an *adj* or *pp*) very: *I shall be ～ too pleased to get home. The news was ～ too true,* was really true, and not, as might be hoped or expected, untrue. *if ～,* expressing a wish or assumption. ⇨ if(8).

only³ /'əʊnlɪ/ *conj* but then; it must, however, be added that: *The book is likely to be useful, ～ it's rather expensive. He's always ready to promise help, ～ he never keeps his promises. ～ that,* with the exception that; were it not that: *He would probably do well in the examination, ～ that he gets rather nervous.*

ono·mato·poeia /ˌɒnəˌmætə'pɪə/ *n* [U] formation of words in imitation of the sounds associated with the thing concerned (as *cuckoo* for the bird that utters this cry).

on·rush /'ɒnrʌʃ/ *n* strong, onward rush or flow.

on·set /'ɒnset/ *n* attack; vigorous start: *at the first ～; the ～ of a disease.*

on·shore /'ɒnʃɔː(r)/ *adj, adv* toward the shore.

on·slaught /'ɒnslɔːt/ *n* [C] furious attack (*on*).

onto /*before consonants:* 'ɒntə; *before vowels or finally:* 'ɒntuː/ *prep* ⇨ on¹(2).

on·tol·ogy /ɒn'tɒlədʒɪ/ *n* [U] department of metaphysics concerned with the nature of existence; [C] specific theory of this.

onus /'əʊnəs/ *n* the ～, responsibility for, burden of, doing sth: *The ～ of proof rests with you,* It is for you to supply proof.

on·ward /'ɒnwəd/ *adj, adv* forward: *an ～ march/ movement.* □ *adv* (also ～**s**) towards the front; forward: *move ～(s).*

onyx /'ɒnɪks/ *n* [U] (sorts of) quartz in layers of different colours, used for ornaments, etc.

oodles /'uːdlz/ *n pl* (sl) ～ **of,** great amounts or sums: ～ *of money.*

oomph /ʊmf/ *n* (sl) energy; sex-appeal.

ooze /uːz/ *n* [U] soft liquid mud, esp on a riverbed, the bottom of a pond, lake, etc. □ *vi, vt* **1** [VP2C] (of moisture, thick liquids) pass slowly through small openings: *Blood was still oozing from the wound.* (fig) *Their courage was oozing away.* **2** [VP6A] pass out; emit: *He was oozing sweat.* **oozy** *adj* of or like ～; slimy.

opac·ity /əʊ'pæsətɪ/ *n* [U] (quality of) being opaque.

opal /'əʊpl/ *n* semi-precious stone in which changes of colour are seen, often used as a gem. **opal·escent** /ˌəʊpə'lesnt/ *adj* like an ～.

opaque /əʊ'peɪk/ *adj* not allowing light to pass through; that cannot be seen through; dull. ～·**ly** *adv* ～·**ness** *n*

op art /'ɒp ɑːt/ *n* form of modern abstract art using geometrical patterns which produce optical illusions.

open¹ /'əʊpən/ *adj* **1** not closed; allowing (things, persons) to go in, out, through: *sleep with ～ windows; leave the door ～.* ～-'**eyed** *adj* with ～ eyes; watchful; surprised. ～-'**mouthed** /-'maʊðd/ *adj* (a) showing greed (for food, etc). (b) showing great surprise or stupidity. ～ **vowel,** one made with the roof of the mouth and the tongue fairly wide apart, eg /ɑː, ɒ/. '～-**work** *n* [U] pattern (in metal, lace, etc) with spaces: ～-*work lace;* ～-*work stockings.* **2** not enclosed, fenced in, barred or blocked: *the ～ country,* land affording wide views, without forests, etc. **the ～ sea,** not a bay or harbour, not closed in by land. **an ～ river,** not barred by ice, mudbanks, etc. ～ **water,** navigable, free from ice. **an ～ prison,** one with fewer restrictions than usual, esp one where prisoners with good records come and go freely to work outside. **3** not covered in or over: *an ～ boat,* one without a deck; *an ～ car,* with no roof, or a roof that is folded back; *an ～ drain/sewer,* in the form of a ditch, not in pipes under the ground: *an ～ sandwich,* single slice of bread with meat, etc on top; *in the ～ 'air,* out of doors. '～-**air** *attrib adj* taking place out of doors; fond of life in the ～ air: *an ～-air 'theatre.* **4** spread out; unfolded: *The flowers were all ～. The book lay ～ on the table. His mind was/His thoughts were an ～ book,* It was easy to read his thoughts. **with ～ hands,**

generously. Hence, ⚋-'**handed** adj generous; giving freely. ⚋-'**hearted** adj sincere; frank. **with ⚋ arms,** with affection or enthusiasm. ⚋ **order,** (of troops), with wider space than usual between ranks. **5** public; free to all; not limited to any special persons, but for anyone to enter: an ⚋ competition/championship/scholarship; tried in ⚋ court, of a law case, the public being freely admitted to hear the trial. The position is still ⚋, No one has yet been chosen to fill it. **the ⚋ door,** policy of free trade or freedom from tariffs; admission of foreign traders. ⚋ **shop,** workshop, factory, etc where members and non-members of trade unions work on equal terms. ⇨ closed shop at close³(2). **keep ⚋ house,** offer hospitality to all comers. **6** not settled or decided: leave a matter ⚋. ⚋-'**ended** adj (of a discussion, a subject for debate, etc) having a variety of possible solutions; on which no decision or agreement is reached, expected or required. **an ⚋ question,** with no decision, answer. **an ⚋ verdict,** jury's verdict of the fact and cause of a death, but not saying whether it is natural, accidental, suicide or murder. **have/keep an ⚋ mind (on sth),** be ready to consider sth further, to listen to new evidence, agreements, etc. Hence, ⚋-'**minded** adj unprejudiced. **7** ready for business or for the admission of the public: Are the shops ⚋ yet? Doors ⚋ at 7.00pm, eg of a theatre. **8** known to all; not secret or disguised; frank: an ⚋ quarrel/scandal; an ⚋ character/countenance. Let me be quite ⚋ (= frank) with you. **an ⚋ letter,** one that is addressed to an individual or group but sent to and published in a periodical, usu in protest against sth. **9** unprotected; unguarded; vulnerable. **be/lay oneself ⚋ to sth,** behave so that one is vulnerable to sth: Don't lay yourself ⚋ to ridicule/attack. **10** not settled, finished or closed: keep one's account ⚋ at a bank; be ⚋ to an offer, willing to consider one. **11** (phrases) '⚋-**cast** adj surface: ⚋-cast coal; ⚋-cast mining, from strata near the earth's surface (contrasted with production from deep mines). **an ⚋ cheque,** one that is not crossed and which may be cashed at the bank on which it is drawn. **the '⚋ season,** (fishing and shooting) when there are no restrictions. ⇨ close¹(12). **an ⚋ secret,** sth supposed to be a secret but in fact known to all people. **the O⚋ University,** (GB) university (founded in 1971) whose students live at home and get tuition by correspondence, textbooks and special radio and TV programmes. ⚋ **weather, an ⚋ winter,** free from severe frost and snow, so that it is possible to get about. □ n the ⚋, the ⚋ air. ⇨ 3 above. **come (out) into the ⚋,** (fig) come into public view; make one's ideas, plans, etc, known. ⚋-**ly** adv without secrecy; frankly; publicly: speak ⚋ly; go ⚋ly into a place, eg where one might be expected to go secretly. ⚋-**ness** n [U].

open² /'əʊpən/ vt,vi **1** [VP6A,14,16A,12C] make ⚋ or cause to be open; unfasten: ⚋ a box. He ⚋ed the door for me to come in/to let me in. O⚋ the window a fraction/crack/bit, please. ⚋ one's eyes, express surprise. ⚋ (sb's) eyes to sth, cause him to realize sth, eg how he has been deceived. **2** [VP6A,15A,B] cut or make an opening in or a passage through: ⚋ a mine/a well; ⚋ a new road through a forest; O⚋ up! command to ⚋ a door, etc. ⚋ **sth up,** make ⚋; make accessible; make possible the development of: ⚋ up a wound/a mine/undeveloped land/a new territory to

trade. **3** [VP6A,15A,B] spread out; unfold: ⚋ one's hand/a book/a newspaper/a parcel; ⚋ out a folding map. ⚋ one's mind/heart to sb, make known one's ideas/feelings. **4** [VP6A] start: ⚋ an account, eg at a bank, shop; ⚋ a debate/a public meeting. ⚋ the bidding, make the first bid (at an auction, at bridge). ⚋ fire (at/on), start shooting. **5** [VP6A] declare, indicate, that business, etc may now start: ⚋ a shop; ⚋ Parliament. **6** [VP2A,C] become open; be ⚋ed; allow of being ⚋ed: The flowers are ⚋ing. This shop does not ⚋ on Sundays. The door ⚋ed and a man came in. Does this door ⚋ inwards or outwards? The two rooms ⚋ into one another, have a door between them. This door ⚋s on to the garden. **7** [VP3A] ⚋ with, start: The story ⚋s with a murder. **8** [VP2A,C] ⚋ (out), become visible: The view ⚋ed (out) before our eyes. ⚋er n person or thing that ⚋s: (chiefly in compounds) 'pew-⚋er; 'tin-⚋er; 'bottle-⚋er. '**eye-opener,** ⇨ eye¹(3).

open·ing /'əʊpənɪŋ/ n **1** open space; way in or out: an ⚋ in a hedge. **2** beginning: the ⚋ of a book/speech. **the ⚋ night,** eg on which a new play/film is performed/shown for the first time, and to which dramatic critics are invited. '⚋ **time,** eg at which public houses open and begin to serve drinks. **3** process of becoming open: watch the ⚋ of a flower. **4** position (in a business firm) which is open or vacant; opportunity: an ⚋ in an advertising agency. □ adj first: his ⚋ remarks.

op·era /'ɒprə/ n **1** [C] dramatic composition with music, in which the words are sung. **comic ⚋,** humorous, with spoken dialogue and a happy ending. **grand ⚋,** serious, with no spoken dialogue. **light ⚋,** not serious. ⇨ cantata, oratorio. **2** [U] dramatic works of this kind as entertainment: fond of ⚋; the ⚋ season. '⚋-**cloak** n lady's cloak for wearing with evening dress. '⚋-**glasses** n pl small binoculars for use in a theatre. '⚋-**hat** n man's tall, black silk hat, made so that it folds flat. '⚋-**house** n theatre for performances of ⚋s. **op·er·atic** /ˌɒpə'rætɪk/ adj of or for an ⚋: ⚋tic music/singers.

op·er·ate /'ɒpəreɪt/ vt,vi **1** [VP6A,2A,C,4A] (cause to) work, be in action, have an effect; manage: ⚋ a machine; machinery that ⚋s night and day. The company ⚋s three factories and a coal-mine. The lift was not operating properly. The lift is ⚋d by electricity. This new law ⚋s (= produces an effect) to our advantage. Several causes ⚋d to bring about the war. **2** [VP2A,3A] ⚋ (on sb) (for sth), perform a surgical operation: The doctors decided to ⚋ at once. '**operating-table/-theatre** n for use in surgical operations. **3** [VP2A,C] (of an army) carry out various movements: operating on a large scale. **4** [VP2A,C] (of a stockbroker) buy and sell, esp in order to influence prices. **op·er·able** /'ɒpərəbl/ adj that can be treated by means of a surgical operation.

op·er·ation /ˌɒpə'reɪʃn/ n **1** [U] working; way in which sth works. **be in/bring sth into/come into ⚋,** be/cause to be/become effective: When does the plan come into ⚋? Is this rule in ⚋ yet? **2** [C] piece of work; sth (to be) done: begin ⚋s; the ⚋s of nature, changes brought about by natural forces. **3** (usu pl; colloq abbr **ops**) movements of troops, ships, aircraft, etc in warfare or during manoeuvres. '⚋s **room,** from which ⚋s are controlled; (sing) in code names for military campaigns (O⚋ Overlord) and, by extension, for planned campaigns in industry, commerce, etc: *building/ banking* ~*s;* ~*s research,* to promote greater efficiency in industry. **4** [C] *an* ~ *(on sb) (for sth),* act performed by a surgeon on any part of the body, esp by cutting to take away or deal with a diseased part: *an* ~ *for appendicitis.* **5** (maths) addition, subtraction, multiplication, division, etc. ~**al** /-ʃənl/ *adj* **1** of, for, used in, ~s. ~**al costs/ expenditure,** needed for operating (machines, aircraft, etc). ~**al research,** into the best ways of using, improving, etc new weapons, machinery, etc. **2** ready for use: *When will the newly designed airliner be* ~*al?*

op·er·at·ive /ˈɒpərətɪv US: -reɪt-/ *adj* **1** operating; having an effect: *This law became* ~ *on 1 May.* **2** ~ **words,** those having legal effect in a deed, etc; (loosely) most significant words. **3** of surgical operations: ~ *treatment.* □ *n* worker; mechanic: *cotton* ~*s.*

op·er·ator /ˈɒpəreɪtə(r)/ *n* **1** person who operates or works sth: *telephone/telegraph* ~*s; private* ~*s in civil aviation,* privately owned companies (contrasted with state-owned corporations). **2** (sl) confident, efficient man (in business, love affairs, etc): *He's a smooth/slick* ~.

op·er·etta /ˌɒpəˈretə/ *n* one-act, or short, light musical comedy.

oph·thal·mia /ɒfˈθælmɪə/ *n* [U] inflammation of the eye. **oph·thal·mic** /-mɪk/ *adj* of the eyes; afflicted with ~. **oph·thal·mo·scope** /ɒfˈθælməskəʊp/ *n* instrument with a mirror (having a hole in the centre) through which the eye may be examined.

opi·ate /ˈəʊpɪət/ *n* [C] drug containing opium, used to relieve pain or to help sb to sleep.

opine /əˈpaɪn/ *vt* [VP9] ~ *that,* (formal) have or express the opinion.

opin·ion /əˈpɪnɪən/ *n* **1** [C] belief or judgement not founded on complete knowledge: *political* ~*s. What's your* ~ (= view) *of the new President? Those are my* ~*s about the affair.* **in my, your, etc** ~; **in the** ~ **of sb,** it is my, your, etc view that...: *In my* ~*/In the* ~ *of most people, the scheme is unsound.* **act up to one's** ~*s,* act according to them. **be of the** ~ *that....,* feel, believe, that.... **have a good/bad/high/low** ~ **of sb/sth,** think well/badly, etc of. **2** [U] views, beliefs, of a group: *O~ is shifting in favour of stiffer penalties for armed robbery.* **public** ~, what the majority of people think: *Public* ~ *is against the proposed change.* '~ **poll,** ⇨ poll¹(2). **3** [C] professional estimate or advice: *get a lawyer's* ~ *on the question. You had better have another* ~ *before you let that man take out all your teeth.* ~**·ated** /-eɪtɪd/, ~**·at·ive** /-ətɪv US: -eɪtɪv/ *adjj* obstinate in one's ~s; dogmatic.

opium /ˈəʊpɪəm/ *n* [U] substance prepared from poppy seeds, used to relieve pain, cause sleep, and as a narcotic drug. '~**-den** *n* place where ~ smokers can obtain and use this drug.

opos·sum /əˈpɒsəm/ (also **possum** /ˈpɒsəm/) *n* kinds of small American animal that lives in trees.

op·po·nent /əˈpəʊnənt/ *n* person against whom one fights, struggles, plays games, or argues.

op·por·tune /ˈɒpətjuːn US: -tuːn/ *adj* **1** (of time) suitable, favourable; good for a purpose: *arrive at a most* ~ *moment.* **2** (of an action or event) done, coming, at a favourable time: *an* ~ *remark/ speech.* ~**·ly** *adv*

op·por·tun·ism /ˌɒpəˈtjuːnɪzəm US: -ˈtuːn-/ *n* [U]

being guided by what seems possible, or by circumstances, in determining policy; preferring what can be done to what should be done. **op·por·tun·ist** /-ɪst/ *n* person who acts on this principle; person who is more anxious to gain an advantage for himself than to consider whether he is trying to get it fairly.

op·por·tun·ity /ˌɒpəˈtjuːnətɪ US: -ˈtuːn-/ *n* (*pl* -ties) [C,U] ~ **(for sth/of doing sth/to do sth),** favourable time or chance: *to make/find/get an* ~; *have few opportunities of meeting interesting people; have no/little/not much* ~ *for hearing good music. I had no* ~ *to discuss the matter with her. The* ~ *came early one morning.*

op·pose /əˈpəʊz/ *vt* **1** [VP6A] set oneself, fight, against (sb or sth): ~ *the Government;* ~ *a scheme. I am very much* ~*d to your going abroad, I am against the plan.* **2** [VP14] ~ **(against/to),** put forward as a contrast or opposite; set up against: ~ *your will against mine/your views to mine;* ~ *a vigorous resistance to the enemy.* **as** ~**d to,** in contrast with.

op·po·site /ˈɒpəzɪt/ *adj* **1** ~ **(to),** facing; front to front or back to back (with): *the house* ~ (*to*) *mine; on the* ~ *side of the road.* **2** entirely different; contrary: *in the* ~ *direction.* **3** similarly placed elsewhere. **one's** ~ **number,** person occupying the same or a similar position in another group, etc: *The British Foreign Minister is in Washington discussing problems with his* ~ *number.* □ *n* word or thing that is ~: *Black and white are* ~*s. I thought quite the* ~.

op·po·si·tion /ˌɒpəˈzɪʃn/ *n* **1** [U] the state of being opposite or opposed: *The Socialist Party was in* ~, formed the O~. ⇨ **2** below. **be in** ~ **to,** opposing: *We found ourselves in* ~ *to our friends on this question.* **2** (*sing*) MP's of the political party or parties opposing the Government: *Her Majesty's O~; the leader of the O~; the O~ benches. We need a stronger O~.* **3** [U] resistance: *Our forces met with strong* ~ *all along the front.*

op·press /əˈpres/ *vt* [VP6A] **1** rule unjustly or cruelly; keep down by unjust or cruel government. **2** (fig) weigh heavily on; cause to feel troubled, uncomfortable: ~*ed with anxiety/with a foreboding of misfortune; feel* ~*ed with the heat.* ~**or** /-sə(r)/ *n* person who ~es; cruel or unjust ruler. **op·pres·sion** /əˈpreʃn/ *n* **1** [U] the condition of being ~ed: *a feeling of* ~*ion.* **2** [U] ~ing or being ~ed: *victims of* ~*ion.* [C] instance of this; cruel or unjust act. **op·pres·sive** /əˈpresɪv/ *adj* **1** unjust: ~*ive laws/rules.* **2** hard to endure; over-powering: ~*ive weather/heat/taxes.* **op·pres·ive·ly** *adv*

op·pro·bri·ous /əˈprəʊbrɪəs/ *adj* (formal) (of words, etc) showing scorn or reproach; abusive. ~**·ly** *adv* **op·pro·brium** /-brɪəm/ *n* (formal) [U] scorn; disgrace; public shame.

op·pugn /əˈpjuːn/ *vt* [VP6A] (formal) call in question; be contrary to.

opt /ɒpt/ *vi* **1** [VP3A] **opt for sth,** choose; decide on: *Fewer students are opting for science courses nowadays.* **2 opt out of,** choose to take no part in: *young people who have opted out of society,* chosen not to be conventional members of society.

op·tat·ive /ˈɒptətɪv/ *adj,* *n* (of) verbal form expressing desire: ~ *mood,* eg in Greek, but not in English.

op·tic /ˈɒptɪk/ *adj* of the eye or the sense of sight: *the* ~ *nerve,* from the eye to the brain. ⇨ the illus at eye. ~**s** *n* (with *sing v*) science of light and the

laws of light.
op·tical /ˈɒptɪkl/ adj 1 of the sense of sight. **an ∼ illusion,** sth by which the eye is deceived: *A mirage is an ∼ illusion.* 2 for looking through; to help eyesight: *∼ instruments,* eg microscopes, telescopes; *∼ glass,* the kind used for *∼* instruments. *∼·ly* /-klɪ/ adv
op·ti·cian /ɒpˈtɪʃn/ n person who makes or supplies optical instruments, esp lenses and spectacles.
op·ti·mism /ˈɒptɪmɪzəm/ n [U] (opp of *pessimism*) belief that in the end good will triumph over evil; tendency to look upon the bright side of things; confidence in success. **op·ti·mist** /-mɪst/ n person who is always hopeful and looks upon the bright side of things, who believes that all things happen for the best. **op·ti·mis·tic** /ˌɒptɪˈmɪstɪk/ adj expecting the best; confident: *an optimistic view of events.* **op·ti·mis·ti·cally** /-klɪ/ adv
op·ti·mum /ˈɒptɪməm/ n (attrib) best or most favourable: *the ∼ temperature for the growth of plants.*
op·tion /ˈɒpʃn/ n 1 [U] right or power of choosing. **have no/little, etc ∼,** have no/little, etc choice: *I haven't much ∼ in the matter, cannot choose. I had no ∼,* was forced to act as I did. *He was given six months' imprisonment without the ∼ of a fine.* **local ∼,** right of people in (some towns, districts) to decide, by voting, whether or not to have or allow sth, eg the sale of alcoholic liquor. 2 [C] thing that is or may be chosen: *None of the ∼s is satisfactory.* **leave one's ∼s open,** not commit oneself. 3 [C] (comm) right to buy or sell sth at a certain price within a certain period of time: *have an ∼ on a piece of land.* **∼al** /-ʃənl/ adj which may be chosen or not as one wishes; not compulsory: *∼al subjects at school.* **∼·ally** /ˈɒpʃənəlɪ/ adv
opu·lence /ˈɒpjʊləns/ n [U] (formal) wealth; abundance. **opu·lent** /-ənt/ adj rich; wealthy; luxuriant: *∼ vegetation.* **op·u·lent·ly** adv
opus /ˈəʊpəs/ n (pl opera /ˈɒpərə/, rarely used) separate musical composition (abbr **op,** used in citing a composition by number, as *Beethoven, Op 112*). **magnum ∼,** great artistic undertaking, completed or in course of being completed.
or /ɔː(r)/ conj 1 (introducing an alternative): *Is it green or blue? Are you coming or not?* **either... or,** ⇨ either. **whether... or:** *I don't care whether he stays or goes.* **or else,** otherwise: *Hurry up or else you'll be late. Pay up, or else!* (as a threat). 2 (introducing all but the first of a series of alternatives): *I'd like it to be black,* (or) *white or grey.* 3 (introducing a word that explains, or means the same as, another): *an English pound, or one hundred pence; a dugout, or a canoe made by hollowing out a tree trunk; geology, or the science of the earth's crust.* 4 **or so,** (often equivalent to *about*) suggesting vagueness or uncertainty about quantity: *There were twenty or so.* **or somebody/ something/somewhere; somebody/ something/somewhere or other,** (colloq) (expressing uncertainty about who/what/where): *I put it in the cupboard or somewhere,* ie somewhere, perhaps in the cupboard. *'Who told you?'—'Oh, somebody or other, I've forgotten who.'*
or·acle /ˈɒrəkl US: ˈɔːr-/ n 1 (in ancient Greece) (answer given at) place where questions about the future were asked of the gods; priest(ess) giving the answers: *consult the ∼.* 2 person considered able to give reliable guidance. **oracu·lar** /əˈrækjʊlə(r)/ adj of or like an *∼;* with a hidden meaning: *orac-*

ular utterances.
oral /ˈɔːrəl/ adj 1 using the spoken, not the written, word: *an ∼ examination.* 2 (anat) of, by, for, the mouth: *∼ contraceptives,* ⇨ pill(2). □ n (colloq) *∼* examination. **∼·ly** /ˈɔːrəlɪ/ adv by spoken words; by the mouth: *not to be taken ∼ly,* (eg of medical preparations) not to be swallowed; for external use only.
or·ange /ˈɒrɪndʒ US: ˈɔːr-/ n, adj [C] ⇨ the illus at fruit. (evergreen tree with a) round, thick-skinned juicy fruit, green and usu changing to a colour between yellow and red; [U] usual colour of this fully-ripened fruit. **∼·ade** /ˌɒrɪndʒˈeɪd US: ˌɔːr-/ n [U] drink made of *∼* juice.
Or·ange·man /ˈɒrɪndʒmæn US: ˈɔːr-/ n (pl -men) member of a Protestant political society in Ulster, Northern Ireland.
orang-outang /ɔːˌræŋ uːˈtæŋ US: əˌræŋ əˈtæŋ/ (also **-utan, -outan** /-ˈtæn/) n large, long-armed ape of Borneo and Sumatra. ⇨ the illus at ape.
orate /ɔːˈreɪt/ vi [VP2A] speak publicly.
ora·tion /ɔːˈreɪʃn/ n [C] formal speech made on a public occasion: *a funeral ∼.*
ora·tor /ˈɒrətə(r) US: ˈɔːr-/ n person who makes speeches (esp a good speaker). **∼·i·cal** /ˌɒrəˈtɒrɪkl US: ˌɔːrəˈtɔːr-/ adj of speech-making and *∼s:* *∼ical phrases/gestures; an ∼ical contest.*
ora·torio /ˌɒrəˈtɔːrɪəʊ US: ˌɔːr-/ n (pl *∼s*) [C] musical composition for solo voices, chorus and orchestra, usu with a religious subject: *the ∼s of Handel;* [U] musical compositions of this kind collectively: *Do you like ∼?* ⇨ cantata, opera.
ora·tory[1] /ˈɒrətrɪ US: ˈɔːrətɔːrɪ/ n (pl -ries) [C] small chapel for private worship or prayer.
ora·tory[2] /ˈɒrətrɪ US: ˈɔːrətɔːrɪ/ n [U] (art of) making speeches; rhetoric.
orb /ɔːb/ n globe, esp the sun, moon or one of the planets; jewelled globe with a cross on top, part of a sovereign's regalia. ⇨ the illus at regalia.
or·bit /ˈɔːbɪt/ n path followed by a heavenly body, eg a planet, the moon, or a man-made object, eg a spacecraft, round another body: *the earth's ∼ round the sun. How many satellites have been put in ∼ round the earth?* □ vt,vi [VP6A,2A,C] put into, (cause to) move, in *∼: When was the first man-made satellite ∼ed? How many spacecraft have orbited the moon?* **∼al** /ˈɔːbɪtl/ adj of an *∼: a spacecraft's ∼al distance from the earth.* **∼ velocity,** minimal velocity needed to place sth in *∼.*
or·chard /ˈɔːtʃəd/ n [C] piece of ground (usu enclosed) with fruit-trees: *apple-∼s.*
or·ches·tra /ˈɔːkɪstrə/ n 1 group of persons playing musical instruments together: *a dance/string/ symphony ∼.* ⇨ brass band at brass(3). 2 *∼* (**pit**), place in a theatre for an *∼.* **∼ stalls,** front seats on the floor of a theatre. 3 semicircular space in front of the stage of a theatre in ancient Greece, where the chorus sang and danced. **or·ches·tral** /ɔːˈkestrəl/ adj of, for, by, an *∼: orchestral instruments/performances.*
or·ches·trate /ˈɔːkɪstreɪt/ vt [VP6A] compose, arrange, score, for orchestral performances. **or·ches·tra·tion** /ˌɔːkɪˈstreɪʃn/ n
or·chid /ˈɔːkɪd/ (also **or·chis** /ˈɔːkɪs/) n [C] sorts of plant of which the English wild kinds (usu *orchis*) have tuberous roots, and the tropical kinds (usu *orchid*) have flowers of brilliant colours and fantastic shapes. ⇨ the illus at flower.
or·dain /ɔːˈdeɪn/ vt 1 [VP6A,23] make (sb) a priest or minister: *He was ∼ed priest.* 2 [VP9] *∼ that,*

(of God, law, authority) decide; give orders (that); destine: *God has ~ed that all men shall die.*

or·deal /ɔːˈdiːl/ *n* severe test of character or endurance: *pass through terrible ~s.*

or·der¹ /ˈɔːdə(r)/ *n* **1** [U] way in which things are placed in relation to one another: *names in alphabetical ~; in chronological ~,* ie according to dates. *in ~ of,* arranged according to: *in ~ of size/merit/importance, etc.* **2** [U] condition in which everything is carefully arranged; working condition. *(not) in ~,* (not) as it should be: *Is your passport in ~,* Has it all the necessary entries to satisfy the authorities? *He put/left his affairs/ accounts/papers in ~ before he left the country. Get your ideas into some kind of ~ before beginning to write. in good ~,* without any confusion: *The troops retired in good ~,* Their retreat was orderly, disciplined. *in good/bad/running/ working ~,* (esp of machines) working well/ badly/smoothly, etc: *The engine has been tuned and is now in perfect running ~. out of ~,* (of a machine, a bodily organ) not functioning properly: *The lift/phone is out of ~. My stomach is out of ~.* **3** [U] (condition brought about by) good and firm government, obedience to law, rules, authority: *The army restored law and ~. It is the business of the police to keep ~. Some teachers find it difficult to keep ~ in their classes/to keep their classes in ~.* ⇨ disorder. **4** [U] rules usual at a public meeting; rules accepted, eg in Parliament, committee meetings, by members and enforced by a president, chairman, or other officer. *call (sb) to ~,* (of the Speaker in the House of Commons, the chairman of a meeting, etc) request (a member, etc) to obey the rules, the usual procedures. *be in ~ to do sth,* be according to the rules, etc: *Is it in ~ to interrupt? on a point of ~,* on a point (= question) of procedure. *O~! O~!* (used to call attention to a departure from the usual rules of debates or procedures). *~ of the day,* programme of business to be discussed. '*~-paper n* written or printed ~ of the day. *standing ~s,* ⇨ standing *adj*(1). **5** [C] command given with authority: *Soldiers must obey ~s. He gave ~s for the work to be started/that the work should be started at once. be under ~s (to do sth),* have received ~s: *He is under ~s to leave for Finland next week. by ~ of,* according to directions given by proper authority of: *by ~ of the Governor. under the ~s of,* commanded by. *under starters' ~s,* ⇨ start²(10). **6** [C] request to supply goods; the goods (to be) supplied: *an ~ for two tons of coal; give a tradesman an ~ for goods; fill an ~,* supply the goods asked for. *The butcher has called for ~s,* to ask what is wanted. *on ~,* requested but not yet supplied. *made to ~,* made according to the customer's special requirements or instructions. ⇨ *ready-made* at ready. *a large/tall ~,* (colloq) sth difficult to do or supply. '*~-book n* one in which a tradesman, commercial traveller, manufacturer, etc writes down ~s for goods: *The company has full ~-books,* orders for large quantities of goods. '*~-form n* printed form with blank spaces to be filled in by the customer. **7** [C] written direction to a bank ('*banker's ~*) or post office ('*postal ~*) to pay money, or giving authority to do sth: *an ~ on O'Reilly's Bank; a postal ~ for £9; an ~ to view,* eg from an estate-agent to inspect a house that is for sale. **8** [U] purpose, intention. *in ~ to do sth,* with the purpose of doing sth, with a view to doing sth: *in ~ (for you) to see clearly. in ~*

that, with the intention that; so that: *in ~ that he may/might/shall/should arrive in time.* **9** [C] group of people belonging to or appointed to a special class (as an honour or reward): *the O~ of Merit/of Knights/of the Bath/of the Golden Kite, etc;* badge, sign, etc worn by members of such an ~: *wearing all his ~s and decorations.* **10** (*pl*) authority given by a bishop to perform church duties. *be in/take (holy) ~s,* be/become a priest. **11** [C] class of persons on whom holy ~s have been conferred: *the O~ of Deacons/Priests/Bishops.* **12** [C] group of persons living under religious rules: *the monastic ~s; the ~ of Dominicans.* **13** [C] method of treating architectural forms, esp of columns (pillars) and capitals, esp the classical ~s (*Doric, Ionic, Corinthian*). ⇨ the illus at column. **14** (biol) [C] highest division under *class* in the grouping of animals, plants, etc: *The rose and the bean families belong to the same ~.* **15** [C] kind; sort: *intellectual ability of a high ~.* **16** [U] arrangement of military forces: *advance in review ~,* on parade; *advance in extended ~,* in battle. *advance in open/close ~,* with wide/with only slight spaces between the men, etc.

or·der² /ˈɔːdə(r)/ *vt* **1** [VP6A,9,12B,13B,15A,B,17] give an order(5,6,7) *to* (sb) or *for* sth: *The doctor ~ed me to (stay in) bed. The disobedient boy was ~ed out of the room. The chairman ~ed silence. The regiment was ~ed to the front. The judge ~ed that the prisoner should be remanded. The doctor has ~ed me absolute quiet. She ~ed herself two dozen oysters and a pint of stout. I've ~ed lunch for 1.30. The regiment was ~ed up (to the front). ~ sb about,* keep on giving orders to him. **2** [VP6A,15A] arrange; direct: *~ one's life according to strict rules. ~-ing n* (from **2** above) arrangement.

or·der·ly /ˈɔːdəlɪ/ *adj* **1** well arranged; in good order; tidy: *an ~ room/desk;* methodically inclined: *a man with an ~ mind.* **2** well behaved; obedient to discipline: *an ~ crowd.* **3** (army use, attrib only) concerned with carrying out orders: *the ~ officer,* the officer on duty for the day; *the '~ room,* room in barracks where the clerical work is done. □ *n* (*pl -lies*) (army) officer's messenger. *medical ~,* attendant in a military hospital. **or·der·li·ness** *n*

or·di·nal /ˈɔːdɪnl US: -dənl/ *n, adj* [C] (number) showing order or position in a series. *~ numbers,* eg *first, second, third.* ⇨ cardinal; App 4.

or·di·nance /ˈɔːdɪnəns/ *n* [C] order, rule, statute, made by authority or decree: *the ~s of the City Council.*

or·di·nand /ˌɔːdɪˈnænd US: ˈɔːrdənænd/ *n* candidate for ordination.

or·di·nary /ˈɔːdɪnrɪ US: ˈɔːrdəneri/ *adj* normal; usual; average: *an ~ day's work; in ~ dress. in an ~ way,* if the circumstances were ~ or usual. *in the ~ way,* in the usual or customary way. *in ~,* by permanent appointment, not temporary or extraordinary: *physician in ~ to Her Majesty. out of the ~,* unusual. *~ seaman,* (abbr **OS**) one who has not yet received the rank of *able seaman* (abbr *AB*). **or·di·nar·ily** /ˈɔːdɪnərəlɪ US: ˌɔːdnˈerəlɪ/ *adv* in an ~ way: *behave quite ordinarily.*

or·di·na·tion /ˌɔːdɪˈneɪʃn US: -dnˈeɪʃn/ *n* [U] ceremony of ordaining (a priest or minister); [C] instance of this.

ord·nance /ˈɔːdnəns/ *n* [U] artillery; munitions. **Royal Army 'O~ Corps,** (US = **O~ Corps**) that which is responsible for military supplies. **the O~**

Survey, (the preparation of) accurate and detailed maps of GB.

or·dure /'ɔːdjʊə(r) *US:* -dʒər/ *n* [U] excrement; dung; filth.

ore /ɔː(r)/ *n* [C,U] (kinds of) rock, earth, mineral, etc from which metal can be mined or extracted: *iron ore; a district rich in ores.*

or·gan /'ɔːgən/ *n* **1** any part of an animal body or plant serving an essential purpose: *the ~s of speech*, the tongue, teeth, lips, etc; *the 'nasal ~*, the nose; *the reproductive ~s.* ⇨ the illus at alimentary, ear, eye, respire, reproduce. **2** means of getting work done; organization: *Parliament is the chief ~ of government.* **3** means for making known what people think: *~s of public opinion*, newspapers, radios, TV, etc. **4** musical instrument from which sounds are produced by air forced through pipes, played by keys pressed with the fingers and pedals pressed with the feet (in US also called a **'pipe-~**). ⇨ the illus at church. **'reed/A'merican ~**, harmonium (with reeds instead of pipes). **'~-blower** *n* person who works the bellows of an ~. ⇨ **'~-grinder** *n* person who plays a barrel-~. ⇨ barrel. **'~-loft** *n* gallery (in some churches, etc) where the ~ is placed. **'~-ist** /-ɪst/ *n* person who plays an ~(4).

or·gan·die (US also **-dy**) /ɔː'gændɪ/ *n* [U] kind of fine translucent muslin.

or·ganic /ɔː'gænɪk/ *adj* **1** of an organ or organs of the body: *~ diseases*, affecting the structure of these organs, not only their functions. **2** (opp *inorganic*) having bodily organs: *~ life.* **~ chemistry**, dealing with carbon compounds. **3** made of related parts; arranged as a system: *an ~* (ie organized) *whole; an ~* (ie structural) *part.* **or·gani·cally** /-klɪ/ *adv*

or·gan·ism /'ɔːgənɪzəm/ *n* [C] living being with parts which work together; individual animal or plant; any system with parts dependent upon each other: *the social ~.*

or·gan·iz·ation /ˌɔːgənaɪ'zeɪʃn *US:* -nɪ'z-/ *n* **1** [U] act of organizing; condition of being organized: *He is engaged in the ~ of a new club. An army without ~ would be useless.* **2** [C] organized body of persons; organized system: *The human body has a very complex ~.*

or·gan·ize /'ɔːgənaɪz/ *vt* [VP6A] **1** put into working order; arrange in a system; make preparations for: *~ an army/a government/a political party/an expedition to the South Pole/one's work/oneself.* **2** (of workers) form into, join, a trade union. **or·gan·ized** *adj* **1** ordered; orderly. **2** furnished with organs; made into a living organism: *highly ~d forms of life.* **3** (of workers) in a trade union. **or·gan·izer** *n* person who ~s things.

or·gasm /'ɔːgæzəm/ *n* [C] violent (esp erotic) excitement; the climax of sexual excitement.

or·gi·as·tic /ˌɔːdʒɪ'æstɪk/ *adj* of the nature of an orgy; frenzied.

orgy /'ɔːdʒɪ/ *n* [C] (*pl* **orgies**) **1** occasion of wild merry-making; (*pl*) drunken or licentious revels. **2** (colloq) excessive amount of: *an ~ of parties/concerts/spending.*

oriel /'ɔːrɪəl/ *n* **1** part of a room projecting from an upper storey and supported from the ground or on corbels and having a window in it. **2 ~ (window)**, window of an ~. ⇨ the illus at window.

orient¹ /'ɔːrɪənt/ *n* **the O~**, (liter) the countries of the East, ie Asia, contrasted with *the Occident.* □ *adj* (poet) Eastern; (of the sun) rising: *the ~ sun.*

orient² /'ɔːrɪənt/ *vt* = orientate.

orien·tal /ˌɔːrɪ'entl/ *adj* of the Orient: *~ civilization/art/rugs.* □ *n* **O~**, inhabitant of the Orient, esp China and Japan. **~·ist** /-ɪst/ *n* person who studies the languages, arts, etc of ~ countries.

orien·tate /'ɔːrɪənteɪt/ *vt* [VP6A] **1** place (a building, etc) so as to face east; build (a church) with the chancel end due east. **2** place or exactly determine the position of (sth) with regard to the points of the compass; (fig) bring into clearly understood relations: *~ oneself*, make oneself familiar with a situation, determine how one stands in relation to one's surroundings, etc. **orien·ta·tion** /ˌɔːrɪen'teɪʃn/ *n* [U] orientating or being ~d.

ori·fice /'ɒrɪfɪs *US:* 'ɔːr-/ *n* outer opening; mouth (of a cave, etc).

ori·gin /'ɒrɪdʒɪn *US:* 'ɔːrədʒɪn/ *n* [C,U] starting-point: *the ~ of a quarrel; the ~(s) of civilization; a man of humble ~*, parentage; *words of Latin ~.*

orig·inal /ə'rɪdʒənl/ *adj* **1** first or earliest: *the ~ inhabitants of the country: The ~ plan was better than the plan we followed. ~ sin*, ⇨ sin. **2** newly formed or created; not copied or imitated: *~ ideas; an ~ design.* **3** able to produce new ideas, etc; inventive: *an ~ thinker/writer; an ~ mind.* □ *n* **1** [C] that from which sth is copied: *This is a copy; the ~ is in the Prado in Madrid.* **2 the ~**, language in which sth was first composed: *read Homer in the ~*, in ancient Greek; *study Don Quixote in the ~*, in Spanish. **3** [C] person with an original(3) mind. **~·ly** /-nəlɪ/ *adv* **1** in an ~ manner: *speak/think/write ~ly.* **2** from or in the beginning: *The school was ~ly quite small.* **~·ity** /əˌrɪdʒə'nælətɪ/ *n* [U] state or quality of being ~(2): *work that lacks ~ity*, is copied or imitated.

orig·inate /ə'rɪdʒɪneɪt/ *vi,vt* **1** [VP2C,3A] **~ from/in sth; ~ from/with sb,** have as a cause or beginning: *The quarrel ~d in rivalry between two tribes. With whom did the scheme ~?* **2** [VP6A] be the author or creator of: *~ a new style of dancing.* **orig·in·ator** /-tə(r)/ *n*

ori·ole /'ɔːrɪəʊl/ *n* (**golden**) *~*, kinds of bird with black and yellow feathers.

ori·son /'ɒrɪzn *US:* 'ɔːr-/ *n* [C] (archaic) prayer.

or·lop /'ɔːlɒp/ *n* **~ (deck),** lowest deck of a ship with three or more decks.

or·molu /'ɔːməluː/ *n* [U,C] (article made of, or decorated with) gilded bronze or a gold-coloured alloy of copper, zinc and tin: *an ~ clock.*

or·na·ment /'ɔːnəmənt/ *n* **1** [U] adorning or being adorned; that which is added for decoration: *add sth by way of ~; an altar rich in ~.* **2** [C] sth designed or used to add beauty to sth else: *a shelf crowded with ~s*, eg small vases, statuettes, pieces of china. **3** [C] person, act, quality, etc that adds beauty, charm, etc: *He is an ~ to his profession.* □ *vt* /'ɔːnəment/ [VP6A,14] be an ~ to; make beautiful: *~ a dress with lace.* **or·na·men·tal** /ˌɔːnə'mentl/ *adj* of or for *~.* **or·na·men·ta·tion** /ˌɔːnəmen'teɪʃn/ *n* [U] *~ing* or being *~ed*; that which *~s: a church with no ~ation.*

or·nate /ɔː'neɪt/ *adj* richly ornamented; (of liter style) full of flowery language; not simple in style or vocabulary. **~·ly** *adv* **~·ness** *n*

or·nery /'ɔːnərɪ/ *adj* (US colloq) ill-tempered; perverse and stubborn.

or·ni·thol·ogy /ˌɔːnɪ'θɒlədʒɪ/ *n* [U] scientific study of birds. **or·ni·thol·ogist** /-dʒɪst/ *n* expert in *~.* **or·ni·tho·logi·cal** /ˌɔːnɪθə'lɒdʒɪkl/ *adj*

oro·tund /'ɔːrəʊtʌnd/ *adj* (formal) **1** imposing; dignified. **2** pompous; pretentious.

or·phan /'ɔːfn/ n person (esp a child) who has lost one or both of his parents by death: (attrib) an ∼ child. □ vt [VP6A] cause to be an ∼: ∼ed by war. ∼·age /-ɪdʒ/ n home for ∼s.

or·ris·root /'ɒrɪsruːt US: 'ɔːr-/ n fragrant root of some kinds of iris, used in perfumes and cosmetics.

or·tho·dox /'ɔːθədɒks/ adj (having opinions, beliefs, etc which are) generally accepted or approved: an ∼ member of the Church; ∼ beliefs; ∼ behaviour. ⟹ heterodox. **the O∼ Church**, the Eastern Church, recognizing the Patriarch of Constantinople (= Istanbul) as chief bishop; the communion of the autonomous churches of the Soviet Union, Romania, Greece, etc. ∼y /'ɔːθədɒksɪ/ n (pl ∼ies) [U] being ∼; [C] ∼ belief, character, practice.

or·tho·gra·phy /ɔː'θɒɡrəfɪ/ n [U] (system of) spelling; correct or conventional spelling. **or·tho·graphic** /ˌɔːθə'ɡræfɪk/ adj

or·tho·paedic (also **-pedic**) /ˌɔːθə'piːdɪk/ adj of the curing of deformities and diseases of bones: ∼ surgery. **or·tho·paed·ics** (also **-ped·ics**) n (with sing v) branch of surgery dealing with bone deformities and diseases.

or·to·lan /'ɔːtələn/ n small wild bird valued as a table delicacy.

oryx /'ɒrɪks US: 'ɔːr-/ n African antelope with long, straight or arching horns.

Os·car /'ɒskə(r)/ n the annual US award for what is judged to be a great achievement in cinema: be nominated for/win an ∼.

os·cil·late /'ɒsɪleɪt/ vi,vt **1** [VP2A] swing backwards and forwards as the pendulum of a clock does; (fig) waver or change between extremes of opinion, etc. **2** [VP6A] cause to swing to and fro. **3** (electr, of current) undergo high frequency alternations; (of radio receivers) radiate electro-magnetic waves; experience interference (in reception) from this. **oscillating current**, current whose direction is periodically reversed. **os·cil·la·tion** /ˌɒsɪ'leɪʃn/ n [U] oscillating or being ∼d; [C] one swing of a pendulum or other object or of an electric charge. **os·cil·lator** /-tə(r)/ n (esp) device for producing electric oscillations (eg for wireless telegraphy).

os·cillo·graph /ə'sɪləɡrɑːf US: -ɡræf/ n (electr) instrument for recording oscillations.

os·cillo·scope /ə'sɪləskəʊp/ n (electr) instrument which shows on the screen of a cathode ray tube (like a TV screen) variations of current as a wavy line.

osier /'əʊzɪə(r) US: 'əʊʒər/ n [C] kind of willowtree, the twigs of which are used in basket-work.

os·prey /'ɒsprɪ/ n (pl ∼s) large kind of hawk that preys on fish. ⟹ the illus at water.

oss·eous /'ɒsɪəs/ adj consisting of bone; having a bony skeleton.

oss·ify /'ɒsɪfaɪ/ vt,vi (pt,pp -fied) [VP6A,2A] (formal) make or become hard like bone; change into bone; (fig) make or become rigid, unprogressive, unable to change. **ossi·fi·ca·tion** /ˌɒsɪfɪ'keɪʃn/ n [U] ∼ing or being ossified; that part of a structure that is ossified.

os·ten·sible /ɒ'stensəbl/ adj (of reasons, etc) put forward in an attempt to hide the real reason; apparent. **os·ten·sibly** /-əblɪ/ adv

os·ten·ta·tion /ˌɒsten'teɪʃn/ n [U] display (of wealth, learning, skill, etc) to obtain admiration or envy: the ∼ of the newly rich.

os·ten·ta·tious /ˌɒsten'teɪʃəs/ adj fond of, show-

ing, ostentation: ∼ jewellery; in an ∼ manner. ∼·ly adv

os·te·opathy /ˌɒstɪ'ɒpəθɪ/ n [U] treatment of certain diseases by manipulation of the bones and muscles. **os·teo·path** /'ɒstɪəpæθ/ n person who practises ∼.

os·tler /'ɒslə(r)/ n (old use) stableman (man who looks after horses) at an inn.

os·tra·cize /'ɒstrəsaɪz/ vt [VP6A] **1** shut out from society; refuse to meet, talk to, etc: People who hold very unorthodox opinions are sometimes ∼d. **2** (in ancient Greece) banish by popular vote for ten or five years. **os·tra·cism** /-sɪzəm/ n [U] ostracizing or being ∼d.

os·trich /'ɒstrɪtʃ/ n fast-running bird, the largest in existence, unable to fly, bred for its valuable tail feathers: have the digestion of an ∼, be able to digest almost anything. ⟹ the illus at rare.

other /'ʌðə(r)/ adj, pron (person or thing) not already named or implied. **1 the ∼**, (sing) the second of two: The twins are so much alike that people find it difficult to tell (the) one from the ∼. One of them is mine; the ∼ is my sister's. The post office is on the ∼ side of the street. Where are the ∼ boys? **on the '∼ hand**, used (sometimes, but not always, after on the one hand) to introduce sth in contrast to an earlier statement, etc: It's cheap, but on the ∼ hand the quality is poor. **2 the ∼s**, (pl) when the reference is to two or more: Six of them are mine; the ∼s are John's. Where are the ∼s? **3** (with the indef art, written and printed as one word, **an∼** /ə'nʌðə(r)/) an additional (one); a different one. ⟹ another. Will you have an∼ cup of tea? I won't say an∼ word about it. I don't like this one; can you show me an∼? (The pl of an∼ is some/any ∼s or some/any more): I don't like these. Have you any ∼s/any more? Please let me see some ∼s/some more. **4** (when one member of a group is compared with any ∼ member of the group, other is usu used): Green is far better as a bowler than any ∼ member of the team. **5** (phrases) **each ∼**, ⟹ each(4). **every ∼**, (a) all the ∼s: John is stupid; every ∼ boy in the class knows the answer. (b) alternate: Write only on every ∼ line. **one an∼**, ⟹ one[3](3). **one after the ∼; one after an∼**, in succession, not together. **...or ∼**, used to suggest absence of certainty or precision: I shall be coming again some day or ∼, one of these days. I'll get there somehow or ∼, by one means if not by an∼. Someone or ∼ (= Some unknown person) has left the gate open. **∼ things being equal**, if conditions are/were the same or alike except for the point in question: O∼ things being equal, Alice would marry Jim, not Tom, but Jim is poor and Tom is rich. **the ∼ day**, a few days ago. **6** different: I do not wish her ∼ than she is. The question must be decided by quite ∼ considerations. **∼·worldly** /ˌʌðə'wɜːldlɪ/ adj concerned with, thinking of, another world, of sth mystic rather than this world. □ adv (= otherwise) in a different way: I could not do it ∼ than hurriedly.

other·wise /'ʌðəwaɪz/ adv **1** in another or different way: You evidently think ∼. He should have been working but he was ∼ engaged, but he was doing sth different. **2** in other or different respects; in different conditions: The rent is high, but ∼ the house is satisfactory. □ conj if not; or else: Do what you've been told; ∼ you will be punished.

oti·ose /'əʊʃɪəʊs/ adj (formal) serving no practical purpose; not required; functionless.

ot·ter /'ɒtə(r)/ n [C] fur-covered, fish-eating aquatic animal with four webbed feet and a flat tail; [U] its fur. ⇨ the illus at **small**.

ot·to·man /'ɒtəmən/ n long cushioned seat without back or arms, often used as a box, eg for storing bedding.

ou·bli·ette /ˌuːblɪ'et/ n secret dungeon (underground prison) with an entrance only by a trapdoor in the roof.

ouch /aʊtʃ/ int used to express sudden pain.

ought /ɔːt/ anom fin [VP7B] ∼ **to,** (defective; no infinitive, no particles, no inflected forms; ought not is contracted to oughtn't /'ɔːtnt/; for past time, ought is used with a perfect infinitive; in reported speech, the perfect infinitive is not always necessary; ought to = should as found at **shall(3,8,9)**). **1** (indicating duty or obligation): You ∼ to start at once. Such things ∼ not to be allowed, ∼ they? 'O∼ I to go'—'Yes, I think you ∼ (to)'. You ∼ to have done that earlier. I told him (that) he ∼ to do it, ie now, or in future. I told him (that) he ∼ to have done it, ie in the past. **2** (indicating what is advisable, desirable or right): There ∼ to be more buses during the rush hours. You ∼ (ie I advise you) to see that new film at the Odeon. Coffee ∼ to be drunk while it is hot. Your brother ∼ to have been a doctor, He would probably have been a good doctor. **3** (indicating probability): If he started at nine, he ∼ to be here now. That ∼ to be enough fish for three people, I think. Harry ∼ to win the race.

ouija /'wiːdʒə/ n '∼(-board), board lettered with the alphabet and with other signs, used in seances to obtain messages said to come from the spirits of the dead.

ounce /aʊns/ n (abbr oz) unit of weight, one sixteenth of a pound avoirdupois or one twelfth of a pound troy. ⇨ **App 5.**

our /ɑː(r), 'aʊə(r)/ adj of or belonging to us, that we are concerned with, etc: We have done our share. **Our Father,** God. **Our Lady,** the Virgin Mary. **Our Lord,** Jesus Christ.

ours /ɑːz, 'aʊəz/ pron, pred adj (the one or ones) belonging to us: This house is ∼. Don't stay at their house; stay at ∼. O∼ is larger than theirs. Let me show you some of ∼. This dog of ∼ never wins any prizes. The land became ∼ by purchase.

our·selves /ɑː'selvz, aʊə'-/ pron **1** (reflex): It's no use worrying ∼ about that. We shall give ∼ the pleasure of visiting you soon. **2** (emphat): We ∼ have often made that mistake/We've often made that mistake ∼. We'd better go and see the house (for) ∼, not be content to rely upon what others say. **(all) by ∼, (a)** without help. **(b)** alone, without company: Come in; we're all by ∼, there are no visitors, etc.

oust /aʊst/ vt [VP6A,14] ∼ **sb (from),** drive or push (sb) out (from his employment, position, etc): ∼ a rival from office.

out /aʊt/ adv part (For special uses in combination with vv, ⇨ the v entries. Specimens only are given here.) **1** away from, not in or at, a place, the usual or normal conditions, etc: go out; run out; walk out; take sb out; find one's way out; lock sb out; throw sth out. Out you go! Go out! Out with it! Bring it out! Say it! **2** (with be, various meanings): Mrs White is out, not at home. The manager is out, not in the office. The dockers are out again, on strike. The book I wanted was out, ie had been borrowed; was not in the library. The tide is out, low.

The ship was four days out from Lisbon, had sailed from Lisbon four days earlier. The Socialist party was out, out of office; not in power. Short skirts are out, not fashionable. **be out and about,** (of a person who has been in bed through illness or injury) able to get up, go outdoors, etc. **3** (in various phrases to indicate absence from home): We don't go out much. Let's have an evening out, eg at a cinema or discotheque, or having dinner at a restaurant, etc. **4** (with advv and adv phrases, to emphasize the idea of distance): He lives out in the country. My brother is out in Australia. He lived out East for many years. The fishing boats are all out at sea. What are you doing out there? **5** (indicating liberation from confinement or restraint; into the open; exposed; discovered): The secret is out, discovered, known. The apple blossom is out, open. The sun is out, not hidden by cloud. His new book is out, published. There's a warrant out (ie issued) against him. Out with it! Tell the news! Explain it! etc, according to context. It's the best game out, the best ever invented. **6** (indicating exhaustion, extinction): The fire/gas/candle, etc is out, not burning. The fire has burnt out. The lease/copyright is out, has reached the end of its term. The warships steamed towards the enemy with all lights out. Put that cigarette out! The wind blew the candles out. The candle blew out. **7** (to or at an end; completely) (used with many vv, as): hear sb out; work out a problem; supplies running out; fight it out, settle the dispute by fighting. I'm tired out. He'll be here before the week is out. Let her have her sleep out, have all the sleep she needs. **cry one's 'eyes out,** continue crying until this brings relief. **have it out with sb,** ⇨ have⁴(9). **out and out,** thorough(ly); surpassing(ly): He's a crook out and out/an out-and-out crook. **out and away,** by far: I was out and away the handsomest man in the room. **8** (indicating error): I'm out in my calculations/reckoning. We're ten pounds out in our accounts. You're not far out, not much in error; almost right. Your guess was a long way out, badly in error. You've put me out, distracted me, upset the thread of my ideas, etc. My watch is five minutes out (more usu five minutes slow or fast). **9** (indicating clearness or loudness): call/cry/shout out; say sth out loud, in a loud voice; speak out, clearly, or without hesitation; bring out (= make clearer) the meaning of a paragraph by paraphrasing it; tell sb sth straight out/right out, without keeping anything back, without ambiguity. **10** (in phrases) **be out for,** be engaged in seeking, interested in obtaining: I'm not out for compliments. He's out for your blood, anxious to attack you. **out to + inf,** trying or hoping to: I'm not out (= It is not my aim) to reform the world. The firm is out to capture the Canadian market. **all out,** exerting the maximum power or effort: His new car does 80 miles an hour when it's going all out. What is needed is an all-out effort. **11** (cricket) (of a batsman) no longer batting; having been bowled, caught, etc: The captain was out for three. Kent all out, 137, innings ended for 137 runs. **12 out of,** prep (contrasted with in and into. ⇨ the n and v entries for special uses, eg out of date at date¹(3), out of the way at way(2).) **(a)** (of place): Fish cannot live out of water. Mr Green is out of town this week. This plant is not found out of (= is found only in) a small area in Central Asia. **(b)** (of movement): He walked out of the shop. He jumped *out of bed. We pulled the cart out of the ditch.* (c) (indicating motive or cause): *It was done out of mischief/spite. They helped us out of pity/kindness. She asked only out of curiosity.* (d) from among: *Choose one out of these ten. It happens in nine cases out of ten. This is only one instance out of several.* (e) by the use of; from: *The hut was made out of old planks. She made a hat out of bits of old material. Can good ever come out of evil?* (f) without: *out of breath,* breathless; *out of work,* unemployed; *out of patience;* (*born*) *out of wedlock,* of unmarried parents. *We're out of tea/petrol,* We have no tea/petrol left. *This book is out of stock,* There are no copies left in the shop. (g) (indicating condition): *out of fashion; out of control; out of order; out of danger.* ⇨ the *n* entries. (h) (indicating origin or source): *a scene out of a play; drink out of a cup/a bottle; copy sth out of a book; steps cut out of the solid rock; paid for out of the housekeeping money; a dog and a cat eating out of the same dish.* (i) (indicating result): *talk sb out of doing sth,* talk to him with the result that he does not do it; *reason sb out of his fears; cheat sb out of his money;* (colloq) *be done* (= cheated) *out of sth; frighten sb out of his wits.* (j) (at a certain distance from): *The ship sank ten miles out of Singapore. out of it,* (a) not invited to be a member of a party, etc; sad for this reason: *She felt out of it as she watched the others set off on the picnic.* (b) not concerned with, not involved in, sth: *It's a dishonest scheme and I'm glad to be out of it.* 13 (used as *n*) *the ins and (the) outs,* (a) those in office and those out of office; the Government and the Opposition. (b) the details (of procedure, etc). □ *vt* (sl or colloq) eject by force.

out·back /'aʊtbæk/ *adj, n* (eg in Australia) (of) the more remote and sparsely populated areas.

out·bal·ance /ˌaʊt'bæləns/ *vt* [VP6A] weigh down; outweigh.

out·bid /ˌaʊt'bɪd/ *vt* (-dd-) (*pt,pp* -bid) [VP6A] go beyond in bidding; bid higher than (another person) at an auction, etc.

out·board /'aʊtbɔːd/ *attrib adj* placed on or near the outside of a ship or boat. **~ motor** *n* detachable engine that is mounted at the stern, outside the boat.

out·bound /'aʊtbaʊnd/ *adj* (of a ship) outward bound; going away from a home port.

out·brave /aʊt'breɪv/ *vt* [VP6A] defy: *~ the storm.*

out·break /'aʊtbreɪk/ *n* [C] breaking out: *an ~ of anger/fever/hostilities.*

out·build·ing /'aʊtbɪldɪŋ/ *n* building, eg a shed or stable, separate from the main building: *a tenroomed farmhouse, with useful ~s.*

out·burst /'aʊtbɜːst/ *n* [C] bursting out (of steam, energy, laughter, anger, etc).

out·cast /'aʊtkɑːst *US:* -kæst/ *n, adj* (person or animal) driven out from home or society; homeless and friendless.

out·caste /'aʊtkɑːst *US:* -kæst/ *n, adj* (eg in India) (person) having lost, or been expelled from, or not belonging to, a caste.

out·class /ˌaʊt'klɑːs *US:* -'klæs/ *vt* [VP6A] be much better than; surpass: *He was ~ed from the start of the race,* His competitors were much better.

out·come /'aʊtkʌm/ *n* [C] effect or result of an event, or of circumstances.

out·crop /'aʊtkrɒp/ *n* [C] that part of a layer or vein (of rock, etc) which can be seen above the surface of the ground.

out·cry /'aʊtkraɪ/ *n* (*pl* -cries) 1 [C] loud shout or scream (of fear, alarm, etc). 2 [C,U] public protest (*against* sth).

out·dated /aʊt'deɪtɪd/ *adj* made out of date (by the passing of time).

out·dis·tance /aʊt'dɪstəns/ *vt* [VP6A] travel faster than, and leave behind: *Tom ~d all his competitors in the mile race.*

out·do /ˌaʊt'duː/ *vt* (*3rd person sing pres t* -does /-'dʌz/, *pt* -did /-'dɪd/, *pp* -done /-'dʌn/) [VP6A] do more or better than: *Not to be outdone* (ie not wanting to let someone do better than he himself had done), *he tried again.*

out·door /'aʊtdɔː(r)/ *attrib adj* done, existing, used, outside a house or building: *leading an ~ life,* eg of a person fond of open-air activities and sport; *~ dress/clothes,* worn outside the house; *~ sports* (cf *indoor games*).

out·doors /ˌaʊt'dɔːz/ *adv* in the open air; outside: *It's cold ~. In hot countries it's possible to sleep ~. Farm workers spend most of their time ~.*

outer /'aʊtə(r)/ *adj* of or for the outside, ⇨ inner; farther from the middle or inside: *~ garments.* ⇨ underwear; *the ~ suburbs; journeys to ~ space,* eg to the planet Mars; *the ~ man,* his personal appearance, dress, etc. '**~·most** /-məʊst/ *adj* farthest from the inside or centre.

out·face /ˌaʊt'feɪs/ *vt* [VP6A] face boldly; stare at (sb) until he turns his eyes away; cause (sb) to be embarrassed.

out·fall /'aʊtfɔːl/ *n* place where water falls or flows out (of a lake, river, etc); outlet; river mouth.

out·field /'aʊtfiːld/ *n* (usu **the ~**) (cricket and baseball) part of the field farthest from the batsmen; the fielders there. **~·er** *n*

out·fight /ˌaʊt'faɪt/ *vt* (*pt,pp* -fought /-'fɔːt/) [VP6A] fight better than: *The champion outfought his opponent.*

out·fit /'aʊtfɪt/ *n* [C] all the clothing or articles needed for a purpose: *a camping ~,* tent, etc; *a boy's ~ for school; a carpenter's ~,* his tools, etc. □ *vt* (-tt-) fit out (chiefly in the *pp* ~ted). **~·ter** *n* shopkeeper selling clothes.

out·flank /ˌaʊt'flæŋk/ *vt* [VP6A] go or pass round the flank of (the enemy): *an ~ing movement.*

out·flow /'aʊtfləʊ/ *n* [C] flowing out: *an ~ of water/bad language; the ~ of gold bullion.*

out·fox /ˌaʊt'fɒks/ *vt* [VP6A] get the better of by being cunning.

out·go /'aʊtgəʊ/ *n* (*pl* ~es /-gəʊz/) (opp of *income*) that which goes out or is paid out; expenditure.

out·go·ing /'aʊtgəʊɪŋ/ *adj* (attrib only) going out; leaving: *the ~ tenant,* the one who is giving up the house, etc; *an ~ ship/tide.* **out·go·ings** *n pl* expenditure; outlay.

out·grow /ˌaʊt'grəʊ/ *vt* (*pt* -grew /-'gruː/, *pp* -grown /-'grəʊn/) [VP6A] grow too large or too tall for, eg one's clothes; grow faster or taller than, eg one's brother; leave behind, as one grows older (bad habits, childish interests, opinions, etc): *~ one's strength,* grow too quickly (during childhood), so that the health suffers.

out·growth /'aʊtgrəʊθ/ *n* [C] 1 natural development or product. 2 that which grows out of sth; offshoot: *an ~ on a tree.*

out-herod /ˌaʊt'herəd/ *vt* [VP6A] *~ Herod,* be more cruel, violent, etc than King Herod (ruler of Palestine when Jesus Christ was born).

out·house /'aʊthaʊs/ *n* (*pl* -houses /-haʊzɪz/)

small building adjoining the main building (eg a shed, barn, or stable); (US) outdoor lavatory.

out·ing /'aʊtɪŋ/ n [C] holiday away from home; pleasure trip: *go for an* ~; *an* ~ *to the seaside.*

out·land·ish /aʊt'lændɪʃ/ adj looking or sounding odd, strange or foreign: ~ *dress/behaviour/ideas.* ~·ly adv ~·ness n

out·last /ˌaʊt'lɑːst US: -'læst/ vt [VP6A] last or live longer than.

out·law /'aʊtlɔː/ n (hist) person punished by being placed outside the protection of the law; criminal. □ vt [VP6A] make (sb) an ~; drive out from society. ~ry /'aʊtlɔːrɪ/ n [U] being an ~; being ~ed.

out·lay /'aʊtleɪ/ n [U] ~ (on), spending; laying out money; [C] sum of money that is spent: *a large* ~ *on/for scientific research.*

out·let /'aʊtlet/ n ~ (for), 1 way out for water, steam, etc: *an* ~ *for water; the* ~ *of a lake.* 2 (fig) means of or occasion for releasing (one's feelings, energies, etc): *Children need an* ~ *for their energies.*

out·line /'aʊtlaɪn/ n [C] 1 line(s) showing shape or boundary: *an* ~ *map of Great Britain; draw sth in* ~. 2 statement of the chief facts, points, etc: *an* ~ *for an essay/a lecture; An O*~ *of European History*, title of a book with a summary of the chief events, etc. □ vt [VP6A] draw in ~; give an ~ of: ~ *Napoleon's Russian campaign.*

out·live /ˌaʊt'lɪv/ vt [VP6A] 1 live longer than: ~ *one's wife.* 2 live until sth is forgotten: ~ *a disgrace.*

out·look /'aʊtlʊk/ n 1 view on which one looks out: *a pleasant* ~ *over the valley; an* ~ *on to roofs and chimneys.* 2 what seems likely to happen: *a bright* ~ *for trade;* (weather forecast): *further* ~, *dry and sunny.* 3 person's way of looking at sth: *a man with a narrow* ~ *on life.*

out·lying /'aʊtlaɪɪŋ/ adj far from the centre: ~ *villages, with poor communications.*

out·man·oeuvre (US = -ma·neu·ver) /ˌaʊtmə'nuːvə(r)/ vt [VP6A] overcome, get the better of, by being superior in manoeuvring.

out·march /ˌaʊt'mɑːtʃ/ vt [VP6A] surpass by marching faster or longer.

out·match /ˌaʊt'mætʃ/ vt [VP6A] be more than a match for; excel: *be* ~*ed in skill and endurance.*

out·moded /ˌaʊt'məʊdɪd/ adj out of fashion.

out·most /'aʊtməʊst/ adj = outermost.

out·num·ber /ˌaʊt'nʌmbə(r)/ vt [VP6A] be greater in number than.

out-of-date /'aʊt əv deɪt/ adj not modern; not fashionable: ~ *styles/methods/slang.*

out-of-door /ˌaʊt əv 'dɔː(r)/ attrib adj = outdoor.

out-of-doors /ˌaʊt əv 'dɔːz/ adv = outdoors.

out-of-the-way /ˌaʊt əv ðə 'weɪ/ adj 1 remote; secluded: *an* ~ *cottage.* 2 not commonly known: ~ *items of knowledge.*

out·patient /'aʊtpeɪʃnt/ n person visiting a hospital for treatment but not staying there.

out·play /ˌaʊt'pleɪ/ vt [VP6A] play better than: *The English team was* ~*ed by the Brazilians.*

out·point /ˌaʊt'pɔɪnt/ vt [VP6A] (in boxing, etc) score more points than; defeat on points: *The British champion was* ~*ed by the Mexican.*

out·port /'aʊtpɔːt/ n port or harbour away from a central custom-house or centre of trade.

out·post /'aʊtpəʊst/ n 1 (soldiers in an) observation post at a distance from the main body of troops. 2 any distant settlement: *an* ~ *of the Roman Empire.*

out·pour·ing /'aʊtpɔːrɪŋ/ n [C] pouring out; (usu pl) expression of feeling: ~*s of the heart.*

out·put /'aʊtpʊt/ n (sing only) 1 quantity of goods, etc, produced: *the* ~ *of a gold mine/a factory; the literary* ~ *of the year*, the books, etc published. 2 power, energy, etc produced; information produced from a computer. ⇨ input.

out·rage /'aʊtreɪdʒ/ n [U,C] 1 (act of) extreme violence or cruelty: *never safe from* ~; ~*s committed by a drunken mob. Would the use of H-bombs be an* ~ *against humanity?* 2 act that shocks public opinion. □ vt [VP6A] treat violently; be guilty of an ~ upon; violate: ~ *public opinion;* ~ *one's sense of justice.*

out·rage·ous /aʊt'reɪdʒəs/ adj shocking; very cruel, shameless, immoral: ~ *behaviour; an* ~ *price/remark.* ~·ly adv

out·range /ˌaʊt'reɪndʒ/ vt [VP6A] have a greater range than: *Our guns were* ~*d by those of the enemy's cruisers.*

out·rank /ˌaʊt'ræŋk/ vt [VP6A] rank higher than.

outré /'uːtreɪ US: uː'treɪ/ adj outside the bounds of what is conventionally correct; contrary to what is decorous: ~ *behaviour.*

out·ride /ˌaʊt'raɪd/ vt (pt -rode /-'rəʊd/, pp -ridden /-'rɪdn/) [VP6A] ride better or faster than: ~ *one's pursuers.*

out·rider /'aʊtraɪdə(r)/ n person on horseback, a motor-cycle, etc, accompanying a vehicle, as an attendant or guard.

out·rig·ger /'aʊtrɪgə(r)/ n (boating) beam, spar or structure projecting from or over the side of a boat for various purposes (eg for the rowlock in a racing shell, or to give stability to a canoe or yacht). **out·rigged** /'aʊtrɪgd/ adj (of a boat) having an ~ or ~s.

out·right /'aʊtraɪt/ adj 1 thorough; positive: *an* ~ *denial;* ~ *wickedness; an* ~ *manner*, ie thoroughly frank. 2 clear; unmistakable: *On the voting for secretary, Smith was the* ~ *winner.* □ adv 1 openly, with nothing held back: *tell a man* ~ *what one thinks of his behaviour.* 2 completely; at one time; *buy a house* ~, ie not by instalments; *be killed* ~ *by a blow.*

out·rival /ˌaʊt'raɪvl/ vt (-ll-, US also -l-) [VP6A] be or do better than (sb) as a rival.

out·run /ˌaʊt'rʌn/ vt (pt -ran /-'ræn/, pp -run; -nn-) [VP6A] run faster or better than; go beyond: *His ambition outran his ability*, He was ambitious to do more than he was able to do.

out·sail /aʊt'seɪl/ vt [VP6A] sail faster than.

out·set /'aʊtset/ n start. **at/from the** ~, at/from the beginning: *at the* ~ *of his career.*

out·shine /ˌaʊt'ʃaɪn/ vt (pt,pp -shone /-'ʃɒn/) [VP6A] shine more brightly than.

out·side /ˌaʊt'saɪd/ n (contrasted with *inside*) 1 the other side or surface; the outer part(s): *The* ~ *of the house needs painting. Don't judge a thing from the* ~, from the external appearance. 2 **at the (very)** ~, at the most; at the highest reckoning: *There were only fifty people there at the* ~, certainly not more than fifty. *He earns £10000 a year at the* ~. □ /'aʊtsaɪd/ adj (or attrib use of n) 1 of or on, nearer, the ~: ~ *repairs*, ie to the ~ of a building; ~ *measurements*, eg of a box; *an* ~ *broadcast*, from a place ~ the studios. 2 greatest possible or probable: *an* ~ *estimate/price.* 3 not connected with or included in a group, organization, etc: *We shall need* ~ *help* (= extra workers) *for this job. She doesn't like meeting the* ~ *world,* people not belonging to the close circle of her family and friends. □ *adv* on or to the ~: *The house is painted green* ~. *The car is waiting* ~. □ *prep* **1** at or on the outer side of: ~ *the house; a ship moored* ~ *the harbour*. **2** beyond the limits of: *We cannot go* ~ *the evidence. He has no occupation* ~ *his office work.*

out·sider /ˌaʊt'saɪdə(r)/ *n* **1** person who is not, or who is not considered to be, a member of a group, society, etc; (colloq) ill-mannered person not socially acceptable. **2** (racing) horse that is thought to have little chance of winning a race.

out·size /'aʊtsaɪz/ *adj* (esp of articles of clothing, etc) larger than the usual size.

out·skirts /'aʊtskɜːts/ *n pl* borders or outlying parts (esp of a town): *on the* ~ *of Lille.*

out·smart /ˌaʊt'smɑːt/ *vt* [VP6A] (colloq) be smarter (= cleverer, more cunning) than.

out·span /ˌaʊt'spæn/ *vi, vt* (-nn-) [VP6A,2A] (S Africa) unyoke; unharness.

out·spoken /ˌaʊt'spəʊkən/ *adj* saying freely what one thinks; frank: ~ *comments; be* ~ *in one's remarks.* ~·**ly** *adv* ~·**ness** *n*

out·spread /ˌaʊt'spred/ *adj* spread or stretched out: *with* /~'*arms; with arms* ~.

out·stand·ing /ˌaʊt'stændɪŋ/ *adj* **1** in a position to be easily noticed; attracting notice: *the* ~ *features of the landscape; an* ~ *landmark. The girl who won the scholarship was quite* ~. **2** (of problems, work, payments, etc) still to be attended to: ~ *debts/liabilities; a good deal of work still* ~. **3** /'aʊtstændɪŋ/ sticking out: *a boy with big,* ~ *ears.* ~·**ly** *adv* to a high degree: ~*ly intelligent.*

out·station /'aʊtsteɪʃn/ *n* remote station(2).

out·stay /ˌaʊt'steɪ/ *vt* [VP6A] stay longer than: ~ *the other guests.* ~ *one's welcome,* stay too long, until one is no longer a welcome guest.

out·stretched /ˌaʊt'stretʃt/ *adj* stretched or spread out: *with* ~ *arms; lie* ~ *on the grass.*

out·strip /ˌaʊt'strɪp/ *vt* (-pp-) [VP6A] do better than; pass (sb) in a race, etc: *The hare was* ~*ped by the tortoise.*

out·vie /ˌaʊt'vaɪ/ *vt* [VP6A] do better than in competition.

out·vote /ˌaʊt'vəʊt/ *vt* [VP6A] win, obtain, more votes than.

out·ward /'aʊtwəd/ *adj* **1** of or on the outside: *the* ~ *appearance of things; the* ~ *man* (contrasted with the spiritual nature, the soul). **2** going out: *during the* ~ *voyage.* □ *adv* (also **out·wards** /-wədz/) towards the outside; away from home or the centre: *The two ends must be bent* ~*s. The ship is* ~ *bound,* sailing away from its home port. ~·**ly** *adv* on the surface; apparently: *Though badly frightened she appeared* ~*ly calm.*

out·wear /ˌaʊt'weə(r)/ *vt* (*pt* -wore /-'wɔː(r)/ *pp* -worn /-'wɔːn/) [VP6A] **1** last longer than: *Well-made leather shoes will* ~ *two pairs of these cheap rubber shoes.* **2** wear out; use up; exhaust (esp in the *pp* when attrib): *outworn quotations,* used so often that they no longer strike the listener or reader; *outworn* (= out-of-date) *practices in industry.*

out·weigh /ˌaʊt'weɪ/ *vt* [VP6A] be greater in weight, value or importance than: *Do the disadvantages* ~ *the advantages?*

out·wit /ˌaʊt'wɪt/ *vt* (-tt-) [VP6A] get the better of by being cleverer or more cunning than: *The thief* ~*ted the police and got away with his loot.*

out·work /'aʊtwɜːk/ *n* part of a military defence system away from the centre: *the* ~*s of a castle.*

out·wore /ˌaʊt'wɔː(r)/, **out·worn** /aʊt'wɔːn/ ⇨ outwear.

ouzel /'uːzl/ *n* kinds of small bird of the thrush family.

ouzo /'uːzəʊ/ *n* [U] aniseed-flavoured Greek liqueur, drunk with water.

ova /'əʊvə/ *n pl* of ovum.

oval /'əʊvl/ *n, adj* (plane figure or outline that is) egg-shaped; shaped like an ellipse.

ovary /'əʊvərɪ/ *n* (*pl* -ries) either of the two reproductive organs in which ova are produced in female animals; seed-vessel in a plant. ⇨ ovum. ⇨ the illus at flower; reproduce.

ova·tion /əʊ'veɪʃn/ *n* [C] enthusiastic expression of welcome or approval: *The leader was given a standing* ~, The audience stood to clap, etc.

oven /'ʌvn/ *n* **1** enclosed box-like space which is heated for cooking food: *Bread is baked in an* ~. **2** small furnace or kiln used in chemistry, etc. '~·**ware** /-weə(r)/ *n* [U] heat-proof dishes for use in an ~: ~*ware pottery.*

over[1] /'əʊvə(r)/ *adv* (⇨ the *v* entries for special combinations, eg *give over.* Specimens only are given here.) **1** (indicating movement from an upright position, from one side to the other side, or so that a different side is seen, etc): *He fell* ~ *on the ice. Don't knock that vase* ~. *A slight push would send it* ~. *He gave me a push and* ~ *I went,* I fell. *Turn the patient* ~ *on his face and rub his back. Turn* ~ *the page. It rolled* ~ *and* ~, made a series of revolutions. *He turned* ~ *in bed.* **2** (indicating motion upwards and outwards): *The milk boiled* ~. *He was boiling* ~ *with rage.* **3** from beginning to end; through: *I'll look the papers* ~, look or read through them. *You should think it* ~, consider the matter carefully. **4** (indicating repetition) again: *Count them* ~, a second time. (*all*) ~ *again,* a second time (from the beginning): *He did the work so badly that I had to do it all* ~ *again myself.* ~ *and* ~ *again,* repeatedly; many times: *I've warned you* ~ *and* ~ *again not to do that.* **5** across (a street, an open space, a distance, etc): *Take these letters* ~ *to the post office. Let me row you* ~ *to the other side of the lake. Ask him* ~, Ask him to come here/to pay a visit. *He's* ~ *in/has gone* ~ *to France. Come* ~ *and see me some time,* Come to visit me some time. *Some wild geese have just flown* ~. ~ *against,* (lit or fig) (**a**) opposite to. (**b**) in contrast with. **6** remaining; not used after part has been taken or used: *Seven into thirty goes four times and two* ~. *If there's any meat* (*left*) ~, *give it to the dog. I've paid all my debts and have £15* ~. **7** in addition; in excess; more: *children of fourteen and* ~; *10 metres and a bit* ~. **8** ended; finished; done with: *The meeting will be* ~ *before we arrive if we don't hurry. The storm is* ~. *His sufferings will soon be* ~. *It's all* ~ *with him,* He's ruined, sure to die soon, etc, according to context. **9** more than is right, usual, wise, etc: ~ *anxious;* ~ *polite. If she grieves* ~ *much, she may fall ill. He's not* ~ *strong,* not so strong as is desirable. *He hasn't done it* ~ *well,* He has done it rather badly. ⇨ over- below. **10** (indicating transference or change from one person, party, etc to another): *He has gone* ~ *to the enemy,* joined them. *He made his business* ~ *to his son,* made his son the owner. *Hand that weapon* ~ *to me. Over (to you)!* (in radio telegraphy, vessel) It is now your turn to speak. **11** on the whole surface; in all parts: *He was aching all* ~. *This pianist is famous all the world* ~.

Your clothes are all ∼ *dust/are dusty all* ∼*. Paint the old name* ∼, cover it with paint. *That's Smith all* ∼, It's characteristic of him, what he might be expected to do.

over² /'əʊvə(r)/ *prep* 1 resting on the surface of and covering, partly or completely (not, in this sense, replaceable by *above*): *He spread his handkerchief* ∼ *his face to keep the flies off. Spread a cloth* ∼ *the table. Tie a piece of paper firmly* ∼ *the top of the jar. I knocked the man's hat* ∼ *his eyes,* so that he couldn't see. 2 at or to a level higher than, but not touching (in this sense often replaceable by *above*): *Attendants held a large umbrella* ∼/*above the chief's head. The sky is* ∼/*above our heads. These telegraph wires* ∼ *the streets are ugly. The balcony juts out* ∼ *the street. There was a lamp* ∼ *the table.* 3 (indicating superiority in rank, authority, etc): *He reigns* ∼ *a great empire. He has jurisdiction* ∼ *three provinces. These people need a firm ruler* ∼ *them. He has no command* ∼ *himself/*∼ *his passions. Mr White is* ∼ *me in the office.* 4 in or across every part of: *Snow is falling* ∼ *the north of England. He is famous all* ∼ *the world.* ⇨ over¹(11). *He has travelled all* ∼ *Europe.* 5 from one side to the other of; to or at the other side of: *He escaped* ∼ *the frontier. She spoke to me* ∼ *her shoulder. Look* ∼ *the hedge. We heard voices from* ∼ *the fence. Who lives in that house* ∼ *the way,* on the opposite side of the road or street? 6 (of time): *Can you stay* ∼ *Sunday,* until Monday? 7 so as to be ∼ and on the other side of: *climb* ∼ *a wall; jump* ∼ *a brook.* 8 (opp of *under*) more than: *He spoke for* ∼ *an hour. He stayed in London (for)* ∼ *a month. She is* ∼ *40 inches round the waist. The river is* ∼ *fifty miles long. He's* ∼ *fifty.* ∼ *and above,* besides; in addition to: *The waiters get good tips* ∼ *and above their wages.* 9 in connection with; while engaged in; concerning: *He went to sleep* ∼ *his work,* while doing it. *How long will he be* ∼ *it?* How long will it take him to do it, get there, etc? *We had a pleasant chat* ∼ *a cup of tea,* while drinking tea. *We all laughed* ∼ *the affair.*

over³ /'əʊvə(r)/ *n* (cricket) number of balls bowled in succession by each bowler in turn.

over- /ˌəʊvə(r)/ *pref* too (much): /ˌ∼-po'lite; ˌ∼-'tired; ˌ∼-'heated.* (Note: compounds not entered below have the same stress pattern as the examples below.) The meanings of the *adjj* below may be obtained by putting *too* in place of *over.*

ˌ∼-a'bundant	ˌ∼-ex'cited
ˌ∼-'active	ˌ∼-fa'miliar
ˌ∼-am'bitious	ˌ∼-'fond
ˌ∼-'anxious	ˌ∼-'full
ˌ∼-'bold	ˌ∼-'generous
ˌ∼-'busy	ˌ∼-'greedy
ˌ∼-'careful	ˌ∼-'hasty
ˌ∼-'cautious	ˌ∼-'jealous
ˌ∼-'confident	ˌ∼-'modest
ˌ∼-'credulous	ˌ∼-'nervous
ˌ∼-'critical	ˌ∼-'proud
ˌ∼-'curious	ˌ∼-'ripe
ˌ∼-'delicate	ˌ∼-'sensitive
ˌ∼-'eager	ˌ∼-'serious
ˌ∼-e'motional	ˌ∼-sus'picious
ˌ∼-en,thusi'astic	ˌ∼-'zealous

The meanings of the *nn* below may be obtained by putting *too much* in place of *over.*

ˌ∼-a'bundance	ˌ∼-in'dulgence
ˌ∼-an'xiety	ˌ∼-'payment
ˌ∼-'confidence	ˌ∼-,popu'lation
ˌ∼-cre'dulity	ˌ∼-pro'duction
ˌ∼-ex'ertion	ˌ∼-'strain
ˌ∼-ex'posure	ˌ∼-'tolerance

The meaning of the *vv* below may be obtained by putting *too much* after the *v* in place of *over.*

ˌ∼-'burden	ˌ∼-'heat
ˌ∼-'cook	ˌ∼-in'dulge
ˌ∼-'eat	ˌ∼-'praise
ˌ∼-'emphasize	ˌ∼-pro'duce
ˌ∼-'estimate	ˌ∼-'simplify
ˌ∼-ex'ert	ˌ∼-'strain
ˌ∼-ex'pose	ˌ∼-'value

over·act /ˌəʊvər'ækt/ *vi,vt* [VP2A,6A] act²(4) in an exaggerated way: ∼*ing* (*in*) *his part.*

over·all¹ /ˌəʊvər'ɔːl/ *adj* including everything; containing all: *the* ∼ *measurements of a room; coal burnt at an* ∼ *efficiency of only 18 per cent.*

over·all² /'əʊvərɔːl/ *n* 1 (GB) loose-fitting garment that covers other garments (eg as worn by small children during play). 2 (*pl*) loose-fitting trousers, with the front extended above the waist, with shoulder straps, and made of heavy, strong material, worn over other clothes to protect them from dirt, etc.

over·arch /ˌəʊvər'ɑːtʃ/ *vt,vi* [VP6A,2A] form an arch (over): *Trees* ∼*ed the road.*

over·arm /'əʊvərɑːm/ *adj, adv* (sport, eg cricket) with the arm swung over the shoulder: *bowling* ∼; *an* ∼ *bowler.*

over·awe /ˌəʊvər'ɔː/ *vt* [VP6A] awe completely; awe through great respect, etc: ∼ *sb into submission.*

over·bal·ance /ˌəʊvə'bæləns/ *vt,vi* 1 [VP6A,2A] (cause to) lose balance; fall over: *He* ∼*d and fell into the water. Don't* ∼ *the canoe.* 2 [VP6A] outweigh: *The gains* ∼ *the losses.*

over·bear /ˌəʊvə'beə(r)/ *vt* (*pt* -bore /-'bɔː(r)/, *pp* -borne /-'bɔːn/) [VP6A] overcome (by forcible arguments, strong force, or authority): *My objections were overborne in the argument.* ∼*ing adj* masterful; forcing others to one's will: *an* ∼*ing manner.* ∼*ing·ly adv*

over·bid /ˌəʊvə'bɪd/ *vt,vi* (*pt,pp* -bid; -dd-) 1 [VP6A] (at an auction) bid higher than (another person). 2 [VP6A,2A] bid more than the value of (sth offered for sale). 3 [VP6A,2A] (bridge) make a higher bid than (one's partner) or than one's hand is worth. □ *n* /'əʊvəbɪd/ act of ∼ding.

over·blown /ˌəʊvə'bləʊn/ *adj* (of flowers) too fully open; past their best.

over·board /'əʊvəbɔːd/ *adv* over the side of a ship or boat into the water: *fall/jump* ∼; *throw sb* ∼, (fig) get rid of him, stop supporting him, etc.

over·bore /ˌəʊvə'bɔː(r)/, **over·borne** /ˌəʊvə'bɔːn/ ⇨ overbear.

over·bur·den /ˌəʊvə'bɜːdn/ *n* [U] surface soil, etc which must be moved away to get at coal, etc underneath. □ *vt* [VP6A] burden too heavily: ∼*ed with grief.*

over·call /ˌəʊvə'kɔːl/ *vt,vi* = overbid(3).

over·capi·tal·ize /ˌəʊvə'kæpɪtəlaɪz/ *vt* fix or estimate the capital of (a company) too high. **over·capi·tal·iz·ation** /ˌəʊvəˌkæpɪtəlaɪ'zeɪʃn US: -lɪ'z-/ *n*

over·cast /ˌəʊvə'kɑːst US: -'kæst/ *adj* (of the sky) darkened (as) by clouds; (fig) gloomy; sad. □ *n* (*sing* only) cloud-covered sky: *Breaks in the* ∼ *will give sunny periods.*

over·charge /ˌəʊvə'tʃɑːdʒ/ *vt,vi* 1 [VP6A,2A]

charge (sb) too high a price: *We were ~d for the eggs. That grocer never ~s.* 2 [VP6A] fill or load too heavily: *~ a gun; ~ an electric circuit.* □ *n* /'əʊvətʃɑːdʒ/ [C] charge that is too high or great, eg of electric current, explosive or for a purchase.

over·coat /'əʊvəkəʊt/ *n* long coat worn out of doors over ordinary clothes in cold weather.

over·come /ˌəʊvə'kʌm/ *vt* (*pt* -came /-'keɪm/, *pp* -come) [VP6A] 1 get the better of; be too strong for: *~ the enemy; ~ a bad habit; ~ temptation.* 2 make weak: *be ~ by fatigue/emotion/liquor/ fumes.*

over·crop /ˌəʊvə'krɒp/ *vt* (-pp-) [VP6A] take too many crops from (land) (so that it loses fertility).

over·crowd /ˌəʊvə'kraʊd/ *vt* [VP6A] crowd too much: *~ed buses/trains; the ~ing of large cities.*

over·do /ˌəʊvə'duː/ *vt* (*pt* -did /-'dɪd/, *pp* -done /-'dʌn/) [VP6A] 1 do too much; exaggerate; overact: *The comic scenes in the play were overdone. He overdid his part in the play.* ~ *it,* (a) work, etc too hard: *You should work hard, but don't ~ it and make yourself ill.* (b) exaggerate; go too far in order to achieve one's object: *He showed sympathy for us, but didn't he rather ~ it?* 2 cook too much: *overdone beef.*

over·dose /'əʊvədəʊs/ *n* too great an amount (of a drug) taken at one time: *take an ~; die of an ~ of morphine.* □ /ˌəʊvə'dəʊs/ *vt* [VP6A,14] ~ *sb (with sth),* give him an ~ (of sth).

over·draft /'əʊvədrɑːft US: -dræft/ *n* amount of money by which a bank account is overdrawn.

over·draw /ˌəʊvə'drɔː/ *vt,vi* (*pt* -drew /-'druː/, *pp* -drawn /-'drɔːn/) [VP6A,2A] 1 draw a cheque for a sum in excess of (one's credit balance in a bank): *an ~n account.* 2 exaggerate: *The characters in this novel are rather ~n,* are not true to life.

over·dress /ˌəʊvə'dres/ *vt,vi* [VP6A,2A] dress (oneself, etc) too richly or more showily than is suitable for the occasion.

over·drive /'əʊvədraɪv/ *n* mechanism fitted into the normal gear-box of a motor vehicle to reduce the power output while maintaining the driving speed.

over·due /ˌəʊvə'djuː US: -'duː/ *adj* beyond the time fixed (for arrival, payment, etc): *The train is ~,* is late. *These bills are all ~,* ought to have been paid before now. *The baby is two weeks ~,* still not born two weeks after the expected date of birth.

over·flow /ˌəʊvə'fləʊ/ *vt,vi* (*pt,pp* ~ed) 1 [VP6A,2A] flow over; flow over the edges or limits; flood; spread beyond the ordinary or usual area: *The river ~ed its banks. The lake is ~ing. The crowds were so big that they ~ed the barriers.* 2 [VP3A] ~ *with,* be more than filled: *a heart ~ing with gratitude; a friend ~ing with kindness.* □ *n* /'əʊvəfləʊ/ [C] flowing over of liquid; flood; that which flows over or is too much for the space, area, etc available: *new suburbs for the ~ of population; an ~ meeting,* one held for those unable to find room in the hall, etc where the principal meeting is held.

over·grown /ˌəʊvə'grəʊn/ *adj* 1 having grown too fast: *an ~ boy.* 2 covered with sth that has grown over: *a garden ~ with weeds; walls ~ with ivy.*

over·growth /'əʊvəgrəʊθ/ *n* 1 [U,C] that which has grown over: *an ~ of weeds.* 2 [U] growth that is too fast or excessive: *weakness due to ~.*

over·hand /'əʊvəhænd/ *adj* (cricket, etc) overarm; (in swimming) with the hand and arm raised out of the water: *the ~ stroke.*

over·hang /ˌəʊvə'hæŋ/ *vt,vi* (*pt,pp* -hung /-'hʌŋ/) [VP6A,2A] 1 hang over; be over, project over, like a shelf: *The cliffs ~ the stream. The ledge ~s several feet.* 2 threaten; be likely to come: *~ing dangers.* □ *n* /'əʊvəhæŋ/ part that ~s: *the ~ of a roof/cliff.*

over·haul /ˌəʊvə'hɔːl/ *vt* 1 examine thoroughly in order to learn about the condition of: *have the engine of a car ~ed;* (colloq) *go to one's doctor to be ~ed,* physically examined. 2 overtake; catch up with: *The fast cruiser soon ~ed the old cargo boat.* □ *n* /'əʊvəhɔːl/ [C] examination for the purpose of repairing, cleaning, etc.

over·head /ˌəʊvə'hed/ *adv* above one's head; in the sky: *the people in the room ~; the stars ~.* □ *adj* /'əʊvəhed/ 1 raised above the ground: *~ wires/ cables; an ~ railway,* built at a level higher than that of the streets. 2 (business): *~ expenses/ charges* (or, *n pl,* ~s), those expenses, etc needed for carrying on a business, eg rent, advertising, salaries, light, heating, not manufacturing costs.

over·hear /ˌəʊvə'hɪə(r)/ *vt* (*pt,pp* -heard /-'hɜːd/) [VP6A,18A,19A] hear without the knowledge of the speaker(s); hear what one is not intended to hear; hear by chance.

over·joyed /ˌəʊvə'dʒɔɪd/ *adj* greatly delighted (*at* one's success, etc).

over·kill /'əʊvəkɪl/ *n* capacity exceeding what is needed to destroy.

over·land *adj* /'əʊvəlænd/, *adv* /ˌəʊvə'lænd/ across the land (contrasted with the sea): *the ~ route used by Marco Polo; travel ~.*

over·lap /ˌəʊvə'læp/ *vt,vi* (-pp-) [VP6A,2A] 1 partly cover by extending beyond one edge: *tiles that ~ one another; ~ping shingles; ~ping boards.* 2 (fig) partly coincide; involve duplication: *His duties/authority and mine ~. His visit and mine ~ped.* □ *n* /'əʊvəlæp/ [C] ~ping part; [U] fact or process of ~ping.

over·lay /ˌəʊvə'leɪ/ *vt* (*pt,pp* -laid /-'leɪd/) put a coating over the surface of: *wood overlaid with gold.* □ *n* /'əʊvəleɪ/ thing laid over sth.

over·leaf /ˌəʊvə'liːf/ *adv* on the other side of the leaf (of a book, etc).

over·leap /ˌəʊvə'liːp/ *vt* (*pt,pp* ~ed or -leapt /-'lept/) [VP6A] leap over; (fig) go too far, attempt too much: *Ambition often ~s itself.*

over·load /ˌəʊvə'ləʊd/ *vt* [VP6A] put too great a load on; (electr) put too great a charge into.

over·look /ˌəʊvə'lʊk/ *vt* [VP6A] 1 have a view of from above: *From my study window I ~ the bay and the headlands. Our garden is ~ed from the neighbours' windows,* They can look down on to our garden from their windows. 2 fail to see or notice; pay no attention to: *~ a printer's error. His services have been ~ed by his employers,* They have not properly rewarded him. 3 pass over without punishing: *~ a fault.* 4 superintend; supervise.

over·lord /'əʊvəlɔːd/ *n* (in feudal times) nobleman in relation to his vassals; superior from whom men held land and to whom they owed service.

over·ly /'əʊvəlɪ/ *adv* to an excessive degree: *~ cautious.* Cf *overcautious.*

over·man·tel /'əʊvəmæntl/ *n* structure (wood or stone, carved or decorated) over a mantlepiece.

over·mas·ter /ˌəʊvə'mɑːstə(r) US: -'mæs-/ *vt* [VP6A] overcome, overpower: *an ~ing passion,* a passion so strong that it is difficult to subdue it.

over·much /ˌəʊvə'mʌtʃ/ *adj, adv* too great(ly): *give students ~ homework; an author who has* *been praised* ∿.

over·night /ˌəʊvə'naɪt/ *adv* **1** on the night before: *get everything ready for the journey* ∿; *make preparations* ∿. **2** for, during, the night: *stay* ∿ *at a friend's house*, sleep there for the night. *The situation changed* ∿. □ /'əʊvənaɪt/ *adj* during or for the night: *an* ∿ *journey*; *an* ∿ *stop at Rome*.

over·pass /'əʊvəpɑːs *US:* -pæs/ *n* bridge or road that carries a road over a highway or motorway. ⇨ **flyover, underpass**.

over·pay /ˌəʊvə'peɪ/ *vt* (*pt,pp* -paid /-'peɪd/) [VP6A,14] pay too much or too highly: *Has Jack been overpaid for his work?*

over·play /ˌəʊvə'pleɪ/ *vt* ∿ *one's hand*, (gambling, cards) take risks that are not justified (by overestimating one's own strength).

over·plus /'əʊvəplʌs/ *n* [C] amount which is surplus or in excess.

over·power /ˌəʊvə'paʊə(r)/ *vt* [VP6A] overcome; be too strong for; defeat by greater strength or numbers: *The criminals were easily* ∿*ed by the police. He was* ∿*ed by the heat.* ∿*·ing adj* too strong; very powerful: *an* ∿*ing stink;* ∿*ing grief.*

over·print /ˌəʊvə'prɪnt/ *vt* [VP6A] print additional matter on (an already printed surface, eg of postage stamps). □ *n* /'əʊvəprɪnt/ *thing* ∿*ed.*

over·rate /ˌəʊvə'reɪt/ *vt* [VP6A] put too high a value on: ∿ *sb's abilities; an* ∿*d book.*

over·reach /ˌəʊvə'riːtʃ/ *vt* [VP6A] **1** get the better of (by trickery). **2** ∿ *oneself*, fail in one's object, damage one's own interests, by being too ambitious.

over·ride /ˌəʊvə'raɪd/ *vt* (*pt* -rode /-'rəʊd/, *pp* -ridden /-'rɪdn/) [VP6A] prevail over (sb's opinions, decisions, wishes, claims, etc): *They overrode my wishes*, set them aside without consideration.

over·rule /ˌəʊvə'ruːl/ *vt* [VP6A] decide against (esp by using one's higher authority): ∿ *a claim or objection. The judge* ∿*d the previous decision. We were* ∿*d by the majority.*

over·run /ˌəʊvə'rʌn/ *vt* (*pt* -ran /-'ræn/, *pp* -run) [VP6A] **1** spread over and occupy or injure: *a country* ∿ *by enemy troops; warehouses* ∿ *with rats; a garden* ∿ *with weeds.* **2** go beyond (a limit): *speakers who* ∿ *the time allowed them. The broadcast overran the allotted time.*

over·sea(s) /ˌəʊvə'siː(z)/ *adv* (at, to, from, for, places) across the sea: ∿(s) *trade; an* ∿(s) *broadcast programme.* □ *adv. go/live* ∿(s), across the sea; abroad.

over·see /ˌəʊvə'siː/ *vt* (*pt* -saw /-'sɔː/, *pp* -seen /-'siːn/) [VP6A] look after, control (work, workmen). **over·seer** /'əʊvəsɪə(r)/ *n* foreman; person whose duty it is to take charge of work and see that it is properly done.

over·sexed /ˌəʊvə'sekst/ *adj* having sexual desire in excess of what is normal; obsessed by sex.

over·shadow /ˌəʊvə'ʃædəʊ/ *vt* [VP6A] throw a shade over; (fig) render less conspicuous; cause to seem less important.

over·shoe /'əʊvəʃuː/ *n* [C] rubber shoe worn over an ordinary one for protection against wet and mud. ⇨ **galoshes**.

over·shoot /ˌəʊvə'ʃuːt/ *vt* (*pt,pp* -shot /-'ʃɒt/) [VP6A] shoot over or beyond (a mark); (lit, fig) go too far: *The aircraft overshot the runway.*

over·shot /ˌəʊvə'ʃɒt/ *adj* ∿ *wheel*, water wheel driven by the pressure of water falling on to it from above.

over·side /'əʊvəsaɪd/ *adv* over the side (of a ship, etc): *discharge cargo* ∿, eg into lighters, not on to the quay.

over·sight /'əʊvəsaɪt/ *n* **1** [U] failure to notice sth; [C] instance of this: *Through an unfortunate* ∿ *your letter was left unanswered.* **2** [U] watchful care: *under the* ∿ *of a nurse.*

over·sim·plify /ˌəʊvə'sɪmplɪfaɪ/ *vt,vi* [VP6A,2A] state (problem, fact, etc) too simply for the truth to be fully told. **over·sim·pli·fi·cation** /ˌəʊvəˌsɪmplɪfɪ'keɪʃn/ *n* [U,C] (instance of) oversimplifying.

over·skirt /'əʊvəskɜːt/ *n* one worn over a skirt.

over·sleep /ˌəʊvə'sliːp/ *vi* (*pt,pp* -slept /-'slept/) [VP2A] sleep too long; continue sleeping after the proper time for waking: *He overslept and was late for work.*

over·spill /'əʊvəspɪl/ *n* sth that spreads into surrounding areas; (esp) excess population: *build new towns for London's* ∿.

over·state /ˌəʊvə'steɪt/ *vt* [VP6A] express or state too strongly; state more than is true about: *Don't* ∿ *your case.* ∿*·ment* /'əʊvəsteɪtmənt/ *n* [U] exaggeration; [C] exaggerated statement.

over·stay /ˌəʊvə'steɪ/ *vt* [VP6A] stay too long. ∿ *one's welcome*, stay until one is no longer a welcome guest.

over·step /ˌəʊvə'step/ *vt* (-pp-) [VP6A] go beyond: ∿ *one's authority.*

over·stock /ˌəʊvə'stɒk/ *vt* [VP6A] supply with too large a stock: ∿ *a farm with cattle*, with more cattle than there is food or space for.

over·strung /ˌəʊvə'strʌŋ/ *adj* **1** (of a person, his nerves) intensely strained; easily excited; too sensitive. **2** (of a piano) with strings crossing obliquely to save space.

over·sub·scribed /ˌəʊvəsəb'skraɪbd/ *adj* (fin) (of an issue of shares, etc) with applications in excess of what is offered.

overt /'əʊvɜːt *US:* əʊ'vɜːrt/ *adj* done or shown openly, publicly: ∿ *hostility.* ∿*·ly adv* ⇨ **covert**.

over·take /ˌəʊvə'teɪk/ *vt* (*pt* -took /-'tʊk/, *pp* -taken /-'teɪkən/) [VP6A] **1** come or catch up with; outstrip: ∿ *other cars on the road;* ∿ *arrears of work.* **2** (of storms, troubles, etc) come upon (sb) suddenly, by surprise: *be* ∿*n by/with fear/surprise/events; be* ∿*n by a storm.*

over·tax /ˌəʊvə'tæks/ *vt* [VP6A] tax too heavily; put too heavy a burden or strain on: ∿ *one's strength/sb's patience.*

over·throw /ˌəʊvə'θrəʊ/ *vt* (*pt* -threw /-'θruː/, *pp* -thrown /-'θrəʊn/) [VP6A] defeat; put an end to; cause to fall or fail: ∿ *the government.* □ *n* /'əʊvəθrəʊ/ ruin; defeat; fall.

over·time /'əʊvətaɪm/ *n* [U], *adv* (time spent at work) after the usual hours: *working* ∿; *be paid extra for* ∿; *be on* ∿, ie working ∿; ∿ *pay.*

over·tone /'əʊvətəʊn/ *n* (music) higher note more faintly heard than the main note produced from a than; rise above: ∿*ped by the new skyscraper.*

over·trump /ˌəʊvə'trʌmp/ *vt* [VP6A] (whist, bridge) play a higher trump than.

over·ture /'əʊvətjʊə(r)/ *n* **1** (often *pl*) approach made (*to* sb) with the aim of starting discussions: *peace* ∿*s; make* ∿*s to sb.* **2** musical composition played as an introduction to an opera, or as a separate item at a concert.

over·turn /ˌəʊvə'tɜːn/ *vt,vi* [VP6A,2A] (cause to) turn over; upset: *He* ∿*ed the boat. The boat* ∿*ed.*

over·ween·ing /ˌəʊvə'wiːnɪŋ/ *adj* having, marked by, excessive self-confidence or conceit: ∿

ambition/vanity.

over·weight /'əʊvəweɪt/ *n* [U] excess of weight above what is usual or legal: *Shopkeepers rarely give* ~. □ *adj* /ˌəʊvə'weɪt/ exceeding the weight allowed or normal: *an* ~ *bag. If your luggage is* ~ *you'll have to pay extra. Your suitcase is five kilograms* ~. ⇨ underweight. ~**ed** /ˌəʊvə'weɪtɪd/ *part adj* carrying too much weight: ~*ed with packages.*

over·whelm /ˌəʊvə'welm *US*: -'hwelm/ *vt* [VP6A] weigh down; submerge, cover completely by flowing over or pouring down on; crush; destroy; cause to feel confused or embarrassed: *be* ~*ed by the enemy/by superior forces; an* ~*ing victory;* ~*ing sorrow; be* ~*ed by a flood; be* ~*ed with grief/ gratitude.*

over·work /ˌəʊvə'wɜːk/ *vt, vi* [VP6A,2A] (cause to) work too hard or too long: ~ *oneself;* ~ *a horse. It's foolish to* ~. □ *n* /'əʊvəwɜːk/ [U] working too much or too long: *ill through* ~.

over·wrought /ˌəʊvə'rɔːt/ *adj* tired out by too much excitement; in a state of nervous excitement.

ovi·duct /'əʊvɪdʌkt/ *n* (also called *Fallopian tube*) either of two tubes through which ova pass from the ovary to the uterus. ⇨ the illus at reproduce.

ovip·ar·ous /əʊ'vɪpərəs/ *adj* producing young from eggs which hatch outside the body.

ovoid /'əʊvɔɪd/ *adj,* n egg-shaped (object).

ovum /'əʊvəm/ *n* (*pl* ova /'əʊvə/) female germ or sex cell in animals, capable of developing into a new individual when fertilized by male sperm.

owe /əʊ/ *vt, vi* 1 [VP6A,12A,13A,2A,3A] **owe sb sth; owe sth to sb; owe for sth,** be in debt to (sb) (for sth): *He owes his father £50. He owes £50 to his father. I have paid all that was owing. He still owes for the goods he had last month.* 2 [VP12A,13A] be under an obligation to, feel the necessity of gratitude to: *I owe a great deal to my parents and teachers. I owe it to you that I am still alive.* 3 [VP12A,13A] be bound to give as a duty: *owe reverence and obedience to the Pope.* 4 [VP14] **owe sth to sb,** be indebted to as the source of: *He owes his success to good luck more than to ability. To whom do we owe the discovery of penicillin?* ·

ow·ing /'əʊɪŋ/ *adj* still to be paid: *large sums still* ~. ~ **to** *prep* because of; on account of: *O*~ *to the rain the match was cancelled.*

owl /aʊl/ *n* night-flying bird that lives on small birds and animals, eg mice. ⇨ the illus at prey. **ow·let** /'aʊlɪt/ *n* young owl. **owl·ish** /'aʊlɪʃ/ *adj* of or like an owl; looking, or trying to look, solemn and wise. **owl·ish·ly** *adv*

own¹ /əʊn/ *adj, pron* 1 (used with possessives, either attributively or predicatively, to give emphasis to the idea of personal possession, to the peculiar or individual character of sth): *I saw it with my own eyes. It was her own idea. This is my own house/This house is my own,* belongs to me, is not rented. *This fruit has a flavour all its own,* is not to be compared to the flavour of any other fruit. *May I have it for my very own,* Are you willing to let me be the sole owner, so that I need not share it? *My time is my own,* I can spend it as I wish. *For reasons of his own* (= For particular reasons, reasons perhaps only known to him), *he refused to join the club.* **(be) (all) on one's own, (a)** alone: *I'm all on my own today. She lives on her own,* alone, not with family or friends. **(b)** independently of an employer; without supervision: *He's* (*working*) *on his own. He can be left to work on his own.*

(c) outstanding; excellent: *For craftsmanship, Smith is on his own,* has no equal. **own brother/ sister,** with both parents the same, not a half-brother/sister. **be one's own man/master,** be independent; be self-employed. **come into one's own,** receive what rightly belongs to one, the credit, fame, etc that one deserves: *Along unpaved and rutted tracks, this sturdy car really comes into its own,* shows what it is capable of. **,get one's 'own back,** have one's revenge. **,hold one's 'own (against sb/sth), (a)** maintain one's position against attack; not be defeated. **(b)** not lose strength: *The patient is holding her own.* 2 (used to indicate the idea of personal activity; done or produced by and for oneself): *She makes all her own clothes. I can cook my own meals. It's unwise to try to be your own lawyer.*

own² /əʊn/ *vt, vi* 1 [VP6A] possess; have as property: *This house is mine; I own it. Who owns this land,* To whom does it belong? 2 [VP6A,9,2C,3B] ~ **(to)** agree; confess; recognize: *own that a claim is justified; own to having told a lie; own one's faults; own oneself* (*to be*) *defeated; own the force of an argument. The man refused to own the child,* would not admit that he was its father. *I must own myself no* (= confess that I am not a) *supporter of reform.* **own up (to sth),** confess fully and frankly.

owner /'əʊnə(r)/ *n* person who owns sth: *Who's the* ~ *of this house?* ~-'**occupied** *adj* (of a house, etc) lived in by the ~ (not rented to sb else). ~- '**occupier** *n* one who owns the house he lives in. ~-'**driven** *adj* (of a vehicle) driven regularly by the ~. ~-'**driver** *n* motorist who drives a car which he owns. ~-**less** *adj* without an ~, not known to belong to anyone: ~*less dogs.* '~-**ship** /-ʃɪp/ *n* [U] state of being an ~; right of possessing: *land of uncertain* ~*ship.*

ox /ɒks/ *n* (*pl* oxen /'ɒksn/) 1 general name for domestic cattle. ⇨ bull¹(1), bullock, cow¹(1). ⇨ the illus at domestic. 2 (esp) fully grown castrated bullock, used as a draught animal. '**ox-eye** *n* name (often used *attrib*) of several kinds of plants (daisies, wild chrysanthemums, etc). ,**ox-'eyed** *adj* with large, round eyes like those of an ox. '**ox-tail** *n* tail of ox, much used for soup, etc.

Ox·bridge /'ɒksbrɪdʒ/ *n* (invented name for) Oxford and/or Cambridge (contrasted with *Redbrick,* ⇨ red(3)).

Ox·ford /'ɒksfəd/ *n* university city in England. ~ **bags,** trousers with very wide legs. ~ **blue,** dark, purplish blue. **the** ~ **Movement,** religious movement (19th c) advocating the revival of Catholicism within the Anglican church. ~ **shoes,** low shoes lacing over the instep.

ox·ide /'ɒksaɪd/ *n* [C,U] compound of oxygen: *iron* ~; ~ *of tin.* **oxi·dize** /'ɒksɪdaɪz/ *vt, vi* [VP6A,2A] (cause to) combine with oxygen; make or become rusty. **oxi·diz·ation** /ˌɒksɪdaɪ'zeɪʃn *US*: -dɪ'z-/ *n*

Ox·on·ian /ɒk'səʊnɪən/ *n, adj* (member) of the University of Oxford.

oxy·acety·lene /ˌɒksɪə'setəliːn/ *adj, n* (of a) mixture of oxygen and acetylene: ~ *torch/blowpipe,* tool burning ~; ~ *welding,* by means of a hot flame of ~.

oxy·gen /'ɒksɪdʒən/ *n* [U] chemical element (symbol **O**), gas without colour, taste, or smell, present in the air and necessary to the existence of all forms of life. '~ **mask,** mask placed over the nose and mouth to supply ~, eg in an aircraft at a

oxyacetylene welding

great altitude. '~ **tent,** small tent or canopy placed over the head and shoulders of a patient who needs an extra supply of ~. '~·**ate** /-eɪt/, '~·**ize** /-aɪz/ *vt* supply, treat, or mix, with ~.

oyez /əʊˈjez/ (also **oyes** /əʊˈjes/) *int* cry meaning 'Listen', repeated three times by (hist) a town-crier, or (in a law court) by an usher to demand silence and attention.

oy·ster /ˈɔɪstə(r)/ *n* kinds of shellfish much used as food, usu eaten uncooked. ⇨ the illus at **bivalve.** '~-**bar** *n* counter (in a restaurant, etc) where ~s are served. '~-**bed,** '~-**bank** *nn* part of the sea-bottom where ~s breed or are bred. '~-**catcher** *n* wading seabird.

ozone /ˈəʊzəʊn/ *n* [U] form of oxygen with a sharp and refreshing smell; (fig) exhilarating influence; (colloq) pure refreshing air as at the seaside.

Pp

P, p /piː/ (*pl* P's, p's /piːz/) the 16th letter of the English alphabet. **mind one's p's and q's,** be careful not to offend against propriety.

pa /pɑː/ *n* (colloq) short for papa.

pabu·lum /ˈpæbjʊləm/ *n* [U] food (usu fig): *mental* ~, food for thought.

pace /peɪs/ *n* [C] **1** (distance covered by the foot in a) single step in walking or running. **2** rate of walking or running, or (fig) progress. **go at a good** ~, go fast. **go the** ~, (a) go at great speed. (b) (fig) spend money freely (esp on pleasure or in dissipated ways). **keep** ~ (**with sb/sth**), (lit or fig) go forward at the same rate: *He finds it hard to keep* ~ *with all the developments in nuclear physics.* **set the** ~ (**for sb**), set a speed for sb. '~-**maker** *n* (a) (also '~-**setter**) rider, runner, etc who sets the ~ for another in a race. (b) electronic device (with radioactive core) to correct weak or irregular heart beats. **3** *(esp of horses)* way of walking, running, etc. **put a person through his** ~**s,** test his abilities, etc. □ *vi,vt* **1** [VP2A,C] walk with slow or regular steps: ~ *up and down;* (of a horse) amble; go at an easy, unhurried ~. **2** [VP6A] move across in this way: ~ *a room; pacing the station platform.* **3** [VP15B] ~ *sth off/out,* measure it by taking ~s: ~ *off a distance of 30 metres;* ~ *out a room.* **4** [VP6A] set the ~ for (a rider or runner in a race).

pachy·derm /ˈpækɪdɜːm/ *n* (kinds of) thick-skinned, four-footed animal, eg an elephant.

pa·ci·fic /pəˈsɪfɪk/ *adj* peaceful; making or loving peace. **pa·ci·fi·cally** /-klɪ/ *adv*

paci·fi·ca·tion /ˌpæsɪfɪˈkeɪʃn/ *n* [U] making or becoming peaceful; bringing about a state of peace.

paci·fism /ˈpæsɪfɪzəm/ *n* [U] principle that war should and could be abolished. **paci·fist** /-ɪst/ *n* believer in ~.

pac·ify /ˈpæsɪfaɪ/ *vt* (*pt,pp* -fied) [VP6A] calm and quieten; end violence in.

pack¹ /pæk/ *n* **1** bundle of things tied or wrapped up together for carrying; (US) packet: *a* ~ *of cigarettes.* '~-**horse,** '~-**animal** *nn* one used for carrying ~s. '~-**saddle** *n* one with straps for supporting ~s. '~-**thread** *n* [U] strong thread for sewing or tying up ~s or canvas bags. **2** number of dogs kept for hunting (*a* ~ *of hounds*) or of wild animals that go about together: *Wolves hunt in* ~s. **3** (usu contemptuous) number of things or persons: *a* ~ *of thieves/liars/lies.* **4** complete set (usu 52) of playing-cards. **5** (Rugby football) a side's forwards. **6** '~-**ice** *n* [U] mass of large pieces of float-ing ice in the sea. **7** quantity of fish, meat, fruit, etc packed in a season: *this year's* ~ *of salmon.* ⇨ pack²(5).

pack² /pæk/ *vt,vi* [VP6A,14,15A,B,2A,C] ~ (*up*) (*in/into*), put (things) into a box, bundle, bag, etc; fill (a bag, box, etc) with things; get ready for a journey by doing this: ~ *clothes into a trunk;* ~ *a trunk with clothes. Have you* ~*ed* (*up*) *your things? You must begin* ~*ing at once. These books* ~ *easily,* It is easy to ~ them. *Her husband takes a* ~*ed lunch* (eg sandwiches, etc ~ed into a box or other container) *to work every day.* ~ **one's bags,** (lit or fig) prepare to leave. ~ **it in,** (sl) give up doing sth; end it. ~ **up,** (colloq) put one's tools, etc away; stop working: *It's time to* ~ *up. One of the aircraft's engines* ~*ed up,* (sl) failed. **2** [VP14,3D] ~ **into,** crush or crowd together (into a place or period of time): ~*ing people into an already over-crowded bus; crowds* ~*ing into the cinemas on a wet day. She managed to* ~ *a lot of sightseeing into the short time she had in London.* **3** [VP6A,15A] put soft material into or round (sth) to keep it safe, or to prevent loss or leakage: *glass* ~*ed in straw;* ~ *a leaking joint.* **4** ~ *sb off; send sb* ~*ing,* send him away quickly and unceremoniously (because he is troublesome, etc): *I wish you'd* ~ *yourself off,* go away. **5** [VP6A] prepare and put (meat, fruit, etc) in tins for preservation. ⇨ pack¹(7). **6** [VP6A] choose (the members of a committee, etc) so that their decisions are likely to be in one's favour. ~**er** *n* person or machine that ~s; (esp, usu *pl*) person who ~s meat, fruit, etc for market.

pack·age /ˈpækɪdʒ/ *n* [C] parcel of things, packed together; (fig, colloq) detailed plan. ~ **deal/offer** *n* (colloq) number of proposals for discussion or acceptance. '~ **tour,** (colloq) holiday tour with many details arranged in advance by travel agents and sold at a fixed price. □ *vt* place in a ~; make a ~ of.

packet /ˈpækɪt/ *n* **1** small parcel or bundle: *a* ~ *of letters; a postal* ~; *a* ~ *of 20 cigarettes.* **2** '~(-**boat),** mailboat. **3** (sl) considerable sum of money: *make/cost a* ~. **4** (army sl) trouble of some sort: *catch/stop/get a* ~, (esp) be severely wounded.

pack·ing /ˈpækɪŋ/ *n* [U] process of packing (goods); materials used in packing(3), eg for closing a leaking joint. '~-**case** *n* one of rough boards in which goods are packed for shipment. '~-**needle** *n* large needle used for sewing up canvas packages, etc.

pact /pækt/ n compact; agreement: *the P~ of Locarno; a new Peace P~.*

pad[1] /pæd/ n **1** mass of, container filled with, soft material, used to prevent damage, give comfort or improve the shape of sth. **2** guard for the leg or other parts of the body (in cricket and other games). ⇨ the illus at cricket. **3** number of sheets of writing-paper fastened together along one edge. **4** (also **'ink-pad**) absorbent material (usu in an oblong box) used for inking rubber stamps. **5** soft, fleshy underpart of the foot (of a dog, fox, etc). **6** (usu **'launching pad**) platform from which missiles are launched into outer space. ⇨ the illus at rocket. **7** (sl) bed; room to sleep in; apartment. □ vt (-dd-) **1** [VP6A] put pads(1) in or on (to prevent injury, to give comfort, or to fill out hollow spaces, etc): *a jacket with padded shoulders; a padded cell*, one with padded walls (in a mental hospital). **2** [VP6A,15B] **pad sth out**, make (a sentence, essay, book, etc) longer by using unnecessary material: *an essay padded out with numerous quotations*. **pad·ding** /'pædɪŋ/ n [U] material used for making pads(1) or for padding(v, 2).

pad[2] /pæd/ vi,vt (-dd-) [VP2A,C] travel on foot: *padding along;* [VP6A] tramp (the roads) on foot: *He lost all his money and had to pad it home.*

paddle[1] /'pædl/ n **1** short oar with a broad blade at one or (*double ~*) at both ends, used (without a rowlock) to propel a canoe through the water. ⇨ the illus at canoe. **2** (in rowing) act or period of propelling a boat with light, easy strokes. **3** '**~-box** n wooden covering for the upper part of a ~-wheel. '**~-steamer** n steam vessel propelled by ~-wheels. '**~-wheel** n one of a pair of wheels, each with boards round the circumference which press backwards against the water and propel a ~-steamer. **4** ~-shaped instrument (eg one used for beating, stirring or mixing things). □ vt,vi [VP6A,2A] send (a canoe) through the water by using a ~ or ~s; row with light, easy strokes. ~ **one's own canoe**, (colloq) depend on oneself alone.

paddle[2] /'pædl/ vi [VP2A] walk with bare feet in shallow water (as children do at the seaside): *a 'paddling pool*, shallow pool (eg in a public park) where children ~. □ n act or period of paddling.

pad·dock /'pædək/ n **1** small grass field, esp one used for exercising horses. **2** (at a race-course) enclosed area of grassland where horses are assembled and paraded before a race.

paddy[1] /'pædɪ/ n [U] rice that is still growing; rice in the husk. '**~-field** n rice-field.

paddy[2] /'pædɪ/ n (pl -dies) (colloq) rage; fit of bad temper: *She's in one of her paddies*, one of the fits of bad temper to which she is subject.

Paddy /'pædɪ/ n (nickname for an) Irishman. '**~-wagon**, (US sl) police van for taking persons suspected of crime into custody.

pad·lock /'pædlɒk/ n lock of the kind shown here. □ vt [VP6A] fasten with a ~: *The gate was ~ed.*

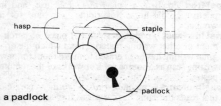
a padlock

padre /'pɑːdreɪ/ n (army and navy colloq) chaplain; (GB colloq) priest; parson.

paean, (US) **pean** /'piːən/ n song of thanksgiving, praise or triumph.

paed·er·asty /'pedəræstɪ/ n = pederasty.

paedi·at·rics /ˌpiːdɪ'ætrɪks/=pediatrics.

pae·ony /'piːənɪ/ n = peony.

pa·gan /'peɪgən/ n, adj (person who is) not a believer in any of the chief religions of the world. ~**ism** /-ɪzəm/ n [U] beliefs, practices, of ~s.

page[1] /peɪdʒ/ n one side of a leaf of paper in a book, periodical, etc; entire leaf of a book, etc: *Several ~s have been torn out.* □ vt number the ~s of.

page[2] /peɪdʒ/ n **1** (also '**~ boy**) boy servant, usu in uniform, in a hotel, club, etc. **2** (in the Middle Ages) boy in training for knighthood and living in a knight's household. □ vt [VP6A] call by name, by means of, or as if by means of (eg over a loudspeaker), a page(1).

pag·eant /'pædʒənt/ n **1** public entertainment, usu outdoors, in which historical events are acted in the costume of the period. **2** public celebration, esp one in which there is a procession of persons in fine costumes (eg a coronation). ~**ry** /'pædʒəntrɪ/ n [U] rich and splendid display.

pagi·na·tion /ˌpædʒɪ'neɪʃn/ n [U] (figures used for the) numbering of the pages of a book.

pagodas

pa·goda /pə'gəʊdə/ n (in India, Nepal, Ceylon, Burma, China, Japan, etc) religious building, typically a sacred tower of pyramidal form (Hindu temple), or of several storeys (Buddhist tower).

pah /pɑː/ int expressing disgust.

paid /peɪd/ ⇨ pay[2].

pail /peɪl/ n vessel, usu round and open, of metal or wood, for carrying liquid: *a ~ of milk.* '**~·ful** /-fʊl/ n as much as a ~ holds.

pail·lasse, **pail·liasse** /'pælɪæs US: ˌpælɪ'æs/ nn mattress filled with straw.

pain /peɪn/ n **1** [U] suffering of mind or body: *be in (great) ~; cry with ~; feel some/no/not much/a great deal of ~.* '**~-killer** n medicine for lessening ~. **2** [C] particular or localized kind of bodily suffering: *a ~ in the knee; ~s in the back; stomach ~s. a ~ in the neck,* (sl) irritating person. **3** [U,C] (old use) punishment; penalty: *(legal phrase) ~s and penalties.* **on/under ~ of death,** at the risk of being sentenced to death. □ vt [VP6A] cause ~ to: *Doesn't your laziness ~ your parents? My foot is still ~ing me. ~ed adj distressed: She looked ~ed when I refused to help. She had a ~ed look.* '**~-ful** /-fl/ adj causing ~: *This duty is ~ful to me.* '**~-fully** /-fəlɪ/ adv ~**-less** adj without ~; causing no ~: *~less extractions,* (of teeth). ~**-less·ly** adv

pains /peɪnz/ n pl trouble; effort: *work hard and get very little for all one's ~*. *be at ~ to do sth*, make a great effort, work hard, to do it. *spare no ~*, do everything possible. *take (great) ~ (over sth/to do sth)*, take great trouble: *take great ~ to please one's lover*. '~·**taking** adj careful; industrious.

paint /peɪnt/ n **1** [U] solid colouring matter (to be) mixed with oil or other liquid and used to give colour to a surface: *give the doors two coats of ~*. **2** [U] material used to colour the face. **3** (pl) collection of tubes or cakes of colouring materials. '~·**box** n box with such a collection. '~·**brush** n brush for applying ~. ⇨ the illus at palette. □ vt,vi **1** [VP6A,22] coat with paint: ~ *a door*; ~ *the gate green*. ~ *the town red*, (colloq) go out and have a lively, exciting time esp when celebrating sth. **2** [VP6A,15A,B,2A,C] make a picture (of) with paint: ~ *flowers/a landscape*; ~ *in oils/in watercolours*. ~ *sth in*, add to a picture: ~ *in the foreground*. ~ *sth out*, cover up or hide by using paint. **3** [VP6A,22] (fig) describe vividly in words. *not so black as one is ~ed*, not so bad as one is represented to be.

painter¹ /'peɪntə(r)/ n **1** person who paints pictures; artist. **2** workman who paints woodwork, walls, buildings, ships, etc.

painter² /'peɪntə(r)/ n rope fastened to the bow of a boat by which it may be tied to a ship, pier, etc. ⇨ the illus at sail. *cut the ~*, **(a)** set (a boat, etc) adrift. **(b)** (fig), effect a separation; become independent.

paint·ing /'peɪntɪŋ/ n **1** [U] using paint; occupation of a painter. **2** [C] painted picture.

pair /peə(r)/ n **1** two things of the same kind (to be) used together: *a ~ of shoes/gloves; two ~s of socks*. **2** single article with two parts always joined: *a ~ of trousers/tights/scissors/tongs*. **3** two persons closely associated, eg an engaged or married couple: *the happy ~*, eg two newly married persons. *in ~s*, in twos. **4** two animals of opposite sex; two horses harnessed together. **5** (in Parliament) two persons of opposite political parties who absent themselves from a division(6) by mutual agreement; one member willing to do this: *The member for Lewisham couldn't find a ~*. □ vt,vi [VP6A,15B,2A,C] form a ~ or ~s; join in ~s; (of animals) mate. ~ *off*, put in ~s; go off in ~s; (in Parliament) make a ~(5).

pais·ley /'peɪzlɪ/ n [U] (soft wool fabric with) curved patterns in bright colours: *a ~ shawl*.

pa·ja·mas /pə'dʒɑːməz/ n pl ⇨ pyjamas.

pal /pæl/ n (colloq) comrade; friend. □ vi (-ll-) *pal up (with sb)*, become friendly. **pally** /'pælɪ/ adj (colloq) friendly.

pal·ace /'pælɪs/ n **1** official residence of a sovereign, archbishop or bishop; any large and splendid house; large, splendid building for entertainment. **2** *the ~*, influential persons at the ~ of a sovereign ruler. ~ *revolution*, overthrow of sb in a position of great power, eg a President, by high-ranking colleagues or close subordinates.

pala·din /'pælədɪn/ n any of the twelve Peers of the court of Emperor Charlemagne /'ʃɑːləmeɪn/, AD 742—814; knight errant; notable champion.

palaeo- /'pælɪəʊ- US: 'peɪlɪəʊ-/ pref (in compounds, etc) = paleo-.

palan·quin, palan·keen /ˌpælən'kiːn/ nn covered litter for one person, carried on poles by two or more men, as formerly used in India and other Eastern countries.

pal·at·able /'pælətəbl/ adj agreeable to the taste or (fig) to the mind.

pala·tal /'pælətl/ n, adj (sound) made by placing the tongue against or near (usu the hard) palate (eg /j, 3, ʃ, dʒ/); of the palate.

pal·ate /'pælət/ n **1** roof of the mouth: *the hard/soft ~*, its front/back part. ˌ**cleft** '~, ⇨ cleave¹(3). ⇨ the illus at mouth. **2** sense of taste: *have a good ~ for fine wines*.

pa·la·tial /pə'leɪʃl/ adj of or like a palace; magnificent: *a ~ residence*.

pal·at·in·ate /pə'lætɪnət US: -tənət/ n territory ruled over by an earl or count having some royal privileges.

pal·aver /pə'lɑːvə(r) US: -'læv-/ n [C] (hist) talk or conference, esp one between traders or explorers and the people of the country; [U] idle talk; [U,C] (colloq) bother. □ vi [VP2A] talk idly for a long time.

pale¹ /peɪl/ adj (-r, -st) **1** (of a person's face) having little colour; bloodless: *He turned ~ at the news. You're looking ~ today*. '~·**face** n name said to have been used by N American Indians for a European white person. **2** (of colours) not bright; faintly coloured: ~ *blue*. □ vi [VP2A,C] grow ~; lose colour. ~ *before/by the side of*, (fig) be far outdone by; appear weak when seen with. ~·**ly** /'peɪllɪ/ adv ~·**ness** n

pale² /peɪl/ n pointed piece of wood used for fences; stake. ⇨ paling.

pale³ /peɪl/ n (hist) area around Dublin (in Ireland) controlled by the English. Now, only in: *beyond/outside the ~*, socially unacceptable or unreasonable: *His remarks put him quite outside the ~*.

paleo·lithic (also **palaeo-**) /ˌpælɪəʊ'lɪθɪk US: ˌpeɪl-/ adj of the period marked by the use of primitive stone implements.

pale·on·tol·ogy (also **palae-**) /ˌpælɪɒn'tɒlədʒɪ US: ˌpeɪl-/ n [U] study of fossils as a guide to the history of life on earth. **pale·on·tol·ogist** (also **palae-**) /-ədʒɪst/ n

pal·ette /'pælɪt/ n board (with a hole for the thumb) on which an artist mixes his colours. '~·**knife** n thin steel blade with a handle, used (by artists) for mixing (and sometimes spreading) oil colours, (by potters) for moulding clay, and in cookery.

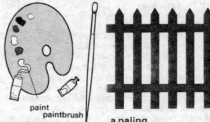

paint
paintbrush
a palette   a paling

pal·frey /'pɔːlfrɪ/ n (pl -freys) (old use, and in poetry) saddle-horse for riding, esp one for a woman.

pal·imp·sest /'pælɪmpsest/ n [C] piece of parchment or other writing material from which the original writing has been erased to make room for new writing, esp as a source for lost works of the remote past.

pal·in·drome /'pælɪndrəʊm/ n word, verse, etc that reads the same backwards as forwards, eg ma-

dam.

pal·ing /'peɪlɪŋ/ *n* fence made of pales².

pali·sade /ˌpælɪ'seɪd/ *n* **1** fence of strong, pointed wooden stakes (eg as used to defend a building in former times). **2** (*pl*) (US) line of high, steep cliffs (esp along a river). □ *vt* [VP6A] enclose or fortify with a ∼(1).

pal·ish /'peɪlɪʃ/ *adj* somewhat pale.

pall¹ /pɔːl/ *n* **1** heavy cloth spread over a coffin. '∼-bearer *n* person who helps to carry, or who walks alongside, a coffin at a funeral. **2** (fig) any dark, heavy covering: *a* ∼ *of smoke.*

pall² /pɔːl/ *vi* [VP2A,3A] ∼ (*on/upon*), become distasteful or boring because done, used, etc for too long a time: *pleasures that* ∼ *after a time; a long lecture that* ∼*ed upon most of the listeners.*

pal·let /'pælɪt/ *n* **1** straw-filled mattress for sleeping on. **2** large tray or platform for moving loads (by means of slings, etc), eg from a lorry into a train or on to a ship, and so save handling of separate items.

pal·li·asse /'pælɪæs US: ˌpælɪ'æs/ *n* = paillasse.

pal·li·ate /'pælɪeɪt/ *vt* [VP6A] (formal) lessen the severity of (pain, disease); excuse the seriousness of (a crime, etc). **pal·li·ation** /ˌpælɪ'eɪʃn/ *n* [U] the act of palliating; the state of being ∼d; [C] that which ∼s; excuse. **pal·li·ative** /'pælɪətɪv/ *n, adj* (sth) serving to ∼.

pal·lid /'pælɪd/ *adj* pale; ill-looking. ∼·ly *adv* ∼·ness *n*

pal·lor /'pælə(r)/ *n* [U] paleness, esp of the face.

pally ⇨ pal.

palm¹ /pɑːm/ *n* inner surface of the hand between the wrist and the fingers. ⇨ the illus at arm. *grease/oil sb's* ∼, give him a bribe. *have an itching* ∼, be always ready to receive a bribe. □ *vt* [VP6A,15B] hide (a coin, card, etc) in the hand when performing a trick. ∼ *sth off* (*on/upon sb*), get him to accept it by fraud, misrepresentation, etc.

palm² /pɑːm/ *n* **1** sorts of tree growing in warm climates, with no branches and a mass of large wide leaves at the top: *the* '*date-*∼; *the* '*coconut* ∼. '∼-oil *n* [U] oil obtained from the nuts of a W African ∼. '∼ wine *n* [U] W African alcoholic drink, the sap of ∼ trees. *P*∼ '**Sunday**, the Sunday before Easter. **2** leaf of a ∼ as a symbol of victory. *bear/carry off the* ∼, be victorious. *yield the* ∼ (*to sb*), admit defeat (by sb). ∼**y** *adj* (-ier, -iest) flourishing; prosperous: *in my* ∼*y days.* ∼**er** *n* (formerly) pilgrim returning from the Holy Land with a ∼-leaf.

COCONUT PALM

DATE PALM

coconut

date

palms

palm·ist /'pɑːmɪst/ *n* person who claims to tell a person's future by examining the lines on his palm. **palm·is·try** /'pɑːmɪstrɪ/ *n* art of doing this.

pal·metto /pæl'metəʊ/ *n* (*pl* ∼s or ∼es /-təʊz/)

kinds of small palm with fan-shaped leaves, common in the West Indies and the SE coast of the US.

pal·pable /'pælpəbl/ *adj* that can be felt or touched; clear to the mind: *a* ∼ *error.* **pal·pably** /-əblɪ/ *adv*

pal·pi·tate /'pælpɪteɪt/ *vi* [VP2A,C] (of the heart) beat rapidly and irregularly; (of a person, his body) tremble (with terror, etc). **pal·pi·ta·tion** /ˌpælpɪ'teɪʃn/ *n* palpitating of the heart (from disease, great efforts, etc).

palsy /'pɔːlzɪ/ *n* [U] paralysis: *suffering from cerebral* ∼. ⇨ spastic. □ *vt* paralyse.

pal·ter /'pɔːltə(r)/ *vi* [VP3A] ∼ *with,* be insincere when dealing with; trifle with: *Don't* ∼ *with the question,* Do treat it seriously.

pal·try /'pɔːltrɪ/ *adj* (-ier, -iest) worthless; of no importance; contemptible.

pam·pas /'pæmpəs US: -əz/ *n pl* extensive, flat, grassy, treeless plains of S America. ⇨ prairie, savanna, steppe, veld. '∼-grass *n* [U] tall grass with sharp-edged blades and a silvery plume-like flower.

pam·per /'pæmpə(r)/ *vt* [VP6A] indulge too much; be unduly kind to: *a* ∼*ed poodle. She sometimes* ∼*s herself and has a day in bed.*

pamph·let /'pæmflɪt/ *n* [C] small paper-covered book, esp on a question of current interest. ∼·eer /ˌpæmflɪ'tɪə(r)/ *n* writer of ∼s.

pan¹ /pæn/ *n* **1** flat dish, usu shallow and without a cover, used for cooking and other domestic purposes. '**pancake** *n* (a) batter cooked on both sides until brown and (usu) eaten hot. '**Pancake Day,** Shrove Tuesday. (b) **pancake landing,** emergency landing in which the aircraft drops flat to the ground. (c) cosmetic face-powder pressed into a flat cake, used without a foundation cream. **2** receptacle with various uses: *the pan* (= bowl) *of a lavatory; a* '*bedpan,* ⇨ bed¹(6). **3** (natural or artificial) depression in the ground: *a* '*salt-pan,* where salt water is evaporated. **4** '**brain-pan,** upper part of the skull, enclosing the brain. **5** either of the dishes on a pair of scales. ⇨ the illus at balance. **6** open dish for washing gravel, etc to separate gold ore or other metals. **7** (in flintlock guns) cavity in the lock that holds the gunpowder. *a flash in the pan,* ⇨ flash¹(1). **8** [U] ('**hard-**)**pan,** hard subsoil. **9** (sl) face. □ *vt,vi* (-nn-) **1** [VP15B,3A,2C] *pan sth off/out,* wash (gold-bearing gravel, etc) in a pan. *pan for,* wash gravel, etc for eg gold. ∼ *out,* (a) yield gold. (b) (fig) succeed; turn out: *How did things pan out? The scheme panned out well.* **2** [VP6A] (colloq) criticize harshly.

pan² /pæn/ *vi,vt* (cinema and TV) turn a camera right or left to follow a moving object or get a panoramic effect. ⇨ zoom(2).

pan- *pref* ⇨ App 3.

pana·cea /ˌpænə'sɪə/ *n* remedy for all troubles, diseases, etc.

pa·nache /pæ'næʃ US: pə-/ *n* [U] confident and flamboyant manner: *There was an air of* ∼ *about everything he did.*

pa·nama /'pænəmɑː/ *n* ∼ (**hat**), hat made from fine pliant straw-like material from the leaves of a plant of S and Central America.

pana·tella /ˌpænə'telə/ *n* [C] long slender cigar.

pan·chro·matic /ˌpænkrə'mætɪk/ *adj* (photo) equally sensitive to all colours: ∼ *film.*

pan·creas /'pæŋkrɪəs/ *n* [C] gland near the stomach, discharging a juice which helps digestion. ⇨ the illus at alimentary. **pan·cre·atic**

/ˌpæŋkrɪˈætɪk/ *adj* of the ~.

panda /ˈpændə/ *n* bear-like mammal of Tibet, with black legs and a black and white body. '**P~ car** *n* (GB) police patrol car. '**P~ crossing** *n* (GB) road crossing controlled by flashing lights, operated by pedestrians who press a button on a post.

pan·demic /pænˈdemɪk/ *n, adj* (disease) prevalent over the whole of a country or continent.

pan·de·mo·nium /ˌpændɪˈməʊnɪəm/ *n* [C,U] (scene of) wild and noisy disorder.

pan·der /ˈpændə(r)/ *vi* [VP3A] ~ **to, 1** give help or encouragement (to sb, to his passions and desires): *newspapers that ~ to the public interest in crime; ~ to low tastes.* **2** act as a go-between (eg to sb's sexual desires). ⇨ procure(3), the more usu word now. □ *n* person who ~s(2).

pane /peɪn/ *n* single sheet of glass in (a division of) a window. ⇨ the illus at window.

pan·egyric /ˌpænɪˈdʒɪrɪk/ *n* [C] speech, piece of writing, praising a person or event.

panel /ˈpænl/ *n* **1** separate part of the surface of a door, wall, ceiling, etc usu raised above or sunk below the surrounding area. **2** piece of material of a different kind or colour inserted in a dress. **3** board or other surface for controls and instruments: '*instrument* ~, of an aircraft or motor-vehicle; *con'trol* ~, on a radio or TV set. **4** list of names, eg of men who may be summoned to serve on a jury. **5** group of speakers, esp one chosen to speak, answer questions, take part in a game, before an audience, eg of listeners to a broadcast: (attrib) *a '~ discussion/game.* □ *vt* (-ll-, US -l-) furnish or decorate with ~s(1,2): *a ~led room/wall/wainscot.* **~·ling** *n* [U] series of ~s on a wall, etc.

pang /pæŋ/ *n* sharp, sudden feeling of pain, remorse, etc.

panga /ˈpæŋɡə/ *n* large chopping knife used by African workers.

pan·handle /ˈpænhændl/ *n* (US) narrow strip of land projecting from a larger area. □ *vi* (US colloq) beg, esp on the streets.

panic /ˈpænɪk/ *n* [C,U] **1** unreasoning, uncontrolled, quickly spreading fear: *There is always danger of (a) ~ when a cinema catches fire.* '**~stricken** *adj* terrified; overcome by ~: *The crowd was ~-stricken,* filled with ~. **2** (attrib) unreasoning: ~ *fear.* □ *vi* (-ck-) be affected with ~: *Don't ~! There's no danger!* **pan·icky** /ˈpænɪkɪ/ *adj* (colloq) easily affected by ~; in a state of ~.

pan·jan·drum /pænˈdʒændrəm/ *n* name applied jokingly to an exalted personage or to a pompous official.

pan·nier /ˈpænɪə(r)/ *n* one of a pair of baskets placed across the back of a horse or donkey; one of a pair of bags on either side of the back of a (motor-)cycle.

pan·ni·kin /ˈpænɪkɪn/ *n* (GB) small metal cup; its contents.

pan·oply /ˈpænəplɪ/ *n* (*pl* -plies) complete suit of armour; (fig) splendid array. Hence, **pan·oplied** /ˈpænəplɪd/ *adj* provided with a ~.

pan·op·tic /pænˈɒptɪk/ *adj* giving a complete view, eg by diagram, illustration, of sth.

pan·or·ama /ˌpænəˈrɑːmə *US*: -ˈræmə/ *n* wide, uninterrupted view; constantly changing scene: *the ~ of London life.* **pan·or·amic** /ˌpænəˈræmɪk/ *adj*

pan·pipes /ˈpæn paɪps/ *n pl* musical instrument made of a series of reeds or pipes, played by blowing across the open ends.

pansy /ˈpænzɪ/ *n* (*pl* -sies) **1** flowering herbaceous plant. **2** ⚠ (derog, offensive term for) effeminate man; homosexual.

pant /pænt/ *vi, vt* **1** [VP2A,C] take short, quick breaths; gasp: *The dog ~ed along behind its master's horse.* **2** [VP6A,15B] say while ~ing: *He ~ed out his message.* **3** [VP3A] ~ **for,** (old use) have a strong wish for. □ *n* short, quick breath; gasp. **~·ing·ly** *adv*

pan·ta·loon /ˌpæntəˈluːn/ *n* **1** (in pantomime) foolish character upon whom the clown plays tricks. **2** (*pl*) (now hum, or US) = pants.

pan·tech·ni·con /pænˈteknɪkən/ *n* (GB) large van for removing furniture.

pan·the·ism /ˈpænθɪɪzəm/ *n* [U] belief that God is in everything and that everything is God; belief in and worship of all gods. **pan·the·ist** /-ɪst/ *n* believer in ~. **pan·the·is·tic** /ˌpænθɪˈɪstɪk/ *adj* of ~.

pan·theon /ˈpænθɪən *US*: -ˈθɪɒn/ *n* temple dedicated to all the gods: *the P~ in Rome;* all the gods of a nation collectively: *the (ancient) Egyptian ~;* building in which the illustrious dead are buried or have memorials.

pan·ther /ˈpænθə(r)/ *n* black leopard; (US) puma. ⇨ the illus at cat.

pan·ties /ˈpæntɪz/ *n pl* **1** short trousers worn by children. **2** (woman's or girl's) close-fitting short drawers.

pan·tile /ˈpæntaɪl/ *n* curved roof tile: (attrib) *a ~ roof.*

panto /ˈpæntəʊ/ *n* (colloq abbr of) pantomime.

pan·to·graph /ˈpæntəɡrɑːf *US*: -græf/ *n* **1** device for copying a plan, etc on a different scale. **2** device for carrying electric current to a vehicle from overhead wires.

pan·to·mime /ˈpæntəmaɪm/ *n* **1** [C,U] (example of a) kind of English drama based on a fairy tale or traditional story, with music, dancing and clowning. **2** [U] acting without words.

pan·try /ˈpæntrɪ/ *n* (*pl* -tries) **1** room (in a large house, hotel, ship, etc) in which silver, glass, table-linen, etc are kept. '**~·man** /-mən/ *n* (*pl* -men) butler or his assistant. **2** larder; room (in a house) in which food is kept.

pants /pænts/ *n pl* **1** (GB) underpants; (US) trousers. *bore/scare/talk, etc the '~ off one,* bore, etc one extremely. *catch sb with his '~ down,* find him in an unprepared state.

panty-hose /ˈpæntɪ həʊz/ *n* = tights.

pan·zer /ˈpæntsə(r)/ *attrib adj* (G) armoured: '*~ divisions/troops.*

pap /pæp/ *n* [U] soft or semi-liquid food for very young children or invalids; (fig) easy, trivial reading matter.

papa /pəˈpɑː *US*: ˈpɑːpə/ *n* (child's word for) father.

pa·pacy /ˈpeɪpəsɪ/ *n* (*pl* -cies) position of, author-

cycle panniers | donkey panniers

ity of, the Pope; system of government by Popes.
pa·pal /'peɪpl/ adj of the Pope or the ∼.

pa·paw, paw·paw /pəˈpɔː *US:* ˈpɔːpɔː/ n 1 tropical tree with a straight trunk like that of a palm; its large edible fruit with yellow pulp inside. ⇨ the illus at fruit. 2 small N American evergreen tree with small fleshy edible fruit (also called *custard apple*).
pa·paya /pəˈpaɪə/ n = papaw.

pa·per /'peɪpə(r)/ n 1 [U] substance manufactured from wood fibre, rags, etc in the form of sheets, used for writing, printing, drawing, wrapping, packing, etc: *a sheet of* ∼; *a* ∼ *bag. (be/look) good on* ∼, (be/look) good when judged from written or printed evidence, eg plans, proposals, diplomas, testimonials: *a good scheme on* ∼ (but not yet tested). *This applicant looks good on* ∼, has good ∼ qualifications. *put pen to* ∼, (dated for) begin to write, eg a letter. '∼-backed adj (of books) bound in paper covers. Hence, '∼-back n such a book and such a form: *Has the book appeared in* ∼*back?* '∼-chase n ⇨ hare and hounds, at hare. '∼-clip n = clip¹(1). '∼-hanger n man whose trade is to paste ∼ on the walls of rooms. '∼-knife n one for cutting open the leaves of books, opening envelopes, etc. '∼-mill n one where ∼ is made. ∼ 'tiger n person, group of persons, etc which seems to be, but is not, powerful. '∼-weight n weight placed on loose ∼s to prevent them from being blown away. '∼-work n [U] written work (in an office, etc, eg filling in forms, correspondence, contrasted with practical affairs, dealing with people): *He's good at* ∼*-work.* 2 [C] newspaper: *today's* ∼*s; the evening* ∼. 3 [U] ∼ money, banknotes, etc used as currency. 4 (pl) documents showing who sb is, what authority he has, etc: *send in one's* ∼*s,* (mil) resign. 5 [C] set of printed examination questions on a given subject: *The biology* ∼ *was difficult.* 6 [C] essay, esp one to be read to a learned society: *a* ∼ *on currency reform.* □ vt [VP6A,15B] paste ∼ on (walls, etc): ∼ *the dining-room;* cover with ∼. ∼ *over the cracks,* (fig) cover up, conceal, faults, etc. ∼ *the house,* (fig) issue free tickets for a theatre, etc (to give the impression of success).
pa·pier-mâché /ˌpæpɪeɪ ˈmæʃeɪ *US:* ˌpeɪpər məˈʃeɪ/ n [U] paper pulped and used as a plastic material for making trays, boxes, etc.
pa·pist /'peɪpɪst/ n, adj (unfriendly word, as used by some Protestants) (member) of the Roman Catholic Church.
pa·poose /pəˈpuːs *US:* pæˈpuːs/ n (word used by Indians of N America for a) baby; framed bag (like a rucksack) for carrying a young baby on sb's back.
pap·rika /'pæprɪkə *US:* ˈpæˈpriːkə/ n [U] sweet red pepper used in cooking. ⇨ the illus at vegetable.
pa·py·rus /pəˈpaɪərəs/ n 1 [U] (kind of paper made in ancient Egypt from) tall water plant or reed. 2 [C] (pl papyri /pəˈpaɪəraɪ/) manuscript written on this paper.
par¹ /pɑː(r)/ n [U] average or normal amount, degree, value, etc. *above/below/at par,* (of shares, bonds, etc), above/below/at the original price or face value. *on a par (with),* equal (to). *up to par,* (colloq) as good/well as usual. *par of exchange,* normal rate of exchange between two currencies, eg the £ and the US $. *par value,* nominal or face value of a share. 2 (golf) number of strokes considered necessary for a good player to complete a hole or course.
par² /pɑː(r)/ ⇨ parr.

par·able /'pærəbl/ n simple story designed to teach a moral lesson: *speak in* ∼*s. Jesus taught in* ∼*s.*
para·boli·cal /ˌpærəˈbɒlɪkl/ adj of, expressed in, ∼s.
par·ab·ola /pəˈræbələ/ n plane curve formed by cutting a cone on a plane parallel to its side, so that the two arms get farther away from one another. **para·bolic** /ˌpærəˈbɒlɪk/ adj of, like, a ∼.
para·chute /'pærəʃuːt/ n apparatus used for a jump from an aircraft or for dropping supplies, etc: (attrib) '∼ *troops/flares/mines.* □ vt,vi [VP2A,C,6A,15A,B] drop, descend, from an aircraft by means of a ∼: *men* ∼*d behind the enemy lines.* **para·chut·ist** /-ɪst/ n person who jumps with a ∼.
par·ade /pəˈreɪd/ vt,vi 1 [VP6A,2A] (of troops) (cause to) gather together for drilling, inspection, etc; march in procession. 2 [VP6A] make a display of; try to attract attention to: ∼ *one's abilities.* □ n 1 [U] parading of troops: *be on* ∼; [C] instance of this. 2 [C] '∼-ground, area of ground on which ∼s are held. 3 [C] display or exhibition. *make a* ∼ *of one's virtues,* try to impress people by showing them. 4 [C] public promenade; wide, often ornamented pathway, esp on a seafront.
para·digm /'pærədaɪm/ n example or pattern, esp of the declension of a noun, the conjugation of a verb, etc.
para·dise /'pærədaɪs/ n 1 the Garden of Eden, home of Adam and Eve. ,bird of '∼, bird (of New Guinea) with beautiful feathers. 2 Heaven. 3 [C] any place of perfect happiness; [U] condition of perfect happiness. *a fool's* ∼, ⇨ fool¹(1). **para·dis·iac** /ˌpærəˈdɪzɪæk/, **para·disia·cal** /ˌpærədɪˈzaɪəkl/ adj j of or like ∼: *Adam and Eve in their paradisiac state,* in their pristine innocence.
para·dox /'pærədɒks/ n [C] statement that seems to say sth opposite to common sense or the truth, but which may contain a truth (eg 'More haste, less speed'). ∼**i·cal** /ˌpærəˈdɒksɪkl/ adj ∼**i·cally** /-klɪ/ adv
par·af·fin /'pærəfɪn/ n [U] 1 '∼ (oil), (GB) oil obtained from petroleum, coal, etc used as a fuel (in lamps, heating and cooking-stoves). (US = *kerosene*). 2 ∼ (wax), wax-like substance used for making candles. 3 (,liquid) '∼, odourless, tasteless form of ∼ used as a laxative.
para·gon /'pærəgən *US:* -gɒn/ n model of excellence; apparently perfect person or thing: *I make no claim to be a* ∼ *of virtue.*
para·graph /'pærəgrɑːf *US:* -græf/ n [C] 1 division (usu a group of several sentences dealing with one main idea) of a piece of writing, started on a new line (and usu inset); the mark (¶) used to show where a new ∼ is to begin, and as a mark of reference. 2 small item of news in a newspaper. □ vt divide into ∼s.
para·keet /'pærəkiːt/ n small, long-tailed parrot of various kinds. ⇨ the illus at rare.
par·al·lel /'pærəlel/ adj (of lines) continuing at the same distance from one another; (of one line) having this relation (*to* or *with* another): *a road running* ∼ *to/with the railway; in a* ∼ *direction* (*with*...). ∼ 'bars, pair of ∼ bars on posts for gymnastic exercises. □ n 1 ∼ of latitude, line on a map ∼ to, and passing through all places the same distance north or south of, the equator. ⇨ the illus at projection. *in* ∼, (of the components of an electrical circuit) with the supply of current taken to each component independently, not in series). ⇨

series. **2** [U,C] person, event, etc precisely similar: *a brilliant career without (a)* ~ *in modern times*. **3** comparison: *draw a* ~ *between....* □ *vt* (-l- or (GB) -ll-) [VP6A] **1** quote, produce or mention sth ~ or comparable. **2** be ~ to: *His experiences* ~ *mine in many instances. The street* ~*s the railway.* ~·ism /-ɪzəm/ *n* (lit or fig) being ~. ~o·gram /ˌpærəˈleləgræm/ *n* four-sided plane figure whose opposite sides are ~. ⇨ the illus at quadrilateral.

par·al·y·sis /pəˈræləsɪs/ *n* [U] loss of feeling or power to move in any or every part of the body; (fig) state of utter powerlessness. para·lyt·ic /ˌpærəˈlɪtɪk/ *n, adj* **1** (person) suffering from ~: *a paralytic stroke;* (fig) helpless: *paralytic laughter.* **2** (person who is) very drunk. para·lyse, (US = -lyze) /ˈpærəlaɪz/ *vt* [VP6A] **1** affect with ~. **2** make helpless: *paralysed with fear.*

par·ameter /pəˈræmɪtə(r)/ *n* characteristic or determining feature.

para·mili·tary /ˌpærəˈmɪlɪtrɪ US: -terɪ/ *adj* having a status or function ancillary or similar to that of regular military forces: ~ *organizations.*

para·mount /ˈpærəmaʊnt/ *adj* (formal) supreme, superior in power: ~ *chiefs;* pre-eminent: *of* ~ *importance;* superior. ~cy /-tsɪ/ *n*

para·mour /ˈpærəmʊə(r)/ *n* (archaic) illicit partner of a married man or woman.

para·noia /ˌpærəˈnɔɪə/ *n* [U] mental disorder (usu incurable), marked by fixed delusions, eg of persecution or grandeur. para·noiac /ˌpærəˈnɔɪæk/, para·noid /ˈpærənɔɪd/ *nn, adjj* (person) suffering from ~.

para·pet /ˈpærəpɪt/ *n* **1** (usu low) protective wall at the edge of a flat roof, side of a bridge, etc. **2** defensive bank of earth, stone, etc along the front edge of a trench (in war).

para·pher·nalia /ˌpærəfəˈneɪlɪə/ *n* [U] numerous small possessions, tools, instruments, etc esp concerning sb's hobby or technical work.

para·phrase /ˈpærəfreɪz/ *vt* [VP6A], *n* (give a) restatement of the meaning of (a piece of writing) in other words.

para·ple·gia /ˌpærəˈpliːdʒə/ *n* [U] (path) paralysis of the lower part of the body, including both legs, caused by injury to the spinal cord. para·plegic /ˌpærəˈpliːdʒɪk/ *n, adj* (person) suffering from ~.

para·site /ˈpærəsaɪt/ *n* **1** animal (eg *louse, hookworm*) or plant (eg *mistletoe*) living on or in another and getting its food from it. **2** person supported by another and giving him nothing in return. para·sitic /ˌpærəˈsɪtɪk/, para·siti·cal /ˌpærəˈsɪtɪkl/ *adjj* caused by, living as, a ~.

para·sol /ˈpærəsɒl US: -sɔːl/ *n* umbrella used to give shade from the sun.

para·troops /ˈpærətruːps/ *n pl* troops trained for being dropped by parachute. para·trooper /ˈpærətruːpə(r)/ *n* one of these.

para·typhoid /ˌpærəˈtaɪfɔɪd/ *n* [U] kind of fever in some ways like typhoid but milder and caused by a different bacterium.

par·boil /ˈpɑːbɔɪl/ *vt* [VP6A] boil (food) until partially cooked; (fig) make uncomfortably hot.

par·cel /ˈpɑːsl/ *n* [C] **1** thing or things wrapped and tied up for carrying, sending by post, etc: *She left the shop with an armful of* ~*s.* '~ post *n* [U] system, method, etc of carrying ~s by post. **2** *part and* ~ *of,* an essential part of. *a* ~ *of land,* an area of land (esp part of an estate). □ *vt* (-ll-, US also -l-) [VP6A,15B] ~ *out,* divide into portions.

~ *up,* make (books, etc) into a ~.

parch /pɑːtʃ/ *vt* [VP6A] **1** (of heat, the sun, etc) make hot and dry: *the* ~*ed deserts of N Africa.* **2** dry or roast by heating: ~*ed peas.*

parch·ment /ˈpɑːtʃmənt/ *n* **1** [C,U] (manuscript on) writing surface prepared from the skin of a sheep or goat. **2** [U] kind of paper resembling ~.

par·don /ˈpɑːdn/ *n* **1** [U] forgiveness: *ask for* ~; [C] instance of this. **2** [U] indulgence; forbearance. *beg sb's* ~, excuse oneself, eg for disagreeing with what sb says, or apologize, eg for not hearing or understanding what sb says: *I beg your* ~! ⇨ excuse[1](3); sorry(2). **3** (archaic) indulgence(3). □ *vt* [VP6A,12B,13B] ~ *sb for sth;* ~ *sb sth,* forgive; excuse; overlook: ~ *sb for doing wrong;* ~ *sb an offence. P*~ *me for/P*~ *my contradicting you.* ~·able /ˈpɑːdnəbl/ *adj* that can be ~ed. ~·ably /-əblɪ/ *adv* (formal) in a way that can be ~ed: *She was* ~*ably proud of her wonderful cooking.* ~er *n* (in the Middle Ages) person who had been licensed to sell papal indulgences(3).

pare /peə(r)/ *vt* [VP6A,15B] cut away the outer part, edge or skin of: ~ *one's (finger~) nails;* ~ *the claws of an animal;* ~ (= peel) *an apple;* (fig) ~ *down* (= reduce) *one's expenses.* par·ings /ˈpeərɪŋz/ *n pl* that which is ~d off: '*nail-parings.*

par·egoric /ˌpærəˈgɒrɪk US: -ˈgɔːr-/ *n* [U] soothing medicine containing opium and flavoured with aniseed.

par·ent /ˈpeərənt/ *n* father or mother; ancestor: *the* ~ *birds; the* ~ *plant. May I introduce you to my* ~*s?* ie to my father and mother. ~ company, (comm) one that controls another, eg by owning more than half its shares or because of the composition of its Board of Directors. '~·age /-ɪdʒ/ *n* [U] fatherhood or motherhood; origin; birth: *of unknown* ~*age,* having unknown ~s. ~al /pəˈrentl/ *adj* of ~(s): ~*al anxieties; children who lack* ~*al care.* ~·ally /-təlɪ/ *adv*

par·enth·esis /pəˈrenθəsɪs/ *n* (*pl* -eses /-əsiːz/) sentence within another sentence, marked off by commas, dashes or brackets; (*sing* or *pl*) round brackets () for this. ⇨ bracket[2]. ⇨ App 9. *in* ~, between parentheses; (fig) taking (sth) separately. par·en·thetic /ˌpærənˈθetɪk/, par·en·theti·cal /-ɪkl/ *adjj* of, relating to, used as, a ~. par·en·theti·cally /-klɪ/ *adv*

par ex·cel·lence /ˌpɑːr ˈeksəlɑːns US: ˌeksəˈlɑːns/ *adv* (F) by virtue of special excellence; in the highest degree.

pa·riah /pəˈraɪə/ *n* (India) person of low caste or of no caste; (fig) social outcast. '~-dog *n* (India) ownerless dog of mixed breed.

pari-mu·tuel /ˌpærɪ ˈmjuːtjʊel US: ˈmjuːtʃʊəl/ *n* (F) form of betting (on races) in which the winners divide the stakes of the losers, less a percentage for management expenses.

pari passu /ˌpærɪ ˈpæsuː/ *adv* (Lat) simultaneously and equally; at an equal rate of progress.

par·ish /ˈpærɪʃ/ *n* (GB) division of a county with its own church and priest: *the* ~ *church; the* ~ *council.* ~ clerk, official with various duties connected with the ~ church. ~ 'pump, (usu attrib) of local interest only: ~*-pump affairs/politics.* ~ regis·ter, book with records of christenings, marriages and burials. civil ~, division of a county for local government. ~ioner /pəˈrɪʃənə(r)/ *n* inhabitant of a ~.

Pa·ris·ian /pəˈrɪzɪən US: -ʒn/ *n, adj* (native, inhabitant) of Paris.

par·ity /'pærətɪ/ n [U] equality; being equal; being at par: *Should teachers in secondary schools and teachers in primary schools receive ~ of pay? The two currencies have now reached ~*, are at par. **~ of ex'change**, rates of currency exchange officially determined by Governments.

park¹ /pɑːk/ n **1** public garden or public recreation ground in a town. **'ball ~**, (US) playing-field. **2** area of grassland (usu with trees) round a large country house or mansion. **3 'car-~**, place where motor-vehicles may be left for a time. **4 ,national '~**, area of natural beauty, eg mountains, forests, lakes, set apart by the State for public enjoyment, and where industrial and urban development is forbidden or limited. **5** place used by the military for artillery, stores, etc.

park² /pɑːk/ vt,vi **1** [VP6A,2A] put (a motor-vehicle) for a time, unattended: *Where can we ~ (the car)?* **2** [VP6A,15A] (colloq) put (sth or sb) somewhere: *Where can I ~ my luggage? P~ yourself in that chair while I make you a cup of tea.*

parka /'pɑːkə/ n (US) waterproof jacket with a hood attached (as worn for skiing, mountain-climbing, etc). (GB = *anorak*).

parking /'pɑːkɪŋ/ n [U] (area for the) ~ of motor-vehicles: *No ~ between 9am and 6pm*. **'~ lot**, (US) area for the ~ of motor-vehicles. **'~ meter**, coin-operated meter beside which a car may be parked in a public place, eg a street. **'~ orbit**, temporary orbit for a spacecraft.

Parkinson's /'pɑːkɪnsnz/ adj **'~ disease**, (path) chronic progressive disease of old people, with muscular tremors, muscular rigidity and general weakness. **'~ law**, (hum) suggestion that work will always last as long as the time available for it.

parky /'pɑːkɪ/ adj(sl) (of the air, weather) chilly.

par·lance /'pɑːləns/ n use or choice of words; way of speaking: *common/ legal ~*.

par·ley /'pɑːlɪ/ n (pl ~s) [C] conference, esp between leaders of two opposed forces. □ vi [VP2A,3A] ~ *(with sb)*, discuss terms, hold a conference.

par·lia·ment /'pɑːləmənt/ n (in countries with representative government) supreme law-making council or assembly, esp of GB, formed of the House of Commons and the House of Lords: *enter P~; ,Members of 'P~; summon/adjourn P~; P~ sits/rises; open P~*, (of the Sovereign) declare it open with traditional ceremonial. **par·lia·men·tarian** /,pɑːləmən'teərɪən/ n person skilled in the rules and procedures of ~, who is a good debater, etc. **par·lia·men·tary** /,pɑːlə'mentrɪ/ adj of ~: *~ary debates; ~ary language*, polite, civil language, as required in ~ary debates.

par·lour (US = **-lor**) /'pɑːlə(r)/ n **1** ordinary sitting-room for the family in a private house (now more usu called sitting-room or living-room). **'~ games**, games played in the home (competitions, guessing, etc). **2** official room for the reception of visitors: *the Mayor's ~*, in a town hall, etc. **3** (esp US) room for customers and clients: *a 'beauty ~; a 'hairdresser's ~*. **'~-car** n (US) luxurious railway coach with individual reserved seats.

par·lous /'pɑːləs/ adj(formal) perilous.

Par·me·san /'pɑːmɪzæn/ n kind of cheese made at Parma and elsewhere in N Italy.

par·ochial /pə'rəʊkɪəl/ adj of a parish; (fig) limited, narrow: *a ~ outlook/mind/point of view*. **~·ly** /-kɪəlɪ/ adv **~·ism** /-ɪzəm/ n

par·ody /'pærədɪ/ n (pl -dies) **1** [C,U] (piece of)

writing intended to amuse by imitating the style of writing used by sb else. **2** [C] weak imitation. □ vt [VP6A] make a ~ of: *~ an author/a poem*. **par·odist** /-ɪst/ n person who writes parodies.

pa·role /pə'rəʊl/ n [U] prisoner's solemn promise, on being given certain privileges, that he will not try to escape. **on ~**, liberated after making such a promise. **break one's ~**, (try to) escape while on ~. □ vt [VP6A] set (a prisoner) free on ~.

paro·quet /'pærəkiːt/ n = parakeet.

par·ox·ysm /'pærəksɪzəm/ n [C] sudden attack or outburst (of pain, anger, laughter, etc).

par·quet /'pɑːkeɪ *US:* pɑːr'keɪ/ n flooring of wooden blocks fitted together to make a pattern.

parr, par /pɑː(r)/ n young salmon.

par·ri·cide /'pærɪsaɪd/ n [C,U] (person guilty of the) murder of one's father or near relation.

par·rot /'pærət/ n **1** sorts of bird with a hooked bill and (usu) brightly coloured feathers, some kinds of which can be trained to imitate human speech. ⇨ the illus at rare. **'~ fever**, = psittacosis. **2** person who repeats, often without understanding, what others say.

parry /'pærɪ/ vt (pt,pp -ried) [VP6A] turn aside (a blow); (fig) evade (a question). □ n [C] act of ~ing, esp in fencing and boxing.

parse /pɑːz *US:* pɑːs/ vt [VP6A] describe (a word) grammatically; point out how the words of a sentence are related.

Par·see /pɑː'siː/ n member of a religious group in India, the members being descended from Persians who settled in India in the 8th c.

par·si·mony /'pɑːsɪmənɪ *US:* -məʊnɪ/ n [U] (formal) (usu as a bad quality) excessive carefulness in using money or (fig) immaterial things. **par·si·moni·ous** /,pɑːsɪ'məʊnɪəs/ adj too economical; miserly.

pars·ley /'pɑːslɪ/ n [U] garden plant with crinkled green leaves, used in seasoning and sauces and for garnishing food.

pars·nip /'pɑːsnɪp/ n [C] long, white or pale-yellow root, cooked as a vegetable.

par·son /'pɑːsn/ n parish priest; (colloq) any clergyman. **~'s nose**, (colloq) rump of a cooked fowl. **'~·age** /-ɪdʒ/ n ~'s house.

part¹ /pɑːt/ n [C] **1** (often *sing* without *indef art*) some but not all of a thing or a number of things; something less than the whole: *We spent (a) ~ of our holiday in France/in a ~ of the country we had never visited before. P~s of the book are interesting. The greater ~ of what you heard is only rumour*. **for the 'most ~**, in most cases; mostly. **in ~**, in some degree. **,~-'owner** n person who owns sth in common with others. **,~-'time** adj, adv for only a ~ of the working day or week: *be employed ~-time; ~-time teaching*, eg two days a week. Hence, **,part-'timer** n. **2** (pl) region; district: *in these/those ~s*. **3** any one of a number of equal divisions: *A minute is the sixtieth ~ of an hour*. **4** person's share in some activity; his duty or responsibility; what an actor in a play, film, etc says and does: *a man with a ~ in a play/in a conference. He spoke/acted his ~ very well. Do the actors all know their ~s? I had only a small ~ in these events.* **play a (big, small, etc) ~ (in sth)**, be concerned in sth, make a contribution: *He had an important ~ to play in ensuring the success of the scheme.* **take ~ (in)**, have a share (in); help: *Are you going to take ~ in the discussion, Do you intend to speak?* **5** side in a dispute, transaction, agreement, mutual arrangement, etc. **take sb's ~;** **take the ~ of sb,** support sb: *He always takes his brother's ~.* **for 'my ~,** as far as I am concerned: *For my ~ I am quite happy about the division of the money.* **on 'my/'his/'your, etc ~; on the ~ of (Mr A, etc),** proceeding from, done by, me/him/you/Mr A, etc: *There was no objection on his ~/on the ~ of the owner of the land,* He did not object. *The agreement has been kept on my ~ but not on his.* **6 take sth in good ~,** not be offended at it. **7** division of a book; each issue of a work published in instalments: *a new encyclopaedia to be issued in monthly ~s.* **8** essential piece or section of sth. **(spare) ~,** extra piece, etc to be used when needed, when sth breaks or wears: *When can I get a ~ for my pump?* **9** (music) each of the melodies that make up a harmony; the melody for a particular voice or instrument: *orchestral ~s; sing in three ~s.* **'~-singing, '~-song** *n* singing, song, with three or more voice ~s. **10** (gram) **~ of 'speech,** one of the classes of words, eg noun, verb, adjective. **11 a man/woman of (many) ~s,** of (many) abilities; talented. □ *adv* (usu ~... ~...) in some degree: *made ~ of iron and ~ of wood.* **~·ly** *adv* in some degree.

part² /pɑːt/ *vt, vi* **1** [VP6A, 2A, D] (cause to) separate or divide: *The policemen ~ed the crowd. We tried to ~ the two fighters. Let us ~ friends,* leave each other with no feeling of enmity. *The crowd ~ed and let us through.* **~ company (with sb), (a)** end a relationship. **(b)** leave; separate from. **(c)** disagree: *On that question I am afraid I must ~ company with you.* **2** [VP3A] **~ with,** give up, give away: *He hates to ~ with his money,* doesn't like to spend it or give it away. **3** [VP6A] **~ one's hair,** make a dividing line by combing the hair in opposite ways. **~·ing** *n* **1** [C] line where the hair is combed in opposite ways. **2** [C,U] departure; leave-taking: (attrib) *his ~ing injunctions,* those given on taking leave. **at the ~ing of the ways,** at the point where the road divides or forks; (fig) when one has to choose between courses of action. **~·ing shot** = *Parthian shot,* ⇨ Parthian.

par·take /pɑːˈteɪk/ *vi, vt* (*pt* -took /-ˈtʊk/, *pp* -taken /-ˈteɪkən/) [VP3A] **~ of sth,** (dated formal) **1** take a share in: *They partook of our triumph. They were partaking of our simple meal.* **2** have some of (the nature or characteristics of): *His manner ~s of insolence.*

par·terre /pɑːˈteə(r)/ *n* **1** (in a garden) level space with lawns and flower-beds. **2** (in a theatre) part of the auditorium behind the orchestra.

par·theno·gen·esis /ˌpɑːθɪnəʊˈdʒenəsɪs/ *n* [U] reproduction of offspring without fertilization by sexual union.

Par·thian /ˈpɑːθɪən/ *adj* of Parthia /ˈpɑːθɪə/, ancient country of NE Iran conquered by the Persians in AD 226. **~ shot/shaft,** (fig) sth said or done as a final reply, argument, etc at the moment of parting.

par·tial /ˈpɑːʃl/ *adj* **1** forming only a part; not complete: *a ~ success; a ~ eclipse of the sun.* **2 ~ (towards),** showing too much favour to one person or side: *examiners who are ~ towards pretty women students.* **3 ~ to,** having a liking for: *~ to French cuisine.* **~·ly** /ˈpɑːʃəlɪ/ *adv* **1** partly; not completely. **2** in a ~(2) manner. **~·ity** /ˌpɑːʃɪˈælətɪ/ *n* **1** [U] being ~(2) in treatment of people, etc; bias; favouritism. **2 ~ity for,** [C] fondness: *a ~ity for moonlight walks.*

par·tici·pate /pɑːˈtɪsɪpeɪt/ *vi* [VP2A, 3A] **~ (in),** **1**

have a share, take part (in): *~ in sb's suffering/in a plot.* **par·tici·pant** /pɑːˈtɪsɪpənt/ *n* person who ~s (*in* sth). **par·tici·pa·tion** /pɑːˌtɪsɪˈpeɪʃn/ *n* [U] act of participating.

par·ti·ciple /ˈpɑːtɪsɪpl/ *n* (gram) verbal *adj* qualifying *nn* but retaining some properties of a *v.* 'Hurrying' and 'hurried' are the present and past ~s of 'hurry'. **par·ti·cip·ial** /ˌpɑːtɪˈsɪpɪəl/ *adj* of a ~: *a participial adjective,* eg 'loving' in 'a loving mother'.

par·ticle /ˈpɑːtɪkl/ *n* **1** very small bit: *~s of dust;* smallest possible quantity: *She hasn't a ~ of sense.* **elementary ~,** (phys) one of the constituents of an atom, not yet known to be composed of simpler ~s, eg an electron. **2** (gram) minor part of speech, eg an article (*a, an, the*), a preposition or adverb (*up, in, out*), a conjunction (*or*), an affix (*un-, in-, -ness, -ly*).

parti-col·oured, (US = **-col·ored**) /ˈpɑːtɪ kʌləd/ *adj* differently coloured in different parts.

par·ticu·lar /pəˈtɪkjʊlə(r)/ *adj* **1** relating to one as distinct from others: *in this ~ case.* **2** special; worth notice; outstanding: *for no ~ reason. He took ~ trouble to get it right.* **in ~,** especially: *I remember one of them in ~.* **3** very exact; scrupulous: *a full and ~ account of what we saw.* **4 ~ (about/over),** hard to satisfy; fastidious: *She's ~ about what she wears. He's too ~ over what he will eat and drink.* □ *n* detail. **go into ~s,** give details. **~·ly** *adv* in a ~ manner: *His good humour was ~ly noticeable. I ~ly mentioned that point.* **~·ity** /pəˌtɪkjʊˈlærətɪ/ *n* [U] exactness; attention to detail. **~·ize** /-aɪz/ *vt, vi* [VP6A, 2A] name specially or one by one.

part·ing /ˈpɑːtɪŋ/ ⇨ part².

par·ti·san /ˌpɑːtɪˈzæn *US*: ˈpɑːrtɪzn/ *n* **1** person devoted to a party, group or cause. **2** (esp) member of an armed resistance movement in a country occupied by enemy forces: *~ troops.* □ *adj* uncritically devoted to a cause: *His loyalties are too ~.* **'~-ship** /-ʃɪp/ *n*

par·ti·tion /pɑːˈtɪʃn/ *n* **1** [U] division into parts: *the ~ of India in 1947.* **2** [C] that which divides, esp a thin wall between rooms, etc. **3** [C] part formed by dividing; section. □ *vt* [VP6A, 15B] **~ (sth off),** divide into sections, etc; separate by means of a ~(2).

par·ti·tive /ˈpɑːtɪtɪv/ *n, adj* (word) denoting part of a collective whole: *'Some' and 'any' are ~s.*

part·ner /ˈpɑːtnə(r)/ *n* **1** person who takes part with another or others in some activity, esp one of the owners of a business: *~s in crime; profits shared equally among all the ~s; active ~,* one taking part in the affairs of the business. **sleeping ~,** ⇨ sleep²(1). **2** one of two persons dancing together, playing tennis, cards, etc together; husband or wife. □ *vt* [VP6A, 15A] be a ~ to; bring (people) together as ~s. **'~-ship** /-ʃɪp/ *n* [U] state of being a ~; [C] joint business: *enter into ~ship (with* sb); *be in ~ship.*

par·took /pɑːˈtʊk/ ⇨ partake.

par·tridge /ˈpɑːtrɪdʒ/ *n* [C] sorts of bird of the same family as the pheasant; [U] its flesh as food. ⇨ the illus at fowl.

par·tur·ition /ˌpɑːtjʊˈrɪʃn *US*: -tʃʊ-/ *n* [U] childbirth.

party /ˈpɑːtɪ/ *n* (*pl* -ties) **1** [C] group of persons united in policy and opinion, in support of a cause, esp in politics: *the Conservative, Liberal and Socialist parties.* **2** [U] (esp attrib use) government

based on political parties: *the '~ system; ~ politics*, politics of and within a ~, eg manoeuvres designed to win influence or power; *Should a politician put public interest before ~ interest?* **follow
the ~ line; ~ line**, ⇨ line¹(11). **~ machine**, ⇨
machine(2). **~-'spirit**, enthusiasm for, devotion
to, a (political) ~. Hence, **~-'spirited** *adj* 3 one
of the persons or sides in a legal agreement or dispute. **~-'wall**, one that divides two properties and
is the joint responsibility of the owners of these
properties. 4 group of persons travelling or working together, or on duty together: *a 'firing-~*, of
soldiers, at a military funeral or execution. 5
gathering of persons, by invitation, for pleasure: *a
'dinner/'birthday ~; give a ~*, arrange one and be
the host(ess); (attrib) *a ~ dress.* **lack the ~ spirit**,
be without enthusiasm for a ~. **make up a ~**, join
together to form a ~. 6 person taking part in and
approving of or being aware of what is going on: *a
~ to a conspiracy; an innocent ~.* 7 (hum) person:
Who's the old ~ in blue, the old person dressed in
blue? 8 **'~-coloured**, = parti-coloured.
par·venu /'pɑ:vənju: *US:* -nu:/ *n* person who has
suddenly reached higher economic or social status
from a low status.
pas·chal /'pæskl/ *adj* 1 of the Jewish Passover. 2
of Easter.
pasha /'pɑːʃə *US:* 'pæʃə/ *n* (hist) title of honour
placed after the name of a Turkish officer of high
rank or the governor of a province.
pass¹ /pɑːs *US:* pæs/ *n* 1 success in an examination, esp (in university degree examinations) success in satisfying the examiners but without distinction or honours¹(7): *get a ~; a '~ degree.* 2
come to/reach a pretty/sad/strange, etc ~,
reach such a state or condition. 3 **bring to ~**, accomplish, carry out. **come to ~**, happen: *How exactly did that come to ~?* 4 (paper, ticket, etc giving) permission or authority to travel, enter a building, occupy a seat in a cinema, etc: *a free ~*, ticket
giving free travel on the railways, etc. *All ~es to
be shown at the barrier*, eg in a station. *No admittance without a ~.* ⇨ ~-book below. 5 act of
kicking, throwing, or hitting the ball from one
player to another player (of the same team): *a clever ~ to the forward.* 6 movement of the hand over
or in front of sth (as in conjuring or juggling, or in
mesmerism). 7 forward movement, blow (in fencing, etc). **make a ~ at sb**, (sl) make (possibly unwelcome) amorous advances. 8 narrow way over
or through mountains; such a way viewed as the
entrance to a country. ⇨ the illus at mountain.
hold the ~, (fig) defend a cause. **sell the ~**, (fig)
betray a cause; yield up a position. 9 (card games)
act of passing. ⇨ pass²(15). 10 (compounds) **'~-
book** *n* (a) book supplied by a bank to a customer
with records of his account. (b) (S Africa) booklet,
document, allowing a black African person to be in
a certain area. **'~-key** *n* private key to a gate, etc;
key which opens a number of locks; master key.
'~-word *n* secret word or phrase which enables a
person to be recognized as a friend by sentries:
give/demand the ~word.
pass² /pɑːs *US:* pæs/ *vi,vt* (*pp* ~ed, or, as *adj*
past /pɑːst *US:* pæst/) (For special uses with *advv*
and *preps*, ⇨ 19 below.) 1 [VP2A,C] move towards and beyond, proceed (*along, through,
down, etc*): *~ through a village. Please let me ~.
The road was too narrow for cars to ~. The two
ships ~ed each other during the night. I glanced at*

her and ~ed on. He ~ed in front of/behind me.
They ~ed by, went past. Hence, **~er-'by** *n* (*pl
passers-by*) person who ~es sb or sth: *The purse
was picked up by a ~er-by.* 2 [VP6A] leave (a person, place, object, etc) on one side or behind as one
goes forward: *Turn right after ~ing the Post Office. I ~ed Miss Green in the street.* 3 [VP6A] go
through, across, over or between: *The ship ~ed
the channel. No complaints ~ed her lips.* 4 [VP2A]
(of time) go by; be spent: *Six months ~ed and still
we had no news of them. The time ~ed pleasantly.*
5 [VP6A] spend (time): *How shall we ~ the evening? What can we do to ~ the time?* 6 [VP3A] *~
(from...) (to/into...),* change from one state of
things to another; change into another state of
things: *Water ~es from a liquid to a solid state
when it freezes. When water boils it ~es into
steam.* 7 [VP6A,15B,12A,13A] give by handing:
*Please ~ (me) the butter. The letter was ~ed on/
round to all the members of the family. The note
was ~ed round the table.* 8 [VP6A] utter: *~ a remark*, say sth. *~ the time of day with sb*, engage
them in light conversation. 9 [VP6A,2A,C] (cause
to) circulate: *He was imprisoned for ~ing forged
banknotes. He ~es under the name of Mr Green*, is
known and accepted as Mr Green. 10 [VP6A,2A]
examine and accept; be examined and accepted:
*Parliament ~ed the Bill. The Bill ~ed and became
law. The examiners ~ed most of the candidates.
The candidates ~ed (the examination). Will the
play ~ the censor? We have to ~ the Customs before we leave.* 11 [VP2A,C] take place; be said or
done (between persons): *Did you see/hear what
was ~ing? Tell me everything that ~ed between
you.* 12 [VP6A] be beyond the range of: *a story that
~es belief. It ~es my comprehension.* 13 [VP14]
~ sth on sth/sb, give (an opinion, judgement,
sentence on sth or sb): *~ sentence on an accused
man. I can't ~ an opinion on your work without
seeing it.* 14 [VP2A] be accepted without rebuke or
blame; go unnoticed or unreproved: *His rude remarks ~ed without comment. I don't like it, but I'll
let it ~*, will not make objections, etc. *Such conduct may ~ in certain circles but cannot be tolerated here. ~ muster*, ⇨ muster. 15 [VP2A] (card
games) let one's turn go by without playing a card
or making a bid. 16 [VP15A] move; cause to go:
*He ~ed his hand across his forehead/his fingers
through his hair. I ~ed a rope round the barrel.
Will you please ~ your eye (= glance) over this
note. ~ water*, (euphem) urinate. 17 (in football,
hockey, etc) kick, hand or hit (the ball) to a player
of one's own side. 18 [VP6A,15A] cause (troops) to
go by: *~ troops in review.* 19 [VP2C,15B] (special
uses with *adverbial particles* and *preps*):
pass away, (euphem) die: *He ~ed away peacefully.*
pass sb/sth by, pay no attention to; disregard: *I
can't ~ the matter by without a protest.*
pass for sb/sth, be accepted as: *In this small village, he ~ed for a learned man. Do I speak French
well enough to ~ for a Frenchman?*
pass in; pass into sth, gain admission (to): *He
~ed into the Military College with no difficulty.*
pass off, (a) (of events) take place, be carried
through: *The meeting of the strikers ~ed off quietly.* (b) (of pain, a crisis) end: *Has your toothache
~ed off yet? ~ sth off*, turn attention from: *~ off
an awkward situation. ~ sth/sb off as sth/sb*,
represent falsely to be: *He tried to ~ himself off as*

a qualified doctor.
pass on, (euphem) die: *I'm grieved to learn that your dear mother has ~ed on.* **~ sth on,** hand or give it (to sb else, to others).
pass out, (colloq) faint; lose consciousness. **~ out (of sth),** leave college, etc having ~ed one's examinations. Hence, **~ing-'out (ceremony/ parade),** esp for cadets who have completed their training.
pass sb over, overlook; fail to notice: *They ~ed me over* (eg failed to promote me) *in favour of young Hill.*
pass through sth, experience it.
pass sth up, (colloq) neglect it; not take advantage of it: *~ up an opportunity.*
pass·able /'pɑːsəbl US: 'pæs-/ adj 1 (of roads, etc) that can be passed over or crossed: *Are the Alpine roads ~ yet?* 2 that can be accepted as fairly good but not excellent: *a ~ knowledge of German.* **pass·ably** /-əblɪ/ adv
pas·sage /'pæsɪdʒ/ n 1 [U] passing; act of going past, through or across; right to go through: *the ~ of time.* **bird of ~,** (a) migratory bird. (b) person who passes through a place without staying there long. 2 [C] voyage; journey from point to point by sea or air: *book one's ~ to New York.* **work one's ~,** ⇨ work²(4). 3 [C] way through: *force a ~ through a crowd.* 4 [C] **'~·(way),** corridor in a house. 5 [C] short extract from a speech or piece of writing, quoted or considered separately. 6 passing of a Bill so that it becomes law. 7 (*pl*) what passes between two persons in conversation: *have angry ~s with an opponent during a debate.* 8 **,~ of 'arms,** (lit, fig) combat; dispute.
pass·book n⇨ pass¹(10).
passé /'pæseɪ US: pæ'seɪ/ adj (fem **passée**) (F) past his/her/its best; no longer current; out of date.
pas·sen·ger /'pæsɪndʒə(r)/ n 1 person being conveyed by bus, taxi, tram, train, ship, aircraft, etc. 2 (colloq) member of a team, crew, etc who does no effective work.
passe·par·tout /,pæspɑː'tuː/ n 1 master-key. 2 kind of adhesive tape used eg as a mounting for a picture, etc (to form a frame).
passer-by /,pɑːsə 'baɪ US: 'pæsər/ ⇨ pass²(1).
pas·sim /'pæsɪm/ adv (Lat) (of allusions, phrases, etc to be found in a book or author) frequently; in every part: *This occurs in Milton ~.*
pas·sing /'pɑːsɪŋ US: 'pæs-/ adj going by; not lasting: *the ~ years.* □ adv (old use) very: *~ rich.* □ n [U] the act of going by: *the ~ of the old year,* ie on New Year's Eve.
passion /'pæʃn/ n 1 [U,C] strong feeling or enthusiasm, esp of love, hate or anger: *be filled with ~* (ie love) *for sb; choking with ~,* ie anger or hate; *~s were running high,* people were filled with strong feeling. 2 a **~,** outburst of strong feeling: *fly into a ~,* become very angry; *be in a ~;* 3 **the P~,** the suffering and death of Jesus. **,P~ 'Sunday,** the fifth Sunday in Lent. **'P~ Week,** the week between P~ Sunday and Palm Sunday. **'P~ play,** drama dealing with the P~. **'~-flower** n kinds of (usu climbing) plants with flowers that are thought to resemble the crown of thorns placed on the head of Jesus. **'~ fruit,** edible fruit of the ~-flower. **~·less** adj
passion·ate /'pæʃənət/ adj easily moved by passion; filled with, showing, passion; *a ~ nature; ~ language.* **~·ly** adv in a ~ manner: *She is ~ly fond of tennis.*

pass·ive /'pæsɪv/ adj 1 acted upon but not acting; not offering active resistance: *~ obedience.* In spite of my efforts the boy remained *~,* showed no signs of interest, activity, etc. **,~ re'sistance,** resistance that takes the form of not obeying orders, the law, etc but without active measures of opposition. **,~ re'sister,** person who practises this. 2 **the ~ (voice),** (gram) the form in italic type in the sentence 'The letter *was written* yesterday,' ie the verb phrase containing *be + pp.* ⇨ active. □ *n ~* voice. **~·ly** adv. **~·ness, pass·iv·ity** /pæ'sɪvətɪ/ nn [U] the state or quality of being ~.
pass·key n⇨ pass¹(10).
Pass·over /'pɑːsəʊvə(r) US: 'pæs-/ n Jewish religious festival commemorating the liberation of the Jews from slavery in Egypt. ⇨ Exod 12.
pass·port /'pɑːspɔːt US: 'pæs-/ n government document to be carried by a traveller abroad, giving personal particulars; (fig) sth that enables one to win or obtain sth: *Is flattery a ~ to success?*
pass·word n⇨ pass¹(10).
past¹ /pɑːst US: pæst/ adj (Cf *passed, pp* of pass²) of the time before the present; gone by in time: *for the ~ few days/weeks, etc; during the ~ week; in times ~; for a long time ~; ~ generations; the ~ tense; a ~ participle,* eg passed, taken, gone. **~ master,** one who has a thorough mastery (*of or in a* subject, *at* doing sth). □ *n* 1 **the ~,** time: *We cannot change the ~. Memories of the ~ filled her mind.* 2 person's *~* life or experiences, esp when these are not reputable: *We know nothing of his ~. She's a woman with a ~.*
past² /pɑːst US: pæst/ prep 1 beyond in time; after: *half ~ two; ten (minutes) ~ six; buses every twenty minutes ~ the hour,* ie at 1.20, 2.20, 3.20, etc; *stay out until ~ 11 o'clock; an old man ~ seventy; a woman ~ middle age.* 2 beyond in space; up to and farther than: *He walked ~ the house. He hurried ~ me without stopping to speak. The driver took the bus ~ the traffic signal.* 3 beyond the limits, power or range of: *The old man is ~ work,* too old, weak, etc to work. *She's ~ child-bearing,* too old to bear a child. *The pain was almost ~ bearing,* too severe to be endured. *He's ~ praying for,* There's no hope of cure, improvement, etc. *She's ~ caring what happens,* has reached the stage of complete indifference, is quite resigned to ill fortune, etc. **be/get ~ it,** (colloq) be no longer able to do the things one could formerly do: *My gardener is over seventy-five and I'm afraid he's getting past it.* **wouldn't put sth '~ sb,** consider him capable of doing sth disreputable, unusual, etc: *You may say that he is honest but I wouldn't put it ~ him to run off with the money.* □ adv (in the sense of 2 above): *walk/march/go/ run/hurry ~.*
pasta /'pæstə US: 'pɑːstə/ n [U] (I) (dish of food prepared from a dough of) flour, eggs and water mixed and dried, eg macaroni, spaghetti, ravioli.
paste /peɪst/ n [U] 1 soft mixture of flour, fat, etc for making pastry. 2 preparation of foodstuffs, cut up and pounded to a soft, moist mass: *'anchovy ~; 'fish-~.* 3 mixture of flour and water used for sticking things together, esp paper on walls and boards: *a bottle of ~.* **'~-board** n [U] stiff board-like material made by pasting sheets of paper together; cardboard. 4 substance (a glass-like material) used in making artificial diamonds, etc □ *vt* 1 [VP6A,15A,B] stick with ~(3). **~ sth down,** fasten down with ~. **~ sth up,** (a) fasten with ~

to a surface: ~ *up a notice.* **(b)** seal or cover using ~: ~ *up cracks with paper.* **(c)** fasten sheets or strips of paper on larger sheets, eg to design pages for a magazine, book, etc. Hence, '~-**up** *n.* **2** [VP6A] (colloq) thrash; beat. Hence, **past·ing** *n* (colloq) severe beating: *Get/Give sb a pasting.*

pas·tel /'pæstl US: pæ'stel/ *n* **1** (picture drawn with) coloured chalk made into crayons. **2** (attrib) ~ *shades,* soft, light, delicate shades of colour.

pas·tern /'pæstən/ *n* part of a horse's foot between the fetlock and the hoof. ⇨ the illus at domestic.

pas·teur·ize /'pæstʃəraɪz/ *vt* [VP6A] rid (milk, etc) of disease-producing bacteria by using the heating method of Louis Pasteur /pæ'stɜ:(r)/, 1822—1895, French chemist. **pas·teur·iz·ation** /ˌpæstʃəraɪ-'zeɪʃn US: -rɪ'z-/ *n*.

pas·tiche /pæ'sti:ʃ/ *n* [C] literary or other work of art composed in the style of another author, etc; musical composition made up from various sources.

pas·tille /'pæstɪl US: pæ'sti:l/ *n* [C] small flavoured tablet to be sucked, eg one containing medicine for the throat.

pas·time /'pɑ:staɪm US: 'pæs-/ *n* [C] anything done to pass time pleasantly; game: *Photography is her favourite* ~.

pas·tor /'pɑ:stə(r) US: 'pæs-/ *n* minister(3), esp of a nonconformist church.

pas·toral /'pɑ:stərəl US: 'pæs-/ *adj* **1** of shepherds and country life: ~ *poetry.* **2** of a pastor; (esp) of a bishop: *a* ~ *letter,* one to the members of a bishop's diocese; ~ *staff,* bishop's emblem, like a shepherd's crook, carried by or before bishops ceremonially. **3** of (duties towards) a priest's or a minister's flock: ~ *care/responsibilities.* □ *n* ~ poem, play, letter, etc.

pas·tor·ate /'pɑ:stərət US: 'pæs-/ *n* **1** office of a pastor; time during which he holds it. **2** body of pastors.

pas·try /'peɪstrɪ/ *n* (*pl* -tries) **1** [U] paste of flour, fat, etc baked in an oven; pie-crust. **2** [C] article of food made wholly or partly of this, eg a pie or tart; [U] such articles collectively: *eat less* ~. '~-**cook** *n* person who makes ~, esp for public sale.

pas·ture /'pɑ:stʃə(r) US: 'pæs-/ *n* [U] grassland for cattle; grass on such land, ⇨ meadow; [C] piece of land of this kind. □ *vt,vi* **1** [VP6A] (of persons) put (cattle, sheep, etc) to graze: ~ *one's sheep on the village common;* (of cattle, etc) eat down grassland. **2** [VP2A] graze. **pas·tur·age** /-ɪdʒ/ *n* [U] (right to graze cattle on) ~ land.

pasty¹ /'peɪstɪ/ *adj* (-ier, -iest) like paste(1): *a* ~ *complexion,* white and unhealthy.

pasty² /'pæstɪ/ *n* (*pl* -ties) pie of meat, jam, etc enclosed in paste and baked without a dish: *a Cornish* ~.

pat¹ /pæt/ *adv* at the right moment; at once and without hesitation: *The answer came pat. He had his excuse pat.* **stand pat,** stick to one's decision; refuse to change.

pat² /pæt/ *vt,vi* (-tt-) **1** [VP6A,15A] tap gently with the open hand or with sth flat: *pat a dog; pat a ball,* so that it bounces up and down. *pat sb/oneself on the back,* (fig) express approval, congratulate, etc. **2** [VP2A] carry out the action of patting. □ *n* [C] **1** tap with the open hand, eg as a caress or to show sympathy. **2** small mass of sth, esp butter, formed by patting. **3** light sound made by striking sth with a flat object.

patch¹ /pætʃ/ *n* **1** small piece of material put on

over a hole or a damaged or worn place: *a coat with* ~*es on the elbows; a* ~ *on the inner tube of a tyre.* ~-'**pocket** *n* one made by sewing a piece of cloth on to the outside of a garment. **2** piece of plaster put over a cut or wound. **3** pad worn to protect an injured eye. **4** small, irregular, differently coloured part of a surface: *a dog with a white* ~ *on its neck.* **5** small area (of ground, esp for garden vegetables): *the* '*cabbage* ~; small area of anything: ~*es of fog; small* ~*es of blue in a cloudy sky.* **6** *not a* ~ *on,* not nearly so good as. **7** *go through/hit/strike a bad* ~, be in/reach a period of bad luck, difficulty, unhappiness. '~-**work** *n* [U] **1** piece of material made up of bits of cloth of various sizes, shapes and colours: (attrib) *a* ~*work quilt.* **2** (fig) piece of work made up of odds and ends.

patch² /pætʃ/ *vt* [VP6A] **1** put a patch on; (of material) serve as a patch for. **2** [VP15B] ~ *up,* repair; make roughly ready for use: *an old,* ~*ed-up motor-cycle;* (fig) ~ *up a quarrel,* settle it for a time. ~**y** *adj* (-ier, -iest) made up of ~es; not regular or uniform; of uneven quality: ~*y work/ knowledge. The fog was* ~*y.* ~·**ily** /-ɪlɪ/ *adv* ~·**i-ness** *n*

patch·ouli /'pætʃʊlɪ/ *n* [U] (perfume derived from an) Asiatic plant.

pate /peɪt/ *n* (colloq) head: *a bald* ~.

pâté /'pæteɪ US: pɑ:'teɪ/ *n* **1** pie; patty. **2** paste. ~ *de foie gras* /ˌ- də fwɑ: 'grɑ:/, (F) (patty of) goose-liver paste.

pa·tel·la /pə'telə/ *n* (anat) kneecap.

pat·ent¹ /'peɪtnt US: 'pætnt/ *adj* **1** evident, easily seen: *It was* ~ *to everyone that he disliked the idea.* **2** ,**letters** '~ /'pætnt/, government authority to manufacture sth invented and protect it from imitation. **3** protected by letters ~: ~ *medicines,* made by one firm or person only. **4** ~ **leather,** leather with a hard, smooth, shiny surface. ~·**ly** *adv* clearly; obviously.

pat·ent² /'peɪtnt US: 'pætnt/ *n* [C] **1** (privilege granted by) letters patent: *take out a* ~ *to protect a new invention.* **P**~ (usu /'pætnt/) **Office,** government department which issues ~s. **2** that which is protected by letters ~; invention or process. □ *vt* [VP6A] obtain a ~ for (an invention or process). ~**ee** /ˌpeɪtn'ti: US: ˌpætn-/ *n* person to whom a ~ is issued.

pater·fa·mil·ias /ˌpeɪtəfə'mɪlɪæs US: ˌpæt-/ *n* (hum) father or head of a family.

pa·ter·nal /pə'tɜ:nl/ *adj* **1** of or like a father: ~ *care.* **2** related through the father: *my* ~ *grand-father.* ~**ly** /-nəlɪ/ *adv* ~·**ism** /-ɪzəm/ *n* [U] (practice of) governing or controlling people in a ~ way (providing for their needs but giving them no responsibility).

pa·ter·nity /pə'tɜ:nətɪ/ *n* [U] fatherhood; being a father; origin on the father's side: *of unknown* ~.

pater·nos·ter /ˌpætə'nɒstə(r)/ *n* (Lat for 'Our Father') **1** (recital of) the Lord's Prayer. **2** bend in a rosary at which the Lord's Prayer is repeated. **3** lift(2) with a series of doorless cars(3) moving on a continuous belt so that passengers can step on or off at each floor.

path /pɑ:θ US: pæθ/ *n* (*pl* ~s /pɑ:ðz US: pæðz/) **1** '~·(way), ('foot)·~, way, track made (across fields, through woods, etc) by or for people walking: *Keep to the* ~ *or you may lose your way.* '~·**finder** *n* explorer; sb sent on ahead to find a route, etc; pioneer. **2** track specially made for foot or cycle racing (usu *cinder track*). **3** line along which sth or sb moves: *the moon's ~ round the earth; the 'flight ~ of a spacecraft; the ~ of a tornado.* ~**less** *adj* having no ~s: ~*less jungles.*

pa·thetic /pə'θetɪk/ *adj* **1** able to be considered sad, pitiful, or (colloq) contemptible: *a ~ sight; ~ ignorance.* **2 the ~ fallacy,** the error of imaginatively endowing inanimate objects with life, human feelings, etc. **pa·theti·cally** /-klɪ/ *adv*

pa·thol·ogy /pə'θɒlədʒɪ/ *n* [U] science of diseases. **path·ol·ogist** /pə'θɒlədʒɪst/ *n* student of, expert in, ~. **path·o·logi·cal** /ˌpæθə'lɒdʒɪkl/ *adj* of ~; of the nature of disease. **path·o·logi·cally** /-klɪ/ *adv*

pa·thos /'peɪθɒs/ *n* [U] quality in speech, writing, etc which arouses a feeling of pity, sympathy or tenderness.

pa·tience /'peɪʃns/ *n* [U] **1** (power of) enduring trouble, suffering, inconvenience, without complaining; ability to wait for results, to deal with problems calmly and without haste: *I haven't the ~ to hear your complaints again. She has no ~ with people who are always grumbling,* cannot endure them. **be out of ~ (with),** be unable to endure further. **the ~ of Job,** very great ~: *His behaviour would try* (= test) *the ~ of Job.* **2** (GB) kind of card game, usu for one player (US = *solitaire*).

pa·tient[1] /'peɪʃnt/ *adj ~ (with sb),* having or showing patience (with him): *be ~ with a tired child. be ~ of sth,* (archaic) **(a)** be able to endure it ~ly. **(b)** admit(5). ~**ly** *adv: wait/sit/listen ~ly.*

pa·tient[2] /'peɪʃnt/ *n* [C] person who has received, is receiving, or is on a doctor's list for, medical treatment: *The Smiths are ~s of Dr Quack.*

pat·ina /'pætɪnə/ *n* (usu) green, glossy surface formed on old bronze or copper; glossiness of old woodwork, etc.

patio /'pætɪəʊ/ *n* (*pl* ~s /-əʊz/) **1** courtyard, open to the sky, within the walls of a Spanish or Spanish American house. **2** (modern use) paved area near a house, used for recreation.

pa·tis·serie /pə'tiːsərɪ/ *n* (F) shop, bakery, specializing in (French) pastry and cakes.

pat·ois /'pætwɑː/ *n* dialect of the common people of a district, differing from the standard language of the country.

pa·trial /'peɪtrɪəl/ *n* person who has qualifications which give him the right to be considered legally a British citizen.

patri·arch /'peɪtrɪɑːk *US:* 'pæt-/ *n* **1** venerable old man. **2** male head of a family or tribe. **3** bishop among the early Christians; (in the RC Church) high-ranking bishop; (in Eastern Churches) bishop of highest honour: *the P~ of Antioch/Jerusalem.* ~**al** /ˌpeɪtrɪ'ɑːkl *US:* ˌpæt-/ *adj* of or like a ~. '~**ate** /-eɪt/ *n* position, see [2], residence, of a Church ~.

pa·tri·cian /pə'trɪʃn/ *n, adj* (person) of noble birth (esp in ancient Rome); aristocrat(ic).

pat·ri·cide /'pætrɪsaɪd/ *n* [U] killing of one's own father; [C] instance of this; [C] person guilty of this.

pat·ri·mony /'pætrɪmənɪ *US:* -məʊnɪ/ *n* (*pl* -nies) [C] property inherited from one's father or ancestors; endowment. **pat·ri·mo·nial** /ˌpætrɪ'məʊnɪəl/ *adj* of a ~.

pa·triot /'pætrɪət *US:* 'peɪt-/ *n* person who strongly supports his country. '~**ism** /-ɪzəm/ *n* [U] the feelings and qualities of a ~. ~**ic** /ˌpætrɪ'ɒtɪk *US:* ˌpeɪt-/ *adj* having, showing, the qualities of a ~. ~**i·cally** /-klɪ/ *adv*

pa·trol /pə'trəʊl/ *vt,vi* (-ll-) [VP6A,2A] go round (a camp, town, the streets, roads, etc) to see that all is well, to look out (for wrongdoers, persons in need of help, the enemy, etc). □ *n* **1** [U] the act of ~ling: *soldiers on ~; maintain a constant sea and air ~,* eg looking for submarines during a war; (attrib) *a police '~ car,* eg on a motorway. **2** [C] person(s), ship(s) or aircraft on ~ duties: *We were helped by an AA* (= Automobile Association) *~(man),* scout. **3** (US) '~ **wagon** *n* one used by the police for conveying prisoners or persons who have been arrested. '~**·man** /-mən/ (*pl* -men) (esp) policeman who ~s an area.

pa·tron /'peɪtrən/ *n* **1** person who gives encouragement, moral or financial support, to a person, cause, the arts, etc: *Modern artists have difficulty in finding wealthy ~s. ~ 'saint,* saint regarded as the special protector (*of* a church, town, travellers, etc). **2** regular customer at a shop. '~**·ess** /-ɪs/ *n* woman ~.

pa·tron·age /'pætrənɪdʒ *US:* 'peɪt-/ *n* [U] **1** support, encouragement, given by a patron: *with/ under the ~ of the Duke of X.* **2** right of appointing sb to a benefice or office, to grant privileges, etc: *He's an influential man, with a great deal of ~ in his hands.* **3** customer's support (to a shopkeeper, etc): *take away one's ~ because of poor service.* **4** patronizing manner. ⇨ patronize(2).

pa·tron·ize /'pætrənaɪz *US:* 'peɪt-/ *vt* [VP6A] **1** act as patron towards: *~ a young musician/a dressmaker.* **2** treat (sb whom one is helping, talking to, etc) as if he were an inferior person; be condescending towards. **pat·ron·iz·ing** *adj* **pat·ron·iz·ing·ly** *adv*

pat·ro·nymic /ˌpætrə'nɪmɪk/ *n, adj* (name) derived from that of a father or ancestor, eg *Robertson; MacNeil; O'Neil.*

pat·ten /'pætn/ *n* clog, wooden shoe, mounted on a metal framework to keep the wearer's foot above the mud.

pat·ter[1] /'pætə(r)/ *n* [U] **1** kind of talk used by a particular class of people: *thieves' ~; the ~ of an auctioneer.* **2** rapid talk of a conjuror or comedian; rapid speech introduced into a song (*a* '~ *song*). □ *vt,vi* [VP6A] recite, say, repeat (prayers, etc) very quickly or in a mechanical way; [VP2A] talk fast or glibly.

pat·ter[2] /'pætə(r)/ *n* [U] sound of quick, light taps or footsteps: *the ~ of rain on a roof; the ~ of footsteps.* □ *vi* [VP2A,C] make this sound: *rain ~ing on the window-panes.*

pat·tern /'pætn/ *n* [C] **1** excellent example; sb or sth serving as a model: *She's a ~ of all the virtues.* (attrib) *He has a ~ (model* is the usu word) *wife.* **2** sth serving as a model, esp shape of a garment, cut out in paper, used as a guide in dressmaking, etc; model from which sth is to be cast and from which a mould is made (in a foundry, etc): '~**·maker;** '~**·shop,** in a foundry. **3** sample, esp a small piece of cloth: *a bunch of ~s from the tailor.* **4** ornamental design, eg on a carpet, on wallpaper, curtain material: *a ~ of roses; geometrical ~s.* **5** way in which sth happens, develops, is arranged, etc: *new ~s of family life,* eg when married women, instead of keeping house, go out to work and add to the family income. □ *vt* **1** [VP14] *~ sth/oneself upon/after sth/sb,* model: *a dress ~ed upon a Paris model. He ~s himself upon his father.* **2** decorate with a ~.

patty /'pætɪ/ *n* (*pl* -ties) little pie or pasty: *oyster* *patties.* '∼**-pan** *n* pan for baking a ∼ in.

pau·city /'pɔːsətɪ/ *n* [U] (formal) smallness of number or quantity.

Paul /pɔːl/ *n* **rob Peter to pay** ∼, ⇨ Peter. ∼ **Pry**, an inquisitive person.

paunch /pɔːntʃ/ *n* belly, esp if fat: *a* ∼ *like that of Falstaff. He was getting quite a* ∼, getting wide round the waist. ∼**y** *adj* having a large ∼. ∼**i-ness** *n*

pau·per /'pɔːpə(r)/ *n* person with no means of livelihood, esp one who is supported by charity. '∼**-ism** /-ɪzəm/ *n* [U] state of being a ∼; existence of ∼s: *abolish* ∼*ism.* '∼**-ize** /-aɪz/ *vt* [VP6A] bring to the state of being a ∼. ∼**-iz·ation** /ˌpɔːpəraɪ'zeɪʃn US: -rɪ'z-/ *n*

pause /pɔːz/ *n* **1** short interval or stop (while doing or saying sth): *during a* ∼ *in the conversation; a* ∼ *to take breath. give* ∼ *to,* cause (a person) to hesitate, to stop and think. **2** (music) sign (⌒ or ⌣) over or under a note or rest to show that it is to be prolonged. □ *vi* [VP2A,4A] make a ∼: ∼ *to look round.*

pave /peɪv/ *vt* [VP6A] put flat stones, bricks, etc on (a path, etc): *a path* ∼*d with brick;* (fig) *a career* ∼*d with* (= full of) *good intentions.* ∼ **the way for,** make conditions easy or ready for. '**paving-stone,** slab of stone for paving.

pave·ment /'peɪvmənt/ *n* **1** (GB) paved way at the side of a street for people on foot (US = *sidewalk*). '∼ **artist,** one who draws pictures on a ∼ with coloured chalks (to get money from passers-by). **2** (US) hard surface for streets, roads, etc. **crazy** ∼, ⇨ crazy(4).

pa·vil·ion /pə'vɪlɪən/ *n* **1** building on a sports ground for the use of players, spectators, etc. **2** ornamental building for concerts, dancing, etc. **3** large tent, eg as used for a flower exhibition.

paw /pɔː/ *n* animal's foot that has claws or nails (contrasted with *hoof*): *a dog's paw;* (colloq, hum) hand. ⇨ the illus at dog. □ *vt* [VP6A,15B] **1** (of animals) feel or scratch with the paw(s); (of a horse) strike (the ground) with a hoof. **2** (of persons) touch with the hands, awkwardly, rudely or with improper familiarity.

pawky /'pɔːkɪ/ *adj* (Scot) sly; arch: ∼ *humour.* **pawk·ily** /'pɔːkɪlɪ/ *adv*

pawl /pɔːl/ *n* **1** lever with a catch for the teeth of a ratchet wheel or rod, to prevent slipping or movement in the opposite direction. **2** short bar used to prevent a capstan or windlass from recoiling.

pawn[1] /pɔːn/ *n* least valuable piece in the game of chess; person made use of by others for their own advantage. ⇨ the illus at chess.

pawn[2] /pɔːn/ *vt* [VP6A] **1** deposit (clothing, jewellery, etc) as a pledge for money borrowed: *The medical student* ∼*ed his microscope to pay his rent.* **2** (fig) pledge: ∼ *one's life/honour.* □ *n* [U] *in* ∼, in a state of being ∼ed: *My watch is in* ∼. '∼**-broker** *n* person licensed to lend money at interest on the security of goods left with him. '∼**-shop** *n* ∼broker's place of business. '∼**-ticket** *n* ∼broker's receipt for goods pledged with him.

paw·paw /pɔ'pɔː US: 'pɔːpɔː/ *n* = papaw.

pax /pæks/ *n* (in church) kiss or sign of peace. **Pax Romana** /ˌpæks rəʊ'mɑːnə/, peace enforced on states in the ancient Roman Empire.

pay[1] /peɪ/ *n* [U] money paid for regular work or services, esp in the armed forces (*Pay* is used instead of *wages* and *salary* in the Navy, Army and Air Force): *draw one's pay; get an increase in pay.*

in the pay of, employed by (often with a suggestion of dishonour, eg *in the pay of the enemy.* '**pay-claim** *n* = *wage-claim,* ⇨ wage. '**pay-day** *n* (**a**) day on which wages, salaries, etc are (to be) paid. (**b**) day (on the Stock Exchange) on which transfer of stock has to be paid for. '**pay-dirt** *n* [U] (US) earth in which there is ore of a grade high enough to make mining profitable. '**pay-load** *n* (**a**) that part of the load (of a ship, aircraft, etc) for which payment is received, eg passengers and cargo, but not fuel. (**b**) bomb in a missile. (**c**) crew and instruments of a spacecraft. '**pay-master** *n* official responsible for paying troops, workers, etc. ˌ**pay-master 'general,** officer at the head of a department of the Treasury. '**pay-off** *n* (colloq) (time of) full and final settlement of accounts or of final retribution or revenge. '**pay-packet** *n* envelope or packet containing pay. '**pay-phone/-station** *nn* (US) coin-operated telephone call-box. '**pay-roll/ -sheet** *nn* (**a**) list of persons to be paid and the amounts due to each. (**b**) total amount of wages, salaries, etc to be paid to them. '**pay-slip** *n* slip of paper included in a pay-packet, showing how pay has been calculated, deductions for tax, etc.

pay[2] /peɪ/ *vt,vi* (*pt,pp* paid /peɪd/) (For special uses with *adverbial particles* and *preps,* ⇨ 6 below.) **1** [VP6A,12B,13B,14,3A] **pay sb; pay for sth; pay sb for sth; pay sb sth; pay sth (to sb) (for sth),** give (sb) money for goods, services, etc: *You must pay me what you owe. You must pay for what you eat and drink. Have you paid the milkman this month? I paid you the money last week. He paid £600 to a dealer for that car. I pay £5 a week for guitar lessons.* **2** [VP2A,14,12B,13B] give (sb) reward or recompense: *He says that sheep farming doesn't pay,* that it isn't profitable. *He has been amply paid for his trouble. They say it pays to advertise.* **3** [VP6A] settle (debts, etc): *Have you paid all your debts yet? He has paid his bills/dues/ subscriptions/taxes.* **put** '**paid to sth,** (colloq) settle it; end it so that it gives no more trouble. **4** [VP6A,12A,13A] ∼ (**to**), give, eg attention, respect, etc to sb: *Please pay more attention to your work. He has called to pay* (= offer) *his respects. He seldom pays his wife any compliments,* seldom compliments her. *I look forward to paying you a visit* (= visiting you) *next week.* **5** (phrases) **pay one's way,** not get into debt. **pay through the nose,** ⇨ nose[1](1). ˌ**pay-as-you-'earn,** (abbr **PAYE**), method of collecting income tax (in GB) by requiring employers to deduct it from earnings. **pay·able** /'peɪəbl/ *adj* which must or may be paid. **payee** /peɪ'iː/ *n* person to whom sth is (to be) paid. **payer** *n* person who pays or who is to pay. **6** [VP15B,3A] (special uses with *adverbial particles* and *preps*):

pay sth back, return (money, etc) that has been borrowed. **pay sb back/out (for sth),** punish him; have one's revenge: *I've paid him out for the trick he played on me.*

pay for, (a) ⇨ 1 above. (**b**) suffer pain or punishment for: *He'll have to pay for this foolish behaviour.*

pay sth in; pay sth into sth, deposit (money) with a bank, to one's own or another's account: *Please pay this sum into my/my wife's account.*

pay sb off, (a) pay sb his wages and discharge him. (**b**) pay in full and be free from obligation: *pay off one's creditors; pay off the crew of a ship.* ⇨ *pay-off* at pay[1].

pay sth out, (a) give money, eg in settlement of expenses: *When you move into a new house you really have to start paying out* (*money*). (b) (naut) allow (rope) to run out freely through the hands; slacken (rope) so that it runs freely.
pay up, pay in full what is owing: *If you don't pay up, I'll take you to court.*
pay·ment /'peɪmənt/ n 1 [U] paying or being paid: *demand prompt* ~; *a cheque in* ~ *for services rendered.* 2 [C] sum of money (to be) paid: *£50 cash down and ten monthly* ~s *of £5.* 3 [C,U] (fig) reward; punishment.
pay·nim /'peɪnɪm/ n (archaic) pagan; heathen; (esp during the Crusades to the Holy Land) Saracen.
pea /piː/ n [C] plant with seeds in pods, used for food. ⇨ the illus at **vegetable.** **as like as two peas (in a pod),** exactly alike. '**pea-chick,** '**pea-fowl,** '**pea-hen** nn ⇨ peacock. '**pea-flour** n [U] meal made from dried peas. '**pea-green** adj, n bright light-green colour of young peas. '**pea-shooter** n (toy) tube from which dried peas are shot by blowing through the tube. ,**pea-'soup** n thick soup made from dried peas. ,**pea-'souper** n (colloq) thick yellow fog.
peace /piːs/ n [U] (not used in pl, but see examples for use of *indef art*) 1 state of freedom from war: *be at* ~ *with neighbouring countries. After a brief* ~ (= a brief period of ~) *war broke out again.* **make** ~ **(with),** bring about ~ (with). 2 (often P~) treaty of ~: *P~/A P~ was signed between the two countries.* 3 freedom from civil disorder. **break the** ~, cause civil disorder, rioting, etc. **keep the** ~, obey the laws and refrain from disorder and strife. **breach of the** ~, a disturbance or riot. **the King's/Queen's** ~, the general ~ of the country, as secured by law. **Justice of the P~,** (abbr **JP**) magistrate. 4 rest; quiet; calm: *the* ~ *of the countryside;* ~ *of mind.* **at** ~ **(with),** in a state of friendship or harmony: *He's never at* ~ *with himself,* is always restless. **in** ~, peacefully: *live in* ~ *with one's neighbours.* **hold one's** ~, keep silence; stop talking or arguing. **make one's** ~ **(with sb),** settle a quarrel. '~**-maker** n person who restores friendly relations. '~**-offering** n sth offered to show that one is willing to make ~.
peace·able /'piːsəbl/ adj not quarrelsome; free from fighting or uproar. **peace·ably** /-əblɪ/ adv
peace·ful /'piːsfl/ adj 1 loving peace: ~ *nations.* 2 calm; quiet: *a* ~ *evening; a* ~ *death.* ~**ly** /-fəlɪ/ adv ~**·ness** n
peach¹ /piːtʃ/ n 1 (tree with) juicy, round fruit with delicate yellowish-red skin and a rough stone-like seed; yellowish-red. ⇨ the illus at **fruit.** 2 (sl) person or thing greatly admired.
peach² /piːtʃ/ vi,vt [VP2A,3A,6A] ~ **(against/ on/upon) (sb),** (sl) inform (against); betray.
pea·cock /'piːkɒk/ n large male bird noted for its fine tail feathers. ⇨ the illus at **rare.** ~**-'blue** adj, n bright blue (colour). '**pea-chick** n young pea-fowl. '**pea-fowl** n ~ or pea-hen. '**pea-hen** n female of the ~.
pea-jacket /'piː dʒækɪt/ n short double-breasted overcoat of thick woollen cloth, as worn by sailors.
peak¹ /piːk/ n 1 pointed top, esp of a mountain; point, eg of a beard. ⇨ the illus at **mountain.** '**P~ District,** area in Derbyshire, England, having many ~s. 2 pointed front part of a cap; projecting brim (to shade the eyes). 3 narrow part of a ship's hold at the bow ('*fore*~) or stern ('*after*~). 4 highest point in a record of figures that fluctuate: ~

hours of traffic, times when the traffic is heaviest; *industry's* ~ *hours,* when consumption of electric current, etc is highest; *off-* ~ *periods,* when traffic, consumption of current, etc is light; *off-* ~ *flights to Rome,* during the less busy times, eg during hours of darkness. **peaked** adj having a ~: ~*ed cap/roof.*
peak² /piːk/ vi [VP2A] 1 reach the highest point, value, etc: *property prices have* ~*ed.* 2 ~ **and pine,** waste away. **peaked** pp sharp-featured; thin, pale and weak-looking. **peaky** adj = peaked.
peal /piːl/ n [C] 1 loud ringing of a bell or of a set of bells with different notes; changes rung upon a set of bells; set of bells tuned to each other. 2 loud echoing noise: *a* ~ *of thunder;* ~s *of laughter.* □ vi,vt 1 [VP2A,C] sound forth in a ~; ring out loudly. 2 [VP6A] cause to ring or sound loudly.
pean /'piːən/ (US) = paean.
pea-nut /'piːnʌt/ n groundnut. ,~ '**butter,** paste of roasted ground ~s. ,~ '**oil,** oil pressed from ~s, used in cooking, etc. ~**s,** (sl, derog) small amount of money.
pear /peə(r)/ n [C] (tree with) sweet, juicy fruit, usu tapering towards the stalk. ⇨ the illus at **fruit.**
pearl /pɜːl/ n 1 silvery-white or bluish-white spherical formation found inside the shells of some oysters, valued as a gem: *a necklace of* ~s; *a* ~ *necklace.* '~**-diver** n one who dives for ~-oysters. '~**-fishery** n place where ~-oysters are fished up. '~**-oyster** n kind in which ~s are found. 2 = mother-of-~: ~ *buttons.* ⇨ mother. 3 small round fragment of various substances. ,~-'**barley/-'sago** nn barley/sago rubbed into small ~-like grains. 4 sth that looks like a ~, eg a dew-drop; sb or sth very precious: *She's a* ~ *among women.* **cast** ~s **before swine,** (prov) offer sth valuable or beautiful to those who cannot appreciate it. □ vi fish for ~s: *go* ~*ing.* ~**y** adj of, like, ornamented with, ~s. **P~y King/Queen,** costermonger wearing pearlies. ~**-ies** n pl (the now festive) dress of some London costermongers, ornamented with many mother-of-~ buttons.
pear-main /'peəmeɪn/ n variety of apple.
peas·ant /'peznt/ n (not GB or US) countryman working on the land, either for wages or on a very small farm which he either rents or owns: (attrib) ~ *labour,* ⇨ for GB, *smallholder,* at small and, for US, *sharecropper* at share¹(1). ~**ry** /'pezntrɪ/ n the ~s of a country; ~s as a class.
pease /piːz/ n ~**-pudding** n pudding of boiled peas.
peat /piːt/ n [U] plant material partly decomposed by the action of water, found in bogs, used in horticulture, and as a fuel: *a bag/bale of* ~; *a* '~*-bog,* a marshy place where ~ is found; *a* ~ *fire,* one on which cut pieces of ~ are burnt as fuel. ~**y** adj of, like, smelling of, ~.
pebble /'pebl/ n small stone made smooth and round by the action of water, eg in a stream or on the seashore. **peb·bly** /'peblɪ/ adj covered with ~s: *a pebbly beach.*
pe·can /pɪ'kæn US: pɪ'kɑːn/ n [C] (nut of a) kind of hickory tree growing in the Mississippi region of the USA.
pec·cable /'pekəbl/ adj (formal) liable to sin.
pec·ca·dillo /,pekə'dɪləʊ/ n (pl ~es or ~s /-ləʊz/) small weakness in a person's character; small sin or fault.
pec·cary /'pekərɪ/ n (pl -ries) kind of wild pig

found in America.

peck¹ /pek/ n measure of capacity for dry goods (= 2 gallons or approx 9 litres): a ~ of beans; (fig) a lot: a ~ of troubles. ⇨ App 5.

peck² /pek/ vi,vt 1 [VP2A,C,3A,6A] ~ (at), (try to) strike with the beak: hens ~ing at the corn; cocks ~ing (at) the hens; (colloq) ~ at one's food, (of a person) eat only small bits of food; eat without appetite. '~·ing order, order (within a flock of poultry) in which each bird submits to ~ing and domination by stronger birds and itself ~s and dominates weaker birds; any similar arrangement in a group of human beings: Poor Tom! He's at the bottom of the ~ing order, is dominated by all the members of his group. 2 [VP6A] get or make by striking with the beak: ~ corn. The hens ~ed a hole in the sack. 3 (colloq) kiss hurriedly from habit or a sense of duty rather than from affection. □ n 1 stroke with the beak; mark made by this. 2 (colloq) hurried, unemotional kiss. ~er n (GB sl) human nose; (fig) courage; spirits. ˌkeep your '~·er up, stay cheerful; don't let your spirits droop. '~·ish /-ɪʃ/ adj (colloq) hungry.

pec·tin /'pektɪn/ n [U] (chem) compound similar to sugar, formed in fruits by ripening process and by heating, eg when fruit is made into jam. **pec·tic** /'pektɪk/ adj of ~; producing ~: pectic acid.

pec·toral /'pektərəl/ adj 1 of, for, the chest or breast: a ~ muscle/fin. 2 worn on the chest or breast: a ~ cross, as worn by a bishop.

pecu·late /'pekjʊleɪt/ vi,vt embezzle. **pecu·la·tion** /ˌpekjʊ'leɪʃn/ n [U] peculating; [C] instance of this.

pe·cu·liar /pɪ'kjuːlɪə(r)/ adj 1 ~ (to), belonging exclusively; used, adopted, practised, only by: customs ~ to these tribes; a style ~ to the 18th century. 2 strange; unusual; odd. 3 particular; special: a matter of ~ interest. ~·ly adv in a ~ manner: ~ly annoying, more than usually annoying. ~·ity /pɪˌkjuːlɪ'ærətɪ/ n (pl -ties) 1 [U] the quality of being ~. 2 [C] sth distinctive or characteristic. 3 [C] sth odd or strange: ~ities of speech/dress/behaviour.

pe·cuni·ary /pɪ'kjuːnɪərɪ US: -ɪerɪ/ adj (formal) of money: ~ aid; work without ~ reward.

peda·gogue (US also **-gog**) /'pedəɡɒɡ/ n (formal) schoolmaster; (colloq) pedantic teacher. **peda·gogy** /'pedəɡɒdʒɪ/ n [U] science of teaching. **peda·gog·ic** /ˌpedə'ɡɒdʒɪk/, **peda·gogi·cal** /-ɪkl/ adjj of pedagogy.

pedal¹ /'pedl/ n lever (eg on a bicycle, sewing-machine, organ or piano) worked by the foot or feet: (attrib) ~ cyclist; ~ boat, propelled by ~s. ⇨ the illus at bicycle, church, key. □ vi, vt (-ll-, US also -l-) [VP2A,C,6A] use a ~ or ~s (for playing an organ, riding a bicycle, etc); move or work by the use of a ~ or ~s: The boy ~led away on his tricycle.

pedal² /'pedl/ adj (zool) of the foot or feet.

ped·ant /'pednt/ n person who lays too much stress on book-learning, technical knowledge, rules and adherence to rules. **~·ry** /'pedntrɪ/ n [U] tiresome and unnecessary display of learning; too much insistence upon formal rules; [C] instance of this. **pe·dan·tic** /pɪ'dæntɪk/ adj of or like a ~. **pe·dan·ti·cally** /-klɪ/ adv

peddle /'pedl/ vi,vt 1 [VP2A] be a pedlar; go from house to house trying to sell small articles. 2 [VP6A] deal out in small quantities: She loves to ~ gossip round the village. **ped·dler** n =· pedlar. **ped·dling** adj petty; trivial: peddling details.

ped·er·asty /'pedəræstɪ/ n [U] amorous or sexual relations between a man and a boy. **ped·er·ast** n man who practices ~.

ped·estal /'pedɪstl/ n base of a column; base for a statue or other work of art; each of the two supports of a knee-hole writing-desk. Hence, '~ desk. **knock sb off his ~,** show that he is no longer highly regarded. **set sb on a ~,** make him an object of high regard.

pe·des·trian /pɪ'destrɪən/ n person walking in a street, etc: ~s killed in traffic accidents. ~ **crossing,** street crossing specially marked, where ~s have priority over traffic. ~ **precinct,** ⇨ precinct. □ adj 1 connected with walking. 2 (of writing, a person's way of making speeches, etc) prosaic; dull; uninspired.

pedi·at·rics /ˌpiːdɪ'ætrɪks/ n (with sing v) branch of medicine concerned with children and their illnesses. **pedia·tric·ian** /ˌpiːdɪə'trɪʃn/ n physician who specializes in ~.

pedi·cab /'pedɪkæb/ n (in some Asian countries) tricycle with one seat for the man in charge and a seat behind for two passengers, used as a form of public transport.

pedi·cure /'pedɪkjʊə(r)/ n treatment of the feet, esp toe-nails, corns, bunions, etc.

pedi·gree /'pedɪgriː/ n 1 [C] line of ancestors: proud of their long ~s; [U] ancestry, esp ancient descent. 2 (attrib) having a line of descent that has been recorded: ~ cattle; a ~ poodle.

pedi·ment /'pedɪmənt/ n (in Gk architecture) triangular part over the front of a building; similar part over the portico of a building in other styles of architecture. ⇨ the illus at column.

ped·lar, ped·dler /'pedlə(r)/ n person who travels about selling small articles.

ped·ometer /pɪ'dɒmɪtə(r)/ n device which measures the number of steps taken by a walker, and the approximate distance he walks.

pee /piː/ vi [VP2A] (colloq) urinate: Do you want to pee? □ n [U] urine: a puddle of pee; [C] act of urinating: I must go for/must have a pee.

peek /piːk/ vi ~ at, peep at. □ n quick look: have a quick ~ over the fence.

peek-a-boo /ˌpiːk ə 'buː/ n game for amusing a small child, in which one covers and then uncovers the face, repeatedly, saying '~!' as one does this.

peel /piːl/ vt,vi ~ (off), 1 [VP6A,15B] take the skin off (fruit, etc): ~ a banana; ~ potatoes. 2 [VP2A,C] come off in strips or flakes: These potatoes ~ easily, the skin comes off them easily. The wallpaper is ~ing off. After a day in the hot sun my skin began to ~/my face ~ed. The bark of plane-trees ~s off regularly. It was so hot that we all ~ed off (= undressed) and jumped into the lake. □ n [U] skin of fruit, some vegetables, young shoots, etc. ⇨ the illus at fruit. **candied ~,** ⇨ candy. **~er** n (in compounds) device used for ~ing, eg potatoes. **~·ings** n pl parts ~ed off (esp of potatoes).

peep¹ /piːp/ n 1 short, quick look, often one taken secretly or inquisitively; incomplete view: have a ~ at sb through the window. '~-hole n small opening in a wall, partition, etc through which one can have a ~. '~-show n exhibition of small pictures to be seen through a magnifying lens in a small opening. 2 the first light (of day): ~ of day, dawn. □ vi [VP2A,C] 1 ~ (at), take a ~ (at); look slyly or cautiously: ~ through a keyhole at sth; neighbours ~ing at us from behind curtains.

~ing 'Tom, name used of a prurient person who spies on people who think they are alone; voyeur. **2** come slowly or partly into view: *The moon ~ed out from behind the clouds.* ~er *n* **1** person who ~s. **2** (sl) eye.

peep² /piːp/ *n* [C] weak, shrill sound made by mice, young birds, etc □ *vi* make this sound.

pee·pul, pi·pal /'piːpəl/ *n* large Indian fig-tree.

peer¹ /pɪə(r)/ *n* **1** equal in rank, merit or quality: *It will not be very easy to find his* ~. **2** (in GB) member of one of the degrees of nobility, eg duke, marquis, earl, viscount, baron. ~ **of the realm,** person with the right to sit in the House of Lords. **'life** ~, one elected to the House of Lords for life only (contrasted with a **he'reditary** ~). ~**·ess** /'pɪərəs/ *n* woman ~; wife of a ~(2). ~**·less** *adj* without a ~(1); without equal.

peer² /pɪə(r)/ *vi* [VP2A,3A] ~ **(at/into),** look closely, as if unable to see well: ~ *into dark corners;* ~*ing at her over his spectacles.*

peer·age /'pɪərɪdʒ/ *n* **1** the whole body of peers; rank of peer(2). **raise sb to the** ~, elect sb to the ~. **2** book containing a list of peers(2) with their ancestry.

peeve /piːv/ *vt* (colloq) vex; annoy. ~**d** *adj* (colloq) annoyed.

pee·vish /'piːvɪʃ/ *adj* irritable. ~**·ly** *adv* ~**·ness** *n*

pee·wit /'piːwɪt/ = pewit.

peg¹ /peg/ *n* **1** wooden or metal pin or bolt, usu pointed at one end, used to fasten parts of woodwork together. **a square peg in a round hole,** a person unsuited to the position he fills. **2** pin driven into the ground to hold a rope (*a* 'tent-peg), or fastened to a wall or door ('*hat and* 'coat *pegs*), or to mark a position or boundary. **(buy sth) off the peg,** (colloq) (buy clothes) ready-made (as if off a peg in a shop). **3** '**clothes-peg,** device for holding laundered clothes in place on a line. **4** (fig) theme, pretext or excuse: *a peg on which to hang a speech.* **5** wooden screw for tightening or loosening the string of a violin, etc. ⇨ the illus at string. **,take sb 'down a peg (or two),** humble him. **6** piece of wood for stopping the vent of a cask, etc. **7** (colloq) wooden leg.

pegs

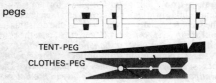

TENT-PEG

CLOTHES-PEG

peg² /peg/ *vt,vi* (-gg-) **1** [VP6A,15B] **peg sth (down),** fasten with pegs: *peg a tent down.* **peg sb down,** (fig) make him keep to a certain line of action, restrict him to the rules, etc. **2** [VP15B] **peg sth out,** mark by means of pegs fixed in the ground; show (a score, esp at cribbage) by means of pegs. **level pegging,** (often fig) making progress at the same rate. **3** [VP6A,15B] (comm) keep (prices, etc) steady by buying and selling (stocks) freely at fixed prices; keep (wages) steady: *wage-pegging efforts that failed.* **4** [VP2C] **peg away at,** keep on working at. **peg out,** (colloq) die.

peig·noir /'peɪnwɑː(r)/ *n* woman's loose dressing gown.

pe·jor·at·ive /pɪ'dʒɒrətɪv US: -'dʒɔːr-/ *adj* depreciatory; disparaging; deteriorating in use or meaning. ~**·ly** *adv*

peke /piːk/ *n* short for *pekinese* (*dog*).

pe·kin·ese /ˌpiːkɪ'niːz/ *n* small Chinese dog with long, silky hair. ⇨ the illus at dog.

pe·koe /'piːkəʊ/ *n* [U] high grade of black tea.

pelf /pelf/ *n* [U] (usu contemptuous use) money.

peli·can /'pelɪkən/ *n* large water-bird with a large bill under which hangs a pouch for storing food. ⇨ the illus at water.

pe·lisse /pe'liːs/ *n* mantle.

pel·let /'pelɪt/ *n* **1** small ball of sth soft, eg wet paper, bread, made, for example, by rolling between the fingers. **2** slug of small shot, eg as used from an air-gun. **3** pill.

pell-mell /ˌpel 'mel/ *adv* in a hurrying, disorderly manner.

pel·lu·cid /pe'luːsɪd/ *adj* (lit, fig) very clear. ~**·ly** *adv*

pel·met /'pelmɪt/ *n* strip (of wood, cloth, etc) above a window or door to conceal a curtain rod.

pe·lota /pə'ləʊtə/ *n* [U] ball game popular in Spain, Latin America and the Philippines, the players using a long basket strapped to the wrist to hit the ball against a wall.

pelt¹ /pelt/ *n* animal's skin with the fur or hair on it.

pelt² /pelt/ *vt,vi* **1** [VP6A,14] ~ **sth (at sb);** ~ **sb (with sth),** attack by throwing things at: ~ *sb with stones/snowballs/mud.* **2** [VP2C] (of rain, etc) beat down; fall heavily: *It was* ~*ing with rain. The rain was* ~*ing down. The hail was* ~*ing against the roof.* □ *n* ~ing. **at full** ~, (running) as fast as possible.

pel·vis /'pelvɪs/ *n* (*pl* ~es or pelves /'pelviːz/) (anat) bony frame within the hip-bones and the lower part of the backbone, holding the kidneys, rectum, bladder, etc. ⇨ the illus at skeleton. **pelvic** /'pelvɪk/ *adj* of the ~.

pem·mi·can /'pemɪkən/ *n* [U] dried lean meat beaten and mixed into cakes (as by N American Indians).

pen¹ /pen/ *n* **1** (formerly) quill-feather, pointed and split at the end, for writing with ink; (mod use) instrument with a pointed piece of split metal ('*pen-nib*) fixed into a holder ('*pen-holder*) of wood or other material; ballpoint-pen; fountain-pen, ⇨ *ball(point)-pen* at ball¹(1) and *fountain-pen* at fountain. **2** (style of) writing: *make a living with one's pen.* **3** ,**pen-and-'ink,** (attrib) drawn with these: *a pen-and-ink sketch.* '**pen-friend** *n* person (eg in another country) with whom one has a friendship through exchanges of letters. '**pen-knife** *n* small folding knife, usu carried in the pocket. **pen·man·ship** /'penmənʃɪp/ *n* [U] art or style of handwriting. '**pen-name** *n* name used by a writer instead of his real name. '**pen-pusher** *n* (derog) clerk. □ *vt* (-nn-) write (a letter, etc).

pen² /pen/ *n* **1** small enclosure for cattle, sheep, poultry, etc or other purposes. **2** ('**play**)-**pen,** portable enclosure for a very small child to play in safety. **3** bomb-proof shelter for submarines. □ *vt* (-nn-) [VP15A,B] **pen up/in,** shut up in, or as in, a pen.

penal /'piːnl/ *adj* connected with punishment: ~ *laws; a* ~ *offence,* one for which there is legal punishment. ~ '**servitude,** imprisonment with hard labour. '~ **settlement/colony,** one used as a place of punishment. ~**ly** /'piːnəlɪ/ *adv*

pe·nal·ize /'piːnəlaɪz/ *vt* **1** [VP6A] make (sth) penal; declare to be punishable by law. **2** [VP6A,14] ~ **sb (for sth),** place at a disadvantage; give a penalty(2) to (a player, competitor, etc). **pe·nal·iz·ation** /ˌpiːnəlaɪˈzeɪʃn *US:* -lɪˈz-/ *n*

pen·alty /ˈpenltɪ/ *n* (*pl* -ties) **1** [U] punishment for wrongdoing, for failure to obey rules or keep an agreement; [C] what is imposed (imprisonment, payment of a fine, etc) as punishment; (fig) suffering which a wrongdoer brings upon himself or others: *Spitting forbidden:* ~ *£5. The* ~ (eg in a business agreement) *for non-performance of contract is heavy.* '~ **clause,** (comm) clause in a contract requiring payment for breaking it. **on/under** ~ **of (death, etc),** with (death, etc) as the ~: *forbidden under* ~ *of death.* **2** (in sport, competitions, etc) disadvantage to which a player or team must submit for breaking a rule: *The referee awarded a* ~. '~ **area,** (football) part of the ground in front of the goal where a breach of the rules by defenders gives the opposing team the right to a free kick (*a* '~ *kick*) at the goal. **3** handicap imposed upon a player or team for winning a previous contest.

pen·ance /ˈpenəns/ *n* [U] **1** punishment which one imposes upon oneself to show repentance, eg upon the advice of a priest. *do* ~ *(for sth),* perform an act of ~ (for sth). **2** (RC Church) name for the sacrament that includes contrition, confession and penance.

pence /pens/ *n* ⇨ penny.

pen·chant /ˈpɑːnʃɑːn *US:* ˈpentʃənt/ *n* (F) *a* ~ *(for),* taste, liking, inclination: *have a* ~ *for marshmallows.*

pen·cil /ˈpensl/ *n* instrument for drawing or writing with, esp of graphite or coloured chalk enclosed in wood or fixed in a metal holder; stick of cosmetic material: *an* 'eyebrow ~. □ *vt* (-ll-, US also -l-) [VP6A] write, draw, mark, with a ~: ~*led eyebrows.*

pen·dant /ˈpendənt/ *n* **1** ornament which hangs down, esp one attached to a necklet, bracelet, etc; lustre attached to a chandelier, etc. **2** (naut) = pennant.

pen·dent /ˈpendənt/ *adj* (formal) **1** hanging; overhanging: ~ *rocks.* **2** = pending.

pend·ing /ˈpendɪŋ/ *adj* waiting to be decided or settled: *The lawsuit was then* ~. □ *prep* **1** during: ~ *these discussions.* **2** until: ~ *his decision.*

pen·du·lous /ˈpendjʊləs *US:* -dʒʊləs/ *adj* (formal) hanging down loosely so as to swing freely: *the* ~ *nests of the weaver-birds.*

pen·du·lum /ˈpendjʊləm *US:* -dʒʊləm/ *n* weighted rod hung from a fixed point so that it swings freely, esp one to regulate the movement of a clock. *the swing of the* ~, (fig) the movement of public opinion from one extreme to the other.

pen·etrable /ˈpenɪtrəbl/ *adj* (formal) that can be penetrated. **pen·etra·bil·ity** /ˌpenɪtrəˈbɪlətɪ/ *n*

pen·etrate /ˈpenɪtreɪt/ *vt,vi* **1** [VP6A,3A] ~ *(into/ to/through),* make a way into, etc; (fig) see into, etc: *The cat's sharp claws* ~*d my skin. The mist* ~*d (into) the room. He* ~*d their thoughts. Our eyes could not* ~ *the darkness. We soon* ~*d his disguise,* saw through it, knew who he really was. **2** *be* ~*d with,* be filled with: *be* ~*d with a desire for mystical experiences.* **pen·etrat·ing** *adj* **1** (of a person, his mind) able to see and understand quickly and deeply. **2** (voices, cries, etc) piercing; loud and clear. **pen·etrat·ing·ly** *adv*

pen·etra·tion /ˌpenɪˈtreɪʃn/ *n* [U] **1** penetrating: *peaceful* ~, acquiring influence, control, etc without the use of force, eg by trade, supplying a country with capital. **2** mental quickness; ability to grasp ideas.

pen-friend /ˈpen frend/ ⇨ pen¹(3).

pen·etra·tive /ˈpenɪtrətɪv *US:* -treɪtɪv/ *adj* able to penetrate; intelligent.

pen·guin /ˈpeŋgwɪn/ *n* seabird of the Antarctic with wings used for swimming. ⇨ the illus at water.

peni·cil·lin /ˌpenɪˈsɪlɪn/ *n* [U] antibiotic drug that, by changing the chemical environment of germs, prevents them from surviving or multiplying.

pen·in·sula /pəˈnɪnsjʊlə *US:* -nsələ/ *n* area of land, eg Italy, almost surrounded by sea and projecting far into the sea. **pen·in·su·lar** /-lə(r)/ *adj* of or like a ~.

pe·nis /ˈpiːnɪs/ *n* organ of urination and copulation of a male animal.

peni·tence /ˈpenɪtəns/ *n* [U] ~ *(for),* sorrow and regret (for wrongdoing, sin).

peni·tent /ˈpenɪtənt/ *adj* feeling regret; showing regret or remorse. ~·**ly** *adv*

peni·ten·tial /ˌpenɪˈtenʃl/ *adj* of penitence or penance. ~·**ly** /-ʃəlɪ/ *adv*

peni·ten·tiary /ˌpenɪˈtenʃərɪ/ *n* (*pl* -ries) (US) prison for persons guilty of serious crimes, esp one in which reform of the prisoners is the main aim. □ *adj* of reformatory treatment.

pen-name /ˈpen neɪm/ ⇨ pen¹(3).

pen·nant /ˈpenənt/ *n* flag (usu long and narrow) used on a ship for signalling, identification, etc. ⇨ the illus at barque.

pen·ni·less /ˈpenɪlɪs/ *adj* without any money: *I'm* ~ *until pay-day.*

pen·non /ˈpenən/ *n* **1** long, narrow (usu triangular) flag, as used by a knight on his lance, by soldiers in lancer regiments, and on ships, eg in signalling. **2** (US) flag of this shape as a school banner, with the school's name or initials on it.

penn'orth /ˈpenəθ/ *n* = pennyworth; ⇨ penny(5).

penny /ˈpenɪ/ *n* (*pl* pence /pens/ when combined with numbers, as in 'sixpence, 'tenpence, ˌeighteen 'pence; *pl* pennies /ˈpenɪz/ when used of individual coins: *Please give me ten pennies for this tenpence piece.*) ⇨ App 5. **1** (until 1971) British bronze coin (abbr **d**) worth one twelfth of a shilling. **2** (since decimal coinage was introduced, 1971) British bronze coin (abbr **p**) worth one hundredth of a pound: *These cigarettes are 70 pence a packet.* **3** (US colloq) cent. **4** (phrases, all pre-1971 in origin) *(cost) a pretty* ~, a large sum of money. *in for a* ~, *in for a pound,* sth that one has begun must be finished, whatever the cost may be. ~-*wise and pound foolish,* careful in small matters and wasteful in large matters. *turn an honest* ~, earn a little money honestly. **5** (compounds) ˌ~ 'dreadful, (colloq) cheap, sensational, popular novel, etc. '~ pincher, (colloq) miser. '~ pinching *adj* mean; miserly. '~-weight *n* 24 grains, one-twentieth of an ounce Troy. ⇨ App 5. ˌ~ 'whistle, simple, cheap musical pipe. '~-worth (also penn'orth /ˈpenəθ/) *n* as much as can be bought for a ~. *a good/bad* ~worth, a good/bad bargain. **6** (from the use of pennies in coin-operated machines, locks on doors, etc). *spend a* ~, (colloq) urinate. *The* ~ *dropped,* The desired result was achieved, the meaning of a remark, etc was understood.

pe·nol·ogy /piːˈnɒlədʒɪ/ *n* [U] study of the problems of legal punishment and prison management.

pen·sion¹ /ˈpenʃn/ *n* [C] regular payment made by the State to sb old (*Re'tirement P*~, or *old-'age* ~), disabled (eg 'war ~) or widowed, or by a former employer to an employee after long service. **draw a/one's** ~, receive it on one occasion or regularly. **on (a)** ~, receiving a ~: *be/go/retire on (a)* ~. □ *vt* [VP15B] ~ **sb off**, grant or pay a ~ to; dismiss or allow to retire with a ~. ~**·able** /-əbl/ *adj* (of services, posts, age, work, etc) entitling one to a ~. ~**er** *n* person who is receiving a ~.

pen·sion² /'pɒnsɪɒn/ *n* (in Europe, but not GB) boarding-house at which fixed rates are charged (by the week or month). **en** ~ /ɒn 'pɒnsɪɒn/, as a boarder.

pen·sive /'pensɪv/ *adj* deep in thought; seriously thoughtful: *a* ~ *look; look* ~. ~**·ly** *adv* ~**·ness** *n*

pen·stock /'penstɒk/ *n* flood-gate; sluice.

pen·ta·gon /'pentəgən *US:* -gɒn/ *n* plane figure with five sides and five angles. **the P·**~, building in Arlington, Virginia, headquarters of the US Armed Forces. **pen·tag·on·al** /pen'tægənl/ *adj*

pen·tam·eter /pen'tæmɪtə(r)/ *n* (in English verse) line of five iambic feet.

Pen·ta·teuch /'pentətjuːk/ *n* **the** ~, the first five books of the Bible.

pen·tath·lon /pen'tæθlən/ *n* (modern Olympic Games) contest in which each competitor takes part in five events (running, horseback riding, swimming, fencing and shooting with a pistol).

Pente·cost /'pentɪkɒst *US:* -kɔːst/ *n* [U] **1** Jewish harvest festival, fifty days after the Passover. **2** (esp US) Whit Sunday, the seventh Sunday after Easter. ~**al** /,pentɪ'kɒstl *US:* -'kɔːstl/ *adj*

pent·house /'penthaʊs/ *n* **1** sloping roof supported against a wall, esp one for a shelter or shed. **2** apartment built on the roof of a tall building.

pent-up /,pent 'ʌp/ *adj* repressed: ~ *feelings/fury.*

pen·ul·ti·mate /pen'ʌltɪmət/ *n, adj* (word, syllable, event, etc which is) the one before the last one.

pen·um·bra /pɪ'nʌmbrə/ *n* partly shaded region around the shadow of an opaque body (esp round the total shadow of the moon or earth in eclipse).

pen·uri·ous /pɪ'njʊərɪəs *US:* -'nʊr-/ *adj* (formal) poor; grudging; stingy: *a man who is* ~ *in his habits.* ~**·ly** *adv* ~**·ness** *n*. **pen·ury** /'penjʊərɪ/ *n* (formal) [U] poverty: *living in penury; reduced to penury.*

peon /'piːən/ *n* **1** (in Latin America) unskilled farm worker, esp one who is not wholly free. **2** (in India and Pakistan) office messenger; orderly. '~**·age** /-ɪdʒ/ *n* [U] system of employing ~s(1); (legal) use of indebtedness to compel sb to work.

peony /'piːənɪ/ *n* (*pl* -nies) [C] garden plant with large round pink, red or white flowers.

people /'piːpl/ *n* [U] (collective, with *pl v.* Note that for one human being, it is preferable to use *man, woman, boy, girl* and not *person*, which, although useful in definitions, may be derogatory or formal). **1** persons in general: *streets crowded with* ~. *Some* ~ *are very inquisitive.* **2** those persons belonging to a place, or forming a social class: *The* ~ *in the village like the new doctor. Some* ~ *spend a lot of money on clothes.* **3** all the persons forming a State: *government of the* ~, *by the* ~, *for the* ~; *the P*~*'s Republic of China,* (official name). **4** those persons who are not nobles, not high in rank, position, etc. **5** (colloq) one's near relations: *You must come home with me and meet my* ~, *darling.* **6** [C] (not collective) race, tribe, nation: *the* ~*s of Asia; a brave and intelligent* ~. □ *vt* [VP6A] fill with ~; put ~ in: *a thickly* ~*d district.*

pep /pep/ *n* [U] (sl) vigour; spirit. '**pep pill,** one

that stimulates the nervous system (usu one containing amphetamine). '**pep talk,** one intended to fill the listener(s) with spirit and energy. □ *vt* (-pp-) [VP15B] **pep up,** give energy to; liven up.

pep·per /'pepə(r)/ *n* **1** [U] hot-tasting powder made from the dried berries of certain plants, used to season food. ,~**-and-'salt** *n* (colour of) cloth of dark and light wools woven together, with small dark and light dots. '~**·corn** *n* the dried, black berry of the plant; (fig) this as a nominal rent. '~**·mill** *n* container in which ~corns are ground to powder and sprinkled on food. '~**·mint** *n* **(a)** [U] kind of mint grown for its essential oil, used in medicine and confectionery. **(b)** [C] sweet of boiled sugar flavoured with ~mint. '~**-pot** *n* small container with a perforated top from which ~ is sprinkled on food. **2** (garden plant with a) red or green seed pod (eg capsicum) which is used as a vegetable: *stuffed* ~*s.* □ *vt* [VP6A] **1** put ~ on (food). **2** pelt (sb) (with stones, shot, questions, etc). ~**y** *adj* tasting of ~; (fig) hot-tempered: *a* ~*y old colonel.*

pep·sin /'pepsɪn/ *n* [U] liquid (an enzyme) produced in the stomach for helping to digest food. **pep·tic** /'peptɪk/ *adj* digestive; of digestion or the digestive system: *a peptic ulcer.*

per /pɜː(r); *weak form* pə(r)/ *prep* **1** (when comparing two amounts; when quoting a *rate¹*(1)) for each: *per annum* /'ænəm/, for each year; *per diem* /'diːem/, for each day; *per pound; 15 rounds of ammunition per man; interest at 6 per cent,* (6%); *30 miles per gallon,* (abbr **mpg**). ⇨ **to¹** (12). **2** by means of: *per post/rail.* **as per,** (colloq) following: *as per instructions.* **as per usual,** (colloq) as usual.

per·ad·ven·ture /,pɜːrəd'ventʃə(r)/ *adv* (archaic) **1** perhaps. **2** (after *if* and *lest*) by chance: *If* ~ *you fail.*

per·am·bu·late /pə'ræmbjʊleɪt/ *vi,vt* [VP6A,2A] (liter) walk through or over; walk up and down. **per·am·bu·la·tion** /pə,ræmbjʊ'leɪʃn/ *n*

per·am·bu·lator /pə'ræmbjʊleɪtə(r)/ *n* (common colloq abbr **pram** /præm/) four-wheeled carriage, pushed by hand, for a baby; baby-carriage (the usu word in US).

per·ceive /pə'siːv/ *vt* [VP6A,8,9,10,18A,19A,25] (formal) become aware of, esp through the eyes or the mind: *On entering his house, we at once* ~*d him to be/*~*d that he was a man of taste.* **per·ceiv·able** /-əbl/ *adj*

per·cen·tage /pə'sentɪdʒ/ *n* **1** rate or number per cent (= for each hundred). **2** proportion: *What* ~ *of his income is paid in income tax?*

per·cep·tible /pə'septəbl/ *adj* (formal) that can be perceived. **per·cep·tibly** /-əblɪ/ *adv* **per·cep·ti·bil·ity** /pə,septə'bɪlətɪ/ *n*

per·cep·tion /pə'sepʃn/ *n* [U] (formal) process by which we become aware of changes (through the senses of sight, hearing, etc); act or power of perceiving.

per·cep·tive /pə'septɪv/ *adj* (formal) having, connected with, perception; able to perceive; discerning. ~**·ly** *adv*

perch¹ /pɜːtʃ/ *n* (*pl* unchanged) kinds of freshwater fish with spiny fins, used as food.

perch² /pɜːtʃ/ *n* **1** bird's resting-place, eg a branch; bar or rod provided, eg in a bird-cage, a hen-roost, for this purpose. **2** (colloq) high position occupied by a person; elevated and secure position: *come off your* ~, (colloq) stop being so superior (in manner, etc); *knock sb off his* ~, stop sb being too confident

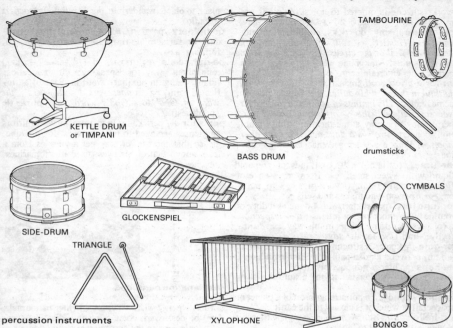

TAMBOURINE

KETTLE DRUM
or TIMPANI

BASS DRUM

drumsticks

CYMBALS

SIDE-DRUM

GLOCKENSPIEL

TRIANGLE

percussion instruments

XYLOPHONE

BONGOS

and superior. **3** (also *pole, rod*) measure of length, esp for land, 5½ yds; *square ~*, 30½ sq yds. ⇨ App 5. □ *vi,vt* **1** [VP2C] alight: *The birds ~ed upon the television aerial.* **2** [VP2C] (of a person) take up a position (usu on sth high): *~ed on stools at the bar.* **3** (chiefly in *pp*) (of buildings) be situated (on sth high): *a castle ~ed on a rock.*

per·chance /pə'tʃɑːns *US:* -'tʃæns/ *adv* (archaic) by chance; possibly.

per·cipi·ent /pə'sɪpɪənt/ *adj* (formal) perceiving (quickly and keenly).

per·co·late /'pɜːkəleɪt/ *vi,vt* [VP6A,2A,3A] *~ (through),* (of liquid) (cause to) pass slowly; filter: *Water ~s through sand. I make coffee by percolating boiling water through ground coffee. I'll ~ some coffee.* **per·co·lator** /-tə(r)/ *n* (esp) kind of coffee pot in which boiling water ~s through coffee (in a container near the top).

per·cussion /pə'kʌʃn/ *n* the striking together of two (usu hard) objects; sound or shock produced by this. **the '~ (section),** musical instruments played by ~, eg drums, cymbals. '~ **cap,** ⇨ cap *n*(4). **~·ist** /-ɪst/ *n* player of ~ instruments.

per·di·tion /pə'dɪʃn/ *n* [U] (formal) complete ruin; everlasting damnation.

per·egri·na·tion /ˌperɪgrɪ'neɪʃn/ *n* [U] (formal) travelling; [C] journey.

per·emp·tory /pə'remptərɪ *US:* 'perəmptɔːrɪ/ *adj* (formal) (of commands) not to be disobeyed or questioned; (of a person, his manner) (too) commanding; insisting upon obedience. **~ writ,** (legal) one that compels a defendant to appear in court. **per·emp·torily** /-trəlɪ *US:* -tɔːrəlɪ/ *adv*

per·en·nial /pə'renɪəl/ *adj* **1** continuing throughout the whole year. **2** lasting for a very long time. **3** (of plants) living for more than two years. □ *n ~* plant: *hardy*(1) *~s.* **~·ly** /-nɪəlɪ/ *adv*

per·fect¹ /'pɜːfɪkt/ *adj* **1** complete with everything needed. **2** without fault; excellent: *a ~ performance of a play.* **3** exact; accurate: *a ~ circle.* **4** having reached the highest point in training, skill, etc: *~ in the performance of one's duties.* **5 ~ tenses,** those composed of *have* + *pp,* eg 'He has/had/will have written the letter' (present, past, future *~*). **6** (attrib only) complete; utter unqualified: *a ~ stranger/fool; ~ nonsense.* **~·ly** *adv* (a) quite; quite well; completely: *~ly happy/satisfied.* (b) in a *~* way: *Your trousers fit ~ly.*

per·fect² /pə'fekt/ *vt* [VP6A] make *~*: *She's ~ing her Arabic before taking up her job in Cairo.* **~·ible** /-əbl/ *adj* that can be *~ed.* **~·i·bil·ity** /pəˌfektə'bɪlətɪ/ *n*

per·fec·tion /pə'fekʃn/ *n* [U] **1** perfecting or being perfected: *busy with the ~ of detail.* **2** perfect quality or example: *It was the very ~ of beauty.* **3** best possible state; highest point attainable: *bring something to ~.* **4** (with *pl*) accomplishment(3). **~·ist** /-ɪst/ *n* **1** person who believes that moral *~* may be attained, that it is possible to live without sinning. **2** (colloq) person who is satisfied with nothing less than what he thinks to be perfect.

per·fer·vid /pɜː'fɜːvɪd/ *adj* (formal) extremely zealous or eager.

per·fidi·ous /pə'fɪdɪəs/ *adj* (formal) treacherous; faithless (*to*). **~·ly** *adv* **~·ness** *n*

per·fidy /'pɜːfɪdɪ/ *n* [U] (*pl* -dies) (formal) treachery; breaking of faith; [C] instance of this.

per·for·ate /'pɜːfəreɪt/ *vt* [VP6A] make a hole or holes in; make rows of tiny holes (in paper) so that part may be torn off easily: *a ~d sheet of postage stamps; a ~ed ulcer.* **per·for·ation** /ˌpɜːfə'reɪʃn/ *n* **1** [U] perforating or being ~d. **2** [C] series of small holes made in paper, etc eg as between postage stamps.

per·force /pə'fɔːs/ *adv* of necessity.

per·form /pə'fɔːm/ *vt,vi* **1** [VP6A] do (a piece of

work, sth one is ordered to do, sth one has promised to do): ~ *a task.* **2** [VP6A,2A] act (a play); play (music); sing, do tricks, etc before an audience: ~ *'Hamlet'*; ~ *skilfully on the flute. The seals* ~*ed well at the circus. Do you enjoy seeing* ~*ing animals?* ~**er** *n* one who ~s, esp at a concert or other entertainment.

per·form·ance /pə'fɔːməns/ *n* **1** [U] performing: *faithful in the* ~ *of his duties.* **2** [C] notable action; achievement: *His innings of 150 was a fine* ~. *Are you satisfied with the* ~ *of your new car?* **3** [C] performing of a play at the theatre; public exhibition; concert: *two* ~*s a day; tickets for the afternoon* ~. *What a* ~*!* (derog) What shocking behaviour!

per·fume /'pɜːfjuːm/ *n* [C,U] (kinds of prepared liquid with) sweet smell, esp from an essence of flowers. □ *vt* /pə'fjuːm/ [VP6A] give a ~ to; put ~ on. ~**r** *n* person who makes and sells ~s.

per·func·tory /pə'fʌŋktərɪ/ *adj* **1** done as a duty or routine but without care or interest: *a* ~ *inspection.* **2** (of persons) doing things in this way. **per·functorily** /-trəlɪ *US:* -tɔːrəlɪ/ *adv*

per·gola /'pɜːgələ/ *n* structure of posts (forming an arbour, or over a garden path) for climbing plants.

per·haps /pə'hæps/ *adv* possibly; maybe.

peri /'pɪərɪ/ *n* (in Persian myth) beautiful girl or woman; fairy; elf.

peri·gee /'perɪdʒiː/ *n* point in an orbit of a planet or spacecraft at which it is closest to the earth.

peri·helion /ˌperɪ'hiːlɪən/ *n* point in a planet's orbit at which it is nearest to the sun.

peril /'perəl/ *n* **1** [U] serious danger: *in* ~ *of one's life; do sth at one's* ~, at one's own risk. **2** [C] sth that causes danger: *the* ~*s of the ocean,* storm, shipwreck, etc. □ *vt* (-ll-, *US* also -l-) (liter, poet) (= *imperil,* which is more usu) put or bring into danger. ~**ous** /'perələs/ *adj* dangerous; full of risk. ~**·ous·ly** *adv*

per·imeter /pə'rɪmɪtə(r)/ *n* [C] (length of the) outer boundary of a closed figure, a military position, an airfield, etc.

per·iod /'pɪərɪəd/ *n* [C] **1** length or portion of time marked off by events that recur, eg hours, days, months and years, fixed by events in nature: *20 teaching* ~*s a week; a lesson* ~ *of 45 minutes.* **2** portion of time in the life of a person, a nation, a stage of civilization, etc; division of geological time: *the* ~ *of the French Revolution. The actors will wear costumes of the* ~/~ *costumes,* ie of the time when the events of the play took place. *The house is 18th century and has* ~ *furniture,* ie of the same century. **3** full pause at the end of a sentence; full stop (.) marking this in writing and print: *put a* ~ *to sth,* bring it to an end. ⇨ App 9. **4** (gram) complete sentence or statement, usu complex; (*pl*) rhetorical or flowery language. **5** time during which a disease runs its course; stage in the course of a disease: *the* ~ *of incubation,* the time during which it is latent. **6** (astron) time taken to complete one revolution. **7** occurrence of menstruation.

peri·odic /ˌpɪərɪ'ɒdɪk/ *adj* occurring or appearing at regular intervals: ~ *attacks of malaria; the* ~ *revolution of a heavenly body.* ~ **'table,** (chem) tabular arrangement of the elements according to their atomic weights and common properties. **peri·odical** /-kl/ *adj* = ~. □ *n* magazine or other publication which appears at regular intervals, eg monthly, quarterly. **peri·od·ically** /-klɪ/ *adv*

peri·pa·tetic /ˌperɪpə'tetɪk/ *adj* going about from

place to place; wandering: *the* ~ *religious teachers of India.*

pe·riph·ery /pə'rɪfərɪ/ *n* (*pl* -ries) external boundary or surface. **pe·riph·eral** /-ərəl/ *adj* of, on, forming, a ~.

pe·riph·ra·sis /pə'rɪfrəsɪs/ *n* (*pl* -ases /-əsiːz/) roundabout way of speaking; circumlocution; (gram) using an auxiliary word in place of an inflected form, eg *'It does work'* for *'It works', 'the word of God'* for *'God's word'.* **peri·phras·tic** /ˌperɪ'fræstɪk/ *adj* of ~.

peri·scope /'perɪskəʊp/ *n* instrument with mirrors and lenses arranged to reflect a view down a tube, etc so that the viewer may get a view as from a level above that of his eyes; used in submarines, trenches, etc.

a submarine periscope

per·ish /'perɪʃ/ *vi,vt* **1** [VP2A,C] (liter or journalism) be destroyed, come to an end, die: *Hundreds of people* ~*ed in the earthquake. I shall do it or* ~ *in the attempt.* **P**~ *the thought!* May even the thought die! **2** [VP6A] (of cold or exposure; usu passive) reduce to distress or inefficiency: *We were* ~*ed with cold/hunger.* **3** [VP6A,2A] (cause to) lose natural qualities; decay: *The rubber belt on this machine has* ~*ed,* has lost its elasticity. *Oil on your car tyres will* ~ *them.* ~**·able** /-əbl/ *adj* (esp of food) quickly or easily going bad. ~**·ables** *n pl* (esp) goods that go bad if delayed in transit, eg fish, fresh fruit. ~**er** *n* (sl) person who is unpleasant and disliked; naughty child.

peri·style /'perɪstaɪl/ *n* (archit) row of columns surrounding a temple, court, etc; space so surrounded.

per·ito·ni·tis /ˌperɪtə'naɪtɪs/ *n* [U] inflammation of the membrane lining the walls of the abdomen.

peri·wig /'perɪwɪg/ *n* = wig.

peri·winkle[1] /'perɪwɪŋkl/ *n* creeping, evergreen plant with light-blue flowers.

peri·winkle[2] /'perɪwɪŋkl/ *n* [C] edible sea snail with a spiral shell. ⇨ the illus at mollusc.

per·jure /'pɜːdʒə(r)/ *vt* [VP6A] (reflex) ~ *oneself,* knowingly make a false statement after taking an oath to tell the truth. ~**r** /'pɜːdʒərə(r)/ *n* person who has ~d himself. **per·jury** /'pɜːdʒərɪ/ *n* [U] act of perjuring oneself; [C] (*pl* -ries) wilful false statement.

perk[1] /pɜːk/ *vi,vt* **1** [VP2C] ~ *up,* (of a person) become lively and active (after depression, illness, etc). **2** [VP15B] ~ *sb/sth up,* smarten; raise (head); make (sb) lively: ~ *oneself up. The horse* ~*ed up its head,* lifted its head as a sign of interest. ~**y** *adj* (-ier, -iest) **1** lively; showing interest or confidence. **2** self-assertive; impudent. ~**·ily** /-ɪlɪ/ *adv* ~**·i·ness** *n*

perk[2] /pɜːk/ *vi,vt* (colloq) percolate (coffee): *Is the coffee* ~*ing yet? We* ~*ed some coffee.*

perk[3] /pɜːk/ *n* (colloq; usu *pl*) perquisite: *an executive's salary with the usual* ~*s.*

perm /pɜːm/ n (colloq abbr for) **1** permanent wave: *go to the hairdresser's for a ~.* **2** permutation (in football pools) □ vt give a ~ to.

per·ma·frost /'pɜːməfrɒst US: -frɔːst/ n permanently frozen subsoil (in the polar regions).

per·ma·nence /'pɜːmənəns/ n [U] state of being permanent. **per·ma·nency** /-nənsɪ/ n (pl -cies) **1** [U] = permanence. **2** [C] permanent thing, person or position: *Is your new job a permanency or merely temporary?*

per·ma·nent /'pɜːmənənt/ adj not expected to change; going on for a long time; intended to last: *my ~ address; a ~ position in the Civil Service.* ⇨ temporary. *~ wave,* style of hairdressing in which artificial waves or curls are put in the hair so that they last several months. **~·ly** adv

per·manga·nate /pə'mæŋgəneɪt/ n ~ of potash, potassium ~, (KMnO₄) dark-purple crystalline salt which is used, dissolved in water, as an antiseptic and disinfectant.

per·meate /'pɜːmɪeɪt/ vt,vi [VP6A,3A] ~ (through/among), pass, flow or spread into every part of: *water permeating (through) the soil; new ideas that have ~d (through/among) the people. The smell of cooking ~d (through) the flat.* **per·meation** /ˌpɜːmɪ'eɪʃn/ n [U] permeating or being ~d. **per·meable** /'pɜːmɪəbl/ adj that can be ~d by fluids; porous. **per·mea·bil·ity** /ˌpɜːmɪə'bɪlətɪ/ n

per·mis·sible /pə'mɪsəbl/ adj that may be permitted. **per·mis·sibly** /-əblɪ/ adv

per·mis·sion /pə'mɪʃn/ n [U] act of allowing or permitting; consent: *with your ~, if you will allow me; give sb ~ to do sth. You have my ~ to leave. By whose ~ did you enter this building?*

per·miss·ive /pə'mɪsɪv/ adj giving permission: ~ *legislation,* that gives powers to do sth but does not order that it shall be done. **the ~ society,** (in GB, 1967 onwards) term used for social changes, including greater sexual freedom, homosexual law reform, abolition of censorship in the theatre, frank discussion of hitherto taboo subjects, etc. **~·ness** n

per·mit /pə'mɪt/ vt,vi (-tt-) **1** [VP6A,C,17,19C] allow: *weather ~ting. Smoking not ~ted in this cinema. Circumstances do not ~ me to help you/ do not ~ my helping you.* **2** [VP3A] ~ of, (formal) admit of: *The situation does not ~ of any delay,* There must be no delay. □ n /'pɜːmɪt/ [C] written authority to go somewhere, do sth, etc: *You won't get into the atomic research station without a ~.*

per·mu·ta·tion /ˌpɜːmjuː'teɪʃn/ n (maths) [U] change in the order of a set of things arranged in a group; [C] any one such arrangement: *The ~s of x, y and z are xyz, xzy, yxz, yzx, zxy, zyx.*

per·mute /pə'mjuːt/ vt [VP6A] change the order of.

per·ni·cious /pə'nɪʃəs/ adj ~ (to), harmful, injurious: ~ *habits; ~ to the welfare of society; ~ anaemia,* a severe kind, often fatal. **~·ly** adv **~·ness** n

per·nick·ety /pə'nɪkətɪ/ adj (colloq) fussy; worrying about trifles.

per·or·ation /ˌperə'reɪʃn/ n (formal) last part of a speech; summing up.

per·ox·ide /pə'rɒksaɪd/ n (hydrogen ~; ~ of hydrogen (H₂O₂)) colourless liquid used as an antiseptic and to bleach hair. ~ **blonde,** person with hair bleached with ~.

per·pen·dicu·lar /ˌpɜːpən'dɪkjʊlə(r)/ adj **1** ~ (to), at an angle of 90° (to another line or surface). **2** upright; crossing the horizontal at an angle of 90°;

(archit; **P~**) of the style of English Gothic architecture of the 14th and 15th cc, marked by vertical lines in the tracery of its windows. □ n [C] ~ line; [U] ~ position: *The wall is a little out of the ~.* **~·ly** adv

per·pe·trate /'pɜːpɪtreɪt/ vt [VP6A] commit (a crime, an error); be guilty of (sth wrong or sth considered outrageous): ~ *a crime/a blunder/a frightful pun.* **per·pe·tra·tor** /-tə(r)/ n **per·pe·tra·tion** /ˌpɜːpɪ'treɪʃn/ n

per·pet·ual /pə'petʃʊəl/ adj **1** never-ending; going on for a long time or without stopping. ~ **'mo·tion,** the motion of a machine, if such could be invented, which would go on for ever without an external source of energy. **2** continual; often repeated: *She's tired of their ~ chatter.* **~·ly** /-ʃʊəlɪ/ adv

per·petu·ate /pə'petʃʊeɪt/ vt [VP6A] preserve from being forgotten or from going out of use: ~ *the memory of a great statesman by erecting a statue of him.* **per·petu·ation** /pəˌpetʃʊ'eɪʃn/ n

per·petu·ity /ˌpɜːpɪ'tjuːətɪ US: -'tuː-/ n (pl -ties) **1** [U] state of being perpetual. **in ~,** for ever. **2** [C] (legal) perpetual annuity or possession.

per·plex /pə'pleks/ vt [VP6A,14] ~ (with), **1** puzzle; bewilder: ~ *sb with questions.* **2** make more complex or intricate. *Don't ~ the issue.* **~ed** adj puzzled; complicated. **~·ed·ly** /-ɪdlɪ/ adv **~·ity** /-ətɪ/ n (pl -ties) **1** [U] ~ed condition; mental difficulty caused by doubt: *He looked at us in ~ity.* **2** [C] perplexing thing; cause of bewilderment.

per·qui·site /'pɜːkwɪzɪt/ n [C] profit, allowance, etc given or looked upon as one's right, in addition to regular wages or salary: *The salesman's ~s include the use of his firm's car out of business hours. Politics in Britain used to be the ~ of the great landowners.* ⇨ perk³.

perry /'perɪ/ n [U] drink made from the fermented juice of pears. ⇨ cider.

per se /ˌpɜː 'seɪ/ adv (Lat) (of sth) considered alone.

per·se·cute /'pɜːsɪkjuːt/ vt **1** [VP6A] punish, treat cruelly, esp because of religious beliefs. **2** allow no peace to; worry: ~ *a man with questions.* **per·se·cu·tor** /-tə(r)/ n **per·se·cu·tion** /ˌpɜːsɪ'kjuːʃn/ n [U] persecuting or being ~d: *suffer persecution for one's religious beliefs.* **2** [C] instance of this (in history, etc): *the numerous persecutions of the Jews.*

per·se·vere /ˌpɜːsɪ'vɪə(r)/ vi [VP2A,3A] ~ (at/in/ with), keep on steadily, continue (esp sth difficult or tiring): ~ *in one's studies.* **per·se·ver·ing** adj **per·se·ver·ing·ly** adv **per·se·ver·ance** /-rəns/ n [U] constant effort to achieve sth: steadfastness.

Per·sian /'pɜːʃn US: 'pɜːrʒn/ n, adj (inhabitant) of Persia (now Iran); language of the people of Persia (now Iran): ~ *carpets; ~ cats,* with long, silky hair.

per·si·flage /'pɜːsɪflɑːʒ/ n [U] banter; light, good-humoured teasing.

per·sim·mon /pə'sɪmən/ n (tree bearing) soft yellow fruit which becomes sweet when completely ripe, esp when softened by frost.

per·sist /pə'sɪst/ vi **1** [VP3A] ~ in sth/in doing sth, refuse, in spite of argument, opposition, failure, etc to make any change in (what one is doing, one's beliefs, etc): *She ~s in wearing that old-fashioned hat.* ~ *with,* continue to work hard at. **2** [VP2A] continue to exist: *The fog is likely to ~ in most areas.* **~·ence** /-əns/ n [U] ~ing or being ~ent: *The ~ence of a high temperature in the patient puzzled the doctor.* **~·ent** /-ənt/ adj ~ing;

continuing; occurring again and again: ~*ent attacks of malaria.* ~-**ent·ly** *adv*

per·son /'pɜːsn/ *n* **1** man, woman (which are the preferred words; *people* is preferred to ~s for the *pl*; ~ is often derog except when official or impersonal): *Who is this* ~? *There's a young* ~ *to see you. Any* ~ (= Anyone) *leaving litter in the park will be prosecuted.* **in the** ~ **of,** in the man/woman who is: *She found a good friend in the* ~ *of her landlady,* Her landlady became her good friend. ~**-to-**'~ **call,** (of a telephone call) made (via the operator) to a particular ~ and charged for only from the time that ~ answers the phone. **2** living body of a human being: *Offences against the* ~ (eg assaults, bodily attacks) *are punished severely.* **in** ~, physically present: *I shall be present at the meeting in* ~, I shall be there myself (instead of sending sb to represent me). *Will you apply for the position by letter or in* ~? **3** (gram) each of three classes of personal pronouns: *the first* ~ (I, we), *the second* ~ (you) *and the third* ~ (he, she, it, they).

per·sona /pɜːˈsəʊnə/ *n* (psych) role that a person assumes to show his conscious intentions to himself and others. ~ **'grata** /'grɑːtə/, (Lat) person who is acceptable, esp a diplomat who is acceptable to a foreign government. ~ **ˌnon 'grata** /ˌnɒn 'grɑːtə/, one who is not acceptable in this way.

per·son·able /'pɜːsənəbl/ *adj* handsome; pleasing in manner.

per·son·age /'pɜːsənɪdʒ/ *n* (important) person; person of distinction.

per·sonal /'pɜːsənl/ *adj* **1** private; individual; of a particular person: *my* ~ *affairs/needs/opinions; your* ~ *rights. I have something* ~ *to discuss with you,* either my own or your intimate affairs. '~ **column,** (in a newspaper, etc) column in which private messages or advertisements appear. **2** done or made by a person himself: *a* ~ *interview. The Prime Minister made a* ~ *appearance at the meeting,* appeared himself, instead of sending one of his colleagues. **3** done or made for a particular person: *provide a* ~ *service for sb; give sb one's* ~ *attention. He did me a* ~ *favour,* one directed to me and by him. ~ **as'sistant** (abbr **PA**), one who helps an official, etc in an office, government department, etc usu doing more than a secretary, eg by making travel arrangements, interviewing people. **4** of the body: *P*~ *cleanliness is important to health as well as to appearance.* **5** of the nature of a human being: *Do you believe in a* ~ *God?* **6** of or about a person in a critical or hostile way: *I object to such highly* ~ *remarks. Let's not be too* ~. **7** ~ **'property/e'state,** (legal) temporal or movable property, not land. ⇨ *real estate* at real¹(2). **8** ~ **'pronoun,** pronoun for the three persons(3): *I, we; you; he, she, it; they.* □ *n* [C] short newspaper item about a particular person. ~**ly** /-ənəlɪ/ *adv* **1** in one's own person, not through an agent: *He conducted me* ~*ly through the mansion. She likes* ~*ly conducted tours,* holiday tours with a courier or guide who accompanies those making the tour. **2** speaking for oneself; for one's own part: *P*~*ly I see no objection to your joining us.*

per·son·al·ity /ˌpɜːsəˈnælətɪ/ *n* (*pl* -ties) **1** [U] state of being a person; existence as an individual: *respect the* ~ *of a child.* **2** [C,U] qualities that make up a person's character: *a man with little* ~; *a woman with a strong* ~. *They both have striking personalities.* **3** [C] (mod use) person, esp one who

is well known in certain circles (though perhaps quite unknown in other circles): *personalities of the stage and screen; a TV* ~, sb known to television viewers. '~ **cult,** practice of giving fervent admiration, devotion, etc to a ~, esp a political leader. **4** (*pl*) impolite remarks about sb's looks, habits, etc: *indulge in personalities,* utter such remarks.

per·son·al·ize /'pɜːsənəlaɪz/ *vt* [VP6A] have (sth) printed with one's address (~*ed stationery*) or given a monogram (with one's initials) (~*d shirts, handkerchiefs*).

per·son·alty /'pɜːsənltɪ/ *n* [U] (legal) personal estate.

per·son·ate /'pɜːsəneɪt/ *vt* [VP6A] **1** play the part of (a character in a drama). **2** = impersonate (the more usu word). **per·son·ation** /ˌpɜːsəˈneɪʃn/ *n*

per·son·ify /pəˈsɒnɪfaɪ/ *vt* (*pt,pp* -fied) [VP6A] **1** regard or represent (sth) as a person: ~ *the sun and moon,* by using 'he' and 'she'. **2** be an example of (a quality): *That man personifies avarice/is avarice personified.* **per·soni·fi·ca·tion** /pəˌsɒnɪfɪˈkeɪʃn/ *n* **1** [U] ~ing or being personified; [C] instance of this. **2** *the* ~ *of,* a striking example of the quality of: *He's the personification of selfishness.*

per·son·nel /ˌpɜːsəˈnel/ *n* (with *sing* or *pl v*) staff; persons employed in any work, esp public undertakings and the armed forces: *There were five airline* ~ *on the plane that crashed.* '~ **officer/ manager,** one employed to deal with relationships between individual employees, their problems, grievances, etc.

per·spec·tive /pəˈspektɪv/ *n* **1** [U] the art of drawing solid objects on a flat surface so as to give the right impression of their relative height, width, depth, distance, etc; [C] drawing so made. **in/out of** ~, drawn/not drawn according to the rules of ~. **2** [U] apparent relation between different aspects of a problem. **in the/its right/wrong** ~, in the right/wrong relationship; with/without exaggeration or neglect of any aspects: *You must get the story in (its right)* ~. *He sees things in their right* ~. **3** [C] (lit, fig) view; prospect: *a distorted* ~ *of the nation's history.*

front elevation   side elevation

top elevation   perspective drawing

perspective and elevation

per·spex /'pɜːspeks/ *n* [U] (P) tough plastic material that will not splinter, used as a substitute for glass (eg in the windscreens of cars).

per·spi·ca·cious /ˌpɜːspɪˈkeɪʃəs/ *adj* (formal) quick to judge and understand. **per·spi·cac·ity** /ˌpɜːspɪˈkæsətɪ/ *n* [U].

per·spicu·ous /pəˈspɪkjʊəs/ *adj* (formal) expressed clearly; expressing things clearly. ~**·ly** *adv* ~**·ness** *n* **per·spi·cu·ity** /ˌpɜːspɪˈkjuːətɪ/ *n*

per·spire /pəˈspaɪə(r)/ *vi* [VP2A] sweat. **per·spir·ation** /ˌpɜːspəˈreɪʃn/ *n* [U] sweat; sweating.

per·suade /pə'sweɪd/ vt 1 [VP11,14] ~ sb that...; ~ sb of sth, convince (sb): How can I ~ you of my sincerity/that I am sincere? 2 [VP17] cause (sb) by reasoning (to do sth): We ~d him/He was ~d to try again. 3 [VP14] ~ sb into/out of (doing) sth, cause sb to do/stop doing sth: Can you ~ her out of her foolish plans? Who ~d you into writing that letter? **per·suad·able** /-əbl/ adj

per·sua·sion /pə'sweɪʒn/ n 1 [U] persuading or being persuaded; power of persuading. 2 [U] conviction; belief (the usu word): It is my ~ that.... 3 [C] group or set holding a particular belief: men of various (religious) ~s.

per·sua·sive /pə'sweɪsɪv/ adj able to persuade; convincing: She has a ~ manner. ~·ly adv ~·ness n

pert /pɜːt/ adj 1 saucy; not showing proper respect: a ~ child/answer. 2 (US) lively; sprightly. ~·ly adv ~·ness n

per·tain /pə'teɪn/ vi [VP3A] ~ to, (formal) belong as a part or accessory; have reference; be appropriate: the enthusiasm ~ing to youth; the mansion and the lands ~ing to it.

per·ti·na·cious /ˌpɜːtɪ'neɪʃəs US: -tn'eɪʃəs/ adj (formal) not easily giving up (what has been started); determined. ~·ly adv **per·ti·nac·ity** /ˌpɜːtɪ'næsətɪ US: -tn'æ-/ n [U].

per·ti·nent /'pɜːtɪnənt US: -tənənt/ adj ~ (to), (formal) referring directly; relevant: remarks not ~ to the subject under discussion; a ~ reply. ~·ly adv **per·ti·nence** /-əns/ n [U].

per·turb /pə'tɜːb/ vt [VP6A] (formal) trouble; make anxious: ~ing rumours; a man who is never ~ed. **per·tur·ba·tion** /ˌpɜːtə'beɪʃn/ n [U] ~ing or being ~ed.

pe·ruke /pə'ruːk/ n long wig.

pe·ruse /pə'ruːz/ vt [VP6A] (formal) read carefully. **pe·rusal** /pə'ruːzl/ n [C,U] act of reading carefully.

Peru·vian /pə'ruːvɪən/ adj of Peru: ~ bark, of the cinchona tree, the source of quinine. □ n native of Peru.

per·vade /pə'veɪd/ vt [VP6A] spread through every part of: The subversive ideas that ~ all these periodicals may do great harm. **per·va·sion** /pə'veɪʒn/ n [U] pervading or being ~d.

per·va·sive /pə'veɪsɪv/ adj tending to pervade: ~ influences. ~·ly adv ~·ness n

per·verse /pə'vɜːs/ adj 1 (of persons) wilfully continuing in wrongdoing; wilfully choosing a wrong course. 2 (of circumstances) contrary (to one's wishes). 3 (of behaviour) contrary to reason. ~·ly adv ~·ness n

per·ver·sion /pə'vɜːʃn US: -ʒn/ n 1 [U] perverting or being perverted. 2 [C] turning from right to wrong; change to sth abnormal, unnatural, etc: a ~ of justice; a ~ of the appetite, eg a desire to eat grass, as Nebuchadnezzar had; sexual ~s.

per·ver·sity /pə'vɜːsətɪ/ n (pl -ties) [U] being perverse; [C] perverse act.

per·vert /pə'vɜːt/ vt [VP6A] 1 turn (sth) to a wrong use. 2 cause (a person, his mind) to turn away from right behaviour, beliefs, etc: ~ (the mind of) a child. Did Socrates really ~ the youth of Athens? Do pornographic books ~ those who read them? □ n /'pɜːvɜːt/ ~ed person; person whose behaviour deviates from what is normal, eg in sexual practices.

pe·seta /pə'seɪtə/ n (pl ~s) unit of currency in Spain.

pesky /'peskɪ/ adj (colloq) troublesome; annoying.

peso /'peɪsəʊ/ n (pl ~s) unit of currency in many Latin American countries and the Philippines.

pes·sary /'pesərɪ/ n (pl -ries) (med) any of various devices placed and left to dissolve in the vagina.

pessi·mism /'pesɪmɪzəm/ n [U] (opp of optimism) tendency to believe that the worst thing is most likely to happen, that everything is essentially evil. **pes·si·mist** /-ɪst/ n person subject to ~. **pessi·mis·tic** /ˌpesɪ'mɪstɪk/ adj **pessi·mis·ti·cally** /-klɪ/ adv.

pest /pest/ n troublesome or destructive thing, animal, etc; (colloq) person who is a nuisance: garden ~s, eg insects, mice, snails; '~ control, the use of various methods to get rid of ~s. **pes·ti·cide** /'pestɪsaɪd/ n substance used to destroy ~s, esp insects.

pes·ter /'pestə(r)/ vt [VP6A,17,14] ~ sb (with sth/for sth/to do sth), annoy; trouble: be ~ed with flies/with requests for help; ~ sb for money; ~ sb to help.

pes·tif·er·ous /pe'stɪfərəs/ adj causing disease; morally dangerous.

pes·ti·lence /'pestɪləns/ n [C,U] (any kind of) fatal epidemic disease, esp bubonic plague. **pes·ti·lent** /-ənt/, **pes·ti·len·tial** /ˌpestɪ'lenʃl/ adjj 1 like a ~; carrying infection. 2 (colloq) extremely annoying or objectionable: These pestilential flies/children give me no peace.

pestle /'pesl/ n stick with a thick end used in a mortar for pounding or crushing things. □ vt crush in (or as in) a mortar.

pet¹ /pet/ n 1 (often attrib) animal, etc kept as a companion, treated with care and affection, eg a cat or a dog: a 'pet shop, one where pets, eg dogs, canaries, tortoises are sold. 2 person treated as a favourite: Mary is the teacher's pet. 3 sb specially loved or lovable: make a pet of a child. She's a perfect pet, (colloq) has very winning ways, is very lovable. **pet aversion**, sth or sb most disliked: Cowboy films are her pet aversion. **'pet name**, name other than the real name, used affectionately. □ vt (-tt-) fondle; treat with affection; kiss and caress: silly women petting their poodles.

pet² /pet/ n fit of ill temper, esp about sth trifling: in one of her pets.

petal /'petl/ n one of the leaf-like divisions of a flower: 'rose ~s. ⇨ the illus at flower. **pet·al·led** (US **pet·aled**) /'petld/ adj having ~s.

pe·tard /pe'tɑːd/ n kind of bomb used in former times to break down doors, gates, walls, etc. **hoist with one's own ~**, (prov) caught or injured by what one intended as a snare for others.

peter /'piːtə(r)/ vi [VP2C] ~ out, (of supplies, etc) come gradually to an end.

Peter /'piːtə(r)/ n **rob ~ to pay 'Paul**, take from one to give to another. **,blue 'peter**, blue flag with a white square, flown by a ship before leaving port.

pe·tit bour·geois /ˌpetɪ 'bʊəʒwɑː/ n (F) member of the lower middle class: (attrib) ~ habits/opinions. ⇨ middle class at middle(3); ⇨ bourgeois.

pe·tite /pə'tiːt/ adj (of a person) small, slender, neat and dainty.

pe·ti·tion /pɪ'tɪʃn/ n [C] 1 prayer; earnest request; appeal (esp a written document signed by a large number of people). 2 formal application made to a court of law. □ vt,vi 1 [VP6A,17,11,14] ~ sb (for sth/to do sth/that...), make a ~ to, eg the authorities: ~ Parliament to redress grievances. 2 [VP3A] ~ for, ask earnestly or humbly: ~ for a retrial. ~er n one who ~s, esp the plaintiff in a divorce suit.

pet·rel /'petrəl/ n long-winged black and white seabird. ⇨ the illus at water. **stormy ~**, (fig) person whose coming causes (eg social or industrial) unrest.

pet·rify /'petrɪfaɪ/ vt,vi (pt,pp -fied) [VP6A,2A] (cause to) change into stone; (fig) take away power to think, feel, act, etc (through terror, surprise, etc): *petrified with terror*. **pet·ri·fac·tion** /ˌpetrɪ'fækʃn/ n ~ing or being petrified; petrified substance.

petro- /ˌpetrəʊ-/ pref of rocks or of petroleum. **~-chemical** n chemical substance derived from petroleum or natural gas.

pet·rol /'petrəl/ n [U] refined petroleum used as a fuel in internal combustion engines (US = *gasoline*): *fill up with ~; stop at the next'~ station; the '~ tank*.

pe·tro·leum /pɪ'trəʊlɪəm/ n [U] mineral oil (vegetable in origin, from forests in prehistoric times) found underground and obtained from wells; used in various forms (petrol, paraffin, etc) for lighting, heating and driving machines. **~ 'jelly** n [U] semi-solid substance obtained from ~, used as a lubricant and in ointments.

pe·trol·ogy /pɪ'trɒlədʒɪ/ n [U] the study of rocks.

pet·ti·coat /'petɪkəʊt/ n woman's under-skirt.

pet·ti·fog·ging /'petɪfɒgɪŋ/ adj (of a person) worrying about small and unimportant details; (of a method) unnecessarily concerned with small matters.

pet·tish /'petɪʃ/ adj 1 (of a person) having short and often repeated fits of ill temper, like a spoiled child. 2 (of a remark, act) said or done in a fit of ill temper. **~·ly** adv **~·ness** n

petty /'petɪ/ adj (-ier, -iest) 1 small; unimportant: **~ troubles/details**; **~ regulations enforced by ~ officials**. 2 on a small scale: **~ farmers/shopkeepers**. 3 having or showing a narrow mind; mean: **~ spite**. 4 **~ cash**, (business) money for or from small payments. **~ larceny**, theft of articles of little value. **~ officer**, highest rank of non-commissioned officer in the navy. **pet·tily** /'petɪlɪ/ adv **pet·ti·ness** n

petu·lant /'petjʊlənt US: -tʃʊ-/ adj unreasonably impatient or irritable. **~·ly** adv **petu·lance** /-əns/ n [U].

pe·tu·nia /pɪ'tjuːnɪə US: -'tuː-/ n [C] garden plant with funnel-shaped flowers of various colours.

pew /pjuː/ n bench with a back, usu fixed to the floor, in a church: *empty pews at morning service*; (colloq) seat: *Take a pew!* ⇨ the illus at church. **'pew-opener** n person who conducted persons to their seats when, in former times, family pews were enclosed and had doors.

pe·wit, pee·wit /'piːwɪt/ n lapwing; kind of mountain plover, named after its cry.

pew·ter /'pjuːtə(r)/ n [U] grey alloy of lead and tin; kitchen vessels made of this: *a good collection of ~*; (attrib) **~ mugs/dishes**.

pe·yote /peɪ'əʊtɪ/ n Mexican cactus from which is derived a drug (*mescaline*) which causes hallucinations.

pfen·nig /'fenɪg/ n German copper coin, one hundredth of a mark.

phae·ton /'feɪtn US: 'feɪətən/ n (hist) light, four-wheeled open carriage, usu drawn by a pair of horses.

phago·cyte /'fægəsaɪt/ n sort of leucocyte (blood cell) capable of guarding the system against infection by absorbing microbes.

phal·anx /'fælæŋks/ n (pl ~es or phalanges /fə'lændʒiːz/) 1 (in ancient Greece) body of soldiers in close formation for fighting. 2 number of persons banded together for a common purpose. 3 (anat) bone in a finger or toe. ⇨ the illus at skeleton.

phal·lus /'fæləs/ n image of the erect penis, as a symbol of generative power. **phal·lic** /'fælɪk/ adj of a ~: *phallic symbols/emblems*.

phan·tasm /'fæntæzəm/ n phantom. **phan·tas·mal** /fæn'tæzməl/ adj of or like a ~. **phan·tas·ma·goria** /ˌfæntæzmə'gɒrɪə US: -'gɔːrɪə/ n changing group of images, real or imagined figures, etc eg as seen in a dream.

phan·tasy /'fæntəsɪ/ n = fantasy.

phan·tom /'fæntəm/ n [C] ghost; sth without reality, as seen in a dream or vision: (attrib) **~ ships**.

Phar·aoh /'feərəʊ/ n title of the kings of ancient Egypt.

Phari·see /'færɪsiː/ n member of an ancient Jewish sect known for strict obedience to written laws and for pretensions to sanctity; (small **p**) hypocritical and self-righteous person. **phari·saic** /ˌfærɪ'seɪɪk/, **phari·sai·cal** /-kl/ adjj of or like a ~ or the ~s.

phar·ma·ceuti·cal /ˌfɑːmə'sjuːtɪkl US: -'suː-/ adj of, engaged in, pharmacy; of medicinal drugs: *the ~ industry*.

phar·ma·cist /'fɑːməsɪst/ n person professionally qualified to prepare medicines. ⇨ chemist, druggist.

phar·ma·col·ogy /ˌfɑːmə'kɒlədʒɪ/ n [U] science of pharmacy. **phar·ma·col·ogist** /-ədʒɪst/ n expert in, student of, ~.

phar·ma·co·poeia /ˌfɑːməkə'piːə/ n (officially published) book with list of medicinal preparations and directions for their use.

phar·macy /'fɑːməsɪ/ n (pl -cies) 1 [U] preparation and dispensing of medicines and drugs. 2 [C] dispensary; (part of a) shop where medical goods are sold (US = *drug-store*).

pharos /'feərɒs/ n lighthouse; beacon for sailors.

phar·ynx /'færɪŋks/ n cavity (with the muscles, etc that enclose it) at the back of the mouth, where the passages to the nose, mouth and larynx begin. ⇨ the illus at head. **phar·yn·gi·tis** /ˌfærɪn'dʒaɪtɪs/ n [U] inflammation of the mucous membrane of the ~.

phase /feɪz/ n [C] 1 stage of development: *a ~ of history; the critical ~ of an illness; enter upon a new ~ of one's career*; stage in a cycle. **in/out of ~**, having/not having the same ~ at the same time; in/out of harmony. 2 (of the moon) amount of bright surface visible from the earth (new moon, full moon, etc). □ vt [VP6A,15B] plan, carry out, by ~s: *a ~d withdrawal*, one made by stages. **~ in**, introduce, one stage at a time. **~ out**, withdraw, one stage at a time.

crescent   half moon   gibbous   full moon

the phases of the moon

pheas·ant /'feznt/ n [C] long-tailed game bird; [U] its flesh as food. ⇨ the illus at fowl.

pheno·bar·bi·tone /ˌfiːnəʊ'bɑːbɪtəʊn/ n [U] drug

used to calm the nerves and induce sleep.

phen·ol /'fi:nɒl/ *n* [U] (comm, science) carbolic acid (as used in disinfectants).

phe·nom·enal /fɪ'nɒmɪnl/ *adj* **1** perceptible to the senses. **2** concerned with phenomena. **3** prodigious; extraordinary. ~**ly** /-nəlɪ/ *adv*

phe·nom·enon /fɪ'nɒmɪnən US: -nɒn/ *n* (*pl* -ena /-ɪnə/) **1** thing that appears to or is perceived by the senses: *the phenomena of nature.* **2** remarkable or unusual person, thing, happening, etc.

phew /fju:/ *or a less precise puffing noise/ int* natural cry indicating astonishment, impatience, discomfort, disgust, etc according to context.

phial /'faɪəl/ *n* small bottle, esp one for liquid medicine; vial.

phil·an·der /fɪ'lændə(r)/ *vi* [VP2A] be in the habit of making love without serious intentions; flirt. ~**er** *n* person who does this.

phil·an·thropy /fɪ'lænθrəpɪ/ *n* [U] love of mankind; practical sympathy and benevolence. **phil·an·thro·pist** /-ɪst/ *n* person who helps others, esp those who are poor or in trouble. **phil·an·thropic** /ˌfɪlən'θrɒpɪk/ *adj* of ~; benevolent; kind and helpful: *philanthropic institutions,* eg for blind people or orphans. **phil·an·thropi·cally** /-klɪ/ *adv*

phil·at·ely /fɪ'lætəlɪ/ *n* postage-stamp collecting. **phil·at·el·ist** /-ɪst/ *n* person who collects postage-stamps; person with expert knowledge of them.

phil·hel·lene /fɪl'heli:n/ *n, adj* (person) friendly to the Greeks. **phil·hel·lenic** /ˌfɪlhe'li:nɪk US:* -'lenɪk/ *adj*

Phi·lis·tine /'fɪlɪstaɪn US:* -sti:n/ *n* **1** (Biblical) one of the warlike people in Palestine who were the enemies of the Israelites. **2** (mod use; small **p**) uncultured person; person whose interests are material and commonplace: (attrib) ~ *neighbours.*

phil·ol·ogy /fɪ'lɒlədʒɪ/ *n* [U] study of the development of language, or of particular languages. ⇨ linguistics. **phil·ol·ogist** /fɪ'lɒlədʒɪst/ *n* student of, expert in, ~. **philo·logi·cal** /ˌfɪlə'lɒdʒɪkl/ *adj* of ~.

phil·os·opher /fɪ'lɒsəfə(r)/ *n* **1** person studying or teaching philosophy, or having a system of philosophy. **2** person whose mind is untroubled by passions and hardships; person who lets reason govern his life. ~**'s stone,** substance which, alchemists believed, could change any metal into gold; elixir.

phil·os·ophy /fɪ'lɒsəfɪ/ *n* (*pl* -phies) **1** [U] the search for knowledge, esp the nature and meaning of existence. **moral** ~, the study of the principles underlying the actions and behaviour of men; ethics. **natural** ~, (old use) physics. **2** [C] system of thought resulting from such a search for knowledge: *conflicting philosophies; a man without a* ~, with no views upon the problems of life. **3** [U] calm, quiet attitude towards life, even in the face of unhappiness, danger, difficulty, etc. **philo·sophi·cal** /ˌfɪlə'sɒfɪkl/ *adj* **1** of, devoted to, guided by, ~. **2** resigned; of or like a philosopher(2). **philo·sophi·cally** /-klɪ/ *adv* **phil·os·ophize** /fɪ'lɒsəfaɪz/ *vi* [VP2A] think or argue like a philosopher; discuss, speculate about, a theory in ~.

philtre (US = **phil·ter**) /'fɪltə(r)/ [C] love-potion.

phleb·itis /flɪ'baɪtɪs/ *n* [U] inflammation of a vein.

phlegm /flem/ *n* [U] **1** thick, semi-fluid substance forming abnormally in the respiratory passages, and brought up by coughing. **2** quality of being slow to act, or to feel, show emotion or interest. **phleg·matic** /fleg'mætɪk/ *adj* having the quality of ~(2): *Not all English people are* ~*atic.* **phleg-**

mat·i·cally /-klɪ/ *adv*

phlox /flɒks/ *n* [U] kinds of garden plant with clusters of flowers in various colours.

pho·bia /'fəʊbɪə/ *n* morbid or pathological fear and dislike; aversion.

phoe·nix /'fi:nɪks/ *n* mythical bird which, after living hundreds of years in the Arabian desert, burnt itself on a funeral pile and rose from the ashes young again, to live for another cycle.

phone[1] /fəʊn/ *n, vt,vi* (colloq abbr for) telephone. '~**·booth** *n* telephone kiosk; call-box. '~**·call** *n* telephone call. '~**-in** *n* radio/television programme in which listeners/viewers participate by telephone.

phone[2] /fəʊn/ *n* (linguistics) single speech-sound (vowel or consonant).

pho·neme /'fəʊni:m/ *n* [C] (ling) unit of the system of sounds of a language: *English has 24 consonant* ~*s.* **pho·nemic** /fə'ni:mɪk/ *adj* (of transcriptions) providing one symbol for each ~ of the language transcribed (as with the pronunciations in this dictionary). **pho·nem·ics** *n* (with *sing v*) study and description of the phonemic systems of languages.

pho·netic /fə'netɪk/ *adj* (ling) **1** concerned with the sounds of human speech. **2** (of transcriptions) providing not only a symbol for each phoneme of the language transcribed but with additional symbols for differences between variations of the same phoneme in different situations. **3** (of a language) having a system of spelling that approximates closely to the sounds represented by the letters used: *Spanish spelling is* ~. **pho·net·ics** *n* (with *sing v*) study and science of speech sounds, their production, and the signs used to represent them. **pho·neti·cally** /-klɪ/ *adv* **pho·neti·cian** /ˌfəʊnɪ'tɪʃn/ *n* expert in ~s.

pho·ney, phony /'fəʊnɪ/ *adj* (colloq) sham; unreal; not genuine. □ *n* ~ person: *He's a complete* ~.

pho·nic /'fɒnɪk/ *adj* of sound; of vocal sounds. ~**s** *n* (with *sing v*) the use of elementary phonetics in the teaching of reading.

pho·no·graph /'fəʊnəɡrɑ:f US:* -ɡræf/ *n* (US) record player.

pho·nol·ogy /fə'nɒlədʒɪ/ *n* [U] (linguistics) scientific study of the organization of speech sounds (including phonemes), esp in particular languages. **pho·no·logi·cal** /ˌfəʊnə'lɒdʒɪkl/ *adj*

phooey /'fu:ɪ/ *int* exclamation of contempt, disbelief or disappointment.

phos·gene /'fɒzdʒi:n/ *n* [U] colourless gas ($COCl_2$), used as a poison gas and in industry.

phos·phate /'fɒsfeɪt/ *n* any salt of phosphoric acid, esp one of the numerous artificial fertilizers containing or composed of various salts of this kind, used widely in agriculture.

phos·pho·res·cence /ˌfɒsfə'resns/ *n* [U] the giving out of light without burning, or by gentle burning without heat that can be felt. **phos·pho·res·cent** /-snt/ *adj* giving out light without burning.

phos·phorus /'fɒsfərəs/ *n* [U] yellowish, nonmetallic, poisonous wax-like element (symbol **P**) which catches fire easily and gives out a faint light in the dark; red, non-poisonous form used in the manufacture of safety matches. **phos·phoric** /fɒs'fɒrɪk US:* -'fɔ:r-/, **phos·phor·ous** /'fɒsfərəs/ *adj* relating to or containing ~.

photo /'fəʊtəʊ/ *n* (*pl* ~s /-təʊz/) (colloq abbr for) photograph.

photo- /'fəʊtəʊ/ *pref* of light or of photography.

'~·copy vt, n [VP6A] (make a) copy of (a document, etc) by a photographic method. Hence, '~-copier n ,~·e'lectric adj: ~electric cell, cell or device which emits an electric current when light falls on it, used for many purposes, eg to measure light for photography, to cause a door to open when someone approaches it, to count objects passing before it. ,~ 'finish n (horse-racing) finish so close that only a photograph of the horses as they pass the winning-post can decide the winner. ,~·'genic /-'dʒenɪk/ adj suitable for being photographed; photographing well or effectively. ,~·'sensitize vt make (sth) sensitive to light.

photo·graph /'fəʊtəgrɑːf US: -græf/ n [C] picture recorded by means of the chemical action of light on a specially prepared glass plate or film in a camera, transferred to specially prepared paper. □ vt 1 [VP6A] take a ~ of. 2 ~ well/badly, come out well/badly when ~ed. photo·grapher /fə'tɒgrəfə(r)/ n person who takes ~s: amateur and professional ~ers. Cf camera man, for cinema and TV. photo·gra·phy /fə'tɒgrəfi/ n [U] art or process of taking ~s. photo·graphic /ˌfəʊtə'græfɪk/ adj of, related to, used in, taking ~s: photographic apparatus/goods/periodicals, etc. photo·graphi·cally /-klɪ/ adv

photo·gra·vure /ˌfəʊtəgrə'vjʊə(r)/ n [U] process of producing a picture on a metal plate from a photographic negative so that the plate can be used in printing; [C] picture printed from such a plate.

photo·li·tho·gra·phy /ˌfəʊtəʊlɪ'θɒgrəfɪ/ n [U] process of reproducing on plates (stone or zinc) by means of photography.

photo·meter /fəʊ'tɒmɪtə(r)/ n device for measuring the intensity of light.

photon /'fəʊtɒn/ n (phys) unit of quantity of energy in light.

photo·stat /'fəʊtəstæt/ vt, n (P) = photocopy.

photo·syn·thesis /ˌfəʊtəʊ'sɪnθəsɪs/ n [U] process by which the energy of sunlight is used by a green plant to keep it growing.

phrase /freɪz/ n [C] 1 group of words (often without a finite v) forming part of a sentence, eg in the garden, in order to. '~-book n one containing and explaining (or giving equivalents of in another language) ~s of a language: an English-Polish ~-book. 2 striking, clever way of saying sth. 3 (music) short, independent passage forming part of a longer passage. □ vt [VP6A] express in words: a neatly ~d compliment. phrasal /'freɪzl/ adj in the form of a ~: phrasal verbs, eg go in for, fall over, blow up. phras·eol·ogy /ˌfreɪzɪ'ɒlədʒɪ/ n [U] choice of words; wording.

phren·etic /frə'netɪk/ adj = frenetic.

phren·ol·ogy /frə'nɒlədʒɪ/ n [U] the judging of a person's character, capabilities, etc from an examination of the shape of his skull. phren·ol·ogist /-ɪst/ n person who practises ~.

phthi·sis /'θaɪsɪs/ n [U] tuberculosis of the lungs.

phut /fʌt/ adv go ~, (lit or fig) (colloq) collapse; break down: My record player has/holiday plans have gone ~.

phylum /'faɪləm/ n (biol) highest division in the animal kingdom.

physic /'fɪzɪk/ n 1 (archaic) medicine. 2 (pl) = physics.

physi·cal /'fɪzɪkl/ adj 1 of material (contrasted with moral and spiritual) things: the ~ world/universe; ~ force. 2 of the body; bodily: ~ exercise, eg walking, playing football; ~ education. 3 of the

laws of nature: It's a ~ impossibility to be in two places at once. 4 of the natural features of the world: ~ geography, of the earth's structure. ~ly /-klɪ/ adv

phys·ician /fɪ'zɪʃn/ n person qualified to practise both medicine and surgery.

physi·cist /'fɪzɪsɪst/ n expert in, student of, physics.

phys·ics /'fɪzɪks/ n (with sing v) group of sciences dealing with matter and energy (eg heat, light, sound), but usu excluding chemistry and biology: P~ is taught by Professor Molecule.

physi·og·nomy /ˌfɪzɪ'ɒnəmɪ US: -'ɒgnəʊmɪ/ n (pl -mies) [C,U] (art of judging character from the features of) the face; general features of a country.

physi·ol·ogy /ˌfɪzɪ'ɒlədʒɪ/ n [U] science of the normal functions of living things, esp animals. physi·ol·ogist /-ɪst/ n expert in, student of, ~. physio·logi·cal /ˌfɪzɪə'lɒdʒɪkl/ adj

physio·ther·apy /ˌfɪzɪəʊ'θerəpɪ/ n [U] treatment of disease by means of exercise, massage, the use of light, heat, electricity and other natural forces. physio·thera·pist n person trained to give such treatment.

phy·sique /fɪ'ziːk/ n [U,C] structure and development of the body: a man of strong ~.

pi /paɪ/ n the Greek letter p (π), esp (maths) as a symbol of the ratio of the circumference of a circle to its diameter (ie 3·14159). ⇨ App 4.

pi·ano¹ /'pjɑːnəʊ/ adv, adj (music) soft(ly). pia·nis·simo /pjæ'nɪsɪməʊ/ adv, adj very soft(ly).

pi·ano² /pɪ'ænəʊ/ n (pl ~s /-nəʊz/) musical instrument in which stretched metal strings are struck by hammers operated by keys. ⇨ the illus at keyboard. cottage ~, small upright ~. grand ~, ~ with horizontal strings. upright ~, one with vertical strings. pia·nist /'pɪənɪst/ n person who plays the ~. piano·forte /pɪˌænəʊ'fɔːtɪ US: pɪ'ænəfɔːrt/ n (full name, now formal, for) ~. pia·nola /pɪə'nəʊlə/ n (P) ~ operated mechanically.

pi·astre (US = pi·as·ter) /pɪ'æstə(r)/ n unit of currency in some countries in the Middle East.

pi·azza /pɪ'ætsə/ n 1 public square or market-place, esp in an Italian town. 2 (US) veranda.

pi·broch /'piːbrɒk/ n piece of martial music for the bagpipes.

pica /'paɪkə/ n printer's unit for the size of type¹(3).

pica·dor /'pɪkədɔː(r)/ n man (mounted on a horse) who uses a lance to incite and weaken bulls in the sport of bull-fighting.

pic·ar·esque /ˌpɪkə'resk/ adj (of a style of fiction) dealing with the adventures of rogues and vagabonds.

pic·ca·lilli /ˌpɪkə'lɪlɪ/ n [U] kind of hot-tasting pickle made of chopped vegetables, spices in mustard, vinegar, etc.

pic·ca·ninny /ˌpɪkə'nɪnɪ US: 'pɪkənɪnɪ/ n (pl -nies) (old use) small child, esp a Negro baby.

pic·colo /'pɪkələʊ/ n (pl ~s /-ləʊz/) small flute producing notes an octave higher than those of the ordinary flute. ⇨ the illus at brass.

pick¹ /pɪk/ n picking; selection. the ~ of, the best (part) of a collection of things or people.

pick² /pɪk/ n 1 '~ (-axe), heavy tool with an iron head having two pointed ends, used for breaking up hard surfaces. ⇨ the illus at tool. 2 small, sharp-pointed instrument: an 'ice-~; a 'tooth~.

pick³ /pɪk/ vt, vi (For special uses with adverbial particles and preps, ⇨ 7 below.) 1 [VP6A] take up, remove, pull away, with the fingers: ~ flowers, gather flowers; ∼ *fruit,* take fruit from the bush or tree; ∼ *a thread from one's coat;* ∼ *one's nose,* remove bits of dried mucus from the nostrils. ∼ *sb's brains,* get ideas and information from sb. ∼ *sb's pocket,* steal sth from it. Hence, '∼-**pocket** *n* person who ∼s pockets. ∼ **and steal,** pilfer. **2** [VP6A] tear or separate; use a pointed instrument to clean, etc: ∼ *rags,* tear them to small pieces; ∼ *one's teeth,* get bits of food from the spaces between them, etc by using a pointed stick of wood (a '*toothpick*); ∼ *a lock,* use a pointed tool, a piece of wire, etc to unlock it without a key; ∼ *a bone,* get all the meat from it. **have a 'bone to ∼ with sb,** ⇨ bone(1). **3** [VP6A] choose; select: ∼ *only the best;* ∼ *one's words,* choose those words that express one's meaning best, that will not cause offence, etc (according to context); ∼ *one's way along a muddy road;* ∼ *sides,* choose players for the two teams in a game (of football, cricket, etc) or competition; ∼ *the winning horse/*∼ *the winner,* make a successful guess at the winner (before the race). ∼ *a quarrel with sb,* bring about a quarrel intentionally. **4** [VP6A] make by ∼ing: ∼ *holes in sth.* ∼ *holes in an argument,* (fig) find its weak points. **5** [VP6A] (of birds) take up (grain, etc) in the bill; peck; (of persons) eat (food, etc) in small amounts; [VP3A] ∼ *at,* eat without interest or appetite: *She only* ∼*ed at her food.* **6** (US) pluck (the strings of): ∼ *a banjo/the strings of a banjo.* **7** [VP3A,15B] (special uses with *adverbial particles* and *preps*):

pick at sb, (colloq) nag at; find fault with: *Why are you always* ∼*ing at the poor child?*

pick sth off, take or pluck off. ∼ *sb off,* shoot him with deliberate aim: *A sniper behind the bushes* ∼*ed off three of our men.*

pick on sb, single out, esp for sth unpleasant: *Why should you* ∼ *on me to do the chores?*

pick sb/sth out, (a) choose. (b) distinguish from surrounding persons, objects, etc: ∼ *out one's friends in a crowd.* ∼ *sth out,* (a) make out, see, (the meaning of a passage, etc) by careful study. (b) play (a tune) by ear on a piano, etc. (c) relieve (one colour, the ground colour) with touches of a different colour: *green panels* ∼*ed out with brown.*

pick sth over, examine and make a selection from: ∼ *over a basket of strawberries,* eg to throw out any that are bad.

pick sth up, (a) break up (ground) with a pickaxe. (b) take hold of and lift: ∼ *up one's hat/ parcels, etc.* (c) gain; acquire: ∼ *up a foreign language,* learn it without taking lessons or studying; ∼ *up a livelihood by selling things from door to door;* ∼ *up bits of information;* ∼ *up a bargain at an auction sale. The locomotive* ∼*s up current from a third rail.* (d) succeed in seeing or hearing (by means of apparatus): *enemy planes* ∼*ed up by our searchlights/radar installations, etc.* (e) recover; regain: *You'll soon* ∼ *up health when you get to the seaside.* ∼ *sb up,* (a) make the acquaintance of casually: *a girl he* ∼*ed up on the street.* (b) take (persons) along with one: *He stopped the car to* ∼ *up a young girl who was hitch-hiking across Europe. The escaped prisoner was* ∼*ed up* (= seen and arrested) *by the police at Hull.* ∼ *oneself up,* raise (oneself) after a fall: *She slipped and fell, but quickly* ∼*ed herself up.* ∼ *up (health),* recover health; improve: *He's beginning to* ∼ *up now.* ∼ *up speed,* gain speed. ∼ *up with sb,* make acquaintance with: *Where did you* ∼ *up*

with that queer fellow? '∼-**up** *n* (*pl* ∼-ups) (**a**) that part of a record-player that holds the stylus. (**b**) small general-purpose van or truck, open and with low sides, (eg as used by builders, farmers, etc, for carrying merchandise). (**c**) (sl) person whose acquaintance is made casually. (**d**) acceleration: *an engine/car with a good* ∼-*up.* ∼-**me-up** /'pɪk mɪ ʌp/ *n* sth, eg a drink, that gives new strength and cheerfulness.

picka·back /'pɪkəbæk/ *adv* (eg of the way a child is carried) on the shoulders or back like a bundle.

picker /'pɪkə(r)/ *n* person or thing that picks (chiefly in compounds): '*hop*–∼*s;* '*rag*–∼*s.*

pick·erel /'pɪkərəl/ *n* (*pl* unchanged) young pike.

picket /'pɪkɪt/ *n* **1** pointed stake, etc set upright in the ground (as part of a fence, or to tether a horse to). **2** small group of men on police duty, or sent out to watch the enemy. **3** worker, or group of workers, stationed at the gates of a factory, dockyard, etc during a strike, to try to persuade others not to go to work: *a* '∼ *line,* line of ∼s, eg outside a factory. **flying** ∼, ∼ formed of workers who do not work at the place where the ∼ is stationed. □ *vt,vi* [VP6A,2A] **1** put ∼s(1) round; tether (a horse) to a ∼(1). **2** place ∼s(2) in or round; station (men) as ∼s. **3** place ∼s(3) at: ∼ *a factory;* act as a ∼(3).

pick·ing /'pɪkɪŋ/ *n* **1** [U] act of picking. ∼ **and stealing,** stealing cheap things. **2** (*pl*) things left over from which profits may be made; these profits; profits made from stealing cheap things.

pickle /'pɪkl/ *n* **1** [U] salt water, vinegar, etc for keeping meat, vegetables, etc, in good condition. **have a rod in** ∼ **for sb,** ⇨ rod. **2** (usu *pl*) vegetables kept in ∼: *onion* ∼*s.* **3** *in a sad/sorry/nice* ∼, in a sad, etc plight. □ *vt* [VP6A] **1** preserve in ∼: ∼*d onions/walnuts.* **2** ∼**ed** *pp* (sl) drunk.

pic·nic /'pɪknɪk/ *n* **1** pleasure trip on which food is carried to be eaten outdoors: *have/go for a* ∼; (attrib) *a* '∼ *hamper,* one for holding food, dishes, etc. **2** (colloq) sth easy and enjoyable: *It's no* ∼, is not an easy job. □ *vi* (-ck-) take part in a ∼: ∼ *in the woods.* **pic·nicker** *n* person who ∼s.

pic·ric /'pɪkrɪk/ *adj* ∼ **acid,** acid used in dyeing, explosives and antiseptics.

pic·tor·ial /pɪk'tɔːrɪəl/ *adj* of, having, represented in, pictures: *a* ∼ *record of the wedding.* □ *n* periodical in which pictures are the main feature.

pic·ture /'pɪktʃə(r)/ *n* **1** painting, drawing, sketch, of sth, esp as a work of art. '∼-**book** *n* book consisting mainly of ∼s, esp one for children. '∼-**card** *n* (in playing cards) court-card; one with a king, queen or knave on it. '∼-**gallery** *n* room or building in which ∼s are exhibited. '∼ **hat,** woman's hat with a very wide brim. **2** beautiful scene, object, person, etc. **3** type or embodiment. **be the** ∼ **of health,** appear to have it in a high degree. **4** (fig) account or description that enables sb to see in his mind an event, etc. **be/put sb in the** ∼, be/cause sb to be well informed, aware of all the facts of a situation. **5** film (to be) shown in a cinema. **the** ∼**s,** the cinema: *We don't often go to the* ∼*s.* **6** what is seen on a television screen: *a set free from* ∼ *distortion.* □ *vt* **1** [VP6A] make a ∼ of; paint. **2** [VP14] ∼ *sth to oneself,* imagine: *He* ∼*d to himself what it might be like to live in Java.*

pic·tur·esque /ˌpɪktʃə'resk/ *adj* **1** having the quality of being like, or of being fit to be, the subject of a painting: *a* ∼ *village.* **2** quaint; vivid; graphic: ∼ *language.* **3** (of a person, his character) striking;

original. ~·ly adv ~·ness n

piddle /'pɪdl/ vi, n (colloq) (pass) urine.

pid·dling /'pɪdlɪŋ/ adj trifling; insignificant: ~ jobs.

pidgin /'pɪdʒɪn/ n **1** any of several languages resulting from contact between European traders and local peoples, eg in West Africa and the Far East, containing elements of the local language(s) and English, French or Dutch, still used for internal communication. **2** 'one's ~, (colloq) one's job or concern: Don't ask me; that's your ~.

pie /paɪ/ n [C,U] meat or fruit covered with pastry and baked in a deep dish: fruit pies; a meat pie; eat too much pie. ⇨ flan, tart². **have a finger in the/ every pie,** be concerned in the/every matter (esp in an officious way). **as easy as pie,** (sl) very easy. **pie in the sky,** happiness in Heaven; unrealistic hopes. '**pie-crust** n [U] baked pastry of a pie.

pie·bald /'paɪbɔːld/ adj (of a horse) having white and dark patches of irregular shape.

piece¹ /piːs/ n **1** part or bit of a solid substance (complete in itself, but broken, separated or made from a larger portion): a ~ of paper/wood/glass/ chalk. Will you have another ~ (= slice) of cake? This ~ of string is too short. **(be) in ~s,** broken; dismantled: The vase is in ~s. **break (sth) to ~s,** be in ~s as the result of an accident: The teapot fell and was broken to ~s. **come/take (sth) to ~s,** divide (sth) into the parts which make it up: Does this machine come/take to ~s? **go (all) to ~s,** (colloq) (of a person) break up physically, mentally or morally. **a ~ of cake,** (sl) sth very easy. **~ by ~,** one at a time. **of a ~ (with sth),** (fig) of the same character (as); consistent (with); in keeping (with). **2** separate instance or example: a ~ of news/luck/advice/information, etc; single article: a ~ of furniture. **give sb a ~ of one's mind,** tell him candidly what one thinks of him. **say one's ~,** say what one has to say, sth one has learnt to say, eg a poem to be recited. **3** standard length or quantity in which goods are prepared for distribution: a ~ of wallpaper (usu 12 yds); a ~ of cloth; sold only by the ~. '**~-goods** n pl textile fabrics (esp cotton and silk) made in standard lengths. **4** single composition (in art, music, etc): a fine ~ of work/music/poetry; a dramatic ~. **5** single thing out of a set: a dinner service of 50 ~s; one of the wooden, metal, etc objects moved on a board in such games as chess. **6** coin: a ten-pence ~; a five cent ~; a ~ of eight, an old Spanish silver coin. **7** gun: a fixed-~, field-gun; a 'fowling-~, for shooting game. **8** (fixed or agreed) amount of work (to be) done: pay a workman by the ~, according to the work produced (not by the time taken). Hence, '~-work n ⇨ time-work at time¹(13). **9** (in compounds) **(a)** (player of a) musical instrument: a six-~ jazz group. **(b)** item in collection: a 25-piece dinner service, ⇨ service(7).

piece² /piːs/ vt [VP6A,15A,B] ~ (together), put (parts, etc) together; make by joining or adding (pieces) together: ~ together odds and ends of cloth; ~ a quilt, make one by putting ~s together; ~ one thing to another. **~ sth out,** make (a story, theory, etc) complete by connecting the parts.

piece·meal /'piːsmiːl/ adv piece by piece; a part at a time: work done ~. □ adj coming, done, etc piece by piece.

pied /paɪd/ adj of mixed colours, of black and white, eg of birds.

pied-à-terre /ˌpjeɪd ɑː 'teə(r)/ n (F) extra room(s)

or house which one keeps for use when needed: He lives in the county, and has a ~ in London.

pier /pɪə(r)/ n **1** structure of wood, iron, etc built out into the sea as a landing-stage; similar structure for walking on for pleasure (often with a pavilion, restaurant, etc). **2** pillar supporting a span of a bridge, etc. **3** wall between windows or other openings. '**~-glass** n large, long mirror in which one can see the whole of oneself.

a pier

pierce /pɪəs/ vt,vi **1** [VP6A] (of sharp-pointed instruments) go into or through; make (a hole) by doing this: The arrow ~d his shoulder. She had her ears ~d in order to be able to wear earrings. **2** [VP6A] (fig, of cold, pain, sounds, etc) force a way into or through; affect deeply: Her shrieks ~d the air. A ray of light ~d the darkness. **3** [VP2C] penetrate (through, into, etc): Our forces ~d through the enemy's lines. **~·ing** adj (esp of cold, voices) sharp; penetrating: a piercing wind. **~· ing·ly** adv: a piercingly cold wind.

pier·rot /'pɪərəʊ/ n **1** character in French pantomime. **2** member of a group of entertainers (esp at seaside resorts), dressed in loose white clothes and with a whitened face.

pietà /ˌpiːeɪˈtɑː/ n (I) painting or sculpture of the Virgin Mary holding the dead body of Jesus in her lap.

piety /'paɪətɪ/ n **1** [U] devotion to God and good works; being pious. **filial ~,** correct behaviour towards a parent. **2** [C] (pl -ties) act, etc that shows ~.

piffle /'pɪfl/ n [U] (colloq) nonsense. □ vi talk ~. **pif·fling** /'pɪflɪŋ/ adj trivial; worthless.

pig /pɪg/ n **1** [C] domestic and wild animal, ⇨ the illus at domestic; ⇨ boar, hog, sow¹, swine; [U] its flesh (esp roast pig) as meat. ⇨ bacon, ham, pork. **bring one's pigs to the wrong market,** fail in an undertaking (to sell sth). **buy a pig in a poke,** buy sth without seeing it or knowing its value, which turns out to be worth less than one paid for it. **pigs might fly,** (expressing disbelief) wonders might happen. '**pig-boat** n (US sl) submarine. ˌpig-'**headed** adj stubborn. ˌpig-'**headedly** adv ˌpig-'**headedness** n '**pig-skin** n [U] (leather made of a) pig's skin; (sl) saddle. '**pig-sticking** n [U] the sport of hunting wild boars with spears. '**pig-sty** /-staɪ/ n **(a)** small building for pigs. **(b)** dirty hovel. '**pig-tail** n plait of hair hanging down over the back of the neck and shoulders. '**pig-wash, 'pig-swill** nn [U] waste food (from a brewery or kitchen) given to pigs as food. **2** (colloq) dirty, greedy or ill-mannered person. **make a 'pig of oneself,** eat or drink to excess. '**pig-iron** n [U] oblong mass of iron extracted from ore and shaped in a mould. □ vi (-gg-) **pig it; pig together,** live or herd together in dirty conditions. '**pig-gish** /-ɪʃ/ adj like a pig; dirty, greedy. '**pig-gish·ly** adv **pig·gish·ness** n **pig-gery** /'pɪgərɪ/ n (pl -ries) pig-breeding establishment; pig-farm.

piggy /'pɪgɪ/ n little pig. □ adj (colloq) greedy.

'piggyback, (US) = pickaback. **'piggy bank** *n* model (of a pig) with a slot for coins, used by a child for saving coin money.

pigeon /'pɪdʒɪn/ *n* **1** bird, wild or tame, of the dove family: **'carrier-∼, 'homing-∼,** kind trained to carry messages or bred for sport. ⇨ the illus at bird. **'∼-breasted** *adj* (of a person) having a bulging, convex chest. **'∼-toed** *adj* (of a person) having the toes turned inwards. **'∼-hole** *n* one of a set of small open boxes for keeping papers in. □ *vt* put (papers, etc) in a ∼hole and ignore or forget them; postpone consideration of: *The scheme was ∼holed.* **2 clay ∼,** disc thrown up into the air as a mark for shooting. **3** simpleton; easily deceived person. **4** (**'stool-**)**∼,** ⇨ stool. **5 'one's ∼,** = *one's pidgin,* ⇨ pidgin(2).

pig-iron /'pɪg aɪən/ *n* ⇨ pig(3).

pig·let /'pɪglɪt/ *n* young pig.

pig·ment /'pɪgmənt/ *n* **1** [U] colouring matter for making dyes, paint, etc; [C] particular substance used for this. **2** [U] the natural colouring matter in the skin, hair, etc of living beings. **pig·men·ta·tion** /ˌpɪgmen'teɪʃn/ *n* colouring of tissues by ∼.

pigmy /'pɪgmɪ/ *n* = pygmy.

pike¹ /paɪk/ *n* long wooden shaft with a spearhead, formerly used by soldiers fighting on foot. **'∼-staff** *n* wooden shaft of a ∼. **as plain as a ∼staff,** quite plain; easy to see or understand.

pike² /paɪk/ *n* (*pl* unchanged) large, fierce, fresh-water fish.

pike³ /paɪk/ *n* **1** turnpike road. **2** toll-bar; toll.

pike⁴ /paɪk/ *n* (dialect, N of England) peaked top of a hill: *Langdale P∼.*

pi·laf(f) /pɪ'læf US: -'lɑːf/ = pilau.

pi·las·ter /pɪ'læstə(r)/ *n* rectangular column, esp an ornamental one that projects from a wall into which it is set.

pi·lau /pɪ'laʊ/ (also **pi·laf(f)** /pɪ'læf US: -'lɑːf/) *n* [U] oriental dish of steamed rice with meat, etc.

pil·chard /'pɪltʃəd/ *n* small sea-fish resembling the herring.

pile¹ /paɪl/ *n* [C] heavy beam of timber, steel, concrete, etc driven into the ground, esp under water, as a foundation for a building, a support for a bridge, etc. **'∼-driver** *n* machine for driving ∼s into the ground. **'∼-dwelling** *n* (also called *lake-dwelling*) house resting on ∼s, esp at the side of a lake. □ *vt* [VP6A] supply with ∼s.

pile² /paɪl/ *n* **1** number of things lying one upon another: *a ∼ of books.* **2 funeral ∼,** heap of wood, etc on which a corpse is burnt. **3** (colloq) large amount of money. **make a/one's ∼,** earn a lot of money. **4** large high building or group of buildings. **5** dry battery for producing electric current. **atom·ic ∼,** apparatus for the controlled release of atomic energy; nuclear reactor.

pile³ /paɪl/ *vt, vi* **1** [VP6A,15A,B] make into a ∼; put on or in a ∼: *∼ logs; ∼ up dishes on a table; ∼ a table with dishes; ∼ more coal on (the fire).* **∼ arms,** place (usu four) rifles together with butts on the ground and muzzles touching. **∼ it on,** (colloq) exaggerate. **∼ on the agony,** (colloq) make a ∼ description of a painful event more agonizing than is necessary. **2** [VP2C] **∼ up,** (a) accumulate: *My work keeps piling up,* There is more and more work for me to do. **(b)** (of a number of vehicles) crash into each other, forming a ∼. Hence, **'∼-up** *n*: *another bad ∼-up on the motorway during thick fog.* **3 ∼ into/out of sth,** enter/leave in a disorderly way: *They all ∼d into/out of the car/*

cinema.

pile⁴ /paɪl/ *n* [U] soft, thick, hair-like surface of velvet, some carpets, etc.

piles /paɪlz/ *n* [U] hemorrhoids.

pil·fer /'pɪlfə(r)/ *vt, vi* [VP6A,2A] steal, esp in small quantities: *∼ed during transit by rail.* **∼er** *n* **∼age** /-ɪdʒ/ *n* [U] act of ∼ing; loss by ∼ing.

pil·grim /'pɪlgrɪm/ *n* person who travels to a sacred place as an act of religious devotion: *∼s to Mecca; the Canterbury ∼s,* in England, during the Middle Ages. **the P∼ Fathers,** English Puritans who went to America in 1620 and founded the colony of Plymouth, Massachusetts. **∼·age** /-ɪdʒ/ *n* journey of a ∼: *go on a ∼age to Benares.*

pill /pɪl/ *n* **1** small ball or tablet of medicine for swallowing whole. **a bitter ∼ (to swallow),** ⇨ bitter. **sugar/sweeten the ∼,** make sth disagreeable seem less so. **'∼-box** *n* **(a)** small cylindrical box for holding ∼s. **(b)** (army use) small (often partly underground) concrete fort. **2 the ∼,** oral contraceptive. **be/go on the ∼,** be taking/start to take such ∼s regularly.

pil·lage /'pɪlɪdʒ/ *n, vt* plunder, esp in war. **pil·lager** /-ɪdʒə(r)/ *n* one who ∼s.

pil·lar /'pɪlə(r)/ *n* **1** upright column, of stone, wood, metal, etc as a support or ornament. ⇨ the illus at church, column. **from ∼ to post,** (fig) from one resource to another, to and fro. **2** (fig) **∼ of,** strong and important supporter: *a ∼ of the establishment.* **3 '∼-box** *n* cylindrical container (in GB, scarlet) about 5 feet high, standing in a public place, in which letters are posted. **4** sth in the shape of a ∼, eg a column of fire, smoke, cloud or, in a coalmine, of coal left to support the roof.

pil·lion /'pɪlɪən/ *n* seat for a second rider behind the rider of a horse; seat for a passenger behind the driver of a motor-bike: *riding ∼; the ∼ passenger.*

pil·lory /'pɪlərɪ/ *n* (*pl* -ries) wooden framework in which the head and hands of wrongdoers were, in olden times, secured whilst they were ridiculed.

pil·low /'pɪləʊ/ *n* soft cushion for the head, esp when lying in bed. **'∼-case/-slip** *n* washable cover for a ∼. **'∼-fight** *n* child's game of fighting with ∼s. □ *vt* [VP6A] rest, support, on or as on a ∼; serve as a ∼ for.

pi·lot /'paɪlət/ *n* **1** person trained and licensed to take ships into or out of a harbour, along a river, through a canal, etc. **drop the ∼,** (fig) dismiss a trusted adviser. **2** person trained to operate the controls of an aircraft. **P∼ Officer,** lowest commissioned rank in the Royal Air Force, below that of Flying Officer. **3** (attrib) experimental; used to test how sth on a larger scale will work, how it may be improved, etc: *a '∼ census/survey/scheme; a '∼ plant,* for a manufacturing process; *a '∼ tunnel.* **4** (compounds) **'∼-boat** *n* one which takes ∼s to ships. **'∼-cloth** *n* [U] blue woollen cloth used for overcoats, etc. **'∼-engine** *n* railway engine that goes in advance (eg to check for safety). **'∼-fish** *n* small fish which often swims in company with larger fish, eg sharks, or sometimes ships. **'∼-light/-burner** *n* small flame in a gas cooker or lamp, kept burning continuously, which lights large burners, etc when the gas is turned on. □ *vt* [VP6A,15A] act as a ∼ to: *∼ ships through the Panama Canal.*

pi·mento /pɪ'mentəʊ/ *n* (*pl* ∼s /-təʊz/) **1** [U] dried aromatic berries of a West Indian tree, also called *Jamaica pepper* and *all-spice.* **2** [C] tree that produces the berries.

pimp /pɪmp/ n pander(2). □ vi [VP2A,3A] ~ *(for sb)*, act as a ~.

pim·per·nel /'pɪmpənel/ n small annual plant growing wild in wheatfields and on waste land, with scarlet, blue or white flowers.

pimple /'pɪmpl/ n small, hard, inflamed spot on the skin. **pim·pled** adj having ~s. **pim·ply** /'pɪmplɪ/ adj (-ier, -iest) having ~s: *a pimply boy/face.*

pin[1] /pɪn/ n 1 short, thin piece of stiff wire with a sharp point and a round head, used for fastening together parts of a dress, papers, etc. *don't care a pin,* don't care at all. *neat as a new pin,* very neat. *pins and needles,* tingling sensation in a part of the body caused by blood flowing again after its circulation has been checked for a time. 2 similar piece of wire with an ornamental head for special purposes: *a 'tie-pin; a 'hat-pin.* **'safety-pin,** pin bent with a guard at one end to protect and hold fast the point at the other end. ⇨ the illus at safety. 3 peg of wood or metal for various purposes. ⇨ *drawing-pin* at drawing, *hairpin* at hair(2), ninepins, *rolling-pin* at roll[2](11); peg round which a string of a musical instrument is fastened. **'pin-ball** n game played with a small ball which has to be electrically struck against one of several upright knobs, and guided into one of several numbered holes on a sloping board. **'pin-table** n table used in pin-ball. 4 (pl) (sl) legs: *He's quick on his* ~s. 5 (compounds) **'pin-cushion** n pad into which (a dressmaker's) pins are stuck. **'pin-head** n (colloq) very stupid person. **'pin-money** n [U] money allowance to, or money earned by, a woman for dress, small personal necessities, etc. **'pin-point** n sth very small; (attrib of targets) requiring accurate and precise bombing or shelling. □ vt find, hit, such a target with the required accuracy: *Our planes pin-pointed the target.* **'pin-prick** n (fig) small act, remark, etc causing annoyance. **'pin-stripe** adj (of dress material) with many very narrow stripes.

pin[2] /pɪn/ vt (-nn-) [VP15A,B] 1 fasten (things *together, up, to* sth, etc) with a pin or pins: *pin papers together; pin up a notice,* eg with drawing-pins on a notice-board. *pin sth on sb,* make him appear responsible; place the blame for sth on sb. *pin one's hopes on sb,* have strong hope that he will help; rely on him unquestioningly. **'pin-up** n picture of a favourite or much admired person, pinned up on a wall: (attrib) *a 'pin-up girl.* 2 make unable to move: *He was pinned under the wreckage/the wrecked car. He pinned his assailant against the wall,* held him there and prevented him from moving. *The troops were pinned down by accurate fire,* were unable to advance or withdraw. *pin sb down,* (fig) get him to commit himself, to state his intentions, etc: *He's a difficult man to pin down. pin sb down to sth,* get him to agree to keep, eg a promise, an agreement.

pina·fore /'pɪnəfɔː(r)/ n loose article of clothing worn over a dress to keep it clean.

pince-nez /'pæns neɪ/ n pair of spectacles with a spring to clip the nose (instead of a frame that fits round the ears).

pin·cers /'pɪnsəz/ n pl (pair of) ~s, 1 instrument for gripping things, pulling nails out of wood, etc. ⇨ the illus at tool. **'pincer movement,** (mil) attack by two converging forces. 2 pincer-shaped claws of certain shellfish. ⇨ the illus at crustacean.

pinch /pɪntʃ/ vt,vi 1 [VP6A,15A,B] take in a tight grip between the thumb and finger; have in a tight grip between two hard things which are pressed together: *He* ~*ed the boy's cheek. He* ~*ed the top of the plants off/*~*ed out the side shoots. I* ~*ed my finger in the doorway.* 2 [VP6A,2A] be too tight; hurt by being too tight: *These shoes* ~ (*me*). *(see, etc) where the shoe* ~*es,* (fig) where the difficulty or hardship lies. 3 (in passive) suffer; feel the effects of: *be* ~*ed with cold/poverty. be* ~*ed for money,* be short of money. 4 [VP6A] (colloq) steal; take without permission: *Who's* ~*ed my dictionary?* 5 [VP2A] be niggardly; be very mean; live sparingly or economically: *parents who have to* ~ *and scrape in order to save money for a child's clothes.* 6 (sl) (of the police) take into custody; arrest: *You'll be* ~*ed if you're not careful.* □ n 1 act of ~ing; painful squeeze: *He gave her a spiteful* ~. 2 (fig) stress: *feel the* ~ *of poverty.* 3 amount which can be taken up with the thumb and finger: *a* ~ *of salt/snuff. take sth with a* ~ *of salt,* ⇨ salt. *4 at a* ~; *if it comes to the* ~, if there is need and if there is no other way: *We can get six people round the table at a* ~.

pinch·beck /'pɪntʃbek/ n alloy of copper and zinc, simulating gold, used in cheap jewellery, etc. □ adj sham.

pine[1] /paɪn/ n [C] kinds of evergreen tree with needle-shaped leaves ('~-needles) and cones ('~-cones); [U] the wood of this tree. ⇨ the illus at tree.

pine[2] /paɪn/ vi 1 [VP2A,C] waste away through sorrow or illness: *pining from hunger.* 2 [VP3A,4C] ~ *for sth;* ~ *to do sth,* have a strong desire: *exiles pining for home/to return home.*

pin·eal /'paɪnɪəl/ adj shaped like a pine-cone: ~ *gland,* gland in the brain.

pine-apple /'paɪnæpl/ n [C] (tropical plant with) sweet, juicy fruit; [U] this as food: ~ *juice; tinned* ~. ⇨ the illus at fruit.

ping /pɪŋ/ n short, sharp, ringing sound as of elastic being stretched and released or a rifle bullet in the air or striking a hard substance. □ vi make this sound.

ping-pong /'pɪŋpɒŋ/ n (colloq) table tennis.

pin·ion[1] /'pɪnɪən/ n 1 bird's wing, esp the outer joint; flight-feather of a bird. 2 (poet) wing: *an eagle's* ~s. □ vt [VP6A] 1 cut off a ~ of (a wing or bird) to hamper flight. 2 [VP15A,B] ~ *(to/ together),* bind the arms of (a person); bind (sb's) arms; bind (sb) fast (to sth).

pin·ion[2] /'pɪnɪən/ n small cogwheel with teeth fitting into those of a larger cogwheel. ⇨ the illus at gear.

pink[1] /pɪŋk/ n 1 [U] pale red colour of various kinds (*rose* ~, *salmon* ~). ~ *gin,* portion of gin with angostura. 2 [C] garden plant with sweet-smelling white, ~, crimson or variegated flowers. *3 in the* ~ *(of health),* (colloq) very well. □ adj 1 of pale red colour. 2 (colloq) inclined to be left wing in politics. ⇨ red. ~*·ish* /-ɪʃ/ adj rather ~.

pink[2] /pɪŋk/ vt 1 [VP6A] pierce with a sword. 2 [VP6A,15B] ~ *(out),* decorate (leather, cloth) with small holes, etc. **'~·ing scissors/shears** n pl sewing scissors with serrated edges, used to prevent edges of cloth from fraying.

pink[3] /pɪŋk/ vi (of an internal combustion engine) make high-pitched explosive sounds; knock(3).

pin·nace /'pɪnɪs/ n big ship's small motor-boat.

pin·nacle /'pɪnəkl/ n 1 tall, pointed ornament built on to a roof or buttress. ⇨ the illus at church. 2

high, slender mountain peak. **3** (fig) highest point: *at the* ∼ *of his fame.* □ *vt* set (as) on a ∼; supply with ∼s.

pin·nate /'pɪneɪt/ *adj* (bot) (of a leaf) formed of small leaves on opposite sides of a stem.

pinny /'pɪnɪ/ *n* (*pl* -nies) (child's name for a) pinafore.

pint /paɪnt/ *n* unit of measure for liquids and certain dry goods, one-eighth of a gallon or about ·57 of a litre: *a* ∼ *of milk/beer/lentils.* ⇨ App 5.

pion·eer /ˌpaɪə'nɪə(r)/ *n* **1** person who goes into a new or undeveloped country to settle or work there; first student of a new branch of study, etc; explorer. **2** (mil) one of an advance party of soldiers (eg clearing or making roads). □ *vi, vt* [VP2A] act as a ∼; [VP6A] open up (a way, etc); show (new methods, etc) to others.

pious /'paɪəs/ *adj* **1** having, showing, deep devotion to religion. **2** (old use) dutiful to parents. ∼·ly *adv*

pip¹ /pɪp/ *n* seed, esp of a lemon, orange, apple or pear. ⇨ the illus at fruit.

pip² /pɪp/ *n* **the pip**, disease of poultry; (sl) fit of depression or irritation. *have/get/give sb the pip*: *That man gives me the pip.*

pip³ /pɪp/ *n* note of a time-signal on the telephone or radio: *The last of the six pips gives the time to the second.*

pip⁴ /pɪp/ *n* **1** each spot on playing-cards, dice and dominoes. **2** (GB colloq) star (1 to 3 according to rank) on an army officer's shoulder-strap.

pip⁵ /pɪp/ *vt* (-pp-) [VP6A] (GB colloq) hit with a gunshot. *pipped at the post,* defeated at the last moment.

pi·pal /'pi:pəl/ ⇨ peepul.

pipe¹ /paɪp/ *n* **1** tube through which liquids or gases can flow: '*water*-∼*s;* '*gas*-∼*s;* '*drain*-∼*s.* '∼·**line** *n* line of connected ∼s, often underground, for conveying eg petroleum to distant places. *in the* ∼*line,* (of any kind of goods or proposals) on the way; about to be delivered in a schedule, list, etc to receive attention. **2** musical wind-instrument (a single tube with holes stopped by the fingers); each of the tubes from which sound is produced in an organ; (*pl*) bag∼s. **3** (sound of the) whistle used by a boatswain. **4** song or note of a bird. **5** tubular organ in the body: '*wind*∼. **6** (**to'bacco**) ∼, tube with a bowl, used for smoking tobacco; quantity of tobacco held in the bowl: *smoke a* ∼. *Give me a* ∼ *of tobacco, please.* *Put 'that in your* ∼ *and smoke it,* (colloq) That is sth for you to reflect upon and accept if you can. '∼·**clay** *n* [U] fine, white clay formerly used for making tobacco ∼s, and (by soldiers) for whitening leather belts and other pieces of equipment. '∼·**dream** *n* plan, idea, etc that is fantastic and impracticable. '∼·**rack** *n* rack for tobacco ∼s. **7** cask for wine (equal to about 105 gallons). '∼·**ful** /-fʊl/ *n* as much as a ∼(6) holds.

pipe² /paɪp/ *vi, vt* **1** [VP6A, 15A] convey (water, etc) through pipes: ∼ *water into a house.* **2** [VP6A, 2A] play (a tune) on a pipe; whistle; utter or sing in a thin, treble voice. [VP2C] ∼ *up,* (colloq) begin to play, sing or speak. ∼ *down,* (colloq) be quiet; be less noisy or cocksure. **3** [VP15A] (naut) summon (sailors) by blowing a boatswain's pipe: ∼ *all hands on deck;* lead or welcome (sb) by the sound of a boatswain's pipe: ∼ *the captain on board.* **4** [VP6A] trim (a dress), ornament (a cake, etc) with piping. ⇨ piping(2).

piper /'paɪpə(r)/ *n* one who plays on a pipe, esp a player of the bagpipes. *pay the* ∼ *(and call the tune),* bear the cost of an undertaking (and have control of what is done).

pip·ette /pɪ'pet/ *n* slender tube for transferring small quantities of liquid, esp in chemistry.

pip·ing /'paɪpɪŋ/ *n* [U] **1** length of pipes(1), esp for water and drains: *ten feet of lead* ∼. **2** narrow cord-like material used to ornament the edges of some garments; cord-like lines of icing-sugar used to decorate cakes, etc. **3** action of playing on a pipe; sound produced from a pipe. □ *adj* like the sound from a pipe(2): *a* ∼ *voice.* *the* ∼ *time(s) of peace,* time(s) when there is peaceful music instead of martial music. □ *adv* ∼ *hot,* (of liquids, food) hissing or steaming hot.

pip·pin /'pɪpɪn/ *n* kinds of apple.

pip·squeak /'pɪpskwi:k/ *n* (sl) insignificant or contemptible person or thing.

pi·quant /'pi:kənt/ *adj* pleasantly sharp to the taste: *a* ∼ *sauce;* (fig) pleasantly exciting to the mind: *a* ∼ *bit of gossip.* ∼·**ly** *adv* **pi·quancy** /-ənsɪ/ *n* the quality of being ∼.

pique /pi:k/ *vt* [VP6A] **1** hurt the pride or self-respect of. **2** stir (the curiosity); stir the curiosity of (sb). **3** ∼ *oneself on sth,* pride oneself on; feel proud about: *He* ∼*d himself on being punctual.* □ *n* [U,C] pride; feeling one has when one's curiosity is unsatisfied; resentment: *go away in a fit of* ∼; *take a* ∼ *against sb.*

pi·quet /pɪ'ket/ *n* card game for two players with a pack of 32 cards.

pi·ranha /pɪ'rɑːnjə/ *n* (kinds of) tropical American freshwater fish, noted for attacking and eating live animals.

pi·rate /'paɪərət/ *n* **1** sea-robber; sea-robber's ship. **2** person who infringes another's copyright, who broadcasts without a licence, usurps trading rights, etc. □ *vt* [VP6A] use, reproduce (a book, a recording, another's work, etc) without authority and for one's own profit. **pi·rati·cal** /ˌpaɪə'rætɪkl/ *adj* of a ∼, in the manner of, a ∼. **pi·rati·cally** /-klɪ/ *adv* **pi·racy** /'paɪərəsɪ/ *n* (*pl* -cies) [U] robbery by ∼s; pirating of books, etc; [C] instance of either of these.

pir·ou·ette /ˌpɪru'et/ *n* [C] ballet-dancer's rapid turn on the ball of the foot or on the point of the toe. □ *vi* dance a ∼ or ∼s.

pis al·ler /ˌpi:z 'æleɪ *US:* ˌpi:z æ'leɪ/ *n* (F) the·last resort; course of action taken because there seems to be nothing better.

pis·ca·tor·ial /ˌpɪskə'tɔːrɪəl/ *adj* of fishing; addicted to fishing.

Pis·ces /'paɪsi:z/ *n* twelfth sign of the zodiac (also called *the fish*). ⇨ the illus at zodiac.

piss /pɪs/ *vt, vi* ⚠ (not in polite use) pass urine; discharge (blood) with urine; wet with urine. *P*∼ *off!* (vulg) Go away! ∼*ed* (vulg) very drunk. ∼*ed off,* (vulg) annoyed. □ *n* urine.

pis·ta·chio /pɪ'stɑːtʃɪəʊ *US:* - æʃɪəʊ/ *n* (*pl* ∼s /-ʃɪəʊz/) (tree yielding) nut with a green edible kernel; colour of this kernel.

pis·til /'pɪstl/ *n* seed-producing part of a flower. ⇨ the illus at flower.

pis·tol /'pɪstl/ *n* [C] small firearm held and fired in one hand. *hold a* ∼ *to sb's head,* try, by using threats, to make him do what one wants.

pis·ton /'pɪstən/ *n* round plate or short cylinder of wood or metal, fitting closely inside another cylinder or tube in which it moves up and down or backwards and forwards, used in engines, pumps, etc to impart or receive motion by means of a rod, called a '~-rod. ⇨ the illus at motor. '~ en-gined, (of aircraft) having engines with ~s (contrasted with jet engines). '~ ring n split metal ring used in a ~ to make a gas-tight joint.

pit¹ /pɪt/ n 1 hole in the earth, usu with steep sides, esp one from which material is dug out (a 'chalk-pit; a 'clay-pit; a 'coal-pit) or for industrial purposes (a 'saw-pit). 'pit-head n entrance of a coal-mine: pithead baths. 'pit-man /-mən/ n (pl-men) collier; worker in a coal-pit. 'pit pony n pony kept underground in coalmines. 'pit-prop n prop used to support the roof of a gallery in a mine pit. 'pit-saw n saw used in a saw-pit. ⇨ saw². 2 covered hole as a trap for wild animals, etc. 'pit-fall n covered pit as a trap for animals; (more usu, fig) unsuspected snare or danger. 3 hollow in an animal or plant body. the pit of the stomach, the depression in the belly between the ribs. ⇨ also armpit at arm¹(1). 4 scar left on the body after smallpox. 5 (GB, not US) seats on the ground floor of a theatre behind the stalls; people occupying these seats. 6 (US) part of the floor of an exchange used for a special commodity: the 'wheat-pit. 7 the pit, (rhet, biblical) hell. 8 hole in the floor (of a garage, workshop) from which the underside of a motor-vehicle can be examined and repaired; place (at a race-course) at which racing cars stop for fuel, new tyres, etc, during a race. 9 = cockpit. □ vt 1 [VP6A] mark with pits(4) or with hollows in the ground: a face pitted with smallpox; the surface of the moon, pitted with craters. 2 [VP14] ~ against, cause to struggle against: pit one's wits against the Income Tax Office.

pit² /pɪt/ n (US) hard, stone-like seed (of such fruits as cherries, plums, peaches, dates). □ vt (-tt-) (US) remove pits from.

pit-a-pat /ˌpɪt ə 'pæt/ adv with quick beating, with the sound of light, quick taps or steps: Her heart/ feet went ~.

pitch¹ /pɪtʃ/ n 1 place where sb (esp a street trader) usu does business, where a street entertainer usu performs. queer sb's ~, upset his plans; thwart him. 2 (cricket) part of the ground between the wickets; manner in which the ball is delivered in bowling; (baseball) manner or act of pitching the ball; (football) ground, field (the usual words) on which the game is played. 3 act of pitching or throwing anything; distance to which sth is thrown. 4 (music and speech) degree of highness or lowness; quality of sound. 5 degree: at the lowest ~ of his (ill) fortune. Excitement rose to fever ~. 6 amount of slope (esp of a roof). 7 (of a ship) process of pitching(5).

pitch² /pɪtʃ/ n [U] black substance made from coal-tar, turpentine or petroleum, sticky and semi-liquid when hot, hard when cold, used to fill cracks or spaces, eg between planks forming a floor or ship's deck, make roofs waterproof, etc. as black/dark as ~, completely black/dark. ,~-'black/-'dark adj adj completely black/dark. '~-blende n [U] black, shining mineral ore (oxide of uranium) yielding radium. '~ pine n specially resinous kinds of pine-tree or its wood.

pitch³ /pɪtʃ/ vt,vi 1 [VP6A] set up, erect (a tent, camp); [VP2A] set up one's tent or camp. 2 [VP6A,15A,B] throw (a ball, etc); throw (sb or sth out, aside, etc), esp with impatience or energetic dislike: Let's ~ the drunkard out. The men were ~ing hay, lifting it, eg into a wagon, with forks.

'~-fork n long-handled fork with sharp prongs for lifting hay, etc. □ vt lift or move with a fork; (fig) thrust (a person) forcibly (into a position, etc). 3 [VP15A] (music) set in a certain pitch(4) or key: ~ a tune too high/in a lower key. This song is ~ed too low for me. 4 [VP2C,15A,B] (cause to) fall heavily forwards or outwards: He ~ed on his head. The carriage overturned and the passengers were ~ed out. 5 [VP2A,C] (of a ship) move up and down as the bows rise and fall. ⇨ roll²(6). 6 ~ in, set to work with energy. ~ into, (a) attack violently: They ~ed into him. (b) get busy with: We ~ed into the work. The hungry boy ~ed into the meat-pie, began to eat it. ~ upon, select by chance; light or pick upon: ~ upon the most suitable man for the job. 7 ~ed battle, one that is fought with troops arranged in prepared positions, not a casual encounter. 8 [VP15B,22] (cricket) (cause the ball to) strike the ground near or around the wicket: ~ the ball short; ~ the ball up a bit; (baseball) throw (the ball) to the batter. ~ wickets, (cricket) fix the stumps in the ground with the bails in place. 9 (sl) tell (a yarn, a story). 10 ,~-and-'toss n game of skill and chance in which coins are ~ed at a mark.

pitchers

pitcher¹ /'pɪtʃə(r)/ n large (usu earthenware) vessel with a handle and lip for holding liquids; large jug.

pitcher² /'pɪtʃə(r)/ n (baseball) player who throws the ball. ⇨ the illus at baseball.

pit-eous /'pɪtɪəs/ adj arousing pity. ~-ly adv

pit-fall /'pɪtfɔːl/ ⇨ pit¹(2).

pith /pɪθ/ n [U] 1 soft substance that fills the stems of some plants (eg reeds); similar substance lining the rind of oranges, etc. '~ hat/helmet, light sun hat made of dried ~. 2 (fig) essential part: the ~ of his argument/speech, etc. 3 vigour; force. ~y adj (-ier, -iest) 1 of, like, full of, ~. 2 forcible; full of meaning: ~y sayings. ~-ily /-ɪlɪ/ adv

piti-able /'pɪtɪəbl/ adj exciting pity; deserving only contempt: a ~ attempt. piti-ably /-əblɪ/ adv

piti-ful /'pɪtɪfl/ adj 1 feeling pity; compassionate. 2 causing pity: a ~ sight. 3 arousing contempt. ~ly /-fəlɪ/ adv

piti-less /'pɪtɪlɪs/ adj showing no pity. ~-ly adv

pi-ton /'piːtɒn/ n metal spike driven into rock, with a hole for rope, used as a hold in mountain climbing.

pit-tance /'pɪtŋs/ n low, insufficient payment or allowance (for work, etc): work all day for a mere ~.

pitter-patter /'pɪtə pætə(r)/ n patter: the ~ of rain on the roof.

pi-tu-itary /pɪ'tjuːɪtərɪ US: -'tuːətərɪ/ adj '~ gland, small ductless gland at the base of the brain, secreting hormones that influence growth, etc. □ n ~ gland.

pity /'pɪtɪ/ n (pl -ties) 1 [U] feeling of sorrow for the troubles, sufferings, etc of another person: be *filled with/feel* ～ *for sb.* **have/take** ～ **on sb,** help sb in trouble, etc. *for* ～**'s sake,** (used as a form of entreaty): *For* ～*'s sake try to stop this persecution.* **out of** ～, because of a feeling of ～: *give a beggar a few coins out of* ～. **2** (with *indef art,* but not in *pl* except as below) (event which gives) cause for regret or sorrow: *What a* ～ (= How unfortunate) (*.that*) *you can't come with us! It's a* ～ (*that*) *he can't swim. The* ～ *is that...*, The thing to be regretted is that.... *It's a thousand pities that...*, is most unfortunate that.... □ *vt* (*pt,pp* -tied) [VP6A] feel genuine ～ for; feel contemptuous ～ for: *He is much to be pitied. I* ～ *you if you think that you deserve to be helped.* ～**-ing** *adj* expressing ～. ～**ing·ly** *adv*

pivot /'pɪvət/ *n* **1** central pin or point on which sth turns, ⇨ the illus at balance; (fig) sth on which an argument or discussion depends. **2** (mil) man or unit on whom a body of troops turns or wheels when changing front or direction. □ *vt,vi* **1** [VP3A] ～ **on,** turn as on a ～. **2** [VP6A] place on a ～; supply with a ～. ～**al** /-tl/ *adj* of, forming, a ～; (fig) of great importance because other things depend upon it.

pixi·lated /'pɪksɪleɪtɪd/ *adj* (dial) slightly crazy.

pixy, pixie /'pɪksɪ/ *n* (*pl* -xies) small elf or fairy.

pizza /'piːtsə/ *n* (I) dish of food made by baking a layer of dough covered with a mixture of tomatoes, cheese, etc.

piz·zi·cato /ˌpɪtsɪ'kɑːtəʊ/ *adj, adv* (I) (music) (played) by plucking the strings (of a violin, etc) instead of using the bow.

plac·ard /'plækɑːd/ *n* written or printed announcement (to be) publicly displayed; poster. □ *vt* [VP6A] put ～s on (walls, etc); make known by means of ～s.

pla·cate /plə'keɪt US: 'pleɪkeɪt/ *vt* [VP6A] soothe; pacify.

place¹ /pleɪs/ *n* **1** particular part of space occupied by sb or sth: *I can't be in two* ～s *at once.* **2** city, town, village, etc: *visit* ～s *and see things,* travel as a tourist. '*go* ～s, (colloq) have increasing success. '～**-name** *n* name of a city, town, village, hill, lake, etc: *an expert on the origin of* ～*-names.* **3** building or area of land used for some particular purpose that is specified: *a* ～ *of worship,* a church, etc; ～s *of amusement,* theatres, discotheques, cinemas, etc; *a* '*market–*～; *a* ～ *of business.* **4** particular ～ on a surface: *a sore* ～ *on my neck.* **5** passage, part, in a book, etc: *I've lost my* ～, can't find the ～ *where I stopped reading. Use a book-mark to keep your* ～ *instead of turning down the corner of the page.* **6** rank or station (in society, etc): *keep/know one's* ～. **7** (in a race) position among those competitors who are winners: *Whose horse got the first* ～? *I shall back* (= bet some money on) *the favourite for a* ～, ie to be one of the first three past the winning-post. Hence, '～**-bet** *n* **8** (maths) position of a figure in a series as indicating its value in decimal or other notation: *calculated to five* ～s *of decimals/to five decimal* ～s, eg 6·57132. **9** single step or stage in an argument, etc. *in the first/second, etc* ～, firstly/secondly, etc. **10** proper or natural position: *A tidy person likes to have a* ～ *for everything and everything in its* ～. *Please take your* ～s, eg ready for a dance. *Go back to your* ～, eg your seat. *There's always a* ～ *for you around our table,* You will always be a welcome guest. *in* ～, (a) in the right or proper ～: *I like to have everything in* ～. (b) (fig) suitable; ap-

propriate: *The proposal is not quite in* ～. *out of* ～, (a) not in the right or proper ～. (b) (fig) unsuitable; inappropriate: *Your remarks were rather out of* ～. *in* ～ *of,* instead of. *give* ～, yield. *give* ～ *to,* be succeeded by. *make* ～ *for,* (a) make room (which is the more usu word) for. (b) yield precedence to. (c) be superseded by. *put sb in his (proper)* ～; *put oneself in sb's/sb else's* ～, ⇨ put¹(2). *take the* ～ *of,* be substituted for: *Who will take the* ～ *of Mr X/take Mr X's* ～? *Plastics have taken the* ～ *of many materials. take* ～, happen: *The wedding/party/celebration took place yesterday. pride of* ～, position of superiority. **11** office, employment, esp a government appointment; duties of an office-holder: *It's your* ～ *to see that the junior members of the staff do not arrive late. He will get a* ～ *in the Oxford boat,* will be chosen to be a member of the crew. '～**·man,** '～**seeker,** man looking for a favoured position, eg in government. **12** estate; house; home: *He has a nice little* ～ *in the country. Come round to my* ～ *one evening.* **13** (in proper names) alternative name for *Street, Square,* etc in a town: *St James's P*～. **14** '～**-kick** *n* (Rugby football) kick made when the ball is previously placed for that purpose on the ground.

place² /pleɪs/ *vt* [VP6A,15A,B] **1** put (sth) in a certain place; arrange (things) in their proper places: *P*～ *them in the right order.* **2** appoint (sb) to a post; put in office or authority: *He was* ～*d in command of the Second Army.* **3** put, invest (money): ～ *£500 in Saving Bonds;* ～ *£100 to sb's credit in the bank.* **4** put (an order for goods, etc) with a business firm: ～ *an order for books with Blackwell's.* **5** dispose of (goods) to a customer: *How can we* ～ *all this surplus stock?* **6** have, fix, repose: ～ *confidence in a leader.* **7** recognize or estimate (sb) by connecting him with past experience; fully identify: *I know that man's face, but I can't* ～ *him. He's a difficult man to* ～. **8** (racing) state the position of runners (in a race), contestants (in an athletic contest). *be* ～*d,* be among the first three: *The Duke's horse wasn't* ～*d.*

pla·cebo /plə'siːbəʊ/ *n* (*pl* ～s) sth not containing medicine given to soothe, not to cure, a patient.

pla·centa /plə'sentə/ *n* (zool) organ lining the womb during pregnancy, by which the foetus is nourished. It is expelled with the foetus and the umbilical cord following birth. ⇨ the illus at reproduce.

pla·cid /'plæsɪd/ *adj* calm; untroubled; (of a person) not easily irritated. ～**·ly** *adv* ～**·ity** /plə'sɪdətɪ/ *n* [U].

placket /'plækɪt/ *n* opening in a woman's skirt to make it easier to put on and take off; pocket inside this.

plage /plɑːʒ/ *n* (F) sea beach (esp at a fashionable seaside resort).

pla·giar·ize /'pleɪdʒəraɪz/ *vt* [VP6A] take and use sb else's ideas, words, etc as if they were one's own. **pla·giar·ism** /-ɪzəm/ *n* [U] plagiarizing; [C] instance of this. **pla·giar·ist** /-ɪst/ *n* person who ～s.

plague /pleɪg/ *n* **1** *the* ～, = *bubonic plague,* ⇨ bubonic. '～**-spot** *n* (a) spot on the skin characteristic of ～. (b) district infected with ～. (c) centre, source or symptom of moral evil. **2** cause of trouble, annoyance or disaster: *a* ～ *of locusts/flies. What a* ～ *that boy is! What a nuisance he is!* □ *vt* [VP6A,14] ～ (*with*), annoy (esp with repeated requests or questions). **plaguy** /'pleigi/ adj (colloq) annoying. **pla·guily** /-ɪlɪ/ adv annoyingly; provokingly.

plaice /pleɪs/ n (pl unchanged) edible flatfish. ⇨ the illus at fish.

plaid /plæd/ n 1 [C] long piece of woollen cloth worn over the shoulders by Scottish Highlanders. 2 [U] cloth, usu with a chequered or tartan pattern, used for this article of dress.

plain¹ /pleɪn/ adj (-er, -est) 1 easy to see, hear or understand: ~ English; in ~ speech; ~ language, (of telegrams, etc) not in code. The meaning is quite ~. ~ 'sailing, (fig) course of action that is simple and free from difficulties: After we engaged a guide, everything was ~ sailing. 2 simple; ordinary; without luxury or ornament: a ~ blue dress, of blue material without a design on it, or without trimmings, etc; in ~ clothes, (esp of policemen) in ordinary clothes, not in uniform; ~ food/cooking; a ~ cook, one who can prepare ~ meals. 3 (of persons, their thoughts, actions, etc) straightforward; frank: in ~ words, frankly; ~ dealing, honesty, sincerity. to be '~ with you, to speak openly. ,~-'spoken adj frank in speech. 4 (of a person's appearance) not pretty or handsome. 5 '~-song/-chant n music for a number of voices in unison, used in the Anglican and Roman Catholic Church services. □ adv clearly: learn to speak ~; entirely: You are ~ wrong. ~·ly adv clearly: The rock stuck out ~ly; obviously: You are ~ly wrong. ~·ness n

plain² /pleɪn/ n area of level country: the wide ~s of Canada. '~s·man /-zmən/ n (pl -men) inhabitant of a ~.

plain³ /pleɪn/ n simple stitch in knitting. ⇨ purl¹. □ vt, vi knit this stitch.

plaint /pleɪnt/ n 1 (legal) charge; accusation. 2 (poet) complaint; lamentation.

plain·tiff /'pleɪntɪf/ n person who brings an action at law. ⇨ defendant.

plain·tive /'pleɪntɪv/ adj sounding sad; sorrowful. ~·ly adv ~·ness n

plait /plæt/ vt [VP6A] weave or twist (three or more lengths of hair, straw, etc) under and over one another into one rope-like length. □ n sth made by ~ing: wearing her hair in a ~.

plan /plæn/ n 1 outline drawing (of or for a building) showing the relative sizes, positions, etc of the parts, esp as if seen from above: ~s for a new school. ⇨ elevation(5); ⇨ the illus at perspective. 2 diagram (of the parts of a machine). 3 diagram showing how a garden, park, town or other area of land has been, or is to be, laid out. Cf map for a large area of land. 4 arrangement for doing or using sth, considered in advance: make ~s for the holidays; a ~ to encourage saving; a five-year ~, eg for a country's economic and industrial development. (go) according to ~, (happen) as planned. □ vt (-nn-) 1 [VP6A] make a ~ of or for: ~ a house/garden. 2 [VP7A] ~ to do sth, make ~s: We're ~ning to visit Europe this summer. 3 [VP6A,15B] ~ (out), consider and arrange in advance: ~ (out) a military campaign. a ~ned economy, economic system ~ned by government authorities. ⇨ town(2). ~·ner n one who makes ~s. ~·less adj without a ~.

plan·chette /plɑːnˈʃet US: plænˈʃet/ n small board supported by two castors, with a vertical pencil said to trace marks on paper at spiritualistic seances without conscious direction by hand.

plane¹ /pleɪn/ n '~(-tree), one of several kinds of tree with spreading branches, broad leaves and thin bark, which comes off in flakes.

plane² /pleɪn/ n tool for trimming the surface of wood by taking shavings from it. ⇨ the illus at tool. □ vt, vi [VP2A,15B,2D,22] use a ~; make smooth with a ~: ~ sth smooth. ~ away/down, remove irregularities with a ~.

plane³ /pleɪn/ n 1 flat or level surface; surface such that the straight line joining any points on it is touching it at all points; imaginary surface of this kind; (attrib) ~ ge'ometry, geometry of figures on a ~. ~ 'sailing, the art of determining a ship's position on the theory that the ship is moving on a ~. ⇨ plain sailing at plain¹(1). 2 main supporting surface of an aeroplane. 3 (fig) level or stage (of development, etc): on the same ~ as a savage; on a higher social ~. □ vi ~ (down), (of aeroplanes) travel, glide.

plane⁴ /pleɪn/ n (colloq abbr for) aeroplane.

planet /'plænɪt/ n one of the heavenly bodies (eg Mars, Venus) which moves round a star such as the sun and is illuminated by it. **plan·et·ary** /'plænɪtrɪ US: -terɪ/ adj relating to, moving like, a ~. **plan·et·ar·ium** /ˌplænɪˈteərɪəm/ n (building with a) device for representing the movements of the stars and ~s by projecting spots of light on the inner surface of a large dome that represents the sky.

plan·gent /'plændʒənt/ adj (formal) (of sounds) resounding; vibrating.

plank /plæŋk/ n 1 long, flat piece of timber, 2 to 6 inches thick, 9 or more inches wide; board. '~-bed n one of boards, without mattresses. walk the ~, ⇨ walk²(4). 2 basic principle in a political platform. □ vt 1 [VP6A] furnish with ~s; cover (a floor, etc) with ~s. 2 [VP15B] ~ sth down, (colloq) put down (esp money); pay at once. ~·ing n [U] ~s put down to form a floor.

plank·ton /'plæŋktən/ n [U] the (chiefly microscopic) forms of organic life that drift in or float on the water of the oceans, lakes, rivers, etc.

plant¹ /plɑːnt US: plænt/ n 1 living organism which is not an animal, esp the kind smaller than trees and shrubs: garden ~s; a tobacco ~. '~-louse n kinds of insect pest that attack ~s, esp aphis. 2 [U] apparatus, fixtures, machinery, etc used in an industrial or manufacturing process: We get our tractors and bulldozers from a ~-hire firm. The farm has its own lighting ~, eg a generator for producing electric current. 3 [U] (US) factory; buildings and equipment of an institution. 4 (sl) planned swindle; hoax; person who joins a gang of criminals to get evidence against them.

plant² /plɑːnt US: plænt/ vt [VP6A,15A,B] 1 put ~s, bushes, trees, etc in (a garden, etc): ~ a garden with rose-bushes; set up a monument and ~ it round with trees/~ trees round it. 2 put (plants, trees, etc) in the ground to grow; (fig) cause (an idea) to take root in sb's mind: ~ (out) strawberry runners/pansies. ⇨ sow². 3 place firmly in position; take up a position or attitude: He ~ed his feet firmly on the ground. He ~ed himself in front of the fire. He ~ed his feet wide apart. 4 establish, found (a community, colony, etc); settle (a person) in a place as a colonist, etc. 5 deliver (a blow, etc) with deliberate aim: ~ a blow on sb's ear. 6 (sl) hide (esp in order to deceive sb, to cause an innocent person to seem guilty, etc): ~ stolen goods on sb. ~·er n 1 person who grows crops on a plantation: 'tea/'rubber-~ers. 2 machine for ~ing.

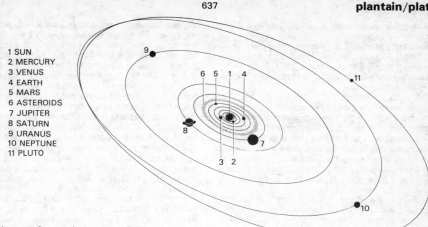

1 SUN
2 MERCURY
3 VENUS
4 EARTH
5 MARS
6 ASTEROIDS
7 JUPITER
8 SATURN
9 URANUS
10 NEPTUNE
11 PLUTO

the planets of our solar system

plan·tain¹ /'plæntɪn/ n tree-like tropical plant bearing fruit similar to that of the banana-palm; its fruit. ⇨ the illus at vegetable.

plan·tain² /'plæntɪn/ n common wild plant with broad leaves and seeds much used for cage-birds.

plan·ta·tion /plæn'teɪʃn/ n **1** area of land planted with trees: ∼s of fir and pine. **2** large estate on which tea, cotton, sugar, tobacco or other commercial crop is cultivated: '∼ songs, songs sung by Negroes who formerly worked as slaves on cotton ∼s in N America.

plaque /plɑːk US: plæk/ n flat metal or porcelain plate fixed on a wall as an ornament or memorial.

plash /plæʃ/ n (sing only) light splashing sound: the ∼ of oars in water. □ vt,vi [VP6A] strike the surface of (water) gently; splash.

plasm/'plæzəm/ n [U] genetic material of a cell.

plasma/'plæzmə/ n ('blood) ∼, [U] clear, yellowish fluid in which the blood-cells are carried.

plas·ter /'plɑːstə(r) (US): 'plæs-/ n **1** [U] soft mixture of lime, sand, water, etc used for coating walls and ceilings. ∼ of 'Paris n [U] white paste made from gypsum that becomes very hard when dry, used for making moulds, etc. '∼ cast n (a) mould made with gauze and ∼ of Paris to hold a broken or dislocated bone in place. (b) mould (eg for a small statue) made of ∼ of Paris. '∼-board n [U] board made of gypsum and thick paper or cardboard, used for inside walls and ceilings instead of plastering. **2** [C] piece of fabric spread with a medicinal substance, for application to part of the body, to relieve pain, cover a wound, etc. **3** ('sticking-)∼, [U,C] material treated with some substance so that it will stick to the skin, used for covering a cut, blister, burn, for holding a bandage in position, etc. □ vt [VP6A,14] **1** cover (a wall, etc) with ∼(1); put a ∼(2) on (the body). **2** ∼ sth with sth; ∼ sth on sth, cover thickly: hair ∼ed with oil; an old suitcase ∼ed with hotel labels. ∼ed adj (colloq) drunk. ∼er n workman who ∼s walls and ceilings.

plas·tic /'plæstɪk/ adj **1** (of materials) easily shaped or moulded: Clay is a ∼ substance; (of goods) made of such materials, esp synthetic resinous substances: ∼ raincoats/flowers/cups/spoons. ∼ ex-'plosive, kind that is easily moulded around the object it is to destroy. ∼-'bomb, one made of such explosive. **2** of the art of modelling: the ∼

arts. ∼ 'surgery, for the restoration of deformed or diseased parts of the body (by grafting skin, etc). **3** (fig) easily influenced or changed: the ∼ mind of a child. □ n [C] ∼ substance. ∼s n pl (a) ∼ substances (esp synthetic, resinous) moulded under pressure while heated, or drawn into filaments for use in textiles. (b) (with sing v) science of making ∼ substances. ∼·ity /plæ'stɪsəti/ n [U] state or quality of being ∼.

plas·ti·cine /'plæstɪsiːn/ n [U] (P) plastic substance resembling clay but remaining soft for a long time, used for modelling in schools.

plate¹ /pleɪt/ n **1** [C] shallow, usu circular, almost flat dish, made (usu) of earthenware or china, from which food is served or eaten: a dinner/soup/dessert ∼; contents of this: a ∼ of beef and vegetables. **hand/give sb sth on a ∼**, (colloq) give, allow sb to have, sth without his having to make any effort. **on one's ∼**, to occupy one's time: He has enough/a lot/too much on his ∼. '∼-rack n rack in which ∼s are kept or placed to drain after being washed. **2** [C] similar vessel or dish (usu of metal) used for collection of money in churches: put only a dime in the ∼. **3** [U] (collective) gold or silver articles, eg spoons, dishes, bowls, for use at meals: a fine piece of ∼, one of these articles. ⇨ plate²(2). '∼-powder n [U] powder for cleaning and polishing ∼. **4** [C] flat, thin sheet of metal, glass, etc, eg steel ∼s for building ships: 'boiler ∼s. ∼-'glass n [U] thick and very clear glass in sheets for windows, mirrors, doors etc. **5** [U,C] sheet of glass coated with sensitive film for photography: 'whole-∼, 'half-∼, 'quarter-∼, the usual sizes. **6** [C] oblong piece of metal (usu brass) with a person's name, etc on it, fixed to the door or gate (as used by doctors, solicitors and other professional persons). **7** sheet of metal, plastic, rubber, etc from which the pages of a book are printed; book illustration (usu photographic) printed separately from the text. **8** 'dental ∼, (also called a denture) thin piece of plastic material, moulded to the shape of the gums, with artificial teeth attached to it. **9** [C] silver or gold cup as a prize for a horse-race; the race. **10** (in baseball) (also home ∼) home base of the batting side. '∼-ful /-fʊl/ n amount that a ∼ holds.

plate² /pleɪt/ vt [VP6A,14] ∼ (with), **1** cover (esp a ship) with metal plates(4). **2** cover (another metal) with gold, silver, copper or tin: *gold-~d dishes; silver-~d spoons.*

pla·teau /'plætəʊ US: plæ'təʊ/ n (pl ~s or ~x /-təʊz/) expanse of level land high above sea-level. ⇨ the illus at mountain.

plate·layer /'pleɪtleɪə(r)/ n workman who lays and repairs railway tracks.

plat·form /'plætfɔːm/ n 1 flat surface built at a higher level than the track in a railway station, used by travellers: *Which ~ does the Bournemouth train leave from?* 2 flat structure raised above floor-level for speakers in a hall or in the open air, teachers in a classroom, etc; space at the entrance of a bus or tram (for the conductor). 3 programme of a political party, esp as stated before an election.

plat·ing /'pleɪtɪŋ/ n [U] (esp) thin coating of gold, silver, etc. ⇨ plate²(2).

plati·num /'plætɪnəm/ n [U] grey untarnishable metal (symbol **Pt**) used for jewellery and alloyed with other metals for use in industry. ,~ **'blonde,** (colloq) woman with silvery-white hair (but not used of a hair that has turned white with age).

plati·tude /'plætɪtjuːd US: -tuːd/ n 1 [C] statement that is obviously true, esp one often heard before, but uttered as if it were new. 2 [U] quality of being commonplace. **plati·tudi·nous** /,plætɪ'tjuːdɪnəs US: -'tuːdənəs/ adj commonplace: *platitudinous remarks.*

Pla·tonic /plə'tɒnɪk/ adj of Plato or his teachings: *~ love/friendship,* between two people without a desire for physical love.

pla·toon /plə'tuːn/ n body of soldiers, subdivision of a company, acting as a unit and commanded by a lieutenant.

plat·ter /'plætə(r)/ n 1 (US) large, shallow dish for serving food, esp meat and fish. 2 (archaic in GB) flat dish, often of wood.

platy·pus /'plætɪpəs/ n (pl ~es /-pəsɪz/) (,**duck-billed**) '~, (also called *duckbill*) small Australian animal which suckles its young but lays eggs (called *duckbilled* because it has a bill like that of a duck). ⇨ the illus at small.

plau·dit /'plɔːdɪt/ n (usu pl) cry, clapping or other sign of approval: *gratified at the ~s of the audience.*

plaus·ible /'plɔːzəbl/ adj 1 seeming to be right or reasonable: *a ~ excuse/explanation.* 2 (of persons) clever at producing convincing arguments, etc: *a ~ rogue.* **plaus·ibly** /-əblɪ/ adv **plausi·bil·ity** /,plɔːzə'bɪlətɪ/ n [U] state of being ~; [C] (pl -ties) ~ excuse, argument, etc.

play¹ /pleɪ/ n 1 [U] (what is done for) amusement; recreation: *The children are at ~,* engaged in playing. *What I said was only in ~,* not intended to be taken seriously. *a ~ on words,* a pun. '**child's-~** n [U] sth simple and easy. '**~-box** n box to hold toys. '**~-boy** n rich young man chiefly interested in enjoying himself. '**~-fellow/mate** nn companion in ~. '**~-ground** n piece of ground used for ~, eg one at a school or in a public park (cf *playing-field* below). '**~-group** n = ~-school. '**~-pen** n portable enclosure in which a baby or small child may be left to ~. '**~-room** n one in a house for children to ~ in. '**~-school** n group of young children who play together regularly under supervision. '**~-suit** n loose garment(s) to be worn (eg on a beach) by a child while playing. '**~-thing** n toy; (fig) sb treated as a mere toy. '**~-time** n period for ~. 2 [U] the playing of a game; manner of playing: *There was a lot of rough ~ in*

the football match yesterday. That was expert ~/ an expert bit of ~! in/out of ~, (of the ball in football, cricket, etc) in/not in a position where the rules of the game allow it to be played. **fair ~,** (fig) justice, equal conditions and treatment for all: *I will see fair ~,* I will ensure that both sides are treated justly. **foul ~,** ~ contrary to the rules; (fig) treachery; violence: *Do the police suspect foul ~?* 3 [U] turn or move in a game (eg chess): *It's your ~,* You are to make the next move. 4 [U] gaming; gambling: *lose £50 in one evening's ~; high ~,* ie for high stakes. 5 [C] drama for the stage: *the ~s of Shakespeare. Let's go to a ~* (=theatre) *this evening.* **as good as a ~,** amusing, interesting. '**~-actor** n (old use) actor. '**~-acting** n [U] n performance of ~s; (fig) pretence. '**~-bill** n bill announcing the performance of a ~. '**~-goer** /-gəʊə(r)/ n person who often goes to the theatre. '**~-house** n theatre. '**~-wright** n dramatist. 6 [U] light, quick, fitful movement: *the ~ of sunlight upon water.* 7 [U] (space for) free and easy movement; scope for activity: *allow full ~ to one's curiosity; give free ~ to one's fancy/emotions; a knot with too much ~,* one that is not tight enough. *Give the rope more ~,* keep it less taut. 8 [U] activity; operation: *the ~ of forces.* **be in full ~,** be fully operating or active. **bring sth into ~,** make use of it; bring it into action. **come into ~,** begin to operate or be active.

play² /pleɪ/ vt,vi (pt,pp ~ed /pleɪd/) (For special uses with *adverbial particles* and *preps,* ⇨ 15 below.) 1 [VP2A,B,C] (contrasted with *work*) have fun; do things to pass the time pleasantly, as children do: *The children are ~ing in the park. Let's go out and ~. ~ with,* amuse oneself with: *~ with the kitten.* 2 [VP3A,6A] ~ (**at doing sth**), pretend, for fun, to be sth or do sth: *Let's ~ (at being) pirates. The children were ~ing at keeping shop.* 3 [VP6A,14,12C] ~ **a joke/prank/trick (on sb),** trick him. 4 [VP6A,2A,C,3A] (be able to) take part in a game, eg of cricket, football, golf, cards: *Do you ~ cricket? He ~s (football) for Stoke/ England. On Saturday France ~s (Rugby) against Wales/~s Wales at Rugby. They were ~ing bridge. Will you ~ me at chess/ ~ chess with me? He went on ~ing* (= gambling) *until he had lost everything.* 5 [VP2C] ~ (**as/at**), fill a particular position in a team: *I've never ~ed (as/at) centre-forward before. Who's ~ing in goal/as goal-keeper?* [VP6A,15A,16B] ~ **sb (as/at),** include in a team: *I think we should ~ Smith in the next match. Who shall we ~ as goalkeeper?* 6 [VP15A,B] (cricket, football, etc) strike (the ball) in a specified manner: *~ the ball to mid-on; ~ (the ball) on to one's own wicket* (and so put oneself out). *In soccer only the goal-keeper may ~ the ball with his hands.* ~ **ball (with),** (fig, colloq) be ready to act in partnership; co-operate: *The French President refused to ~ ball,* eg to co-operate with the leader of another country. [VP2C] (cricket, of the ground) be in good, poor, etc condition for ~ing: *The pitch is ~ing well/badly.* 7 [VP6A] move (a piece) in chess: *~ a pawn;* take (a playing-card) from one's hand (in whist, bridge, etc) and lay it down face upwards when one's turn comes: *~ one's ace of hearts/a trump. ~ one's cards well/badly,* (fig) make good/bad use of opportunities. 8 ~ **fair,** fairly; in accordance with the rules. ~ **hard,** (of a player) ~ vigorously. ~ **the ball, not the man,** kick the ball, not one's op-

ponent. ~ **the game,** observe the rules of the game; (fig) be fair and honest; observe the code of honour. **9** [VP6A,2A,12B,13B] perform on (a musical instrument); perform (music); cause (music) to be heard (by operating a record-player or tape-recorder): ~ *the piano/flute/violin, etc;* ~ *a Beethoven sonata. Won't you please* ~ *me some Chopin/* ~ *some Chopin for me? He was* ~*ing an old tune on his guitar. We* ~*ed a lot of reggae at our party. P*~ *me Pat Simon's latest disc.* [VP15B] ~ **sth back,** reproduce (music, speech, etc) from a tape or disc after it has been recorded: *The discussion was recorded on tape and then* ~*ed back.* Hence, '~**-back** *n* (a) the device on a tape-recorder which ~s back recorded material. (b) occasion when this is done. ~ **second fiddle (to sb),** ⇨ fiddle. ~ **sth by ear/at sight,** ⇨ ear¹(2), *at/on sight* at sight¹(2). ~ **it cool,** ⇨ cool¹(5). **10** [VP6A,2A] perform (a drama on the stage); act (a part in a drama); (of a drama) be performed: ~ *'Twelfth Night';* ~ *Shylock; the National Theatre, where 'Hamlet' is now* ~*ing,* = being ~ed. ~ **the fool,** act foolishly. ~ **the man,** act like a man; be manly. ~ **a (big/small, etc) part (in sth),** ⇨ part¹(4). **11** [VP2A,C,15A] move about in a light or capricious manner; direct (light) (*on, over, along,* etc sth): *sunlight* ~*ing on the water. They* ~*ed coloured lights over the dance floor. A smile* ~*ed on her lips. His fancy* ~*ed round the idea of entering a monastery. They* ~*ed searchlights on the clouds/along the road.* **12** [VP2A,6A,15A] operate continuously; discharge in a steady stream: *The fountains in the park* ~ *on Sundays. The firemen* ~*ed their hoses on the burning building.* **13** [VP14,3A] ~ **(sth) on/upon sth,** fire: *We* ~*ed our guns on the enemy's lines. Their guns* ~*ed on the fort.* **14** ~ **a fish,** (when angling with a rod and line) allow a fish to exhaust itself by pulling against the line. **15** [VP2C,3A,15B] (special uses with *adverbial particles* and *preps*):
play at sth, (a) ⇨ 2,5 above. (b) engage in sth in a trivial or half-hearted way, or merely for pleasure: *Go for him properly—you're only* ~*ing at boxing!*
play sth back, ⇨ 9 above.
play down to sb, deliberately talk to or behave towards sb so that he does not feel inferior, in order to win support or favour. ~ **sth down,** deliberately minimize its importance.
play sb in; play sb into a place, ~ music while he is entering (the place). **play into sb's hands/ the hands of sb,** act so as to give him an advantage or benefit: *My opponent* ~*ed into my hands.*
play one person off against another, oppose him against another, esp for one's own advantage; stimulate rivalry between them. ~ **(sth) off,** ~ again (eg a football match that was drawn): ~ *off a draw/tie. Leeds and Liverpool* ~ *off (their tie) to-morrow.* Hence, '~**-off** *n* such a match.
play on/upon sth, try to rouse or make use of (sb's feelings, incredulity, etc): *He tried to* ~ *on her sympathies.* ~ **on/upon words,** make puns.
play sth out, ~ it to the end (usu fig): *The long struggle between the strikers and their employers is not yet* ~*ed out.* **be** ~**ed out,** be exhausted of energy or usefulness; be out of date: *His horse was* ~*ed out when the day's hunting was over. Is that theory* ~*ed out,* no longer worth considering?
play up, (a) (esp in the imper) (sport) ~ vigorously, energetically. (b) (colloq) behave mischievously: *Don't let the children* ~ *up.* ~ **sth up,** give ex-

cessive importance to: *Don't let him* ~ *up his illness,* eg by making it an excuse for doing nothing. ~ **(sb) up,** (colloq) give trouble (to): *This sciatica has been* ~*ing me up again.* ~ **up to sb,** (a) act in a drama so as to support another actor. (b) (colloq) flatter (to win favour for oneself): *He always* ~*s up to his political bosses.*
play with sb, (a) ⇨ 1 and 4 above. (b) trifle with; consider lightly: *It's wrong for a man to* ~ *with a woman's affections. He's* ~*ing with the idea of emigrating to Canada.*
player /'pleɪə(r)/ *n* **1** one who plays a game. **2** actor. **3** person who plays a musical instrument; mechanical device for producing musical sounds: *a 'record-* ~. '~**-piano** *n* piano fitted with a mechanism which enables the piano to be played automatically.
play·ful /'pleɪfl/ *adj* full of fun; in a mood for play; not serious: *as* ~ *as a kitten; a* ~ *manner.* ~**ly** /-fəlɪ/ *adv* ~**·ness** *n*
play·ing /'pleɪɪŋ/ *n* '~**-card,** ⇨ card¹(3). '~**-field** *n* field for such games as football and cricket; field for children's games.
play·let /'pleɪlɪt/ *n* short dramatic piece.
plaza /'plɑːzə *US:* 'plæzə/ *n* market-place; open square (esp in a Spanish town).
plea /pli:/ *n* [C] **1** (legal) statement made by or for a person charged in a law court. **2** request: ~*s for mercy.* **3** reason or excuse offered for wrongdoing or failure to do sth, etc: *on the* ~ *of ill health.*
pleach /pli:tʃ/ *vt* [VP6A] interlace: ~*ed hedges,* made by intertwining growing branches.
plead /pli:d/ *vt,vi* (*pt,pp* ~ed, or, (US) pled, /pled/) **1** [VP3A] (legal) ~ **for/against sb,** address a court of law as an advocate on behalf of either the plaintiff or the defendant. ~ **guilty/not guilty,** admit/deny that one is guilty: *'How do you* ~?'—'Not guilty, my Lord'.* **2** [VP6A] (legal) (of a lawyer) present the case of (to a court of law); put forward as a plea: *You should get a lawyer to* ~ *your case. Her Counsel* ~*ed insanity,* declared that his client was insane, and therefore not legally responsible for her actions. **3** [VP3A] ~ **(with sb) (for sth/to do sth),** ask earnestly: ~ *(with sb) for mercy. He* ~*ed with his son to be less trouble to his mother.* **4** [VP6A] offer as an explanation or excuse: *The thief* ~*ed poverty. She* ~*ed ignorance of the law.* **5** [VP6A] argue in favour of; advance reasons for (a cause, etc): ~ *the cause of the political prisoners.* ~**·ings** *n pl* (legal) formal (usu written) statements, replies to accusations, etc, made by the parties in a legal action. ~**·ing·ly** *adv*
pleas·ance /'plezns/ *n* [C] (archaic) pleasure; pleasure-ground.
pleas·ant /'pleznt/ *adj* giving pleasure; agreeable; friendly: *a* ~ *afternoon/taste/wine/surprise/ companion; make oneself* ~ *to visitors;* ~ *to the taste.* ~**·ly** *adv* ~**·ness** *n* [U].
pleas·ant·ry /'plezntrɪ/ *n* (*pl* -tries) **1** [U] being jocular; humour. **2** [C] humorous or joking remark: *The girls smiled dutifully at the headmistress's pleasantries.*
please /pli:z/ *vi,vt* **1** (imper) (abbr of *if you* ~) (used as a polite form of request): *Come in,* ~. *P*~ *come in. Two coffees,* ~. *P*~ *don't do that.* **2** [VP6A] give satisfaction to; be agreeable to: *That will* ~ *you. It's difficult to* ~ *everybody. Are you* ~*d with your new clothes? We're very* ~*d to see you here. I shall be* ~*d to come.* ,*P*~ **your'self,** Do as you like. **3** [VP2A] think fit; choose: *I shall do*

as I ~. *Take as many as you* ~. *You may do as you* ~. **4** *if you* ~, (used with the ironical implication that nothing could be more reasonable): '*And now, if you* ~, *I'm to get nothing for all my work!*' ~ **God**, if it be pleasing to God: *War may be abolished one day,* ~ *God.* ~**d** *adj* glad; feeling or showing satisfaction: *He looked* ~*d with himself. I'm very (much)* ~*d with what he has done.* **pleas·ing** *adj* affording pleasure (*to*); agreeable. **pleas·ing·ly** *adv*

pleas·ure /'pleʒə(r)/ *n* **1** [U] feeling of being happy or satisfied: *It gave me much* ~ *to hear of your success. Is this a* ~*-seeking age? Has he gone abroad for* ~ *or on business? May we have the* ~ *of your company for lunch? 'Will you join us?'*—'*Thank you, with* ~'. *His life is given to* ~, to sensuous enjoyments. **take (no/great, etc)** ~ **in sth,** experience (no, etc) enjoyment: *Some boys take great* ~ *in teasing their little sisters.* '~-**boat/-craft** *n* one used for* ~ *only.* '~-**ground** *n* amusement park; recreation ground. **2** [U] will; desire: *We await your* ~. *We needn't consult his* ~. *You may go or stay at your* ~, as you wish. **3** [C] thing that gives happiness: *the* ~*s of friendship.* **pleas·ur·able** /'pleʒərəbl/ *adj* giving ~. **pleas·ur·ably** /-əblɪ/ *adv*

pleat /pli:t/ *n* fold made by doubling cloth on itself. □ *vt* [VP6A] make ~s in: *a* ~*ed skirt.*

pleb /pleb/ *n* (colloq abbr for) plebeian.

pleb·eian /plɪ'bi:ən/ *n, adj* (person who is) of the lower social classes (originally in ancient Rome); coarse; ignoble.

plebi·scite /'plebɪsɪt *US*: -saɪt/ *n* [C] (decision made upon a political question by) the votes of all qualified citizens.

plec·trum /'plektrəm/ *n* small piece of metal, bone or ivory attached to the finger for plucking the strings of some stringed instruments, eg the mandolin, guitar.

pled /pled/ ⇨ plead.

pledge /pledʒ/ *n* **1** [C] sth left with sb to be kept by him until the giver has done sth which he is under an obligation to do; article left with a pawnbroker. **2** [U] state of being left with sb on these conditions: *goods lying in* ~; *put/hold sth in* ~; *take sth out of* ~. **3** [C] sth given as a sign of love, approval, etc: *a* ~ *of friendship;* (fig) *the* ~ *of their youthful love,* their child. **4** [U] agreement; promise: *under* ~ *of secrecy.* **take/sign the** ~, (esp) make a written promise to abstain from alcoholic drink. □ *vt* [VP6A] **1** give as security; put in pawn. **2** give; engage; make an undertaking (to do sth): *be* ~*d to secrecy;* ~ *one's word/honour.* **3** drink the health of: ~ *the bride and bridegroom.*

ple·nary /'pli:nərɪ/ *adj* **1** (of powers, authority) unlimited; absolute. **2** (of meetings) attended by all who have a right to attend: *a* ~ *session.* **plen·ar·ily** /'pli:nərəlɪ/ *adv*

pleni·po·ten·tiary /ˌplenɪpə'tenʃərɪ/ *n* (*pl* -ries), *adj* (person, eg a representative, an ambassador) having full power to act, make decisions, etc (on behalf of his government, etc).

pleni·tude /'plenɪtjuːd *US*: -tuːd/ *n* (*sing* only) (formal) fullness; abundance: *in the* ~ *of his powers.*

plen·teous /'plentɪəs/ *adj* (chiefly poet) plentiful. ~·**ly** *adv*

plen·ti·ful /'plentɪfl/ *adj* in large quantities or numbers; abundant. ~·**ly** /-fəlɪ/ *adv*

plenty /'plentɪ/ *n* [U] ~ **(of),** as much as or more

than is needed or desired; a large number or quantity: *There are* ~ *of eggs in the house. There's* ~ *more (of it). We must get to the station in* ~ *of time. Six will be* ~, as many as I need. *I've had* ~, thank you. **in** ~, in a large quantity: *There was food and drink in* ~. □ *adv* (colloq) quite: *It's* ~ *big enough.*

pleo·nasm /'plɪənæzəm/ *n* [C,U] (instance of the) use of more words than are needed to express the meaning, eg 'each of the *two* twins'; 'divide sth into *four* quarters'.

pleth·ora /'pleθərə/ *n* (formal) **1** glut; (over-) abundance. **2** (med) unhealthy condition of the body marked by an excess of red corpuscles in the blood.

pleur·isy /'plʊərəsɪ/ *n* [U] serious illness with inflammation of the delicate membrane of the thorax and the lungs, marked by pain in the chest or sides.

plexus /'pleksəs/ *n* (*pl* ~es /-səsɪz/ or ~) (anat) network of fibres or vessels in the body: *the solar* ~, in the abdomen.

pli·able /'plaɪəbl/ *adj* easily bent, shaped or twisted; (of the mind) easily influenced; open to suggestions. **pli·abil·ity** /ˌplaɪə'bɪlətɪ/ *n* [U].

pli·ant /'plaɪənt/ *adj* pliable. ~·**ly** *adv* **pli·ancy** /'plaɪənsɪ/ *n*

pli·ers /'plaɪəz/ *n pl* (**pair of**) ~, kind of pincers with long, flat jaws, used for holding, bending, twisting or cutting wire, etc. ⇨ the illus at tool.

plight¹ /plaɪt/ *n* serious and difficult condition: *His affairs were in a terrible* ~. *What a* ~ *to be in!*

plight² /plaɪt/ *vt* [VP6A] (archaic) **1** pledge, promise: *one's* ~*ed word.* **2** ~ **one's troth;** ~ **oneself,** engage oneself to be married.

Plim·soll /'plɪmsəl/ *n* '~ **line/mark,** line on the hull of a ship to mark how far it may legally go down in the water when loaded.

plim·solls /'plɪmsəlz/ *n pl* rubber-soled canvas shoes (US = *sneakers*).

plinth /plɪnθ/ *n* square base or block on which a column or statue stands. ⇨ the illus at column.

plod /plɒd/ *vi,vt* (-dd-) [VP2C] continue walking, working, etc slowly and wearily but without resting: ~ *on one's way;* ~ *away at a dull task.* ~·**der** *n* person who ~s; slow but earnest person. ~·**ding** *adj* ~·**ding·ly** *adv*

plonk¹ /plɒŋk/ *n* sound of sth dropping (esp into liquid). □ *adv* with a ~. □ *vi* ~ **(down),** drop sth with a ~ing sound: ~ *the fish down on the table.*

plonk² /plɒŋk/ *n* [U] (sl) cheap wine.

plop /plɒp/ *n* [C] sound (as) of a small smooth object dropping into water without a splash. □ *adv* with a ~. □ *vi* (-pp-) make a ~; fall with a ~.

plo·sive /'pləʊsɪv/ *n, adj* (phon) (consonant sound) with a complete closing of the air passage followed by an audible release of the air compressed behind the closure, eg /t/ and /p/ in *top.*

plot¹ /plɒt/ *n* piece of ground (usu small): *a building* ~; *a* ~ *of vegetables.* □ *vt* (-tt-) **1** [VP6A] make a plan, map or diagram of; mark (the position of sth) on a diagram by connecting points on a graph: ~ *a temperature curve;* ~ *aircraft movements by radar.* **2** [VP6A,15B] ~ **(out),** divide into ~s.

plot² /plɒt/ *n* [C] **1** secret plan (good or bad); conspiracy: *a* ~ *to overthrow the government.* **2** plan or outline (of the events of a story, esp of a novel or drama). □ *vt,vi* (-tt-) [VP2A,3A,4,6A,8,10] make secret plans; form, take part in, a ~: ~ *with sb against the government.* ~·**ter** *n* person who ~s;

conspirator.

plough (US = **plow**) /plaʊ/ n **1** implement for cutting furrows in soil and turning it up, drawn by animals or (more usually) a tractor. *put one's hand to the* ∼, (fig) undertake a task. '∼·boy n boy who leads the horses that pull a ∼. '∼·man /-mən/ n (pl -men) man who guides a ∼. '∼·share n broad blade of a ∼. **2** kinds of implement resembling a ∼. '**snow·**∼ n one for clearing away snow from roads and railways. **3** [U] ploughed land: *100 acres of* ∼. **4 the P**∼, (astron) the group of stars called *Charles's Wain, the Big Dipper* or *the Great Bear*. □ vt,vi **1** [VP6A,15B] ∼ *(back)*, break up (land) with a ∼: ∼ *a field;* (fig) ∼ *back the profits of a business,* reinvest them. ∼ *a lonely furrow,* (fig) work without help or support. ∼ *the sand,* (fig) do useless work. **2** [VP3A] ∼ *through,* force a way through; advance laboriously: *a ship* ∼*ing through the heavy waves;* ∼ *(one's way) through the mud;* ∼ *through a dull textbook.* **3** [VP6A] (sl) reject (a candidate) in an examination: *The examiners* ∼*ed half the candidates.*

tractor

plough

furrows

a plough

plover /'plʌvə(r)/ n sorts of long-legged, short-tailed land bird that frequents marshy ground near the sea, esp (in England) the golden ∼, the green ∼, and the lapwing or peewit.

plow /plaʊ/ (US) = plough.

ploy /plɔɪ/ n [C] manoeuvre; sth said or done, eg in a game, to win an advantage over one's opponent.

pluck /plʌk/ vt,vi **1** [VP6A] pull the feathers off (a hen, goose, etc). *Has this goose been* ∼*ed?* **2** [VP6A] pick (flowers, fruit, etc). [VP15B] ∼ *sth out/up,* pull (weeds, etc, up or out). **3** [VP3A] ∼ *at,* snatch at; take hold of and pull: *The child was* ∼*ing at its mother's skirt.* **4** ∼ *up courage,* summon one's courage; overcome one's fears. **5** [VP6A] (sl) swindle (esp a young or inexperienced person, eg in gambling). □ n **1** [U] courage; spirit. **2** [U] that which is ∼ed out, esp the heart, liver and lungs of an animal that has been killed. **3** [C] short, sharp pull. ∼**·y** adj (-ier, -iest) brave; having ∼(1). ∼**·ily** /-ɪlɪ/ adv

plug /plʌg/ n **1** piece of wood, metal, rubber etc used to stop up a hole (eg in a barrel, wash-basin, bath, cistern, etc) (US = *stopper*). '∼**-hole,** hole for a ∼ (US = *drain*). **2** device for making a connection with a supply of electric current: *a three-/two-pin* ∼; *put the* ∼ *in the socket/outlet.* ⇨ also *sparking-*∼ at spark¹. **3** cake of pressed or twisted tobacco; piece of this cut off for chewing. **4** (sl) piece of favourable publicity (eg in a radio or TV programme) for a commercial product. ⇨ **5** below. □ vt,vi (-gg-) **1** [VP6A,15B] ∼ *(up),* stop or fill (up) with a ∼: ∼ *a leak.* **2** [VP2C] (colloq) ∼ *away at,* work hard at. **3** [VP2C,15B] ∼ *(sth) in,* make a connection with a ∼(2): ∼ *in the TV set.* **4** [VP6A] (US, sl) hit; shoot. **5** [VP6A] (sl) cause (sth) to be widely known by giving repeated pub-

licity: ∼ *a new song,* eg on radio or TV.

plum /plʌm/ n **1** (tree having) soft round, smooth-skinned fruit with a stone-like seed. ⇨ the illus at fruit. **2** ∼ '**cake,** kind containing dried raisins, currants, etc. ∼ '**duff,** boiled pudding containing dried raisins, currants, etc. ∼**-'pudding,** rich boiled pudding containing dried fruits and spices, part of traditional Christmas food. **2** (colloq) sth considered good and desirable, esp a well-paid position.

plum·age /'pluːmɪdʒ/ n [U] bird's feathers: *tropical birds in their brightly coloured* ∼.

plumb /plʌm/ n ball or piece of lead tied to the end of a cord or rope (a '∼**-line**) for finding the depth of water or testing whether a wall is vertical. *out of* ∼, not vertical. □ adv **1** exactly. **2** (US, colloq) quite: ∼ *crazy.* □ vt [VP6A] (fig) get to the root of: ∼ *the depths of a mystery.*

plum·bago /plʌm'beɪɡəʊ/ n [U] black substance, graphite, used for pencils, etc and mixed with clay for making crucibles.

plum·bago² /plʌm'beɪɡəʊ/ n (pl ∼s /-ɡəʊz/) blue-flowered plant.

plumber /'plʌmə(r)/ n workman who fits and repairs water-pipes, water-tanks, cisterns, etc in a building.

plumb·ing /'plʌmɪŋ/ n [U] **1** the work of a plumber. **2** the water-pipes, water-tanks, cisterns, etc in a building: *The* ∼ *is out of order.*

plume /pluːm/ n feather, esp a large one used as a decoration; ornament of feathers; sth suggesting a feather by its shape: *a* ∼ *of smoke/steam.* ⇨ the illus at rare. *borrowed* ∼*s,* (fig) finery displayed as one's own but borrowed from someone. □ vt [VP6A] (of a bird) smooth (its feathers); preen (itself, its wings). ∼ *oneself (on sth),* (fig) congratulate oneself.

plum·met /'plʌmɪt/ n (weight attached to a) plumb-line; weight attached to a fishing-line to keep the float upright. □ vi (-tt-) [VP2A] fall, plunge, steeply: *Share prices have* ∼*ted.*

plummy /'plʌmɪ/ adj (-ier, -iest) (colloq) good; desirable: ∼ *jobs;* affected, snobbish: *a* ∼ *voice.*

plump¹ /plʌmp/ adj (esp of an animal, a person, parts of the body) rounded; fat in a pleasant-looking way: *a baby with* ∼ *cheeks.* □ vt,vi [VP6A,2A,15B,2C] ∼ *out/up,* make or become rounded: *His cheeks are beginning to* ∼ *up/out. She* ∼*ed up the pillows.*

plump² /plʌmp/ vi,vt **1** [VP2C,15B] ∼ *(sb/oneself/sth) down,* (cause to) fall or drop, suddenly and heavily: ∼ *(oneself) down in a chair;* ∼ *down a heavy bag.* **2** [VP3A] ∼ *for,* vote for, choose, with confidence: ∼ *for the Liberal candidate.* □ n abrupt, heavy fall. □ adv **1** suddenly, abruptly: *fall* ∼ *into the hole.* **2** bluntly: *I told him* ∼ *that....* □ adj unqualified; direct: *give sb a* ∼ *'No' for an answer.*

plun·der /'plʌndə(r)/ vt,vi [VP6A,14,2A] ∼ *(of),* rob (people), esp during war or civil disorder; take goods from (places) by force: ∼ *a palace of its treasures;* ∼ *the citizens of a conquered town.* □ n [U] ∼*ing;* goods taken: *live by* ∼; *wagon-loads of* ∼. ∼**·er** n

plunge /plʌndʒ/ vt,vi **1** [VP6A,14,2A,C] ∼ *(into),* put (sth), or go suddenly and with force, into: ∼ *one's hand into cold water/a hole;* ∼ *a country into war;* ∼ *a room into darkness,* eg by cutting off the current; ∼ *into a swimming-pool;* ∼ *into an argument; be* ∼*d into grief.* **2** [VP2A,C] (of a horse) move forward and downward quickly; (of a ship) thrust its bows into the water; (sl) gamble deeply; run into debt. □ *n* act of plunging (eg from a diving-board into water); violent thrust or other movement. **take the ~,** (fig) take a critical step; do sth decisive. **plunger** *n* (esp) part of a mechanism that moves with a plunging motion, eg the piston of a pump; suction device for clearing a blocked pipe.

plunk /plʌŋk/ = plonk¹.

plu·per·fect /ˌpluːˈpɜːfɪkt/ *n, adj* (gram) (tense) expressing action completed before some past time stated or implied (and in English conveyed by *had* and a *pp*, as in 'As he *had* not *received* my letter, he did not come').

plu·ral /ˈplʊərəl/ *n, adj* (form of word) used with reference to more than one: 'The ~ of *child* is *children*'. **~ society,** one with more than one race, eg Kenya, with Africans, Asians and Europeans. **~ voter,** person who has a vote in more than one constituency.

plu·ral·ism /ˈplʊərəlɪzəm/ *n* [U] the quality of being plural; the holding of more than one office at one time. **plu·ral·ist** /-ɪst/ *n* supporter of ~.

plu·ral·ity /plʊəˈrælətɪ/ *n* (*pl* -ties) **1** [U] state of being plural; [C] large number; majority (*of* votes, etc). **2** [U] holding of more than one office at a time; [C] office held with another.

plus /plʌs/ *prep* with the addition of: *Two ~ five is seven,* 2 + 5 = 7. **~-'fours** *n pl* wide, loose knickerbockers. □ *adj* positive: *a ~ quantity,* one greater than zero. ⟹ minus. □ *n* the sign +; (colloq, fig) positive quality.

plush /plʌʃ/ *n* [U] kind of silk or cotton cloth with a soft nap. □ *adj* (also **~y** (-ier, -iest)) (sl) smart; sumptuous: *a ~(y) restaurant.*

Pluto /ˈpluːtəʊ/ *n* **1** (Roman myth) god of the underworld. **2** (astron) planet farthest from the sun. ⟹ the illus at **planet.**

plu·toc·racy /pluːˈtɒkrəsɪ/ *n* (*pl* -cies) [C,U] (government by a) rich and powerful class. **plu·to·crat** /ˈpluːtəkræt/ *n* person who is powerful because of his wealth. **plu·to·cratic** /ˌpluːtəˈkrætɪk/ *adj* of ~ or a plutocrat.

plu·to·nium /pluːˈtəʊnɪəm/ *n* [U] (artificially produced) radioactive element (symbol **Pu**) derived from uranium, used in nuclear reactors and weapons.

ply¹ /plaɪ/ *n* [C] **1** layer of wood or thickness of cloth: *three-ply wood,* made by sticking together three layers with the grain of each at a right angle to that of the next. **'ply·wood** *n* [U] board(s) made by gluing together thin layers of wood. **2** one strand in wool, rope, etc: *four-ply wool for knitting socks.*

ply² /plaɪ/ *vt,vi* (*pt,pp* plied /plaɪd/) **1** [VP6A] (formal) work with (an instrument): *ply one's needle,* work busily with it. **2** [VP2C] (of ships, buses, etc) go regularly to and fro: *ships that ply between Glasgow and New York; ferry-boats plying across the Channel.* **3** *ply a trade,* work at it. **ply sb with sth,** keep him constantly supplied with (food and drink); attack him constantly with (questions, arguments, etc).

pneu·matic /njuːˈmætɪk *US:* nuː-/ *adj* worked or driven by compressed air: ~ *drills;* filled with compressed air: ~ *tyres.* **pneu·mati·cally** /-klɪ/ *adv*

pneu·monia /njuːˈməʊnɪə *US:* nuː-/ *n* [U] serious illness with inflammation of one or both lungs.

poach¹ /pəʊtʃ/ *vt* [VP6A] cook (an egg) by cracking the shell and dropping the contents into boiling water; simmer (eg fish) in liquid (eg wine).

poach² /pəʊtʃ/ *vt,vi* [VP6A,2A,3A] ~ **(on/for), 1** (go on sb else's property and) take (hares, pheasants, salmon, etc) illegally: ~ *hares;* ~ *for salmon; go out ~ing;* ~ *on a neighbour's land.* **2** (fig) be active in some kind of work that properly belongs to another (or that he considers to be his preserve): *Don't ~ on my preserves.* **~er** *n*

pock /pɒk/ *n* spot on the skin caused by smallpox. **'~-marked,** with marks left after smallpox. **~ed** *adj* be **~ed with,** have holes or depressions in: *The moon's surface is ~ed with small craters.*

pocket /ˈpɒkɪt/ *n* **1** small bag sewn into and forming part of an article of clothing, for carrying things in: *trouser/waistcoat, etc* ~. **pick sb's** ~, steal from sb's ~. **put one's pride in one's** ~, do sth that would normally make one feel mortified. **put one's hand in one's** ~, be ready to spend or give money. **'~-book** *n* (a) notebook. (b) (US) leather case for paper money (GB = *wallet*). (c) (US) woman's purse or handbag. **~-'handkerchief** *n* one to be carried in the ~; (attrib) of small size: *a ~-handkerchief rug.* **'~-knife** *n* small knife with one or more folding blades. **'~-money** *n* [U] money for small needs, esp money given to children. **2** money resources; money: *He will suffer in his* ~, will lose financially. **in/out of** ~, having gained/lost money as the result of doing sth: *The deal left him hundreds of dollars out of* ~. **out-of-~ expenses,** actual outlay incurred; what one has actually spent. **3** bag, hollow, cavity, eg a string pouch at the corner of a billiard or pool table; small cavity in the ground or in rock, containing gold or ore; partial vacuum in the atmosphere (*an 'air-~*) affecting the flight of an aircraft; cavity of air (*an 'air-~*) in a mine²(1), where a shaft is flooded; isolated area: *enemy ~s,* eg occupied by enemy forces; ~s *of resistance;* ~s *of unemployment in the Midlands.* **4** (attrib) of a size suitable for a ~: *a ~ guide/dictionary/edition; a ~-size camera.* **'~-ful** /-fʊl/ *n* amount which a ~ holds. □ *vt* [VP6A] **1** put into one's ~: *He ~ed the money.* ~ **an insult,** endure it without protest. ~ **one's pride,** suppress or hide one's feelings of mortification. **2** appropriate for oneself (usu but not necessarily dishonestly): *He ~ed half the profits. He was given £5 for expenses, but ~ed most of it.* **3** send (a ball) into a ~ on a billiard or pool table.

pod /pɒd/ *n* [C] long seed-vessel of various plants, esp peas and beans. ⟹ the illus at **vegetable.** □ *vt,vi* (-dd-) **1** [VP6A] take (peas, etc) out of pods. **2** [VP2A,C] ~ **(up),** form pods: *The peas are podding (up) well.*

podgy /ˈpɒdʒɪ/ *adj* (-ier, -iest) (of a person) short and fat.

podi·atry /pəˈdaɪətrɪ/ *n* [U] (US) = chiropody.

po·dium /ˈpəʊdɪəm/ *n* platform, eg for the conductor of an orchestra, a lecturer, etc.

poem /ˈpəʊɪm/ *n* [C] piece of creative writing in verse form, esp one expressing deep feeling or noble thought in beautiful language, composed with the desire to communicate an experience; piece of prose writing in elevated style: *a* 'prose ~.

po·esy /ˈpəʊɪzɪ/ *n* [U] (archaic) poetry.

poet /ˈpəʊɪt/ *n* writer of poems. ~ **'laureate,** ⟹ laureate. **'poet·ess** /-es/ *n* woman ~.

po·etic /pəʊˈetɪk/ *adj* of poets and poetry: *in* ~ *form;* ~ *genius.* ~ **'justice,** ideal justice, with proper distribution of rewards and punishments. ~

'licence, ⇨ licence. **po·eti·cal** /-kl/ adj = ∼: the ∼al works of Keats, his poetry. **po·eti·cally** /-klɪ/ adv

po·etry /'pəʊɪtrɪ/ n [U] **1** the art of a poet; poems. **2** quality that produces feelings as produced by poems: the ∼ of motion, eg in ballet or some kinds of athletics.

po·grom /'pɒgrəm US: pə'grɒm/ n [C] organized persecution or killing and plunder (of a group or class of people).

poign·ant /'pɔɪnjənt/ adj distressing to the feelings; deeply moving; keen: ∼ sorrow/regret/ memories. ∼·ly adv **poign·ancy** /-ənsɪ/ n [U] state or quality of being ∼.

poin·set·tia /pɔɪn'setɪə/ n tropical plant with small, greenish-yellow flowers surrounded by large scarlet leaves.

point¹ /pɔɪnt/ n **1** [C] sharp tip (of a pin, pencil, knife, etc). **not to put too fine a ∼ on it,** to speak bluntly, to tell the plain truth. **2** [C] tapering end; tip: the ∼ of the jaw, eg as the place for a knockout in boxing; headland or promontory; piece of land that stretches out into the sea, a lake, etc: a ∼ of land; Pagoda P∼, in Burma. **3** dot made by or as with the ∼ of a pen, etc: a decimal ∼; four ∼ six (4·6); a full ∼, a full stop, the sign . **4** [C] real or imaginary mark of position, in space or time: a ∼ of departure. **a/the ∼ of no return,** ⇨ return¹(1). ∼ **of view,** position from which sth is viewed; (fig) way of looking at a question. ⇨ angle¹(2) (US). **at 'this ∼,** at this place or moment. **be at the ∼ of death,** be dying. **be on the ∼ of doing sth,** be about to do sth. **if/when it comes to the ∼,** if/when the moment for action or decision comes: When it came to the ∼, he refused to help. **'∼-duty** n [U] duty of a policeman stationed at a particular ∼ to control traffic. **'turning-∼,** ⇨ turning. **,∼-to-'∼ race,** race (by persons riding horses) across country, from one ∼ to another (these being recognized by certain landmarks). **5** [U] (printing) unit of measurement for type: 6—∼ is small and 18–∼ is large. Is this sentence printed in 8–∼? **6** [C] mark on a scale; unit of measuring; degree: the 'boiling-∼ of water; the 'melting-∼ of lead. The cost of living went up several ∼s last month, eg from 105 to 110, with 100 as a standard fixed earlier. Oil shares rose several ∼s (ie on the Stock Exchange) yesterday. **Possession is nine ∼s** (= nine-tenths) **of the law,** is strong evidence in favour of the person in possession of sth. **7** [C] unit of scoring in some games and sports, in measuring the quality, etc of exhibits in a show: score twenty ∼s. **give sb ∼s; give ∼s to sb,** be able to offer him advantages and still win: He can give me ∼s at golf, give me odds; is a better player. **score a ∼ (against/off/over sb),** ⇨ score²(3). **win/be beaten on ∼s,** (boxing) win/ be beaten by the ∼s awarded, there being no knockout. **8** [C] one of the thirty-two marks on the circumference of a compass; one of the divisions (11° 15′) between two such consecutive marks. ⇨ the illus at compass. **9** [C] chief idea of sth said, done or planned; single item, detail or particular: There are ∼s on which we've agreed to differ. Let me explain the theory ∼ by ∼. What was the first ∼ in his argument? **carry/gain one's ∼,** persuade sb to agree to one's objective. **come to/get to/ reach the ∼,** give the essential fact or part of what one is trying to say, ignoring what is irrelevant. **get/see/miss the ∼ of sth,** see/fail to see what

sb is trying to make clear, etc: I don't quite get the ∼. She missed the ∼ of the story/joke. **make one's ∼,** win acceptance for an argument, establish what one is proposing. **make a ∼ of doing sth,** regard or treat it as important or necessary. **stretch a ∼,** go beyond what is normally allowable on a question of principle, etc: Can't you stretch a ∼ in my favour? **take sb's ∼,** (during a discussion) understand, appreciate what sb is proposing, etc. **(get/wander) away from/off the ∼,** (say sth) not relevant to what is being discussed. **a case in ∼,** one connected with the subject being discussed: Let me give you a case in ∼, an example that illustrates my argument. **in ∼ of fact,** in reality; indeed. **a ∼ of honour/conscience,** sth of great importance to one's honour/conscience. **on a ∼ of order,** ⇨ order¹(4). **10** [U] reason. **no/not much ∼ in doing sth,** no good reason, little reason, for doing it: There's very little ∼ in protesting, It won't help much. **What's the ∼?** Why bother? (It's irrelevant, useless, etc). **11** [C] marked quality; characteristic: What are her best ∼s as a secretary? He has many good ∼s and few bad ∼s. Singing is not my best ∼, I don't sing well. **12** [C] (GB) socket or outlet for electric current. **13** (pl) tapering movable rails by which a train can move from one track to another. **'∼s·man** /-mən/ n (pl -men) worker in charge of ∼s on a railway, to keep them in order, see that they are moved as needed, etc. **14** [U] effectiveness; urgency: His remarks lack ∼.

point² /pɔɪnt/ vt,vi **1** [VP2A,3A] ∼ (to), direct attention to; show the position or direction of; be a sign of: The needle of a compass ∼s to the north. He ∼ed to the door. It's rude to ∼. Both the hour hand and the minute hand ∼ed to twelve, It was noon. All the evidence ∼s to his guilt. **2** [VP14] ∼ sth at/towards, aim or direct (at, towards): ∼ a gun at sb; ∼ a telescope at the moon; ∼ing his forefinger at me reprovingly. **3** [VP15B] ∼ sth out, show; call or direct attention to: ∼ out a mistake; ∼ out to sb the stupidity of his behaviour. Can you ∼ (me) out the man you suspect? He ∼ed out the finest pictures to me. I must ∼ out that delay is unwise. **4** [VP6A] make a point on (eg a pencil); (fig) give force to (advice, a moral). **5** [VP6A] fill in the joints of (brickwork, etc) with mortar or cement, using a trowel to smooth the material. **6** (of a dog) take up a position with the body steady and the head ∼ing in the direction of game. ⇨ pointer(3). **∼ed** adj **1** (fig) directed clearly against a particular person or his behaviour: a ∼ed reproof. Jack was showing ∼ed attentions to the glamorous film star. **2** (of wit) incisive. **∼·ed·ly** adv

point-blank /,pɔɪnt 'blæŋk/ adj **1** (of a shot) aimed, fired, at very close range: fired at ∼ range. **2** (fig, of sth said) in a manner that leaves no room for doubt: a ∼ refusal. □ adv in a ∼ manner: fire ∼ at sb; ask sb ∼ whether he intends to help; refuse ∼ to help.

pointer /'pɔɪntə(r)/ n **1** stick used to point to things on a map, etc. **2** indicator on a dial or balance. **3** large, short-haired hunting dog trained to stand still with its nose pointing in the direction of game it scents.

point·less /'pɔɪntlɪs/ adj **1** (fig) with little or no sense, aim or purpose: It seemed ∼ to go on until they were certain of being on the right road. **2** without points scored: a ∼ draw. ∼·ly adv

poise /pɔɪz/ *vt,vi* **1** [VP2C] be or keep balanced; (fig) be ready: ~d *in mid-air/on the brink/for action*. **2** [VP6A,15A] balance; support in a particular place or manner: *He* ~d *himself on his toes*. Note the way he ~s *his head*. □ *n* **1** [U] balance, equilibrium; [C] way in which one carries oneself, holds one's head, etc. **2** [U] quiet self-confidence; self-possession.

poi·son /'pɔɪzn/ *n* [C,U] **1** substance causing death or harm if absorbed by a living thing (animal or plant): '*rat-*~; ~ *for killing weeds on gravel paths; commit suicide by taking* ~. ~-'**gas** *n* deadly gas used in warfare. ,~-'**ivy** *n* N American shrub or vine which causes painful spots if brought into contact with a person's skin. '~ **pen**, person who writes anonymous letters full of malice, slander, etc. ~ '**pen letter**, letter of this kind. **2** (fig) evil principle, teaching, etc considered harmful to society. □ *vt* [VP6A] **1** give ~ to; put ~ on or in; kill with ~; infect: ~ *a cat;* ~ *the wells; a* ~*ed hand*, inflamed because of an infected cut, etc. **2** injure morally: ~ *a person's mind against sb; an experience which* ~*ed his whole life*, which spoilt or ruined his life. ~**er** *n* (esp) person who murders by means of ~. ~·**ous** /'pɔɪznəs/ *adj* **1** acting as ~; causing death or injury if taken into the system: ~*ous plants*. **2** morally injurious: *a* ~*ous play/ novel/doctrine; a man with a* ~*ous tongue*, one who spreads evil reports, wicked scandal, etc. ~·**ous·ly** *adv*

poke¹ /pəʊk/ *vt,vi* **1** [VP6A,15A,B] push sharply, jab (with a stick, one's finger, etc): ~ *a man in the ribs*, nudge him in a friendly way; ~ *the fire*, move the coals, to make the fire burn up. **2** [VP15A] put, move (sth) in a given direction, with a sharp push: *Don't* ~ *your umbrella through the bars of the lion's cage. She* ~*d a toffee into my mouth. Don't let your boy* ~ *his head out of the (train) window— —it's dangerous!* ~ **fun at sb**, ridicule him. ~ **one's nose into sth,** (colloq) interfere in (sb's business, affairs). **3** [VP2C] ~ **(about)**, search, feel about: *He was poking (about) at the rubbish. Who's that poking about in the attic?* **4** [VP6A,15A] make (a hole) by poking: ~ *a hole in a paper screen*. □ *n* [C] act of poking; nudge: *give the fire a* ~; *give sb a* ~ *in the ribs*.

poke² /pəʊk/ *n* sack (now dial, except in) *buy a pig in a* ~, ⇨ pig.

poke-bonnet /,pəʊk 'bɒnɪt/ *n* bonnet with a broad projecting brim.

poker¹ /'pəʊkə(r)/ *n* strong metal rod or bar for stirring or breaking up the coal in the fire.

poker² /'pəʊkə(r)/ *n* [U] card game for two or more persons in which the players bet on the value of the cards they hold. '~-**face** *n* (colloq) (person with a) face that betrays no emotion.

poky /'pəʊkɪ/ *adj* (-ier, -iest) (of a place) small; limited in space: *a* ~ *little room*.

po·lar /'pəʊlə(r)/ *adj* **1** of or near the North or South Pole: *the* ~ *circles*, the Arctic and Antarctic Circles. '~ **bear**, the white kind living in the north ~ regions. ⇨ the illus at bear. **2** directly opposite. ~-**ity** /pəʊ'lærətɪ/ *n* [U,C] state in which there are two opposite, conflicting or contrasting qualities, principles or tendencies.

po·lar·ize /'pəʊləraɪz/ *vt* [VP6A] cause to concentrate about two opposite, conflicting or contrasting positions. **po·lar·iz·ation** /,pəʊlərəɪ'zeɪʃn US: -rɪ'z-/ *n* act of polarizing; state of being ~d.

Po·lar·oid /'pəʊlərɔɪd/ *n* [U] (P) thin transparent film used in sun-glasses, car windows, etc to lessen sun glare: ~ *camera*, one able to produce positive prints within seconds after the picture has been taken.

pole¹ /pəʊl/ *n* **1** North/South P~, either of the two ends of the earth's axis. **2** North/South Magnetic P~, either of the two points near the North P~ or South P~ to which the compass needle points. **3** North/South P~, (astron) either of the two points in the celestial sphere about which the stars appear to turn. '~-**star** *n* the North Star or Polaris /pəʊ'lærɪs/, almost coinciding with the true north of the celestial sphere. **4** either of the two ends of a magnet or the terminal points of an electric battery: *the negative/positive* ~. **5** (fig) either of two opposite, conflicting or contrasting principles, etc. **be** ~**s apart,** be widely separated: *The employers and the trade union leaders are still* ~*s apart*, are far from reaching an agreement or compromise, eg about wages.

pole² /pəʊl/ *n* **1** long, slender, rounded piece of wood or metal, esp as a support for a tent, telegraph wires, etc or for flying a flag. **under bare** ~**s,** (naut) with all sails furled. **up the** ~, (sl) (a) in a difficulty. (b) slightly mad; eccentric. '~-**jumping** *n* (athletic contest) jumping with the help of a long ~ held in the hands. '~-**vault** *n* jump of this kind over a bar which can be raised or lowered. **2** measure of length (also called *rod* or *perch*), 5½ yds or about 5 metres. ⇨ App 5.

Pole /pəʊl/ *n* native of Poland.

pole-axe, pole-ax /'pəʊl æks/ *n* **1** (hist) axe for use in war, with a long handle. **2** butcher's implement for slaughtering cattle. □ *vt* [VP6A] strike down with a ~; (fig) slaughter; destroy.

pole·cat /'pəʊlkæt/ *n* small, dark-brown, fur-covered animal of the weasel family which gives off an unpleasant smell, native of Europe.

pol·emic /pə'lemɪk/ *n* [C] (formal) dispute; argument; (*pl*) art or practice of carrying on arguments. □ *adj* of ~s. **pol·emi·cally** /-klɪ/ *adv*

po·lice /pə'li:s/ *n* (collective, always *sing* in form, used with *pl v*) **(the)** ~, men and women belonging to a department of government concerned with the keeping of public order: *Several hundred* ~ *were on duty at the demonstration. Extra* ~ *are needed here. The* ~ *have not made any arrests.* ~ '**con-stable** *n* ~-officer of ordinary rank. '~ **dog** *n* dog trained to track or attack suspected criminals. '~ **force** *n* body of ~-officers of a country, district or town. '~-**man** /-mən/ *n* (*pl* -men) male member of the ~ force. '~-**office** *n* headquarters of the ~ in a city or town. '~-**officer** *n* ~man or ~woman. '~ **state** *n* one controlled by political ~, usu a totalitarian state. '~-**station** *n* office of a local ~ force: *The drunken driver was taken to the* ~-*station*. '~-**woman** *n* (*pl* -women) female member of the ~ force. □ *vt* [VP6A] keep order in (a place) with ~ or as with ~; control: *United Nations forces* ~*d the Gaza strip for a long period.*

pol·icy¹ /'pɒləsɪ/ *n* (*pl* -cies) **1** [U,C] plan of action, statement of aims and ideals, esp one made by a government, political party, business company, etc: *British·foreign* ~, official relations between the British government and other governments. *Is honesty the best* ~? **2** [U] wise, sensible conduct; art of government.

pol·icy² /'pɒləsɪ/ *n* written statement of the terms of a contract of insurance: *a 'fire-insurance* ~; *a* '~-*holder*.

po·lio /'pəʊlɪəʊ/ n [U] (colloq abbr for) poliomyelitis: '~ *victims;* ,anti-'~ *injections.*

polio·my·eli·tis /ˌpəʊlɪəʊˌmaɪə'laɪtɪs/ n [U] infectious, virus-caused disease with inflammation of the grey matter of the spinal cord, often resulting in physical disablement; formerly called 'infantile paralysis'.

polish /'pɒlɪʃ/ vt,vi 1 [VP6A,15B,2A] ~ *(up),* make or become smooth and shiny by rubbing (with or without a chemical substance): ~ *furniture/shoes;* ~ *sth up. This wood won't* ~. 2 [VP6A] (usu in *pp*) improve in behaviour, intellectual interests, etc; make refined or elegant: *a* ~*ed speech/performance.* 3 [VP15B] ~ *sth off,* finish quickly: ~ *off a large plateful of pie;* ~ *off arrears of correspondence.* □ n 1 [U,C] (shiny surface, etc obtained by) ~ing: *shoes/tables with a good* ~. 2 [U,C] substance used for ~ing: '*shoe/'furniture/'floor* ~; *a tin of metal* ~. 3 [U] (fig) refinement; elegance. ~**er** n workman skilled in ~ing wood or metal.

Pol·ish /'pəʊlɪʃ/ adj of Poland or the Poles. □ n [U] language of the Poles.

pol·it·buro /'pɒlɪtbjʊərəʊ/ n (pl ~s /-rəʊz/) chief executive committee of a political (esp the Communist) party.

pol·ite /pə'laɪt/ adj 1 having, showing the possession of, good manners and consideration for other people: *a* ~ *boy; a* ~ *remark.* 2 refined: ~ *society;* ~ *literature.* ~**ly** adv ~**ness** n

poli·tic /'pɒlətɪk/ adj 1 (of persons) acting or judging wisely; prudent. 2 (of actions) well judged; prudent: *follow a* ~ *course; make a* ~ *retreat.* 3 **the ,body** '~, the state as an organized group of citizens.

pol·iti·cal /pə'lɪtɪkl/ adj 1 of the State; of government; of public affairs in general: ~ *liberties; for* ~ *reasons.* ~ **a'sylum,** protection given by a State to sb who has left his own country for ~ reasons: *a sailor who deserted his ship and asked for* ~ *asylum.* ~ **e'conomy,** study of the ~ problems of government. ~ **ge'ography,** dealing with boundaries, communications, etc. Cf *physical* and *economic* geography. ~ **'prisoner,** one who is imprisoned because he opposes the (system of) government. 2 of politics: *a* ~ *crisis.* ~**ly** /-klɪ/ adv

poli·ti·cian /ˌpɒlɪ'tɪʃn/ n person taking part in politics or much interested in politics; (in a bad sense) person who follows politics as a career, regardless of principle: *party* ~s. *Is your leader a* ~ *or a statesman?*

pol·iti·cize /pə'lɪtɪsaɪz/ vt,vi [VP6A,2A] become or cause to become politically conscious or organized.

poli·tick /'pɒlətɪk/ vi [VP2A] engage in politics.

poli·tics /'pɒlətɪks/ n pl (with *sing* or *pl v*) the science or art of government; political views, affairs, questions, etc: *party* ~; *local* ~. *What are your* ~? 'P~ *is much more difficult than physics',* said Einstein.

pol·ity /'pɒlətɪ/ n (pl -ties) [U] form or process of government; [C] society as an organized State.

polka /'pɒlkə US: 'pəʊlkə/ n [C] (piece of music, of E European origin, for a) lively kind of dance. '~ **dots,** regular pattern of large dots on cloth: (attrib) *a* ~-*dot scarf.*

poll[1] /pəʊl/ n 1 voting at an election; list of voters; counting of the votes; place where voting takes place: *a light/heavy* ~, voting by a small/large proportion of the voters; *awaiting the result of the* ~; *go to the* ~s (= ~ing-booths), vote; *exclude people from the* ~; *be successful at the* ~; *head the* ~, have the largest number of votes; *declare the* ~, announce the result. 2 survey of public opinion by putting questions to a representative selection of persons: *a public opinion* ~; *the Gallup* ~. ⇨ *straw vote* at straw. 3 (old use) head: (hum) *a grey* ~, a grey-haired person. '~-**tax** n tax levied on every person in a community.

poll[2] /pəʊl/ vt,vi 1 [VP2A,C] vote at an election; [VP6A] receive (a certain number of) votes; take the votes of electors in (a constituency): *Mr Hill* ~*ed over 3000 votes. The constituency was* ~*ed thoroughly.* '~**-ing-booth/-station** nn place where voters go to record votes. '~**-ing-day** n day appointed for a ~. 2 [VP6A] cut off the top of (the horns of cattle): ~*ed cattle;* cut off the top of (a tree) (= pollard).

poll[3] /pɒl/ n (also '~*parrot*) conventional name for a parrot.

pol·lard /'pɒləd/ vt [VP6A] cut off the top of (a tree) so that a thick head of new branches grows out. □ n ~ed tree.

pol·len /'pɒlən/ n [U] fine powder (usu yellow) formed on flowers which fertilizes other flowers when carried to them by the wind, insects, etc. '~ **count,** figure of the ~ in the atmosphere in a given volume of air during 24 hours, from deposits on slides, as a guide to possible attacks of hay fever, etc.

pol·lin·ate /'pɒlɪneɪt/ vt [VP6A] make fertile with pollen. **pol·li·na·tion** /ˌpɒlɪ'neɪʃn/ n [U].

poll·ster /'pəʊlstə(r)/ n (colloq) person who conducts public opinion polls.

pol·lute /pə'luːt/ vt [VP6A] make dirty; destroy the purity or sanctity of: *rivers* ~*d with filthy waste from factories;* ~*d water,* unfit to drink. **pol·lu·tant** /-ənt/ n anything that ~s, eg exhaust fumes from motor-vehicles. **pol·lu·tion** /pə'luːʃn/ n [U] polluting or being ~d; that which ~s.

polo /'pəʊləʊ/ n [U] ball game played on horseback with mallets. '**water-~** n game played by swimmers with a large ball. '~**-neck** adj = turtleneck(ed), ⇨ turtle[1].

pol·on·aise /ˌpɒlə'neɪz/ n (piece of music for a) slow processional dance of Polish origin.

po·lony /pə'ləʊnɪ/ n [U] sausage of partly cooked pork.

pol·ter·geist /'pɒltəgaɪst/ n [C] (in folklore, etc) noisy, mischievous spirit(2).

pol·troon /pɒl'truːn/ n coward. ~**ery** /-ərɪ/ n cowardice.

poly /'pɒlɪ/ n (colloq abbr for) polytechnic.

poly·an·dry /'pɒlɪændrɪ/ n [U] custom of having more than one husband at the same time. **poly·an·drous** /ˌpɒlɪ'ændrəs/ adj 1 of, practising, ~. 2 (bot) (of plants) having numerous stamens.

poly·an·thus /ˌpɒlɪ'ænθəs/ n (pl ~es /-θəsɪz/ for individual plants) kinds of cultivated primrose with several flowers on one stalk.

poly·gamy /pə'lɪɡəmɪ/ n [U] custom of having more than one wife at the same time. **poly·ga·mist** /-ɪst/ n man who practises ~. **poly·ga·mous** /pə'lɪɡəməs/ adj of, practising, ~.

poly·glot /'pɒlɪɡlɒt/ adj knowing, using, written in, many languages. □ n ~ person or book.

poly·gon /'pɒlɪɡən US: -ɡɒn/ n plane figure with many (usu five or more) straight sides.

poly·mor·phous /ˌpɒlɪ'mɔːfəs/, (also **poly·mor·phic** /-fɪk/) adj having, passing through, many stages (of development, growth, etc).

polyp /'pɒlɪp/ n (zool) very simple form of animal life found in water; polypus.

poly·ph·ony /pə'lɪfənɪ/ n [U] (music) counterpoint. **poly·phonic** /ˌpɒlɪ'fɒnɪk/ adj (music) contrapuntal.

poly·pus /'pɒlɪpəs/ n (pl ~es /-pəsɪz/, -pi /-paɪ/) (path) kinds of tumour (eg in the nose) usu with many stems like tentacles, extending down into the tissue.

poly·sty·rene /ˌpɒlɪ'staɪriːn/ n [U] type of light, firm plastic material (a good insulator), used esp for making boxes etc.

poly·syl·lable /'pɒlɪsɪləbl/ n word of several (usu more than three) syllables. **poly·syl·labic** /ˌpɒlɪsɪ'læbɪk/ adj

poly·tech·nic /ˌpɒlɪ'teknɪk/ n (colloq abbr **poly** /'pɒlɪ/) institution for advanced full-time and part-time education, esp in scientific and technical subjects.

poly·theism /'pɒlɪθiːɪzəm/ n [U] belief in, worship of, more than one god. **poly·theis·tic** /ˌpɒlɪθiː'ɪstɪk/ adj

poly·thene /'pɒlɪθiːn/ n [U] plastic material widely used for waterproof packaging, insulation, etc.

pom /pɒm/ n (abbr) = pommy.

po·made /pə'mɑːd US: pəʊ'meɪd/ n [U] perfumed ointment for use on the hair. □ vt put ~ on.

pom·egran·ate /'pɒmɪgrænɪt/ n (tree with) thick-skinned round fruit which, when ripe, has a reddish centre full of seeds.

pom·elo /'pɒmɪləʊ/ n (pl ~s /-ləʊz/) kind of large grapefruit; shaddock.

pom·mel /'pɒml/ n 1 the rounded part of a saddle which sticks up at the front. ⊳ the illus at harness. 2 rounded knob on the hilt of a sword. □ /'pʌml/ vt (-ll-, US also -l-) = pummel.

pommy /'pɒmɪ/ n (pl -mies) (sl) British immigrant in Australia or New Zealand; British person.

pomp /pɒmp/ n [U] splendid display, magnificence, esp at a public event: the ~ and ceremony of the State Opening of Parliament.

pom·pon /'pɒmpɒn/ n ornamental tuft or bunch of feathers, silk, ribbon, etc worn on a hat or dress or shoes; ball of wool worn on eg a soldier's cap.

pom·pous /'pɒmpəs/ adj full of, showing, self-importance: a ~ official; ~ language, full of high-sounding words. **pom·pos·ity** /pɒm'pɒsətɪ/ n [U] being ~; [C] (pl-ties) instance of this.

ponce /pɒns/ n man who lives with a prostitute and lives on her earnings.

pon·cho /'pɒntʃəʊ/ n (pl ~s /-tʃəʊz/) large piece of cloth with a slit in the middle for the head, worn as a cloak; similar garment in waterproof material used by hikers, cyclists, etc.

pond /pɒnd/ n small area of still water, esp one used or made as a drinking place for cattle.

pon·der /'pɒndə(r)/ vt,vi [VP6A,2A,8,10,3A] ~ (over), consider; think over: We ~ed many things. He ~ed over the incident.

pon·der·able /'pɒndərəbl/ adj (phys) that can be weighed or measured. □ n pl events, conditions, etc that can be taken into account and estimated.

pon·der·ous /'pɒndərəs/ adj 1 heavy; bulky; unwieldy: ~ movements, eg of a heavy man. 2 (of style) dull; laboured. ~·ly adv

pone /pəʊn/ n (also 'corn ~) maize bread, esp as made by N American Indians.

pon·iard /'pɒnjəd/ n (archaic or poet) dagger.

pon·tiff /'pɒntɪf/ n 1 the Pope. 2 (old use) bishop;

high priest; chief priest.

pon·tifi·cal /pɒn'tɪfɪkl/ adj 1 of or relating to the Pope or a bishop. 2 authoritative (in a pompous way). □ n pl vestments and insignia used by bishops and cardinals at some church functions and ceremonies.

pon·tifi·cate /pɒn'tɪfɪkət/ n office of a pontiff, esp of the Pope; period of this. □ vi /-keɪt/ [VP2A] assume airs of infallibility.

pon·toon /pɒn'tuːn/ n flat-bottomed boat; one of a number of such boats, or a floating hollow metal structure, supporting a roadway over a river: a ~ bridge. ⊳ the illus at bridge.

pon·toon /pɒn'tuːn/ n [U] kind of card game.

pony /'pəʊnɪ/ n (pl -nies) 1 horse of small breed. '~-tail n style of girls' hairdressing which became popular in the 1950's with long hair tied in a bunch at the back of the head. '~-trekking n [U] the making of a journey for pleasure by riding on ponies. 2 (GB sl) £25. 3 (US sl) = crib²(2).

poodle /'puːdl/ n kind of dog with thick curling hair, often clipped and shaved into fantastic patterns. ⊳ the illus at dog.

poof /puːf/ n = pouf(2).

pooh /puː/ int expressing impatience or contempt or disgust at a bad smell.

pooh-pooh /ˌpuː'puː/ vt [VP6A] treat (an idea, etc) with contempt.

pool /puːl/ n 1 small area of still water; esp one naturally formed: After the rainstorm there were ~s on the roads. 2 quantity of water or other liquid lying on a surface: The corpse was lying in a ~ of blood. 3 ('swimming-)~, large paved hole filled with water to swim in. 4 part of a river where the water is quiet and deep.

pool /puːl/ n 1 (gambling) total of money staked by a number of gamblers. **the ('football) ~s,** organized gambling on the results of football matches: hoping to win a fortune on the ~s. 2 arrangement by business firms to share business and divide profits, to avoid competition and agree on prices. 3 common fund, supply or service, provided by or shared among many: a 'typing ~, arrangement by which many persons share the services of typists instead of each having the services of his or her own typist. 4 [U] (US) game for several players played on a billiard-table with six pockets (GB = snooker): to shoot (= play) ~. '~-room n place, room, in which the game of ~ is played. □ vt [VP6A] share in common; put (money, resources, etc) together for the use of all who contribute: They ~ed their savings and bought a used car.

poop /puːp/ n (raised deck at the) stern of a ship. ⊳ the illus at barque.

poor /pʊə(r)/ adj (-er, -est) 1 having little money; not having and not able to get the necessaries of life. **the ~ n pl** ~ people. '~-box n (formerly, in a church) box in which money may be placed to be given to the ~. '~-house n (formerly) building where ~ people were maintained at the public expense. '~ law n (formerly) group of laws relating to the relief and care of the ~ (now replaced by Social Security Services). '~-rate n (formerly) rate (= local tax) for the relief of the ~. ~ 'white, (in southern US and S Africa) one of a class of socially inferior white people. 2 deserving or needing help or sympathy: The ~ little puppy had been abandoned. 3 (often hum or ironic) humble; of little value: in my ~ opinion. 4 small in quantity: a ~ supply of well-qualified science teachers; a *country* ~ *in minerals.* **5** low in quality: ~ *soil;* ~ *food; in* ~ *health.* ~-**'spirited** *adj* lacking in courage; timid.

poor·ly /'pʊəlɪ/ *pred adj* (colloq) unwell: *He's rather* ~ *this morning.* □ *adv* **1** in a poor manner; badly; with little success: ~ *lighted streets;* ~ *dressed.* **2** ~ *off,* having very little money: *She's been* ~ *off since her husband died.*

poor·ness /'pʊənɪs/ *n* [U] lack of some desirable quality or element (note that *poverty* is usu for being poor(1)): *the* ~ *of the soil.*

pop[1] /pɒp/ *n* **1** short, sharp, explosive sound: *the pop of a cork.* **2** [U] (sl) bottled drink with gas in it: *ginger pop,* ginger beer; *a bottle of pop.* **3** (sl) *in pop,* in pawn. □ *adv* with the sound of popping: *I heard it go pop. Pop went the cork!*

pop[2] /pɒp/ *n* (US abbr for) poppa.

pop[3] /pɒp/ *adj* (colloq abbr for) popular: '*pop music;* '*pop singers;* '*pop groups,* (singers and players) (esp) those whose records sell in large numbers and who are most popular on radio, TV and in discotheques. '**pop art,** the depiction of scenes of everyday life, using comic strips, commercial technique, etc. '**pop concert,** of popular music. '**pop festival,** large, usu outdoor, gathering of people to hear pop singers and musicians. □ *n* [U] (colloq) pop music, pop art, etc; [C] pop song: *top of the pops,* disc, etc which (calculated by sales) is most popular during a given period of time.

pop[4] /pɒp/ *vt,vi* (-pp-) **1** [VP6A,15B,2C] (cause to) make a sharp, quick sound (as when a cork comes out of a bottle): *Champagne corks were popping (away) on all sides. pop the question,* (sl) propose marriage. '**pop-eyed** *adj* having bulging eyes or eyes very wide open (with surprise, etc). '**pop-gun** *n* child's toy gun which fires a cork with a popping sound. **2** [VP15A,B,2A,C] (uses with *adverbial particles* and *preps*) *pop across to,* ▷ pop over below. *pop in/out (of),* (cause to) go or come in/out quickly (giving the idea of rapid or unexpected movement or activity): *He popped his head in at the door. Pop in and see me some time. The neighbours' children are always popping in and out,* are very frequent visitors. *His eyes almost popped out (of his head) in surprise. pop sth into sth,* quickly put it there: *She popped the gin bottle into the cupboard as the vicar entered the room. pop off,* (**a**) go away. (**b**) (sl) die: *I don't intend to pop off yet. pop over/across to,* make a quick, short visit to: *She has just popped over/across to the grocer's.* **3** (sl) [VP2C] shoot: *They were popping away at the pigeons.* **4** (sl) pawn: *I'll pop my watch and take you to the cinema.* **5** (US) parch (maize) until it bursts open and puffs out. '**pop-corn** *n* maize treated in this way.

Pope /pəʊp/ *n* (often **the** ~) the Bishop of Rome as chief bishop of the Roman Catholic Church. **pop·ery** /'pəʊpərɪ/ *n* [U] (in hostile use) Roman Catholicism; papal system. **pop·ish** /'pəʊpɪʃ/ *adj* (in hostile use) of popery. **pop·ish·ly** *adv*

pop·in·jay /'pɒpɪndʒeɪ/ *n* conceited person, esp one who is vain about clothes.

pop·lar /'pɒplə(r)/ *n* [C] tall, straight, fast-growing tree; [U] its wood.

pop·lin /'pɒplɪn/ *n* [U] (formerly) cloth of silk and wool with a ribbed surface; (now, usu) kind of strong, shiny cotton cloth used for shirts, etc.

poppa /'pɒpə/ *n* (US) = papa.

pop·pet /'pɒpɪt/ *n* (GB) used as a term of endearment (usu to a child): *Isn't she a* ~ *? And how's my little* ~ *this morning?*

poppy /'pɒpɪ/ *n* (*pl* -pies) sorts of plant, wild and cultivated, with large flowers, esp red, and a milky juice: '*opium* ~, kind from which opium is obtained.

poppy·cock /'pɒpɪkɒk/ *n* [U] (sl) nonsense.

popu·lace /'pɒpjʊləs/ *n* (formal) the common people; the general public; the masses.

popu·lar /'pɒpjʊlə(r)/ *adj* **1** of or for the people: ~ *government,* by the elected majority of all those who have votes. ~ '**front,** (in politics) coalition of parties opposed to reaction and fascism. **2** suited to the tastes, needs, educational level, etc of the general public: ~ *science; meals at* ~ (= low) *prices.* **3** liked and admired: *a* ~ *hero;* ~ *film stars; a man who is* ~ *with his neighbours.* ▷ pop[3]. ~·**ly** *adv*

popu·lar·ity /,pɒpjʊ'lærətɪ/ *n* [U] quality of being popular(3): *win* ~; *the* ~ *of baseball in Japan.*

popu·lar·ize /'pɒpjʊləraɪz/ *vt* [VP6A] make popular: ~ *a new method of teaching spelling.* **popu·lar·iz·ation** /,pɒpjʊləraɪ'zeɪʃn US: -rɪ'z-/ *n*

popu·late /'pɒpjʊleɪt/ *vt* [VP6A] supply with people; inhabit; form the population of: *thinly* ~*d; the densely* ~*d parts of India.*

popu·la·tion /,pɒpjʊ'leɪʃn/ *n* (number of) people living in a place, country, etc or a special section of them: *a fall/rise in* ~; *the* ~ *of London; the working-class* ~.

popu·lism /'pɒpjʊlɪzəm/ *n* [U] government or politics based on an appeal to popular sentiments or fears. **popu·list** /-ɪst/ *n* supporter or promoter of ~.

popu·lous /'pɒpjʊləs/ *adj* thickly populated.

por·ce·lain /'pɔːsəlɪn/ *n* [U] (articles, eg cups and plates, made of a) fine china with a coating of translucent material called *glaze.*

porch /pɔːtʃ/ *n* **1** built-out roofed doorway or entrance to a building. **2** (US, also) veranda.

por·cine /'pɔːsaɪn/ *adj* of or like a pig.

por·cu·pine /'pɔːkjʊpaɪn/ *n* small rat-like animal covered with spines that the animal can stick out if attacked.

pore[1] /pɔː(r)/ *n* tiny opening (esp in the skin of an animal body) through which fluids (eg sweat) may pass: *He was sweating at every* ~.

pore[2] /pɔː(r)/ *vi* [VP3A] ~ *over sth,* study it with close attention: ~ *over a letter/book.*

pork /pɔːk/ *n* [U] flesh of a pig (usu fresh, not salted or cured) used as food: *a leg of* ~; *a* ~ *chop; roast* ~. ▷ bacon, ham(1). '~-**barrel** *n* (US, sl) money from State or Federal taxes, etc spent to confer local benefits for political reasons. '~-**butcher** *n* one who kills pigs for sale as food, makes ~ sausages, ~ pies, etc. ~ '**pie** *n* minced ~, highly seasoned, in a container of pie-crust. ~**er** *n* pig raised for food, esp one fattened for killing.

porn /pɔːn/ *n* (colloq abbr of) pornography. '~ **shop** *n* shop where pornographic books, etc are sold.

por·nogra·phy /pɔː'nɒgrəfɪ/ *n* [U] treatment of obscene subjects, in writing, pictures, etc; such writings, etc. **por·nogra·pher** /pɔː'nɒgrəfə(r)/ *n* person who makes or deals in ~. **por·no·graphic** /,pɔːnə'græfɪk/ *adj*

po·rous /'pɔːrəs/ *adj* **1** full of pores. **2** allowing liquid to pass through: *Sandy soil is* ~. ~·**ness,** **po·ros·ity** /pɔː'rɒsətɪ/ *nn* quality or condition of being ~.

por·phyry /'pɔːfɪrɪ/ *n* [U] hard, red kind of rock

with red and white crystals bedded in it, polished and made into ornaments.

por·poise /'pɔːpəs/ n sea animal rather like a dolphin or small whale. ⇨ the illus at **sea**.

por·ridge /'pɒrɪdʒ US: 'pɔːr-/ n [U] soft food made by boiling a cereal, eg oatmeal, in water or milk: a bowl/plate of ∼.

por·rin·ger /'pɒrɪndʒə(r) US: 'pɔːr-/ n small bowl with a handle (for a child) from which porridge, soup, etc is eaten.

port¹ /pɔːt/ n **1** harbour: a naval ∼; reach ∼. **2** town or city with a harbour, esp one where customs officers are stationed. **free** ∼, one open for the merchandise of all countries to load and unload in; one where there is exemption of duties for imports or exports. **3** (fig) refuge. **any** ∼ **in a storm**, in time of difficulty help or safety may be sought anywhere. ∼ **after stormy seas**, rest after struggles.

port² /pɔːt/ n (naut) opening in the side of a ship for entrance, or for loading and unloading cargo; ∼hole(b). '∼·hole n (a) opening in a ship's side for admission of light and air. (b) small glass window in the side of a ship or aircraft.

port³ /pɔːt/ n left-hand side of a ship or aircraft as one faces forward: put the helm to ∼; (attrib) on the ∼ bow/quarter. ⇨ starboard; ⇨ the illus at **ship**. □ vt [VP6A] turn (the ship's helm) to ∼.

port⁴ /pɔːt/ n [U] strong, sweet, dark-red or white wine of Portugal.

port⁵ /pɔːt/ n **at the** ∼, (mil) position of a rifle on porting arms. □ vt carry (a rifle or other weapon) diagonally across and close to the body ready for inspection by an officer: P∼ arms! command for this to be done.

port·able /'pɔːtəbl/ adj that can be carried about; not fixed: ∼ radios/typewriters. **port·abil·ity** /ˌpɔːtə'bɪlətɪ/ n [U] being ∼: The portability of my tape-recorder is exaggerated.

port·age /'pɔːtɪdʒ/ n [C,U] (cost of) carrying goods, esp when (eg in forest country in Canada) goods have to be carried overland between two rivers or parts of a river; place where this is done.

por·tal /'pɔːtl/ n doorway, esp an imposing one of a large building.

port·cul·lis /ˌpɔːt'kʌlɪs/ n (hist) iron grating that could be raised or lowered to protect the gateway of a castle. ⇨ the illus at **drawbridge**.

porte-cochère /ˌpɔːt kə'ʃeə(r)/n (F)gateway at the entrance to a building to give shelter to persons entering or leaving cars, etc.

por·tend /pɔː'tend/ vt [VP6A] (formal) be a sign or warning of (a future event, etc): This ∼s war.

por·tent /'pɔːtent/ n thing, esp sth marvellous or mysterious, that portends sth; omen. **por·ten·tous** /pɔː'tentəs/ **1** ominous; threatening. **2** marvellous; extraordinary. **por·ten·tous·ly** adv

por·ter¹ /'pɔːtə(r)/n **1** person whose work is to carry luggage, etc at railway stations, airports, hotels, etc. **2** person carrying a load on his back or head (usu in country where there are no roads for motor-vehicles). '∼·age /-ɪdʒ/ n [U] (the charge for) carrying of luggage, etc by a ∼.

por·ter² /'pɔːtə(r)/ n doorkeeper (at a hotel, public building, etc): The hotel ∼ will call a taxi for you. (US = doorman). ∼'s lodge, ⇨ lodge¹(3).

por·ter³ /'pɔːtə(r)/ n [U] dark-brown bitter beer.

por·ter·house /'pɔːtəhaʊs/ n ∼ (steak), choice cut of beefsteak.

port·folio /pɔːt'fəʊlɪəʊ/ n (pl ∼s /lɪəʊz/) **1** flat

case (usu leather) for keeping loose papers, documents, drawings, etc. **2** position and duties of a minister of state: He resigned his ∼. Mr X is minister without ∼, not in charge of any particular department. **3** list of securities and investments (stocks, shares, etc) owned by an individual, a bank, etc.

port·hole n ⇨ port².

port·ico /'pɔːtɪkəʊ/ n (pl ∼es or ∼s /kəʊz/) roof supported by columns, esp at the entrance of a building.

a portico

port·ière /ˌpɔːtɪ'eə(r)/ n (F) heavy curtain hung over a door(way).

por·tion /'pɔːʃn/ n **1** part, esp a share, (to be) given when sth is distributed: (of a railway ticket) this ∼ to be given up; (of a railway train) the through ∼ for Liverpool, the coaches for Liverpool (passengers in which will not need to change trains); a marriage ∼, dowry. **2** quantity of any kind of food served in a restaurant: a generous ∼ of roast duck. **3** (sing) one's lot or fate: Brief life is here our ∼. □ vt **1** [VP15B] ∼ sth out (among/between), divide into ∼s, share. **2** [VP14] ∼ sth to sb, provide a ∼ of (sth to sb).

Port·land /'pɔːtlənd/ n ∼ stone, yellowish-white limestone (quarried near ∼, Dorset), used for building. ∼ cement, cement used for concrete that resembles ∼ stone in colour.

port·ly /'pɔːtlɪ/ adj (usu of elderly persons) stout; round and fat: a ∼ city councillor.

port·man·teau /pɔːt'mæntəʊ/ n (pl ∼s or ∼x /-təʊz/) oblong, square-shouldered leather case for clothes, opening on a hinge into two equal parts. ∼ word, one made by using two or more words and combining their meanings, eg shamateur (from sham and amateur).

por·trait /'pɔːtrɪt/ n **1** painted picture, drawing, photograph, of a person or animal. **2** vivid description in words. '∼·ist /-ɪst/ n maker of ∼s. '∼·ure /-tʃə(r) US: -tʃʊə(r)/ n [U] art of making ∼s; ∼.

por·tray /pɔː'treɪ/ vt [VP6A] **1** make a picture of. **2** describe vividly in words. **3** act the part of (in a play). ∼al /pɔː'treɪəl/ n [U] ∼ing; [C] description.

pose /pəʊz/ vt,vi **1** [VP6A] put (sb) in a desired position before making a portrait, taking a photograph, etc: The artist ∼d his model carefully. All the subjects are well ∼d. **2** [VP2A,3A] ∼ (for), take up a position (for a portrait, etc): Are you willing to ∼ for me? **3** [VP6A] put forward for discussion; create; give rise to: The increase in student numbers ∼s many problems for the universities. **4** [VP2C] ∼ as, set oneself up as, claim to be: ∼ as an expert on old coins. **5** [VP2A] behave in an affected way, hoping to impress people: She's always posing, is never natural in her behaviour. □ n **1** position taken up for a portrait, photograph, etc: a striking and unusual ∼. **2** attitude, unnatural way of behaving, intended to impress people; affectation: *That rich man's socialism is a mere ~.* **poser** *n* awkward or difficult question.

po·seur /pəʊˈzɜː(r)/, (fem) **po·seuse** /pəʊˈzɜːz/ *n* person who poses(5); affected person.

posh /pɒʃ/ *adj* (colloq) smart; first-class: *a ~ hotel; ~ clothes; her ~ friends.* □ *vt* [VP15B] *~ up,* make *~: We must ~ ourselves up for the party.*

posit /ˈpɒzɪt/ *vt* [VP6A] postulate.

po·si·tion /pəˈzɪʃn/ *n* **1** [C] place where sth or sb is or stands, esp in relation to others: *fix a ship's ~,* eg by observation of the sun or stars; *secure a ~ where one will get a good view of the procession; storm the enemy's ~s,* the places they occupy. *in/out of ~,* in/not in the right place. **2** [U] state of being advantageously placed (in war or any kind of struggle): *They were manoeuvring for ~.* **3** [C] way in which sb or sth is placed; attitude or posture: *sit/lie in a comfortable ~.* **4** [C] person's place or rank in relation to others, in employment, in society, etc: *a pupil's ~ in class; a high/low ~ in society.* **5** [C] job; employment: *apply for the ~ of assistant manager.* **6** [C] condition; circumstance: *placed in an awkward ~. I regret I am not in a ~* (= am unable) *to help you.* **7** [C] attitude; opinion: *What's your ~ on this problem?* □ *vt* [VP6A] place (sth or sb) in *~*; determine the *~* of.

posi·tive /ˈpɒzətɪv/ *adj* **1** definite; sure; leaving no room for doubt: *give a man ~ orders/instructions; ~ knowledge.* **2** (of persons) quite certain, esp about opinions: *Are you ~ (that) it was after midnight? Can you be ~ about what you saw?* **3** practical and constructive; that definitely helps: *a ~ suggestion; ~ help; ~ criticism.* **4** (colloq) downright; out and out: *That man is a ~ fool/nuisance. It's a ~ crime to drink and drive.* **5** (maths) greater than zero: *the ~ sign* (+). **6** (of electricity) of the sort produced by rubbing glass with silk; of the sort caused by deficiency of electrons: *a ~ charge. ~ pole,* anode. **7** (photo) showing light and shadows as in nature, not reversed (as in a *negative*). **8** (gram, of *adjj* and *advv*) of the simple form, not the comparative or superlative. □ *n ~* degree, adjective, quantity, etc; photograph printed from a (negative) plate or film. *~·ly adv* definitely; certainly. *~·ness n* [U] confidence.

posi·tiv·ism /ˈpɒzɪtɪvɪzəm/ *n* [U] philosophical system of Auguste Comte /kɔːnt/ 1798—1857, French philosopher, based on observable phenomena and positive facts rather than speculation. **logical ~,** modern (20th c) development of this philosophy mainly concerned with linguistic analysis and verification of empirical statements by observation. **posi·tiv·ist** /-ɪst/ *n*

posse /ˈpɒsɪ/ *n* (chiefly US) body of constables or other men having authority who can be summoned by a sheriff to help him in maintaining order, etc.

pos·sess /pəˈzes/ *vt* [VP6A] **1** own, have; *~ nothing; lose all that one ~es.* **2** keep control over: *~ one's soul in patience,* be patient. *⇨ self-~ed* at self-. **3** *~ oneself of,* (old use) become the owner of. *be ~ed of,* have: *He is ~ed of great natural ability.* **4** *be ~ed,* be mad, be controlled by an evil spirit: *She is surely ~ed. He fought like one ~ed,* like a person having a devil inside him. **5** occupy (the mind); dominate: *What ~ed you to do that? What influenced or dominated your mind and caused you to do that? He is ~ed with the idea that someone is persecuting him.* *~or* /-sə(r)/ *n* owner;

person who *~es* sth.

pos·ses·sion /pəˈzeʃn/ *n* **1** [U] possessing; ownership: *come into ~ of a large estate; get ~ of sth,* succeed in getting *~* of it. *The players fought for/won ~ of the ball. Who is in ~ of the property? The information in my ~ is strictly confidential. You can't take ~ of the house* (= move into it) *until all the papers have been signed. Is the woman in full ~ of her senses?* Is she quite sane? **2** [C] (often *pl*) sth possessed; property: *lose all one's ~s; a man of great ~s. Most of Britain's ~s overseas* (= her former colonies, etc) *are now independent countries.*

pos·sess·ive /pəˈzesɪv/ *adj* **1** of possession or ownership: *He has a ~ manner,* seems to assert claims, eg to the attention of people. *She has a ~ nature,* is eager to acquire things or wants the whole of (someone's) love or attention. **2** (gram) showing possession: *the ~ case,* eg *Tom's, the boy's, the boys'; ~ pronouns,* eg *yours, his. ~·ly adv*

pos·set /ˈpɒsɪt/ *n* drink of warm milk with ale or wine and spices in it, formerly much used as a remedy for colds.

pos·si·bil·ity /ˌpɒsəˈbɪlətɪ/ *n* (*pl* -ties) **1** [U] state of being possible; (degree of) likelihood: *Is there any/much ~ of your getting to London this week? I admit the ~ of your being right. Help is still within the bounds of ~.* **2** [C] sth that is possible: *I see great possibilities in this scheme,* It can have great success in many ways. *Don't neglect the ~ that his train has been delayed/the ~ of an accident.*

poss·ible /ˈpɒsəbl/ *adj* **1** that can be done; that can exist or happen: *Come as quickly as ~. Frost is ~, though not probable, even at the end of May. Are you insured against all ~ risks?* **2** that is reasonable or satisfactory: *a ~ answer to a problem,* one that may be accepted, though not, perhaps, the best. *He is the only ~ man for the position.* □ *n ~* person or thing: *A trial game was arranged between ~s and probables.* **poss·ibly** /-əblɪ/ *adv* **1** in accordance with what is *~: I will come as soon as I possibly can. Can you possibly lend me £5?* **2** perhaps: *'Will they put your salary up?'—'Possibly.'*

pos·sum /ˈpɒsəm/ *n* (colloq abbr of) opossum. *play ~,* pretend to be asleep, unaware, etc so as to deceive sb (from the *~*'s habit of feigning death when attacked).

post¹ /pəʊst/ *n* [C] **1** place where a soldier is on watch; place of duty: *The sentries are all at their ~s.* **2** place occupied by soldiers, esp a frontier fort; the soldiers there. *⇨* outpost. **3** trading station, esp one in a country where law and order are not yet firmly established: *trading ~s in northern Canada a hundred years ago.* **4** position or appointment; job: *get a better ~; be given a ~ as general manager.* □ *vt* [VP6A, 15A] **1** put at a *~*(1): *~ sentries at the gates of the camp.* **2** send to a *~*(1,2,4): *~ an officer to a unit. I hope to be ~ed to Damascus next year.*

post² /pəʊst/ *n* (mil) bugle-call sounded at sunset: (esp) **the first/last ~.** (The last *~* is also sounded at military funerals.)

post³ /pəʊst/ *n* **1** (hist) one of a number of men placed with horses at intervals, the duty of each being to ride with letters, etc to the next stage; letter-carrier; mail-cart. *~-'chaise n* (hist) travelling carriage hired from stage to stage or drawn by *~*-horses hired from stage to stage. '*~-horse n* (hist) horse kept at inns, etc for the use of men carrying letters, etc and for other travellers. **2 (GB)** transport and delivery of letters, etc; one collection of letters, etc; one delivery or distribution of letters, etc (US = *mail*): *miss/catch the* ~, be too late/in time for one of the regular clearances of letters. *Has the* ~ *come yet?* Has there been a delivery of letters, etc? *I will send you the book by* ~. *Please reply by return of* ~, by the next ~ (from your town, etc to mine). **the P~ (Office)**, public corporation set up to perform these duties, responsible to the Ministry of ~s and Telecommunications. **3 the** ~, ~ box or ~ office: *take letters to the* ~. **4** (compounds) '~-**bag** *n* = mailbag. '~-**box**, box into which letters are dropped for collection. '~-**card** *n* card, one side of which is usu a photograph or picture, used instead of a letter. '~-**code**, (US = *zipcode*) group of letters and numbers, eg W1X4AH, used to make the sorting and delivery of mail easier (by use of a computer). ~-'**free** *adj, adv* carried free of charge by ~, or with postage prepaid; (of a price) including the charge for postage. '~-**man** /-mən/ *n* (*pl*-men) man employed to deliver letters, etc (US = *mailman*). '~-**mark** *n* official mark stamped on letters, cancelling postage stamp(s) and giving the place, date, and time of collection. □ *vt* mark (an envelope, etc) with this. '~-**master**, '~-**mistress** *nn* official in charge of a ~ office. '~ **office** *n* office, building, etc where ~al business is carried on, together with the business of telegraphs and telephones, payment of state pensions, etc. '~ **office** (abbr **PO**) **box** *n* numbered box in a ~ office for ~ addressed to an individual or company. ~-'**paid** *adj, adv* with postage already paid.

post⁴ /pəʊst/ *vt, vi* **1** [VP6A] put (letters, etc) into a postbox or take (them) to a post office to be forwarded (US = *mail*). **2** [VP3A] (hist) travel (*from/to*) by stages, using relays of horses. ⇨ **post³(1)**. ~-'**haste** *adv* in great haste. **3** [VP6A,15B] ~ (*up*), (book-keeping) write items in (a ledger); transfer (items) from a day-book to a ledger: ~ (*up*) *export sales;* ~ *up a ledger.* **keep** *sb* ~**ed**, (fig) keep him supplied with news.

post⁵ /pəʊst/ *n* upright piece of wood, metal, etc supporting or marking sth: '*gate~s; the* '*starting/* '*winning~*, marking the starting and finishing points in a race; '*bed~s* (in the old-fashioned kind of bed which had curtains round it); '*lamp~s*, poles in towns, etc with electric lamps for street-lighting. □ *vt* [VP6A,15A,B] **1** ~ (*up*), display publicly in a public place by means of a paper, placard, etc: *P~ no bills* (warning that notices, advertisements, etc, must not be pasted on the wall, etc). *The announcement was* ~*ed up on the wall of the town hall.* **2** ~ (*over*), cover with bills, placards, etc: ~ *a wall* (*over*) *with placards.* **3** make known by means of a ~ed notice: *a ship* ~*ed as missing.*

post- /pəʊst/ *pref* after. ⇨ App 3.

post·age /'pəʊstɪdʒ/ *n* [U] payment for the carrying of letters, etc: *What is the* ~ *for an air-letter?* '~ **stamp** *n* stamp (to be) stuck on letters, etc with a specified value, showing the amount of ~ paid.

postal /'pəʊstl/ *adj* of the post³(2): '~ *rates;* '~ *workers; a* ~ *vote*, sent by post to decide a ballot; ~ *union*, agreement by governments of most countries for the regulation of international postal business. '~ **order**, ⇨ order¹(7).

post·date /ˌpəʊst'deɪt/ *vt* [VP6A] **1** put (on a letter, cheque, etc) a date later than the date of writing. **2**

give (to an event) a date later than its actual date.

poster /'pəʊstə(r)/ *n* **1** placard displayed in a public place (announcing or advertising sth); large printed picture. **2** ('**bill-**)~, person who posts bills or placards on walls, hoardings, etc.

poste res·tante /ˌpəʊst 'restɑːnt *US:* re'stænt/ *n* [U] (F) post office department to whose care letters may be addressed, to be kept until called for.

pos·terior /pɒ'stɪərɪə(r)/ *adj* **1** ~ (*to*), later in time or order. ⇨ prior¹. **2** placed behind. □ *n* (hum) buttocks: *kick his* ~.

pos·ter·ity /pɒ'sterətɪ/ *n* [U] **1** person's descendants (his children, their children, etc). **2** future generations: *plant trees for the benefit of* ~.

pos·tern /'pɒstən/ *n* side way or entrance; (esp, in former times) concealed entrance to a castle or fortress: (attrib) ~ *door/gate.*

Post Exchange /ˌpəʊst ɪk'stʃeɪndʒ/ *n* (abbr **PX**) (US) store at a military base where personnel and their families may buy services and tax-free goods.

post·gradu·ate /ˌpəʊst 'grædʒʊət/ *adj* (of studies, etc) done after taking a first academic degree. □ *n* person engaged in ~ studies.

post·hum·ous /'pɒstjʊməs/ *adj* **1** (of a child) born after the death of its father. **2** coming or happening after death: ~ *fame; a* ~ *novel*, published after the author's death; *the* ~ *award of a Victoria Cross.* ~·**ly** *adv*

pos·til·ion (also **pos·til·lion**) /pɒ'stɪlɪən/ *n* man riding on one of the two or more horses pulling a carriage or coach.

post·mas·ter /'pəʊstmɑːstə(r) *US:* -mæs-/ *n* ,P~ '**General**, the Minister at the head of a country's Post Office Department. ⇨ post³(2).

post meri·diem /ˌpəʊst mə'rɪdɪəm/ *adv* (abbr **pm**) time between noon and midnight: *7.30pm.* ⇨ *am* at ante meridiem; ⇨ App (6).

post-mor·tem /ˌpəʊst 'mɔːtəm/ *n, adj* **1** (medical examination) made after death: *A* ~ *showed that the man had been poisoned.* **2** (colloq) review of an event, etc in the past.

post·pone /pə'spəʊn/ *vt* [VP6A,C] put off until another time: ~ *a meeting;* ~ *sending an answer to a request.* ~·**ment** *n* [U] postponing; [C] instance of this: *after numerous* ~*ments.*

post·pran·dial /ˌpəʊst'prændɪəl/ *adj* (usu hum) after dinner: ~ *oratory.*

post·script /'pəʊsskrɪpt/ *n* **1** (abbr **PS**) sentence(s) added (*to* a letter) after the signature. **2** additional or final information.

pos·tu·lant /'pɒstjʊlənt *US:* -tʃʊ-/ *n* candidate, esp for admission to a religious order. ⇨ novice.

pos·tu·late /'pɒstjʊleɪt *US:* -tʃʊ-/ *vt* [VP6A] demand, put forward, take for granted, as a necessary fact, as a basis for reasoning. □ *n* sth ~d; sth that may be considered axiomatic: *the* ~*s of Euclidean geometry*, eg the possibility of drawing a straight line between any two points.

pos·ture /'pɒstʃə(r)/ *n* **1** [C] attitude of, way of holding, the body: *The artist asked his model to take a reclining* ~. *Good* ~ *helps you to keep well.* **2** [U] state or condition: *in the present* ~ *of public affairs.* **3** frame of mind; attitude: *Will the Government alter its* ~ *over aid to the railways?* □ *vt, vi* [VP6A] put or arrange in a ~: ~ *a model.* **2** [VP2A] adopt a vain, pretentious ~: *The vain girl was posturing before a tall mirror.* **pos·tur·ing** *n* [U,C] (from the v(2)) *All this posturing must stop!*

posy /'pəʊzɪ/ *n* (*pl*-sies) small bunch of cut flowers.

pot¹ /pɒt/ n **1** round vessel of earthenware, metal or glass, for holding liquids or solids, for cooking things in, etc; contents of such a vessel: a '*jam-pot; eat a whole pot of jam; a '*teapot; a '*coffee-pot; a '*flower-pot; a '*chamber-pot*. ⇨ the nn forming the first element of such compounds. **2** (phrases and provs) **go to pot,** (sl) be ruined or destroyed. **keep the '*pot boiling,** earn enough money to buy one's food, etc; keep sth, eg a children's game, going briskly. **take ,pot 'luck,** whatever is available (without choice); whatever is being prepared for a meal: *Come home with me and take pot luck*. **the ,pot calling the ,kettle '*black,** the accuser having the same fault as the accused. **3** (colloq) large sum: *make a pot/pots of money*. **4 a big pot,** (colloq) an important person. **5** (colloq) prize in an athletic contest, esp a silver cup: *all the pots he won when he was young*. **6** (sl) marijuana. **7** (compounds) '*pot-belly** n (person with a) large, prominent belly. ,pot-'*bellied** adj (of a person) having a pot-belly; (of a stove) having a rounded container in which fuel, eg wood, burns. '*pot-boiler** n book, picture, etc produced merely to bring in money. '*pot-bound** adj (of a plant) having roots that have filled its pot. '*pot-boy, '*pot-man** /-mən/ (pl -men) nn (hist) one who helps in a public house by filling pots with beer, etc. '*pot hat** n (sl) bowler hat. '*pot-head** n (sl) habitual marijuana user. '*pot-herb** n plant, etc whose leaves or stems, or whose roots or tubers, are used in cooking. '*pot-hole** n (a) hole in a road made by rain and traffic. (b) deep cylindrical hole worn in rock (eg in limestone caves) by water. '*pot-holer** n person who explores pot-holes in caves. '*pot-hook** n (a) hook, often S-shaped, which can be raised or lowered on a metal bar, for holding pots, etc over a fireplace. (b) curved or wavy stroke made by children when learning to write their letters. '*pot-house** n (old use) low-class public house; ale-house: *pot-house manners*, vulgar manners. '*pot-hunter** n (a) sportsman who shoots anything he comes across, thinking only of food for the pot or profit. (b) person who takes part in contests merely for the sake of the prizes. ⇨ **5** above. '*pot roast** n beef, etc browned in a pot and cooked slowly with very little water. '*pot-shot** n shot aimed at a bird or animal that is near, so that careful aim is not needed; random shot. '*pot-trained** adj (of a small child) trained to use a chamber pot.

pot² /pɒt/ vt,vi (-tt-) **1** [VP6A] put (meat, fish paste, etc) in a pot to preserve it: *potted shrimps/ ham*. **2** [VP6A,15B] *pot (up),* plant in a flower-pot: *pot (up) chrysanthemum cuttings*. **3** [VP6A] kill with a pot-shot: *pot a rabbit;* [VP3A] *pot at,* shoot at: ∼ *a hare*. **4** (billiards) drive a ball into a pocket. **5** (colloq) put (a baby) on a chamber-pot.
pot·able /'pəʊtəbl/ adj fit to drink.
pot·ash /'pɒtæʃ/ n [U] common name for various potassium salts, used in the manufacture of fertilizers, soap, and various chemicals.
po·tass·ium /pə'tæsɪəm/ n [U] soft, shining, white metallic element (symbol **K**), vital to all living matter, occurring in the form of mineral salts and in rocks.
po·ta·tion /pəʊ'teɪʃn/ n (liter) drink.
po·tato /pə'teɪtəʊ/ n (pl ∼es /-təʊz/) plant with rounded tubers eaten as a vegetable; one of the tubers: *baked ∼es; mashed ∼(es) ; ∼ soup;* (US) ∼ *chips* (= GB *crisps*). ⇨ the illus at **vegetable.** ,**sweet '∼,** tropical plant with long tuberous roots

used for food. '∼ **beetle,** beetle that destroys the leaves of ∼ plants.
po·teen /pɒ'tiːn/ n [U] Irish whisky from an illicit still.
po·tent /'pəʊtnt/ adj (not of persons or machines) powerful: ∼ *reasons/arguments/charms/drugs/ remedies;* (of males) not sexually impotent. ∼·ly adv **po·tency** /-nsɪ/ n
po·ten·tate /'pəʊtnteɪt/ n powerful person; monarch; ruler.
po·ten·tial /pə'tenʃl/ adj **1** that can or may come into existence or action: ∼ *wealth/resources;* ∼ *energy* (waiting to be released); *the* ∼ *sales of a new book*. **2** ∼ *mood,* (gram) indicating possibility. □ n **1** [C] that which is ∼; possibility; [U] what sb or sth is capable of: *He hasn't realized his full* ∼ *yet*. **2** (gram) ∼ mood. **3** (electr) energy of an electric charge, expressed in volts: *a current of high* ∼. ∼·ly /-ʃəlɪ/ adv a ∼*ly rich country,* eg one with rich but undeveloped natural resources. ∼·ity /pə,tenʃɪ'ælətɪ/ n (pl -ties) power or quality which is ∼, and needs development; latent capacity: *a situation/a country with great potentialities*.
pother /'pɒðə(r)/ n trouble; commotion.
po·tion /'pəʊʃn/ n [C] dose of liquid medicine or poison, or of sth used in magic: a '*love* ∼.
pot-pourri /,pəʊ 'pʊərɪ: US: pə'ri:/ n **1** mixture of dried rose-petals and spices, kept in a jar for its perfume. **2** musical or literary medley.
pot·sherd /'pɒt-ʃɜːd/ n broken piece of pottery (esp in archaeology).
pot·tage /'pɒtɪdʒ/ n (old use) thick soup.
potted /'pɒtɪd/ adj **1** ⇨ pot². **2** (of a book, etc) inadequately summarized: *a* ∼ *version of a classical novel*.
pot·ter¹ /'pɒtə(r)/ (US = **put·ter** /'pʌtər/) vi [VP2A,C] **1** work with little energy; move about from one little job to another: ∼*ing about in the garden*. **2** waste (time) in ∼*ing:* ∼ *away a whole afternoon*. ∼·er n person who ∼s.
pot·ter² /'pɒtə(r)/ n maker of pots. ∼'s **wheel,** horizontal revolving disc on which pots are shaped.
pot·tery n (pl -ries) [U] earthenware; pots; [C] ∼'s workshop. **the Potteries,** district in Staffordshire, England where ∼y is the chief industry.

a potter's wheel

potty¹ /'pɒtɪ/ adj (-ier, -iest) (GB dated colloq) **1** petty; unimportant; insignificant: ∼ *little details/ jobs*. **2** ∼ *(about sb/sth),* (of a person) foolish, crazy: *She's quite* ∼, mad. *He's* ∼ *about his new gramophone*.
potty² /'pɒtɪ/ n (pl -ties) child's chamber-pot.
pouch /paʊtʃ/ n **1** small bag carried in the pocket (*a to'bacco-*∼) or fastened to the belt (a soldier's ,ammu'nition-∼). **2** bag-like formation, eg that in which a female kangaroo carries her young. ⇨ the illus at **large. 3** puffy area of skin, eg under the eyes of a sick or old person. □ vt **1** [VP6A] put into a ∼. **2** [VP6A] make (part of a dress, etc) like a ∼;

[VP2A] hang like a ∼.

pouf, pouffe /puːf/ *n* **1** large, thick cushion used as a seat. **2** /puf/ ⚠ (derog sl) male homosexual.

poul·terer /'pəʊltərə(r)/ *n* (GB) dealer in poultry and game, eg hares.

poul·tice /'pəʊltɪs/ *n* [C] soft heated mass of eg linseed, mustard, spread on a cloth, and put on the skin to relieve pain, etc. □ *vt* [VP6A] put a ∼ on.

poul·try /'pəʊltrɪ/ *n* (collective *n*) **1** (with *pl v*) large domestic fowl (eg hens, ducks, geese, turkeys) kept for eating or for egg-laying: *The* ∼ *are being fed.* **2** (with *sing v*) these considered as food: *P∼ is expensive this Christmas.* ⇨ the illus at fowl.

pounce /paʊns/ *vi* [VP3A] ∼ **on/at,** make a sudden attack or downward swoop on: *The hawk* ∼*d on its prey. The tiger* ∼*d savagely on the goat.* (fig) *He* ∼*d at* (= seized) *the first opportunity to inform against his colleague.* □ *n* such an attack.

pound¹ /paʊnd/ *n* (⇨ App 5) **1** unit of weight, 16 ounces avoirdupois, 12 ounces troy. **2** ∼ **(sterling),** British unit of money: *five* ∼*s,* written £5; *a five-*∼ *note,* banknote for £5. *penny wise,* ∼ *foolish; in for a penny, in for a* ∼, ⇨ penny. **3** monetary unit of various other countries.

pound² /paʊnd/ *n* **1** enclosed area in a village where, in olden times, cattle that had strayed were kept until claimed by their owners. **2** (mod use) place where stray dogs and cats, and motor-vehicles left in unauthorized places, are kept until claimed.

pound³ /paʊnd/ *vt,vi* [VP6A,15A,2C,3A] ∼ *(away) (at/on),* **1** strike heavily and repeatedly; thump: *Our heavy guns* ∼*ed (away at) the walls of the fort. Who is* ∼*ing (on) the piano? Someone was* ∼*ing at the door with a heavy stick. I could hear feet* ∼*ing on the stairs. She could feel her heart* ∼*ing as she finished the 100 metres race.* **2** crush to powder; break to pieces: ∼ *crystals in a mortar; a ship* ∼*ing/being* ∼*ed to pieces on the rocks.* **3** [VP2C] ride, run, walk, heavily: *He* ∼*ed along the road.*

pound·age /'paʊndɪdʒ/ *n* [U] commission or fee of so much (eg 5p) per pound sterling (£1) or payment of so much (eg 3oz) per pound weight (1 lb).

pounder /'paʊndə(r)/ *n* (usu in compounds) sth weighing so many pounds: *a three-*∼, eg a fish weighing 3 lb; gun that fires a shot of so many pounds: *an eighteen-*∼.

pour /pɔː(r)/ *vt,vi* **1** [VP6A,12B,13B,15A,B,14] cause (a liquid or a substance that flows like a liquid) to flow in a continuous stream: *P∼ yourself another cup of tea. Please* ∼ *a cup of tea for me, too. He* ∼*ed the coffee out of the saucepan into the jug.* (fig) *He* ∼*ed out his tale of misfortunes. The Underground stations* ∼ *thousands of workers into the streets between 8 and 9.30 each morning.* ∼ *cold water on sth,* discourage (a person's plan, zeal or enthusiasm). ∼ *oil on troubled waters,* try to calm a disturbance or quarrel with soothing words. **2** [VP2C] flow in a continuous stream; come freely (*out/off, etc*): *The sweat was* ∼*ing off him. Tourists* ∼ *into London during the summer months. The crowds were* ∼*ing out of the football ground. Letters of complaint* ∼*ed in.* **3** (of rain) come down heavily: *The rain* ∼*ed down. It was a* ∼*ing wet day. It never rains but it* ∼*s,* a saying used when (usu unwelcome) things come or events happen in quick succession.

pout /paʊt/ *vt,vi* [VP6A,2A] (as a sign of dis-

pleasure) push out (the lips). □ *n* such a pushing out of the lips. ∼*·ing·ly* *adv* sulkily.

pov·erty /'pɒvətɪ/ *n* [U] state of being poor: *live in* ∼; *fall into* ∼; lack, inferiority: *an essay which shows* ∼ *of ideas.* '∼**-stricken** *adj* affected by ∼: ∼*-stricken homes.*

pow·der /'paʊdə(r)/ *n* **1** [C,U] (kind of) substance that has been crushed, rubbed or worn to dust; special kind of this, eg for use on the skin (*a tin of* '*talcum-*∼), or as a medicine (*take a* ∼ *every morning*), for cleaning things ('*soap-*∼, '*bleaching-*∼), or for cooking ('*baking-*∼). '∼-**puff** *n* soft, pad used for applying cosmetic ∼ to the skin. '∼**-room** *n* ladies' room in an hotel, restaurant, cinema, etc with wash-basins and lavatories. **2** = gunpowder, ⇨ gun. *not worth* ∼ *and shot,* not worth fighting for. '∼**-magazine** *n* place where gun∼ is stored. '∼**-flask/-horn** *n* (hist) for carrying gun∼. □ *vt,vi* [VP6A] put ∼ on (the face, etc). **2** [VP2A] use face-powder. ∼*ed adj* reduced to ∼; dehydrated: ∼*ed milk/eggs.* ∼*y adj* of, like, covered with, ∼: ∼*y snow; a* ∼*y nose.*

power /'paʊə(r)/ *n* **1** [U] (in living things, persons) ability to act or do: *It is not within/It is beyond/outside my* ∼ *to help you,* I am unable, or am not in a position, to do so. *This animal, the chameleon, has the* ∼ *of changing its colour. I will do everything in my* ∼ *to help.* **2** (*pl*) faculty of the body or mind: *His* ∼*s are failing,* He is becoming weak. *You are taxing your* ∼*s too much. He's a man of great intellectual* ∼*s.* **3** [U] strength; force: *the* ∼ *of a blow. More* ∼ *to your elbow!* (phrase used to encourage sb). **4** [U] energy of force that can be used to do work: '*water* ∼; *e*'*lectric* ∼. '**horse**∼, ⇨ horse. (attrib) '∼**-lathe/-loom/-mill,** operated by mechanical ∼, not by hand labour. '∼**-boat,** one with an engine; motorboat (esp one used for racing; or towing water-skiers). '∼**-dive** *vt, n* (put an aircraft into a) steep dive with the engines working. '∼**-house/-station,** building where electric ∼ is generated for distribution. '∼**-point,** socket on a wall, etc for a plug to connect an electric circuit. **5** [U] right; control; authority: *the* ∼ *of the law; the* ∼ *of Congress; have a person in one's* ∼, be able to do what one wishes with him; *have* ∼ *over sb; Spain at the height of her* ∼; *fall into sb's* ∼. *in* ∼, (of a person or political party) in office. ∼ *politics,* diplomacy backed by force. **6** [C] right possessed by, or granted to, a person or group of persons: *Are the* ∼*s of the Prime Minister defined by law? The President has exceeded his* ∼*s,* has done more than he has authority to do. **7** [C] person or organization having great authority or influence: *Is the press a great* ∼ *in your country?* Are the newspapers influential, etc? *the* ∼*s that be,* (hum) those who are in authority. **8** [C] State having great authority and influence in international affairs. **the Great P∼s,** the largest and strongest States. **9** [C] (maths) result obtained by multiplying a number or quantity by itself a certain number of times: *the second, third, fourth, etc* ∼ *of x* (= x^2, x^3, x^4, etc); *the fourth* ∼ *of 3* (= 3 × 3 × 3 × 3 = 81). **10** [U] capacity to magnify: *the* ∼ *of a lens; a telescope of high* ∼. **11** (colloq) large number or amount: *This brandy is doing me a* ∼ *of good!* **12** [C] god, spirit, etc: *Preserve us from the* ∼*s of darkness.* **pow·ered** *adj* having, able to exert or produce, mechanical energy: *a new aircraft* ∼*ed by Rolls Royce engines; a high-*∼*ed car;* (fig) *a* *high*–∼*ed salesman,* one with great ∼s of persuasion.

power·ful /'paʊəfl/ *adj* having or producing great power: *a* ∼ *blow/enemy; a* ∼ *remedy for constipation.* ∼**ly** /-fəlɪ/ *adv*

power·less /'paʊəlɪs/ *adj* without power; unable (*to do* sth): *render sb* ∼*; be* ∼ *to resist.* ∼**·ly** *adv*

pow·wow /'paʊwaʊ/ *n* conference of N American Indians; (colloq) any other kind of conference. □ *vi* hold a conference (*about* sth).

pox /pɒks/ *n* (colloq, usu **the** ∼) syphilis: *catch/ give sb the pox.*

prac·ti·cable /'præktɪkəbl/ *adj* that can be done or used or put into practice: *methods that are not* ∼*; a mountain pass that is* ∼ *only in summer.* **prac·ti·cably** /-əblɪ/ *adv* **prac·ti·ca·bil·ity** /ˌpræktɪkə'bɪlətɪ/ *n*

prac·ti·cal /'præktɪkl/ *adj* **1** concerned with practice (contrasted with *theoretical*): *overcome the* ∼ *difficulties of a scheme; a suggestion/proposal with little* ∼ *value; a* ∼ *joke,* ⇨ joke. **2** (of persons, their character, etc) clever at doing and making things; preferring activity and action to theorizing: *a* ∼ *young wife; ideas that appeal to* ∼ *minds.* **3** useful; doing well what it is intended to do: *Your invention is ingenious, but not very* ∼. ∼**ly** /-klɪ/ *adv* **1** in a ∼ manner. **2** almost: *We've had* ∼*ly no fine weather this month. He says he is* ∼*ly ruined.* ∼**·ity** /ˌpræktɪ'kælətɪ/ *n* (*pl* -ties): *Let's get down to* ∼*ities,* to considering ∼ proposals.

prac·tice /'præktɪs/ *n* **1** [U] performance; the doing of sth (contrasted with *theory*): *put a plan into* ∼, carry it out, do what has been planned. *The idea would never work in* ∼, may seem good theoretically, but would be useless if carried out. **2** [C] way of doing sth that is common or habitual; sth done regularly: *the* ∼ *of closing shops on Sundays; Christian/Protestant/Catholic* ∼*s,* ceremonies or observances; *an aperitif before dinner, as is my usual* ∼. **make a** ∼ **of (sth),** do it habitually: *boys who make a* ∼ *of cheating at examinations.* **3** [U] frequent or systematic repetition, repeated exercise, in doing sth (esp an art or craft): *Piano-playing needs a lot of* ∼. *That is a stroke,* eg in golf, *that needs a lot of* ∼. *It takes years of* ∼ *to acquire the skill of an expert.* (attrib) *Let's have a* ∼ *game.* **in/out of** ∼, having/not having given enough time recently to ∼: *Please don't ask me to play the piano for you: I'm out of* ∼. **4** [U] work of a doctor or lawyer: *retire from* ∼*; no longer in* ∼; [C] (collective) (number of) persons who regularly consult a doctor or lawyer: *a doctor with a large* ∼*; sell one's* ∼, sell (to another doctor) the connection one has (of regular patients); *a doctor in general* ∼, ⇨ general practitioner at practitioner. **5** sharp ∼, [U] not strictly honest or legal ways of doing business.

prac·ti·cian /præk'tɪʃn/ *n* = practitioner.

prac·tise (US = **-tice**) /'præktɪs/ *vt,vi* [VP6A,C,2A,B] **1** do sth repeatedly or regularly in order to become skilful: ∼ *the piano;* ∼ *making a new vowel sound;* ∼ *(for) two hours every day.* **2** make a habit of: ∼ *early rising.* ∼ **what one preaches,** make a habit of doing what one advises others to do. **3** exercise or follow (a profession, etc): ∼ *medicine/the law,* work as a doctor/ lawyer. **4** [VP3A,4A] ∼ **on/upon;** ∼ **to do sth,** (old use) take advantage of (sb's incredulity, etc); set oneself: ∼ *to deceive.* ∼**d** (US = **-ticed**) *adj* skilled; having had much practice.

prac·ti·tioner /præk'tɪʃənə(r)/ *n* **1** one who practises a skill or art. **2** professional man, esp in medicine and the law. **general** '∼ (abbr **GP**), doctor who is qualified in both medicine and minor surgery (also called *a family doctor*) who sees patients either in his surgery or in their homes.

prae·sid·ium /prɪ'sɪdɪəm/ *n* = presidium.

prae·tor (also **pre·tor**) /'priːtə(r)/ *n* annually elected magistrate in ancient Rome. **prae·tor·ian** /prɪ'tɔːrɪən/ *adj* of, having the rank of, a ∼; of the bodyguard of a Roman commander or Emperor.

prag·matic /præg'mætɪk/ *adj* concerned with practical results and values; treating things in a matter-of-fact or practical way. **prag·mati·cally** /-klɪ/ *adv*

prag·ma·tism /'prægmətɪzəm/ *n* [U] **1** (phil) belief or theory that the truth or value of a conception or assertion depends upon its practical bearing upon human interests. **2** dogmatism; officiousness; pedantry. **prag·ma·tist** /-tɪst/ *n* believer in ∼(1).

prairie /'preərɪ/ *n* wide area of level land with grass but no trees, esp in N America. ⇨ pampas, savanna, steppe, veld.

praise /preɪz/ *vt* [VP6A] **1** speak with approval of; say that one admires: ∼ *a man for his courage. Our guests* ∼*d the meal as the best they had had for years.* ∼ *give honour and glory to (God).* □ *n* **1** [U] act of praising: *His heroism is worthy of great* ∼*/is beyond* (= too great for) ∼. *The leader spoke in* ∼ *of the man who had given his life for the cause.* **2** (*pl*) **sing sb's/one's own** ∼**s,** ∼ him/ oneself enthusiastically. **3** [U] worship; glory: *P*∼ *be to God. P*∼ *be!* Thank goodness! '∼·**worthy** /-wɜːðɪ/ *adj* deserving ∼. '∼·**worth·ily** /-ɪlɪ/ *adv* '∼·**worthi·ness** *n*

pram /præm/ *n* (GB) (short for, and the usu word for) perambulator.

prance /prɑːns *US*: præns/ *vi* [VP2A,C] ∼ **(about), 1** (of a horse) move forwards jerkily, by raising the forelegs and springing from the hind legs. **2** (fig) move, carry oneself, in an arrogant manner; dance or jump happily and gaily. □ *n* prancing movement.

prank /præŋk/ *n* [C] playful or mischievous trick: *play* ∼*s on sb.*

prate /preɪt/ *vi* [VP2A,C] talk (foolishly); talk too much: *a silly young fellow prating about a subject of which he knows nothing.*

prattle /'prætl/ *vi* [VP2A,C] (of a child) talk in a simple, artless way; (of adults) talk in a childish, simple way; chatter. □ *n* [U] such talk. **prat·tler** /'prætlə(r)/ *n* one who ∼s.

prawn /prɔːn/ *n* [C] edible shellfish like a large shrimp: *a dish of curried* ∼*s.* □ *vi* fish for ∼s: *go* ∼*ing.*

pray /preɪ/ *vt,vi* **1** [VP2A,3A] ∼ **(to God) (for sth),** commune with God; offer thanks, make requests known: ∼ *to God for help. They knelt down and* ∼*ed. The farmers are* ∼*ing for rain. He's past* ∼*ing for,* There now seems to be little hope for his recovery, eg from illness, or from some fault, etc. **2** [VP17,14,11] ∼ **sb for sth/to do sth,** (liter, rhet) ask sb as a favour: *I* ∼ *you to think again. We* ∼ *you for mercy/to show mercy. We* ∼ *you that the prisoner may be set free.* **3** (formal request equivalent to) please: *P*∼ *don't speak so loud.*

prayer /preə(r)/ *n* **1** [U] act of praying to God: *He knelt down in* ∼. **2** [U] form of church worship: *Morning/Evening P*∼. **3** [C] form of words used in praying: *the Lord's P*∼. ⇨ lord; request or petition (spoken or unspoken) to God: *say one's ~s; family ~s; a ~ for rain.* **'~-book** *n* book containing ~s for use in church services, etc. **the 'P~ Book,** (also called *Book of Common P~*) the one used in Church of England services. **'~-meeting** *n* meeting at which those present offer up ~s to God in turn. **'~-rug/-mat** *n* small rug used by Muslims to kneel on when they pray. **'~-wheel** *n* revolving cylinder inscribed with or containing ~s, used by the Buddhists of Tibet.

pre- /pri:/ *pref* before; beforehand: *pre-war; a pre-amplifier; pre-natal; pre-arrange.* ⇨ App 3.

preach /pri:tʃ/ *vt,vi* 1 [VP6A,2A,B,C,3A] ~ *(to),* deliver (a sermon); make known (a religious doctrine, etc); give a talk (esp in church) about religion or morals: ~ *the gospel;* ~ *Buddhism;* ~ *against covetousness;* ~ *for two hours.* 2 [VP3A,12A,13A] ~ *(to),* give moral advice: *the headmaster* ~*ing to his pupils. Don't* ~ *me a sermon about being lazy now, please.* 3 [VP6A] urge; recommend (as right or desirable): *The Dictator* ~*ed war as a means of making the country great.* ~**er** *n* one who ~es (esp sermons). **'~-ify** /-ɪfaɪ/ *vi* (*pt,pp* -**fied**) ~, esp (2); moralize in a tedious way.

pre·amble /pri:'æmbl/ *n* introduction or preliminary statement (esp to a formal document).

pre·arrange /ˌpri:ə'reɪndʒ/ *vt* arrange in advance. ~**·ment** *n*

preb·end /'prebənd/ *n* (eccles) part of the revenue of a church granted as a stipend to a priest. **preb·en·dary** /'prebəndrɪ *US:* -derɪ/ *n* (*pl* -**ries**) priest who receives a ~.

pre·cari·ous /prɪ'keərɪəs/ *adj* (formal) uncertain; unsafe; depending upon chance: *make a* ~ *living as an author.* ~**·ly** *adv*

pre·cast /ˌpri:'kɑːst *US:* -'kæst/ *adj* (of concrete) cast into blocks ready for use in building.

pre·caution /prɪ'kɔːʃn/ *n* [U] care taken in advance to avoid a risk; [C] instance of this: *take an umbrella as a* ~; *take* ~s *against fire; insure one's house as a measure of* ~. ~**·ary** /prɪ'kɔːʃənərɪ *US:* -nerɪ/ *adj* for the sake of ~.

pre·cede /prɪ'si:d/ *vt,vi* [VP6A,2A] come or go before (in time, place or order): *the calm that* ~*d the storm; the Mayor,* ~*d by the mace-bearer; in the preceding paragraph/the paragraph that* ~*s.* **pre·ced·ing** *adj* existing or coming before.

pre·ced·ence /'presɪdəns/ *n* [U] (right to a) priority, or to a senior place. *have/take* ~ *(over): questions which take* ~ *over all others,* which must be considered first.

pre·ced·ent /'presɪdənt/ *n* earlier happening, decision, etc taken as an example or rule for what comes later. *set/create/establish a* ~ *(for sth): Is there a* ~ *for what you want me to do?* ~*ed adj* having, supported by, a ~.

pre·cen·tor /prɪ'sentə(r)/ *n* (eccles) person in general control of the singing.

pre·cept /'pri:sept/ *n* 1 [U] moral instruction: *Example is better than* ~. 2 [C] rule or guide, esp for behaviour.

pre·cep·tor /prɪ'septə(r)/ *n* (formal) teacher; instructor.

pre·cession /prɪ'seʃn/ *n* ~ *of the equinoxes,* change by which the equinoxes occur earlier in each successive year.

pre·cinct /'pri:sɪŋkt/ *n* [C] 1 space enclosed by outer walls or boundaries, esp of a cathedral or church: *within the sacred* ~s. 2 (US) subdivision of a county or city or ward: *an e'lection* ~; *a po-*

'lice ~. 3 (*pl*) neighbourhood or environs (of a town). 4 boundary: *within the city* ~s. 5 area of which the use is in some way restricted. **pedes·trian** ~, where vehicles are not allowed. **'shop·ping** ~, for shops only.

pre·ci·os·ity /ˌpreʃɪ'ɒsətɪ/ *n* [U] over-refinement; being precious(4); [C] (*pl* -**ties**) instance of this.

precious /'preʃəs/ *adj* 1 of great value and beauty: *the* ~ *metals,* gold, platinum; ~ *stones,* diamonds, rubies, etc. 2 highly valued; dear: *Her children are very* ~ *to her.* 3 (colloq) (as in intensive) complete: *a* ~ *fool. It cost a* ~ *sight more than I could afford,* very much more. 4 (of language, workmanship, etc) over-refined; affected. □ *adv* (colloq) very: *I have* ~ *little* (= hardly any) *money left.* ~**·ly** *adv* ~**·ness** *n*

preci·pice /'presɪpɪs/ *n* vertical or very steep face of a rock, cliff or mountain.

pre·cipi·tate /prɪ'sɪpɪteɪt/ *vt* [VP6A,14] 1 throw or send (sb or sth) violently down from a height. ~ *sb/sth into sth,* thrust violently into (a condition): ~ *the country into war.* 2 cause (an event) to happen suddenly, quickly, or in haste: ~ *a crisis; events that* ~*d his ruin.* 3 (chem) separate (solid matter) from a solution. 4 condense (vapour) into drops which fall as rain, dew, etc. □ *n* that which is ~d as solid matter, rainfall, etc. □ *adj* /prɪ'sɪpɪtət/ violently hurried; hasty; (doing things, done) without enough thought. ~**·ly** *adv*

pre·cipi·ta·tion /prɪˌsɪpɪ'teɪʃn/ *n* 1 (esp) fall of rain, sleet, snow or hail; amount of this: *the annual* ~ *in the Lake District; a heavy* ~. 2 [U] violent haste or being violently hurried: *act with* ~, without enough thought or consideration of the consequences. 3 act of precipitating.

pre·cipi·tous /prɪ'sɪpɪtəs/ *adj* (formal) like a precipice; very steep. ~**·ly** *adv*

pré·cis /'preɪsiː *US:* preɪ'siː/ *n* (*pl* unchanged in spelling, pronunciation /-i:z/) restatement in shortened form of the chief ideas, points, etc of a speech or piece of writing. □ *vt* make a ~ of.

pre·cise /prɪ'saɪs/ *adj* 1 exact; correctly and clearly stated; free from error: ~ *measurements;* ~ *orders; at the* ~ *moment when I lifted the receiver.* 2 taking care to be exact, not to make errors: *a very* ~ *man;* too careful, fussy, about details: *prim and* ~ *in his manner.* ~**·ly** *adv* 1 in a ~ manner; exactly: *state the facts* ~*ly; at 2 o'clock* ~*ly.* 2 (as a response, agreeing with sb) quite so. ~**·ness** *n*

pre·ci·sion /prɪ'sɪʒn/ *n* [U] accuracy; freedom from error: (attrib) ~ *instruments/tools,* those, used in technical work, that are very precise (for measuring, etc); ~ *bombing.*

pre·clude /prɪ'kluːd/ *vt* [VP6A,C,14] ~ *sb from doing sth,* prevent; make impossible: ~ *all doubt/misunderstanding.* **pre·clu·sion** /prɪ'kluːʒn/ *n*

pre·co·cious /prɪ'kəʊʃəs/ *adj* 1 (of a person) having developed certain faculties earlier than is normal: *a* ~ *child,* eg one who reads well at the age of three. 2 (of actions, knowledge, etc) marked by such development. ~**·ly** *adv* ~**·ness,** **pre·coc·ity** /prɪ'kɒsətɪ/ *nn* [U] being ~.

pre·cog·ni·tion /ˌpriːkɒg'nɪʃn/ *n* [U] knowledge of sth before it occurs.

pre·con·ceive /ˌpriːkən'siːv/ *vt* [VP6A] form (ideas, opinions) in advance (before getting knowledge or experience): *visit a foreign country with* ~*d ideas.* **pre·con·cep·tion** /ˌpriːkən'sepʃn/ *n* [U,C] ~d idea.

pre·con·certed /ˌpriːkən'sɜːtɪd/ *adj* (formal) agreed

in advance: *following* ~ *plans*.
pre·con·di·tion /ˌpriːkənˈdɪʃn/ *n* = prerequisite.
pre·cur·sor /ˌpriːˈkɜːsə(r)/ *n* [C] (formal) person or thing coming before, as a sign of what is to follow.
pre·cur·sory /-sərɪ/ *adj* preliminary; anticipating.
preda·tory /ˈpredətrɪ US: -tɔːrɪ/ *adj* (formal) **1** (of people) plundering and robbing: ~ *tribesmen/ habits*; ~ *incursions*, raids made for plunder. **2** (of animals) preying upon others. **pred·ator** /-tə(r)/ *n* ~ *animal*.
pre·de·cease /ˌpriːdɪˈsiːs/ *vt* (legal) die before (another person).
pre·de·cessor /ˈpriːdɪsesə(r) US: ˈpredɪ-/ *n* **1** former holder of any office or position: *Mr Green's* ~ *in office*. **2** thing to which another has succeeded: *Is the new proposal any better than its* ~*?*
pre·des·ti·nate /ˌpriːˈdestɪneɪt/ *adj* foreordained by God; fated. □ *vt* = predestine(1).
pre·des·ti·na·tion /ˌpriːdestɪˈneɪʃn/ *n* **1** theory or doctrine that God has decreed from eternity that part of mankind shall have eternal bliss and part eternal punishment. **2** destiny; doctrine that God has decreed everything that comes to pass.
pre·des·tine /ˌpriːˈdestɪn/ *vt* **1** [VP17,14] (often passive) ~ *sb to sth/to do sth*, (of God, fate) decide, ordain, beforehand; cause (sb) to behave, etc in a certain way. **2** [VP17] ~ *sb to do sth*, decide or make inevitable: *Everything took place as if he was* ~*d to succeed. These events were clearly* ~*d (to happen)*.
pre·de·ter·mine /ˌpriːdɪˈtɜːmɪn/ *vt* (formal) **1** [VP6A] decide in advance: *The social class into which a child is born often seems to* ~ *his later career*. **2** [VP17] ~ *sb to do sth*, persuade or impel sb in advance to do sth: *Did an unhappy childhood* ~ *him to behave as he did?* **pre·de·ter·mi·na·tion** /ˌpriːdɪˌtɜːmɪˈneɪʃn/ *n*
pre·dica·ment /prɪˈdɪkəmənt/ *n* difficult or unpleasant situation from which escape seems difficult: *be in an awkward* ~.
predi·cate¹ /ˈpredɪkət/ *n* (gram) part of a statement which says sth about the subject, eg 'is short' in 'Life is short'.
predi·cate² /ˈpredɪkeɪt/ *vt* (formal) **1** [VP6A,17,9] declare to be true or real: ~ *of a motive that it is good*; ~ *a motive to be good*. **2** [VP6A] make necessary as a consequence: *These policies were* ~*d by Britain's decision to join the Common Market*.
pre·di·cat·ive /prɪˈdɪkətɪv US: ˈpredɪkeɪtɪv/ *adj* (gram, of an *adj* or *n*, opposed to *attrib*) forming part or the whole of the predicate. ~ **adjective**, one used only in the predicate, eg *asleep, alive*.
pre·dict /prɪˈdɪkt/ *vt* [VP6A,9,10] say, tell in advance: ~ *a good harvest*; ~ *that there will be an earthquake*. **pre·dic·tion** /prɪˈdɪkʃn/ *n* [U] ~ing; [C] sth ~ed; prophecy. ~**·able** /-əbl/ *adj* that can be ~ed. ~**·or** /-tə(r)/ *n* instrument or device that ~s, eg one used in war to determine when to open anti-aircraft fire. ~**·a·bil·ity** /prɪˌdɪktəˈbɪlətɪ/ *n*
pre·di·gest /ˌpriː-/ *vt* treat (food) so that it is easily digested: ~*ed food for babies*.
pre·di·lec·tion /ˌpriːdɪˈlekʃn US: ˌpredlˈek-/ *n* [C] *a* ~ *for*, special liking, mental preference.
pre·dis·pose /ˌpriːdɪˈspəʊz/ *vt* [VP14,17] ~ *sb to sth/to do sth*, (formal) cause (sb) to be inclined or liable before the event: *His early training* ~*d him to a life of adventure/to travel widely. I find myself* ~*d in his favour*, inclined to favour him.
pre·dis·po·si·tion /ˌpriːdɪspəˈzɪʃn/ *n* [C] ~ *to sth/*

to do sth, state of mind or body favourable to: *a* ~ *to arthritis; a* ~ *to find fault*.
pre·domi·nant /prɪˈdɒmɪnənt/ *adj* ~ *(over)*, (formal) having more power or influence than others; prevailing, conspicuous: *The* ~ *feature of his character was pride*. ~**·ly** *adv* in a ~ manner: *a* ~*ly brown-eyed race*. **pre·domi·nance** /-əns/ *n* [U] superiority in strength, numbers, etc; state of being ~.
pre·domi·nate /prɪˈdɒmɪneɪt/ *vi* [VP2A,3A] ~ *(over)*, (formal) have or exert control (over); be superior in numbers, strength, influence, etc: *a forest in which oak-trees* ~.
pre·emi·nent /ˌpriːˈemɪnənt/ *adj* excelling others; best of all: ~ *above all his rivals*. ~**·ly** *adv* **pre·emi·nence** /-əns/ *n* [U].
pre·empt /ˌpriːˈempt/ *vt* [VP6A] (formal) **1** obtain by pre-emption. **2** (US) occupy (public land) so as to have the right of pre-emption. **pre·emp·tion** /ˌpriːˈempʃn/ *n* [U] (formal) purchase by one person, etc before others are offered the chance to buy; right to purchase in this way; the obtaining of sth in advance. **pre·emp·tive** /-tɪv/ *adj* relating to pre-emption: *a* ~ *bid*, (in bridge) one intended to be high enough to prevent further bidding; *a* ~*'air strike*, eg by bombing, against forces considered likely to attack.
preen /priːn/ *vt* **1** [VP6A] (of a bird) smooth (itself, its feathers) with its beak. **2** [VP6A,14] (of a person) tidy (oneself). ~ *oneself on*, (fig) pride oneself (on); show self-satisfaction.
pre·exist /ˌpriːɪgˈzɪst/ *vi* [VP2A] exist beforehand; live a life before this life. ~**·ence** /-əns/ *n* life of the soul before entering its present body or this world. ~**·ent** /-ənt/ *adj* existing in a former life or previously.
pre·fab /ˈpriːfæb US: ˌpriːˈfæb/ *n* [C] (colloq abbr of) pre-fabricated house.
pre·fab·ri·cate /ˌpriːˈfæbrɪkeɪt/ *vt* [VP6A] manufacture the parts, eg roofs, walls, fitments, of a building, a ship, etc before they are put together on the site, in the yards, etc: ~*d houses; a* ~*d school*. **pre·fab·ri·ca·tion** /ˌpriːfæbrɪˈkeɪʃn/ *n*
pref·ace /ˈprefɪs/ *n* [C] author's explanatory remarks at the beginning of a book; preliminary part of a speech: *write a* ~ *to a book*. □ *vt* [VP14] ~ *sth with sth/by doing sth*, provide with a ~; begin (a talk, etc) with a ~: *The chairman* ~*d his remarks with some sharp raps on the table*. **prefa·tory** /ˈprefətrɪ US: -tɔːrɪ/ *adj* of or in the nature of a ~: *after a few prefatory remarks*.
pre·fect /ˈpriːfekt/ *n* **1** (in ancient Rome) title of various civil and military officers; governor. **2** (in France, Japan) title of the chief administrative officer of a department; head of the Paris police. **3** (in some English schools) one of a number of senior pupils given responsibility, eg for keeping order.
pre·fec·ture /ˈpriːfektjʊə(r) US: -tʃər/ *n* **1** administrative area in some countries, eg France, Japan. ⇨ county (in GB). **2** (in France) place or office where a prefect(2) works; his official residence. **3** position of a prefect(1); period of office. **pre·fec·tural** /ˌpriːˈfektʃərəl/ *adj* of a ~: *the prefectural offices*.
pre·fer /prɪˈfɜː(r)/ *vt* (-rr-) **1** [VP6A,D,7A,9,14,17] ~ *(to)*, choose rather; like better: *Which would you* ~*, tea or coffee? I* ~ *walking to cycling. He* ~*s to write his letters rather than dictate them. I should* ~ *to wait until evening. I should* ~ *you not to go/that you did not go there alone*. **2** [VP6A,14]

~ *a charge/charges (against sb),* put forward, submit: ~ *a charge against a motorist,* ie accuse him of sth. 3 [VP6A,14] ~ *sb (to sb),* appoint (sb) (to a higher position). ~·**able** /'prefrəbl/ *adj* (not used with *more*) ~ *(to),* superior; to be ~red. ~·**ably** /'prefrəblɪ/ *adv*

pref·er·ence /'prefrəns/ *n* 1 [C,U] act of preferring: *have a ~ for French novels. I should choose this in ~ to any other.* 2 [C] that which is preferred: *What are your ~s?* 3 [U] the favouring of one person, country, etc more than another (in business relations, etc esp by admitting imports at a lower import duty); [C] instance of this: *give sb ~ (over others).* 4 '**P~ Stock,** stock on which dividend payments must be made before profits are distributed to holders of Ordinary Stock.

pref·er·en·tial /ˌprefə'renʃl/ *adj* of, giving, receiving, preference; (eg of import duties, etc) favouring particular countries: *get ~ treatment.*

pre·fer·ment /prɪ'fɜːmənt/ *n* [U] act of preferring(3); promotion or advancement: ~ *to a directorship.*

pre·fig·ure /ˌpriː'fɪɡə(r) US: -ɡjər/ *vt* (formal) 1 [VP6A] represent beforehand; show (what is coming). 2 [VP6A,9,10] imagine, picture to oneself, beforehand.

pre·fix /'priːfɪks/ *n* 1 (abbr *pref* in this dictionary) word or syllable, eg *pre-, co-,* placed in front of a word to add to or change its meaning. ⇨ **App 3.** 2 word used before a person's name, eg Mr, Dr. □ *vt* /ˌpriː'fɪks/ [VP6A,14] ~ *sth (to sth),* add a ~ to or in front of; add at the beginning: ~ *a new paragraph to Chapter Ten.*

preg·nant /'pregnənt/ *adj* 1 (of a woman or female animal) having in the uterus offspring in a stage of development before birth. 2 (of words, actions) significant; full of promise. ~ *with,* filled with: *words ~ with meaning;* certain or likely to have: *political events ~ with consequences.* **preg·nancy** /-nənsɪ/ *n* [U] the state of being ~; (fig) fullness; depth; significance; [C] instance of being ~: *She's had six pregnancies in six years.*

pre·hen·sile /ˌpriː'hensaɪl US: -sl/ *adj* (of a foot or tail, eg a monkey's) able to seize and hold.

pre·his·toric /ˌpriːhɪ'stɒrɪk US: -'tɔːrɪk/, **-tori·cal** /-kl/ *adjj* of the time before recorded history. **pre·his·tory** /ˌpriː'hɪstrɪ/ *n*

pre·judge /ˌpriː'dʒʌdʒ/ *vt* [VP6A] make up one's mind about a person, cause, action, etc before hearing the evidence, making a proper inquiry, etc. ~·**ment** *n*

preju·dice /'predʒʊdɪs/ *n* 1 [U] opinion, like or dislike, formed before one has adequate knowledge or experience; [C] instance of this: *have a ~ against/in favour of modern jazz; listen to new poems without ~; racial ~,* against members of other races. 2 [U] (legal) injury that may or does arise from some action or judgement: *to the ~ of sb's rights,* with (possible) injury to them. *without ~ (to),* without injury to any existing right or claim. □ *vt* [VP6A,15A] ~ *sb (against/in favour of sb/sth),* 1 cause sb to have a ~(1). 2 injure or weaken (sb's interests, etc): *He ~d his claim by asking too much.* **preju·di·cial** /ˌpredʒʊ'dɪʃl/ *adj* ~ *(to),* causing ~ or injury.

prel·acy /'prelәsɪ/ *n* (*pl* -cies) 1 office, rank, see, of a prelate. 2 **the ~,** the whole body of prelates.

prel·ate /'prelət/ *n* bishop or other churchman of equal or higher rank.

pre·lim /prɪ'lɪm/ *n* (colloq abbr for) (a) preliminary

examination. (b) /'priːlɪmz/ (*pl*) pages (with title, contents, etc) preceding the actual text (in a book).

pre·limi·nary /prɪ'lɪmɪnərɪ US: -nerɪ/ *adj* coming first and preparing for what follows: *a ~ examination; after a few ~ remarks.* □ *n* (*pl*-ries) (usu *pl*) ~ actions, measures, etc: *the usual preliminaries to a Geneva conference,* eg the wrangling about procedures and agenda.

prel·ude /'preljuːd/ *n* [C] ~ *to,* action, event, etc that serves as an introduction to (another); (music) introductory movement (to a fugue or as part of a suite). □ *vt* [VP6A] serve as, be, a ~ to.

pre·mari·tal /ˌpriː'mærɪtl/ *adj* before marriage.

pre·ma·ture /'premətjʊə(r) US: ˌpriːmə'tʊər/ *adj* done, happening, doing sth, before the right or usual time: ~ *decay of the teeth;* ~ *birth; a ~ baby,* one born at less than 38 weeks of pregnancy. ~·**ly** *adv*

pre·medi·tate /ˌpriː'medɪteɪt/ *vt* [VP6A] consider, plan, (sth) in advance: *a ~d murder.* **pre·medi·ta·tion** /ˌpriːmedɪ'teɪʃn/ *n* [U].

pre·mier /'premɪə(r) US: 'priːm-/ *adj* first in position, importance, etc. □ *n* prime minister; head of the government. '~·**ship** /-ʃɪp/ *n*

pre·mière /'premɪeə(r) US: prɪ'mɪər/ *n* first performance of a play or (*'film-~*) first public showing of a cinema film.

prem·ise, prem·iss /'premɪs/ *n* 1 statement on which reasoning is based. 2 each of the two first parts of a syllogism: *the major ~,* eg 'Boys like fruit'; *the minor ~,* eg 'You are a boy'; the conclusion being 'Therefore you like fruit'. 3 (*pl*) house or building with its outbuildings, land, etc: *business ~s,* the building(s), offices, etc where a business is carried on; *to be consumed on the ~s,* eg of alcoholic drinks in a public house or hotel which has no 'off-licence'. 4 (*pl*) (legal) details of property, names of persons, etc in the first part of a legal agreement. □ *vt* [VP6A,9] ~ *(sth/that...),* state by way of introduction.

pre·mium /'priːmɪəm/ *n* (*pl* ~s) 1 amount or instalment paid for an insurance policy. 2 reward; bonus: *a ~ for good conduct.* '**P~ Bond,** (GB) government bond that offers the chance of prizes (in a draw) instead of the more usual interest¹(6). *put a ~ on sth,* make it advantageous for sb (to behave in a certain way, to do sth): *Does high taxation put a ~ on business dishonesty?* 3 addition to ordinary charges, wages, rent, etc; bonus: *He had to pay the agent a ~ before he could rent the house,* an extra sum above the rent. 4 fee (to be) paid by a pupil to a professional man, eg an accountant or architect, for instruction and training. 5 (of stocks and shares) amount above par value: *The shares are selling at a ~. at a ~,* (fig) highly valued or esteemed.

pre·mon·ition /ˌpriːmə'nɪʃn/ *n* [C] feeling of uneasiness considered as a warning (of approaching danger, etc): *have a ~ of failure.* **pre·moni·tory** /prɪ'mɒnɪtərɪ US: -tɔːrɪ/ *adj*

pre·natal /ˌpriː'neɪtl/ *adj* preceding birth.

pren·tice /'prentɪs/ *n* (old use, short for *apprentice*) *try his ~ hand,* make an unskilled or novice's attempt.

pre·oc·cu·pa·tion /ˌpriːɒkjʊ'peɪʃn/ *n* [U] state of mind in which sth takes up all a person's thoughts; [C] the subject, etc that takes up all his thoughts: *His greatest ~ was how to find money for a holiday in Europe.*

pre·oc·cupy /priː'ɒkjʊpaɪ/ *vt* (*pt,pp*-pied) [VP6A]

take all the attention of (sb, his mind) so that attention is not given to other matters: *preoccupied by family troubles; preoccupied with thoughts of the coming holidays.*

pre·or·dain /ˌpriːɔːˈdeɪn/ *vt* [VP6A,9] decree or determine in advance.

prep /prep/ *n* (schoolboy slang for) (**a**) preparation(3). (**b**) preparatory school.

pre·pack·aged /ˌpriː ˈpækɪdʒd/, **pre·packed** /ˌpriːˈpækt/ *adjj* (of products) wrapped, packed, before being supplied to shops, etc where they are to be sold.

prep·ara·tion /ˌprepəˈreɪʃn/ *n* **1** [U] preparing or being prepared: *The meal is in ∼. We're getting things together in ∼ for the journey. Don't try to do it without ∼.* **2** [C] (usu *pl*) things done to get ready for sth: *∼s for war; make ∼s for a voyage.* **3** [U] (colloq abbr *prep*) homework. **4** [C] kind of medicine, food, etc specially prepared: *pharmaceutical ∼s.*

pre·para·tory /prɪˈpærətrɪ US: -tɔːrɪ/ *adj* introductory; needed for preparing: *∼ measures/training. ∼ to*, in readiness for; before. '*∼ school*, (esp in England) private school where pupils are prepared for entry to a higher school (esp a public school); (US) (usu private) school where pupils are prepared for college.

pre·pare /prɪˈpeə(r)/ *vt,vi* **1** [VP6A,7,14,3A] *∼ (for)*, get or make ready: *∼ a meal/one's lessons/a sermon; ∼ pupils for an examination*, coach them; *∼ for an attack*, get ready to repel an attack; *∼ to attack*, get ready to make an attack; *be ∼d for anything to happen.* **2** *be ∼d to*, be able and willing to: *We are ∼d to supply the goods you ask for. ∼d·ness* /prɪˈpeəɪdnɪs/ *n* [U] being *∼d*: *Everything was in a state of ∼dness.*

pre·pay /ˌpriːˈpeɪ/ *vt* (*pt,pp* -paid /-ˈpeɪd/) [VP6A] pay in advance: *send a telegram with reply prepaid.*

pre·pon·der·ant /prɪˈpɒndərənt/ *adj* (formal) greater in weight, number, strength, etc. *∼·ly adv* **pre·pon·der·ance** /-əns/ *n*

pre·pon·der·ate /prɪˈpɒndəreɪt/ *vi* [VP2A,C] (formal) be greater in weight, number, strength, influence, etc: *reasons that ∼ over other considerations.*

prep·osi·tion /ˌprepəˈzɪʃn/ *n* word or group of words (eg *in, from, to, out of, on behalf of*) often placed before a *n* or *pron* to indicate place, direction, source, method, etc. *∼al* /-ˈʃənl/ *adj* of, containing, a *∼*. *∼al phrase*, (**a**) phrase made up of a group of words used as a *∼*, eg *in front of, on top of.* (**b**) *∼* + the *n* or *n phrase* following it, eg *in the night; on the beach.*

pre·pos·sess /ˌpriːpəˈzes/ *vt* [VP6A,15A] (formal) give (a person) a feeling (about sth), usu favourable; fill (a person *with* or *by* an idea, a feeling): *I was ∼ed by his appearance and manners,* They made a favourable impression upon me. *∼·ing adj* attractive; making a good impression: *a girl of ∼ing appearance.* **pre·pos·session** /ˌpriːpəˈzeʃn/ *n* [C] favourable feeling experienced in advance.

pre·pos·ter·ous /prɪˈpɒstərəs/ *adj* completely contrary to reason or sense; absurd. *∼·ly adv*

pre·puce /ˈpriːpjuːs/ *n* (anat) foreskin.

pre·re·cord /ˌpriːrɪˈkɔːd/ *vt* [VP6A] record, eg a radio or TV programme, in advance on tape or discs.

pre·requi·site /ˌpriːˈrekwɪzɪt/ *n, adj* (thing) required as a condition for sth else: *Three passes at*

'*A' level are a ∼ for university entrance/are ∼ for university entrance.*

pre·roga·tive /prɪˈrɒgətɪv/ *n* [C] special right(s) or privilege(s), esp of a ruler: *the ∼ of pardon*, eg to pardon a condemned criminal. **the Royal P∼**, (GB) the (theoretical) right of the sovereign to act independently of Parliament.

pre·sage /ˈpresɪdʒ/ *n* [C] (formal) presentiment; sign looked upon as a warning. □ *vt* /prɪˈseɪdʒ/ [VP6A] foretell; be a sign of: *The clouds ∼ a storm.*

pres·by·ter /ˈprezbɪtə(r)/ *n* elder (person in authority) in some Protestant churches, esp the Presbyterian Church.

Pres·by·terian /ˌprezbɪˈtɪərɪən/ *adj ∼ Church*, one governed by elders, all of equal rank (in England, since 1972, united with the Congregational Church to form the United Reformed Church) (⇨ episcopal, governed by bishops). □ *n* member of the *∼* Church. *∼·ism* /-ɪzəm/ *n* the *∼* system of church government; the beliefs of *∼s.*

pres·by·tery /ˈprezbɪtrɪ US: -terɪ/ *n* (*pl* -ries) [C] **1** (in a church) eastern part of the chancel beyond the choir; sanctuary. **2** (regional) administrative court of the Presbyterian Church. **3** residence of a Roman Catholic parish priest.

pre·sci·ent /ˈpresɪənt/ *adj* (formal) knowing about, able to see into, the future. *∼·ly adv* **pre·sci·ence** /-əns/ *n*

pre·scribe /prɪˈskraɪb/ *vt,vi* **1** [VP6A,14] *∼ sth (for sth)*, advise or order the use of: *∼d textbooks,* books which pupils are required to use. *The doctor ∼d a long rest. What do you ∼ for this illness?* **2** [VP6A,8,10,21,2A,3A] say, with authority, what course of action is to be followed: *penalties ∼d by the law. Complete the ∼d form.*

pre·script /ˈpriːskrɪpt/ *n* ordinance; command.

pre·scrip·tion /prɪˈskrɪpʃn/ *n* [U] act of prescribing; [C] that which is prescribed; (esp) doctor's written order or direction for the making up and use of a medicine; the medicine itself: *∼ charges*, (in GB) charges made under National Health Service requirements for *∼s.*

pre·scrip·tive /prɪˈskrɪptɪv/ *adj* giving orders or directions; authorized; prescribed by custom: *a ∼ grammar of the English language*, one telling the reader how he ought to use the language. ⇨ descriptive.

pres·ence /ˈprezns/ *n* [U] **1** being present in a place, etc: *in the ∼ of his friends*, with his friends there. *Your ∼ is requested at the annual general meeting*, Please be there. *He was calm in the ∼ of danger. ∼ of mind*, ⇨ mind¹(2). **2** bearing; person's way of carrying himself: *a man of noble ∼.*

pres·ent¹ /ˈpreznt/ *adj* **1** being in the place in question: *the Smiths, and other people ∼* (= who were *∼*). *Were you ∼ at the ceremony? ∼ company excepted,* (colloq) used to show that one's remarks do not apply to anyone who is *∼.* ⇨ absent¹(1). **2** being discussed or dealt with; now being considered: *in the ∼ case*, this case. **3** existing now: *the ∼ government.* **4** *∼ to*, felt, remembered by: *∼ to the mind/imagination.* **5** (archaic) ready at hand: '*a very ∼ help in trouble'.* □ *n* **1** the *∼*, the *∼* time, the time now passing: *the past, the ∼, and the future;* (gram) the *∼* tense. *at ∼*, now: *We don't need any more at ∼. for the ∼*, for the time being, as far as the *∼* is concerned: *That will be enough for the ∼.* **2** *by these ∼s*, (legal) by this document.

pres·ent² /'preznt/ *n* gift: '*birthday* ∼*s; I'm buying it for a* ∼ (= as a gift), *so please wrap it up nicely.* **make sb a** ∼ **of sth,** give sb sth: *I'll make you a* ∼ *of my old car.*

pre·sent³ /prɪ'zent/ *vt* **1** [VP14,15A] ∼ **sth to sb;** ∼ **sb with sth,** give; offer; put forward; submit: ∼ *the village with a bus-shelter/*∼ *a bus-shelter to the village; the clock that was* ∼*ed to me when I retired;* ∼ *a petition to the Governor;* ∼ *a cheque at the bank,* ie for payment; ∼ *one's compliments/greetings, etc to sb,* (polite phrase). **2** [VP6A,14,15A] ∼ **sb to sb,** introduce formally. **3** [VP15A] (reflex) appear; attend: ∼ *oneself at a friend's house;* ∼ *oneself for trial/for examination.* **4** [VP6A] show; reveal: *He* ∼*ed a bold front to the world,* showed that he was facing his difficulties, etc bravely. *This case* ∼*s some interesting features. A good opportunity has* ∼*ed itself for doing what you suggested.* **5** [VP6A] (of a theatrical manager or company) produce (a play): cause (an actor) to take part in a play: *The Mermaid Company will* ∼ '*Hamlet' next week/will* ∼ *Tom Hill as Brutus in 'Julius Caesar'.* **6** [VP14] ∼ **sth at sb,** aim (a weapon) at him; hold out (a weapon) in position for aiming at him: *The intruder* ∼*ed a pistol at me.* **7** [VP6A] hold (a rifle, etc) vertically in front of the body as a salute, etc. **P**∼ **arms!** (the order to do this). □ *n* position of a weapon in a salute: *at the* ∼, with the weapon held in a perpendicular position.

pre·sent·able /prɪ'zentəbl/ *adj* fit to appear, be shown, in public: *Is this old suit still* ∼? *Is the girl he wants to marry* ∼, the sort of girl he can introduce to his friends and family? **pre·sent·ably** /-əblɪ/ *adv*

pres·en·ta·tion /ˌprezn'teɪʃn *US:* ˌpriː:zen-/ *n* [U] presenting or being presented; [C] sth presented: *the* ∼ *of a new play; a* ∼ *copy,* a book given as a present, esp by the author. *The cheque is payable on* ∼, ie at the bank.

pre·sen·ti·ment /prɪ'zentɪmənt/ *n* [C] (formal) vague feeling that sth (esp unpleasant or undesirable) is about to happen.

pres·ent·ly /'prezntlɪ/ *adv* **1** soon: *I'll be with you* ∼. **2** (US) at the present time: *The Secretary of State is* ∼ *in Africa.*

pres·er·va·tion /ˌprezə'veɪʃn/ *n* [U] **1** act of preserving: *the* ∼ *of food/one's health; the* ∼ *of peace; the* ∼ *of wild life.* **2** condition of sth preserved: *old paintings in an excellent state of* ∼.

pre·serv·ative /prɪ'zɜːvətɪv/ *n, adj* (substance) used for preserving: *fresh cream free from* ∼*s,* with no substances added to preserve the cream.

pre·serve /prɪ'zɜːv/ *vt* [VP6A,14] ∼ *(from),* **1** keep safe from harm or danger: *social activities preserving old people from the loneliness of old age. God* ∼ *us all!* **2** keep from decay, risk of going bad, etc (by pickling, making into jam, etc): ∼ *fruit/eggs, etc.* **3** keep from loss; retain (qualities, etc): ∼ *one's eyesight; a well-*∼*d old man,* one who shows few signs of the usual weaknesses of old age. **4** care for and protect land, rivers, lakes, etc with the animals, birds and fish, esp to prevent these from being taken by poachers: *The fishing in this stream is strictly* ∼*d.* **5** keep alive (sb's name or memory); keep extant: *Few of his early poems are* ∼*d.* □ *n* **1** (usu *pl*) jam. **2** woods, streams, etc where animals, birds and fish are ∼*d: a* '*game* ∼. **poach on an-other's** ∼, (fig) take a share in activities, interests, etc looked upon as associated especially with sb

else. **pre·serv·able** /-əbl/ *adj* that can be ∼*d.* ∼**r** *n* person or thing that ∼*s.*

pre·side /prɪ'zaɪd/ *vi* [VP2A,C,3A] ∼ *at,* be chairman: *The Prime Minister* ∼*s at meetings of the Cabinet.* ∼ *over,* be the head or director of: *The city council is* ∼*d over by the mayor.*

presi·dency /'prezɪdənsɪ/ *n* (*pl*-cies) **1 the** ∼, the office of president. **2** term of office as a president: *during the* ∼ *of Lincoln.*

presi·dent /'prezɪdənt/ *n* **1** (elected) head of the government in the US and other modern republics. **2** head of some government departments (*P*∼ *of the Board of Trade*), of some business companies, colleges, societies, etc. **presi·den·tial** /ˌprezɪ'denʃl/ *adj* of a ∼ or his duties: *the* ∼*ial election; the* ∼*ial year,* (in US) the year of the ∼ial elections.

pre·sid·ium /prɪ'sɪdɪəm/ *n* executive committee of the administration, and of various organisations, in some socialist countries; group of presiding persons.

press¹ /pres/ *n* **1** act of pressing: *a* ∼ *of the hand; give sth a light* ∼. **2** machine or apparatus for pressing: *a* '*wine-*∼; *a* '*cider-*∼; *keep one's (tennis) racket in a* ∼; *a hydraulic* ∼. **3** (usu **the** ∼), printed periodicals; the newspapers generally; journalists: *The book was favourably noticed by the* ∼/*had a good* ∼, was favourably reviewed by the literary critics. *There was a* ∼ *campaign against him,* He was attacked in the newspapers. *The liberty/freedom of the* ∼ (= The right of newspapers to report events, express opinions, etc freely) *is a feature of democratic countries.* '∼**-agent** *n* person employed by a theatre, actor, musician, etc to arrange for publicity in the newspapers. Hence, '∼**-agency** *n.* '∼**-box** *n* place reserved for reporters at a football or cricket match, etc. '∼**-conference** *n* one of newspaper reporters, convened by a minister, government official, etc who talks about policy, achievements, etc. '∼**-cutting/-clipping** *nn* paragraph, article, etc cut out from a newspaper or other periodical. '∼**-gallery** *n* gallery reserved for reporters, esp in the House of Commons. '∼**-lord** *n* powerful newspaper proprietor. '∼**-photographer** *n* newspaper photographer. **4** business for printing (and sometimes publishing) books or periodicals: *Oxford University P*∼; (also '**printing-**∼) machine for printing: *in the* ∼, being printed; *send a manuscript to the* ∼, send it to be printed; *go to* ∼, start printing; *correct the* ∼, correct errors in printing, be a proof-reader. **5** crowd: *lost in the* ∼; *fight one's way through the* ∼. **6** pressure: *the* ∼ *of modern life; because of the* ∼ *of business.* **7** cupboard with shelves for clothes, books, etc usu in a recess in a wall. '∼**-mark** *n* mark or number in a book showing its place in a library shelf. **8** ∼ *of sail/canvas,* (naut) as much sail as the wind will allow.

press² /pres/ *vt,vi* **1** [VP6A,15B] push steadily against: ∼ *the trigger of a gun;* ∼ *(down) the accelerator pedal* (of a car); ∼ *the button,* eg of an electric bell. '∼**-up** *n* (*pl* ∼**-ups**) exercise in which one stretches out face down on the floor, the arms being straightened and bent by ∼ing against the floor with the palms of one's hands to raise and lower one's body. '∼**-stud** ⇨ snap(5). **2** [VP6A,15B,22] use force or weight to get sth smooth or flat, to get sth into a smaller space, to get juice out of fruit, etc: ∼ *a suit/skirt, etc,* with an iron, to remove creases, etc; ~ *grapes,* when making wine; ~ *the juice out of an orange;* ~*ed beef,* beef that has been boiled and pressed into shape for packing in tin boxes. **3** [VP6A,15A,B] keep close to and attack; bear heavily on: ~ *the enemy hard,* attack with determination; ~ (*home*) *an attack,* carry it out with determination; ~ *a point* (in an argument, debate) *home,* (fig) obtain support, agreement, etc by a determined, articulate speech; *be hard* ~*ed,* be under determined attack. **4** ~ *for,* make repeated requests for; demand urgently: ~ *for an inquiry into a question.* **5** *be* ~*ed for,* have barely enough of: ~*ed for time/money/space.* **6** [VP2C] push, crowd, with weight or force: *crowds* ~*ing against the barriers/*~*ing round the royal visitors.* **7** [VP3A,4A,14,17] ~ (*sb*) *for sth;* ~ (*sb*) *to do sth,* urge; insist on: ~ (*sb*) *for an answer;* ~ *sb for a debt/to pay a debt. He did not need much* ~*ing. They are* ~*ing for a decision to be made.* ~ *sth on/upon sb,* insist that sb takes it: *He* ~*ed the money on me,* insisted on my accepting it. *Don't* ~ *your opinions upon her,* Don't insist that she should accept them. **8** [VP2A] demand action or attention: *The matter is* ~*ing,* is urgent. **9** *Time* ~*es,* There is no time to lose. **10** [VP6A,15A] squeeze (sb's hand, arm, etc) as a sign of affection or sympathy; draw (sb) to oneself in an embrace: *He* ~*ed her to his side.* **11** [VP2C] ~ (*down*) *on/upon sb,* weigh; oppress: *His responsibilities* ~ *heavily upon him. The new taxes* ~*ed down heavily on the people.* **12** [VP2C] ~ *on/ forward* (*with sth*), hurry, continue in a determined way: ~ *on with one's work. It was getting dark, so the travellers* ~*ed forward.* ~*·ing* n one of many identical gramophone records made from the same matrix: *make and sell 10000* ~*ings of a symphony.* □ *adj* **1** urgent; requiring immediate attention: ~*ing business.* **2** (of persons, their requests, etc) insistent: *a* ~*ing invitation; as you are so* ~*ing.* ~*·ing·ly adv*

press³ /pres/ *vt* [VP15A] **1** (hist) force (a man) to serve in the navy or army. '~**-gang** *n* (hist) body of men employed to ~ men. **2** take (sth) for public use; requisition. ~ *into service,* make use of because of urgent need: *Even my thirty-year-old car was* ~*ed into service.*

press·ure /'preʃə(r)/ *n* [C,U] pressing; (the amount of) force exerted continuously on or against sth by sth which touches it: *a* ~ *of 6 lb to the square inch; see that the tyre* ~ *is right; atmospheric* ~*/the* ~ *of the atmosphere,* the ~ of weight of air, as measured by a barometer. '**blood-**~ *n* tension of the blood-vessels. '~ **cabin** *n* cabin (in an aircraft) that is pressurized. '~**-cooker** *n* airtight container for cooking quickly with steam under ~. '~**- gauge** *n* apparatus or device for measuring the ~ of a liquid or gas at a given point. **2** compelling force or influence: *He pleaded* ~ *of work/family* ~*s and resigned his place on the committee. be/ come under* ~, feel/be caused to feel strongly compelled (to act): *He's under strong* ~ *to vote with the government on this issue. He always works best under* ~, when he has to. *bring* ~ *to bear on sb* (*to do sth*); *put* ~ *on sb/put sb under* ~ (*to do sth*), use force or influence on sb. '~ **group,** organized group, eg an association of manufacturers such as brewers, farmers, which tries to exert influence or lobby for the benefit of its members. **3** sth that oppresses or weighs down: *the* ~ *of taxation; under the* ~ *of poverty/necessity.* **4** (**at**) *high*

~, (with) great energy and speed: *work at high* ~; *a high-*~ *salesman.* □ *vt* = pressurize.

press·ur·ize /'preʃəraɪz/ *vt* **1** [VP6A] apply pressure to. **2** [VP6A,14,17] ~ *sb* (*into doing sth/to do sth*), use force (of persuasion, influence, etc) to make him do it: ~ *the President into resigning/to resign.* **3** (usu *pp*) (of an aircraft, a submarine, etc) construct so that the internal air pressure can be controlled and kept normal: *a* ~*d cabin.*

pres·ti·di·gi·ta·tor /ˌprestɪ'dɪdʒɪteɪtə(r)/ *n* juggler; conjuror. **pres·ti·di·gi·ta·tion** /ˌprestɪˌdɪdʒɪ'teɪʃn/ *n*

pres·tige /pre'stiːʒ/ *n* [U] **1** respect that results from the good reputation (of a person, nation, etc); power or influence coming from this: *behaviour that would mean loss of* ~. **2** distinction, glamour, that comes from achievements, success, possessions, etc: (attrib) *the* ~ *value of living in a fashionable district/of owning a Rolls-Royce.* **pres·tig·ious** /pre'stɪdʒəs/ *adj* bringing ~.

pres·tis·simo /pre'stɪsɪməʊ/ *adj, adv* (I; music) very quick(ly); as quickly as possible.

presto /'prestəʊ/ *adj, adv* (I; music) quick(ly). *Hey* ~! words used by a conjuror when performing a trick.

pre·stressed /ˌpriː'strest/ *adj* (of concrete) strengthened by having stretched cables inserted.

pre·sum·able /prɪ'zjuːməbl/ *US:* -'zuː-/ *adj* that may be presumed. **pre·sum·ably** /-əblɪ/ *adv*

pre·sume /prɪ'zjuːm/ *US:* -'zuːm/ *vt, vi* **1** [VP6A,9,25] take for granted; suppose (to be true): *In Britain an accused man is* ~*d* (*to be*) *innocent until he is proved guilty. Let us* ~ *that...; Dr Livingstone, I* ~. **2** [VP7A] venture; take the liberty: *I won't* ~ *to disturb you. May I* ~ *to advise you?* **3** [VP3A] ~ *upon sth,* (formal) make a wrong use of, take an unfair advantage of: ~ *upon sb's good nature,* take advantage of it by asking for help, etc; ~ *upon a short acquaintance,* treat sb familiarly even though one has known him for only a short time. **pre·sum·ing** *adj* having, showing, a tendency to ~, to take liberties.

pre·sump·tion /prɪ'zʌmpʃn/ *n* **1** [C] sth presumed(1); sth which seems likely although there is no proof: *on the false* ~ *that the firm was bankrupt; the* ~ *that he was drowned.* **2** [U] arrogance; behaviour that is too bold: *If you will excuse my* ~, *I should like to contradict what you have just said.*

pre·sump·tive /prɪ'zʌmptɪv/ *adj* based on presumption(1): ~ *evidence; the* ~ *heir/the heir* ~, person who is heir (to the throne, etc) until sb with a stronger claim is born. ~*·ly adv*

pre·sump·tu·ous /prɪ'zʌmptʃʊəs/ *adj* (formal) (of behaviour, etc) too bold or self-confident. ~*·ly adv*

pre·sup·pose /ˌpriːsə'pəʊz/ *vt* [VP6A,9] **1** assume beforehand. **2** imply; require as a condition: *Sound sleep* ~*s a mind at ease.* **pre·sup·po·si·tion** /ˌpriːsʌpə'zɪʃn/ *n* [C] sth ~d; [U] presupposing.

pre·tence (*US* = **-tense**) /prɪ'tens/ *n* **1** [U] pretending; make-believe: *do sth under the* ~ *of friendship/religion/patriotism. It's all* ~. **2** [C] pretext or excuse; false claim or reason: *He calls for the night porter on the slightest* ~. *It is only a* ~ *of friendship. false* ~*s,* (legal) acts intended to deceive: *obtain money by/on/under false* ~*s.* **3** [C] claim (to merit, etc); [U] ostentation: *a man without* ~.

pre·tend /prɪ'tend/ *vt, vi* **1** [VP7A,9] make oneself appear (to be sth, to be doing sth), either in play or to deceive others: ~ *to be asleep; boys* ~*ing that* *they are pirates. Let's ~ we are cowboys. They ~ed not to see us.* 2 [VP6A] say falsely that one has (as an excuse or reason, or to avoid danger, difficulty, etc): *~ sickness. He ~ed ignorance, hoping to avoid being fined for breaking the law.* 3 [VP3A] *~ to,* put forward a claim to: *There are not many persons who ~ to an exact knowledge of the subject. Surely he does not ~ to intelligence! The young man ~ed to the throne,* claimed it (falsely). *~·ed·ly* adv *~er* n person whose claim (to a throne, a title, etc) is disputed.

pre·tense /prɪ'tens/ ⇨ pretence.

pre·ten·sion /prɪ'tenʃn/ n 1 [C] (often pl) (statement of a) claim: *He makes no ~s to expert knowledge of the subject. Has he any ~s to being considered a scholar? She has some social ~s,* claims some place in high society. 2 [U] being pretentious.

pre·ten·tious /prɪ'tenʃəs/ adj claiming (without justification) great merit or importance: *a ~ author/book/speech; use ~ language.* *~·ly* adv *~·ness* n

pret·er·ite (also **-erit**) /'pretərɪt/ n, adj ~ (**tense**), (gram) (tense) expressing a past action or state.

pre·ter·natu·ral /ˌpriːtə'nætʃrəl/ adj out of the regular course of things; not normal or usual. *~·ly* adv. *~ly* solemn.

pre·text /'priːtekst/ n [C] false reason (*for* an action, etc): *On/Under the ~ of asking for my advice, he called and borrowed £10 from me. Can we find a ~ for refusal/refusing the invitation?*

pre·tor /'priːtə(r)/ n = praetor.

pret·tify /'prɪtɪfaɪ/ vt (pt,pp **-fied**) [VP6A] make pretty, esp in an insipid way.

pretty /'prɪtɪ/ adj (-ier, -iest) 1 pleasing and attractive without being beautiful or magnificent: *a ~ girl/garden/picture/piece of music.* '*~~* adj (colloq) superficially ~ or charming. 2 fine; good: *a ~ wit. A ~ mess you've made of it!* (ironic). 3 (colloq) considerable in amount or extent. *a ~ penny,* quite a lot: *It will cost you a ~ penny.* **come to/reach a ~ pass,** reach a difficult position. *a* '*~ kettle of fish,* ⇨ fish¹(1). □ adv fairly, moderately: *The situation seems ~ hopeless. It's ~ cold outdoors today. ~ much,* very nearly: *The result of the ballot is ~ much what we expected. ~ nearly,* almost: *The car is new, or ~ nearly so,* almost new. *~ well,* almost: *We've ~ well finished the work.* **sitting ~,** (colloq) well off; favourably placed for future developments, etc. □ n (pl -ties) *my ~,* my ~ one (used of a child). **pret·tily** /'prɪtɪlɪ/ adv in a ~ or charming way. **pret·ti·ness** n

pret·zel /'pretsl/ n (G) crisp, salt-flavoured biscuit, made in the shape of a knot or stick.

pre·vail /prɪ'veɪl/ vi 1 [VP2A,3A] *~ (over/ against),* gain victory (over); fight successfully (against): *Truth will ~. We ~ed over our enemies.* 2 [VP2A] be widespread; be generally seen, done, etc: *the conditions now ~ing in Africa. The use of opium still ~s in the south.* 3 [VP3A] *~ on/upon sb to do sth,* persuade: *~ upon a friend to lend you £10. ~·ing* adj most frequent or usual: *the ~ing winds/fashions in dress.*

preva·lent /'prevələnt/ adj (formal) common, seen or done everywhere (at the time in question): *the ~ fashions; the ~ opinion on the proposed reforms. Is malaria still ~ in that country?* **preva·lence** /-əns/ n [U] being ~: *I'm shocked at the prevalence of bribery among these officials.*

pre·vari·cate /prɪ'værɪkeɪt/ vi [VP2A] (formal) make untrue or partly untrue statements; try to

evade telling the (whole) truth. **pre·vari·ca·tion** /prɪˌværɪ'keɪʃn/ n [U] prevaricating; [C] instance of this.

pre·vent /prɪ'vent/ vt 1 [VP6A,14,19C] *~ sb (from doing sth); ~ sth (from happening),* stop or hinder: *~ a disease from spreading. Who can ~ us from getting married/~ our getting married now that you are of age? Your prompt action ~ed a serious accident.* 2 (old use) go before as a guide: '*P~ us, O Lord, in all our doings'. ~·able* /-əbl/ adj that can be ~ed.

pre·ven·ta·tive /prɪ'ventətɪv/ adj, n = preventive.

pre·ven·tion /prɪ'venʃn/ n [U] act of preventing: *the Society for the P~ of Cruelty to Animals. P~ is better than cure.*

pre·ven·tive /prɪ'ventɪv/ adj serving or designed to prevent; precautionary. *~ custody,* imprisonment of sb considered unlikely to be reformed, so that he may not commit further crimes. *~ detention,* detention without trial because a person is thought likely to commit crime or (in some countries) oppose the government. *~ medicine,* research into means of warding off disease, illness, eg hygiene, working conditions. □ n sth (eg medicine) to prevent or ward off sth.

pre·view /'priːvjuː/ n [C] view of a film, play, etc before it is shown to the general public. □ vt have/ give a ~ of.

pre·vi·ous /'priːvɪəs/ adj 1 coming earlier in time or order: *on a ~ occasion; ~ convictions,* convictions for earlier offences, taken into account by a judge when passing sentence upon sb convicted of a further offence. *I regret that a ~ engagement prevents me from accepting your kind invitation.* 2 too hasty: *Aren't you rather ~ in supposing that I will marry you?* 3 *~ to,* before. *~·ly* adv

pre·vi·sion /ˌpriː'vɪʒn/ n [U] foresight; [C] instance of this: *have a ~ of danger.*

prey /preɪ/ n (sing only) animal, bird, etc hunted for food: *The eagle was devouring its ~.* **be/fall a ~ to,** (a) be seized, caught by: *The zebra fell a ~ to the lion.* (b) be greatly troubled by: *be a ~ to anxiety and fears.* ˌ**beast/ˌbird of** '*~,* one that kills and eats others, eg tigers, eagles. □ vi [VP3A] *~ on/upon,* 1 take, hunt, as *~*(1): *hawks ~ing on small birds.* 2 steal from; plunder: *Our coasts were ~ed upon by Viking pirates.* 3 (of fears, etc) trouble greatly: *anxieties/losses that ~ upon my mind.*

price /praɪs/ n 1 [C] sum of money for which sth is (to be) sold or bought; that which must be done, given or experienced to obtain or keep sth: *What ~ are you asking? P~s are rising/falling/going up/ going down. I won't buy it at that ~. He sold the house at a good ~. Loss of independence was a high ~ to pay for peace. at a ~,* at a fairly high ~: *There's fresh asparagus in the shops—at a ~! Every man has his ~,* can be bribed. **put a** '*~ on sb's head,* offer a reward for his capture (dead or alive). '**asking ~,** (for a house, etc) price stated by the vendor: *accept an offer of £200 below the asking ~.* '*~-control* n control or fixing of ~s by authorities, manufacturers, etc. Hence, '*~-controlled* adj. '*~-list* n list of current ~s of goods for sale. '**list-~** n ~ recommended by the manufacturer, etc but not always compulsory. 2 [U] value; worth: *a pearl of great ~.* **beyond/ above/without ~,** so valuable that buying is impossible. 3 [C] (betting) odds. *What ~...?* (sl) (a) What is the chance of...? (b) (used to sneer at the failure of sth): *What ~ peace now?* **'starting ~**, odds offered by a bookmaker as a race is about to start. □ vt **1** [VP6A] fix, ask about, the ~ of sth; mark (goods) with a ~: *All our goods are clearly ~d.* **2 ~ oneself/one's goods out of the market,** (of manufacturers, producers) fix ~s so high that sales decline or stop. **~y** /'praɪsɪ/ *adj* (sl) expensive. **~·less** *adj* **1** too valuable to be ~d: *~less paintings.* **2** (sl) absurd: *a ~less old fellow;* very amusing: *a ~less joke.*

prick¹ /prɪk/ *n* **1** small mark or hole caused by the act of pricking: *~s made by a needle.* **2** pain caused by pricking: *I can still feel the ~. He feels the ~ of conscience/remorse,* mental uneasiness. **'pin-~**, (fig) sth small that irritates. **3** (old use) goad for oxen. **kick against the ~s,** (fig) hurt oneself by useless resistance. **4** ⚠ (vulg) penis; (vulg) term of abuse: *He's a stupid ~!*

prick² /prɪk/ *vt, vi* **1** [VP6A] make a hole or a mark in (sth) with a sharp point: *~ a toy balloon; ~ a blister,* on the skin; *~ holes in paper.* **2** [VP6A] hurt, cause pain to, with a sharp point or points: *~ one's finger with/on a needle. The thorns on these roses ~ed my fingers.* (fig) *His conscience ~ed him.* **3** [VP2A] feel sharp pain: *My fingers are ~ing.* **4** [VP15B] **~ sth out/off,** put (seedlings) in the earth (in holes made with a pointed stick, etc): *~ out young cabbage plants.* **5** [VP15B] **~ up one's ears,** (esp of dogs, horses) raise the ears; (fig, of persons) pay sharp attention to sth being said. **~er** *n* person who, thing which, ~s; instrument for piercing holes, eg a bradawl. **~·ing** *n* act of ~ing; ~ing sensation.

prickle /'prɪkl/ *n* [C] (usu small) pointed growth on the stem, etc of a plant, or on the skin of some animals, eg hedgehogs; thorn. □ *vt, vi* give or have a pricking sensation. **prick·ly** /'prɪklɪ/ *adj* **1** covered with ~s. **prickly pear,** cactus covered with ~s and having pear-shaped fruit. **2 prickly heat,** inflammation of the sweat glands, marked by a pricking

sensation, common in the tropics during the hot-weather season. **3** (colloq) easily irritated or angered: *You're a bit prickly today.*

pride /praɪd/ *n* **1** [U] feeling of satisfaction arising from what one has done, or from persons, things, etc one is concerned with: *look with ~ at one's garden.* **take (a) ~ in sb/sth; take no/little, etc ~ in sb/sth,** have some/no/little, etc ~ about him/it: *take (a) great ~ in one's achievements/in the success of one's children. ~ of place,* a position of superiority. **2** [U] (also **proper ~**) self-respect; knowledge of one's worth and character: *He has no ~. His ~ prevents him from doing anything dishonourable. Don't say anything that may wound his ~.* **false ~,** mistaken feeling of this kind; vanity. **3** [U] object of ~(1): *a girl who is her mother's ~ and joy.* **4** [U] too high an opinion of oneself, one's position, possessions, etc; arrogance: *the sin of ~; be puffed up with ~.* **P~ goes before a fall,** (prov) ⇨ go before at go¹(28). **5 the ~ of,** the prime, flower, of: *in the full ~ of youth.* **6** [C] group: (esp) *a ~ of lions/peacocks.* □ *vt* (reflex) **~ oneself on/upon sth,** take ~ in; be pleased and satisfied about: *He ~s himself upon his skill as a pianist.*

prie-dieu /'priː djɜː/ *n* small piece of furniture at which to kneel when praying to God.

priest /priːst/ *n* **1** ordained minister of a Christian Church, esp one who is between a deacon and a bishop in the Anglican, Orthodox or Roman Catholic Church. ⇨ the illus at **vestment.** *Clergyman* is usu the Anglican Church, except in official use, *minister* in the non-conformist Churches. **'~-ridden** *adj* ruled by, under the subjection of, ~s. **2** (of non-Christian religions) person trained to perform special acts of religion, to serve the deity, give advice, etc. **~·ess** /'priːstes/ *n* woman ~(2). **'~·craft** *n* [U] ambitious or worldly policy of ~s. **~·hood** /-hʊd/ *n* the whole body of ~s of a Church: *the Irish ~hood.* **~·ly, ~·like**

birds of prey

adjj of or for a ∼; like a ∼.

prig /prɪg/ *n* [C] smug, self-satisfied, self-righteous person. ∼-**gish** /-ɪʃ/ *adj* behaving like, typical of, a ∼; full of self-satisfaction. ∼-**gish·ly** *adv* ∼-**gish·ness** *n*

prim /prɪm/ *adj* (-mmer, -mmest) neat; formal: *a* ∼ *garden;* (of persons, their manner, speech, etc) disliking, showing a dislike of, anything rough, rude, improper: *a very* ∼ *and proper old gentleman.* □ *vt* (-mm-) put (the face, lips) into a ∼ expression. ∼-**ly** *adv* ∼-**ness** *n*

prima /ˈpriːmə/ *adj* (I) first. ∼ ˌ**balleˈrina** /ˌbælɪˈriːnə/, leading woman performer in ballet. ∼ ˈ**donna** /ˈdɒnə/, leading woman singer in opera; (colloq) arrogant, temperamental person.

pri·macy /ˈpraɪməsɪ/ *n* (*pl* -cies) 1 pre-eminence. 2 position of an archbishop.

pri·mae·val /praɪˈmiːvl/ *adj* ⇨ primeval.

prima facie /ˌpraɪmə ˈfeɪʃiː/ *adv, adj* (Lat) (based) on the first impression: *have* ∼ *a good case.* ∼ **evidence,** (legal) sufficient to prove something (unless refuted).

pri·mal /ˈpraɪml/ *adj* (formal) primeval; chief; first in importance.

pri·mary /ˈpraɪmərɪ US: -merɪ/ *adj* 1 leading in time, order or development: *of* ∼ (= chief) *importance;* a ∼ *school,* (GB) for junior pupils (5 to 11 years); ∼ *rocks,* of the lowest series of strata; *the* ∼ *meaning of a word,* the earliest and original meaning. 2 ∼ **colours,** red, blue and yellow, from which all other colours can be obtained by mixing two or more. □ *n* (*pl* -ries) (US) meeting of electors to name candidates for a coming election. **pri·mar·ily** /ˈpraɪmərəlɪ US: praɪˈmerəlɪ/ *adv* in the first place; essentially.

pri·mate¹ /ˈpraɪmeɪt/ *n* archbishop.

pri·mate² /ˈpraɪmeɪt/ *n* one of the highest order of mammals (including men, apes, monkeys and lemurs).

prime¹ /praɪm/ *adj* 1 chief; most important: *his* ∼ *motive.* **P**∼ **Minister,** chief minister of a Government. 2 excellent; first-rate: ∼ (*cuts of*) *beef.* 3 fundamental; primary. ∼ **cost,** cost of production not including overhead charges, margin for profit, etc. ∼ **meridian,** the zero meridian, that of Greenwich. ∼ **mover,** primary source of motive power, eg wind, water; (fig) person who initiates a plan, action, etc. ∼ **number,** (maths) one which cannot be divided exactly except by itself and the number 1 (eg 7, 17, 41).

prime² /praɪm/ *n* [U] 1 state of highest perfection; the best part: *in the* ∼ *of youth; in the* ∼ *of life. When is a man in his* ∼? *He is past his* ∼. 2 first or earliest part: *the* ∼ *of the year,* spring. 3 church service at 6am or sunrise.

prime³ /praɪm/ *vt* [VP6A] 1 get ready for use or action: ∼ *a gun,* (hist) put in gunpowder, etc; ∼ *a pump,* wet it, pour in water, to get it started. ∼ *the pump,* (fig) put money into an inactive industry, etc or into the economy, to stimulate it to growth. 2 supply with facts, etc: *The witness had been* ∼*d by a lawyer. The Socialist candidate had been well* ∼*d with facts by Party headquarters.* 3 (colloq) fill (a person) with food or drink: *well* ∼*d with liquor.* 4 cover (a surface) with the first coat of paint, oil, varnish, etc.

primer¹ /ˈpraɪmə(r)/ *n* first school textbook: *a Latin* ∼.

primer² /ˈpraɪmə(r)/ *n* [C] 1 small quantity of explosive, contained in a cap or cylinder, for igniting

the powder in a cartridge, bomb, etc. ⇨ the illus at cartridge. 2 priming (of paint).

pri·meval (also **-mae·val**) /praɪˈmiːvl/ *adj* 1 of the earliest time in the world's history. 2 very ancient: ∼ *forests,* natural forests in which no trees have ever been felled.

prim·ing /ˈpraɪmɪŋ/ *n* 1 gunpowder used to fire the charge of a gun, bomb, mine, etc. 2 mixture used by painters for a first coat.

primi·tive /ˈprɪmɪtɪv/ *adj* 1 of the earliest times; of an early stage of social development: ∼ *man;* ∼ *culture.* 2 simple; old-fashioned; having undergone little development: ∼ *weapons,* eg bows and arrows, spears. □ *n* painter or sculptor of the period before the Renaissance; example of his work. ∼-**ly** *adv* ∼-**ness** *n*

pri·mo·geni·ture /ˌpraɪməʊˈdʒenɪtʃə(r) US: -tʃʊər/ *n* fact of being the firstborn of the children of the same parents. **right of** ∼, (legal) system by which all real estate passes on from a father to the eldest son.

pri·mor·dial /praɪˈmɔːdɪəl/ *adj* in existence at or from the beginning; primeval.

primp /prɪmp/ *vt* = prink.

prim·rose /ˈprɪmrəʊz/ *n* [C] common wild plant with pale yellow flowers; the flower; its colour. *the* ∼ *way/path,* (fig) the pursuit of reckless pleasure.

prim·ula /ˈprɪmjʊlə/ *n* kinds of perennial herbaceous plants with flowers of various colours and sizes (including the primrose and polyanthus).

pri·mus /ˈpraɪməs/ *n* (*pl* ∼es /-məsɪz/) (P) kind of cooking stove that burns vaporized oil.

prince /prɪns/ *n* 1 ruler, esp of a small state. 2 male member of a royal family, esp (in GB) a son or grandson of the Sovereign. 3 **the** ∼ **of darkness,** Satan. **the P**∼ **of Peace,** Jesus. **P**∼ **Consort,** husband of a reigning queen. ∼-**dom** /-dəm/ *n* rank or dignity of, or area ruled by, a ∼(1). ∼-**ly** *adj* (-ier, -iest) (worthy) of a ∼; splendid; generous: *a* ∼*ly gift.* **prin·cess** /prɪnˈses/ *n* wife of a ∼; daughter or granddaughter of a sovereign.

prin·ci·pal /ˈprɪnsəpl/ *adj* highest in order of importance: *the* ∼ *rivers of Europe; the* ∼ *food of the people of Java.* ∼ **boy,** person (traditionally, in GB, an actress, not an actor) who takes the leading part in a pantomime. □ *n* 1 title of some heads of colleges and of some other organizations. 2 person for whom another acts as agent in business: *I must consult my* ∼. 3 main girder or rafter in a roof. 4 (fin) money lent, put into a business, etc on which interest is payable. 5 (legal) person directly responsible for a crime (distinguished from an abetter or accessory). ∼-**ly** /-plɪ/ *adv* for the most part; chiefly.

prin·ci·pal·ity /ˌprɪnsɪˈpælətɪ/ *n* (*pl* -ties) country ruled by a prince. **the P**∼, Wales.

prin·ciple /ˈprɪnsəpl/ *n* [C] 1 basic truth; general law of cause and effect: *the (first)* ∼*s of geometry/political economy/navigation.* 2 guiding rule for behaviour: *moral* ∼*s;* ∼*s of conduct; live up to one's* ∼*s;* (collective *sing*) *a man of high* ∼. *in* ∼, (contrasted with *in detail*) in general. *on* ∼, from conviction, from a settled moral motive: *He refused on* ∼ *to understate his income for taxation purposes.* 3 general law shown in the working of a machine, etc: *These machines work on the same* ∼. ∼*d adj* (in compounds) following, having, the kind of ∼(2) indicated: *a most high-*∼*d woman, unhappily married to a low-*∼*d man.* ⇨ unprincipled.

prink /priŋk/ vt ~ *oneself (up)*, make oneself look smart or spruce.

print[1] /prɪnt/ n **1** [U] mark(s), letters, etc in printed form: *clear* ~; *in large/small* ~. *in* ~, (of a book) printed and on sale. *out of* ~, (of a book) no more printed copies available from the publisher. *rush into* ~, (of an author) hasten to publish sth he has written. **2** [C] (usu in compounds) mark left on a surface preserving the form left by the pressure of sth: '*finger—*~s; '*foot—*~s. **3** [U] printed cotton fabric: (attrib) *a* ~ *dress*. **4** [C] picture, design, etc made by ~ing from a block, plate, etc: *old Japanese* ~s; photograph ~ed from a negative. '**blue-**~, ⇨ blue[2](7). '~-**seller** n man who sells engravings, etchings, etc. '~-**shop** n shop of a ~-seller. **5** [C] (now chiefly US) ~ed publication, esp a newspaper.

print[2] /prɪnt/ vt,vi **1** [VP6A] make marks on (paper), etc by pressing it with inked type, etc; make books/pictures, etc in this way; (of a publisher, an editor, an author) cause to be ~ed: ~ *6000 copies of a novel. Do you intend to* ~ *your lectures/have your lectures* ~ed? (fig) *The incidents* ~ed *themselves on her memory.* '~ed **matter/papers,** (as on envelopes, wrappers, etc) circulars, prospectuses, etc to be charged for postage at a reduced rate. '~-**out** n the ~ed output of a computer. **2** [VP6A] shape (one's letters), write (words), in imitation of ~ed characters (instead of ordinary joined handwriting). **3** [VP6A,15B] ~ *(off)*, make (a photograph) on paper, etc from a negative film or plate: *How many copies shall I* ~ *(off) for you from this negative?* **4** [VP2A] (of a plate or film) produce a picture; be produced as the result of ~ing(3): *This film/plate/picture hasn't* ~ed *very well.* **5** [VP6A] mark (a textile fabric) with a coloured design. ~-**able** /-əbl/ adj that can be ~ed, or ~ed from; fit to be ~ed. ~-**er** n workman who ~s books, etc; owner of a ~ing business. ~-**ing** n (in verbal senses): '~-**ink,** kind of ink used for ~ing books, etc. '~-**ing-machine,** '~-**ing-press** nn machine for ~ing books, etc. '~-**ing office** n place where ~ing is done.

prior[1] /'praɪə(r)/ adj ~ *(to)*, earlier in time, order or importance: *have a* ~ *claim to sth.* ~ *to*, prep (formal) before: ~ *to any discussion of this matter. The house was sold* ~ *to auction*, before the day of the auction.

prior[2] /'praɪə(r)/ n head of a religious order or house; (in an abbey) next below an abbot. ~ess /'praɪərɪs/ n woman ~. ~y /'praɪərɪ/ n religious house governed by a ~ or ~ess.

pri·or·ity /praɪ'ɒrətɪ US: -'ɔːr-/ n (pl -ties) **1** [U] ~ *(over)*, being prior; right to have or do sth before others: *I have* ~ *over you in my claim. The proceeds of the sale* (eg of the property of a bankrupt) *will be distributed according to* ~. **2** [C] claim to consideration; high place among competing claims: *Road building is a first* ~ (or, colloq, *a top* ~). *The Government gave* ~ *to housing after the war.*

prise /praɪz/ vt = prize[3].

prism /'prɪzəm/ n **1** solid figure with similar, equal and parallel ends, and with sides which are parallelograms. **2** body of this form, usu triangular and made of glass, which breaks up white light into the colours of the rainbow.

pris·matic /prɪz'mætɪk/ adj **1** like, having the shape of, a prism. **2** (of colours) brilliant and

varied.

prison /'prɪzn/ n [C] building in which wrongdoers are kept locked up; place where a person is shut up against his will; [U] confinement in such a building: *escape/be released from* ~; *be in/go to/send sb to* ~, '~-**breaking** n the illegal act of escaping from ~. ~-**er** n person kept in ~ for crime or until tried in a law court; person, animal or bird kept in confinement: *a bird kept* ~er *in a cage.* ~-**er of 'conscience,** political ~er, ⇨ political(1). ~-**er of 'war,** person captured in war and (usu) kept in a camp for the duration of the war.

pris·tine /'prɪstiːn/ adj (formal) primitive; of early times; unchanged by later developments; fresh as if new: *Who would want to get back to the* ~ *simplicity of Anglo-Saxon days?*

prithee /'prɪðɪ/ int (archaic) I pray thee; please: *P~, keep silent. Tell me,* ~,....

priv·acy /'prɪvəsɪ US: 'praɪv-/ n [U] **1** state of being away from others, alone and undisturbed: *the invasion of* ~ *by the press and TV. I should hate to live in a household where* ~ *was impossible. I don't want my* ~ *disturbed.* **2** secrecy (opp to *publicity*): *They were married in strict* ~.

pri·vate /'praɪvɪt/ adj **1** (opp of *public*) of, for the use of, concerning, one person or group of persons, not people in general: *a* ~ *letter*, about personal matters; *for* ~ *reasons*, not to be explained to everybody. ~ '**enterprise,** the management of industry, etc by ~ individuals, companies, etc (contrasted with State ownership or control). ~ '**means,** income not earned as a salary, etc but coming from personal property, investments, etc. ~ '**school,** one at which fees are paid (contrasted with a school financially supported by the State, etc). **2** secret; kept secret; *a letter marked 'P~'*; *have* ~ *information about sth.* ~ **parts,** external sex organs. **3** having no official position; not holding any public office: *do sth in one's* ~ *capacity*, not as an official, etc; *his* ~ *life*, the life he leads away from business or public affairs. *retire into* ~ *life*, retire after a public career. ~ **member** (of the House of Commons), one who is not a member of the Government. **4** ~ **(soldier),** ordinary soldier without rank: *P~ Dodd.* □ n **1** ~ soldier. **2** *in* ~, ~ly, not in public, ~·**ly** adv

pri·va·teer /praɪvə'tɪə(r)/ n (formerly) armed vessel under private ownership, allowed to attack enemy shipping in time of war; commander or member of the crew of such a vessel.

pri·va·tion /praɪ'veɪʃn/ n **1** [U,C] lack of the necessaries of life; destitution: *fall ill through* ~; *suffering many* ~s. **2** [C] state of being deprived of sth (not necessarily sth essential): *He found it a great* ~ *not being allowed to smoke in prison.*

privet /'prɪvɪt/ n [U] evergreen shrub, bearing small white flowers, much used for garden hedges: *clipping the* ~ *hedges.*

pri·vi·lege /'prɪvəlɪdʒ/ n **1** [C] right or advantage available only to a person, class or rank, or the holder of a certain position, etc: *the* ~s *of birth*, eg

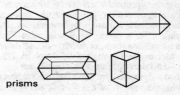

prisms

that come because one is born into a wealthy family. **2** [C] special favour or benefit: *grant sb the ~ of fishing in a privately owned trout stream. It was a ~ to hear her sing.* **3** [C,U] right to do or say things without risk of punishment, etc (as when Members of Parliament may say things in the House of Commons which might result in a libel case if said outside Parliament). **~d** /'prɪvəlɪdʒd/ *adj* having, granted, a ~ or ~s. **the ~d classes,** those who enjoy the advantages of the best education, of wealth, and secure social position. **,under-'~d,** suffering from poverty.

privy /'prɪvɪ/ *adj* **1** (old use, except legal) secret; private. **~ to,** having secret knowledge of: *charged with having been ~ to the plot against the prince.* **2 the P~ Council,** committee of persons appointed by the Sovereign, advising on some State affairs, but membership now being chiefly a personal dignity. **P~ Councillor/Counsellor,** member of the P~ Council. **P~ Purse,** allowance of money from the public revenue for the Sovereign's private expenses. **P~ Seal,** State seal affixed to documents of minor importance. □ *n* (*pl* -vies) (old use) water-closet. **priv·ily** /-ɪlɪ/ *adv* privately; secretly.

prize¹ /praɪz/ *n* **1** sth (to be) awarded to one who succeeds in a competition, lottery, etc: *be awarded a ~ for good conduct; draw a ~-winning ticket in a lottery; carry off most of the ~s at the village flower show; win first ~ on the pools; consolation ~s,* given to console those who do not win the good ~s; *~ cattle,* cattle that have been awarded ~s; *a ~ scholarship,* one awarded as a ~. **2** (fig) anything struggled for or worth struggling for: *the ~s of life.* **3** '**~-fight** *n* boxing match for money. Hence '**~-fighter,** '**~-fighting** *nn* '**~-ring** *n* the enclosed area (now usu a square) in which boxing-matches are fought; the sport of ~-fighting. **4** '**~-man** /-mən/ *n* (*pl* -men) winner of a ~ (usu with the name of the ~ or scholarship prefixed). □ *vt* value highly: *my most ~d possessions.*

prize² /praɪz/ *n* [C] sth, esp a ship or its cargo, captured at sea during a war. '**~-money** *n* money realized by the sale of a ~ (and divided up among those who captured it).

prize³ (also **prise**) /praɪz/ *vt* [VP15A,B] use force to get sth, eg a box, lid, *open/up/off.*

pro¹ /prəʊ/ *n* [C] (usu only in) **the ~s and cons** *(of sth),* the arguments for and against (sth). □ *adv* **pro and con,** for and against: *argue pro and con.*

pro² /prəʊ/ *n* (*pl* pros) (colloq) (short for) professional (player): *a golf pro.*

pro- /ˌprəʊ/ *pref* supporting; favouring: *pro-British;* acting for: *pro-consul; pro-vice-chancellor.* ⇨ App 3.

prob·abil·ity /ˌprɒbə'bɪlətɪ/ *n* (*pl* -ties) **1** [U] quality of being probable. **in all ~,** most probably. **2** [U] likelihood: *There is no/little/not much ~ of his succeeding/that he will succeed.* **3** [C] (most) probable event or outcome: *What are the probabilities?*

prob·able /'prɒbəbl/ *adj* likely to happen or to prove true or correct: *the ~ result; a ~ winner. Rain is possible but not ~ before evening. It seems ~ that....* □ *n* person who will most likely be chosen, eg for a team, or do sth; ~ candidate, winner, etc. **prob·ably** /-əblɪ/ *adv* most likely: *Jim's late—he's probably stuck in a traffic jam.*

pro·bate /'prəʊbeɪt/ *n* **1** [U] the official process of proving the validity of a will: *take out ~ of a will;*

grant ~ of a will. **2** [C] copy of a will with a certificate that it is correct. □ *vt* (US) establish the validity of a will (GB = *prove*).

pro·ba·tion /prə'beɪʃn US: prəʊ-/ *n* [U] **1** testing of a person's conduct, abilities, qualities, etc before he is finally accepted for a position, admitted into a society, etc: *two years on ~,* ie undergoing such testing; *an officer on ~.* **2 the ~ system,** (legal) that by which (esp young) offenders are allowed to go unpunished for their first offence while they continue to live without further breaking of the law: *three years' ~ under suspended sentence of one year's imprisonment.* '**~ officer,** one who watches over the behaviour of offenders who are on ~. **~·ary** /prə'beɪʃnrɪ US: prəʊ'beɪʃənerɪ/ *adj* relating to ~. **~er** *n* **1** hospital nurse receiving training and still on ~(1). **2** wrongdoer who has been released on ~(2).

probe /prəʊb/ *n* **1** slender instrument with a blunt end, used by doctors for learning about the depth and direction of a wound, etc. **2** (journalism) investigation (*into* a scandal, etc). □ *vt* [VP6A] **1** examine with a ~. **2** investigate or examine thoroughly (sb's thought, the causes of sth).

prob·ity /'prəʊbətɪ/ *n* [U] (formal) uprightness of character; integrity.

prob·lem /'prɒbləm/ *n* [C] question to be solved or decided, esp sth difficult: *mathematical ~s; the ~s of youth.* '**~ child,** one whose behaviour offers a difficult ~ to his parents, teachers, etc. ~ **pic·ture,** one in which the artist's intention is obscure. **~ play/novel,** one dealing with a social or moral ~. **~·atic** /ˌprɒblə'mætɪk/ *adj* (esp of a result) doubtful; that cannot be seen or foretold. **~·ati·cally** /-klɪ/ *adv*

pro·bos·cis /prə'bɒsɪs/ (*pl* ~es /-sɪsi:z/) *n* **1** elephant's trunk. **2** elongated part of the mouth of some insects.

pro·cedure /prə'si:dʒə(r)/ *n* [C,U] (the regular) order of doing things, esp legal and political: *the usual ~ at committee meetings; stop arguing about (questions of) ~ and get down to business.* **pro·cedural** /prə'si:dʒərəl/ *adj* of ~.

pro·ceed /prə'si:d/ *vi* **1** [VP2A,3A,4C] **~ to sth/to do sth,** go forward; go on: *Let us ~ to business/to the next item on the agenda. He ~ed to inform me that.... They ~ed* (more usu *went*) *from London to Leeds.* **~ with sth,** start or continue with it: *Please ~ with your explanation.* **2** [VP3A] **~ from sth,** come, arise from: *famine, plague and other evils that ~ from war.* **3** [VP3A] **~ against sb,** take legal action. **4** [VP3A] **~ to sth,** go on from a lower university degree: *~ to the degree of MA.*

pro·ceed·ing /prə'si:dɪŋ/ *n* **1** [U] course of action; (way of) behaving: *What is our best way of ~?* **2** [C] sth done; piece of conduct: *What he did was a rather high-handed ~. The ~s at the meeting were rather disorderly. There have been suspicious ~s in committee meetings.* **3** (*pl*) **take/start legal ~s (against sb),** take legal action. **4** (*pl*) records (of the activities of a society, etc); minutes: *the ~s of the Kent Archaeological Society.*

pro·ceeds /'prəʊsi:dz/ *n pl* financial results, profits, of an undertaking: *hold a bazaar and give the ~ to local charities.*

pro·cess¹ /'prəʊses US: 'prɒses/ *n* **1** [C] connected series of actions, changes, etc esp such as are involuntary or unconscious: *the ~es of digestion, reproduction and growth.* **2** [C] series of operations deliberately undertaken: *Unloading the cargo was* *a slow* ~. **3** [C] method, esp one used in manufacture or industry: *the 'Bessemer* ~, in steel manufacture. **4** [U] forward movement; progress: *The glasses were broken during the* ~ *of removal. in* ~ *of,* during: *a building in* ~ *of construction; in* ~ *of time,* as time goes on. *in* ~, in course of being done. **5** [C] (legal) action at law; formal commencement of this; summons or writ ordering a person to appear in a law court. '~-**server** *n* sheriff's officer who delivers writs. □ *vt* [VP6A] treat (material) in order to preserve it: ~ *leather;* put (esp food) through a special ~(**3**): ~*ed cheese;* (photo) ~ *film,* develop it, etc; (computers) ~ *tape/information,* put it through the system in order to obtain the required information.

pro·cess² /prə'ses/ *vi* walk in or as if in procession.

pro·ces·sion /prə'seʃn/ *n* [C] number of persons, vehicles, etc moving forward and following each other in an orderly way: *a 'funeral* ~; [U] act of moving forward in this way: *walking in* ~ *through the streets.*~**al** /-ʃənl/ *adj* of, for, used in, ~s: *a* ~*al chant,* sung by persons taking part in a religious ~.

pro·claim /prə'kleɪm/ *vt* [VP6A,9,23,25] **1** make known publicly or officially: ~ (= declare) *war/ peace;* ~ *a public holiday;* ~ *a republic;* ~ *a man* (*to be*) *a traitor/*~ *that he is a traitor. He* ~*ed Anne his heir.* **2** reveal, show: *His accent* ~*ed him a Scot/that he was a Scot.* **proc·la·ma·tion** /ˌprɒklə'meɪʃn/ *n* [U] act of ~ing: *by public proclamation;* [C] that which is ~ed: *issue/make a proclamation.*

pro·cliv·ity /prə'klɪvətɪ/ *n* (*pl* -ties) [C] ~ (*to/ towards sth/to do sth*), (formal) tendency, inclination.

pro·con·sul /ˌprəʊ'kɒnsl/ *n* (in ancient Rome) governor of a Roman province; (rhet, mod use) governor of a colony or dominion. **pro·con·su·lar** /ˌprəʊ'kɒnsjʊlə(r) *US:* -səl-/ *adj* **pro·con·su·late** /-lət/ *n* position of a ~; his term of office.

pro·cras·ti·nate /prəʊ'kræstɪneɪt/ *vi* [VP2A] (formal) delay action; keep on putting off: *He* ~*d until it was too late.* **pro·cras·ti·na·tion** /prəʊˌkræstɪ'neɪʃn/ *n* [U]: *Procrastination is the thief of time,* (prov) procrastinating wastes time.

pro·create /'prəʊkrɪeɪt/ *vt* [VP6A] beget, generate (offspring). **pro·cre·ation** /ˌprəʊkrɪ'eɪʃn/ *n*

proc·tor /'prɒktə(r)/ *n* **1** (at Oxford and Cambridge) university official with various duties, including the maintenance of discipline among students. **2 Queen's/King's P**~, official whose duty is to watch the parties in certain kinds of legal cases, eg divorce, and to intervene if there are irregularities, eg collusion or suppression of facts.

procu·ra·tor /'prɒkjʊreɪtə(r)/ *n* **1** agent, esp one who has a power of attorney. **2** ~ **fiscal,** public prosecutor of a district in Scotland.

pro·cure /prə'kjʊə(r)/ *vt* [VP6A,12B,13B] **1** obtain, esp with care or effort: *Can you* ~ *me some specimens? The book is out of print and difficult to* ~. **2** (old use) bring about; cause: ~ *sb's death by poison.* **3** obtain clients for a prostitute. **pro·cur·able** /-əbl/ *adj* obtainable. ~-**ment** *n* procuring: *the* ~*ment of military supplies.* ~**r** *n* (esp) pander. **pro·cur·ess** /-rɪs/ *n* woman ~r.

prod /prɒd/ *vt,vi* (-dd-) [VP6A,3A] ~ (*at*), push or poke with sth pointed; (fig) urge (to action): *The cruel boys were* ~*ding* (*at*) *the bear·through the bars of the cage.* □ *n* poke or thrust: *She gave the man a* ~ *with her umbrella.*

prodi·gal /'prɒdɪgl/ *adj* ~ (*of*), wasteful; spending or using too much: *a* ~ *administration,* spending public funds too freely. *Nature is* ~ *of her gifts.* **the** ~ **son,** wasteful and improvident man (in one of the parables of Jesus) who repents of his actions. ⇨ Luke 15:11. □ *n* [C] person who is wasteful. ~-**ly** /-gəlɪ/ *adv* in a ~ manner: *a man who gives* ~*ly to charities.* ~-**ity** /ˌprɒdɪ'gælətɪ/ *n* [U] (in a good sense) being ~: *the* ~*ity of the sea,* ie in supplying fish; (in a bad sense) extravagance; wasteful spending.

pro·di·gious /prə'dɪdʒəs/ *adj* enormous; surprisingly great; wonderful: *a* ~ *sum of money.* ~-**ly** *adv*

prod·igy /'prɒdɪdʒɪ/ *n* (*pl* -gies) sth wonderful because it seems to be contrary to the laws of nature; person who has unusual or remarkable abilities or who is a remarkable example of sth: *a* ~ *of learning; prodigies of nature.* **infant** ~, extremely talented child, eg one who plays the piano well at six.

pro·duce /prə'dju:s *US:* -'du:s/ *vt,vi* [VP6A,2A] **1** put or bring forward to be looked at or examined: ~ *proofs of a statement;* ~ *one's railway ticket when asked to do so. The conjuror* ~*d a rabbit from his hat.* **2** manufacture; make; grow; create: ~ *woollen goods; fields which* ~ *heavy crops. We must* ~ *more food for ourselves and import less. This artist* ~*s very little.* **3** give birth to; lay (eggs). **4** cause; bring about: *success* ~*d by hard work and enthusiasm; a film that* ~*d a sensation.* **5** (maths) make (a line) longer (*to* a point). **6** bring before the public: ~ *a new play,* organize it and put it on the stage; *a well-*~*d book,* one that is well printed, bound, etc. □ *n* /'prɒdju:s *US:* -du:s/ [U] that which is ~d, esp by farming: *garden/farm/ agricultural* ~.

pro·ducer /prə'dju:sə(r) *US:* -'du:-/ *n* **1** person who produces goods (contrasted with the *consumer*). **2** person responsible for presenting a play in the theatre or for the production of a film (apart from the directing of the actors); person in charge of a broadcast programme (radio or TV). ⇨ **director. 3** '~ **gas,** gas obtained by passing air through red-hot carbon or air and steam through hot coal or coke.

prod·uct /'prɒdʌkt/ *n* [C] **1** sth produced (by nature or by man): '*farm* ~*s; the chief* ~*s of Scotland; the* ~*s of genius,* eg great works of art. **2** (maths) quantity obtained by multiplication; (chem) substance obtained by chemical reaction.

pro·duc·tion /prə'dʌkʃn/ *n* **1** [U] process of producing: *the* ~ *of crops/manufactured goods, etc.* **mass** ~, ⇨ **mass. 2** [U] quantity produced: *increase* ~ *by using better methods and tools; a fall/increase in* ~. **3** [C] thing produced: *epic* ~*s at the cinema; his early* ~*s as a writer,* his first novels, plays, etc.

pro·duc·tive /prə'dʌktɪv/ *adj* **1** able to produce; fertile: ~ *land.* **2** ~ *of,* tending to produce; resulting in: ~ *of happiness; discussions that seem to be* ~ *only of quarrels.* **3** producing things of economic value: ~ *labour.* ~-**ly** *adv*

pro·duc·tiv·ity /ˌprɒdʌk'tɪvətɪ/ *n* [U] being productive; power of being productive: *increase* ~, increase efficiency and the rate at which goods are produced; *a* ~ *bonus for workers.* '~ **agreement,** (as part of a wage settlement) better pay and conditions for an increased output.

pro·fane /prə'feɪn *US:* prəʊ-/ *adj* **1** (contrasted

with *sacred, holy*) worldly: ∼ *literature*, (opp *biblical*). **2** having or showing contempt for God and sacred things: ∼ *language/words/practices; a ∼ man.* □ *vt* [VP6A] treat (sacred or holy places, things) with contempt, without proper reverence: ∼ *the name of God.* ∼·ly *adv*∼·ness *n* **profa·na·tion** /ˌprɒfəˈneɪʃn/ *n* [C,U] instance of profaning.

pro·fan·ity /prəˈfænətɪ *US:* prəʊ-/ *n* (*pl* -ties) **1** [U] ∼ conduct or speech; use of ∼ language. **2** (*pl*) ∼ phrases, utterances: *A string of profanities came from his lips.*

pro·fess /prəˈfes/ *vt,vi* **1** [VP6A] declare that one has (beliefs, likes, ignorance, interests, etc): *He ∼es a distaste for modern music. He ∼ed a great interest in my welfare.* **2** [VP6A] affirm one's faith in, allegiance to, (a religion, Christ): ∼ *Islam.* **3** [VP6A] (formal) have as one's profession or business: ∼ *law/medicine;* teach as a professor: ∼ *history/modern languages.* **4** [VP6A,7A,9,25] claim; represent oneself: *I don't ∼ to be an expert on that subject. He ∼ed himself satisfied. She ∼ed that she could do nothing unaided.* ∼ed *adj* **1** self-acknowledged; *a ∼ed atheist.* **2** falsely claiming to be: *a ∼ed friend.* **3** having taken religious vows: *a ∼ed nun.* ∼·ed·ly /-ɪdlɪ/ *adv* according to one's own claims or admissions: *He is ∼edly a Communist.*

pro·fes·sion /prəˈfeʃn/ *n* [C] **1** occupation, esp one requiring advanced education and special training, eg the law, architecture, medicine, accountancy: *He is a lawyer by ∼.* **2** ∼ *of,* statement or declaration of belief, feeling, etc: ∼*s of faith/loyalty. She does not believe in his ∼s of passionate love.* **3** **the ∼**, the body of persons engaged in a particular ∼(1).

pro·fes·sional /prəˈfeʃnəl/ *adj* **1** of a profession(1): ∼ *skill;* ∼ *etiquette,* the special conventions, forms of politeness, etc associated with a certain profession; ∼ *men,* eg doctors, lawyers. **2** doing or practising sth as a full-time occupation or for payment or to make a living (opp of *amateur*): ∼ *football;* ∼ *tennis-players; a ∼ politician.* □ *n* (contrasted with *amateur*) **1** (often abbr to *pro* /prəʊ/) person who teaches or engages in some kind of sport for money. **2** person who does sth for payment that others do (without payment) for pleasure: ∼ *musicians.* **turn ∼,** become a ∼. ∼·ly /-nəlɪ/ *adv* in a ∼ manner or capacity. ∼·ism /-əlɪzəm/ *n* **1** mark or qualities of a profession(1). **2** the practice of employing ∼s to play games.

pro·fes·sor /prəˈfesə(r)/ *n* **1** university teacher of the highest grade, holding a chair of some branch of learning; (in US, also) teacher or instructor. **2** title assumed by instructors of various subjects: *P∼ Pate, the renowned phrenologist.* **3** one who makes a public profession(2): *a ∼ of pacifism/ Catholicism.* **prof·es·sorial** /ˌprɒfɪˈsɔːrɪəl/ *adj* relating to a ∼: *his ∼ial duties.* ∼·ship /-ʃɪp/ *n* ∼'s post at a university: *be appointed to a ∼ship.*

prof·fer /ˈprɒfə(r)/ *vt* [VP6A,7] offer. □ *n* offer.

pro·fi·cient /prəˈfɪʃnt/ *adj* ∼ (*in*), skilled; expert. ∼·ly *adv* **pro·fi·ciency** /-nsɪ/ *n* **proficiency (in),** [U] being ∼: *a certificate of proficiency in English.*

pro·file /ˈprəʊfaɪl/ *n* **1** [U,C] side view, esp of the head: *a portrait drawn in ∼.* **2** edge or outline of sth seen against a background. **3** brief biography, as given in an article in a periodical or a broadcast talk. □ *vt* draw, show, in ∼: *a line of hills ∼d against the night sky.*

profit[1] /ˈprɒfɪt/ *n* **1** [U] advantage or good obtained

from sth: *gain ∼ from one's studies; study sth to one's ∼.* **2** [C,U] money gained in business, etc: *make a ∼ of ten pence on every article sold; sell sth at a ∼; do sth for ∼.* ↗ *and* '**loss account,** (book-keeping) one that shows the trading ∼ or loss for a definite period. '∼-**margin** *n* difference between cost of purchase or production and selling price. '∼-**sharing** *n* [U] the sharing of ∼s between employers and employees: *start a ∼-sharing scheme.* ∼·**less** *adj*∼·**less·ly** *adv*

profit[2] /ˈprɒfɪt/ *vt,vi* **1** [VP3A] ∼ *from/by,* (of persons) be benefited or helped: *Have you ∼ed by the experience? I have ∼ed from your advice.* **2** [VP6A,13A] (old use) (of things) be of advantage to: *What can it ∼ him? It ∼ed him nothing.*

prof·it·able /ˈprɒfɪtəbl/ *adj* bringing profit; beneficial: ∼ *investments; a deal that was ∼ to all of us.* **prof·it·ably** /-əblɪ/ *adv*

profi·teer /ˌprɒfɪˈtɪə(r)/ *vi* [VP2A] make large profits, esp by taking advantage of times of difficulty or scarcity, eg in war. □ *n* person who does this.

prof·li·gate /ˈprɒflɪgət/ *adj* **1** (of a person, his behaviour) shamelessly immoral. **2** (of the spending of money) reckless; very extravagant: ∼ *inheritance.* □ *n* ∼(1) person. **prof·li·gacy** /ˈprɒflɪgəsɪ/ *n* [U] being ∼.

pro forma /ˌprəʊ ˈfɔːmə/ *adj, adv* (Lat) as a formality only. ∼ **invoice,** one that notifies the value of goods dispatched but does not ask for payment.

pro·found /prəˈfaʊnd/ *adj* **1** deep: *a ∼ sleep/ sigh/bow; take a ∼ interest in sth; listen with ∼ interest.* **2** needing, showing, having, great knowledge: ∼ *books/authors/thinkers; a man of ∼ learning.* **3** needing much thought or study to understand: ∼ *mysteries.* ∼·ly *adv* in a ∼ manner: ∼*ly* (= deeply) *grateful/disturbing.* **pro·fun·dity** /prəˈfʌndətɪ/ *n* (*pl* -ties) [U] depth: *the profundity of his knowledge;* [C] (chiefly in non-material senses) that which is deep or abstruse; (*pl*) depths of thought or meaning.

pro·fuse /prəˈfjuːs/ *adj* **1** very plentiful or abundant: ∼ *gratitude.* **2** ∼ *in,* lavish or extravagant: *He was ∼ in his apologies,* apologized almost to excess. ∼·ly *adv*∼·ness *n* **pro·fu·sion** /prəˈfjuːʒn/ *n* [U] abundance; great supply: *roses growing in profusion; make promises in profusion.*

pro·geni·tor /prəʊˈdʒenɪtə(r)/ *n* (formal) ancestor (of a person, animal or plant); (fig) political or intellectual predecessor.

progeny /ˈprɒdʒənɪ/ *n* (formal) (collective *sing*) offspring; descendants, children.

prog·no·sis /prɒgˈnəʊsɪs/ *n* (*pl* -noses /-nəʊsiːz/) (med) forecast of the probable course of a disease or illness. ⇨ **diagnosis.**

prog·nos·tic /prɒgˈnɒstɪk/ *adj* (formal) predictive (*of*). □ *n* pre-indication (*of*): *a ∼ of failure.*

prog·nos·ti·cate /prɒgˈnɒstɪkeɪt/ *vt* [VP6A,9] (formal) foretell; predict: ∼ *trouble.* **prog·nos·ti·ca·tion** /prɒgˌnɒstɪˈkeɪʃn/ *n* [U] prognosticating; [C] sth which ∼s.

pro·gramme (also **-gram**) /ˈprəʊgræm/ *n* **1** list of items, events, etc, eg for a concert, or to be broadcast for radio or TV, or for a sports meeting; list of names of actors in a play, singers in an opera, etc. '∼ **music,** music designed, in sound, to suggest to the listener a known story, picture, etc. '∼ **note,** short account, in a ∼, eg of a musical work, a performer, etc. **2** plan of what is to be done: *a political ∼. What's the ∼ for tomorrow?* What are we/you going to do? **3** coded collection of information, data, etc fed into an electronic computer. □ *vt* [VP6A] make a ∼ of or for; supply (a computer) with a ∼; plan. **∼d course,** (education) one in which the material to be learnt is presented (in books or a machine) in small, carefully graded amounts. **∼d learning,** self-instruction using such courses. **pro·gram·mer** *n* person who prepares a computer ∼.

prog·ress /'prəʊgres *US:* 'prɒg-/ *n* **1** [U] forward movement; advance; development: *making fast ∼; make ∼ in one's studies; ∼ in civilization. An inquiry is now in ∼,* being made. *The patient is making good ∼,* is improving. **2** [C] (old use) state journey: *a royal ∼ through Cornwall.* □ *vi* /prə'gres/ [VP2A,C] make ∼: *The work is ∼ing steadily. She is ∼ing in her studies.*

pro·gres·sion /prə'greʃn/ *n* **1** [U] progress; moving forward: *modes of ∼,* eg crawling, walking. **2** (maths) ⇨ arithmetic, geometry.

pro·gress·ive /prə'gresɪv/ *adj* **1** making continuous forward movement. **the ∼ tenses,** (gram) forms of the verb (using the ending *-ing*) that express action that continues over a period of time, as in 'I am/was/will be/have been writing.' (Also called *continuous tenses.*) **2** increasing by regular degrees or advancing in successive stages: *∼ education/ schools; ∼ taxation,* with an increase of the rate of tax as the incomes increase; *∼ cancer,* becoming steadily worse. **3** undergoing improvement; getting better, eg in civilization; supporting or favouring progress: *a ∼ policy; a ∼ political party.* □ *n* person supporting a ∼ policy. **∼·ly** *adv* **∼·ness** *n*

pro·hibit /prə'hɪbɪt *US:* prəʊ-/ *vt* [VP6A,14] ∼ *sb (from doing sth),* forbid (esp by rules or regulations); say that sth must not be done, that sb must not do sth: *Smoking strictly ∼ed. Children are ∼ed from buying cigarettes.*

pro·hib·ition /ˌprəʊɪ'bɪʃn/ *n* **1** [U] prohibiting; (esp) prohibiting by law the making or sale of alcoholic drinks (esp, US, the period 1920—33): *the ∼ law(s); in favour of/opposed to ∼.* **2** [C] edict or order that forbids: *a ∼ against the sale of cigarettes to children.* **∼·ist** /-ɪst/ *n* person who favours the ∼ of sth, esp the sale of alcoholic drink.

pro·hibi·tive /prə'hɪbətɪv *US:* prəʊ-/ *adj* tending to, intended to, prevent the use or abuse or purchase of sth: *a ∼ tax; books published at ∼ prices.*

pro·hibi·tory /prə'hɪbɪtərɪ *US:* prəʊ'hɪbɪtɔːrɪ/ *adj* designed to prohibit sth: *∼ laws.*

pro·ject¹ /'prɒdʒekt/ *n* [C] (plan for a) scheme or undertaking: *a ∼ to establish a new national park; form/carry out/fail in a ∼.*

pro·ject² /prə'dʒekt/ *vt,vi* **1** [VP6A] make plans for: *∼ a new dam/waterworks.* **2** [VP6A,14] ∼ *sth (on (to) sth),* cause a shadow, an outline, a picture from a film, slide, etc to fall on a surface, etc: *∼ a picture on a screen; ∼ a beam of light on to sth.* **3** [VP14] ∼ *sth on to sb,* attribute unconsciously (usu unpleasant feelings such as guilt, inferiority) to other people (often as a means of self-justification or self-defence): *She always ∼s her own neuroses on to her colleagues,* describes them as suffering from them. **4** [VP6A] make known the characteristics of: *Do the BBC External Services adequately ∼ Great Britain,* give listeners right ideas about British life, etc? **5** [VP6A,15A] throw; hurl: *an apparatus to ∼ missiles into space.* **6** [VP6A] represent (a solid thing) on a plane surface by drawing straight lines through every point of it from a centre; make (a map) in this way. **7**

[VP2A,C] stick out; stand out beyond the surface nearby: *∼ing eyebrows; a balcony that ∼s over the street.*

pro·jec·tile /prə'dʒektaɪl *US:* -tl/ *n* sth (to be) shot forward, esp from a gun; self-propelling missile, eg a rocket. □ *adj* able to send sth, or be sent, forward through air, water, etc: *a ∼ missile/torpedo.*

pro·jec·tion /prə'dʒekʃn/ *n* [U] the act of projecting (all senses); [C] sth that projects or has been projected; prominence. '∼ **room,** (in a cinema) room from which pictures are projected on to the screen. ⇨ Mercator's projection. **∼·ist** /-ɪst/ *n* (in a cinema) person who projects the pictures on to the screen.

pro·jec·tor /prə'dʒektə(r)/ *n* [C] apparatus for projecting pictures by rays of light on to a screen: *a 'cinema/'slide ∼.*

pro·lapse /prəʊ'læps/ *vi* (med, eg of the bowel or uterus) slip forward or down out of place. □ *n* /'prəʊlæps/ such a movement.

prole /prəʊl/ *n* (colloq) member of the proletariat.

pro·let·ariat /ˌprəʊlɪ'teərɪət/ *n* **1** the whole body of wage-earners (esp manual workers) contrasted with the owners of industry (the bourgeoisie): *the dictatorship of the ∼,* as a Communist aim or ideal. **2** (in ancient Rome) the lowest class of the community. **pro·let·arian** /-ən/ *n, adj* (member) of the ∼.

pro·lif·er·ate /prə'lɪfəreɪt *US:* prəʊ-/ *vi,vt* **1** [VP2A] grow, reproduce, by rapid multiplication of cells, new parts, etc. **2** [VP6A] reproduce (cells, etc). **pro·lif·er·ation** /prəˌlɪfə'reɪʃn *US:* prəʊ-/ *n.* **non-proliferation treaty,** eg one for controlling the spread of nuclear weapons to States not having them.

pro·lific /prə'lɪfɪk/ *adj* (formal) producing much or many: *a ∼ author,* one who writes many books, etc; *as ∼ as rabbits,* producing numerous offspring.

pro·lix /'prəʊlɪks *US:* prəʊ'lɪks/ *adj* (formal) (of a speaker, writer, speech, etc) tedious; tiring because too long. **pro·lix·ity** /prəʊ'lɪksətɪ/ *n.*

pro·logue /'prəʊlɒg *US:* -lɔːg/ *n* **1** introductory part of a poem; poem recited at the beginning of a play: *the 'P∼' to the 'Canterbury Tales'.* **2** (fig) first of a series of events.

pro·long /prə'lɒŋ *US:* -'lɔːŋ/ *vt* [VP6A] make longer: *∼ a visit/a line.* **∼ed** *adj* continuing for a long time: *after ∼ed questioning.* **pro·lon·ga·tion** /ˌprəʊlɒŋ'geɪʃn *US:* -lɔːŋ-/ *n* [U] making longer; the state of being made longer; [C] that which is added in order to ∼.

prom /prɒm/ *n* (colloq abbr of) **1** (GB) seaside promenade; promenade concert. **2** (US) promenade(2).

prom·en·ade /ˌprɒmə'nɑːd *US:* -'neɪd/ *n* **1** (place suitable for, specially made for, a) walk or ride taken in public, for exercise or pleasure, esp a broad road along the water-front at a seaside resort, or a part of a theatre where people may walk about during the intervals, etc. '∼ **concert,** one at which parts of the concert hall have no seats and are used by listeners who stand. '∼ **deck,** upper deck of a liner, where passengers may walk. **2** (US) formal dance or ball (for a class in a high-school or college). □ *vi,vt* [VP2A,C] go up and down a ∼; [VP6A,15A] take (sb) up and down a ∼: *∼ one's children/one's husband along the sea-front.*

promi·nent /'prɒmɪnənt/ *adj* **1** standing out; easily seen: *∼ cheek-bones; the most ∼ feature in the*

map projection

Lines of Latitude run in the same direction as the equator

Lines of Longitude run from Pole to Pole

CONICAL PROJECTION

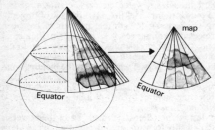

map

Equator

Equator

MERCATOR'S PROJECTION

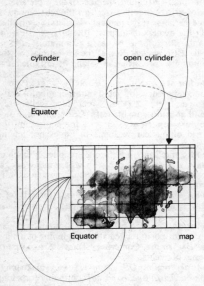

cylinder

open cylinder

Equator

Equator   map

ZENITHAL PROJECTION

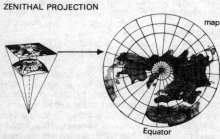

map

Equator

landscape. **2** (of persons) distinguished; eminent: ~ *politicians/scientists.* **3** important; conspicuous: *occupy a ~ position; play a ~ part in civic life.* ~·ly *adv* **promi·nence** /-əns/ *n* **1** [U] the state of being ~. **bring sth/come into prominence,** (cause to) become ~. **2** [C] ~ part or place: *a ~ in the middle of a plain.*

pro·mis·cu·ous /prə'mɪskjʊəs/ *adj* **1** confused and disorderly; unsorted: *in a ~ heap.* **2** indiscriminate; casual: ~ *friendships,* made without careful choice; ~ *sexual intercourse.* ~·ly *adv* **prom·is·cu·ity** /ˌprɒmɪ'skjuːətɪ/ *n* (state of) being ~; confusion caused by being ~.

prom·ise¹ /'prɒmɪs/ *n* **1** [C] written or spoken undertaking to do, or not to do, sth: ~*s of help; make/give/keep/carry out/break a ~; under a ~ of secrecy.* **2** [C] that which one undertakes to do: *I claim your ~,* require you to do what you said you would do. **3** [U] (sth that gives) hope of success or good results: *boys who don't show much ~,* do not seem likely to succeed: *a writer of ~; the land of ~.*

prom·ise² /'prɒmɪs/ *vt,vi* **1** [VP6A,7A,9,11,12A,13A,17] make a promise(1) to: *They ~d an immediate reply. He ~d (me) to be here/that he would be here at 6 o'clock. I ~d myself a quiet weekend. 'Will you come?'—'Yes, I ~'.* **the P~d Land,** the land of promise: **(a)** the fertile country ~d to the Israelites by God; Canaan: **(b)** any state of future happiness. **2** [VP6A,2A] give cause for expecting: *The clouds ~ rain. It ~s to be warm this afternoon.* ~ **well,** show signs of success. **prom·is·ing** *adj* full of promise(3); seeming likely to succeed, have good results, etc.

prom·iss·ory /'prɒmɪsərɪ US: -sɔːrɪ/ *adj* conveying a promise. '~ **note,** signed promise to pay a stated sum of money to a specified person or to the bearer on a specified date or on demand.

prom·on·tory /'prɒməntrɪ US: -tɔːrɪ/ *n* [C] headland; high point of land standing out from the coastline.

pro·mote /prə'məʊt/ *vt* **1** [VP6A,14] ~ **(to),** give (sb) a higher position or rank: *He was ~d sergeant/to sergeant/to the rank of sergeant.* **2** [VP6A] help to organize and start; help the progress of; help to found or organize: ~ *a new business company;* ~ *a bill in Parliament; try to ~ good feelings (between...).* **pro·mo·ter** *n* (esp) person who ~s new trading companies, professional sports, etc.

pro·mo·tion /prə'məʊʃn/ *n* **1** [U] promoting or being promoted: *win/gain ~. Ought ~ to go by seniority or by merit and abilities?* **2** [C] instance of promoting or being promoted: *He resigned from the firm because ~s were few and far between.* **3** encouragement by publicity, etc: *the ~ of a new commercial product/a new book; sales ~,* advertising, publicising one's products.

prompt¹ /prɒmpt/ *adj* acting, done, sent, given, without delay: *a ~ reply;* ~ *payment; men who are ~ to volunteer; at 6pm ~ (= ~ly).* ~·ly *adv* ~·ness *n*

prompt² /prɒmpt/ *vt* **1** [VP6A,17A] be the reason causing (sb to do sth): *He was ~ed by patriotism. What ~ed him to be so generous?* **2** [VP6A] follow the text of a play and, when an actor forgets his words, say quietly some of these to him. □ *n* action of ~ing (an actor): *wait for a ~.* '~-**box** *n* place where the ~er sits. '~-**copy** *n* text of a play, used by a ~er. ~**er** *n* person who ~s actors.

promp·ti·tude /'prɒmptɪtjuːd US: -tuːd/ *n* [U] promptness; readiness to act.

prom·ul·gate /'prɒmʌlgeɪt/ *vt* [VP6A] **1** make public, announce officially (a decree, a new law, etc). **2** spread widely beliefs, knowledge, opinions, etc. **prom·ul·ga·tion** /ˌprɒmʌl'geɪʃn/ *n* [U].

prone /prəʊn/ *adj* **1** (stretched out, lying) face

downwards; prostrate: *in a ~ position; fall ~.* **2 ~ to,** liable, inclined: *~ to accidents/error/anger/ idleness/superstition* (and other generally undesirable things). **'accident-~** *adj* often experiencing accidents: *Some people seem to be accident ~.* **~-ness** *n*

prong /prɒŋ *US:* prɔːŋ/ *n* each one of the long, pointed parts of a fork. **~ed** *adj* (in compounds) having the kind or number of *~s* indicated: *a ,three-~ed 'fork; a ,three-~ed at'tack,* (mil) one made by three attacking forces.

pro·nomi·nal /prəʊ'nɒmɪnl/ *adj* of (the nature of) a pronoun.

pro·noun /'prəʊnaʊn/ *n* word used in place of a *n* or *n phrase,* eg *he, it, hers, me, them.*

pro·nounce /prə'naʊns/ *vt, vi* **1** [VP6A,9,22,25] declare, announce (esp formally, solemnly or officially): *The doctors ~d him to be/~d that he was out of danger. Has judgement been ~d yet?* **2** [VP9,25] declare as one's opinion: *The wine was tasted and ~d excellent. He ~d himself in favour of the plan.* **3** [VP3A] *~ for/against sb,* (legal) pass judgement (in a law court). *~ on/upon,* give one's opinion on, eg a proposal. **4** [VP6A,2A] utter, make the sound of (a word, etc): *He ~s badly. How do you ~ p-h-l-e-g-m? The 'b' in 'debt' is not ~d.* **~·able** /-əbl/ *adj* (of sounds, words) that can be *~d.* *~d* *adj* definite; strongly marked: *a man of ~d opinions.* **~·ment** *n* [C] formal statement or declaration.

pronto /'prɒntəʊ/ *adv* (sl) quickly; at once.

pro·nun·cia·mento /prə,nʌnsɪə'mentəʊ/ *n* (*pl* ~s /-təʊz/) manifesto or proclamation.

pro·nun·ci·ation /prə,nʌnsɪ'eɪʃn/ *n* **1** [U] way in which a language is spoken: *lessons in ~; study the ~ of English.* **2** [U] person's way of speaking a language, or words of a language: *His ~ is improving.* **3** [C] way in which a word is pronounced: *Which of these three ~s do you recommend?*

proof¹ /pruːf/ *n* **1** [U] evidence (in general), or [C] a particular piece of evidence, that is sufficient to show, or helps to show, that sth is a fact: *We shall require ~(s) of that statement. Is there any ~ that the accused man was at the scene of the crime? They gave him a gold watch as (a) ~ of their regard. Can you give ~ of your nationality/~ that you are British?* **2** [U] demonstrating; testing of whether sth is true, a fact, etc: *Is life on the planet Mars capable of ~? He produced documents in ~ of his claim.* **3** [C] test, trial, examination: *put sth to the ~,* test it. *It has stood the ~,* has passed the test. *The ~ of the pudding is in the eating,* (prov) The real test is practical, not theoretical. **4** [C] trial copy of sth printed or engraved, for approval before other copies are printed: *pass the ~s for press,* approve them, agree that printing may be begun. **'~-read** *vi, vt* [VP2A,6A] read and correct *~s.* **'~-reader** *n* person employed to read and correct *~s.* **5** [U] standard of strength of distilled alcoholic liquors: *This rum is 30 per cent below ~.* *~ spirit,* alcoholic mixture which is up to standard.

proof² /pruːf/ *adj ~ (against),* giving safety or protection; able to resist or withstand: *~ against bullets;* '*bullet-~;* '*water~;* '*sound~;* '*splinter-~;* '*shatter-~;* (fig) *~ against temptation.* **'fool-~** *adj* incapable of failure; involving no risk. □ *vt* [VP6A] make (sth) *~* (esp make a fabric water*~*).

prop¹ /prɒp/ *n* **1** support used to keep sth up: '*pit-~s,* supporting the roof in a coalmine; *a 'clothes-*

~, holding up a line on which laundered clothes are drying. **2** person who supports sth or sb: *He is the ~ of his parents in their old age* □ *vt* (-pp-) [VP6A,15A,B,22] *~ sth (up),* support; keep in position: *Use this box to ~ the door open. The nurse ~ped her patient (up) on the pillows. I ~ped the ladder against the wall.* (fig) *He can't always expect his colleagues to ~ him up.*

prop² /prɒp/ *n* (colloq abbr of) propeller. ⇨ turboprop.

prop³ /prɒp/ *n* (colloq abbr of) (stage) property: *Who's in charge of the ~s?* ⇨ property(5).

propa·ganda /,prɒpə'gændə/ *n* [U] information; (derog) doctrines, opinions, official statements: *~ by government departments for public health, better driving, etc; political ~;* (attrib) *~ plays/films.* **the Congregation/College of the P~,** a committee of RC cardinals in charge of foreign missions. **propa·gan·dist** /-dɪst/ *n* person who spreads *~.* **propa·gan·dize** /-daɪz/ *vi* spread *~.*

propa·gate /'prɒpəgeɪt/ *vt, vi* (formal) **1** [VP6A] increase the number of (plants, animals, diseases) by natural process from the parent stock: *~ plants by taking cuttings. Trees ~ themselves by seeds.* **2** [VP6A] spread more widely: *~ news/knowledge.* **3** [VP6A] transmit; extend the operation of: *vibrations ~d through rock.* **4** [VP2A] (of animals and plants) reproduce; multiply. **propa·ga·tor** /-tə(r)/ *n* **propa·ga·tion** /,prɒpə'geɪʃn/ *n* [U] propagating: *the propagation of disease by insects/of plants by cuttings.*

pro·pane /'prəʊpeɪn/ *n* [U] colourless gas (C_3H_8) (in natural gas and petroleum) used as a fuel.

pro·pel /prə'pel/ *vt* (-ll-) [VP6A,15A] drive forward: *mechanically ~led vehicles; a boat ~led by oars; a ~ling pencil,* with lead that is ~led forward as the outer case is turned. **~·lant, ~·lent** /-ənt/ *adj, n ~ling* (agent); explosive substance that ~s a bullet from a firearm; fuel that burns to ~ a rocket, etc. **~·ler** *n* two or more spiral blades, fixed to a revolving shaft, for driving a ship or aircraft. ⇨ *air-screw* and the illus at air¹.

pro·pen·sity /prə'pensətɪ/ *n* [C] (*pl* -ties) *~ to/ towards sth/to do sth/for doing sth,* natural tendency: *a ~ to exaggerate; a ~ for getting into debt.*

proper /'prɒpə(r)/ *adj* **1** right, correct, fitting, suitable: *clothes ~ for such an occasion; not a ~ time for merrymaking. Are you doing it the ~ way? Is this the ~ tool for the job? We must do the ~ thing by him,* treat him in the right way, be fair or loyal to him. **2** in conformity with, paying regard to, the conventions of society; respectable: *~ behaviour. He's not at all a ~ person for a young girl to know. That's not a ~ thing to do in the public park.* **3** *~ to,* (formal) belonging especially; relating distinctively: *the books ~ to this subject; the psalms ~ to this Sunday.* **4** (placed after the *n*) strictly so called; genuine: *architecture ~,* excluding, for example, the question of water-supply, electric current, etc. **5** (colloq) great; thorough: *We're in a ~ mess. He gave the burglar a ~ hiding,* beat him thoroughly. *~ fraction,* (eg $\frac{1}{2}$, $\frac{3}{4}$) one in which the number above the line is smaller than that below the line. *~ noun/name,* (gram) name used for an individual person, town, etc eg *Mary, Prague.* **~·ly** *adv* **1** in a *~* manner: *behave ~ly. Do it ~ly or not at all. He is not ~ly* (= strictly) *speaking a chemist.* **2** (colloq) thoroughly: *The American boxer was ~ly beaten by the new world champion.*

prop·erty /'prɒpətɪ/ n (pl -ties) **1** [U] (collectively) things owned; possessions: *Don't interfere with these tools—they're not your* ∼. **man of** ∼, wealthy man. **common** ∼, known to, possessed by, many people. **personal** ∼, movable belongings. **real** ∼, land, buildings. **2** [C] estate; area of land or land and buildings: *He has a small* ∼ (ie land and a house) *in Kent.* **3** [U] ownership; the fact of owning or being owned: *There is no* ∼ *in the seashore*, it cannot be privately owned. *P*∼ *has its obligations*, eg if you own farmland, etc, you have the duty of keeping it free from weeds, etc. **4** [C] special quality that belongs to sth: *the chemical properties of iron; herbs with healing properties.* **5** (theatre) (abbr *prop*) article of dress or furniture or other thing (except scenery) used on the stage in the performance of a play. '∼-**man**/-**master**, (also '**props-man**/-**master**), *n* man in charge of stage properties. **prop·er·tied** /'prɒpətɪd/ *adj* owning ∼, esp land: *the propertied classes*, the landowners.

proph·ecy /'prɒfəsɪ/ *n* (*pl* -cies) **1** [U] power of telling what will happen in the future: *have the gift of* ∼. **2** [C] statement that tells what will happen: *His* ∼ *was fulfilled.*

proph·esy /'prɒfɪsaɪ/ *vt,vi* (*pt,pp* -sied) **1** [VP6A,9,10] foretell; say (what will happen in the future): ∼ *war/that war will break out.* **2** [VP2A,C] speak as a prophet: *He prophesied of strange things to come. Does he ever* ∼ *right?*

prophet /'prɒfɪt/ *n* **1** person who teaches religion and claims that his teaching comes to him directly from God: *the* ∼ *Isaiah; Muhammad, the P*∼ *of Islam.* **the P**∼**s**, the prophetical books of the Old Testament. **2** pioneer of a new theory, cause, etc; advocate: *William Morris, one of the early* ∼*s of socialism.* **3** person who tells, or claims to tell, what will happen in the future: *I'm not a good weather*∼. ∼**·ess** /-es/ *n* woman ∼.

pro·phetic /prə'fetɪk/ *adj* of a prophet or prophecy; containing a prophecy: *accomplishments which were* ∼ *of her future greatness.* **pro·pheti·cal** /-kl/ *adj* = ∼. **pro·pheti·cal·ly** /-klɪ/ *adv*

pro·phy·lac·tic /ˌprɒfɪ'læktɪk/ *n, adj* [C] (substance, treatment, action) serving or tending to protect from disease or misfortune. **pro·phy·lax·is** /-'læksɪs/ *n* [U] preventive treatment of disease.

pro·pin·quity /prə'pɪŋkwətɪ/ *n* [U] (formal) nearness (in time, place, relationship); similarity (of ideas).

pro·pi·ti·ate /prə'pɪʃɪeɪt/ *vt* [VP6A] (formal) do sth to take away the anger of: *offer a sacrifice to* ∼ *the gods.* **pro·pi·ti·ation** /prəˌpɪʃɪ'eɪʃn/ *n* [U] propitiating; atoning. **pro·pi·ti·atory** /prə'pɪʃɪətrɪ US: -tɔːrɪ/ *adj* serving to, intended to, ∼: *With a propitiatory smile he offered her a large bunch of roses.*

pro·pi·tious /prə'pɪʃəs/ *adj* ∼ **to sb/for sth**, favourable; well-disposed: ∼ *omens; weather that was* ∼ *for our enterprise.* ∼**·ly** *adv*

pro·pon·ent /prə'pəʊnənt/ *n* person who proposes sth: *a* ∼ *of a theory/a course of action.*

pro·por·tion /prə'pɔːʃn/ *n* **1** [U] relation of one thing to another in quantity, size, etc; relation of a part to the whole: *The* ∼ *of imports to exports* (= The excess of imports over exports) *is worrying the government.* **in** ∼ **to**, relative to: *wide in* ∼ *to the height; payment in* ∼ *to work done, not in* ∼ *to the time taken to do it.* **get sth/be out of (all/any)** ∼ **(to)**, (make sth) bear no relation (to): *His earnings are out of all* ∼ *to his skill and ability*, He earns much more than is right for his skill and ability.

When you're angry, you may get things out of ∼, have an exaggerated or distorted view of things. **2** (often *pl*) the correct relation of parts or of the sizes of the several parts: *a room of good* ∼*s. The two windows are in admirable* ∼. **3** (*pl*) size; measurements: *a ship of majestic* ∼*s; build up an export trade of substantial* ∼*s.* **4** [C] part; share: *You have not done your* ∼ *of the work.* **5** (maths) equality of relationship between two sets of numbers; statement that two ratios are equal (eg 4 is to 8 as 6 is to 12. ⅜ and ⅒ are in ∼). □ *vt* [VP6A,14] ∼ **(to)**, put into ∼ or right relationship: *Do you* ∼ *your expenditure to your income? What a well-*∼*ed room!* ∼**·able** /-ʃənəbl/ *adj* = ∼al.

pro·por·tional /prə'pɔːʃənl/ *adj* ∼ **(to)**, (formal) in proper proportion; corresponding in degree or amount: *payment* ∼ *to the work done; compensation* ∼ *to his injuries.* ∼ **represen'tation**, ⇨ *representation* at represent[1]. ∼**·ly** /-ənəlɪ/ *adv*

pro·por·tion·ate /prə'pɔːʃənət/ *adj* (formal) = proportional. ∼**·ly** *adv*

pro·po·sal /prə'pəʊzl/ *n* **1** [U] proposing. **2** [C] sth proposed; plan or scheme: *a* ∼ *for peace;* ∼*s for increasing trade between two countries.* **3** offer (esp of marriage): *a girl who had five* ∼*s in one week.*

pro·pose /prə'pəʊz/ *vt,vi* **1** [VP6A,D,7A,9] offer or put forward for consideration, as a suggestion, plan or purpose: *I* ∼ *starting early/an early start/to start early/that we should start early. We* ∼ *leaving at noon. The motion was* ∼*d by Mr X and seconded by Mr Y.* ∼ **a toast/sb's health**, ask persons to drink sb's health or happiness. **2** [VP6A,2A] ∼ **(marriage) (to sb)**, offer marriage. **3** [VP6A,14] ∼ **sb (for sth)**, put forward (sb's name) for an office/for membership of a club, etc: *I* ∼ *Mr Smith for chairman. Will you please* ∼ *me for your club?* **pro·poser** *n*

prop·osi·tion /ˌprɒpə'zɪʃn/ *n* [C] **1** statement; assertion: *a* ∼ *so clear that it needs no explanation.* **2** question or problem (with or without the answer or solution): *a* ∼ *in Euclid. Tunnelling under the English Channel is a big* ∼. **3** proposal; suggestion. **4** (colloq) matter to be dealt with. **a tough** ∼, (colloq) sb or sth difficult to deal with. □ *vt* [VP6A] (colloq) make a (esp illegal or immoral) ∼(3) to.

pro·pound /prə'paʊnd/ *vt* [VP6A] (formal) put forward or offer for consideration or solution: ∼ *a theory/a riddle.*

pro·pri·etary /prə'praɪətrɪ US: -terɪ/ *adj* **1** (abbr (P) used in this dictionary) owned or controlled by sb; held as property: ∼ *medicine*, patented; ∼ *rights; a* ∼ *name*, eg Kodak for cameras and films. **2** of or like a proprietor or owner: *He walked round his estate with* ∼ *solicitude.*

pro·pri·etor /prə'praɪətə(r)/ *n* owner, esp of a hotel, store, land or patent: *the* ∼*s of the hotel/this patent medicine.* **pro·pri·e·tress** /prə'praɪətrɪs/ *n* woman ∼.

pro·pri·ety /prə'praɪətɪ/ *n* (*pl* -ties) (formal) **1** [U] state of being correct in behaviour and morals: *a breach of* ∼; (*pl*) details of correct social behaviour: *observe the proprieties; offend against the proprieties.* **2** [U] reasonableness; fitness: *I question the* ∼ *of granting such a request*, doubt whether it is right to do so.

pro·pul·sion /prə'pʌlʃn/ *n* [U] propelling force. **jet** ∼, by means of jet engines. **pro·pul·sive** /prə'pʌlsɪv/ *adj* propelling; serving to propel.

pro rata /ˌprəʊ 'rɑːtə/ *adv* (Lat) in proportion; according to the share, etc of each.

pro·rogue /prəʊˈrəʊg/ vt [VP6A] bring (a session of Parliament) to an end without dissolving it (so that unfinished business may be taken up again in the next session). **pro·ro·ga·tion** /ˌprəʊrəˈgeɪʃn/ n

pro·saic /prəˈzeɪk/ adj dull; uninteresting; commonplace: a lively woman with a ~ husband; the ~ life of the ordinary housewife. **pro·sai·cally** /-klɪ/ adv

pro·scenium /prəˈsiːnɪəm/ n (in a theatre) that part of the stage between the curtain and the orchestra. ~ **arch**, arch above this space.

pro·scribe /prəˈskraɪb US: prəʊ-/ vt [VP6A] **1** (old use) publicly put (a person) out of the protection of the law. **2** denounce (a person, practice, etc) as dangerous. **pro·scrip·tion** /prəˈskrɪpʃn US: prəʊ-/ n [U] proscribing or being ~d; [C] instance of this.

prose /prəʊz/ n [U] language not in verse form: (attrib) the ~ writers of the 19th century. ⇨ poetry.

pros·ecute /ˈprɒsɪkjuːt/ vt [VP6A] (formal) continue with: ~ a war/one's studies/an inquiry. **2** [VP6A,14] ~ **sb (for sth)**, start legal proceedings against: ~d for exceeding the speed limit. Trespassers will be ~d. **pros·ecu·tor** /ˈprɒsɪkjuːtə(r)/ n person who ~s(2). **Public 'Prosecutor**, legal official who ~s criminal cases on behalf of the State or the public.

pros·ecu·tion /ˌprɒsɪˈkjuːʃn/ n **1** [U] act of prosecuting(1): In the ~ of his duties he had to interview people of all classes. **2** [U] prosecuting or being prosecuted(2): make oneself liable to ~; [C] instance of this: start a ~ against sb. **the Director of Public P~s**, Public Prosecutor, ⇨ prosecute. **3** (collective) person who prosecutes(2), together with his advisers: the case for the ~. ⇨ defence(3).

pros·elyte /ˈprɒsəlaɪt/ n person who has been converted from his religious, political or other opinions or beliefs to different ones. **pros·elyt·ize** /ˈprɒsəlɪtaɪz/ vt,vi [VP6A,2A] make, try to make, converts to a religion or cause; make a ~ of (sb).

pros·ody /ˈprɒsədɪ/ n [U] science of verse rhythms or metres; (of a language) rhythm, pause, tempo, stress and pitch features.

pros·pect[1] /ˈprɒspekt/ n **1** [C] wide view over land or sea or (fig) before the mind, in the imagination. **2** (pl) sth expected, hoped for, looked forward to: The ~s for the wine harvest are poor this year. The manager held out bright ~s to me if I would accept the position. **3** [U] expectation; hope: I see no/little/not much ~ of his recovery. Is there no ~ of your visiting us soon? He is out of work and has nothing in ~ (= no expectation of finding work) at present. **4** [C] possible customer or client; sb from whom one hopes to gain something: He's a good/ bad ~.

pros·pect[2] /prəˈspekt US: ˈprɒspekt/ vi [VP2A,3A] ~ **(for)**, search (for): ~ing for gold. **pros·pec·tor** /-tə(r)/ n person who explores a region looking for gold or other valuable ores, etc.

pros·pec·tive /prəˈspektɪv/ adj hoped for; looked forward to; which or who will or may be: ~ advantages/wealth; a ~ buyer; my ~ bride; the ~ Labour candidate.

pros·pec·tus /prəˈspektəs/ n (pl ~es /-təsɪz/) printed account giving details of and advertising sth, eg a university, a new business enterprise, a book about to be published.

pros·per /ˈprɒspə(r)/ vi,vt **1** [VP2A] succeed; do

well: The business ~ed. Is your son ~ing? **2** [VP6A] (liter or rhet) (of God) cause to ~: May God ~ you!

pros·per·ity /prɒˈsperətɪ/ n [U] state of being successful; good fortune: a life of happiness and ~; live in ~. The ~ of this industry depends upon a full order book.

pros·per·ous /ˈprɒspərəs/ adj successful; flourishing: a ~ business; ~ years. **~·ly** adv

pros·tate /ˈprɒsteɪt/ n ~ **(gland)**, (anat) gland in male mammals at the neck of the bladder.

pros·ti·tute /ˈprɒstɪtjuːt US: -tuːt/ n person who offers herself/himself for sexual intercourse for payment. □ vt **1** [VP6A] (reflex) make a ~ of (oneself). **2** [VP6A] put to wrong or unworthy uses: ~ one's energies/abilities; ~ one's honour, lose it for money basely gained. **pros·ti·tu·tion** /ˌprɒstɪˈtjuːʃn US: -ˈtuːʃn/ n [U] practice of prostituting oneself, one's talents, etc.

pros·trate /ˈprɒstreɪt/ adj **1** lying stretched out on the ground, usu face downward, eg because exhausted, or to show submission, deep respect. **2** (fig) overcome (with grief, etc); conquered; overthrown. □ vt /prɒˈstreɪt US: ˈprɒstreɪt/ **1** [VP6A] cause to be ~: trees ~d by the gale. **2** [VP6A] (reflex) make (oneself) ~: The wretched slaves ~d themselves before their master. **3** (usu passive) overcome; render helpless: Several of the competitors were ~d by the heat. She is ~d with grief. **pros·tra·tion** /prɒˈstreɪʃn/ n **1** [U] state of extreme physical weakness; complete exhaustion: Two of the runners in the Marathon race collapsed and were carried off in a state of prostration. **2** [C] act of bowing or lying face downwards to show submission or humility.

prosy /ˈprəʊzɪ/ adj (-ier, -iest) (of authors, speakers, books, speeches, style, etc) dull; tedious; unimaginative. **pros·ily** /-əlɪ/ adv **prosi·ness** n

pro·tag·on·ist /prəˈtægənɪst/ n (formal) chief person in a drama; (by extension) chief person in a story or factual event.

pro·tean /ˈprəʊtɪən/ adj versatile; easily and quickly changing (like Proteus /ˈprəʊtɪəs/, the Greek sea-god who took various shapes).

pro·tect /prəˈtekt/ vt [VP6A,14] ~ **sb/sth (from/against)**, **1** keep safe from danger, enemies; against attack; guard: well ~ed from the cold/ against the weather. **2** guard (home industry) against competition by taxing imports.

pro·tec·tion /prəˈtekʃn/ n [U] **1** protecting or being protected: travel under the ~ of a number of soldiers. These tender plants need ~ against the weather. '~ **(money)**, money demanded by or paid to, gangsters for ~ against acts of violence, etc. **2** [U] system of protecting home industry against foreign competition. **3** [C] person or thing that protects: wearing a heavy overcoat as a ~ against the cold. **~·ism** /-ɪzəm/ n [U] system of giving ~(2) to home industry. **~·ist** /-ɪst/ n supporter of, believer in, ~ism.

pro·tec·tive /prəˈtektɪv/ adj **1** giving protection: a ~ covering; a ~ tariff, ie on imported goods; ~ sheath, ⇨ sheath. **~ 'clothing**, clothes that safeguard the wearer against such risks as burns, contamination and radiation. **~ 'colouring**, ie of animals, birds, insects, causing them to be seen with difficulty in their natural surroundings, thus protecting them from their enemies. **~ 'foods**, foods that safeguard health, eg kinds with a good supply of essential vitamins. **2** ~ **(towards)**, (of persons) with a wish to protect: *A mother naturally feels ~ towards her children.* **~·ly** *adv*

pro·tec·tor /prə'tektə(r)/ *n* **1** person who protects; sth made or designed to give protection. **2** (GB hist) **the P~**, official title of Oliver and Richard Cromwell.

pro·tec·tor·ate /prə'tektərət/ *n* **1** country under the protection of another. **2 the P~**, period (1653—59) of rule of Oliver and Richard Cromwell.

pro·tégé (fem **-gée**) /'prɒtɪʒeɪ *US:* ˌprəʊtɪ'ʒeɪ/ *n* (F) person to whom another gives encouragement and help (usu over a long period).

pro·tein /'prəʊtiːn/ *n* [U,C] body-building substance essential to good health, in such foods as milk, eggs, meat.

pro tem·pore /ˌprəʊ 'tempərɪ/ *adv* (Lat) (often shortened to **pro tem**) for the time being; for the present only: *I am in charge of the office pro tem.*

pro·test[1] /'prəʊtest/ *n* **1** [C,U] (statement of) disapproval or objection: *make/lodge/enter a ~ (against sth). The Government's policy gave rise to vigorous ~s. He paid the tax demand under ~,* unwillingly and after declaring that what he was doing was not right or just. *He gave way without ~,* without making any objection. **2** (attrib) expressing ~: *a '~ movement; a '~ march,* eg by persons objecting to official policy.

pro·test[2] /prə'test/ *vt, vi* **1** [VP6A,9] affirm strongly; assert against opposition: *He ~ed that he had never been near the scene of the crime. He ~ed his innocence,* asserted his innocence by ~ing. **2** [VP2A,3A] ~ **(against),** raise an objection, say sth *(against): I ~ against being called an old fool. The children ~ed loudly* (= cried out in disapproval) *when they were told to go to bed early.* **~·er** *n* **~·ing·ly** *adv*

Prot·es·tant /'prɒtɪstənt/ *n, adj* (member) of any of the Christian bodies that separated from the Church of Rome at the time of the Reformation (16th c), or of their later branches. **~·ism** /-ɪzəm/ *n* [U] systems, beliefs, teaching, etc of the ~s; ~s as a body.

prot·es·ta·tion /ˌprɒte'steɪʃn/ *n* [C] (formal) solemn declaration: *~s of innocence/friendship.*

pro·to·col /'prəʊtəkɒl *US:* -kɔːl/ *n* **1** [C] first or original draft of an agreement (esp between States), signed by those making it, in preparation for a treaty. **2** [U] code of behaviour; etiquette as practised on diplomatic occasions: *Were the seating arrangements for the dinner party according to ~,* Were rules of precedence, etc properly observed?

pro·ton /'prəʊtɒn/ *n* positively charged particle forming part of an atomic nucleus. ⇨ **electron.**

pro·to·plasm /'prəʊtəplæzəm/ *n* [U] colourless, jelly-like substance which is the material basis of life in animals and plants.

pro·to·type /'prəʊtətaɪp/ *n* [C] first or original example, eg of an aircraft, from which others have been or will be copied or developed.

pro·to·zoa /ˌprəʊtə'zəʊə/ *n pl* (division of the animal kingdom consisting of) animals of the simplest type formed of a single cell (and usu microscopic).

pro·tract /prə'trækt *US:* prəʊ-/ *vt* [VP6A] prolong; lengthen the time taken by: *a ~ed visit/argument.* **pro·trac·tion** /prə'trækʃn *US:* prəʊ-/ *n* lengthening out.

pro·trac·tor /prə'træktə(r) *US:* prəʊ-/ *n* instrument, usu in the form of a semicircle, and graduated (0° to 180°), for measuring and drawing angles.

pro·trude /prə'truːd *US:* prəʊ-/ *vi, vt* [VP2A,6A] (cause to) stick out or project: *a shelf that ~s from a wall; protruding eyes/teeth.* **pro·tru·sion** /prə'truːʒn *US:* prəʊ-/ *n* [U] protruding; [C] sth that ~s. **pro·trus·ive** /prə'truːsɪv *US:* prəʊ-/ *adj* protruding.

pro·tu·ber·ant /prə'tjuːbərənt *US:* prəʊ'tuː-/ *adj* (formal) curving or swelling outwards; bulging. **pro·tu·ber·ance** /-əns/ *n* [U] being ~; [C] sth that is ~; bulge or swelling.

proud /praʊd/ *adj* (-er, -est) **1** (in a good sense) having or showing a proper pride or dignity: *~ of their success/of being so successful; ~ to belong/that they belonged to such a fine team.* **2** (in a bad sense) arrogant; having or showing too much pride: *He was too ~ to join our party.* **3** arousing justifiable pride; of which one is or may be properly ~; splendid; imposing: *soldiers in ~ array. It was a ~ day for the country when its team won the championship. His rose garden was a ~ sight.* **4** ~ **flesh,** overgrown flesh round a healing wound. **5** (compounds) **'house-~,** of one's house, of the care with which it is looked after, cleaned, etc. **'purse-~,** arrogant because of one's wealth. **6** (*adv* use; colloq) **do sb ~,** honour greatly, entertain splendidly. **~·ly** *adv* in a ~ manner; splendidly.

prove /pruːv/ *vt, vi* (*pp* ~d, or, as 1 below, ~n /'pruːvn/) **1** [VP6A,9,14,25] ~ **(to),** supply proof of; show beyond doubt to be true: *~ sb's guilt/that he is guilty. His guilt was clearly ~d. I shall ~ to you that the witness is quite unreliable. Can you ~ it to me?* **The exception ~s the rule,** shows that the rule is valid in most cases. **not ~n,** (in a criminal trial in Scotland) jury's decision that as the charge cannot be ~d, the accused may be released (although he may not be innocent). **2** [VP6A] establish the genuineness of: *~ a will;* test the quality or accuracy of: *~ a man's worth.* **3** [VP4D,25] ~ **(oneself) (to be),** be seen or found in the end (to be): *The new typist ~d (to be) useless. He ~d (himself) to be a coward. Our wood supply ~d (to be) insufficient.* **prov·able** /-əbl/ *adj* that can be ~d.

prov·enance /'prɒvənəns/ *n* [U] (place of) origin: *antique furniture of doubtful ~,* eg that may not be genuinely antique.

prov·en·der /'prɒvɪndə(r)/ *n* [U] food, eg hay, oats, for horses and cattle; (colloq) food of any kind.

prov·erb /'prɒvɜːb/ *n* **1** popular short saying, with words of advice or warning, eg 'It takes two to make a quarrel'. **2 (the Book of) P~s,** one of the books of the Old Testament. **3** sb or sth so well known that he/it has become notorious: *He is a ~ for meanness. His meanness is a ~.* **~·ial** /prə'vɜːbɪəl/ *adj* **1** of or expressed in a ~: *~ sayings/wisdom.* **2** widely known and talked about; admitted by everyone: *His stupidity is ~ial.* **~·ially** *adv: He is ~ially stupid.*

pro·vide /prə'vaɪd/ *vi, vt* **1** [VP3A] ~ **for sb/sth,** make ready, do what is necessary, for: *He has a large family to ~ for. We must ~ for our visitors,* get in supplies of food, etc. *He died without providing for his widow,* leaving nothing for her to live on. ~ **against sth,** take steps to guard against: *Have you ~d against a coal shortage next winter?* **2** [VP6A,14] ~ **sth (for sb);** ~ **sb with sth,** give, supply (what is needed, esp what a person needs in order to live): *~ one's children with food and clothes; ~ food and clothes for one's family.* **3**

[VP9] stipulate: *A clause in the agreement ~s that the tenant shall bear the cost of all repairs to the building.* **~r** *n* person who provides.

pro·vid·ed /prə'vaɪdɪd/ *conj* ~ *(that)*, on condition (that).

pro·vid·ing /prə'vaɪdɪŋ/ *conj* ~ *(that)*, = provided (that): *I will go* ~ *(that) my expenses are paid.*

provi·dence /'prɒvɪdəns/ *n* **1** [U] (old use) thrift; being provident or prudent (about future needs, etc). **2 P~**, God; God's care for human beings and all he has created; (small *p*) particular instance of this care: *the mysterious working of divine* ~. *A special* ~ *preserved him from the tragic fate of his companions.*

provi·dent /'prɒvɪdənt/ *adj* (careful in) providing for future needs or events, esp in old age: *Our firm has a* ~ *fund for the staff.* **~·ly** *adv*

provi·den·tial /ˌprɒvɪ'denʃl/ *adj* of, by, through, coming from, Providence(2): *a* ~ *escape.* **~·ly** /-ʃəlɪ/ *adv*

prov·ince /'prɒvɪns/ *n* **1** large administrative division of a country. **2 the ~s**, all the country outside the capital: *people from the* ~*s visiting London. The pop group is now touring the* ~*s.* **3** district under an archbishop. **4** area of learning or knowledge; department of activity: *That is outside my* ~, not sth with which I can or need deal. *Doesn't your question fall outside the* ~ *of science?*

prov·in·cial /prə'vɪnʃl/ *adj* **1** of a province(1): ~ *taxes;* ~ *government.* **2** of the provinces(2): ~ *roads.* **3** narrow in outlook; having, typical of, the speech, manners, views, etc of a person living in the provinces (esp in former times when communications were poor): *a* ~ *accent.* □ *n* person from the provinces; countrified person. **~·ly** /-ʃəlɪ/ *adv* **~·ism** /-ɪzəm/ *n* [C] example of ~ manners, speech, behaviour, etc; [U] attachment to one's province and its customs, etc rather than to one's country.

pro·vi·sion /prə'vɪʒn/ *n* **1** [U] providing, preparation (esp for future needs): *the* ~ (= supply) *of water and gas to domestic consumers; make* ~ *for one's old age,* eg by saving money; *make* ~ *against sth,* guard against it. **2** [C] amount (*of* sth) provided: *issue a* ~ *of meat to the troops.* **3** (*pl*) food; food supplies: *lay in a store of* ~*s;* (attrib, sing) *a* ~ *merchant,* a grocer; *a wholesale* ~ *business.* **4** [C] condition in a legal document, eg a clause in a will: *if there is no* ~ *to the contrary.* □ *vt* [VP6A] supply with ~s(3) and stores: ~ *a ship for a voyage to the Antarctic.*

pro·vi·sional /prə'vɪʒənl/ *adj* of the present time only, and to be confirmed or changed or replaced later: *a* ~ *government/contract, etc.* **~·ly** /-nəlɪ/ *adv*

pro·viso /prə'vaɪzəʊ/ *n* (*pl* ~s, US also ~es /-zəʊz/) (clause containing a) limitation, esp in a legal document: *with the* ~ *that,* on condition that; *subject to this* ~, with this limitation. **pro·vi·sory** /prə'vaɪzərɪ/ *adj* depending upon a ~.

Provo /'prəʊvəʊ/ *n* (*pl* ~s /-əʊz/) (colloq) member of a group *(the Provisional IRA)* fighting for the political unification of Ireland.

provo·ca·tion /ˌprɒvə'keɪʃn/ *n* **1** [U] provoking or being provoked: *wilful* ~ *of public disorder; do sth under* ~, when provoked. *She flares up at/on the slightest* ~, Very little things make her anger break out. **2** [C] sth that provokes or annoys.

pro·voca·tive /prə'vɒkətɪv/ *adj* causing, likely to cause, anger, argument, interest, etc: ~ *remarks; a* ~ *dress.* **~·ly** *adv*

pro·voke /prə'vəʊk/ *vt* **1** [VP6A] make angry; vex: *He was* ~*d beyond endurance. If you* ~ *the dog, it will attack you.* **2** [VP6A] cause; arouse: ~ *laughter/a smile/a riot.* **3** [VP17,14] ~ *sb to do sth/into doing sth,* cause or compel them: *His impudence* ~*d her into slapping his face. He was* ~*d to answer rudely.* **pro·vok·ing** *adj* annoying: *provoking of sb to be late.* **pro·vok·ing·ly** *adv*

pro·vost /'prɒvəst *US:* 'prəʊ-/ *n* **1** title of some heads of university colleges, etc. **2** (in Scotland) head of a municipal corporation or burgh (= mayor). **3** ~ **marshal** /prəˌvəʊ 'mɑːʃl *US:* ˌprəʊvəʊ-/, head of the military police.

prow /praʊ/ *n* pointed front of a ship or boat. ⇨ the illus at barque.

prow·ess /'praʊɪs/ *n* [U] bravery; valour; unusual skill or ability.

prowl /praʊl/ *vi,vt* **1** [VP2A,C] go about cautiously looking for a chance to get food (as wild animals do), or to steal, etc. **2** [VP6A] go about (the streets) in this way. □ *n be on the* ~, ~ing. '~ *car,* (US) ⇨ *squad car* at squad. **~·er** *n* animal or person that ~s.

prox /prɒks/ ⇨ proximo.

proxi·mate /'prɒksɪmət/ *adj* (formal) nearest, before or after.

prox·im·ity /prɒk'sɪmətɪ/ *n* [U] (formal) nearness: *in* (*close*) ~ *to,* (very) near to (which is usu preferable). ~ *fuse,* one that explodes the shell to which it is fitted when near the target, eg an enemy aircraft.

prox·imo /'prɒksɪməʊ/ *adj* (abbr **prox**) (comm or official style, better avoided) of next month: *on the 22nd prox.*

proxy /'prɒksɪ/ *n* (*pl* -xies) [C] (document giving) [U] authority to represent or act for another (esp in voting at an election); [C] person given a ~: *vote by* ~; *make one's wife one's* ~.

prude /pruːd/ *n* person of extreme or exaggerated propriety (often affected) in behaviour or speech.

pru·dery /'pruːdərɪ/ *n* (*pl* -ries) [U] extreme propriety; [C] prudish act or remark. **prud·ish** /'pruːdɪʃ/ *adj* of or like a ~; excessively modest; easily shocked. **pru·dish·ly** *adv*

pru·dent /'pruːdnt/ *adj* careful; acting only after careful thought or planning: *a* ~ *housekeeper.* **~·ly** *adv* **pru·dence** /-dns/ *n* [U] being ~; careful forethought.

pru·den·tial /pruː'denʃl/ *adj* relating to, marked by, prudence.

prune[1] /pruːn/ *n* dried plum; (colloq) silly person.

prune[2] /pruːn/ *vt* [VP6A,14,15B] ~ *sth from sth;* ~ *sth off sth;* ~ *sth away,* cut away parts of (trees, bushes, etc) in order to control growth or shape; (fig) take out unnecessary parts from: ~ *the rose-bushes;* ~ *away unwanted growth;* ~ *an essay of superfluous matter;* ~ *away unnecessary adjectives.* **prun·ing** *n* [U]: *The roses need pruning,* ought to be ~d. **'pruning-knife/-hook/saw/-scissors/-shears,** kinds of tool used for pruning. **pruners** *n pl* pruning-scissors.

pru·ri·ent /'prʊərɪənt/ *adj* having, showing, an excessive and unhealthy interest in matters of sex. **~·ly** *adv* **pru·ri·ence** /-əns/, **pru·ri·ency** /-ənsɪ/ *nn* state of being ~.

Prus·sian /'prʌʃn/ *n, adj* (inhabitant, native) of Prussia. ~ **blue,** deep blue colour.

prus·sic /'prʌsɪk/ *adj* ~ '**acid,** violent and deadly poison.

pry[1] /praɪ/ vi (pt,pp **pried** /praɪd/) [VP2A,3A] **pry (into),** inquire too curiously (into other people's affairs); [VP2C] **pry about,** look or peer (about) inquisitively. **pry·ing·ly** adv

pry[2] /praɪ/ vt [VP22,15A,B] (= **prize**[3]) get (sth open) (eg with a lever); lift (sth up): (fig) **pry a secret out of sb.**

psalm /sɑːm/ n sacred song or hymn, esp (**the P~s**) those in the Bible. **~·ist** /-ɪst/ n person who writes ~s, esp **the P~ist,** David, said to be the author of ~s in the Bible. **~·ody** /'sɑːmədɪ/ n (pl -dies) 1 [U] practice or art of singing ~s. 2 [C] arrangement of ~s for singing; book of ~s with their musical settings.

psal·ter /'sɔːltə(r)/ n Book of Psalms; copy of the Psalms, esp one designed for use in public worship.

psal·tery /'sɔːltərɪ/ n (pl -ties) musical instrument (ancient and medieval times) with strings over a sound-board, played by plucking the strings.

pse·phol·ogy /se'fɒlədʒɪ US: siː-/ n scientific study of election trends, eg by means of opinion polls. **pse·phol·ogist** /-ɪst/ n

pseud /sjuːd US: suːd/ n (colloq) = pseudo(n).

pseudo /'sjuːdəʊ US: 'suː-/ adj (colloq) sham; insincere: I've always found him very ~. □ n sham person.

pseudo- /ˌsjuːdəʊ US: ˌsuː-/ pref false; spurious: ~-scientific. ⇨ App 3.

pseu·do·nym /'sjuːdənɪm US: 'suːdənɪm/ n name taken, esp by an author, instead of his real name. **pseud·ony·mous** /sjuː'dɒnɪməs US: suː-/ adj writing, written, under an assumed name.

pshaw /pfɔ or similar 'burst' of noise/ int exclamation to indicate contempt or impatience.

psit·ta·co·sis /ˌsɪtə'kəʊsɪs/ n [U] (also called '**parrot fever**) contagious virus disease (caught from parrots and related birds) producing fever and other complications (as in pneumonia).

psyche /'saɪkɪ/ n 1 human soul or spirit. 2 human mind; mentality.

psyche·delic /ˌsaɪkɪ'delɪk/ adj 1 (of drugs) hallucinatory: Mescalin and LSD are ~ drugs. 2 (of visual and sound effects) acting on the mind like ~ drugs: ~ music.

psy·chia·try /saɪ'kaɪətrɪ US: sɪ-/ n [U] the study and treatment of mental illness. **psy·chia·trist** /-ɪst/ n expert in ~. **psy·chi·atric** /ˌsaɪkɪ'ætrɪk/ adj of ~: a psychiatric clinic.

psy·chic[1] /'saɪkɪk/ n [C] person apparently, or claiming to be, responsive to occult powers; (popular term for a) medium(4).

psy·chic[2] /'saɪkɪk/, **psy·chi·cal** /'saɪkɪkl/ adjj 1 of the soul or mind. 1 of phenomena and conditions which appear to be outside physical or natural laws: ~ research, the study and investigation of such phenomena, eg telepathy, second sight.

psy·cho·an·aly·sis /ˌsaɪkəʊ ə'næləsɪs/ n [U] 1 method of healing mental·illnesses by tracing them, through interviews, to events in the patient's early life, and bringing those events to his consciousness. 2 body of doctrine based on this method concerned with the investigation and treatment of emotional disturbances. **psy·cho·ana·lyst** /ˌsaɪkəʊ 'ænəlɪst/ n person who practises ~. **psy·cho·ana·lytic(al)** /ˌsaɪkəʊ ˌænə'lɪtɪk(l)/ adj relating to ~. **psy·cho·ana·lyse** (US = -lyze) /ˌsaɪkəʊ 'ænəlaɪz/ vt treat (sb) by ~.

psy·chol·ogy /saɪ'kɒlədʒɪ/ n [U] 1 science, study, of the mind and its processes: abnormal/animal/ child/industrial ~, branches of this science. 2 [C] (colloq, unscientific, use) mental nature, processes, etc of a person: She understands her husband's ~ very well. **psy·chol·ogist** /-ɪst/ n student of, expert in, ~. **psy·cho·logi·cal** /ˌsaɪkə'lɒdʒɪkl/ adj of ~; of the mind. **the psychological moment,** the most appropriate time; the time when one is most likely to achieve the desired end. **psychological warfare,** waged by trying to influence people's ideas and beliefs. **psy·cho·logi·cally** /-klɪ/ adv

psy·cho·path /'saɪkəʊpæθ/ n person suffering from severe emotional derangement, esp one who is aggressive and antisocial, with little or no moral sense. **~ic** /ˌsaɪkəʊ'pæθɪk/ adj of, suffering from, severe emotional or mental disorder.

psy·cho·sis /saɪ'kəʊsɪs/ n (pl -choses /-'kəʊsiːz/) severely abnormal or diseased mental state.

psy·cho·so·matic /ˌsaɪkəʊsə'mætɪk/ adj (of disease) caused by mental stress; (of medicine) concerned with such disease.

psy·cho·therapy /ˌsaɪkəʊ'θerəpɪ/ n [U] treatment by psychological methods of mental, emotional and nervous disorders.

ptar·mi·gan /'tɑːmɪgən/ n bird of the grouse family with black or grey feathers in summer and white in winter.

ptero·dac·tyl /ˌterə'dæktɪl/ n extinct flying reptile.

pto·maine /'təʊmeɪn/ n (sorts of) poison which is found in decaying food: ill with ~ poisoning.

pub /pʌb/ n (abbr for) public house: go round to the pub for a drink. '**pub-crawl,** ⇨ crawl n(1).

pu·berty /'pjuːbətɪ/ n [U] stage at which a person becomes physically able to become a parent; maturing of the sexual functions: reach the age of ~.

pu·bic /'pjuːbɪk/ adj of the lower part of the abdomen: ~ hair.

pub·lic /'pʌblɪk/ adj (opp of private) of, for, connected with, owned by, done for or done by, known to, people in general: a ~ library/park; a matter of ~ knowledge, sth known to everyone; enter ~ life, engage in the affairs or service of the people, eg in government; ~ elementary and secondary schools, government-controlled schools providing free education. **~-ad'dress system** n (abbr **PA system**) system of microphones and loud speakers for broadcasting in ~ areas. **~ 'bar,** ordinary bar in a ~ house or hotel. ⇨ saloon bar at saloon. **~ ,corpo'ration,** (legal) corporation providing services for the public, eg in GB the British Broadcasting Corporation, the BBC. **~ 'enemy,** person thought to be a danger to the ~, to the whole community. **~ 'house** n (GB) (formal) (colloq abbr **pub** /pʌb/) house (not a club, hotel, etc) licensed to sell alcoholic drinks to be consumed on the premises but not offering accommodation. **~ 'nuisance,** (legal) illegal act harmful to people in general rather than to an individual; (colloq) sb who is a nuisance to a community. **~ o'pinion poll,** ⇨ poll[1](2). **~ 'ownership,** ownership by the State, eg of the railways. **P~ 'Prosecutor,** ⇨ prosecutor at prosecute. **~ re'lations** (abbr **PR**) n pl (esp) relations between a government department or authority, business organization, etc with the general ~, usu through the distribution of information. **~ re'lations officer** (abbr **PRO**) person employed in ~ relations. **~ 'school,** (a) (GB) private school for older fee-paying pupils, usu a boarding school, supported partly by endowments and managed by a board of governors. ⇨

preparatory school (for younger pupils) at preparatory. **(b)** (US and Scot) school providing free education, supported by ~ funds. ~ **'spirit,** readiness to do things that are for the good of the community. Hence, ~-**'spirited** *adj* ~ **'transport,** transport systems (road and rail) owned by ~ corporations, eg city and town authorities: *travel by* ~ *transport,* contrasted with privately owned systems, one's own car, etc. ~ **trustee,** ⇨ trustee. ~ **u'tilities,** organizations which supply services and commodities, eg water, gas, electricity, transport, communications, to the general ~. **go** ~, (of a business organization) offer shares for purchase (on the Stock Exchange) by the ~: *Rolls-Royce, after its bankruptcy in 1971, went* ~ *in 1972.* □ *n* **1** the ~, members of the community in general: *the British* ~. *The* ~ *are not admitted. The* ~ *is/are requested not to leave litter in the park. in* ~, openly, not in private. **2** particular section of the community: *the theatre-going* ~, those who attend theatres; *the reading* ~, those who read books, etc; *a book that will appeal to a large* ~, to many readers. ~**·ly** /-klɪ/ *adv*

pub·li·can /'pʌblɪkən/ *n* **1** (GB) keeper of a public house. **2** (in Roman times and in the New Testament) tax-gatherer.

pub·li·ca·tion /ˌpʌblɪ'keɪʃn/ *n* **1** [U] act of making known to the public, of publishing sth: *the* ~ *of a report; date of* ~. **2** [C] sth published, eg a book or a periodical.

pub·li·cist /'pʌblɪsɪst/ *n* newspaper man who writes on current topics of public interest, eg a political journalist; person who publicizes.

pub·lic·ity /pʌb'lɪsətɪ/ *n* [U] **1** the state of being known to, seen by, everyone: *an actress who seeks/avoids* ~; *heads of state who live their lives in the full blaze of* ~. **2** (business of) providing information to win public interest: *give a new book/ play, etc wide* ~; *conduct a* '~ *campaign.* '~ **agent,** person employed to keep the name of a person, eg an actor, or product constantly before the public.

pub·li·cize /'pʌblɪsaɪz/ *vt* [VP6A] give publicity to; bring to the attention of the public.

pub·lish /'pʌblɪʃ/ *vt* [VP6A] **1** have (a book, periodical, etc) printed and announce that it is for sale. **2** make known to the public: ~ *the news;* ~ *the banns of marriage,* announce formally in a church the names of persons shortly to be married. ~**er** *n* person whose business is the ~ing of books.

puce /pjuːs/ *n* [U] purple-brown.

puck¹ /pʌk/ *n* (in folklore) mischievous sprite or goblin. ~**·ish** /-ɪʃ/ *adj* mischievous: *a* ~*ish smile.* ~**·ish·ly** *adv*

puck² /pʌk/ *n* hard rubber disc used instead of a ball in ice-hockey. ⇨ the illus at hockey.

pucker /'pʌkə(r)/ *vt,vi* [VP6A,15B,2A,C] ~ **up,** draw or come together into small folds or wrinkles: ~ *up one's brows/lips. This coat* ~*s* (*up*) *at the shoulders.* □ *n* wrinkle.

pud /pʊd/ *n* [U] (sl) pudding.

pud·den /'pʊdn/ *n* (colloq) (only in) '~**-head** *n* slow, stupid person.

pudding /'pʊdɪŋ/ *n* [C,U] **1** (dish of) food, usu a soft, sweet mixture, served as part of a meal, generally eaten after the meat course: *milk* ~*s,* of some kind of grain, eg rice, cooked with milk and flavourings, '~**-face,** large fat face. **2** kind of sausage. **black** ~, intestine of pig stuffed with oat-

meal, blood, etc. **3** sth like a ~ in appearance. **4** '~ **stone,** rock composed of rounded pebbles in a kind of stone like concrete.

puddle /'pʌdl/ *n* **1** [C] small pool of water. **2** [U] wet clay and sand mixed to a paste, used as a watertight covering for embankments, etc. □ *vt* **1** mix (wet clay and sand) into a thick paste. **2** stir (molten iron) to produce wrought iron by expelling carbon. **pud·dler** /'pʌdlə(r)/ *n* worker who ~s clay, etc or molten iron.

pu·denda /pjuː'dendə/ *n pl* (formal) external genital organs, esp of the female.

pudgy /'pʌdʒɪ/ *adj* (-ier, -iest) short, thick and fat: ~ *fingers.*

pueblo /'pwebləʊ/ *n* (*pl* ~s /-ləʊz/) communal village dwelling of adobe and stone, as built by American Indians in Mexico and the south-western US.

puer·ile /'pjʊəraɪl *US:* -rəl/ *adj* trivial; suitable only for a child: *ask* ~ *questions.* **puer·il·ity** /ˌpjʊə'rɪlətɪ/ *n* [U] childishness; foolishness; [C] childish or foolish act, idea, utterance, etc.

pu·er·peral /pjuː'ɜːpərəl/ *adj* of, due to, childbirth: ~ *fever.*

puff¹ /pʌf/ *n* [C] **1** (sound of a) short, quick sending out of breath, air, etc; amount of steam, smoke, etc sent out at one time: ~*s from a steam-engine; have a* ~ *at a pipe.* **2** ('**powder-**)~, piece or ball of soft material, for putting powder on the face. **3** round, soft mass of material used on an article of dress as an ornament: ~ *sleeves,* swelling out like balloons. **4** ~ **pastry,** light, flaky pastry. **5** quantity of ~ pastry filled with jam, whipped cream, etc: *jam* ~*s.* **6** review of a book, play, etc, praising it extravagantly. **7** '~**-adder** *n* poisonous African viper which inflates the upper part of its body when excited. '~**-ball** *n* kind of fungus shaped like a ball which when ripe breaks open and sends out ~s of dust-like spores. ~**y** *adj* (-ier, -iest) short of breath; easily made short of breath (by running, climbing, etc); swollen: *a red face,* ~*y under the eyes.* ~**i·ness** *n* [U] state of being ~y.

puff² /pʌf/ *vi,vt* **1** [VP2A,C] move along with puffs(1); breathe quickly (as after running); (of smoke, steam, etc) come out in puffs: *The old steam-engine* ~*ed out of the station. He was* ~*ing hard when he jumped on to the bus. He was* ~*ing* (*away*) *at his cigar. Smoke* ~*ed up from the crater of the volcano.* **2** [VP15A,B] send out in puffs: *He* ~*ed smoke into my face. He managed to* ~ *out a few words. He was rather* ~*ed* (= out of breath) *after running to the bus stop.* ~*ed up,* filled with pride; conceited. **3** [VP15B] ~ **sth out, (a)** blow out: *He* ~*ed out the candle.* **(b)** cause to swell with air: *He* ~*ed out his chest with pride.* **4** [VP6A] praise (a book, etc) in an advertisement or review, esp in an exaggerated way.

puf·fin /'pʌfɪn/ *n* N Atlantic seabird with a large bill. ⇨ the illus at water.

pug /pʌg/ *n* (also '**pug-dog**) small breed of pugnosed dog. '**pug-nose(d)** *adj, n* (with a) short, squat or snub nose.

pu·gil·ist /'pjuːdʒɪlɪst/ *n* (formal) boxer. **pu·gil·ism** /-ɪzəm/ *n* [U] boxing. **pu·gil·is·tic** /ˌpjuːdʒɪ'lɪstɪk/ *adj* of ~s or pugilism.

pug·na·cious /pʌg'neɪʃəs/ *adj* (formal) fond of, in the habit of, fighting. ~**·ly** *adv* **pug·nac·ity** /pʌg'næsətɪ/ *n* [U].

puis·sant /'pjuːɪsnt/ *adj* (archaic) having great power or influence. **puis·sance** /-sns/ *n* [U] strength.

puke /pjuːk/ *vi, vt, n* [U] (sl) vomit.

pukka /'pʌkə/ (dated sl) genuine; authentic; superior.

pul·chri·tude /'pʌlkrɪtjuːd *US:* -tuːd/ *n* [U] (formal) physical beauty. **pul·chri·tudi·nous** /ˌpʌlkrɪ'tjuːdɪnəs *US:* -'tuːdənəs/ *adj*

pule /pjuːl/ *vi* [VP2A] (eg of a baby) cry feebly; whimper.

pull¹ /pʊl/ *n* **1** [C] act of pulling: *give a ~ at a rope;* [C] act of deep drinking: *take a ~ at a bottle,* drink deeply from it. **2** [C,U] attraction: *the ~ of the life of a sailor/singer/tramp.* **3** [C] effort of moving: *a hard/long ~ up the hill.* **4** [C,U] (colloq) power to get help or attention through influence, eg with people in high positions: *He has a strong ~/a great deal of ~ with the Managing Director.* **5** handle, etc which is to be pulled. **6** (printing) proof; single impression.

pull² /pʊl/ *vt, vi* (For special uses with *adverbial particles* and *preps,* ⇨ **7** below.) **1** [VP6A,15A,B,22,2A] (contrasted with *push*) use force upon (sth or sb) so as to draw towards or after one, or in the direction indicated: *The horse was ~ing a heavy cart. How many coaches can that locomotive ~? Would you rather push the barrow or ~ it? The baby was ~ing its father's beard. P~ your chair up to the table. She ~ed her tights/gloves on/off. He ~ed my ears/~ed me by the ears. I'm going to the dentist to have a bad tooth ~ed out. Stop ~ing, please! ~ sth to pieces,* use force to separate its parts or to break it up into parts; (fig) criticize severely by pointing out the weak points or faults: *He ~ed my proposals/theory to pieces.* **2** [VP6A,15A,B,2A,C] move (a boat) by ~ing an oar or a pair of oars; (of a boat) be rowed (by): *Now, all ~ together, please! The men/boat ~ed for the shore. ~ together,* (fig) work together; co-operate. *~ one's weight,* exert oneself so as to do a fair share of the work: *Either you ~ your weight or we replace you.* **3** [VP3A] *~ at/on sth,* (a) give a tug: *~ at/on a rope.* (b) draw or suck: *~ing at his pipe,* drawing in breath and smoke through his (tobacco) pipe; *~ at a bottle,* have a drink from one. ⇨ pull¹(1). **4** *~ a 'fast one,* (colloq) deceive sb. *~ a muscle,* strain it. *~ a proof,* take an impression (from type); print a proof. For other uses with *nn,* ⇨ the *n* entries, eg *~ a face/faces; ~ sb's leg; ~ one's punches; ~ strings; ~ wires; ~ the 'wool over sb's eyes.* **5** (in games, sport) (golf) hit (the ball) wrongly to the left. Cf *slice*(4); (cricket) strike (the ball) forward and to the left of the wicket, by striking across the ball's path; (horse-racing) *~* in the reins (of a horse) to prevent it from winning. **6** (sl) raid; rob: *~ a bank;* steal: *~ a few thousand quid.* **7** [VP15B,2C] (special uses with *adverbial particles* and *preps*):

pull sb/sth about, *~* in different directions; treat roughly.

pull sth apart, tear or *~* into its parts.

pull sth down, destroy or demolish, eg an old building. **pull sb down,** (of illness, etc) weaken; lower the spirits of: *An attack of influenza soon ~s you down.*

pull in, (a) (of a train) enter a station: *The express from Rome ~ed in on time.* **(b)** (of a motor-vehicle or boat) move in towards: *The boat ~ed in to the bank/shore. The lorry driver ~ed in to the side of the road.* Hence, **'~-in** *n* place at which to *~* in

(also ⇨ *~-up* below). *~ sb in,* (a) attract, draw: *The new play at the National Theatre is ~ing in large audiences.* (b) (colloq, of the police) detain; arrest: *He was ~ed in for questioning/loitering. ~ sth in,* (a) (colloq) earn: *How much money is he ~ing in, do you think? ~ oneself in* draw in the stomach muscles (so as to be upright, less flabby).

pull sth off, (a) drive a motor-vehicle into a layby or hard shoulder. Hence, **'~-off** *n* (US) = layby. **(b)** succeed in a plan, in winning sth: *~ off a good speculation; ~ off some good wins at the races,* make successful bets.

pull out, (a) move or row out: *The boat ~ed out into midstream. The driver of the car ~ed out from behind the lorry.* **(b)** detach, eg from a periodical: (attrib) *a '~-out supplement,* part of a magazine, etc which can be ~ed out and kept separately. Hence, **'~-out** *n = out of sth,* leave: *The train ~ed out of Euston right on time. Sam ~ed out of the scheme at the last moment. ~ (sb) out (of sth),* (cause to) leave a place or situation which is too difficult to manage: *Troops are being ~ed out/are ~ing out of these troubled areas.* Hence, **'~-out** *n: The ~-out was planned to spread over a month.*

pull (sth) over, (cause a vehicle, boat, etc to) move or steer to one side, eg to let another vehicle or boat pass: *P~ (your car) over and let me pass!*

pull (sb) round, (help to) recover from illness, weakness, a faint, etc: *You'll soon ~ round here in the country. Have this brandy; it will ~ you round.*

pull through, (a) = *~ round.* **(b)** succeed in avoiding difficulties, dangers, etc; avoid failure. *~ sb through,* (a) help to recover from illness, etc: *The doctors ~ed me through.* (b) help to avoid failure, help to pass an examination, etc: *David's tutor did what he could to ~ him through.* **'~-through** *n* oily rag attached to a cord, ~ed through the barrel of a rifle, etc to clean it.

pull together, ⇨ 2 above. *~ oneself together,* get control of oneself, of one's feelings, etc.

pull (sth) up, bring or come to a stop: *The driver ~ed up when he came to the traffic lights. He ~ed up his car at the entrance.* Hence, **'~-up** *n* place at which to ~ up: *'Good ~-up for lorry-drivers',* eg as a sign outside a roadside café (also ⇨ *~-in* above). *~ sb up,* check; reprimand: *He was ~ed up by the chairman. ~ up to/with sb/sth,* improve one's relative position (in a race, etc): *The favourite soon ~ed up with the other horses.*

pul·let /'pʊlɪt/ *n* young hen, esp at the time she begins to lay eggs.

pul·ley /'pʊlɪ/ *n* (*pl ~s*) grooved wheel(s) for ropes or chains, used for lifting things. **'~-block** *n* wooden block in which a ~ is fixed.

Pull·man /'pʊlmən/ *n* **1** (also **'~ car**) sleeping-car on a railway train. **2** especially comfortable railway carriage.

pull·over /'pʊləʊvə(r)/ *n* knitted outer garment, with or without sleeves, pulled on over the head. ⇨ jersey, jumper, sweater.

pul·lu·late /'pʌljʊleɪt/ *vi* breed, multiply, rapidly; swarm.

pul·mon·ary /'pʌlmənərɪ *US:* -nerɪ/ *adj* of, in, connected with, the lungs: *~ diseases; the ~ arteries,* conveying blood to the lungs.

pulp /pʌlp/ *n* **1** [U] soft, fleshy part of fruit: *'apple ~.* **2** [U,C] soft mass of other material, esp of wood fibre as used for making paper: *reduce to (a)*

~, destroy the shape of by beating up and making soft. ~ **magazines/literature,** (term applied disparagingly to) cheap, popular periodicals, etc. □ vt,vi [VP6A,2A] make into, become like, ~; remove ~ from: ~ *old books.* ~y *adj* (-ier, -iest) like or consisting of ~.

pul·pit /'pʊlpɪt/ *n* (usu small) raised and enclosed structure in a church, used by a clergyman, esp when preaching. **the** ~, the clergy. ⇨ the illus at **church.**

pul·que /'puːlkeɪ/ *n* [U] fermented milky drink made in Mexico from some kinds of agave.

pul·sar /'pʌlsɑː(r)/ *n* star (in a galaxy) detected by pulsating radio signals only.

pul·sate /pʌl'seɪt *US:* 'pʌlseɪt/ *vt,vi* **1** [VP2A] beat or throb; expand and contract rhythmically; vibrate; quiver. **2** [VP6A] cause to vibrate; agitate; **pul·sa·tion** /pʌl'seɪʃn/ *n* **1** [C] single beat or throb; heartbeat. **2** [U] pulsating; throbbing.

pulse[1] /pʌls/ *n* **1** the regular beat of the arteries, eg as felt at the wrist, as the blood is pumped through them by the heart: *The patient has a weak/strong/low/irregular* ~. **feel sb's** ~, feel the artery at the wrist and count the number of beats per minute. **2** (fig) throb or thrill of life or emotion: *an event that stirred my* ~s, roused my emotion, excited me. □ *vi* [VP2C] beat; throb: *the life pulsing through a great city; news that sent the blood pulsing through his veins.*

pulse[2] /pʌls/ *n* [U] (collective *sing,* sometimes with *pl v*) seeds growing in pods, eg peas, beans and lentils, used as food.

pul·ver·ize /'pʌlvəraɪz/ *vt,vi* **1** [VP6A] grind to powder; smash completely: (fig) ~ *an opponent's arguments.* **2** [VP2A] become powder or dust.

puma /'pjuːmə/ *n* large brown American animal of the cat family (also called a *cougar* and *mountain lion).* ⇨ the illus at cat.

pum·ice /'pʌmɪs/ *n* [U] '~(-**stone**), light, porous stone (lava) used for cleaning and polishing.

pum·mel /'pʌml/ *vt* (-ll-, US also -l-) [VP6A,15B] beat repeatedly with the fists: *give sb a good* ~*ling.*

pump[1] /pʌmp/ *n* machine or device for forcing liquid, gas or air into, out of or through sth, eg water from a well, petrol from a storage tank, air into a tyre, oil through a pipe-line: *a row of*'*petrol* ~*s; a* '*bicycle* ~. ⇨ the illus at bicycle. ⇨ also *parish-pump* at parish. '~-**room** *n* (at a spa) room where medicinal water is dispensed. □ *vt,vi* **1** [VP6A,15A,B,22] force, eg water, etc *out/up/into/through* sth, by using a ~: ~ *water up/out;* ~ *a well dry,* ~ until there is no water left in the well; ~ *air into a tyre;* ~ *up the tyres;* (fig) ~ *information out of sb;* ~ *facts into the heads of dull pupils; a* '~*ing station,* eg on a pipe-line carrying petroleum. **2** [VP2A,C] use a ~: *He was* ~*ing away.*

pump[2] /pʌmp/ *n* kind of light, soft shoe worn for sport, dancing, etc; (US) woman's low-heeled shoe without a fastening.

pum·per·nickel /'pʌmpənɪkl/ *n* [U] wholemeal rye bread.

pump·kin /'pʌmpkɪn/ *n* large, round orange-yellow fruit with many seeds in it, used as a vegetable and (US) as a filling for pies.

pun /pʌn/ *n* [C] humorous use of different words which sound the same or of two meanings of the same word, eg 'A cannon-ball took off his *legs,* so he laid down his *arms.*' □ *vi* (-nn-) [VP2A,3A] ~ **(on/upon),** make a pun or puns (on/upon a word).

punch[1] /pʌntʃ/ *n* **1** tool or machine for cutting holes in leather, metal, paper, etc; tool for forcing nails beneath a surface, or bolts out of holes. **2** tool for stamping designs on surfaces. □ *vt* **1** [VP6A] make a hole (in sth) with a ~: ~ *holes in a sheet of metal;* ~ *a train-ticket;* ~*ed cards,* as used in filing systems or computers; ~*d (paper) tape,* used by computer programmers. **2** [VP15B] ~ **sth in/out,** drive sth in or out with a ~.

punch[2] /pʌntʃ/ *n* [U] drink made of wine or spirits mixed with hot water, sugar, lemons, spice, etc: *rum* ~. '~-**bowl** *n* bowl in which ~ is mixed.

punch[3] /pʌntʃ/ *vt* [VP6A,15A] strike hard with the fist: ~ *a man on the chin. He has a face I'd like to* ~. □ *n* **1** [C] blow given with the fist: *give sb a* ~ *on the nose; a boxer with a strong* ~, the ability to deliver strong ~es. **pull one's** ~**es,** attack less vigorously than one is able to. '~-**ball,** '~-**ing-ball** *nn* inflated or stuffed ball hung up and ~ed with the fists for exercise. ~-'**drunk** *adj* (in boxing) dazed by ~es received in a fight; (fig) confused. '~ **line** *n* climax of a story (where the point is made, where laughter comes). '~-**up** *n* (colloq) fight with the fists: *The quarrel ended in a* ~-*up.* **2** [U] (fig) energy: *a speech with plenty of* ~ *in it.*

Punch /pʌntʃ/ *n* grotesque hump-backed figure in the traditional puppet-show called **P**~ **and Judy.** **as pleased/proud as P**~, greatly pleased/very proud.

punc·tilio /pʌŋk'tɪlɪəʊ/ *n* (*pl* ~s /-lɪəʊz/) **1** [C] particular point of good conduct, ceremony, honour. **2** [U,C] formality; (point of) etiquette (esp when it is not really important): *stand upon* ~s, insist too much upon protocol(2).

punc·tili·ous /pʌŋk'tɪlɪəs/ *adj* (formal) very careful to carry out correctly details of conduct and ceremony; careful in performing duties. ~-**ly** *adv* ~-**ness** *n*

punc·tual /'pʌŋktʃʊəl/ *adj* neither early nor late; coming, doing sth, at the time fixed: *be* ~ *for the appointment/in payment of one's rent.* ~**ly** /-ʊəlɪ/ *adv* in a ~ manner: *The train arrived* ~*ly.* ~-**ity** /ˌpʌŋktʃʊ'ælətɪ/ *n* [U] being ~.

punc·tu·ate /'pʌŋktʃʊeɪt/ *vt* **1** [VP6A] put full-stops, commas, etc, (eg .,;:?!) into a piece of writing. **2** [VP15A] interrupt from time to time: *a speech* ~*d with cheers;* ~ *one's remarks with thumps on the table.* **punc·tu·ation** /ˌpʌŋktʃʊ'eɪʃn/ *n* [U] punctuating; art or practice of punctuating. ⇨ App 9.

punc·ture /'pʌŋktʃə(r)/ *n* [C] small hole made by sth sharp, esp one made accidentally in a pneumatic tyre. □ *vt,vi* **1** [VP6A] make a ~ in: ~ *an abscess/a motor-car tyre;* (fig) deflate: *She likes to* ~ *her husband's ego,* lessen his self-conceit. **2** [VP2A] experience a ~: *Two of my tyres* ~*d while I was on that stony road.*

pun·dit /'pʌndɪt/ *n* very learned Hindu; authority on a subject; (hum) learned teacher; pedant.

pun·gent /'pʌndʒənt/ *adj* (of smells, tastes; fig of remarks) sharp; biting; stinging: *a* ~ *sauce;* ~ *remarks/satire/criticism.* ~-**ly** *adv* **pun·gency** /-nsɪ/ *n* [U] ~ quality.

Pu·nic /'pjuːnɪk/ *adj* of ancient Carthage and its people. **the** ~ **Wars,** the wars between Rome and Carthage. ~ **faith,** treachery.

pun·ish /'pʌnɪʃ/ *vt* [VP6A,14] ~ **sb (with/by sth) (for sth),** **1** cause (sb) suffering or discomfort for wrongdoing; cause suffering or discomfort to sb (for wrongdoing): ~ *a man with/by a fine. How* *would you ~ stealing/sb for stealing/sb who steals?* **2** treat roughly; knock about: *The champion ~ed his opponent severely,* (boxing) gave him severe blows. *Chapman ~ed the bowling,* (cricket) scored freely (from poor or weak bowling). **3** (colloq) eat, drink, use up, deal with, etc, much of: *~ the cold beef/the cider cask.* **~·able** /-əbl/ *adj* that can be ~ed (by law). **~·ment** *n* [U] ~ing or being ~ed: *escape without ~ment.* [C] penalty inflicted for wrongdoing: *make the ~ment fit the crime; inflict severe ~ments on criminals.*

pu·ni·tive /'pju:nɪtɪv/ *adj* (intended for) punishing: *a ~ expedition,* a military expedition with the purpose of punishing rebels, etc.

punk /pʌŋk/ *n* **1** [U] (US) partly decayed wood; rotten wood used as tinder. **2** [U] (colloq) worthless stuff; rubbish: *He talked a lot of ~.* **~ rock** *n* [U] (late 1970's) loud, fast, violent style of rock[3] music. **3** [C] (sl) worthless person. **4** [C] (late 1970's) fan[3] (of bizarre appearance) of ~ rock music.

pun·kah /'pʌŋkə/ *n* (India) large piece of cloth on a frame, kept moving by means of a cord and pulley, used to keep the air in movement (as an electric fan does).

pun·net /'pʌnɪt/ *n* small basket, made of very thin wood, plastic, etc esp as a measure for fruit: *strawberries, 20p a ~.*

pun·ster /'pʌnstə(r)/ *n* person who has the habit of making puns.

punt[1] /pʌnt/ *n* flat-bottomed, shallow boat with square ends, moved by pushing the end of a long pole against the river-bed. □ *vt, vi* [VP6A, 2A] move (a ~) in this way; carry (sb or sth) in a ~; go in a ~. **punter** *n*

punt[2] /pʌnt/ *vt* [VP6A] kick (a football) after it has dropped from the hands and before it reaches the ground. □ *n* such a kick.

punt[3] /pʌnt/ *vi* [VP2A] (in some card-games) lay a stake against the bank; bet on a horse, etc. **~er** *n* person who ~s or bets.

puny /'pju:nɪ/ *adj* (-ier, -iest) small and weak: *What a ~ little creature! My ~ efforts are not worth much.* **pun·ily** /'pju:nɪlɪ/ *adv*

pup /pʌp/ *n* **1** young dog; young of some other animals, eg the seal. *sell sb a pup,* (colloq) swindle him, esp by selling him sth which, he is made to believe, may have greatly increased value in the future. **2** conceited young man.

pupa /'pju:pə/ *n* (*pl* ~s, or ~e /-pi:/) chrysalis. ⇨ the illus at butterfly.

pu·pil[1] /'pju:pl/ *n* person who is learning in school or from a private teacher.

pu·pil[2] /'pju:pl/ *n* (anat) circular opening in the centre of the iris of the eye, regulating the passage of light. ⇨ the illus at eye.

GLOVE-PUPPET

MARIONETTE

puppets

pup·pet /'pʌpɪt/ *n* **1** doll, small figure of an animal, etc with jointed limbs moved by wires or strings, used in plays or shows called '~*-plays/-shows;* marionette; ('*glove-~*) doll of which the body can be put on the hand like a glove, the arms and head

being moved by the fingers of the operator. **2** person, group of persons, whose acts are completely controlled by another: (attrib) *a ~ government/ State.*

puppy /'pʌpɪ/ *n* (*pl* -pies) **1** young dog. '*~ love* *n* [U] first love affair(s). '*~ fat* *n* [U] the kind of fat that boys and girls sometimes have before adolescence. **2** conceited young man.

pur·blind /'pɜ:blaɪnd/ *adj* partly or nearly blind; (fig) stupid.

pur·chase[1] /'pɜ:tʃəs/ *n* **1** [U] buying: '*~-money,* price (to be) paid. '*~ tax* *n* (US = *sales tax*) tax on the retail price of goods, collected by the retailer and paid by him to the State (GB since 1973 replaced by value-added tax.) ⇨ value. **2** [C] sth bought: *He filled the car with his ~s. I have some ~s to make.* **3** (*sing* only) firm hold or grip (for pulling or raising sth, or to prevent sth from slipping: *get a/any/some ~ on sth.* **4** [U] value or worth, esp as reckoned in annual yield or return: *sold at thirty years' ~,* (of land, etc) sold for the equivalent of thirty years' rent. *His life is not worth a day's ~,* He is on the point of death.

pur·chase[2] /'pɜ:tʃəs/ *vt* [VP6A] buy (which is much more usu): *a dearly ~d victory,* eg a battle in which many lives are lost. **pur·chas·able** /-əbl/ *adj* that can be ~d. **~r** *n* buyer.

pur·dah /'pɜ:də/ *n* [U] (esp in Muslim communities) curtain for, convention of, keeping women from the sight of strangers, esp men: *live/be in ~.*

pure /pjʊə(r)/ *adj* (-r, -st except 5,6 below) **1** unmixed with any other substance, etc: *~ water/ milk/gold; ~ air,* free from smoke, fumes, etc. **2** of unmixed race: *~ blood; a ~ Negro; a ~bred* (= *thoroughbred* which is more usu) *Alsatian dog.* **3** clean; without evil or sin: *~ in body and mind; ~ thoughts; the ~ in heart.* **4** (of sounds) clear and distinct: *a ~ note.* **5** dealing with, studied for the sake of, theory only (not *applied*): *~ mathematics/science.* **6** mere; nothing but: *~ mischief; a ~ waste of time; spread unkind gossip out of ~ malice.* **sth ~ and simple,** it alone: *laziness ~ and simple,* sheer laziness. **~·ly** *adv* (esp) entirely; completely; merely: *~ly by accident; a ~ly formal request.* **~·ness** *n* = purity (which is more usu).

pu·rée /'pjʊəreɪ *US:* pjʊə'reɪ/ *n* thick liquid made of vegetables, etc boiled to a pulp and pressed through a sieve; fruit similarly treated.

pur·ga·tion /pɜ:'geɪʃn/ *n* [U] (formal) **1** purging or purification.

pur·ga·tive /'pɜ:gətɪv/ *n, adj* (substance) having the power to purge or cleanse the bowels.

pur·ga·tory /'pɜ:gətrɪ *US:* -tɔ:rɪ/ *n* (*pl* -ries) **1** (esp in RC doctrine) condition after death in which the soul is purified in preparation for heaven; place where souls are so purified. **2** any place of temporary suffering or expiation. **pur·ga·torial** /,pɜ:gə'tɔ:rɪəl/ *adj* of ~.

purge /pɜ:dʒ/ *vt* [VP6A,14,15A,B] *~ sb (of/from sth); ~ sth (away) (from sb),* **1** make clean or free (of physical or moral impurity): *be ~d of/from sin; ~ away one's sins.* **2** empty (the bowels) of waste matter by means of medicine. **3** clear (oneself, a person, of a charge, of suspicion); (legal) atone for (an offence, etc) by submission: *~ one's contempt,* (legal) do what is right after showing contempt of court. **4** rid (a political party, etc) of members who are considered undesirable. □ *n* [C] **1** purging, clearing out or away: *the political*

~s that followed the overthrow of the government. **2** medicine used for purging(2).

pu·rify /'pjʊərɪfaɪ/ vt (pt,pp -fied) [VP6A,14] ~ **sth (of)**, make pure; cleanse: an air-~ing plant (eg for providing pure air in a factory). **pu·ri·fi·ca·tion** /ˌpjʊərɪfɪˈkeɪʃn/ n [U] ~ing, eg as a religious ceremony.

pu·rist /'pjʊərɪst/ n person who pays great attention to correct procedures (eg in the arts).

puri·tan /'pjʊərɪtən/ n **1** P~, (16th and 17th cc, in England) member of a division of the Protestant Church which wanted simpler forms of church ceremony. **2** person who is strict in morals and religion, who looks upon fun and pleasure as sinful, and who believes that all people should work hard always. □ adj of or like a ~. ~**ism** /-ɪzəm/ n practices and beliefs of a P~ or a ~. **puri·tani·cal** /ˌpjʊərɪˈtænɪkl/ adj very strict and severe, like a ~. **puri·tani·cally** /-klɪ/ adv

pu·rity /'pjʊərətɪ/ n [U] state or quality of being pure.

purl[1] /pɜːl/ n (knitting) inverted stitch, which produces a ribbed appearance (the opp of plain). □ vt,vi invert (stitches); invert stitches of (sth being knitted).

purl[2] /pɜːl/ vi (poet) (of a small stream) flow with a murmuring sound. □ n this sound.

pur·lieus /'pɜːljuːz/ n pl outskirts; outlying parts: the ~ of the camp.

pur·loin /pɜːˈlɔɪn/ vt [VP6A] (formal) steal.

purple /'pɜːpl/ n, adj (colour) of red and blue mixed together: a ~ sunset; become ~ with rage. **the ~**, the ~ robes of a Roman emperor or a cardinal. **born in the ~**, a member of a royal family. **raise sb to the ~**, make him a cardinal. **~ 'heart** n **(a)** (GB) heart-shaped tablet containing amphetamine, used as a stimulant. **(b)** (US **P~ Heart**) medal awarded to a soldier wounded in battle. **pur·plish** /'pɜːpəlɪʃ/ adj somewhat ~.

pur·port /'pɜːpət/ n [U] (formal) general meaning or intention of sth said or written; likely explanation of a person's actions: the ~ of what he said. □ vt /pəˈpɔːt/ **1** [VP6A,9] seem to mean: The statement ~s that.... **2** [VP7A] claim: The book ~s to be an original work but is really a compilation.

pur·pose /'pɜːpəs/ n **1** [C] that which one means to do, get, be, etc; plan; design; intention: For what ~(s) do you want to go to Canada? I wouldn't go to London for/with the mere ~ of buying a new tie. This van is used for various ~s. This is a novel with a ~, one written eg to explain or defend a doctrine, not merely to amuse. ~**·'built** adj made to serve a particular function. **2** [U] determination; power of forming plans and keeping to them: weak of ~; wanting in ~. **3** (phrases) **on ~**, by intention, not by chance: You sometimes hurt yourself by accident but you don't hurt yourself on ~. He has left the book here on ~ for you to read. He came here on ~ to borrow money from you. She sometimes does things on ~ just to annoy me. **of set ~**, deliberately; not accidentally. **to the ~**, useful for one's ~; relevant: The reply was so little to the ~ that it was not worth our consideration. **to little/no/some ~**, with little/no/some result or effect. **serve/answer one's ~**, be satisfactory; do what is required. □ vt [VP6A,D,7,9] (liter) have as one's ~: They ~ (making/to make) a further attempt. ~**·ful** /-fl/ adj having a conscious ~; full of meaning. ~**·fully** /-fəlɪ/ adv ~**·less** adj lacking ~; having no object in view. ~**·less·ly** adv. ~**·ly**

adv on ~; intentionally. **pur·pos·ive** /'pɜːpəsɪv/ adj having, serving, done with, a ~: purposive movements; (of a person, his conduct) having, showing, ~ and determination.

purr /pɜː(r)/ vi,vt **1** [VP2A,C] (of a cat) make a low, continuous vibrating sound expressing pleasure; (of a car engine) make a vibrating sound; (fig, of a person) indicate contentment by using a pleasant tone: Mrs Black ~ed with delight on receiving the invitation to dine with the duchess. **2** [VP6A] express (contentment, etc) thus: She ~ed her approval of the suggestion. □ n ~ing sound.

purse /pɜːs/ n **1** small bag for money (originally closed by drawing strings together, now usu closed with a clasp): That big car is beyond my ~, costs more than I can afford. ~**-proud** adj ⇨ proud(5). **hold the '~-strings**, have control of expenditure. **tighten/loosen the '~-strings**, reduce/increase expenditure; be economical/generous. **2** money; funds. **privy P~**, ⇨ privy. **the public ~**, the national treasury. **3** sum of money collected or offered as a prize, gift, etc: make up a ~; give/put up a ~, eg for the winner of a boxing match. **4** (US) handbag. □ vt [VP6A,15B] ~ **(up)**; ~ **(up) the lips**, draw the lips together in tiny folds or wrinkles.

purser /'pɜːsə(r)/ n officer responsible for a ship's accounts and stores, esp in a passenger liner.

pur·su·ance /pəˈsjuːəns US: -ˈsuː-/ n in ~ of, (formal) in the carrying out of or the performance of (one's duties, a plan, etc). **pur·su·ant** /-ənt/ adj **pursuant to**, (formal) in accordance with; in agreement with: pursuant to your instructions.

pur·sue /pəˈsjuː US: -ˈsuː/ vt [VP6A] **1** go after in order to catch up with, capture or kill: pursuing a robber/a bear; make sure that you are not being ~d. **2** (fig) (of consequences, penalties, etc) persistently follow: His record as a criminal ~d him wherever he went. He has been ~d by misfortune. **3** go on with; work at: ~ one's studies after leaving school. **4** have as an aim or purpose: ~ pleasure. ~**r** n person who ~s(1).

pur·suit /pəˈsjuːt US: -ˈsuːt/ n **1** [U] (in) ~ (of), act of pursuing: a dog in ~ of rabbits; a fox with the hounds in hot ~; in his ~ of happiness; (attrib) a ~ plane, one that pursues and fights enemy planes. **2** [C] sth at which one works or to which one gives one's time: engaged in scientific/literary ~s.

pursy[1] /'pɜːsɪ/ adj (old use) (of a person) fat and short-winded.

pursy[2] /'pɜːsɪ/ adj (old use) puckered: ~ eyes. ⇨ purse, v.

puru·lent /'pjʊərələnt/ adj of, containing, discharging, pus. **puru·lence** /-əns/ n

pur·vey /pəˈveɪ/ vt,vi **1** [VP6A,14] ~ **(to)**, (formal) provide, supply (food, as a trader): A butcher ~s meat to his customers. **2** [VP3A] ~ **for**, supply provisions for: a firm that ~s for the Navy. ~**or** /-ə(r)/ n person whose business is to supply provisions on a large scale, eg for the Army or Navy, for large public dinners. ~**·ance** /-əns/ n

pur·view /'pɜːvjuː/ n (formal) range or operation or activity; scope; extent: These are questions that lie outside/that do not come within the ~ of our inquiry.

pus /pʌs/ n [U] thick yellowish-white liquid formed in and coming out from a poisoned place in the body: It is unwise to squeeze a boil to force the pus out.

push[1] /pʊʃ/ n **1** [C] act of pushing: Give the door a hard ~. *He opened the gate with/at one* ~. **2** [C] vigorous effort: *We must make a* ~ *to finish the job this week. The enemy made a* ~ (= an attack in force) *to capture the city.* **3 get the** ~, (sl) be dismissed (from one's employment, etc). **give sb the** ~, (sl) dismiss him. **4** [U] determination to make one's way in life, to attract attention, etc: *He hasn't enough* ~ *to succeed as a salesman.* **5 at a** ~, if compelled by need or circumstances: *We can sleep seven or eight people in the house at a* ~. **if/ when/until it comes to the** ~, if/when/until one is compelled by need or circumstances, when an effort is needed: *He seemed a satisfactory man until it came to the* ~; *then he failed us.*

push² /pʊʃ/ *vt,vi* (For special uses with *adverbial particles* and *preps,* ⇨ **9** below.) **1** [VP6A,15A,B,22,2A,C] (contrasted with *pull*) use force on (sth/sb) to cause forward movement; exert pressure against: *Please* ~ *the table nearer to the wall. If you'll* ~ *the car, I'll steer it. You can pull a rope, but you can't* ~ *it! We had to* ~ *our way* (= go forward by ~ing) *through the crowd. Stop* ~*ing at the back! He* ~*ed the door open. The football crowds* ~*ed past me.* **2** [VP6A] persuade others to recognize, eg claims, or buy, eg goods: *Unless you* ~ *your claims you'll get no satisfaction. You must* ~ *your wares if you want better sales. Haven't you a friend who can* ~ *you,* use his influence to help you? ~ **oneself,** show energy, etc to win recognition: *You'll never get anywhere if you don't* ~ *yourself.* ⇨ also ~ *oneself forward* in **9** below. **3** [VP6A] (sl) sell (illicit drugs) by acting as a link between large suppliers and the drug addicts. ⇨ pusher below. **4** [VP14] ~ **sb for sth,** press sb hard (to get sth): *We're* ~*ing them for payment/an answer to our request.* **be** ~**ed for sth,** have difficulty in finding: *I'm rather* ~*ed for money/time just now.* **5** [VP14,17] ~ **sb/oneself to sth/to do sth,** drive or urge: *Tony had to* ~ *himself to go on doing such dull work. She'll* ~ *him to the verge of suicide.* **6** [VP6A] press: ~ *a button,* eg to ring a bell; ~*button warfare,* war in which missiles, eg with atomic war-heads, are fired by pressing buttons. **7 be** ~**ing thirty/forty, etc,** (colloq) be nearing the age indicated: *She wouldn't like you to think so, but she's* ~*ing thirty.* **8** (compounds) '~**bike** *n* one that is worked by pedalling (not a *moped* or *motor-bike*). '~**cart** *n* small cart ~ed by a man. '~**chair** *n* carriage for a child, like a chair on wheels (used when a child is old enough to sit up). ~**er** *n* **1** (colloq) person who ~es himself/herself forward: *Isn't she a* ~*er!* (said of someone who takes every opportunity of gaining an advantage for herself). **2** (sl) pedlar of illicit drugs. ~**ful** /-fl/, ~**ing** *adj* having a tendency to ~ oneself: *He's too* ~*ing with strangers,* tries too much to force himself upon their attention. ⇨ **3** above. **9** [VP15A,B,3A] (special uses with *adverbial particles* and *preps*):
push along, (colloq) leave sb/a place: *I'm afraid it's time I was* ~*ing along,* time for me to go.
push sb around, (colloq) bully him; order him about: *I'm not going to be* ~*ed around by you or anybody!*
push forward/on (to a place), go on resolutely with a journey, one's work, etc: *It's getting dark; we must* ~ *on to our destination. We must* ~ *on with our work,* hurry and finish it. ~ **oneself forward,** ambitiously draw attention to oneself, eg at work, in society: *He never* ~*es himself forward,* is

modest, doesn't try to attract attention.
push off, (colloq) leave; go away: *Tell that rude fellow to* ~ *off! It's time we* ~*ed off.* ~ **(a boat, etc) off,** (of sb in a boat) ~ against the bank, etc, eg with an oar or pole, to get the boat moving in the current, etc.
push (a boat, etc) out, ~ off.
push sb/sth over, cause to fall; overturn: *Don't* ~ *me over! Several children were* ~*ed over in the stampede.* '~**over** *n* (sl) sth very easy to do; person who is easily overcome or controlled.
push sb through (sth), enable sb (esp sb needing help) to succeed in sth: ~ *a weak student through an exam.* ~ **sth through,** bring sth to the final stage by special efforts: ~ *legislation through,* get it passed. *We must* ~ *the matter through.*
push sth up, force, eg prices, to rise. ~ **up the daisies,** (sl) be buried in a grave.

pu·si·lani·mous /ˌpjuːsɪˈlænɪməs/ *adj* (formal) timid; easily frightened. **pu·sil·la·nim·ity** /ˌpjuːsɪləˈnɪmətɪ/ *n* [U].

puss /pʊs/ *n* **1** cat; word used to call a cat. **2** (colloq) girl: *She's a sly* ~. ~**y** /ˈpʊsɪ/ *n* (*pl* -sies) (also '~**y-cat**) (child's word for a) cat. '~**foot** *vi* [VP2A,C] (colloq) move about in a quiet, stealthy way (as a cat does): *Was that you* ~*footing about in the corridor last night?* (fig) act too cautiously or timidly. '~**y willow** *n* tree with soft silky catkins.

pus·tule /ˈpʌstjuːl US: -tʃuːl/ *n* (med) pimple or blister, esp one filled with pus.

put¹ /pʊt/ *vi,vt* (*pt,pp* put, *pres part* -tt-) (For special uses with *adverbial particles* and *preps,* ⇨ **11** below.) **1** [VP6A,15A] move (sth) so as to be in a certain place or position: *He put the book on the table. He put his hands in(to) his pockets. He put the corpse down the well. Did you put milk in my tea? It's time to put the baby to bed. Will you please put* (= sew) *a patch on these trousers? He put* (= fastened) *a new handle on to the knife. He put* (= pushed) *a knife into me/between my ribs. I'll put a bullet through your head, kill you. They've put a satellite into orbit round Mars. They've put men on the moon. He put* (= pushed) *his fist through the window, broke it by doing this. He put his pen through the word, struck the word out.* **put pen to paper,** start writing. **put one's foot in it,** ⇨ foot¹(1). **2** [VP15A] cause (sb/ oneself) to be in some relationship, eg as an employee, client, with sb. **put oneself/sth in/into sb's hands,** let him deal with one's problems, etc: *I put myself entirely in your hands. I shall put the matter into the hands of my solicitors.* **put sb in his (proper) place,** make him humble. **put oneself in sb's/sb 'else's' position,** imagine oneself in his position: *How would you feel (about the matter)?—Just put yourself in my/her position!* **3** [VP14] make sb bear (the particular nervous or moral strain indicated). **put the blame on sb,** blame him: *Don't put all the blame on me.* **put pressure on sb (to do sth),** strongly urge him: *They're putting great pressure on him* (= pressing him hard) *to resign.* **put (a) strain on sb/sth,** make him/it suffer from hard work or use: *All this work is putting (a) great strain on him.* **4** [VP15A] affect the progress of. **put an end/a stop to sth,** end or abolish it. **put an end to one's life,** commit suicide. **put the brake(s) on sth,** (fig, colloq) slow it down. **5** [VP15A] cause to pass into or suffer the emotional, physical etc state indicated by the phrase that follows. *put oneself to death,* commit suicide. *put sb to death,* kill him. *put sb at his ease,* cause him to feel relaxed, free from anxiety, etc. *put sb to (great) expense,* cause him to spend (a lot). *put sb to (great) inconvenience,* cause him inconvenience. *put sb to the indignity of doing sth,* cause him to do sth involving loss of dignity. *put sb in mind of sb/sth,* recall or remind him of sb/sth. *put sb/sth out of his/its misery,* relieve him/it of anxiety, pain, etc; kill (eg an animal in pain). *put sb on (his) oath,* make sb swear on oath; bind him to tell the truth. *put sb/sth to the test,* test him/it. *put sb in the wrong,* cause him to appear to be wrong. 6 [VP22] cause sb/sth to become (what is indicated by the adj): *That picture on the wall is crooked—I must put it straight. put sth right,* correct it: *A short note put the matter right,* ended any misunderstanding. *put sb right/straight,* correct an error he has made; give him correct information: *We had taken a wrong turning, but a policeman put us right,* told us which way to go. 7 [VP15A] write; indicate; mark: *put a tick against a name/a price on an article/one's signature to a will.* 8 [VP14] *put sth to sb; put it to sb (that),* submit; propound; express: *put a proposal to the Board of Directors; put a question to the vote/a resolution to the meeting; I put it to you that...,* invite you to agree with me that.... *You have put the case very clearly. Put it* (= submit the matter) *to her so as not to offend her. How can I put it,* express it? *How would you put* (= express, translate) *this in Danish? That can all be put in a few words. Please put all questions to the chairman. put the question,* ⇨ question ¹(2). 9 [VP14] *put a price/value/valuation on sth,* state or estimate the value: *The experts refused to put a price on the Rubens painting. What value do you put on her advice? put sth at (a figure),* say that, eg sb's age, sth's value, weight, is: *I would put her age at about sixty. I put her fur coat at £200.* 10 [VP6A] throw with an upward and outward movement of the arm. *put the shot,* ⇨ shot ¹(3). Hence, '*shot-put* n this as an event at an athletic meeting. 11 [VP15B,2C,14] (special uses with *adverbial particles* and *preps*): *put (a ship) about,* (cause to) change direction: *The captain put the ship about. put oneself about,* (chiefly Scots) trouble, distress, oneself: *He was very much put about by these false allegations. put sth about,* spread, eg rumours: *Don't believe all these stories that are being put about.*

put sth across (to sb), (a) communicate sth successfully: *a teacher who quickly puts his ideas across to his students.* (b) (colloq) make a success of: *Put a business deal across* (more usu *through*). *put sth across sb,* colloq) deceive; trick: *You can't put that across me,* make me believe or accept it.

put sth aside, (a) lay down: *put aside one's book; put one's work aside.* (b) save: *He has put aside a good sum of money.* (c) disregard; ignore: *Put aside for a moment the fact that the man has been in prison.*

put sth away, (a) put in the usual place of storage, eg a drawer, box: *Put your books/toys away.* (b) save: *put money away for one's old age.* (c) (colloq) eat or drink (to excess): *How can that boy put away so much pie and ice-cream?* (d) give up; renounce: *He's had to put away all ideas of becoming a concert pianist. put sb away,* (a) (colloq)

put into confinement, eg in a mental home: *He was acting so strangely that he had to be put away.* (b) (colloq, of pets) put to death (because of age, illness): *The dog was so old and weak that it had to be put away.*

put back, (naut) return: *The ship/We put back to harbour. put sth back,* (a) replace: *Put the reference books back on the shelf when you've finished with them.* (b) move backwards: *That clock is fast; I'd better put it back five minutes,* move the minute hand back. (c) (fig) check the advance of, cause delay to: *put back the efforts of the reformers. The strike at the car factory put back production badly. put sth by,* save for future use: *Has she any money put by?*

put (sth) down, (a) land: *He put down (his glider) in a field.* (b) set or place down: *Put down that gun!* (c) press down: *When you get on the motorway, you can really put your foot down,* press the accelerator pedal down. *put one's foot down,* ⇨ foot ¹(1). (d) place in storage: *put down eggs,* eg by packing in isinglass. *He has put down a good supply of port and claret.* (e) suppress by force or authority: *put down a rebellion; put down gambling and prostitution.* (f) write down; make a note of: *Here's my address—put it down before you forget it. put sb down,* (a) allow to alight: *The bus stopped to put down passengers.* (b) snub; reduce to silence: *put down hecklers at a political meeting.* Hence, '*put-down* n snub. (c) make humble: (biblical) *put down the mighty from their seats. put sb down as,* consider that sb is: *They put me down as a fool. put sb down for,* write his name on a list as willing to give, eg to a charity or other fund: *You can put me down for £5;* put sb's name down as an applicant, participant, etc: *They put him down for Eton/the school football team. put sth down to sth,* (a) charge to an account: *Put the shoes down to my account. You can put the cost of the petrol down to business expenses.* (b) attribute to: *The cholera outbreak was put down to bad drinking water. Can we put it down to his ignorance?*

put sth forth, (formal) send out: *The trees are putting forth new leaves.*

put sth forward, (a) advance; put before people for consideration: *put forward a new theory.* (b) move on: *put forward the hands of a clock,* eg when it is stopped or slow. *put sb forward,* propose: *put oneself/a friend forward as a candidate.*

put in, exclaim (often as an interruption): '*But what about us?' he put in. put in/into,* (naut) (of a boat, its crew) enter: *The boat put in at Malta/put into Malta for repairs. put in for sth,* apply formally for: *put in for the position of manager. put in for leave,* request permission to be absent from duty, work, etc. *put sth in,* (a) cause to be in: *He put his head in at the window.* (b) submit; present formally: *put in a claim for damages; put in a document* (in a law case); *put in a plea of not guilty.* (c) manage to strike or utter: *put in a blow/word. put sth in/into sth,* devote; give: *put a lot of work into improving one's French. put sb in for sth,* recommend sb for promotion, an award, etc: *The commanding officer is putting Sergeant Green in for the Victoria Cross. put in a good word for sb,* say sth on his behalf, to help him. (d) do, perform: *put in an hour's work before breakfast; put in an hour's piano practice.* (e) pass (time): *There's still an hour to put in before the pubs open. put sb in,* (a) give duties to: *put in a caretaker/*

bailiff. (b) elect to office: *Which party will be put in at the next general election?* **put sb in mind of sb/sth,** ⇨ 5 above. ⇨ the *n* entries for **put in an appearance; put the boot in; put one's oar in; put a sock in it.**

put off, (of a boat or crew) leave: *We put off from the pier.* **put sth off,** (a) postpone: *put off a meeting; put off going to the dentist.* (b) (usu of non-material things, *take off* being usual for clothes) get rid of: *You must put off your doubts and fears.* **put sb off (sth),** (a) put to a later date an arrangement, etc: *We shall have to put the Smiths off till next week.* (b) make excuses and try to avoid, eg sth one has promised to do, a duty: *He tried to put me off with vague promises. I won't be put off with such flimsy excuses,* won't accept them. **put sb off (sth),** hinder or distract him (from sth): *put sb off his game,* eg distract him when he is about to strike the ball at golf. *The mere smell of garlic put him off his supper,* caused him not to want supper. **put sb off his stroke,** distract him; cause him to pause.

put sth on, (a) (contrasted with *take off*) clothe oneself with: *put one's hat/shoes, etc on.* (b) assume; pretend to have: *put on an air of innocence. Her modesty is all put on,* she's only pretending to be modest, eg about her ability or skill. (c) increase; add: *put on more steam/pressure; put on speed. He's putting on weight/flesh,* is getting heavier/fatter. *Marks and Sparks put on sixty runs,* (cricket) together added sixty to the score. (d) add to: *This policy will put pounds on the cost of living,* will make it much higher. (e) arrange for; make available: *put on extra trains during the rush hours; put a play on,* arrange for it to be shown at a theatre. (f) advance: *put the clock on one hour,* move the hands forward, eg for Summer Time. **put sb on,** (colloq) deceive them: *He's not really interested; he's putting you on.* Hence, **'put-on** *n* deception: *What a put-on!* **put it on,** (colloq) (a) exaggerate a show of feeling; pretend to be more important, etc than is justified or warranted; talk or behave in a pretentious way. (b) overcharge: *Some of the hotels put it on during the holiday season.* **put sb on (to bowl),** (cricket) arrange for him to bowl at least one over. **put money on sb/sth,** stake (horse-racing, etc): *I've put a pound on the favourite.*

put out (from), (naut) (of a boat or crew) move out, leave, eg from harbour. **put sth out,** (a) extinguish; cause to stop burning: *put out the lights/ the candle/the gas/the gas-fire. The fireman soon put the fire out.* (b) cause to be out of joint; dislocate: *She fell off a horse and put her shoulder out.* (c) give (sth) to be done off the premises: *All repairs are done on the premises and not put out. We put out the washing,* send it to a laundry instead of having it done at home. (d) lend (money) at interest: *He has £1000 put out at 5 per cent.* (e) produce: *The firm puts out 1000 bales of cotton sheeting every week.* ⇨ output. (f) issue; broadcast: *The Health Department has put out a warning about dangerous drugs.* **put one's hand out,** hold it out in welcome, for caning as a punishment, etc. **put one's tongue out,** show it, eg for a doctor, or at sb, as a rude act. **put sb out,** (a) disconcert; cause to be confused or worried: *The least thing puts him out,* he is easily upset. *She was very much put out by your rudeness.* (b) inconvenience: *Would it put you out to lend me £5 until Friday? He was very much put out by the late arrival of his*

guests. **put sb out (of),** expel; drive out.

put over, (naut) (of a boat or crew) move over: *put over to the other side of the harbour.* **put sth over to sb,** (colloq) = put sth across to sb.

put sth through, carry it out: *put through a business deal.* **put sb/sth through,** connect (by telephone): *Please put me/this call through to the Manager.* **put sb through sth,** cause him to undergo, eg an ordeal, a test: *The police put him through a severe examination. The trainees were put through an assault course.* **put a person through his paces,** ⇨ pace *n*(3). **put sb 'through it,** (colloq) test or examine him thoroughly, eg by giving him a medical examination, or by inflicting suffering on him to get a confession.

put sth to sb, ⇨ 8 above. **be hard 'put to it to do sth,** find difficulty in doing sth: *I'd be hard put to it to say exactly why I disliked him. He was hard put to it to satisfy his creditors.*

put sth together, construct (a whole) by combining parts: *It's easier to take a machine to pieces than to put it together again. I must put my thoughts/ideas together before I go on the platform,* collect my ideas, etc before I give my address, speech, etc. **put our/your/their 'heads together,** consult one another. **put two and two together,** ⇨ two.

put up (at), obtain lodging and food: *put up (at an inn) for the night.* **put up (for sth),** offer oneself for election: *Are you going to put up for Finchley again,* ie as a prospective member of Parliament? **put sth up,** (a) raise; hold up: *put up one's hands,* eg over one's head, as a sign that one is ready to surrender, or with fists clenched, ready to fight; *put up a flag/a sail.* **put one's 'hair up,** (of long hair) wear it coiled on the head instead of letting it fall over the neck and shoulders. (b) build, erect: *put up a shed/a tent.* (c) publish (banns); place so as to be seen: *put up a notice.* (d) raise, increase: *put up the rent by 50p (a week).* (e) pack (in parcels, boxes, etc): *herrings put up in barrels. The hotel will put us up some sandwiches,* prepare and pack some for us. (f) offer, make: *put up a stout resistance/a good fight.* (g) supply (a sum of money for an undertaking): *I will supply the skill and knowledge if you will put up the £2000 capital.* (h) (old use) sheathe (a sword). (i) cause (wild birds or animals) to leave shelter or cover: *put up a partridge.* **put sb's back up,** ⇨ back¹(1). **put sth up for auction/sale,** offer it to be auctioned/sold: *Has the house been put up for auction?* **a put-up 'job,** sth done in order to give a false impression, to swindle sb, etc. **put sb up,** provide lodging and food (for): *We can put you up for the weekend.* **put sb up (for sth),** propose, nominate sb for a position: *She was put up for the position of secretary,* eg of a society; *put sb up for a club.* **put sb 'up to sth,** suggest sth to sb, esp urge him to do sth mischievous or wrong: *Who put you up to all these tricks?* **put 'up with sb/sth,** endure without protest; bear patiently: *There are many inconveniences that have to be put up with when you are camping.*

put² /pʌt/ *n, vi, vt* = putt.

pu·ta·tive /'pjuːtətɪv/ *adj* commonly reputed to be: *his ~ father.*

pu·trefy /'pjuːtrɪfaɪ/ *vt, vi* (*pt,pp* -fied) [VP6A,2A] (cause to) become putrid. **pu·tre·fac·tion** /ˌpjuːtrɪ'fækʃn/ *n* ~ing; sth which has putrefied.

pu·tres·cent /pjuː'tresnt/ *adj* becoming putrid; in

the process of rotting. **pu·tres·cence** /-sns/ *n*

pu·trid /'pju:trɪd/ *adj* **1** having become rotten; decomposed and ill-smelling: ∼ *fish*. **2** (sl) very distasteful or unpleasant: ∼ *weather*. **∼·ity** /pju:'trɪdətɪ/ *n* [U] decomposed matter; ∼ state.

putsch /pʊtʃ/ *N* (G) revolutionary attempt; insurrection.

putt /pʌt/ *vi,vt* [VP2A,6A] strike (a golf-ball) gently with a club so that it rolls across the ground towards or into a hole: *spend an hour practising* ∼*ing*. '∼·**ing-green** *n* smooth area of lawn around a hole. '∼·**ing-iron** *n* club for ∼ing. □ *n* stroke as described above.

put·tee /'pʌtɪ/ *n* long band of cloth wound round the leg from ankle to knee, for protection and support.

put·ter /'pʌtə(r)/ *vt,vi* = potter.

putty /'pʌtɪ/ *n* [U] soft paste of white powder and oil used for fixing glass in window frames, etc. □ *vt* [VP6A,15B] fill or make fast with ∼: ∼ *up a hole*.

puzzle /'pʌzl/ *n* [C] **1** question or problem difficult to understand or answer. **2** problem (eg *a* '*crossword-*∼) or toy (eg *a* '*jig-saw-*∼) designed to test a person's knowledge, skill, patience or temper. **3** (*sing* only) state of bewilderment or perplexity: *be in a* ∼ *about sth*. □ *vt,vi* **1** [VP6A] cause (sb) to be perplexed; make hard thought necessary to (sb): *This letter* ∼*s me. He was* ∼*d what to do next/how to answer the letter. He* ∼*d his brains* (= thought hard) *to find the answer*. **2** [VP3A] ∼ *over sth*, think deeply about it. **3** [VP15B] ∼ *sth out*, (try to) find the answer or solution by hard thought. ∼·**ment** *n* state of being ∼d. **puzz·ler** *n* puzzling question: *ask sb a few* ∼*rs. That's a real* ∼*r!*

pygmy, pigmy /'pɪgmɪ/ *n* (*pl* -mies) **1** P∼, member of a dwarf people in Equatorial Africa. **2** very small person; dwarf. **3** (attrib) very small.

py·ja·mas (US = **pa·ja·mas**) /pə'dʒɑ:məz *US:* -'dʒæm-/ *n pl* **1** (also **a pair of** ∼) loose-fitting jacket and trousers for sleeping in (*sing* when attrib): *pyjama top/jacket/bottom/trousers*. **cat's** ∼ = *cat's whiskers*, ⇨ whisker(2). **2** loose trousers

tied round the waist, worn by Muslims of both sexes in India and Pakistan.

py·lon /'paɪlon/ *n* **1** tower (steel framework) for carrying overhead high-voltage electric cables. **2** gateway to an ancient Egyptian temple; tall structure erected as a support, boundary or decoration.

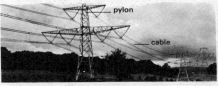

pylons

py·or·rhoea (also **-rhea**) /ˌpaɪə'rɪə/ *n* [U] inflammation of the gums causing them to shrink, with loosening of the teeth.

pyra·mid /'pɪrəmɪd/ *n* structure with a triangular or square base and sloping sides meeting at a point, esp one of those built of stone in ancient Egypt; pile of objects in the shape of a ∼. ⇨ the illus at Sphinx. ∼ **selling**, (comm) method of selling goods whereby distributors pay a premium for the right to sell a company's goods and then sell part of that right to other distributors.

pyre /'paɪə(r)/ *n* large pile of wood for burning, esp a funeral pile for a corpse.

py·rites /ˌpaɪə'raɪti:z *US:* pɪ'r-/ *n* [U] **copper** ∼, sulphide of copper and iron. **iron** ∼, either of two sulphides of iron, gold in colour.

pyro·tech·nics /ˌpaɪrə'teknɪks/ *n pl* art of making or using fireworks; public display of fireworks; (fig, often ironic) brilliant display of oratory, wit, etc. **py·ro·tech·nic** *adj* of ∼.

Pyr·rhic /'pɪrɪk/ *adj* ∼ **victory**, one gained at too great a cost.

py·thon /'paɪθn/ *n* large snake that kills its prey by twisting itself round it and crushing it. ⇨ the illus at snake.

pyx /pɪks/ *n* (eccles) vessel in which consecrated bread used at Holy Communion is kept.

Qq

Q, q /kju:/ (*pl* Q's, q's /kju:z/) the seventeenth letter of the English alphabet. *mind one's p's and q's*, ⇨ P,p. *on the qt*, ⇨ quiet(5).

qua /kweɪ/ *conj* (Lat) as; in the character or capacity of.

quack[1] /kwæk/ *vi, n* [VP2A] (make the) cry of a duck. '∼·∼ *n* (child's name for a) duck.

quack[2] /kwæk/ *n* person dishonestly claiming to have knowledge and skill (esp in medicine); (attrib) of, used by, sold by, such persons: *a* ∼ *doctor;* ∼ *remedies*. '∼·**ery** /-ərɪ/ *n* [U] methods, practices, etc of ∼s; (*pl*) instances of the use of such methods, etc.

quad /kwod/ *n* (colloq abbr of) **1** quadrangle. **2** quadruplet.

quad·rangle /'kwodræŋgl/ *n* **1** plane figure with four sides, esp a square or a rectangle. **2** (abbr *quad*) space in the form of a ∼, wholly or nearly surrounded by buildings, esp in a college, esp at Oxford. Cf *court* at Cambridge. **quad·ran·gu·lar** /kwo'dræŋgjʊlə(r)/ *adj* in the form of a ∼.

quad·rant /'kwodrənt/ *n* **1** fourth part of a circle or its circumference. ⇨ the illus at circle. **2** graduated strip of metal, etc shaped like a quarter-circle, for use in measuring angles (of altitude) in astronomy and navigation.

quad·ratic /kwo'drætɪk/ *adj* (maths) ∼ **equation**, one in which the second and no higher power of an unknown quantity is used, eg $x^2 + 2x - 8 = 0$.

quad·ri·lat·eral /ˌkwodrɪ'lætərəl/ *adj, n* four-sided (plane figure).

qua·drille /kwə'drɪl/ *n* [C] (music for an) old--fashioned square dance for four couples.

quad·ril·lion /kwo'drɪlɪən/ *n* **1** (GB) fourth power of one million (1 followed by 24 ciphers). **2** (US) fifth power of one thousand (1 followed by 15 ciphers). ⇨ App 4.

quad·ro·phony /kwo'drofənɪ/ *n* [U] recording or reproduction of sound using four channels. **quad·ro·phonic** /ˌkwodrə'fonɪk/ *adj*

quad·ru·ped /'kwodrʊped/ *n* four-footed animal.

quad·ru·ple /'kwodru:pl *US:* kwo'dru:pl/ *adj* **1**

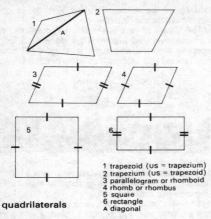

1 trapezoid (US = trapezium)
2 trapezium (US = trapezoid)
3 parallelogram or rhomboid
4 rhomb or rhombus
5 square
6 rectangle
A diagonal

quadrilaterals

made up of four parts. 2 agreed to by four persons, parties, etc: *a ~ alliance*, of four Powers. □ *n* number or amount four times as great as another: *20 is the ~ of 5*. □ *vt,vi* /kwɒˈdruːpl/ [VP6A,2A] multiply by 4: *He has ~d his income/His income has ~d in the last four years.*

quad·ru·plet /ˈkwɒdruːplet *US:* kwɒˈdruːp-/ *n* (common abbr *quad*) one of four babies at a birth (usu *pl: one of the ~s* is commoner than *one ~*).

quad·ru·pli·cate /kwɒˈdruːplɪkət/ *adj* four times repeated or copied. □ *n in ~*, in four exactly similar examples or copies. □ *vt* /kwɒˈdruːplɪkeɪt/ [VP6A] make four quadruplicate copies.

quaff /kwɒf *US:* kwæf/ *vt,vi* [VP6A,15B,2A] (liter) drink deeply: *~ (off) a glass of wine.*

quagga /ˈkwægə/ *n* (now extinct) S African quadruped related to the ass and the zebra.

quag·mire /ˈkwægmaɪə(r)/ *n* [C] area of soft, wet land; bog; marsh.

Quai d'Or·say /ˌkeɪ dɔːˈseɪ/ *n* (F) (used for) French Foreign Office; French foreign policy.

quail[1] /kweɪl/ *n* small bird, similar to a partridge, valued as food: (unchanged in the collective *pl*) *shoot ~ and duck.* ⇨ the illus at fowl.

quail[2] /kweɪl/ *vi* [VP2A,3A] *~ (at/before)*, feel or show fear: *His heart ~ed. He ~ed at the prospect before him. His eyes ~ed before her angry looks.*

quaint /kweɪnt/ *adj* (-er, -est) attractive or pleasing because unusual or old-fashioned; whimsical: *American visitors to England admire our ~ villages/customs. ~·ly adv ~·ness n*

quake /kweɪk/ *vi* [VP2A,C] 1 (of the earth) shake: *The ground ~d under his feet.* 2 (of persons) tremble: *quaking with fear/cold.* □ *n* (colloq abbr for) earthquake.

Quaker /ˈkweɪkə(r)/ *n* member of the Society of Friends, a Christian group that holds informal meetings instead of formal church services and is opposed to violence or war under any circumstances.

quali·fi·ca·tion /ˌkwɒlɪfɪˈkeɪʃn/ *n* 1 [U] act of qualifying, modifying or limiting; [C] sth which modifies, restricts or limits: *You can accept his statement without ~/with certain ~s.* 2 [C] training, test, etc that qualifies(1) a person; degree, diploma, etc awarded at the end of such training: *a doctor's ~s.*

qual·ify /ˈkwɒlɪfaɪ/ *vt,vi* (*pt,pp* -fied) 1 [VP2C,6A,14,17,16B] *~ sb (for sth/to do sth/as sth)*, be equipped, equip (sb) by training: *He's qualified for this post. His training qualifies him as a teacher of English. He's not qualified to teach French. A qualifying examination* (= one at which candidates must reach certain standards for a profession, etc) *will be held next week.* 2 [VP17,4,3A] *~ sb to do sth*, entitle: *He's the manager's son but that does not ~ him to criticize my work. ~ for sth*, be entitled to: *Do you ~ for the vote/to vote?* 3 [VP6A] limit; make less inclusive, less general: *The statement 'Boys are lazy' needs to be qualified*, eg by saying 'Some boys' or 'Many boys'. 4 [VP6A] (gram) limit the meaning of; name the qualities of: *Adjectives ~ nouns.* 5 [VP16B] *~ sb as*, describe: *~ a man as an ambitious self-seeker.* **quali·fied** *adj* 1 having the necessary qualifications: *a qualified doctor.* 2 limited: *give a scheme one's qualified approval.* **quali·fier** /-faɪə(r)/ *n* (gram) *~ing word*, eg an adjective or adverb.

quali·tat·ive /ˈkwɒlɪtətɪv *US:* -teɪt-/ *adj* relating to quality: *~ analysis.* ⇨ quantitative.

qual·ity /ˈkwɒlətɪ/ *n* (*pl* -ties) 1 [C,U] (degree, esp high degree, of) goodness or worth: *goods of first-rate ~. Poor ~ goods won't sell easily. We aim at ~ rather than quantity*, aim to produce superior goods, not large quantities. *We manufacture goods of various qualities. He is a man with many good qualities. Give us a taste of your ~*, show us what accomplishments you have. 2 [C] sth that is special in, or that distinguishes, a person or thing: *One ~ of pine-wood is that it can be sawn easily. He has the ~ of inspiring confidence.* 3 [U] (archaic) high social position: *a lady of ~.*

qualm /kwɑːm/ *n* [C] 1 feeling of doubt (esp about whether one is doing or has done right); misgiving: *He felt no ~s about borrowing money from friends.* 2 temporary feeling of sickness in the stomach: *~s which spoilt his appetite during the first few days of the voyage.*

quan·dary /ˈkwɒndərɪ/ *n* [C] (*pl* -ries) state of doubt or perplexity: *be in a ~ about what to do next.*

quango /ˈkwæŋɡəʊ/ *n* quasi-autonomous nongovernmental organisation.

quan·tify /ˈkwɒntɪfaɪ/ *vt* [VP6A] express or measure the quantity of.

quan·ti·tat·ive /ˈkwɒntɪtətɪv *US:* -teɪt-/ *adj* relating to quantity: *~ analysis.* ⇨ qualitative.

quan·tity /ˈkwɒntətɪ/ *n* (*pl* -ties) 1 [U] the property of things which can be measured, eg size, weight, number: *I prefer quality to ~. Mathematics is the science of pure ~.* 2 [C] amount, sum or number: *There's only a small ~* (ie not much or not many) *left. What ~ do you want?* 3 (often *pl*) large amount or number: *We've had quantities of rain this summer. He buys things in ~/in large quantities.* 4 *an unknown ~*, (maths) symbol (usu *x*) representing an unknown ~ in an equation; (fig) person or thing whose action, ability etc cannot be foreseen. *~ surveyor*, expert who estimates quantities of materials needed in building, their cost, etc. *bill of ~*, one prepared by a *~* surveyor.

quan·tum /ˈkwɒntəm/ *n* (*pl* quanta /-tə/) amount required or desired. *'~ theory,* (phys) the hypothesis that in radiation the energy of electrons is discharged not continuously but in certain fixed amounts (or *quanta*).

quar·an·tine /ˈkwɒrəntiːn *US:* ˈkwɔːr-/ *n* [U] (med) (period of) separation from others until it is known that there is no danger of spreading disease: *be in* ~ *for a week; be out of* ~; (attrib) of the system of ~: *the* ~ *regulations. How long will my dog be kept in* ~? □ *vt* [VP6A] put in ~: ~*d because of yellow fever.*

quark /kwɑːk/ *n* (phys) kind of elementary particle.

quar·rel /'kwɒrəl *US:* 'kwɔːrəl/ *n* [C] **1** angry argument; violent disagreement: *have a* ~ *with sb about sth. They made up their* ~, ended it and became friendly. *He's always fighting other people's* ~*s,* helping them, eg to get social justice. **2** cause for being angry; reason for protest or complaint: *I have no* ~ *with/against him.* **pick a** ~ **(with sb),** find or invent some occasion or excuse for disagreement, etc. □ *vi* (-ll-, US also -l-) **1** [VP2A,C,3A] ~ **(with sb) (about sth),** have, take part in, a ~: *The thieves* ~*led with one another about how to divide the loot.* **2** [VP3A] ~ **with,** disagree with; refuse to accept; complain about: *It's not the fact of examinations I'm* ~*ling with; it's the way they're conducted.* '~·**some** /-səm/ *adj* quick-tempered; fond of ~s.

quarry[1] /'kwɒrɪ *US:* 'kwɔːrɪ/ *n* (*pl*-ries) (usu *sing*) animal, bird, etc which is hunted; anything eagerly pursued.

quarry[2] /'kwɒrɪ *US:* 'kwɔːrɪ/ *n* [C] (*pl*-ries) place (not underground like a mine) where stone, slate, etc is obtained (for building, road-making, etc). □ *vt,vi* **1** [VP6A,15A,B] get from a ~: ~ *limestone;* ~ (*out*) *a block of marble;* (fig) search for (facts, etc) in old books, records, etc. **2** [VP2A,C] engage in work of this kind: ~ *in old manuscripts.* '~-**man** /-mən/ *n* (*pl*-men) man who works in a ~.

quart /kwɔːt/ *n* measure of capacity equal to two pints or about 1·14 litre. ⇨ App **5**: *drink a* ~ *of beer.* **put a** ~ **into a pint pot,** make the less contain the greater; attempt the impossible.

quar·ter /'kwɔːtə(r)/ *n* **1** fourth part (⅟₄); one of four equal or corresponding parts: *a* ~ *of a mile; a mile and a* ~; *a* ~ *of an hour,* 15 minutes; *an hour and a* ~; *the first* ~ *of this century,* ie 1901—25. *We've come a* ~ *of the distance now. Divide the apples into* ~*s.* **a bad** ~ **of an hour,** a short but unpleasant experience (eg in a dentist's chair). **2** point of time 15 minutes before or after any hour: *a* ~ *to* (US = *of*) *six; a* ~ *past six. It isn't the* ~ *yet. This clock strikes the hours, the half-hours, and the* ~*s.* **3** three months, esp as a period for which rent and other payments are made: *owe several* ~*s' rent; pay one's rent at the end of each* ~. '~-**day** *n* first day of a legal ~ of the year, on which rents and other three-monthly accounts are paid (in England, 25 Mar; 24 June; 29 Sept; 25 Dec). '~ **sessions,** ⇨ *court of* ~ *sessions* at court[1](1). **4** (US) 25 cents; a ~ of a dollar. **5** joint of meat including a leg: *a* ~ *of beef;* also used of the living animal (usu in compounds, as '*fore*-~*s;* '*hind*-~*s*). **6** direction; district; source of supply, help, information, etc: *men running from all* ~*s/ from every* ~; *travel in every* ~ *of the globe,* everywhere. *From what* ~ *does the wind blow? As his father was penniless, he could expect no help from that* ~. *The suggestion did not find favour in the highest* ~*s,* was not welcomed by those at the head of affairs. **7** division of a town, esp one of a special class of people, etc: *the Chinese* ~ *of San Francisco; the manufacturing/residential* ~. **8** one-fourth of a lunar month; the moon's phase at the end of the first or third week; *the moon at the first* ~/*in its last* ~. ⇨ the illus at phase. **9** (*pl*)

lodging; (mil) place where soldiers, etc are lodged or stationed: *take up* ~*s,* lodge; *return to* ~*s.* ⇨ *headquarters* at head[1](20). **married** ~**s,** place where soldiers, etc lodge with their families. **single** ~**s,** place where unmarried soldiers, etc lodge. **10** *at close* ~**s,** (seen) from very near. **11** (*pl*) positions taken up by sailors on duty on a ship, esp for fighting: *Officers and men at once took up their* ~*s.* **12** [U] **ask for/give** ~, mercy to an enemy; life granted to a defeated enemy who is willing to surrender: *No* ~ *was asked for and none given,* there were no prisoners. **13** (naut) rear part of a ship's side: *on the port/starboard* ~. '~-**deck** *n* part of the upper deck between the stern and the aftermast of a warship, reserved for officers; officers of a warship or navy. ⇨ *lower deck* at low[1](13), forecastle. **14** (GB) fourth part of a hundredweight, 28 lb; (US) 25 lb; grain-measure of eight bushels. ⇨ App **5**. **15** one of the four parts of a shield used in armorial bearings. **16** (compounds) ~-'**final** *n* (sport) one of four competitions or matches, the winners of which play in the semi-finals. '~-**light** *n* triangular section at the front or back window of a car, opened to admit air. '~-**master** *n* (**a**) (army) (abbr **QM**) officer in charge of the stores, etc of a battalion. (**b**) (navy) petty officer in charge of steering the ship, signals, etc. ~-**master-**'**general** *n* (abbr **QMG**) staff officer in charge of supplies for a whole army. '~-**plate** *n* photographic plate 3¼ inches × 4½ inches; photograph made from it. '~-**staff** *n* strong pole, 6 to 8 ft long, formerly used as a weapon and in a rough kind of fencing. □ *vt* **1** [VP6A] divide into ~s: ~ *an apple;* (in former times) divide (a traitor's body) into ~s: *condemned to be hanged, drawn* (= *disembowelled*) *and* ~*ed.* **2** [VP6A,15A] find lodgings for (troops); place (troops) in lodgings: ~ *troops in the villages.* ~-**ing** *n* method of arranging two or more coats of arms, to show alliances with or descent from various families; coat of arms resulting from this.

quar·ter·ly /'kwɔːtəlɪ/ *adj, adv* (happening) once in each three months: ~ *payments/subscriptions; to be paid* ~. □ *n* (*pl*-lies) periodical published ~.

quar·tet /kwɔː'tet/ *n* (piece of music for) four players or singers: *a string* ~, for (usu) two violins, viola and cello; *a piano* ~, for piano and three stringed instruments.

quarto /'kwɔːtəʊ/ *n* (*pl* ~s /-təʊz/) (also written **4to**) size given by folding a sheet of paper twice (making four leaves or eight pages); book made of sheets so folded (usu about 9 by 12 in): *the first* ~ *of 'Hamlet'.*

quartz /kwɔːts/ *n* [U] sorts of hard mineral (esp crystallized silica), including agate and other semi-precious stones. ~ **clock,** one of very great accuracy, with ~ oscillators.

quasar /'kweɪzɑː(r)/ *n* (astron) very distant source of radio or light waves.

quash /kwɒʃ/ *vt* [VP6A] put an end to, annul, reject as not valid (by legal procedure): ~ *a verdict/decision.*

quasi- /'kweɪsaɪ/ *pref* (with a *n* or *adj*) to a certain extent; seeming(ly): *a* ~-*official position.* ⇨ App **3**.

quas·sia /'kwɒʃə/ *n* [U] (bitter drug used medicinally and obtained from) wood or bark of a S American tree; the tree.

quat·er·cen·ten·ary /ˌkwɒtəsen'tiːnərɪ *US:* -'sentənerɪ/ *n* 400th anniversary: *the* ~ *celebrations* *in 1964 of Shakespeare's birth.*

quat·rain /'kwɒtreɪn/ *n* verse of four lines, usu rhyming *a b a b.*

quat·tro·cento /ˌkwætrəʊ'tʃentəʊ/ *n* (I) the 15th century as a period of Italian art and literature.

qua·ver /'kweɪvə(r)/ *vt, vi* 1 [VP2A] (of the voice or a sound) shake; tremble: *in a ~ing voice; in a voice that ~ed.* 2 [VP6A, 15B] say or sing in a shaking voice: *She ~ed (out/forth) her little song.* □ *n* [C] 1 ~ing sound. 2 musical note with one-half the time value of a crotchet. ▷ the illus at notation.

quay /kiː/ *n* solid, stationary landing-place usu built of stone or iron, alongside which ships can be tied up for loading and unloading.

queasy /'kwiːzɪ/ *adj* (-ier, -iest) 1 (of food) causing a feeling of sickness in the stomach. 2 (of the stomach) easily upset. 3 (of a person) easily made sick; feeling sick. 4 (fig, of a person or his conscience) over-scrupulous, tender or delicate. **queas·ily** /-ɪlɪ/ *adv* **queasi·ness** *n*

queen /kwiːn/ *n* 1 woman ruler in her own right: *the Q~ of England; Q~ Elizabeth II.* 2 wife of a king: *King George VI and Q~ Elizabeth.* 3 ~ *dowager,* widow of a king. ~ **mother,** ~ dowager who is the mother of a reigning Sovereign. 4 woman regarded as chief of a group: *the ~ of the May;* '*May Q~,* girl chosen as ~ in old-time May Day ceremonies; town or place regarded as occupying a leading position: *Venice, the ~ of the Adriatic.* '**beauty ~,** winner of a beauty contest. 5 ~ **ant/bee/wasp,** fertile, egg-producing ant etc. 6 (chess) most powerful piece for attack or defence; ▷ the illus at **chess;** (cards)`one with the picture of a ~: *the ~ of spades/hearts.* 7 ⚠ (GB derog sl) effeminate male homosexual. □ *vt ~ it (over sb),* act like a ~; assume the leadership. ~-**ly** *adj* like a ~; fit for a ~; majestic; generous: *~ly robes; her ~ly duties.*

queer /kwɪə(r)/ *adj* 1 strange; unusual: *a ~ way of talking.* 2 causing doubt or suspicion: *a ~ character;* ~ *noises in the attic.* 3 (colloq) unwell; faint: *feel very ~.* 4 ⚠ (derog sl) homosexual. 5 *in* '*Q~ street,* (GB sl) in debt; in trouble. □ *n* ⚠ (derog sl) homosexual. □ *vt* [VP6A] (sl) put out of order; cause to go wrong, esp ~ *sb's pitch,* ▷ pitch¹(1). ~-**ly** *adv* ~-**ness** *n*

quell /kwel/ *vt* [VP6A] (poet and rhet) suppress, subdue (a rebellion, rebels, opposition).

quench /kwentʃ/ *vt* [VP6A] 1 put out (flames, fire). 2 satisfy (thirst). 3 put an end to (hope). 4 cool in water: ~ *steel.* ~-**less** *adj* (liter) that cannot be, or is never, ~ed: *a ~less flame.*

quern /kwɜːn/ *n* hand-mill for grinding corn; small hand-mill for pepper, etc.

queru·lous /'kwerʊləs/ *adj* full of complaints; fretful: *in a ~ tone.* ~-**ly** *adv* ~-**ness** *n*

query /'kwɪərɪ/ *n* [C] (*pl* -ries) 1 question, esp one raising a doubt about the truth of sth: *raise a ~.* 2 the mark (?) put against sth, eg in the margin of a document, as a sign of doubt. □ *vt* 1 [VP10] ~ *whether/if,* inquire: *I ~ whether his word can be relied on.* 2 [VP6A] express doubt about: ~ *a person's instructions.* 3 [VP6A] put the mark (?) against.

quest /kwest/ *n* [C] (rhet) search or pursuit: *the ~ for gold. in ~ of,* (old or liter use) seeking for, trying to find: *He went off in ~ of food.* □ *vi* [VP3A] ~ *for,* (esp of dogs) look for; (rhet) go about in ~ of: *~ing for further evidence.*

ques·tion¹ /'kwestʃən/ *n* 1 sentence which by word-order, use of interrogative words (*who, why,* etc) or intonation, requests information, an answer, etc: *ask a lot of ~s; put a ~ to sb.* '~-**mark** *n* the mark (?). ▷ App 9. '~-**master** *n* (in panel games) chairman. '~ **time,** (in the House of Commons) period of time during which ministers answer ~s put to them by members. 2 sth about which there is discussion; sth which needs to be decided; inquiry; problem; affair: *a difficult/vexed ~; economic ~s. Success is only a ~ of time,* will certainly come sooner or later. *The ~ is...,* What we want to know, what we must decide, is.... *That's not the ~,* not the matter being discussed. *in ~,* being talked about: *Where's the man in ~? out of the ~,* impossible; not to be discussed at all: *We can't go out in this weather; it's out of the ~. be some/no, etc ~ of,* some/no, etc discussion of: *There was no ~ of my being invited to become Chairman,* that was not discussed or proposed. *beg the ~,* ▷ beg(2). *come into ~,* be discussed, become of practical importance: *If sending me in a spacecraft to the moon ever comes into ~, I shall refuse without hesitation.* Q~! (at a public meeting) used to warn a speaker that he is not keeping to the subject being discussed, or (less correctly) to express doubt about the truth of sth he has said. *put the ~,* (at a meeting) ask those present to record their votes for or against the proposal. 3 [U] (the putting forward of) doubt, objection: *There is no ~ about/some ~ as to his honesty. There is no ~ but that he will* (= he will undoubtedly) *succeed. beyond (all)/without ~,* certain(ly); without doubt. *His integrity is beyond all ~. Without ~, he's the best man for the job. call sth in ~,* raise objections to, express doubt about, it: *No one has ever called my honesty in ~. His conduct was called in ~.*

ques·tion² /'kwestʃən/ *vt* 1 [VP6A] ask a ~ or ~s of; examine: *a two-hour ~ing session. He was ~ed by the police. They ~ed the Conservative candidate on his views.* 2 [VP6A, 10] ~ *(whether/if),* express or feel doubt about: ~ *sb's veracity;* ~ *the value* (or *importance*) *of compulsory games at school. I ~ whether his proposal will be approved.* ~-**able** /-əbl/ *adj* which may be ~ed(2): *a ~able assertion.* ~-**ably** /-əblɪ/ *adv* ~-**er** *n* person who ~s(1). ~-**ing·ly** *adv* in a ~ing manner.

ques·tion·naire /ˌkwestʃə'neə(r)/ *n* list of (usu printed) questions to be answered by a group of people, esp to get facts or information, or for a survey.

quet·zal /'kwetsl *US:* ket'sæl/ *n* beautiful bird of Central America; monetary unit of Guatemala.

queue /kjuː/ *n* 1 line of people waiting for their turn (eg to enter a cinema, get on a bus, buy sth): *form a ~; stand in a ~. jump the ~,* ▷ jump²(6). 2 line of vehicles waiting to proceed: *a ~ of cars held up by the traffic lights.* 3 plait of hair hanging down over the back of the neck (eg part of a wig, as worn by men in Europe in former times). □ *vi* [VP2A, C, 3A] ~ *(up) (for sth),* get into, be in, a ~: *~ing for a bus; ~ up to buy tickets for the film.*

quibble /'kwɪbl/ *n* [C] evasion of the main point of an argument, attempt to escape giving an honest answer, by using a secondary or doubtful meaning of a word or phrase. □ *vi* ~ *(over),* use ~s; argue about small points or differences: ~ *over triviali-*

687 **quiche/quit**

ties. **quib·bler** *n* **quib·bling** *adj*

quiche /kiːʃ/ *n* open tart with savoury filling; flan.

quick /kwɪk/ *adj* (-er, -est) **1** moving fast; able to move fast and do things in a short time; done in a short time: *a ~ train/worker; walking at a ~ pace; have a ~ meal; find ~ ways of doing sth/getting somewhere. Be ~ about it!* Hurry up! *Try to be a little ~er. She's as ~ as lightning. The flashes of lightning came in ~ succession,* at very short intervals of time; *We just have time for a ~ one,* (usu = a ~ (alcoholic) drink). *(in) ~ time,* (at) the ordinary rate of marching for soldiers (about four miles an hour). *~ march int* (command to) begin marching in ~ time. '*~·step n* ballroom dance with both quick and slow steps. ,*~-'change attrib adj* (of an actor, etc) ~ly changing his appearance, costume, etc to play another part: *a ~-'change artist.* '*~-freeze vt* freeze (food) very ~ly so as to keep the natural flavours unchanged: *~-frozen foods.* **2** lively; bright; active; prompt: *~ to understand; a ~ ear for music; ~ to make up one's mind/to seize an opportunity; ~ at figures; a ~* (= intelligent) *child; not very ~,* (colloq, of a child) rather dull or stupid; *a ~ temper,* soon aroused.   ,*~-'eared/-'eyed/-'sighted/* '*tempered/-'witted adjj* having ~ ears/eyes/ sight, etc. **3** (old use) living. *the ~ and the dead.* □ *n* [U] tender or sensitive flesh below the skin, esp the nails: *bite one's nails to the ~. cut/touch sb to the ~,* hurt his feelings deeply. □ *adv* (-er, -est) (common in colloq use for *quickly,* always placed after the *v*). **1** *You're walking too ~ for me. Can't you run ~er? He wants to get rich ~. I don't know any get-rich-~ methods.* **2** (in compounds, for ~ly): *a ~-firing gun.* *~·ly adv* in a ~ manner: *You speak too ~ly. He ~ly changed his clothes.* *~·ness n*

quicken /'kwɪkən/ *vt,vi* [VP6A,2A] **1** make or become quick(er): *We ~ed our pace. Our pace ~ed.* **2** make or become more lively, vigorous or active: *Good literature ~s the imagination. His pulse ~ed. The child ~ed in her womb,* She felt its movement for the first time.

quickie /'kwɪkɪ/ *n* (colloq) sth made or done very quickly.

quick·lime /'kwɪklaɪm/ *n* unslaked lime. ⇨ lime¹(1).

quick·sand /'kwɪksænd/ *n* [C] (area of) loose, wet, deep sand which sucks down men, animals, vehicles, etc that try to cross it.

quick·set /'kwɪkset/ *adj* (of hedges) formed of living plants, esp hawthorn, set in the ground to grow.

quick·sil·ver /'kwɪksɪlvə(r)/ *n* [U] mercury.

quick·step /'kwɪkstep/ *n*⇨ quick(1).

quid¹ /kwɪd/ *n* lump of chewing tobacco.

quid² /kwɪd/ *n* (GB, sl; *pl* unchanged) pound: *earning fifty quid* (= £50) *a week.*

quid pro quo /ˌkwɪd prəʊ 'kwəʊ/ *n* (Lat) sth given or returned as the equivalent of sth else.

qui·esc·ent /kwaɪ'esnt/ *adj* at rest; motionless; passive. *~·ly adv* **qui·esc·ence** /-sns/ *n*

quiet /'kwaɪət/ *adj* (-er, -est) **1** with little or no movement or sound: *a ~ sea; a ~ evening; ~ footsteps.* **2** free from excitement, trouble, anxiety: *live a ~ life in the country; have a ~ mind; ~ times.* **3** gentle; not rough (in disposition, etc): *~ children; a ~ old lady.* **4** (of colours) not bright. **5** not open or revealed: *harbouring ~ resentment.* *keep sth ~,* keep it secret. *on the ~,* (or, sl, *on the qt* /ˌkjuː 'tiː/), secretly: *have a drink on the ~;*

tell sb sth on the ~, in confidence. □ *n* [U] state of being ~ (all senses): *in the ~ of the night; have an hour's ~,* an hour free from activity, disturbance, etc; *live in peace and ~; a period of ~ after an election,* free from all the activity, etc that usu accompanies an election. □ *vt,vi* (more usu ~en /'kwaɪətn/) [VP6A,15B,2C] make or become ~: *~(en) a fretful child; ~(en) sb's fears/suspicions. The city ~ed/~ened down after the political disturbances.* *~·ly adv ~·ness n*

quiet·ism /'kwaɪətɪzəm/ *n* [U] (as a form of religious mysticism) the abandoning of all desire, with a passive acceptance of whatever comes. **quiet·ist** /-ɪst/ *n* person who follows this principle.

quiet·ude /'kwaɪətjuːd US: -tuːd/ *n* (liter) stillness; tranquillity.

qui·etus /kwaɪ'iːtəs/ *n* (formal) final settlement (eg of a debt); release from life; extinction: *give sb his ~,* put an end to his life.

quiff /kwɪf/ *n* lock of hair brushed up above the forehead.

quill /kwɪl/ *n* **1** '*~(-feather),* large wing or tail feather; (hollow stem of) such a feather as formerly used for writing with: *a ~ pen.* **2** long, sharp, stiff spine of a porcupine.

quilt /kwɪlt/ *n* thick bed-covering of two layers of cloth padded with soft material kept in place by crossed lines of stitches. ⇨ duvet. □ *vt* make in the form of a ~, ie with soft material between layers of cloth: *a ~ed dressing-gown.*

quin /kwɪn/ *n* (colloq abbr of) quintuplet.

quince /kwɪns/ *n* (tree with) hard, acid, pear-shaped fruit, deep yellow when ripe, used in jams and jellies.

quin·cen·ten·ary /ˌkwɪnsen'tiːnərɪ US: -'sentənerɪ/ *adj, n* (of the) 500th anniversary.

quin·ine /kwɪ'niːn US: 'kwaɪnaɪn/ *n* [U] bitter liquid made from the bark of a tree and used as a medicine for fevers and a flavouring in drinks.

Quin·qua·ges·ima /ˌkwɪŋkwə'dʒesɪmə/ *n* the Sunday before Lent.

quinsy /'kwɪnzɪ/ *n* [U] inflammation of the throat with discharge of pus from the tonsils.

quin·tal /'kwɪntl/ *n* unit of weight, 100 or 112 lb or 100 kilograms.

quin·tes·sence /kwɪn'tesns/ *n* **1** perfect example: *the ~ of virtue/politeness.* **2** essential part.

quin·tet /kwɪn'tet/ *n* (piece of music for) group of five players or singers: *piano ~,* string quartet and piano; *string ~,* string quartet and an additional cello or viola; *wind ~,* bassoon, clarinet, flute, horn and oboe.

quin·tu·plet /'kwɪntjuːplet US: kwɪn'tuːplɪt/ *n* (common abbr *quin*) one of five children at a birth (usu *pl: two of the ~s* is commoner than *two ~s*).

quip /kwɪp/ *n* clever, witty or sarcastic remark or saying; quibble. □ *vi* (-pp-) make ~s.

quire /'kwaɪə(r)/ *n* twenty-four sheets of writing-paper: *buy/sell paper by the ~/in ~s.*

quirk /kwɜːk/ *n* habit or action peculiar to sb/sth; foible: *One of his ~s is sleeping with his socks on.*

quis·ling /'kwɪzlɪŋ/ *n* person who co-operates with the authorities of an enemy country who are occupying his country.

quit¹ /kwɪt/ *pred adj* free, clear: *We are well ~ of him,* fortunate to be rid of him.

quit² /kwɪt/ *vt* (-tt-, US also -t-; *pt,pp* ~ted or ~) **1** [VP6A,2A] go away from; leave: *I ~ted him in disgust. We've had notice to ~,* a warning that we must give up the house we rent. *I've given my sec-*

retary notice to ∼, told her that she must leave my service. **2** [VP6A,D] stop: ∼ *work when the siren sounds;* ∼ *grumbling. Q*∼ *that!* Stop doing that! **3** (old use; reflex) acquit: *They* ∼*ted themselves like heroes.* ∼**-ter** *n* (colloq) person who does not finish what he has started, esp sth undertaken as a duty.

quite /kwaɪt/ *adv* **1** completely; altogether: *He has* ∼ *recovered from his illness. I* ∼ *agree/ understand. She was* ∼ *alone. See that your watch is* ∼ (= exactly) *right. That man is not* ∼ *acceptable. It was* ∼ (= at least) *six weeks ago. That's* ∼ *another* (ie a completely different) *story.* ∼ *the thing,* (colloq). what is considered correct, fashionable, etc: *These Italian dress materials are* ∼ *the thing this summer.* **2** to a certain extent; more or less; in some degree: (preceding articles and *adjj*) ∼ *a good player. It's* ∼ *warm today. He was* ∼ *polite, but he wasn't ready to help me. She* ∼ *likes him, but not enough to marry him.* **3** really; truly: *They are both* ∼ *young. She's* ∼ *a beauty. I believe they're* ∼ *happy together.* **4** (used to indicate agreement, understanding, polite acquiescence): A: *'It's a difficult situation'.* B: *'Q*∼ (*so*)!' A: *'I'm so sorry; I'm afraid I've taken your seat'.* B: *'Oh, that's* ∼ *all right'.*

quits /kwɪts/ *pred adj be* ∼ *(with sb),* be on even terms (by repaying a debt of money, punishment, etc): *We're* ∼ *now. I'll be* ∼ *with him,* will have my revenge. **call it** ∼, agree that things are even, that a dispute or quarrel may cease. **double or** ∼, ⇨ **double**³(1).

quit·tance /'kwɪtns/ *n* (document giving) release from an obligation or debt.

quiver¹ /'kwɪvə(r)/ *n* archer's sheath for carrying arrows.

quiver² /'kwɪvə(r)/ *vt,vi* [VP6A,2A] (cause to) tremble slightly or vibrate: *a* ∼*ing leaf. The moth* ∼*ed its wings.* □ *n* ∼*ing* sound or movement.

qui vive /kiː 'viːv/ *n* (only in) **on the** ∼, on the alert; watchful.

quix·otic /kwɪk'sɒtɪk/ *adj* generous, unselfish, imaginative, in a way that disregards one's own welfare. **quix·oti·cally** /-klɪ/ *adv*

quiz /kwɪz/ *vt* (-zz-) [VP6A] **1** ask questions of, as a test of knowledge. **2** (archaic) make fun of; tease; stare at. □ *n* **1** general knowledge test; (broadcasting) game in which members of a panel undergo such a test. '∼**-master,** = question–master. **2** (archaic) amused, supercilious look.

quiz·zi·cal /'kwɪzɪkl/ *adj* questioning and teasing: *a* ∼ *smile.* ∼**ly** /-klɪ/ *adv*

quoin /kɔɪn/ *n* exterior angle in the brickwork or stonework of a building; cornerstone.

quoit /kɔɪt *US:* kwɔɪt/ *n* ring (of metal, rubber, rope) to be thrown at a peg so as to encircle it; (*pl*) this game (as often played on the deck of a ship).

Quonset /'kwɒnsɪt/ *n*'∼ (**hut**), (US) (P) large prefabricated hut, usu of corrugated iron, semicircular at each end and with a rounded roof, similar to, but much larger than, a Nissen hut.

quo·rum /'kwɔːrəm/ *n* (*pl* ∼s) number of persons who must, by the rules, be present at a meeting (of a committee, etc) before its proceedings can have authority: *have/form a* ∼.

quota /'kwəʊtə/ *n* (*pl* ∼s) limited share, amount or number, esp a quantity of goods allowed to be manufactured, sold, etc or number, eg of immigrants allowed to enter a country: *The village was unable to raise its* ∼ *of men for the army. The* ∼ *of immigrants for this year has already been filled.*

quo·ta·tion /kwəʊ'teɪʃn/ *n* **1** [U] quoting(1). **2** [C] sth quoted(1): ∼*s from Shakespeare.* '∼ **marks,** the marks '''' or '' enclosing words quoted. ⇨ App **9. 3** [C] statement of the current price of an article, etc: *the latest* ∼*s from the Stock Exchange.* **4** [C] estimate of the cost of a piece of work: *Can you give me a* ∼ *for building a garage?*

quote /kwəʊt/ *vt* **1** [VP6A,14] ∼ *(from),* repeat, write (words used by another); repeat or write words (from a book, an author, etc): ∼ *a verse from the Bible;* ∼ *the Bible. Is Shakespeare the author most frequently* ∼*d from? He is* ∼*d as having said that there will be an election this autumn.* **2** [VP6A,13] give (a reference, etc) to support a statement: *Can you* ∼ (*me*) *a recent instance?* **3** [VP6A] name, mention (a price): *This is the best price I can* ∼ *you. The shares are* ∼*d on the Stock Exchange at 80p.* □ *n* (colloq) sth ∼d, esp sth witty, unusual, etc; quotation (2,3,4). **quot·able** /-əbl/ *adj* that can be, or deserves to be, ∼d. **quo·ta·bil·ity** /ˌkwəʊtə'bɪlətɪ/ *n* [U].

quoth /kwəʊθ/ *vt* (1st and 3rd person *sing, pt* only) (archaic) said: ∼ *I/he/she. Q*∼ *the raven, 'Nevermore!'*

quo·tid·ian /kwəʊ'tɪdɪən/ *adj* (of fevers) recurring every day.

quo·tient /'kwəʊʃnt/ *n* (maths) number obtained by dividing one number by another.

Rr

R, r /ɑː(r)/ (*pl* R's, r's) the eighteenth letter of the English alphabet. **the three R's,** reading, (w)riting and (a)rithmetic as the basis of an elementary education.

rabbi /'ræbaɪ/ *n* teacher of the Jewish law; (title of a) spiritual leader of a Jewish congregation. **rab·bini·cal** /rə'bɪnɪkl/ *adj* of ∼s, their learning, writings, etc.

rab·bit /'ræbɪt/ *n* **1** small burrowing animal of the hare family, brownish–grey in its natural state, black or white or bluish-grey in domestic varieties. ⇨ the illus at **small.** '∼**-hole/-burrow** *nn* hole in which wild ∼s live. '∼**-hutch** *n* wooden cage for domestic ∼s. '∼**-punch** *n* punch on the back of

the neck. '∼**-warren** *n* area of land full of ∼-burrows; (fig) area of narrow, winding streets or rooms and passages. **Welsh** ∼, = rarebit. **2** (colloq) poor performer at any game, esp tennis. □ *vi* (-tt-) hunt ∼s: *go* ∼*ting.*

rabble /'ræbl/ *n* **1** disorderly crowd; mob. '∼**-rousing** *adj* inciting, designed to rouse, the passions of the mob: ∼*-rousing speeches/speakers.* **2** **the** ∼, (contemptuous) the lower classes of the populace.

Rab·elais·ian /ˌræbə'leɪzɪən *US:* -eɪʒn/ *adj* of or like the writings, marked by coarse humour and satire, of Rabelais /'ræbəleɪ/, 1490—1553, French writer.

rabid /'ræbɪd/ *adj* **1** affected with rabies; mad. **2**

furious; fanatical; violent: ~ *hate; a* ~ *Socialist/ Conservative,* one with extreme views, violently expressed.

ra·bies /'reɪbiːz/ *n* [U] infectious disease causing madness in wolves, dogs and other animals; hydrophobia.

rac·coon = racoon.

race[1] /reɪs/ *n* [C] **1** contest or competition in speed, eg in running, swimming or to see who can finish a piece of work, or get to a certain place, first: *a* '*horse*-~; *a* '*boat*-~; *a half-*'*mile* ~; *run a* ~ *with sb; a* ~ *for a train,* an effort to catch it. *a* ~ *against time,* an effort to do sth before a certain time or possible event. '~-**card** *n* programme of a ~-meeting with a list of ~s and names of horses. '~-**course** *n* ground where horse-~s are run. '~-**horse** *n* horse specially bred for running ~s. '~-**meeting** *n* occasion when a number of horse-~s are held on a certain ~-course on a certain day, or a number of successive days: *the Epsom* ~-*meeting.* **the** ~**s,** ~-meeting. **2** strong, fast current of water in the sea, a river, etc: *a* '*mill*-~, the channel carrying water to the wheel of a water-mill. **3** (liter) course of the sun or moon, or (fig) of life: *His* ~ *is nearly run,* He is near the end of his life. □ *vi,vt* **1** [VP2A,C,3A,4A] ~ *(with/against sb),* compete in speed, have a ~; move at full speed: ~ *along;* ~ *over the course; boys racing home from school;* ~ *to see what is happening;* ~ *against time;* ~ *with sb for a prize. I'll* ~ *you home,* (colloq) ~ against you to get home first. **2** [VP2A,6A] own or train horses for racing and take part in ~-meetings; cause (a horse) to compete in ~s: *He* ~*s at all the big meetings. Are you going to* ~ *your horse at Newmarket next week?* **3** [VP6A,15A] cause (sth or sb) to move at full speed: *He* ~*d me to the station in his car. The Government* ~*d the bill through the House,* pushed it through the House of Commons at great speed. *Don't* ~ *your engine,* cause the engine to run very fast when it is not doing any work. [VP2A] *Don't let the engine* ~. **rac·ing** *n* [U] (esp) the hobby, sport or profession of running horses or motor-cars in races: *a* '*racing man; keep a racing stable; a* '*racing car/yacht,* designed for racing. ~**r** *n* horse, boat, car, etc designed for racing.

race[2] /reɪs/ *n* **1** [C,U] any of several subdivisions of mankind sharing certain physical characteristics, esp colour of skin, colour and type of hair, shape of eyes and nose: *the Caucasian/Mongolian/Negroid* ~; *people of mixed* ~; *people of the same* ~ *but different culture.* **2** [C] (used loosely for) group of people having a common culture, history and/or language: *the* ,*Anglo-*'*Saxon* ~; *the* '*German* ~. **3** (attrib) of, between, ~s(1,2): *Can* ~ *relations be improved by legislation?* **4** [U] ancestry; descent: *a man of ancient and noble* ~. **5** [C] main division of any living creatures: *the human* ~, mankind; *the* '*feathered* ~, (joc) birds; *the* '*finny* ~, (joc) fish.

ra·ceme /'ræ'siːm *US:* reɪ-/ *n* (botany) flower cluster with the separate flowers on short equal stalks springing from a main central stem, the lowest flowers opening first.

racial /'reɪʃl/ *adj* relating to race[2](1,2): ~ *conflict/hatred/pride;* ~ *minorities;* ~ *discrimination.* ~**·ly** /-ʃəlɪ/ *adv* ~**·ism** /-ʃəlɪzəm/ *n* [U] tendency to ~ conflict; antagonism between different races; belief that one's own race is superior. ~**·ist** /-ɪst/ *n* person who stirs up ~ism. **rac·ily, raci·ness** ⇨ racy.

rac·ism /'reɪsɪzəm/ *n* racialism; belief that human abilities are determined by race. **rac·ist** /-ɪst/ *n* racialist; believer in racialism or racism.

rack[1] /ræk/ *n* **1** wooden or metal framework for holding food (esp hay) for animals (in a stable or in the fields). **2** framework with bars, pegs, etc for holding things, hanging things on, etc: *a* '*plate*-~; *a* '*hat*-~; *a tool*-~. **3** shelf over the seats of a railway-carriage, air-liner, bus, etc for light luggage: *a* '*luggage*-~. **4** rod, bar or rail with teeth or cogs into which the teeth on a wheel (or pinion) fit (as used on special railways up a steep hill-side). ⇨ the illus at gear. '~-**railway** *n* one with a third rail with cogs between the two rails on which the wheels of trains are supported.

rack[2] /ræk/ *n* (usu **the** ~) instrument of torture consisting of a frame with rollers to which a person's wrists and ankles were tied so that his joints were stretched when the rollers were turned. **on the** ~, undergoing severe suffering (physical or mental). □ *vt* [VP6A,15A] **1** torture by placing on the ~; (of a disease or of mental agony) inflict torture on: ~*ed with pain; a* ~*ing headache;* ~*ed with a bad cough;* ~*ed by remorse.* **2** ~ *one's brains (for),* make great mental efforts (for, in order to find, an answer, method, etc). **3** oppress (tenants) with excessive rent. Hence, '~-**rent** *n* exorbitant rent.

rack[3] /ræk/ *n* [U] **1** (liter) drifting cloud.

rack[4] /ræk/ *n* (only in) **go to** ~ **and ruin.** fall into a ruined state.

racket[1] /'rækɪt/ *n* **1** (*sing* only, with *indef art* or [U]) uproar, loud noise: *What a* ~*! The drunken men in the street kicked up no end of a* ~, were very noisy and boisterous. **2** [U] (time of) great social activity, hurry and bustle: *the* ~ *of a politician's life.* **3** [C] (colloq) dishonest way of getting money (by deceiving or threatening people, selling worthless goods, etc): *be in on a* ~, have a share in it, be one of those who make money from it. **4** [C] ordeal or trying experience. **stand the** ~, **(a)** come successfully through a test (of sth). **(b)** accept, be responsible for, the consequences (of sth); take the blame, pay the costs. □ *vi* [VP2A,C] ~ *(about),* make a ~(1,2). ~**·eer** /,rækə'tɪə(r)/ *n* person who is engaged in a ~(3). ~**·eer·ing** *n* [U] the actions of ~eers.

racket[2], **rac·quet** /'rækɪt/ *n* **1** light bat used for hitting the ball in tennis, badminton, etc. ⇨ the illus at badminton, tennis. **2** (*pl*) ball-game for two or four players in a court with four walls.

rac·on·teur /,rækɒn'tɜː(r)/ *n* person who tells anecdotes or stories with skill and wit: *a good* ~.

rac·oon, rac·coon /rə'kuːn *US:* ræ-/ *n* small, flesh-eating animal of N America with a bushy, ringed tail; (US) its fur.

rac·quet = racket[2].

racy /'reɪsɪ/ *adj* (-ier, -iest) **1** (of speech or writing) vivid; spirited; vigorous: *a* ~ *style.* **2** having strongly marked qualities: *a* ~ *flavour.* ~ *of the soil,* showing traces of origin; direct, lively and stimulating. **rac·ily** /-ɪlɪ/ *adv* **raci·ness** *n*

radar /'reɪdɑː(r)/ *n* [U] (the use of) apparatus that indicates on a screen (by means of radio echoes) solid objects that come within its range, used (eg by pilots of ships, aircraft or spacecraft) in fog or darkness and which gives information about their position, movement, speed, etc: *follow the flight of an aircraft by* ~; (attrib) '~ *installation; on the* '~ *screen.*

radial /'reɪdɪəl/ *adj* relating to a ray, rays or a radius; (of spokes in a bicycle wheel, etc) from a centre; arranged like rays or radii. □ *n* ~ (**tyre**), tyre designed (by having the material inside the tyre wrapped in a direction ~ to the hub of the wheel) to give more grip on road surfaces, esp when cornering or when roads are wet. ~**ly** /-ɪəlɪ/ *adv*

radi·ant /'reɪdɪənt/ *adj* **1** sending out rays of light; shining: *the* ~ *sun*. **2** (of a person, his looks, eyes) bright; showing joy or love: *a* ~ *face; the* ~ *figures in the paintings of Renoir*. **3** (phys) transmitted by radiation: ~ *heat/energy*. ~**ly** *adv* **radi·ance** /-əns/ *n* [U] ~ quality.

radi·ate /'reɪdɪeɪt/ *vt, vi* **1** [VP6A] send out rays of (light or heat): *a stove that* ~*s warmth;* (fig) spread abroad, send out: *a woman who* ~*s happiness; an orator who* ~*s enthusiasm for the cause he supports.* **2** [VP2A, 3A] ~ *(from)*, come or go out in rays; show: *heat that* ~*s from a stove/a fireplace; the happiness that* ~*s from her eyes*. **3** [VP2A, 3A] ~ *(from)*, spread out like radii: *the avenues that* ~ *from the Arc de Triomphe in Paris.*

radi·ation /ˌreɪdɪ'eɪʃn/ *n* **1** [U] radiating; the sending out of energy, heat, etc in rays. '~ **sickness**, illness caused by gamma rays or rays from radioactive dust (as from nuclear weapons). **2** [C] sth radiated: ~*s emitted by an X-ray apparatus.*

radi·ator /'reɪdɪeɪtə(r)/ *n* [C] **1** apparatus for radiating heat, esp heat from steam or hot water supplied through pipes or from electric current. **2** device for cooling the cylinders of the engine of a motor-vehicle: *This car has a fan-cooled* ~. ⇨ the illus at motor.

rad·ical /'rædɪkl/ *adj* **1** of or from the root or base; fundamental: ~ (= thorough and complete) *reforms; make* ~ *changes in a scheme*. **2** (politics) favouring fundamental reforms; advanced in opinions and policies: *a member of the R*~ *Party*. **3** (maths) relating to the root of a number or quantity: *the* ~ *sign* (√). □ *n* **1** person with ~(2) opinions; member of the R~ Party. **2** (maths) the ~ sign; a quantity expressed as the root of another. ~**ly** /-klɪ/ *adv* ~**ism** /-kəlɪzəm/ *n* beliefs and policies of ~(2) people. ~**ize** /-kəlaɪz/ *vt* [VP6A] cause to become ~(2).

rad·icle /'rædɪkl/ *n* embryo root (eg of a pea or bean).

radii /'reɪdɪaɪ/ ⇨ radius.

radio /'reɪdɪəʊ/ *n* (*pl* ~s /-dɪəʊz/) **1** [U] (communication by) use of electromagnetic waves without a connecting wire: *send a message by* ~. **2** [U] broadcasting by this means: *hear something on the* ~; *talk over the* ~; (attrib) *the* ~ *programme*. **3** [C] '~(**-set**), apparatus, eg on ships, aircraft, for transmitting and receiving ~ messages or (as in the home) for receiving sound broadcast programmes: *a portable* ~; *the latest types of* ~*s/*~*-sets*. **4** '~ **beacon**, station for transmitting signals to help aircraft pilots. '~ **beam**, beam of ~ signals from a ~ beacon. '~ **frequency**, frequency between 10 kilocycles per second to 300000 megacycles per second. '~ **link**, (sound broadcasting) programme in which speakers in widely separated towns are linked by the same programme.

radio- /ˌreɪdɪəʊ/ *pref* of rays or radium. ~**·'ac·tive** *adj* (of such metals as radium and uranium) having atoms that break up and, in so doing, send out rays in the form of electrically charged particles capable of penetrating opaque bodies and of producing electrical effects: ~*active carbon;* ~*active dust,*

dust (eg as carried by winds) from explosions of nuclear bombs, etc; ~*active waste*, waste material from nuclear power stations, etc. Hence, ~**·ac·'tiv·ity** *n* [U]. '~**-gram** *n* (**a**) (abbr of): ~ gramophone. (**b**) X-ray photograph. ~**·'gramophone** *n* combined ~ receiver and record-player. '~**-graph** *n* X-ray photograph. ˌ**radi·'ogra·phy** /ˌreɪdɪ'ɒgrəfɪ/ *n* [U] production of X-ray photographs. ˌ**radi·'ogra·pher** *n* person trained to take ~graphs. ~**·'iso·tope** *n* ~active form of an element, used in medicine, industry, etc to study the path and speed of substances through bodies and objects. ˌ~**-lo'cation** *n* radar. ˌ**radi·'ol·ogy** /ˌreɪdɪ'ɒlədʒɪ/ *n* [U] scientific study of X-rays and other radiation (esp as used in medicine). ˌ**radi·'ologist** *n* expert in ~logy. ~**·'telescope** *n* apparatus that detects stars by means of ~ waves from outer space and tracks spacecraft. ~**·'therapy** *n* treatment of disease by means of X-rays or other forms of radiation, eg of heat. ~**·'therapist** *n* expert in ~-therapy.

dish

a radio telescope

rad·ish /'rædɪʃ/ *n* salad plant with a white or red edible root.

radium /'reɪdɪəm/ *n* [U] radioactive metallic element (symbol **Ra**) used in the treatment of some diseases, eg cancer.

radius /'reɪdɪəs/ *n* (*pl* -dii /-dɪaɪ/) **1** (length of a) straight line from the centre of a circle or sphere to any point on the circumference or surface. ⇨ the illus at circle. **2** circular area measured by its ~: *The police searched all the fields and woods within a* ~ *of two miles*. **3** (anat) outer of the two bones in the forearm. ⇨ the illus at skeleton.

raf·fia /'ræfɪə/ *n* [U] fibre from the leaf-stalks of a kind of palm-tree, used for making baskets, hats, mats, etc.

raff·ish /'ræfɪʃ/ *adj* disreputable; dissipated: *a* ~ *young man; with a* ~ *air*. ~**·ly** *adv*

raffle /'ræfl/ *n* [C] sale of an article by a lottery, often for a charitable purpose: *buy* '~ *tickets/tickets for a* ~. □ *vt* [VP6A, 15B] ~ *sth.(off)*, sell in a ~: ~ *(off) a motor-scooter.*

raft /rɑːft US: ræft/ *n* **1** number of tree trunks fastened together to be floated down a river. **2** ('**life-**) ~, flat, floating structure of rough timber, barrels, etc as a substitute for a boat or for the use of swimmers: *The sailors got away from the wrecked ship on a* ~. □ *vt, vi* **1** [VP6A, 15A, B] carry on a ~; cross (a stream) on a ~. **2** [VP2C] go on a ~: ~ *down the stream*. ~**er**, '**rafts·man** /-mən/ (*pl* -men) *nn* man who ~s timber.

rafter /'rɑːftə(r) US: 'ræf-/ *n* one of the sloping beams of the framework on which the tiles or slates of a roof are supported. **raft·ered** /'rɑːftəd US: 'ræf-/ *adj* provided with ~s: *a* ~*ed roof,* (esp) one of which the ~s are visible from beneath, eg in a hall that has no ceiling.

rag [1] /ræg/ n [C] **1** odd bit of cloth: *a rag to polish the car with.* **2** piece of old and torn cloth; (*pl*) old and torn clothes: *dressed in rags; My coat was worn to rags.* **the 'rag trade,** (sl) the business of making and selling clothes. **'glad rags,** ⟹ glad. **3** scrap; irregular piece. **'rag-bag** n **(a)** bag in which scraps of fabric are stored. **(b)** motley collection; confused mass. **(c)** (sl) untidily dressed person. **4** (*pl*) old, waste pieces of cloth from which a good quality of paper ('*rag paper*) is made. **5** (used contemptuously for a) newspaper: *Why do you read that worthless rag?*

rag [2] /ræg/ vt (-gg-) [VP6A] (colloq) tease; play practical jokes on; be noisy and boisterous. □ n (colloq) rough, noisy disturbance; carnival with side-shows, a procession of amusing floats [1](3), etc, eg as held by college students. **'rag-day,** day (usu annually) on which students hold a rag, and often collect money for charity.

raga-muf-fin /'rægəmʌfɪn/ n dirty, disreputable person, esp a small boy dressed in rags.

rage /reɪdʒ/ n **1** [C,U] (outburst of) furious anger; violence: *livid with* ~; *the* ~ *of the sea,* its violence during a storm. **be in/fly into a** ~, be, become, violently angry. **2** [C] ~ (*for*), strong desire: *He has a* ~ *for collecting butterflies.* **3 be (all) the** ~, (colloq) sth for which there is a widespread but temporary enthusiasm; sth very fashionable: *The new musical comedy at Drury Lane is all the* ~. *These white handbags from Italy are (all) the* ~ *this summer.* □ vi [VP2A,C] be violently angry; (of storms, etc) be violent: *He* ~d *and fumed against me for not letting him have his own way. The storm* ~d *all day. The wind* ~d *round the house. Flu* ~d *through the country.*

ragged /'rægɪd/ adj **1** (with clothes) badly torn or in rags: *a* ~ *coat; a* ~ *old man.* **2** having rough or irregular edges or outlines or surfaces: *a dog with a* ~ *coat of hair; a sleeve with* ~ *edges/which is* ~ *at the cuff;* ~ *rocks;* ~ *clouds driven by the gale.* **3** (of work, etc) imperfect; lacking smoothness or uniformity: *a* ~ *performance,* eg of a theatrical rôle, a piece of music. **~-ly** adv **~-ness** n

rag-lan /'ræglən/ n (usu attrib) sweater or coat without shoulder seams (so that the seams for the sleeves go up from the armpit to the neckline).

ra-gout /'ræɡu: US: ræ'ɡu:/ n (dish of) meat and vegetable stew.

rag-tag /'rægtæg/ n **(the)** ~ **and 'bobtail,** the riff-raff; disreputable people.

rag-time /'rægtaɪm/ n [U] (1920's) popular music and dance of US Negro origin, the accent of the melody falling just before the regular beat of the accompaniment.

rah /rɑː/ int hurrah (as used, in US) in cheers at a sports meeting, etc: *Rah, rah, rah!*

raid /reɪd/ n **1** surprise attack made by troops, ship(s) or aircraft: *make a* ~ *upon the enemy's camp; killed in an 'air-*~ (attack by aircraft). **2** sudden visit by police to make arrests: *a* ~ *on a gambling-den.* **3** sudden attack or inroad for the purpose of taking money: *a* ~ *on a bank by armed men; a* ~ *on the bank's reserves,* when they are to be used by the directors for expansion, etc. □ vt,vi [VP6A,2A] make a ~ on or into; carry out a ~: *Boys have been* ~ing *my orchard,* visiting it to steal fruit. **~er** n person, ship, aircraft, etc that makes a ~.

rail [1] /reɪl/ n **1** horizontal or sloping bar or rod or continuous series of bars or rods, of wood or metal, as part of a fence, as a protection against contact or falling over: *wooden* ~s *round a field; metal* ~s *round a monument; build a* ~ *fence. He was leaning on the ship's* ~, *looking over the water. One of the horses was forced to the* ~s, (in a horse-race) pressed so close to the ~s of the race-course that it was at a disadvantage. **2** similar bar or rod placed for things to hang on: *a 'towel-*~, eg at the side of a wash-basin. **3** steel bar or continuous line of such bars, laid on the ground as one side of a track for trains or trams: *send goods by* ~, by ~way; *a* ~ *strike,* of railway workers. **off the** ~s, (of a train) off the track; (fig) out of order, out of control; disorganized; (colloq) eccentric; neurotic; mad. **'**~-**road** n (US) = ~way. □ vt (colloq) [VP15A,B] rush (sb or sth) unfairly (*to, into, through, etc*): ~road *a bill through Congress.* **'**~-**way** n **(a)** road or track laid with ~s on which trains run: *build a new* ~way. **(b)** system of such tracks, with the locomotives, cars, wagons, etc and the organization controlling the system: *work on the* ~way. *The* ~ways *in many countries are owned by the State.* **(c)** (attrib) '~way *station/bridge/carriage/ engineer/contractors/transport,* etc. **'**~-**car** n single coach or car, with its own motive power, used on a ~way. **'**~-**head** n farthest point reached by a ~way under construction. □ vt [VP6A,15B] ~ **off/in,** put ~s(1) round; shut (in, off) separate, by means of ~s(1): ~ *off a piece of ground; fields that are* ~ed *off from the road.* ~-**ing** n [C] (often pl) fence made with ~s, eg as a protection at the side of a series of steps.

rail [2] /reɪl/ vi [VP2A,3A] ~ **(at/against),** (liter) find fault; utter reproaches: *It's no use your* ~ing *at fate.* ~-**ing** n [U] act of finding fault, complaining, protesting, etc: (*pl*) utterances of this kind.

rail-lery /'reɪlərɪ/ n [U] (liter) good-humoured teasing; [C] (*pl*-ries) instance of this.

rai-ment /'reɪmənt/ n [U] (liter) clothing.

rain [1] /reɪn/ n **1** [U] condensed moisture of the atmosphere falling in separate drops; fall of such drops: *It looks like* ~, as if there will be a fall of ~. *Don't go out in the* ~. *Come in out of the* ~. *The farmers want* ~. ~ *or shine,* whether the weather is wet or sunny. ~-**bow** /'reɪnbəʊ/ n arch containing the colours of the spectrum, formed in the sky opposite the sun when ~ is falling or when the sun shines on mist or spray. '~-**bow trout,** food fish with reddish bands and black spots. '~-**coat** n light coat of waterproof or tightly-woven material. '~-**drop** n single drop of ~. '~-**fall** n amount of ~ falling within a given area in a given time, (eg measured in cm of depth per annum). '~ **forest,** hot, wet forest in tropical areas, where ~fall is heavy and there is no dry season. '~-**gauge** n instrument for measuring ~fall. '~-**proof** adj able to keep ~ out. '~-**water** n water that has fallen as ~ and has been collected as ~ (contrasted with *well-water,* etc); soft water. **2** *a* ~ + *adj* + ~, fall or shower of ~: *There was a heavy* ~ *last night.* **the** ~s, the season in tropical countries when there is heavy and continuous ~. **3** (usu **a** ~) descent of sth that comes like ~: *a* ~ *of arrows/ bullets; a* ~ *of ashes,* eg from a volcano; (fig) *a* ~ *of congratulations.*

rain [2] /reɪn/ vi,vt **1** (impers): *It was* ~ing, ~ *was falling. It has* ~ed *itself out,* has stopped ~ing. ~ **cats and dogs,** ~ *very hard. It never* ~s *but it*

pours, (prov) Things, usu unwelcome, do not come singly but in numbers, eg if one disaster happens, another will follow. **2** [VP2C] fall in a stream: *Tears ~ed down her cheeks. Misfortunes have ~ed heavily upon the old man.* **3** [VP14] ~ **sth on/upon,** send or come down on: *He ~ed blows/Blows ~ed on the door. The people ~ed gifts upon the heroes returning from the war.*

rainy /'reɪnɪ/ adj (-ier, -iest) having much rain: ~ *weather; a ~ day/climate; the '~ season.* **save/ provide/put away/keep sth for a ~ day,** save (esp money) for a time when one may need it.

raise /reɪz/ vt [VP6A,15A,B] **1** lift up; move from a low(er) to a high(er) level; cause to rise: ~ *a sunken ship to the surface of the sea; ~ one's hat to sb,* as a sign of respect; ~ *one's glass to one's lips;* ~ *prices;* ~ (= build, erect) *a monument.* ~ **one's glass to sb,** drink his health. ~ **one's hand to sb,** move as if to give him a blow. ~ **sb's hopes,** make him more hopeful. ~ **a man to the peerage,** make him a peer. ~ **the temperature, (a)** make a place warmer. **(b)** (fig) increase tension, eg by losing one's temper. ~ **one's voice,** speak more loudly or in a higher tone: *voices ~d in anger.* **2** cause to be upright: ~ *a man from his knees;* ~ *the standard of revolt.* ~ **sb from the dead,** restore him to life. **3** cause to rise or appear: ~ *a cloud of dust;* ~ *the spirits of the dead; shoes that* ~ *blisters on my feet; a story that might* ~ *a blush on a young girl's cheeks; a long, hot walk that ~d a good thirst,* caused the walker to be thirsty. ~ **a dust/commotion,** (fig) cause a disturbance. ~ **a laugh,** do sth to cause laughter. ~ **Cain/hell/the devil/the roof,** (sl) cause an uproar; start a big row or disturbance. **4** bring up for discussion or attention: ~ *a new point/a question/a protest/an objection.* **5** grow or produce (crops); breed (sheep, etc); rear, bring up (a family). `6 get or bring together; manage to get: ~ *an army;* ~ *a loan;* ~ *money for a new undertaking;* ~ *funds for a holiday,* eg by pawning one's jewels. **7** ~ **a siege/blockade,** end it. ~ **an embargo,** remove it. **8** ~ **land,** (naut) come in sight of (land that appears to rise above the horizon): *The ship ~d land the next morning.* □ *n* (esp US, cf GB, *rise*) increase in salary, etc. ~**r** *n* (in compounds) one who, that which, ~s (in various senses): '*cattle-~s;* '*curtain-~r,* short introductory play; '*fire-~rs,* arsonists.

raisin /'reɪzn/ *n* [C] dried sweet grape, as used in cakes, etc.

raison d'être /ˌreɪzɒn 'detrə/ *n* (*sing* only) (F) reason for, purpose of, a thing's existence.

raj /rɑːdʒ/ *n* sovereignty: *the ending of the British raj in India.*

ra·jah /'rɑːdʒə/ *n* Indian prince; Malayan chief.

rake¹ /reɪk/ *n* **1** long-handled tool with prongs used for drawing together straw, dead leaves, etc or for smoothing soil or gravel, ⇨ the illus at tool; similar kinds of tool on wheels, drawn by a horse or tractor. **2** implement used by a croupier for drawing in money or chips at a gaming-table. □ *vt,vi* **1** [VP6A,22] use a ~ (on); make smooth with a ~: ~ *garden paths;* ~ *the soil smooth for a seedbed.* **2** [VP6A,15A,B,14] get (sth *together, up, out, etc*) with or as with a ~: ~ *together dead leaves;* ~ *out a fire,* get the ashes or cinders out from the bottom of a grate, etc; ~ *up hay;* ~ *the dead leaves off the lawn.* ~ **sth in,** (fig) earn, make, much money: *The firm is very successful—they're raking it in/ raking in the money.* '~**-off** *n* (sl) (usu suggesting

dishonesty) commission; share of profits: *If I put this bit of business in your way, I expect a ~-off.* ~ **sth up,** (esp) bring to people's knowledge (sth forgotten, esp sth which it is better not to recall to memory): ~ *up old quarrels/accusations/ slanders/grievances. Don't* ~ *up the past.* **3** [VP6A,15A,B,2C,3A] ~ **(over/through) sth,** search for facts, etc: ~ *through old manuscripts for information;* ~ *one's memory;* ~ *about among old documents.* **4** [VP6A,15A] fire with guns at, from end to end: ~ *a ship;* ~ *a trench with machine-gun fire.*

rake² /reɪk/ *n* dissolute man.

rake³ /reɪk/ *vi,vt* [VP2A,6A] (of a ship, or its bow or stern) project beyond the keel; (of the funnel, masts) (cause to) slope towards the stern; (of the stage of a theatre) slope down (towards the audience. □ *n* degree of slope: *the ~ of a ship's masts/ of the stage of a theatre.*

rak·ish¹ /'reɪkɪʃ/ *adj* **1** of or like a rake²; dissolute: *a ~ appearance.* **2** jaunty: *set one's hat at a ~ angle* (from *rake³*). ~·**ly** *adv* in a ~ manner: *with his hat tilted ~ly.* ~·**ness** *n*

rak·ish² /'reɪkɪʃ/ *adj* (of a ship) looking smart and as if built for speed (and therefore, in olden times, suggesting that she might be a pirate ship).

ral·len·tando /ˌrælən'tændəʊ/ *adj, adv* (music) gradually slower. ⇨ accelerando.

rally¹ /'rælɪ/ *vt,vi* (*pt,pp* -lied) [VP6A,15A,2A,C] **1** (cause to) come together, esp after defeat or confusion, or in the face of threats or danger, to make new efforts: *The troops rallied round their leader. The leader rallied his men. My supporters are ~ing round me again. They rallied to the support of the Prime Minister.* **2** give new strength to; (cause to) recover health, strength, firmness: ~ *one's strength/spirits;* ~ *from an illness. The boy rallied his wits. The market rallied,* eg of the Stock Exchange, prices stopped dropping and became firm. □ *n* (*pl* -lies) [C] **1** act or process of ~ing; coming together after being dispersed; recovery of strength; improvement during illness. **2** (tennis) exchange of several strokes before a point is scored. **3** gathering or assembly, esp to encourage fresh effort: *a po'litical ~: a 'peace ~,* one to urge the necessity of ending or avoiding war. **4** competition of motor vehicles over public roads.

rally² /'rælɪ/ *vt* (*pt,pp* -lied) [VP6A] tease; chaff good-humouredly.

ram /ræm/ *n* **1** uncastrated male sheep. **2** one of various implements or devices for striking or pushing with great force, eg the falling weight of a pile-driving machine; form of water-pump in which a heavy fall of water is used to force a smaller quantity to a higher level. **3** ⇨ *battering-ram* at batter¹. **4** metal projection on a warship's bow for piercing the side of an enemy ship. □ *vt* (-mm-) **1** [VP6A,15A,B] strike and push heavily: *ram down the soil,* eg when building roads or embankments; *ram piles into a river bed; ram a charge home/into a gun;* (colloq) *ram one's clothes into a suitcase.* **ram sth down sb's throat,** (fig) say sth repeatedly so as to impress it upon sb, get him to learn it or recognize its truth. **2** [VP6A] (of a ship) strike with a ram(4): *ram and sink a submarine.* **3** '**ram-jet** *n* jet engine in which the air is rammed or forced through the engine and compressed by the speed of flight. '**ram-rod** *n* iron rod for ramming the charge into old (muzzle-loading) guns.

Rama·dan /ˌræmə'dɑːn *US:* -'dæn/ *n* ninth month

of the Muslim year, when Muslims fast between sunrise and sunset.

ramble /'ræmbl/ *vi* [VP2A,C] **1** walk for pleasure, with no special destination; (fig) wander in one's talk, not keeping to the subject. **2** (of plants) grow with long shoots that trail or straggle. □ *n* rambling walk: *go for a country* ∼. **ram·bler** *n* person or thing that ∼s: (attrib) *∼r roses*. **ram·bling** *adj* **1** (esp of buildings, streets, towns), extending in various directions irregularly, as if built without planning. **2** (of a speech, essay, etc) disconnected.

ram·bunc·tious /ræm'bʌŋkʃəs/ *adj* boisterous.

ram·ify /'ræmɪfaɪ/ *vi,vt* (*pt,pp* -fied) [VP2A,6A] form or produce branches; make or become a network: *a ramified system*. **rami·fi·ca·tion** /ˌræmɪfɪ'keɪʃn/ *n* [C] subdivision of sth complex or like a network: *the widespread ramifications of trade/a plot/an argument*.

ram·jet ⇨ ram(3).

ramp¹ /ræmp/ *n* sloping way from one level to another, eg instead of, or in addition to, stairs or steps in a hospital, so that beds can be wheeled from one floor to another, or, at a kerb in a many-storeyed garage, so that cars can be driven up and down; change of level during road repairs.

ramp² /ræmp/ *n* (GB, sl) dishonest attempt to obtain an exorbitant price; swindle.

ramp³ /ræmp/ *vt* [VP2C] ∼ *about,* (now usu joc) storm, rage or rush.

ram·page /ræm'peɪdʒ/ *vi* [VP2A] rush about in excitement or rage. □ *n* /'ræmpeɪdʒ/ *be/go on the* ∼, be/go rampaging. **ram·pa·geous** /ræm'peɪdʒəs/ *adj* excited and noisy.

ram·pant /'ræmpənt/ *adj* **1** (of plants, etc) rank; luxuriant: *Rich soil makes some plants too* ∼, causes them to spread too thickly, to have too much foliage, etc. **2** (of diseases, social evils, etc) unchecked; beyond control: *Cholera was* ∼ *among them.* **3** (of animals, esp of a lion in heraldry) on the hind legs. ∼·**ly** *adv*

ram·part /'ræmpɑːt/ *n* [C] **1** wide bank of earth, often with a wall, built to defend a fort or other defensive work. **2** (fig) defence; protection.

ram·rod /'ræmrɒd/ ⇨ ram(3).

ram·shackle /'ræmʃækl/ *adj* almost collapsing; nearly at breaking-point: *a* ∼ *house; a* ∼ *old bus; their* ∼ *empire.*

ran /ræn/ *pt* of run².

ranch /rɑːntʃ *US:* ræn-/ *n* (US) large farm, esp one with extensive lands for cattle, but also for fruit, chickens, etc. '∼ **house,** (US) rectangular bungalow type of house. '∼ **wagon,** (US) = station wagon. ∼·**er** *n* person who owns, manages or works on, a ∼.

ran·cid /'rænsɪd/ *adj* with the smell or taste of stale, decaying fat or butter; (of fat) having gone bad; ill smelling: *This butter smells* ∼*/has gone* ∼.

ran·cour (US = **-cor**) /'ræŋkə(r)/ *n* [U] deep and long-lasting feeling of bitterness; spitefulness: *full of* ∼ (*against sb*). **ran·cor·ous** /'ræŋkərəs/ *adj*

rand /rænd/ *n* monetary unit of the Republic of S Africa, divided into 100 cents.

ran·dom /'rændəm/ *n* **1** *at* ∼, without aim or purpose: *shooting/dropping bombs at* ∼; *hit out at* ∼. **2** (attrib) done, made, taken, at ∼: ∼ *remarks; a* ∼ *sample/selection;* ∼ *sampling.*

randy /'rændɪ/ *adj* (-ier, -iest) **1** (Scot) boisterous; aggressively noisy. **2** full of sexual lust.

ranee, rani /'rɑːniː/ *n* Hindu queen or princess; wife of a rajah.

rang /ræŋ/ *pt* of ring².

range¹ /reɪndʒ/ *n* [C] **1** row, line or series of things: *a magnificent* ∼ *of mountains; a* '*mountain-*∼; *a long* ∼ *of cliffs.* **2** area of ground with targets for shooting at: *a* '*rifle-*∼; area in which rockets and missiles are fired. **3** distance to which a gun will shoot or to which a shell, etc can be fired: *at a* ∼ *of five miles; in/within/out of/ beyond* ∼; distance between a gun, etc and the target: *fire at short/long* ∼. '∼-**finder** *n* (a) instrument for finding the distance of sth to be fired at. (b) device fitted in some cameras for measuring distances. **4** distance at which one can see or hear, or to which sound will carry. **5** extent; distance between limits: *the annual* ∼ *of temperature,* eg from − 10°C to 40°C; *a long-*∼ *weather forecast,* for a long period; *a narrow* ∼ *of prices; cotton fabrics in a wide* ∼ *of colours; the* ∼ *of her voice,* ie between her top and bottom notes; (fig) *a subject that is outside my* ∼, one that I have not studied; *a wide* ∼ *of interests.* **6** (US) area of grazing or hunting ground. **7** area over which plants are found growing or in which animals are found living: *What is the* ∼ *of the nightingale in this country?* **8** cooking-stove, usu with ovens, a boiler, and a surface with openings or hot-plates for pans, kettles, etc: *a kitchen* ∼.

range² /reɪndʒ/ *vt,vi* **1** [VP6A,15A] place or arrange in a row or rows; put, take one's place in a specified situation, order, class or group: *The general* ∼*d his men along the river bank. They were* ∼*d against us/among the rebels. The spectators* ∼*d themselves along the route of the procession.* **2** [VP2C,3A,6A] ∼ *(through/over),* go, move, wander: *animals ranging through the forests;* ∼ *over the hills;* ∼ *the seas/hills, etc;* (fig) *researches that* ∼*d over a wide field; a speaker who* ∼*d far and wide,* spoke on many topics; *a wide-ranging discussion.* **3** [VP2C] extend, run in a line: *a boundary that* ∼*s north and south/from A to B.* **4** [VP2C] vary between limits: *prices ranging from £7 to £10/between £7 and £10.* **5** (of guns, projectiles) carry: *This gun* ∼*s over six miles,* can fire to this distance.

ranger /'reɪndʒə(r)/ *n* **1** (US) forest guard. **2** (US) one of a body of mounted troops employed as police (eg in thinly populated areas). **3** (US) commando. **4** (GB) keeper of a royal park, who sees that the forest laws are observed.

rani /'rɑːniː/ ⇨ ranee.

rank¹ /ræŋk/ *n* **1** [C] line of persons or things: *a* '*cab-*∼. *Take the taxi at the head of the* ∼, the first one in the line. **2** number of soldiers placed side by side (on parade, usu in three lines, called the *front, centre* and the *rear* ∼s). **keep/break** ∼, remain/ fail to remain in line. **3** the ∼s; the ∼ and file; other ∼s, ordinary soldiers, ie privates, corporals, etc contrasted with officers. **be reduced to the** ∼s, (of a non-commissioned officer, eg a sergeant) made an ordinary private soldier (as a punishment). **rise from the** ∼s, (of an ordinary soldier) be given a commission as an officer. **4** [C,U] position in a scale; distinct grade in the armed forces; category or class: *promoted to the* ∼ *of captain; above/below a major in* ∼; *officers of high* ∼; *hold the* ∼ *of colonel; persons of high* ∼, of high social position; *people of all* ∼s *and classes; be in the* ∼s *of the unemployed; a painter of the first* ∼; *a second-*∼ (more usu *second-rate*) *dancer.* **pull** ∼ **on sb,** use one's superior position

to gain an advantage over them. □ *vt,vi* **1**
[VP6A,15A,16B] put or arrange in a ~ or ~s; put
in a class: *Where/How do you* ~ *Addison as an
essayist? Would you* ~ *him among the world's
great statesmen?* **2** [VP3A] have a place: *Does he*
~ *among/with the failures? A major* ~s *above a
captain. Will my shares* ~ *for the next dividend?* **3**
~ing officer, (US) the officer of highest ~
present.
rank[2] /ræŋk/ *adj* **1** (of plants, etc) growing too luxuriantly, with too much leaf: ~ *grass; roses that
grow* ~; (of land) choked with weeds or likely to
produce a lot of weeds: ~ *soil; a field that is* ~
with nettles and thistles. **2** smelling or tasting bad;
offensive: ~ *tobacco.* **3** unmistakably bad; possessing a bad quality to an extreme degree: *a* ~
traitor; ~ *injustice. These fungi are* ~ *poison.*
~·ly *adv* ~·ness *n*
ranker /'ræŋkə(r)/ *n* commissioned officer who has
risen from the ranks. ⇨ rank[1](3).
rankle /'ræŋkl/ *vi* [VP2A] continue to be a painful
or bitter memory: *The insult* ~d *in his mind.*
ran·sack /'rænsæk US: ræn'sæk/ *vt* **1**
[VP6A,14,16A] ~ *sth (for sth/to do sth),* search
(a place) thoroughly (for sth): ~ *a drawer;* ~ *a
dictionary to find just the right word.* **2** [VP6A,14]
~ *sth (of sth),* rob; plunder: *The house had been
~ed of all that was worth anything.*
ran·som /'rænsəm/ *n* [U] freeing of a captive on
payment; [C] sum of money, etc, paid for this.
hold a man to ~, keep him as a captive and ask
for ~. *worth a king's* ~, worth a very large sum
of money. □ *vt* [VP6A] obtain the freedom of (sb),
set (sb) free, in exchange for ~: ~ *a kidnapped diplomat.*
rant /rænt/ *vi,vt* [VP2A,6A] use extravagant, boasting language; say or recite (sth) noisily and theat-
rically: *an actor who* ~s *his part.* □ *n* piece of
~ing talk. ~·er *n* person who ~s.
rap[1] /ræp/ *n* [C] **1** (sound of a) light, quick blow: *I
heard a rap on the door. give sb a rap on/over
the knuckles,* reprove him. **2** (colloq) blame; consequences. *take the rap (for sth),* be reproved or
reprimanded (esp when innocent). **3** (US sl) conversation; discussion. □ *vt,vi* (-pp-)
[VP6A,15B,2A,C] **1** give a rap to; make the sound
of a rap: *rap (on) the table; rap (at) the door.* **2**
rap sth out, (a) say sth suddenly or sharply: *rap
out an oath.* (b) (of spirits at a seance) express by
means of raps: *rap out a message.* **3** (US sl) talk;
discuss.
rap[2] /ræp/ *n not care/give a rap,* not care at all.
ra·pa·cious /rə'peɪʃəs/ *adj* (formal) greedy (esp for
money). ~·ly *adv* **ra·pac·ity** /rə'pæsəti/ *n* [U]
greed; avarice.
rape[1] /reɪp/ *n* [U] plant grown as food for sheep
and pigs; plant grown for the oil obtained from its
seeds.
rape[2] /reɪp/ *vt* [VP6A] **1** seize and carry off by
force. **2** commit the crime of forcing sexual intercourse on (a woman or girl). □ *n* act of raping.
rap·ist /'reɪpɪst/ *n*
rapid /'ræpɪd/ *adj* **1** quick; moving, occurring,
with great speed: *a* ~ *decline in sales; a* ~ *pulse/
river/worker;* (of action) done quickly: ~-*fire
questions,* in ~ succession. **2** (of a slope) steep;
descending steeply. □ *n* (usu *pl*) part of a river
where a steep slope causes the water to flow fast.
~·ly *adv* **rap·id·ity** /rə'pɪdəti/ *n* [U].
rapier /'reɪpɪə(r)/ *n* light sword used for thrusting in

duels and the sport of fencing. '~-thrust, (fig) a
delicate or witty retort.

a rapier

rap·ine /'ræpaɪn US: 'ræpɪn/ *n* (liter or rhet) [U]
plundering.
rap·port /ræ'pɔː(r) US: -'pɔːrt/ *n* [U,C] sympathetic
relationship. *be in* ~ *(with),* (or, as in French, *en*
/ɑːn/ ~), in close relationship or sympathy (with).
rap·proche·ment /ræ'prɒʃmɒŋ US:
ˌræprəʊʃ'mɒŋ/ *n* [C] coming together again (of persons, parties, States) in friendly relations; renewal
of friendship.
rap·scal·lion /ræp'skæliən/ *n* (old use) rascal;
rogue.
rapt /ræpt/ *adj* so deep in thought, so carried away
by feelings, that one is unaware of other things; en-
raptured: *listening to the orchestra with* ~ *attention;* ~ *in contemplation of the scenery;* ~ *in a
book.*
rap·ture /'ræptʃə(r)/ *n* **1** [U] state of being rapt; ec-
static delight: *gazing with* ~ *at the face of the girl
he loved.* **2** (*pl*) *be in/go into/be sent into* ~s
(over/about), be/become extremely happy, full of
joy and enthusiasm: *She went into* ~s *over the
dresses they showed her.* **rap·tur·ous** /'ræptʃərəs/
adj inspiring or expressing ~. **rap·tur·ous·ly** *adv*
rare[1] /reə(r)/ *adj* (-r, -st) **1** unusual; uncommon;
not often happening, seen, etc: *a* ~ *occurrence; a
~ book,* one of which few copies are obtainable. *It
is very* ~ *for her to arrive late.* **2** (dated colloq)
unusually good: *We had a* ~ *time/* ~ *fun.* **3** (of a
substance, esp the atmosphere) thin; not dense: *the
~ air of the mountains in the Himalayas.* ~·ly *adv*
1 seldom: *I* ~ly *eat in restaurants. He visits us
only* ~ly *nowadays.* **2** excellently.
~·ness *n*
rare[2] /reə(r)/ *adj* (of meat) underdone; cooked so
that the redness and juices are retained: ~ *steak.*
rare·bit /'reəbɪt/ *n* [C] Welsh ~ (also, colloq, *rabbit*), melted or toasted cheese on toasted bread.
rarefy /'reərɪfaɪ/ *vt,vi* (*pt,pp* –fied) [VP6A,2A]
make or become less dense; purify: *the rarefied air
of the mountain tops;* refine; make subtle: *rarefied
ideas/theories.* **rare·fac·tion** /ˌreərɪ'fækʃn/ *n* [U]
~ing.
rar·ing /'reərɪŋ/ *adj* (colloq) full of eagerness:
They're ~ *to go.*
rar·ity /'reərəti/ *n* (*pl* –ties) **1** [U] rareness. **2** [C]
sth rare, uncommon or unusual; sth valued because
rare: *Rain is a* ~ *in Upper Egypt.*
ras·cal /'rɑːskl US: 'ræskl/ *n* **1** dishonest person. **2**
(playfully) mischievous person (esp a child), fond
of playing tricks. ~·ly /-kəlɪ/ *adj* of or like a ~;
mean; dishonest: *a* ~ly *trick.*
rase /reɪz/ *vt* ⇨ raze.
rash[1] /ræʃ/ *n* (breaking out of, patch of) tiny red
spots on the skin: *a* '*heat-*~; '*nettle-*~; (fig) *a* ~
*of new red brick bungalows on a country road. If a
~ appears, the child may have* (*the*) *measles.*
rash[2] /ræʃ/ *adj* too hasty; overbold; done, doing
things, without enough thought of the consequences: *a* ~ *act/statement; a* ~ *young man.* ~·ly
adv ~·ness *n*
rasher /'ræʃə(r)/ *n* slice of bacon or ham (to be)
fried: *eat three* ~s *and two fried eggs for breakfast.*
rasp /rɑːsp US: ræsp/ *n* [C] metal tool like a coarse

file with a surface or surfaces having sharp points, used for scraping; rough, grating sound produced by this tool. □ *vt,vi* **1** [VP6A,15A,B,22] ~ *sth (away/off)*, scrape with a ~; scrape. **2** [VP6A] (fig) grate upon, have an irritating effect upon: ~ *sb's feelings/nerves.* **3** [VP15B] ~ *out*, utter in a way that grates or sounds like the noise of a ~: ~ *out orders/insults.* **4** [VP2A,C] make a harsh, grating sound: *a learner ~ing (away) on his violin; a ~ing voice.* ~**ing·ly** *adv*

rasp·berry /'rɑːzbrɪ *US:* 'ræzberɪ/ *n* (*pl* -ries) **1** bush with small, sweet, yellow or red berries, wild or cultivated: (attrib) ~ *jam/canes;* one of these berries. **2** (sl) contemptuous noise made with the tongue and lips, or a gesture indicating dislike, derision or disapproval: *give/blow sb a ~; get a ~.*

rat /ræt/ *n* **1** animal like, but larger than, a mouse; person who deserts a cause that he thinks is about to fail (from the belief that rats desert a ship that will sink or be wrecked). ⇨ the illus at small. **smell a rat**, suspect that sth wrong is being done. **(look) like a drowned rat**, wet and miserable; soaked to the skin. **the 'rat race**, ceaseless and undignified competition for success in one's career, social status, etc as among office workers, etc. **2** (fig) cowardly traitor; strike-breaker. **Rats!** (dated sl, as an exclamation) Nonsense! □ *vt* (-tt-) **1** hunt rats: *go ratting.* **2** [VP2A,3A] ~ *(on sb)*, break a promise, withdraw from an undertaking. **rat·ter** *n* man, dog or cat that catches rats: *Are terriers good ratters?* **rat·ty** *adj* (-ier, -iest) (colloq) irritable; snappish.

rat·able, rate·able /'reɪtəbl/ *adj* liable to payment of municipal rates: ~ *property; the ~ value of a house,* its value as assessed for the levying of rates.

rat·abil·ity, rate·abil·ity /ˌreɪtə'bɪlətɪ/ *n* [U].
rat·an /ræ'tæn/ ⇨ rattan.
rat-a-tat-tat /ˌræt ə ˌtæt 'tæt/ ⇨ rat-tat.
ratch /rætʃ/ *n* = ratchet.
ratch·et /'rætʃɪt/ *n* toothed wheel provided with a catch (*pawl*) that prevents the wheel from slipping back and allows it to move in only one direction.
rate[1] /reɪt/ *n* **1** [C] standard of reckoning, obtained by bringing two numbers or amounts into relationship: *walk at the ~ of 3 miles an hour; a train travelling at a/the ~ of 50 miles an hour; an aircraft with a good ~ of climb; at a great/fearful, etc ~,* at great speed; *buy things at the ~ of 55p a hundred. What is the airmail letter ~ to Peru?* ⇨ per; to[1] (12). **'birth/'marriage/'death, etc ~**, the number of births, etc in relationship to a period of time and a number of people: *a death-~ of 2·3 per 1000 (per year).* **~ of exchange**, relationship between two currencies (eg US dollars and F francs). **the 'discount ~, the 'bank ~**, the officially announced percentage at which a country's central bank is prepared to discount Bills. **2** (phrases) **at 'this/'that ~**, if this/that is true, if we may assume that this/that is the case; if this/that state of affairs continues. **at 'any ~**, in any case; whatever happens. **3** (the) ~**s**, (GB) tax on property (land and buildings), paid to local authorities for local purposes: *an extra penny on the ~s for the public library,* ie a charge of one penny on each pound of the assessment. **~s and taxes**, payments to local authorities and taxes levied by the national government. **'~-payer** *n* person liable to have ~s exacted from him. ⇨ also *water-~* at water[1](7). **4** (with ordinal numbers) class or grade: *first ~,* excellent; *second ~,* fairly good; *third ~,* (rather) poor; (at-

PARROT

feather

beak

OSTRICH

PEACOCK

PARAKEET

COCKATOO

EMU

KIWI

TOUCAN

MYNAH

rare or exotic birds

trib, with a hyphen) *a first-~ teacher*. Hence, *,first-'rater, ,second-'rater, etc.*

rate² /reɪt/ *vt,vi* **1** [VP6A,14,15A,16B] ~ *(at)*, judge or estimate the value or qualities of: *What do you ~ his fortune at? He was a man whom all his friends ~d as kind and hospitable. Do you ~* (= consider) *Mr X among your friends?* **2** [VP6A,14] ~ *sth (at)*, (GB) value (property) for the purpose of assessing rates(2) on: *My property was ~d at £100 per annum. Should private houses be more heavily ~d than factories?* **3** [VP16B] ~ *sb as*, (naut) place in a certain class: *He was ~d as a midshipman.* **4** [VP2D,C] (colloq) be ~ed: *he ~s high/as a midshipman.*

rate·able /'reɪtəbl/ *adj* ⇨ **ratable**.

rather /'rɑːðə(r)/ *US:* 'ræ-/ *adv* **1** more willingly; by preference or choice (usu *would/had* ~... *than*; also with inversion: ~ *than... would*): *I would ~ you came tomorrow than today. She would ~ have the small one than the large one. Wouldn't you ~ be liked than feared? He resigned ~ than take part in such a dishonest transaction. A: 'Will you join us in a game of cards?'—B: 'Thank you, but I'd ~ not.'* **2** more truly, accurately or precisely: *He arrived very late last night or ~ in the early hours this morning.* **3** (to be distinguished from *fairly²*; note that *fairly* is not used with comparatives, *too*, *nn*, and *vv*) in a certain degree or measure; more (so) than not; somewhat; **(a)** (with *adjj*, preceding or following the *indef art*, following the *def art*): *a ~ surprising result/~ a surprising result; the ~ tall boy in the corner.* **(b)** (with comparatives): *My brother is ~ better today. This hat is ~ more expensive than that.* **(c)** (with *too*): *This book is ~ too difficult for the juniors and ~ too easy for the seniors.* **(d)** (with *nn*): *It's ~ a pity, ~ regrettable. She's ~ a dear, ~ lovable. £100 is ~ a lot to pay for a dress, isn't it?* **(e)** (with *vv* and *pp*): *I ~ think you may be mistaken. The rain ~ spoiled our holiday. We were all ~ exhausted when we got to the top of the mountain.* **(f)** (with *advv*): *You've done ~ well/~ better than I had expected.* **4** (colloq; GB /,rɑː'ðɜː(r)/) (in answers) most certainly.

rat·ify /'rætɪfaɪ/ *vt* (*pt,pp* -fied) [VP6A] confirm (an agreement) by signature or other formality. **rati·fi·ca·tion** /,rætɪfɪ'keɪʃn/ *n* ~ing or being ratified.

rat·ing /'reɪtɪŋ/ *n* **1** [C] act of valuing property for the purpose of assessing rates, ⇨ rate²(2); amount or sum fixed as the municipal rate. **2** [C] class, classification, eg of yachts by tonnage, motor-cars by engine capacity or horse-power; popularity of radio or TV programmes as estimated by asking a selected group. **3** (navy) person's position or class as recorded in the ship's books; non-commissioned sailor: *officers and ~s.*

ra·tio /'reɪʃɪəʊ/ *n* (*pl* ~s /-ʃɪəʊz/) [C] relation between two amounts determined by the number of times one contains the other: *The ~s of 1 to 5 and 20 to 100 are the same.*

rati·oc·in·ation /,rætɪ,ɒsɪ'neɪʃn *US:* ,ræʃɪ-/ *n* [U] the process of methodical reasoning, esp by the use of syllogisms.

ration /'ræʃn/ *n* fixed quantity, esp of food, allowed to one person; (*pl*) fixed allowance served out to, eg members of the armed forces: *go and draw ~s.* '~ **card/book**, one that entitles the holder to ~s, eg for a civilian when there is a food shortage during or immediately after a war. **be on**

short ~**s**, be allowed or able to have less than the usual quantity of food. □ *vt* **1** [VP6A] limit (sb) to a fixed ~. **2** [VP6A,15B] ~ *(out)*, limit (food, water, etc): *We'll have to ~ the water. He ~ed out* (= distributed ~s of) *the bread.*

ra·tional /'ræʃnəl/ *adj* **1** of reason or reasoning. **2** able to reason; having the faculty of reasoning. **3** sensible; that can be tested by reasoning: ~ *conduct/explanations.* ~**ly** /-ʃnəlɪ/ *adv* ~·**ity** /,ræʃə'nælətɪ/ *n* quality of being ~; reasonableness.

ration·ale /,ræʃə'nɑːl/ *n* fundamental reason, logical basis (of sth).

ration·al·ism /'ræʃnəlɪzəm/ *n* [U] the practice of treating reason as the ultimate authority in religion as in other subjects of study. **ration·al·ist** /-ɪst/ *n* person who accepts reason as the ultimate authority in religion, ethics, etc. **ration·al·is·tic** /,ræʃnə'lɪstɪk/ *adj* of ~ or rationalists.

ration·al·ize /'ræʃnəlaɪz/ *vt* **1** [VP6A] bring into conformity with reason; (attempt to) treat or explain in a rational manner: ~ *one's fears/ behaviour.* **2** [VP6A] reorganize (an industry, etc) so as to lessen or get rid of waste (in time, labour, materials, etc). **ration·al·iz·ation** /,ræʃnəlaɪ'zeɪʃn *US:* -lɪ'z-/ *n*

rat·lin, rat·line /'rætlɪn/ (usu *pl*) small rope fixed across the shrouds of a ship (like a rung on a ladder) used as a step by a sailor climbing up or down.

rat·tan, ratan /ræ'tæn/ *n* **1** [C] (East Indian palmtree with a) cane-like stem. **2** [C] walking-stick or cane made from a ~ stem. **3** [U] ~ stems (collectively), as used for building, basketwork, furniture, etc: *a chair with a ~ seat.*

rat-tat /ræ 'tæt/ (also **rat-a-tat-tat** /,ræt ə ,tæt 'tæt/) *n* sound of a rapping or knocking, esp on a door.

rattle /'rætl/ *vt,vi* **1** [VP6A,15A,2A,C] (cause to) make short, sharp sounds quickly, one after the other: *The wind ~d the windows. The windows were rattling in the wind. The hailstones ~d on the tin roof. The old bus ~d along over the stony road.* **2** [VP2C,15B] ~ *away;* ~ *sth off*, talk, say or repeat (sth) quickly and in a thoughtless or lively way: *The boy ~d off the poem he had learnt. The children ~d away merrily.* □ *n* **1** [U] rattling sound: *the ~ of bottles from a milkman's van; the ~ of hail on the window-panes.* **2** [C] baby's toy for producing a rattling sound; similar device whirled (eg by spectators at a football match) to make a noisy clatter. **3** [U] lively flow of talk; chatter. **4** [C] series of horny rings in a ~snake's tail. '~**-snake** *n* poisonous American snake that makes a rattling noise with its tail. ⇨ the illus at **snake**. **5** ('**death-**)~, rattling sound sometimes produced in the throat immediately before death. **6** '~**-brain**, '~**-pate** *nn* person with an empty head; silly chatterer. Hence, '~**-brained,** '~**-pated** *adjj* **rat·tler** /'rætlə(r)/ *n* person or thing that ~s, esp a ~snake.

rat·tling /'rætlɪŋ/ *adj* (sl) quick(-moving); firstrate; excellent: *travelling at a rattling rate; a rattling breeze; have a rattling* (= enjoyable) *time.* □ *adv* (sl) very: *a rattling good speech.*

ratty /'rætɪ/ *adj* ⇨ rat.

rau·cous /'rɔːkəs/ *adj* (of sounds) harsh; rough; hoarse: *the ~ cries of the crows; a ~ voice; ~ laughter.* ~·**ly** *adv*

rav·age /'rævɪdʒ/ *vt,vi* [VP6A] **1** destroy; damage badly: *forests ~d by fire; a face ~d by disease,* eg covered with marks after smallpox. **2** (of armies, etc) rob, plunder, with violence: *They had* ~*d the countryside* □ *n* **1** [U] destruction; devastation. **2** (*pl*) ~*s of*, destructive effects: *the* ~*s of time*, eg on a woman's looks; *the* ~*s of torrential rains*.

rave /reɪv/ *vi* **1** [VP2A,C,3A] ~ (*at/against/about sth*), talk wildly, violently, angrily: *The patient* (eg someone with a high fever) *began to* ~. *When he was accused of stealing he* ~*d wildly against me*. **2** [VP3A] ~ *about sb/sth*, talk or act with (often) excessive enthusiasm: *She* ~*d about the food she had had in France*. **3** [VP15B] ~ *it up*, (sl) take part in a very noisy, enjoyable party. Hence, '~-**up** *n* lively party. □ *n* **1** (colloq, often attrib) enthusiastic praise: *a* ~ *review*, eg of a book. **2** (sl) wild, exciting party, dance, outing, etc. **3** (sl) great enthusiasm: *be in a* ~ *about sb*. **raver** *n* (colloq) sb who ~s(3). **rav·ing** *adj* talking wildly: *a raving lunatic*. □ *adv* to the point of talking wildly: *You're raving mad!* **rav·ings** *n pl* foolish or wild talk: *the ravings of a madman*.

ravel /'rævl/ *vt,vi* (-ll-, US also -l-) **1** [VP2A,C] (of knitted or woven things) separate into threads; become untwisted; fray: *Bind the edge of the rug so that it won't* ~. **2** [VP6A] cause (threads, hair, etc) to be twisted together, knotted, etc; (fig) make confused. **3** [VP6A,15B] ~ (*out*), disentangle: ~ (*out*) *a rope's end*. ⇨ unravel.

raven /'reɪvn/ *n* **1** large, black bird like a crow, popularly regarded as a bird of ill omen. **2** (attrib) glossy, shining black: ~ *locks*, black hair.

rav·en·ing /'rævənɪŋ/ *adj* fierce; savage; crazy for food: *a* ~ *wolf*.

rav·en·ous /'rævənəs/ *adj* **1** very hungry. **2** greedy: *a* ~ *appetite*; ~ *hunger*; ~ *for power*. ~**ly** *adv* hungrily; greedily: *eat* ~*ly*.

ra·vine /rə'viːn/ *n* deep, narrow valley.

ra·vi·oli /ˌrævɪ'əʊlɪ/ *n* (I) dish of small cases of pasta containing chopped meat, etc usu served with a sauce.

rav·ish /'rævɪʃ/ *vt* [VP6A] **1** fill with delight; enchant: *a* ~*ing view*; ~*ed by the view*; ~*ed with her beauty*. ~**ing·ly** *adv* ~**ment** *n* ~ing or being ~ed. **2** (archaic or poet) seize and carry off: ~*ed from the world by death*. **3** (archaic) rape (a woman or girl).

raw /rɔː/ *adj* **1** uncooked: *raw meat; eat oysters raw*. **2** in the natural state, not manufactured or prepared for use: *raw hides*, not yet tanned; *raw sugar*, not yet refined; *the raw materials of industry*, eg coal, ores; *raw spirit*, undiluted alcohol. *in the raw*, unrefined; in the natural state; (fig) naked. '**raw·hide** *adj* made of untanned hide: *rawhide boots*. **3** (of persons) untrained; unskilled; inexperienced: *raw recruits*, for the army, etc. **4** (of the weather) damp and cold: *a raw February morning; raw winds*. **5** (of wounds) unhealed; bloody; (of a place on the flesh) with the skin rubbed off; sore and painful. ,**raw-'boned** *adj* having little flesh on the bones: *a raw-boned horse*. **6** artistically crude: *His literary style is still rather raw*. **7** (colloq) harsh; unjust; (esp) *a raw deal*, harsh or cruel treatment. □ *n* raw place on the skin, esp on a horse's skin. *touch sb on the raw*, (fig) wound a person's feelings, wound him on the question, topic, etc on which he is most sensitive.

ray¹ /reɪ/ *n* [C] **1** line, beam, of radiant light, heat, energy: *the rays of the sun*; '*X-rays*; '*heat-rays*; (fig) *a ray of hope*. **2** any one of a number of lines coming out from a centre. □ *vi,vt* send out or come out in rays.

ray² /reɪ/ *n* kinds of large sea-fish with a broad, flat body, eg *skate*.

rayon /'reɪɒn/ *n* [U] silk-like material made from cellulose: (attrib) ~ *shirts*.

raze, rase /reɪz/ *vt* destroy (towns, buildings) completely, esp by making them level with the ground: *a city* ~*d by an earthquake*.

razor /'reɪzə(r)/ *n* instrument with a sharp blade or cutters (some electrically driven) used for shaving hair from the skin. '**safety** ~ *n* kind in which a thin blade is fitted between metal guards. '~-**back** *n* kind of whale. '~-**backed** *adj* having a thin, sharp back: *a* ~-*backed pig*. '~-**blade** *n* disposable blade for a safety ~. ,~-'**edge** *n* sharp line of division; critical situation. □ *vt* (rare, except in *pp*): *a well-*~*ed chin*, well shaved.

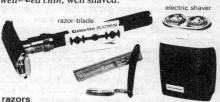

razor-blade · Gillette PLATINUM · WILKINSON RAZOR · electric shaver

razors

razzle /'ræzl/ *n* (also ~-'**dazzle**) *be/go on the* ~, (sl) be/go on a spree. ~ *spree*.

re¹ /riː/ *prep* (in legal style) in the matter of; concerning.

re² /reɪ/ *n* second note in the musical octave.

re- /riː-/ *pref* **1** again: *reappear, refloat, replay*. **2** in a different way: *rearrange*. ⇨ App 3.

reach /riːtʃ/ *vt,vi* **1** [VP2C,3C,15B] ~ (*out*) (*for*), stretch out: *He* ~*ed out his hand for the knife, but it was too far away. He* ~*ed* (*out*) *for the dictionary*. **2** [VP6A,15B,12B,13B] stretch out the hand for and take (sth); get and give (sth) to: *Can you* ~ *that book for your brother? Please* ~ *me that book. He* ~*ed down the atlas from the top shelf*. **3** [VP6A] (lit or fig) get to, go as far as: ~ *London*; ~ *the end of the chapter. Can you* ~ *the branch with those red apples? Our hands can't* ~ *our ears*. **4** [VP2C] extend; go; pass: *My land* ~*es as far as the river. The speaker's voice did not* ~ *to the back of the hall. I haven't been able to reach Kate for days*, ie get into contact with her, eg by telephone. *as far as the eye can* ~, to the horizon. **5** '~-**me-downs** *n pl* (sl) second-hand clothes. □ *n* **1** (*sing* only) act of ~ing or stretching out (a hand, etc): *get sth by a long* ~. **2** [U] extent to which a hand, etc can be ~ed out, a movement carried out or one's mental powers extended or used: *This boxer has a long* ~. *within/out of/beyond* ~: *I like to have my reference books within my* ~/*within easy* ~, so near that I can get them quickly and easily. *Put that bottle of weed-killer out of the children's* ~/*out of* ~ *of the children. The hotel is within easy* ~ *of the beach. The village is within* ~ *of London. He was beyond* ~ *of human aid*, No one could do anything to help him. **3** [C] continuous extent, esp of a river or canal, that can be seen between two bends or locks. ⇨ lock²(3): *one of the most beautiful* ~*es of the Thames*.

re·act /rɪ'ækt/ *vi* **1** [VP2A,3A] ~ *on/upon*, have an effect (on the person or thing acting): *Applause* ~*s upon a speaker*, eg has the effect of giving him confidence. **2** [VP3A] ~ *to*, respond; behave differently, be changed, as the result of being acted upon: *An orator* ~*s to applause. Do children* ~ *to* *kind treatment by becoming more self-confident?* **3** [VP3A] ~ **against,** respond to sth with a feeling: *Will the people one day ~ against the political system that oppresses them?* **4** [VP3A] ~ **on,** (chem) (of one substance applied to another) have an effect: *How do acids ~ on metals?*

re·ac·tion /rɪ'ækʃn/ *n* [C,U] **1** action or state resulting from, in response to, sth, esp a return to an earlier condition after a period of the opposite condition: *action and ~. After these days of excitement there was a ~,* eg a period when life seemed dull. *Higher wages affect costs of production and then comes the ~ of costs on prices.* **2** retrograde tendency, esp in politics; opposition to progress: *The forces of ~ made reform difficult.* **3** responsive feeling: *What was his ~ to your proposal?* **4** (science) action set up by one substance in another; change within the nucleus of an atom. ~·**ary** /rɪ'ækʃənrɪ US: -ənerɪ/ *n* (*pl* -ries), *adj* (person) opposing progress or reform.

re·ac·tor /rɪ'æktə(r)/ *n* **nuclear** ~, apparatus for the controlled production of nuclear energy; atomic pile.

read /ri:d/ *vt,vi* (*pt,pp* read /red/) **1** [VP6A,2A] (used in the simple tenses or with *can/be able*) look at and (be able to) understand (sth written or printed): *Can you ~ Chinese characters/French/a musical score? A motorist must be able to ~ traffic signs. Can the child ~ the time/the clock yet? I can't ~ your shorthand notes. The boy can neither ~ nor write.* **2** [VP6A,12A,13A,15B,2A,C] (simple or continuous tenses) reproduce mentally or vocally the words of (an author, book, etc): *R~ the letter aloud, please. She was ~ing the letter silently/to herself. She was ~ing a story to the children. I haven't enough time to ~/for ~ing. He ~ the letter through six times. Please ~ me the letter. She ~ out the letter to all of us. The old man ~ me a lesson/~ me a severe lecture,* reproved me. *The play was ~* (ie each actor ~ his part aloud) *before the cast went on the stage.* **3** [VP6A,15A,B] study (a subject, esp at a university): *He's ~ing physics/~ing for a degree in physics/~ing for a physics degree at Cambridge. He's ~ing for the Bar,* studying law in order to become a barrister. *You had better ~ the subject up,* make a special study of it. **4** [VP6A] interpret mentally; learn the significance of: ~ *a riddle/dream;* ~ *sb's thoughts. The gipsy offered to ~ my hand/palm,* tell me about myself and the future by examining the lines on the palm of my hand. **5** [VP2C] give a certain impression; seem (good, etc) when ~: *The play ~s better than it acts,* is better for ~ing than for performance on the stage. **6** [VP16B] assume, find implications in (what is read, etc): *Silence mustn't always be ~ as consent,* We must not always assume that a person means 'Yes' when no answer is given to a request, etc. ~ **into,** add more than is justified: *You have ~ into her letter more sympathy than she probably feels.* ~ **between the lines,** look for or discover meanings that are not actually expressed. **7** [VP2B] (of instruments) indicate: *What does the thermometer ~?* **8** [VP15A] bring into a specified state by ~ing: *She ~ herself to sleep.* **9** (*pp* with an *adv*) having knowledge gained from books, etc: *a well-~ man; deeply ~ in the classics.* □ *n* period of time given to ~ing: *have a good ~ in the train; have a quiet ~.* ~·**able** /'ri:dəbl/ *adj* **1** that is easy or pleasant to ~. **2** that can be ~. ⇨ legible, the more usu

word. ~·**abil·ity** /ˌri:də'bɪlətɪ/ *n*

re·ad·dress /ˌri: ə'dres/ *vt* [VP6A] change the address on (a letter, etc).

reader /'ri:də(r)/ *n* **1** person who reads, esp one who spends much time in reading; (*publisher's* ~) person employed to read MSS offered for publication and say whether they are good, etc; printer's proof-corrector; (*lay* ~) person appointed to read aloud parts of a service in church. **2** (GB) university teacher of a rank immediately below a professor: *R~ in English Literature.* **3** textbook for reading in class; book with selections for reading by students of a language: *a Latin R~.* **4** person who can interpret what is hidden or obscure, esp *a* '*mind/'thought~.* '~·**ship** /-ʃɪp/ *n* **1** position of a ~(2). **2** (of a periodical) number of persons who read it (which may be larger than its circulation).

read·ily, readi·ness ⇨ ready.

read·ing /'ri:dɪŋ/ *n* **1** [U] act of one who reads. '~ **desk,** lectern. '~·**glasses** *n* glasses for ~ (contrasted with glasses for long-distance use). '~·**lamp** *n* shaded table-lamp used to read by. '~·**room** *n* room (eg in a club or public library) set apart for ~. **2** [U] knowledge, esp of books: *a man of wide ~.* **3** [C] way in which sth is interpreted or understood: *my solicitor's ~ of this clause in the agreement,* what he says it means. **4** [C] figure of measurement, etc as shown on a dial, scale, etc: *The ~s on my thermometer last month were well above the average.* **5** [C] variant reading of a text that occurs in copying or printing from time to time: *The ~ of the First Folio is the true one.* **6** [C] entertainment in which sth is read to an audience; passage so read: *R~s from Dickens.* '**play~,** recital of the text of a play by a group. **7** [C] (in Parliament) one of the three stages through which a Bill must pass before it is ready for royal assent.

re·ad·just /ˌri: ə'dʒʌst/ *vt* [VP6A,3A,15A] ~ (*oneself*) (*to*), adjust again: *It's sometimes difficult to ~ (oneself) to life in Britain after working abroad.* ~·**ment** *n* ~ing or being ~ed; [C] instance of this.

ready /'redɪ/ *adj* (-ier, -iest) **1** (*pred* only) ~ (*for sth/to do sth*), in the condition needed for use; in the condition for doing sth; willing: ~ *for work; get ~ for a journey; be ~ to start. He's always ~ to help his friends.* **make** ~, prepare. **2** quick; prompt: *Don't be so ~ to find fault. He always has a ~ answer. You are too ~ with excuses. He has a ~ wit.* **3** within reach; easily procured: *keep a revolver ~,* near at hand. ~ **money,** money in the form of coins or notes, which can be used for payment at the time when goods are bought (contrasted with *credit*). ~ **reckoner,** book of answers to various common calculations needed in business, etc. **4** (*adv* use, with *pp*) prepared beforehand: *buy food ~ cooked.* ~·'**made** *adj* (a) ~ to wear or use: ~·*made clothes,* made in standard sizes, not to measurements of customers. (b) (fig) not original; of standard pattern, etc: *come to a subject with* ~·*made ideas.* □ *n* (only in) *at the* ~, (of a rifle) in the position for aiming and firing. **read·ily** /-ɪlɪ/ *adv* **1** without showing hesitation or unwillingness. **2** without difficulty. **readi·ness** /'redɪnɪs/ *n* [U] **1** *in readiness (for),* in a ready or prepared state: *have everything in readiness for an early start.* **2** willingness: *a surprising readiness to accept the proposal.* **3** promptness; quickness: *readiness of wit.*

re·af·firm /ˌri: ə'fɜ:m/ *vt* [VP6A,9] affirm again;

repeat an affirmation: ~ *one's loyalty.*
re‑af·for·est /ˌriː: əˈfɒrɪst US: ‑ˈfɔːr‑/, (US = **re‑for·est** /ˌriːˈfɒrɪst US: ‑ˈfɔːr‑/) vt replant (an area of land) with forest trees. **re‑af·for·est·ation** /ˌriː: əfɒrɪˈsteɪʃn US: ‑ˌfɔːr‑/, (US = **re·for·est·ation** /ˌriː:ˌfɒr‑ US: ‑ˌfɔːr‑/) n
re·agent /riːˈeɪdʒənt/ n [C] (chem) substance used to detect the presence of another by reaction; reactive substance or force.
real[1] /rɪəl/ adj **1** existing in fact; not imagined or supposed; not made up or artificial: *Is this ~ gold or pinchbeck? Is this ~ silk or rayon? Was it a ~ man you saw or a ghost? The doctors could not effect a ~* (= genuine, complete) *cure. Things that happen in ~ life are sometimes stranger than things that occur in fiction. Who is the ~ manager of the firm? Tell me the ~* (= true) *reason.* ~ **ale,** (GB 1970s) ale that is made, stored and served in traditional, careful ways. **2** '~ **estate,** (legal) immovable property consisting of land, any natural resources, and buildings (contrasted with *personal estate*). **3** (US colloq, as *adv*) really, very: *We had a ~ good time. I'm ~ sorry.* ~**ly** /ˈrɪəlɪ/ adv **1** in fact; without doubt; truly: *What do you ~ly think about it? It was ~ly not my fault. I'm ~ly sorry.* **2** (as an expression of interest, surprise, mild protest, doubt, etc according to context): *'We're going to Mexico next month.'—'Oh, ~ly!'* (or) *'Not ~ly?' You ~ly shouldn't say that about her!*
real[2] /reɪˈɑːl/ n [C] silver coin and unit of currency formerly used in Spanish‑speaking countries.
real·ism /ˈrɪəlɪzəm/ n [U] **1** (in art and literature) showing of real life, facts, etc in a true way, omitting nothing that is ugly or painful, and idealizing nothing. **2** behaviour based on the facing of facts and disregard of sentiment and convention. **3** (phil) theory that matter has real existence apart from our mental perception of it. ⇨ **idealism.** ~**ist** /‑ɪst/ n person who believes in ~ in art, philosophy, social problems, etc; person who believes himself to be without illusions. ~**is·tic** /ˌrɪəˈlɪstɪk/ adj **1** marked by, relating to, ~ in philosophy or art. **2** practical; not moved by sentiment: *realistic politics.* ~**is·ti·cally** /‑klɪ/ adv
re·al·ity /rɪˈælətɪ/ n (pl ‑ties) **1** [U] the quality of being real; real existence; that which underlies appearance: *belief in the ~ of miracles; the search after God and ~.* **bring sb back to ~,** get him to stop dreaming, being sentimental, etc. *in ~,* really, in actual fact. **2** [C] sth real; sth actually seen or experienced: *the grim realities of war,* contrasted with romantic ideas, etc. **3** [U] realism(1).
real·ize /ˈrɪəlaɪz/ vt **1** [VP6A,9,10] be fully conscious of; understand: *Does he ~ his error yet/~ that you must have help?* **2** [VP6A] convert (a hope, plan, etc) into a fact: *~ one's hopes/ambitions.* **3** [VP6A] exchange (property, business shares, etc) for money: *Can these shares/bonds, etc, be ~d at short notice?* **4** [VP6A,14] ~ *(on),* (of property, etc) obtain as a price for or as a profit: *The furniture ~d a high price at the sale. How much did you ~ on the paintings you sent to the sale?* **real·iz·able** /‑əbl/ adj that can be ~d. **real·iz·ation** /ˌrɪəlaɪˈzeɪʃn US: ‑ɪˈz‑/ n [U] realizing (of a plan, one's ambitions or hopes); act of exchanging property for money.
realm /relm/ n **1** (poet, rhet or legal use) kingdom: *the defence of the R~; a Peer of the R~.* **2** region (fig): *the ~ of the imagination; in the ~s of fancy.*
Re·al·tor /ˈrɪəltə(r)/ n (US) person engaged in real

estate business who is a member of the National Association of Real Estate Boards and subscribes to its standards of ethical conduct (GB = *estate agent).*
re·alty /ˈrɪəltɪ/ n (pl ‑ties) (legal) real estate.
ream /riːm/ n measure for paper, 480 (or US 500) sheets or 20 quires; (colloq, pl) great quantity (of writing): *She has written ~s of verse.*
re·ani·mate /riːˈænɪmeɪt/ vt [VP6A] fill with new strength, courage or energy.
reap /riːp/ vt,vi [VP6A,2A] cut (grain, etc); gather in a crop of grain from (a field, etc): *~ a field of barley; ~ the corn;* (fig) *~ the reward of virtue; ~ where one has not sown,* profit from work done by others. **(sow the wind and)** ~ **the whirlwind,** (prov) suffer for one's foolish conduct. '~**ing‑hook** n sickle. ~**er** n **1** person who ~s. **2** ~**ing‑machine** for cutting grain (and in some cases binding it into sheaves).
re·appear /ˌriːəˈpɪə(r)/ vi [VP2A] appear again (esp after disappearing). ~**ance** /‑rəns/ n
re·apprais·al /ˌriːəˈpreɪzl/ n new examination and judgement: *a ~ of our relations with China.*
rear[1] /rɪə(r)/ n **1** back part: *The kitchen is in the ~ of the house. The garage is at the ~ of* (US *in the ~ of*) *the house.* **2** (attrib) in or at the ~: *the ~ wheels/lamps,* of a car, etc; *leave the bus by the ~ entrance; a ~‑view mirror,* driving mirror (in a motor‑vehicle) for seeing out of the back window. **3** last part of any army, fleet, etc: *attack the enemy in the ~.* **bring up the ~,** come/be last. **4** ,~‑'admiral** /ˌrɪər ˈædmərəl/ n naval officer below a vice‑admiral. '~‑**guard** n body of soldiers given the duty of guarding the ~ of an army. *a ~guard action,* fight between an army in retreat and the enemy. ~‑**most** /ˈrɪəməʊst/ adj farthest back. ~‑**ward** /ˈrɪəwəd/ n: *to ~ward of,* some distance behind; *in the ~ward,* at the back. **~‑wards** /ˈrɪəwədz/ adv towards the ~.
rear[2] /rɪə(r)/ vt,vi **1** [VP6A] cause or help to grow; bring up: *~ poultry/cattle; ~ a family* (US usu *raise a family).* **2** [VP2A,C] (esp of a horse) rise on the hind legs. **3** [VP6A,15B] raise; lift up: *The snake ~ed its head. The horse ~ed itself up.* **4** [VP6A] set up: *~ a monument.*
re·arm /ˌriːˈɑːm/ vt,vi [VP6A,2A] supply (an army, etc) with weapons again, or with weapons of new types, etc. **re·arma·ment** /riːˈɑːməmənt/ n
rea·son[1] /ˈriːzn/ n **1** [C,U] (fact put forward or serving as) cause of or justification for sth: *There is ~ to believe that he is dishonest. Is there any ~ why you should not help? He complains with ~* (= rightly) *that he has been punished unfairly. Give me your ~s for doing it. My ~ is that the cost will be too high. The ~ why he's late is that/because there was a breakdown on the railway.* **by ~ of,** because of: *He was excused by ~ of his age.* **2** [U] power of the mind to understand, form opinions, etc: *Only man has ~.* **lose one's ~,** go mad: *The poor old fellow has lost his ~.* **3** [U] what is right or practicable; common sense; sensible conduct: *He's not amenable to ~.* **bring sb to ~,** persuade him to give up foolish activities, useless resistance, etc. **do anything in/within ~,** anything sensible or reasonable: *I'm willing to do anything in ~.* **listen to/hear ~,** allow oneself to be persuaded; pay attention to common‑sense, advice, etc. **lose all ~,** become irrational, illogical. **without rhyme or ~,** ⇨ rhyme(1). **It stands to ~ (that...),** is obvious to sensible people (that...); most people

will agree (that...). ~·less adj lacking ~.

rea·son² /'riːzn/ vi, vt 1 [VP2A] make use of one's reason(2); exercise the power of thought: Man's ability to ~ makes him different from the animals. 2 [VP3A] ~ with sb, argue in order to convince him: She ~ed with me for an hour about the folly of my plans. 3 [VP9] ~ that..., say by way of argument: He ~ed that if we started at dawn, we could arrive before noon. 4 [VP6A] express logically or in the form of an argument: a well-~ed statement/manifesto. ~ sth out, find an answer by considering successive arguments, etc: ~ out the answer to a question. 5 [VP14] ~ sb into/out of sth, persuade by argument to do/not to do sth: ~ a person out of his fears, show him that his fears are groundless; ~ sb out of a false belief; ~ sb into a sensible course of action. ~·ing n [U] process of reaching conclusions by using one's reason: He surpasses most of us in power of ~ing, is better at drawing conclusions from facts, etc. There's no ~ing with that woman, She won't listen to reason.

rea·son·able /'riːznəbl/ adj 1 having ordinary common sense; able to reason; acting, done, in accordance with reason; willing to listen to reason: You're not very ~ if you expect a child to understand sarcasm. Is the accused guilty beyond ~ doubt? 2 moderate; neither more or less than seems right or acceptable: a ~ price/offer. 3 fair; just; not absurd: a ~ excuse; be ~ in one's demands. ~·ness n rea·son·ably /-əblɪ/ adv

re·as·sure /ˌriːəˈʃʊə(r)/ vt [VP6A] remove the fears or doubts of: She felt ~d after the police had told her that her children were safe. re·as·sur·ance /-rəns/ n [U,C]. re·as·sur·ing adj comforting: a reassuring glance/word/pat. re·as·sur·ing·ly adv

re·bar·ba·tive /rɪˈbɑːbətɪv/ adj (formal) stern; repellent.

re·bate /'riːbeɪt/ n [C] sum of money by which a debt, tax, etc may be reduced; discount: There is a ~ of £1.50 if the account is settled before 31 Dec.

rebel¹ /'rebl/ n 1 person who takes up arms against, or refuses allegiance to, the established government; person who resists authority or control: a ~ in the home, eg a child who resists the authority of its parents. 2 (attrib) relating to ~s; of the nature of a rebellion: the ~ forces.

re·bel² /rɪˈbel/ vi (-ll-) [VP2A,3A] ~ (against), 1 take up arms to fight (against the government). 2 show resistance; protest strongly: The prisoners ~led against having no physical exercise. Such treatment would make anyone ~.

re·bel·lion /rɪˈbelɪən/ n [U] ~ (against), rebelling, esp against a government: rise in ~; [C] instance of this: five ~s in two years; a ~ against the dictator.

re·bel·li·ous /rɪˈbelɪəs/ adj 1 acting like a rebel; taking part in a rebellion: ~ subjects; ~ behaviour. 2 not easily controlled: a child with a ~ temper. ~·ly adv ~·ness n

re·bind /ˌriːˈbaɪnd/ vt (pt,pp -bound /-ˈbaʊnd/) [VP6A] put a new binding on (a book, etc).

re·birth /ˌriːˈbɜːθ/ n 1 spiritual change, eg by conversion or englightenment, causing a person to lead a new kind of life. 2 revival: the ~ of learning.

re·born /ˌriːˈbɔːn/ adj (fig) born again, ie spiritually.

re·bound /rɪˈbaʊnd/ vi [VP2A,3A] 1 ~ (from), spring or bounce back after hitting sth: The ball ~ed from the wall into the lily pond. 2 ~ on/upon, (fig) come back upon the agent; happen as the consequence of one's own action: The evil you do may ~ upon yourselves. □ n /ˈriːbaʊnd/ on the ~, (a) while bouncing back: hit a ball on the ~. (b) (fig) while still reacting to depression or disappointment: She quarrelled with Paul and then married Peter on the ~. 3 pt,pp of rebind.

re·buff /rɪˈbʌf/ n [C] meet with/suffer a ~ (from sb), unkind or contemptuous refusal of, or show of indifference to (an offer of or request for help, friendship, etc); snub. □ vt [VP6A] give a ~ to.

re·build /ˌriːˈbɪld/ vt (pt,pp -built /-ˈbɪlt/) [VP6A] build or put together again: a rebuilt typewriter.

re·buke /rɪˈbjuːk/ vt [VP6A,14] ~ sb (for sth), reprove; speak severely to (officially or otherwise): ~ a subordinate for being impudent. □ n [C] reproof: administer ~s to sb. re·buk·ing·ly adv

re·bus /'riːbəs/ n puzzle in which a word or phrase has to be guessed from pictures or diagrams that suggest the syllables that make it.

re·but /rɪˈbʌt/ vt (-tt-) [VP6A] prove (a charge, piece of evidence, etc) to be false; refute. ~·tal /-tl/ n act of ~ting; evidence that ~s a charge, etc.

re·cal·ci·trant /rɪˈkælsɪtrənt/ adj disobedient; resisting authority or discipline. re·cal·ci·trance /-əns/, re·cal·ci·trancy /-ənsɪ/ nn [U] being ~.

re·call /rɪˈkɔːl/ vt 1 [VP6A,14] ~ sb (from/to), summon back: ~ an ambassador (from his post/to his own country). 2 [VP6A,C,8,9,10,19C] bring back to the mind; recollect: I don't ~ his name/face/meeting him/where I met him. Can you ~ your schooldays? 3 [VP6A] take back; revoke (an order, a decision). □ n 1 summons to return; (esp) summons to an ambassador to return to his own country: letters of ~. 2 [U] ability to remember: a man gifted with instant ~; possibility of recalling. beyond/past ~, that cannot be brought back or revoked. 3 [C] signal, eg a bugle call, to troops, etc to return: sound the ~.

re·cant /rɪˈkænt/ vt,vi [VP6A,2A] give up (an opinion, a belief); take back (a statement) as being false: The torturers could not make the man ~, give up his beliefs, eg religious or political. re·can·ta·tion /ˌriːkænˈteɪʃn/ n [U] ~ing; [C] instance of this; statement disavowing former beliefs.

re·cap¹ /'riːkæp/ vt,vi, n (colloq abbr of) recapitulate, recapitulation.

re·cap² /ˌriːˈkæp/ vt (-pp-) (US) retread (a tyre).

re·cap·itu·late /ˌriːkəˈpɪtʃʊleɪt/ vt,vi [VP6A,2A] repeat, go through again, the chief points of (sth that has been said, discussed, argued about, etc). re·cap·itu·la·tion /ˌriːkəˌpɪtʃʊˈleɪʃn/ n [U] recapitulating; [C] instance of this.

re·cap·ture /ˌriːˈkæptʃə(r)/ vt [VP6A] 1 capture again. 2 recall: try to ~ the past.

re·cast /ˌriːˈkɑːst US: -ˈkæst/ vt [VP6A] 1 cast or fashion anew: ~ a gun/a bell; ~ (= rewrite) a sentence/paragraph/chapter. 2 change the cast of a play, ie find different actors or give actors different parts.

recce /'rekɪ/ n (mil; colloq abbr of) reconnaissance.

re·cede /rɪˈsiːd/ vi [VP2A,3A] ~ (from), 1 (appear to) go back from the observer or from an earlier position: As the tide ~d we were able to explore the rocky pools on the beach. As our ship sailed out to sea the coast slowly ~d. 2 slope away from the front or from the observer: a receding chin/forehead.

re·ceipt /rɪˈsiːt/ n 1 [U] receiving or being received: on ~ of the news. I am in ~ of your letter of the 3rd, (pompous for) I have received.... 2 (pl) money received (in a business, etc, contrasted with *expenditure*). **3** [C] written statement that sth (money or goods) has been recei√.d: *get a ~ for money spent; sign a ~; a '~ book*, one with forms and counterfoils for writing out ~s. □ *vt* [VP6A] write out and sign or stamp a ~(3): *~ a hotel bill*, put 'Paid' or 'Received with thanks' on it.

re·ceiv·able /rɪ'siːvəbl/ *adj* **1** that can be received; fit to be received. **2** (comm; of bills, accounts, etc) on which money is to be received. **bills** ~, contrasted with *bills payable*.

re·ceive /rɪ'siːv/ *vt,vi* [VP6A,2A] **1** accept, take, get (sth offered, sent, etc): *When did you ~ the letter/news/telegram, etc? He ~d a good education. We ~d nothing but insults. You will ~ a warm welcome when you come to England. He was caught receiving* (ie taking possession of stolen property) *soon after his release from prison.* **re'ceiving-set** *n* radio receiver. **2** allow to enter; (formally) see, welcome or entertain (friends, guests, etc): *The hotel is now open to ~ guests. He was ~d into the Church*, admitted as a member. *Lady Snooks ~s on Monday afternoons*, is at home to her friends and acquaintances then. **~d** *adj* widely accepted as correct: *the ~d version/text/view/opinion/pronunciation*.

re·ceiver /rɪ'siːvə(r)/ *n* **1** person who receives, esp who knowingly receives stolen goods. **2 (Official) R~**, official appointed to take charge of the property and affairs of a bankrupt, or to administer property in dispute. **3** part of an apparatus for receiving sth, eg that part of a telephone that is held to the ear; apparatus for receiving broadcast signals: *a 'radio-~. ~·ship* /-ʃɪp/ *n* office of a ~(2); his period of office.

re·cent /'riːsnt/ *adj* (having existed, been made, happened) not long before; begun not long ago: *~ news; a ~ event; within ~ memory. Ours is a ~ acquaintance*, We have been acquainted for only a short time. **~·ly** *adv* lately; not long ago: *until quite ~ly*.

re·cep·tacle /rɪ'septəkl/ *n* container or holder in which things may be put away or out of sight.

re·cep·tion /rɪ'sepʃn/ *n* **1** [U] receiving or being received: *prepare rooms for the ~ of guests; '~ area/camp/centre*, one where persons, eg evacuees, refugees, are received and accommodated: *a '~ committee. The house has two ~ rooms* (rooms for the ~ of guests, but this usu means livingrooms), *a kitchen, and three bedrooms. '~-desk*, (in a hotel) counter where guests are received, where they ask for rooms, etc. *'~ clerk*, (US) person at a ~-desk, who attends to inquiries from guests. **2** [C] formal party or welcome: *Mrs X holds a ~ every Monday. There was a ~ after the wedding ceremony.* **3** [C] welcome or greeting of a specified kind; demonstration of feeling toward sb or sth: *The new book had a favourable ~*, was welcomed by the critics, the public, etc. *The President was given an enthusiastic ~.* **4** [U] receiving of radio, etc signals; degree of efficiency of this: *Is radio ~ good in your district? R~ of TV programmes is unsatisfactory here. ~·ist* /-ɪst/ *n* person employed in a hotel, or by a hair-dresser, dentist or other professional person, to receive clients.

re·cep·tive /rɪ'septɪv/ *adj* quick or ready to receive suggestions, new ideas, etc: *a ~ mind; ~ to new ideas. ~·ly adv* **re·cep·tiv·ity** /ˌriːsep'tɪvətɪ/ *n*

re·cess /rɪ'ses US: 'riːses/ *n* **1** (US = *vacation*) period of time when work or business is stopped,

eg when Parliament, the law courts, are not in session. **2** part of a room where the wall is set back from the main part; alcove or niche: *a ~ with a writing-desk and a chair in it.* **3** secret place; place difficult of access: *the dark ~es of a cave; a mountain ~;* (fig) *in the innermost ~es of the heart/mind.* □ *vt* [VP6A] **1** place in a ~; set back: *~ a wall/a ~ed wall.* **2** provide with ~es.

re·ces·sion /rɪ'seʃn/ *n* **1** [U] withdrawal; act of receding. **2** [C] slackening of business and industrial activity: *The ~ caused a lot of unemployment.*

re·ces·sional /rɪ'seʃənl/ *n ~* **(hymn)**, hymn sung while the clergy and choir withdraw after a church service. □ *adj* **1** of a recession: *'~ music.* **2** relating to a Parliamentary recess.

re·ces·sive /rɪ'sesɪv/ *adj* **1** having a tendency to recede or go back. **2** (biol) exhibiting weak characteristics (the stronger ones are called *dominant*) which are passed on by means of genes to later generations, eg blue eyes and blond hair.

ré·chauffé /reɪ'ʃəʊfeɪ US: ˌreɪʃəʊ'feɪ/ *n* dish of food warmed up again; rehash.

re·cher·ché /rə'ʃeəʃeɪ/ *adj* devised or selected with (too much) care; too studied or far-fetched.

re·cidi·vist /rɪ'sɪdɪvɪst/ *n* person who habitually relapses into crime; one who apparently cannot be cured of criminal tendencies; persistent offender. **re·cidi·vism** /-ɪzəm/ *n*

recipe /'resəpɪ/ *n* [C] *~* **(for)**, direction for preparing (a cake, a dish of food, a medical remedy) or for getting (any result): *a ~ for a fruit cake. Have you a ~ for happiness?*

re·cipi·ent /rɪ'sɪpɪənt/ *n* person who receives sth.

re·cip·ro·cal /rɪ'sɪprəkl/ *adj* **1** given and received in return; mutual: *~ affection/help.* **2** corresponding, but the other way round: *a ~ mistake*, eg I thought he was a waiter and he thought I was a guest, but I was a waiter and he was a guest. **3** (gram) *~* **pro·nouns**, those expressing mutual action or relation, eg *each other, one another. ~·ly* /-klɪ/ *adv*

re·cip·ro·cate /rɪ'sɪprəkeɪt/ *vt,vi* [VP6A,2A] **1** give in return; give and receive, each to and from each: *I ~ your good wishes. He ~d by wishing her a pleasant journey.* **2** (of parts of a machine) (cause to) move backwards and forwards in a straight line (eg the piston of an engine): *a reciprocating engine/saw.* ⇨ **rotatory.** **re·cip·ro·ca·tion** /rɪˌsɪprə'keɪʃn/ *n* [U].

reci·proc·ity /ˌresɪ'prɒsətɪ/ *n* [U] principle or practice of give and take, of making mutual concessions; the granting of privileges in return for similar privileges: *~ in trade* (*between two countries*).

re·cital /rɪ'saɪtl/ *n* [C] **1** detailed account of a number of connected events, etc: *We were bored by the long ~ of his adventures.* **2** performance of music by a soloist or small group, or of the works of one composer: *a pi'ano ~; a ~ of songs.*

reci·ta·tion /ˌresɪ'teɪʃn/ *n* **1** [U] the act of reciting(2): *the ~ of his grievances.* **2** [U] public delivery of passages of prose or poetry learnt by heart; [C] instance of this: *a 'Dickens ~*, of dramatic extracts from the novels. **3** [C] piece of poetry or prose (to be) learnt by heart and recited. **4** (US) [U] repetition of a prepared lesson by a pupil to his teacher; [C] instance of this.

reci·ta·tive /ˌresɪtə'tiːv/ *n* **1** [U] style of music between singing and talking, many words being spoken or sung on the same note, used for the narrative and dialogue parts of some operas. **2** [C] passage (in an opera or oratorio) (to be) rendered thus.

re·cite /rɪ'saɪt/ vt,vi [VP6A,15A,2A] **1** say (esp poems) aloud from memory: *The mayor ~d to the Queen a long and tedious speech of welcome.* **2** give a list of, tell one by one (names, facts, etc): ~ *one's grievances;* ~ *the names of all the capital cities of Europe.*

reck·less /'reklɪs/ adj ~ *(of)*, rash; not thinking of the consequences: *a* ~ *spender;* ~ *of danger/the consequences; fined £10 for* ~ (= dangerous) *driving.* ~·ly adv ~·ness n

reck·on /'rekən/ vt,vi **1** [VP6A,15B,2A] calculate; find out (the quantity, number, cost, etc) by working with numbers: ~ *the cost of a holiday. Hire charges are* ~ed *from the date of delivery. The child can't* ~ *yet.* ~ *sth in*, include, take into account, when ~ing: *Did you* ~ *in the cost of a taxi across London?* ~ *sth up*, find the total of: ~ *up the bill.* **2** ~ *with sb*, (a) deal with; settle accounts with: *When the fighting is over, we'll* ~ *with the enemy's sympathizers.* (b) take into account; consider: *He is certainly a man to be* ~ed *with*, a man who cannot be ignored, who may be a serious competitor, opponent, etc (according to context). ~ *without sb*, not take into account; not consider. **3** ~ *on/upon sb/sth*, depend on, base one's hopes on: *I* ~ *on your help. The proprietors of the Casino* ~ *on human foolishness and greed*, can depend, for making profit, on the foolishness and greed of those who gamble. *He's the sort of man you can* ~ *on in a crisis.* **4** [VP9,16B,25,7A] ~ *sb/sth as/to be;* ~ *that...*, be of the opinion, suppose; consider: *One-quarter of the country is* ~ed *as unproductive. She was* ~ed (*to be*) *the prettiest girl in the village. Do you still* ~ *him among/as one of your friends? I* ~ *he is rather too old to marry again.* **5** [VP9,7A] estimate; calculate: *I* ~ *to arrive in Delhi at noon.* **6** [VP9] (US colloq) assume: *I* ~ *we'll go next week.* ~er /'rekənə(r)/ n person or thing that counts. **ready** ~er, ⇨ ready. ~·ing /'rekənɪŋ/ n (esp) **1** [C] (totalled) account of items to be paid for, eg at a hotel or restaurant: *pay the* ~ing. *There'll be a heavy* ~ing *to pay if he continues this wild life*, He will have to suffer for it. *day of* ~ing, time when sth must be atoned for. **2** [U] calculation, eg of a ship's position by observation of the sun, stars, etc. *dead* ~ing, method of calculating the position of a ship or aircraft from a known earlier position, and later course and distance, when observations of the sun, etc are impossible. *out in one's* ~ing, mistaken in one's calculations.

re·claim /rɪ'kleɪm/ vt [VP6A] **1** bring back (waste land, etc) to a useful condition, a state of cultivation, etc. **2** reform (a person): ~ *a man from error/vice; a* ~ed *drunkard.* **3** demand that sth be given back. **rec·la·ma·tion** /ˌreklə'meɪʃn/ n [U].

re·cline /rɪ'klaɪn/ vi,vt [VP2A,C,15A] place oneself, be, in a position of rest; put (one's arms, etc) in a resting position; lie back or down: ~ *on a couch;* ~ *one's arms on the table; a reclining chair*, one with a back that tilts.

re·cluse /rɪ'kluːs/ n person who lives alone and avoids other people: *live the life of a* ~, live like a hermit, avoiding meeting people.

rec·og·ni·tion /ˌrekəg'nɪʃn/ n [U] recognizing or being recognized: ~ *signals; aircraft* ~. *He was given a cheque for £25 in* ~ *of his services. R~ of the new State is unlikely*, It is unlikely that diplomatic relations will be established with it. *alter/ change beyond/out of (all)* ~, change so much

that ~ *is impossible: The town has changed out of all* ~ *since I was there ten years ago.*

re·cog·ni·zance /rɪ'kɒgnɪzns/ n [C] (legal) **1** bond by which a person is bound to appear before a court of law at a certain time, or to observe certain conditions, and to forfeit a certain sum if he fails to do so. *enter into* ~*s*, sign such a bond. **2** sum of money (to be) paid as surety for observing such a bond.

rec·og·nize /'rekəgnaɪz/ vt **1** [VP6A,16A] know, (be able to) identify again (sb or sth) that one has seen, heard, etc before: ~ *a tune/an old acquaintance.* **2** [VP6A] be willing to accept (sb or sth) as what he or it claims to be or has been in the past: *refuse to* ~ *a new government/* ~ *sb as lawful heir.* **3** [VP6A,9] be prepared to admit; be aware: *He* ~d *that he was not qualified for the post/* ~d *his lack of qualifications.* **4** [VP6A,9,25] acknowledge: *Everyone* ~d *him to be the greatest living authority on ancient Roman coins. His services to the State were* ~d, eg he was made a knight. **rec·og·niz·able** /'rekəgnaɪzəbl/ adj that can be ~d. **rec·og·niz·ably** /-əblɪ/ adv

re·coil /rɪ'kɔɪl/ vi **1** [VP2A,3A] ~ *(from)*, draw or jump back; shrink: ~ *from doing sth* (in fear, horror, disgust, etc). **2** [VP2A] (of a gun) kick back (when fired). **3** [VP3A] ~ *on/upon* (fig) rebound; react: *His meanness* ~ed *upon his own head. Revenge may* ~ *upon the person who takes it.* □ n act of ~ing.

rec·ol·lect /ˌrekə'lekt/ vt,vi [VP6A,C,8,10,9,2A] call back to the mind; succeed in remembering: ~ *childhood days;* ~ *meeting the King;* ~ *how to do sth/how sth was done. As far as I* ~,....

rec·ol·lec·tion /ˌrekə'lekʃn/ n **1** [U] act or power of recollecting: *scenes which arise in quiet* ~ *of the past; to the best of my* ~, so far as I can recollect, if I remember correctly. **2** [U] time over which the memory goes back: *Such a problem has never arisen within my* ~. **3** [C] sth recollected; that which is remembered: *The old letters brought many* ~*s to my mind.*

rec·om·mend /ˌrekə'mend/ vt **1** [VP6A,14,12A,13A,16A] ~ *sth (to sb) (for sth);* ~ *sb sth;* ~ *sb (for sth/as sth)*, speak favourably of; say that one thinks sth is good (for a purpose) or that sb is fitted (for a post, etc, as...): *I can* ~ *this soap. He has been* ~ed *for first class honours. What would you* ~ *for getting ink stains from my blouse? Can you* ~ *me a good novel? Can you* ~ *Miss Hill as a good typist?* **2** [VP17,6C,9] suggest as wise or suitable; advise: *I have been* ~ed *to try these pills for sea-sickness. I* ~ *you not to/that you do not disobey your officers. Do you* ~ *raising the school-leaving age?* **3** [VP6A,14] ~ *sb (to sb)*, (of a quality, etc) cause to be or appear pleasing, satisfactory; make acceptable: *Behaviour of that sort will not* ~ *you.* **4** [VP14] ~ *sb to sb*, commend (the more usu word): ~ *oneself/one's soul to to God;* ~ *a child to sb's care.* **rec·om·men·da·tion** /ˌrekəmen'deɪʃn/ n **1** [U] ~ing: *speak in* ~ation *of sb or sth; buy sth on the* ~ation *of a friend*, because he has ~ed it. **2** [C] statement that ~s sb or sth: *My bank manager has sent me a list of* ~ations, eg names of stocks which he ~s me to buy. *The jury brought in a verdict of guilty, with a* ~ *to mercy.* **3** [C] sth which causes a person to be well thought of: *Is a sweet disposition a* ~ation *in a wife?*

rec·om·pense /'rekəmpens/ vt [VP6A,14] ~ *sb*

(for sth), reward or punish; make payment to: ~ *sb for his trouble;* ~ *good with evil;* ~ *sb for a loss.* □ *n* [C,U] reward; payment; satisfaction given for injury: *receive a* ~ *for one's services; work hard without* ~; *in* ~ *for your help.*

rec·on·cile /'rekənsaɪl/ *vt* **1** [VP6A,14] ~ *sb (with sb),* cause (persons) to become friends after they have quarrelled: *We became* ~*d. He refused to become* ~*d with his brother.* **2** [VP6A] settle, arrange (a quarrel, difference of opinion, etc). **3** [VP6A,14] ~ *sth (with sth),* bring into harmony with; cause to agree with: *How can this decision be* ~*d with justice? I can't* ~ *what you say with the facts of the case.* **4** [VP14] ~ *oneself to sth; be* ~*d to sth,* overcome one's objections to; resign oneself to: *You must* ~ *yourself to a life of hardship and poverty.* **rec·on·cil·able** /-əbl/ *adj* **rec·on·cili·ation** /ˌrekən͵sɪlɪ'eɪʃn/ *n* [U] reconciling or being ~*d;* [C] instance of this: *bring about a reconciliation between friends who have quarrelled.*

rec·on·dite /'rekəndaɪt/ *adj* **1** (of subjects of knowledge) out of the way; little known; abstruse: ~ *studies.* **2** (of an author) having ~ knowledge.

re·con·di·tion /ˌriːkən'dɪʃn/ *vt* [VP6A] put into good condition again: *a car with a* ~*ed engine.*

re·con·nais·sance /rɪ'kɒnɪsns/ *n* **1** [U] act of reconnoitring: ~ *in force,* made with sufficient troops to resist any enemy forces that may be encountered. **2** [C] instance of reconnoitring; survey, made by troops or a group of scouting vessels or aircraft, of an enemy's position or whereabouts; (fig) survey of any kind of work before it is started: *make a* ~ *of the work to be done.*

re·con·noitre (US = **-ter**) /ˌrekə'nɔɪtə(r)/ *vt, vi* [VP6A,2A] go to or near (a place or area occupied by enemy forces) to learn about their position, strength, etc: ~ *the ground.*

re·con·struct /ˌriːkən'strʌkt/ *vt* [VP6A] **1** construct again. **2** build up a complete structure or description of (sth of which one has only a few parts or only partial evidence): ~ *a ruined abbey. The detective tried to* ~ *the crime,* picture to himself how it had been committed. **re·con·struc·tion** /ˌriːkən'strʌkʃn/ *n*

rec·ord¹ /'rekɔːd *US:* 'rekərd/ *n* **1** [C] written account of facts, events, etc: *a* ~ *of school attendances/of road accidents; the* (ˌPublic) 'R~ *Office,* one in London where public documents with accounts of events, official acts, etc written down at the time they occur, are stored. **2** [U] state of being ~*ed* or preserved in writing, esp as authentic evidence of sth: *a matter of* ~, sth that is established as fact by being ~*ed.* **be/go/put sb on** ~: *It is on* ~ *that the summer was the wettest for 50 years. I don't want to go on* ~/*don't want you to put me on* ~ *as saying that I think the Prime Minister a fool.* **off the** ~, (colloq) not for publication or for recording: *What the President said at his press conference was off the* ~, not to be repeated by the newspaper men there, and not to be used in their reports or articles. **3** [C] facts known about the past of sb or sth: *He has an honourable* ~ *of service/a good* ~. *Your* ~ *is in your favour,* What we know about your past is favourable to you. *That airline has a bad* ~, eg has had many accidents to its aircraft. **4** [C] sth that provides evidence or information: *Our museums are full of* ~*s of past history. R*~*s of ancient civilizations are still being excavated.* **5** [C] disc on which sound has been registered; what is ~*ed* on such a disc:

'gramophone ~*s.* ⇨ recording. '~-player *n* instrument for reproducing sound from discs (often one connected to an external loud-speaker). **6** [C] limit, score, point, attainment, mark, etc (high or low), not reached before; (esp in sport) the best yet done: *Which country holds the* ~ *for the marathon? Two* ~*s fell during the sports meeting at Oslo last week.* (attrib) *Hill made a* ~ *score in the match against Kent,* (cricket) scored a total that was a ~. *There was a* ~ *rice crop in Thailand that year.* **break/beat the** ~, do better than has been done before. Hence, '~-breaking *adj*

re·cord² /rɪ'kɔːd/ *vt* [VP6A] **1** set down in writing for reference; preserve for use, by writing or in other ways, eg on a disc, magnetic tape, video-tape, film, etc: *This volume* ~*s the history of the regiment. The programme was* ~*ed.* Cf a *'live' broadcast. The tape-recorder has* ~*ed his voice and the camera has* ~*ed his features.* ~**ing angel,** angel who, it is said, ~*s* men's good and bad actions. **2** (of an instrument) mark or indicate on a scale: *The thermometer* ~*ed 40 °C.*

re·corder /rɪ'kɔːdə(r)/ *n* **1** (GB) judge with a certain criminal and civil jurisdiction. **2** apparatus that records. 'tape-~, one that records sound on magnetic tape. 'video tape-~, one that records vision and sound on magnetic tape. **3** wooden musical instrument with finger holes, played by blowing it at one end. ⇨ the illus at brass.

re·cord·ing /rɪ'kɔːdɪŋ/ *n* (esp in sound or TV broadcasting, and for record-players, etc) programme, piece of music, etc registered on a disc, magnetic tape, film, etc for reproduction: *It wasn't a 'live' performance but a BBC* ~. *I have a good* ~ *of this opera on three discs.* ⇨ the illus at tape.

re·count /rɪ'kaʊnt/ *vt* [VP6A] give an account of; tell: *He* ~*ed to them the story of his adventures in Mexico.*

re·count /ˌriː 'kaʊnt/ *vt* [VP6A] count again: ~ *the votes.* □ *n* /'riː kaʊnt/ another count: *One of the candidates demanded a* ~.

re·coup /rɪ'kuːp/ *vt* [VP6A,14] ~ *(for),* compensate (sb, oneself, *for* a loss, etc); make up for: ~ *one's losses;* ~ *oneself for one's losses.*

re·course /rɪ'kɔːs/ *n* [U] **1** *have* ~ *to,* turn to for help; seek help from: *I don't advise you to have* ~ *to the money-lenders.* **2** sth turned to for help: *Your only* ~ *is legal action against them.*

re·cover /rɪ'kʌvə(r)/ *vt, vi* **1** [VP6A] get back (sth lost, etc); get back the use of: ~ *what was lost;* ~ *consciousness* (after fainting); ~ *one's sight/hearing. I am* ~*ing my strength,* getting well (after an illness). *We soon* ~*ed lost time. They have* ~*ed their losses.* **2** [VP2A,3A] ~ *(from),* become well; get back to a former position of prosperity, state of health, mental condition, etc: *He is slowly* ~*ing from his illness. I doubt whether he will* ~. *I haven't yet* ~*ed from my astonishment. Has the country* ~*ed from the effects of the war yet?* **3** [VP6A] regain control of oneself; become calm or normal: *He almost fell, but quickly* ~*ed (himself). He* ~*ed his balance/composure.* ~**·able** /-əbl/ *adj* that can be ~*ed*(1): *Is the deposit I've paid* ~*able?* **re·cov·ery** *n* [U] ~*ing* or being ~*ed: make a quick* ~*y,* get well again quickly or quickly regain one's position after losing for a time in a game, athletic match, etc: ~*y from influenza; the* ~*y of a lost article,* getting it back again.

re·cover /ˌriː 'kʌvə(r)/ *vt* [VP6A] supply with a new cover: *This cushion/quilt needs to be* ~*ed.*

rec·re·ant /'rekrɪənt/ adj, n (liter) cowardly, unfaithful or traitorous (person): a ~ lover.

rec·re·ation /ˌrekrɪ'eɪʃn/ n [C,U] (form of) play or amusement; refreshment of body and mind; sth that pleasantly occupies one's time after work is done: walk and climb mountains for ~. Is gardening a ~ or a form of hard work? Flirting is an innocent ~, perhaps. '~ ground, land, eg in a public park, set aside for games, etc. ~al /-ʃənl/ adj of ~: provide more ~al facilities, eg sports grounds, swimming pools.

re·crimi·na·tion /rɪˌkrɪmɪ'neɪʃn/ n [C,U] accusation made in return for one already made; countercharge: indulge in ~(s). **re·crimi·nate** /rɪ'krɪmɪneɪt/ vi [VP2A,3A] ~ (against sb), accuse (sb) in return. **re·crimi·na·tory** /rɪ'krɪmɪnətrɪ US: -tɔːrɪ/ adj of ~.

re·cru·des·ence /ˌriːkruː'desns/ n (of disease, violence, etc) new outburst; breaking out again: a ~ of civil disorder; the ~ of influenza.

re·cruit /rɪ'kruːt/ n new member of a society, group, etc, esp a soldier in the early days of his training: gain a few ~s to one's party, eg in politics; ~s being drilled on the parade ground. □ vt, vi 1 [VP6A] get ~s for; enlist (persons) as ~s (for the army, a cause, etc): a '~ing officer; ~ a new political party from the middle classes. Were men for the Navy ~ed from men on merchant ships? 2 [VP6A] get a sufficient quantity or store of; bring back to what is usual or normal: ~ supplies; ~ one's health/strength. ~·ment n

rec·tal /'rektəl/ adj of the rectum.

rec·tangle /'rektæŋgl/ n [C] plane four-sided figure with four right angles, esp one with adjacent sides unequal. ⇨ the illus at quadrilateral. **rec·tangu·lar** /rek'tæŋgjʊlə(r)/ adj in the shape of a ~.

rec·tify /'rektɪfaɪ/ vt (pt,pp -fied) [VP6A] 1 put right; take out mistakes from: ~ abuses; mistakes that cannot be rectified. 2 purify or refine by repeated distillation or other process: rectified spirits. **rec·ti·fier** n person or thing that rectifies; (electr) device which converts alternating current to direct current. **rec·tifi·ca·tion** /ˌrektɪfɪ'keɪʃn/ n [U] ~ing or being rectified: the rectification of errors/alcohol; [C] instance of this; sth that has been rectified.

rec·ti·lin·ear /ˌrektɪ'lɪnɪə(r)/ adj in or forming a straight line; bounded by, characterized by, straight lines.

rec·ti·tude /'rektɪtjuːd US: -tuːd/ n [U] honesty; upright or straightforward behaviour.

recto /'rektəʊ/ n (pl ~s /-təʊz/) any right-hand page of a book. ⇨ verso.

rec·tor /'rektə(r)/ n 1 (C of E) clergyman in charge of a parish, the tithes of which were not withdrawn, (eg to a college), at or after the time when the English Church separated from the Church of Rome. ⇨ vicar. 2 head of certain universities, colleges, schools or religious institutions. ~y /'rektərɪ/ n (pl -ries) ~'s residence.

rec·tum /'rektəm/ n lower and final part of the large intestine. ⇨ the illus at alimentary.

re·cum·bent /rɪ'kʌmbənt/ adj (esp of a person) lying down: a ~ figure on a tomb, statue or carving in a ~ position.

re·cu·per·ate /rɪ'kuːpəreɪt/ vt, vi [VP6A,2A] make or become strong again after illness, exhaustion or loss: ~ one's health; go to the seaside to ~. **re·cu·per·ation** /rɪˌkuːpə'reɪʃn/ n recuperating. **re·cu·per·at·ive** /rɪ'kuːpərətɪv/ adj helping, relating

to, recuperation.

re·cur /rɪ'kɜː(r)/ vi (-rr-) 1 [VP2A] come, happen, again; be repeated: a problem which ~s periodically; ~ring decimals, figures in decimal fractions that ~ in the same order, as 3·999... (written 3·9̇), 4·014014... (written 4·0̇1̇4̇). 2 [VP3A] ~ to, go back (to sth) in words or thought: ~ring to what you said yesterday; if I may ~ to your idea. 3 [VP3A] ~ to, (of ideas, events etc) come back: My first meeting with her often ~s to my memory. **re·cur·rence** /rɪ'kʌrəns/ n [C,U] ~ring; repetition: Let there be no ~rence of this error. The frequent ~rence of these headaches made her life miserable. **re·cur·rent** /-ənt/ adj (of events, fevers etc) ~ring frequently or regularly: allow £35 a month for ~rent expenses, eg rent, lighting and heating.

re·curve /ˌriː'kɜːv/ vt, vi curve or bend backwards or downwards.

recu·sant /'rekjʊznt/ n, adj (person) refusing to submit to authority or to comply with regulations, esp (hist) a Roman Catholic who refused to attend Church of England services. **recu·sancy** /-znsɪ/ n [U].

re·cycle /ˌriː'saɪkl/ vt [VP6A] treat (substances already used for industry, etc) so that further use is possible: ~ old newspapers, by de-inking and pulping them.

red /red/ adj (-der, -dest) 1 of the colour of fresh blood, rubies, human lips, the tongue, maple leaves in autumn, post-office pillar boxes in GB;· of shades varying from crimson to bright brown (as of iron rust): red with anger/embarrassment, flushed in the face; with red hands, with hands stained with blood; with red eyes, eyes red with weeping. ~ 'carpet, one laid out for the reception of an important visitor. **paint the town red,** go on a spree and indulge in noisy, rough behaviour. **see red,** lose control of oneself through anger, or indignation. 2 Russian; Soviet; Communist: The Red Army. 3 (various uses in compounds, etc): '**red·breast** n (also robin redbreast) bird called the robin. '**Red·brick** adj (GB) name applied to the English universities founded near the end of the 19th c (contrasted chiefly with Oxford and Cambridge—known as Oxbridge). '**red·cap** n (GB) member of the military police; (US) railroad porter. '**red·coat** n (old name for) British soldier. ,**Red 'Crescent** n (emblem of an) organization in Muslim countries corresponding to the Red Cross. ,**Red 'Cross** n (emblem of the) international organization concerned with the relief of suffering caused by natural disasters, etc and for helping the sick and wounded and those taken prisoner in war. ,**red 'deer** n kind of deer native to the forests of Europe and Asia. ,**red 'ensign** (or colloq, ,red '**duster**) n red flag with the Union Jack in one corner, used by British merchant ships. ,**red 'flag** n (a) flag used as a symbol of danger (eg on railways, by workers on the roads). (b) symbol of revolution. (c) **the** ,**Red 'Flag,** revolutionary socialist song. **(catch sb)** ,**red-'handed** adj in the act of committing a crime. ,**red 'hat** n cardinal's hat. '**red-head** n person having red hair. ,**red 'herring** n (a) smoke-cured herring. (b) (fig) irrelevant matter introduced to distract attention from the subject being discussed. **neither fish, flesh, nor good red herring,** of a doubtful or ambiguous nature, which cannot be defined. **draw a red herring across the trail,** introduce irrelevant matter to distract attention from the subject being discussed. ,**red-'hot** adj (of a metal) heated until it is red; (fig) highly excited, furious: *red-hot enthusiasm*. **‚Red 'Indian** *n* (old use, now impolite) American Indian. **‚red 'lead** *n* [U] pigment made from red oxide of lead. **‚red-'letter day**, important or memorable day. **‚red 'light** *n* **(a)** danger signal on railways, etc; 'stop' signal on roads. *see the red light*, realize the nearness of danger or disaster. **(b)** *red-light district*, part of a town where there are brothels. **‚red 'meat** *n* [U] beef and mutton (contrasted with *white* meat, ie veal, pork, poultry). **‚red 'pepper** *n* red fruit of the capsicum plant. **‚red 'rag** *n like a red rag to a bull*, sth that excites a person's anger or passion. **'red-skin** *n* (old use, now impolite) American Indian. **the ‚Red 'Star**, symbol of the USSR and other Communist States. **‚red 'tape** *n* [U] (fig) excessive use of formalities in public business; too much attention to rules and regulations: *red tape in government offices.* **'red-wing** *n* name used of kinds of thrush and other birds with red wing-feathers. **'red-wood** *n* name used of kinds of tree with reddish wood, esp an evergreen Californian tree, some of which are of great height. □ *n* **1** [C,U] (shade of) red colour: *too much red in the painting; the reds and browns of the woods in autumn,* the red and brown shades of the leaves. **2** red clothes: *dressed in red.* **3** (colloq) person favouring or supporting Communism or the Soviet system. **4 the red**, debit side of business accounts. *be in/get into the red*, have/get liabilities that exceed assets. *be/get out of the red*, reach the position when one is no longer in the red. ⇨ black *n*(5).

re-dact /rɪˈdækt/ *vt* [VP6A] (formal) edit. **re-dac-tion** /rɪˈdækʃn/ *n* [U,C].

red-den /ˈredn/ *vt,vi* [VP6A,2A] make or become red; blush.

red-dish /ˈredɪʃ/ *adj* rather red.

re-deem /rɪˈdiːm/ *vt* [VP6A,14] ~ *(from),* **1** get (sth) back by payment or by doing sth: ~ *a pawned watch/a mortgage;* ~ *one's honour.* **2** perform (a promise or obligation). **3** set free by payment; rescue: ~ *a slave/prisoner;* (by Jesus) make free from sin. **4** compensate; make amends for: *his* ~*ing feature,* the feature or quality that balances his faults, etc. *The acting barely* ~*s the play,* The play is poor and the acting not very good. ~**-able** /-əbl/ *adj* that can be ~ed. **(the) Re-dee-mer** *n* Jesus Christ.

re-demp-tion /rɪˈdempʃn/ *n* [U] redeeming or being redeemed: *the* ~ *of a promise;* deliverance or rescue (esp from evil ways): *past/beyond* ~, too bad to be redeemed.

re-demp-tive /rɪˈdemptɪv/ *adj* serving to redeem; relating to redemption.

re-de-ploy /ˌriːdɪˈplɔɪ/ *vt* [VP6A] (of troops, workers in industry, etc) withdraw and rearrange so as to use more efficiently. ~**-ment** *n* [U,C] ~ing: *the* ~*ment of labour.*

re-dif-fu-sion /ˌriːdɪˈfjuːʒn/ *n* [U] system of using broadcast programmes (sound and television) in public places (eg cinemas).

re-do /ˌriːˈduː/ *vt* (*pt* -did /-ˈdɪd/, *pp* -done /-ˈdʌn/) [VP6A] do again: *We must have the walls redone,* repapered, recoloured, etc according to context.

redo-lent /ˈredələnt/ *adj* ~ *of,* (formal) having a strong smell, esp one that is reminiscent of sth: *bed sheets* ~ *of lavender;* (fig) *a town* ~ *of age and romance.* **redo-lence** /-əns/ *n*

re-double /rɪˈdʌbl/ *vt,vi* [VP6A,2A] **1** make or become greater or stronger: *They* ~*d their efforts. Her zeal* ~*d.* **2** (bridge) double again a bid already doubled by an opponent. ⇨ double⁴(6).

re-doubt /rɪˈdaʊt/ *n* [C] strong point in a system of fortifications: *attack and capture a* ~.

re-doubt-able /rɪˈdaʊtəbl/ *adj* (liter) to be feared; formidable: *those* ~ *ladies, the suffragettes.*

re-dound /rɪˈdaʊnd/ *vi* [VP3A] ~ *to,* (formal) contribute greatly in the end; promote: *Your success will* ~ *to the fame of the college. It* ~*s to your honour.*

re-dress /rɪˈdres/ *vt* [VP6A] **1** set (a wrong) right again; make up for, do sth that compensates for (a wrong): *You should confess and* ~ *your errors.* **2** ~ *the balance,* make things equal again. *r.* [U] act of ~ing or correcting (abuses, etc); sth that ~es: *seek* ~; *go to a lawyer to get legal* ~.

re-duce /rɪˈdjuːs *US:* -ˈduːs/ *vt,vi* [VP6A,14] ~ *(to),* **1** make less; make smaller in size, number, degree, price, etc: ~ *speed/pressure/costs;* ~ *one's expenses;* ~ *one's weight by ten pounds/ from X pounds to Y pounds. He is* ~*d almost to a skeleton,* has become very thin. [VP2A,B] (colloq): *She has been reducing for the last few weeks,* has been dieting (or trying other methods) in order to ~ her weight. **2** bring or get to a certain condition, way of living, etc: ~ *a class of noisy children to order;* ~ *sb to silence,* cause him to stop talking; ~ *sth to order;* ~ *the rebels to submission;* ~ *a sergeant to the ranks. They were* ~*d to begging or starving,* They became so poor that they had either to beg or go hungry. *They are living in* ~*d circumstances,* in (comparative) poverty. **3** change (to another form): ~ *an equation/argument/statement to its simplest form;* ~ *water by electrolysis,* separate it into oxygen and hydrogen; ~ *(sth) to an absurdity,* make, eg a scheme or argument, appear absurd by removing whatever hides its real nature; ~ *wood logs to pulp.* **re-duc-ible** /-əbl/ *adj* that can be ~d.

reductio ad absurdum /rɪˌdʌktɪəʊ ˌæd əbˈsɜːdəm/ (Lat) the disproof of a proposition by showing that its conclusion can only be absurd.

re-duc-tion /rɪˈdʌkʃn/ *n* **1** [U] reducing or being reduced; [C] instance of this: *a* ~ *in/of numbers; great* ~*s in prices; price* ~*s.* **2** [C] copy, on a smaller scale, of a picture, map, etc.

re-dun-dant /rɪˈdʌndənt/ *adj* superfluous; not needed: *a paragraph without a* ~ *word;* ~ *labour,* unneeded or surplus workers. *With the decreasing demand for coal many thousands of miners may become* ~. **re-dun-dance** /-əns/, **re-dun-dancy** /-ənsɪ/ *nn* [U] being ~: *redundancy among clerks caused by the increasing use of computers;* [C] (*pl* -cies) instance of this: *more redundancies in the docks.* **re'dundancy pay**, money paid by an employer to a ~ worker, the sum depending upon age and length of service.

re-dupli-cate /rɪˈdjuːplɪkeɪt *US:* -ˈduː-/ *vt* [VP6A] double; repeat. **re-dupli-ca-tion** /rɪˌdjuːplɪˈkeɪʃn *US:* -ˌduː-/ *n*

re-echo /riː ˈekəʊ/ *vi* [VP2A] echo again and again. □ *n* (*pl* ~es /-əʊz/) echo of an echo.

reed /riːd/ *n* [C] **1** (tall, firm stem or stalk of) kinds of coarse, firm-stemmed, jointed grasses growing in or near water; [U] (collective) mass of such grasses growing together; (*pl*) dried stalks used for thatching. *a broken* ~, (fig) an unreliable person or thing. **2** (in some wind-instruments, eg the oboe, ‛bassoon, clarinet and in some organ-pipes) strip of metal, etc that vibrates to produce sound. **the ~s**, ~ instruments of this sort. **~y** adj **1** abounding in ~s(1). **2** (of sounds, voices) shrill; piping.

reef¹ /ri:f/ n that part of a sail which can be rolled up or folded so as to reduce its area: *take in a ~*, shorten sail; (fig) go forward more cautiously. **'~-knot** n ordinary double knot (= US *square knot*). ⇨ the illus at knot. □ vt [VP6A] reduce the area of (a sail) by rolling up or folding a part.

reef² /ri:f/ n ridge of rock, shingle etc just below or above the surface of the sea: *wrecked on a coral ~*. ⇨ the illus at atoll.

reefer /'ri:fə(r)/ n **1** close-fitting double-breasted jacket of thick cloth, as worn by sailors. **2** (sl) kind of cigarette containing marijuana.

reek /ri:k/ n [U] **1** strong, bad smell: *the ~ of stale tobacco smoke*. **2** (liter and Scot use) thick smoke or vapour: *the ~ of a peat fire*. □ vi **1** [VP3A] *~ of*, smell unpleasantly of: He ~s of whisky/garlic. The room ~ed of stale cigar smoke. **2** *~ with*, be covered (with sweat, blood, etc); show signs or traces of: *a horse ~ing with sweat; a murderer whose hands still ~ed with blood.*

reel¹ /ri:l/ n **1** cylinder, roller or similar device on which cotton, thread, wire, photographic film, magnetic tape, hose (for water, etc), a fishing line, is wound. **(straight) off the ~**, (colloq) without a hitch or pause, in rapid succession. **2** (cinema) length of positive film rolled on one ~: *a six-~ film*, a complete film on six ~s. ⇨ spool. □ vt [VP6A,15A,B] roll or wind (thread, a fishing line etc) on to, or with the help of, a ~; wind (thread, etc) *off*: ~ *in the line; ~ up a fish; ~ the silk thread off cocoons.* ~ *sth off*, tell, say or repeat sth without pause or apparent effort: ~ *off the verses of a long poem; ~ off a list of names.*

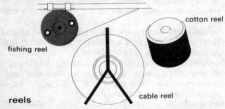

fishing reel

cotton reel

reels

cable reel

reel² /ri:l/ vi [VP2A,C] **1** be shaken (physically or mentally) by a blow, a shock, rough treatment, etc: *His mind ~ed when he heard the news.* **2** walk or stand unsteadily, moving from side to side; sway: *He ~ed like a drunken man. He went ~ing down the road.* **3** seem to sway; appear to move or shake: *The street ~ed before his eyes.*

reel³ /ri:l/ n [C] (music for a) lively Scottish dance, usu for two couples.

re-en·try /ˌri: 'entrɪ/ n (pl -ries) act of re-entering; return of a spacecraft into the earth's atmosphere.

reeve /ri:v/ n **1** (hist) chief magistrate of a town or district. **2** (Canada) president of a village or town council.

re·face /ˌri:'feɪs/ vt put a new surface on.

re·fec·tion /rɪ'fekʃn/ n [U] refreshment in the form of food and drink; [C] light meal.

re·fec·tory /rɪ'fektərɪ/ n (pl -ries) dining-hall (in a monastery, convent or college).

re·fer /rɪ'fɜ:(r)/ vt,vi (-rr-) **1** [VP14,15B] *~ sb/sth (back) (to sb/sth)* send, take, hand over (*to, back to*) to be dealt with, decided etc: *The dispute was ~red to the United Nations. I was ~red to the Manager/to the Inquiry Office. The question was ~red back*, was deferred. **2** [VP3A] *~ to*, (of a speaker, what is said, etc) speak of, allude to; apply to: *When I said that some people are stupid I wasn't ~ring to you. Don't ~ to this matter again, please. What I have to say ~s to all of you. Does that remark ~ to me?* **3** [VP3A] *~ to*, turn to, go to, for information, etc: *The speaker often ~red to his notes.* **ref·er·able** /rɪ'fɜ:rəbl/ adj that can be ~rred.

ref·eree /ˌrefə'ri:/ n **1** person to whom disputes, eg in industry, between workers and employers, are referred for decision. **2** (in football, boxing, etc) person who controls matches, judges points in dispute, etc. ⇨ umpire. □ vt,vi [VP6A,2A] act as ~: *~ a football match.*

ref·er·ence /'refrəns/ n **1** [C,U] (instance of) referring: *You should make ~ to a dictionary. The book is full of ~s to places that I know well.* **'~ book**, **book of ~**, one that is not read through but consulted for information, eg a dictionary or encyclopaedia. **'~ library**, one containing ~ books, to be consulted there but not to be taken away. **terms of ~**, (of a commission, etc) scope or range given to an authority: *Is this question outside our terms of ~*, one that we are not required to investigate? **2** [C] (person willing to make a) statement about a person's character or abilities: *excellent ~s from former employers. The shop will open a credit account for you if you supply a banker's ~*, a note from your bank stating that your financial position is sound. **3** [C] note, direction, etc telling where certain information may be found: *He dislikes history books that are crowded with ~s to other books.* **'~ marks**, marks, eg *, †, ‡, §, used to refer the reader to the place, eg a footnote, where information may be found. **,cross-'reference**, ⇨ cross-~. **4** [U] *in/with ~ to*, concerning; about. *without ~ to*, irrespective of; having no connection with. **ref·er·en·tial** /ˌrefə'renʃl/ adj having ~ to.

ref·er·en·dum /ˌrefə'rendəm/ n (pl ~s; -da /-də/) [C] the referring of a political question to a direct vote of the electorate.

re·fill /ˌri:'fɪl/ vt fill again. □ n /'ri:fɪl/ that which is used to ~; a container: *two ~s for a ball-point pen.*

re·fine /rɪ'faɪn/ vt,vi **1** [VP6A,2A] free from other substances; make or become pure: ~ *sugar/oil/ores.* **2** [VP6A] cause to become more cultured, polished in manners; get rid of what is coarse or vulgar: ~ *a language; ~d language/manners/speech/taste.* **3** *~ upon*, improve by giving great attention to details: ~ *upon one's methods.*

re·fine·ment /rɪ'faɪnmənt/ n **1** [U] refining or being refined. **2** [U] purity of feeling, taste, language, etc; delicacy of manners: *a lady of ~; lack of ~*, ie vulgarity; *aim at acquiring ~.* **3** [C] ingenious or remarkable example of such purity of tastes, etc; delicate or clever development of sth: ~s *of meaning/cruelty; all the ~s of the age.*

re·finer /rɪ'faɪnə(r)/ n **1** person whose business is to refine sth: *sugar ~s.* **2** machine for refining metals, sugar, etc. **~y** /-nərɪ/ n place, building, etc where sth is refined: *a 'sugar ~y; an 'oil ~y.*

re·fit /ˌri:'fɪt/ vt,vi (-tt-) [VP6A] make (a ship, etc) ready for use again by renewing or repairing parts; [VP2A] (of a ship) be made fit for further voyages: *The ship put into Cardiff to ~.* □ n /'ri:fɪt/ refitting.

re·flate /ˌriːˈfleɪt/ vt [VP6A] restore to a previous economic or currency state; *plans to ∼ the economy.*

re·fla·tion /riːˈfleɪʃn/ n [U] inflation of currency after a deflation, to restore the system to its previous condition.

re·flect /rɪˈflekt/ vt, vi 1 [VP6A] (of a surface) throw back (light, heat, sound); (of a mirror) send back an image of: *The sunlight was ∼ed from the water. Look at the trees ∼ed in the lake. The moon shines with ∼ed light. The sight of my face ∼ed in the mirror never pleases me.* '∼-ing **telescope**, one in which the image is ∼ed in a mirror and magnified. 2 [VP6A] express; show the nature of: *Her sad looks ∼ed the thoughts passing through her mind. Does the literature of a nation ∼ its politics?* 3 [VP14] ∼ sth **on/upon** sb, (of actions, results) bring (credit or discredit upon): *The results ∼ the greatest credit upon all concerned. Such behaviour can only ∼ discredit upon you.* 4 [VP3A] ∼ **on/ upon,** bring discredit upon; hurt the good reputation of: *I do not wish to ∼ upon your sincerity,* suggest that you are not sincere. *Your rude behaviour ∼s only upon yourself,* You are the only person whose reputation is hurt by it. 5 [VP2A,3A,9,8,10] ∼ **(on/upon),** consider; think on: *I must ∼ upon what answer to give/how to answer that question. He ∼ed how difficult it would be to escape.*

re·flec·tion (GB also **re·flexion**) /rɪˈflekʃn/ n 1 [U] reflecting or being reflected: *the ∼ of heat.* 2 [C] sth reflected, esp an image reflected in a mirror or in still water: *see one's ∼ in a mirror; the ∼ of trees in (the water of) a lake.* 3 [U] thought; (re-)consideration: *lost in ∼; do sth without sufficient ∼. on ∼,* after reconsidering the matter. 4 [C] expression of a thought in speech or writing; idea arising in the mind: *∼s on the pleasures of being idle.* 5 [C] expression of blame: *I intended no ∼ on your character,* did not want to suggest that you are blameworthy. *How dare you cast ∼s on my motives?* 6 [C] sth that brings discredit: *This is a ∼ upon your honour.*

re·flec·tive /rɪˈflektɪv/ adj thoughtful; in the habit of reflection(5). ∼·**ly** adv

re·flec·tor /rɪˈflektə(r)/ n sth that reflects heat, light or sound, esp a piece of glass or metal for reflecting light, etc in a required direction. '∼ **studs,** (GB) studs inserted in a road surface to help drivers by reflecting light from headlamps (colloq *cat's eyes*). ⇔ the illus at **bicycle.**

re·flex /ˈriːfleks/ adj 1 '∼ **action,** action that is independent of the will, being an involuntary response to a stimulation of the nerves, eg shivering, sneezing. 2 '∼ **camera,** hand camera in which, by means of a mirror, the reflected image of the object or scene to be photographed can be seen and focused up to the moment of exposure. □ n ∼ action.

re·flex·ion /rɪˈflekʃn/ n = reflection.

re·flex·ive /rɪˈfleksɪv/ n, adj (word or form) showing that the agent's action is upon himself. ∼ **verb,** eg He *cut* himself. ∼ **pronoun,** eg *myself, themselves.*

re·float /ˌriːˈfləʊt/ vt, vi [VP6A,2A] cause (sth) to float again after it has gone aground, been sunk, etc; float again.

re·flux /ˈriːflʌks/ n flowing back; ebb: *flux and ∼.*

re·for·est /ˌriːˈfɒrɪst/ US: -ˈfɔːr-/ vt ⇔ reafforest.

re·for·es·ta·tion /riːˌfɒrɪˈsteɪʃn/ US: -ˌfɔːr-/ n

re·form /rɪˈfɔːm/ vt, vi [VP6A,2A] make or become better by removing or putting right what is bad or wrong: *∼ a sinner/one's character/the world; ∼ oneself; a ∼ed man,* one who has given up his bad ways and is now living a good life. □ n 1 [U] ∼ing; removal of vices, imperfections, etc: *agitate for social or political ∼; the Re'form Bill of 1832,* (GB) that which extended the franchise and improved parliamentary representation. 2 [C] instance of ∼; change made in order to remove imperfections: *a ∼ in teaching methods.* ∼**er** n person actively engaged in advocating or carrying our ∼s.

re-form /ˌriː ˈfɔːm/ vt, vi form again; (of soldiers) get into ranks, etc again. **re-for·ma·tion** /ˌriː fɔːˈmeɪʃn/ n

ref·or·ma·tion /ˌrefəˈmeɪʃn/ n 1 [U] reforming¹ or being reformed¹; [C] radical change for the better in social, political or religious affairs. 2 **the R∼,** the 16th-century movement for reform of the Roman Catholic Church, resulting in the establishment of the Reformed or Protestant Churches.

re·forma·tory /rɪˈfɔːmətrɪ US: -tɔːrɪ/ adj tending or intending to produce reform. □ n (pl -ties) (formerly) school or institution for reforming young offenders against the law by means of special training, mental, moral and physical (usu, in GB, called an *approved school* or *community house*).

re·fract /rɪˈfrækt/ vt [VP6A] cause (a ray of light) to bend aside where it enters, eg water, glass, obliquely: *Light is ∼ed when it passes through a prism.* **re·frac·tion** /rɪˈfrækʃn/ n ∼ing or being ∼ed.

re·frac·tory /rɪˈfræktərɪ/ adj 1 resisting control, discipline, etc; wilful: *as ∼ as a mule;* (of diseases) not yielding to treatment. 2 (of substances, esp metals) hard to melt, fuse or work.

re·frain¹ /rɪˈfreɪn/ n [C] lines of a song which are repeated, esp at the end of each verse: *Will you all join in singing the ∼, please?*

re·frain² /rɪˈfreɪn/ vi [VP2A,3A] ∼ **(from),** hold oneself back: *Please ∼ from spitting in public places. Let's hope they will ∼ from hostile action.*

re·fresh /rɪˈfreʃ/ vt [VP6A] 1 give new strength to; make fresh: *∼ oneself with a cup of tea/a warm bath.* 2 ∼ **one's memory,** call things back to the memory by referring to notes, etc. 3 take sth to eat or drink: *They stopped at a pub to ∼ themselves. They felt much ∼ed.* ∼·**ing** adj 1 strengthening; giving rest and relief: *a ∼ing breeze/sleep.* 2 welcome and interesting because rare or unexpected: *∼ing innocence,* eg of children to older, sophisticated persons. ∼·**ing·ly** adv

re·fresher /rɪˈfreʃə(r)/ n 1 (legal) extra fee paid to counsel1¹(3) while a case is proceeding in the law courts. 2 (colloq) drink. 3 (attrib) '∼ **course,** course providing instruction, eg to teachers already in service, on modern methods, newer professional techniques, etc.

re·fresh·ment /rɪˈfreʃmənt/ n 1 [U] refreshing or being refreshed: *feel ∼ of mind and body.* 2 [U] (often pl) that which refreshes, esp food and drink: *order some light ∼(s),* snacks; '∼ **room,** one where one can buy food and drink, eg at a railway station. *R∼s were provided during the interval.*

re·frig·er·ate /rɪˈfrɪdʒəreɪt/ vt [VP6A] make cool or cold; keep (food) in good condition by making and keeping it cold. **re·frig·er·ant** /-ənt/ n, adj (substance) serving to ∼, eg liquid carbon dioxide. **re·frig·er·ation** /rɪˌfrɪdʒəˈreɪʃn/ n (esp) the cooling or freezing of food in order to preserve it: *the refrigeration industry.* **re·frig·er·ator** /rɪˈfrɪdʒəreɪtə(r)/ n [C] (colloq abbr *fridge*) cabinet or room in which food is kept cold.

reft /reft/ *pp* = bereft.

re·fuel /ˌriːˈfjuːəl/ *vt,vi* (-ll-; US also -l-) [VP6A,2A] supply with, take on, a fresh quantity of fuel: *The plane came down to ~.*

ref·uge /ˈrefjuːdʒ/ *n* [C,U] (place giving) shelter or protection from trouble, danger, pursuit, etc: *seek ~ from the floods; take ~ in the cellar;* (fig) *take ~ in silence,* eg to avoid answering impertinent questions. *Books are a ~ of the lonely.*

refu·gee /ˌrefjʊˈdʒiː/ US: ˈrefjʊdʒiː/ *n* person who has been forced to flee from danger, eg from floods, war, political persecution: (attrib) *,refu·gee camps.*

re·ful·gent /rɪˈfʌldʒent/ *adj* (formal) shining; brilliant. **re·ful·gence** /- əns/ *n* [U].

re·fund /rɪˈfʌnd/ *vt* [VP6A] pay back (money to sb): *~ the cost of postage.* □ *n* /ˈriːfʌnd/ [C,U] repayment: *obtain a ~ of a deposit.*

re·fur·bish /ˌriːˈfɜːbɪʃ/ *vt* [VP6A] make clean or bright again; make (as if) like new.

re·fusal /rɪˈfjuːzl/ *n* **1** [U] act of refusing; [C] instance of this: *the ~ of an invitation; his ~ to do what I asked.* **2 (the)** *~,* right of deciding whether to accept or refuse sth before it is offered to others: *If you ever decide to sell your car, please give me (the) first ~.*

ref·use¹ /ˈrefjuːs/ *n* [U] waste or worthless material: *a¹~ dump,* eg place where town *~* (collected from houses, etc) is dumped. *'~-collector* *n* dustman.

re·fuse² /rɪˈfjuːz/ *vt,vi* [VP6A,7A,12C,2A] say 'no' to (a request or offer); show unwillingness to accept (sth offered), to do (sth that one is asked to do): *~ a gift; ~ one's consent; ~ to help. They ~d me permission. I was ~d admittance.*

re·fute /rɪˈfjuːt/ *vt* [VP6A] prove (statements, opinions, etc) to be wrong or mistaken; prove (sb) wrong in his opinions: *~ an argument/an opponent.* **re·fut·able** /-əbl/ *adj* that can be *~d.* **refu·ta·tion** /ˌrefjuːˈteɪʃn/ *n* [U] refuting; [C] counter-argument.

re·gain /rɪˈgeɪn/ *vt* [VP6A] **1** get possession of again: *~ consciousness; ~ one's freedom.* **2** get back to (a place or position): *~ one's footing,* recover one's balance after slipping or falling.

re·gal /ˈriːgl/ *adj* of, for, fit for, by, a monarch; royal: *~ dignity/splendour/power.* *~ly* /-gəlɪ/ *adv*

re·gale /rɪˈgeɪl/ *vt* [VP6A,14] *~ oneself/sb (with/on sth),* give pleasure or delight to: *~ oneself with a cigar; regaling themselves and their friends on caviar and champagne.*

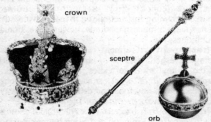

crown

sceptre

orb

regalia

re·galia /rɪˈgeɪlɪə/ *n pl* [C] (often with a *sing v*) **1** emblems (crown, orb, sceptre, etc) of royalty, as used at coronations. **2** emblems or decorations of an order(10), eg of the freemasons.

re·gard¹ /rɪˈgɑːd/ *n* **1** (liter or old use) long, steady

or significant look. **2** [U] point attended to; relation. *in 'this ~,* in respect of (= regarding) this point. *in/with ~ to,* with respect to; concerning. **3** [U] attention; concern; consideration: *You'll get into trouble if you continue to behave without ~ to decency. He has very little ~ for the feelings of others. More ~ must be paid to safety on the roads.* **4** [U] esteem; consideration; respect: *hold sb in high/low ~; have a high/low ~ for sb's judgement.* **5** (*pl*) kindly thoughts and wishes: (at the end of a letter) *with kind ~s, yours sincerely,.... Please give my kind ~s to your brother. ~-ful* /-fl/ *adj ~ful (of),* full of *~*(3): *Be more ~ful of your own interests. ~·less adj ~less of,* paying no attention to: *~less of the consequences; ~less of expense.*

re·gard² /rɪˈgɑːd/ *vt* **1** [VP6A] (liter or old use) look closely at. **2** [VP16B] *~ sb/sth as,* consider: *~ sb as a hero; ~ sth as a crime. He's ~ed as the best dentist in town.* **3** [VP6A,14] *~ (with),* look upon mentally: *I ~ his behaviour with suspicion/horror. How is he ~ed locally? He is ~ed with disfavour/ unfavourably.* **4** [VP6A] pay attention to (chiefly neg and interr): *He seldom ~s my advice. Why do you so seldom ~ my wishes?* **as ~s,** *~ing prep* with reference to; concerning.

re·gatta /rɪˈɡætə/ *n* meeting for boat races (rowing boats or yachts).

re·gency /ˈriːdʒənsɪ/ *n* (*pl* -cies) the office of a regent; regent's period of office. **the R~,** (in GB) the period 1810—20.

re·gen·er·ate /rɪˈdʒenəreɪt/ *vt,vi* [VP6A,2A] **1** reform spiritually; raise morally. **2** give new strength or life to; restore lost qualities to. **3** grow again. □ *adj* /rɪˈdʒenərət/ spiritually reborn: *a ~ society.* **re·gen·er·ation** /rɪˌdʒenəˈreɪʃn/ *n* [U] being *~d.*

re·gent /ˈriːdʒənt/ *n* **1** person appointed to perform the duties of a ruler who is too young, old, ill, etc or who is absent. **2** (US) member of a governing board (eg of a State university). □ *adj* (following the *n*) performing the duties of a *~: the Prince R~.*

reg·gae /ˈreɡeɪ/ *n* [U] West Indian popular music and dance with strong rhythms.

regi·cide /ˈredʒɪsaɪd/ *n* [U] crime of killing a king; [C] person who kills, or takes part in the killing of, a king.

ré·gime, re·gime /reɪˈʒiːm/ *n* [C] **1** method or system of government or of administration; prevailing system of things: *under the old ~,* before the changes were made, etc (according to context). **2** = regimen.

regi·men /ˈredʒɪmən/ *n* [C] set of rules for diet, exercise, etc for promoting one's health and physical well-being.

regi·ment /ˈredʒɪmənt/ *n* [C] (cavalry and artillery) unit divided into squadrons or batteries and commanded by a colonel; (GB infantry) organization usu based on a city or county, with special traditions and dress, represented in the field by battalions: *the 1st battalion of the Manchester R~. ~ of,* large number: *whole ~s of starlings.* □ *vt* [VP6A] organize; discipline: *~ the workers of a country.* **reg·i·men·ta·tion** /ˌredʒɪmenˈteɪʃn/ *n* [U] subjection to control; strict political discipline (as in a police state).

regi·men·tal /ˌredʒɪˈmentl/ *adj* of a regiment: *the ~ tie,* in the colours of the regiment. □ *n* (*pl*) dress worn by the men of a regiment; military uniform: *in full ~s,* in full dress.

Re·gina /rɪ'dʒaɪnə/ n (abbr **R**) reigning queen: (used in signatures to proclamations) *Elizabeth* ∼; (legal) (used in titles of lawsuits): ∼ v *Hay*, the Crown against Hay. ⇨ **Rex**.

re·gion /'riːdʒən/ n [C] area or division with or without definite boundaries or characteristics: *the Arctic* ∼s; *the forest* ∼; *the lower* ∼s, hell; *the* ∼ *of metaphysics; the abdominal* ∼. ∼**al** /-nl/ adj of a ∼: *the* ∼*al wines of France; a* ∼*al geography.* ∼**·ally** /-nəlɪ/ adv

reg·is·ter [1] /'redʒɪstə(r)/ n [C] **1** (book containing a) record or list: *a parish* ∼, one with records of baptisms, marriages and funerals; *Lloyd's* ∼, of shipping; *the R*∼ *of voters, the Parliamentary R*∼, of persons qualified to vote at elections. **2** range of the human voice or of a musical instrument; part of this range: *the upper/middle* ∼; *the lower* ∼ *of the clarinet.* **3** mechanical device for indicating and recording speed, force, numbers, etc. '**cash** ∼, as used for recording cash payments in shops, etc. ⇨ the illus at **cash**. **4** adjustable metal plate or grating for widening or narrowing the size of an opening and so regulating the passage of air, etc through it: *a hot-air* ∼, one controlling the flow of hot air, eg in a building heated from a basement furnace. **5** = **registry**. **6** (linguistics) vocabulary, grammar, etc used by speakers in particular circumstances or contexts, eg legal, commercial.

reg·is·ter [2] /'redʒɪstə(r)/ vt,vi [VP2A,3A,6A,14] ∼ **(sth/oneself) (with sth/sb) (for sth)**, **1** make a written and formal record of, in a list: ∼ *one's car/the birth of a child/a new trade-mark; a State R*∼*ed Nurse*, one who is officially ∼ed. *I am a foreigner here; must I* ∼ *(myself) with the police? Where can I* ∼ *for the Arabic course?* **2** put or get (sb's name, one's own name) on a register. **3** (of instruments) indicate; record: *The thermometer* ∼*ed only two degrees above freezing-point.* **4** (of sb's face) show (emotion, etc): *Her face* ∼*ed surprise.* **5** send (a letter or parcel) by special post, paying an extra charge which ensures compensation if it is lost: *It's wise to* ∼ *letters containing banknotes.*

reg·is·trar /ˌredʒɪ'strɑː(r)/ n person whose duty is to keep records or registers, eg for a town council or a university.

reg·is·tra·tion /ˌredʒɪ'streɪʃn/ n **1** [U] registering; recording: ∼ *of letters/luggage;* ∼ *of students for an examination/an academic course; the* '∼ *number* (of a car). **2** [C] entry; record of facts.

reg·is·try /'redʒɪstrɪ/ n (pl -tries) **1** (sometimes *register*) place where registers are kept: *a ship's port of* ∼; *married at a* '∼ *office*, before a registrar (without a religious ceremony). **2** [U] = registration.

reg·nant /'regnənt/ adj reigning: *Queen* ∼, one who is ruling in her own right and not as a consort.

re·gress /rɪ'gres/ vi [VP2A] return to an earlier or more primitive form or state. **re·gression** /rɪ'greʃn/ n ∼ing. **re·gressive** adj tending to ∼.

re·gret [1] /rɪ'gret/ n **1** [U] feeling of sadness at the loss of sth, or of annoyance or disappointment because sth has or has not been done: *express* ∼ *at not being able to help; hear with* ∼ *that a friend is ill. Much to my* ∼ *I am unable to accept your kind invitation.* **2** (pl) (in polite expressions of refusal, etc): *Please accept my* ∼s *at having to refuse. He refused with many* ∼s/*with much* ∼. *I have no* ∼s, do not feel sorry (about what I did, etc). ∼**·ful** /-fl/ adj sad; sorry; ∼**·fully** /-fəlɪ/ adv sadly; with ∼.

re·gret [2] /rɪ'gret/ vt (-tt-) [VP6A,D,7A,9] **1** be sorry for the loss of; wish to have again: ∼ *lost opportunities. He died* ∼*ted by all.* **2** feel sorry for; be sorry (*to say, etc; that...*): *I* ∼ *being unable to help/*∼ *that I cannot help. I* ∼ *to say that.... It is to be* ∼*ted that...*, is a pity that.... *I* ∼ *my child's ignorance.* ∼**·table** /-əbl/ adj to be ∼ted: ∼*table failures.* ∼**·tably** /-əblɪ/ adv. *a* ∼*tably small attendance.*

re·group /ˌriː'gruːp/ vt,vi [VP6A,2A] form again into groups; form into new groups.

regu·lar /'regjʊlə(r)/ adj **1** evenly arranged; symmetrical; systematic: ∼ *teeth;* ∼ *features*, eg of the face; *a* ∼ *figure; a* ∼ *nomenclature.* **2** coming, happening, done, again and again at even intervals: *a man with* ∼ *habits*, doing the same things at the same times every day; *keep* ∼ *hours*, eg leaving and returning home, getting up and going to bed, at the same times every day; ∼ *breathing; have a* ∼ *pulse; walking up and down with* ∼ *steps. He has no* ∼ *work*, no continuous occupation. **3** properly qualified; recognized; trained; full-time or professional: ∼ *soldiers*, not volunteers or militia; *the* ∼ *army*, made up of ∼ soldiers. **4** conforming to a standard of etiquette; in agreement with what is considered correct procedure or behaviour: *I doubt whether your procedure would be considered* ∼ *by the authorities.* **5** (gram, of vv, nn, etc) having normal inflections: *The verb 'go' is not* ∼. **6** (eccles) bound by, living under, religious rule (opp of *secular*): *the* ∼ *clergy*, eg monks but not parish priests. **7** (colloq) thorough; complete: *He's a* ∼ *hero/rascal.* **8** ordinary; normal: *Do you want king size cigarettes or* ∼ *size?* **9** (colloq) likeable; good: *He's a* ∼ *guy.* □ n **1** soldier of the ∼ army. **2** (colloq) ∼ customer or client, eg at a hairdresser's or a pub. ∼**·ly** adv in a ∼ manner; at ∼ intervals or times: *a garden* ∼*ly laid out; as* ∼*ly as clockwork.* ∼**·ity** /ˌregjʊ'lærətɪ/ n [U] state of being ∼: *win a prize for* ∼*ity of attendance.*

regu·lar·ize /'regjʊləraɪz/ vt [VP6A] make lawful or correct: ∼ *the proceedings.* **regu·lar·iz·ation** /ˌregjʊləraɪ'zeɪʃn US: -rɪ'z-/ n

regu·late /'regjʊleɪt/ vt [VP6A] **1** control systematically; cause to obey a rule or standard: ∼ *one's conduct/expenditure;* ∼ *the traffic. Accidents happen even in the best* ∼*d families.* **2** adjust (an apparatus, mechanism) to get the desired result: ∼ *a clock;* ∼ *the speed of a machine.* **regu·la·tor** /-tə(r)/ n person or thing that ∼s, eg a device that ∼s a mechanical movement, esp in a clock.

regu·la·tion /ˌregjʊ'leɪʃn/ n **1** [U] regulating or being regulated: *the* ∼ *of affairs/of a clock.* **2** [C] rule; order; authoritative direction: '*safety* ∼s, eg in factories; '*traffic* ∼s, made by the police for drivers of vehicles; *contrary to* ∼s; *Queen's/ King's* ∼s, those governing the conduct of the armed forces. **3** (attrib) as required by rules; correct: ∼ *dress/uniform; application forms of the* ∼ *size.*

re·gur·gi·tate /rɪ'gɜːdʒɪteɪt/ vi,vt [VP6A,2A] (of liquid, etc) gush back; bring (swallowed food) up again to the mouth.

re·ha·bili·tate /ˌriːə'bɪlɪteɪt/ vt [VP6A] **1** restore (eg old buildings) to a good condition. **2** restore (sb) to former rank, position or reputation: *He has been* ∼*d in public esteem.* **3** bring back (sb who is physically disabled or delinquent) to a normal life by special treatment. **re·ha·bili·ta·tion**

/ˌriːəˌbɪlɪ'teɪʃn/ n rehabilitating: *a rehabilitation centre*, place where persons are ~d(3).

re·hash /ˌriː'hæʃ/ vt take (eg old literary material) and use again in a new form: ~ *last term's lectures for the coming term.* □ n /'riːhæʃ/ [C] ~ed material.

re·hear /ˌriː'hɪə(r)/ vt [VP6A] hear, consider, again (a case, plea etc in a law court). **re·hear·ing** n instance of this.

re·hearse /rɪ'hɜːs/ vt,vi [VP6A,2A] **1** practise (a play, music, programme, etc) for public performance: ~ *the parts in a play;* ~ *an opera.* **2** say over again; give an account of: ~ *the events of the day;* ~ *one's grievances.* **re·hearsal** /-sl/ n **1** [U] rehearsing: *put a play into rehearsal.* **2** [C] trial performance of a play or other entertainment: *a 'dress rehearsal*, one in which the actors wear the costumes and use the props as for public performances.

re·house /ˌriː'haʊz/ vt [VP6A] provide with a new house (esp in place of one officially condemned): *The people in these slums will have to be ~d.*

Reich /raɪk/ n the German Commonwealth as a whole. **the First R~**, the Holy Roman Empire, 9th c to 1806. **the Second R~**, 1871—1918. **the Third R~**, the Nazi regime, 1933—45.

reign /reɪn/ n [C] (period of) sovereignty, rule; dominance: *during five successive ~s;* in the ~ *of King Alfred; the ~ of law/reason; the R~ of Terror*, (in France, 1793—94, during the Revolution). □ vi [VP2A,3A] ~ *(over)*, **1** hold office as a monarch: *The king ~ed but he did not rule or govern. He ~ed over the country for ten years.* **2** be influential; prevail: *the ~ing beauty*, woman acknowledged to be most beautiful for the time in question. *Silence ~ed everywhere.*

re·im·burse /ˌriːɪm'bɜːs/ vt [VP6A,12A,13A,14] ~ *sth (to sb);* ~ *sb (for) sth*, pay back (sb who has spent money, the money spent): *We must* ~ *him the costs of the journey. You will be ~d (for) your expenses.* ~·ment n [C,U] repayment (of expenses).

rein /reɪn/ n (often *pl* in the same sense as the *sing*) long, narrow strap fastened to the bit of a bridle for controlling a horse. ⇨ the illus at **harness**. *assume/drop the ~s of government*, enter upon/give up office. *draw* ~, (lit and fig) pull up; go slower. *give free ~/the ~s to sb/sth*, (lit and fig) allow freedom to: *give a horse the ~s; give the* ~*(s) to one's imagination*, allow it great freedom. *hold/take the ~s*, (lit and fig) have/take control: *hold the ~s of government. keep a tight* ~ *on sb/sth*, (lit and fig) be firm with; allow little freedom to. □ vt [VP6A,15B] control with, or as with, ~s: ~ *in a horse*, restrain it; check it; ~ *up/back a horse*, pull it up or back with the ~s.

re·in·car·nate /ˌriːɪn'kɑːneɪt/ vt give a new body to (a soul). □ adj /ˌriːɪn'kɑːneɪt/ born again in a new body. **re·in·car·na·tion** /ˌriːɪnkɑː'neɪʃn/ n [U] religious doctrine that the soul enters, after death, into another (human or animal) body; [C] instance of this; new body inhabited by the soul.

rein·deer /'reɪndɪə(r)/ n (pl unchanged) kind of large deer with branched antlers, used in Lapland for transport and kept in herds for its milk, flesh and hide. ⇨ the illus at **large**.

re·in·force /ˌriːɪn'fɔːs/ vt [VP6A] make stronger by adding or supplying more men or material; increase the size, thickness, of sth so that it supports more weight, etc: ~ *an army/a fleet;* ~ *a garment*, by adding an extra thickness of cloth in places; ~ *a bridge.* ~d **concrete**, concrete strengthened with steel bars or metal netting embedded in it. ~·ment n [U] reinforcing or being ~d; (esp *pl*) that which ~s; (esp) men, ships, etc sent to ~.

re·in·state /ˌriːɪn'steɪt/ vt [VP6A,14] ~ *sb (in)*, replace (sb) (in a former position or condition): ~ *sb in his former office.* ~·ment n

re·in·sure /ˌriːɪn'ʃʊə(r)/ vt [VP6A] insure again (esp of an underwriter who relieves himself of some or all of a risk by taking out an insurance with another underwriter or insurance company. **re·in·sur·ance** /-rəns/ n

re·is·sue /ˌriː'ɪʃuː/ vt [VP6A] issue again after temporary discontinuance: ~ *stamps/books.* □ n sth ~d, esp a reprint of a book with a change of format or price. Cf **new edition**, in which changes are made in the text.

re·iter·ate /riː'ɪtəreɪt/ vt [VP6A] say or do again several times: ~ *a command.* **re·iter·ation** /riːˌɪtə'reɪʃn/ n [U] act of reiterating; [C] instance of this; repetition.

re·ject[1] /'riːdʒekt/ n sth ~ed: *export ~s*, articles made for export but ~ed because of a flaw or imperfection.

re·ject[2] /rɪ'dʒekt/ vt [VP6A] **1** put aside, throw away, as not good enough to be kept: ~ *fruit that is over-ripe.* **2** refuse to accept: ~ *an offer of help;* ~ *a heart transplant*, (of the body) fail to adapt to the new heart; *a ~ed suitor. The army doctors ~ed him*, would not accept him as medically fit. **re·jec·tion** /rɪ'dʒekʃn/ n [U] ~ing or being ~ed; [C] instance of this; sth ~ed: '~ion slip*, printed or written note from an editor or publisher ~ing an offered article, novel etc.

re·jig /ˌriː'dʒɪg/ vt (-gg-) [VP6A] supply (a factory, etc) with new mechanical equipment.

re·joice /rɪ'dʒɔɪs/ vt,vi **1** [VP6A] make glad; cause to be happy: *The boy's success ~d his mother's heart.* **2** [VP2A,C,3B,4C] ~ *(at/over)*, feel great joy; show signs of great happiness: ~ *over a victory;* ~ *at sb's success. I* ~ *to hear that you are well again/~ that you have recovered so quickly. He ~s in the name of Bloggs*, humorous for 'His name is Bloggs'. Note: in colloq style 'be glad' and 'be pleased' are commoner than 'rejoice'. **re·joic·ing** n [U] happiness; joy; (pl) celebrations; merry-making.

re·join[1] /rɪ'dʒɔɪn/ vt,vi [VP6A,2A] answer; reply; (legal) answer a charge or plea. ~·der /-də(r)/ n [C] what is said in reply; retort.

re·join[2] /ˌriː'dʒɔɪn/ vt join the company of again: ~ *one's regiment/ship.*

re·join[3] /ˌriː'dʒɔɪn/ vt [VP6A] join (together) again.

re·ju·ven·ate /riː'dʒuːvəneɪt/ vt,vi [VP6A,2A] make or become young or vigorous again in nature or appearance. **re·ju·ven·ation** /riːˌdʒuːvə'neɪʃn/ n

re·kindle /ˌriː'kɪndl/ vt,vi [VP6A,2A] kindle again: ~ *a fire. Our hopes ~d.*

re·laid /ˌriː'leɪd/ pt,pp of **relay**[2].

re·lapse /rɪ'læps/ vi [VP2A,3A] ~ *(into)*, fall back again (into bad ways, error, illness, silence etc): *He ~d into smoking twenty cigarettes a day.* □ n [C] falling back, esp after recovering from illness: *The patient has had a ~.*

re·late /rɪ'leɪt/ vt,vi **1** [VP6A,14] ~ *(to)*, (formal) tell (a story, etc to sb); give an account of (facts, adventures etc): *He ~d to his wife some amusing stories about his employer. Strange to ~, I once met Christopher in Katmandu.* **2** [VP14] ~ *to/*

with, connect in thought or meaning: *It is difficult to ∼ these results with/to any known cause.* **3** [VP3A] **∼ to,** have reference (to): *She is a girl who notices nothing except what ∼s to herself.* **4 be ∼d (to),** be connected by family (to): *I am not ∼d to him in any way. He and I are not ∼d. She says she is ∼d to the royal family.*

re·la·tion /rɪ'leɪʃn/ *n* **1** [U] the act of relating(1,2), narrating or telling: *the ∼ of his adventures;* [C] *that which is narrated; tale or narrative.* **2** [U] (= ∼ship) connection; what there is between one thing, person, idea, etc and another or others: *the ∼ between mother and child/between weather and the crops. The effort and expense needed for this project bore no ∼/were out of all ∼ to the results,* were not proportional to the results. *in/with ∼ to,* as regards; concerning. **3** (usu *pl*) dealings; affairs; what one person, group, country etc, has to do with another: *have business ∼s with a firm in Stockholm; the friendly ∼s between my country and yours; diplomatic ∼s. I have broken off all ∼s with that fellow, I have nothing to do with him now.* ˌpublic reˈlations officer, ⇨ public, *adj*(1). **4** [U] kinship (now usu ∼ship); [C] kinsman or kinswoman; relative(2): *He's a near ∼ of mine. She's a ∼ by marriage.* ∼·ship /-ʃɪp/ *n* **1** ∼(2): *He admitted his affair with Susan could never develop into a lasting ∼ship.* **2** [U] (= ∼(4)) condition of belonging to the same family; being connected by birth or marriage. **3** [C] instance of being related; particular connection or ∼ (*between/to/with*).

rela·tive /'relətɪv/ *adj* **1** comparative: *the ∼ advantages of two methods/of gas and electricity for heating. They are living in ∼ comfort,* ie compared with other people or with themselves at an earlier time. **2** ∼ **to,** referring to; having a connection with: *the facts ∼ to this problem; the papers ∼ to the case.* **3** (gram) ∼ **adverb** (eg *where* in 'the place where the accident occurred'). ∼ **clause,** one joined by a ∼ *pron* or *adv* to the antecedent of the ∼ word. ∼ **pronoun** (eg *whom* in 'the man whom we saw'). □ *n* [C] **1** ∼ word, esp a ∼ pronoun. **2** person to whom one is related (eg an uncle or aunt, a cousin, a nephew or niece). ∼·ly *adv* comparatively; in proportion to: *In spite of her dull husband she is ∼ly happy. The matter is unimportant,* ∼*ly speaking,* if we think of this matter in proportion to other matters.

rela·tiv·ity /ˌrelə'tɪvətɪ/ *n* [U] (esp) Einstein's theory of the universe, based on the principle that measures of motion, space and time are relative.

re·lax /rɪ'læks/ *vt,vi* **1** [VP6A] cause or allow to become less tight, stiff, strict or rigid: *∼ one's grip/hold on sth; ∼ the muscles; ∼ discipline; a ∼ed throat,* a form of sore throat; *a ∼ing climate,* (opp of *bracing*) one that causes an inclination to feel sluggish, lacking in energy. **2** [VP2A,C] become less tense, rigid, energetic, strict: *His severity ∼ed. His face ∼ed in a smile. Let's stop working and ∼ for an hour. He's feeling ∼ed now,* free from nervous anxiety, disturbing tensions, etc. ∼·ation /ˌriːlæk'seɪʃn/ *n* **1** [U] ∼ing or being ∼ed: *∼ation of the muscles.* **2** [U] recreation; [C] sth done for recreation: *Fishing and mountain-climbing are his favourite ∼ations.*

re·lay¹ /'riːleɪ/ *n* [C] **1** supply of fresh horses to take the place of tired horses; gang or group of men, supply of material, similarly used: *working in/by ∼s.* '∼ **race** *n* one between teams, each member of the team running, swimming, etc one section of the

total distance. **2** (telegraphy, broadcasting) device which receives messages, radio programmes, etc and transmits them with greater strength, thus increasing the distance over which they are carried. '∼ **station,** place from which radio programmes are broadcast after being received from another station. **3** (short for) ∼ race; ∼ed broadcast programme. □ *vt* /rɪ'leɪ/ (*pt,pp* ∼ed) send out (a broadcast programme received from another station).

re·lay² /ˌriː'leɪ/ *vt* (*pt,pp* -laid /-'leɪd/) lay (a cable, carpet, etc) again.

re·lease /rɪ'liːs/ *vt* [VP6A,14] ∼ *(from),* **1** allow to go; set free; unfasten: *∼ one's hold of sth; ∼ a man from prison/from a promise; ∼ a bomb (from an aircraft),* allow it to fall; *∼ a monk from his vows; ∼ sb from his suffering; ∼ the handbrake (of a car).* **2** allow (news) to be known or published; allow (a film) to be exhibited or (goods) to be placed on sale: *recently ∼d films/discs.* **3** (legal) give up or surrender (a right, debt, property) to another. □ *n* **1** [U] releasing or being ∼d; [C] instance of this: *obtain (a) ∼ from an obligation; an order for sb's ∼ from prison; the ∼ of a film for public exhibition; a'press ∼,* ie to the newspapers; *a feeling of ∼,* ie of freedom; *the newest ∼s,* eg films/discs; *on general ∼,* (of cinema films) available for seeing at the usual network of local cinemas. **2** [C] handle, lever, catch, etc that ∼s part of a machine: *the 'carriage ∼* (on a typewriter); (attrib) '∼ *gear; the '∼ button/knob.*

rel·egate /'relɪgeɪt/ *vt* [VP14] ∼ *sth/sb to sth,* **1** delegate². **2** dismiss to a lower position or condition: *He ∼d his wife to the position of a mere housekeeper.* (League football) *Will our team be ∼d to the second division?* **rel·ega·tion** /ˌrelɪ'geɪʃn/ *n* [U].

re·lent /rɪ'lent/ *vi* [VP2A] become less severe; give up unkind or cruel intentions: *At last their mother ∼ed and allowed the children to stay up and watch TV.* ∼·**less** *adj* without pity: *∼less persecution.* ∼·**less·ly** *adv*

rel·evant /'reləvənt/ *adj* ∼ *(to),* (closely) connected with what is happening, being discussed, done, etc: *have all the ∼ documents ready; supply the facts ∼ to the case.* ∼·**ly** *adv* **rel·evance** /-əns/, **rel·evancy** /-ənsɪ/ *nn*

re·liable /rɪ'laɪəbl/ *adj* that may be relied or depended upon: *∼ tools/assistants/information/ witnesses.* **re·li·ably** /-əblɪ/ *adv* **re·lia·bil·ity** /rɪˌlaɪə'bɪlətɪ/ *n* [U] state or quality of being ∼.

re·li·ance /rɪ'laɪəns/ *n* **1** [U] ∼ *on/upon,* trust; confidence: *Do you place much ∼ on your doctor? There is little ∼ to be placed on his promises.* **2** person or thing depended upon. **re·li·ant** /-ənt/ *adj* having ∼; trusting.

relic /'relɪk/ *n* [C] **1** part of the body, dress, etc of a saint or sth that belonged to him or was connected with him, kept after his death, as an object of reverence, and in some cases said to have miraculous powers. **2** sth that has survived from the past and that serves to keep memories alive: *a ∼ of early civilization,* eg a stone implement; *∼s of superstition.* **3** (*pl*) person's dead body or bones; what has survived destruction or decay.

re·lict /'relɪkt/ *n* (legal) widow: *Alice, ∼ of Arthur Williams.*

re·lief¹ /rɪ'liːf/ *n* [U] (used with the *indef art* as in examples, but not normally in the *pl*) **1** lessening or ending or removal of pain, distress, anxiety, etc:

The doctor's treatment gave/brought some/not much ~. *A doctor's task is to work for the* ~ *of suffering. She heaved a sigh of* ~ *when she was told that the child's life was not in danger. To my great* ~ *the difficulties were all overcome. It was a great* ~ *to find the children safe.* **2** that which brings ~(1); help given to those in need; food, clothes, money, etc for persons in trouble: *send* ~ *to people made homeless by floods; provide* ~ *for refugees; a'* ~ *fund; a'* ~ *road,* alternative road for one that has heavy traffic. **3** sth that makes a change from monotony or that relaxes tension: *We crossed wide stretches of moorland without* ~, with no change of scenery. *Shakespeare introduced comic scenes into his tragedies by way of* ~. **4** ~ *(of),* reinforcement of a besieged town; raising (of a siege): *The general hastened to the* ~ *of the fortress.* **5** (replacing of a person, persons, on duty by a) person or persons appointed to go on duty: *on duty from 8am to 8pm with only two hours'* ~; *happy to know that the* ~ *is on the way;* (attrib) *a '* ~ *driver.*

re·lief² /rɪ'liːf/ n ⇨ bas-~. **1** [U] method of carving or moulding in which a design stands out from a flat surface: *a profile of Julius Caesar in* ~; *in high/low* ~, with the background cut out to a deep/shallow degree. **2** [C] design or carving made in this way. **3** [U] (in drawing, etc) appearance of being done in ~ by the use of shading, colour, etc. '~ **map,** one showing hills, valleys, etc by shading or other means, not only by contour lines. **4** [U] (lit or fig) vividness; distinctness of outline. *be/stand out in* ~ *against,* be in contrast to: *The hills stood out in sharp* ~ *against the morning sky. His behaviour stood out in strong* ~ *against his declared principles.*

re·lieve /rɪ'liːv/ vt [VP6A] **1** give or bring relief¹ to; lessen or remove (pain or distress): *We were* ~d *to hear that you had arrived safely. The fund is for relieving distress among the flood victims.* ~ *one's feelings,* provide an outlet for them (eg by shedding tears, or by using strong language, behaving violently). ~ *oneself,* empty the bladder or bowels. ⇨ relief¹(3). **2** take one's turn on duty: ~ *the guard/the watch/a sentry. You will be* ~d *at noon.* ⇨ relief¹(5). **3** ~ *sb of sth,* **(a)** take it from him: *Let me* ~ *you of your suitcase,* carry it for you (which is more usu). **(b)** (joc) steal from: *The thief* ~d *him of his watch.* **(c)** dismiss from: *He was* ~d *of his post.* **4** bring into relief²; make (sth) stand out more clearly (*against* a dark background, etc).

re·lig·ion /rɪ'lɪdʒən/ n **1** [U] belief in the existence of a supernatural ruling power, the creator and controller of the universe, who has given to man a spiritual nature which continues to exist after the death of the body. **2** [C] one of the various systems of faith and worship based on such belief: *the great* ~s *of the world,* eg Christianity, Islam, Buddhism. **3** [U] life as lived under the rules of a monastic order: *Her name in* ~ *is Sister Mary,* This is her name as a nun. **4** matter of conscience; sth that one considers oneself bound to do: *She makes a* ~ *of keeping her house clean and tidy.*

re·lig·ious /rɪ'lɪdʒəs/ adj **1** of religion. **2** (of a person) devout; God-fearing. **3** of a monastic order: *a* ~ *house,* a monastery or convent. **4** scrupulous; conscientious: *do one's work with* ~ *care/ exactitude.* □ n a ~, person bound by monastic vows; monk or nun; (*pl,* unchanged in form) *the/*

some/several ~, persons bound by monastic vows. ~·*ly adv*

re·line /ˌriː'laɪn/ vt put a new lining in, eg a garment.

re·lin·quish /rɪ'lɪŋkwɪʃ/ vt **1** [VP6A] give up: ~ *a hope/a habit/a belief.* ~ *one's hold of/over sb/ sth,* give up control. **2** [VP14] ~ *sth (to sb),* surrender: ~ *one's rights/shares to a partner.*

reli·quary /'relɪkwərɪ US: -kwerɪ/ n (pl -ries) box, casket, or other receptacle for a relic or relics.

rel·ish /'relɪʃ/ n **1** [C,U] (sth used to give, or which has, a) special flavour or attractive quality: *Hunger is the best* ~ *for food. Some pastimes lose their* ~ *when one grows old.* **2** [U] liking (*for*); zest: *I have no further* ~ *for active pursuits now that I am 90.* □ vt [VP6A,D] enjoy; get pleasure out of: *I would* ~ *a lobster and a bottle of wine. She won't* ~ *having to get up before dawn to catch that train.*

re·live /ˌriː'lɪv/ vt live through, undergo, again: *That was an experience I should not like to* ~.

re·lo·cate /ˌriː'ləʊ'keɪt US: ˌriː'ləʊkeɪt/ vt,vi establish, become established, in a new place or area.

re·lo·ca·tion /ˌriː'ləʊ'keɪʃn/ n [U] putting in, moving to, a new place or area: *the relocation of industry; the relocation of population;* compulsory evacuation of persons from military areas during a war, with resettlement in a new area.

re·luc·tant /rɪ'lʌktənt/ adj ~ *(to do sth),* (slow to act because) unwilling or disinclined; offering resistance: ~ *helpers; a* ~ *recruit into the army. He seemed* ~ *to help us.* ~·*ly adv* **re·luc·tance** /-əns/ n [U].

rely /rɪ'laɪ/ vi (pt,pp -lied) [VP3A] ~ *on/upon,* depend upon with confidence, look to for help: *He can always be relied upon for help. You may* ~ *upon my early arrival. You may* ~ *upon it that he will be early.*

re·main /rɪ'meɪn/ vi **1** [VP2A] be still present after a part has gone or has been away: *After the fire, very little* ~ed *of my house. If you take 3 from 8, 5* ~s. *Much* ~s *to be settled.* **2** [VP2A,B,C,4A] continue in some place or condition; continue to be: *How many weeks shall you* ~ (= stay) *here? Let things* ~ *as they are. He* ~ed *silent. I shall* ~ (*stay* is more usu) *to see the end of the game. Man* ~ed *a hunter for thousands of years,* ie before beginning to cultivate crops, etc.

re·main·der /rɪ'meɪndə(r)/ n that which remains; persons or things that are left over: *Twenty people came in and the* ~ (= the rest, the others) *stayed outside.*

re·mains /rɪ'meɪnz/ n pl **1** what is left: *the* ~s *of a meal; the* ~s (= ruins) *of an old abbey/of ancient Rome.* **2** dead body; corpse: *His mortal* ~s *are buried in the churchyard.*

re·make /ˌriː'meɪk/ vt (pt,pp -made /-'meɪd/) make again. □ n /'riː'meɪk/ sth made again: *a* ~ *of a film.*

re·mand /rɪ'mɑːnd US: -'mænd/ vt [VP6A] send (an accused person) back (from a court of law) into custody so that more evidence may be obtained: ~ed *for a week.* □ n [U] ~ing or being ~ed: *detention on* ~. '~ *centre/home,* institution to which law-breaking children and adolescents are sent while inquiries are being made, or until the courts have decided their future treatment.

re·mark /rɪ'mɑːk/ vt,vi **1** [VP6A,9] say (*that*): *He* ~ed *that he would be absent the next day. 'I thought it was curious', he* ~ed. **2** [VP3A] ~ *on/ upon,* say sth by way of comment. *It would be* *rude to* ∼ *upon her appearance.* **3** [VP6A,9,10] (formal, old use) notice; see: *Did you* ∼ *the similarity between them?* □ *n* **1** [C] comment; sth said: *pass rude* ∼*s about sb; make a few* ∼*s,* give a short talk. **2** [U] notice; looking at: *There was nothing worthy of* ∼ *at the Flower Show.* ∼·**able** /-əbl/ *adj* out of the ordinary; deserving or attracting attention: *a* ∼*able event; a boy who is* ∼*able for his stupidity.* ∼·**ably** /-əblɪ/ *adv*

re·marry /ˌriːˈmærɪ/ *vt,vi* (*pt,pp* -ried) marry again. **re·mar·riage** /ˌriːˈmærɪdʒ/ *n*

rem·edy /ˈremədɪ/ *n* [C,U] (*pl* -dies) ∼ (*for*), cure (for a disease, evil, etc), method of, sth used for, putting right sth that is wrong: *a good* ∼ *for colds. The* ∼ *seems to be worse than the disease. Your only* ∼ (= way to get redress) *is to go to law. The evil is past/beyond* ∼, cannot be cured. □ *vt* [VP6A] put right; provide a ∼ for (evils, defects): *Your faults of pronunciation can be remedied.* **re·medial** /rɪˈmiːdɪəl/ *adj* providing, or intended to provide, a ∼: *remedial measures; remedial education/classes,* eg for children suffering disadvantages. **re·medi·able** /rɪˈmiːdɪəbl/ *adj* that can be remedied.

re·mem·ber /rɪˈmembə(r)/ *vt,vi* **1** [VP6A,C,7A,8,9,10,14,16B,19C] have or keep in the memory; call back to mind the memory of: *I can't* ∼ *his name. I* ∼*ed* (= did not forget) *to post your letters. I* ∼ *posting your letters* (= have the memory of that act in my mind). *I* ∼ *having heard you speak on that subject. Do you* ∼ *where you put the key? I* ∼ *her* (= picture her in my mind) *as a slim young girl. Please don't* ∼ *this unfortunate affair against me,* don't bear it in mind and, for that reason, be unfriendly to me. *'Have you ever met my brother?'—'Not that I* ∼.*'* I don't ∼ having met him. **2** [VP6A] make a present to: *Please* ∼ *the waiter,* don't forget to tip him. *I hope you'll* ∼ *me in your will,* leave me sth. **3** [VP14] ∼ **sb to sb,** convey greetings: *Please* ∼ *me to your brother.*

re·mem·brance /rɪˈmembrəns/ *n* **1** [U] remembering or being remembered; memory: *to the best of my* ∼; *have no* ∼ *of sth; a service in* ∼ *of those killed in the war.* **R**∼ **Day/Sunday,** (GB) Nov 11th, or the nearest Sunday, on which those killed in the two World Wars are commemorated. **2** [C] sth given or kept in memory of sb or sth: *He sent us a small* ∼ *of his visit.* **3** (*pl*) regards; greetings (⇨ regard¹(5)): *Give my kind* ∼*s to your parents.*

re·mili·tar·ize /ˌriːˈmɪlɪtəraɪz/ *vt* [VP6A] provide, occupy, again with armed forces and military equipment. **re·mili·tar·iz·ation** /ˌriːˌmɪlɪtəraɪˈzeɪʃn US: -rɪˈz-/ *n*

re·mind /rɪˈmaɪnd/ *vt* [VP6A,11,14,17,20,21] ∼ *sb* (*to do sth/that...*); ∼ *sb of sth/sb,* cause (sb) to remember (to do sth, etc); cause (sb) to think (of sth): *Please* ∼ *me to answer that letter. Travellers are* ∼*ed that inoculation against yellow fever is advisable. He* ∼*s me of his brother. This* ∼*s me of what we did together during our holidays. That* ∼*s me,...,* What you have just said ∼s me..., I've just remembered..., etc. ∼·**er** *n* sth (eg a letter) that helps sb to remember sth: *He hasn't paid me that money yet—I must send him a* ∼*er,* ie a letter to ∼ him about it.

remi·nisce /ˌremɪˈnɪs/ *vi* [VP2A,3A] ∼ (*about*), think or talk about past events and experiences.

remi·nis·cence /ˌremɪˈnɪsns/ *n* ∼ (*of*), **1** [U] reminiscing; recalling of past experiences. **2** (*pl*) remembered experiences; narrative, spoken or

written, of what sb remembers: ∼*s of my days in the Navy.* **3** sth that is suggestive (*of* sth else): *There is a* ∼ *of his father in the way he walks.*

remi·nis·cent /ˌremɪˈnɪsnt/ *adj* ∼ (*of*), **1** reminding one of; suggestive of: *Your face is* ∼ *of your mother's.* **2** recalling past experiences: *become* ∼. ∼·**ly** *adv*

re·miss /rɪˈmɪs/ *adj* ∼ **in,** careless of duty: *You have been* ∼ *in your duties.* ∼ *of,* negligent, lax: *That was very* ∼ *of you.* ∼·**ness** *n* [U].

re·mission /rɪˈmɪʃn/ *n* **1** [U] pardon or forgiveness (of sins, by God). **2** [U] freeing (from debt, punishment, etc): ∼ *of a claim;* [C] instance of this: ∼ (from a prison sentence) *for good conduct; No* ∼*s of examination fees are allowed.* **3** [U] lessening or weakening (of pain, efforts, etc): ∼ *of a fever.*

re·mit /rɪˈmɪt/ *vt,vi* (-tt-) **1** [VP6A] (of God) forgive (sins). **2** [VP6A] excuse (sb) payment (of a debt, a punishment): *The taxes have been* ∼*ted. Your fees cannot be* ∼*ted.* **3** [VP12A,13A,2C] send (money, etc) by post: *When can you* ∼ *me the money? Kindly* ∼ *by cheque,* send a cheque for the sum owing. **4** [VP6A] make or become less: ∼ *one's efforts.* **5** [VP14] ∼ **sth to sb,** take or send (a question to be decided) (to some authority): *The matter has been* ∼*ted to a higher tribunal.* ∼·**tance** /-ns/ *n* [U] the ∼ting, of money; [C] sum of money sent.

re·mit·tent /rɪˈmɪtnt/ *adj* (esp of a fever) that abates in severity at intervals.

rem·nant /ˈremnənt/ *n* [C] **1** small part that remains: ∼*s of a banquet;* ∼*s of former glory.* **2** (esp) length of cloth offered at a reduced price after the greater part has been sold: *a* ∼ *sale.*

re·mon·strance /rɪˈmɒnstrəns/ *n* [U] remonstrating (*with*); [C] protest (*against*).

re·mon·strate /ˈremənstreɪt/ *vi* [VP2A,3A] ∼ **with sb (about sth/that...),** make a protest; argue in protest: ∼ *with sb about his foolish behaviour;* ∼ *against cruelty to children.*

re·morse /rɪˈmɔːs/ *n* [U] **1** ∼ (*for*), deep, bitter regret for wrongdoing: *feel/be filled with* ∼ *for one's failure to help sb; in a fit of* ∼. **2** compunction: *without* ∼, merciless(ly). ∼·**ful** /-fl/ *adj* feeling ∼. ∼·**fully** /-fəlɪ/ *adv* ∼·**less** *adj* without ∼. ∼·**less·ly** *adv*

re·mote /rɪˈməʊt/ *adj* (-r, -st) ∼ (*from*), **1** far away in space or time: *in the* ∼*st parts of Asia; live in a house* ∼ *from any town or village; in the* ∼ *past/future.* ∼ **control,** control of apparatus, eg in an aircraft, a rocket, from a distance by means of radio signals. **2** widely separated (in feeling, interests, etc *from*): *Some of your statements are rather* ∼ *from the subject we are discussing.* **3** distant in manner; aloof. **4** (esp in the superl) slight: *a* ∼ *possibility; have not the* ∼*st idea of what sth means.* ∼·**ly** *adv* in a ∼ manner: *Gillian and I are* ∼*ly related.* ∼·**ness** *n*

re·mount¹ /ˌriːˈmaʊnt/ *vt,vi* [VP6A,2A] get on (a horse, bicycle, etc) again; go up (a ladder, hill, etc) again.

re·mount² /ˌriːˈmaʊnt/ *vt* [VP6A] **1** supply (a man, a regiment) with a fresh horse or horses. **2** put (a photograph, etc) on a new mount. □ *n* /ˈriːmaʊnt/ fresh horse; supply of fresh horses.

re·move¹ /rɪˈmuːv/ *vt,vi* **1** [VP6A,14] ∼ (*from*), take off or away from the place occupied; take to another place: ∼ *one's hat/coat;* ∼ *one's hand from sb's shoulder;* ∼ *the cloth from the table;* ∼ *a boy from school,* eg because of ill health. **2** [VP6A,14] ∼ (*from*), get rid of: ∼ *doubts/fears.*

What do you advise for removing grease/ink stains, etc from clothes? **3** [VP6A,14] ~ *(from),* dismiss: ~ *a man from office;* ~ *a Civil Servant.* **4** [VP2A,C] go to live in another place (move is more usu): *We're removing into the country next week/ removing from London to the country.* **5** ~*d from,* distant or remote from: *a dialect equally* ~*d from French and Spanish; an explanation far* ~*d from the truth.* **6** ~*d,* (of cousins) different by a generation: *first cousin once* ~*d,* first cousin's child. **re·mov·able** /-əbl/ *adj* that can be ~d (esp of a magistrate or other official who can be ~d from office at any time). ~r *n* **1** (esp) person who follows the business of moving furniture when people ~(4). **2** (in compounds) sth that ~s(2): *superfluous hair* ~*r.* **re·moval** /-vl/ *n* [U] act of removing: *the removal of furniture;* (attrib) *a re'moval van* (for furniture); *the removal of dissatisfaction;* [C] instance of removal.

re·move² /rɪ'muːv/ *n* stage or degree: *only a few* ~*s from....*

re·mun·er·ate /rɪ'mjuːnəreɪt/ *vt* [VP6A,14] ~ *sb (for sth),* pay (sb) (for work or services); reward. **re·mun·er·ation** /rɪ,mjuːnə'reɪʃn/ *n* [U] payment; reward. **re·mun·er·ative** /rɪ'mjuːnərətɪv *US:* -nəreɪtəv/ *adj* profitable.

re·nais·sance /rɪ'neɪsns *US:* 'renəsɑːns/ *n* **1 the R~,** (period of) revival of literature, painting, etc in Europe in the 14th, 15th and 16th cc, based on ancient Greek learning: (attrib) ~ *art.* **2** [C] any similar revival.

re·nal /'riːnl/ *adj* (anat) of or in the (region of the) kidneys: ~ *artery.*

re·name /,riː'neɪm/ *vt* [VP6A] give a new name to; name again.

re·nas·cence /rɪ'næsns/ *n* = renaissance(2). **re·nas·cent** /-snt/ *adj* springing up anew; reviving; being reborn.

rend /rend/ *vt* (*pt,pp* rent /rent/) [VP6A,14,15A] (liter) **1** pull or divide forcibly; penetrate: *a country rent (in two) by civil war. Loud cries rent the air.* **2** tear or pull (*off, away*) violently: *Children were rent from their mothers' arms by the brutal soldiers.*

ren·der /'rendə(r)/ *vt* **1** [VP6A,14,12A,13A,15A,B] ~ *sth (to sb),* give in return or exchange, or as sth due: ~ *thanks to God;* ~ *good for evil;* ~ *help to those in need;* ~ *a service to sb/*~ *sb a service;* ~ *up* (= surrender) *a fort to the enemy; a reward for services* ~*ed.* **2** [VP6A] present; offer; send in (an account for payment): *an account* ~*ed,* previously presented but not yet paid. *You will have to* ~ *an account of your expenditure.* ~ *an account of oneself/one's behaviour,* explain, justify oneself/it. **3** [VP22] cause to be (in some condition): ~*ed helpless by an accident.* **4** [VP6A,14] give a performance of (eg a drama, a character in a drama); express in another language: *The piano solo was well* ~*ed. 'Othello' was* ~*ed rather poorly. There are many English idioms that cannot be* ~*ed into other languages.* **5** [VP6A,15B] ~ *sth (down),* melt and make clear: ~ *down fat/lard.* **6** [VP6A] cover (stone, brick) with the first layer of plaster. ~·**ing** /'rendərɪŋ/ *n* (a) [C] way of performing, playing, translating, sth. ⇨ ~(4). (b) [U] first layer of plaster. ⇨ ~(6).

ren·dez·vous /'rɒndɪvuː/ *n* (*pl* ~ /-z/) [C] **1** (place decided upon for a) meeting at a time agreed upon. **2** place where people often meet: *This café is a* ~ *for writers and artists.* □ *vi* [VP2A,C] meet at a ~:

~ *in a café/beside a lake.*

ren·di·tion /ren'dɪʃn/ *n* [C] interpretation or rendering (of a song, etc).

ren·egade /'renɪgeɪd/ *n* [C] person who changes his religious beliefs; person who deserts his political party; traitor: (attrib) *a* ~ *priest.* □ *vi* turn ~.

re·nege, re·negue /rɪ'niːɡ/ *vi* **1** (in card games) revoke(2). **2** [VP3A] ~ *on,* fail to keep (one's word).

re·new /rɪ'njuː *US:* -'nuː/ *vt* [VP6A] **1** make (as good as) new; put new life and vigour into; restore to the original condition: ~ *one's youth; with* ~*ed enthusiasm.* **2** get, make, say or give, again: ~ *a lease/contract;* ~ *one's subscription to a periodical;* ~ *an attack;* ~ *one's complaints.* **3** replace (with the same sort of thing, etc): *We must* ~ *our supplies of coal. Snakes cast off and* ~ *their skins.* ~·**able** /-əbl/ *adj* that can be ~ed. ~**al** /-'njuːəl *US:* -'nuːəl/ *n* [U] ~ing or being ~ed: *delighted at the* ~*al of negotiations; urban* ~*al,* eg slum clearance for the provision of better housing. [C] sth ~ed.

ren·net /'renɪt/ *n* [U] preparation used in curdling milk for making cheese, etc.

re·nounce /rɪ'naʊns/ *vt* [VP6A] **1** declare formally that one will no longer have anything to do with, that one no longer recognizes (sb or sth having a claim to one's care, affection, etc): ~ *one's faith/ religion;* ~ *the world,* give up meeting people socially, begin to lead the life of a hermit, etc. **2** consent formally to give up (a claim, right, possession): ~ *one's claim to the throne/a peerage.* **3** disown; refuse to recognize: *He* ~*d his sons because they were criminals.*

reno·vate /'renəveɪt/ *vt* [VP6A] restore, eg old buildings, oil paintings, to good or strong condition. **reno·va·tor** /-tə(r)/ *n* person who ~s. **reno·va·tion** /,renə'veɪʃn/ *n* [U] renovating; [C] instance of this: *costly renovations of old college buildings at Oxford.*

re·nown /rɪ'naʊn/ *n* [U] fame: *win* ~; *a man of high* ~. **re·nowned** *adj* famous; celebrated: ~*ed as a portrait painter;* ~*ed for his skill.*

rent¹ /rent/ *n* [C,U] regular payment for the use of land, a building, a room or rooms, machinery, etc; sum of money paid in this way: *owe three weeks'* ~ *for one's house; live in a house free of* ~, without paying ~; *pay a heavy/high* ~ *for farming land; collect the* ~*s.* '~**-collector** *n* person who goes from house to house to collect ~s for the owner(s). ,~-'**free** *adj, adv: a* ~*-free house,* for which no ~ is charged to the tenant; *occupy a house* ~*-free.* ,~-'**rebate** *n* rebate, based on earnings and the amount of ~ payable, given by a local government authority on ~ paid, esp by council tenants. '~**-roll** *n* (a) register of a person's land and buildings with the ~s due from them. (b) total income from ~s. □ *vt,vi* **1** [VP6A,14] ~ *(from/to),* occupy or use (land, buildings, etc) for ~; allow (land, buildings, etc) to be used or occupied in return for ~: *We don't own our house, we* ~ *it from Mr Gay. Mr Hill* ~*s this land to us at £50 a year.* **2** [VP2A,C] be ~ed: *The building* ~*s at £150 a year.* ~·**able** *adj* that may be ~ed; able to yield a ~. ~**al** /'rentl/ *n* [C] amount of ~ paid or received; income from ~s.

rent² /rent/ *n* [C] **1** torn place in cloth, etc; split: ~ *in his shirt.* **2** (fig) division or split (in a political party, etc).

rent³ /rent/ *pt,pp* of rend.

rent·ier /'rɒntieɪ/ *n* person whose income comes

from investments and/or rents from property.

re·nunci·ation /rɪˌnʌnsɪ'eɪʃn/ n [U] renouncing, self-denial.

re·open /riː'əʊpən/ vt,vi [VP6A,2A] open again after closing or being closed: ~ a shop; ~ a discussion. School ~s on Monday.

re·or·gan·ize /riː'ɔːgənaɪz/ vt,vi organize again or in a new way.

re·orien·tate /riː'ɔːrɪənteɪt/ (also **re·orient** /riː'ɔːrɪənt/) vt,vi orient(ate) again or anew.

rep¹, repp /rep/, **reps** /reps/ n [U] textile fabric used in upholstery.

rep² /rep/ n (colloq abbr of) representative(n(2)) of a commercial firm; commercial traveller.

rep³ /rep/ n (colloq abbr of) repertory company or theatre: act in rep.

re·pair¹ /rɪ'peə(r)/ vt [VP6A] 1 restore (sth worn or damaged) to good condition: ~ the roads/a puncture/a watch/a shirt. 2 put right again: ~ an error. □ n 1 [U] ~ing or being ~ed: road under ~. 2 (pl) work or process of ~ing: The shop will be closed during ~s. The ~s needed before we can occupy the house will be considerable. 3 [U] relative condition for using or being used: The machine is in a bad state of ~/in good ~. ~·able /-əbl/ adj that can be ~ed. ~·er n one who ~s things: boot and shoe ~ers.

re·pair² /rɪ'peə(r)/ vi [VP3A] ~ to, (formal) go to (esp go frequently, go in large numbers to): ~ to the seaside resorts for the summer.

rep·ar·able /'repərəbl/ adj (of a loss, etc) that can be made good.

rep·ar·ation /ˌrepə'reɪʃn/ n [U] act of compensating for loss or damage; (pl) compensation for war damages, demanded from a defeated enemy.

rep·ar·tee /ˌrepɑː'tiː/ n [C] witty, clever retort; [U] the making of such retorts: He's good at ~.

re·past /rɪ'pɑːst US: -'pæst/ n (formal) meal: The guests partook of a luxurious ~ in the banqueting hall.

re·pat·ri·ate /riː'pætrɪeɪt US: -'peɪt-/ vt [VP6A] send or bring (sb) back to his own country: ~ refugees after a war. □ n ~d person. **re·pat·ri·ation** /ˌriː'pætrɪ'eɪʃn US: -ˌpeɪt-/ n

re·pay /rɪ'peɪ/ vt,vi (pt,pp -paid /-'peɪd/) 1 [VP6A] pay back (money): If you'll lend me 75p, I'll ~ you next week. 2 [VP6A,14] ~ sth; ~ sb (for sth), give in return: ~ sb's kindness; ~ sb for his kindness. I have been repaid (for the help I gave) only with ingratitude. 3 [VP2A] give equal favour (or justice) in return: God will ~, eg will punish injustice. ~·able /-əbl/ adj that can or must be repaid. ~·ment n [U] ~ing; [C] instance of this: bonds due for ~ment.

re·peal /rɪ'piːl/ vt [VP6A] revoke, annul (a law, etc) □ n ~ing.

re·peat /rɪ'piːt/ vt,vi 1 [VP6A,9] say or do again: ~ a word/a mistake. I ~ that I cannot undertake the task. Don't ~ yourself, say or do the same thing more than once (usu without being aware of doing so). Does history ~ itself, Do similar events or situations recur? '~ing watch/rifle, ⇨ repeater below. 2 [VP6A] say (what sb else has said or what one learnt by heart): You must not ~ what I've told you; it's very confidential. His language won't bear ~ing, eg contained too many curses, swear words, etc. 3 [VP6A] (of food) continue to be tasted after being eaten: Do you find that onions ~? 4 [VP2A] (of numbers, eg decimals) recur: The last two figures ~. 5 [VP6A] (comm) supply a further

consignment of: We regret that we cannot ~ this article. □ n 1 [C] ~ing (eg of an item in a programme) of a performance: (attrib) a ~ performance; a ~ order, (comm) an order for a further consignment of goods similar to an earlier one. There will be a ~ (= another broadcast) of this talk on Friday. 2 (music) mark indicating a passage intended to be repeated. ~·ed part adj: ~ed questioning/banging. ~·ed·ly adv again and again. ~er n revolver or rifle which can be fired a number of times without being reloaded (now usu a (semi-)automatic or self-loading rifle).

re·pel /rɪ'pel/ vt (-ll-) [VP6A] 1 drive back or away; refuse to accept: ~ the enemy/temptation; ~ a young man's advances, discourage him. 2 cause a feeling of dislike in: His long, rough beard ~led her. ~·lent /-ənt/ adj tending to ~; unattractive; uninviting: ~lent work/food. His manner is rather ~lent. □ n [U] sth that ~s, esp a preparation that ~s insects: Smear some of this mosquito ~lent on your legs.

re·pent /rɪ'pent/ vi,vt [VP2A,3A,6A,D] ~ (of), think with regret or sorrow of; be full of regret (about); wish one had not done (sth): He ~ed of what he had done. Don't you ~ (of) having wasted your money so foolishly? He has bitterly ~ed his folly. Have you nothing to ~ of? ~·ance /-əns/ n [U] regret for wrongdoing: show ~ance (for sth). ~·ant /-ənt/ adj feeling or showing ~ance: a ~ant sinner; ~ant of his folly; the righteous and the ~ant. ~·ant·ly adv

re·per·cussion /ˌriːpə'kʌʃn/ n 1 [U] springing back; driving or throwing back; [C] sth thrown or driven back; echoing sound: the ~ of the waves from the rocks. 2 [C] (usu pl) far-reaching and indirect effect (of an event, etc): The assassination of the President was followed by ~s throughout the whole country.

rep·er·toire /'repətwɑː(r)/ n [C] all the plays, songs, pieces, etc which a company, actor, musician, etc, is prepared to perform, etc: She has a large ~ of songs.

rep·er·tory /'repətrɪ US: -tɔːrɪ/ n (pl -ries) [C] 1 = repertoire. '~ company/theatre, (common abbr rep) one in which the actors/plays are changed regularly (instead of having long runs as in most London theatres). 2 store or collection, esp of facts, information, etc: My father is a ~ of useful information.

rep·eti·tion /ˌrepɪ'tɪʃn/ n 1 [U] repeating or being repeated; [C] instance of this: after numerous ~s. 2 [C] further recurrence: Let there be no ~ of this, Don't do it again. 3 [C] piece (of poetry, etc) set to be learnt by heart and repeated. **rep·eti·tious** /ˌrepɪ'tɪʃəs/, **re·peti·tive** /rɪ'petətɪv/ adjj characterized by ~: the repetitive work of a factory's production line.

re·pine /rɪ'paɪn/ vi [VP2A,3A] ~ (at), (formal) be discontented with: ~ at misfortune. ~ against, fret against: ~ against Providence.

re·place /rɪ'pleɪs/ vt [VP6A,15A] 1 put back in its place: ~ a dictionary on the shelf; ~ the receiver, ie after telephoning. 2 [VP6A] take the place of: Have buses ~d trams in your town? Can anything ~ a mother's love and care? 3 [VP14] ~ sb/sth by/with, supply as a substitute for: ~ coal by/with oil. ~·able /-əbl/ adj that can be ~d. ~·ment n [U] replacing or being ~d: the ~ment of worn-out parts; [C] sb or sth that ~s: get a ~ment (ie sb to do one's work) while one is away on holiday.

re·play /ˌriːˈpleɪ/ vt [VP6A] play (eg a football match that was drawn) again. □ n /ˈriːpleɪ/ [C] ~ed match; ~ing of a record, etc.

re·plen·ish /rɪˈplenɪʃ/ vt [VP6A,14] ~ (with), fill up (sth) again; get a new supply of or for: I must ~ my wardrobe. ~·ment n

re·plete /rɪˈpliːt/ adj ~ (with), (formal) filled with; holding as much as possible: ~ with food; feeling ~; a home ~ with every modern convenience. **re·ple·tion** /rɪˈpliːʃn/ n [U] (formal) state of being ~: Is it wrong to eat to repletion?

rep·lica /ˈreplɪkə/ n [C] exact copy (esp one made by an artist of one of his own pictures): make a ~ of a painting.

re·ply /rɪˈplaɪ/ vi,vt (pt,pp -plied) [VP2A,3A,B] ~ (to), give as an answer to, in words or action: He failed to ~ (to my question). 'Certainly not,' he replied. He replied that I could please myself. The enemy replied to our fire, fired in return. David Jones rose to ~ for (= speak on behalf of) the guests. □ n act of ~ing; what is replied: He made no ~. What did he say in ~?, ~-'paid, (of a telegram, letter, etc) with the cost of the ~ prepaid by the sender.

re·point /riːˈpɔɪnt/ vt [VP6A] point (brickwork, etc) again. ⇨ point²(5).

re·port¹ /rɪˈpɔːt/ n 1 [C] account of, statement about, sth heard, seen, done, etc: ~s on the state of the roads, eg from an automobile association; the annual ~ of a business company; the chairman's ~, ⇨ chairman at chair; 'law ~s, ie of trials, etc, in the law courts; a school ~, eg by teachers about a pupil, with his examination marks, etc; newspaper ~s. 2 [U] common talk; rumour; [C] piece of gossip: R~ has it that..., People are saying that.... We have only ~(s) (ie no reliable news) to go on. Don't listen to idle ~s. 3 [U] (formal) repute; way a person or thing is spoken about: of good/evil ~. 4 [C] sound of an explosion: the ~ of a gun. It went off with a loud ~.

re·port /rɪˈpɔːt/ vt,vi 1 [VP6A,D,9,25,3A,15B] give an account of (sth seen, heard, done, etc); give as news: The discovery of a new planet has been ~ed. It is ~ed that another earth satellite has been put into orbit. They ~ed the enemy to be ten miles away. He ~ed having seen the escaped convict. ~ on sth, give news about or comment on it: Jim's been sent to Hong Kong to ~ on the situation there. ~ sth out, (US) return it with comment: The committee ~ed the proposal out in record time. ~ progress, state what has been done so far. ~ed·ly adv according to report(s). 2 [VP6A,2A] take down (eg in shorthand) the words of speeches, etc for newspapers, etc: ~ a speech/a Parliamentary debate; ~ for 'The Times', be a correspondent on its staff. ~ed speech, = indirect speech. ⇨ indirect. 3 [VP3A,14,15A] ~ (oneself) (to sb/ sth) (for sth), go (somewhere), and announce that one has come, that one is ready for work, duty, etc: ~ for duty at the office; ~ to the Manager. The officer was told to ~ (himself) to headquarters. 4 [VP6A,14] ~ sb/sth (to sb) (for sth), make a complaint against sb (to authorities): ~ an official for insolence. I shall have to ~ your unpunctuality to the Manager. ~·age /ˌrepɔːˈtɑːʒ/ n [U] (typical style of) ~ing events for newspapers. ~er n person who ~s for a newspaper, for radio or TV.

re·pose¹ /rɪˈpəʊz/ vt [VP14] ~ sth in sth/sb, (formal) place (trust, confidence, etc) in: Don't ~ too much confidence in that man/in his honesty/his promises, etc.

re·pose² /rɪˈpəʊz/ vt,vi (formal) 1 [VP6A,15A,2A,C] rest; give rest or support to: a girl reposing in a hammock; ~ one's head on a cushion; ~ oneself. Below this stone ~ the mortal remains of.... 2 [VP3A] ~ on, be based or supported on. □ n [U] (formal) 1 rest; sleep: earn a night's ~; disturb sb's ~. Her face is beautiful in ~. 2 peaceful, restful or quiet behaviour or appearance: His attitude lacked ~, ease of manner. ~·ful /-fl/ adj calm; quiet.

re·posi·tory /rɪˈpɒzɪtrɪ US: -tɔːrɪ/ n [C] (pl -ries) place where things are or may be stored: The drawers in my desk are repositories for all sorts of useless papers. My grandfather is a ~ of interesting facts.

re·pot /ˌriːˈpɒt/ vt transfer (a plant) from one pot to another (usu larger) pot.

rep·re·hend /ˌreprɪˈhend/ vt [VP6A] rebuke, reprove: ~ sb's conduct. **rep·re·hen·sible** /ˌreprɪˈhensəbl/ adj deserving to be ~ed.

rep·re·sent¹ /ˌreprɪˈzent/ vt 1 [VP6A] be, give, make, a picture, sign, symbol or example of: Phonetic symbols ~ sounds. This painting ~s a hunting scene. The new ambassador ~s the best traditions of his country. 2 [VP16A,25,9] declare to be; describe (as); allege (that...): He ~ed himself as an expert. I am not what you have ~ed me to be. 3 [VP6A,9,14] ~ sth (to sb), explain; make clear: Let me try to ~ my ideas to you in another way/in different terms. 4 [VP6A,14,9] ~ sth (to sb), convey; express: They ~ed their grievances to the Governor. I will ~ to him the risks he is running. He ~ed to the magistrates that the offender was only a child. 5 [VP6A] act or speak for; be MP for; be agent for: members (ie MP's) ~ing Welsh constituencies. Many countries were ~ed by their ambassadors at the Independence Day celebrations. Our firm is ~ed in India and Pakistan by Mr Hall. 6 [VP6A] act (a play, etc); play the part of, on the stage. **rep·re·sen·ta·tion** /ˌreprɪzenˈteɪʃn/ n 1 [U] ~ing or being ~ed; [C] that which is ~ed: no taxation without ~ation, ie citizens should not be taxed without being ~ed (in Parliament, etc); an unusual ~ation of 'Hamlet'. **proportional ~ation**, an electoral system designed so that minority parties, etc are ~ed (in a legislative assembly) in proportion to their strength. 2 [C] (esp) polite protest or remonstrance: make ~ations to the Inspector of Taxes about an excessive assessment.

re·pre·sent² /ˌriːprɪˈzent/ vt submit again: Your cheque has been returned; please ~ it when you have funds in your account.

rep·re·sen·ta·tive /ˌreprɪˈzentətɪv/ adj 1 ~ (of), serving to portray or show; serving as an example of a class or group; containing examples of a number of classes or groups: manuscripts ~ of monastic life; a ~ collection of domestic utensils of the Middle Ages. 2 consisting of elected deputies; based on representation by such elected deputies: ~ government/institutions. □ n [C] ~ (of), 1 example; typical specimen (of a group or class). 2 person elected or appointed to represent or act for others: send a ~ to a conference; sole ~s of the XYZ Petrol Company in Cardiff; ~s of the press, newspaper reporters; our ~ (= MP) in the House of Commons. **the House of R~s**, the lower house of the US Congress or of a state legislature.

re·press /rɪˈpres/ vt [VP6A] keep or put down or under; prevent from finding an outlet: ~ a revolt;

~ *sedition;* ~ *a sneeze;* ~ *an impulse;* ~*ed emotions.* ~*ed* *adj* suffering from repression (b). **re·pres·sion** /rɪ'preʃn/ *n* (a) [U] ~ing or being ~ed. (b) [U] (psych) forcing into the unconscious of impulses and desires, esp those in conflict with accepted standards of conduct, often resulting in abnormal behaviour; [C] impulse or instinct ~ed in this way. **re·pres·sive** /rɪ'presɪv/ *adj* serving or tending to ~: ~*ive legislation. The* ~*ive measures taken by the police were condemned in Parliament.*

re·prieve /rɪ'priːv/ *vt* [VP6A] postpone or delay punishment (esp the execution of sb condemned to death); (fig) give relief for a short time (from danger, trouble, etc). □ *n* [C] (order giving authority for) postponement or remission of punishment (esp by death); (fig) delay or respite: *grant (sb) a* ~.

re·pri·mand /'reprɪmɑːnd *US:* -mænd/ *vt* [VP6A] rebuke (sb) severely and officially (for a fault, etc). □ *n* [C] official rebuke.

re·print /ˌriː'prɪnt/ *vt* [VP6A] print again; print a new impression of: *The book is* ~*ing,* being ~ed. □ *n* /'riːprɪnt/ [C] new impression of sth printed (usu without alterations). ⇨ edition.

re·prisal /rɪ'praɪzl/ *n* **1** [U] paying back injury with injury: *do sth by way of* ~. **2** (*pl*) acts of retaliation, esp of one country on another during a war.

re·proach /rɪ'prəʊtʃ/ *vt* [VP6A,14] ~ *sb (for/with sth),* find fault with (sb, usu with a feeling of sorrow, or suggesting the need for sorrow): ~ *sb with extravagance/for being late. We have nothing to* ~ *ourselves with,* have done nothing we need regret. □ *n* **1** [U] ~ing: *a term/look of* ~. **2** [C] instance of ~ing; word, phrase, etc that ~es: *She heaped* ~*es upon her sister.* **3** [U] state of disgrace or discredit: *bring* ~ *upon oneself.* **above/beyond** ~, perfect; blameless. **4** [C] ~ *(to),* sth that brings disgrace or discredit (to): *slums that are a* ~ *to the city council.* ~*·fully* /-flɪ/ *adj* full of ~; expressing ~: *a* ~*ful look.* ~*·fully* /-fəlɪ/ *adv*

rep·ro·bate /'reprəbeɪt/ *vt* [VP6A] express or feel strong disapproval of. □ *n* depraved person; person with no respect for moral behaviour. **rep·ro·ba·tion** /ˌreprə'beɪʃn/ *n* [U].

re·pro·duce /ˌriːprə'djuːs *US:* -'duːs/ *vt,vi* **1** [VP6A] cause to be seen, heard, etc again: ~ *music from*

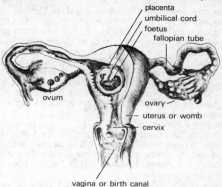

placenta
umbilical cord
foetus
fallopian tube
ovum
ovary
uterus or womb
cervix
vagina or birth canal

the female reproductive organs in early pregnancy

magnetic tape. This record/record-player ~*s every sound perfectly. The artist has* ~*d your features very well in this portrait.* **2** [VP6A,2A] bring forth as offspring; bring about a natural increase: ~ *one's kind; plants that* ~ *by spores,* eg ferns. **3** [VP6A] grow anew (a part that is lost, etc): *Can lizards* ~ *their tails? Human beings cannot* ~ *lost limbs.* ~**r** *n* one who, that which, ~s. **re·pro·duc·ible** /-əbl/ *adj* that can be ~d. **re·pro·duc·tion** /ˌriːprə'dʌkʃn/ *n* [U] process of reproducing; [C] sth ~d; copy of sth, esp a work of art. **re·pro·duc·tive** /ˌriːprə'dʌktɪv/ *adj* reproducing; for, relating to, reproduction: *reproductive organs.*

re·proof[1] /rɪ'pruːf/ *n* **1** [U] blame; finding fault: *a glance of* ~; *conduct deserving of* ~. **2** [C] expression of blame or disapproval: *administer sharp* ~s.

re·proof[2] /ˌriː'pruːf/ *vt* [VP6A] make (a coat, etc) waterproof again.

re·prove /rɪ'pruːv/ *vt* [VP6A,14] ~ *sb (for sth),* find fault with; say sharp words to: *The priest* ~*d the people for not attending church services.* **re·prov·ing·ly** *adv*

rep·tile /'reptaɪl *US:* -tl/ *n* cold-blooded egg-laying animal that creeps or crawls, eg *a lizard, tortoise, crocodile, snake.* ⇨ the illus here and at

reptiles

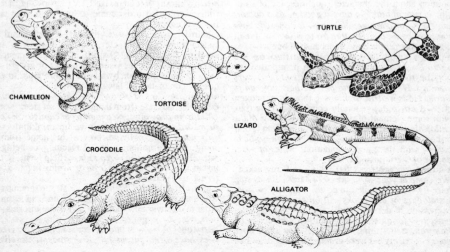

CHAMELEON

TORTOISE

TURTLE

LIZARD

CROCODILE

ALLIGATOR

snake. rep·til·ian /rep'tɪlɪən/ adj of, or like a ~.

re·pub·lic /rɪ'pʌblɪk/ n 1 (country with a) system of government in which the elected representatives of the people are supreme, with an elected head (the President), as eg in the US, France, India. (in France) the First R~, 1789—1804; the Second R~, 1848—1852; the Third R~, 1871—1940; the Fourth R~, 1947—58; the Fifth R~, from 1958. 2 any society in which the members have equal rights and privileges: the ~ of letters, literary men as a class.

re·pub·li·can /rɪ'pʌblɪkən/ adj of, relating to, supporting the principles of, a republic. □ n 1 person who favours ~ government. 2 R~, member of one of the two main political parties in the US (the other is Democrat). ~·ism /-ɪzəm/ n [U] (adherence to) ~ principles.

re·pudi·ate /rɪ'pju:dɪeɪt/ vt [VP6A] 1 disown; say that one will have nothing more to do with: ~ an old friend/a wicked son. 2 refuse to accept or acknowledge: ~ the authorship of an article, declare that one did not write it. 3 refuse to pay (an obligation or debt). re·pudi·ation /rɪ,pju:dɪ'eɪʃn/ n

re·pug·nant /rɪ'pʌgnənt/ adj ~ (to), distasteful; causing a feeling of dislike or opposition: I find his views/proposals ~. All food was ~ to me during my illness. re·pug·nance /-nəns/ n [U] ~ (to), strong dislike or distaste: a great repugnance to accept charity; the repugnance she has to writing letters.

re·pulse /rɪ'pʌls/ vt [VP6A] 1 repel; drive back (the enemy); resist (an attack) successfully. 2 (not replaceable by repel) refuse to accept (sb's help, friendly offers, etc); discourage (a person) by unfriendly treatment. □ n repulsing or being ~d. re·pul·sion /rɪ'pʌlʃn/ n [U] 1 feeling of dislike or distaste: feel repulsion for sb. 2 (phys) (opp of attraction) tendency of bodies to repel each other.

re·pul·sive /rɪ'pʌlsɪv/ adj 1 causing a feeling of disgust: a ~ sight; a ~-looking beggar. 2 (phys) repelling; exercising repulsion(2): ~ forces. ~·ly adv in a ~ manner; ~ly ugly.

repu·table /'repjʊtəbl/ adj respected; of good repute: ~ occupations; a ~ wine merchant. repu·tably /-əblɪ/ adv

repu·ta·tion /,repjʊ'teɪʃn/ n [U,C] the general opinion about the character, qualities, etc of sb or sth: a man of high ~; have a good ~ as a doctor; have a ~ for courage; make a ~ for oneself; have the ~ of being a miser. live up to one's ~, live in the way that people expect (because of one's ~).

re·pute /rɪ'pju:t/ vt [VP25] (usu passive) be ~d as/to be, be generally considered or reported (to be), be thought of as: He is ~ed (to be) very wealthy. He is ~d (as/to be) the best surgeon in Paris. He is well/ill/highly ~d, thought or spoken of. ~d attrib adj generally considered to be (but with some element of doubt): the ~d father of the child; his ~d learning. □ n [U] 1 reputation (good or bad): know a man by ~; be held in high ~; be in bad ~ with sb. 2 good reputation: wines of ~; a doctor of ~. re·put·ed·ly adv

re·quest /rɪ'kwest/ n 1 [U] asking or being asked: We came at your ~/at the ~ of Mr X. Buses stop here by ~, if signalled to do so. This is a ~ stop. Catalogues of our books will be sent on ~. 2 [C] expression of desire for sth: repeated ~s for help; make a ~ for quiet; your ~ that I should lecture on Pakistan. 3 [C] thing asked for: You shall have your ~. All my ~s were granted. 4 [U] state of be-

ing in demand, sought after. in ~, often asked for. □ vt [VP6A,9,17] ~ sth (from/of sb); ~ sb to do sth, make a ~: Visitors are ~ed not to touch the exhibits, as a notice in a museum, etc. All I ~ of you is that you should be early. I ~ed him to use/ ~ed that he (should) use his influence on my behalf.

requiem /'rekwɪəm/ n [C] (musical setting for a) special mass for the repose of the soul of a dead person.

re·quire /rɪ'kwaɪə(r)/ vt 1 [VP6A,D,9] need; depend on for success, fulfilment, etc: We ~ extra help. Does this machine ~ much attention? The situation there ~s that I should be present. 2 [VP6A,9,14,17] ~ sth (of sb); ~ sb to do sth; ~ that..., (often passive) (formal) order; demand; insist upon as a right or by authority: Students are ~d to take three papers in English literature. What do you ~ of me? It is ~d that you arrive at 8am. I have done all that is ~d by law. These books are ~d reading, must be read, eg for an examination. ~·ment n sth ~d or needed: fulfil the ~ments of the law; meet sb's ~ments, do what he wants done.

requi·site /'rekwɪzɪt/ n, adj ~ (for), (thing) needed or required by circumstances or for success: We supply every ~ for travel/all travelling ~s. They lack the ~ capital for expanding their business.

requi·si·tion /,rekwɪ'zɪʃn/ n [U] act of requiring or demanding; [C] formal and usu written demand (for sth or that sth should be done): a ~ for supplies, eg by army authorities during a war; make a ~ on the citizens for stores. The hotel bus was in constant ~ (= was needed all the time) for bringing visitors from, and taking them back to, the railway station. □ vt [VP6A,14] ~ (for), make a ~ for: ~ food for the troops; ~ sb's services; ~ a town for supplies/lodgings, eg during a war.

re·quite /rɪ'kwaɪt/ vt [VP6A,14] ~ sth/sb (with sth), (formal) 1 repay; give in return: ~ kindness with ingratitude; ~ an obligation. Will she ever ~ my love? 2 take vengeance on. re·qui·tal /-tl/ n [U] repayment: receive food and lodging in requital for/of one's services; make full requital.

rere·dos /'rɪədɒs US: 'rerədɒs/ n (pl ~es /-dɒsɪz/) [C] ornamental screen covering the wall at the back of a church altar.

re·run /'ri:rʌn/ n (cinema and TV) reshowing of a film or recorded programme. □ vt (-nn-) show a film, etc again.

re·scind /rɪ'sɪnd/ vt [VP6A] (legal) repeal, annul, cancel (a law, contract, etc).

re·script /'ri:skrɪpt/ n [C] 1 official announcement, esp an edict or decree issued by a ruler or government. 2 decision made by a Pope (esp in reply to a question on matters of law or morality).

res·cue /'reskju:/ vt [VP6A,14] ~ sb from sth/sb, deliver, make safe (from danger, etc); set free: ~ a child from drowning; ~ a man from captivity; ~ a drunkard, persuade him to give up drinking; ~ sb's name from oblivion, prevent his name from being quite forgotten. □ n [U] rescuing or being ~d. come/go to the ~/to sb's ~, help them; [C] instance of this: three ~s from drowning in one afternoon. res·cuer n

re·search /rɪ'sɜ:tʃ US: 'ri:sɜ:tʃ/ n [U,C] (not usu with many or numerals) investigation undertaken in order to discover new facts, get additional information, etc: be engaged in ~; busy with ~ work; carry out (a) ~/~es into the causes of cancer. His ~es have been successful. R~ students usually *supplement their income by teaching.* R~ *workers are examining the problem.* □ *vi* [VP2A,3A] ~ *(into),* make ~s (into a problem, etc). ~**er** *n*

re·seat /ˌriːˈsiːt/ *vt* [VP6A] **1** supply with a new seat: ~ *an old pair of trousers/a cane chair.* **2** sit on a seat again: *She stood up and then* ~*ed herself more comfortably.*

re·sem·blance /rɪˈzembləns/ *n* **1** [U] likeness; similarity: *There's very little* ~ *between them.* **2** [C] point or degree of likeness or similarity: *The boys show great* ~*s—are they twins?*

re·semble /rɪˈzembl/ *vt* [VP6B] be like; be similar to: *She* ~*s her mother. They* ~ *each other in shape but not in colour.*

re·sent /rɪˈzent/ *vt* [VP6A,19C] feel bitter, indignant or angry at: ~ *criticism. Does he* ~ *my being here?* ~**·ful** /-fl/ *adj* feeling or showing ~ment; inclined to ~. ~**·fully** /-fəlɪ/ *adv* ~·**ment** *n* [U] feeling that one has when insulted, ignored, injured, etc: *bear/feel no* ~*ment against anyone; walk away in* ~*ment.*

res·er·va·tion /ˌrezəˈveɪʃn/ *n* **1** [U] keeping or holding back; failure or refusal to express sth that is in one's mind; [C] that which is kept or held back: *accept sth without* ~, wholeheartedly, completely; *accept a plan with* ~*s,* with limiting conditions; *the central* ~ *of a motorway,* land dividing the two carriageways. **2** [C] (US) area of land reserved for a special purpose. ⇨ **reserve¹**(5). **3** [C] (esp US) travel arrangement to keep sth for sb, eg a seat in a train or aircraft, a passage on a ship, a room in a hotel: *My travel agents have made all the* ~*s for my journey.* ⇨ **book²**(2), for GB usages. **4** R~ **of the Sacrament,** practice of keeping back part of the bread used in the Eucharist for later use, eg at the home of a sick person.

re·serve¹ /rɪˈzɜːv/ *n* **1** [C] sth that is being or has been stored for later use: *a* ~ *of food; the bank's* ~*s,* ie of money; *the company's* ~*s,* its undivided profits; *the 'gold* ~, ie to cover the issue of notes; (attrib) *a '*~ *fund; his* ~ *strength.* **2** [C] (mil) military forces kept back for use when needed. **3** the R~, forces outside the regular Navy, Army and Air Force, liable to be called out if needed. **4** [U] *in* ~, kept back unused, but available if needed: *have/hold a little money in* ~. **5** [C] place or area reserved for some special use or purpose: *a '* game ~, eg in Africa, for the preservation of wild animals; *a 'forest* ~. **6** [C,U] (instance of) limitation or restriction; condition that limits or restricts: *We accept your statement without* ~, believe it completely. *He has put a* ~ *price on his house,* has fixed a price less than which will not be accepted. *He has placed a* ~ *on the painting,* ie a ~ price. **7** [U] self-control in speech and behaviour; keeping silent or saying little; not showing one's feelings: ~ *of manner; break through sb's* ~, get him to talk and be sociable. **re·serv·ist** /rɪˈzɜːvɪst/ *n* soldier or sailor belonging to the Army or Navy R~. ⇨ 3 above.

re·serve² /rɪˈzɜːv/ *vt* [VP6A,14] **1** store, keep back, for a later occasion: *R*~ *your strength for the climb. The judge* ~*d his judgement,* deferred announcing it until a future time. **2** keep for the special use of, or for a special purpose: *The first three rows of the hall are* ~*d for special guests.* **3** secure possession of, or the right to use, eg by advance payment: ~ *rooms at a hotel. All seats* ~*d,* ie the seats (in a theatre, concert hall, etc) can be obtained only by booking them in advance. *All*

rights ~*d,* (legal) secured or kept (for the owners of property, etc). **4** set apart, destine: *A great future is* ~*d for you.* ~**d** *adj* (of a person, his character) slow to reveal feelings or opinions; uncommunicative: *He is too* ~*d to be popular.* ~**d·ly** /rɪˈzɜːvɪdlɪ/ *adv*

res·er·voir /ˈrezəvwɑː(r)/ *n* [C] **1** place (often an artificial lake) where water is stored, eg for supplying a town; anything for holding a liquid: *the* ~ *of a fountain-pen/an oil lamp.* **2** (fig) supply (of facts, knowledge, etc).

re·set /ˌriːˈset/ *vt* (*pt,pp* reset; -tt-) [VP6A] **1** sharpen again: ~ *a saw.* **2** place in position again: ~ *a diamond in a ring;* ~ *a broken bone.* **3** (printing) set the type again. ⇨ **set²**(9).

re·settle /ˌriːˈsetl/ *vt,vi* [VP6A,2A] (esp of refugees) (help to) settle again in a new country: ~ *war refugees in Canada.* ~·**ment** *n*

re·shuffle /ˌriːˈʃʌfl/ *vt* [VP6A] shuffle again: ~ *the cards.* □ *n* shuffling again: *a Cabinet* ~, a redistribution of Cabinet posts among the same persons.

re·side /rɪˈzaɪd/ *vi* **1** [VP2C,3A] ~ *(in/at),* live (the more usu word), have one's home: ~ *abroad;* ~ *at 10 Railway Terrace.* **2** [VP3A] ~ *in,* (of power, rights, etc) be the property of, be present in: *The supreme authority* ~*s in the President.*

resi·dence /ˈrezɪdəns/ *n* **1** [U] residing: *take up one's* ~ *in a new house,* go and live in it. *in* ~, **(a)** (of an official, etc) living in the house officially provided for him. **(b)** (of students, etc) residing in a college, etc: *The students are not yet in* ~. **2** place where one resides; house (esp a large or dignified one): (as used by house-agents) *town and country* ~*s; this desirable family* ~ *for sale.*

resi·dency /ˈrezɪdənsɪ/ *n* [C] (*pl* -cies) official residence of a Resident(2).

resi·dent /ˈrezɪdənt/ *adj* residing: *the* ~ *population of the town* (contrasted with visitors, tourists, etc); *a* ~ *tutor,* one who lives in the household as a member of the family; *a* ~ *physician,* one who lives in the hospital, etc where he works. □ *n* **1** person who resides in a place (contrasted with a visitor). **2** R~, official sent to another country to act as adviser to the administration, etc.

resi·den·tial /ˌrezɪˈdenʃl/ *adj* **1** of residence: *the* ~ *qualifications for voters,* ie requiring that they should reside in the constituency. **2** of, with, private houses: *a* ~ *suburb;* ~ *parts of the town* (contrasted with business or industrial parts).

re·sid·ual /rɪˈzɪdjʊəl US: -dʒʊ-/ *adj* remaining; of, forming, a residue.

re·sid·u·ary /rɪˈzɪdjʊərɪ US: -dʒʊerɪ/ *adj* of a residue; (legal) relating to the residue of an estate: *the* ~ *legatee,* the person to whom the residue of an estate is left.

resi·due /ˈrezɪdjuː US: -duː/ *n* [C] that which remains after a part is taken or used; (legal) that part of an estate which is left after all particular bequests, debts, etc have been settled.

re·sign /rɪˈzaɪn/ *vt,vi* **1** [VP6A,2A,3A] ~ *(from),* give up (a post, position, etc): ~ *one's job;* ~ *one's position as secretary of the club;* ~ *from the Cabinet. The Minister of Education has* ~*ed.* **2** [VP14] ~ *sb/oneself to sb/sth,* hand over: *I* ~ *my children to your care/myself to your guidance.* **3** [VP14] ~ *oneself to sth/be* ~*ed to sth,* be ready to accept or endure uncomplainingly: *be* ~*ed to one's fate. We must* ~ *ourselves to leaving the country.* ~**ed** *adj* having or showing patient acceptance of sth: *with a* ~*ed look.* ~·**ed·ly** /-ɪdlɪ/

adv in a ~ed manner.

res·ig·na·tion /ˌrezɪgˈneɪʃn/ *n* **1** [U] resigning(1); [C] instance of this; letter (to one's employers, superior, etc) stating this: *offer/send in/hand in one's* ~. **2** [U] state of being resigned to conditions, etc; uncomplaining acceptance or endurance: *accept failure with* ~.

re·sil·ience /rɪˈzɪlɪəns/, **re·sil·iency** /-nsɪ/ *nn* [U] quality or property of quickly recovering the original shape or condition after being pulled, pressed, crushed, etc: *the* ~ *of rubber;* (fig) power of recuperating quickly; buoyancy: *the* ~ *of the human body.* **re·sil·ient** /-nt/ *adj* having or showing ~; (of persons) buoyant in disposition.

resin /ˈrezɪn US: ˈrezn/ *n* [C,U] sticky substance that flows out from most plants when cut or injured, esp from fir and pine trees, hardening in air, used in making varnish, lacquer, etc; kind of similar substance (plastics) made chemically, widely used in industry. ⇨ **rosin**. **res·in·ated** /ˈrezɪneɪtɪd US: -zən-/ *adj* flavoured, permeated, with ~. **re·sin·ous** /ˈrezɪnəs US: ˈrezənəs/ *adj* of or like ~.

re·sist /rɪˈzɪst/ *vt,vi* [VP6A,C,2A] **1** oppose; use force against in order to prevent the advance of: ~ *the enemy/an attack/authority/the police. He could* ~ *no longer.* **2** be undamaged or unaffected by: *a kind of glass dish that* ~s *heat,* that does not break or crack in a hot oven. **3** try not to yield to; keep oneself back from: ~ *temptation. She can't* ~ *chocolates. She couldn't* ~ *making jokes about his baldness.* ~**er** *n* person who ~s: *passive* ~ers. ~**·less** *adj* that cannot be ~ed; inevitable: *a* ~less *impulse.*

re·sis·tance /rɪˈzɪstəns/ *n* ~ *(to),* **1** [U] (power of) resisting: *break down the enemy's* ~; *make/offer no/not much* ~ *to the enemy's advance; drug* ~; *passive* ~, ⇨ **passive**. '~ **movement,** (in an enemy-occupied country) effort made by groups of unconquered people to resist the invaders. **2** [U] opposing force: *An aircraft has to overcome the* ~ *of the air.* **line of least** ~, direction in which a force meets least opposition; (fig) easiest way or method. **3** [C,U] antagonism; desire to oppose: '*sales/consumer* ~, unwillingness of the public to buy goods offered for sale. *A good advertisement should not arouse* ~ *in the public.*

re·sis·tant /rɪˈzɪstənt/ *adj* ~ *(to),* offering resistance: *insects that have become* ~ *to DDT;* ~ *strains of mosquitoes.*

re·sis·tor /rɪˈzɪstə(r)/ *n* device to provide resistance in an electric circuit.

re·sole /ˌriːˈsəʊl/ *vt* [VP6A] put a new sole on (a shoe).

res·ol·ute /ˈrezəluːt/ *adj* fixed in determination or purpose; firm: *a* ~ *man;* ~ *for peace.* ~**·ly** *adv* ~**·ness** *n*

res·ol·ution /ˌrezəˈluːʃn/ *n* **1** [U] quality of being resolute; fixity or boldness of determination: *show great/not much* ~; *a man who lacks* ~. **2** [C] sth that is resolved(1); formal expression of opinion by a legislative body or a public meeting; proposal for this: *pass/carry/adopt/reject a* ~ *(for/against/in favour of/that...).* **3** [C] resolve; sth one makes up one's mind to do: *make good* ~s; *her* ~ *never to marry; a New Year* ~ *(sth one resolves to do in a new year, eg to give up smoking).* **4** [U] resolving, solution (of a doubt, question, discord, etc). ⇨ **resolve**(3). **5** process of separating into constituents: *the* ~ *of white light into the colours of the spectrum.*

re·solve /rɪˈzɒlv/ *vt,vi* **1** [VP7A,9,3A] ~ *to do sth;* ~ *that...;* ~ *on/upon (doing) sth,* decide; determine: *He* ~d *that nothing should hold him back/*~d *to be held back by nothing. He* ~d *on making an early start. He* ~d *to succeed.* **2** [VP9] (of a committee, public meeting, legislative body) pass by formal vote the decision (*that*): *The House of Commons* ~d *that.... R*~d, *that this meeting is in favour of.../opposed to.../views with alarm...,* etc. **3** [VP6A] put an end to (doubts, difficulties, etc) by supplying an answer. **4** [VP6A,14] ~ *sth (into sth),* break up, separate (into parts); convert, be converted: ~ *a problem into its elements. The House of Commons* ~d *itself into a committee. A powerful telescope can* ~ *a nebula into stars.* □ *n* **1** [C] sth that has been determined on; mental resolution(3): *make a* ~ *to do sth; keep one's* ~. **2** (liter) resolution(1): *deeds of high* ~. **re·solv·able** /-əbl/ *adj* that may be ~d.

res·on·ant /ˈrezənənt/ *adj* **1** (of sound) resounding; continuing to resound: ~ *notes; a deep,* ~ *voice.* **2** (of rooms, etc) tending to prolong sounds by vibration: ~ *walls which echo and re-echo sound; a* ~ *hall.* **3** (of places) resounding: *Alpine valleys* ~ *with the sound of church bells.* **res·on·ance** /-əns/ *n* [U] quality of being ~. **res·on·ate** /ˈrezəneɪt/ *vt,vi* produce or show resonance. **res·ona·tor** /-tə(r)/ *n* appliance or system for increasing sound by resonance.

re·sort /rɪˈzɔːt/ *vi* [VP3A] ~ *to,* **1** make use of for help or to gain one's purpose, etc: *If other means fail, we shall* ~ *to force. I'm sorry you have* ~ed *to deception.* **2** frequently visit: *The police watched the cafés where the wanted man was known to* ~. □ *n* **1** [U] recourse; ~ing(1): *Can we do it without* ~ *to compulsion/force?* **in the last** ~; **as a last** ~, when all else has failed, as a last means of finding help or relief. **2** sb or sth that is ~ed(1) to: *An old taxi was the only* ~ *left.* **3** [C] place ~ed(2) to: '*seaside/*'*summer/*'*health* ~s.

re·sound /rɪˈzaʊnd/ *vi,vt* **1** [VP2A,3A] ~ *(with),* (of a voice, instrument, sound) echo and re-echo; fill a place with sound; send back (sound); (of a place) ring or echo: *The organ* ~ed. *The hall* ~ed *with cries of dissent.* **2** [VP2C] (fig, of fame, an event) be much talked of; spread far and wide: *His success* ~ed *through all Asia. The film was a* ~ing *success.* ~**·ing·ly** *adv*

re·source /rɪˈsɔːs US: ˈriːsɔːrs/ *n* **1** (*pl*) wealth, supplies of goods, raw materials, etc which a person, country, etc has or can use: *Our* ~s *in men and ammunition were inadequate for the defence of the town. We must exploit the natural* ~s *of our country, its mineral wealth, potential water power, the productivity of the soil,* etc. *I am at the end of my* ~s, have nothing left to use. *We must make the most of our* ~s, use what we have to the best advantage. **2** [C] sth which helps in doing sth, that can be turned to for support, help, consolation: *He has no inner* ~s *of character/no inner* ~s *to fall back on. Leave him to his own* ~s, Leave him to amuse himself, find his own way of passing the time. **3** [U] skill in finding ~s(2); quick wit: *a man of* ~. ~**·ful** /-fl/ *adj* good or quick at finding ~s(2). ~**·fully** /-fəlɪ/ *adv*

re·spect[1] /rɪˈspekt/ *n* **1** [U] ~ *(for),* honour; high opinion or regard; esteem for a person or quality: *The Prime Minister is held in the greatest* ~. *Children should show* ~ *for their teachers. He has no* ~ *for his promises,* does not think it necessary to

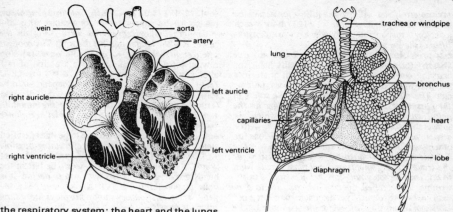

the respiratory system: the heart and the lungs

keep them. **2** [U] ~ *(for)*, consideration; attention: *We must have ~ for the needs of the general reader*, think about his requirements or preferences. **pay ~ to, (a)** consider. **(b)** honour. **~ for persons,** unfair discrimination, on the basis of wealth, social position, etc. **3** [U] reference; relation. *with ~ to*, concerning. *without ~ to*, paying no attention to, leaving out of the question. **4** [C] detail; particular aspect. *in ~ of,* as regards: *Your essay is admirable in ~ of style but unsatisfactory in other ~s. in some/any/no, etc ~s*, with regard to some aspect(s), detail(s): *They resemble one another in some/all/no/a few ~s.* **5** *(pl)* regards; polite greetings: *Give him my ~s. My father sends you his ~s.* **pay one's ~s to sb,** visit, etc sb as a sign of ~ for him.

re∙spect² /rɪ'spekt/ *vt* [VP6A] have ~ for; treat with consideration: *He is ~ed by everyone. We must ~ his wishes. I ~ your opinions. I wish people would ~ my (desire for) privacy. Do you ~ the laws of your country? Do you ~ oneself,* have proper ~ for one's own character and conduct: *If you don't ~ yourself, how can you expect others to ~ you?* **~er** *n* (only in) *no ~er of persons,* person or thing paying little or no attention to wealth, social rank, etc: *Death is no ~er of persons.* **~ing** *prep* relating to; concerned with: *legislation ~ing property.*

re∙spect∙able /rɪ'spektəbl/ *adj* **1** (of persons) of good character and good social position; having the qualities associated with such social position; (of clothes, appearance, behaviour, etc) suitable for such persons: *Are these clothes ~ enough for Mrs Whitehouse's party? It is not considered ~ in this country to spit in public.* **2** (ironic use) (of behaviour, appearances, etc) conventional; likely to satisfy conventional people: *Need we worry quite so much about being ~?* **3** of some size, merit, importance, etc; deserving respect: *do sth from ~ motives. He has quite ~ talents. There was a ~ attendance at the meeting this morning. He earns a ~ income.* **re∙spect∙ably** /-əblɪ/ *adv* in a ~ manner: *Go and get respectably dressed.* **re∙spect∙abil∙ity** /rɪ,spektə'bɪlətɪ/ *n* (*pl* -ties) **1** [U] quality of being socially ~(2,3).

re∙spect∙ful /rɪ'spektfl/ *adj* ~ *(to)*, showing respect: *They stood at a ~ distance from the President.* **~ly** /-fəlɪ/ *adv*

re∙spect∙ive /rɪ'spektɪv/ *adj* for, belonging to, each of those in question: *The three men were given work according to their ~ abilities. The party ended and we all went off to our ~ rooms, each of us went to his or her own room.* **~ly** *adv* separately or in turn, and in the order mentioned: *Training colleges for miners and fishermen are to be built at Leeds and Hull ~ly,* ie for miners at Leeds and for fishermen at Hull.

res∙pir∙ation /,respə'reɪʃn/ *n* [U] breathing; [C] single act of breathing, ie breathing in and breathing out.

res∙pir∙ator /'respəreɪtə(r)/ *n* [C] apparatus for breathing through, eg by aviators at high altitudes to warm the air inhaled, by firemen, to filter the air of smoke and fumes.

re∙spire /rɪ'spaɪə(r)/ *vi* [VP2A] (formal) breathe; breathe in and out. **re∙spir∙atory** /rɪ'spaɪərətrɪ US: 'respɪrətɔːrɪ/ *adj* of breathing: *the respiratory organs/system; respiratory diseases*, eg bronchitis, asthma.

res∙pite /'respaɪt US: 'respɪt/ *n* **1** [C,U] ~ *(from)*, time of relief or rest (from toil, suffering, anything unpleasant): *work without (a) ~.* **2** [C] postponement or delay permitted in the suffering of a penalty or the discharge of an obligation; reprieve. □ *vt* [VP6A] give a ~ to: *~ a murderer.*

re∙splen∙dent /rɪ'splendənt/ *adj* very bright; splendid: *~ in cornation robes.* **~ly** *adv* **re∙splen∙dence** /-əns/, **re∙splen∙dency** /-ənsɪ/ *nn* [U].

re∙spond /rɪ'spɒnd/ *vi* **1** [VP2A,3A,B] ~ *(to),;* (of people at a church service) make the usual answers or responses to the priest. **2** [VP2C] act in answer to, or because of, the action of another: *When Jack insulted Jill, she ~ed with a kick.* **3** [VP3A] ~ *(to),* react (to); be affected (by): *~ to kindness. The illness quickly ~ed to treatment. The plane ~s well to the controls.*

re∙spon∙dent /rɪ'spɒndənt/ *n* (legal) defendant (esp in a divorce case).

re∙sponse /rɪ'spɒns/ *n* **1** [C] answer: *My letter of inquiry brought no ~. She made no ~. In ~ to your inquiry....* **2** [C] (in a church service) part of the liturgy said or sung by the congregation alternately with the priest. **3** [C,U] reaction: *My appeal to her pity met with no/little/some ~.*

re∙spon∙si∙bil∙ity /rɪ,spɒnsə'bɪlətɪ/ *n* (*pl* -ties) **1** [U] being responsible; being accountable: *You did it on your own ~, without being told or ordered to do it. You have a post of great ~. I will lend you* *my camera if you will assume full* ~ *for it*, pay me the cost of any damage or loss. **2** [C] sth for which a person is responsible; duty: *the heavy responsibilities of the President.*

re·spon·sible /rɪˈspɒnsəbl/ *adj* **1** ~ *(to sb)* *(for sb/sth)*, (of a person) legally or morally liable for carrying out a duty, for the care of sth or sb, in a position where one may be blamed for loss, failure, etc: *The pilot of an airliner is* ~ *for the safety of the passengers. You are* ~ *to the Manager for the petty cash.* ~ **government,** one which is answerable to the electors for its actions. **2** ~ *(for sth)*, involving the obligation to make decisions for others and bear the blame for their mistakes: *The President has a* ~ *position. I've made you* ~ *for the travel arrangements and you must decide what to do. Isn't he too young for such a* ~ *job?* **3** trustworthy; to be relied upon: *Give the task to a* ~ *man.* **4 be** ~ **for sth,** be the cause or source of: *Bad workmanship was* ~ *for the collapse of the block of flats. Who's* ~ *for this mess in the kitchen?* **re·spon·sibly** /-əblɪ/ *adv*

re·spon·sive /rɪˈspɒnsɪv/ *adj* **1** answering: *a* ~ *gesture;* ~ *(to)*, answering easily or quickly: *a* ~ *nature;* ~ *to affection/treatment.*

rest¹ /rest/ *n* **1** [U] condition of being free from activity, movement, disturbance; sleep: *R*~ *is necessary after hard work. She had a good night's* ~, *sleep. We had several* ~*s/stops for* ~ *on the way up the mountain. Sunday is a day of* ~ *for many people. Let's stop and take/have a* ~. *at* ~, **(a)** still; not troubled; free from movement or agitation. **(b)** dead. *be laid to* ~, be buried. *come to* ~, (of a moving body) stop moving. *set sb's mind/fears at* ~, calm him; relieve him of doubt, anxiety, etc. '~**-cure** *n* course of treatment for persons suffering from nervous disorders. '~**-day** *n* day spent in ~. '~**-home** *n* place where old or convalescent people are cared for. '~**-house** *n* house or bungalow for the use of travellers (esp in areas where there are no hotels). '~ **room,** (US) public lavatory; cloak-room. **2** [C] that on which sth is supported: *a* ~ *for a billiard cue/a telescope; an* '*arm*-~; *a* '*neck*-~. **3** [C] (music) (sign marking an) interval of silence. ~**·ful** /-fl/ *adj* quiet; peaceful; giving ~ or a feeling of ~: *a* ~*ful scene; colours that are* ~*ful to the eyes.* ~**·fully** /-fəlɪ/ *adv* ~**·ful·ness** *n* ~**·less** *adj* never still or quiet; unable to rest: *the* ~*less waves; spend a* ~*less night. The audience was growing* ~*less,* showing signs of impatience, wishing to leave, etc. ~**·less·ly** *adv* ~**·less·ness** *n*

rest² /rest/ *n* **the** ~, **1** what remains; the remainder: *Take what you want and throw the* ~ *away. Her hat was red, like the* ~ *of her clothes. and (all) the* ~ *(of it)*, and everything else that might be mentioned. *for the* ~, as regards other matters. **2** (with *pl v*), the others: *John and I are going to play tennis; what are the* ~ *of you going to do?*

rest³ /rest/ *vi,vt* **1** [VP2A,B,C] be still or quiet; be free from activity, movement, disturbance, etc: *We* ~*ed (for) an hour after lunch. He* ~*s* (= is buried) *in the churchyard. His last* ~*ing-place* (= place of burial) *is on the hillside there. He will not* ~ (= will have no peace of mind) *until he knows the truth. The matter cannot* ~ *here,* We must investigate it further. *We shall let this field* ~ *for a year,* let it lie fallow. **2** [VP6A] give rest or relief to: *He stopped to* ~ *his horse. These dark glasses* ~ *my eyes. May God* ~ *his soul,* give repose to his

soul. **3** [VP14,3A] ~ *(sth) on/upon/against,* (cause to) be supported (on or against sth): *She* ~*ed her elbows/Her elbows were* ~*ing on the table. R*~ *the ladder against the wall. The roof* ~*s upon eight columns.* ~ *on one's oars,* **(a)** stop rowing for a time. **(b)** (fig) have a period of rest after any kind of work or effort. **4** [VP14,3A] ~ *(sth) on/upon,* lie, spread out, depend or rely (on); (of sight, etc) fall (on), be steadily directed (on): *Look at those clouds* ~*ing upon the mountain top. Her eyes/gaze* ~*ed on me. She let her glance* ~ *on me.*

rest⁴ /rest/ *vi* **1** [VP2D] continue to be in a specified state: *You may* ~ *assured that everything possible will be done. The affair* ~*s* (= remains, the usu word) *a mystery.* **2** [VP3A] ~ *with,* be left in the hands or charge of: *It* ~*s with you to decide,* It is your responsibility. **3** [VP3A] ~ *on/upon,* depend, rely: *His fame* ~*s upon his plays more than upon his novels.*

re·state /ˌriːˈsteɪt/ *vt* [VP6A] state again or in a different way. ~**·ment** *n*

res·taur·ant /ˈrestrɒnt *US:* -tərənt/ *n* place where meals can be bought and eaten. **res·taura·teur** /ˌrestərəˈtɜː(r)/, **res·taur·an·teur** /ˌrestrɒnˈtɜː(r) *US:* -tərən-/ *n* manager of a ~.

res·ti·tu·tion /ˌrestɪˈtjuːʃn *US:* -ˈtuː-/ *n* [U] **1** restoring (of sth stolen, etc) to its owner: *make* ~ *of sth to sb;* ~ *of property.* **2** = reparation.

res·tive /ˈrestɪv/ *adj* **1** (of a horse or other animal) refusing to move forward; moving backwards or sideways. **2** (of a person) reluctant to be controlled or disciplined. ~**·ly** *adv* ~**·ness** *n*

re·stock /ˌriːˈstɒk/ *vt* [VP6A] put fresh stock into: ~ *a lake with trout.*

res·to·ra·tion /ˌrestəˈreɪʃn/ *n* **1** [U] restoring or being restored: ~ *to health and strength;* ~ *of stolen property.* **2 the R**~, (the period of) the re-establishment of the monarchy in England in 1660, when Charles II became king: *R*~ *poetry/comedy.* **3** [C] model representing the supposed original form of an extinct animal, ruined building, etc; building formerly ruined and now rebuilt: *The castle is a mere* ~, ie there is very little of the original left. *Closed during* ~*s,* ie while rebuilding is in progress.

re·stora·tive /rɪˈstɔːrətɪv/ *adj* tending to restore health and strength. □ *n* [C,U] ~ *food, medicine,* etc.

re·store /rɪˈstɔː(r)/ *vt* [VP6A,14] ~ *(to)*, **1** give back: ~ *stolen property/borrowed books.* **2** bring back into use; reintroduce: ~ *old customs.* **3** make well or normal again; bring back (to a former condition): *quite* ~*d to health; feel completely* ~*d. Law and order were quickly* ~*d after the attempted revolution.* **4** repair; rebuild as before; reconstruct (sth) so that it is like the original: ~ *a ruined abbey;* ~ *a text,* try to make it as it was originally by supplying missing words and phrases, getting rid of errors made by copyists, etc. **5** place in or bring back to the former position, etc: ~ *an employee to his old post/an officer to his command.* ~*r n* one who, that which, ~*s,* eg an expert who cleans old oil paintings: '*hair*-~*r,* preparation that, it is claimed, will ~ hair to a bald head.

re·strain /rɪˈstreɪn/ *vt* [VP6A,14] ~ *(from)*, hold back; keep under control; prevent (sb or sth from doing sth): ~ *a child from (doing) mischief;* ~ *one's anger/laughter.* ~*ed adj* (esp) not emotional or wild; kept under control. ~*t* /rɪˈstreɪnt/ *n* **1** [U]

~ing or being ~ed: *submit to* ~*t; break loose from all* ~*t.* **be put under** ~*t,* (esp of a mentally ill person) be placed in a mental home. *without* ~*t,* freely; without control. 2 [U] (in art, literature, etc) avoidance of excess or exaggeration. 3 [C] that which ~s; check; controlling influence: *the* ~*ts of poverty.*

re·strict /rɪ'strɪkt/ *vt* [VP6A,14] ~ *(to),* limit; keep within limits: *Discussion at the meeting was* ~*ed to the agenda. We are* ~*ed to a speed of 30 miles an hour in built-up areas. The trees* ~ *our vision. Is the consumption of alcohol* ~*ed by law in your country?* **re·stric·tion** /rɪ'strɪkʃn/ *n* 1 [U] ~ing or being ~ed: ~*ion of expenditure.* 2 [C] instance of this; sth that ~s: *place* ~*ions on foreign trade/on the sale of alcohol; currency* ~*ions,* eg on the sums that a person may use for foreign travel. ~**ive** /rɪ'strɪktɪv/ *adj* ~ing; tending to ~. ~**ive practices,** (in industry) practices that hinder the most effective use of labour, technical resources, etc and tend to damage productive efficiency. ~**ive·ly** *adv*

re·struc·ture /ˌriː'strʌktʃə(r)/ *vt* [VP6A] give new structure or arrangement to: ~ *an organisation/a proposal/the plot of a novel.*

re·sult /rɪ'zʌlt/ *vi* 1 [VP2A,3A] ~ *(from),* come about, happen, as a natural consequence: *Any damage* ~*ing from negligence must be paid for by the borrower.* 2 [VP3A] ~ *in,* bring about; have as a consequence: *Their dispute* ~*ed in war.* 3 end in a specified manner: *Their efforts* ~*ed badly.* □ *n* 1 [C,U] that which is produced by an activity or cause; outcome; effect: *work without* (*much*) ~*; obtain good* ~*s; announce the* ~*s of a competition,* the names of prize-winners, etc; '*football* ~*s,* the scores. *His limp is the* ~ *of a car accident last year.* 2 [C] sth found by calculation; answer (to a mathematical problem, etc). ~**·ant** /-ənt/ *adj* coming as a ~, esp as the total outcome of forces or tendencies from different directions. □ *n* [C] product or outcome (*of* sth).

re·sume /rɪ'zjuːm* US*: -'zuːm/ *vt* 1 [VP6A,D] go on after stopping for a time: ~ *one's work/a story;* ~ *the thread of one's discourse,* take up an interrupted discourse. 2 [VP6A] take or occupy again: ~ *one's seat.*

ré·sumé /'rezjuːmeɪ* US*: ˌrezʊ'meɪ/ *n* [C] summary; abstract(3); (US) = *curriculum vitae,* ⇨ curriculum.

re·sump·tion /rɪ'zʌmpʃn/ *n* [U] resuming; [C] instance of this.

re·sur·face /ˌriː'sɜːfɪs/ *vt,vi* 1 [VP6A] put a new surface on (a road, etc). 2 [VP2A] (of a submarine) come to the surface again.

re·sur·gent /rɪ'sɜːdʒənt/ *adj* reviving; coming back to activity, vigour, etc (after defeat, destruction, etc): ~ *nationalism;* ~ *hopes.* **re·sur·gence** /-əns/ *n*

res·ur·rect /ˌrezə'rekt/ *vt,vi* 1 [VP6A] bring back into use; revive the practice of: ~ *an old word/ custom.* 2 [VP6A] take from the grave; (colloq) dig up: *My dog* ~*ed an old bone in the garden.* 3 [VP6A,2A] (rare) bring or come back to life again. **res·ur·rec·tion** /ˌrezə'rekʃn/ *n* [U] 1 **the R**~, (a) the rising of Jesus from the tomb; anniversary of this. (b) the rising of all the dead on the Last Day. 2 revival from disuse, inactivity, etc: *the* ~ *of hope.*

re·sus·ci·tate /rɪ'sʌsɪteɪt/ *vt,vi* [VP6A,2A] bring or come back to consciousness: ~ *a person who has been nearly drowned.* **re·sus·ci·ta·tion**

/ˌrɪˌsʌsɪ'teɪʃn/ *n* [U].

ret /ret/ *vt* (-tt-) [VP6A] soften (flax, hemp, etc) by soaking or exposing to moisture: *Coconut shells are buried in wet sea-sand to ret the coir fibre.*

re·tail /'riːteɪl/ *n* [C] sale of goods (usu in small quantities) to the general public, not for resale: *sell goods* (*by*) ~; (attrib) ~ *dealers/prices; the* '~ *department.* ⇨ wholesale. □ *adv* by ~: *Do you buy wholesale or* ~*?* □ *vt,vi* 1 [VP6A,3A] ~ *(at),* sell (goods) by ~; (of goods) be sold ~: *an article that is* ~*ed at/that* ~*s at seventy pence.* 2 [VP6A] repeat (what one has heard, esp gossip) bit by bit or to several persons in turn: ~ *a slander.* ~**er** *n* tradesman who sells by ~.

re·tain /rɪ'teɪn/ *vt* [VP6A] 1 keep; continue to have or hold; keep in place: *This vessel won't* ~ *water. This dyke was built to* ~ *the flood waters. The* ~*ing wall* (ie one built to support and confine a mass of earth or water) *collapsed. He is 90 but still* ~*s the use of all his faculties. She* ~*s a clear memory of her schooldays.* 2 get the services of (esp a barrister) by payment (*a* ~*ing fee*). ~**er** *n* 1 (legal) fee paid to ~ the services of, eg a barrister. 2 (old use) servant.

re·take /ˌriː'teɪk/ *vt* (*pt* -took /-'tʊk/, *pp* -taken /-'teɪkən/) [VP6A] take, capture, photograph, again. □ *n* /'riːteɪk/ (esp, cinema, TV) rephotographed scene.

re·tali·ate /rɪ'tælɪeɪt/ *vi* [VP2A,3A] ~ *(against/ on/upon),* return the same sort of ill treatment that one has received: ~ *upon one's enemy. He* ~*d by kicking the other boy on the ankle. If we raise our import duties on their goods, they may* ~ *against us.* **re·tali·ation** /rɪˌtælɪ'eɪʃn/ *n* [U] retaliating: *in retaliation for.* **re·tali·at·ive** /rɪ'tælɪətɪv* US*:-lɪeɪt-/, **re·tali·at·ory** /rɪ'tælɪətrɪ* US*: -tɔːrɪ/ *adj* returning ill treatment for ill treatment; of or for retaliation: *retaliatory measures.*

re·tard /rɪ'tɑːd/ *vt* [VP6A] check; hinder: ~ *progress/development; a mentally* ~*ed child,* one whose mental or emotional development has been checked. **re·tar·da·tion** /ˌriːtɑː'deɪʃn/ *n*

retch /retʃ/ *vi* [VP2A] make (involuntarily) the sound and physical movements of vomiting but without bringing up anything from the stomach.

re·tell /ˌriː'tel/ *vt* (*pt,pp* -told /-'təʊld/) [VP6A] tell again; tell in a different way or in a different language: *old Greek tales retold for children.*

re·ten·tion /rɪ'tenʃn/ *n* [U] retaining or being retained: *suffering from* ~ *of urine,* inability to pass it out from the bladder.

re·ten·tive /rɪ'tentɪv/ *adj* ~ *(of),* having the power of retaining(1) things: *a memory that is* ~ *of details; a* ~ *soil,* one that retains water, does not dry out quickly. ~**·ly** *adv* ~**·ness** *n*

re·think /ˌriː'θɪŋk/ *vt,vi* (*pt,pp* -thought /-'θɔːt/) [VP2A,6A] think about again; reconsider: *They will have to* ~ *their policy towards China. A good deal of* ~*ing is needed on this question.* □ *n* /'riːθɪŋk/ (colloq) thinking again: *If that's your decision, you'd better have a* ~.

reti·cent /'retɪsnt/ *adj* in the habit of saying little; not saying all that is known or felt; reserved: *She was* ~ *about/on what Tom had said to her.* ~**·ly** *adv* **reti·cence** /-sns/ *n* [U] being ~; [C] instance of this: *His reticences are often more revealing than what he says.*

re·ticu·late /rɪ'tɪkjʊleɪt/ *vt,vi* [VP6A,2A] divide, be divided, in fact or in appearance into a network of small squares or intersecting lines. □ *adj*

/rɪˈtɪkjʊlət/ covered with such a network. **re·ticu·la·tion** /rɪˌtɪkjʊˈleɪʃn/ n (often pl) net-like mark or structure.
reti·cule /ˈretɪkjuːl/ n (archaic) woman's small handbag.
ret·ina /ˈretɪnə US: ˈretənə/ n (pl ~s or -nae /-niː/) [C] layer of membrane at the back of the eyeball, sensitive to light. ⇨ the illus at eye.
reti·nue /ˈretɪnjuː US: ˈretənu:/ n [C] number of persons (servants, officers, etc) travelling with a person of high rank.
re·tire /rɪˈtaɪə(r)/ vi,vt 1 [VP2A,3A] ~ (from) (to), withdraw; go away: He ~d to his bedroom. The batsman ~d hurt, left the pitch and went back to the pavilion, because hurt. 2 ~ (to bed) (formal for) go to bed: My wife usually ~s at 10 o'clock. 3 [VP2A,C] (of an army) withdraw; go back: Our forces ~d to prepared positions. Cf The enemy retreated. 4 [VP2A,C] give up one's work, position, business, etc: He will ~ on a pension at 65; reach retiring age; a retiring allowance, one given to a person when he ~s. 5 [VP6A] cause (sb) to ~(3,4): ~ the head clerk. 6 ~ from the world, enter a monastery or become a hermit; become a recluse. ~ into oneself, become unsociable because one is wrapped up in one's own thoughts. □ n signal to troops to ~: sound the ~, ie on the bugle. ~d adj 1 having ~d(4): a ~d civil servant; the '~d list, of officers (of the Army, etc) who have ~d; '~d pay, pension. 2 secluded; quiet: a ~d valley; live a ~d life in a small village. **re·tir·ing** adj (of persons, their way of life, etc) inclined to avoid society; reserved: a girl of a retiring disposition. ~·ment n 1 [U] retiring or being ~d; seclusion: ~ment from the world, eg in a convent. 2 [U] condition of being ~d: be/live in ~ment. go into ~ment, retire (esp 4 and 6 above). 3 [C] instance of retiring or being ~d: There have been several ~ments in my office recently. '~ment pension, = old-age pension. ⇨ pension.
re·tool /ˌriːˈtuːl/ vt [VP6A] equip (a factory, etc) with new machine tools.
re·tort¹ /rɪˈtɔːt/ n [C] 1 vessel with a long narrow neck turned downwards, used for distilling liquids. 2 receptacle used in the purification of mercury, and in the making of gas.
re·tort² /rɪˈtɔːt/ vt,vi 1 [VP6A,9,2A] answer back quickly, wittily or angrily (esp to an accusation or challenge): 'It's entirely your fault,' he ~ed. 2 [VP14] (formal, rare) get equal with sb by returning (what has been received) in kind: ~ insult for insult; ~ an argument/affront. □ n [U] ~ing: say sth in ~; [C] ~ing answer: make an insolent ~.
re·touch /ˌriːˈtʌtʃ/ vt [VP6A] improve (a photograph, painting, etc) by a few touches of a brush, etc.
re·trace /riːˈtreɪs/ vt [VP6A] 1 go back over or along: ~ one's steps. 2 go over (past actions, etc) in the mind.
re·tract /rɪˈtrækt/ vt,vi 1 [VP6A,2A] take back or withdraw (a statement, offer, opinion, etc); take back a statement: The prisoner of war ~ed his parole. Even when confronted with proof the accused man refused to ~, would not acknowledge the error of what he had said. 2 [VP6A,2A] draw in or back; move back or in; be capable of doing this: A cat can ~ its claws and a snail its horns. A cat's claws can ~. ~·able /-əbl/ adj that can be ~ed: a ~able undercarriage, (in an aircraft) wheels, etc which can be drawn up into the body of the aircraft

during flight. **re·trac·tile** /rɪˈtræktaɪl US: -tl/ adj that can be drawn in: the retractile claws of a cat. **re·trac·tion** /rɪˈtrækʃn/ n [U] ~ing; [C] instance of this.
re·tread /ˌriːˈtred/ vt (pt,pp ~ed) furnish (an old tyre) with a new tread. ⇨ tread, n(3). □ n /ˈriːtred/ tyre that has been ~ed (US = recap).
re·treat /rɪˈtriːt/ vi 1 [VP2A,C,3A] ~ (from) (to), (esp of an army) go back; withdraw: force the enemy to ~; ~ on (ie towards) the capital. 2 recede (which is more usu): a ~ing forehead. □ n 1 [U] act of ~ing: The army was in full ~. We made good our ~, ~ed safely. 2 [U] signal for ~ing: sound the ~, eg on a drum or bugle. 3 [C] instance of ~ing: after many advances and ~s. beat a (hasty) ~, (fig) withdraw from, abandon, an undertaking. 4 [C,U] (place for a) period of quiet and rest: a quiet country ~. go into ~, eg temporary retirement for religious exercises.
re·trench /rɪˈtrentʃ/ vt,vi [VP6A,2A] cut down (expenses); make economies: We must ~ this year in order to have a good holiday next year. ~·ment n [U] ~ing; [C] instance of this.
re·trial /ˌriːˈtraɪəl/ n act of trying again in a law court; new trial.
ret·ri·bu·tion /ˌretrɪˈbjuːʃn/ n [U] deserved punishment: R~ for evil does not always come in this life. There will be a day of ~. **re·tri·bu·tive** /rɪˈtrɪbjʊtɪv/ adj coming as ~; inflicted or coming as a penalty for wrongdoing.
re·trieve /rɪˈtriːv/ vt,vi 1 [VP6A] get possession of again: ~ a lost piece of luggage. 2 [VP6A] put or set right; make amends for: ~ an error/a loss/disaster/defeat. 3 [VP6A,14] ~ (from), rescue from; restore to a flourishing state: ~ sb from ruin; ~ one's honour/fortunes; ~ oneself. 4 [VP6A,2A] (of specially trained dogs) find and bring in (killed or wounded birds, etc). **re·triev·able** /-əbl/ adj **re·trieval** /-vl/ n [U] 1 act of retrieving: the retrieval of one's fortunes. 2 possibility of recovery: beyond/past retrieval. **re·triever** n breed of dog used for retrieving(4). ⇨ the illus at dog.
retro·ac·tive /ˌretrəʊˈæktɪv/ adj (of laws, etc) = retrospective(2). ~·ly adv
retro·grade /ˈretrəɡreɪd/ adj 1 directed backwards: ~ motion. 2 deteriorating; likely to cause worse conditions: a ~ policy. □ vi [VP2A] decline; revert; grow worse.
retro·gress /ˌretrəˈɡres/ vi [VP2A] go or move backwards.
retro·gression /ˌretrəˈɡreʃn/ n return to a less advanced state; decline. **retro·gres·sive** /ˌretrəˈɡresɪv/ adj returning, tending to return, to a less advanced state; becoming worse.
retro·rocket /ˈretrəʊrɒkɪt/ n jet engine fired to slow down or alter the course of a missile, spacecraft, etc.
retro·spect /ˈretrəspekt/ n [U] view of past events. in ~, looking back at past events, etc. **retro·spec·tion** /ˌretrəˈspekʃn/ n [U] action of looking back at past events, scenes, etc; [C] instance of this. **retro·spec·tive** /ˌretrəˈspektɪv/ adj 1 relating to retrospection; looking back on past events, etc: a ~ive exhibition of a painter's work, one that traces his development from his early to his latest work. 2 (of laws, payments, etc) applying to the past; not restricted to the future: ~ive legislation; a ~ive (= back-dated) wage increase. **retro·spec·tive·ly** adv
re·troussé /rəˈtruːseɪ US: ˌretrʊˈseɪ/ adj (of a nose)

turned up at the end.
ret·ro·ver·sion /ˌretrəʊ'vɜːʃn US: -ʒn/ n state of being turned backwards; turning or tilting backward.
ret·sina /ret'siːnə US: 'retsmə/ n [U] resinated Greek wine.
re·turn¹ /rɪ'tɜːn/ n **1** [C,U] ~ing or being ~ed; coming, going, giving, sending, putting, back: *a ~ home; on my ~, when I got/get back; a poor ~ for kindness,* (eg) ungrateful behaviour; *the ~ of spring; have a ~ of the symptoms* (of an illness). **by ~,** by the next post out: *Please send a reply by ~.* **in ~ (for),** as repayment (for). **Many happy ~s (of the day),** phrase used as a greeting on sb's birthday. **on sale or ~,** (of goods in commerce) supplied (to retailers) on the understanding that they may be ~ed to the wholesaler or manufacturer if not sold. **a/the point of no ~,** (on a long voyage, flight across an ocean, etc) point at which fuel supplies, etc are insufficient for a ~ to the starting-point, so that continuation of the voyage, etc is essential; (fig) stage of negotiations at which no further progress seems possible. **2** (attrib) involving going back or coming back, etc: *the ~ voyage.* ~ **fare,** needed for the journey both there and back. ~ **half,** the half of a ~ ticket for the journey back. ~ **match,** one played between teams which have already played one match. '~ **ticket,** one giving a traveller the right to go to a place and back to his starting-point (US = *two-way ticket*). ,**day-'~,** ~ ticket available only for the day of issue: *Two day-~s to London, please.* **3** (often *pl*) profit on an investment or undertaking: *get a good ~ on an investment; small profits and quick ~s,* motto for shops that rely on large sales and quick turnover. **4** [C] official report or statement, esp one that is compiled by order: *make one's ~ of income* (to the Inspector of Taxes for purposes of income tax); *the e'lection ~s,* figures of the voting at an election.
re·turn² /rɪ'tɜːn/ vi,vt **1** [VP2A,C,3A,4A] ~ **(to) (from),** come or go back: ~ *home;* ~ *to London;* ~ *from a journey;* ~ *to Paris from London. He ~ed to collect his money. I shall ~ to this point later in my lecture.* **2** [VP3A] ~ **to,** pass or go back to a former state: *He has ~ed to his old habits. After death animal bodies ~* (= change) *to dust.* **3** [VP6A] (rare) reply; retort: *'Not this time', he ~ed.* **4** [VP6A,12A,13A] give, put, send, pay, carry, back: *When will you ~* (*me*) *the book I lent you? In case of non-delivery,* ~ *to* (*the*) *sender,* often written on letters sent by post. *All books are to be ~ed to the library before Friday. He ~ed the blow* (ie hit back) *smartly. She ~ed the compliment,* said sth pleasant after a compliment had been paid to her. ~ **thanks,** express thanks, esp by saying grace before a meal, or in response to a toast. ~**ed empties,** empty bottles, crates, etc ~ed to the sender for re-use. **5** [VP6A,16A] (of a constituency) send (sb) as representative to Parliament. '~·**ing officer** n official in charge of a Parliamentary election and announcing the name of the person elected. **6** [VP6A,15A] state or describe officially, esp in answer to a demand: ~ *the details of one's income* (for taxation purposes); *liabilities ~ed at £2000. The prisoner was ~ed guilty. The jury ~ed a verdict of guilty.* **7** [VP6A] give as a profit: *an investment that ~s a good interest.* ~-**able** /-əbl/ *adj* that can be, or is to be, ~ed.
re·un·ion /ˌriː'juːnɪən/ n [U] reuniting or being reu-

nited; [C] (esp) meeting of old friends, former colleagues, etc after separation: *a family ~ at Christmas.*
re·unite /ˌriːjuː'naɪt/ vt,vi [VP6A,2A] bring or come together again: ~*d after long years of separation.*
rev /rev/ vt,vi (-vv-) [VP2A,6A,2C,15B] **rev (up),** (colloq) increase the speed of revolutions in (an internal-combustion engine): *Don't rev* (*up*) (*the engine*) *so hard.* □ *n* revolution: *You're driving at maximum revs.*
re·value /ˌriː'væljuː/ vt [VP6A] value again or anew; (esp) increase the value of a currency. **re·valu·ation** /ˌriːvæljuː'eɪʃn/ n revaluing: *revaluation of the German mark.*
re·vamp /ˌriː'væmp/ vt [VP6A] (colloq) patch up; reconstruct; renew: ~ *an old comedy;* ~ *agriculture in a backward country,* try to improve it.
re·veal /rɪ'viːl/ vt [VP6A,14,9,25] ~ **(to), 1** allow or cause to be seen; display: *His worn jacket ~ed his elbows.* **2** make known: ~ *a secret. One day the truth about these events will be ~ed. The doctor did not ~ to him his hopeless condition. Research has ~ed him to be/~ed that he was the father of twelve children.* ~**ed religion,** religion believed to be taught to mankind directly by God.
re·veille /rɪ'vælɪ US: 'revəlɪ/ n (in the armed forces) bugle signal to men to get up in the morning: *sound the ~.*
revel /'revl/ vi (-ll-; US -l-) **1** [VP2A,B,C,15B] make merry; have a gay, lively time: *They ~led until dawn. They ~led away the time.* **2** [VP3A] ~ **in,** take great delight in: ~ *in one's freedom; people who ~ in gossip.* □ *n* [C,U] (occasion of) lively, happy festivity: *Our ~s now are ended.* ~**·ler,** (US = ~**er**) /'revələ(r)/ *n* person who ~s.
rev·el·ation /ˌrevə'leɪʃn/ n **1** [U] revealing; making known of sth secret or hidden; [C] that which is revealed, esp sth that causes surprise: *truths which man knows only by ~,* ie from God. *It was a ~ to John when Mary said she had married him only for his money.* **2** R~, the last book of the New Testament, called *The R~ of St John the Divine,* or (less correctly) *R~s.*
rev·elry /'revlrɪ/ n [U] (or *pl;* -ries) noisy, joyous festivity and merrymaking: *when the ~/revelries ended.*
re·venge /rɪ'vendʒ/ vt **1** [VP6A] do sth to get satisfaction for (an offence, etc to oneself or another): ~ *an injustice/insult;* ~ *one's friend,* inflict injury (deliberately) on the person who injured one's friend. **2** **be ~d on sb;** ~ **oneself on sb,** get satisfaction by deliberately inflicting injury in return for injury inflicted on oneself. ⇨ avenge. □ *n* [U] **1** deliberate infliction of injury upon the person(s) from whom injury has been received: *thirsting for ~; nurse thoughts of ~.* **get/take one's ~; take ~ on sb (for sth); have/get one's ~ (on sb) (for sth); do sth in/out of ~ (for sth).* **2** [U] vindictiveness. **3** (in sport) opportunity given for reversing an earlier result by a return match, etc. **give sb his ~; get/take one's ~.** ~**·ful** /-fl/ *adj* feeling or showing a desire for ~. ~**·fully** /-fəlɪ/ *adv*
rev·enue /'revənjuː US: -ənuː/ n **1** [U] income, esp the total annual income of the State; government department which collects money for public funds: *a '~ officer,* a customs and excise officer; *a '~ cutter,* boat used to detect and prevent smuggling. **Inland R~,** income from taxation, etc. '~ **tax,** one designed to produce ~ (contrasted with taxes designed to protect a country's trade and commerce).

2 (*pl*) separate items of ~ put together: *the ~s of the City Council.*

re·ver·ber·ate /rɪ'vɜ:bəreɪt/ *vt, vi* [VP6A,2A] (esp of sound) send or throw back, be sent back, again and again: *The roar of the train ~d/was ~d in the tunnel. His voice ~d from the walls of the cave.* **re·ver·ber·ant** /-ənt/ *adj* resounding **re·ver·ber·ation** /rɪ,vɜ:bə'reɪʃn/ *n* [U] reverberating or being ~d; (*pl*) echoes; repercussions.

re·vere /rɪ'vɪə(r)/ *vt* [VP6A] have deep respect for; regard as sacred, with great respect: ~ *virtue; my ~d grandfather.*

rev·er·ence /'revərəns/ *n* [U] deep respect; feeling of wonder and awe: *hold sb/sth in ~; have/show ~ for sb/sth.* □ *vt* [VP6A] treat with ~.

rev·er·end /'revərənd/ *adj* 1 deserving to be treated with respect (because of age, character, etc). **2 the R~**, (usu shortened in writing to *the Rev* or *Revd*), used as a title of a clergyman: *the Rev John Smith* or *the Rev J Smith* (but not *the Rev Smith*); *the Very R~* (of a dean); *the Right R~* (of a bishop); *the Most R~* (of an archbishop); *the R~ Father* (of a RC priest). **R~ Mother**, Mother Superior of a convent. □ *n* (usu *pl*) clergyman: *a crowd of ~s and right ~s at the Lambeth Conference.*

rev·er·ent /'revərənt/ *adj* feeling or showing reverence. **~·ly** *adv*

rev·er·en·tial /,revə'renʃl/ *adj* caused or marked by reverence. **~·ly** /-ʃəlɪ/ *adv*

rev·erie /'revərɪ/ *n* 1 [C,U] (instance/occasion of a) condition of being lost in dreamy, pleasant thoughts: *lost in ~; indulge in ~s about the future.* **2** [C] piece of dreamy music.

re·vers /rɪ'vɪə(r)/ *n* (*pl* ~ /-ɪəz/) turned-back edge of a coat, etc showing the reverse side, as on a lapel.

re·ver·sal /rɪ'vɜ:sl/ *n* 1 [U] reversing or being reversed: *the ~ of the seasons in the two hemispheres.* **2** [C] instance of this: *a ~ of procedure.*

re·verse¹ /rɪ'vɜ:s/ *adj* ~ (*to/of*), contrary or opposite in character or order; inverted: *this is the ~ direction to that; the ~ side of a length of cloth; the ~ side of a coin or disc.* **in ~ order**, from the end to the start, or in the opposite order; in the ~ direction. **~·ly** *adv*

re·verse² /rɪ'vɜ:s/ *n* 1 [U] **the ~** (*of*), opposite; contrary: *do the ~ of what one is expected to do. Your remarks were the ~ of polite*, were impolite. **2** [C] **the ~** (*of*), (sth on the) reverse side (of a coin, medal, disc, etc): *On the ~ of this 50p coin there is a design showing a lion wearing a crown.* ⇨ reverse¹. **3** [U,C] mechanism or device that reverses: *Most typewriters have an automatic ribbon ~. Most cars have three forward gears and* (*a*) ~. *Put the car into ~.* **4** [C] defeat; change to bad fortune: *Our forces have suffered a slight ~. These financial ~s will prevent my taking a holiday.*

re·verse³ /rɪ'vɜ:s/ *vt, vi* [VP6A] **1** turn (sth) the other way round or up or inside out: ~ *a procedure;* ~ *one's policy.* **a ~d charge**, charge for a telephone call (to be) paid by the person to whom the call is made instead of by the person who makes it. ~ **arms**, (mil) hold the rifle with the muzzle pointing down (as at military funerals). **2** [VP6A,2A] (cause to) go in the opposite direction: ~ *one's car into the garage* (*back* is the more usu word). **3** [VP6A] change the order, position, etc of: *Their conditions are now ~d: A is poor and B is rich.* **4** [VP6A] revoke, annul: ~ *the decision of a*

lower court; ~ *a decree.* **re·vers·ible** /-əbl/ *adj* that can be ~d, eg of cloth, either side of which can be used on the outside. **re·versi·bil·ity** /rɪ,vɜ:sə'bɪlətɪ/ *n*

re·ver·sion /rɪ'vɜ:ʃn *US:* -ʒn/ *n* ⇨ revert.

re·vert /rɪ'vɜ:t/ *vi* [VP2A,3A] ~ (*to*), **1** return (to a former state, condition, topic, etc): *The fields have ~ed to moorland*, have gone out of cultivation, etc. *R~ing to your original statement, I think.... Garden plants sometimes ~ to type*, go back to the wild kind from which they were developed. *Mental patients sometimes ~*, ie to their condition before treatment started. **2** (legal) (of property, rights, etc) return at some named time or under certain conditions (to the original owner, the State, etc): *If he dies without an heir, his property will ~ to the state.* **~·ible** /-əbl/ *adj* that may ~. **re·ver·sion** /rɪ'vɜ:ʃn *US:* -ʒn/ *n* 1 [U] ~ing (of property, etc). ⇨ 2 above. **2** [C] right to possess property in certain circumstances; land, property, etc to which one has such a right; **3** [U] ~ing(1): *reversion of plants, etc* (ie to ancestral types). **re·ver·sion·ary** /rɪ'vɜ:ʃənərɪ *US:* -ʒənerɪ/ *adj* of reversion(2).

re·vet·ment /rɪ'vetmənt/ *n* retaining wall; facing of masonry, concrete, etc on an embankment, etc.

re·view /rɪ'vju:/ *vt, vi* 1 [VP6A] consider or examine again; go over again in the mind: ~ *the past;* ~ *last week's lesson.* **2** [VP6A] inspect formally (troops, a fleet, etc). **3** [VP6A,2A,C] write an account of (new books, etc) for newspapers and other periodicals: *His new novel has been favourably ~ed. Mr Hay ~s for 'The Spectator'.* □ *n* 1 [U] act of ~ing(1). **come under ~**, be considered or examined. [C] instance of such ~ing: *a ~ of the year's sporting events.* **2** [C] inspection of military, naval, etc forces: *hold a ~.* **3** [C] article that critically examines a new book, etc: *write ~s for the monthly magazines; a ~ copy of a book*, one presented by the publishers to the editor of a periodical for ~. **4** [C] periodical with articles on current events, ~s of new books, etc. **~er** *n* person who writes ~s (of books, etc).

re·vile /rɪ'vaɪl/ *vt, vi* [VP6A,3A] ~ *at/against*, swear at; abuse: ~ *at/against corruption;* ~ *one's persecutors.*

re·vise /rɪ'vaɪz/ *vt* [VP6A] reconsider; read carefully through, esp in order to correct and improve: ~ *one's estimates;* ~ *one's opinion of sb. She's revising her notes for the exams*, going through them in preparation for them. **the R~d Version**, the Version of the Bible made in 1870—84 as a Revision of the translation published in 1611, known as *the Authorized Version.* □ *n* [C] (printing) proof-sheet in which errors marked in an earlier proof have been corrected. **re·viser** *n* person who ~s.

re·vi·sion /rɪ'vɪʒn/ *n* [U] revising or being ~d; [C] instance of this: *after two revisions;* [C] that which has been ~d; corrected version. **re·vi·sion·ist** /rɪ'vɪʒənɪst/ *n* person who supports a review of the fundamental tenets of a political ideology. **re·vi·sion·ism** /-ɪzəm/ *n*

re·vital·ize /ri:'vaɪtəlaɪz/ *vt* put new life into; restore vitality. **re·vital·iz·ation** /ri:,vaɪtəlaɪ'zeɪʃn *US:* -lɪ'z-/ *n*

re·vival /rɪ'vaɪvl/ *n* 1 [U] reviving or being revived; bringing or coming back into use or knowledge; [C] instance of this: *the ~ of an old custom; a ~ of a play by Maugham; a ~ of trade.* **the R~ of Learning**, the Renaissance. **2** [C] (series of meetings intended to produce an) increase of interest in religion: *a religious* ∼; ∼ *meetings.* ∼·ist /-vəlɪst/ *n* person who organizes or conducts religious ∼ meetings.

re·vive /rɪ'vaɪv/ *vi,vt* [VP6A,2A] 1 come or bring back to consciousness, strength, health or an earlier state: ∼ *a person who has fainted;* ∼ *an old play,* produce it for the theatre after many years. *The flowers will* ∼ *in water. Our hopes* ∼*d.* 2 come or bring into use again: *customs which* ∼/*are* ∼*d.*

re·viv·ify /rɪ:'vɪvɪfaɪ/ *vt* (*pt,pp* -fied) restore to animation; give new life or liveliness to.

re·vo·ca·ble /'revəkəbl/ *adj* that can be revoked. revo·ca·tion /ˌrevə'keɪʃn/ *n* [U] revoking or being revoked; [C] instance of this.

re·voke /rɪ'vəʊk/ *vt,vi* 1 repeal; cancel; withdraw (a decree, consent, permission, etc): ∼ *an order/a driving licence.* 2 [VP2A] (of a player at such card games as whist and bridge) fail to follow suit (ie not play a card of the same suit as that led by another player although he could do so). □ *n* failure of this kind.

re·volt /rɪ'vəʊlt/ *vi,vt* 1 [VP2A,3A] ∼ (*against*), rise in rebellion: *The people* ∼*ed against their oppressors.* 2 [VP3A] ∼ *against/at/from,* be filled with disgust or horror: *Human nature* ∼*s at/from/ against such a crime. This is a doctrine from which sensitive persons must* ∼. 3 [VP6A] fill with disgust or horror: *scenes that* ∼*ed all who saw them.* □ *n* [U] act of ∼ing; state of having ∼ed(1): *a period of* ∼; *break out in* ∼; *stir the people to* ∼; [C] instance of this; rebellion or rising: ∼*s against oppression.*

re·volt·ing /rɪ'vəʊltɪŋ/ *adj* disgusting: ∼ *behaviour;* ∼ *to our ideas of morality.* ∼·ly *adv* in a way that disgusts: *a* ∼*ly dirty room.*

rev·ol·ution /ˌrevə'lu:ʃn/ *n* 1 [C] act of revolving or journeying round: *the* ∼ *of the earth round the sun;* [C] complete turn of a wheel, etc: *sixty-five* ∼*s* (or, colloq *revs*) *a minute.* 2 [C,U] (instance of) complete change (in conditions, ways of doing things, esp in methods of government when caused by the overthrow of one system by force): *the French R*∼ (in 1789); *prefer evolution to* ∼ *in politics;* ∼*s in our ideas of time and space;* ∼*s in our ways of travelling,* eg as the result of travel by air. ∼·ary /-ʃənərɪ US: -nerɪ/ *adj* of a ∼(2); bringing, causing, favouring, great (and perhaps violent) changes: ∼*ary ideas; a* ∼*ary society; imprisoned for advocating* ∼*ary principles.* □ *n* supporter of a (political) ∼. ∼·ize /-naɪz/ *vt* [VP6A] 1 fill with ∼*ary* principles. 2 make a complete change in; cause to be entirely different: *The use of atomic energy will* ∼*ize the lives of coming generations.*

re·volve /rɪ'vɒlv/ *vt,vi* 1 [VP6A,2A,3A] ∼ (*about/around*), (cause to) go round in a circle: *A wheel* ∼*s about/round its axis. The earth* ∼*s round/about the sun. This theatre has a revolving stage.* 2 [VP6A] turn over in the mind; think about all sides of (a problem, etc): ∼ *a problem in one's mind.*

re·volver /rɪ'vɒlvə(r)/ *n* pistol with a revolving mechanism that makes it possible to fire it a number of times without reloading.

re·vue /rɪ'vju:/ *n* [C] theatrical entertainment which consists of a medley of dialogue, dance and song, usu holding up current events, fashions, etc, to satire; [U] this form of entertainment: *to appear/ perform in* ∼.

re·vul·sion /rɪ'vʌlʃn/ *n* [U] (no *pl*) 1 sudden and complete change of feeling: *There was a* ∼ *of pub-*

lic feeling in favour of the accused woman. 2 ∼ (*against/from*), feeling of reaction.

re·ward /rɪ'wɔ:d/ *n* 1 [U] recompense for service or merit: *work without hope of* ∼; *the* ∼ *of virtue; get very little in* ∼ *for one's hard work.* 2 [C] that which is offered, given or obtained in return for work or services, or the restoration of lost or stolen property, the capture of a criminal, etc: *offer a* ∼ *of £100 for information about a stolen painting.* □ *vt* [VP6A,14] ∼ *sb* (*for sth*), give a ∼ to (sb for sth): *Is that how you* ∼ *me for my help?*

re·wire /ˌri:'waɪə(r)/ *vt* provide, eg a building, with new wiring (for electric current).

re·word /ˌri:'wɜ:d/ *vt* [VP6A] express again in different words: *If we* ∼ *the telegram we can save one-third of the cost.*

re·write /ˌri:'raɪt/ *vt* [VP6A] write again in a different style, etc. □ /'ri:raɪt/ *n* (colloq) sth rewritten: (attrib) *a '*∼ *man,* one employed to ∼ articles, books, etc in a form suitable for publication.

Rex /reks/ *n* (abbr **R**) reigning king (used as Regina is used).

rhap·sody /'ræpsədɪ/ *n* [C] (*pl* -dies) 1 enthusiastic expression of delight (in speech, poetry, etc): *Everyone went into rhapsodies over Helen's wedding dress.* 2 (music) composition in irregular form: *Liszt's Hungarian Rhapsodies.* rhap·so·dize /'ræpsədaɪz/ *vi* [VP2A,3A] rhapsodize (*about/ over/on*), talk or write with great enthusiasm.

rhea /rɪə/ *n* three-toed ostrich of S America.

Rhen·ish /'renɪʃ/ *adj* of the River Rhine and the districts on its banks: ∼ *wine,* hock.

rheo·stat /'ri:əstæt/ *n* instrument for regulating the strength of an electric current by means of different resistances in the circuit, eg as in the volume control of a radio receiver.

rhe·sus /'ri:səs/ *n* small monkey with a short tail, common in N India, often used in biological experiments. ⇨ the illus at ape.

rhet·oric /'retərɪk/ *n* [U] 1 (art of) using words impressively in speech and writing. 2 language with much display and ornamentation (often with the implication of insincerity and exaggeration): *the* ∼ *of the politicians.*

rhe·tori·cal /rɪ'tɒrɪk/ US: -'tɔ:r-/ *adj* in, using, a style designed to impress or persuade; artificial or exaggerated in language: *a* ∼ *speech.* a ∼ *question,* one asked for the sake of effect, to impress people, no answer being needed or expected. ∼·ly /-klɪ/ *adv*

rhet·or·ician /ˌretə'rɪʃn/ *n* person skilled in rhetoric or fond of rhetorical language.

rheum /ru:m/ *n* [U] watery discharge from the nose or eyes.

rheu·matic /ru:'mætɪk/ *adj* relating to, causing, caused by, rheumatism; suffering from, liable to have, rheumatism: ∼ *joints.* ∼ *fever,* serious fever with inflammation of joints, chiefly in children. □ *n* 1 person who suffers from rheumatism. 2 (*pl* colloq) ∼ pains.

rheu·ma·tism /'ru:mətɪzəm/ *n* [U] (kinds of) painful disease with stiffness and inflammation of the muscles and joints.

rheu·ma·toid /'ru:mətɔɪd/ *adj* of rheumatism. ∼ **arthritis,** chronic form of arthritis.

rhi·nal /'raɪnl/ *adj* (anat) of the nose or nostrils.

Rhine /raɪn/ *n* German river: ∼ *wine,* = hock. '∼·stone *n* kind of rock-crystal; paste gem made in imitation of a diamond.

rhino /'raɪnəʊ/ *n* (*pl* ∼s /-nəʊz/) (colloq abbr of)

rhinoceros.

rhi·noc·er·os /raɪ'nɒsərəs/ n (pl ~es /-əsɪz/ or, collectively, ~) thick-skinned, heavily built animal of Africa and Asia with one or two horns on the snout. ⇨ the illus at large.

rhi·zome /'raɪzəʊm/ n [C] (bot) thick, horizontal stem of some plants, eg iris, on or just below the ground, from which new roots grow.

rho·do·den·dron /ˌrəʊdə'dendrən/ n [C] kinds of evergreen shrub with large flowers growing in clusters.

rhomb /rɒm/, **rhom·bus** /'rɒmbəs/ nn four-sided figure with equal sides, and angles which are not right angles (eg diamond or lozenge shape). ⇨ the illus at quadrilateral. **rhom·boid** /'rɒmbɔɪd/ adj of the shape of a ~. □ n rhombus with only its opposite sides equal. ⇨ the illus at quadrilateral.

rhu·barb /'ruːbɑːb/ n [U] **1** (garden plant with) thick, juicy stalks which are cooked and eaten like fruit. **2** (colloq) nonsense; (US) angry disagreement.

rhyme (US also **rime**) /raɪm/ n **1** [U] sameness of sound of the endings of two or more words at the ends of lines of verse, eg say, day, play; measure, pleasure; puff, rough. **without ~ or reason**, without meaning; nonsensical(ly). **2** [C] ~ (for/ to), word which provides a ~: Is there a ~ to/for 'hiccups'? **3** [C] verse or verses with ~. **'nursery ~**, verse for small children. **4** [U] the employment of ~: The story should be told in ~, in verse with ~s. □ vt,vi **1** [VP6A] put together to form a ~: Can we ~ 'hiccups' and 'pick-ups'? **2** [VP2A,3A] ~ (with), (of words or lines of verse) be in ~: 'Piebald' doesn't ~ with 'ribald'. **rhyming slang**, eg 'trouble and strife' for 'wife'. **3** [VP2A] write verse(s) with ~. **rhymed** adj having ~s: ~d verse. **~·ster** /'raɪmstə(r)/ n (usu contemptuous) person who writes ~s or verses.

rhythm /'rɪðəm/ n **1** [U] regular succession of weak and strong stresses, accents, sounds or movements (in speech, music, dancing, etc); regular recurrence of events, processes, etc: the ~ of the tides, their regular rise and fall. **2** [C] particular kind of such regular succession or recurrence. **rhyth·mic** /'rɪðmɪk/, **rhyth·mi·cal** /'rɪðmɪkl/ adjj marked by ~; having ~: the ~ical tread of marching soldiers.

rib /rɪb/ n [C] **1** any one of the 12 pairs of curved bones extending from the backbone round the chest to the front of the body in man; ⇨ the illus at skeleton; corresponding bone in an animal. **dig/ poke sb in the ribs**, poke him to draw his attention (good-naturedly) to sth or to show enjoyment of a joke. **2** (of various things like ribs) vein of a leaf; mark left on sand on the sea-shore by waves; (in a wooden boat) one of the curved pieces of timber to which planks are secured; raised line in a piece of knitting; long, narrow, raised ridge on cloth; hinged rod of an umbrella-frame. □ vt (-bb-) [VP6A] **1** supply with, mark off in, ribs: ribbed cloth, having rib-like marks. **2** (US, colloq or sl) tease.

rib·ald /'rɪbld/ adj (of a person) using indecent or irreverent language or humour; (of language, laughter, etc) coarse; mocking: ~ jests/songs. □ n person who uses ~ language. **~·ry** /-drɪ/ n [U] ~ language; coarse jesting.

rib·and /'rɪbənd/ n (old use) ribbon.

rib·bon /'rɪbən/ n **1** [C,U] (piece or length of) silk or other material woven in a long, narrow strip or

band, used for ornamenting, for tying things, etc: Her hair was tied up with a ~. Typewriter ~s may be all black or black and red. **2** [C] piece of ~ of a special design, colour, etc worn to indicate membership of an order, as a symbol of a military decoration (when medals are not worn). **3** [C] long, narrow strip: His clothes were hanging in ~s, were torn or worn to strips. The shirts were torn to ~s in the washing machine. **4** ~ **de'velopment** n (the building of) long lines of houses along main roads leading out of a large town (considered to spoil the countryside).

ri·bo·fla·vin /ˌraɪbəʊ'fleɪvɪn/ n [U] growth-producing factor in the vitamin B_2 complex, found in meat, milk, some vegetables, and produced synthetically.

rice /raɪs/ n [U] (plant with) pearl-white grain used as a staple food everywhere: polished ~, with the husks removed; brown ~, unpolished ~; ground ~, ~ ground to a fine powder. ⇨ the illus at cereal. **'~-paper** n kind of thin paper used by Chinese artists for painting on; edible kind used in cooking and for packing cakes, sweets, etc.

rich /rɪtʃ/ adj (-er, -est) **1** having much money or property: the ~ and the poor, ~ people and poor people. **2** costly; splendid; luxurious: ~ clothes/ jewels/furniture. **3** ~ in, producing or having much or many; abundant: ~ in minerals; an art gallery ~ in paintings by the Dutch masters. **4** (of food) containing a large proportion of fat, oil, butter, eggs, etc: a ~ fruit cake; a ~ diet. **5** (of colours, sounds, etc) full; deep; mellow; strong: the ~ colours of the begonias; ~ tones; the ~ voice of the baritone. **6** (colloq) highly entertaining; giving opportunities for humour: a ~ joke; a ~ incident. That's ~! (often ironic). **~·ly** adv **1** in a ~ manner: ~ly dressed. **2** (esp) **~·ly deserved**, thoroughly; fully: He ~ly deserved the punishment he received. **~·ness** n [U] quality or state of being ~ (but not usu in sense of **1** above).

riches /'rɪtʃɪz/ n pl wealth; being rich: the enjoyment of ~; amass great ~.

rick¹ /rɪk/ n [C] mass of hay, straw, corn, etc regularly built up (and usu thatched or otherwise covered to protect it from the rain). □ vt [VP6A] make (hay, etc) into a ~.

rick² /rɪk/ = wrick.

rick·ets /'rɪkɪts/ n (with sing or pl v) disease of childhood, marked by softening and malformation of the bones, caused by deficiency of vitamin D as found in fresh food, eg milk, butter.

rick·ety /'rɪkətɪ/ adj weak, esp in the joints; likely to break and collapse: ~ furniture; a ~ old car.

rick·shaw /'rɪkʃɔː/ n two-wheeled covered vehicle for one or two passengers, pulled by a man. **'cycle ~**, three-wheeled bicycle with ~ seating attached behind the driver.

rico·chet /'rɪkəʃeɪ US: ˌrɪkə'ʃeɪ/ n [U] jumping or skipping movement (of a stone, bullet, etc) after hitting the ground, a solid substance or the surface of water; [C] hit made by sth after such a jumping or skipping movement. □ vi,vt (-t- or -tt-) (pt,pp -che(t)ted /-ʃeɪd/) [VP6A,2A] (of a shot, etc) (cause to) rebound, skip or bound off: The bullet ~ed off the wall.

rid /rɪd/ vt (pt,pp rid) [VP14] **rid of**, make free: rid oneself of debt/lice; rid a country of terrorists/a house of mice. **be/get rid of**, be/become free of: We were glad to be rid of our overcoats. These shoes are difficult to get rid of, (eg of articles in a shop) difficult to sell. *How can we get rid of this unwelcome visitor*, How can we manage to make him leave?

rid·dance /'rɪdns/ n [U] (usu *good* ~) welcome clearing away; state of being rid of sth unwanted or undesirable: *Their departure was a good* ~, it brought satisfaction because we wanted to be rid of them.

rid·den /'rɪdn/ (*pp* of ride²) (esp in compounds) oppressed or dominated by: '*priest*-~; *po'lice*-~.

riddle¹ /'rɪdl/ n [C] 1 puzzling question, statement or description, intended to make a person use his wits: *ask sb a* ~; *know the answer to a* ~. 2 puzzling person, thing, situation, etc: *the* ~ *of the universe/of existence*. □ *vt* ~ *me this*, solve this ~ (as a challenge).

riddle² /'rɪdl/ n [C] coarse sieve (for stones, earth, gravel, cinders etc). □ *vt* 1 [VP6A] pass (soil, ashes, corn etc) through a ~; agitate (a grate, eg in a stove) in order to force ashes, small cinders, etc, through. 2 [VP6A,14] ~ (*with*), make many holes in (sth), eg by firing bullets into it: ~ *a ship with shot*; ~ *a man with bullets*; ~ *an argument*, refute it by bringing many facts, etc against it. *be* ~*d with*, be filled or permeated with: *a murder* ~*d with puzzles.*

ride¹ /raɪd/ n [C] 1 period of riding; journey on horseback, on a bicycle, etc or in a public conveyance (cf *go for a drive* in a privately owned car, etc): *go for a* ~ *before breakfast. 'Give me a* ~ *on your shoulders, Daddy.' It's a fivepenny* ~ *on a bus.* *take sb for a* ~, (colloq) deceive, swindle or humiliate him. 2 road or track (usu unpaved), esp one through a wood or forest for the use of persons on horseback and not normally used by vehicles.

ride² /raɪd/ vi,vt (*pl* rode /rəʊd/, *pp* ridden /'rɪdn/) 1 [VP2A,B,C,4A] sit on a horse, etc and be carried along; sit on a bicycle, etc and cause it to go forward: *He jumped on his horse and rode off/away. He was riding fast.* ~ *for a fall*, ride recklessly; (fig) act in such a way that failure or disaster is probable. 2 [VP6A] sit on and control: ~ *a horse/pony/bicycle.* 3 [VP2A,C,4A] be in, and be carried on, a cart, bus or other vehicle: ~ *in a bus*; ~ *in/on a cart.* 4 [VP6A] compete in, on horseback, etc: ~ *a race.* 5 [VP2C,3A] ~ *on*, sit or go or be on sth, move astride, as if on a horse: *The boy was riding on his father's shoulders.* 6 [VP15A] allow (sb) to ~(5): *Shall I* ~ *you on my shoulders/knees?* 7 [VP2A] go out regularly on horseback (as a pastime, for exercise, etc): *I've given up riding.* ~ *to hounds*, go fox-hunting. 8 [VP6A] go through or over on horseback, etc: ~ *the prairies/the desert.* 9 [VP2B] (of a jockey or other person) weigh when ready for riding: *He* ~*s 9 stone, 6 pounds.* 10 [VP2D] (of ground, etc) be in a specified condition for riding on (usu on horseback): *The heavy rain made the course* ~ *soft. The ground rode hard after the frost.* 11 [VP6A,2C] float on: *a ship riding the waves*; float on water: *a ship riding at anchor*; be supported by: *an albatross riding (on) the wind. The moon was riding high*, appeared high as if floating. ~ *out a storm*, (of a ship) come safely through it; (fig) come safely through trouble, attack, controversy, etc. *let sth* ~, (colloq) take no action on it; leave things to take their natural course. 12 ~ *sb down*, (a) chase (on horseback) and catch up with. (b) direct one's horse at sb so as to let the horse knock him down: ~ *down a fugitive.* 13 [VP2C] ~ *up*, eg of an ar-

ticle of clothing, shift or move upwards, out of place. 14 ridden *pp* tyrannized, dominated: *ridden by fears/prejudices*; '*pest-ridden.*

rider /'raɪdə(r)/ n 1 person who rides, esp one who rides a horse: *Miss White is no* ~. ⇨ also *di'spatch*-~ at dispatch¹(2). 2 additional observation following a statement, verdict, etc: *The jury added a* ~ *to their verdict recommending mercy.* ~*less* adj without a ~: *a* ~*less horse careering round the race-course.*

ridge /rɪdʒ/ n [C] 1 raised line where two sloping surfaces meet: *the* ~ *of a roof.* '~*pole* n horizontal pole of a long tent; strong horizontal main beam at the apex of a roof. '~*tile* n tile for the ~ of a roof. 2 long, narrow stretch of high land along the tops of a line of hills; long mountain range or watershed. 3 (in ploughed land) raised part between two furrows. □ *vt* [VP6A] make into, cover with, ~s.

ridi·cule /'rɪdɪkjuːl/ n [U] making or being made fun of; derision; mockery: *pour* ~ *on a scheme*; *an object of* ~. *hold a man up to* ~, make fun of him. *lay oneself open to* ~, behave so that people are likely to make fun of one. *vt* [VP6A] make fun of; cause (sb or sth) to appear foolish: *Why do you* ~ *my proposal?*

rid·icu·lous /rɪ'dɪkjʊləs/ adj deserving to be laughed at; absurd: *You look* ~ *in those tight jeans. What a* ~ *idea!* ~*ly* adv

rid·ing¹ /'raɪdɪŋ/ n [U] (from ride²) '~*breeches* n pl used for riding on horseback. '~*habit* n woman's long skirt and tight-fitting coat (worn when riding a horse). '~*light/-lamp* n light in the rigging of a ship which is at anchor. '~*master* n man who teaches horse-~. '~*school* n one for teaching and practising horse-~.

rid·ing² /'raɪdɪŋ/ n (GB until 1974) one of the three administrative divisions of Yorkshire: *the North/East/West R*~ since 1974 replaced by *Humberside* and *North/South/West Yorkshire*).

Ries·ling /'riːslɪŋ/ n dry, white wine.

rife /raɪf/ adj (*pred* only) 1 wide-spread; common: *Is superstition still* ~ *in the country?* 2 ~ *with*, full of: *The country was* ~ *with rumours of war.*

riff /rɪf/ n repeated phrase in jazz or pop music.

riffle /'rɪfl/ vt,vi 1 [VP6A] shuffle playing cards by holding part of the pack in each hand and releasing the edges so that they fall haphazardly into one pack again. 2 [VP6A] turn over (the pages of a book, periodical, etc) quickly. [VP3A] ~ *through sth*, shuffle (a pack of cards); turn over quickly or casually (the pages of a newspaper, a periodical, etc).

riff-raff /'rɪf ræf/ n *the* ~, ill-behaved people of the lowest class; the rabble; disreputable persons: *Is it only the* ~ *who leave litter about in the parks?*

a rifle

rifle¹ /'raɪfl/ vt [VP6A] cut spiral grooves in (a gun, its barrel or bore). □ n gun with a long ~d barrel, to be fired from the shoulder; large gun with such spiral grooves; (*pl*) troops armed with ~s: *the Royal Irish R*~*s.* '~*range* n (a) place where men practise shooting with ~s. (b) distance that a ~ bullet will carry: *within/out of* ~*range.* '~*shot* *n* (a) = ~-range(b). (b) good marksman with a ~. '~-man /-mən/ *n* (*pl*-men) soldier of a ~ regiment.

rifle² /'raɪfl/ *vt* [VP6A] search thoroughly in order to steal from: *The thief ~d every drawer in the room/~d the drawers of their contents.*

rift /rɪft/ *n* [C] **1** split or crack: *a ~ in the clouds.* '~-valley *n* steep-sided valley caused by subsidence of the earth's crust. **2** (fig) dissension (eg between two friends, friendly groups, parties, etc).

rig¹ /rɪg/ *vt,vi* (-gg-) **1** [VP6A,14,2A,C] *rig (with),* supply (a ship) with masts, spars, rigging, sails, etc; (of a ship) be supplied with these things; prepare for sea in this way: *rig a ship with new sails. The schooner is rigging for another voyage.* **2** [VP14,15B] *rig sb (out) (in/with sth),* (a) provide with necessary clothes, equipment, etc. (b) (colloq) dress up: *She was rigged out in her best clothes. He rigged himself out as a sailor/tramp.* '**rig-out** *n* (colloq) person's clothes, etc: *What a queer rig-out!* **rig sth up,** (a) assemble or adjust parts of. (b) make, put together, quickly or with any materials that may be available: *The climbers rigged up a shelter for the night on a narrow ledge. They rigged up some scaffolding for the workmen.* (c) = rig sth out. □ *n* [C] **1** way in which a ship's masts, sails, etc, are arranged: *the fore-and-aft rig of a schooner.* **2** equipment put together for a special purpose: *an* '*oil-rig/'drilling-rig,* ⇨ oil; *a* '*test-rig,* on which motor-vehicles are tested for fitness. **3** (colloq) style of dress: *a bizarre rig.* **rigging** *n* [U] all the ropes, etc which support a ship's masts and sails. **rig-ger** *n* person who rigs ships, etc; (esp) one whose work is to assemble and adjust the parts of aircraft.

rig² /rɪg/ *vt* (-gg-) [VP6A] manage or control fraudulently, eg for private profit: *rig the market,* cause prices (of stocks, shares, etc) to go up (or down) by trickery; *a rigged election.*

right¹ /raɪt/ *adj* (contrasted with *wrong*) **1** (of conduct, etc) morally good; required by law or duty: *Always do what is ~ and honourable. It seems only ~ to tell you that…. You were quite ~ to refuse. You were ~ in deciding not to go/were ~ in your decision.* **2** true; correct; satisfactory: *What's the ~ time? Your account of what happened is not quite ~. Have you got the ~* (= exact) *fare?* **get sth ~,** understand sth clearly, so that there is no error or misunderstanding: *Now let's get this ~ before we pass on to the next point.* **put/set sth ~,** restore to order, good health, a good condition, etc: *put a watch ~,* ie to the correct time. *It is not your business to put me ~,* to correct my errors. *This medicine will soon put you ~.* ,*R~ you* '*are!/* ,*R~-*'*ol/R~!* *int* (colloq) used to indicate agreement to an order, request, proposal, etc. ,*All* '~ !/ **Alright!** /,ɔːl'raɪt/ *int* used to indicate agreement, approval, etc: ,~-'**minded** *adj* having opinions or principles based on what is ~: *All ~-minded people will agree with me when I say….* **3** most suitable; best in view of the circumstances, etc; preferable: *Are we on the ~ road? Which is the ~ way to Exeter? He is the ~ man for the job. Which is the ~ side* (ie the side meant to be seen or used) *of this cloth? Have you got it the ~ side up? He's still on the ~ side of fifty,* is still under 50 years old. **get on the ~ side of sb,** win his favour. **4** (*all*) ~, in good or normal condition; sound; sane: *Do you feel all ~? not (quite) ~ in the/one's head,* (colloq) not sane; foolish. *not in one's ~*

mind, in an abnormal mental state. ~ *as rain/as a trivet,* (colloq) perfectly sound or healthy. **5** (of an angle) of 90° (ie neither acute nor obtuse). *at* '~ *angles/at a ~ angle (to),* at an angle of 90° (to). ⇨ the illus at angle. '~-**angled** *adj* having a ~ angle: *a ~-angled triangle.* ~·**ly** *adv* justly; justifiably; correctly; truly: *act ~ly. R~ly or wrongly, I think the man should not be punished. She has been sacked, and ~ly so. Am I ~ly informed?* ~·**ness** *n*

right² /raɪt/ *adv* **1** straight; directly: *Put it ~ in the middle. The wind was ~ in our faces.* ~ *away/off,* at once, without any delay. ~ *now,* at this very moment. ~ *on! int* (colloq) used to indicate approval or encouragement. **2** all the way (*to/round, etc*); completely (*off/out, etc*): *Go ~ to the end of this winding road, and then turn left. He slipped ~ to the bottom of the icy slope. There's a veranda ~ round the building. The pear was rotten ~ through. The prisoner got ~ away. He turned ~ round.* **3** justly; correctly; satisfactorily; properly: *if I remember ~* (cf *if I am ~ly informed*); *Have I guessed ~ or wrong? Nothing seems to go ~ with him,* Everything he does is a failure. *It serves sb ~,* It is what he deserves, he has been ~ly punished, etc. **4** (old or dial use) to the full; very: *We were ~ glad to hear that…. He knew ~ well that….* '~-**down** *adj, adv* (dial; more usu *downright*) thorough(ly). **5** *R~* **Honourable,** ⇨ honourable. *R~* **Reverend,** ⇨ reverend.

right³ /raɪt/ *n* **1** [U] that which is right¹(1), good, just, honourable, true, etc: *know the difference between ~ and wrong. May God defend the ~. be in the ~,* have justice and truth on one's side. **2** [U] proper authority or claim; the state of being justly entitled to sth; [C] sth to which one has a just claim; sth one may do or have by law: *He has a ~/no ~/not much ~ to do that. What gives you the ~ to say that? by ~(s),* if justice were done; justly; correctly: *The property is not mine by ~(s). by ~ of,* because of: *The Normans ruled England by ~ of conquest.* **in one's own ~,** because of a personal claim, qualification, etc not depending upon another person: *She's a peeress in her own ~,* ie not only by marriage. ~ *of way,* (a) ~ of the general public to use a path, road, etc esp a ~ which has existed from ancient times through land that is privately owned: *Is there a ~ of way across these fields?* (b) (in road traffic) ~ to use the carriageway before others; precedence: *It's my ~ of way, so that lorry must stop or slow down until I've passed it. human ~s,* those ~s that all people are or should be entitled to, eg a fair trial in a court of law, access to medical care and education, freedom of religion. ⇨ *the four freedoms* at freedom. *women's ~s,* (esp) of equality with men (in political, economic, social, etc affairs). ⇨ lib. *stand on/assert one's ~s,* say what one's ~s are and declare that they will not be surrendered. **3** (*pl*) true state. *put/set things to ~s,* put them in order. ~*s and wrongs,* true facts: *What are the ~s and wrongs of the case?* ⇨ right¹(2).

right⁴ /raɪt/ *vt* [VP6A] put, bring or come back, into the right or an upright condition; make sth right again: *The ship ~ed herself after the big wave had passed. That fault will ~ itself,* will be corrected without help. *The driver quickly ~ed the car after it skidded.* ~ *the helm,* put it amidships, ie neither to port nor to starboard.

right⁵ /raɪt/ *adj* (contrasted with *left*) of the side of the body which is toward the east when a person faces north: *my ∼ hand/leg. In Great Britain traffic keeps to the left, not the ∼, side of the road. The ∼ bank of a river is on the ∼ side as you look in the direction it is flowing.* **one's ∼ hand/arm,** (fig) one's most reliable helper. **one's ∼ hand** all one's energy: *put one's ∼ hand to the work,* work hard. **'∼-hand** *adj* (to be) placed on the ∼ hand: *a ∼-hand glove.* **,∼-'handed** *adj* (a) (of a person) using the ∼ hand more, or with more ease, than the left. (b) (of a blow, etc) given with the ∼ hand. **,∼-'hander** *n* (a) ∼-handed person. (b) ∼-handed blow. **,∼-'turn** *n* turn into a position at ∼ angles (90°) with the original one. **,∼-about 'turn/'face,** ∼ turn continued until one is faced in the opposite direction. □ *adv* to the ∼ hand or side: *He looked neither ∼ nor left. Eyes ∼!* as a military command. *The crowd divided ∼ and left.* **∼ and left,** everywhere: *He owes money ∼ and left,* owes money everywhere. □ *n* [U] **1** side or direction on one's ∼ hand: *Take the first turning to the ∼. Our troops attacked the enemy's ∼,* ∼ *wing or flank.* **2** (politics; usu **R∼**) conservative or reactionary party or parties: *members of the R∼.* **∼·ist** */-ɪst/ n* member of a ∼ wing political party. □ *adj* of such a party: *∼ist sympathizers.*

right·eous /'raɪtʃəs/ *adj* **1** doing what is morally right; obeying the law: *the ∼ and the wicked,* good and bad people. **2** morally justifiable: *∼ anger.* **∼·ly** *adv* **∼·ness** *n*

right·ful /'raɪtfl/ *adj* **1** according to law and justice: *the ∼ king; the ∼ owner of the land.* **2** (of actions, etc) fair; justifiable. **∼·ly** */-fəlɪ/ adv* **∼·ness** *n*

rigid /'rɪdʒɪd/ *adj* **1** stiff; unbending; that cannot be bent: *a ∼ support for a tent.* **2** firm; strict; not changing; not to be changed: *a ∼ disciplinarian; practise ∼ economy.* **∼·ly** *adv* **ri·gid·ity** /rɪ'dʒɪdətɪ/ *n* [U] **1** stiffness; inflexibility: *the ∼ity of his religious beliefs.* **2** strictness; sternness.

rig·ma·role /'rɪɡmərəʊl/ *n* [C] **1** long, wandering story or statement that does not mean much; incoherent account or description. **2** confusing and tiring procedure.

rigor mor·tis /ˌrɪɡə 'mɔːtɪs/ *n* (Lat) the stiffening of the muscles after death.

rig·or·ous /'rɪɡərəs/ *adj* **1** stern; strict; severe: *∼ discipline; a ∼ search for dutiable goods.* **2** harsh; severe: *a ∼ climate.* **∼·ly** *adv*

rig·our (US = **rigor**) /'rɪɡə(r)/ *n* **1** [U] sternness; strictness; strict enforcement (of rules, etc): *punish sb with the utmost ∼ of the law.* **2** (often *pl*) severe conditions: *the ∼s of prison life; the ∼(s) of the winter in Canada,* the severe climatic conditions.

rile /raɪl/ *vt* [VP6A] (colloq) annoy; rouse anger in: *It ∼d him that no one would believe his story.*

rill /rɪl/ *n* small stream; rivulet.

rim /rɪm/ *n* [C] circular edge of the framework of a wheel, on which the tyre is fitted; ⇨ the illus at bicycle. border (of steel, gold, etc) round the lenses of spectacles (hence *rimless spectacles,* having lenses without rims); edge, border or margin of sth circular: *the rim of a cup/bowl;* frame of a sieve. **,red-'rimmed** *adj* (of eyes) having red rims, eg from weeping. □ *vt* (-mm-) [VP6A] provide with a rim; be a rim for.

rime¹ /raɪm/ *n* (liter) hoarfrost. ⇨ hoar. □ *vt* [VP6A] cover with or as with ∼.

rime² /raɪm/ *n* = rhyme.

rind /raɪnd/ *n* [U] hard, outside skin or covering (of some fruits, eg melons, or of bacon and cheese);

[C] piece or strip of this skin; tough covering of one fruit.

rin·der·pest /'rɪndəpest/ *n* [U] contagious virus disease of cattle.

ring¹ /rɪŋ/ *n* [C] **1** circular band (often of gold or platinum, and set with a gem or gems) worn round a finger as an ornament, or as a token: *an en'gagement ∼; a 'wedding ∼;* similar band for other parts of the body: *an 'ear∼, a 'nose-∼.* **'∼-finger** *n* third of the left hand. **2** circular band of any kind of material, eg metal, wood, ivory: *a 'napkin ∼; a 'key-∼,* one of split metal, for carrying keys on. **'∼-mail/-armour** *nn* = chain-armour. ⇨ chain(4). **3** circle: *a ∼ of light round the moon; the ∼s of a tree,* seen in concentric circles of wood when the trunk is cut across, showing the tree's age; *puff out 'smoke-∼s* (of cigarette smoke). *The men were standing in a ∼.* **make/run '∼s round sb,** move, do things, much faster than he does. **4** combination of persons working together for their own advantage: *a ∼ of revolutionaries/smugglers.* **5** ('circus-)∼, circular enclosure or space for circus-riding. **'∼-master** *n* man who directs performances in a circus-∼. **6** space for the showing of cattle, dogs, etc (at farming exhibitions, etc). **7** betting at race meetings: **the ∼,** book-makers collectively. ⇨ book¹(8). **8** the 'prize-∼, ⇨ prize¹(3). **9** (compounds) **'∼-leader** *n* person who leads others in a rising against authority. **'∼-road** *n* road round and through the outskirts of a town, for the use of through traffic and designed to avoid congestion in the centre. Cf *by-pass,* a new road specially constructed. **'∼-worm** *n* [U] contagious disease of the skin, esp of children, causing round, red patches. **'∼-side** *n* place near to the ring of a circus, prize-fight, etc: *have a ∼side seat,* be favourably placed for seeing an event, etc. □ *vt,vi* (*pt,pp* ∼ed) **1** [VP6A,15B] surround: *∼ed about with enemies; ∼ cattle,* hem them into one place. **2** [VP6A] put a ∼ in the nose of (a bull, etc) or on the leg of (a bird, eg a homing pigeon). **3** [VP6A] (in games) toss or throw a ring or a horseshoe round, eg a mark, peg, etc; make a ring round (sth), eg with a pencil, or by shooting holes round a target. **4** [VP2A] (of a hunted fox) take a circular course.

ring² /rɪŋ/ *vt,vi* (*pt* rang /ræŋ/, *pp* rung /rʌŋ/) **1** [VP2A,B,C] give out a clear, musical sound as when metal vibrates: *How long has that telephone (bell) been ∼ing? Start work when the bell ∼s.* A shot rang out, The noise of a shot was heard. **2** [VP2D] produce a certain effect when heard: *His words rang hollow,* What he said seemed insincere. *His words rang true. The coin rang true/ false,* seemed, when tested by being thrown down, to be genuine/counterfeit. **3** [VP2A,3A] ∼ **(for sb/sth),** cause a bell to sound, as a summons, warning, etc: *She rang for the porter. Did you ∼, sir? Someone is ∼ing at the door,* ∼ing for admittance or attention. The cyclist didn't ∼. **4** [VP6A] cause sth, esp a bell, to ∼: ∼ *the bells;* ∼ *the bell for the steward;* ∼ *a coin,* test its genuineness by throwing it down on sth and listening to the sound. **∼ a bell,** (colloq) bring sth vaguely back to mind: *Ah! That ∼s a bell!* ∼ **the bell,** (colloq) be successful in sth. **5** [VP3A] ∼ **(with sth),** resound; re-echo: *The children's playground rang with happy shouts. The village rang with the praises of the brave girl.* **6** [VP2C] linger in one's hearing or memory: *His last words are still ∼ing in my ears.* **7** [VP2A,3A] ∼ **(with),** (of the ears) be filled with a ringing or humming sound: *My ears are still ~ing.* **8** ~ **sb (up)**, get into communication with sb by telephone: *I'll ~ you (up) this evening.* (US = *call sb (up)*.) ~ *off*, end a telephone conversation. **9** [VP6A] (of a chime of bells) announce (the hour, etc); strike the hours: *The bell ~s the hours, but not the quarters.* **10** [VP6A,15B] give a signal by ~ing a bell, etc: ~ *the knell of sth*, announce its end or downfall; ~ *an alarm*, give one by ~ing bells. ~ *the curtain up/down,* (in a theatre) give the signal for it to be raised/lowered. **11** [VP6A] sound (a peal, etc with a bell or bells). ~ *the changes (on),* (of church bells) ring the bells in different orders which are possible; (fig) put or arrange things, do things, in as many different ways as possible. **12** [VP15A] announce or celebrate the beginning or end of sth by ~ing bells. ~ *out the Old (year) and ~ in the New.* □ *n* **1** (*sing* only) resonant sound produced by a bell or piece of metal when it is struck: *This coin has a good ~.* **2** (*sing* only) loud and clear sound: *the ~ of happy voices. There was a ~ of sincerity in his promise.* **3** [C] act of ~ing; sound of a bell: *There was a ~ at the door. I'll give you a ~ this evening,* will ~ you up (by telephone). *~er n* bell-ringer.

ring·let /'rɪŋlɪt/ *n* [C] small curl of hair: *Her hair hung down in ~s.*

rink /rɪŋk/ *n* [C] specially prepared sheet of ice for skating or hockey, or floor for roller-skating.

rinse /rɪns/ *vt* [VP6A,15A,B] ~ **sth (out);** ~ **sth out of sth, 1** wash with clean water in order to remove unwanted substances, etc: ~ *soap out of the clothes;* ~ *the clothes,* to get soapy water out; ~ (*out*) *the teapot;* ~ *the tea-leaves out of the pot;* ~ (*out*) *the mouth,* eg while being treated by a dentist. **2** ~ *sth down,* help (food) down with a drink: *R~ it down with a glass of beer.* □ *n* **1** act of rinsing: *Give your hair a good ~ after you've shampooed it.* **2** solution for tinting the hair: *the blue ~ used by some elderly women.*

riot /'raɪət/ *n* **1** [C] violent outburst of lawlessness by the people in a district: *put down a ~ by force. R~s during the election were dealt with by the police.* **the 'R~ Act,** act dealing with the prevention of ~s and the breaking up of disorderly crowds. **read the 'R~ Act,** (**a**) read part of this Act officially to disorderly persons after which, if they do not disperse, they can be arrested for felony. (**b**) (joc, eg of parents) give a warning that noisy and unruly behaviour must stop. **2** [U] noisy, unontrolled behaviour (not lawless). **run ~,** throw off all discipline; (of plants) be out of control by growing fast and luxuriantly. **3** *a riot (of),* profusion; luxuriance: *The flower-beds were a ~ of colour.* **4** *a ~ (of),* unrestrained indulgence in or display of sth: *a ~ of emotion.* **5** *a ~,* (colloq) occasion of wild enthusiasm (as indicating great success): *His latest play was a ~ when it was produced in New York.* □ *vi* [VP2A,B,C] **1** take part in a ~(1,2): *The voters were ~ing all night after the election.* **2** [VP3A] ~ *in,* indulge or revel (in): *The tyrant ~ed in cruelty. ~er n* person who ~s. *~ous* /-əs/ *adj* likely to cause a ~; unruly; disorderly; running wild: *a ~ous assembly; charged with ~ous behaviour. ~ous·ly adv*

rip /rɪp/ *vt,vi* (-pp-) **1** [VP6A,15A,B,22] pull, tear or cut (sth) quickly and with force (to get it off, out, open, etc): *rip open a letter; rip the cover off; rip the seams of a garment; rip a piece of cloth in two;* make a long cut or tear in: *rip a tyre,* eg on a

rocky road. *My poor cat had its ear ripped open by a dog. rip sth/sb off,* (sl) steal (it); defraud (him). Hence, **'rip-off** *n* sth stolen; instance of stealing or defrauding. **'rip-cord** *n* cord which, when pulled during a descent, releases a parachute from its pack; cord pulled to release gas from a balloon. **2** [VP6A] saw (wood, etc) with the grain. **'rip-saw** *n* saw used for this. **3** [VP2A] (of material) tear; be ripped. **4** [VP2A,C] go forward, rush along. *Let her/it rip,* (colloq) (of a boat, car, machine, etc) allow it to go at its maximum speed. *let things rip,* cease to exercise control; let things take their natural course. □ *n* [C] torn place; long cut: *The rips in my tent were made by the horns of that angry bull.*

ri·par·ian /raɪˈpeərɪən/ *adj* of, on, the bank(s) of a river or lake: ~ *rights,* eg to catch fish in the river; ~ *property.*

ripe /raɪp/ *adj* **1** (of fruit, grain, etc) ready to be gathered and used: ~ *fruit; cherries not ~ enough to eat;* ~ *corn;* ~ *lips,* red and soft like ~ fruit. **2** matured and ready to be eaten or drunk: ~ *cheese/wine.* **3** fully developed: ~ *judgement/ scholarship; a person of ~ age,* a mature and experienced person; *a person of ~(r) years,* past the stage of youth. **4** ~ *for,* ready, fit, prepared: ~ *for mischief/revolt; land that is ~ for development,* eg for building houses or factories. *~·ly adv ~·ness n*

ripen /'raɪpən/ *vt,vi* [VP6A,2A] make or become ripe.

ri·poste /rɪˈpɒst/ *n* **1** quick return thrust in fencing (after parrying). **2** quick, sharp reply or retort. □ *vi* deliver a ~.

ripple /'rɪpl/ *n* [C] (sound of) small movement(s) on the surface of water, etc, eg made by a gentle wind; (sound of) the rise and fall of voices or laughter: *A long ~ of laughter passed through the audience.* □ *vt,vi* [VP6A,2A] (cause to) move in ~s; (cause to) rise and fall gently: *The wheat ~d in the breeze. The breeze ~d the corn-fields. The tide ~d the sand,* caused a wavy surface on the sand.

rip-tide /'rɪp taɪd/ *n* tide causing strong currents and rough water.

rise¹ /raɪz/ *n* **1** small hill; upward slope: *a ~ in the ground; a cottage situated on a ~.* **2** upward progress; increase (in value, temperature, etc): *a ~ in prices/social position, etc; have a ~ in wages* (US = *raise*); *the ~ and fall of the tide.* **3** (liter) coming up (of the sun, etc): *at ~ of sun/day,* (more usu *sunrise*). **4** movement of fish to the surface of water: *not a sign of a ~. I fished two hours without getting a ~. get/take a/the ~ out of sb,* cause him to show petulance or weakness (often by good-natured teasing). **5** origin; start: *The river has/takes its ~ among the hills. give ~ to,* cause; suggest: *Such conduct might give ~ to misunderstandings. ~r n* **1** *early/late ~r,* person who gets up early/late. **2** vertical part of a step, connecting two treads of a staircase.

rise² /raɪz/ *vi* (*pt* rose /rəʊz/, *pp* risen /'rɪzn/) [VP2A,B,C,3A,4A] ~ **(up), 1** (of the sun, moon, stars) appear above the horizon: *The sun ~s in the East. Has the moon ~n yet?* ⇨ set²(1). **2** get up from a lying, sitting or kneeling position: *He rose to welcome me. The wounded man fell and was too weak to ~. The horse rose on its hind legs. On rising from table...,* leaving the table at the end of the meal.... *Parliament will ~ on Thursday next,* cease to sit for business, start the recess. *The*

House rose at 10pm, ended its discussions, etc. **3** get out of bed; get up (which is commoner): *He* ∼*s very early.* **4** come to life (*again, from the dead*): *Jesus Christ rose* (*again*) *from the dead. Christ is* ∼*n* (as an Easter greeting). *He looks as though he had* ∼*n from the grave.* **5** go, come, up or higher; reach a high(er) level or position: *The smoke from our fire rose straight up in the still air. The river/ flood, etc has* ∼*n two feet. His voice rose in anger/excitement, etc*, became high, shrill. *Sugar has* ∼*n a penny a pound. Prices continue to* ∼. *The mercury in the barometer is rising. The bread won't* ∼, The dough will not swell with the yeast. *New office blocks are rising in our town.* '**high**-∼ *attrib adj* having many storeys: *high-*∼ *flats/ office-blocks.* ⇨ **skyscraper** at **sky(1)**. **the rising generation,** young people who are growing up. **rising twelve, etc,** (of a person) nearing the age of twelve, etc. **6** develop greater intensity or energy: *The wind is rising. His colour rose,* He became flushed. **7** come to the surface: *The fish were rising*, coming to the surface for food. *They say a drowning man* ∼*s three times. Bubbles rose from the bottom of the lake.* **8** become or be visible above the surroundings: *A range of hills rose on our left.* **9** reach a higher position in society; make progress (in one's profession, etc): ∼ *in the world;* ∼ *to greatness;* ∼ *from the ranks*, ie to be an officer; *a rising young politician/lawyer.* **10** ∼ **to,** develop powers equal to. ∼ **to the occasion/ challenge/task, etc,** prove oneself able to deal with an unexpected problem, a difficult task, etc. **11** slope upwards: *rising ground.* **12** have as a starting-point: *Where does the Nile* ∼*? The quarrel rose from a mere trifle.* **13** ∼ **against,** rebel (against the government, etc). **ris·ing** *n* (esp) armed outbreak; rebellion.

ris·ible /ˈrɪzəbl/ *adj* of laughing and laughter; inclined to laugh; causing laughter, ludicrous. **risibil·ity** /ˌrɪzəˈbɪlətɪ/ *n* [U] disposition to laugh.

risk /rɪsk/ *n* **1** [C,U] (instance of) possibility or chance of meeting danger, suffering loss, injury, etc: *There's no/not much* ∼ *of your catching cold if you wrap up well.* **run/take** ∼*s/a* ∼, put oneself in a position where there is ∼: *She's too sensible to take a* ∼ *when she's driving.* To succeed in business one must be prepared to run ∼*s.* **run/take the** ∼ **of doing sth,** do sth which may involve ∼: *We'll take the* ∼ *of being late. He was ready to run the* ∼ *of being taken prisoner by the enemy.* **at the** ∼ **of/at** ∼ **to,** with the possibility of (loss, etc): *He was determined to get there even at the* ∼ *of his life. at* ∼, threatened by uncertainties (such as failure, loss, etc): *Is the Government's income policy seriously at* ∼*? at one's own* ∼, accepting responsibility, agreeing to make no claims, for loss, injury, etc. *at owner's* ∼, (of goods sent by rail, etc) the owner to bear any loss there may be. **2** [C] (insurance) amount for which sb or sth is insured; the person or thing insured. *He's a good/poor* ∼. ⇨ also *security* ∼ at **security**. □ *vt* **1** [VP6A] expose to ∼; ∼ *one's health/fortune/neck* (ie life), etc. **2** [VP6A,C] take the chances of: ∼ *failure. We must* ∼ *getting caught in a storm.* **risky** *adj* (-ier, -iest) **1** full of ∼: *a* ∼*y undertaking.* **2** = risqué. ∼·**ily** /-ɪlɪ/ *adv* ∼·**i·ness** *n*

ri·sotto /rɪˈzɒtəʊ/ *n* [C] dish of rice cooked with butter, cheese, onions, etc.

ris·qué /ˈriːskeɪ *US:* rɪˈskeɪ/ *adj* (of a story, remark, situation in a drama, etc) likely to offend against

propriety; on the borderline of indecency.

ris·sole /ˈrɪsəʊl/ *n* [C] small ball of minced meat, fish, etc mixed with potato, eggs, breadcrumbs, etc and fried.

rite /raɪt/ *n* [C] act or ceremony (esp in religious services): '*burial* ∼*s;* ∼*s of baptism;* ¡*niti'ation* ∼*s. He died after receiving the* ∼*s of the church*, eg the sacraments of Penance, the Eucharist, and Extreme Unction.

rit·ual /ˈrɪtʃʊəl/ *n* [U] all the rites or forms connected with a ceremony; way of conducting a religious service: *the* ∼ *of the Catholic Church;* [C] particular form of ∼; any procedure regularly followed, as if it were a ∼: *He went through the* ∼ *of rolling his own cigarette slowly and carefully.* (*pl*) ceremonial observances: *initiation* ∼*s.* □ *adj* of religious rites; done as a rite: ∼ *laws; the* ∼ *dances of an African tribe.* ∼·**ism** /-ɪzəm/ *n* [U] fondness for, insistence upon, ∼; study of ∼. ∼·**ist** /-ɪst/ *n* person who has expert knowledge of ∼ practices and religious rites; person who supports strict observance of ∼. ∼·**is·tic** /ˌrɪtʃʊəˈlɪstɪk/ *adj* relating to ∼ism and ∼ists.

ritzy /ˈrɪtsɪ/ *adj* (sl) luxurious; elegant.

ri·val /ˈraɪvl/ *n* person who competes with another (because he wants the same thing, or to be or do better than the other): '*business* ∼*s;* ∼*s in love;* (attrib) ∼ *business firms.* □ *vt* (-ll-, *US* also -l-) [VP6A,14] ∼ (*in*), be a ∼ of; seem or claim to be (almost) as good as: *Cricket cannot* ∼ *football in excitement.* ∼·**ry** /ˈraɪvlrɪ/ *n* [C,U] (*pl* -ries) (instance of) being ∼*s*; competition: *enter into* ∼*ry with other shops;* ∼*ry between two schools,* eg in sport; *the rivalries between political parties.*

rive /raɪv/ *vt,vi* (*pt* ∼d, *pp* riven /ˈrɪvn/) [VP6A,15A,B] (archaic or poet) break or tear away violently; split: *trees riven by lightning;* (fig) *a heart riven by grief.*

river /ˈrɪvə(r)/ *n* [C] **1** natural stream of water flowing in a channel to the sea or to a lake, etc or joining another ∼: *the R*∼ *Thames.* ⇨ the illus at delta, estuary. **sell sb down the** ∼, (fig) betray him. **2** (attrib) '∼-**basin** *n* area drained by a ∼ and its tributaries. '∼-**bed** *n* ground over which a ∼ flows in its channel. '∼-**side** *n* ground along a ∼ bank: *a* ∼*side villa.* **3** great flow: *a* ∼ *of lava;* ∼*s of blood*, great bloodshed (in war).

rivet /ˈrɪvɪt/ *n* [C] metal pin or bolt for fastening metal plates (eg in a ship's sides), the plain end being hammered flat to prevent slipping. □ *vt* [VP6A,15A,B] **1** fasten with a ∼ or ∼*s*; flatten (the end of a bolt) to make it secure. **2** fix or concentrate (one's eyes, attention) on: *He* ∼*ed his eyes on the scene.* **3** take up, secure (attention, etc): *The scene* ∼*ed our attention.*

Rivi·era /ˌrɪvɪˈeərə/ *n* **the** ∼, stretch of the Mediterranean coast (of SE France and NW Italy), used as a holiday resort.

rivu·let /ˈrɪvjʊlɪt/ *n* small stream.

roach[1] /rəʊtʃ/ *n* (*pl* unchanged) fresh-water fish of the carp family.

roach[2] /rəʊtʃ/ *n* (*pl* -es) (colloq) = cockroach.

road /rəʊd/ *n* [C] **1** specially prepared way, publicly or privately owned, between places for the use of pedestrians, riders, vehicles, etc: *main and minor* ∼*s;* (attrib) '∼ *junctions; a* '∼-*map of Great Britain* (Cf a *street*-map of London); '∼ *accidents;* ∼ *works in progress,* ∼*s* under construction or repair. **on the** ∼, travelling: *How long were you on the road?* How long did your journey take? **rule of**

the ~, custom which regulates the side to be taken by vehicles, ships, etc when meeting or passing each other. **take the ~,** start a journey. **take to the ~,** become a tramp. '**~ safety,** safety from traffic dangers: *a campaign for ~ safety,* for preventing ~ accidents. **2** (compounds) '**~-bed** *n* foundation of rock, stones, etc on which the surface of a ~ is laid. '**~-block** *n* barricade built across a ~ to stop or slow down traffic (eg by police to catch an escaped prisoner or by military authorities during a period of political disturbances). '**~-book** *n* book describing the ~s of a country, with itineraries (for tourists, etc). '**~-hog** *n* (colloq) motorist who is reckless and inconsiderate of others. '**~-house** *n* building(s) on a main ~, often one with facilities for meals, dancing, etc used by people who travel by car. '**~-man** /-mæn/, '**~-mender** *nn* man who repairs ~s. '**~-metal** *n* stone used for making and repairing ~s. '**~-sense** *n* capacity for intelligent behaviour on ~s, eg the avoidance of accidents: *Harry/ Harry's dog has no ~ sense.* '**~ show** *n* (US) theatrical performance by a touring company. '**~-side** *n* bordering of a ~: (attrib) *~side flowers/ inns.* '**~-way** *n* (usu with *def art*) central part used by wheeled traffic (contrasted with the footpath, etc): *Dogs should be kept off the ~way.* '**~-worthy** *adj* (of a motor-vehicle, etc) fit for use on the ~s. **3** one's way or route: *You're in the/my ~,* in my way, obstructing me. **4** ~ **to,** (fig) way of getting to: *Is excessive drinking the ~ to ruin? There's no royal ~ to wisdom,* no easy way, ⇨ royal. **5** (in proper names) **(a) the ... R~,** name of a ~ leading to the town, etc named: *the Oxford R~,* leading to Oxford; *the Great West R~,* from London to the West of England. **(b)** ... **R~/Rd,** street of buildings: *35 York Rd, London, SW 16.* **6** (usu *pl*) stretch of water near the shore in which ships can ride at anchor: *anchored in the ~s.* **7** (US) = railway. **~-less** *adj* having no ~s. '**~-stead** /-sted/ *n* = road(6).

road·ster /'rəʊdstə(r)/ *n* [C] open motor-car, usu for two persons.

roam /rəʊm/ *vi,vt* [VP2A,C,6A] walk or travel without any definite aim or destination over or through (a country, etc): *go ~ing; ~ about the world; ~ the seas; settle down after years of ~ing.*

roan¹ /rəʊn/ *adj* (of animals) with a coat of a mixed colour, esp brown with white or grey hairs in it. □ *n* ~ horse or cow.

roan² /rəʊn/ *n* [U] soft sheepskin leather sometimes used for binding books.

roar /rɔː(r)/ *n* [C] loud, deep sound as of a lion, of thunder, of a person in pain, etc: *the ~s of a tiger; the ~ of the sea/of waves breaking on the rocks; the ~ of London's traffic; with a ~ of rage; ~s of laughter; set the table/room in a ~,* cause everyone to laugh loudly. □ *vt,vi* **1** [VP2A,C,3A] make such loud, deep sounds: *lions ~ing in the distance. Several lorries ~ed past; ~ with laughter/pain/ rage; ~ for mercy.* **2** [VP6A,15B] ~ **sth out,** say, sing, loudly: *~ out an order; ~ out a drinking song.* **3** [VP22,15B] ~ **oneself hoarse, etc,** make oneself hoarse, etc by ~ing. **~ sb down, ~** in order to drown the words of a speaker so that he has to give up. **~-ing** *adj* **1** noisy; rough. **2** stormy: *a ~ing night; the ~ing forties,* part of the Atlantic between 40° and 50° N latitude, often very stormy. **3** brisk; healthy: *do a ~ing trade; be in ~ing health.* □ *adv* extremely: *~ing drunk.*

roast /rəʊst/ *vt,vi* [VP6A,2A] **1** (of meat, potatoes, etc) cook, be cooked, in a hot oven, or over or in front of a hot fire, eg on a spit, the meat, etc being basted periodically with the fat and juices that come out: *~ a joint. The meat was ~ing in the oven. You've made a fire fit to ~ an ox,* a very large, hot fire. **2** heat, be heated: *~ coffee-beans.* **3** expose for warmth to heat of some kind: *~ oneself in front of the fire; lie in the sun and ~.* □ *attrib adj* that has been ~ed: *~ beef/pork.* □ *n* **1** [C] joint of ~ed meat; [U] slices from such a joint: *cold ~ on Monday.* **2** operation of ~ing: *give sth a good ~.* **~er** *n* kind of oven for ~ing; apparatus for ~ing coffee-beans; article of food, eg a chicken, sucking pig, suitable for ~ing. **~·ing** *n* (from the dated use of ~ meaning criticize harshly) **give sb a good ~ing,** (fig) scold or ridicule him harshly.

rob /rɒb/ *vt* (-bb-) [VP6A,14] **rob sb/sth (of sth),** **1** deprive (sb) of his property; take property from (a place) unlawfully (and often by force): *I was robbed of my watch.* Cf I had my watch *stolen. The bank was robbed last night. The village boys rob my orchard.* Cf They *steal* apples from my orchard. **2** deprive a person of (what is due to him, etc): *be robbed of the rewards of one's labour.* **rob·ber** *n* person who robs; thief. **rob·bery** /'rɒbəri/ *n* [C,U] (*pl* -ries) (instance of) robbing: *robbery with violence; three robberies in one week.* **,daylight 'robbery,** (colloq) charging of excessive prices: *50p for a cup of coffee is daylight robbery!*

robe /rəʊb/ *n* [C] **1** long, loose outer garment. '**bath-~** (US) dressing-gown. **2** (often *pl*) long, loose garment worn as a sign of rank or office: *the ,Coro'nation ~s,* of a king or queen; *magistrates/ judges in their black ~s.* □ *vt,vi* [VP6A,14,2A] ~ **(in),** put a ~ or ~s on: *professors ~d in their bright-coloured gowns; ~d in the scarlet of a cardinal.*

robin /'rɒbɪn/ *n* **1** small, brownish bird with red breast-feathers (also called ,~ 'redbreast). ⇨ the illus at bird. **2** (name given to kinds of) small bird outside the British Isles (eg the American ~, a red-breasted thrush). ,**R~ 'Goodfellow** *n* type of mischievous but good-natured goblin or elf in English folklore (also called *Puck*).

ro·bot /'rəʊbɒt/ *n* [C] machine made to act like a man; machine-like person.

ro·bust /rəʊ'bʌst/ *adj* vigorous; healthy: *a ~ young man; a ~ appetite.* **~·ly** *adv* **~·ness** *n*

roc /rɒk/ *n* gigantic bird of Eastern tales.

rock¹ /rɒk/ *n* **1** [U] solid stony part of the earth's crust: *a house built upon ~.* ⇨ bed-rock at bed¹(4). ⇨ the illus at stratify. **2** [C,U] mass of ~ standing out from the earth's surface or from the sea. **as firm/solid as a ~,** immovable; (fig) (of persons) sound; dependable. **on the ~s,** (of a ship) wrecked on ~s; (fig, of a person) very short of money; (of a marriage) likely to end in divorce or separation. **see ~s ahead,** see danger of shipwreck (or fig, any kind of danger). **the R~ of Ages,** Jesus Christ. **3** [C] large, detached stone or boulder: *~s rolling down the side of a mountain;* (US) = stone¹(2). **4** [U] (GB) kind of hard, sticky sweet, usu made in long cylindrical pieces: *a stick of ~; almond ~.* **5 on the ~s,** (US) (of whisky) served on ice-cubes without water. **6** (compounds) ,**~-'bottom** *n* [U] lowest point: *Prices have reached ~-bottom;* (attrib) *~-bottom prices.* '**~-cake** *n* [C] small cake or bun with a hard, rough surface. '∼-climbing *n* the climbing of masses of ∼ on mountain-sides (with the help of ropes, etc). '∼-crystal *n* pure natural transparent quartz. '∼-garden *n* artificial or natural bank or mound with ∼s and stones and ∼-plants growing among them. '∼-plant *n* kinds of plant found growing among ∼s, esp on mountains and cultivated in ∼-gardens, etc. ∼-'salmon *n* (trade name for) dog-fish. '∼-salt *n* common salt as found in mines in crystal form. ∼ery /'rɒkərɪ/ *n* [C] (*pl* -ies) = ∼-garden.

rock² /rɒk/ *vt,vi* [VP6A,15A,2A] (cause to) sway or swing backwards and forwards, or from side to side: ∼ *a baby to sleep;* ∼ *a baby in its cradle. The town was* ∼*ed by an earthquake. He sat* ∼*ing* (*himself*) *in his chair. Our boat was* ∼*ed by/was* ∼*ed on the waves.* ∼ **the boat,** (fig) do sth that upsets the smooth progress of an undertaking, etc. '∼-ing-chair *n* one fitted with rockers on which it rests. '∼-ing-horse *n* wooden horse with rockers for a child to ride on. ∼er *n* **1** one of the curved pieces of wood on which a ∼ing-chair or ∼ing-horse rests. **2** (US) ∼ing-chair. **3** R∼er, (GB, 1960's) member of a teenage gang, wearing leather jackets and riding motor-bikes. **4** *off one's* ∼*er,* (sl) crazy; out of one's mind.

rock³ /rɒk/ *n* (also ∼-'n-roll /ˌrɒk ən 'rəʊl/) [U] highly rhythmic popular music for dancing, played on electric guitars, etc. □ *vi* dance to this music.

rock-'n-roll /ˌrɒk ən 'rəʊl/ *n* ⇨ rock³.

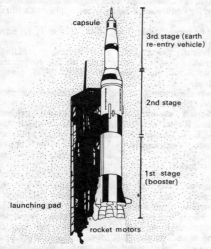

capsule

3rd. stage (Earth re-entry vehicle)

2nd stage

1st stage (booster)

launching pad

rocket motors

a rocket launching a spacecraft

rocket /'rɒkɪt/ *n* **1** [C] tube-shaped case filled with fast-burning material, which launches itself into the air (as a firework, as a signal of distress, or as a self-propelled projectile or missile; also used to launch an aircraft or spacecraft or, attached to an aircraft, to give it higher speed and range): ∼ *propulsion;* ∼-*propelled.* ⇨ also retro∼. '∼-base *n* military base for ∼ missiles. '∼-range *n* area used for experiments with missiles propelled by ∼s. **2** (colloq) severe scolding: *get/give sb a* ∼. □ *vi* [VP2A] go up fast like a ∼: (colloq) *Prices* ∼*ed after the war.* ∼ry /-trɪ/ *n* [U] (art or science of) using ∼s for projectiles, space missiles, etc.

rocky /'rɒkɪ/ *adj* (-ier, -iest) **1** of rock, full of or

abounding in rocks; hard like rock: *a* ∼ *road;* ∼ *soil.* **2** (colloq) shaky; unsteady: *The table is rather* ∼*. His business is very* ∼.

ro-coco /rə'kəʊkəʊ/ *adj* (of furniture, architecture, etc) with much elaborate ornament (with scrolls, foliage, etc) as in Europe in the late 18th c.

rod /rɒd/ *n* **1** thin, straight piece of wood or metal: '*curtain-rods; a* '*fishing-rod; fishing with rod and line.* **2** stick used for punishing. **make a rod for one's own back,** prepare trouble for oneself. ˌspare the 'rod and ˌspoil the 'child, (prov) A child who is not punished will become undisciplined and unruly. **have a rod in** '**pickle for sb,** be saving up severe punishment for him when the opportunity comes. **3** (US, sl) revolver. **4** measure of length equal to 5½ yds or 5.03 metres (also called *pole* or *perch*). **5** metal bar; shaft, etc: '*piston-rods.*

rode /rəʊd/ *pt* of ride².

ro-dent /'rəʊdnt/ *n* animal, eg a *rat, rabbit, squirrel* or *beaver,* which gnaws things with its strong teeth specially adapted for this purpose.

ro-deo /rəʊ'deɪəʊ US: 'rəʊdɪəʊ/ *n* (*pl* ∼s /-əʊz/) [C] **1** (on the plains of Western US) rounding up of cattle. **2** contest of skill in lassoing cattle, riding untamed horses, etc.

rodo-mon-tade /ˌrɒdəmɒn'teɪd/ *n* [U] (formal) boastful, bragging talk.

roe¹ /rəʊ/ *n* [C,U] (mass of) eggs or sperm in a fish: *salted cod's-roe for Friday's supper.*

roe² /rəʊ/ *n* (*pl* roes or, collectively, roe) small kind of European and Asiatic deer. '**roe-buck** *n* male roe.

Roent-gen /'rɒntjən US: 'rentgən/ = röntgen.

ro-ga-tion /rə'geɪʃn/ *n* (usu *pl*) litany of the saints chanted on the three days before Ascension Day: '*R*∼ *week,* the week including these days; *R*∼ *Sunday,* the Sunday before Ascension Day.

roger /'rɒdʒə(r)/ *int* (in radio communication) message heard and understood.

Rog-er /'rɒdʒə(r)/ *n* **the Jolly** ∼, pirates' black flag. **Sir** ∼ **de Coverley** /sə ˌrɒdʒə də 'kʌvəlɪ/, country-dance and tune.

rogue /rəʊg/ *n* [C] **1** scoundrel; rascal. ∼'s **gallery,** collection of photographs of known criminals. **2** (playfully or humorously) person fond of playing tricks, teasing people. **3** wild animal (esp ˌ∼-'**elephant**) driven or living apart from the herd and of a savage temper. **ro-guery** /'rəʊgərɪ/ *n* (*pl* -ries) **1** [C,U] (instance or example of the) conduct of a ∼. **2** [U] playful mischief; (*pl*) mischievous acts.

ro-guish /'rəʊgɪʃ/ *adj* **1** dishonest; of the nature of a ∼. **2** mischievous: ∼ *eyes.* ∼·ly *adv* ∼·ness *n*

roist-erer /'rɔɪstərə(r)/ *n* rough, noisy merrymaker.

role, rôle /rəʊl/ *n* [C] actor's part in a play; person's task or duty in an undertaking: *play the* '*title-*∼ *in 'Hamlet',* play the part of Hamlet.

roll¹ /rəʊl/ *n* **1** sth made into the shape of a cylinder by being rolled: *a* ∼ *of cloth/newsprint/carpet/photographic film, etc;* sth in this shape, made by rolling or otherwise: *a man with* ∼*s of fat on his neck; a bread* ∼, a small quantity of bread baked in the shape of a ball; ∼*s of butter; a sausage* ∼, a sausage rolled in pastry and then baked. ∼-**top** '**desk** *n* desk with a flexible cover that slides back into a compartment at the top. **2** turned-back edge: *a* ∼-'*collar,* large collar made by turning back the edge of the material. **3** rolling movement: *The slow, steady* ∼ *of the ship made us sick. He walks* with a nautical ~, like a sailor. *The young foal was enjoying a ~ on the grass.* **4** official list or record, esp of names. **call the ~,** read the names (to check who is present and who absent). Hence, **'~-call** *n* calling of names. **,~ of 'honour,** list of those who have died for their country in war. **strike off the ~s,** take (a solicitor's name) off the list of those who eg have the right to practise, eg when a solicitor has been proved guilty of dishonesty. **5** rolling sound: *the distant ~ of thunder/drums.*

roll² /rəʊl/ *vt,vi* (For special uses with *adverbial particles* and *preps,* ⇨ **11** below.) **1** [VP6A,15A,B,2A,C] (cause to) move along on wheels or by turning over and over: *The man ~ed the barrel into the yard. Rocks and stones were ~ing down the hillside. The coin fell and ~ed under the table. The bicycle hit me and sent me ~ing/~ed me over. The child was ~ing a hoop.* **heads will roll,** (colloq) some people will be dismissed or disgraced. **2** [VP6A,12B,13B,15B] ~ **(up),** cause to revolve between two surfaces; make (sth) by doing this; make into the shape of a ball or a cylinder: *Please ~ me a cigarette/~ a cigarette for me. R~ the string/wool (up) into a ball. R~ up the carpet/that map on the wall. He ~ed up* (= furled) *his umbrella. He ~ed* (= wrapped by turning over) *himself (up) in the blanket.* ⇨ **sleeve. 3** [VP2C] come or go in some direction: *The clouds ~ed away as the sun rose higher. The years ~ed on/by,* passed. *The tears were ~ing* (= flowing) *down her cheeks.* **4** [VP2A,C] turn about in various directions: *a porpoise ~ing in the water.* **5** [VP6A,22] make or become flat, level or smooth by pressing with a ~ing cylinder of wood, metal, etc or by passing between two such cylinders: ~ *a lawn/a road surface;* ~ *sth flat. This dough ~s well,* is of the sort that one can ~ easily. **~ed gold,** thin coating of gold on the surface of another metal, applied by ~ing. **6** [VP2A,B,C] (cause to) sway or move from side to side; walk with a side-to-side movement: *The ship was ~ing heavily. We ~ed and pitched for two days after leaving Lisbon. Some sailors have a ~ing gait. The drunken man ~ed up to me.* **7** [VP2A] (of surfaces) have long slopes that rise and fall: *miles and miles of ~ing country; a ~ing plain.* **8** [VP2A,C] move with a rise and fall; be carried with rise-and-fall motion: *The waves ~ed in to the beach.* **9** [VP2A,C,6A,15A,B] make, utter, be uttered with, long, deep, vibrating or echoing sounds: *The thunder ~ed in the distance. The drums ~ed. He ~ed out his words/song, etc.* ~ **one's r's,** utter them with the tongue making a rapid succession of taps against the palate. **10** [VP2A,C,14] ~ **(at),** (of the eyes) (cause to) move from side to side, change direction: *His eyes ~ed strangely at me. Don't ~ your eyes at me!* **~-ing** *n* (compounds) **'~ing-mill** *n* mill where metal is ~ed out into sheets, bars, etc. **'~ing-pin** *n* cylinder of wood, glass, etc usu about a foot long, for ~ing out dough, etc. **'~ing-stock** *n* railway's coaches, wagons, etc; all the stock that is on wheels. **11** [VP2C,15B] (special uses with *adverbial particles* and *preps*):

roll sth back, turn or force back, eg enemy forces.
roll in, come, arrive, in large numbers or quantities: *Offers of help are ~ing in.* **be '~ing in sth,** have a large quantity of it: *He's ~ing in money/ property.*
roll on, (a) be capable of being put on by ~ing. **(b)** (of time) pass steadily: *Time ~ed on.* **(c)** (of time,

chiefly *imper*) come soon: *R~ on the day when I retire from this dull work!* ~ **sth on,** put on by ~ing, eg over a part of the body: *She ~ed her stockings on.* **'~-on** *n* (woman's) elastic foundation garment ~ed on to the hips.
roll sth out, (a) cause it (ie sth that is ~ed up) to become flat, level or smooth, by opening it out: ~ *out a map/carpet.* ~ **out the red carpet,** (fig) give an important visitor a special welcome. ⇨ *red carpet* at **red**(1). **(b)** flatten it by ~ing: ~ *out pastry.* ⇨ *~ing pin* at **10** above.
roll up, (of a vehicle) arrive and stop; (of a person) arrive: *Raymond always ~s up late. R~ up! R~ up!,* used as an invitation to join others, eg possible customers at a street stall. ~ **sth up, (a)** ⇨ **2** above. **(b)** (mil) drive the flank of (an enemy line) back and round.

roller /'rəʊlə(r)/ *n* [C] **1** cylinder-shaped object of wood, metal, rubber, etc, usu part of a machine, for pressing, smoothing, crushing, printing, etc: *a* **'garden-~,** for use on a lawn; *the ~s of a mangle,* (between which articles are passed to press out water); *a* **'road-~,** used for making roads level, by crushing rock, etc. **2** cylinder of wood, metal, etc placed beneath an object to make movement easy, or round which sth may be rolled easily: *a* **'~-blind,** on which a window blind (US = *shade*) is rolled; *a* **'~-towel,** an endless towel on a ~. **'~-skate** (often **pair of ~-skates**), *n, vi* (use a) skate¹ with small wheels for use on a smooth surface. **3 '~ bandage,** long surgical bandage rolled up for convenience before being applied to a limb, etc. **4** long, swelling wave.
rol·lick·ing /'rɒlɪkɪŋ/ *adj* noisy, jolly and gay: *have a ~ time.*
roly-poly /ˌrəʊlɪ 'pəʊlɪ/ *n* **1** (GB) (also ~ *pudding*) pudding made of paste spread with jam, etc formed into a roll and boiled. **2** (colloq) short, plump child.
Ro·maic /rəʊ'meɪɪk/ *adj, n* (of, in) modern vernacular Greek (more usu called *demotic*).
Ro·man /'rəʊmən/ *adj* **1** of Rome /rəʊm/, esp ancient Rome: *the ~ Empire.* **the ~ alphabet,** the ABC. ~ **letters/type,** the plain, upright kind, not italic. ~ **numerals,** ⇨ App 4(1). **2** of the Rome of the Popes, esp = Roman Catholic: *the ~ rite* (contrasted eg with Greek or Russian Orthodox). ⇨ **catholic**(2); **pope; Protestant.** □ *n* **1** citizen of ancient Rome; (*pl*) Christians of ancient Rome: *the Epistle to the ~s* (in the NT). **2** Roman Catholic.
ro·mance /rəʊ'mæns/ *n* **1** [C] story or novel of adventure; love story, esp one in which the events are quite unlike real life; [U] class of literature consisting of such stories. **2** [C] **R~,** medieval story, usu in verse, relating the adventures of some hero of chivalry. **3** [C] real experience, esp a love-affair, considered to be remarkable or worth description; (colloq) any love-affair. **4** [U] state of mind which welcomes stories of the marvellous, etc; the qualities characteristic of stories of love and adventure: *travel abroad in search of ~. There was an air of ~ about the old castle.* **5** [C,U] exaggerated description; picturesque falsehood. □ *vi* [VP2A] (more usu *romanticize*) exaggerate by adding interesting or attractive details when telling a story, recounting events, etc.
Ro·mance /rəʊ'mæns/ *adj* ~ **languages,** French, Italian, Spanish, Portuguese, Rumanian and others developed from Latin.
Ro·man·esque /ˌrəʊmə'nesk/ *n* [U] style of archi-

tecture, with round arches and thick walls (in Europe between the ancient classical and the Gothic periods).

ro·man·tic /rəʊˈmæntɪk/ *adj* **1** (of persons) having ideas, feelings, etc remote from experience and real life; given to romance(4); visionary. **2** of, like, suggesting, romance: ∼ *scenes/adventures/tales/ situations; a* ∼ *old castle.* **3** (in art, literature and music) marked by feeling rather than by intellect; preferring grandeur, passion, informal beauty, to order and proportion (opp of *classic* and *classical*): *the* ∼ *poets,* eg Shelley, Keats. □ *n* **1** person with ∼(3) ideals. **2** (*pl*) ∼ ideas; extravagantly visionary feelings, expressions, etc. **ro·man·ti·cally** /-klɪ/ *adv* **ro·man·ti·cism** /-tɪsɪzəm/ *n* [U] ∼ tendency in literature, art and music (contrasted with *realism* and *classicism*); ∼ spirit; quality of allowing full play to the imagination. **ro·man·ti·cist** /-tɪsɪst/ *n* follower of romanticism in literature or art, eg Wordsworth. **ro·man·ti·cize** /-tɪsaɪz/ *vt,vi* [VP6A,2A] treat in a ∼ way; make ∼; use a ∼ style in writing, etc; be ∼.

Rom·any /ˈrɒmənɪ/ *n* (*pl* -nies) **1** [C] Gypsy. **2** [U] language of the Gypsies. □ *adj* Gypsy.

Rom·ish /ˈrəʊmɪʃ/ *adj* (usu disparaging) of the Roman Catholic Church.

romp /rɒmp/ *vi* [VP2A,C] **1** (esp of children) play about, esp running, jumping and being rather rough. **2** win, succeed, quickly or without apparent effort: (in a horse-race) *The favourite* ∼*ed home,* won easily. *John just* ∼*s through his examinations,* passes them easily. □ *n* [C] child fond of ∼ing; period of ∼ing: *have a* ∼; *a game of* ∼*s.* ∼**er** *n* (*sing* or *pl*) loose-fitting garment worn by a child: *a pair of* ∼*ers; a'* ∼*er suit.*

ron·deau /ˈrɒndəʊ/, **ron·del** /ˈrɒndl/ *nn* poem of thirteen or ten lines with two rhymes throughout and the opening words used twice as a refrain.

rondo /ˈrɒndəʊ/ *n* (*pl* ∼s /-dəʊz/) piece of music in which the principal theme returns from time to time.

Ro·neo /ˈrəʊnɪəʊ/ *n* (P) machine that duplicates letters, circulars, etc. □ *vt* duplicate on a ∼ machine.

Rönt·gen /ˈrɒntjən *US:* ˈrentgən/ ∼ **rays** *n pl* = X-rays.

rood /ruːd/ *n* **1** (old use) '∼(-tree) cross on which Jesus was put to death. **2** crucifix, esp one raised on the middle of a wooden or stone carved screen (a '∼-*screen*) separating the nave and choir of a church. **3** (GB) measure of land, one-fourth of an acre.

roof /ruːf/ *n* **1** top covering of a building, tent, bus, car, etc: *How can you live under the same* ∼ *as that woman,* in the same building? *raise the* ∼, (colloq) create an uproar; make a great noise (indoors). '∼-*garden n* garden on the flat ∼ of a building. '∼-*tree n* strong horizontal main beam at the apex of a ∼. **2** highest part: *the* ∼ *of heaven,* the sky; *the* ∼ *of the world,* a high mountain range; *the* ∼ *of the mouth,* the palate. □ *vt* (*pt,pp* ∼ed /ruːft/) [VP6A,15A,B] supply with a ∼; be a ∼ for: *a shed* ∼*ed over with strips of bark.* ∼-*less adj* having no ∼; (fig, of persons) homeless; lacking shelter. ∼-*ing n* (also '∼*ing material*) material used for ∼s (eg slates, shingles).

rook¹ /rʊk/ *n* large black bird like a crow. ∼-*ery* /-ərɪ/ *n* (*pl* -ries) **1** place (a group of trees) where many ∼s have their nests; colony of ∼s. **2** colony of penguins or seals.

rook² /rʊk/ *n* person who makes money by cheat-

ing at dice and cards, playing with inexperienced gamblers. □ *vt* [VP6A] win money from (sb) at cards, etc by cheating; swindle; charge (a customer) a ridiculously high price.

rook³ /rʊk/ *n* chess piece (also called a *castle*). ⇨ the illus at chess.

rookie /ˈrʊkɪ/ *n* (army sl) inexperienced recruit.

room /ruːm/ *n* **1** [C] part of a house or other building enclosed by walls or partitions, floor and ceiling. **-roomed** /ruːmd/ *adj: a ten-*∼*ed house* one having ten ∼s. **2** (*pl*) set of ∼s occupied by a person or family; apartments: *Come and see me in my* ∼*s one evening.* '∼-*mate n* one of two or more persons sharing a ∼. **3** [U] ∼ *(for sb/sth);* ∼ *(to do sth),* space that is or might be occupied, or that is enough for a purpose: *Is there* ∼ *for me in the car? This table takes up too much* ∼. *There was* ∼ *in the bus to stand but not to sit. Standing* ∼ *only!* eg in a bus, theatre. *Can you make* ∼ *on that shelf for some more books? There's no* ∼ *for doubt,* We can be quite certain about it. **4** [U] scope; opportunity: *There's* ∼ *for improvement in your work,* It is not as good as it could be. □ *vi* [VP2C] (US) lodge; occupy a ∼ or ∼s: *He's* ∼*ing with my friend Rodney.* '∼-*ing house,* (US) building where a number of independent ∼s can be rented (usu without service). ∼**er** *n* (US) person who lives in a rented ∼ in sb else's house; lodger. ∼-*ful* /-fʊl/ *n* amount (of furniture, etc), number of persons, that fills a ∼. ∼-*y adj* (-ier, -iest) having plenty of space: *a* ∼*y cabin; a* ∼*y raincoat,* one that is loose-fitting. ∼-*ily* /-ɪlɪ/ *adv*

roost /ruːst/ *n* [C] branch, pole, etc on which a bird rests, esp one for hens to sleep or rest on; henhouse, or that part of it, where fowls rest at night: *at* ∼, *on a* ∼. *come home to* ∼, (of words) take effect upon the one who utters them. *rule the* ∼, be the leader or master. □ *vi* [VP2A] (of birds) settle down for the night's sleep.

rooster /ˈruːstə(r)/ *n* domestic cock.

root¹ /ruːt/ *n* [C] **1** that part of a plant, tree, etc which is normally in the soil and which takes water and food from it: *pull up a plant by the* ∼*s. He has no* ∼*s in society,* (fig) is not settled, does not belong to any particular group or place. *pull up one's* ∼*s,* (fig) move from a settled home, job, etc to start a new life elsewhere. *put down new* ∼*s,* (fig) establish oneself in another place after leaving a place where one has been established. *take/ strike* ∼, (a) (eg of a cutting) send out a ∼ or ∼s; begin to grow. (b) (fig) become established. ∼ *and branch,* (fig) thoroughly; completely: *This tyrant and his henchmen must be destroyed* ∼ *and branch.* **2** ∼s, '∼-*crop,* plant with a ∼ that is used as food, eg *carrots, turnips, parsnips.* ∼ *beer,* (US) non-alcoholic drink made from the ∼s of various plants. **3** that part of a hair, tooth, the tongue, a finger-nail, etc that is like a ∼ in position, function, etc. **4** (fig) that from which sth grows; basis; source; essential substance: *the* ∼ *of the trouble. Is money the* ∼ *of all evil? get at/to the* ∼ *of sth,* tackle it at its source. *the* ∼ *cause,* the fundamental cause. **5** (gram) (also *base form*) form of a word on which other forms of that word are said to be based: *'Walk' is the* ∼ *of 'walks', 'walked', 'walking', and 'walker'.* **6** (arith) quantity which, when multiplied by itself a certain number of times, produces another quantity: *4 is the square* (= second) ∼ *of 16* (√16 = 4), *the cube* (= third) ∼ *of 64* (∛64 = 4), *the fourth* ∼ *of 256*

($\sqrt[3]{256} = 4$).

root² /ruːt/ *vt,vi* **1** [VP6A,2A] (of plants, cuttings, etc) (cause to) send out ~s and begin to grow: ~ *chrysanthemum cuttings in sand and peat. Some cuttings ~ easily.* **2** [VP6A,15A] cause to stand fixed and unmoving: *Fear ~ed him to the ground. He stood there ~ed to the spot.* **3** (of ideas, principles, etc) establish firmly (chiefly in *pp*): *She has a ~ed objection to cold baths. Her affection for him is deeply ~ed.* **4** [VP15B] ~ **sth out,** get rid of, exterminate (an evil, etc). ~ **sth up,** dig or pull up with the ~s. **~-less** *adj* having no ~s; (of a person) without ~s in society. ⇨ root¹(1).

root³ /ruːt/ *vi,vt* **1** [VP2C,15B] ~ **about (for),** (of pigs) turn up the ground with the snout in search of food; (of persons) search for; turn things over when searching: *~ing about among piles of papers for a missing document.* ~ **sth out,** find by searching: *I managed to ~ out a copy of the document.* **2** [VP2A,3A] ~ **(for),** (US sl) cheer: *~ing for the college baseball team.*

rootle /ˈruːtl/ *vi* [VP2C] ~ **about for,** (of pigs, etc) dig about (with the snout) for food, etc.

rope /rəʊp/ *n* **1** [C,U] (piece or length of) thick strong cord or wire cable made by twisting finer cords or wires together: *tie sb's arms behind his back with (a) ~. The climbers were on the ~,* fastened together with a ~ (while climbing on a difficult and dangerous surface). **the ~,** noose for hanging a condemned person. **the ~s,** those that enclose the prize-ring or other place used for sport or games. *show sb/know/learn the ~s,* the conditions, the rules, the procedure (in some sphere of action). *give sb (plenty of) ~,* freedom of action. *Give sb enough ~ and he'll hang himself,* (prov) Let a fool follow his own devices and he will come to ruin. **2** (compounds) **~-dancer** *n* performer on a tight-~. **,~-ladder** *n* ladder made of two long ~s connected by rungs of ~. **'~-walk/ -yard** *n* long piece of ground or long, low shed where ~ is made. **'~-walker** *n* = ~-dancer. **'~-way** *n* means of carrying goods in buckets, etc suspended from overhead steel cables: (attrib) **'~way** *buckets.* **'~-yarn** *n* [U] material (esp when unpicked) of which ~s are made. **3** [C] number of things twisted, strung or threaded together: *a ~ of onions.* ☐ *vt* [VP15A,B] **1** fasten or bind with ~: ~ *a man to a tree;* ~ *climbers together,* connect them at intervals with a ~ for safety. **2** ~ **sth off,** enclose or mark off with a ~: *Part of the field was ~d off.* **3** ~ **sb in,** persuade him to help in some activity. **~y** /ˈrəʊpɪ/ *adj* (sl) very inferior in quality.

Roque·fort /ˈrɒkfɔː(r) *US:* ˈrəʊkfərt/ *n* [U] kind of French cheese made of goats' and ewes' milk.

ro·sary /ˈrəʊzərɪ/ *n* (*pl* -ries) **1** form of prayer used in the RC Church; book containing this. **2** string of beads for keeping count of these prayers, which are said while meditating; such beads used by a person of another religion. **3** rose-garden.

rose¹ /rəʊz/ *pt* ⇨ rise².

rose² /rəʊz/ *n* **1** (shrub or bush with prickles or thorns on its stems and bearing a) beautiful and usu sweet-smelling flower (red, pink, white, cream, yellow), ⇨ the illus at flower; one of various flowering plants: *the 'rock-~; 'Christmas ~. a bed of ~s,* a pleasant, easy condition of life. *not all ~s,* not perfect; having some discomfort and disadvantages. *no ~ without a thorn,* complete, pure happiness cannot be found. *gather life's ~s,*

seek the pleasures of life. **2** [U] pinkish-red colour. *see things through ~-coloured/-tinted spectacles,* take an optimistic view of them (perhaps without good reason). **3** (of various things thought to resemble a ~ in shape) **(a)** sprinkling nozzle of a watering can or hose: *Use a fine-~d can* (one fitted with such a nozzle) *for watering seedlings.* **(b)** bunch of ribbons; rosette. **(c)** ~-shaped conventional design, the national emblem of England (as the shamrock is used for Ireland). **4** (compounds) **'~-bed** *n* bed in which ~ bushes are grown. **'~-bud** *n* bud of a ~; (attrib) *a ~bud mouth,* having this shape. **'~-leaf** *n* petal from a ~ flower. **,~-'red** *adj* red as a ~. **'~-water** *n* perfume made from ~s. **,~ 'window** *n* ornamental circular window (usu in a church, esp one with a pattern of small sections radiating from the centre). ⇨ the illus at window. **'~-wood** *n* [U] hard, dark red wood obtained from several varieties of tropical tree (so named for their fragrance): *a ~wood piano.*

ro·seate /ˈrəʊzɪət/ *adj* rose-coloured; pinkish-red.

rose·mary /ˈrəʊzmərɪ *US:* -merɪ/ *n* [U] evergreen shrub with fragrant leaves used in making perfumes.

ro·sette /rəʊˈzet/ *n* [C] small rose-shaped badge or ornament, eg of silk or ribbon; carved rose on stonework.

rosin /ˈrɒzɪn *US:* ˈrɒzn/ *n* [U] resin, esp in solid form, as used on the strings of violins, etc and on the bow with which violins are played. ☐ *vt* [VP6A] rub with ~.

ros·ter /ˈrɒstə(r)/ *n* list of names of persons showing duties to be performed by each in turn.

ros·trum /ˈrɒstrəm/ *n* (*pl* ~s or -tra /-trə/) platform or pulpit for public speaking.

rosy /ˈrəʊzɪ/ *adj* (-ier, -iest) **1** of the colour of red roses: ~ *cheeks,* indicating good health. **2** (fig) causing optimism; encouraging: ~ *prospects.*

rot /rɒt/ *vi,vt* (-tt-) **1** [VP2A,C] decay by processes of nature: *A fallen tree soon rots. The shed had fallen in, and the wood was rotting away. One of the branches had rotted off,* decayed and broken off. **2** [VP2A,C] (fig, of a society, etc) gradually perish from lack of vigour or activity; (of prisoners, etc) waste away: *left to rot in a deep dungeon.* **3** [VP6A] cause to decay or become useless: *Oil and grease will rot the rubber of your tyres.* **'rot-gut** *n* [U] strong alcoholic liquor, esp inferior spirit, that is harmful to the stomach. ☐ *n* [U] **1** decay; rotting; condition of being bad: *a tree affected by rot. Rot has set in,* decay has begun. *We have dry rot in the floor.* ⇨ dry¹(13). **2** (usu **the rot**) liver disease of sheep. **'foot-rot,** foot disease of sheep. **3** (,tommy-)'rot,** (sl) nonsense; foolishness; rubbish: *Don't talk rot! His speech was all rot.* **4** succession of failures: *A rot set in. How can we stop the rot?*

rota /ˈrəʊtə/ *n* (*pl* ~s) (GB) list of persons who are to do things in turn; list of duties to be performed in turn.

ro·tary /ˈrəʊtərɪ/ *adj* **1** (of motion) moving round a central point. **2** (of an engine) worked by ~ motion: a ~ printing machine/press, that prints from curved metal plates on to a continuous roll of paper. **3** **'R~ Club,** (branch of an) international association of professional and business men in a town. **Ro·tarian** /rəʊˈteərɪən/ *n* member of a R~ Club. ☐ *n* (US) = roundabout(2).

ro·tate /rəʊˈteɪt *US:* ˈrəʊteɪt/ *vi,vt* [VP6A,2A]

(cause to) move round a central point; (cause to) take turns or come in succession: ∼ *crops*, ⇨ rotation(2). *The office of Chairman* ∼*s.*

ro·ta·tion /rəʊ'teɪʃn/ *n* **1** [U] rotating or being rotated: *the* ∼ *of the earth;* [C] complete turning: *five* ∼*s an hour.* **2** [C,U] the regular coming round of things or events in succession: *'crop-*∼, ∼ *of crops,* varying the crops grown each year on the same land to avoid exhausting the soil. *in* ∼, in turn; in regular succession.

ro·ta·tory /'rəʊtətərɪ *US:* -tɔːrɪ/ *adj* relating to, causing, moving in, rotation: ∼ *movement.*

rote /rəʊt/ *n* (only in) *by* ∼, by heart, from memory without thinking: *do/say/know/learn sth by* ∼.

ro·tis·se·rie /rəʊ'tiːsərɪ/ *n* cooking device with a rotating spit on which meat, etc is roasted; shop or restaurant providing food cooked in this way.

roto·gra·vure /ˌrəʊtəʊgrə'vjʊə(r)/ *n* **1** [U] process of printing from an engraved copper cylinder on which illustrations, etc have been etched. **2** [C] illustration, etc printed by this process.

ro·tor /'rəʊtə(r)/ *n* [C] rotary part of a machine; (esp) assembly of horizontally rotating blades of a helicopter propellor.

rot·ten /'rɒtn/ *adj* **1** decayed; having gone bad: ∼ *eggs. The sails were* ∼ *and so were the ropes.* **2** (sl) disagreeable; very unpleasant or undesirable: *What* ∼ *luck! I'm feeling* ∼ *today,* unwell, tired. ∼**·ly** *adv* ∼**·ness** *n*

rot·ter /'rɒtə(r)/ *n* (dated sl) worthless, objectionable person.

ro·tund /rəʊ'tʌnd/ *adj* **1** (of a person, his face) round and plump; (of the voice) full-sounding; rich and deep. **2** (of speech, liter style) grandiloquent. ∼**·ly** *adv* ∼**·ity** /-ətɪ/ *n* [U] state of being ∼.

ro·tunda /rəʊ'tʌndə/ *n* round building, esp one with a domed roof.

rouble /'ruːbl/ *n* unit of currency in the USSR (= 100 kopecks).

roué /'ruːeɪ *US:* ruː'eɪ/ *n* (esp elderly) dissolute man; rake².

rouge /ruːʒ/ *n* [U] fine red powder or other cosmetic substance for colouring the cheeks; powder for cleaning silver plate. □ *vt,vi* [VP6A,2A] use ∼ on (the face); use ∼.

rough¹ /rʌf/ *adj* (-er, -est) **1** (of surfaces) not level, smooth or polished; (of roads) of irregular surface, not easy to walk or ride on: ∼ *paper; a fruit with a* ∼ *skin; cloth that is* ∼ *to the touch.* **2** not calm or gentle; moving or acting violently: ∼ *children;* ∼ *behaviour; a* ∼ (= stormy) *sea; have a* ∼ *crossing from Dover to Calais. Keep away from the* ∼ *quarter of the town,* the part where disorderly and violent people live. *This suitcase has had some* ∼ *handling,* has been treated violently, thrown about, etc. *He has a* ∼ *tongue,* a habit of speaking rudely or sharply. *be* ∼ *on sb, be* unpleasant or unlucky for: *It's rather* ∼ *on her, having to live in a caravan. give sb the* ∼ *side of one's tongue,* speak to sb rudely and/or severely. *give sb/have a* ∼ *time,* (cause sb to) experience hardship, be treated severely, etc (according to context). '∼ *house,* (colloq) noisy quarrelling with exchange of blows, etc. '∼**-house** *vt,vi* [VP6A,2A] handle (sb) violently; act violently. ∼ *luck,* worse luck than is deserved. **3** made or done without attention to detail, esp as a first attempt: *a* ∼ *sketch/translation;* lacking refinement, delicacy or finish; *a* ∼ *draft,* eg of a letter; ∼ *accommoda-*

tion at a small country inn; lead a ∼ *life away from civilization. a* ∼ *diamond,* (fig) an uneducated or uncouth person, lacking social graces, but good-hearted and good-natured. ∼ *and ready,* good enough for ordinary purposes, occasions, etc; not particularly efficient, etc: ∼ *and ready methods.* **4** (of sounds) harsh; discordant: *a* ∼ *voice.* **5** (compounds) ∼**-and-'tumble** *adj, n* disorderly and violent (fight or struggle). '∼**-neck** *n* (US colloq) rowdy person; hooligan. '∼**-rider** *n* person who is expert at breaking in untamed horses. ∼**·ly** *adv* **1** in a ∼ manner: *treat sb* ∼*ly; a* ∼*ly made table,* not finely finished. **2** approximately: *at a cost of* ∼*ly £5;* ∼*ly speaking,* with no claim to accuracy. ∼**·ness** *n* quality or state of being ∼.

rough² /rʌf/ *adv* **1** in a rough manner: *play* ∼, be (rather) violent (in games, etc); *treat sb* ∼. *cut up* ∼, (colloq) become angry. *live* ∼, live in the open (as a vagrant may do). *sleep* ∼, (of homeless persons) sleep out of doors or wherever there is some shelter, eg under a bridge, in the open air. **2** (compounds) '∼**-cast** *n* coarse plaster containing gravel or pebbles for the surfaces of outside walls. □ *vt* coat (a wall) with this mixture. '∼**-dry** *vt* dry (laundered clothes) without ironing them. '∼**-hewn** *adj* shaped or carved ∼ly: *a* ∼*-hewn statue.* '∼**-shod** *adj* (of a horse) having shoes with the heads of the nails projecting to prevent slipping. *ride* '∼*shod over sb,* treat him harshly, inconsiderately or contemptuously. ,∼**-'spoken** *adj* addicted to, using, unrefined or harsh language.

rough³ /rʌf/ *n* **1** [U] rough state; rough ground; rough surface; unpleasantness; hardship. *take the* ∼ *with the smooth,* (fig) accept what is unpleasant with what is pleasant. **2** [U] the ∼, unfinished state: *I've seen his new statue only in the* ∼. *in* ∼, (eg of sth written) as a rough draft. **3** [U] **the** ∼, (golf) part of a course (not the fairway or a green) where the ground is uneven and the grass uncut: *lose one's ball in the* ∼. **4** man or boy ready for lawless violence; hooligan: *He was set on by a gang of* ∼*s who knocked him down and took all his money.*

rough⁴ /rʌf/ *vt* **1** [VP6A,15B] ∼ *sth (up),* make untidy or uneven: *Don't* ∼ (*up) my hair!* ∼ *sb up,* (sl) treat him roughly, with physical violence: *He was* ∼*ed up by hooligans.* ∼ (more usu *rub*) *sb up the wrong way,* ⇨ rub(3). **2** [VP15B] ∼ *sth in,* make a first rough sketch of; sketch in outline. **3** ∼ *it,* live without the usual comforts and conveniences of life: *The explorers had to* ∼ *it when they got into the jungle.*

rough·age /'rʌfɪdʒ/ *n* [U] coarse, rough foodstuff, esp bran of cereals, supplying bulk, not nourishment, and taken to stimulate bowel movements.

roughen /'rʌfn/ *vt,vi* make or become rough.

rou·lette /ruː'let/ *n* [U] gambling game in which a small ball falls by chance into one of the compartments of a revolving wheel or disc. **Russian** ∼, stunt in which a person holds to his head a revolver, of which only one (unknown) chamber contains a bullet, and then pulls the trigger.

round¹ /raʊnd/ *adj* **1** shaped like a circle or a ball: *a* ∼ *plate/window/table; a* ∼*-table conference,* at which there is no position of importance at the head of the table, everyone being apparently of equal importance; ∼ *cheeks/arms/limbs,* plump and curved. *a* '∼ *game,* one in which there are no teams or partners and in which the number of players is not fixed. **the R**∼ **Table,** the order of knighthood founded by King Arthur. **2** done with, involving, a circular motion. ~ **brackets**, parentheses. '~ **dance**, one in which the dancers form a circle, with revolving movements. ~ **robin**, petition with signatures in a circle to conceal the order in which they were written. ~ **trip**, (GB) circular trip or tour; (US) journey to a place and back again over the same route. **3** entire; continuous; full: *a ~ dozen/score*, that number and not less; *a good, ~ sum*, a considerable sum. *in ~ figures/numbers*, given in 10's, 100's, 1000's, etc; not troubling about smaller denominations; (hence) roughly correct. **4** full; plain: *at a ~ pace/trot*, vigorous; *a ~ oath*, unmistakably an oath; *a ~ voice*, full-toned and mellow; *scold sb in good, ~ terms*, outspokenly; *a ~ unvarnished tale*, the plain truth. **5** (compounds) '~-arm *adj, adv* (cricket) with the arm swung ~ at the height of the shoulder: *~-arm bowling; bowl ~-arm.* ,~-'**backed** *adj* having the back curved or humped. ,~-'**eyed** *adj* with the eyes wide open: *staring/listening in ~-eyed wonder.* '~-hand *n* [U] (a) style of handwriting with the letters well rounded and clearly written. (b) = ~-arm (bowling). '**R~-head** *n* member of the Parliament side in the Civil War in the 17th c in England, so called from his close-cut hair. '~-**house** *n* (a) cabin or set of cabins on the after part of the quarter deck (of old sailing ships). (b) building (with a turn-table in the middle) where locomotives are stored and repaired. (c) (in former times) place where people were locked up as prisoners. '~-**shot** *n* cannon ball (contrasted with a shell). ~-'**shouldered** *adj* having the shoulders bent forward. ~-ish /-ɪʃ/ *adj* rather ~. ~-ly *adv* in a thorough-going way; pointedly: *tell sb ~ly that he is not wanted; be ~ly cursed.* ~-**ness** *n*

round² /raʊnd/ *adv part* (may be replaced by *around*, except in special idiomatic uses; for special uses with *vv*, ⇨ the *v* entries; specimens only are given here) **1** in a circle or curve to face the opposite way: *Turn your chair ~ and face me.* **2** with a return to the starting-point: *The hour hand of a clock goes right ~ in twelve hours. Christmas will soon be ~ again. I shall be glad when spring comes ~ again.* ~ *and* ~, with repeated revolutions. *all ~; right ~,* completely ~: *We walked right ~ the lake. all (the) year ~,* at all seasons of the year. **3** in circumference: *Her waist is only twenty-four inches ~.* **4** (so as to be) in a circle: *A crowd soon gathered ~. The garden has a high wall all ~.* **5** from one (place, point, person, etc) to another: *Please hand these papers ~,* ie distribute them. *The news was soon passed ~. Tea was served/handed ~. go ~,* supply everybody: *Have we enough food to go ~? Will the meat go ~,* ie be enough for everybody? *look ~,* visit and look at: *Let's go into the town and look ~/have a look ~,* ie see the places of interest, etc. *taking it all ~,* considering the matter from all points of view. **6** by a longer way or route; not by the direct route: *If you can't jump over the stream, you'll have to go ~ by the bridge. The taxi-driver brought us a long way ~.* **7** to a place where sb is or will be: *Come ~ and see me this evening. The Whites have asked me to go ~ this evening,* ie to visit them. **8** ~ (*about*), in the neighbourhood: *all the country ~; everybody for a mile ~; in all the villages ~ about.*

round³ /raʊnd/ *n* **1** sth round; a slice made by a complete cut across the end of a loaf: *two ~s (= sandwiches) of ham and one of beef; a ~ of toast.*

2 [U] (sculpture) solid form, enabling an object to be viewed from all sides (contrasted with *relief*). *in the ~,* (arts) made so that it can be viewed from all sides: *a statue in the ~. theatre in the ~,* with the audience on (nearly) all sides of the stage. **3** regular series or succession or distribution: *the daily ~,* the ordinary occupations of the day; *the earth's yearly ~,* the cycle of the four seasons; *the doctor's ~ of visits* (to the homes of his patients); *a ~ of pleasures/gaiety,* a succession of parties, gay events, etc; *the postman's ~,* the route he takes to deliver letters. *go the ~s; make one's ~s,* make one's usual visits, esp of inspection: *The night watchman makes his ~s every hour. go the ~ of,* be passed on (to): *The news quickly went the ~ of the village.* **4** (in games, contests, etc) one stage: *a boxing-match of ten ~s; knocked out in the third ~; the semi-final ~ of the League Championship; the sixth ~ of the FA Cup,* the quarter-finals of this soccer contest; *have a ~ of cards; a ~ of golf,* to all the 9 or 18 holes of the course. **5** allowance of sth distributed or measured out; one of a set or series: *pay for a ~ of drinks,* drinks for every member of the company; *another ~ of wage claims,* by trade unions for higher wages for their members; *~ after ~ of cheers,* successive bursts of cheering; *have only three ~s of ammunition left,* enough to fire three times. **6** song for several persons or groups, the second singing the first line while the first is singing the second line, etc. **7** dance in which the dancers move in a circle.

round⁴ /raʊnd/ *prep* (may be replaced by *around*, except in special idiomatic uses) **1** (expressing movement) in a path that passes on all sides of and comes back to the starting-point: *The earth moves ~ the sun. Drake sailed ~ the world. (sleep/work) ~ the clock,* all day and all night. ~-**the-clock** *attrib adj* kept up continuously for 24 hours: *~-the-clock dancing.* **2** (expressing movement) in a path changing direction, from one side to another side of: *follow sb/walk ~ a corner. ~ the bend,* (sl) mad. **3** (expressing position) so as to be on all sides of: *They were sitting ~ the table. He had a scarf ~ his neck.* **4** in various or all directions: *He looked ~ the room. Shall I show you ~ the house,* ie take you to the various rooms, etc? **5** to or at various points away from the centre: *The captain stationed his fielders ~ the pitch. We haven't time to go ~ (= to visit) the museums and art galleries.* **6** ~ (*about*), (fig) approximate(ly): *Come ~ about 2 o'clock. He's ready to pay somewhere ~ £1000 for a car.*

round⁵ /raʊnd/ *vt,vi* **1** [VP6A] make or become round: *~ the lips,* eg when making the sound /uː/; *stones ~ed by the action of water.* **2** [VP6A] go round: *~ a corner.* **3** [VP15B,2C,3A] *~ sth off,* bring it to a satisfactory conclusion, add a suitable finish: *~ off a sentence; ~ off one's career by being made a Minister. ~ out,* (cause to) become round: *Her figure is beginning to ~ out. ~ sb/sth up,* drive, bring or collect, together: *The courier ~ed up the tourists and hurried them back into the coach. ~ up (a figure/price),* bring it to a whole number: *The price had been ~ed up from £647.50 to £650. The cowboy ~ed up the cattle.* Hence, '~-**up** *n* a driving or bringing together: *a ~-up of criminals* (by police); *a ~-up of cattle. ~ upon sb,* turn on him and attack him (in words or action).

round-about /'raʊndəbaʊt/ *attrib adj* not going or

coming by, or using, the shortest or most direct route: *I heard the news in a ～ way. We came by a ～ route. What a ～ way of doing things!* □ *n* [C] **1** (= *merry-go-round*) revolving circular platform with wooden horses, etc on which children ride for fun (at fairs, etc). *You lose on the swings what you make on the ～s,* (prov) have losses and profits which are about equal. **2** circular road junction causing traffic to go round instead of directly across (US = *traffic circle* or *rotary*).

roun·del /'raʊndl/ *n* small disc, esp a decorative medallion; small circular panel (eg as used on military aircraft to indicate the country they belong to).

roun·de·lay /'raʊndɪleɪ/ *n* short, simple song with a refrain.

roun·ders /'raʊndəz/ *n pl* game for two teams, played with bat and ball, the players running through a number of bases arranged in a square, similar to baseball.

Roundhead /'raʊndhed/ ➪ round¹(5).

rounds·man /'raʊndzmən/ *n* (*pl*-men) tradesman or his employee going round to ask for orders and deliver goods.

rouse /raʊz/ *vt,vi* **1** [VP6A] wake up: *I was ～ed by the ringing of a bell.* **2** [VP6A,15A] ～ *sb (from sth/to sth),* cause (sb) to be more active, interested, etc (from inactivity, lack of confidence, etc): ～ *sb/oneself to action;* ～ *sb from indolence;* ～*d to anger by insults; rousing cheers. He's terrifying when he's ～d,* when his passions have been stirred. **3** [VP2A] (= ～ oneself) wake; become active.

rout¹ /raʊt/ *n* **1** utter defeat and disorderly retreat: *The defeat became a ～. put to ～,* defeat completely. **2** (old use) large festive gathering of people; large evening party or reception. **3** (old use, or legal) disorderly, noisy crowd. □ *vt* [VP6A] defeat completely; put to ～: ～ *the enemy.*

rout² /raʊt/ *vt* [VP15B] ～ *sb out (of),* get or fetch him up, out of bed, etc: *We were ～ed out of our cabins before breakfast for passport examination.*

route /ruːt/ *n* **1** way taken or planned from one place to another: *The climbers tried to find a new ～ to the top of the mountain. He flew from Europe to Tokyo by the ～ across the Pole. en ～ /,*on 'ruːt/, on the way. **2** [U] (mil) *column of ～,* marching formation. *'～-march,* long march made by soldiers in training. □ *vt* plan a ～ for; send by a specified ～: *We were ～d to France by way of Dover.*

rou·tine /ruː'tiːn/ *n* [C,U] fixed and regular way of doing things: *business ～; a question of ～.* □ *adj* usual; ordinary: *the ～ procedure; my ～ duties,* those performed regularly, as if by rule.

rove /raʊv/ *vi,vt* **1** [VP2C,6A] roam (the more usu word); wander: ～ *over sea and land;* ～ *the moors. a roving commission,* duties that take one from one place to another frequently. **2** [VP2A] (of the eyes, one's affections) be directed first one way, then another. ～*r n* **1** wanderer. **2** (old use) *'sea-～r,* pirate. **3** (formerly) Venture Scout.

row¹ /raʊ/ *n* [C] number of persons or things in a line: *a row of books/houses/desks; plant a row of cabbages; sitting in a row/in rows; a front-row seat,* eg in a theatre. *a hard row to hoe,* a difficult task.

row² /raʊ/ *vt,vi* [VP6A,2A,B,C,15A,B] propel (a boat) by using oars; carry or take (sb or sth) in a boat with oars; be an oarsman in a boat: *Can you row (a boat)? Shall I row you up/down/across the river? They rowed forty (strokes) to the minute. He*

rows *No 5* (= has this position) *in the Oxford crew. Let's row a race. The crew were rowed out* (= exhausted by rowing) *at the end of the race.* **'row-boat** *n* (US) rowing-boat. □ *n* journey or outing in a boat moved by oars; period of this; distance rowed: *go for a row; a long and tiring row.* **row·ing** *n* (compounds) **'rowing-boat** *n* one moved by the use of oars. **'rowing-club** *n* one for persons who row. ～*er n* person who rows a boat.

a rowing-boat

row³ /raʊ/ *n* **1** [U] uproar; noisy disturbance: *How can I study with all this row going on outside my windows?* **2** [C] noisy or violent argument or quarrel: *have a row with the neighbours. That man is always ready for a row,* he has a quarrelsome nature. *kick up/make a row,* start a noisy quarrel or scene. **3** [C] instance of being in trouble, scolded, etc: *get into a row for being late at the office.* □ *vt,vi* **1** [VP6A] scold; reprimand. **2** [VP2A,3A] *row (with),* quarrel noisily (with): *He's always rowing with his neighbours.*

rowan /'raʊən US: 'raʊən/ *n* '～(-tree), small tree of the rose family, also called *mountain ash.* '～(-berry), one of the scarlet berries of this tree.

rowdy /'raʊdɪ/ *adj* (-ier, -iest) rough and noisy: *The ～ element in the audience continually interrupted the speaker. There were ～ scenes at the elections.* □ *n* (*pl* -dies) ～ person. **row·dily** /-ɪlɪ/ *adv* **row·di·ness,** *nn* ～·**ism** /-ɪzəm/ [U] ～ behaviour.

rowel /'raʊəl/ *n* [C] revolving disc with sharp teeth at the end of a spur.

row·lock /'rɒlək US: 'raʊlɒk/ *n* [C] pivot for an oar or scull on the side (gunwale) of a boat (US = *oar-lock*). ➪ the illus at row.

royal /'rɔɪəl/ *adj* of, like, suitable for, supported by, belonging to the family of, a king or queen: *His R～ Highness; the ～ family; the R～ Society; the R～ Navy/Air Force; a ～ welcome,* one fit for a king, etc; splendid. ～ *road to,* (fig) easiest way of getting (to): *Practice is the ～ road to success when learning a language.* **R～ Commission,** one officially appointed to hold an enquiry and issue a report. ～**ly** /'rɔɪəlɪ/ *adv* in a ～ or splendid manner: *We were ～ly entertained.* ～·**ist** /'rɔɪəlɪst/ *n* supporter of a king or queen or of ～ government; supporter of the ～ side in a civil war.

roy·alty /'rɔɪəltɪ/ *n* (*pl* -ties) **1** [U] royal persons: *The play was performed in the presence of ～. The hotel has been patronized by ～.* **2** [U] position, rank, dignity, power, etc of a royal person. **3** [C] sum paid by a mining or oil company to the owner of the land: *oil royalties;* sum paid to the owner of a copyright or patent: *a ～ of 10 per cent of the price of the book on all copies sold.*

rub¹ /rʌb/ *n* **1** period of rubbing: *give the spoons/ table, etc a good rub.* **2** (esp in the phrase *There's the rub*) difficulty; point at which doubt or difficulty arises.

rub² /rʌb/ *vt,vi* (-bb-) (For special uses with *ad-*

verbial particles and *preps*, ⇨ **3** below.) **1** [VP6A,15A,22] move (one thing) backwards and forwards on the surface of (another); make (sth *clean, dry*, etc) by doing this: *He was rubbing his hands together. Rub this oil on your skin. He rubbed his hands with the soap. You've rubbed your coat against some wet paint. Rub the surface dry.* **rub shoulders with,** meet and mix with (people). **2** [VP2A,C] come into, or be in, contact with, by a sliding or up and down movement: *What is the wheel rubbing on/against?* **3** [VP2C,15B] (special uses with *adverbial particles* and *preps*): **rub along,** (colloq) (of a person) manage to exist, pass one's time, without too much difficulty. **rub along with sb/together,** (of two or more persons) live without quarrelling, etc: *I manage to rub along with her. We manage to rub along together.* **rub-ber** *n* ⇨ rubber¹(4).

rub sb/oneself/a horse down, rub thoroughly, vigorously, eg with a towel, to make dry and clean: *He rubbed himself down after his bath.* **rub sth down,** make sth smooth or level by rubbing: *Rub the walls down well before applying new paint.* Hence, **'rub-down** *n*. *Give the horse/the walls a good rub-down.*

rub sth in; rub sth into sth, (a) force (ointment, etc) into sth, eg the skin, by rubbing: *Rub the ointment well in/into the skin.* (b) force (a lesson, a humiliating or unpleasant fact) into sb's mind: *The moral needs to be well rubbed in.* **rub it in,** (esp) remind sb repeatedly of a fault, failure, etc: *I know I behaved foolishly but you needn't rub it in.*

rub sth off, remove sth (from a surface) by rubbing: *How did you rub the skin off your knees? The nap of this cloth has been rubbed off.*

rub sth out, remove (marks, writing, etc) by rubbing: *rub out a word/pencil marks/mistakes. The stains won't rub out,* can't be rubbed out. **rub sb out,** (US sl) murder him.

rub sth up, polish by rubbing: *rub up the silver spoons.* Hence, **'rub-up** *n*. **rub sb (up) the right/wrong way,** placate/irritate him.

rub-a-dub /ˌrʌb ə 'dʌb/ *n* [U] sound made by beating a drum.

rub-ber¹ /'rʌbə(r)/ *n* **1** [U] tough elastic substance made from the milky liquid that flows from certain trees when the bark is cut, used for making tyres, tennis balls, etc: (attrib) '~ *trees; the* '~ *plantations of Malaysia;* ~ *bands,* elastic bands for keeping things together; *a* ~ *stamp.* ˌ~-'**stamp** *vt* (colloq) approve or endorse (a proposal, etc) without giving it proper consideration. '~-**neck** *n* (US colloq) tourist or sightseer of the kind who constantly turns his head to see as much as possible. □ *vi* look at sights in this way. **2** [C] piece of ~ material for rubbing out pencil marks, etc: *a pencil with a* ~ *at one end.* **3** (*pl*) overshoes (galoshes) made of ~. **4** [C] person or thing that rubs, eg a part of a machine that applies friction. □ *vt* [VP6A] cover or coat with ~. ~-**ize** /-aɪz/ *vt* cover or treat with ~. ~-**y** *adj* made of ~.

rub-ber² /'rʌbə(r)/ *n* [C] (in such card games as whist and bridge) **1** three successive games between the same sides or persons: *Let's play another* ~. **2** the winning of two games out of three; the third game when each side has won one: *game and* ~, (We have won) the third game and (therefore) the ~.

rub-bing /'rʌbɪŋ/ *n* impression of sth, eg a brass over a grave, by rubbing paper laid over it with wax, chalk or charcoal.

rub-bish /'rʌbɪʃ/ *n* [U] **1** waste material; that which is, or is to be, thrown away as worthless; refuse. **2** nonsense; worthless ideas: *This book is all* ~. **3** (as an exclamation) Nonsense! ~**y** *adj* worthless.

rubble /'rʌbl/ *n* [U] bits of broken stone, rock or brickwork: *buildings reduced to* ~ *by bombing; build roads with a foundation of* ~.

Ru-bi-con /'ruːbɪkən *US*: -kɒn/ *n* **cross the** ~, commit oneself to an enterprise from which one cannot turn back.

ru-bi-cund /'ruːbɪkənd/ *adj* (of a persons's face or complexion) ruddy; high-coloured.

ru-bric /'ruːbrɪk/ *n* [C] **1** title or heading printed in red or special type. **2** rule; direction; explanation.

ruby /'ruːbɪ/ *n* [C] (*pl* -bies) red jewel. □ *adj, n* deep red (colour).

ruck¹ /rʌk/ *n* **the** ~, **the common** ~, ordinary commonplace things or persons: *He was ambitious to get out of the* ~, to escape from being thought of as ordinary, commonplace, etc.

ruck² /rʌk/ *n* [C] irregular fold or crease (esp in cloth). □ *vi, vt* [VP2A,C,6A,15B] ~ *(up),* be pulled into ~s; make into ~s: *The sheets on my bed have* ~*ed up.*

ruck-sack /'rʌksæk/ *n* [C] canvas bag strapped on the back from the shoulders, used by people on a walking holiday, etc; haversack, knapsack.

ruc-tions /'rʌkʃnz/ *n pl* angry words or protests; noisy argument: *There'll be* ~ *if you don't do what you're told.*

rud-der /'rʌdə(r)/ *n* [C] **1** flat, broad piece of wood or metal hinged vertically at the stern of a boat or ship for steering. ⇨ the illus at sail. **2** similar structure on an aircraft. ⇨ the illus at air.

ruddle /'rʌdl/ *n* [U] red ochre, esp the kind used for marking ownership of sheep. □ *vt* put ~ on sheep.

ruddy /'rʌdɪ/ *adj* (-ier, -iest) **1** (of the face) red, as showing good health: ~ *cheeks; in* ~ *health,* having ~ cheeks indicating good health. **2** red or reddish: *a* ~ *glow in the sky.* **3** (sl; euphem for) bloody(3): *What the* ~ *hell are you doing?*

rude /ruːd/ *adj* (-r, -st) **1** (of a person, his speech, behaviour) impolite; not showing respect or consideration: *It's* ~ *to interrupt/to point at people. What a* ~ *reply! Would it be* ~ *to ask when you are likely to leave?* eg to a guest who stays too long. **2** startling; violent; rough: *get a* ~ *shock. a* ~ *awakening,* a sudden realization of sth unpleasant. **3** primitive; without refinement: *our* ~ *forefathers.* **4** roughly made; simple: *a* ~ *wooden plough.* **5** vigorous: *in* ~ *health.* **6** in the natural state; crude, raw (the more usu words): ~ *ore/ produce; cotton in its* ~ *state.* ~**ly** *adv* in a ~ manner: *a* ~*ly* (ie in a primitive manner) *fashioned craft; be* ~*ly awakened.* ⇨ **2** above. ~**ness** *n* [U]

ru-di-ment /'ruːdɪmənt/ *n* **1** (*pl*) first steps or stages (of an art or science): *learn the* ~*s of chemistry/ grammar.* **2** earliest form on which a later development is or might have developed; imperfectly developed part: *Certain fossils reveal the* ~ *of a thumb. A new-born chicken has only the* ~*s of wings.* **ru-di-men-tary** /ˌruːdɪ'mentrɪ/ *adj* **1** elementary: *a* ~*ary knowledge of mechanics.* **2** undeveloped; existing in an imperfect or undeveloped form.

rue¹ /ruː/ *n* [U] small evergreen plant with bitter-tasting leaves formerly used in medicine.

rue² /ruː/ *vt* [VP6A] (dated or liter) repent of; think of with sadness or regret: *You'll live to rue it,* will one day regret it. *You'll rue the day when.... rue-ful* /'ru:fl/ *adj* showing, feeling, expressing regret: *a rueful smile.* **rue·ful·ly** /'ru:fəlɪ/ *adv*

ruff[1] /rʌf/ *n* **1** ring of differently coloured or marked feathers round a bird's neck, or of hair round an animal's neck. **2** wide, stiff frill worn as a collar in the 16th c. ⇨ the illus at doublet.

ruff[2] /rʌf/ *vi,vt* trump (in a card game). □ *n* act of trumping.

ruf·fian /'rʌfɪən/ *n* violent, cruel man. **∼·ly** *adj* like a ∼; lawless. **∼·ism** /-ɪzəm/ *n* [U] rough, brutal conduct.

ruffle /'rʌfl/ *vt,vi* **1** [VP6A,15B] **∼ (up),** disturb the peace, calm or smoothness of: *The bird ∼d up its feathers. A sudden breeze ∼d the surface of the lake. Who's been ruffling your hair? Anne is easily ∼d,* easily annoyed, put out of temper. **2** [VP2A] become **∼d:** *You ∼ too easily.* □ *n* [C] **1** strip of material gathered into folds; frill used to ornament a garment at the wrist, neck or breast. **2** ruffling or being ∼d(1).

rug /rʌg/ *n* **1** floor mat of thick material (usu smaller than a carpet): = *a 'hearth-rug.* **2** thick, usu woollen, covering or wrap: *a 'travelling-rug* (for putting round one's knees in a car, etc).

Rugby /'rʌgbɪ/ *n* ∼ **(football),** (GB) kind of football using an oval-shaped ball which may be handled: ∼ *League,* form of ∼ with thirteen players and allowing professionalism; ∼ *Union,* with fifteen players and having amateur teams only.

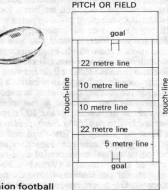

PITCH OR FIELD

ball

goal
22 metre line
touch-line   10 metre line   touch-line
10 metre line
22 metre line
5 metre line
goal

Rugby Union football (rugger)

rug·ged /'rʌgɪd/ *adj* **1** rough; uneven; rocky: *a ∼ coast;* ∼ *country.* **2** having furrows or wrinkles: *a ∼ face;* ∼ *features.* **3** not refined or gentle: *a ∼ character;* ∼ *manners.* **∼·ly** *adv* **∼·ness** *n*

rug·ger /'rʌgə(r)/ *n* [U] (colloq) Rugby football.

ruin /'ru:ɪn/ *n* **1** [U] destruction; overthrow; serious damage: *the ∼ of her hopes; the impulse that led to my ∼; brought to ∼ by gambling and drink.* **2** [U] state of being decayed, destroyed, collapsed: *The castle has fallen into ∼.* **go to rack and ∼,** ⇨ rack[4]. [C] sth which has decayed, been destroyed, etc: *The building is in ∼s. The abbey is now a ∼.* **3** [U] cause of ∼: *Gambling was his ∼* (= was the ∼ of him). □ *vt* [VP6A] cause the ∼ of: *You will ∼ your prospects if you continue to be so foolish. The storm ∼ed the crops. He's bankrupt and ∼ed,* has lost all his money, property, etc. **∼·ation** /ˌruːɪ'neɪʃn/ *n* [U] being ∼ed; bringing to ∼: *These late frosts mean ∼ation to the fruit farmers.* **∼·ous** /-əs/ *adj* **1** causing ∼: *∼ous expenditure/folly.* **2**

in ∼s: *live in a ∼ous old house.* **∼·ous·ly** *adv*

rule /ru:l/ *n* **1** [C] law or custom which guides or controls behaviour or action; decision made by an organization, etc about what must or must not be done: *obey the ∼s of the game. There is a ∼ that.... It's against the ∼s to handle the ball in soccer.* **∼(s) of the road,** ⇨ road(1). **by/according to ∼,** according to ∼s and regulations: *He does everything by ∼,* never uses his own judgement. **work to ∼,** pay exaggerated attention (deliberately) to ∼s and regulations and so slow down output: *Instead of coming out on strike, the men decided to work to ∼.* '∼ **book,** book (issued to workers) containing such ∼s and regulations. ∼ **of thumb,** ⇨ thumb. **2** [C] sth that is the usual practice; habit: *My ∼ is to get up at seven and have breakfast at eight. Rainy weather is the ∼ here during April. He makes it a ∼ to do an hour's work in the garden every day. She makes a ∼ of going for a walk every afternoon.* **as a ∼,** usually; more often than not. **3** [U] government; authority: *the ∼ of the people; countries that were once under French ∼. The ∼ of law; mob ∼,* state that exists when a mob takes over. **4** [C] strip of wood, metal, etc, used to measure: *a 'foot-∼; a 'slide-∼.* □ *vi,vt* **1** [VP2A,B,6A,3A] ∼ **(over),** govern; have authority (over): *King Charles I ∼d (England) for eleven years without a parliament. An emperor is a monarch who ∼s over an empire.* **2** (usu in the *passive*) be guided or influenced by; have power or influence over: *Don't be ∼d by your passions/by hatred.* **3** [VP6A,9,15A,B,25] give as a decision: *The chairman ∼d the motion out of order/that the motion was out of order.* ∼ **sth out,** declare that it cannot be considered, that it is out of the question: *That's a possibility that can't be ∼d out,* It is something we must bear in mind. **4** [VP6A,15A,B] make (a line or lines) on paper (with a ruler); make parallel lines on (paper): *∼d notepaper;* ∼ *a line across the sheet.* ∼ **sth off,** separate it by ruling a line: ∼ *off a column of figures.* **5** [VP2C] (comm, of prices) have a certain general level: *Prices ∼d high,* were, for the most part, high.

ruler /'ru:lə(r)/ *n* **1** person who rules or governs. **2** straight length of wood, plastic, metal, etc usu flat, used in drawing straight lines, or, if graduated, for measuring.

rul·ing /'ru:lɪŋ/ *adj* that rules; pre-dominating; prevalent; *his ruling passion,* that which governs his actions. □ *n* [C] (esp) decision made by sb in authority, eg a judge.

rum[1] /rʌm/ *n* [U] alcoholic drink made from sugar-cane juice; (US) (any kind of) alcoholic liquor. '**rum-runner** *n* (US) person or ship engaged in the illegal importation of alcoholic liquor.

rum[2] /rʌm/ *n* [U] *adj* (rummer, rummest) (colloq) queer; odd: *What a rum fellow he is!* **rummy** *adj* = rum[2].

rumba /'rʌmbə/ *n* [C] (music for a) ballroom dance that originated in Cuba.

rumble /'rʌmbl/ *vi,vt* **1** [VP2A,C] make a deep, heavy, continuous sound: *thunder/gun-fire rumbling in the distance;* move with such a sound: *heavy carts rumbling along the street;* (of the bowels) make sounds as gas moves through them. **2** [VP15B] **out,** utter, say, in a deep voice: ∼ *out a few remarks.* □ *n* **1** [U] deep, heavy, continuous sound: *the ∼ of thunder.* **2** [C] (old use) place at the back of a carriage for a person or for luggage, etc; (= dickey-seat; US, also '∼-seat) extra, open

seat at the back of an (old-fashioned) automobile.
rum·bus·tious /rʌm'bʌstɪəs/ *adj* boisterous.
ru·mi·nant /'ruːmɪnənt/ *n, adj* (animal) which chews the cud, eg cows, deer.
ru·mi·nate /'ruːmɪneɪt/ *vi* [VP2A,B,C] meditate; turn over in the mind: ∼ *over/about/on recent events;* (of animals) chew the cud. **ru·mi·na·tive** /'ruːmɪnətɪv *US:* -neɪtɪv/ *adj* inclined to meditate. **ru·mi·na·tion** /,ruːmɪ'neɪʃn/ *n* [U].
rum·mage /'rʌmɪdʒ/ *vi,vt* **1** [VP2A,B,C,3A] ∼ *(among/in/through)*, turn things over, move things about, while looking for sth: ∼ *in/through a desk drawer;* ∼ *about among old papers.* **2** [VP6A,15B] ∼ *(through)*, search thoroughly: ∼ *a ship,* eg by Customs officers who suspect that there is contraband. □ *n* [U] **1** search (esp of a ship by Customs officers). **2** things found by rummaging; miscellaneous old clothes, old stock, etc. '∼ **sale,** = jumble (the more usu word) sale.
rummy¹ /'rʌmɪ/ *adj* ⇨ rum².
rummy² /'rʌmɪ/ *n* [U] card game for two or more players, using one or two packs of cards.
ru·mour (US = **ru·mor**) /'ruːmə(r)/ *n* [U] general talk, gossip, hearsay, [C] (statement, report, story) which cannot be verified and is of doubtful accuracy: *R*∼ *has it/There is a* ∼ *that there will be a General Election in the autumn. All sorts of* ∼*s are going round. There is a* ∼ *of the Loch Ness monster having been seen/a* ∼ *that the... has been seen.* '∼**-monger** *n* person who spreads ∼s. □ *vt* (usu passive) report by way of ∼: *It is* ∼*ed that.... He is* ∼*ed to have escaped to Dublin.*
rump /rʌmp/ *n* [C] **1** animal's buttocks; tail-end of a bird; (joc, of a human being) bottom. ∼**-'steak** *n* beefsteak cut from near the ∼. **2** (contemptible) remnant of a larger group.
rumple /'rʌmpl/ *vt* [VP6A] crease; crumple; make rough: *Don't play too violently or you'll* ∼ *your dress. I've just done my hair, so please don't* ∼ *it.*
rum·pus /'rʌmpəs/ *n* (*sing* only; colloq) disturbance; noise; uproar: *have a* ∼ *with sb. What's all this* ∼ *about?* **kick up/make a** ∼, cause a ∼.
run¹ /rʌn/ *n* **1** act of running on foot: *go for a short run across the fields;* (in fox-hunting) period of chasing a fox. **at a run,** running: *He started off at a run but soon tired and began to walk.* **on the run, (a)** in flight: *He's on the run from the police. We have the enemy on the run,* We have caused them to run away. **(b)** continuously active and moving about: *I've been on the run ever since I got up.* **give sb/get a (good) run for his/one's money, (a)** obtain (sth) in return for his efforts, expenditure. **(b)** provide him with strong competition. *We must give him a good run for his money.* **2** [C] excursion or visit: *a run to Paris; have a run in the country,* eg by car; outing or journey in a car, train, etc: *How many hours' run is Leeds from London by train? Can we have a trial run in the new car?* **3** [C] distance travelled by a ship in a specified time: *make bets on the day's run,* on the distance travelled in 24 hours. **4** route taken by vehicles, ships, etc: *The boat was taken off its usual run.* **5** quick fall: *Prices/The temperature came down in/with a run.* **6** series of performances: *The play had a long run/a run of six months.* **7** period; succession: *a run of bad luck,* a series of misfortunes. **a run on sth,** sudden demand by many people for it: *a run on the bank,* a demand by many customers together for immediate repayment. **in the 'long run,** ultimately: *It pays in the long run to buy*

goods of high quality. **8** (usu large, enclosed) space for domestic animals, fowls, etc: *a*'*chicken-run; a*'*sheep-run,* area of pasture for sheep. **9** (cricket and baseball) unit of scoring, made by running over a certain course. **10** common, average or ordinary type or class: *the common run of mankind,* ordinary, average people; *an hotel out of the common run,* different from, and better than, the kind one usually finds. **,run-of-the-'mill,** ordinary; average. **11** (colloq) permission to make free use (of). **give sb/get the run of sth,** the permission to use it: *I have the run of his library.* **12** way in which things tend to move; general direction or trend: *The run of events is rather puzzling. The run of the cards* (= The cards that were dealt to me during the evening) *favoured me.* **13** (music) series of notes sung or played quickly and in the order of the scale. **14** shoal of fish in motion: *a run of salmon,* eg on their way upstream. **15** (US) ladder(2).
run² /rʌn/ *vi,vt* (*pt* ran /ræn/, *pp* run; -nn-) (For special uses and *adverbial particles* and *preps,* ⇨ 26 below; for special uses of *running, part adj,* ⇨ running.) **1** [VP2A,B,C,E,4A] (of men and animals) move with quick steps, faster than when walking: *run three miles; run fast; run (out) to see what's happening; run upstairs. She came running to meet me. She ran to meet us. We ran to his aid/ran to help him. The dog was running behind its master.* ⇨ run after in 26 below. *Don't run across the road until you're sure it's safe.* **take a running jump,** run up to the point where one starts a jump; (sl, imper) go away, you are being foolish, etc. **2** [VP2A,B,C] escape or avoid by going away; take to flight: *As soon as we appeared the boys ran off. Run for your lives!* ie run if you want to save your life. **run for it,** avoid sth, eg getting wet in a storm, by running. **cut and run,** (sl) escape by taking to flight. **a running fight,** a fight between a retreating ship/fleet, etc and those in pursuit. **3** [VP2A,B,C] practise running for exercise or as a sport; compete in races on foot: *He used to run when he was at college. Is he running in the 100 metres? Is your horse likely to run in the Derby?* '**also ran,** used of a horse not among the first three past the winning post: *Hyperion also ran.* Hence, '**also-ran** *n* [C] person or animal unsuccessful in a race or other form of competition. **4** [VP3A] ∼ **for,** (esp US) compete for (an elected office). Cf *stand for,* the more usu GB usage: *run for President/for mayor.* **5** [VP6A,15A] cause to compete (in a race); present or nominate (for an office): *run two horses in the Derby. How many candidates is the Liberal Party running in the General Election?* **6** [VP2D,15A] (cause to) reach a certain condition or place as the result of running: *He ran second in the race.* **run oneself out (of breath),** ⇨ run out in 26 below. **run sb (clean) off his feet/legs,** (colloq) keep him going until he is exhausted. **run oneself/sb into the ground,** exhaust oneself/sb by hard work or exercise. **7** [VP6A] make one's way quickly to the end of, or through or over (sth). **run its course,** develop in the usual or normal way: *The disease ran its course.* **run a race,** take part in one. **run the rapids,** (of a boat, men in a boat) move rapidly over or through them. ⇨ shoot²(4), the more usu word. **run the streets,** (of children) spend time playing (esp without supervision) in the streets. **8** [VP6A] expose oneself to: be open to. **run the chance/danger of sth:** *You run the chance of being suspected of theft.* **run risks/a risk/the risk of**

sth, ⇨ risk. **9** [VP15A] chase; compete with. **run sb/sth to earth,** pursue until caught or found: *run a fox to earth,* chase it until it goes to its earth(4); (fig) *run a quotation to earth,* find, after searching, where it occurs. **run sb/sth close/hard,** be almost equal to, as good as, in merit, etc: *We run our competitors close for price and quality. It was a close run thing,* (of competition, etc) The result was very close. **10** [VP2A,C] (of ships, etc) sail or steer; (of fish) swim: *The ship was running before the wind. Our ship ran aground/on the rocks/ ashore. We ran into port for supplies. The two ships ran foul of each other,* collided. *The salmon are running,* swimming upstream from the sea. **11** [VP2C] go forward with a sliding, smooth or continuous motion; advance on, or as if on, wheels: *Trams run on rails; buses don't run on rails. Sledges run well over frozen snow. The train ran past the signal.* **12** [VP2A,C] be in action; work freely; be in working order: *Don't leave the engine of your car running. The sewing-machine doesn't run properly. The works have ceased running,* The factory has closed, is no longer producing goods. *His life has run smoothly up to now.* **13** [VP2A,C] (of public conveyances, eg buses, ferry-boats) ply; journey to and fro: *The buses run every ten minutes. The 9.05 train is not running today. There are frequent trains running between London and Brighton.* **14** [VP6A] organize; manage; cause to be in operation: *run a business/a theatre/a bus company; run extra trains during the rush hours. Can I run* (= operate) *my electric sewing-machine off the light circuit? I can't afford to run a car* (= own and use one) *on my small salary. Mr Green is run by his secretary,* She is the dominant personality and tells him what to do, etc. **run the show,** (colloq) be boss in an undertaking; have control. **15** [VP6A,15A,B] convey; transport: *I'll run you up to town/run you back home,* drive you there in my car. **run errands/messages (for sb),** make journeys to do things, carry messages, etc. **run arms/guns,** convey them into a country unlawfully. Hence, **'arms-∼ner** *n* person who does this. **run liquor/contraband,** smuggle it into a country; get it past the coastguards secretly. **16** [VP14,15A] cause to move quickly (in a certain direction or into a certain place): *run a car into a garage; run one's fingers/a comb through one's hair; run one's eyes over a page; run one's fingers over the keys of a piano.* **17** [VP2C] (of thoughts, feelings, etc, eyes, exciting news, etc) pass or move briefly or quickly: *The thought kept running through my head. Mary's eyes ran critically over her friend's new dress. The pain ran up my arm. A shiver ran down his spine. The news ran like wildfire. A whisper ran through the crowd.* **18** [VP15A] cause (sth) to penetrate (intentionally or by accident) or come into contact with; penetrate or pierce (sb/sth) with sth: *run a sword through a man/run a man through with a sword; run a splinter into one's finger; run one's head against a glass door in a dark corridor. The drunken driver ran his car into a tree.* **19** [VP2A,B,C] (of liquids, grain, sand, etc) flow, drip; (of surfaces) be wet (with); (of colours, eg dyes) flow and spread: *Rivers run into the sea. The tears ran down my cheeks. Who has left the tap/ water running? The tide was running strong. The beggar's legs were covered with running sores. Your nose is running—use your hanky,* ie wipe your nose clean. *Water was running all over the*

bathroom floor. The floor was running with water. Will the colours run if the dress is washed? **20** [VP6A,15A,B] cause (a liquid, molten metal, etc) to flow: *Run some hot water into the bowl. Run the water off,* (= let it flow out) *when you've had your bath. The molten metal was run into a mould.* **21** [VP2D] become; pass into (a specified condition): *The rivers are running dry,* ceasing to flow. *Supplies are running short/low. I have run short of money. Feelings/Passions ran high,* became stormy or violent. *My blood ran cold,* I was filled with horror. **run riot,** (a) behave in a wild and lawless way. (b) (of plants, etc) grow unchecked. **run wild,** be without control, restraint, discipline, etc: *The garden is running wild. She lets her children run wild.* **run a temperature,** (colloq) be feverish. **22** [VP2A,B,C] extend; have a certain course or order; be continued or continuous; *shelves running round the walls; a scar that runs across his left cheek; a road that runs across the plain; a fence running round the property. It happened several days running,* several days in succession. *He hit the target seven times running. The play ran (for) six months,* was kept on the stage, was performed, during this period of time. *The lease of my house has only a year to run.* **a running commentary,** account of an event as it occurs by a broadcaster: *a running commentary of a football match.* **'running costs,** continuous costs for producing goods, etc (as opposed to costs of original manufacture. **23** [VP2C,D] have a tendency or common characteristic; have as an average price or level: *This author runs to sentiment. Blue eyes run in the family. Our apples run rather small this year. Prices for fruit are running high this season.* **24** [VP2A] be told or written: *So the story ran,* that is what was told or said. *The story runs that...,* It is said that.... *The agreement runs in these words. I forget how the next verse runs,* how the words or notes follow one another. **25** [VP2A] (of woven or knitted material) become unwoven or unravelled; drop stitches through several rows: *Nylon tights sometimes run.* ⇨ ladder, the more usu word with reference to stockings. **26** [VP2C,3A,15B] (special uses with *adverbial particles* and *preps*):

run across, pay a short informal visit: *run across to a neighbour's flat to borrow some sugar.* **run across sb/sth,** meet or find by chance: *I ran across my old friend Jean in Paris last week.*

run after sb/sth, (a) try to catch: *The dog was running after a rabbit.* (b) seek the society of; go after in order to get the attention of: *She runs after every good-looking man in the village.*

run against sb, compete with him by running in a race; (esp US) compete with him (for an elected office).

run along, (colloq) go away, be off: *Now, children, run along!*

run away, leave rapidly; flee; escape: *Don't run away—I want your advice. The boy ran away and went to sea,* left home and became a sailor. Hence, **run·away** /ˈrʌnəweɪ/ *n* person who has run away. ⊡ *adj* **runaway success, etc,** great, immediate success, etc. **run away with sb,** (b) go at a speed too high for control: *Don't let your horse/car run away with you.* (c) destroy the self-control of: *Don't let your temper run away with you.* **run away with sth,** (a) use up: *This new scheme will run away with a lot of the ratepayers' money.* (b) carry off; steal: *The maid ran away with the du-*

chess's jewels. (c) get a clear win over: *The girl from Peru ran away with the first set,* eg in a tennis tournament. **run away with the idea/notion that,** assume too hastily that sth is the case: *Don't run away with the idea that I can lend you money every time you need help.*
run back over sth, review past events, etc: *run back over the past. I'll run back over the procedure again.* **run sth back,** rewind (film, tape, etc) (after it has been looked at, listened to).
run down, (a) (of a clock or other mechanism worked by weights) stop because it needs winding up. (b) (of a battery) become weak or exhausted: *The battery is/has run down; it needs recharging.* **(be/feel/look) run down,** (of a person, his health) exhausted or weak from overwork, mental strain, etc. **run sb/sth down,** knock down or collide with: *The liner ran down a fishing-boat during the dense fog. The cyclist was run down by a big lorry.* **run sb down,** (a) say unkind things about; disparage: *That man doesn't like me; he's always running me down.* (b) pursue and overtake: *run down an escaped prisoner.* **run sth down,** allow to become less active or occupied: *run down the ship's boilers; run down a naval dockyard,* do less work and employ fewer workers. Hence, '**run-down** *n* 1 reduction: *the run-down of the coal industry.* 2 (colloq) detailed explanation or listing. □ *adj* (of a place) decayed; dilapidated; not cared for.
run for sth, (a) ⇨ 2 above. (b) ⇨ 4 above.
run in, = *run across.* **run sb in,** (colloq of the police) arrest and take to a police station: *The drunken man was run in for creating a public disturbance.* **run sth in,** bring (new machinery, esp the engine of a car) into good condition by running it carefully for a time or distance: *He's still running in his new car and doesn't exceed fifty miles an hour.*
run into sb, meet unexpectedly: *run into an old friend in a pub.* **run into sth,** (a) collide with: *The bus got out of control and ran into a wall.* (b) fall into: *run into debt/danger/difficulties.* (c) reach (a level or figure): *a book that has run into six editions. His income runs into five figures,* is now ten thousand (pounds, dollars, etc) or more. **run sb into sth,** cause (sb) to fall into (a certain state): *My wife has run me into despair.* **run sth into sth,** cause sth to collide or connect with sth: *run one's car into a wall.*
run off with sb/sth, (a) steal and take away: *The treasurer has run off with all the club's funds.* (b) elope with: *My mother has run off with her bank manager.* **run sth off,** (a) cause to flow away: *run off the water from a tank,* empty the tank. (b) write or recite fluently, eg a list of names: *run off an article for the local (news)paper.* (c) print; produce: *run off a hundred copies on the duplicating machine.* (d) decide (a race) after a tie, or trial heats; cause to be run or played: *run off a heat. When will the race be run off?* Hence, '**run-off** *n* deciding race, etc after a dead heat or tie. ⇨ **dead.** **run off sb (like water off a duck's back),** have no effect on him: *Her warnings ran off him like water off a duck's back.*
run on, (a) talk continuously: *He will run on for an hour if you don't stop him.* (b) elapse: *Time ran on.* (c) (of a disease) continue its course. **run (sth) on,** (a) (of written letters of the alphabet) join, be joined, together: *When children are learning to write, they should let the letters run on, not write*

them separately. *They should run the letters on.* **run on/upon sth,** (a) (of thoughts, etc) be concerned with: *That boy's thoughts are always running on food. His thoughts were running upon the past/on recent events in India.* (b) (of ship) strike: *The ship ran upon the rocks.*
run out, (a) go out: *The tide is running out.* (b) (of a period of time) come to an end: *When does the lease of the house run out?* (c) (of stocks, supplies) come to an end, be exhausted; (of persons) become short of (supplies, etc): *Our provisions are running out. Her patience is running out. The sands are running out,* (with reference to the sand in an hour-glass) the time allowed to us (before something unwelcome comes) is coming to an end. (d) jut out; project: *a pier running out into the sea.* **run (rope/string) out,** pass (it) out; be passed out: *The rope ran out smoothly. The sailor ran the rope out neatly.* **run out of sth,** reach an end of (stocks, supplies): *We're fast running out of beer/cigarettes.* **be run out,** (cricket, of a batsman) have his innings ended because, while trying to make a run, he fails to reach his crease before the wicketkeeper or one of the fielders returns the ball and removes the bails or stump(s): *Smith was run out before he had scored.* **run oneself out (of breath),** exhaust oneself: *He's completely run out.* **run out on sb,** (sl) abandon, desert: *Poor Jane! Her husband has run out on her.*
run over, (a) (of a vessel or its contents) overflow. (b) = *run across.* **run over sth,** (a) review; recapitulate: *Let's run over our parts again,* eg when learning and rehearsing parts in a play. (b) read through quickly: *He ran over his notes before starting his lecture.* **run over sb; run sb over,** (of a vehicle) (knock down and) pass over (sb or sth lying on the ground): *The bus ran over his legs. He was run over and had to be taken to hospital.*
run round, = *run across.*
run sth through sth, draw a line, one's pen, through sth. **run sb through,** pierce with a sword, bayonet, etc. **run through sth,** (a) use up (a fortune, etc) esp by foolish or reckless spending: *He soon ran through the money he had won at poker.* (b) examine quickly; deal with in rapid succession: *run through one's mail during breakfast.* Hence, '**run-through** *n* quick examination or discussion: *give sth a quick run-through.* (c) rehearse. Hence, '**run-through** *n* rehearsal.
run to sth, (a) reach (an amount, number, etc): *That will run to a pretty penny,* will cost a lot of money. (b) have money for; (of money) be enough for: *We can't/Our funds won't run to a holiday abroad this year. I can't run to that,* can't afford it. (c) extend to: *His new novel runs for 900 pages/ has already run to three impressions.* **run to fat,** (of persons) tend to put on too much fat. **run to ruin,** fall into ruin. **run to seed,** (of plants) tend to develop chiefly seed instead of new growth of leaves, etc. **run to waste,** (eg of water) be wasted.
run up, (cricket; of a bowler) gather speed by running, before releasing the ball; (of athletes in some field events) gather speed before jumping, throwing a javelin, etc. Hence, '**run-up** *n* (a) (length or manner of a) bowler's or athlete's approach: *a long/short run-up.* (b) period leading up (to sth): *the run-up to the General Election,* the period when candidates are busy seeking support, etc. **run sth up,** (a) raise; hoist: *run up a flag on the mast.* (b) erect, make or construct quickly or in an unsub-

stantial way: *run up a dress/a garden shed.* (c) add up (a column of figures). (d) cause to grow quickly in amount: *run up a big bill at a hotel; run up the bidding at an auction,* force others to bid higher, force up prices. **run up against, sth,** meet by chance or unexpectedly: *run up against difficulties.* **run up to,** amount, extend to (a figure): *Prices ran up to £5 a ton.*

run-away /'rʌnəweɪ/ *n, adj* ⇨ *run away* at run(26).

rune /ruːn/ *n* any letter of an old alphabet used in N Europe, esp of the Scandinavians and Anglo-Saxons (from AD 200); similar mark of a mysterious or magic sort. **runic** /'ruːnɪk/ *adj* of ~s; written in, inscribed with, ~s.

rung¹ /rʌŋ/ *n* [C] **1** crosspiece forming a step in a ladder: *start on the lowest/reach the highest* ~ (*of the ladder*), (fig) a particular level in society, one's employment, etc. **2** crosspiece joining the legs of a chair to strengthen it.

rung² /rʌŋ/ *pp* of *ring²*.

run-nel /'rʌnl/ *n* **1** brook. **2** open gutter (for rainwater) at a roadside, etc.

run-ner /'rʌnə(r)/ *n* **1** person, animal, etc that runs: *How many* ~*s were there in the Derby?* ~-'**up** *n* person or team taking the second place in a competition. **2** messenger, scout, collector, etc: *Bow Street* ~, (hist) police-officer. **3** (in compounds) smuggler: '*gun*-~*s*; '*rum*-~*s*. **blo'ckade-**~, person who tries to get through the forces that are blockading a port, etc. **4** part on which sth slides or moves along: *the* ~*s of a sledge*. **5** long piece of cloth (for a table, etc); long piece of carpet, eg for stairs. **6** stem coming from a strawberry plant and taking root; kinds of twining bean-plant: *scarlet* ~*s*; ~ *beans*. ⇨ the illus at vegetable.

run-ning /'rʌnɪŋ/ *n* [U] **1** act of a person or animal that runs, esp in racing. **make the** ~, set the pace (lit or fig). **take up the** ~, take the lead. **in/out of the** ~, (of competitors) having some/no chance of winning. **2** '~-**board** *n* (now old-fashioned) footboard on either side of a car. '~ **mate,** (a) horse used to set the pace for another horse in a race. (b) candidate for the lesser of two associated political offices, eg for the Vice-Presidency of the US. □ *adj* **1** done, made, carried on, while or immediately after running: *a* ~ *kick/jump/fight.* ⇨ *run²*(1,2). **2** continuous; uninterrupted: *a* ~ *fire of questions,* coming in a continuous stream; *a* ~ *hand,* (of handwriting) with the letters joined. *a* ~ **commentary,** ⇨ run²(22). **3** (after a *pl n*) in succession: *win three times* ~. **4** (of water) flowing; coming from a mains supply: *All bedrooms in this hotel have hot and cold* ~ *water,* coming when taps are turned. **5** (of sores, etc) with liquid or pus coming out. **6** a '~ **knot,** one that slips along a rope and so makes the noose larger or smaller. ⇨ the illus at knot.

runny /'rʌnɪ/ *adj* (colloq) semi-liquid; tending to run(18) or flow: *a* ~ *nose. The jam is rather* ~; *you'd better boil it again.*

runt /rʌnt/ *n* (colloq) undersized or stunted plant, animal (esp the smallest of a litter), or (derog) person.

run-way /'rʌnweɪ/ *n* **1** specially prepared surface along which aircraft take off and land. **2** way made for rolling felled trees and logs down a hillside.

ru-pee /ruː'piː/ *n* [C] monetary unit of India, Pakistan, Sri Lanka, Nepal, Mauritius, etc.

ru-piah /ruː'piːə/ *n* monetary unit of Indonesia.

rup-ture /'rʌptʃə(r)/ *n* **1** [U] breaking apart or bursting; [C] instance of this. **2** [C,U] (instance of) ending of friendly relations. **3** [C] swelling in the abdomen caused by the breaking of some organ or tissue through the wall of its retaining cavity. ⇨ hernia. □ *vt,vi* [VP6A,2A] break or burst, eg a blood-vessel or membrane; end (a connection, etc).

ru-ral /'rʊərəl/ *adj* in, of, characteristic of, suitable for, the countryside (opp of *urban*): ~ *scenery; live in* ~ *seclusion.*

Ru-ri-tan-ian /ˌrʊərɪ'teɪnɪən/ *adj* (of a State, its politics) full of plots and intrigues (as in a melodramatic story about an imaginary country called Ruritania).

ruse /ruːz/ *n* [C] deceitful way of doing sth, getting sth, etc; trick; stratagem.

rush¹ /rʌʃ/ *n* **1** [U] rapid, headlong movement; sudden swift advance; [C] instance of this: *I don't like the* ~ *of city life. He was swept away by the* ~ *of the current and drowned. Why all this* ~, this hurry and excitement? *There were several* ~*es to the refreshment tent during the afternoon. There was the usual Easter* ~, ie of traffic to the holiday resorts, etc. '**gold**-~, ⇨ gold. **2** [C] sudden demand: *a* ~ *for raincoats,* eg when there is heavy rain; sudden or intense activity: *the Christmas* ~, the period before Christmas when crowds of people go shopping. **the** '~-**hour,** when crowds of people are travelling to or from work in a large town: (attrib) *We were caught in the* ~-*hour traffic.* **3** (cinema, often *pl*) first print of a film before cutting and editing.

rush² /rʌʃ/ *n* [C] (tall stem of one of numerous varieties of) marsh plant with slender leafless stems containing pith, often dried and used for making seats or chairs, for weaving into baskets, etc, and, in olden times, for strewing floors. '~-**light** *n* kind of candle made by dipping the pith of a ~ into tallow. **rushy** *adj* full of, abounding with, ~es: *a* ~*y ditch.*

rush³ /rʌʃ/ *vi,vt* **1** [VP6A,15A,B,2A,C,4A] ~ *(away/off/out),* (cause to) go or come, do sth, with violence or speed: *The children* ~*ed out of the school gates. They* ~*ed (away/off/out) to see the procession. The bull* ~*ed at me. They* ~*ed more troops to the front.* ~ **to conclusions,** form them hastily. ~ **into print,** publish sth without proper care, consideration, etc. ~ **sth through,** do sth at high speed: *The order for furniture was* ~*ed through* (= The goods were packed and sent off) *in two days. The new Bill was* ~*ed through Parliament.* **2** [VP6A] capture by a sudden attack; get through, over, into, etc by pressing eagerly or violently forward: ~ *the enemy's trenches;* ~ *the gates of the football ground. The panic-stricken passengers tried to* ~ *the life-boats,* force their way into them quickly. **3** [VP6A,15A] force into hasty action: *I must think things over, so don't* ~ *me.* ~ **sb off his feet,** succeed in forcing him into hasty action with no time for thought; exhaust him. **4** ~ **(for sth),** (sl) charge an exorbitant price: *How much did they* ~ *you for this?*

rusk /rʌsk/ *n* [C] piece of bread baked hard and crisp; kind of crisp biscuit: '*teething* ~*s.*

rus-set /'rʌsɪt/ *n* **1** [U] yellowish or reddish brown. **2** [C] kind of rough-skinned ~-coloured apple. □ *adj* of the colour of ~.

Rus-sian /'rʌʃn/ *adj* of or from Russia. **R~ roulette,** ⇨ roulette. □ *n* **1** native of Russia. **2** the principal language of the Soviet Union.

rust /rʌst/ n [U] **1** reddish-brown coating formed on iron by the action of water and air; similar coating on other metals: ~-covered machinery; rub the ~ off sth. **2** (plant-disease with ~-coloured spots caused by) kinds of fungus; mildew; blight. □ vt, vi [VP6A,2A,C] (cause to) become covered with ~; (fig) become poor in quality because not used: Don't leave the lawn-mower out in the garden to ~. It's better to wear out than to ~ out, to become worn through use than to lose value by ~ing. ~-less adj that does not ~: ~less steel, used for stainless cutlery, etc. **rusty** adj (-ier, -iest) **1** covered with ~: ~y needles. **2** in need of practice; out-of-date: My German is rather ~y, hasn't been used for a long time and needs to be practised. **3** (of black cloth) discoloured by age; dingy or shabby. ~i-ness n [U].

rus·tic /'rʌstɪk/ adj **1** (in a good sense) characteristic of country people; simple; unaffected: ~ simplicity. **2** rough; unrefined: ~ speech/manners, contrasted with the speech, etc of smart, city people. **3** of rough workmanship: a ~ bench/bridge, made or rough, unplaned timber and untrimmed branches. □ n countryman; peasant. ~-ity /rʌ'stɪsətɪ/ n [U] being ~ in appearance or character.

rus·ti·cate /'rʌstɪkeɪt/ vi, vt **1** [VP2A] lead a rural life. **2** [VP6A] (GB) send (a student) temporarily away from the university as a punishment.

rustle /'rʌsl/ vi, vt **1** [VP2A,C] make a gentle, light sound (like dry leaves blown by the wind, or of silk clothes in motion); move along making such a sound: Did you hear something rustling through the undergrowth? **2** [VP6A] cause to make this sound: I wish people wouldn't ~ their programmes while the orchestra is playing. **3** [VP6A] (US, colloq) steal (cattle or horses). **4** [VP15B] ~ sth up, get together, provide: ~ up some food for an unexpected guest. □ n [U] gentle light sound as of dry leaves blown by the wind, of silk clothes, etc: the ~ of paper. **rust·ler** /'rʌslə(r)/ n (US, colloq) cattle thief. **rust·ling** /'rʌslɪŋ/ n [U] sound made by sth that ~s: the rustling of dry leaves/of sweet wrappings; (pl) repetitions of such sounds: mysterious rustlings at night.

rut[1] /rʌt/ n [C] **1** line or track made by wheel(s) in soft ground. **2** (fig) way of doing sth, behaving, living, etc that has become established. be in/get into a rut, a fixed (and boring) way of living so that it becomes difficult to change. □ vt (usu in pp) mark with ruts: a deeply rutted road.

rut[2] /rʌt/ n [U] periodic sexual excitement of male animals, esp deer. □ vi [VP2A] be affected with this: the rutting season.

ruth·less /'ruːθlɪs/ adj cruel; without pity; showing no mercy. ~·ly adv ~·ness n

rye /raɪ/ n [U] **1** (plant with) grain used for making flour, and as a food for cattle. ⇨ the illus at cereal. **'rye-bread** n bread made with flour from rye. **2** kind of whisky made from rye.

Ss

S, s /es/ (pl S's, s's /'esɪz/) the nineteenth letter of the English alphabet.

sab·ba·tarian /ˌsæbə'teərɪən/ n Christian who advocates strict observance of Sunday (eg by opposing the opening of places of entertainment, the playing of games, etc on Sundays). ⇨ Sabbath. □ adj of the principles of ~s.

Sab·bath /'sæbəθ/ n day of rest, Saturday for Jews, Sunday for Christians: break the ~, work or play on the ~; keep the ~, spend it in worship of God and in rest.

sab·bati·cal /sə'bætɪkl/ adj of or like the Sabbath: After this uproar there came a ~ calm. ~ (year), year of freedom from routine duties given to some university teachers to enable them to travel or undertake special studies.

sa·ber /'seɪbə(r)/ ⇨ sabre.

sable /'seɪbl/ n [C] **1** small animal valued for its beautiful dark fur; [U] fur of this animal: a ~ coat/stole. **2** ~ antelope, large, horned, dark African antelope. □ adj (liter) black; gloomy.

sa·bot /'sæbəʊ US: sæ'bəʊ/ n [C] shoe hollowed out of a single piece of wood; wooden-soled shoe with a band of leather across the instep.

sab·otage /'sæbətɑːʒ/ n [U] the wilful damaging of machinery, materials, etc or the hindering of an opponent's activity, during an industrial or political dispute, or during war. □ vt [VP6A] perform an act of ~ against. **sab·oteur** /ˌsæbə'tɜː(r)/ n person who commits ~.

sabre (US = sa·ber) /'seɪbə(r)/ n heavy cavalry sword with a curved blade. **'~-rattling** n aggressive display of military strength. **'~-toothed** adj having (usu two) ~-like teeth: a ~-toothed tiger (now extinct). □ vt strike with a ~.

sac /sæk/ n bag-like membrane enclosing a cavity in an animal or plant. ⇨ the illus at flower.

sac·char·in /'sækərɪn/ n [U] very sweet substance made from coal-tar, used in place of sugar. **sac·char·ine** /-riːn/ adj resembling sugar; very sweet; too sweet.

sac·er·do·tal /ˌsæsə'dəʊtl/ adj connected with priests. ~·ism /-ɪzəm/ n [U] system of government in which priests (claiming to be mediators between God and mankind) have a great part or exercise great power.

sachet /'sæʃeɪ US: sæ'ʃeɪ/ **1** small perfumed bag. **2** [C,U] (packet of) sweet-smelling dried lavender or other substance for laying among clothes, etc. **3** small packet, containing eg shampoo.

sack[1] /sæk/ n **1** (quantity held by a) large bag of strong material (eg coarse flax, hemp, stiffened paper) for storing and carrying heavy goods, eg cement, coal, flour, potatoes: coal £3 a ~; two ~s of potatoes. **'~-race** n one between competitors each of whom has his legs tied into a sack and moves by short jumps. **'~-cloth** n [U] coarse material made of flax or hemp. ~cloth and ashes, (a) regret for wrongdoing; penitence. (b) mourning. 2 short loose dress. ~-ing n = ~cloth.

sack² /sæk/ n **give sb/get the ~,** (colloq) dismiss sb/be dismissed from employment: *He got the ~ for petty thieving.* □ vt [VP6A] dismiss from employment.

sack³ /sæk/ vt [VP6A] (of a victorious army) plunder violently (a captured city, etc). □ n the ~, ~ing of a captured town, etc.

sack⁴ /sæk/ n (sl) bed. *hit the ~*, go to bed.

sack⁵ /sæk/ n [U] (hist) kinds of white wine imported from Spain and the Canary Islands.

sack·but /'sækbʌt/ n medieval musical wind instrument with a slide like that of a trombone.

sac·ra·ment /'sækrəmənt/ n [C] solemn religious ceremony in the Christian Church, eg Baptism, Confirmation, Matrimony, believed to be accompanied by great spiritual benefits; (esp) **the Blessed/Holy S~,** Holy Communion, the Eucharist. **sac·ra·men·tal** /ˌsækrə'mentl/ adj of, connected with, ~s: ~al wine.

sacred /'seɪkrɪd/ adj 1 of God; connected with religion: *a ~ building,* eg a church, mosque, synagogue or temple; ~ *music,* for use in religious services; ~ *writings,* eg the Koran, the Bible; ~ *to the memory of...,* phrase seen on tombstones and memorials to the dead. 2 solemn: *a ~ promise; hold a promise ~; regard sth as a ~ duty.* 3 (to be) treated with great respect or reverence: *In India the cow is a ~ animal. Nothing is ~ to these wild youths,* They respect nothing. ~ *cow,* (colloq) sth to be regarded with reverence, and as immune from reasonable criticism. **~·ly** adv **~·ness** n

sac·ri·fice /'sækrɪfaɪs/ n 1 [U] the offering of sth precious to a god; [C] instance of this; [C] the thing offered: *the ~ of an ox to Jupiter; kill a sheep as a ~.* 2 [C,U] the giving up of sth of great value to oneself for a special purpose, or to benefit sb else; [C] sth given up in this way: *He gave his life as a ~ for his country,* eg of a soldier killed in war. *Parents often make ~s* (eg go without things) *in order to educate their children. Is the ~ of one's health to money-making worth while?* □ vt,vi [VP6A,14,3A,16A] ~ *(sth) (to),* 1 make a ~(1): ~ *a lamb to the gods;* ~ *to idols.* 2 give up as a ~(2,3): *He ~d his life to save the drowning child. Do you approve of sacrificing comfort to appearance,* eg by wearing formal clothes during hot weather? *She has ~d herself/her life/her pleasures and pastimes to her husband's interests and welfare.* **sac·ri·fi·cial** /ˌsækrɪ'fɪʃl/ adj of or like a ~.

sac·ri·lege /'sækrɪlɪdʒ/ n [U] disrespectful treatment of, injury to, what should be sacred: *It would be ~ to steal a crucifix from a church altar.* **sac·ri·legious** /ˌsækrɪ'lɪdʒəs/ adj

sac·ris·tan /'sækrɪstən/ n (RC Church) sexton.

sac·risty /'sækrɪstɪ/ n (pl -ties) (RC Church) room in a church where vestments and articles used in church worship are kept; vestry.

sac·ro·sanct /'sækrəʊsæŋkt/ adj (to be) protected from all harm, because sacred or holy; (fig, often ironic) not to be violated: *He regards his privileges as ~.*

sad /sæd/ adj (-der, -dest) 1 unhappy; causing unhappy feelings: *John is sad because his dog has died. It was a sad day for Mary when her mother died. Why is he looking so sad?* 2 shameful; deplorably bad: *a sad case of total callousness.* **sad·ly** adv **sad·ness** n **sad·den** /'sædn/ vt,vi [VP6A,2A] make or become sad.

saddle /'sædl/ n 1 leather seat for a rider on a horse, donkey or bicycle; part of a horse's back on which the seat is placed. ⇨ the illus at bicycle, harness. *in the ~,* on horseback; (fig) in a position of control or power. **'~-bag** n (a) one of a pair of bags laid over the back of a horse or donkey. (b) small bag hung behind a bicycle ~. **'~-sore** adj (of a rider) having sores caused by chafing from the ~. ~ *of mutton/venison,* joint of meat from the back of the animal, together with part of the backbone and ribs. 2 line or ridge of high land rising at each end to a high point. ⇨ the illus at mountain. □ vt 1 [VP6A] put a ~ on (a horse). 2 [VP14] ~ *sb with sth,* put a heavy responsibility on him; put a burden, etc, on him: *be ~d with a wife and ten children;* ~ *sb with heavy tasks.* **sad·dler** /'sædlə(r)/ n maker of ~s and leather goods for horses. **sad·dlery** /'sædlərɪ/ n [U] goods made by a saddler; [C] (pl -ries) saddler's business.

sadhu /'sɑːduː/ n Hindu holy man who leads an ascetic life.

sa·dism /'seɪdɪzəm/ n [C] 1 getting sexual pleasure from cruelty to one's partner. 2 (loosely) (delight in) excessive cruelty. **sa·dist** /-ɪst/ n person displaying ~. **sa·dis·tic** /sə'dɪstɪk/ adj of ~.

sado·maso·chism /ˌseɪdəʊ'mæsəkɪzəm/ n [U] sadism and masochism found or treated together. **ˌsado-'masochist** /-kɪst/ n person displaying ~.

sa·fari /sə'fɑːrɪ/ n [C,U] hunting expedition, overland journey, esp in E and Central Africa: *on ~; return from ~;* (by extension) organized tour (for people on holiday) to game reserves, etc.

safe¹ /seɪf/ adj (-r, -st) 1 ~ *(from),* free from, protected from, danger: ~ *from attack.* 2 unhurt and undamaged. ~ *and sound,* secure and unharmed: *return ~ and sound from a dangerous expedition.* 3 not causing or likely to cause harm or danger: *Is 120 kilometres an hour ~ on this wide road? Is your dog ~? Are these toys ~ for small children?* 4 (of a place, etc) giving security: *Keep it in a ~ place. Is this beach ~ for bathing? Is the bathing ~ here? Is this a ~ seat for the Tories,* Is it certain that the Tory candidate will be elected? 5 cautious; not taking risks: *a ~ statesman. They appointed a ~ man as Headmaster. be on the '~ side,* take more precautions than may be necessary: *Although the sun was shining he took his raincoat and umbrella to be on the ~ side.* 6 certain (to do, be, become): *Mr Hill is ~ to win the seat,* will certainly be elected. 7 (compounds) **,~-'conduct** n (document giving the) right to visit or pass through a district without the risk of being arrested or harmed (esp in time of war). **'~-deposit** (US = **~-de'posit**) n building containing strong-rooms and safes which persons may rent separately for storing valuables. **'~-guard** n object, condition, circumstance, etc that tends to prevent harm, give protection (*against*): *smear one's skin with sun-tan lotion as a ~guard against sun-burn.* □ vt [VP6A,14] **~guard (against),** protect, guard: ~*guard one's house against burglars,* eg with a burglar-alarm. **,~-'keeping** n [U] care; custody: *Leave your jewels in the bank for ~-keeping while you are on holiday.* **~·ly** adv **~·ness** n or a feeling of ~ness.

safe² /seɪf/ n 1 fireproof and burglar-proof box in which money and other valuables are kept. 2 cool, airy cupboard in which food is kept to protect it from flies, etc: *a '~meat~.*

safety /'seɪftɪ/ n [U] 1 being safe; freedom from

danger: *do nothing that might endanger the* ~ *of other people; seek* ~ *in flight; ensure sb's* ~; *play for* ~, avoid taking risks in a game (or fig). **S~ First,** motto used to warn that ~ is important. **road** ~, ~ from traffic dangers. **2** (compounds) '~-**belt**, = seat belt. '~-**bolt/-catch/-lock**, device that gives ~ against a possible danger (eg to prevent a gun from being fired by accident or a door being opened without the proper key). '~-**curtain** *n* fireproof curtain that can be lowered between the stage and auditorium of a theatre. '~ **glass** *n* glass that does not shatter or splinter. '~-**lamp** *n* miner's lamp in which the flame is protected so as not to ignite dangerous gases. '~-**match** *n* one that lights only when rubbed on a special surface (on the side of the box). '~-**pin** *n* one with a guard for the point. '~-**razor** *n* razor with a guard to prevent the blade from cutting the skin. '~-**valve** *n* (a) valve which releases pressure (in a steam boiler, etc) when it becomes too great. (b) (fig) way of releasing feelings of anger, excitement, etc harmlessly. **sit on the ~-valve**, follow a policy of repression.

a safety-pin

saf·fron /'sæfrən/ *n* orange powder obtained from flowers of the autumn crocus, used as a dye and for flavouring; colour of this (bright orange-yellow).

sag /sæg/ *vi* (-gg-) [VP2A] **1** sink or curve down in the middle under weight or pressure: *a sagging roof. Prices are sagging,* falling. **2** hang down unevenly; hang sideways: *His cheeks are beginning to sag.* □ *n* [C] (degree of) sagging: *There is a bad sag in the seat of this chair.*

saga /'sɑːgə/ *n* [C] **1** mediaeval story of heroic deeds of Icelandic or Norwegian heroes. **2** long narrative, eg a number of connected books (esp novels) about a family, social group, etc: *the Forsyte S~.* **3** (colloq) long description of an eventful experience: *the ~ of Caroline's trip up the Amazon.*

sa·gacious /sə'geɪʃəs/ *adj* showing good judgement, common sense or (of animals) intelligence. ~·**ly** *adv*

sa·gac·ity /sə'gæsətɪ/ *n* [U] sound judgement; wisdom of a practical kind: *S~, unlike cleverness, may increase with age.*

sage[1] /seɪdʒ/ *n* wise man; man who is believed to be wise. □ *adj* wise; having the wisdom of experience; (often ironic) wise-looking. ~·**ly** *adv*

sage[2] /seɪdʒ/ *n* [U] herb with dull greyish-green leaves, used to flavour food: ~ *and onions,* stuffing used for a goose, duck, etc. ~-'**green** *n, adj* the colour of ~ leaves.

Sag·it·ta·rius /ˌsædʒɪ'teərɪəs/ *n* ninth sign of the zodiac. ⇨ the illus at **zodiac**.

sago /'seɪgəʊ/ *n* [U] starchy food, in the form of hard, white grains, from the pith of certain palm-trees ('~ *palms*).

Sa·hib /sɑːɪb/ *US*: /sɑːɪb/ *n* (old use, in India and Pakistan, used *after* a title or name) sir: *Colonel ~; Churchill ~.*

said /sed/ **1** *pt, pp* of **say. 2** = *aforesaid,* ⇨ **afore.**

sail[1] /seɪl/ *n* **1** [C,U] sheet of canvas spread to catch the wind and move a boat or ship forward: *hoist/ lower the ~s; in full ~,* with all the ~s spread or

set. **under ~,** (moving) with ~s spread. **set ~ (from/to/for),** begin a voyage. **take in ~,** reduce the area of sails spread; (fig) become less ambitious or active. **take the wind out of sb's ~s,** ⇨ **wind**[1](1). '~-**cloth** *n* [U] canvas for ~s. **2** [C] set of boards attached to the arm of a windmill to catch the wind. **3** (*pl* unchanged) ship: *a fleet of twenty ~. There wasn't a ~ in sight. S~ ho!* (cry announcing that a ship is in sight). **4** (rarely *pl*) voyage or excursion on water for pleasure: *go for a ~;* voyage of a specified duration: *How many days' ~ is it from Hull to Oslo?*

sail[2] /seɪl/ *vi, vt* **1** [VP2A,B,C] move forward across the sea, a lake, etc by using ~s or engine-power, move forward (in sport) across ice or a sandy beach, by means of a sail or sails: ~ *up/along the coast; ~ into harbour; go ~ing. ~ close/near to the wind,* **(a)** (naut) sail near to the direction in which the wind is blowing. **(b)** (fig) nearly, but not quite, break a law or offend against a moral principle. '~-**ing-boat/-ship/-vessel**, *n* boat, etc moved by sails. **2** [VP2A,C,3A] ~ *(for/from/to),* (of a ship or persons on board) begin a voyage; travel on water by use of sails or engines: *When does the ship ~? He has ~ed for New York. Here is a list of ~ings* (= ships that ~, with dates) *from London. The captain has received his ~ing orders,* instructions concerning the voyage. **3** [VP6A] voyage across or on: ~ *the sea/the Pacific.* **4** [VP6A,2A] (be able to) control (a boat): *He ~s his own yacht. Do you ~?* '~-**ing-master** *n* officer who navigates a yacht. **5** [VP2C] move smoothly like a ship with sails: *The moon/clouds ~ed across the sky. The duchess ~ed into the room,* entered in a stately manner. **6** ~ *in,* begin sth with energy and confidence. ~ *into sb,* scold; attack.

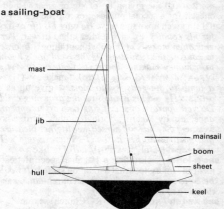

a sailing-boat

mast

jib

mainsail

boom

sheet

hull

keel

sailor /'seɪlə(r)/ *n* **1** seaman; member of a ship's crew. '~ **hat/blouse/suit**, hat, etc eg to be worn by a child, made in imitation of the kind worn by a ~. **2 good/bad ~**, person seldom/often seasick in rough weather.

saint /seɪnt; *GB weak form immediately before names:* snt/ *n* **1** holy person. **2** person who, having died, is among the blessed in Heaven. **3** (abbr **St**) person who has been declared by the Church to have won by holy living on earth a place in Heaven and veneration on earth. **4** unselfish or patient person. **5** '~'**s-day** *n* Church festival in memory of a ~. **St 'Andrew's Day**, 30th November (patron ~

of Scotland). **St 'David's Day,** 1st March (patron
~ of Wales). **St 'George's Day,** 23rd April (patron ~ of England). **St 'Patrick's Day,** 17th March
(patron ~ of Ireland). **St 'Valentine's Day,** ⇨
Valentine. **6 St Bernard** /snt 'bɜːnəd US: ˌseɪnt
bərˈnɑːrd/ n large, powerful breed of dog, originally bred by monks in the Swiss Alps, trained to rescue travellers lost in snowstorms. **St ˌVitus's**
/ˌvaɪtəsɪz/ **'dance** n nervous disorder with convulsive, involuntary movements. ~**ed** adj declared to
be, regarded as, a ~. ~**-hood** /-hʊd/ n [U]. ~**-**
like, ~**-ly** adj very holy or good; like a ~; of a ~:
a ~ly expression on his face. ~**-li-ness** n [U] holiness of life; condition of being ~ly.
saith /seθ/ old form of says, ⇨ say.
sake /seɪk/ n **for the ~ of sb/sth; for sb's/sth's**
~, for the welfare or benefit of; because of an interest in or desire for: do sth for the ~ of one's
family. I'll help you for your sister's ~, because I
want to save your sister trouble, help her, etc. We
must be patient for the ~ of peace. He argues for
the ~ of arguing, only because he likes arguing.
for God's/goodness'/pity's/mercy's, etc ~,
used to make an imperative request emphatic.
saké /'sɑːkɪ/ n [U] Japanese fermented liquor made
from rice.
sa-laam /sə'lɑːm/ n **1** [C] Muslim greeting (from an
Arabic word) meaning 'Peace'. **2** [C] low bow. □ vi
make a low bow (to sb).
sal-able, sale-able /'seɪləbl/ adj fit for sale; likely
to find buyers.
sa-lacious /sə'leɪʃəs/ adj (of speech, books, pictures, etc) obscene; indecent; likely to arouse sexual excitement. ~**-ly** adv ~**-ness** n **sa-lac-ity**
/sə'læsətɪ/ n
salad /'sæləd/ n **1** [C,U] (cold dish of) sliced (and
usu uncooked) vegetables such as lettuce, endive,
cucumber, tomatoes, seasoned with oil, vinegar,
etc eaten with, or including, cheese, cold meat,
fish, etc: prepare/mix a ~; a chicken/lobster ~;
cold beef and ~. '~**-days** n pl period of inexperienced youth. '~**-dressing** n mixture of oil,
vinegar, herbs, etc used with ~. '~**-oil** n oil used
for ~-dressing. **2 fruit** ~, mixture of fruits, sliced
or cut up, eaten cold. **3** [U] lettuce, endive or other
green vegetable suitable for eating raw.
sala-man-der /'sæləmændə(r)/ n lizard-like animal once supposed to be capable of living in fire.
sa-lami /sə'lɑːmɪ/ n [U] Italian sausage salted and
flavoured with garlic.
sal-ary /'sælərɪ/ n [C] (pl -ries) (usu monthly) payment for regular employment on a yearly basis: a
~ of £2000 per annum. Cf a weekly wage. **sal-ar-**
ied adj receiving a ~; (of employment) paid for by
means of a ~; the salaried classes; salaried posts.
sale /seɪl/ n **1** [U] exchange of goods or property for
money; act of selling sth: The ~ of his old home
made him sad. **(up) for** ~, intended to be sold (usu
by or on behalf of the owners): Is the house for ~?
I shall put these goods up for ~, announce that
they may be bought. **on** ~, (of goods in shops, etc)
offered for purchase. **on** ~ **or return,** (of goods
sent to a retailer) either to be sold or, if unsold or
unsatisfactory, to be returned. ˌ**bill of** '~, (comm)
document which transfers the title(3) of personal
chattels, etc to another person although the goods
remain with the person making the transfer (used as
a method of borrowing money). **2** [C] instance of
selling sth: I haven't made a ~ all week. He finds a
ready ~ for the strawberries he grows. His straw-

berries find a ready ~, are quickly sold. **S~s are**
up/down this month, more/fewer goods have been
sold. '~**s clerk,** (US) shop assistant. '~**s depart-**
ment, that part of a business company that is concerned with selling goods (contrasted with manufacture, dispatch, etc). '~**s resistance,** reluctance
of the public to buy goods. '~**s talk,** (colloq '~**s**
chat), talk (to a prospective customer) to boost the
~s of goods. '~**s tax,** tax payable on the sum
received for articles sold by retail. **3** [C] the offering of goods at low prices for a period (to get rid of
old stock, etc): the winter/summer ~s; buy goods
at the ~s; '~ price, low price at a ~. **4** [C] occasion when goods, property, etc are put up for ~ by
auction: get bargains by attending ~s. '~**-room,**
room where goods, etc are sold by public auction.
5 ~ **of work,** ~ of articles (eg clothing) made by
members of a church, etc for charity. ⇨ jumble.
'~**s-man** /-mən/, '~**s-woman** /-wʊmən/ nn person selling goods in a shop or (on behalf of whole-
salers) to shopkeepers. '~**s-man-ship** /-mənʃɪp/ n
[U] skill in selling goods. ~**-able** /-əbl/ adj =
salable.
sa-li-ent /'seɪlɪənt/ adj **1** outstanding; prominent;
easily noticed; the ~ points of a speech. Honesty is
his most ~ characteristic. **2** (of an angle) pointing
outwards. □ n ~ angle; forward wedge driven into
the enemy's battle front.
sa-line /'seɪlaɪn US: -liːn/ adj containing salt; salty:
a ~ solution, eg as used for gargling; ~ springs. □
n **1** [U] solution of salt and water. **2** [C] ~ lake,
marsh, well, spring, etc. **sa-lin-ity** /sə'lɪnətɪ/ n [U]
quality of being ~.
sal-iva /sə'laɪvə/ n [U] the natural liquid present in
the mouth; spittle. **sali-vary** /'sælɪvərɪ US: -verɪ/
adj of or producing ~: the '~ry glands. ⇨ the illus
at alimentary. **sali-vate** /'sælɪveɪt/ vi secrete too
much ~.
sal-low /'sæləʊ/ adj (-er, -est) (of the human skin
or complexion) of an unhealthy yellow colour. □
vt, vi make or become ~: a face ~ed by years of
residence in the tropics.
sally /'sælɪ/ n (pl -lies) [C] **1** sudden breaking out
by soldiers who are surrounded by the enemy:
make a successful ~. **2** lively, witty remark, esp
one that is a good-humoured attack on sb or sth. □
vi [VP2A,C] **1** make a ~(1): ~ out against the besiegers. **2** ~ out/forth, go out on a journey or for
a walk.
salmon /'sæmən/ n [C] (pl unchanged) large fish,
valued for food and the sport of catching it with rod
and line; [U] its flesh as food; the colour of its
flesh, orange-pink. ~ **trout,** (kinds of) fish like
~, esp (kinds of) trout.
salon /'sælɒn US: sə'lɒn/ n **1** assembly, as a regular event, of notable persons at the house of a lady
of fashion (esp in Paris); reception room used for
this purpose. **2 the S~,** annual exhibition of pictures by living artists in a French town. **3** establishment offering services connected with fashion, etc:
a 'beauty-~.
sa-loon /sə'luːn/ n **1** room for social use in a ship,
hotel, etc: the ship's 'dining-~. '~ **bar,** most
comfortable bar in a public house or inn. ⇨ public
bar at public. **2** public room or rooms for a specified purpose: a 'billiards/'hairdressing ~. **3** (US)
place where alcoholic drinks may be bought and
drunk (GB = pub); bar. **4** ('~)**-car,** (GB) motor-
car with wholly enclosed seating space for 4—7
passengers (US = sedan).

sal·sify /'sælsɪfaɪ/ n [U] (plant with a) long, fleshy root cooked as a vegetable.

salt /sɔːlt/ n **1** [U] (often *common* ⁓) white substance obtained from mines, present in sea-water and obtained from it by evaporation, used to flavour and preserve food; sodium chloride (**NaCl**): *too much* ⁓ *in the soup;* '*table* ⁓, powdered for convenient use at table. **not/hardly worth one's** ⁓, not deserving one's pay. **take (a statement, etc) with a grain/pinch of** ⁓, feel some doubt whether it is altogether true. **the** ⁓ **of the earth,** the finest citizens; persons with very high qualities. **2** (chem) chemical compound of a metal and an acid. **3 a** ⁓, **an old** ⁓, an experienced sailor. **4** (*pl*) medicine used to empty the bowels: *take a dose of* (*Epsom*) ⁓*s*, (sl) very fast. ⇨ also *smelling*-⁓*s* at smell²(4). **5** (fig) sth that gives flavour or zest: *Adventure is the* ⁓ *of life to some men.* **6** (compounds) '⁓-**cellar** n small container (open, or with a hole or holes at the top) for ⁓ at table. '⁓-**lick** n place where animals come to lick earth with ⁓ in it. '⁓-**pan** n hollow place (natural or artificial) near the sea where ⁓ is obtained by evaporation of sea-water. '⁓-**shaker** n (US) small container (with a hole or holes at the top for sprinkling) for ⁓ at table. '⁓-**water** adj of the sea. '⁓-**works** n (*sing or pl*) place where ⁓ is manufactured. □ vt [VP6A] put ⁓ on or in (food) to season it; [VP6A, 15B] ⁓ **sth (down)**, preserve (food) with ⁓: ⁓ (*down*) *cod;* ⁓*ed meat.* ⁓ **sth away,** (colloq) put money away for the future: *He's got quite a bit* ⁓*ed away.* □ adj **1** containing, tasting of, preserved with, ⁓: ⁓ *beef;* ⁓ *water.* **2** (of land) impregnated with ⁓: ⁓ *marshes; the* '⁓ *flats of Utah.* ⁓**y** adj (-ier, -iest) containing, tasting of, ⁓. ⁓**i·ness** n

salt·petre (US = **-pe·ter**) /sɔːlt'piːtə(r)/ n salty white powder (potassium nitrate, nitre) used in making gunpowder, for preserving food and as medicine.

sa·lu·bri·ous /sə'luːbrɪəs/ adj (esp of climate) health-giving: *the* ⁓ *mountain air of Switzerland.*

salu·tary /'sæljʊtrɪ US: -terɪ/ adj having a good effect (on body or mind): ⁓ *exercise/advice.*

salu·ta·tion /ˌsælju'teɪʃn/ n [C,U] (act or expression of) greeting or goodwill (eg a bow or a kiss): *He raised his hat in* ⁓; (in a letter, etc) introductory phrase, eg *Dear Sir.*

sa·lute /sə'luːt/ n **1** sth done to welcome sb or to show respect or honour, esp (eg in the armed forces) the raising of the hand to the forehead, the firing of guns, the lowering and raising of a flag: *give a* ⁓; *fire a* ⁓ *of ten guns; stand at the* ⁓, stand with the right hand raised to the forehead. **take the** ⁓, acknowledge the ⁓s of a body of soldiers who march past and give ⁓s. **2** friendly greeting such as a bow, raising of the hat (by a man). □ vt,vi [VP6A, 2A] greet; give a ⁓ (to): *The soldier* ⁓*d smartly.*

sal·vage /'sælvɪdʒ/ n [U] **1** the saving of property from loss (by fire or other disaster, eg a wrecked ship): *a* '⁓ *company,* one whose business is to bring wrecked ships to port, raise valuables from a ship that has sunk, etc; *a* '⁓ *tug,* for towing a disabled ship to port. **2** property so saved. **3** payment given to those who save property. **4** (saving of) waste material that can be used again after being processed: *collect old newspapers and magazines for* ⁓. □ vt [VP6A] save from loss, fire, wreck, etc.

sal·va·tion /sæl'veɪʃn/ n [U] **1** the act of saving,

a samovar

the state of having been saved, from sin and its consequences. ˌS⁓ '**Army,** religious and missionary Christian organization on a semi-military model. **2** that which saves sb from loss, disaster, etc: *Government loans have been the* ⁓ *of several shaky business companies.* **work out one's own** ⁓, find, by one's own efforts, how to save oneself.

salve /sælv US: sæv/ n **1** [C,U] (kinds of) oily medicinal substance used on wounds, sores or burns: '*lip*-⁓. **2** (fig) sth that comforts wounded feelings or soothes an uneasy conscience. □ vt [VP6A] soothe; put a ⁓ on; be a ⁓ to: ⁓ *one's conscience by giving stolen money to charity.*

sal·ver /'sælvə(r)/ n metal household tray.

salvo /'sælvəʊ/ n (*pl* ⁓s, ⁓es /-vəʊz/) **1** the firing of a number of guns together as a salute. **2** round of applause.

sal vol·a·tile /ˌsæl və'lætəlɪ/ n [U] solution of ammonium carbonate (smelling salts) used medically when a person feels faint or becomes unconscious.

Sa·mari·tan /sə'mærɪtən/ n **Good** ⁓, person who pities and gives practical help to persons in trouble. ⇨ Luke 10: 33.

samba /'sæmbə/ n (music for a) ballroom dance that originated in Brazil.

same /seɪm/ adj, pron (always **the** ⁓, except as noted in 6 below) **1** not different; unchanged: *He is the* ⁓ *age as his wife. We have lived in the* ⁓ *house for fifty years. We are all going the* ⁓ *way.* **2 the** ⁓... **that; the** ⁓... **as**: *She uses the* ⁓ *scent that you do/the* ⁓ *scent as you.* ⇨ as²(13). **3** (with a relative clause introduced by *that, where, who,* etc. As replaces *that* if the *v* is omitted): *Put the book back in the* ⁓ *place where you found it. Our eggs are sold the* ⁓ *day that/as they come in. The price is the* ⁓ *as last year. Are these the* ⁓ *people* (*whom*) *we saw here last week?* **4** (as *pron*) the same thing: *We must all say the* ⁓. *I would do the* ⁓ *again.* **be all/just the** ⁓ **to,** make no difference to; be a matter of indifference to: *You can do it now or leave it till later; it's all the* ⁓ *to me.* **5** (in phrases) **come/amount to the** ⁓ **thing,** have the ⁓ result, meaning, etc: *You may pay in cash or cheque; it comes to the* ⁓ *thing.* **the very** ⁓, (emph): *You've made the very* ⁓ *mistake again!* **one and the** ⁓, absolutely the ⁓: *Dr Jekyll and Mr Hyde were one and the* ⁓ *person.* **at the** ⁓ **time, (a)** together: *Don't all speak at the* ⁓ *time. She was laughing and crying at the* ⁓ *time.* **(b)** (introducing a fact, etc that is to be borne in mind) yet; still; nevertheless: *At the* ⁓ *time you must not forget that....* **6** (with *this, that, these, those*) already thought of, mentioned or referred to: *I stayed at home on Monday, and on that* ⁓ *day, the office was wrecked by a bomb.* **7** (as *pron*, often without the *def art;* comm use only): *To dry-cleaning suit, £3; to repairing* ⁓, *£2.* □ adv in the ⁓ way: *Old people do not feel the* ⁓ *about these things as the younger generation.* **all the** ⁓, nevertheless: *He's not very reliable, but I like him all the* ⁓. ⁓**·ness** n [U] the condition of being the ⁓, of being uninteresting through lack of variety.

samo·var /'sæməvɑː(r)/ n metal urn with an interior tube, used in Russia for boiling water for tea.

sam·pan /'sæmpæn/ n small, flat-bottomed boat used along the coasts and rivers of China.

sample /'sɑːmpl US: 'sæmpl/ n [C] specimen; one of a number, part of a whole, taken to show what the rest is like (esp as offered by a dealer in goods sold by weight or measure). **up to ~,** (comm) (of goods) equal in quality to the ~ offered. □ vt [VP6A] take a ~ or ~s of; test a part of: *spend an hour at the wine-shop, sampling* (= making a random sampling of) *the wines.*

sam·pler /'sɑːmplə(r) US: 'sæm-/ n piece of cloth embroidered to show skill in needlework, often displayed on a wall.

sam·urai /'sæmʊraɪ/ n **1 the ~,** the military caste in feudal Japan. **2** member of this caste.

sana·tor·ium /ˌsænə'tɔːrɪəm/ (US also **sana·tar·ium** /ˌsænə'teərɪəm/) n establishment for the treatment of invalid or convalescent people.

sanc·tify /'sæŋktɪfaɪ/ vt (pt,pp -fied) [VP6A] make holy; set apart as sacred. **sanc·ti·fi·ca·tion** /ˌsæŋktɪfɪ'keɪʃn/ n

sanc·ti·moni·ous /ˌsæŋktɪ'məʊnɪəs/ adj making a show of being devout. **~·ly** adv

sanc·tion /'sæŋkʃn/ n **1** [U] right or permission given by authority to do sth: *a book that was translated without the ~ of the author and publisher.* **2** [U] approval, encouragement (of behaviour, etc), by general custom or tradition. **3** [C] penalty intended to maintain or restore respect for law or authority, esp as adopted by several States together against a country violating international law: *apply arms/economic ~s against an aggressor country.* **4** [C] reason for obeying a rule, etc: *The best moral ~ is that of conscience; the worst ~ is the fear of punishment.* □ vt [VP6A] give a ~ to; agree to: *Would you ~ flogging as a punishment for crimes of violence?*

sanc·tity /'sæŋktətɪ/ n (pl -ties) **1** [U] holiness; sacredness; saintliness: *violate the ~ of an oath.* **2** (pl) sacred obligations, feelings, etc: *the sanctities of the home.*

sanc·tu·ary /'sæŋktʃʊərɪ US: -ʊerɪ/ n (pl -ries) **1** holy or sacred place, esp a church, temple or mosque. **2** chancel of a church. **3** sacred place (eg the altar of a church) where, in former times, a person running away from the law or his creditors was secure, by Church law, against arrest or violence. **4** [U] (right of offering) freedom from arrest: *to seek/take/be offered ~.* **5** place of refuge: *Great Britain has always been a ~ of political refugees from many parts of the world.* **6** area where by law it is forbidden to kill birds, rob their nests, etc to shoot animals, etc: *a 'bird-~.*

sanc·tum /'sæŋktəm/ n **1** holy place. **2** (colloq) person's private room or study.

sand /sænd/ n **1** [U] (mass of) finely crushed rock as seen on the seashore, in river-beds, deserts, etc: *mix ~ and cement to make concrete.* **2** (often pl) expanse of ~ (on the seashore or a desert): *children playing on the ~(s).* **3** (pl) *The ~s are running out,* (with reference to the ~ running through an hour-glass, etc) There is not much time left; time is passing. **4** (compounds) '**~·bag** n bag filled with ~ used as a defence (in war, against rising flood-water, etc). '**~·bank** n bank or shoal of ~ in a river or the sea. '**~·bar** n bank of ~ at the mouth

a sampan

of a river or harbour. '**~·blast** vt [VP6A] send a jet of ~ against sth, eg stonework, to clean it, or against metal or glass to cut or make a design on it. '**~·boy** n (now used only in) *as happy as a ~boy,* very happy. '**~ dune** n mound of ~, formed by the wind. '**~·fly** n (pl -flies) kind of midge common on seashores. '**~·glass** n glass with two connected bulbs containing enough ~ to take a definite time, eg five minutes, one hour, in passing from one bulb to the other. '**~·paper** n [U] strong paper with ~ glued to it, used for rubbing rough surfaces smooth. □ vt [VP6A] make smooth with ~paper. '**~·piper** n small bird living in wet, sandy places near streams. ⇨ the illus at water. '**~·pit** n unroofed enclosure filled with ~, for children to play in. '**~·shoes** n pl canvas shoes with rubber or hemp soles for wearing on sandy sea-shores. '**~·stone** n rock formed of compressed ~. '**~·storm** n storm in a sandy desert with clouds of ~ raised by the wind. □ vt [VP6A] cover, sprinkle or scrub with ~. **sandy** adj (-ier, -iest) **1** covered with or consisting of ~: *a ~y bottom,* eg of part of the sea. **2** (of hair, etc) yellowish-red. □ n (colloq) nickname given to a person with yellowish-red hair.

san·dal /'sændl/ n kind of open shoe made of a sole and heel with straps to hold it on the foot. **~·led** /'sændld/ adj wearing ~s.

san·dal·wood /'sændlwʊd/ n [U] hard, sweet-smelling wood used for making fans, caskets, etc.

sand·wich /'sænwɪdʒ US: -wɪtʃ/ n [C] two slices of buttered bread with meat, etc between: *ham/chicken/cheese, etc ~es.* '**~·man** /-mæn/ n (pl -men) man who walks about the streets with two advertisement boards, one hanging over his chest and the other over his back. '**~·board** n one of such boards. '**~ course,** course of training with alternating periods of theoretical and practical study. □ vt [VP6A,14] ~ **(between),** put (one thing or person) between two others, esp when there is little space: *I was ~ed between two very fat men on the bus.*

sane /seɪn/ adj (-r, -st) **1** healthy in mind; not mad. **2** sensible; balanced: *a ~ policy; ~ views/judgement.* **~·ly** adv

sang /sæŋ/ pt of sing.

sang froid /ˌsɒŋ'frwɑː/ n [U] (F) calmness in face of danger or in an emergency; composure.

san·gui·nary /'sæŋgwɪnərɪ US: -nerɪ/ adj (formal, old use) **1** with much bloodshed: *a ~ battle.* **2** fond of bloodshed; delighting in cruel acts: *a ~ ruler.*

san·guine /'sæŋgwɪn/ adj (formal) **1** hopeful; optimistic: *~ of success; ~ that we shall succeed.* **2** having a red complexion.

sani·tarium /ˌsænɪ'teərɪəm/ n (US) sanatorium; health resort.

sani·tary /'sænɪtrɪ US: -terɪ/ adj **1** clean; free from dirt which might cause disease: *poor ~ conditions in a camp.* **2** of, concerned with, the protection of health: *a '~ inspector,* official whose duty it is to see that regulations for the protection of health are obeyed. '*~ towel/napkin,* absorbent pad used during menstruation.

sani·ta·tion /ˌsænɪˈteɪʃn/ *n* [U] arrangements to protect public health, esp for the efficient disposal of sewage.

san·ity /ˈsænətɪ/ *n* [U] **1** health of mind. **2** soundness of judgement.

sank /sæŋk/ *pt* of sink².

sans /sænz/ *prep* (colloq) without: *S~ teeth, ~ eyes, ~ taste, ~ everything.*

San·skrit /ˈsænskrɪt/ *n* the ancient language of India; the literary language of Hinduism.

Santa Claus /ˈsæntə klɔːz/ *n* (also *Father Christmas*) person who, small children are told, puts toys in their stockings by night at Christmas.

sap¹ /sæp/ *vt* (-pp-) [VP6A] weaken; drain away the life and strength of: *sapped by disease/an unhealthy climate.*

sap² /sæp/ *n* [C] tunnel or covered trench made to get nearer to the enemy (eg in a military strongpoint or, formerly, a beseiged town). '**sap-head** *n* end of a sap nearest to the enemy. □ *vt, vi* (-pp-) [VP6A, 2A] make a sap or saps; weaken (a wall, etc) by digging under it; (fig) destroy or weaken (sb's faith, confidence, etc). **sap·per** *n* soldier engaged in making saps or (mod use) in engineering, eg road and bridge building.

sap³ /sæp/ *n* (dated sl) silly person.

sap⁴ /sæp/ *n* [U] **1** liquid in a plant, carrying food to all its parts: *The sap is beginning to rise in the maple-trees.* **sap·wood** /ˈsæpwʊd/ *n* soft, outer layers of wood. **2** (fig) (anything that provides) vigour or energy. **sap·less** *adj* without sap; dry; lacking vigour. **sap·ling** /ˈsæplɪŋ/ *n* young tree; (fig) young person. **sappy** *adj* (-ier, -iest) full of sap; young and vigorous.

sa·pi·ent /ˈseɪpɪənt/ *adj* (liter) wise. **~·ly** *adv* **sa·pi·ence** /-əns/ *n* (often ironic) wisdom.

Sap·phic /ˈsæfɪk/ *adj* of the Greek lesbian poetess Sappho. **~ verse/stanza/ode,** (prosody) with three lines that rhyme and one short line.

sap·phire /ˈsæfaɪə(r)/ *n* **1** [C] clear, bright blue jewel. **2** [U] bright blue colour.

sara·band /ˈsærəbænd/ *n* [C] (piece of music for a) stately old Spanish dance.

Sara·cen /ˈsærəsn/ *n* (name used by later Greeks and Romans for) Arab or Muslim of the time of the Crusades.

sar·casm /ˈsɑːkæzəm/ *n* [U] (use of) bitter remarks intended to wound the feelings; [C] such a remark; taunt that is ironically worded. **sar·cas·tic** /sɑːˈkæstɪk/ *adj* of, using, ~. **sar·cas·ti·cally** /-klɪ/ *adv*

sar·copha·gus /sɑːˈkɒfəgəs/ *n* (*pl* -gi /-gaɪ/, ~es /-gəsɪz/) stone coffin (esp as used in ancient times). ⇨ the illus at mummy.

sar·dine /sɑːˈdiːn/ *n* small fish (a young pilchard), usu preserved and tinned in oil or tomato sauce. *packed like ~s,* closely crowded together.

sar·donic /sɑːˈdɒnɪk/ *adj* mocking; scornful: *a ~ smile/laugh/expression.* **sar·doni·cally** /-klɪ/ *adv*

sari /ˈsɑːrɪ/ *n* (*pl* ~s) length of cotton or silk cloth draped round the body, worn by Hindu women.

sa·rong /səˈrɒŋ US: -ˈrɔːŋ/ *n* long strip of cotton or silk material worn as a skirt round the middle of the body, tucked round the waist, the national garment

of Malays and Indonesians (men and women).

sar·sa·pa·rilla /ˌsɑːspəˈrɪlə/ *n* [U] (tonic drink made from the roots of a) tropical American plant.

sar·tor·ial /sɑːˈtɔːrɪəl/ *adj* concerned with (the making of) clothes: *~ elegance.*

sash¹ /sæʃ/ *n* [C] long strip of cloth worn round the waist or over one shoulder for ornament or as part of a uniform.

sash² /sæʃ/ *n ~* **window,** one that slides up and down (instead of opening outwards like a casement). ⇨ the illus at window. '*~-cord/-line* **n** strong cord (with a weight at one end) running over a pulley to keep the window balanced in any desired position.

Sas·sen·ach /ˈsæsənæk/ *n* (derog or hum) (name used by the Scots for an) English person.

sassy /ˈsæsɪ/ *adj* (US colloq) lively; stylish.

sat /sæt/ *pt, pp* of sit.

Satan /ˈseɪtn/ *n* the Evil One, the Devil. **~ic** /səˈtænɪk US:* seɪ-/ *adj* **1** of ~: *His ~ic Majesty,* (hum) Satan. **2** (small **s**) wicked; evil.

satchel /ˈsætʃl/ *n* small bag for carrying light articles, esp school books.

sate /seɪt/ *vt* [VP6A] = satiate.

sat·el·lite /ˈsætəlaɪt/ *n* **1** comparatively small body moving in orbit round a planet; moon; artificial object, eg a spacecraft, put in orbit round a celestial body: *com,muni'cations ~,* for relaying back to the earth telephone messages, radio and TV signals. **2** (fig, often attrib) person, state, depending upon and taking the lead from another. '*~ town,* one built to take the excess population of another.

sati·able /ˈseɪʃəbl/ *adj* (formal) that can be fully satisfied.

sati·ate /ˈseɪʃɪeɪt/ *vt* [VP6A] (formal) satisfy fully; cloy; weary (oneself) with too much: *be ~d with food/pleasure.*

sati·ety /səˈtaɪətɪ/ *n* [U] (formal) condition or feeling of being satiated: *indulge in pleasure to/the point of ~.*

satin /ˈsætɪn US:* ˈsætn/ *n* [U] silk material smooth and shiny on one side: (attrib) *~ dresses/ribbons.* □ *adj* smooth like ~.

sat·in·wood /ˈsætɪnwʊd US:* ˈsætn-/ *n* [U] smooth, hard wood of a tropical tree, used for furniture.

sat·ire /ˈsætaɪə(r)/ *n* **1** [U] form of writing holding up a person or society to ridicule, or showing the foolishness or wickedness of an idea, customs, etc. **2** [C] piece of writing that does this; sth that exposes false pretensions: *Are our lives sometimes a ~ upon our religious beliefs?* **sa·tiri·cal** /səˈtɪrɪkl/ *adj* containing, expressing, ~; mocking. **sa·tiri·cally** /-klɪ/ *adv* **sat·ir·ist** /ˈsætərɪst/ *n* person who writes ~s. **sat·ir·ize** /ˈsætəraɪz/ *vt* [VP6A] attack with ~(s); describe satirically.

a sari   a sarong   a kimono

sat·is·fac·tion /ˌsætɪsˈfækʃn/ n 1 [U] the state of being satisfied, pleased or contented; act of satisfying: *feel ~ at having one's ability recognized; have the ~ of being successful in life; pass an examination to one's own ~ and to the ~ of one's friends: the ~ of one's hopes/desires/ambitions.* 2 (with *indef art,* but rarely *pl*) sth that satisfies: *Your success will be a great ~ to your parents. It is a ~ to know that he is well again.* 3 [U] (opportunity of getting) revenge or compensation for an injury or insult: *give sb/demand/obtain ~. The angry man demanded ~ but the other refused it,* would neither apologize nor fight.

sat·is·fac·tory /ˌsætɪsˈfæktərɪ/ adj giving pleasure or satisfaction; satisfying a need or desire; good enough for a purpose: *The result of the experiment was ~. We want ~ reasons for your failure to help.* **sat·is·fac·tor·ily** /-tərəlɪ/ adv in a ~ manner: *The patient is getting on satisfactorily.*

sat·isfy /ˈsætɪsfaɪ/ vt, vi (pt, pp -fied) 1 [VP6A,2A] make contented; give (sb) what he wants or needs: *Nothing satisfies him; he's always complaining. Riches do not always ~. ~ the examiners,* just reach the lowest standard needed for passing an examination. 2 [VP6A,2A] be enough for (one's needs); be equal to (what one hopes for or desires): *~ one's hunger.* 3 [VP6A,11,14] ~ *sb (that.../of sth),* convince; make free from doubt: *He satisfied me that he could do the work well. Have you satisfied yourself of the truth of the report?* **~·ing** adj giving satisfaction: *a ~ing meal.* **~·ly** adv

sa·trap /ˈsætræp US: ˈseɪtræp/ n governor of a province in the ancient Persian empire.

sat·suma /ˈsæt'suːmə/ n tangerine.

satu·rate /ˈsætʃəreɪt/ vt [VP6A,14] ~ *(with/in),* 1 make thoroughly wet; soak with moisture; cause to take in as much as possible of sth: *We were caught in the rain and came home ~d. They lay on the beach and were ~d with sunshine. He is ~d with Greek history.* 2 be unable to take any more: *The market for used cars is ~d.* 3 (chem) cause (one substance) to absorb the greatest possible amount of another: *a ~d solution of salt.* **satu·ra·tion** /ˌsætʃəˈreɪʃn/ n [U] state of being ~d. **saturation bombing,** bombing so that everything in the target area is totally destroyed, **satu'ration point,** (chem) the stage at which, if more of one substance is added to another, they will not unite completely: *The saturation point of a hot liquid is higher than that of a cold one,* eg more sugar can be dissolved in hot tea than in cold tea; (fig) stage at which no more can be absorbed or accepted.

Sat·ur·day /ˈsætədɪ/ n the seventh and last day of the week.

Sat·urn /ˈsætən/ n 1 (astron) large planet encircled by rings. ⇨ the illus at planet. 2 (myth) ancient Roman god of agriculture.

sat·ur·na·lia /ˌsætəˈneɪlɪə/ 1 n pl S~, yearly festival of the god Saturn, held in ancient Rome in December, a time of wild merry-making. 2 [C] time of wild revelry or disorder.

sat·ur·nine /ˈsætənaɪn/ adj (liter) gloomy.

satyr /ˈsætə(r)/ n 1 (Gk and Roman myth) god of the woods, half man and half animal. 2 man with uncontrolled sexual desires. **sa·tyric** /səˈtɪrɪk/ adj of or like ~s.

sauce /sɔːs/ n 1 [C,U] (kind of) liquid or semi-liquid preparation served with some kinds of food to give a relish or flavour; *spaghetti with tomato ~; fruit pudding and brandy ~. What is ~ for*

the goose is ~ for the gander, (prov) what applies in one case must apply in an identical or similar case. '**~-boat** n vessel in which ~ is served at table. 2 [U] (colloq) impudence (usu amusing rather than annoying): *None of your ~! Don't be impertinent. What ~!* How impudent! □ vt [VP6A] (colloq) be impudent to: *How dare you ~ your mother?* **saucy** adj (-ier, -iest) 1 impudent. 2 (colloq) smart-looking: *a saucy little hat.* **sauc·ily** adv **sauci·ness** n

sauce·pan /ˈsɔːspən US: -pæn/ n deep metal cooking pot, usu round and with a lid and a handle.

saucer /ˈsɔːsə(r)/ n 1 small curved dish on which a cup stands. '**~-eyed** adj with large, round, wide-opened eyes, eg as the result of surprise. ,**flying '~,** ⇨ flying. 2 ~-shaped disc (also called a *dish*) of a radio telescope. 3 depression in the ground.

sauer·kraut /ˈsaʊəkraʊt/ n [U] (G) cabbage cut up, salted and allowed to ferment until sour.

sauna /ˈsaʊnə/ n steam bath or bath-house as in Finland.

saun·ter /ˈsɔːntə(r)/ vi [VP2A,C] walk in a leisurely way: *~ along Oxford Street window-shopping.* □ n quiet, unhurried walk or pace: *come at a ~. ~er* n person who ~s.

saur·ian /ˈsɔːrɪən/ n, adj (one) of the order of lizards including crocodiles, lizards and some extinct kinds.

saus·age /ˈsɒsɪdʒ US: ˈsɔːs-/ n [U] chopped up meat, etc flavoured and stuffed into a casing or tube of thin skin; some kinds sliced and eaten raw, others cooked and eaten hot; [C] one section of such a tube. '**~-dog,** (GB colloq) dachshund. '**~-meat** n meat minced for making ~s. ,**~-'roll** n ~ in a covering of pastry.

sauté /ˈsəʊteɪ US: səʊˈteɪ/ adj (F) (of food) quickly fried in a little fat: *~ potatoes.* □ vt fry food in this way.

sav·age /ˈsævɪdʒ/ adj 1 in a primitive or uncivilized state: *~ customs.* 2 fierce; cruel: *a ~ dog; make a ~ attack on sb; ~ criticism.* 3 (colloq) very angry. □ n ~ person, esp a member of a primitive tribe living by hunting and fishing. □ vt [VP6A] attack, bite, trample on: *The man was badly ~d by his mare.* **~·ly** adv **~·ness** n **~ry** /ˈsævɪdʒrɪ/ n [U] the state of being ~; ~ behaviour: *living in ~ry; treat conquered enemies with great ~ry.*

sa·van·na(h) /səˈvænə/ n [C] treeless, grassy plain, in tropical and subtropical America and E and W Africa. ⇨ pampas, prairie, steppe, veld.

sa·vant /ˈsævənt US: sæˈvɑːnt/ n person of great learning.

save¹ /seɪv/ vt, vi 1 [VP6A,14] ~ *(from),* make or keep safe (from loss, injury, etc): *~ sb from drowning; ~ sb's life; ~ a person from himself,* from the results of his own foolishness. ~ *one's bacon,* ⇨ bacon. ~ *one's face,* ⇨ face¹(4). ~ *one's skin,* avoid, often by cowardice, the risk of loss, injury, etc. ~ *the situation,* deal successfully with a situation which seems hopeless. 2 [VP2A,C,3A,6A,12B,13B,14,15B] ~ *(up) (for sth);* ~ *sth (up) (for sth),* keep for future use: *~ (up) money for a holiday; ~ part of one's salary each month; ~ some of the meat for tomorrow; ~ me some ice-cream/~ some ice-cream for me; ~ for one's old age. He has never ~d,* never put money by for the future. *He is saving himself/ saving his strength for the heavy work he'll have to do this afternoon. ~ for a rainy day,* ⇨ rainy. 3

[VP6A,D,12C] make unnecessary; relieve (sb) from the need of using: *If you walk to the office every morning, you'll* ~ *spending money on bus fares. That will* ~ *you 50 pence a week. That will* ~ *us a lot of trouble. We've been* ~*d a lot of expense by doing the work ourselves. Do you use modern labour-saving devices in your home?* ie machines that make work (eg cleaning, cooking) in the home quicker and easier. **4** [VP6A,14,2A] ~ *sb (from sth),* (in the Christian religion) set free from the power of (or the eternal punishment for) sin: *Jesus Christ came into the world to* ~ *sinners from their sins.* **5** [VP6A] make a reservation concerning (sth): *a saving clause,* one that stipulates an exemption, etc. □ *n* (in football, etc) act of preventing the scoring of a goal: *Banks made a brilliant* ~. ~*r n* person who ~s: *a* ~*r of souls,* eg a priest; means of saving: *This device is a useful 'time–*~*r. Some machines are* ~*rs of labour.* **sav·ing** *adj* (esp) that redeems or compensates. **saving grace,** good quality that redeems a person whose other qualities are not all good: *He has the saving grace of humour.* □ *n* **1** way of saving; amount ~d: *a useful saving of time and money.* **2** (*pl*) money ~d up: *keep one's savings in the Post Office.* **'savings account** *n* (with a bank) on which interest is paid. **'savings-bank** *n* bank which holds, and gives interest on, small savings.

save² /seɪv/ (also **sav-ing** /'seɪvɪŋ/) *prep* except: *all save him. We know nothing about him save that he was in the army during the war.*

sav·eloy /'sævəlɔɪ/ *n* [C] kind of highly-seasoned pork sausage.

sav·ing /'seɪvɪŋ/ *prep* = save².

sav·iour (US = **-ior**) /'seɪvjə(r)/ *n* person who rescues or saves sb from danger. **The S**~, **Our S**~, Jesus Christ.

savoir-faire /ˌsævwɑː 'feə(r)/ *n* [U] (F) social tact; knowledge of how to behave in any situation.

sa·vory /'seɪvərɪ/ *n* [U] herb of the mint family used in cooking; (US) = savoury.

sa·vour (US = **-vor**) /'seɪvə(r)/ *n* [C,U] ~ *of*, taste or flavour (of sth); suggestion (of a quality): *soup with a* ~ *of garlic. His political views have a* ~ *of fanaticism.* □ *vt,vi* **1** [VP6A] (lit or fig) appreciate the taste or flavour or character of: *He* ~*ed the wine/the joke.* **2** [VP3A] ~ *of,* suggest the presence: *Such a proposal* ~*s of impertinence.*

sa·voury (US = **-vory**) /'seɪvərɪ/ *adj* having an appetizing taste or smell; (of food dishes) having a salt or sharp, not a sweet, taste: *a* ~ *omelette.* □ *n* [C] (*pl* -ries) ~ dish, esp one taken at the start or end of a meal.

sa·voy /sə'vɔɪ/ *n* [C,U] (kind of) winter cabbage with wrinkled leaves.

savvy /'sævɪ/ *v* (sl) know, understand. *no* ~, I do not know/understand. □ *n* [U] (sl) wits; understanding: *Where's your* ~?

saw¹ /sɔː/ *pt* of see¹.

saw² /sɔː/ *n* [C] (kinds of) tool with a sharp-toothed edge, for cutting wood, metal, stone, etc worked by hand or mechanically. **'saw·dust** *n* [U] tiny bits of wood falling off when wood is being sawn. **'saw-horse** *n* frame of wood for supporting wood that is being sawn. **'saw-mill** *n* mill with power-operated saws. **'saw-pit** *n* pit in which a man stands guiding the lower part of a large hand-saw (= *pit-saw*) for sawing logs, the upper part being guided by another man at an upper level. □ *vt,vi* (*pt* sawed, *pp* sawn /sɔːn/ and (US) sawed) **1**

[VP6A,15A,B,2A] cut with a saw; make (boards, etc) with a saw; use a saw: *saw wood; saw a log into planks; saw a log in two.* **saw sth off,** cut off with a saw: *saw a branch off a tree; a sawn-off shotgun,* one with (most of) the barrel sawn off (as used by criminals for ease of concealment and carrying). **saw sth up,** cut into pieces with a saw: *sawn-up timber,* timber that has been sawn into planks (contrasted with logs). **2** [VP2A,C,6A] move backward and forward: *sawing at his fiddle,* using his bow as if it were a saw. **3** [VP2A] capable of being sawn: *This wood saws easily.* **saw·yer** /'sɔːjə(r)/ *n* man whose work is sawing wood.

saw³ /sɔː/ *n* [C] proverbial saying.

sax /sæks/ *n* (abbr of) saxophone.

saxi·frage /'sæksɪfrɪdʒ/ *n* [U] kinds of Alpine or rock plant with white, yellow or red flowers.

Saxon /'sæksn/ *n, adj* (member, language) of a people once living in NW Germany, some of whom conquered and settled in Britain in the 5th and 6th cc.

saxo·phone /'sæksəfəʊn/ *n* (colloq abbr *sax*) musical wind instrument with a reed in the mouthpiece and keys for the fingers, made of brass. ⊏> the illus at brass. **sax·ophon·ist** /sæk'sɒfənɪst US: 'sæksəfəʊnɪst/ *n* ~ player.

say /seɪ/ *vt,vi* (*3rd pers, pres t* says /sez/, *pt,pp* said /sed/) [VP6A,14,9,10] **1 say sth (to sb),** utter; make (a specified word or remark); use one's voice to produce (words, sentences): *Be polite and say 'Please' and 'Thank you'. Did you say anything? He said that his friend's name was Sam. Everyone was saying what a handsome couple they made. Everyone said how well I was looking. I've something to say to you,* to tell you. *I wouldn't say no to a glass of beer,* would accept one willingly. *You may well say so,* You are right. *So you say* (implying that the speaker may be mistaken). *go without saying,* be obvious: *It goes without saying that country life is healthier than town life.* **have nothing/anything to say for oneself,** ie in one's own defence: *Well, what have you to say for yourself,* What can you say to explain or defend your conduct? **say the word,** express agreement: *You've only to say the word* (eg say 'Yes') *and the money's yours,* ie I will let you have it. **say a good word for sb/sth,** commend; praise: *He hasn't a good word to say for anybody.* **say one's say,** finish what one has to say: *Have you said your say yet? that is to say,* in other words: *three weeks tomorrow, that's to say, the 10th of May.* **What do you say (to sth/doing sth)?** What do you think (about...): *What do you say to a walk/to going round to my mother's? I say,* exclamation used to draw attention, open a conversation or express surprise. **They say; It's said,** forms used to introduce reports, rumours, etc: *They say/It's said that he's a miser.* **2** (also [VP10] esp neg and interr) suppose; estimate; form and give an opinion concerning: *There is no saying when this war will end. And so say all of us,* that is the opinion of all of us. *You may learn to play the violin in, let's say, three years.* □ *n* (only in the following) **have/say one's say,** express one's opinion; state one's views: *Let him have his say.* **have a/no/not much, etc 'say in the matter,** have some/no/not much right or opportunity to share in a discussion, decision, express one's opinions, etc: *He didn't have much say in deciding where they should spend their holidays.*

say·ing /'seɪɪŋ/ *n* remark commonly made; well-known phrase, proverb, etc: *'More haste, less speed'*, as the saying goes.

scab /skæb/ *n* **1** [C] dry crust formed over a wound or sore. **2** [U] (= *scabies*) skin disease (esp of sheep). **3** [C] (colloq) workman who refuses to join a strike, or his trade union, or who takes a striker's place; blackleg. **scabby** *adj* covered with scabs(1).

scab-bard /'skæbəd/ *n* sheath for the blade of a sword, dagger or bayonet. ⇨ the illus at **sword**.

sca-bies /'skeɪbiːz/ *n* [U] kind of skin disease causing itching.

sca-bi-ous /'skeɪbɪəs/ *n* kinds of wild and cultivated plant with delicately coloured flowers.

scab-rous /'skeɪbrəs *US:* 'skæb-/ *adj* **1** (of animals, plants, etc) having a rough surface. **2** (of subjects) difficult to write delicately about. **3** indelicate; salacious: *a ~ novel.*

scads /skædz/ *n* (*sing* or *pl*) *~ (of),* (US colloq) large quantity (of): *~ of money/people.*

scaf-fold /'skæfəʊld/ *n* [C] **1** structure put up for workmen and materials around a building which is being erected or repaired. **2** platform on which criminals are executed: *go to the ~,* be executed. *~ing* /'skæfəldɪŋ/ *n* [U] (materials for a) *~*(1) (eg poles and planks, or, *tubular ~ing,* metal tubes to be bolted together).

scal-a-wag /'skæləwæg/ *n* (US) = scallywag.

scald /skɔːld/ *vt* [VP6A] **1** burn with hot liquid or steam: *~ one's hand with hot fat. He was ~ed to death when the boiler exploded. ~ing tears,* tears of deep and bitter grief. **2** clean (dishes, etc) with boiling water or steam. **3** heat (milk) almost to boiling-point. □ *n* injury to the skin from hot liquid or steam: *an ointment for burns and ~s.*

scale[1] /skeɪl/ *n* **1** [C] one of the thin overlapping plates of hard material that cover the skin of many fish and reptiles: *scrape the ~s off a herring.* ⇨ the illus at **fish**. **2** [C] scale-like outer piece on an organic or other object, eg a flake of skin that loosens and comes off the body in some diseases; a flake of rust on iron. *remove the ~s from sb's eyes,* (fig) enable sb who has been deceived to realize the true state of affairs. **3** [U] chalky deposit inside boilers, kettles, waterpipes, etc (from the lime in hard water); deposit of tartar on teeth. □ *vt,vi* **1** [VP6A,15A,B] cut or scrape *~s* from (eg fish) (but *de~* a boiler or kettle). **2** [VP2C] *~ off,* come off in flakes: *paint/plaster scaling off a wall.* **scaly** *adj* covered with *~* or *~s*; coming off in *~s*: *a kettle scaly with rust.*

scale[2] /skeɪl/ *n* [C] **1** series of marks at regular intervals for the purpose of measuring (as on a ruler or a thermometer): *This ruler has one ~ in centimetres and another in inches.* **2** ruler or other tool or instrument marked in this way. **3** system of units for measuring: *the 'decimal ~.* **4** arrangement in steps or degrees: *a ~ of wages; a person who is high in the social ~; sink in the ~,* fall to a lower level. **sliding ~,** ⇨ slide[2](4). **5** proportion between the size of sth and the map, diagram, etc which represents it: *a map on the ~ of ten kilometres to the centimetre; drawn to ~,* with a uniform reduction or enlargement. **6** relative size, extent, etc. *on a large/small, etc ~,* to a large, etc extent/degree: *They are preparing for war on a large ~.* **7** (music) series of tones arranged in order of pitch, esp a series of eight starting on a keynote: *the ~ of F,* beginning with F as the keynote; *practise ~s on the piano.* ⇨ octave. □ *vt* **1** [VP6A] make a copy or representation of, according to a

certain *~*: *~ a map/building.* **2** [VP15B] *~ up/down,* increase/decrease by a certain proportion: *All wages/marks were ~d up by 10 per cent.*

scale[3] /skeɪl/ *n* [C] **1** one of the two pans on a balance. **(pair of) ~s,** simple balance or instrument for weighing. ⇨ the illus at **balance**. *hold the ~s even,* judge fairly (between). *turn the ~(s),* decide the result of sth which is in doubt: *The arrival of reinforcements turned the ~(s) in our favour. turn the ~(s) at,* (colloq) weigh: *The jockey turned the ~(s) at 80 lb.* **2** any machine for weighing: *bathroom ~s,* for measuring one's weight. □ *vi* [VP2B] weigh: *~ 10 lb.*

scale[4] /skeɪl/ *vt* [VP6A] climb up (a wall, cliff, etc). **'scaling-ladder** *n* one used for scaling high walls, eg of a fortified town in former times.

scal-lop /'skɒləp/ *n* **1** kind of bivalve mollusc with a shell divided into grooves. ⇨ the illus at **bivalve**. **'~-shell** *n* one half of this shell, used as a utensil in which a savoury dish is cooked and served. **2** (*pl*) ornamental edging of *~*-shaped projections cut in pastry, cloth, etc. □ *vt* [VP6A] **1** cook (eg oysters) in a *~*-shell. **2** decorate the edge of (sth) with *~s.*

scal-ly-wag /'skælɪwæg/ (US = **scal-a-wag** /'skæləwæg/) *n* (hum) scamp; rascal.

scalp /skælp/ *n* [C] skin and hair of the head, excluding the face; this skin, etc from an enemy's head as a trophy of victory (a former practice of some American Indians). *out for ~s,* (fig) making efforts to win trophies of victory over opponents. □ *vt* [VP6A] cut the *~* off.

scal-pel /'skælpəl/ *n* small, light knife used by surgeons.

scamp[1] /skæmp/ *n* (often used playfully) rascal; worthless person.

scamp[2] /skæmp/ *vt* [VP6A] do (work, etc), make sth, carelessly, hastily or without interest.

scam-per /'skæmpə(r)/ *vi* [VP2A,C] (esp of small animals, eg mice, rabbits, when frightened, or of children and dogs at play) run quickly. □ *n* short, quick run: *take the dog for a ~.*

scampi /'skæmpɪ/ *n pl* large prawns.

scan /skæn/ *vt,vi* (-nn-) **1** [VP6A] look at attentively; run the eyes over every part of: *The shipwrecked sailor ~ned the horizon anxiously every morning.* **2** [VP6A] glance at quickly but not very thoroughly: *He ~ned the newspaper while having his breakfast.* **3** [VP6A] test the metre of (a line of verse) by noting the division into feet, as in:

> 'Never /'seek to /'tell thy /'love
> 'Love that /'never /'told can /'be.

4 [VP2A] (of verse) fit a metrical pattern; be composed so that it can be *~*ned: *This line does not/ will not ~. The verses ~ well.* **5** [VP6A] (TV) resolve (a picture) into its elements of light and shade for transmission; (radar) traverse an area with electronic beams in search of sth. **~-sion** /'skænʃn/ *n* [U] the *~*ning of verse; the way verse *~s.*

scan-dal /'skændl/ *n* **1** [C,U] (action, piece of behaviour, etc that causes a) general feeling of indignation; [C] shameful or disgraceful action: *cause (a) ~. A series of ~s caused the Government to fall. It is a ~ that the accused man was declared innocent. If she leaves her husband she will certainly create (a) ~ in the village.* **2** [U] harmful gossip; careless or unkind talk which damages sb's reputation: *Don't talk/listen to ~. Most of us enjoy a bit of ~.* **'~-monger** /-mʌŋgə(r)/ *n* person who spreads *~s*(2). **~-monger-ing** /-mʌŋgərɪŋ/ *n* [U] the spreading of ~s(2). **~·ize** /'skændəlaɪz/ vt [VP6A] shock; offend the moral feelings or the ideas of etiquette of: ~ize the neighbours by sunbathing on the lawn in the nude. **~·ous** /'skændələs/ adj **1** disgraceful; shocking. **2** (of reports, rumours) containing ~. **3** (of persons) fond of spreading ~. **~·ous·ly** adv

Scan·di·na·vian /ˌskændɪ'neɪvɪən/ n, adj (native) of Scandinavia (Denmark, Norway, Sweden, Iceland).

scan·sion /'skænʃn/ ⇨ scan.

scant /skænt/ adj ~ (of), (having) hardly enough: ~ of breath; pay ~ attention to sb's advice. □ vt [VP6A] skimp; make ~; cut down: Don't ~ the butter when you make a cake. **~y** adj (-ier, -iest) (opp of ample) small in size or amount; barely large enough: a ~y rice crop; a ~y bikini. **~·ily** /-ɪlɪ/ adv in a ~y manner: ~ily dressed. **~·i·ness** n

scant·ling /'skæntlɪŋ/ n small beam or piece of timber; board not more than 5 inches wide.

scape-goat /'skeɪpgəʊt/ n person blamed or punished for the mistake(s) or wrong-doing of another or others.

scape-grace /'skeɪpgreɪs/ n (often used playfully) person who constantly gets into trouble.

scap·ula /'skæpjʊlə/ n (anat) shoulder-blade. ⇨ the illus at skeleton.

scar /skɑː(r)/ n mark remaining on the surface (of skin, furniture, etc) as the result of injury or damage: a long ~ across his cheek; (fig) grief that left a ~ (on the heart). □ vt,vi (-rr-) **1** [VP6A] mark with a ~ or ~s: a face ~red by smallpox; war~red towns. **2** [VP2C] heal over (with a ~); form ~s: The cut on his forehead ~red over.

scarab /'skærəb/ n kinds of beetle, esp one regarded as sacred in ancient Egypt; carving in the shape of a ~ (as an ornament or charm).

scarce /skeəs/ adj **1** (opp of plentiful) not available in sufficient quantity; not equal to the demand: Eggs are ~ and expensive this month. **2** rare; seldom met with: a ~ book. **make oneself ~,** (colloq) keep out of the way, go away. **scarc·ity** /'skeəsətɪ/ n [U] state of being ~; smallness of supply compared with demand: The scarcity of fruit was caused by the drought. [C] (pl -ties) instance or occasion of scarcity.

scarce·ly /'skeəslɪ/ adv barely; not quite; almost not: There were ~ a hundred people present. I ~ know him. S~ had he entered the room when the phone rang.

scare /skeə(r)/ vt,vi [VP6A,15A,B,2A] frighten; become frightened: He was ~d by the thunder. They were ~d at the strange noise. The dogs ~d the thief away. He ~s easily/is easily ~d. ~ sb stiff, (colloq) alarm sb, make sb nervous: He's ~d stiff of women. ~ sb out of his wits, make him extremely frightened: The sound of footsteps outside ~d her out of her wits. □ n [C] feeling of alarm; state of widespread fear: The news caused a war ~, a fear that war might break out. You did give me a ~, did frighten me. **'~-crow** n figure of a man dressed in old clothes, set up to ~ birds away from crops. **'~ headline** n sensational newspaper headline in heavy black print. **'~·monger** /-mʌŋgə(r)/ n person who spreads alarming news and starts a ~. **scary** /'skeərɪ/ adj (colloq) causing alarm.

scarf /skɑːf/ n (pl ~s /skɑːfs/ or scarves /skɑːvz/) long strip of material (silk, wool, etc) worn over

the shoulders, round the neck or (by women) over the hair. **'~-pin** n ornamental pin worn on a ~.

scar·ify /'skærɪfaɪ/ vt (pt,pp -fied) [VP6A] **1** (in surgery) make small cuts in, cut off skin from. **2** (fig) hurt by severe criticism. **3** loosen (the surface of the soil or a road) by using an agricultural tool or a machine with prongs.

scar·let /'skɑːlət/ n, adj bright red: the ~ pillarboxes in Great Britain. **~ 'fever,** infectious disease with ~ marks on the skin. **~ 'hat,** cardinal's hat. **~ 'runner,** ~-flowered kind of bean plant. **~ 'woman,** (old use) prostitute.

scarp /skɑːp/ n steep slope; escarpment.

scat /skæt/ int (sl) Go away!

scath·ing /'skeɪðɪŋ/ adj (of criticism, ridicule, etc) severe; harsh: a ~ retort; a ~ review of a new book. **~·ly** adv

scat·ter /'skætə(r)/ vt,vi **1** [VP6A,15A,B,2A,C] send, go, in different directions: The police ~ed the crowd. The crowd ~ed. **2** [VP6A,15A] throw or put in various directions, or here and there: ~ seed; ~ gravel on an icy road. **'~-brain** n person who cannot keep his thoughts on one subject for long. Hence, **'~-brained** adj. □ n that which is ~ed; sprinkling: a ~ of hailstones. **~ed** (pp as an) adj lying in different directions; not situated together; wide apart: a few ~ed fishing villages; a thinly ~ed population.

scatty /'skætɪ/ adj (-ier, -iest) (colloq) **1** mad; feeble-minded: That man would drive any woman ~! **2** scatter-brained; absent-minded.

scav·en·ger /'skævɪndʒə(r)/ n **1** animal or bird, eg a vulture, that lives on decaying flesh. **2** person who searches among discarded or refuse material. **scav·enge** /'skævɪndʒ/ vi [VP2A,3A] ~ (for), act as a ~.

scen·ario /sɪ'nɑːrɪəʊ US: -'nær-/ n (pl ~s /-rɪəʊz/) written outline of a play, an opera, a film, with details of the scenes, etc; imagined sequence of future events. **scen·arist** /sɪ'nɑːrɪst US: -'nær-/ n writer of ~s.

scene /siːn/ n [C] **1** place of an actual or imagined event: the ~ of a great battle. The ~ of the novel is laid/set in Scotland. **2** description of an incident, or of part of a person's life; incident in real life suitable for such a description: 'S~s of Clerical Life', tales by George Eliot. There were distressing ~s when the earthquake occurred. **3** (incident characterized by an) emotional outburst: She made a ~/We had a ~ when I criticized her. **4** view; sth seen; sth spread out to view (indoors or outdoors, in a town or in the country, with or without action; cf scenery, which is used of natural features on land): The boats in the harbour make a beautiful ~. They went abroad for a change of ~. **5** (abbr Sc) one of the parts, shorter than an act, into which some plays and operas are divided; episode within such a part: 'Macbeth', Act II, Sc 1; the 'duel ~ in 'Hamlet'. **6** place represented on the stage of a theatre; the painted background, woodwork, canvas, etc representing such a place: The first ~ of 'Lotus Blossom' is a tropical garden. The ~s are changed during the intervals. **behind the ~s, (a)** out of sight of the audience; behind the stage. **(b)** (fig, of a person) influencing events secretly; (of an event) in secret, not known to the public. **be/come on the ~,** (fig) be present/appear. **'~-painter** n (theatre) person who paints scenery(2). **'~-shifter** n (theatre) person who changes the ~s. **7** (colloq) area of what is currently fashionable or notable: the

,enter·tainment ~ in the West End of London; the 'drug ~ in our big cities. **be on/make the ~,** (colloq) be part of/present in such a ~.

scen·ery /'si:nərɪ/ n [U] **1** general natural features of a district, eg mountains, plains, valleys, forests: mountain ~; stop to admire the ~. Cf town scenes. **2** the furnishings, painted canvas, woodwork, etc used on the stage of a theatre.

scenic /'si:nɪk/ adj having fine natural scenery: the ~ splendours of the Rocky Mountains; a ~ highway across the Alps. **sceni·cally** /-klɪ/ adv

scent /sent/ n **1** [U] smell, esp of sth pleasant coming from or belonging to sth: the ~ of new-mown hay; a rose that has no ~; [C] particular kind of smell: ~s of lavender and rosemary. **2** [U] (usu liquid) preparation distilled from flowers, etc; perfume: a bottle of ~; a '~-bottle. She uses too much ~. **3** (usu sing) smell left by an animal; the track of an animal: follow up/lose/recover the ~. The ~ was strong/poor/hot/cold, easy/difficult, etc for the hounds to follow. **on the ~,** having, following, a clue. **off the ~,** having, following, no clue or the wrong clue. **put/throw sb off the ~,** (fig) mislead him by giving false information. **4** [U] sense of smell (in dogs): hunt by ~. □ vt [VP6A] **1** learn the presence of by smell: The dog ~ed a rat. **2** begin to suspect the presence or existence of: ~ a crime; ~ treachery/trouble. **3** put ~ on; make fragrant: ~ a handkerchief; roses that ~ the air. **~·less** adj having no ~: ~less flowers.

scep·ter /'septə(r)/ n = sceptre.

scep·tic (US = **skep·tic**) /'skeptɪk/ n person who doubts the truth of a particular claim, theory, etc; person who doubts the truth of the Christian religion or of all religions. **scep·ti·cal** (US = **skep-**) /-kl/ adj inclined not to believe; in the habit of questioning the truth of claims, statements, etc. **scep·ti·cally** (US = **skep-**) /-klɪ/ adv **scep·ti·cism** (US = **skep-**) /'skeptɪsɪzəm/ n [U] doubting state of mind; ~al attitude of mind.

sceptre (US = **scep·ter**) /'septə(r)/ n rod or staff carried by a ruler as a sign of power or authority. **scep·tred** (US = **-tered**) adj having a ~. ⇨ the illus at regalia.

sched·ule /'ʃedju:l US: 'skedʒʊl/ n [C] list or statement of details, esp of times for doing things; programme or timetable for work: a production ~, eg in a factory; a full ~, a busy programme. **on/behind ~,** on/not on time: The train arrived on ~, on time, punctually. **(according) to ~,** as planned. □ vt [VP6A,7A,14] ~ **(for),** make a ~ of; put in a ~; (esp US) enter in a list of arrangements: ~d services, (eg of aircraft) flying according to announced time-tables (Cf charter flights.) The President is ~d to make a speech tomorrow. His arrival is ~d for Thursday.

sche·matic /skɪ'mætɪk/ adj of the nature of a scheme or plan; (shown) in a diagram or chart. **sche·mati·cally** /-klɪ/ adv

scheme /ski:m/ n [C] **1** arrangement; ordered system: a'colour ~, eg for a room, so that colours of walls, rugs, curtains, etc are in harmony. **2** plan or design (for work or activity): a ~ for manufacturing paper from straw; a ~ (= syllabus) for the term's work. **3** secret and dishonest plan: a ~ to defraud a widow. □ vi,vt **1** [VP2A,3A,4A] ~ **for sth/to do sth,** make a (esp dishonest) ~ or ~s: He ~d to keep his rivals in ignorance of his plans. They ~d for the overthrow of the government. **2** [VP6A] make plans for (esp sth dishonest); a

scheming (= crafty) thief. ~r n person who ~s or intrigues.

scherzo /'skeətsəʊ/ n (pl ~s /-səʊz/) (I) lively, vigorous passage in music.

schism /'sɪzəm/ n [U] (offence of causing the) division of an organization (esp a Church) into two or more groups, usu through difference of opinion; [C] instance of such separation. **schis·matic** /sɪz'mætɪk/ adj tending to or inclined to ~; guilty of ~.

schist /ʃɪst/ n kinds of rock which splits easily into thin plates.

schizo·phrenia /ˌskɪtsəʊ'fri:nɪə/ n type of mental disorder (colloq split personality) marked by lack of connection between thoughts, feelings, and actions. **schizo·phrenic** /ˌskɪtsəʊ'frenɪk/ adj of ~. □ n (colloq abbr schizo) person suffering from ~.

schmal(t)z /ʃmɔːlts/ n (colloq) sickly sentimentality. **schmal(t)zy** adj

schnapps /ʃnæps/ n [U] strong alcoholic spirit distilled from grain.

schnit·zel /'ʃnɪtsl/ n veal cutlet covered with breadcrumbs and fried in butter.

schnor·kel /'snɔːkl/ n = snorkel.

scholar /'skɒlə(r)/ n **1** (dated use) boy or girl at school. **2** student who, after a competitive examination or other means of selection, is awarded money or other help so that he may attend school or college, or pursue further education: British Council ~s. **3** person with much knowledge (usu of a particular subject, and esp one who gives careful attention to evidence, method, etc). **schol·ar·ly** adj having or showing much learning; of suitable, or right for a ~(3); fond of learning: a ~ly translation; a ~ly young woman.

schol·ar·ship /'skɒləʃɪp/ n **1** [U] learning or knowledge obtained by study; proper concern for scholarly methods. **2** [C] payment of money, eg a yearly grant to a scholar(2) so that he may continue his studies: win a ~ to the university.

schol·as·tic /skə'læstɪk/ adj **1** of schools and education: the '~ profession, that of teaching; a '~ post, a position as a teacher; a '~ agency, private one that finds positions for teachers and teachers for schools. **2** connected with the learning of the Middle Ages, esp when men argued over small points of dogma. **schol·as·ti·cism** /skə'læstɪsɪzəm/ n [U] the system of philosophy taught in the universities in the Middle Ages.

school[1] /sku:l/ n **1** [C] institution for educating children: 'primary and'secondary ~s; 'evening ~s; 'Sunday ~s; ~ doctors, medical officers responsible for the health of school children; (US) college, university. '~-board n (US) local education authority. '~-book n book used in ~s; textbook. '~-boy n boy at ~: (attrib) ~boy slang. '~-days n pl time of being at ~: look back upon one's ~-days. '~-fellow n member, past or present, of the same ~. '~-girl n girl at ~. '~-house n building of a ~ esp a small one in a village. '~-man /-mən/ n (pl -men) teacher in a European university in the Middle Ages; theologian dealing with religious teachings by the use of Aristotle's logic. '~-master/·mistress n school teacher. '~-mate n = ~fellow. '~-time n lesson time at ~. **2** [U] (not with def art) process of being educated in a ~: '~ age, between the ages of starting and finishing ~; ~-leaving age, age at which children leave ~. The ~-leaving age has been raised to 16. Is he old enough for ~/to go to ~? He left ~ when he was *fifteen. My boys are still at* ∼. **3** [U] (not with *def art*) time when teaching is given; lessons: *S*∼ *begins at 9am. There will be no* ∼ (= no lessons) *tomorrow. Will you come for a walk after* ∼? **4** (with *def art*) all the pupils in a ∼: *The whole* ∼ *hopes that its football team will win the match.* **5** department or division of a university for the study of a particular subject: *The S*∼ *of Oriental and African Studies,* in the University of London; *the* '*Law/*'*Medical S*∼; *the S*∼ *of Dentistry;* (GB) branch of study for which separate examinations are given in a university: *the* '*History* ∼; hall in which these examinations are held; (*pl*) these examinations. **6** [C] (fig) circumstances or occupation that provides discipline or instruction: *the hard* ∼ *of experience/adversity.* **7** (*pl*) **the** ∼**s,** medieval universities, their professors, teaching, and arguments. ⇨ also ∼*man* in 1 above. **8** [C] group of persons who are followers or imitators of an artist, a philosopher, etc, or of persons having the same principles or characteristics: *the Dutch/Venetian, etc* ∼ *of painting; the Hegelian* ∼, of philosophers; *a gentleman of the old* ∼, who retains the traditions, manners, etc of older times. ∼ *of thought,* way of thinking shared by a group of persons. □ *vt* [VP6A,15B,16A] ∼ **sb (in sth/to do sth),** train; control; discipline: ∼ *a horse;* ∼ *oneself in patience/to be patient.* ∼**·ing** *n* [U] education: *He had very little* ∼*ing. Who's paying for her* ∼*ing?*

school[2] /'sku:l/ *n* [C] large number (*of* fish) swimming together; shoal.

schoo·ner /'sku:nə(r)/ *n* **1** kind of sailing-ship with two or more masts and fore and aft sails. **2** tall drinking-glass.

schot·tische /ʃɒ'ti:ʃ/ *n* (music for a) kind of polka.

schwa /ʃwɑ:/ *n* symbol /ə/ used in phonetic notation for central vowels or diphthong elements as in /ə'gəʊ/ for *ago.*

sci·atic /saɪ'ætɪk/ *adj* of the hip: *the* ∼ *nerve,* nerve extending through the hip and thigh. **sci·atica** /saɪ'ætɪkə/ *n* [U] neuralgia of the ∼ nerve.

science /'saɪəns/ *n* **1** [U] knowledge arranged in an orderly manner, esp knowledge obtained by observation and testing of facts; pursuit of such knowledge. *S*∼ *is an exact discipline.* ⇨ art[1](2). **the natural** ∼**s,** eg botany, zoology. **the physical** ∼**s,** eg physics, chemistry. **social** ∼**(s),** eg psychology, politics. **the applied** ∼**s,** eg engineering. ∼ '**fiction,** fiction dealing with recent or imagined scientific discoveries and advances (usu fantasies). **3** [U] expert's skill (opp of strength): *In judo* ∼ *is more important than strength.* **scien·tist** /'saɪəntɪst/ *n* person expert in one or more of the natural or physical ∼s.

scien·tific /ˌsaɪən'tɪfɪk/ *adj* **1** of, for, connected with, used in, science; guided by the rules of science: ∼ *methods;* ∼ *farming;* ∼ *instruments.* **2** having, using, needing, skill or expert knowledge: *a* ∼ *boxer.* **scien·tifi·cally** /-klɪ/ *adv*

scimi·tar /'sɪmɪtə(r)/ *n* short, curved, single-edged sword, formerly used by Arabs, Persians, Turks.

a scimitar

scin·tilla /sɪn'tɪlə/ *n* [C] spark; atom; shred; iota: *not a* ∼ *of truth in the story; not a* ∼ *of evidence,* none at all.

scin·til·late /'sɪntɪleɪt US: -təleɪt/ *vi* [VP2A] sparkle; be brilliant: *scintillating with wit.* **scin·til·la·tion** /ˌsɪntɪ'leɪʃn US: -tl'eɪʃn/ *n*

scion /'saɪən/ *n* **1** young member of a (esp old or noble) family. **2** shoot of a plant, esp one cut for grafting or planting.

scis·sors /'sɪzəz/ *n pl* (**pair of**) ∼, cutting instrument with two blades which cut as they come together: *Where are my* ∼? ∼ **and paste,** (of articles, books, etc) compiled from parts of others: *This article's a* ∼ *and paste job.*

scler·osis /sklə'rəʊsɪs/ *n* [U] diseased condition in which soft tissue (eg walls of the arteries) hardens.

scoff[1] /skɒf US: skɔ:f/ *vi* [VP2A,3A] ∼ **(at),** speak contemptuously, mock (at): ∼ *at dangers;* ∼ *at religion.* □ *n* **1** taunt; ∼ing remark. **2** object of ridicule. ∼**er** *n* person who ∼s. ∼**·ing·ly** *adv*

scoff[2] /skɒf US: skɔ:f/ *vt* (sl) eat greedily: *Who has* ∼*ed all the pastries?* □ *n* **1** act of ∼ing: *have a good* ∼. **2** [U] (sl) food: *Where's all the* ∼ *gone?*

scold /skəʊld/ *vt, vi* [VP2A,6A,14] ∼ **(sb) (for sth),** blame with angry words; find fault noisily: ∼ *a child for being lazy.* □ *n* person who ∼s. ∼**·ing** *n* [C] severe rebuke: *give sb/get a* ∼*ing for being late.*

scol·lop /'skɒləp/ *n, vt* = scallop.

sconce /skɒns/ *n* bracket fixed to a wall for a candle (or, today, any other form of light).

scone /skɒn US: skəʊn/ *n* [C] soft, flat cake of barley meal or wheat flour baked quickly.

scoop /sku:p/ *n* [C] **1** (sorts of) deep, shovel-like, short-handled tool for taking up and moving quantities of grain, flour, sugar, etc; long-handled, ladle-shaped tool for dipping out liquid. **2** motion of, or as of, using a ∼: *at one* ∼, in one single movement of a ∼: (fig) *He won £50 at one* ∼. **3** (colloq) piece of news obtained and published by one newspaper before its competitors; (comm) large profit made by anticipating competitors. □ *vt* **1** [VP15B] ∼ **sth out/up,** lift with, or as with, a ∼. **2** [VP6A,15B] ∼ **(out),** make (a hole, groove, etc) with, or as with, a ∼: ∼ *out a hole in the sand.* **3** [VP6A] (colloq) get (news, a profit, etc) as a ∼(3). ∼**·ful** /-fʊl/ *n* as much as a ∼ holds.

scoot /sku:t/ *vi* (either imper or inf) (colloq, hum) run away quickly: *S*∼! *Tell him to* ∼. ⇨ scram.

scooters

scooter /'sku:tə(r)/ *n* **1** ('**motor-**)∼ light motorcycle with small wheels and a low seat. **2** child's toy, an L-shaped vehicle with small wheels, one foot being used to move it by pushing against the ground.

scope /skəʊp/ *n* [U] **1** opportunity; outlet: *work that gives* ∼ *for one's abilities.* **2** range of action or observation: *Ought politics to be within the* ∼ *of a trade union's activities? Economics is a subject beyond the* ∼ *of my mind.*

scor·bu·tic /skɔ:'bju:tɪk/ *adj* of, affected with, scurvy.

scorch /skɔ:tʃ/ *vt, vi* **1** [VP6A] burn or discolour the surface of (sth) by dry heat; cause to dry up or wither: *The long, hot summer ~ed the grass. You ~ed my shirt when you ironed it.* ⁓**ed 'earth policy,** policy of burning crops, and destroying buildings, etc that might be useful to enemy forces occupying a district. **2** [VP2A] become discoloured, etc with heat. **3** [VP2A,C] (colloq, of cyclists, motorists, etc) travel at very high speed. □ *n* [C] mark on the surface of sth (esp cloth) made by dry heat. ⁓**er** *n* sth or sb that ⁓es: *Yesterday was a ~er,* a very hot day. ⁓**ing** *adj* very hot. □ *adv:* ⁓*ing hot,* extremely hot.

score¹ /skɔː(r)/ *n* [C] **1** cut, scratch or notch made on a surface: *~s on rock,* eg made during the Ice Age; *~s on a slave's back* (made by whipping). **2** (from the old custom of chalking lines on a board in inns, to record what a customer owed for drinks, etc) account or record of money owing: *run up a ~,* get into debt. **pay/settle/wipe off old ~s,** (fig) get even with sb for past offences; have one's revenge: *I have some old ~s to settle with that fellow.* **3** (record of) points, goals, runs, etc made by a player or team in sport: *The ~ in the tennis final was 6—4, 3—6, 7—5. The half-time ~* (eg football) *was 2—1.* **keep the ~,** keep a record of the ~ as it is made. **'~-board/-book/-card,** one on which the ~ (eg in cricket) is recorded (during play). **4** reason; account. **on the ~ of,** on account of, in consideration of: *rejected on the ~* (*grounds* is more usu) *of ill health.* **on more ~s than one,** for more than one reason. **on 'that ~,** as far as that point is concerned: *You need have no anxiety on that ~.* **5** copy of orchestral, etc music showing what each instrument is to play, each voice to sing: *follow the ~ while listening to music.* **6** twenty; set of twenty: *a ~ of people; three ~ and ten,* 70, the normal length of human life according to the Bible. *I've been there ~s of times,* very often. **7** (sl) remark or act by which a person gains an advantage for himself in an argument, etc: *a politician who is clever at making ~s off hecklers at public meetings,* clever at making them appear foolish. ⇨ score²(4).

score² /skɔː(r)/ *vt,vi* **1** [VP6A,15A,B] mark with cuts, scratches, lines, etc: *The mountain side is ~d by torrents,* shows where torrents of water have washed away soil, etc. *Don't ~ the floor by pushing heavy furniture about. The composition was ~d with corrections in red ink.* ⁓ *out,* draw a line or lines through: *Three words had been ~d out.* ⇨ score¹(1). **2** [VP6A,2A,15B] ~ (**up**), make or keep a record (esp for games): *~ up runs,* in cricket. *Who's going to ~?* **3** [VP6A,2A] make as points in a game: *~ a goal; ~ a century,* 100 runs at cricket; *a batsman who failed to ~,* who made no runs; *~ no tricks,* ie whist or bridge. *~ an advantage/a success,* win one; have good fortune. *~ a point (against/off/over sb),* = ~ off sb. **4** [VP3A] ~ **off sb,** (colloq) humiliate him; defeat him in an argument; make a clever retort to sth he says. **5** [VP15B] ~ **sth up (against sb),** enter as a record: *That remark will be ~d up against you,* will be remembered (and, perhaps, be revenged). **6** [VP6A] orchestrate; write instrumental or vocal parts for a musical composition: *~d for violin, viola and cello.* ⇨ score¹(5). ⁓**r** *n* **1** person who keeps a record of points, goals, runs, etc ~d in a game. **2** player who ~s runs, goals, etc.

scorn /skɔːn/ *n* [U] **1** contempt; feeling that sb or sth deserves no respect: *be filled with ~ for a pro-*

posal; *dismiss a suggestion with ~.* **laugh sb/sth to ~,** treat with contemptuous laughter. **2** object of contempt: *He was the ~ of the village.* □ *vt* [VP6A,D,7A] feel or show contempt for; refuse (to do sth as being unworthy): *We ~ a liar. He ~ed my advice. She ~s lying/telling lies/to tell a lie.* ⁓**ful** /-fl/ *adj* showing or feeling ~; *a ~ful smile; ~ful of material things.* ⁓**fully** /-fəlɪ/ *adv*

Scor·pio /'skɔːpɪəʊ/ *n* eighth sign of the zodiac. ⇨ the illus at zodiac.

scor·pion /'skɔːpɪən/ *n* small animal of the spider group with a poisonous sting in its long, jointed tail. ⇨ the illus at arachnid.

scot /skɒt/ *n* (only in) **pay ~ and lot,** share financial burdens. **get off/escape ~-'free,** unharmed, unpunished.

Scot /skɒt/ *n* native of Scotland.

Scotch /skɒtʃ/ *adj* of Scotland or its people: ~ *whisky,* the kind distilled in Scotland. **~ 'terrier,** small, rough-haired, short-legged kind of terrier. □ *n* **1** the ~, *n pl* natives of Scotland. **2** [U] ~ whisky. **'~-man** /-mən/, **'~-woman** *nn* = Scotsman, Scotswoman (which are the preferred terms).

scotch /skɒtʃ/ *vt* [VP6A] **1** (archaic) wound without killing: *~ a snake.* **2** put an end to; frustrate (a plan, idea, etc).

Scot·land Yard /ˌskɒtlənd 'jɑːd/ *n* (now *New S~ Y~*) (used for) the London police; headquarters of the Criminal Investigation Department: *They called in ~,* asked for the help of this Department.

Scots /skɒts/ *adj* = Scotch. **the ~** *n pl* natives of Scotland. **'~-man** /-mən/, **'~-woman** /-wʊmən/ *nn* native of Scotland.

Scot·tish /'skɒtɪʃ/ *adj* = Scotch.

scoun·drel /'skaʊndrəl/ *n* wicked person with no principles or scruples; villain; rascal. ⁓**ly** /-rəlɪ/ *adj* of or like a ~.

scour¹ /'skaʊə(r)/ *vt,vi* **1** [VP6A,15A,B] make (a dirty surface) clean or bright by friction: *~ the pots and pans; ~ out a saucepan,* clean the inside (with a ~er). **2** [VP6A,15B] ~ **sth (away/off),** get rid of (rust, marks, etc) by rubbing or with a strong jet of water: *~ the rust off.* **3** [VP6A,15A] clear out (a channel, etc) by flowing over or through it: *The torrent ~ed a channel down the hillside.* □ *n* act of ~ing: *give a dirty saucepan a good ~.* ⁓**er** *n* (esp) pad of stiff nylon or wire for ~ing pots and pans.

scour² /'skaʊə(r)/ *vt,vi* [VP6A] go rapidly into every part of (a place) looking for: *~ the woods. The police ~ed London for the thief.* **2** [VP2C] ~ **about after/for sb/sth,** go quickly in search or pursuit of.

scourge /skɜːdʒ/ *n* **1** (old use) whip for flogging persons. **2** cause of suffering; person regarded as an instrument of vengeance or punishment: *After the ~ of war came the ~ of disease.* □ *vt* [VP6A] **1** (old use) use a ~ on. **2** (fig) cause suffering to.

scout¹ /skaʊt/ *n* **1** person (not a spy), ship or small, fast aircraft, sent out to get information of the enemy's movements, strength, etc. **2** (**Boy**) **S~,** member of an organization (**the S~ Association**) intended to develop character and teach self-reliance, discipline and public spirit. Cf *Girl Guide* (US = *Girl S~*). **'~-master** *n* officer who leads a troop of Boy S~s. **3** patrol-man on the roads, helping motorists who are members of the Automobile Association or Royal Automobile Club. **4** person employed to look out for talented performers (in sport, the theatre, etc) and recruit them for his employer(s): *a 'talent* ~. **5** (at Oxford) college servant. □ *vi* [VP2C] ~ **about/around (for sb/ sth)**, go about as a ~(1,4): ~ *about/around for...,* go about looking for....

scout² /skaʊt/ *vt* [VP6A] dismiss (an idea, suggestion, etc) as worthless or ridiculous.

scow /skaʊ/ *n* large flat-bottomed boat used for carrying sand, rock, rubbish, etc.

scowl /skaʊl/ *n* [C] bad-tempered look (on the face). □ *vi* [VP2A,3A] ~ **(at)**, look in a bad-tempered way: *The prisoner ~ed at the judge.*

scrabble¹ /'skræbl/ *n* [U] (P) game in which words are built up on a board (marked with squares) from letters printed on counters or blocks.

scrabble² /'skræbl/ *vi* **1** [VP2A] scrawl, scribble. **2** [VP2C] ~ **about (for sth)**, grope about to find or collect sth: ~ *about for sth dropped under the table.* □ *n* act of scrabbling.

scrag /skræg/ *n* **1** lean, skinny person or animal. **2** ~(-'end), bony part of a sheep's neck, used for making soup and stews. □ *vt* (-gg-) put to death by strangling; twist the neck of. **scraggy** *adj* (-ier, - iest) thin and bony: *a long,* ~*gy neck.*

scram /skræm/ *vi* (either *imper* or *inf*) (sl) go away: *I told him to* ~.

scramble /'skræmbl/ *vi,vt* **1** [VP2A,C,4A] climb, clamber or crawl (over steep or rough ground): ~ *up the side of a cliff/over a rocky hillside.* **2** [VP3A,4A] ~ **(for)**, struggle with others to get sth, or as much or as many as possible of sth, from competitors: *The players* ~*d for/*~*d to get possession of the ball. The children* ~*d for the coins that were thrown to them.* **3** [VP6A] cook (eggs) by beating them and then heating them in a saucepan with butter and milk. **4** [VP6A] make a message sent by telephone, etc unintelligible (by changing the wave frequency) without a special receiver. □ *n* [C] **1** climb, walk, motor-bike competition or trial, over or through obstacles, rough ground, etc. **2** rough struggle: *There was a* ~ *for the best seats.* **scram-bler** /'skræmblə(r)/ *n* device for scrambling telephone messages. ⇨ **4** above.

scrap¹ /skræp/ *n* **1** [C] small (usu unwanted) piece: ~*s of paper/broken porcelain;* (fig) small amount: *not a* ~ *of evidence to support the charge; not even a* ~ *of comfort in the news.* **2** [U] waste or unwanted articles, esp those of value only for the material they contain: *A man comes round regularly collecting* ~. '~-heap *n* pile of waste or unwanted material or articles. '~-iron *n* [U] articles made of iron, to be melted down for re-use. **throw sth/sb on the** ~-heap, discard sth, dismiss sb, as no longer wanted. **3** (*pl*) odds and ends; bits of un-eaten food: *Give the* ~*s to the dog.* **4** [C] picture or paragraph cut out from a periodical, etc for a collection. '~-book *n* book of blank pages on which to paste these. □ *vt* (-pp-) [VP6A] throw away as useless or worn-out: *You ought to* ~ *that old bicycle and buy a new one.* ~py *adj* (-ier, -iest) made up of bits or ~s; not complete or properly arranged. ~·ily /-ɪlɪ/ *adv* ~·i-ness *n*

scrap² /skræp/ *n* (colloq) fight, quarrel, esp one that is not planned or premeditated: *He had a bit of a* ~ *with his brother.* □ *vi* (-pp-) fight; quarrel: *Tell those boys to stop* ~*ping.*

scrape /skreɪp/ *vt,vi* **1** [VP6A,14,15A,B,22] ~ *sth* **(from/off sth)**; ~ *sth* **(away/off)**, make clean, smooth or level by drawing or pushing the hard edge of a tool, or sth rough, along the surface; re-move (mud, grease, paint, etc) in this way: ~ *out a*

sticky saucepan; ~ *the rust off sth;* ~ *paint from a door;* ~ *a dish clean. The ship's bottom needs to be* ~*d,* eg in order to remove barnacles. **2** [VP6A,14] ~ *sth* **(from/off sth)**, injure or damage by harsh rubbing, etc: *The boy fell and* ~*d his knee/*~*d the skin off his knee. He* ~*d the side of his car/*~*d the paintwork off his car.* **3** [VP6A,15B] ~ *sth* **(out)**, make by scraping: ~ (*out*) *a hole.* **4** [VP2C,3A] go, get, pass along, touching or almost touching: ~ *along a wall; branches that* ~ *against the window panes.* ~ **along,** (fig) manage to live in spite of difficulties. ~ **through (sth)**, only just pass: *The boy just* ~*d through (his exams). bow and* ~, bow awkward-ly while drawing one foot along the floor; (fig) be-have with exaggerated respect. **5** [VP6A,15B] ~ **sth/sb together**, obtain by being careful, or with effort: *We managed to* ~ *together an audience of fifty people/enough money for a short holiday.* ~ **(up) an acquaintance with sb**, force one's ac-quaintance upon sb; push oneself into a person's company in order to get acquainted with him. ~ **a living**, with difficulty make enough money for a living. □ *n* **1** act or sound of scraping: *the* ~ *of sb's pen on paper/of the teacher's fingernail on the blackboard.* **2** place that is ~d: *a bad* ~ *on the el-bow,* eg as the result of a fall. **3** awkward situation resulting from foolish or thoughtless behaviour: *That boy is always getting into* ~*s. Don't expect me to get you out of your* ~*s.* ~r *n* tool used for scraping, eg for scraping mud from one's shoes at the entrance to a building, or for scraping paint from woodwork. **scrap-ing** *n* (esp *pl*) small bits produced by scraping: *scrapings from the bottom of the barrel.*

scrappy /'skræpɪ/ *adj* ⇨ scrap¹.

scratch¹ /skrætʃ/ *vt,vi* **1** [VP6A,2A] make lines on or in a surface with sth pointed or sharp, eg finger-nails, claws: *The cat* ~*ed me. Does your cat* ~? *Who has* ~*ed the paint?* ~ **the surface,** (fig) deal with a subject without being thorough, without get-ting deeply into it: *The lecturer merely* ~*ed the surface of the subject.* **2** [VP6A] get (oneself, a part of the body) ~*ed* by accident: *He* ~*ed his hands badly while pruning the rose-bushes.* **3** [VP15B] ~ **sth out,** draw a line or lines through a word or words, a name, etc: ~ *out Smith/his name from the list. The essay contained a lot of scratched-out words/*~*ings-'out.* **4** [VP6A,2A] withdraw (a horse, a candidate, oneself) from a competition; take out (the name of a horse, a candidate) from a list of entries for a race or competition: *The horse was* ~*ed,* Its name was withdrawn. *I hope you're not going to* ~ (= withdraw, decline) *at the last moment.* **5** [VP6A,2A] scrape or rub (the skin), esp to relieve itching: ~ *mosquito bites. Stop* ~*ing* (*yourself*). ~ **one's head,** show signs of being perplexed. **If you'll** ~ **,my back, I'll** ~ **'yours,** (fig) If you'll help, flatter, etc me, I'll do the same for you. **6** [VP6A,15B] ~ **sth (out),** make by ~ing: ~ (*out*) *a hole.* **7** [VP6A] write hurriedly; scribble: ~ *a few lines to a friend.* '~-pad *n* scrib-bling pad. **8** [VP2A] make a scraping noise: *This pen* ~*es.* **9** [VP2C,15B] ~ **about (for sth);** ~ **sth up,** tear or dig with the claws, fingernails, etc in search of sth: *The chickens were* ~*ing about in the yard. The dog* ~*ed up a bone.* **10** [VP15B] scrape(5): ~ *up/together a few pounds.*

scratch² /skrætʃ/ *n* **1** [C] mark, cut, injury, sound, made by scratching(1): *Her hands were covered* *with* ~*es after she had pruned her rose-bushes. It's only a* ~, a very slight injury. *He escaped without a* ~, quite unhurt. **a ~ of the pen,** a few words quickly and easily written; a signature. **2** (*sing* only) act or period of scratching(5): *The dog enjoys having a good* ~. **3** (*sing* only; no article) starting line for a race. **start from** ~, start from this line; (fig) start without being allowed any advantage(s); (fig) begin (sth) without preparation. **be/come/bring sb up to** ~, (fig) be ready/get sb ready to do what is expected or required: *Will your teachers manage to bring you up to* ~ *before you take the examination,* get you ready for it? **4** (attrib) (sport) without a handicap: ~ *players.* '~**-race** *n* one in which all competitors start from ~, on equal terms. **5** (attrib) collected by chance; brought together, done, made, with whatever is available: *a* ~ *crew/team; a* ~ *dinner,* prepared from what happens to be in the house. ~**y** *adj* **1** (of writing, drawings) done carelessly or unskilfully. **2** (of a pen) making a scratching noise.

scrawl /skrɔːl/ *vi, vt* [VP6A,2A,C] write or draw quickly or carelessly; make meaningless or illegible marks: *Who has* ~*ed all over this wall? He* ~*ed a few words on a postcard to his wife.* □ *n* **1** [C] piece of bad writing; hurried note of letter. **2** (*sing* only) shapeless, untidy handwriting: *What a* ~*! His signature was an illegible* ~.

scrawny /'skrɔːnɪ/ *adj* (-ier, -iest) bony, scraggy: *the* ~ *neck of a turkey.*

scream /skriːm/ *vi, vt* **1** [VP2A,C,6A,15A,B,22] ~ *(out),* (of human beings, birds, animals) give a loud, sharp cry or cries of, or as of, fear or pain; cry (sth) in a loud shrill voice: *She* ~*ed in anger. The baby has been* ~*ing for an hour. This parrot* ~*s but does not talk. The child* ~*ed itself red in the face. She* ~*ed out that there was a burglar under the bed. We all* ~*ed with laughter,* laughed noisily. ~ **one's 'head off,** ~ very loudly (and for a long time). **2** [VP2A,C] (of the wind, machines, etc) make a loud, shrill noise: *The wind* ~*ed through the trees.* □ *n* [C] **1** loud, shrill, piercing cry or noise: *the* ~ *of a peacock;* ~*s of pain/ laughter.* **2** (colloq) sb or sth that causes ~s of laughter: *He/It was a perfect* ~. ~**ing·ly** *adv* (esp): ~*ingly funny,* so funny as to cause ~s of laughter.

scree /skriː/ *n* [C,U] (part of a mountain-side covered with) small loose stones which slide down when trodden on. ⇨ the illus at mountain.

screech /skriːtʃ/ *vi, vt* [VP2A,C,6A,15A,B] ~ *(out),* **1** make a harsh, piercing sound: *jet planes* ~*ing over the house-tops. The brakes* ~*ed as the car stopped.* **2** scream in anger or pain; cry out in high tones: *monkeys* ~*ing in the trees. She* ~*es out her top notes instead of singing them.* □ *n* [C] ~*ing cry or noise: the* ~ *of tyres,* eg when a car is cornering fast. '~**-owl** *n* kind of owl that ~*es* instead of hooting.

screed /skriːd/ *n* [C] long (and usu uninteresting) piece of writing; long monotonous speech.

screen /skriːn/ *n* [C] (often movable) upright framework (some made so as to fold), used to hide sb or sth from view, or to protect from draughts or from too much heat, light, etc. **2** (in a church) structure of wood or stone separating (but not completely) the main part of the church and the altar, or the nave of a cathedral and the choir. **3** anything that is or can be used to give shelter or protection from observation, the weather, etc: *a* ~ *of trees,*

hiding a house from the road; *a* '*smoke-*~, used in war to hide ships, etc from the enemy; *a* ~ *of indifference,* an appearance of indifference that hides interest. **4** white or silver surface on to which slides, film transparencies, cinema films, TV pictures, etc are projected; surface upon which an image is seen on a cathode ray tube. Hence, (attrib, = *cinema*) *a* ~ *play,* the script of a film; ~ *actors/stars; a* '~ *test,* test of a person's suitability for acting in films. **5** frame with fine wire netting ('*window* ~, '*door* ~) to keep out flies, mosquitoes, etc. **6** large sieve or riddle used for separating coal, gravel, etc into different sizes. **7** (cricket) one of two large movable erections of white wood or canvas placed near the boundary line to help batsmen to see the ball. □ *vt, vi* **1** [VP6A,14,15A,B] ~ *(off) (from),* shelter, hide, protect from view, with a ~: *The trees* ~ *our house from public view. One corner of the room was* ~*ed off. You should* ~ *the lens of your camera from direct sunlight. We have* ~*ed our house (ie doors and windows) against mosquitoes.* **2** [VP6A,14] ~ *(from),* (fig) protect from blame, discovery, punishment: *I'm not willing to* ~ *your faults/* ~ *you from blame.* **3** [VP6A] separate (coal, etc) into different sizes by passing through a ~(6): ~*ed coal,* from which dust has been removed. **4** [VP6A] investigate (sb's) past history, eg the political antecedents of a refugee or displaced person, sb applying for a position in government service, in order to judge his loyalty, dependability, etc; examine (sb) to judge his qualifications for a post, etc. **5** [VP6A] show (an object, a scene) on a ~(4); make a cinema film of. [VP2C] ~ **well/badly,** (of a stage play, an actor, etc) be suitable/unsuitable for filming.

thread   types of head

screws

screw /skruː/ *n* **1** metal peg with slotted head and a spiral groove cut round its length, driven into wood, metal, etc by twisting under pressure, for fastening and holding things together. *a* '~ *loose,* (fig) sth wrong or out of order: *There's a* ~ *loose somewhere. He has a* ~ *loose,* is a little stupid. '~**-driver** *n* tool for turning ~s. ⇨ the illus at tool. ~**-'topped** *adj* (of jars, etc) having a top or lid with a spiral groove, put on or taken off by twisting. '~**-ball** *n, adj* (US, sl) crazy (person). ~ sth that is turned like a screw and is used for exerting pressure, tightening, etc. **put the** ~**(s) on** '**sb; give (sb) another turn of the** ~, use one's power, a threat of force, etc to force him to do sth. '**thumb**~ *n* ⇨ thumb. **3** action of turning; turn: *This isn't tight enough yet; give it another* ~. **4** '~**(-propeller)** propeller of a ship: *a twin-*~ *ship.* ('*air*)~, propeller of an aircraft. ⇨ the illus at air. **5** [C,U] (in games, eg billiards) spin given to a ball to make it curve or change direction. **6** small, twisted piece of paper and its contents: *a* ~ *of tea/tobacco.* **7** (colloq) miser. **8** (GB, sl) amount of salary or wages: *He's paid a good* ~. **9** (GB, sl) (= *turnkey*) prison warder. **10** ⚠ act of or partner in sexual intercourse. □ *vt, vi* **1** [VP6A,15A,B] fasten or tighten with a ~ or ~s: ~ *a lock on a door;* ~ *down the lid of a coffin;* ~ *up a door,* so that it cannot be opened. **have one's head** ~**ed on (the right**

way), be sensible, have good judgement. **2** [VP6A,15A,B] twist round; make tight, tense or more efficient: ～ *a lid on/off a jar;* ～ *one's head round,* in order to look over one's shoulder; ～ *up one's face/features/eyes,* contract the muscles, eg when going out into bright sunshine from a dark room. ～ *up one's courage,* overcome one's fears. **3** [VP6A,15A,B] exert pressure on; force (out of): ～ *water out of a sponge/more taxes out of the people.* **4** (sl) *be* ～*ed,* be drunk. **5** [VP6A,2A] ⚠ have sexual intercourse with. ～**y** *adj* (GB colloq) eccentric; crazy; (US colloq) ludicrously odd; absurd.

scribble /'skrɪbl/ *vt, vi* [VP6A,2A] write hastily or carelessly; make meaningless marks on paper, etc. **'scribbling-block** *n* pad of cheap paper making notes. □ *n* [U] hasty, careless handwriting; [C] sth ～d. **scrib·bler** /'skrɪblə(r)/ *n* person who ～s; (colloq) inferior author.

scribe /skraɪb/ *n* **1** professional letter-writer; person who, before the invention of printing, made copies of writings, eg in monasteries. **2** (Jewish hist) maker and keeper of records; teacher of Jewish law (at the time of Jesus Christ).

scrim·mage /'skrɪmɪdʒ/ *n* **1** [C] confused struggle or fight. **2** (US football) the play that takes place when two teams are lined up for the players to begin or resume play. **3** = scrum(mage). □ *vi, vt* engage in a ～(1); put (the ball) in a ～.

scrimp /skrɪmp/ *vt, vi* = skimp (which is more usu).

scrip /skrɪp/ *n* [C] document, the possession of which entitles the holder to a formal certificate for ownership of stock in a business company, etc on completion of formalities; [U] such documents collectively.

script /skrɪpt/ *n* **1** [U] (opp of *print*) handwriting; printed cursive characters in imitation of handwriting. **2** [C] (short for) manuscript or typescript (esp of an actor's part in a play, a talk, discussion, drama, etc to be broadcast, etc). **'～-writer** *n* person who writes ～s for films or broadcast programmes. ～**ed** *adj* read from a ～: *Un～ed discussions are usually livelier than ～ed discussions,* eg in a broadcast programme.

scrip·ture /'skrɪptʃə(r)/ *n* **1** (Holy) **S～,** The (Holy) **S～s,** the Bible; (attrib) taken from, relating to, the Bible: *a '～ lesson.* **2** sacred book of a religion other than Christianity. **scrip·tural** /'skrɪptʃərəl/ *adj* based on the Bible.

scrof·ula /'skrɒfjʊlə/ *n* [U] tuberculous disease in which there are swellings of the lymphatic glands. **scrofu·lous** /'skrɒfjʊləs/ *adj*

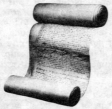

a scroll

scroll /skrəʊl/ *n* **1** roll of paper or parchment for writing on; ancient book written on a ～. **2** ornamental design cut in stone; flourish in writing, suggesting by its curves a ～ of parchment.

Scrooge / skru:dʒ/ *n* mean-spirited miser.

scro·tum /'skrəʊtəm/ *n* pouch of skin enclosing the

testicles in mammals.

scrounge /skraʊndʒ/ *vi, vt* [VP2A,6A] (colloq) get what one wants by taking it without permission or by trickery. ～**r** *n* person who ～s.

scrub¹ /skrʌb/ *n* **1** [U] (land covered with) trees and bushes of poor quality; stunted forest growth: (attrib) '～-pine, '～-oak, dwarf or stunted kinds. **2** [C] anything below the usual size. ～**by** /'skrʌbɪ/ *adj* (-ier, -iest) **1** small, stunted; mean. **2** rough and bristly: *a ～by chin.*

scrub² /skrʌb/ *vt, vi* (-bb-) [VP6A,15B,22,2A,C] ～ *(out),* clean by rubbing hard, esp with a stiff brush, soap and water: ～ *the floor;* ～ *out a pan;* ～ *the walls clean;* cancel; ignore: ～ *(out) an order.* '～-**bing-brush** *n* stiff brush for ～bing floors, etc. ⇨ the illus at brush. □ *n* act of ～bing: *The floor needs a good～.*

scruff /skrʌf/ *n* (only in) *the ～ of the neck,* the back of the neck, the nape, when used for grasping or lifting: *seize/take an animal by the ～ of the neck.*

scruffy /'skrʌfɪ/ *adj* (-ier, -iest) (colloq) dirty, untended and untidy looking.

scrum /skrʌm/ *n* (abbr of) scrummage. **scrum half,** the half-back who puts the ball into the ～.

scrum·mage /'skrʌmɪdʒ/ *n* the play in Rugby football when the forwards of both sides pack together with their heads down while the ball is thrown into the middle of them and they then try to kick the ball back to their own team; all those forwards when such play occurs.

scrump·tious /'skrʌmpʃəs/ *adj* (colloq, chiefly of food) delightful: ～ *food.*

scrunch /skrʌntʃ/ *n, vt* = crunch(2).

scruple /'skru:pl/ *n* **1** [C] weight-unit of 20 grains. ⇨ App 5. **2** [C,U] (hesitation caused by) uneasiness of conscience: *Have you no ～s about borrowing things without permission? He will tell lies without ～.* □ *vi* [VP4C] ～ *to do sth,* hesitate owing to ～s: (usu neg) *He doesn't ～ to tell a lie if he thinks it useful.*

scru·pu·lous /'skru:pjʊləs/ *adj* careful to do nothing morally wrong; paying great attention to small points (esp of conscience): *He is not ～ in his business dealings. A solicitor must act with ～ honesty.* ～**ly** *adv* in a ～ manner: ～*ly exact/ careful.*

scru·ti·neer /ˌskru:tɪ'nɪə(r) *US:* -tn'ɪər/ *n* official who examines ballot papers to see that they are not filled in irregularly.

scru·ti·nize /'skru:tɪnaɪz *US:* -tənaɪz/ *vt* [VP6A] make a detailed examination of.

scru·tiny /'skru:tɪnɪ *US:* -tənɪ/ *n* (*pl* -nies) **1** [U] thorough and detailed examination; [C] instance of this. **2** [C] official examination of votes, esp a recount of votes at an election when the result of the first count is very close: *demand a ～.*

scud /skʌd/ *vi* (-dd-) [VP2A,C] go straight and fast, with smooth motion: *The clouds ～ded across the sky. The yacht was ～ding along before the wind.* □ *n* [C] act of ～ding; [U] vapoury clouds driven by the wind.

scuff /skʌf/ *vi, vt* **1** [VP2A,C] walk without properly lifting the feet from the ground; shuffle. **2** [VP6A,15A,B] wear out or injure (shoes, etc) by walking in this way: ～ *one's shoes.*

scuffle /'skʌfl/ *vi* [VP2A,C], *n* (take part in a) rough, confused fight or struggle: *There was a ～ between the police and some demonstrators.*

scull /skʌl/ *n* **1** one of a pair of oars used together

by a single rower, one in each hand. **2** oar worked
at the stern of a boat with twisting strokes. □ *vt, vi*
[VP6A,2A] propel (a boat) with a ～; row (a boat)
with ～s; use a ～ or ～s. ～**er** *n* person who ～s.

scul·lery /'skʌlərɪ/ *n* (*pl* -ries) room usu in a large
house next to the kitchen, where dishes, pots, etc
are washed up.

scul·lion /'skʌlɪən/ *n* (hist) boy or man who did
rough work in the kitchen of a large house, etc.

sculpt /skʌlpt/ *vt, vi* = sculpture.

sculp·tor /'skʌlptə(r)/ *n* artist who sculptures.

sculp·tress /'skʌlptrɪs/ *n* woman ～.

sculp·ture /'skʌlptʃə(r)/ *n* **1** [U] art of making representations in stone, wood, metal, etc by carving
or modelling. **2** [C,U] (piece of) such work. □ *vt, vi*
1 [VP6A] represent in ～; decorate with ～: ～ *a
statue out of stone;* ～*d columns.* **2** [VP2A] be a
sculptor; do ～. **sculp·tural** /'skʌlptʃərəl/ *adj* of,
like, connected with, ～: *the sculptural arts.*

scum /skʌm/ *n* [U] **1** froth which forms on the surface of some boiling liquids; dirt on the surface of a
pond or other area of still water. **2** *the* ～ *(of),* (fig)
worthless person(s) (of a place). *the* ～ *of the
Earth,* worthless person(s). ～**my** *adj* of, like,
having or containing, ～.

scup·per /'skʌpə(r)/ *n* opening in a ship's side to
allow water to run off the deck. □ *vt* sink a ship deliberately; (colloq, usu passive) ruin; disable:
We're ～*ed!*

scurf /skɜːf/ *n* [U] small bits of dead skin, esp on
the scalp, loosened as new skin grows; dandruff:
monkeys searching each other's fur for ～. ～**y** *adj*
having, covered with, ～.

scur·ri·lous /'skʌrɪləs/ *adj* using, full of, violent
and taunting words of abuse: ～ *attacks upon the
Prime Minister.* **scur·ril·ity** /skə'rɪlətɪ/ *n* [U] ～
language; (*pl*; -ties) ～ remarks: *indulge in scurri-
lities.*

scurry /'skʌrɪ/ *vi* (*pt,pp* -ried) [VP2A,C,3A] ～
(about) (for/through), run with short, quick
steps; hurry: *The rain sent everyone* ～*ing for
shelter. Don't* ～ *through your work.* □ *n* **1** [U] act
or sound of ～ing; anxious or excited bustle and
movement: *the* ～ *and scramble of town life. There
was a* ～ *towards the refreshments.* **2** [C] ～ *(of),*
windy shower (of snow); cloud (of dust).

scurvy /'skɜːvɪ/ *n* [U] diseased state of the blood
caused (esp among sailors in former times) by eating too much salt meat and not enough fresh vegetables and fruit. □ *adj* (sl) dishonourable, contemptuous: *That was a* ～ *trick to play on an old lady.*
scurv·ily /-ɪlɪ/ *adv*

scut /skʌt/ *n* [C] short, erect tail, esp of a rabbit,
hare or deer.

scutch·eon /'skʌtʃən/ *n* = escutcheon.

scuttle¹ /'skʌtl/ *n* ('coal-)～, container for a supply
of coal at the fireside.

scuttle² /'skʌtl/ *vi* [VP2A,C] ～ *(off/away),*
scurry. □ *n* hurried flight or departure; cowardly
avoidance of, or running away from, difficulties
and dangers: *The Opposition leader accused the
Government of a policy of* ～.

scuttle³ /'skʌtl/ *n* small opening with a lid, in a
ship's side or deck, or in a building's roof or wall.
□ *vt* [VP6A] cut holes in, open valves in, a ship's
sides or bottom to sink it: *The captain* ～*d his ship
to avoid its being captured by the enemy.*

Scylla /'sɪlə/ *n* (myth) (six-headed monster living
on) a dangerous rock opposite a whirlpool (called
Charybdis /kə'rɪbdɪs/) (in the Strait of Messina, S

Italy). *between* ～ *and Charybdis,* between two
great dangers.

scythe /saɪð/ *n* tool with a slightly curved blade on
a long wooden pole with two short handles, for
cutting long grass, grain, etc. □ *vt* [VP6A,15A] cut
with a ～.

scything

sea /siː/ *n* **1** *the sea,* expanse of salt water that
covers most of the earth's surface and encloses its
continents and islands; any part of this (in contrast
to areas of fresh water and dry land): *Ships sail on
the sea. Fish swim in the sea. The sea covers nearly three-fourths of the world's surface. Let's go for
a swim in the sea. follow the sea,* be a sailor. *on
the sea,* (of a place) on the coast: *Brighton is on
the sea.* **2** *seas,* same sense as 1 above. *beyond/
over the sea(s),* abroad; to or in countries separated by the sea (note that *overseas* is more usu).
the high seas, parts which are not near the land,
esp outside the territorial limits over which the
nearest country has or claims jurisdiction. *the
freedom of the seas,* the right to carry on sea-
trade without interference. **3** (in proper names)
particular area of sea which is smaller than an
ocean: *the Mediterranean Sea; the Caribbean Sea;
the South China Sea;* inland body of water; lake:
*the Caspian Sea; the Sea of Galilee. the Seven
Seas,* (liter or poet) the Arctic, the Antarctic, the N
and S Pacific, the N and S Atlantic and the Indian
Oceans: *He has sailed the Seven Seas.* **4** (in various phrases without articles) *at sea,* away from,
out of sight of, the land: *He was buried at sea. all/
completely at sea,* (fig) puzzled; at a loss: *He
was all at sea when he began his new job. by sea,*
in a ship: *travel by sea and land. go to sea,* become a sailor. *put to sea,* leave port or land. **5** [C]
local state of the sea; swell of the ocean; big wave
or billow: *There was a heavy sea,* large waves. *The
ship was struck by a heavy sea,* a large wave. *The
seas were mountains high. half seas over,* having
drunk too much; intoxicated. **6** [C] large quantity
or expanse (*of*): *a sea of up-turned faces,* eg
crowds of people looking upwards; *a sea of flame.*
7 (attrib and in compounds): ,**sea 'air** *n* air at the
seaside, considered to be good for health: *enjoy the
sea air.* '**sea-anemone** *n* ⇨ the illus at anemone.
'**sea-animal** *n* animal inhabiting the sea, eg fish,
mammals, molluscs, etc. '**sea-bathing** *n* bathing
in the sea. '**sea-bed** *n* floor of the sea. '**sea-bird** *n*
any of several species of bird which live close to
the sea, ie on cliffs, islands, etc. ⇨ the illus at
water. '**sea-board** *n* coast region; line of coast.
'**sea-boat** *n* ship with the sea-going qualities specified: *a good/bad sea-boat,* one that sails well/
badly. '**sea-borne** *adj* (of trade) carried in ships:
sea-borne commerce/goods. '**sea-breeze** *n* breeze
blowing landward from the sea, esp during the day
in alternation with a land-breeze at night. Cf *a* ,**sea
'breeze,** any kind of breeze at sea. '**sea-coal** *n*

(hist) coal brought from Newcastle to London by sea (opp of *charcoal*). **'sea-cow** *n* kind of warm-blooded creature living in the sea and feeding its young with milk. **'sea-dog** *n* (a) old sailor, esp the captains of English ships during the reign of Elizabeth I. (b) dogfish. (c) seal. **'sea-faring** /-feəriŋ/ *adj* of work or voyages on the sea: *a 'seafaring man*, a sailor. **'sea-fish** *n* fish living in the sea (opp to *freshwater-fish*). **'sea fog** *n* fog along the coast, caused by difference between land and sea temperatures. **'sea-food** *n* edible fish or shellfish from the sea: *a 'seafood restaurant; a seafood cocktail.* **'sea-front** *n* part of a town facing the sea: *The best hotels are on the sea-front.* **'sea-girt** *adj* (poet) surrounded by the sea. **'sea-god** *n* god living in or having power over the sea, eg *Neptune.* **'sea-going** *adj* (of ships) built for crossing the sea, not for coastal voyages only; (of a person) seafaring. **,sea-'green** *adj, n* bluish-green as of the sea. **'sea-gull** *n* = gull. **'sea-horse** *n* kind of small fish. **,sea-island 'cotton** *n* fine quality of long-stapled cotton. **'sea-kale** *n* plant whose young white shoots are used as a vegetable. **'sea-legs** *n pl* ability to walk on the deck of a rolling ship: *get/ find one's sea-legs.* **'sea-level** *n* level of sea halfway between high and low tide as the basis for measuring height of land and depth of sea: *100 metres above/below sea level.* **'sea-lion** *n* large seal of the N Pacific Ocean. **'Sea Lord** *n* one of four naval members of the Board of Admiralty

(London). **'sea-man** /-mən/ *n* (*pl* -men) (a) (in the Navy) sailor who is not an officer. (b) person expert in nautical matters. Hence, **'sea-man-like** /-mənlaɪk/ *adj* **'sea-man-ship** /-mənʃɪp/ *n* skill in managing a boat or ship. **'sea mile** *n* nautical mile. **'sea-plane** *n* aircraft constructed so that it can come down on and rise from water. **'sea-port** *n* town with a harbour used by sea-going ships. **'sea-power** *n* ability to control and use the seas (by means of naval strength). **'sea-rover** *n* pirate; pirate's ship. **'sea-scape** *n* picture of a scene at sea. ⇨ landscape. **'sea-shell** *n* shell of any mollusc inhabiting the sea. **'sea-shore** *n* land bordering on the sea; beach: *children playing on the sea-shore;* (legal) between high and low-water marks. **'sea-sick** *adj* sick, inclined to vomit, from the motion of a ship. **'sea-sick-ness** *n* **'sea-side** *n* (often attrib) place, town, etc by the sea, esp a holiday resort: *go to the seaside for one's summer holidays; own a house by the seaside; a seaside town.* **'sea-snake** *n* (kinds of) (usu venomous) snake living in the sea. **'sea-urchin** *n* small sea-animal with a shell covered with sharp points. **,sea-'wall** *n* wall built to check the encroachment of the sea on the land. **'sea-water** *n* water from the sea. **'sea-way** *n* (a) progress of a ship through the water. (b) inland waterway, eg a river, series of lakes, joined by canals and locks, used by sea-going ships: *the St Lawrence S~way* (connecting the Atlantic and the Great Lakes between Canada and the US). **'sea-**

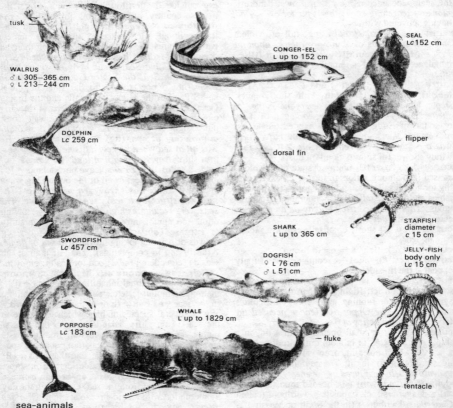

tusk

WALRUS
♂ L 305—365 cm
♀ L 213—244 cm

CONGER-EEL
L up to 152 cm

SEAL
Lc 152 cm

DOLPHIN
Lc 259 cm

flipper

dorsal fin

SWORDFISH
Lc 457 cm

SHARK
L up to 365 cm

STARFISH
diameter
c 15 cm

DOGFISH
♀ L 76 cm
♂ L 51 cm

JELLY-FISH
body only
Lc 15 cm

PORPOISE
Lc 183 cm

WHALE
L up to 1829 cm

fluke

tentacle

sea-animals

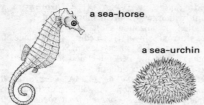

a sea-horse

a sea-urchin

weed n [C,U] kinds of plant growing in the sea, esp on rocks washed by the sea. '**sea·ward** /-wəd/ adj towards the sea; in the direction of the sea. '**sea·wards** /-wədz/ adv '**sea·worthy** adj (of a ship) fit for a voyage; well built and in good repair. **seal**[1] /si:l/ n kinds of fish-eating sea-animal hunted for its oil and skin and the fur of some species. ⇨ the illus at sea. '**∼·skin** n skin of a fur-seal; garment made of this. □ vi [VP2A] hunt ∼s: go ∼ing; a ∼ing expedition. **∼er** n person or ship engaged in hunting ∼s.
seal[2] /si:l/ n 1 piece of wax, lead, etc stamped with a design, attached to a document to show that it is genuine, or to a letter, packet, box, bottle, door, etc to guard against its being opened by unauthorized persons. **given under my hand and ∼**, (legal) signed and sealed by me. **under ∼ of secrecy**, (fig) what has been said must be kept secret because secrecy has been stipulated or is obligatory. 2 sth used instead of a ∼(1), eg a paper disc stuck to, or an impression stamped on, a document.

seals

3 piece of metal, etc on which is a design and which is used to stamp the ∼ on wax, etc. '**∼-ring**, finger-ring with a ∼ (often with the design cut on a gem). 4 ∼ **of,** (fig) act, event, etc regarded as a confirmation or guarantee (of sth) or giving approval (of sth): By visiting Drake's ship, Queen Elizabeth I put/set the ∼ of approval on his piratical voyages. □ vt 1 [VP6A,15A,B] ∼ **(up),** put a ∼(1) on: ∼ a letter; fasten or close tightly: ∼ up a drawer so that it cannot be opened; ∼ a jar of fruit, make it air-tight so that the fruit will keep; ∼ up a window, eg by pasting paper over all the crevices. ∼ **sth in,** keep it in by ∼ing: Our special canning process ∼s the flavour in. ∼ **sth off,** block it: ∼ off an area of land, block all means of entering it, eg one where, after military use, there may be unexploded shells, etc. **One's lips are ∼ed,** One must not speak; the matter must be kept secret. **∼ed orders,** instructions given to a ship's captain (or other person in authority), esp in wartime, in a ∼ed envelope to be opened only at a certain time or place. '**∼·ing-wax** n kind of wax that melts quickly when heated and quickly hardens when cooled, used to ∼ letters, etc. 2 [VP6A] settle; decide: ∼ a bargain; His fate is ∼ed.
seal·skin /si:lskɪn/ ⇨ seal[1].
Sealy·ham /si:liəm US: -lihæm/ n kind of terrier with a long body and short legs.
seam /si:m/ n [C] 1 line where two edges, esp of cloth or leather, are turned back and sewn together:

searching for a lost coin in the ∼s of his trousers. 2 line where two edges, eg of boards forming a ship's deck, meet. 3 layer of coal, etc between layers of other materials, eg rock, clay. 4 line or mark like a ∼(1) (eg a wrinkle on the face). □ vt (esp in the pp, of the face) **∼ed with,** marked with (lines, scars, etc). **∼·less** adj without a ∼; made in a single piece.
seam·stress /si:mstrɪs/, **semp·stress** /sempstrɪs/ nn woman who makes a living by sewing.
seamy /si:mɪ/ adj (-ier, -iest) (chiefly fig, esp in) **the '∼ side (of life),** the less attractive aspects of life; poverty, crime, etc.
sé·ance /seɪɑːns/ n meeting for the study of spiritualistic phenomena, eg communicating with the spirits of the dead through a medium.
sear[1] /sɪə(r)/ vt [VP6A] 1 burn or scorch the surface of, esp with a heated iron; cauterize. '**∼·ing-iron** one used for cauterizing. 2 (fig) make (sb's heart, conscience, etc) hard and without feeling: His soul had been ∼ed by injustice.
sear[2], **sere** /sɪə(r)/ adj (liter) dried up; withered (esp of flowers, leaves).
search /sɜːtʃ/ vt,vi 1 [VP6A,14,15A,B,2A,3A] ∼ **(sb/sth) (for sb/sth);** ∼ **sb/sth out,** examine, look carefully at, through, or into (in order to find sth or sb): ∼ a criminal to see what he has in his pockets. He ∼ed and ∼ed through all the drawers for the missing papers. I've ∼ed my memory but can't remember that man's name. Do you spend much time ∼ing through dictionaries for words to use? ∼ **out,** look for: ∼ out an old friend. ∼ **one's heart/conscience,** examine carefully one's own beliefs and conduct. **,S∼ 'me!** (colloq) I have no idea, no knowledge (of what you are asking about)! 2 [VP6A] (liter) go deeply into; go into every part of: The cold wind ∼ed the streets. □ n [C,U] act of ∼ing: go in ∼ of a missing child; a ∼ for a missing aircraft; make a ∼ for contraband. **right of ∼,** right of the warships of a country at war to stop and examine a neutral ship (for contraband, etc). '**∼·light** n powerful light with a beam that can be turned in any direction, as used for discovering enemy movements, etc in war. '**∼·party** n number of persons looking for sb or sth that is lost. '**∼·warrant** n official authority to enter and ∼ a building (eg for stolen property). 3 (legal) investigation (eg by lawyers, from local authorities) into possible reasons (eg planned demolition) why one should not buy land or property. **∼er** n person who ∼es. **∼·ing** adj (of a look) taking in all details; (of a test, etc) thorough. **∼·ing·ly** adv
sea·son /si:zn/ n [C] 1 one of the divisions of the year according to the weather, eg spring, summer, etc; the '**dry ∼,** the '**rainy ∼.** 2 period suitable or normal for sth, or closely associated with sth: the '**football ∼;** the '**nesting ∼,** when birds build nests and lay eggs; the '**dead ∼,** the '**off ∼,** (in hotels at holiday resorts, etc) the time when there are very few guests; the '**holiday/'tourist ∼;** Christmas, the ∼ of goodwill. **the ∼'s greetings,** (as written on a Christmas card). **in/out of ∼,** (a) (of food) normally available/not available: Oysters/ Strawberries are out of ∼ now. (b) at the time when most people take/do not take their holidays: Hotel charges are lower out of ∼. **,in (∼) and 'out of ∼,** at all times. **a word in ∼,** advice at a time when it is likely to be useful. '**close/the 'open ∼,** ⇨ close[1](12), open[1](11). '**∼(-ticket)** n (a) one

that gives the owner the right to travel between places over a specified route as often as he wishes during a stated period of time: *a three-month* ~(-*ticket*). Cf US *commutation ticket.* (**b**) ticket that gives the owner the right to attend a place of amusement, etc, eg a concert hall, as often as he wishes (for the concerts, etc specified on the ticket) during a certain period. □ *vt,vi* **1** [VP6A,2A] make or become suitable for use; cause to be acclimatized, etc: *Has this wood been well* ~*ed*, dried and hardened? *The soldiers were not yet* ~*ed to the rigorous climate.* **2** [VP6A,14] ~ *(with)*, flavour (food) (with salt, pepper, etc): *mutton* ~*ed with garlic; highly* ~*ed dishes;* (fig) *conversation* ~*ed with wit.* **3** [VP6A] (liter) soften; moderate: *'when mercy* ~*s justice'*, ⇨ Mer of Ven, Act IV, Sc 1. ~·**ing** *n* [C,U] sth used to ~ food: *There's not enough* ~*ing in the sausage. Salt and pepper are* ~*ings.*

sea·son·able /'si:znəbl/ *adj* **1** (of the weather) of the kind to be expected at the time of year. **2** (of help, advice, gifts, etc) coming at the right time; opportune.

sea·sonal /'si:zənl/ *adj* dependent upon a particular season; hanging with the seasons: ~ *occupations*, eg fruit-picking; *a* ~ *trade*, eg the selling of Christmas cards. ~·**ly** /-nəlɪ/ *adv*

seat /si:t/ *n* **1** sth used or made for sitting on, eg a chair, box, bench, the floor: *There are no more chairs; you'll have to use that box for a* ~. *The back* ~ *of the car is wide enough for three people.* **keep one's** ~, remain in one's ~: *There's no danger—keep your* ~*s, please*, ie don't panic. **lose one's** ~, have one's ~ taken by someone else. ⇨ **4** below. **take a** ~, sit down: *Won't you take a* ~? **take one's** ~, sit down in one's place, eg in a hall or theatre. **take a back** ~, ⇨ back⁴(2). '~-**belt** *n* safety strap (worn as a belt) fastened to the sides of a ~ in a passenger vehicle or aircraft. ⇨ the illus at motor. **2** that part of a chair, stool, bench, etc on which one sits (contrasted with the back, legs, etc): *a' chair-*~. **3** part of the body (the buttocks) on which one sits; part of a garment covering this: *a hole in the* ~ *of one's trousers.* **4** place in which one has a right to sit: *I have four* ~*s* (ie tickets for them) *for 'Swan Lake' at Covent Garden. Mr Smith has a* ~ *in the House of Commons*, is a member. **take one's** ~, assume one's membership (in the House of Commons). **win a** ~; **lose one's** ~, win/be defeated in a Parliamentary election. **5** place where sth is, or where sth is carried on: *In the US, Washington is the* ~ *of government and New York City is the chief* ~ *of commerce. A university is a* ~ *of learning.* **6** (,**country-**)'~, large house in the country, usu the centre of a large estate: *He is rich enough to have a country-*~*/a* ~ *in the country as well as a large house in London.* **7** manner of sitting, esp on a horse: *That rider has a good* ~, rides his horse well. □ *vt* [VP6A] **1** ~ **oneself; be** ~*ed*, (formal) sit down: *Please be* ~*ed, ladies and gentlemen.* **2** have ~*s* for: *a hall that* ~*s 500. Are the* ~*ing arrangements* (= the arrangements for providing and placing ~*s) in the hall satisfactory?* '~·**ing-room** *n* [U] seats: *We have* ~*ing-room for thirty pupils in this classroom.* **3** (usu re~) repair the ~ or bottom of: ~ *a chair/an old pair of trousers.*

sec /sek/ *n* (sl abbr of) second³(2). ⇨ mo.

seca·teurs /'sekətɜ:z/ *n pl* pair of clippers used by gardeners for pruning bushes, etc.

se·cede /sɪ'si:d/ *vi* [VP2A,3A] ~ *(from)*, (of a group) withdraw (from membership of a state, federation, organization, etc).

se·cession /sɪ'seʃn/ *n* [U] seceding; [C] instance of this (as in the US when eleven Southern States withdrew from the Federal Union in 1860—61). ~·**ist** /-ʃənɪst/ *n* supporter of ~.

se·clude /sɪ'klu:d/ *vt* [VP6A,14,15A] ~ *sb/oneself (from)*, keep (a person, oneself) apart from the company of others: ~ *oneself from society; keep women* ~*d in the harem.* ~**d** *adj* (esp of a place) quiet; solitary. **se·clu·sion** /sɪ'klu:ʒn/ *n* [U] secluding or being ~*d*; ~*d* place; retirement: *live in seclusion; in the seclusion of one's own home.*

sec·ond¹ /'sekənd/ *adj* **1** (abbr **2nd**) next after the first (in place, time, order, importance, etc): *February is the* ~ *month of the year. Tom is the* ~ *son—he has an elder brother. Osaka is the* ~ *city/the* ~ *largest city in Japan.* ,~-'**best** *adj* next after the best: *my* ~*-best suit.* □ *n, adv: I won't accept/put up with* ~*-best.* **come off** ~*-best*, get the worst of sth. ,~-'**class** *adj, adv* (**a**) (of the) class next after the first: *a* ~*-class hotel;* ~*-class compartments*, in a railway carriage, etc; ~*-class mail*, sent at a cheaper rate. (**b**) class below the first in examination results: *take a* ~*-class (degree)* in law. (**c**) (regarded or treated as) inferior: ~*-class citizens.* □ *adv: go/travel* ~*-class.* ~ **floor** *n* the one above the first (in GB two floors, in US one floor, above the ground): (attrib) *a* ~*-floor apartment.* ,~-'**hand** *adj* (**a**) previously owned by someone else: ~*-hand furniture/books; a* ~*-hand bookshop*, shop for ~*-hand books.* Cf *used* cars. (**b**) (of news, knowledge) obtained from others, not based on personal observation, etc: *get news* ~*-hand.* ~ **lieutenant** *n* lowest commissioned rank in the Army. ,~-'**rate** *adj* not of the best quality; inferior: *a man with* ~*-rate brains.* Hence, ,~-'**rater** *n* person with ~-rate intelligence or abilities: *a Cabinet made up mainly of* ~*-raters.* ~·'**sight** *n* power to see future events, or events happening at a distance, as if present. Hence, ,~-'**sighted** *adj* having this power. ,~ '**teeth** *n* those which grow after a child's first teeth are out. ,~ '**wind**, ⇨ wind¹(3). ~ **to none**, surpassed by no other. **2** additional; extra: *You will need a* ~ *pair of shoes.* **3** ,S~ '**Advent/'Coming**, the return of Jesus Christ at the Last Judgement. ,~ '**ballot**, a method used in some elections by which, if the winner of the first ballot receives less than half the votes cast, a new ballot is taken, in which only he and the next candidate are voted for. ,~ '**chamber** *n* upper house in a legislature: *The House of Lords is the* ~ *chamber of Parliament in Great Britain.* ,~ '**nature** *n* acquired tendency that has become instinctive: *Habit is* ~ *nature.* ,~'**thoughts**, opinion or resolution reached after reconsideration: *On* ~ *thoughts I will accept the offer. I'm having* ~ *thoughts* (= am not so sure) *about buying that house.* **4** of the same kind as one that has gone before; subordinate: *This fellow seems to think he's a* ~ *Napoleon!* ,~ '**childhood** *n* old age when accompanied by weakening of the mental powers. ,~ '**cousin** *n* child of a first cousin of either of one's parents. **play** ,~ '**fiddle (to sb)**, be of only secondary importance (to sb else). □ *adv* in the ~ place; ~ in order or in importance: *The English swimmer came (in)* ~. ~·**ly** *adv* in the next place; furthermore.

sec·ond² /'sekənd/ *n* **1** person or thing that comes

next to the first: *the* ∼ *of May; George the S*∼, King George II. **get a** ∼, get a ∼ class in an examination. **2** another person or thing besides the person or thing previously mentioned: *You are the* ∼ *to ask me that question.* **3** (*pl*) goods below the best in quality. **4** (*pl*) second helping of food. **5** person chosen by the principal in a duel to support him; supporter of a boxer in a boxing-match.

sec·ond³ /'sekənd/ *n* **1** (indicated by the mark ") 60th part of a minute (of time or of an angle, ⇨ App 5): *winning time 1 minute, 5* ∼*s; 1° 6' 10″ = one degree, six minutes, and ten* ∼*s.* '∼**-hand** *n* extra hand in some watches and clocks recording ∼s. ⇨ also *second-hand* at **second**¹(1). **2** moment; short time: *I shall be ready in a* ∼ *or two/in a few* ∼*s.*

se·cond⁴ /'sekənd/ *vt* [VP6A] **1** support (esp in a duel or a boxing-match). **2** (of a member of a debating body) rise or speak formally in support of a motion to show that the proposer is not the only person in favour of it: *Mr Smith proposed, and Mr Green* ∼*ed, a vote of thanks to the lecturer.* ∼**er** *n* person who ∼s a proposal at a meeting.

se·cond⁵ /sɪ'kɒnd *US:* 'sekənd/ *vt* [VP6A, 15A] (official GB use, esp mil) take (sb) from his ordinary duty and give him special duty: *Captain Smith was* ∼*ed for service on the General's staff.* ∼**·ment** *n* ∼ing or being ∼ed.

sec·ond·ary /'sekəndrɪ *US:* -derɪ/ *adj* coming after, less important than, what is first or chief: ∼ *education/schools*, for children over eleven; *a* ∼ *stress*, eg on the first syllable of 'sacrificial' /ˌsækrɪ'fɪʃl/. **sec·ond·ar·ily** /-drəlɪ *US:* -derəlɪ/ *adv*

se·crecy /'siːkrəsɪ/ *n* [U] keeping of secrets; ability to keep secrets; habit of keeping secrets; state of being kept secret: *rely on sb's* ∼; *prepare sth in* ∼, secretly; *do sth with great* ∼. **swear/bind sb to** ∼, make him promise to keep sth secret.

se·cret /'siːkrɪt/ *adj* **1** (to be) kept from the knowledge or view of others; of which others have no knowledge: *a* ∼ *marriage; keep sth* ∼ *from one's family. He escaped through a* ∼ *door.* **the** ∼ '**service,** government department concerned with espionage and counter-espionage. ˌ∼ '**agent** *n* member of this department (called a 'spy' if he works for a foreign government and 'secret agent' if he works for one's own government). **2** (of places) secluded; quiet. **3** (of persons) secretive (the more usu word). □ *n* **1** [C] sth ∼. **keep a** ∼, not tell anyone else: *Can you keep a* ∼? *in the* ∼, among those who are allowed to know it: *Is your brother in the* ∼? **let sb into a/the** ∼, share it. **(be) an open** ∼, (of sth which is said to be ∼) be (in fact) widely known. **2** [C] hidden cause; explanation, way of doing or getting sth, that is not known to some or most people: *What is the* ∼ *of his success?* **3** [U] secrecy: *I was told about it in* ∼. **4** [C] mystery; sth hard to learn about or understand: *the* ∼*s of nature.* ∼**·ly** *adv*

sec·re·tariat /ˌsekrə'teərɪət/ *n* staff or office of the Secretary-General of a large organization: *get a position on the* ∼ *of UNO in New York.*

sec·re·tary /'sekrətrɪ *US:* -rəterɪ/ *n* (*pl* -ries) **1** employee in an office, who deals with correspondence, keeps records, makes arrangements and appointments for a particular member of the staff (and often called *private* ∼). **2** official who has charge of the correspondence, records, and other business affairs of a society, club or other organization: *honorary* ∼, (abbr *hon sec*) unpaid ∼ of a society,

etc which is not conducted for profit. **3** (GB) **S**∼ **of State,** minister in charge of a Government office: *the S*∼ *of State for Foreign and Commonwealth Affairs/Home Affairs/Scotland/Defence, etc.* (US) *S*∼ *of State,* head of the Foreign Affairs Department; *S*∼ *of the Treasury,* head of the Treasury Department. **Permanent S**∼, senior official in the Civil Service. ˌ**S**∼-'**General,** principal executive office of a large organisation (eg of UNO). **sec·re·tar·ial** /ˌsekrə'teərɪəl/ *adj* of (the work of) secretaries: *secretarial duties/training/ colleges.*

se·crete /sɪ'kriːt/ *vt* [VP6A] **1** produce by secretion(1). **2** put or keep in a secret place. **se·cre·tion** /sɪ'kriːʃn/ *n* **1** [U] process by which certain substances in a plant or animal body are separated (from sap, blood, etc) for use, or as waste matter; [C] substance so produced, eg *saliva, bile*. **2** act of secreting: *the secretion of stolen goods.*

se·cret·ive /'siːkrətɪv/ *adj* having the habit of keeping things secret; tending to hide one's thoughts, feelings, intentions, etc. ∼**·ly** *adv* ∼**·ness** *n*

sect /sekt/ *n* [C] group of people united by (esp religious) beliefs or opinions that differ from those more generally accepted.

sec·tarian /sek'teərɪən/ *n, adj* (member, supporter) of a sect or sects: ∼ *jealousies*, eg between one sect and another; ∼ *politics*, in which the advantage of a sect is considered more important than the public welfare. ∼**·ism** /-ɪzəm/ *n* [U] tendency to split up into sects, work in the interest of sects, etc.

sec·tion /'sekʃn/ *n* [C] **1** part cut off; slice; one of the parts into which sth may be divided: *the* ∼*s of an orange.* **2** one of a number of parts which can be put together to make a structure: *fit together the* ∼*s of a complete prefabricated building*. **3** subdivision of an organized body of persons (*the* '*Postal S*∼), or of a piece of writing (often indicated by the '∼ *mark §,* as § 21), or of a town, county, country or community: ˌ*resi'dential/'shopping* ∼*s* (*area* is more usu). **4** view or representation of sth seen as if cut straight through; thin slice of sth, eg tissue, suitable for examination under a microscope: ∼**al** /-ʃənl/ *adj* **1** made or supplied in ∼s(2): *a* ∼*al fishing-rod;* ∼*al furniture.* **2** of a ∼ of ∼s of a community, etc: ∼*al interests,* the different and often conflicting interests of various ∼s of a community; ∼*al jealousies.* ∼**·al·ism** /-ʃənəlɪzəm/ *n* [U] devotion to ∼al interests instead of to those of the community as a whole.

sec·tor /'sektə(r)/ *n* [C] **1** part of a circle lying between two straight lines drawn from the centre to the circumference. ⇨ the illus at circle. **2** one of the areas into which a battle area is divided for the purpose of controlling operations. **3** branch (of industry, etc): *the public and private* ∼*s of industry*, those parts publicly owned and those privately owned.

secu·lar /'sekjʊlə(r)/ *adj* **1** worldly or material, not religious or spiritual: ∼ *education;* ∼ *art/music; the* ∼ *power,* the State contrasted with the Church. ⇨ sacred. **2** living outside monasteries: *the* ∼ *clergy*, parish priests, etc. ∼**·ism** /-ɪzəm/ *n* [U] the view that morality and education should not be based on religion. ∼**·ist** /-ɪst/ *n* believer in, supporter of, ∼ism. ∼**·ize** /-aɪz/ *vt* [VP6A] make ∼: ∼*ize church property/courts; a* ∼*ized Sunday*, eg when professional sporting events are permitted.

se·cure /sɪ'kjʊə(r)/ *adj* **1** free from anxiety: *feel* ∼ *about one's future.* **2** certain; guaranteed: *Our vic-*

tory is ~. *He has a* ~ *position in the Civil Service.*
3 unlikely to involve risk; firm: *Don't go higher up
the cliff unless you find* ~ *footholds. Are you sure
the doors and windows are* ~? *Is that ladder* ~? **4**
~ *(from, against),* safe: *Are we* ~ *from
interruption/attack, etc?* □ *vt* **1** make fast: ~ *all
the doors and windows before leaving the house.* **2**
[VP6A,14] ~ **sth (against/from),** make certain,
firm or safe: *By strengthening the embankments
they* ~*d the village against/from floods.* **3**
[VP6A,12B,13B] succeed in getting (sth for which
there is a great demand): *Can you* ~ *me two good
seats for the concert? She has* ~*d a good job.* ~**·ly**
adv

Se·curi·cor /sɪ'kjʊərɪkɔː(r)/ *n* (P) commercial organization for the secure transportation of money
and other valuables (eg to and from banks, offices), for guarding property, etc: '~ *van,* one used
for this purpose.

se·cur·ity /sɪ'kjʊərətɪ/ *n* (*pl* -ties) **1** [C,U] (sth that
provides) safety, freedom from danger or anxiety:
children who lack the ~ *of parental care; cross the
street in* ~ *at a pedestrian crossing. Is there any* ~
from/against H-bombs? **the Se'curity Council,**
the permanent peace-keeping organ of the United
Nations (with five permanent and ten elected members). '~ **police/forces,** those policemen or soldiers whose duty it is to protect important people or
places, and to see that secret agents of foreign
powers do not operate successfully. '~ **risk,** a person who, because of his political affiliations, etc
may be a danger to the security of the State. **2**
[C,U] sth valuable, eg a life-insurance policy,
given as a pledge for the repayment of a loan or the
fulfilment of a promise or undertaking: *lend money
on* ~; *give sth as* (*a*) ~. **3** [C] document, certificate, etc showing ownership of property (esp
bonds, stocks and shares): *government securities,*
for money lent to a government.

se·dan /sɪ'dæn/ *n* **1** ~(-'chair), enclosed seat for
one person, carried on poles by two men, used in
the 17th and 18th cc. **2** saloon car for four or more
persons.

a sedan-chair

se·date /sɪ'deɪt/ *adj* (of a person, his behaviour)
not lively or agitated; composed. ~**·ly** *adv* ~**·ness**
n

se·da·tion /sɪ'deɪʃn/ *n* [U] treatment by sedatives;
condition resulting from this: *The patient is under*
~.

seda·tive /'sedətɪv/ *n, adj* (medicine, drug) tending
to calm the nerves and reduce stress: *After taking a*
~ *she was able to get to sleep. Tobacco has a* ~
effect on some people. ⇨ *tranquillizer* at tranquil.

sed·en·tary /'sedntrɪ US: -terɪ/ *adj* (of work) done
sitting down (at a desk, etc); (of persons) spending
much of their time seated: *lead a* ~ *life.*

sedge /sedʒ/ *n* [U] forms of grasslike plant grow-

ing in marshes or near wet places. **sedgy** *adj*
covered or bordered with ~.

sedi·ment /'sedɪmənt/ *n* [U] matter (eg sand, dirt,
gravel) that settles to the bottom of a liquid, eg
mud left on fields after a river has been in flood
over them. **sedi·men·tary** /ˌsedɪ'mentrɪ/ *adj* of the
nature of ~; formed from ~: ~*ary rocks,* eg slate,
sandstone, limestone.

se·di·tion /sɪ'dɪʃn/ *n* [U] words or actions intended
to make people rebel against authority, disobey the
government, etc: *incitement to* ~. **se·di·tious**
/sɪ'dɪʃəs/ *adj* of the nature of ~: *seditious
speeches/writings.*

se·duce /sɪ'djuːs US:* -'duːs/ *vt* [VP6A,14] ~ *sb
(from/into sth),* **1** persuade (sb) to do wrong;
tempt (sb) into crime or sin: ~ *a man from his
duty;* ~*d by the offer of money into betraying one's
country.* **2** by charm, knowledge of the world, etc
persuade sb less experienced to have sexual intercourse: *How many women did Don Juan* ~? *Po-
tiphar's wife tried to* ~ *young Joseph.* **se·ducer** *n*
person who ~s, esp (2).

se·duc·tion /sɪ'dʌkʃn/ *n* **1** [U] seducing or being
seduced; [C] instance of this. **2** sth very attractive
and charming; sth likely to lead a person astray (but
often with no implication of immorality): *surrender to the* ~*s of country life.* **se·duc·tive** /sɪ'dʌktɪv/
adj alluring; captivating: *seductive smiles; a seductive offer.* **se·duc·tive·ly** *adv*

sedu·lous /'sedjʊləs US:* 'sedʒʊləs/ *adj* persevering; done with perseverance: *He paid her* ~ *attention,* was persevering in his attempt to please her.
~**·ly** *adv*

see[1] /siː/ *vi,vt* (*pt* saw /sɔː/, *pp* seen /siːn/) (For
special uses with *adverbial particles* and *preps,* ⇨
11 below.) **1** [VP2A,B,C,4A] (often with *can,
could;* not usu in the progressive tenses) have or
use the power of sight: *If you shut your eyes you
can't see. It was getting dark and I couldn't see to
read. On a clear day we can see (for) miles and
miles from this hill-top. Move aside, please: I
can't see through you! He'll never be able to see
again,* He has gone blind. **seeing is believing,**
(prov) What one sees oneself is the most satisfactory evidence. **be 'seeing things,** have hallucinations, ie see things that are not there or that do not
exist, as a drunken man may: *You're seeing
things—there's nobody there!* **2**
[VP6A,8,9,10,18A,19A,24A] (often with *can,
could,* esp when an effort of perception is needed;
not in the progressive tenses) be aware of by using
the power of sight: *Can/Do you see that ship on the
horizon? I looked out but saw nothing. I saw him
put the key in the lock, turn it and open the door.
The suspected man was seen to enter the building.
I saw two men struggling for the knife. He was seen
running away from the scene of the crime. Have
you ever seen a man hanged? I saw that the box
was empty. If you watch carefully you will see how
to do it/how I do it/how it is done.* **see the back of
sb,** get rid of him; see him for the last time: *That
fellow's a nuisance; I shall be glad to see the back
of him.* **see the last of sb/sth,** have done with; see
for the last time: *I shall be glad to see the last of
this job,* get to the end of it. **see the sights,** visit
notable places, etc as a sightseer. **see stars,** have
dancing lights before the eyes, eg as the result of a
blow on the head. **see visions,** be a seer. **see
one's way (clear) to doing sth,** see how to manage to do it, feel disposed to doing it: *He didn't see*

his way to lending me the money I needed. **3** [VP6A,2A] (in the *imper*) look (at): *See, here he comes! See page 4.* **4** [VP6A,9,10,2A] (not in the progressive tenses) understand; learn by search or inquiry or reflection: *He didn't see the joke/the point of the story. We saw that the plan was unwise. Do you see what I mean? As far as I can see...,* To the best of my understanding... *I think I'll be able to help, but I'll have to see,* wait until I know more. *Go and see if/whether the postman has been yet.* **see for oneself,** find out in order to be convinced or satisfied: *If you don't believe me, go and see for yourself!* **not see the use/good/fun/ advantage etc of doing sth,** feel doubt about whether it is useful, etc to do it. **you see,** (used parenthetically) (**a**) as you no doubt know or understand. (**b**) as I must now tell you or explain to you. **seeing that,** in view of the fact that; considering. **5** [VP9] learn from the newspaper or other printed sources: *I see that the Prime Minister has been in Wales.* **6** [VP6A,22,24A] have knowledge or experience of; have (sth) presented to one's attention: *This coat of mine has seen hard wear,* ie has been worn for a long time. *He has seen a good deal in his long life. I never saw such grief. I want to see you happy/settled before I leave,* I don't want to leave until I know that you are happy/ settled. **will never see thirty/forty, etc again,** is already past that age. **have seen the day/time when...,** used to call attention to a past state of affairs: *He had seen the day when there were no cars on the roads,* was living before there were cars. **have seen better days,** have now declined, lost former prosperity, etc. **see sb damned/in hell first,** used to express an absolute refusal to do what one is asked, etc. **see service in sth; see (good) service,** ⇨ service. **7** [VP15A,6A] give an interview to; visit; receive a call from: *Can I see you on business? You ought to see a doctor about that cough. She's too ill to see anyone at present. The manager can see you for five minutes.* Note: The progressive tenses are used for this sense: *I'm seeing my solicitor this afternoon. I shall be seeing them tomorrow.* **Be'seeing you/,See you 'soon,** (colloq) used as an equivalent for 'Goodbye!'. **8** [VP18A,15A,24A] allow to; look on without protest or action: *You can't see people starve without trying to help them, can you? You wouldn't see me left here all alone?* **9** [VP9] attend to; take care; make provision: *See that the windows and doors are fastened.* **10** [VP16B,19A] call up a picture of; imagine: *He saw himself as the saviour of his country. I can't see myself allowing people to cheat me.* **11** (special uses with *adverbial particles* and *preps*):

see about sth, deal with: *He promised to see about the matter.* **see sb about sth,** consult sb, take advice (on sth): *I must see a builder about these tiles that have fallen from the roof.*

see sb across sth, guide, conduct, help sb across (a road, etc): *That man's blind—I'd better see him across the street.*

see (sb) around (sth), = see (sb) over (sth). **See you around!** (sl) Goodbye!

see sb back/home, accompany sb: *May I see you home? Tom's had too much to drink—we'd better see him back/home.*

see sb off, go to a railway station, an airport, the docks, etc with sb about to start on a journey: *I was seen off by many of my friends.* **see sb off sth,** go

with him until he is at the door, outside, etc: *I don't want this fellow here; please see him off the premises,* get rid of him.

see sb out (of sth), accompany sb until he is out of a building: *My secretary will see you out.* **see sth out,** = see sth through.

see over sth, visit and examine or inspect carefully: *see over a house that one wishes to buy or rent.* **see sb over (sth),** show him around (a place). **see (sb) round (sth),** = see (sb) over (sth).

see through sb/sth, not be deceived by: *I see through your little game,* am aware of the trick you are trying to play on me. *We all saw through him,* knew what kind of man he really was. **'see-through** *adj* (esp of clothing) that can be seen through; transparent. **see sb through (sth),** give him support, encouragement, until the end: *You'll have a difficult time, but I'll see you safely through.* **see sth through,** not give up an undertaking until the end is reached: *He said that whatever happened he would see the struggle through.*

see to sth, attend to sth: *This machine is out of order; get a mechanic to see to it. Will you see to the arrangements for the next meeting of the committee?*

see² /si:/ *n* district under a bishop; bishop's position, office, jurisdiction: *the See of Canterbury; the Holy See/the See of Rome,* the Papacy.

seed /si:d/ *n* (*pl* ~s or ~, unchanged) **1** flowering plant's unit of reproduction, from which another plant can grow: *a packet of* ~(*s*). ⇨ the illus at flower, fruit. *Sow the* ~ *in May or June. Its* ~s *are/Its* ~ *is very small.* **run/go to** ~, stop flowering as ~ is produced; (fig) become careless of one's appearance and clothes. **'~-bed** *n* bed of fine soil in which to sow ~. **'~-cake** *n* cake containing ~s, eg caraway, as a flavouring. **'~-corn** *n* grain kept for ~. **'~s-man** /-mən/ *n* (*pl* -men) dealer in ~s. **'~-time** *n* sowing season. **2** [U] (old use) offspring: *the* ~ *of Abraham,* the Hebrews. **3** cause, origin (*of* a tendency, development, etc): *sow the* ~s *of virtue in young children.* **4** [U] semen. **5** **'~-potato** *n* potato kept and allowed to sprout before being planted. **'~-pearls** *n pl* small pearls. **6** (sport) ~ed player: *England's No. 1* ~ (in a championship). ⇨ **4** below. □ *vi,vt* **1** [VP2A] (of a plant) produce ~ when full grown; let ~ fall. **2** [VP6A] sow with ~: ~ *a field with wheat; a newly-~ed lawn.* **3** [VP6A] remove ~ from: ~ed *raisins.* **4** [VP6A] (esp in tennis) separate those players well tested and known to be stronger from the weaker players (in order to have good matches later in a tournament): ~ed *players.* **~-less** *adj* having no ~: ~*less raisins.* **~-ling** /'si:dlɪŋ/ *n* young plant newly grown from a ~.

seedy /'si:dɪ/ *adj* (-ier, -iest) **1** full of seed: *as* ~ *as a dried fig.* **2** shabby-looking; in worn clothes: *a* ~ *boarding-house; a* ~-*looking person.* **3** (colloq) unwell: *feel* ~. **seed·ily** /-ɪlɪ/ *adv* **seedi-ness** *n*

seek /si:k/ *vt* (*pt,pp* sought /sɔːt/) (formal) **1** [VP2A,15A] look for; try to find: ~ *shelter from the rain;* ~ *safety in flight. The reason is not far to* ~, is found near at hand, quickly found. *Are you* ~*ing a quarrel,* trying to start one? *He is going to Canada to* ~ *his fortune,* to try to become rich. **2** [VP6A] ask for: *I will* ~ *my doctor's advice.* **3** [VP7A] try; attempt: *They sought to kill him.* **4** [VP3A] ~ *for,* try to win: *unsought-for fame,* fame which came without being looked for. *(much)* **sought after,** (much) in demand.

seem /siːm/ *vi* [VP4D,E,2A] have or give the impression or appearance of being or doing; appear to be: *Things far off ～ (to be) small. What ～s easy to some people ～s difficult to others. There ～ to be no objections to the proposal. He ～s to think so. I shall act as ～s best (= as it ～s best to me). The book ～s (to be) quite interesting. The child ～s to be asleep. It ～s that no one knew what had happened. I can't ～ (= I ～ unable) to get out of that bad habit. It would ～ that...,* (a cautious way of saying 'It ～s that...'). *'I've been out in the rain–'—'So it ～s'*, ie from your wet clothes it appears that you've been out in the rain. **～·ing** *adj* apparent but perhaps not real or genuine: *In spite of his ～ing friendship he gave me no help.* **～·ing·ly** *adv* in appearance; apparently.

seem·ly /'siːmlɪ/ *adj* (-ier, -iest) (formal) **1** (of behaviour) proper or correct (for the occasion or circumstances): *It isn't ～ to praise oneself.* **2** decent; decorous: *Strip-tease is not a ～ occupation for any girl.* **seem·li·ness** *n*

seen /siːn/ *pp* of see¹

seep /siːp/ *vi* [VP2C] (of liquids) ooze out or through; trickle: *water ～ing through the roof of the tunnel.* **～·age** /'siːpɪdʒ/ *n* [U] slow leaking through.

seer /sɪə(r)/ *n* person claiming to see into the future; prophet.

seer·sucker /'sɪəsʌkə(r)/ *n* [U] thin fabric with a striped pattern and a crinkled surface: *a ～ table-cloth.*

see·saw /'siːsɔː/ *n* [C,U] (game played on a) long plank with a person astride each end which can rise and fall alternately; up-and-down or to-and-fro motion: *play at ～.* □ *vi* play at ～; move up and down or to and fro; (fig) vacillate: *～ between two opinions.*

seethe /siːð/ *vi,vt* **1** [VP2A,3A] **～ (with),** boil, bubble over; be crowded, agitated (esp fig): *～ with anger; a country seething with discontent; streets seething with people.* **2** [VP6A,2A] (old use) cook by boiling.

seg·ment /'segmənt/ *n* [C] **1** part cut off or marked off by a line: *a ～ of a circle.* **2** division or section: *a ～ of an orange.* ⇨ the illus at fruit. □ *vt,vi* /seg'ment/ divide, become divided, into ～s. **seg·men·ta·tion** /ˌsegmən'teɪʃn/ *n* division into ～s.

seg·re·gate /'segrɪgeɪt/ *vt* [VP6A] put apart from the rest; isolate: *～ the sexes; ～ people with infectious diseases.* **seg·re·ga·tion** /ˌsegrɪ'geɪʃn/ *n* segregating or being ～d: *a policy of racial segregation.* ⇨ *integration* at integrate.

seign·ior /'seɪnjə(r)/ *US:* 'siːnjər/ *n* feudal lord; landowner in feudal times.

seine /seɪn/ *n* [C] large fishing-net which hangs like a curtain, with floats along the top edge and sinkers (weights) along the bottom edge, used to encircle fish, and usu hauled ashore. □ *vt,vi* fish, catch (fish), with a ～.

seis·mic /'saɪzmɪk/ *adj* of earthquakes. **seis·mo·graph** /'saɪzməgrɑːf *US:* -græf/ *n* instrument which records the strength, duration and distance away of earthquakes. **seis·mol·ogy** /saɪz'mɒlədʒɪ/ *n* [U] science of earthquakes. **seis·mol·ogist** /saɪz'mɒlədʒɪst/ *n*

seize /siːz/ *vt,vi* **1** [VP6A,15A] take possession of (property, etc) by law: *～ sb's goods for payment of debt.* **2** [VP6A,15A] take hold of, suddenly and

violently: *～ a thief by the collar.* **3** [VP6A,3A] *～ (on/upon),* see clearly and use: *～ (upon) an idea/a chance/an opportunity.* **4** [VP2A,C] *～ (up),* (of moving parts of machinery) become stuck or jammed, eg because of too much heat or friction.

seiz·ure /'siːʒə(r)/ *n* **1** [U] act of seizing or taking possession of by force or the authority of the law; [C] instance of this: *seizure of contraband by Customs officers.* **2** [C] sudden attack of apoplexy; heart attack.

sel·dom /'seldəm/ *adv* (usu placed with the *v*) not often; rarely: *I have ～ seen such large apples. She ～ goes out. She goes out very ～. His wife ～, if ever, has a holiday. He ～ or never gives his wife a present.*

se·lect /sɪ'lekt/ *vt* [VP6A,15A,16] choose (as being the most suitable, etc): *～ a book/a Christmas present for a child. Who has been ～ed to lead the delegation?* □ *adj* **1** carefully chosen; *～ passages from Milton.* **2** (of a school, society, etc) of or for carefully chosen persons, not for all: *a ～ club; shown to a ～ audience.* *～* **committee,** (in the House of Commons) small committee appointed for a special investigation. **se·lec·tor** /-tə(r)/ *n* one who, that which, ～s, eg a member of a committee ～ing a national sports team, etc.

se·lec·tion /sɪ'lekʃn/ *n* **1** [U] choosing: '*～* **committee,** one appointed to select, eg new members for a sports team. **natural** *～,* (Darwin's theory of) the process in nature by which certain plants and animals flourish and multiply while others are less suited to their surroundings and die out. **2** [C] collection or group of selected things or examples; number of things from which to select: *～s from 18th-century English poetry. That shop has a good ～ of denim jeans.*

se·lec·tive /sɪ'lektɪv/ *adj* having the power to select; characterized by selection. *～* **service,** (US) selection, for compulsory military service, of men with certain requirements, abilities, etc. **～·ly** *adv* **sel·ec·tiv·ity** /ˌsɪlek'tɪvətɪ/ *n* [U] (esp) power (of a radio) to receive broadcasts from one station without interference from other stations.

se·le·nium /sɪ'liːnɪəm/ *n* non-metallic element (symbol **Se**) whose power to conduct electric current increases with the intensity of the light reaching it. *～* **cell,** one containing a strip of ～, used in photo-electric devices, eg the exposure meter of a camera.

self /self/ *n* (*pl* selves /selvz/) **1** [U] person's nature, special qualities; one's own personality: *one's better/worse ～,* one's nobler nature/base nature; *one's former ～,* oneself as one formerly was; *analysis of the ～; the conscious ～.* **2** [U] one's own interests or pleasure: *She has no thought of ～,* thinks only of the interests, welfare, etc of others. **3** (comm, dated style, or joc): myself, yourself, etc: *pay to ～,* (on a cheque) pay to the person whose signature appears on it; *a room for ～ and wife. Let us drink a toast to our noble selves.*

self– /self/ *pref* short for *itself, myself, himself, oneself,* etc: *～·'taught,* taught by oneself; *～·'governing colonies,* colonies that govern themselves. **～·a'basement** *n* [U] humiliation of oneself. **～·ab'sorbed** *adj* having one's attention taken up by one's own interests, thoughts, etc; unaware of other person. **～·'acting** *adj* automatic. **～·ad'dressed** *adj* addressed to oneself: *I enclose a stamped ～·addressed envelope.* **～·'activating** *adj* (eg of an explosive device) made so as to acti-vate itself without external control. ⏢-ap'pointed *adj* chosen or declared by oneself; unsanctioned (and perhaps unqualified): *a ⏢-appointed arbiter/expert.* ⏢-as'sertion *n* [U] the putting forward of one's own claims in a determined manner; the putting forward of oneself in an effort to be noticed by everyone. ⏢-as'sertive *adj* ⏢-as'surance *n* [U] confidence in oneself. ⏢-as'sured *adj* ⏢-'centred *adj* interested chiefly in oneself and one's own affairs. ⏢-col'lected *adj* (of persons) having or showing presence of mind and composure; calm. ⏢-'coloured *adj* of the same colour all over. ⏢-com'mand *n* [U] power of controlling one's feelings. ⏢-com'placency *n* [U] state of being too easily pleased with oneself. ⏢-con'fessed *adj* on one's own confession: *a ⏢-confessed thief.* ⏢-'confidence *n* [U] belief in one's own abilities. ⏢-'confident *adj* ⏢-'conscious *adj* aware of one's own existence, thoughts and actions; (colloq) shy; embarrassed. ⏢-'consciousness *n* [U]. ⏢-con'tained *adj* (a) (of a person) not impulsive or communicative. (b) (esp of a flat) complete in itself (not sharing the kitchen, bathroom, etc with occupants of other flats) and (usu) with its own private entrance. ⏢-con'trol *n* [U] control of one's own feelings, behaviour, etc: *exercise ⏢-control; lose one's ⏢-control.* ⏢-de'fence *n* [U] defence of one's own body, property, rights, etc: *kill sb in ⏢-defence,* while defending oneself against attack; *the art of ⏢-defence,* boxing. ⏢-de'nial *n* [U] going without things one would like to have in order to help others: *practise ⏢-denial to help the children.* ⏢-de'nying *adj* ⏢-de,termi'nation *n* [U] (a) (in politics) decision, made by a people having the characteristics of a nation, whether they shall be independent or (continue to) be part of another state: *the right of all peoples to ⏢-determination.* (b) the making of one's own decisions; the guidance, by the individual, of his own conduct. ⏢-'educated *adj* educated without (much) help from schools or teachers. ⏢-ef'facing *adj* keeping oneself in the background; not trying to get attention. ⏢-em'ployed *adj* working, eg as a shopkeeper, a jobbing gardener, without an employer. ⏢-e'steem *n* [U] good opinion of oneself; (sometimes) conceit; *injure one's ⏢-esteem,* lower one's opinion of oneself. ⏢-'evident *adj* clear without proof or more evidence. ⏢-ex,ami'nation *n* [U,C] examining one's own behaviour, motives, moods, etc. ⏢-ex'planatory *adj* clear without (further) explanation. ⏢-'help *n* [U] use of one's own powers to achieve success, etc. ⏢-im'portant *adj* pompous; having too high an opinion of oneself. ⏢-im'portance *n* [U]. ⏢-im'posed *adj* (of a duty, task, etc) imposed on oneself. ⏢-in'dulgent *adj* giving way too easily to desires for one's own comfort, pleasures, etc. ⏢-in'dulgence *n* [U]. ⏢-'interest *n* [U] one's own interests and personal advantage. ⏢-'locking *adj* locking automatically when closed. ⏢-'made *adj* having succeeded by one's own efforts, esp after beginning life without money, education or influence. ⏢-o'pinionated *adj* over-certain that one's own opinions are correct; having strong opinions not firmly based. ⏢-'pity *n* [U] (exaggerated) pity for oneself. ⏢-pos'sessed *adj* calm, cool, confident. ⏢-pos'session *n* [U] coolness; composure: *lose/regain one's ⏢-possession.* ⏢-,preser'vation *n* [U] keeping oneself from harm or destruction: *the*

instinct of ⏢-preservation. ⏢-'raising *adj* (of flour) not needing the addition of baking-powder (when bread, etc is being made). ⏢-re'liant *adj* having or showing confidence in one's own powers, judgement, etc. ⏢-re'liance *n* [U] ⏢-re'spect *n* [U] feeling that one is behaving and thinking in ways that will not cause one to be ashamed of oneself: *lose all ⏢-respect.* ⏢-re'specting *adj* having ⏢-respect: *No ⏢-respecting man could agree to do such a thing.* ⏢-'righteous *adj* convinced of one's own goodness and that one is better than others. ⏢-'rule *n* = ⏢-government. ⏢-'sacrifice *n* [U,C] the giving up of one's own interests and wishes for the sake of other people. ⏢-'sacrificing *adj'* ⏢-same *adj* very same; identical: *Tom and I reached Paris on the ⏢-same day.* ⏢-'sealing *adj* (of a fuel tank, pneumatic tyre, etc) having a substance (eg soft rubber) that automatically seals a puncture made in it. ⏢-'seeker *n* person who is too much concerned with gaining advantages for himself. ⏢-'seeking *n, adj* ⏢-'service (a) (of a canteen, restaurant), one at which persons collect their own food and drink from counters and carry it to tables. (b) (of a shop) one at which customers collect what they want from counters or shelves and pay as they leave. (c) (of a garage) one at which customers fill their cars with petrol and then go and pay the charge at a counter. ⏢-'sown *adj* (of plants) coming from seed that has dropped from the plant (not sown by a gardener). ⏢-'starter *n* device (usu electric) for starting an engine. ⏢-'styled *adj* using a name, title, etc which one has given oneself and to which one has no right: *The ⏢-styled 'Dr' Smith had never been awarded a degree of any kind.* ⏢-suf'ficient *adj* (a) needing no help from others: *The country has now become ⏢-sufficient in woollen goods,* no longer has to import them. (b) over-confident. ⏢-suf'ficiency *n* [U]. ⏢-suf'ficing *adj* = ⏢-sufficient: *a ⏢-sufficing economic unit.* ⏢-sup'porting *adj* (of a person) earning enough money to keep oneself: *now that my children are ⏢-supporting;* (of a business, etc) paying its way; not needing a subsidy. ⏢-'will *n* [U] wilfulness; determined to do as one wishes and not be guided by others. ⏢-'willed *adj* obstinate; refusing advice or guidance. ⏢-'winding *adj* (of a watch) winding itself automatically (from movements of the wrist, etc).

self·ish /'selfɪʃ/ *adj* chiefly thinking of and interested in one's own needs and welfare; without care for others: *act from ⏢ motives.* ⏢·ly *adv* ⏢·ness *n*

sell /sel/ *vt,vi* (*pt,pp* sold /səʊld/) **1** [VP6A,12A,13A,15B] ⏢ *sth (to sb);* ⏢ *sb sth,* give in exchange for money: ⏢ *fruit;* ⏢ *sth by auction;* ⏢ *sth at a good price;* ⏢ *oranges at fivepence each;* ⏢ *a man into slavery. I'll* ⏢ *it to you for £5. Will you* ⏢ *me your bicycle?* ⏢ *sth off,* ⏢ (a stock of goods) cheaply. ⏢ *sth out,* (a) ⏢ part or all of one's share in a business: *He sold out his share of the business and retired.* (b) ⏢ all of one's stock of sth: *We are sold out of small sizes. The book you ask for is sold out,* There are no copies left. ⏢ (*sb*) *out,* (colloq) be treacherous; betray sb. '⏢-out *n* (a) event, eg a concert, for which all tickets are sold. (b) (colloq) betrayal. ⏢ *sb up,* ⏢ (a person's goods and property) for payment of debt: *I went bankrupt and was sold up.* ⏢ (*sb*) *short,* ⇨ short²(3). **2** [VP6A] keep stocks for sale; be a deal-

semaphore
(thin line = left arm; thick line = right arm)

A&1   B&2   C&3   D&4   E&5   F&6   G&7   H&8   I&9

J&direction   K   L   M   N   O   P   Q   R

multiple
e's=error

S   T   U&attention   V   W   X   Y   Z   numeral
sign

er in: *Do you ~ needles? This little shop ~s a wide variety of goods.* '~-ing price, price to be paid by the customer; cash price. Cf *cost* price. 3 [VP2A,C] (of goods) be sold; find buyers: *Ice-cream sells best in summer. His new novel is ~ing well. These articles ~ at 20p apiece. Your house ought to ~ for at least £20000.* 4 [VP6A] cause to be sold: *It is not the low prices but their quality which ~s our goods.* 5 (fig uses): *~ one's life dearly,* kill or wound a number of one's attackers before being killed. '~ oneself,* (a) present oneself to others in a convincing way (eg when applying for a job). (b) do sth dishonourable for money or reward. *~ the pass,* (prov) do sth that weakens one's country or side; be a traitor. 6 (usu passive) cheat; disappoint by failure to keep an agreement, etc: *I've been sold! Sold again!* I've been tricked, let down, etc! 7 **be sold on sth,** (colloq) accept it, believe that it is good, etc: *Are the workers sold on the idea of profit-sharing?* □ *n* (colloq, from 6 above) disappointment: *What a ~!* **hard/soft ~,** aggressive/ persuasive ~ing technique. **~er** *n* 1 person who ~s: *a 'book~er.* **a ~ers' market,** (comm) situation when goods are scarce and money plentiful, so that ~ers are favoured. 2 sth that is sold. **,best-'~** *n* ⇨ best ²(2).

sel·vage, sel·vedge /'selvɪdʒ/ *n* edge of cloth woven so that threads do not unravel.

selves /selvz/ *pl* of self.

sem·an·tic /sɪ'mæntɪk/ *adj* relating to meaning in language; of ~s. **se·man·tics** *n* (with *sing v*) branch of linguistics concerned with studying the meanings of words and sentences.

sema·phore /'seməfɔ:(r)/ *n* [U] 1 system for sending signals by using arms on a post or flags held in the hands, with various positions for the letters of the alphabet: *send a message by ~.* 2 mechanical device with red and green lights on mechanically moved arms, used for signalling on railways. □ *vt,vi* [VP6A,2A] send (messages) by ~(1).

sem·blance /'sembləns/ *n* [C] likeness; appearance: *put on a ~ of gaiety.*

se·men /'si:mən/ *n* [U] fertilizing sperm-bearing fluid of male animals. **se·minal** /'semɪnl/ *adj* of seed or semen or reproduction; embryonic; (fig) providing a basis for development: *seminal ideas.*

sem·es·ter /sɪ'mestə(r)/ *n* (esp in Germany and US) each of the two divisions of an academic year. Cf *term* in GB.

semi- /'semɪ/ *prep* 1 half of. '~-circle *n* half a circle. ⇨ the illus at circle. **,~-'circular** *adj* (having the shape of a) half a circle; '~-breve (US = *whole note*), the longest written musical note in common use. '~-quaver, half a quaver. ⇨ the illus at notation. '~-tone *n* half a tone in a musical scale, the smallest interval in normal Western music. 2 on one of two sides. **,~-de'tached** *adj* (of a

house) joined to another on one side only (by one wall in common). 3 little better than: **,~-bar'barian; ,~-'barbarism.** 4 (various). **~-'colon** (US = **'semi-colon**) the punctuation mark (;) used in writing and printing, between a comma and a full stop in value. ⇨ App 9. **,~-'conscious** *adj* partly conscious. **,~-'final** *n* match or round that precedes the final (eg in football matches). **~-'finalist** *n* player, team, in the ~-finals. **,~-of'ficial** *adj* (esp of announcements, etc made to newspaper reporters by officials, with the stipulation that they must not be considered as coming from an official source). **,~-'rigid** *adj* (esp of airships) having a rigid keel attached to a flexible gas-bag. **,~-'tropical** *adj* of regions near but not in the tropics. '~-vowel *n* (letter representing a) sound with a vowel quality but a consonant function (eg /w/, /j/). 5 occurring, published, etc twice in (a year, etc) (*bi-* is more usu): **,~-'annual; a ,~-'weekly.**

semi·nal /'semɪnl/ ⇨ semen.

sem·inar /'semɪnɑ:(r)/ *n* class of students, etc studying a problem and meeting for discussion with a tutor or professor.

sem·inary /'semɪnərɪ *US:* -nerɪ/ *n* (*pl* -ries) 1 Roman Catholic training college for priests. 2 (formerly used as a pretentious name for a) place of education: *a ~ for young ladies.* **semin·ar·ist** /'semɪnərɪst/ *n* man trained in a ~(1).

Sem·ite /'si:maɪt/ *n, adj* (member) of any of the group of peoples that includes the Hebrews and Arabs and formerly the Phoenicians and Assyrians. **Se·mitic** /sɪ'mɪtɪk/ *adj* of the ~s or their languages: *a Semitic people.*

semo·lina /,semə'li:nə/ *n* [U] hard grains of wheat meal, used for pasta, and in milk puddings, etc.

semp·stress /'sempstrɪs/ ⇨ seamstress.

sen·ate /'senɪt/ *n* [C] 1 (in ancient Rome) highest council of state. 2 (in modern times) Upper House (usu the smaller) of the legislative assembly in various countries, eg France, US. 3 governing council of some universities. **sena·tor** /'senətə(r)/ *n* member of ~(1,2). **sena·torial** /,senə'tɔ:rɪəl/ *adj* of a ~ or senator: *senatorial rank/powers; a senatorial district,* (US) one entitled to elect a senator.

send /send/ *vt,vi* (*pt,pp* sent) (For special uses with *adverbial particles* and *preps,* ⇨ 5 below.) 1 [VP12A,13A,6A,15A] **~ sb/sth; ~ sth to sb,** cause sb or sth to go or be carried without going oneself: *~ a telegram; ~ a message to sb/~ sb a message. The children were sent to bed. John was sent to school with an older child.* ⇨ take¹(4). 2 [VP19B] use force to cause sb/sth to move sharply or rapidly: *The earthquake sent the crockery and cutlery crashing to the ground. Mind how you go —you nearly sent me flying,* ie you nearly knocked me over. **~ sb packing/about his business,**

(colloq) dismiss him at once, without formality: *His incompetent typist was sent packing.* S~ *that fellow about his business—he's no use to anybody!* ⇨ bring. **3** [VP22,6A] cause to become: *This noise is* ~*ing me crazy. This music/This gorgeous girl really* ~*s me,* (sl) excites me intensely, rouses me to ecstasy. **4** (old use, of God, Providence): *Heaven* ~ *that he arrives safely,* may God grant this. *'S~ her victorious'* (in the British national anthem) May God grant that the Sovereign may be victorious. **5** [VP15B,2C,3A] (special use with *adverbial particles* and *preps*): **send sb away,** dismiss. ~ *away for sth,* order (goods) from a distance, to be delivered by rail, post, etc: *When we lived in the country, we had to* ~ *away for many things we needed.* **send sb down,** (esp) expel a student from a university (for misconduct, etc). ~ *sth down,* cause to fall: *The good harvest sent the prices down. The storm sent the temperature down.* **send for sb/sth (to do sth),** ask or order sb/sth to come, for sth to be delivered: ~ *for a doctor/taxi. We must* ~ *for a man to repair the TV. Please keep these things until I* ~ *for them.* **send sth forth,** (formal) produce, issue: ~ *forth leaves.* **send sth in** (for sth, eg a competition, exhibition): ~ *in one's name for a contest;* ~ *in two oil paintings;* ~ *in a report for consideration.* ~ *one's name in,* cause one's name to be made known. **send sb off,** (more usu *see sb off)* go with sb to the place from which he will start a journey: *Many of his friends went to the airport to* ~ *him off.* Hence, *'*~*-off* n: *He was given a good* ~*-off.* ~ *sth off,* dispatch: *Please see that these parcels are sent off at once.* **send sth on,** (a) ~ it in advance. (b) (of letters) readdress and repost: *I asked my wife to* ~ *all my letters on while I was away from home.* **send sth out,** (a) distribute; give out: *The sun* ~*s out light and warmth.* (b) produce: *The trees* ~ *out new leaves in spring.* **send sb/sth up,** tease; parody; show that sb/sth is ridiculous or false. Hence, *'*~*-up* n mocking imitation or parody. ~ *sth up,* cause to rise: *The heavy demand for beef sent the price up.*

send·er /'sendə(r)/ n person or thing that sends: *If lost, return to* ~ (ɒg on a letter).

se·nes·cent /sɪ'nesnt/ adj showing signs of old age: *I may be* ~, *but I'm not yet senile.* **se·nes·cence** /-sns/ n [U].

sen·eschal /'senɪʃl/ n (in the Middle Ages) important official (steward or major-domo) in the castle of a noble.

se·nile /'si:naɪl/ adj suffering from bodily or mental weakness because of old age: *caused by old age:* ~ *decay.* **sen·il·ity** /sɪ'nɪlətɪ/ n [U] weakness (of body or mind) in old age.

sen·ior /'si:nɪə(r)/ adj (opp of *junior*) **1** ~ *(to),* older in years; higher in rank, authority, etc: *He is ten years* ~ *to me. Smith is the* ~ *partner in* (= the head of) *the firm.* ~ *'citizen,* (euphem for) person over the age of retirement; old age pensioner. **2** (after a person's name, esp when a father and his son have the same name; abbr **Sen**): *John Brown* (*Sen*). ⇨ major. □ n **1** ~ person: *He is my* ~ *by ten years. The* ~*s* (= members of the ~ class) *defeated the juniors by 3—1.* **2** (US) student in his/her fourth year at high school or college. ~**ity** /ˌsi:nɪ'ɒrətɪ US: -'ɔ:r-/ n [U] condition of being

~ (in age, rank, etc): *Should promotion be through merit or through* ~*ity? Remember the precedence due to* ~*ity.*

senna /'senə/ n [U] dried leaves of the cassia plant, used as a laxative.

se·ñor /se'njɔ:(r)/ n (pl señores /se'njɔ:reɪz/) used of or to a Spanish-speaking man; Mr; sir. (**S**~ when prefixed to a name.) **se·ñora** /se'njɔ:rə/ n used of or to a Spanish-speaking woman; Mrs; Madam. **se·ñorita** /ˌsenjɔ:'ri:tə/ n used of or to an unmarried Spanish-speaking woman or girl; Miss.

sen·sa·tion /sen'seɪʃn/ n **1** [C,U] ability to feel; feeling: *lose all* ~ *in one's legs; have a* ~ *of warmth/dizziness/falling.* **2** [C,U] (instance of, sth that causes, a) quick and excited reaction: *Our popular newspapers deal largely in* ~. *The news created a great* ~. ~*al* /-ʃənl/ adj **1** causing a ~(2): *a* ~*al murder.* **2** (of newspapers, etc) presenting news in a manner designed to cause ~(2): *a* ~*al writer/newspaper.* ~**ally** /-ʃənəlɪ/ adv ~**al·ism** /-ʃənəlɪzəm/ n [U] the deliberate rousing of ~(2): *the* ~*alism of the cinema; avoid* ~*alism during an election campaign.* ~**al·ist** /-ʃənəlɪst/ n

sense /sens/ n **1** any one of the special powers of the body by which a person is conscious of things (ie sight, hearing, smell, taste and touch): *be in the enjoyment of all one's* ~*s; have a keen* ~ *of hearing.* '~-**organ** n part of the body, eg the ear or eye, concerned in producing sensation. ˌ**sixth** '~, ⇨ six. **2** (pl) normal state of mind (as when a person has the five ~s of **1** above): *in one's (right)* ~*s,* sane; *out of one's* ~*s,* insane; *frighten sb out of his* ~*s,* frighten him so that he behaves in an excited way. **bring sb to his** ~*s,* cause him to give up behaving foolishly or wildly. **come to one's** ~*s,* stop behaving like a fool or madman. **take leave of one's** ~*s,* become mad; start behaving irrationally. **3** (a/the) ~ (of), appreciation or understanding of the value or worth (of): *a* ~ *of humour; my* ~ *of duty; the moral* ~; *a* ~ *of locality/direction,* ie recognition of places, landmarks, directions, etc. **4** (a/the) ~ (of), consciousness (of): *have no* ~ *of shame; a* ~ *of one's own importance/responsibility.* **5** [U] power of judging; judgement; practical wisdom: *Haven't you* ~ *enough to come in out of the rain? There's a lot of* ~ *in what he says. There's no* ~ *in doing that,* It's pointless. *What's the* ~ *of doing that? Now you're talking* ~. ⇨ also *common* ~ at common¹(2). **6** [C] meaning: *a word with several* ~*s. In what* ~ *are you using the word? The* ~ *of the word is not clear.* **in a** ~, if the statement, etc is taken in a particular way: *What you say is true in a* ~. **make** ~, have a meaning that can be understood: *What you say doesn't make* ~*/makes no* ~, means nothing. **make** ~ **of sth,** find a meaning in it: *Can you make* ~ *of this poem?* **in the strict/ literal/figurative/full/best** (= most favourable)/ **proper, etc** ~, interpreting (the statement, etc) strictly/literally, etc. **7** [U] general feeling or opinion among a number of people: *take the* ~ *of a public meeting,* ask questions in order to learn the general sentiment or opinion. □ vt [VP6A,9] feel; be vaguely aware of; realize: *He* ~*d that his proposals were unwelcome.*

sense·less /'senslɪs/ adj **1** foolish: *a* ~ *idea. What a* ~ *fellow he is!* **2** unconscious: *fall* ~ *to the ground.* ~**·ly** adv ~**·ness** n

sen·si·bil·ity /ˌsensə'bɪlətɪ/ n (pl -ties) [U,C]

power of feeling; (esp) power or receiving or feeling delicate emotional impressions; such feeling(s): *the ~ of a poet. Her sensibilities are easily wounded.*

sen·sible /'sensəbl/ *adj* **1** having or showing good sense(5); reasonable; practical: *a ~ woman; ~ shoes for mountain climbing; ~ clothing,* functional, not merely for appearance or ornament; *~ ideas. That was ~ of you.* **2** *~ of,* (old use) aware of: *He is ~ of the danger of his position.* **3** (old use) that can be perceived by the senses(1); perceptible (the usu word now): *a ~ fall in the temperature; ~ phenomena.* **sen·sibly** /-əblɪ/ *adv* in a ~ way: *sensibly dressed for hot weather.*

sen·si·tive /'sensətɪv/ *adj* ~ **(to), 1** quickly or easily receiving impressions: *The eyes are ~ to light. A ~ skin is easily hurt by too much sunshine. A ~ nerve in a tooth can cause great pain.* **2** easily hurt in the spirit; easily offended: *Children are usually ~ to blame. An author must not be too ~ to criticism. He is very ~ about his ugly appearance.* **3** (of instruments, and institutions thought of as measuring things) able to record small changes: *~ thermometers/scales. The Stock Exchange is ~ to political disturbances.* **4** (of photographic film, paper, etc) affected by light. **~·ly** *adv* **sen·si·tiv·ity** /ˌsensə'tɪvətɪ/ *n* [U] quality, degree, of being ~: *The dentist gave her an injection to reduce the sensitivity of the nerves.* **sen·si·tize** /'sensɪtaɪz/ *vt* [VP6A] make sensitive; (photo) make (film, paper, etc) ~ to light (for use in photography).

sen·sory /'sensərɪ/ *adj* of the senses(1) or sensation: *~ organs/nerves.*

sen·sual /'senʃʊəl/ *adj* of, given up to, the pleasures of the senses; self-indulgent in regard to food and drink and sexual enjoyment: *~ enjoyment; a ~ life; ~ lips,* giving the impression that a person is ~. **~·ism** /-ɪzəm/ *n* ~ ity. **~·ist** /-ɪst/ *n* ~ person. **~·ity** /ˌsenʃʊ'ælətɪ/ *n* [U] love of, indulgence in, ~ pleasures, esp of the body.

sen·su·ous /'senʃʊəs/ *adj* affecting, noticed by, appealing to, the senses(1): *~ music/painting.* (Note that ~ is free of the sense of 'self-indulgence' in *sensual*). **~·ly** *adv* **~·ness** *n*

sent /sent/ *pt,pp* of send.

sen·tence /'sentəns/ *n* [C] **1** (statement by a judge, etc, of) punishment: *pass ~ (on sb),* declare what the punishment is to be; *under ~ of death. The ~ of the court was three years' imprisonment.* **2** (gram) the largest grammatical unit, consisting of phrases and/or clauses, used to express a statement, question, command, etc. □ *vt* [VP6A,14,17] state that (sb) is to have a certain punishment: *~ a thief to six months' imprisonment. He had been ~d to pay a fine of £10.*

sen·ten·tious /sen'tenʃəs/ *adj* **1** (old use) in the habit of saying or writing things in a short and witty manner. **2** (mod use) having, putting on, an air of wisdom; dull and moralizing: *a ~ speaker/speech.* **~·ly** *adv*

sen·ti·ent /'senʃnt/ *adj* having, able to have, feeling; experiencing sensation.

sen·ti·ment /'sentɪmənt/ *n* **1** [C] mental feeling, the total of what one thinks and feels on a subject; [U] such feelings collectively as an influence: *The ~ of pity is made up of the feeling of sympathy and of a desire to help and protect. A true statesman is animated by lofty ~s. Should reason be guided by ~? What are your ~s towards my sister,* Do you love her or is it sth less than love? **2** [U] (tendency

to be moved by) (display of) tender feeling (contrasted with reason): *There's no place for ~ in business.* **3** expression of feeling; opinions or point of view: *The ambassador explained the ~s of his government on the question.*

sen·ti·men·tal /ˌsentɪ'mentl/ *adj* **1** having to do with the feelings; emotional: *do sth for ~ reasons; have a ~ attachment to one's birthplace. The bracelet had only ~ value,* eg because it belonged to one's mother. **2** (of things) tending to arouse, expressing (often excessive, inappropriate or false) feelings: *~ music; ~ novelettes;* (of persons) having such feelings: *She's far too ~ about her cats.* **~·ly** /-təlɪ/ *adv* **~·ist** *n* person who is ~(1). **~·ity** /ˌsentɪmen'tælətɪ/ *n* [U] the quality of being weakly or foolishly ~. **~·ize** /-təlaɪz/ *vt,vi* [VP6A,2A] (cause to) become ~(2).

sen·ti·nel /'sentɪnl/ *n* = sentry (now the usu word): *stand ~ (over),* (liter) keep guard (over).

sen·try /'sentrɪ/ *n* (*pl* -ries) soldier posted to keep watch and guard. **'~-box** *n* hut or cabin for a ~. **'~-go** *n* duty of pacing up and down as a ~: *be on ~-go.*

se·pal /'sepl/ *n* (bot) one of the divisions of the calyx of a flower. ⇨ the illus at flower.

sep·ar·able /'sepərəbl/ *adj* that can be separated. **sep·ar·ably** /-əblɪ/ *adv* **sep·ar·abil·ity** /ˌseprə'bɪlətɪ/ *n*

sep·ar·ate¹ /'seprət/ *adj* **1** divided; not joined or united: *Cut it into three ~ parts.* **2** forming a unit which is distinct and which exists apart:*The children sleep in ~ beds,* Each of them has his own bed. *Mr Green and his wife are living ~* (= apart) *now. Keep these ~ from those.* □ *n* (trade use, *pl*) ~ garments which may be worn in a variety of combinations, eg jerseys, blouses and skirts. **~·ly** *adv* in a ~ manner: *Tie them up ~ly.*

sep·ar·ate² /'sepəreɪt/ *vt,vi* **1** [VP6A,14,15B] ~ **(from),** make, be, ~ from: *S~ the good ones from the bad. England is ~d from France by the Channel. ~ sth (up) into,* divide into: *The land was ~d (up) into small fields.* **2** [VP2A] (of a number of people) go in different ways: *We talked until midnight and then ~d.* **sep·ar·at·ist** /'sepərətɪst/ *n* (opp of *unionist*) member of a group which wants (esp political or ecclesiastical) separation. **sep·ar·ator** /'sepəreɪtə(r)/ *n* (esp) device for separating cream from milk.

sep·ar·ation /ˌsepə'reɪʃn/ *n* **1** [U] (state of) being separated or separate; act of separating: *S~ from his friends made him sad.* **judicial ~,** (commonly called *legal ~*) arrangement (ordered by a court of law) which does not end a marriage, but which requires married persons no longer to live together. ⇨ divorce¹(1). **2** [C] instance of, period of, separation: *after a ~ of five years; ~s of husbands and wives in time of war.*

se·pia /'si:pɪə/ *n* [U] dark brown (ink or paint): *a '~-drawing,* one done in ~.

sep·sis /'sepsɪs/ *n* [U] contamination from a festering wound.

Sep·tem·ber /sep'tembə(r)/ *n* the ninth month of the year.

sep·tet /sep'tet/ *n* (musical composition for a) group of seven voices or instruments.

sep·tic /'septɪk/ *adj* of sepsis; causing, caused by, infection (with disease germs): *~ poisoning. A dirty wound may become ~,* affected by bacteria. **~ tank,** one in which sewage is disposed of by bacterial activity.

sep·ti·cemia /ˌseptɪ'siːmɪə/ *n* blood-poisoning.

sep·tua·gen·ar·ian /ˌseptjʊədʒɪ'neərɪən *US:* -tʃʊdʒə-/ *n* person 70 to 79 years old.

Sep·tua·gint /'septjʊədʒɪnt *US:* -tʊ-/ *n* Greek version of the Old Testament and the Apocrypha made about 270 BC.

sep·ul·chre (*US* = **sep·ul·cher**) /'seplkə(r)/ *n* [C] tomb, esp one cut in rock or built of stone. **the Holy S~**, that in which Jesus Christ was laid. **whited ~** *n* hypocrite. ⇨ Matt. 23: 27. **sep·ul·chral** /sɪ'pʌlkrəl/ *adj* 1 of a ~; of burial. 2 deep and gloomy; suggestive of burial: *sepulchral looks; in a sepulchral voice.*

sep·ul·ture /'seplt∫ʊə(r)/ *n* [U] burying; putting in the tomb or grave.

se·quel /'siːkwəl/ *n* [C] 1 that which follows or arises out of (an earlier happening): *Famine has often been the ~ of war. Her action had an unfortunate ~*, later on; as things developed afterwards. 2 story, film, etc with the same character of an earlier one.

se·quence /'siːkwəns/ *n* [U] succession; [C] connected line of events, ideas, etc: *deal with events in historical ~; the ~ of events,* the order in which they occur; *a ~ of bad harvests; a ~ of clubs* (in playing cards), three or more next to each other in value, eg Ace, King, Queen, or 10, 9, 8. **~ of tenses,** (gram) principles according to which the tenses of subordinate clauses are suited to the tenses of principal clauses. **se·quent** /-ənt/ *adj* (formal) following in order or time; resulting. **se·quen·tial** /sɪ'kwenʃl/ *adj* following in order of time or place; following as a result.

se·ques·ter /sɪ'kwestə(r)/ *vt* [VP6A] 1 keep (sb) away or apart from other people; withdraw to a quiet place: *~ oneself from the world; lead a ~ed life.* 2 (legal) = sequestrate. **~ed** *adj* (of places) quiet; secluded.

se·ques·trate /sɪ'kwestreɪt/ *vt* [VP6A] 1 (legal) take temporary possession of (a debtor's property, estate, etc) until debts are paid or other claims met. 2 confiscate. **se·ques·tra·tion** /ˌsiːkwe'streɪʃn/ *n*

se·quin /'siːkwɪn/ *n* 1 tiny metal disc of silver, jet, etc sewn on to a dress, etc as an ornament. 2 (hist) gold coin once used in Venice.

se·quoia /sɪ'kwɔɪə/ *n* large evergreen coniferous tree of California (the *redwood*) of great height.

se·ra·glio /se'rɑːlɪəʊ/ *n* (*pl ~s* /-lɪəʊz/) harem; (hist) Turkish ruler's walled palace with government offices, etc.

ser·aph /'serəf/ *n* (*pl ~s* or *~im* /-fɪm/) (biblical) one of the highest order of angels. ⇨ **cherub. ~ic** /se'ræfɪk/ *adj* angelic; happy and beautiful as a ~.

sere /sɪə(r)/ = sear².

ser·en·ade /ˌserə'neɪd/ *n* (piece of) music (to be) sung or played outdoors at night. □ *vt* [VP6A] sing or play a ~ to (sb).

ser·en·dip·ity /ˌserən'dɪpətɪ/ *n* (talent for) making fortunate and unexpected discoveries by chance.

ser·ene /sɪ'riːn/ *adj* clear and calm; tranquil: *a ~ sky; a ~ look; a ~ smile.* **~·ly** *adv* **ser·en·ity** /sɪ'renətɪ/ *n* [U].

serf /sɜːf/ *n* (hist) person who was not allowed to leave the land on which he worked; (fig) person treated almost like a slave; drudge. **~·dom** /-dəm/ *n* [U] 1 social and economic system in which land was cultivated by ~s. 2 ~'s condition of life.

serge /sɜːdʒ/ *n* [U] hard-wearing woollen cloth: (attrib) *a blue ~ suit.*

ser·geant /'sɑːdʒənt/ *n* 1 non-commissioned army

officer above a corporal and below a ~-major. **,~-'major** *n* highest grade of non-commissioned army officer. 2 police-officer with rank below that of an inspector.

ser·ial /'sɪərɪəl/ *adj* 1 of, in or forming a series: *the ~ number of a banknote or cheque.* 2 (of a story, etc) appearing in parts (in a periodical, on radio, TV, etc): *An exciting new ~ story will begin in our next week's issue.* □ *n ~* play, story, etc. **~·ly** /-ɪəlɪ/ *adv* **~·ize** /-laɪz/ *vt* [VP6A] publish or produce in ~ form.

seri·atim /ˌsɪərɪ'eɪtɪm/ *adv* (Lat) point by point; taking subjects, etc after one another in order: *deal with arguments ~.*

seri·cul·ture /'serɪkʌltʃə(r)/ *n* (breeding of silkworms for) the production of silk. **seri·cul·tural** /ˌserɪ'kʌltʃərəl/ *adj* **ser·i·cul·tur·ist** /-tʃɔrɪst/ *n*

series /'sɪərɪːz/ *n* (*pl* unchanged) number of things, events, etc each of which is related in some way to the others, esp to the one before it: *a ~ of stamps/ coins,* eg of different values, but issued at one time; *a ~ of brilliant statesmen; a ~ of good harvests; a 'Television ~,* a number of programmes, each complete in itself, linked by cast, theme, etc. **in ~,** in an orderly arrangement; (of the components of an electrical circuit) with the supply of current fed directly through each component. ⇨ *in parallel* at parallel.

serio·comic /ˌsɪərɪəʊ'kɒmɪk/ *adj* serious in intention but appearing to be comic (or vice versa); having both serious and comic elements.

seri·ous /'sɪərɪəs/ *adj* 1 solemn; thoughtful; not given to pleasure-seeking: *a ~ mind/ appearance/face; look ~.* 2 important because of possible danger: *a ~ illness/mistake. The international situation looks ~.* 3 in earnest; sincere: *a ~ worker/lover. Please be ~ about your work.* **~·ly** *adv* in a ~ manner: *speak ~ly to sb; be ~ly ill.* **~·ness** *n* state of being ~: *the ~ness of the country's financial situation.* **in all ~ness,** very ~ly; not at all in a light-hearted way: *I tell you this in all ~ness.*

ser·jeant /'sɑːdʒənt/ *n* **,S~-at-'arms,** official with ceremonial duties or who keeps order in a court, legislature, etc.

ser·mon /'sɜːmən/ *n* [C] spoken or written address on a religious or moral subject, esp one given from a pulpit in a church; serious talk reproving a person for his faults, etc. **~·ize** /-aɪz/ *vt,vi* [VP6A,2A] preach or talk seriously to: *Stop ~izing,* lecturing to me on my faults, etc!

serous /'sɪərəs/ *adj* of or like serum.

ser·pent /'sɜːpənt/ *n* snake (which is the more usu word); (fig) sly, treacherous person: *the old S~,* the Devil.

ser·pen·tine /'sɜːpəntaɪn *US:* -tiːn/ *adj* twisting and curving like a snake: *the ~ course of the river.*

ser·rated /sɪ'reɪtɪd *US:* 'sereɪtɪd/ *adj* having notches on the edge like a saw; having a toothed edge: *~ leaves.*

ser·ried /'serɪd/ *adj* (of lines or ranks of persons) close together, shoulder to shoulder: *in ~ ranks.*

serum /'sɪərəm/ *n* 1 [U] watery fluid in animal bodies; thin, transparent part of blood. 2 (dose of) such a fluid taken from the blood of an animal which has been made immune to a disease, used for inoculations.

ser·vant /'sɜːvənt/ *n* 1 (**domestic**) ~, person who works in a household for wages, food and lodging: *have a large staff of ~s; engage/dismiss a ~.* 2

public ~, person who works for the public, eg a police officer, member of the Fire Service. **civil** ~, government employee, member of the civil service. **your humble** ~, form sometimes used preceding the signature in an official letter. **3** person devoted to sb or sth: *a ~ of Jesus Christ,* eg a Christian priest. **4** sth useful thqt should be treated as a means but not as an end: *Fire is a good ~ but a bad master.*

serve /sɜːv/ *vt, vi* **1** [VP6A, 15A, 2A, C] be a servant to (sb); work for (sb): *She ~d the Ambassador for ten years. He ~s as gardener and also as chauffeur.* **2** [VP6A, 15A, 2A, B, 3A] perform duties (for): *~ one's country,* eg in Parliament; *~ a year in the Army. Can I ~ you in any way,* Is there anything I can do for you? *~ on sth,* be a member of: *~ on a committee.* *~ under sb,* be in the armed forces under the command of: *My grandfather ~d under Montgomery.* *~ two masters,* (fig) be divided in one's loyalty, or between two opposite principles. **3** [VP6A, 2A, 14, 15B] *~ sth (to sb);* *~ sb (with sth);* *~ sth (out),* attend to (customers in a shop, etc); supply (with goods and services); place (food, etc) on the table for a meal; give (food, etc) to people at a meal: *There was no one in the shop to ~ me. We are well ~d with gas/electricity, etc in this town. Rations were ~d (out) to the troops. Roast pork is often ~d with apple sauce. Dinner is ~d,* is ready. *S~ the coffee in the next room, please.* **4** [VP6A, 2A, C, 4A] *~ sb (for/as sth),* be satisfactory for a need or purpose: *This box will ~ for a seat. It isn't very good but it will ~ me. That excuse will not ~ you/That will not ~ you as an excuse,* will not be accepted. *This accident ~s to show the foolishness of not being prepared.* *~ sb's needs/purpose(s),* meet his requirements: *The house will ~ his needs admirably.* **as occasion ~s,** when there is a suitable or convenient occasion or opportunity. **5** [VP15A, B] act towards, treat (sb in a certain way): *They have ~d me shamefully,* behaved very badly towards me. *I hope I shall never be ~d such a trick again,* have such a trick played on me. *It ~s him right,* His failure, misfortune, etc is deserved; he does not merit sympathy. **6** [VP6A] pass the usual or normal number of years (learning a trade, etc); go through one's term of office: *~ one's time;* *~ one's apprenticeship.* **7** [VP6A] *~ a sentence;* *~ time,* undergo a period of imprisonment. *He has ~d five years of his sentence.* **8** [VP14] *~ a summons/writ/warrant on sb;* *~ sb with a summons/writ/warrant,* (legal) deliver (a summons, etc) to the person named in it. **9** [VP6A, 2A] (tennis, etc) put the ball into play by striking it to an opponent: *~ a ball;* *~ well/badly.* **10** [VP6A] of a male animal, eg a bull, ram or boar, copulate with. **11** [VP2A, 6A] help a priest at Mass: *~ Mass.* □ *n* (tennis, etc) first stroke; turn for striking and putting the ball into play: *Whose ~ is it?* *~r n* **1** person who ~s, eg one who helps a priest at Mass or ~s at tennis. **2** tray for dishes; salver. **3** utensil used in serving out food: *'salad-~rs.* **serv·ing** *n* quantity of food (to be) served to one person: *This recipe will be enough for four servings.*

ser·vice /'sɜːvɪs/ *n* **1** [U] being a servant; position as a servant. *be in/go into/go out to ~,* be employed as a domestic servant. **2** [C] department or branch of public work, government employment, etc: *the ˌCivil 'S~; the ˌDiplo'matic S~; the fighting ~s,* the Navy, Army, Air Force; *~ men and*

women, members of the fighting ~s. **on active ~,** performing duties required by membership of the fighting ~s in time of war. **see ~ in sth,** serve (in the armed forces): *He saw ~ in both World Wars. He has seen ~ in many parts of the world.* **have seen (good) ~,** have served one well: *These old climbing-boots have seen good ~ on my numerous holidays in the Alps.* **3** [C] sth done to help or benefit another or others: *His ~s to the State have been immense. Do you need the ~s of a doctor/lawyer? do sb a ~,* help him: *She did me a great ~ by driving me to the airport.* **4** [U] benefit, use, advantage: *Can I be of ~ to you,* help you in any way? *I am at your ~,* ready to help you. *My car is at your ~,* ready for you to use when you want to. **5** [C] system or arrangement that supplies public needs, esp for communications: *a 'bus/'train ~; the 'telephone ~; a good 'postal ~.* '~ **road** *n* minor road, off a main road, giving access to houses, etc. **6** [C] form of worship and prayer to God: *three ~s every Sunday; attend morning/evening ~; 'marriage/'burial/com'munion ~.* **7** [C] complete set of plates, dishes, etc for use at table: *a 'tea/'dinner ~ of 30 pieces.* **8** [U] serving of food and drink (in hotels, etc); work done by domestic servants, hotel staff, etc: *The food is good at this hotel, but the ~ is poor. The waiter added 10 per cent to the bill for ~,* eg to a bill at a restaurant, instead of getting a tip. *Do you make a '~ charge at this hotel,* eg add 10%? '~ **flat** *n* one (usu furnished) of which the rent includes a charge for ~. **9** [U] expert help or advice given by manufacturers or their agents after the sale of an article: *send the car in for ~ every 3000 miles,* eg for greasing, checking of brakes, etc: (attrib) '~ **de·partment.** '~ **station** *n* petrol station which also offers general servicing facilities. **10** (legal) serving of a writ, summons, etc. **11** (tennis, etc) act of serving the ball; manner of doing this; person's turn to serve: *Her ~ is weak. Whose ~ is it?* □ *vt* [VP6A] maintain or repair (a car, radio, machine, etc) after sale (⇨ **9** above): *have the car ~d regularly.* **~·able** /-əbl/ *adj* **1** suited for ordinary wear and use; strong and durable: *~able clothes for schoolchildren.* **2** of use; capable of giving good service.

ser·vi·ette /ˌsɜːvɪ'et/ *n* [C] table napkin: *I prefer a linen napkin to a paper ~.*

ser·vile /'sɜːvaɪl US: -vl/ *adj* **1** (archaic) of or like a slave. **2** lacking in the spirit of independence; obsequious: *~ flattery; ~ to public opinion,* paying excessive attention to it. **~·ly** /-aɪllɪ/ *adv.* **ser·vil·ity** /sɜː'vɪlətɪ/ *n* [U] ~ behaviour or attitude.

ser·vi·tor /'sɜːvɪtə(r)/ *n* (old use) servant; attendant.

ser·vi·tude /'sɜːvɪtjuːd US: -tuːd/ *n* [U] condition of being forced to work for others and having no freedom. ⇨ **penal.**

servo- /'sɜːvəʊ/ *pref* (of machinery) using a system that automatically controls a larger system: '~-**motor,** controlling motor in such a system; *~-*as'sisted **brakes,** eg in a large car; *~-*'mechanism, general name for the controlling system.

ses·ame /'sesəmɪ/ *n* **1** plant with seeds used in various ways as food and giving an oil used in salads. **2** *Open ~!* magic words used, in one of the Arabian Nights stories, to cause a door to open; hence, easy way of securing access to what is usu inaccessible: *an open ~ to high society.*

ses·qui·ped·alian /ˌseskwɪpɪ'deɪlɪən/ *adj* (of a word) having many syllables; (fig) tedious; long-winded.

session /'seʃn/ *n* [C] **1** (meeting of a) law court, law-making body, etc; time occupied by discussions at such a meeting: *the autumn* ∼ (= sitting) *of Parliament; have a long* ∼; *go into secret* ∼. **Court of S**∼, supreme civil court of Scotland. **petty** ∼**s**, courts held by magistrates to hear certain offences without a jury. **2** (Scot and US) university term. **3** single, uninterrupted meeting for other purposes: *a re'cording* ∼, period of time during which material is recorded (on discs or tapes, eg for broadcasts).

set¹ /set/ *n* **1** [C] number of things of the same kind, that belong together because they are similar or complementary to each other: *a set of golfclubs/the novels of Dickens/Albanian stamps; a 'tea-set and 'dinner-set,* (= service (7), the more usu word); *a new set of false teeth.* **2** [C] number of persons who associate, or who have similar or identical tastes and interests: *the 'racing/'literary/ 'golfing set; the 'smart set,* those who consider themselves leaders in society; *the 'fast set,* those who gamble, etc; *the 'jet set,* rich pleasure-loving people, flying from one holiday resort to another. **3** radio or television receiving apparatus: *an ,all- 'mains set; a transistor set.* **4** (not *pl*) direction (of current, wind, etc); tendency (of opinion): *the set of the tide.* **5** (not *pl*) position or angle; posture: *I recognize him by the set of his head/shoulders.* **6** way in which a garment conforms to the shape of the body: *I don't like the set of this coat,* the way it fits (or doesn't fit). ⇨ set²(14). **7** [U] (poet) sunset: *at set of sun.* **8** (tennis, etc) group of games counting as a unit to the side that wins more than half the games in it. **9** the act of pointing at game (birds, animals) by a setter. ⇨ set²(15). **make a dead set at,** (a) combine to attack vigorously, by argument or ridicule. (b) (of a person) try to win the attention and affection of (another person to whom one is attracted). **10** [C] granite paving stone (as used for road surfaces). **11** [C] built-up scenery on the stage of a theatre, or in a studio or outdoors for a film: *everyone to be on the set by 7am.* **12** [C] young plant, cutting, bulb, etc ready to be planted: *get the onion sets in.* **13** badger's burrow. **14** setting of the hair: *shampoo and set, £4.* ⇨ set²(9).

set² /set/ *vt,vi* (-tt-, *pt,pp* set) (For special uses with *adverbial particles* and *preps,* ⇨ 19 below.) **1** [VP2A] (of the sun, moon, stars) go down below the horizon: *It will be cooler when the sun has/is set.* His star has set, (fig) The time of his power, greatness, etc is over. **2** [VP14] **set sth to sth,** move or place sth so that it is near to or touching sth else: *set a glass to one's lips/one's lips to a glass.* **set the axe to,** cut down (a tree); (fig) start to destroy (sth). **set fire/a match/(a) light to sth,** cause it to begin burning. **set pen to paper,** begin to write. **set one's seal to sth; set the seal on sth,** authorize or confirm it. **set one's shoulder to the wheel,** ⇨ shoulder. **3** [VP22,16A] cause (sb/sth) to be in, or reach, a specified state or relation. **set sb/sth at defiance/naught/nought,** ⇨ defiance; nought. **set sb at his ease,** make him feel free from embarrassment, feel comfortable, etc. **set sb/sth on his/its feet,** (a) help him to get to his feet after a fall. (b) help sb/sth to gain strength, financial stability, etc: *Foreign aid set the country on its feet after the war.* **set sth on fire,** (= set fire to sth) cause it to begin burning. *,not/ ,never ,set the 'Thames on fire,* not/never do/be

anything wonderful, extraordinary. **set sb free/at liberty,** free (prisoners, etc). **set people at loggerheads/variance,** cause them to argue and dispute. **set sth in order,** arrange, organize (one's papers, affairs, etc) properly. **,set one's ('own) 'house in order,** (fig) order one's own affairs, one's own life (before criticizing others). **set sb's mind at ease/rest; set sb's doubts/fears/mind at rest,** help him to be free from worry, free him from anxiety. **set sb's 'teeth on edge,** jar his nerves: *That noise sets my teeth on edge.* **set sb right,** (a) correct his errors; put him on the right road. (b) cause him to feel well and fit again. **set sth right/to rights,** correct, remedy (faults, grievances). **set sb on his way,** (old use) go part of the way with him (when he starts out on foot). **be all set (for sth/to do sth),** be quite ready (for the start of a race, etc). **be set on doing sth,** be determined to do it: *My Uncle Ernest is set on swimming the English Channel.* **4** [VP19B] cause sb/sth to begin to do sth: *It's time we set the machinery going,* start operations. *What has set the dog barking? The news set me thinking. My joke set everyone laughing. 'Blow, bugles, blow, set the wild echoes flying!'* **5** [VP6A,15A] (usu with an *adv* or *adv phrase;* ⇨ 19 below for combinations of *set* and adverbial particles with special meanings) put, place, lay, stand: *She set the dishes on the table. We set food and drink before the travellers. He set the stake in the ground.* **6** [VP6A,14,12C] **set (for),** put forward (as (material to be dealt with as a task, a pattern, etc): *The teacher set the children a difficult problem,* gave them one to be solved. *I have set myself a difficult task. Who will set the papers for the examination,* draw up the examination questions? *What books have been set for the Cambridge Certificate next year,* What books are to be studied? Hence, **,set 'book,** book on which examinations are to be given. **set (sb) a (good) example,** offer a good standard for others to follow: *You should set the younger boys a good example.* **set the fashion,** start a fashion to be copied by others. **set the pace,** fix it by leading (in a race, etc); (fig) fix a standard for an activity, style of living, etc: *The Joneses set the pace and their neighbours try to keep up with them.* **set the stroke,** (rowing) fix the number of strokes per minute. **7** [VP17A] **set (sb/oneself) to do sth,** give sth (to sb/oneself) as a task: *He set the farm labourer to chop wood. I set myself to study the problem. I've set myself* (= have resolved) *to finish the job by the end of May.* **,Set a ,thief to 'catch a thief,** (prov) Use illegal methods to uncover illegal actions. **8** [VP6A,15A] (with various grammatical objects, the *nn* in alphabetical order) **set one's cap at sb,** ⇨ cap. **set eyes on sb,** see him: *I hope I never set eyes on that fellow again.* **set one's face against sth,** steadfastly oppose sth. **set one's heart/hopes/mind on sth,** be filled with strong desire for, determination to get; direct one's hopes towards: *The boy has set his heart on becoming an engineer.* **set a price on sth,** declare what it will be sold for. **set a price on sb's head,** offer a specified reward to anyone who kills him. **set much/great/little/no store by sth,** value sth highly/little/not at all. **9** [VP6A,15A] put in a certain state or condition for a particular purpose: *set a (broken) bone,* bring the parts together so that they may unite. **set a butterfly,** arrange it with wings outspread (in a glass case) as a specimen. **set a clock/watch,** put the hands to the correct time (or, for an alarm clock, to sound at the desired time): *set one's watch by the time-signal on the radio.* **set eggs,** place them (to be hatched) under a hen, etc in a nest. **set one's hair,** arrange it (when damp) so that when it is dry, it is in the required style. *She's having her hair set for this evening's party.* **set a hen,** place it over eggs (to hatch them). **set a saw,** sharpen the teeth with a file and put them (alternately) at the right outward angle. **set the scene,** describe a place and the people taking part in an activity, eg in a play, novel or sporting event: *Our commentator will now set the scene in the stadium. The scene is now set for the tragedy,* Events leading up to the tragedy have taken place and the tragedy will follow. *The scene is now set for a direct confrontation between the major powers.* **set sail (from/to/for),** begin a voyage. **set the table,** lay it ready with plates, cutlery, etc: *She set the table for five people.* **set one's teeth,** clench them; (fig) become determined and inflexible (against some course of action, etc). **set a trap (for sth/sb), (a)** adjust one to catch a mouse, rat, etc. **(b)** do sth to discover a dishonest person, etc: *set a trap to catch a thief/for a boy who cheats.* **set (up) type,** arrange it ready for printing sth. **10** [VP6A,14] **set sth in sth; set sth with sth,** put, fix, one thing firmly in another: *set a diamond in gold; a crown set with jewels; a gold ring set with gems; a heavy lathe set* (= embedded) *in concrete; glass panes set in lead,* ie strips of lead, as in old lattice windows. *The tops of the walls were set with broken glass,* ie to discourage persons from climbing over them. *The sky seemed to be set with diamonds,* the stars looked like diamonds. **11** [VP2A,C] (of tides, currents) move or flow along; gather force; (fig) show or feel a tendency: *A strong current sets through the channel. The current sets in towards the shore. The wind sets from the west. The tide has set in his favour,* (fig) He is winning public support and approval. *Public opinion is setting against the proposal.* **12** [VP6A,14] **set sth (to sth),** provide with music, usu composed for the purpose: *set a poem to music; set new words to an old tune.* **13** [VP6A,2A] (of plants, fruit trees, their blossom) form or develop fruit as the result of fertilization: *The apple-blossom hasn't/The apples haven't set well this year. This liquid, if sprayed on the flowers, helps to set the tomatoes.* **14** [VP2C] (of a garment) adapt itself to the shape of the body; sit (which is the more usu word): *A well-tailored jacket ought to set well. That dress sets rather badly.* **15** [VP2A,C] (of a sporting dog) stop and stand with the muzzle pointing, to indicate presence of game; (of dancers) take positions facing partners: *set to partners.* **16** [VP6A,2A] (cause to) become firm, solid, rigid (from a liquid or soft state): *Some kinds of concrete set more quickly than others. The jelly is/has not set yet. Heat sets eggs and cold sets jellies.* **17** [VP6A,2A] (rare) (cause to) develop into definite lines and shapes, become mature: *His body has/is set,* is fully developed. *Too much exercise may set a boy's muscles prematurely. His character has/is set,* is no longer pliant, is already formed. **18** (*pp*) **(a)** unmoving, fixed: *a set smile/look/purpose.* **(b)** pre-arranged; *at a set time; set lunches £2.50,* (eg at a restaurant, there being no choice of dishes); *a set piece,* a large and elaborate firework set on a platform or scaffold; (attrib) *a set-piece attack,* ie carefully planned in advance. **(c)** unchanging: *set*

in one's ways, having fixed habits; *a man of set opinions,* unable or unwilling to change them. **(d)** regular; fixed or planned in advance: *set phrases; a set speech; set forms of prayers.* **(e) set fair,** (of the weather) fine and with no signs of change. **19** [VP15A,2C,3A] (special uses with *adverbial particles* and *preps*):

set about sth, start; take steps towards: *I must set about my packing,* begin to pack my clothes, etc. *I don't know how to set about this job,* how to make a start on it. **set about sb,** (colloq) attack: *They set about each other fiercely,* began to exchange blows. **set sth about,** spread (rumours, etc): *Who set (put* is more usu) *it about that he is resigning?*

set sb against sb, cause him to compete with, struggle against, sb. **set one thing against another,** regard it as compensating for, balancing, another.

set sth apart/aside, (a) put on one side for future use. **(b)** disregard: *Let's set aside my personal feelings.* **(c)** (legal) reject: *set a claim aside.*

set sth back, (a) move back: *set back the hands of a clock. The horse set back its ears.* **(b)** be placed away, at a distance, from: *The house is well set back from the road.* **set sb/sth back, (a)** hinder or reverse the progress of: *All our efforts at reform have been set back.* Hence, **'set-back** *n* (*pl* set-backs) check to progress or development: *meet with many set-backs; have a set-back in one's career/business.* **(b)** (sl) cost: *That haircut set me back £5.*

set sth down, (a) put down: *set down a load.* **(b)** write down on paper. **set sb down,** (of a vehicle, its driver) allow (a passenger) to get down or out: *The bus stopped to set down an old lady. I'll set you down at the corner of your street.* **set sb/oneself down as,** (*put* is more usu) explain or describe as: *How should I set myself down in the hotel register—as a journalist or as an author? We must set him down as either a criminal or a fool.* **set sth down to sth,** (*put* is more usu), attribute sth to, say that sth is the result of: *set one's success down to hard work.*

set forth, begin a journey (*set out* is more usu). **set sth forth,** (formal) make known; declare: *set forth one's political views. Is this condition set forth* (= included) *in the agreement?*

set in, (a) start and seem likely to continue: *The rainy season has set in. It set in to rain. Go to your dentist before decay of the teeth sets in.* **(b)** (of tides, winds; ⇨ 11 above) begin to flow: *The tide is setting in,* flowing towards the shore.

set off, start (a journey, race, etc): *They've set off on a journey round the world.* **set sth off, (a)** explode a mine, firework, etc. **(b)** make more striking by comparison: *Use blue eye-shadow to set off your green eyes. This gold frame sets off the painting very well.* **(c)** balance; compensate: *set off gains against losses.* **(d)** mark off: *set off a clause by a comma.* **set sb off (doing sth),** cause to start (doing sth): *Don't set him off talking politics or he'll go on all evening.*

,set 'on, (formal) go forward; advance to the attack. **'set on/upon sb,** attack: *She was set on by a savage dog.* **be'set on/upon doing sth,** be determined to do it: *My daughter is set on becoming an airline pilot.*

set out, begin (a journey, venture): *They set out at dawn. He set out with the best intentions.* **set out to do sth,** have sth as an aim or intention: *He set* *out to break the record for the Channel swim/to make his first million in five years.* **set sth out,** (a) declare; make known: *set out one's reasons (for sth).* (b) show; put on display: *The women set out their chickens and ducks on the market stalls. He sets out his ideas clearly in this essay.* (c) plant out: *Set the young plants out one foot apart.*

set sb over sb, put sb in control/command of sb.

,set 'to, (a) begin doing sth: *The engineers set to and repaired the bridge. They were all hungry and at once set to,* began eating. (b) (usu with *pl* subject) begin to fight, struggle, quarrel, etc. Hence, **,set-'to** *n* struggle; quarrel.

set sth up, (a) place sth in position: *set up a post/ statue/memorial.* (b) establish (an institution, business, argument, etc): *set up a tribunal. What defence did his counsel set up in the trial?* Hence, **'set-up** *n* (colloq) arrangement of an organization, group of people, etc: *What's the set-up here? How's your business, etc organized?* (c) cause: *I wonder what has set up this irritation in my throat/this rash on my face?* (d) utter loudly: *set up a yell.* (e) make ready for printing: *set up type/a book.* **set sb up,** restore after illness: *Her holiday in the country has set her up again.* **set (oneself) up as,** (a) go into business as: *He has set (himself) up as a bookseller.* (b) have pretensions to being: *I've never set myself up as a scholar.* **set sb up (as sth),** get sb started or established, eg by supplying capital: *set up one's son in business. His father set him up as a bookseller.* **set up house,** start living in one, eg after being in lodgings. **set up house with sb/together,** (of two persons) begin living together. **be well set up,** (a) have a body well developed by exercises, etc: *He has a well set up figure. What a well set up young woman!* (b) be well provided with: *be well set up with clothes/reading matter.*

set-square /'set skweə(r)/ *n* [C] triangular plate of wood, plastic, metal, etc with angles of 90°, 60° and 30° (or 90°, 45°, 45°), used for drawing lines at these angles.

sett /set/ *n* = set¹(10).

set·tee /se'ti:/ *n* [C] long, soft seat like a sofa, with sides and back, for two or more persons.

set·ter /'setə(r)/ *n* **1** (breeds of) long-haired dog trained to stand motionless on scenting game. ⇨ set¹(9). **2** (in compounds) person who, thing which, sets (various meanings): *a 'bone-~; a 'type-~.*

set·ting /'setɪŋ/ *n* [C] **1** framework in which sth is fixed or fastened: *the ~ of a jewel;* (by extension) surroundings, environment: *a beautiful natural ~ for a play,* eg the grounds of an old castle. **2** music composed for a poem, etc. ⇨ set²(12). **3** descent (of the sun, moon, etc) below the horizon.

settle¹ /'setl/ *n* [C] long, wooden seat with a high back and arms, the seat often being the lid of a chest.

settle² /'setl/ *vt, vi* (For special uses with *adverbial particles* and *preps,* ⇨ 10 below.) **1** [VP2C,6A] make one's home in (permanently, as a colonist); establish colonists in: *The Dutch ~d in South Africa. By whom was Canada ~d?* **2** [VP2C] make one's home in; live in (not as a colonist): *~ in London/in Canada/in the country.* **3** [VP2A,3A] *~ (on sth),* come to rest (on); stay for some time (on): *The bird ~d on a branch. The dust ~d on everything. The cold has ~d on my chest.* **4** [VP6A,15A] cause (sb) to become used to, or com-

fortable in, a new position or posture (after a period of restless movement or activity: *The nurse ~d her patient for the night,* made him/her comfortable, gave him/her medicine, etc. *Then the nurse ~d herself in an armchair in the next room.* **5** [VP6A,2C] make or become calm, untroubled, composed: *The thunderstorm will perhaps ~ the weather. We want a period of ~d weather for the harvest. Wait until the excitement has ~d. Things are settling into shape,* becoming orderly, normal. *Have a brandy—it will ~ your nerves.* **6** [VP6A,7,8,10] make an agreement about; decide; determine: *That ~s the matter. It's time you ~d the dispute/argument. Nothing is ~d yet. You ought to ~ your affairs* (eg by making your Will) *before you go into hospital for that lung operation. The lawsuit was ~d amicably/out of court/ between the parties,* a decision was reached by the parties themselves (and their lawyers) instead of by the court. *What have you ~d to do about it? Have they ~d where to go/where they'll spend their holiday.* **7** [VP6A,2A,C] pay: *~ a bill. Will you ~ for all of us,* pay what is owing for all of us, eg at a restaurant? **8** [VP6A,2A] (of dust, etc in the air, particles of solid substances in a liquid, etc) (cause to) sink; (of a liquid) become clear as solid particles sink: *We need a shower to ~ the dust. Stir the coffee to ~ the grounds. The grounds settled and the coffee was clear.* **9** [VP2A,C] (of the ground, the foundation of a building, etc) sink gradually to a lower level: *The road-bed ~d. The ship was settling down by the stern,* tending to sink. **10** [VP2C,14,15B,2A] (special uses with *adverbial particles* and *preps*):

settle down, sit or lie comfortably (after a period of movement or activity): *He ~d down in his armchair to read a new novel. ~ (sb) down,* make or become calm and peaceful: *Wait until the children have ~d down before you start your lesson. The chairman tried to ~ the audience down,* get them to stop talking, etc. *~ (down) to sth,* overcome distractions, etc and give one's attention to one's work: *It's terrible—I can't ~ (down) to anything today,* am too restless to do my work, etc. *~ down (to sth),* become established (in a new way of life, new work, etc): *~ down well in a new career/job. ~ down to married life; marry and ~ down,* live the regular routine life said to be typical of married persons.

settle for sth, accept, although not altogether satisfactory: *I had hoped to get £1000 for my old car but had to ~ for £650.*

settle (sb) in, (help sb to) move into a new house, flat, job, etc and put things in order: *We haven't ~d in yet. You must come and see our new house when we're/we've ~d in.*

settle sth on/upon sb, (legal) give sb (property, etc) for use during his/her lifetime: *~ part of one's estate on one's son; ~ an annuity on a nephew.* ⇨ settlement(2). *~ on/upon sth,* decide to take; choose: *Which of the recordings have you ~d on? We must ~ on a place to meet.*

settle (up) (with sb), pay what one owes to sb: *I shall ~ (up) with you at the end of the month. I've already settled up with the waiter,* paid for our meal. *Now to ~ with you!* Now I'll deal with you (according to context, pay, fight with you, get rid of you, etc). **,have an ac'count to ~ with sb,** (colloq) have some unpleasant business, a quarrel, etc to discuss.

settled /'setld/ adj **1** fixed; unchanging; permanent: ~ *weather; a man of* ~ *convictions;* ~ *melancholy.* **2** (written on a paid bill) payment is acknowledged.

settle·ment /'setlmənt/ n **1** [U] the act of settling (a dispute, debt, etc); [C] instance of this: *The terms of* ~ *seem just. We hope for a lasting* ~ *of all these troubles. The strikers have reached a* ~ *with the employers. I enclose a cheque in* ~ *of your account.* **2** [C] (statement of) property settled(10) on sb: *a*'*marriage* ~, one made by a man in favour of his wife. **3** [U] process of settling people in a colony; [C] new colony; group of colonists: *empty lands awaiting* ~; *Dutch and English* ~s *in North America; penal* ~s *in Australia.*

set·tler /'setlə(r)/ n colonist; person who has come to live in a newly developing country: *Welsh* ~s *in Argentina.*

seven /'sevn/ n, adj the number 7. ⇨ App 4. '~**fold** /-fəʊld/ adj, adv ~ times as much or as many; ~ times as great. **sev·enth** /'sevnθ/ n, adj *in the/one's* ~**th heaven,** extremely happy. **the** **S**~**th Day,** Saturday, the Sabbath of the Jews. **sev·enth·ly** adv in the 7th place. ~**·teen** /ˌsevn'tiːn/ n, adj the number 17. ~**·teenth** /ˌsevn'tiːnθ/ n, adj 17th; next after 16, one of ~teen parts. ~**·ty** /'sevntɪ/ n, adj the number 70. **the** ~**ties** n pl 70-79. ~**·ti·eth** /'sevntɪəθ/ n, adj

sever /'sevə(r)/ vt, vi **1** [VP6A,15A] cut: ~ *a rope;* ~ *the head of a sheep from the body;* (fig) break off: ~ *one's connections with sb.* **2** [VP2A] break: *The rope* ~*ed under the strain.* ~**·ance** /'sevərəns/ n [U] severing or being ~ed: *the severance of diplomatic relations/of communications.*

sev·eral /'sevrəl/ adj **1** three or more; some but not many: *You will need* ~ *more. I've read it* ~ *times.* **2** (formal) (with *pl nn* only) separate; individual: *They went their* ~ *ways.* Each went his own way. □ pron a few; some: *S*~ *of us decided to walk home.* ~**ly** /'sevrəlɪ/ adv separately.

se·vere /sɪ'vɪə(r)/ adj **1** stern, strict: ~ *looks; be* ~ *with one's children; be too* ~ *on a pupil.* **2** (of the weather, attacks of disease, etc) rigorous; violent: *a* ~ *storm;* ~ *pain; a* ~ *attack of toothache.* **3** making great demands on skill, ability, patience and other qualities: ~ *competition. The pace was too* ~ *to be kept up for long.* **4** (of style, etc) simple; without ornament. ~**·ly** adv **se·ver·ity** /sɪ'verətɪ/ n (pl -ties) **1** [U] quality of being ~: *punish sb with severity; acts of severity; the severity* (= extreme cold) *of the winter in Canada.* **2** (pl) ~ treatment or experiences: *the severities of the winter campaign.*

sew /səʊ/ vt, vi (pt sewed, pp sewn /səʊn/ or sewed)`[VP6A,15B,2A,B,C] work with a needle and thread; fasten with stitches; make (a garment) by stitching: *sew a button on; sew a dress. The garment is* ,*hand-*'*sewn/sewn by hand. She has been sewing all evening.* **sew sth up,** (a) join (at the edges) with stitches: *The corpse was sewn up in a sack and thrown into the river.* (b) (colloq) arrange; complete: *All the details of the project are sewn up. The deal is sewn up.* **sewer** /'səʊə(r)/ n **sew·ing** n [U] work (clothes, etc) being sewn. '**sewing-machine** n machine for sewing.

sew·age /'sjuːɪdʒ US: suː-/ n [U] foul liquid material, waste organic matter, etc carried off in sewers; the disposal of ~. '~**-farm/works** nn place where ~ is treated and disposed of.

sewer¹ /'sjuːə(r) US: suː-/ n [C] underground chan-

nel (pipeline, or construction of brick, concrete, etc) to carry off sewage and rainwater to centres (sewage-farms) for treatment, or to a natural waterway for disposal. '~**-gas** n bad-smelling gas formed in ~s. '~**-rat** n brown rat commonly found in ~s. ~**·age** /-ɪdʒ/ n system of ~s; drains.

sewer² /'səʊə(r)/ n ⇨ sew.

sewn /səʊn/ pp of sew.

sex /seks/ n **1** being male or female: *What is its sex? Help them all, without distinction of race, age or sex.* **2** males or females as a group. **3** [U] differences between males and females; consciousness of these differences: '*sex antagonisms.* **4** [U] the activities surrounding, centring on and leading to coitus: *a film/novel with lots of sex in it; the* '*sex instinct;* '*sex appeal,* sexual attractiveness. **5** [U] sexual intercourse: *have sex with sb.* □ vt [VP6A] determine the sex of. **sexed** part adj having a (specified) sexual nature: *highly/weakly* ~*ed.* **sex·less** adj neither male nor female; displaying neither masculine nor feminine characteristics. '**sex-starved** adj (colloq) deprived of sexual gratification. **sexy** adj (-ier, -iest) (colloq) of or about sex; sexually attractive.

sexa·gen·ar·ian /ˌseksədʒɪ'neərɪən/ n, adj (person) between 59 and 70 years of age.

sex·ism /'seksɪzəm/ n [U] unfair or unreasonable discrimination between the sexes; unreasonable maintaining of traditional sexual roles (eg that men are strong and women are weak). **sex·ist** /'seksɪst/ adj of ~: *sexist attitudes; sexist words,* eg *baby, bird, chick, doll,* used to mean a woman. □ n person who displays or approves of ~. ⇨ *male chauvinist* at chauvinism.

using a sextant

sex·tant /'sekstənt/ n instrument used for measuring the altitude of the sun, etc (in order to determine a ship's position, etc).

sex·tet, sex·tette /seks'tet/ n [C] (piece of music for) six voices, instruments or players in combination.

sex·ton /'sekstən/ n man who takes care of a church buildings, digs graves in the churchyard, rings the church bell, etc.

sex·ual /'seksjʊəl/ adj of sex or the sexes: ~ *inter-*

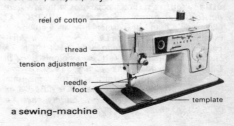

reel of cotton

thread

tension adjustment

needle
foot

template

a sewing-machine

course = coitus. ~**ity** /ˌsekʃʊˈælətɪ/ *n* [U] ~ nature or characteristics.

sh (also **ssh, shh**) /ʃ/ *int* be quiet! be silent!

shabby /ˈʃæbɪ/ *adj* (-ier, -iest) **1** in bad repair or condition; much worn; poorly dressed: *wearing a* ~ *overcoat. You look rather* ~ *in those clothes.* ˌ~-**gen'teel** *adj* having evidence of former gentility but now ~; trying to keep up appearances. **2** (of behaviour) mean; unfair: *a* ~ *excuse; play a* ~ *trick on sb.* **shab·bily** /ˈʃæbɪlɪ/ *adv* **shab·bi·ness** *n*

shack /ʃæk/ *n* [C] small, roughly built shed, hut or house (usu of wood). □ *vi* [VP2C] ~ **up (with sb/ together),** (sl) live together.

shackle /ˈʃækl/ *n* [C] one of a pair of iron rings joined by a chain for fastening a prisoner's wrists or ankles; (*pl*) fetters; (fig) sth that prevents freedom of action: *the* ~*s of convention.* □ *vt* [VP6A] put ~s on; prevent from acting freely.

shad /ʃæd/ *n* (*pl* unchanged) large edible fish of the N Atlantic coast of N America.

shad·dock /ˈʃædək/ *n* (tropical tree with a) large edible fruit related to the grapefruit; pomelo.

shade /ʃeɪd/ *n* **1** [U] (with *adj, v* and *indef art*) comparative darkness caused by the cutting off of direct rays of light; (fig) comparative obscurity: *a temperature of 35°C in the* ~*. Keep in the* ~*; it's cooler. The trees give a pleasant* ~*.* **put sb/sth in/into the** ~*,* cause to appear small, unimportant, etc, by contrast: *You are so clever and brilliant that my poor efforts are put into the* ~*.* '~-**tree** *n* (esp US) tree planted to give ~. **2** [U] darker part(s) of a picture, etc; reproduction of the darker part of a picture: *There is not enough light and* ~ *in your drawing.* **3** [C] degree or depth of colour: *dress materials in several* ~*s of blue.* **4** [C] degree of difference: *a word with many* ~*s of meaning. She is a* ~ *better today.* **5** sth that shuts out light or lessens its brilliance: *an 'eye*~*; a 'lamp*~*; a 'window*~*.* ⟹ **blind³**. (*pl*) (US colloq) sunglasses. **6** (*pl;* liter) darkness: *the* ~*s of evening.* **7** [C] unreal or unsubstantial thing; soul after death. **the** ~*s,* the abode of spirits; the Greek underworld. □ *vt,vi* **1** [VP6A,15A] keep direct rays of light from: *He* ~*d his eyes with his hands.* **2** [VP6A] screen (a light, lamp, etc) to reduce brightness. **3** [VP6A] darken with parallel pencil lines, etc (parts of a drawing, etc), to give the appearance of light and ~. **4** [VP2C] change by degrees: *scarlet shading off into pink; a colour that* ~*s from blue into green.* **shad·ing** *n* **1** [U] use of black, etc to give light and shade to a drawing. **2** [C] slight difference or variation.

shadow /ˈʃædəʊ/ *n* **1** [C] area of shade, dark shape, thrown on the ground, a wall, floor, etc by sth which cuts off the direct rays of light: *The earth's* ~ *sometimes falls on the moon.* **be afraid of one's own** ~*,* be very timid. *Coming events cast their* ~*s before them,* give warning of their coming. **2** [U] area of shade of indefinite shape or extent: *Her face was in deep* ~*.* **3** [C] sth unsubstantial or unreal: *catch at* ~*s, run after a* ~*,* try to get hold of sth unreal. *He is only the* ~ *of his former self,* is very thin and weak. *worn to a* ~*,* (of a person) weakened, exhausted. '~-**boxing,** sparring against an imaginary opponent (for practice). **4** (*pl*) partial darkness: *the* ~*s of evening.* **5** [C] dark patch or area: *have* ~*s under/round the eyes,* such areas thought to be caused by lack of sleep, illness, etc. **6** (*sing* only) slightest trace: *without/ beyond a* ~ *of (a) doubt.* **7** person's constant

attendant or companion. ~ **cabinet,** (GB) group formed from the leaders of the Parliamentary Opposition, i e those who might form a new cabinet if there is a change of government after a general election. □ *vt* [VP6A] **1** darken; overspread with ~. **2** keep a secret watch on; follow closely and watch all the movements of: *The suspected spy was* ~*ed by detectives.* **shad·owy** *adj* **1** having ~ of shade; shady(1): *cool,* ~*y woods.* **2** like a ~; indistinct: *a* ~*y outline.*

shady /ˈʃeɪdɪ/ *adj* (-ier, -iest) **1** giving shade from sunlight; situated in shade: *the* ~ *side of the street.* **2** of doubtful honesty: *a* ~ *transaction/financier; a* ~-*looking customer,* (colloq) person who appears to be a rogue. *Politics has its* ~ *side.*

shaft /ʃɑːft US: ʃæft/ *n* [C] **1** (long, slender stem of an) arrow or spear; (fig) ~*s of envy/ridicule,* expressions of envy, etc. **2** long handle of an axe or other tool. **3** one of the pair of bars (wooden poles) between which a horse is harnessed to pull a cart, etc. **4** main part of a column (between the base and the capital). ⟹ the illus at **column**. **5** long, narrow space, usu vertical, eg for descending into a coalmine, for a lift in a building, or for ventilation. **6** bar or rod joining parts of a machine, or transmitting power. **7** ray (of light); bolt (of lightning).

shag /ʃæg/ *n* [U] coarse kind of cut tobacco.

shagged /ʃægd/ *pred adj* ~ **(out),** (GB sl) very tired.

shaggy /ˈʃægɪ/ *adj* (-ier, -iest) **1** (of hair) rough, coarse and untidy. **2** covered with rough, coarse hair: ~ *eyebrows; a* ~ *dog.* ~-**'dog story,** long joke that is funny because it is so boring and its punch-line is so weak. **shag·gily** /-ɪlɪ/ *adv.* **shag·gi·ness** *n.*

shah /ʃɑː/ *n* (title of a) former ruler of Iran.

shake¹ /ʃeɪk/ *vt,vi* (*pt* **shook** /ʃʊk/, *pp* **shaken** /ˈʃeɪkən/) **1** [VP6A,15A,15B,2A,C] (cause to) move from side to side, up and down etc: ~ *a rug;* ~ *a man by the shoulder;* ~ *the dice* (in a box, etc before throwing them on to a table): ~ *one's head* (*at sb*), to indicate 'No', or doubt, disapproval, etc; ~ *one's finger at sb,* to indicate disapproval or as a warning; ~ *one's fist at sb,* to show defiance. *His sides were shaking with laughter. He was shaking with cold. He was shaking in his shoes,* trembling with fear. *The earth shook under us,* eg in an earthquake. ~ **hands (with sb),** ⟹ hand¹(1). **2** [VP6A] shock; trouble; weaken: ~ *sb's faith/ courage. They were badly* ~*n by the news. The firm's credit has been badly* ~*n.* **3** [VP2A,C] (of sb's voice) tremble; become weak or faltering: *Her voice shook with emotion.* **shak·ing** *n* = shake: *give sth a good shaking,* shake it well; *get a shaking,* be ~*n.* **shaker** *n* one who, that which, ~*s;* container in which or from which sth is ~*n: a* 'cocktail~*r; a 'flour~r.* **4** [VP14,15B,C] (special uses with *adverbial particles* and *preps*).

shake down, (colloq) **(a)** get into harmony, become adjusted to new conditions: *The new staff are shaking down well.* **(b)** lie down for sleep: ~ *down on the beach/floor.* ~ **sb down,** (US) get money from him by threats, violence, etc. ~ **sb/sth down,** (US) search him/it thoroughly. ~ **sth down,** give it a ~-down (d). '~-**down** *n* (colloq) **(a)** temporary or makeshift bed. **(b)** (US) extortion of money. **(c)** (US) thorough search. **(d)** final test (eg of a new ship, aircraft): *a* ~-*down voyage/flight.*

shake sth from/out of sth, get from/out of by

shaking: ~ *apples from a tree;* ~ *sand out of one's shoes.*
shake sb off, free oneself from: *The thief ran fast and soon shook off his pursuers.* ~ **sth off,** get rid of: ~ *off a cold/a fit of depression.*
shake out, (mil) spread; disperse: *The troops were ordered to* ~ *out when crossing open country.* ~ **sth out,** spread so as to be out by shaking: ~ *out a sail/tablecloth.* '~-**out** *n* process or act of making workers redundant: *a new* ~-*out in the shipbuilding industry.*
sth sth up, (a) mix well by shaking: ~ *up a bottle of medicine.* (b) restore sth to shape by shaking: ~ *up a cushion.* ~ **sb up,** restore from apathy or lethargy: *Some of these managers need shaking up—they're asleep on the job.* Hence, '~-**up** *n*: *We need a good* ~-*up in our firm—the management are completely out of touch with the facts of modern life.*
shake² /ʃeɪk/ *n* [C] **1** shaking or being shaken: *a* ~ *of the head,* to indicate 'No'; *give sth a good* ~. **2** (colloq) moment: *in two* ~*s; in half a* ~, almost at once. **3** (*pl*) **great** ~*s,* (sl) not very good or efficient. **4** '**egg-**~, '**milk-**~, etc, glass of milk and egg or milk alone, flavoured and shaken up.
Shake·spear·ian /ʃeɪkˈspɪərɪən/ *adj* (in the style) of Shakespeare /ˈʃeɪkspɪə(r)/, 1564—1616. ⇨ App 8.
shaky /ˈʃeɪkɪ/ *adj* (-ier, -iest) **1** (of a person, his movements, etc) weak; unsteady: ~ *hands; speak in a* ~ *voice; be* ~ *on one's legs; feel very* ~. **2** unsafe; unreliable: *a* ~ *table. My French is rather* ~. **shak·ily** /-ɪlɪ/ *adv* **shaki·ness** *n*
shale /ʃeɪl/ *n* [U] soft rock that splits easily into layers. '~-**oil** *n* oil obtained from bituminous ~.
shall /*weak form* ʃl; *strong form* ʃæl/ *anom fin* (*shall not* is often shortened to **shan't** /ʃɑːnt *US:* ʃænt/; with *thou* the old form **shalt** /ʃælt/ occurred; *pt* form **should** /ʃʊd/; *weak form* ʃəd/; *should not* is often shortened to **shouldn't** /ˈʃʊdnt/) **1** (used as an *aux v* to express the future tense, used with the first person, affirm and interr, and second person, interr only. Note that *will* is often used for *shall* in colloq style. *I'll* and *We'll* are used for *I/We shall*.): *We* ~ *arrive tomorrow. S*~ *we be back in time? He said I was not to go, but I certainly* ~. (The use of *should* in place of ~ indicates either future in the past, or a conditional statement, with an *if*-clause expressed or understood): *I told him that I should see him the next day. I should have bought it if I had had enough money.* **2** (used with the second and third persons to form a future or conditional statement expressing the speaker's will or intention; with stress on ~, *should,* this expresses obligation or compulsion; without special stress on ~, *should,* it expresses a promise or a threat): *You say you will not do it, but I say you* ~ *do it. He says he won't go, but I say he* ~. *You* ~ *not catch me so easily next time. If you work well, you* ~ *have higher wages.* **3** (used with all persons to form statements or questions expressing the ideas of duty, command, obligation, conditional duty, and (in the *neg*) prohibition): *S*~ *I* (= Do you want me to) *open the window? S*~ *the boy* (= Do you want the boy to) *wait?* (Note that *Will I/he* is not used here, but that '*Would you like us/him to',* is the usu equivalent.) *I asked the man whether the boy should wait. You shan't have it; it's mine! You should* (= ought to) *have been more careful. He shouldn't* (= oughtn't to) *do things*

like that. **4** (used with all persons in clauses expressing purpose, equivalent to *may* or *might,* thus forming a subjunctive equivalent): *I lent him the book so that he should study the subject.* **5** (used with all persons as a subjunctive equivalent): *I'm anxious that it* ~/*should be done at once. It is surprising that he should be so foolish.* **6** (in reported speech) ~, *should* are used when reporting the first person to other persons (eg *He said: 'I* ~ *do it'—he said he should do it,* but *will, would* are now commoner), or when reporting from other persons to the first person (eg *He said to me: 'You will succeed'—he told me that I should succeed*). **7** (*should* is used after *how, why,* and (occasionally) other interrogative words): *How should I know? Why should you/he think that?* **8** (*should* is used to express probability or expectation): *They should be there by now, I think,* ie I expect they are there; they are probably there. **9** (*should* is used to express what is advisable or desirable): *You should drink your coffee while it's hot. You should see the new film that's on at the Odeon.* (also ⇨ **ought**).
shal·lot /ʃəˈlɒt/ *n* sort of small onion with cloves like, but not so strong-tasting as, those of garlic.
shal·low /ˈʃæləʊ/ *adj* of little depth: ~ *water; a* ~ *saucer/dish;* (fig) not earnest, sound or serious: *a* ~ *argument;* ~ *talk.* □ *n* (often *pl*) ~ place in a river or in the sea; shoal. □ *vi* become ~.
sha·lom /ʃæˈlɒm/ *int* (Hebrew word) (used as a greeting and on parting) Peace!
shalt /ʃælt/ ⇨ **shall.**
sham /ʃæm/ *vi,vt* (-mm-) [VP2A,D,6A] pretend to be; simulate: *He* ~*med dead/death. He's only* ~*ming.* □ *n* **1** person who ~*s:* sth intended to deceive: *His love was a mere* ~; *what he really wanted was her money. He's a* ~, an impostor. **2** [U] pretence: *What he says is all* ~. □ *adj* false; pretended: ~ *piety; a* ~ *battle* (as in military training); *,*~-'*Tudor,* imitating the Tudor style of architecture.
shamble /ˈʃæmbl/ *vi* [VP2A,C] walk unsteadily as if unable to lift the feet properly: *The old man* ~*d up to me.* □ *n* shambling walk.
shambles /ˈʃæmblz/ *n sing* **1** (archaic) scene of bloodshed: *The place became a* ~. **2** (colloq) (scene of) muddle or confusion: *His flat is a complete* ~. *He made a* ~ *of the job.*
shame /ʃeɪm/ *n* [U] **1** distressed feeling, loss of self-respect, caused by wrong, dishonourable or foolish behaviour, failure, etc (of oneself, one's family, etc): *feel* ~ *at having told a lie/at failing in an examination; hang one's head in/for* ~. *To my* ~, *I must confess that....* '~-**faced** *adj* showing ~; looking distressed through ~. Hence, '~-**faced·ly** /ˈʃeɪmfeɪstlɪ/ *adv* '~-**making** *adj* (colloq) causing a feeling of ~. **2** capacity for experiencing ~: *He has no* ~/*is quite without* ~/*is lost to* ~. *(For)* ~! an appeal to sb not to disregard this feeling (used as a reproof to sb who does wrong and does not show ~). **3** [U] dishonour. **bring** ~ **on sb/oneself,** dishonour sb/oneself. **cry** ~ **on sb,** say that he is disgraceful, ought to be ashamed of himself. **put sb to** ~, disgrace him (eg by showing superior qualities). **S**~ **on you!** You should be ashamed of yourself! **4 a** ~, sth unworthy; sth that causes ~; sth or sb that is wrong or regrettable: *What a* ~ *to deceive the girl! It's a* ~ *to take the money for doing such easy work. He's a* ~ *to his family.* □ *vt* **1** [VP6A] cause ~ to; cause sb to feel ~; bring disgrace on: ~ *one's family.* **2** [VP14] ~

sb into/out of doing sth, frighten or force (sb to do/not to do sth) by ~: ~ *a man into apologizing.*
~·ful /-fl/ *adj* causing or bringing ~: ~*ful conduct.* ~·fully /-fəlɪ/ *adv* ~·less *adj* without ~; immodest. ~·less·ly *adv* ~·less·ness *n*

shammy /'ʃæmɪ/ *n* '~ **(leather),** ⇨ chamois.

sham·poo /ʃæm'puː/ *n* [C,U] (special soap, liquid, powder, etc for a) washing of the hair: *give sb a* ~; *a* ~ *and set.* □ *vt* [VP6A] wash (the hair of the head).

sham·rock /'ʃæmrɒk/ *n* clover-like plant with (usu) three leaves on each stem (serving) as the national emblem of Ireland).

shandy /'ʃændɪ/ *n* [U] mixed drink of beer and ginger-beer or lemonade.

shang·hai /ʃæŋ'haɪ/ *vt* (sl) make (a man) unconscious (with drink or drugs) and then carry him off to be a seaman on an outgoing ship; trick (a person) into an awkward situation.

shank /ʃæŋk/ *n* **1** leg, esp the part between the knee and the ankle; shin-bone. *go on* ~*'s mare/pony,* on one's own legs (not riding a horse, etc). **2** straight, slender part of an anchor, key, spoon, etc; smooth part of the stem of a screw.

shan't /ʃɑːnt *US:* ʃænt/ = shall not.

shan·tung /ʃæn'tʌŋ/ *n* [U] kind of heavy silk, usu undyed.

shanty[1] /'ʃæntɪ/ *n* [C] (*pl* -ties) poorly made hut, shed or cabin. '~·**town** *n* slum area of a town, or on the outskirts of a town, consisting of huts or shanties.

shanty[2] (US = **chant(e)y**) /'ʃæntɪ/ *n* (*pl* -ties) (often '**sea** ~) song sung by sailors in rhythm with their movements while working.

shape[1] /ʃeɪp/ *n* **1** [C,U] outer form; total effect produced by the outlines of sth: *There were clouds of different* ~*s in the sky. The garden is in the* ~ *of a square/oblong/crescent. What's the* ~ *of his nose? That hat hasn't much* ~*/has a queer* ~. *get/put sth into* ~, give definite form to; arrange in an orderly way: *get/put one's ideas into* ~. *give* ~ *to,* express (clearly): *He has some difficulty in giving* ~ *to his ideas. knock sth into/out of* ~, put sth into/out of the right ~. *take* ~, become definite in form or outline: *The new building is beginning to take* ~, One begins to see what the final ~ will be. *take* ~ *in,* find expression in: *His intentions took* ~ *in action,* were realized in action. *in* ~, in form, outline or appearance: *What a fat fellow! He's like a barrel in* ~*! He looks like a devil/monster in human* ~. **2** sort, description: *I've had no proposals from him in any* ~ *or form,* none of any sort. **3** condition: *Her affairs are in good* ~, are satisfactory. *Ali is in good* ~ *for his forthcoming fight,* is physically fit. **4** [C] sth indistinctly seen; vague form; apparition: *Two* ~*s could be discerned in the darkness. A huge* ~ *loomed up through the fog.* **5** [C] pattern or mould on which sth is given ~, eg a block on which hats are made.

shape[2] /ʃeɪp/ *vt,vi* **1** [VP6A,15A] give a shape or form to: ~ *a pot on a wheel;* ~ *clay into an urn,* on a potter's wheel or lathe; ~ (= direct) *one's course for home;* (*pp*) ~*d like a pear,* having the shape of a pear. **2** [VP2A,C] take shape; give signs of future shape or development: *Our plans are shaping well,* giving promise of success. *The students are shaping satisfactorily,* making good progress. ~·**less** *adj* ~·**less·ly** *adv* ~·**less·ness** *n*

shape·ly /'ʃeɪplɪ/ *adj* (-ier, -iest) (esp of a person's form, or of limbs) well-formed; having a pleasing

shape: *a* ~ *pair of legs.*

shard /ʃɑːd/ *n* (old use, but still used by gardeners and archaeologists for a) piece of broken earthenware, eg one placed over the hole in a flower-pot.

share[1] /ʃeə(r)/ *n* **1** [C] part or division which sb has in, receives from, or gives to, a stock held by several or many persons, or which he contributes to a fund, expenses, etc: *Please let me take a* ~ *in the expenses,* pay sth towards them. *We shall all have a* ~ *in the profits. go* ~*s (with sb) (in sth),* divide (profits, costs, etc) with others; become part owner (with others); pay (a part of an expense): *Let me go* ~*s with you in the taxi fare.* '~·**cropper** *n* (in some countries, not in GB) tenant farmer who pays a ~ of his crop as rent to the owner of the land. **2** [U] part taken or received by sb in an action, undertaking, etc, eg of responsibility, blame: *What* ~ *did he have in their success? You must take your* ~ *of the blame. You're not taking much* ~ *in the conversation,* are saying little. **3** [C] one of the equal parts into which the capital of a company is divided, entitling the holder of the ~ to a proportion of the profits: *hold 500* ~*s in a shipping company; £1* ~*s are now worth £1.75.* '**ordinary** ~, on which dividends are paid according to profits after payments on preference ~s. '**preference** ~, one on which a fixed dividend is guaranteed before payments are made on others. '~ **certificate,** document proving ownership of ~s. '~·**holder** *n* owner of (business) ~s. '~ **index** *n* number used to show how ~ prices have fluctuated, based on prices of ~s selected for this purpose: *The Financial Times* ~ *index went up/down five points yesterday.* □ *vt,vi* **1** [VP6A,14,15B] ~ *sth (out) (among/between),* give a ~ of to others; divide and distribute: ~ (*out) £100 among five men,* eg by giving them £20 each; ~ *the sweets between you.* Hence, '~·**out** *n* distribution. ~ *sth with sb,* give part of it to him: *He would* ~ *his last pound with me.* **2** [VP6A,14] ~ *sth (with sb),* have or use (with); have in common: *He hated having to* ~ *the hotel bedroom with a stranger.* **3** [VP6A,3A] ~ *(in) sth,* have a ~: *I will* ~ *(in) the cost with you. She* ~*s (in) my troubles as well as (in) my joys.* ~ *and* ~ *alike,* have equal ~s with others in the use, enjoyment, expense, etc of sth.

share[2] /ʃeə(r)/ *n* blade of a plough.

shark /ʃɑːk/ *n* **1** sea-fish, some kinds of which are large and dangerous to bathers, etc. ⇨ the illus at sea. '~·**skin** *n* textile fabric with a smooth and shiny surface, used for outer clothing: *a* ~·*skin jacket/suit.* **2** swindler; usurer.

sharp /ʃɑːp/ *adj* (-er, -est) **1** with a fine cutting edge; not blunt: *a* ~ *knife;* with a fine point, able to make holes: *a* ~ *pin/needle.* **2** well-defined; clear-cut; distinct: *a* ~ *outline; a* ~ *image,* (in photography) one with clear contrasts between light and shade. **3** (of curves, slopes, bends) abrupt; changing direction quickly: *a* ~ *bend in the road; a* ~ *turn to the left;* ~·'**featured,** (of a person) having angular features. **4** (of sounds) shrill; piercing: *a* ~ *cry of distress.* **5** quickly aware of things; acute: ~ *eyes/ears; a* ~ *intelligence; a* ~ *sense of smell; keep a* ~ *look-out; a* ~ *child;* ~ *at arithmetic.* '~·**shooter** *n* man skilled at shooting with a rifle, placed where accurate shooting (in war) is required. Hence, ~·'**eyed/-'sighted/ -'witted** *adjj* **6** (of feelings, taste) producing a physical sensation like cutting or pricking: *a* ~ *pain; a* ~ *flavour; a* ~ *frost.* **7** harsh; severe: ~

words; *a ~ rebuke; a ~ tongue*, of a person who speaks sarcastically, bitterly. **8** quick; brisk; lively: *go for a ~ walk; a ~ struggle/contest. That was ~ work*, was finished or done quickly and energetically. **9** quick to take advantage; unscrupulous: *a ~ lawyer. He was too ~ for me*, He got the better of me by being unscrupulous. **~ practice**, business dealings that are not altogether honest. **10** (music) above the normal pitch; (of a note) raised half a tone in pitch: *C ~* (= C#), ⇨ flat ²(5). ⇨ the illus at notation. □ *n* (music) *~* note; the symbol # used to indicate a *~* note. □ *adv* **1** punctually: *at seven* (*o'clock*) *~.* **2** suddenly; abruptly: *turn ~ to the left.* **3** (music) above the true pitch: *sing ~.* **4** *look ~*, waste no time; hurry. **5** '*~-set adj* hungry. **~en** /'ʃɑːpən/ *vt,vi* [VP6A,2A] make or become *~*: *~en a pencil. This knife needs ~ening. The walk has ~ened my appetite.* **~·ener** /'ʃɑːpnə(r)/ *n* sth that *~*ens: *a 'pencil-~ener; a 'knife-~ener.* **~er** *n* swindler, esp ('**card-~er**) person who makes a living by cheating at cards. **~·ly** *adv* in a *~* manner: *a ~ly pointed pencil; a ~ly defined image; to answer ~ly.* **~·ness** *n*

shat /ʃæt/ *pt,pp* of shit.

shat·ter /'ʃætə(r)/ *vt,vi* [VP6A,2A] break suddenly and violently into small pieces: *The explosion ~ed every window in the building. Our hopes were ~ed. What a nerve-~ing noise!* eg that of pneumatic drills or jet engines. '**~·proof**, ⇨ proof ².

shave /ʃeɪv/ *vt,vi* (*pt,pp* ~d or, chiefly as *adj*, *~n* /'ʃeɪvn/) **1** [VP6A,2A,15B] *~* (*off*), cut (hair) off the chin, etc with a razor: *Do you ~ yourself or go to the barber's? He has ~d off his beard. He doesn't ~ every day.* '**shaving-brush** *n* brush for spreading lather over the face before shaving. **2** [VP15B] *~ sth off*, pare off (a thin layer, etc). **3** [VP6A,15A] pass very close to, almost but not touching: *The bus just ~d me by an inch.* **4** *~n* (*pp* as *adj*) **,clean-'~n, ,well-'~n**, having been *~*d clean, well. □ *n* [C] **1** shaving (of the face): *A sharp razor gives a close ~. How much does a ~ cost?* **2** close approach without touching. (only in) *a close/narrow ~*, a narrow escape from injury, danger, etc. **~r** *n* **1** (**electric**) **~r**, razor with an electric motor, operated from the mains or by a battery. ⇨ the illus at razor. **2** (joc, usu *young ~r*) lad, youngster. **shav·ings** *n pl* thin parings of wood *~*d off (esp with a plane): *The floor of the carpenter's shop was covered with shavings.*

Shav·ian /'ʃeɪvɪən/ *adj, n* (in the manner) (devotee) of G B Shaw /ʃɔː/, 1856—1950, Irish dramatist and critic.

shawl /ʃɔːl/ *n* [C] large (usu square or oblong) piece of material worn about the shoulders or head of a woman, or wrapped round a baby.

she /ʃiː/ *pron* (⇨ her) **1** female person, etc already referred to or implied: *My sister says she is going for a walk. This cat's a she, not a he.* **2** (pref) female: *a' she-goat/-ass, etc.*

sheaf /ʃiːf/ *n* (*pl* sheaves /ʃiːvz/) **1** bundle of corn, barley, etc stalks tied together after reaping. **2** bundle of papers, arrows, etc laid lengthwise and tied together.

shear /ʃɪə(r)/ *vt* (*pt ~ed, pp* shorn /ʃɔːn/ or *~ed*) [VP6A] cut the wool off (a sheep) with shears; (fig) strip bare of; deprive of: *They'll be ~ing* (*the sheep*) *next week.* **shorn of**, having lost completely: *The gambler came home shorn of his money.*

shears /ʃɪəz/ *n pl* (**pair of**) *~*, large cutting instrument shaped like scissors, used for shearing sheep,

cutting cloth, etc. ⇨ the illus at tool.

sheath /ʃiːθ/ *n* (*pl*~s /ʃiːðz/) **1** cover for the blade of a weapon or tool: *Put the dagger back in its ~.* '**~-knife** *n* knife with a fixed blade, that fits into a *~.* **2** *~*-like cover (of tissue, skin, etc) fitting over part of an animal or plant (eg the '*wing-~* of some insects). (**protective**) *~*, contraceptive device used on the penis. **3** (attrib; dressmaking) close-fitting: *a ~ corset/gown.*

sheathe /ʃiːð/ *vt* [VP6A] **1** put into a sheath: *~ the sword*, stop fighting. **2** protect with a casing or covering: *~ a ship's bottom with copper.* **sheathing** *n* protective layer of boards, metal plates, etc eg on parts of a building, the underpart of a ship's hull.

sheaves /ʃiːvz/ ⇨ sheaf.

she·bang /ʃɪ'bæŋ/ *n* **the whole** *~*, the whole collection of facts or things; the whole situation, or-ganization.

she·been /ʃɪ'biːn/ *n* unlicensed public house (esp in Ireland and S Africa).

shed ¹ /ʃed/ *n* building, roughly made structure, used for storing things ('*tool-~*, '*wood-~*, '*coal-~, etc*), for sheltering animals ('*cattle-~*), vehicles, etc ('*engine-~*, '*bicycle-~*).

shed ² /ʃed/ *vt* (*pt,pp ~; -dd-*) [VP6A] **1** let (leaves, etc) fall; let come off: *Trees ~ their leaves and flowers ~ their petals. Some kinds of deer ~ their horns.* **~** (**one's**) **blood**, (a) be wounded or killed: *~ one's blood for one's country.* (b) cause the blood of others to flow. Hence, '**blood-~**. **n. ~ tears**, weep. **2** throw or take off; get rid of: *People in the park began to ~ their clothes as it got hotter and hotter.* **3** spread or send out: *a fire that ~s warmth; a woman who ~s happiness around her; a lamp that ~s a soft light.* **~ light on**, (fig) make clear to the mind. **4** '**load-~ding**, ⇨ load ¹(3).

she'd /ʃiːd/ = *she had; she would.*

sheen /ʃiːn/ *n* [U] brightness; shiny quality: *the ~ of silk. That girl's hair has a ~ like gold.*

sheep /ʃiːp/ *n* (*pl* unchanged) grass-eating animal kept for its flesh as food (mutton) and its wool. ⇨ the illus at domestic. ⇨ ewe, lamb and ram. *separate the ~ from the goats*, separate good from bad persons. ⇨ Matt 25: 33. *cast/make ~'s eyes at*, look at in an amorous but foolish way. *a wolf in ~'s clothing*, a wicked man who pretends to be good. *as well be hanged for a ~ as a lamb*, commit a big crime rather than a small one if the punishment is the same. **,black '~,** ⇨ black(4). '**~-dog** *n* dog trained to help a shepherd to look after *~.* ⇨ the illus at domestic. '**~-fold** *n* enclosure for *~.* '**~-run** *n* tract of land (esp in Australia) on which *~* are pastured. '**~-skin** *n* (a) rug of a *~'s* skin with the wool on it; garment made of two or more such skins. (b) leather of *~'s* skin used in book-binding, etc. (c) parchment made from such skin; (esp US) diploma written on such parchment. '**~-ish** /-ɪʃ/ *adj* **1** awkwardly self-conscious: *a ~ish-looking boy.* **2** (feeling) foolish or embarrassed by consciousness of a fault. **~·ish·ly** *adv* **~·ish·ness** *n*

sheer ¹ /ʃɪə(r)/ *adj* **1** complete; thorough; absolute: *~ nonsense; a ~ waste of time; by ~ chance.* **2** (of textiles, etc) finely woven and almost transparent: *stockings of ~ nylon.* **3** without a slope; (almost) perpendicular: *a ~ drop of 50 feet; a ~ rock.* □ *adv* straight up or down: *a cliff that rises ~ from the beach. He fell 500 feet ~.*

sheer ² /ʃɪə(r)/ *vi* [VP2C] **1** *~ away/off*, (esp of a ship) deviate from course. **2** ~ **off,** (colloq) go away (from sb one dislikes, sb by whom one had been offended).

sheet¹ /ʃiːt/ n [C] **1** large rectangular piece of linen or cotton cloth, as used in pairs for sleeping between: *put clean ~s on the bed.* **2** broad, flat piece (of some thin material): *a ~ of glass/tin/ wrapping-paper/note-paper, etc; ~ copper/iron, etc,* rolled or hammered into thin ~s; *'~ music,* published in ~s, not in book form. *The book is in ~s,* ie in ~s of paper ready for binding. **3** wide expanse (of water, ice, snow, flame, etc): *The rain came down in ~s,* very heavily. '~-**lightning** n lightning that comes in sheet-like flashes of diffused brightness (not in zigzags, etc). ~**ing** n [U] material used for making ~s(1).

sheet² /ʃiːt/ n cord fastened at the lower corner of a sail to hold it and control the angle at which it is set. ⇨ the illus at sail. '~-**anchor** n (usu fig) sth on which one depends for security as a final resort when other things have failed.

sheik(h) /ʃeɪk US: ʃiːk/ n Arab chieftain; head of an Arab village, tribe, etc. ~**dom** /-dəm/ n

shekel /ˈʃekl/ n ancient silver coin used by the Jews; (pl) money, riches.

shel·drake /ˈʃeldreɪk/ n (kinds of) fish-eating wild duck with brightly coloured feathers.

shelf /ʃelf/ n (pl shelves /ʃelvz/) **1** flat, rectangular piece of wood, metal, glass or other material, fastened at right angles to a wall or in a cupboard, bookcase, cabinet, etc. **on the ~, (a)** put aside as done with, eg of a person too old to continue working. **(b)** (colloq, of a woman) unmarried and considered as being unlikely to be asked to marry. **2** ~-like projection of rock on a cliff face, etc (as used by rock-climbers).

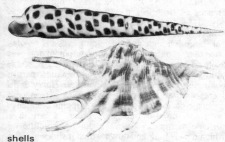

shells

shell /ʃel/ n [C] **1** hard outer covering of bird's eggs, nuts (eg walnuts, coconuts), some seeds (eg peas) and fruits, and of some animals (eg oysters, lobsters, snails) or parts of them. ⇨ the illus at mollusc. **go/retire into one's ~; come out of one's ~,** become/cease to be shy, reserved, uncommunicative. '~-**fish** n kinds of molluscs (oysters, etc) and crustaceans (crabs, shrimps, etc) having ~s. **2** walls, outer structure, of an unfinished building, ship, etc or of one of which the contents have been destroyed (eg by fire): *Only the ~ of the factory was left when the fire had been extinguished.* **3** (US = cartridge) metal case filled with explosive, to be fired from a large gun. Cf cartridge for rifles, shot-guns. ⇨ the illus at cartridge. '~-**proof** adj so thickly or strongly built that a ~ cannot pierce it. '~-**shock** n nervous or mental disorder caused by the noise and blast of bursting ~s. **4** light racing-boat propelled by oarsmen. □ vt,vi **1** [VP6A] take out of a ~(1) (cf US *shuck*):

It's as easy as ~ing peas, is very easy. *These peas ~ easily,* = are easily ~ed. **2** [VP6A] fire ~s(3) at: ~ *the enemy's trenches.* **3** ~ *out,* [VP15B,2C] (colloq) pay up (money, a required sum): *I shall be expected to ~ out (the money) for the party.*

she'll /ʃiːl/ = she will; she shall.

shel·lac /ʃəˈlæk/ n [U] resinous substance in the form of thin sheets used in making varnish and (formerly) gramophone records. □ vt varnish with ~.

shel·ter /ˈʃeltə(r)/ n **1** [U] condition of being kept safe, eg from rain, danger: *take ~ from the rain,* eg under a tree; *get under ~,* eg when bombs are dropping during an air raid. **2** [C] sth that gives safety or protection, esp a hut, etc built to keep off wind and rain: *a 'bus ~* (in which people wait for buses); *a taxi-drivers' ~,* one where they wait until called by phone, etc; *an 'air-raid ~.* □ vt,vi **1** [VP6A,14] ~ *(from),* give ~ to; protect: *trees that ~ a house from cold winds;* ~ (= hide, protect) *an escaped prisoner; dig trenches to ~ the men from gunfire;* ~ *sb from blame;* ~ed *trades,* those which (like building and inland transport) are not exposed to foreign competition. **2** [VP2A,C] take ~: ~ *from the rain;* ~ *under the trees.*

shelve¹ /ʃelv/ vt [VP6A] **1** put (books, etc) on a shelf. **2** (fig, of problems, plans, etc) postpone dealing with; defer consideration of. **3** cease to employ (a person).

shelve² /ʃelv/ vi [VP2A,C] (of land) slope gently: *The shore ~s down to the sea.*

shelves /ʃelvz/ pl of shelf.

shep·herd /ˈʃepəd/ n man who takes care of sheep. **the Good S~,** Jesus Christ. ~**'s pie,** [U] minced meat baked under mashed potatoes. ~**'s plaid,** small black and white check pattern in cloth. □ vt [VP6A,15A] take care of; guide or direct (people) like sheep: *The passengers were ~ed across the tarmac to the airliner.* ~**ess** /ˌʃepəˈdes US: ˈʃepədəs/ n woman ~ (esp as idealized in pastoral poetry).

Shera·ton /ˈʃerətən/ n [U] 18th-century style of furniture (in GB): (attrib) ~ *chairs.*

sher·bet /ˈʃɜːbət/ n [C,U] (glass of) cooling drink of sweetened fruit juices, sometimes effervescent (made from powder); (US) water-ice.

sher·iff /ˈʃerɪf/ n **1** (usu High S~) chief officer of the Crown in counties and certain cities, with legal and ceremonial duties. **2** (US) chief law-enforcing officer of a county.

sherry /ˈʃerɪ/ n [U] yellow or brown fortified wine of S Spain; similar kinds of wine from S Africa, Cyprus, etc.

she's /ʃiːz/ = she is; she has.

Shet·land /ˈʃetlənd/ n (also the ~s) group of islands NNE of Scotland. ~ **pony,** small, hardy breed. ~ **wool,** soft, fine kind spun in the S~s.

shew /ʃəʊ/ ⇨ show.

shib·bol·eth /ˈʃɪbəleθ/ n [C] **1** custom whose use is regarded as a criterion for distinguishing membership of a group. **2** old-fashioned and now generally abandoned custom which was at one time considered to be essential: *the outworn ~s of the past.*

shied /ʃaɪd/ ⇨ shy², shy³.

shield /ʃiːld/ n [C] **1** piece of armour (metal, leather, wood) carried on the arm, to protect the body when fighting; representation of a ~, eg carved on a stone gateway, showing a person's coat of arms. ⇨ arms. ⇨ the illus at armour. **2** (fig) person or thing that protects. **3** (in machinery, etc) protective plate or screen; sth designed to keep out dust, wind, etc. (US *wind*~ = GB *windscreen*.) □ *vt* [VP6A,15A] protect; keep safe; save (sb) from punishment or suffering: ~ *one's eyes with one's hand;* ~ *a friend from censure.*

shift[1] /ʃɪft/ *n* **1** change of place or character; substitution of one thing for another: *a* ~ *in emphasis,* placing the emphasis differently. **2** [C] group of workmen who start work as another group finishes; period for which such a group works: *on the day/ night* ~; *an eight-hour* ~; *working in* ~s. **3** dodge, trick, scheme, way of evading a difficulty, of getting sth: *resort to dubious* ~s *in order to get some money. As a last desperate* ~, *he pawned his wife's wedding ring.* **make** ~ **(with sth/to do sth),** manage or contrive, be able somehow or other: *We must make* ~ *with the money we have. He must make* ~ *without help.* ⇨ **make**~ at make[1](29). **4** woman's narrow dress without a waistline; (old use) chemise. **5** ('**gear-**)~, (motoring) mechanism for gear change: *Do you prefer a manual to an automatic gear*~? ~**·less** *adj* without ability to find ways of doing things; unable to get on in life.

shift[2] /ʃɪft/ *vt,vi* **1** [VP6A,14,15A,2A,C] ~ **sth (from/to),** change position or direction; transfer: ~ *a burden from one shoulder to the other;* ~ *the blame (on) to sb else. Will you help me to* ~ *the furniture about/round, please? The wind has* ~*ed to the north. The cargo has* ~*ed,* has been shaken out of place by the movement of the ship. *Don't try to* ~ *the responsibility on to me.* ~ **one's ground,** take up a new position, approach the subject in a different way, during an argument. **2** (motoring) change (gears): ~ *into second/third gear.* **3** ~ **for oneself,** manage as best one can (to make a livelihood, get sth done) without help: *When their father died the children had to* ~ *for themselves.* **shifty** *adj* (-ier, -iest) untrustworthy; deceitful; not straightforward: *a* ~*y customer;* ~*y behaviour;* ~*y eyes.* ~**·ily** /-ɪlɪ/ *adv* ~**·i·ness** *n*

shil·ling /ˈʃɪlɪŋ/ *n* **1** (until 1971) British coin with the value of twelve pennies, one-twentieth of a pound. ⇨ App 4. **2** basic monetary unit of Kenya, Uganda and Tanzania, equal to 100 cents.

shilly-shally /ˈʃɪlɪ ʃælɪ/ *vi* [VP2A] be unable to make up one's mind; be undecided. □ *n* [U] indecision.

shim·mer /ˈʃɪmə(r)/ *vi* [VP2A,C], *n* [U] (shine with a) wavering soft or faint light: *moonlight* ~*ing on the lake; the* ~ *of pearls.*

shin /ʃɪn/ *n* front part of the leg below the knee. ⇨ the illus at leg. '~**-guard** *n* pad worn on the ~ at football. '~**-bone** *n* tibia. ⇨ the illus at skeleton. □ *vi* (-nn-) [VP3A] ~ **up,** climb up (using arms and legs to grip sth): ~ *up a tree.*

shin·dig /ˈʃɪndɪɡ/ *n* (sl) **1** lively and noisy party. **2** (= *shindy*) brawl.

shindy /ˈʃɪndɪ/ *n* [C] (*pl* -dies) (colloq) brawl; noisy disturbance: *kick up a* ~.

shine /ʃaɪn/ *vi,vt* (*pt,pp* shone /ʃɒn US: ʃəʊn/ but ⇨ 2 below) **1** [VP2A,C] give out or reflect light; be bright (lit or fig); excel in some way: *The moon is shining. The sun shone out,* suddenly began to ~ (as clouds moved). *His face shone with excitement. He does not* ~ *in conversation,* is not a good talker. *I don't* ~ *at tennis.* **2** [VP6A] (colloq, and with *pp* ~d) polish (which is more usu); make bright: ~ *shoes. Have you* ~*d your shoes/the brass?* □ *n* **1** (*sing* only) polish; brightness: *Give your shoes a*

good ~. *How can I take the* ~ *out of the seat of my trousers?* **2** [U] **come rain or** ~, whatever the weather may be; (fig) whatever may happen. **shiny** *adj* (-ier, -iest) polished; rubbed bright: *a shiny coat,* one with the nap rubbed off (so that the surface ~s).

shingle[1] /ˈʃɪŋɡl/ *n* [U] small, rounded pebbles on the seashore. **shin·gly** /ˈʃɪŋɡlɪ/ *adj* of ~: *I prefer a sandy beach to a shingly beach.*

shingle[2] /ˈʃɪŋɡl/ *n* [C] **1** small, flat square or oblong piece of wood used (like tiles and slates) on roofs, spires and walls. **2** (US colloq) small, wooden signboard (used by lawyers, dentists, etc): *put up one's* ~, set up for the first time, eg as a doctor. □ *vt* cover (a roof, etc) with ~s: *a* ~*d church spire.*

shingle[3] /ˈʃɪŋɡl/ *vt* [VP6A] cut (a woman's hair) so that it is short at the back but longer at the sides. □ *n* this kind of haircut.

shingles /ˈʃɪŋɡlz/ *n* (with *sing v*) skin disease forming a band of inflamed spots (often round the waist).

ship[1] /ʃɪp/ *n* **1** sea-going vessel of considerable size: *a* '*sailing-*~; *a* '*merchant-*~; *a* '*war*~, etc; *take* ~, go on board a ~; *the* ~'s *company,* the entire crew; *the* ~'s *articles,* the terms on which seamen are engaged; *the* ~'s *papers,* the documents showing ownership, nationality, nature of the cargo, etc. ⇨ the illus at barque. **when my** '~ **comes in/home,** when I have made my fortune. **on** '~**·board,** on board ~. **2** (colloq) spacecraft; (US colloq) aircraft. **3** (compounds) '~**-breaker** *n* contractor who buys and breaks up old ~s (for scrap). '~**-broker** *n* agent of a shipping company who does a ~'s business in port; one who buys, sells and charters ~s; agent for marine insurance. '~**-builder** *n* one whose business is building ~s. Hence, '~**-building** *n* [U]: '~*building yard,* = ~yard. '~('s) **biscuit,** hard, coarse biscuit used, in former times, during long voyages. '~**-canal** *n* canal large enough for sea-going vessels. '~'s**-chandler** *n* one who deals in equipment for ~s. '~**-load** *n* as much cargo, or as many passengers, as a ~ can carry. '~**-mate** *n* fellow sailor; person belonging to the same ~ as another: *Harry and I were* ~*mates in 1962.* '~**-owner** *n* person who owns a ~ or ~s, or shares in a shipping company. '~**-shape** *adj* tidy; in good order. □ *adv* in a ~shape manner. '~**-way** *n* sloping structure on which a ~ is built and down which it slides into the water. '~**-wreck** *n* [U] loss or destruction of a ~ at sea by storm, collision, etc: *suffer* ~*wreck.* [C] instance of this. □ *vi* cause to suffer ~wreck; destroy by ~wreck. '~**-wright** *n* ~ builder. '~**-yard** *n* place where ~s are built.

ship[2] /ʃɪp/ *vt,vi* (-pp-) **1** [VP6A,15A,B] put, take, send, in a ship: ~ *gold to India;* (comm) take, send, by train, road, etc: ~ *goods by express train.* ~ **off,** send: ~ *off young men to the war.* **2** [VP6A] ~ **oars,** take them out of the water into the boat. ~ **water;** ~ **a sea,** be flooded by water breaking over the side. **3** [VP6A,15A,2C] engage for service on a ship: ~ *a crew for a voyage round the world. He* ~*ped* (= took service) *as a steward on an Atlantic liner.* ~**-ment** *n* [U] putting of goods, etc on a ship; [C] quantity of goods ~ped. ~**-per** *n* person who arranges for goods to be ~ped. ~**-ping** *n* [U] all the ships of a country, part, etc. '~**-ping-agent** *n* shipowner's representative at a port. '~**-ping-office** *n* ~ping-agent's office; office where

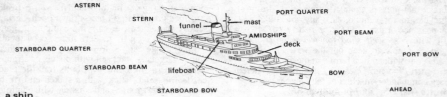

ASTERN

STERN   funnel   mast   PORT QUARTER

AMIDSHIPS   PORT BEAM

deck   PORT BOW

STARBOARD QUARTER

STARBOARD BEAM   lifeboat   BOW

STARBOARD BOW   AHEAD

a ship

seamen are engaged.

shire /ʃaɪə(r)/ n [C] county (now chiefly used as a suffix in the names of certain counties, and usu pronounced /-ʃə(r)/): *Hampshire, Yorkshire.* ⇨ App 6. **the ~s,** certain midland counties of England and parts of these well known for fox-hunting. '**~ horse,** powerful breed of horse used for pulling carts and wagons.

shirk /ʃɜːk/ vt,vi [VP6A,D,2A] avoid, try to escape (doing sth, responsibility, duty, etc): *~ going to the dentist; ~ work/school. He's ~ing. ~er* n

shirt /ʃɜːt/ n **1** man's loose-fitting garment for the upper part of the body (of cotton, linen, silk, etc) usu worn under a jacket, with long sleeves or ('*sports ~*) half sleeves. *in one's '~-sleeves,* not wearing a jacket or coat. *keep one's ~ on,* (sl) keep one's temper. *put one's ~ on* (a horse, etc), bet all one has on. '**~-front** n usu stiffened and starched breast of a white ~. '**~-waister** (US '**~-waist**) woman's blouse or dress that buttons down the front. **~-ing** n material for making ~s. **~y** adj (-ier, -iest) (sl) ill-tempered.

shish kebab /ʃɪʃ kəˈbæb US: ˈʃɪʃ kəbæb/ n dish of pieces of meat roasted and served on skewers.

shit /ʃɪt/ (⚠, not in polite use) n[U] **1** excrement. **2** (sl) hashish. **3** (contemptuous for a) person: *You big ~! □ vi (-tt-) (pt,pp ~ted* or *shat /ʃæt/)* [VP2A,3A] empty the bowels of excrement. **~ on sb,** (vulg sl) **1** severely scold or find fault with him. **2** report on him, esp to the police. □ *int* ⚠ (vulg) (as an expression of irritation or objection) Bother! Rubbish!

shiver¹ /ˈʃɪvə(r)/ vi [VP2A,C] tremble, esp from cold or fear: *~ing all over with cold; ~ing like a leaf.* □ n **1** trembling that cannot be controlled: *The sight sent cold ~s down my back. A ~ ran down her back.* **2** (pl) *get/have/give sb the ~s,* (colloq) get/give sb ~ing movements, a feeling of fear or horror. **~y** adj inclined to ~; having or causing a feeling of cold, fear, horror.

shiver² /ˈʃɪvə(r)/ n (usu pl) one of the many small pieces into which sth is broken: *break sth to ~s; burst into ~s.* □ vt,vi [VP15A,2C] break into ~s.

shoal¹ /ʃəʊl/ n [C] great number of fish swimming together; great number (of people, things): *a ~ of herring; swimming in ~s.* □ vi (of fish) form ~s.

shoal² /ʃəʊl/ n [C] shallow place in the sea, esp where there are sandbanks; (pl; fig) hidden dangers. □ vi [VP2A] become shallow(er).

shock¹ /ʃɒk/ n **1** [C] violent blow or shaking (eg as caused by a collision or explosion): *the ~ of a fall; earthquake ~s.* '**~ absorber** n kinds of device fitted to motor-vehicles, aircraft, etc to lessen ~s and add to the cushioning effects of tyres, springs, etc. '**~ tactics,** use of massed forces to attack (in war). '**~ troops,** troops specially trained for violent assaults. '**~-brigade,** '**~-workers,** (esp in USSR) body of workers engaged in specially arduous work. '**~ wave,** region of intensely high air pres-

sure caused by an atomic explosion or an aircraft moving at supersonic speed. **2** [C] effect caused by the passage of an electric current through the body: *If you touch that live wire you'll get a ~.* **3** [C] sudden and violent disturbance of the feelings or the nervous system (caused by bad news, severe injury, etc); [U] condition caused by such a disturbance: *The news of her mother's death was a terrible ~ to her. The stock market quickly recovered from the ~ of the election results. It gave me quite a ~ to learn that he had married again. She died of ~ following an operation on the brain.* ⇨ shell-~ at shell(3). '**~ treatment/therapy,** treatment of (esp mental) disorder by using electric ~s or drugs on the nervous system. □ vt [VP6A] cause ~(3) to; fill with surprised disgust, horror, etc: *I was ~ed at the news of her death. He was ~ed to hear his daughter swearing. I'm not easily ~ed, but that book really is obscene.* **~er** n **1** person who ~s: *He's a ~er,* a ~ingly bad person. **2** sth that ~s, eg a sensational novel; bad specimen of sth. **~-ing** adj **1** very bad or wrong: *~ing behaviour.* **2** causing ~(3): *~ing news,* eg of a flood that causes great loss of life. **3** (colloq) bad: *a ~ing dinner; ~ing handwriting.* □ adv (colloq, as an intensive) very: *a ~ing bad cold.* **~-ing-ly** adv **1** badly: *You're playing ~ingly.* **2** extremely: *How ~ingly expensive!*

shock² /ʃɒk/ n number of sheaves of grain placed together and supporting each other in a field to dry during harvest.

shock³ /ʃɒk/ n (usu ~ of hair) rough, untidy mass of hair (on sb's head). **~-'headed** adj having such hair.

shod /ʃɒd/ ⇨ shoe v.

shoddy /ˈʃɒdɪ/ n [U] (cloth of poor quality, made from) fibre from old cloth, etc. □ adj (-ier, -iest) of poor quality; made to seem better than it is: *~ cloth; a ~ piece of work.*

shoe /ʃuː/ n **1** (often *pair of ~s*) outer covering for the foot, esp one which does not reach above the ankle (⇨ boot): *put on/take off one's ~s. be in/ put oneself in 'sb's ~s,* occupy, imagine oneself to be in, his position; be in his plight: *I wouldn't be in your ~s for a thousand pounds. know where the ~ pinches,* understand from one's own experience all about hardships, etc. **2** (compounds) '**~-black** n boy or man who polishes ~s of passers-by. '**~-horn** n device with a curved blade for getting the heel easily into a ~. '**~-lace** n cord for fastening the edges of a shoe's uppers. '**~-leather** n leather suitable for making ~s. '**~-maker** n person who makes and/or repairs ~s and boots. '**~-making** n [U] trade of a ~maker. '**~-string** n(US) = ~lace. *do sth on a ~string.* do sth (eg start a business) on a very small amount of capital. '**~-tree** n thin, flexible, shaped block for inserting in a shoe to keep its shape. **3** (horse-)~ /ˈhɔːʃuː/, metal band nailed to the hoof of a horse:

His horse cast/threw a ~, lost one. **4** part of a brake that presses against the wheel or drum (of a bicycle, motor-vehicle, etc); any object like a ~ in appearance or use. □ *vt* (*pt,pp* shod /ʃɒd/) [VP6A] fit with ~s: *well shod for wet weather,* having good ~s able to keep out the wet; *an iron-shod stick,* one with an iron ferrule at the end.

sho·gun /'ʃəʊguːn US: -gʌn/ *n* (until 1867) hereditary commander-in-chief of the Japanese army.

shone /ʃɒn US: ʃəʊn/ *pt,pp* of shine.

shoo /ʃuː/ *int* cry used for driving away birds, etc. □ *vt* (*pt,pp* ~ed) [VP15B] ~ *sth/sb away/off,* drive away by making this cry.

shook /ʃʊk/ *pt* of shake.

shoot¹ /ʃuːt/ *n* [C] **1** new, young growth on a plant or bush: *train the new* ~*s of a vine.* **2** = chute(1,2). **3** party of people shooting for sport; area of land over which birds, etc are shot: *rent a* ~ *for the season.*

shoot² /ʃuːt/ *vi,vt* (*pt, pp* shot /ʃɒt/) **1** [VP2C,15A,B] move, come, go, send, suddenly or quickly (*out, in, up, forth,* etc): *The snake's tongue shot out. The snake shot its tongue out. Flames were* ~*ing up from the burning house. The meteor shot across the sky. The horse stumbled and the rider was shot over its head. As the car hit the tree the occupants were shot out. At the half-way mark,* Hill *shot ahead,* (in a race) came on quickly and passed his competitors. *They shot angry glances at us. Rents have shot up,* (= risen suddenly) *in the last few months.* Tom *is* ~*ing up fast,* quickly growing tall. *She shot an angry look at him/shot him an angry look.* ~ *a bolt,* send a bolt (of a door, etc) into (or out of) its fastening. ~ *one's bolt,* make one's last effort. ~ *dice,* throw dice. ~ *rubbish,* let it slide from a cart, etc (on to a heap or dump). ~*ing* '*star,* meteor which burns up as it passes into and through the earth's atmosphere. **2** [VP2A,C] (of plants, bushes) sprout; send out new twigs or branches from a stem: *Rose bushes* ~ *again after being cut back.* **3** [VP2A,C] (of pain) pass with a stabbing sensation suddenly and swiftly: *The pain shot up his arm. I have a* ~*ing pain in my left leg.* **4** [VP6A] (of boats) move, be moved, rapidly over, through, etc: ~ *the rapids;* ~ *the bridge,* pass under it rapidly with the current. **5** [VP6A,15A,B,2A,C,4A] aim and fire with a gun or revolver; aim with a bow and send an arrow at; hit with a shell, bullet, arrow, etc; wound or kill (a person, animal, etc) by doing this: *They were* ~*ing at a target. He* ~*s well. He shot an arrow from his bow. Can you/Does your gun* ~ *straight? The soldier was shot* (= executed by ~*ing*) *for desertion. The police did not* ~ *to kill,* They used their weapons only to frighten the people (eg by firing over their heads). *He's in Africa* ~*ing lions. He neither rides,* ~*s nor fishes,* does not take part in these sports. *He fell like a shot rabbit,* like a rabbit that had been shot. ~ *away,* (more usu *fire away*) (a) begin and continue ~*ing.* (b) (fig) go ahead; begin. ~ *sth away,* (more usu *fire sth away*) get rid of by ~*ing:* ~ *away all one's ammunition.* ~ *sth down,* bring to the ground by ~*ing: The bomber was shot down in flames.* ~ *sth off,* sever by ~*ing: He had his arm shot off.* ~ *a covert/an estate, etc,* ~ the game in it. ~ *a line,* (sl) exaggerate; lie; deceive. ~ *one's* '*mouth off,* (US sl) talk indiscreetly or wildly. ~ *a place up,* (US sl) terrorize (a town, district, etc) by going through it and shooting at random, firing at houses,

etc. '~*ing-box* *n* house used by sportsmen in the ~ing season (eg one on moorlands). '~*ing-brake* *n* (former times) large horse-drawn open carriage used by sportsmen (for carrying equipment, game that was shot, etc); (in modern times, occasionally used for) estate car. '~*-ing-gallery* *n* place where ~ing at targets is practised with pistols or airguns. '~*-ing-range* *n* ground with butts for rifle practice. '~*-ing-stick,* stick with a spiked end (to be pushed into the ground) and a handle which unfolds to form a seat. **6** [VP6A,2A] (cinema) photograph (a scene): *a* ~*ing script,* one to be used while a film is being shot (giving the order in which scenes are photographed, etc). **7** [VP2A] (football, hockey, etc) (chiefly imper) make a shot at scoring a goal. ~*ing* *n* [U] (esp) (right of) ~ing (game) over an area of land: *sell the* ~*ing on an estate.* ⇨ also 6 above.

shooter /'ʃuːtə(r)/ *n* (in compounds) shooting implement: *a* '*pea-*~*: a* ,six-~, revolver firing six shots without reloading.

shop /ʃɒp/ *n* **1** (US = *store*) building or part of a building where goods are shown and sold retail: *a butcher's/chemist's* ~; *a* '*fruit-*~. *come/go to the wrong* ~, (colloq) to the wrong place/person (for help, information, etc). *keep* ~, be on duty (eg in a small ~): *Mr Green got a friend to keep* ~ *for him while he went to his wife's funeral. keep a* ~, be a shopkeeper, own and manage a ~. *set up* ~, set up in business as a retail trader. '~*-assistant* *n* employee in a ~. '~*-bell* *n* bell (on the door of a small ~) which rings when a customer enters, warning the ~-keeper. '~*-girl/-boy* *n* young ~-assistant. '~*-front* *n* frontage of a ~ with its window display, etc. ~ *hours* *n pl* hours during which a ~ is, or may legally be, open for business. '~*-keeper* *n* owner of (usu a small) ~. '~*-lift* *vi,vt* [VP2A,6A] steal (sth) from a shop while pretending to be a customer. Hence, '~*-lifter* *n* person who does this; '~*-lifting* *n* [U] doing this. '~*-soiled/-worn* *adjj* damaged or dirty as the result of being put on view or handled in a ~. '~*-walker* *n* person who directs customers (in a large ~ or department store) to the right counters, departments, etc. ,~·'*window* *n* window used for the display of wares, etc. *put all one's goods in the* ~*window,* (fig) make a display of all one's knowledge, ability, etc and have nothing in reserve (used of a superficial person). **2** [U] one's profession, trade, business, things connected with it. *talk* ~, talk about one's work, profession, etc with other people who do the same work. *shut up* ~, (colloq) stop doing sth (not necessarily connected with buying and selling). **3** *all* '*over the* ~, (sl) (a) in disorder, scattered in confusion; *My belongings are all over the* ~. (b) in every direction: *I've looked for it all over the* ~. **4** (= *work*~) place where manufacturing or repairing is done: *an* ,*engi'neering-*~; *a* ma'*chine-*~; *the men on the* ~ *floor,* the workers (contrasted with the management). ~*-'steward* *n* member of a local branch committee of a trade union, chosen by his fellow workers to represent them. ,*closed* '~ *n* system of compulsory membership of trade unions or other professional associations. □ *vi* (-pp-) [VP2A,C] **1** go to ~s to buy things (usu *go* ~*ping*). ~ *around,* (colloq) visit various ~s, markets, etc to obtain the best value for one's money, etc. **2** ~ *on sb,* (sl) inform against, esp to the police. ~*-ping* *n* [U] *do one's* ~*ping; a* '~*ping street,* one with many ~s;

a '*~ping bag/basket,* in which to carry purchases. '*~ping centre* *n* part of a town where there are ~s, markets, etc close together and often where cars are not allowed. '*window-~ping* *n* [U] visiting a ~ping centre, street, etc to look at the displays in the ~windows. ~·*per* *n* person who is ~ping: *crowds of Christmas ~pers.*

shore[1] /ʃɔː(r)/ *n* [U,C] stretch of land bordering on the sea or a large body of water: *a house on the ~(s) of Lake Geneva; go on ~* (from a ship).

shore[2] /ʃɔː(r)/ *n* [C] wooden support set against a wall, tree, etc to keep it up; prop set against the side of a ship while it is being built or repaired out of the water. □ *vt* [VP15B] *~ sth up,* support, prop up (with a wooden beam, etc).

shore[3] /ʃɔː(r)/, **shorn** /ʃɔːn/ ⇨ shear.

short[1] /ʃɔːt/ *adj* (-er, -est) **1** (opp of *long*) measuring little from end to end in space or time; (opp of *tall*) below the average height: *a ~ stick; a ~ way off,* not far away; *a ~ man; ~ grass; a ~ holiday; a ~ time ago. You've cut my hair very ~. She walked with ~, quick steps. The coat is a little ~ in the sleeves. The days are getting ~er now that autumn is here. **a ~ ball,** (cricket) not bowled on a correct length. '*~ cut* *n* way of getting somewhere, doing sth, etc (thought to be) quicker than the usual or ordinary way: *They took a ~ cut across the fields instead of going by the road.* ~· '*circuit* *n* accidental fault in wiring enabling an electric current to flow without going through the resistance of the complete circuit. ~·'*circuit* *vt, vi* cause, make or take a ~ circuit in; cut off current from (sth) in this way; (fig) shorten or simplify (a procedure, etc): *The system has ~-circuited.* '*~ list* *n* list of candidates (for a position, etc) that has been reduced to a small number from which a final selection is to be made. Hence, '*~-list* *vt: the candidates who have been ~-listed,* whose names have been put on a ~ list (perhaps for interviews). ~·'*lived* /'lɪvd US: 'laɪvd/ *adj* lasting for a ~ time; brief: *a ~-lived triumph.* ~·'*range* *adj* (*a*) (of plans, etc) designed for a limited period of time. (**b**) (of missiles, etc) with a comparatively limited range[1](3). **have a ~ temper,** be lacking in self-control, so that one quickly or easily becomes angry; hence, ~·'*tempered* *adj.* ~·'*term attrib adj* limited to, due to be repaid in, a ~ period of time: *~-term loans.* **2** not reaching the usual, stated or required (amount, distance, weight, etc): *The shopkeeper was fined for giving ~ weight/ measure. The factory is/The workmen are on ~ time,* working fewer hours per day, or days per week, than usual. *These goods are in ~ supply,* The supply is not equal to the demand (*are scarce* is more usu). ⇨ also commons(2). *You've given me ~ change,* less than the correct change. Hence, ~·'*change* *vt* cheat (sb) by giving less than the correct change. **be ~ of,** (**a**) not have enough of: *~ of money/time.* (**b**) be distant from: *The car broke down when we were still five miles ~ of our destination.* **little/nothing ~ of,** nothing/little less than: *Our escape was little ~ of miraculous,* was almost a miracle. **make ~ work of,** deal with, dispose of, eat or drink, quickly. *~ of breath,* panting, eg after running fast. '*~-coming* *n* (usu *pl*) failure (to reach a required standard, to develop properly, to do one's duty). '*~ drink* *n* [C] (or, colloq a ~) whisky, gin, etc in comparatively small glasses or small portions at a time (contrasted with a long drink such as a glass of beer). ~-

'*handed* *adj* having not enough workmen or helpers. *~ 'sight,* *n* [U] inability to see clearly things that are distant, or (fig) to see into the future. Hence, ~·'*sighted* *adj: The Government's policy is ~-sighted,* does not take into account future needs, developments, etc. ~·'*winded* *adj* easily and quickly becoming breathless after exertion; unable to run for long. **3** (in comm) maturing early; to be paid or met soon: *a ~ bill/paper; ~ date,* early date for maturing of a bill, bond, etc. Hence, ~·'*dated* *adj.* ~ '*bond* *n* one which matures within a period of five years. ~·*term* '*capital,* capital raised for short periods. **4** (of a person) saying very little, or saying much in few words; (of what he says, his manner of speaking) expressed in few words; curt; abrupt: *He/His answer was ~ and to the point. He was very ~ with me.* **for ~,** as a ~er form; for brevity's sake: *Benjamin, called 'Ben' for ~.* **in ~,** in a few words; to sum up briefly (after a long description, etc). **the long and the ~ of it,** all that can or need be said. **5** (of cake, pastry) easily breaking or crumbling. ~ '*pastry* *n* [U] made with much butter or fat. '*~-bread/cake* *nn* easily crumbled dry cake made with flour, sugar and much butter. **6** (of vowels or syllables) taking the less of two usual durations; *the ~ vowel in 'pull' and the long vowel in 'pool'.* **7** (other compounds and special uses). '*~-fall* *n* deficit. '*~-hand* *n* [U] system of rapid writing using special signs; stenography. **by a ~ head,** (**a**) (racing) by a distance of less than the length of a horse's head: *Fly-by-Night won by a ~ head.* (**b**) (fig) by only a little. '*~-horn* *n* [C] name of a breed of cattle with ~ curved horns. ~ **leg/slip** *n* (cricket) ⇨ the illus at cricket. '*~ wave* *n* (radio telegraphy) one having a wave-length of from 10 to 100 metres. ~·*ly adv* **1** soon; in a ~ time; ~*ly after*(*wards*); ~*ly before noon. He is ~ly to leave for Mexico.* **2** briefly; in a few words. **3** sharply; curtly: *answer rather ~ly.* ~·*ness* *n*

short[2] /ʃɔːt/ *adv* **1** abruptly; suddenly: *stop ~. bring/pull/take sb up ~,* interrupt or check him abruptly. **~ of,** leaving out of question; except: *They would commit every crime ~ of murder.* **2** before the natural or expected time. **come/fall ~ of,** be insufficient, inadequate, disappointing (expectations, etc): *The box-office receipts fell ~ of the manager's expectations.* **cut sth/sb ~,** (**a**) interrupt; bring to an end before the usual or natural time: *The chairman had to cut ~ the proceedings.* (**b**) make ~(er). **go ~ (of),** do without; deprive oneself (of): *I don't want you to go ~* (of money, etc) *in order to lend me what I need.* **run ~ (of),** reach the end: *Our supplies ran ~. We're running ~ of paraffin.* **be taken ~,** (colloq) have a sudden motion of the bowels necessitating a hurried visit to the lavatory. **3** *sell ~,* (comm) sell for future delivery (stocks, shares, commodities, etc that one does not own) in the expectation of being able to buy more cheaply before the date agreed upon for delivery. **sell sb ~,** betray, cheat, belittle, them.

short[3] /ʃɔːt/ *n* (colloq) short circuit, ⇨ short[1](1); short drink. □ *vi, vt* short-circuit.

short·age /'ʃɔːtɪdʒ/ *n* [C,U] (amount of) deficiency; condition of not having enough: '*food ~s; a ~ of rice; owing to ~ of staff; a ~ of 50 tons.* ⇨ glut, *n*

shorten /'ʃɔːtn/ *vt, vi* [VP6A,2A] make or become shorter: *The days are beginning to ~,* eg in autumn. *The captain ordered his men to ~ sail,* re-

duce the area of sail spread to the wind. **~-ing**
/'ʃɔːtnɪŋ/ *n* [U] fat used for making pastry light and
flaky. ⇨ short¹(5).

shorts /ʃɔːts/ *n pl (pair of)* ~, short trousers extending to or above the knees, as worn by children,
by adults for games, informal wear (on the beach,
etc).

shot¹ /ʃɒt/ *n* **1** [C] (sound of the) firing of a gun,
etc: *hear ~s in the distance; the first ~s in the
campaign,* the start of the attack. *At each ~ he got
nearer to the centre of the target.* **(do sth) like a
~,** at once; without hesitation. **off like a ~,** off at
great speed. **2** [C] attempt to hit sth, hitting of sth;
attempt to do sth, answer a question, etc; throw,
stroke, hit, etc in certain games: *Good ~, Sir!
That remark was a ~ at me,* was aimed at me. **a ~
in the dark,** a wild or random guess. **have a ~ (at
sth),** try to do sth: *Have a ~ at solving the problem. The striker had a ~ at goal,* tried to score. *Let
me have a ~ at it. He made several lucky ~s at the
examination questions.* **a ꞌlong ~,** an attempt to
solve a problem, etc with little evidence, few facts
to go on: *It's a long ~ but I think John must have
known about the murder. ꞏnot by a ꞌlong ~,* not
even if circumstances were most favourable. **3** [C]
that which is fired from a gun, esp (formerly stone,
later metal) non-explosive projectile for old-
-fashioned cannon. ⇨ **shell**(3); heavy iron ball
thrown in athletic competition (called the 'ꞓ~-*put*):
putting the ~. **4 lead ~,** [U] quantity of tiny balls
(or pellets) of lead contained in the cartridge of a
sporting gun (instead of a single bullet), used
against birds and small animals. ⇨ the illus at cartridge. 'ꞓ~-**gun** *n* sporting gun with a smooth bore
firing cartridges containing ~. 'ꞓ~-**tower** *n* tower
in which ~ is made from molten lead poured
through a sieve at the top and falling into water. **5**
[C] person who shoots, with reference to his skill:
He's a first-class/good/poor, etc ~. **6** [C] photograph, or one of a series of photographs, taken with
a cine-camera: *The exterior ~s were taken in Ber-
muda.* '**long ~,** (opp of *close-up*) taken with a
long distance between the camera and the subject.
7 (esp US) injection from a hypodermic needle (of
a drug): *have a ~ in the arm.* **have/get/give sb a
~ in the arm, (a)** have/give sb an injection. **(b)**
have/give sb/sth that revives or restores, eg the
economy. **8 a ꞌbig ~,** (sl) an important person, esp
a conceited one.

shot² /ʃɒt/ *n* share of a reckoning or of expense:
pay one's ~.

should /ʃʊd/ *weak form* ʃəd/ *v*⇨ **shall.**

shoul·der /'ʃəʊldə(r)/ *n* **1** that part of the body of a
human being or animal where an arm or foreleg is
joined to the trunk (⇨ the illus at **trunk**), or where
the wing of a bird joins its neck; curve from this
point to the neck: *This coat is narrow across the
~s. He has one ~ a little higher than the other. ~
to ~,* side by side and touching; (fig) united. **give
sb the cold ~,** ⇨ cold¹(1). **put one's ~ to the
wheel,** work energetically at a task. **stand head
and ~s above** (others), be considerably taller (or,
fig, mentally or morally better) than. **straight
from the ~,** (fig, of criticism, rebukes, etc) frankly put. 'ꞓ~-**blade** *n* either of the flat bones of the
upper back, behind and below the neck. ⇨ the illus
at skeleton. 'ꞓ~-**strap** *n* **(a)** narrow strap on the ~
of a military uniform (with badges of rank, etc) **(b)**
ribbon which passes over a woman's ~ and supports a garment. 'ꞓ~-**flash** *n* strip of material on the

~ of a military uniform, with a coloured patch as
the distinguishing emblem of a division, etc. **2** (*pl*)
part of the back between the two ~s(1): *give a
child a ride on one's ~s; shift the blame to other
~s,* let others take the blame. **have broad ~s,** be
able to bear much weight or (fig) responsibility. **3**
~-like part of a bottle, tool, mountain, etc. **hard
~,** hard surface at the side of a roadway (esp a motorway). □ *vt* **1** [VP6A] take on the ~(s) (lit and
fig): *~ a burden/a task/the responsibility for sth.
~ arms,* (mil) move the rifle to an upright position
in front of the right ~. **2** [VP15A] push with the ~;
make (one's way) thus: *~ people aside; be ~ed to
one side; ~ one's way through a crowd.*

shout /ʃaʊt/ *n* [C] loud call or cry: *~s of joy; a ~
of alarm. They greeted him with ~s of 'Long live
the President'.* □ *vi, vt* ~ *(out),* **1**
[VP2A,B,C,4B,22] speak or cry out in a loud voice:
*Don't ~ at me! He ~ed to attract attention. He
~ed with pain. He ~ed himself hoarse.* **2**
[VP6A,15A,B,3A] say in a loud voice: *~ (out)
one's orders. They ~ed their disapproval,*
expressed it by ~ing. *He ~ed to me/~ed for me to
come. 'Go back!' he ~ed.* ~ **sb down,** to
prevent sb from being heard: *The crowd ~ed the
speaker down.* **~-ing** *n* [U] ~s. **It's all over but/
bar the ~ing,** The struggle, fight, etc is over and
the praise, cheers, etc will follow.

shove /ʃʌv/ *vt, vi* [VP6A,15A,B,2A,C] (colloq)
push (usu heavily): *~ a boat into the water. Stop
shoving! ~ off,* **(a)** start from the shore in a boat
(by pushing the shore, etc). **(b)** (sl) leave (a place):
I'm sick of this place; let's ~ off. □ *n* [C] vigorous
push: *Give it a ~.* ꞏ-**ha'penny** /ʃʌv 'heɪpnɪ/ *n* =
shovel-board.

shovel /'ʃʌvl/ *n* spade-like tool, used for moving
coal, sand, snow, etc ⇨ the illus at tool; large device used for the same purpose, mechanically operated from a crane in a vehicle. □ *vt* (-ll-, US -l-) **1**
[VP6A,15A,B] lift, move, with a ~: *~ up coal; ~
the snow away from the garden path.* **2**
[VP6A,15A] clear or clean with a ~: *~ a path
through the snow.* **~-ful** /-fʊl/ *n* as much as a ~
will hold.

shovel-board /'ʃʌvl bɔːd/ *n* [U] game in which
discs or coins are pushed along a board to a mark.

show¹ /ʃəʊ/ *n* **1** [U,C] showing (chiefly in): *by (a)
~ of hands,* (voting) by the raising of hands for or
against (a proposal). **2** [C] collection of things publicly displayed, esp for competition, or as a public
entertainment: *a ꞌflower/ꞌhorse/ꞌcattle ~; the ꞌmo-
tor ~,* = exhibition; *the Lord Mayor's ~,* a
procession through the City of London when a new
Lord Mayor is installed; *a travelling ~,* eg of circus animals. **on ~,** exhibited. **3** [C] (colloq) natural display; sth to be seen: *a fine ~ of blossom in
the Kent orchards.* **4** [C] (colloq) kind of public entertainment, eg circus, theatre, radio, TV, etc:
Have you seen any good ~s lately? 'ꞓ~-**business,**
(colloq) 'ꞓ~-**biz** /bɪz/ *n* the public entertainment
business. **5** [C] (colloq) performance (not theatrical, etc): *put up a good ~,* do sth creditably; *a poor
~,* sth done badly. **steal the ~,** attract all the attention: *Good ~!* used to express approval of sth
done well. **6** [C] (colloq) organization; undertaking; business; something that is happening: *Who's
running this ~,* Who controls or manages it? **give
the (whole)ꞌ~ away,** let people know what is being done or planned: *I wish she wouldn't talk and
give the ~ away.* **7** (*sing* only; dated colloq use)

opportunity of doing sth, defending oneself, etc: *Give the man a fair* ~. *He had no* ~ *at all.* **8** outward appearance; impression: *a claim with some* ~ *of·justice; with a* ~ *of reason. He didn't offer even a* ~ *of resistance.* **9** [U] pomp; display; ostentation: *a house furnished for* ~, *not comfort. They're fond of* ~. **10** (compounds) '~**-boat** *n* river steam-boat on which theatrical performances were given (esp on the Mississippi, US). '~**-case** *n* case with glass sides and (or) top, for showing and protecting articles in a shop, museum, etc; (fig) special exhibition of sth, esp sth new. '~**-down** *n* (colloq) full and frank declaration of one's strength, intentions, etc: *call for a* ~*-down*, ask (opponents, rivals, etc) for such a declaration; *if it comes to a* ~*-down*, if such a declaration is (or has to be) made. '~**-girl** *n* girl who sings or dances (or is merely decorative) in a musical play, revue, etc. '~**-jumping** *n* display of skill in riding horses over fences, barriers, etc. '~**-man** /-mən/ *n* (*pl* -men) (**a**) organizer of public entertainments (esp circuses). (**b**) person (esp in public life) who uses publicity, etc to attract attention to himself: *Some politicians are great* ~*men and very little else.* '~**-man·ship** /-mənʃɪp/ *n* art of attracting, ability to attract, public attention, eg to what one is trying to sell. '~**-place** *n* one that tourists go to see: *old palaces, castles and other* ~ *places.* '~**-room**/ **window** *n* one in which goods are kept for display, inspection, etc. ~**y** *adj* (-ier, -iest) likely to attract attention; (often contemptuous) (too) decorated or ornamented; (too) brightly coloured: ~*y flowers*, eg some kinds of dahlia; *a* ~*y dress; the* ~*y patriotism of persons hoping for titles.* ~**·ily** /-ɪlɪ/ *adv* ~**i·ness** *n*

show² (archaic **shew**) /ʃəʊ/ *vt,vi* (*pt* ~ed; *pp* ~n /ʃəʊn/, rarely ~ed) **1** [VP6A, 12A,13A,15A,19B,24A] ~ *sth* (*to sb*); ~ *sb sth*, bring before the sight: *You must* ~ *your ticket at the barrier. What films are they* ~*ing at the local cinema this week? He won several prizes for the roses he* ~*ed*, exhibited. *He* ~*ed me his pictures. He has* ~*n them to all his friends. The photograph* ~*s him sitting/seated at his desk.* **2** [VP6A] allow to be seen: *That frock* ~*s your petticoat*, is too short to cover it. *A dark suit will not* ~ *the dirt. My shoes are* ~*ing signs of wear.* **3** [VP2A,C] be visible or noticeable: *Your petticoat is* ~*ing, Jane. Does the mark of the wound still* ~? *The pink of the apple-blossom is beginning to* ~. *His fear* ~*ed in his eyes.* **4** [VP6A] ~ *itself*, be visible: *His annoyance* ~*ed itself in his looks.* ~ *oneself*, be present (at a meeting, etc): *Ought we to* ~ *ourselves at the Evans's party tonight?* ~ *one's face*, appear before people: *He's ashamed to* ~ *his face in the street.* ~ *fight*, give signs of being ready to fight. ~ *one's hand/cards*, (fig) make known one's intentions or plans. ~ *a leg*, (colloq) get out of bed. ~ *one's teeth*, (fig) look angry. *have nothing to* ~ *for it/sth*, have nothing that is evidence of what one has achieved or tried to achieve. **5** [VP6A,14,12A,13A] give; grant: ~ *mercy on sb. He* ~*ed me great kindness.* **6** [VP6A,25] give evidence or proof of having or being: *He* ~*s no sign of intelligence. She* ~*ed great courage. His new book* ~*s him to be a first-rate novelist.* **7** [VP15A,B] direct; conduct. ~ *sb in*; ~ *sb into sth*; ~ *sb out*; ~ *sb out of sth*, direct or conduct sb into/out of a place: *Please* ~ *this gentleman out. We were* ~*n into the living-room.*

~ *sb over/around/round, sth*, take sb round a place: *The guide* ~*ed us over the old castle.* ~ *sb the door*, require him to leave and go with him to the door to see that he does so. ~ *sb the way*, explain which way to go; (fig) set an example. **8** [VP6A,9,10,20,21,25] make clear; cause (sb) to understand; prove: *He* ~*ed me how to do it/how he had done it. He* ~*ed his annoyance/that he was annoyed/how annoyed he was. That* ~*s how little you know. We have* ~*n the falsity of the story/that the story is false/the story to be false.* **9** [VP2C,15B] ~ *sb/sth off*, display (sth) to advantage: *a swim-suit that* ~*s off her figure well; mothers who like to* ~ *off their daughters*, display their daughter's good looks, abilities, accomplishments, etc. ~ *off*, make a display of one's wealth, learning, abilities, etc in order to impress people: *a man who is always* ~*ing off.* Hence, '~*-off* *n* person who ~*s off: He's an irritating* ~*-off*, is always trying to show his abilities, etc. ~ *sb/sth up*, make the truth about (sb or sth dishonest, disreputable, etc) known: ~ *up a fraud/a rogue/an impostor.* ~ *up*, (**a**) be conspicuous, easily visible: *Her wrinkles* ~*ed up in the strong sunlight.* (**b**) [VP2A] (colloq) put in an appearance; be present (*at* sth); *Only three of the people we invited to the party didn't* ~ *up.* ~*ing* *n* (usu *sing*) (act of) displaying or pointing out; appearance; evidence: *a firm with a poor financial* ~*ing*, whose financial accounts do not appear to be good; *on present/past* ~*ing*, on present/past evidence. *on one's own* ~*ing*, by one's own admission.

shower /'ʃaʊə(r)/ *n* [C] **1** brief fall of rain, sleet or hail; sudden sprinkle of water: *be caught in a* ~; *a* ~ *of spray.* '~*(-bath)* *n* (washing one's body by using a) device by which water comes down in a ~ through a plate with numerous small holes: *have a* ~*(-bath) every morning.* **2** large number of things arriving together: *a* ~ *of blows/stones/blessings/ insults; sparks falling in a* ~*/in* ~*s.* **3** (US) party at which presents are given to a woman about to become a bride. □ *vt,vi* **2** [VP14] ~ *sth upon sb*; ~ *sb with sth*, send or give it to him in a ~: *They* ~*ed honours upon the hero/*~*ed the hero with honours. Questions were* ~*ed upon the new arrival.* **2** [VP2C] fall in a ~: *Good wishes* ~*ed (down) upon the bridegroom.* ~**y** *adj* (of the weather) with frequent ~s.

shown /ʃəʊn/ *pp* of **show².**

shrank /ʃræŋk/ *pt* of **shrink.**

shrap·nel /'ʃræpnəl/ *n* [U] fragments of shell or bullets packed inside a shell which is designed to explode and scatter these contents over a wide area: *hit by (a piece of)* ~.

shred /ʃred/ *n* [C] strip or piece scraped, torn or broken off sth; fragment: (fig) *not a* ~ *of truth in what she says; not a* ~ *of evidence against me. tear to* ~*s*, (lit or fig) destroy: *They have torn her reputation to* ~*s.* □ *vt* (-dd-) [VP6A] tear or scrape into ~s.

shrew /ʃruː/ *n* **1** bad-tempered, scolding woman. **2** '~*(-mouse)*, small mouse-like animal that feeds on insects. ~**·ish** /-ɪʃ/ *adj* scolding; sharp-tongued. ~**·ish·ly** *adv* ~**·ish·ness** *n*

shrewd /ʃruːd/ *adj* (-er, -est) **1** having, showing, sound judgement and common sense: ~ *business-men;* ~ *arguments.* **2** astute; discriminating: *make a* ~ *guess*, one likely to be correct; *a* ~ *blow/ thrust*, one carefully made and likely to be effective. ~**·ly** *adv* ~**·ness** *n*

shriek /ʃriːk/ *vi,vt* ~ *(out)*, 1 [VP2A,C] scream shrilly. 2 [VP6A,15B] utter in a shrill, screaming voice: ~ *out a warning;* ~ *with laughter.* □ *n* [C] shrill scream: ~*s of girlish laughter; the* ~ (= whistle) *of a railway engine.*

shrift /ʃrɪft/ *n* [U] (archaic) confession (of sins) to a priest; confession and absolution. *give sb/get short* ~, give him/get curt treatment, brief and unwilling attention.

shrike /ʃraɪk/ *n* (kinds of) bird (also called 'butcher-bird) with a strong, hooked bill and the habit of fastening its prey (small birds and insects) on thorns.

shrill /ʃrɪl/ *adj* (of sounds, voices, etc) sharp; piercing; high-pitched: ~ *cries; a* ~ *voice/ whistle.* ~y /ʃrɪlɪ/ *adv* ~·ness *n*

shrimp /ʃrɪmp/ *n* [C] small marine shellfish used for food, ⇨ the illus at crustacean; (hum) very small person. □ *vi* catch ~s: (usu) *go* ~*ing.*

shrine /ʃraɪn/ *n* [C] 1 tomb or casket containing holy relics; altar or chapel of special associations or hallowed by some memory. 2 building or place associated with sth or sb deeply respected or venerated: *a Shinto* ~, in Japan. *worship at the* ~ *of Mammon*, give excessive devotion to wealth and money-making. □ *vt* = enshrine (the usu word).

shrink /ʃrɪŋk/ *vi,vt* (*pt* shrank /ʃræŋk/, or shrunk /ʃrʌŋk/, *pp* shrunk, or, as *adj* shrunken /ʃrʌŋkən/) 1 [VP6A,2A] make or become less, smaller (esp of cloth through wetting): *Will this soap* ~ *woollen clothes? Those jeans will* ~ *in the wash. How your gums have shrunk since your teeth were extracted!* 2 [VP2A,C3A] ~ *(back) (from)*, move back, show unwillingness to do sth (from shame, dislike, etc): *A shy man* ~*s from meeting strangers. She shrank back from the horrifying spectacle.* '~·age /-ɪdʒ/ *n* [U] process of ~ing; degree of ~ing: *Make the pullover a little longer, and allow for* ~*age. The* ~*age in our export trade/in the value of our currency is serious.*

shrive /ʃraɪv/ *vt* (*pt* ~d or shrove /ʃrəʊv/, *pp* ~d or shriven /ʃrɪvn/) [VP6A] (archaic, of a priest) hear the confession of a penitent sinner and absolve him from the spiritual consequences of his sin(s).

shrivel /ʃrɪvl/ *vt,vi* (-ll-, US also -l-) [VP6A,15B,2A,C] ~ *(up)*, (cause to) become dried or curled (through heat, frost, dryness or old age): *The heat* ~*led up the leaves/the leather. He has a* ~*led face,* with the skin wrinkled.

shriven /ʃrɪvn/ ⇨ shrive.

shroud /ʃraʊd/ *n* [C] 1 (also called 'winding-sheet) cloth or sheet (to be) wrapped round a corpse: *You'll have no pockets in your* ~. 2 sth which covers and hides: *a* ~ *of mist.* 3 (*pl*) ropes supporting a ship's masts, ⇨ the illus at barque; ropes linking a parachute and the harness which is strapped to the parachutist. □ *vt* [VP6A,15A] 1 wrap (a corpse) in a ~. 2 cover; hide: ~*ed in darkness/ mist; a crime* ~*ed in mystery.*

shrove /ʃrəʊv/ ⇨ shrive.

Shrove Tues·day /ʃrəʊv 'tjuːzdɪ *US:* 'tuːz-/ *n* day before the beginning of Lent, on which, and on preceding days (**Shrove·tide**), it was formerly the custom to be shriven.

shrub /ʃrʌb/ *n* [C] plant with woody stem, lower than a tree, and (usu) with several separate stems from the root. ~·bery /ʃrʌbərɪ/ *n* (*pl*-ries) place, eg part of a garden, planted with ~s.

shrug /ʃrʌɡ/ *vt* (-ɡɡ-) [VP6A,15B] lift (the shoulders) slightly (to show indifference, doubt, etc). ~

sth off, dismiss it as not deserving attention, as sth trivial. □ *n* [C] such a movement: *with a* ~ *of the shoulders/a* ~ *of despair.*

shrunk(en) /ʃrʌŋk, 'ʃrʌŋkən/ ⇨ shrink.

shuck /ʃʌk/ *n* (US) husk; pod; outer covering; (fig) sth of little value. **S~s!** *int* (US) (exclamation of disbelief, regret, or irritation) □ *vt* [VP6A] remove the ~s from: ~ *peanuts/maize.*

shud·der /ʃʌdə(r)/ *vi* [VP2A,C,4C] shake convulsively; tremble with fear or disgust: ~ *with cold/ horror;* ~ *at the sight of blood. The ship* ~*ed as she struck the rocks. He* ~*ed to think of it.* □ *n* [C] uncontrollable shaking: *a* ~ *passed over her. It gives me the* ~*s,* (colloq) terrifies me.

shuffle /ʃʌfl/ *vi,vt* 1 [VP2A,C,6A] walk without raising the feet properly. ~ *one's feet,* slide or drag them on the ground when walking, or when standing or sitting. 2 [VP6A,15A,B,2A] slide or move (playing-cards, etc) one over the other to change their relative positions: ~ *the dominoes. He* ~*d the papers together in a drawer.* 3 [VP2C,15B] do sth in a careless way; slip (sth *off, on*) casually: ~ *through one's work;* ~ *one's clothes on/off;* (fig) ~ *off responsibility upon others,* get rid of it by passing it to others. 4 [VP2A] keep shifting one's position; be unstraightforward; try to avoid giving a certain answer, etc: *Don't* ~; *give a clear answer.* □ *n* [C] 1 shuffling movement; shuffling dance: ,soft-shoe '~; shuffling of cards: *Give the cards a good* ~. 2 general change of relative positions: *a* ~ *of the Cabinet; a Cabinet* ~, giving members different portfolios. 3 piece of dishonesty; misleading statement or action. **shuf·fler** *n* one who ~s.

shufty /ʃʌftɪ/ *n* (GB sl) *take/have a* ~ *(at sth/sb),* have a (quick) look (at it/him).

shun /ʃʌn/ *vt* (-nn-) [VP6A,D] keep away from; avoid: ~ *temptation/publicity/society.*

'shun /ʃʌn/ *int* (abbr of) attention(3) (as a word of command).

shunt /ʃʌnt/ *vt,vi* 1 [VP6A,15B] send (railway wagons, coaches, etc) from one track to another, esp to keep a track clear for important traffic: ~ *a train on to a siding.* 2 [VP2A] (of a train) be ~ed to a siding. 3 [VP6A,15A] (fig, colloq) divert; postpone or evade discussion of (sth): *She* ~*ed the conversation on to less morbid topics.* 4 [VP6A,15A] (fig) lay aside (a project); leave (sb) unoccupied, or inactive. ~**er** *n* (esp) railway employee who ~s wagons, etc.

shush /ʃʊʃ/ *vi,vt* 1 = hush. 2 = sh.

shut /ʃʌt/ *vt,vi* (*pt,pp* shut; -tt-) (For special uses with *adverbial particles* and *preps,* ⇨ 5 below.) 1 [VP6A,15A] move (a door, one's lips, etc) into position to stop an opening: ~ *the doors and windows;* ~ *a drawer;* ~ *one's mouth. He* ~ *his ears to all appeals for help,* refused to listen to them. *He* ~ *his eyes to* (= deliberately refused to notice) *her faults. Why have you* ~ *the door upon further negotiations,* refused to consider them? *They* ~ *the door against her/on her/in her face,* refused to receive or admit her. '~**-eye** *n* (colloq) nap; sleep: *It's time for half an hour's* ~*-eye.* 2 [VP2A] become closed; be able to be closed: *The window* ~*s easily. The door won't* ~. 3 [VP6A] bring the folding parts of (sth) together: ~ (= *close,* the more usu word) *a book/a clasp-knife.* 4 [VP15A] catch or pinch by shutting sth: ~ *one's fingers/dress, etc in the door,* ie between the door and the door-post. 5 [VP2C,15B] (special uses with *adverbial par*-

ticles and *preps*):

shut (sth) down, (of a factory, etc) stop working; end activity: *The workshop has* ~ *down and the workers are unemployed. They've* ~ *down their factory.* Hence, **'~-down** *n* (temporary or permanent) closing of a factory, etc.

shut sb in, confine or enclose: *We're* ~ *in by hills here,* surrounded by hills which make access difficult and which prevent us from seeing far. *They* ~ *the boy in the cellar,* kept him there as a prisoner.

shut sth off, stop the supply or flow of, eg gas, steam, water.

shut sb/sth out, keep out; exclude; block: ~ *out immigrants/competitive goods. Don't* ~ *me out,* Don't close the door(s) so that I must stay out. *These trees* ~ *out the view.*

shut sth up, (a) close and secure all the doors and windows: ~ *up a house before going away for a holiday. It's time to* ~ *up shop,* close the shop and stop doing business. **(b)** put away for safety: ~ *up one's jewels in the safe.* ~ **(sb) up,** (colloq) (cause sb to) stop talking: *Tell him to* ~ *up. Can't you* ~ *him up?*

shut·ter /'ʃʌtə(r)/ *n* [C] **1** movable cover (wooden panel or iron plate, hinged or separate and detachable) for a window, to keep out light or thieves: *The shop-front is fitted with rolling* ~*s.* **put up the** ~**s,** stop doing business (for the day, or permanently). **2** device that opens to admit light through the lens of a camera. □ *vt* [VP6A] provide with ~s; put up the ~s of.

shuttle /'ʃʌtl/ *n* **1** (in a loom) cigar-shaped instrument with two pointed ends by which thread of weft is carried between threads of warp; (in a sewing-machine) sliding holder which carries the lower thread to meet the upper thread to make a stitch. **2** (compounds) '~-cock *n* round-based cork with feathers in it, struck to and fro across a net in the games of battledore and ~cock and badminton. ⇨ the illus at badminton. ~ **diplomacy,** diplomatic negotiation requiring the diplomat(s) to travel to and fro between the groups involved. '~ **service,** service (of trains, buses, etc) to and fro between places not far apart. □ *vt,vi* [VP6A,15A,2C] (cause to) move backwards and forwards, to and fro, like a ~.

shy¹ /ʃaɪ/ *adj* (-er, -est) **1** (of persons) self-conscious and uncomfortable in the presence of others; (of behaviour, etc) showing this: *He's not at all shy with women. She gave him a shy look/ smile.* **2** (of animals, birds, fish, etc) easily frightened; unwilling to be seen. **3 shy of,** chary of; hesitating about: *They're shy of speaking to one another. Don't be shy of telling me what you want.* **fight shy of,** ⇨ fight²(1). **shy·ly** *adv* **shy·ness** *n*

shy² /ʃaɪ/ *vi* (*pt,pp* shied /ʃaɪd/) [VP2A,3A] **shy (at sth),** (of a horse) turn aside from in fear or alarm: *The horse was shying at a white object in the hedge.*

shy³ /ʃaɪ/ *vt* (*pt,pp* shied /ʃaɪd/) (colloq) [VP6A,15A] throw: *shying stones at a bottle.* □ *n* (*pl* shies /ʃaɪz/) throw: *fivepence a shy,* eg throwing balls at coconuts at a fair; (colloq) any kind of attempt: *have a shy at a task/an examination.*

shy·ster /'ʃaɪstə(r)/ *n* (US, colloq) person without professional honour, esp an unscrupulous lawyer.

Sia·mese /ˌsaɪə'miːz/ *adj* of Siam (now *Thailand*). ~ **twins,** two persons joined together from birth. ~ **(cat),** oriental breed of cat with blue eyes and short-haired coat of cream, fawn or light grey hair.

□ *n* (now *Thai*) native of Siam; language of Siam. ⇨ App 6.

Si·berian /saɪ'bɪərɪən/ *adj* of, coming from, Siberia /saɪ'bɪərɪə/ (the NE part of the USSR).

sibi·lant /'sɪbɪlənt/ *adj* having, making, a whistling kind of sound. □ *n* sound such as one of the six English sounds /s, z, ʃ, ʒ, tʃ, dʒ/.

sib·ling /'sɪblɪŋ/ *n* one of two or more persons having the same parents; brother or sister.

sibyl /'sɪbl/ *n* one of several women in ancient times who, it was believed, could see the future and give out messages from the gods; (hence, contemptuous or hum) fortune-teller; prophetess. ~**line** /'sɪbəlam/ *adj* uttered by, characteristic of, a ~; mysteriously prophetic.

sic /sɪk/ *adv* (Lat) thus (placed in brackets to indicate that the preceding word, statement, etc is correctly quoted even though this seems unlikely or is clearly incorrect).

Si·cil·ian /sɪ'sɪlɪən/ *n, adj* (native) of Sicily /'sɪsɪlɪ/.

sick /sɪk/ *adj* **1** (*pred* only) **be** ~, throw up food from the stomach. **feel** ~, feel that one is about to do this. **'air-/car-/sea-**~ *adj* vomiting or inclined to vomit because of the motion of a plane/car/ship. Hence, **'air-/car-/sea-**~**ness** *n: I was sea*~ *on the first day of the voyage.* **2** unwell; ill (in GB *ill* and *unwell* are polite usage, in US *sick* is normal usage): *He's been* ~ *for six weeks. He's a* ~ *man.* **be off** ~ **(with sth),** be away from one's work because of bad health or disease: *Kate's off* ~ *with flu/a bad back.* **fall** ~, become ill. **go/report** ~, (mil use) report to the doctor for medical treatment. **the** ~, (*pl*) those who are ill. **'~-bay** *n* **(a)** (Navy) part of a ship for those who are ill. **(b)** medical centre on a university campus, etc. **'~-bed** *n* bed of a sick person. **'~-benefit** *n* ⇨ sickness. **'~-berth** *n* = ~-bay(a). **'~-headache** *n* bilious headache. **'~-leave** *n* [U] permission to be away from duty or work because of illness: *on* ~-*leave.* **'~-list** *n* list of those who are ill (eg in a regiment, on a warship, etc). **'~-parade** *n* (mil) parade of those who are reporting ~. **'~-pay** *n* [U] pay to an employee who is absent from work because he is ill. **'~-room** *n* room occupied by, or kept ready for, sb who is ill. **3** ~ **(and tired/to death) of,** (colloq) tired of, disgusted with: *I'm* ~ *to death, of being blamed for everything that goes wrong.* **4** ~ **at heart,** deeply sad. ~ **at/about sth,** (colloq) unhappy, filled with regret about it: ~ *at failing to pass the examination.* **5** ~ **for,** filled with a longing for: ~ *for home/old happy times.* **6** (sl) morbid; perverted: ~ *humour/jokes; a* ~ *mind.* □ *vt* ~ *sth up,* (colloq) vomit; throw up from the stomach.

sicken /'sɪkən/ *vi,vt* **1** [VP2A,3A] ~ **(for sth),** be in the first stages of (an illness): *The child is* ~*ing for something.* **2** [VP6A] cause to feel disgusted: *Cruelty* ~*s most of us. Their business methods* ~ *me.* **3** [VP3A,4C] ~ **at sth/to see sth,** feel sick to see: *They* ~*ed at the sight of so much slaughter/* ~*ed to see so many people slaughtered.* ~ **of sth,** become tired of, disgusted with: *He* ~*ed of trying to bring about reforms.* ~**·ing** /'sɪkənɪŋ/ *adj* disgusting: ~*ing smells/cruelty.* ~**·ing·ly** *adv*

sick·ish /'sɪkɪʃ/ *adj* somewhat sick or sickening: *feel* ~; *a* ~ *smell.*

sickle /'sɪkl/ *n* [C] short-handled tool with a curved blade for cutting grass, grain, etc. ⇨ the illus at tool.

sick·ly /'sɪklɪ/ *adj* (-ier, -iest) **1** frequently ill; often in poor health: *a ~ child.* **2** having the appearance of sickness or ill health; pale: *These plants are/ look rather ~.* **3** weak; faint; suggesting unhappiness: *a ~ smile.* **4** causing, or likely to cause, a feeling of sickness or distaste: *a ~ smell/taste; ~ sentiments.*

sick·ness /'sɪknɪs/ *n* **1** [U] illness; ill health: *Is there much ~ in the village now? They were absent because of ~.* '~ **benefit,** insurance payment to sb absent from work through illness. **2** [C,U] (an) illness or disease: *suffering from* '*mountain ~/'sea-~/'air-~.* **3** [U] inclination to vomit; vomiting.

side[1] /saɪd/ *n* [C] (except **13** below) **1** one of the flat or fairly flat surfaces of a solid object: *the six ~s of a cube.* **2** one of the surfaces which is not the top or the bottom: *A box has a top, a bottom, and four ~s.* **3** one of the surfaces which is not the top, bottom, front or back: (attrib) *the ~ entrance of the house* (contrasted with the *front* or *back* entrance). **4** (maths) one of the lines bounding a plane figure such as a rectangle or triangle. **5** either of the two surfaces of a thin, flat object or of material such as paper, cloth, anything manufactured in sheets: *Write on one ~ of the paper only. Which is the right ~ of the cloth,* the ~ intended to be seen? **6** inner or outer surface of sth vertical, sloping, round or curved: *the ~ of a mountain; put one's socks on the wrong ~ out* (= inside out, the usu phrase); *prehistoric paintings on the ~s* (= walls) *of a cave.* **7** one of the two halves of a person on his left or right, esp from armpit to hip: *wounded in the left ~. Come and sit by/at my ~. ~ by ~,* close together, for mutual support. *split/burst one's ~s (laughing/with laughter),* laugh heartily. Hence, '~-**splitting** *adj* causing hearty laughter. *by the ~ of; by one's ~,* close to and compared with: *She looks small by the ~ of her companion.* **8** one of the two halves of an animal from foreleg to hindleg, esp as part of a carcass: *a ~ of beef/ bacon.* **9** part of an object, area, space, etc away from, at a distance from, a real or imaginary central line: *the left/right/shady/sunny ~ of the street; the east ~ of the town; the debit/credit ~ of an account. He crossed to the far/the other ~ of the room. on/from all ~s; on/from every ~,* in/ from all directions; everywhere. *take sb on one ~,* take him aside, apart, eg to speak to him in confidence. *on the right/wrong ~ of (fifty, etc),* below/above (50 years of age, etc). *(do sth) on the ~,* **(a)** as a ~line. ⇨ sideline below. **(b)** secretly, discreetly: *He lived with his wife but regularly saw Julia on the ~. put sth on one ~,* **(a)** put it aside, apart. **(b)** postpone dealing with it. **10** one of two groups or parties of people who are opposed (in games, politics, war, etc) or who uphold beliefs, opinions, etc against the other: *be on the winning/losing ~; faults on both ~s; to pick* (= choose) *~s. Austria has a strong ~,* eg a good football team. *be on sb's ~,* be a supporter of him: *Whose ~ are you on, anyway?* = Aren't you supposed to be supporting me? *Both countries claimed that God was on their ~,* eg in a war. *let the* '~ *down,* give an inferior performance and disappoint one's colleagues, team-mates, etc. *take ~s (with),* support (sb, a party) in a dispute. ⇨ side[2]. *off/on ~,* (football, hockey) in a position (for receiving or playing the ball) that is/is not contrary to the rules. **11** aspect or view that is not complete; aspect different from or opposed to other aspects: *look on the dark/bright/gloomy, etc ~ of*

things/life, etc; *study all ~s of a question; a man with many ~s to his character. There are two ~s to the story,* two aspects. *on the* '*high/*'*low, etc ~,* rather high/low, etc: *Prices offered for fat cattle were on the high ~.* **12** line of descent through a parent: *a cousin on my father's ~.* **13** [U] (colloq) behaviour suggesting that one is better than other people; arrogance. *have no/be without ~,* make no pretence, assumption, of being superior or important. *put on ~,* claim to be, behave as if one is, superior. **14** (compounds, etc) '~-**arms** *n pl* swords or bayonets, worn at the left ~ by soldiers. '~-**board** *n* table, usu with drawers and cupboards, placed against the wall of a dining-room. '~-**burns/-boards** *n pl* ~-whiskers. '~-**car** *n* small one-wheeled car fastened to the ~ of a motor-cycle. '~-**chapel** *n* one in the aisle or at one ~ of a church. ⇨ the illus at church. '~-**dish** *n* extra dish or course at a meal. '~-**drum** *n* small, double-sided drum, (originally hung at the drummer's ~) in a jazz or military band. '~ **effect** *n* secondary or indirect effect, eg an undesirable effect of a drug used for a specific purpose. '~-**face** *adv* in profile: *photograph sb ~-face.* '~-**glance** *n* look to or from one ~. '~ **issue** *n* question of less importance (in relation to the main one). '~-**light** *n* light from or at the ~; (fig) incidental illumination, eg of a person's character, of a problem, etc. '~-**line** *n* class of goods sold in addition to the chief class of goods; occupation which is not one's main work. '~-**lines** *n pl* (space immediately outside) lines bounding a football pitch, tennis-court, etc at the ~s. *on the ~-lines,* (fig) merely as a spectator, not taking part. '~-**long** *adj, adv* (directed) to or from one ~: *look ~long at sb; a ~long glance.* '~-**road** *n* minor road branching off a main road. '~-**saddle** *n* woman's saddle, made so that both feet may be on the same ~ of the horse. □ *adv on a ~-saddle: In former times most women used to ride ~-saddle.* '~-**show** *n* **(a)** small show at a fair or exhibition. **(b)** activity of small importance in relation to the main activity. '~-**slip** *n* **(a)** (motoring) skid. **(b)** (flying) movement to one ~ instead of forward. □ *vi* (-pp-) make a ~-slip. '~·**s·man** /-zmən/ *n* (*pl* -men) church helper who shows people to their seats, takes up the collection, etc. '~·**step** *n* step taken to one ~ (eg to avoid a blow in boxing). □ *vt,vi* (-pp-) [VP6A] avoid (a blow, etc) by stepping to one ~; evade (a question); [VP2A] step to one ~. '~-**stroke** *n* (kinds of) stroke used in swimming in which one ~ is above and the other below the water. '~-**track** *n* railway siding; branch road. □ *vt* [VP6A] turn (a train) into a siding; (fig) turn (a person) from his purpose; postpone consideration of (a proposal, etc). '~-**view** *n* view obtained from the ~. '~-**walk** *n* (chiefly US; GB = *pavement*) path at the ~ of a street for persons on foot. '~-**whiskers** *n pl* hair on the ~s of the face down to, but excluding, the chin. ⇨ beard. -**sided** /-saɪdɪd/ *suff* having a specified number of ~s: *a 'five-~d figure.* ~-**wards** /-wədz/, ~**ways** /-weɪz/ *advv* to, towards, from, the ~; with the ~ or edge first: *look ~ways at sb; walk/carry sth ~ways through a narrow opening;* (attrib) directed to one ~.

side[2] /saɪd/ *vi* [VP3A] ~ **with,** take part, be on the same side (as sb in an argument or quarrel): *It is safer to ~ with the stronger party.*

sid·er·eal /saɪ'dɪərɪəl/ *adj* of the stars and their measurements: ~ *time,* measured by the stars; *the*

~ **year**, 365 days, 6 hours, 10 minutes.

sid·ing /'saɪdɪŋ/ n [C] short railway track to and from which trains may be shunted.

sidle /'saɪdl/ vi [VP2C] ~ **along/off;** ~ **away from/up to sb,** move in a shy or nervous way: *The little girl ~d up to me.*

siege /si:dʒ/ n [C,U] (period of) operations of armed forces who surround and blockade a town or fortress in order to capture it: *a ~ of 50 days. Before the ~ ended, the citizens were almost starving.* **lay ~ to (a town, etc),** surround and blockade it. **raise a ~,** end it by forcing the enemy's forces to withdraw. '~ **artillery/guns,** big guns used in ~s (too heavy, in former times, for use in the field).

si·en·na /sɪ'enə/ n [U] kind of earth used as a colouring matter: *burnt ~,* reddish-brown; *raw ~,* brownish-yellow.

si·er·ra /sɪ'erə/ n [C] long mountain chain with sharp slopes and edges (esp in Spain and Spanish America).

si·es·ta /sɪ'estə/ n [C] period of rest or sleep taken in the early afternoons, as is customary in hot countries.

sieve /sɪv/ n [C] utensil with wire network or gauze for separating finer grains, etc from coarse grains, etc or solids from liquids. **have a head/memory like a ~,** be incapable of remembering anything. □ vt [VP6A] put through, sift with, a ~.

sift /sɪft/ vt,vi 1 [VP6A,14,15A,B] ~ **(out) (from),** put, separate by putting, through a sieve: ~ *the cinders;* ~ *(out) ashes from the cinders/the wheat from the chaff.* 2 [VP6A,15A] shake through a sieve: ~ *flour;* ~ *sugar on to a cake.* 3 [VP6A] (fig) examine carefully: ~ *the evidence.* 4 [VP2C] fall, pass, come through, as from a sieve. ~**er** n small sieve-like utensil, chiefly used in cooking: *a 'flour~er.*

sigh /saɪ/ vi,vt 1 [VP2A] take and exhale a deep breath that can be heard (indicating sadness, tiredness, relief, etc); (of the wind) make a sound like ~ing. 2 [VP3A] ~ **for sth,** feel a longing (for): ~ *for the good old days to return.* 3 [VP6A,15B] ~ **(out),** express, utter, with ~s: ~ *out a prayer.* □ n [C] act of ~ing; sound of ~ing: *utter/heave a ~; with a ~ of relief.*

sight¹ /saɪt/ n 1 [U] power of seeing: *lose one's ~,* become blind; *have long/short* or *far/near ~,* be able to see things well only at long/short range; *have good/poor ~* (= eyesight). **know sb by ~,** know him by appearance only, not as an acquaintance. **second ~,** ⇨ second¹(1). 2 [U, but sometimes with *indef art*] seeing or being seen: *Their first ~ of land came after three days at sea.* **catch ~ of; have/get a ~ of,** begin to see; succeed in seeing: *If you ever catch ~ of Ted Clark anywhere, call the police.* **keep ~ of; keep sb/sth in ~,** remain near enough to see or watch. **lose ~ of,** see no longer; fail to pay further attention to; forget about: *I've lost ~ of that bird. We must not lose ~ of the fact that....* **at/on ~,** as soon as (sb or sth) is seen: *play music at ~,* from printed music without previous study or practice; *a draft payable at ~/a '~ draft,* to be paid at once when presented. *The sentry had orders to shoot at/on ~,* as soon as he saw any suspicious person, etc. **at first ~,** when first seen; without study, examination, etc: *At first ~ the problem seemed insoluble. He fell in love with her at first ~.* **at (the) ~ of,** on seeing: *At ~ of the police officers the men ran off. They all*

laughed at the ~ of old Percy dancing with a girl of sixteen. 3 [U] range of seeing; distance within which seeing is possible: *in/within/out of (one's) ~,* (of objects, etc) visible/invisible. *The train was still in ~/was not yet out of ~. Victory was not yet in ~. in/within/out of ~ of sth,* (of the viewer) where sth can/cannot be seen: *We are not yet out of ~ of land,* can still see it. *We are now within ~ of the end of this boring task,* can look forward to reaching the end. **come into/go out of ~,** come near enough/go too far away to be visible. **keep out of ~,** stay where one cannot be seen. **keep out of sb's ~,** stay where he cannot see you. 4 [U] opinion; way of looking at sth: *Do what is right in your own ~. All men are equal in the ~ of God.* 5 [C] sth seen or to be seen, esp sth remarkable; (*pl*) noteworthy buildings, places, features, etc of a place or district: *The Grand Canyon is one of the ~s of the world. Our tulips are a wonderful ~ this year/are a ~ to see. Come and see the ~s of London.* Hence, '~**-seeing** n going about to see places, etc. '~**-seer** /-si:ə(r)/ n person who goes to see the ~s. **a ~ for sore eyes,** person or thing that enjoys seeing; sb or sth very welcome. 6 **a ~,** (colloq) person or thing that excites ridicule or unfavourable comment: *What a ~ she looks in that old dress! What a ~ you are! She 'does look a ~!* 7 [C] (often *pl*) device that helps to aim or observe when using a rifle, telescope, etc: *the ~s of a rifle;* aim or observation taken with such a device: *take a careful ~ before firing; take a ~ with a compass/ quadrant; take a ~ at the sun,* eg to determine a ship's position. 8 **a ~,** (sl) great quantity: *It cost him a ~ of money/trouble. He's a ~* (adverbial, = very much) *too clever to be caught by the police.* **not by a 'long ~,** not nearly. –~**ed** suff (with *adjj*) having the kind of ~(1) indicated: 'weak-/ 'long-/far-~ed.

sight² /saɪt/ vt [VP6A] 1 get sight of, esp by coming near: *After many months at sea, Columbus ~ed land.* 2 observe (a star, etc) by using sights(7); adjust the sights(7) of a gun; furnish (a gun, etc) with sights: *a '~ing shot,* one to get the range. ~**·ing** n occasion on which sth is ~ed: *new ~ings of the Loch Ness monster.*

sight·less /'saɪtlɪs/ adj blind.

sign¹ /saɪn/ n [C] 1 mark, object, symbol, used to represent sth: *mathematical ~s,* eg +, −, ×, ÷. 2 word or words, design, etc, on a board or plate to give a warning, or to direct sb towards sth: 'traffic ~s, eg for a speed limit, a bend in the road. '~**-post** n post at or near crossroads with names of places on each road (and often distances). □ vt provide with ~posts: *The road is well ~-posted.* 3 sth that gives evidence, points to the existence or likelihood of sth: *the ~s of suffering on his face. Are dark clouds a ~ of rain? Violence is a ~ of weakness or fear, not a ~ of strength or confidence.* ~ **and counter~,** secret sentences, etc by which friends can be distinguished from enemies or from those who do not share a secret. 4 movement of the hand, head, etc used with or instead of words; signal: *a '~-language,* eg one used by deaf and dumb persons; *the ~ of the cross,* a movement with the hand outlining a cross, as a blessing, or with a prayer. 5 '~**(-board),** device (often painted on a board) displayed by traders and shopkeepers ('shop-~), and by inns ('inn-~), to advertise their business: *at the ~ of the Red Lion,* at the inn of this name. '~**-painter** n person who paints

~boards.

sign² /saɪn/ vt,vi [VP6A,15B,2A,2C] write one's name on (a letter, document, etc) to show that one is the writer or that one accepts or agrees with the contents: ~ a letter/a Will and Testament/a cheque; ~ one's name, write it for this purpose. Please ~ on the dotted line. ~ sth away, give up (rights, property, etc) by ~ing one's name. ~ (sb) in/out, write one's/sb's name as a record of arrival/departure. ⇨ clock in/out at clock¹(2). ~ on, (colloq) (of an unemployed worker) become formally registered for money on social security, ⇨ social(2). ~ on/up, (of a worker, etc), ~ an agreement about employment: The seaman ~ed on for a voyage to Valparaiso and back. ~ sb on/up, (of an employer, etc) ~ an agreement about employment: The firm ~ed on fifty more workers last week. The manager, ie of a football team, has ~ed up some new players. ~ sth over (to sb), confirm the sale of sth (to sb) by ~ing legal papers. 3 [VP3A,6A] ~ (to/for) sb (to do sth), make known (to sb) an order or request by making signs(4): The policeman ~ed (for) them to stop. He ~ed to me to be quiet. 4 [VP2C] ~ on/off, (radio) indicate the beginning/end of a broadcast, eg by means of a few bars of a tune or by other sound effects. ⇨ signature(2).

sig·nal¹ /'sɪgnəl/ n [C] 1 (making of a) movement, (showing of a) light, (sending of a) message, device used, to give a warning, an order or information, esp to sb at a distance; order, warning, etc, conveyed in this way: 'traffic ~s, for cars, etc in the streets; 'hand ~s, made with the hand by the driver of a motor-vehicle to show which way it will turn, etc; give the ~ for an attack. A red light is usually a ~ of danger. A train must not pass a ~ that is at danger. '~-box n building on a railway from which ~s and movements of trains are controlled. '~-man /-mən/ n (pl -men) person who operates ~s on a railway; man who sends and receives ~s (in the army and navy). '~ gun n one fired as a ~ in case of distress, eg on a wrecked ship. 2 event which is the immediate cause of general activity, etc: The arrival of the President was the ~ for an outburst of cheering. 3 electronic impulse in radio, TV, etc; sound or TV image, transmitted or received: an area with a poor/excellent TV signal. □ vt,vi (-ll-, US, -l-) [VP6A,9,17,2A,C] make a ~ or ~s to; send by ~; make use of ~(s): ~ a message; ~ (to) the commanding officer (that...); ~ (to) the waiter to bring the menu; ~ that one is about to turn left. Sailors ~ with flags by day and with lights at night. ~·ler (US = ~er) /'sɪgnələ(r)/ n person who ~s, esp a soldier (cf Navy, '~·man) specially trained in sending and receiving messages.

sig·nal² /'sɪgnəl/ attrib adj remarkable; outstanding: a ~ victory/success/achievement. ~·ly /-nəlɪ/ adv in a ~ manner: fail ~ly.

sig·nal·ize /'sɪgnəlaɪz/ vt [VP6A] make (an event) noteworthy or conspicuous.

sig·na·tory /'sɪgnətrɪ US: -tɔːrɪ/ n [C] (pl -ries) (person, country, etc) that has signed an agreement; the signatories to the Treaty; (attrib) the ~ powers.

sig·na·ture /'sɪgnətʃə(r)/ n [C] 1 person's name signed by himself: put one's ~ to a letter; send letters in to the manager for ~, for him to sign. 2 '~ tune, tune (a few bars of a piece of music) identifying a broadcasting station or a particular pro-

gramme or performer. '**key** ~, (music) indication of a (change of) key.

sig·net /'sɪgnɪt/ n [C] private seal used with or instead of a signature. '~-ring, finger ring with a ~ set in it. **Writer to the S**~, Scottish law officer.

sig·nifi·cance /sɪg'nɪfɪkəns/ n [U] meaning; importance; understand the ~ of a remark; a matter/speech of great/little ~; a look of deep ~.

sig·nifi·cant /sɪg'nɪfɪkənt/ adj ~ (of), having a special or suggestive meaning; important: a ~ speech. Few things are more ~ of a man's interests than the books on his shelves. ~·ly adv

sig·nifi·ca·tion /ˌsɪgnɪfɪ'keɪʃn/ n [C] (intended) meaning (of a word, etc).

sig·nifi·cat·ive /sɪg'nɪfɪkətɪv US: -keɪtɪv/ adj ~ (of), offering evidence (of).

sig·nify /'sɪgnɪfaɪ/ vt,vi (pt,pp -fied) 1 [VP6A,9,15A] make known (one's views, intentions, purpose, etc); be a sign of; mean: He signified his agreement/that he agreed by nodding. His wife signified her approval. Do dark clouds ~ rain? What does this phrase ~? 2 [VP2A,C] matter; be of importance: It doesn't ~. It signifies much/little.

si·gnor /'siːnjɔː(r)/, **si·gnora** /sɪ'njɔːrə/, **si·gnor·ina** /ˌsiːnjɔː'riːnə/ nn S~, titles used of or to Italians, corresponding to Mr, Mrs and Miss or (with a small s) Sir, Madam and young lady.

Sikh /siːk/ n member of a monotheistic Hindu sect founded in the 16th c in the Punjab.

si·lage /'saɪlɪdʒ/ n [U] green fodder stored in a silo or pit without drying (to feed cattle in winter).

si·lence /'saɪləns/ n [U] 1 condition of being quiet or silent; absence of sound: the ~ of night/of the grave. 2 condition of not speaking, answering (questions, spoken or written), or making comments, etc; (with indef art) period (of saying nothing): Your ~ on recent events surprises me. There was a short ~ and then uproar broke out. **S~ gives consent**, (prov) If nothing is said in answer to a proposal or suggestion we may suppose that it is agreed to. **reduce sb to ~**, (esp) refute his arguments so that he has to stop talking. **in ~**, silently: listen to sb in ~. We should not pass over this disgraceful affair in ~, We ought to protest, etc. □ vt [VP6A] make (sb or sth) silent; cause to be quiet(er): ~ a baby's crying; ~ one's critics/the enemy's guns. **si·lencer** n device that reduces the noise made by the exhaust of a petrol engine, the report of a gun, etc.

si·lent /'saɪlənt/ adj 1 making no or little sound; still; not accompanied by any sound: a ~ prayer; with ~ footsteps; the ~ running of a Rolls Royce car; a ~ film, without a sound track. 2 saying little or nothing; giving no answer, views, etc: Do you know when to keep ~, say nothing, keep a secret? You'd better be ~ about what happened. Her husband is the strong, ~ type. '~ partner, (US) = sleeping partner. ⇨ sleep²(1). 3 written but not pronounced: a ~ letter, eg b in doubt, w in wrong. ~·ly adv

sil·hou·ette /ˌsɪluː'et/ n picture in solid black showing only the outline; outline of sb or sth seen against a light background: see sth in ~. □ vt (usu passive) show, exhibit, in ~: ~d against the eastern sky at dawn. ⇨ the illus at hansom.

sil·ica /'sɪlɪkə/ n [U] silicon dioxide (SiO₂), occurring as ~ sand (used in glass-making) in quartz, and as the principal constituent of sandstone and other rocks.

sili·cate /'sɪlɪkeɪt/ n [U] one of a great number of compounds containing silica: ∼ of soda.

sili·con /'sɪlɪkən/ n [U] non-metallic element (symbol **Si**) found combined with oxygen in quartz, sandstone, etc. ∼ **'chip** n chip made of ∼, used to make an integrated circuit. ➪ **integrate(1)**.

sili·cone /'sɪlɪkəʊn/ n [U] (kinds of) complex organic compounds of silicon used in paints, varnish and lubricants.

sili·co·sis /ˌsɪlɪ'kəʊsɪs/ n [U] disease caused by breathing in quartz dust (eg in a coalmine).

silk /sɪlk/ n 1 [U] fine, soft thread from the cocoons of certain insects; material made from this; (attrib) made of this: raw ∼; ∼ stockings; a ∼ shirt. **'∼-screen (printing)**, method of printing by forcing the colour(s) through a stencil of ∼ or other finely woven material. **'∼·worm** n caterpillar that spins ∼ to form a cocoon. 2 (pl) garments of ∼: dressed in ∼s and satins, wearing rich clothes. 3 [C] (in England) Queen's/King's Counsel (abbr **QC, KC**). ➪ **counsel¹(3)**. **take** ∼, become a QC/KC.

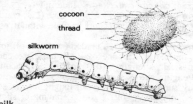

cocoon ———
thread ———
silkworm
silk

silken /'sɪlkən/ adj 1 soft and smooth; soft and shining: a ∼ voice; ∼ hair. 2 (old use, or liter) made of silk: ∼ dresses.

silky /'sɪlkɪ/ adj (-ier, -iest) soft, shiny, smooth, like silk: a ∼ (= suave) manner; a ∼ voice. **silki·ness** n

sill /sɪl/ n [C] flat shelf or block of wood or stone at the base of a window (= **'window-sill**) or (rarely) of a doorway. ➪ the illus at window.

sil·la·bub (US = **syll-**) /'sɪləbʌb/ n [C,U] soft, sweet dish of food made of cream or milk mixed with wine into curd, etc.

silly /'sɪlɪ/ adj (-ier, -iest) foolish; weak-minded: say ∼ things; a ∼ little boy. Don't be ∼! How ∼ of you to do that! □ n (pl -lies) (chiefly used to or by children) ∼ person. **sil·li·ness** n

silo /'saɪləʊ/ n (pl ∼s /-ləʊz/) [C] airtight structure (either a tall cylindrical tower or a pit) in which green food (silage) is stored for farm animals.

silt /sɪlt/ n [U] sand, mud, etc carried by moving water (and left at the mouth of a river, in a harbour, etc). □ vt,vi [VP2C,15B] ∼ (sth) up, (cause to) become stopped with ∼: The harbour has ∼ed up. The sand has ∼ed up the mouth of the river.

sil·van /'sɪlvən/ = sylvan.

sil·ver /'sɪlvə(r)/ n [U] 1 shining white precious metal (symbol **Ag**) used for ornaments, coins, utensils, etc: 'table ∼, spoons, forks, etc. ∼ **plate**, metal articles coated with ∼. **be born with a ∼ 'spoon in one's mouth**, be born into a wealthy family. 2 ∼ coins: £20 in notes and £5 in ∼; a handful of ∼; a ∼ collection, to which ∼ coins are to be given. Have you any ∼ on you? 3 ∼ vessels, dishes, articles, eg candlesticks, trays: have all one's ∼ taken by burglars; sell one's ∼ to pay the mortgage interest. 4 (attrib) the colour of ∼: the ∼ moon; (of sounds) soft and clear: He has a ∼ tongue/is ˌ∼-'tongued, is eloquent. ∼ **grey**, lust-

rous grey. **the ∼ screen**, cinema; cinema screen. 5 (in art and literature) second best: the ∼ age, ➪ golden(2). 6 (compounds) ˌ∼ 'birch n common white birch with ∼-coloured bark. '∼-fish n (kinds of) small wingless insect that damages book bindings, clothes, etc. ∼ **'paper**, (colloq) thin, light foil made of tin or aluminium (as used for packing chocolates, cigarettes, etc). ∼-**side** n best side of a round of beef. '∼-**smith** n manufacturer of ∼ articles; merchant who sells these. ˌ∼ 'wedding n 25th anniversary. □ vt,vi 1 [VP6A] coat with ∼ or with sth that looks like ∼; make (sth) bright like ∼: The years have ∼ed her hair. 2 [VP2A] become white or ∼ colour. Her hair had ∼ed. ∼y adj like ∼: the ∼y notes of a temple bell.

sil·vern /'sɪlvən/ adj (archaic) silver: Speech is ∼ but silence is golden, it is better to be silent than to speak.

sim·ian /'sɪmɪən/ adj, n (of, like, a) monkey or ape.

simi·lar /'sɪmɪlə(r)/ adj ∼ (to), like; of the same sort: My wife and I have ∼ tastes in music. Gold is ∼ in colour to brass. ∼·ly adv /ˌsɪmə'lærətɪ/ n [C] (pl -ties) likeness; state of being ∼; [C] point or respect in which there is likeness: points of ∼ity between the two men. Are there any ∼ities between China and Japan?

sim·ile /'sɪmɪlɪ/ n [C,U] (use of) comparison of one thing to another, eg 'He is as brave as a lion.' 'Childhood is like a swiftly passing dream': He uses interesting ∼s. His style is rich in ∼.

sim·ili·tude /sɪ'mɪlɪtjuːd US: -tuːd/ n 1 [U] (formal) resemblance (in general details but not in everything). 2 [C] comparison; simile: talk in ∼s.

sim·mer /'sɪmə(r)/ vi,vt 1 [VP2A,B,6A,15A] be, keep (sth), almost at boiling-point: Let the soup ∼ for a few minutes. S∼ the stew for an hour. 2 [VP2C] be filled with (anger, etc), which is only just kept under control: ∼ with rage/laughter/ annoyance. ∼ **down**, (fig) become calm (after being angry or excited). □ n (sing only) **keep sth at a ∼/on the ∼**, ∼ing.

sim·ony /'sɪmənɪ/ n [U] (hist) offence of accepting or offering money for a position in the Church.

si·moom /sɪ'muːm/, **si·moon** /sɪ'muːn/ n hot, dry, dust-laden wind blowing in a straight track in the Sahara and the deserts of Arabia.

sim·per /'sɪmpə(r)/ vi [VP2A], n (give a) silly, self-conscious smile. ∼-**ing·ly** /'sɪmprɪŋlɪ/ adv

simple /'sɪmpl/ adj (-r, -st) 1 unmixed; not divided into parts; having only a small number of parts: a ∼ substance; a ∼ machine; a ∼ sentence, one without subordinate clauses. ∼ **interest**, on capital only, not on accumulated interest. ➪ compound¹(3). 2 plain; not much decorated or ornamented: ∼ food/cooking; a ∼ style of architecture; the ∼ life, a way of living without luxuries, servants or artificial pastimes, or in the country, contrasted with cities. 3 not highly developed: ∼ forms of life. 4 easily done or understood; not causing trouble: written in ∼ English; a ∼ task. 5 innocent; straight-forward: behave in a pleasant and ∼ way; as ∼ as a child; ∼ folk. ˌ∼-'hearted adj frank. ∼-'minded adj (a) frank; unsophisticated. (b) feeble-minded. 6 inexperienced; easily deceived: Are you ∼ enough to believe everything your newspapers tell you? I'm not so ∼ as to suppose you like me. She's a ∼ soul, innocent of guile. 7 with nothing added; absolute: a ∼ fact. **pure and ∼**, (colloq) absolute(ly), unquestionably: *It's a case of kill or be killed, pure and* ∼. □ *n* [C] (old use) herb used medicinally. **sim·ply** /'sɪmplɪ/ *adv* **1** in a ∼(2) manner: *live simply; dress simply; simply dressed.* **2** completely; absolutely: *His pronunciation is simply terrible,* is very bad indeed. *She looks simply lovely.* **3** only; merely; nothing more nor less than: *This drink consists simply of fresh oranges. You must believe me simply on my word,* with nothing more than my assertion, without proof or evidence. *It is simply a matter of working hard.*

simple·ton /'sɪmpltən/ *n* foolish, weak-minded person, esp one who is easily deceived.

sim·plic·ity /sɪm'plɪsətɪ/ *n* [U] the state of being simple: *the* ∼ *of the problem; speak with* ∼. *be* ∼ *itself,* (colloq) be extremely easy.

sim·plify /'sɪmplɪfaɪ/ *vt* (*pt,pp* -fied) [VP6A] make simple; make easy to do or understand: *a simplified reader/text. That will* ∼ *my task.* **sim·pli·fi·ca·tion** /ˌsɪmplɪfɪ'keɪʃn/ *n* [U] act or process of ∼ing; [C] instance of ∼ing; sth simplified.

simu·lac·rum /ˌsɪmjʊ'leɪkrəm/ *n* (*pl* -cra /-krə/) sth made in the likeness of a person or object; shadowy likeness that deceives.

simu·late /'sɪmjʊleɪt/ *vt* [VP6A] **1** pretend to be; pretend to have or feel: ∼*d innocence/enthusiasm.* **2** counterfeit: *insects that* ∼ *dead leaves.* **simu·la·tion** /ˌsɪmjʊ'leɪʃn/ *n* [U] pretence; imitation. **simu·la·tor** /-tə(r)/ *n* (esp) apparatus designed to provide (for testing purposes) conditions (eg non-gravity, for simulating weightlessness) like those which are encountered in real operations.

sim·ul·ta·neous /ˌsɪml'teɪnɪəs US: ˌsaɪm-/ *adj* ∼ *(with),* happening or done at the same time as. ∼·**ly** *adv* ∼·**ness, sim·ul·ta·ne·ity** /ˌsɪmltə'niːətɪ US: ˌsaɪm-/ *nn*

sin /sɪn/ *n* **1** [U] breaking of God's laws; behaviour that is against the principles of morality, ⇨ *crime;* [C] instance of this; immoral act such as telling a lie, stealing, murder: *confess one's sins to a priest; ask for one's sins to be forgiven.* **live in sin,** (dated or hum use) live together as if married. **original sin,** proneness to commit sin which, some Christians believe, is part of mankind's nature. **deadly/ mortal sin,** one that is fatal to salvation of the soul. *the seven deadly sins,* pride, covetousness, lust, anger, gluttony, envy, sloth. **2** [C] (colloq) offence against convention; sth considered contrary to common sense: *It's a sin to give the children so much homework. It's a sin to stay indoors on such a fine day.* □ *vi* (-nn-) [VP2A,3A] *sin (against),* commit sin; do wrong: *We are all liable to sin. Is it sinning against society to have a very large family?* **sin·ful** /-fl/ *adj* wrong; wicked. **sin·ful·ness** *n* **sin·less** *adj* free from sin; innocent. **sin·less·ness** *n* **sin·ner** /'sɪnə(r)/ *n* person who sins/has sinned.

since /sɪns/ *adv* **1** (with the perfect tenses) after a date, event, etc in the past; before the present time; between some time in the past and the present time, or the time referred to: *The town was/had been destroyed by an earthquake ten years ago/earlier and has/had* ∼ *been rebuilt. He left home in 1970 and has not been heard of* ∼. *ever* ∼, throughout the whole of a period of time referred to and up to the present: *He went to Turkey in 1956 and has lived there ever* ∼. **2** (with the simple tenses) ago (which is the usu word): *He did it many years* ∼. *How long* ∼ *is/was it?* □ *prep* (with the perfect tenses in the main clause) after; during a period of time after: *S*∼ *last seeing you I have been ill. She*

hasn't/hadn't been home ∼ *her marriage.* □ *conj* **1** (with the perfect tenses in the main clause) from the past time when: *Where have you been* ∼ *I last saw you?* (with the simple present tense in the main clause): *How long is it* ∼ *you were in London? It is just a week* ∼ *we arrived here.* **2** seeing that; as: *S*∼ *we've no money, we can't buy it.*

sin·cere /sɪn'sɪə(r)/ *adj* **1** (of feelings, behaviour) genuine; not pretended: *It is my* ∼ *belief that.... Are they* ∼ *in their wish to disarm?* **2** (of persons) straightforward; not in the habit of expressing feelings that are pretended. ∼·**ly** *adv* in a ∼ manner. *Yours* ∼*ly,* commonly used before a signature at the end of a letter to a friend or acquaintance. **sin·cer·ity** /sɪn'serətɪ/ *n* [U] the quality of being ∼; honesty: *speaking in all sincerity,* very ∼ly and honestly.

sin·ecure /'saɪnɪkjʊə(r)/ *n* [C] position for which one receives credit or payment but which does not entail work or responsibility.

sine die /ˌsaɪnɪ 'daɪiː/ *adv* (Lat) without a date fixed: *adjourn a meeting* ∼, indefinitely.

sine qua non /ˌsaɪneɪ kwɑː 'nəʊn/ *n* (Lat) condition or qualification that cannot be done without; essential condition.

sinew /'sɪnjuː/ *n* [C] **1** tendon (strong cord) joining a muscle to a bone. **2** (*pl*) muscles; energy; physical strength; (fig) means of acquiring strength. *the* ∼*s of war,* money (with which to buy supplies). **sin·ewy** *adj* tough; having strong ∼s: ∼*y arms;* (fig) vigorous; having or showing nervous strength.

sing /sɪŋ/ *vi,vt* (*pt* sang /sæŋ/, *pp* sung /sʌŋ/) **1** [VP2A,C,3A,6A,12B,13B,15A] make musical sounds with the voice; utter words to a tune: *She* ∼*s well. He was* ∼*ing a Malay song. He was* ∼*ing to the guitar/to a piano accompaniment. She sang the baby to sleep. You're not* ∼*ing in tune. You're* ∼*ing out of tune. Will you* ∼ *me a song/*∼ *a song for me?* ∼ *another tune,* behave or speak in a different way, eg with less confidence or presumption. ∼ *small,* (colloq) speak or behave humbly (after being reproved, etc). **2** [VP2A,C] make a humming, buzzing or ringing sound: *The kettle was* ∼*ing (away) on the cooker. My ears are* ∼*ing,* are affected with buzzing sounds. **3** [VP6A,3A] ∼ *(of) sth,* (liter) celebrate in verse: ∼ *(of) sb's exploits.* ∼ *sb's praises,* praise him with enthusiasm. **4** ∼ *out (for),* shout (for). ∼ *sth out,* shout sth: ∼ *out an order.* ∼ *up,* ∼ with more force, ∼ more loudly: *S*∼ *up, girls, and let's hear you.* ∼**er** *n* person who ∼s, esp one who does this in public. ∼**ing** *n* (esp) art of the ∼er: *teach* ∼*ing; my '*∼*ing-master; take '*∼*ing lessons.* ∼·**able** /-əbl/ *adj* that can be sung: *Some of this modern music is not* ∼*able.*

singe /sɪndʒ/ *vt,vi* (*pres part* singeing) **1** [VP6A] burn off the tips or ends (esp of hair, as may be done at the hair-dresser's): *have one's hair cut and* ∼*d.* **2** [VP6A] blacken the surface of by burning; burn slightly: *If the iron is too hot you'll* ∼ *that dress. She was busy* ∼*ing the poultry,* burning the downy feathers off the birds (after they had been killed). **3** [VP2A] become ∼d or scorched. □ *n* slight burn or scorch (on cloth, etc).

single /'sɪŋgl/ *adj* **1** one only; one and no more: *a* ∼ *cherry hanging from the tree. in* ∼ *file,* (moving, standing) one behind the other in a line. ∼-'**breasted** *adj* (of a coat) having only one row of buttons down the front. ∼ '**combat,** fight with

weapons, one man against another man. ,~-
'**handed** adj, adv done by one person without help
from others. ,~-'**minded** adj having, intent on,
only one purpose. '~-**stick** n [C,U] (fencing with a)
stick about the length of a sword. ~ **ticket** n ticket
for a journey to a place, not there and back. Cf US
one-way ticket. ~ **track** n (on a railway) one line
only, with traffic in one direction only at one time.
2 not married: ~ men and women; remain ~; the
~ state/life, that of an unmarried person. **3** for the
use of, used for, done by, one person: a ~ bed;
reserve (at a hotel) two ~ rooms and one double
room. **4** (bot) having only one set of petals. ⇨
double¹(5): a ~ tulip. □ n [C] **1** (tennis and golf)
game with one person on each side: play a ~; the
men's/women's ~s at Wimbledon; (cricket) hit for
which one run is scored: run a quick ~; (baseball)
base hit. **2** (short for a) ~ ticket: two second-class
~s to Leeds. □ vt [VP15B] ~ **sb/sth out,** select
from others (for special attention, etc): Why have
you ~d out this incident for criticism? **sing·ly**
/'sɪŋglɪ/ adv one by one; by oneself. ~·**ness** n [U]
quality of being ~. ~**ness of purpose,** complete
devotion to one purpose only.
sin·glet /'sɪŋglɪt/ n (GB) sleeveless garment worn
for games or under a shirt; vest.
single·ton /'sɪŋgltən/ n [C] (in card games) single
card of any suit held in one hand (of 13 cards): a ~
in hearts.
sing·song /'sɪŋsɒŋ/ n **1** meeting of friends to sing
songs together; impromptu vocal concert: have a
~ round the camp fire. **2** in a ~, (of a voice) in a
rising and falling way; in a monotonous rhythm:
(attrib) in a ~ voice/manner.
sin·gu·lar /'sɪŋgjʊlə(r)/ adj **1** (liter) uncommon;
strange: Isn't it unwise to make yourself so ~ in
your dress, to be so unconventional? **2** (formal)
outstanding: a man of ~ courage and honesty. **3**
(gram) of the form used in speaking or writing of
one person or thing. □ n the ~ number: What is the
~ of children? ~·**ly** adv outstandingly; strangely;
peculiarly. ~·**ity** /,sɪŋgjʊ'lærətɪ/ n (pl -ties) [C]
strangeness; [C] sth unusual or strange. '~·**ize**
/-aɪz/ vt make ~(1).
Sin·ha·lese, Sin·gha·lese /,sɪnhə'li:z, ,sɪŋhə'li:z/
adj of the larger of the communities in Sri Lanka
and their language. ⇨ Tamil. □ n member, language, of this community.
sin·is·ter /'sɪnɪstə(r)/ adj **1** suggesting evil or the
likelihood of coming misfortune: a ~ beginning. **2**
showing ill will: a ~ face; ~ looks. **3** (in heraldry)
on the left side of the shield (regarded from the
bearer's point of view). **bar** ~, mark on a shield
showing illegitimate descent.
sink¹ /sɪŋk/ n [C] **1** fixed basin (of stone, porcelain,
steel, etc) with a drain for taking off water, usu under water taps in a kitchen or scullery, used for
washing dishes, cleaning vegetables, etc: She complains that she spends half her life at the kitchen ~,
seldom gets away from dull domestic work. **2** cess-
pool. **3** (fig) place where evil people and evil practices collect: That part of the town is a ~ of iniquity.
sink² /sɪŋk/ vi, vt (pt sank /sæŋk/, pp sunk /sʌŋk/,
and, as adj, sunken /'sʌŋkən/) **1** [VP2A,C] go
down, esp below the horizon or the surface of water or other liquid or a soft substance, eg mud: The
sun was ~ing in the west. Wood does not ~ in
water, it floats. The ship sank, went to the bottom.
~ or swim, phrase used of running great risks

when the alternatives are complete loss or failure
and safety or success. **2** [VP2A,C] slope downwards; become lower or weaker: The foundations
have sunk. The ground ~s to the sea. The soldier
sank to the ground badly wounded. (fig) His heart
sank at the thought of failure. **3** [VP6A,15A] make
by digging: ~ a well; place (sth) in a hole made by
digging: ~ a post one foot deep in the ground. **4**
[VP2C,3A] ~ in; ~ into sth, (of liquids, and fig)
go down deep: The rain sank into the dry ground.
Let this warning ~ into your mind. The lesson
hasn't sunk in, (fig) has not been learnt or fully understood. **5** [VP2C,3A] ~ in; ~ into/to sth, come
to a lower level or state (physical or moral): ~ into
a deep sleep; ~ into vice; ~ into insignificance; ~
in the estimation of one's friends. He was sunk in
thought/despair. He is ~ing fast, will soon die.
The old man has sunken cheeks. His cheeks have
sunk in. His voice sank to a whisper. **6** [VP6A,15A]
cause or allow to ~: ~ a ship. He sank (=
lowered) his voice to a whisper. Let us ~ our differences (= put them out of our thoughts, forget
them), and work together. **7** [VP6A,14] ~ (in), invest (money), esp so that it is not easy to withdraw
it: He has sunk half his fortune in a new business
undertaking. '~·**able** /-əbl/ adj that can be sunk.
sinker /'sɪŋkə(r)/ n [C] (esp) lead weight attached
to a fishing line or net to keep it under the water.
hook, line and ~, ⇨ hook(1).
sink·ing /'sɪŋkɪŋ/ n (gerund) (esp) a '~ **feeling,**
feeling in the stomach caused by fear or hunger.
'~-**fund** n money from revenue put aside by a
government, business company, etc for gradual repayment of a debt.
Sinn Fein /,ʃɪn 'feɪn/ n political movement and organization founded in Ireland in 1905 for independent republican government.
Si·nol·ogy /saɪ'nɒlədʒɪ/ n [U] knowledge, study, of
the Chinese language and culture. **Si·nol·ogist**
/-dʒɪst/ n expert in ~.
sinu·ous /'sɪnjʊəs/ adj winding; full of curves and
twists. **sinu·os·ity** /,sɪnjʊ'ɒsətɪ/ n (pl -ties) [U] being ~; [C] curve or twist.
sinus /'saɪnəs/ n (pl ~es) [C] hollow in a bone,
esp one of several air-filled cavities in the bones of
the skull, communicating with the nostrils. ~·**itis**
/,saɪnə'saɪtɪs/ n [U] inflammation of a ~. ⇨ the illus at skeleton.
Sioux /su:/ n member of a N American Indian
tribe.
sip /sɪp/ vt, vi (-pp-) [VP6A,15B,2A] drink, taking a
very small quantity at a time: sip (up) one's coffee.
□ n [C] (quantity taken in a) sipping: drink brandy
in sips, not gulps.
si·phon /'saɪfən/ n [C] **1** bent or curved tube, pipe,
etc so arranged (like an inverted U) that liquid will
flow up through it and then down. **2** bottle from
which soda-water can be forced out by the pressure
of gas in it. □ vt, vi [VP15B] ~ **sth off/out,** draw
(liquid) out or off through or as if through a ~:
Who has ~ed off all the petrol from the tank of my
car?
sir /sɜ:(r)/ n **1** polite form used in addressing a man
to whom one wishes to show respect: Yes, sir.
Dinner is served, sir. Sir, it is my duty to inform
you that. . . . **2 Sir,** used at the beginning of a formal
letter: Dear Sir/Sirs. **3 Sir** /sə(r)/, title used before
the first name of a knight or baronet: Sir 'Edward;
Sir ,John 'Jackson.
sir·dar /'sɜ:dɑ:(r)/ n (in some Asian countries) of-

ficer or leader of high, esp military, rank.

sire /'saɪə(r)/ n 1 (old use) father or male ancestor. 2 (old use) title of respect used when addressing a king or emperor. 3 male parent of an animal: *race-horses with pedigree* ∼*s.* □ *vt* [VP6A] (esp of horses) be the ∼ of: *a Derby winner* ∼*d by Pegasus.*

si·ren /'saɪərən/ n 1 (Gk myth) one of a number of winged women whose songs charmed sailors and caused their destruction; (hence) woman who attracts and is dangerous to men. 2 ship's whistle for sending warnings and signals; device for producing a loud shrill noise (as a warning, etc): *an 'air-raid* ∼; *an ambulance/a fire-engine racing along with its* ∼*s wailing.*

sir·loin /'sɜːlɔɪn/ n [C,U] best part of loin of beef.

sir·occo /sɪ'rɒkəʊ/ n (pl ∼s /-kəʊz/) [C] hot, moist wind reaching Italy from Africa.

sir·rah /'sɪrə/ n (contemptuous; archaic) sir.

sirup /'sɪrəp/ = syrup.

si·sal /'saɪsl/ n [U] plant (⇨ agave) with fleshy leaves which provide strong fibre used for making rope: (attrib) ∼ *grass/fibre/rope.*

sissy /'sɪsɪ/ n (colloq; derog) effeminate or cowardly person. **sis·si·fied** /'sɪsɪfaɪd/ adj effeminate or cowardly.

sis·ter /'sɪstə(r)/ n 1 daughter of the same parents as oneself or another person: *my/your/his* ∼. '**half–**∼ n related by one parent only. ⇨ also step-∼ at step-. '∼**-in-law** n (pl ∼s-in-law) ∼ of one's wife or husband; wife of one's brother. 2 person who behaves towards one as a ∼ does: *She was like a* ∼ *to him.* 3 (GB) senior hospital nurse. 4 member of certain religious orders; nun: *S*∼*s of Mercy,* a nursing sisterhood. 5 (attrib) of the same design or type: ∼ *ships/organisations.* ∼**·ly** adj of or like a ∼: ∼*ly love; a* ∼*ly kiss.* ∼**·hood** /-hʊd/ n [C] society of women who devote themselves to charitable works, nursing, etc or live together in a religious order.

sit /sɪt/ vi,vt (pt,pp sat /sæt/, -tt-) (For special uses with *adverbial particles* and *preps,* ⇨ 8 below.) 1 [VP2A,C] take or be in a position in which the body is upright and supported by the buttocks (resting on the ground or on a seat): *sit on a chair/ on the floor/in an armchair/at a table or desk/on a horse, etc. The child is not big enough to sit at table yet. sit to an artist,* have one's portrait painted by him (while sitting). *sit (for) an examination,* take one. *sit for one's portrait,* have one's portrait painted while sitting before an artist. *sit tight,* (a) remain firmly in one's place, esp in the saddle. (b) (colloq) stick firmly to one's purpose, opinions, etc. *sit for (a borough, etc),* represent it in Parliament. Hence, *sitting member,* the candidate (at a general election) who held the seat before the dissolution of Parliament. 2 [VP6A] cause to sit; place in a sitting position: *He lifted the child and sat* (= seated) *her at a little table; (reflex): Sit yourself down,* be seated. 3 [VP2A] (of Parliament, a law court, a committee, etc) hold meetings: *The House of Commons was still sitting at 3am.* 4 [VP6A] keep one's seat on (a horse, etc): *She sits her horse well. He couldn't sit his mule.* 5 [VP2A,C] (of birds) perch: *sitting on a branch.* ,**sitting 'duck,** an easy target or victim. ,**sitting 'tenant,** one who is actually in occupation (of a house, flat, etc, contrasted with a prospective tenant): *greedy owners who want to get rid of sitting tenants and then charge higher rents to new te-*

nants. 6 [VP2A] (of domestic fowls) remain on the nest in order to hatch eggs: *That hen wants to sit.* 7 [VP2C] (of clothes) suit, fit, hang: *That dress sits well/loosely, etc on her. The coat sits badly across the shoulders. His new dignity sits well on him,* (fig) suits him well. 8 [VP2C,3A,15B] (special uses with *adverbial particles* and *preps*):

sit back, (a) settle oneself comfortably back, eg in a chair. (b) (fig) take one's ease (after strenuous activity, etc); take no action.

sit down, (a) take a seat: *Please sit down, all of you.* ,**sit–down 'strike,** strike by workers who refuse to leave the factory, etc until their demands are considered or satisfied. *sit down under (insults, etc),* suffer without protest or complaint.

sit in, (of workers, students, etc) demonstrate by occupying a building (or part of it) and staying there until their grievances are considered or until they themselves are ejected: *There are reports of students sitting in at several universities.* Hence, '**sit-in** n such a demonstration. *sit in on sth,* attend (a discussion, etc) as an observer, not as a participant.

sit on/upon sth, (a) (of a person) be a member of (a jury, committee, etc). (b) (colloq) neglect to deal with: *They've been sitting on my application for a month. sit on/upon sth,* (of a jury, etc) inquire into, investigate (a case). *sit on/upon sb,* (colloq) repress; snub: *That impudent fellow needs to be sat on.*

sit out, sit outdoors: *It's hot indoors—let's sit out in the garden, shall we? sit sth out,* (a) stay to the end of (a performance, etc): *sit out a boring play.* (b) take no part in (esp a particular dance): *I think I'll sit out the next dance.*

sit up, not go to bed (until later than the usual time): *I shall be late getting back, so please don't sit up for me. The nurse sat up with her patient all night. Ought children to sit up late looking at TV programmes? sit (sb) up,* (cause to) take an upright position after lying flat or sitting badly: *The patient is well enough to sit up in bed now. Just sit me up a little,* help me to sit up. *sit up straight!* Don't lean back! Don't sprawl! *make sb sit up (and take notice),* (colloq) alarm or frighten him; rouse him from lethargy to activity.

si·tar /sɪ'tɑː(r)/ n Hindu stringed musical instrument. ⇨ the illus at string.

site /saɪt/ n [C] place where sth was, is, or is to be: *built on the* ∼ *of an old fort; a* ∼ *for a new school; deliver materials to a 'building* ∼. □ *vi* [VP6A] locate; place: *Where have they decided to* ∼ *the new factory?*

sit·ter /'sɪtə(r)/ n 1 person who is sitting for a portrait. 2 hen that sits(5): *a good/poor* ∼. 3 bird or animal that is sitting and therefore easy to shoot; (hence) easy shot; sth easily done. 4 ⇨ *baby-*∼ at baby.

sit·ting /'sɪtɪŋ/ n 1 time during which a court of law, Parliament, etc is ∼ continuously: *during a long* ∼. 2 period of time during which one is engaged continuously in a particular occupation: *finish reading a book at one* ∼. 3 act of ∼ for a portrait: *The artist wants you to give him six* ∼*s,* sit for him six times. 4 occasion of ∼ (for a meal, etc): *In the dining-room of this hotel 100 people can be served at one* ∼, ie at the same time, together. 5 collection of eggs on which a hen sits. 6 '∼**-room** n room for general use (contrasted with a dining-room, bedroom, etc).

situ·ated /'sɪtʃʊeɪtɪd/ *pred adj* **1** (of a town, building, etc) placed: *The village is ~ in a valley.* **2** (of a person) in (certain) circumstances: *Having six children and no income, the widow was badly ~. I'm awkwardly ~ just now,* in difficult circumstances.

situ·ation /ˌsɪtʃʊ'eɪʃn/ *n* [C] **1** position (of a town, building, etc). **2** condition, state of affairs, esp at a certain time: *be in an embarrassing ~.* **3** work, employment: *S~s vacant, S~s wanted,* headings of newspaper notices of employment offered and asked for; *be in/out of a ~,* be employed/ unemployed.

six /sɪks/ *n adj* the number 6, ⇨ App 4. **(It is) six of one and half a dozen of the other,** There is very little difference between the one and the other. *in sixes,* in groups of six at a time. *at sixes and sevens,* in confusion. **,six-'footer** *n* (colloq) person six feet in height; thing six feet long. **'six-pence** *n* **(a)** former GB coin value (formerly) six pennies (*6d*), or (since 1971) 2½p. **(b)** the sum of six pennies, either 6*p* or 6*d*. ⇨ App 5. **'six-penny** *adj* costing 6*d* or 6*p*. **,six-'shooter** *n* revolver with six chambers. **'six-fold** /-fəʊld/ *adj, adv* six times as much or as many; six times as great. **six·teen** /sɪk'sti:n/ *n, adj* the number 16. **six·teenth** /si:k'sti:nθ/ *n, adj* **sixth** /sɪksθ/ *n, adj* **'sixth form** *n* (in secondary schools, GB) form (= class) for pupils being prepared for A-level examinations. ⇨ level²(3). **'sixth-former** *n* pupil in this form. **,sixth 'sense** *n* power to be aware of things independently of the five senses; intuition. **sixth·ly** *adv* **six·ti·eth** /'sɪkstɪəθ/ *n, adj* **sixty** /'sɪkstɪ/ *n, adj* the number 60. **the sixties** *n pl* 60–69.

size¹ /saɪz/ *n* **1** [U] degree of largeness or smallness: *a building of vast ~; about the ~ of* (= about as large as) *a duck's egg; of some ~,* fairly large. *They're both of a ~,* are the same ~. *That's about the ~ of it,* (colloq) That's a fair account of

the affair, situation, etc. **2** [C] one of the standard and (usu) numbered classes in which articles of clothing, etc are made: *a ~ fifteen collar; trousers three ~s too large; all ~s of gloves. I take ~ nine shoes.* □ *vt* [VP6A] **1** arrange in ~s or according to ~. [VP15B] *~ sb/sth up,* (colloq) form a judgement or opinion of. **-sized** /-saɪzd/ *suff* (in compounds) having a certain ~: *medium-sized.* **'siz(e)·able** /-əbl/ *adj* fairly large.

size² /saɪz/ *n* [U] sticky substance used to glaze textiles, paper, plaster, etc. □ *vt* [VP6A] stiffen or treat with ~.

sizzle /'sɪzl/ *vi* [VP6A], *n* (colloq) (make the) hissing sound as of sth cooking in fat: *sausages sizzling in the pan;* (fig) *a sizzling hot day.*

ice-skating

skate¹ /skeɪt/ *n* ('ice-)~, one of a pair of sharp-edged steel blades to be fastened to a boot for moving smoothly over ice. ⇨ the illus at hockey. ⇨ also *roller-~s* at roller(2). □ *vi* [VP2A,C] move on ~s: *~ over/round a difficulty/a delicate problem,* make only passing and cautious reference to it. *~ on thin ice,* talk about a subject that needs great tact. **'~-board** *n* narrow board for standing on, about 50cm long, mounted front and back on two pairs of roller-skate wheels, used in sport over a

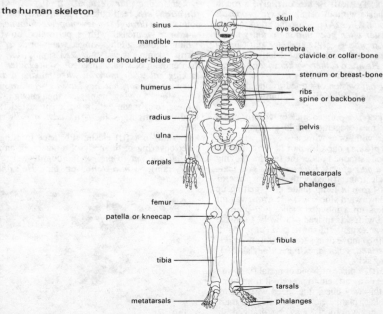

the human skeleton

sinus — skull
— eye socket
mandible —
— vertebra
scapula or shoulder-blade — — clavicle or collar-bone
— sternum or breast-bone
humerus —
— ribs
— spine or backbone
radius —
— pelvis
ulna —
carpals —
— metacarpals
— phalanges
femur —
patella or kneecap —
— fibula
tibia —
— tarsals
metatarsals — — phalanges

smooth surface (eg for racing, demonstrating skill). '∼-boarder n person using a ∼board. '∼-boarding n [U] sport of using a ∼board. 'skat-ing n sport of using ∼s. 'skat-ing-rink n specially prepared surface for skating. ∼r n person who ∼s.

skate² /skeɪt/ n large, flat, long-tailed sea-fish, valued as food.

ske-daddle /skɪˈdædl/ vi [VP2A] (GB, colloq, usu imper) run away.

skeet /skiːt/ n (kind of) clay-pigeon shooting. ⇨ pigeon(2).

skein /skeɪn/ n [C] length of silk or wool yarn or thread coiled loosely into a bundle.

skel-eton /ˈskelɪtn/ n [C] 1 bony framework of an animal body; bones of an animal body in the same relative positions as in life; hard framework of woody fibre containing a vegetable body: He looks like a living ∼. reduced to a ∼, (of an animal, a human being) very thin as the result of hunger, illness, etc. the ∼ in the cupboard; the family ∼, sth of which a family is ashamed and which it tries to keep secret. 2 framework of a building, organization, plan, theory, etc; outline to which details are to be added: the steel ∼ of a new building. 3 (attrib) '∼ key, one that will open a number of different locks. a ∼ staff/crew/service, etc, one reduced to the smallest possible number needed for maintenance.

skep /skep/ n (kinds of) wicker basket; straw or wicker bee-hive.

skep-tic /ˈskeptɪk/ ⇨ sceptic.

sketch /sketʃ/ n [C] 1 rough, quickly made drawing: make a ∼ of a face/place. '∼-book/-block nn book or pad of sheets of drawing-paper for making ∼es on. '∼-map n one with outlines but little detail. 2 short account or description; rough draft or general outline, without details: He gave me a ∼ of his plans for the expedition. 3 short, humorous play or piece of writing. □ vt,vi 1 [VP6A] make a ∼ of; [VP15B] ∼ sth out, give a rough plan of; indicate without detail: ∼ out proposals for a new road. 2 [VP2A] practise the art of making ∼es: My sister often goes into the country to ∼. ∼er n person who ∼es(2). sketchy adj (-ier, -iest) 1 done roughly and without detail or care. 2 incomplete: He has a rather ∼y knowledge of geography. ∼ily /-ɪlɪ/ adv ∼i-ness n

skew /skjuː/ adj twisted or turned to one side; not straight. '∼-eyed adj (colloq) squinting. on the ∼, (colloq) ∼.

skewer /ˈskjʊə(r)/ n pointed stick of wood or metal for holding meat together while cooking. □ vt [VP6A] fasten with, or as with, a ∼.

ski /skiː/ n (pl skis) one of a pair of long, narrow strips of wood, strapped under the feet for moving over snow: a pair of skis; bind on one's skis. 'ski-bob n bicycle frame fitted with skis in place of wheels. 'ski-jump n jump made after getting up speed on a downward slope. 'ski-lift n ropeway for carrying skiers up a mountain side. 'ski-plane n aircraft fitted with skis instead of wheels, to enable it to land on an expanse of snow. □ vi (pt,pp ski'd, pres part skiing) move over snow on ski(s): go skiing in Switzerland; go in for skiing. skier /ˈskiːə(r)/ n person using ski(s).

skid /skɪd/ n [C] 1 piece of wood or metal fixed under the wheel of a cart, etc to prevent it from turning, and in this way check the speed when going downhill. 2 log, plank, etc used to make a track over which heavy objects may be dragged or

rolled. ∼ row /rəʊ/ n (US) slum area where vagrants live. 3 slipping movement, often sideways, of the wheels of a car, etc on a slippery or icy road, or caused by excessive speed while turning a corner: How would you get out of/correct a ∼? '∼-pan n surface specially prepared to cause ∼s, used for practice in controlling vehicles which ∼. put the ∼s under sb, (sl) do sth to make him hurry. □ vi (-dd-) [VP2A] (of a car, etc) move or slip sideways, etc; have a ∼(3).

skies /skaɪz/ pl of sky.

skiff /skɪf/ n small, light boat, esp one rowed or sculled by a single person.

skiffle /ˈskɪfl/ n [U] (1950's) mixture of jazz and folksong, with improvised instruments and a singer who usu has a guitar or a banjo. '∼-group, group of such players.

skil-ful (US = skillful) /ˈskɪlfl/ adj having or showing skill: He's not very ∼ with his chopsticks/at using chopsticks. ∼ly /-fəlɪ/ adv

skill /skɪl/ n [U] ability to do sth expertly and well; [C] particular kind of ∼: Is learning a foreign language a question of learning new ∼s, or a question of acquiring new knowledge? ∼ed adj 1 trained; experienced; having ∼; ∼ed workmen; ∼ed in doing sth. 2 needing ∼: ∼ed work.

skil-let /ˈskɪlɪt/ n 1 small metal cooking-pot with a long handle and (usu) feet. 2 (US) frying-pan.

skilly /ˈskɪlɪ/ n [U] thin broth or soup (usu oatmeal and water flavoured with meat).

skim /skɪm/ vt,vi (-mm-) 1 [VP6A,15B,14] ∼ (off) (from), remove floating matter from (the surface of a liquid): ∼ milk; remove (cream, scum, etc) from the surface of a liquid: ∼ the cream from the milk; ∼ off the fat from the soup. '∼-med-milk n milk from which the cream has been ∼med. 2 [VP2C,15A] move lightly over (a surface), not touching, or only lightly or occasionally touching (it): The swallows were ∼ming (over) the water/ ∼med along the ground. 3 [VP6A,3A] ∼ (through) sth, read quickly, noting only the chief points: ∼ (through) a newspaper/catalogue, etc. ∼-mer n 1 utensil with a perforated bowl for ∼ming liquids. 2 long-winged water-bird.

skimp /skɪmp/ vt,vi [VP6A,2A] supply, use, less than enough of what is needed: ∼ the butter when making cakes/the material when making a dress. They are so poor that they have to ∼. skimpy adj (-ier, -iest) 1 giving, using, less than enough. 2 (of a dress, etc) made with insufficient material; too small; too tight. ∼ily /-ɪlɪ/ adv. a ∼ily made dress.

skin /skɪn/ n 1 [U] elastic substance forming the outer covering of the body of a person or animal: We all got wet to the ∼, thoroughly wet (eg in heavy rain). ∼ and bone, very thin: He's only ∼

skiing

and bone. **by the ~ of one's teeth,** by a narrow margin; narrowly. **get under one's ~,** (fig) annoy, irritate, anger one; infatuate one. **get sb under one's skin,** be infatuated with him. **have a thin/thick ~,** (fig) be sensitive/insensitive; be easily/not easily hurt by unkindness, criticism, rebuke, etc. Hence, ,thin-/,thick-'~ned *adjj* **save one's ~,** avoid being hurt, etc; escape safely. '~-diving *n* form of sport in which a person dives into and swims under the water without a diving-suit, with goggles to protect the eyes and a snorkel or aqualung to help breathing. ,~-'deep *adj* (of beauty, feelings, etc) only on the surface; not deep or lasting. '~-flint *n* miser. '~ game *n* fraudulent gambling game; swindle. '~-graft *n* surgical process of grafting ~ from one part of a person's body (or from another person's body) on to a part which has been damaged, eg by burning. 'skin-head *n* (GB, early 1970's) young gangster with closely-cut hair. ,~-'tight *adj* (of a garment) fitting closely to the body. 2 [C] animal ~ with or without the hair or fur; hide; pelt: '*rabbit-~s.* 3 [C] vessel for storing or carrying liquid, made of the whole ~ of an animal: '*wine-~s.* 4 [C,U] outer covering of a fruit, or plant: *slip on a ba'nana ~;* '*grape ~s.* ⇨ the illus at fruit. Cf *peel* for potatoes, apples, etc; the *bark* of a tree. 5 thin layer that forms on boiled milk: *the ~ on a milk pudding.* □ *vt,vi* (-nn-) 1 [VP6A] take the ~ off: ~ *a rabbit.* **keep one's 'eyes ~ned,** (colloq) be alert, watchful. 2 [VP6A,14] (colloq) swindle; fleece: *He was ~ned of all his money by confidence tricksters.* 3 [VP2C] ~ **over,** become covered with ~: *The wound ~ned over.* ~ny *adj* (-ier, -iest) with little flesh; (colloq) mean; miserly. ⇨ skinflint above.

skint /skɪnt/ *adj* (GB sl) without money; penniless.

skip¹ /skɪp/ *vi,vt* (-pp-) 1 [VP2A,C] jump lightly and quickly: ~ *over an obstacle/over a brook/out of the way of a bus. The lambs were ~ping about in the fields,* jumping about, gambolling. 2 [VP2A] jump over a rope which is turned over the head and under the feet as one jumps. '~-ping-rope *n* length of rope (usu with two wooden handles) used in the children's game of ~ping. 3 [VP2C] go from one place (or, fig, subject) to another quickly or casually: ~ *over/across to Paris for the weekend. He ~ped off* (= left) *without saying anything to any of us. He ~ped from one subject to another.* 4 [VP6A,2A] make omissions, go from one part (of a book, etc) to another without reading, paying attention, etc: *He ~ped the dull parts of the book. We'll ~ the next chapter. Do you read without ~ping?* □ *n* [C] ~ping movement: *a hop, a ~ and a jump.*

skip² /skɪp/ *n* cage or bucket in which men or materials are raised and lowered in mines and quarries; large metal container for carrying away builders' refuse, etc.

skip-per /'skɪpə(r)/ *n* captain, esp of a small merchant ship or fishing-boat; (colloq) captain of a team in games such as football and cricket.

skirl /skɜːl/ *n* shrill, piercing sound: *the ~ of the bagpipes.*

skir-mish /'skɜːmɪʃ/ *n* [C] (often unpremeditated) fight between small parts of armies or fleets; (hence) short argument or contest of wit, etc. □ *vi* [VP2A,C] engage in a ~. ~**er** *n* one who ~es, esp a member of a force sent out from the main body of troops to hide its movements, or to learn about the movement of the enemy.

skirt /skɜːt/ *n* 1 woman's garment that hangs from the waist. 2 part of a dress or other garment (eg a long coat or shirt) that hangs below the waist. 3 (*pl*) (= outskirts) border; extreme parts: *on the ~s of the town.* □ *vt,vi* [VP6A,2C] be on, pass along, the edge of: *Our road ~ed the forest. Our path ~ed along the moor.* ~ **round sth,** be indirect about it; avoid direct reference to it: *He ~ed round the subject of his family.* '~-ing-board *n* strip or line of boards fixed round the walls of a room close to the floor.

skit /skɪt/ *n* [C] short piece of humorous writing, short play, mimicking and making fun of sth or sb: *a ~ on Wagner/on 'Macbeth'.*

skit-tish /'skɪtɪʃ/ *adj* (of horses) excitable; lively; difficult to control; (of a person) lively and coquettish, fond of flirting, etc. ~**-ly** *adv* ~**-ness** *n*

skittle /'skɪtl/ *n* (*pl* ~s, with *sing v*) game in which a ball is bowled along an alley ('~-alley) with the purpose of knocking down a number of bottle-shaped pieces of wood (called ~s or '~-pins). ⇨ ninepins, tenpins. **(all) beer and ~s,** amusement; fun: *Life is not all beer and ~s.* □ *vt* [VP15B] ~ **out,** (cricket) dismiss easily: *The whole side was ~d out for 100 runs.*

skivvy /'skɪvɪ/ *n* (*pl* -vies) (GB sl) (pej) servant who is required to do all sorts of work.

skua /'skjuːə/ *n* large kind of seagull.

skulk /skʌlk/ *vi* [VP2A,C] hide, move secretly, through cowardice, or to avoid work or duty, or with an evil purpose. ~**er** *n*

skull /skʌl/ *n* bony framework of the head. ⇨ the illus at skeleton. **have a thick ~,** be stupid. ~ **and 'cross-bones,** picture of a ~ and two thigh-bones crossed below it (as an emblem of death or danger, and formerly used on a flag by pirates). '~-cap *n* close-fitting (often velvet) cap worn indoors by old or bald men, by Popes and cardinals. **-skulled** *suff* (with *adj* prefixed): ,thick-'~ed, having a thick ~.

skull-dug-gery /skʌl'dʌgərɪ/ *n* (colloq) clever deception; trickery.

skunk /skʌŋk/ *n* 1 small, bush-tailed N American animal able to send out a strong, unpleasant smell as a defence when attacked; [U] its fur. 2 detestable or contemptible person.

skyscrapers

sky /skaɪ/ *n* (*pl* skies /skaɪz/) 1 (usu **the sky; a sky** when modified by an *adj*, often *pl* in the same sense) the space we look up to from the earth, where we see the sun, moon and stars: *under the open sky,* out of doors; *a clear, blue sky; a starry sky/(the) starry skies.* **praise/extol/laud sb to the skies,** praise him very highly. ,**sky-'blue** *adj, n* (of) the bright blue colour of the sky on a cloudless day. ,**sky-'high** *adv* so as to reach the sky; as high as the sky: *When the bomb exploded, the bridge was blown sky-high.* '**sky-light** *n* window in a sloping roof. **'sky-line** *n* outline of hills, buildings, etc, defined against the sky: *the skyline of New York.* **'sky-lark** *n* small bird that sings as it flies up into the sky. □ *vi* = lark¹. **'sky pilot** *n* (sl) parson (esp, among sailors, a chaplain on a warship). **'sky-rocket** *vi* (of prices) soar; go up steeply. **'sky-scraper** *n* very tall building. **'sky-writing** *n* [U] (making of) smoke-trails forming legible words in the sky (by aircraft for advertising purposes). **2** (often *pl*) climate: *the sunny skies of southern Italy.* □ *vt* hit (eg a ball) high up. **sky-ward(s)** /'skaɪwəd(z)/ *adj, adv* toward(s) the sky; upward(s).

slab /slæb/ *n* thick flat (usu square or rectangular) piece of stone, wood or other solid substance: *paved with* ∿s *of stone; a* ∿ *of cheese/cooking chocolate; a mortuary* ∿.

slack¹ /slæk/ *adj* **1** giving little care or attention to one's work; having or showing little energy: *Don't get* ∿ *at your work. She feels* ∿ (= lacking in energy) *this morning.* **2** dull; inactive; with not much work to be done or business being done: *Trade/Business is* ∿ *this week. There is only a* ∿ *demand for S African mining shares.* **3** loose, not tight: *a* ∿ *rope.* **keep a** ∿ **rein on sth**, control sth negligently, (fig) govern carelessly. **4** slow-moving; sluggish: *periods of* ∿ *water,* when the tide is neither ebbing nor flowing. □ *vi* [VP2A,C] **1** ∿ **(off)**, be lazy or careless in one's work: *Don't* ∿ *off in your studies.* **2** ∿ **up**, reduce speed: *S*∿ *up before you reach the cross-roads.* **3** ∿ **off/away**, make loose (a rope, etc). ∿**er** *n* (colloq) lazy person; person who avoids his proper share of work. ∿**·ly** *adv* ∿**·ness** *n*

slack² /slæk/ *n* **1** the ∿, that part of a rope, etc that hangs loosely. **take up the** ∿, pull a rope so that it is taut; (fig) regulate industry so that it is active and productive. **2** (*pl*) loose-fitting trousers, not part of a suit, eg as informal wear for men or women. **3** [U] coal dust.

slacken /'slækən/ *vt, vi* [VP6A,2A] **1** make or become slower, less active, etc: ∿ *speed. The ship's speed* ∿*ed. The gale is* ∿*ing a little.* **2** make or become loose(r): ∿ *the reins. S*∿ *away/off!* eg as an order to loosen ropes.

slag /slæg/ *n* [U] waste matter remaining when metal has been extracted from ore. **'∿-heap** *n* hill of ∿ (dumped from a mine).

slain /sleɪn/ *pp* of slay.

slake /sleɪk/ *vt* [VP6A] **1** satisfy or make less strong (thirst, desire for revenge). **2** change the chemical nature of (lime) by adding water. ⇨ calcium.

sla·lom /'slɑːləm/ *n* ski-race along a zigzag course marked out by poles with flags.

slam /slæm/ *vt, vi* (-mm-) **1** [VP6A,15A,B,22] ∿ **(to)**, shut violently and noisily: ∿ *the door* (*to*); ∿ *the window shut;* ∿ *the door in sb's face.* **2** [VP2A,C] ∿ **(to)**, be shut violently: *The door* ∿*med* (*to*). **3** [VP15A,B] put, throw or knock with force: *She* ∿*med the box down on the table. The batsman* ∿*med the ball into the grand-stand.* □ *n* **1** noise of sth being ∿med: *the* ∿ *of a car door.* **2** (in whist, bridge) **a grand** ∿, taking of 13 tricks. **a small** ∿, taking of 12 tricks.

slan·der /'slɑːndə(r)/ *US*: 'slæn-/ *n* [C,U] (offence of making a) false statement that damages a person's reputation: *bring a* ∿ *action against sb,* charge him with ∿ *in a court of law.* □ *vt* [VP6A] utter ∿ about (sb). ∿**er** *n* ∿**·ous** /-əs/ *adj* uttering or containing ∿.

slang /slæŋ/ *n* [U] (abbr *sl* used in this dictionary) words, phrases, meanings of words, etc commonly used in talk among friends or colleagues, but not suitable for good writing or formal occasions, esp the kind used by and typical of only one class of persons: *army* ∿; *prison* ∿; (attrib) ∿ *words and expressions. The use of out-of-date* ∿ *is sometimes a feature of foreigners' English.* ⇨ colloquial. □ *vt* [VP6A] use violent language to; abuse: *Stop* ∿*ing me.* **a'** ∿*ing match,* a long exchange of insults and accusations. ∿**y** *adj* (-ier, -iest) using, in the nature of, ∿. ∿**·ily** /-ɪlɪ/ *adv* ∿**·i·ness** *n*

slant /slɑːnt *US*: slænt/ *vi, vt* **1** [VP2A,C,6A] slope: *His handwriting* ∿*s from right to left.* **2** [VP6A] ∿ *the news,* present it so that it is seen from, and supports, a particular point of view, eg of the writer's newspaper or government. □ *n* **1** [C] slope. **on a/the** ∿, in a sloping position. **2** (colloq) point of view (sometimes prejudiced or biased) when considering sth: *get a new* ∿ *on the political situation.* ∿**·ing·ly,** ∿**·wise** /-waɪz/ *advv* in a ∿ing position or direction.

slap /slæp/ *vt* (-pp-) **1** [VP6A,15A] strike with the palm of the hand; smack: *She* ∿*ped his face/*∿*ped him on the face. I don't like being* ∿*ped on the back as a greeting.* **2** [VP15B] ∿ *sth down,* put sth down with a ∿ping noise: *He* ∿*ped the book down on the table.* □ *n* [C] quick blow with the palm of the hand or with sth flat. **get/give sb a** ∿ **in the face,** (fig) a rebuff or snub. □ *adv* straight; directly; full: *The car ran* ∿ *into the wall.* ∿**-'bang** *adv* violently; headlong. '∿**-dash** *adj, adv* careless(ly); impetuous(ly): *a* ∿*dash worker; do one's work* ∿*dash/in a* ∿*dash manner.* '∿**-happy** *adj* (colloq) impetuous, carefree. '∿**-stick** *n* [U] low comedy of the roughest kind; fun arising from violence: (attrib) ∿*stick comedy.* '∿**-up** *adj* (sl) first-class; extremely good: *be treated to a* ∿*-up dinner at a* ∿*-up restaurant.*

slash /slæʃ/ *vt, vi* **1** [VP6A,2C] make a cut or cuts in or at sth with sweeping strokes; strike with a whip: *His face had been* ∿*ed with a razor-blade. Don't* ∿ *your horse in that cruel way. He* ∿*ed at the tall weeds with his stick.* **2** [VP6A] condemn vigorously and outspokenly: *a* ∿*ing attack on the government's policy;* ∿ *a new book/play,* criticize it adversely. **3** [VP6A] (colloq) cut, reduce drastically: ∿ *prices/taxes/salaries.* **4** (usu passive) make long, narrow gashes in (for ornament, etc): ∿*ed sleeves,* the lining or other material being seen through the ∿es. □ *n* **1** act of ∿ing; long cut or gash. **2** (vulg sl) act of urinating.

slat /slæt/ *n* long, thin narrow piece of wood, metal or plastic material, eg as in Venetian blinds or louvred doors. ∿**·ted** *adj* made with, having, ∿s.

slate /sleɪt/ *n* **1** [U] kind of blue-grey stone that splits easily into thin, flat layers; [C] one of these layers, square or oblong, used for roofs: *hit on the head by a falling* ∿; *a* ∿*-covered roof;* '∿*-coloured,* blue-grey; *a'* ∿ *quarry.* **2** [C] sheet of ∿ in a wooden frame for writing on (as formerly used by school-children). **a clean** ∿, (fig) a good record: *start with a clean* ∿, (fig) make a new start with past errors, enmities, etc, forgotten. '∿**-club** *n* (GB) club collecting small weekly contributions of money, usu saved until Christmas, when the total is distributed to members. ∿**-'pencil** *n* thin rod of soft ∿, used for writing on ∿s(2). □ *vt* **1** [VP6A] cover (a roof, etc) with ∿s. **2** (US, colloq) propose (sb) for an office, a position, etc: (newspaper head-

line) *Green ~d for the Presidency.* **3** [VP6A]
(colloq) criticize severely (esp in a newspaper notice of a book, play, etc). **slaty** *adj* of or like ~;
containing ~: *slaty coal.* **slat·ing** *n* adverse criticism: *give sb a sound slating.*
slat·tern /'slætən/ *n* dirty, untidily dressed woman.
~·ly *adj* (of women) dirty and untidy. ~·li·ness *n*
slaugh·ter /'slɔːtə(r)/ *n* [U] **1** killing of animals
(esp for food). '~-house *n* place where animals
are butchered for food. **2** killing of many people at
once; massacre: *the ~ on the roads,* the killing of
people in road accidents. □ *vt* [VP6A] kill (animals,
people) in large numbers. ~er *n*
Slav /slɑːv/ *n* member of a race spread over most of
Eastern Europe, including Russians, Czechs,
Poles, Bulgarians, etc. □ *adj* of the ~s.
slave /sleɪv/ *n* **1** person who is the property of another and bound to serve him. '~-driver *n* overseer of ~s at work; person who makes those who
are under him work very hard. '~ ship *n* ship used
in the ~-trade. '~ States *n pl* southern States of N
America in which there was slavery before the Civil War. '~-trade/-traffic *n* capturing, transportation, buying and selling, of ~s. **2** person
compelled to work very hard for someone else:
You mustn't make a ~ of your au pair girl. **3** sb
completely in the power of, under the control of, an
impulse, habit, etc: ~s *of fashion,* eg persons who
feel compelled to dress in the latest fashions; *a ~
to duty/passion/convention/drink.* □ *vi*
[VP2A,B,C,3A] ~ *(away) (at sth),* work hard:
Poor Jane! She's been slaving away (= cooking)
over a hot stove for three hours! ~r *n* '~-trader;
'~ ship. **slav·ery** /'sleɪvərɪ/ *n* [U] **1** condition of
being a ~: *sold into* ~ry. **2** custom of having ~s:
men who worked for the abolition of ~ry. **3** hard or
badly paid work. **slav·ish** /'sleɪvɪʃ/ *adj* lacking in
independence or originality; abject(2): *a slavish
imitation,* an exact copy showing no originality.
slav·ish·ly *adv*
slaver /'slævə(r)/ *vi* [VP2A,C] ~ *(over),* let spit
run from the mouth (because of hunger): ~*ing over
a plate of spaghetti;* (fig) ~*ing over a travel brochure.* □ *n* [U] spit; saliva. also ⇨ *slaver* at slave.
slavey /'sleɪvɪ/ *n* (*pl*-veys) (sl) young servant.
Slav·onic /slə'vɒnɪk/ *adj* of the Slavs or their languages.
slaw /slɔː/ *n* [U] (often 'cole-~) sliced cabbage,
raw or cooked, served with a dressing.
slay /sleɪ/ *vt* (*pt* slew /sluː/, *pp* slain /sleɪn/)
[VP6A] (liter, or rhet) kill, murder. ~er *n* (journalism) murderer.
sleazy /'sliːzɪ/ *adj* (-ier, -iest) (colloq) uncared-
for, dirty, untidy: *a ~ hotel/appearance.*
sled /sled/ *n* = sledge.
sledge¹ /sledʒ/ *n* vehicle with runners (long, narrow strips of wood or metal) instead of wheels,
used on snow, larger types being pulled by horses
or dogs and smaller types used in sport for travelling downhill at speed. □ *vi,vt* (-dd-) travel or carry
by ~: *go sledging.*
sledge² /sledʒ/ *n* '~(-hammer), heavy hammer
with a long handle, used for driving posts into the
ground, and by blacksmiths.
sleek /sliːk/ *adj* (of hair, an animal's fur, etc) soft,
smooth and glossy; (of a person) having such hair.
as ~ as a cat, (fig) having smooth manners (perhaps over-anxious to please). □ *vt* [VP6A] make ~:
~ *a cat's fur.* ~·ly *adv* ~·ness *n*
sleep¹ /sliːp/ *n* **1** [U] condition of the body and

mind such as recurs regularly every night, in which
the eyes are closed and the muscles, nervous
system, etc are relaxed: *How many hours' ~ do
you need? He didn't get much ~. Do you ever talk
in your ~? get to ~,* manage to fall asleep, succeed in passing into the condition of ~: *I couldn't
get to ~ last night. go to ~,* fall asleep. **have
one's '~ out,** continue ~ing until one wakes up
naturally: *Don't wake her up—let her have her ~
out. put sb to ~,* cause him to fall asleep. *put (a
pet animal) to ~,* (euphem) deliberately kill it
(because of illness, etc). **2 a** ~, period of ~: *have
a short/good/restful, etc ~; a ~ of three hours.*
'~-walker *n* person who walks while asleep. ~-
less *adj* without ~: *pass a* ~*less night.* ~·less·ly
adv ~·less·ness *n*
sleep² /sliːp/ *vi,vt* (*pp,pt* slept /slept/) **1**
[VP2A,B,C] rest in the condition of ~, be or fall
asleep: *We go to bed to ~. He ~s well/badly. She
slept (for) eight hours.* ~ *like a top/log,* ~ very
soundly. ~ *round the clock;* ~ *the clock round,*
~ for twelve hours continuously. **2** [VP6A] provide
beds for: *This hotel ~s 300 guests.* ~·ing *n* (in
compounds) '~·ing-bag *n* warmly lined and
waterproof bag in which to ~ when out of doors
(eg on holiday) or in a tent. '~-ing-car *n* railway
coach fitted with beds or berths. '~-ing-draught/
-pill *n* one that contains a drug to help sb to ~. ~-
ing partner *n* (US = *silent partner*) person who
provides a share of the capital of a business but
does not share in the management.'~·ing-
sickness *n* [U] disease caused by the tsetse-fly; it
results in weakening of the mental powers and
(usu) death. ~er *n* **1** person who ~s: (with *adjj*) *a
heavy/light* ~*er,* one whom it is hard/easy to wake
up; *a good/bad* ~*er.* **2** (US = *tie*) heavy beam of
wood (or similarly shaped piece of other material)
on a railway track, used etc supporting the rails. **3** (bed
or berth in a) ~*ing-car* on a train. **3**
[VP2C,15B,3A] (with *adverbial particles* and
preps):
sleep around, (colloq) be promiscuous.
sleep in/out, ~ at/outside one's place of employment: *Does the housekeeper ~ in?*
sleep sth off, recover from sth by ~ing: ~ *off a
bad headache/a hangover.*
sleep on, continue to sleep: *Don't wake him
up—let him ~ on for another hour.* ~ *on sth,* (often ~ *on it*), leave the answer, solution, to a problem, etc to the next day.
sleep through sth, not be woken up by (a noise,
the alarm-clock, etc).
sleep with sb, (euphem for) have sexual intercourse with.
sleepy /'sliːpɪ/ *adj* (-ier, -iest) **1** needing, ready
for, sleep: *feel/look ~.* '~-head *n* (esp as a form
of address to sb) a ~ or inattentive person. **2** (of
places, etc) quiet; inactive: *a ~ little village.* **3** (of
some kinds of fruit) over-ripe: ~ *pears/bananas,*
soft and brown inside. **sleep·ily** /-ɪlɪ/ *adv* **sleepiness** *n*
sleet /sliːt/ *n* [U] falling snow or hail mixed with
rain: *squalls of ~.* □ *vi* [VP2A] *It was* ~ing, S~
was falling. **sleety** *adj*
sleeve /sliːv/ *n* **1** part of a garment that covers all or
part of the arm: *roll up the ~s of one's shirt/one's
'shirt—~s.* **have sth up one's ~,** have an idea,
plan, etc which one keeps secret for future use.
laugh up one's ~, be secretly amused. **roll up
one's ~s,** prepare to work or fight. **wear one's**

heart on one's ~, allow one's feelings (of love for sb) to be seen; fail to show proper reserve. **2** stiff envelope for a disc of recorded sound, often with notes on the composer, player(s), etc. **3** wind-sock. ⇨ wind¹(8). **-sleeved** suff: '*short*/ '*loose--*~*d*. ~**-less** adj without ~s.

sleigh /sleɪ/ n sledge, esp one drawn by a horse: *go for a* '~-*ride/a ride in a* ~. '~-**bell** n one of several small tinkling bells commonly attached to a ~ or to the harness of the horse pulling the ~. □ vi,vt [VP2A,6A] travel in a ~; carry (goods) by ~.

sleight /slaɪt/ n (usu in) ~ *of hand*, great skill in using the hand(s) in performing tricks, juggling, etc.

slen·der /'slendə(r)/ adj **1** small in width or circumference compared with height or length: ~ *fingers; a* ~ *waist; a wineglass with a* ~ *stem*. **2** (of persons) slim; not stout: *a* ~ *girl*, slight and graceful; *a woman with a* ~ *figure*. **3** slight; scanty; inadequate: *a* ~ *income;* ~ *means/hopes*. ~**·ly** adv~·**ness** n ~**·ize** /-aɪz/ vt,vi [VP6A] (US) make, cause to appear, become, ~(2).

slept /slept/ pt,pp of sleep.

sleuth /slu:θ/ n (colloq) detective. '~-**hound** n bloodhound; dog that follows a scent.

slew¹ /slu:/ pt of slay.

slew² (US = **slue**) /slu:/ vi,vt [VP2C,15B] ~ (sth) round, force or turn round in a new direction: *The crane* ~*ed round. The driver* ~*ed his crane round*.

slice /slaɪs/ n [C] **1** thin, wide, flat piece cut off sth, esp bread or meat: *S*~*s of cold beef between* ~*s of bread make good sandwiches*. **2** part; share: *a* ~ *of good luck. Smith took too large a* ~ *of the credit for our success*. **3** utensil with a wide, flat blade for cutting, serving or lifting (eg cooked fish, fried eggs). **4** (in games such as golf) bad stroke that causes the ball to go spinning off in a direction different from that desired, ie to the right of a right-handed player. □ vt,vi **1** [VP6A,15A,B,22,3A] cut into ~s: *into/through a cake;* ~ (*up*) *a loaf. S*~ *the beef thin. The butcher* ~*d off a thick steak*. **2** [VP6A] (golf): ~ *the ball*, strike with a ~(4).

slick /slɪk/ adj (colloq) **1** smooth; slippery: *The roads were* ~ *with wet mud*. **2** carried through smoothly and efficiently, perhaps with some trickery: *a* ~ *business deal;* (of a person) doing things in a ~ way: *a* ~ *salesman*. □ n [C] '*oil* ~, film of thick oil covering an area of the sea, etc (eg from an oil-tanker after a collision). □ adv directly, completely: *hit a man* ~ *on the jaw*. ~**er** n (US colloq) **1** long, loose, waterproof coat. **2** ~ person. ⇨ 2 above: *city* ~*ers*.

slide¹ /slaɪd/ n **1** act of sliding(1); smooth stretch of ice, hard snow, etc on which to slide: *have a* ~ *on the ice*. **2** smooth slope down which persons or things can slide (eg for felled timber down a mountain slope, or a wooden or metal slope made for children to play on). **3** picture, diagram, etc on photographic film (and usu mounted in a frame); (formerly) such a picture on a glass plate, to be slid into a projector and shown on a screen. **4** glass plate on which is placed sth to be examined under a microscope. **5** part of a machine, etc that slides (eg the U-shaped part of a trombone). **6** ('*land*)~, ⇨ land¹(6). **7** ('*hair*)~, ⇨ hair(2).

slide² /slaɪd/ vi,vt (pt,pp slid /slɪd/) **1** [VP2A,C,6A,15A] (cause to) move smoothly over, slip along, a polished surface: *children sliding on the ice. The book slid* (= slipped, which is more

usu) *off my knee. Let's* ~ *down this grassy slope. The drawers of this desk* ~ *in and out easily. S*~ *the drawer into its place*. ~ *over sth*, pass over (a delicate subject, etc) quickly; barely touch upon it. *let things* ~, not trouble about them, be negligent. **2** [VP3A] ~ *into*, pass gradually, without being fully aware, into (a condition, etc): ~ *into dishonesty/bad habits*. **3** [VP2A,15A] (cause to) move quickly, or so as to avoid observation: *The thief slid behind the curtains. She slid a coin into his hand*. **4** (compounds) '~-*rule* n device of two rulers with logarithmic scales, one of which ~s in a groove, used for rapid calculations. **slid·ing door** n one that is pulled across an opening (instead of turning on hinges). **slid·ing scale** n scale by which one thing, eg wages, goes up or down in relation to changes in sth else, eg the cost of living. **slid·ing seat** n seat on runners, esp in a racing boat, to lengthen the stroke of the rower or sculler.

slight¹ /slaɪt/ adj (-er, -est) **1** slim; slender; frail-looking: *a* ~ *figure; supported by a* ~ *framework*. **2** small; not serious or important: *a* ~ *error; a* ~ *headache; do sth without the* ~*est difficulty*, with no difficulty at all. *She takes offence at the* ~*est thing*, is very easily offended. *not in the* ~*est*, not at all: *You didn't embarrass me in the* ~*est*. ~**·ly** adv **1** slenderly: *a* ~*ly built boy*. **2** to a ~ degree; somewhat: *The patient is* ~*ly better today. I know her* ~*ly*. ~**·ness** n

slight² /slaɪt/ vt [VP6A] treat without proper respect or courtesy; neglect in a marked manner: *She felt* ~*ed because no one spoke to her*. □ n [C] marked failure to show respect or courtesy: *put a* ~ *on sb; suffer* ~*s*. ~**·ing·ly** adv

slim /slɪm/ adj (-mer, -mest) **1** slender: *a* ~ *waisted girl*. **2** (colloq) small; insufficient: ~ *hopes/chances of success; condemned upon the* ~*est* (*of*) *evidence*. □ vi (-mm-) eat less, diet, take exercise, etc with the object of reducing one's weight and becoming ~(1): ~*ming exercises*. ~**·ly** adv ~**·ness** n

slime /slaɪm/ n [U] **1** soft, nasty, thick, sticky mud. **2** sticky substance from snails, etc: *a trail of* ~.

slimy /'slaɪmɪ/ adj (-ier, -iest) of, like, covered with, ~; hard to hold because slippery with ~; (fig) disgustingly dishonest, meek, flattering, obsequious, etc: *a slimy(-tongued) coward*.

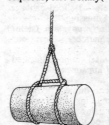

slings

sling¹ /slɪŋ/ n [C] **1** band of material, length of rope, chain, etc looped round an object, eg a barrel, a broken arm, to support or lift it. **2** strip of leather used (held in the hand in a loop) to throw stones to a distance. **3** act of throwing. □ vt,vi (pt,pp slung /slʌŋ/) **1** [VP6A,15A,B] throw with force: *naughty boys* ~*ing stones at street lamps*. ~ *one's hook*, (sl) go away: *Tell him to* ~ *his hook*. ~ *mud at sb*, (fig) abuse him. ~ *sb out*, throw sb out; expel him by force. **2** [VP6A,15A,B] support (sth) so that it can swing, be lifted, etc: ~ *a hammock between two tree-trunks;* ~ *(up) a barrel; with his rifle slung over his shoulder.* ~**er** /ˈslɪŋə(r)/ *n* person armed with a ~(2).

sling² /slɪŋ/ *n* drink made of gin, rum, etc sweetened with fruit juices (esp lime).

slink /slɪŋk/ *vi* (*pt,pp* slunk /slʌŋk/) [VP2C] go or move (*off, away, in, out, by*) in a secret, guilty or sneaking manner.

slip¹ /slɪp/ *n* [C] **1** act of slipping; false step; slight error caused by carelessness or inattention: *make a* ~. *a* ~ *of the tongue/pen,* error in speaking/ writing. *give sb the* ~; *give the* ~ *to sb,* escape from, get away from (one's pursuers, etc). *There's many a* ~ *'twixt (the) cup and (the) lip,* (prov) Something may easily go wrong before a plan is fully carried out. **2** (ˈpillow-~) loose cover for a pillow; loose sleeveless garment worn under a dress; (ˈgym-~) girl's garment for gymnastic exercises. **3** narrow strip of paper; printer's proof on such a strip. **4** cutting (short length of stem) taken from a plant for planting or grafting (to grow a new plant, etc). **5** young, slender person: *a* (*mere*) ~ *of a boy/girl,* a slim boy/girl. **6** (usu *pl*; also 'ˈ~**·way**) sloping way (of stone or timber) down to the water, on which ships are built, or pulled up out of the water for repairs: *The ship is still on the* ~s. **7** (*pl*) (more usu *wings*) parts of the stage of a theatre from which the scenery is pushed on, and where actors stand before going on to the stage: *watch a performance from the* ~s. **8** (cricket) one of the fielders: *first/second/leg* ~; (*pl*) part of the ground where these fielders stand. ⇨ the illus at cricket. **9** [U] semi-fluid clay for coating earthenware or making patterns on it.

slip² /slɪp/ *vi,vt* (-pp-) **1** [VP2A,C] lose one's balance; fall or almost fall as the result of this: *He* ~*ped on the icy road and broke his leg.* **2** [VP2A,C] go or move quietly or quickly, esp without attracting attention: *She* ~*ped away/out/past without being seen. The years* ~*ped by.* **3** [VP2A,C] move, get away, escape, fall, by being difficult to hold, or by not being held firmly: *The fish* ~*ped out of my hand. The blanket* ~*ped off the bed. The knife* ~*ped and cut my hand. let sth* ~, **(a)** allow sth to fall from one's hands, escape, or be neglected: *Don't let the opportunity* ~. **(b)** accidentally reveal (a secret, etc): *let* ~ *a secret.* ~ *through one's fingers,* (lit or fig) fail to grasp, keep a hold on. ~ *one's mind,* (of a name, address, message, etc) be forgotten (because one is in a hurry, busy, etc). **4** [VP15A,B,2C] put, pull on or push off, with a quick, easy movement: ~ *a coat on/off;* ~ *into/out of a dress;* ~ *a coin into the waiter's hand.* **5** [VP2C] allow (small mistakes, etc) to enter, esp by carelessness: *errors that have* ~*ped into the text;* make a small error. ~ *up,* (colloq) make a mistake. Hence, 'ˈ~**-up** *n* [C] mistake. **6** [VP2C] move smoothly and effortlessly; go with a gliding motion: *The ship* ~*ped through the water.* **7** [VP6A] get free from; let go from restraint: ~ *greyhounds from the leash;* ~ *anchor,* detach a ship from the anchor; (of a cow) ~ *her calf,* give birth to it prematurely; ~ *a stitch,* (knitting) move a stitch from one needle to the other without knitting it. *The dog* ~*ped its collar,* got out of it. *The point* ~*ped my attention.* **8** (compounds) 'ˈ~**-carriage/coach** *nn* one at the end of a train which can be detached without stopping the

train. 'ˈ~**-cover** *n* detachable cover for a piece of furniture. ⇨ **2** above. 'ˈ~**-knot** *n* **(a)** knot which slips along the cord round which it is made to tighten or loosen the loop. **(b)** knot which can be undone by a pull. ⇨ the illus at knot. 'ˈ~**-on/over** *n* shoe or garment to be slipped easily or or over sth. 'ˈ~**-road** *n* road for joining or leaving a motorway (US = *access-road*); minor or local by-pass road. 'ˈ~**-stream** *n* stream of air from the propeller or jet engine of an aircraft.

slip·per /ˈslɪpə(r)/ *n* (often *pair of* ~s) loose-fitting light shoe worn in the house. ~**ed** *adj* wearing ~s.

slip·pery /ˈslɪpərɪ/ *adj* (-ier, iest) **1** (of a surface) smooth, wet, polished, etc so that it is difficult to hold, to stand on, or to move on: ~ *roads;* ~ *under foot;* (fig) (of a subject) needing care: *We're on* ~ *ground when dealing with this subject. be on a* ~ *slope,* (fig) on a course of action which may lead to failure or disgrace. **2** (fig, of persons) unreliable; unscrupulous: *a* ~ *customer,* a rogue. *He's as* ~ *as an eel,* is untrustworthy, difficult to manage. **slip·peri·ness** *n*

slippy /ˈslɪpɪ/ *adj* (colloq) **1** slippery. **2** (dated) quick: *Be* ~ *about it! Look* ~!

slip·shod /ˈslɪpʃɒd/ *adj* slovenly; careless: *a* ~ *piece of work; a* ~ *style.*

slit /slɪt/ *n* [C] long, narrow cut, tear or opening: *the* ~ *of a letter-box* (through which letters are put); *eyes like* ~s. □ *vt* (*pt,pp* slit; -tt-) **1** [VP6A,15A,22] make a ~ in; open (by ~ting): ~ *a man's throat;* ~ *an envelope open;* ~ *cloth into strips/a sheet of leather into thongs.* **2** [VP2A,C] be cut or torn lengthwise: *The shirt has* ~ *down the back.*

slither /ˈslɪðə(r)/ *vi* [VP2A,C] slide or slip unsteadily: ~ *down an ice-covered slope.* ~**y** *adj* slippery.

sliver /ˈslɪvə(r)/ *n* [C] small, thin strip of wood; splinter; thin piece pared off a large piece: *a* ~ *of cheese.* □ *vt,vi* [VP6A,2A] break off as a ~; break into ~s; splinter.

slob /slɒb/ *n* (sl) unpleasantly dirty or rude person.

slob·ber /ˈslɒbə(r)/ *vi,vt* **1** [VP2A,3A] let saliva run from the mouth (as a baby does). ~ *over sb,* show excessive and maudlin love or admiration for (eg by giving wet kisses). **2** [VP6A] make wet with saliva: *The baby has* ~*ed its bib.* □ *n* [U] saliva running from the mouth; maudlin talk, etc.

sloe /sləʊ/ *n* [C] small, bluish-black, very bitter wild plum, fruit of the blackthorn; the blackthorn bush. ˌ~-ˈgin *n* liqueur made from ~s steeped in gin.

slog /slɒg/ *vi,vt* (-gg-) [VP6A,2C,3A] ~ (*at*), hit hard and wildly, esp in boxing and cricket; walk or work hard and steadily: ~ (*at*) *the ball;* ~*ing away at one's work;* ~*ing along the road.* ~**·ger** *n* person who ~s, eg at cricket; hard worker.

slo·gan /ˈsləʊgən/ *n* [C] striking and easily remembered phrase used to advertise sth, or to make clear the aim(s) of a group, organization, campaign, etc: *political* ~s.

sloop /sluːp/ *n* small one-masted sailing-ship with fore-and-aft rig.

slop¹ /slɒp/ *vi,vt* (-pp-) **1** [VP2A,C] (of liquids) spill over the edge: *The tea* ~*ped (over) into the saucer.* **2** ~ *over sb,* = slobber over sb. **3** [VP6A,15A] cause to spill: ~ *beer over the counter of a pub;* splash. **4** ~ *out,* empty ~s(1). **5** [VP6A,15A] make a mess with: ~ *paint all over* *the floor.* **6** [VP2C] splash: *Why do some children love ~ping about in puddles?* □ *n* ~**s, 1** dirty waste water from the kitchen or from bedrooms (where there are no basins with running water and drains); urine, excrement (in pails, as in a prison cell). **'~-basin** *n* basin into which dregs from teacups are emptied at table. **'~-pail** *n* one in which bedroom ~s are removed. **2** liquid food, eg milk, soup, esp for people who are ill; swill (for pigs).

slop² /slɒp/ *n* (esp as supplied to sailors in the Navy, usu *pl*) cheap, ready-made clothing; bedding. **'~-shop** *n* shop where ~s are sold.

slope /sləʊp/ *n* **1** [C,U] slanting line; position or direction at an angle, less than 90°, to the earth's surface or to another flat surface: *the ~ of a roof; a slight/steep ~; a ~ up/down; a hill with a ~ of 1 in 5.* **2** area of rising or falling ground: *'mountain ~s; 'ski ~s.* **3** position of a (soldier with his) rifle on the shoulder: *with his rifle at the ~.* □ *vi,vt* **1** [VP2A,C] have a ~; slant: *Our garden ~s (down) to the river. Does your handwriting ~ forward or backward?* **2** [VP6A] cause to ~. **~ arms,** (mil) place and hold the rifle in a sloping position on the left shoulder. **3** [VP2C] (colloq) **~ off,** (also *do a ~*), go off or away (to evade sb, or escape doing sth). **slop·ing·ly** *adv*

sloppy /'slɒpɪ/ *adj* (-ier, -iest) **1** wet or dirty with rain, etc; full of puddles; (of a table, etc) wet with slops: *The melting snow made the roads ~.* **2** (of food) consisting of slops. ⇨ slop¹ *n*(2). **3** (colloq) unsystematic; not done with care and thoroughness: *a ~ piece of work.* **4** (colloq) foolishly sentimental; weakly emotional: *~ sentiment; ~ talk about girlfriends and boyfriends.* **slop·pily** /-ɪlɪ/ *adv* in a ~ manner: *sloppily* (= carelessly) *dressed.* **slop·pi·ness** *n*

slosh /slɒʃ/ *vt,vi* **1** [VP6A,15A] (sl) hit: *~ sb on the chin.* **2** [VP3A] **~ about,** flounder about in slush or mud. **3** [VP15B] **~ sth about,** throw water or other liquid or semi-liquid substance about. **~ed** *adj* (sl) drunk.

slot /slɒt/ *n* [C] **1** narrow opening through which sth is to be put; slit for a coin in a machine (**'~-machine** or *vending-machine*) that automatically delivers sth, eg tickets, cigarettes, packets of sweets. **2** slit, groove or channel into which sth fits or along which sth slides. **3** (colloq) right or suitable place for sth (in a broadcast programme, scheme, etc): *find a ~ for a talk on bee-keeping.* □ *vt* (-tt-) [VP6A,15A] provide with ~s; make a ~ or ~s in: *~ a song recital into a radio programme; ~ 30000 graduates a year into jobs,* find jobs for them.

sloth /sləʊθ/ *n* **1** [U] laziness; idleness. **2** [C] S American mammal which lives in the branches of trees and moves very slowly. **~·ful** /-fl/ *adj* inactive; lazy.

slouch /slaʊtʃ/ *vi* [VP2A,C] stand, sit or move, in a lazy, tired way: *louts who ~ about at street corners all day.* □ *n* ~ing attitude or way of walking: *walk with a ~.* **,~-'hat** *n* soft hat with a turned-down brim. **~·ing·ly** *adv*

slough¹ /slaʊ/ *n* [C] *in US topography*: slu:/ swamp; marsh.

slough² /slʌf/ *n* [C] cast-off skin of a snake; any dead part of an animal dropped off at regular periods. □ *vt,vi* [VP6A,15B,2A] **~ (off),** put, come or throw off: *~ (off) bad habits; a snake that has ~ed its skin.*

sloven /'slʌvn/ *n* person who is untidy, dirty, careless or slipshod in his appearance, dress, habits, etc. **~·ly** *adj* of or like a ~: *a ~ly appearance; ~ in his dress.* **~·li·ness** *n*

slow¹ /sləʊ/ *adj* (-er, -est) **1** not quick; taking a long time: *a ~ runner; a ~ train,* eg one that stops at all or almost all stations, contrasted with an express train; *a ~ journey.* **2** at less than the usual rate or speed. *a ~ march,* eg at a military funeral. *in ~ motion,* (of a cinema film) with the number of exposures per second greatly increased (so that when the film is shown at normal rate the action appears to be ~); Hence, *a ~-motion film.* **3** not quick to learn; dull: *a ~ child;* not acting immediately; acting only after a time: *~ poison. He is ~ to anger/~ to make up his mind/~ of speech/~ at accounts/not ~ to defend himself.* **'~-coach** *n* person who is ~ in action, or who is dull, or who has out-of-date ideas. **4** (usu *pred*; of watches and clocks) showing a time behind the correct time (eg 1.55 when it is 2.00): *That clock is five minutes ~.* **5** not sufficiently interesting or lively: *We thought the party was rather ~.* **6** (of a surface) of such a nature that what moves over it (esp a ball) tends to do so at a reduced speed: *a ~ running track/cricket pitch/billiard table.* **~·ly** *adv* in a ~ manner: *walk/speak/learn ~ly. He ~ly opened the door. S~ly the door opened.* ⇨ slow² below. **~·ness** *n*

slow² /sləʊ/ *adv* (-er, -est) (Note that *slowly* may precede the finite *v* as in 'He slowly walked up the path', or follow, as in 'He walked slowly up the path', or have front position, as in 'Slowly he walked up the path', whereas ~ follows the *v*, except when used with *how*, or in participial compounds as in **2** below.) **1** at a low speed; slowly: *Tell the driver to go ~er. How ~/How slowly the time passes! S~ astern!* (a command to go astern slowly). **go ~, (a)** (of workers in a factory, etc) work slowly as a protest, or in order to get attention to demands, etc. Hence, **go-'~** *n.* **(b)** be less active: *You ought to go ~ until you feel really well again.* **2** (compounds) **,~-'going/-'moving/ 'spoken,** going/moving/speaking slowly.

slow³ /sləʊ/ *vi,vt* [VP3C,15B] **~ (sth) up/down,** (cause to) go at a slower speed: *S~ up/down before you reach the crossroads. You should ~ up a bit* (= stop working so hard) *if you want to avoid a breakdown. All this conversation ~s down the action of the play.* **'~-down** *n* (esp) intentional decrease of industrial production by labour or management.

slow-worm /'sləʊ wɜːm/ *n* small, limbless non-poisonous reptile.

sludge /slʌdʒ/ *n* [U] **1** thick, greasy mud; slush. **2** sewage. **3** thick, dirty oil or grease.

slue /slu:/; ⇨ slew².

slug¹ /slʌg/ *n* slow-moving creature like a snail but without a shell, a garden pest destructive to seedlings and plants. ⇨ the illus at mollusc.

slug² /slʌg/ *n* **1** bullet of irregular shape. **2** strip of metal with a line of type along one edge.

slug³ /slʌg/ *vt,vi* (-gg-) (US) = slog.

slug·gard /'slʌgəd/ *n* lazy, slow-moving person.

slug·gish /'slʌgɪʃ/ *adj* inactive; slow-moving: *a ~ river/pulse/liver.* **~·ly** *adv* **~·ness** *n*

sluice /slu:s/ *n* [C] **1** **'~(-gate/-valve),** apparatus, contrivance, for regulating the level of water by controlling the flow into or out of (a canal, lake, etc): *open the ~-gates of the reservoir.* **2** **'~(-way),** artificial water channel, eg one made by gold-miners for rinsing gold from sand and dirt. **3** flow of water above, through or below a floodgate. □ *vt,vi* **1** [VP6A] send a stream of water over; wash with a stream of water: ~ *ore*, to separate it from gravel, etc. **2** [VP6A,15B] ~ *(out)*, wash or flood with water from a ~. **2** [VP3A] ~ *out*, (of water) rush out as from a ~.

slum /slʌm/ *n* **1** court, alley or street of small, badly-built, dirty, crowded houses: *live in a ~*. **2** the ~s, part(s) of a town where there are such houses. ~ **clearance**, the demolishing of ~s and the rehousing of the people living in them. □ *vi* (-mm-) **1** visit the ~s to give charitable aid to the people in them. **2** (colloq) live very cheaply. ~**my** *adj* of ~s: *a ~my part of the town*.

slum·ber /'slʌmbə(r)/ *vi,vt* (liter and rhet) **1** [VP2A] sleep, esp sleep peacefully or comfortably. **2** [VP15B] pass (time) in ~: ~ *away a hot afternoon*. □ *n* (often *pl*) sleep: *fall into a troubled ~; disturb sb's* ~(*s*). ~**er** *n* one who ~s. ~·**ous** /-əs/ *adj* sleepy.

slump /slʌmp/ *vi* **1** [VP2A,C] drop or fall heavily: *Tired from his walk, he ~ed into a chair. The bullet entered his chest and he ~ed down to the floor.* **2** [VP2A] (of prices, trade, business activity) fall steeply or suddenly. □ *n* [C] general drop in prices, trade activity, etc; business depression.

slung /slʌŋ/ *pt,pp* of sling.

slunk /slʌŋk/ *pt,pp* of slink.

slur /slɜː(r)/ *vt,vi* (-rr-) **1** [VP6A] join (sounds, letters, words) so that they are indistinct; (music) sing or play legato. **2** [VP3A] ~ *over sth*, deal quickly with in an attempt to conceal: *He ~red over the dead man's faults and spoke chiefly of his virtues.* □ *n* **1** [U,C] reproach; suggestion of wrongdoing: *cast a ~ on sb's reputation; keep one's reputation free from* ~. **2** [C] act of ~ring sounds. **3** [C] (music) the mark ⌢ or ⌣ used to show that two or more notes are to be sung to one syllable or performed legato. ⇨ the illus at notation.

slurry /'slʌrɪ/ *n* [U] thin semi-liquid mixture of cement, clay, mud, etc.

slush /slʌʃ/ *n* [U] soft, melting snow; soft mud; (fig) foolish sentiment. '~ **fund** *n* (comm) fund of money used by a business company for the purpose of bribing public officials, etc. ~**y** *adj*

slut /slʌt/ *n* slovenly woman; slattern. ~·**tish** /-ɪʃ/ *adj*

sly /slaɪ/ *adj* (-er, -est) **1** deceitful; keeping or doing things secretly; seeming to have, suggesting, secret knowledge: *a sly look. a sly dog*, secretive person. **on the sly**, secretly. **2** playful, mischievous. **sly·ly** *adv* **sly·ness** *n*

smack / smæk/ *n* [C] **1** (sound of a) blow given with the open hand on sth with a flat surface; sound of the lips parted suddenly or of a whip: *with a ~ of the lips*, with this sound (suggesting enjoyment of food or drink); *give sb a ~ on the lips*, a loud kiss. *I heard the ~* (= crack) *of a whip*. **2** slap, blow: *give the ball a hard ~*, hit it hard (eg in cricket). **get a ~ in the eye**, (colloq) experience a setback; suffer a sharp disappointment. **have a ~ at sth**, (colloq) have a try to do it. □ *vt* [VP6A] **1** strike with the open hand: ~ *a naughty child*. **2** ~ **one's lips**, part the lips with a ~ing sound to show pleasure (at food or drink, or in anticipation of other sensual pleasures). □ *adv* in a sudden and violent way: *run ~ into a brick wall; hit sb ~ in the eye*. ~**er** *n* (colloq) **1** loud kiss. **2** pound (£) or dollar. ~·**ing** *n* act or occasion of hitting with the

palm of the hand: *The child needs a good ~ing*.

smack² / smæk/ *n* small sailing-boat for fishing.

smack³ / smæk/ *vi* [VP3A], *n* ~ *of*, (have a) slight flavour or suggestion (of): *opinions that ~ of heresy; medicine that ~s of sulphur; have a ~ of obstinacy in one's character*.

small /smɔːl/ *adj* (-er, -est) (opp of *big* or *large*; *also* ⇨ little) **1** not large in degree, size, etc: *a ~ town/room/audience/sum of money, etc; a ~ pony*, Cf *a nice little pony*, 'little' being preferred when there are emotive implications; ~ *children*, Cf *charming/nice/naughty, etc little children*. **2** not doing things on a large scale: ~ *farmers/ business men/shopkeepers*. **3** unimportant, trifling. **be thankful for ~ mercies**, for trifling pieces of good fortune. '~ **talk**, conversation about everyday and unimportant social matters. **4** (attrib only) *a ~ eater*, person who eats ~ quantities of food. **5** morally mean; ungenerous: *Only a ~ man/a man with a ~ mind would behave so badly*. Hence, ,~-'**minded** *adj*. **6** of low social position; humble: *great and ~*, all classes of people. **7 in a ~ way**, modestly, unpretentiously: *He has contributed to scientific progress in a ~ way. They live in quite a ~ way*, simply and without social ambitions. **8** little or no: *have ~ cause for gratitude. He failed, and ~ wonder*, It is not surprising. **9** (compounds and special uses) '~-**arms** *n pl* weapons light enough to be carried in the hand by a single soldier, eg rifles, revolvers. ~ **change** (a) coins of ~ denominations: *Can you give me ~ change for this note.* (b) (fig) trivial remarks; light conversation. '~ **fry** *n* ⇨ fry². '~-**holding** *n* (in GB) piece of land under fifty acres in extent let or sold to sb for cultivation. '~-**holder** *n* person owning or renting a ~holding. **the ~ hours** *n pl* ⇨ hour(1). ~ **letters** *n pl* not capitals. '~-**pox** *n* [U] serious contagious disease which leaves permanent scars on the skin. '~-**time** *adj* (colloq) of minor importance; third-rate. **the still, ~ voice**, the voice of conscience. **on the '~ side**, somewhat too small. **look/feel ~**, be humiliated. □ *adv* **sing ~**, ⇨ sing(1). □ **n the ~ of**, the slenderest part of: *the ~ of the back.* ~**s**, (colloq) ~ articles of clothing (for laundering). ~·**ness** *n*

smarmy /'smɑːmɪ/ *adj* (GB, colloq) ingratiating; trying to win favour by flattery, etc.

smart¹ /smɑːt/ *adj* (-er, -est) **1** bright; newlooking; clean; well-dressed: *a ~ hat/suit/car. You look very ~. Go and make yourself ~ before we call on the Joneses*. **2** fashionable; conspicuous in society: *the '~ set; ~ people*. **3** clever; skilful; having a good, quick brain; showing ingenuity: *a ~ student/officer; a ~ retort/saying; ~ dealing*, clever and intelligent, but perhaps dishonest. **4** quick; brisk: *go for a ~ walk; start out at a ~ pace.* **Look ~!** Hurry! **5** severe: ~ *punishment; a ~ rebuke; a ~ box on the ear.* ~·**ly** *adv* ~·**ness** *n* ~**en** /'smɑːtn/ *vt,vi* [VP6A,15B,2C] ~**en (oneself) (up)**, make or become ~(1,4): ~**en** *oneself up to receive visitors. She has ~ened up since I met her last.*

smart² /smɑːt/ *vt* [VP2A,C,3A] feel or cause a sharp pain (of body or mind): *The smoke made my eyes ~. He was ~ing under an injustice/under his father's rebukes. She was ~ing with vexation.* ~ **for**, suffer the consequences of, be paid out for: *He will make you ~ for this impudence.* □ *n* [U] sharp pain, bodily or mental: *The ~ of his wound kept him awake.*

BADGER
Lc 91cm

MONGOOSE
Lc 45cm

RABBIT
Lc 40cm

BEAVER
Lc 73cm

MOLE
Lc 12cm

ARMADILLO
Lc 76cm

BAT
Lc 5cm

FOX
Lc 104cm

OTTER
Lc 76cm

RAT
Lc 20cm

SQUIRREL
Lc 25cm

GUINEA-PIG
Lc 17cm

DUCKBILLED PLATYPUS
Lc 51cm

KOALA
Lc 60cm

HEDGEHOG
Lc 17cm

small wild animals

smash /smæʃ/ *vt,vi* **1** [VP6A,15A,B,22,2A,C] break, be broken, violently into small pieces: ∼ *a window. The drunken man* ∼*ed up all the furniture. The firemen* ∼*ed in/down the doors. Don't* ∼ *the door open; I have a key!* ∼**-and-'grab raid,** one in which a thief ∼es a shop-window, eg a jeweller's, and grabs valuables from behind it. **2** [VP2A,C] rush, force a way, violently (*into, through, etc*): *The car* ∼*ed into a wall.* **3** [VP6A] deal a heavy blow to; defeat: *give sb a* ∼*ing blow;* ∼ *the enemy;* ∼ *a record,* (in sport, etc) set up a far better record. **4** [VP6A] (tennis) hit (a ball) downwards over the net with a hard, overhand stroke. **5** [VP2A] (of a business firm) go bankrupt. □ *n* [C] ∼ing; breaking to pieces. '∼(**-up**), violent collision: *The teapot fell with an awful* ∼*. He fell and hit his head an awful* ∼ *on the kerbstone. There has been a terrible* ∼(*-up*) *on the railway. When the banks failed, many businesses were ruined in the* ∼ *that followed.* **go** ∼, be ruined. **2** (tennis) stroke in which the ball is brought swiftly down. **3** *a* ∼ **hit,** (colloq) sth (esp a new play, song, film, etc) which is at once very successful. □ *adv* with a ∼: *go/run* ∼ *into a wall.* ∼**er** *n* (sl) (**a**) violent blow. (**b**) sth or sb considered to be remarkably fine, attractive, etc. ∼**ing** *adj* (sl) remarkably fine, attractive, etc: *John Travolta's* ∼*ing!*
smat·ter·ing /'smætərɪŋ/ *n* (usu *a* ∼ (*of*)) slight knowledge (*of* a subject).

smear /smɪə(r)/ *vt,vi* **1** [VP14] ∼ *sth on/over/ with,* cover or mark with sth oily or sticky; spread (sth oily, etc) on: ∼ *one's hands with grease;* ∼ *grease on one's hands; hands* ∼*ed with blood.* **2** [VP6A] make dirty, greasy marks on; (fig) defame or sully (sb's reputation). *a* '∼(*ing*) *campaign,* one that aims at damaging sb's reputation (by spreading rumours, etc). **3** [VP6A] blot; obscure the outline of: ∼ *a word.* **4** [VP2A] become ∼ed. □ *n* [C] stain; mark made by ∼ing: *a* ∼ *of paint;* ∼*s of blood on the wall.* '∼**-word** *n* word (eg *communist* in US) suitable for ∼ing (sb's reputation).
smell¹ /smel/ *n* **1** [U] that one of the five senses which is special to the nose: *Taste and* ∼ *are closely connected. S*∼ *is more acute in dogs than in men.* **2** [C,U] that which is noticed by means of the nose; quality that affects this sense: *What a nice/horrible/unusual* ∼*! There's a* ∼ *of cooking. I like the* ∼ *of thyme.* **3** [C] (without an *adj*) bad or unpleasant quality that affects the nose: *What a* ∼*!* **4** [C] (usu *a* ∼) act of breathing in through the nose to get the ∼(2) of sth: *Have/Take a* ∼ *of this egg and tell me whether it's bad.*
smell² /smel/ *vt,vi* (*pt,pp* sme**l**t /smelt/) **1** [VP6A,19A] (not in the progressive tenses; often with *can, could*) be aware of through the sense of smell: *Can/Do you* ∼ *anything unusual? The camels smelt the water a mile off. I can* ∼ *something burning.* ∼ *a rat,* ⇨ rat. **2** [VP6A,15B,2A,C]

(with progressive tenses possible) use one's sense of smell in order to learn sth; inhale the odour of: *S~ this and tell me what it is. The dog was ~ing (at) the lamp-post.* **~ round/about,** go here and there ~ing, to get information (liter and fig). **~ sth out,** discover, hunt out, by means of the sense of smell or (fig) by intuition. **3** [VP2A] (not in the progressive tenses) have the sense of smell: *Do/ Can fishes ~?* **4** [VP2A,D,3A] **~ (of sth),** give out a smell (of the kind specified by an *adj* or *adv*); suggest or recall the smell (of): *The flowers ~ sweet. The dinner ~s good. The lamb ~s of garlic. Your breath ~s of brandy.* (Note that if there is no *adj*, the suggestion is usu sth unpleasant): *Fish soon ~s in summer if it is not kept on ice. His breath ~s.* **~ of the lamp,** (of work) seem to have been composed late at night, with much hard work. **'~-ing-salts** *n pl* sharp-smelling substances to be sniffed as a cure for faintness, etc; sal volatile. **'~-ing-bottle** *n* one containing ~ing-salts. **smelly** *adj* (-ier, -iest) (colloq) having a bad ~.

smelt¹ /smelt/ *vt* [VP6A] melt (ore); separate (metal) from ore by doing this: *a copper-~ing works.*

smelt² /smelt/ *n* small fish valued as food.

smelt³ *pp,pt* of **smell²**.

smi·lax /'smaɪlæks/ *n* [U] kind of plant with trailing vines much used in decoration.

smile /smaɪl/ *n* [C] pleased, happy, amused or other expression on the face, with (usu a parting of the lips and) loosening of the face muscles: *There was a pleasant/ironical/amused, etc ~ on her face. He was all ~s,* looked very happy. *His face was wreathed in ~s.* □ *vi,vt* **1** [VP2A,B,4B,3A] **~ (at/on/upon),** give a ~ or ~s; show pleasure, amusement, sympathy, contempt, irony, etc by this means: *He never ~s. What/who are you smiling at? Fortune has not always ~d upon* (= favoured) *me. He ~d to see her so happy.* **2** [VP6B] express by means of a ~: *Father ~d his approval. She ~d her thanks.* **3** [VP6B] give the kind of ~ indicated: *~ a bitter ~.* **smil·ing·ly** *adv* with a ~ or ~s.

smirch /smɜːtʃ/ *vt* [VP6A] make dirty; (fig) dishonour. □ *n* [C] (fig) blot or stain.

smirk /smɜːk/ *vi* [VP2A], *n* (give a) silly, self-satisfied smile.

smite /smaɪt/ *vt,vi* (*pt* smote /sməʊt/, *pp* smitten /'smɪtn/) (archaic, or, in mod use, hum or liter) **1** [VP6A] strike; hit hard: *He smote the ball into the grandstand. His conscience smote him,* he was conscience-stricken. *He was smitten with remorse/smitten with that pretty girl.* **2** [VP6A] defeat utterly: *God will ~ our enemies.* **3** [VP2A,C] strike; come forcibly: *A strange sound smote upon our ears.*

smith /smɪθ/ *n* worker in iron or other metals: *'black~.* ⇨ **black, gold, silver, tin.** **smithy** /'smɪðɪ/ *n* black~'s workshop.

smith·er·eens /ˌsmɪðə'riːnz/ *n pl* small fragments: *smash sth to/into ~.*

smit·ten /'smɪtn/ *pp* of **smite.**

smock /smɒk/ *n* loose garment (with smocking on it) like an overall. **~·ing** *n* [U] kind of ornamentation on a garment made by gathering the cloth tightly with stitches.

smog /smɒg/ *n* [U] mixture of fog and smoke.

smoke¹ /sməʊk/ *n* **1** [U] visible vapour with particles of carbon, etc coming from a burning substance: *~ pouring from factory chimneys; ˌciga rette/ciˈgar ~.* **end up in ~,** come to, end in,

nothing. **go up in ~,** be burnt up; (fig) be without result, leave nothing solid or worth while behind. **There is no ~ without fire,** (prov) ⇨ fire¹(1). **'~-bomb** *n* one that sends out clouds of ~ (used to conceal military operations, etc). **'~-cured/dried** *adj* (of ham, certain kinds of fish, etc) dried and cured in wood ~. **'~-screen** *n* clouds of ~ made to hide military or naval operations; (fig) explanation, etc designed to mislead people about one's real intentions, etc. **'~-stack** *n* (a) outlet for ~ and steam from a steamship (and, US, from a steam locomotive). (b) tall chimney. **2** [C] act of smoking tobacco: *stop working and have a ~;* (colloq) cigar or cigarette: *pass the ~s round.* **~-less** *adj* **1** that burns without ~: *~less fuel.* **2** free from ~: *a ~less zone,* where ~ is prohibited; *the ~less atmosphere of the countryside.* **smoky** *adj* (-ier, -iest) **1** giving out much ~; full of ~: *smoky chimneys/fires; the smoky atmosphere of an industrial town.* **2** like ~ in smell, taste or appearance.

smoke² /sməʊk/ *vi,vt* **1** [VP2A] give out smoke, or sth thought to resemble smoke, eg visible vapour or steam: *a smoking volcano. That oil-lamp ~s badly.* **2** [VP2A] (of a fire or fireplace) send out smoke into the room (instead of up the chimney): *This fireplace ~s badly.* **3** [VP2A,6A] draw in and let out the smoke of burning tobacco or other substance: *~ a pipe/cigar, etc. Do you ~? If you ~ opium, give it up.* **4** [VP22] bring (*oneself*) into a specific state by smoking tobacco, etc: *He ~d himself sick.* **5** [VP2A,C] (of pipes, cigars, etc, with passive force): *This pipe ~s well,* is satisfactory when ~d. *A good cigar will ~* (= can be ~d) *for at least half an hour.* **6** [VP6A] dry and preserve (meat, fish) with smoke (from wood fires): *~d ham/salmon.* **7** [VP6A] stain, darken, dry, with smoke: *a ~d ceiling; a sheet of ~d glass,* eg through which to look at the sun. **8** [VP6A,15B] send smoke on to (plants, insects): *~ the plants in a greenhouse,* to kill insects. **~ sth out,** force to leave by smoking: *~ out snakes from a hole.* **smok·ing** *n* [U] (*gerund,* in compounds) **'smoking-carriage/-car/-compartment** *nn* one for smokers on a railway train. **'smoking-mixture** *n* blend of tobaccos for smoking in pipes. **'smoking-room** *n* room (in a hotel, etc) where smoking is permitted. **smoker** *n* **1** person who habitually ~s tobacco. **2** smoking-carriage on a train.

smol·der /'sməʊldə(r)/ ⇨ **smoulder.**

smooth¹ /smuːð/ *adj* (-er, -est) **1** having a surface like that of glass; free from roughness or (fig) difficulty: *~ paper/skin; a ~ road; a ~ sheet of ice; ~ to the touch; a ~ sea,* calm, free from waves; *make things ~ for sb,* (fig) remove difficulties for him. *The way is now ~,* is no longer difficult. **take the rough with the ~,** take things (both the good and the bad things of life) as they come. **'~-bore** *adj* (of a gun) having no rifling in the barrel. **~-'faced** *adj* (fig) friendly but hypocritical. **2** (of movement) free from shaking, bumping, etc: *a ~ ride in a good car; a ~ flight in a jet airliner; a ~ crossing,* eg by sea from England to France. **3** (of a liquid mixture) free from lumps; well beaten or mixed: *a ~ paste.* **4** free from harshness of sound or taste: flowing easily: *~ verse; a ~ voice; ~ claret/ whisky.* **5** (of a person, his manner) flattering, polite, unruffled, conciliatory: *a ~ temper; ~ manners; a ~ face,* often used to suggest hypocrisy. Hence, **~-'faced/-'spoken/-'tongued** *adjj* (all having a suggestion of insincerity). **∼·ly** *adv* in a ∼ manner: *a ∼ly running engine. Things are not going very ∼ly,* There are troubles, obstacles, interruptions, etc. **∼·ness** *n*

smooth² /smuːð/ *vt,vi* **1** [VP6A,15B] ∼ **sth** *(down/out/away/over),* make smooth: ∼ *down one's dress;* ∼ *away/over obstacles/difficulties/ perplexities, etc,* get rid of them. ∼ **sb's path,** (fig) make progress easier. **2** [VP2C] become smooth or quiet: *The sea has ∼ed down.* **3** (compounds) '∼·ing-iron *n* (*iron* is the usu word) flatiron used (heated) to ∼ linen, clothes, etc. '∼-ing-plane *n* small plane for finishing the planing of wood. □ *n* act of ∼ing: *give one's hair a ∼.*

smor·gas·bord /ˈsmɔːɡəsbɔːd/ *n* [U] (Swedish) meal with a variety of dishes served from a buffet.

smote /sməʊt/ *pt* of smite.

smother /ˈsmʌðə(r)/ *vt* **1** [VP6A] cause the death of, by stopping the breath of or by keeping air from; kill by suffocation. **2** [VP6A] put out (a fire); keep (a fire) down (so that it burns slowly) by covering *with* ashes, sand, etc. **3** [VP14] ∼ **sth/sb with sth,** cover, wrap up, overwhelm with: ∼ *a grave with flowers/a child with kisses/one's wife with kindness; be ∼ed with/in dust by passing cars.* **4** [VP6A,15B] suppress; hold back: ∼ *a yawn/one's anger/feelings of resentment;* ∼ *up a scandal,* try to conceal it. □ *n* (usu **a** ∼) cloud of dust, smoke, steam, spray, etc.

smoul·der (US = **smol-**) /ˈsmuːldə(r)/ *vi* [VP2A,C] burn slowly without flame; (fig, of feelings, etc) exist or operate unseen, undetected, suppressed, etc: ∼*ing discontent/hatred/rebellion.* □ *n* [U] ∼ing burning: *The ∼ became a blaze.*

smudge /smʌdʒ/ *n* [C] **1** dirty mark; blotted or blurred mark: *You've got a ∼ on your cheek. Wash you hands or you'll make ∼s on the writing-paper.* **2** (chiefly US) outdoor fire with thick smoke made to keep away insects. □ *vt,vi* **1** [VP6A] make a ∼ or ∼s on; make a ∼ on (when writing a letter or word). **2** [VP2A] (of ink, paint, etc) become blurred or smeared: *Ink ∼s easily.*

smug /smʌɡ/ *adj* (-gg-) self-satisfied; having, showing, a character that is satisfied although without ambition, imagination, broadmindedness: *a ∼ smile; a life of ∼ respectability; ∼ optimism; ∼ rich men.* **∼·ly** *adv* **∼·ness** *n*

smuggle /ˈsmʌɡl/ *vt* [VP6A,14,15A,B] **1** get (goods) secretly and illegally (*into, out of,* a country, *through* the customs, *across* a frontier): ∼

Swiss watches into England. **2** take (sth or sb) secretly and in defiance of rules and regulations: ∼ *a letter into a prison.* **smug·gler** /ˈsmʌɡlə(r)/ *n*

smut /smʌt/ *n* **1** [C] (mark or stain made by a) bit of soot, dirt, etc. **2** [U] disease of corn (wheat, etc) that causes the ears to turn black. **3** [U] (colloq) indecent or obscene words, stories: *Don't talk ∼.* □ *vt* (-tt-) [VP6A] mark with ∼s(1). **∼·ty** *adj* (-ier, -iest) **1** dirty with ∼s. **2** containing ∼(3): *∼ty stories.* **∼·tily** /-ɪlɪ/ *adv* **∼·ti·ness** *n*

snack /snæk/ *n* light usu hurriedly eaten meal. '∼-bar/-counter *nn* bar/counter where ∼s may be eaten.

snaffle¹ /ˈsnæfl/ *n* '∼(-bit) horse's bit without a curb.

snaffle² /ˈsnæfl/ *vt* [VP6A] (GB sl) take without permission; pinch(4).

snag /snæɡ/ *n* [C] **1** rough or sharp object, root of a tree, hidden rock, which may be a source of danger. **2** (colloq) hidden, unknown or unexpected difficulty or obstacle: *strike/come upon a ∼. There's a ∼ in it somewhere.*

snail /sneɪl/ *n* kinds of small, soft animal, most of them with a spiral shell. ⇨ the illus at mollusc. **at a** '∼'s **pace,** very slowly.

snake /sneɪk/ *n* kinds of long, legless, crawling reptile, some of which are poisonous; (fig) (often ∼ *in the grass*) treacherous person who pretends to be a friend. **see ∼s,** have hallucinations. '∼-charmer *n* person who can control ∼s with music. □ *vi* [VP2C] move in twists and glides: *The road ∼s through the mountains.* **snaky** *adj* of or like a ∼; (fig) venomous, ungrateful, treacherous.

snap /snæp/ *vt,vi* (-pp-) **1** [VP6A,15B,2A,3A] ∼ *(at) (sth),* (try to) snatch with the teeth: *The dog ∼ped at my leg. The fish ∼ped at the bait. They ∼ped at the offer,* (fig) offered eagerly to accept it. ∼ *sth up,* buy eagerly: *The cheapest articles were quickly ∼ped up.* **2** [VP6A,14,15A,B,22,2A,C] break with a sharp crack; open or close with, make a sudden, sharp sound; say (sth), speak, sharply: *He stretched the rubber band till it ∼ped. The rope ∼ped. He ∼ped down the lid of the box. He ∼ped his whip. Her whip ∼ped down on the pony's back. The sergeant ∼ped out his orders.* ∼ *at sb,* speak to sb sharply: *I'm sorry I ∼ped at you just now.* ∼ *one's finger at sb/in sb's face,* make a cracking noise by flicking a finger audibly against the thumb (usu to show contempt). ∼ *sb's* 'nose/'head off, speak angrily to; interrupt rudely or impatiently. **3**

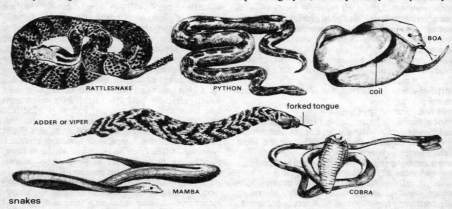

RATTLESNAKE PYTHON BOA coil

forked tongue

ADDER or VIPER

MAMBA COBRA

snakes

[VP6A] take a ∼shot (⇨ 8 below) of. **4** (sl) ∼ '*to it,* start moving, get going, quickly. ∼ '*out of it,* get out of a mood, habit, etc. □ *n* **1** [C] act or sound of ∼ping: *The dog made an unsuccessful* ∼ *at the meat. The lid shut with a* ∼. *The oar broke with a* ∼. *S*∼ *went the oar,* (adverbial use) It broke with a ∼ping noise. **2** [C] **cold** ∼, sudden, short period of cold weather. **3** [U] (colloq) energy, dash, vigour, liveliness: *Put some* ∼ *into it.* ⇨ snappy below. **4** [C] kinds of small, crisp cake: (usu in compounds) '*ginger-*∼*s.* **5** [C] (usu in compounds) catch, device for fastening things, closed by pressing. '∼-**fasteners** (also *press-stud*) fastening device used on dresses, gloves, etc. **6** = ∼shot ⇨ 8 below. **7** (attrib) done quickly and with little or no warning: *a* ∼ *election; take a* ∼ *vote; a* ∼ *division,* in the House of Commons. **8** (compounds, etc) '∼-**dragon** *n* [C] (= antirrhinum) kinds of plant with flowers that are like bags and can be made to open (like lips) when pressed. '∼-**shot** *n* quickly taken photograph with a hand camera (and usu by an amateur). ∼**py** *adj* (-ier, -iest) bright; lively: *Make it* ∼**py***! Look* ∼**py***!* (sl) Be quick about it! ∼**pish** /-ɪʃ/ *adj* inclined to ∼, to be ill-tempered or irritable. ∼**pish·ly** *adv* ∼**pish·ness** *n*

snare /sneə(r)/ *n* [C] **1** trap, esp one with a noose, for catching small animals and birds. **2** (fig) sth that tempts one to expose oneself to defeat, disgrace, loss, etc: *His promises are a* ∼ *and a delusion.* **3** string of gut stretched across the bottom of side-drum to produce a sharp, rattling sound. '∼-**drum** *n* side-drum with ∼s attached. □ *vt* [VP6A] catch in a ∼: ∼ *a rabbit.*

snarl[1] /snɑːl/ *vi,vt* [VP2A,3A] ∼ *(at),* (of dogs) show the teeth and growl (at); (of persons) speak in a harsh voice. □ *n* act or sound of ∼ing: *answer with a* ∼.

snarl[2] /snɑːl/ *n* tangle; confused state: *the traffic* ∼*s in a big town.* □ *vt,vi* [VP6A,15B,2A,C,3A] ∼ *(up),* (cause to) become jammed: *The traffic (was)* ∼*ed up.* Hence, '∼-**up** *n* = traffic jam. ⇨ traffic.

snatch /snætʃ/ *vt,vi* [VP6A,2A,15A,B] **1** put out the hand suddenly and take: *He* ∼*ed the letter from me/*∼*ed the letter out of my hand. It's rude to* ∼. *He* ∼*ed at* (ie tried to seize) *the letter but was not quick enough. He* ∼*ed up his gun and fired.* **2** get quickly or when a chance occurs: ∼ *an hour's sleep/a meal;* ∼ *a kiss.* □ *n* [C] **1** act of ∼ing; sudden attempt to get sth by stretching out the hand: *make a* ∼ *at sth;* (attrib) *a* ∼ *decision,* one that is ∼ed(2). **2** short outburst or period: *short* ∼*es of music; overhear* ∼*es of conversation; work in* ∼*es,* not continuously. ∼**er** *n*

snaz·zy /'snæzɪ/ *adj* (sl) smart; fine.

sneak /sniːk/ *vi,vt* **1** [VP2A,3A] ∼ *(on sb),* go quietly and furtively (*in, out, away, back, past,* etc). **2** [VP2A] (school sl) go to the teacher and tell him about the faults, wrongdoing, etc of another. **3** [VP6A] (sl) steal. □ *n* (sl) **1** cowardly, treacherous person. '∼-**thief** *n* petty thief; person who steals things from open doors and windows. **2** (school sl) boy or girl who ∼s(2). ∼**ing** *adj* furtive: *have a* ∼*ing respect/sympathy, etc for sb,* respect, etc which is not shown openly; *a* ∼*ing suspicion,* a vague, puzzling one. ∼**ing·ly** *adv* **sneaky** *adj* = ∼ing. ∼**ers** *n pl* (chiefly US) (also *a pair of* ∼**ers**) rubber-soled canvas shoes; plimsolls.

sneer /snɪə(r)/ *vi* [VP2A,3A] ∼ *(at),* show contempt by means of a derisive smile; utter contemp-

tuous words: ∼ *at religion.* □ *n* ∼ing look, smile, word or utterance: *You should ignore their* ∼*s at your efforts.* ∼**·ing·ly** *adv*

sneeze /sniːz/ *n* [C] sudden, uncontrollable outburst of air through the nose and mouth: *Coughs and* ∼*s spread diseases.* □ *vi* [VP2A] make a ∼: *Use a handkerchief when you* ∼. *not to be* ∼*d at,* (colloq) not to be despised; passable: *A prize of £50 in the lottery is not to be* ∼*d at.*

snick /snɪk/ *vt,vi,* *n* **1** (make a) small cut in sth. **2** (cricket) (make a) slight deflection of the ball with the bat: ∼ *a ball through the slips.*

snicker /'snɪkə(r)/ *vi, n* whinny; snigger.

snide /snaɪd/ *adj* sneering; slyly critical: ∼ *remarks.*

sniff /snɪf/ *vi,vt* **1** [VP2A] draw air in through the nose so that there is a sound: *They all had colds and were* ∼*ing and sneezing.* **2** [VP2A,3A] ∼ *(at),* ∼(1) to show disapproval or contempt: *The offer* (eg to buy a good car for £4000) *is not to be* ∼*ed at.* **3** [VP2A,3A,6A,15B] ∼ *(at) sth;* ∼ *sth up,* draw in through the nose as one breathes: ∼ *the sea-air;* ∼ *(at) a rose; a preparation* (eg for catarrh) *to be* ∼*ed up through the nostrils. The dog was* ∼*ing (at) the lamp-post.* □ *n* [C] act or sound of ∼ing; breath (of air, etc): *get a* ∼ *of sea air. One* ∼ *of this stuff is enough to kill you.* ∼**y** *adj* (colloq) **1** contemptuous. **2** (of sth that should have no smell) ill smelling.

sniffle /'snɪfl/ *vi* = snuffle.

snif·ter /'snɪftə(r)/ *n* (dated sl) small portion of strong alcoholic drink.

snig·ger /'snɪɡə(r)/ *n* [C] half-suppressed laugh (esp at sth improper, or in a cynical manner). □ *vi* [VP2A,C] ∼ *(at/over),* laugh in this way.

snip /snɪp/ *vt,vi* (-pp-) [VP6A,15B,3A] ∼ *(at) sth;* ∼ *sth up,* cut with scissors or shears, esp in short, quick strokes: ∼ *off the ends of sth;* ∼ *a hole in sth;* ∼ *cloth/paper.* □ *n* **1** cut made by ∼ping; sth ∼ped off. **2** (colloq) profitable bargain: *Only 50p! It's a* ∼*!* ∼**ping** *n* small piece of material ∼ped off a larger piece.

snipe[1] /snaɪp/ *n* (*pl* unchanged) bird which frequents marshes, with a long bill. ⇨ the illus at water.

snipe[2] /snaɪp/ *vi,vt* [VP2A,3A] ∼ *(at),* fire shots (at) from a hiding-place, usu at long range; [VP6A] kill or hit thus. **sniper** *n* person who ∼s.

snip·pet /'snɪpɪt/ *n* small piece cut off; (*pl*) bits (of information, news, etc).

snitch /snɪtʃ/ *vt,vi* **1** [VP6A] (sl) steal (usu sth of little or no value). **2** [VP2A,3A] ∼ *(on sb),* sneak, inform (on sb).

snivel /'snɪvl/ *vi* (GB -ll-; US -l-) [VP2A] cry from pretended grief, sorrow or fear; complain in a miserable, whining way: *a harassed woman with six* ∼*ling children.* ∼**·ler** (US = ∼**er**) *n* person who ∼s.

snob /snɒb/ *n* person who pays too much respect to social position or wealth, or who despises persons who are of lower social position: '∼ *appeal,* power to attract the interest of ∼s. ∼**·bish** /-ɪʃ/ *adj* of or like a ∼. ∼**·bish·ly** *adv* ∼**·bish·ness,** ∼**·bery** /'snɒbərɪ/ *nn* [U] state, quality, of being ∼bish; (*pl*) ∼bish acts or utterances.

snood /snuːd/ *n* ornamental net worn by a woman to keep her hair in place.

snook /snuːk/ *n* (only in) **cock a** ∼ *(at sb),* (lit or fig) show impudent contempt by placing the thumb to the nose and spreading out the fingers towards him.

snooker /'snu:kə(r)/ n game (a variety of *pool*) played with 15 red balls and six balls of other colours on a billiard-table. **be** ~**ed**, (colloq) be placed in a difficult position.

snoop /snu:p/ vi [VP2A,C,3A] (colloq) ~ (about/ around), search, examine (eg to find error, the breaking of rules, etc) in a secretive way. ~ **into**, pry into matters one is not properly concerned with. ~**er** n person who ~s.

snooty /'snu:tɪ/ adj (-ier, -iest) (colloq) supercilious; snobbish. **snoot·ily** /-ɪlɪ/ adv

snooze /snu:z/ vi [VP2A], n (sl) (take a) short sleep (esp in the daytime): *have a* ~ *after lunch.*

snore /snɔ:(r)/ vi [VP2A,C] breathe roughly and noisily while sleeping: *Does my snoring bother you?* □ n sound of snoring: *His* ~s *woke me up.* **snorer** n person who ~s.

snor·kel, schnor·kel /'snɔːkl, 'ʃn-/ n tube that enables a submarine to take in air while submerged; device for enabling a swimmer to take in air while under water. ⇨ the illus at frog.

snort /snɔːt/ vi,vt 1 [VP2A,C] force air violently out through the nose; do this to show impatience, contempt, etc: ~ *with rage* (*at* sb or sth); (colloq) indicate amusement with a burst of loud laughter. 2 [VP6A,15B] express by ~ing: ~ *defiance at sb;* ~ *out a reply. 'Never!', he* ~*ed.* □ n 1 act or sound of ~ing: *give a* ~ *of contempt.* 2 snorkel (of a submarine). ~**y** adj (colloq) ill-tempered. ~**er** n (colloq) 1 sb or sth that is violent or outstanding in some way: *This problem is a real* ~*er*, very difficult. 2 strong gale.

snot /snɒt/ n [U] (vulg) mucus of the nose. ~**ty** adj 1 (vulg) running with, wet with, ~. 2 '~(-nosed), (sl) superior; snooty: *You* ~*-nosed little bastard!*

snout /snaʊt/ n nose (and sometimes the mouth or jaws) of an animal (esp a pig); pointed front of sth, thought to be like a ~. ⇨ the illus at domestic, fish.

snow[1] /snəʊ/ n 1 [U] frozen vapour falling from the sky in soft, white flakes; mass of such flakes on the ground, etc: *a heavy fall of* ~; *roads deep in* ~; (*pl*) falls or accumulation of ~. 2 (compounds) '~**·ball** n (a) mass of ~ pressed into a hard ball for throwing in play. (b) sth that increases quickly in size as it moves forward. □ vt,vi (a) throw ~balls (at). (b) grow quickly in size, importance, etc: *Opposition to the war* ~*balled.* '~**·berry** n garden shrub with white berries. '~**·blind** adj (temporarily) unable to see because the eyes are tired by the glare of the sun on ~. Hence, '~**·blind·ness** n '~**·bound** adj unable to travel because of heavy falls of ~. '~**-capped/-clad/-covered** adjj covered with ~: ~*-capped mountains;* ~*-covered roofs.* '~**·drift** n bank of ~ heaped up by the wind: *The train ran into a* ~*drift.* '~**·drop** n bulb plant with small white flowers at the end of winter or in early spring. ⇨ the illus at flower. '~**·fall** n [C] amount of ~ that falls on one occasion or in a period of time, eg one winter, one year. '~**·field** n permanent wide expanse of ~, eg on high mountains. '~**·flake** n one of the feather-like collections of small crystals in which ~ falls. '~**-line** n level (in feet or metres) above which ~ lies permanently at any place: *climb above the* ~*-line.* '~**·man** /-mæn/ n (*pl*-men) figure of a man made of ~ by children for amusement. '~**·plough** (US '~**·plow**) n device for pushing ~ from roads and railways. '~**-shoes** n pl frames with leather straps for

walking on deep ~ without sinking in. '~**·storm** n heavy fall of ~, esp when accompanied by strong wind. ,~-'**white** adj pure, bright white in colour.

snow[2] /snəʊ/ vi,vt 1 [VP2A,B] (of snow) come down from the sky: *It* ~*ed all day.* 2 [VP2C] ~ **in**, come in large numbers or quantities: *Gifts and messages* ~*ed in on her birthday.* 3 **be** ~**ed** '**in**/ '**up**, be prevented by heavy snow from going out. **be** ~**ed** '**under** (**with**), (fig) be overwhelmed: ~*ed under with work/with invitations to dinner parties.* ~**y** adj (-ier, -iest) 1 covered with snow: ~*y roofs.* 2 characterized by snow: ~*y weather.* 3 as white or fresh as newly fallen snow: *a* ~*y tablecloth.*

snub[1] /snʌb/ vt (-bb-) [VP6A] treat (esp a younger or less senior person) with cold behaviour or contempt; reject (an offer) in this way; *be/get* ~*bed by a civil servant.* □ n [C] ~bing words or behaviour: *suffer a* ~.

snub[2] /snʌb/ adj (only in) **a** ~ **nose**, short, stumpy, turned up; hence, '~**-nosed** adj

snuff[1] /snʌf/ n [U] powdered tobacco to be taken up into the nose by sniffing: *take a pinch of* ~. **up to** ~, (colloq) (a) shrewd; not childishly innocent. (b) in normal health. '~**-box** n box for ~. '~**-colour(ed)** adj, n (of) dark yellowish-brown.

snuff[2] /snʌf/ vi, n = sniff.

snuff[3] /snʌf/ vt,vi 1 [VP6A,15B] cut or pinch off the burnt black end of the wick of (a candle). ~ *sth out*, (lit or fig) put out, extinguish (the light of a candle): *His hopes were nearly* ~*ed out.* 2 [VP2C] ~ **out**, (sl) die. ~**·ers** n pl scissors with a kind of box to catch the burnt wick of candles when they are ~ed.

snuffle /'snʌfl/ vi [VP2A] make sniffing sounds; breathe noisily (as when the nose is partly stopped up while one has catarrh). □ n act or sound of snuffing: *speak in/with a* ~, nasally.

snug /snʌg/ adj (-gg-) 1 sheltered from wind and cold; warm and comfortable: ~ *and cosy by the fireside;* ~ *in bed;* a ~ *woollen vest.* 2 neat and tidy; rightly or conveniently placed or arranged: *a* ~ *cabin*, on a ship. 3 good enough for modest needs: *a* ~ *little income.* 4 closely fitting: *a* ~ *jacket*; (as an adv) *a* ~*-fitting coat.* □ n = snuggery. ~**·ly** adv ~**·ness** n

snug·gery /'snʌgərɪ/ n (*pl*-ries) snug place, esp a private room planned for comfort.

snuggle /'snʌgl/ vi,vt [VP2C] ~ (**up**) (**to sb**), lie or get (close to sb) for warmth, comfort or affection: *The child* ~*d up to its mother/*~*d into its mother's arms. The children* ~*d up* (*together*) *in bed. She* ~*d down in bed*, made herself comfortable. 2 [VP14] ~ *sb to sb*, draw close (to one): *She* ~*d the child close to her.*

so[1] /səʊ/ adv of degree to such an extent. 1 (in the pattern: **not** + **so** + *adj/adv* + **as**): *It is not so big as I thought it would be. We didn't expect him to stay so long*, (as, in fact, he did stay). *He was not so much angry as disappointed.* 2 (in the pattern: **so** + *adj* + **as** + **to** + *inf*): *Would you be so kind as to help me*, ie will you please help me? *He is not so stupid as to do that.* 3 (in the pattern: **so** + *adj/adv* + **that**): *He was so ill that we had to send for a doctor. There were so many that we didn't know where to put them all. He was so angry that he couldn't speak.* (Colloq: *He couldn't speak, he was so angry*). 4 (If the *adj* modifies a sing n, the *indef art* is placed between the *adj* and the *n*. It is often better to use *such*): *He is not so clever a* *boy* (= such a clever boy) *as his brother.* **5** (used, colloq style, with exclamatory emphasis for *very*. 'Ever so* is colloq): *I'm 'so glad to see you! It was 'so kind of you! There was 'so much to do! That's 'ever so much better!* **6** (in phrases) 'so far*, up to this/that time, point or extent: *Now that we've come so far, we may as well go all the way. Everything is in order so far.* so 'far as*, to the extent or degree that: *So far as I know/as I'm concerned...* ,So far, so 'good*, Up to this point all is satisfactory. so 'far from*, instead of; quite contrary to: *So far from being a help, he was a hindrance.* so 'long as*, on condition that; provided that: *You may borrow the book so long as you keep it clean.* 'so much/many*, an unspecified quantity/number: *So much butter, so much sugar, so many eggs,.... ,Twelve dinners, at so much a head.* not so 'much as: *He didn't so much as* (= didn't even) *ask me to sit down. He is not so much unintelligent as uneducated,* ie he lacks education, not intelligence. ⇨ much¹. 'so much* (nonsense, etc), all, merely: *What you have written is so much nonsense.* 'so much for*, that is all that need be said, done, etc, about: *So much for the first stage of our journey.* ,so much 'so that*, to such an extent that: *He is rich—so much so that he does not know what he is worth.*

so² /səʊ/ *adv of manner* **1** in this/that way; thus: *So, and so only, can it be done. Stand just so. So it was* (= That is how) *I became a sailor. As X is to Y, so Y is to Z. As you treat me, so I shall treat you.* **2** (in phrases) 'so-called*, called or named thus but perhaps wrongly or doubtfully: *Your so-called friends won't help you in your troubles.* 'so that,* (a) in order that: *Speak clearly, so that they may understand you.* (b) with the result that: *Nothing more was heard of him, so that people thought that he was dead.* 'so... that,* (a) with the intent that: *We have so arranged matters that one of us is always on duty.* (b) with the result that; in a way that: *It so happened that I couldn't attend the meeting.* 'so as to do sth*, in order to; in such a way that: *Don't let your television blare so as to disturb your neighbours. I will have everything ready so as not to keep you waiting.* ⇨ as²(15). **3** (used as a substitute for a word, phrase or situation): *I told you so!* That is what I told you! *I could scarcely believe it, but it was so,* ie that was the state of affairs, etc. *So I believe/hope/suppose, etc.* **4** (used to express agreement, in the pattern: *so + pron + aux v*): A: *'It was cold yesterday.'* B: *'So it was.'* A: *'Tomorrow will be Friday.'* B: *'So it will.'* A: *'We have all worked hard.'* B: *'So we have.'* **5** (used meaning 'also' in the pattern: *so + aux v + (pro)n*): *You are young and so am I,* ie I also am young. *Tom speaks French and so does his brother.* A: *'I went to the cinema yesterday.'* B: *'Oh, did you? So did I.'* **6** (various uses) or so* (unstressed), about: *He must be forty or so,* about forty years old. *It will be warmer in another month or so,* in about a month from now. and 'so on (and 'so forth),* and other things of the same kind; et cetera. ,just 'so,* (a) used to express agreement. (b) neat and tidy: *Eric likes everything to be just so.* 'so to say/speak*, used as an apology for an unusual use of a word or phrase, an exaggeration, etc. 'so-so,* ⇨ this entry below. 'so-and-so /'səʊ ən səʊ/ (*pl* so-and-so's) (colloq) **(a)** person or thing not needing to be named: *Don't worry about what old so-and-so says.* **(b)** (derog) unpleasant person.

so³ /səʊ/ *conj* **1** therefore; that is why: *The shops were closed so I couldn't buy anything. She asked me to go, so I went. They cost a lot of money, so use them carefully.* **2** (exclamatory) *So you're back again! So you've lost your job, have you? So you're not coming! So there you are!*

so⁴, soh /səʊ/, sol /sɒl/ *n* fifth note in the musical octave.

soak /səʊk/ *vt,vi* **1** [VP2A] become wet through by being in liquid or by absorbing liquid: *The clothes are ~ing in soapy water.* **2** [VP6A,14A] ~ sth (in sth),* cause sth to absorb as much liquid as possible: ~ *dirty clothes in water/bread in milk. S~ the cloth in the dye for one hour.* **3** [VP15A,B] ~ sth up*, absorb; take in (liquid): *Blotting-paper ~s up ink.* ~ oneself in sth,* (fig) absorb: ~ *oneself in the atmosphere of a place.* **4** [VP6A,15B] (of rain, etc) ~ sb (through),* make him very wet: *We all got ~ed (through).* be ~ed to the skin,* get wet right through one's clothes. **5** [VP3A] ~ through sth,* penetrate; enter and pass through: *The rain had ~ed through the roof/his overcoat.* **6** [VP6A] (sl) extract money from by charging or taxing very heavily: *Are you in favour of ~ing the rich?* **7** [VP2A] (colloq) drink alcohol excessively (and habitually). □ *n* **1** act of ~ing: *Give the sheets a good ~. in ~,* being ~ed: *The sheets are in ~.* **2** (sl, usu old ~) person greatly addicted to alcoholic drink. ~er *n* **1** (colloq) heavy fall of rain: *What a ~er!* **2** drunkard.

soap /səʊp/ *n* [U] substance made of fat or oil and an alkali, used for washing and cleaning: *a bar/cake of ~;* '~-flakes;* '~-powder; use plenty of ~ and water.* 'soft ~,* ⇨ soft(15). '~-box *n* improvised stand for an orator (in a street, park, etc): ~-box oratory,* of the kind heard from demagogues. '~-bubble *n* filmy ball of ~y water with changing colours, full of air. '~-opera *n* (US) radio or TV serial drama dealing with domestic problems, etc in a sentimental or melodramatic way. '~-suds *n pl* frothy lather of ~ and water. □ *vt* **1** [VP6A,15B] apply ~ to; rub with ~: ~ oneself down.* **2** [VP6A] (colloq) flatter; try to please. soapy *adj* (-ier, -iest) **1** of or like ~: *This bread has a ~y taste.* **2** (fig) over-anxious to please: *He has a ~y voice/manner.*

soar /sɔː(r)/ *vi* [VP2A,C] fly or go up high in the air; hover in the air without flapping of wings; rise: ~ *like an eagle; a ~ing flight,* eg in a sailplane: *a cathedral nave that ~s up to the vaulted roof; the ~ing spire of Salisbury cathedral. Prices ~ed when war broke out.*

sob /sɒb/ *vi,vt* (-bb-) **1** [VP2A,C] draw in the breath sharply and irregularly from sorrow or pain, esp while crying; [VP15A,B]: *She sobbed her heart out,* sobbed bitterly. *She sobbed herself to sleep.* **2** [VP15B] sob sth out,* tell while doing this: *She sobbed out the story of her son's death in a traffic accident.* □ *n* [C] act or sound of sobbing: *The child's sobs gradually died down.* 'sob-stuff *n* [U] (colloq) the sort of writing, film, etc which is full of pathos and sentiment. sob-bing-ly *adv*

so-ber /'səʊbə(r)/ *adj* **1** self-controlled; temperate; serious in thought, etc; calm: *be in ~ earnest; make a ~ estimate of what is possible; exercise a ~ judgement; be ~-minded,* serious; ~ colours,* not bright; *in ~ fact,* in fact (contrasted with what is fancied or imagined). '~-sides *n* (dated colloq) serious and sedate person. **2** avoiding drunkenness; not drunk: *Does he ever go to bed ~?* □ *vt,vi*

[VP6A,15B,2C] **1** ~ *(sb) down,* make or become ~(1): *The bad news ~ed all of us. I wish those noisy children would ~ down,* become less excited, etc. **2** ~ *(sb) up,* make or become ~(2): *Put him to bed until he ~s up. Throw a pail of water over him—that'll ~ him up.* ~·ly *adv*
so·bri·ety /sə'braɪətɪ/ *n* [U] quality or condition of being sober(1,2).
so·bri·quet /'səʊbrɪkeɪ/ *n* [C] nickname.
soc·cer /'sɒkə(r)/ *n* [U] (colloq) (as used by those who play Rugby football for) association football.
so·cia·ble /'səʊʃəbl/ *adj* fond of the company of others; friendly; showing friendliness. **so·cia·bly** /-əblɪ/ *adv* **so·cia·bil·ity** /ˌsəʊʃə'bɪlətɪ/ *n* [U]
so·cial /'səʊʃl/ *adj* **1** (of animals, etc) living in groups, not separately: ~ *ants/wasps. Man is a ~ animal.* **2** of people living in communities; of relations between persons and communities: ~ *customs/reforms/welfare.* ¡S~ 'Democrat, (in politics) person who wishes society to move, by peaceful, democratic changes, to a system of socialism. ¡~ se'curity, government provisions for helping people who are unemployed, ill, disabled, etc: *The family is on a ~ security,* receiving such help. **(the)** ¡~ 'services *n pl* organised government service providing help and advice (eg in matters of health, housing, mental illness, law-breaking) to people who are in need or trouble. '~-work *n* [U] the profession of those who work in the ~ services. '~ worker *n* person who works in the ~ services. **3** of or in society: *one's ~ equals,* persons of the same class as oneself in society; ~ *advancement,* improvement of one's position in society; ~ *climbers,* persons trying to obtain ~ advancement. **4** for companionship: *a '~ club; spend a ~ evening,* in the company of friends. **5** = sociable. □ *n* ~ gathering, party, organized by a club. ~ly /-ʃəlɪ/ *adv*
so·cial·ism /'səʊʃəlɪzəm/ *n* [U] philosophical, political and economic theory that land, transport, the chief industries, natural resources eg coal, water-power, etc, should be owned and managed by the State or by public bodies, and wealth equally distributed. **so·cial·ist** *n* supporter of, believer in ~. □ *adj* of, tending towards, ~: *a Socialist Party,* political party which advocates and works for ~. **so·cial·ize** /-aɪz/ *vt* [VP6A] make social(1) or socialist; govern on socialist principles. **socialized medicine,** (US) the provision of free medical services by the Government. **so·ciali·zation** /ˌsəʊʃəlaɪ'zeɪʃn US: -lɪ'z-/ *n*
so·cial·ite /'səʊʃəlaɪt/ *n* (colloq) person prominent in fashionable society.
so·ciety /sə'saɪətɪ/ *n* (*pl* -ies) **1** [U] social way of living; customs, etc of a civilized community; system whereby people live together in organized communities: *a danger to ~,* person, idea, etc that endangers the bodily or moral welfare of the members of a community; *pests of ~,* persons who prey on the community and contribute nothing to its welfare. **2** [C] social community: *modern industrial societies;* certain grouping of humanity, eg Western Christendom, the people of Islam. **3** [U] company; companionship: *spend an evening in the ~ of one's friends.* **4** [U] people of fashion or distinction in a place, district, country, etc; the upper classes: *leaders of ~; high* (ie the most wealthy, influential, etc) *~; the customs of polite ~;* (attrib) *a '~ man/woman;* ~ *weddings,* of fashionable persons; ~ *gossip/news,* as printed in newspapers,

etc. **5** [C] organization of persons formed with a purpose; club; association: *the school de'bating ~; a co-'operative ~; the S~ of Friends.*
socio- /ˌsəʊsɪəʊ-/ *pref* of society or sociology.
so·ci·ol·ogy /ˌsəʊsɪ'ɒlədʒɪ/ *n* [U] science of the nature and growth of society and social behaviour. **so·ci·ol·ogist** /-dʒɪst/ *n* student of, expert in ~. **so·cio·logi·cal** /ˌsəʊsɪə'lɒdʒɪkl/ *adj* of ~. **so·cio·logi·cally** /-klɪ/ *adv*
sock¹ /sɒk/ *n* **1** (often **pair of** ~s) short stocking not reaching the knee. **pull one's ~s up,** (colloq) improve oneself, one's performance. **put a ~ in it,** (sl) be quiet; stop speaking. **2** loose sole used inside a shoe. ⇨ *wind-~* at wind¹(8).
sock² /sɒk/ *n* (sl) blow given with the fist or sth thrown: *Give him a ~ on the jaw!* Hit him hard! □ *vt* [VP6A,15A] (sl) give (sb) such a blow: *S~ him on the jaw! S~ a brick at him! S~ it to him!* □ *adv* (sl) squarely: *(hit sb) ~ in the eye.*
socket /'sɒkɪt/ *n* natural or artificial hollow into which sth fits or in which sth turns: *the 'eye-~s; a ~ for an electric light bulb/a candle.*
So·cratic /sə'krætɪk US: səʊ-/ *adj* characteristic of Socrates, /'sɒkrətiːz/, the Greek philosopher (died 399 BC). **the ~ method,** examining an idea, theory, etc, by question and answer between two or more people.
sod¹ /sɒd/ *n* [U] upper layer of grassland including the grass with its roots and earth; [C] square or oblong piece of this pared off; turf.
sod² /sɒd/ *n* ⚠ (vulgar term of abuse, used in annoyance and sudden anger): *You sod!* □ *vi* ⚠ *Sod (it)!* Damn (it)! *Sod off!* Go away! **sod·ding** *attrib adj* ⚠ (used as an intensive) *What a sodding mess!*
soda /'səʊdə/ *n* [U] common chemical substance used in soap-making, glass manufacture, etc: 'washing-~ (sodium carbonate, Na_2CO_3), used for softening water, etc; 'baking-~ (sodium bicarbonate, $NaHCO_3$), used in cooking. '~-biscuit/cracker *n* biscuit from dough containing baking-~ and sour milk. '~-fountain *n* counter, bar, from which ~-water, ices, etc are served. '~ pop (US colloq) soft drink of ~-water, flavoured sometimes with ice-cream. '~-water *n* water charged with carbon dioxide gas to make it bubble.
sod·den /'sɒdn/ *adj* **1** soaked through: *clothes ~ with rain.* **2** (of bread, etc) heavy and dough-like; moist or sticky because undercooked. **3** (often 'drink-~) stupid through too much drinking of alcoholic liquor.
so·dium /'səʊdɪəm/ *n* [U] silver-white metal (symbol **Na**) occurring naturally only in compounds: ~ *chloride,* **(NaCl)** common salt. ⇨ soda.
sod·omy /'sɒdəmɪ/ *n* [U] anal sexual intercourse, esp between males. **sod·om·ite** /'sɒdəmaɪt/ *n* person practising ~.
so·ever /səʊ'evə(r)/ *suff* (formal, used with *relative pronouns, advv* and *adjj*) any kind or extent of: 'how~, 'who~, etc.
sofa /'səʊfə/ *n* long seat with raised ends and back, on which several persons can sit or one person can lie.
soft /sɒft US: sɔːft/ *adj* **1** (opp of *hard*) changing shape easily when pressed; not resisting pressure; ~ *soil/ground/mud. Warm butter is ~. She likes a ~ pillow and a hard mattress.* **a ~ landing,** (eg of a spacecraft on the moon) one that avoids damage or destruction. Hence, ¡~·'land *v* land in this way. **2** (of surfaces) smooth and delicate: *as ~ as velvet;*

~ *fur;* ~ *furnishings,* curtains, hangings, etc; ~ *goods,* textiles. **3** (of light, colours) opp of glaring; restful to the eyes: *lampshades that give a* ~ *light.* **4** (of sounds) subdued; not loud: ~ *music;* ~ *murmurs/whispers; in a* ~ *voice.* **5** (of outlines) indistinct. **6** (of answers, words, etc) mild; gentle; intended to please: *a* ~ *answer; have a* ~ *tongue.* **7** (of the air, weather) mild: *a* ~ *breeze/wind;* ~ *weather.* **8** (of water) free from mineral salts and therefore good for washing: *as* ~ *as rainwater.* **9** (of certain sounds) not a plosive: *C is* ~ *in 'city' and hard in 'cat'. G is* ~ *in 'gin' and hard in 'get'.* **10** easy: *have a* ~ *job,* (sl) an easy, well-paid job; business deal with easily earned money. **11** feeble; lacking in strength and determination: *muscles that have got* ~ *through lack of exercise; a* ~ *generation,* eg of young people. **12** sympathetic; considerate: *have a* ~ *heart.* **have a** ~ **spot for sb,** a liking or fondness for him. **13** (colloq) feebleminded: *He's not as* ~ *as he looks. He's gone* ~. *Jack is* ~ (= sentimentally silly) *about Anne.* **14** (various uses; compounds) ~-'**boiled** *adj* (of eggs) boiled so that the egg is ~. ~ '**coal** *n* coal that burns with yellow, smoky flames. ~ '**currency** *n* one that is not convertible to gold, or into certain other currencies which are more in demand. ~ '**drink** *n* [C] cold, sweet, non-alcoholic drink, eg fruit juice (often charged with gas). '~ **drug** *n* [C] drug (eg marijuana) that is mildly habit-forming (as opposed to a *hard drug,* eg heroin, which is addictive). ~-'**footed** *adj* (of a person) moving with quiet, gentle steps. ~-'**headed** *adj* idiotic; foolish. ~-'**hearted** *adj* sympathetic; kind. ~ '**option** *n* alternative which is thought to involve little work. ~ '**palate** *n* back part of the roof of the mouth. ~-'**pedal** *vi, vt* play (music, the piano) with the ~ pedal down; (fig) make (a statement, etc) less definite or confident. ~ **soap** *n* semi-liquid soap made with potash; (fig) flattery. ~-'**soap** *vt* flatter. ~-'**solder** *n* kinds of solder used for easily fusible metal. ~-'**solder** *vt* solder with these soft kinds. ~-'**spoken** *adj* having a gentle voice; saying pleasant, friendly things. '~-**ware** *n* data, programmes, etc not forming parts of a computer but used for its operation. ⇨ *hardware* at *hard*[1](9). ~-'**witted** *adj* foolish. '~-**wood** *n* [C,U] (kinds of) easily sawn wood such as pine and other coniferous trees. '~-**ish** /-ɪʃ/ *adj* somewhat ~. ~-**ly** *adv* in a ~ manner: *tread/speak* ~ly. *She* ~ly *pressed his hand.* ~-**ness** *n* ~y *n* stupid person; feeble person.

sof·ten /'sɒfn *US:* 'sɔːfn/ *vt, vi* [VP6A,2A] make or become soft: *curtains that* ~ *the light; people who are* ~ed *by luxurious living.* ~ **sb up,** weaken (enemy positions) by shelling, bombing, etc; make (persons) unable or less able to resist (attack, salesmanship, etc). ~**er** *n* [C] sth used to ~, esp a chemical substance (or apparatus using this) for ~ing hard water.

soggy /'sɒgɪ/ *adj* (-ier, -iest) (esp of ground) heavy with water. **sog·gi·ness** *n*

soh /səʊ/ *n* ⇨ so[4].

Soho /'səʊhəʊ/ *n* district in the West End of London noted for its foreign restaurants, food shops and night clubs.

soi·gné /'swɑːnjeɪ *US:* swɑːˈnjeɪ/ *adj* (F) (fem - **née**) (of a person's way of dressing, etc) carefully finished or arranged, with attention to detail.

soil /sɔɪl/ *n* [C,U] **1** ground; earth, esp the upper layer of earth in which plants, trees, etc grow:

good/poor/alluvial/sandy, etc ~; *clay* ~s. '~-**pipe** *n* pipe from a water-closet pan to the drains. **2** *one's native* ~, one's native country; *a man of the* ~, one who works on the land (and is devoted to it). □ *vt, vi* **1** [VP6A] make dirty: ~ed *linen/ underwear, etc,* that has been used and is to be laundered. *He refused to* ~ *his hands,* refused to do dirty work. **2** [VP2A,C] admit of being ~ed: *material that* ~s *easily,* is easily ~ed.

soi·rée /'swɑːreɪ *US:* swɑːˈreɪ/ *n* social gathering in the evening, esp for music, conversation, etc, and often to help the aims of a society(5).

so·journ /'sɒdʒən *US:* səʊˈdʒɜːrn/ *vi* [VP2C], *n* (liter) (make a) stay (*with* sb, *at* or *in*) for a time. ~**er** *n*

sol /sɒl/ *n* ⇨ so[4].

Sol /sɒl/ *n* (hum) (often *old Sol*) the sun.

sol·ace /'sɒlɪs/ *n* [C,U] (that which gives) comfort or relief (when one is in trouble or pain): *The invalid found* ~ *in music.* □ *vt* [VP6A,15A] give ~ to: *The unhappy man* ~d *himself with whisky.*

so·lar /'səʊlə(r)/ *adj* of the sun. **a** ~ **cell,** device (as used in satellites) which converts the energy of sunlight into electric energy. **the** '~ **system,** the sun and the planets which revolve round it. ~ '**plexus** /'pleksəs/ *n* complex of nerves at the pit of the stomach. **the** ~ **year,** time occupied by the earth to complete one revolution round the sun, about 365 days, 5 hours, 48 minutes and 46 seconds.

so·lar·ium /səʊˈleərɪəm/ *n* (*pl* -ria /-rɪə/) place enclosed with glass for enjoyment of the sun's rays, esp one for the medical use of sunlight.

sold /səʊld/ *pt, pp* of sell.

sol·der /'sɒldə(r) *US:* 'sɒdər/ *n* [U] easily melted alloy used, when melted, to join harder metals, wires, etc. □ *vt* [VP6A,15A,B] join with ~. '~-**ing-iron** *n* tool used for this work.

sol·dier /'səʊldʒə(r)/ *n* member of an army: *three* ~s, *two sailors and one civilian. The children were playing at* ~s. **private** ~, one who is not a commissioned or non-commissioned officer. ~ **of fortune,** man who will take service under any State or person who will hire him; mercenary. □ *vi* [VP2A] serve as a ~: (chiefly in) *go/enjoy* ~ing; *be tired of* ~ing. ~ **on,** continue bravely with one's work, etc in the face of difficulties. ~-**ly,** '~-**like** *adjj* like a ~; smart; brave. ~**y** *n* (*sing* only, *collective n*) ~s of a specified character: *the undisciplined* ~y; *brutal, licentious* ~y.

sole[1] /səʊl/ *n* flat sea-fish with a delicate flavour.

sole[2] /səʊl/ *n* under surface of a human foot, or of a sock, shoe, etc, other than the heel. □ *vt* [VP6A] put a ~ on (a shoe, etc): *send a pair of shoes to be* ~d *and heeled.* -**soled** *suff* (with *n* or *adj* prefixed) '*rubber-*~d *boots;* '*thin-*~d *shoes.*

sole[3] /səʊl/ *adj* **1** one and only; single: *the* ~ *cause of the accident.* **2** restricted to one person, company, etc: *We have the* ~ *right of selling the article.* ~-**ly** *adv* alone; only: ~ly *responsible;* ~ly *because of you.*

sol·ecism /'sɒlɪsɪzəm/ *n* [C] error in the use of language; offence against good manners; mistake in etiquette.

sol·emn /'sɒləm/ *adj* **1** performed with religious or other ceremony; causing deep thought or respect: *a* ~ *silence as the coffin was carried out of the church; a* ~ *duty;* ~ *music; a* ~ *oath,* grave and important. **2** serious-looking; grave: ~ *faces; look as* ~ *as a judge.* ~-**ly** *adv* ~-**ness** *n*

sol·em·nity /sə'lemnəti/ *n* (*pl* -ties) **1** [U] seriousness; gravity. **2** [U] (but also *pl*) solemn ceremony: *The Queen was crowned with all ~/with all the proper solemnities.*

sol·em·nize /'sɒləmnaɪz/ *vt* [VP6A] perform (a religious ceremony, esp a wedding) with the usual rites; make solemn. **sol·em·niz·ation** /ˌsɒləmnaɪ'zeɪʃn US: -nɪ'z-/ *n* [U].

sol-fa /ˌsɒl 'fɑː *US*: ˌsəʊl/ *n* = *tonic* ~, ⇨ tonic.

sol·icit /sə'lɪsɪt/ *vt,vi* **1** [VP6A,14] ~ *sb (for sth)*, ask (for) earnestly: make requests (for): *Both the candidates ~ed (me for) my vote. The tradesmen are all ~ing us for our custom*, asking us to deal with them. **2** [VP6A,2A] (of a prostitute) make a sexual offer (to), esp in a public place: *I was openly ~ed at Piccadilly Circus.* **sol·ici·ta·tion** /səˌlɪsɪ'teɪʃn/ *n* [U] ~ing; [C] instance or occasion of this.

sol·ici·tor /sə'lɪsɪtə(r)/ *n* **1** (GB) lawyer who prepares legal documents, eg wills, sale of land or buildings, advises clients on legal matters, and speaks on their behalf in lower courts. ⇨ advocate, attorney, barrister. **So,licitor-'General**, one of the principal law officers in the British Government, advising on legal matters. **2** (US) person who solicits trade, support, etc; canvasser (eg for votes).

sol·ici·tous *adj* ~ *(for/about sth/sb)*; ~ *(to do sth)*, anxious, concerned about (sb's welfare, etc) or to help/serve sb: ~ *to please*; ~ *for her comfort.* ~·ly *adv* **sol·ici·tude** /sə̩lɪsɪ'tjuːd *US*: -tuːd/ *n* [U] being ~; concern or anxiety: *my deep solicitude for your welfare.*

solid /'sɒlɪd/ *adj* **1** not in the form of a liquid or gas: ~ *fuels*, eg coal, wood, ~*-fuelled rockets. When water freezes and becomes* ~, *we call it ice.* ˌ~-'state *adj* (of electronic devices) totally transistorized, ie without valves: *a ~-state amplifier.* **2** compact; substantial; heavy: *a man with good* ~ *flesh on him;* ~ *food*, not slops. **3** without holes or spaces; not hollow: *a* ~ *sphere.* **4** of strong or firm material or construction; able to support weight or resist pressure: ~ *buildings/furniture; build on* ~ *foundations; a man of* ~ *build; on* ~ *ground; steps cut in the* ~ *rock.* **5** that can be depended on: ~ *arguments; a* ~ (= financially sound) *business firm; a man of* ~ *character.* **6** alike all through; of the same substance throughout: *made of* ~ *gold.* **7** unanimous; undivided: *We are* ~ *for peace. The miners are* ~ *on this issue. There was a* ~ *vote in favour of the proposal.* **8** continuous; without a break: *wait for a* ~ *hour; sleep ten* ~ *hours/ten hours* ~. **9** (maths) having length, breadth and thickness: *a* ~ *figure*, eg a cube; ~ *geometry*, of ~, not plane, figures. □ *n* [C] **1** body or substance which is ~, not a liquid or a gas. **2** (geom) figure of three dimensions. ~·ly *adv* **sol·id·ity** /sə'lɪdəti/, ~·ness *nn* [U] quality of being ~: *the* ~*ity of a building/argument, etc.*

soli·dar·ity /ˌsɒlɪ'dærəti/ *n* [U] unity resulting from common interests or feelings: *national* ~ *in the face of danger.*

sol·id·ify /sə'lɪdɪfaɪ/ *vt,vi* (*pt,pp* -fied) [VP6A,2A] make or become solid, hard or firm. **sol·idi·fi·ca·tion** /səˌlɪdɪfɪ'keɪʃn/ *n*

sol·il·oquy /sə'lɪləkwɪ/ *n* (*pl* -quies) [C,U] (instance of) speaking one's thoughts aloud; (in drama) speech in which a character speaks his thoughts without addressing a listener. **sol·il·oquize** /sə'lɪləkwaɪz/ *vi* [VP2A] talk to oneself; think aloud.

sol·ip·sism /'sɒlɪpsɪzəm/ *n* (metaphysics) theory that one can have knowledge only of the self.

soli·taire /ˌsɒlɪ'teə(r) *US*: 'sɒlɪteə(r)/ *n* **1** (ornament such as an earring having a) single gem or jewel. **2** (also called *patience*) kinds of card-game for one player.

soli·tary /'sɒlɪtrɪ *US*: -terɪ/ *adj* **1** (living) alone; without companions; lonely: *a* ~ *life; a* ~ *walk.* ~ **confinement**, prison punishment by which a person is isolated in a separate cell. *in* ~, in ~ confinement. **2** only one: *not a* ~ *instance of sth*, not even one instance of it. **3** seldom visited: *a* ~ *valley.* **soli·tar·ily** /'sɒlɪtrəlɪ *US*: ˌsɒlɪ'terəlɪ/ *adv*

soli·tude /'sɒlɪtjuːd *US*: -tuːd/ *n* **1** [U] being without companions; solitary state: *live in* ~; *not fond of* ~. **2** [C] lonely place: *spend six months in the* ~*s of the Antarctic.*

solo /'səʊləʊ/ *n* (*pl* ~s /-ləʊz/) **1** piece of music (to be) performed by one person: *a violin/piano* ~. **2** any performance by one person; (as *adv*) *fly* ~; (attrib) *his first* ~ *flight.* **3** [U] kind of whist in which one player opposes others. '~·ist /-ɪst/ *n* person who gives a ~(1).

So·lon /'səʊlɒn/ *n* (the name of an Athenian lawgiver, hence) wise legislator.

sol·stice /'sɒlstɪs/ *n* [C] either time (*summer* ~, about 21 June; *winter* ~, about 22 Dec) at which the sun is farthest N or S of the equator.

sol·uble /'sɒljʊbl/ *adj* **1** ~ *(in)*, that can be dissolved. **2** (= solvable) that can be solved or explained. **solu·bil·ity** /ˌsɒljʊ'bɪlətɪ/ *n*

sol·ution /sə'luːʃn/ *n* **1** [C] ~ *(to/for/of)*, answer (to a question, etc); way of dealing with a difficulty: *Recourse to arms is not the best* ~ *to a quarrel between two countries. Might economy be the* ~ *to/for/of your financial troubles?* **2** [U] process of finding an answer or explanation: *problems that defy* ~, cannot be solved. **3** [U] process of dissolving a solid or a gas in liquid: *the* ~ *of sugar in tea.* **4** [C,U] liquid that results from this process: *a* ~ *of salt in water.*

solve /sɒlv/ *vt* [VP6A] find the answer to (a problem, etc): ~ *a crossword puzzle/an equation*; find a way out of a difficulty, etc: *Help me to* ~ *my financial troubles.* **solv·able** /-əbl/ *adj* that can be ~d or explained.

sol·vent /'sɒlvənt/ *adj* **1** of the power of dissolving or forming a solution: *the* ~ *action of water.* **2** having money enough to meet one's debts. □ *n* [C] substance (usu a liquid) able to dissolve another substance (usu specified): *grease* ~, eg petrol. **sol·vency** /-nsɪ/ *n* [U] being ~(2).

so·matic /səʊ'mætɪk/ *adj* of the body.

sombre (US = **som·ber**) /'sɒmbə(r)/ *adj* dark-coloured; gloomy; dismal: *a* ~ *January day;* ~ *clothes; a* ~ *picture of the future of mankind.* ~·ly *adv* ~·ness *n*

som·brero /sɒm'breərəʊ/ *n* (*pl* ~s /-rəʊz/) broad-brimmed hat (as worn in Latin American countries).

some[1] /sʌm; *weak form* səm, *used only in the adjectival sense of* 'consisting of an undefined amount or number of'/ *adj* **1** (used in affirm sentences; usually replaced by *any* in interr and neg sentences, in conditional clauses, and in sentences where doubt or negation is implied. *S*~ and *any* are used with material *nn* to indicate an amount or quantity that is either unknown or not given, with abstract *nn* to indicate a certain degree, and with *pl* common *nn* to indicate a certain number (three or more). *S~* and *any* are *pl* equivalents of the numeral article *a/an* (⇨ a²), of numeral *one*, and the *indef pron* 'one'): *Please give me* ~ *milk.* Cf *Have you any sugar? We haven't any tea. There are* ~ *children outside.* Cf *There is a child outside. They haven't any children. Are there any stamps in that drawer? I wonder whether Mr Black has any flowers in his garden. I doubt whether there are any flowers in Mr Green's garden. I don't like a garden without any flowers in it. There are scarcely/hardly any flowers in this garden. S~* (= S~ people) *say that....* **2** *S~* is used in sentences that are interr in form if the speaker expects, or wishes to suggest, an affirm answer: *Aren't there* ~ *stamps in that drawer?* Cf *There are* ~ *stamps in that drawer, aren't there? Didn't he give you* ~ *money?* Cf *He gave you* ~ *money, didn't he?* (*S~* is used in sentences that are interr in form if these sentences are really invitations or requests: *Will you have* ~ *cake?* Cf *Please have* ~ *cake. Will you please buy me* ~ *stamps when you go out?* Cf *Please buy me* ~ *stamps.*) **3** (After *if*, introducing a supposition, either *some* or *any* may be used): *If we had* ~/*any money, we could buy it. If we find* ~/*any, we'll share them with you.* **4** (*S~* and *any* are used with *more*): *Give me* ~ *more /sə* 'mɔ:(r)/*. Do you want any more? I haven't any more. Won't you have* ~ *more?* **5** (*S~* (always /sʌm/) is often contrasted with *the rest, other*(*s*), and *all*): *S~ children learn languages easily* (*and others with difficulty*). *All work is not dull;* ~ *work is pleasant.* **6** (*S~* (always /sʌm/) is used before *sing common nn* to indicate that the person, place, object, etc is unknown, or when the speaker does not wish to be specific. The words *or other* are often added): *He's living at* ~ *place in East Africa. I've read that story before in* ~ *book or other. S~ man at the door is asking to see you.* **7** (*S~* (always stressed) is used with *nn* meaning 'a considerable quantity or number of'): *I shall be away for* ,~ '*time*, a fairly long time. *Mr Green spoke at* ~ (= considerable) *length. We went* ~ (= several) *miles out of our way. The railway station is at* ~ *distance* (= quite a long way) *from the village.* **8** (*S~* (always stressed) is also used with *nn* meaning 'to a certain extent or degree'): *That is* ~ *help* (ie It helps to a certain extent) *towards understanding the problem.* □ *adv* (*S~* (always /sʌm/) is used adverbially, meaning *about* or *approximately*, before numbers): *That was* ~ *twenty years ago. There were* ~ *fifteen people there.* ~ **few**, ⇨ few(3).

some² /sʌm/ *pron* (*S~* as a *pron* is used in the same ways as ~, *adj*, (**1,2** and **3**). *S~ of* and *any of* are equivalent to *a few of, a little of, part of*): *S~ of these books are quite useful. I don't want any of these* (*books*). *I don't want any of this* (*paper*). *I agree with* ~ (= part) *of what you say. Scotland has* ~ *of the finest scenery in the world.*

some·body /'sʌmbədɪ/, **some·one** /'sʌmwʌn/ *pron* **1** (replaced by *anybody* in *interr, neg, etc* sentences) some person: *There's* ~ *at the door. Is there anyone at home? That must be* ~ *from the Department of Education.* **2** (often with the *indef art*; also in the *pl*) a person of some importance: *If you had studied harder at college you might have become* (*a*) ~. *He's nobody here in town but I suppose he's a* ~ *in his own village.*

some·how /'sʌmhaʊ/ *adv* **1** in some way (or other); by one means or another: *We must find*

money for the rent ~ (*or other*). *We shall get there* ~. **2** for some (vague) reason (or other): *She never liked me,* ~. *S~ I don't trust that man.*

some·one /'sʌmwʌn/ *n* = somebody.

some·place /'sʌmpleɪs/ *adv* (US colloq) somewhere: *I've left my bag* ~. *He lives* ~ *between Baltimore and Washington. Let's go* ~ *else.*

som·er·sault /'sʌməsɔ:lt/ *n* [C] leap or fall in which one turns heels over head before landing on one's feet: *turn/throw a* ~. □ *vi* [VP2A] turn a ~.

some·thing /'sʌmθɪŋ/ *pron* **1** (replaced by *anything* in *interr, neg, etc* sentences) some thing, object, event, etc (of an indefinite nature): *There's* ~ *on the floor. Is there anything in that box? I want* ~ *to eat. There's* ~ (= some truth, some point) *in what he says. It's* ~ (= some satisfaction, some comfort) *to be home again without an accident. He is* ~ (= has some position or other) *in the Department of the Environment.* **2** *or* ~, (colloq) indicates absence of precise information: *Mr Green is a shopkeeper or* ~, is engaged in trade of some kind. *I hear he has broken an arm or* ~, met with some sort of accident and has broken a limb, etc. *He struck a match too near the petrol tank or* ~, or did something equally foolish and dangerous. **3** ~ *of*, used to indicate an indefinite degree: *The soldier found himself* ~ *of a hero* (= was greeted as a hero to some extent) *when he returned to his village. He's* ~ *of a liar,* (= is not wholly truthful), *don't you think? I'm* ~ *of a carpenter,* I have some ability as a carpenter. □ *adv* ~ *like,* (**a**) rather like; having some resemblance to: *The airship was shaped* ~ *like a cigar.* (**b**) approximately: *He left* ~ *like ten thousand,* ie died leaving about £10000. (**c**) (colloq) *Now that's* ~ *like it,* (used to denote satisfaction).

some·time /'sʌmtaɪm/ *adv* **1** at some time: *I saw him* ~ *in May. It was* ~ *last summer. I will speak to him about it* ~. *I hope you will come* ~ *soon.* (Do not confuse with *some time* meaning 'for some period of time', as in: I have been waiting some time). **2** (also as *adj*) former(ly): *The Rev Thomas Atkins,* ~ *priest of this parish; Mr Snuffle,* ~ *fellow of Trinity College.*

some·times /'sʌmtaɪmz/ *adv* at some times; now and then; from time to time: *I* ~ *have letters from him. I have* ~ *had letters from him. S~ we go to the cinema and at other times we go for a walk.* (When ~ is used in a contrasting statement, or when it is repeated, it may follow the *v*): *She likes* ~ *the one and* ~ *the other. He says* ~ *the one thing and at other times the exact opposite.*

some·way /'sʌmweɪ/ *adv* (US colloq) = somehow.

some·what /'sʌmwɒt US: -hwɒt/ *adv* **1** rather; in some degree: *I was* ~ *surprised/disappointed, etc. He answered* ~ *hastily. We've arrived* ~ *late, I'm afraid.* **2** ~ *of,* rather: *He was* ~ *of a liar. I found it* ~ *of a difficulty.*

some·where /'sʌmweə(r) US: -hweər/ *adv* (in *interr, neg, etc* sentences replaced by *anywhere*) in, at, to, some place: *It must be* ~ *near here. Is it anywhere near here? I didn't go anywhere yesterday. He lost it* ~ *between his office and the station. You will find the text* ~ *in the Bible.*

som·nam·bu·lism /sɒm'næmbjʊlɪzəm/ *n* [U] sleep-walking. **som·nam·bu·list** /-ɪst/ *n* sleep-walker.

som·nol·ent /'sɒmnələnt/ *adj* sleepy; almost asleep; causing sleep. ~·**ly** *adv* **som·nol·ence** /-əns/

n [U] sleepiness.

son /sʌn/ *n* **1** male child of a parent. *the Son of God; the Son of Man,* Jesus Christ. *the sons of men,* mankind. **'son-in-law** *n* (*pl* sons-in-law) husband of one's daughter. **2** (used as a form of address, eg by an older man to a young man, a priest to a penitent): *my son.* **3** *son of,* person having the qualities, etc indicated: *sons of freedom,* those who have inherited freedom from their ancestors; *a son of the soil,* one whose father worked on the land and who follows his father's occupation.

so-nar /'səʊnɑ:(r)/ *n* device or system for detecting and locating objects submerged in water by means of reflected sound waves.

so-nata /sə'nɑ:tə/ *n* (*pl* ~s /-təz/) musical composition for one instrument (eg the piano), or two (eg piano and violin), normally with three or four movements.

song /sɒŋ US: sɔ:ŋ/ *n* **1** [U] singing; music for the voice: *burst into ~; the ~* (= musical cry) *of the birds.* **'~-bird** *n* bird (eg blackbird, thrush) noted for its ~. **2** [U] poetry; verse: *renowned in ~.* **3** [C] short poem or number of verses set to music and intended to be sung: *a marching ~; popular ~s.* **'~-book** *n* collection of ~s (with both words and music). **buy sth for a ~/an old ~; go for a ~,** buy sth/be sold for a small amount. **nothing to make a ~ and dance about,** (colloq) of little or no importance. *a ~ and dance,* (colloq) fuss. **~-ster** /-stə(r)/ *n* singer; ~-bird. **~-stress** /-strɪs/ *n* female singer.

sonic /'sɒnɪk/ *adj* relating to sound, sound-waves or the speed of sound: *a ~ bang/boom,* noise made when an aircraft exceeds the speed of sound; *the ~ barrier,* ⇨ *sound barrier* at sound²(3). ⇨ super-er~, ultra~.

son-net /'sɒnɪt/ *n* kind of poem containing 14 lines, each of 10 syllables, and with a formal pattern of rhymes. **~-eer** /ˌsɒnɪ'tɪə(r)/ *n* (usu derog) writer of ~s.

sonny /'sʌnɪ/ *n* (*pl* -nies) familiar form of address to a young boy.

son-or-ous /sə'nɔ:rəs/ *adj* **1** having a full, deep sound: *a ~ voice; the ~ note of the temple bell.* **2** (of language, words, etc) impressive; imposing: *~ titles; a ~ style of writing.* **~-ly** *adv* **son-or-ity** /sə'nɒrətɪ US: -'nɔ:r-/ *n*

sonsy /'sɒnsɪ/ *adj* (Scot) *a ~ lass,* a plump, merry, cheerful girl.

soon /su:n/ *adv* **1** not long after the present time or the time in question; in a short time. (*S~* may occupy mid-position with the *v,* or, esp if modified by *too, very* or *quite,* end position): *We shall ~ be home. We shall be home quite ~ now. He'll be here very ~. It will ~ be five years since we came to live in London. ~ after,* a short time after: *He arrived ~ after three.* (The opposite of *~ after* is *a little before.*) **2** early: *How ~ can you be ready? Must you leave so ~? We reached the station half an hour too ~. He will be here ~er than you expect.* **3** **as/so ~ as,** at the moment that; when; not later than: *He started as ~ as he received the news. I'll tell him the news as ~ as I see him. We didn't arrive so/as ~ as we had hoped.* **no ~er... than,** immediately when or after: *He had no ~er/No ~er had he arrived home than he was asked to start on another journey. No ~er said than done,* ie done immediately. **4** (in double comparative constructions): *The ~er you begin the ~er you'll finish. The ~er the better.* **~er or later,** one day

whether ~ or (much) later. **5** (suggesting comparison) *(just) as ~... (as),* with equal readiness or willingness... (as): *I would (just) as ~ stay at home as go for a walk. ~er than,* rather than: *He would ~er resign than take part in such dishonest business deals. S~er than marry that man, she would earn her living as a waitress. as ~ as not,* (most) willingly: *I'd go there as ~ as not.*

soot /sʊt/ *n* [U] black powder in smoke, or left by smoke on surfaces: *sweep the ~ out of the chimney.* **~y** *adj* black with ~; black like ~. □ *vt* cover with ~.

sooth /su:θ/ *n* (archaic) truth. *in ~,* truly. **'~-say-er** /-seɪə(r)/ *n* fortune-teller.

soothe /su:ð/ *vt* [VP6A] **1** make (a person, his nerves, passions) quiet or calm: *~ a crying baby; ~ sb's anger; a soothing voice.* **2** make (pains, aches) less sharp or severe: *~ an aching tooth; a soothing lotion for the skin,* eg against sunburn. **sooth-ing-ly** *adv*

sop /sɒp/ *n* **1** piece of bread, etc soaked in milk soup, etc. **2** *a sop to sb,* sth offered to prevent trouble or to give temporary satisfaction: (*throw*) *a sop to Cerberus,* (do) sth to pacify or bribe a troublesome person. □ *vt* (-pp-) [VP6A,15B] soak (bread, etc in broth, etc). *sop sth up,* take up liquid, etc: *Sop up the water with this towel.* **sop-ping,** *adv* soaking (wet): *sopping (wet) clothes.*

soph-ism /'sɒfɪzəm/ *n* [C,U] false reasoning or argument, intended to deceive.

soph-ist /'sɒfɪst/ *n* person who uses clever but misleading arguments.

soph-is-ti-cated /sə'fɪstɪkeɪtɪd/ *adj* **1** having learnt the ways of the world and having lost natural simplicity; showing this: *a ~ girl; a girl with ~ tastes.* **2** complex; with the latest improvements and refinements: *~ modern weapons; ~ devices used in spacecraft.* **3** (of mental activity) refined; complex; subtle: *a ~ discussion/argument.* **soph-is-ti-ca-tion** /səˌfɪstɪ'keɪʃn/ *n*

soph-is-try /'sɒfɪstrɪ/ *n* (*pl* -tries) [U] use of sophisms; [C] instance of this.

sopho-more /'sɒfəmɔ:(r)/ *n* (US) person in his second year at a four-year college.

sop-or-ific /ˌsɒpə'rɪfɪk/ *n, adj* (substance, drink, etc) producing sleep.

sop-ping /'sɒpɪŋ/ *adj* ⇨ sop.

soppy /'sɒpɪ/ *adj* (-ier, -iest) **1** very wet. **1** (colloq) foolishly sentimental.

so-prano /sə'prɑ:nəʊ US: -'præn-/ *n* (*pl* ~s /-nəʊz/), *adj* (person having the) highest singing voice of women and girls and boys.

sorbet /'sɔ:bət/ *n* = sherbet.

sor-cerer /'sɔ:sərə(r)/ *n* man who practises magic with the help of evil spirits. **sor-cer-ess** /'sɔ:sərɪs/ *n* woman ~. **sor-cery** /'sɔ:sərɪ/ *n* (*pl* -ries) [U] witchcraft; (*pl*) evil acts done by a ~.

sor-did /'sɔ:dɪd/ *adj* **1** (of conditions) wretched; shabby; comfortless: *a ~ slum; living in ~ poverty.* **2** (of persons, behaviour, etc) contemptible; prompted by self-interest or meanness: *~ motives.* **~-ly** *adv* **~-ness** *n*

sore /sɔ:(r)/ *adj* **1** (of a part of the body) tender and painful; hurting when touched or used: *a ~ knee/ throat.* **like a bear with a ~ head,** ill tempered, grumpy. *a sight for ~ eyes,* sb or sth welcome, pleasant. **2** filled with sorrow; sad: *a ~ heart.* **3** causing sorrow or annoyance. *a ~ point/subject,* one that hurts the feelings when talked about. **4** irritated; aggrieved: *feel ~ about not being invited to the party.* **5** (old use; also adverbial) grievous(ly); severe(ly): *in ~ distress; in ~ need of help; ~ oppressed.* □ *n* [C] **1** ~ place on the body (where the skin or flesh is injured): *treat/bandage/heal a ~.* **2** (fig) ~ subject; painful memory: *Let's not recall old ~s.* ~·ly *adv* **1** severely: *~ly tempted/ afflicted.* **2** greatly: *More financial help is ~ly needed.* ~·ness *n*

sor·ghum /'sɔːgəm/ *n* [U] kinds of millet.

sor·or·ity /sə'rɒrəti US: -'rɔːr-/ *n* (*pl* -ties) (US) women's social club in a college or university.

sor·rel[1] /'sɒrəl US: 'sɔːrəl/ *n* kinds of herb with sour-tasting leaves used in cooking.

sor·rel[2] /'sɒrəl US: 'sɔːrəl/ *adj, n* (of a) reddish-brown colour; horse of this colour.

sor·row /'sɒrəʊ/ *n* [C,U] (cause of) grief or sadness; regret: *express ~ for having done wrong; to my great ~; to the ~ of all who were present; in ~ and in joy,* when we are sad and also when we are happy. *His ~s had turned his hair white.* **more in ~ than in anger,** with more regret than anger for what was done, etc. *the Man of S~s,* Jesus. □ *vi* [VP2A,C] ~ *(at/for/over),* feel ~ (at/for/over sth): *~ing over her child's death.* ~·ful /-fl/ *adj* feeling, showing, causing, ~. ~·fully /-fəli/ *adv*

sorry /'sɒri/ *adj* **1** (*pred* only) feeling regret or sadness: *We're ~ to hear of your father's death. I should be ~ for you to think/if you were to think that I dislike you. I was ~ to hear that you thought I disliked you.* **be/feel ~ (about/for sth),** feel regret or repentance: *Aren't you ~ for/about what you've done? If you'll say you're ~* (= that you repent), *we'll forget the incident.* **be/feel ~ for sb,** (a) feel sympathy: *I feel ~ for anyone who has to drive in weather like this.* (b) feel pity or mild contempt: *I'm ~ for you, but you've been rather foolish, haven't you? If he doesn't realize that he must make sacrifices, I'm ~ for him.* **2** (used to express mild regret or an apology): *'Can you lend me a pound?'—'(I'm) S~, but I can't.'* ⇨ excuse[2](3), pardon(2). **3** (attrib) (-ier, -iest) pitiful: *in a ~ state;* worthless; shabby: *a ~ excuse.*

sort[1] /sɔːt/ *n* [C] **1** group or class of persons or things which are alike in some way: *Pop music is the ~ she likes most. What ~ of people does he think we are? We can't approve of this ~ of thing/these ~ of things/things of this ~.* **of a ~;** **of ~s,** used (colloq) to suggest that what is referred to does not fully deserve the name: *They served coffee of a ~/coffee of ~s/a ~ of coffee.* ~ **of,** (colloq) rather; to some extent: *I sort of thought* (= had a vague idea) *this would happen.* ⇨ *kind of* at kind[2](2). **2** *after a ~;* *in a ~,* to a certain extent. **3** *a good ~,* (esp) a person who is likable, who has good qualities. **4** *out of ~s,* (colloq) feeling unwell, out of spirits.

sort[2] /sɔːt/ *vt, vi* **1** [VP6A,15B] ~ *sth (out),* arrange in groups; separate things of one sort from things of other sorts: *The boy was ~ing/~ing out/over the foreign stamps he had collected. We must ~ out the good apples from the bad.* ~ *sth out,* (colloq) put in good order; solve: *I'll leave you to ~ that out,* find a solution. *Let's leave that pair to ~ themselves out,* clear up their problems, misunderstandings, etc. **2** ~ *well/ill with,* (liter) be in/out of harmony with: *His heroic death ~ed well with his character.* ~·er *n* (esp) post-office worker who ~s letters.

sor·tie /'sɔːtiː/ *n* [C] **1** attack made by besieged sol-

diers on their besiegers. **2** flight made by one aircraft during military operations: *The four planes each made two ~s yesterday.*

SOS /ˌes əʊ 'es/ *n* [C] **1** message for help (sent by radio, etc) from a ship, aircraft, etc when in danger. Cf *mayday call.* **2** urgent call for help, eg a broadcast to find relatives of a person seriously ill.

so–so /ˌsəʊ 'səʊ/ *pred adj, adv* (colloq) not very good: *'How are you feeling today?'—'Oh, only so-so.'*

sot /sɒt/ *n* habitual drunkard, esp one whose mind has become dulled. **sot·tish** /'sɒtɪʃ/ *adj* habitually drunk and, for this reason, dull or stupid. **sot·tish·ly** *adv* **sot·tish·ness** *n*

sotto voce /ˌsɒtəʊ 'vəʊtʃɪ/ *adv* (I) in a low voice, aside.

sou /suː/ *n* former French coin of low value; (fig) very small amount of money: *He hasn't a sou,* is penniless.

sou·brette /suː'bret/ *n* maidservant (usu pert, coquettish, fond of intrigue) in a comedy for the theatre; actress taking such a part.

sou·bri·quet /'suːbrɪkeɪ/ *n* = sobriquet.

souf·flé /'suːfleɪ US: suː'fleɪ/ *n* [C] (F) dish of eggs, milk, etc beaten to a froth, flavoured (with cheese, etc) and baked.

sough /sʌf US: saʊ/ *vi* [VP2A], *n* (make a) murmuring or whispering sound (as of wind in trees).

sought /sɔːt/ *pt, pp* of seek.

soul /səʊl/ *n* [C] **1** non-material part of a person, believed to exist for ever: *believe in the immortality of the ~; commend one's ~ to God,* (when at the point of death). *He eats hardly enough to keep body and ~ together,* to keep him alive. *She has a ~ above material pleasures.* **2** (often without *indef art*) emotional, moral and intellectual energy: *This music has no soul. He is a man without a soul,* is unfeeling, selfish. *He put his heart and ~ into the work.* **3 the life and ~ of the party, etc,** (person looked upon as the) liveliest person present at the party, etc. **4** person regarded as the pattern or personification of some virtue or quality: *He is the ~ of honour/discretion.* **5** spirit of a dead person: ,*All 'S~s' Day,* 2 Nov. **6** person: *There wasn't a ~ to be seen,* No one was in sight. *The ship sank with 200 ~s.* **7** (expressing familiarity, pity, etc according to context): *He's a cheery ~,* a cheerful man. *Be a good ~ and lend me a dollar. She's lost all her money, poor ~.* **8** (US colloq) all those qualities that enable a person to be in harmony with himself and others, used esp by Afro-Americans and expressed through their music and dancing. ~ **brother/sister,** fellow Afro-American; person who thinks and feels in the same way as oneself. ~ **music,** modern Afro-American popular blues music with strong rhythm for dancing. **9** (compounds) '~**-destroying** *adj* killing the ~ or spirit: *~-destroying work.* '~**-stirring** *adj* exciting, etc. ~**ful** /-fl/ *adj* having, affecting, showing, deep feeling: *~ful eyes/music/glances.* ~**fully** /-fəli/ *adv* ~**less** *adj* without higher or deeper feelings. ~**less·ly** *adv*

sound[1] /saʊnd/ *adj* **1** healthy; in good condition; not hurt, injured or decayed: ~ *fruit/teeth; have a ~ constitution. a ~ mind in a ~ body,* good mental and physical health. ~ *in wind and limb,* (colloq) physically fit. **2** dependable; based on reason; prudent: *a ~ argument/policy; ~ advice; a ~ business firm. Is he ~ on national defence? Are his views, etc reasonable, well-founded?* **3**

capable, careful: *a ~ tennis player*. **4** thorough; complete: *have a ~ sleep*, a deep and peaceful sleep; *be a ~ sleeper; give sb a ~ thrashing*. □ *adv* **be/fall ~ asleep**, be/become deeply and peacefully asleep. **~·ly** *adv* in a ~ manner; thoroughly: *a ~ly based argument; sleep ~ly; be ~ly beaten at tennis*. **~·ness** *n*

sound² /saʊnd/ *n* [C,U] **1** that which is or can be heard: *within ~ of the guns*, near enough to hear them; '*vowel* ~*s*, eg /uː, ʌ, ə/ *and* '*consonant* ~*s*, eg /p, b, ʃ, ʒ/. *We heard the ~ of voices*. **2** (*sing* only) mental impression produced by sth stated (or read): *The news has a sinister ~*, seems to be sinister. *I don't like the ~ of it*. **3** (compounds, etc) ~ '**archives** *n pl* recordings on disc or magnetic tape of broadcasts considered to deserve being kept for future use: *the BBC ~ archives*. '~ **barrier** *n* point at which an aircraft's speed equals that of ~-waves, causing sonic booms: *break the ~ barrier*, exceed the speed of sound. '~-**box** *n* part of an old-fashioned gramophone containing a diaphragm and into which the needle that moves over a record is fixed (corresponding to the pick-up of an electrical reproducer). '~ **effects** *n pl* sounds (recorded on discs, magnetic tape, film, etc) for use in broadcasts, in making films, etc or produced when needed (in a studio, etc). '~-**film** *n* cinema film with dialogue, music, etc recorded on it. '~-**proof** *adj* constructed so that ~(s) cannot pass through or into: *a ~proof studio*. Hence, '~-**proof** *vt* [VP6A] make ~proof. '~-**recording** *n* (contrasted with *video-recording*) sth recorded in ~ only. '~-**track** *n* (music, etc on a) track or band at the side of a cinema film which has the recording ~. '~-**wave** *n* vibration made in the air or other medium by which ~ is carried. **~·less** *adj* ~·**less·ly** *adv*

sound³ /saʊnd/ *vt,vi* **1** [VP6A] produce sound from; make (sth) produce sound: *~ a trumpet*. **2** [VP6A] utter: *~ a note of alarm/danger*. **3** [VP6A] pronounce: *Don't ~ the 'h' in 'hour' or the 'b' in 'dumb'*. **4** [VP6A] give notice of: *~ the alarm*, eg by ringing a bell; *~ the retreat*, by blowing a bugle. **5** [VP2A] give forth sound: *The trumpet ~ed. This black key* (eg on the piano) *won't ~*, No sound is produced when the key is struck. **6** [VP6A] test, examine (the wheels of a railway carriage, etc by striking them; a person's lungs by tapping the chest). **2** [VP2C,D] give an impression when heard (often fig): *How sweet the music ~s! It ~s to me as if there's a tap running somewhere*, I think I can hear water running from a tap. *His explanation ~s all right*, seems reasonable enough. *Her excuse ~s very right*, is unconvincing. **8** '~-**ing-board** *n* canopy placed over a platform to direct the ~ of the speaker's voice towards his listeners; thin plate of wood on a musical instrument, for magnifying its ~; (fig) way of causing an opinion, plan, etc to be widely heard.

sound⁴ /saʊnd/ *vt,vi* **1** [VP6A,2A] test the depth of (the sea, etc) by letting down a weighted line (called a '~*ing-line* or ~*ing apparatus*); find the depth of water in a ship's hold (with a '~*ing-rod*); get records of temperature, pressure, etc in (the upper atmosphere) (by sending up instruments in a '~*ing-balloon*). **2** [VP6A,15A,B] *~ sb (out) (about/on sth)*, try (esp cautiously or in a reserved manner) to learn sb's views, sentiments, etc: *I will ~ the manager about/on the question of holidays. Have you ~ed him out yet*, tried to learn his views? **~·ings** *n pl* **1** measurements obtained by ~ing(1).

2 reactions obtained by ~ing(2). **3** place or area near enough to the shore to make it possible to ~(1): *We are in ~ings/have come into ~ings*.

sound⁵ /saʊnd/ *n* [C] narrow passage of water joining two larger areas of water; strait.

soup¹ /suːp/ *n* [U] liquid food made by cooking meat, vegetables, etc in water: *chicken/pea/tomato ~. in the ~*, (colloq) in trouble. '~-**kitchen** *n* public establishment for supplying ~ to persons who are poor, or after a calamity such as an earthquake or flood.

soup² /suːp/ *vt* [VP15B] *~ sth up*, (sl) fit (a motor-vehicle, its engine) with a supercharger (to increase the power output, and so its speed): *a ~ed-up car*.

soup·çon /'suːpsɒn *US:* suːp'sɒn/ *n* (F) (usu *a ~ of*) small amount; trace: *a ~ of garlic in the salad/of malice in his remarks*.

sour /'saʊə(r)/ *adj* **1** having a sharp taste (like that of vinegar, a lemon or an unripe plum, apple, etc). *~ grapes* ⇨ grape. **2** having a taste of fermentation: *~ milk; a ~ smell*, ie of sth that has fermented. **3** (fig) bad-tempered; sharp-tongued: *made ~ by disappointments. What a ~ face she has!* □ *vt,vi* [VP6A,2A] turn or become ~ (liter, fig): *The hot weather has ~ed the milk. Her personality has ~ed. The old man has been ~ed by poverty*. **~·ly** *adv* ~·**ness** *n*

source /sɔːs/ *n* [C] **1** starting-point of a river: *the ~s of the Nile. Where does the Rhine have its ~?* **2** place from which sth comes or is got: *The news comes from a reliable ~. Is that well the ~ of infection for these cases of typhoid?* **3** (*pl*) original documents, etc serving as material for a study, eg of sb's life, a period of history: (attrib) *~ materials*.

souse /saʊs/ *vt* [VP6A] **1** throw into water; throw water on. **2** put (fish, etc) into salted water, vinegar, etc to preserve it: *~d herrings*. **3** ~d (*pp*) (sl) drunk.

sou·tane /suː'tɑːn/ *n* (F) (in the RC Church) priest's cassock.

south /saʊθ/ *n* **1** ⇨ the illus at **compass**. one of the four cardinal points of the compass, on the right of a person facing the sunrise; part of any place, country, etc lying farther in this direction than other parts: *the ~ of London/England. Mexico is to the ~ of the US*. **2** (attrib) situated in, living in, pertaining to, coming from, the ~: *S~ Wales; S~ America; the S~ Pacific; a room with a ~ aspect*, with windows facing ~; *grow roses on a ~ wall; the S~ Pole*. □ *adv* to or towards the ~: *The ship was sailing due ~*. **~·'east, ~·'west** (abbr **SE, SW**), *nn, adjj, advv* (sometimes, esp naut, **sou'-east** /ˌsaʊ 'iːst/, **sou'-west** /ˌsaʊ 'west/) (regions) midway between ~ and east, ~ and west. **~·~·'east, ~·~·'west** (abbr **SSE, SSW**) *nn, adjj, advv* (sometimes, esp naut, **sou'-sou'-'east, sou'-sou'-'west**) (regions) midway between ~ and ~east, ~west. **~·'easter** *n* [C] strong wind blowing from the ~east. **~·'easter·ly** *adj* (of wind) from the ~east; (of direction) towards the ~east. **~·'wester, sou'-wester** /ˌsaʊ 'westə(r)/ *n* (a) strong ~west wind. (b) (always *sou'wester*) waterproof (usu oilskin) hat with a wide flap at the back to protect the neck. **~·'wester·ly** *adj* (of wind) from the ~west; (of direction) towards the ~west. **~·'eastern** /-'iːstən/ *adj* of, from, situated in, the ~east. **~·'western** /-'westən/ *adj* of, from, situated in the ~west. **~·ward(s)**

/'saʊθwədz/ *adv* towards the ~.

south·er·ly /'sʌðəlɪ/ *adj, adv* **1** (of winds) blowing from the south. **2** towards the south: *The plane flew off in a* ~ *direction.*

south·ern /'sʌðən/ *adj* in or of the south: ~ *Europe; the S~ States of the U.S.A.* ~**er** *n* person from the ~ part of the country, esp from the S~ States (US). '~·**most** /-məʊst/ *adj* farthest south.

sou·venir /ˌsuːvə'nɪə(r) *US:* 'suːvənɪər/ *n* [C] sth taken, bought or received as a gift, and kept as a reminder of a person, place or event.

sou'·wester /ˌsaʊwestə(r)/ ⇨ south(2).

sov·er·eign /'sɒvrɪn/ *adj* **1** (of power) highest; without limit; (of a nation, state, ruler) having ~ power: *become a* ~ *state,* fully self-governing and independent in foreign affairs. **2** excellent; effective: *Is there a* ~ *remedy for cancer?* □ *n* **1** ~ ruler, eg a king, queen or emperor. **2** British gold coin not now in circulation (face value one pound). ~**ty** /'sɒvrəntɪ/ *n* [U] ~ power.

so·viet /'səʊvɪət/ *n* [C] one of the councils of workers, etc in any part of the USSR (the Union of S~ Socialist Republics); any of the higher groups to which these councils give authority, forming part of the system of government (*the Supreme S~*) of the whole of the USSR: *S~ Russia; the S~ Union.* '~·**ize** /-aɪz/ *vt* convert to the ~ system of government.

sow¹ /saʊ/ *n* fully grown female pig. ⇨ boar, hog, swine.

sow² /səʊ/ *vt, vi* (*pt* sowed, *pp* sown /səʊn/ or sowed) [VP6A,15A,2A] put (seed) on or in the ground or in soil (in pots, seed-boxes, etc); plant (land *with* seed): *sow grass; sow a plot of land with grass;* (fig) *sow the seeds of hatred. It's too soon to sow yet.* ~·**er** *n* one who sows.

soy /sɔɪ/, **soya** /'sɔɪə/ *n* '**soy(a) bean,** bean grown as food and for the oil obtained from its seeds. ,**soy 'sauce,** sauce made by fermenting soy beans in brine.

soz·zled /'sɒzld/ *adj* (GB, sl) very drunk.

spa /spɑː/ *n* (place where there is a) spring of mineral water having medicinal properties.

space /speɪs/ *n* **1** [U] that in which all objects exist and move: *The universe exists in* ~. *Travel through* ~ *to other planets interests many people today.* '~·**capsule,** '~·**craft,** '~·**helmet,** '~·**rocket,** '~·**ship,** '~·**suit/-vehicle** *nn* of the kind needed for travel beyond the earth's atmosphere. ⇨ the illus at capsule, rocket. ~·'**time** *n* (also known as 'the fourth dimension') fusion of time and the three dimensions of ~, as a concept much used in modern physics and philosophy. **2** [C,U] interval or distance between two or more objects: *the* ~*s between printed words; separated by a* ~ *of ten feet; put as much* ~ *as possible between the lines; leave a blank* ~ *for sth to be added.* '~·**bar** *n* bar in a typewriter, tapped to make ~s between words. **3** [C,U] area or volume: *open* ~*s,* (esp) land, in or near a town, not built on. *Clear a* ~ *on the platform for the speakers.* '~·**heater** *n* heating apparatus (electric, or oil-burning) designed to warm a room by radiation or convection. **4** [U] limited or unoccupied place or area; room(3): *There isn't enough* ~ *in this classroom for thirty desks. Have you enough* ~ *to work in?* **5** (*sing* only) period of time: *a* ~ *of three years.* □ *vt* [VP6A,15B] ~ **sth (out),** set out with regular ~s between: ~ *out the posts three feet apart;* ~ *out the type more;* ~ (= spread) *out payments* (eg for

a house) *over twenty years: a well-~d family,* one in which children are born at planned intervals of time. ,~**ed 'out** *adj* (US sl) drugged; drunk. ,**single-/,double-'spacing** *n* [U] the arrangement of typed material with single/double ~s between the lines.

spacious /'speɪʃəs/ *adj* having much space; roomy. ~·**ly** *adv* ~·**ness** *n*

spade /speɪd/ *n* **1** tool for digging. ⇨ the illus at tool. '~·**work** *n* (fig) hard work (to be) done at the start of an undertaking. *call a* ~ *a* ~, speak plainly. **2** (one of a) suit of playing-cards: *the five of* ~*s.* ⇨ the illus at card. □ *vt* [VP6A,15B] ~ **sth (up),** dig (up) with a ~. '~·**ful** /-fʊl/ *n* amount that is taken up by a ~.

spa·ghetti /spə'getɪ/ *n* [U] Italian pasta of narrow long rods, cooked by boiling.

spake /speɪk/ (old or poet) *pt* of speak.

spam /spæm/ *n* [U] (P) chopped or minced ham, spiced, cooked, sold tinned in the form of a loaf, and usu eaten cold.

span /spæn/ *n* [C] **1** distance between the tips of a person's thumb and little finger when stretched out (esp as a measure, = 9 inches). **2** distance or part between the supports of an arch: *The bridge crosses the river in a single* ~. *The arch has a* ~ *of 60 metres.* **3** length in time, from beginning to end: *the* ~ *of life; for a short* ~ *of time.* **4** (S Africa) pair of horses or mules; yoke of oxen. **5** ~ **roof** *n* one with two inclined roofs (contrasted with a lean-to roof): *a* ~*-roof greenhouse.* □ *vt* (-nn-) [VP6A] **1** extend across (from side to side): *The Thames is* ~*ned by many bridges. His life* ~*ned almost the whole of the 19th c.* **2** measure by ~s(1).

spangle /'spæŋgl/ *n* [C] tiny disc of shining metal, esp one of many, as used for ornament on a dress, etc. □ *vt* (esp in *pp*) cover with, or as with, ~s. **the Star-S~d Banner,** ⇨ star(2).

Span·iard /'spænɪəd/ *n* native of Spain.

span·iel /'spænɪəl/ *n* sorts of dog with short legs, long, silky hair and large, drooping ears.

Span·ish /'spænɪʃ/ *adj* of Spain; of the Spaniards, or their language. ~ **onion,** mild flavoured, yellow-skinned variety. **the S~ Main,** (hist) the NE coast of S America and the Caribbean Sea, near this coast. □ *n* the ~ language.

spank /spæŋk/ *vt, vi* **1** [VP6A] punish (a child) by slapping on the buttocks with the open hand or a slipper, etc. **2** [VP2C] ~ (*along*), (esp of a horse or a ship) move along at a good pace. ~·**ing** *n* slapping on the buttocks: *give a child a* ~*ing.* □ *adj* (dated colloq) first-rate; excellent: *have a* ~*ing time; a* ~*ing* (= strong) *breeze.*

span·ner /'spænə(r)/ *n* (US = **wrench**) tool for gripping and turning nuts on screws, bolts, etc. ⇨ the illus at tool. *throw a* '~ *in/into the works,* sabotage a scheme, etc.

spar¹ /spɑː(r)/ *n* strong metal or wooden, pole used as a mast, yard, boom, etc. ⇨ the illus at barque.

spar² /spɑː(r)/ *vi* (-rr-) [VP2A,C] make the motions of attack and defence with the fists (as in boxing); (fig) dispute or argue. '~·**ring-match** *n* demonstration boxing match; (fig) dispute or argument. '~·**ring-partner** *n* man with whom a boxer ~s as part of his training.

spar³ /spɑː(r)/ *n* kinds of non-metallic mineral, easily cleavable.

spare¹ /speə(r)/ *adj* **1** additional to what is usually needed or used; in reserve for use when needed; (of time) for leisure; unoccupied: *I have no/very little* ∼ *time/money*, no time/money that I cannot use. *Surely you carry a* ∼ *wheel in the back of your car? We have no* ∼ *room/We don't have a* ∼ *room* (= extra bedroom, eg for a guest) *in our house.* ∼ **part**, part to replace a broken or worn-out part of a machine, etc. **2** (of persons) thin; lean: *a tall,* ∼ *man; a* ∼ *figure;* ∼ *of build.* **3** (attrib only) small in quantity: *a* ∼ *meal; on a* ∼ *diet.* ,∼-'**rib**, rib of pork with most of the meat cut off. □ *n* [C] ∼ part (for a machine, etc). ∼·**ly** *adv* in a ∼(2,3) manner: ∼*ly built.* ∼·**ness** *n*

spare² /speə(r)/ *vt,vi* **1** [VP6A,12A,13A] refrain from hurting, damaging or destroying; show mercy to: ∼ *sb's life,* ∼ *sb his life,* not kill him or have him killed. *We may meet again if we are* ∼*d,* if our lives are ∼d by Providence. *He doesn't* ∼ *himself,* is severe with himself, does not refrain from making great demands upon himself (his energies, time, etc). ∼ *sb's feelings,* avoid hurting his feelings. *S*∼ *the rod and spoil the child,* (prov) If you refrain from punishing the child, you will spoil its character. **2** [VP12B,13B,6A] ∼ *sth (for sb/sth),* ∼ *sb sth;* afford to give (time, money, etc) to sb, or for a purpose: *Can you* ∼ *me a few litres of petrol? Can you* ∼ *one of them for me? Can you* ∼ *me a few minutes (of your time)? I can't* ∼ *the time for a holiday at present. We have enough and to* ∼, more than we need. **3** [VP6A] use in small quantities, rarely or in a saving manner. *no expense(s)/pains* ∼*ed,* with no economy in money or effort: *I'm going to redecorate the house, no expense* ∼*d.* **spar·ing** *adj sparing of,* economical, frugal, careful (of): *You should be more sparing of your energy.* **spar·ing·ly** *adv*

spark¹ /spɑːk/ *n* [C] tiny glowing bit thrown off from a burning substance or still present in ashes, etc or produced by striking flint or hard metal and stone together; flash of light produced by the breaking of an electric current; (fig) sign of life, energy, etc; flash of wit: *The firework burst into a shower of* ∼*s. He hasn't a* ∼ *of generosity in him.* □ *vt,vi* [VP2A,15B] give out ∼s. ∼ *sth off,* (fig) lead to; be the immediate cause of: *His statement* ∼*ed off a quarrel between them.* '∼(-ing)-plug *n* device for firing the gas in a petrol engine by means of an electric ∼. ⇨ the illus at motor.

spark² /spɑːk/ *n* (colloq) gay and elegant person.

sparkle /'spɑːkl/ *vi* [VP2A,C] send out flashes of light: *Her diamonds* ∼*d in the bright light. Her eyes* ∼*d with excitement.* □ *n* spark; glitter. **spark·ler** /'spɑːklə(r)/ *n* sth that ∼s, eg a kind of firework; (sl, esp among criminals, often *pl*) diamond. **spark·ling** /'spɑːklɪŋ/ *adj* (esp) (of wines) giving out tiny bubbles of carbonic acid gas when the bottle is opened. ⇨ still¹(2).

spar·row /'spærəʊ/ *n* small brownish-grey bird common in many parts of the world, esp the 'house-∼, European kind found around buildings. ⇨ the illus at bird.

sparse /spɑːs/ *adj* **1** thinly scattered: *a* ∼ *population.* **2** not dense, thick or crowded: *a* ∼ *beard.* ∼·**ly** *adv: a* ∼*ly furnished room,* one with little furniture. ∼·**ness, spar·sity** /'spɑːsətɪ/ *nn* [U].

Spar·tan /'spɑːtn/ *n, adj* (person) caring little for the ordinary comforts of life, unafraid of pain and hardship; (of living conditions) hard because very simple: *live a* ∼ *life; in* ∼ *simplicity.*

spasm /'spæzəm/ *n* [C] **1** sudden and involuntary tightening of a muscle or muscles: *asthma* ∼*s.* **2**

sudden, convulsive movement: *in a* ∼ *of pain/excitement/grief; a* ∼ *of coughing.* **3** sudden burst (of energy).

spas·modic /spæz'mɒdɪk/ *adj* **1** taking place, done, at irregular intervals. **2** caused by, affected by, spasms: ∼ *asthma.* **spas·modi·cally** /-klɪ/ *adv*

spas·tic /'spæstɪk/ *n, adj* (person) suffering from cerebral palsy, physically disabled because of faulty links between the brain and motor nerves, causing spasmodic movements through difficulty in controlling voluntary muscles.

spat¹ /spæt/ *n* (a pair of) ∼s, cloth cover worn over the upper part of a shoe and round the ankle.

spat² /spæt/ *pt,pp* of spit.

spat³ /spæt/ *vi,vt* (-tt-), *n* (US) (have a) slight quarrel; (give a) light slap (to).

spat⁴ /spæt/ *n* spawn of oysters. □ *vi* (-tt-) (of oysters) spawn.

spatch·cock /'spætʃkɒk/ *n* fowl killed and cooked at once. □ *vt* [VP6A,14] ∼ *(in/into),* (colloq) insert (words): *He* ∼*ed into his speech a curious passage about....*

spate /speɪt/ *n* **1** strong current of water at abnormally high level (in a river): *After the storm the rivers were all in* ∼. **2** sudden rush of business, etc: *a* ∼ *of orders; a* ∼ *of new cars on the market.*

spa·tial /'speɪʃl/ *adj* of, in relation to, existing in, space. ∼·**ly** /-ʃəlɪ/ *adv*

spat·ter /'spætə(r)/ *vt,vi* [VP6A,14] ∼ *sth (on/over sth);* ∼ *sth (with sth),* splash, scatter, in drips: ∼ *grease on one's clothes/*∼ *one's clothes with grease. As the bus went by it* ∼*ed us with mud.* **2** [VP2C] fall or spread out in drops: *We heard the rain* ∼*ing down on the tin roof of the hut.* □ *n* [C] sprinkling; shower: *a* ∼ *of rain/bullets.*

spat·ula /'spætjʊlə US: 'spætʃʊlə/ *n* tool with a wide, flat, flexible blade used for mixing or spreading various substances.

spavin /'spævɪn/ *n* [U] disease of horses in which a bony swelling forms at the hock, causing lameness. **spav·ined** *adj* affected with ∼.

spawn /spɔːn/ *n* [U] **1** eggs of fish and certain water animals, eg frogs. ⇨ the illus at amphibian. **2** threadlike matter from which mushrooms and other fungi grow. □ *vt,vi* [VP6A,2A] lay or produce in great numbers: *departments which* ∼ *committees and sub-committees.*

spay /speɪ/ *vt* [VP6A] remove the ovaries of (a female animal).

speak /spiːk/ *vi,vt* (*pt* spoke /spəʊk/, archaic spake /speɪk/, *pp* spoken /'spəʊkən/) **1** [VP2A,C] make use of language in an ordinary, not a singing, voice: *Please* ∼ *more slowly.* **2** [VP2B,C,3A] ∼ *(to/with sb) (about sth): I was* ∼*ing to him about plans for the holidays.* ∼ *for sb,* (a) state the views, wishes, etc of; act as spokesman for. (b) give evidence on behalf of. ∼ *for oneself,* (a) express one's views, etc in one's own way. (b) (usu *S*∼ *for yourself!*) not presume to ∼ for others. ∼ *to sb,* admonish: *Your secretary was late again this morning—you'd better* ∼ *to her about it.* ∼ *to sth,* ∼ in confirmation of or in reference to: *Is there anyone here who can* ∼ *to his having been at the scene of the crime,* who can say that he was there? *You must* ∼ *to the subject,* not wander away from it. ∼ *of the devil!* said when, just after being spoken about, sb is seen, heard, etc. *nothing to* ∼ *of,* nothing worth mentioning; not much. ∼ *out/up,* (a) ∼ loud(er). (b) give one's opinions, etc without hesitation or fear. *not be on* '∼*ing terms*

with sb, (a) not know him well enough to ∼ to him. (b) no longer ∼ to him because one has quarrelled with him. **so to** ∼, as one might say; if I may use this expression, etc. '∼-ing-trumpet *n* (now replaced by *hearing-aids*) trumpet-shaped device held to the ear by a deaf person to help him to hear. '∼-ing-tube *n* tube that carries the voice from one place to another, eg from a ship's bridge to the engine-room. **3** [VP2C,15A] give evidence (of), convey ideas (not necessarily in words): *Actions* ∼ *louder than words. The portrait* ∼*s/is a* ∼*ing likeness,* is excellent, tells us well what the sitter was like. ∼ **volumes for,** be strong evidence of: *This evidence* ∼*s volumes for his honesty.* ∼ **well for,** be evidence in favour of. **4** [VP6A] know and be able to use (a language): *He* ∼*s several languages. Is English spoken here?* **5** [VP2A,B] address an audience; make a speech: *He spoke for forty minutes. Are you good at* ∼*ing in public?* **6** [VP6A] make known; utter: ∼ *the truth.* ∼ **one's mind,** express one's views frankly or bluntly. **7** (in the pattern, *adv* (in *-ly*) and *pres part*): *strictly/ roughly/generally, etc* ∼*ing,* using the word(s) in a strict/rough/general, etc sense. **8** [VP6A] (naut) hail and exchange information with (by flag signals, etc): ∼ *a passing ship.* **9** [VP2A] (of a gun, musical instrument, etc) make sounds. **10** '∼-easy *n* illicit liquor shop (esp in the US during the period of prohibition). ∼er *n* **1** person who makes speeches (in the manner indicated): *He's a good/ poor, etc* ∼*er.* **2** (short for) *loud-*∼*er.* **3 the S**∼**er,** presiding officer of the House of Commons and other legislative assemblies. '∼-er-ship /-ʃɪp/ *n* office of the S∼er; period of office of a S∼er.

spear /spɪə(r)/ *n* weapon with a metal point on a long shaft, used in hunting, or (formerly) by men fighting on foot. □ *vt* [VP6A] pierce, wound, make (a hole) in, with a ∼. '∼-head *n* (usu fig) individual or group chosen to lead an attack. □ *vt* act as ∼-head for: *armoured vehicles that* ∼-*head the offensive.*

spear·mint /'spɪəmɪnt/ *n* aromatic variety of mint used for flavouring; chewing-gum flavoured with this.

spec /spek/ *n* (colloq abbr of) speculation: *Those mining shares turned out a good* ∼, proved profitable. **on** ∼, as a speculation; as a guess.

special /'speʃl/ *adj* **1** of a particular or certain sort; not common, usual or general; of or for a certain person, thing or purpose: *He did it for her as a* ∼ *favour. What are your* ∼ *interests? Newspapers send* ∼ *correspondents to places where important events take place. On holidays the railways put on* ∼ *trains,* run extra trains for ∼ purposes. ∼ **constable,** man enrolled to help the ordinary police in time of need. ∼ **delivery,** delivery of mail (a letter, package, etc) by a ∼ messenger instead of by the usual postal services. ∼ **licence,** licence which allows a marriage to take place at a time or place other than those legally authorized. **2** exceptional in amount, degree, etc: *Why should we give you* ∼ *treatment? You've taken no* ∼ *trouble with your work for us.* □ *n* ∼ constable, ∼ train, ∼ edition of a newspaper, etc. ∼·ly /-ʃəlɪ/ *adv* particularly: *I came here* ∼*ly* (= on purpose) *to see you.* ∼·ist /-ʃəlɪst/ *n* person who is an expert in a ∼ branch of work or study, esp medicine: *an* '*eye* ∼*ist; a* ∼*ist in plastic surgery.*

spe·ci·al·ity /ˌspeʃɪ'ælətɪ/ *n* [C] (*pl* -ties) **1** special quality or characteristic of sb or sth. **2** (also **spe-**

cialty /'speʃəltɪ/ (*pl* -ties)) special pursuit, activity, product, operation, etc; thing to which a person (firm, etc) gives special attention or for which a place is well known: *Embroidery is her* ∼. *Wood-carvings are a* ∼ *of this village.*

spe·cial·ize /'speʃəlaɪz/ *vi,vt* **1** [VP2A,3A] ∼ *(in sth),* be or become a specialist; give special or particular attention to: ∼ *in oriental history. After his first degree he wishes to* ∼. '**2** (usu *pp*) adapt for a particular purpose: *a hospital with* ∼*d wards,* (cf *general wards*); ∼*d knowledge,* (cf *general knowledge*). **spe·cial·iz·ation** /ˌspeʃəlaɪ'zeɪʃn US: -lɪ'z-/ *n*

spe·cialty /'speʃəltɪ/ *n* (*pl* -ties) ⇨ speciality(2).

specie /'spiːʃiː/ *n* [U] (store of, consignment of) money in the form of coins: ∼ *payments; payment in* ∼.

spe·cies /'spiːʃiːz/ *n* (*pl* unchanged) **1** (biol) group having some common characteristics (division of a genus) able to breed with each other but not with other groups: *the human* ∼, mankind. **2** sort: *Blackmail is a* ∼ *of crime hated by all decent folk.*

spe·ci·fic /spə'sɪfɪk/ *adj* **1** detailed and precise: ∼ *orders. What are your* ∼ *aims?* **2** relating to one particular thing, etc, not general: *The money is to be used for a* ∼ *purpose.* ∼ **gravity,** mass of any substance relative to that of an equal volume of water. ∼ **name,** (biol) distinguishing name of the species. ∼ **remedy,** one for a particular disease. □ *n* [C] ∼ remedy: *Quinine is a* ∼ *for malaria.* **spe-cifi·cally** /-klɪ/ *adv* in a ∼ manner: *You were* ∼*ally warned by your doctor not to eat lobster.*

spec·ifi·ca·tion /ˌspesɪfɪ'keɪʃn/ *n* **1** [U] specifying. **2** (often *pl*) details, instructions, etc for the design, materials, of sth to be made or done: ∼*s for* (*building*) *a garage; the technical* ∼*s of a new car.*

spec·ify /'spesɪfaɪ/ *vt* (*pt,pp* -fied) [VP6A,9] state or name definitely; include in the specifications: *The contract specifies red tiles, not slates, for the roof. The regulations* ∼ *that you may use a dictionary in the examination.*

speci·men /'spesɪmɪn/ *n* [C] **1** one as an example of a class: ∼*s of rocks and ores.* **2** part taken to represent the whole: *a publisher's catalogue with* ∼ *pages of books.* **3** sth to be tested, etc for definite or special purposes: *supply a* ∼ *of one's urine.* **4** (colloq) unusual thing or person regarded with contempt or amusement: *What a queer* ∼ *(of humanity) he is!*

spe·cious /'spiːʃəs/ *adj* seeming right or true, but not really so: *a* ∼ *argument/person.* ∼·ly *adv* ∼·ness *n*

speck /spek/ *n* [C] small spot or particle (of dirt, etc) stain; discoloured spot on fruit (showing rottenness); dot: *Do you ever seem to see* ∼*s in front of your eyes? The ship was a mere* ∼ *on the horizon.* ∼ed *adj* marked with ∼s: ∼*ed apples.* ∼·less *adj*

speckle /'spekl/ *n* [C] small mark or spot, esp one of many, distinct in colour, on the skin, feathers, etc. ∼d *adj* marked with ∼s: *a* ∼*d hen;* ∼*d plumage.*

specs /speks/ *n pl* (colloq) spectacles(3).

spec·tacle /'spektəkl/ *n* [C] **1** public display, procession, etc, esp one with ceremony: *The ceremonial opening of Parliament was a fine* ∼. **2** sth seen; sth taking place before the eyes, esp sth fine, remarkable or noteworthy: *The sunrise as seen from the top of the mountain was a tremendous* ∼.

The poor drunken man was a sad ~. Don't make a ~ of yourself, don't draw attention to yourself by dressing, behaving, etc ridiculously. **3 ~s; a pair of ~s,** pair of lenses in a frame, resting on the nose and ears, to help the eyesight (or to protect the eyes from bright sunlight) (*glasses* is the more usu name). *see everything through rose-coloured ~s,* take a cheerful, optimistic view of things. **~d** *adj* wearing ~s.

spec·tac·u·lar /spek'tækjʊlə(r)/ *adj* making a fine spectacle(1,2); attracting public attention: *a ~ display of fireworks.* □ *n* [C] spectacle; ~ show: *a Christmas TV ~.* **~·ly** *adv*

spec·ta·tor /spek'teɪtə(r) *US:* 'spekteɪtər/ *n* onlooker (esp at a show or game): (attrib) ~ *sports,* those which draw crowds of ~s, eg football.

spectre (US = **spec·ter**) /'spektə(r)/ *n* [C] ghost; haunting fear of furure trouble. **spec·tral** /'spektrəl/ *adj* **1** of or like a ~. **2** of spectra or the spectrum: *spectral colours.*

spec·tro·scope /'spektrəskəʊp/ *n* instrument for producing and examining the spectra of a ray of light. **spec·tro·scopic** /ˌspektrə'skɒpɪk/ *adj* of, by means of, a ~: *spectroscopic analysis.*

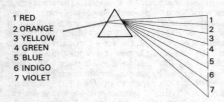

1 RED	1
2 ORANGE	2
3 YELLOW	3
4 GREEN	4
5 BLUE	5
6 INDIGO	6
7 VIOLET	7

the colours of the spectrum

spec·trum /'spektrəm/ *n* (*pl* -tra /-trə/) image of a band of colours (as seen in a rainbow and usu described as red, orange, yellow, green, blue, indigo and violet) formed by a ray of light which has passed through a prism; (fig) wide range or sequence: *the whole ~ of recent philosophical enquiry.*

specu·late /'spekjʊleɪt/ *vi* [VP2A,C] **1** consider, form opinions (without having complete knowledge); guess ~ *about/upon the future of the human race;* ~ *as to what sort of man one will marry.* **2** buy and sell goods, stocks and shares, etc with risk of loss and hope of profit through changes in their market value: ~ *in oil shares/wheat.* **specu·la·tor** /-tə(r)/ *n* person who ~s(2).

specu·la·tion /ˌspekjʊ'leɪʃn/ *n* **1** [U] speculating(1); meditation; [C] opinion reached by this means; guess. **2** [U] speculating(2): ~ *in rice;* [C] transaction, business deal, of this kind: *make some bad ~s; buy mining shares as a ~.*

specu·lat·ive /'spekjʊlətɪv *US* -leɪtɪv/ *adj* **1** concerned with speculation(1): ~ *philosophy.* **2** concerned with speculation(2): ~ *purchase of grain;* ~ *housing,* the building of houses as a speculation(2). **~·ly** *adv*

sped /sped/ *pt,pp* of speed.

speech /spiːtʃ/ *n* **1** [U] power, act, manner, of speaking: *Man is the only animal that has the faculty of ~. Our thoughts are expressed by ~. They say that ~ is silver but silence is golden. His indistinct ~ made it impossible to understand him.* ~ **therapy,** remedial treatment for defective speech, eg for stuttering. **2** [C] talk or address given in public: *make a ~ on/about the Common Market to a*

receptive audience. **'~-day** *n* annual school celebration with ~es and distribution of certificates and prizes. **~·less** *adj* **1** unable to speak, esp because of deep feeling: ~*less with surprise. Anger left him ~less.* **2** that causes a person to be unable to speak: ~*less rage.* **~·less·ly** *adv* **~·ify** /'spiːtʃɪfaɪ/ *vi* (*pt,pp* -fied) make ~es; talk as if making ~es (usu implying that this is done unnecessarily or badly): *town councillors ~ifying at the unveiling of a statue/at a welcome to the Queen.*

speed /spiːd/ *n* **1** [U] swiftness; rapidity of movement. *More haste, less ~,* (prov) Too much haste may result in delay. **2** [C,U] rate of motion or moving: *travelling at full/top ~; at a ~ of thirty miles an hour. It's dangerous to corner at ~,* to go round corners (in a vehicle) at a high ~. **3** (sl) amphetamine used as a drug to produce euphoria. **4** (compounds) **'~-boat** *n* motor-boat designed for high ~s. **'~-cop** *n* (sl) police motor-cyclist who checks the ~ of motorists. **'~-indicator** *n* = ~ometer. ⇨ below. **'~-limit** *n* ~ which must not be exceeded, eg in a built-up area. **'~ merchant,** (sl) person who drives a car or motor-bike extremely fast. **'~-way** *n* (a) track, for fast driving and racing, esp by motor-bikes. (b) (US) road for fast traffic; expressway. □ *vt,vi* (*pt,pp* sped) **1** [VP2A,C] move along, go, quickly: *cars ~ing past the school. He sped down the street.* **2** [VP6A,14] cause to move or go quickly: ~ *an arrow from the bow.* **3** (archaic) give success to: *God ~ you,* May God make you prosper. **4** [VP15B,2C] (*pt,pp* ~ed) ~ (*sth*) *up,* increase the ~ (of). *They have ~ed up production/the train service. He ~ed the engine up. The train soon ~ed up.* Hence, **'~-up** *n* ~ing up the rate of production, etc. **~·ing** *n* (of motorists) travelling at an illegal or dangerous ~: *fined £30 for ~ing.* **~om·eter** /spiː'dɒmɪtə(r)/ *n* instrument showing the ~ of a motor-vehicle, etc. ⇨ the illus at motor. **~·y** *adj* (-ier, -iest) quick; coming, done, without delay: *wish sb a ~y recovery from illness.*

outboard motor
55

a speed-boat

speed·well /'spiːdwel/ *n* kinds of small, wild plant with bright blue flowers.

spelae·ol·ogy (also **spele-**) /ˌspiːlɪ'ɒlədʒɪ/ *n* [U] the scientific study and exploration of caves. **spelae·ol·ogist** (also **spele-**) /-dʒɪst/ *n* expert in, student of, ~.

spell[1] /spel/ *n* [C] **1** words used as a charm, supposed to have magic power: *cast a ~ over sb; put a ~ on sb; be under/lay sb under a ~.* **'~-bound** /-baʊnd/ *adj* with the attention held by, or as by, a ~: *The speaker held his audience ~bound.* **'~-binder** /-baɪndə(r)/ *n* speaker who can hold audiences ~bound. **2** attraction, fascination, exercised by a person, occupation, etc: *under the ~ of her beauty; the mysterious ~ of the music of Delius.*

spell² /spel/ *n* **1** period of time: *a long ~ of warm weather; a cold ~ in January; rest for a (short) ~.* **2** period of activity or duty, esp one at which two or more persons take turns: *take ~s at the wheel,* eg of two persons making a long journey by car. □ *vt ~ sb (at sth),* take turns with sb: *Will you ~ me at rowing the boat?*

spell³ /spel/ *vt,vi* (*pt,pp* ~ed /speld/ or spelt /spelt/) **1** [VP6A] name or write the letters of (a word): *How do you ~ your name?* '~·ing pro-nunciation, one suggested by the written form of the word (eg /'nefju:/ instead of /'nevju:/ for ne-phew). **2** [VP6A] (of letters) form when put to-gether in a particular order: *C-A-T ~s cat.* **3** [VP15B] *~ sth out,* (a) make out (words, writing) laboriously, slowly: *It took the boy an hour to ~ out a page of German.* (b) make clear and easy to understand; explain in detail: *My request seems simple enough—do you want me to ~ it out for you?* **4** [VP6A] have as a consequence: *Does lazi-ness always ~ failure?* **5** [VP2A,6A] place the let-ters of words in the correct or accepted order: *These children can't ~. Why don't you learn to ~ my name (correctly)? ~er n* person who ~s: *a good/poor ~er. ~·ing n* [C] way a word is spelt: *Which is the better ~ing: Tokio or Tokyo? Do you use English or American ~ing(s)?*

spelt¹ ⇨ spell³.

spelt² /spelt/ *n* [U] kind of wheat giving very fine flour.

spend /spend/ *vt,vi* (*pt,pp* spent /spent/) **1** [VP6A,14,2A] *~ money (on sth),* pay out (money) for goods, services, etc: *~ all one's money; ~ too much money on clothes; ~ £30 a week. He's always ~ing. '~·thrift n* person who ~s money extravagantly. **2** [VP6A,14,19B] *~ sth (on sth/(in) doing sth),* use up; consume: *~ a lot of time on a project/(in) explaining a plan; ~ all one's energies. They went on firing until all their ammunition was spent.* **3** [VP6A,19B] pass: *~ a weekend in London/one's spare time gardening. How do you ~ your leisure? ~er n* person who ~s money (usu in the way indicated by the *adj*): *an ex-travagant ~er.* **spent** (*pp* as *adj*) exhausted; used up: *a spent runner/swimmer/horse; a spent cartridge/bullet,* one that has been fired and is now useless.

sperm /spɜ:m/ *n* [U] fertilizing fluid of a male ani-mal. '~·whale *n* whale producing spermaceti.

sper·mato·zoon /ˌspɜ:mətə'zəʊən/ *n* (*pl* -zoa /-'zəʊə/) male fertilizing element contained in sperm (fusing with an ovum to produce new off-spring).

sper·ma·ceti /ˌspɜ:mə'seti/ *n* [U] white, waxy, fatty substance contained in solution in the heads of sperm-whales, used for ointments, candles, etc.

spew /spju:/ *vt,vi* [VP6A,15B,2A] vomit.

sphag·num /'sfægnəm/ *n* (*pl* ~s) kinds of moss growing in peat and bogs, used in packing and medicinally.

sphere /sfɪə(r)/ *n* **1** solid figure that is entirely round; form of a ball or globe. *music of the ~s,* (myth) music produced by the movement of heavenly bodies, inaudible to mortals. **2** globe rep-resenting the earth or the sky. **3** person's interests, activities, surroundings, etc: *a woman who is dis-tinguished in many ~s,* eg in literary and artistic circles, and in the political world. *Skiing lies out-side the ~ of my activities.* **4** range, extent: *a ~ of influence,* area over which a country claims certain

rights or is recognized as having them. **spheri·cal** /'sferɪkl/ *adj* shaped like a ~. **sphe·roid** /'sfɪərɔɪd/ *n* body that is almost spherical.

sphinx /sfɪŋks/ *n* stone statue (esp **the S~**) in Egypt with a lion's body and a man's head; per-son who keeps his thoughts and intentions secret; enigmatic person.

a pyramid and the Sphinx

spice /spaɪs/ *n* **1** [C,U] sorts of substance, eg ging-er, nutmeg, cinnamon, cloves, used to flavour food: *a dealer in ~* (collective); *mixed ~(s); too much ~ in the cake.* ⇨ herb. **2** [U] (and with *indef art*) (fig) interesting flavour, suggestion, or trace (of): *a story that lacks ~. She has a ~ of wildness in her character.* □ *vt* [VP6A] add flavour to (sth) with ~, or as with ~: *~d with humour.* **spicy** *adj* (-ier, -iest) of, flavoured with, ~; (fig) exciting or interesting because somewhat improper: *spicy de-tails of the film star's love life.* **spic·ily** /-ɪlɪ/ *adv* **spici·ness** *n*

spick /spɪk/ *adj* (only in) *~ and span,* bright, clean and tidy.

spi·der /'spaɪdə(r)/ *n* sorts of creature with eight legs, many species of which spin webs for the cap-ture of insects as food. ⇨ the illus at arachnid. ~y *adj* (esp of handwriting) with long, thin strokes.

spied /spaɪd/ *pt,pp* of spy.

spiel /ʃpi:l US: spi:l/ *vi,vt* (sl) talk, say (sth) glibly and at length. □ *n* long voluble talk (usu intended to persuade sb).

spigot /'spɪgət/ *n* **1** (usu wooden) plug or peg which can be used to stop the hole of a cask or bar-rel. **2** valve for controlling the flow of water or other liquid from a tank, barrel, etc.

spike /spaɪk/ *n* **1** sharp point; pointed piece of metal, eg on iron railings or on running-shoes. **~ heel,** (also *stiletto heel*) thin, pointed heel on a (woman's) shoe. **2** ear of grain, eg barley; long, pointed cluster of flowers on a single stem: *~s of lavender.* □ *vt* [VP6A] **1** put ~s (on shoes, etc): *~d running-shoes.* **2** pierce or injure with a ~; (of cannon in former times) make useless by driving a ~ into the opening where the powder was fired. Hence, *~ sb's guns,* spoil his plans. **spiky** *adj* (-ier, -iest) having ~s or sharp points; (fig, of per-sons) difficult to manage because unwilling to yield.

spike·nard /'spaɪknɑ:d/ *n* [U] (costly ointment for-merly made from a) tall, perennial, sweet-smelling plant.

spill¹ /spɪl/ *vt,vi* (*pt,pp* spilt /spɪlt/ or ~ed) **1** [VP6A,2A,C] (of liquid or powder) (allow to) run over the side of the container: *Who has spilt/~ed the milk? The ink has spilt on the desk. ~ the beans,* ⇨ bean. *~ blood,* be guilty of wounding or killing sb. **2** [VP6A] (of a horse, cart, etc) upset; cause (the rider, passenger, etc) to fall: *His horse spilt him. The horse shied and we were all spilt* (= thrown out of the cart, etc) *into the ditch.* □ *n* fall from a horse, out of a cart, etc: *have a nasty ~.*

'**∼·over** n (often attrib) (of population) excess: *new towns for London's* ∼*over* (*population*). '∼·**way** n passage for surplus water from a reservoir, river, etc.

spill² /spɪl/ n [C] thin strip of wood, rolled or twisted strip of paper, used to light candles, tobacco in a pipe, etc.

spilt /spɪlt/ ⇨ spill¹.

spin /spɪn/ vt,vi (pt spun /spʌn/ or span /spæn/, pp spun) (-nn-) **1** [VP6A,14,2A] ∼ (*into/from*), form (thread) by twisting wool, cotton, silk, etc; draw out and twist (wool, cotton, etc) *into* threads; make (yarn) *from* wool etc in this way; engage in the occupation of ∼ning thread: ∼*ning wool/ thread/yarn.* ∼·**ning jenny** n early kind of machine for ∼ning more than one thread at a time.

a spinning-wheel

∼·**ning-wheel** n simple household machine for ∼ning thread continuously on a spindle turned by a large wheel, usu worked by a treadle. **2** [VP6A] form by means of threads: *spiders* ∼*ning their webs; silkworms* ∼*ning cocoons.* **3** [VP6A,15B] (fig) produce, compose (a narrative). ∼ *a yarn,* tell a story: *The old sailor loves to* ∼ *yarns about his life at sea.* ∼ *sth out,* make it last as long as possible: ∼ *out the time by talking; economize in order to make one's money* ∼ *out until next payday.* **4** [VP6A] cause (sth) to go round and round: ∼ *a top,* ⇨ top³; ∼ *a coin,* send it up in the air, revolving as it goes up, to decide sth (by 'heads or tails'); ∼ *the ball,* (in cricket, tennis). ∼·'**drier** n device that uses centrifugal force to dry what is placed in it (eg laundered clothes). ∼·'**dry** vt (pt,pp dried) dry in a ∼-drier. '∼-**off** n incidental benefit or product (from a larger enterprise, or from research for such an enterprise). **5** [VP2A,C] move round rapidly: *The top was* ∼*ning merrily. The collision sent the car* ∼*ning across the roadway. The blow sent him* ∼*ning to the wall. The bicycle was* ∼*ning along* (= moving along) *at a good speed.* **6 spun glass,** glass made into threads (by being spun when heated). **spun silk,** cheap material of short-fibred and waste silk, often mixed with cotton. □ n **1** [U] turning or ∼ning motion, esp as given to the ball in some games, eg cricket, baseball: *The pitcher gave* (a) ∼ *to the ball.* **2** short ride for pleasure in a motor-car, on a bicycle, etc: *go for/have a* ∼. **3** fast ∼ning movement of an aircraft during a diving descent: *get into/out of a* ∼. *in a flat* ∼, in a panic.

spin·ach /'spɪnɪdʒ US: -ɪtʃ/ n [U] common garden plant with green leaves, cooked and eaten as a vegetable.

spi·nal /'spaɪnl/ adj of or to the spine: *the* ∼ *column,* the backbone; *the* ∼ *cord,* nerve-fibres in the spine; *a* ∼ *injury.*

spindle /'spɪndl/ n **1** (in spinning) thin rod for twisting and winding thread by hand. ⇨ the illus at

spin. **2** bar or pin which turns round, or on which sth turns (eg an axle or a shaft). '∼-**legged**/ **shanked** adj having long, thin legs. '∼-**shanks** n person with such legs. '∼-**berry/-tree** n small tree with deep-pink berries and hard wood, used for ∼s. **spin·dly** /'spɪndlɪ/ adj long and thin; too tall and thin.

spin·drift /'spɪndrɪft/ n [U] foam or spray blown along the surface of the sea.

spine /spaɪn/ n **1** backbone. ⇨ the illus at skeleton. **2** one of the sharp needle-like parts on some plants, eg a cactus, and animals, eg a porcupine. **3** part of a book's cover that is visible when it is in a row on a shelf, usu with the book's title on it. ∼-**less** adj having no ∼(1); (fig) cowardly; timid. **spiny** adj (-ier, -iest) having ∼s(2).

spinet /spɪ'net US: 'spɪnɪt/ n old type of keyboard instrument like a harpsichord. ⇨ the illus at keyboard.

spin·na·ker /'spɪnəkə(r)/ n large triangular sail carried on the main-mast of a racing yacht on the side opposite the mainsail when running before the wind.

spin·ney /'spɪnɪ/ n (pl ∼s) thicket; small wood with thick undergrowth, esp (in England) one used for sheltering game¹(6).

spin·ster /'spɪnstə(r)/ n (usu offical or legal use) unmarried woman; woman who remains single after the conventional age for marrying. '∼-**hood** /-hʊd/ n the state of being a ∼.

spi·ral /'spaɪərəl/ adj, n (in the form of an) advancing or ascending continuous curve winding round a central point: *A snail's shell is* ∼. *The rocket went up in a* ∼. *A* ∼ *nebula is a group of stars that has the appearance of a* ∼. ⇨ also *inflationary* ∼ at inflate. ⇨ the illus at whorl. □ vi (-ll-, US also -l-) [VP2A,C] move in a ∼: *The smoke* ∼*led up. Prices are still* ∼*ling.*

spirals

spire /'spaɪə(r)/ n pointed structure like a tall cone or pyramid rising above a tower (esp of a church). ⇨ the illus at church.

spirit /'spɪrɪt/ n **1** [C,U] soul; immaterial, intellectual or moral part of man: *He was vexed in* ∼, inwardly. *I shall be with you in* (the) ∼, My *thoughts will be with you even though I am not with you in the flesh. The* ∼ *is willing but the flesh is weak,* One is willing to do sth, but physically unable to do it. **the Holy S**∼, the Third Person of the Trinity. **2** the soul thought of as separate from the body; disembodied soul: *the abode of* ∼s, where the ∼s of the dead are; *believe in* ∼s; *raise a* ∼. '∼-**rapper** n person who claims to receive messages from the dead by means of raps on a table. **3** [C] sprite; elf; goblin. **4** [U] life and consciousness not associated with a body; disembodied soul: *God is pure* ∼. **5** [C] (always with an adj) person considered from the intellectual, moral or emotional point of view: *What a noble/ generous, etc* ∼ *he is! He was one of the leading* ∼s *of the Reform Movement. moving* ∼, person who is the originator and sustainer of an idea, project, etc. **6** [U] quality of courage, vigour, liveliness: *Put a little more ~ into your work. You haven't the ~ of a mouse.* 7 (*sing* only) mental or moral attitude: *in a ~ of mischief. Whether it was unwise or not depends upon the ~ in which it was done.* 8 [U] real meaning or purpose underlying a law, etc (contrasted with the apparent meaning of the words, etc): *obey the ~, not the letter, of the law. Have you followed out the ~ of his instructions?* 9 (*pl*) state of mind (as being happy, hopeful, etc or the opposite): *in high ~s,* cheerful; *in poor/low ~s,* out of ~s, depressed, unhappy. *Have a glass of brandy to keep up your ~s.* 10 (*sing* only) influence or tendency that rouses or causes development: *The wind of change is blowing and we cannot resist the ~ of the times.* 11 [U] industrial alcohol. '~-lamp/-stove *n* one in which ~ is burned. '~-level *n* glass tube partly filled with water or alcohol, with a bubble of air which, when centred, shows that a surface is horizontal. 12 (*pl*) solution in alcohol: *~s of camphor/turpentine;* ~(*s*) *of salt,* hydrochloric acid. 13 (usu *pl*) strong alcoholic drink (eg whisky, brandy, gin, rum): *a glass of ~s and water. She drinks no ~ but vodka.* □ *vt* [VP15B] *~ sb/sth away/off,* take sb/sth rapidly, secretly or mysteriously: *She has disappeared as completely as if she had been ~ed away to another planet.* ~ed /'spiritid/ *adj* 1 full of ~(6); lively; courageous: *a ~ed attack/defence/reply; a ~ed horse; a ~ed conversation.* 2 (in compounds) having the kind of spirits(9) indicated: ,*high-/,low-/,poor-'~ed,* etc. ~-less *adj* without ~(6); not having or showing energy or courage; depressed.

spiri·tual /'spiritʃuəl/ *adj* 1 of the spirit(1) or soul(1); of religion, not of material things; of, from, God: *concerned about sb's ~ welfare.* 2 of spirits(2); supernatural. 3 caring much for things of the spirit(1). 4 of the church: *lords ~,* (GB) bishops and archbishops in the House of Lords. □ *n* (**Negro**) ~, religious song as sung by Negroes in the US. ~ly /-tʃʊli/ *adv* ~·ity /,spiritʃʊ'æləti/ *n* [U] ~ quality; devotion to ~ things.

spiri·tu·al·ism /'spiritʃuəlizəm/ *n* [U] belief in the possibility of receiving messages from the spirits of the dead; practice of attempting to do this. **spiri·tu·al·ist** /-ist/ *n* believer in ~. **spiri·tu·al·is·tic** /,spiritʃuə'listik/ *adj* of ~ or spiritualists.

spiri·tu·al·ize /'spiritʃuəlaiz/ *vt* [VP6A] make pure or spiritual. **spiri·tu·al·iz·ation** /,spiritʃuəlai'zeiʃn US: -li'z-/ *n* [U].

spiri·tu·ous /'spiritʃuəs US: -tʃuəs/ *adj* (of liquids) containing alcohol: *~ liquors,* distilled liquors such as whisky, not (usu) fermented liquors such as beer.

spirt /spɜːt/ *vi* [VP2C,2A], *n* = spurt.

spit¹ /spit/ *n* 1 long thin metal spike to which meat, etc is secured for roasting. 2 small, narrow point of land running out into a body of water. □ *vt* (-pp-) put a ~ through (a chicken, piece of meat, etc); pierce with the point of a sword, spear, etc.

spit² /spit/ *vt,vi* (*pt,pp* spat /spæt/) (-tt-) 1 [VP2A,C,3A] *~ (at/on/upon sb/sth),* send liquid (saliva) out from the mouth; do this as a sign of contempt or hatred: *If you ~ in a London bus you may be fined £5. He spat in the man's face/spat at him. The cat spat (= made an angry or hostile ~ting noise) at the dog.* 2 [VP6A,15B] *~ sth (out),* send out from the mouth; (fig) utter angrily or sharply: *The baby spat out the nasty pill. After the tooth had been extracted the boy spat a lot of*

blood. *She spat (out) curses at me. ~ it out,* (colloq) say what you have to say, quickly. 3 [VP2A,6A] (of a fire, candle, gun, etc) throw out; make the noise of ~ting: *The engine was ~ting. The guns were ~ting fire.* '~·fire *n* hot-tempered person. 4 [VP2A] (of rain or snow) fall lightly: *It's not raining heavily, only ~ting.* □ *n* 1 [U] saliva. 2 act of ~ting. *~ and polish,* the cleaning and polishing of equipment (by soldiers, etc). 3 *the dead ~ of; the ~ and image of* /,spit n 'imidʒ/; *the ~ting image of,* exact counterpart or likeness of: *He's the dead ~/the ~ting image of his father.* 4 frothy secretion of some insects (seen on plants, etc).

spit³ /spit/ *n* (*pl ~* or *~s*) spade's depth: *Dig the patch two ~(s) deep.*

spite /spait/ *n* 1 [U] ill will; desire to cause pain or damage: *do sth out of/from ~.* 2 (with *indef art*) grudge: *have a ~ against sb; do sth to satisfy a private ~.* 3 (*prep* phrase) *in ~ of,* not to be prevented by; notwithstanding: *They went out in ~ of the rain. In ~ of all his efforts he failed.* □ *vt* [VP6A] injure or annoy because of ~: *The neighbours let their radio blare every afternoon just to ~ us.* ~·ful /-fl/ *adj* having, showing, ~. ~·fully /-fəli/ *adv* ~·ful·ness *n*

spittle /'spitl/ *n* [U] liquid of the mouth; saliva.

spit·toon /spi'tuːn/ *n* container to spit into.

spiv /spiv/ *n* (GB sl) person not in regular employment but who makes money by dubious business methods, and who goes about smartly dressed and having a good time.

splash /splæʃ/ *vt,vi* 1 [VP6A,15B,14] *~ sth (about) (on/over sth); ~ sth/sb (with sth),* cause (a liquid) to fly about in drops; make (sb or sth) wet: *~ water on/over the floor; ~ the floor with water; ~ water about. The children love to ~ water over one another.* 2 [VP2A] (of a liquid) fly about and fall in drops: *fountains ~ing in the park. This tap is a bad one—it ~es.* 3 [VP2C] move, fall, so that there is ~ing: *We ~ed (our way) across the stream/into the lake, etc. Look at that hippo ~ing about in the river. The spacecraft ~ed down in the Pacific.* Hence, '~-down *n* landing of a spacecraft in the sea. 4 [VP15B] *~ money/news about,* spend/display it freely, prominently. □ *n* [C] 1 (sound, spot, mark, made by) ~ing: *He jumped into the swimming pool with a ~. There are some ~es of mud on your trousers.* 2 patch of colour: *Her dog is brown with white ~es.* 3 (colloq) small quantity of soda-water etc: *a whisky and ~.* 4 *make a ~,* (colloq, fig) attract attention by making a display of (esp) one's wealth.

splay /splei/ *vt,vi* make opposite sides (of an opening) diverge; cause to slant or slope: *a ~ed window,* eg one in a very thick wall, so that the opening in the wall is wider on one side than the other; (of an opening) be constructed in this way. *The plumber ~ed the end of the pipe before fitting it over the next section.* □ *n* sloping side of a window opening, etc. □ *adj* (esp of feet) broad, flat and turned outwards. Hence, '~-foot *n.* '~-footed *adj* having ~ feet.

spleen /spliːn/ *n* 1 [C] bodily organ in the abdomen which causes changes in the blood. ⇨ the illus at alimentary. 2 [U] lowness of spirits; bad temper: *in a fit of ~; vent one's ~ on sb.*

splen·did /'splendid/ *adj* 1 magnificent: *a ~ sunset/house/victory; ~ jewellery.* 2 (colloq) very satisfactory; excellent: *a ~ dinner/idea.* ~·ly *adv*

splen·dif·er·ous /splen'dɪfərəs/ adj (colloq, often hum or ironic) splendid.

splen·dour (US = **-dor**) /'splendə(r)/ n **1** [U] magnificence; brightness: the ~ of stained glass windows. **2** (sometimes pl) grandeur, glory.

sple·netic /splɪ'netɪk/ adj ill-tempered; peevish.

splice /splaɪs/ vt [VP6A] **1** join (two ends of rope) by weaving the strands of one into the strands of the other; join (two pieces of wood, magnetic tape, film) by fastening them at the ends. **2** get ~d, (sl) get married. □ n joint made by splicing. ~r n device for joining two pieces of paper or magnetic tape, film, etc.

splint /splɪnt/ n strip of wood, etc bound to an arm, leg, etc to keep a broken bone in the right position: put an arm/a limb in ~s.

splin·ter /'splɪntə(r)/ n sharp-pointed or sharp-edged bit of hard material (wood, metal, glass, etc) split, torn or broken off a larger piece: get a ~ into one's finger. **a** '~ **group/party**, (in politics) group of persons who have broken off from their party. '~-**proof** adj (eg of glass) that will not ~; giving protection against ~s, eg of broken glass, or from a bomb. □ vt, vi [VP2C,15B] ~ (off), break into ~s; come off as a ~. ~y adj apt to ~; full of ~s; like ~s.

split /splɪt/ vt, vi (pt, pp split; -tt-) **1** [VP6A,14,2A,C] ~ (into), break, cause to break, be broken, into two or more parts, esp from end to end along the line of natural division: ~ting logs. Some kinds of wood ~ easily. Only a skilled workman can ~ slate into layers. **2** [VP2D,22] ~ (open), break open by bursting: His coat has ~ at the seams. **3** [VP6A,15A,B,2A,C] ~ (up) (into), (cause to) break into parts; divide: ~ the atom; ~ (up) a compound into its parts. The party ~ up into small groups. Let's ~, (mod colloq) leave (a party, etc). Let's ~ the cost of the meal, share it. Joe and Jenny have ~ up, (of a couple) separated from each other. ~ **the difference**, (when making a bargain) compromise (on the price, cost, etc). **a** ~ting **headache**, so severe that it feels that one's head may crack. ~ **hairs**, make very fine distinctions (in an argument, etc). Hence, '**hair-**~**ting** adj. ~ **an infinitive**, place an adverb between to and the infinitive (as in 'to quickly read a book'). ~ **level** adj (of houses, housing) in which adjoining rooms are in a level midway between successive storeys of other parts. **a** ~ **mind/personality**, person who behaves sometimes with one set of actions, emotions, etc, and sometimes with another set; also ⇨ schizophrenia; Jekyll and Hyde. ~ **peas**, dried peas ~ into halves. **a** ~ **ring**, one split along its length, as used for keeping keys on. **a** ~ **second**, a brief instant of time. ~ **one's sides (with laughter)**, laugh with movements of the sides. Hence, '**side-**~**ting** adj **4** [VP2A,3A] ~ **(on sb)**, (sl) give away the secret of (usu an accomplice); give information about him (to his disadvantage. **5** [VP2A] (US sl) leave (a place). □ n [C] **1** splitting; crack or tear made by splitting: sew up a ~ in a seam. **2** separation or division resulting from splitting: a ~ in the Labour Party. **3** (colloq) half-bottle of soda water, etc. **4** the ~s, acrobat's feat of sinking to the floor by extending the legs laterally with the trunk upright: do the ~s.

splosh /splɒʃ/ vt = splash(4).

splotch /splɒtʃ/, **splodge** /splɒdʒ/ nn [C] daub or smear (of ink, dirt, etc); irregular patch (of colour, light, etc).

splurge /splɜːdʒ/ vi, n (colloq) (make a) noisy display or effort (intended to attract attention); show off.

splut·ter /'splʌtə(r)/ vi, vt **1** [VP2A,C] speak quickly and confusedly (from excitement, etc). **2** [VP6A,15B] ~ sth (out), say quickly, confusedly, indistinctly; ~ out a few words/a threat. **3** [VP2A] make a series of spitting sounds; sputter(1): The swimmers dived and came ~ing to the surface. □ n [U] ~ing sound.

Spode /spəʊd/ n [U] type of English porcelain.

spoil /spɔɪl/ vt, vi (pt, pp ~t or ~ed) **1** [VP6A] make useless or unsatisfactory: fruit ~t by insects; holidays ~t by bad weather; ~t ballot papers, made invalid because the voters have not marked them as required by regulations. Don't ~ your appetite by eating sweets just before dinner. '~-**sport** n person who does things that interfere with the enjoyment of other people. **2** [VP6A] harm the character or temperament of by wrong upbringing or lack of discipline: parents who ~ their children. **3** [VP6A] pay great attention to the comfort and wishes of: He likes having a wife who ~s him. **4** [VP2A] (of food, etc) become bad, unfit for use: Some kinds of food soon ~. **5** be ~ing for (a fight, etc), be eager for. **6** [VP6A,14] ~ sb (of sth), (old use, or liter; pt, pp always ~ed, never ~t) plunder, rob by force or stealth: financiers who ~ed (= despoiled) widows of their money. □ n **1** (either [U] or pl, not with numerals) stolen goods; plunder: The thieves divided up the ~(s). **2** (pl) profits, profitable positions, gained from political power: the ~s of office; the '~s system, (in some countries) system by which positions in the public service (their salaries and other advantages) are given to supporters of the political party which wins power. **3** [U] earth, unwanted material, etc thrown or brought up in excavating, draining, etc.

spoke¹ /spəʊk/ n **1** any one of the bars or wire rods connecting the hub (centre) of a wheel with the rim (outer edge). ⇨ the illus at bicycle. **put a '~ in sb's wheel**, hinder him; prevent him from carrying out his plans. **2** rung of a ladder.

spoke², **spoken** /spəʊk, 'spəʊkən/ pt and pp of speak.

spokes·man /'spəʊksmən/ n (pl -men) person speaking, chosen to speak, on behalf of a group.

spo·li·ation /ˌspəʊlɪ'eɪʃn/ n [U] plunder, esp of neutral merchant ships by countries at war.

spon·dee /'spɒndiː/ n (prosody) metrical foot of two long or stressed syllables, used in poetry to vary other metres. **spon·daic** /spɒn'deɪɪk/ adj

sponge /spʌndʒ/ n **1** [C] kinds of simple sea animal with light structures of elastic material full of holes and able to absorb water easily; one of these, or sth of similar texture (eg porous rubber), used for washing, cleaning, etc. **pass the ~ over**, wipe out, agree to forget (an offence, etc). **throw up/in the ~**, admit defeat or failure. **2** piece of absorbent material, eg gauze, used in surgery; mop used in cleaning the bore of a gun, etc. **3** '~-**cake** n soft, light yellow cake made of eggs, sugar and flour. □ vt, vi **1** [VP6A,15B] ~ sth (out), wash, wipe or clean with a ~: ~ a wound/a child's face; ~ out a memory, wipe it out, end it. **2** [VP15B] ~ sth up, take up (liquid) with a ~: ~ up the mess. **3** [VP3A] ~ on/upon sb, (colloq) live at his expense, get money from him, without giving, or intending to give, anything in return: ~ (up)on one's friends;

[VP6A,14] ~ *sth (from sb)*, get by sponging: ~ *a dinner;* ~ *a fiver* (= £5) *from an old acquaintance.* ~**r** *n* person who ~s(3). **spongy** *adj* (-ier, -iest) soft, porous and elastic like a ~: *spongy, moss-covered land.* **spongi-ness** *n*

spon-sor /'spɒnsə(r)/ *n* **1** person (eg a godfather) making himself responsible for another. **2** person who first puts forward or guarantees a proposal; person, firm, etc paying for a commercial radio or TV programme (usu in return for advertising of products). □ *vt* [VP6A] act as a ~ for.

spon-ta-neous /spɒn'teɪnɪəs/ *adj* done, happening, from natural impulse, not caused or suggested by sth or sb outside: *He made a* ~ *offer of help. Nothing he says is* ~—*he always thinks carefully before he speaks.* ~ **combustion**, burning caused by chemical changes, etc inside the material, not by the application of fire from outside. ~**ly** *adv* ~**ness**, **spon-ta-neity** /ˌspɒntə'niːətɪ/ *nn*

spoof /spuːf/ *vt*, *n* (sl) hoax; trick; swindle: *You've been* ~*ed*, You've been hoaxed.

spook /spuːk/ *n* (hum) ghost. ~**y** *adj* (-ier, -iest) of, suggesting, ~s: *a* ~*y* (= haunted) *house.*

spool /spuːl/ *n* reel (for thread, wire, photographic film, typewriter ribbon, paper or magnetic tape, etc). ⇨ the illus at **tape**.

spoon[1] /spuːn/ *n* utensil with a shallow bowl on a handle, used for stirring, serving and taking up food; named according to use, as: *des'sert-/ 'soup-/'table/'tea/'egg-*~. **be ˌborn with a ˌsilver '~ in one's mouth,** ⇨ **silver**(1). '~**-feed** *vt* (a) feed (a baby, etc) from a ~. (b) (fig) give (sb) excessive help or teaching: *Some teachers* ~*-feed their pupils.* □ *vt* [VP15B] ~ *sth up/out*, take up a ~: ~ *up one's soup;* ~ *out the peas,* serve them. '~**-ful** /-fʊl/ *n* (*pl* ~fuls) as much as a ~ can hold.

spoon[2] /spuːn/ *vi* [VP2A] (dated colloq) behave in a way that shows that one is in love.

spoon-er-ism /'spuːnərɪzəm/ *n* [C] confusion of two or more words by wrong placing of the initial sounds, eg *well-boiled icicle* for *well-oiled bicycle.*

spoor /spʊə(r)/ *n* [C] track or trail of a wild animal, enabling it to be followed.

spor-adic /spə'rædɪk/ *adj* occurring, seen, only here and there or occasionally: ~ *raids/firing.* **spor-adi-cally** /-klɪ/ *adv*

spore /spɔː(r)/ *n* [C] germ, single cell, by which a flowerless plant (eg moss, a fern) reproduces itself.

spor-ran /'spɒrən/ *n* pouch, usu fur-covered, worn by Scottish Highlanders in front of the kilt. ⇨ the illus at **kilt**.

sport /spɔːt/ *n* **1** [U] amusement, fun: *say sth in* ~, not seriously; *make* ~ *of sb*, make him seem ridiculous. **2** [U] ⇨ the illus at base, cricket, football, hockey, rugby, tennis. activity engaged in, esp outdoors, for amusement and exercise; [C] particular form of such activity: *fond of/devoted to* ~; *country* ~s, eg hunting, fishing, shooting, horse-racing; *athletic* ~s, eg running, jumping; '~s *coverage/reporting on TV.* **3** (*pl*) meeting for athletic contests: *the school* ~s; *inter-university* ~s. **4** (compounds, etc) '~s**-car** *n* small motor-car designed for high speeds. '~s**-coat/-jacket,** informal jacket. '~s**-editor** *n* newspaper editor responsible for reports of ~s and games. '~s**-man** /-mən/ *n* (*pl* -men) (a) person who takes part in, is fond of, ~. (b) (also ~) person who plays fairly, who is willing to take risks, and is not down-hearted if he loses. Hence, '~s**-man-ship** /-ʃɪp/ *n*

'~s**-man-like** *adj.* **5** (colloq) = ~sman; agreeable, easy-going person: *Come on, be a* ~*!* **6** [C] plant or animal that deviates in a striking way from the normal type. □ *vi*, *vt* **1** [VP2C] play about, amuse oneself: *seals* ~*ing about in the water.* **2** [VP6A] (colloq) have or wear for proud display: ~ *a moustache/a diamond ring/a flower in the buttonhole of one's jacket.* ~**-ing** *adj* **1** connected with ~, interested in ~. **2** willing to take a risk of losing; involving a risk of losing: *make sb a* ~*ing offer; give sb a* ~*ing chance.* **3** ~smanlike. It's very ~ing of you to give me such an advantage. ~**-ing-ly** *adv*

sport-ive /'spɔːtɪv/ *adj* playful; merry. ~**-ly** *adv* ~**-ness** *n*

spot /spɒt/ *n* **1** small (esp round) mark different in colour from what it is on: *white dress material with red* ~s. *Which has* ~s, *the leopard or the tiger?* **2** dirty mark or stain: ~s *of mud on your boots.* **3** small, red mark, blemish, on the skin; pimple: *This ointment won't clear your face of* ~s. **4** (fig) moral blemish: *There isn't a* ~ *on her reputation.* **5** drop: *Did you feel a few* ~s *of rain?* **6** particular place or area: *the* (*very*) ~ *where he was murdered.* **TV/radio** ~, place in a TV/radio programme for an item or a commercial advertisement. ⇨ **slot**(3). **7** (phrases) **a** ~ **check,** a quickly-made investigation, esp one made suddenly and without warning. **a tender** ~, (fig) a subject on which a person's feelings are easily hurt. **in a** ~, (colloq) in a difficult situation. **knock** ~s **off** *sb,* easily surpass, do better than, him. **on the** ~, (a) at the place where one is needed: *The police were on the* ~ *within a few minutes of hearing about the crime.* (b) then and there; immediately: *He fell dead on the* ~. *The bullet struck his head and he was killed on the* ~. (c) (sl) in trouble. Cf 'on the carpet'. **the person on the** ~, the man at the place in question (who, presumably, is acquainted with local conditions, happenings, etc and able to deal with them): *Let's leave the decision to the man/the men/the people on the* ~. **put sb on the** ~, (a) place sb in danger or difficulty: *You've put me on the* ~ *here: I can't answer your question.* (b) (of gangsters) decide to kill (eg a rival gangster). **put one's finger on/find sb's weak** ~, find the point (of character, etc) where he is most open to attack. **8** (comm) ~ **cash,** payment on delivery of goods. ~ **prices,** prices quoted for such payment. **9** (GB colloq) small quantity of anything: *I need a* ~ *of brandy. What about doing a* ~ *of work? He's having a* ~ *of bother with his brother,* a quarrel. □ *vt*, *vi* (-tt-) **1** [VP6A,2A] mark, become marked, with ~s: *a table* ~*ted with ink; material that* ~s *easily,* easily becomes ~ted. **2** [VP6A] pick out, recognize, see (one person or thing out of many): ~ *a friend in a crowd;* ~ *the winner in a race,* pick out the winner before the start. **3** [VP2A] (colloq) rain slightly: *It's beginning to* ~*/is* ~*ting with rain.* ~**-ted** *adj* marked with ~s, eg of such animals as the leopard and panther, and of birds with ~s of different colour on their plumage, of textile material with ~s. ~**-ted 'fever** *n* form of meningitis; form of typhus. ~**-less** *adj* free from ~s; clean: *a* ~*less kitchen/reputation.* ~**-less-ly** *adv.* ~*lessly clean.* ~**ty** *adj* (-ier, -iest) **1** marked with ~s (esp on the skin): *a* ~*ty complexion; windows that are* ~*ty with fly marks.* **2** of varying quality: *a* ~*ty piece of work,* done unevenly. ~**-ter** *n* person who ~s(2), eg 'aircraft-~*ter,* person who, eg during a war, looks for and identifies different types of aircraft; '**train-~ter**, (usu) schoolboy who looks for and notes different types of railway-engines.

spot·light /'spotlaɪt/ n [C] (projector or lamp used for sending a) strong light directed on to a particular place or person, eg on the stage of a theatre: *He likes to be in the/to hold the* ~, (fig) be the centre of attention. □ vt [VP6A] direct a ~ on to.

spouse /spaʊz US: spaʊs/ n (legal or archaic) husband or wife.

spout /spaʊt/ n [C] **1** pipe or lip through or from which liquid pours, eg for carrying rain-water from a roof, or tea from a teapot. **2** stream of liquid coming out with great force. ⇨ *water-~* at water¹(7). **3** *up the* ~, (sl) **(a)** in pawn. **(b)** in difficulties, broken, etc according to context. **(c)** pregnant. □ vt,vi **1** [VP2A,C,6A] ~ *(out)*, (of liquid) come or send out with great force: *water ~ing (out) from a broken water-main; blood ~ing from a severed artery; a broken pipe ~ing water. The whales were ~ing,* sending up jets of water. **2** [VP2A,6A] (colloq) speak, recite (verses, etc) pompously: *~ing unwanted advice.*

sprain /spreɪn/ vt [VP6A] injure (a joint, eg in the wrist or ankle) by twisting violently so that there is pain and swelling: ~ *one's wrist; suffering from a ~ed ankle.* □ n [C] injury so caused.

sprang /spræŋ/ pt of spring³.

sprat /spræt/ n small European sea-fish used as food.

sprawl /sprɔːl/ vi **1** [VP2A,C] sit or lie with the arms and legs loosely spread out; fall so that one lies in this way: ~*ing on the sofa; be sent ~ing in the mud.* **2** (of plants, handwriting, fig of large towns) spread out loosely and irregularly over much space: *suburbs that ~ out into the country-side.* □ n [U,C] ~ing position or movement; widespread untidy area, esp of buildings: *London's suburban ~.*

spray¹ /spreɪ/ n small branch of a tree or plant, esp a graceful one with leaves and flowers as an ornament; artificial ornament in a similar form: *a ~ of diamonds.*

spray² /spreɪ/ n **1** [U] liquid sent through the air in tiny drops (by the wind, or through an apparatus): '*sea-~,* ~ blown from waves; *the ~ of a waterfall.* **2** [C,U] kinds of liquid preparation, eg a perfume, disinfectant or insecticide, to be applied in the form of ~ through an atomizer or other apparatus. **3** [C] atomizer, etc used for applying such a liquid. '**~-gun** n apparatus using pressure to spread cellulose, paint, varnish, etc over surfaces. □ vt [VP6A,14] ~ *sth/sb (with sth);* ~ *sth (on sth/sb),* scatter ~ on: ~ *mosquitoes/fruit-trees;* ~ *the enemy with bullets.* **~er** n **1** person who ~s. **2** apparatus for ~ing.

spread /spred/ vt,vi (pt,pp ~) **1** [VP6A,14,15B] ~ *sth on/over sth;* ~ *sth with sth;* ~ *sth (out),* extend the surface or width of sth by unfolding or unrolling it; cover (sth) by doing this: ~ *a cloth on a table/a table with a cloth;* ~ *out a map;* ~ *(out) one's arms. The bird ~ its wings.* **2** [VP14] ~ *sth on sth;* ~ *sth with sth,* put (a substance) on a surface and extend its area by flattening, etc; cover (a surface) by doing this: ~ *butter on bread/a slice of bread with butter.* **3** [VP6A,15A,B,2A,C] (cause to) become more widely extended or distributed: ~ *knowledge. Flies ~ disease. The water ~ over the floor. The rumour quickly ~ through the village.*

The fire ~ from the factory to the houses near by. ~ *oneself,* **(a)** occupy much space, eg by lying with the limbs extended. **(b)** talk or write at length (on a subject). **(c)** let oneself go, eg by being generous in hospitality. **4** [VP2A,B,C] show an extended surface: *a desert ~ing for hundreds of miles.* **5** [VP6A,15B] extend in time: *a course of studies ~ over three years; instalments/payments ~ over twelve months.* **6** ,~'**eagle** n figure of an eagle with the legs and wings extended (as seen on coins). □ vt (reflex) take up a lying position with arms and legs extended to form a cross: *sunbathers ~eagled on the grass/sands.* '**~-over** n arrangement in an industry by which hours of work are adjusted to special needs. □ n (rarely pl) **1** extent; breadth: *the ~ of a bird's wings.* **2** extension; spreading(3): *the ~ of disease/knowledge/education.* **3** (colloq) table ~ with good things to eat and drink: *What a ~!* **4** sth that is ~(1) (usu in compounds) *a 'bed~,* a cover ~ over the bed-clothes. *He's developing (a) middle-age ~,* (colloq) is getting big round the waist (as some persons do in middle age). **5** name used for various kinds of paste (to be) ~ on bread, etc. **~er** n one who, that which, ~s, eg a '*flame-~er* in an oil-stove; an implement used for ~ing paste, etc on bread.

spree /spriː/ n lively frolic: *have a ~,* have a lively, merry time. *be on the ~; go out on a ~,* be having, go out to enjoy, a ~. *a* '**spending**/'**buying** ~, an occasion of (extravagant or unusual) spending of money.

sprig /sprɪg/ n **1** small twig (of a plant or bush) with leaves, etc: *a ~ of mistletoe for Christmas.* **2** (usu contemptuous) young person. **~-ged** adj ornamented with designs of ~s: ~*ged muslin.*

spright·ly /'spraɪtlɪ/ adj (-ier, -iest) lively; brisk. **spright·li·ness** n

spring¹ /sprɪŋ/ n **1** act of springing or jumping up. **2** (place where there is) water coming up from the ground: '*hot-~;* '*mineral-~; a hot-'~ resort;* (attrib) ~ *water.* **3** device of twisted, bent or coiled metal or wire which tends to return to its shape or position when pulled or pushed or pressed: *the ~s of a motor-car; the ~ of a watch.* ,~-'**balance** n device that measures weight by the tension of a ~. '**~-board** n board to give a ~ing motion to sb jumping from it. '**~-gun** n one that goes off when a trespasser comes against a wire which is attached to the trigger. ,~-'**mattress** n one containing spiral ~s in a rigid frame. ~ *tide* n (two words; ⇨ ~*tide,* ~*time* at spring²) tide with the greatest rise or fall, occurring shortly after new and full moon in each month; ⇨ *neap-tide* at neap. **4** [U] elastic quality: *rubber bands that have lost their ~. The old man's muscles have lost their ~.* **5** (often pl) cause or origin: *the ~s of human conduct.* '**~-less** adj without ~s(3): *a ~less cart.* ~**y** adj (-ier, -iest) (of movement or substances) elastic; that springs: *walk with a youthful, ~y step.*

spring² /sprɪŋ/ n [U,C] season of the year in which vegetation begins; season between winter and summer (in GB from about 21 March to 22 June): *in (the) ~;* (attrib) ~ *flowers/weather.* '**~-time** (also, poet '**~-tide**) nn season of ~. ,~-'**clean** vt clean (a house, a room) thoroughly. Hence, ,~-'**cleaning** n. '**~-like** adj: ~*like weather.*

spring³ /sprɪŋ/ vi,vt (pt sprang /spræŋ/, pp sprung /sprʌŋ/) **1** [VP2C] jump suddenly from the ground; move suddenly (*up, down, out,* etc) from

rest, concealment, etc: *He sprang to his feet/ sprang out of bed/sprang forward to help me/ sprang up from his seat. The branch sprang back and hit me in the face.* 2 [VP2C] ~ *(up),* appear; grow up quickly from the ground or from a stem: *A breeze has sprung up. Weeds were* ~*ing up every-where. The wheat is beginning to* ~ *up.* (fig) *A suspicion/doubt sprang up in her mind.* 3 [VP3A] ~ *from,* arise or come from: *He is sprung from royal blood,* is of royal ancestry. *Where have you sprung from,* suddenly and unexpectedly appeared from? 4 [VP14] ~ *sth on sb,* bring forward sud-denly: ~ *a surprise on sb;* ~ *a new theory/ proposal on sb.* 5 [VP6A] cause to operate by means of a mechanism: ~ *a mine,* cause it to ex-plode; ~ *a trap,* cause it to go off. 6 [VP6A,2A] (of wood) (cause to) warp, split, crack: *My cricket bat has sprung. I have sprung my tennis racket.* ~ *a leak,* (of a ship) crack or burst so that water enters.
spring-bok /'sprɪŋbɒk/ *n* small S African gazelle.
sprinkle /'sprɪŋkl/ *vt* [VP6A,14] ~ *sth (on/with sth),* direct, throw, a shower of (sth) on to (a sur-face): ~ *water on a dusty path;* ~ *a dusty path with water;* ~ *the floor with sand.* **sprink-ler** /'sprɪŋklə(r)/ *n* (esp) apparatus or device for sprinkling water (eg on to a lawn) or (permanently installed in buildings) for fighting fire. **sprink-ling** *n* small quantity or number here and there: *There was a sprinkling of hooligans in the crowd.*
sprint /sprɪnt/ *vi* [VP2A,C] run a short distance at full speed: *He* ~*ed past his competitors just before reaching the tape.* □ *n* such a run; (esp) burst of speed at the end of a race. ~**er** *n*
sprit /sprɪt/ *n* small spar reaching from a mast to the upper outer corner of a sail. ⇨ the illus at barque. **'~-sail** *n* sail extended by a ~.
sprite /spraɪt/ *n* fairy; elf.
sprocket /'sprɒkɪt/ *n* each of several teeth on a wheel connecting with the links of a chain or holes in a movie film, paper or magnetic tape. **'~-wheel** *n* such a wheel, eg as on a bicycle.
sprout /spraʊt/ *vi,vt* 1 [VP2A,C] ~ *(up),* put out leaves; begin to grow: *Peter has really* ~*ed up in the past year.* 2 [VP6A] cause to grow: *The conti-nuous wet weather has* ~*ed the barley,* eg after it has been cut and left in the field. 3 [VP6A] deve-lop, produce: *When do deer first* ~ *horns? Tom has* ~*ed a moustache.* □ *n* [C] shoot, newly ~ed part, of a plant. ⇨ Brussels ~s.
spruce¹ /spruːs/ *adj* neat and smart in dress and ap-pearance. □ *vt,vi* [VP6A,15B,2C] ~ *(sb/oneself) (up),* make oneself ~: *Go and* ~ *yourself up. They were all* ~*d up for the party.* ~**·ly** *adv* ~**·ness** *n*
spruce² /spruːs/ *n* ~ *(fir),* kinds of fir-tree grown in plantations for its wood, used for making paper.
sprung /sprʌŋ/ *pp* of spring³.
spry /spraɪ/ *adj* (-er, -est) lively; nimble: *still* ~ *at eighty.* **look** ~, be quick.
spud /spʌd/ *n* [C] 1 (colloq) potato. 2 short spade with a narrow blade for digging or cutting up weeds.
spue /spjuː/ *vt,vi* = spew.
spume /spjuːm/ *n* [U] foam; froth.
spun /spʌn/ *pp* of spin.
spunk /spʌŋk/ *n* [U] (colloq) courage; mettle; spirit: *have no* ~; *a boy with plenty of* ~; (sl) semen. ~**·y** *adj* having ~.
spur /spɜː(r)/ *n* 1 one of a pair of sharp-toothed wheels, worn on the heels of a rider's boots and used to make the horse go faster. **win one's** ~**s,**

(hist) gain knighthood; (fig) win honour and repu-tation. 2 (fig) sth that urges a person on to greater activity: *the* ~ *of poverty.* **act on the** ~ **of the moment,** on a sudden impulse. 3 sharp, hard projection on a cock's leg. ⇨ the illus at bird. 4 ridge extending from a mountain or hill. □ *vt,vi* (-rr-) 1 [VP6A,15B] ~ *sb/sth (on),* urge on with, or as with, ~s: *It's foolish to* ~ *on a willing horse. He was* ~*red on by ambition.* 2 [VP2C] ride fast or hard: *The rider* ~*red on/forward to his destina-tion.*
spu·ri·ous /'spjʊərɪəs/ *adj* false; not genuine: ~ *coins/credentials/arguments.* ~**·ly** *adv* ~**·ness** *n*
spurn /spɜːn/ *vt* [VP6A] reject or refuse contemptu-ously; have nothing to do with (an offer, a person or his advances).
spurt /spɜːt/ *vi* 1 [VP2C,3A] ~ *(out) (from),* (of liquids, flame, etc) come out in a sudden burst: *Blood* ~*ed (out) from the wound.* 2 [VP2A] make a sudden, short and violent effort, esp in a race or other contest: *The runner* ~*ed as he approached the winning-post.* □ *n* [C] sudden bursting forth; sudden burst of energy: ~*s of water/flame/energy; a* ~ *of anger; put on a* ~ (= increase speed) *to-wards the end of a race.*
sput·nik /'spʊtnɪk/ *n* artificial unmanned satellite put into space by means of rocket propulsion (esp the first, launched from the Soviet Union in 1957).
sput·ter /'spʌtə(r)/ *vi,vt* 1 [VP2A,C] make a series of spitting sounds: *The sausages were* ~*ing in the frying-pan.* ~ *out,* stop burning after making spit-ting sounds: *The candle* ~*ed out.* 2 = splut-ter(1,2).
spu·tum /'spjuːtəm/ *n* [U] saliva; matter coughed up from the throat (esp as indicating the nature of an illness).
spy /spaɪ/ *n* (*pl* spies) 1 person who tries to get secret information, esp about the military affairs of other countries (called a 'secret agent' if he is em-ployed by one's own government and a 'spy' if he is working for other countries). 2 person who keeps a secret watch on the movements of others: *police spies,* persons employed by the police to watch suspected criminals; *industrial spies,* employed to learn trade secrets, etc. □ *vi,vt* 1 [VP2A,3A,15B] ~ *(into/on/upon sth);* ~ *sth out,* act as a spy on, watch secretly: *spy on the enemy's movements; spy out the land; spy into other people's affairs.* 2 [VP6A,19A] observe; see; discover: *I spy someone coming up the garden path. You are quick at spy-ing her faults.* **'spy-glass** *n* small telescope. **'spy-hole** *n* peep-hole.
squab /skwɒb/ *n* 1 young bird, esp an unfledged pigeon: ~ *pie,* pigeon pie. 2 (comm) soft seat or cushion, esp as a seat in a car.
squabble /'skwɒbl/ *vi* [VP2C] engage in a petty or noisy quarrel: *Tom was squabbling with his sister about who should use the bicycle.* □ *n* [C] noisy quarrel about sth trivial.
squad /skwɒd/ *n* small group of persons, eg of sol-diers, working or being trained together: *Scotland Yard's flying* ~, number of special police cars and men always ready for prompt action, eg on reports of burglaries, etc. **'~ car,** (US) police patrol car.
squad·ron /'skwɒdrən/ *n* 1 sub-unit of a cavalry, armoured, or engineer regiment (120—200 men). 2 number of warships or military aircraft forming a unit. **'S~ Leader** *n* RAF rank, next below Wing Commander.
squalid /'skwɒlɪd/ *adj* dirty, mean, uncared for:

living in ~ *conditions/houses.* ~·**ly** *adv*

squall /skwɔːl/ *n* [C] **1** loud cry of pain or fear (esp from a baby or child). **2** sudden violent wind, often with rain or snow: *look out for* ~*s*, (often fig) be on one's guard against danger or trouble. □ *vi* [VP2A] utter ~s(1): ~*ing babies. The boy* ~*s as soon as he sees the dentist.* ~**y** *adv* having, marked by, ~s(2): *a* ~*y February day.*

squalor /'skwɒlə(r)/ *n* [U] squalid state: *born in* ~; *the* ~ *of the slums.*

squan·der /'skwɒndə(r)/ *vt* [VP6A] waste (time, money). '~·**mania** /-meɪnɪə/ *n* [U] (craze for) extravagant spending of money.

square¹ /skweə(r)/ *adj* **1** having the shape of a square²(1): *a* ~ *table.* **a** ~ **peg in a round hole,** ⇨ peg¹(1). '~ **dance/game,** one in which the dancers/players face inwards from four sides. **2** having or forming (exactly or approx) a right angle: ~ *corners; a* ~ *jaw/chin,* with angular, not curved, outlines. ,~ **'brackets** *n pl* the marks [ ]. ⇨ bracket(2). ,~-**'built** *adj* (of a person) of comparatively broad shape. ,~-**'rigged** *adj* (of a sailing ship) having the principal sails set at right angles to the mast. Cf *fore-and-aft.* ,~-**'shouldered** *adj* with the shoulders at right angles to the neck, not sloping. '~-**toed** *adj* (of shoes) having a ~ toe-cap; (fig, of persons) formal; prim. '~-**toes** *n* formal or prim person. '~-**toes** *n* formal or prim person. **3** level or parallel (*with*); balanced; settled: *get one's accounts* ~, settled. **be** *(all)* ~, **(a)** (golf) have equal scores: *all* ~ *at the ninth hole.* **(b)** with neither person in debt to the other: *Let's call it all* ~, *shall we?* **get** ~ **with sb,** settle accounts; (fig) have one's revenge on him. **4** of a number multiplied by itself: *a* ~ *metre,* surface area of a ~ which has sides of one metre in length; *nine* ~ *cm. The* ~ *root of x⁴ is x²/9 is 3. A carpet 6 metres* ~ *has an area of 36* ~ *metres.* ~ **measure,** expressed in ~ feet, metres, etc. **5** thorough; uncompromising: *meet with a* ~ *refusal.* **a** ~ **meal,** one that is satisfactory because there is plenty of good food. **6** fair, honest: ~ *dealings,* in business; *play a* ~ *game,* in sport. *(get/give sb) a* ~ **deal,** a fair bargain, fair treatment, equality of opportunity. **7** ~ **leg,** ⇨ the illus at cricket. □ *adv* **1** in a ~(2) manner: *stand/sit* ~; *hit a man* ~ *on the jaw.* **2 fair and** ~, in a ~(6) manner. ~·**ly** *adv* **1** so as to form a right angle. **2** fairly; honestly: *act* ~*ly.* **3** directly opposite: *He faced me* ~*ly across the table.* ~·**ness** *n*

square² /skweə(r)/ *n* [C] **1** plane figure with four equal sides and four right angles, ie □. ⇨ the illus at quadrilateral. **back to** ~ **one,** (from the use of ~s on board games, played by throwing dice, and with penalties for certain numbered ~s) back to the starting-point and forced to start again. **2** anything having the shape of a ~. **3** four-sided open area, eg in a town, used as a garden or for recreation, or one enclosed by streets and buildings: *listening to the band playing in the* ~. '**barrack** ~ *n* such an open space in a military barracks. '~-**bashing** (sl) military drill (esp marching, etc). **4** buildings and streets surrounding a ~(4): *He lives at No 95 Russell S*~. **5** block of buildings bounded by four streets; distance along one side of such a block (the word *block* being more usu, esp US). **6** result when a number or quantity is multiplied by itself: *The* ~ *of 7 is 49. What is the* ~ *of x²?* **7** L-shaped or ('T-~) T-shaped instrument for drawing or testing right angles. **out of** ~, not at right angles. **8 on the** ~, fair(ly), honest(ly): *Can we trust them to*

act on the ~? *Is their business on the* ~? **9** body of infantry drawn up in a ~ form. **10** '**word** ~, number of words arranged so that they read alike forwards and downwards. **11** (sl) person (considered to be) out of touch with new ideas, styles, etc: *I'm not even a* ~, *I'm a cube!* I'm rigidly conventional and old-fashioned.

square³ /skweə(r)/ *vt,vi* **1** [VP6A] make square; give a square shape to. ~ *the circle,* attempt sth that is impossible. **2** [VP6A] cause one line or side to make a right angle with another: ~ *timber,* give it rectangular edges. **3** [VP6A] make straight or level: ~ *one's shoulders.* **4** [VP6A] multiply a number by itself; get the square(6) of a number: *Three* ~*ed is nine. x² = x* ~*ed.* **5** [VP6A,15B] ~ *sth off,* mark (off) in squares. **6** [VP2C,14,15B] ~ *(sth) (up) (with sb),* settle, balance: ~ *accounts with sb,* settle one's debts; (fig) have one's revenge on him. *It's time I* ~*ed up with you/time we* ~*ed up,* settled our accounts. **7** [VP6A] bribe; get the (dishonest) co-operation of: *All the officials had to be* ~*ed before they would do anything for us. He has been* ~*ed to hold his tongue.* **8** [VP14,3A] ~ *(sth) with,* make or be consistent: *You should* ~ *your practice with your principles. It would be convenient if the facts* ~*ed with the theory, but they do not.* **9** [VP2C] ~ *up to sb,* take up the attitude of a boxer (ready to begin fighting).

squash¹ /skwɒʃ/ *vt,vi* **1** [VP6A,15A,B,22] crush; press flat or into a small space: ~ *too many people into a bus. Don't sit on my hat; you'll* ~ *it flat.* **2** [VP2A] become ~ed or pressed out of shape: *Soft fruits* ~ *easily.* **3** [VP2C] squeeze or crowd: *Don't all try to* ~ *into the lift together. They* ~*ed through the gate into the football ground.* **4** [VP6A] (colloq) silence (sb) with a crushing retort; snub. *He was/felt completely* ~*ed.* **5** [VP6A] (colloq) subdue (a rebellion). □ *n* (rarely *pl*) **1** crowd of persons ~ed together: *There was a violent* ~ *at the gate.* **2** (sound of) sth ~ing or being ~ed: *The ripe tomato hit the speaker in the face with a* ~. **3** [C,U] drink (cold, usu bottled) made from fruit juice: *orange/lemon* ~. **4** '~(-**rackets**), game played with rackets and a rubber ball in a walled, roofed court. ~**y** *adj* easily ~ed; soft and wet.

squash² /skwɒʃ/ *n* (*pl* unchanged) kinds of gourd, like a pumpkin, eaten as a vegetable.

squat /skwɒt/ *vi* (-tt-) **1** [VP2A,C] sit on one's heels, or on the ground with the legs drawn under or close to the body; [VP6A,15B] put (oneself) in this position: *The old man* ~*ted in front of the fire. He* ~*ted (himself) down.* **2** [VP2A,C] (of animals) crouch with the body close to the ground. **3** [VP2A,C] (colloq) sit: *Find somewhere to* ~. **4** [VP2A] settle on land without permission, esp publicly owned and unoccupied land (in order to acquire ownership); occupy empty (usu deserted, derelict) buildings without authority. □ *adj* short and thick: *a* ~ *man;* dumpy: *a* ~ *teapot.* ~·**ter** *n* **1** person who ~s(4); (in Australia) sheep-farmer. **2** person who takes unauthorized possession of unoccupied premises.

squaw /skwɔː/ *n* N American Indian woman or wife.

squawk /skwɔːk/ *vi* [VP2A,C], *n* (chiefly of birds) (utter a) loud, harsh cry, as when hurt or frightened; (colloq) (make a) loud complaint; (sl) betray: *The old man* ~*ed (to the police).* ~**er** *n*

squeak /skwiːk/ *n* [C] **1** short, shrill cry, eg made by a mouse, or similar sound, eg from an unoiled

hinge. 2 a narrow ~, a narrow escape from danger or failure. □ *vi,vt* **1** [VP2A] make a ~: *These new shoes* ~. **2** [VP6A,15B] ~ *sth (out),* utter in a ~ing voice: ~ *out a few frightened words.* **3** [VP2A,C] (colloq) become an informer. ~**er** *n* (colloq) informer. ~**y** *adj* (-ier, -iest) ~ing: *a* ~*y floor; in a* ~*y voice.*

squeal /skwi:l/ *n* [C] shrill cry or sound, longer and louder than a squeak, often indicating terror or pain: *the* ~ *of brakes,* eg on lorries. □ *vi,vt* **1** [VP2A,C] make a ~: *The pigs were* ~*ing. He* ~*ed like a pig.* **2** [VP6A,15B] utter with a ~; say in a ~ing voice. **3** [VP2A,C] (colloq) become an informer. ~**er** *n* **1** animal that ~s. **2** informer.

squeam·ish /'skwi:mɪʃ/ *adj* **1** having a delicate stomach and easily made sick; feeling sick. **2** easily disgusted or offended; too modest, scrupulous or proper. ~**·ly** *adv* ~**·ness** *n*

squee·gee /ˌskwi:'dʒi:* US: 'skwi:dʒi:/ *n* implement with a rubber edge, fastened to a long handle, used for pushing water, etc off a smooth surface; similar implement with a short rubber roller for pressing water from photographic prints. □ *vt* [VP6A] use a ~ on.

squeeze /skwi:z/ *vt,vi* **1** [VP6A,15A,22] press on from the opposite side or from all sides; change the shape, size, etc of sth by doing this: ~ *sb's hand;* ~ *a sponge;* ~ *a lemon dry;* ~ *one's fingers,* eg by catching them in a doorway; ~ *paste into a ball.* **2** [VP6A,14,15A,B] ~ *sth (from/out of sth);* ~ *sth out,* get (water, juice, etc) out of sth by pressing hard; ~ *(the juice out of) a lemon;* ~ *the water out.* **3** [VP15A,B,2C] force (sb, oneself) into or through a narrow passage or small space: ~ *(one's way) into a crowded bus;* ~ *(oneself) through a gap in a hedge:* ~ *(one's way) through a crowd. Can you* ~ *in?* eg into a crowded lift. **4** [VP15B] ~ *sth out of sth/sb,* get by extortion, entreaty, etc: ~ *more money out of the public,* eg by increasing taxes; *blackmailers who* ~ *the last penny out of their victims.* **5** [VP2A] yield to pressure: *Sponges* ~ *easily.* □ *n* [C] **1** act of squeezing; condition of being ~d; sth obtained by squeezing: *give sb a hug and a* ~; *a'* ~ *bottle,* plastic container that ejects the contents, eg scent, liquid detergent, when ~d. *It was a tight* ~, We were ~d tightly, eg in a crowd. *Add a* ~ *of lemon to your drink.* ⇨ also credit¹(3). **2** *close/narrow/tight* ~, narrow escape. **3** [U] (colloq) policy of high taxation, high interest rates, etc aimed at deflation; [U] money obtained by squeezing(4). ~**r** *n* one who, that which, ~s, eg a device for squeezing out juice: *a'lemon*~*r.*

squelch /skweltʃ/ *vi,vt* [VP2A,C] make a sucking sound as when feet are lifted from stiff, sticky mud: *cows* ~*ing through the mud. The water* ~*ed in my boots.* □ *n* ~ing sound; act of ~ing.

squib /skwɪb/ *n* **1** small firework of the kind thrown by hand, one that first hisses and then explodes. **damp** ~, unsuccessful attempt to do sth impressive. **2** short satirical attack on sb, spoken or (more usu) written.

squid /skwɪd/ *n* kind of cuttle-fish with ten arms round the mouth (smaller kinds used as bait). ⇨ the illus at mollusc.

squiffy /'skwɪfɪ/ *adj* (sl) slightly drunk.

squiggle /'skwɪgl/ *n* small twisty line or scrawl: *Is this* ~ *supposed to be his signature?* **squig·gly** /'skwɪglɪ/ *adj*

squint /skwɪnt/ *vi* **1** [VP2A] have eyes that do not turn together but look in different directions at once; be cross-eyed. **2** [VP3A] ~ *at/through,* look at sideways or with half-shut eyes or through a narrow opening. □ *n* **1** ~ing position of the eyeballs: *a man with a* ~. '~-**eyed** *adj* having a ~; cross-eyed; (fig) malignant; disapproving. **2** (colloq) look or glance: *Let me have a* ~ *at it.*

squire /'skwaɪə(r)/ *n* **1** (in England) chief landowner in a country parish. **2** (hist) young man who was a knight's attendant until he himself became a knight. **3** (often hum) man who escorts a woman; man who is attentive to women and frequents their company. **4** (US) justice of the peace or local judge. **5** (GB sl) fellow. □ *vt* [VP6A,15A] (of a man) attend upon, escort (a woman). '~-**ar·chy** /-ɑːkɪ/ *n* (*pl*-chies) (in England) great landowners (before 1832); these men as a class.

squirm /skwɜːm/ *vi* [VP2A,C] twist the body, wriggle (from discomfort, shame or embarrassment). □ *n* ~ing movement.

squir·rel /'skwɪrəl/ *n* (kinds of) small, tree-climbing, bushy-tailed animal with red or grey fur. ⇨ the illus at small.

squirt /skwɜːt/ *vt,vi* [VP6A,15A,B,2A,C] (of liquid, powder) force out, be forced out, in a thin stream or jet: ~ *soda-water into a glass. The water* ~*ed all over me.* □ *n* **1** thin stream or jet (of liquid, powder, etc). **2** sth from which liquid, etc can be ~ed, eg a syringe, as a child's toy. **3** (colloq, as a term of abuse) insignificant but self-assertive person.

stab /stæb/ *vt,vi* (-bb-) **1** [VP6A,15A,3A] ~ *(at),* pierce or wound with sharp-pointed weapon or instrument; push (a knife, etc) into (sb); aim a blow (at sb) with such a weapon: ~ *a man in the back;* ~ *sb to the heart. His conscience* ~*bed (at) him,* (fig) caused him to feel regret. **2** [VP2A] produce a sensation of being ~bed: ~*bing pains in the back.* □ *n* [C] **1** ~*bing blow; pain inflicted by this. a* ~ *in the back,* (fig) a treacherous attack, eg on sb's reputation. **2** (colloq) try, attempt (= colloq 'go' or 'shot'): *Let me have a* ~ *at it,* try to do it. ~·**ber** *n*

stable¹ /'steɪbl/ *adj* firm; not likely to move or change: *What we needis a* ~ *Government. He needs a job.* **sta·bil·ity** /stə'bɪlətɪ/ *n* [U] quality of being ~. **sta·bil·ize** /'steɪbəlaɪz/ *vt* [VP6A] make ~: *stabilize prices and wages.* **sta·bi·lizer** *n* person or thing that stabilizes; (esp) device to keep a ship or aircraft steady, free from rolling or pitching. **sta·bil·iz·ation** /ˌsteɪbəlaɪ'zeɪʃn* US: -lɪ'z-/ *n* making or becoming ~.

stable² /'steɪbl/ *n* building in which horses are lodged and fed; number of horses (esp race-horses) belonging to one particular owner and kept in one set of ~s. '~-**boy/-man** *nn* boy/man employed in a ~. '~-**companion/-mate** *n* horse of the same ~; (fig) member of same group. □ *vt* put, keep, in a ~: *Where did you* ~ *your horse?* **stab·ling** /'steɪblɪŋ/ *n* [U] accommodation for horses: *The house has stabling for 20 horses.*

stac·cato /stə'kɑːtəʊ/ *adj, adv* (musical direction) (to be played) with each successive note clear and detached.

stack /stæk/ *n* [C] **1** circular or rectangular pile of hay, straw, grain, etc usu with a sloping, thatched top, for storage in the open. **2** group of rifles arranged in the form of a pyramid; pile or heap (of books, papers, wood, etc); (colloq) large amount: *I have* ~*s of work waiting to be done.* **3** (brickwork or stonework enclosing a) number of chimneys. ⇨ *smoke-~* at **smoke**¹(1). **4** rack with shelves for books (in a library or bookshop). **5** number of aircraft circling at different heights while waiting for instructions to land. □ *vt* **1** [VP6A,15B] ~ *(up)*, make into a ~ or ~s; pile up: ~ *hay/wood;* ~ *up the dishes on the draining-board.* **2** (US) arrange (playing-cards) unfairly. **have the cards ~ed a'gainst one,** be at a great disadvantage. **3** [VP6A] arrange aircraft in a ~(5).

sta·dium /'steɪdɪəm/ *n* (*pl* ~s) enclosed area of land for games, athletic competitions, etc, usu with stands for spectators: *build a new ~ for the Olympic Games.*

an Olympic stadium

staff /stɑːf *US:* stæf/ *n* **1** strong stick used as a support when walking or climbing, or as a weapon; (now usu fig): *the ~ of life,* bread. *He is the ~ of my old age,* eg a son who supports his old father. **2** such a ~ as a sign of office or authority: *a pastoral ~,* eg an ornamental one carried by or before a bishop, etc. **3** pole serving as a support: *a'flag~.* **4** group of assistants working together under a manager or head: *the headmaster and his ~,* ie the teachers; *'office-~; be on the ~. A large ~* (collective *n, sing v*) *of advisers has been employed for the President. The school ~* (= Members of the ~, *pl v*) *are expected to supervise school meals.* '**~-office,** personnel office. ⇨ personnel. **5** group of senior army officers engaged in planning and organization: *the General S~;* (attrib) '~ *officers.* **6** (music) (*pl* staves /'steɪvz/) set of five parallel lines on or between which notes are placed to indicate their pitch. ⇨ the illus at notation. □ *vt* [VP6A] provide with, act as, a ~(4): ~ *a new school; a well-~ed hotel/hospital; an under-~ed office.*

stag /stæg/ *n* **1** male deer. '**~-party** *n* (colloq) party for men only (eg one for a man about to get married). **2** person who buys newly issued stocks and shares hoping that prices will rise and enable him to sell at a profit.

stage /steɪdʒ/ *n* **1** (in a theatre) raised platform or structure of boards on which the actors appear. **2** **the ~,** theatrical work; the profession of acting in theatres. *be/go on the ~,* be/become an actor or actress. '**~-craft** *n* [U] skill or experience in writing or directing plays. '~ **direction** *n* printed direction in a play to actors about their positions, movements, etc. ~ '**door** *n* entrance at the back of a theatre, used by actors and workmen. '~ **fright** *n* [U] nervousness felt when facing an audience. ~ '**manager** *n* person who superintends the production of a play, supervises the rehearsals, etc. '~-**struck** *adj* having a strong desire to become an actor or actress. ~-'**whisper** *n* whisper that is meant to be overheard. **3** (fig) scene of action; place where events occur. **4** point, period or step in development: *at an early ~ in our history. The baby*

has reached the '*talking ~,* is learning to talk. **5** any of two or more successive periods on the journey of a rocket vehicle when one part has been jettisoned: *a multi-~ rocket.* **6** journey, distance, between two stopping-places along a road or route; such a stopping-place: *travel by easy ~s,* for only a short distance at a time. '~(-**coach**) *n* (hist) horse-drawn public vehicle carrying passengers (and often mail) along a regular route. '**fare-~** *n* section along the route of a bus or tram for which there is a fixed fare. **7** structure with tiers or shelves, eg for plants. ⇨ also staging below, and *landing-~* at landing. □ *vt,vi* **1** [VP6A] put on the ~(1); put before the public: ~ *'Hamlet',* (fig) arrange to take place dramatically. ~ **a'come-back,** come back (to a sport, eg to the boxing ring) from retirement or after having failed. **2** [VP2C] ~ *well/badly,* (of a drama) be well/badly suited for the theatre.

stager /'steɪdʒə(r)/ *n* (only in) **an old ~,** a person of long experience; an old hand. ⇨ hand¹(6).

stag-fla·tion /ˌstæg'fleɪʃn/ *n* [U] (fin) (word formed from *stagnation* + *inflation*) monetary inflation without growth of industrial production.

stag-ger /'stægə(r)/ *vi,vt* **1** [VP2A,C] walk or move unsteadily (from weakness, a heavy burden, drunkenness, etc): *The man ~ed along/to his feet/across the room/from side to side of the road.* **2** [VP6A] (of a blow or shock) cause to walk or move unsteadily; (of news, etc) shock deeply; cause worry or confusion to: *receive a ~ing blow. I was ~ed to hear/on hearing/when I heard who the group's leader was.* **3** [VP6A] arrange (times of events) so that they do not all occur together: ~ *office hours,* so that employees are not all using buses, trains, etc, at the same time; ~ *the annual holidays.* □ *n* **1** (*sing*) ~ing movement. **2 the ~s,** giddiness; nervous disease of cattle and horses, marked by ~ing. **~er** *n*

stag-ing /'steɪdʒɪŋ/ *n* **1** [C,U] stage(6); (platform or working area on) scaffolding for men on constructional work, eg building. **2** [U] (method of) presenting a play on the stage of a theatre.

stag-nant /'stægnənt/ *adj* **1** (of water) without current or tide; still and stale: *water lying ~ in ponds and ditches.* **2** (fig) unchanging; inactive: *Business was ~ last week.* **stag-nancy** /-nənsɪ/ *n*

stag-nate /stæg'neɪt *US:* 'stægneɪt/ *vi* [VP2A] be stagnant; (fig) be or become dull or sluggish through disuse, inactivity, etc. **stag-na·tion** /stæg'neɪʃn/ *n* [U].

stagy /'steɪdʒɪ/ *adj* theatrical in style, manner or appearance. **stag-ily** /-ɪlɪ/ *adv* **stagi-ness** *n*

staid /steɪd/ *adj* (of persons, their appearance, behaviour, etc) conservative, quiet and serious. **~-ly** *adv* **~-ness** *n*

stain /steɪn/ *vt,vi* **1** [VP6A] (of liquids, other substances) change the colour of; make coloured patches or dirty marks on: *fingers ~ed with nicotine; blood-~ed hands; a tablecloth ~ed with gravy;* (fig) *a guilt-~ed reputation.* **2** [VP6A,22] colour (wood, fabrics, etc) with a substance that penetrates the material: *He ~ed the wood brown. The scientist ~ed his specimen before examining it under the microscope.* **~ed glass,** glass made by mixing into it transparent colours during the process of manufacture: *~ed glass windows in a church.* **3** [VP2A] (of material) become discoloured or soiled: *Does this material ~ easily?* □ *n* **1** [U] liquid used for ~ing wood, etc. **2** [C] ~ed place;

dirty mark or patch of colour: '**ink**-/'**blood**-~s; (fig) a ~ on one's reputation; without a ~ on your character. ~**-less** adj 1 without a ~: a ~less reputation. 2 (esp of a kind of steel alloy) that resists rust and corrosion: ~less steel cutlery.

stair /steə(r)/ n [C] (any one of a) series of fixed steps leading from one floor of a building to another. ⇨ downstairs, upstairs. The child was sitting on the bottom ~. She always runs up/down the ~s. I passed her on the ~s. **below** ~s, in the basement of a house (in large houses, formerly the part used by servants): Their affairs were being discussed below ~s, by the servants. **a flight of** ~s, a set of ~s in a continuous line, or from one landing, eg halfway between two floors, to another. **at the foot/head of the** ~s, at the bottom/top of a flight of ~s. '~**-carpet** n strip of carpet for laying on ~s. '~**-rod** n rod for keeping a ~-carpet in the angle between two steps. '~**-case** n series of ~s (often with banisters) inside a building: Many old Edinburgh houses have spiral ~cases, ie winding round a central pillar. '~**-way** n = ~case.

stake /steɪk/ n [C] 1 strong, pointed length of wood or metal (to be) driven into the ground as a post (eg for a fence) or as a support for sth, eg plants, young trees. 2 post, as used in olden times, to which a person was tied before being burnt to death as a punishment (for heresy): condemned to the ~; suffer at the ~. **go to the** ~, be burned at the ~; (fig) suffer the consequences of an ill-advised action. 3 sum of money risked on the unknown result of a future event, eg a horse-race; interest or concern (in sth); sum of money invested in an enterprise: He has a ~ in the country, is concerned in its welfare, is interested in its prosperity, etc (eg because he is a landowner). **at** ~, to be won or lost; risked, depending, upon the result of sth: (fig) His reputation/His life itself was at ~. '~**-holder** n person with whom ~s are deposited until the result is known. 4 (pl) money to be contended for, esp in a horse-race; such a race: the trial ~s at Newmarket. □ vt 1 [VP6A] support with a ~: ~ newly planted trees. 2 [VP6A,15B] ~ sth (out/off), mark (an area) with ~s: ~ out a claim (to land in a new country, etc; also fig). 3 [VP6A,14] ~ sth on sth, risk (money, one's hopes, etc): ~ £5 on the favourite, eg in a horse-race. I'd ~ my all/my life on it, am very confident about it.

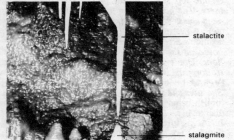
stalactite

stalagmite

stal·ac·tite /'stæləktaɪt US: stə'læk-/ n [C] pencil-shaped or cone-shaped formation of lime hanging from the roof of a cave as water drips from it. **stal·ag·mite** /'stæləgmaɪt US: stə'læg-/ n [C] similarly shaped growth mounting upwards from the floor of a cave as water containing lime drips

from the roof.

stale /steɪl/ adj 1 (of food) dry and unappetizing because not fresh: ~ bread. 2 uninteresting because heard before: ~ news/jokes. 3 (of athletes, pianists, etc) no longer able to perform really well because of too much playing, training, practice, etc: become ~. □ vi [VP2A] become ~: Are there any kinds of pleasure that never ~? ~**·ness** n

stale·mate /'steɪlmeɪt/ n [C,U] 1 position of the pieces in chess from which no further move is possible. 2 (fig) any stage of a dispute at which further action by either side seems to be impossible. □ vt [VP6A] (chess) reduce a player to a ~; (fig) bring to a standstill.

stalk[1] /stɔːk/ n [C] non-woody part of a plant that supports a flower or flowers, a leaf or leaves, or a fruit or fruits; stem.

stalk[2] /stɔːk/ vt,vi 1 [VP2C,6A] walk with slow, stiff strides, esp in a proud, self-important or grim way: ~ out of the room; ~ along (the road). Famine ~ed (through) the land. 2 [VP6A] move quietly and cautiously towards (wild animals, etc) in order to get near: ~ deer. '~**-ing-horse** n horse behind which a hunter hides; (more usu, fig) pretext; means of hiding one's real intentions. ~**er** n person who ~s animals: a'deer-~er.

stall /stɔːl/ n 1 compartment for one animal in a stable or cattle shed. '~**-fed** adj kept and fattened in a ~, not in the fields. 2 small, open-fronted shop; table, etc used by a trader in a market, on a street, in a railway-station, etc: a'book-/'flower-/'coffee-~. 3 (usu pl) (not US) seat in the part of a theatre nearest to the stage. 4 fixed seat in a church (usu enclosed at sides and back, often in carved wood) for the special use of a clergyman (usu in the choir or chancel): canon's/dean's ~. 5 ('finger)~, ⇨ finger. 6 condition of an aircraft when its speed has decreased to the point at which it no longer answers to the controls. □ vt,vi 1 [VP6A] place or keep (an animal) in a ~(1), esp for fattening: ~ed oxen. 2 [VP2A] (eg of an internal combustion engine) fail to keep going through insufficient power or speed; [VP2A,6A] (of a driver) cause an engine to stop from such a cause. 3 [VP6A,2A] (of an aircraft) cause to be, become, out of control through loss of speed. 4 [VP2A] avoid giving a clear answer to a question (in order to get more time): ~ for time; ~ off creditors. Quit ~ing!

stal·lion /'stæliən/ n uncastrated fully grown male horse, esp one used for breeding.

stal·wart /'stɔːlwət/ adj tall and muscular; solidly built; firm and resolved: ~ supporters. □ n loyal supporter of a political party, etc.

sta·men /'steɪmən/ n male part of a flower, bearing pollen. ⇨ the illus at flower.

stam·ina /'stæmɪnə/ n [U] vigour, energy, enabling a person or animal to work hard for a long time, to survive a serious illness, exposure, etc; (fig) mental toughness; moral strength.

stam·mer /'stæmə(r)/ vi,vt 1 [VP2A] speak haltingly with a tendency to repeat rapidly the same sound or syllable, as in 'G-g-give me that b-b-book'. 2 [VP6A,15B] ~ sth (out), say sth in this confused or halting way: ~ out a request. □ n (tendency to) ~ing talk. ~**er** n person who ~s. ~**ing·ly** adv

stamp[1] /stæmp/ vt,vi 1 [VP6A,3A,2C,22,15B] put (one's foot) down with force (on sth): ~ one's foot; ~ the ground; ~ on a spider; move (about, etc) doing this: ~ about/out of the room; ~ upstairs; flatten by doing this: ∼ the soil flat. ∼ **sth out**, crush, destroy, end: ∼ out a fire in the grass/a rebellion/an epidemic disease. '∼-**ing-ground** n (a) place where specified animals, eg elephants, may usually be found. (b) place where specified people often gather: Soho, the ∼ing-ground in London of those who enjoy exotic food and entertainment. 2 [VP6A,14] ∼ **sth (on/with sth)**, print (a design, lettering, the date, etc) on paper, cloth or other surface: ∼ one's name and address on an envelope/∼ an envelope with one's name and address: a manufacturer's goods ∼ed with his trademark. The library assistant forgot to ∼ my library books, ∼ the date on which they were taken out (or should be returned). 3 [VP6A] put a postage ∼ on (a letter, etc), an insurance ∼ on (a card): I enclose a ∼ed and addressed enve-lope for your reply. Your insurance card is insuffi-ciently ∼ed. 4 [VP6A,15B] ∼ **sth (out)**, give shape to sth (eg pieces of metal) with a die or cut-ter. 5 [VP6A,15A] (fig uses) impress: He ∼ed his authority/personality on the game, eg of a great footballer. [VP16B] mark out: These actions ∼ him as a man of high principles.

stamp² /stæmp/ n 1 act of stamping with the foot: a ∼ of impatience. 2 that with which a mark or de-sign is made on a surface: a rubber ∼, one on which a design, words, etc are cut (used for print-ing dates, signatures, addresses, etc). 3 design, word(s), etc made by stamping on a surface. 4 ('**postage-**)∼, piece of printed paper (usu with perforated edges) stuck on letters, etc to show the postage, insurance dues, etc paid, or the duty paid on legal documents. '∼-**album** n one in which a collector of postage-∼s keeps his specimens. '∼-**collector** n person who collects ∼s. '∼-**dealer** n person who buys and sells ∼s for collectors. '∼-**duty** n tax imposed on certain kinds of legal docu-ments. 5 (usu sing) characteristic mark or quality: He bears the ∼ of genius. Her face bears the ∼ of suffering. 6 (usu sing) kind; class: men of that ∼.

stam·pede /stæm'pi:d/ n [C] sudden rush of fright-ened people or animals. □ vi,vt 1 [VP2A,6A] take part in a ∼; cause to do this. 2 [VP14] ∼ **sb into sth/doing sth**, hustle or frighten sb into rash ac-tion: Don't be ∼d into buying the house.

stance /stæns/ n (golf, cricket) position taken for a stroke; pose; person's (intellectual, moral, etc) at-titude.

stanch /stɑ:ntʃ US: stæntʃ/ = staunch.

stan·chion /'stɑ:nʃən US: 'stæntʃ-/ n upright post for supporting sth (eg bars for confining cattle in stalls).

stand¹ /stænd/ n 1 stopping of motion or progress: come/be brought to a ∼ (or, more usu ∼still), stop, be stopped. 2 **make a** ∼, be ready to resist or fight: make a ∼ against the enemy; make a ∼ for one's principles. 3 position taken up: He took his ∼ near the window. **take one's** ∼, declare one's position, opinion, etc. I take my ∼ upon sound precedents, use these to support my claim, etc. 4 small article of furniture, support, etc on or in which things may be placed: a 'music-/'hat-/um'brella-∼. ⇨ also hand∼ at hand¹(16), ink∼ at ink, wash-∼ at wash-. 5 structure from which things are sold: a 'news∼; area, structure(s), for the exhibition of goods, etc: the British ∼ at the Hanover Fair. 6 place where vehicles may stand in line in a street, etc while waiting for passengers: a 'cab-∼; a ∼ for six taxis. 7 structure, usu sloping,

where people may stand or sit to watch races, sports-meetings, etc: open ∼s; the 'grand∼. 8 halt made by a theatrical company when touring the country. ,**one-night** '∼, theatrical performance on one evening only; (fig) an (esp sexual) encounter that will not be repeated. 9 (US) witness-box (in a law court): take the ∼. 10 growing crop in a cer-tain area: a good ∼ of wheat/timber. 11 (com-pounds) '∼-**pipe** n vertical pipe (connected with a water-main and used as a hydrant). '∼-**point** n point of view: from the ∼point of the consumer. '∼-**still** n stop; halt: be at/come to/bring sth to a ∼still; (attrib) a ∼still agreement, one that agrees to no change, eg in wage rates or hours of work.

stand² /stænd/ vi,vt (pt,pp stood /stʊd/) (For special uses with adverbial particles and preps, ⇨ 11 below.) 1 [VP2A,B,C,4A] have, take, keep, an upright position; balance, support, the body on the feet: He was too weak to ∼. A chair will not ∼ on two legs. We had to ∼ all the way back in the bus. S∼ing room only, all seats are occupied, eg in a bus or cinema. His hair stood on end, ie with terr-or. He ∼s six foot two, is of this height when ∼ing. Don't ∼ there arguing about it. He stood looking over my shoulder. S∼ still while I take your photograph. S∼ and deliver! (command given by a highwayman) Stop and give me your valuables, etc! 2 [VP2A,C,4A] ∼ (**up**), rise to the feet: S∼ up, please. Everyone stood (up) when the Queen entered. We stood (up) to see better. 3 [VP2A,C] remain without change: Let the words ∼, don't alter them or take them out. The agree-ment must ∼, cannot be altered or cancelled. The house has stood two hundred years and will ∼ an-other century. ∼ **firm/fast**, not give way, retreat, change one's views, etc. 4 [VP2C] be in a certain condition or situation: The emergency services ∼ (= are) ready to help if called on. The matter ∼s thus, this is the state of affairs. As affairs now ∼..., As they are at present.... He ∼s (= is) in need of help. Who ∼s (= is) first on the list? Will you ∼ (= be) godmother to the child? He stood convicted of treachery. I ∼ corrected, accept the correction of my views, etc. He ∼s alone among his colleagues, None of them equals him in ability, etc. ∼ **clear (of sth)**, move away: S∼ clear of the gates, eg as a warning when they are about to be closed. ∼ **easy/at ease**, ⇨ easy, ease. 5 [VP2C] have a certain place; be situated: These dishes ∼ on the top shelf. A tall poplar tree once stood there. The house ∼s on the hill. Where does Tom ∼ in class, What is his position (in order of ability, etc)? 6 [VP15A] cause to be placed in an upright position. S∼ the ladder against the wall. S∼ the bottle on the table. S∼ the empty barrels on the floor. Don't ∼ this tin of petrol near the fire. The traitor was stood up against the wall and shot. 7 [VP6A,C] endure; bear: He can't ∼ hot weather. She says she will ∼ no nonsense, not put up with foolish behaviour. I can't ∼ that woman, strongly dislike her. She can't ∼ being kept waiting. ∼ **one's ground**, maintain one's position, eg in bat-tle; (fig) not give way in an argument. ∼ (**one's**) **trial**, be tried (in a court of law). 8 [VP6A,12A] ∼ **sb sth**, provide at one's expense: ∼ sb a good din-ner; ∼ drinks all round, pay for drinks for every-one. Will he ∼ us champagne? ∼ **treat**, pay the costs of entertaining sb or others. 9 (phrases) ∼ **a (good/poor, etc) chance**, (of success, etc) have a (good/poor, etc) prospect (of success, etc). ∼ **sb**

in good stead, ⇨ stead. ∼ *on ceremony,* ⇨
ceremony. *It* ∼*s to reason that,* ⇨ reason ¹(3).
∼ *to win/gain/lose sth,* be in a position where
one is likely to win, etc: *What do we* ∼ *to gain by
the agreement?* **10** [VP2C,3,15B] (special uses with
adverbial particles and *preps*):
stand aside, **(a)** be inactive, do nothing: *He's a
man who never* ∼*s aside when there's something
that needs doing.* **(b)** move to one side: ∼ *aside to
let someone pass.* **(c)** withdraw one's name (as a
candidate): ∼ *aside in favour of a better man.*
stand at, be at a certain level (on a scale, etc): *The
appeal fund* ∼*s at £10000. The temperature stood
at 30℃.*
stand back, **(a)** move back: *The policeman ordered us to* ∼ *back.* **(b)** be situated away from: *The
house* ∼*s back from the road.*
stand by, **(a)** be a bystander; look on without doing anything: *How can you* ∼ *by and see such
cruelty?* **(b)** be ready for action: *The troops are
*∼*ing by.* ∼ *by sb,* support, side with, sb; show
oneself to be a good friend: *I'll* ∼ *by you whatever
happens.* ∼ *by sth,* be faithful to (a promise, one's
word, etc). Hence, '∼*·by* *n* **(a)** state of readiness:
The troops are on 24-hour ∼*by,* ready to move at
24 hours' notice. **(b)** sb or sth that one may depend
upon: (attrib) *a* ∼*by generator,* one for use in an
emergency, eg for use when electric current from
the mains is cut off. *Aspirin is a good* ∼*by for
headaches.*
stand down, retire from a witness-box or similar
position; (of a candidate) withdraw (in favour of sb
else).
stand for sth, **(a)** represent: *PO* ∼*s for Post Office
or postal order. I condemn fascism and all it* ∼*s
for.* **(b)** support, contend for: ∼ *for racial tolerance.* **(c)** (GB) be a candidate for: ∼ *for Parliament.* **(d)** (colloq; ⇨ **8** above) tolerate: *She says
she's not going to* ∼ *for her own children disobey-
ing her.*
stand in (with sb), take a share in: *Let me* ∼ *in
with you if it's expensive.* ∼ *in (for sb),* take the
place of, eg a principal actor or actress until filming begins. Hence, '∼*-in* *n* person who does this.
stand off, remain at a distance; move away. ∼ *sb
off,* dispense with the services of, eg workers,
temporarily. ∼*-'off·ish* *adj* reserved; cold and distant in behaviour. Hence, ∼*-'off·ish·ly* *adv* ∼*-
'off·ish·ness* *n*
stand out, **(a)** be easily seen above or among
others: *Does your work* ∼ *out from that of others,
Is it obviously better?* ⇨ outstanding. ∼ *out a
mile,* be extremely obvious. **(b)** continue to resist:
*The troops stood out against the enemy until their
ammunition was exhausted.*
stand over, be postponed: *Let the matter* ∼ *over
until the next meeting.* ∼ *over sb,* supervise,
watch closely: *Unless I* ∼ *over him he makes all
sorts of foolish mistakes.*
stand to, (mil) take up positions to resist possible
attack: *The company* (*was*) *stood to for half an
hour.* Hence, '∼*-to* *n* army signal to be on the
alert.
stand up, ⇨ **2** above. '∼*-up* *adj* **(a)** (of collars)
upright (opp of *turn-down*). **(b)** (of a meal) eaten
while ∼ing: *a* ∼*-up buffet.* **(c)** (of a fight) violent
and hard-hitting. ∼ *sb up,* (colloq) not keep a rendezvous with him: *First she agreed to come out
with me, then she stood me up.* ∼ *up for sb,* support; take the part of; defend. ∼ *up to sb,* defend

oneself with courage against him. ∼ *up to sth,* (of
materials) remain in good condition after long or
hard use, etc: *metals that* ∼ *up well to high temperatures.*
stand (well) with sb, be on (good) terms with, be
(well) thought of: *How do you* ∼ *with your boss?
He* ∼*s well with his bank manager* (and may,
therefore, get an overdraft without difficulty).
stan·dard /'stændəd/ *n* **1** distinctive flag, esp one
to which loyalty is given or asked: *the royal* ∼, eg
as flown to show that the Queen is in residence.
raise the ∼ *of revolt,* (fig) begin a struggle and
call for support. '∼*-bearer* *n* person who carries a
∼; (fig) prominent leader in a cause. **2** (often attrib) sth used as a test or measure for weights,
lengths, qualities or for the required degree of excellence: *the* ∼ *yard/pound, etc;* ∼ *weights and
measures; the* ∼ *of height required for recruits to
the police force; set a high* ∼ *for candidates in an
examination; conform to the* ∼*s of society,* live and
behave as society expects; *a high* ∼ *of living,* one
with plenty of material comforts, etc; *a high moral
*∼; ∼ *authors,* accepted as good. *be up to/below
*∼, be equal to/not so good as, what is normal, re-
quired, etc: *Their work is not up to* ∼. ∼ *time,*
time officially adopted for a country or part of it. **3**
(former) grade of classification in primary schools
(now usu *class*): *boys in S*∼ *One.* **4** **monetary** ∼,
proportion of weight of fine metal and alloy in gold
and silver coin. **the** '**gold** ∼, system by which the
value of money is based on that of gold.
abandon/go off the gold ∼, abandon such a
system. **5** (often attrib) upright support; pole or
column; vertical water- or gas-pipe. '∼ **lamp,**
lamp on a tall support with its base on the floor. **6**
tree or shrub that has been grafted on an upright
stem (contrasted with a bush or climbing plant): ∼
roses.
stan·dard·ize /'stændədaɪz/ *vt* [VP6A] make of one
size, shape, quality, etc according to fixed standards: *The parts of motor-vehicles are usually* ∼*d.
S*∼*d products are usually cheaper than hand-
made articles.* **stan·dard·iz·ation**
/,stændədaɪ'zeɪʃn US: -dɪ'z-/ *n* [U] standardizing;
making regular: *the problem of the standardization
of the use of hyphens in compounds.*
stand·ing /'stændɪŋ/ *n* **1** [U] duration: *a debt/
dispute of long* ∼. **2** [C,U] position or reputation;
(if there is no *adj*) established position: *men of
*(*high*) ∼; *a member in full* ∼. □ *adj* **1** established
and permanent; ready for use: *a* ∼ *army; a* ∼ *committee,* a permanent one that meets regularly; *a* ∼
order for newspapers and periodicals, to be delivered regularly; *a* ∼ *order to a bank,* customer's
order for payments that recur regularly, eg rent,
rates; *a* ∼ *joke,* sth that regularly causes amusement. ∼ *orders,* (*pl*) rules and regulations which
remain in force until repealed by the proper authorities. **2** ∼ **corn,** not yet cut (harvested). ∼
jump, made without a preliminary run.
stank /stæŋk/ *pt* of stink.
stan·za /'stænzə/ *n* (*pl* ∼s) [C] group of rhymed
lines forming a division in some forms of poem.
staple¹ /'steɪpl/ *n* U-shaped metal bar with pointed
ends hammered or pressed into a surface, to hold
sth, eg flexible wire for electric current, in position; hoop-shaped bar hammered into wood, etc to
take the point of a hook, or the hasp of a padlock,
⇨ the illus at padlock; piece of wire for fastening
sheets of paper together (as in some periodicals). □

vt [VP6A] fasten or fit with a ~. **'sta·pling-machine** *n* one used for fastening sheets of paper together with ~s. **sta·pler** /'steɪpɔ(r)/ *n* small hand-operated device for fastening papers together.

staple² /'steɪpl/ *n* **1** [C] chief sort of article or goods produced or traded in: *Cotton is one of the* ~*s of Egypt.* **2** chief material or element (*of* sth): *The weather forms the* ~ *of their conversation.* **3** [U] fibre of cotton, wool, etc (as determining its quality): *cotton of short/fine, etc* ~; *long-* ~ *cotton.* **4** (attrib) forming the ~(2): *Is coffee still the* ~ *product of Brazil? Rice is the* ~ *food in many Asian countries.*

star /stɑː(r)/ *n* **1** any one of the bodies seen in the sky at night as distant points of light. **fixed** ~ *n* one which is not a planet. **shooting** ~ *n* ⇨ shoot²(1). '~·**fish** *n* ~-shaped sea-animal. ⇨ the illus at sea. '~·**light** *n* [U] light from the ~s: *walk home by* ~*light;* (attrib) *a* ~*light night.* '~·**lit** *adj* lighted by the ~s: *a* ~*lit scene.* **2** figure or design with points round it, suggesting a ~ by its shape; an asterisk (*): *a five-* ~ *hotel,* given five ~s (in guide-books, etc) to show its grading; badge of rank (worn by officers on the shoulder-strap). **see** ~**s,** seem to see flashes of lights, eg as the result of a blow in the eye(s). **the ,S~-Spangled 'Banner,** (a) the national flag of the US. (b) the national anthem of the US. **the S~s and Stripes** *n sing* the national flag of the US. **3** planet or heavenly body regarded as influencing a person's fortune, etc: *born under a lucky* ~. *What do the* ~*s fortell? You may thank your lucky* ~*s you were not killed in that accident.* '~·**gazer** *n* (hum) astrologer or astronomer. **4** person famous as a singer, actor, actress, etc: *the* ~*s of stage and screen;* '*film*~*s; an all-* ~ *cast,* in which leading players are all ~s; *the* ~ *turn,* the principal item in an entertainment or performance. □ *vi,vt* (-rr-) **1** [VP6A] mark or decorate with, or as with, a ~ or ~s, eg an asterisk to direct attention to sth: *a lawn* ~*red with daisies.* **2** [VP3A,14] ~ (*sb*) *in,* be a ~(4) (*in* a play, film, etc); present (sb) as a ~(4): *She is to* ~*/to be* ~*red in a new film.* '~·**dom** /-dəm/ *n* status of being a ~(4). ~·**let** /-lɪt/ *n* young actress on the way to ~dom. ~·**less** *adj* with no ~s to be seen: *a* ~*less sky/night.* ~·**ry** /'stɑːrɪ/ *adj* lighted by, shining like, ~s: *a* ~*ry night;* ~*ry eyes.* ~**ry-'eyed** *adj* (colloq) visionary but impractical: ~*ry-eyed reformers.*

star·board /'stɑːbəd/ *n* right side of a ship or aircraft from the point of view of a person looking forward. ⇨ port: *alter course to* ~; *on the* ~ *bow.* ⇨ the illus at ship. □ *vt* turn to ~: ~ *the helm,* turn the helm to ~.

starch /stɑːtʃ/ *n* [U] **1** white, tasteless, carbohydrate food substance, plentiful in potatoes, grain, etc. **2** this substance prepared in powdered form and used for stiffening cotton clothes, etc; (fig) stiffness of manner; formality. □ *vt* [VP6A] make, eg shirt collars, stiff with ~; (fig, in *pp*) *a* ~*ed manner.* ~**y** *adj* of or like ~; containing ~: ~*y foods.*

stare /steə(r)/ *vi,vt* **1** [VP2A,B,C,3A] ~ (*at*), look fixedly; (of eyes) be wide open: *Do you like being* ~*d at? She was staring into the distance. They all* ~*d with astonishment. He gazed at the scene with staring eyes.* **make sb** ~, surprise him. **2** [VP15B] ~ *sb out (of countenance),* ~ until he becomes nervous, etc. ~ *sb out/down,* ~ at him longer

than he is able to ~ at you. ~ *one in the face,* (a) ~ at sb's face. (b) be right in front of one: *The book I was looking for was staring me in the face. Defeat was staring them in the face,* was clearly inevitable. □ *n* [C] staring look: *give sb a rude* ~; *with a* ~ *of horror/astonishment; with a vacant* ~, suggesting an empty mind; *with a glassy* ~, suggesting indifference. **star·ing** *adj* (of colours, etc) too bright or conspicuous: *His tie was a staring red.* □ *adv* (only in) **stark staring mad,** completely mad.

stark /stɑːk/ *adj* **1** stiff, esp in death. **2** complete; downright: ~ *madness/folly.* □ *adv* completely: ~ *naked.* ~**ers** /'stɑːkəz/ *pred adj* (GB sl) completely naked.

star·ling /'stɑːlɪŋ/ *n* common bird (with black, brown-spotted plumage) which nests near buildings and is a good mimic.

starry /'stɑːrɪ/ ⇨ star.

start¹ /stɑːt/ *n* **1** [C] beginning of a journey, activity, etc: *make an early* ~; *the* ~ *of a race; after several false* ~*s; from* ~ *to finish.* **2** [U,C] (no *pl*) amount of time or distance by which one person starts in front of competitors; advantageous position: *The small boys were given a* ~ *of ten yards. They didn't give me much/any* ~. *He got the* ~ *of* (= gained an advantage over) *his rivals. He got a good* ~ (= a position of advantage) *in life/business.* **a ,head '**~ *n* (lit or fig) advantageous position: *give sb/have/get a head* ~ (*over sb*). **3** [C] sudden movement of surprise, fear, etc: *He sat up with a* ~. *The news gave me a* ~, surprised me. **by fits and** ~**s,** ⇨ fit³(3).

start² /stɑːt/ *vi,vt* (Note: *begin* may replace *start* only as in 2 below) **1** [VP2A,C] ~ (*out*), leave; set out: *We must* ~ (*out*) *early. We* ~*ed at six. At last the bus* ~*ed.* **2** [VP6A,D,7A] begin: ~ *work. It* ~*ed raining. It's* ~*ing to rain. Have you* ~*ed working yet?* **3** [VP6A,3A] ~ (*on*) *sth,* make a beginning: ~ (*on*) *one's journey home. Have you* ~*ed on your next book yet,* begun to read (or write) it? **4** [VP2A,C] ~ (*up*), make a sudden movement (from pain, surprise, fear, etc) or change of position; jump: *He* ~*ed up from his seat. He* ~*ed at the sound of my voice.* **5** [VP2C] move, rise, spring, suddenly: *Tears* ~*ed to her eyes, suddenly came to her eyes. His eyes nearly* ~*ed out of his head,* suddenly opened wide (in surprise, etc). **6** [VP2A,C,6A] (of timbers) (cause to) spring out of position; make or become loose: *The ship has* ~*ed at the seams. The planks have* ~*ed. The damp has* ~*ed the timbers.* **7** [VP6A,15A,19B] set going; originate, bring into existence; cause or enable to begin: *This news* ~*ed me thinking. The smoke* ~*ed her coughing. He decided to* ~ *a newspaper. A rich uncle* ~*ed him in business,* helped him, eg by supplying capital. *She has* ~*ed a baby,* (colloq) become pregnant. **8** [VP3C] (with *adverbial particles*) ~ *back,* begin to return: *It's time we* ~*ed back.* ~ *in (on sth/to do sth),* (colloq) begin to do it: *Poor Jane! She's* ~*ed in on a huge pile of ironing.* ~ *off,* begin to move: *The horse* ~*ed off at a steady trot.* ~ *out (to do sth),* (colloq) begin; take the first steps: ~ *out to write a novel.* ~ *up,* (a) rise suddenly; jump. ⇨ 4 above. (b) come into existence suddenly or unexpectedly: *Many difficulties have* ~*ed up.* ~ *sth up,* put (an engine, etc) in motion: *We couldn't* ~ *up the car.* **9 to** ~ **with,** (a) in the first place: *To* ~ *with, we haven't enough money, and secondly we haven't enough time.* (b) at the beginning: *We had only six members to* ~ *with.* **10** '~-ing-gate *n* barrier where horses ~ a race, raised when the time comes for them to ~. '~-ing-point *n* place at which a start is made. '~-ing-post, place from which competitors ~ in a race. '~-ing-prices *n pl* (in horse-racing) the odds just before the start of a race. ~er *n* **1** person, horse, etc that takes part in a race: *There were only five* ~*ers in the last race.* **2** person who gives the signal for a race to ~. **under** ~*er's orders,* (of horses, athletes, etc lined up for a race) awaiting the starter's order or signal to ~ the race. **3** device for causing an engine to ~ working; ignition. ⇨ *self-*~*er* at **self-**. **4** (colloq) first course of a meal. **for** ~*ers,* (sl) = to ~ with, ⇨ **9** above.

startle /'stɑːtl/ *vt* [VP6A,15A] give a shock of surprise to; cause to move or jump: ~*d out of one's sleep;* ~*d out of one's wits,* suffered a sudden great shock. *She was* ~*d to see him looking so ill. What startling news!*

starve /stɑːv/ *vi,vt* **1** [VP6A,15A,2A,C] (cause to) suffer or die from hunger: ~ *to death. The proud man said he would* ~ *rather than beg for food. They tried to* ~ *the army into surrender/*~ *them out,* force them to surrender by preventing them from getting supplies of food. *be* ~*d of/*~ *for,* (fig) long for, be in great need of: *The motherless children were* ~*ed of/were starving for affection.* **2** (colloq) feel very hungry: *What's for dinner?—I'm starving!* **star·va·tion** /stɑː'veɪʃn/ *n* [U] suffering or death caused by lack of food; *die of starvation; starvation wages,* too low to buy adequate supplies of food; *be on a starvation diet,* a diet that is inadequate for health. ~·ling /'stɑːvlɪŋ/ *n* starving or ill-fed person or animal.

stash /stæʃ/ *vt* [VP15B] ~ *sth away,* (sl) put it safely; hide it.

state¹ /steɪt/ *n* **1** (*sing* only) condition in which sth or sb is (in circumstances, appearance, mind, health, etc): *The house was in a dirty* ~. *These buildings are in a bad* ~ *of repair,* need to be repaired. *She's in a poor* ~ *of health. What a* ~ *he's in!* How anxious, dirty, untidy, etc he is, according to context. *Now don't get into a* ~, (colloq) Don't get excited or anxious! ~ *of play,* **(a)** (cricket) score. **(b)** (fig) how parties in dispute stand in relation to one another (as likely to win or lose). **2** (often S~) organized political community with its apparatus of government; territory in which this exists; such a community forming part of a federal republic: *Railways in Great Britain belong to the S*~. *How many S*~*s are there in the United States of America? The President's 'Message to the Union' is not addressed to individual S*~*s but to the Union as a whole/to the nation.* **the** (United) S~s (also the US), (colloq) the United States of America (the USA). **Head of S**~, ⇨ head¹(12). ⇨ also *police* ~, *totalitarian* ~ at police, totalitarian. **3** (attrib) of, for, concerned with, the S~(2): *S*~ *documents/records/archives; S*~ *forests,* belonging to the S~, not privately owned; *bring industries under S*~ *control; S*~ *socialism,* policy of ~ control of industry etc. **the 'S~ De-partment,** (US) Government Ministry of Foreign Affairs. ,~'s '**evidence,** (US) evidence for the state in criminal cases. Cf *King's/Queen's* evidence in GB. '**S~-house,** building in which a S~ Legislature sits. '**S~** '**Legislature,** representative law-making assembly of a ~ within a federation, eg that of the S~ of Madras in India. Cf *the*

National Assembly for the whole of India. ,**S**~**s'** '**rights,** (US) all rights which are not delegated to the Federal Government in Washington. **4** [U] civil government: *Church and S*~; *S*~ *schools,* contrasted with Church schools. **5** [U] rank; dignity: *persons in every* ~ *of life. He lived in a style befitting his* (high or low) ~. **6** [U] pomp; ceremonial formality: *The Queen was in her robes of* ~. *in* ~, with ceremonial formality: *The President was driven in* ~ *through the streets of Peking.* **7** (attrib) of or for ceremony and formality: *the* ~ *coach,* eg as used by the Queen on ceremonial occasions; *the* ~ *apartments at the palace; a* ~ *call,* (colloq) formal visit. **8** *lie in* ~, (of a dead person) be placed on view in a public place before burial. **9** '~-room *n* private cabin (or sleeping-compartment) on a ship (and, in US, in a railway-carriage). ~·ly *adj* (-ier, -iest) impressive; dignified: *a* ~*ly dowager; the* ~*ly homes of England,* those of the nobility, etc; *with* ~*ly grace.* ~·li·ness *n.* '~·craft *n* [U] = ~smanship. ⇨ below. ~·less *adj* (of a person) not recognized as a citizen or national of any country: ~*less persons,* eg some political refugees.

state² /steɪt/ *vt* [VP6A,9] express in words, esp carefully, fully and clearly: ~ *one's views. I have seen it* ~*d that.... He* ~*d positively that he had never seen the accused man.* ~*d adj* made known; announced: *at* ~*d times/intervals.* ~·ment *n* **1** [U] expression in words: *Clearness of* ~*ment is more important than beauty of language.* **2** [C] stating of facts, views, a problem, etc; report: *issue a* ~*ment; a 'bank* ~*ment; make a* ~*ment (in court),* give a formal account in a law court setting out the cause of a legal action or its defence. *My bank sends me monthly* ~*ments of the state of my bank account.*

states·man /'steɪtsmən/ *n* (*pl* -men) person taking an important part in the management of State affairs; disinterested political leader. '~·like *adj* gifted with, showing, wisdom and a broad-minded outlook in public affairs. '~·ship /-ʃɪp/ *n* [U] skill and wisdom in managing public affairs.

static /'stætɪk/ *adj* at rest; in a state of balance: ~ *water,* not flowing (eg water in a tank, needing to be pumped); ~ *electricity,* as accumulated on an insulated body. **stat·ics** *n* [U] (*pl* with *sing v*) **1** branch of knowledge dealing with bodies remaining at rest or with forces which balance one another. ⇨ dynamic. **2** (radio, TV) atmospherics.

sta·tion /'steɪʃn/ *n* [C] **1** place, building, etc where a service is organized and provided: *a 'bus/po'lice/'broadcasting/'radar/'fire*~. **2** [U] position, or relative position, to be taken up or maintained by sb/sth: *One of the cruisers was out of* ~, not in its correct position relative to other ships. **3** stopping-place for railway trains; the buildings, offices, etc, connected with it: *a 'goods* ~, one for merchandise. '~-master *n* man in charge of a railway ~. **4** social position, rank: *people in all* ~*s of life.* **5** (Australia) (usu extensive) sheep or cattle ranch. **6** military or naval base; those living there. **7** S~s of the Cross, fourteen crosses, usu with images telling the story of the sufferings and death of Jesus, for religious devotions, set up in a church or along a path. **8** '~-wagon *n* (US) estate car. ⇨ estate(5). ▢ *vt* [VP6A,15A] put (sb, oneself, a military or naval force, etc) at or in a certain place: *The detective* ~*ed himself among the bushes,* hid there. *HMS Tiger has been* ~*ed at Hong Kong for the last two years.*

sta·tion·ary /'steɪʃənrɪ US: -nerɪ/ adj 1 not intended to be moved from place to place: a ~ crane/ engine. ⇨ mobile(1). 2 not moving or changing: remain ~; collide with a ~ van.

sta·tioner /'steɪʃnə(r)/ n dealer in ~y. ~y /'steɪʃənrɪ US: -nerɪ/ n [U] writing materials, etc. **Her Majesty's/the 'S~y Office** (abbr **HMSO**), government department which publishes and distributes government papers, books, etc.

stat·is·tics /stə'tɪstɪks/ n 1 (with pl v) collection of information shown in numbers: S~ suggest that the population of this country will be doubled in ten years' time. **vital ~,** ⇨ vital. 2 (with sing v) the science of ~. **stat·is·ti·cal** /stə'tɪstɪkl/ adj of ~: statistical tables/experts. **stat·is·ti·cally** /-klɪ/ adv **stat·is·ti·cian** /ˌstætɪ'stɪʃn/ n person who is expert in ~.

statu·ary /'stætʃʊərɪ US: -ʊerɪ/ adj of or for statues: ~ marble. □ n [U] sculpture; statues.

statue /'stætʃuː/ n figure of a person, animal, etc in wood, stone, bronze, etc, usu of life size or more than life size. ⇨ the illus at discus. **statu·ette** /ˌstætʃʊ'et/ n small ~. **statu·esque** /ˌstætʃʊ'esk/ adj like a ~ in having clear-cut outlines, in being motionless, etc.

stat·ure /'stætʃə(r)/ n [U] (person's) natural bodily height: short of ~; (fig) mental or moral quality; calibre.

status /'steɪtəs/ n [U] person's legal, social or professional position in relation to others: have no official ~, no official rank, eg in the Civil Service. Many young people desire ~ (= an established social position) and security. **'~ symbol,** sth which the ownership of is thought to be evidence of social rank, wealth, etc, eg a better car than one's neighbours, a yacht, a colour TV.

status quo /ˌsteɪtəs 'kwəʊ/ (Lat) social situation as it is now: conservatives who defend the ~. **~ 'ante** /'æntɪ/, social situation as it was before a recent change.

stat·ute /'stætʃuːt/ n [C] (written) law passed by Parliament or other law-making body. **'~ law** n all the ~s (contrasted with case-law and common law). ⇨ case ¹(2), common ¹(1). **'~-book** n book(s) containing the ~ law. **statu·tory** /'stætʃʊtrɪ US: -tɔːrɪ/ adj fixed, done, required, by ~: statutory control of prices and incomes.

staunch¹ /stɔːntʃ/ (US also **stanch** /stɑːntʃ US: stæntʃ/) vt [VP6A] stop the flow of (esp blood); check the flow of blood from (a wound): ~ blood/a wound.

staunch² /stɔːntʃ/ adj (of a friend, supporter, etc) trustworthy; loyal; firm. **~·ly** adv **~·ness** n

stave¹ /steɪv/ n 1 one of the curved pieces of wood used for the side of a barrel or tub. 2 (music) = staff(6). 3 stanza; verse.

stave² /steɪv/ vt,vi (pt,pp ~d or stove /stəʊv/) 1 [VP15B] ~ sth in, break, smash, make a hole in: The side of the yacht was ~d in by the collision. [VP3A] ~ in, become or get broken or smashed: The boat stove in when it struck the rocks. 2 [VP15B] ~ sth off, keep off, delay (danger, disaster, bankruptcy, etc).

stay¹ /steɪ/ vi,vt 1 [VP2A,B,C,4A] be, remain, continuously in a place or condition (for a long or short time, permanently or temporarily, as specified by the context): ~ in the house/at home/in bed; ~ (= be a guest) at a hotel/with friends. I'm too busy to ~/I can't ~, I must leave now. I can only ~ a few minutes. I ~ed to see what would

happen. Why don't you ~ with us (as a guest) when you next visit Oxford? Jenny's ~ing in Dublin (eg at a hotel, or with friends) for a few weeks, but she now lives/is living (= has her home) in Belfast. **~ for (an event/meal); ~ to (a meal),** remain for it: Won't you ~ for/to supper? **~ in,** (a) not go outdoors: The doctor advised me to ~ in for a few days. (b) remain in school after hours: The teacher made the boy ~ in and do his exercises again. **~ out,** (a) remain outdoors: Tell the children they mustn't ~ out after dark. (b) remain on strike: The miners ~ed out for several weeks. **~ up,** not go to bed: I ~ed up reading until midnight. I'll be late home, but please don't ~ up for me. **be ,here to'~; have ,come to'~,** (colloq) be permanent: I hope that the principle of equality of opportunity for men and women has come to ~/is here to ~. **come to ~ (with sb),** (of a person) visit sb (ie temporarily); start to live with sb (ie permanently): Sue is coming to ~ for a week next month. Since my wife's mother came to ~ with us last year, the TV has been on more or less continuously. **'~-at-home** n person who seldom goes anywhere; unadventurous person. 2 [VP2C] continue in a certain state: ~ single, not marry. That fellow never ~s sober for long, frequently gets drunk. **~ put,** (colloq) remain where placed: I wish this earring would ~ put instead of falling out every time. 3 [VP6A] stop, delay, postpone, check: ~ the progress of a disease; ~ one's hand, refrain from doing sth; ~ (= delay) judgement/ proceedings. 4 [VP2A,6A] be able to continue (work, etc); show endurance: The horse lacks '~ing power. **~ the course,** be able to continue to the end of the race, (fig) the struggle, etc. 5 (usu in imper; archaic or lit) pause: S~! (= Stop!) You've forgotten your overcoat! 6 [VP6A] satisfy for a time: have a sandwich to ~ one's hunger. □ n 1 period of ~ing; visit: make a short ~ in Karachi; a fortnight's ~ with my rich uncle. 2 (legal) delay; postponement. **~ of execution,** order that a court judgement need not be carried out for the time being. **~er** n person or animal able to ~(4): The horse that won the race is a good ~er.

stay² /steɪ/ n [C] 1 rope or wire supporting a mast, pole, etc. ⇨ the illus at barque. 2 (fig) support: the ~ of his old age, person who helped him, eg by giving him a home, looking after him. 3 (pl) (old-fashioned name for) kind of corset reinforced with strips of stiff material (bone or plastic). □ vt [VP6A,15B] ~ (up), support by means of a wire, rope or prop.

stead /sted/ n [U] **in sb's ~,** in his place; instead of him. **stand sb in good ~,** be useful or helpful to him in time of need: My anorak has stood me in good ~ this winter.

stead·fast /'stedfɑːst US: -fæst/ adj firm and unchanging; keeping firm (to): a ~ gaze; ~ in adversity; be ~ to one's principles. **~·ly** adv **~·ness** n

steady /'stedɪ/ adj (-ier, -iest) 1 firmly fixed or supported; balanced; not likely to fall over: make a table ~, eg by repairing a leg; on a ~ foundation; not very ~ on one's legs, eg of sb after a long illness. 2 regular in movement, speed, direction, etc: a ~ wind/speed/rate of progress/improvement. 3 regular in behaviour, habits, etc: a ~ young man; a ~ worker. 4 constant, unchanging: a ~ faith/ purpose. 5 (in exclamations) Keep her ~! (naut) Keep the ship on her course unchanged. **S~ (on)!**

(colloq, used as a warning) Control yourself! □ *adv* = steadily. **go** ~, (colloq) go about regularly with sb of the opposite sex, though not being engaged to marry: *Are Tony and Jane going* ~? □ *n* (sl) regular boy-friend or girl-friend. □ *vt,vi* [VP6A,2A] make or become ~; keep ~: ~ *a boat/table-leg;* ~ *oneself by holding on to the rail*, eg on the deck of a ship that is rolling. *Prices are* ~*ing*. **stead-ily** /'stedɪlɪ/ *adv* in a ~ manner: *work steadily. His health is getting steadily worse*. **steadi-ness** *n*

steak /steɪk/ *n* [U,C] (thick slice of) meat or fish for (usu) frying or grilling: *fillet/rump* ~; *two tuna* ~*s*.

steal /stiːl/ *vt,vi* (*pt* stole /stəʊl/, *pp* stolen /'stəʊlən/) **1** [VP6A,14,2A] ~ *sth (from sb)*, take (sb else's property) secretly, without right, unlawfully: *Someone has stolen my watch. I have had my watch stolen*. Cf I have been *robbed of* my watch. *It is wrong to* ~. **2** [VP6A,15A] obtain by surprise or a trick: ~ *a kiss from sb;* ~ *a glance at sb in the mirror*. ~ *a march on sb*, do sth before him and so gain an advantage. **3** [VP2C] move, come, go (*in, out, away, etc*) secretly or quietly: *He stole into the room. A tear stole down her cheek. The morning light was* ~*ing through the shutters*.

stealth /stelθ/ *n* [U] (only used in) **by** ~, secretly and quietly: *enter a house by* ~. ~**y** *adj* (-ier, -iest) doing things, done, quietly and secretly: ~*y footsteps*. ~**-ily** /-ɪlɪ/ *adv*

steam /stiːm/ *n* [U] **1** gas or vapour into which boiling water changes; power obtained from ~: ~*-covered windows; a building heated by* ~. *The ship was able to proceed under her own* ~, using her own engines and not needing to be towed. **Full** ~ **ahead!** order to go forward at full speed. **get up/raise** ~, provide ~ at a higher pressure in the boilers, etc: *The stokers got up* ~. **2** (fig uses; colloq) energy. **get up** ~, collect one's energy; become excited or angry. **let off** ~, release surplus energy or emotion; become less excited. **run out of** ~, become exhausted: *Is there a danger of the housing programme running out of* ~, losing its impetus? **under one's own** ~, without help from others. **3** (compounds) '~**-boat** *n* vessel propelled by ~. ~**-'boiler** *n* vessel in which ~ is generated (to work an engine). ~ **brake/hammer/whistle/ winch, etc** *nn* worked by ~. ~**-'coal** *n* coal used for heating in ~-boilers. '~**-engine** *n* locomotive or stationary engine worked or driven by pressure of ~. ~**-'heat** *n* heat given out by ~ from radiators, pipes, etc. □ *vt:* ~*-heated buildings*, kept warm by ~-heat. ~ '**radio** *n* (sl) sound broadcasting (contrasted with TV). '~**-roller** *n* heavy, slow-moving locomotive with wide wheels used in roadmaking. □ *vt* [VP6A] crush as with a ~-roller: ~*-roller all opposition*. '~**-ship** *n* ship driven by ~. □ *vi, vt* **1** [VP2A,C] give out ~ or vapour: ~*ing hot coffee. The kettle was* ~*ing (away) on the stove*. **2** [VP2C] move, work, etc under (or as if under) the power of ~: *a ship* ~*ing up the Red Sea;* ~ *at ten knots. The train* ~*ed into the station*. **3** [VP6A,22] cook, soften, clean, by the use of ~; ~ *fish;* ~ *open an envelope*, use steam to soften the gum on the flap. **4** ~ **up**, become misty with condensed ~: *The windows* ~*ed up*. **be/get (all)** ~**ed up**, (colloq) become excited and perhaps violent: *Now don't get all* ~*ed up over nothing!* ~**er** *n* **1** ~-ship. **2** vessel in which food is cooked by being ~ed. ~**y** *adj* of, like, full of, ~: ~*y windows; the* ~*y heat of the rainy season in the trop-*

ics.

steed /stiːd/ *n* (liter or hum) horse.

steel /stiːl/ *n* [U] **1** strong, hard alloy of iron and carbon, used for knives, tools, machinery, etc. ~ **band** *n* (as, orig, in Trinidad) band of musicians who use empty oil drums as percussion instruments. '~**-clad** *adj* covered with ~ armour. ~**-'plated** *adj* covered with ~ plates; armoured. ~ **wool**, fine ~ shavings (used for scouring and polishing). '~**-works** *n pl* (often with *sing v*) factory where ~ is made. **2** ~ weapon, eg a sword, contrasted with a firearm: *an enemy worthy of one's* ~, (rhet or fig) one who will fight well. **cold** ~, ⇨ **cold**[1](1). □ *vt* [VP6A,15A,16A] harden: ~ *oneself/one's heart (against pity/to do sth)*. ~**y** *adj* like ~ in hardness, polish, brightness, etc.

a steel band

steel-yard /'stiːljɑːd/ *n* balance(1) with an arm in two parts, the longer side being graduated for a weight which slides along it.

steen-bok /'stiːnbɒk/ *n* kind of small S African antelope.

steep[1] /stiːp/ *adj* (-er, -est) **1** (of a slope) rising or falling sharply: *a* ~ *gradient/path/descent; a* ~ *roof*, with a ~ pitch. **2** (colloq, of a demand) unreasonable; excessive: *It's a bit* ~ *that I should pay for all of you! £10 for this dictionary—isn't that a bit* ~? *That story's rather* ~, difficult to believe, exaggerated. ~**-ly** *adv* ~**-ness** *n* ~**en** /'stiːpən/ *vt,vi* [VP6A,2A] make or become ~ or ~er. '~**-ish** /-ɪʃ/ *adj* rather ~.

steep[2] /stiːp/ *vt,vi* [VP6A,14,2A] ~ *sth (in sth)*, **1** soak or bathe in liquid: ~ *onions in vinegar*, to pickle them. **2** (fig) pervade with; get a thorough knowledge of: ~*ed in ignorance/prejudice; a scholar* ~*ed in the literature of ancient Greece and Rome*.

steeple /'stiːpl/ *n* high tower with a spire, rising above the roof of a church. ⇨ the illus at **church**. '~**-chase** *n* cross-country horse-race or race on foot with obstacles such as fences, hedges and ditches. ⇨ **flat racing** at **flat**[2](1). '~**-jack** *n* man who climbs ~s, tall chimney-stacks, etc to do repairs.

steer[1] /stɪə(r)/ *n* young (usu castrated) male of an animal of the ox family, raised for beef. ⇨ **bull**[1](1), **bullock, heifer, ox**.

steer[2] /stɪə(r)/ *vt,vi* [VP6A,2A,C] direct the course of (a boat, ship, car, etc): ~ *north;* ~ *by the stars;* (with passive force): *a ship that* ~*s* (= ·is ~ed) *well/easily/badly*. ~ *clear of*, (fig) avoid. '~**ing-gear** *n* [U] (of a ship) rudder and the mechanism controlling it. '~**-ing-wheel** *n* (a) (on a ship) wheel turned to control for rudder. (b) (on a motor-vehicle) wheel for ~ing (mounted on the

'~ing-column). ⇨ the illus at motor. **~·s·man** /-zmən/ n (pl -men) person who ~s a vessel.

steer·age /'stɪərɪdʒ/ n [U,C] (sing only, or attrib) **1** act or effect of steering. **2** that part of a ship nearest the rudder; this section formerly used for providing for passengers travelling at the lowest fares. '~**way** n forward progress needed by a vessel to enable her to be controlled by the helm.

stele /'sti:lɪ/ n (also **stela** /'sti:lə/, pl stelae /-li:/) (Gk archaeology) upright slab or pillar, usu with a sculptured design or inscription.

stel·lar /'stelə(r)/ adj of stars: ~ light.

stem[1] /stem/ n **1** part of a plant coming up from the roots; part of a leaf, flower or fruit that joins it to the main stalk or twig. ⇨ the illus at flower. **~·med** suff (with adjj) ,long-'~med, ,short-'~med, ,thick-'~med, having long, short, thick, ~s. **2** ~-shaped part, eg the slender part of a wine-glass, between the base and the bowl, the part of a tobacco pipe between the mouthpiece and the bowl. **3** root or main part of a noun or verb from which other words are made by additions (esp inflectional endings). **4** main upright timber at the bow of a ship. **from ~ to stern**, throughout the whole length of a ship. □ vi (-mm-) [VP3A] ~ **from**, arise from; have as origin.

stems

stem[2] /stem/ vt (-mm-) [VP6A] **1** check, stop, dam up (a stream, a flow of liquid, etc). **2** make headway against the resistance of: ~ the tide/ current; (fig) ~ the tide of popular indignation.

stench /stentʃ/ n [C] horrid smell.

sten·cil /'stensl/ n [C] thin sheet of metal, cardboard, waxed paper, etc with letters or designs cut through it; lettering, design, etc printed by inking paper, etc through a stencil: cut a ~, eg by typing without the ribbon on a waxed sheet. □ vt (-ll-, US also -l-) [VP6A] produce (a pattern, wording, etc) by using a ~.

Sten gun /'sten gʌn/ n small kind of machine-gun, usu fired from the hip.

sten·ogra·phy /stə'nɒɡrəfɪ/ n (US) shorthand. **sten·ogra·pher** /-fə(r)/ n (US) writer of shorthand (GB = ,shorthand-'typist).

sten·torian /sten'tɔːrɪən/ adj (of a voice) loud and strong.

step[1] /step/ vi, vt (-pp-) **1** [VP2C] move the foot, or one foot after the other (forward, or in the direction indicated): ~ across a stream; ~ into a boat; ~ on to/off the platform; ~ across to a neighbour's, cross (the road) to his house. ~ **this way**, (polite invitation to) follow sb somewhere, eg into a room. ~ **on the gas**; ~ **on it**, (a) (gas = gasoline) press down the accelerator pedal of a motor vehicle to increase speed. (b) (sl) hurry. '~**·ping-stone** n (a) one of a number of flat stones placed in a shallow stream, so that it can be crossed with dry feet. (b) (fig) means of attaining sth: a first ~ping-stone to success. '~**-ins** n pl (colloq) woman's undergarment or shoes, put on by being ~ped into. **2**

[VP2C,15B] (uses with adverbial particles):

step aside, (a) move to one side. (b) (fig) allow sb else to take one's place.

step down, (fig) resign (to make way for sb else).

step in, (fig) intervene (either to help or hinder): If the police hadn't ~ped in during the demonstration there would have been a violent struggle.

step sth off/out, measure by taking steps: ~ out a distance of ten metres.

step out, (a) walk faster, walk briskly. (b) (colloq) have a gay time, a busy social life.

step sth up, (a) (naut) fix (the foot of a mast) in its socket. (b) increase: ~ up production; ~ up the doses (of medicine); ~ up the campaign, put more effort into it.

step[2] /step/ n **1** act of stepping once; distance covered by doing this: He was walking with slow ~s. The water was deeper at every ~. We must retrace our ~s, go back. It's only a few ~s farther. We have made a long ~ (fig, much progress) towards success. **watch one's** ~, be careful or cautious. ~ **by** ~, gradually; by degrees. '**one-~**, '**two-~** nn names of dances. **2** ('**foot·**)~, sound made by somebody walking; way of walking (as seen or heard): We heard (foot)~s outside. That's Lucy—I recognize her ~. **3** **be/get in/out of** ~ **(with)**, (a) put/not put the right foot to the ground at the same time as others (in walking, marching, dancing). (b) conform/not conform with other members of a group: He's out of ~ with the rest of us. **keep** ~ **(with)**, walk or march in ~ (with). **break** ~, get out of ~. **4** one action in a series of actions with a view to effecting a purpose: take ~s to prevent the spread of influenza; a false ~, a mistaken action. What's the next ~, What are we to do next? That would be a rash ~ to take. **5** place for the foot when going from one level to another: Mind the ~s when you go down into the cellar. They had to cut ~s in the ice as they climbed. The child was sitting on the bottom ~. ~**s, a pair of** ~**s, a** '~**-ladder** nn portable folding ladder with ~s, not rungs and usu a small platform at the top. **6** grade, rank; promotion: When do you get your next ~ up? When will you be promoted?

a step-ladder   a stethoscope

step- /step/ pref (used to show a relationship not by blood but by a later marriage) '~**·child/·son/·daughter** nn child of an earlier marriage of one's wife or husband. '~**·brother/·sister** nn child of an earlier marriage of one's stepfather or stepmother. '~**·father/·mother/·parent** nn one's parent's later husband or wife.

steppe /step/ n [C] level, grassy treeless plain, esp in SE Europe and central Asia. ⇨ pampas, prairie, savanna, veld.

stereo /'sterɪəʊ/ n (abbr of ~phonic) ~phonic record-player, apparatus, sound, etc.

stereo·phonic /ˌsterɪəˈfɒnɪk/ adj (of broadcast and recorded sound, using two separately placed loudspeakers) giving the effect of naturally distributed sound; (of apparatus) designed for recording or reproducing sound in this way: *a ~ recording.*

stereo·scope /ˈsterɪəskəʊp/ n [C] apparatus by which two photographs of sth, taken from slightly different angles, are seen as if united and with the effect of depth and solidity. **stereo·scopic** /ˌsterɪəˈskɒpɪk/ adj of, by means of, a ~.

stereo·type /ˈsterɪətaɪp/ n [C,U] 1 (process of printing from a) printing-plate cast from a mould of a piece of printing set in movable type. 2 fixed, formalized or standardized (and therefore perhaps false) phrase, idea, belief. □ vt [VP6A] 1 make ~s of; print by the use of ~s. 2 (fig) (of phrases, ideas, etc) fix in form; use and repeat without thought or change: *~d greetings,* eg 'Good morning', 'How d'you do'?

ster·ile /ˈsteraɪl US: ˈsterəl/ adj 1 not producing, not able to produce, seeds or offspring. 2 (of land) barren. 3 (fig) having no result; producing nothing: *a ~ discussion.* 4 free from living germs. **ste·ril·ity** /stəˈrɪlətɪ/ n [U] being ~. **ster·il·ize** /ˈsterəlaɪz/ vt [VP6A] make ~: *The surgeon carefully sterilized his instruments.* **ster·il·iz·ation** /ˌsterəlaɪˈzeɪʃn US: -lɪˈz-/ n [U].

ster·ling /ˈstɜːlɪŋ/ adj 1 (abbr **stg**) (of gold and silver) of standard value or purity: *plates of ~ gold.* 2 (fig) of solid worth; genuine: *~ sense/ qualities.* □ n British money: *the pound ~* (= £); *payable in ~.* the *'~ area,* group of countries which keep their reserves in British ~ currency and between which money can be transferred freely.

stern¹ /stɜːn/ adj (-er, -est) 1 demanding and enforcing obedience: *a ~ taskmaster.* 2 severe; strict: *a ~ face; ~ looks; ~ treatment/rebukes.* **~·ly** adv **~·ness** n

stern² /stɜːn/ n [C] rear end of a ship or boat: *move out of dock ~ foremost.* ⇨ the illus at ship. **~·'wheeler** n steamer with a larger paddle-wheel at the ~ (instead of paddle-wheels at the sides).

ster·num /ˈstɜːnəm/ n (anat) narrow bone in the front of the chest (also called *'breast-bone*) connecting the collar-bone and the top seven pairs of ribs. ⇨ the illus at skeleton.

ster·tor·ous /ˈstɜːtərəs/ adj (of breathing or a person breathing) making a loud snoring sound. **~·ly** adv

stet /stet/ vi (Lat) direction to a printer, etc to disregard a correction in a MS or proof.

stetho·scope /ˈsteθəskəʊp/ n instrument used by doctors for listening to the beating of the heart, sounds of breathing, etc. ⇨ the illus at step².

stet·son /ˈstetsn/ n man's hat with a high crown and a wide brim.

steve·dore /ˈstiːvədɔː(r)/ n man whose work is loading and unloading ships.

stew /stjuː US: stuː/ vt,vi [VP6A,15A,2A,C] cook, be cooked, in water or juice, slowly in a closed dish, pan, etc: *~ed chicken/fruit; '~ing pears,* suitable for ~ing but not for eating uncooked. *let sb ~ in his own 'juice,* do nothing to help him (when he is in trouble for which he is himself responsible). *~ in one's own 'juice,* suffer from trouble's of one's own making. *let sb ~,* let him continue suffering from the consequences of his own stupidity without offering help or sympathy. □ n 1 [C,U] (dish of) *~ed* meat, etc: *have mutton ~ for supper; prepare a ~.* 2 *be in/get into a ~*

(about sth), (colloq) a nervous, excited condition. **stewed** adj (sl) intoxicated.

stew·ard /stjʊəd US: ˈstuː-/ n 1 man who arranges for the supply of food, etc in a club, college, etc. 2 man who attends to the needs of passengers in a ship or airliner: *the 'baggage/'cabin/'deck, etc ~.* 3 man responsible for organizing details of a dance, race-meeting, public meeting, show, etc: *~s of the Jockey Club. The hecklers were thrown out by the ~s.* 4 man who manages another's property (esp a large house or estate). 5 **shop ~,** ⇨ shop(3). **~·ess** /ˌstjʊəˈdes US: ˈstuːədɪs/ n woman ~ (esp 2 above). **~·ship** /-ʃɪp/ n rank and duties of a ~(4); period of office.

stick¹ /stɪk/ n 1 thin branch broken, cut or fallen, from a bush, tree, etc: *gather dry ~s to make a fire; cut ~s to support the peas in the garden.* 2 such a branch cut to a convenient length, piece of cane cut, shaped, etc for a special purpose: *The old man cannot walk without a ~. We have only a few ~s of furniture,* only a few very roughly made articles of furniture of the simplest kind. *give sb the ~,* beat him with a cane, as punishment; (fig) punish him. *get hold of the ,wrong end of the '~,* be confused; misunderstand things completely. *the big ~,* (fig) threat of the use of force, eg in relationships between countries: *a policy of the big ~.* **hockey ~,** ⇨ hockey. 3 slender, rod-shaped piece (of chalk, sealing-wax, charcoal, dynamite, celery, etc). 4 (colloq) person, esp one who is dull, stiff and reserved: *He's a dull/dry old ~.* 5 the **~s,** (colloq) the backwoods; rural areas far from cities. *out in the ~s,* away from the centre of things. □ vt (pt,pp ~ed) [VP6A] support with ~s(1): *Have you ~ed your peas yet?*

stick² /stɪk/ vt,vi (pt,pp stuck /stʌk/) (For special uses with *adverbial particles* and *preps,* ⇨ 7 below.) 1 [VP6A,15A,B] ~ *sth (in),* push (sth pointed) (into, through, etc): *S~ the fork into the potato/S~ it in. The cushion was stuck full of pins. ~ a pig,* (in sport) kill one with a spear. 2 [VP2C] (of sth pointed) be, remain, in a position by the point: *The needle stuck in my finger. I found a nail ~ing in the tyre.* 3 [VP15A,B,2A,C] (cause to) be or become joined or fastened with, or as with, paste, glue or other substance: *~ a stamp on a letter/a placard on a hoarding. These stamps have stuck (together). be/get stuck with sb/sth,* (colloq) become permanently involved with him/it; be/become unable to escape from him/it: *It looks as if I'm stuck with the job of clearing up this mess. '~-ing-plaster* n [U] plaster for ~ing on and protecting a cut, injury, etc. 4 [VP15A] (colloq) put (in some position or place), esp quickly or carelessly: *He stuck his pen behind his ear/his hands in his pockets/the papers in a drawer.* 5 [VP2A,C] (also in the passive) ~ *(in),* be or become fixed (in); fail to work properly: *The key stuck in the lock,* could not be turned or withdrawn. *The bus (was) stuck in the mud. Don't get stuck in the bog. The door has stuck,* eg as the result of being newly painted. ~ *in one's throat,* (of a proposal, etc) be difficult to accept; (of words) be difficult to utter (because of unwillingness, etc). *'~-in-the-mud* attrib adj resistant to change: *~-in-the-mud ideas.* □ n person of this kind: *My grandfather is an old ~-in-the-mud.* 6 [VP6A] (colloq) bear; endure: *How can you ~ that fellow? I can't ~ it any longer.* ⇨ 7, ~ it out, below. *S~ to it!* (used as a cry of encouragement meaning 'Bear the conditions bravely', etc. **7** [VP2C,3A,15B] (special uses with *adverbial particles* and *preps*):

stick around, (sl) (of a person) stay in or near a place: *S~ around; we may need you.*

stick at sth, (a) stop short of, hesitate at: *Don't ~ at trifles. He ~s at nothing,* allows no feelings of doubt, no scruples, to stop him. (b) keep on with sth: *He ~s at his work ten hours a day.*

stick sth down, (a) (colloq) put down: *S~ it down anywhere you like.* (b) (colloq) write down. (c) fasten with paste, etc: *~ down (the flap of) an envelope.*

stick on sth, remain on: *Can you ~ on a horse? ~ sth on,* fasten to with paste, etc: *~ on a label.* Hence, '*~-on* attrib adj: *~-on* labels (as contrasted with *tie-on* labels). *~ it on,* (sl) make very high charges: *The hotel keepers ~ it on during the (busy) season.*

stick sth out, (cause to) project, stand out: *with his chest stuck out; a rude boy ~ing his tongue out at his sister. Don't ~ your head out of the car window. ~ it/sth out,* (colloq) endure hardship, etc until the end. ⇨ **6** above. *~ one's neck out,* ⇨ neck(1). *~ out for sth,* refuse to give way until one gets (sth demanded): *They're ~ing out for higher wages.*

stick to sb/sth, (a) be faithful to (one's ideals, a friend, etc); remain determined: *~ to a resolution.* (b) continue at: *~ to a task until it is finished; ~ to a timetable,* make no changes in what has been agreed. *~ to one's guns,* ⇨ gun(1).

stick together, (colloq) (of persons) remain loyal or friendly to one another.

stick up, be upright, project upwards: *The branch was ~ing up out of the water. ~ sb/sth up,* (sl) threaten to shoot sb in order to rob him/it: *~ up a bank.* Hence, '*~-up* n. *~ your 'hands up; ~ 'em 'up,* raise your hands (so that resistance is not intended). *~ up for sb/oneself/sth,* defend, support: *~ up for one's friends.*

stick with sb/sth, remain loyal to, continue to support: *~ with a friend/an ideal.*

sticker /'stɪkə(r)/ *n* **1** one who, or that which, sticks, eg a persevering person. ⇨ stick²(7). **2** adhesive label to be stuck on sth.

stick-ler /'stɪklə(r)/ *n ~ for sth,* person who insists upon the importance of sth (eg accuracy, discipline, formality, etc).

sticky /'stɪkɪ/ *adj* (-ier, -iest) **1** that sticks or tends to stick to anything that touches it: *~ fingers/ toffee; a ~ road,* eg deep in wet mud. *a ~ wicket,* (cricket) soft wet area which makes batting difficult. *be on a ~ wicket,* (fig) in a situation that is difficult to deal with. **2** (sl) unpleasant; difficult: *have a ~ time. come to a ~ end,* die in an unpleasant and painful way. **3** (colloq) making, likely to make, objections, be unhelpful, etc: *The bank manager was ~ about letting her have an overdraft. stick-ily* /-ɪlɪ/ *adv* **stick-ness** *n*

stiff /stɪf/ *adj* **1** not easily bent or changed in shape: *a ~* (ie starched) *collar; a sheet of ~ cardboard; have a ~ leg/back,* not easily bent; *feel ~ after a long walk,* have *~* muscles and joints; *lying ~ in death. keep a ~ upper lip,* show firmness of character (by not complaining when in pain or trouble). *,~-'necked adj* obstinate. **2** hard to stir, work, move, etc: *stir the flour and milk to a ~ paste;* hard to do; difficult: *a ~ climb/ examination. The book is ~ reading.* **3** (of manners, behaviour) formal, unfriendly, haughty: *get a*

~ reception; be rather ~ with one's neighbours; give sb a ~ bow. **4** great in degree: *a ~* (= strong) *breeze; a ~* (= high) *price; a ~ glass of rum/a ~ drink,* strong in alcoholic content. □ *adv* thoroughly; to the point of exhaustion: *It bored me ~,* bored me very much. *She was scared ~,* very badly scared. □ *n* (sl) **1** corpse. **2** (sl) fool. *~ly adv ~ ness* *n.* *~en* /'stɪfn/ *vt,vi* [VP6A,2A] make or become *~.* *~en-ing* /'stɪfnɪŋ/ *n* [U] material used to *~en* a substance or object. *~ener* /'stɪfnə(r)/ *n* sth used to *~en.*

stifle /'staɪfl/ *vt,vi* **1** [VP6A,2A] give or have the feeling that breathing is difficult: *They were ~d by the heat. The heat was stifling. The smoke filled the building and almost ~d the firemen.* **2** [VP6A] suppress; put down; keep back: *~ a rebellion; ~ a yawn/a cry/one's laughter.*

stigma /'stɪgmə/ *n* [C] **1** (*pl ~s* /-məz/) (fig) mark of shame or disgrace: *the ~ of illegitimacy.* **2** (*pl ~ta* /-tə/) marks resembling those made by the nails on the body of Jesus at his crucifixion, said to have appeared on the body of St Francis of Assisi and others. **3** (*pl ~s*) that part of the pistil of a flower which receives the pollen. ⇨ the illus at flower.

stig·ma·tize /'stɪgmətaɪz/ *vt* [VP16B] describe (sb) scornfully (*as*): *be ~d as a coward and a liar.*

stile /staɪl/ *n* arrangement of steps or rungs to enable persons on foot to get over or through a fence, hedge, wall, etc but keeping cattle out. ⇨ turnstile at turn²(6). *help a lame dog over a ~,* ⇨ dog¹(2).

sti·letto /stɪ'letəʊ/ *n* (*pl ~s, ~es* /-təʊz/) small dagger with a narrow tapering blade. *~ heel,* (on a woman's shoes) high, thin and (usu) made of metal.

still¹ /stɪl/ *adj, adv* (-er, -est) **1** without movement or sound; quiet: *Please keep/stay ~ while I take your photograph. How ~ everything is! the ~ small voice,* the voice of conscience. *,~-'life n* [U] representation of non-living things (eg fruit, flowers, etc) in painting; [C] (*pl ~-lifes*) painting of this kind. '*~-birth n* child or foetus dead at birth. ⇨ *live-birth* at live¹(4). '*~-born adj* (of a child) dead at birth. **2** (of wines) not sparkling; not containing gas. □ *n* **1** [U] (poet) deep silence: *in the ~ of the night.* **2** [C] ordinary photograph selected from, and contrasted with, a cinema film: *~s from a new film,* eg as used for advertising in the press. □ *vt* [VP6A] cause to be *~* or at rest; make calm. *~y adj* (poet) calm; quiet. *~ness n*

still² /stɪl/ *adv* **1** (usu mid position, but may occur after a direct object) even to this or that time: *He is ~ busy. He ~ hopes/is ~ hoping for a letter from her. Will he ~ be here when I get back? In spite of his faults she ~ loved him/loved him ~.* Cf *still* and *yet: Is your brother here yet,* Has he arrived? *Is your brother ~ here,* Has he left? **2** (with a comp) even; yet; in a greater degree: *Tom is tall but Mary is ~ taller/is taller ~. That would be better ~/be ~ better.* **3** nevertheless; admitting that: *He has treated you badly; ~, he's your brother and you ought to help him.*

still³ /stɪl/ *n* [C] apparatus for making liquors (brandy, whisky, etc) by distilling. '*~-room n* house-keeper's storeroom in a large house.

stilt /stɪlt/ *n* (often (*pair of*) *~s*) one of a pair of poles, each with a support for the foot at some distance from the bottom, used to raise the user from the ground: *walk on ~s.*

stilted /'stɪltɪd/ adj (of liter style, talk, behaviour, etc) stiff and unnatural; too formal. ∼·ly adv

Stil·ton /'stɪltən/ n rich, white, creamy cheese with a green-blue mould in it.

stimu·lant /'stɪmjʊlənt/ n [C] drink (eg coffee, brandy), drug, etc that increases bodily or mental activity; sth that spurs one on (eg praise, hope of gain).

stimu·late /'stɪmjʊleɪt/ vt [VP6A,14,17] ∼ sb (to sth/to do sth), excite; rouse; quicken thought or feeling: ∼ sb to further efforts; ∼ sb to make greater efforts. **stimu·lat·ing** adj

stimu·lus /'stɪmjʊləs/ n (pl -li /-laɪ/) [C] sth that stimulates: work harder under the ∼ of praise; a ∼ to further exertions.

sting¹ /stɪŋ/ n 1 [C] sharp, often poisonous, pointed organ of some insects (eg bees, wasps, gnats): The ∼ of a scorpion is in its tail. '∼-ray n broad, flat, tropical fish which can cause severe wounds with its sharp spines. 2 hair projecting from the surface of the leaf of a plant (esp a '∼ing-nettle), which causes pain to the fingers, etc when touched. 3 [C] sharp pain caused by the ∼ of an insect or by nettles, etc; place of a wound made by a ∼: Her face was covered with ∼s. Have you any ointment to put on these ∼s? 4 [C,U] any sharp pain of body or mind: the ∼ of a whip/the northeast wind/hunger/remorse. His service (in tennis) has no ∼ in it, is weak.

sting² /stɪŋ/ vt, vi (pt, pp stung /stʌŋ/) 1 [VP6A,2A] prick or wound with a sting or as with a sting; have the power to ∼: A hornet stung me on the cheek. The blows of the cane stung the boy's fingers. Not all nettles ∼. 2 [VP6A,14,15A] ∼ sb (to/into sth/doing sth), cause sharp pain to; anger: He was stung by his enemy's insults. Anger stung (= roused) him to action/into fighting. 3 [VP2A] (of parts of the body) feel sharp pain: His fingers were still ∼ing from the caning he had had. 4 ∼ sb (for sth), (colloq) charge him an excessive price (for sth); swindle sb: He was stung for £5, had to pay this sum. How much did they ∼ you for? ∼er n (esp) smart, painful blow. ∼·less adj having no ∼.

stingy /'stɪndʒɪ/ adj (-ier, -iest) spending, using or giving unwillingly; niggardly; miserly: Don't be so ∼ with the sugar! **stin·gily** /-dʒɪlɪ/ adv **stin·gi·ness** n

stink /stɪŋk/ vi,vt (pt stank /stæŋk/ or stunk /stʌŋk/, pp stunk) 1 [VP2A,3A] ∼ (of sth), have a horrid and offensive smell: That fish ∼s. Her breath stank of garlic. **cry** ∼ing fish, condemn one's own goods, etc. 2 [VP15B] ∼ sb/sth out, (a) drive out by means of sth evil-smelling: ∼ out a fox, eg by sending smoke into its hole. (b) fill a place with ∼s: You'll ∼ the place out with your cheap cigars! □ n [C] horrid smell. **raise/kick up a** ∼ (about sth), (colloq) cause trouble or annoyance, eg by complaining. ∼er n (sl) 1 letter intended to convey strong disapproval, reproach, etc. 2 person who arouses strong dislike. 3 (colloq) sth difficult: The biology paper (ie in an examination) was a ∼er.

stint /stɪnt/ vt,vi [VP6A,14] ∼ sb (of sth), restrict (sb) to a small allowance: She ∼ed herself of food in order to let the children have enough. Don't ∼ the food. □ n 1 (usu) without ∼, without limit, without sparing any effort. 2 [C] fixed or allotted amount (of work): do one's daily ∼.

sti·pend /'staɪpend/ n [C] (esp clergyman's) salary.

sti·pen·di·ary /staɪ'pendɪərɪ US: -dɪerɪ/ adj receiving a ∼, not working without pay: a ∼iary magistrate, paid magistrate in a large town (appointed by the Home Secretary) dealing with police court cases. □ n (pl -ries) ∼iary magistrate.

stipple /'stɪpl/ vt [VP6A] draw or paint with dots instead of lines.

stipu·late /'stɪpjʊleɪt/ vt,vi 1 [VP6A,9] state, put forward, as a necessary condition: It was ∼d that the goods should be delivered within three days. 2 [VP3A] ∼ for sth, insist upon (as part of an agreement): ∼ for the best materials to be used. **stipu·la·tion** /ˌstɪpjʊ'leɪʃn/ n [C] sth ∼d; condition: on the stipulation that....

stir /stɜ:(r)/ vi,vt (-rr-) 1 [VP6A,2A,C] be moving; cause to move: Not a leaf was ∼ring, There was no wind to move the leaves. A breeze ∼red the leaves. Nobody was ∼ring in the house, Everyone was resting. She is not ∼ring yet/has not ∼red yet, is still in bed. You had better ∼ yourself, get busy, be active. I haven't ∼red out all morning, haven't left the house. **not** ∼ **an eyelid**, remain unmoved, showing no alarm or concern. **not** ∼ **a finger**, make no effort to do things; give no help. ∼ **one's stumps**, (colloq) make haste, walk faster. 2 [VP6A,15B] ∼ sth (up), move a spoon, etc round and round in liquid, etc in order to mix it thoroughly: ∼ one's tea; ∼ the porridge; ∼ milk into a cake mixture. ∼ the fire, use the poker in it. 3 [VP6A,14,15B] ∼ sb to sth; ∼ sth (up), excite: The story ∼red the boy's imagination. Discontented men ∼red the crew to mutiny/∼ed up trouble among the crew. He wants ∼ring up, needs to be roused from lethargy. ∼ the blood, rouse to excitement or enthusiasm. 4 [VP2A,C] be roused: Pity ∼red in his heart. □ n (usu a ∼) commotion; excitement: The news caused quite a ∼ in the village. ∼·ring adj exciting: ∼ring tales of adventure; live in ∼ring times. ∼·ring·ly adv

stir·rup¹ /'stɪrəp/ n [C] foot-rest, hanging down from a saddle, for the rider of a horse. ⇨ the illus at harness. '∼-cup n drink (of wine, etc) offered to sb mounted on a horse ready for departure.

stir·rup² /'stɪrəp/ n (anat) bone in the ear. ⇨ the illus at ear.

stitch /stɪtʃ/ n 1 [C] (in sewing) the passing of a needle and thread in and out of cloth, etc; (in knitting) one complete turn of the wool, etc over the needle. 2 the thread, etc seen between two consecutive holes made by a needle; result of a single movement with a threaded needle, knitting-needle, etc: make long/neat, etc ∼es; put a few ∼es in a garment; drop a ∼, allow a loop to slip off the end of a knitting-needle; put ∼es into/take ∼es out of a wound. **have not a** ∼ **on**, (colloq) be naked. **A** ∼ **in time saves nine**, (prov) A small piece of work done now may save a lot of work later. 3 (in compounds) particular kind of ∼: a 'button-hole ∼; a 'chain-∼, etc. 4 (sing only) sharp pain in the side (as caused sometimes by running too soon after a meal). □ vt,vi [VP6A,15A,B,2A,C] sew; put ∼es in or on.

stoat /stəʊt/ n small furry animal larger than a rat; weasel; ermine (in its summer coat of brown).

stock¹ /stɒk/ n 1 [C,U] store or goods available for sale, distribution or use, esp goods kept by a trader or shopkeeper. **(be) in/out of** ∼, be available/not available: The book is in/out of ∼. Have you any linen sheets in ∼? '∼-list n list of goods, etc available. '∼-room n room in which ∼ is kept. **take**

~, examine and make a list of goods in ~; Hence, '~-taking n: The annual ~-taking starts tomorrow, eg in a draper's shop. take ~ of sth/sb, (fig) review (a situation); estimate (sb's abilities, etc). ,~-in-'trade n [U] everything needed for a trade or occupation. 2 (attrib use, from 1 above) usually kept in ~ (and therefore usually obtainable): ~ sizes in hats, commonly or regularly used; hackneyed: ~ arguments/comparisons; ~ questions/ answers. She's tired of her husband's ~ jokes. ~ company, company of actors who have a ~ (or repertoire) of plays which they perform. 3 [C,U] supply of anything: a good ~ of information; get in ~s of coal and coke for the winter. '~-piling n purchase (esp by a Government) of ~s of raw materials or goods not easily available from local sources (eg tin, rubber, needed in war). 4 [U] ('live-)~, farm animals: 'fat ~, ~ fit for slaughter as food: fat~ prices. '~-breeder/farmer n farmer who breeds or raises cattle. '~-car n (US) railway truck for carrying cattle. '~-car racing n racing of ordinary models of motor-cars as sold generally. '~-yard n enclosure where cattle are kept temporarily, eg at a market, or before being slaughtered. 5 [C,U] money lent to a government in return for interest; shares in the capital of a business company: have £5000 in the ~s; invest one's money in (a) safe ~. '~-broker n man whose business is the buying and selling of ~(s). '~ ex-change n place where ~s and shares are publicly bought and sold. '~-holder n (chiefly US) shareholder. '~-jobber n member of a ~ exchange from whom a ~broker buys and to whom he sells. '~-list n publication with current prices of ~s(5) and shares. 6 [U] line of ancestry: a woman of Irish ~/of Puritan/farming, etc ~. 7 ~s and stones, lifeless things. ,~-'still adv motionless. 'laughing-~, target or object of ridicule. 8 [U] raw material ready for manufacture: 'paper ~, eg rags, etc to be made into paper. 9 [U] liquid in which bones, etc have been stewed; juices of meat and vegetables, used for making soup, gravy, etc. '~-cube n cube of dehydrated ~. '~-fish n fish (esp cod) split open and dried in the air without salt, a staple food in some countries. '~-pot n one in which ~(9) is made or stored. 10 [C] base, support, or handle of an instrument, tool, etc: the ~ of a rifle/plough/whip; the ~ of an anchor, the crossbar. lock, ~ and barrel, (fig) completely. 11 [C] lower part of a tree trunk. 12 [C] growing plant into which a graft is inserted. 13 (pl) framework supporting a ship while it is being built or repaired. on the ~s, under construction; in preparation. 14 (pl) wooden framework with holes for the feet in which wrongdoers were formerly locked in a sitting position. 15 [C] wide band of stiff linen worn around the neck by men in former times (like the modern tie). 16 sort of garden plant with single or double brightly coloured sweet-smelling flowers.

stock² /stɒk/ vt [VP6A,14] ~ (with), supply or equip with; have a stock of; keep in stock: ~ a shop with goods; well ~ed with the latest fashions. Do you ~ raincoats? He has a memory well ~ed with facts. ~-ist /-ɪst/ n one who ~s (certain goods) for sale.

stock·ade /stɒ'keɪd/ n [C] line or wall of upright stakes, built as a defence. □ vt (usu pp) defend with a ~.

stock·in·ette /,stɒkɪ'net/ n [U] elastic machine-made knitted fabric (esp as used for underclothing).

stock·ing /'stɒkɪŋ/ n [C] (often (pair of) ~s) tight-fitting covering of nylon, silk, cotton, wool, etc for the foot and leg, reaching to or above the knee. in one's ~ feet, wearing ~s or socks but not shoes. ⇨ tights.

stocky /'stɒkɪ/ adj (-ier, -iest) (of persons, animals, plants) short, strong and stout. stock·ily adv in a ~ manner: a stockily built man.

stodge /stɒdʒ/ n [U] (sl) heavy and solid food. stodgy /'stɒdʒɪ/ adj 1 (of food) heavy and solid: a stodgy meal. 2 (of books, etc) written in a heavy, uninteresting way (overweighted with facts, details, etc); (of persons) having a heavy personality; dull and unenterprising.

stoep /stʊp/ n (S Africa) terraced veranda; porch or steps outside the front entrance of a house.

stoic /'stəʊɪk/ n person who has great self-control, who bears pain and discomfort without complaint. sto·ical /-kl/ adj of or like a ~. sto·ically /-klɪ/ adv sto·icism /'stəʊɪsɪzəm/ n [U] patient and uncomplaining endurance of suffering, etc.

stoke /stəʊk/ vt,vi [VP6A,15B,2A,C] ~ (sth) (up), put (coal, etc) on the fire of (an engine, furnace, etc); attend to a furnace: ~ (up) the furnace; ~ (up) twice a day. '~-hole/-hold nn place where a ship's furnaces are ~d. ~r n workman who ~s a furnace, etc; mechanical device for feeding a furnace with fuel.

stole¹ /stəʊl/ n 1 strip of silk or other material worn (round the neck with the ends hanging down in front) by priests of some Christian Churches during services. ⇨ the illus at vestment. 2 woman's wrap worn over the shoulders.

stole², stolen pt,pp of steal.

stolid /'stɒlɪd/ adj not easily excited; slow to show the feelings. ~·ly adv, ~·ness, sto·lid·ity /stɒ'lɪdɪtɪ/ nn [U].

stom·ach /'stʌmək/ n 1 [C] bag-like part of the alimentary canal into which food passes to be digested: It is unwise to swim on a full ~/to work on an empty ~. ⇨ the illus at alimentary. '~-ache n pain in the ~ or the bowels. '~-pump n pump with a flexible tube, inserted into the ~ through the mouth (for use, eg in a case of poisoning). 2 [U] appetite. have no ~ for sth, be disinclined to do or agree with sth, (because one disapproves of it): have no ~ for bull-fighting. □ vt [VP6A] (usu neg or interr) endure; put up with: How could you ~ the violence in that film?

stomp /stɒmp/ vi [VP2C] ~ about, stamp, tread, heavily. □ n (jazz music for a) dance with a heavy beat.

stone /stəʊn/ n 1 [U] (often attrib) solid mineral matter which is not metallic; rock (often with a defining word as prefix, as 'sand~, 'lime~): a wall made of ~; ~ walls/buildings; ~ jars, made of '~ware, ⇨ below; have a heart of ~, (fig) be hard-hearted. the 'S~ Age, period of culture when weapons and tools were made of ~ (before the use of metals was known). ~-'blind/-'cold/-'dead/-'deaf/-'sober adjj completely blind, etc. '~-breaker n person who breaks up ~, esp for road-making; machine for crushing ~. '~-mason n man who cuts, prepares and builds with ~. '~-pit n quarry for ~. ,~-'wall vt (cricket) be excessively cautious when batting so that runs come slowly; (fig) (in Parliament) obstruct progress by making long speeches, etc. Hence, ,~-'walling n. ,~-'waller n person given to this. '~-ware n [U] pottery made from clay and flint. '~-work n [U] masonry; part(s) of a building made of ∾. 2 [C] piece of ∾(1) of any shape, usu broken off: *a road covered with* ∾*s; a fall of* ∾*s down a hillside.* **leave no** ∾ **unturned (to do sth),** try every possible means (to do it). **throw** ∾*s at,* (fig) attack the character of: *Those who live in glass houses should not throw* ∾*s,* (prov) If your own character is not beyond reproach you should not attack the character of others. **within a'**∾**'s throw (of),** very close (to). 3 [C] **(precious)** ∾, jewel. 4 [C] piece of ∾ of a definite shape, for a special purpose (usu in compounds): *a* '*grave*∾, ⇨ grave²; '*stepping*-∾*s,* ⇨ step¹; '*tomb*∾*s,* ⇨ tomb; '*mill*∾*s,* ⇨ mill¹. 5 [C] sth round and hard like a ∾, esp **(a)** the hard shell and nut or seed of such fruits as the apricot, peach, plum and cherry. ⇨ the illus at fruit. '∾-**fruit** *n* fruits of this kind. **(b)** (usu '**hail**∾) small frozen drop of rain: *hail with* ∾*s as big as peas.* **(c)** small hard object that has formed in the bladder or kidney: *have an operation for* ∾. '**gall**∾, ⇨ gall¹(1). 6 (not US; *pl* unchanged) unit of weight, 14 lb: *two* ∾ *of flour.* □ *vt* 1 [VP6A,15A] throw ∾s at: *Christian martyrs who were* ∾*d to death.* 2 [VP6A] take the ∾s(5a) out of (fruit): ∾*d dates.* ∾-**less** *adj* (esp of ∾-fruit, ⇨ 5(a) above) without ∾s. **stoned** *adj* (colloq) under the influence of (usu) soft drugs; very drunk.

stony /'stəʊnɪ/ *adj* (-ier, -iest) 1 having many stones: ∾ *soil/ground;* covered with stones: *a* ∾ *path/road.* 2 hard, cold and unsympathetic: *a* ∾ *heart;* ∾-'*hearted; a* ∾ *stare;* ∾ *politeness.* 3 (sl) ∾(-'**broke**), completely without money; penniless. **ston·ily** /-ɪlɪ/ *adv* in a ∾(2) manner: *stonily polite.*

stood /stʊd/ *pt,pp* of stand².

stooge /stuːdʒ/ *n* person who, in variety entertainment, is made fun of by a comedian; (colloq) person used as an assistant (to perform unpleasant jobs or duties that may incur blame, punishment, etc). □ *vi* ∾ **for sb,** act as a ∾.

stool /stuːl/ *n* 1 seat without a back or arms, usu for one person: *sitting on* ∾*s at the bar drinking beer; a pi'ano*∾. **fall between two** ∾**s,** lose an opportunity through hesitating between two courses of action. 2 ('**foot**)∾, low support on which to rest the feet. 3 [U] (med) solid excrement: *send a specimen of one's* ∾*s to the doctor,* eg to be tested for amoebic infection. 4 '∾-**pigeon** *n* pigeon used as a decoy; (fig) person acting as a decoy, eg one employed by the police to trap a criminal.

stoop¹ /stuːp/ *vi,vt* 1 [VP2A,C,4A,6A] bend the body forwards and downwards; bend the neck so that the head is forward and down: ∾*ing with old age;* ∾ *to pick sth up;* ∾ *one's head to get into a car.* 2 [VP3A] ∾ **to sth,** (fig) lower oneself morally: ∾ *to folly/cheating. He's a man who would* ∾ *to anything,* who has no moral scruples. □ *n* (usu *sing*) ∾ing position of the body: *walk with a* ∾, as when very old or ill.

stoop² /stuːp/ *n* (in N America) porch or unroofed platform or set of steps at the entrance to a house. ⇨ stoep.

stop¹ /stɒp/ *n* [C] 1 stopping or being stopped: *The train came to a sudden* ∾. *This train goes from London to Leeds with only two* ∾*s.* **put a** ∾ **to sth; bring sth to a** ∾, cause it to ∾ or end: *I'll put a* ∾ *to this nonsense. Traffic was brought to a complete* ∾. 2 place at which buses, trams, etc stop regularly or (*re*'*quest* ∾) when requested to do so: *Where's the nearest* '*bus*-∾? 3 (music) key or

lever (eg in a flute) for regulating pitch; row of pipes (in an organ) providing tones of one quality; knob or lever working such a row of pipes. ⇨ the illus at church, key. **pull out all the** ∾**s,** (fig) appeal to all the emotions; make a great effort. 4 mark of punctuation, esp *full* ∾ (·). 5 (in a camera) device for regulating the size of the aperture through which light reaches the lens. 6 (in phonetics) consonant produced by the sudden release of air which has been held back (eg /p, b, k, g, t, d/). 7 device that stops the movement of sth at a fixed point, eg a peg of wood to prevent an ill-fitting window from rattling. 8 (compounds) '∾-**cock** *n* valve inserted in a pipe by which the flow of liquid or gas through the pipe can be regulated: *A water-pipe has burst—where's the* ∾*cock?* '∾-**gap** *n* temporary substitute. '∾ **press** *n* [U] (not US) latest news inserted in a newspaper already on the printing machines. '∾-**watch** *n* watch with a hand that can be started and stopped when desired, used to time events such as races to a fraction of a second. ∾-**page** /'stɒpɪdʒ/ *n* [C] 1 state of being stopped up, ⇨ stop²(6); obstruction. 2 stopping(7): ∾*page of leave/pay,* (esp in the armed forces, eg as a form of punishment). 3 interruption of work (in a factory, etc as the result of strike action.) ∾-**per** *n* object which fits into and closes an opening, esp the mouth of a bottle or pipe; (US) plug(1). ⇨ the illus at decanter. **put a** ∾**per/the** ∾**pers on (sth),** (fig) bring it to an end; suppress it.

stop² /stɒp/ *vt,vi* (-pp-) 1 [VP6A] put an end to (the movement or progress of a person, thing, activity, etc: ∾ *a car/a train/a runaway horse. The earthquake* ∾*ped all the clocks.* 2 [VP6A,B,14] ∾ *sb (from) (doing sth),* prevent; hinder: *What can* ∾ *our going/*∾ *us from going if we want to go? Can't you* ∾ *the child (from) getting into mischief? He will certainly go—there's no one to* ∾ *him.* 3 [VP6A,C] leave off; discontinue (doing sth): ∾ *work. We* ∾*ped talking. Why doesn't he* ∾ *beating his wife?* **S**∾ **it!** (imper) ∾ doing that (sth disliked or disapproved of). 4 [VP2A,3A,4A] ∾ **(at),** break off; discontinue: *The rain has* ∾*ped. The clock/His heart has* ∾*ped. It has* ∾*ped raining. We* ∾*ped to have a rest. We* ∾*ped (in order) to talk.* Cf *We* ∾*ped talking.* 5 [VP2A,3A,4A] ∾ **(at),** come to rest; halt: *The train* ∾*ped. Does this train* ∾ *at Crewe?* ∾ *dead,* ∾ suddenly. ∾ **short at sth,** limit one's actions, etc: *Will our neighbours* ∾ *short at war?* 6 [VP6A,15A,B] ∾ **sth (up),** fill or close (a hole, opening, etc): ∾ *a leak in a pipe;* ∾ *up a mouse-hole; have a tooth* ∾*ped,* have a cavity filled; ∾ *one's ears,* (fig) refuse to listen; ∾ *the way,* prevent progress. 7 [VP6A,14] cut off; keep back or refuse to give (sth normally supplied): ∾ *(payment of) a cheque,* order the bank not to cash it; ∾ *sb's wages. The bank has* ∾*ped payment,* is unable to meet its obligations. ∾ **sth out of sth,** deduct sth from (wages, salary, etc). 8 [VP2A,B,C] (colloq) stay: ∾ *at home. Are you* ∾*ping at this hotel?* ∾ **off (at/in),** break a journey for a short period: ∾ *off at a store to buy sth.* ∾ **off/over (at/in),** break a journey for a stay: ∾ *off overnight in Edinburgh.* '∾-**over** *n* [C] break in a journey; place where one does this; (attrib): '∾-*over ticket,* one that permits a journey to be broken in this way. ∾ **up (late),** stay up, not go to bed until late. 9 (music) produce desired note(s) by pressing fingers on strings (eg of a violin), or over holes (eg in a flute). **~·ping** *n* filling for a dental cavity. ⇨ 6 above.

stor·age /'stɔ:rɪdʒ/ *n* [U] (space used for, money paid for) the storing of goods: *put one's furniture in ~; keep fish in cold ~;* (attrib) '~ *tanks,* eg for oil; '~ *heater,* electric radiator which stores heat (accumulated during off-peak periods).

store /stɔ:(r)/ *n* **1** [C] quantity or supply of sth kept for use as needed: *lay in ~s of coal for the winter; have a good ~ of provisions in the house.* **2** [U] *in ~,* (a) kept ready for use; for future use: *That's a treat in ~,* a pleasure still to come. (b) destined (*for*); coming to: *Who knows what the future has in ~ for us?* **3** (*pl*) goods, etc of a particular kind, or for a special purpose: *naval and military ~s; marine ~s* (but note: ,*marine-'~ dealer*). **4** [C] '~(*-house*), place where goods are kept; warehouse: *The book is a ~-house of information.* '~·**room** *n* one in which household supplies are kept. **5** [C] (chiefly US but ⇨ 6 below) shop: *a 'clothing ~; ~ clothes,* bought from a ~, ready to wear, not tailor-made. **6** (*pl*) shop selling many varieties of goods: *the big department ~s of London; the ,Army and 'Navy S~s; a general ~s,* (esp) village shop selling a variety of goods. ⇨ also *chain-~* at chain(4). **7** [U] *set great/little/no/not much ~ by,* consider of great/little, etc value or importance. □ *vt* [VP6A,15B] ~ *sth (up),* **1** collect and keep for future use: *Do all squirrels ~ up food for the winter?* **2** put (furniture, etc) in a warehouse, etc, for safe keeping. **3** furnish, equip, supply: *a mind well ~d with facts.*

storey (US = story) /'stɔ:rɪ/ *n* (*pl* ~s, (US) -ries) floor or level in a building: *a house of two ~s,* ie with rooms on the ground floor and one floor upstairs. **-storeyed** (US = **stor·ied**) /-'stɔ:rɪd/ *adj* having the number of ~s indicated by the prefixed number: *a six-~ed building.*

stor·ied /'stɔ:rɪd/ *adj* (liter) made famous in legend or stories: *the ~ Rhine.*

stork /stɔ:k/ *n* large, long-legged, usu white wading-bird (some of which build their nests on the tops of high buildings). ⇨ the illus at water.

storm /stɔ:m/ *n* **1** [C] occasion of violent weather conditions: *a 'thunder-/'wind-/'rain-/'dust-/'sand-~; cross the Channel in a ~. The forecast says there will be ~s. a ~ in a teacup,* much excitement about sth trivial. '~-**beaten** *adj* damaged by ~s. '~-**bound** *adj* unable to continue a journey, voyage, etc unable to go out, because of ~s. '~-**centre** *n* centre of a ~ or (fig) of a disturbance or trouble. '~-**cloud** *n* heavy rain-cloud accompanying, or showing the likelihood of, a ~. '~-**cone**/-**signal** *n* one hoisted as a warning of high wind. '~-**lantern** *n* one for use outdoors, made so that the light is well protected from wind. '~-**proof** *adj* able to resist ~s. '~-**tossed** *adj* damaged or blown about by ~s. **2** violent outburst of feeling: *a ~ of protests/cheering/applause/abuse. bring a '~ about one's ears,* do or say sth that rouses strong opposition, indignation, etc. **3** *take by ~,* capture by a violent and sudden attack. '~-**troops** *n pl* troops trained for violent attacks. '~-**trooper** *n* one of these. □ *vi,vt* **1** [VP2A,3A] ~ (*at*), give violent expression to anger; shout angrily. **2** [VP15A,B,2C] force (a way) into a building, etc; [VP6A] capture (a place) by sudden and violent attack: *The men ~ed (their way) into the fort/~ed the fort.* ~·**y** *adj* (-ier, -iest) **1** marked by strong wind, heavy rain or snow or hail: *~y weather; a*

~*y night/crossing.* **2** marked by strong feelings of indignation, anger, etc: *a ~y discussion/meeting; ~y scenes during the debate.* ~·**ily** /-ɪlɪ/ *adv*

story[1] /'stɔ:rɪ/ *n* [C] (*pl* -ries) **1** account of past events: *the ~ of Columbus; stories of ancient Greece.* **2** account of imaginary events: *a 'ghost ~; a children's '~-book; a ~-book ending,* a happy one (as in most stories for children). *The ~ goes that...,* People are saying that.... '~-**teller** *n* person who tells stories. **3** (journalism) any descriptive article in a newspaper; an event, situation, etc suitable for such an article. **4** untrue statement: *Don't tell stories, Tom.*

story[2] /'stɔ:rɪ/ *n* ⇨ storey.

stoup /stu:p/ *n* **1** (old use) drinking-vessel; flagon. **2** stone basin for holy water on the wall of a church or near the porch.

stout /staʊt/ *adj* **1** strong, thick, not easily broken or worn out: *~ shoes for mountain-climbing.* **2** determined and brave: *offer a ~ resistance to the enemy; a ~ fellow; a ~ heart.* Hence, ,~-**'hearted** *adj* courageous. **3** (of a person) rather fat; tending to fatness: *She's growing too ~ to walk far.* □ *n* [U] strongest kind of dark beer. ~·**ly** *adv* ~·**ness** *n*

stove[1] /staʊv/ *n* [C] closed apparatus burning wood, coal, gas, oil or other fuel, used for warming rooms, cooking, etc. '~-**pipe** *n* pipe for carrying off smoke from a ~.

stove[2] /staʊv/ ⇨ stave[2].

stow /staʊ/ *vt* [VP6A,15A,B] ~ *sth (away); ~ sth into/with sth,* pack, esp carefully and closely: *~ cargo in a ship's holds; ~ things away in the attic; ~ clothes into a trunk/~ a trunk with clothes.* '~-**away** *n* person who hides himself in a ship or aircraft (at least until after it starts) in order to make a journey without paying.

straddle /'strædl/ *vt,vi* **1** [VP6A] sit or stand across (sth) with the legs widely separated: *~ a ditch/a seat/a horse/a fence.* **2** [VP2A] stand with the legs wide apart.

strafe /strɑ:f US: streɪf/ *vt* [VP6A] (colloq) **1** bombard. **2** punish; scold.

straggle /'strægl/ *vi* [VP2A,C] **1** grow, spread, in an irregular or untidy manner: *a straggling village; vines straggling over the fences.* **2** drop behind while on the march; stray from the main body. **strag·gler** /'stræglə(r)/ *n* person who ~s(2). **strag·gly** /'stræglɪ/ *adj* straggling.

straight[1] /streɪt/ *adj* **1** without a bend or curve; tending in one direction only: *a ~ line/road; ~ hair,* with no curls in it. **2** parallel to (sth else, esp the horizon); level: *Put the picture ~. Is my hat on ~? 3* in good order; tidy: *put a room ~. put sth ~,* make it tidy: *Please put your desk ~ before you leave the office. put the record ~,* give an accurate account of events, etc. **4** (of a person, his behaviour, etc) honest, frank, upright: *give a ~ answer to a question,* answer frankly; *keep ~,* avoid wrongdoing, live as a good citizen. *He is perfectly ~ in all his dealings. His wife will keep him ~* (= help him to live honestly) *when he is released from prison.* ⇨ straight[2](4). **5** (colloq) (of a person) conventional; heterosexual. **6** (phrases) **a ~ fight,** (in politics) one in which there are only two candidates. **a ~ play,** an ordinary drama (contrasted with variety). **a ~ tip,** (eg about the likely winner of a race, an investment in shares), one (said to come) from a direct and reliable source. *keep a ~ face,* refrain from smiling or laughing. *vote the* ~ *ticket,* ⇨ ticket(3). **7** (of alcoholic drinks) neat, ie without added(soda-) water, etc: *Two* ~ *whiskies, please.* □ *n* [C] (colloq) conventional or heterosexual person. ~**en** /'streɪtn/ *vt,vi* ~**en** *(out/up),* [VP6A,15B,2A,C] make or become ~: ~*en a piece of wire/one's tie/one's skirt.* ~**ness** *n*

straight² /streɪt/ *adv* **1** directly; not in a curve or at an angle: *The smoke rose* ~ *up. Keep* ~ *on. Look* ~ *ahead. The drunken man couldn't walk* ~. *Can you shoot* ~, aim accurately? **2** by a direct route; without turning aside; without delay: *Come* ~ *home. He went* ~ *to Rome without staying in Paris. He went* ~ *from school into the navy.* **come** ~ *to the point,* make a prompt and clear statement of what is meant, wanted, etc. **3** ~ *away/ off,* immediately. ~ *out,* without hesitation or deliberation: *I told him* ~ *out that I thought he was mistaken.* **4** *go* ~, (fig) live an honest life (esp after having been dishonest).

straight³ /streɪt/ *n* (usu **the** ~) condition of being straight; straight part of sth, esp the final part of a track or race-course, near the winning-post: *The two horses were together as they entered the final* ~.

straight·for·ward /ˌstreɪt'fɔːwəd/ *adj* **1** honest; without evasion: *a* ~ *explanation.* **2** easy to understand or do: *written in* ~ *language; a* ~ *problem in algebra.* ~**·ly** *adv*

straight·way /ˌstreɪt'weɪ/ *adv* (archaic) at once; immediately.

strain¹ /streɪn/ *n* **1** [C,U] condition of being stretched; force exerted: *The rope broke under the* ~. *Engineers calculate the* ~*s and stresses of a bridge. What is the breaking* ~ *of this cable, the* ~ *that will break it?* **2** [C,U] sth that tests and strains one's powers; severe demand on one's strength, etc: *the* ~ *of sleepless nights. The payment of the lawyer's bills was a great* ~ *on my resources. Do you suffer from the* ~ *of modern life? He has been under severe* ~. **3** [U] exhaustion; fatigue: *suffering from mental/nervous* ~. **4** [C] sprain; injury caused by twisting a joint, etc. **5** (poet; usu *pl*) music, song, verse (of the kind indicated): *the* ~*s of an organ; the martial* ~*s of the band of the Royal Marines.* **6** [C] manner of speaking or writing: *in a lofty/cheerful/dismal* ~; *and much more in the same* ~, the same general tendency. **7** tendency in a person's character: *There is a* ~ *of insanity in the family/of mysticism in her.* **8** breed (of animals, insects, etc); line of descent: ~*s of mosquitoes that are resistant to DDT; a spaniel of good* ~.

strain² /streɪn/ *vt,vi* **1** [VP6A,15A] stretch tightly by pulling (*at*): ~ *a rope to breaking-point; a dog* ~*ing at its lead.* **2** [VP6A,16A] make the greatest possible use of; exert one's powers: ~ *every nerve* (*to do sth*), do one's utmost; ~ *one's eyes/ears/ voice,* look/listen/speak to the best of one's power. ⇨ **3** below. **3** [VP6A] injure or weaken by ~*ing*(2): ~ *a muscle;* ~ *one's heart,* injure it by over-exertion; ~ *one's eyes,* by using them too much, or on small print, in poor light, etc; ~ *one's voice,* by speaking or singing too long or too loudly. **4** [VP2A,3A] ~ *(at/on),* make an intense effort; *The wrestlers* ~*ed and struggled. We* ~*ed at the oars.* ~ *after effects,* make exaggerated efforts to get effects: *There is no* ~*ing after effects in this writer's work.* **5** [VP6A] (fig) stretch the meaning of: force beyond a limit or what is right: ~ *the belief/ credulity of one's listeners;* ask too much of it; ~

one's authority/rights, apply them in a way that is beyond what is allowable or reasonable; ~ *the meaning of a word.* **6** [VP15A] (liter) hold tightly; squeeze: *She* ~*ed the boy to her bosom.* **7** [VP6A,15B] ~ *(off/out),* pass (liquid) through a cloth, or a network of fine wire, etc; separate solid matter in this way: ~ *the soup;* ~ *off the water from the vegetables.* **8** ~ *at sth,* be too scrupulous or hesitant about accepting sth. **9** ~*ed* (*pp*) (esp of feelings and behaviour) forced; unnatural; as if forced: ~*ed cordiality; a* ~*ed laugh.* ~**ed relations,** marked by loss of patience, irritability, risk of quarrelling. ~**er** *n* sieve or other device by means of which solid matter is separated from liquid: *a 'tea~er,* for keeping back tea-leaves when tea is poured out from a teapot.

strait¹ /streɪt/ *adj* (old use) narrow (rare except in: ~ *gate,* ⇨ Matt 7: 14). '~**·jacket,** long-sleeved jacket used to bind the arms of a mentally ill person to the body and prevent him from struggling; (fig) sth that prevents growth or development. ~- '**laced** *adj* severely virtuous; having a strict attitude towards moral questions; puritanical. ~**en** /'streɪtn/ *vt* (usu in *pp*) *in* ~*ed circumstances,* in poverty.

strait² /streɪt/ *n* **1** narrow passage of water connecting two seas or two large bodies of water (*pl* or *sing* with proper names): *the S~s of Gibraltar; the Magellan S~.* **2** (usu *pl*) trouble; difficulty: *be in financial* ~*s; in great* ~*s.*

strand¹ /strænd/ *n* (poet or rhet) sandy shore of a lake, sea or river. □ *vi,vt* **1** [VP6A,2A] (of a ship) (cause to) run aground. **2** *be (left)* ~*ed,* (of a person) be left without means of transport, in a difficult position, without money or friends: *be* ~*ed in a foreign country.*

strand² /strænd/ *n* [C] **1** any of the threads, hairs, wires, etc twisted together into a rope or cable, or in a textile material; tress of hair. **2** (fig) line of development (in a story, etc): *May I pick out one* ~ *in that narrative?*

strange /streɪndʒ/ *adj* (-r, -st) **1** not previously known, seen, felt or heard of; (for this reason) surprising: *hear a* ~ *noise; in a* ~ *land. What* ~ (= unusual) *clothes you're wearing! Truth is* ~*r than fiction. She says she feels* ~, not in her usual condition, perhaps rather dizzy, etc. ~ *to say...,* It is surprising that.... **2** (*pred*) ~ *to sth,* fresh or unaccustomed to: *The village boy was* ~ *to city life. He is still* ~ *to the work,* has not yet learnt his new job. ~**·ly** *adv* ~**·ness** *n*

stran·ger /'streɪndʒə(r)/ *n* person one does not know; person in a place or in company that he does not know: *The dog always barks at* ~*s. You're quite a* ~, (colloq) It's a long time since we met. *I am a* ~ *in this town,* do not know my way about. *He is no* ~ *to misfortune,* (fig) has had experience of it.

strangle /'stræŋgl/ *vt* [VP6A] kill by squeezing the throat of; hinder the breathing of: *This stiff collar is strangling me,* is so tight that it squeezes my neck. '~**·hold** *n* (usu fig) deadly grip: *The new tariffs have put a* ~*hold on our trade with them.* **stran·gu·la·tion** /ˌstræŋgjʊ'leɪʃn/ *n* [U] strangling or being ~d.

strap /stræp/ *n* strip of leather or other flexible material (often with a buckle) to fasten things together or to keep sth (eg a wrist-watch) in place. '~**·hanger** *n* standing passenger in a bus, train, etc who holds on to a ~ with a loop (hanging from the roof) when all the seats are occupied. □ *vt* (-pp-) **1** [VP6A,15B] ~ *sth (on/up),* fasten or hold in place with a ~: ~ *on a wrist-watch;* ~ *up a suitcase,* using ~s and buckles. **2** beat with a ~. ~·**ping** *adj* big, tall, healthy-looking: *a* ~*ping girl.*

strata /'strɑːtə *US:* 'streɪtə/ *pl* of stratum.

strat·agem /'strætədʒəm/ *n* [C,U] (use of a) trick or device to deceive sb (esp the enemy in war).

stra·tegic /strə'tiːdʒɪk/, **stra·tegi·cal** /-kl/ *adj* of, by, serving the purpose of, strategy: *a* ~ *retreat; a* ~ *link in a line of defence;* ~ *bombing,* eg of industrial areas and communications; ~ *materials,* those essential for war. **stra·tegi·cally** /-klɪ/ *adv* **stra·tegics** *n* [U] science or art of strategy.

strat·egy /'strætədʒɪ/ *n* [U] the art of planning operations in war, esp of the movements of armies and navies into favourable positions for fighting; skill in managing any affair. ⇨ tactic(2). **strat·egist** /-dʒɪst/ *n* person skilled in ~.

strat·ify /'strætɪfaɪ/ *vt,vi* (*pt,pp* -fied) **1** [VP6A] arrange in strata: *stratified rock. English society is highly stratified.* **2** [VP2A] form into strata. **strat·ifi·ca·tion** /ˌstrætɪfɪ'keɪʃn/ *n* arrangement in strata.

stratified rock

strato·sphere /'strætəsfɪə(r)/ *n* layer of atmospheric air between about 10 and 60 km above the earth's surface.

stra·tum /'strɑːtəm *US:* 'streɪtəm/ *n* (*pl* -ta /-tə/) horizontal layer of rock, etc in the earth's crust; social class or division: *Students in Britain come from various strata in society.*

straw /strɔː/ *n* **1** [U] dry cut stalks of wheat, barley, rice and other grains, as material for making hats, mats, etc or bedding for cattle, or thatching roofs, etc: *a* ~ *mattress,* one stuffed with ~. **make bricks without** ~, make sth without all the necessary materials. ⇨ Exod 5: 7. *a man of* ~, imaginary person, easily overcome, set up as an opponent. '~·**board** *n* [U] coarse cardboard made of ~ pulp. '~·**coloured** *adj* pale yellow. **2** [C] single stalk or piece of ~; thin tube of other material for sucking up liquid: *suck lemonade through a* ~. **catch at a** ~; **clutch at** ~s, try any expedient, however useless (like a drowning man clutching at a ~). **not care a** ~, not at all. **not worth a** ~, worth nothing. *a* ~ *in the wind,* a slight hint that shows which way things may develop; hence, a ~ **vote,** attempt to discover public opinion on a topic of current interest by an unofficial poll (eg as made by a newspaper). **the last** ~, an addition to a task, burden, etc, that makes it intolerable. □ *vt* spread ~ on; cover with ~.

straw·berry /'strɔːbrɪ *US:* -berɪ/ *n* (*pl* -ries) [C] (perennial, low-growing plant having) juicy red fruit with tiny yellow seeds on its surface, eaten raw and in jam. ⇨ the illus at fruit. '~ **mark,** reddish birthmark on the skin.

stray /streɪ/ *vi* (*pt,pp* ~ed) [VP2A,C] wander (from the right path, from one's companions, etc); lose one's way: *Don't* ~ *from the point.* □ *n* **1** ~ed animal or person (esp a child). **waifs and** ~s, homeless children. **2** (attrib) having ~ed: ~ *cats and dogs; killed by a* ~ *bullet,* killed by chance, not purposely; occasional; seen or happening occasionally: *The streets were empty except for a few* ~ *taxis.*

streak /striːk/ *n* [C] **1** long, thin, usu irregular line or band: ~*s of lean and fat,* eg in meat; *like a* ~ *of lightning,* very fast. **2** trace or touch (*of*): *There's a* ~ *of vanity/cruelty in his character.* **3** brief period: *The gambler had a* ~ *of good luck,* won for a time. **hit a winning** ~, have a series of successes (in gambling, etc). □ *vt,vi* [VP6A,15A] **1** mark with ~s: *white marble* ~*ed with brown.* **2** [VP2C] (colloq) move very fast (like a ~ of lightning): *The children* ~*ed off as fast as they could.* ~**y** *adj* (-ier, -iest) marked with, having, ~s: ~*y bacon,* with ~s of fat and lean in it.

stream /striːm/ *n* **1** river or brook; current. **go up/down** ~, move up/down the river. **go with the** ~, (fig) do or think as the majority of people do, be carried along by the course of events. **2** steady flow (of liquid, persons, things, etc): *a* ~ *of blood/curses. S*~*s of people were coming out of the railway station.* ~ **of consciousness,** continuous conscious experience of an individual; (in literature) technique of writing novels to indicate this, eg as in James Joyce's *Ulysses.* **3** (education) (division of a) class of children in age groups according to ability and intelligence: *bright boys and girls in the* 'A-*stream.* □ *vi* **1** [VP2A,C] flow freely; move continuously and smoothly in one direction: *Sweat was* ~*ing down his face. His face was* ~*ing with sweat.* **2** [VP2C] float or wave (in the wind): *The flag/Her long hair* ~*ed in the wind.* **3** [VP6A] place (children) in ~s(3). ~**er** *n* **1** long narrow flag; long narrow ribbon of paper. ~**er headline,** (US) = banner headline. ⇨ banner. **2** column of light shooting out in the aurora. ~·**let** /-lɪt/ *n* small ~ or brook.

stream·line /'striːmlaɪn/ *vt* make more efficient (by simplifying, getting rid of, wasteful methods, etc); ~ *production,* eg in a factory. '~**d** *adj* (a) having a shape that offers least resistance to the flow of air, water, etc: ~*d cars.* (b) having nothing likely to impede progress: ~*d controls/methods.*

street /striːt/ *n* town or village road with houses on one side or both: *meet a friend in the* ~; *cross the* ~; *a* '~-*map/-plan of York.* Cf *a road-map of Yorkshire.* '~-**car** *n* (esp US) tram-car. ~ **door** *n* door which opens (usu directly) on to the ~. (If there is a garden *front door* is preferred). **the man in the** ~, typical citizen. **not in the same** ~ **(as),** not nearly so good (as). ~**s ahead of,** (colloq) far ahead of. **(right) up one's** ~, (colloq) within one's area of knowledge, interests, etc. **go on the** ~**s,** earn one's living by prostitution. '~-**girl,** '~-**walker** *nn* prostitute.

strength /streŋθ/ *n* [U] **1** quality of being strong: *a man/horse of great* ~; *the* ~ *of a rope,* its ability to resist strain; *the* ~ *of our army; get back one's health and* ~ *after an illness. She hasn't the* ~/ *hasn't* ~ *enough to walk upstairs. How is the* ~ *of alcoholic liquors measured?* **on the** ~ **of,** encouraged by, relying upon: *I employed the boy on the* ~ *of your recommendation.* **2** that which helps to make sb or sth strong: *God is our* ~. **3** power measured by numbers of persons present or persons who can be used: *The enemy were in (great)* ∼, *Their numbers were great. The police force is 500 below* ∼, needs 500 more men. **bring sth/be up to** ∼, reach/be the required number: *We must bring the police force up to* ∼. ∼**en** /'streŋθn/ *vt,vi* [VP6A,2A] make or become strong(er).

strenu·ous /'strenjʊəs/ *adj* using or needing great effort; energetic: ∼ *work;* ∼ *workers; make* ∼ *efforts; lead a* ∼ *life.* ∼·**ly** *adv* ∼·**ness** *n*

strep·to·coc·cus /ˌstreptə'kɒkəs/ *n* (*pl* -cocci /-'kɒkaɪ/) any of a group of bacteria which causes serious infections and illnesses.

strep·to·my·cin /ˌstreptə'maɪsɪn/ *n* antibiotic medical preparation.

stress /stres/ *n* **1** [U] pressure; condition causing hardship, disquiet, etc: *times of* ∼, of trouble and danger; *driven into harbour by* ∼ *of weather; under the* ∼ *of poverty/fear/excitement.* **2** [U] (also with *indef art*) weight or force: *a school that lays (a)* ∼ *on foreign languages.* **3** [C,U] (result of) extra force, used in speaking, on a particular word or syllable: *In 'strategic' the* ∼ *is on the second syllable. S*∼ *and rhythm are important in speaking English. You must learn where to place the* ∼*es.* '∼-**mark** *n* mark (eg ' (principal or main ∼) and , (secondary ∼) as used in this dictionary) that indicates the ∼ on a syllable. **4** [C,U] (in mechanics) tension; force exerted between two bodies that touch, or between two parts of one body. □ *vt* [VP6A] put ∼ or emphasis on: *He* ∼*ed the point that....*

stretch /stretʃ/ *vt,vi* **1** [VP6A,15A,B,16A,22] make wider, longer or tighter, by pulling; be or become wider, etc when pulled: ∼ *a rope tight;* ∼ *a rope across a path;* ∼ *a pair of gloves/shoes,* eg to make them fit better; ∼ *one's neck,* eg to see over the heads of people in a crowd; ∼ *one's arms/legs/oneself/one's muscles,* extend the limbs, etc and thus tighten the muscles; ∼ *out one's arm for a book.* ∼ *one's legs,* exercise oneself by walking as a relief from sitting or lying. **2** ∼ *(oneself) out (on),* lie on at full length: *They were* ∼*ed out on the lawn. He* ∼*ed himself out on the beach.* **3** [VP6A] make (a word, law, etc) include or cover more than is strictly right; exert beyond what is right: ∼ *the law/one's principles/a point in sb's favour,* ⇨ point¹(9); strain to the utmost; ∼ *one's powers,* work very hard or too hard. **be fully** ∼**ed,** working to the utmost of one's powers. **4** [VP2A,B,C] extend: *forests* ∼*ing for hundreds of miles; a road* ∼*ing away across the desert.* □ *n* [C] **1** act of ∼ing or being ∼ed: *by a* ∼ *of language/ the law/one's principles.* ⇨ **3** above. *The cat woke and gave a* ∼. *He got up with a* ∼ *and a yawn.* **by 'any/'no** ∼ **of the imagination,** however much one may try to imagine sth. **at full** ∼, fully ∼ed(3): *The factory was/The workers were at full* ∼. **2** unbroken or continuous period of time or extent of country, etc: *a beautiful* ∼ *of wooded country;* (sl) *do a two-year* ∼ *in prison.* **at a** ∼, continuously: *Can you work for six hours at a* ∼? **3** straight side of a track or course (for racing). ∼**er** *n* **1** framework of poles, canvas, etc for carrying a sick, injured or wounded person. '∼**er-bearer** *n* person who helps to carry a ∼er. '∼**er-party** *n* number of persons with ∼ers (to carry an injured or wounded person). **2** device for ∼ing things (eg gloves, shoes).

strew /struː/ *vt* (*pt* ∼ed, *pp* ∼ed or strewn

/struːn/) [VP6A,14] ∼ *sth (on/over sth);* ∼ *sth with sth,* scatter (sth) over a surface; (partly) cover (a surface) (with sth scattered): ∼ *flowers over a path;* ∼ *a path with flowers.*

strewth /struːθ/ = struth.

stri·ated /straɪ'eɪtɪd US: 'straɪeɪtɪd/ *adj* striped; furrowed.

stricken /'strɪkən/ *adj* (*pp* of strike; used pred) affected or overcome: '*grief-/panic-/terror-*∼, overcome by grief/panic/terror; ∼ *with fever/ malaria/cancer;* '*cancer-*∼. ∼ *in years,* (archaic) old and feeble.

strict /strɪkt/ *adj* (-er, -est) **1** stern; demanding obedience or exact observance: *a* ∼ *father;* ∼ *discipline; be* ∼ *with one's children; keep a* ∼ *hand over the children; a* ∼ *rule against smoking,* eg at a petrol station. **2** clearly and exactly defined; precisely limited: *tell sb sth in* ∼*est confidence; in the* ∼ *sense of the word; the* ∼ *truth.* ∼·**ly** *adv* in a ∼ manner: *Smoking is* ∼*ly prohibited.* ∼·**ness** *n*

stric·ture /'strɪktʃə(r)/ *n* [C] **1** (often *pl*) severe criticism or blame: *pass* ∼*s on sb.* **2** (med) contraction of a tube-like part of the body, causing a diseased condition.

stride /straɪd/ *vi,vt* (*pt* strode /strəʊd/, *pp* (rare) stridden /'strɪdn/) **1** [VP2C] walk with long steps: ∼ *along the road;* ∼ *off/away.* **2** ∼ *over/across sth,* pass over in one step: ∼ *over a ditch.* **3** [VP6A] = bestride. □ *n* [C] (distance covered in) one long step: *walk with vigorous* ∼*s.* **make great** ∼**s,** make good and rapid progress. **take sth in one's** ∼, do it without special effort.

stri·dent /'straɪdnt/ *adj* (of sound) loud and harsh; shrill: *the* ∼ *notes of the cicadas.* ∼·**ly** *adv*

stridu·late /'strɪdjʊleɪt US: 'strɪdʒʊleɪt/ *vi* [VP2A] make shrill grating sounds (esp of insects such as crickets). **stridu·la·tion** /ˌstrɪdjʊ'leɪʃn US: -dʒ-/ *n*

strife /straɪf/ *n* [U] quarrelling; state of conflict: *industrial* ∼ (between workers and employers).

strike¹ /straɪk/ *n* **1** act of striking(5): *the numerous* ∼*s in the coalmines; a* ∼ *of bus-drivers;* (attrib) *take* ∼ *action.* **be/go on** ∼; **be/come/go out on** ∼, be engaged in, start, a ∼. **a general** ∼, by workers in all or most trades, etc; also ⇨ hunger, lightning, sympathetic, unofficial. '∼-**bound** *adj* unable to function because of a ∼: *The docks were* ∼*-bound for a week.* '∼-**breaker** *n* worker brought in or coming in to take the place of a striker. '∼ **fund** *n* special fund to supplement ∼-pay. '∼-**leader** *n* worker or official who leads a ∼. '∼-**pay** *n* money paid to strikers from trade-union funds (during a ∼ officially recognized by a union). **2** act of striking (oil, etc) in the earth. **lucky** ∼, fortunate discovery. **3** sudden attack by aircraft.

strike² /straɪk/ *vt,vi* (*pt,pp* struck /strʌk/) (also ⇨ stricken, above) (For special uses with *adverbial particles* and *preps,* ⇨ **17** below.) **1** [VP6A,12C,14,2A,C,3A] hit; give a blow or blows to; aim a blow *at: He struck me on the chin* (note use of *def art*). *He struck the table with a heavy blow. He struck his knee with his hand/struck his hand on his knee. He seized a stick and struck at me. Who struck the first blow,* started the fight? *The ship struck a rock. That tree was struck by lightning.* ∼ *at the root of sth,* attack trouble, evil, etc at its source. *S*∼ *while the iron is hot,* (prov) Act promptly while action is likely to get results. *a* '∼/ *striking force,* military force ready to attack at short notice. *within* '*striking distance,*

near enough to reach or attack easily. **2** [VP6A,2A] produce (a light) by striking or scraping: ~ *sparks from a flint;* ~ *a match,* cause it to burst into flame by scraping it on a surface; ~ *a light,* produce one in this way. *These matches are damp—they won't* ~. **3** [VP6A] come upon, discover (by mining, drilling, etc): *to* ~ *gold.* ~ *oil,* (a) discover oil by drilling. **(b)** (fig) have good fortune; find a means of getting rich. ~ *it rich,* win wealth suddenly. **4** [VP6A,2A] (cause to) sound: ~ *a chord on the piano. This clock* ~*s the hours. The clock has just struck (four). The/His hour has struck,* (fig) the critical moment has come or gone. ~ *a note of,* give an impression (of the kind indicated): *The President struck a note of warning against over-optimism.* **5** [VP2A,3A] ~ *(for/against),* (of workers, etc) stop working for an employer (in order to get more pay, shorter hours, better conditions, etc or as a protest against sth): ~ *for higher pay/against bad working conditions.* ⇨ strike¹(1). **6** [VP6A,16A] impress; have an effect upon the mind: *How does the idea/suggestion* ~ *you? The plan* ~*s me as ridiculous. What struck me* (= The impression I had) *was that he was not telling the truth. An idea suddenly struck me,* came to me, with an immediate response. **7** [VP16A, or 2D with object and *as* omitted] have an effect on the body or mind: *The room* ~*s you as warm and comfortable when you enter. The prison cell struck cold and damp,* was felt as cold and damp by anyone entering it. **8** [VP6A] produce by stamping or punching: ~ *a coin/medal/medallion.* **9** [VP6A] achieve, arrive at, by reckoning or weighing: ~ *an average;* ~ *a balance between anarchy and authoritarian rule/between licence and repression.* ~ *a bargain (with sb),* reach one by agreement; conclude one. **10** [VP6A] come upon; find: ~ *the track/the right path.* **11** [VP2A,C] ~ *(off/out),* set out, go (in a certain direction): *We struck (off)* (= turned and went) *into the woods. The boys struck (out) across the fields. The explorers struck out* (= started, set out) *at dawn.* **12** [VP22] cause (sb) to be, suddenly and as if by a single stroke: *be struck blind/dumb/silent.* **13** [VP14] ~ *fear/terror/alarm into sb,* fill, afflict, with fear, etc: *Attila struck terror into the people of eastern Europe. The bombing attack struck fear into their hearts.* **14** [VP6A] lower or take down (sails, tents). ~ *one's flag,* lower it (as a signal that one surrenders a ship, fortress, etc to the enemy). ~ *tents/camp,* pack up tents, etc. **15** [VP6A] ~ *a cutting,* take a cutting from a plant and insert it in soil to ~ root. ~ *root,* put out roots. **16** [VP6A] hold or put the body in a certain way to indicate sth: ~ *an attitude of defiance;* ~ *a pose.* **17** [VP2C,3,15B] (special uses with *adverbial particles* and *preps*):
strike sb down, (formal) hit him so that he falls to the ground; (of a disease, etc) attack him: *He was struck down in the prime of life,* eg of sb who was assassinated.
strike sth off, (a) cut off with a blow, eg of an axe. **(b)** print: ~ *off 1000 copies of a book.* ~ *sth off (sth),* remove: ~ *sb's name off a list. The doctor's name was struck off the Medical Register,* was cancelled, eg because of professional misconduct.
strike on/upon sth, get or find suddenly or unexpectedly: ~ *on an idea/a plan.*
strike out, (a) use the arms and legs vigorously in swimming: ~ *out for the shore.* **(b)** aim vigorous blows: *He lost his temper and struck out wildly.* **(c)**

follow a new or independent path, a new form of activity: ~ *out on one's own/in a new direction.* ~ *sth out/through,* cross out, put a line or lines through: ~ *out a word/name/item.*
strike (sth) up, begin to play: *The band struck up (a tune).* ~ *up sth (with sb),* begin (perhaps casually) a friendship or acquaintance: *The two boys quickly struck up a friendship. She struck up an acquaintance with a fellow passenger during the cruise.*
striker /'straɪkə(r)/ *n* (a) worker who strikes(5). **(b)** (football) player in an attacking position.
strik·ing /'straɪkɪŋ/ *adj* **1** attracting attention; arousing great interest. **2** that strikes(4): *a* ~ *clock.* ~*ly adv* in a ~ manner: *a* ~*ly beautiful woman.*
string¹ /strɪŋ/ *n* **1** [C,U] (piece or length of) fine cord for tying things, keeping things in place, etc; narrow strip of other material used for the same purposes: *a ball of* ~; *a piece of* ~; ~ *and brown paper for a parcel.* **tied to one's mother's/wife's apron-**~**s,** ⇨ apron. (US) **'shoe** ~**s,** ⇨ lace(2). **2** [C] = bow~, ⇨ bow¹(1). **have two** ~**s to one's bow,** have an alternative means of achieving one's purpose. **the first/second** ~, the first/the alternative person or thing relied upon for achieving one's purpose. **3** [C] tightly stretched length of cord, gut or wire, eg in a violin or guitar, for producing musical sounds. **keep harping on one** ~**/on the same** ~, keep talking or writing on one subject. **the** ~**s,** the instruments of the violin family in an orchestra. ~ **'orchestra/'band** *n* one composed of ~ed instruments only. ~ **quar'tet** *n* (music for a) quartet of four ~ed instruments. **4** [C] ~ used for causing puppets to move. ⇨ the illus at puppet. **have sb on a** ~, have him under one's control. **pull** ~**s,** exert a (hidden) influence: *pull* ~*s to get sb a job/to have sb dismissed.* **pull the** ~**s,** control events, or the actions of other people (as if they were puppets on ~s). **no** ~**s (attached); without** ~**s,** (colloq; of help, esp of money, eg given by one country to another) without conditions about how the help is to be used. **5** [C] series of things threaded on a ~: *a* ~ *of beads/pearls/onions;* number of things in, or as in, a line: *a* ~ *of abuses/curses/lies; a* ~ *of horses,* number of horses kept for racing. ⇨ stud². **6** tough fibre or ~-like substance. ~ **bean,** kind of bean of which the pod is used as a vegetable. **'heart**~**s,** ⇨ heart(7). ~**y** *adj* (-ier, -iest) like ~; having tough fibres: ~*y meat,* tough.
string² /strɪŋ/ *vt,vi* (*pt,pp* strung /strʌŋ/) **1** [VP6A] put a string or strings on (a bow, violin, tennis racket, etc). ~**ed instrument** *n* musical instrument with ~s(3). **2** (*pp*) **strung (up),** (of a person, his senses, nerves) made tense, ready, excited, etc: *The athlete was strung up before the important race.* **highly strung,** very nervous or tense. **3** [VP6A] put (pearls, etc) on a string. **4** [VP15A,B] ~ **(up),** tie or hang on a string, etc: ~ *up lanterns among the trees/lamps across a street.* **5** [VP2C,15B] (special uses with *adverbial particles*):
string sb along, deliberately mislead him into the belief that he will benefit, etc: *He doesn't intend to marry the girl—he's just* ~*ing her along.* ~ *along with sb,* maintain a relationship with sb for as long as it suits one, without making genuine commitments.
string out, be, become, spread out at intervals in a line. ~ *sth out,* cause this to happen: *horses*

strung out towards the end of a long race.

string sb up, (sl) put him to death by hanging. ∼ **sth up**, ⇨ 4 above.

strin-gent /ˈstrɪndʒənt/ *adj* **1** (of rules) strict, severe; that must be obeyed: *a* ∼ *rule against smoking.* **2** (of the money-market) tight; difficult to operate because of scarcity of money. ∼**·ly** *adv* **strin·gency** /-nsɪ/ *n*

strip /strɪp/ *vt, vi* (-pp-) **1** [VP2A,C,6A,14,15B,22] ∼ *(off)*; ∼ *sth/sb (off)*; ∼ *sth (from/off sth)*; ∼ *sth/sb (of sth)*, take off (coverings, clothes, parts, etc): ∼ *a machine*, dismantle it; ∼ *paint from a surface/* ∼ *a surface of paint*, remove the paint; ∼ *the bark off a tree/* ∼ *a tree of its bark. The bandits* ∼*ped him naked/* ∼*ped him of his clothes. They* ∼*ped the house of all its furnishings. They* ∼*ped,/* ∼*ped off,/* ∼*ed off their clothes, and jump-ed into the lake.* ∼ *sth down*, (eg of an engine) remove detachable parts (for overhaul, etc). ˈ∼**-tease**, ˈ∼**-show** *nn* dance, cabaret or theatrical entertainment in which a woman takes off her garments one by one. Hence, ˈ∼**per** *n* woman who does this. ˌ∼**-ˈpoker** *n* game of poker in which the loser of each hand must take off one garment. **2** [VP14] ∼ *sb of sth*, deprive him of property, etc: ∼ *a man of his possessions/titles, etc.* **3** [VP6A] tear parts from: ∼ *a gear/screw*, tear the cogs/thread from it (by misuse, etc). **4** [VP6A] squeeze out the last milk from (a cow's udder); obtain (milk) in this way. □ *n* [C] **1** long narrow piece (of material, land, etc): *a* ∼ *of garden behind the house; a* ∼ *of paper; an* ˈair∼, ⇨ air¹(7). ˈ∼**-lighting** *n* method of lighting, using long tubes in-stead of bulbs. ∼ **cartoon** *n* sequence of small drawings in a row, telling a story. ⇨ *comic* ∼ at comic. **2** (colloq) clothes worn by players in a team: *the colourful* ∼ *of many football teams.*

stripe /straɪp/ *n* [C] **1** long, narrow band (usu of the same breadth throughout) on a surface different in colour, material, texture, etc: *a white tablecloth* with red ∼s; *the tiger's* ∼s. **the Stars and S∼s**, the national flag of the US. **2** (often a V-shaped) badge worn on a uniform, showing rank, eg of a soldier: *How many* ∼s *are there on the sleeve of a sergeant?* **3** (old use) blow with a whip (*stroke* is now the usu word). ∼**d** /straɪpt/ *adj* marked with ∼s(1): ∼*d material*, eg for clothing. **stripy** *adj* having ∼s: *a stripy tie.*

strip-ling /ˈstrɪplɪŋ/ *n* youth.

strive /straɪv/ *vi* (*pt* strove /strəʊv/, *pp* striven /ˈstrɪvn/) **1** [VP2A,3A] ∼ *(with/against sth/sb)*, struggle. **2** [VP3A,4A] ∼ *for sth/to do sth*, make great efforts. ∼**r** *n* person who tries hard.

strobe /strəʊb/ *n, adj* ˈ∼ **(light)**, (light) that goes on and off very fast.

strode /strəʊd/ *pt* of stride.

stroke¹ /strəʊk/ *n* [C] **1** (act of striking or dealing a) blow: *kill a man with one* ∼ *of a sword; the* ∼ *of a hammer; 20* ∼s *of the lash.* **2** one of a series of regularly repeated movements, esp as a way of swimming or rowing: *swimming with a slow* ∼; ˈbreast-/ˈback-∼; *a fast/slow* ∼ (in rowing). **3** (in a rowing crew) oarsman nearest the boat's stern who sets the rate of striking the oars. ⇨ the illus at eight; ⇨ bow³(2). **4** single movement of the upper part of the body and arm(s), esp in games, eg cricket, golf. **5** single effort; result of this: *That was a good* ∼ *of business. I haven't done a* ∼ *of work today. What a* ∼ *of luck!* What a piece of good fortune! **at a/one** ∼, with one effort and im-mediately. **put sb off his** ∼, ⇨ put off at put ²(11). **6** (mark made by a) single movement of a pen or brush: *with one* ∼ *of the pen; thin/thick* ∼s. **7** sound made by a bell striking the hours: *on the* ∼ *of three*, at three o'clock. *He was here on the* ∼, punctually at the time appointed. **8** sudden attack of illness in the brain, with loss of feeling, power to move, etc: *a paralytic* ∼. ⇨ also *sun*∼ at sun(4). □ *vt* (*pt, pp* ∼d) [VP6A] act as ∼(3) to.

stroke² /strəʊk/ *vt* [VP6A,15B] pass the hand along

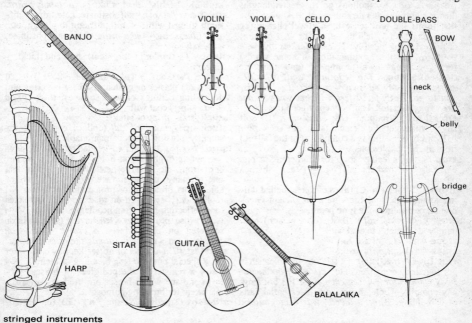

stringed instruments

a surface, usu again and again: ∼ *a cat/one's beard.* ∼ *sb the wrong way,* irritate him instead of soothing him. ∼ *sb down,* mollify him, cause him to be no longer irritated. □ *n* act of stroking; stroking movement.

stroll /strəʊl/ *n* [C] quiet, unhurried walk: *have/go for a* ∼. □ *vi* [VP2A,C] go for a ∼. ∼**er** *n*

strong /strɒŋ US: strɔːŋ/ *adj* (-nger /-ŋɡə(r)/, -ngest /-ŋɡɪst/) 1 (opp of *weak*) having power to resist; not easily hurt, injured, broken, captured, etc; having great power of body or mind: *a* ∼ *stick,* not easily broken; *a* ∼ *fort,* not easily captured; *a* ∼ *wind; a* ∼ *will/imagination/determination; have* ∼ *nerves,* be not easily frightened, worried, etc; ∼ *eyes; feel quite* ∼ *again,* in good health after an illness; *a* ∼ *army; an army 500000* ∼, numbering 500000; *a* ∼ *candidate,* one likely to be well supported, etc; ∼ (= deeply held or rooted) *beliefs/convictions.* **as** ∼ **as a horse,** physically powerful. **one's** ∼ **point,** that which one does well. '∼**-arm,** (of methods, tactics, etc) violent; bullying. '∼**-box** *n* one that is ∼ly built for keeping valuables. '∼**-hold** /-həʊld/ *n* (a) fort. (b) (fig) place where a cause or idea has ∼ support: *a* ∼*hold of Protestantism.* ∼**-'minded** /'maɪndɪd/ *adj* having a mind that is capable and vigorous. '∼**-room** *n* one built with thick walls and (usu) a thick steel door (eg in a bank) for storing valuables. **2** having a large proportion of the flavouring; etc element: ∼ *tea/coffee; a* ∼ *whisky,* whisky with very little water, etc. **3** having a considerable effect on the mind or the senses: *the* ∼ *light of the tropics; a* ∼ *smell of gas;* ∼ *bacon/butter/cheese/ onions. His breath is rather* ∼, is ill-smelling. ∼ **language** *n* forcible expressions, esp words that are blasphemous or abusive. **4** ∼ **drink,** containing alcohol, eg gin, rum. ⇨ *soft drink* at soft(9). **5** (*adverbial* use) *going* ∼, (colloq) continuing (the race, activity, etc) vigorously; continuing in good health: *aged 90 and still going* ∼. *come/go it* (*rather/a bit*) ∼, (colloq) go to greater lengths than is right; exaggerate somewhat. **6** ∼ **verb,** one that forms the past tense by a vowel change (eg *sing, sang*), not by adding *-d, -ed* or *-t.* **7** (comm; of prices) rising steadily: *Prices/Markets are* ∼. **8** '∼ **form,** (of the pronunciation of some words) form occurring in a prominent (and therefore stressed) position: *The* ∼ *form of 'and' is* /ænd/. ⇨ weak(5). ∼**-ly** *adv* in a ∼ manner: *I* ∼*ly advise you to go. I* ∼*ly feel/I feel* ∼*ly that you've made the wrong decision,* I am ∼ly convinced that...

stron·tium /'strɒntɪəm US: -nʃɪəm/ *n* [U] soft silver-white metallic element (symbol **Sr**). ∼ **90** *n* [U] variety of ∼ that is a component of the fall-out from nuclear explosions.

strop /strɒp/ *n* leather strap for sharpening razors, eg as used by barbers. □ *vt* (-pp-) [VP6A] sharpen on a ∼.

strophe /'strəʊfɪ/ *n* [C] (lines of verse recited during a) movement of the chorus in ancient Greek drama; one section of a lyric poem.

stroppy /'strɒpɪ/ *adj* (GB sl) (of a person) bad-tempered; difficult to deal with.

strove /strəʊv/ *pt* of strive.

struck /strʌk/ *pt,pp* of strike².

struc·ture /'strʌktʃə(r)/ *n* **1** [U] way in which sth is put together, organized, etc: *the* ∼ *of the human body; molecular* ∼; *sentence* ∼. **2** [C] building; any complex whole; framework or essential parts of a building: *The Parthenon was a magnificent*

marble ∼. **struc·tural** /'strʌktʃərəl/ *adj* of a ∼, esp the framework: *structural alterations to a building,* eg combining two rooms into one; *structural steel,* ie bars, beams, girders, for use in building. **struc·tur·ally** /-ərəlɪ/ *adv.* *The building is structurally sound.*

stru·del /'struːdl/ *n* kind of tart made of fruit, etc rolled up in puff pastry and baked: *a slice of apple* ∼.

struggle /'strʌɡl/ *vi* [VP2A,B,3A,4A] ∼ (*against/with*), fight, make great efforts: ∼ *against difficulties;* ∼ *for influence/power. The thief* ∼*d in the policeman's arms/*∼*d to get free.* □ *n* [C] struggling; contest: *the* ∼ *for freedom; not surrender without a* ∼.

strum /strʌm/ *vi,vt* (-mm-) [VP2A,B,C,3A,6A] ∼ (*on*), play music, play (on a musical instrument) carelessly or monotonously (and esp without skill): ∼ (*on*) *the banjo;* ∼ *a tune on the piano.* □ *n* sound of ∼ing: *the* ∼ *of a guitar.*

strum·pet /'strʌmpɪt/ *n* (archaic) prostitute.

strung /strʌŋ/ *pt,pp* of string².

strut[1] /strʌt/ *n* [C] piece of wood or metal inserted in a framework and intended to strengthen it by bearing weight or resisting pressure in the direction of its length.

strut[2] /strʌt/ *vi* (-tt-) [VP2A,C] walk (*about, along, in, out, into a room, etc*) in a stiff, self-satisfied way. □ *n* such a way of walking.

strych·nine /'strɪkniːn/ *n* [U] strong poison (used in very small doses to stimulate the nerves).

stub /stʌb/ *n* [C] **1** short remaining end of a pencil, cigarette or similar object: *The dog has only a* ∼ *of a tail,* a very short one. **2** counterfoil: *the* ∼*s of a cheque-book.* □ *vt* (-bb-) **1** [VP6A] ∼ *one's toe,* strike it against sth. **2** [VP15B] ∼ *sth out,* extinguish (esp a cigarette) by pressing it against sth hard.

stubble /'stʌbl/ *n* [U] short stalks of grain plants left in the ground after harvest; sth suggesting this, eg a short stiff growth of beard: *three days'* ∼ *on his chin.* **stub·bly** /'stʌblɪ/ *adj* of or like ∼: *a stubbly beard.*

stub·born /'stʌbən/ *adj* obstinate; determined; difficult to deal with: ∼ *soil,* difficult to plough, etc; *a* ∼ *illness.* **as** ∼ **as a mule,** extremely obstinate. ∼**·ly** *adv* ∼**·ness** *n*

stubby /'stʌbɪ/ *adj* (-ier, -iest) short and thick: ∼ *fingers.*

stucco /'stʌkəʊ/ *n* (*pl* ∼s, ∼es /-kəʊz/) [C,U] (kinds of) plaster or cement used for covering and decorating ceilings or wall surfaces. □ *vt* (*pt,pp* ∼ed; ∼ing) coat with ∼.

stuck /stʌk/ *pt,pp* of stick².

stuck-up /ˌstʌk 'ʌp/ *adj* (colloq) conceited; insolently refusing to be companionable.

stud[1] /stʌd/ *n* **1** small two-headed button-like device put through button-holes to fasten a collar, shirt-front, etc. **2** large-headed nail or knob, usu one of many, on the surface of sth (eg a gate or shield), as ornament or protection. **re'flector** ∼, (colloq *cat's eye*) used on roads to mark out lanes (and reflecting light from headlamps at night). □ *vt* (-dd-) (usu *pp*) ∼*ded with,* having (sth) set in or scattered on the surface: *a crown* ∼*ded with jewels; a sea* ∼*ded with islands/the sails of yachts.*

stud[2] /stʌd/ *n* number of horses kept by one owner for a special purpose (esp breeding or racing). '∼**-book** *n* register of the pedigrees of horses. '∼**-farm** *n* place where horses are bred. '∼**-mare** *n* mare kept for breeding purposes.

stu·dent /'stjuːdnt US: 'stuː-/ *n* **1** (GB) (undergraduate or postgraduate) person who is studying at a college, polytechnic or university: '*medical* ~*s;* (US also) boy or girl attending school. **2** anyone who studies or who is devoted to the acquisition of knowledge: *a* ~ *of bird-life/nature/theology.*

stu·dio /'stju:dɪəʊ *US:* 'stu:-/ *n* (*pl* ~s /-dɪəʊz/) **1** well-lit workroom of a painter, sculptor, photographer, etc. ~ **couch,** couch that can be used as a bed. **2** room or hall where cinema films are acted and photographed; (*pl*) all the ~s of a cinema company, with the office buildings, etc. **3** room from which radio or TV programmes are regularly broadcast or in which recordings are made. ~ **audience,** audience in a ~, to provide applause, laughter, etc.

stu·di·ous /'stju:dɪəs *US:* 'stu:-/ *adj* **1** having or showing the habit of learning. **2** painstaking; deliberate: *with* ~ *politeness.* ~·**ly** *adv* ~·**ness** *n*

study[1] /'stʌdɪ/ *n* (*pl* -dies) **1** [U and in *pl*] devotion of time and thought to getting knowledge of, or to a close examination of, a subject, esp from books: *fond of* ~; *give all one's leisure time to* ~; *make a* ~ *of the country's foreign trade. My studies show that....* **2** [C] sth that attracts investigation; that which is (to be) investigated: *scientific studies. The proper* ~ *of mankind is man. His face was a* ~, was well worth observing closely. **3** *be in a brown* ~, musing, unaware of people, happenings, etc near one. **4** room used by sb (eg in his home) for reading, writing, etc: *You will find Mr Green in the/his* ~. **5** sketch etc made for practice or experiment; piece of music played as a technical exercise. **6** [U] (old use) earnest effort.

study[2] /'stʌdɪ/ *vt,vi* (*pt,pp* -died) **1** [VP6A,8,15A,2A,B,4A] give time and attention to learning or discovering sth: ~ *medicine. He was* ~*ing for the medical profession/*~*ing to be a doctor.* **2** [VP6A] examine carefully: ~ *the map.* **3** [VP6A,4A] give care and consideration to: ~ *the wishes of one's friends/only one's own interests.* **4** (*pp*) **studied,** intentional, deliberate: *a studied insult.*

stuff[1] /stʌf/ *n* **1** [C,U] material or substance of which sth is made or which may be used for some purpose (often fig); [U] material of which the name is uncertain, unknown or unimportant; material of (a certain) quality: *We're short of* '*green/*'*garden* ~, vegetables. *He is not the* ~ *heroes are made of,* is not likely to be a hero, to act heroically. *Do you call this* ~ *beer? We must find out what* ~ *he is made of,* what sort of man he is, what his character is. *S*~ *and nonsense!* That's foolish talk! **2** (sl uses) *That's the* ~ *to give 'em,* That's how to treat them, etc. *Do your* ~, Show what you can do, etc. *know one's* ~, be expert in what one claims to be able to do, etc. **3** [U] (old use) woollen cloth: *a* ~ *gown.*

stuff[2] /stʌf/ *vt* **1** [VP6A,14,15B] ~ *sth with/into sth;* ~ *sth up,* fill tightly with; press tightly into: ~ *a bag with feathers;* ~ *feathers into a bag;* ~ *oneself with food,* overeat; *a head* ~*ed with facts/ silly romantic ideas;* ~ (*up*) *one's ears with cotton-wool;* ~ *up a hole. My nose is* ~*ed up,* full of mucus (as when one has a cold). *a* ~*ed shirt,* (colloq) a pretentious or pompous person. **2** [VP6A,14] ~ (*with*), (colloq) make (sb) believe what is not true: *He's* ~*ing you with silly ideas.* **3** [VP6A,14] put chopped up and specially flavoured food into (a bird, etc) before cooking it: *a* ~*ed turkey;* ~*ed veal.* **4** [VP6A] fill the empty carcass of

(a bird, an animal, etc) with enough material to restore it to its original shape, eg for exhibition in a museum: *a* ~*ed tiger/owl.* **5** [VP2A,6A] overeat: *When will that boy stop* ~*ing* (*himself*)? **6** ~ *it/ sth,* (sl) do what one likes with it: *If you don't like it you can* ~ *it,* will just have to put up with it/do what you like with it. **7** ⚠ (vulg sl) have sexual intercourse (with a woman). ~·**ing** *n* [U] material for ~ing, eg cushions, birds, ⇨ **3,4** above. *knock the* '~*ing out of sb,* (a) take away his conceit or self-confidence. (b) (of an illness, etc) weaken; make tired.

stuffy /'stʌfɪ/ *adj* (-ier, -iest) **1** (of a room) badly ventilated. **2** (colloq) sulky; ill-tempered. **3** (colloq, of a person) easily shocked or offended. **4** dull; formal. **stuff·ily** /-ɪlɪ/ *adv* **stuffi·ness** *n*

stul·tify /'stʌltɪfaɪ/ *vt* (*pt,pp* -fied) [VP6A] cause to seem foolish or to be useless; reduce to absurdity: ~ *efforts to reach agreement.* **stul·ti·fi·ca·tion** /ˌstʌltɪfɪ'keɪʃn/ *n*

stumble /'stʌmbl/ *vi* [VP2A,C,3A] **1** strike the foot against sth and almost fall: ~ *over the root of a tree. The child* ~*d and fell.* ~ *across/upon sth,* find unexpectedly or by accident. '**stumbling-block** *n* obstacle; sth that causes difficulty or hesitation. **2** ~ *about/along/around,* move or walk in an unsteady way. **3** speak in a hesitating way, with pauses and mistakes: ~ *over one's words;* ~ *through a recitation.* ◻ *n* act of stumbling.

stump /stʌmp/ *n* [C] **1** part of a tree remaining in the ground when the trunk has fallen or has been cut down. ~ *oratory/speeches,* political speeches to persuade or rouse the audience. *on the* ~, (colloq) engaged in political speech-making, agitation, etc. **2** anything remaining after the main part has been cut or broken off or has worn off, eg an amputated limb, a worn-down tooth, the useless end of a pencil, cigar, etc; (hum) leg. *stir one's* ~*s,* (colloq) move quickly. **3** (cricket) one of the three upright pieces of wood at which the ball is bowled: *send the middle* ~ *flying. draw* ~*s,* end play. ⇨ the illus at cricket. ◻ *vi,vt* **1** [VP2C] walk (*along, about, etc*) with stiff, heavy movements. **2** [VP6A] (colloq) be too hard for; leave at a loss: *All the examination candidates were* ~*ed by the second question.* **3** [VP6A] go about (a district, the country) making ~ speeches ⇨ the *n*, **1** above. **4** [VP6A] (cricket) end the innings of (a batsman) by touching the ~s with the ball while he is out of his crease. ⇨ crease(2). **5** [VP15B,2C] ~ *money up,* (sl) pay or give a sum of money; produce (a sum of money): *Mr Green has had to* ~ *up* (£50) *for his son's debts.* ~·**er** *n* (colloq) question that ~s(2); difficult or embarrassing question.

stumpy /'stʌmpɪ/ *adj* (-ier, -iest) short and thick: *a* ~ *little man; a* ~ *umbrella.*

stun /stʌn/ *vt* (-nn-) [VP6A] **1** make unconscious by a blow, esp one on the head; knock senseless: *The blow* ~*ned me.* **2** shock; confuse the mind of: *He was* ~*ned by the news of his father's death.* ~·**ning** *adj* (colloq) splendid; ravishing: *What a* ~*ning figure!* ~·**ning·ly** *adv* ~·**ner** *n* (colloq) delightful, attractive person, object, etc.

stung /stʌŋ/ *pt,pp* of sting[2].

stunk /stʌŋk/ *pp* of stink.

stunt[1] /stʌnt/ *n* [C] (colloq) sth done to attract attention; *advertising* ~*s,* eg sky-writing by an aircraft; ~ *flying,* aerobatics. *That's a good* ~, a clever idea (for getting publicity, etc). '~ *man,* person employed to perform ~s (involving risk, etc) as a stand-in for an actor in films, etc.

stunt² /stʌnt/ vt [VP6A] check the growth or development of: ~ed trees; a ~ed mind.

stu·pefy /'stjuːpɪfaɪ US: 'stuː-/ vt (pt,pp -fied) [VP6A] make clear thought impossible: stupefied with drink/amazement. He was stupefied by what happened. **stu·pe·fac·tion** /ˌstjuːpɪ'fækʃn US: ˌstuː-/ n [U] state of being stupefied.

stu·pen·dous /stjuː'pendəs US: stuː-/ adj tremendous; amazing (in size, degree): a ~ error/ achievement. What ~ folly!~·ly adv

stu·pid /'stjuːpɪd US: 'stuː-/ adj 1 slow-thinking; foolish: Don't be ~ enough to believe that. 2 in a state of stupor. □ n (colloq) ~ person: I was only teasing, ~! ~·ly adv ~·ity /stjuː'pɪdəti US: stuː-/ n [U] being ~; [C] (pl -ties) ~ act, utterance, etc.

stu·por /'stjuːpə(r) US: 'stuː-/ n [C,U] almost unconscious condition caused by shock, drugs, alcohol, etc: in a drunken ~.

sturdy /'stɜːdɪ/ adj (-ier, -iest) strong and solid; vigorous: ~ children; offer a ~ resistance; ~ common sense. **stur·dily** /-ɪlɪ/ adv. a sturdily built bicycle. **stur·di·ness** n

stur·geon /'stɜːdʒən/ n kinds of large fish valued as food, from which caviare is obtained.

stut·ter /'stʌtə(r)/ vi,vt n = stammer. ~**er** n person who ~s. ~**·ing·ly** adv

sty¹ /staɪ/ n (pl sties) pigsty. ⇨ pig(1).

sty² (also **stye**) /staɪ/ n (pl sties, styes) inflamed swelling on the edge of the eyelid.

Styg·ian /'stɪdʒɪən/ adj (as) of the River Styx or Hades (the lower world in Gk myth); hence, dark; gloomy.

style /staɪl/ n 1 [C,U] manner of writing or speaking (contrasted with the subject matter); manner of doing anything, esp when it is characteristic of an artist or of a period of art: written in an irritating ~. The ~ in this book is more attractive than the matter. What do you know about the Norman/ decorated/perpendicular, etc ~s of English architecture? 2 [C,U] quality that marks sth done or made as superior, fashionable or distinctive: living in a ~ beyond his means, in a way that he cannot afford. Did they live in European ~ when they were in Japan? in ~, in a grand or elegant way: do things in ~, not in a commonplace way; live in (grand) ~, with servants, luxuries, etc; drive up in ~, eg in a very fine car, not a taxi. 3 [C,U] fashion in dress, etc: the latest ~s in trousers/in hairdressing. 4 [C] general appearance, form or design; kind or sort: made in all sizes and ~s; this ~, £18.50. 5 [C] right title (to be) used when addressing sb: Has he any right to assume the ~ of Colonel? 6 [C] implement used in ancient times for scratching letters on wax-covered surfaces. 7 [C] (bot) part of the seed-producing part of a flower. ⇨ the illus at flower. □ vt [VP6A] 1 describe by a specified ~(5): Should he be ~d 'Right Honourable' or 'Mister'? 2 design: new cars ~d by the Italian experts; an electric cooker brilliantly re~d, redesigned. **styl·ish** /-ɪʃ/ adj having ~(2,3); fashionable: stylish clothes. **sty·lish·ly** adv. stylishly dressed. **styl·ish·ness** n

sty·list /'staɪlɪst/ n 1 person, esp a writer, who achieves a good or original literary style. 2 (comm, etc) person who is concerned with the styles of decorating, clothes, etc: a 'hair-~, a hairdresser. **sty·lis·tic** /staɪ'lɪstɪk/ adj of style in writing. **sty·lis·ti·cally** /-klɪ/ adv

sty·lize /'staɪəlaɪz/ vt represent or treat (art forms,

etc) in a particular style.

sty·lus /'staɪləs/ n (pl ~es /-ləsɪz/) sharp point (made of diamond or sapphire) used to cut the groove of a gramophone record, or to reproduce sound by following this groove.

sty·mie /'staɪmɪ/ n (in golf) situation on the green when an opponent's ball is between one's own ball and the hole; (fig, colloq) check; obstruction. □ vt [VP6A] put (one's opponent or his ball, or oneself) in this difficulty; (fig) check; obstruct.

styp·tic /'stɪptɪk/ n, adj (substance) checking the flow of blood: a ~ pencil, stick of this (eg as used on a cut made while shaving).

Styx /stɪks/ n (Gk myth) river that encircles Hades, where the spirits of the dead exist. cross the ~, die.

sua·sion /'sweɪʒn/ n [U] (formal) persuasion. moral ~, persuasion based on moral grounds, not force.

suave /swɑːv/ adj smooth and gracious (but possibly insincere) in manner. ~·ly adv. **suav·ity** /-ətɪ/ n [U] quality of being ~; (pl) instances of being ~; ~ utterances, etc.

sub¹ /sʌb/ n (colloq, abbr of) 1 submarine. 2 subscription. 3 sub-lieutenant. 4 sub-editor.

sub² /sʌb/ vi,vt 1 [VP2A,3A] ~ (for sb), (colloq) act as a substitute (for him). 2 [VP6A] (colloq abbr of) subedit.

sub- /sʌb/ pref⇨ App 3.

sub·al·tern /'sʌbltən US: sə'bɔːltərn/ n (GB) (formerly) commissioned army officer of lower rank than a captain.

sub·atomic /ˌsʌbə'tomɪk/ adjof, relating to, any of the particles smaller than an atom.

sub·com·mit·tee /'sʌb kəmɪtɪ/ n committee formed from members of a main committee.

sub·con·scious /ˌsʌb'kɒnʃəs/ adj of one's mental activites of which one is not (wholly) aware: the ~ self. □ n the ~, ~ thoughts, desires, impulses, etc collectively. ~·ly adv ~·ness n

sub·con·ti·nent /ˌsʌb'kɒntɪnənt/ n mass of land large enough to be regarded as a separate continent but forming part of a larger mass: India is often called the S~.

sub·con·tract /ˌsʌb'kɒntrækt/ n contract which is for carrying out a previous contract or a part of it. □ vt,vi /ˌsʌbkən'trækt US: -'kɒntrækt/ [VP6A,2A] give or accept a ~. ~**or** /ˌsʌbkən'træktə(r) US: -'kɒntræk-/ n person who accepts a ~.

sub·cu·taneous /ˌsʌbkjuː'teɪnɪəs/ adj under the skin; ~ parasites, living under the skin; a ~ injection.

sub·di·vide /ˌsʌbdɪ'vaɪd/ vt,vi [VP6A,2A] divide into further divisions. **sub·di·vi·sion** /ˌsʌbdɪ'vɪʒn/ n [U] subdividing; [C] sth produced by subdividing.

sub·due /səb'djuː US: -'duː/ vt [VP6A] 1 overcome; bring under control: ~ the tropical jungle/one's passions. 2 make quieter, softer, gentler: (esp pp) ~d voices/lights; a tone of ~d satisfaction in his voice.

sub·edit /sʌb'edɪt/ vt act as an assistant editor of (a newspaper, etc) **sub·edi·tor** /-tə(r)/ n

sub·fusc /'sʌbfʌsk/ adj rather dark in colour; (fig colloq) unimpressive.

sub·head·ing /'sʌbhedɪŋ/ n [C] words showing the contents of part of an article, etc eg in a newspaper.

sub·hu·man /ˌsʌb'hjuːmən/ adj less than human; more like an animal than a human being.

sub·ject¹ /'sʌbdʒɪkt/ adj 1 under foreign govern-

ment, not independent: *a ~ province; ~ peoples.*
2 be ~ to, owe obedience (to): *We are ~ to the
law of the land.* **3 ~ to,** having a tendency (to);
prone to: *Are you ~ to colds? The trains are ~ to
delays when there is fog.* **4 ~ to,** *(adj, adv)* condi-
tional(ly) upon: *The plan is ~ to confirmation. The
arrangement is made ~ to your approval.* **~ to
contract,** *(legal)* conditional upon the signing of a
contract. **~ to prior sale,** conditional upon no sale
having been made before a further offer is made,
before the date of the auction, etc.
sub·ject² /'sʌbdʒɪkt/ *n* **1** any member of a State except the supreme ruler: *British ~s; French by birth
and a British ~ by marriage.* ⇨ *citizen,* (usu
preferred in republics). **2** sth (to be) talked or written about or studied: *an interesting ~ of conversation; a ~ for an essay; the ~ of a poem/picture.*
change the ~, talk about sth different. *on the ~
of,* concerning, dealing with: *While we are on the
~ of money, may I ask when you will repay that
loan?* '*~ matter n* [U] the content of a book,
speech, etc (contrasted with style). **3** person, animal or thing (to be) treated or dealt with, to be
made to undergo or experience sth: *a ~ for
experiment/dissection.* **4 ~ for sth,** circumstance,
etc that gives cause for it: *a ~ for pity/ridicule/
congratulation.* **5** person with the tendencies (usu
undesirable) specified: *a hysterical ~.* **6** (gram)
(contrasted with predicate¹) word(s) in a sentence
about which sth is predicated; (contrasted with ob-
ject¹(4)) *n* or *n* equivalent which carries out the action of a *v,* and which must agree(6) with the *v, eg
book* in 'There was a book lying on the table' and
they in 'Did they come early?' **7** (music) theme on
which a composition (or one of its movements) is
based.
sub·ject³ /səb'dʒekt/ *vt* [VP14] **~ to, 1** bring, get
(a country, nation, person) under control: *Ancient
Rome ~ed most of Europe to her rule.* **2** cause to
undergo or experience; expose: *~ oneself/one's
friends to criticism/ridicule; ~ a man to torture.
As a test the metal was ~ed to great heat.* **sub-
jec·tion** /səb'dʒekʃn/ *n* [U] *~ing* or being *~ed:
The ~ion of the rebels took several months. The
people lived in a state of ~ion/were kept/held in
~ion for half a century.*
sub·jec·tive /səb'dʒektɪv/ *adj* **1** (of ideas, feelings,
etc) existing in the mind, not produced by things
outside the mind; not objective: *Did he really see a
ghost or was it only a ~ impression?* **2** (of art and
artists, writing, etc) giving the personal or individual point of view or feeling (opp to realistic art,
writing, etc). **3** (gram) of the subject. *~·ly adv* in a
~ manner: *An examination paper in arithmetic
can be marked objectively, but a literary essay can
be marked only ~ly,* ie on the personal impression
of the examiner. **sub·jec·tiv·ity** /ˌsʌbdʒek'tɪvəti/ *n*
[U].
sub·join /ˌsʌb'dʒɔɪn/ *vt* [VP6A] (formal) add at the
end: *~ a postscript to a letter.*
sub judice /ˌsʌb 'dʒuːdɪsɪ/ (Lat) under judicial consideration, not yet decided (and for this reason, in
GB, not (by law) to be commented upon).
sub·ju·gate /'sʌbdʒʊgeɪt/ *vt* [VP6A] subdue; conquer. **sub·ju·ga·tion** /ˌsʌbdʒʊ'geɪʃn/ *n* [U].
sub·junc·tive /səb'dʒʌŋktɪv/ *adj* (gram) expressing
a condition, hypothesis, possibility, etc. □ *n* [U,C]
the *~* mood; form of a verb in this mood.
sub·lease /ˌsʌb'liːs/ *vt, vi* [VP6A,2A] lease to another person (a house, land, etc which one has

oneself leased); sublet. □ *n* lease of this kind.
sub·let /ˌsʌb'let/ *vt, vi* (-tt-) [VP6A,2A] **1** rent to sb
else (a room, house, etc of which one is a tenant). **2**
give part of (a contract, eg for building a factory) to
sb else.
sub·lieu·ten·ant /ˌsʌblə'tenənt *US:* -luː't-/ *n*
naval officer with rank next below that of a lieutenant.
sub·li·mate /'sʌblɪmeɪt/ *vt* [VP6A] **1** (chem) convert from a solid state to vapour by heat and allow
to solidify again (in order to purify it). **2** (psych)
unconsciously change (emotions and activities
arising from the instincts) into higher or more desirable channels. □ *n, adj* (substance) refined by
being *~d.* **sub·li·ma·tion** /ˌsʌblɪ'meɪʃn/ *n*
sub·lime /sə'blaɪm/ *adj* **1** of the greatest and
highest sort; causing wonder or reverence: *~
scenery/heroism/self-sacrifice.* **2** extreme; as-
tounding (as of a person who does not fear the consequences): *What ~ conceit/impudence/
indifference!* □ *n* the *~,* that which fills one with
awe or reverence. *(go) from the ~ to the ridiculous,* (pass) from what is beautiful, noble, etc to
what is trivial, inferior, absurd, etc: *To find a
snack bar at the top of Mount Olympus would be to
go from the ~ to the ridiculous. ~·ly adv* in a *~*
manner: *He was ~ly unconscious* (= completely
ignorant) *of how foolish he looked.* **sub·lim·ity**
/sə'blɪmətɪ/ *n* [U and in *pl;* -ties] *~* quality or
qualities: *the sublimity of the Alps; the sublimities
of great art.*
sub·lim·inal /ˌsʌb'lɪmɪnl/ *adj* below the threshold
of consciousness; of which one is not consciously
aware: *~ advertising,* as when an advertisement is
projected on to a cinema or TV screen for a fraction
of a second and is noted only by the subconscious
mind.
sub·mar·ine /ˌsʌbmə'riːn *US:* 'sʌbməriːn/ *adj* existing, designed for use, under the surface of the sea:
~ plant life; a ~ cable. □ *n* ship which can be submerged to operate under water. **sub·mar·iner**
/sʌb'mærɪnə(r)/ *n* member of a *~'s* crew.

a submarine

sub·merge /səb'mɜːdʒ/ *vt, vi* **1** [VP6A] put under
water; cover with a liquid. **2** [VP2A] sink out of
sight; (of a submarine) go down under the surface.
sub·merged *adj* under the surface of the sea, etc:
~d rocks; a wreck that is ~d at high tide. **sub-
merg·ence** /səb'mɜːdʒəns/, **sub·mer·sion**
/səb'mɜːʃn *US:* -ʒn/ *nn* [U] submerging or being
~d. **sub·mers·ible** /səb'mɜːsəbl/ *adj* capable of
submerging.
sub·mission /səb'mɪʃn/ *n* **1** [U] act of submitting;
acceptance of another's power or authority: *The
rebels made their ~ to the army. The enemy were
starved into ~,* compelled to submit by hunger. **2**
[U] obedience; humility: *with all due ~,* with profound respect. **3** [C,U] (legal) theory, opinion, etc
submitted to a judge or jury: *My ~ is that.../In my
~,... I submit(3) that....*
sub·miss·ive /səb'mɪsɪv/ *adj* yielding to the con-

trol or authority of another: ~ *to advice. Marian is not a ~ wife.* ~·ly *adv* ~·ness *n*

sub·mit /səb'mɪt/ *vt, vi* (-tt-) **1** [VP6A,14] ~ *oneself to sb/sth,* put (oneself) under the control of another: ~ *oneself to discipline. Should a wife ~ herself to her husband?* **2** [VP14] ~ *sb to sth,* cause him to endure it: ~ *a prisoner to torture/ interrogation.* **3** [VP6A,14] ~ *sth (to sb/sth),* put forward for opinion, discussion, decision, etc: ~ *plans/proposals, etc to a city council;* ~ *proofs of identity.* **4** [VP9] (legal) suggest, argue: *Counsel* ~*ted that there was no case against his client.* **5** [VP3A] ~ *to sb/sth,* surrender; give in; abstain from resistance: ~ *to the enemy/ill treatment/ separation from one's family.*

sub·nor·mal /ˌsʌb'nɔːml/ *adj* below normal: ~ *temperatures;* less than normal: *a child of* ~ *intelligence.* □ *n* person of ~ intelligence.

sub·or·bital /ˌsʌb'ɔːbɪtl/ *adj* of less duration or distance than one orbit.

sub·or·di·nate /sə'bɔːdɪnət *US:* -dənət/ *adj* **1** ~ *(to),* junior in rank or position; less important: *in a* ~ *position.* **2** ~ *clause,* (gram) dependent clause; clause which, introduced by a conjunction, serves as a *noun, adj* or *adv.* ⇨ co-ordinate. □ *n* person in a ~ position; person working under another. □ *vt* /sə'bɔːdɪneɪt *US:* -dəneɪt/ [VP6A,14] ~ *sth (to),* treat as ~; make ~ (to). **subordinating conjunction,** (gram) one that introduces a ~ clause, eg *because, if, as.* **sub·or·di·na·tion** /səˌbɔːdɪ'neɪʃn *US:* -dən'eɪʃn/ *n* subordinating or being ~d. **sub·or·di·na·tive** /sə'bɔːdɪnətɪv *US:* -dəneɪtɪv/ *adj* subordinating.

sub·orn /sə'bɔːn/ *vt* [VP6A] induce (a person) by bribery or other means to commit perjury or other unlawful act. **sub·or·na·tion** /ˌsʌbɔː'neɪʃn/ *n* [U].

sub·poena /sə'piːnə/ *n* (*pl* ~s) [C] (legal) written order requiring a person to appear in a law court. □ *vt* (*pt, pp* -naed) [VP6A] summon with a ~: *be* ~*ed as a witness.*

sub rosa /ˌsʌb 'rəʊzə/ (Lat) (of communications, etc) in strict confidence.

sub·scribe /səb'skraɪb/ *vi, vt* **1** [VP2A,3A,6A,14] ~ *(sth) (to/for),* (agree to) pay (a sum of money) in common with other persons (to a cause, for sth): *He* ~*s liberally to charities. He* ~*ed £5 to the flood relief fund. How many shares did you* ~ *for in the new company?* **2** [VP3A] ~ *to sth,* (a) agree to take (a newspaper, periodical, etc) regularly for a specified time. (b) agree with, share (an opinion, view, etc). ~ *for a book,* agree before it is published to buy a copy or copies. **3** [VP6A] (formal) write (one's name, etc) at the foot of a document: ~ *one's name to a petition.* ~r *n* person who ~s (esp to funds, newspapers). **sub·scrip·tion** /səb'skrɪpʃn/ *n* **1** [U] subscribing or being ~d: *The monument was erected by public subscription.* **2** [C] sum of money ~d (for charity, for receiving a newspaper, magazine, etc), or paid for membership of a club. **sub'scription concert,** one whose seats are all paid for in advance.

sub·se·quent /ˈsʌbsɪkwənt/ *adj* ~ *(to),* later; following: ~ *events;* ~ *to this event.* ~·ly *adv* afterwards.

sub·serve /səb'sɜːv/ *vt* [VP6A] serve as a means in helping or promoting (an end, a purpose).

sub·ser·vi·ent /səb'sɜːvɪənt/ *adj* ~ *to,* **1** giving too much respect to: ~ *shopkeepers.* **2** useful as a means to a purpose; subordinate or subject to. ~·ly *adv* **sub·ser·vi·ence** /-əns/ *n* [U].

sub·side /səb'saɪd/ *vi* [VP2A] **1** (of flood water) sink to a lower or to the normal level. **2** (of land) sink, eg because of mining operations. **3** (of buildings) settle lower down in the ground, eg because of a clay subsoil that shrinks in a dry season. **4** (of winds, passions, etc) become quiet(er) after being violent: *The storm began to* ~. **5** (hum) (of a person) go down slowly: ~ *into a chair.* **sub·sid·ence** /səb'saɪdns/ *n* [C,U] act or process of subsiding(2,3); instance of this.

sub·sidi·ary /səb'sɪdɪərɪ *US:* -dɪerɪ/ *adj* ~ *(to),* serving as a help or support but not of first importance: *a* ~ *company,* one that is controlled by a larger one. □ *n* (*pl* -ries) ~ company; ~ thing or person.

sub·sidy /ˈsʌbsədɪ/ *n* [C] (*pl* -dies) money granted, esp by a government or society, to an industry or other cause needing help, or to an ally in war, or (eg *food subsidies*) to keep prices at a desired level. **sub·si·dize** /ˈsʌbsɪdaɪz/ *vt* [VP6A] give a ~ to: *subsidized industries.* **sub·si·diz·ation** /ˌsʌbsɪdaɪ'zeɪʃn *US:* -dɪ'z-/ *n* [U].

sub·sist /səb'sɪst/ *vi* [VP2A,3A] ~ *(on),* exist; be kept in existence on: ~ *on a vegetable diet/on charity.* **sub·sis·tence** /-təns/ *n* [U] existence; means of existing: *a* ~*ence wage,* one that is only just enough to enable a worker to exist; *my means of* ~*ence,* how I make a living; '~*ence crops,* those grown for consumption (contrasted with '*cash crops,* those sold for money); *on a '*~*ence level,* on a standard of living only just adequate for remaining alive.

sub·soil /ˈsʌbsɔɪl/ *n* [U] layer of soil that lies immediately beneath the surface layer.

sub·sonic /ˌsʌb'sɒnɪk/ *adj* (of speed) less than that of sound; (of aircraft) flying at ~ speed. ⇨ supersonic.

sub·stance /ˈsʌbstəns/ *n* **1** [C,U] (particular kind of) matter: *Water, ice and snow are not different* ~*s; they are the same* ~ *in different forms.* **2** [U] most important part, chief or real meaning, of sth: *an argument of little* ~; *the* ~ *of a speech. I agree in* ~ *with what you say, but differ on some small points.* **3** [U] firmness; solidity: *This material has some* ~, is fairly solid or strong. **4** [U] money; property: *a man of* ~, eg a property owner; *waste one's* ~, spend one's money unwisely.

sub·stan·dard /ˌsʌb'stændəd/ *adj* below average standard.

sub·stan·tial /səb'stænʃl/ *adj* **1** solidly or strongly built or made. **2** large; considerable: *a* ~ *meal/ improvement/loan.* **3** possessing considerable property; well-to-do: *a* ~ *business firm;* ~ *farmers.* **4** essential; virtual: *We are in* ~ *agreement.* **5** real; having physical existence: *Was what you saw something* ~ *or only a ghost?* ~·ly /-ʃəlɪ/ *adv.* *Your efforts contributed* ~*ly* (= considerably) *to our success.*

sub·stan·ti·ate /səb'stænʃɪeɪt/ *vt* [VP6A] give facts to support (a claim, statement, charge, etc). **sub·stan·ti·ation** /səbˌstænʃɪ'eɪʃn/ *n*

sub·stan·ti·val /ˌsʌbstən'taɪvl/ *adj* (gram) of the nature of a substantive: *a* ~ *clause,* a clause functioning as a noun.

sub·stan·tive /ˈsʌbstəntɪv/ *adj* having an independent existence; real; actual: *Almost all of Great Britain's colonies now have the status of* ~ *nations.* **a** ~ **motion,** (in a debate) an amendment which, having been carried, becomes the subject of further discussion. ~ /səb'stæntɪv/ **rank,** (GB)

permanent rank (in the army, etc). □ *n* (gram) noun.
sub·sta·tion /ˈsʌbsteɪʃn/ *n* branch or subordinate station, eg for the distribution of electric current.
sub·sti·tute /ˈsʌbstɪtjuːt *US:* -tuːt/ *n* person or thing taking the place of, acting for or serving for another: *Is chicory a satisfactory ~ for coffee? S~s for rubber can be made from petroleum.* □ *vt, vi* [VP6A,14,3A] ~ **(sth/sb) (for),** put, use or serve as a ~: *~ margarine for butter. Mr X ~d for the teacher who was in hospital.* **sub·sti·tu·tion** /ˌsʌbstɪˈtjuːʃn *US:* -ˈtuːʃn/ *n* [U].
sub·stra·tum /ˌsʌbˈstrɑːtəm *US:* -ˈstreɪt-/ *n* (*pl* -ta /-tə/) **1** level lying below another: *a ~ of rock.* **2** foundation: *The story has a ~ of truth,* is based upon facts (though perhaps at first sight seeming false).
sub·struc·ture /ˈsʌbstrʌktʃə(r)/ *n* foundation; supporting part. ➪ superstructure.
sub·sume /səbˈsjuːm *US:* -ˈsuːm/ *vt* [VP6A,14] ~ **(under),** include (an example, etc) under a rule or in a particular class.
sub·tend /səbˈtend/ *vt* (geom) (of a chord, the side of a triangle) be exactly opposite to (an arc or angle).

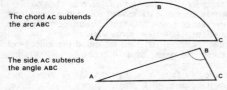

The chord AC subtends the arc ABC

The side AC subtends the angle ABC

sub·ter·fuge /ˈsʌbtəfjuːdʒ/ *n* [C] trick, excuse, esp one used to evade trouble or sth unpleasant; [U] trickery.
sub·ter·ranean /ˌsʌbtəˈreɪnɪən/ *adj* underground: *a ~ passage; ~ fires.*
sub·title /ˈsʌbtaɪtl/ *n* secondary title (of a book); translation of the dialogue of a foreign language film, printed on the film.
subtle /ˈsʌtl/ *adj* **1** difficult to perceive or describe because fine or delicate: *a ~ charm/flavour; ~ humour; a ~ distinction.* **2** ingenious; complex: *a ~ argument/design.* **3** quick and clever at seeing or making delicate differences; sensitive: *a ~ observer/critic.* **sub·tly** /ˈsʌtlɪ/ *adv.* **~ty** /ˈsʌtltɪ/ *n* (*pl* -ties) [U] the quality of being ~; [C] ~ distinction, etc.
sub·topia /ˌsʌbˈtəʊpɪə/ *n* [U] (part of the country where there is a) monotonous urban sprawl of standardized buildings, etc; (result of such a) tendency to urbanize the country.
sub·tract /səbˈtrækt/ *vt* [VP6A,14] ~ **(from),** take (a number, quantity) away from (another number, etc): *~ 6 from 9; 6 ~ed from 9 gives 3,* ie 9 − 6 = 3. **sub·trac·tion** /səbˈtrækʃn/ *n* [U] the process of ~ing; [C] instance of this: *Two from five is a simple ~ion.*
sub·tropi·cal /ˌsʌbˈtrɒpɪkl/ *adj* bordering on the tropics; nearly tropical; of ~ areas: *a ~ climate; ~ plants.*
sub·urb /ˈsʌbɜːb/ *n* [C] outlying residential district of a town or city. **the ~s,** all these districts collectively. **sub·ur·ban** /səˈbɜːbən/ *adj* **1** of or in a ~: *~an shops.* **2** (derog) having the good qualities of neither town nor country people; narrow in interests and outlook. **sub·ur·bia** /səˈbɜːbɪə/ *n* [U] (usu derog) (kind of life lived by, characteristic

outlook of, people in) ~s (collectively).
sub·ven·tion /səbˈvenʃn/ *n* subsidy; grant of money in aid.
sub·vers·ive /səbˈvɜːsɪv/ *adj* tending to subvert: *speeches that are ~ of peace and order; ~ propaganda.*
sub·vert /sʌbˈvɜːt/ *vt* [VP6A] destroy, overthrow (religion, a government) by weakening people's trust, confidence, belief: *~ the monarchy.* **sub·ver·sion** /səbˈvɜːʃn *US:* -ʒn/ *n* [U].
sub·way /ˈsʌbweɪ/ *n* **1** [C] underground passage or tunnel, eg one to enable people to get from one side of a busy street to another: *Cross by the ~.* **2** (the) ~, (US) underground railway in a town (GB = *the Underground* or, colloq, *the tube*) : *take the ~; travel by ~.*
suc·ceed /səkˈsiːd/ *vi,vt* [VP2A,3A] ~ **(in),** do what one is trying to do; gain one's purpose: *~ in life; ~ in (passing) an examination. The attack ~ed.* **2** [VP6A,16B] come next after and take the place of: *Who ~ed Churchill as Prime Minister?* **3** [VP2A,3A] ~ **(to),** inherit; have (a title, position, etc) on the death of sb: *~ to an estate. On George VI's death, Elizabeth II ~ed (to the throne).*
suc·cess /səkˈses/ *n* **1** [U] succeeding; the gaining of what is aimed at: *meet with ~. Nothing succeeds like ~,* (prov) S~ in one case is likely to be followed by ~ in other cases. **2** [U] good fortune; prosperity: *have great ~ in life.* **3** [C] sb or sth that succeeds; example of succeeding: *The plan was a great ~. He has had three ~es and one failure,* eg of a dramatist. *The army has had several ~es* (= victories) *recently.* **~·ful** /-fl/ *adj* having ~: *~ful candidates; ~ in everything.* **~·fully** /-fəlɪ/ *adv*
suc·cession /səkˈseʃn/ *n* **1** [U] the coming of one thing after another in time or order: *the ~ of the seasons. in ~,* one after the other: *five wet days in ~.* **2** [C] number of things in ~: *a ~ of wet days/ defeats.* **3** [U] (right of) succeeding to a title, the throne, property, etc; person having this right: *Who is first in ~ to the throne?* **the Apostolic S~,** the unbroken passing of spiritual authority through the bishops from the Apostles of Jesus, and through the Popes from St Peter. **'~ duty,** tax on inherited property.
suc·cess·ive /səkˈsesɪv/ *adj* coming one after the other in an uninterrupted sequence: *The school team won five ~ games.* Cf *five games in succession,* and *five games running.* **~·ly** *adv*
suc·cessor /səkˈsesə(r)/ *n* person or thing that succeeds another: *the ~ to the throne; appoint a ~ to a headmaster.*
suc·cinct /səkˈsɪŋkt/ *adj* expressed briefly and clearly; terse. **~·ly** *adv* **~·ness** *n*
suc·cour (*US* = **-cor**) /ˈsʌkə(r)/ *n* [U] (liter) help given in time of need. □ *vt* [VP6A] give help to (sb in danger or difficulty).
suc·cu·bus /ˈsʌkjʊbəs/ *n* female demon supposed to have sexual intercourse with a sleeping man. ➪ incubus.
suc·cu·lent /ˈsʌkjʊlənt/ *adj* **1** (of fruit and meat) juicy; tasting good: *a ~ steak.* **2** (of stems, leaves) thick and fleshy; (of plants) having ~ stems and leaves. □ *n* [C] ~ plant, eg a cactus. **suc·cu·lence** /-əns/ *n* [U].
suc·cumb /səˈkʌm/ *vi* [VP2A,3A] ~ **(to),** yield (to temptation, flattery, etc); die: *~ to one's injuries.*
such /sʌtʃ/ *adj* (no comp or superl; not placed between the *indef art* and its *n*; note, in the examples, the place of *such* after *no, some, many, all*) **1** of

the same kind or degree (as): ∼ *a word* (*as that*); ∼ *words* (*as those*); *no* ∼ *words* (*as those*); *poets* ∼ *as Keats and Shelley;* ∼ *poets as Keats and Shelley;* ∼ *people as these; people* ∼ *as these; on* ∼ *an occasion as this; on an occasion* ∼ *as this; Harrison, or some* ∼ *name. Some* ∼ *plan was in his mind. All* ∼ *possibilities must be considered. I have met many* ∼ *people. I've never heard of* ∼ *a thing! I hope I never have* ∼ *an experience again.* 2 ∼ **as it is,** used to suggest that sth is of poor quality, of little value, etc: *You can use my bicycle,* ∼ *as it is.* ∼ **as to** + *inf,* of a degree or kind that would or might: *Your stupidity is* ∼ *as to fill me with despair. His illness is not* ∼ *as to cause anxiety.* 3 ∼ **that;** ∼ ... **that:** *His behaviour was* ∼ *that everyone disliked him. S*∼ *was the force of the explosion/The force of the explosion was* ∼ *that all the windows were broken.* 4 (Cf the positions of ∼ and *so* in these examples): *Don't be in* ∼ *a hurry,* in so much of a hurry, in so great a hurry. *I haven't had* ∼ *an enjoyable evening* (= so enjoyable an evening) *for months.* 5 (intensive, esp in exclamatory sentences): *It was* ∼ *a long time ago! You gave me* ∼ *a fright! We've had* ∼ *a good time!* Cf What a fright you gave me! What a good time we've had! 6 (pred use) this, that, these, those (as already stated, etc): *S*∼ *is not my intention. S*∼ *were his words. S*∼ *was her reward. S*∼ *is life!* Life is like that, life is as these circumstances show it to be! □ *pron* ∼ person(s) or thing(s); that/those: *I may have hurt her feelings but* ∼ (= that) *was certainly not my intention. He is a brilliant scholar and is everywhere recognized as* ∼, as a brilliant scholar. *Down with anarchists and all* ∼, all persons of that kind! **as** ∼, properly so called; in every way: *I didn't have a nervous breakdown as* ∼, *it was more a reaction to overwork.* ∼ **as,** those that: *I haven't many specimens but I will send you* ∼ *as I have.* '∼**·like** *adj* (colloq) of the same kind; similar: *I have no time for concerts, theatres, cinemas and* ∼*like.*

suck /sʌk/ *vt,vi* 1 [VP6A,15A,B] ∼ *sth* **(in/out/ up/through, etc) (from/out of, etc),** draw (liquid) into the mouth by the use of the lip muscles: ∼ *the juice from an orange;* ∼ *poison out of a wound;* (fig) ∼ *in knowledge.* 2 [VP6A,22] draw liquid or (fig) knowledge, information, etc from: *a baby* ∼*ing its mother's breast.* Cf The mother was nursing her baby at the breast. *She* ∼*ed the orange dry.* ∼ *sb's brains,* = pick (now the usu word) sb's brains. '∼**·ing-pig** *n* young pig still taking its mother's milk. 3 [VP6A] hold (sth) in the mouth and lick, roll about, squeeze, etc with the tongue: ∼ *a toffee. The child still* ∼*s its thumb.* 4 [VP2C] perform the action of ∼ing: *The baby was* ∼*ing away at the empty feeding-bottle. The old man was* ∼*ing at his pipe.* 5 [VP6A,15B] ∼ *sth* **(up),** absorb: *plants that* ∼ *up moisture from the soil.* 6 [VP15A,B] (of a whirlpool, etc) engulf, pull in: *The canoe was* ∼*ed* (*down*) *into the whirlpool.* 7 [VP2C] ∼ *up (to),* (sl) try to please by flattery, offers of service, etc. □ *n* act or process of ∼ing: *have/take a* ∼ *at a lollipop.* **give** ∼ **to,** allow (a baby) to ∼ at the breast (but *nurse* and *suckle* are more usu).

sucker /'sʌkə(r)/ *n* [C] 1 one who, that which, sucks. 2 organ in some animals enabling them to rest on a surface by suction. 3 rubber device, eg a concave rubber disc, that adheres by suction to a surface (and can be used to cause articles to adhere

in this way). 4 unwanted shoot (new growth) coming up from the roots of a tree, shrub, etc. 5 (colloq) person foolish enough to be deceived by unscrupulous tricksters, advertisements, etc.

suckle /'sʌkl/ *vt* [VP6A] feed with milk from the breast or udder. **suck·ling** /'sʌklɪŋ/ *n* baby or young animal still being ∼d. *babes and suck-lings,* innocent children. ⇨ mouth¹.

suc·tion /'sʌkʃn/ *n* [U] 1 action of sucking; removal of air, liquid, etc from a vessel or cavity so as to produce a partial vacuum and enable air-pressure from outside to force in liquid or dust: *Some pumps and all vacuum-cleaners work by* ∼. 2 similar process, eg in a rubber disc with a concave surface, a fly's foot, causing two surfaces to be held together.

sud·den /'sʌdn/ *adj* happening, coming, done, unexpectedly, quickly, without warning: *a* ∼ *shower; a* ∼ *turn in the road.* □ *n* (only in) *all of a* ∼, unexpectedly. ∼**·ly** *adv* ∼**·ness** *n*

suds /sʌdz/ *n pl* froth, mass of tiny bubbles, on soapy water.

sue /sju:/ *vt,vi* **sue (for),** 1 [VP6A,14] make a legal claim against: *sue a person for damages,* for money in compensation for loss or injury. 2 [VP14,3A] beg; ask: *sue (the enemy) for peace; suing for mercy; sue for a divorce,* in a law court.

suede /sweɪd/ *n* [U] kind of soft leather made from the skin of goats, with the flesh surface rubbed into a soft nap: (attrib) ∼ *shoes/gloves.*

suet /'su:ɪt/ *n* [U] hard fat round the kidneys of sheep and oxen, used in cooking. ∼**y** *adj* like, containing, ∼.

suf·fer /'sʌfə(r)/ *vi,vt* 1 [VP2A,3A] ∼ *(from),* feel or have pain, loss, etc: ∼ *from* (= often have) *headaches;* ∼*ing from loss of memory. His business* ∼*ed while he was ill,* His business did not do well. *You will* ∼ (= be punished) *one day for your insolence!* 2 [VP6A] experience, undergo (sth unpleasant): ∼ *pain/defeat/adversity;* ∼ *death,* lose one's life, eg as a condemned criminal or as a martyr. 3 [VP17A] allow, permit (which are the more usu words). 4 [VP6A] tolerate; put up with: *How can you* ∼ *such insolence?* ∼ *fools gladly,* be patient with foolish people. ∼**er** /'sʌfərə(r)/ *n* person who ∼s. ∼**·able** /'sʌfərəbl/ *adj* bearable. ∼**·ing** *n* 1 [U] pain of body or mind: *How much* ∼*ing is there in the world?* 2 (*pl*) feelings of pain, unhappiness, etc: *They laughed at the prisoner's* ∼*ings.*

suf·fer·ance /'sʌfərəns/ *n* [U] **on** ∼, with permission implied by the absence of objection: *He's here on* ∼, allowed to be here but not wanted.

suf·fice /sə'faɪs/ *vi,vt* 1 [VP2A,3A] ∼ *(for),* be enough (which is more usu): *Will £10* ∼ *for the trip? Your word will* ∼, I am content to accept your promise. *S*∼ *it to say that...* (= It ∼s to say), I will content myself by saying that.... 2 [VP6A] meet the needs of: *One meal a day won't* ∼ *a growing boy.*

suf·fi·cient /sə'fɪʃnt/ *adj* enough: *Is £10* ∼ *for the expenses of your journey? Have we* ∼ *food for ten people?* ∼**·ly** *adv* **suf·fi·ciency** /-nsɪ/ *n* (usu *a sufficiency of sth*) ∼ quantity: *a sufficiency of fuel for the winter.*

suf·fix /'sʌfɪks/ *n* (abbr *suff* used in this dictionary) letter(s), sound(s) or syllable(s) added at the end of a word to make another word, eg *y* added to *rust* to make *rusty,* or as an inflexion, eg *-en* in *oxen.* ⇨ prefix and App 3.

suf·fo·cate /'sʌfəkeɪt/ *vt,vi* 1 [VP6A,2A,C] cause

or have difficulty in breathing: *The fumes almost ~d me. He was suffocating with rage.* **2** [VP6A] kill, choke, by making breathing impossible. **suf-fo-ca-tion** /ˌsʌfəˈkeɪʃn/ n

suf-fra-gan /ˈsʌfrəgən/ n ~ **bishop, bishop** ~, bishop who is consecrated to help the bishop of a see by managing part of the diocese.

suf-frage /ˈsʌfrɪdʒ/ n **1** [C] (formal) vote; consent expressed by voting. **2** [U] franchise; right of voting in political elections: *When was the ~ extended to all women in Great Britain? Is there universal ~ in your country,* Have all adults the right to vote? **suf-fra-gette** /ˌsʌfrəˈdʒet/ n woman who, in the early part of the 20th c, agitated for women's ~ in GB.

suf-fuse /səˈfjuːz/ vt [VP6A] (esp of colours, tears) spread slowly over the surface of: *eyes ~d with tears; the evening sky ~d with crimson.* **suf-fu-sion** /səˈfjuːʒn/ n [U].

sugar /ˈʃʊgə(r)/ n [U] sweet substance obtained from the juices of various plants, esp ('**cane-~**) from '**~-cane** and ('**beet-~**) from '**~-beet**, used in cooking and for sweetening tea, coffee, etc. **~-'coated** adj coated with ~: *~-coated pills;* (fig) superficially attractive: *~-coated promises.* '**~-daddy** n (colloq) rich, usu elderly, man who is generous to a young woman in return for sexual favours or friendship. '**~-loaf** n hard lump of ~ in the form of a cone, as sold in former times. '**~-lump** n small cube of ~, used to sweeten a cup of tea, coffee, etc. '**~-refinery** n establishment where raw ~ is refined. '**~-tongs** n pl small tongs for taking lumps (cubes) of ~ at table. □ vt [VP6A] sweeten or mix with ~. ⇨ pill(1). **sugary** adj tasting of ~; (fig) too sweet: ~y *compliments/music.*

sug-gest /səˈdʒest US: səgˈdʒ-/ vt **1** [VP6A,C,9,10,14] ~ **sth** (**to sb**); ~ (**to sb**) **that...**; ~ **doing sth,** propose; put forward for consideration, as a possibility: *I ~ed a visit. I ~ed going home/that we should go home. I ~ we go to the theatre. What did you ~ to the manager? Can you ~ where I could park my car?* **2** [VP6A] bring (an idea, possibility, etc) into the mind: *Your wheezing breathing ~s asthma or bronchitis,* causes me to think that these are what you may be suffering from. **3** [VP14] (reflex) come into the mind: *An idea ~s itself to me,* has occurred to me. **~-ible** /-əbl/ adj that can be influenced by ~ion; that can be ~ed. **sug-ges-tion** /səˈdʒestʃən US: səgˈdʒ-/ n **1** [U] ~ing: *at the ~ion of my brother; on your ~ion. S~ion is often more effective than persuasion.* **2** [C] idea, plan, etc that is ~ed: *These ~ions didn't appeal to me.* **3** [C] slight indication: *He speaks English with a ~ion of a French accent.* **4** [U] process of bringing an idea into the mind through association with other ideas. **hypnotic ~ion,** putting ideas or impulses into the mind of a person who is hypnotized. **sug-ges-tive** /səˈdʒestɪv US: səgˈdʒ-/ adj **1** tending to bring ideas, etc into the mind: *~ive remarks.* **2** tending to ~ sth improper or indecent: *~ive jokes.* **sug-ges-tive-ly** adv

sui-cide /ˈsjuːɪsaɪd/ n **1** [U] self-murder: *commit ~;* [C] instance of this: *three ~s last week;* [C] person who commits ~. **2** [U] action destructive to one's interests or welfare: *political ~,* that makes continuance in office, etc, impossible; *economic ~,* eg adoption of policies that ruin the country's economy. **sui-cidal** /ˌsjuːɪˈsaɪdl/ adj of ~; very harmful to one's own interests: *a man with suicidal ten-*

dencies; *a suicidal policy.*

suit¹ /suːt/ n **1** [C] set of articles of outer clothing of the same material: *a ~ of armour; a man's ~,* jacket, (waistcoat) and trousers; *a woman's ~,* coat and skirt; a '*trouser-~,* woman's ~ of jacket and trousers; *a two-/three-piece ~,* of two/three garments; a '*dress ~,* a man's formal evening ~. '**~-case** n portable flat-sided case for clothes, used when travelling. **2** [C] (formal) request made to a superior, esp to a ruler: *grant sb's ~; press one's ~,* beg persistently. **3** [C] (liter or old use) asking a woman's hand in marriage: *plead/press one's ~ with a young woman.* **4** ('**law-**)**~,** case in a law court; prosecution of a claim: *bring a ~ against sb; be a party in a ~; a criminal/civil ~.* **5** [C] any of the four sets of cards (*spades, hearts, diamonds, clubs*) used in many card games. ⇨ the illus at card. **a long ~,** many cards of one ~, eg ace, king, 10, 8, 6; one player's hand. **follow ~, (a)** play a card of the ~ that has been led. **(b)** (fig) do what sb else has done. **~-ing** n (shop term for) material for clothing: *gentlemen's ~ings,* material for men's suits.

suit² /suːt/ vt,vi **1** [VP6A,2A] satisfy; meet the needs of; be convenient to or right for: *The seven o'clock train will ~ us very well. Does the climate ~ you/your health? Will Thursday ~ (you),* be convenient? ~ **oneself,** do what one chooses to do; act according to one's own wishes. ~ **sb down to the ground,** ~ him very well. **2** [VP6B] (esp of articles of dress, styles of dressing the hair, etc) look well; be appropriate for: *Does this skirt ~ me? That colour does not ~ your complexion. It doesn't ~ you to have your hair cut short.* **3** ~ **sth to,** make fit or appropriate: ~ *the punishment to the crime;* ~ *one's style to one's audience.* ~ **the action to the word,** carry out the promise (threat, etc) at once. **4** (pp) **be ~ed (to/for),** be fitted, have the right qualities: *Is Western democracy ~ed to/for the nations of Asia and Africa? That man is not ~ed for teaching/to be a teacher. Jack and his wife seem well ~ed to one another,* likely to be and remain on good terms.

suit-able /ˈsuːtəbl/ adj right for the purpose or occasion: *clothes ~ for cold weather; a ~ place for a picnic; a ~ case for* (medical, psychiatric, etc) *treatment.* **suit-ably** /-əblɪ/ adv **suit-abil-ity** /ˌsuːtəˈbɪlətɪ/ n ~**-ness** n

suite /swiːt/ n [C] **1** group of personal attendants of an important person (eg a ruler). **2** complete set of matching articles of furniture: *a dining-room ~,* ie a table, chairs, a sideboard; *a lounge/bedroom ~.* **3** complete set of rooms (eg in a hotel, a bedroom, a sitting-room and a bathroom). **4** complete set of objects that belong together: *a computer suite,* all the machinery needed to run a computer. **5** (music) orchestral composition made up of three or more related parts.

suitor /ˈsuːtə(r)/ n **1** person bringing a lawsuit. ⇨ suit¹(4). **2** man courting a woman. ⇨ suit¹(3).

sulfa /ˈsʌlfə/ adj (US) = sulpha. ⇨ sulphonamides.

sul-fate (US) = sulphate.

sul-fide (US) = sulphide.

sul-fona-mides (US) = sulphonamides.

sul-fur, sul-fur-ic, sul-fur-ous, etc (US) = sulphur, sulphuric, sulphurous, etc.

sulk /sʌlk/ vi [VP2A,C] be in a bad temper and show this by refusing to talk. **the ~s** n pl condition of ~ing: *be in the ~s; have (a fit of) the ~s.*

~y adj (-ier, -iest) having a tendency to ~; unsociable: as ~y as a bear; be/get ~y with sb about a trifle. ~·ily /-ɪlɪ/ adv i·ness n

sulky /'sʌlkɪ/ n (pl -kies) light two-wheeled carriage for one person, drawn by one horse.

sul·len /'sʌlən/ adj 1 silently bad-tempered; unforgiving: ~ looks. 2 dark and gloomy; dismal: a ~ sky. ~·ly adv ~·ness n

sully /'sʌlɪ/ vt (pt,pp -lied) [VP6A] (usu fig) stain or discredit: ~ sb's reputation.

sulpha (US = **sulfa**) /'sʌlfə/ n ⇨ sulphonamides.

sul·phate (US = **sulfate**) /'sʌlfeɪt/ n [C,U] salt of sulphuric acid: ~ of copper/copper ~, chemical (CuSO₄) used in water to kill algae and fungi; ~ of magnesium, Epsom salts.

sul·phide (US = **sulfide**) /'sʌlfaɪd/ n [C,U] compound of sulphur and another element: hydrogen ~, (H₂S) sulphuretted hydrogen, a gas with a smell like that of rotten eggs.

sul·phona·mides (US =sul·fo-) /sʌl'fɒnəmaɪdz/ n pl group of drugs (synthetic chemical compounds, also called the 'sulpha drugs) acting as anti-bacterial agents.

sul·phur (US = **sul·fur**) /'sʌlfə(r)/ n light-yellow non-metallic element (symbol **S**) that burns with a bright flame and a strong smell, used in medicine and industry. ~·etted /'sʌlfjʊretɪd/ adj having ~ in combination: ~etted hydrogen, (H₂S). **sul·phureous** (US = **sul·fu-**) /sʌl'fjʊərɪəs/ adj of, like, containing ~. **sul·phu·ric** (US = **sul·fu-**) /sʌl'fjʊərɪk/ adj ~**ic acid**, oily, colourless, very strong acid (H₂SO₄) important in many industries. ~·ous /-əs/ adj of, containing, ~.

sul·tan /'sʌltən/ n Muslim ruler, esp of the former Ottoman Empire. ~·ate /'sʌltəneɪt/ n position, period of rule of, a ~; territory ruled by a ~. **sul·tana** /sʌl'tɑːnə US: -ænə/ n wife, mother, sister or daughter of a ~.

sul·tana /sʌl'tɑːnə US: -ænə/ n [C] kind of small seedless raisin used in puddings and cakes.

sul·try /'sʌltrɪ/ adj (-ier, -iest) (of the atmosphere, the weather) hot and oppressive; (of a person's temper) passionate. **sul·trily** /-trəlɪ/ adv **sul·triness** n

sum /sʌm/ n 1 (also **sum total**) total obtained by adding together items, numbers or amounts. 2 problem in arithmetic: good at sums; do a sum in one's head. 3 amount of money: win a large sum at the Casino; save a nice little sum out of one's wages each week. 4 **in sum**, in a few words. □ vt,vi (-mm-) [VP15B,2C] **sum (sb/sth) up, (a)** give the total of. **(b)** express briefly (the chief points of what has been said); The judge summed up (the evidence). **(c)** form a judgement or opinion of: He summed up the situation at a glance, realized it at once. She quickly summed him up, judged his character, etc. ,summing-'up n (pl summings-up) judge's review of evidence, arguments, etc, in a law-case.

su·mac(h) /'ʃuːmæk/ n (kinds of) shrub or small tree, the dried leaves being used in tanning and dyeing.

sum·mary /'sʌmərɪ/ adj 1 brief; giving the chief points only: a ~ account. 2 done or given without delay or attention to small matters: ~ justice/punishment/methods. □ n (pl -ries) brief account giving the chief points. **sum·mar·ily** /'sʌmərəlɪ US: sə'merəlɪ/ adv **sum·mar·ize** /'sʌməraɪz/ vt [VP6A] be or make a ~ of.

sum·mat /'sʌmət/ n (sl and dial) something.

sum·ma·tion /sʌ'meɪʃn/ n 1 addition. 2 summing up.

sum·mer /'sʌmə(r)/ n [U,C] (in countries outside the tropics) the warmest season of the year, May or June to August in the northern hemisphere: in (the) ~; in the ~ of 1999; this/next/last ~; (attrib) ~ weather; the ~ holidays; a ~ cottage/house, for use during the ~; a girl of ten ~s, (liter) ten years of age. It's been an unusually hot ~. '~-house n shelter with seats in a garden, park, etc. '~ school n course of lectures, often at a university, during the ~ vacation. '~-time n the season of ~. '~ time n time as recognized in some countries where clocks are put forward one hour so that darkness falls an hour later, giving long light evenings during the ~ months. ⇨ daylight saving at daylight. **Indian** ~, ⇨ Indian(3). □ vi [VP2C] spend the ~: ~ at the seaside/in the mountains. ~y adj characteristic of, suitable for, ~: a ~y dress.

sum·mit /'sʌmɪt/ n [C] highest point; top: reach the ~, of a mountain; (fig) the ~ of his ambition/power; talks at the ~. '~ **talk/meeting**, discussion between heads of States.

sum·mon /'sʌmən/ vt 1 [VP6A,14,17] ~ **sb (to sth/to do sth)**, demand the presence of; call or send for: ~ shareholders to a general meeting; ~ sb to appear as a witness, eg in a law court. The debtor was ~ed, ie to appear in a law court. The Queen has ~ed Parliament, ordered members to assemble. 2 [VP15B] ~ **sth up**, gather together; call up: ~ up one's courage/energy/nerve for a task/to do sth.

sum·mons /'sʌmənz/ n (pl ~es) [C] 1 order to appear before a judge or magistrate; document with such an order: issue a ~. The ~ was served by a bailiff. 2 command to do sth or appear somewhere. □ vt [VP6A] serve a ~(1) on.

sump /sʌmp/ n 1 inner casing of a petrol engine containing lubricating oil. 2 hole or low area into which waste liquid drains.

sump·ter /'sʌmptə(r)/ n (old use) (often '~-horse, '~-mule) horse or mule for carrying burdens; pack-animal.

sump·tu·ary /'sʌmptjʊərɪ US: -tʃʊerɪ/ adj (attrib only) (of laws) controlling or limiting private expenditure of money (on what is considered extravagant, etc).

sump·tu·ous /'sʌmptʃʊəs/ adj magnificent; costly-looking: a ~ feast; ~ clothes. ~·ly adv ~·ness n

sun /sʌn/ n 1 (the)sun, the heavenly body from which the earth gets warmth and light. ⇨ the illus at planet. **rise with the sun,** get up at dawn. **the midnight sun,** the sun as seen in the arctic and antarctic regions. 2(the)sun, light and warmth from the sun: sit in the sun; have the sun in one's eyes; draw the curtains to shut out/let in the sun. **under the sun,** (anywhere) in the world: the best wine under the sun. **give sb/have a place in the sun,** (fig) space and conditions favourable to development. 3 [C] any fixed star: There are many suns larger than ours. 4 (compounds) '**sun-baked** adj made hard by the heat of the sun: sunbaked fields. '**sun-bathe** vi expose one's body to sunlight, eg to give a pale skin a tan. ⇨ sunburn below. '**sunbeam** n ray of sunshine; (colloq) cheerful and happy person (esp a child). '**sun-blind** n window shade, esp an awning outside a window. '**sunbonnet/-hat** nn hat or (usu linen) bonnet made so as to shade the face and neck from the sun. **'sun-burn** *n* [C,U] (place where there is a) darkening of the skin caused by the sun, or reddening and blistering caused by too much exposure to the sun. **'sun-burnt, 'sun-burned** *adjj* having sunburn. **'sun-burst** *n* sudden burst of sunlight (through broken clouds) **'sun-dial** *n* device that shows the time by the shadow of a rod or plate on a scaled dial. **'sun-down** *n* [U] sunset. **'sun-downer** *n* (a) (in Australia) tramp who habitually arrives (at a sheep farm, etc) at nightfall. **(b)** (colloq) drink (usu of sth alcoholic) at sundown. **'sun-drenched** *adj* exposed to great light and heat from the sun: *sun-drenched beaches along the Riviera.* **'sun-dried** *adj* (of fruit, etc) dried naturally, by the sun, not by artificial heat. **'sun-fish** *n* large fish almost spherical in shape. **'sun-flower** *n* tall garden plant with large golden-rayed flowers. ⇨ the illus at flower. **'sun-glasses** *n pl* glasses of dark-coloured glass to protect the eyes from bright sunshine. **'sun-god** *n* sun worshipped as a god. **'sun-helmet** *n* hat specially made to protect the head from the sun in the tropics. **'sun-lamp** *n* lamp that gives out ultra-violet rays with effects like those of the sun, used for artificial sun-bathing. **'sun-light** *n* [U] the light of the sun. **'sun-lit** *adj* lighted by the sun: *a sunlit landscape.* **'sun-lounge,** or, less usu **'sun-parlour/-porch** *nn* made with glass sides and so situated as to admit much sunlight. **'sun-ray** *n* ultra-violet ray used on the body: (attrib) *'sun-ray treatment.* **'sun-rise** *n* [U] (time of) the sun's rising: *start at sunrise.* **'sun-roof** (or, less usu **'sunshine-roof'**) *n* panel on the roof of a saloon car which slides back to admit sunshine. **'sunset /-set/** *n* [U] (time of) the sun's setting. **'sun-shade** *n* parasol (like an umbrella) to keep off the sun; awning of a shop window. **'sun-shine** *n* [U] light of the sun. **'sun-spot** *n* (astron) dark patch on the sun at times, often causing electrical disturbances and interfering with radio communications; (colloq) place that has a sunny climate (eg for holidays). **'sun-stroke** *n* [U] illness caused by too much exposure to the sun, esp on the head. **'sun-tan** *n* [U,C] browning of the skin from exposure to sunlight: *'suntan lotion/oil.* **'sun-trap** *n* warm sunny place (sheltered from wind). **'sun-up** *n* [U] (colloq) sunrise. **'sun-worship** *n* [U] worship of the sun as a deity; (colloq) fondness for sun-bathing. □ *vt* (-nn-) [VP6A] put in, expose (*oneself*) to, the rays of the sun: *The cat was sunning itself on the path.* **sun-less** *adj* receiving little or no sunlight; without sun; dark: *a sunless day/room.* **sunny** *adj* (-ier, -iest) **1** bright with sunlight: *a sunny room; sunny days.* **,sunny-side 'up,** (US) (of an egg) fried on one side only. **2** cheerful: *a sunny smile/ disposition/welcome.*   **sun-ni-ly** /-ɪlɪ/ *adv*

a sundial

sun-dae /'sʌndeɪ *US:* -dɪ/ *n* portion of ice-cream with crushed fruit, fruit-juice, nuts, etc.

Sun-day /'sʌndɪ/ *n* the first day of the week, a day of rest and worship among Christians. **one's ~ clothes/best,** (colloq, joc) one's best clothes, not

used for working in. **'~ school,** one (in a church, etc) attended by children on ~s for religious teaching. *a month of* ~*s,* a long period of time.

sun-der /'sʌndə(r)/ *vt* (old use, or liter) [VP6A] keep apart; sever. □ *n* (only in) *in* ~, = asunder.

sun-dries /'sʌndrɪz/ *n pl* various small items not separately named.

sun-dry /'sʌndrɪ/ *adj* various: *on ~ occasions.* **all and ~,** (colloq) everyone; everything.

sung /sʌŋ/ *pp* of sing.

sunk /sʌŋk/ *pt* of sink².

sunk-en /'sʌŋkən/ *pp* of sink² esp (5).

sunny /'sʌnɪ/ *adj* ⇨ sun.

sup¹ /sʌp/ *vi,vt* (-pp-) [VP2A,C,6A,15B] *sup (up),* (esp Scot and N Eng) drink in small amounts; take (liquid) into the mouth a little at a time: *Sup (up) your broth.* □ *n* small quantity (of liquid): *a sup of ale. I've had neither bite nor sup* (= neither food nor drink) *for six hours.*

sup² /sʌp/ *vi* (-pp-) [VP3A] *sup on/off,* (rare) eat (on, off): *sup on bread and cheese. He that sups with the devil must have a long spoon,* (prov) Caution is needed in dealings with someone of doubtful character.

super /'su:pə(r)/ *n* (colloq) supernumerary; superintendent (of police). □ *adj* (colloq) excellent; splendid.

super-abun-dant /ˌsu:pərə'bʌndənt/ *adj* very abundant; more than enough. **super-abun-dance** /-əns/ *n*

super-an-nu-ate /ˌsu:pər'ænjʊeɪt/ *vt* **1** [VP6A] give a pension to (an employee) when he is old or unable to work; dismiss (an employee) because of age or weakness. **2** (*pp,* ~**d,** as *adj*) too old for work or use; (colloq) old-fashioned or out of date. **super-an-nu-ation** /ˌsu:pərˌænjʊ'eɪʃn/ *n*

su-perb /su:'pɜ:b/ *adj* magnificent; first class. ~**·ly** *adv*

super-cargo /'su:pəkɑ:gəʊ/ *n* (*pl* ~es /-gəʊz/) person on a merchant ship who manages the sale of the cargo, etc.

super-charger /'su:pətʃɑ:dʒə(r)/ *n* device used in an internal-combustion engine to force extra oxygen into the cylinders. **'super-charged** *adj* fitted with a ~.

super-cili-ous /ˌsu:pə'sɪlɪəs/ *adj* showing contemptuous indifference: *nose high in the air, looking like a ~ camel.* ~**·ly** *adv* ~**·ness** *n*

super-ego /'su:pəregəʊ *US:* -i:gəʊ/ *n* [U] **(the)** ~, (psych) the part of the mind that responds to conscience and morality. ⇨ ego, id.

super-ero-gation /ˌsu:pərˌerə'geɪʃn/ *n* [U] the doing of more than is required or expected: *a work of* ~.

super-fat-ted /ˌsu:pə'fætɪd/ *adj* (chiefly of soap) containing a larger than usual proportion of fat.

super-fi-cial /ˌsu:pə'fɪʃl/ *adj* **1** of or on the surface only: *a ~ wound; ~ area.* **2** not thorough or profound: *a ~ book; have only a ~ knowledge of a subject; a ~ mind.* ~**·ly** /-ʃəlɪ/ *adv* ~**·ity** /ˌsu:pəˌfɪʃɪ'ælətɪ/ *n* [U].

super-fi-cies /ˌsu:pə'fɪʃi:z/ *n* (*pl* unchanged) **1** surface; surface area. **2** outward appearance.

super-fine /'su:pəfaɪn/ *adj* **1** unusually fine in quality. **2** unnecessarily refined or subtle: *a ~ distinction.*

super-flu-ous /su:'pɜ:fluəs/ *adj* more than is needed or wanted. ~**·ly** *adv* **super-flu-ity** /ˌsu:pə'flu:ətɪ/ *n* (*pl* -ties) [C,U] (an amount that is) more than is needed: *have a superfluity of good things.*

super·hu·man /ˌsuːpəˈhjuːmən/ adj exceeding ordinary human power, size, knowledge, etc: by a ～ effort; an apparition of ～ size.

super·im·pose /ˌsuːpərɪmˈpəʊz/ vt [VP6A,14] put (one thing) on top of sth else: a map of Great Britain ～d on a map of Texas, eg to show comparative size.

super·in·tend /ˌsuːpərɪnˈtend/ vt,vi [VP6A,2A] manage; watch and direct (work, etc). **～·ence** /-əns/ n [U] **～ing**: under the personal ～ence of the manager. **～·ent** /-ənt/ n person who ～s; manager; police officer above a chief inspector in rank.

su·perior /suːˈpɪərɪə(r)/ adj **1** better than the average: ～ cloth; a girl of ～ intelligence; ～ grades of coffee. **2** greater in number: The enemy attacked with ～ forces/were ～ in numbers. **3** ～ to, (a) better than: This cloth is ～ to that. (b) higher in rank or position than. (c) not influenced by; not giving way to: ～ to flattery; rise (= be) ～ to temptation. **4** priggish; supercilious: 'I never apologize', he said, with a ～ air. □ n **1** person of higher rank, authority, etc than another, or who is better, etc than another (in sth): my ～s in rank/in expertise. Napoleon had no ～ as a general. **2** (in titles) head of a religious community: the Father S～, eg an abbot; the Mother S～, eg an abbess. **～·ity** /suːˌpɪərɪˈɒrətɪ US: -ˈɔːr-/ n [U] state of being ～: the ～ity of one thing to another; his ～ity in talent. '**～·ity complex**, (pop use) aggressive or domineering attitude as a defence against a feeling of inferiority.

su·per·la·tive /suːˈpɜːlətɪv/ adj **1** of the highest degree or quality: a wine of ～ bouquet and flavour. **2** (gram) the ～ degree, the form of an adj or adv expressing the highest degree, eg best, worst, slowest, most foolish(ly). □ n ～ form of an adj or adv. **speak in ～s**, use language expressing extreme opinions and feelings; exaggerate.

super·man /ˈsuːpəmæn/ n (pl -men) man having more than ordinary human powers and abilities, eg as imagined by sb writing about the future of mankind.

super·mar·ket /ˈsuːpəmɑːkɪt/ n large self-service store selling food, household goods, etc.

su·per·nal /suːˈpɜːnl/ adj (liter) heavenly; divine: ～ loveliness.

super·natu·ral /ˌsuːpəˈnætʃrəl/ adj spiritual; of that which is not controlled or explained by physical laws: ～ beings, eg angels and devils. **the ～**, ～ agencies, phenomena, etc. **～·ly** /-ˈnætʃrəlɪ/ adv

super·nor·mal /ˌsuːpəˈnɔːml/ adj beyond what is normal.

super·nu·mer·ary /ˌsuːpəˈnjuːmərərɪ US: -ˈnuːmərerɪ/ n (pl -ries), adj (person or thing) in excess of the normal number; (esp) person engaged for odd jobs; actor who has only a small part, eg in crowd scenes.

super·scrip·tion /ˌsuːpəˈskrɪpʃn/ n [C] word(s) written at the top of or outside sth, eg the address on the envelope of a letter.

super·sede /ˌsuːpəˈsiːd/ vt [VP6A] take the place of; put or use sb or sth in the place of: Motorways have ～d ordinary roads for long-distance travel. **super·session** /ˌsuːpəˈseʃn/ n

super·sonic /ˌsuːpəˈsɒnɪk/ adj (of speeds) greater than that of sound; (of aircraft) able to fly at ～ speed.

super·sti·tion /ˌsuːpəˈstɪʃn/ n [C,U] (idea, practice, etc founded on) unreasoning belief in magic, witchcraft, etc; irrational fear of what is unknown or mysterious: sunk in ignorance and ～. **super·sti·tious** /ˌsuːpəˈstɪʃəs/ adj of, showing, resulting from, ～; believing in ～s: superstitious beliefs/ ideas/people. **super·sti·tious·ly** adv

super·struc·ture /ˈsuːpəstrʌktʃə(r)/ n structure built on the top of sth else; parts of a ship above the main deck.

super·tax /ˈsuːpətæks/ n [C,U] tax on, or the taxation of, incomes (additional to income tax) above a certain level.

super·vene /ˌsuːpəˈviːn/ vi [VP2A] (formal) come or happen as a change from or interruption of (a condition or process).

super·vise /ˈsuːpəvaɪz/ vt,vi [VP6A,2A] watch and direct (work, workers, an organization). **super·vi·sor** /-zə(r)/ n person who ～s. **super·vi·sion** /ˌsuːpəˈvɪʒn/ n supervising: under the supervision of, ～d by. **super·vis·ory** /ˌsuːpəˈvaɪzərɪ/ adj supervising: supervisory duties.

su·pine /ˈsuːpaɪn US: sʊˈpaɪn/ adj **1** lying flat on the back, face upwards. ⇨ prone(1). **2** inactive; slow to act; indolent. **～·ly** adv

sup·per /ˈsʌpə(r)/ n [C,U] last meal of the day, when this is less large or less formal than a dinner: have cold meat for ～; eat very little ～; have a good ～; late ～s after the theatre. **～·less** adj without ～: go to bed ～less.

sup·plant /səˈplɑːnt US: -ˈplænt/ vt [VP6A] **1** take the place of (sth): Trams in London have been ～ed by buses. **2** take the place of (sb), esp after getting him out of office: The Prime Minister was ～ed by his rival. She has been ～ed in his affections by another woman. **～·er** n person who ～s another.

supple /ˈsʌpl/ adj easily bent or bending; not stiff: the ～ limbs of a child; a ～ mind, quick to respond to ideas. **～·ness** n

supple·ment /ˈsʌplɪmənt/ n [C] **1** sth added later to improve or complete, eg a dictionary. **2** extra and separate addition to a newspaper or other periodical: The Times Literary S～; the Observer colour ～. □ vt /ˈsʌplɪment/ [VP6A,15A] make an addition or additions to: ～ one's ordinary income by writing books.

supple·men·tary /ˌsʌplɪˈmentrɪ/ adj **1** additional; extra: ～ estimates, eg for additional expenditure: ～ benefit, (in GB) extra money granted by the State to people in need. **2** (of an angle) making with another a total of 180°.

sup·pli·ant /ˈsʌplɪənt/ n, adj (formal) (person) asking humbly for sth: kneel as a ～ at the altar, ie praying to God; in a ～ attitude.

sup·pli·cate /ˈsʌplɪkeɪt/ vt,vi [VP6A,14,17,2C] (formal and liter) make a humble petition to sb: ～ sb to help; ～ sb's protection; ～ for pardon. **sup·pli·cant** /ˈsʌplɪkənt/ n person who ～s; suppliant. **sup·pli·ca·tion** /ˌsʌplɪˈkeɪʃn/ n [C,U] humble prayer.

supply /səˈplaɪ/ vt (pt,pp -lied) [VP6A,14] **～ sth to sb; ～ sb with sth, 1** give or provide (sth needed or asked for): ～ gas/electricity to domestic consumers; ～ consumers with gas, etc. **2** meet (a need): Should the government ～ the need for more houses, (help to) provide them (eg by building them, or giving subsidies or making loans)? □ n **1** [U] ～ing; [C] (pl -lies) that which is supplied; stock or amount of sth which is obtainable: Have you a good ～ of reading matter for the train journey, plenty of books, magazines, etc? We shall be receiving new supplies of shoes next week, (eg of a shop) new stocks. ~ *and demand,* quantities available and quantities asked for (thought of as regulating prices). *in short* ~, scarce (which is the more usu word). **2 supplies,** (esp) stores necessary for some public need, eg the armed forces: '*medical supplies.* **3** *be/go on* ~, work as a temporary substitute, eg for a teacher or clergyman: (attrib) *a* '~ *teacher.* **4 supplies,** (GB) grant of money by Parliament for the cost of government. **S~ Day,** (in the House of Commons) day on which approval of the Estimates (of expenditure) is asked for. **5 supplies,** allowance of money to a person: *Tom's father cut off the supplies.* **sup·pli·er** n person or firm ~ing goods, etc.

sup·port /sə'pɔ:t/ vt [VP6A] **1** bear the weight of; hold up or keep in place: *Is this bridge strong enough to* ~ *heavy lorries? He hurt his ankle, so he had to be* ~*ed home,* someone had to help him to walk home. **2** strengthen; help (sb or sth) to continue: ~ *a claim/a political party;* ~ *a football team,* eg by regularly watching it play; ~*ing troops,* held in reserve to help those who are fighting; *a hospital* ~*ed by voluntary contributions; a theory that is not* ~*ed by the facts; an accusation not* ~*ed by proofs; a* '~*ing actor,* one who takes a part secondary to that of the leading actor; *a*'~*ing film,* secondary to the main feature film. **3** provide for (financially, etc): *He has a large family to* ~. **4** endure: *I can't* ~ *your jealousy any longer.* □ n **1** [U] ~ing or being ~ed: *This bridge needs more* ~. *I hope to have your* ~ *in the election. The proposal obtained no/little/not much* ~. *Mr X spoke in* ~ *of the motion. The divorced wife claimed* ~ (ie a regular financial contribution) *for her children from her ex-husband, but he was found to be without visible means of* ~, with no apparent resources (money, work) on which to live. *in* ~, (of troops) in reserve, ready to give ~. *(be) in* ~ *of sb/sth,* (be) ~ing him/it. **2** [C] sb or sth that ~s: *Dick is the chief* ~ *of the family,* earns the money for the family. '*price* ~*s,* (US) subsidies, eg paid by the government to farmers. ~**·able** /-əbl/ *adj* that can be ~ed; endurable. ~**·er** n person or device that ~s. ~**·ive** *adj* ~ing; giving help, encouragement.

sup·pose /sə'pəʊz/ vt **1** [VP9,6A,25] let it be thought that; take it as a fact that: *Let us* ~ (*that*) *the news is true. S~ the world were flat. Everyone is* ~*d to know the rules,* It is assumed, taken for granted, that we all know the rules. *I don't* ~ *for one/a minute that...,* I don't believe that.... **2** [VP9,6A,25] guess; think: *What do you* ~ *he wanted? All her neighbours* ~*d her to be/*~*d that she was a widow. You'll be there, I* ~. '*Will he come?'*—'*Yes, I* ~ *so'/*'*No, I* ~ *not'/*'*No, I don't* ~ *so'. I* ~ *you want to borrow money again!* **3** [VP6A] (forming an imper, or used to make a suggestion or proposal): *S~ we go* (= Let's go) *for a swim.* **4** [VP6A] require as a condition; imply: *Creation* ~*s a creator.* **5** *be* ~*d to,* (a) be expected or required to (by customs, duty, etc): *Is he* ~*d to clean the outside of the windows or only the inside?* (b) (colloq) (in the neg) not be allowed to: *We're not* ~*d to play football on Sundays.* **sup·pos·ing** *conj* if: *Supposing it rains, what shall you do?* ~*d* accepted as being so: *his* ~*d generosity. The* ~*d beggar was really a police officer in disguise.* **sup·pos·ed·ly** /-ɪdlɪ/ *adv* according to what is/may ~*d.*

sup·po·si·tion /ˌsʌpə'zɪʃn/ n **1** [U] supposing: *This newspaper article is based on* ~, on what the writ-

er supposes to be the case, not on fact; *We mustn't condemn him on mere* ~. **2** [C] sth supposed; guess: *Our* ~*s were fully confirmed. on this* ~; *on the* ~ *that...,* supposing that this is the case.

sup·posi·tory /sə'pɒzɪtrɪ US: -tɔ:rɪ/ n (pl -ries) medical preparation (in a soluble capsule) inserted into the rectum or vagina and left to dissolve.

sup·press /sə'pres/ vt [VP6A] **1** put an end to the activity or existence of: ~ *a rising/the slave trade.* **2** prevent from being known or seen: ~ *the truth/a yawn/one's feelings;* ~ *a newspaper,* prevent its publication. ~**ion** /sə'preʃn/ n ~ing: *a policy of* ~*ion,* eg of ~ing movements for independence or for freedom. ~**ive** *adj* tending to ~; designed to ~. ~**or** /-sə(r)/ n sth that ~es; (esp) a device fitted to electric apparatus to prevent interference with radio and television reception: *fit a* ~ *to an electric motor.*

sup·pu·rate /'sʌpjʊreɪt/ vi [VP2A] (formal) form pus, fester. **sup·pu·ra·tion** /ˌsʌpjʊ'reɪʃn/ n

supra /'su:prə/ *adv* (Lat; formal) above; earlier on (in a book, etc): *See* ~, *p 21,* See p 21 earlier on in this book.

supra·na·tional /ˌsu:prə'næʃnəl/ *adj* above nations or states: *a* ~ *authority,* one that might be created for world government.

su·preme /su:'pri:m/ *adj* **1** highest in degree or rank or authority: *the S~ Commander; the S~ Court,* highest in one of the States of the US or in the whole of the US; *the S~ Soviet,* the legislature of the USSR; *the S~ Being,* God. **2** most important; greatest: *make the* ~ *sacrifice,* lay down one's life (eg in war). ~**·ly** *adv* in a ~ manner: ~*ly happy.* **su·prem·acy** /sʊ'preməsɪ/ n [U] *supremacy over,* being ~ over; highest authority: *His supremacy was unchallenged.*

sur·charge /'sɜ:tʃɑ:dʒ/ n **1** payment demanded in addition to the usual charge, eg as a penalty for a letter with insufficient postage paid on it. **2** excessive or additional load. **3** mark overprinted on a postage-stamp changing its value. □ vt **1** [VP6A] overload. **2** [VP6A,15A] demand a ~(1) on or in.

surd /sɜ:d/ n (math) quantity, esp a root (√), that cannot be expressed in finite terms of ordinary numbers or quantities.

sure /ʃʊə(r)/ *adj* (-r, -st) **1** (pred only) free from doubt; having confidence; knowing and believing; having, seeming to have, good reason for belief: *I think he's coming, but I'm not quite* ~. *You're* ~ *of* (= certain to receive) *a welcome. I'm not* ~ *whether I have a copy/where I left my copy/when I lost it. I'm not* ~ *why he wants it. be/feel* ~ *(about sth),* have no doubts (about): *I think the answer's right, but I'm not* ~ *(about it). Smith's a good man for the job, but I'm not so* ~ *about Robinson. be/feel* ~ *of sth/that...,* have confidence: *Are you* ~ *of your facts? Can we be* ~ *of his honesty/that he's honest? be/feel* ~ *of oneself,* have self-confidence. *be* ~ *to do sth;* (colloq) *be* ~ *and do sth,* don't fail to: *Be* ~ *to write and give me all the news. to be* ~, it is admitted, granted: *She's not pretty, to be* ~, *but she's very intelligent. Well, to be* ~! *make* ~ *that.../of sth,* (a) feel ~: *I made* ~ *he would be here.* (b) satisfy oneself; do what is necessary in order to feel ~ to get sth, etc: *I think there's a train at 5.15, but you'd better make* ~, eg by looking up trains in a timetable. *There aren't many seats left for this concert; you'd better make* ~ *of one/make* ~ *that you get one today.* **2** (attrib and pred) proved or tested; reliable; trustworthy: *no* ~ *remedy for colds;* ~ *proof; send a letter by a* ~ *hand/a* ~ *messenger.* ~-'footed *adj* not likely to stumble or slip. □ *adv* 1 ~ enough, certainly, in fact: *I said it would happen, and* ~ *enough it did happen.* for ~, (usu colloq) certainly. 2 as ~ as, as certain as: *as* ~ *as fate; as* ~ *as my name's Bob.* 3 (colloq, esp US) certainly: *It* ~ *was cold.* ~-ness *n*

sure·ly /'ʃʊəlɪ/ *adv* 1 (usu placed with the *v*) with certainty: *He will* ~ *fail. He was working slowly but* ~. 2 (placed either with the subject, usu preceding it, or at the end of the sentence, often indicating either confidence or incredulity) if experience or probability can be trusted: *S*~ *this wet weather won't last much longer! You didn't want to hurt his feelings,* ~! *S*~ *I've met you before somewhere.* 3 (esp US) (in answers) certainly; undoubtedly: *'Would you be willing to help?'—'S*~!' (*Certainly* is more usu in GB usage.)

surety /'ʃʊərətɪ US: 'ʃʊərtɪ/ *n* (*pl* -ties) [C,U] (sth given as a) guarantee; person who makes himself responsible for the conduct or debt(s) of another person: *stand* ~ *for sb.*

surf /sɜːf/ *n* [U] waves breaking in white foam on the seashore, on sand-banks or reefs. '~-ing, '~-riding *nn* sport in which one balances oneself on a long narrow board while being carried along by heavy ~. '~-board *n* board used for this sport. '~-boat *n* boat specially built for use in ~.

surf-board—

surfing

sur·face /'sɜːfɪs/ *n* [C] 1 the outside of any object, etc; any of the sides of an object: *Glass has a smooth* ~. *A cube has six* ~s. 2 top of a liquid, esp of a body in water, eg the sea: *The submarine rose to the* ~. *Most people consider* ~ *vessels* (= ordinary ships) *to be more vulnerable than submarines.* 3 '~ mail, mail sent by vehicles or ships moving on the earth's ~: *S*~ *mail is cheaper than airmail.* ~-to-'air, (of missiles, etc) fired or launched from the ground or from ships, and aimed at aircraft. 4 outward appearance; what is seen or learnt from a quick view or consideration: *You must not look only at the* ~ *of things. His faults are all on the* ~. *When you get below the* ~, *you find that he is warm-hearted and considerate.* 5 (attrib) of the ~ only: ~ *politeness;* ~ *impressions,* received quickly or casually, with no depth of thought, observation, etc; '~ noise, eg from a gramophone record, made by the stylus. □ *vt,vi* 1 [VP6A] give a ~ to: ~ *a road with gravel/tarmac.* 2 [VP6A,2A] (of a submarine, skin-diver, etc) (cause to) come to the ~.

sur·feit /'sɜːfɪt/ *n* (usu *a* ~ (*of*)) too much of anything, esp food and drink: *have a* ~ *of curry while in Madras;* feeling of discomfort resulting from a ~. □ *vt* [VP6A,14] ~ sb/oneself (with), (cause to) take too much of anything: ~ *oneself with fruit;*

be ~ed *with pleasure.*

surge /sɜːdʒ/ *vi* [VP2C] move forward, roll on, in or like waves: *The floods* ~d *over the valley. The crowds* ~d *out of the sports stadium. Anger* ~d (*up*) *within him.* □ *n* [C] forward or upward movement; onrush: *the* ~ *of the sea; a* ~ *of anger/pity.*

sur·geon /'sɜːdʒən/ *n* 1 doctor who performs operations. dental ~ *n* dentist qualified in surgery. 'house ~ *n* one of the staff of a hospital. 2 medical officer in the navy: ~-com'mander.

sur·gery /'sɜːdʒərɪ/ *n* (*pl* -ries) 1 [U] the science and practice of treating injuries and disease by manual and instrumental operations: *qualified in both* ~ *and medicine.* 2 [C] (GB) doctor's or dentist's room where patients come to consult him: ~ *hours, 4pm to 6pm; political* ~, (colloq) where constituents can consult their member of Parliament.

sur·gi·cal /'sɜːdʒɪkl/ *adj* of, by, for, surgery: ~ *treatment;* ~ *instruments; a* ~ *boot,* one specially designed to fit a deformed foot. ~-ly /-klɪ/ *adv*

sur·ly /'sɜːlɪ/ *adj* (-ier, -iest) bad-tempered and unfriendly. sur·lily /-ɪlɪ/ *adv* sur·li·ness *n*

sur·mise /sə'maɪz/ *vt,vi* [VP6A,9,2A] (formal) guess, conjecture: *She* ~d *as much.* □ /'sɜːmaɪz/ *n* [C] guess: *You were right in your* ~.

sur·mount /sə'maʊnt/ *vt* 1 [VP6A] overcome (difficulties); get over (obstacles). 2 (passive) be ~ed by/with, have on or over the top: *a spire* ~ed *by a weather-vane.* ~-able /-əbl/ *adj* that can be overcome or conquered.

sur·name /'sɜːneɪm/ *n* [C] person's hereditary family name: *Smith is a very common English* ~. ⇨ *given name* at give¹(11), *Christian name* at Christian, and forename.

sur·pass /sə'pɑːs US: -'pæs/ *vt* [VP6A,15A] do or be better than; exceed; excel: ~ *sb in strength/speed/skill. The beauty of the scenery* ~ed *my expectations.* ~-ing *adj* matchless: *of* ~ing *beauty.* ~-ing·ly *adv* in a way that is not ~ed: ~ingly ugly.

sur·plice /'sɜːplɪs/ *n* loose-fitting (usu white) gown with wide sleeves worn by (some) priests (over a cassock) during church services. ⇨ the illus at vestment. sur·pliced *adj* wearing a ~.

sur·plus /'sɜːpləs/ *n* 1 [C] amount (of money) that remains after needs have been supplied; excess of receipts over expenditure, ⇨ deficit; amount (of anything) in excess of requirements: *Brazil had a* ~ *of coffee last year.* 2 (attrib) exceeding what is needed or used: ~ *labour,* workers for whom there are no jobs; *a sale of* ~ *stock;* ~ *population,* in excess of what is thought desirable, or for which there is not enough food, employment, etc; 'surplus store, (GB) shop where ~ items (eg military clothing) are sold.

sur·prise /sə'praɪz/ *n* 1 [C,U] (feeling caused by) sth sudden or unexpected: *His failure did not cause much* ~/*was not a great* ~. *What a* ~! *To my* ~/ *To the* ~ *of everyone, his plan succeeded. We have some* ~s *in store for you. He looked up in* ~. take sb by ~, catch him unprepared, at a time when he is not expecting to be seen, etc. take a fort/town, etc by ~, capture it by making an unexpected attack. 2 (attrib) unexpected; made, done, etc, without warning: *a* ~ *visit/attack.* □ *vt* 1 [VP6A] give a feeling of ~ to: *You* ~ *me! She was more* ~d *than frightened.* 2 be ~d, experience ~: *We were* ~d *at the news/*~d *to hear the news. I'm* ~d (*to learn that*) *he didn't come. We were* ~d *at* finding the house empty. It's nothing to be ~d about/at. I shouldn't be ~d if it rained this afternoon, It seems to me likely that it will rain. **3** [VP6A] come upon suddenly, without previous warning; take by ~: ~ the enemy, attack them when they are off their guard; ~ a burglar in the act of breaking into a house. **4** ~ sb into doing sth, hurry him into doing sth, eg by making a sudden challenge. **sur·pris·ing** adj causing ~. **sur·pris·ing·ly** adv **sur·prised** adj showing or feeling ~. **sur·pris·ed·ly** /-ɪdlɪ/ adv in a ~d manner.

sur·real·ism /sə'rɪəlɪzəm/ n [U] 20th-century movement in art and literature that aims at expressing what there is in the subconscious mind (so that a painting may depict a number of unrelated objects as seen in a dream). **sur·real·ist** /-ɪst/ n artist, writer, etc of this movement. **sur·real·is·tic** /sərɪə'lɪstɪk/ adj of ~; fantastic.

sur·ren·der /sə'rendə(r)/ vt,vi **1** [VP6A,14,2A] ~ **(to),** give up (oneself, a ship, a town, etc) to the enemy, the police, etc): We shall never ~. We advised the hijackers to ~ (themselves) to the police. **2** [VP6A] yield up under pressure or from necessity; abandon possession of: We shall never ~ our liberty. He ~ed his insurance policy, gave up his rights under the policy in return for a lump sum of money (called the ~ value of the policy). **3** [VP14] ~ **(oneself) to,** yield or give way to (a habit, emotion, influence, etc): He ~ed (himself) to despair and committed suicide. □ n ~ing or being ~ed: demand the ~ of a town/of all fire-arms; ~ value, ⇨ 2 above. No ~!Let us not ~!

sur·rep·ti·tious /ˌsʌrəp'tɪʃəs/ adj (of actions) done secretly or stealthily. ~**ly** adv

sur·ro·gate /'sʌrəgeɪt/ n deputy, esp of a bishop. ⇨ suffragan.

sur·round /sə'raʊnd/ vt [VP6A] be, go, all round, shut in on all sides: a house ~ed with trees. We are ~ed with/by dangers. The troops were ~ed, had enemy forces all round them. □ n floor between the walls and the carpet; its covering: a linoleum ~. ~**ing** adj which is around about: York and the ~ing countryside. ~**ings** n pl everything around and about a place; conditions that may affect a person: living in pleasant ~ings. You don't see animals in their natural ~ings at a zoo.

sur·tax /'sɜːtæks/ n [C,U] (levying of) additional tax on personal incomes beyond a certain level. □ vt impose ~ on.

sur·veil·lance /sɜː'veɪləns/ n [U] close watch kept on persons suspected of wrongdoing, etc: under police ~.

sur·vey /sə'veɪ/ vt [VP6A] **1** take a general view of: ~ the countryside from the top of a hill. **2** examine the general condition of: The Prime Minister, in his speech at the Guildhall, ~ed the international situation. **3** measure and map out the position, size, boundaries, etc of (an area of land, a country, coast, etc): ~ a parish/a railway. **4** examine the condition of (a building, etc): Have the house ~ed before you offer to buy it. ~**ing** n [U] the work of ~ing(3,4): 'land-~ing; a '~ing ship, used for ~ing coasts; instruction in the principles of making surveys(3). □ n /'sɜːveɪ/ [C] **1** general view: make a general ~ of the situation/subject. **2** piece of land-surveying; map or record of this: an aerial ~ of East Africa, made by photography from aircraft; the ordnance ~ of Great Britain, ⇨ ordnance. ~**or** /sə'veɪə(r)/ n **1** person who ~s(3) land, etc. **2** person who ~s and values buildings, etc. **3** official

inspector: ~or of weights and measures; the ~or of highways. **quantity** ~**or,** ⇨ quantity.

sur·vival /sə'vaɪvl/ n **1** [U] state of continuing to live or exist; surviving: ~ after death, of the spirit after the death of the body; the ~ of the fittest, the continuing existence of those animals and plants which are best adapted to their surroundings, etc; (attrib) a '~ kit, package of necessities for a person after a disaster, etc (eg at sea). **2** [C] person, custom, belief, etc that has survived but is looked upon as belonging to past times.

sur·vive /sə'vaɪv/ vt,vi [VP6A,2A] continue to live or exist; live or exist longer than; remain alive after: ~ an earthquake/shipwreck; those who ~d. The old lady has ~d all her children. I hope I shall never ~ my usefulness, continue to live (or to hold a position) after I have ceased to be useful. **sur·viv·or** /-və(r)/ n person who has ~d: send help to the survivors of the earthquake.

sus·cep·tible /sə'septəbl/ adj **1** easily influenced by feelings; impressionable: a girl with a ~ nature; a ~ young man, one who easily falls in love. **2** ~ **to,** sensitive to; easily affected by: ~ to flattery/kind treatment; ~ to pain. **3** ~ **of,** (formal) capable of, that can receive or be given: Is your statement ~ of proof? **sus·cep·ti·bil·ity** /sə,septə'bɪlətɪ/ n (pl -ties) **1** [U] sensitiveness: ~ to hay fever/hypnotic influences. **2** (pl) sensitive points of a person's nature: We must avoid wounding their susceptibilities, not say or do anything that might hurt their feelings.

sus·pect /sə'spekt/ vt **1** [VP6A,9,25] have an idea or feeling (concerning the possibility or likelihood of sth): He ~ed an ambush. She has more intelligence than we ~ed her to possess. I ~ (that) he's a liar (less usu ~ him to be a liar). **2** [VP6A] feel doubt about: ~ the truth of an account. **3** [VP6A,14] ~ **sb (of sth),** have a feeling that sb may be guilty (of): He is ~ed of telling lies. □ n /'sʌspekt/ person ~ed of wrongdoing, disloyalty, etc: Are political ~s kept under police observation in your country? □ pred adj /'sʌspekt/ of doubtful character; possibly false; ~ed: His statements are ~.

sus·pend /sə'spend/ vt **1** [VP6A,14] ~ **sth (from),** hang up (from): lamps ~ed from the ceiling. **2** (passive) (of solid particles, in the air or other fluid medium) be or remain in place: dust/smoke ~ed in the still air. **3** [VP6A] stop for a time; delay; keep in an undecided state for a time: ~ payment, stop payment (eg when bankrupt); ~ a rule; ~ judgement, postpone giving one; (of a person) in a state of ~ed animation, alive but unconscious, (fig, joc; of institutions, committees, etc) temporarily inactive. He was fined £50 with a ~ed sentence/~ed execution of sentence, the payment of the fine being not required for a time, ie while he continues to observe the law. **4** [VP6A] announce that (sb) cannot be allowed to perform his duties, enjoy privileges, etc for a time: ~ a (professional) football player, eg because of repeated breaches of the rules.

sus·pend·er /sə'spendə(r)/ n **(pair of)** ~**s, 1** (GB) garter. '~ **belt,** light garment worn round the waist, with clasps for keeping up women's stockings. **2** (US) pair of straps (braces in GB) worn over the shoulders to keep up trousers.

sus·pense /sə'spens/ n [U] uncertainty, anxiety (about news, events, decisions, etc): We waited in great ~ for the doctor's opinion. **keep sb in ~,**

delay telling him what he is eager to know: *They've kept me in* ~ *for five days already.*

sus·pen·sion /sə'spenʃn/ n [U] suspending or being suspended: *the* ~ *of a member of Parliament,* eg for abuse of Parliamentary privileges; ⇨ suspend(4); *the* ~ *of a motor-vehicle,* the means by which it is supported on its axles (springs, shock absorbers, etc). '~ **bridge** n bridge suspended on or by means of steel cables supported from towers. ⇨ the illus at bridge.

sus·pi·cion /sə'spɪʃn/ n 1 [C,U] feeling that a person has when he suspects; suspecting or being suspected; feeling that sth is wrong: *I have a* ~ *that he is dishonest. I resent your* ~s *about my motives. He was looked upon with* ~. *He was arrested on* (*the*) ~ *of having stolen the money. His behaviour aroused no* ~. *Don't lay yourself open to* ~. *Don't let* ~ *fall on you/Don't fall under* ~. *above* ~, of such good reputation that ~ is out of the question. **2 a** ~ (*of*), slight taste or suggestion: *There was a* ~ *of sadness in her voice/of garlic in the stew.*

sus·pi·cious /sə'spɪʃəs/ adj having, showing or causing suspicion: *The affair looks* ~ *to me. He's a* ~ *character,* There is reason to suspect that he's dishonest, etc. (*be/become/feel*) ~ *about/of sb/sth,* have suspicions about: *The policeman became increasingly* ~ *of his movements.* ~·ly adv

suss /sʌs/ vt [VP15B] ~ *sth out,* (colloq) 1 discover. 2 reconnoitre.

sus·tain /sə'steɪn/ vt [VP6A] 1 keep from falling or sinking: *Will this light shelf* ~ (*the weight of*) *all these books?* 2 (enable to) keep up, maintain: ~*ing food,* that gives strength; ~ *an argument/attempt;* ~ *a note,* continue to sing or play the note without faltering; *make a* ~*ed effort.* 3 suffer; undergo: ~ *a defeat. The pilot* ~*ed severe injuries when his plane crashed.* 4 (legal) uphold; give a decision in favour of: *The court* ~*ed his claim/*~*ed him in his claim.*

sus·ten·ance /'sʌstɪnəns/ n [U] (nourishing quality of) food or drink; nourishment: *There's more* ~ *in cocoa than in tea.*

sut·tee /'sʌti:/ n Hindu widow who cremated herself on the funeral pyre of her husband; practice (now illegal) of doing this.

su·ture /'su:tʃə(r)/ n seam formed in sewing up a wound; thread used for this.

su·ze·rain /'su:zəreɪn US: -rɪn/ n State or ruler in relation to a country over which it or he has some control or authority; (formerly) feudal overlord. ~ty /'su:zərəntɪ/ n: *under the* ~*ty of.*

svelte /svelt/ adj (F) (of a person) slender and graceful.

swab /swɒb/ n 1 mop or pad for cleaning, eg floors, decks. 2 sponge, bit of absorbent material, etc for medical use, eg taking a specimen from the throat for testing infection; specimen (eg of mucus) so taken: *take* ~s *from children suspected of having diphtheria.* □ vt (-bb-) [VP6A,15B] clean with a ~: ~ *down the decks;* ~ *up water that has been upset on the floor.*

swaddle /'swɒdl/ vt [VP6A] bind (a baby) with long narrow strips of cloth (as was formerly the custom). '**swaddling-clothes,** the strips of cloth used: *still in his swaddling-clothes,* (fig) still not free from restraining influences.

swag /swæg/ n [U] 1 (sl) stolen goods; things obtained dishonestly. 2 (Australia) bundle of personal belongings carried by a vagrant.

swag·ger /'swægə(r)/ vi [VP2A,C] walk or behave

in a self-important or self-satisfied manner. □ n ~ing walk or way of behaving: *with a* ~. □ adj (sl) very chic. ~er n

swain /sweɪn/ n (poet or archaic) young rustic man (esp regarded as a lover): *lasses and their* ~s; (joc) lover.

swal·low¹ /'swɒləʊ/ n kinds of small, swift-flying insect-eating bird with a forked tail, which migrates to warm countries, eg to England every summer, and is associated with the beginning of summer. ⇨ the illus at bird. **One** ~ **doesn't make a summer,** (prov) It is unwise to form a judgement on the basis of a single instance. '~ **dive** n dive with the arms outspread till close to the water. '~-**tailed** adj (of butterflies, birds) with a deeply forked tail; (of a man's coat) with long tails (as of an evening dress coat).

swal·low² /'swɒləʊ/ vt,vi [VP6A,15B,2C] 1 ~ (*up*), cause or allow to go down the throat: ~ *one's food,* eat it quickly; work the muscles of the throat as when ~ing sth (to give relief to some kind of emotion): *He* ~*ed hard,* eg as if ~ing an insult; ⇨ 3 below. 2 ~ (*up*), take in; exhaust; cause to disappear; use up: *earnings that were* ~*ed up by lawyers' bills. The earth seemed to* ~ *them up,* They suddenly disappeared. *The aircraft was* ~*ed* (*up*) *in the clouds.* 3 (fig uses) ~ *an insult/affront,* accept it meekly; ~ *sth whole,* believe it without argument, doubt; ~ *one's words,* take them back, express regret for them; ~ *a story,* believe it too easily; ~ *the bait,* (of a person) accept a proposal, an offer, etc made to tempt one to do sth. □ n act of ~ing; amount ~ed at one time.

swam /swæm/ pt of swim.

swami /'swɑːmɪ/ n Hindu religious teacher; (loosely) mystic, yogi.

swamp /swɒmp/ n [C,U] (area of) soft wet land; marsh. □ vt 1 [VP6A] flood, soak, with water: *A big wave* ~*ed the boat. Everything in the boat was* ~*ed.* 2 [VP14] ~ *with,* (fig) overwhelm: *We are* ~*ed with work. The firm is* ~*ed with orders,* ie for their goods. ~y adj (-ier, -iest).

swan /swɒn/ n large, graceful, long-necked (usu white) water-bird. ⇨ the illus at water. '~ **dive,** (US) = swallow-dive. '~-**song** n (from the old belief that a swan sang sweetly when about to die) last performance, appearance, work before death of a poet, musician, etc. '~'s-**down** n [U] (a) soft underfeathers of ~s. (b) kind of thick cotton cloth with a soft nap on one side. □ vi (-nn-) [VP2C] (colloq) ~ *off/around, etc* move, go in a leisured, often aimless manner, esp of a privileged person or one who need not work: *I suppose you're* ~*ning off to Paris for the weekend. The boys are* ~*ning around Austria on a mountaineering holiday.*

swank /swæŋk/ vi [VP2A,C] (colloq) swagger; behave or talk in a boastful way; show off. □ n [U] ~ing behaviour: *wear a gold wrist-watch just for* ~; [C] person who ~s. ~y adj smart; characteristic of a person who ~s: *a* ~y *sports car; Jill and her* ~y *friends.*

swap /swɒp/ vt,vi (-pp-) = swop.

sward /swɔːd/ n [U] (liter) turf.

swarm¹ /swɔːm/ n [C] colony, large number, of insects, birds, etc moving about together: *a* ~ *of ants/locusts; a* ~ *of bees,* cluster of honeybees when migrating with a queen bee to establish a new colony; ~s *of children in the parks.* □ vi 1 [VP2A] (of bees) move or go in large numbers round a queen bee for emigration to a new colony. 2

[VP3A] **be ~ing with;** **~ with,** (of places) be overrun or crowded: *The beaches were ~ing with bathers. The stables ~ed with flies.* **3** [VP2C] be present in large numbers; move in a ~: *When the rain started the crowd ~ed back into the hotel. Beggars ~ed round the rich tourists.*
swarm² /swɔːm/ *vt* [VP6A,15B] **~ (up),** climb by clinging with the arms and legs.
swarthy /'swɔːðɪ/ *adj* having a dark complexion.
swash·buck·ler /'swɒʃbʌklə(r)/ *n* bully; boastful fellow who behaves recklessly. **swash·buck·ling** /'swɒʃbʌklɪŋ/ *adj* reckless and boastful. □ *n* [U] behaviour of a ~.
swas·tika /'swɒstɪkə/ *n* [C] kind of cross emblematic of the sun, good fortune or Nazism. ⇨ the illus at cross.
swat /swɒt/ *vt* (-tt-) slap with a flat object: *~ a fly.* □ *n* **1** slap of this kind: *Give that fly a ~.* **2** flexible device on a handle for ~ting (flies, etc): *a 'fly-~* (also '*fly-swatter*).
swath /swɔːθ/, **swathe** /sweɪð/ *n* **1** ridge of grass, wheat, barley, etc lying after being cut. **2** space left clear after one passage of a mower.
swathe¹ /sweɪð/ *vt* [VP6A,15A] wrap or bind up: *He came out of hospital with his leg still ~d in bandages.* □ *n* bandage; wrapping.
swathe² /sweɪð/ *n* ⇨ swath.
sway /sweɪ/ *vi,vt* **1** [VP2A,C,6A,15A] (cause to) move, first to one side and then to the other; swing: *The branches of the trees were ~ing in the wind. Do you sway your hips when you walk?* **2** [VP6A] control or influence; govern the direction of: *~ed by his feelings; a speech that ~ed the voters.* □ *n* [U] **1** ~ing movement. **2** rule or control: *the peoples who were under the ~ of Rome,* were ruled by Rome (in ancient times).
swear /sweə(r)/ *vt,vi* (*pt* swore /swɔː(r)/, *pp* sworn /swɔːn/) **1** [VP6A,7A,9] say solemnly or emphatically: *He swore to tell the truth/swore that he would tell the truth. I could have sworn that there was somebody in the next room, I felt certain of this.* **2** [VP6A,15A,B] take an oath; cause (sb) to take an oath. **~ sb in,** cause him to take the oath of office. **~ sb to secrecy,** make him ~ to keep sth secret. **~ a witness,** administer the oath to him. **sworn enemies,** enemies who can never be reconciled. **sworn friends/brothers,** very close friends. **3** [VP3A] **~ by sth,** (a) appeal to as a witness or witnesses: *~ by all the gods that...;* **~ by** *all that one holds dear.* (b) (colloq) use and have great confidence in: *He ~s by quinine for malaria.* **~ off sth,** (colloq) declare that one will give up, stop using: *He swore off smoking when the doctors said it caused lung cancer.* **~ to sth,** say emphatically: *He swore to having paid for the goods,* said emphatically that he had done so (when accused of not having done so). *I think I've met that man somewhere but I wouldn't ~ to it,* am not very confident of having met him. **4** [VP6A,14] make an affirmation after having taken an oath: *~ an accusation/a charge against sb; sworn evidence/statements.* **5** [VP2A,B,C,3A,22] **~ (at sb),** use obscene etc words to insult, or for emphasis (⇨ section on *stylistic values* in Introduction): *The foreman swore at his workers. He gave vent to his anger by ~ing loudly. He swore himself hoarse,* continued ~ing until he was hoarse. '**~-word** *n* word used in ~ing. **~er** *n* person who ~s(5).
sweat /swet/ *n* **1** [U] moisture that is given off by the body through the skin: *wipe the ~ off one's*

brow. '**~-band** *n* (a) band of absorbent material inside a hat. (b) cloth tied round the forehead, wrist, etc to absorb ~. '**~ shirt** *n* cotton sweater with sleeves, worn esp by athletes before and after exercise. **2 a ~,** condition of a person or animal (esp a horse) when covered with ~: *be in a ~. They say that a good ~ will cure a cold.* **be in a cold ~,** in a state of fear or anxiety. **all of a ~,** (colloq) wet with ~; (fig) anxious or frightened. **3** (colloq, *sing* only) hard work: *This job is a frightful ~.* **4** [C] **an old ~,** (sl) soldier with many years' service; (by extension) person with many years' experience of his job. **5** [U] moisture on the surface of anything, eg condensation on an inner wall. □ *vt,vi* **1** [VP2A] give out ~(1,5): *The long hot climb made him ~.* **2** [VP6A,15B] give out (sth that comes out of a surface). **~ blood,** (fig) work like a slave. **~ out a cold,** get rid of it by ~ing. **3** [VP6A] (cause to) ~: *The doctor ~ed his patient. Don't ~ your horse.* **4** [VP6A,2A,C] (cause to) work hard: *~ one's workers.* **~ed goods,** produced by ~ed labour. **~ed labour,** the labour of underpaid workers. '**~-shop** *n* workshop where ~ed labour is used. **~y** *adj* (-ier, -iest) **1** damp with ~: *~y underwear.* **2** causing one to ~: *~y work.*
sweater /'swetə(r)/ *n* knitted garment usu of thick wool with long sleeves, worn by athletes before or after exercise; similar woolly garment (not necessarily thick or heavy) worn for warmth. ⇨ jersey, jumper, pullover.
swede /swiːd/ *n* kind of turnip.
sweep¹ /swiːp/ *n* **1** '**~(-up/-out),** act of sweeping with, or as with, a broom, etc: *Give the room a good ~. Let's have a thorough ~-up/out.* **make a clean ~ (of sth),** get rid of (what is unwanted) completely: *They made a clean ~ of their old furniture and replaced it with brand new pieces. In forming his new Cabinet the Prime Minister has made a clean ~.* **2** sweeping movement: *with a ~ of his arm/scythe.* **3** space covered by a sweeping movement; range of such a movement: *The knight killed everyone who came within the ~ of his sword.* **4** long unbroken stretch, esp curved, on a road, river, coast, etc or of sloping land: *a fine ~ of country.* **5** steady uninterrupted flow: *the ~ of the tide.* **6** ('**chimney-)~,** man whose work is sweeping soot from chimneys. **7** long oar worked by a rower who stands, for steering or moving a boat, eg a sailing-boat when there is no wind. **8** long pole mounted as a lever for raising a bucket from a well. **9** '**~(-stake),** form of gambling on horse-races, the money staked by all those who take part being divided among those who have drawn numbered tickets for the winners (usu the first three).
sweep² /swiːp/ *vt,vi* (*pt,pp* swept /swept/) **1** [VP6A,15A,B,22,2A] **~ sth (from sth); ~ sth (free) of sth; ~ sth up/away, etc** clear (dust, dirt, etc) away with, or as with, a brush or broom; clean by doing this: *~ the dust from the carpets; ~ the carpets/the floor/the yard; ~ the chimney (free of soot); ~ up dead leaves from the garden paths; ~ up the crumbs; ~ the crumbs under the carpet/ into a corner/into a dustpan.* **2** [VP6A,15A,B] clean or clear away as with a broom; push away: *~ the seas of pirates. The current swept the logs along. The wind swept my hat off/the clouds away. Many bridges were swept away by the floods. We were almost swept off our feet by the waves. ~ all*

before one, have complete uninterrupted success. **~ the board,** (a) win all the money on the table when gambling. (b) win all the prizes; have every possible success. *be swept off one's feet,* (fig) be overcome by feeling, filled with enthusiasm, eg an audience by a great singer. **,swept-'back** *adj* (a) (of aircraft wings) attached so that they are at an acute angle to the axis of the aircraft. (b) (of hair) arranged so that it is combed or brushed away from the face. **3** [VP2C,6A] pass over or along, esp so as to overcome obstacles; move quickly over or with a rush: *A huge wave swept over the deck. A blizzard swept the country. The big tanks swept over the enemy's trenches. The wind swept along the street.* **4** [VP2C] move in a dignified or stately manner; go majestically: *She swept out of the room. The big car swept up the drive to the entrance of the palace.* **5** [VP2C] extend in an unbroken line, curve or expanse: *The road ~s round the lake. The coast ~s northwards in a wide curve.* **6** [VP6A] pass over (as if) to examine or survey: *The searchlights swept the sky. Her eyes swept the room.* **7** [VP6A] move along lightly and quickly: *His fingers swept the keys of the piano. Her dress swept the ground.* **8** [VP12A] make (a bow, curtsey) with a ~ing movement: *She swept him a curtsey.* **~er** *n* **1** person or thing that ~s: '*street ~ers; a* '*carpet-~er.* **2** (football) defender who covers the backs, tackling any opponent who passes them. **~ing** *adj* far-reaching; taking in very much: *~ing changes/reforms; a ~ing statement/ generalization,* with no limitations or exceptions; *a ~ing* (= complete) *victory; ~ing* (= very great) *reductions in prices,* eg at a sale. **~ing·ly** *adv* **~ings** *n pl* dust, rubbish, scraps, etc, collected by ~ing: *a heap of 'street ~ings.*

sweet /swiːt/ *adj* **1** (opp of *sour*) tasting like sugar or honey: *Do you like your tea ~? It tastes ~,* has a ~ taste. *have a ~ tooth,* like things that taste ~. ~ **wine,** wine with a ~ or fruity flavour (contrasted with *dry* wine). **2** fresh and pure: ~ *milk; keep a room clean and ~;* ~ *breath;* ~ *water,* fit to drink (contrasted with brackish water, etc). **3** having a fragrant smell, like roses: *The garden is ~ with thyme. Don't the roses smell ~!* ,~-'**scented** *adj* having a ~ smell. **4** pleasant or attractive: *a ~ face; a ~ voice; a ~ singer,* sb having a ~ voice; *a ~ little girl; a ~ temper;* ,~-'**tempered.** *It was ~ to hear people praise me so much. What a ~ little poodle you have! Isn't the baby ~!* **5** (phrases) *at one's own ~ will,* as and when one pleases, with no one to give orders or advice. *be ~ on (sb),* (colloq) very fond of, in love with. **6** (compounds) '~·**bread** *n* pancreas of a calf or lamb used as food. ,~-'**briar/**-'**brier** *n* wild rose with ~-scented leaves and single pink flowers. '~·**heart** *n* either of a pair of lovers: *David and his* ~**heart.** '~·**meat** *n* piece of ~-tasting food (usu made of sugar or chocolate); fruit preserved in sugar. ,~ '**pea** *n* garden plant (an annual) with brightly-coloured, ~-scented flowers. ,~ '**potato** *n* tropical climbing plant with thick edible roots, cooked as a vegetable. ,~ '**william** *n* garden plant with flowers in close clusters, often parti-coloured. □ *n* [C] **1** (US = *candy*) small piece of ~-tasting food (eg boiled flavoured sugar, chocolate, etc). **2** (US = *dessert*) dish of ~ food (eg a pudding, tart, jelly, trifle, etc) as one of the courses of a meal. (In GB *dessert* usu means a course of fresh fruit, nuts, etc.) **3** (*pl*) delights; pleasures: *taste the ~s of suc-*

cess; enjoy the ~s of life while one is young. **4** (as a form of address) darling: *Yes, my ~.* ~·**ly** *adv* ~·**ness** *n* ~·**ish** /-ɪʃ/ *adv* rather ~. ~**en** /'swiːtn/ *vt,vi* [VP6A,2A] make or become ~. ⇨ pill(1). ~**en·ing** /'swiːtnɪŋ/ *n* [C,U] that which ~ens; sth ~ used in cooking, etc.

swell /swel/ *vi,vt* (*pt* ~**ed** /sweld/, *pp* swollen /'swəʊlən/, rarely ~**ed**) **1** [VP6A,14,15B,2A,C] ~ **(up) (with),** (cause to) become greater in volume, thickness or force: *Wood often ~s when wet. The river was swollen with melted snow. His face began to ~ up,* eg from toothache. *He/His heart was ~ing with pride. The boy's eyes were swollen up with tears. These small items help to ~ the total. have/suffer from a swollen head,* be conceited. Hence, ,**swollen-'headed** *adj* **2** [VP2A,C,6A,15B] ~ **(out),** have, cause to have, a curved surface: *The sails ~ed out in the wind. The wind ~ed the sails.* □ *n* **1** gradual increase in the volume of sound: *the ~ of an organ.* **2** (*sing* only) slow rise and fall of the sea's surface after a storm (with large but unbroken waves): *There was a heavy ~ after the storm.* **3** (US colloq) smartly dressed person; person of distinction or ability: *What a ~ you look in that new suit! come the heavy ~ over sb,* (sl) try to appear great and important and in this way impress him. □ *adj* (US colloq) **1** smart, fashionable: *Who are your ~ friends? He took her to a ~ dinner party.* **2** excellent; first-rate: *He's a ~ tennis player.* ~·**ing** *n* [U,C] **1** swollen place on the body, eg the result of a knock or blow or toothache. **2** increase in size.

swel·ter /'sweltə(r)/ *vi* [VP2A] be uncomfortably warm; suffer from the heat: *a ~ing hot day.*

swept /swept/ *pt,pp* of sweep².

swerve /swɜːv/ *vi,vt* [VP2A,C,4A,6A] (cause to) change direction suddenly: *The car ~d to avoid knocking the boy down. Don't ~ from your purpose.* □ *n* [C] swerving movement; (esp) turn or curve of a ball in the air.

swift[1] /swɪft/ *adj* (-er, -est) quick; fast; prompt: ~ *of foot;* (liter) able to run fast; *a ~ revenge;* ~ *to anger,* (formal) quickly becoming angry. ~·**ly** *adv* ~·**ness** *n*

swift[2] /swɪft/ *n* sorts of small insect-eating bird with long wings, similar to a swallow. ⇨ the illus at bird.

swig /swɪɡ/ *vt,vi* (-gg-) [VP6A,15B,2A,C] ~ **(down/off),** (colloq) take drinks of: *~ging beer;* ~ *off a glass of rum.* □ *n* long drink: *take a ~ at a bottle of beer,* have a drink direct from the bottle.

swill /swɪl/ *vt,vi* **1** [VP6A,15B] ~ *sth (out),* rinse, wash by pouring liquid into, over or through: ~ *out a dirty tub.* **2** [VP6A] (colloq) drink greedily: *The workmen were ~ing tea when they ought to have been working.* □ *n* **1** [C] rinsing: *Give the bucket a good ~ out.* **2** [U] waste food, mostly liquid, eg as given to pigs.

swim /swɪm/ *vi,vt* (*pt* swam /swæm/, *pp* swum /swʌm/) (-mm-) **1** [VP2A,B,C] move the body through water by using arms, legs, fins, the tail, etc: *Fishes ~. We swam all afternoon. Let's go ~ming. He swam across the river. When the boat sank they had to ~ for it,* save themselves by ~ming. ~ *with the tide/the stream,* do as the majority do (taking the easiest course). '~·**ming-bath/-pool** *n* indoor or outdoor, large or small, pool for ~ming in. '~·**ming-costume,** '~·**suit** *nn* garment worn for ~ming. '~·**ming-trunks** *n pl* garment worn by boys and men for ~ming. **2**

[VP6A] cross by ~ming: ~ *the English Channel;* take part in (a race) in this way; compete with (sb) in this way: ~ *a race;* ~ *two lengths of the pool;* cause (an animal) to ~: ~ *one's horse across a river.* **3** [VP3A] ~ **with;** ~ **in/on,** be covered or overflowing (with); be (as if) floating (in or on): *eyes ~ming with tears; meat ~ming in gravy; strawberries ~ming in cream.* **4** [VP2A] seem to be moving round and round; have a dizzy feeling: *The room swam before his eyes. His head swam.* □ *n* **1** act or period of ~ming: *have/go for a ~.* **2 the ~,** main current of affairs. · *be in/out of the ~,* be/not be taking part in, aware of, current affairs. **~·mer** *n* person who ~s. **~·ming·ly** *adv* easily and without trouble: *We're getting along ~mingly. Everything went ~mingly,* without obstruction or delay of any kind.

swindle /'swɪndl/ *vt,vi* [VP6A,14] ~ *sth out of sb;* ~ *sb out of sth,* cheat; get (money, etc out of sb) by cheating: ~ *money out of sb;* ~ *sb out of his money. Some people are easily ~d.* □ *n* [C] piece of swindling; sth sold, etc that is less valuable than it is described to be: *This new radio set is a ~,* the quality of the sound is bad. **swin·dler** /'swɪndlə(r)/ *n* person who ~s.

swine /swaɪn/ *n* (*pl* unchanged) **1** (old use, or liter) pig. '**~·herd** *n* man who (formerly) looked after ~ (when they were out in the woods, etc). **2** △ (abusive, derog) disgusting person. **swin·ish** /-ɪʃ/ *adj* beastly and disgusting.

swing /swɪŋ/ *vi,vt* (*pt,pp* swung /swʌŋ/) **1** [VP2A,B,C,6A,15A,B,22] (of sth having one end or one side fixed and the other free) move, cause to move, forwards and backwards or in a curve: *His arms swung as he walked. He was ~ing his arms. The door swung shut/swung to. The big ape swung (itself) from branch to branch.* ~ *for sb/sth,* (colloq) be hanged (for murder). *no room to ~ a cat in,* (of an enclosure) very small; having very little space for movement. ~ *the lead,* ⇨ lead¹(3). **2** [VP6A,C] walk or run with a free easy movement (the arms ~ing freely): *The soldiers advanced at a ~ing trot.* **3** [VP2A] dance to or play ~ music; (sl) be lively, gay and up-to-date. **4** [VP2C,15A,B] turn, cause to turn, in a curve: *He swung (= turned quickly) round and faced his accusers. The car swung round the corner.* □ *n* **1** ~ing movement: *the ~ of the pendulum.* **2** strong rhythm. *in full ~,* active; in full operation. *go with a ~,* **(a)** (of music, poetry) have a good rhythm. **(b)** (fig) (of an entertainment, event, etc) proceed smoothly, without delays, etc. ~ **(music),** (1930's) orchestral jazz, usu played by big bands. **3** [C] seat held by ropes or chains for ~ing on; act, period, of ~ing on such a seat. **~·ing** *adj* (sl) lively; gay; up-to-date; enjoyable.

swinge /swɪndʒ/ *vt* (archaic) strike hard. **~·ing** *part adj* huge; very forcible: *~ing damages,* eg awarded by a judge in a law suit; *~ing taxation.*

swipe /swaɪp/ *vt* (colloq) **1** [VP6A,15A,3A] hit hard: *The batsman ~d the ball into the grandstand. He ~d at the ball and missed it.* **2** [VP6A] (colloq, usu hum) steal. □ *n* swinging blow: *have/take a ~ at the ball.*

swirl /swɜːl/ *vi,vt* [VP2C,15B] (of water, air, etc) (cause to) move or flow at varying speeds, with twists and turns: *dust ~ing about the streets;* carry (sth) *off, away,* in this way. □ *n* **1** ~ing movement; eddy: *a ~ of dust.* **2** (US) twist or curl: *a hat with a ~ of lace round it.*

swish /swɪʃ/ *vt,vi* **1** [VP6A,15B] ~ *sth (off),* move (sth) through the air with a hissing or brushing sound; cut (sth off) in this way: *The horse ~ed its tail. He ~ed his whip/~ed off the tops of the thistles with his whip.* **2** [VP2A] make, move with, a sound like that of sth moving through the air: *Her long silk dress ~ed as she came in.* □ *n* sound of, sound suggesting, sth being ~ed: *We heard the ~ of a cane.* □ *adj* (colloq) smart; expensive and fashionable: *a ~ restaurant.*

switch /swɪtʃ/ *n* [C] **1** device for making and breaking a connection at railway points (to allow trains to go from one track to another). '**~·man** /-mən/ *n* (*pl* -men) man in charge of railway ~es. **2** device for making and breaking an electric circuit: *a two-way ~,* one of a pair that can be used for turning electric current on or off from two points (eg at the bottom making connections by telephone or operating electric circuits. **3** thin twig or easily bent shoot cut from a tree, eg as used for urging a horse on. **4** bunch of false hair used by a woman to make her hair appear thicker or longer. **5** '**~·back** *n* **(a)** ~*back (railway),* one that twists and turns up and down steep slopes, esp the kind seen in amusement parks (US = *roller-coaster*). **(b)** ~*back (road),* road with numerous ups and downs. **6** transfer; change-over: *a ~ from glass bottles to plastic cartons.* □ *vt,vi* **1** [VP15B] ~ *sth on/off,* use a ~(1) to turn (electric current) on/off: ~ *the light/radio, etc on. Don't ~ off yet, please.* **2** ~ *sb on,* (sl, esp pp) cause sb to feel happy, excited; *That music really ~es me on! He's really ~ed on!* **3** [VP6A,15B] move (a train, tram, etc) on to another 'track: ~ *a train into a siding.* **4** [VP6A,15A] ~ *(to);* ~ *(over to),* shift; change: ~ *the conversation (to a less embarrassing subject);* ~ *over to modern methods.* **5** [VP6A] whip or flick with a ~(3). **6** [VP6A,15A] swing (sth) round suddenly; snatch suddenly: *The cow ~ed (more usu swished) her tail. He ~ed it out of my hand.*

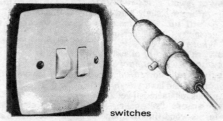

switches

swivel /'swɪvl/ *n* ring and pivot or ring with a linked hook to a chain joining two parts so that one can turn round without turning the other: *a '~-chain/-hook,* provided with a ~; *a '~-chair/-gun,* one that can rotate on a pivot. □ *vt,vi* (-ll-, US also -1-) [VP6A,15B,2A,C] turn on or as on a ~: *He ~led round in his chair/~led his chair round to see who had come in.*

swiz /swɪz/ *n* (sl) bitter disappointment; fraud.

swizzle /'swɪzl/ *n* (colloq) (kinds of) mixed alcoholic drink served in a tall glass. '**~-stick** *n* glass rod for stirring such a drink.

swob /swɒb/ *n, vt* (-bb-) = swab.

swol·len /'swəʊlən/ *pp* of swell, esp as *adj*: *a ~ ankle.*

swoon /swuːn/ (archaic) *vi* [VP2A] faint. □ *n* fainting fit.

swoop /swuːp/ *vi,vt* **1** [VP2A,C] ~ *(down) (on),*

come down on with a rush: *The eagle ~ed down on its prey. The soldiers ~ed down on the bandits,* attacked them suddenly. 2 [VP15B] ~ *sth up,* grab, snatch it. □ *n* ~ing movement; sudden attempt to snatch and carry off sth. *at one (fell) ~,* in one sudden swift attack or movement.

swop (also **swap**) /swɒp/ *vt,vi* (-pp-) [VP6A,15A,2A] (colloq) exchange by barter: ~ *foreign stamps;* ~ *yarns,* tell one another stories (of adventure, etc). ~ *places with sb,* exchange seats. *Don't ~ horses in mid-stream,* (prov) If changes are needed, make them before the crisis is reached. □ *n* exchange by barter: *I think your hat would suit me—shall we try a ~?*

sword /sɔːd/ *n* long steel blade fixed in a hilt, used as a weapon, or worn by army officers, etc as part of a uniform or as court dress. *cross ~s with sb,* (fig) dispute with him. *draw/sheathe the ~,* (rhet) begin/end a war. *put to the ~,* (rhet) kill. *at the point of the ~,* under threat of violence. '**~-cane/-stick** *n* ~-blade enclosed in a hollow walking-stick. '**~-cut** *n* (scar left by a) wound given with a ~-edge. '**~-dance** *n* dance over ~s laid on the ground, or one in which ~s are waved or clashed. '**~-fish** *n* large sea-fish with a long ~-like upper jaw. ⇨ the illus at sea. '**~-play** *n* [U] fencing; (fig) repartee; lively arguing. '**~s-man** /-zmən/ *n* (*pl* -men) man skilled in the use of a ~ (usu with *adjj*): *a good ~sman.* '**~s-man-ship** /-mənʃɪp/ *n*

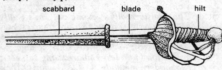

scabbard   blade   hilt

a sword

swore, sworn ⇨ swear.

swot /swɒt/ *vi,vt* (-tt-) [VP2A,C,3A,15B] (not US) ~ *(for sth),* study hard (for an examination, etc). ~ *sth up,* work hard at; revise: ~ *up one's geometry.* □ *n* 1 person who ~s. 2 hard work: *What a ~!*

swum /swʌm/ *pp* of swim.

swung /swʌŋ/ *pt,pp* of swing.

syb·ar·ite /'sɪbəraɪt/ *n* person who is devoted to comfort and luxury. **syb·ar·itic** /ˌsɪbə'rɪtɪk/ *adj* luxurious; characteristic of a ~.

syca·more /'sɪkəmɔː(r)/ *n* 1 [C] large tree valued for its wood (in GB a kind of maple-tree; in US a kind of plane-tree, also called a 'buttonwood'; in Egypt and Syria a kind of fig-tree). 2 [U] valuable hard wood of the ~.

syco·phant /'sɪkəfænt/ *n* person who tries to win favour by flattering rich or powerful people. **~ic** /ˌsɪkə'fæntɪk/ *adj*

syl·lable /'sɪləbl/ *n* minimum rhythmic unit of spoken language, consisting of a vowel or sustained consonant, often preceded or followed by unsustained consonant(s); similar unit of written language: *'Arithmetic' is a word of four ~s.* **-syl-labled** *adj* having a stated number of ~s: *'Syco-phant' is a three-~d word.* **syl·la·bary** /'sɪləbərɪ US: -berɪ/ *n* [C] (*pl* -ries) list of characters (eg in Japanese) representing ~s. **syl·labic** /sɪ'læbɪk/ *adj* (**a**) of or in ~s. (**b**) (of consonant) making a ~. **syl·labi·cate** /sɪ'læbɪkeɪt/, **syl·labify** /sɪ'læbɪfaɪ/ (*pt,pp* -fied), **syl·la·bize** /'sɪləbaɪz/ *vvt* divide into

~s. **syl·labi·ca·tion** /sɪˌlæbɪ'keɪʃn/, **syl·labi·fi·ca·tion** /sɪˌlæbɪfɪ'keɪʃn/ *nn* (system of) division into ~s.

syl·la·bus /'sɪləbəs/ *n* (*pl* ~es /-bəsɪz/ or -bi /-baɪ/) outline or summary of a course of studies; programme of school studies.

syl·lo·gism /'sɪlədʒɪzəm/ *n* [C] reaching a conclusion from two statements, eg: *All men must die; I am a man; therefore I must die.* ⇨ premise(2). **syl·lo·gis·tic** /ˌsɪlə'dʒɪstɪk/ *adj* in the form or nature of a ~.

sylph /sɪlf/ *n* one of a class of female nature spirits believed to inhabit the air (cf *nymph,* spirit of the woods, etc); (hence) slender, graceful girl or woman. '**~-like** *adj* slender and graceful.

syl·van, sil·van /'sɪlvən/ *adj* (liter) of trees and woodland: ~ *scenes; a ~ retreat,* eg a cottage in a forest.

sym·bio·sis /ˌsɪmbɪ'əʊsɪs/ *n* [U] (biol) harmonic association of different organisms, etc: *the tall Dingas of the southern Sudan, living in ~ with their magnificent cattle.*

sym·bol /'sɪmbl/ *n* [C] sign, mark, object, etc looked upon as representing sth: *mathematical ~s,* eg ×, ÷, +, −; *phonetic ~s. Red is a symbol of danger. The Cross is the ~ of Christianity.* **~ic** /sɪm'bɒlɪk/, **~i·cal** /-kl/ *adjj* of, using, used as, a ~. **~i·cally** /-klɪ/ *adv* **~·ize** /'sɪmbəlaɪz/ *vt* [VP6A] be a ~ of; make use of a ~ or ~s for. **~·iz·ation** /ˌsɪmbəlaɪ'zeɪʃn US: -lɪ'z-/ *n* **~·ism** /'sɪmbəlɪzəm/ *n* 1 [U] representation of ideas by the use of ~s; literary and artistic movement (late 19th c) that used artistic invention to express sensually ideas, emotions, abstractions in place of realism. 2 [C] system of ~s used to represent a particular group of ideas.

sym·me·try /'sɪmətrɪ/ *n* [U] (beauty resulting from the) right correspondence of parts; quality of harmony or balance (in size, design, etc) between parts: *The bump on the left side of her forehead spoilt the ~ of her face.* **sym·met·ric** /sɪ'metrɪk/, **sym·met·ri·cal** /-kl/ *adjj* having ~; (of a design) having (usu two) exactly similar parts on either side of a dividing line. **sym·met·ri·cally** /-klɪ/ *adv*

sym·path·etic /ˌsɪmpə'θetɪk/ *adj* having or showing sympathy; caused by sympathy: ~ *looks; words; a ~ face/heart; a ~ audience; be/feel ~ to/towards sb.* ~ *strike n* strike[1](1) by workers purely to show support for other workers who are on strike. **sym·path·eti·cally** /-klɪ/ *adv*

sym·path·ize /'sɪmpəθaɪz/ *vi* [VP2A,3A] ~ *(with),* feel or express sympathy (with): ~ *with sb in his afflictions. Tom's parents do not ~ with his ambition to become an actor,* do not give him their approval and encouragement. **sym·path·izer** *n* person who ~s, eg one who supports a cause or political party.

sym·pathy /'sɪmpəθɪ/ *n* (*pl* -thies) 1 [U] (capacity for) sharing the feelings of others, feeling pity and tenderness: *send sb a letter of ~; feel ~ for sb; have no ~ with sb's foolish opinions. I have some ~ with their views,* share them to some extent. *in ~ with,* agreeing with, approving of: *We are all in ~ with your proposals. Will the bus workers strike in ~ with* (= to show their ~ for) *the railway workers?* 2 (*pl* in a few usages): *a man of wide sympathies,* with a great capacity for fellow-feeling. *You have my sympathies,* my feelings of ~. *My sympathies are with the miners in this dispute,* I'm on their side.

sym·phony /'sɪmfənɪ/ *n* [C] (*pl* -nies) (long and large-scale) musical composition in (usu) three or four parts (called *movements*) for (usu a large) orchestra. **sym·phonic** /sɪm'fɒnɪk/ *adj* of, having the character of, a ∼.

sym·po·sium /sɪm'pəʊzɪəm/ *n* (*pl* ∼s or -sia /-zɪə/) collection of essays, etc (eg forming a book) by several persons on a problem or subject; conference for discussion of a subject.

symp·tom /'sɪmptəm/ *n* **1** change in the body's condition that indicates illness: *A persistent cough may be a* ∼ *of tuberculosis.* **2** sign of the existence of sth: *The Government must not ignore these* ∼*s of discontent among their own supporters.* **symp·to·matic** /ˌsɪmptə'mætɪk/ *adj* serving as a ∼: *A headache may be* ∼*atic of brain fever.* **symp·to·mati·cally** /-klɪ/ *adv*

syna·gogue /'sɪnəgɒg/ *n* [C] (building used for an) assembly of Jews for religious teaching and worship.

inside a synagogue

syn·chro·flash /ˌsɪŋkrəʊ'flæʃ/ *n* (usu attrib) device for simultaneous flashlight and opening of the shutter of a camera: ∼ *photography/attachments for a camera.*

syn·chro·mesh /ˌsɪŋkrəʊ'meʃ/ *n* system of gear-changing (esp in motor-vehicles) so that the parts revolve at the same speed and so change smoothly.

syn·chron·ize /'sɪŋkrənaɪz/ *vt, vi* [VP6A,2A] (cause to) happen at the same time, agree in time, speeds, etc: ∼ *the sound-track of a film with the movements seen;* ∼ *all the clocks in a building.* **syn·chron·iz·ation** /ˌsɪŋkrənaɪ'zeɪʃn US: -nɪ'z-/ *n*

syn·chro·tron /'sɪŋkrəʊtrɒn/ *n* apparatus for accelerating electrons.

syn·co·pate /'sɪŋkəpeɪt/ *vt* [VP6A] (music) change the rhythm of; displace the normal beats or accents of, eg as in some jazz. **syn·co·pa·tion** /ˌsɪŋkə'peɪʃn/ *n*

syn·cope /'sɪŋkəpɪ/ *n* (med term for) fainting; brief loss of consciousness from fall of blood-pressure.

syn·dic /'sɪndɪk/ *n* member of a committee (for business purposes) of a university or other organization).

syn·di·cal·ism /'sɪndɪkəlɪzəm/ *n* [U] theory that political power should be in the hands of trade unions and that these unions should own and manage the industries in which their members work. **syn·di·cal·ist** /-ɪst/ *n* supporter of ∼.

syn·di·cate /'sɪndɪkət/ *n* **1** business association that supplies articles, cartoons, etc to periodicals. **2** combination of commercial firms associated to forward a common interest. □ *vt* /'sɪndɪkeɪt/ [VP6A] publish (articles, strip-cartoons, etc) in numerous periodicals through a ∼(1). **syn·di·ca·tion** /ˌsɪndɪ'keɪʃn/ *n*

syn·drome /'sɪndrəʊm/ *n* (med) number of symptoms which collectively indicate an often abnormal condition of the body or mind; (fig) particular combination of a person's actions, opinions, etc that can be expected to occur together.

synod /'sɪnəd/ *n* [C] meeting of church officers to discuss and decide questions of policy, government, teaching, etc.

syn·onym /'sɪnənɪm/ *n* word with the same meaning as another in the same language but often with different implications and associations. **syn·ony·mous** /sɪ'nɒnɪməs/ *adj*

syn·op·sis /sɪ'nɒpsɪs/ *n* (*pl* -opses /-siːz/) summary or outline (of a book, play, etc). **syn·op·tic** /sɪ'nɒptɪk/ *adj* giving a ∼: *the synoptic Gospels,* those of Matthew, Mark and Luke (similar in contents, order, etc). **syn·op·ti·cally** /-klɪ/ *adv*

syn·tax /'sɪntæks/ *n* [U] (gram) (rules for) sentence-building. **syn·tac·tic** /sɪn'tæktɪk/ *adj* of ∼. **syn·tac·ti·cally** /-klɪ/ *adv*

syn·thesis /'sɪnθəsɪs/ *n* (*pl* -theses /-siːz/) [C,U] combination of separate parts, elements, substances, etc into a whole or into a system; that which results from this process: *produce rubber from petroleum by* ∼. **syn·thesize** /'sɪnθəsaɪz/ *vt* [VP6A] produce a whole by this process: *synthesize diamonds/rubber.* **syn·thetic** /sɪn'θetɪk/ *adj* **1** produced by ∼: *synthetic rubber,* artificially made. **2** pertaining to ∼: *synthetic chemistry.* **3** (of a language) containing, tending to form, many compound words: *German is a synthetic language.* **syn·theti·cally** /-klɪ/ *adv.* ⇨ analysis.

syph·ilis /'sɪfɪlɪs/ *n* [U] infectious venereal disease. **syphi·litic** /ˌsɪfɪ'lɪtɪk/ *adj* pertaining to, suffering from, ∼. □ *n* person affected with ∼.

syphon *n* = siphon.

syr·inga /sɪ'rɪŋgə/ *n* shrub with strong-scented white flowers (popularly called the mock-orange); botanical name of the lilac genus.

syr·inge /sɪ'rɪndʒ/ *n* kinds of device for drawing in liquid by suction and forcing it out again in a fine stream, used for washing out wounds, injecting liquids into the body, in spraying plants, etc: *a hypodermic* ∼; *a garden* ∼. □ *vt* [VP6A,15B] clean, inject liquid into, with a ∼; apply (liquid) with a ∼.

needle

a hypodermic syringe

syrup /'sɪrəp/ *n* [U] thick sweet liquid made from sugar-cane juice or by boiling sugar with water: *pineapple tinned in* ∼; 'cough ∼, ∼ *with medicine in it to relieve a cough; fruit* ∼, ∼ *flavoured with fruit juices.* ∼**y** *adj* of or like ∼; (fig, eg of music) too sweet.

sys·tem /'sɪstəm/ *n* **1** group of things or parts working together in a regular relation: *the 'nervous* ∼; *the di'gestive* ∼; *a 'railway* ∼. *The poison has passed into his* ∼, *his body as a whole. Too much alcohol is bad for the* ∼. **2** ordered set of ideas, theories, principles, etc: *a* ∼ *of philosophy; a* ∼ *of government; a good* ∼ *of teaching languages;* '∼*-building/*'∼*-built houses,* built of prefabricated sections, put together on the site. **3** [U] orderliness: *You mustn't expect good results if you work* *without* ~. ~·**atic** /ˌsɪstə'mætɪk/ *adj* methodical; based on a ~: *a* ~*atic attempt*. ~·**ati·cally** /-klɪ/ *adv* ~·**atize** /'sɪstəmətaɪz/ *vt* [VP6A] arrange ac-

cording to a ~; make into a ~. ~·**atiz·ation** /ˌsɪstəmətaɪ'zeɪʃn *US:* -tɪ'z-/ *n*

Tt

T, t /tiː/ (*pl* T's, t's /tiːz/) the twentieth letter of the English alphabet; used before names of various objects shaped like the letter T: *a* '*T-bandage; a* '*T-shirt*, short-sleeved, close-fitting, collarless and buttonless usu cotton shirt worn informally; *a* '*T-square*. ⇨ square²(7). *to a T*, ⇨ tee.

ta /tɑː/ *int* (colloq) thank you.

tab /tæb/ *n* **1** small piece or strip of cloth, etc fixed to a garment, etc as a badge or distinguishing mark or (as a loop) for hanging up a coat, etc; binding at the end of a shoelace, etc. **2** (colloq) account; check. *keep a tab/tabs on sth/sb*, keep an account of, keep under observation: *keep a tab on the expenses.*

tab·ard /'tæbəd/ *n* (hist) short, sleeveless outer garment (worn eg by a knight over his armour, or by a herald).

tabby /'tæbɪ/ *n* (*pl* -bies) '~(-cat), cat with grey or brown stripes.

tab·er·nacle /'tæbənækl/ *n* **1** (in the Bible) **the T~**, the portable structure used by the Israelites as a sanctuary during their wanderings before they settled in Palestine. **2** (eccles) receptacle for a pyx. **3** place of worship, eg a Baptist Church or Mormon temple.

table /'teɪbl/ *n* [C] **1** piece of furniture consisting of a flat top with (usu four) supports (called legs): *a* '*dining-~; a* '*kitchen-~; a* '*billiard-~. at* ~, having a meal: *They were at* ~ *when we called.* '~*-cloth* *n* one (to be) spread on a ~. '~*-knife* *n* steel knife for use at ~. '~*-lifting/-rapping/ turning* *nn* lifting/rapping, etc of a ~, apparently without physical exertion, occurring while people sit at a ~ during a spiritualistic seance. '~*-linen* *n* [U] ~*-cloths*, napkins, etc. '~*-mat* *n* one to be placed under a hot dish on a ~. '~*-spoon* *n* large spoon for serving food at ~ from a dish, etc. '~*-spoon·ful* *n* as much as a ~spoon holds. '~*-talk* *n* conversation during a meal. '~ *tennis* *n* game (sometimes called *ping-pong*) played with bats and balls, similar to tennis, on a ~. '~*-ware* *n* [U] dishes, silver, cutlery, etc used for meals. **2** (*sing* only) people seated at a ~: *a* ~ *of card-players; King Arthur and his Round T~*, his knights; *jokes that amused the whole* ~. **3** (*sing* only) food provided at ~: *He keeps a good* ~, provides good meals. **4** '~(-land), plateau; extensive area of high, level land. **5** [C] list, orderly arrangement, of facts, information, etc (usu in columns): *a* ~ *of contents*, summary of what a book contains; *multiplication* ~*s; a railway* '*time~*. **6** (phrases) *lay sth on the* ~, (in Parliament) postpone (a measure, report, etc) indefinitely. *turn the* ~*s on sb*, gain a position of superiority after having been defeated or in a position of inferiority. **7** [C] (in the Bible) flat slab of stone, wood, etc; tablet(1); what is written or inscribed on such a ~: *the* ~*s of the law*, the ten commandments given to Moses by God. □ *vt* [VP6A] **1** submit for discussion: ~ *a motion/Bill/amendment.* ⇨ 6 above. **2** (esp US) postpone (a proposal, etc) indefinitely. **3** put in the form of a ~(5).

tab·leau /'tæbləʊ/ *n* (*pl* ~x /-ləʊz/) (often ~ **vi·vant** /'viːvɑːn *US:* viː'vɑːn/) representation by living persons of a picture or scene, without words or action, esp on a stage or platform; dramatic situation suddenly brought about.

table d'hôte /ˌtɑːbl 'dəʊt/ *adj, adv* (F) (of a restaurant meal) at an inclusive fixed price: *a* ~ *lunch*. ⇨ à la carte.

tab·let /'tæblɪt/ *n* **1** flat surface with words cut or written on it, eg one fixed to a wall in memory of sth or sb. **2** number of sheets of writing-paper fastened together along one edge. **3** lump of hard soap; small ˌflattened pellet of compressed medicine: *two* ~*s of aspirin;* flat, hard sweet: *throat* ~*s*, to be sucked to relieve a cough, sore throat, etc. **4** (hist) flat sheet of wood, stone, etc for cutting words on (eg as used in ancient Rome).

tab·loid /'tæblɔɪd/ *n* small size newspaper with many pictures, strip cartoons, etc and with its news presented in simplified form: (attrib) ~ *journalism.*

ta·boo /tə'buː *US:* tæ'buː/ *n* **1** [C,U] (among some peoples) something which religion or custom regards as forbidden, not to be touched, spoken of, etc: *That tree is under* (*a*) ~. **2** [C] general agreement not to discuss sth, do sth. □ *adj* under ~: *Questions and problems that were once* ~ *are now discussed openly. Unkind gossip ought to be* ~. '~ *words*, those which convention avoids or prohibits (eg most of those marked ⚠ in this dictionary). □ *vt* [VP6A] forbid, esp on moral or religious grounds.

ta·bor /'teɪbə(r)/ *n* small drum, esp one used to accompany a pipe or fife.

tabu·lar /'tæbjʊlə(r)/ *adj* arranged or displayed in tables(5): *a report in* ~ *form.*

tabu·late /'tæbjʊleɪt/ *vt* [VP6A] arrange (facts, figures, etc) in tables(5), in lists or columns. **tabu·la·tor** /-tə(r)/ *n* machine, device, that ~s. **tabu·la·tion** /ˌtæbjʊ'leɪʃn/ *n*

tacho·graph /'tækəʊgrɑːf/ *n* device that records the speed and duration of a journey in a motor-vehicle.

tacit /'tæsɪt/ *adj* unspoken; understood without being put into words: ~ *consent/agreement.* ~·**ly** *adv*

taci·turn /'tæsɪtɜːn/ *adj* (in the habit of) saying very little. ~·**ly** *adv* **taci·tur·nity** /ˌtæsɪ'tɜːnətɪ/ *n* [U].

tack /tæk/ *n* **1** small, flat-headed nail (eg as used for securing some kinds of carpet or linoleum to a floor): '*tin-~*, of iron coated with tin; '*thumb-~* (US) = drawing-pin. **2** long, loose stitch used in fastening pieces of cloth together loosely or temporarily. **3** sailing-ship's direction as fixed by the direction of the wind and the position of the sails: *on the port/starboard* ~, with the wind on the port/starboard side. *on the right/wrong* ~, (fig) following a wise/unwise course of action. **4** [U] (hard) ~, hard ship's biscuits. □ *vt,vi* **1** [VP6A,15A,B] fasten with ~s(1): ~ *down the carpet.* **2** [VP6A,15A,B] fasten with ~s(2): ~ *a ribbon on to a hat;* ~ *down a fold;* (fig) ~ *an appeal for money on to a speech*, add one. **3** [VP2A,C] sail in a zigzag course; make a ~ or ~s(3): ~*ing about;* ~ *to port.*

tackle /'tækl/ *n* **1** [C,U] set of ropes and pulleys for working a ship's sails, or for lifting weights, etc. ⇨ the illus at pulley. **2** [U] equipment, apparatus, for doing sth: '*fishing* ~, a rod, line, hooks, etc. **3** [C] act of seizing and bringing down an opponent with the ball (in Rugby and American-style football). □ *vt,vi* **1** [VP6A,14] deal with, attack (a problem, a piece of work): *I don't know how to* ~ *this problem,* how to start on it. ~ *sb about/over sth,* speak to sb frankly (about a matter). **2** [VP6A,2A] seize, lay hold of, sb, eg a thief, a player who, in Rugby, has the ball: *He* ~*s fearlessly.*

tacky /'tæki/ *adj* **1** sticky; not yet dry: *The paint/ varnish is still* ~. **2** (US) = tatty.

tact /tækt/ *n* [U] (use of) skill and understanding shown by sb who handles people and situations successfully and without causing offence: *show* ~*/have great* ~ *in dealing with people.* ~·ful /-fl/ *adj* having or showing ~. ~·fully /-fəlɪ/ *adv* ~·less *adj* lacking ~. ~·less·ly *adv* ~·less·ness *n*

tac·tic /'tæktɪk/ *n* **1** expedient; means of achieving an object. **2** (*pl* often with *sing v*) art of placing or moving fighting forces for or during battle. ⇨ strategy; (fig) plan(s) or method(s) for carrying out a policy: *win by surprise* ~*s; These* ~*s are unlikely to help you.* **tac·ti·cal** /-kl/ *adj* of ~s: ~*al exercises; a* ~*al error.* ⇨ strategic. **tact·i·cally** /-klɪ/ *adv* **tac·ti·cian** /tæk'tɪʃn/ *n* expert in ~s.

tac·tile /'tæktaɪl *US:* -təl/, **tac·tual** /'tæktʃʊəl/ *adjj* of, experienced by, the sense of touch: *a* ~ *organ/reflex.*

tad·pole /'tædpəʊl/ *n* form of a frog or toad from the time it leaves the egg to the time when it takes its adult form. ⇨ the illus at amphibian.

taf·feta /'tæfɪtə/ *n* [U] thin, shiny, rather stiff silk material; similar material of linen, rayon, etc.

taff·rail /'tæfreɪl/ *n* rail round a ship's stern.

Taffy /'tæfɪ/ *n* (colloq) Welshman.

taffy /'tæfɪ/ *n* **1** (US) toffee. **2** insincere flattery.

tag /tæg/ *n* **1** metal or plastic point at the end of a shoe-lace, string, etc. **2** label (eg for showing prices, addresses) fastened to or stuck into sth. **3** phrase or sentence often quoted: *Latin tags.* **4** any loose or ragged end. '**question tags,** (gram) phrases such as *isn't it? won't you? are there?* added to statements. **5** [U] game in which one child chases and tries to touch another. □ *vt,vi* (-gg-) **1** [VP6A] fasten a tag(2) to. **2** [VP14] *tag sth on (to)*, fasten, attach. **3** [VP2C] *tag along/behind/after,* follow closely: *children tagging after their mother. Tag along with us* (= Come with us) *if you like.* **4** [VP15A,B] join: *tag old articles together to make a book.*

tail /teɪl/ *n* **1** movable part (from the end of the backbone) at the end of the body of a bird, animal, fish or reptile: *Dogs wag their* ~*s when they are pleased.* **turn** ~, run away. ~*s up,* (of persons) in good spirits. **2** ⇨ the illus at aircraft. sth like a ~ in position: *the* ~ *of a kite/comet/aircraft/cart/ procession;* (attrib) *a* ~ (= following) *wind.* '~·**board** *n* board, usu on hinges, forming the back part of a cart or truck. ~·'**coat,** ~**s** *n* man's evening coat, long, divided and tapered at the back. ~·'**end** *n* (usu with *the* ~*-end (of)* final part: *at the* ~*-end of the procession.* '~·**gate** *n* door or flap at the rear of a motor-vehicle which can be opened for loading and unloading. '~·**light** *n* light at the end of a train, tram or other vehicle. '~·

piece *n* **(a)** (in a book, etc) decoration printed in the blank space at the end of a chapter, etc. **(b)** sth added at the end of sth. '~·**spin** *n* spiral dive of an aircraft in which the ~ makes wider circles than the front. **the** ~ **of the eye**, the outer corner: *watching me from the* ~ *of his eye.* **3** ~**s,** side of a coin opposite to that in which there is the head of sb. ⇨ head¹(3). **4** ~**s,** (colloq) ~·coat: *Am I to wear a dinner-jacket or* ~*s?* **5** (colloq) sb employed to follow and watch sb, eg a suspected criminal: *put a* ~ *on sb.* □ *vt,vi* **1** [VP3A] ~ *after sb,* follow close behind. **2** [VP6A] ~ *a person,* follow him closely, eg because he is suspected to be a criminal. **3** [VP2C] ~ *off/away,* **(a)** become smaller in number, size, etc. **(b)** (of remarks, etc) end in a hesitating or inconclusive way. **(c)** fall behind or away in a scattered line. ~·**tailed** /-teɪld/ *adj* (in compounds) *,long-¹*~*ed, ,short-¹*~*ed,* having a long/short ~. ~·**less** *adj* having no ~: *a* ~*less cat.*

tailor /'teɪlə(r)/ *n* maker of (esp outer) garments: *go to the* ~'*s to be measured for a suit/an overcoat.* ~·'**made** *adj* made by a ~, with special attention to exact fit; (fig) appropriate, well-suited: *He seems* ~*-made for the job.* □ *vt* **1** [VP6A] cut out and sew: *a well-*~*ed suit.* **2** [VP15A] adapt: ~*ed for a special purpose/to a particular audience.*

taint /teɪnt/ *n* [C,U] trace of some bad quality, decay or infection: *There was a* ~ *of insanity in the family. Is the meat free from* ~? □ *vt,vi* [VP6A,2A] make or become infected: ~*ed meat.* ~·**less** *adj* without ~; pure.

take¹ /teɪk/ *vt,vi* (*pt* took /tʊk/, *pp* taken /'teɪkən/) (For uses with a large number of *nn,* ⇨ **15** below. For special uses with *adverbial particles* and *preps* ⇨ **16** below.) **1** [VP6A,15A] get or lay hold of with the hand(s) or any other part of the body, eg the arms, teeth or with an instrument (Cf *let go* of or *release,* as opposite in meaning): ~ *sb's hand;* ~ *sth on one's back;* ~ *a man by the throat;* ~ *sb in one's arms,* put one's arms round him, embrace him; ~ *sth up* (= pick it up) *with one's fingers/with a pair of tongs;* ~ *a person's arm,* put, rest, one's hand on his arm, eg to support him or be supported by him. ~ *hold of sth,* grasp or seize it. **2** [VP6A,15A,2A] capture; catch (sb or sth) by surprise or pursuit; win (in a contest, etc): ~ *a town/a fortress,* in war; ~ *500 prisoners; be* ~*n prisoner/captive,* be caught and be made a prisoner. *The rabbit was* ~*n in a trap. The major's bull took* (= was awarded) *the first prize at the agricultural show. How many tricks did you* ~, ie win, eg at a card game such as whist or bridge? *Be careful not to* ~ *cold,* become ill with a cold (*catch cold* is more usu). ~ *sb's fancy,* please, delight: *The new dance has really taken the public's fancy.* ~ *sb at a disadvantage,* be approached, attacked, etc when unready, in a unfavourable situation, etc. *be* ~*n ill,* (passive only) become ill, catch an illness. ~ *sb unawares/by surprise,* approach or discover sb doing sth when he is unaware of one's presence, that one sees him, etc. **3** [VP6A] use; use or borrow without permission; steal; avail oneself of: *Someone has* ~*n my hat,* ie by mistake. *Who has* ~*n my bicycle,* borrowed or stolen it? *He* ~*s whatever he can lay his hands on.* **4** [VP6A,15A,B,12A,13A,19B] carry (sth), accompany (sb), away from a place: ~ *letters to the post;* ~ *the luggage upstairs;* ~ *a friend home in one's car;* ~ *the dog out for a walk;* ~ *one's wife to the* *cinema;* ~ *the children swimming /for a swim. Please* ~ *these things in/out/away/back/home, etc. Shall I* ~ *your message to her/*~ *her your message? T*~ *her some flowers. He took me a new way to the coast,* by a route that was new to me. **'~-home wages/pay,** (colloq) net sum after deduction of national insurance contribution, income tax, etc. **5** [VP6A,15A] get, have; eat or drink; allow oneself: ~ *a holiday/a walk/a bath/a quick look round/a deep breath;* ~ *a chair/a seat,* sit down; ~ *medical/legal advice,* get the advice of a doctor/lawyer; ~ *driving lessons;* ~ (= hire) *a taxi;* ~ (= rent) *a cottage at the seaside for the holidays. Let's go into the garden and* ~ *the air,* have some fresh air. *Will you* ~ *tea or coffee? I'll* ~ (= buy) *2 lb of your Kenya coffee. Why don't you* ~ *a wife,* (old use) marry? *You should* ~ *a partner into the business/*~ *your brother into the business.* **6** [VP6A,15A,16B] accept; receive: *Will you* ~ *£1500 for the car,* sell it for this sum? *This small café* ~*s £500 a week,* This is the total of the receipts. ⇨ takings below. (From the C of E marriage service) *Do you* ~ *this man to be your lawful wedded husband? You must* ~ *us as you find us,* not expect exceptional treatment, consideration, etc (while you are with us). *He will* ~ *no nonsense,* will not allow any. *I'm not taking any more or your insults,* I refuse to listen to them. ~ **one's chance,** trust to one's luck; accept whatever may come or happen: *She'll have to* ~ *her chance with the other applicants for the job.* ~ **a chance (on sth),** accept the possibility of not getting sth: *I'm ready to* ~ *a chance on finding him at home,* will call hoping to find him there. ~ **one's chance,** attempt sth though aware of the possibility of failing. ~ *it from me;* ~ *my word for it,* believe me when I say: *T*~ *it from me, there'll be some big changes made in the coming year.* **be able to** ~ **it; can** ~ **it,** be able to endure suffering, punishment, attack, etc without showing weakness, readiness to admit defeat, etc. **7** [VP6A] subscribe to; receive and pay for regularly: *Which newspapers do you* ~? **8** [VP6A,15A,B] ~ **(down),** make a record of: ~ *notes of a lecture;* ~ *sth down in shorthand;* ~ *a letter,* from dictation; ~ (*down*) *a broadcast on tape,* ie using a tape-recorder; ~ *a photograph.* [VP2A] *He does not* ~ *well,* It is difficult to ~ good photographs of him. **9** [VP2B,6B,15A] need, require: *The work took four hours. These things* ~ *time. How long will this job* ~ *you/How long will you* ~ *over this job? The wound took a long time to heal.* ~ **one's time (over sth),** (a) not hurry; use as much time as one needs: *Take your time over the job, and do it well.* (b) (ironic) use more time than is reasonable: *The workmen are certainly taking their time over the job.* **It** ~*s* **'two to make a quarrel,** (prov) suggesting that both parties to a quarrel are at fault. ~ **a lot of doing,** need much effort, skill, etc. **10** [VP14,22] ~ **sb/sth for...;** ~ **sb/sth to be...,** suppose; conclude; infer; consider: *I took you to be an honest man. Do you* ~ *me for a fool? Even the experts took the painting for a genuine Rembrandt.* ~ **it (from sb) that...,** assume: *I* ~ *it that we are to come early. You may* ~ *it from me that...,* be confident because I tell you....* ~ **sb/sth for granted,** ⇨ grant v(2). **11** [VP6A] find out (by inquiry, measurement, etc): *The doctor took my temperature. Has the tailor* ~*n your measurements for that new suit? Did the police* ~ *your name and address?* **12** [VP22,16B]

treat or regard in a specified way: ~ *it/things easy,* not work too hard or too fast; ~ *things coolly/calmly,* not get excited; ~ *sth ill/amiss,* resent it. *I should* ~ *it kindly* (= be grateful to you) *if.... Don't* ~ *it so seriously,* Don't treat the matter with such seriousness. ~ **sth as** + *pp,* assume it to be: ~ *an apology as given/an objection as answered.* ~ **sth as read,** agree that it is unnecessary to read it, eg the minutes of the previous meeting. ~ **(it) as read (that...),** assume it, assume that...: *We can* ~ (*it*) *as read that an apology was given.* **13** [VP6A] accept responsibility for: ~ *evening service,* (at church) conduct it; ~ *a class,* be in charge, give the class its lesson, etc. **14** [VP2A] be successful: *George Green's second novel did not* ~, did not become popular; have the required effect: *That smallpox injection did not* ~. *The dye doesn't* ~ *in cold water,* is ineffective. **15** (with *nn*) (For other examples, ⇨ the *n* entries) ~ **account of,** (= ~ sth into account), ⇨ account[1](7). ~ **advantage of sb/sth,** ⇨ advantage. ~ **aim,** ⇨ aim[1](2). ~ **the biscuit/the cake,** ⇨ biscuit, cake. ~ **care,** ⇨ care[1](2). ~ **a chair,** ⇨ 5 above. ~ **a/one's chance,** ⇨ 6 above. ~ **charge (of),** ⇨ charge[1](5). ~ **courage,** ⇨ courage. ~ **a degree,** obtain a degree(5). ~ **(a) delight/an interest/(a) pleasure/(a) pride in sth,** be, show that one is, delighted/interested, etc in it. ~ **a dislike to sb,** ⇨ dislike. ~ **effect,** ⇨ effect(1). ~ **an examination,** be tested on one's knowledge or ability. ~ **exception to,** ⇨ exception(3). **not/never take one's eyes off,** ⇨ 16 below. ~ **a fancy to;** ~ **the fancy of,** ⇨ fancy[1](3). ~ **fright (at sth),** become frightened. ~ **a gamble (on sth),** do sth knowing it is risky. ~ **a hand at,** ⇨ hand[1](13). ~ **sb in hand,** accept responsibility for him (esp to improve his behaviour). ~ **(fresh) heart;** ~ **sth to heart,** ⇨ heart(2). ~ **heed,** pay attention. ~ **a/the hint,** ⇨ hint. ~ **(one's) leave (of sb),** ⇨ leave[2](3). ~ **the liberty of;** ~ **liberties with,** ⇨ liberty(2). ~ **a liking to,** become fond of. ~ **the measure of sb,** ⇨ measure[1](1). ~ **one's/sb's mind off (sth),** ⇨ mind[1](2). ~ **no notice (of),** ⇨ notice(3). ~ **an oath,** ⇨ oath(1). ~ **objection to,** ⇨ objection(1). ~ **offence (at sth),** ⇨ offence(2). ~ **the opportunity of doing/to do sth,** recognize a favourable moment and act. ~ **(holy) orders,** become a priest, etc. ~ **(great) pains (over sth/to do sth),** ⇨ pains. ~ **part (in),** ⇨ part[1](4). ~ **place;** ~ **the place of,** ⇨ place[1](10). ~ **the risk of;** ~ **risks,** ⇨ risk(1). ~ **a seat,** ⇨ 5 above. ~ **silk,** ⇨ silk(3). ~ **stock,** ⇨ stock[1](1). ~ **one's time (over sth),** ⇨ 9 above. ~ **trouble (over sth);** ~ **the trouble to do sth,** ⇨ trouble, *n*(3). ~ **umbrage (at),** ⇨ umbrage. ~ **my word for it,** ⇨ 6 above. **16** [VP3A,2C,15B] (special uses with *adverbial particles* and *preps*): **be taken aback,** ⇨ aback).

take after sb, resemble (esp a parent or relation) in features or character: *Your daughter does not* ~ *after you in any way.*

take sth apart, separate sth (machinery, etc) into its (component) parts.

take (away) from, lessen, weaken, diminish: *That foolish indiscretion took away from his public image. These faults to some extent* ~ (*away*) *from his credit as a biographer.* ~ **sth/sb away (from sb/sth),** remove: *Not to be* ~*n away,* eg books from a library. *The child was* ~*n away from* school, not allowed to attend. *What ~s you away so early,* Why are you leaving so early? *'Sandwiches to ~ away'* (eg as a sign outside a shop, = '...to be ~n away'), Sandwiches may be bought here and eaten elsewhere. Hence, '**~-away** *attrib* to be ~n away: *~-away hamburgers; a ~-away restaurant,* one that sells food that may be ~n away.

take sth back, (a) retreat or withdraw (what one has said) as an admission of error, as an apology, etc: *I ~ back what I said.* (b) agree to receive back: *Shopkeepers will not usually ~ back goods after they have been paid for.* **~ sb back (to),** carry or conduct to an earlier period: *These stories took him back to his childhood days,* (fig) brought them back to his mind.

take sth down, (a) write down: *The reporters took down the speech.* (b) lower; get by lifting down from (a shelf, etc): *~ down a book from the top shelf; ~ down the curtains/pictures from the walls; ~ down a mast.* (c) dismantle; pull down; get into separate parts: *~ down a crane/the scaffolding round a building; ~ down a partition.* **sb 'down a peg (or two),** humble; lower the pride of: *That fellow needs to be ~n down a peg.*

take from, ⇨ take (*away*) *from* above.

take sth in, (a) receive (work) to be done in one's own house for payment: *The poor widow earns money by taking in washing/sewing.* (b) (⇨ 7 above) pay for and receive regularly: *~ in journals/periodicals.* (c) reduce the size, area, length or width of (a garment, sail, etc): *This dress needs to be ~n in* (= made smaller) *at the waist. Orders were given to ~ in sail.* ⇨ *~ up the slack* at slack²(1). (d) comprise; include, eg in one's journey or route: *a motor-coach tour that ~s in six European capitals.* (e) take (territory, common land, etc) into one's possession; (re)claim: *A good deal of Romney Marsh was ~n in from the sea by monks.* (f) understand; absorb; digest mentally: *They listened to my lecture, but how much did they ~ in, I wonder? We need more time to ~ in the situation,* form a correct idea of it. (g) see at a glance; see at once: *She took in every detail of the other woman's clothes. He took in the scene at a glance.* (h) listen to, watch, with excitement: *The children took in the whole spectacle openmouthed.* **~ sb in,** (a) receive, admit: *make a living by taking in guests/lodgers; ~ a traveller in for the night.* (b) deceive; get the better of by a trick: *Don't let yourself be ~n in by these politicians. He was badly ~n in when he bought that second-hand car.*

take sth into account, ⇨ account(7). **~ a person into one's confidence,** ⇨ confidence(1). **~ sth into one's head,** ⇨ head ¹(19).

take off, (a) make a start in jumping. (b) (of an aircraft) leave the ground and rise: *The plane took off despite the fog.* Hence, '**~-off** *n* (a) (also *jump-off,* esp in show jumping) place at which the feet leave the ground in jumping. (b) (of aircraft) leaving the ground and rising: *a smooth ~-off.* ⇨ *touch–down* at touch²(11). **~ sth off,** (a) remove: *~ off one's shirt. Why don't you ~* (= shave) *off that silly little moustache? The surgeon took off* (= amputated) *his leg.* **~ one's hat off to sb,** ⇨ hat. (b) withdraw (from service): *The 7am express to Bristol will be ~n off next month,* will not run. **~ sth off (sth),** (a) lift and move to another position: *T~ your hand off my shoulder.* (b) deduct: *~ 50p off*

the price. **~ sb off,** (a) conduct; lead away somewhere: *He was ~n off to prison. She took me off to see her garden.* **~ sb off sth,** remove him from it: *The crew were ~n off* (= rescued from) *the wrecked ship by the lifeboat.* (b) ridicule by imitation; mimic; burlesque: *Alice is clever at taking off the headmistress.* Hence, '**~-off** *n* caricature; burlesque imitation of sb's behaviour: *a good ~-off of the Prime Minister.* **not/never ~ one's eyes off sth/sb,** look at constantly: *He never took his eyes off his small daughter while she was swimming in the sea.* **~ one's mind off (sth),** ⇨ mind ¹(2).

take on, (a) (colloq) become excited or agitated; make a fuss: *She took on something dreadful when I said she'd told a pack of lies.* (b) (colloq) become popular; have a vogue: *We introduced a new sports car last year but it never took on.* **~ sth on,** (a) undertake; charge oneself with: *~ on extra work/ heavy responsibilities. You've ~n on too much.* (b) assume; put on (a quality, appearance): *The chameleon can ~ on the colours of its background.* **~ sb on,** (a) accept as an opponent: *~ sb on at golf/billiards; ready to ~ on all comers,* play against, fight, anyone who accepts a challenge. (b) engage: *~ on twenty more workers.* (c) (of a train, etc) allow to enter: *The bus stopped to ~ on some children.* (d) (of trains, etc) carry too far, past the destination: *I fell asleep in the train and was ~n on to York.*

take sth out, (a) extract; remove: *have one's appendix/a tooth ~n out. How can I ~ out* (= remove) *these inkstains from my blouse?* (b) obtain; procure (sth issued): *~ out an insurance policy/a driving licence/a summons/a patent.* **~ sb out,** (a) conduct; accompany: *~ the children out for a walk; ~ one's wife out for dinner,* ie at a restaurant. (b) (in bridge): *~ one's partner out,* make a higher bid (than that which he has made). **~ it out in sth,** accept as recompense or compensation: *The innkeeper couldn't pay me the £10 he owed me but let me ~ it out in drinks and cigars.* **~ it out of sb,** leave him weak and exhausted: *His recent illness/All that hard work has ~n it out of him.* **~ it out on sb,** vent one's anger, disappointment, etc on (usu) sb else: *He came home angry at losing his job and took it out on his wife.*

take sb over (to), carry from one place to another: *Mr White took me over to the island in his launch.* **~ sth over (from sb),** assume control of; succeed to the management or ownership of (a business, etc): *Was it in 1948 that the Government took over the railways in Great Britain,* nationalized them? *When Mr Green retired his son took over the business from him.* Hence, '**~-over** *n* change of control of a firm or company, eg after another has made a successful bid to buy its stock: *a '~over bid.* **~ over (from sb),** accept duties, responsibilities, etc: *The new Chancellor took over* (ie *from* his predecessor) *yesterday.*

take to sth, (a) adopt as a practice or hobby, as a means of livelihood; get into a habit: *~ to gardening when one retires; ~ to drink(ing),* get into the habit of taking alcoholic liquor; *~ to the road,* become a tramp (or, in former times a highwayman); (of a circus, etc) go on tour from town to town giving shows. (b) take refuge in; use as a means of escape: *~ to flight,* run away; *~ to the woods/the jungle/the heather,* go to the woods, etc, to avoid capture. *The crew took to the boats when the torpedo struck the ship.* **~ to one's heels,** ⇨ heel ¹(1).

~ **to sth/sb,** conceive a liking for: *Has the baby ~n to its new nursemaid? That boy will never ~ to cricket.*

take sth up, (a) lift up; raise: ~ *up one's pen/book/gun;* ~ *up a carpet.* **(b)** (of trains, taxis, etc; more usu ~ *on*) stop to allow (passengers) to enter. **(c)** absorb (a liquid): *Blotting-paper ~s up ink.* **(d)** dissolve (solids): *How much water is needed to ~ up a pound of salt?* **(e)** interest oneself in; engage in (sth) (as a hobby, business, etc): ~ *up photography/market gardening.* **(f)** pursue further; begin afresh (sth left off, sth begun by sb else): *Harry took up the tale at the point where John had left off.* **(g)** occupy (time, space): *This table ~s up too much space. My time is fully ~n up with writing.* **(h)** (comm) advance money (on a mortgage); accept (a Bill of Exchange); subscribe for (shares, etc) at the time of issue. **(i)** catch the end of and make secure: ~ *up a dropped stitch.* **'~-up spool** *n* (on a ciné projector, tape-recorder, etc) spool on to which film, tape, etc is wound from the spool having the film, tape, etc that is being used. ~ **sth up (with sb),** speak or write (to him) about it: *I will ~ the matter up with the Ministry,* eg by asking for information, or by making a protest. ~ **sb up,** make a protegé of; help: *The young soprano was ~n up by the famous conductor,* He encouraged and helped her in her career. ~ **sb 'up on sth,** accept from him his offer, challenge, bet, etc: *why don't you take Jim up on his offer to lend you £50?* **be ~n up with sb/sth,** be much interested in: *He seems to be very much ~n up with that tall Swedish girl.* ~ **sb up sharp/short,** interrupt and correct (a speaker): *He took me up short when I suggested that....* ~ **up one's residence at,** (formal) proceed to occupy: *The new ambassador has ~n up his residence* (in the Embassy).

take sth upon/on oneself, assume responsibility; undertake: *You mustn't ~ upon yourself the right to make decisions.*

take² /teɪk/ *n* **1** amount (of money) taken. **2** (film industry) scene that has been or is to be photographed. **3** act of taking.

taker /'teɪkə(r)/ *n* one who, that which, takes, esp one who takes a bet: *There were no ~s,* no one willing to take bets.

tak·ing /'teɪkɪŋ/ *adj* attractive; captivating. □ *n (pl)* money taken in business; receipts.

talc /tælk/ *n* [U] soft, smooth mineral that can be split into thin transparent plates. **'~ powder** *n* perfumed powder to rub on the body, made from ~.

tal·cum /'tælkəm/ *n* **'~ powder,** = talc powder.

tale /teɪl/ *n* [C] **1** story: **'fairy-~s;** ~*s of adventure. It tells its own ~,* explains itself, requires no comment or explanation. **2** report; account. **tell ~s,** tell sth about another person that he wishes to be kept secret, eg his wrongdoing. Hence, **'~-bearer/-teller** *nn* person who tells ~s.

tal·ent /'tælənt/ *n* **1** [C,U] (particular kind of) natural power to do sth well: *a man of great ~; local ~,* (usu amateur) musicians, actors, etc of a district; *a '~ scout,* (colloq) person who watches out for persons of ~ for films, the theatre, sports, etc; *have a ~ for music/not much ~ for painting; an exhibition of local ~,* of works, eg paintings, by people of a district or locality. **2** [C] measure of weight, unit of money, used in ancient times among the Greeks, Romans, Assyrians, etc. **~ed** *adj* having ~; gifted: *a ~ed musician.*

tal·is·man /'tælɪzmən US: -ɪsm-/ *n* [C] (*pl ~s*)

sth that is thought to bring good luck, eg a trinket or ring.

talk¹ /tɔːk/ *n* **1** [C,U] talking; conversation; discussion: *I've had several ~s with the headmaster about my boy. There's too much ~* (= ~ing) *and not enough work being done.* **2** [C] informal speech: *give a ~ to the Women's Institute on one's travels in Asia.* **3** (phrases) **the ~ of the town,** sth or sb everyone is ~ing about. **be all ~,** said of sb who ~s a lot but does not get results. **'small ~,** conversation on everyday but not important topics.

talk² /tɔːk/ *vi,vt* (*pt,pp* ~ed) **1** [VP2A,B,C,3A,15B] ~ **(to/with sb) (about/of sth),** say things; speak to give information; discuss sth, etc: *He was ~ing to* (less often *with*) *a friend. What are they ~ing about* (less often *of*)*? We ~ed all afternoon/for two hours. Were they ~ing in Spanish or in Portuguese?* **be/get oneself ~ed about,** (in some contexts) be made the subject of gossip: *You'll get yourself ~ed about if you go on being so foolish.* ~ **at sb,** speak to sb without paying attention to his replies: *I don't like people who ~ at me instead of with me.* ~ **away,** continue ~ing: *They were still ~ing away at midnight.* ~ **back (to sb),** (often *answer back*) reply defiantly. ~ **big,** brag; boast. ~ **sb down,** silence him by talking loudly at him. ~ **down an aircraft,** ~ by radio to the pilot while he is about to make a landing, giving him instructions, etc. ~ **down to sb,** ~ in a way that suggests that the speaker is superior, eg by using condescendingly simple words, etc: *It's unwise for a lecturer to ~ down to his audience.* ~**ing of,** while on the subject of: *T~ing of travel, have you been to Munich yet?* ~ **sth over,** discuss it. ~ **round sth,** ~ about a subject without reaching the point or a conclusion. ~ **to sb,** (colloq) scold; reprove. Hence, **'~-ing-to** *n* scolding: *The teacher gave the lazy boy a good ~ing-to.* **2** [VP2A] have the power of speech: *Can the baby ~ yet?* **3** [VP6A] be able to use (a language): ~ *English/Spanish.* **4** [VP6A] discuss: ~ *business,* ~ *shop,* ⇨ shop(2). *We ~ed music all evening.* **'~-ing-point,** topic likely to cause discussion; argument likely to persuade or convince sb. **5** [VP6A] express in words: ~ *sense/nonsense/treason.* **6** [VP14,22] bring into a certain condition by ~ing: ~ *oneself hoarse,* ~ *until one is hoarse.* ~ **sb into/out of doing sth,** persuade sb to do/not to do sth: *She ~ed her husband into having a holiday in France. He ~ed his wife out of buying a new car.* ~ **sb over/round,** persuade sb to agree to or to accept sth: *We ~ed them over to our way of thinking.* **7** [VP2A] (various uses): *Don't do anything indiscreet—you know how people ~,* gossip. *Has the accused man ~ed yet,* given information, eg under coercion or threats? *Some parrots can ~,* imitate the sounds of human speech. **~a·tive** /'tɔːkətɪv/ *adj* fond of ~ing. **~er** *n* **1** (esp with an *adj*) person who ~s: *a good/poor, etc ~er. What a ~er that woman is!* How fond she is of ~ing! **2** person who ~s a lot but does not get results: *He's a mere ~er.*

talkie /'tɔːkɪ/ *n* [C] (dated colloq term for a) cinema film with spoken dialogue (used when these were a novelty). **the ~s,** (colloq) cinema films with spoken dialogue.

tall /tɔːl/ *adj* (-er, -est) **1** (of persons) of more than average height; (of objects such as a ship's mast, a flagpole, a church spire, a tree whose height is greater than its width, but not of mountains) higher than the average or than surrounding objects: *She is*

~er *than her sister. She wears high heels to make herself look ~er. That yacht has a very ~ mast.*
'~·boy (GB; US = **highboy**) *n* bedroom chest of drawers 5 or 6 ft high. **2** of a specified height: *Tom is six foot ~.* **3** (colloq) excessive, exorbitant. **a ~ order,** an unreasonable request; a task difficult to perform. **a ~ story,** one that it is difficult to believe. **~·ish** /-ɪʃ/ *adj* rather ~.

tal·low /'tæləʊ/ *n* [U] hard (esp animal) fat used for making candles, etc.

tally /'tælɪ/ *n* [C] (*pl* -lies) **1** score; reckoning: *keep the ~.* **2** ticket, label, etc used for identification. **'~·clerk** *n* clerk who checks cargo, etc eg at the docks. **'~·man** /-mæn/ *n* (*pl* -men) person who sells goods and collects weekly payments. □ *vi* (*pt,pp* -lied) [VP2A,3A] ~ (*with*), (*of stories, amounts, etc*) *correspond; agree: The two lists do not ~. Does your list ~ with mine? The stories of the two men tallied.*

tally-ho /ˌtælɪ 'həʊ/ *int* huntsman's cry on catching sight of the fox.

Tal·mud /'tælmʊd US: 'tɑːl-/ *n* compendium of Jewish law and teaching.

talon /'tælən/ *n* claw of a bird of prey, eg an eagle.

talus /'teɪləs/ *n* (geol) sloping mass of fragments at the foot of a cliff or precipice.

ta·male /tə'mɑːlɪ/ *n* Mexican dish of chopped meat, red peppers, etc steamed in corn (= maize) husks.

tam·ar·ind /'tæmərɪnd/ *n* (edible fruit of a) tropical tree.

tam·ar·isk /'tæmərɪsk/ *n* [C] evergreen shrub with feathery branches, often planted in sandy soil near the sea.

tam·bour /'tæmbʊə(r)/ *n* rolling front for a TV set or the top of a writing-desk, made of narrow strips of wood glued to canvas.

tam·bour·ine /ˌtæmbə'riːn/ *n* small, shallow drum with metal discs in the rim, played by striking with the knuckles and shaking it at the same time. ⇨ the illus at **percussion.**

tame /teɪm/ *adj* (-r, -st) **1** (of animals) brought under control and/or accustomed to living with human beings; not wild or fierce: *a ~ monkey. The deer in the park are very ~.* **2** (of a person) spiritless; submissive; docile: *Her husband is a ~ little man.* **3** dull: *a ~ baseball match. The story/film, etc has a ~ ending.* □ *vt* [VP6A] make ~: *~ a lion.* **tamer** *n* (usu in compounds) person who ~s: *a 'lion—~r.* **tam·able** /-əbl/ *adj* that can be ~d, converted from a savage state. **~·ly** *adv* **~·ness** *n*

Tam·many /'tæmənɪ/ *n* ~ (**Hall**), central organization of the Democratic Party in New York City; (attrib) of its politics, members, etc.

tam-o'-shan·ter /ˌtæm ə 'ʃæntə(r)/, **tammy** /'tæmɪ/ *nn* round, woollen or cloth cap fitting closely to the forehead.

tamp /tæmp/ *vt* [VP15B] ~ **sth down,** tap or drive down by repeated light blows: *He ~ed down the tobacco in his pipe.*

tam·per /'tæmpə(r)/ *vi* [VP3A] ~ **with,** meddle or interfere with; make unauthorized changes in: *Someone has been ~ing with the lock/the seal of this letter.*

tan /tæn/ *n, adj* yellowish brown; brown colour of sunburnt skin: *tan leather shoes/gloves; get a good tan* (on one's skin). □ *vt,vi* (-nn-) [VP6A,2A] **1** (of an animal's skin) make, be made, into leather (by treatment with tannic acid, etc). *tan sb's hide,* (sl) give him a good beating. **2** make or become brown with sunburn: *return from the holidays with a*

tanned *face. Some people tan quickly.* **tan·ner** *n* workman who tans skins. **tan·nery** /'tænərɪ/ *n* (*pl* -ries) place where skins are tanned.

tan·dem /'tændəm/ *n* bicycle made for two persons to ride on, one behind the other, with pedals for both. □ *adv* (*in*) ~, (of horses in harness or two persons on a ~ bicycle) one behind the other: *drive/ride in ~.*

tang /tæŋ/ *n* sharp taste or flavour, esp one that is characteristic of sth: *the salt ~ of the sea air.* **tangy** *adj:* *a ~y aroma/sauce.*

tan·gent /'tændʒənt/ *n* straight line touching but not cutting a curve. ⇨ the illus at **circle.** *go/fly off at a ~,* (fig) change suddenly from one line of thought, action, etc to another.

tan·ger·ine /ˌtændʒə'riːn US: 'tændʒəriːn/ *n* [C] small, sweet-scented, loose-skinned orange.

tan·gible /'tændʒəbl/ *adj* **1** that can be perceived by touch. **2** clear and definite; real: *~ proof; the ~ assets,* eg of a business company, its buildings, machinery, etc but not its goodwill. **tan·gibly** /-əblɪ/ *adv* **tan·gi·bil·ity** /ˌtændʒə'bɪlətɪ/ *n*

tangle[1] /'tæŋgl/ *n* [C] **1** confused mass (of string, hair, etc): *brush the ~s out of a dog's hair. The kitten has made a ~ of my ball of wool.* **2** confused state: *The traffic was in a frightful ~.* □ *vt,vi* **1** [VP6A,15B,2A,C] make or become confused, disordered: *~d hair.* **2** [VP3A] ~ **with sb,** (colloq) be/become involved in a fight or quarrel with: *I shouldn't ~ with Peter—he's bigger than you.*

tangle[2] /'tæŋgl/ *n* [U] (kinds of) seaweed with long leathery fronds.

tango /'tæŋgəʊ/ *n* (*pl* ~s /-gəʊz/) (music for a) S American dance with strongly marked rhythm.

tank /tæŋk/ *n* **1** (usu large) container for liquid or gas: *the 'petrol-~ of a car; a 'rain-water ~,* eg for storing rain-water from roofs; *a ship's ~s,* the compartments into which the double hull is divided, to contain fuel-oil, fresh water, etc. **'~·car,** large (usu cylindrical) ~ for carrying petroleum, etc by rail. **2** (in India, Pakistan, etc) large, artificial (usu rectangular) pool for storing water. **3** armoured fighting vehicle with guns, moving on caterpillar tracks. **'~ trap,** deep ditch or other obstruction built to hinder or stop the advance of ~s. □ *vi* ~ **sth up,** fill up the ~ of a vehicle, etc. *be/get ~ed up,* (sl) be/get drunk. **~er** *n* ship or aircraft with ~s for carrying liquid as freight; heavy road vehicle with a large cylindrical ~ for carrying oil, milk or other liquid in bulk.

a tank

tank·ard /'tæŋkəd/ *n* large drinking mug, esp one for beer.

tan·ner[1] /'tænə(r)/ *n* (sl) former British silver coin, value sixpence (6d, = 2½p).

tan·ner[2] /'tænə(r)/ **tan·nery,** ⇨ tan.

tan·nic /'tænɪk/ *adj* ~ **acid,** = tannin.

tan·nin /'tænɪn/ *n* [U] acid obtained chiefly from

the bark of oak and other trees, and used in preparing leather, dyeing, the manufacture of ink, etc.

.tan·noy /'tænɔɪ/ n (P) type of loudspeaker or loudspeaker system, eg as used for public-address systems.

tansy /'tænzɪ/ n herb with yellow flowers and bitter leaves, used in medicine and cooking.

tan·ta·lize /'tæntəlaɪz/ vt [VP6A] raise hopes that cannot (yet) be realized; keep just out of reach sth that sb desires: *a tantalizing smell of food.*

tan·ta·mount /'tæntəmaʊnt/ adj ∼ **to,** equal in effect to: *The Queen's request was ∼ to a command.*

tan·trum /'tæntrəm/ n [C] fit of bad temper or anger: *He's in one of his ∼s again.*

tap¹ /tæp/ n **1** device for controlling the flow of liquid or gas from a pipe, barrel, etc. (Cf *valve* for controlling flow *through* a pipe; cf *faucet,* the usu word in the US): *turn the tap on/off. Don't leave the taps running,* ie turn them off. **on tap,** (of beer, etc) in a barrel with a tap, ready to be drawn off; (hence, fig) available when needed. '**tap·room** n (in an inn, etc) room in which barrels are stored and cheaper drinks sold. '**tap-root** n chief descending root of a plant, tree, etc (going straight down for moisture). **2** plug used to close the opening of a cask. □ vt (-pp-) [VP6A,14,15B] *tap (off) sth (from sth).* **1** draw out liquid through the tap of a (barrel): *tap a cask of cider; tap (off) cider from a cask;* cut (the bark of a tree) and get (the sap, etc): *tap rubber-trees; tap sugar-maples,* eg in Canada. **2** extract or obtain (sth from sb or sth): *tap a man for money/information; tap a telephone/wire/line,* make a connection so as to intercept messages. *My phone is being tapped.* **3** furnish (a cask, etc) with a tap.

tap² /tæp/ n [C] **1** quick, light blow: *a ∼ on the window/at the door.* '**tap-dancing** n stage-dancing with rhythmical tapping of the foot, toe or heel. **2 taps,** (US armed forces) last signal of the day (by drum or bugle) for lights to be put out. □ vt,vi (-pp-) [VP6A,15A,2A,C] give a tap or taps (to): *tap a man on the shoulder; tap at/on the door; tap one's foot on the floor impatiently.*

tape /teɪp/ n [C,U] **1** (piece, length of) narrow strip of material used for tying up parcels, etc or in dressmaking: *three yards of linen ∼; do up the ∼s of an apron into neat bows.* '**∼-measure** n length of ∼ or strip of thin, flexible metal or of strengthened cloth graduated for measuring things with. '**∼·worm** n kinds of many-jointed, long, flat worm that lives during its adult stage as a parasite in the intestines of man and other animals. **2** ('**ticker-**)∼, narrow strip of paper on which telegraph instruments automatically print news, etc. '**insulating** ∼, strip of sticky cloth used for insulating electrical connections, etc. **magnetic** ∼, strip of a plastic material magnetized to record sound or vision. **red** ∼, ⇨ red, adj(3). '**∼ deck,** ∼ recorder (without amplifiers or speakers) as a component in a hi-fi system. '**∼-recorder** n apparatus for recording sound on, and playing sound back from, this kind of ∼. **3** length of ∼ stretched between the winning-posts on a race-track: *breast the ∼,* reach and pass this ∼. □ vt [VP6A] **1** fasten, tie together, with ∼. **2** record (sound) on magnetic ∼. **3** (colloq) *have sth/sb ∼d,* understand it/him thoroughly.

taper¹ /'teɪpə(r)/ n [C] length of thread with a covering of wax, burnt to give a light; very slender candle.

taper² /'teɪpə(r)/ vt,vi [VP6A,15B,2A,C] make or become gradually narrower towards one end: *One end ∼s/is ∼ed off to a point.*

tap·es·try /'tæpɪstrɪ/ n (pl -ries) [C,U] (piece of) cloth into which threads of coloured wool are woven by hand to make designs and pictures, used for covering walls and furniture. **tap·es·tried** adj hung, decorated, with ∼: *tapestried walls.*

tapi·oca /ˌtæpɪ'əʊkə/ n [U] starchy food (in the form of hard, white grains) from the root of the cassava plant.

ta·pir /'teɪpə(r)/ n pig-like animal of Central and S America with a long, flexible nose.

taps /tæps/ ⇨ tap²(2).

tap·ster /'tæpstə(r)/ n person employed to draw and serve beer, spirits, etc. ⇨ *tap-room* at tap¹(1).

tar¹ /tɑ:(r)/ n [U] black substance, hard when cold, thick and sticky when warm, obtained from coal, etc used to preserve timber (eg in fences and posts), in making roads, etc. **tar-macadam** = tarmac. □ vt (-rr-) [VP6A] cover with tar. *tar and feather sb,* put tar on him and then cover with feathers as a punishment. *tarred with the same brush,* having the same faults.

tar² /tɑ:(r)/ n (Jack) tar, (dated colloq) sailor.

tara·diddle /'tærədɪdl US: ˌtærə'dɪdl/ n (colloq) untruth; fib.

tar·an·tella /ˌtærən'telə/, **tar·an·telle** /-'tel/ nn [C] (music for a) rapid, whirling Italian dance for two persons.

ta·ran·tula /tə'ræntjʊlə US: -tʃʊlə/ n large, hairy, poisonous spider of S Europe; other kinds of spider.

tar·boosh /tɑ:'bu:ʃ/ n brimless felt cap like a fez, worn by some Muslim men.

tardy /'tɑ:dɪ/ adj (-ier, -iest) **1** slow; slow-moving; coming or done late: *∼ progress/repentance; ∼ in offering help.* **2** (US) late: *be ∼ for school.* **tar·dily** /-ɪlɪ/ adv **tar·di·ness** n

tare¹ /teə(r)/ n (Biblical; usu pl) weed growing among corn.

tare² /teə(r)/ n allowance made to a purchaser for the weight of the vehicle carrying the commodity he has brought or for the weight of the container in which the commodity is packed, in cases where the commodity is weighed together with the vehicle or container; weight of a motor-vehicle, etc without fuel.

tar·get /'tɑ:gɪt/ n **1** sth to be aimed at in shooting-practice; any object aimed at. ⇨ the illus at archery. **2** thing, plan, etc against which criticism is directed: *This book will be the ∼ of bitter criticism.* **3** objective (set for savings, production, etc);

recording tape spool

measuring tape

ticker tape

recording tape cassette

tapes

885 tariff/tattoo

total which it is desired to reach.

tar·iff /'tærɪf/ n [C] **1** list of fixed charges, esp for meals, rooms, etc at a hotel; price-list. **2** list of taxes on goods imported or (less often) exported; tax on a particular class of imported goods: *raise ~ walls against foreign goods*, (try to) exclude them by means of import taxes; *~ reform*, movement (esp in GB, 19th century) to get rid of inequalities in ~s.

tar·mac /'tɑːmæk/ n [U] mixture of tar and gravel, as used for the surfaces of paths, roads, aircraft runways, etc.

tarn /tɑːn/ n small mountain lake.

tar·nish /'tɑːnɪʃ/ vi,vt [VP6A,2A] (esp of metal surfaces) lose, cause the loss of, brightness: *The damp atmosphere has ~ed the gilt. Chromium does not ~ easily. His reputation is ~ed.* □ n dullness; loss of polish.

taro /'tɑːrəʊ/ n (pl ~s /-rəʊz/) kinds of tropical plant with a starchy root used as food, esp in the Pacific islands.

tar·pau·lin /tɑː'pɔːlɪn/ n [C,U] (sheet or cover of) canvas made waterproof, esp by being tarred: *cover the goods on the lorry with a ~.*

tar·pon /'tɑːpɒn US: -pən/ n large fish found in the warmer parts of the Atlantic Ocean.

tar·ra·gon /'tærəgən US: -gɒn/ n [U] herb with sharp-tasting leaves, used in salads and for flavouring vinegar (*~ vinegar*).

tarry¹ /'tɑːrɪ/ adj covered, sticky, with tar.

tarry² /'tærɪ/ vi (archaic or liter) [VP2A,B,C] **1** stay, remain, lodge: *~ a few days at/in a place; ~ (behind) for sb.* **2** be slow in coming, going, appearing.

tar·sal /'tɑːsl/ adj (anat) of the bones in the ankle. □ n (anat) bone in the ankle. ⇨ the illus at skeleton.

tar·sus /'tɑːsəs/ n (pl tarsi /-saɪ/) (anat) collection of seven small bones in the ankle.

tart¹ /tɑːt/ adj acid; sharp in taste; (fig) sharp: *~ fruit; a ~ flavour; ~ humour; a ~ manner/disposition. ~·ly adv ~·ness n*

tart² /tɑːt/ n **1** fruit pie. **2** circle of pastry cooked with fruit or jam on it.

tart³ /tɑːt/ n (derog sl) prostitute. □ vt [VP15B] *~ sth/sb up*, (colloq) make gaudy; add superficial attractions to; smarten.

tar·tan /'tɑːtn/ n [U] Scottish woollen fabric woven with coloured crossing stripes; [C] particular pattern of ~, eg of a Scottish clan. ⇨ the illus at kilt.

tar·tar¹ /'tɑːtə(r)/ n [U] **1** chalk-like substance deposited on the teeth. **2** substance deposited on the sides of casks from fermented wine. *cream of ~*, purified form of this, used with baking soda to make baking powder. *~ic* /tɑː'tærɪk/ *acid*, acid of ~, found in the juice of grapes, oranges, etc (used in making baking powder, etc).

tar·tar² /'tɑːtə(r)/ n rough, violent, troublesome person. *catch a ~*, have to deal with a person of this kind, esp one who is more than one's match.

tar·tar³ /'tɑːtə(r)/ n *~ sauce*, cold mayonnaise with chopped onions, herbs, gherkins, pickles, etc.

task /tɑːsk US: tæsk/ n [C] piece of (esp hard) work (to be) done: *set a boy a ~. She finds housekeeping an irksome ~. take sb to ~ (about/for sth)*, scold him: *take sb to ~ for arriving late.* '*~-force* n specially organized unit (of warships, etc) for a special purpose. (*hard*) '*~-master/-mistress* nn (strict) overseer. □ vt [VP6A] (of a ~) put a strain on: *Mathematics ~s that boy's brain.*

tas·sel /'tæsl/ n bunch of threads, etc tied together

at one end and hanging (from a flag, hat, etc) as an ornament. ⇨ the illus at kilt. *~·led* (US = *~ed*) adj having a ~ or ~s.

taste¹ /teɪst/ n **1 the ~**, sense by which flavour is known: *sweet/sour to the ~.* '*~ bud* n group of cells in the tongue for this sense. ⇨ the illus at mouth. **2** [C,U] quality of a substance made known by this sense, eg by putting some on the tongue: *Sugar has a sweet ~. I don't like the ~ of this mixture. This medicine has no/very little/not much/a queer ~. leave a bad/nasty '~ in the mouth.* (lit or fig) be followed by a feeling of dislike or disgust. **3** (usu *a ~ (of)*)small quantity (of sth to eat or drink, or fig): *Won't you have a ~ of this cake/wine? Give him a ~ of the whip*, enough to be a sample of what it feels like to be whipped. **4** [C,U] *~ (for)*, liking or preference for: *He has a ~ for French cigarettes. She has expensive ~s in clothes. There's no accounting for ~s*, We cannot explain why different people like different things. *Abstract art is not to his ~/not to the ~ of everyone.* **5** [U] ability to enjoy beauty, esp in art and literature; ability to form judgements about these; ability to behave in the most appropriate and pleasing way: *She has excellent ~ in dress/dresses in perfect ~. It would be bad ~ to refuse their invitation. (be) in good/bad/poor/excellent, etc ~*, (be, be done, etc) showing this ability well/badly, etc. *(be) in the best/worst of ~*, (be, be done, etc) showing this ability in the best/worst way. *~·ful* /-fl/ adj showing good ~(5). *~·fully* /-fəlɪ/ adv in a ~ful manner: *~fully decorated with flowers. ~·less* adj **1** (of food) having no ~ or flavour. **2** without ~(5); in bad ~(5). *~·less·ly* adv *tasty* adj (-ier, -iest) having a pleasant flavour; pleasing to the ~. *tast·ily* /-ɪlɪ/ adv

taste² /teɪst/ vt,vi **1** [VP6A,2A] (not in the progressive tenses; often with *can, could*) be aware of the taste of sth: *Can you ~ anything strange in this soup? If you have a bad cold you cannot ~ (anything).* **2** [VP3A,2D] *~ (of)*, have a particular taste or flavour: *~ sour/bitter/sweet. It ~s too much of garlic/spice.* **3** [VP6A] test the ~ of: *The cook ~d the soup to see whether he had put enough salt in it.* **4** [VP6A] (fig) experience: *~ happiness/the joys of freedom. ~ of*, (liter) know; experience. *~r* n person who is employed to judge teas, wines, etc by ~: *A wine-~r doesn't swallow what he ~s.*

tat¹ /tæt/ vi,vt (-tt-) do tatting; make by tatting.

tat² /tæt/ n [U] quality of being tatty; tatty person or thing.

tat³ /tæt/ n ⇨ tit².

ta ta /,tɑ 'tɑː/ int (baby language) goodbye.

tat·ter /'tætə(r)/ n (usu pl) rag; piece of cloth, paper, etc torn off or hanging loosely from sth: *in ~s*, in tags or torn strips; *tear sb's reputation to ~s*, (fig) destroy it. *~ed* adj ragged. *~·de·malion* /,tætədə'meɪlɪən/ n sb dressed in ~s.

tat·ting /'tætɪŋ/ n [U] (art or process of making a) kind of handmade knotted lace-work used for trimming.

tattle /'tætl/ vi,vt [VP2A] chatter, gossip, prattle. □ n [U] idle talk. *tat·tler* /'tætlə(r)/ n person who ~s.

tat·too¹ /tə'tuː US: tæ'tuː/ n (pl ~s) **1** (sing only) beating of drum(s) to call soldiers back to quarters; hour at which a ~ is sounded: *beat/sound the ~.* **2** [C] continuous tapping: *beat a ~ on the table with his fingers.* **3** [C] public entertainment, usu at night (often *torchlight ~*) with music and marching, by soldiers.

tat·too² /tə'tu:/ *US:* tæ'tu:/ *vt* [VP6A] mark (sb's skin) with a permanent picture or pattern by pricking it and putting in dyes or stains; put (a picture or pattern) on the skin thus: *The sailor had a ship ~ed on his arm.* □ *n* [C] (*pl ~s*) picture or pattern of this kind.

tatty /'tætɪ/ *adj* (-ier, -iest) (sl) untidy and shabby looking; tawdry. **tat·tily** /-ɪlɪ/ *adv*

taught /tɔ:t/ *pt,pp* of teach.

taunt /tɔ:nt/ *n* [C] remark intended to hurt sb's feelings; contemptuous reproach: *endure the ~s of a successful rival.* □ *vt* [VP6A,14] ~ **sb** (**with sth**), attack (sb) with ~s: *They ~ed the boy with cowardice/with being a coward.* ~**·ing·ly** *adv*

Taurus /'tɔ:rəs/ *n* (astrol) second sign of the zodiac. ⇨ the illus at zodiac.

taut /tɔ:t/ *adj* (of ropes, wires, etc) tightly stretched; (of muscles and (fig) of nerves) tense. ~**·ly** *adv* ~**·ness** *n*

taut·ol·ogy /tɔ:'tɒlədʒɪ/ *n* [U] the saying of the same thing again in different ways without making one's meaning clearer or more forceful; needless repetition; [C] (*pl* -gies) instance of this. **tauto·logi·cal** /ˌtɔ:tə'lɒdʒɪkl/ *adj*

tav·ern /'tævən/ *n* (archaic or liter) inn or public house.

taw·dry /'tɔ:drɪ/ *adj* (-ier, -iest) showy; brightly coloured or decorated, but cheap or in bad taste: ~ *jewellery/dresses.* **taw·drily** /-əlɪ/ *adv* **taw·dri·ness** *n*

tawny /'tɔ:nɪ/ *adj* brownish yellow.

tawse /'tɔ:z/ *n* [C] (Scot) leather strap for punishing children.

tax /tæks/ *n* **1** [C,U] (sum of) money (to be) paid by citizens (according to income, value of purchases, etc) to the government for public purposes: *state/ local taxes; levy a tax on sth; direct taxes,* ie on income; *indirect taxes,* eg paid when one buys goods. *How much income tax did you pay last year? He paid £50 in taxes.* **'tax-collector** *n* official who collects taxes. **'tax-payer** *n* person who pays taxes. **ˌtax-'free** *adj* (a) not subject to taxation. (b) (of dividends or interest) on which tax has been deducted before distribution. **2** *a tax on,* sth that is a burden or strain: *a tax on one's strength/ health/patience.* □ *vt* **1** [VP6A] put a tax(1) on; require (a person) to pay a tax: *tax luxuries/ incomes/rich and poor alike.* **2** [VP6A] be a tax(2) on: *tax a person's patience,* eg by asking him many silly questions. **3** [VP14] *tax sb with sth,* accuse him of it: *tax sb with neglect of/with having neglected his work.* **4** (legal) examine and decide, eg costs of a lawsuit. **tax·able** /-əbl/ *adj* capable of being taxed. **tax·abil·ity** /ˌtæksə'bɪlətɪ/ *n* **tax·ation** /tæk'seɪʃn/ *n* [U] (system of) raising money by taxes; taxes (to be) paid: *reduce taxation; grumble at high taxation.*

taxi /'tæksɪ/ *n* (*pl ~s*) (also '~**·cab,** usu abbr to *cab,* esp in US) motor-car, esp one with a ~meter, which may be hired for journeys. '~**·meter** *n* (usu abbr to *meter*) device which automatically records the fare during a journey in a ~. '~ **rank,** place where ~s wait to be hired. □ *vi,vt* [VP2C,15A] (of an aircraft) (cause to) move on wheels along the ground (or on floats, etc on the surface of water): *The plane ~ed/was taxiing along the runway.*

taxi·dermy /'tæksɪdɜ:mɪ/ *n* [U] art of preparing and stuffing the skins of animals, birds and fish so that they look as they did when living. **taxi·der·mist**

/ -ɪst/ *n* person who practises ~.

tax·on·omy /tæk'sɒnəmɪ/ *n* [U,C] (principles of) classification.

tea /ti:/ *n* **1** [U] (dried leaves of an) evergreen shrub of eastern Asia, Africa, etc; drink made by pouring boiling water on these leaves: *a pound of tea; Ceylon/China, etc tea; a cup of tea; make (the) tea,* prepare it. *not my cup of tea,* (fig) not the sort of thing I like. **'tea-bag** *n* small porous bag holding enough tea-leaves for use in a teacup or teapot. **'tea-break** *n* (in an office, factory, etc) short period when work is stopped for tea drinking. **'tea-caddy** *n* (*pl* -dies) air-tight box in which to keep a supply of tea for daily use. **'tea-cake** *n* small, flat, sweetened cake, usu eaten hot with butter at tea. **'tea-chest** *n* large wooden box in which tea is packed for export. **'tea-cloth** *n* (a) cloth to be spread on a tea-table or tea-tray. (b) tea-towel. **'tea-cosy** *n* cover for keeping the contents of a teapot warm. **'tea-cup** *n* cup in which tea is served. *a storm in a teacup,* a lot of fuss about sth trivial. **'tea-garden** *n* (a) garden in which tea and other refreshments are served to the public. (b) tea plantation. **'tea-house** *n* (in Japan and China) restaurant where tea is served. **'tea-kettle** *n* one in which water is boiled for making tea. **'tea-leaf** *n* (usu *pl;* -leaves) one of the leaves in a teapot after tea has been made, or left in a teacup: *tell sb's fortune from the tea-leaves in her cup.* **'tea-party** *n* social gathering for afternoon tea. **'tea-pot** *n* vessel in which tea is made. **'tea-room** *n* restaurant in which tea and light refreshments may be obtained. **'tea-service/-set** *nn* set of cups, saucers, plates, with a teapot, milk-jug, etc. **'tea-spoon** *n* small spoon for stirring tea. **'tea-spoon·ful** /-fʊl/ *n* as much as a teaspoon can hold. **'tea-strainer** *n* device for keeping back tea-leaves when pouring tea into a cup. **'tea-table** *n* (usu small) table at which tea is served: (attrib) *tea-table conversation.* **'tea-things** *n pl* (colloq) tea-set as needed for a meal: *put the tea-things on the table.* **'tea-time** *n* [U] time at which tea is usu taken in the afternoon. **'tea-towel** *n* cloth for drying washed crockery, cutlery, etc. **'tea-tray** *n* one on which a tea-set is used or carried. **'tea-trolley** *n* tea-wagon. **'tea-urn** *n* urn in which water is boiled for making tea in quantity, eg in a café. **'tea-wagon** *n* small table on wheels, used for serving tea. **2** [C,U] occasion (in the late afternoon) at which tea is drunk: *We have tea at/Tea is at half-past four. They were having/ at tea when I called. The waitress has served twenty teas since four o'clock.* **high tea,** meal taken between lunch and supper if a dinner is not taken in the evening (usu a more substantial meal than afternoon tea as taken by people who have dinner in the evening).

teach /ti:tʃ/ *vt,vi* (*pt,pp* taught /tɔ:t/) [VP6A,11,12A,13A,17,20,21,2A,B,C] give instruction to (sb); cause (sb) to know or be able to do sth; give to sb (knowledge, skill, etc); give lessons (at school, etc); do this for a living: ~ *children;* ~ *French/history, etc;* ~ *a child (how) to swim. He has taught his dog to perform some clever tricks. Who taught you German? She is ~ing the piano to several of the village children. He ~es for a living. He has been ~ing four hours already this morning. I'll ~ you (not) to...,* (colloq, used as a threat) I'll show the risk or penalty of.... '~**-in** *n* (colloq) discussion of a subject of topical interest (as held in a college, with students, staff and other speakers).

∼·**able** /-əbl/ *adj* that can be taught. ∼**er** *n* person who ∼es. ∼**ing** *n* **1** [U] work of a ∼er: *earn a living by* ∼*ing*. **2** [U,C] that which is taught: *the* ∼*ing(s) of Buddha*.

teak /ti:k/ *n* tall, evergreen tree of India, Burma, Malaysia, etc; [U] its hard wood, used for making furniture, in shipbuilding, etc.

teal /ti:l/ *n* (*pl* unchanged) kinds of small wild duck living on rivers and lakes.

team /ti:m/ *n* [C] **1** two or more oxen, horses, etc pulling a cart, plough, etc together. **2** number of persons playing together and forming one side in some games, eg football, cricket, hockey, and in some sports, eg relay races; group of people working together: *the players in my* ∼, my fellow players. '∼**-work** *n* [U] combined effort; organized co-operation: *succeed by means of good* ∼*-work*. ∼ **spirit**, spirit in which each member of a ∼ thinks of the success, etc of the ∼ and not of personal advantage, glory, etc. □ *vi* [VP2C] ∼ **up (with sb)**, (colloq) make an effort in co-operation (with); work together (with). ∼·**ster** /'ti:mstə(r)/ *n* driver of a ∼ of animals; (US) truck-driver.

tear¹ /tɪə(r)/ *n* [C] drop of salty water coming from the eye: *Her eyes filled with* ∼s. *The sad story moved us to* ∼s, made us cry. *The girl burst into* ∼s, ∼s *began to flow from her eyes. They all laughed till* ∼s *came*. '∼**-drop** *n* single ∼. '∼**-gas** *n* [U] gas that causes severe watering of the eyes: '∼*-gas bombs*, as used by the police to disperse a mob of demonstrators, unruly crowds, etc. ∼·**ful** /-fl/ *adj* crying; wet with ∼s: *a* ∼*ful face;* ∼*ful looks*. ∼·**fully** /-fəlɪ/ *adv* ∼·**less** *adj* without ∼s, not weeping: *The mother stared at her dead baby in* ∼*less grief*, grief that was too deep for ∼s.

tear² /teə(r)/ *vt,vi* (*pt* tore /tɔ:(r)/, *pp* torn /tɔ:n/) **1** [VP6A,15A,B,22,3A] pull sharply apart or to pieces; make (a rent in sth), damage, by pulling sharply: ∼ *a sheet of paper in two/*∼ *it to pieces/to bits;* ∼ *sth up,* ∼ *it into small pieces:* ∼ *one's dress on a nail;* ∼ *a hole in one's jacket; wearing old and torn clothes;* ∼ (= hurt, injure, cause to bleed) *one's hand on a nail. He tore* (= pulled violently) *at the wrapping of the parcel. He tore* (= pulled at) *his hair with rage. He tore the parcel open*. **2** [VP6A,15A,B] cause (sth) to be out of place (*down, off, away, etc*) by pulling sharply: ∼ *a page out of a book/a notice down from a notice-board/a leaf from a calendar.* ∼ *oneself away (from),* leave; stop doing sth: *She could scarcely* ∼ *herself away from the scene*, make up her mind to leave. *He could not* ∼ *himself away from his book*, couldn't put it down. **3** [VP6A] (usu passive) destroy the peace of: *a country torn by civil war; a heart torn by grief.* **torn between,** painfully distracted by having to choose between (conflicting demands, wishes, etc). **4** [VP2A] become torn: *This material* ∼s *easily. As I pulled the sheet out of the typewriter it tore*. **5** [VP2C] go in excitement or at great speed: *The children tore out of the school gates/were* ∼*ing about in the playground. He tore down the hill*. '∼**-away** *adj, n* (colloq) impetuous (person). □ *n* [C] torn place in sth, eg cloth, paper.

tease /ti:z/ *vt* **1** [VP6A,15A] make fun of (sb) playfully or unkindly; worry with questions, etc; annoy: *She* ∼*d her father about his bald head. You must never* ∼ *a child because he stutters. Molly was teasing the cat*, eg by pulling its tail. **2** [VP6A,15B] pick into separate fibres; fluff up the surface of (cloth, etc) by doing this: ∼ *flax/wool*. □ *n* person who is fond of teasing others: *What a* ∼ *she is!* ∼**r** *n* **1** person who often ∼s or who is fond of teasing. **2** (colloq) difficult question or task; puzzling problem. **teas·ing·ly** *adv* in a teasing manner; in order to ∼.

tea·sel, tea·zel, teazle /'ti:zl/ *n* (kinds of plant with) large prickly flower with hooked points (used formerly for teasing cloth, etc).

teat /ti:t/ *n* nipple(2). ⇨ the illus at domestic.

tec /tek/ *n* (sl abbr for) detective.

tech /tek/ *n* (colloq abbr for) technical college.

tech·ni·cal /'teknɪkl/ *adj* **1** of, connected with, the execution of a work of art (as contrasted with general considerations of the form of the work): ∼ *difficulties; a pianist who has* ∼ *skill but not much feeling*. **2** of, connected with, a particular art, craft, science, etc: ∼ *terms/training*. ∼ **college,** (former name for a) polytechnic. ∼**ly** /-klɪ/ *adv* ∼·**ity** /ˌteknɪ'kælətɪ/ *n* (*pl* -ties) ∼(2) word, phrase, point, etc: *The two architects were discussing building* ∼*ities. The judge explained the legal* ∼*ities of the case to the jury*.

tech·ni·cian /tek'nɪʃn/ *n* expert in the technique(s) of a particular art, etc; highly skilled craftsman or mechanic.

Tech·ni·color /'teknɪkʌlə(r)/ *n* (P) process of colour photography used for cinema films.

tech·nique /tek'ni:k/ *n* **1** [U] technical(1) or mechanical skill in music, painting, etc. **2** [C] method of doing sth expertly; method of artistic expression in music, painting, etc.

tech·noc·racy /tek'nɒkrəsɪ/ *n* [C,U] (*pl* -cies) (state where there is) organization and management of a country's industrial resources by technical experts. **tech·no·crat** /'teknəkræt/ *n* supporter, member, of a ∼.

tech·nol·ogy /tek'nɒlədʒɪ/ *n* [U] study, mastery and utilization of manufacturing and industrial methods; systematic application of knowledge to practical tasks in industry: *the* ∼ *of computers/printing/plastics, etc*. **tech·nol·ogist** /-dʒɪst/ *n* expert in, student of, ∼. **tech·no·logi·cal** /ˌteknə'lɒdʒɪkl/ *adj* of ∼: *technological advances/problems*.

techy /'tetʃɪ/ = tetchy.

teddy bear /'tedɪ beə(r)/ *n* child's toy bear stuffed with soft material.

Teddy boy /'tedɪ bɔɪ/, (also colloq **Ted** /ted/) *n* (GB) teenager (in the 1950's and early 1960's), who expressed opposition to authority by engaging in vicious gang fights and wore clothes like those worn during the reign of Edward VII (1901—10).

Te Deum /ˌti: 'di:əm/ *n* (music for a) Latin hymn beginning *Te Deum laudamus* (meaning 'We praise you, God'), sung at morning service and on special occasions of thanksgiving.

tedi·ous /'ti:dɪəs/ *adj* tiresome; wearying; uninteresting: *a* ∼ *lecture(r);* ∼ *work*. ∼·**ly** *adv* ∼·**ness** *n*. **te·dium** /'ti:dɪəm/ *n* [U] ∼ness; monotony; boredom.

tee /ti:/ *n* **1** (golf) place from which a player starts in playing a hole; small pile of sand, or specially shaped piece of wood, plastic, etc, on which the ball is placed before the player drives, used instead of such a pile of sand. '**tee-shirt** *n* = *T-shirt*, ⇨ T. **2** mark aimed at in certain games, such as quoits. **to a tee/T**, perfectly; exactly. □ *vt,vi* **1** [VP2C,15B] **tee (the ball) up**, put (the ball) on a tee(1). **2** [VP2A] **tee off**, drive from a tee.

teem¹ /tiːm/ vi **1** [VP2C] be present in large numbers: *Fish ~ in this river.* **2** [VP3A] ~ **with**, have in great numbers: *The lakeside ~ed with gnats and mosquitoes. His head is ~ing with bright ideas.*

teem² /tiːm/ vi [VP2A,C,3A] ~ **(down) (with)**, (of rain, etc) fall heavily; pour: *It was ~ing with rain/a ~ing wet day. The rain was ~ing down.*

teens /tiːnz/ n pl the ages of 13 to 19: *girls in their ~,* between the ages of 13 and 19 inclusive. *She's still in/not yet out of her ~,* is under 20. **teen-age** /'tiːneɪdʒ/ adj of or for a ~ager: *~age fashions/ problems.* **teen-ager** /'tiːneɪdʒə(r)/ n boy or girl in his or her ~; (loosely) young person up to 21 or 22 years of age: *a club for teenagers.*

teeny /'tiːnɪ/ adj = tiny.

teeny-bop-per /'tiːnɪbɒpə(r)/ n young, fashion-conscious teenager.

tee-ter /'tiːtə(r)/ vi [VP2C] stand or walk unsteadily: *~ing on the edge of disaster.*

teeth /tiːθ/ pl of tooth.

teethe /tiːð/ vi [VP2A] (used only in progressive tenses, and as gerund and pres part) (of a baby) be getting its first teeth. **'teething troubles**, discomfort, slight illnesses, etc of a baby while its first teeth are coming through; (fig) troubles which may occur during the early stages of an enterprise.

tee-total /tiːˈtəʊtl/ US: 'tiːtəʊtl/ adj not drinking, opposed to the drinking of, alcoholic liquor. ~**-ler** (US also ~**er**) /-tlə(r)/ n person who abstains completely from alcoholic liquor.

tee-totum /tiːˈtəʊtəm/ n top spun with the fingers, esp a four-sided one with letters on it.

tegu-ment /'tegjʊmənt/ n [C] (more usu *integument*) natural covering of (part of) an animal body, eg a turtle's shell.

tele-cast /'telɪkɑːst US: -kæst/ n, vt broadcast by television.

tele-com-muni-ca-tions /ˌtelɪkəmjuːnɪˈkeɪʃnz/ n pl communications by cable, telegraph, telephone, radio or TV.

tele-gram /'telɪgræm/ n [C] message sent by telegraphy.

tele-graph /'telɪgrɑːf US: -græf/ n means of, apparatus for, sending messages by the use of electric current along wires or by wireless. '~**-post/-pole** nn post supporting ~ wire(s). '~**-line/-wire** n wire along which messages (including telephone messages) travel. **bush** ~ n sending of messages over long distances by smoke signals, beating of drums, etc. □ vi,vt [VP6A,12A,13A,11,2A] send (news, etc) by ~: *Shall I ~ or telephone? He ~ed (to) his brother.* (Note: *send a telegram* and *send a cable* are commoner than the use of the v.) **tel-egra-pher** /tɪˈlegrəfə(r)/ n skilled operator whose work is to send and receive messages by ~. ~**ic** /ˌtelɪˈgræfɪk/ adj sent by, suitable for, connected with, the ~: *a ~ic address*, abbreviated address or brief registered address, for use in telegrams. ~**i-cally** /-klɪ/ **tel-egra-phese** /ˌtelɪgrəˈfiːz/ n [U] style of language used in telegrams (with unessential words omitted). **tel-egra-phist** /tɪˈlegrəfɪst/ n = ~**er**. **tel-egra-phy** /tɪˈlegrəfɪ/ n [U] art, science, process, of sending and receiving messages by ~, of constructing ~ic apparatus, etc.

te-lem-etry /tɪˈlemɪtrɪ/ n [U] automatic transmission and measurement of data from a distance, usu by radio.

tele-ol-ogy /ˌtelɪˈɒlədʒɪ/ n theory, teaching, belief, that events and developments are due to the purpose or design that they are serving (as opposed to

the mechanistic theory of the universe, ⇨ mechanistic). **teleo-logi-cal** /ˌtelɪəˈlɒdʒɪkl/ adj **teleol-ogist** /telɪˈɒlədʒɪst/ n believer in ~.

tel-epa-thy /tɪˈlepəθɪ/ n [U] **1** transference of thoughts or ideas from one mind to another without the normal use of the senses. **2** (colloq) ability to be immediately aware of the thoughts and feelings of others. **tele-pathic** /ˌtelɪˈpæθɪk/ adj. **tel-epa-thist** /tɪˈlepəθɪst/ n person who studies or believes in ~ or who claims to have telepathic powers.

tele-phone /'telɪfəʊn/ (usu abbr *phone* in colloq speech) n [U] means, system, of transmitting the human voice by electric current, through wires (usu called *telegraph wires*, not ~ *wires*) supported by poles (usu called *telegraph poles*, not ~ *posts*), or by radio (*radio-~*); [C] apparatus (with receiver and mouthpiece) for this purpose: *You're wanted on the phone. Mr Green is on the phone just now,* is using the ~. *Will you answer the phone, please,* pick up the receiver and answer. '~ **booth**, (also '*phone-booth* or '*call-box*), small enclosure with a coin-operated public ~. '~ **directory**, (also '*phone-book*) list of names with numbers and addresses. '~ **exchange**, place where ~ connections are made. □ vt,vi [VP6A,12A,13A,11,12,2A,4A] send (a message to sb) by ~: *I'll phone you tomorrow. He phoned (through) to say that.... It's Mary's birthday today—we must phone her a greetings telegram,* send her a greeting ('Happy Birthday') by asking for such a telegram to be sent (and usu received by ~). **tel-eph-ony** /tɪˈlefənɪ/ n [U] method, process, of sending and receiving messages by ~. **tel-ephon-ist** /tɪˈlefənɪst/ n operator in a ~ exchange.

tele-photo /ˌtelɪˈfəʊtəʊ/ n **1** ~ **lens**, = telescopic lens. **2** (colloq abbr of) ~**graph**. ~**-graph** /-grɑːf US: -græf/ n (a) photograph made with a ~ lens. (b) picture transmitted and received by ~graphy. **tele-pho-togra-phy** /ˌtelɪfəˈtɒgrəfɪ/ n [U] **1** process of photographing distant objects, etc using a ~ lens. **2** process of transmitting and receiving charts, pictures, etc over a distance.

tele-prin-ter /'telɪprɪntə(r)/ n telegraph instrument for sending messages (typed by an operator at the sending end), which are re-typed automatically and almost simultaneously by machine at the other end.

tele-promp-ter /'telɪprɒmptə(r)/ n TV device by which a speaker can read in front of him an enlargement of his script, so that he seems to speak spontaneously.

tele-scope /'telɪskəʊp/ n tube-like instrument with lenses for making distant objects appear nearer and larger. **,radio-**'~, ⇨ radio-. □ vt,vi [VP6A,2A] make or become shorter by means of or in the manner of sections that slide one within the other: *When the trains collided, the first two cars of one of the trains ~d/were ~d.* **tele-scopic** /ˌtelɪˈskɒpɪk/ adj **1** of, containing, able to be seen with, a ~: *a telescopic lens,* extra lens attached to a camera to enable distant objects and scenes to be photographed (and now often called a *telephoto lens*); *a telescopic sight,* (on a rifle, to magnify the target); *a telescopic view of the moon,* seen through a ~. **2** having sections which slide one within the other: *a telescopic aerial,* eg as part of a portable radio receiver.

tele-type-writer /ˌtelɪˈtaɪpraɪtə(r)/ n (US) = teleprinter.

tele-vi-sion /'telɪvɪʒn/ n **1** [U] (abbr **TV**, or colloq **telly** /'telɪ/) process of transmitting a view of events, plays, etc (while these are taking place, or from films or tapes on which a record has been made) by radio to a distant ~ receiving set with synchronized sound: *Did you see the boat race on (the)* ~? **2** [C] '~ (**set**), apparatus for receiving and showing this transmission. **tele·vise** /'telɪvaɪz/ *vt* [VP6A] send views of by ~: *The Olympic Games were televised.*

tel·fer /'telfə(r)/ = **telpher.**

telex /'teleks/ *n* system of communication using teleprinters.

tell /tel/ *vt,vi* (*pt,pp* told /təʊld/) **1** [VP6A,13A,12A,11,20,21] ~ **sth (to sb),** ~ **sb sth,** make known (in spoken or written words); give information concerning or a description of: *He told the news to everybody in the village. I told him my name. T~ me where you live. I can't ~ you how happy I am,* can't find words that are adequate. *He told me (that) he was coming. So I've been told,* I've already been told that. *If he asks,* ~ *him. Don't ~ me it's too late!* (used to express surprise or alarm) *I'll ~ you what...,* used meaning 'Here's a suggestion, idea, etc that may help'. *I ~* (= assure) *you, he's thoroughly dishonest!* **I told you so,** I warned you that this would happen, etc and now you see that I'm right: *Things have gone wrong but please don't say 'I told you so!'* **You're ~ing 'me!** I fully agree with you. *T~ me another!* I don't believe you. ~ **the world,** (colloq) ~ everybody: *We all know you're clever, but do you have to ~ the world,* be so emphatic about it? **2** [VP6A,13A,12A,15A] utter; express with words: ~ *a lie;* ~ *the children a tale/story.* '*When in doubt,* ~ *the truth', said Mark Twain.* ~ **the tale,** (colloq) ~ a pitiful story in order to get sympathy, etc. ~ **tales about/on sb,** make known sb's secrets, misconduct, etc in a malicious way. ~**·tale** /'telteɪl/ *n* person who ~s about another's private affairs, makes known a secret, etc; circumstances, etc that reveal a person's thoughts, activities, etc (often attrib): *a ~tale blush; the ~tale cigarette ash on the carpet,* that made known the fact that someone had been smoking a cigarette. **3** [VP17] order; direct: *Do what I ~ you. You must do what you're told.* T~ *him to wait. He was told to start at once.* **4** [VP6A,14] (esp with *can/could/be able to*) **sb/sth (from sb/sth),** know apart; distinguish: *Can you ~ Tom from his twin brother? They look exactly the same—how can you ~ which is which?* **5** [VP6A,8,10,2A] learn by observation; make out; become aware (of sth): *How do you ~ which of these buttons to press?* ~ **the time,** (be able to) read (or say) the time from a clock, etc: *Can Mary ~ the time yet? Can you ~ me what time it is?* **You can never ~; You never can ~,** you can never be sure, eg because appearances are often deceptive. **there is/was, etc no ~ing,** it is impossible or difficult to know: *There's no ~ing what may happen/where she's gone/what he's doing, etc.* **6** [VP6A,15B] (old use) count. ~ **one's beads,** say one's prayers (counting beads on a rosary) ~ **sb off (for sth/to do sth),** (**a**) count one by one and give orders: *Ten men were told off for special duty/to clean the latrines.* (**b**) (colloq) give a list of sb's misdoings; scold him: *That fellow needs to be told off. She told the typist off for making so many careless mistakes.* **7** [VP2A,3A] ~ (**on/upon sb),** have a marked effect on; influence the result of: *All this hard work is ~ing on him,* is affecting his health. *Every blow ~s.* ~**·ing** *adj* effective; im-

pressive: *a ~ing speech/argument/blow.* ~**·ing·ly** *adv.* **8** [VP2A,3A] ~ (**on sb),** (colloq) reveal a secret; inform against: *John told on his sister.* ⇨ **tale-bearer** at **tale**(2). *You promised not to ~ and now you've done so!*

tel·ler /'telə(r)/ *n* **1** person who receives, and pays out, money over a bank counter. **2** man who counts votes, eg in the House of Commons.

telly /'telɪ/ *n* (colloq abbr for) television.

tel·pher /'telfə(r)/ *n* conveyance for goods, suspended from overhead wire cables, usu driven by electricity; transportation system of this kind, eg for rock from a quarry.

Tel·star /'telstɑː(r)/ *n* (P) communications satellite used (commercially) for the transmission of telephone messages and TV.

te·mer·ity /tɪ'merətɪ/ *n* [U] rashness.

tem·per[1] /'tempə(r)/ *n* **1** condition of the mind and emotions: *in a good ~,* calm and pleasant; *in a bad ~,* angry, impatient, etc. **get/fly into a ~,** become angry. **keep/lose one's ~,** keep/fail to keep one's ~ under control. **out of ~ (with),** angry (with). -**tem·pered** /'tempəd/ *adj* (in compounds) having or showing a certain kind of ~: *a ,good-/ ,sweet-/,fiery-/,hot-, etc '~ed man.* -**tem·per·ed·ly** *adv* (in compounds) *good-/~edly.* **2** [U] degree of hardness, toughness, elasticity, of a substance, esp of steel.

tem·per[2] /'tempə(r)/ *vt,vi* **1** [VP6A] give the required temper(2) to (eg steel) by heating and cooling; bring (eg clay) to the required condition by moistening, mixing, kneading, etc; [VP2A] come to the required condition as the result of treatment. **2** [VP6A,15A] soften or modify; mitigate: ~ *justice with mercy,* be merciful when giving a just punishment.

tem·pera /'tempərə/ *n* [U] = distemper, esp as used in fresco painting.

tem·pera·ment /'temprəmənt/ *n* **1** [C,U] person's disposition or nature, esp as this affects his way of thinking, feeling and behaving: *a girl with a nervous/an artistic ~. The two brothers have entirely different ~s. Success often depends on ~.* **2** [U] (without an *adj*) kind of disposition that is easily excited, passionate, not easily controlled or restrained, eg as in some actresses and opera singers. **tem·pera·men·tal** /temprə'mentl/ *adj* **1** caused by ~: *a ~al dislike for study.* **2** subject to quickly changing moods: *a ~al tennis player,* one whose playing changes according to his mood. **tem·pera·men·tally** /-təlɪ/ *adv*

tem·per·ance /'tempərəns/ *n* [U] **1** moderation, self-control, in speech, behaviour and (esp) in the use of alcoholic drinks. **2** total abstinence from alcoholic drinks: (attrib) *a '~ society,* one for the restriction or abolition of the use of alcoholic drinks.

tem·per·ate /'tempərət/ *adj* **1** showing, behaving, with temperance(1): *Be more ~ in your language, please.* **2** (of climate, parts of the world) free from extremes of heat and cold: *the north '~ zone,* between the Tropic of Cancer and the arctic zone. ~**·ly** *adv* ~**·ness** *n*

tem·pera·ture /'temprətʃə(r) *US:* 'tempərtʃʊər/ *n* [C,U] degree of heat and cold: *In Hawaii there are no extremes of ~. The nurse took the ~s of all the patients,* measured their body ~s with a thermometer. **have/run a ~,** have a fever.

tem·pest /'tempɪst/ *n* [C] violent storm; (fig) violent agitation: *A ~ of laughter swept through* the crowd. '∼-swept/-tossed adjj (liter) swept, etc by ∼s. tem·pes·tu·ous /tem'pestʃʊəs/ adj (of the weather and fig) violent; stormy: in a ∼uous mood; a ∼uous political meeting.

tem·plate, tem·plet /'templɪt/ nn pattern or gauge (usu a thin board or metal plate) used as a guide in cutting or drilling metal, wood, etc.

temple¹ /'templ/ n 1 building used for the worship of a god (esp ancient Greek, Roman, Egyptian and modern Hindu, Buddhist, etc). 2 (applied occasionally to a) place of Christian worship (church and chapel being the usu words): a Mormon ∼. 3 any of the three successive religious centres of the Jews in ancient Jerusalem. 4 the Inner/Middle T∼, two Inns of Court in London. ⇨ inn(2).

a Hindu temple

temple² /'templ/ n flat part of either side of the forehead. ⇨ the illus at head.

tem·plet /'templɪt/ n ⇨ template.

tempo /'tempəʊ/ n (pl ∼s or, in music, tempi /-piː/) (I) 1 rate of movement or activity: the tiring ∼ of city life. This long strike has upset the ∼ of production. 2 speed at which music is (to be) played.

tem·poral /'tempərəl/ adj 1 of, existing in, time: (gram) ∼ conjunctions, eg when, while. 2 of earthly human life; of this physical life only, not spiritual: the ∼ power of the Pope, ie as head of the Vatican State; the lords ∼ (= the peers of the realm) and the lords spiritual (= the bishops). ∼ity /ˌtempə'rælətɪ/ n (usu pl; -ties) secular possessions: the temporalities of the Church. ∼ty /'tempərəltɪ/ n laity.

tem·por·ary /'tempʀərɪ US: -pərerɪ/ adj lasting for, designed to be used for, a short time only: ∼ employment; a ∼ bridge. tem·por·ar·ily /'tempʀərəlɪ US: ˌtempə'rerəlɪ/ adv tem·por·ari·ness n

tem·por·ize /'tempəraɪz/ vi [VP2A] delay making a decision, giving an answer, stating one's purpose, etc; act so as gain time: a temporizing politician/ answer.

tempt /tempt/ vt [VP6A,17,14] ∼ (to sth/into doing sth), 1 (try to) persuade (sb) to do sth wrong or foolish: Nothing could ∼ him to such a course of action/to take such a step. He was ∼ed into making a false step, doing sth unwise. 2 attract (sb) to have or do sth: The warm weather ∼ed us to go for a swim. She ∼ed the child to have a little more soup. What a ∼ing (= attractive) offer! 3 (old use, biblical) test. ∼ Providence, take a risk. ∼·ing·ly adv. ∼er n person who ∼s; (esp) the T∼er, Satan, the Devil. temp·tress /'temptʀɪs/ n woman who ∼s.

temp·ta·tion /temp'teɪʃn/ n 1 [U] tempting or being tempted: the ∼ of easy profits; yield/give way to ∼; put ∼ in sb's way. 2 [C] that which tempts or attracts: The sight of the purse on the table was a strong ∼ to the poor child. Clever advertisements are ∼s to spend money.

ten /ten/ n, adj the number 10. ⇨ App 5. ten to one, very probably: Ten to one he will arrive late. tenth /tenθ/ n, adj the next after the 9th; one of 10 equal parts. tenth·ly adv 'ten·fold adv ten times as many or much. 'ten·pence n (GB decimal coin with the) value of ten pennies.

ten·able /'tenəbl/ adj 1 that can be defended successfully: His theory is hardly ∼. 2 (of an office or position) that can be held (by sb for a time): The lectureship is ∼ for a period of three years. ten·abil·ity /ˌtenə'bɪlətɪ/ n

ten·acious /tɪ'neɪʃəs/ adj holding tightly, refusing to let go: a ∼ memory; ∼ of our rights. ∼·ly adv ∼·ness n ten·ac·ity /tɪ'næsətɪ/ n

ten·ant /'tenənt/ n person who pays rent for the use of land, a building, a room, etc: evict ∼s for non-payment of rent; ∼ farmers, who cultivate farms which they do not own. □ vt (usu passive) occupy as a ∼: houses ∼ed by railway workers. ten·ancy /-ənsɪ/ n 1 [U] use of land, etc as a ∼: during his tenancy of the farm. 2 [C] length of time during which a ∼ uses land, etc: hold a life tenancy of a house. ten·an·try /'tenəntrɪ/ n (collective sing) all the ∼s occupying land and houses on one estate.

tench /tenʃ/ n edible European freshwater fish; carp.

tend¹ /tend/ vt [VP6A] watch over; attend to: shepherds ∼ing their flocks; (esp US) ∼ the store, serve customers.

tend² /tend/ vi [VP2C,4A] be inclined to move; have a direction: Prices are ∼ing upwards. He ∼s to pitch the ball too high. He ∼s towards atheism. ten·dency /'tendənsɪ/ n [C] (pl -cies) turning or inclination, leaning: Business is showing a ∼ency to improve. There was a strong upward ∼ency in oil shares yesterday, prices ∼ed upwards.

ten·den·tious /ten'denʃəs/ adj (of a speech, a piece of writing, etc) having an underlying purpose, aimed at helping a cause; not impartial: Countries at war often send out ∼ reports, reports designed to show their cause in a favourable light, win sympathy, etc. ∼·ly adv ∼·ness n

ten·der¹ /'tendə(r)/ adj 1 delicate; easily hurt or damaged; quickly feeling pain: ∼ blossoms, eg easily hurt by frosts; touch sb on a ∼ spot, one that hurts when touched; a ∼ subject, (fig) one that has to be dealt with carefully to avoid hurting people's feelings; a person of ∼ age/years, young and immature; have a ∼ conscience; a ∼ heart, easily moved to pity, hence, ∼-'hearted adj. '∼-foot n (pl -foots) new-comer to the sort of country where there is rough living, hardship, etc. 2 (of meat) easily chewed; not tough: a ∼ steak. '∼-loin n [U] ∼ part of the loin of beef or pork; undercut of sirloin. 3 kind, loving: ∼ looks; ∼ care; ∼ parents; bid sb a ∼ farewell. ∼·ly adv ∼·ness n

ten·der² /'tendə(r)/ n 1 person who looks after, watches over, sth: a ma'chine-∼; a 'bar-∼, ⇨ bar¹(13). 2 small ship attending a larger one, to carry stores, put on or take off passengers, etc. 3 wagon for fuel and water behind a steam locomotive.

ten·der³ /'tendə(r)/ vt, vi 1 [VP6A,12A,13A] offer; present: ∼ money in payment of a debt. He ∼ed

*his resignation to the Prime Minister/his services
to the Government.* **2** [VP2A,3A] ~ *(for),* make an
offer (to carry out work, supply goods, etc) at a
stated price: ~ *for the construction of a new motorway.* □ *n* **1** [C] statement of the price at which
one offers to supply goods or services, or to do sth:
invite ~*s for a new bridge; put in/make/send in a
~ for sth; accept the lowest* ~. **2 legal** ~, form of
money which must, by law, be accepted in payment of a debt: *Are copper coins legal* ~ *for a sum
in excess of £10?*

ten·don /'tendən/ *n* [C] tough, thick cord that joins
muscle to bone; sinew.

ten·dril /'tendrəl/ *n* [C] thread-like part of a plant,
eg a vine, that twists round any nearby support. ⇨
the illus at ivy.

ten·ement /'tenəmənt/ *n* [C] **1** '~(-house), large
building with apartments for the use of many families at low rents. **2** (legal) any dwelling-house; any
kind of permanent property.

tenet /'tenɪt/ *n* [C] principle; belief; doctrine.

ten·ner /'tenə(r)/ *n* (colloq) ten pounds in GB
money; ten-pound note.

ten·nis /'tenɪs/ *n* [U] game for two or four players
who hit a ball backwards and forwards across a net.
'~-court *n* marked area on which ~ is played.
,~-'elbow *n* inflammation of the elbow caused by
playing ~.

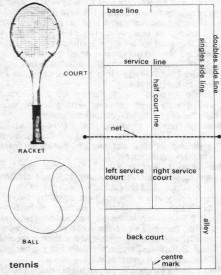

tennis

tenon /'tenən/ *n* end of a piece of wood shaped to
go into a mortise to make a joint.

tenor[1] /'tenə(r)/ *n* (usu **the** ~ *(of)*) general routine
or direction *(of* one's life): *interrupt sb's even* ~;
general meaning; thread, drift (*of* a speech, etc):
She knew enough Spanish to get the ~ *of what was
being said.*

tenor[2] /'tenə(r)/ *n* **1** (music for, singer with, the)
highest normal adult male voice: (attrib) ~ *voice;
the* ~ *part.* **2** (of instruments) with a range about
that of the ~ voice: *a* ~ *horn/saxophone.*

ten·pin /'tenpɪn/ *n* **1** (*pl* with **sing** *v*) game like
ninepins with ten skittles instead of nine. **2** pin
used. **3** (attrib) ~ *bowling.*

tense[1] /tens/ *adj* (lit or fig) tightly stretched;

strained to stiffness: ~ *nerves; faces* ~ *with anxiety; a moment of* ~ *excitement. We were* ~ *with
expectancy,* Our nerves were ~, keyed up. *There
was a* ~ *atmosphere,* People had a feeling of nervous strain and an attitude of expectancy. □ *vt,vi*
[VP6A,2A] make or become ~; stiffen: *He* ~*d his
muscles for the effort.* **be/get** ~*d up,* feel nervous
strain: *He's always* ~*d up before a game/an exam.*
~·ly *adv* ~·ness *n*

tense[2] /tens/ *n* (gram) verb form that shows time:
the present/past, etc ~.

ten·sile /'tensaɪl US: 'tensl/ *adj* **1** of tension:
measure the ~ *strength of wire,* eg to find the load
it will support without breaking. **2** capable of being
stretched.

ten·sion /'tenʃn/ *n* [U] **1** state of, degree of, being
tense: *If you increase the* ~ *of that violin string it
will break.* **2** stretching or being stretched. **3** mental, emotional or nervous strain; condition when
feelings are tense, when relations between persons,
groups, states, etc are strained: *racial* ~(*s*) *in Africa;·political* ~. **4** voltage: *Keep away from those
high* ~ *wires or you'll be electrocuted.* **high** ~
battery, one made up of a number of small batteries connected in series. ⇨ series. **5** expansive
force of gas or vapour.

tens·ity /'tensəti/ *n* = *tenseness.* ⇨ tense[1].

tent /tent/ *n* (usu portable) shelter made of canvas
supported by poles and ropes,. esp as used by
campers, scouts, soldiers, etc. **'oxygen** ~, airtight
cover (over a bed) for a person who is being given
extra oxygen. '~-peg *n* wooden peg used to secure
a rope to the ground.

ten·tacle /'tentəkl/ *n* [C] long, slender, flexible,
snake-like, boneless growth on the head or round
the mouth of certain animals used for touching,
feeling, holding, moving, etc. ⇨ the illus at mollusc.

ten·ta·tive /'tentətɪv/ *adj* made or done as a trial, to
see the effect: *only a* ~ *suggestion; come to a* ~
conclusion; make a ~ *offer.* ~·ly *adv*

ten·ter·hooks /'tentəhʊks/ *n pl* (only in) **on** ~, in
a state of anxious suspense.

tenth /tenθ/ *n, adj*⇨ ten.

tenu·ous /'tenjʊəs/ *adj* thin; slender: *the* ~ *web of
a spider;* (of distinctions) subtle. **ten·uity** /tɪ'njuːəti
US:* teˈnuː-/ *n*

ten·ure /'tenjʊə(r) US: -jə(r)/ *n* [C,U] (period,
time, condition of) holding (eg political office) or
using (land): *The farmers want security of* ~, to be
secure in their tenancies. *The* ~ *of office of the
President is four years.*

tepee /'tiːpiː/ *n* cone-shaped tent of skins or bark of
the American Indians; wigwam.

tepid /'tepɪd/ *adj* lukewarm (lit or fig). ~·ly *adv*
~·ness *n* ~·ity /teˈpɪdəti/ *n*

ter·cen·ten·ary /ˌtɜːsenˈtiːnəri US: tɜːˈsentəneri/,
ter·cen·ten·nial /ˌtɜːsenˈtenɪəl/ *nn* 300th anniversary: (attrib) ~ *celebrations.*

ter·gi·ver·sate /'tɜːdʒɪvəseɪt/ *vi* (formal) make a
complete change in one's opinions, principles, etc;
make conflicting statements. **ter·gi·ver·sa·tion**
/ˌtɜːdʒɪvəˈseɪʃn/ *n*

term /tɜːm/ *n* [C] **1** fixed or limited period of time:
a long ~ *of imprisonment; during his* ~ *of office
as President.* **2** (of schools, universities, etc) one of
the periods (usu three or four) into which the
academic year is divided: *the summer* ~; *end-of-
* ~ *examinations; during* '~(-time). **3** (legal)
period during which a Court holds session. **4** (*pl*)

conditions offered or agreed to: *enquire about* ~s (ie prices) *for a stay at a hotel;* ~*s of surrender,* eg offered to a defeated enemy; ~*s of reference,* ⇨ reference(1). **come to** ~*s/make* ~**s (with sb),** reach an agreement (with him). **come to** ~**s with sth,** accept, become resigned to it. **come to** ~*s with a difficult situation.* **do sth on one's own** ~**s/sb else's** ~**s,** on conditions that one/sb else decides: *If he agrees to help, it will be on his own* ~*s.* **5** (*pl*) relations. **be on good/friendly/bad** ~**s (with sb),** be friendly, etc (with him): *I didn't know you and she were on such good* ~*s,* were such good friends. **on equal** ~**s,** as equals. **not be on 'speaking** ~**s with sb,** ⇨ speak(2). **6** words used to express an idea, esp a specialized concept: *technical/scientific/legal* ~*s. In box-office* ~*s* (as expressed in financial, or box-office receipts) *the film was a failure.* **7** (*pl*) mode of expression: *He referred to your work in* ~*s of high praise/in flattering* ~*s. How dare you speak of her in such abusive* ~*s?* **a contradiction in** ~**s,** a statement that contradicts itself. **8** (maths) part of an expression joined to the rest by + or −: *The expression* a^2 + $2ab$ + b^2 *has three* ~*s.* □ *vt* [VP23] name; apply a ~ to: *He has no right to* ~ *himself a professor.*

ter·ma·gant /'tɜːməgənt/ *n* noisy, quarrelsome woman; shrew.

ter·min·able /'tɜːmɪnəbl/ *adj* that may be terminated.

ter·minal /'tɜːmɪnl/ *adj* **1** of, taking place, each term(1,3): ~ *examinations/accounts.* **2** of, forming, the point or place at the end: ~ *cancer,* not curable; ending in death; *the '*~ *ward,* (in a hospital) for persons who cannot be cured and must soon die. □ *n* **1** end of a railway line, bus line, etc; centre (in a town) used by passengers departing for, or arriving from, an airport: *the ,West ,London 'Air T*~*.* **2** point of connection in an electric circuit: *the* ~*s of a battery.* **ter·min·ally** *adv*

ter·min·ate /'tɜːmɪneɪt/ *vt,vi* [VP6A,2A,15A] (formal) bring to an end; come to an end: ~ *sb's contract;* ~ *a pregnancy.*

ter·mi·na·tion /ˌtɜːmɪˈneɪʃn/ *n* **1** [C,U] ending: *the* ~ *of a contract;* ~ *of pregnancy,* abortion. **2** [C] final syllable or letter of a word (as in inflexion or derivation).

ter·mi·nol·ogy /ˌtɜːmɪˈnɒlədʒɪ/ *n* [C,U] (*pl* -gies) (science of the) proper use of terms(6); terms used in a science or art: *problems of* ~; *medical/grammatical* ~. **ter·mi·no·logi·cal** /ˌtɜːmɪnəˈlɒdʒɪkl/ *adj* of ~: *a terminological inexactitude,* (hum) an untruth.

ter·mi·nus /'tɜːmɪnəs/ *n* [C] (*pl* ~es /-nəsɪz/) station at the end of a railway line; end of a tram, bus or air route.

ter·mite /'tɜːmaɪt/ *n* insect (popularly but wrongly called *white ant*), found chiefly in tropical areas, very destructive to timber, textiles, etc and which makes large hills of hard earth. ⇨ the illus at insect.

tern /tɜːn/ *n* sea-bird like a gull, but usu smaller and swifter in flight.

Terp·si·chorean /ˌtɜːpsɪkəˈriːən/ *adj* of dancing: *the* ~ *art.*

ter·race /'terəs/ *n* **1** level(led) area of ground with a vertical or sloping front or side; a series of these, separated by sloping banks, rising one above the other, eg as a method of irrigation on a hillside. **2** flight of wide, shallow steps (eg for spectators at a sporting event such as a football match, or on the

banks of the Ganges at Benares, used by bathers). **3** continuous row of houses in one block (often as part of a postal address): *6 Olympic T*~, *Glasgow.* **4** (US) porch, paved area, adjacent to a house, used as an outdoor living area. □ *vt* [VP6A] (usu *pp*) form into ~s; make ~s in: *a* ~*d lawn;* ~*d houses,* (long line of) houses joined together, sometimes with an alley in the rear for access to the backyards.

terra-cotta /ˌterə ˈkɒtə/ *n* [U] hard, reddish-brown pottery (used for vases, small statues, ornamental building material, etc): (attrib) *a* ~ *vase;* the colour reddish-brown.

terra firma /ˌterə ˈfɜːmə/ *n* [U] (Lat) dry land, solid land (contrasted with water): *glad to be on* ~ *again.*

terra in·cog·nita /ˌterə ɪnˈkɒgnɪtə/ *n* (Lat) unknown territory, eg on maps of unexplored areas.

ter·rain /teˈreɪn *US:* təˈ-/ *n* stretch of land, esp with regard to its natural features: *difficult* ~ *for heavy armoured vehicles.*

ter·ra·pin /'terəpɪn/ *n* kinds of fresh-water tortoise and turtle of N America: (esp) *the diamond-back* ~, valued as food.

ter·res·trial /tɪˈrestrɪəl/ *adj* **1** of, on, living on, the earth or land: *the* ~ *parts of the world.* **2** of the earth (opposed to *celestial*): *a* ~ *globe,* representing the earth.

ter·rible /'terəbl/ *adj* **1** causing great fear or horror: *a* ~ *war/accident. He died in* ~ *agony.* **2** causing great discomfort; extreme: *The heat is* ~ *in Baghdad during the summer.* **3** (colloq) extremely bad: *My room was in a* ~ *state of disorder. What* ~ *food they gave us!* **ter·ribly** /-əblɪ/ *adv* (colloq) extremely: *How terribly boring he is!*

ter·rier /'terɪə(r)/ *n* kinds of small and active dog, esp the kind that digs into burrows to pursue its prey. ⇨ the illus at dog.

ter·rific /təˈrɪfɪk/ *adj* **1** causing fear; terrible. **2** (colloq) very great; extreme: *driving at a* ~ *pace.* **ter·rifi·cally** /-klɪ/ *adv* (colloq) extremely.

ter·rify /'terɪfaɪ/ *vt* (*pt,pp* -fied) [VP6A,15A] fill with fear: *The child was terrified of being left alone in the house. She was terrified out of her wits. What a* ~*ing experience!*

ter·ri·torial /ˌterɪˈtɔːrɪəl/ *adj* **1** of land, esp land forming a division of a country: ~ *possessions; have* ~ *claims against a State,* claim part of its territory. ~ *waters,* the sea near a country's coast, over which special rights are claimed, eg for fishing. **2** T~, of any of the US Territories: *T*~ *laws.* **3** (GB) (often *T*~) of the force of mostly non-professional soldiers organized for the defence of Great Britain and trained in their spare time: *the T*~ *Army.* □ *n* member of the T~ Army.

ter·ri·tory /'terɪtrɪ *US:* -tɔːrɪ/ *n* (*pl* -ries) **1** [C,U] (area of) land, esp land under one ruler or Government: *Turkish* ~ *in Europe.* **2** [C] land or district; [U] extent of such land, etc: *This salesman travels over a large* ~. *How much* ~ *does he travel over?*

irrigation terraces

Mating blackbirds will defend their ∼ (= the area which they regard as belonging to themselves) *against intruders.* **3** (US) district not admitted as a State but having its own law-making body: *Until 1959 Hawaii was a T*∼, *not a State.*

ter·ror /'terə(r)/ *n* **1** [U] great fear: *run away in* ∼; *be in* ∼ *of one's life,* fear that one will lose one's life. *strike* ∼ *into sb,* fill him with ∼. Hence, '∼**-struck,** '∼**-stricken** *adjj* struck, filled, with ∼. **2** [C] instance of great fear; (sth or sb that causes) great fear: *have a* ∼ *of fire. This added to our* ∼*s.* **3** [C] (colloq) troublesome person: *This child is a perfect* ∼, a great nuisance. ∼**·ism** /-ɪzəm/ *n* use of violence and intimidation, esp for political purposes. ∼**·ist** /-ɪst/ *n* supporter of, participant in, ∼ism. ∼**·ize** /-aɪz/ *vt* [VP6A] fill with ∼ by threats or acts of violence.

terse /tɜːs/ *adj* (of speech, style, speakers) brief and to the point; concise. ∼**·ly** *adv* ∼**·ness** *n*

ter·tian /'tɜːʃn/ *adj* (of fever) marked by paroxysms which occur every other day.

ter·ti·ary /'tɜːʃərɪ US: -ʃɪerɪ/ *adj* third in rank, order, occurrence, importance: *the T*∼ *period,* (geol) the third period in the formation of rocks; ∼ *burns/syphilis,* a severe stage.

tery·lene /'terəliːn/ *n* [U] (GB) (P) (fabric made from) kinds of man-made fibre.

tes·sel·lated /'tesəleɪtɪd/ *adj* formed of small, flat pieces of stone of various colours (as used in mosaic): *a* ∼ *pavement.*

test /test/ *n* [C] (often attrib) examination or trial (of sth) to find its quality, value, composition, etc; trial or examination (of sb, his powers, knowledge, skill, etc): *methods that have stood the* ∼ *of time; an endurance* ∼, eg for a new aero-engine; *a* '*blood* ∼, eg at a hospital, for infection, etc. *a* '∼ *bore,* hole bored into the ground or sea-bed to learn whether there is mineral ore, oil, etc: ∼ *bores in the North Sea; a* ∼ *in arithmetic; an intelligence* ∼. **a** '∼ *case,* (in law) one that shows the principle involved (even though it may not be important in itself). '∼ *drive n* drive in a car one thinks of buying, to judge its qualities, worth, etc. Hence, '∼**-drive** *vt.* '∼ *pilot n* one who flies newly built aircraft to try their qualities, performance, etc. **a** '**driving** ∼, an examination of one's ability to drive a car in the way required by law. *put sth to the* ∼, submit it to conditions, etc, that will show its qualities, etc. '∼ *match n* one of the matches in any of the cricket or Rugby tours arranged between certain countries. '∼**-tube** *n* slender glass tube, closed at one end, used in chemical ∼s and experiments. '∼**-tube baby,** baby whose early development took place in a laboratory (after artificial insemination) and is later implanted in the womb. □ *vt* [VP6A,15A] put to the ∼; examine: *have one's eyesight* ∼*ed;* ∼ *ore for gold; a well-*∼*ed remedy. The long climb* ∼*ed* (= was a ∼ of) *our powers of endurance.*

tes·ta·ment /'testəmənt/ *n* **1** [C] (often *last Will and T*∼) statement in writing saying how sb wishes his property to be distributed after his death. **2** *Old T*∼, *New T*∼, the two main divisions of the Bible. ⇨ App 10. **tes·ta·men·tary** /ˌtestə'mentrɪ/ *adj* of, connected with, given in, a ∼(1).

tes·tate /'testeɪt/ *n, adj* (person) who has made a testament (and died leaving it in force). **tes·ta·tor** /te'steɪtə(r) US: 'testeɪtər/ *n* man who has made a testament. **tes·ta·trix** /te'steɪtrɪks/ *n* woman testator.

tes·ticle /'testɪkl/ *n* each of the two glands of the male sex organ that secrete spermatozoa.

tes·tify /'testɪfaɪ/ *vt,vi* (*pt,pp* -fied) **1** [VP2A,3A,9] ∼ *that...;* ∼ *to sth;* ∼ *against/in favour of sth,* bear witness, give evidence: *He testified under oath that he had not been at the scene of the crime. The teacher testified to the boy's ability. Two witnesses will* ∼ *against her and three will* ∼ *on her behalf.* **2** [VP6A] serve as evidence of: *Her tears testified her grief.*

tes·ti·mo·nial /ˌtestɪ'məʊnɪəl/ *n* **1** written statement testifying to a person's merits, abilities, qualifications, etc eg as sent with an application for a position. **2** sth given to sb to show appreciation of services, usu sth subscribed for by several or many colleagues.

tes·ti·mony /'testɪmənɪ US: -məʊnɪ/ *n* [U] **1** declaration, esp in a law court, testifying that sth is true: *The witness's* ∼ *is false. Several men were called in to bear* ∼ *to what the police officer said.* **2** declarations; statements: *According to the* ∼ *of the medical profession, the health of the nation is improving.*

tes·tis /'testɪs/ *n* (*pl*-tes /-tiːz/) = testicle.

testy /'testɪ/ *adj* (-ier, -iest) quickly or easily annoyed; impatient. **tes·tily** /-ɪlɪ/ *adv* **tes·ti·ness** *n*

teta·nus /'tetənəs/ *n* [U] disease marked by stiffening and tightening of some or all of the muscles which are normally under conscious control: ∼ *of the lower jaw* (colloq called *lockjaw*).

tetchy /'tetʃɪ/ *adj* (-ier, -iest) peevish; irritable. **tetch·ily** /-ɪlɪ/ *adv* **tetchi·ness** *n*

tête-à-tête /ˌteɪt ɑː 'teɪt/ *n* private meeting between two persons; their talk: *have a* ∼ *with sb; have a* ∼ *talk.* □ *adv* in a ∼: *He dined* ∼ *with the Prime Minister.*

tether /'teðə(r)/ *n* rope or chain by which an animal is fastened while grazing. *at the end of one's* ∼, (fig) at the end of one's powers, resources, endurance, etc. □ *vt* [VP6A,15A] fasten with a ∼: *He* ∼*ed his horse to the fence.*

Teu·ton /'tjuːtən US: 'tuːtn/ *n* member of any of the Teutonic nations. ∼**ic** /tjuː'tɒnɪk US: tuː-/ *adj* of the Germanic (ie Anglo-Saxon, Dutch, German and Scandinavian) peoples.

text /tekst/ *n* **1** [U] main body of a book or printed page (contrasted with notes, diagrams, illustrations, etc): *too much* ∼ *and not enough pictures.* **2** [C] original words of an author, apart from anything else in a book: *a corrupt* ∼, one that, perhaps because of mistakes in copying, is no longer in its original form. **3** [C] short passage, sentence, esp of Scripture, as the subject of a sermon or discussion. **4** ∼(**·book**) /'tekstbʊk/ book giving instruction in a branch of learning: *an algebra* ∼*book.* **tex·tual** /'tekstʃʊəl/ *adj* of, in, a ∼: ∼*ual errors;* ∼*ual criticism.*

tex·tile /'tekstaɪl/ *attrib adj* of the making of cloth: ∼ *processes; the* ∼ *industry;* woven; suitable for weaving: ∼ *fabrics/materials.* □ *n* [C] ∼ material.

tex·ture /'tekstʃə(r)/ *n* [C,U] **1** the arrangement of the threads in a textile fabric: *cloth with a loose/ close* ∼. **2** arrangement of the parts that make up sth: *the* ∼ *of a mineral.* **3** tissue: *a skin of fine/ coarse* ∼. ∼**d** *pp* (in compounds): *ˌcoarse-/ˌthin-* '∼*d.*

thal·ido·mide /θə'lɪdəmaɪd/ *n* [U] (P) sedative drug which caused some women to give birth to deformed babies (esp with undeveloped limbs).

than /ðən; *rarely heard strong form:* ðæn/ *conj* **1**

(introducing the second part of a comparison): *John is taller ～ his brother. I have never met anyone more stupid ～ you.* **different than,** ⇨ different. **2** (with a *transitive v* the form of a *pron* after *than* depends upon the sense of the complete sentence. Note the words in parenthesis in these examples): *I know you better ～ he* (*does*), ie ～ he knows you. *I know you better ～ him,* ie ～ I know him. *I like her no better ～ he* (*does*), ie ～ he likes her. *I like her no better ～ him,* ie ～ I like him. **3** (with an *intransitive v* the *pron* after *than* is often in the object form, in both colloquial and written English, even though the subject form is required by formal grammar. This is esp so when the *pron* is followed by *all*): *He is several years older ～ me/～ I am. He can run faster ～ me/～ I can. He is wiser ～ us all.* **4** (in phrases) *no other ～,* (used as an equivalent to a construction with an emphatic *pron*): *It was no other ～ my old friend John,* ie it was John himself. *nothing else ～,* only, entire(ly): *His failure was due to nothing else ～* (= was entirely due to) *his own carelessness. What he told you was nothing else ～ nonsense,* was complete nonsense. *rather ～,* ⇨ rather(1). *sooner ～,* ⇨ soon(3,5).

thane /θeɪn/ *n* (hist) man who gave military service in return for land.

thank /θæŋk/ *vt ～ sb (for sth),* **1** [VP6A,14] express gratitude to: *～ a person for his help. There's no need to ～ me.* '*T～ you,* the usual formula for 'I ～ you.' ,*No,* '*～ you,* formula used to decline an offer. (Note that the 'No' is essential; '*T～ you*' is used for acceptance and may mean 'Yes, please.') [VP11] *T～ Heaven* (*that*) *you've come. T～ God she's safe.* **2** [VP14,17] (in peremptory requests, future tense): *I'll ～ you for that book,* please give it to me. *I'll ～ you to be a little more polite/to mind your own business.* □ *n* (now only in *pl* except in *～-offering* and with suffixes as below): (expression of) gratitude: *give ～s to God. T～s/No ～s,* colloq formulas of gratitude/refusal. *～s to,* as the result of; owing to: *T～s to your help we were successful. small ～s to,* used ironically: *We were successful, but small ～s to you,* you gave us no help. '*～-offering n* offering made, eg to a charity, a religious organization, as an expression of gratitude. *～s-'giving n* (a) expression of gratitude, esp to God; form of prayer for this. (b) (US) (also ,*T～s-'giving Day*) day set apart each year for giving ～s to God (usu the fourth Thursday in November). *～-ful* /-fl/ *adj* grateful: *Be ～ful for small mercies. You should be ～ful to have/that you have escaped with minor injuries.* *～-fully* /-fəlɪ/ *adv* *～-ful-ness n* *～-less adj* not feeling or expressing gratitude; (of actions) not arousing gratitude or winning appreciation: *a ～less task,* one which brings no ～s, appreciation or reward.

that ¹ /ðæt/ *n* (*no weak form*)/ (*pl* those /ðəʊz/) *adj, pron* (contrasted with *this, these.* *～/those* and *this/these* are used to make a person or thing specific. *this/these* are used when the person or thing is near to the speaker.) **1** *Look at ～ man/those men there. What's ～ over there? What are those? What was ～ noise? What noise was ～? Is ～ you, Mary? Are those children yours? Is ～ what you really think? T～'s what he told me. This book is much better than ～* (*one*). *These are much better than those. Life was easier in those days/at ～ time,* then, during that period. *So ～'s ～!* (formula used to indicate finality, the end of a discussion, an argument, etc). **2** (as antecedent to a *rel pron,*

expressed or omitted): *All those* (*that*) *I saw were old. Those who do not wish to go need not go. It's a different kind of car from ～* (= kind of car) (*which*) *I am used to. Throw away all those* (*which are*) *unfit for use. Those* (= People who were) *present at the ceremony were.... There are those who say* (= some people who say)*.... ** 3** (with a *pl n,* considered as a collective *sing*): *What about ～ five pounds you borrowed from me last month? When do you intend to repay ～ sum of five pounds?* **4** (*That* and a possessive cannot be used together. Note the construction used when ～ and a possessive are both needed): *I don't like ～* new *secretary of his. Well, how's ～ bad leg of yours getting on?* □ *adv* (colloq) to such a degree; so: *I can't walk ～ far,* = as far as ～. *I've done only ～ much,* ie as much as is shown, indicated, etc. *It's about ～ high,* ie as high as ～. *I was ～* (= so) *angry I could have hit him,* ie I wanted to hit him. *It isn't all ～ cold,* eg not so cold that a fire/ overcoat, etc is needed.

that ² /(*usual form:* ðət; *strong form:* ðæt; *conj* **1** introducing *n* clauses, but often omitted: *She said* (*～*) *she would come. It so happens ～ I know the man. The trouble is ～ we are short of money. I will see to it ～ everything is ready.* **2** *so ～; in order ～,* (introducing clauses of purpose): *Bring it nearer* (*so*) *～ I may see it better. I will give up my claim so ～/in order ～ you may have the property.* **3** (introducing clauses of result): *His behaviour was such ～/was so bad ～ we all refused to receive him in our homes.* **4** (introducing clauses of condition): *supposing ～...; on condition ～....* **5** (introducing clauses of reason or cause) ⇨ not(4), and now, *conj.* **6** (rhet) in exclamations: *Oh, ～ I could be with you again! How I wish...! Oh, ～ I should live to see my own son sent to prison as a thief! How sad it is ～...!*

that ³ /(*usual form:* ðət; *strong form:* ðæt/ *rel pron* (*pl* unchanged; used in defining or restrictive clauses; not preceded by a pause or a comma; often preferred to *which* for things; often preferred to *whom* and often used in place of *who*) (a) (as the subject of the *v* in a clause): *The letter ～ came this morning is from my father. Those dogs ～ attacked your sheep ought to be shot. The man ～* (*who* is preferred) *sold you that camera is a rogue. The man ～* (*who* is preferred) *cycled past you is nearly ninety.* (b) (Although *who* is usually preferred to *that, that* is preferred to *who* after superlatives, *only, all, any,* and *it is* or *it was*): *Newton was one of the greatest men ～ ever lived. He's the cleverest man ～ I ever met. You're the only person ～ can help me. Anyone ～ wants to succeed must work hard. It's you ～ I want to speak to, not Paul.* (c) (as the object of the *v* in the clause; *whom* is to be avoided; the *pron* ～ is often omitted): *The watch* (*～*) *you gave me is working perfectly. Is this the best* (*～*) *you can do? The girl* (*～*) *you met yesterday wants to see you again.* (d) (after an expression of time. Cf *when, rel adv*): *the year* (*～*) *my father died; the week* (*～*) *we went camping.* (e) (as the object of a *prep; whom* is to be avoided; *that* is often omitted, and the *prep* follows the *v*): *All the people* (*～*) *I invited have agreed to come. The photographs* (*～*) *you were looking at were taken by my brother. The man* (*～*) *I was talking to had just arrived from Canada. Where's the man* (*～*) *you borrowed it from?*

thatch /θætʃ/ *n* [U] (roof covering of) dried straw,

reeds, etc; (colloq) thick hair of the head. □ *vt* [VP6A] cover (a roof, etc) with ∽.

thaw /θɔː/ *vi,vt* [VP6A,15B,2A,C] ∽ *(out)*, **1** *It is* ∽*ing*, The temperature has risen above freezing-point (so that snow and ice begin to melt). **2** (cause anything frozen to) become liquid or soft again: ∽ *out the radiator,* (of a car); *leave frozen food to* ∽ *before cooking it.* **3** (of persons, their behaviour) (cause to) become less formal, more friendly: *After a good dinner he began to* ∽. *A bottle of wine helped to* ∽ (*out*) *our guests.* □ *n* (usu *sing*) (state of the weather causing) ∽*ing: Let's go skating before the* ∽*/a* ∽ *sets in.*

the /*before consonants:* ðə; *before vowels:* ðɪ; *strong form:* ðiː/ *def art* **1** (used as a less specific form of *this, these, that, those,* applied to person(s), thing(s), event(s), etc already referred to or being discussed. Note the changes from the *indef art* to the *def art* in these sentences): *An old man and an old woman once lived in a small hut by a river near a forest. One day the old man left the hut and went into the forest to gather wood. The old woman went to the river to wash clothes.* **2** (used when who or what is referred to is quite obvious): *Please take these letters to the post office,* ie the post office near by, the post office of this district. *Please close the window,* ie the window that is open. *Shall we have a walk by the river?* eg in London, the River Thames. **3** (used with a *n* when it stands for sth unique): *the sun; the moon; the year 1939; the universe.* **4** (used with *nn* such as *sea, sky, wind* (as in **2** above) when there is no *adj*): *The sea was calm. There's an aeroplane in the sky. Isn't the wind strong!* (Note that the use of an *adj* to describe the sea, wind, etc may make the use of the *indef art* possible: *There was a calm sea* (cf *The sea was calm*) *when I crossed from Dover to Calais. What a stormy-looking sky! There was a cold wind* (cf *The wind was cold*). **5** (used with a *n* if it is modified by a phrase or clause that makes it unique): *the back of the house; the left side of the road.* (In many phrases the *def art* is or may be omitted: *from beginning to end; from* (*the*) *top to* (*the*) *bottom; in* (*the*) *future.*) **6** (used with the superl): *the best way to get there; the tallest of the five men; the most interesting book I have ever read.* (The *def art* is not needed in the predicate after the *v* '*be*' when the superl is used without a *n*: *It is wisest* (= *The* wisest plan is) *to avoid the centre of the town.* When *most* means 'very', the *def art* is not used: *The story was most exciting. This is a most useful reference book.*) ⇨ most²(3). **7** used before (**a**) names of seas and oceans: *the Mediterranean, the Red Sea; the Atlantic* (*Ocean*), *the Indian Ocean.* (**b**) names of rivers and canals: *the Nile; the river Thames; the Suez Canal.* (**c**) *pl* geographical names: *the Alps; the Philippines; the West Indies; the Netherlands.* (**d**) in a few geographical names: *the Sudan; the Sahara.* **8** (used with *adjj* and participles to denote all members of a class: *the rich, the young, and the beautiful; the dead, the dying, and the wounded,* eg after a battle. **9** the + *adj,* (equivalent to an abstract *n*): *the sublime,* sublimity. **10** (used formerly with names of diseases, now usually omitted except with colloq or sl *pl*): *She's got the creeps/the fidgets/the blues.* Survivals of the older use: *The child has* (*the*) *measles.* **11** Note: *to play the piano/the violin/the banjo, etc,* but (with names of games): *to play tennis/football/cards/chess/billiards. etc.* **12** (used

with a *sing common n* to denote the whole class, eg of animals or plants): *Is it true that the owl cannot see well in daylight?* (In colloq style, the use of the *pl,* without the *def art,* is more usu: *Is it true that owls cannot...?*). **13** (used in a similar way with names of inventions. In this case the use of the *def art* with the *sing n* is usu in both liter and colloq styles): *We don't know who invented the wheel. The telephone is a most useful invention.* **14** (used with *nn* expressing a unit): *This car does thirty miles to the gallon,* ie to each gallon of petrol. *These apples are small; there are seven or eight to the kilo,* ie to each kilo. *I get paid by the hour,* ie I earn so much for each hour's work. □ *adv* by so much; by that amount; (used before an *adj* or *adv* in the comparative degree to indicate that two things increase or decrease in a parallel way, or that one increases in a degree equal to that by which another decreases): *The more he gets the more he wants. The more he reads the less he understands.*

the-atre (US = **the-ater**) /'θɪətə(r)/ *n* **1** building or arena (*open-air* ∽) for the performance of plays, for dramatic spectacles, etc: *go to the* ∽ *to see a Shakespeare play.* '∽-**goer** *n* person who frequently goes to ∽s. **2** hall or room with seats in rows rising one behind another for lectures, scientific demonstrations, etc. '**operating** ∽, room (in a hospital, etc) where surgical operations are performed. **3** scene of important events: *Belgium has often been a* ∽ *of war.* **4** [U] dramatic literature or art; the writing and acting of plays, esp when connected with one author, country, period, etc: *a book about the Greek* ∽. *Do Henry James's plays make good* ∽, are they satisfactory when presented on the stage? **the-atri-cal** /θɪ'ætrɪkl/ *adj* **1** of or for the ∽: *theatrical scenery/performances; a theatrical company,* of actors. **2** (of behaviour, manner, way of speaking, persons, etc) designed for effect; showy, not natural. □ *n* (usu *pl*) (usu amateur) dramatic performance. **the-atri-cally** /-klɪ/ *adv*

thee /ðiː/ *pron,* ⇨ thou.

theft /θeft/ *n* [C,U] (the act of, an instance of) stealing.

their /ðeə(r)/ *adj* of them: *They have lost* ∽ *dog. They have a house of* ∽ *own.* **theirs** /ðeəz/ *pron* of them: *That dog is* ∽s, *not ours. It's a habit of* ∽s, one of ∽ habits.

the-ism /'θiːɪzəm/ *n* [U] belief in the existence of a revealed God, creator and ruler of the universe. ⇨ deism. **the-ist** /'θiːɪst/ *n* believer in ∽. **the-is-tic** /θiː'ɪstɪk/, **the-is-ti-cal** /-kl/ *adjj*

them /ðəm; *strong form:* ðem/ *pron,* ⇨ they.

them-atic /θɪ'mætɪk/ *adj* (music) of a theme(**3**) or themes.

theme /θiːm/ *n* [C] **1** topic; subject of a talk or a piece of writing. **2** (esp US) (subject set for a) student's essay. **3** (music) short melody which is repeated, expanded, etc eg in a sonata or symphony. '∽ **song,** one that is often repeated in a musical play, film, etc.

them-selves /ðəm'selvz/ *pron* **1** (reflex): *They hurt* ∽. *They kept some for* ∽. *They did the work by* ∽, without help. *They were by* ∽ (= alone, without company) *when I called.* **2** (emphat): *They* ∽ *have often made that mistake.*

then /ðen/ *adv* **1** at the time (past or future): *We were living in Wales* ∽. *I was still unmarried* ∽. (*every*) *now and* ∽, ⇨ now(3). ∽ *and there; there and* ∽, ⇨ there¹(5). **2** (used to modify a *n*): *the* ∽ *Lord Mayor,* the Lord Mayor at that time. **3**

(used after a *prep*): *from* ~ (= from that time) *on-wards; until* ~; *since* ~. **4** next; after that; after-wards: *We'll have fish first, and* ~ *roast chicken. We had a week in Rome and* ~ *went to Naples.* **5** (usu at the beginning or end of a sentence) in that case; that being so: *A: 'It isn't here.'—B: 'It must be in the next room,* ~.' *You say you don't want to call a doctor.—T*~ *what do you want to do?* **6** fur-thermore; and also: *T*~ *there's Mrs Green—she must be invited to the wedding. And* ~, *you must remember....* **7** '**Now** ~, used to call attention, or to express a warning, make a protest, etc: *Now* ~, *who's been smoking?*

thence /ðens/ *adv* (formal) from there; for that reason. ~**·forth** /ˌðens'fɔ:θ/, ~**·for·ward** /ˌðens'fɔ:wəd/ *advv* from that time onwards.

the·oc·racy /θɪ'ɒkrəsɪ/ *n* [C,U] (*pl* -cies) (country with a) system of government in which the laws of the State are believed to be the laws of God; (hence) government by priests or a priestly class. **theo·cratic** /ˌθɪə'krætɪk/ *adj*

the·odo·lite /θɪ'ɒdəlaɪt/ *n* instrument used by sur-veyors for measuring horizontal and vertical angles.

the·ol·ogy /θɪ'ɒlədʒɪ/ *n* **1** [U] formal study of the nature of God and of the foundations of religious belief. **2** [C] theological system or interpretation: *rival theologies; a/the* ~ *of sex.* **theo·lo·gian** /ˌθɪə'ləudʒən/ *n* expert in or student of ~. **theo·logi·cal** /ˌθɪə'lɒdʒɪkl/ *adj* **theo·logi·cally** /-klɪ/ *adv*

the·orem /'θɪərəm/ *n* **1** statement which logical reasoning shows to be true. **2** (maths) statement for which a reasoned proof is required.

the·or·etic, the·or·eti·cal /θɪə'retɪk, -ɪkl/ *adjj* based on theory, not on practice or experience. **the·or·eti·cally** /-klɪ/ *adv*

the·ory /'θɪərɪ/ *n* (*pl* -ries) **1** [C,U] (explanation of the) general principles of an art or science (con-trasted with practice): *Naval officers must under-stand both the* ~ *and practice of navigation. Your plan is excellent in* ~, *but would it succeed in practice?* **2** [C] reasoned supposition put forward to explain facts or events: *Darwin's* ~ *of evolution.* **3** [C] sth conjectured, not necessarily based on reasoning: *He has a* ~ *that wearing hats makes men bald. In* ~, *three things could happen,* There are three possibilities. **the·or·ist** /'θɪərɪst/ *n* person who forms theories. **the·or·ize** /'θɪəraɪz/ *vi* [VP2A,3A] ~ (*about sth*), form theories.

the·os·ophy /θi:'ɒsəfɪ/ *n* [U] any of several systems of philosophy which aim at a direct know-ledge of God by means of spiritual ecstasy and contemplation. **the·os·oph·ist** /-fɪst/ *n* believer in ~. **theo·sophi·cal** /ˌθi:ə'sɒfɪkl/ *adj*

thera·peutic, -i·cal /ˌθerə'pju:tɪk, -ɪkl/ *adj* con-nected with the art of healing, the cure of disease: *take* ~ *baths at a spa.* **thera·peutic(s)** /ˌθerə'pju:tɪk(s)/ *n* (usu with *sing v*) branch of med-icine concerned with curing disease.

ther·apy /'θerəpɪ/ *n* [U] curative treatment, esp of a kind indicated by a preceding word: *radio-*~, treatment by x-rays; *psycho-*~, treatment by psychoanalytic methods; *occupational* ~, treat-ment by means of work that exercises certain muscles. **thera·pist** /'θerəpɪst/ *n* specialist in ~.

there[1] /ðeə(r)/ *adv of place and direction* (con-trasted with *here*) **1** in, at or to, that place: *We shall soon be* ~. *We're nearly* ~, have nearly ar-rived. *Put the box* ~, in that corner. *I've never been to Rome but I hope to go* ~ *next year.* **2** (front

position, in exclamatory style; always stressed, and not to be confused with *there* + *be/appear/seem, etc*, dealt with at there[2] below; ⇨ here(2); used with inversion of subject and *v* if the subject is a *n*, but not if the subject is a *pers pron*): *T*~ *goes the last bus! T*~ *it goes! T*~ *come the rest of the party! T*~ *they come!* **3** (used to call attention; al-ways stressed): *T*~*'s the bell ringing for church. T*~*'s a fine stroke!* (used to give praise or encour-agement.) *You have only to turn the switch and* ~ *you are,* ie you get the desired result. *T*~*'s a fine, ripe pear for you!* See what a fine, ripe pear that is! *T*~*'s gratitude for you!* Note how grateful he, she, etc is! (used either sincerely or ironically). **4** at, in connection with, that point (in an action, story, ar-gument, etc): *Don't stop* ~! *T*~ (ie on that point) *I disagree with you. T*~ *you are mistaken. T*~ *comes the difficulty.* **5** (in phrases): **all** ~, ⇨ all[2](1). **here and** ~, ⇨ here(5). ~ **and back,** to a place and back again: *Can I go* ~ *and back in one day?* **over** ~, (indicating a place farther than is in-dicated by ~ alone): *I live here, Mr Green lives* ~, *and Mr Brown lives over* ~, on the other side of the river. **then and** ~; ~ **and then,** at that time and place. Cf here and now. **6** (in colloq style only, after a *n* or *pron*, for emphasis): *Hi! You* ~! *That woman* ~ *is eating a lot!* **7** (used after *preps* and *advv*): *Put them in/under/near, etc* ~. *Pass along* ~, *please!* (used to request people to move along in a crowded street, bus, etc).

there[2] /usual form: ðə(r); strong form: ðeə(r)/ *adv* (used to introduce a sentence in which the *v* (esp '*be*') normally precedes its subject, which is usu indef, ⇨ [VP1,2A,4E]) **1** (with the *v* '*be*'): *T*~*'s a man at the door.* Cf *The man is at the door. T*~ *can be no doubt about it. I don't want* ~ *to be any misunderstanding. T*~*'s no stopping him,* It is impossible to stop him. **2** (with other *vv*, esp *seem* and *appear*): *T*~ *seems* (*to be*) *no doubt about it. T*~ *appeared to be no one who could answer our inquiries. T*~ *comes a time when....*

there[3] /ðeə(r)/ *int* (always stressed) **1** (used, chief-ly to children, to soothe or comfort): *T*~! *T*~! *Never mind, you'll soon feel better.* **2** (used to sug-gest that the speaker was right in sth, or to indicate triumph, dismay, etc according to the context): '*T*~, *now! What did I tell you,* You now see that I was right! *T*~! *You've woken the baby!*

there·about(s) /'ðeərəbaut(s)/ *adv* (usu preceded by *or*) near that place, number, quantity, degree, etc: *in Rye or* ~; *£5/15 lb/3 o'clock or* ~.

there·after /ðeər'ɑ:ftə(r) *US:* -'æf-/ *adv* (formal) afterwards.

there·by /ðeə'baɪ/ *adv* (formal) by that means; in that connection.

there·fore /'ðeəfɔ:(r)/ *adv* for that reason.

there·in /ðeər'ɪn/ *adv* (formal) in that place; in that respect; in that particular.

there·in·after /ˌðeərɪn'ɑ:ftə(r) *US:* -'æf-/ *adv* (chiefly legal) in that part which follows.

there·of /ðeər'ɒv/ *adv* (formal) of that; from that source.

there·to /ðeə'tu:/ *adv* (formal) to that; in addition to that.

there·under /ðeər'ʌndə(r)/ *adv* (formal) under that.

there·upon /ˌðeərə'pɒn/ *adv* (formal) then; as the result of that.

there·withal /'ðeəwɪðɔ:l/ *adv* (archaic) in addition; besides.

therm /θɜːm/ n [C] (100000 GB thermal units as a) unit of heat as used for measuring the consumption of gas (coal-gas or natural gas).

ther·mal /'θɜːml/ adj of heat: ~ springs, of warm or hot water; the '~ barrier, barrier to the use of high speeds (in flying) caused by increased friction of the air on the surfaces of the aircraft; a ,~ 'power station, one using heat (from coal, oil) (contrasted with a hydro–electric power station). ~ capacity, (phys) number of units of heat needed to raise the temperature of a body by one degree. ~ unit, (phys) unit of measure of heat. British ~ unit (abbr BTU), amount of heat needed to raise 1lb of water by 1°F. □ n rising current of warm air (as needed by a glider to gain height).

ther·mi·onic /ˌθɜːmɪ'ɒnɪk/ adj of that branch of physics that deals with the emission of electrons at high temperatures. ~ valve (US = ~ tube) n system of electrodes arranged in a glass or metal envelope exhausted of air.

thermo- /ˌθɜːməʊ/ (in compounds) of heat. ,~-dy'nam·ics n pl [U] (usu with sing v) science of the relations between heat and mechanical work. ,~-'nu·clear adj (eg of weapons) of, using, the high temperatures released in nuclear fission: the ~-nuclear bomb, the hydrogen bomb. ~-'plas·tic n, adj (substance) which can at any time be made plastic by the application of heat. ,~-'set·ting adj (of plastics) becoming permanently hard after being heated and shaped. '~-stat /'θɜːməstæt/ n [C] device for automatically regulating temperature by cutting off and restoring the supply of heat (eg in central heating, refrigerators, air-conditioning). ~-static /ˌθɜːmə'stætɪk/ adj of a ~stat: ~static control.

ther·mom·eter /θə'mɒmɪtə(r)/ n instrument for measuring temperature. ⇨ App 5.

ther·mos /'θɜːməs/ n (also '~ flask) (P) vacuum flask. ⇨ vacuum.

the·sau·rus /θɪ'sɔːrəs/ n (pl ~es /-rəsɪz/) dictionary of words and phrases grouped together according to similarities in their meanings.

these /ðiːz/ ⇨ this.

the·sis /'θiːsɪs/ n (pl theses /'θiːsiːz/) statement or theory (to be) put forward and supported by arguments, esp a lengthy written essay submitted (as part of the requirements) for a university degree.

Thes·pian /'θespɪən/ adj (liter) connected with the drama. □ n actor or actress.

thews /θjuːz/ n pl (liter) muscles: ~ and sinews, bodily strength.

they /ðeɪ/ pers pron (subject form, pl, of he, she, it): T~ (= People in general) say that the government will have to resign. What a lot of questions ~ (= those in authority) ask in this tax form! them /ðəm/ strong form: ðem/ pers pron (object form of they): Give them to me. It was very kind of them, They were very kind.

they're /ðeə(r)/ = they are.

thick /θɪk/ adj (-er, -est) 1 (opp of thin) of relatively great or a specified measurement in diameter, from one side to the other, or from the front to the back: a ~ slice of bread; a ~ line; ice three inches ~; ~ print, of ~ lines. ~-'skinned adj (fig) not sensitive to reproach or insults. 2 having a large number of units close together: ~ hair; a ~ forest; in the ~est part of the crowd. The corn was ~ in the fields. ~-'set adj (a) having a short, stout body; solidly built. (b) (of a hedge) with bushes, etc closely planted. 3 ~ with, abounding or

packed with: The air was ~ with dust/snow. 4 (of liquids) semi-solid: ~ soup; (of vapour, the atmosphere) not clear; dense: a ~ fog. 5 (of voices) obstructed, eg because one has a cold. 6 (colloq) stupid; dull. ,~-'headed adj stupid. 7 (colloq) intimate: John is very ~ with Anne now. as ~ as thieves, very friendly. 8 (various colloq uses) a bit ~; rather ~, beyond what is reasonable or endurable: Three weeks of heavy rain is a bit ~. give sb a ~ ear, give him a blow that causes his ear to swell. lay it on ~, (sl) be profuse, esp in paying compliments. □ n [U] 1 most crowded part; part where there is greatest activity: in the ~ of the fight. We were in the ~ of it. through ~ and thin, under any kind of conditions, good or bad. 2 ~ part of anything: the ~ of the thumb. □ adv~ly: You spread the butter too ~. The snow/dust lay ~ everywhere. His blows came ~ and fast, rapidly and in large numbers. ~·ly adv in a ~ manner: cut the bread/spread the butter ~ly. ~·en /'θɪkən/ vt,vi make or become ~: ~en the gravy. The plot ~ens, becomes more complex. ~·en·ing /'θɪkənɪŋ/ n [U] material or substance used to ~en sth; process of becoming ~(er) or making sth ~(er). ~·ness n 1 [U] quality or degree of being ~: four centimetres in ~ness; a ~ness of four centimetres. 2 [C] layer: one ~ness of cotton-wool and two ~nesses of felt.

thicket /'θɪkɪt/ n [C] mass of trees, shrubs, undergrowth, growing thickly together.

thief /θiːf/ n (pl thieves /θiːvz/) person who steals, esp secretly and without violence. ⇨ bandit, burglar, robber at rob. **thieve** /θiːv/ vi,vt [VP2A] be a ~; [VP6A] steal (sth). **thiev·ery** /'θiːvərɪ/ n theft. **thiev·ish** /-ɪʃ/ adj having the habit of stealing; thief-like. **thiev·ish·ly** adv

thigh /θaɪ/ n [C] 1 part of the human leg between the knee and the hip. ⇨ the illus at leg. '~-bone n bone of this part of the leg; femur. 2 corresponding part of the hind legs of other animals.

thimble /'θɪmbl/ n cap (of metal, etc) used to protect the end of the finger when pushing a needle through cloth, etc. ~·ful /-fʊl/ n (colloq) sip, very small quantity (of a liquid).

thin /θɪn/ adj (-ner, -nest) 1 (opp of thick) having opposite surfaces close together; of small diameter: a ~ slice of bread; a ~ sheet of paper; ~ boards; a ~ piece of string; a ~ stroke, of the pen, etc. ~-'skinned adj (fig) sensitive to criticism; easily offended. 2 lacking density: a ~ mist. ~ air, invisibility; nothingness: He seemed to vanish into ~ air, disappear mysteriously without leaving a trace. 3 (opp of fat) having not much flesh: rather ~ in the face. Your illness has left you very ~. 4 not full or closely packed: a ~ audience, with more seats empty than occupied. 'Your hair's getting rather ~ on top, sir', said the barber. 5 (of liquids) lacking substance; watery: ~ beer/wine, lacking body; weak. 6 lacking in some important ingredient; poor: ~ humour; a ~ excuse, not very convincing; a ~ disguise, easily seen through; a ~ story, one that contains nothing very exciting; one that does not convince (as an excuse, etc). 7 (colloq) have a ~ time, an uncomfortable, distasteful one. □ adv so as to be ~: You've spread the butter very thin. □ vt,vi (-nn-) [VP6A,15B,2A,C] make or become ~. ~ (down), make (a liquid) less dense: ~ down paint with turpentine. ~ (out), make or become less dense, or fewer in number: War and disease had ~ned (out) the population.

He ⁓*ned out the seedlings,* pulled up some of them to allow the others to grow better. *We had better wait until the fog* ⁓*s out. At last the crowd/traffic* ⁓*ned out.* ⁓**·ly** *adv* in a ⁓ manner: *Sow the seed* ⁓*ly.* ⁓**·ness** /'θɪnnɪs/ *n*

thine /ðaɪn/ ⇨ **thy.**

thing /θɪŋ/ *n* **1** any material object: *What are those* ⁓*s on the table? There wasn't a* ⁓ (= nothing) *to eat. She's too fond of sweet* ⁓*s,* sweet kinds of food. **2** (*pl*) belongings; articles of which the nature is clear (or thought to be clear) from the context: *Bring your swimming* ⁓*s* (= your swimming-suit, towel, etc) *with you. Have you packed your* ⁓*s* (= clothes, etc) *for the journey? Put your* ⁓*s* (= coat, hat, etc) *on and let's leave.* **3** subject: *There's another* ⁓ (= something else) *I want to ask you about.* **4** that which is non-material: *He values* ⁓*s of the mind more than* ⁓*s of the body.* **be 'seeing** ⁓*s,* have hallucinations. **5** circumstance; event; course of action: *That only makes* ⁓*s* (= the situation) *worse. You take* ⁓*s* (= happenings) *too seriously. I must think* ⁓*s over,* consider what has happened, what has to be done, etc. *What's the next* ⁓ *to do,* What must be done next? *It's just one of those* ⁓*s,* sth that can't be helped, explained, remedied, etc (according to context). *T*⁓*s* (= The state of affairs) *are getting worse and worse. Well, of 'all* ⁓*s!* (expressing surprise, indignation, etc, at what has been done, suggested, etc). **for 'one** ⁓, used to introduce a reason: *For one* ⁓, *I haven't any money; for another....* **Taking one** ⁓ **with another,** considering various circumstances, etc. **6** (used of a person or an animal, expressing an emotion of some kind): *She's a sweet little* ⁓/*a dear old* ⁓. *Poor* ⁓, *he's been ill all winter.* **7 the** ⁓, just what will be best in the circumstances: *A holiday in the mountains will be the best* ⁓ *for you. That's not the* ⁓ *to do,* is unsuitable, inappropriate. *He always says the right/wrong* ⁓, makes the most suitable/unsuitable remark or comment. **quite the** ⁓, fashionable. **8** (phrases) **the** ⁓ '**is,** the question to be considered is: *The* ⁓ *is, can we get there in time? The* ⁓ *is* (= The most important factor is) *to make your views quite clear to everyone.* **first** ⁓, before anything else; early: *I'll do it first* ⁓ *tomorrow morning.* **first** ⁓**s first,** ⇨ first²(1). **the ,general/ ,common/'usual'** ⁓, the common practice. **a near** ⁓, a narrow escape (from an accident, missing a train, etc). **an understood** ⁓, sth that has been/is accepted. **do one's (own)** ⁓, (colloq) do sth which one does well, or which one feels an urge to do; act without inhibition. **have a** ⁓ **about,** (colloq) be obsessed by. **9** (*pl* with an *adj* following) all that can be so described: ⁓*s Japanese,* Japanese customs, art, etc. **10** (legal) ⁓*s personal/ real,* personal/real property.

thing·ummy /'θɪŋəmɪ/, **thing·(u)ma·bob** /'θɪŋ(ə)məbɒb/, **thing·(u)ma·jig** /'θɪŋ(ə)mədʒɪg/ *nn* (colloq) person or thing whose name one forgets or is not known (used in the same way as *what's-his-name, what d'you call it*).

think¹ /θɪŋk/ *vi,vt* (*pt,pp* thought /θɔːt/) (For special uses with *adverbial particles* and *preps,* ⇨ 8 below). **1** [VP2A,B,C,6A,8] (with cognate object) use, exercise, the mind in order to form opinions, come to conclusions: *Are animals able to* ⁓? *You should* ⁓ (= not be hasty) *before doing that. Do you* ⁓ *in English when you speak English, or translate mentally? Let me* ⁓ *a moment,* Give me

time before I answer. *He may not say much but he* ⁓*s a lot.* ⁓ **aloud,** utter one's thoughts as they occur. '⁓**-tank** *n* group or organization that provides advice, ideas, solutions to problems, etc. **2** [VP9,25] consider; be of the opinion: *Do you* ⁓ *it will rain? Yes, I* ⁓ *so. No, I don't* ⁓ *so. It's going to rain, I* ⁓. *I* ⁓ (*that*) *you're very brave. Do you* ⁓ *it likely/that it is likely? I thought I heard a scream. They had been thought (to be) lost. It will be better, don't you* ⁓, *to start early.* ⁓ **fit.** ⇨ fit¹(2). **3** [VP10] (neg with *can/could*) imagine, form a conception of: *I can't* ⁓ *what you mean. I can't* ⁓ *where she has gone off to/how she did it/ why she left. You can't'* ⁓ *how glad I am to see you.* **4** [VP9] have a half-formed intention: *I* ⁓ *I'll go for a swim.* **5** [VP10] reflect: *She was* ⁓*ing (to herself) how cold the room was.* **6** [VP7A,9] expect, intend: *I never thought that I'd see you here! Who would have thought to see you here!* **I thought as much,** That is what I expected or suspected. **7** [VD22] bring into a mental condition by ⁓ing: *Stop worrying or you'll* ⁓ *yourself sick!* **8** [VP3A,15B] (special uses with *adverbial particles* and *preps*):

think about sth, (a) examine, consider (esp a plan, idea, to see whether it is desirable, practicable, etc): *She's* ⁓*ing about emigrating to Canada. Please* ⁓ *about the proposal and let me have your views tomorrow.* (b) recall; reflect upon: *She was* ⁓*ing about her childhood days.*

think of sth, (a) consider; take into account: *We have a hundred and one things to* ⁓ *of before we can decide. You* ⁓ *of everything!* (b) consider, contemplate (without reaching a decision or taking action): *We're* ⁓*ing of emigrating to Canada. I did* ⁓ *of visiting him, but I've changed my mind.* (c) imagine: *Just* ⁓ *of the cost/danger! To* ⁓ *of his not knowing anything about it!* Isn't it surprising! (d) have, entertain, the idea of (often with *could, would, should,* and *not* or *never,* with *dream* as a possible substitute for *think*): *Surrender is not to be thought of. I couldn't* ⁓ *of such a thing. He would never* ⁓ *of letting his daughter marry a fellow like you.* (e) call to mind; recall: *I can't* ⁓ *of his name at the moment.* (f) put forward; suggest: *Who first thought of the idea? Can you* ⁓ *of a good place for a weekend holiday?* ⁓ **highly/well/not much/ little, etc of sb/sth,** (not in the progressive tenses), have a high/good/poor, etc opinion of: *His work is highly thought of by the critics. He* ⁓*s the world of her,* ⁓*s she's wonderful, loves her dearly. *⁓ **nothing of sth/doing sth,** consider (doing) it to be insignificant or unremarkable: *Barbara* ⁓*s nothing of walking 20 miles a day.* ⁓ **nothing 'of it,** (formal) Don't mention it, ⇨ mention. ⁓ **better of sb,** have a higher opinion of (than to...): *I had always thought better of you than to suppose you could be so unkind.* ⁓ **better of sth,** reconsider and give up: *What a foolish idea! I hope you'll* ⁓ *better of it.*

think sth out, consider carefully and make a plan for: *It seems to be a well-thought out scheme. That wants* ⁓*ing out,* needs careful consideration.

think sth over, reflect upon, consider further (before reaching a decision, etc): *Please* ⁓ *over what I've said. I'd like more time to* ⁓ *things over.*

think sth up, devise, conceive, invent (a scheme, etc): *There's no knowing what he'll* ⁓ *up next.*

think² /θɪŋk/ *n* (colloq) occasion of, need for, thinking: *If that's what he wants, he's got another*

~ *coming*, will need to think again.

think·able /'θɪŋkəbl/ *adj* conceivable: *It's not* ~ (more usu *It's un*~) *that*....

thinker /'θɪŋkə(r)/ *n* person who thinks (usu with an *adj*): *a great/shallow* ~.

think·ing /'θɪŋkɪŋ/ *adj* thoughtful; intelligent: *the* ~ *public; all* ~ *people.* □ *n* [U] thought; reasoning: *do some hard* ~, think deeply. *You are of my way of* ~, You think as I do. *He is, to my (way of)* ~ (ie in my opinion), *the best living novelist. Can I bring you round to my way of* ~, get you to think as I do, agree with me? **put one's** '~-**cap on,** (colloq) think about a problem, etc.

third /θɜːd/ *adj, n* (abbr **3rd**) next after the second (in place, time, order, importance, etc); one of the three equal divisions of a whole: *the* ~ *month of the year*, ie March; *on the* ~ *of April; on the* ~ *floor* (US = fourth floor); *every* ~ *day; the* ~ *largest city in France; Edward the T*~, Edward III, the ~ king of this name; *one—*~ *of a litre.* ~ **degree**, prolonged or hard questioning, use of torture (as used by the police in some countries to get confessions or information). **a/the** ~ **party,** another person besides the two principal people. ~-**party insurance,** of a person other than the person insured, which the insurance company undertakes to meet. ~ **rail,** conductor rail, carrying electric current. ~-**'rate** *adj* of £poor quality. ~-**'rater** *n* person who is ~-rate. **the T**~ **World,** the developing countries not aligned with the great power blocs. ~·**ly** *adv*

thirst /θɜːst/ *n* [U, and with *indef art* as in examples] **1** feeling caused by a desire or need to drink; suffering caused by this: *The horse satisfied its* ~ *at the river. This kind of work gives me a* ~. *They lost their way in the desert and died of* ~. **2** (fig) strong desire (*for*, or, liter and biblical, *after*): *a* ~ *for knowledge; satisfy one's* ~ *for adventure.* □ *vt* [VP2A,3A] ~ (*for*), have ~; be eager (for); ~ *for* (liter and biblical, *after*) *revenge.* ~·**y** *adj* (-ier, -iest) having or causing ~: *be/feel* ~y. *Some kinds of food make one* ~y. *Tennis is a* ~y *game on a hot day. The fields are* ~y *for rain.* ~·**ily** /-ɪlɪ/ *adv*

thir·teen /θɜː'tiːn/ *adj, n* the number 13. ⇨ App 4.
thir·teenth /θɜː'tiːnθ/ *adj, n* next after the twelfth; one of ~ equal parts.

thirty /'θɜːtɪ/ *adj, n* the number 30. ⇨ App 4. **the thirties,** 30–39. **thir·ti·eth** /'θɜːtɪəθ/ *adj, n* next after the 29th; one of ~ equal parts.

this /ðɪs/ (*pl* these /ðiːz/) *adj, pron* (contrasted with *that, those.* ~/*these* and *that/those* are used to make a person or thing specific. ~/*these* are used when the person or thing is near in space or time to the speaker.) **1** *Look at* ~ *box/these boxes here. What's* ~ *over here? What are these? Are these books yours? Are these your children? Is* ~ *what you want? T*~ (one) *is larger than that. These are better than those. Do it like* ~, ie in ~ way, as shown here, etc. *Life is difficult these days*, nowadays. *He will be here* ~ *Thursday*, Thursday of ~ week. *What's all* ~? (colloq) What's the trouble? What's happening? **2** (*T*~ and a possessive cannot be used together. Note the construction used when ~ and a possessive are both needed): *T*~ *car of yours needs a thorough overhaul. These new shoes of mine are painfully tight.* **3** (in narrative) a certain: *Then* ~ *funny little man came up to me. We all ended up at* ~ *pub.* □ *adv* (colloq) to ~ degree; so: *It's about* ~ *high. Now that we have come* ~ *far* (= as far as ~).... *Can you spare me* ~ *much*

(= as much as ~)? *I know* ~ *much* (= what I am about to state), *that his story is exaggerated.*

thistle /'θɪsl/ *n* [C] (sorts of) wild plant with prickly leaves and yellow, white or purple flowers. '~-**down** *n* [U] fluff of ~ flowers, carrying the seed.

thither /'ðɪðə(r) US: 'θɪðər/ *adv* (old use) to that place; in that direction. **hither and** ~, here and there; in all directions.

tho' /ðəʊ/ *adv, conj* (informal spelling of) though.

thole /θəʊl/ *n* (also '~-**pin**) pin or peg in the gunwale of a boat to keep an oar secure; one of two pins between which an oar is held. ⇨ rowlock.

thong /θɒŋ US: θɔːŋ/ *n* narrow strip of leather, eg as a fastening, the lash of a whip.

tho·rax /'θɔːræks/ *n* **1** part of an animal's body between the neck and the belly, eg in a man, the chest. **2** middle of the three main sections of an insect (bearing the legs and wings). ⇨ the illus at insect.

thorn /θɔːn/ *n* **1** [C] sharp-pointed growth on the stem of a plant. ⇨ the illus at flower. *a* ~ *in one's flesh/side*, (fig) constant source of annoyance. **2** [C,U] (usu in compounds) kinds of shrub or tree with ~s: '*haw*~; '*black*~. **thorny** *adj* (-ier, -iest) **1** having ~s. **2** (fig) full of trouble and difficulty; causing argument: *a* ~y *problem/subject*.

thor·ough /'θʌrə US: -rəʊ/ *adj* complete in every way; not forgetting or overlooking anything; detailed: *a* ~ *worker; receive* ~ *instruction in English; give a room a* ~ *cleaning; be* ~ *in one's work.* '~-**going** *adj* ~; complete; uncompromising. *a* ~-*going revision.* ~·**ly** *adv* ~·**ness** *n*

thor·ough·bred /'θʌrəbred/ *n, adj* (animal, esp a horse, also fig, person) of pure breed; high-spirited, thoroughly trained.

thor·ough·fare /'θʌrəfeə(r)/ *n* [C] road or street, esp one much used by traffic and open at both ends: *The Strand is one of London's busiest* ~s. *No* ~, (as a sign) Not open to the public; no way through.

those /ðəʊz/ *pl* of that.

thou /ðaʊ/ *pron* (archaic) you (*sing*). **thee** /ðiː/ *pron* object form of ~.

though /ðəʊ/ *conj* **1** (also **al~** /ɔːl'ðəʊ/) in spite of the fact that; notwithstanding the fact that: *Al*~ *it was so cold, he went out without an overcoat* (cf *but: It was very cold, but he...*). *T*~ *they are so poor, they have enough to eat. He passed the examination al*~ *he had been prevented by illness from studying.* **2** (also **al~** and **even** ~) even if: *strange* ~ *it may appear/al*~ *it may appear strange, even if it appears strange. He will never be dishonest even* ~ *he (should) be reduced to poverty.* **3** *what* ~, (liter) what does it matter if: *What* ~ *the way be long,....* **4** *as* ~, ⇨ *as* ~/*as if* at as[2](11). **5** (also **al~**) (introducing an independent statement) and yet; all the same: *He will probably agree,* ~ *you never know*, and yet one can never be certain. *I'll try to come,* ~ *I don't think I shall manage it.* □ *adv* (used absolutely, in the sense 5 above) however: *He will probably agree; you never know,* ~. *He said he would come; he didn't,* ~.

thought[1] /θɔːt/ *pt, pp* of think[1].

thought[2] /θɔːt/ *n* **1** [U] (power, process of) thinking: *He spends hours in* ~. *He was lost/deep in* ~, thinking so deeply as to be unaware of his surroundings, etc. **2** [U] way of thinking characteristic of a particular period, class, nation, etc: *Greek/ working-class/scientific/modern* ~. **3** [U] ~ (*for*), care, consideration: *after serious* ~. *He often acts* *without* ~. *The nurse was full of* ~ *for her patient.* **take** ~ **for,** be concerned about. **4** [C,U] idea, opinion, intention, formed by thinking: *His speech was full of striking* ~s. *Please write and let me have your* ~s *on the matter. That boy hasn't a* ~ *in his head. He keeps his* ~s *to himself,* does not tell anyone what he thinks. *She says she can read my* ~s. *He had no* ~ (= intention) *of hurting your feelings. You must give up all* ~ *of marrying Tom. I had some* ~ *of going* (= had half intended to go) *to Spain this summer.* **on ,second** ' ~s, after further consideration. '~-**reader** *n* person who claims to know people's ~s. '~ **transference,** telepathy. **5 a** ~, a little: *You should be a* ~ *more considerate of other people.* ~-**ful** /-fl/ *adj* **1** full of ~; showing ~: ~*ful looks.* **2** considerate; thinking of, showing ~(3) for, the needs of others: *a* ~*ful friend. It was* ~*ful of you to warn me of your arrival.* ~-**fully** /-fəlɪ/ *adv* ~-**ful·ness** *n* ~-**less** *adj* **1** careless; unthinking: *Young people are often* ~*less for the future.* **2** selfish; inconsiderate (*of* others): *a* ~*less action.* ~-**less·ly** *adv* ~-**less·ness** *n*

thou·sand /'θaʊznd/ *adj, n* the number 1000, ⇨ App 4; (loosely, exaggerated style) a great number: *A* ~ *thanks for your kindness. He made a* ~ *and one excuses.* **a** ,~ **to ' one (chance),** remote (possibility). **one in a** ~, a rare exception. ~**th** /'θaʊznθ/ *adj, n* ~-**fold** /-fəʊld/ *adj, adv* a ~ times (as much or many).

thrall /θrɔːl/ *n* [C,U] (condition of being a) slave: (fig) *He is* (*in*) ~ *to his passions.* **thral·dom** /-dəm/ *n* [U] slavery.

thrash /θræʃ/ *vt,vi* **1** [VP6A] beat with a stick, whip, etc: *Stop* ~*ing that donkey, you cruel boy! He* ~*ed the boy soundly,* gave him a thorough beating. *He threatened to* ~ *the life out of me.* **2** [VP6A] (colloq) defeat (a team, etc) in a contest. **3** [VP15B] ~ **sth out,** (colloq) (a) clear up (a problem, etc) by discussion. (b) arrive at (the truth, a solution, etc) by discussion. **4** [VP6A,15A,2C] (cause to) toss, move violently: *The whale* ~*ed the water with its tail. The swimmer* ~*ed about in the water. The gale made the branches of the trees* ~ *against the windows.* **5** = thresh. ~-**ing** *n* [C] (esp) beating; *give sb/get a good* ~*ing;* defeat, eg in games.

thread /θred/ *n* **1** [C,U] (length of) spun cotton, silk, flax, wool, etc esp for use in sewing and weaving: *a reel of silk* ~; *a needle and* ~; *gold* ~, ~ with gold wire wound round it. *hang by a* ~, (fig) be in a dangerous or precarious state. **2** sth very thin, suggesting a ~: *A* ~ *of light came through the keyhole.* **3** chain or line (connecting parts of a story, etc): *lose the* ~ *of one's argument; gather up the* ~s *of a story,* bring parts of it together and relate them to one another; *pick up/ resume the* ~s, continue (after an interruption). **4** spiral ridge round a screw or bolt. ⇨ the illus at bolt. □ *vt* **1** [VP6A] pass a ~ through the eye of (a needle); put (beads, pearls, etc) on a ~; make (a chain of beads, etc) thus: ~ *a film,* put it in place (eg in a ciné-projector, ready for showing it on a screen). **2** [VP15A] ~ **one's way through,** find, pick, one's way (through a crowd, streets, etc). **3** (of hair) streak: *black hair* ~*ed with silver,* with streaks of silver hair in it. '~-**bare** /-beə(r)/ *adj* **1** (of cloth) worn thin; shabby: *a* ~*bare coat.* **2** (fig) much used and therefore uninteresting or valueless; hackneyed: ~*bare jokes/arguments.* '~-**like** *adj*

resembling a ~; long and slender.

threat /θret/ *n* [C] **1** statement of an intention to punish or hurt sb, esp if he does not do as one wishes: *utter a* ~ (*against sb*); *carry out a* ~; *be under the* ~ *of expulsion,* eg from a university. **2** *a/the* ~ **(to sb/sth) (of sth),** sign or warning of coming trouble, danger, etc: *the* ~ *to the country's economy of inflation. There was a* ~ *of rain in the dark sky.*

threaten /'θretn/ *vt,vi* **1** [VP6A,14,17] ~ **sth;** ~ **sb (with sth);** ~ **to do sth,** announce sth, using a threat; be a threat of sth to sb; use a threat (of sth) against sb: ~ *an employee with dismissal;* ~ *an enemy;* ~ *to murder sb. They* ~*ed revenge. The race was* ~*ed with extinction,* It seemed possible that all people of this race would die. **2** [VP6A,2A] give warning of: *The clouds* ~*ed rain. It* ~s *to rain.* **3** [VP2A] seem likely to occur or come: *Knowing that danger* ~*ed, the sentry kept an extra careful watch.* ~-**ing·ly** *adv*

three /θriː/ *adj, n* the number 3. ⇨ App 4: *a* ~-*act play,* one with ~ acts. ~-'**cornered** *adj* triangular: *a* ~-*cornered contest/fight,* with ~ contestants or competitors, eg in a Parliamentary election. ⇨ *straight fight* at straight '(5). ~-'**D,** (abbr for) ~-*dimensional.* ⇨ below. ~-'**decker** *n* (a) old type of sailing-ship with ~ decks. (b) kind of sandwich with ~ layers of bread and two layers of filling. (c) novel in ~ volumes (common in the 18th and 19th cc). ~-**di'mensional** *adj* (abbr **3-D**) having, or appearing to have, ~ dimensions (length, breadth and depth); stereoscopic. ~-'**figure** *adj* (of numbers) between 100 and 999 (inclusive). ~-**pence** /'θriːpens/ *n* the sum of ~ pence. ~-**penny** /'θriːpenɪ/ *adj* costing or worth ~ pence: *a* ~*penny stamp.* ~-'**lane** *adj* (of a roadway) marked for ~ lanes of traffic. ~-'**legged** /-'legɪd/ *adj* (a) having ~ legs: *a* ~-*legged stool.* (b) (of a race) one in which the competitors run in pairs, the right leg of one runner being tied to the left leg of the other. ~-'**piece** *adj* consisting of ~ pieces: *a* ~-*piece suit,* set of ~ garments (a man's jacket, waistcoat and trousers, or a woman's jacket, skirt/trousers and blouse); *a* ~-*piece suite,* set of ~ pieces of furniture (usu a sofa and two armchairs). ~-'**ply** *adj* (a) (of wool, thread) having ~ strands. (b) (of wood) having ~ layers glued together. ~-'**quarter** *n* (Rugby football) person who plays between the half-backs and the full-back. ⇨ the illus at Rugby. □ *adj* (of a portrait) down to the hips. Cf *a full-length portrait* at full(7). ~-'**score** *adj, n* sixty. '~-**some** /-səm/ *n* group of, or game played by, ~ persons. ~-'**storey(ed)** *adj* (of a building) having ~ storeys. ~-'**wheeled** *adj* having ~ wheels.

thren·ody /'θrenədɪ/ *n* (*pl* -dies) song of lamentation; funeral song.

thresh /θreʃ/ *vt,vi* [VP6A,15A,2A] beat the grain out of (wheat, etc); beat wheat, etc for this purpose: ~ *corn by hand. Have the farmers started* ~*ing yet?* '~-**ing-floor** *n* part on which grain is ~ed out. '~-**ing-machine** *n* one for ~ing grain. ~-**er** *n* **1** ~ing-machine; person who ~es. **2** large shark with a long tail.

thresh·old /'θreʃhəʊld/ *n* [C] **1** stone or plank under an outside doorway; part of an entrance over which one must step: *cross the* ~, enter. **2** (fig) entrance, start, beginning: *He was on the* ~ *of his career. We are at the* ~ *of an era of peace.* **3** (physiol, psych) limit: *a pain* ~, point at which a sensation is felt as pain; *above/below the* ~ *of consciousness*, above/below the limit at which we are aware of things. ⇨ **subliminal.**

threw /θruː/ *pt* of **throw**¹.

thrice /θraɪs/ *adv* (rarely used) three times.

thrift /θrɪft/ *n* [U] care, economy, in the use of money or goods. ~**y** *adj* (-ier, -iest) **1** economical; using ~. **2** (US) thriving; prosperous. ~**·ily** /-ɪlɪ/ *adv* ~**·less** *adj* without ~; wasteful. ~**·less·ly** *adv* ~**·less·ness** *n*

thrill /θrɪl/ *n* [C] (experience causing an) excited feeling passing like a wave along the nerves: *a* ~ *of joy/pleasure/horror. It gave her quite a* ~ *to shake hands with the Princess. This film will give you the* ~ *of a lifetime*, excite you as you have never been excited before. □ *vt,vi* **1** [VP6A] cause a ~ or ~s in: *The film* ~*ed the audience. We were* ~*ed with horror/joy.* **2** [VP2A,C] feel a ~ or ~s: *We* ~*ed at the good news. She* ~*ed with delight when the handsome footballer kissed her. There was a* ~*ing finish to the race.* ~**er** *n* novel, play or film in which excitement and emotional appeal are the essential elements.

thrive /θraɪv/ *vi* (*pt* ~d or (archaic) throve /θrəʊv/, *pp* ~d or (archaic) thriven /'θrɪvn/) [VP2A,3A] ~ **(on sth)**, prosper; succeed; grow strong and healthy: *A business cannot* ~ *without good management. Children* ~ *on good food. He has a thriving business.*

thro' /θruː/ (informal spelling of) **through.**

throat /θrəʊt/ *n* **1** front part of the neck: *grip sb by the* ~; *cut one's* ~, eg intending to commit suicide or (fig) destroy one's own opportunities. ⇨ the illus at **head**. **'cut-**~ *attrib adj* (**a**) (of a razor) having a long movable blade set into the handle, ⇨ the illus at **razor.** (**b**) (of competition, etc) intense and ruthless. **2** passage in the neck through which food passes to the stomach and air to the lungs: *A bone has stuck in my* ~. **force/thrust sth down sb's** ~, (fig) try to make sb accept one's views, beliefs, etc. **stick in one's** ~, (fig) won't be readily acceptable. ~**ed** in compounds: *a red-*~*ed bird.* ~**y** *adj* (-ier, -iest) uttered deep in the ~: *a* ~*y voice*, guttural.

throb /θrɒb/ *vi* (-bb-) [VP2A,C] (of the heart, pulse, etc) beat, esp beat more rapidly than usual: *His head* ~*bed*, He had a bad headache. *His wound* ~*bed with pain. Her heart was* ~*bing with excitement.* □ *n* [C] ~bing or vibration: ~*s of joy/ pleasure; the* ~ *of distant gun-fire.* ~**·bing** *adj* that ~s: *the* ~*bing* (*sound of*) *machinery.*

throe /θrəʊ/ *n* ~**s**, sharp pains, esp of childbirth. **in the** ~**s of sth/of doing sth**, (colloq) struggling with the task of it/doing it: *in the* ~*s of an examination/of packing one's luggage.*

throm·bo·sis /θrɒm'bəʊsɪs/ *n* [U] clot of blood in a blood-vessel or in the heart.

throne /θrəʊn/ *n* [C] **1** ceremonial chair or seat of a king, queen, bishop, etc. **2 the** ~, royal authority: *come to the* ~, become king/queen; *united in loyalty to the T*~, to the Sovereign.

throng /θrɒŋ *US:* θrɔːŋ/ *n* crowd. □ *vt,vi* [VP6A,4A,2C] crowd: *The railway stations were* ~*ed with people going away for their holidays. People* ~*ed to see the new play.*

throstle /'θrɒsl/ *n* song-thrush.

throttle /'θrɒtl/ *vt,vi* **1** [VP6A] seize (sb) by the throat and stop his breathing; choke; strangle: ~ *the nightwatchman and then rob the bank. The tyrant* ~*d freedom in his country.* **2**

[VP6A,15B,2C] ~ **(back/down)**, control the flow of steam, petrol vapour, etc in an engine; lessen the speed of (an engine) by doing this. □ *n* '~**(-valve)**, valve controlling the flow of steam, petrol vapour, etc in an engine: *open out the* ~; *close the* ~; *with the* ~ *full open.*

through¹ /θruː/ *adv* (⇨ the *v* entries; specimens only here) **1** from end to end, beginning to end, side to side: *They wouldn't let us* ~, eg pass ~ the gate. *Did your brother get* ~, eg the examination? *He slept the whole night* ~, all night. *His trousers are* ~ (= have holes or rents in them) *at the knees. Read the book* ~ *carefully. all* ~, all the time (while sth was happening, etc): *I knew all* ~ *that he was lying.* **2** to the very end. **be** ~ **(with)**, (**a**) finish (with): *When will you be* ~ *with your work?* (**b**) (colloq) have had enough of; be tired of: *I'm* ~ *with this job; I must find something more interesting.* **go** ~ **with sth**, continue until it is finished or completed. **see sth** ~, be present at, help in, a series of events, etc until the end. ~ **and** ~, in all parts; completely: *He's a reliable man* ~ *and* ~. *You're wet* ~/~ *and* ~, Your clothes are thoroughly wet. **3** all the way to: *This train goes* ~ *to Paris*, There is no need to change trains. *Book your tickets/luggage* ~ *to Vienna.* **4** (telephoning) (**a**) (GB) connected: *I will put you* ~ *to the manager*, connect you. *You're* ~, Your telephone connection has been made. (**b**) (US) finished; not wishing to continue the call. **5** (used, in the sense of **3** above, to modify *nn*): *a* ~ *train to Paris;* ~ *tickets/passengers/fares;* ~ *traffic*, road traffic which is going ~ a place (contrasted with local traffic). '~**·put** /-pʊt/ *n* [U,C] output; amount of material put ~ a process. '~**·way** *n* ~ express way. ⇨ **express**¹(2).

through² (US in informal writing also **thru**) /θruː/ *prep* **1** (of places) from end to end or side to side of; entering at one side, on one surface, etc and coming out at the other: *The River Thames flows* ~ *London. The burglar came in* ~ *the window. The road goes* ~ *the forest. There is a path* ~ (= across) *the fields. She passed a comb/her fingers* ~ *her hair. He was looking* ~ *a telescope. One can see* ~ *glass.* **2** (fig uses; ⇨ the *v* entries; specimens only here): *He went* ~/*has come* ~ (= experienced) *many hardships. He soon got/went* ~ (= got to the end of, spent the whole of) *his fortune. We must go* ~ (= examine) *the accounts. He got* ~ (= passed) *the examination. He saw* ~ (= was not deceived by) *the trick.* **3** (of time) from beginning to end of: *He won't live* ~ *the night*, The children are too young to sit ~ a long concert. **4** (US) up to and including: *We'll be in London from Tuesday* ~ *Saturday.* **5** (indicating the agency, means or cause): *I learnt of the position* ~ *a newspaper advertisement. The accident happened* ~ *no fault of yours. We lost ourselves* ~ *not knowing the way. It was all* ~ *you* (= It was your fault) *that we were late.* **6** without stopping for: *Don't drive* ~ *a red light.*

through·out /θruː'aʊt/ *adv* right through; in every part; in all ways or respects: *The coat is lined with fur* ~. *The woodwork in the house was rotten* ~. □ *prep* all or right through; from end to end of: ~ *the country;* ~ *the length and breadth of the land;* ~ *the war.*

throve /θrəʊv/ ⇨ **thrive.**

throw¹ /θrəʊ/ *vt,vi* (*pt* threw /θruː/, *pp* thrown /θrəʊn/) (For special uses with *adverbial particles*

and *preps*, ⇨ **12** below) **1**
[VP2A,6A,15A,B,12A,13A] cause (sth) to go
through the air, usu with force, by a movement of
the arm or by mechanical means: *He ~s well. He
can ~ a hundred yards. Don't ~ stones at my dog!
He threw the ball to his sister. Please ~ me that
towel. He threw the ball up and caught it. He
seized the man and threw him to the ground. The
drunken man was thrown out. He threw an angry
look at me/me an angry look.* **2** [VP15A,B] put (articles of clothing) (*on, off, over*, etc) quickly or
carelessly: *~ off one's clothes/disguise: ~ a scarf
over one's shoulders.* **3** [VP15A,B] move (one's
arms, legs, etc) (*out, up, down, about*) violently:
*~ one's chest out; ~ up one's arms; ~ one's head
back. You'll never learn to swim properly while
you ~ your legs and arms about so wildly.* **4**
[VP6A] **(a)** (of a horse) cause the rider to fall to the
ground: *Two of the jockeys were ~n in the second
race.* **(b)** (of a wrestler) force (an opponent) to the
floor. **(c)** (of a snake) cast (its skin). **(d)** (of animals) bring forth (young). **5** [VP6A] (of dice) ~ on
to the table (after shaking them in sth); get by doing
this: *~ three sixes.* **6** [VP6A] twist (silk) into
threads. **7** [VP6A] shape (pottery on a potter's
wheel). **8** [VP6A] (colloq) disturb; distress; distract: *The news of her death really threw me.* **9** (sl)
~ a party, give a party. *~ a fit*, have a fit. ⇨
fit³(2). **10** *~ sth open (to)*, [VP22] **(a)** make (eg a
competition) open to all persons. **(b)** allow the
general public to enter (eg gardens which are usually closed). **11** [VP6A] (with *nn*, to which cross-
references are given): *~ cold water on sth*, ⇨
water¹(1). *~ doubt upon*, ⇨ doubt(1). *~ dust
in sb's eyes*, ⇨ dust¹(1). *~ down the gauntlet*,
⇨ gauntlet. *~ light on*, ⇨ light¹(6). *~ a sop to
Cerberus*, ⇨ sop. *~ one's weight about*, ⇨
weight. **12** [VP15B,3C] (special uses with *adverbial particles* and *preps*):
throw sth about, scatter: *Don't ~ waste paper
about in the park. He's ~ing his money about*,
(fig) spending it recklessly.
throw oneself at, **(a)** rush violently at. **(b)** force
one's attentions on; behave without restraint in an
effort to win the love of.
throw sth away, **(a)** lose by foolishness or neglect: *~ away an advantage. My advice was ~n
away upon him*, wasted. **(b)** (of words spoken by
actors, broadcasters, etc) utter in a casual way,
with conscious under-emphasis. Hence, '*~·away*
n sth that may be ~n away (eg a printed handbill);
sth of small value, discarded after use: (attrib) *a
~-away ballpen; a ~-away line*, sth spoken casually, without emphasis.
throw back, show characteristics of, revert to, a
remote ancestor. Hence, '*~-back n* (example of)
reversion to an ancestral type. *~ sb back on/
upon sth*, (often passive) force sb to go back to
(because nothing else is available): *After this failure to get help we were ~n back upon our own resources.*
throw oneself down, lie down at full length.
throw sth in, **(a)** supply sth extra, without an addition to the price: *You can have the piano for £60,
with the stool ~n in.* **(b)** put in (a remark, etc) casually. **(c)** (football) ~ the ball in after it has gone
out of play. Hence, '*~-in n. ~ in one's hand*,
give up an attempt to do sth; confess one's inability
to do sth. *~ in one's lot with sb*, decide to share
his fortunes. *~ in the towel/sponge*, (colloq)

(from boxing) admit defeat. *~ oneself into sth*,
begin to work vigorously at.
throw sb/sth off, manage to get rid of; become
free from: *~ off a cold/a troublesome
acquaintance/one's pursuers. ~ sth off*, produce
or compose, easily, as if without effort: *~ off a few
lines of verse.*
throw oneself on/upon sb/sth, place one's reliance on: *~ oneself (up)on the mercy of one's
captors/the court/the judge.*
throw sth out, **(a)** utter (esp casually): *~ out a
hint/suggestion; ~ out a challenge.* **(b)** reject (a
Bill in Parliament, etc). **(c)** build as an extension:
~ out a new wing, eg to a hospital or other large
building. *~ sb out*, **(a)** (cricket, of a fielder) get (a
batsman) out by ~ing the ball and hitting the wicket. **(b)** disconcert or distract (sb whose attention is
concentrated on sth) so that he makes an error, has
to stop, etc: *Keep quiet for a while or you'll ~ me
out in my calculations.*
throw sb over, desert, abandon: *~ over an old
friend/one's girlfriend.*
throw sth together, assemble hastily: *That last
textbook of his seems to have been ~n together*,
written or compiled carelessly and hurriedly. *~
people together*, bring together: *Chance had ~n
us together at a skiing resort.*
throw sth up, **(a)** vomit (food). **(b)** resign from: *~
up one's job. ~ sth up*, bring it to notice: *A search
through his pockets threw up a very strange collection of objects. ~ up one's hands (in horror)*, express horror by doing this.
throw² /θrəʊ/ *n* [C] throwing; distance to which
sth is or may be thrown: *a well-aimed ~*, eg cricket, to get a batsman out; *a ~ of the dice; a record
~ with the hammer* (as a competition in athletic
sports). *within a'stone's ~ (of)*, quite near (to).
thru /θru:/ (US informal spelling for) through.
thrum /θrʌm/ *vt,vi* (-mm-) [VP6A,3A] *~ (on)
sth*, play monotonously or idly on (a stringed instrument): *~ (on) a guitar*, ⇨ strum; tap or drum
idly with the fingers: *~ on the table.*
thrush¹ /θrʌʃ/ *n* [C] sorts of song-bird, esp the
kind called '*song-~*, or throstle.
thrush² /θrʌʃ/ *n* internal inflammatory disease.
thrust /θrʌst/ *vt,vi* (*pt,pp ~*) [VP6A,15A,B,2A,C]
push suddenly or violently; make a forward stroke
with a sword, etc: *He ~ his hands into his
pockets/a dagger into his enemy's heart. We had
to ~ our way through the crowd. They ~ themselves forward/past into the bus. Some people have
greatness ~ upon them*, ie obtain renown without
their own effort. *He has ~ himself into a well-paid
position*, obtained one by ruthless methods. □ *n* **1**
[C] act of ~ing; (in war) strong attempt to push
forward into the enemy's positions; (in debate, etc)
attack in words; hostile remark aimed at sb. **2** [U]
stress or pressure on a neighbouring part of a structure (eg an arch); force directed forward in a jet-
engine as a reaction to the ejection rearward of
gases. *~er n* (esp) person who ~s himself forward
(to win an advantage, etc).
thud /θʌd/ *n* dull sound as of a blow on sth soft:
*The bullet entered his brain and he fell with a ~ to
the carpet.* □ *vi* (-dd-) [VP2C] strike, fall, with a
~: *Bullets ~ded into the sandbags behind which
we were sheltering.*
thug /θʌg/ *n* violent criminal; murderous ruffian.
~-gery n [U].
thumb /θʌm/ *n* short, thick finger set apart from

the other four. ⇨ the illus at **arm**. *(one's fingers)* **be all ~s; have ten ~s,** be very clumsy. *rule of* **~,** method or procedure based on experience and practice. **under sb's ~,** under his influence and control. **~s up/down,** (phrase signifying success/failure). **~-nail sketch,** portrait on a small scale; hasty word-picture. '**~-screw** *n* (a) (also '**~-nut**) one that can be turned easily with the ~ and a finger. (b) old instrument of torture which squeezed the ~s. '**~-stall** *n* sheath to cover an injured ~. '**~-tack** *n* (US) drawing-pin. □ *vt* 1 [VP6A] turn over (pages, etc); make dirty by doing this: ~ *the pages of a dictionary; a well-~ed book.* 2 ~ *a lift,* ask for (and get) a free ride in a motor-vehicle (by signalling to the driver). ⇨ hitch-hike. ~ *one's nose at sb,* cock a snook at him. ⇨ snook.

thump /θʌmp/ *vt,vi* [VP6A,15A,22,2A,C,3A] strike heavily, esp with the fists; deliver heavy blows: *He ~ed (on) the door. She ~ed the cushion flat. His heart was ~ing with excitement. The two boys began to ~ one another. He was ~ing the keys of the piano/~ing out a tune on the piano,* playing noisily. □ *n* [C] (noise of, or as of, a) heavy blow (esp one given with the fist): *I dislike being given a friendly ~ on the back. The baby fell out of its cot with a ~.* **~-ing** *adj* (colloq) of great size. ⇨ *adv* (colloq) extremely: *What a ~ing great lie!*

thun·der /'θʌndə(r)/ *n* 1 [U] noise which usu follows a flash of lightning: *a loud crash/a long roll of ~. There's ~ in the air,* T~ *seems likely. We haven't had much ~ this summer.* '**~-bolt** *n* flash of lightning with a crash of ~; (fig) unexpected and terrible event. '**~-clap** *n* crash of ~; sth that comes like ~; sudden, terrible event, bad news, etc. '**~-storm** *n* storm of ~ and lightning, usu with heavy rain. '**~-struck** *adj* (pred; fig) amazed. 2 [U,C] loud noise like or suggesting ~: *the ~ of the guns; ~s of applause.* **steal sb's ~,** spoil his attempt to be impressive by anticipating him. □ *vi,vt* 1 [VP2A,C] (impersonal): *It was ~ing and lightening.* 2 [VP2C] make a noise like ~: *Someone was ~ing at the door,* beating at it. *The train ~ed through the station. The juggernauts ~ed past.* 3 [VP2C,3A,15B] ~ *(out) (against),* speak in a loud voice, attack violently sounding like, ~: *~ous applause.* **~y** /-dərɪ/ *adj* (of weather) giving signs of ~.

thu·rible /'θjʊərəbl *US:* 'θʊər-/ *n* = censer.

Thurs·day /'θɜːzdɪ/ *n* fifth day of the week.

thus /ðʌs/ *adv* in this way; so: ~ *far,* to this point.

thwack /θwæk/ *vt, n* = whack.

thwart[1] /θwɔːt/ *n* seat across a rowing-boat for an oarsman.

thwart[2] /θwɔːt/ *vt* [VP6A] obstruct, frustrate: ~ *sb's plans; be ~ed in one's ambitions/aims.*

thy /ðaɪ/ *adj* (archaic) your. **thine** /ðaɪn/ *adj* (archaic) (before a vowel sound) your. □ *pron* yours. **thy·self** /ðaɪ'self/ *reflex, emph pron* (archaic) yourself.

thyme /taɪm/ *n* [U] kinds of herb with fragrant aromatic leaves, growing wild and in gardens, used in cookery.

thy·roid /'θaɪrɔɪd/ *n* ~ **(gland),** gland in the front part of the neck, producing a substance which affects the body's growth and activity. ⇨ the illus at head.

ti /tiː/ *n* seventh note in the musical octave.

ti·ara /tɪ'ɑːrə/ *n* [C] 1 coronet for a woman. 2 triple

crown worn by the Pope.

tibia /'tɪbɪə/ *n* (*pl* ~e /-biː/) (anat) shin-bone; inner and thicker of the two bones between the knee and the foot. ⇨ the illus at skeleton.

tic /tɪk/ *n* involuntary, spasmodic twitching of the muscles (esp of the face).

tick[1] /tɪk/ *n* [C] 1 light, regularly repeated sound, esp of a clock or watch. **~-'tock** *n* ~ing sound (of a clock, etc). 2 (colloq) moment: *I'll be with you in two ~s. Half a ~!* Just a moment! 3 small mark (often √) put against names, figures, etc in a list or to show that sth is correct. 4 '**~-tack** *n* system of signalling (a kind of hand semaphore) used by bookmakers' assistants on race-courses. □ *vi,vt* 1 [VP2A,C] (of a clock, etc) make ~s(1): *The child put the watch to its ear and listened to it ~ing. The taxi's meter was ~ing away. What makes sb/sth ~,* (colloq) What makes him/it function, act, behave, etc in the way he/it does? 2 [VP15B] ~ **away,** (of a clock): ~ *away the minutes,* mark their passing with ~s(1). 3 [VP2C] ~ **over,** (of an internal-combustion engine) operate slowly with gears disconnected (and the vehicle stationary). 4 [VP6A,10] ~ **sth (off),** put a ~(3) against: ~ *off a name/the items on a list.* ~ **sb off,** (colloq) rebuke, scold him: *get ~ed off; give sb a good ~ing-'off.*

tick[2] /tɪk/ *n* small spider-like parasite that fastens itself on the skin, eg of dogs, and sucks blood. ⇨ the illus at arachnid.

tick[3] /tɪk/ *n* 1 [C] outside cover of stout striped linen for a mattress, bolster or pillow. 2 [U] (also ~-ing) material used for ~s.

tick[4] /tɪk/ *n* [U] (colloq) credit(1): *buy goods on ~; get ~.*

ticker /'tɪkə(r)/ *n* [C] 1 telegraphic machine which automatically prints news (esp stock market prices) on paper tape (called '**~-tape**): *get a ~-tape reception,* eg in New York City, of a visiting celebrity in a procession through the streets, be welcomed with streamers of ~-tape thrown from office windows, etc. ⇨ the illus at tape. 2 (colloq) watch. 3 (sl) heart: *a dicky ~,* a weak heart.

ticket /'tɪkɪt/ *n* [C] 1 written or printed piece of card or paper giving the holder the right to travel in a train, bus, ship, etc or to a seat in a cinema, concert hall, etc: *Do you want a single or a return ~* (US = *one-way* or *round-trip ~)? Admission by ~ only,* (as a notice outside a hall, etc). '**~-collector** *n* person who collects ~s (esp railway ~s). 2 piece of card or paper, label, attached to sth and giving information, eg about the price, size of clothing, etc. 3 (US) list of candidates to be voted on, belonging to one political party: *vote the straight ~,* cast the ballot on strict party lines. 4 printed notice of an offence against traffic regulations (eg a parking offence): *get a ~.* 5 **the ~,** (dated sl) the proper thing to do. 6 ~ **of leave,** (archaic) parole. 7 certificate listing the qualifications of a pilot, a ship's mate, etc. □ *vt* [VP6A] put a ~(2) on; mark with a ~.

tick·ing /'tɪkɪŋ/ *n* ⇨ tick[3].

tickle /'tɪkl/ *vt,vi* 1 [VP6A,2A] excite the nerves of the skin by touching lightly, esp at sensitive parts, often so as to cause laughter: ~ *sb in the ribs. The rough blanket ~s (me).* 2 [VP6A] please (one's sense of humour, etc): *The story ~d her fancy. I was ~d to death/~d pink,* (colloq, very amused and delighted) *at the news. They ~d his vanity by praising his work to the skies.* 3 [VP2A,6A] have, feel, cause, an itching or tingling sensation: *Pepper ~s if it gets into the nose. My nose ~s. It ~d my nose.* **tick·ler** /'tɪklə(r)/ *n* (colloq) puzzle. **tick·lish** /'tɪklɪʃ/ *adj* 1 (of a person) easily made to laugh or wriggle when ~d. 2 (of a problem, piece of work, etc) needing delicate care or attention: *a ticklish question; in a ticklish situation.*

ti·dal /'taɪdl/ *adj* of a tide or tides: *a ~ river/ estuary/harbour,* in which the tide rises and falls. '~ **wave** *n* great ocean wave, often destructive of life and property, eg one that is (thought to be) caused by an earthquake; (fig) great wave of popular feeling (enthusiasm, indignation, etc).

tid·bit /'tɪdbɪt/ *n* (US) = titbit.

tid·dler /'tɪdlə(r)/ *n* (colloq) 1 very small fish. 2 young small child.

tid·dley /'tɪdlɪ/ *adj* (colloq) 1 small; negligible. 2 tipsy; slightly drunk.

tid·dly·winks /'tɪdlɪwɪŋks/ *n* [U] game in which players try to make small discs or counters jump into a tray or cup in the centre of a table by pressing them on the edge with a larger disc.

tide /taɪd/ *n* 1 [C,U] regular rise and fall in the level of the sea, caused by the attraction of the moon: *at high/low ~; washed up by the ~(s); spring* (= maximum) *and neap* (= minimum) *~s.* '~**mark** *n* highest point reached by a ~ on a beach. '~**way** *n* channel where ~s run; ebb or flow in such a channel. 2 [C] flow or tendency of (public opinion, feeling, etc): *We must not ignore the rising ~ of public discontent. The Socialists hoped for a turn of the ~,* that public opinion might turn in their favour. 3 (old use) season (now only in compounds, as '*Easter~,* '*even~,* '*Whitsun~*) □ *vt* [VP14,15B] ~ *sb over (sth),* get over; help him to get through or survive (a period of difficulty, etc): *He sold his car to ~ himself over his period of unemployment,* to provide money for his needs. *She needs more coal to ~ her over the winter. Will £5 ~ you over until you get your wages?*

tid·ings /'taɪdɪŋz/ *n pl* (archaic) news: *Have you heard the glad ~?*

tidy /'taɪdɪ/ *adj* (-ier, -iest) 1 arranged neatly and in order; having the habit of placing and keeping everything in its right place: *a ~ room/desk; a ~ boy; ~ habits.* 2 (colloq) considerable; fairly large (esp of money): *a ~ sum of money; cost a ~ penny,* quite a lot of money. □ *n* (pl -dies) receptacle for odds and ends: *a '*hair*~,* eg on a dressing-table for hair from a hair-brush; *a '*sink*~,* for bits of kitchen waste. □ *vt,vi* [VP6A,15B,2A,C] ~ *(up),* make ~: *I must ~ myself,* make myself look ~. *You'd better ~ up (the room) before the guests arrive.* **ti·dily** /'taɪdɪlɪ/ *adv* **ti·di·ness** *n*

tie[1] /taɪ/ *n* [C] 1 sth used for fastening; rod or beam holding parts of a structure together; (US) railway sleeper, ⇨ *sleeper*(2) at sleep[2]; (fig) sth that holds people together: *the ties of friendship; family ties; ties of blood.* 2 sth that takes up one's attention and limits one's freedom of action: *Mothers often find their small children a tie.* 3 equal score in a game, etc: *The game ended in a tie, 2—2. The tie will be played off* (= will be replayed) *on Saturday.* 4 (music) curved line joining two notes of the same pitch that are to be played or sung as one. ⇨ the illus at notation. 5 = necktie.

tie[2] /taɪ/ *vt,vi* (*pres p* tying, *pt,pp* tied) 1 [VP6A,15A,B] fasten or bind (with string, rope, wire, etc): *tie a man's feet together; tie up a*

parcel; *tie a branch down; tie a dog to the street railings.* **tie sb down,** restrict sb's freedom: *He's not in a hurry to get married; he doesn't want to get tied down. Young children do tie a woman down, don't they?* **tie sb down to sth,** restrict sb to (the terms of a contract, etc). **tie oneself down to sth,** accept limits to one's freedom of action. **tie (sth) in with sth,** link, be linked, with: *Doesn't this tie in with what we were told last week?* Aren't the two things linked, connected? **tie sth up,** (a) invest (capital) so that it is not easily available, eg because of legal restrictions. (b) ensure that (property, eg land, buildings) can be used, sold, etc only under certain (usu legal) conditions. **be/ get tied up (with sth/sb),** (a) be, get, involved (with sth/sb) so that one has no time for other things: *I'm afraid I can't help you now—I'm too tied up with other things.* (b) be, become, linked with: *Isn't this company tied up with Vickers-Armstrong?* Hence, '**tie-up** *n* link; merger; partnership. **tied house,** (GB) public house controlled by a particular brewery. ⇨ *free house* at free[1](3). 2 [VP6A,15B] **tie sth (on),** fasten by means of the strings, etc of: *tie an apron (on); tie on a label.* Hence, '**tie-on,** *attrib adj: a tie-on label.* 3 [VP6A,15A] arrange (a ribbon, etc) in the form of a bow or knot: *tie one's shoelaces; tie a ribbon/ scarf; tie the ribbon in(to) a bow.* 4 [VP6A,15A] make by tying: *tie a knot in a piece of string.* 5 [VP2A] be fastened: *Does this sash tie in front or at the back?* 6 [VP2A,3A] **tie (with) (for),** (of players, teams, candidates in a competitive examination) make the same score (as); equal in points, marks, etc: *The two teams tied. They tied for first place (in the examination). We tied with Arsenal in the last game.*

tier /tɪə(r)/ *n* row (esp of seats), shelf, etc esp one of a number parallel to and rising one above another, eg in a theatre or stadium: *a first/second ~ box,* in a theatre.

tiff /tɪf/ *n* slight quarrel (between friends or acquaintances): *Alice has had a ~ with her boyfriend.*

ti·ger /'taɪɡə(r)/ *n* large, fierce animal of the cat family, yellow-skinned with black stripes, found in Asia. ⇨ the illus at cat. '~**-lily** *n* garden lily with orange flowers spotted with black or purple. ~**·ish** /-ɪʃ/ *adj* like, cruel as, a ~. **ti·gress** /'taɪɡrɪs/ *n* female ~.

tight /taɪt/ *adj* (-er, -est) 1 fastened, fixed, fitting, held, closely: *a ~ knot. I can't get the cork out of the bottle—it's too ~. The drawer is so ~ that I can't open it. These shoes are so ~ that they hurt.* '~**-'lipped** *adj* keeping the lips firmly together; saying little or nothing; (fig) grim-looking. 2 closely or firmly put together; put together in a small space: *a ~ joint;* (esp in compounds) made so that sth cannot get out or in: '*water-/'air-~.* 3 packed so as to occupy the smallest possible space or to get in as much as possible: *Make sure that the bags are filled/packed ~.* 4 (colloq) having had too much alcoholic drink: *He gets ~ every payday.* 5 fully stretched: *a ~ rope.* '~**-rope** *n* one on which acrobats perform feats. 6 produced by pressure; causing difficulty. *in a ~ corner/spot,* (usu fig) in a difficult or dangerous situation. ~ **schedule,** one that it is difficult to keep to. ~ **squeeze,** condition of being uncomfortably crowded: *We got everyone into the bus, but it was a ~ squeeze.* 7 (of money) not easily obtainable, eg on loan from banks: *Money is* ~. *The money-market is* ~, It is possible to borrow money only by paying a high rate of interest. **8** ~-**'fisted** *adj* stingy; miserly. ~-**'laced** *adj* = *strait-laced.* ⇨ strait¹. '~-**wad** /-wɒd/ *n* (sl) stingy person. □ *adv* = ~ly: *squeeze/hold sth* ~. *sit* ~, ⇨ sit(1). (Note that ~ *adv* is not used before a *pp*; ~ly must be used in this position: *packed* ~, but ~*ly packed*). ~·**ly** *adv* in a ~ manner: *squeeze/hold sth* ~*ly*; ~*ly packed together*; ~*ly sealed.* ~·**ness** *n.* ~**en** /'taɪtn/ *vt,vi* [VP6A,15B,2A,C] make or become ~(er): ~**en** (*up*) *the screws*; ~**en** *the ropes of the tent. It needs* ~**ening** *up.* ~**en** *one's belt,* go without food (when there is little or none available); become frugal.

tights /taɪts/ *n pl* **1** close-fitting garment covering the hips, legs and feet, as worn by girls and women. **2** skin-tight garment covering the legs and body, worn by acrobats, ballet-dancers, etc.

tike /taɪk/ *n* = tyke.

tilde *n* **1** /'tɪldə/ the mark ~ placed over Spanish *n* when it is pronounced *ny/*nj/ (as in *cañon*). **2** /tɪld/ the mark (~) as used in this dictionary to indicate the use of a headword in an entry.

tile /taɪl/ *n* (usu square or oblong) plate of baked clay for covering roofs, walls, etc, often, eg Dutch, Italian and Portuguese ~s, painted with designs or pictures. *be* (*out*) *on the* ~*s*, (sl) be merry-making. *have a*'~ (more usu *screw*) *loose,* (sl) be rather mad. □ *vt* [VP6A] cover (a roof, etc) with ~s.

till¹ /tɪl/ (also *until* /ʌn'tɪl/) (*until* is more formal than *till*; *until* is preferred when its clause or phrase comes first) *conj* up to the time when: *Go straight on until you come to the post-office and then turn left. Let's wait* ~ *the rain stops. Until you told me, I had heard nothing of what happened. She won't go away* ~ *you promise to help her.* □ *prep* up to (the time when): *I shall wait* ~ *ten o'clock/next Monday, etc. Goodbye* ~ *tomorrow. Until now I knew/Until then I had known nothing about it. He works from morning* ~ *night, day after day. He lived at home until soon after his father's death.*

till² /tɪl/ *n* money-drawer, eg in a cash-register: *The boy was caught with his hand in the* ~, *caught stealing.*

till³ /tɪl/ *vt* [VP6A] cultivate (land). ~**age** /'tɪlɪdʒ/ *n* [U] act or process of ~ing; ~ed land. ~**er** *n* person who ~s.

tiller /'tɪlə(r)/ *n* lever (like a long handle) used to turn the rudder of a small boat. ⇨ the illus at sail.

tilt /tɪlt/ *vt,vi* **1** [VP6A,15A,B,2A,C] (cause to) come into a sloping position (as by lifting one end); tip: *Don't* ~ *the table. T*~ *the barrel* (*up*) *to empty it. The table* ~ed (*over*) *and the plates slid off it to the floor.* **2** [VP2A,3A] ~ (*at*), (hist, of men on horseback) ride (at another) with a lance; (fig) attack in speech or writing: *The reformer* ~*ed at the tax and property laws.* ~ *at windmills,* fight imaginary enemies (from the story of Don Quixote). □ *n* [C] **1** ~ing; sloping position. **2** act of ~ing with a lance: *have a* ~ *at sb,* (fig) attack him (in a friendly way) in a debate, etc. (*at*) *Quixote*). □ *n* [C] **1** ~ing; sloping position. **2** act of ~ing with a lance: *have a* ~ *at sb,* (fig) attack him (in a friendly way) in a debate, etc. (*at*) *full* ~, at great speed; with great force: *The boy ran full* ~ *into me.* '~-**yard** *n* place where ~ing was practised in former times.

tilth /tɪlθ/ *n* depth of soil affected by cultivation;

tilled land: *rake a seed-bed to a good* ~, until there is a depth of fine, crumbly soil.

tim·ber /'tɪmbə(r)/ *n* **1** [U] wood prepared for use in building, etc: '~-*merchants; a* '~-*yard,* place where ~ is stored, bought and sold, etc; *dressed* ~, sawn, shaped and planed ready for use. **2** [U] growing trees (sometimes *standing* ~) thought of as containing wood suitable for building, carpentry, etc: *cut down/fell* ~; *put a hundred acres of land under* ~, plant with trees for ~. *The fire destroyed thousands of acres of* ~. **3** [C] large piece of shaped wood, beam, forming a support (eg in a roof or a ship). **4** [U] (in fox-hunting) wooden fences and gates. ~**ed** /'tɪmbəd/ *adj* (of buildings) made of ~ or with a framework of ~.

timbre /'tæmbrə US: 'tɪmbər/ *n* characteristic quality of sound produced by a particular voice or instrument.

tim·brel /'tɪmbrəl/ *n* tambourine.

time¹ /taɪm/ *n* **1** [U] all the days of the past, present and future: *past, present and future* ~. *The world exists in space and* ~. **2** [U] the passing of all the days, months and years, taken as a whole (sometimes personified as (*old*) *Father T*~): *T*~ *will show who is right. T*~ *waits for no man,* (prov). **3** [U] (also *a* + *adj* + ~) portion or measure of ~: *Six o'clock is a point of* ~; *six hours is a period of* ~. *What a* (*long*) ~ *you've been! I had a most unpleasant* ~ *at the dentist's. That will take* ~, cannot be done soon or quickly. *I have no/not much* ~ *for sport. We have no* ~ *to lose,* we must hurry. *He spent a lot of* ~ (*in*) *getting ready. Take your* ~ *over it,* Don't hurry. *We were pressed for* ~, had not enough ~, were forced to hurry. *behind* ~, (a) late: *The train is ten minutes behind* ~. (b) behindhand: *He's always behind* ~ *with his payments. for the* ~ *being,* ⇨ be³(4). *on* ~, up to ~, not late, punctual(ly): *The train is/came in on* ~. *in* '*no* ~, very soon; very quickly. (*from/since*) ~ *immemorial;* (*from/since*) ~ *out of mind,* for a period of ~ longer than any one can remember. *gain* ~, obtain extra ~ by making excuses, deliberately using slow methods, etc. *all the* ~, (a) during the whole of the ~ in question: *I looked all over the house for that letter, and it was in my pocket all the* ~, while I was searching. (b) at all times; first and last: *He's a business man all the* ~, has no other interests in life. '*half the* ~, (a) half of the ~ available: *He did the work in four hours; I could have done it in half the* ~, in two hours. (b) for long periods of ~; (loosely) very often; nearly always: *He says he works hard, but he's day-dreaming half the* ~. **4** [U] point of ~ stated in hours and minutes of the day: *What* ~ *is it? What is the* ~? *The child can now tell the* ~. **5** [U] ~ measured in units (years, months, hours, etc): *The winner's* ~ *was 11 seconds. He ran the mile in record* ~, in a period of ~ shorter than that of any previous runner. *keep good/bad* ~, (of a clock or watch) show the hour correctly/incorrectly. *the* ~ *of day,* the hour as shown by a clock. *pass the* ~ *of day* (*with...*), exchange a greeting, say 'Good morning!', etc. **6** [U] point or period of ~ associated with, or available or suitable for, a certain event, purpose, etc: *at the* ~ *you're speaking of; by the* ~ *we reached home; last* ~ *I was there; every* ~ *I looked at her. It is*'*lunch-*~. *There is a* ~ *for everything. Now's your* ~ (= opportunity). *It's* ~ *I was going/*~ *for me to go,* I ought to leave now. *It's* ~ *somebody taught you to behave your-*

self I must bide my ∼, be patient, wait for a suitable ∼. T∼ *is up*, The ∼ allowed for something is ended. *(work, etc) against* ∼, with the greatest speed (because only a limited amount of ∼ is available). *at the same* ∼, (a) together: *to laugh and cry at the same* ∼. (b) notwithstanding; nevertheless: *He's slightly mad; at the same* ∼, *he's one of the kindest men I know. at* ∼*s; from* ∼ *to* ∼, occasionally; now and then. *at* '*all* ∼*s*, always. *at* '*your*/'*his, etc* ∼ *of life*, at your/his, etc age. *in* ∼, (a) not late; early enough: *We were in* ∼ *for the train/to catch the train. We arrived in good* ∼, with ∼ to spare. (b) sooner or later; after the passing of an indefinite period of ∼: *You will learn how to do it in* ∼. *in the nick of* ∼, ⇨ nick¹(2). *near her* ∼, (of a woman) soon to give birth to a child. *do* ∼, (colloq) undergo a period of imprisonment. *serve one's* ∼, (a) work as an apprentice for an agreed number of years: *The boy has served half his* ∼. (b) = *do* ∼, ⇨ above. *My/His, etc* ∼ *is drawing near*, I am/He is, etc near a ∼ of crisis, of some important happening, etc (according to the context). ∼ *and motion*, ⇨ motion(1). **7** [C] (Cf *twice*) occasion: *this/that/next/another* ∼; *the* ∼ *before last; for the first/last* ∼. *He failed five* ∼*s. I've told you a dozen* ∼*s* (= very often, repeatedly) *not to do that. at* '*one* ∼, during a period of past ∼, known but not mentioned: *At one* ∼ *I used to go mountain-climbing every summer. at other* ∼*s*, on other occasions. ∼ *and again;* ∼*s without number*, again and again; repeatedly. '*many a* ∼; '*many* ∼*s*, often; on many occasions. *one/two, etc at a* ∼, one/two, etc on each occasion; separately: *Hand them to me two at a* ∼. **8** (*pl*) used to indicate multiplication (but note that *twice* is used instead of *two* ∼*s*). *Three* ∼*s five is/are fifteen*, 3 × 5 = 15. *Yours is ten* ∼*s the size of mine/ten* ∼*s as large as mine*. **9** [C] (often *pl*) period of ∼, more or less definite, associated with certain events, circumstances, persons, etc: *in* '*Stuart* ∼*s*, when the Stuart kings ruled; *in the* ∼(*s*) *of the Stuarts; in* '*ancient*/*prehistoric* ∼*s. Mr Curtis was the manager in* '*my* ∼, when I was working there. *The house is old but it will last my* ∼, will serve me for the rest of my life. **10** [C] (often *pl*) the conditions of life, the circumstances, etc of a period characterized by certain qualities, etc: *We lived through terrible* ∼*s during the war years. T*∼*s are good/bad*, (often meaning that it is easy/difficult to make a living). *ahead of one's* ∼; *born before one's* ∼, having ideas too much in advance of, too enlightened for, the period in which one lives. *(even) at the* '*best of* ∼*s*, even when conditions are good: *He's an irritating fellow even at the best of* ∼*s. behind the* ∼*s*, antiquated; having out-of-date ideas, etc. *have a good* ∼, enjoy oneself. *have the* ∼ *of one's life*, (colloq) experience a period of exceptional happiness or enjoyment. **11** [U] **Greenwich/local/summer/standard** ∼, ⇨ these words. **12** [U] (music) style of rhythm depending upon the number of beats in the successive bars of a piece of music: '*common* ∼, two or four beats in a bar; '*waltz* ∼, three or six beats in a bar; also, the rate (or *tempo*) at which a piece of music is to be played. *in/out of* ∼, in/not in accordance with the ∼ of the music. *in double-quick* ∼, very quickly. *beat* ∼, show the ∼ (*tempo*, etc) by movements made with the hand or a stick (*baton*). *keep* ∼, sing or dance in ∼. **13** (compounds) '∼*-ball n* one

which slides down a staff (at an observatory to show a fixed ∼, usu noon or 1pm). '∼**-bomb** *n* designed to explode at some ∼ after being dropped, placed in position, etc. '∼**-card/-sheet** *n* one for a record of workmen's hours of work. '∼**-expired** *adj* (of soldiers and sailors) having completed the period of service. '∼**-exposure** *n* exposure of a photographic film for a ∼ longer than half a second. '∼**-fuse** *n* one that has been made to burn for a given ∼, eg to explode a bomb. '∼**-honoured** (US = **-honored**) *adj* respected because of its antiquity. '∼**-keeper** *n* (a) one who, or that which, records the ∼ spent by workers at their work. (b) (of a watch, etc) one that keeps ∼ well, etc; *a good/bad* ∼*keeper*. '∼**-lag** *n* interval of ∼ between two connected phenomena or events (eg between a flash of lightning and the thunder, or between a decision to do sth and its accomplishment). '∼**-limit** *n* limited period of ∼; last moment of this: *set a* ∼*-limit for the completion of a job*. '∼**-piece** *n* clock. '∼**-saving** *adj* serving to save ∼: *a* ∼*-saving idea*. '∼**-server** *n* one who acts, not according to principles, but according to self-interest, esp one who is always trying to please powerful people. '∼**-serving** *adj* behaving as a ∼-server: ∼*-serving politicians*. '∼**-signal** *n* signal (eg a series of pips) indicating the ∼. '∼ **slip** *n* = *time warp*. '∼**-switch** *n* switch set to operate at a desired ∼ (eg to turn a heating system on or off). '∼**-table** *n* list showing the days or hours at which events will take place, work will be done, trains etc will depart. '∼ **warp** *n* (in science fiction) breaking of past or future ∼ into present ∼. '∼**-work** *n* [U] work (esp manual work) paid for by the hour or day (contrasted with *piece-work*).

time² /taɪm/ *vt* **1** [VP6A,15A] choose the time or moment for; arrange the time of: *He* ∼*d his journey so that he arrived before dark. The remark was well/ill* ∼*d*, made at a suitable/an unsuitable moment. **2** [VP6A] measure the time taken by or for (a race, runner, an action or event). **3** [VP6A] regulate: ∼ *one's steps* (in dancing) *to the music;* ∼ *the speed of a machine.* **tim·ing** *n* [U] act of determining or regulating the (order of) occurrence of an action, event, etc to achieve the desired results: *a* '*timing device;* (theatre) speed of dialogue/cues, etc: *The timing in last night's performance was excellent.* ∼**·less** *adj* (liter) unending; not to be thought of as having duration.

time·ly /'taɪmlɪ/ *adj* (-ier, -iest) occurring at just the right time; opportune. **time·li·ness** *n* [U].

timid /'tɪmɪd/ *adj* easily frightened; shy: *That fellow is as* ∼ *as a rabbit.* ∼**·ly** *adv* ∼**·ity** /tɪ'mɪdətɪ/, ∼**·ness** *nn* [U].

tim·or·ous /'tɪmərəs/ *adj* (liter) timid. ∼**·ly** *adv*

tim·othy /'tɪməθɪ/ *n* [U] '∼ **(grass)**, grass grown as fodder for cattle.

tim·pani /'tɪmpənɪ/ *n pl* set of kettledrums (eg of an orchestra). ⇨ the illus at percussion. **tim·pan·ist** /'tɪmpənɪst/ *n* player of a kettledrum.

tin /tɪn/ *n* **1** [U] soft, white metal (symbol Sn) used in alloys and for coating iron sheets. '**tin-foil** *n* [U] tin in the form of foil (thin pliable sheets), used for wrapping and packing. (**little**) **tin god**, (colloq) sth or sb mistakenly given great veneration or worship. ∼ **hat**, (sl) steel helmet (as worn by soldiers in modern times). '**tin-plate** *n* [U] sheet iron coated with tin (used in the canning industry). '**tin-smith** *n* worker in tin-plate. '**tin-tack** *n* short nail of tinned iron. **2** [C] tin-plated container for food, etc esp one made so as to be air-tight (US = can): *a tin of sardines/oil.* (Cf *a can of beer).* **'tin-opener** *n* device for opening tins. □ *vt* (-nn-) [VP6A] **1** put a coating of tin on. **2** pack (food, etc) in tins(2) (US = can): *tinned peaches.* **tinny** *adj* of or like tin (eg in sound): *a tinny piano.*

tinc·ture /'tɪŋktʃə(r)/ *n* **1** medical substance dissolved in alcohol: ~ *of iodine/quinine.* **2 a** ~ *(of),* slight flavour or suggestion (of). □ *vt* give a ~(2) of (sth) to: *teachings* ~*d with heresy.*

tin·der /'tɪndə(r)/ *n* [U] material (eg dry, scorched linen, etc) that easily catches fire from a spark. '~**-box** *n* box containing ~, flint and steel (as used in former times for kindling fire).

tine /taɪn/ *n* point, prong (eg of a fork, harrow, etc); branch of a deer's antler. ⇨ the illus at large. ~*d* /-taɪnd/ *suff* (in compounds) having the number or kind of ~s indicated: *a three-*~*d hayfork.*

ting /tɪŋ/ *vi,vt, n* (cause to make, make, a) clear, ringing sound.

tinge /tɪndʒ/ *vt* [VP6A,14] ~ *sth (with),* **1** colour slightly (with red, etc). **2** (esp in *pp*) affect slightly: *admiration* ~*d with envy.* □ *n* slight colouring or mixture (*of*): *There was a* ~ *of sadness in her voice/of irony in his remark.*

tingle /'tɪŋgl/ *vi* [VP2A,C] have a pricking or stinging feeling in the skin; (fig) be stirred: *His cheek* ~*d from the slap she had given him. His fingers* ~*d with the cold. The children were tingling with excitement.* □ *n* tingling feeling: *have a* ~ *in one's finger-tips.*

tin·ker /'tɪŋkə(r)/ *n* **1** worker with metal who travels from place to place and repairs kettles, pans, etc. **not care/give a** ~**'s cuss/damn,** not care in the least. **2** ~ing: *have an hour's* ~ *at the radio set,* try to mend it. □ *vi* [VP2A,C,3A] ~ *(at/ with),* work in an amateurish or inexpert way (at): ~ *(away) at a broken machine. Please don't* ~ *with my car engine.*

tinkle /'tɪŋkl/ *vi,vt* [VP2A,C,6A] (cause to) make a succession of light, ringing sounds, eg of a small bell. □ *n* (*sing*) such sounds: *the* ~ *of a bell/of falling glass/of ice being stirred round in a glass.*

tinny /'tɪnɪ/ *adj* ⇨ tin.

tin pan alley /,tɪn pæn 'ælɪ/ *n* composers, players and publishers of popular music (as a group).

tin·sel /'tɪnsl/ *n* [U] **1** glittering metallic substance made in sheets, strips and threads, used for ornament: *trim a Christmas tree/a dress with* ~. **2** superficial; cheap, showy brilliance. ~**ly** /-səlɪ/ *adj* trimmed with, suggesting, ~. □ *vt* (-ll-, US also -l-) trim with ~.

tint /tɪnt/ *n* (esp pale or delicate) shade or variety of colour: ~s *of green in the sky at dawn; an artist who excels at '*flesh-~s. □ *vt* [VP6A,22] give a ~ to; put a ~ on; tinge.

tin·tin·nab·u·la·tion /,tɪntɪn,æbjʊ'leɪʃn/ *n* [U] tinkling of bells.

tiny /'taɪnɪ/ *adj* (-ier, -iest) very small.

tip¹ /tɪp/ *n* [C] **1** pointed or thin end of sth: *the tips of one's fingers/one's '*finger-tips*; the tip of one's nose; asparagus tips. The bird measured 12 inches from tip to tip,* from the tip of one wing to the tip of the other. **(have sth) on the tip of one's tongue,** (be) just going to say (it). **,tip-'top** *adj, adv* (dated colloq) first-rate: *a tip-top hotel/dinner. You've done tip-top.* **2** small piece put at the end of sth: *cigarettes with filter-tips.* □ *vt* (-pp-) supply with a tip(2): *filter-tipped cigarettes.*

tip² /tɪp/ *vt,vi* (-pp-) **1** [VP6A,15A,B,2A,C] tip

(sth) (up), (cause to) rise, lean or tilt on one side or at one end: *The table tipped up. Tip the barrel up and empty it.* **tip sth** *(over),* (cause to) overbalance or overturn: *Careful! You'll tip the canoe over.* **tip the scale (at),** (**a**) be just enough to cause one scale or pan (of a balance) to go lower than the other; (fig) be the deciding factor (for or against). (**b**) weigh: *He tipped the scale at 140 lb.* **tip-up seat,** seat with a hinge, eg the kind used in cinemas, etc to allow people to pass freely. **2** [VP6A,15A,B] **tip sth (out); tip sth (out of sth) (into sth),** empty (the contents of sth) out/out of/into: *No rubbish to be tipped (out) here,* a warning put up in open spaces. *She tipped the slops out of the bucket into the sink. He was tipped out of the cart into the ditch. Which is better, to incinerate the rubbish from our towns or to tip it into disused quarries?* □ *n* (not US) place where rubbish may be tipped(2): *the municipal '*refuse tip*;* hill of waste material from a coalmine, etc; (colloq) untidy place: *They live in a tip.*

tip³ /tɪp/ *vt* (-pp-) [VP6A] **1** touch or strike lightly: *His bat just tipped the ball.* **,tip-and-'run** *adj* (of a raid by robbers, etc) in which there is a brief attack followed by a quick escape. **2** [VP6A,12C] give a tip to (1,2 below): *tip the porter 50p.* **tip sb off,** (colloq) give him a warning or a hint. Hence, **'tip-off** *n* hint or warning: *give the police a tip-off.* **tip sb the wink,** (colloq) give him special information; warn him secretly. **tip the winner,** name the winner (usu of a horse-race) before the event takes place. □ *n* [C] **1** gift of money to a porter, waiter, taxi-driver, etc for personal services: *leave a 50p tip,* eg at a restaurant. **2** piece of advice on how to do sth, esp information about the probable winner of a horse-race, on the future value of shares (on the Stock Exchange, etc): *a tip for the Derby. If you take my tip* (= advice) *you'll make a lot of money.* **3** light blow; tap.

tip·pet /'tɪpɪt/ *n* (archaic) scarf or long fur worn by a woman round the neck and shoulders with the ends hanging down to the waist in front; similar article of dress worn by judges, clergy, etc. ⇨ the illus at vestment.

tipple /'tɪpl/ *vi,vt* **1** [VP2A] be in the habit of drinking alcoholic liquor. **2** [VP6A] drink (wine, spirits, etc). □ *n* [U] alcoholic drink; (hum) any kind of drink: *John's favourite* ~ *is lager; mine is sherry.* **tip·pler** *n*

tip·staff /'tɪpstɑ:f US: -stæf/ *n* sheriff's officer.

tip·ster /'tɪpstə(r)/ *n* person who gives tips about races. ⇨ tip³(2).

tipsy /'tɪpsɪ/ *adj* (colloq) slightly drunk.

tip·toe /'tɪptəʊ/ *adv* on ~, on the tips of one's toes: *be/wait on* ~ *with excitement.* □ *vi* [VP2A,C] walk quietly on ~: *She* ~*d to the bedside of the sleeping child.*

ti·rade /taɪ'reɪd/ *n* long, angry or scolding speech.

tire¹ /'taɪə(r)/ *n* (US) = tyre.

tire² /'taɪə(r)/ *vt,vi* [VP6A,15B,2A,3A] ~ *(sb) (out);* ~ *of,* make or become weary, or in need of rest, or uninterested: *The long walk* ~*d the child/* ~*d him out/made him* ~*d. The long lecture* ~*d the audience. She never* ~*s of talking about that clever son.* **be** ~*d of,* have had enough of, be exhausted with: *I'm* ~*d of boiled eggs, I've had too many of them, or too often.* ~*d* /'taɪəd/ *adj* weary in body or mind: *He was a* ~*d man when he got back from the long climb.* ~*d out,* completely exhausted. ~*d-ness* *n* ~*-less* *adj* **1** not easily ~*d: a*

~less worker. 2 ceaseless; continuing a long time: ~less energy. ~·less·ly adv ~·some /-səm/ adj troublesome; tedious. tir·ing adv making ~d: a tiring journey/argument.

tiro, tyro /'taɪərəʊ/ n (pl ~s /-rəʊz/) beginner; person with little experience.

tis·sue /'tɪʃu:/ n 1 [C,U] (any kind of) woven fabric. 2 [C,U] mass of cells and cell-products in an animal body: muscular/connective ~. 3 '~ paper, thin, soft paper for wrapping things, protecting delicate articles, etc: 'toilet ~, soft paper for use in the WC; 'face/'facial ~s, for use in wiping off lipstick, face-cream, etc. 4 [C] (fig) web or network; series: a ~ of lies.

tit¹ /tɪt/ n kinds of small bird: titmouse; titlark; tomtit; long-tailed tit, etc. ⇨ the illus at bird.

tit² /tɪt/ n (only in) tit for tat, blow in return for blow; (fig) equal retaliation.

tit³ /tɪt/ n △ (vulg sl) teat; nipple; woman's breast.

ti·tan /'taɪtn/ n 1 T~, (Gk myth) one of a family of giants who once ruled the world. 2 person of super-human size, strength, intellect, etc. ~ic /taɪ'tænɪk/ adj immense.

tit·bit /'tɪtbɪt/ n [C] choice and attractive bit (of food, news, gossip, etc).

tithe /taɪð/ n [C] 1 (hist) tenth part of farm produce given for the support of (Church of England) parish priests. '~-barn n barn in which ~s were stored. 2 (rhet) tenth part.

tit·il·late /'tɪtɪleɪt/ vt [VP6A] stimulate or excite pleasantly. tit·il·la·tion /ˌtɪtɪ'leɪʃn/ n

titi·vate (also tit·ti-) /'tɪtɪveɪt/ vt,vi [VP6A,2A] (colloq) adorn; make smart: She was titivating (herself) before the mirror.

tit·lark /'tɪtlɑːk/ n ⇨ tit¹.

title /'taɪtl/ n 1 [C] name of a book, poem, picture, etc. '~-page n page at the front of a book giving the ~, the author's name, etc. '~-role n part in a play that gives the play its name: a performance of 'Othello' with Olivier in the ~-role, with Olivier as Othello. 2 [C] word used to show a person's rank, occupation, status, etc, eg Lord, Prince, Professor, Dr. 3 [C,U] ~ to sth/to do sth, (legal) right or claim, esp right to the possession of a position, property: What ~ has he to the throne? Has he any ~ to the land? '~-deed n document proving a ~ to property. 4 'credit ~s, (or credits), names of persons (eg script-writers, producers, camera men) responsible for a cinema film or TV production, shown at the beginning or end of the film, etc. ~d /'taɪtld/ adj having a ~ of nobility: a ~d lady, eg a duchess.

tit·mouse /'tɪtmaʊs/ n (pl -mice /-maɪs/) ⇨ tit¹.

tit·ter /'tɪtə(r)/ vi [VP2A], n (give a) silly, half-suppressed little laugh.

tittle /'tɪtl/ n not one jot or ~, not a particle; not even a very little bit.

tittle-tattle /'tɪtl tætl/ n, vi gossip.

titu·lar /'tɪtjʊlə(r) US: -tʃʊ-/ adj 1 held by virtue of a title(3): ~ possessions. 2 existing in name but not having authority or duties: the ~ ruler; ~ sovereignty.

tizzy /'tɪzɪ/ n be in a ~, (colloq) in a nervous state.

T-junction /'tiː dʒʌŋkʃn/ n one where two roads, wires, pipes, etc meet to form a T.

TNT /ˌtiː en 'tiː/ n (= trinitrotoluene) powerful explosive.

to¹ /usual form before consonants: tə; before vowels: tʊ or tu:; strong form or finally: tu:/ prep 1 in the direction of; towards: walk to work; go to the pub; fall to the ground; off to London; point to sth; hold sth (up) to the light; on the way to the station; twenty miles to Dover; sitting with his feet to the fire; turn to the right; going from town to town/place to place, etc. Scotland is to the north of England. 2 (fig uses) towards (a condition, quality, etc); to reach the state of: a tendency to laziness/fat, to be lazy/fat; all to no purpose, without any, or a satisfactory, results; stir sb to action; bring/move/reduce sb to tears. The mother sang her baby to sleep, sang until the baby slept. He tore the letter to pieces, eg in anger. Don't start moving until the traffic lights change from red to green. 3 (introducing the indirect object, as in VP13A): To whom did you give it? Who did you give it to? The man I gave it to has left. 4 as far as: from beginning to end; from first to last; faithful to the end/last; fight to the last gasp; wet to the skin; frozen to the marrow; count (up) to ten; shades of colour from red to violet; push sb to violent action. 5 before: a quarter to six; ten to two. ⇨ past. 6 until: from Saturday to Monday; from morning to night. I didn't stay to the end of the meeting. He was conscious to the last. 7 (indicating comparison, ratio, reference): He's quite rich now, compared to what he used to be. It's nothing to what it might be. I prefer walking to climbing. We won by six goals to three. The picture is true to life/nature. This is inferior/superior to that. Draw it to scale. 8 against; touching: dance cheek to cheek; march shoulder to shoulder. 9 for; of: the key to the door; a secretary to the managing director; the words to a tune; be/hear/say etc sth to one's/sb's advantage/liking, etc. 10 forming; making: 100p to the pound/100c to the dollar, ie £1 = 100p/$1 = 100c. 11 in honour of: drink (a health) to sb; erect a monument to (the memory of) the soldiers who died in the war. ⇨ health(4); monument(1). 12 (when comparing two amounts; when quoting a rate) for each; per: petrol consumption of 30 miles to the gallon; a tax of 10p to the pound. ⇨ per; rate¹(1). 13 causing: To my surprise/annoyance/delight/sorrow, etc, the Liberals were defeated in the election, Their defeat caused surprise, etc, in me. To my shame, I completely forgot our date, I am ashamed that I forgot it. 14 (used with verbs of perception like seem, appear, feel, look, smell, sound, etc) in the judgement of; according to: It feels/looks/smells/sounds, etc to me like velvet/gold/ammonia/crying, etc.

to² /usual form before consonants: tə; before vowels and strong form: tu:/ particle, marking the infinitive, used immediately before the v 1 (⇨ VP7,17; used after many vv but not after can, do, may, must, shall, will): He wants to go. He wants me to go. 2 (with adverbial functions of purpose, result, outcome): They came (in order) to help me. He lived to be ninety. We make our goods to last, ie so that they will last. 3 (limiting the meanings of adjj and advv): I'm ready to help. The book is easy to understand. He's old enough to go to school. She's too young to marry. This coffee's too hot to drink, to be drunk. 4 (indicating a subsequent fact; ⇨ VP4B): The good old days have gone never to return, and will never return. He awoke to find himself (= and found himself) in a strange room. 5 (with an adjectival function): John was the first to arrive, who arrived first. 6 (used with an inf as a n): It is wrong to steal. To err is human, to forgive divine. 7 (as a substitute for the inf): We didn't *want to go but we had to. I intended to go, but for-got to. He often does things you wouldn't expect him to.*

to³ /tu:/ (*no weak form*)/ **1** to or in the usual or re-quired position, esp to a closed or almost closed position: *Push the door 'to. Leave the door 'to,* al-most closed. **2 to and fro,** ⇨ fro. **3 bring 'to; come 'to; fall 'to,** ⇨ bring(6); come(15); fall²(14).

toad /təʊd/ *n* rough-skinned, frog-like animal that lives on land except when breeding. ⇨ the illus at amphibian. **,~-in-the-'hole** *n* sausages baked in batter. **'~-stool** *n* kinds of umbrella-shaped fun-gus, some of them poisonous. ⇨ the illus at fungi.

toady /'təʊdɪ/ *n* obsequious flatterer. □ *vi* [VP2A,3A] ~ *(to sb),* flatter in the hope of advan-tage or gain: ~ *to the boss.*

toast¹ /təʊst/ *n* [U] (slice of) bread made brown and crisp by heating at a fire, etc: *a poached egg on ~; two slices of buttered ~.* **'~-rack** *n* for holding slices of ~. □ *vt, vi* [VP6A,2A] **1** make or become brown and crisp by heating. **'~-ing-fork** *n* fork with a long handle used for holding bread in front of a fire. **2** warm (oneself, one's toes, etc) before a fire. ~**er** *n* device (usu electric) for ~ing bread.

toast² /təʊst/ *vt* [VP6A] wish happiness, success, etc to (sb or sth) while raising a full drinking-glass: ~ *the bride and bridegroom.* □ *n* [C] act of ~ing; person, etc ~ed: *propose a ~ to the bridesmaids; drink a ~; respond/reply to the ~,* eg of the speeches made after a wedding to and by the bride and bridegroom. **'~-master** *n* person who an-nounces the ~s at a banquet at which there are dis-tinguished guests.

to-bacco /tə'bækəʊ/ *n* [U] (plant having) leaves which are dried, cured and used for smoking (in pipes, cigars, cigarettes) or as snuff; (*pl,* for kinds of ~ leaf): *This is a mixture of the best ~s.* ~**-nist** /tə'bækənɪst/ *n* dealer in ~.

to-bog-gan /tə'bɒgən/ *n* long, narrow sledge, curved up in front, used for going downhill on snow. □ *vi* [VP2A,C] go down a snow- or ice-covered slope on a ~.

tobogganing

toby-jug /'təʊbɪ dʒʌg/ *n* drinking-mug shaped like a man, wearing a three-cornered hat.

toc-cata /tə'kɑːtə/ *n* (music) composition for a key-board instrument (organ, piano, etc) in a free style, designed to show the performer's technique.

toc-sin /'tɒksɪn/ *n* [C] (bell rung to give a) signal of alarm (now usu fig).

to-day /tə'deɪ/ *adv, n* [U] **1** (on) this day: *T~ is Sunday. Have you seen ~'s newspaper? We're leaving ~ week/a week ~,* in one week's time. **2** (at) this present age or period: *the writers/the young people of ~.*

toddle /'tɒdl/ *vi* [VP2A,C] walk with short, uncer-tain steps as a baby does; (colloq) walk: ~ *off/*

round to see a friend. **tod-dler** /'tɒdlə(r)/ *n* baby who can ~.

toddy /'tɒdɪ/ *n* (*pl* -dies) **1** [C,U] (drink of) alco-holic spirits (esp whisky) and hot water. **2** [U] fresh or fermented sap of some kinds of palm-trees.

to-do /tə 'duː/ *n* ado; fuss; commotion: *What a ~!* What a lot of excitement and talk!

toe /təʊ/ *n* **1** each of the five divisions of the front part of the foot; similar part of an animal's foot: *turn one's toes in/out,* ie in walking. ⇨ the illus at leg. **tread/step on sb's toes,** (fig) offend his feelings or prejudices. *from top to toe,* from head to foot, completely. *on one's toes,* (fig) alert, ready for action. **'toe-cap** *n* outer covering of the toe of a shoe or boot. **'toe-hold** *n* small, insecure foothold (eg when climbing a cliff). **'toe-nail** *n* nail of the toe of a human being. **2** part of a sock, shoe, etc covering the toes. □ *vt* [VP6A] touch, reach, with the toes. *toe the line,* (a) stand with a toe on the starting-line ready for a race. (b) (fig) obey orders given to one as a member of a group or party.

toff /tɒf/ *n* (dated GB *sl*) well-dressed or distinguished-looking person.

toffee /'tɒfɪ *US:* 'tɔːfɪ/ *n* (*pl* ~s) (US = *taffy* /'tæfɪ/) [C,U] (piece of) hard, sticky sweet made by boiling sugar, butter, etc.

tog /tɒg/ *vt* (-gg-) [VP15B] *tog oneself up/out (in),* (colloq) put on smart clothes. **togs** *n pl* (colloq) clothes: *put on one's best togs.*

toga /'təʊgə/ *n* loose flowing outer garment worn by men in ancient Rome.

to-gether /tə'geðə(r)/ *adv* **1** in company: *They went for a walk ~. We are working ~. ~ with,* as well as; in addition to; and also: *These new facts, ~ with the evidence you have already heard, prove the prisoner's innocence.* **2** so as to be in the same place, to be in contact, to be united: *Tie the ends ~. He nailed the boards ~ and made a crate. Stand the two boys ~ and see who is taller. The leader called his men ~. be ~; get sth/it ~,* (*sl*) (cause it to) be, become organised, under control. *put your/our, etc heads ~,* consult with each other (to find a solution to sth, make plans, etc). **3** at the same time: *All his troubles seemed to come ~.* **4** without interruption; in continuous succes-sion: *They sat talking for hours ~. He has been away from school for weeks ~ through illness.* ~**ness** *n* [U] comradeship; feeling of unity.

togs /tɒgz/ *n pl* ⇨ tog.

toggle /'tɒgl/ *n* short piece of wood (like a peg) (to be) put through a loop (to fasten two things to-gether, eg as used instead of a button on a coat).

toil /tɔɪl/ *vi* [VP2A,B,C,3A,4A] ~ *(at),* work long or hard (at a task); move with difficulty and trouble: ~ *at one's studies; ~ up a steep hill.* □ *n* [U,C] labour; hard work: *after long ~.* ~**er** *n* hard worker. ~**-some** /-səm/ *adj*

toilet /'tɔɪlɪt/ *n* **1** process of dressing, cleaning, ar-ranging the hair, face, body, etc: *She spent only a few minutes on her ~.* **2** (attrib) *a '~ set, '~ ar-ticles,* such things as a hair-brush, comb, hand-mirror, etc. **'~-powder** *n* [U] talc. **'~-table** *n* dressing-table (with a mirror or mirrors). **3** water-closet. **'~-paper** *n* for use in a water-closet. **'~-roll** *n* roll of ~-paper.

toils /tɔɪlz/ *n pl* nets; snares: (usu fig) *caught in the ~ of the law.*

To-kay /təʊ'keɪ/ *n* [U] kind of sweet, rich Hun-garian wine.

to·ken /'təʊkən/ n [C] **1** sign, evidence, guarantee or mark: *A white flag is used as a ~ of surrender. I am giving you this jewel as a ~ of my esteem/ affection.* **in ~ of,** as evidence of. **'book/'record/ 'gift ~,** receipt (usu on an attractive card) for payment of money, exchangeable for a book/record, etc of the value stated. **2** (attrib) serving as a preliminary or small-scale substitute: *The enemy offered only a ~ resistance,* did not resist seriously. **'~ money,** coins of low intrinsic value, but exchangeable for money of standard value. **~ payment,** payment of a small part of what is owed, made to show that the debt is recognized. **~ strike,** for a few hours only (as a warning that a long strike may follow). **~ vote,** Parliamentary vote of money for government purposes, it being understood that a larger sum may be taken without further discussion or voting.

told /təʊld/ pt,pp of tell.

tol·er·ate /'tɒləreɪt/ vt [VP6A,C] **1** allow or endure without protest: *I won't ~ your selfishness/your doing that.* **2** endure the society of: *How can you ~ that pompous idiot?* **tol·er·able** /'tɒlərəbl/ adj that can be ~d; fairly good: *tolerable food; in tolerable health.* **tol·er·ably** /-əblɪ/ adv in a tolerable manner or degree: *feel tolerably* (= fairly) *certain about sth.* **tol·er·ance** /'tɒlərəns/ n [U] quality of tolerating opinions, beliefs, customs, behaviour, etc different from one's own: *religious/racial tolerance.* **tol·er·ant** /-rənt/ adj having or showing tolerance: *Mr X is not very tolerant of criticism/ contradiction,* does not endure it easily. **tol·er·ant·ly** adv **tol·er·ation** /ˌtɒləˈreɪʃn/ n [U] tolerance.

toll[1] /təʊl/ n [C] **1** payment required for the use of a road, bridge, harbour, etc. **'~-bar/-gate** n bar/ gate across a road at which a ~ is payable. **'~-house** n house for the man in charge of a ~-bar. **2** (fig) sth paid, lost or suffered: *the ~ of the roads, deaths and injuries from traffic accidents. The war took a heavy ~ of the nation's manhood.* **3** '~ **call** n telephone call for which the rates are higher than for local calls.

toll[2] /təʊl/ vt,vi [VP6A,2A] (of a bell) (cause to) ring with slow, regular strokes: *The funeral bell ~ed solemnly. Whose death is being ~ed?* □ n (sing only) ~ing stroke, of a bell.

toma·hawk /'tɒməhɔːk/ n light axe used as a tool and a weapon by N American Indians. □ vt strike with a ~.

tom·ato /təˈmɑːtəʊ *US:* təˈmeɪtəʊ/ n (pl ~es /-təʊz/) [C] (plant with) soft, juicy, red or yellow fruit usu eaten with meat, in salads, and in sauces: (attrib) '~ *juice.* ⇨ the illus at **vegetable.**

tomb /tuːm/ n place dug in the ground, cut out of rock, etc for a dead body, esp one with a monument over it. **'~-stone** n stone set over a ~.

tom·bola /tɒmˈbəʊlə/ n [C] (pl ~s) (now usu called *bingo*) kind of lottery with sums of money or small fancy articles as prizes.

tom·boy /'tɒmbɔɪ/ n girl who likes rough, noisy games and play.

tom·cat /'tɒmkæt/ n male cat.

tome /təʊm/ n large, heavy book.

tom·fool /ˌtɒmˈfuːl/ n stupid person; (attrib) stupid: *a ~ speech.* **~·ery** /-ərɪ/ n [U] senseless behaviour; [C] (pl -ries) stupid joke.

tommy-gun /'tɒmɪ ɡʌn/ n submachine-gun (light kind that can be carried and used by one man).

tommy-rot /ˌtɒmɪˈrɒt/ n (colloq) utter foolishness: *You're talking ~. That's all ~.*

to·mor·row /təˈmɒrəʊ/ adv, n [U] (on) the day after today: *If today is Monday, ~ will be Tuesday and the day after ~ will be Wednesday. Don't wait until ~. Where will he be ~ morning/afternoon/ evening/night? The announcement will appear in ~'s newspapers. What will the men and women of ~* (= of the next few years) *think of us? ~ week,* eight days hence.

tom-tit /'tɒm tɪt/ n kind of small bird. ⇨ tit[1].

tom-tom /'tɒmtɒm/ n (kind of) African or Asian drum, esp a long and narrow kind, beaten with the hands.

ton /tʌn/ n **1** measure of weight (2240 lb in GB, 2000 lb in the US). **metric ton,** = tonne. ⇨ App 5. **2** measure of the internal capacity (100 cu ft) or carrying capacity (40 cu ft) of a ship. **3** (colloq) large weight, quantity or number: *He has tons of money.* **4 the ton,** (sl) speed of 100 mph: *Can your motor-bike do the ton?* □ vi [VP2C] **ton up,** drive (a motor-cycle) for sport at a high speed.

to·nal /'təʊnl/ adj of tone or tones; of ~ity. **~·ity** /təʊˈnælətɪ/ n (pl -ties) (music) character of a melody, depending upon the scale in which it is written, the key in which it is developed, etc.

tone[1] /təʊn/ n **1** [C] sound, esp with reference to its quality, pitch, duration, feeling, etc: *the sweet ~(s) of a violin; speak in an angry/entreating ~. The doctor's ~ was serious.* **,~-'deaf** adj unable to distinguish between differences of pitch. **'~-poem** n musical composition for an orchestra, illustrating a poetic idea, legend, etc. **2** [C] the pitch aspect of a (usu stressed) syllable; rise, fall, etc of the pitch of the voice in speaking: *In 'Are you ill?' there is usu a rising ~ on 'ill'; in 'He's ill', there is usu a falling ~ on 'ill'.* **3** (sing only) general spirit, character, morale, of a community, etc: *The ~ of the country is buoyant. The next speaker gave a serious/flippant ~ to the discussion. There was a ~ of quiet elegance in the room,* The furnishings, etc gave this impression. **4** [C] shade (of colour); degree (of light): *a carpet in ~s of brown; a picture in warm ~s,* in shades suggesting warmth. **5** (music) any one of the five larger intervals between one note and the next which, together with two semi-~s, make up an octave. **6** [U] proper and normal condition of (parts of) the body: *good muscular ~; recover mental ~.* **-toned** adj having a particular kind of ~(1): *silver-~d trumpets.* **~-less** adj lacking colour, spirit, etc; dull: *answer in a ~less voice.* **~·less·ly** adv

tone[2] /təʊn/ vt,vi [VP6A] give a particular tone of sound or colour to. **2** [VP15B,2C] **~ (sth) down,** make or become less intense: *The excitement ~d down. The artist ~d down the cruder colours in his painting. You'd better ~ down some of the offensive statements in your article. ~ (sth) up,* make or become more vigorous, intenser, brighter, etc: *Exercise ~s up the muscles.* **3** ~ **in (with),** (esp of colours) be in harmony: *These curtains ~ in well with your rugs.*

tongs /tɒŋz/ n pl (**pair of**) ~, one of various kinds of usu hinged tool for taking up and holding sth: *'sugar ~; 'coal ~; 'ice ~. be/go at it hammer and ~,* ⇨ hammer(1).

tongue /tʌŋ/ n **1** [C] movable organ in the mouth, used in talking, tasting, licking, etc: *The doctor asked me to put out my ~. Don't put your ~ out at me, you cheeky girl!* ⇨ the illus at mouth, snake. **have sth on the tip of one's ~,** ⇨ tip[1](1). **find one's ~,** become able to speak again (after being too shy to do so). **have/say sth with/speak with one's ~ in one's cheek,** say sth that one does not intend to be taken seriously. Hence, **~-in-'cheek** *adj, adv:* ~-*in-cheek remarks; speak* ~-*in-cheek.* **have lost one's ~,** be too shy to speak. **have a ready ~,** be fluent, quick to answer questions, etc. **hold one's ~,** be silent, saying nothing. **keep a civil '~ in one's head,** not be rude. **'~-tied** *adj* silent; unable or unwilling to speak through shyness, fear, etc. **'~-twister** *n* word or succession of words difficult to utter quickly and correctly. **2** [C] language: *one's mother* ~, one's native language; *the German* ~. **3** [C,U] animal's ~ as an article of food: *boil an 'ox-~; ham and* ~ *sandwiches.* **4** sth like a ~ in shape or function, eg the clapper of a bell, the strip of leather under the laces of a shoe, a jet of flame (which licks things), a long promontory (*a* ~ *of land*). **-~d** *adj* (in compounds) having a ~ of the kind indicated: *a sharp-~d woman.*

tonic /'tɒnɪk/ *n, adj* **1** (sth, eg, medicine) giving strength or energy: *the* ~ *quality of sea air; get a bottle of* ~ *from the doctor. Praise can be a fine* ~. *The good news acted as a* ~ *on us all,* cheered us up. **'~ (water),** bottled, carbonated water with quinine: *a gin and* ~ (as a drink). **2** (music) keynote. **~ ˌsol-'fa** /ˌsɒl 'fɑː: *US:* ˌsəʊl 'fɑː/ *n* (in teaching singing) method of showing musical notes by syllables, eg *sol, fa, do.* ⇨ **do**[5].

to·night /tə'naɪt/ *adv, n* [U] (on) the night of today: *last night,* ~, *and tomorrow night; after* ~; ~*'s radio news.*

ton·nage /'tʌnɪdʒ/ *n* **1** internal cubic capacity of a ship (1 ton = 100 cu ft). **2** cargo-carrying capacity of a ship stated in tons (of 40 cu ft). **3** total ~(1) of a country's merchant shipping. **4** charge per ton on cargo, etc for transport.

tonne /tʌn/ *n* metric ton, = 1000 kilograms. ⇨ App 5.

ton·sil /'tɒnsl/ *n* either of two small oval masses of tissue at the sides of the throat, near the root of the tongue: *have one's* ~*s out,* have them removed by a surgeon. ⇨ the illus at head. **~·litis** /ˌtɒnsɪ'laɪtɪs/ *n* [U] inflammation of the ~s.

ton·sorial /tɒn'sɔːrɪəl/ *adj* (often hum, eg *the* ~ *art*) of a hairdresser and his work.

ton·sure /'tɒnʃə(r)/ *n* shaving of the top of the head of a person about to become a monk or priest; part of the head that has been shaved in this way. □ *vt* give the ~ to.

ton·tine /'tɒntiːn/ *n* annuity shared by subscribers to a loan, the shares increasing as the subscribers die, till the last subscriber gets all that is left.

too /tuː/ *adv* **1** also; as well, in addition (usu in end position but placed immediately after the word it modifies if there is a risk of ambiguity): *I, too, have been to Paris,* eg I, as well as he, you, etc. *I've been to Paris, too,* eg to Paris as well as to Rome, Milan, etc. *She plays the piano, and sings, too,* plays the piano and also sings. *Sally, too,* (= Sally, as well as Mary, etc) *plays the piano.* (Cf the construction in negative sentences: *I know the answer, too.* Neg: *I don't know the answer, either.*) **2** moreover; nevertheless: *There was frost last night, and in May too!* **3** (*adv of degree,* modifying *adjj* and *advv*) in a higher degree than is allowable, required, etc: *We've had too much rain lately. You're driving too fast for safety. These shoes are much too small for me. It's too hot for work/too hot to work. It's too difficult a task for me. That's too small a box/That box is too small to hold all these*

things. (Note that *too* is used to modify a participle that is adjectival, but that with a participle that is purely verbal, *too much* is preferred in formal style. Cf: *He was too tired to go any farther. I hope you were not too* (much) *disturbed by all the noise we made. I'm not too* (much) *bothered by his criticisms.*) **4** (phrases) **carry sth/go too far,** ⇨ far[2](2). **all too soon/quickly, etc,** sooner, more quickly, etc than is desired: *The holidays ended all too soon.* **none too soon, etc,** not at all too soon, etc: *We were none too early for the train,* We caught the train with very little time to spare. **one too many,** ⇨ many(1). **have one too many,** take more than one can drink and remain sober. **be too much for,** ⇨ much[1]. **only too** (+ *adj*), ⇨ only[2](2).

took /tʊk/ *pt* of take[1].

tool /tuːl/ *n* **1** instrument held in the hand(s) and used by workmen, eg gardeners and carpenters. **ma·chine '~** *n* ⇨ machine. **2** person used by another for dishonest purposes: *He was a mere* ~ *in the hands of the dictator.* □ *vt* **1** [VP6A] ornament (the edges of a book-cover) with designs pressed on with a heated ~. **2** [VP2C] ~ **up,** provide a factory with machine-~s (eg as needed for a particular kind of work).

toot /tuːt/ *n* [C] short, sharp warning sound from a horn, whistle, trumpet, etc. □ *vi,vt* [VP2A,6A] (cause to) give out a ~ or ~s.

tooth /tuːθ/ *n* (*pl* teeth /tiːθ/) **1** each of the hard, white, bone-like structures rooted in the gums, used for biting and chewing: *have a* ~ *out* (US = *have a* ~ *pulled*), ie by a dentist; *have all one's own teeth/a fine set of artificial teeth.* ⇨ the illus at mouth. **armed to the teeth,** completely and elaborately armed. **cast sth in a person's teeth,** reproach him with it. **escape by the skin of one's teeth,** have a narrow escape. **fight** ~ **and nail,** fiercely, with a great effort. **get one's teeth into sth,** attack (a job) vigorously. **have a sweet** ~, be fond of sweet food. **lie in one's teeth/throat,** lie shamelessly. **long in the** ~, (originally of horses, because gums recede with age) old. **show one's teeth,** take up a threatening attitude. **in the teeth of,** against the full force of; in opposition to. **(a/ the) '~-ache** *n* pain in a ~ or teeth. **'~-brush** *n* one for cleaning the teeth. ⇨ the illus at brush. **'~-paste/-powder** *n* [U] for cleaning the teeth. **'~-pick** *n* short, pointed piece of wood, etc, for removing bits of food from between the teeth. **2** ~-like part, esp of a comb, saw or rake. ⇨ the illus at gear. **ˌfine-'~ comb,** one with fine teeth set closely together. **go over/through sth with a ˌfine-~ comb,** examine it closely and thoroughly. **3** (*pl,* colloq) effective force: *When will the new legislation be given some teeth,* be made effective? **~ed** /tuːθt/ (attrib) having teeth (eg of the kind named): *a saw-~ed wheel.* **~·less** *adj* without teeth. **~·some** /-səm/ *adj* (liter) (of food) pleasant to the taste.

tootle /'tuːtl/ *vi, n* toot softly or continuously, as on a flute.

top[1] /tɒp/ *n* (usu **the top (of)**) **1** highest part or point: *at the top of the hill; the hilltop; at the top of the page; line 5 from the top.* **on top,** above: *The green book is at the bottom of the pile and the red one is on top.* **on (the) top of,** (a) over, resting on: *Put the red book on top of the others.* (b) in addition to: *He borrowed £50 from me for the journey and then, on top of that, asked me if he could*

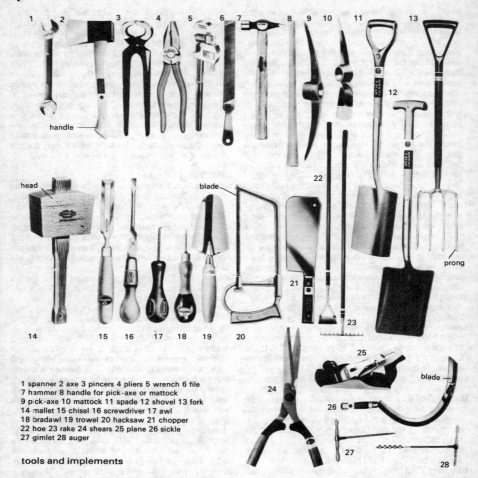

1 spanner 2 axe 3 pincers 4 pliers 5 wrench 6 file
7 hammer 8 handle for pick-axe or mattock
9 pick-axe 10 mattock 11 spade 12 shovel 13 fork
14 mallet 15 chisel 16 screwdriver 17 awl
18 bradawl 19 trowel 20 hacksaw 21 chopper
22 hoe 23 rake 24 shears 25 plane 26 sickle
27 gimlet 28 auger

tools and implements

borrow my car. **from top to bottom,** completely. **from top to toe,** from head to foot. **blow one's top,** (colloq) explode in rage. **off the top of one's head,** (of sth said) without careful thought or preparation. **2** upper surface, eg of a table: *polish the top of a table/the 'table top;* put the luggage on the top of the car. **go over the top,** (mil) go over the front of a trench to attack the enemy; (fig) act quickly after a period of doubt or hesitation. **on top of the world,** (colloq) extremely happy, satisfied with everything: *I'm feeling on top of the world today!* **3** highest rank, foremost (or most important) place: *He came out at the top of the list,* eg of examination results. *Our host placed us at the top* (= the upper end) *of the table,* the part for honoured guests. **come to the top,** (fig) win fame, success, etc. **reach/be at the top of the ladder/ tree,** the highest position in a profession, career, etc. **4** utmost height or degree. **shout at the top of one's voice,** ⇨ voice, *n*(3); **to the top of one's bent,** ⇨ bent¹. **5** (motoring) **in top,** in top (the highest) gear: *What will the car do in top?* **6** (often *pl*) leaves, etc of a plant grown chiefly for its root: *'turnip tops.* **7 the big top,** very large circus tent. **8**

(attrib, and in compounds) highest in position or degree: *on the top shelf; at top speed; in top gear; the top right-hand corner; charge top prices.* **'top-boot** *n* boot with a high top, usu reaching to just below the knee. **'top-coat** *n* overcoat. **be top dog,** (sl) victor, master. ⇨ underdog. **,top- 'drawer** *n* the highest social class: *She's out of the top drawer/is very top drawer.* **,top-'dress** *vt* apply (manure, etc) to the surface of (ground) instead of ploughing or digging it in; hence, **,top- 'dressing** *n.* give a field a top-dressing of lime. **,top-'flight/-'notch** *attrib adjj* (colloq) first-rate; best possible: *top-flight French authors.* **,top- 'gallant** *adj, n* mast, sail, etc immediately above the topmast and topsail. ⇨ the illus at barque. **,top- 'hat** *n* tall silk hat. **,top-'heavy** *adj* over-weighted at the top so as to be in danger of falling. **,top- 'hole** *adj* (dated sl) excellent; first-rate. **'top-knot** *n* knot of hair, bunch of feathers, etc on the top of the head. **'top-mast** *n* upper mast (clamped to the mainmast). **'top-most** /-məʊst/ *adj* highest. **,top 'people,** those at the top of their profession, holding the highest positions, etc: *Not all top people read 'The Times'.* **,top-'ranking** *adj* of the highest rank. **'top·sail** *n* square sail next above the lowest. ⇨ the illus at barque. **,top 'secret,** most secret.

top·less *adj* (of a woman's garment) leaving the breasts bare: *a topless dress/swimsuit;* (of a woman) wearing such a garment: *topless waitresses in California.*

top² /tɒp/ *vt* (-pp-) [VP6A] **1** provide a top for; be a top for; be a top to: *a church topped by/with a steeple.* **2** [VP6A] reach the top of; be at the top of: *When we topped the hill we had a fine view.* **3** *top (sth) up,* fill up (a partly empty container): *top up a car battery,* add distilled water to raise the level to what is normal; *top up with oil,* add lubricating oil; *top up a drink,* refill a partly emptied glass. *top (sth) out,* mark the completion of a tall building (a tower block, etc) with drinks, speeches, etc: *a ,topping-'out ceremony.* **4** surpass, be taller or higher than: *Our exports have just topped the £80000000 mark. to 'top it all,* to crown all, add the last (and surprising, etc) touch. **5** cut the tops off: *lift and top beets/turnips,* take them from the ground and cut off the leaves; *top and tail gooseberries,* remove the ends from the berries.

top³ /tɒp/ *n* toy that spins and balances on a point, set in motion by hand, or by winding round it a string which is pulled away, and (in some cases) kept in motion by being whipped. *sleep like a top,* soundly.

to·paz /'təʊpæz/ *n* [U] transparent yellow mineral; [C] gem cut from this.

tope /təʊp/ *vi,vt* [VP2A,6A] (dated) drink (alcoholic liquors) to excess; drink habitually. **toper** *n* person who ~s.

topi /'təʊpi US:* təʊ'piː/ *n* sun-helmet.

topi·ary /'təʊpɪərɪ US:* -ɪerɪ/ *n* [U], *adj* (concerned with) the clipping of shrubs, eg yew, into ornamental shapes, eg birds, animals: *the ~ art; a ~ garden.*

topic /'tɒpɪk/ *n* subject for discussion. **topi·cal** /-kl/ *adj* of present interest; of ~s of the day: *a ~al 'news film,* of current events. **topi·cally** /-klɪ/ *adv*

top·ogra·phy /tə'pɒɡrəfɪ/ *n* [U] (description of the) features, eg rivers, valleys, roads, of a place or district. **topo·graphi·cal** /,tɒpə'ɡræfɪkl/ *adj* **topo·graphi·cally** /-klɪ/ *adv*

top·per /'tɒpə(r)/ *n* (colloq) top hat.

top·ping /'tɒpɪŋ/ *adj* (colloq) excellent. **~·ly** *adv*

topple /'tɒpl/ *vi,vt* [VP2A,C,6A,15B] (cause to) be unsteady and overturn: *The chimney ~d and fell. The pile of books ~d over/down. The dictator was ~d from power.*

tops /tɒps/ *n pl* (usu **the tops**) (colloq) the very best.

topsy-turvy /,tɒpsɪ 'tɜːvɪ/ *adj, adv* (colloq) in confusion; upside down: *The whole world is/has turned ~.* **~·dom** /-dəm/ *n* condition of being ~.

toque /təʊk/ *n* (woman's) small, brimless, close-fitting hat.

tor /tɔː(r)/ *n* small hill, rocky peak (esp in place-names on Dartmoor, SW England): *Hay Tor.*

torch /tɔːtʃ/ *n* **1** piece of wood, twisted flax, etc treated with oil, soaked in tallow, etc for carrying or using as a flaming light; (fig) sth that gives enlightenment: *the ~ of learning; hand on the ~,* keep knowledge, etc alive. *carry a ~ for sb,* have (esp unrequited) love for him. **'~-light** *n* [U] light of a ~ or ~es: *a ~light procession/tattoo,* one in which lighted ~es are used. **'~-race** *n* (in ancient Greece) performance of runners who handed light-

ed ~es to others in relays. **'~-singer** *n* woman who sings sentimental love-songs. **2** (GB) electric hand-light (US = *flashlight);* (US) blow-lamp (for welding, etc).

tore /tɔː(r)/ *pt* of tear².

tor·ea·dor /'tɒrɪədɔː(r) US:* 'tɔːr-/ *n* Spanish bull-fighter (usu mounted on a horse).

tor·ment /'tɔːment/ *n* [C,U] (sth that causes) severe bodily or mental pain or suffering: *be in ~; suffer ~(s) from an aching tooth; the ~s of jealousy. What a little ~ that child is!* (because it worries, asks constant questions, etc). □ *vt* /tɔː'ment/ [VP6A,15A] cause severe suffering to; annoy: *~ed with neuralgia/hunger/mosquitoes. Stop ~ing your father by asking silly questions.* **tor·men·tor** /tɔː'mentə(r)/ *n* sb or sth that ~s.

torn /tɔːn/ *pp* of tear².

tor·nado /tɔː'neɪdəʊ/ *n* (*pl ~es /-dəʊz/)* violent and destructive whirlwind.

tor·pedo /tɔː'piːdəʊ/ *n* (*pl ~es /-dəʊz/)* cigar-shaped self-propelling shell filled with explosives, aimed at ships (from surface ships, submarines and aircraft), and launched to travel below the surface of the sea. **'~-boat** *n* small, fast warship from which ~es are fired. **'~-tube** *n* tube from which ~es are discharged. □ *vt* [VP6A] attack or destroy with a ~ or ~es; (fig) attack (a policy, institution, etc) and make it ineffective: *Who ~ed the Disarmament Conference?*

tor·pid /'tɔːpɪd/ *adj* **1** dull and slow; inactive. **2** (of animals that hibernate) not moving or feeling. **~·ly** *adv.* **~·ness, ~·ity** /tɔː'pɪdətɪ/ *nn* [U] ~ condition.

tor·por /'tɔːpə(r)/ *n* [U,C] torpid condition.

torque /tɔːk/ *n* **1** [C] necklace, collar or arm-band of twisted metal, as worn by the ancient Britons and Gauls. **2** [U] twisting force causing rotation, eg as exerted on a ship's propeller shaft.

tor·rent /'tɒrənt US:* 'tɔːr-/ *n* [C] **1** violent, rushing stream of liquid (esp water): *mountain ~s; ~s of rain; rain falling in ~s.* **2** (fig) violent outpouring: *a ~ of words/abuse/insults.* **tor·ren·tial** /tə'renʃl/ *adj* of, like, caused by, a ~: *~ial rain.*

tor·rid /'tɒrɪd US:* 'tɔːr-/ *adj* (of the weather, a country) very hot; tropical: *the '~ zone,* part of the earth's surface between the tropics(1). **~·ity** *n* [U] extreme heat.

tor·sion /'tɔːʃn/ *n* [U] act or process of twisting; state of being twisted.

torso /'tɔːsəʊ/ *n* (*pl ~s)* (statue of a) human body without head, arms and legs.

tort /tɔːt/ *n* (legal) private or civil wrong for which the wronged person may get redress in a law court.

tor·tilla /tɔː'tiːjə/ *n* pancake omelette (Mexican style).

tor·toise /'tɔːtəs/ *n* slow-moving, four-legged land (and fresh-water) varieties of turtle with a hard shell. ⇨ the illus at reptile. **'~-shell** *n* [U] outer shell, esp the kind with yellow and brown markings, of some sea-turtles.

tor·tu·ous /'tɔːtʃʊəs/ *adj* full of twists and bends: *a ~ path;* (fig) not straightforward; devious: *a ~ argument/policy/politician.* **~·ly** *adv*

tor·ture /'tɔːtʃə(r)/ *vt* [VP6A,16A] cause severe suffering to: *~ a man to make him confess sth; ~d with anxiety.* □ *n* **1** [U] torturing; infliction of severe bodily or mental suffering: *put a man to the ~, ~* him (esp to get a confession or to make him supply information); *instruments of ~.* **2** [C,U] pain so inflicted or suffered; method of torturing: *suffer ~ from toothache; the ~s of the damned,* ie in Hell. **tor·turer** n

Tory /'tɔːrɪ/ n (pl -ries) = Conservative.

tosh /tɒʃ/ n (sl) nonsense.

toss /tɒs/ US: tɔːs/ vt,vi **1** [VP6A,12A,13A,15B] throw up into or through the air; jerk: ∼ a ball to sb; ∼ sth aside/away. The horse ∼ed its rider, caused the rider to fall to the ground. He ∼ed the beggar a coin/∼ed a coin to the beggar. The horse ∼ed its head. She ∼ed her head back, ie with a suggestion of contempt, indifference, etc. He was ∼ed by the bull. ∼ **(up) a coin;** ∼ **(sb) for sth;** ∼ **up,** send a coin spinning up in the air and guess which side will be on top when it falls; use this method to decide sth (with sb): Who's to pay for the drinks? Let's ∼ up/Let's ∼ for it. '∼-**up** n such ∼ing of a coin; (hence) sth about which there is doubt: It's a ∼-up whether he will get here in time. **2** [VP2C,6A,15A,B] (cause to) move restless-ly from side to side or up and down: The ship (was) ∼ed about on the stormy sea. The sick child ∼ed about in its sleep all night. The branches were ∼ing in the wind. **3** ∼ **sth off, (a)** drink sth straight down. **(b)** produce sth quickly and without much thought or effort: ∼ off a newspaper article. □ n [C] **1** ∼ing movement: a contemptuous ∼ of the head; take a ∼, (esp) be thrown from the back of a horse. **2 win/lose the** ∼, guess correctly/incorrectly when a coin is ∼ed up (esp at the be-ginning of a game).

tot¹ /tɒt/ n **1** (often **tiny tot**) very small child. **2** (colloq) small glass of liquor.

tot² /tɒt/ vt,vi (-tt-) [VP15B,2C] **tot (sth) up,** (colloq) add up: expenses totting up to £5; tot up a column of figures.

to·tal /'təʊtl/ adj complete; entire: ∼ silence; be in ∼ ignorance of sth. What are your ∼ debts? There was a ∼ eclipse of the sun. ∼ **war,** war in which all the resources of a country (manpower, industry, etc) are involved. □ n [C] ∼ amount: Our expenses reached a ∼ of £20. What does the ∼ come to? □ vt,vi (-ll-, US also -l-) [VP6A,2C] find the ∼ of; reach the ∼ of; amount to: The visitors to the ex-hibition ∼led 15000. It ∼s up to £16. ∼**ly** /'təʊtəlɪ/ adv completely: ∼ly blind. ∼·**ity** /təʊ'tælətɪ/ n entirety; (esp) period during which an eclipse is ∼.

to·tali·tar·ian /ˌtəʊtælɪ'teərɪən/ adj of a political system in which only one political party and no ri-val loyalties are permitted: a ∼ State, eg Germany under Hitler. ∼·**ism** /-ɪzəm/ n

to·tal·iz·ator /'təʊtəlaɪzeɪtə(r) US: -lɪz-/ n machine for registering bets (eg on horses) with a view to dividing the total amount among those who bet on the winners.

tote¹ /təʊt/ n (colloq abbr of) totalizator.

tote² /təʊt/ vt [VP6A] (sl) carry (esp a gun): He ∼s a six-shooter.

to·tem /'təʊtəm/ n [C] natural object, esp an ani-mal, considered, esp by N American Indians, to have a close connection with a family group. '∼-**pole** n one on which is carved or painted a series of ∼s.

tot·ter /'tɒtə(r)/ vi [VP2A,C] **1** walk with weak, un-steady steps; get up unsteadily: The wounded man ∼ed to his feet. **2** be almost falling; seem to be about to collapse: The tall chimney-stack ∼ed and then fell. ∼·**y** adj unsteady; insecure.

tou·can /'tuːkæn/ n kinds of tropical American bird with brightly coloured feathers and an immense beak. ⇨ the illus at rare.

touch¹ /tʌtʃ/ n **1** [C] act or fact of touching: I felt a ∼ on my arm. Even the slightest ∼ will break a soap-bubble. **at a** ∼, if touched, however lightly. **2** [U] (sense giving) feeling by touching: soft/rough to the ∼, when touched; the cold ∼ of mar-ble. '∼·**stone** n sth used as a test or standard (of purity, etc); criterion. **3** [C] stroke made with a brush, pen, etc: add a few finishing ∼es (to a drawing or any piece of work); give a horse a ∼ of the spurs. **4** [C] **a** ∼ **(of),** slight quantity, trace: a ∼ of frost in the air; have a ∼ of the sun, slight sunstroke; a ∼ of irony/bitterness in his remarks; have a ∼ (= a slight attack) of rheumatism. **5** [C] style or manner of touching the keys, strings, etc of a musical instrument, etc of workmanship (in art): the ∼ of a master, expert style, eg in painting; a sculpture with a bold ∼; have a light ∼, eg on a piano, a typewriter; the (eg) 'Nelson ∼, the bold way of dealing with a situation characteristic of (eg) Nelson. '∼-**type** vi [VP2A] type without looking at the typewriter keyboard (because famili-ar with it). **6** [U] communication. **in/out of** ∼ **(with),** in/not in regular communication (with); having/not having information about: keep in ∼ with old friends; be out of ∼ with the political si-tuation. **lose** ∼ **(with),** be out of ∼ (with): If we correspond regularly we shan't lose ∼. **7** (football and Rugby) part of the pitch outside the side-lines: The ball is in/out of ∼. '∼-**line** n side line of the field of play. ⇨ goal-line at goal; ⇨ the illus at football, Rugby. **8 a near** ∼, a narrow escape. ˌ∼-**and-'go** adj (colloq) risky; of uncertain result: It was ∼-and-go whether the doctor would arrive in time. It was ∼-and-go with the sick man, uncer-tain whether he would live. **9 a soft/easy** ∼, (sl) sb from whom one can beg or borrow easily. ⇨ ∼ sb for sth, at touch ²(11).

touch² /tʌtʃ/ vt,vi (For special uses with adverbial particles and preps, ⇨ **11** below.) **1** [VP6A,15A,B,2A] (cause to) be in contact with; be separated from at one or more points by no space or object; bring a part of the body (esp the hand) into contact with: One of the branches is ∼ing the wat-er. The two farms ∼ (each other), have, in part, a common boundary. Can you ∼ (= reach with your hand) the top of the door? The mountains seemed to ∼ the clouds. Visitors (eg in a museum) are re-quested not to ∼ the exhibits. He ∼ed me on the arm/shoulder, eg to attract my attention. I merely ∼ed the eggs together and they cracked. The ther-mometer ∼ed 35°C yesterday. ∼ **bottom, (a)** reach the bottom: The water isn't deep here; I can just ∼ bottom, ie with my feet. **(b)** (fig) reach the lowest point of misfortune, depravity, etc. ∼ **wood,** ∼ sth made of wood in the belief that one will avert ill luck: I've never been in a road ac-cident—∼ wood. **2** [VP6A] apply a slight or gentle force to: He ∼ed the bell, rang it by pressing the button. He ∼ed the keys of the piano. **3** [VP6A] (usu in neg) compare with; be equal to: No one can ∼ him as an actor of tragic roles. There's nothing to ∼ mountain air for giving you an appetite. **4** [VP6A] (usu neg) take (food, drink): He hasn't ∼ed food for two days. **5** [VP6A] affect (a person or his feelings); concern: The sad story ∼ed us/our hearts. We were all ∼ed with remorse/pity when we heard what had happened. **6** [VP6A] have to do with: What you say does not ∼ the point at issue. The question ∼es your interests closely. **7** [VP6A] injure slightly: The apple-blossom was ∼ed by the

frost. The valuable paintings were not ~ed by the fire. **8** (*pp* ~**ed**) (colloq) slightly mad or deranged: *He seems to be a bit ~ed.* **9** [VP6A,15A] rouse painful or angry feeling in; wound: *You've ~ed his self-esteem. You've ~ed him on a tender place* (lit or fig). ⇨ **quick(***n***). 10** [VP6A] deal with; cope with; get a result from: *Nothing I have used will ~* (= get rid of) *these grease spots. She couldn't ~* (= even begin to answer) *the first two questions in the biology paper,* ie in an examination. **11** [VP3A,2C,15B] (special uses with *adverbial particles* and *preps*):
touch at, (of a ship) call at: *Our steamer ~ed at Naples.*
touch down, (a) (Rugby) ~ the ball on the ground behind the opponent's goal line. **(b)** (of aircraft) come down to land; alight. Hence, '~**-down** *n*
touch sb for sth, (sl) get money from (by begging): *He ~ed me for a fiver* (ie £5).
touch sth off, discharge (a cannon, etc); (fig) cause to start: *The arrest of the men's leaders ~ed off a riot.*
touch on/upon sth, treat (a subject) briefly.
touch sth up, make small changes in (a picture, a piece of writing, etc) to improve it, give the finishing touches, etc.
touch·able /'tʌtʃəbl/ *adj* that may be touched.
touch·ing /'tʌtʃɪŋ/ *adj* pathetic; arousing pity or sympathy. □ *prep* concerning. ~·**ly** *adv*
touchy /'tʌtʃɪ/ *adj* (-ier, -iest) easily or quickly offended. **touch·ily** /-ɪlɪ/ *adv* **touchi·ness** *n*
tough /tʌf/ *adj* (-er, -est) **1** (of meat) hard to cut or get one's teeth into. **2** not easily cut, broken or worn out: *as ~ as leather. T~ rubber is needed for tyres.* **3** strong; able to endure hardships: ~ *soldiers.* **4** (of persons) rough and violent: *a ~ criminal.* ~ **customer,** (colloq) person likely to cause trouble, unlikely to submit to control or discipline. **5** stubborn; unyielding. **be/get ~ (with sb)**: *The employers got ~ with/adopted a get-~ policy towards their workers.* **6** hard to carry out; difficult: *a ~ job/problem.* **7** ~ **luck,** (colloq) bad luck. □ *n* (also ~**ie** /'tʌfɪ/) (colloq) ~(**4**) person. ~·**ly** *adv* ~·**ness** *n* ~**en** /'tʌfn/ *vt,vi* make or become ~.
tou·pee /'tu:peɪ *US:* tu:'peɪ/ *n* patch of false hair worn to cover a bald spot; small wig.
tour /tʊə(r)/ *n* **1** journey out and home again during which several or many places are visited: *a round-the-world ~; a coach ~ of France;* conducted ~s, made by a group conducted by a guide. **2** brief visit to or through: *a ~ of the palace/house.* **3** period of duty (at a military or naval station overseas); interval between passage-paid home leaves (⇨ **leave²(1)**) in service abroad: *a ~ of three years as a lecturer in the University of Ibadan.* **4** round of (official) visits to institutions, units, etc: *The Director leaves tomorrow on a ~ of overseas branches.* **5** number of visits to places made by a theatrical company, etc. **on tour,** visiting in this way: *be/go on ~; take a company on ~ to perform three of Shakespeare's plays.* □ *vt,vi* [VP6A,2A,C] make a ~ (of): ~ *Mexico. They are ~ing in Spain. The play will ~ the provinces in the autumn.* ~·**ing** *n, adj: a* '~*ing car,* one suitable for ~ing; *a* '~*ing party.* ~**ist** /-ɪst/ *n* **1** person making a ~ for pleasure: *London is full of ~ists in summer.* **2** (attrib) of or for ~s: *a* '~*ist agency; a* '~*ist ticket,* one issued on special terms, eg at a lower price; '~ *class,* (on liners, airliners) second

class ~**ism** /'tʊərɪzəm/ *n* [U] organized ~ing: *Some countries obtain large sums of foreign exchange from ~ism,* from the money brought in by ~ists.
tour de force /ˌtʊə də 'fɔːs/ *n* (F) feat of strength or skill.
tour·na·ment /'tɔːnəmənt *US:* 'tɜːrn-/ *n* [C] **1** series of contests of skill between a number of players: *a* '*tennis*/'*chess* ~. **2** (in the Middle Ages) contest between knights on horseback, armed with blunted weapons.
tour·ney /'tɜːnɪ/ *n* = tournament(2).
tour·ni·quet /'tʊənɪkeɪ *US:* 'tɜːnɪkɪt/ *n* device for stopping a flow of blood through an artery by twisting sth tightly around a limb.
tousle /'taʊzl/ *vt* [VP6A] put (esp the hair) into disorder by pulling it about, rubbing it, etc; make untidy: *a girl with ~d hair.*
tout /taʊt/ *n* person who worries others to buy sth, use his services, etc, esp one who sells information about race-horses: *a* '*ticket* ~, eg selling tickets for a major football match at a greatly inflated price. □ *vi* [VP2A,3A] ~ **(for),** act as a ~: *There were men outside the railway station ~ing for the hotels.*
tout en·sem·ble /ˌtuːt ɒn'sɒmbl/ *n* (F) sth viewed as a whole; its general effect.
tow¹ /təʊ/ *vt* [VP6A,15A,B] pull along by a rope or chain: *tow a damaged ship into port; tow a broken-down car to the nearest garage.* '**tow(-ing)-line/-rope** *nn* one used in towing. '**tow(-ing)-path** *n* path along the bank of a river or canal for use in towing, eg by horses pulling canal boats. □ *n* [C,U] towing or being towed? *have/take a boat in tow. Can we give you a tow? The lorry was on tow. He usually has his family in tow,* (colloq) has them with him.
tow² /təʊ/ *n* [U] coarse and broken fibres of flax, hemp, etc (for making rope).
to·ward(s) /tə'wɔːd(z) *US:* tɔːrd(z)/ *prep* **1** approaching; in the direction of: *walking ~ the sea; sit with one's back turned ~ the window; drifting ~ war; first steps ~ the abolition of armaments.* **2** as regards; in relation to: *Are his feelings ~ us friendly? What will the Government's attitude be ~ the plan?* **3** for the purpose of (helping): *We must save money ~ the children's education.* **4** (of time) near: ~ *the end of the century;* ~ *evening.*
towel /'taʊəl/ *n* [C] piece of cloth or absorbent paper for drying or wiping sth wet (eg one's hands or body): *a* '*bath* ~; *a* '*roller*~, an endless one on a revolving bar. '~**-rack/-horse** *nn* wooden frame for hanging ~s on. '~**-rail** *n* (usu metal) rail for a ~ (eg near a wash-basin). **throw in the** ~, ⇨ throw¹(11). □ *vt* (-ll-, *US* -l-) dry or rub (oneself) with a ~. ~·**ling** (*US* = ~·**ing**) *n* [U] material for ~s.
tower /'taʊə(r)/ *n* **1** tall, usu equal-sided (esp square) or circular building, either standing alone (eg as a fort, *the T~ of London*) or forming part of a church, castle or other large building (eg a college). ⇨ the illus at church. **2** (fig) *a* ~ *of strength,* a person who can be relied upon for protection, strength or comfort in time of trouble. **3** '**water** ~, ~ that supports a large tank for the storage and distribution of water at high pressure: '~**block** *n* high block of flats or offices. □ *vi* [VP2C] rise to a great height, be very tall, esp in relation to the height of the surroundings: *the skyscrapers that ~ over New York.* ~ **above sb,** (fig, of eminent persons) greatly exceed in ability, in intellectual or

moral qualities: *a man who ~s above his contemporaries.* ~·**ing** *adj* (esp): *in a ~ing rage*, violently angry.

town /taʊn/ *n* **1** centre of population larger than a village, smaller than, or not created, a city (and often used in contrast to *country*): *Would you rather live in a ~ or in the country?* (In GB the word ~ is used much more frequently than *city*, even when the place actually is a city, the word *city* being used chiefly in connection with local government affairs.) ⇨ city(1). *be/go out on the ~*, be/go out to enjoy the entertainment facilities of a ~. *paint the ~ red,* ⇨ red(1). **2** (attrib) ~ **centre**, area around which public buildings, eg the town hall, the public library, are grouped. ~ **clerk**, official who keeps ~ or city records. ~ **council**, governing body of a ~. ~ **councillor**, member of a ~ council. '~-**gas** *n* manufactured gas for domestic and industrial use. ~ **hall**, building with offices of local government and usu a hall for public events (meetings, concerts, etc). '~ **house**, house in ~, belonging to sb who also has a house in the country. ~ **planning**, preparation of plans for the regulated growth and improvement of ~s. **3** (preceded by a *prep*, and without the *def* or *indef art*) the business, shopping, etc part of a ~ (contrasted with the suburbs, etc): *go to ~ to do some shopping. He's in ~ today. I'm going down ~ this afternoon.* ⇨ downtown. *go to ~,* (sl) act, behave, without inhibitions, eg by spending lavishly, having a spree. **4** (without the *def* or *indef art*) the chief city or ~ in the neighbourhood (esp, in England, London): *He is spending the weekend in ~. He went up to ~ from Leeds. Mr Green is not in ~/is out of ~. man about ~,* fashionable man who spends much time amusing himself. **5 the ~,** the people of a ~: *The whole ~ was talking about it. the talk of the ~,* ⇨ talk¹(3). **6 the ~,** ~s in general: *Farm workers are leaving the country in order to get better paid work in the ~.* **7** '~s-**folk** *n pl* (a) (with *def art*) the people of the ~ referred to. **(b)** (without *def art*) people who live in ~s. '~s-**people** *n pl* = ~sfolk. '~s-**man** /-zmən/ *n* (*pl*-men) **(a)** man who lives in a ~. **(b)** (often *fellow*-'~*sman*) person who lives in one's own ~. **tow·nee** /taʊ'ni:/ *n* (derog) person who lives in a ~ and is ignorant of rural things.

town·ship /'taʊnʃɪp/ *n* **1** (US, Canada) subdivision of a county having certain powers of government; district six miles square in US surveys of land. **2** (S Africa) area, suburb, for houses, etc, of non-Europeans. **3** (Australia) site laid out for a town.

tox·aemia (also **tox–emia**) /tɒk'si:mɪə/ *n* [U] blood-poisoning.

toxic /'tɒksɪk/ *adj* of, caused by, a toxin; poisonous. ~·**ity** /tɒk'sɪsəti/ *n* [U] quality or degree of being ~: *study the ~ity of insecticides.* **toxi·col·ogy** /ˌtɒksɪ'kɒlədʒɪ/ *n* [U] branch of medical science dealing with the nature and effects of poisons. **toxi·col·ogist** /-dʒɪst/ *n* student of, expert in, toxicology.

toxin /'tɒksɪn/ *n* [C] poisonous substance, esp one formed by bacteria in plants and animals and causing a particular disease.

toy /tɔɪ/ *n* **1** child's plaything; small thing meant for amusement rather than for serious use. **2** (attrib) *toy dog/spaniel, etc*, small kinds kept as pets; *toy soldier*, one made as a toy(1). '**toy-shop** *n* shop where toys are sold. □ *vi* [VP3A] *toy with sth,* **1** amuse oneself (with); think not very seriously

about: *He toyed with the idea of buying a yacht.* **2** handle carelessly or absent-mindedly: *toying with a pencil.*

trace¹ /treɪs/ *n* **1** [U,C] mark, sign, etc showing that sb or sth has been present, that sth has existed or happened: *~s of an ancient civilization. The police were unable to find any ~ of the thief. We've lost all ~ of them,* don't know where they are. **2** [C] very small amount: *The post-mortem showed ~s of arsenic in the intestines.* '~ **element**, element of which a ~ is necessary for the development of animal or plant life and without which growth is poor (eg manganese in the soil, for wheat and oats).

trace² /treɪs/ *vt,vi* **1** [VP6A,15B] ~ *sth (out),* draw, sketch, the course, outline, etc, of: ~ *out the site of an old castle;* ~ (*out*) *one's route on a map;* (fig) ~ *out a policy,* give its outlines. **2** [VP6A] copy (sth), eg by drawing on transparent paper the lines, etc on (a map, design, etc) placed underneath. **3** [VP6A] write slowly and with difficulty: *He ~d the words laboriously.* **4** [VP6A,15A,B] follow or discover (sb or sth) by observing marks, tracks, bits of evidence, etc: *The criminal was ~d to Glasgow. I cannot ~* (= cannot find, do not think I received) *any letter from you dated 1st June.* ~ (*sth/sb*) *back (to sth),* (a) find the origin of by going back in time: *He ~s his descent back to an old Norman family. His fear of dogs ~s back/can be ~d back to a childhood experience.* (b) find the origin of by going back through evidence: *The rumour was ~d back to a journalist,* It was discovered that he had started it. **5** [VP6A] discover the position, size, etc of (sth) from its remains: *Archaeologists have ~d many Roman roads in Britain.* ~·**able** /-əbl/ *adj* capable of being ~d (*to*). ~r *n* **1** person who ~s(2). **2** (often '~r *bullet/ shell*) projectile whose course is made visible by a line of flame or smoke left behind it. '~r **element,** radioactive element which, when introduced into sth, can be ~d by the use of a Geiger counter. **trac·ing** *n* reproduction (of a map, design, etc) made by tracing(2). '**tracing–paper** *n* [U] strong transparent paper on which tracings are made.

trace³ /treɪs/ *n* [C] either of the leather straps, ropes, etc by which a wagon, carriage, cart, etc is pulled by a horse. ⇨ the illus at **harness.** *kick over the ~s,* (fig) become undisciplined; refuse to accept control.

tracery /'treɪsərɪ/ *n* [C,U] (*pl*-ries) ornamental arrangement of designs (eg as made by frost on glass, or of stonework in a church window); decorative pattern. ⇨ the illus at window.

tra·chea /trə'kɪə *US:* 'treɪkɪə/ *n* (*pl* ~e /-kɪi:/) (anat) windpipe. ⇨ the illus at respiratory.

tra·choma /trə'kəʊmə/ *n* [U] contagious eye disease causing inflammation of the inner surfaces of the eyelids.

track /træk/ *n* [C] **1** line or series of marks left by a vehicle, person, animal, etc in passing along; path or rough road made by persons/animals: ~*s in the snow,* eg footprints; *follow the ~s left by a bear;* '*sheep–~s across the moor; a ~ through the forest. be on sb's ~/on the ~ of sb,* be in pursuit of: *The police are on the ~ of the thief. I'm on his ~. cover up one's ~s,* conceal one's movements or activities. *go off/keep to the beaten ~,* ⇨ beaten. *have a ,one–~ 'mind,* habitually follow the same line of thought; give all one's attention to one topic. *keep/lose ~ of sb/sth,* keep in/lose touch with; follow/fail to follow the course or development of: *read the newspapers to keep ~ of current events.* **make ~s,** (colloq) depart (usu in a hurry); run away. **make ~s for,** (colloq) go towards: *It's time we made ~s for home.* **in one's ~s,** (sl) where one stands, there and then: *He fell dead in his ~s.* **off the ~,** (fig) away from the subject; following a wrong line of action. **go off/keep to the beaten ~,** ⇨ beaten. **2** course; line taken by sth (whether marked or not): *the ~ of a storm/comet/spacecraft.* **3** set of rails for trains, etc: *single/double ~,* one pair/two pairs of rails: *The train left the ~,* was derailed. **on/from the wrong side of the ~s,** (US) on/from the part of a town that is socially inferior, the part lived in by poor people. **4** path prepared for racing (eg made of cinders, clinkers, etc): *a 'motor-racing/ 'cycling/'running ~;* (attrib) *'~-racing; '~ events,* eg running races, contrasted with field events such as jumping, throwing the discus. **'~ suit** *n* loose-fitting warm suit worn by an athlete while not taking part in ~ events. **5** endless belt used instead of wheels on some tractors, military tanks, etc. □ *vt* **1** [VP6A,15A,B] follow the ~ of: *~ an animal to its den.* **'~-ing station** *n* one which, by radar or radio, maintains contact with space-vehicles, etc. **~ sb/sth down,** find by searching: *~ down a bear/a reference.* **~ out,** trace (the course or development of sth) by examining ~s. **2** (cinema, TV) move a camera (mounted on a mobile platform) while taking a long shot (called *a '~ing shot*). **~ed** *adj* having ~s(5): *~ed vehicles.* **~er** *n* person, esp a hunter, who ~s wild animals. **'~er dog,** dog used in pursuing persons escaping from justice. **~less** *adj* having no ~s(1): *~less forests.*

tract[1] /trækt/ *n* **1** stretch or area (*of* forest, farmland, etc): *the wide ~s of desert in N Africa.* **2** system of related parts in an animal body: *the di'gestive/re'spiratory ~.*

tract[2] /trækt/ *n* short printed essay on sth, esp a moral or religious subject.

tract·able /'træktəbl/ *adj* easily controlled or guided. **trac·ta·bil·ity** /ˌtræktə'bɪləti/ *n*

trac·tion /'trækʃn/ *n* [U] (power used in) pulling or drawing sth over a surface: *electric/steam ~.* **'~-engine** *n* engine used for pulling heavy loads.

trac·tor /'træktə(r)/ *n* powerful motor-vehicle used for pulling agricultural machinery (ploughs, drills, etc), or other heavy equipment. ⇨ the illus at plough.

trad /træd/ *n* [U] (colloq abbr of) traditional; (esp) jazz (of the 1920's and 1930's) played by a small group with simple rhythms and much improvisation.

trade[1] /treɪd/ *n* **1** [U] buying and selling of goods; exchange of goods for money or other goods; [C] particular branch of this: *Great Britain does a lot of ~ with some countries and not much with others. T~ was good last year. He's in the 'cotton/ 'furniture/'book, etc ~.* ˌstock-in-'~, ⇨ stock[1](1). **the ~,** (colloq) those engaged in the manufacture and sale of a certain commodity. **'~-mark** *n* design, special name, etc used to distinguish a manufacturer's goods from others; (fig) distinguishing characteristics: *He leaves his ~mark on all his undertakings.* **'~ name** *n* name given to manufacturers to a proprietary article. **'~ price** *n* the price charged by a manufacturer or wholesaler to a retailer. **~(s)-'union** *n* organized association

of workers in a ~ or group of ~s, formed to protect their interests, improve their conditions, etc. **~-'unionism** *n* [U] this system of association. **~-'unionist** *n* member of a ~-union. **T~s Union Congress,** (abbr **TUC**) association of British ~ unions. **'~-wind** *n* strong wind blowing always towards the equator from the SE and NE. **the T~s,** these winds. **2** occupation; way of making a living, esp a handicraft: *He's a weaver/mason/ carpenter/tailor by ~. Shoemaking is a useful ~. The college teaches many useful ~s.* **'~s-folk, '~s-people** *nn* persons engaged in ~; shopkeepers (and their families). **'~s·man** /-zmən/ *n* (*pl* men) shopkeeper.

trade[2] /treɪd/ *vi,vt* **1** [VP2A,C,3A] ~ **(in) (with),** engage in trade(1); buy and sell: *~ in furs and skins; ships that ~ between London and ports in the Mediterranean. Britain ~s with many European countries.* **'trad·ing estate,** (usu large) planned industrial area rented to manufacturers. **'trad·ing stamp,** (= gift coupon) coupon given to customers with purchases, exchangeable for various articles or cash. **2** [VP14] ~ **sth for sth,** exchange; barter: *The boy ~d his knife for a cricket bat.* **3** [VP15B] ~ **sth in,** hand over (a used article) in part payment for a new purchase: *He ~d in his old car for a new model.* Hence, **'~-in** *n* [C] sth sold in this way. **4** [VP3A] ~ **on/upon,** take a wrong advantage of, use, in order to get sth for oneself: *~ upon sb's sympathy; ~ upon one's past reputation.* **5** (US) shop: *Which stores do you ~ at,* do your shopping? **~r** *n* merchant.

tra·di·tion /trə'dɪʃn/ *n* [U] (handing down from generation to generation of) opinions, beliefs, customs, etc; [C] opinion, belief, custom, etc handed down: *The stories of Robin Hood are based mainly on ~(s). It is a ~ in that family for the eldest son to enter the army and for the second son to become a lawyer.* **~al** /-ʃənl/ *adj* **~·ally** /-ʃənəlɪ/ *adv* **~-al·ism** /-ʃənəlɪzəm/ *n* (excessive) respect for ~, esp in religious matters. **~·al·ist** /-ʃənəlɪst/ *n* person who attaches great importance to ~.

tra·duce /trə'djuːs *US:* -'duːs/ *vt* [VP6A] (formal) slander. **tra·ducer** *n* slanderer.

traf·fic /'træfɪk/ *n* [U] **1** (movement of) people and vehicles along roads and streets, of aircraft in the sky: *There was a lot of/not much ~ on the roads yesterday. T~ in large towns is controlled by ~ lights. The ~ control tower at an airport uses radar screens.* **'~ circle,** (US) = roundabout. **'~ indicator** = trafficator. ⇨ the illus at motor. **'~ jam,** condition in which many road vehicles are prevented from moving forward. **'~ light(s),** mechanical signal controlling road ~ (esp at junctions) by coloured lights (red, amber, green). **'~ warden,** ⇨ warden. **2** transport business done by road, rail, ship, air, etc. **3** illicit trading: *the ~ in liquor; illegal drug ~.* □ *vi* (-ck-) [VP3A] ~ **in sth (with sb),** trade: *~ in hides (with...).* **traf·ficker** *n* (usu in a bad sense) trader: *a 'drug ~ker.*

traf·fi·ca·tor /'træfɪkeɪtə(r)/ *n* device (usu a flickering amber light) used on a motor-vehicle to indicate the direction in which the vehicle is about to turn.

tra·gedy /'trædʒədɪ/ *n* (*pl* -dies) **1** [C] play for the theatre, cinema, TV, of a serious or solemn kind, with a sad ending; [U] branch of the drama with this kind of play. **2** [C,U] very sad event, action, experience, etc, in real life. **tra·gedian** /trə'dʒiːdɪən/ *n* writer of, actor in, ~. **tra·gedi-**

enne /trəˌdʒiːˈdɪˈen/ *n* actress in ~.

tra·gic /ˈtrædʒɪk/ *adj* of tragedy: *a ~ actor/event.* **tragi·cally** /-klɪ/ *adv*

tragi-com·edy /ˌtrædʒɪˈkɒmədɪ/ *n* (*pl* -dies) drama, event, that is a mixture of tragedy and comedy. **ˌtragi-ˈcomic** /ˈkɒmɪk/ *adj*

trail /treɪl/ *n* [C] **1** line, mark or series of marks, drawn or left behind by sb or sth that has passed by: *a ~ of smoke,* (from a railway steam-engine); *ˈvapour ~s,* as left in the sky by high-flying aircraft; *a ~ of destruction,* eg left by a violent storm. *The wounded tiger left a ~ of blood.* **2** track or scent followed in hunting. *hot on the ~ (of),* (lit or fig) close behind. **3** path through rough country. *blaze a ~,* ⇨ blaze³. □ *vt,vi* **1** [VP6A,15A,B,2A,C] pull, be pulled, along: *The child was ~ing a toy cart. Her long skirt was ~ing along/on the floor.* **2** [VP6A,15A] follow the ~ of: *~ a wild animal/a criminal.* **3** [VP2C] (of plants) grow over or along the ground, etc: *roses ~ing over the walls;* (of persons) walk wearily: *The wounded soldiers ~ed past us. The tired children ~ed along behind their father. ~er n* **1** transport-vehicle hauled by a tractor or truck; van or caravan drawn by a motor-vehicle (used for living in when parked). **2** ~ing plant. **3** series of short extracts from a cinema or TV film to advertise it in advance.

train¹ /treɪn/ *n* **1** [C] (locomotive and) number of railway coaches, wagons, etc joined together: *ˈpassenger/ˈgoods/ˈfreight ~s; take the 1.15am ~ to town; travel by ~; get into/out of a ~; get on/ off a ~; have lunch on the ~. The ~ is in/is waiting,* is at the station. *He missed/just caught his ~.* *ˈ~ ferry,* for carrying ~s over water (eg from England to France). *ˈ~·man* /-mən/ *n* (*pl* -men) (US) member of the crew operating a ~. **2** number of persons, animals, carriages, etc, moving in a line: *a ~ of camels; the ˈbaggage ~; persons in the king's ~,* in his retinue of attendants. **3** series or chain: *A knock at the door interrupted my ~ of thought. What an unlucky ~ of events! War often brings disease in its ~.* **4** part of a long dress or robe that trails on the ground behind the wearer. *ˈ~-bearer n* attendant who holds up, or helps to hold up, such a ~. **5** line of gunpowder leading to a place where material has been placed for an explosion (eg in a mine), to be lit at a safe distance. *in ~,* in readiness; being prepared.

train² /treɪn/ *vt,vi* **1** [VP6A,14,17,2C,3A] ~ *(for),* give teaching and practice to (eg a child, a soldier, an animal) in order to bring to a desired standard of behaviour, efficiency or physical condition: ~ *children to be good citizens; ~ a horse for a race/ performing seals for a circus. Very little escapes his ~ed eye. He was ~ed for the law/to be a lawyer. There is a shortage of ~ed nurses. They are ~ing for the boat-race.* **2** [VP6A,15A] cause to grow in a required direction: ~ *roses against/over a wall.* **3** [VP6A,14] ~ *sth on/upon sth,* point, aim: ~ *a gun upon the enemy's positions. ~ee* /treɪˈniː/ *n* person undergoing some form of (usu industrial) ~ing. *~er n* **1** person who ~s (esp athletes, horses for races, animals for the circus, etc). **2** aircraft used for ~ing pilots. *~·ing n* [U] ~ing or being ~ed. *in/out of ~ing,* in/not in good physical condition (eg for athletic contests). *go into ~ing,* ~ oneself. *ˈ~-ing-college n* college for ~ing people for a trade, profession, etc. *ˈ~-ing-ship n* one for ~ing boys in seamanship.

traipse /treɪps/ *vi* [VP2A,B,C] (colloq) walk weari-

ly: ~ *round the shops buying food for the family.*

trait /treɪt/ *n* [C] distinguishing quality or characteristic: *Two ~s in the American character are generosity and energy.*

trai·tor /ˈtreɪtə(r)/ *n* ~ *(to),* person who betrays a friend, is disloyal to a cause, his country, etc. *turn* ~, become a ~. *~·ous* /-əs/ *adj* treacherous; of or like a ~: *~ous conduct. ~·ous·ly adv* **traitress** /ˈtreɪtrɪs/ *n* woman ~.

tra·jec·tory /trəˈdʒektərɪ/ *n* (*pl* -ries) curved path of a projectile (eg a bullet, missile).

tram /træm/ *n* **1** (also *ˈ~-car* or *ˈtrolley-bus*) electric car used for public transport, running on rails along public streets (US = *ˈstreet-car* or *ˈtrolley-car*). *ˈ~-line n* line of rails for ~s; route served by ~s. **2** four-wheeled car used in coalmines.

tram·mel /ˈtræml/ *vt* (-ll-; US -l-) [VP6A] hamper; make progress difficult. □ *n pl ~s,* sth that ~s: *the ~s of routine/etiquette/superstition.*

tramp /træmp/ *vi,vt* **1** [VP2A,C] walk with heavy steps: *He ~ed up and down the platform waiting for the train.* **2** [VP2A,B,C,6A] walk through or over (esp for a long distance): ~ *through the mountains of Wales; ~ over the moors. They ~ed (for) miles and miles/~ed all day. He enjoys ~ing the hills.* □ *n* **1** *the ~ of,* sound of heavy footsteps: *I heard the ~ of marching soldiers.* **2** long walk: *go for a ~ in the country.* **3** person (usu homeless) who goes from place to place and does no regular work: *There's a ~ at the door begging for food.* **4** *ˈ~(-steamer),* cargo boat which goes to any port(s) where cargo can be picked up.

trample /ˈtræmpl/ *vt,vi* **1** [VP6A,15B] ~ *sth (down),* tread heavily on with the feet; crush under the feet: *The children have ~d (down) the flowers/~d the grass down. You wouldn't like to be ~d to death by elephants.* **2** [VP3A] ~ *on,* tread heavily on: ~ *on sb's toes/feelings.* **3** [VP2C] ~ *about,* walk about heavily. □ *n* sound, act, of trampling.

tram·po·line /ˈtræmpəliːn/ *n* [C] sheet of strong canvas on a spring frame, used by gymnasts for acrobatic leaps.

trance /trɑːns *US:* træns/ *n* **1** sleep-like condition: *be/fall/go into a ~.* **2** abnormal, dreamy state; hypnotic state: *send sb into a ~.*

tran·quil /ˈtræŋkwɪl/ *adj* calm; quiet: *a ~ life in the country. ~·ly* /-wɪlɪ/ *adv* *~·lity* (US also *~-ity*) /træŋˈkwɪlətɪ/ *n* [U] ~ state. *~·lize* (US also *~-ize*) /-aɪz/ *vt* [VP6A] make ~ (esp by means of a drug). *~·li·zer* (US also *~·izer*) *n* drug that ~lizes; sedative.

trans·act /trænˈzækt/ *vt* [VP6A,14] ~ *sth (with sb),* conduct, carry through (business, etc with sb).

trans·ac·tion /trænˈzækʃn/ *n* **1** [U] *the ~ of,* transacting: *the ~ of business.* **2** [C] piece of business: *cash ~s; the bank's ~s in stocks and shares.* **3** (*pl*) (records of the) proceedings of (esp a learned society, eg its meetings, lectures): *the ~s of the Kent Archaeological Society.*

trans·al·pine /trænˈzælpaɪn/ *n, adj* (person living) beyond the Alps (esp as viewed from Italy).

trans·at·lan·tic /ˌtrænzətˈlæntɪk/ *adj* beyond the Atlantic; crossing the Atlantic: *a ~ voyage/flight;* concerning (countries on) both sides of the Atlantic: *a ~ treaty/trade agreement.*

tran·scend /trænˈsend/ *vt* [VP6A] go or be beyond or outside the range of (human experience, reason, belief, powers of description, etc).

tran·scen·dent /trænˈsendənt/ *adj* surpassing; ex-

celling: *a man of* ~ *genius.* **tran·scen·dence**
/-dəns/, **tran·scen·dency** /-dənsɪ/ *nn*
tran·scen·den·tal /ˌtrænsen'dentl/ *adj* **1** not based
on experience or reason; going beyond human
knowledge; that cannot be discovered or understood by practical experience; known by intuition.
⇨ **empirical. 2** (colloq) vague; not clear to ordinary minds. ~·**ly** /-təlɪ/ *adv* ~·**ism** /-təlɪzəm/ *n*
[U] ~ philosophy; doctrine that knowledge may be
obtained by a study of the mental processes, apart
from experience. ~·**ist** /-təlɪst/ *n* believer in
~ism.
trans·con·ti·nen·tal /ˌtrænzkɒntɪ'nentl/ *adj* crossing a continent: *a* ~ *railway.*
tran·scribe /træn'skraɪb/ *vt* [VP6A] copy in writing, esp write (sth) in full from shorthand notes.
tran·script /'trænskrɪpt/ *n* [C] sth ~d. **tran·scrip-
tion** /træn'skrɪpʃn/ *n* **1** [U] transcribing: *errors in
transcription.* **2** [C] sth ~d, esp into a special form
of writing: *phonetic transcriptions.* **3** (broadcast
made from a) recording (on a disc or tape): *the
BBC transcription service.*
tran·sept /'trænsept/ *n* [C] (archit) (either end of
the) transverse part of a cross-shaped church: *the
north/south* ~ *of the cathedral.* ⇨ the illus at
church.
trans·fer[1] /'trænsfɜ:(r)/ *n* [C,U] (instance of) transferring; document that transfers sth or sb; drawing,
plan, etc transferred from one surface to another;
ticket that allows a passenger to continue his journey on another bus, etc. '~ **fee**, sum paid for a ~
(esp of a professional footballer to another club).
trans·fer[2] /træns'fɜ:(r)/ *vt,vi* (-rr-) [VP6A,14,3A]
~ **(sb/sth) (from) (to), 1** change position, move:
The head office has been ~*red from York to London. He has been* ~*red from the Manchester
branch to the London branch. The dog has* ~*red
its affection to its new master.* **2** hand over the possession of (property, etc to): ~ *rights to sb.* **3** convey (a drawing, design, pattern, etc) from one surface to another (eg from a wooden surface to canvas). **4** change from one train, bus, etc to another;
move from one occupation, position, etc to another: *He has* ~*red from the warehouse to the accounts office.* ~·**able** /-əbl/ *adj* that can be ~red:
~*able accounts,* of money that may be ~red from
one currency to another. *Railway tickets are not*
~*able.* ~·**abil·ity** /ˌtrænsˌfɜːrə'bɪlətɪ/ *n* [U]. ~·
ence /'trænsfərəns US:* træns'fɜːrəns/ *n* ~ing or
being ~red, esp from one job to another.
trans·fig·ure /træns'fɪgə(r) US:* -gjər/ *vt* [VP6A]
change the shape and appearance of, esp so as to
make glorious, exalted or idealized. **trans·figur-
ation** /ˌtrænsfɪgə'reɪʃn US:* -gjə'r-/ *n* [U,C] change
of this sort, esp **the Transfiguration**, that of Jesus, as described in the Bible. ⇨ Matt 17.
trans·fix /træns'fɪks/ *vt* [VP6A] **1** pierce through:
~ *a leopard with a spear.* **2** cause (sb) to be unable
to move, speak, think, etc; paralyse the faculties
of: *He stood* ~*ed with fear/horror/amazement.*
trans·form /træns'fɔːm/ *vt* [VP6A,14] ~ *sth (into
sth),* change the shape, appearance, quality or nature of: *Success and wealth* ~*ed his character. A
steam-engine* ~*s heat into energy. A caterpillar is
* ~*ed into a butterfly.* ~·**able** /-əbl/ *adj* that can be
~ed. **trans·form·ation** /ˌtrænsfə'meɪʃn/ *n* [U]
~ing or being ~ed; [C] instance of this: *His character has undergone a* ~*ation since his brain
operation.* ~·**er** *n* sb or sth that ~s, esp apparatus
that increases or decreases the voltage of an electric

power supply.
trans·fuse /træns'fjuːz/ *vt* [VP6A] transfer (sth, esp
the blood of one person to another). **trans·fusion**
/træns'fjuːʒn/ *n* [U] act or process of transfusing;
[C] instance of this: *The injured man was given a
' blood transfusion.*
trans·gress /trænz'gres/ *vt,vi* **1** [VP6A] go beyond
(a limit or bound): ~ *the bounds of decency.* **2**
[VP6A] break (a law, treaty, agreement). **3** [VP2A]
sin; offend against a moral principle. **trans·gress-
ion** /trænz'greʃn/ *n* [U] ~ing; [C] instance of this;
sin. ~·**or** /-sə(r)/ *n* person who ~es; sinner.
tran·si·ent /'trænzɪənt US:* 'trænʃnt/ *adj* lasting for
a short time only; brief: ~ *happiness; a* ~ *success.*
□ *n* (US) guest (in a hotel, boarding-house, etc)
who is not a permanent resident. **tran·si·ence**
/-əns/, **tran·si·ency** /-nsɪ/ *nn*
tran·sis·tor /træn'zɪstə(r)/ *n* [C] **1** small electronic
device, often used in place of a thermionic valve,
used in radio sets, hearing aids and other kinds of
electronic apparatus: (attrib) *a portable* ~ *(set).* **2**
~ **set;** ~ **radio.** ~·**ized** /-aɪzd/ *adj* fitted with ~s
instead of valves: *a* ~*ized computer.*
tran·sit /'trænsɪt/ *n* [U] **1** conveying or being conveyed, across, over or through: *goods lost/delayed
in* ~, while being carried from one place to another. '~ **camp,** one for the use of persons (eg refugees, soldiers) who are in ~ from one place to
another. '~ **visa,** visa allowing passage through
(but not a stay in) a country. **2** apparent passage of
a heavenly body, eg a planet, across the disc of another one, eg of Venus across the sun.
tran·si·tion /træn'zɪʃn/ *n* [C,U] changing, change,
from one condition or set of circumstances to another: *the period of* ~ *in Africa,* eg when colonial
countries there were becoming self-governing
states. *Adolescence is the* ~ *period/the period of
* ~ *between childhood and adulthood. The frequent
* ~*s from cold to warm weather this spring have
caused much illness.* ~·**al** /-ʃnl/ *adj* ~·**ally**
/-ʃnəlɪ/ *adv*
tran·si·tive /'trænsətɪv/ *adj* (gram) (of a verb) taking a direct object. ~·**ly** *adv*
tran·si·tory /'trænsɪtrɪ US:* -tɔːrɪ/ *adj* transient.
trans·late /trænz'leɪt/ *vt* [VP6A,14] ~ *sth (from)
(into),* **1** give the meaning of (sth said or written) in
another language: ~ *an English book into French;
* ~*d from (the) Italian. The poems don't* ~ *well.* **2**
remove (a bishop) to a different see; (in the Bible)
take to heaven without death. **trans·lat·able** /-əbl/
adj **trans·la·tor** /-tə(r)/ *n* person who ~s (esp sth
written). Cf *interpreter* for sth spoken. **trans·la-
tion** /-'leɪʃn/ *n* [U] translating: *errors in translation;* [C] sth ~d: *make/do a translation into
French.*
trans·lit·er·ate /trænz'lɪtəreɪt/ *vt* [VP6A,14] ~ *sth
(into),* write (a word, passage) in the characters of
a different language or system: ~ *Greek into Roman letters;* ~ *English words into phonetic
symbols.* **trans·lit·er·ation** /ˌtrænzlɪtə'reɪʃn/ *n*
[C,U] transliterating; sth ~d.
trans·lu·cent /trænz'luːsnt/ *adj* allowing light to
pass through but not transparent (as ordinary glass
is): *Frosted glass is* ~. **trans·lu·cence** /-sns/,
trans·lu·cency /-snsɪ/ *nn*
trans·mi·gra·tion /ˌtrænzmaɪ'greɪʃn/ *n* [U] migra-
tion; (esp) ~ *of the soul,* the passing of the soul at
death into another body.
trans·mission /trænz'mɪʃn/ *n* **1** [U] transmitting or
being transmitted: *the* ~ *of news/disease/a radio*

or TV programme. **2** [C] clutch, gears and drive which transmit power from the engine to (usu) the rear axle (of a motor-vehicle).

trans·mit /trænz'mɪt/ *vt* (-tt-) [VP6A,14] ～ **sth** *(to),* **1** pass or hand on; send on: ～ *a message by radio;* ～ *a disease. Parents* ～ *some of their characteristics to their children.* **2** allow through or along: *Iron* ～*s heat.* ～**·ter** *n* sb or sth that ～s, esp (part of a) telegraph or radio apparatus for sending out signals, messages, music, etc.

trans·mog·rify /trænz'mɒgrɪfaɪ/ *vt* (*pt,pp* -fied) [VP6A] cause to change completely in appearance or character, esp in a magical or surprising way. **trans·mog·ri·fi·ca·tion** /ˌtrænzmɒgrɪfɪ'keɪʃn/ *n*

trans·mute /trænz'mjuːt/ *vt* [VP6A,14] ～ **sth** *(into),* change the shape, nature or substance of: *We cannot* ～ *base metals into gold.* **trans·mut·able** /-əbl/ *adj* that can be ～d. **trans·mu·ta·tion** /ˌtrænzmjuː'teɪʃn/ *n*

trans·oceanic /ˌtrænzˌəʊʃɪ'ænɪk/ *adj* beyond or crossing an ocean: *the* ～ *migrations of birds.*

tran·som /'trænsəm/ *n* horizontal bar of wood over the top of a door or window. '～(-**window**), hinged window over a door or other window; (US) fanlight.

trans·par·ent /træns'pærənt/ *adj* **1** allowing light to pass through so that objects (or at least their outlines) behind can be distinctly seen: ～ *window-panes;* ～ *silk.* ⇨ translucent. **2** about which there can be no mistake or doubt: *a* ～ *lie; a man of* ～ *honesty.* **3** clear; easily understood: *a* ～ *style of writing.* ～**·ly** *adv* **trans·par·ence** /-rəns/ *n* [U] state of being ～. **trans·par·ency** /-rənsɪ/ *n* (*pl* -cies) **1** [U] = *transparence.* **2** [C] diagram, picture, etc (usu in a frame) on photographic film, made visible by light behind it (so that it may be projected on to a screen).

tran·spire /træn'spaɪə(r)/ *vi,vt* **1** [VP2A] (of an event, a secret) become public; come to be known: *It* ～*d that the President had spent the weekend golfing.* **2** [VP2A] (colloq) happen. **3** [VP6A] (of the body, plants) give off, pass off (moisture, vapour). **tran·spi·ra·tion** /ˌtrænspɪ'reɪʃn/ *n* transpiring(3); loss of water vapour, eg from the surface of leaves.

trans·plant /træns'plɑːnt *US:* -'plænt/ *vt,vi* **1** [VP6A,2A] take up (plants, etc) with their roots and plant in another place: ～ *young cabbage plants. Some seedlings do not* ～ *well.* **2** transfer (tissue, or an organ, eg a heart or kidney) from one body to another. **3** [VP6A] (fig, of people) move from one place to another. □ *n* /'trænsplɑːnt *US:* -plænt/ instance of ～ing(2): *a* '*kidney* ～. **trans·plan·ta·tion** /ˌtrænsplɑːn'teɪʃn *US:* -plæn-/ *n*

trans·po·lar /ˌtrænz'pəʊlə(r)/ *adj* across the polar regions: ～ *flights from London to Tokyo.*

trans·port[1] /'trænspɔːt/ *n* **1** [U] conveying or being conveyed; means of conveyance: *the* ～ *of troops by air; road* ～*; water-borne* ～, by ship. *My car is being repaired so I am without* ～*/without means of* ～ *at present.* **2** (attrib) of or for carrying, conveying: *London's* ～ *system;* ～ *charges.* '～ **café**, one used by long-distance lorry drivers, etc. **3** [C] (**'troop**-), ship or aircraft for carrying troops and supplies. **4** (often *pl*) **in a** ～**/in** ～**s of,** (liter) filled with, carried away by, strong feelings of (delight, rage, etc).

trans·port[2] /træn'spɔːt/ *vt* **1** [VP6A,15A] carry (goods, persons) from one place to another: ～ *goods by lorry.* **2** [VP6A,15A] (hist) send (a crimi-

nal) to a distant colony as a punishment: ～*ed to Australia.* **3 be** ～**ed with,** (liter) be overcome with, carried away by (strong emotion): *On hearing of the victory, the nation was* ～*ed with joy.* ～**·able** /-əbl/ *adj* that can be ～ed or conveyed. **trans·por·ta·tion** /ˌtrænspɔː'teɪʃn/ *n* [U] ～ing or being ～ed: *The criminal was sentenced to* ～*ation for life.*

trans·porter /træn'spɔːtə(r)/ *n* person or thing that transports, eg a travelling crane, or a long vehicle for carrying motor-vehicles from a factory, or a conveyor belt. '～ **bridge**, bridge with a movable deck or car used to convey passengers and goods from one end to the other.

trans·pose /træn'spəʊz/ *vt* [VP6A,14] **1** cause (two or more things) to change places. **2** (music) put into another key. **trans·po·si·tion** /ˌtrænspə'zɪʃn/ *n* [C,U] transposing or being ～d.

trans·sexual /trænz'sekʃʊəl/ *n* (psych) person who belongs physically to one sex, but who feels psychologically that he belongs to the other sex; person who has had a surgical operation, medical treatment, etc, to modify his sexual organs, etc, so that he physically resembles the other sex.

trans·ship /træn'ʃɪp/ *vt* (-pp-) [VP6A] transfer from one ship or conveyance to another. ～**·ment** *n*

tran·sub·stan·ti·ation /ˌtrænsəbˌstænʃɪ'eɪʃn/ *n* (RC Church) doctrine that the bread and wine in the Eucharist are changed into the body and blood of Christ.

trans·verse /'trænzvɜːs/ *adj* lying or placed across: *a* ～ *engine,* one placed parallel, instead of at right angles, to the axles of a car. ～**·ly** *adv*

trans·vest·ism /trænz'vestɪzəm/ *n* [U] (psych) practice of dressing in clothing of the other sex. **trans·ves·tite** /-taɪt/ *n* person who practises ～.

trap /træp/ *n* **1** device for catching animals, etc: *a* '*fly-*～*; a* '*mouse-*～*; caught in a* ～; (fig) plan for deceiving sb; trick or device to make sb say or do sth he does not wish to do or say: *The employer set a* ～ *for the man by putting marked money in the till. Our soldiers pretended to run away and the enemy, in pursuing them, fell into a* ～. **2** U-shaped or other section of a drain-pipe which retains liquid and so prevents return flow of sewer gas (eg under the pan of a lavatory). **3** light, two-wheeled vehicle pulled by a horse or pony. **4** ～('-**door**), hinged door or opening in roof, ceiling, floor or the stage of a theatre. **5** (sl) mouth: *Shut your* ～*!* **6** device (eg a box) from which an animal or object can be released, eg greyhounds at the start of a race, or clay pigeons, balls, etc. '～-**shooting,** the sport of shooting at clay pigeons or balls released by springs into the air. □ *vt* (-pp-) [VP6A,15A] take in a ～; capture by a trick. ～**·per** *n* person who ～s animals, esp fur-bearing animals.

tra·peze /trə'piːz *US:* træ-/ *n* horizontal bar or rod supported by two ropes, used by acrobats and for gymnastic exercises.

tra·pezium /trə'piːzɪəm/ *n* (*pl* ～s) (geom) (GB) four-sided figure having only two sides parallel; (US) = *trapezoid.* ⇨ the illus at quadrilateral.

trap·ezoid /'træpɪzɔɪd/ *n* (geom) (GB) four-sided figure having no sides parallel; (US) = *trapezium.* ⇨ parallelogram. ⇨ the illus at quadrilateral.

trap·pings /'træpɪŋz/ *n pl* (fig) ornaments or decorations, esp as a sign of public office: *He had all the* ～ *of high office but very little power.*

Trap·pist /'træpɪst/ *n* member of an order of monks noted for refraining from speaking and for other austerities.

trash /træʃ/ n [U] **1** worthless material or writing. **2** (US) rubbish; refuse: *a '~-can* (GB = *dustbin*). **~y** adj worthless: *~y novels.*

trauma /'trɔːmə US: 'traʊmə/ n (pl ~s /-məz/) (med) diseased condition of the body produced by a wound or injury; (psych) emotional shock, often leading to neurosis. **trau·matic** /trɔː'mætɪk US: traʊ-/ adj of a wound or injury; of or for the treatment of a wound or injury; (of an experience) distressing and unforgettable.

tra·vail /'træveɪl US: trə'veɪl/ n [U] **1** (liter) laborious effort. **2** (archaic) pains of childbirth.

travel /'trævl/ vi,vt (-ll-; US -l-) **1** [VP2A,B,C,4A] make a (esp long) journey or journeys: *go ~ling; ~ round the world; ~ (for) thousands of miles; (for) three months; ~ (over) the whole world.* '~ **agent,** n person who makes arrangements for ~ing, by selling tickets, reserving accommodation, etc. ~ **agency/bureau** n **~ling fellowship** n grant of money for educational ~ing. .2 [VP3A] ~ **(in sth) (for sb),** go from place to place as a salesman: *He ~s in cotton goods. He ~s* (ie as a salesman) *for a London publisher.* **3** [VP2A,B,C] move; go: *Light ~s faster than sound. Cars are assembled as they ~ from one part of a workshop to another.* **4** [VP2C] pass from point to point: *The general's eyes ~led over the enemy's positions. Her mind ~led over recent events.* **~·ling,** (US = **~·ing**) n [U] (esp attrib): '~ling expenses; a '~ling bag/dress, used or designed for ~ling. □ n **1** [U] ~ling: *T~ was slow and dangerous in olden days. He is fond of ~.* '~ **sickness** n [U] nausea caused by the motion of ~ling. **2** (in compounds) '~-soiled/-stained/-worn, soiled, etc, by ~. **3** (pl) journeys, esp abroad: *write a book about one's ~s.* **4** extent of the movement of a mechanical part, eg the shuttle of a loom. **~-led,** (US = **~ed**) adj **1** having made many long journeys: *a ~led man.* **2** used by people who ~: *a much ~led part of the country.* **~·ler,** (US = **~er**) /'trævlə(r)/ n **1** person on a journey. '~**ler's cheque** (US '~**er's check**), n one issued by a bank, tourist agency, etc, for the convenience of ~lers. **2** (often commercial ~ler) ~ling salesman. **trav·elogue** (also **-log**) /'trævəlɒg US: -lɔːg/ n film or lecture describing ~s.

tra·verse /'trævɜːs US: trə'vɜːs/ vt [VP6A] travel across; pass over: *Searchlights ~d the sky. The railway ~s hundreds of miles of desert.* □ n [C] **1** (mountaineering) sideways movement across the face of a precipice, steep slope of ice, etc from one point where ascent or descent is possible to another; place where this is necessary. **2** change of direction in a trench to prevent the enemy from firing along it.

trav·esty /'trævəstɪ/ n [C] (pl -ties) parody; imitation or description (of sth) that is, often on purpose, unlike and inferior to the real thing: *His trial was a ~ of justice.* □ vt (pt,pp -tied) [VP6A] make or be a ~ of: *~ a person's style of writing.*

trawl /trɔːl/ n [C] **1** '~(-net), large wide-mouthed net to be dragged along the sea-bottom. **2** (US) '~ **line** (also *setline*) long sea-fishing line to which are attached many short lines with hooks. □ vi,vt [VP2A] fish with a ~; [VP6A] drag along the sea-bottom: *~ a net.* **~er** n boat, fisherman, that ~s.

tray /treɪ/ n flat piece of wood, metal, etc with raised edges, for holding light articles, eg *a 'pen-~,* or carrying things, eg *a 'tea-~;* container on a

writing-desk for papers, etc. '**in-/'out-tray,** for papers, letters, etc coming in/ready to go out.

treach·er·ous /'tretʃərəs/ adj **1** false or disloyal (to a friend, cause, etc). **2** deceptive; not to be relied upon: *~ weather. The ice is ~,* appears to be strong but may break. *My memory is ~.* **~·ly** adv **treach·ery** /'tretʃərɪ/ n (pl -ries) [U] being ~; (pl) ~ acts.

treacle /'triːkl/ n [U] thick, sticky, dark liquid produced while sugar is being refined (US = *molasses*). **treacly** /'triːkəlɪ/ adj like ~; thick and sweet; (fig) excessively sweet: *treacly sentiments.*

tread /tred/ vi,vt (pt trod /trɒd/, pp trodden /'trɒdn/ or trod) **1** [VP2C,3A] ~ **(on sth),** walk, put the foot or feet down (on): *~ on sb's toes. Don't ~ on the flower beds. She trod lightly so as not to wake the baby.* **~ on air,** be light-hearted and gay, transported with joy. **~ on sb's corns/ toes,** (fig) offend him. **~ on sb's heels,** (lit or fig) follow closely after. **2** [VP6A,15A,B] ~ **(out/ down),** stamp or crush; push (down, etc) with the feet: *~ out a fire in the grass; ~ grapes,* when making wine; *~ (out) the juice from grapes; ~ (down) the earth round the roots.* **3** [VP6A] make by walking: *The cattle had trodden a path to the pond.* **4** [VP6A] walk along: (fig) *~ a dangerous path,* follow a risky course of action; *~ the boards,* (rhet) be an actor; *~ a measure,* (archaic) dance. **~ water,** keep oneself afloat in deep water by moving the feet up and down (as if working the pedals of a bicycle). □ n **1** way or sound of walking: *with a heavy/loud ~.* **2** part of a step or stair on which the foot is placed. '**~-mill** n appliance or apparatus for producing circular motion by the movements of a person or animal walking on the steps (or treads) of a wheel or a sloping endless belt (eg the kind formerly used in prisons as a punishment); (fig) monotonous routine. **3** grooved part of a tyre which touches the ground: *Good ~s minimize the risk of skidding.* ⇨ retread.

treadle /'tredl/ n pedal or lever that drives a machine, eg a lathe or sewing-machine, worked by pressure of the foot or feet. □ vi [VP2A] work a ~.

trea·son /'triːzn/ n [U] treachery to, betrayal of, one's country or ruler; disloyalty; betrayal of trust. **~·ous** /'triːzənəs/, **~·able** /'triːzənəbl/ adjj ~**ably** /-əblɪ/ adv

treas·ure /'treʒə(r)/ n **1** [C,U] (store of) gold and silver, jewels, etc; wealth: *The pirates buried their ~.* '**~-house** n building where ~ is stored. '**~- trove** n [U] ~ found hidden in the earth and of unknown ownership. **2** highly valued object or person: *The National Gallery has many priceless 'art ~s. She says her new secretary is a perfect ~. My ~!* (as a term of endearment). □ vt **1** [VP6A,15B]

a trawler

~ **sth (up)**, store for future use: ~ *memories of one's holiday in Thailand;* ~ *sth up in one's memory.* **2** [VP6A] value highly: ~ *sb's friendship. He* ~s *the watch his father gave him.* ~r /'treʒərə(r)/ *n* person in charge of money, etc belonging to a club or society.

treas-ury /'treʒərɪ/ *n* (*pl* -ries) **1 the T~**, (in GB) department of State controlling public revenue. **First Lord of the T~**, the Prime Minister. **the 'T~ Board/Lords of the T~**, officers in charge of public revenue (usu the Prime Minister, the Chancellor of the Exchequer, and three others). **the 'T~ Bench**, bench in the House of Commons occupied by members of the Cabinet. **'~ bill**, (GB) bill of exchange issued by the T~ to raise money for temporary needs. **'~ note**, currency note issued by the US T~; (formerly) currency note issued by the British T~ (now replaced by Bank of England notes). **2** place where funds are kept; funds of a society, organization, etc: *The* ~ *of our tennis club is almost empty.* **3** person, book, etc looked upon as containing valuable information or as a valued source: *This dictionary is a* ~ *of information.*

treat /tri:t/ *vt,vi* [VP15A,16B] ~ **(as)**, act or behave towards: *He* ~s *his wife badly. Don't* ~ *me as (if I were) a child. You must* ~ *them with more consideration.* **2** [VP16B] ~ **as**, consider: *We had better* ~ *it as a joke,* instead of taking it seriously. **3** [VP6A] discuss; deal with: *The lecturer* ~ed *his subject thoroughly. The problem has been* ~ed *by numerous experts.* **4** [VP3A] ~ **of**, (formal) be about: *The essay/lecture/book* ~s *of the progress of cancer research.* **5** [VP6A] give medical or surgical care to: *Which doctors are* ~ing *her for her illness? How would you* ~ *a case of rheumatism/* ~ *sb ill with influenza?* **6** [VP6A] put (a substance) through a process (in manufacture, etc): ~ *a substance with acid/wood with creosote.* **7** [VP6A,14] ~ **sb/oneself (to sth)**, supply (food, drink, entertainment, etc) at one's own expense (to): ~ *one's friends to oysters and champagne. I shall* ~ *myself to a good weekend holiday. It's my turn to* ~ *us today.* **8** [VP3A] ~ **with sb**, discuss or arrange with him: ~ *with the enemy for peace. If we are to* ~ *with you, it must be on equal terms.* □ *n* **1** [C] sth that gives pleasure, esp sth not often enjoyed or sth that comes unexpectedly: *What a* ~ *to get into the peace and quiet of the country! It's a great* ~ *for her to go to the ballet.* **2** act of ~ing(7): *This is to be my* ~, I'm going to pay. **stand** ~, (colloq) bear the expense of the entertainment.

treat·ise /'tri:tɪz *US*: -tɪs/ *n* ~ **(on/upon)**, book, etc that deals systematically with one subject: *a* ~ *on racial prejudice.*

treat·ment /'tri:tmənt/ *n* [C,U] (particular way of) treating sb or sth; what is done to obtain a desired result: *Is the* ~ *of political prisoners fair in your country? He soon recovered under the doctor's* ~*. That dog has suffered from cruel* ~*. He has tried many* ~s *for skin diseases. They are trying a new* ~ *for cancer. She is still under* ~ *in hospital.*

treaty /'tri:tɪ/ *n* (*pl* -ties) **1** [C] formal agreement made and signed between nations: *a'peace* ~*; enter into a* ~ *of commerce* (*with*). **'~ port**, one that a country is bound by ~ to keep open for foreign trade. **2** [U] agreement or negotiation between persons: *be in* ~ *with sb for…; sell a house by private* ~, instead of by public auction or other method.

treble[1] /'trebl/ *adj*, *n* three times as much or many (as): *He earns* ~ *my salary.* ~ **'chance**, method

of competing in football pools. □ *vt,vi* [VP6A,2A] make or become ~: *He has* ~d *his earnings/His earnings have* ~d *during the last few years.*

treble[2] /'trebl/ *n* (boy's voice with, instrument that takes, the) highest part in a piece of music. ~ **clef**, ⇨ clef, and the illus at notation.

tree /tri:/ *n* **1** perennial plant with a single self-supporting trunk of wood with (usu) no branches for some distance above the ground: *cut down* ~s *for timber.* ⇨ bush, shrub. **at the top of the** ~, at the top of one's profession. **up a ('gum-)**~, (colloq) cornered; in a position from which escape is difficult. **family** ~, diagram or list showing or giving family descent. **'~-fern** *n* fern that grows to the size of a tree. **2** piece of wood, metal, etc for a special purpose: *a 'boot-/'shoe-*~, for keeping a boot or shoe in shape while not being worn; *an 'axle-*~, connecting two opposite wheels. □ *vt* [VP6A] cause to take refuge up a ~: *The hunter was* ~d *by the bear. The dog* ~d *the cat.* **~-less** *adj* without ~s: *the* ~*less plains of Argentina.*

tre·foil /'trefɔɪl/ *n* kinds of three-leaved plant, eg clover; ornament or design like a threefold leaf, eg as in stonework.

trek /trek/ *vi* (-kk-) [VP2A,B,C] make a long, hard journey. □ *n* long, hard journey.

trel·lis /'trelɪs/ *n* light upright structure of strips of wood, etc esp as used for supporting climbing plants. □ *vt* [VP6A] furnish with, support on, a ~.

tremble /'trembl/ *vi* [VP2A,B,C,4B] **1** shake involuntarily (as from fear, anger, cold, physical weakness, etc): *His voice* ~d *with anger. We were trembling with cold/excitement.* **2** move to and fro: *The bridge* ~d *as the heavy lorry crossed it. The ground* ~d *under our feet.* **3** be in a state of agitation: *I* ~ *to think what has happened to him,* am deeply worried. *She* ~d *for his safety.* **in fear and trembling**, in a state of frightened anxiety. □ *n* shudder; uncontrollable shaking: *There was a* ~ (more usu *a tremor*) *in his voice. He was all of a* ~, (colloq) was trembling all over.

tre·men·dous /trɪ'mendəs/ *adj* **1** very great; enormous; powerful: *a* ~ *explosion; travelling at a* ~ *speed.* **2** (colloq) extraordinary: *He's a* ~ *eater/talker,* eats/talks to an extraordinary degree; splendid, first rate: *a* ~ *concert/performance/meal.* ~**·ly** *adv*

trem·olo /'tremələʊ/ *n* (*pl* ~s /-ləʊz/) (music) trembling or vibrating effect in singing, or in the playing of a bowed musical instrument.

tremor /'tremə(r)/ *n* [C] **1** shaking or trembling: *the* ~ *of a leaf,* eg in a breeze; *'earth* ~s, as during an earthquake. **2** thrill: *A* ~ *of fear went through the audience when the assassin fired at the President.*

tremu·lous /'tremjʊləs/ *adj* **1** trembling: *in a* ~ *voice; with a* ~ *hand.* **2** timid; nervous. ~**·ly** *adv*

trench /trentʃ/ *n* [C] ditch dug in the ground, eg for the draining of water, for a latrine, as a protection for soldiers against the enemy's fire: *dig* ~es *for irrigation;* ~ *warfare,* fought in and from ~es; *a '*~*-coat,* soldier's waterproof coat. □ *vt* [VP6A] surround with a ~; fortify with a ~ or ~es; make ~es in: ~ *a field,* for draining.

trench·ant /'trentʃənt/ *adj* (of language) vigorous; incisive: ~ *wit; a* ~ *speech.* ~**·ly** *adv* **trench·ancy** /-ənsɪ/ *n*

trencher /'trentʃə(r)/ *n* (hist) large wooden plate on which food was formerly served or carved. **'~-man** /-mən/ *n* (*pl* -men) *a good/poor* ~*man*, person who usu eats a lot/a little.

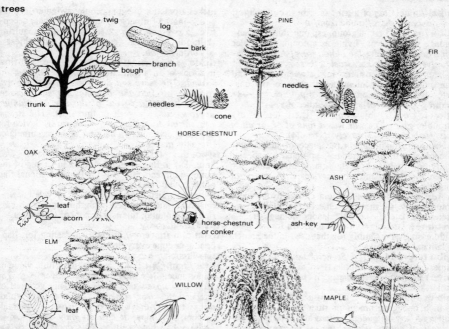

trees

twig

log

bark

branch

bough

trunk

needles

cone

PINE

needles

cone

FIR

HORSE-CHESTNUT

OAK

leaf

acorn

horse-chestnut
or conker

ASH

ash-key

ELM

leaf

WILLOW

MAPLE

trend /trend/ n [C] general direction; tendency: *The ~ of the coastline is to the south. Is the ~ of modern thought away from materialism? The ~ of prices is still upwards.* **set the ~,** start a style, etc which others follow. Hence, **'~-setter,** '**~-setting** nn. **~y** adj (-ier, -iest) (sl, often derog) showing, following, the latest ~s of fashion, etc. □ vi [VP2C] have a certain ~: *The road ~s towards the west.*

tre·pan /trɪˈpæn/ vt (-nn-), n **1** = trephine. **2** bore for drilling a mine shaft.

tre·phine /trɪˈfiːn/ US: -ˈfaɪn/ vt [VP6A] (med) make a small hole in (sb's skull). □ n cylindrical saw used for this.

trepi·da·tion /ˌtrepɪˈdeɪʃn/ n [U] alarm; excited state of mind.

tres·pass /ˈtrespəs/ vi **1** [VP2A,3A] **~ (on/upon),** go on to privately owned land without right or permission: *~ upon sb's (private) property. No ~ing!* (a sign put up on privately owned land as a warning). **2** [VP3A] **~ on/upon,** encroach upon, make too much use of: *~ upon sb's time/ hospitality/privacy.* **3** [VP2A,3A] **~ (against),** (archaic) do wrong; sin: *'as we forgive them that ~ against us.'* □ n **1** [U] **~ing;** [C] instance of this. **2** [C] (old use, and biblical) sin; wrong: *'Forgive us our ~es.'* **~er** n person who ~es(1): *T~ers will be prosecuted.*

tress /tres/ n (poet or liter) **1** (pl) hair (esp of a woman's or girl's head): *her beautiful golden ~es.* **2** plait or braid of hair.

trestle /ˈtresl/ n horizontal beam of wood with two diverging legs at each end, used in pairs to support planks, a table top, a workman's bench, etc. **~-'bridge** n bridge supported by a framework of timber or steel. ⇨ the illus at bridge. **~-'table** n one made by laying planks on ~s.

trews /truːz/ n pl close-fitting tartan trousers.

tri- /traɪ-/ pref three. ⇨ App 3.

triad /ˈtraɪæd/ n group or set of three closely related persons or things.

trial /ˈtraɪəl/ n **1** [U] testing, trying, proving; [C] instance of this: *give sth a ~,* use it to learn about its qualities, value, etc; *give a new worker a ~,* give him a chance to show his skill; *have a ~ of strength with sb,* a contest to learn who is stronger. *We shall put the machine to further ~,* test it further. *The ship performed well during her ~s.* **on ~, (a)** for the purpose of testing: *Take the machine on ~ and then, if you like it, buy it.* **(b)** when tested: *The new clerk was found on ~ to be incompetent.* **~ and error,** method of solving a problem by making tests until error is eliminated. **2** (attrib) for the purpose of testing: *a ~ flight,* eg of a new aircraft; *a ~ trip/voyage; a ~ order,* eg for goods that are to be tested. **3** [C,U] examination in a law court before a judge (or judge and jury): *The judge conducted four ~s in one day. The ~ lasted a week.* **be/go on ~ (for sth),** be tried in a court of law (for an offence). **bring sb to ~; bring sb up for ~; put sb on ~,** cause him to be tried in a court of law. **stand (one's) ~,** be tried. **4** [C] sth or sb troublesome or annoying, esp thought of as a test of one's patience: *That child is a ~ to his parents. Life is full of little ~s.* **~s and tribulations,** irritations and troubles.

tri·angle /ˈtraɪæŋgl/ n **1** plane figure with three straight sides; any three points not in a straight line. **2** musical instrument made of a steel rod in the shape of a ~, struck with another steel rod. ⇨ the illus at percussion. **3** group of three. **the eternal ~,** the situation existing when two persons are both in love with a third. **tri·angu·lar** /traɪˈæŋgjʊlə(r)/ adj **1** in the shape of a ~. **2** in which there are three persons, etc: *a triangular contest in an election,* with three candidates.

tribal /'traɪbl/ adj of a tribe or tribes: ~ loyalties; ~ dances. ~-ism /'traɪbəlɪzəm/ n

tribe /traɪb/ n 1 racial group, esp one united by language and customs, living as a community under one or more chiefs: the Indian ~s of America; the twelve ~s of ancient Israel. 2 (bot, zool) group of plants or animals, usu ranking between a genus and an order. 3 (usu contemptuous) group of persons, etc of one profession: the ~ of politicians. '~s-man /-zmən/ n (pl-men) member of a ~(1).

tribu·la·tion /ˌtrɪbjʊ'leɪʃn/ n [C,U] (cause of) trouble, grief: The war was a time of ~ for all of us. He bore his ~s bravely. ⇨ trial(4).

tri·bu·nal /traɪ'bjuːnl/ n [C] place of judgement; board of officials or judges appointed for special duty, eg to hear appeals against high rents, for exemption from military service: (fig) the ~ of public opinion.

tri·bune¹ /'trɪbjuːn/ n 1 official chosen by the common people of ancient Rome to protect their interests. 2 (later use) popular leader; demagogue.

tri·bune² /'trɪbjuːn/ n raised platform for speakers addressing an assembly (eg that used in the French National Assembly).

tribu·tary /'trɪbjʊtrɪ US: -terɪ/ adj 1 (of a state, ruler, etc) paying tribute(1) to another. 2 (of a river) flowing into another. □ n (pl-ries) ~ state, ruler, river, etc.

trib·ute /'trɪbjuːt/ n [C,U] 1 (usu regular) payment which one government or ruler exacts from another: Many conquered nations had to pay ~ to the rulers of ancient Rome. **lay sb under** ~, force payment of ~ from. 2 sth done, said or given to show respect or admiration: By erecting this statue we have paid (a) ~ to the memory of the founder of our college. The actress received numerous floral ~s, bunches of flowers.

trice¹ /traɪs/ n in a ~, in an instant.

trice² /traɪs/ vt [VP15B] ~ sth up, (naut) haul up and secure (a sail, the boom) in place with rope.

trick /trɪk/ n [C] 1 sth done in order to deceive, to outwit or outdo, sb; sth done to make a person appear ridiculous: The wearing of white clothes is a common ~ of soldiers fighting in snow-covered country. He got the money from me by a ~. **the ~s of the trade**, ways of attracting customers, gaining advantages over rivals, etc. 2 mischievous act, practical joke: The children are always up to amusing ~s. That was an unfair ~. **play a** ~ **on sb**, ⇨ play ²(3). **dirty** ~, a contemptible action. 3 feat of skill or dexterity: conjuring ~s. Does your dog know any ~s? Are you clever at card ~s? **do the** ~, (sl) accomplish one's purpose: One more turn of the screw-driver should do the ~, fasten the screw securely. **a** ~ **worth two of that**, (colloq) a better way of doing it (than yours). **(soon) get/learn the** ~ **of it**, learn the knack (which is the more usu word) of doing it, managing it, etc. 4 strange or characteristic habit, mannerism, etc: He has a ~ of pulling his left ear when he is thinking out a problem. 5 (cards played in) one round (of bridge, etc): take/win a ~, win one round. 6 (naut) period of duty at the helm (usu two hours): take one's ~ at the wheel. □ vt 1 [VP6A,14] ~ sb (into/out of sth), deceive; swindle: You've been ~ed. He ~ed the poor girl out of her money/~ed her into marrying him by pretending that he was rich. 2 [VP15B] ~ sb/sth out/up, decorate, dress, ornament. ~-ery /-ərɪ/ n [U] deception; cheating. ~-ster /-stə(r)/ n person who

makes a practice of ~ing people; swindler. ~y adj (-ier, -iest) 1 (of persons and their actions) deceptive: a ~y politician. 2 (of work, etc) requiring skill; full of hidden or unexpected difficulties: a ~y problem/job.

trickle /'trɪkl/ vi,vt [VP2A,C,15A] (cause to) flow in drops or in a thin stream: Blood ~d from the wound. The tears ~d down her cheeks. He was trickling oil into the bearings of the machine. People began to ~ out of the bar as midnight approached. □ n weak or thin flow: The stream had shrunk to a mere ~. '~ charger, device for the slow continuous charging of an accumulator (from the mains).

tri·col·our (US = **-color**) /'trɪkələ(r) US: 'traɪkʌlər/ n flag of three colours in stripes of the same width, esp, **the T~**, the French national flag of blue, white and red stripes.

tri·cycle /'traɪsɪkl/ n three-wheeled bicycle.

tri·dent /'traɪdnt/ n spear with three points (as carried by Neptune); this as a symbol of sea-power.

tried /traɪd/ ⇨ try¹.

tri·en·nial /traɪ'enɪəl/ n, adj (sth) lasting for, happening or done every, three years.

trier /'traɪə(r)/ n ⇨ try¹.

trifle /'traɪfl/ n 1 thing, event, etc of little value or importance: It's silly to quarrel over ~s. The merest ~ upsets that man, He easily gets out of temper, etc. **not stick at** ~s, not allow small things to interfere with one's plans, etc. 2 small amount of money: It cost me only a ~. 3 **a** ~, (adv) somewhat, a little: This dress is a ~ too short. Isn't the meat a ~ tough? 4 [C,U] sweet dish made of cream, white of eggs, cake, jam, etc: make a ~; eat too much ~. □ vi,vt 1 [VP3A] ~ with, play idly with, behave lightly or insincerely towards: He's not a man to be ~d with, He must be given serious attention. It's wrong of you to ~ with the girl's affections, make her think that you love her when you don't. Don't ~ with your food: either eat it or leave it. 2 [VP15B] ~ sth away, fritter away (which is more usu): ~ away one's time/energies/money. **trif·ling** /'traɪflɪŋ/ adj unimportant: a trifling error; of trifling value. It's no trifling matter, is serious. **trif·ler** /'traɪflə(r)/ n person who ~s.

trig·ger /'trɪgə(r)/ n lever for releasing a spring, esp of a firearm. **be quick on the** ~, quick to shoot. **have one's finger on the** ~, (fig) be in full control, esp of military operations. '~-happy adj (sl) ready to use violence, eg by shooting, at slight provocation. □ vt [VP15B] ~ sth off, be the immediate cause of (sth serious or violent): Who/What ~ed off the rebellion?

trig·on·om·etry /ˌtrɪgə'nɒmətrɪ/ n [U] branch of mathematics that deals with the relations between the sides and angles of triangles.

tri·lat·eral /ˌtraɪ'lætərəl/ adj three-sided: a ~ agreement/treaty.

trilby /'trɪlbɪ/ n (pl-bies) ~ (hat), (man's) soft felt hat.

trill /trɪl/ n [C] 1 quavering sound; shaky or vibrating sound made by the voice or as in bird song. 2 (music) quick alternation of two notes a tone or a semitone apart. 3 speech sound (eg Spanish rr) uttered with a ~. □ vi,vt [VP6A,2A,C] sing or play (a musical note) with a ~; pronounce with a ~: The canary was ~ing away in its cage. Can you ~ the sound 'rr' as in Spanish?

tril·lion /'trɪlɪən/ n, adj (GB) million million million million; (US) million million. ⇨ App 4.

tril·ogy /'trɪlədʒɪ/ *n* [C] (*pl* -gies) group of three plays, novels, operas, etc to be performed, read, etc in succession, each complete in itself but having a common subject.

trim /trɪm/ *adj* (-mmer, -mmest) in good order; neat and tidy: *a ~ ship/cabin; a ~ little garden.* □ *n* [U] ~ state; readiness; fitness: *Everything was in good/proper ~. The crew is in/out of ~ for the boat-race. We must get into (good) ~ for the sports meeting.* □ *vt, vi* (-mm-) **1** [VP6A,15A,22] make ~, esp by taking or cutting away uneven, irregular or unwanted parts: *~ one's beard/the wick of a lamp.* **2** [VP6A,14] ~ *sth (with sth),* decorate or ornament (a hat, dress, etc): *a hat ~med with fur; ~ a dress with lace.* **3** [VP6A] make (a boat, ship, aircraft) evenly balanced by arranging the position of the cargo, passengers, etc; set (sails) to suit the wind. **4** [VP2A] hold a middle course in politics; change one's views, policy, etc in an effort to win popular approval: *a politician who is always ~ming.* **~·mer** *n* person or thing that ~s. **~·ming** *n* [U,C] sth used for ~ming(2): *lace ~ming(s).* **~·ly** *adv*

tri·maran /'traɪməræn/ *n* boat with three parallel hulls. ⇨ catamaran.

tri·nitro·tolu·ene /ˌtraɪˌnaɪtrəʊ'tɒljuːiːn/ *n* [U] (usu **TNT**) /ˌtiː en 'tiː/) powerful explosive.

trin·ity /'trɪnətɪ/ *n* group of three. **the T~,** (in Christian teaching) union of three persons, Father, Son and Holy Spirit, in one God. **T~ House,** British institution which licenses pilots of ships, maintains lighthouses, marks wrecks, etc. **ˌT~ 'Sunday,** Sunday after Pentecost.

trin·ket /'trɪŋkɪt/ *n* ornament or jewel of small value; small fancy article.

trio /'triːəʊ/ *n* (*pl* ~s) group of three; (musical composition for) group of three singers or players.

trip /trɪp/ *vi, vt* (-pp-) **1** [VP2A,C] walk, run or dance with quick, light steps: *She came ~ping down the garden path.* **2** [VP2A,C,3A,15B] ~ *(over)(sth),* catch one's foot, etc in an obstacle and stumble: *He ~ped over the root of a tree. ~ (sb) (up),* (cause to) stumble or make a false step: *He ~ped up and nearly fell. The wrestler ~ped (up) his opponent. That lawyer is always trying to ~ the witness up,* (fig) trying to make him contradict himself, be inaccurate, etc. **3** [VP2A,C] ~ *(out),* (sl) have a ~(3 below). **4** (archaic) ~ *a measure,* dance with quick light steps. □ *n* [C] **1** journey, esp a pleasure excursion: *a ~ to the seaside; a weekend ~; a holiday/honeymoon ~ to Venice.* **2** fall or stumble; (fig) fault or error: *a ~ of the tongue (slip* is more usu). **'~ wire** *n* wire stretched along the ground, working a trap when an animal, etc trips against it. **3** (sl) experience, esp one resulting from taking a hallucinatory drug. **~·per** *n* person making a (usu short) excursion for pleasure: *weekend ~pers.* **~·ping** *adj* light and quick. **~·ping·ly** *adv*

tri·par·tite /ˌtraɪ'pɑːtaɪt/ *adj* **1** in which three parties have a share: *a ~ agreement; ~ talks,* discussion(s) between three (groups of) people. **2** having three parts.

tripe /traɪp/ *n* [U] **1** part of the wall of the stomach of an ox or cow used as food: *a dish of stewed ~ and onions.* **2** (sl) worthless talk, writing, ideas etc: *Stop talking ~!*

triple /'trɪpl/ *adj* made up of three (parts or parties): *the T~ Alliance,* one of several military alliances

(in European history) between three countries; ~ time, (music) of 3 beats to the bar; *the ~ crown,* the Pope's tiara. □ *vt, vi* [VP6A,2A] make, become, be, three times as much or many: *He ~d his income. His income ~d.*

trip·let /'trɪplɪt/ *n* **1** (*pl*) three children born at one birth: *One of the ~s is ill.* **2** set of three.

trip·lex /'trɪpleks/ *adj* triple; threefold. ~ **(glass),** (P) strong glass (as used in motor-cars, etc) made of a sheet of plastic material between two sheets of glass.

trip·li·cate /'trɪplɪkət/ *adj* of which three copies are made. □ *n in ~,* consisting of three like things, esp documents: *drawn up in ~,* consisting of one original and two copies. □ *vt* /'trɪplɪkeɪt/ [VP6A] make in ~.

tri·pod /'traɪpɒd/ *n* three-legged support, eg for a camera; stool, table, etc, resting on three legs.

tri·pos /'traɪpɒs/ *n* examination for an honours degree at Cambridge University: *the History/ Classics, etc ~.*

trip·per /'trɪpə(r)/ *n* ⇨ trip.

trip·tych /'trɪptɪk/ *n* picture or carving on three (usu hinged) panels fixed side by side, eg of religious subjects in a Christian church.

tri·reme /'traɪriːm/ *n* ancient (esp Greek) warship with three tiers of oars on each side.

tri·sect /traɪ'sekt/ *vt* [VP6A] divide (a line, an angle, etc) into three (esp equal) parts.

trite /traɪt/ *adj* (of remarks, ideas, opinions) commonplace; not new. ~·**ly** *adv* ~·**ness** *n*

tri·umph /'traɪʌmf/ *n* **1** [C,U] (joy or satisfaction at a) success or victory: *return home in ~; shouts of ~; score a resounding ~ over one's enemies; recount all one's ~s.* **2** [C] (in ancient Rome) procession and ceremony in honour of a victorious general. □ *vi* [VP2A,3A] ~ *(over),* win a victory (over); show joy because of success: ~ *over opposition/adversity,* overcome it; ~ *over a defeated enemy.* **tri·um·phal** /traɪ'ʌmfl/ *adj* of, for, a ~; expressing ~: *erect a ~al arch,* one built to commemorate a victory. **tri·um·phant** /traɪ'ʌmfnt/ *adj* (rejoicing at) having ~ed. **tri·um·phant·ly** *adv*

tri·um·vir /traɪ'ʌmvə(r)/ *n* (in ancient Rome) each of three men holding an office jointly. **tri·um·vir·ate** /traɪ'ʌmvɪrət/ *n* set of ~s.

tri·une /'traɪjuːn/ *adj* three in one: *the ~ Godhead,* the Trinity.

trivet /'trɪvɪt/ *n* (usu three-legged or three-footed) stand or support for a pot or kettle on or by a fire; iron bracket to be hooked on to the bars of a firegrate. *as right as a ~,* in good condition or health; in satisfactory circumstances.

trivia /'trɪvɪə/ *n pl* trivial, unimportant things.

triv·ial /'trɪvɪəl/ *adj* **1** of small value or importance: *a ~ offence; a ~ loss; raise ~ objections against a proposal.* **2** commonplace; humdrum: *the ~ round,* the ordinary course of everyday events, duties, etc. **3** (of a person) trifling; lacking seriousness; superficial: *Don't marry that ~ young man.* ~·**ly** /-ɪəlɪ/ *adv* ~·**ity** /ˌtrɪvɪ'ælətɪ/ *n* [U] state of being ~; [C] (*pl* -ties) ~ idea, event, etc: *talk/ write ~ities.* ~·**ize** /-aɪz/ *vt* [VP6A] make ~.

tro·chee /'trəʊkiː/ *n* (prosody) metrical foot of one stressed and one unstressed syllable (—◡), as in: *'Life is / 'but an / 'empty / 'dream.* **tro·chaic** /trəʊ'keɪɪk/ *adj*

trod, trod·den /trɒd, 'trɒdn/ *pt,pp* of tread.

trog·lo·dyte /'trɒglədaɪt/ *n* cave-dweller in ancient times.

troika /'trɔɪkə/ n [C] **1** small Russian carriage drawn by a team of three horses abreast. **2** group of three persons (esp political leaders).

Tro·jan /'trəʊdʒən/ n, adj (inhabitant) of ancient Troy: *the ~ war*, between the Greeks and the Trojans, as described by Homer. *work like a ~*, work very hard. *~ horse*, (fig) sb or sth, introduced from outside, that causes the downfall of an enemy from within.

troll¹ /trəʊl/ n (in Scandinavian myth) supernatural being, a giant, or, in later tales, a mischievous but friendly dwarf.

troll² /trəʊl/ vt,vi [VP2A,C] fish with rod and line by pulling bait through the water behind a boat: *~ for pike.*

trol·ley /'trɒlɪ/ n (pl ~s) **1** two- or four-wheeled handcart. **2** small, low truck running on rails, eg one worked by a handlever, used by workers on a railway. **3** (often **'tea-~**) small table on castors (small wheels) used for serving food. **4** small contact-wheel between a tram and an overhead cable. **5** '~(-bus), (US) '~(-car), = tram.

trol·lop /'trɒləp/ n (colloq) slut; prostitute.

trom·bone /trɒm'bəʊn/ n large brass musical instrument with a sliding tube. ⇨ the illus at brass. **trom·bon·ist** /trɒm'bəʊnɪst/ n ~ player.

troop /truːp/ n [C] **1** company of persons or animals. esp when moving: *a ~ of schoolchildren; a ~ of antelope(s)*. **2** (pl) soldiers: *find billets for the ~s.* ⇨ trooper below. '~-carrier n ship or large aircraft for transporting ~s. '~-ship n ship for transporting ~s. **3** unit of cavalry, armoured vehicles or artillery (under the command of a lieutenant). **4** company of boy scouts. □ vi,vt **1** [VP2C] (with pl subject) come or go together in a group: *children ~ing out of school.* **2** ~ *the colour*, (GB, mil) carry the colour (flag) through the ranks of a regiment. *~ing the colour*, such a ceremony (esp as on the Sovereign's birthday). **~er** n **1** soldier in a cavalry or armoured regiment. **2** (US) member of state police force (now using a motorvehicle). *swear like a ~er*, swear fluently.

trope /trəʊp/ n figurative use of a word (as of *tread* in 'The years like great black oxen tread the world').

trophy /'trəʊfɪ/ n [C] (pl -phies) **1** sth kept in memory of a victory or success (eg in hunting, sport, etc). **2** prize, eg for winning a tournament: *'tennis trophies.*

tropic /'trɒpɪk/ n **1** line of latitude 23°27' north (*T~ of Cancer*) or south (*T~ of Capricorn*) of the equator. **2** the ~s, the parts of the world between these two latitudes. **tropi·cal** /-kl/ adj of, or as of, the ~s: *a ~al climate; ~al fruits.* **tropi·cally** /-klɪ/ adv

trot /trɒt/ vi,vt (-tt-) **1** [VP2A,B,C] (of horses, etc) go at a pace faster than a walk but not so fast as a gallop. **2** [VP2A,C] run with short steps; (colloq, hum) go (at an ordinary speed): *Well, I must be ~ting off home. You ~ along!* Go away! **3** [VP15B] ~ *sth out*, (colloq) produce; bring out: *~ out one's knowledge*, eg to get admiration. **4** [VP15A,B] cause to ~: *~ a person off his legs*, take him round, eg sight-seeing, until he is exhausted; *~ sb round*, take him round with one (eg shopping). □ n (sing only) **1** ~ting pace: *go at a steady ~. on the ~*, (sl) one after the other: *five whiskies on the ~. be on the ~; keep sb on the ~*, (a) (colloq) busy on one's feet, moving from one task to another: *I've been (kept) on the ~ all*

morning *and I'm exhausted.* **(b)** (sl) be running away (esp from prison or the police). *be on the ~*, (US = *have the ~s*), (colloq) have diarrhoea. **2** period of ~ting: *go for a ~. ~·ter* n **1** horse bred and trained to ~. **2** (usu pl) pig's or sheep's foot as food.

troth /trəʊθ US: trɔːθ/ n [U] (archaic) *plight one's ~*, pledge one's word; (esp) promise to marry.

trou·ba·dour /'truːbədɔː(r)/ n travelling poet and singer in France and Italy, 11th to 13th cc.

trouble /'trʌbl/ vt,vi **1** [VP6A] cause worry, discomfort, anxiety or inconvenience to: *be ~d by bad news; ~d with a nasty cough. What ~s me is that...* **2** [VP17,14] *~ sb to do sth; ~ sb for sth*, put sb to the inconvenience of doing sth. (a) (with *may/might*, a polite request): *May I ~ you to pass the salt, please. May I ~ you for a match?* **(b)** (with *I'll, I must*, a sarcastic or ironic request): *I'll ~ you to be quiet. I must ~ you to remember your manners.* **3** [VP2A,C,4A] (esp in neg and interr) bother or inconvenience oneself: *Don't ~ to meet me at the station. Don't ~ about that. Oh, don't ~, thanks. Why should I ~ to explain?* **4** [VP6A] agitate; disturb: (esp pp) *a ~d expression; ~d looks. fish in ~d waters*, try to gain an advantage from a confused state of affairs. □ n **1** [C,U] worry; anxiety; discomfort; unhappiness; difficulty; possible punishment: *Her heart was full of ~. She's always making ~ for her friends. He has been through much ~/has had many ~s. He has a lot of family/domestic ~(s). His ~s are over now* (sometimes said of a person who dies). *The ~ is that...,* The difficulty is that.... *What's the ~ now?* What unfortunate thing has happened? *in ~*, suffering, or likely to suffer, misfortune, anxiety, etc, eg because one has done wrong. *'ask/'look for ~*, (colloq) behave in such a way that ~ is likely: *It's asking for ~ to experiment with drugs. get into ~*, do sth that will bring unhappiness, punishment, etc. *get sb into ~*, **(a)** cause sb to be in ~. **(b)** (sl) make (an unmarried woman) pregnant. **2** [C] (sing only) sb or sth that causes ~(1): *I don't want to be any ~* (= nuisance) *to you. Some dishes are very enjoyable to eat but a great ~ to prepare. I find it a great ~ to get up at 6am.* **3** [U] care; attention; (extra) work; inconvenience: *Did the work give you much ~? I don't like putting you to* (= causing you) *so much ~. Thank you for all the ~ you've taken to help my son. It will be no ~*, will not inconvenience me. **4** [C,U] political or social unrest: *'Labour ~(s)* (eg strikes) *cost the country enormous sums last year. They've been having a lot of ~(s) in Southern Africa recently.* **5** [C,U] illness: *'liver ~; 'mental ~; 'children's ~s.* **6** (compounds) '~-maker, person who stirs up discontent (eg in industry). '~-shooter, person employed in conciliating and arbitrating between parties in conflict (eg in industry), or in detecting and correcting faults (esp in machinery). **~-some** /-səm/ adj causing ~: *a ~some child/headache/problem. Her cough is very ~some today.* '~-spot, place where ~(4) often occurs. **troub·lous** /-əs/ adj (liter) disturbed; unsettled: *live in troublous times.*

trough /trɒf US: trɔːf/ n **1** long, open (usu shallow) box for animals to feed or drink from. **2** long open box in which a baker kneads dough for bread. **3** (in the sea, etc) long hollow between two waves. **4** (met) region of lower atmospheric pressure between two regions of higher pressure.

trounce /traʊns/ vt [VP6A] beat; thrash; defeat; reprimand: *Our team was ∼d on Saturday.* **trounc-ing** *n* beating; reprimand: *give sb a good trouncing.*

troupe /truːp/ *n* company, esp of actors or of members of a circus. **∼r** *n* member of a theatrical ∼: *He's a good ∼r,* a loyal, hard-working and uncomplaining colleague.

trouser /ˈtraʊzə(r)/ *n* **1** *(pair of)* **∼s,** two-legged outer garment, reaching from the waist to the ankles. ⇨ **shorts, slacks. 2** (attrib) of or for ∼s: '∼ *buttons/pockets.*

trous-seau /ˈtruːsəʊ/ *n* (*pl* ∼s or ∼x /-səʊz/) outfit of clothing, etc, for a bride.

trout /traʊt/ *n* (*pl* unchanged) freshwater fish valued as food and for the sport of catching it (with rod and line).

trove /trəʊv/ *n* ⇨ treasure(1).

trowel /ˈtraʊəl/ *n* **1** flat-bladed tool for spreading mortar on bricks or stone, plaster on walls, etc. **2** hand-tool with a curved blade for lifting plants, etc. ⇨ the illus at tool.

troy /trɔɪ/ *n* [U] British system of weights, used for gold and silver, in which one pound = 12 ounces: *This spoon weighs 4 oz* ∼. ⇨ App 5.

tru-ant /ˈtruːənt/ *n* **1** child who stays away from school without good reason. *play* ∼, stay away thus. **2** (attrib) (of persons, their conduct, thoughts, etc) wandering; idle; shirking (duty, etc). **tru-ancy** /-ənsɪ/ *n* (*pl* -cies) [U] playing ∼; [C] instance of this.

truce /truːs/ *n* [C] (agreement for the) stopping of fighting for a time (eg to take away the wounded).

truck¹ /trʌk/ *n* **1** (GB) open railway wagon for heavy goods. **2** (US) lorry. **3** porter's two-wheeled barrow (for moving heavy objects).

truck² /trʌk/ *n* [U] **1** barter; exchange. *have no* ∼ *with,* have no dealings with. **2** '*garden*∼, (US) fresh garden produce (vegetables, fruit) grown for the markets. **3** ∼ **(system),** (hist) payment of wages in goods instead of money.

truckle¹ /ˈtrʌkl/ *vi* [VP3A] ∼ *to,* submit in a timid or cowardly way: *This country will never* ∼ *to bullies.*

truckle² /ˈtrʌkl/ *n* '∼-**bed,** low, wheeled bed that can be pushed under another when not in use.

trucu-lent /ˈtrʌkjʊlənt/ *adj* looking for, desiring, a fight; aggressive. ∼·**ly** *adv* **trucu-lence** /-ləns/, **trucu-lency** /-lənsɪ/ *nn*

trudge /trʌdʒ/ *vi* walk wearily or heavily: *trudging through the deep snow. He* ∼*d 20 miles.* □ *n* long tiring walk.

true /truː/ *adj* (-r, -st) **1** in accordance or agreement with fact: *Is it* ∼ *that you are going to Rome? Is the news* ∼*?* **come** ∼, (of a hope, dream) really happen, become fact. **2** ∼ *(to),* loyal, faithful: *be* ∼ *to one's word/promise,* do what one has promised to do. *∼-*'**blue** *n, adj* (person who is) of uncompromising principles, firmly loyal. *∼-*'**hearted** *adj* loyal. '∼-**love** *n* one who loves truly/is truly loved. **3** in accordance with reason or received standards: genuine; rightly so named: *T*∼ *friendship should last for ever. The frog is not a* ∼ *reptile. Who was the* ∼ *heir to the throne?* **4** ∼ *to type,* accurately conforming to its type or class: *Plants grown from seed are not always* ∼ *to type.* **5** accurately fitted or placed: *Is the wheel/post* ∼*?* **6** exact; accurate: *a* ∼ *copy of a document; a* ∼ *pair of scales.* □ *n* (only in) *out of* ∼, not in its exact or accurate position: *The axle/beam/door is out of* ∼.

□ *adv* (with certain *vv*) truly: *aim* ∼; *breed* ∼(4); *tell me* ∼. □ *vt* [VP15B] ∼ *sth up,* make, adjust so as to be ∼(5): ∼ *up a wheel.*

truffle /ˈtrʌfl/ *n* kind of fungus that grows underground, used for flavouring savoury food dishes, paté, etc.

tru-ism /ˈtruːɪzəm/ *n* [C] statement that is obviously true and need not have been made: *It's a* ∼ *to say that your body was once much smaller than it is now.*

truly /ˈtruːlɪ/ *adv* **1** truthfully: *speak* ∼. **2** sincerely: *feel* ∼ *grateful. Yours* ∼ (used at the close of a letter, before the signature). **3** genuinely; certainly: *a* ∼ *beautiful picture; a* ∼ *brave action.*

trump¹ /trʌmp/ *n* [C] **1** (in card games such as whist, bridge) each card of a suit that has been declared as having higher value than the other three suits: *Hearts are* ∼*s.* ⇨ declare(1). *play one's* ∼ *card,* (fig) make use of one's most valuable resource, means of gaining one's ends (esp after trying other means). *turn up* ∼*s,* (colloq) (a) have a better result than was expected. (b) have a stroke of good luck. **2** (colloq) excellent fellow; person who is full of resource, is generous, etc. □ *vt, vi* **1** [VP6A,2A] play a ∼ card (on): ∼ *the ace of clubs.* **2** [VP15B] (usu passive) ∼ *sth up,* invent (an excuse, a false story, etc) in order to deceive sb: *He was arrested on a* ∼*ed-up charge.*

trump² /trʌmp/ *n* (liter) (sound made by a) trumpet. *the last* ∼; *the* ∼ *of doom,* the trumpet call which will, some people believe, be sounded on the Last Day, the day when everyone will be judged by God.

trump-ery /ˈtrʌmpərɪ/ *adj* showy but of little value: ∼ *ornaments.*

trum-pet /ˈtrʌmpɪt/ *n* **1** musical wind instrument of brass. ⇨ the illus at brass. *blow one's own* ∼, (fig) praise oneself. **2** sound (as) of a ∼. **3** sth suggesting a ∼ in shape or use (eg the corona of a daffodil). □ *vt, vi* **1** [VP6A,15B] proclaim, make known; celebrate: ∼ *(forth) sb's heroic deeds.* **2** [VP2A,C] (esp of an elephant) make loud sounds. ∼**er** *n* person who plays a ∼.

trun-cate /trʌŋˈkeɪt *US:* ˈtrʌŋkeɪt/ *vt* [VP6A] shorten by cutting the tip, top or end from: *a* ∼*d cone/ pyramid.*

trun-cheon /ˈtrʌntʃən/ *n* short thick club (esp one used by the police).

trundle /ˈtrʌndl/ *vt, vi* [VP6A,15A,B,2C] (esp of sth heavy or awkward in shape) move or roll: *The porter* ∼*d his barrow along the platform. The child was trundling a hoop along the sidewalk.* '∼ **bed,** (US) = truckle bed.

trunk /trʌŋk/ *n* [C] **1** main stem of a tree (contrasted with the branches). ⇨ the illus at tree. **2** body without head, arms or legs; main part of any structure. **3** large box with a hinged lid, for clothes, etc while travelling. **4** long nose of an elephant. ⇨ the illus at large. **5** (*pl*) = shorts. **6** (US) = boot(2) of a car. **7** (attrib) '∼-**call** *n* telephone call to a distant place, with charges according to distance. '∼-**line** *n* (a) main line of a railway. (b) long-distance telephone line. '∼-**road** *n* main road.

truss /trʌs/ *n* [C] **1** (GB) bundle (of hay, straw). **2** framework supporting a roof, bridge, etc. **3** padded belt worn by a person suffering from hernia. □ *vt* [VP6A,15B] ∼ *sth (up),* **1** tie or fasten up: ∼ *hay;* ∼ *up a chicken,* pin the wings to the body before boiling or roasting it. *The policeman* ∼*ed up the struggling criminal with rope,* tied his arms to his

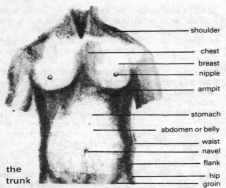

shoulder
chest
breast
nipple
armpit
stomach
abdomen or belly
waist
navel
flank
hip
groin

the trunk

sides. **2** support (a roof, bridge, etc) with a ∼ or ∼es(2).

trust¹ /trʌst/ n **1** [U] ∼ *(in)*, confidence, strong belief, in the goodness, strength, reliability of sth or sb: *put one's* ∼ *in God. A child usually has perfect* ∼ *in its mother. She hasn't/doesn't place much* ∼ *in his promises.* **on** ∼, **(a)** without proof; without close examination: *You'll have to take my statement on* ∼. **(b)** on credit. **2** [U] responsibility: *a position of great* ∼. **3** [C] (legal) property held and managed by one or more persons (*trustees*) for the benefit of another or others; [U] the legal relation between the trustee(s) and the property; the obligation assumed by the trustee(s): *By his will he created* ∼*s for his children. This property is not mine; it is a* ∼. *I am holding the property in* ∼ *for my nephew.* '∼-**money,** '∼ **fund** *nn* money held in ∼. **4** [C] association of business firms for the achievement of various objects, eg reducing competition, maintenance of prices. **5** '**brains** ∼, ⇨ brain. ∼-**ful** /-fl/, ∼-**ing** *adjj* ready to have ∼ in others; not suspicious. ∼-**fully** /-fəli/, ∼-**ing·ly** *advv* '∼-**worthy** *adj* worthy of ∼; dependable. '∼-**wor-thi·ness** *n* ∼y *adj* (archaic or hum) ∼worthy: *a* ∼*y sword/bicycle.*

trust² /trʌst/ *vt,vi* **1** [VP6A] have trust(1) in; believe in the honesty and reliability of: *He's not the sort of man to be* ∼*ed/not a man I would* ∼. *Can you* ∼ *his account of what happened?* **2** [VP3A] ∼ **in sb**, have confidence in; believe that he will act for the best: ∼ *in God.* ∼ **to sth**, have reliance on: *Don't* ∼ *to chance. You* ∼ *to your memory too much.* **3** [VP14] ∼ **sth to sb**, = entrust (the more usu word). **4** [VP15A,B,17] allow (sb) to do sth, have sth, go somewhere, etc without anxiety, knowing that he will act sensibly, etc: *Can I* ∼ *you to get the money safely to the bank? He may be* ∼*ed to do the work well. We can't* ∼ *that boy out of our sight. It's unwise to* ∼ *small children out of doors in a big town,* eg because of traffic dangers. *Should boys of 16 be* ∼*ed with high-powered motor-bikes?* **5** [VP6A] allow credit to a customer: *I wonder whether the newsagent will* ∼ *me; I need some cigarettes and I've no money on me.* **6** [VP7A,9] earnestly hope: *I* ∼ *you're in good health. You're quite well, I* ∼. (comm) *We* ∼ *to receive a cheque from you in settlement of this account.*

trustee /trʌ'stiː/ *n* person who has charge of property in trust(3) or of the business affairs of an institution. **the Public T**∼, state official who executes wills and trusts when asked to do so. ∼-**ship**

/-ʃɪp/ *n* position of a ∼; (esp) responsibility for the administration of a territory, granted to a country by the United Nations Organization: '∼-*ship territories,* eg the Cameroons from 1947 until 1960.

truth /truːθ/ *n* (*pl* ∼s /truːðz/) **1** [U] quality or state of being true: *There's no* ∼/*not a word of* ∼ *in what he says.* **moment of** ∼, time of crisis, test, or revelation. **2** [U] that which is true: *tell the* ∼. **to tell the** ∼,..., (formula used when making a confession): *To tell the* ∼, *I forgot all about your request.* **in** ∼, (liter) truly, really. **3** [C] fact; belief, etc accepted as true: *the* ∼*s of religion/ science.* ∼·**ful** /-fl/ *adj* **1** (of persons) in the habit of telling the ∼. **2** (of statements) true. ∼·**fully** /-fəli/ *adv* ∼·**ful·ness** *n*

try¹ /traɪ/ *vi,vt* (*pt,pp* tried) **1** [VP2A,B,7A] (Note that, in colloq style, *try to* + *inf* is often replaced by *try and* + *inf,* esp in the imperative, and *don't try to* and *didn't try to* are often replaced by *don't try and* and *didn't try and*) make an attempt: *I don't think I can do it, but I'll try. I've tried till I'm tired. He's trying his hardest,* using his utmost efforts. *Try to get here early. Try to/Try and behave better. He didn't try to do it. Don't try and swim across the river.* **2** [VP3A] **try for sth,** make an attempt to get or win (esp a position): *try for a scholarship/a position in the Civil Service.* **3** [VP6A,B,C,10] use sth, do sth, as an experiment or test, to see whether it is satisfactory: *Have you tried sleeping on your back as a cure for snoring? Won't you try* (= buy and use) *this new kind of detergent? Try how far you can jump/whether you can jump across this stream. Try knocking at the back door if nobody hears you at the front door. Please try me for the job,* let me do it as an experiment. ⇨ trial(1). [VP15B] **try sth on, (a)** put on (a garment, show, etc) to see whether it fits, looks well, etc: *I want to try the shoes on before I buy them.* **(b)** (colloq) make a bold or impudent attempt to discover whether sth will be tolerated: *It's no use your trying it/your games/your tricks on with me.* Hence, '**try-on** *n* (colloq) an attempt of this sort. [VP15B] **try sth out,** use it, experiment with it, in order to test it: *The idea seems good but it needs to be tried out.* '**try-out** *n* preliminary test of ability, qualification, etc, eg of an athlete. **try one's hand at sth,** ⇨ hand¹(5). **4** [VP6A,15A] inquire into (a case) in a court of law: *He was tried and found guilty. He will be tried for murder. Which judge will try the case?* ⇨ trial(3). **5** [VP6A] put a strain on; cause to be tired, exhausted, out of patience, etc: *Small print tries the eyes. Don't try his patience too much. His courage was severely tried.* **tried** *adj* that has been tested; reliable: *a tried friend/remedy.* **trier** *n* person who tries hard, who always does his best. **try·ing** *adj* (⇨ 5 above) distressing; putting a strain on, eg the temper, one's patience: *a trying person to deal with; have a trying day,* one during which one's temper, patience, etc are tried; *work that is trying to the eyes.*

try² /traɪ/ *n* **1** attempt: *Let me have a try at it. He had three tries and failed each time.* **2** (Rugby) touching down the ball behind the opponents' goal-line (with a score of three points).

tryst /trɪst/ *n* (archaic) (time and place for, agreement to have, a) meeting, esp between lovers: *keep/break* ∼ *(with* sb*).*

Tsar /zɑː(r)/, **Tsa·rina** /zɑː'riːnə/ *nn* = Czar, Czarina.

tsetse /'tsetsɪ/ *n* '∼(-**fly**) blood-sucking fly (in

tropical Africa) carrying and transmitting (often fatal) disease to men and animals. ⇨ the illus at insect.

T-shirt /'ti:ʃɜːt/ *n* ⇨ T, t.

T-square /'ti: skweə(r)/ ⇨ square²(7).

tub /tʌb/ *n* **1** large open vessel, usu round, made of wood, zinc, etc used for washing clothes, holding liquids, growing plants in, etc: *a rain-water tub.* **'tub-thumper** *n* mob orator. **2** (also **'tub-ful**) as much as a tub holds: *a tub of water.* **3** (colloq) bath-tub; (GB) bath: *have a cold tub before breakfast; prefer a tub to a shower.* **4** (colloq) clumsy slow boat.

tuba /'tju:bə US: 'tu:-/ *n* large musical instrument of brass, of low pitch. ⇨ the illus at brass.

tubby /'tʌbɪ/ *adj* (-ier, -iest) shaped like a tub; fat and round: *a tubby little man.*

tube /tju:b US: tu:b/ *n* **1** long hollow cylinder of metal, glass or rubber, esp for holding or conveying liquids, etc: '**boiler** ∼s; *the* '**inner** ∼ *of a bicycle/car tyre,* of rubber, filled with air at pressure; *tor'pedo* ∼s, from which torpedoes are launched. '∼-**well** *n* metal ∼ placed in the ground to obtain water through perforations in the ∼ near its end. **2** soft metal container with a screw-cap, used for pastes, paints, etc: *a* ∼ *of toothpaste.* **3** [U,C] (in London) underground railway: *travel in to work by* ∼ *every morning; take a/the* ∼ *to Oxford Circus.* **4** (US) thermionic valve as used in electronic apparatus; large ∼ with a screen (*cathode ray* ∼, ⇨ **cathode**) as used in a television set. **5** hollow ∼-shaped organ in the body: *the bronchial* ∼s. **tub-ing** *n* [U] material in the form of a ∼: *five feet of rubber/copper tubing.* **tu-bu-lar** /'tju:bjʊlə(r) US: 'tu:-/ *adj* **1** having the shape of a ∼: *a tubular bridge,* a bridge in the shape of a ∼ through which a railway, etc passes. **2** having, consisting of, ∼s or tubing: *a tubular boiler,* in which water or steam is heated as it passes through many ∼s; *tubular furniture,* with parts made of metal tubing; *tubular scaffolding.* ∼-**less** *adj* having no inner ∼: ∼*less tyres.*

tu-ber /'tju:bə(r) US: 'tu:-/ *n* [C] enlarged part of an underground stem with buds from which new plants will grow, eg a potato, Jerusalem artichoke, yam, etc.

tu-ber-cu-lo-sis /tju:ˌbɜːkjʊ'ləʊsɪs US: tu:-/ *n* [U] (common abbr **TB** /ˌti: 'bi:/) wasting disease affecting various parts of the body's tissues, esp the lungs: *pulmonary* ∼, consumption. **tu-ber-cu-lous** /tju:'bɜːkjʊləs US: tu:-/, **tu-ber-cu-lar** /tju:'bɜːkjʊlə(r) US: tu:-/ *adjj* of, affected by, ∼.

tub-ing, tu-bu-lar ⇨ tube.

tuck /tʌk/ *n* **1** [C] flat, stitched fold of material in a garment, for shortening or for ornament: *make/put in/take out a* ∼ *in a dress/the sleeve of a shirt.* **2** [U] (GB, sl) food, esp the cakes, pastry, etc that children enjoy. '∼-**shop** *n* shop (esp at a school) where ∼ is sold. □ *vt,vi* **1** [VP15A,B] draw together into a small space; put or push into a desired or convenient position: ∼ *one's shirt in,* put the bottom of it inside one's trousers, etc. *She* ∼*ed the ends of her hair into her bathing-cap. He sat with his legs* ∼*ed up under him. The bird* ∼*ed its head under its wing. The map is* ∼*ed away in a pocket at the end of the book. She* ∼*ed the child up in bed,* pulled the bed-clothes up round the child and under the mattress. *She took off her shoes,* ∼*ed up* (= rolled or turned up) *her skirt, and waded across the stream.* **2** [VP2C,3A] ∼ *in,* eat heartily. ∼ *into*

sth, eat it heartily: *He* ∼*ed into the cold ham.* ∼- '**in** *n* full meal: *The boys had a good* ∼*-in.*

tucker /'tʌkə(r)/ *n* piece of lace, linen, etc, worn (in the 17th and 18th cc) to cover a woman's neck and shoulders. *one's best bib and* ∼, (colloq) one's best or finest clothes.

Tues-day /'tju:zdɪ US: 'tu:-/ *n* third day of the week, next after Monday.

tuft /tʌft/ *n* bunch of feathers, hair, grass, etc growing or held together at the base. ∼**ed** *adj* having ∼s; growing in a ∼ or ∼s.

tug /tʌg/ *vt,vi* (-gg-) [VP6A,15A,B,2A,C,3A] **tug** *(at),* pull hard or violently; pull hard (at): *The child was tugging her toy cart round the garden/tugging it along behind. We tugged so hard that the rope broke. The kitten was tugging at my shoe-lace.* □ *n* [C] **1** sudden hard pull: *The naughty boy gave his sister's hair a tug. I felt a tug at my sleeve. Parting from his family was a tug* (*at his heart-strings*), It was difficult to leave them. *tug of war,* contest in which two teams pull against each other on a rope. **2** '**tug(-boat),** small powerful boat for towing ships, etc.

a tug-boat

tu-ition /tju:'ɪʃn US: tu:-/ *n* [U] teaching: *have private* ∼ *in mathematics.*

tu-lip /'tju:lɪp US: 'tu:-/ *n* bulb plant with, in spring, a large bell-shaped or cup-shaped flower on a tall stem.

tulle /tju:l US: tu:l/ *n* [U] soft, fine, silk net-like material for veils and dresses.

tumble /'tʌmbl/ *vi,vt* **1** [VP2A,C] fall, esp quickly or violently: ∼ *down the stairs/off a horse or bicycle/out of a window/over the roots of a tree. The baby is just learning to walk and he's always tumbling over.* **2** [VP2A,C] move up and down, to and fro, in a restless or disorderly way: *The puppies were tumbling about on the floor. The sick man tossed and* ∼*d in his bed. I was so tired that I threw my clothes off and* ∼*d into bed.* **3** [VP2C] be in a weak state (as if ready to fall): *The old barn is tumbling to pieces.* '∼-**down** *attrib adj* dilapidated; likely to collapse: *What a* ∼*-down old house you live in!* **4** [VP15A,B] cause to fall; upset: *The accident* ∼*d us all out of the bus.* **5** [VP6A] put into a state of disorder: ∼ *one's bed-clothes/sb's hair or clothes.* **6** [VP3A] ∼ *to sth,* (colloq) grasp, realize (an idea, etc): *At last he* ∼*d to what I was hinting at.* □ *n* [C] **1** fall: *have a nasty* ∼. **2** confused state: *Things were all in a* ∼. '∼-**weed** *n* (US) plant which grows in desert areas and, when withered, breaks off and is rolled about by the wind.

tum-bler /'tʌmblə(r)/ *n* **1** flat-bottomed drinking-glass without a handle or stem, ⇨ **goblet. 2** part of the mechanism of a lock which must be turned by a key before the lock will open. **3** kind of pigeon that turns over in flight. **4** acrobat.

tum·brel, tum·bril /'tʌmbrəl/ n (hist) cart, esp the kind that carried prisoners to the guillotine during the French Revolution.

tu·mes·cent /tju:'mesnt US: tu:-/ adj swelling; swollen. **tu·mes·cence** /-sns/ n

tu·mid /'tju:mɪd US: 'tu:-/ adj (of parts of the body) swollen; (fig, of a style of writing, etc) bombastic. **~·ity** /tju:'mɪdətɪ US: tu:-/ n

tummy /'tʌmɪ/ n (pl -mies) (colloq) stomach; belly.

tu·mour (US = **tu·mor**) /'tju:mə(r) US: 'tu:-/ n diseased growth in some part of the body.

tu·mult /'tju:mʌlt US: 'tu:-/ n [C,U] 1 uproar; disturbance: the ~ of battle. 2 confused and excited state of mind: in a ~; when the ~ within him had subsided.

tu·mul·tu·ous /tju:'mʌltʃʊəs US: tu:-/ adj disorderly; noisy and violent: a ~ welcome. **~·ly** adv

tu·mu·lus /'tju:mjʊləs US: 'tu:-/ n (pl -li /-lɑːɪ/) mound of earth over a (usu ancient) grave.

tun /tʌn/ n large cask for beer, wine, etc; measure of capacity (252 gallons).

tuna /'tju:nə US: 'tu:nə/ n (pl~ or ~s) = tunny.

tun·dra /'tʌndrə/ n [U,C] wide, treeless plain of the arctic regions (of Russia, Siberia), marshy in summer and frozen hard in winter.

tune /tju:n US: tu:n/ n 1 [C] succession of notes forming a melody (of a song, hymn, etc): whistle a popular ~; ~s that are easy to remember. 2 [U] quality of having a well-marked melody: Some of this modern music has very little ~ in it. 3 [U] in/out of ~, at/not at the correct pitch: sing/play in ~. The piano is out of ~. The piano and the violin are not in ~. 4 [U] (fig) harmony; harmonious adjustment: be in/out of ~ with one's surroundings/companions. 5 (fig uses) change one's ~; sing another ~, change one's way of speaking, behaviour, etc, or one's attitude to others (eg from insolence to respect). to the ~ of, (colloq) to the amount of (usu with the suggestion that the sum is high or exorbitant): He was fined (eg for a motoring offence) to the ~ of £30. □ vt,vi 1 [VP6A] adjust the strings, etc (of a musical instrument) to the right pitch: ~ a guitar. [VP2C] ~ up, (eg of a player or players in an orchestra) ~ a musical instrument: The orchestra were tuning up when we entered the concert-hall. **'tuning-fork** n small steel instrument, which produces a musical note of fixed pitch when struck. 2 [VP2C] ~ in (to), (a) adjust the controls of a radio to a particular frequency/station: ~ in to the BBC World Service. You're not properly ~d in. (b) (fig) be aware of what other people are saying, feeling, etc: He's not very well ~d in to his surroundings. 3 [VP6A] adjust or adapt the engine of a motor-vehicle so that it gives its best, or a special, performance. **~r** n 1 (in compounds) person who ~s musical instruments: a 'piano-tuner. 2 (part of) a radio etc which receives the signals. ⇨ **amplifier** at amplify, loud-speaker at loud(1). **~·ful** /-fl/ adj having a pleasing ~; melodious. **~·fully** /-fəlɪ/ adv **~·ful·ness** n

tung-oil /'tʌŋ ɔil/ n [U] oil (from a tree) used chiefly in varnishing woodwork.

tung·sten /'tʌŋstən/ n [U] grey metal (symbol W) used in making steel and the filaments of electric light bulbs.

tu·nic /'tju:nɪk US: 'tu:-/ n 1 close-fitting jacket as worn by policemen, soldiers, etc. 2 loose blouse or coat for a woman or girl, gathered at the waist with a belt, and reaching down to, or below, the hips. 3 loose, short-sleeved or sleeveless outer garment reaching to the knees, as worn by ancient Greeks and Romans.

tun·nel /'tʌnl/ n underground passage (esp through a hill or mountain, for a road, railway, etc); underwater passage (eg the proposed Channel ~ between England and France). □ vi,vt (-ll-, US also -l-) [VP2A,C,3A,6A] ~ (into/through), dig a ~ (into/through) sth; dig a ~ or ~s through (sth).

tunny /'tʌnɪ/ n (pl -nies or unchanged) large seafish, used as food, and valued for the sport of catching it.

tup /tʌp/ n male sheep; ram.

tup·pence /'tʌpəns/ n (colloq) two pence. **tup·penny** /'tʌpənɪ/ adj costing ~; (fig) of trifling value.

tu quo·que /ˌtju: 'kwəʊkwɪ US: ˌtu: 'kwəʊkweɪ/ n (Lat) (phrase used as a retort) So are you! So did you!

tur·ban /'tɜ:bən/ n 1 headdress made by winding a length of cloth round the head (as worn in some Asian and African countries). 2 close-fitting hat resembling a ~. **~ed** adj wearing a ~: a ~ed Sikh.

tur·bid /'tɜ:bɪd/ adj 1 (of liquids) thick; muddy; not clear: ~ waters/rivers. 2 (fig) disordered; confused: a ~ imagination; ~ thoughts. **~·ness, ~·ity** /tɜ:'bɪdətɪ/ nn

tur·bine /'tɜ:baɪn/ n engine or motor whose driving-wheel is turned by a current of water, steam or air. ⇨ the illus at air.

tur·bo·jet /ˌtɜ:bəʊ'dʒet/ n (aircraft with a) turbine engine that delivers its power in the form of a jet of hot gases (no propellers being needed on the aircraft).

tur·bo·prop /ˌtɜ:bəʊ'prɒp/ n (aircraft with a) turbine engine that uses its power, from hot gases, to turn a propeller.

tur·bot /'tɜ:bət/ n (pl unchanged) large, flat seafish valued as food.

tur·bu·lent /'tɜ:bjʊlənt/ adj violent; disorderly; uncontrolled: ~ waves/passions; a ~ mob. **~·ly** adv **tur·bu·lence** /-ləns/ n

turd /tɜ:d/ n [U,C] (sl) (ball or lump of) excrement: sheep ~s.

tu·reen /tjʊ'ri:n US: tʊ-/ n deep dish with a lid, from which soup, vegetables, etc are served at table.

turf /tɜ:f/ n 1 [U] soil-surface with grass-roots growing in it: strip the ~ off a field; make a lawn by laying ~ (instead of sowing grass-seed). **the ~**, the race-course; the occupation of profession of horse-racing. **'~ accountant, ~ commission agent**, bookmaker, ⇨ book[1](8). 2 (pl ~s or turves /tɜ:vz/) piece of ~ cut out; (in Ireland) (piece of) peat. □ vt 1 [VP6A] cover or lay (a piece of land) with ~. 2 [VP15B] ~ out, (GB sl) throw out.

tur·gid /'tɜ:dʒɪd/ adj 1 swollen; bloated. 2 (of language) pompous; full of high-sounding words. **~·ly** adv **~·ity** /tɜ:'dʒɪdətɪ/ n

Turk /tɜ:k/ n native or inhabitant of Turkey.

tur·key /'tɜ:kɪ/ n (pl ~s) 1 [C] large bird valued as food; [U] its flesh; ⇨ the illus at fowl. 2 (US sl) a flop. **cold ~**, (a) sudden withdrawal from, or hangover after taking, narcotics. (b) frank, determined statement of truth (usu about sth unpleasant). **talk ~**, (US sl) talk frankly and bluntly.

Tur·kish /'tɜ:kɪʃ/ n, adj (language) of Turkey or the

Turks. ~ **bath**, of hot air or steam, followed by a shower and massage. ~ **delight**, sweetmeat of jelly-like substance covered with powdered sugar. ~ **towel**, one made of rough absorbent cloth.

tur·meric /'tɜːmərɪk/ n [U] (E Indian plant with a) root which is used, in powdered form, as a colouring substance and a flavouring (esp in making curries).

tur·moil /'tɜːmɔɪl/ n [C,U] (instance of) trouble, agitation, disturbance: *The town was in (a) ~ during the elections.*

turn [1] /tɜːn/ n 1 act of turning; turning movement: *a few ~s of the handle; a ~ of Fortune's wheel,* a change of fortune. ~ *of the century,* the time when a new century(2) starts. *on the ~,* about to change: *The milk is on the ~,* about to turn sour. *The tide is on the ~.* *done to a ~,* (from the use of a ~spit) cooked just enough, neither underdone nor overdone. 2 change of direction: *sudden ~s in the road.* *at every ~,* (fig) very frequently: *I've been coming across old friends at every ~ during this reunion. He was frustrated at every ~,* every time he tried to achieve his aim. 3 change in condition: *The sick man/My affairs took a ~ for the better/worse. His illness took a favourable ~.* 4 occasion or opportunity for doing sth, esp in one's proper order among others: *It's your ~ to read now, John. Wait (until it is) your ~. My ~ will come* (sometimes meaning 'I shall have my time of success, triumph, revenge, etc', according to context). **(do sth) ~ and ~ about,** (of two or more persons) first one and then the other(s); alternately. **by ~s,** (of persons, groups, actions) in rotation; one after the other: *She went hot and cold by ~s. They laughed and cried by ~s.* **in ~,** (of two persons) = ~ and ~ about; (of more than two persons) in succession: *The boys were summoned in ~ to see the examiner.* **out of ~,** before or after the permitted time: *You mustn't speak out of (your) ~.* **take ~s (at sth); take ~s about,** do it in ~: *Mary and Helen took ~s at sitting up with their sick mother,* Mary sat up first, Helen next, and so on. 5 action regarded as affecting sb. **One good ~ deserves another,** (prov) Help, kind service, etc should be repaid. **do sb a good/bad ~,** be/not be helpful. 6 natural tendency: *a boy with a me chanical ~,* interested in, clever at, mechanical things. *He has a gloomy ~ of mind.* 7 purpose; special need. **serve one's ~,** meet one's requirements: *I think this book will serve my ~.* 8 short period of activity: *I'll take a few ~s* (= have a walk) *round the deck before I go to bed. I'll take a ~ at the oars now if you want a rest.* 9 short performance on the stage (esp of a variety theatre, or similar entertainment for sound or TV broadcasts), eg a song, dance, juggling feat, display of skill. **star ~,** most popular ~. 10 (colloq) nervous shock: *The news gave me quite a ~.*

turn [2] /tɜːn/ vt, vi (For uses with *adverbial particles and preps,* ⇨ 7 below.) 1 [VP6A,15A,B,2A,C,4A] (cause to) move round a point; (cause to) move so as to face in a different direction: *The earth ~s round the sun. The wheels of the car were ~ing slowly. What ~s the wheels? He ~ed away from me. He ~ed his back on me, ⇨ back* [1](1). *He ~ed his back to the wall. He ~ed his head (round) and looked back. He ~ed to look at me. He ~ed (to the) left. It's time we ~ed and went back home. He was idly ~ing the pages of a magazine. The car ~ed (round) the corner. Be careful how you ~*

that corner. Please ~ your eyes (= look) *this way. The mere thought of food ~ed his stomach,* upset his stomach, made him feel ill. *His stomach ~ed at the sight of food. When does the tide ~,* begin to flow in/out? *This tap ~s easily. It's easy to ~ this tap. Nothing will ever ~ him from* (= cause him to change) *his purpose.* ~ *one's mind/thoughts/ attention to sth,* direct one's mind, etc to: *Please ~ your attention to something more important.* ~ *one's hand to sth,* (be able to) undertake (a task, etc): *He can ~ his hand to most jobs about the house,* can deal with them. ~ *sth to account,* ⇨ account [1](3). ~ *a deaf ear to sth,* refuse to listen to: *They ~ed a deaf ear to my request for help.* ~ *sb's flank;* ~ *the flank of sb,* pass round an enemy's position so as to attack it in the flank or rear; (fig) outwit him; defeat him in debate, etc. ~ *the corner,* (fig use) ⇨ corner(1). ~ *the scale(s),* ⇨ scale [3](1). 2 [VP6A,14,15A,B,2A,C,3A] ~ **(sth) (into sth),** (cause to) change in nature, quality, condition, etc: *Frost ~s water into ice. Caterpillars ~ into* (= become) *butterflies. This hot weather has ~ed the milk,* made it sour. *His hair has ~ed grey. Anxiety ~ed his hair white. The leaves are beginning to ~,* change colour (as in autumn). *Could you ~ this piece of prose into verse/this passage into Greek? He has ~ed traitor,* become a traitor. *He's a politician ~ed poet,* who has become a poet. *T~ the dog loose,* let it go free, eg by releasing it from a chain. ~ *sb's brain,* upset him mentally. ~ *sb's head,* unsettle him, make him vain: *The excessive praise the young actor received ~ed his head.* 3 [VP6A] reach and pass: *He has ~ed* (= reach the age of) *fifty. It has just ~ed two,* is just after two o'clock. 4 [VP6A] shape (sth, wood or metal) on a lathe, etc: ~ *brass; a machine-~ed cigarette-case;* ~ *a bowl on a potter's wheel;* (fig) give a graceful form to: ~ *an epigram/a compliment; a well-~ed phrase/sentence; a well-~ed ankle;* (with passive force): *wood/metal that ~s* (= can be ~ed) *easily.* 5 [VP6A] remake (a garment) so that the inner surface becomes the outer surface: *I'll have this old overcoat ~ed.* ~ *one's coat,* ⇨ coat(1). '~-**coat** n person who deserts one party to join another, esp to win profit, advantage, safety, etc. 6 (compounds) '~-**cock** n person employed to ~ water on or off (at the mains). '~-**key** n keeper of the keys in a prison; jailer. '~-**pike** n (hist) gate kept closed across a road and opened on payment of a toll; (US) toll road for fast traffic. '~-**spit** n (hist) dog or servant who turned the spit on which meat, etc used to be roasted. '~-**stile** n revolving gate that admits, lets out, one person at a time. '~-**table** n flat circular platform, eg one on which gramophone discs are played, or on which a railway locomotive is turned round. 7 [VP14,15B,2C,3A] (special uses with *adverbial particles* and *preps*):

turn (sb) about, (cause to) ~ to one side or in a different direction: *About ~!* (as a military command, in drills, etc).

turn sb adrift, send sb away without help or support: *He ~ed his son adrift in the world,* sent him away from home and refused to help him.

turn (sb) against sb, (cause to) become hostile to: *She ~ed against her old friend. He tried to ~ the children against their mother.*

turn (sb) aside (from), (more usu ~ *away*) (cause to) ~ to one side or in a different direction.

turn (sb) away, (cause to) ~ in a different direction so as not to face sb/sth; refuse to look at, welcome, help, admit (to a place): *She ~ed away in disgust. He ~ed away a beggar. We had to ~ away hundreds of people,* eg from a stadium, because all seats were sold.

turn (sb/sth) back, (cause to) return the way one has come: *It's getting dark—we'd better ~ back. We were/Our car was ~ed back at the frontier.*

turn (sth) down, (a) (cause to) fold down: ~ *down one's coat collar; a ~-down collar; ~ down the bed-clothes.* **(b)** reduce (the flame or brilliance of a gas- or oil-lamp, stove, etc) by ~ing a wheel or tap: ~ *down the lamps.* **(c)** place (a playing-card) on the table face downwards. ~ **sb/sth down,** refuse to consider (an offer, a proposal, or the person who makes it): *He tried to join the army but was ~ed down because of poor health. He asked Jane to marry him but she ~ed him down/~ed down his proposal.*

turn in, (colloq) go to bed. ~ **in on oneself/ itself,** withdraw from contact with others; become a recluse; (of a country) become isolationist. ~ **sb in,** (colloq) surrender sb to the police. ~ **(sth) in,** (cause to) fold or slant inwards: *His toes ~ in. He ~ed his toes in.* ~ **sth in,** (colloq) give back to those in authority: *You must ~ in your equipment* (eg uniform) *before you leave.*

turn (sth) inside out, (cause to) become inside out: *The wind ~ed my old umbrella inside out. He ~ed his pockets inside out in search of his keys.*

turn off, change direction; leave (one road) for another: *Is this where we ~ off/where our road ~s off for Hull?* ~ **sth off,** stop the flow of (liquid, gas, current) by ~ing a tap, switch or other control: ~ *off the water/lights/radio/TV.* ~ **(sb) off,** (sl) (cause sb to) lose interest, desire, etc: *He/This music really ~s me off!* Hence, '~-off *n* sth/sb that causes this.

turn sth on, start the flow of (liquid, gas, current) by ~ing a tap, switch, etc: *T~ the lights/radio on. She's fond of ~ing on the charm,* (fig) using her charm to influence people. ~ **(sb) on,** (sl) (cause sb to) have great pleasure or excitement: *Some girls ~ on easily. What kind of music ~s you on? Some drugs ~ you on very quickly,* quickly change your mental or emotional state. Hence, '~-on *n* sth/sb that causes this. ~ **on sth,** depend on: *The success of a picnic usually ~s on the weather.* ~ **on sb,** become hostile to; attack: *The dog ~ed on me and bit me in the leg.*

turn out (well, etc), prove to be; be in the end: *Everything ~ed out well/satisfactory. The day ~ed out wet. As it ~ed out...,* As it happened in the end.... ~ **(sth) out,** (cause to) point outwards: *His toes ~ out. He ~ed his toes out.* ~ **sth out, (a)** extinguish by ~ing a tap, switch, etc: *Please ~ out the lights/gas-fire before you go to bed.* **(b)** empty (a drawer, one's pockets, a room, etc) when looking for sth, when cleaning sth: ~ *out all the drawers in one's desk;* ~ *out the attic,* to get rid of unwanted articles, etc. ~ **sb/sth out,** produce, eg manufactured goods: *Our new factory is ~ing out large quantities of goods. The school has ~ed out some first-rate scholars.* ~ **(sb) out, (a)** (cause him to) assemble for some event, or for duty: *The whole village ~ed out to welcome the princess. Not many men ~ed out for duty.* **(b)** (colloq) (cause sb to) get out of bed. ~ **sb out (of/from sth),** expel by force, threats, etc: ~ *sb out of his*

job/chair; ~ *out a tenant* (= from his house) *for not paying the rent.* ~ **ed out,** (of a person, equipment, etc) dressed, equipped: *a well-~ed out young man. She was beautifully ~ed out,* elegantly dressed. Hence, '~-out *n* **(a)** persons who have ~ed out (assembled): *There was a good ~-out at the meeting.* **(b)** occasion when one ~s out (empties, etc) a drawer, etc: *The drawers in my desk are full of old papers—it's time I had a good ~-out.* **(c)** equipment; way in which sth is equipped; clothes and accessories worn together: *a smart/ sloppy ~-out.* **(d)** output (the more usu word) of manufactured goods, etc.

turn (sb/sth) over, (cause to) fall over, upset; change the position of: *The car (was) ~ed right over,* completely upset. *He ~ed over in bed. The nurse ~ed the old man over and gave him an injection in the left buttock.* ~ **sth over,** do business to the amount of: *His business ~s over £500 a week.* ~ **sth over in one's mind,** think about sth (before making a decision). ~ **sth/sb over (to sb),** give the control or conduct of sth to: *I've ~ed over the management of my affairs to my brother. He's ~ed over his business to his successors. The thief was ~ed* (= handed) *over to the police.* Hence, '~-over *n* **(a)** amount of money ~ed over in business within a period of time or for a particular transaction: *a profit of £1000 on a ~over of £10000; sell goods at low prices hoping for a quick ~over,* quick sales and quick replacement of stock. **(b)** rate of renewal: *There is a higher ~over of the labour force in unskilled trades than in skilled trades,* unskilled workers leave and are replaced more quickly. **(c)** tart made by folding over half of a circular piece of pastry over the other half, with jam, meat, etc inside.

turn (sth/sb) round, (cause to) face another way, be in another direction: *T~ round and let me see your profile. T~ your chair round to the fire.* Hence, '~-round *n* (esp of a ship or aircraft) process of getting it ready for the return voyage or flight: *a ~round of 24 hours in Southampton,* eg for an Atlantic liner.

turn to, get busy: *The design staff ~ed to and produced a set of drawings in twenty-four hours.* ~ **to sb,** go or apply to: *The child ~ed to its mother for comfort. She has nobody to ~ to.*

turn up, (a) make one's appearance; arrive: *He promised to come, but hasn't ~ed up yet. My boss hasn't ~ed up this morning—I hope she isn't ill.* **(b)** be found, esp by chance: *The book you've lost may ~ up one of these days.* **(c)** (of an opportunity, etc) happen; present itself: *He's still waiting for something* (eg a job, a piece of good luck) *to ~ up.* ~ **(sth) up, (a)** (cause to) slope upwards: ~ (= roll) *up one's shirt sleeves.* **(b)** expose; make visible: *The share of a plough ~s up the soil. The ploughman ~ed up some buried treasure/an old skull.* ~ **sb up,** (colloq) cause to vomit; disgust: *The stink from the slaughter-house ~ed me up.* ~ **up one's nose at sth,** (fig) express a superior and critical attitude towards: *She ~ed up her nose at the suggestion.* '~-up *n* **(a)** turned fold at the bottom of a trouser-leg. **(b)** ~-up *(for the book),* surprising and unexpected event: *Fancy seeing you after all these years. What a ~-up for the book!*

turn upon, ⇨ ~ on above, (= attack).

turn·er /'tɜːnə(r)/ *n* person who works at a lathe. ⇨ turn²(4).

turn·ing /'tɜːnɪŋ/ *n* place where a road turns, esp

where one road branches off from another: *Take the first ~ on/to the right.* '**~-point** *n* (fig) point in place, time, development, etc which is critical: *reach a ~-point in history/in one's life. There was a ~-point in the negotiations yesterday.*

tur·nip /'tɜ:nɪp/ *n* [C] (plant with a) large round root used as a vegetable and as food for cattle.

tur·pen·tine /'tɜ:pəntaɪn/ *n* [U] oil obtained from certain trees, used as a solvent in mixing paint and varnish, and in medicine.

tur·pi·tude /'tɜ:pɪtju:d US: -tu:d/ *n* [U] (formal) wickedness; depravity.

turps /tɜ:ps/ *n* [U] (colloq abbr for) turpentine.

tur·quoise /'tɜ:kwɔɪz/ *n* [C] (colour of a) greenish-blue precious stone.

tur·ret /'tʌrɪt/ *n* 1 small tower, esp at a corner of a building or defensive wall. 2 steel structure protecting gunners, often made so as to revolve with the gun(s): *a warship armed with twin-gun ~s.*

turtle[1] /'tɜ:tl/ *n* sea-animal with a soft body protected by a hard shell like that of a tortoise. ⇨ the illus at reptile. **turn ~,** (of a ship) turn upside down; capsize. '**~-neck(ed)** *adj* (of a garment, esp a sweater) having a high, circular, close-fitting collar.

turtle[2] /'tɜ:tl/ *n* (usu) '**~-dove,** kinds of dove, esp a wild kind noted for its soft cooing, and its affection for its mate and young.

turves /tɜ:vz/ *n pl* ⇨ turf.

tusk /tʌsk/ *n* long-pointed tooth, esp one coming out from the closed mouth, as in the elephant, walrus or wild boar. ⇨ the illus at large, sea.

tussle /'tʌsl/ *n, vi* [VP2A,3A] **~ (with),** (colloq) (have a) hard struggle or fight.

tus·sock /'tʌsək/ *n* clump or hillock of growing grass.

tut /tʌt/, **tut-tut** /ˌtʌt 'tʌt/ *int* used to express impatience, contempt, rebuke. □ *vt* (-tt-) [VP6A] express impatience, etc by using this word: *He tut-tutted the idea.*

tu·te·lage /'tju:tɪlɪdʒ US: 'tu:-/ *n* [U] (formal) guardianship: *a child in ~;* (period of) being under ~.

tu·te·lary /'tju:tɪlərɪ US: 'tu:təlrɪ/ *adj* (formal) serving as a guardian or protector; of a guardian: ~ *authority.*

tu·tor /'tju:tə(r) US: 'tu:-/ *n* 1 private teacher, esp one who instructs a single pupil or a very small class, sometimes one who lives with the family of his pupil(s). 2 (GB) university teacher who guides the studies of a number of students. □ *vt* [VP6A,15A,16A] 1 teach as a ~. 2 train, exercise restraint over: ~ *one's passions;* ~ *oneself to be patient.* ~**ial** /tju:'tɔ:rɪəl US:* tu:-/ *adj* of a ~ of his duties: ~*ial classes.* □ *n* period of instruction given by a college ~: *attend a ~ial.*

tutti-frutti /ˌtu:tɪ 'fru:tɪ/ *n* (portion of) ice-cream with chopped nuts and various fruits.

tutu /'tu:tu:/ *n* short skirt with many layers of stiffened fabric worn by women dancers in classical ballet.

tux·edo /tʌk'si:dəʊ/ *n* (*pl* ~s /-dəʊz/) (US) dinner-jacket.

twaddle /'twɒdl/ *n* [U] foolish talk. □ *vi* [VP2A] talk or write ~: *Stop twaddling!*

twain /tweɪn/ *n* (archaic) two.

twang /twæŋ/ *n* 1 sound of a tight string or wire being pulled and released: *the ~ of a guitar.* 2 harsh, nasal tone of voice: *speak with a ~.* □ *vt, vi* [VP6A,2A] (cause to) make this kind of sound: *The*

bow ~ed and the arrow whistled through the air. He was ~ing a banjo.

'**twas** /twɒz; *weak form:* twəz/ (archaic or poet) = it was.

tweak /twi:k/ *vt* [VP6A] pinch and twist: *Wouldn't you like to ~ that rude fellow's nose/ears?* □ *n* act of ~ing.

twee /twi:/ *adj* affectedly or inappropriately dainty or quaint.

tweed /twi:d/ *n* 1 [U] (often attrib) thick, soft, woollen cloth, usu woven of mixed colours: *a ~ hat/coat.* 2 (*pl*) (suit of) clothes made of ~: *dressed in Scottish ~s.*

'**tween** /twi:n/ *adv, prep* (archaic or poet) between, esp '**~-decks,** between decks.

tweet /twi:t/ *n, vi* (of a bird) chirp.

tweeter /'twi:tə(r)/ *n* loudspeaker for reproducing high notes. ⇨ woofer.

tweez·ers /'twi:zəz/ *n pl* (*pair of*) ~, tiny pair of tongs for picking up or pulling out very small things, eg hairs from the eyebrows.

twelfth /twelfθ/ *adj, n* next after the 11th; one of twelve equal parts. ~ **man,** (in cricket) reserve player. '**T~-night,** eve of the festival of Epiphany, celebrated with festivities.

twelve /twelv/ *adj, n* the number 12. ⇨ App 4. **the T~,** the ~ apostles of Jesus. '**~-month** *n* (archaic) year.

twenty /'twentɪ/ *adj, n* the number 20. ⇨ App 4. **the twenties,** 20–29. **twen·ti·eth** /'twentɪəθ/ *adj, n* next after the 19th; one of 20 equal parts.

'**twere** /twɜ:(r)/ (archaic or poet) = it were (= *it would be*).

twerp /twɜ:p/ *n* (sl) contemptible or insignificant person.

twice /twaɪs/ *adv* two times: ~ *as much/as many. I've been there once or ~. He's ~ the man he was,* ~ as well, strong, confident, capable, etc. **think** '**~ about doing sth,** hesitate, think carefully, before deciding to do it. **a** ,**~-told 'tale,** a well-known one.

twiddle /'twɪdl/ *vt, vi* 1 [VP6A] twist or turn idly or aimlessly: ~ *one's thumbs.* 2 [VP3A] **~ with sth,** play idly: ~ *with one's hair/a ring on one's finger.* □ *n* slight twist or turn. **twid·dly** /'twɪdlɪ/ *adj* having a ~.

twig[1] /twɪg/ *n* [C] small shoot on or at the end of a branch (bush, plant). ⇨ the illus at tree. ~**gy** *adj* having many ~s: *support plants with ~gy sticks.*

twig[2] /twɪg/ *vt, vi* (-gg-) [VP6A,2A] (GB colloq) observe; notice; understand: *I soon ~ged what he was up to,* saw the trick he was trying to play.

twi·light /'twaɪlaɪt/ *n* [U] 1 faint half-light before sunrise or after sunset: *go for a walk in the ~.* 2 (fig) remote period about which little is known: *in the ~ of history.* **twi·lit** /'twaɪlɪt/ *adj* dimly lit.

twill /twɪl/ *n* [U] strong cotton cloth woven so that fine diagonal lines or ribs appear on the surface. ~**ed** *adj* (of cloth) woven in this way.

'**twill** /twɪl/ (archaic or poet) = it will.

twin /twɪn/ *n* 1 either of two children born together of the same mother: *one of the ~s;* (attrib) ~ *brothers.* 2 (usu attrib) completely like, closely associated with, another: *a ship with ~ propellers,* two identical propellers; ~ *beds,* two identical single beds; *a* '**~-set,** woman's jumper and long sleeved cardigan of the same colour and style. □ *vt* [VP6A,14] **~ (with),** join closely together; couple; pair. ⇨ twinned.

twine /twaɪn/ *n* [U] thin strings made by twisting

two or more yarns together. □ *vt,vi* [VP15A,B,2A,C] twist; wind: ~ *flowers into a garland; vines that ~ round a tree. She ~d her arms round my neck.*

twinge /twɪndʒ/ *n* [C] sudden, sharp pain: *a ~ of toothache/rheumatism/conscience.*

twinkle /'twɪŋkl/ *vi* [2A,C] **1** shine with a light that gleams unsteadily: *stars that ~ in the sky.* **2** (of eyes) sparkle; (of eyelids, feet in dancing, etc) move rapidly up and down, to and fro: *Her eyes ~d with amusement/mischief.* □ *n* **1** [U] twinkling light: *the ~ of the stars/of a distant light.* **2** sparkle; rapid twitching: *There was a mischievous ~ in her eyes.* **twink·ling** /'twɪŋklɪŋ/ *n* (*sing* only) *in the twinkling of an eye,* in an instant.

twin·ned /twɪnd/ *attrib adj* ~ *(with),* paired (with): *a town in England ~ with a town in France,* (for cultural, educational, etc exchanges).

twirl /twɜːl/ *vt,vi* [VP6A,15B,16A,2A,C] **1** (cause to) turn round and round quickly: *She ~ed the mop to get the water out of it. He sat ~ing his thumbs.* **2** curl: *He ~ed his moustache (up).* □ *n* rapid circular motion.

twist /twɪst/ *vt,vi* **1** [VP6A,15A,B] wind or turn (a number of threads, strands, etc) one around the other: ~ *pieces of straw into a rope. She ~ed the girl's hair round her fingers to make it curl.* **2** [VP6A] make (a rope, a garland, etc) by doing this. **3** [VP6A,15A,B,16A] turn, esp by the use of force; turn the two ends of (sth) in opposite directions; turn one end of (sth): ~ (more usu *wring*) *a wet cloth,* to squeeze out the water; ~ *the cap off a fountain-pen/a tube of toothpaste. If you use too much force, you'll ~ the key,* bend it out of shape. *His features were ~ed* (= distorted) *with pain. He fell and ~ed his ankle. She ~ed her head round as she reversed the car into the garage.* ~ *sth off,* break off by ~ing: ~ *off the end of a piece of wire.* ~ *sb's arm,* (a) force it round to cause pain. (b) (fig, colloq) put (friendly or unfriendly) pressure on him to do sth. ~ *sb round one's little finger,* (colloq) get him to do what one wants him to do. **4** [VP6A,15A] force (sb's words) out of their true meaning: *The police tried to ~ his words into a confession of guilt.* **5** [VP6A,15A,2A,C] give a spiral form to (a rod, column, etc); receive, have, move or grow in, a spiral form: ~ed *columns,* as in architecture. **6** [VP2A,C] turn and curve in different directions; change position or direction: *The road ~s and turns up the side of the mountain. The thief ~ed out of the policeman's grip and ran off. The injured man ~ed about in pain.* **7** [VP6A,2A] (of a ball, esp in billiards) (cause to) take a curved path while spinning. **8** [VP2A] dance the ~, ⇨ **6** below. □ *n* **1** ~ing or being ~ed: *The bully gave the little boy's arm a ~. Give the rope a few more ~s. There are numerous ~s in the road over the pass.* **2** sth made by ~ing: *a rope full of ~s* (= kinks, coils); *a ~ of paper,* a paper packet with screwed-up ends. **3** [C,U] thread, yarn, rope, etc made by ~ing together two or more strands, esp certain kinds of silk thread and cotton yarn; coarse tobacco made by ~ing dried leaves into a roll. **4** motion given to a ball to make it take a curved path. **5** peculiar tendency of mind or character: *He has a criminal ~ in him.* **6** the ~, dance (popular in the 1960's) in which there is ~ing of the arms and hips. ~**er** *n* **1** (colloq) dishonest person. **2** difficult task, problem, etc: *a 'tongue-~er,* word or phrase difficult to pronounce. ~**y** *adj* (-ier, -iest)

1 having many ~s: *a ~y road.* **2** not straightforward: *a ~y politician.*

twit¹ /twɪt/ *vt* (-tt-) [VP6A,14] tease sb (usu in jest) (with or about sth): ~ *a man about the state he was in after a drinking bout.*

twit² /twɪt/ *n* (sl) contemptible fool; idiot.

twitch /twɪtʃ/ *n* [C] **1** sudden, quick, usu uncontrollable movement of a muscle; tic. **2** sudden quick pull: *I felt a ~ at my sleeve.* □ *vi,vt* **1** [VP2A,C,6A] (cause to) move in a ~(1): *The dog's nose ~ed as it passed the butcher's shop. His face ~ed with terror. The horse ~ed its ears.* **2** [VP15A,B] jerk; give a ~(2) to: *The wind ~ed the paper out of my hand.*

twit·ter /'twɪtə(r)/ *vi* [VP15A,B] (of birds) chirp; make a succession of soft short sounds; (of persons) talk rapidly through excitement, nervousness, etc. □ *n* **1** chirping: *the ~ of sparrows.* **2** (of persons) (colloq, esp in) *(all) of a ~,* in an excited state.

'twixt /twɪkst/ *prep* (archaic or poet) = betwixt.

two /tuː/ *n, adj* **1** the number 2. ⇨ App 4. *break/ cut sth in two,* into two parts. *put two and two together,* infer sth from what one sees, hears, learns, etc. *by twos and threes,* two or three at a time. *,Two can play (at) 'that game,* used as a threat of retaliation. **2** (compounds) ,two-'edged *adj* (of a sword) having a cutting edge on each side; (fig, of an argument, etc) having two possible (and contrary) meanings. 'two-,faced *adj* (fig) insincere. 'two-fold *adj, adv* double, doubly. ,two-'handed *adj* (of a sword) needing two hands to use it; (of a saw, etc) to be used by two persons, one at each end. 'two-,pence /'tʌpəns *US:* 'tuːpens/ *n* sum of two pence. 'two-penny /'tʌpənɪ *US:* 'tuːpenɪ/ *adj* costing two pence. ,two-penny 'piece, GB coin worth two pence. ,two-penny-'half-penny /,tʌpnɪ 'heɪpnɪ *US:* ,tuːpenɪ 'hæfpenɪ/ *adj* (colloq) almost worthless; petty. 'two-a-penny *adj* easy to obtain; cheap; almost worthless. ,two-'piece *n* set of garments of similar or matching material, eg skirt and jacket, trousers and jacket; bra and briefs (for swimming); (attrib) *a two-piece suit.* 'two-ply *adj* of two strands or thicknesses: *two-ply wool/ wood.* ,two-'seater *n* car, aircraft, etc with seats for two persons. 'two-timing *adj* (sl) deceitful; engaged in double-crossing. ,two-'way *attrib adj* (a) (of a switch) allowing current to be switched on or off from either of two points. (b) (of a road or street) in which traffic may move in both directions. Cf *one-way street.* (c) (of radio equipment, etc) for both sending and receiving.

'twould /twʊd/ (archaic or poet) = it would.

ty·coon /taɪ'kuːn/ *n* (colloq) wealthy and powerful business man or industrialist: *'oil ~s.*

ty·ing /'taɪɪŋ/ *pres p* of tie².

tyke, tike /taɪk/ *n* cur; (as a term of abuse) low fellow.

tym·pa·num /'tɪmpənəm/ *n* (*pl* ~s or -na /-nə/) (anat) **1** eardrum. **2** middle ear. ⇨ middle; ⇨ the illus at ear.

type¹ /taɪp/ *n* **1** [C] person, thing, event, etc considered as an example of a class or group: *Abraham Lincoln was a fine ~ of the American patriot.* **2** [C] class or group considered to have common characteristics: *men of this ~. Her beauty is of the Italian ~. They claim to make good Burgundy ~ wine/wine of the Burgundy ~ in Australia. true to ~,* representative of that ~: *A cowardly bulldog is not true to ~.* **3** [U] letters, etc cast in blocks of (usu) metal, for use in printing; any fount of these; [C] one of these blocks: *The printers are short of* ~/*certain* ~s. *Wooden* ~ *is/Wooden* ~s *are sometimes used for printing posters. The material is now in* ~, has been set ready for printing. *The examples in this dictionary are in italic* ~. **4** (compounds) '~·**face** *n* style of type(3). ⇨ face¹(3). '~·**script** *n* typewritten copy (prepared for printing, etc). '~·**setter** *n* worker or machine that sets ~ for printing. '~·**writer** *n* machine with which one prints letters on paper, using the fingers on a keyboard. '~·**written** *adj* written using a ~writer: *a* ~*written message.*

type² /taɪp/ *vt, vi* [VP6A,2A] **1** use a typewriter; write with a typewriter: ~ *a letter. She* ~s *well.* **2** [VP6A] determine the type(2) of sth: ~ *a virus;* ~ *a person's blood.* **typ·ist** /'taɪpɪst/ *n* person who ~s.

type·cast /'taɪpkɑːst US: -kæst/ *vt* (*pt,pp* unchanged) [VP6A] (theatre) cast (a person) for a part which he/she has the reputation of doing well or which seems to fit his/her own personality.

ty·phoid /'taɪfɔɪd/ *n* [U] ~ (**fever**), infectious disease which attacks the intestines, caused by bacteria taken into the body with food or drink.

ty·phoon /taɪ'fuːn/ *n* [C] violent hurricane of the kind that occurs in the western Pacific.

ty·phus /'taɪfəs/ *n* [U] infectious disease marked by fever, great weakness and the appearance of purple spots on the body.

typi·cal /'tɪpɪkl/ *adj* ~ (*of*), serving as a type; representative or characteristic. ~·**ly** /-klɪ/ *adv*

typ·ify /'tɪpɪfaɪ/ *vt* (*pt,pp* -fied) [VP6A] be a symbol of; be representative of.

typ·ist /'taɪpɪst/ *n* ⇨ type ².

ty·pog·ra·phy /taɪ'pɒgrəfɪ/ *n* [U] art or style of printing. **ty·pog·ra·pher** /taɪ'pɒgrəfə(r)/ *n* person skilled in ~. **ty·po·graphic** /ˌtaɪpə'græfɪk/ *adj* **ty·po·graphi·cally** /-klɪ/ *adv*

ty·ran·ni·cal /tɪ'rænɪkl/ *adj* of or like a tyrant; acting like a tyrant; obtaining obedience by force or threats.

tyr·an·nize /'tɪrənaɪz/ *vi, vt* [VP6A,3A] ~ (*over*), rule cruelly and unjustly: ~ *over the weak. He* ~s *his family.*

tyr·an·ous /'tɪrənəs/ *adj* = tyrannical.

tyr·anny /'tɪrənɪ/ *n* (*pl* -nies) **1** [U] cruel or unjust use of power; [C] instance of this; tyrannical act. **2** [C,U] (instance of, country with, the) kind of government existing when a ruler has complete power, esp when this power has been obtained by force and is used unjustly: *live under a* ~.

ty·rant /'taɪərənt/ *n* cruel or unjust ruler, esp one who has obtained complete power by force.

tyre (US = **tire**)/'taɪə(r)/ *n* band of solid or inflated rubber on the rim of a wheel, esp (*pneumatic* ~) the kind on bicycle and motor-car wheels. ⇨ the illus at **bicycle**, **motor**.

tyro /'taɪərəʊ/ *n* = tiro.

tzar /zɑː(r)/, **tza·rina** /zɑː'riːnə/ *nn* = czar, czarina.

Uu understüchen - support

U, u /juː/ the 21st letter of the English alphabet. '**U-boat** *n* German submarine. '**U-turn**, one of 180° (by a car, etc): *No U-turns!* (as a traffic notice in towns, on motorways).

ubi·qui·tous /juː'bɪkwɪtəs/ *adj* (formal) present everywhere or in several places at the same time. **ubi·quity** /juː'bɪkwətɪ/ *n* [U] quality of being ~.

ud·der /'ʌdə(r)/ *n* bag of a cow, goat or other animal, from which milk comes, esp a large one with two or more teats. ⇨ the illus at **domestic**.

ugh /*This usu suggests a sound like* ɜ: *made with the lips either spread or rounded very strongly and one's facial expression showing disgust*/ *int* used to indicate disgust. häßlich

ugly /'ʌglɪ/ *adj* (-ier, -iest) **1** unpleasant to look at; hideous: ~ *children/furniture/surroundings.* **2** threatening; unpleasant: *The sky looks* ~, suggests bad weather. *The news in today's newspapers is* ~, suggests unpleasant possibilities, eg of war. ~ **customer**, (colloq) dangerous person; person difficult to deal with. **ug·lify** /'ʌglɪfaɪ/ *vt* (*pt,pp* -fied) make ~. **ug·li·ness** *n*

ukase /juː'keɪs/ *n* (hist) edict of the Czarist Russian government; arbitrary order.

uku·lele /ˌjuːkə'leɪlɪ/ *n* Hawaiian four-stringed guitar.

ul·cer /'ʌlsə(r)/ *n* open sore forming poisonous matter (on the outside or inside surface of the body); (fig) corrupting influence or condition. ~-

ous /-əs/ *adj* ~·**ate** /-eɪt/ *vt, vi* [VP6A,2A] form, convert or be converted into, an ~. ~·**ation** /ˌʌlsə'reɪʃn/ *n*

ulna /'ʌlnə/ *n* (*pl* ~e /-niː/) (anat) inner of the two bones of the forearm. ⇨ the illus at **skeleton**.

ul·ster /'ʌlstə(r)/ *n* long, loose, belted overcoat.

ul·terior /ʌl'tɪərɪə(r)/ *adj* situated beyond; beyond what is first seen or said. ~ **motive**, motive other than what is expressed or admitted.

ul·ti·mate /'ʌltɪmət/ *adj* last, furthest, basic: ~ *principles/truths;* the ~ *cause*, beyond which no other cause is known or can be found; *the* ~ *deterrent* (used of nuclear weapons). ~·**ly** *adv* finally; in the end.

ul·ti·ma·tum /ˌʌltɪ'meɪtəm/ *n* (*pl* ~s, -ta /-tə/) [C] final statement of conditions to be accepted without discussion, eg one sent to a foreign government and threatening war if the conditions are not accepted.

ul·timo /'ʌltɪməʊ/ *adj* (abbr **ult**) (formerly used in business letters) of the month before the current month: *Thank you for your letter of the 10th ult.*

ultra- /'ʌltrə/ *pref* beyond. ⇨ App 3.

ultra·mar·ine /ˌʌltrəmə'riːn/ *adj, n* brilliant pure blue (colour).

ultra·mon·tane /ˌʌltrəmɒn'teɪn/ *adj* (RC Church) favouring the absolute authority of the Pope in matters of faith and discipline.

ultra·sonic /ˌʌltrə'sɒnɪk/ *adj* relating to sound

cutupieder sein mid - to be dissatisfied with

waves beyond the range of normal human audibility.

ultra·vio·let /ˌʌltrə'vaɪələt/ adj of the invisible part of the spectrum beyond the violet. ~ **rays**, invisible rays (in sunlight, light from mercury-vapour lamps, etc) which have an effect upon the skin, curing certain skin diseases, forming vitamins, etc.

ultra vires /ˌʌltrə 'vaɪəriːz/ adj, adv (Lat) beyond the powers or authority granted by law.

ulu·late /'juːljʊleɪt US: 'ʌl-/ vi [VP2A] howl; wail loudly. **ulu·la·tion** /ˌjuːljʊ'leɪʃn US: ˌʌl-/ n

um·ber /'ʌmbə(r)/ adj, n yellowish-green (colouring substance). **burnt** ~, reddish-brown.

um·bili·cal /ʌm'bɪlɪkl/ adj ~ **cord**, cord connecting a foetus at the navel with the placenta. ⇨ the illus at reproduce.

um·brage /'ʌmbrɪdʒ/ n [U] **give/take** ~ **(at sth)**, cause the feeling/feel that one has been treated unfairly or without proper respect.

um·brella /ʌm'brelə/ n **1** folding frame (with a stick and handle), covered with cotton, silk, etc used to shelter the person holding it from rain; (in some countries) such a device, used as a symbol of rank. ⇨ **parasol**; ⇨ **sunshade** at sun(4). **2** (fig) screen of fighter aircraft, eg flying over bombers to protect them against enemy aircraft. **3** protection; patronage: under the ~ of the UNO.

um·laut /'ʊmlaʊt/ n (in Germanic languages) vowel change shown by two dots over the vowel (as in the German plurals Männer, of Mann, and Füsse, of Fuss).

um·pire /'ʌmpaɪə(r)/ n person chosen to act as a judge in a dispute, to see that the rules are obeyed in cricket, baseball, tennis, netball and other games. Cf referee for football and boxing. □ vt, vi [VP6A,2A] act as ~: ~ a cricket match.

ump·teen /'ʌmptiːn/ adj (sl) many. ~**th**/ /'ʌmptiːnθ/ adj: for the ~th time, for I don't know how many times.

'un /ən/ pron (colloq) one: He's a good 'un, a good fellow. That's a good 'un, a good specimen, joke, etc.

un- /ʌn/ pref (⇨ App 3; specimens only here). **1** (before adjj and advv) not: uncertain(ly); unwilling(ly). **2** (before vv) do the opposite of, reverse the action of, what is indicated by the v. unscrew; unroll; undress, unlock. **3** (before nn) indicating absence of: uncertainty; unwillingness.

un·abashed /ˌʌnə'bæʃt/ adj not abashed, embarrassed or awed.

un·abated /ˌʌnə'beɪtɪd/ adj (of a storm, etc) (continuing) as strong, violent, etc as before.

un·able /ʌn'eɪbl/ adj (pred only) ~ **to do sth**, not able to do it.

un·accom·pan·ied /ˌʌnə'kʌmpənɪd/ adj **1** without a companion: ~ luggage, sent separately, the owner not travelling with it. **2** (music) performed without an accompaniment.

un·ac·count·able /ˌʌnə'kaʊntəbl/ adj in a way that cannot be accounted for or explained. **un·ac·count·ably** /-əblɪ/ adv

un·ac·cus·tomed /ˌʌnə'kʌstəmd/ adj **1** ~ **to**, not accustomed to: ~ as I am to speaking in public. **2** not usual; strange: his ~ silence.

un·ad·vised /ˌʌnəd'vaɪzd/ adj without advice; (esp) not discreet or wise; rash. ~**ly** /ˌʌnəd'vaɪzɪdlɪ/ adv rashly.

un·af·fec·ted /ˌʌnə'fektɪd/ adj **1** free from affectation; sincere. **2** ~ **by**, not affected by.

un·alien·able /ʌn'eɪlɪənəbl/ adj that cannot be

taken away or separated: ~ rights.

un·al·loyed /ˌʌnə'lɔɪd/ adj pure; unmixed: ~ joy.

un·al·ter·ably /ʌn'ɔːltərəblɪ/ adv in a way that cannot be changed.

unani·mous /juː'nænɪməs/ adj in, showing, complete agreement: The country is ~ in support of the Government's policy. He was elected by a ~ vote. The proposal was accepted with ~ approval. ~·**ly** adv una·nim·ity /ˌjuːnə'nɪmətɪ/ n [U] complete agreement or unity.

un·an·nounced /ˌʌnə'naʊnst/ adj without having been announced: He walked into the room ~, no one having told the persons there who he was, that he had arrived.

un·an·swer·able /ʌn'ɑːnsərəbl US: -'æn-/ adj (esp) against which no good argument can possibly be brought: His case is ~.

un·an·swered /ʌn'ɑːnsəd US: -'æn-/ adj not replied to: ~ letters; not returned: ~ love.

un·ap·proach·able /ˌʌnə'prəʊtʃəbl/ adj (esp, of a person) difficult to approach (because too stiff or formal): The new manager is an ~ sort of man.

un·armed /ʌn'ɑːmd/ adj without weapons or means of defence.

un·asked /ˌʌn'ɑːskt US: -'æs-/ adj ~ **(for)**, not asked (for), requested, or invited: She's always ready to help and often does so ~. Many of the contributions to the relief fund were ~ for.

un·as·sum·ing /ˌʌnə'sjuːmɪŋ US: -'suː-/ adj not pushing oneself forward; not drawing attention to oneself; modest. ~·**ly** adv

un·at·tached /ˌʌnə'tætʃt/ adj **1** not connected or associated with a particular person, group, organization, etc; independent. **2** not married or engaged to be married.

un·at·tended /ˌʌnə'tendɪd/ adj **1** without attendants or escort. **2** not attended to; with no one to give care or attention to: Would you leave small children at home ~ while you went to the cinema?

un·avail·ing /ˌʌnə'veɪlɪŋ/ adj without effort or success.

un·avoid·able /ˌʌnə'vɔɪdəbl/ adj that cannot be avoided. **un·a·void·ably** /-əblɪ/ adv: He was unavoidably absent.

un·aware /ˌʌnə'weə(r)/ adj (pred) ~ **of sth/ that...**, not knowing; not aware: He was ~ of my presence/that I was present. ~**s** /-'weəz/ adv **1** by surprise; unexpectedly. **take sb** ~**s**, surprise him. **2** without being aware; unconsciously: She probably dropped the parcel ~s.

un·backed /ˌʌn'bækt/ adj **1** (of a proposal, etc) not supported. **2** (of a horse in a race) having no bets placed on it.

un·bal·anced /ˌʌn'bælənst/ adj (esp of a person, the mind) disordered; not sane or normal.

un·bar /ˌʌn'bɑː(r)/ vt (-rr-) remove bars from (a gate, etc); (fig) throw open: ~ all the professions to women.

un·bear·able /ʌn'beərəbl/ adj that cannot be borne or tolerated: I find his rudeness ~. **un·bear·ably** /-əblɪ/ adv in a way that cannot be endured: unbearably hot/rude.

un·beaten /ˌʌn'biːtn/ adj (esp) not having been beaten, defeated or surpassed: an ~ record for the 1000 metres race; an ~ team.

un·be·com·ing /ˌʌnbɪ'kʌmɪŋ/ adj **1** not suited (to the wearer): an ~ dress. **2** ~ **to/for**, not appropriate or befitting. ~**ly** adv

un·be·known /ˌʌnbɪ'nəʊn/, **un·be·knownst** /-nst/ adj, adv (colloq) not known (to), without the knowledge of: *He did it ~st to me,* without my being aware of it.

un·be·lief /ˌʌnbɪ'liːf/ *n* [U] (esp) lack of belief, state of not believing, in God, religion, etc. **un·be·liev·able** *adj* (a) not believable. (b) (colloq) very surprising. **un·be·liev·ably** *adv.* **un·be·liev·ing** *adj* not believing; doubting. **un·be·liev·ing·ly** *adv*

un·bend /ˌʌn'bend/ *vi,vt* (*pt,pp* unbent /-'bent/ or ~ed) **1** [VP2A] behave in a way free from strain, formality; become relaxed: *In the classroom the teacher maintains discipline but after class he ~s.* **2** [VP6A] relax: *~ one's mind.* **~·ing** *adj* (esp) firm in purpose, in not changing decisions, etc: *maintain an ~ing attitude,* make no concessions, etc.

un·bias·sed (also **-biased**) /ˌʌn'baɪəst/ *adj* not biassed; impartial.

un·bid·den /ˌʌn'bɪdn/ *adj* (formal) uninvited; not requested or ordered.

un·bind /ˌʌn'baɪnd/ *vt* (*pt,pp* -bound /-'baʊnd/) [VP6A] free from fastenings, bindings, etc.

un·blush·ing /ˌʌn'blʌʃɪŋ/ *adj* (esp) shameless: *the ~ corruption of some politicians.*

un·born /ˌʌn'bɔːn/ *adj* not yet born; future: *~ generations.*

un·bosom /ʌn'bʊzəm/ *vt* [VP6A,14] *~ oneself (to sb),* tell, reveal (one's sorrows, etc).

un·bounded /ʌn'baʊndɪd/ *adj* boundless; without limits: *~ ambition.*

un·bowed /ˌʌn'baʊd/ *adj* not bowed or bent; not conquered or subdued: *His head is bloody but ~.*

un·bridled /ˌʌn'braɪdld/ *adj* (esp, fig) not controlled: *~ insolence/passions; an ~ tongue.*

un·bro·ken /ˌʌn'brəʊkən/ *adj* (esp) **1** (eg of a horse) not tamed or subdued. **2** not interrupted: *six hours of ~ sleep.* **3** (of records, etc) not beaten or surpassed.

un·buckle /ˌʌn'bʌkl/ *vt* [VP6A] loosen, undo, the buckle(s) of.

un·bur·den /ˌʌn'bɜːdn/ *vt* [VP6A,15A] *~ oneself/ sth (of sth),* relieve of worry, anxiety, etc: *~ one's heart/conscience,* eg by talking about one's troubles, making a confession; *~ oneself to a friend,* find relief by speaking to him about one's feelings, etc: *~ oneself of a secret,* tell it to sb.

un·but·toned /ˌʌn'bʌtnd/ *adj* with the buttons not fastened; (fig) relaxed; (feeling) free from formality.

un·called-for /ʌn'kɔːld fɔː(r)/ *adj* neither desirable nor necessary: *~ insults. Such comments are ~.*

un·canny /ʌn'kænɪ/ *adj* unnatural, mysterious; weird: *an ~ noise; ~ shapes in the darkness.* **un·can·nily** /-ɪlɪ/ *adv*

un·cared-for /ˌʌn'keəd fɔː(r)/ *adj* not looked after; neglected: *~ children; an ~ garden.*

un·ceas·ing /ʌn'siːsɪŋ/ *adj* incessant; going on all the time. **~·ly** *adv*

un·cer·emo·ni·ous /ˌʌnˌserɪ'məʊnɪəs/ *adj* (esp) informal; lacking in courtesy. **~·ly** *adv* **~·ness** *n*

un·cer·tain /ʌn'sɜːtn/ *adj* **1** changeable; not reliable: *~ weather; a man with an ~ temper.* **2** not certainly knowing or known: *be/feel ~ (about) what to do next; ~ of/about/as to one's plans for the future; a woman of ~ age,* one whose age cannot be guessed. **~·ly** *adv* **~·ty** /-tntɪ/ *n* (*pl* -ties) **1** [U] state of being ~. **2** [C] sth which is ~: *the uncertainties of adequate reward in the profession of an actor.*

un·chari·table /ˌʌn'tʃærɪtəbl/ *adj* (esp) severe or harsh (in making judgements of the conduct of

others): *offer an ~ explanation of/put an ~ interpretation on sb's actions.*

un·charted /ˌʌn'tʃɑːtɪd/ *adj* **1** not marked on a map or chart: *an ~ island.* **2** (lit or fig) not explored and mapped: *an ~ sea; ~ emotions.*

un·checked /ˌʌn'tʃekt/ *adj* not checked or restrained: *an ~ advance; ~ anger.*

un·chris·tian /ˌʌn'krɪstʃən/ *adj* **1** not Christian; contrary to Christian principles. **2** (colloq) inconvenient and unreasonable: *Why do you call on me at this ~ hour?* (eg at 5am).

un·civil /ˌʌn'sɪvl/ *adj* (esp) impolite.

un·claimed /ˌʌn'kleɪmd/ *adj* that has not been claimed: *~ letters/parcels* (at the post-office, a lost property office, etc).

uncle /'ʌŋkl/ *n* brother of one's father or mother; husband of one's aunt: *my ~ Charlie.* **U~ Sam,** personification of the US. **U~ Tom,** ⚠ (US, derog) black person who is very friendly to white people. **Dutch U~,** ⇨ Dutch(2).

un·clean /ˌʌn'kliːn/ *adj* (esp, Jewish law) ceremonially impure, eg the pig.

un·clouded /ˌʌn'klaʊdɪd/ *adj* (esp fig) bright; serene: *a life of ~ happiness.* Cf *cloudless,* as in *a cloudless sky.*

unco /'ʌŋkəʊ/ (Scot) *adj* strange; unusual: *an ~ sight.* ▫ *adv* remarkably: (esp) *the ~ good,* religious people who are rigid in their views and behaviour.

un·col·oured (US = **-colored**) /ˌʌn'kʌləd/ *adj* (esp, fig) not exaggerated or heightened in description: *an ~ description of events.*

un·come-at-able /ˌʌnkʌm'ætəbl/ *adj* (colloq) not easy to get to; not accessible.

un·com·fort·able /ʌn'kʌmftəbl/ *US:* -fərt-/ *adj* not comfortable; uneasy: *an ~ chair/feeling.*

un·com·mit·ted /ˌʌnkə'mɪtɪd/ *adj* *~ (to),* not committed or bound (to a course of action, etc); free, independent: *the ~ countries,* those not allied to or bound to either of the power blocs of the modern world.

un·com·mon /ʌn'kɒmən/ *adj* unusual; remarkable. **~·ly** *adv* (esp) remarkably: *a ~ly intelligent child.*

un·com·pro·mis·ing /ʌn'kɒmprəmaɪzɪŋ/ *adj* not ready to make any compromise; unyielding; firm: *an ~ member of the Tory party.*

un·con·cern /ˌʌnkən'sɜːn/ *n* [U] lack of care or interest.

un·con·cerned /ˌʌnkən'sɜːnd/ *adj* **1** *~ in sth,* not involved in. *~ with sth/sb,* not (emotionally) concerned with. **2** free from anxiety; untroubled; uninterested. **un·con·cern·ed·ly** /-'sɜːnɪdlɪ/ *adv*

un·con·di·tional /ˌʌnkən'dɪʃənl/ *adj* absolute; not subject to conditions: *The victors demanded ~ surrender.* **~·ly** /-ʃənlɪ/ *adv*

un·con·di·tioned /ˌʌnkən'dɪʃnd/ *adj* not subject to conditions; (esp) *~ reflex,* instinctive response to a stimulus.

un·con·scion·able /ʌn'kɒnʃənbl/ *adj* unreasonable; not guided by conscience; excessive: *You take an ~ time dressing.*

un·con·scious /ʌn'kɒnʃəs/ *adj* not conscious (all senses): *~ humour,* not intended as humour by the speaker or writer; *be ~ of having done wrong.* ▫ *n* **the ~,** (psych) that part of one's mental activity of which one is unaware, but which can be detected and understood through the skilled analysis of dreams, behaviour, etc. **~·ly** *adv* **~·ness** *n*

un·con·sid·ered /ˌʌnkən'sɪdəd/ *adj* **1** (of words,

remarks) spoken, made, etc without proper consideration or reflection. **2** disregarded (as if of little value or worth).

un·con·ven·tional /ˌʌnkən'venʃənl/ adj not usual or ordinary; not bound by the customs of society: an ~ dress/person/way of life.

un·con·vinc·ing /ˌʌnkən'vɪnsɪŋ/ adj not seeming true, right, or real: an ~ explanation/attempt/disguise.

un·cork /ˌʌn'kɔːk/ vt [VP6A] draw the cork from (a bottle).

un·couple /ˌʌn'kʌpl/ vt [VP6A] unfasten: ~ hounds from the leash/a locomotive from a train.

un·couth /ʌn'kuːθ/ adj (of persons, their behaviour) rough, awkward, not cultured. ~·ly adv ~·ness n

un·cover /ʌn'kʌvə(r)/ vt [VP6A] **1** remove a cover or covering from; (fig) disclose; make known: The police have ~ed a plot against the President. **2** (mil) expose to attack: By a sudden movement we ~ed the enemy's right flank. **3** vi [2A] (archaic) take off one's hat or cap.

un·crossed /ʌn'krɒst US: -'krɔːst/ adj (esp, of a cheque) not crossed. ⇨ cross²(2).

un·crowned /ʌn'kraʊnd/ adj **1** (of a king, etc) not yet crowned. **2** having the power but not the title or name of a king, etc.

unc·tion /'ʌŋkʃn/ n [U] **1** act of anointing with oil, esp as a religious rite. **Extreme U~**, the anointing of a dying person by a priest (of the Orthodox and Roman Catholic Churches). **2** (pretended, insincere) earnestness, smoothness in speech or manner: She related the scandal with a great deal of ~; flattery.

unc·tu·ous /'ʌŋktʃʊəs/ adj (insincerely) earnest, smooth in speech or manner; flattering: ~ tones/assurances. **unc·tu·ous·ly** adv

un·cut /ˌʌn'kʌt/ adj (of a book) with the outer folds of the pages not trimmed or cut; (of a book, film, etc) not abridged or censored.

un·dated /ˌʌn'deɪtɪd/ adj not having a date: an ~ cheque; ~ stocks, with no specified date for redemption.

un·daunted /ˌʌn'dɔːntɪd/ adj not daunted; fearless.

un·de·ceive /ˌʌndɪ'siːv/ vt [VP6A] cause to be no longer deceived or in error.

un·de·cided /ˌʌndɪ'saɪdɪd/ adj not decided; not yet having made up one's mind: She was ~ whether to go to a concert or the cinema.

un·de·clared /ˌʌndɪ'kleəd/ adj **1** (of goods liable to customs duty) not declared or shown to the customs officers. **2** not announced or made known: ~ war.

un·de·fended /ˌʌndɪ'fendɪd/ adj (esp of a lawsuit) in which no defence is offered.

un·de·mon·stra·tive /ˌʌndɪ'mɒnstrətɪv/ adj reserved; not in the habit of showing feelings of affection, interest, etc.

un·de·ni·able /ˌʌndɪ'naɪəbl/ adj that cannot be denied; undoubtedly true: of ~ worth/value. **un·de·ni·ably** /-əblɪ/ adv

un·de·nomi·na·tional /ˌʌndɪˌnɒmɪ'neɪʃənl/ adj not connected with any particular religious sect: ~ education/schools.

un·der¹ /'ʌndə(r)/ adv **1** in or to a lower place, position, etc: The ship went ~, sank. Can you stay ~ (= ~ the water) for two minutes? **down** ~, (used in GB, colloq) (in/to) Australia and New Zealand. **2** (used to modify nn) subordinate; lower in rank, etc: ~-'secretary.

un·der² /'ʌndə(r)/ prep **1** in or to a position lower than: The cat was ~ the table. It is shady ~ the trees. There's nothing new ~ the sun, (prov), nothing new anywhere. We passed ~ several bridges. The soldiers were standing ~ (= at the foot of) the castle wall. The village nestles ~ (= at the foot of) the hill. **2** in and covered by: The part of an iceberg ~ the water is much larger than the part above the water. He hid his face ~ the bedclothes. Her hair came out from ~ her hat. **3** less than; lower (in rank) than: children ~ (opp over-/above) fourteen years of age; books for the ~-'tens (opp over-tens), children under ten; incomes ~ (opp over/above) £3000; run a hundred metres in ~ ten seconds; ~ half an acre; no one ~ (opp above/over) (the rank of) a captain; speak ~ one's breath, in a whisper. ~ **age**, ⇨ age. **4** (indicating various conditions): road ~ repair, being repaired; ~ discussion, being discussed; fifty acres ~ (= planted with) wheat; ~ sentence of (= sentenced to) death; living ~ an assumed name; England ~ the Stuarts, during the times of the Stuart kings and queens; be ~ the impression that..., have the idea or belief that.... The book is listed ~ biology, within that classification. **5** weighed down by (lit and fig): marching ~ a heavy load; sink ~ a load of grief (taxation, etc).

under- /'ʌndə(r)/ pref ⇨ App 3.

under·act /ˌʌndər'ækt/ vt,vi [VP6A,2A] act with too little spirit, energy, emphasis, etc: ~ the part of Hamlet. The star overacted; the other players ~ed.

under·arm /'ʌndərɑːm/ adj, adv (cricket, tennis) with the hand kept below the level of the elbow: ~ bowling; bowl/serve ~.

under·belly /'ʌndəbelɪ/ n (pl -lies) under surface of an animal's body, eg as a cut of meat, esp pork.

under·bid /ˌʌndə'bɪd/ vt (pt,pp unchanged) ⇨ bid¹(1). **1** make a lower bid than (sb else). **2** (card games, bridge) bid less on (a hand of cards) than its strength warrants.

under·brush /'ʌndəbrʌʃ/ n [U] = undergrowth (which is more usu).

under·car·riage /'ʌndəkærɪdʒ/ n landing gear of an aircraft. ⇨ the illus at air.

under·charge /ˌʌndə'tʃɑːdʒ/ vt [VP6A] charge too little for (sth) or to (sb). □ n /'ʌndətʃɑːdʒ/ charge that is too low or small.

under·clothes /'ʌndəkləʊðz/ n pl clothing worn under a shirt, dress, etc next to the skin. **under·cloth·ing** /'ʌndəkləʊðɪŋ/ n [U] = ~.

under·cover /ˌʌndə'kʌvə(r)/ adj secret; surreptitious: an ~ agent, person who associates with suspected criminals, etc to get evidence against them, or who acts as a spy, eg during a war; ~ payments, eg made in order to bribe sb.

under·cur·rent /'ʌndəkʌrənt/ n [U] current of water flowing beneath the surface; (fig) tendency (of thought or feeling) lying below what is apparent: an ~ of opposition/melancholy.

under·cut¹ /'ʌndəkʌt/ n [U] meat cut from the under side of sirloin.

under·cut² /ˌʌndə'kʌt/ vt (pt,pp unchanged; -tt-) [VP6A] (comm) offer (goods, services) at a lower price than competitors.

under·de·vel·oped /ˌʌndədɪ'veləpt/ adj not yet fully developed: ~ muscles/countries.

under·dog /'ʌndədɒg US: -dɔːg/ n (often the ~) poor and helpless person who usu gets the worst of an encounter, a struggle, etc: plead for the ~, for sb who is oppressed.

under·done /ˌʌndə'dʌn/ adj (esp of meat) not completely cooked throughout.

under·esti·mate /ˌʌndər'estɪmeɪt/ vt [VP6A] form too low an estimate of: ~ the enemy's strength. □ n /-mət/ [C] estimate which is too low.

under·ex·pose /ˌʌndərɪk'spəʊz/ vt [VP6A] (photo) expose (a plate or film) for too short a time. **un·der·expo·sure** /-'spəʊʒə(r)/ n

under·fed /ˌʌndə'fed/ adj having had too little food.

under·floor /ˌʌndə'flɔː(r)/ adj (of systems for heating buildings) with the source of heat placed under the floor(s): ~ heating.

under·foot /ˌʌndə'fʊt/ adv under one's feet; on the ground: It is very hard ~, eg when the ground is frozen hard.

under·gar·ment /'ʌndəɡɑːmənt/ n [C] article of underclothing.

under·go /ˌʌndə'ɡəʊ/ vt (pt -went /-'went/, pp -gone /-'ɡɒn US: -'ɡɔːn/) [VP6A] experience; pass through: The explorers had to ~ much suffering. The new aircraft underwent its tests well.

under·grad·uate /ˌʌndə'ɡrædʒʊət/ n university student working for a bachelor's degree: (attrib) '~ work/studies; in his '~ days.

under·ground /'ʌndəɡraʊnd/ attrib adj 1 under the surface of the ground: London's ~ railways; ~ passages/caves. 2 (fig) secret, esp of a secret political movement or one for resisting enemy forces in occupation of another country: ~ workers. □ adv (in the senses of the adj): He went ~ (= into hiding) when he heard the police were after him. □ n (the) ~, (in the senses of the adj): travel in London by ~, ie the ~ railway (US = subway); a member of the French ~, the secret resistance movement during World War Two.

under·growth /'ʌndəɡrəʊθ/ n [U] shrubs, bushes, low trees, growing among taller trees.

under·hand /'ʌndəhænd/ adj; adv secret(ly); deceitful(ly); sly(ly): play an ~ game; ~ methods; behave in an ~ way. ~ed adj = ~.

under·hung /ˌʌndə'hʌŋ/ adj (attrib) (of the lower jaw) projecting beyond the upper jaw.

under·lay /'ʌndəleɪ/ n [U] material (felt, rubber, etc) laid under a carpet or mattress (to preserve its condition).

under·lie /ˌʌndə'laɪ/ vt [VP6A] 1 be or lie under. 2 form the basis of (a theory, of conduct, behaviour, doctrine): the underlying reason/fault/guilt.

under·line /ˌʌndə'laɪn/ vt [VP6A] draw a line under (a word, etc); (fig) emphasize. □ n /'ʌndəlaɪn/ line drawn under a word or words.

under·ling /'ʌndəlɪŋ/ n (usu contemptuous) person in an unimportant position under another or others.

under·man·ned /ˌʌndə'mænd/ adj (of a ship, factory, etc) having not enough men to do all the work that needs to be done.

under·men·tioned /ˌʌndə'menʃnd/ adj mentioned below or later (in an article, etc).

under·mine /ˌʌndə'maɪn/ vt [VP6A] 1 make a hollow or tunnel under; weaken at the base: cliffs ~d by the sea. 2 weaken gradually: His health was ~d by drink. The President's enemies are spreading rumours to ~ his authority.

under·neath /ˌʌndə'niːθ/ adv, prep beneath; below; at or to a lower place.

under·nour·ished /ˌʌndə'nʌrɪʃt/ adj not provided with sufficient food for good health and normal growth. **under·nour·ish·ment** n

under·pants /'ʌndəpænts/ n pl short undergarment

worn by men and boys over the loins. ⇨ panties.

under·pass /'ʌndəpɑːs US: -pæs/ n [C] section of a road that goes under another road or railway. ⇨ overpass, flyover.

under·pay /ˌʌndə'peɪ/ vt (pt,pp -paid /-'peɪd/) [VP6A] pay (workmen, etc) inadequately. ~·ment n

under·pin /ˌʌndə'pɪn/ vt (-nn-) place a support of masonry, etc under (a wall, etc); (fig) support, form the basis for (a case, an argument, etc).

under·popu·lated /ˌʌndə'pɒpjʊleɪtɪd/ adj (of a country or area) having a small population in view of its size or natural resources.

under·privi·leged /ˌʌndə'prɪvəlɪdʒd/ adj not having had the educational and social advantages enjoyed by more fortunate people, social classes, nations, etc.

under·pro·duc·tion /ˌʌndəprə'dʌkʃn/ n [U] production of goods in insufficient quantity or below full capacity.

under·rate /ˌʌndə'reɪt/ vt [VP6A] place too low a value or estimate on: ~ an opponent, fail to realize his abilities, strength, etc.

under·score /ˌʌndə'skɔː(r)/ vt [VP6A] = underline.

under·sec·retary /ˌʌndə 'sekrətrɪ US: -terɪ/ n (pl -ries) assistant secretary, esp (Parliamentary U~) member of the Civil Service and head of a Government Department.

under·sell /ˌʌndə'sel/ vt (pt,pp -sold /-'səʊld/) [VP6A] sell (goods) at a lower price than (competitors).

under·sexed /ˌʌndə'sekst/ adj having less sexual desire or potency than normal.

under·shoot /ˌʌndə'ʃuːt/ vt (pt,pp -shot /-'ʃɒt/) (of an aircraft) ~ the runway, land short of it. ⇨ overshoot.

under·side /'ʌndəsaɪd/ n side that is underneath.

under·sign /ˌʌndə'saɪn/ vt [VP6A] sign (a letter, etc) at the foot: We, the ~ed, We whose signatures appear below.

under·sized /ˌʌndə'saɪzd/ adj of less than the usual size; stunted or dwarfish.

under·slung /ˌʌndə'slʌŋ/ adj (in a vehicle) having springs attached to the axles from below.

under·staffed /ˌʌndə'stɑːft US: -stæft/ adj having too small a staff: The school/hospital is badly ~. ⇨ undermanned.

under·stand /ˌʌndə'stænd/ vt,vi (pt,pp -stood /-'stʊd/) 1 [VP6A,C,8,10,19C,2A] know the meaning, nature, explanation, of (sth): ~ French/figures/a problem. He didn't ~ me/what I said. You don't ~ (= realize) what a difficult position I'm in. A good teacher must ~ children. I cannot ~ his robbing his friend/why he robbed his friend. It is easy to ~ his anger/why he was angry. **make oneself understood**, make one's meaning clear: Can he make himself understood in Russian? (Now), ~ me, phrase often used to preface a warning or threat. ~ **one another**, (of two persons, parties) be clearly aware of one another's views, feelings, intentions: The employers and workers have not reached an agreement yet, but at least they ~ one another. 2 [VP9,17] learn (from information received); infer; take for granted: I ~ that you are now married. Am I to ~ that you refuse? I understood him to say that he would co-operate. **give sb to ~ (that…)**, cause sb to believe or have the idea (that): We were given to ~ that free accommodation would be supplied. 3 [VP6A] supply (a word or phrase) mentally: *In the sentence 'He is taller than I', the verb 'am' is to be understood after 'I'.* ~·able /-əbl/ *adj* that can be understood: *His reluctance to agree is ~able.* ~·ably /-əblɪ/ *adv: He is ~ably furious.* ~·ing *adj* (good at) ~ing or realizing other persons' feelings or points of view; having or showing insight: *with an ~ing smile. Please be ~ing; do not punish the child.* □ *n* **1** [U] power of clear thought. **2** [U] capacity for sympathizing, seeing from another's point of view, etc. **3** (often an ~, but rarely *pl*) agreement; realization of another's views or feelings towards oneself: *reach/come to an ~ing with sb.* **on this ~ing,** on this condition. **on the ~ing that...,** on condition that....

under·state /ˌʌndə'steɪt/ *vt* [VP6A] fail to state fully or adequately; express in excessively restrained language: *They exaggerated the enemy's losses and ~d their own. She ~d her age on the census form.* ~·ment /'ʌndəsteɪtmənt/ *n* [U] understating; [C] statement that expresses an idea, etc, too weakly: *To say that the boy is rather clever is an ~ment,* eg of a boy who is brilliant.

under·stock /ˌʌndə'stɒk/ *vt* [VP6A] equip with less stock than is desirable: *Is the farm ~ed,* Could it support more animals, etc than it now has?

under·study /'ʌndəstʌdɪ/ *n* (*pl* -dies) person learning to, able to, take the place of another (esp an actor). □ *vt* (*pt,pp* -died) learn (a part in a play) for this purpose; act as ~ to (an actor): *He is ~ing Macbeth/~ing the leading actor in the play.*

under·take /ˌʌndə'teɪk/ *vt* (*pt* -took /-'tʊk/, *pp* -taken /-'teɪkən/) **1** [VP6A,7A] ~ **(to do)** *sth,* make oneself responsible for; agree (to do sth): *Gladstone undertook the premiership when he was 82 years old. He undertook to finish the job by Friday.* **2** [VP6A] start (a piece of work). **3** [VP7A,9] affirm; promise: *I can't ~ that you will make a profit.* **under·tak·ing** /ˌʌndə'teɪkɪŋ/ *n* [C] **1** work that one has ~n to do; task or enterprise. **2** promise; guarantee.

under·taker /'ʌndəteɪkə(r)/ *n* one whose business is to prepare the dead for burial or cremation and manage funerals (US = *mortician*). **under·tak·ing** /'ʌndəteɪkɪŋ/ *n* [U] this business.

under-the-counter /ˌʌndə ðə 'kaʊntə(r)/ *adj* ⇨ counter¹.

under·tone /'ʌndətəʊn/ *n* [C] **1** low, quiet, tone: *talk in ~s,* with subdued voices. **2** underlying quality: *an ~ of discontent/hostility/sadness.* **3** thin or subdued colour.

under·took /ˌʌndə'tʊk/ *pt* of undertake.

under·tow /'ʌndətəʊ/ *n* (current caused by the) backward flow of a wave breaking on a beach: *The swimmer was caught in an ~ and carried out to sea.*

under·value /ˌʌndə'væljuː/ *vt* [VP6A] value at less than the true worth. **under·valu·ation** /ˌʌndəˌvæljʊ'eɪʃn/ *n*

under·water /'ʌndəwɔːtə(r)/ *adj* below the surface of the water: *~ swimming,* eg with a snorkel.

under·wear /'ʌndəweə(r)/ *n* [U] underclothing.

under·weight /'ʌndəweɪt/ *n* [U] weight less than what is usual or legal. □ *adj* /ˌʌndə'weɪt/ below the weight that is usual or legal: *an ~ boy. These onions are ~/are ten ounces ~.* ⇨ overweight.

under·went /ˌʌndə'went/ *pt* of undergo.

under·whelm /ˌʌndə'welm US: -'hwelm/ *vt* [VP6A] (colloq, facet) fail to cause enthusiasm,

interest, excitement in: *to ~ an audience; an ~ing argument/speech/performance.*

under·world /'ʌndəwɜːld/ *n* **1** (in Gk myths, etc) place of the departed spirits of the dead. **2** part of society that lives by vice and crime.

under·write /ˌʌndə'raɪt/ *vt* (*pt* -wrote /-'rəʊt/, *pp* -written /-'rɪtn/) [VP6A] undertake to bear all or part of possible loss (by signing an agreement about insurance, esp of ships); engage to buy all the newly issued stock in (a company) not bought by the public. **'under·writer** *n* one who ~s policies of (esp marine) insurance: *an ~r at Lloyd's.*

un·de·served /ˌʌndɪ'zɜːvd/ *adj* not fair or just: *an ~ punishment/reward.*

un·de·sir·able /ˌʌndɪ'zaɪərəbl/ *adj* objectionable; (esp of persons) of a kind not to be welcomed in society. □ *n ~* person.

un·de·ter·red /ˌʌndɪ'tɜːd/ *adj* not deterred or discouraged: *~ by the weather/by failure.*

un·de·vel·oped /ˌʌndɪ'veləpt/ *adj* not developed: *~ land,* not yet used (for agriculture, industry, building, etc).

un·did /ʌn'dɪd/ *pt* of undo.

un·dies /'ʌndɪz/ *n pl* (colloq) underclothes.

un·dig·nified /ʌn'dɪgnɪfaɪd/ *adj* not showing proper dignity; clumsy.

un·dis·charged /ˌʌndɪs'tʃɑːdʒd/ *adj* (of a cargo) not unloaded; (of a debt) (not paid); (esp, of a bankrupt person or firm) not relieved of a further liability to pay money still owing to creditors. ⇨ discharge²(5).

undo /ʌn'duː/ *vt* (*pt* undid /ʌn'dɪd/, *pp* undone /ʌn'dʌn/) [VP6A] **1** untie, unfasten, loosen (knots, buttons, etc): *My shoe-lace has come undone.* **2** destroy the result of; bring back the state of affairs that existed before: *He has undone the good work of his predecessor. What is done cannot be undone.* **un·do·ing** *n* (cause of) ruin: *Drink was his ~ing. He went to the moneylenders, to his complete ~ing.* **un·done** *pred adj* **1** not done; not finished: *leave one's work undone. We have left undone those things which we ought to have done.* **2** (archaic) (of a person) ruined.

un·dock /ʌn'dɒk/ *vt,vi* [VP6A,2A] uncouple (a module, etc) from a spacecraft: *The astronauts had some difficulty in ~ing the lunar module.*

un·doubted /ʌn'daʊtɪd/ *adj* certain; accepted as true: *There is an ~ improvement in the patient's condition.* ~·ly *adv*

un·dreamed /ʌn'driːmd/, **un·dreamt** /ʌn'dremt/ *adjj* (usu) ~-of, not thought of; not imagined: *earn ~-of wealth; ~-of beauties.*

un·dress /ʌn'dres/ *vt,vi* **1** [VP6A] remove the clothes of: *Jane ~ed her doll.* **2** [VP2A] take off one's clothes: *~ and get into bed.* □ *n* [U] **1** uniform for ordinary (non-ceremonial) occasions. **2** state of being partly or not dressed.

un·due /ˌʌn'djuː US: -'duː/ *adj* improper; more than is right: *with ~ haste; exercise an ~ influence upon sb.* **un·duly** /ˌʌn'djuːlɪ US: -'duːlɪ/ *adv* in an ~ manner: *unduly pessimistic.*

un·du·late /'ʌndjʊleɪt US: -dʒʊ-/ *vi* [VP2A,C] (of surfaces) have a wave-like motion or look: *a field of wheat undulating in the breeze; undulating land,* that rises and falls in gentle slopes. **un·du·la·tion** /ˌʌndjʊ'leɪʃn US: -dʒʊ-/ *n* [U] wave-like motion or form; [C] one of a number of wave-like curves or slopes.

un·dy·ing /ˌʌn'daɪɪŋ/ *adj* everlasting; never-ending: *~ love/hatred/fame.*

un·earned /ˌʌn'ɜːnd/ adj **1** not gained by work or service: ∼ *income*, eg from investments, or land or property that is inherited; ∼ *increment*, increase in the value of property, eg houses, land, not due to the owner's expenditure or efforts, eg because of a rise in the value of land. **2** not deserved: ∼ *praise*.

un·earth /ʌn'ɜːθ/ vt [VP6A] discover and bring to light: ∼ *new facts about the life of Shakespeare*; ∼ *a buried treasure. The dog has* ∼*ed some bones.*

un·earth·ly /ʌn'ɜːθlɪ/ adj **1** supernatural. **2** mysterious; ghostly; frightening: ∼ *screams*. **3** (colloq) unreasonable: *Why do you wake me up at this* ∼ *hour?*

un·easy /ʌn'iːzɪ/ adj not easy in body or mind; troubled or anxious: *have an* ∼ *conscience; be* ∼ *in one's mind about the future; pass an* ∼ *night, sleep badly. We grew* ∼ *at their long absence.* **un·eas·ily** /ʌn'iːzɪlɪ/ adv **un·easi·ness, un·ease** /ʌn'iːz/ nn

un·eaten /ʌn'iːtn/ adj (of food, a meal) set out but left unused.

un·edu·cated /ʌn'edʒʊkeɪtɪd/ adj not educated; suggesting lack of education (or the kind of education or social background considered desirable): *He has an* ∼ *mind/voice.*

un·em·ploy·able /ˌʌnɪm'plɔɪəbl/ adj that cannot be employed.

un·em·ployed /ˌʌnɪm'plɔɪd/ adj not being used: ∼ *capital;* not working, not able to get work: ∼ *men.* **the** ∼, those for whom there is no work or who are temporarily without work.

un·em·ploy·ment /ˌʌnɪm'plɔɪmənt/ n [U] **1** state of being unemployed: *U*∼ *is a serious social evil.* **2** amount of unused labour: *There is more* ∼ *now than there was six months ago.* **3** (attrib): ∼ *insurance;* ∼ *pay/benefit,* money paid from insurance funds to a worker who cannot get employment.

un·end·ing /ʌn'endɪŋ/ adj everlasting; unceasing; (colloq) frequently repeated: *She's tired of your* ∼ *grumbles.* ∼·**ly** adv

un·en·dur·able /ˌʌnɪn'djʊərəbl/ adj not able to be endured: ∼ *pain/injustice.*

un·en·light·ened /ˌʌnɪn'laɪtnd/ adj uneducated; not well-informed; (in some contexts) prejudiced or superstitious.

un·equal /ʌn'iːkwəl/ adj ∼ *(to sth),* **1** not equal. **2** (esp of work such as writing) not of the same quality throughout; variable. **3** not strong, clever, etc enough: *I feel* ∼ *to the task.* ∼**ly** /-kwəlɪ/ adv

un·equal·led /ʌn'iːkwld/ adj unmatched; unrivalled.

un·equivo·cal /ˌʌnɪ'kwɪvəkl/ adj clear; having one only possible meaning.

un·err·ing /ʌn'ɜːrɪŋ/ adj accurate: *fire with* ∼ *aim; strike an* ∼ *blow.* ∼·**ly** adv

un·ex·ampled /ˌʌnɪg'zɑːmpld/ adj of which there is no other example that can be compared with it: *the* ∼ *heroism of our soldiers.*

un·ex·cep·tion·able /ˌʌnɪk'sepʃənəbl/ adj beyond criticism; altogether admirable.

un·ex·pected /ˌʌnɪk'spektɪd/ adj not expected: ∼ *guests/questions/results.*

un·fail·ing /ʌn'feɪlɪŋ/ adj never coming to an end; meeting one's expectations at all times: *his* ∼ *good humour/patience; an* ∼ (= loyal) *friend.* ∼·**ly** adv at all times: ∼*ly courteous.*

un·fair /ˌʌn'feə(r)/ adj not right or fair; unjust: ∼ *treatment/competition.* ∼·**ly** adv ∼·**ness** n

un·faith·ful /ˌʌn'feɪθfl/ adj not true to one's duty, a promise, etc; (esp) not faithful to marriage vows:

Her husband is ∼ *to her.* ∼·**ly** /-fəlɪ/ adv ∼·**ness** n

un·fal·ter·ing /ʌn'fɔːltərɪŋ/ adj not wavering or hesitating: *with* ∼ *steps/courage.* ∼·**ly** adv

un·fam·il·iar /ˌʌnfə'mɪlɪə(r)/ adj **1** ∼ *(to),* not well known: *That face is not* ∼ *to me,* I feel that I know it, have seen it before. **2** ∼ *with,* not acquainted with: *He is still* ∼ *with this district.*

un·fath·om·able /ʌn'fæðəməbl/ adj so deep that the bottom cannot be reached; (fig) too strange or difficult to be understood. **un·fath·omed** /ʌn'fæðəmd/ adj (of a person's character) not understood; (of a crime, etc) not solved; (of ocean depths, etc) not measured.

un·feel·ing /ʌn'fiːlɪŋ/ adj **1** hard-hearted; unsympathetic. **2** not able to feel. ∼·**ly** adv

un·feigned /ʌn'feɪnd/ adj not pretended; genuine (which is more usu); sincere: *He showed* ∼ *satisfaction at his son's success.* ∼·**ly** adv openly and sincerely.

un·fit /ˌʌn'fɪt/ adj ∼ *(for sth/to do sth),* not fit or suitable: *He is* ∼ *for business/*∼ *to be a doctor. This road is* ∼ *for heavy traffic. He was rejected* (eg for military service) *as medically* ∼. □ vt (-tt-) [VP14] ∼ *sb for sth,* make ∼ (which is more usu): *A bad attack of lumbago* ∼*ted him for work in the garden.*

un·flag·ging /ˌʌn'flægɪŋ/ adj not showing signs of weariness; uninterrupted: *work with* ∼ *energy.*

un·flap·pable /ˌʌn'flæpəbl/ adj (colloq) unlikely to get into a flap; never upset in a crisis. ➪ **flap** ¹(4).

un·flinch·ing /ˌʌn'flɪntʃɪŋ/ adj fearless; resolute.

un·fledged /ˌʌn'fledʒd/ adj (of a bird) not yet able to fly; (fig, of a person) immature; inexperienced.

un·fold /ʌn'fəʊld/ vt, vi [VP6A,2A,C] **1** (of sth folded) open out: ∼ *a newspaper/a prospectus.* **2** reveal, make known; become known or visible: *as the story* ∼*s* (*itself*). *She* ∼*ed to him her plans for the future. The landscape* ∼*ed before us.*

un·for·get·table /ˌʌnfə'getəbl/ adj that cannot be forgotten: *an* ∼ *experience.*

un·for·tu·nate /ʌn'fɔːtʃʊnət/ adj unlucky: *an* ∼ *expedition;* regrettable: *an* ∼ *remark/lack of good manners.* ∼·**ly** adv: *You're wrong,* ∼*ly.* U∼*ly for you, you're wrong.*

un·founded /ˌʌn'faʊndɪd/ adj without foundation: ∼ *rumours.*

un·fre·quented /ˌʌnfrɪ'kwentɪd/ adj seldom visited.

un·friend·ly /ˌʌn'frendlɪ/ adj not friendly; unfavourable.

un·frock /ˌʌn'frɒk/ vt [VP6A] (of a priest guilty of bad conduct) dismiss from the priesthood.

un·fruit·ful /ʌn'fruːtfl/ adj not bearing fruit; without results or success.

un·furl /ʌn'fɜːl/ vt, vi [VP6A,2A] roll out; spread out: ∼ *the sails.*

un·fur·nished /ˌʌn'fɜːnɪʃt/ adj (esp) without furniture: *rooms/a house to let* ∼.

un·gain·ly /ʌn'geɪnlɪ/ adj clumsy; awkward; ungraceful.

un·gen·er·ous /ʌn'dʒenərəs/ adj not generous; unkind.

un·get-at-able /ˌʌnget'ætəbl/ adj = un-come-at-able.

un·god·ly /ʌn'gɒdlɪ/ adj **1** not religious; not giving reverence to God; sinful. **2** (colloq) annoying; shocking. **3** (colloq) unreasonable: *Why did you phone me at this* ∼ *hour?*

un·gov·ern·able /ʌn'gʌvənəbl/ adj that cannot be controlled: ∼ *passions; a man with an* ∼ *temper.*

un-grate-ful /ʌn'greɪtfl/ adj 1 not showing gratitude. 2 (of a task) not pleasant or agreeable.

un-guarded /ˌʌn'gɑːdɪd/ adj (esp of a person and what he says) careless; indiscreet: In an ~ moment, he gave away most important secrets.

un-guent /'ʌŋgwənt/ n [C,U] any soft substance used as an ointment (eg for soothing skin injuries) or for lubrication.

un-hal-lowed /ʌn'hæləʊd/ adj 1 not made holy: buried in ~ ground, not consecrated by the Church. 2 wicked; impious: with ~ joy.

un-hand /ʌn'hænd/ vt [VP6A] (archaic) let go; take the hands off.

un-happy /ʌn'hæpɪ/ adj (-ier, -iest) 1 not happy. 2 not suitable or tactful: an ~ comment.

un-healthy /ʌn'helθɪ/ adj harmful to bodily or mental health; (colloq) dangerous.

un-heard /ʌn'hɜːd/ adj not heard; not allowed a hearing. go ~, (a) not be heard. (b) have no-one willing to listen to it: Her request for help went ~.

un-heard-of /ʌn'hɜːd ɒv/ adj extraordinary; without an earlier example.

un-hinge /ʌn'hɪndʒ/ vt [VP6A] take (a door, gate, etc) from the hinge(s); cause (sb's mind, brain) to be off its balance: His mind is ~d, He is mentally ill.

un-holy /ʌn'həʊlɪ/ adj 1 wicked; sinful. 2 (colloq) unreasonable.

un-hook /ʌn'hʊk/ vt [VP6A] undo the hooks of (a dress, etc); release from a hook.

un-hoped-for /ʌn'həʊpt fɔː(r)/ adj unexpected: an ~ piece of good fortune.

un-horse /ˌʌn'hɔːs/ vt [VP6A] throw from a horse's back; cause to fall from a horse.

uni-corn /'juːnɪkɔːn/ n (in old stories) horse-like animal with one long horn; (heraldry) representation of this with a lion's tail.

un-iden-ti-fied /ˌʌnaɪ'dentɪfaɪd/ adj which cannot be identified: The dead man is still ~. ~ flying object, (abbr UFO /juː ef 'əʊ/ or /'juːfəʊ/) ⇨ flying saucer at flying.

uni-form /'juːnɪfɔːm/ adj the same; not varying in form, quality, etc: sticks of ~ length; to be kept at a ~ temperature. □ n [C,U] (style of) dress worn by all members of an organization, eg the police, the armed forces: the blue ~(s) of the police; the khaki ~(s) of the army. in ~, wearing such dress: He looks handsome in ~. ~ed adj wearing ~: the ~ed branch of the police, contrasted with those who wear plain clothes, eg detectives. ~-ly adv ~-ity /ˌjuːnɪ'fɔːmətɪ/ n [U] ~ condition; condition of being the same throughout.

unify /'juːnɪfaɪ/ vt (pt,pp -fied) [VP6A] 1 form into one; unite. 2 make uniform. uni-fi-ca-tion /ˌjuːnɪfɪ'keɪʃn/ n [U] ~ing or being unified: work for the unification of Europe.

uni-lat-eral /ˌjuːnɪ'lætrəl/ adj of, on, affecting, done by, one side or party only: a ~ declaration of independence, (abbr UDI); ~ repudiation of a treaty, by one of the parties that signed it, without the consent of the other party or parties. ~-ly /-rəlɪ/ adv

un-im-peach-able /ˌʌnɪm'piːtʃəbl/ adj that cannot be questioned or doubted: ~ honesty; news from an ~ source.

un-in-formed /ˌʌnɪn'fɔːmd/ adj (esp) not having, made without, adequate information: ~ criticism.

un-in-hib-ited /ˌʌnɪn'hɪbɪtɪd/ adj without inhibitions; free from the social and moral restraints usual among conventional people.

un-in-spired /ˌʌnɪn'spaɪəd/ adj without inspiration; dull: an ~ lecture/lecturer.

un-in-ter-ested /ʌn'ɪntrəstɪd/ adj ~ (in), having, showing no interest.

union /'juːnɪən/ n 1 [U] uniting or being united; joining or being joined; [C] instance of this: the ~ of the three towns into one; the Universal Postal U~, of countries for the purpose of interchanging mail services to mutual advantage; the U~ of Soviet Socialist Republics (abbr USSR). the U~, (a) of England and Scotland (in 1707). (b) the United States of America: the President's address to the U~, to all US citizens. the U~ Jack, the British flag. ⇨ the illus at flag. 2 [U] state of being in agreement or harmony: live in perfect ~; [C] instance of this: a happy ~, eg a happy marriage. 3 [C] association formed by the uniting of persons, groups, etc, esp trade ~, ⇨ trade 1(1). 4 (old use; GB) workhouse built by two or more parishes for administration of the poor laws. 5 the U~, general society at some universities, etc. 6 [C] coupling for connecting rods or pipes. 7 ~ suit, (US) combinations(4). ~-ist /-ɪst/ n [C] 1 member of a trade ~; supporter of trade ~s. 2 U~-ist, (a) (GB politics) person who, before the Irish Free State was established, opposed the granting of independence to Ireland. (b) supporter of the Federal Government of the US during the Civil War; opponent of secession.

unique /juː'niːk/ adj having no like or equal; being the only one of its sort. ~-ly adv ~-ness n

uni-sex /'juːnɪseks/ adj (of clothes, etc) of a style designed for both sexes.

uni-son /'juːnɪsn/ n [U] (in) concord or agreement: sing in ~, all singing the same notes, not harmonizing; act in ~ (with others).

unit /'juːnɪt/ n [C] 1 single person, thing or group regarded as complete in itself: (mil) an armoured ~; ~s of the US Sixth Fleet. The family is often taken as the ~ of society. 2 quantity or amount used as a standard of measurement: The metre is a ~ of length. The monetary ~ of Great Britain is the pound. 3 smallest whole number; the number 1. 4 (compounds) 'kitchen ~, article of kitchen equipment, eg a sink, draining board, with cupboards, that can be fitted with others of similar design and appearance along a wall. ~ 'furniture, articles of furniture of similar design, materials, etc, to be used together. '~ trust, trust(3) that invests in a large number and wide variety of stocks and issues certificates (called ~s) on which dividends are payable.

Uni-tar-ian /ˌjuːnɪ'teərɪən/ n member of a Christian church which rejects the doctrine of the Trinity and believes that God is one person. □ adj of the ~s: the U~ Church. ~-ism /-ɪzəm/ n

unite /juː'naɪt/ vt,vi 1 [VP6A,2A] make or become one; join: ~ one country to another; the common interests that ~ our two countries, that bring them together. England and Scotland ~d in 1707. 2 [VP2A,3A,4A] ~ (in sth/to do sth), act or work together: Let us ~ in fighting/~ to fight poverty and disease. ~d adj 1 joined in spirit, by love and sympathy: a ~d family. 2 resulting from association for a common purpose: make a ~d effort; present a ~d front to the enemy; the U~d Nations. 3 joined politically: the U~d Kingdom; the U~d States of Mexico. ~-ly adv

unity /'juːnətɪ/ n (pl -ties) 1 [C,U] the state of being united; (an) arrangement of parts to form a complete whole: *The figure on the left spoils the* ~ *of the painting.* **the dramatic unities; the unities of place, time and action,** (drama) the use of the same scene throughout, the limitation of the duration of the play to one day, or the time taken to act it, and the use of one single plot, with nothing irrelevant to that plot. **2** [U] harmony, agreement (of aims, feelings, etc): *in* ~ *with others; live together in* ~; *political* ~. *National* ~ *is essential in time of war.*

uni·ver·sal /ˌjuːnɪˈvɜːsl/ *adj* of, belonging to, done by, all; affecting all: *War causes* ~ *misery. Television provides* ~ *entertainment.* **a** ~ **joint,** one that permits the turning of connected parts in all directions. **a** ~ **rule,** one with no exceptions. ~ **suffrage,** suffrage extending to all members of a community. ~ **time,** ▷ Greenwich. ~**·ly** /-səlɪ/ *adv* ~**·ity** /ˌjuːnɪvɜːˈsælətɪ/ *n* [U].

uni·verse /ˈjuːnɪvɜːs/ *n* **1 the U~,** everything that exists everywhere; all the galaxies, stars, planets, their satellites, etc; the whole creation and the Creator. **2** [C] system of galaxies: *a new telescope that may reveal new* ~s.

uni·ver·sity /ˌjuːnɪˈvɜːsətɪ/ *n* (*pl* -ties) (colleges, buildings, etc of an) institution for the promotion and dissemination of advanced learning, conferring degrees and engaging in academic research; members of such an institution collectively; (attrib) *a* ~ *student/lecturer; the* ~ *chess team.*

un·kempt /ˌʌnˈkempt/ *adj* untidy; (esp of the hair) uncombed.

un·kind /ʌnˈkaɪnd/ *adj* lacking in, not showing, kindness: *an* ~ *remark.* ~**·ly** *adv* in an ~ manner: *Don't take it* ~*ly if...,* Don't think I intend to be ~ if....

un·know·ing /ʌnˈnəʊɪŋ/ *adj* not knowing; unaware. ~**·ly** *adv* in ignorance; unawares.

un·known /ˌʌnˈnəʊn/ *adj* not known or identified: *the tomb of the* ~ *warrior,* of an ~ soldier (in Westminster Abbey) buried there in memory of those killed in World Wars I and II; *an* ~ *quantity,* of which the value, etc is not known.

un·learn /ˌʌnˈlɜːn/ *vt* [VP6A] get rid of (ideas, habits, etc); learn to give up (sth one has previously learnt).

un·leash /ʌnˈliːʃ/ *vt* [VP6A] let go from a leash: ~ *a dog;* (fig) release; set into action: ~ *one's fury;* ~ *a new atomic weapon.*

un·leav·ened /ˌʌnˈlevnd/ *adj* (of bread) made without yeast.

un·less /ənˈles/ *conj* if not; except when: *You will fail* ~ *you work harder. U*~ *bad weather stops me, I go for a walk every day.*

un·let·tered /ˌʌnˈletəd/ *adj* uneducated; unable to read.

un·like /ˌʌnˈlaɪk/ *pred adj, prep* not like; different from: *His new novel is* ~ *all his previous ones. My son is* ~ *me in every respect.*

un·like·ly /ʌnˈlaɪklɪ/ *adj* not likely to happen or be true: *an* ~ *event/hypothesis.*

un·load /ʌnˈləʊd/ *vt,vi* **1** [VP6A,2A] remove a load from: ~ *a ship;* remove (cargo) from: ~ *cargo. The ship is* ~*ing.* **2** [VP6A,14] ~ **(on to),** (colloq) get rid of (sth not wanted): *She* ~*ed her old car/ her mother-in-law on to me.*

un·looked-for /ʌnˈlʊkt fɔː(r)/ *adj* unexpected; for which one is not prepared.

un·loose /ʌnˈluːs/ *vt* [VP6A] let loose; make free.

un·man /ˌʌnˈmæn/ *vt* (-nn-) [VP6A] weaken the courage and self-control of: *The news of his*

friend's death ~*ned him for a while.*

un·man·ly /ʌnˈmænlɪ/ *adj* **1** weak; cowardly. **2** effeminate.

un·man·ned /ˌʌnˈmænd/ *adj* having no crew: *an* ~ *aircraft with remote control; send an* ~ *spacecraft to Mars.*

un·man·nered /ʌnˈmænəd/, **un·man·ner·ly** /ʌnˈmænəlɪ/ *adjj* discourteous; having bad manners.

un·mask /ʌnˈmɑːsk *US:* -ˈmæsk/ *vt,vi* [VP6A,2A] **1** remove a mask (from): *The revellers* ~*ed at midnight,* took off their masks. **2** [VP6A] show the true character or intentions of: ~ *a traitor/ hypocrite;* ~ *treachery/hypocrisy.*

un·match·able /ʌnˈmætʃəbl/ *adj* that cannot be matched or equalled. **un·matched** /ʌnˈmætʃt/ *adj* without an equal.

un·men·tion·able /ʌnˈmenʃənəbl/ *adj* so bad, shocking, etc that it may not be spoken of.

un·mind·ful /ʌnˈmaɪndfl/ *adj* ~ **(of),** forgetful; oblivious; heedless: ~ *of the time/the need to hurry.*

un·mis·tak·able /ˌʌnmɪˈsteɪkəbl/ *adj* clear; about which no mistake or doubt is possible: *Are black clouds an* ~ *sign of rain?* **un·mis·tak·ably** /-əblɪ/ *adv*

un·miti·gated /ʌnˈmɪtɪɡeɪtɪd/ *adj* complete; absolute: *an* ~ *disaster; an* ~ *evil,* sth which has no accompanying advantages whatever.

un·moved /ʌnˈmuːvd/ *adj* (esp) not moved in feelings; undisturbed; indifferent: *He remained* ~ *by her entreaties for pity.*

un·natu·ral /ʌnˈnætʃrəl/ *adj* not natural or normal: *A mother who is cruel to her children is* ~. ~**·ly** *adv: He expected, not* ~*ly, that his father would help him.*

un·nec·ess·ary /ʌnˈnesəsrɪ *US:* -serɪ/ *adj* not necessary; superfluous. **un·nec·ess·ar·ily** /ˌʌnˈnesəsərəlɪ *US:* ˌʌnˌnesəˈserəlɪ/ *adv* in an ~ manner.

un·nerve /ˌʌnˈnɜːv/ *vt* [VP6A] cause to lose self-control, power of decision, courage.

un·not·iced /ˌʌnˈnəʊtɪst/ *adj* not observed or noticed: *The event passed* ~. *Are you going to let the insult pass* ~?

un·num·bered /ˌʌnˈnʌmbəd/ *adj* **1** more than can be counted. **2** having no number(s): ~ *tickets/ seats,* eg at a concert-hall.

un·ob·trus·ive /ˌʌnəbˈtruːsɪv/ *adj* not too obvious or easily noticeable; discreet.

un·of·fi·cial /ˌʌnəˈfɪʃl/ *adj* not official: *an* ~ *strike,* not authorized by the union; ~ *news,* not officially confirmed.

un·or·tho·dox /ʌnˈɔːθədɒks/ *adj* not in accordance with what is orthodox, conventional, traditional: ~ *teaching methods.*

un·pack /ʌnˈpæk/ *vt,vi* [VP6A,2A] take out (things packed): ~ *one's clothes;* take things out of: ~ *a suitcase.*

un·par·al·leled /ʌnˈpærəleld/ *adj* having no parallel or equal; matchless: *an* ~ *achievement/ disaster.*

un·par·lia·men·tary /ˌʌnˌpɑːləˈmentrɪ/ *adj* (of language, conduct) not suitable (because abusive, disorderly) for Parliament.

un·placed /ˌʌnˈpleɪst/ *adj* (esp) not one of the first three in a race or competition.

un·play·able /ʌnˈpleɪəbl/ *adj* (of a ball, in games) that cannot be played; (of ground) not fit to be played on.

un·pleas·ant /ʌn'pleznt/ adj disagreeable. ~·ness n [U] ~ or disagreeable feeling; bad feeling (between persons); [C] quarrel, disagreement: a slight ~ness.

un·prac·tised /ʌn'præktɪst/ adj having little experience, inexpert; unskilled.

un·prece·dented /ʌn'presɪdentɪd/ adj without precedent; never done or known before. ~·ly adv

un·preju·diced /ʌn'predʒʊdɪst/ adj free from prejudice.

un·pre·ten·tious /ˌʌnprɪ'tenʃəs/ adj modest; not trying to seem important.

un·prin·cipled /ʌn'prɪnsəpld/ adj without moral principles; unscrupulous; dishonest.

un·print·able /ʌn'prɪntəbl/ adj too rude or indecent to be printed.

un·pro·fessional /ˌʌnprə'feʃnəl/ adj (esp of conduct) contrary to the rules or customs of a profession.

un·prompted /ˌʌn'prɒmptɪd/ adj (of an answer, action) spontaneous; not said, done, etc as the result of a hint, suggestion, etc.

un·pro·vided /ˌʌnprə'vaɪdɪd/ adj 1 ~ for, without provision having been made for: The widow was left ~ for, No means of support had been left for her on her husband's death. 2 ~ with, not provided with: schools ~ with books and equipment.

un·pro·voked /ˌʌnprə'vəʊkt/ adj without provocation: ~ aggression/attacks.

un·put·down·able /ˌʌnpʊt'daʊnəbl/ adj (colloq) (of a book, etc) so interesting that the reader cannot put it down until he has finished it.

un·quali·fied /ʌn'kwɒlɪfaɪd/ adj 1 not limited or restricted; absolute: ~ praise; an ~ denial. 2 ~ as sth/to do sth, not qualified: ~ to speak on the subject.

un·ques·tion·able /ʌn'kwestʃənəbl/ adj beyond doubt; certain. **un·ques·tion·ably** /-əblɪ/ adv

un·ques·tioned /ʌn'kwestʃənd/ adj not questioned or disputed: I cannot let your statement pass ~, I must dispute its truth.

un·ques·tion·ing /ʌn'kwestʃənɪŋ/ adj (esp) given, done, without question or protest: ~ obedience.

un·quiet /ʌn'kwaɪət/ adj (formal) restless; uneasy; disturbed: live in ~ times.

un·quote /ʌn'kwəʊt/ (v, imper only) (in a telegram, a telephoned message, etc) end the quotation; close the inverted commas: The rebel leader said (quote) 'We shall never surrender' (unquote).

un·ravel /ʌn'rævl/ vt,vi (-ll-; US -l-) [VP6A,2A] 1 separate the threads of; pull or become separate: The cuff of my jersey has ~led. The baby ~led the knitting that its mother had left on the chair. 2 make clear; solve: ~ a mystery/plot.

un·real /ʌn'rɪəl/ adj imaginary; illusory.

un·reas·on·able /ʌn'ri:znəbl/ adj not governed by reason; immoderate; excessive: make ~ demands.

un·reas·on·ing /ʌn'ri:zənɪŋ/ adj not using or guided by reason.

un·re·lent·ing /ˌʌnrɪ'lentɪŋ/ adj not becoming less in intensity, etc: ~ pressure/attacks. ⇨ relentless at relent.

un·re·li·able /ˌʌnrɪ'laɪəbl/ adj that cannot be relied on; untrustworthy.

un·re·lieved /ˌʌnrɪ'li:vd/ adj (esp) without anything to vary monotony: a plain black dress ~ by a touch of colour or trimming of any kind; ~ boredom/ tedium.

un·re·mit·ting /ˌʌnrɪ'mɪtɪŋ/ adj unceasing: ~

care/efforts. The doctor was ~ in his attention to the case.

un·re·quit·ed /ˌʌnrɪ'kwaɪtɪd/ adj not returned or rewarded: ~ love/service.

un·re·serv·ed·ly /ˌʌnrɪ'zɜ:vɪdlɪ/ adv without reservation or restriction; openly: speak ~; trust sb ~.

un·rest /ʌn'rest/ n [U] (esp) disturbed condition(s): social ~, eg because of widespread unemployment or poverty; political ~.

un·re·strained /ˌʌnrɪ'streɪnd/ adj not checked or held in.

un·re·stricted /ˌʌnrɪ'strɪktɪd/ adj without restriction(s); (esp of a road) not having a speed limit for traffic.

un·ri·valled (US = -ri·valed) /ʌn'raɪvld/ adj having no rival (in courage, etc); unequalled: an ~ reputation.

un·roll /ʌn'rəʊl/ vt,vi [VP6A,2A] roll out; open out by rolling: ~ a carpet/map.My sleeping-bag has ~ed.

un·ruffled /ʌn'rʌfld/ adj calm; not upset or agitated: He remained ~ by all these criticisms.

un·ruly /ʌn'ru:lɪ/ adj (-ier, -iest) not easily controlled; disorderly: an ~ child.

un·said /ˌʌn'sed/ adj not expressed: Some things are better left ~.

un·sa·voury (US = -sa·vory) /ʌn'seɪvərɪ/ adj (esp) nasty; disgusting: ~ stories/scandals; a man with an ~ reputation.

un·say /ʌn'seɪ/ vt (pt,pp -said /-'sed/) [VP6A] (liter) take back (sth that has been said); retract (which is the usu word).

un·scathed /ʌn'skeɪðd/ adj unharmed; unhurt.

un·scramble /ˌʌn'skræmbl/ vt (of a scrambled message) restore to a form that can be understood.

un·scripted /ʌn'skrɪptɪd/ adj (eg of a broadcast talk or discussion) not read from a prepared script.

un·scru·pu·lous /ʌn'skru:pjʊləs/ adj not guided by conscience; not held back (from doing wrong) by scruples. ~·ly adv

un·seas·oned /ˌʌn'si:znd/ adj (of wood) not matured; (of food) not flavoured with seasoning.

un·seat /ˌʌn'si:t/ vt [VP6A] 1 remove from office: Mr Powell was ~ed at the General Election, lost his seat in the House of Commons. 2 throw from a horse: Several riders were ~ed at the water-jump, eg in a steeplechase.

un·seem·ly /ʌn'si:mlɪ/ adj (of behaviour, etc) not suitable or proper.

un·seen /ʌn'si:n/ adj not seen; invisible. □ n 1 the ~, the spiritual world. 2 [C] passage to be translated, without preparation, from a foreign language into one's own language: German ~s.

un·settle /ˌʌn'setl/ vt [VP6A] make troubled, anxious or uncertain: ~d weather, uncertain, changeable weather.

un·sex /ˌʌn'seks/ vt [VP6A] deprive of the attributes of one's sex. ~ed adj not separated according to sex.

un·sight·ly /ʌn'saɪtlɪ/ adj displeasing to the eye: ~ advertisements in the countryside. **un·sight·li·ness** n

un·skilled /ˌʌn'skɪld/ adj (of work) not needing special skill; (of workers) not having special skill or special training.

un·soph·is·ti·cated /ˌʌnsə'fɪstɪkeɪtɪd/ adj naive; inexperienced; simple: ~ children/techniques.

un·sound /ʌn'saʊnd/ adj not in good condition; unsatisfactory: an ~ argument. The structure/ building is ~. of ~ mind, (legal) unbalanced in mind; mentally disordered.

un·spar·ing /ʌnˈspeərɪŋ/ adj liberal; holding nothing back: be ~ in one's efforts; ~ of praise.

un·speak·able /ʌnˈspiːkəbl/ adj that cannot be expressed or described in words: ~ joy/ wickedness; (colloq) very unpleasant: ~ behaviour. **un·speak·ably** adv

un·spot·ted /ʌnˈspɒtɪd/ adj (of reputation) without stain; pure.

un·strung /ˌʌnˈstrʌŋ/ adj (esp) with little or no control over the nerves, mind or emotions.

un·stuck /ˌʌnˈstʌk/ adj not stuck or fastened: The flap of the envelope has come ~. **come (badly)** ~, (colloq) be unsuccessful; fail to work according to plan: Our plan has come ~.

un·stud·ied /ˌʌnˈstʌdɪd/ adj (of behaviour) natural; not aimed at impressing other persons.

un·sung /ˌʌnˈsʌŋ/ adj not celebrated (in poetry or song): an ~ hero.

un·swerv·ing /ʌnˈswɜːvɪŋ/ adj (esp of aims, purposes) not changing; straight: ~ loyalty/devotion; pursue an ~ course. **~·ly** adv

un·syl·labic /ˌʌnsɪˈlæbɪk/ adj 1 not syllabic. 2 (of a consonant) not making a syllable, eg in the word little /ˈlɪtl/ the first /l/ is unsyllabic and the second is syllabic.

un·think·able /ʌnˈθɪŋkəbl/ adj such as one cannot have any real idea of or belief; not to be considered: It's ~ that he should resign now.

un·think·ing /ʌnˈθɪŋkɪŋ/ adj thoughtless; done, said, etc without thought of the effect: in an ~ moment. **~·ly** adv

un·thought-of /ʌnˈθɔːt ɒv/ adj quite unexpected; not imagined.

un·tidy /ʌnˈtaɪdɪ/ adj (-ier, -iest) (of a room, desk, etc) in disorder; (of a person) slovenly; not neat. **un·tidi·ly** adv

un·til /ənˈtɪl/ prep, conj ⇨ till.

un·time·ly /ʌnˈtaɪmlɪ/ adj occurring at a wrong or unsuitable time, or too soon: an ~ remark. He came to an ~ end, died before he had completed his life's work.

un·tir·ing /ʌnˈtaɪərɪŋ/ adj 1 continuing to work without getting tired: She seems to be ~. 2 continuing as if never causing tiredness: his ~ efforts.

unto /ˈʌntuː/ prep (archaic) = to (prep).

un·told /ˌʌnˈtəʊld/ adj (esp) too many or too much to be counted, measured, etc: a man of ~ wealth.

un·touch·able /ʌnˈtʌtʃəbl/ n, adj (member) of the lowest caste in India.

un·to·ward /ˌʌntəˈwɔːd US: ʌnˈtɔːrd/ adj (formal) unfavourable; unfortunate; inconvenient: There were no ~ incidents.

un·truth /ʌnˈtruːθ/ n [U] lack of truth; [C] (pl ~s /-ˈtruːðz/) untrue statement; lie. **~·ful** /-fl/ adv **~·fully** /-fəlɪ/ adv

un·tu·tored /ʌnˈtjuːtəd US: -ˈtuː-/ adj untaught; ignorant.

un·used¹ /ʌnˈjuːzd/ adj not made use of; not put to use; never having been used.

un·used² /ʌnˈjuːst/ adj ~ to, not accustomed to: The children are ~ to city life.

un·usual /ʌnˈjuːʒl/ adj not usual; strange; remarkable: ~ clothes/opinions; a nose of ~ size. **~·ly** /-ʒəlɪ/ adv: **~·ly** small/large/late/early.

un·ut·ter·able /ʌnˈʌtərəbl/ adj unspeakable.

un·var·nished /ʌnˈvɑːnɪʃt/ adj (esp of accounts, descriptions) plain; straightforward: the ~ truth; give an ~ account of what happened.

un·veil /ˌʌnˈveɪl/ vt, vi 1 [VP6A,2A] remove a veil from; remove one's veil. 2 [VP6A] disclose; reveal; (trade use) show publicly for the first time: Several new models were ~ed yesterday at the Motor Show.

un·voiced /ˌʌnˈvɔɪst/ adj (of thoughts, etc) not expressed or uttered.

un·wieldy /ʌnˈwiːldɪ/ adj awkward to move or control because of shape, size or weight. **un·wiel·di·ness** n

un·wind /ˌʌnˈwaɪnd/ vt, vi (pt, pp -wound /-ˈwaʊnd/) 1 [VP6A,2A] wind off (what has been wound up); become unwound. 2 [VP21] (colloq) relax after a period of tension, exhausting work, etc. ⇨ wind⁴(6).

un·wit·ting /ʌnˈwɪtɪŋ/ adj unknowing; unaware; unintentional. **~·ly** adv: If I hurt your feelings it was ~ly.

un·writ·ten /ˌʌnˈrɪtn/ adj not written down: the ~ songs of the countryfolk, folksongs not to be found in writing or print. **an ~ law**, one based on custom or tradition, but not precisely stated anywhere.

un·zip /ˌʌnˈzɪp/ vt (-pp-) unfasten or open by pulling a zip fastener: ~ a handbag.

up /ʌp/ adv part (contrasted with down. ⇨ the v entries for combinations with up. Specimen entries only here.) 1 to or in an erect or vertical position (esp as suggesting readiness for activity): He's already up, out of bed. I was up late (= did not go to bed until late) last night. She was up all night with a sick child. It's time to get up, out of bed. He got up (= stood up) to ask a question. He jumped up (ie to his feet) from his chair. Up with you! Get up! Stand up! Up with them! Put, bring, etc them up! Parliament is up, no longer sitting, no longer in session. His blood was up, His passions were roused. **What's up,** (colloq) What's going on, happening? There's something up, Sth unusual is happening, being planned, etc. **up and about,** out of bed and active (esp of a person recently ill). 2 to or in a high(er) place, position, degree, etc: Lift your head up. Pull your socks up. The tide's up, in. He lives three floors up. Prices are still going up, rising. He's well up in Greek, has made good progress. 3 to a place of importance; (in England) to London; to a place in or to the north: He has gone up to London for the day. He lives up in the Lake District. We're going up to Edinburgh. The case was brought up before the High Court. 4 (used vaguely, in a way similar to the use of down, round, over, across) to the place in question, or in which the speaker is, was, will be: He came up (to me) and asked the time. She went straight up to the door. 5 (with vv to indicate completeness, finality): The stream has dried up, has become completely dry. We've eaten everything up. Time's up, The allowed time is ended. When is your leave up? When must you return to duty? Tear it up. Lock/ Tie/Fasten/Chain/Nail it up, Make it fast, secure, safe, etc by locking, tying, etc. 6 (with vv to indicate an increase in intensity, etc): Speak/Sing up! (ie with more force). Her spirits went up, rose. Blow the fire up. 7 (attrib with nn): the ˈup train (to London); the ˈup line/platform (used by up trains); an ˈup stroke, eg of the pen when writing the letter l. 8 **up against sth,** faced with (difficulties, obstacles, etc). **be up before sb,** appear in court (before a magistrate, etc): He was up before the magistrate for being drunk while driving a car. **up and down,** (a) backwards and forwards; to and fro: walking up and down the station platform. (b) so as to rise and fall: *The float bobbed up and down on the water.* Hence, **ups and downs,** (usu fig) alternations of good and bad fortune. **on the up (and up),** (colloq) steadily improving; becoming more successful. **up for sth,** (a) being tried (for an offence, etc): *up for exceeding the speed limit.* (b) being considered for; on offer: *The contract is up for renewal. The house is up for auction/sale.* **be well up in/on sth,** be well informed about; be expert in: *He's well up on electronic music.* **up to sth,** (a) occupied or busy with: *What's he up to? He's up to no good. What tricks has she been up to,* playing? (b) equal to: *I don't feel up to going to work today. This new book of Hugh Fleetwood's isn't up to his last,* is not as good. *He's not up to his work/to the job,* not good enough for the job. (c) as far as: *up to now/then; count from one up to twenty.* **up to sb,** required, looked upon as necessary, from him: *It's up to us* (= It is our duty) *to give them all the help we can.* **all up (with sb),** ⇨ all ²(2). **up-and-'coming,** (of a person) making good progress, likely to succeed, in his profession, career, etc: *an up-and-coming young MP.* □ *prep* (in the senses of the *adv*): *climb up a mountain; walk up the stairs; sail up* (towards the source of) *a river; travel up country,* away from the coast; *walk up* (= along) *the road.* □ *vi,vt* (-pp-) [VP2A,6A] **1** (hum or colloq use only) rouse oneself: get or jump up: *She upped and threw the teapot at him.* **2** (colloq) increase: *up the price; up an offer.*

up- /ʌp-/ *pref* in an upward direction.
up-beat /'ʌp biːt/ *n* (music) unaccented beat, esp at the end of a bar (eg when the conductor's hand is raised).
up-braid /ʌp'breɪd/ *vt* [VP6A,14] ~ **sb (for doing sth/with sth),** scold, reproach.
up-bring-ing /'ʌpbrɪŋɪŋ/ *n* [U] training and education during childhood: *His* ~ *explains a lot about his attitude towards authority/women.*
up-coun-try /ʌp'kʌntrɪ/ *adj, adv* (esp in a large thinly populated country) towards the interior; inland: ~ *districts; travel* ~.
up-date /ʌp'deɪt/ *vt* [VP6A] bring up-to-date; modernize: ~ *a dictionary/textbook.*
up-grade /ʌp'greɪd/ *vt* [VP6A] raise to a higher grade. □ *n* /'ʌpgreɪd/ (esp) **on the** ~, improving; making progress.
up-heaval /ʌp'hiːvl/ *n* [C] great and sudden change: *a volcanic* ~; *political/social* ~s.
up-held /ʌp'held/ *pt,pp* of uphold.
up-hill /ʌp'hɪl/ *adj* sloping upward; ascending: *an* ~ *road;* (fig) difficult; needing effort. **an** ~ **task,** very difficult one. □ *adv* up a slope: *walk* ~.
up-hold /ʌp'həʊld/ *vt* (*pt,pp* upheld /-'held/) [VP6A] **1** support or approve (a person, his conduct, a practice, etc): *I cannot* ~ *such conduct.* **2** confirm (a decision, a verdict).
up-hol-ster /ʌp'həʊlstə(r)/ *vt* [VP6A] provide (seats, etc) with padding, springs, covering material, etc; provide (a room) with carpets, curtains, cushioned seats, etc: ~ *a settee in tapestry;* ~ed *in/with velvet.* ~er *n* person whose trade is to ~. ~y /-stərɪ/ *n* [U] (materials used in, business of) ~ing.
up-keep /'ʌpkiːp/ *n* [U] (cost of) keeping sth in good order and repair: *£450 for rent and* ~, eg of a house. *The* ~ *of this large garden is more than I can afford.*
up-land /'ʌplənd/ *n* (often *pl*) higher part(s) of a region or country (not necessarily mountainous): (at-

trib) *an* ~ *region.*
up-lift /ʌp'lɪft/ *vt* [VP6A] (fig) raise (spiritually or emotionally): *His soul was* ~ed *by the music.* □ *n* /'ʌplɪft/ [U] socially or mentally elevating influence; moral inspiration.
up-most /'ʌpməʊst/ *adj* = uppermost.
upon /ə'pɒn/ *prep* (formal) = on ²(1-7) (which is more usual. *Upon* is the only normal form in): ~ *my word; once* ~ *a time.*
up-per /'ʌpə(r)/ *adj* (contrasted with *lower*) higher in place; situated above: *the* ~ *lip; the* ~ *arm; one of the* ~ *rooms.* ~ **case,** ⇨ case ²(2), ~ **class,** ⇨ class(3). **the** ~ **crust,** (colloq) the highest social class. **the** ~ **storey,** (fig, colloq) the brain: *wrong in the* ~ *storey,* mentally disordered. **have/get the** ~ **hand (of),** have/get the advantage or control (over). **the U**~ **House,** (in Parliament) the House of Lords. '~-**cut** *n* (boxing) a blow delivered upwards with the arm bent inside an opponent's guard. □ *n* part of a shoe or boot over the sole. **be (down) on one's** ~s, be at the end of one's financial resources. '~-**most** /-məʊst/ *adj* highest; predominant: *Thoughts of the holidays were* ~most *in their minds.* □ *adv* on, to, at, the top or surface: *It's not always wise to say whatever comes* ~most, whatever comes to the top of one's thoughts.
up-pish /'ʌpɪʃ/ *adj* (colloq) self-assertive, conceited: *Don't get* ~ *with me! Don't be too* ~ *about it!* ~**ly** *adv* ~**ness** *n*
up-pity /'ʌpətɪ/ *adj* (colloq) uppish.
up-right /'ʌpraɪt/ *adj* **1** erect; placed vertically (at an angle of 90° to the ground): *an* ~ *post; stand/ hold oneself* ~; *set a post* ~. ~ **piano,** with the strings vertical, not horizontal, as in a grand piano. **2** honourable; straightforward in behaviour: *an* ~ *man/judge; be* ~ *in one's business dealings.* □ *n* [C] ~ support in a structure; ~ post. ~**ly** *adv* ~**ness** *n* [U].
up-ris-ing /'ʌpraɪzɪŋ/ *n* [C] revolt; rebellion.
up-roar /'ʌprɔː(r)/ *n* [U,C] (sing only) (outburst of) noise and excitement; tumult: *The meeting ended in* (*an*) ~. ~**i-ous** /ʌp'rɔːrɪəs/ *adj* very noisy, esp with loud laughter and great good humour: *We were given an* ~ious *welcome. They burst into* ~ious *laughter.* ~**i-ous-ly** *adv*
up-root /ʌp'ruːt/ *vt* [VP6A] pull up by the roots: *The gale* ~ed *numerous trees. After he had lived in New York for fifteen years his firm* ~ed *him and sent him to Chicago.*
up-set /ʌp'set/ *vt,vi* (*pt,pp* upset) (-tt-) **1** [VP6A,2A] tip over; overturn: *Don't* ~ *the boat. The boat* ~. *The cat has* ~ *its saucer of milk.* **2** [VP6A] trouble; cause (sb or sth) to be disturbed: ~ *the enemy's plans;* ~ *one's stomach by eating too much rich food. The sight of physical suffering* ~s *her. She is easily* ~ *emotionally.* □ *n* /'ʌpset/ [C] ~ting or being ~: *have a' stomach* ~. *She's had a terrible* ~, eg an emotional shock. *You can imagine what an* ~ *we have had with the decorators and upholsterers in the house all week.* **2** (sport) unexpected result.
up-shot /'ʌpʃɒt/ *n* **the** ~ **(of sth),** outcome; result: *What will be the* ~ *of it all?*
up-side-down /ʌpsaɪd 'daʊn/ *adv* with the upper side underneath or at the bottom; (fig) in disorder: *The boy pretended he could read, but he was holding the book* ~. *The house was turned* ~ *by the burglars,* Everything was left in disorder.
up-stage /ʌp'steɪdʒ/ *adj* (colloq) uppish; uppity. □

adv (theatre) towards the back of the stage. □ *vt* [VP6A] divert attention from sb else to oneself; put at a disadvantage.

up·stairs /ˌʌp'steəz/ *adv* **1** to or on a higher floor: *go/walk* ∼. **2** (attrib) belonging to, situated on, an upper floor: *an* ∼ *room*.

up·stand·ing /ˌʌp'stændɪŋ/ *adj* standing erect; strong and healthy: *fine* ∼ *children*.

up·start /'ʌpstɑːt/ *n, adj* (person) who has suddenly risen to wealth, power or higher social position, esp one whose behaviour causes resentment: ∼ *officials in government offices*.

up·stream /ˌʌp'striːm/ *adv* up a river; against the stream or current.

up·surge /'ʌpsɜːdʒ/ *n* surging up (of emotion): *an* ∼ *of anger/indignation*.

up·take /'ʌpteɪk/ *n* **quick/slow on the** ∼, (colloq) quick/slow to understand (sth said or hinted at).

up·tight /ˌʌp'taɪt/ *adj* ∼ **(about)**, (sl) **1** extremely tense; nervous: ∼ *about an interview/examination*. **2** uneasy; prejudiced; hostile; fearful.

up-to-date /'ʌp tə deɪt/ *adj* modern; fashionable: ∼ *clothes/ideas/books*.

up·town /ˌʌp'taʊn/ *adj, adv* (US) to or in the upper (the residential or non-business, non-commercial) part (of a town): ∼ *New York; go* ∼.

up·turn /'ʌptɜːn/ *n* upward turn; change for the better: *an* ∼ *in business/employment/production*.

up·ward /'ʌpwəd/ *adj* moving or directed up: *the* ∼ *trend of prices; an* ∼ *glance*. ∼ **(social) mob·il·ity,** ∼ movement of sb from one class(3) to another. □ *adv* ∼**(s)**, towards a higher place, level, etc: *The boat was on the beach, bottom* ∼s, turned upside-down. *Is our civilization moving* ∼? ∼*s of,* more than: ∼*s of a hundred people*.

ura·nium /jʊ'reɪnɪəm/ *n* [U] heavy white metal (symbol **U**) with radioactive properties, a source of atomic energy.

Ura·nus /jʊ'reɪnəs/ *n* (astron) planet seventh in order from the sun. ⇨ the illus at planet.

ur·ban /'ɜːbən/ *adj* of or in a town: *the overcrowded* ∼ *areas of England;* ∼ *guerrillas,* ⇨ guerrilla. ∼**·ize** /-aɪz/ *vt* [VP6A] change from a rural to an ∼ character. ∼**·iz·ation** /ˌɜːbənaɪ'zeɪʃn US: -nɪ'z-/ *n* [U].

ur·bane /ɜː'beɪn/ *adj* polite; polished in manners; elegant. ∼**·ly** *adv* **ur·ban·ity** /ɜː'bænətɪ/ *n* [U] refinement; politeness; (*pl;* -ties) courteous manners.

ur·chin /'ɜːtʃɪn/ *n* mischievous small child; (often 'street-∼) poor destitute child.

Urdu /'ʊədu:/ *adj, n* (of) one of the official languages of Pakistan.

urge /ɜːdʒ/ *vt* **1** [VP6A,15B] ∼ **sb/sth (on/ onward/forward),** push or drive on: *With whip and spur he* ∼*d his horse onward. The foreman* ∼*d his workmen on*. **2** [VP6A,D,9,14,17,19C] ∼ *sb (to sth),* request earnestly; try to persuade; strongly recommend: *The salesman* ∼*d me to buy a new car. Agitators* ∼*d the peasants to revolt/to revolution. He* ∼*d leaving/our leaving/that we should leave/us to leave*. **3** [VP6A,14] ∼ *sth (on/ upon sb),* press it (on him) with requests and arguments: *He* ∼*d on his pupils the importance of hard work. He* ∼*d his youth/the fact that he was young*. □ *n* [U,C] strong desire: *He has/feels an* ∼/*no* ∼ *to travel*.

ur·gent /'ɜːdʒənt/ *adj* **1** needing prompt decision or action: *An SOS is an* ∼ *message. It is most* ∼ *that the patient should get to hospital. The earthquake*

victims are in ∼ *need of medical supplies*. **2** (of a person, his voice, etc) showing that sth is ∼; persistent in making a demand. ∼**·ly** *adv* **ur·gency** /-dʒənsɪ/ *n* [U] need for, importance of, haste or prompt action: *a matter of great urgency*.

uric /'jʊərɪk/ *adj* of urine.

urine /'jʊərɪn/ *n* [U] waste liquid which collects in the bladder and is discharged from the body. **uri·nal** /'jʊərɪnl/ *n* **1** ('*bed urinal*) vessel into which ∼ may be discharged (by sb ill in bed). **2** (*public* '*uri·nal*) place for the convenience of men who need to discharge ∼. **uri·nate** /'jʊərɪneɪt/ *vi* discharge ∼. **uri·nary** /'jʊərɪnrɪ US: -nerɪ/ *adj* of ∼: *a urinary infection*.

urn /ɜːn/ *n* **1** vase, usu with stem and base, esp as used for holding the ashes of a person whose body has been cremated. **2** large metal container in which a drink such as tea or coffee is made or kept hot, eg in cafés and canteens.

urns

us /*weak form:* əs; *strong form:* ʌs/ *pron* object form of *we*.

usage /'juːzɪdʒ US: 'juːs-/ *n* **1** [U] way of using sth; treatment: *Machines soon wear out under rough* ∼. **2** [C,U] body of conventions governing the use of a language (esp those aspects not governed by grammatical rules): *a guide to English grammar and* ∼. *Do you have difficulty in learning the finer points of* ∼? *Such* ∼*s are not characteristic of educated speakers*. **3** [C,U] agreed codes of behaviour: *Industrialization and urbanization influence social* ∼(*s*).

use[1] /juːs/ *n* **1** [U] using or being used; condition of being used: *the use of electricity for lighting; learn the use of tools; a room for the use of women only; for use only in case of fire; bought for use, not for ornament*. **in use,** being used. **out of use,** not being, no longer, used. **come into use,** begin to be used: *When did the word 'transistor' come into common use?* **go/fall out of use,** be no longer used: *The custom has gone out of use*. **make (good/the best) use of,** use (well/in the best way): *You must make good use of any opportunities you have of practising English*. **2** [C,U] purpose for which sth or sb is or may be employed; work that sth or sb is able to do: *a tool with many uses; find a use for sth; put sth to (a) good use; have no further use for sth. I have no use for* (fig, dislike, have no patience with) *people who are always grumbling*. **3** [U] value; advantage: *Is this of any use to you? It's no use your pretending/no use for you to pretend that you didn't know the rules. There isn't much use for that sort of thing nowadays.* ∼ *of,* [U] power of using: *lose the use of one's legs,* become a cripple, unable to walk. **5** [U] right to use: *give a friend the use of one's bike*. **6** [U] usage; familiarity through continued practice: *In these cases use is the best guide*. **use·ful** /'juːsfl/ *adj* **1** helpful; producing good results: *A spade is a useful tool. Are you a useful member of society?* **2**

(colloq) capable, efficient: *He's a useful member of the team.* **use·fully** /-fǝlɪ/ *adv* **use·ful·ness** *n* **use·less** *adj* **1** of no use; worthless: *A car is useless without petrol.* **2** without result; ineffectual: *It's useless to argue with them.* **use·less·ly** *adv* **use·less·ness** *n*

use² / juːz/ *vt* (*pt,pp* used /juːzd/) **1** [VP6A,16A,14] **use (for),** employ for a purpose: *You use your legs when you walk. You use a knife to cut bread. A hammer is used for driving in nails. When persuasion failed they used force. May I use* (= quote) *your name as a reference,* eg in an application for a post. **2** [VP6A,15B] **use sth (up),** consume: *How much coal did we use last winter? He has ~d up all his strength.* **3** [VP15A] behave towards: *Use others as you would like them to use you. He thinks himself ill used,* considers that he is badly treated. **used** /juːzd/ *adj* no longer new: *used cars,* cars offered for sale after they have been used and are no longer in new condition. **us·able** /'juːzǝbl/ *adj* that can be used, that is fit to be used. **user** *n* sb or sth that uses: *There are more telephone users in the USA than in any other country.*

used¹ /juːst/ *anom fin* (neg used not; usedn't/usen't /'juːsnt/; (colloq) didn't use /juːs/) *~ to +* *inf,* (indicating a constant or frequent practice in the past): *That's where I ~ to live when I was a child. Life isn't so easy here as it ~ to be. You ~ to smoke a pipe, use(d)n't you* (or *didn't you*)? *Didn't you use to smoke a pipe?* **there *~ to be,*** (indicating the existence of sth in the past): *There ~ to be some trees in this field, use(d)n't there/ didn't there?*

used² /juːst/ *adj ~ to,* accustomed to: *He's quite ~ to hard work/working hard. I'm not ~ to being spoken to in that rude way. You will soon be/get ~ to it.*

usher /'ʌʃǝ(r)/ *n* **1** person who shows people to their seats in theatres, cinemas, etc. **2** doorkeeper in a law court, etc. □ *vt* **1** [VP15B,14] lead, conduct: *The girl ~ed me to my seat* (in a cinema). **2** [VP15B] *~ sth in,* herald, announce: *The change of government ~ed in a period of prosperity.* **~·ette** /ˌʌʃǝ'ret/ *n* girl or woman *~*(1).

usual /'juːʒl/ *adj* such as commonly happens; customary: *Tea is considered to be the ~ drink of British people. He arrived later than ~. As is ~ with many picnickers, they left a lot of litter behind· them. When the accident happened, the ~ crowd quickly gathered.* **as *~,*** as is *~: You're late, as ~. The meeting was, as ~, badly attended.* **~·ly** /'juːʒǝlɪ/ *adv* in the way that is *~: What do you ~ly do on Sundays? He's ~ly early.*

usurer /'juːʒǝrǝ(r)/ *n* person whose business is usury.

usurp /juː'zɜːp/ *vt* [VP6A] wrongfully take (sb's power, authority, position): *~ the throne.* **~·er** *n* person who does this. **usur·pa·tion** /ˌjuːzɜː'peɪʃn/ *n*

[C,U] (instance of) *~*ing.

usury /'juːʒǝrɪ/ *n* [U] (practice of) lending money, esp at a rate of interest considered to be too high; such high interest. **usuri·ous** /juː'zjʊǝrɪǝs US: -'ʒʊ-/ *adj* of *~: a usurious transaction; a usurious rate of interest.*

uten·sil /juː'tensl/ *n* instrument, tool, etc esp for use in the house: *'household ~s,* eg pots, pans, brushes; *'writing ~s,* eg paper, pens, ink.

uterus /'juːtǝrǝs/ *n* (anat) womb. ⇨ the illus at re-produce. **uter·ine** /'juːtǝraɪn/ *adj* of the *~.*

utili·tar·ian /juːˌtɪlɪ'teǝrɪǝn/ *adj* **1** characterized by usefulness rather than by beauty, truth, goodness. **2** of the U*~*s and their ideas. □ *n* U*~,* supporter of *~*ism. **~·ism** /-ɪzǝm/ *n* [U] political and moral theory that the best rule of life is to aim at 'the greatest happiness of the greatest number,' actions being considered right or wrong according as they help or hinder the achievement of this aim.

util·ity /juː'tɪlǝtɪ/ *n* (*pl* -ties) **1** [U] quality of being useful: (attrib) *'~ van/truck,* one that can be used for various purposes. **2** [C] (**public**) *~,* public service such as the supply of water, electricity, gas, or a bus or railway service.

util·ize /'juːtɪlaɪz US: -tǝlaɪz/ *vt* [VP6A] make use of; find a use for. **util·iz·able** /-ǝbl/ *adj* that can be *~d* or put to a useful purpose. **util·iz·ation** /ˌjuːtɪlaɪ'zeɪʃn US: -tǝlɪ'z-/ *n* [U] utilizing or being *~d.*

ut·most /'ʌtmǝʊst/ *adj* most extreme; greatest: *in the ~ danger; of the ~ importance; with the ~ care.* □ *n* **one's/the *~,*** the most that is possible: *do one's ~; exert/enjoy oneself to the ~. That is the ~ I can do.*

Uto·pia /juː'tǝʊpɪǝ/ *n* [C] imaginary perfect social and political system. **Uto·pian** /-pɪǝn/ *adj* (also **u-**) attractive and desirable but impracticable: *a ~n scheme for giving all old people a pension of £100 a week.*

ut·ter¹ /'ʌtǝ(r)/ *adj* complete; total: *~ darkness; an ~ slander. She's an ~ stranger to me.* **~·ly** *adv* **1** completely. **2** to the depths of one's being: *She ~ly detests him.*

ut·ter² /'ʌtǝ(r)/ *vt* [VP6A] **1** make (a sound or sounds) with the mouth: *~ a sigh/a cry of pain.* **2** say: *the last words he ~ed.* **3** put (false money, etc) into circulation. **~·ance** /'ʌtǝrǝns/ *n* **1** (*sing* only) way of speaking: *a clear/defective/very rapid ~ance.* **2** [C] sth said; spoken word or words. **3** [U] *~*ing: *give ~ance to* (*one's feelings, etc*), express in words.

ut·ter·most /'ʌtǝmǝʊst/ *adj, n* = utmost: *the ~ ends of the earth.*

uvula /'juːvjʊlǝ/ *n* (anat) small piece of fleshy matter hanging from the back of the roof of the mouth. ⇨ the illus at mouth. **uvu·lar** /-lǝ(r)/ *adj* of the.*~.*

ux·ori·ous /ˌʌk'sɔːrɪǝs/ *adj* excessively fond of one's wife. **~·ly** *adv* **~·ness** *n*

Vv

V, v /viː/ *n* (*pl* V's, v's) **1** the 22nd letter of the English alphabet; symbol for the Roman numeral 5. ⇨ App 4. **2** V-shaped thing; *the V sign,* sign made by the hand with the palm outwards and the first and second fingers spread to form a V (for *victory*). **V1, 2** /ˌviː 'wʌn, 'tuː/, flying bomb. ⇨ doodlebug.

vac /væk/ *n* (colloq, abbr of) vacation (= holidays).

va·cancy /'veɪkǝnsɪ/ *n* (*pl* -cies) **1** [U] condition of being empty or unoccupied. **2** [U,C] unoccupied space; blank: *look over the edge of a cliff into ~.* **3** [U] lack of ideas or intelligence; lack of concentration. **4** [C] position in business, etc for which sb is

needed: *good vacancies for typists and clerks.*
va·cant /'veɪkənt/ *adj* **1** empty: *gaze into* ~ *space.*
2 not occupied by anyone: *a* ~ *room,* eg in a hotel;
apply for a ~ *position,* eg in an office. ~ **possession,** phrase used in advertisements of houses, etc
declaring that the buyer can enter into immediate
occupation. **3** (of time) not filled with any activity;
leisured. **4** (of the mind) unoccupied with thought;
(of the eyes) showing no signs of thought or interest: *with* ~ *looks; a* ~ *stare/expression.* ~·**ly**
adv
va·cate /və'keɪt *US:* 'veɪkeɪt/ *vt* [VP6A] **1** give up
living in: ~ *a house/rented rooms.* **2** leave unoccupied: ~ *one's seat.* **3** (formal) give up possession or use of.
va·ca·tion /və'keɪʃn *US:* veɪ-/ *n* **1** [U] (formal) va-
cating: *His* ~ *of a good position in the Civil Service was unwise.* **2** [C] weeks during which universities and law courts stop work: *the long* ~*; the
summer* ~*; the Christmas* ~. **3** [C] (esp US) holi-
day(2); any time or period of rest and freedom from
work. **on** ~, on holiday. □ *vi* [VP3A] ~ **at/in,**
(US) spend a holiday: ~*ing in Florida.* ~·**ist**
/-ʃənɪst/ *n* (US) person on ~(3).
vac·ci·nate /'væksɪneɪt *US:* -səneɪt/ *vt* [VP6A,14]
~ *sb* **(against sth),** protect (sb) (against a disease)
by injecting vaccine. **vac·ci·na·tion** /ˌvæksɪ'neɪʃn/
n [C,U] (instance of) vaccinating or being ~d.
vac·cine /'væksi:n *US:* væk'si:n/ *n* [C,U] substance
injected into the bloodstream, used to protect persons from a disease by causing them to have a
slight, but not dangerous, form of the disease.
vac·il·late /'væsɪleɪt/ *vi* [VP2A,3A] ~ **(between),**
waver; hesitate; be uncertain (in opinion, etc): ~
between hope and fear. **vac·il·la·tion** /ˌvæsɪ'leɪʃn/
n [C,U] (instance of) vacillating.
vacu·ous /'vækjʊəs/ *adj* showing or suggesting absence of thought or intelligence: *a* ~ *expression/
stare/remark/laugh.* ~·**ly** *adv* **vacu·ity** /və'kju:ətɪ/
n (*pl* -ties) [U] state of being ~; (*pl*) ~ remarks,
acts, etc.
vac·uum /'vækjʊəm/ *n* (*pl* ~s or, in science, -uua
/-jʊə/) space completely empty of substance or
gas(es); space in a container from which the air has
been pumped out. '~ **cleaner,** apparatus which
takes up dust, dirt, etc by suction. '~ **flask/bottle,**
one having a ~ between its inner and outer walls,
keeping the contents at an unchanging temperature.
⇨ thermos. '~ **pump,** (a) pump to create a partial
~ in a vessel. (b) pump in which a partial ~ is
used to raise water. '~ **tube/valve,** sealed glass
tube with an almost perfect ~ in it, for observing
the passage of an electric charge.
vade–mecum /ˌveɪdɪ 'mi:kəm/ *n* [C] small handbook which can be carried about and used for reference.
vaga·bond /'vægəbɒnd/ *adj* having no fixed
living-place; habitually wandering: *live a* ~ *life;*
~ *Gypsies.* □ *n* ~ person; tramp.
va·gary /'veɪgərɪ/ *n* [C] (*pl* -ries) strange, unusual
act or idea, esp one for which there seems to be no
good reason: *the vagaries of fashion/of human
emotions.*
va·gina /və'dʒaɪnə/ *n* (anat) passage (in a female
mammal) from the external genital organs to the
womb (colloq '*birth canal*). ⇨ the illus at reproduce. **vag·inal** /və'dʒaɪnl/ *adj*
va·grant /'veɪgrənt/ *adj* leading a wandering life:
~ *tribes/musicians;* wandering: *lead a* ~ *life;* ~
thoughts. □ *n* ~ person; vagabond or tramp. **va-**

grancy /-rənsɪ/ *n* [U] being a ~.
vague /veɪg/ *adj* (-r, -st) **1** not clear or distinct: ~
outlines; ~ *demands. I haven't the* ~*st idea what
they want.* **2** (of persons, their looks, behaviour)
uncertain, suggesting uncertainty (about needs, intentions, etc). ~·**ly** *adv* ~·**ness** *n*
vain /veɪn/ *adj* (-er, -est) **1** without use, value,
meaning or result: *a* ~ *attempt;* ~ *hopes/
promises.* **2** *in* ~, (a) without the desired result: *try
in* ~ *to do sth. All our work was in* ~. (b) without
due reverence, honour or respect: *take the name of
God in* ~, use the word 'God' irreverently; *take a
person's name in* ~, use it lightly, disrespectfully.
3 having too high an opinion of one's looks, abilities, etc; conceited: *He's as* ~ *as a peacock. She's*
~ *of her beauty.* ~·**'glory** *n* extreme vanity or
pride in oneself. ⌒·**'glorious** *adj* full of ~glory;
conceited and boastful. ~·**ly** *adv* **1** in ~. **2** in a
conceited manner.
val·ance, val·ence /'væləns/ *n* short curtain or frill
round the frame or the canopy of a bedstead, above
a window, or under a shelf.
vale /veɪl/ *n* (liter except in place-names) valley.
val·edic·tion /ˌvælɪ'dɪkʃn/ *n* [C] (words used in)
saying farewell.
val·edic·tory /ˌvælɪ'dɪktərɪ/ *adj* relating to, in the
nature of, a farewell: *a* ~ *speech.*
val·ence [1] /'veɪləns/ *n* **1** [U] (chem) capacity of an
atom to combine with, or to be replaced by, another atom. **2** [C] (US) = valency.
val·ence [2] /'væləns/ *n* ⇨ valance.
val·ency /'veɪlənsɪ/ *n* (*pl* -cies) [C] (chem) unit of
valence [1]: *Carbon has 4 valencies.*
val·en·tine /'væləntaɪn/ *n* (letter, card, etc, usu anonymous, sent on St V~'s Day, 14 Feb, to a)
sweetheart.
val·erian /və'lɪərɪən/ *n* [U] kinds of small perennial
plant with strong-smelling pink or white flowers;
root of this used medically.
valet /'vælɪt/ *n* manservant who looks after his
master's clothes; employee in a hotel with similar
duties. □ *vt* [VP6A] act as ~ to: *The hotel has a
good* ~*ing service.*
val·etu·di·nar·ian /ˌvælɪtjuːdɪ'neərɪən *US:* -tuːd-/
adj (formal) of poor health; unduly troubled about,
almost wholly occupied with, the state of one's
health. □ *n* ~ person.
val·iant /'vælɪənt/ *adj* brave. ~·**ly** *adv*
valid /'vælɪd/ *adj* **1** (legal) effective because made
or done with the correct formalities: *a* ~ *claim/
marriage.* **2** (of contracts, etc) having force in law:
~ *for three months; a ticket* ~ *for one single journey between London and Dover.* **3** (of arguments,
reasons, etc) well based; sound: *raise* ~ *objections
to a scheme.* ~·**ly** *adv* ~·**ity** /və'lɪdətɪ/ *n* [U] state
of being ~. **vali·date** /'vælɪdeɪt/ *vt* [VP6A] make
~: ~*ate a claim.*
va·lise /və'liːz *US:* və'liːs/ *n* small leather bag for
clothes, etc during a journey; soldier's kitbag.
val·ley /'vælɪ/ *n* (*pl* -leys) stretch of land between
hills or mountains, often with a river flowing
through it. ⇨ the illus at mountain.
val·our (US = **valor**) /'vælə(r)/ *n* [U] braVery, esp
in war. **val·or·ous** /'vælərəs/ *adj* brave.
valu·able /'væljʊəbl/ *adj* of great value, worth or
use: *a* ~ *discovery.* □ *n* (usu *pl*) sth of much value,
eg articles of gold, jewels.
valu·ation /ˌvæljʊ'eɪʃn/ *n* [U] process of deciding
the value of sth or sb; [C] the value that is decided
upon: *The surveyors arrived at widely different*

~s. *It is unwise to accept a person at his own* ~, the opinion which he has of himself.

value /'vælju:/ n **1** [U] quality of being useful or desirable: *the* ~ *of walking as an exercise.* **2** [U] worth of sth when compared with sth else: *This book will be of great/little/some/no* ~ *to him in his studies.* **3** [C,U] worth of sth in terms of money or other goods for which it can be exchanged: *Is the* ~ *of the American dollar likely to decline? Does this volume give you good* ~ *for your money? The property is going down in* ~ *all the time. Market* ~s *rose sharply last week.* ~-'**added tax,** (abbr **VAT**) tax on the rise in ~ of a product at each stage of manufacture and marketing. **4** [U] what sth is considered to be worth (contrasted with the price obtainable): *I've been offered £500 for my old car but its* ~ *is much higher.* **5** [C,U] **(a)** (in music) full time indicated by a note: *Give the note its full* ~. **(b)** (in painting) relation of light and shade. **(c)** (in language) meaning; effect: *use a word with all its poetic* ~. **(d)** (pl) standards: *moral/artistic* ~s. □ vt [VP6A,15A,16B] **1** estimate the money ~ of: *He* ~d *the house for me at £20000.* **2** regard highly; have a high opinion of: ~ *sb's advice. Do you* ~ *her as a secretary?* ~-**less** adj without ~; worthless. ~**r** n person whose profession is to estimate the money ~ of property, land, etc.

valve /vælv/ n **1** (sorts of) mechanical device for controlling the flow of air, liquid, gas or electrons in one direction only: *the inlet/outlet* ~s *of a petrol or steam engine; the* ~ *of a bicycle tyre.* ⇨ the illus at **bicycle**. **2** structure in the heart or in a blood-vessel allowing the blood to flow in one direction only. **3** ('**radio**) ~, thermionic ~ used in a radio (US = *tube*). ⇨ thermionic. **4** device in musical wind instruments, eg a cornet, for changing the pitch by changing the length of the column of air. **val·vu·lar** /'vælvjʊlə(r)/ adj of the ~s of the heart or blood-vessels: *valvular disease of the heart.*

va·moose /və'mu:s/ vi (US sl) go away quickly.

vamp [1] /væmp/ n upper front part of a boot or shoe. □ vt, vi **1** [VP6A,15B] repair (a boot or shoe) by putting a new ~ on. ~ *sth up*, (fig) make sth from odds and ends: ~ *up some lectures out of old notes.* **2** [VP6A,2A] make up (a tune) for a song; improvise a musical accompaniment to a song or dance.

vamp [2] /væmp/ n seductive woman who uses her attractions to exploit men.

vam·pire /'væmpaɪə(r)/ n **1** (in stories) reanimated corpse that leaves its grave at night and sucks the blood of sleeping persons; ruthless ill-disposed person who preys on others. **2** '~ (**bat**), sorts of blood-sucking bat.

van [1] /væn/ n **1** covered or roofed motor-vehicle for carrying and delivering goods: *the 'baker's van; a 'furniture van.* **2** (GB) roofed railway carriage for goods: *the'luggage van.*

van [2] /væn/ n **1** front or leading part of an army or fleet in battle. **2** = **vanguard.**

Van·dal /'vændl/ n one of a Germanic tribe that overran Gaul, Spain and N Africa in the 4th and 5th cc and sacked Rome in 455 AD. ⇨ **Goth.**

van·dal /'vændl/ n person who wilfully destroys works of art or public and private property, spoils the beauties of nature, etc. ~**ism** /-dəlɪzəm/ n [U] behaviour characteristic of ~s. ~**ize** /-dəlaɪz/ vt [VP6A] wilfully destroy or spoil (as above).

vane /veɪn/ n **1** arrow or pointer on the top of a

building, turned by the wind so as to show its direction. **2** blade of a propeller, sail of a windmill, or other flat surface acted on by wind or water.

van·guard /'vænga:d/ n **1** advance party of an army, etc as a guard against surprise attack. **2** those persons who lead a procession or (fig) a movement: *in the* ~ *of scientific progress.*

va·nilla /və'nɪlə/ n **1** [C] (pods or beans of) plant with sweet-smelling flowers. **2** [U] flavouring substance from ~ beans or synthetic product used for it: ~ *custard; two* ~ *ices.*

van·ish /'vænɪʃ/ vi [VP2A] suddenly disappear; fade away gradually; go out of existence: *Your prospects of success have* ~*ed. The thief ran into the crowd and* ~*ed from sight.* ~ *into thin air,* disappear suddenly and completely. '~**ing cream,** cosmetic cream quickly absorbed into the skin. '~**ing point,** (in perspective) point at which all parallel lines in the same plane appear to meet.

van·ity /'vænətɪ/ n (pl -ties) **1** [U] conceit; having too high an opinion of one's looks, abilities, etc: *do sth out of* ~; *tickle sb's* ~, do or say sth that pleases his conceit; *injured* ~, resentment caused by some slight or humiliation. '~ **bag/case,** bag or case carried by the owner for a small mirror, cosmetics, etc. **2** [U] worthlessness; quality of being unsatisfying, without true value: *the* ~ *of pleasure;* [C] vain, worthless thing or act.

van·quish /'væŋkwɪʃ/ vt [VP6A] (liter) conquer.

van·tage /'va:ntɪdʒ US: 'væn-/ n **1** advantage: '~-*ground; point of* ~. '~-**point** n (lit or fig) place from which one has a (good) view of sth; (advantageous) position. ⇨ **coign.** **2** (in tennis) first point scored after deuce.

vapid /'væpɪd/ adj dull; uninteresting: ~ *conversation; the* ~ *utterances of the clergy.* ~-**ly** adv ~-**ness** n va·**pid·ity** /və'pɪdətɪ/ n [U] state of being ~; (pl; -ties) ~ remarks.

va·por·ize /'veɪpəraɪz/ vt, vi [VP6A,2A] convert into, become, vapour. **va·por·iz·ation** /,veɪpəraɪ'zeɪʃn US: -rɪ'z-/ n

va·por·ous /'veɪpərəs/ adj **1** full of, like, vapour. **2** (fig) full of idle fancies; unsubstantial.

va·pour (US = **va·por**) /'veɪpə(r)/ n **1** [U] steam; mist; gaseous form to which certain substances may be reduced by heat: '*water* ~. '~-**bath** n (enclosed space or apparatus for a) bath in ~ or steam. '~ **trails,** ⇨ trail(1). **2** [C] unsubstantial thing: sth imagined: *the* ~s *of a disordered mind.* **3** the ~s, (archaic) melancholy.

vari·able /'veərɪəbl/ adj varying; changeable: ~ *winds;* ~ *standards;* ~ *costs,* (accounting) costs that go up or down according to the quantity of goods produced. *His mood/temper is* ~. □ n [C] ~ thing or quantity; factor which may vary, eg in an experiment. **vari·ably** /-əblɪ/ adv ~-**ness** n **vari·abil·ity** /,veərɪə'bɪlətɪ/ n [U] quality of being ~; tendency to vary.

vari·ance /'veərɪəns/ n [U] *at* ~ (*with*), in disagreement; having a difference of opinion: *The two sisters have been at* ~ *for years. We are at* ~ *among ourselves/at* ~ *with the others.*

vari·ant /'veərɪənt/ adj different or alternative: ~ *spellings of a word* (eg 'tire' and 'tyre'). □ n ~ form (eg of spelling).

vari·ation /,veərɪ'eɪʃn/ n **1** [C,U] (degree of) varying or being variant: ~(*s*) *of pressure/ temperature;* ~s *in public opinion.* **2** [C] (music) simple melody repeated in a different (and usu more complicated) form: ~s *on a theme by Mo-*

zart. **3** [U] (biol) change in bodily structure or form caused by new conditions, environment, etc; [C] instance of such change.

vari·col·oured (US = **-col·ored**) /'veərɪkʌləd/ *adj* of various colours.

vari·cose /'værɪkəʊs/ *adj* (esp in) ∼ **vein**, vein that has become permanently swollen or enlarged.

var·ied /'veərɪd/ *adj* **1** of different sorts; diverse: ∼ *opinions; the* ∼ *scenes of life*. **2** full of changes or variety: *a* ∼ *career*.

varie·gated /'veərɪgeɪtɪd/ *adj* marked irregularly with differently coloured patches: *The leaves of geraniums/The flowers of pansies are often* ∼. **varie·ga·tion** /ˌveərɪ'geɪʃn/ *n*

var·iety /və'raɪətɪ/ *n* (*pl* -ties) **1** [U] quality of not being the same, or not being the same at all times: *a life full of* ∼. *We demanded more* ∼ *in our food*. **2** (*sing* only) number or range of different things: *for a* ∼ *of reasons; a large* ∼ *of patterns to choose from*. **3** [C] (biol) subdivision of a species. **4** [C] kind or sort which differs from others of the larger group of which it is a part: *rare varieties of early postage stamps. There are now several varieties of spaniel*. **5** [U] kind of entertainment consisting of singing, dancing, acrobatic feats, short plays, etc as given in music-halls (GB), some night-clubs and hotels, and for broadcasting: *a '*∼ *entertainment; a '*∼ *theatre; '*∼ *artists*. (US = *vaudeville*).

vari·form /ˌveərɪ'fɔːm US: 'vær-/ *adj* of various forms.

vari·orum /ˌveərɪ'ɔːrəm/ *adj* (only in) '∼ **edition**, edition, eg of a Shakespeare play, with the notes of various commentators.

vari·ous /'veərɪəs/ *adj* (usu attrib) different; of a number of different sorts: *for* ∼ *reasons; at* ∼ *times; a criminal who is known to the police under* ∼ *names*. ∼·**ly** *adv*

var·let /'vɑːlɪt/ *n* (archaic) rascal.

var·nish /'vɑːnɪʃ/ *n* [C,U] (particular kind of) (liquid used to give a) hard, shiny, transparent coating on the surface of sth, esp woodwork or metalwork; (fig) false or deceiving appearance: *scratch the* ∼ *on a table; a* ∼ *of good manners;* '*nail-*∼, for fingernails. □ *vt* [VP6A] put a coating of ∼ on: ∼ *a piece of furniture/an oil-painting. Some women* ∼ *their toe-nails*.

vars·ity /'vɑːsətɪ/ *n* (*pl* -ties) (colloq) university.

vary /'veərɪ/ *vi,vt* (*pt,pp* -ried) [VP2A,6A] be, become, cause to become, different: ∼*ing prices; prices that* ∼ *with the season. They* ∼ *in weight from 3 lb to 5 lb. You should* ∼ *your diet*.

vas·cu·lar /'væskjʊlə(r)/ *adj* of, made up of, containing, vessels or ducts through which blood, lymph or sap flows: ∼ *tissue*.

vase /vɑːz US: veɪs/ *n* [C] vessel of glass, pottery, etc for holding cut flowers, or as an ornament.

vases

va·sec·tomy /və'sektəmɪ/ *n* (*pl* -mies) simple surgical operation to make a man sterile.

vas·eline /'væsəliːn/ *n* [U] (P) yellowish substance, petroleum jelly, almost without taste or smell, used as an ointment or lubricant.

vas·sal /'væsl/ *n* (hist) person who held land in return for which he vowed to give military service to the owner of the land; feudal tenant; (fig) humble dependant: (attrib) *a* ∼ *state*, one subject to another. '∼·**age** /-səlɪdʒ/ *n* [U] state of being a ∼; servitude.

vast /vɑːst US: væst/ *adj* immense; extensive: ∼ *sums of money; a* ∼ *expanse of desert*. ∼·**ly** *adv* ∼·**ness** *n*

vat /væt/ *n* tank or great vessel for holding liquids, esp in distilling, brewing, dyeing and tanning.

Vati·can /'vætɪkən/ *n* **the** ∼, the residence in Rome of the Pope; centre of Papal government.

vaude·ville /'vɔːdəvɪl/ *n* [U] (US) =variety(5).

vault[1] /vɔːlt/ *n* **1** arched roof; series of arches forming a roof. ⊏> the illus at crypt. **2** underground room or cellar (with or without an arched roof) as a place of storage ('*wine-*∼*s*), or for burials (eg under a church, or in a cemetery), or for safe-keeping of valuables: *keep one's jewels in the* ∼ *at the bank*. **3** ∼-like covering: (poet) *the* ∼ *of heaven*, the sky. ∼**ed** *adj* built with, having, a ∼ or ∼s; in the form of a ∼: *a* ∼*ed roof/chamber*.

vault[2] /vɔːlt/ *vi,vt* [VP2A,B,C,6A] jump in a single movement, with the hand(s) resting on sth, or with the help of a pole: ∼ (*over*) *a fence. The jockey* ∼*ed into the saddle*. '∼·**ing-horse** *n* apparatus for practice in ∼ing. □ *n* jump made in this way. ∼·**er** *n* person who ∼s.

vaunt /vɔːnt/ *vi,vt, n* (liter) boast. ∼·**er** *n* ∼·**ing·ly** *adv*

veal /viːl/ *n* [U] flesh of a calf as food.

veer /vɪə(r)/ *vi* [VP2A,C] (esp of the wind, fig of opinion, talk) change direction: *The wind* ∼*ed round to the north*.

veg·etable /'vedʒtəbl/ *adj* of, from, relating to, plants or plant life: *the* ∼ *kingdom;* ∼ *oils*. □ *n* [C] plant, esp of the sort used for food, eg potatoes, cabbages, beans, onions, carrots, etc.

veg·etar·ian /ˌvedʒɪ'teərɪən/ *n* person who, for humane or religious reasons or for his health's sake, eats no meat: (attrib) *a* ∼ *diet;* ∼ *principles*.

veg·etate /'vedʒɪteɪt/ *vi* [VP2A] live as plants do, without mental effort or intellectual interests; lead a dull life with little activity or interest.

veg·eta·tion /ˌvedʒɪ'teɪʃn/ *n* [U] plants generally and collectively: *the luxuriant* ∼ *of the tropical forests; a desert landscape with no sign of* ∼ *anywhere*.

ve·he·ment /'viːəmənt/ *adj* **1** (of feelings) strong, eager; (of persons, their speech, behaviour, etc) filled with, showing, strong or eager feeling: *a man of* ∼ *character;* ∼ *desires/passions*. **2** violent: *a* ∼ *wind*. ∼·**ly** *adv* **ve·he·mence** /-məns/ *n*

ve·hicle /'viːɪkl/ *n* [C] **1** any conveyance (usu wheeled, eg a cart, lorry, motor-car, but also a sledge) for goods or passengers on land. Cf *craft* for water, space. **2** means by which thought, feeling, etc can be conveyed: *Art may be used as a* ∼ *for/of propaganda*. **ve·hicu·lar** /vɪ'hɪkjʊlə(r)/ *adj* related to, consisting of, conveyed by, ∼s: *The road is closed to vehicular traffic*.

veil /veɪl/ *n* [C] **1** covering of fine net or other material to protect or hide a woman's face, or as part of a headdress: *She raised/dropped/lowered her* ∼. **take the** ∼, become a nun. **2** (fig) sth that hides or disguises: *a* ∼ *of mist; commit murder un-*

der the ~ *of patriotism,* do so under the pretence of patriotism. *draw a* ~ *over sth,* be discreet or secretive about: *Let us draw a* ~ *over what followed.* □ *vt* [VP6A] put a ~ over; (fig) conceal: *Some Muslim women are* ~*ed. He could not* ~ *his distrust.* ~*·ing n* [U] light material used for making ~s; such material used as a ~.

vein /veɪn/ *n* **1** blood-vessel along which blood flows from all parts of the body to the heart. ⇨ the illus at respiratory. ⇨ artery(1). **2** one of the ~-like lines in some leaves or in the wings of some insects; a coloured line or streak in some kinds of stone, eg marble; (fig): *There is a* ~ *of melancholy in his character.* **3** crack or fissure in rock, filled with mineral or ore; lode or seam: *a* ~ *of gold.* **4** mood; train of thought: *in a merry/melancholic/imaginative* ~. *He writes humorous songs when he is in the (right)* ~. ~**ed** /veɪnd/ *adj* having, marked with, ~s: ~*ed marble.*

veld /velt/ *n* [U] flat, treeless grassland of the S African plateau. ⇨ pampas, prairie, savannah, steppe.

vel·lum /ˈveləm/ *n* [U] parchment.

vel·oci·pede /vɪˈlɒsɪpiːd/ *n* early kind of bicycle with pedals on the front wheel; (US) child's tricycle.

vel·oc·ity /vɪˈlɒsətɪ/ *n* [U] **1** speed; quickness. **2** rate of motion: *at the* ~ *of sound;* '*muzzle* ~, the speed of a bullet as it leaves the muzzle of a gun.

ve·lour /vəˈlʊə(r)/ *n* [U] fabric like velvet or felt.

vel·vet /ˈvelvɪt/ *n* [U] cloth with a thick soft nap (⇨ nap²) on one side: (attrib) *a* ~ *frock; a* ~ *tread,* (fig) soft and quiet. *an iron hand in a* ~ *glove,* ruthlessness concealed by good manners, soft speech, etc. ~**·een** /ˌvelvɪˈtiːn/ *n* [U] cheap type of ~. **vel·vety** *adj* smooth and soft like ~.

ve·nal /ˈviːnl/ *adj* **1** (of persons) ready to do sth dishonest (eg using influence or position) for money: ~ *judges/politicians.* **2** (of conduct) influenced by, done for, (possible) payment: ~ *practices.* ~**ly** /-nəlɪ/ *adv* ~**·ity** /vɪˈnælətɪ/ *n* quality of being ~.

vend /vend/ *vt* [VP6A] (chiefly legal) sell; offer for sale (esp small wares). '~**·ing machine,** coin-operated slot machine for the sale of small articles, eg cigarettes and food. ~**er,** ~**or** /-də(r)/ *nn* seller: '*newsvendor,* seller of newspapers.

ven·detta /venˈdetə/ *n* hereditary feud between families in which members of each family commit murders in revenge for previous murders.

ve·neer /vəˈnɪə(r)/ *n* **1** [C,U] (thin layer of) fine quality wood glued to the surface of cheaper wood (for furniture, etc). **2** (fig) surface appearance (of politeness, etc) covering the true nature: *a* ~ *of Western civilization.* □ *vt* [VP6A] put a ~ on: ~ *a deal desk with walnut.*

ven·er·able /ˈvenərəbl/ *adj* **1** deserving respect because of age, character, associations, etc: *a* ~

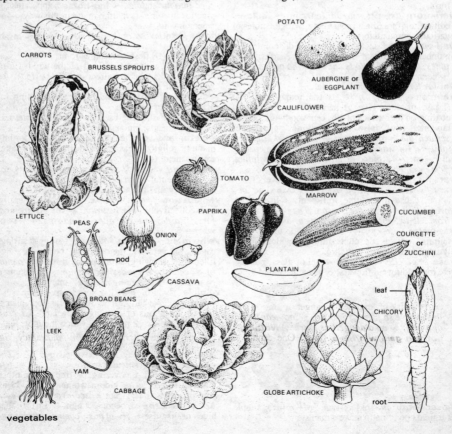

POTATO
CARROTS
BRUSSELS SPROUTS
AUBERGINE or EGGPLANT
CAULIFLOWER
TOMATO
MARROW
CUCUMBER
LETTUCE
PAPRIKA
PEAS
ONION
pod
COURGETTE or ZUCCHINI
CASSAVA
PLANTAIN
BROAD BEANS
leaf
CHICORY
LEEK
YAM
CABBAGE
GLOBE ARTICHOKE
root

vegetables

scholar; the ~ *ruins of the abbey.* **2** (Church of England) title of an archdeacon; (Church of Rome) title of a person in process of being canonized.

ven·er·ate /'venəreɪt/ *vt* [VP6A] regard with deep respect: *They* ~ *the old man's memory.* **ven·er·ation** /ˌvenə'reɪʃn/ *n*

ve·nereal /və'nɪərɪəl/ *adj* of, communicated by, sexual contact: ~ *disease*, (abbr **VD**).

Ve·ne·tian /və'niːʃn/ *adj* of Venice. ~ **blind**, window screen made of many horizontal strips (slats of wood or plastic material) that can be adjusted to let in light and air as desired.

ven·geance /'vendʒəns/ *n* [U] **1** revenge; the return of injury for injury: *seek* ~ *upon sb* (*for an injury*); *take* ~ *on an enemy.* **2** *with a* ~, (colloq) thoroughly; to a greater degree than is normal, expected or desired: *The rain came down with a* ~.

venge·ful /'vendʒfl/ *adj* showing a desire for revenge; vindictive.

ve·nial /'viːnɪəl/ *adj* (of a sin, error, fault) excusable; not serious.

ven·ison /'venɪzn/ *n* [U] deer meat.

venom /'venəm/ *n* [U] poisonous fluid of certain snakes; (fig) hate; spite. ~**ed** /'venəmd/ *adj* (fig) full of malice or hate: ~*ed remarks.* ~**·ous** /'venəməs/ *adj* deadly; spiteful: ~*ous snakes/ criticism.* ~**·ous·ly** *adv*

ve·nous /'viːnəs/ *adj* **1** of the veins: ~ *blood*, (contrasted with arterial blood). **2** (bot) having veins: *a* ~ *leaf.*

vent /vent/ *n* **1** hole serving as an inlet or outlet for air, gas, liquid, etc, eg a hole in the top of a barrel, for air to enter as liquid is drawn out. '~-**hole** *n* hole for the escape of air, smoke, etc. **2** (trade use) slit in the back of a coat or jacket. **3** means of escape: *The floods found a* ~ *through the dykes.* **4** (*sing* only) outlet for one's feelings. **give** ~ **to**, (fig) give free expression to: *He gave* ~ *to his feelings in an impassioned speech.* □ *vt* [VP6A,14] ~ *sth on sb/sth*, find or provide an outlet for: *He* ~*ed his ill-temper upon his long-suffering wife.*

ven·ti·late /'ventɪleɪt US: -təleɪt/ *vt* [VP6A] **1** cause air to move freely through: ~ *a room/the galleries of a coalmine.* **2** (fig) make (a question, a grievance) widely known and cause it to be discussed. **ven·ti·la·tor** /'ventɪleɪtər US: -təl-/ *n* device for ventilating. **ven·ti·la·tion** /ˌventɪ'leɪʃn US: -tə'leɪʃn/ *n* [U] ventilating or being ~d: *the ventilation shaft of a coalmine.*

ven·tricle /'ventrɪkl/ *n* cavity in the body; hollow part of an organ, esp of the heart. ➪ the illus at respiratory.

ven·tril·oquism /ven'trɪləkwɪzəm/ *n* [U] art of producing voice-sounds so that they seem to come from a person or place at a distance from the speaker. **ven·tril·oquist** /-kwɪst/ *n* person skilled in ~.

ven·ture /'ventʃə(r)/ *n* [C,U] undertaking in which there is risk. □ *vt, vi* **1** [VP6A,15A,16A,3A] ~ (*on*), take the risk of, expose to, danger or loss: ~ *one's life to save sb from drowning;* ~ *too near the edge of a cliff;* ~ *on a dangerous journey. Nothing* ~, *nothing gain/win/have*, (prov) One cannot expect to achieve anything if one risks nothing. **2** [VP6A,7A] go so far as, presume, dare: ~ (*to put forward*) *an opinion;* ~ *a guess. I* ~ *to disagree/ to suggest that....* '**V**~ **Scout**, senior Scout. ~**some** /-səm/ *adj* **1** (of persons) ready to take risks; daring. **2** (of acts, behaviour) involving danger; risky. **ven·tur·ous** /'ventʃərəs/ *adj* = adventurous.

venue /'venjuː/ *n* rendezvous; meeting-place; (sport) place fixed for a contest or match.

Venus /'viːnəs/ *n* **1** (Roman myth) goddess of love and beauty. **2** (astron) planet second in order from the sun. ➪ the illus at planet.

ver·acious /və'reɪʃəs/ *adj* (formal) true; truthful. ~**·ly** *adv* **ver·ac·ity** /və'ræsətɪ/ *n* [U] truth; truthfulness.

ve·ran·da(h) /və'rændə/ *n* roofed and floored open space along the side(s) of a house, sports pavilion, etc (US often called *porch*).

verb /vɜːb/ *n* word or phrase indicating what sb or sth does, what state sb or sth is in, what is becoming of sth or sb.

ver·bal /'vɜːbl/ *adj* **1** of or in words: *a* ~ *error;* *have a good* ~ *memory*, be able to remember well the exact words of a statement, etc. **2** spoken, not written: *a* ~ *statement/explanation.* **3** word for word, literal: *a* ~ *translation.* **4** of verbs: *a* ~ *noun* (eg *swimming* in the sentence 'Swimming is a good exercise'). ~**·ly** /'vɜːbəlɪ/ *adv* in spoken words, not in writing.

ver·bal·ize /'vɜːbəlaɪz/ *vt* put into words.

ver·ba·tim /vɜː'beɪtɪm/ *adv, adj* word for word, exactly as spoken or written: *rep·rt a speech* ~*; a* ~ *report.*

ver·bena /vɜː'biːnə/ *n* kinds of herbaceous plant of which garden varieties have flowers of many colours.

ver·bi·age /'vɜːbɪdʒ/ *n* [U] (use of) unnecessary words for the expression of an idea, etc: *The speaker lost himself in* ~.

ver·bose /vɜː'bəʊs/ *adj* using, containing, more words than are needed: *a* ~ *speech/speaker/style.* ~**·ly** *adv* ~**·ness**, **ver·bos·ity** /vɜː'bɒsətɪ/ *nn* [U] state or quality of being ~.

ver·dant /'vɜːdnt/ *adj* **1** (liter) (esp of grass, vegetation, fields) fresh and green: ~ *lawns.* **2** (fig) inexperienced; unsophisticated. **ver·dancy** /-dnsɪ/ *n*

ver·dict /'vɜːdɪkt/ *n* [C] **1** decision reached by a jury on a question of fact in a law case: *The jury brought in* (= announced) *a* ~ *of guilty/not guilty.* **open** ~, ➪ open ¹(6). **2** decision or opinion given after testing, examining, or experiencing sth: *the* ~ *of the electors. The popular* ~ (= The opinion of people in general) *was that it served him right.*

ver·di·gris /'vɜːdɪgrɪs/ *n* [U] green substance formed on copper, brass and bronze surfaces (as rust is formed on iron surfaces).

ver·dure /'vɜːdʒə(r)/ *n* [U] (liter) (fresh green colour of) growing vegetation: *the* ~ *of* (*the trees in*) *spring.*

Verey /'verɪ/ *adj* '~ **light**, ➪ Very.

verge /vɜːdʒ/ *n* **1** [C] edge; border (eg strip of ground at the side of a road, grass edge of a lawn). **2** *be on the* ~ *of*; *bring* (*sb*) *to the* ~ *of*, very close to, on the border of: *The country is on the* ~ *of disaster. She was brought to the* ~ *of bursting into tears.* □ *vi* [VP3A] ~ *on/upon*, approach closely, border upon: *verge on bankruptcy. Such ideas* ~ *on foolhardiness.*

verger /'vɜːdʒə(r)/ *n* **1** (C of E) official with various duties (eg showing people to their seats). **2** officer who carries a staff before a bishop in a cathedral, a vice-chancellor in a university, etc.

ver·ify /'verɪfaɪ/ *vt* (*pt, pp* -fied) [VP6A] **1** test the truth or accuracy of: ~ *a report/statement;* ~ *the figures/details of a report.* **2** (of an event, etc) show the truth of; bear out: *Subsequent events verified my suspicions.* **veri·fi·able** /'verɪfaɪəbl/ *adj* that can be verified. **veri·fi·ca·tion** /ˌverɪfɪ'keɪʃn/ *n* ~ing or being verified; proof or evidence.

ver·ily /'verəlɪ/ *adv* (archaic) really; truly.

veri·si·mili·tude /ˌverɪsɪ'mɪlɪtjuːd *US:* -tuːd/ *n* [U] appearance, semblance, of truth; [C] sth that seems to be true.

veri·table /'verɪtəbl/ *adj* real; rightly named.

ver·ity /'verətɪ/ *n* (*pl* -ties) **1** [U] (old use) truth (*of a statement, etc*). **2** [C] sth that really exists; true statement. *the eternal verities*, fundamental moral principles; laws of God.

ver·mi·celli /ˌvɜːmɪ'selɪ/ *n* [U] paste of white flour made into long slender threads, like spaghetti but much thinner.

ver·mi·form /'vɜːmɪfɔːm/ *adj* worm-like in shape: *the ~ appendix.* ⇨ the illus at **alimentary**.

ver·mil·ion /və'mɪlɪən/ *adj, n* bright red (colour).

ver·min /'vɜːmɪn/ *n* [U] (with *pl v,* but not with numerals) **1** wild animals (eg rats, weasels, foxes) harmful to plants, birds and other animals. **2** parasitic insects (eg lice) sometimes found on the bodies of human beings and other animals. **3** human beings who are harmful to society; persons who prey on others. **~·ous** /-əs/ *adj* **1** infested with fleas, lice, etc: *~ous children.* **2** caused by insect ~: *~ous diseases.*

ver·mouth /'vɜːməθ *US:* vər'muːθ/ *n* [U] fortified white wine flavoured with herbs, drunk as an aperitif (often in cocktails).

ver·nacu·lar /və'nækjʊlə(r)/ *adj* (of a word, a language) of the country in question: *the ~ newspapers in India,* those in the various languages (except English) of India; *a ~ poet,* one who uses a ~ language. □ *n* [C] language or dialect of a country or district: *the ~s of the USA.*

ver·nal /'vɜːnl/ *adj* (liter) of, in, as in, the season of spring. *the ~ equinox,* about 21st March.

ve·ron·ica /və'rɒnɪkə/ *n* kinds of herb or shrub with blue, purple, pink or white flowers.

ver·ruca /və'ruːkə/ *n* small, hard growth on the skin (usu on the bottom of the feet); wart.

ver·sa·tile /'vɜːsətaɪl *US:* -tl/ *adj* interested in and clever at many different things; having various uses: *a ~ inventor; a ~ mind; a ~ tool.* **ver·sa·til·ity** /ˌvɜːsə'tɪlətɪ/ *n*

verse /vɜːs/ *n* **1** [U] (form of) writing arranged in lines, each conforming to a pattern of accented and unaccented syllables: *prose and ~; written in ~; a ~ translation of Homer's 'Odyssey'; blank ~,* without rhymes at the end of the lines. **2** [C] group of lines of this kind forming a unit in a rhyme scheme: *a poem/hymn of five ~s.* **3** [C] one line of (a) ~ with a definite number of feet or accented syllables: *quote a few ~s from Tennyson.* **4** one of the short numbered divisions of a chapter in the Bible. *give chapter and ~ (for sth),* supply the exact reference (for a statement, an authority one quotes, reports, etc).

versed /vɜːst/ *adj* **~ in,** skilled or experienced in: *well ~ in mathematics/the arts.* ⇨ *conversant with* at **conversant**.

ver·sify /'vɜːsɪfaɪ/ *vt, vi* (*pt, pp* -fied) [VP6A] put into verse: *~ an old legend;* [VP2A] write verses. **ver·si·fier** *n* maker of verses. **ver·si·fi·ca·tion** /ˌvɜːsɪfɪ'keɪʃn/ *n* [U] art of ~ing; style in which verse is written; metre.

ver·sion /'vɜːʃn *US:* -ʒn/ *n* [C] **1** account of an event, etc from the point of view of one person:

There were contradictory ~s of what happened/of what the Prime Minister said. **2** translation into another language: *a new ~ of the Bible.*

verso /'vɜːsəʊ/ *n* (*pl* ~s /-səʊz/) any left-hand page of a book (opp of *recto*); reverse side of a medal or coin.

ver·sus /'vɜːsəs/ *prep* (Lat) (in law and sport; often shortened to **v** or **vs** in print) against: (legal) *Robinson v Brown;* (cricket) *Kent vs Surrey.*

ver·te·bra /'vɜːtɪbrə/ *n* (*pl* ~e /-briː/) any one of the segments of the backbone. ⇨ the illus at **skeleton**. **ver·te·brate** /'vɜːtɪbreɪt/ *n, adj* (animal, bird, etc) having a backbone.

ver·tex /'vɜːteks/ *n* (*pl* vertices /-tɪsiːz/) highest point; top; point of a triangle, cone, etc opposite the base.

ver·ti·cal /'vɜːtɪkl/ *adj* (of a line or plane) at a right angle to the earth's surface or to another line or plane: *a ~ cliff; a ~ take-off aircraft,* one that can rise ~ly, not needing a runway. ⇨ horizontal. □ *n ~ line: out of the ~,* not ~. **~·ly** /-klɪ/ *adv*

ver·tices /'vɜːtɪsiːz/ *n pl* ⇨ vertex.

ver·tigo /'vɜːtɪgəʊ/ *n* [U] (formal) dizziness. **ver·ti·gin·ous** /vɜː'tɪdʒɪnəs/ *adj* of, causing, ~.

verve /vɜːv/ *n* [U] enthusiasm, spirit, vigour.

very[1] /'verɪ/ *attrib adj* **1** itself and no other; truly such: *This is the ~ thing I want! At that ~ moment the phone rang. You're the ~ man I want to see.* **2** extreme: *at the ~ end/beginning.* **3** (equivalent to an emphatic or intensive *pron* ending in *-self* or *-selves*): *He knows our ~ thoughts,* ie our thoughts themselves, even our innermost thoughts. *The ~ idea of being sent abroad* (ie the idea alone, quite apart from the reality) *delighted him.*

very[2] /'verɪ/ *adv* **1** (used intensively with *advv, adjj* and *part adjj*): *~ quickly/carefully/soon, etc; ~ much/little; ~ amusing/interesting, etc; ~ small/ cold/useful, etc.* (Note that when the *pp* is part of a passive *v* phrase, *much* or *very much* is preferred; when the *pp* is the complement of *be, seem, feel, ~* is used): *I wasn't much surprised at the news. He wasn't much interested in the news.* Cf *He was/ seemed ~ interested.* **~ well,** often used to indicate agreement or assent (often after persuasion or argument, or in obedience to a command, request, etc): *V~ well, doctor, I'll give up smoking. Oh, ~ well, if you insist.* **2** (with a superl, or *own*) in the highest possible degree: *the ~ best quality; the ~ first to arrive; six o'clock at the ~ latest. You can keep this for your ~ own.*

Very, Verey /'verɪ/ *adj* '~ **light,** (P) coloured signal flare fired from a '~ *pistol,* eg as a signal of distress from a ship.

ves·icle /'vesɪkl/ *n* (anat) small cavity, cyst or swelling. **ves·icu·lar** /və'sɪkjʊlə(r)/ *adj* of ~s: *vesicular disease.*

ves·pers /'vespəz/ *n pl* church service in the evening; evensong.

vessel /'vesl/ *n* [C] **1** hollow receptacle, esp for a liquid, eg a cask, tub, bucket, bowl, bottle, cup. **2** ship or large boat. **3** ⇨ *blood~* at **blood**[1](7).

vest[1] /vest/ *n* [C] **1** (GB) garment worn under a shirt, blouse, etc next to the skin. **2** (trade use in GB; ordinary use in US) short, sleeveless garment worn by men under a jacket (*waistcoat* being the usual name in GB): *coat, ~ and trousers; a ~-pocket* (ie very small) *camera.*

vest[2] /vest/ *vt, vi* **1** [VP14] **~ sth in sb; ~ sb with sth,** furnish or give as a fixed right: *~ a man with authority/rights in an estate. In some countries* *authority is said to be* ~*ed in the people,* ie the people possess final authority on matters of government, etc. *In the United States, Congress is* ~*ed with the power to declare war.* **have a** ~**ed interest in sth,** be likely to gain or lose from it, or be affected in some way by it. ~**ed interests/ rights,** (eg in trade or manufacture) which are by law securely in the possession of a person or a group of persons. **2** [VP3A] ~ *in,* (of property, etc) be ~ed in: *power/authority that* ~*s in the Crown.* **3** [VP6A] (poet or eccles) clothe.

ves·tal /'vestl/ *n* ~ **(virgin),** one of the maidens dedicated to the service of the goddess Vesta in ancient Rome, vowed to chastity. □ *adj* (liter) pure; chaste.

ves·ti·bule /'vestɪbjuːl/ *n* **1** lobby or entrance hall to a building (eg where hats and coats may be left). **2** porch of a church. **3** (US) enclosed space at the end of a railway coach.

ves·tige /'vestɪdʒ/ *n* [C] **1** trace or sign; small remaining bit of evidence of what once existed: *Not a* ~ *of the abbey remains. There is not a* ~ *of truth in the report.* **2** (anat) organ, or part of one, which is a survival of sth that once existed: *A human being has the* ~ *of a tail.* **ves·tigial** /ve'stɪdʒɪəl/ *adj* remaining as a ~.

vest·ment /'vestmənt/ *n* garment, esp one worn by a priest in church; ceremonial robe.

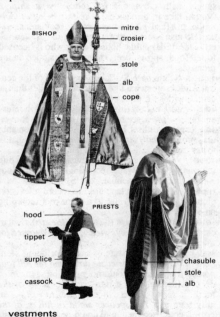

BISHOP

mitre
crosier
stole
alb
cope

PRIESTS

hood
tippet
surplice
cassock

chasuble
stole
alb

vestments

ves·try /'vestrɪ/ *n* (*pl* -tries) **1** part of a church where vestments are kept and where the clergy and members of the choir vest themselves. ⇨ the illus at **church. 2** room in a nonconformist church used for Sunday School, prayer meetings, business meetings, etc. **3** (Anglican Church) (council of) ratepayers of a parish, or their representatives, assembled to discuss parish business. '~·**man** /-mən/ *n* (*pl*-men) member of a ~.

ves·ture /'vestʃə(r)/ *n* (poet) clothing. □ *vt* clothe.

vet /vet/ *n* (colloq abbr for) veterinary surgeon. □ *vt*

(-tt-) [VP6A] (colloq) **1** give (sb) a medical examination. **2** (GB) examine closely and critically, eg sb's past record, qualifications, etc: *He must be thoroughly vetted before he's given the job.*

vetch /vetʃ/ *n* kinds of plant of the bean family used, wild or cultivated, as fodder for cattle.

vet·eran /'vetərən/ *n* **1** person who has had much or long experience, esp as a soldier: ~*s of two World Wars;* (attrib) *a* ~ *teacher;* (of cars) of the years before 1916: *a* ~ *Rolls Royce.* **2** (US) any ex-service man. '**V**~**s Day,** 11th November, commemorating the armistice (1918) in World War I.

vet·erin·ary /'vetrɪnrɪ US: 'vetərɪnerɪ/ *adj* (abbr **vet** /vet/) of or concerned with the diseases of (esp farm and domestic) animals: *a* ~ *surgeon/college.*

veto /'viːtəʊ/ *n* (*pl* ~es) constitutional right of a sovereign, president, legislative assembly or other body, or a member of the United Nations Security Council, to reject or forbid sth; statement that rejects or prohibits sth: *exercise the* ~*; put a* ~ *on sth,* forbid it. □ *vt* [VP6A] put a ~ on: *The police* ~*ed the demonstration that the students wanted. John's parents* ~*ed his plan to buy a motor-cycle.*

vex /veks/ *vt* [VP6A] **1** annoy; distress; trouble: *His silly chatter would vex a saint. She was vexed that I didn't help her. He was vexed at his failure.* **a vexed question,** a difficult problem that causes much discussion. **2** (poet, rhet) put (the sea) into commotion: *vexed by storms.* **vex·ation** /vek'seɪʃn/ *n* [U] state of being vexed; [C] sth that vexes: *the little vexations of life; constant vexations from our neighbours.* **vex·atious** /vek'seɪʃəs/ *adj* annoying: *vexatious rules and regulations.*

via /'vaɪə/ *prep* (Lat) by way of: *travel from London to Paris via Dover.*

vi·able /'vaɪəbl/ *adj* able to exist; capable of developing and surviving without outside help: *Is the newly created State* ~*?* **vi·abil·ity** /ˌvaɪə'bɪlətɪ/ *n*

vi·aduct /'vaɪədʌkt/ *n* long bridge (usu with many spans or arches) carrying a road or railway across a valley or dip in the ground.

vial /'vaɪəl/ *n* small bottle, esp for liquid medicine.

via media /ˌvaɪə 'miːdɪə/ (Lat) middle course between extremes.

vibes /vaɪbz/ *n pl* **1** (colloq abbr for) **vibraphone.** **2** (sl) atmosphere(3).

vi·brant /'vaɪbrənt/ *adj* thrilling; vibrating: *the* ~ *notes of a cello/an electric guitar.*

vi·bra·phone /'vaɪbrəfəʊn/ *n* (music) instrument like a xylophone but with metal bars and tone sustained by electronic resonators.

vi·brate /vaɪ'breɪt US: 'vaɪbreɪt/ *vi, vt* **1** [VP2A,6A] (cause to) move rapidly and continuously backwards and forwards: *The house* ~*s whenever a heavy lorry passes.* **2** [VP2A,C] (of stretched strings, the voice) throb; quiver: *The strings of a piano* ~ *when the keys are struck. His voice* ~*d with passion.* **vi·brator** /-tə(r)/ *n* device that ~s.

vi·bra·tion /vaɪ'breɪʃn/ *n* **1** [U] vibrating movement: *The ship's engines even at full speed cause very little* ~. **2** [C] single movement to and fro when equilibrium has been disturbed: *20* ~*s per second.*

vi·brato /vɪ'brɑːtəʊ/ *n* (music) throbbing or tremulous effect in singing and the playing of stringed and wind instruments with minute and rapid variations in pitch.

vicar /'vɪkə(r)/ *n* **1** (C of E) clergyman in charge of a parish, the tithes of which were partly or wholly payable to another person or body (eg a college) for whom or for which the ∼ acts. ⇨ rector. **2** (RC Church) deputy; representative: *the* ∼ *of Christ,* (sometimes used of) the Pope; *cardinal* ∼, Pope's delegate acting as the bishop of the diocese of Rome. ∼**·age** /'vɪkərɪdʒ/ *n* ∼'s residence.

vi·cari·ous /vɪ'keərɪəs *US:* vaɪ'k-/ *adj* **1** done, undergone, by one person for another or others: *the* ∼ *sufferings of Jesus; a* ∼ *ruler; feel a* ∼ *pleasure/ satisfaction,* eg when sth is done for you or which is sth you would like to do. **2** deputed; delegated: ∼ *authority.* ∼**·ly** *adv*

vice¹ /vaɪs/ *n* [C,U] **1** (any particular kind of) evil conduct or indulgence in depraving practices: *Gluttony is just as much a* ∼ *as drunkenness.* **2** (in a horse) bad habit (eg kicking) which makes control difficult: *He said the horse was free from* ∼/ *had no* ∼*s.*

vice² (*US* = **vise**) /vaɪs/ *n* [C] apparatus with strong jaws in which things can be held tightly while being worked upon: *as firm as a* ∼, immovable.

a vice

vice³ /vaɪs/ *n* (colloq abbr for) vice-president, vice-captain, etc.

vice⁴ /vaɪs/ *prep* (Lat) (formal) in place of: *Mr Smith has been appointed chief accountant* ∼ *Mr Brown, who has retired.*

vice- *pref* ⇨ App 3.

viceroy /'vaɪsrɔɪ/ *n* (eg formerly in India) person governing as the deputy of a sovereign. **vice-reine** /vaɪs'reɪn *US:* 'vaɪsreɪn/ *n* ∼'s wife. **vice-regal** /vaɪs'riːgl/ *adj* of a ∼.

vice versa /,vaɪsɪ 'vɜːsə/ *adv* (Lat) the other way round; with the terms or conditions reversed: *We gossip about them and* ∼, they gossip about us.

vi·cin·ity /vɪ'sɪnətɪ/ *n* (*pl* -ties) **1** [U] nearness; closeness of relationship: *in close* ∼ *to the church.* **2** [C] neighbourhood: *the northern vicinities of the capital. There isn't a good school in the* ∼.

vi·cious /'vɪʃəs/ *adj* **1** of vice¹; given up to vice¹: ∼ *practices/habits; a* ∼ *life.* **2** spiteful; given or done with evil intent: *a* ∼ *kick/look.* **3** (of a horse) having bad habits such as biting, kicking, bolting. **4** having faults, corrupt: *a* ∼ *argument.* ∼ **'circle,** state of affairs in which a cause produces an effect which itself produces the original cause, eg War breeds hate, and hate leads to war again. ∼ **'spiral,** continuous rise in one thing (eg prices) caused by a continuous rise in sth else (eg wages). ∼**·ly** *adv* ∼**·ness** *n*

vi·ciss·itude /vɪ'sɪsɪtjuːd *US:* -tuːd/ *n* [C] change, esp in sb's fortunes: *His life was marked by* ∼*s,* eg changes from wealth to poverty, success to failure.

vic·tim /'vɪktɪm/ *n* **1** living creature killed and of-

fered as a religious sacrifice. **2** person, animal, etc suffering injury, pain, loss, etc because of circumstances, an event, the ill-will of sb, etc: *He is the* ∼ *of his brother's anger/of his own foolishness. A fund was opened to help the* ∼*s of the earthquake. Thousands were* ∼*s of the plague in the Middle Ages.* ∼**·ize** /-aɪz/ *vt* [VP6A] make a ∼ of; single out for ill treatment because of real or alleged misconduct, etc: *Trade union leaders claimed that some of their members had been* ∼*ized,* eg by being dismissed. ∼**·iz·ation** /ˌvɪktɪmaɪ'zeɪʃn *US:* -mɪ'z-/ *n: The strikers said they would return to work if they were promised that there should be no* ∼*ization,* that none of their leaders (or ringleaders) should be ∼ized.

vic·tor /'vɪktə(r)/ *n* person who conquers or wins.

vic·toria /vɪk'tɔːrɪə/ *n* ∼ **plum,** juicy, sweetflavoured plum, changing from green to yellow and red.

Vic·tor·ian /vɪk'tɔːrɪən/ *n, adj* (person) of, living in, the reign of Queen Victoria (1837—1901): ∼ *authors/manners/dress.*

vic·tory /'vɪktərɪ/ *n* [C,U] (*pl* -ries) (instance, occasion, of) success (in war, a contest, game, etc): *gain/win a* ∼ *over the enemy; lead the troops to* ∼; triumphant. **vic·tori·ous** /vɪk'tɔːrɪəs/ *adj* having gained the ∼; triumphant. **vic·tori·ous·ly** *adv*

vict·ual /'vɪtl/ *vt,vi* (-ll-; *US* also -l-) **1** [VP6A] supply with provisions (of food): ∼ *a ship.* **2** [VP2A] take in provisions: *The ship* ∼*led at Colombo.* □ *n* (usu *pl*) food and drink; provisions. ∼**·ler** (*US* also ∼**·er**) /'vɪtlə(r)/ *n* trader in ∼s. **licensed** ∼**·ler,** (GB) public house keeper who is licensed to sell food, spirits, beer, etc to be consumed on the premises.

vi·cuña /vɪ'kjuːnə *US:* -'kuːnə/ *n* animal of the central Andes somewhat like, but much smaller than, a camel, with soft, delicate wool.

vide /'vaɪdɪ/ *v* (Lat) (imperative form used in references). ∼ **'infra,** see below. ∼ **'supra,** see above.

vide·licet /vɪ'diːlɪset *US:* -'del-/ *adv* (common abbr **viz,** pronounced /vɪz/ or spoken as *namely*) that is to say; namely.

video /'vɪdɪəʊ/ *n adj* **1** of television broadcasting (cf *audio*). **2** of ∼**tape** recording. □ *n* **1** (colloq) ∼**tape** recording machine. **2** (US) television. '∼**tape** *n* [U] magnetic tape used to record television pictures and sound. □ *vt* VP6A] make a recording on ∼tape.

vie /vaɪ/ *vi* [VP3A] **vie (with sb) (for sth),** rival or compete: *The two boys vied with one another for the first place.*

view¹ /vjuː/ *n* **1** [U] state of seeing or being seen: field of vision: *Clouds came down and the hill tops passed from our* ∼, *could no longer be seen. in* ∼ *of,* considering, taking into account: *In* ∼ *of the facts, it seems useless to continue. in full* ∼ *of,* fully seen by: *The speaker stood in full* ∼ *of the crowd,* could see them and could be seen by them. *on* ∼, being shown or exhibited: *The latest summer fashions are now on* ∼ *in the big shops. come into* ∼, become visible: *As we rounded the bend the lake came into* ∼. *come in* ∼ *of,* be able to see: *As we rounded the bend, we came in* ∼ *of the lake.* **2** [C] (picture, photograph, etc of) natural scenery, landscape, etc: *a house with fine* ∼*s over valleys and mountains; an album of* ∼*s,* eg photographs. **3** [C] opportunity to see or inspect sth; occasion when there is such an opportunity: *a private* ∼, eg of paintings, before public exhibition. **4** [C] personal opinion; mental attitude; thought or observation (on a subject): *She had/expressed strong ~s on the subject of equal pay for men and women. Your ~s on the situation are not helpful. He holds extreme ~s,* eg in politics. *He took a poor ~ of my conduct,* regarded it unfavourably. **fall in with/ meet sb's ~s,** agree with, accept, his ideas, opinions, etc. **5** aim; intention; purpose. **with a/the ~ to/of,** with the intention or hope: *with a ~ to facilitating research; with the ~ of saving trouble.* **6** (compounds) '**~·point, point of ~,** ⇨ point¹(4). '**~·finder** *n* device in a camera showing the area, etc that will be photographed through the lens.

view² /vjuː/ *vt* [VP6A] look at; examine; consider: *The subject may be ~ed in various ways. Has the matter been ~ed from the taxpayers' standpoint?* **an order to ~,** written authority to look over a house, etc with the idea of buying it: *The house agents gave me an order to ~.* **~·er** /'vjuːə(r)/ *n* (esp) **1** person watching a television programme. **2** device for looking at photographic transparencies. **~·less** *adj* **1** (rhet or poet) invisible. **2** (US) without ~s (= opinions).

vigil /'vɪdʒɪl/ *n* **1** [U] staying awake to keep watch or to pray: *keep ~ over a sick child;* (*pl*) instances of this: *tired out by her long ~s.* **2** eve of a religious festival, esp when observed with prayer and fasting.

vigi·lance /'vɪdʒɪləns/ *n* [U] watchfulness; keeping watch: *exercise ~.* '**~ committee,** (chiefly US) self-appointed group of persons who maintain order in a community where organization is imperfect or has broken down.

vigi·lant /'vɪdʒɪlənt/ *adj* watchful; on the look-out for danger of any kind. **~·ly** *adv*

vigi·lante /,vɪdʒɪ'læntɪ/ *n* member of a vigilance committee.

vi·gnette /viː'njet/ *n* [C] **1** ornamental design, esp on the title-page of a book, or at the beginning or end of a chapter. **2** picture of a person's head and shoulders with the background gradually shaded off. **3** short sketch of a person's character.

vig·our (US = **vigor**) /'vɪgə(r)/ *n* [U] mental or physical strength; energy; forcefulness (of language). **vig·or·ous** /'vɪgərəs/ *adj* strong; energetic. **vig·or·ous·ly** *adv*

Vik·ing /'vaɪkɪŋ/ *n* any of the Scandinavian sea-rovers who raided the coasts of Europe during the 8th, 9th and 10th cc.

vile /vaɪl/ *adj* (-r, -st) **1** shameful and disgusting: *~ habits/language; the ~ practice of bribery.* **2** (colloq) bad: *~ weather.* **3** (old use) valueless: *this ~ body,* ie contrasted with the soul or spirit. **~·ly** /'vaɪllɪ/ *adv* **~·ness** *n*

vil·ify /'vɪlɪfaɪ/ *vt* (*pt,pp* -fied) [VP6A] slander; say evil things about (sb). **vil·ifi·ca·tion** /,vɪlɪfɪ'keɪʃn/ *n*

villa /'vɪlə/ *n* **1** (in GB) (usu as part of the address) detached or semi-detached house or esp one on the outskirts of a town: *No 13 Laburnum Villas.* **2** country house with a large garden, esp in S Europe.

vil·lage /'vɪlɪdʒ/ *n* place smaller than a town, where there are houses and shops, and usu a church and school: (attrib) *the ~ post-office.* **vil·lager** /'vɪlɪdʒə(r)/ *n* person who lives in a ~.

vil·lain /'vɪlən/ *n* **1** wrongdoer; wicked person. **2** = villein. **~·ous** /'vɪlənəs/ *adj* characteristic of a ~; evil. **~·y** *n* (*pl* -nies) [U] evil conduct; (*pl*) evil acts.

vil·lein /'vɪleɪn/ *n* (hist) feudal serf in the Middle Ages. **~·age** /'vɪlnɪdʒ/ *n* [U] state of being a ~;

serfdom.

vim /vɪm/ *n* [U] (colloq) energy: *feel full of vim. Put more vim into it!*

vin·ai·grette /,vɪnɪ'gret/ *n* [U] dressing (for green salads, etc) of vinegar and oil, flavoured with herbs.

vin·di·cate /'vɪndɪkeɪt/ *vt* [VP6A] show or prove the truth, justice, validity, etc (of sth that has been attacked or disputed): *~ a claim/one's title to a privilege; ~ one's veracity/judgement. Events have ~d his judgement/actions.* **vin·di·ca·tion** /,vɪndɪ'keɪʃn/ *n* [U] vindicating or being ~d; [C] instance of this: *speak in vindication of one's conduct.*

vin·dic·tive /vɪn'dɪktɪv/ *adj* unforgiving; having or showing a desire for revenge. **~·ly** *adv* **~·ness** *n*

vine /vaɪn/ *n* [C] climbing plant whose fruit is the grape; any plant with slender stems that trails, eg melons, or climbs (eg peas, hops). **~·yard** /'vɪnjəd/ *n* [C] area of land planted with grape-~s.

vin·ery /'vaɪnərɪ/ *n* (*pl* -ries) greenhouse for ~s.

vin·egar /'vɪnɪgə(r)/ *n* [U] acid liquor (made from malt, wine, cider, etc) used in flavouring food and for pickling. **~·y** /'vɪnɪgərɪ/ *adj* like ~; (fig) sour-tempered.

vino /'viːnəʊ/ *n* (*pl* ~es /-nəʊz/) [U] (colloq) wine.

vi·nous /'vaɪnəs/ *adj* of, like or due to wine.

vin·tage /'vɪntɪdʒ/ *n* **1** (rarely *pl*) (period or season of) grape harvesting: *The ~ was later than usual last year.* **2** [C,U] (wine from) grapes of a particular year: *of the ~ of 1959; rare old ~s; a ~ year,* one in which good wine was made; *~ wines,* from ~ years. **3** (by extension; attrib) of a period in the past and having a reputation for high quality: *a ~ car,* one built between 1916 and 1930, ⇨ veteran; sports car more than 30 years old.

vint·ner /'vɪntnə(r)/ *n* wine-merchant.

vi·nyl /'vaɪnɪl/ *n* (kinds of) tough, flexible plastic, used for clothing, coverings and binding books.

viol /'vaɪəl/ *n* (usu six-)stringed instrument of the Middle Ages from which the modern violin was developed.

vi·ola¹ /vɪ'əʊlə/ *n* tenor violin, of larger size than the ordinary violin. ⇨ the illus at string.

vi·ola² /'vaɪələ/ *n* kinds of plant including pansies of one colour only (not variegated) and violets.

vi·ol·ate /'vaɪəleɪt/ *vt* [VP6A] **1** break (an oath, a treaty, etc); act contrary to (what one's conscience tells one to do, etc). **2** act towards (a sacred place, sb's seclusion, etc) without proper respect: *~ sb's privacy.* **3** rape. **vi·ol·ation** /,vaɪə'leɪʃn/ *n* [U] violating or being ~d: *act in violation of a treaty;* [C] instance of this: *violations of the rights of the citizens/the right of free speech, etc.*

vi·ol·ent /'vaɪələnt/ *adj* **1** using, showing, accompanied by, great force: *~ wind/attack; ~ blows; ~ passions; in a ~ temper; ~ abuse; a ~ (= extreme) contrast.* **2** caused by ~ attack: *meet a ~ death.* **3** severe: *~ toothache.* **~·ly** *adv* **vi·ol·ence** /-əns/ *n* [U] state of being ~; ~ conduct: *crimes/ acts of violence; robbery with violence; an outbreak of violence,* rioting, etc. **do violence to,** (fig) be a breach of: *It would do violence to his principles to eat meat.*

vi·olet /'vaɪələt/ *n* **1** [C] small wild or garden plant with sweet-smelling flowers. **2** [U] bluish-purple colour of wild ~s.

vi·olin /,vaɪə'lɪn/ *n* four-stringed musical instrument played with a bow, ⇨ the illus at string. **~-**

ist /-ɪst/ *n* player of a ∼.

vi·per /'vaɪpə(r)/ *n* kinds of poisonous snake of Africa, Asia, and Europe; (fig) spiteful and treacherous person. **the common** ∼, the adder (the only poisonous snake in GB).

vir·ago /vɪ'rɑːgəʊ/ *n* (*pl* ∼s or ∼es /-gəʊz/) violent and bad-tempered woman who scolds and shouts.

vir·gin /'vɜːdʒɪn/ *n* girl or woman (and in recent use, man) who has not experienced sexual union. **the (Blessed) V∼ (Mary),** (abbr **BVM**), the mother of Jesus Christ. □ *adj* **1** pure and chaste: *the V∼ Queen,* Elizabeth I of England. **the ∼ birth,** the doctrine that Jesus was miraculously conceived by the V∼ Mary. **2** pure and untouched: ∼ *snow.* **3** in the original condition; unused: *a ∼ forest,* one in its natural state, no trees having been felled, planted, etc; ∼ *soil,* soil never before used for crops; (fig) a mind open to receive new ideas. ∼**ity** /və'dʒɪnəti/ *n* [U] state of being a ∼; ∼ condition.

vir·ginal¹ /'vɜːdʒɪnl/ *adj* of, suitable for, a virgin.

vir·ginal² /'vɜːdʒɪnl/ *n* (often *pl*) square spinet without legs used in the 16th and 17th cc (and also called *the ∼s/a pair of ∼s*).

Vir·ginia /və'dʒɪnɪə/ *n* [U] kinds of tobacco produced in the State of V∼, US; ∼ *cigarettes.* ∼ **creeper,** ornamental vine often grown on walls, with large leaves which turn scarlet in the autumn.

Virgo /'vɜːgəʊ/ *n* sixth sign of the zodiac. ⇨ the illus at zodiac.

vir·gule /'vɜːgjuːl/ *n* diagonal mark (/), used to separate alternatives (as in *and/or*).

vir·ile /'vɪraɪl US: 'vɪrəl/ *adj* **1** having or showing strength, energy, manly qualities: ∼ *eloquence; a* ∼ *style (of writing); live to a ∼ old age.* **2** (of men) sexually potent. **vir·il·ity** /vɪ'rɪləti/ *n* [U] masculine strength and vigour; sexual power.

vi·rol·ogy /vaɪə'rɒlədʒɪ/ *n* [U] the study of viruses and virus diseases.

virtu /vɜː'tuː/ *n* (only in) *articles/objects of ∼,* art objects interesting because of fine workmanship, antiquity, rarity, etc.

vir·tual /'vɜːtʃʊəl/ *adj* being in fact, acting as, what is described, but not accepted openly or in name as such: *the ∼ head of the business; a ∼ defeat/confession.* ∼**ly** /-tʃʊəlɪ/ *adv*

vir·tue /'vɜːtʃuː/ *n* **1** [C,U] (any particular kind of) goodness or excellence: *Patience is a ∼. Is patriotism always a ∼? Our climate has the ∼s of never being too hot or too cold.* **make a ∼ of necessity,** do sth pretending it to be an act of ∼ when one really does it under compulsion. **V∼ is its own reward,** (prov) One should not expect a reward for doing sth that is truly virtuous. **the cardinal ∼s,** prudence, fortitude, temperance, justice. **the theological ∼s,** faith, hope, charity. **2** [U] chastity. **3** [U] efficacy; ability to produce a definite result: *Have you any faith in the ∼ of herbs to heal sickness?* **4** [U,C] excellence; advantage: *The great ∼ of the scheme is that it costs very little.* **5 by/in ∼ of,** by reason of; because of: *He claimed a pension in ∼ of his long military service.*

vir·tu·ous /'vɜːtʃʊəs/ *adj* having or showing ∼. **vir·tu·ous·ly** *adv*

vir·tu·oso /ˌvɜːtʃʊ'əʊzəʊ US: -'əʊsəʊ/ *n* (*pl* ∼s or -si /-zi: US: -si:/) person with special knowledge of, or taste for, works of art; person skilled in the methods of an art, esp one who plays a musical instrument with great skill: (attrib) *a ∼ performer.*

vir·tu·os·ity /ˌvɜːtʃʊ'ɒsəti/ *n* [U] skill of a ∼.

viru·lent /'vɪrʊlənt/ *adj* (of poison) strong; deadly; (of ill feeling, hatred) bitter; (of words, etc) full of ill feeling; (of diseases, sores) poisonous. ∼**ly** *adv* **viru·lence** /-ləns/ *n*

vi·rus /'vaɪərəs/ *n* [C] any of various poisonous elements, smaller than bacteria, causing the spread of infectious disease: *the ∼ of rabies; ∼ diseases.*

visa /'viːzə/ *n* [C] stamp or signature put on a passport to show that it has been examined and approved by the officials of a foreign country which the owner intends to visit (*'entrance* or *'entry ∼*) or leave (*'exit ∼*). □ *vt* [VP6A] put a ∼ on: *get one's passport ∼ed* /'viːzəd/ *before going to Poland.*

vis·age /'vɪzɪdʒ/ *n* [C] (liter) face (of a human being). **-vis·aged** /'vɪzɪdʒd/ *suff* (in compounds) having the kind of ∼ indicated: *gloomy-∼d funeral directors.*

vis-à-vis /ˌviːz ɑː 'viː US: ˌviːz ə 'viː/ *adv, prep* **1** facing (one another): *sit ∼ in a train.* **2** (fig) in relation to; compared with.

vis·cera /'vɪsərə/ *n pl* internal organs of the body, esp the intestines. **vis·ceral** /'vɪsərəl/ *adj* of the ∼.

vis·cid /'vɪsɪd/, **vis·cous** /'vɪskəs/ *adj* sticky; semi-fluid. **vis·cos·ity** /vɪs'kɒsəti/ *n* [U] being viscous.

vis·count /'vaɪkaʊnt/ *n* nobleman higher in rank than a baron, lower than an earl. ∼**ess** /-ɪs/ *n* wife of a ∼; woman who is a ∼ in her own right. ∼**cy** /-tsɪ/ *n* (*pl* -cies) title, rank, dignity, of a ∼.

vise /vaɪs/ *n* (US) = vice².

vis·ible /'vɪzəbl/ *adj* that can be seen; that is in sight: *The eclipse will be ∼ to observers in western Europe.* **vis·ibly** /-əblɪ/ *adv* in a ∼ manner: *She was visibly annoyed.* **vis·ibil·ity** /ˌvɪzə'bɪləti/ *n* [U] being ∼; (esp) condition of the atmosphere for seeing things at a distance: *The aircraft turned back because of poor visibility.*

vi·sion /'vɪʒn/ *n* **1** [U] power of seeing or imagining, looking ahead, grasping the truth that underlies facts: *the field of ∼,* all that can be seen from a certain point; *the ∼ of a poet/prophet; a man of ∼.* **2** [C] sth seen, esp by the mind's eye or the power of imagination, or sth seen during sleep or in a trance-like state: *the romantic ∼s of youth. Have you ever had ∼s of great wealth and success?*

vi·sion·ary /'vɪʒənrɪ US: -ʒənerɪ/ *adj* **1** existing only in a vision or the imagination; unpractical; fanciful: ∼ *schemes/scenes/plans.* **2** (of persons) having ∼ ideas; dreamy. □ *n* ∼ person.

visit /'vɪzɪt/ *vt,vi* **1** [VP6A] go to see (sb); go to (a place) for a time: ∼ *a friend;* ∼ *Rome. His rich relatives seldom ∼ him.* [VP2C] (US) stay: ∼*ing in Paris;* ∼*ing at a new hotel.* **2** [VP6A] (chiefly US) go to in order to inspect or examine officially: *Restaurant and hotel kitchens are ∼ed regularly by public health inspectors.* **3** [VP3A] (chiefly US) ∼ **with,** pay a ∼ to; talk with: *She loves ∼ing with her neighbours and having a good gossip.* **4** [VP14] ∼ **sth on sb,** (biblical use) punish. ∼ **the sins of the fathers upon the children,** make the children suffer for their parent's failings. □ *n* act of ∼ing; time of ∼ing: *pay a ∼ to a friend/a patient/a prospective customer; go on a ∼ to the seaside; a ∼ of several hours; during her first ∼ to her husband's parents.* ∼**ing** *n* [U] paying ∼s; making calls (on people): *'∼ing hours at a hospital; We are not on ∼ing terms,* not sufficiently well acquainted to ∼ one another. **visi·tor** /'vɪzɪtə(r)/ *n* person who ∼s; person who stays at a place: *sum-*

mer ~*ors*, eg at a holiday resort; *the* ~*ors' book*, one in which ~ors sign their names, eg at a hotel or a place of public interest.

visi·tant /'vɪzɪtənt/ *n* **1** (liter) visitor, esp an important or supernatural one. **2** migratory bird: *a rare* ~ *to these shores*.

visi·ta·tion /ˌvɪzɪ'teɪʃn/ *n* **1** [C] visit, esp one of an official nature or one made by a bishop or priest: *a* ~ *of the sick*, made by a clergyman as part of his duties. **2** [C] trouble, disaster, looked upon as punishment from God: *The famine was a* ~ *of God for their sins.*

vi·sor /'vaɪzə(r)/ *n* **1** (hist) movable part of a helmet, covering the face. ⇨ the illus at armour. **2** peak of a cap. **3** ('sun-)~, oblong sheet of dark-tinted glass hinged at the top of a windscreen in a car to lessen the glare of bright sunshine.

vista /'vɪstə/ *n* [C] **1** long, narrow view: *a* ~ *of the church spire at the end of an avenue of trees.* **2** (fig) long series of scenes, events, etc which one can look back on or forward to: *the* ~*s of bygone times; a discovery that opens up new* ~*s.*

vis·ual /'vɪʒʊəl/ *adj* concerned with, used in, seeing: ~ *images. She has a* ~ *memory*, is able to remember well things she sees. ~ **aids**, (eg in teaching) eg pictures, film-strips, cinema films. ~**ly** /'vɪʒʊəlɪ/ *adv* ~·**ize** /-aɪz/ *vt* [VP6A] bring (sth) as a picture before the mind: *I remember meeting the man two years ago but can't* ~*ize him*, recall what he looked like. **vis·ual·iz·ation** /ˌvɪʒʊəlaɪ'zeɪʃn US: -lɪ'z-/ *n*

vi·tal /'vaɪtl/ *adj* **1** of, connected with, necessary for, living: *wounded in a* ~ *part.* **the** ~ **force/ principle**, that which is assumed to account for organic life. ~ **statistics**, (a) relating to the duration of life, and to births, marriages and deaths. **(b)** (colloq) woman's measurements at bust, waist and hips. **2** supreme; indispensable: *of* ~ *importance; a* ~ *necessity.* ~**s** *n pl* ~ parts of the body, esp the lungs, heart and brain. ~**ly** /'vaɪtlɪ/ *adv* ~·**ism** /-ɪzəm/ *n* [U] belief that there is a controlling force in living things which is distinct from chemical and physical forces (opp of *mechanism*). ~·**ist** /-ɪst/ *n* person who believes in ~ism.

vi·tal·ity /vaɪ'tælətɪ/ *n* [U] vital power; capacity to endure and perform functions: *Can an artificial language have any* ~?

vi·tal·ize /'vaɪtəlaɪz/ *vt* [VP6A] fill with vitality; put vigour into.

vit·amin /'vɪtəmɪn US: 'vaɪt-/ *n* [C] any of a number of organic substances which are present in certain food-stuffs and are essential to the health of man and other animals: *illnesses* (eg scurvy, rickets) *caused by* ~ *deficiency;* ' ~ *tablets.*

vi·ti·ate /'vɪʃɪeɪt/ *vt* [VP6A] lower the quality of; weaken or destroy the force of: ~*d blood; the* ~*d air of an overcrowded room. This admission* ~*s your argument/claim.*

vit·reous /'vɪtrɪəs/ *adj* of or like glass: ~ *rocks*, hard and brittle; ~ *enamel*, used instead of porcelain.

vit·rify /'vɪtrɪfaɪ/ *vt,vi* (*pt,pp* -fied) [VP6A,2A] change, be changed, into a glass-like substance.

vit·riol /'vɪtrɪəl/ *n* [U] sulphuric acid; any of the salts of sulphuric acid: *blue* ~, copper sulphate; (fig) sarcasm. ~**ic** /ˌvɪtrɪ'ɒlɪk/ *adj* (fig, of words, feelings) biting; full of invective: *a* ~*ic attack on the President;* ~*ic remarks.*

vit·uper·ate /vɪ'tju:pəreɪt US: vaɪ'tu:-/ *vt* [VP6A] abuse in words; curse; revile. **vit·uper·at·ive**

/vɪ'tju:pərətɪv US: vaɪ'tu:pəreɪtɪv/ *adj* abusive. **vit·uper·ation** /vɪˌtju:pə'reɪʃn US: vaɪˌtu:-/ *n* [U] abusive language; severe scolding.

viva /'vaɪvə/ *n* (colloq) = viva voce.

vi·vace /vɪ'vɑ:tʃeɪ/ *adv* (music) briskly.

vi·va·cious /vɪ'veɪʃəs/ *adj* lively; high-spirited; gay: *a* ~ *girl.* ~·**ly** *adv* **vi·vac·ity** /vɪ'væsətɪ/ *n* [U].

viva voce /ˌvaɪvə 'vəʊsɪ/ *adj, adv* oral(ly): *a* ~ *examination.* □ *n* ~ examination or test.

vivid /'vɪvɪd/ *adj* **1** (of colours, etc) intense; bright: *a* ~ *flash of lightning;* ~ *green trousers.* **2** lively; active: *a* ~ *imagination.* **3** clear and distinct: *a* ~ *description of an event; have* ~ *recollections of a holiday in Italy.* ~·**ly** *adv* ~·**ness** *n*

vi·vipar·ous /vɪ'vɪpərəs US: vaɪ-/ *adj* having offspring which develop within the mother's body (not from eggs).

vivi·sect /ˌvɪvɪ'sekt/ *vt* [VP6A] operate or experiment on (living animals) for scientific research. **vivi·sec·tion** /ˌvɪvɪ'sekʃn/ *n* [U] ~ing; [C] instance of this. **vivi·sec·tion·ist** /-ʃənɪst/ *n* person who ~s; person who considers vivisection justifiable.

vixen /'vɪksn/ *n* female fox; bad-tempered quarrelsome woman. ~·**ish** /'vɪksənɪʃ/ *adj* scolding; bad-tempered.

viz /vɪz/ (Lat *videlicet*, usu spoken as *namely*) that is to say; namely.

vi·zier /vɪ'zɪə(r)/ *n* official of high rank in some Muslim countries, esp the old Turkish empire.

vo·cabu·lary /və'kæbjʊlərɪ US: -lerɪ/ *n* (*pl* -ries) **1** total number of words which (with rules for combining them) make up a language: *No dictionary could list the whole* ~ *of a language.* **2** [C,U] (range of) words known to, or used by, a person, in a trade, profession, etc: *a writer with a large* ~. **3** [C] book containing a list of words; list of words used in a book, etc, usu with definitions or translations.

vo·cal /'vəʊkl/ *adj* of, for, with or using, the voice: *the* ~ *cords*, ⇨ cord(2); *the* ~ *organs*, the tongue, lips, etc; ~ *music*, to be sung; *a* ~ *score*, musical score, eg of an opera, giving the vocal parts in full. *Anger made the shy girl* ~, helped her to express her feelings by speaking. ~·**ly** /'vəʊkəlɪ/ *adv* ~·**ist** /'vəʊkəlɪst/ *n* singer. ⇨ **instrumentalist** at instrumental. ~·**ize** /-aɪz/ *vt* say or sing; voice(2).

vo·ca·tion /vəʊ'keɪʃn/ *n* **1** (*sing* only) feeling that one is called to (and qualified for) a certain kind of work (esp social or religious): *The nursing of the sick, said Florence Nightingale, is a* ~ *as well as a profession.* **2** [U] special aptitude (*for*): *He has little or no* ~ *for teaching.* **3** [C] person's trade or profession. ~·**al** /-ʃənl/ *adj* of or for a ~(3): ~*al guidance*, advice on the choice of a ~.

vo·ca·tive /'vɒkətɪv/ *adj, n* (of the) form of a word used when addressing sb: *the* ~ *case.* ⇨ case '(3).

vo·cif·er·ate /və'sɪfəreɪt US: vəʊ-/ *vt, vi* [VP6A,2A] say loudly or noisily; shout. **vo·cif·er·ation** /vəˌsɪfə'reɪʃn US: vəʊ-/ *n* [U] shouting; yelling. **vo·cif·er·ous** /və'sɪfərəs US: vəʊ-/ *adj* noisy; yelling: *a vociferous crowd.*

vodka /'vɒdkə/ *n* [U] strong Russian alcoholic drink distilled from rye and also other vegetable products.

vogue /vəʊg/ *n* **1** current fashion; sth currently being done or used: *Are blue jeans still the* ~*? The* ~*s of the 18th century seem amusing today.* **2** popularity; popular use or acceptance: *Georgette Wheatley's novels had a great* ~ *ten years ago,* *but are not read today.* **be in/come into; be/go out of** ~, be/become (un)fashionable, (un)popular: *When did pointed shoes come into/go out of* ~? **all the** ~, popular everywhere; the latest fashion.

voice /vɔɪs/ *n* **1** [U] sounds made when speaking or singing: *He is not in good* ~, not speaking or singing as well as usual. **2** [C] power of making such sounds: *He has lost his* ~, cannot speak or sing properly, eg because of a bad cold. **3** [C,U] sounds uttered by a person, esp considered in relation to their quality: *in a loud/soft/shrill/rough, etc* ~. *I did not recognize her* ~. *The choir boys have sweet* ~s. *They gave* ~ *to their indignation.* **lift up one's** ~, (old use) sing, speak. **shout at the top of one's** ~, shout as loudly as one can. **with one** ~, (liter) unanimously. **4** *a/some/no, etc* ~ *in sth,* a/some/no, etc right to express an opinion on: *I have no* ~ *in the matter.* **5** [C] anything which may be compared or likened to the human ~ as expressing ideas, feelings, etc: *the* ~ *of Nature; the* ~s *of the night; the* ~ *of God,* conscience. **6** [U] (in phonetics) sound produced by vibration of the vocal cords, not with breath only, as for vowel sounds and the consonants /b, d, ð, z/, etc. **7** (gram) the contrast between *active* and *passive* as shown in the sentences: *The dog ate the meat* and *The meat was eaten by the dog.* □ *vt* [VP6A] **1** put into words: *The spokesman* ~d *the feelings of the crowd.* **2** utter (a sound) with ~(6): ~d *sounds* (eg /d, v, ŋ/). ~d *adj* (in compounds) having the kind of ~ indicated: *rough-*~d. ~**-less** *adj* **1** having no ~; unable to utter words. **2** (of consonants) uttered without ~(6): *The sounds* /p, tʃ, f/ *are* ~*less.*

void /vɔɪd/ *adj* **1** empty; vacant. **2** ~ *of,* without: *a subject* ~ *of interest; a proposal* ~ *of reason.* **3** **null and** ~, (legal) without force; invalid: *The agreement, not having been signed, was null and* ~. □ *n* [C] space: *There was an aching* ~ *in his heart,* (fig) a feeling of sadness caused by the loss of someone he had loved. □ *vt* [VP6A] (legal) make ~(3).

voile /vɔɪl/ *n* [U] thin, light dress material.

vol·atile /'vɒlətaɪl US: -tl/ *adj* **1** (of a liquid) that easily changes into gas or vapour. **2** (of a person, his disposition) lively; changing quickly or easily from one mood or interest to another. **vola·til·ity** /ˌvɒlə'tɪlətɪ/ *n*

vol·cano /vɒl'keɪnəʊ/ *n* (*pl* ~es or ~s /-nəʊz/) hill or mountain with opening(s) (⇨ crater) through which gases, lava, ashes, etc, come up from below the earth's crust (in *an active* ~), or may come up after an interval (in *a dormant* ~), or have long ceased to come up (in *an extinct* ~). **vol·canic** /vɒl'kænɪk/ *adj* of, from, like, a ~.

vole /vəʊl/ *n* rat-like animal: *a 'field-*~, one like a mouse; *a 'water-*~, large water-rat.

vo·li·tion /və'lɪʃn US: vəʊ-/ *n* [U] act, power, of using one's own will, of choosing, making a decision, etc: *do sth of one's own* ~. ~**al** /-ʃənl/ *adj*

vol·ley /'vɒlɪ/ *n* [C] **1** hurling or shooting of a number of missiles (stones, arrows, bullets, etc) together. **2** number of oaths, curses, questions, directed together, or in quick succession, at sb. **3** (tennis) stroke which returns the ball to the sender before it touches the ground. **half-'**~, return of the ball as soon as it touches the ground. **'**~**·ball** *n* game in which players on each side of a high net try to keep a ball in motion by hitting it with their hands back and forth over the net without letting it

touch the ground. □ *vt,vi* **1** [VP2A,C] (of guns) sound together: *The guns* ~*ed on all sides.* **2** [VP6A,2A] return a tennis-ball across the net before it touches the ground.

volt /vəʊlt/ *n* [C] (abbr **v**) unit of electrical force; force that would carry one ampere of current against one ohm resistance. ~**·age** /'vəʊltɪdʒ/ *n* electrical force measured in ~s.

volte-face /ˌvɒlt 'fɑːs/ *n* complete change; act of turning round to the opposite way of standing or to the opposite way of thinking: *make a complete* ~.

vol·uble /'vɒljʊbl/ *adj* talking, able to talk, very quickly and easily; (of speech) fluent. **vol·ubly** /-jʊblɪ/ *adv* **volu·bil·ity** /ˌvɒljʊ'bɪlətɪ/ *n*

vol·ume /'vɒljuːm US: -jəm/ *n* **1** [C] book, esp one of a set of books; number of sheets, papers, periodicals, etc bound together: *an encyclopedia in 20* ~s. **speak** ~s **for,** supply strong evidence of: *His donations to charity speak* ~s *for his generosity.* **2** [U] amount of space (expressed in cubic metres, etc) occupied by a substance, liquid or gas; cubic contents of a container, etc: *the* ~ *of a cask; the* ~ *of wine in a cask.* **3** [C] large mass, amount or quantity: *the* ~ *of business/work, etc;* (esp *pl*) rounded masses of steam or smoke: *V*~s *of black smoke belched out from the chimneys.* **4** [U] (of sound) power; sonority: *a voice of great* ~. *Your radio has a* ~ *control.*

vol·umi·nous /və'ljuːmɪnəs/ *adj* **1** (of writing) great in quantity: *a* ~ *work/history;* (of an author) producing many books. **2** occupying much space: *a* ~ *correspondence;* ~ *skirts.*

vol·un·tary /'vɒləntrɪ US: -terɪ/ *adj* **1** doing or ready to do things, willingly, without being compelled; (sth) done thus: ~ *work/service; a* ~ *statement/confession;* ~ *workers/helpers.* **2** carried on, supported by, ~ work and gifts: *a '*~ *school,* one supported by ~ contributions, not by the State, etc. **3** (of bodily, muscular, movements) controlled by the will (opp of *involuntary*). □ *n* [C] (*pl* -ries) organ solo, esp one played not as part of a church service. **vol·un·tar·ily** /'vɒləntrəlɪ US: ˌvɒlən'terəlɪ/ *adv*

vol·un·teer /ˌvɒlən'tɪə(r)/ *n* **1** person who offers to do sth, esp sth unpleasant or dangerous. **2** soldier who is not conscripted: (attrib) *a* ~ *corps.* □ *vt,vi* [VP6A,7A,2A,3A] ~ *sth/to do sth/for sth,* offer voluntarily; come forward as a ~: *He* ~*ed some information/*~*ed to get some information. How many of them* ~*ed? He* ~*ed for the campaign.*

vol·up·tu·ary /və'lʌptʃʊərɪ US: -ʊerɪ/ *n* person who gives himself up to luxury and sensual pleasures.

vo·lup·tu·ous /və'lʌptʃʊəs/ *adj* of, for, arousing, given up to, sensuous or sensual pleasures: ~ *music/beauty/thoughts/sensations.* ~**·ly** *adv* ~**·ness** *n*

vo·lute /və'ljuːt US: və'luːt/ *n* spiral scroll, esp as on Ionic and Corinthian capitals. ⇨ the illus at column. ~**d** *adj* decorated with, having, ~s: *a* ~d *sea-shell.*

vomit /'vɒmɪt/ *vt,vi* **1** [VP6A,15B,2A] bring back from the stomach through the mouth; throw up from the mouth: *He* ~*ed everything he had eaten. He was* ~*ing blood. He began to* ~. **2** [VP6A] send out in large quantities: *factory chimneys* ~*ing smoke.* □ *n* [U] food that has been ~ed.

voo·doo /'vuːduː/ *n* [U] debased form of religion, made up of sorcery and witchcraft, practised by some in the West Indies, esp Haiti.

vo·racious /vəˈreɪʃəs/ adj very hungry or greedy; desiring much: a ~ appetite; a ~ reader, one who reads many books. ~·ly adv in a ~ manner: He ate his food ~ly. **vo·racity** /vəˈræsətɪ/ n

vor·tex /ˈvɔːteks/ n (pl ~es or vortices /-tɪsiːz/) **1** mass of whirling fluid or wind, esp a whirlpool. **2** (fig) whirl of activity; system, pursuit, viewed as sth that tends to absorb things, engross those who engage in it: be drawn into the ~ of politics/war; the ~ of social life/pleasure.

vo·tary /ˈvəʊtərɪ/ n (pl -ries) person who gives up his time and energy to sth, esp to religious work and service: a ~ of peace/liberation.

vote /vəʊt/ n **1** (right to give an) expression of opinion or will by persons for or against sb or sth, esp by ballot or by putting up of hands: give one's ~ to the more handsome candidate. Do women have the ~ (ie the franchise) in your country? I'm going to the polling-booth to record/cast my ~. Mr X proposed a ~ of thanks to the principal speaker, asked the audience to show, by clapping their hands, that they thanked him. The Government received a ~ of confidence, a majority of ~s was in its favour, to show confidence in its policies, etc. **put sth to the ~,** decide it by asking for ~s. **2** total numbers of ~s (to be) given (eg at a political election): Will the Labour ~ increase or decrease at the next election? **3** money granted, by ~s, for a certain purpose: the Army ~. □ vi, vt **1** [VP3A] ~ **for/against sb/sth,** support/oppose by voting. ~ **on sth,** express an opinion on sth by voting. **2** [VP6A,12B,13B] ~ **sb/sth (for sth),** grant money (to sb): ~ a sum of money for Education. Parliament ~d Charles I £100000 for the Army. **3** [VP15B] ~ **sth down,** defeat by ~s: ~ down (= reject) a proposal. ~ **sth through,** support, approve: ~ a Bill through. **4** [VP25] (colloq) declare, by general opinion: The new teacher was ~d a pompous bore, The children gave this as their opinion. **5** [VP9] suggest, propose: I ~ (that) we avoid him in future. ~r n person who ~s; person who has the right to ~. ~·less adj having no ~; not having the right to ~.

vo·tive /ˈvəʊtɪv/ adj offered or consecrated in connection with the fulfilment of a vow: There were numerous ~ tablets on the walls of the church.

vouch /vaʊtʃ/ vi ~ **for sb/sth,** be responsible for, express one's confidence in (a person, his honesty, the truth of a statement, etc): I am ready to ~ for him/for the truth of his story/for his ability to pay.

voucher /ˈvaʊtʃə(r)/ n receipt or document showing payment of money, correctness of accounts, etc: hotel/meal ~s, (eg as bought from travel agencies) showing that payment has been made in advance. '**gift** ~, supplied with some articles (eg petrol, cigarettes), to be exchanged for gifts. '**luncheon** ~, one supplied by some employers, exchangeable for all or part of a meal (at restaurants which have agreed to accept them).

vouch·safe /vaʊtʃˈseɪf/ vt [VP6A,7A,12C] (formal) be kind enough to give (sth), to do (sth): He ~d (me) no reply. He ~d to help.

vow /vaʊ/ n solemn promise or undertaking: 'marriage vows; a vow of chastity; under a vow of celibacy/silence, having solemnly undertaken not to marry/speak about sth; break a vow; perform a vow, do what one promised. □ vt **1** [VP6A,7A,9] make a vow; promise or declare solemnly: He vowed to avenge the insult/that he would avenge the insult. She vowed never to speak to him again. They were forced to vow obedience. **2** [VP9] (old use) = avow.

vowel /ˈvaʊəl/ n sustainable vocal sound made without audible stopping of the breath, or friction in its passage out through the mouth; letter or symbol used to represent such a sound (eg the letters a, e, i, o, u; the symbols /iː, ɪ, e, æ, ɑː, ɒ, ɔː, ʊ, uː, ʌ, ɜː, ə/). ⇨ diphthong.

vox /vɒks/ n (Lat) voice. **vox populi** /ˌvɒks ˈpɒpjʊlaɪ/, the voice of the people; public opinion.

voy·age /ˈvɔɪdʒ/ n journey by water, esp a long one in a ship: a ~ from Mombasa to Colombo; go on a ~; on the ~ out/home; on the outward/ homeward ~. □ vi [VP2A,C] go on a ~: ~ through the South Seas. ~r /ˈvɔɪədʒə(r)/ n person who makes a ~ (esp of those who, in former times, explored unknown seas).

vo·yeur /vwɑːˈjɜː(r)/ n person who gets pleasure from looking at sexual objects or the sexual activities of others, esp in secret.

vul·can·ite /ˈvʌlkənaɪt/ n [U] hard plastic made from rubber and sulphur. **vul·can·ize** /ˈvʌlkənaɪz/ vt [VP6A] treat (rubber) with sulphur at great heat to harden it. **vul·can·iz·ation** /ˌvʌlkənaɪˈzeɪʃn US: -nɪˈz-/ n

vul·gar /ˈvʌlgə(r)/ adj **1** ill mannered; in bad taste: ~ language/behaviour/ideas; a ~ person; a ~ display of wealth. **2** in common use; generally prevalent: ~ errors/superstitions. ~ **fraction,** one written in the usual way (eg ½), contrasted with a decimal fraction (eg 0·75). **the ~ herd,** (contemptuous) the masses of ordinary people. **the ~ tongue,** the language commonly spoken by the people (formerly, in England, English contrasted with Latin). ~·ly adv **vul·garian** /vʌlˈgeərɪən/ n ~ person, esp a rich person whose manners and tastes are bad. ~·ism /ˈvʌlgərɪzəm/ n [C] word, phrase, expression, etc used only by ignorant persons; [U] ~ behaviour. ~·ity /vʌlˈgærətɪ/ n (pl -ties) [U] ~ behaviour; (pl) ~ acts, utterances, etc. ~·ize /ˈvʌlgəraɪz/ vt [VP6A] make ~. ~·iz·ation /ˌvʌlgəraɪˈzeɪʃn US: -rɪˈz-/ n [U].

Vul·gate /ˈvʌlgeɪt/ n the V~, Latin version of the Bible made in the 4th c.

vul·ner·able /ˈvʌlnərəbl/ adj that is liable to be damaged; not protected against attack: find sb's ~ spot; a position ~ to attack; people who are ~ to criticism. **vul·ner·abil·ity** /ˌvʌlnərəˈbɪlətɪ/ n

vul·pine /ˈvʌlpaɪn/ adj of, like, a fox; crafty.

vul·ture /ˈvʌltʃə(r)/ n **1** large bird, usu with head and neck almost bare of feathers, that lives on the flesh of dead animals. ⇨ the illus at prey. **2** greedy person who profits from the misfortunes of others.

vulva /ˈvʌlvə/ n opening of the female genitals. ⇨ the illus at reproduce.

vy·ing /ˈvaɪɪŋ/ pres p of vie.

W, w /ˈdʌbljuː/ (pl W's, w's) the 23rd letter of the English alphabet.

wad /wɒd/ n 1 lump of soft material for keeping things apart or in place, or to stop up a hole. 2 collection of documents or banknotes folded or rolled together. □ vt (-dd-) stuff with a wad; hold in place with a wad; line (a garment, etc) with soft material (usu cotton or wool): *a wadded jacket/dressing-gown/quilt*. **wad-ding** /'wɒdɪŋ/ n [U] soft material, esp raw cotton or felt, used for packing, lining things, etc.

waddle /'wɒdl/ vi [VP2A,C] walk with slow steps and a sideways roll, as a duck does: *The stout old man ~d across the road.* □ n (sing only) this kind of walk.

wade /weɪd/ vi, vt [VP2A,C,6A] 1 walk with an effort (through water, mud or anything that makes progress difficult); walk across (sth) in this way: *He ~d through the weeds on the bank and then into and across the stream. Can we ~ the brook*, cross it by wading? *The boy ~d* (= read slowly and without interest) *through the dull book*. **'wading bird**, long-legged water-bird that ~s (opp to web-footed birds that swim). 2 ~ *in*, make a vigorous attack. ~ *into sth*, attack sth vigorously. ~r n 1 wading bird (⇒ above). 2 (pl) waterproof boots reaching the hips, used by anglers when wading in streams.

wadi /'wɒdɪ/ n (pl ~s) (in the Middle East, Arabia, northern Africa) rocky watercourse dry except after a heavy fall of rain.

wa-fer /'weɪfə(r)/ n 1 thin flat biscuit (eg as eaten with ice-cream). 2 small round piece of bread used in Holy Communion.

waffle¹ /'wɒfl/ n small cake made of batter baked in a special kind of griddle (a '~-iron) with two parts hinged together.

waffle² /'wɒfl/ vi [VP2A,C] (GB colloq) talk vaguely, unnecessarily, and without much result: *How that man does ~ on! What's she waffling about now?* □ n [U] utterance which (even when it sounds impressive) means little or nothing.

waft /wɒft US: wæft/ vt [VP6A] carry lightly and smoothly through the air or over water: *The scent of the flowers was ~ed to us by the breeze.* □ n [C] 1 breath of air, scent, etc. 2 waving movement.

wag¹ /wæg/ vt, vi (-gg-) [VP6A,2A,C] (cause to) move from side to side or up and down: *The dog wagged its tail. The dog's tail wagged. Don't wag your finger at me*, show disapproval in this way. *The news set tongues/chins/beards wagging*, caused people to talk (esp of sth scandalous). **'wag-tail** n kinds of small bird with a long tail that wags constantly when the bird is standing. □ n wagging movement: *with a wag of the tail*.

wag² /wæg/ n merry person, full of amusing sayings and fond of practical jokes. **wag-gery** /'wægərɪ/ n (pl -ries) [U] behaviour or talk of a wag; (pl) acts, remarks, etc of a wag. **wag-gish** /'wægɪʃ/ adj of or like a wag; done in a joking way: *waggish tricks/remarks*. **wag-gish-ly** adv

wage¹ /weɪdʒ/ n 1 (now usu pl except in certain phrases and when attrib) payment made or received (usu weekly) for work or services: *His ~s are £50 a week. We expect a fair day's ~ for a fair day's work. He takes his ~s/his '~-packet home to his wife every Friday. The postal workers have asked for a '~ increase/rise of £5 a week.* ⇒ fee(1), pay¹, salary. **living ~**, one which allows a man to live without fear of hunger and hardship. **minimum ~**, guaranteed basic level for ~s in an in-

dustry or country. '**~-claim** n ~ demanded from the management for workers by their trade union. '**~-earner** n person who works for ~s (contrasted with the salaried classes). '**~-freeze**, ⇒ freeze, n(2). 2 (old use; pl in form with *sing v*) reward or requital: *The ~s of sin is death.*

wage² /weɪdʒ/ vt [VP6A] carry on, engage in (war, a campaign).

wa-ger /'weɪdʒə(r)/ vt, vi [VP6A,11,14,12C,2A] bet: ~ £5 *on a horse. I'm ready to ~ you a pound that....* □ n bet: *lay/make a ~; take up* (= accept) *a ~.*

waggle /'wægl/ vt, vi = wag¹.

wag-gon (US usu **wagon**) /'wægən/ n 1 four-wheeled vehicle for carrying goods, pulled by horses or oxen. ⇒ cart. **on the ('water) ~**, (colloq) not drinking alcoholic liquors. 2 (US = freight car) open railway truck (eg for coal). '**station-~** n (US) = estate-car. **~er** n man in charge of a ~ and its horses.

wa-gon-lit /ˌvægɒn 'liː/ n (pl **wagons-lit** pronunciation unchanged) sleeping-car (as on European railways).

wag-tail /'wægteɪl/ ⇒ wag¹.

waif /weɪf/ n homeless person, esp a child: *~s and strays*, homeless and abandoned children.

wail /weɪl/ vi, vt [VP2A,B,C,6A] 1 cry or complain in a loud, usu shrill, voice: ~ (over) *one's misfortunes; an ambulance racing through the streets with sirens ~ing. She was ~ing for her lost child.* 2 (of the wind) make sounds like a person ~ing. □ n ~ing cry; lament: *the ~s of a newborn child.*

wain /weɪn/ n (old use, or poet) large farm wagon. **Charles's W~**, the constellation of stars also called the Plough and the Great Bear.

wain-scot /'weɪnskət/ n wooden panelling (usu on the lower half of the walls of a room). **~ed** adj lined with ~: *a ~ed room.*

waist /weɪst/ n 1 part of the body between the ribs and the hips: *wear a sash round the ~; measure 30 inches round the ~. The workmen were stripped to the ~*, were wearing nothing above the ~. *That man has no ~*, is so stout that he has no narrowing at the ~ as in a normal figure. ⇒ the illus at trunk. '**~-band** n band on a garment (eg a skirt) fitting round the ~. **~-'deep** adj, adv up to the ~: *~-deep in the water; wade ~-deep into a stream.* **~-'high** adj, adv high enough to reach the ~: *The wheat was ~-high.* '**~-line** n line round the body at the smallest part of the ~: *a girl with a neat ~-line.* 2 that part of a garment that goes round the ~; (US '*shirt-~*) garment, or part of a garment, covering the body from the shoulders to the ~. 3 middle and narrow part: *the ~ of a ship*, between the forecastle and quarterdeck; *the ~ of a violin/an hour-glass.* **~-coat** /'weɪskəʊt US: 'weskət/ n close-fitting sleeveless garment worn under a coat or jacket, buttoned down the front (called *vest* by tailors, and in the US).

wait¹ /weɪt/ n 1 act or time of waiting: *We had a long ~ for the bus. I don't like these long ~s.* 2 [U] **lie in ~ for**; (less usu) **lay ~ for**, be in hiding in order to attack, etc: *The highwayman lay in ~ for the stage-coach.* 3 (pl) **the ~s**, persons who go from house to house singing carols at Christmas.

wait² /weɪt/ vi, vt 1 [VP2A,B,C,3A,4A] ~ (for), stay where one is, delay acting, until sb or sth comes or until sth happens: *Please ~ a minute.*

W~ *for me, please. How long have you been* ~*ing? We are* ~*ing for the rain to stop. We are* ~*ing for better weather. We* ~*ed* (in order) *to see what would happen. They say that everything comes to those who* ~. **keep sb** ~**ing,** fail to meet him or be ready at the appointed time: *His wife never keeps him* ~*ing.* ~ **up (for sb),** stay up, not go to bed. **No** ~**ing,** warning (indicated by the sign ⊘) that motor-vehicles must not stop at the side of the roadway. **2** [VP6A] (= *await*) ~ *for;* ~ and watch for: *He is* ~*ing his opportunity. He always expects me to* ~ *his convenience,* until it is convenient for him (to do sth). *You must* ~ *your turn,* ~ until it is your turn. **3** [VP6A,14] ~ *(for),* defer, postpone (a meal): *Don't* ~ *dinner for me.* **4** [VP3A] ~ *on/upon sb,* **(a)** act as a servant to, fetch and carry things for. ~ *on* **sb hand and foot,** attend to his every need: *A Japanese wife was formerly expected to* ~ *upon her husband hand and foot.* **(b)** (old use) pay a visit to: *Our commercial agent will* ~ *upon you next Monday.* **5** [VP3A] ~ *at/on,* act as a servant at table, serving food, clearing away dishes, etc: ~ *at table* (US = ~ *on table*). **6** '~**-ing-list,** list of persons who cannot be served, treated, etc now, but who will be served, etc later, if possible: *put sb on a* ~*ing-list for theatre tickets/an appointment, etc.* '~**-ing-room** *n* room in a railway-station, etc used by people who are ~ing for trains; room (eg in a doctor's or dentist's house or office) where people ~ until they can be attended to. ~**er** *n* man who ~s at table in a restaurant, hotel dining-room, etc. ~**-ress** /'weɪtrɪs/ *n* woman ~er.

waive /weɪv/ *vt* [VP6A] (say that one will) not insist on (a right or claim): ~ *a privilege/the age-limit.* ~**r** /'weɪvə(r)/ *n* (legal) (written statement) waiving (a right, etc): *sign a waiver of claims against sb.*

wake¹ /weɪk/ *vi,vt* (*pt* woke /wəʊk/ or ~d, *pp* woken /'wəʊkən/ or ~d) **1** [VP2A,C,4B] ~ *(up),* stop sleeping: *What time do you usually* ~ *(up)? I woke early. Has the baby* ~*d/woken yet? He woke up with a start. The woke to find himself in prison.* **2** [VP6A,15B] ~ *sb (up),* cause to stop sleeping: *Don't* ~ *the baby. The noise woke me (up). They were making enough noise to* ~ *the dead.* **3** [VP6A,15B] ~ *sb (up),* stir up; rouse from inactivity, inattention, etc: *He needs someone to* ~ *him up,* stir him from his sloth, stir him to activity. *The incident* ~*d memories of his schooldays.* **4** [VP6A] disturb with noise; cause to re-echo: ~ *echoes in a mountain valley.* **wak·ing** *adj* being awake: *in his waking hours,* while awake; *waking or sleeping,* while awake or asleep. **waken** /'weɪkən/ *vt,vi* [VP6A,2A] (cause to) ~. ~**·ful** /-fl/ *adj* unable to sleep; with little sleep: *pass a* ~*ful night.*

wake² /weɪk/ *n* **1** (usu *pl*; often **'W~s Week**) annual holiday in N England, esp in the manufacturing towns of Lancashire. **2** (in Ireland) all-night watch by a corpse before burial, with lamentations and drinking of alcoholic liquor.

wake³ /weɪk/ *n* track left by a ship on smooth water, eg as made by propellers. **in the** ~ **of,** after; following: *Traders came in the* ~ *of the explorers.*

wale /weɪl/ *n* alternative spelling (esp US) of weal² or **walk**¹

walk¹ /wɔːk/ *n* [C] **1** journey on foot, esp for pleasure or exercise: *go for a* ~*; have a pleasant* ~ *across the fields. The station is a short* ~*/ten minutes'* ~ *from my house.* **2** manner or style of

walking: *His horse slowed to a* ~, ie after trotting or galloping. *After running for two miles he dropped into a* ~, began to walk. *I recognized him at once by his* ~, his way of walking. **3** path or route for walking: *my favourite* ~*s in the neighbourhood.* **4** ~ *of life,* calling, profession, occupation: *They interviewed people from all* ~*s of life.*

walk² /wɔːk/ *vi,vt* **1** [VP2A,B,C] (of persons) move by putting forward each foot in turn, not having both feet off the ground at once, ⇨ run; (of animals) move at the slowest pace, ⇨ trot, gallop: *We* ~*ed five miles. Shall we ride or* ~*? How old are babies when they learn to* ~*? He was* ~*ing up and down the station platform.* '~**-about** *n* **(a)** (Australian sl, of aborigines in the desert) journey. **(b)** (colloq) occasion when a celebrity ~s round meeting people informally. ~ *away from,* beat easily in a contest: *Smith* ~*ed away from all his competitors,* beat them easily. Hence, '~·**away** *n* easily won contest. (⇨ ~over below). ~ *away with sth,* win sth easily: *Newcombe* ~*ed away with the match.* ~ *off with sth,* (colloq) carry off; take (either on purpose or unintentionally): *Someone has* ~*ed off with my umbrella.* ~ *into,* (sl) **(a)** eat heartily of: ~ *into a meat-pie.* **(b)** abuse; scold. **(c)** (colloq) meet with through inattention: *He just* ~*ed into the ambush.* ~ *on,* play a non-speaking part on the stage: (attrib) *a* ,~*-'on part.* ~ *out,* (colloq) go on strike: *The men in this factory* ~*ed out yesterday.* Hence, '~**-out** *n* (workers') strike. ~ *out on sb,* (sl) abandon or desert him. ~ *out with sb,* (dated colloq) court; have as a sweetheart. ~ *over sb,* defeat him easily. Hence, '~**-over** *n* easy victory; contest in which there is little or no opposition: *The race was a* ~*-over for Jones.* ~ *up,* **(a)** invitation to enter (eg as given by men outside a circus). **(b)** ~ along: *as I was* ~*ing up Oxford Street.* **(c)** ~ upstairs. Hence, *a* '~*-up flat,* one in a building without a lift. **(d)** ~ *up (to sb/sth),* approach: *A stranger* ~*ed up to me and asked me the time.* **2** [VP6A,15A,B] cause to ~: *Horses should be* ~*ed for a while after a race. He* ~*ed his horse up the hill. He put his arm round me and* ~*ed me away/ off.* ~ *sb off his feet/legs,* tire him out by making him ~ far. **3** [VP6A] go over on foot: *I have* ~*ed this district for miles round.* **4** (with various *nn:* ~ *the boards,* be an actor; ~ *the wards,* be a medical student; ~ *the plank,* (of a person captured by pirates in former times) be compelled to ~ blindfolded into the sea along a plank laid over the ship's side; ~ *the streets,* be a prostitute (*a 'street-~er*). ~**er** *n* person who ~s, esp for exercise or enjoyment. ~**·ing** *n* (in compounds) '~*ing-shoes,* strong ones for ~ing in; '~*ing-stick,* stick used in, or carried while, ~ing; '~*ing-tour,* holiday spent ~ing from place to place.

walkie-talkie /ˌwɔːkɪ 'tɔːkɪ/ *n* (colloq) portable two-way radio set.

wall /wɔːl/ *n* **1** continuous, usu vertical, solid structure of stone, brick, concrete, wood, etc forming one of the sides of a building or room, or used to enclose, divide or protect sth (including land): *The castle* ~*s are very thick. Hang the picture on that* ~. *Some old towns have* ~*s right round them. Dry-stone* ~*s* (ie of stones not fixed in mortar) *extend across the moors in some parts of England. Fruit trees are often trained against garden* ~*s for protection and warmth.* **with one's back to the** ~, in a position where retreat or escape is impossible; at bay. **be/go up the** ~, (sl) be/become furious, distracted. **bang/run one's head against a (brick)** ~, attempt to do sth that is clearly impossible. **see through a brick** ~, have wonderful vision or insight. 2 (fig) sth suggesting or resembling a ~: *a* ~ *of fire; a mountain* ~; *the* ~*s of the chest*, the enclosing tissue and ribs; *the abdominal* ~. 3 side (contrasted with the centre) of the street: (chiefly fig) **go to the** ~, be pushed aside as weak or helpless, get the worst of it in competition. **push/drive sb to the** ~, defeat him. 4 (compounds) '~-**flower** *n* (a) common garden plant with (usu) brownish-red or orange sweet-smelling flowers. (b) person who sits out dances because of a lack of partners. '~-**painting** *n* [C] painting on a ~, esp a fresco. '~-**paper** *n* [U] paper, usu with a coloured design, for covering the ~s of rooms. □ *vt* 1 (usu *pp*) surround with a ~ or ~s: ~*ed cities; a* ~*ed garden*. 2 [VP15B] ~ *sth up/off,* fill or close up with bricks, etc: ~ *up a window/opening;* ~ *off part of a room.*

wal·laby /'wɒləbɪ/ *n* (*pl* -bies) sorts of small kangaroo.

wal·lah /'wɒlə/ *n* (sl, in India) person employed about or concerned with sth.

wal·let /'wɒlɪt/ *n* folding pocket-case, usu leather, for papers, banknotes, etc (US = *pocket-book*).

wall-eyed /ˌwɔːl 'aɪd/ *adj* having eyes that show an abnormal amount of white (eg as caused by a squint).

wal·lop /'wɒləp/ *vt* (sl or hum) beat severely; hit hard. □ *n* heavy blow; crash: *Down he went with a* ~*!* ~-**ing** *adj* big; thumping: *What a* ~*ing lie!* □ *n* defeat: *Our football team got a* ~*ing*.

wal·low /'wɒləʊ/ *vi* [VP2A,C] roll about (in mud, dirty water, etc): *pigs* ~*ing in the mire;* (fig) take gross delight in (sth sensual): ~*ing in sensual pleasures.* **be '**~**ing in money,** (colloq) be very rich. □ *n* place to which animals (eg buffaloes) go regularly to ~.

Wall Street /'wɔːl striːt/ *n* (used for) the American money-market: *Shares rose sharply on* ~ *yesterday.*

wal·nut /'wɔːlnʌt/ *n* [C] (tree producing a) nut with an edible kernel in a hard shell; [U] the wood of this tree, used (esp as a veneer) for making furniture.

wal·rus /'wɔːlrəs/ *n* large sea-animal of the arctic regions with two long tusks, ⇨ the illus at sea: *a* ~ *moustache,* (colloq) one of which the ends come downwards like the tusks of a ~.

waltz /wɔːls *US:* wɔːlts/ *n* [C] (music in ¾ time for a) ballroom dance. □ *vi,vt* 1 [VP2A,C] dance a ~: *She* ~*es divinely.* ~ *in/out/into/out of,* dance, run or walk (in, out, etc) gaily: *She* ~*ed into the room and out again.* 2 [VP15A] cause to ~: *He* ~*ed her round the room.*

wam·pum /'wɒmpəm/ *n* [U] shells threaded like beads and used as ornaments by N American Indians (and formerly used as money).

wan /wɒn/ *adj* (-nn-) 1 (of a person, his looks, etc) looking ill, sad, tired, anxious: *a wan smile.* 2 (of light, the sky) pale; not bright. **wan·ly** *adv* **wan·ness** /'wɒnnɪs/ *n*

wand /wɒnd/ *n* 1 slender stick or rod as used by a conjurer, fairy or magician; baton(2). 2 rod or staff carried as a symbol of authority (eg by an usher, steward or sheriff on ceremonial occasions).

wan·der /'wɒndə(r)/ *vi,vt* 1 [VP2A,B,C,6A] go from place to place without any special purpose or

destination: ~ *over the countryside;* ~ *up and down the road aimlessly;* ~ (*through/over*) *the world. Kevin* ~*ed in to see me this morning,* paid me a casual visit. 2 [VP2A,C] leave the right path or direction: *Some of the sheep have* ~*ed away,* are lost. *We* ~*ed (for) miles and miles in the mist.* 3 [VP2A,C] be absent-minded; allow the thoughts to go from subject to subject: *Don't* ~ *from the subject/point. His mind is* ~*ing. Don't let your thoughts* ~. *His mind/thoughts* ~*ed back to his college days.* ~**er** *n* person or animal that ~s. ~**ings** *n pl* 1 long travels; journeys: *tell the story of one's* ~*ings.* 2 confused speech during illness (esp high fever).

wan·der·lust /'wɒndəlʌst/ [U] strong desire to travel.

wane /weɪn/ *vi* [VP2A] 1 (of the moon) show a decreasing bright area after full moon. ⇨ wax²(1). 2 become less or weaker: *His strength/influence/reputation is waning.* □ *n* esp **on the** ~, process of waning.

wangle /'wæŋgl/ *vt* [VP6A] (sl) get, arrange sth, by using improper influence, by trickery, plausible persuasion, etc: ~ *an extra week's holiday.* □ *n* act of wangling: *get sth by a* ~.

wank /wæŋk/ *vi* [VP2A] (GB vulg sl) masturbate. □ *n* [C] instance of masturbation.

wanna /'wɒnə/ (US sl) = *want to.* ⇨ want²(2).

want¹ /wɒnt *US:* wɔːnt/ *n* 1 [U] lack; scarcity; state of being absent: *The earthquake victims are suffering for* ~ *of food and medical supplies. The plants died from* ~ *of water. Your work shows* ~ *of thought/care.* 2 [U] need; absence of some necessary thing: *The house is in* ~ *of repair. We may one day be in* ~, very poor. 3 [C] (usu *pl*) desire for sth as necessary to life, happiness, etc; thing to be desired: *He is a man of few* ~*s. We can supply all your* ~*s. The book meets a long-felt* ~, sth that has been needed for a long time.

want² /wɒnt/ *vt,vi* 1 [VP6A,17,19B,24A] require; be in need of; lack: *You won't be* ~*ed* (= Your services will not be required) *this afternoon. These plants are drooping—they* ~ *water. That man* ~*s a woman to look after him. I don't* ~ (= I object to having) *anyone meddling in my affairs. Do you* ~ (= Would you like to have) *this box opened?* '~-**ad** *n* (colloq) (usu short) advertisement (in a newspaper, etc) for sth ~*ed,* eg a job. 2 [VP6A,7A,17] wish for; have a desire for (⇨ wish *vi,vt*(7); *want* is used for sth which it is possible to obtain; *wish for* is used for sth unlikely to be obtained, or obtainable only in exceptional circumstances): *She* ~*s a holiday. She* ~*s to go to Italy. She* ~*s me to go with her. He is* ~*ed by the police,* ie because he is suspected of wrongdoing. *I don't* ~ *there to be any misunderstanding.* 3 [VP6A,E,7A] need, ought (as in the notes to the examples): *Your hair* ~*s cutting,* needs to be cut. *You* ~ (= ought) *to see your solicitors about that problem. What that naughty boy* ~*s* (= needs to be given) *is a good beating. That sort of thing* ~*s some doing,* (colloq) needs effort, skill, etc (because it is not an easy matter). 4 [VP2A] (progressive tenses only) (with non-human subject) **be** ~**ing,** be missing or lacking: *A few pages of this book are* ~*ing. The infinitive of the verb 'must' is* ~*ing.* **be** ~**ing (in sth),** (with human subject): *He's* ~*ing in courtesy,* is impolite. **be found** ~**ing:** *He was put to the test and found* ~*ing,* inadequate. *He/It was tried and found (to be)* ~*ing,* unequal to a standard or to a need. **5** [VP6A] (impers) fall short by: *It ~s one inch of the regulation length. It ~s half an hour to the appointed time.* **6** [VP2A,3A] be in want (⇨ want ¹(3)): *We mustn't let our soldiers ~* (= suffer poverty or hardship) *in their old age. ~ for nothing,* have all one needs. *~·ing prep* without; in the absence of: *W~ing mutual trust, friendship is impossible.*

wan·ton /'wɒntən/ *US:* 'wɔːn-/ *adj* **1** (liter) playful; irresponsible; capricious: *a ~ breeze; in a ~ mood.* **2** unchecked; luxuriant; wild: *a ~ growth* (of weeds, etc); *in ~ profusion.* **3** wilful; serving no useful purpose: *~ destruction/damage; a ~ insult.* **4** (archaic) immoral; unchaste: *a ~ woman;* lewd, licentious: *~ thoughts.* □ *n* (archaic) unchaste person. □ *vi* [VP2A,C] (liter) be ~ in behaviour: *the wind ~ing with the leaves. ~·ly adv ~· ness n*

war /wɔː(r)/ *n* **1** [C,U] (state created by) the use of armed forces between countries or (*civil war*) rival groups in a nation: *We have had two world wars in this century. at war,* in a state of war: *Ruritania and Utopia are at war again. carry the war into the enemy's camp,* attack (instead of being satisfied to defend). *declare war (on),* announce that a state of war exists (with another state). *go to war (against),* start fighting. *have been in the wars,* (used colloq or hum) have suffered injury (eg as the result of an accident). *make/wage war on,* engage in fighting against. **2** (compounds) **'war-baby** *n* (*pl* -babies) illegitimate child with a soldier as father and attributable to conditions during a war. **'war-bride** *n* bride of a soldier during a war. **'war-cloud(s)** *n* state of affairs that seems to threaten war. **'war-cry** *n* (*pl* -cries) word or cry shouted as a signal in battle; catch-word (eg used by a political party) in any kind of contest. **'war-dance** *n* one by tribal warriors before going into battle, to celebrate a victory, or (in peace) to represent fighting. **'war-god** *n* god (eg Mars) worshipped as giving victory in war. **'war-head** *n* (of a torpedo, shell, etc) explosive head (contrasted with a dummy charge as used in practice, etc). **'war-horse** *n* (rhet) horse used in battle; charger; (fig) veteran soldier, politician, etc. **'war-lord** *n* (rhet) great military leader, esp a Chinese general in the period of civil wars, early 20th c. **'war-monger** *n* person who advocates or stirs up war. **'War Office,** (formerly in GB) State department in charge of the Army, under the Secretary of State of War. (Now named *Ministry of Defence*). **'war-paint** *n* [U] **(a)** paint put on the body before battle by some primitive people; (fig) full, ceremonial dress: *The General was in full war-paint.* **(b)** (sl) make-up (cosmetics). **'war-path** *n* (only in) *on the war-path,* ready for, engaged in, a fight or quarrel. **'war-ship** *n* ship for use in war. **'war-torn** *adj* exhausted by, worn out in, war. **'war-widow** *n* woman whose husband has been killed in war. **3** [U] science or art of fighting, using weapons, etc: *trained for war; the art of war,* strategy and tactics. **4** (fig) any kind of struggle or conflict: *the war against disease; the wars of the elements,* storms, natural calamities; *a war of nerves/words.* □ *vi* (-rr-) fight; make war: *warring for supremacy; warring* (= *rival*) *creeds/ideologies.* **'war-fare** /'wɔːfeə(r)/ *n* [U] making war; condition of being at war; fighting: *the horrors of modern warfare.* **war-like** /'wɔːlaɪk/ *adj* ready for, suggesting, war: *warlike preparations;* fond of war: *a cruel, warlike*

people. **war·time** /'wɔːtaɪm/ *n* [U] time when there is war: *in wartime;* (attrib) *wartime regulations/ rationing.*

warble /'wɔːbl/ *vi,vt* [VP2A,C,6A] (esp of birds) sing, esp with a gentle trilling note: *larks warbling high up in the sky; a blackbird warbling from a branch.* □ *n* warbling; bird's song. **war·bler** /'wɔːblə(r)/ *n* (kinds of) bird that ~s.

ward /wɔːd/ *n* **1** *keep watch and ~,* guard and protect. **2** [U] state of being in custody or under the control of a guardian: *a child in ~;* [C] person under the guardianship of an older person or of law authorities. **3** division of a local government area, each division being represented by one Councillor. **4** division of, separate room in, a building, esp a prison or a hospital: *the fever/isolation/children's ~.* **5** notch in a key; corresponding part in a lock. □ *vt* [VP15B] *~ sth off,* keep away, avoid: *~ off a blow/danger.*

war·den /'wɔːdn/ *n* **1** person having control or authority: *the ~ of a youth hostel.* **'air-raid ~,** (during World War II in GB) member of a civilian organization with various duties during air-raids. **'traffic ~,** (eg in London) person responsible for controlling the parking of cars in streets, squares, etc at parking meters. **2** (old use except in a few cases) title of certain governors or presidents: *the W~ of Merton College, Oxford.* **3** (US) = warder.

war·der /'wɔːdə(r)/ *n* (GB) man acting as guard in a prison; jailer. **war·dress** /'wɔːdrɪs/ *n* woman ~.

ward·robe /'wɔːdrəʊb/ *n* **1** cupboard (*built-in-~*) or movable cupboard-like piece of furniture with pegs, shelves, etc for a person's clothes. **2** stock of clothes: *My ~ needs to be renewed,* I must buy some new clothes. **3** stock of costumes of a theatrical company.

ward-room /'wɔːdrʊm *US:* -ruːm/ *n* living and eating quarters for commissioned officers in a warship except the commanding officer.

ware ¹ /weə(r)/ *n* **1** (in compounds) manufactured goods: *'silver~; 'iron~; 'hard~.* **2** (*pl*) articles offered for sale: *advertise one's ~s. ~·house* /'weəhaʊs/ *n* building for storing goods before distribution to retailers; storehouse for furniture (on behalf of owners). □ *vt* [VP6A] store in a ~house.

ware ² /weə(r)/ *vt* [VP6A] (in imper) look out for; be cautious about; beware of: *W~ wire!* (warning to riders in a fox-hunt that there is barbed wire on a fence, etc).

war·fare /'wɔːfeə(r)/ ⇨ war.

war·ily, wari·ness ⇨ wary.

warm ¹ /wɔːm/ *adj* (-er, -est) **1** having a fairly high degree of heat (between *cool* and *hot*); (of clothing) serving to keep the body ~: *Come and get ~ by the fire. It was ~, but not hot, yesterday. Put your ~est clothes on before you go out in the snow. Red, yellow and orange are called ~ colours. ~ work,* **(a)** work or activity that makes one ~. **(b)** strenuous or dangerous activity or occupation. *make things ~ for sb,* make things unpleasant, make trouble for him; punish him. *~ blood,* that of mammals and birds (ranging from 36°C—42°C). Hence, *~-'blooded adj* **(a)** having ~ blood; not cold-blooded like snakes, etc. **(b)** having feelings and passions that are easily roused. *~ front,* ⇨ front(7). **2** enthusiastic; hearty: *give sb a ~ welcome; a ~ friend/supporter.* **3** sympathetic; affectionate: *He has a ~ heart.* Hence, *~-'hearted adj* kind and sympathetic. **4** (of scent in hunting) fresh; recently made and easily followed by the hounds; (in children's games, when an object is hidden and searched for) close to the object: *You're getting* ~, near to what is being sought. ~·ly *adv* in a ~ manner: ~*ly dressed; thank sb* ~ly. **warmth** /wɔːmθ/ *n* [U] state of being ~: *He was pleased with the* ~*th of his welcome. He answered with* ~*th,* with some emotion (of pleasure, resentment, etc, according to context).

warm² /wɔːm/ *vt,vi* [VP6A,15B,2A,C] ~ *(sth) (up),* make or become warm or warmer: ~ *oneself/one's hands by the fire. Please* ~ *(up) this milk. The milk is* ~*ing (up) on the stove. He* ~*ed up* (= became more animated, enthusiastic) *as he went on with his speech.* ~ *to one's work/task, etc,* become more interested; like it more. '~·**ing-pan** *n* (hist) round metal pan with a lid and a long handle, holding hot coals and used for ~ing the inside of a bed before it was occupied. ~·**er** *n* (usu in compounds) sth which ~s.

warn /wɔːn/ *vt* [VP6A,14,11,15,17] give (sb) notice of possible danger or unpleasant consequences; inform in advance of what may happen: *He was* ~*ed of the danger. We* ~*ed them not to go skating on such thin ice. You've been* ~*ed. He* ~*ed me that there were pickpockets in the crowd/*~*ed me against pickpockets.* ~ *sb off,* give him notice that he must go or stay away, eg from private property. ~·**ing** *adj* that ~s: *He gave me a* ~*ing look. They fired some* ~*ing shots.* □ *n* **1** [C] that which ~s or serves to ~: *He paid no attention to my* ~*ings. Let this be a* ~*ing to you,* Let this accident, misfortune, etc teach you to be careful in future. *There were gale* ~*ings to shipping along the coast.* **2** [U] action of ~ing; state of being ~*ed: You should take* ~*ing* (= be ~*ed) from what happened to me. The speaker sounded a note of* ~*ing,* spoke of possible danger. *The enemy attacked without* ~*ing.*

warp¹ /wɔːp/ *vt,vi* [VP6A,2A] (cause to) become bent or twisted from the usual or natural shape: *The hot sun* ~*ed the boards. His judgement/disposition is* ~*ed,* biased because of possible advantage for himself. □ *n* [C] twisted or bent condition in timber, etc, caused by uneven shrinking or expansion.

warp² /wɔːp/ *n the* ~, the threads over and under which other threads (the *weft* or *woof*) are passed when cloth is woven on a loom.

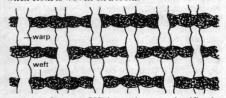

war·rant /'wɒrənt *US:* 'wɔːr-/ *n* **1** [U] justification or authority: *He had no* ~ *for saying so/for what he did.* **2** [C] written order giving official authority for sth: *a* ~ *to arrest a suspected criminal. The 'death-*~ *has been signed. A* ~ *is out for his arrest/against him. Here are the* ~*s for your dividends,* ie on shares. **3** [C] certificate appointing a man as a ~ officer. '~ **officer** *n* highest grade of non-commissioned officer in the army, air force, (GB) marines, (US) navy. □ *vt* **1** [VP6A] be a ~(1) for: *Nothing can* ~ *such insolence. His interference was certainly not* ~*ed.* **2** [VP6A,9,25] assure: *This material is* ~*ed (to be) pure silk. I'll* ~ *him an*

honest and reliable man. I can't ~ it to be/~ that it is genuine. He'll be back, I ~ (= assure) you, when the money's paid out. **war·ran·tee** /ˌwɒrən'tiː: *US:* ˌwɔːr-/ *n* person to whom a warranty is made. **war·ran·tor** /'wɒrəntɔː(r) *US:* 'wɔːr-/ *n* person who makes a warranty. **war·ranty** /'wɒrəntɪ *US:* 'wɔːr-/ *n* [C] (*pl* -ties) authority; (written or printed) guarantee (eg to repair or replace defective goods): *What* ~*y have you for doing this? Can you give me a* ~*y of quality for these goods? The car is still under* ~*y.*

war·ren /'wɒrən *US:* 'wɔːrən/ *n* [C] area of land in which there are many burrows in which rabbits live and breed; (fig) (usu over-populated) building or district in which it is difficult to find one's way about: *lose oneself in a* ~ *of narrow streets.*

war·rior /'wɒrɪə(r) *US:* 'wɔːr-/ *n* (liter, rhet) soldier; fighter: (attrib) *a* ~ *race.*

wart /wɔːt/ *n* small, hard, dry growth on the skin; similar growth on a plant. '~·**hog** *n* kinds of African pig with two large tusks and ~-like growths on the face.

wary /'weərɪ/ *adj* (-ier, -iest) cautious; in the habit of looking out for possible danger or trouble: *be* ~ *of giving offence/of strangers; keep a* ~ *eye on sb; a* ~ *old fox.* **war·ily** /-əlɪ/ *adv* **wari·ness** *n*

was /*weak form:* wəz; *strong form:* wɒz *US:* wʌz/ ⇨ be¹.

wash¹ /wɒʃ *US:* wɔːʃ/ *n* **1** (*sing* only, usu with *indef art*) act of washing; being washed: *Will you give the car a* ~*/a* ˌ~*-'down, please.* **have a** ~ **and brush up,** wash oneself and make oneself tidy. **2** (*sing* only) clothing, sheets, etc to be washed or being washed; place (laundry) where they are being washed: *She has a large* ~ *this week. She was hanging out the* ~. *All my shirts are at the* ~. *When does the* ~ *come back from the laundry?* **3 the** ~ **(of),** movement or flow of water; sound made by moving water: *the* ~ *of the waves; the* ~ *made by a steamer's propeller(s).* **4** [U] thin, weak or inferior liquid: *This soup is a mere* ~, is too watery, has no flavour or substance. **5** [U] kitchen liquid with waste food (eg vegetable peelings and scraps) to be given to pigs. **6** (usu in compounds, ⇨ under the first part) liquid prepared for a special purpose: '*white*~, for putting on walls; '*mouth-*~, for disinfecting the mouth; '*eye*~.

wash² /wɒʃ *US:* wɔːʃ/ *vt,vi* **1** [VP6A,15B,22,2A] make clean with or in water or other liquid: *one's hands/clothes. W*~ *them clean. Go and* ~ *yourself. I must* ~ *before dinner. He never* ~*es* (ie ~es himself) *in cold water.* ~ **one's hands of sth/sb,** say one is no longer responsible for. ~ **one's dirty linen in public,** ⇨ linen. ~ **sth down,** clean by ~ing, esp by using a stream or jet of water (eg from a hose): ~ *down a car/the decks of a ship.* ~ **sth away/off/out,** remove by ~ing: ~ *dirty marks off a wall;* ~ *out blood stains.* **be/ look/feel** ~**ed out,** (fig, colloq) pale and tired; exhausted. ~ **up, (a)** (GB) ~ dishes, cutlery, etc, after a meal. **(b)** (US) ~ one's face and hands. ~ **sth up,** (GB) ~ dishes, cutlery, etc after a meal: ~ *up the dinner things.* Hence, ˌ~·**ing-'up** *n* [U]. (Note: *up* indicates that a number of dishes, etc are to be ~ed. For a single article *up* is not used: *Please* ~ *this plate*). **(all)** ~**ed up,** (colloq) ruined; failed. **2** [VP2A] (of materials) be capable of being ~ed without damage or loss of colour: *Does this material* ~ *well? That argument/excuse will not* ~, (fig) will not bear examination, is weak. **3** [VP6A] (of the sea or a river) flow past or against: *The sea ~es the base of the cliffs.* **4** [VP15B] (of moving liquid) carry away, or in a specified direction: *He was ~ed overboard by a huge wave. All this timber has been ~ed up* (ie carried up on to the beach) *by the waves. The cliffs are being gradually ~ed away by the sea.* **~ sth down (with),** swallow (liquid) with: *My lunch was bread and cheese ~ed down with beer.* **~ed out, (a)** (of games such as cricket, of horse-races, etc) made impossible, cancelled, by heavy rain or flooding. **(b)** (of roads, etc) made impassable by heavy rain, floods, etc. **5** [VP6A,15A] scoop out: *The water had ~ed a channel in the sand.* **6** [VP2C] go flowing, sweeping or splashing (*along, out, in, into, over,* etc): *We heard the waves ~ing against the sides of our boat. Huge waves ~ed over the deck.* **~-able** /-əbl/ *adj* that can be ~ed without being spoiled.

wash- /wɒʃ US: wɔːʃ/ (in compounds; often used as a substitute for *washing*). '**~-basin** *n* basin for holding water in which to wash one's face and hands. '**~-board** *n* board with ridges on it, on which clothes are washed (at home). '**~-bowl** *n* (US) = ~-basin. '**~-cloth** *n* (US) = face-cloth. '**~-day** *n* day on which clothes were washed (at home). '**~-hand-basin** *n* = ~-basin. '**~-drawing** *n* one made with a brush in a black or neutral water-colour. '**~-hand-stand** *n* = ~-stand. '**~-house** *n* room or out-building equipped for washing. '**~-leather** *n* [C,U] (piece of) chamois leather, used for cleaning and polishing windows and other surfaces. '**~-out** *n* **(a)** place in a railway or road where a flood or heavy rain has carried away earth, rock, etc and interrupted communications. **(b)** (colloq) useless or unsuccessful person; complete failure or fiasco. '**~-room** *n* (US) lavatory (esp in a public building, etc). '**~-stand** *n* (now old-fashioned, except in houses where there is no piped supply of water to bathrooms or bedrooms) piece of furniture with a basin, jug, etc for washing in a bedroom. '**~-tub** *n* large wooden tub in which to wash clothes.

washer /'wɒʃə(r) US: 'wɔːʃ-/ *n* **1** machine for washing clothes, or ('*dish-~*) dishes. **2** '**~-woman,** laundress. **3** small flat ring of metal, plastic, rubber or leather for making a joint or screw tight. ⇨ the illus at **bolt**.

wash·ing /'wɒʃɪŋ US: 'wɔː-/ *n* [U] **1** washing or being washed. **2** clothes being washed or to be washed: *hang out the ~ on the line to dry.* '**~-day** *n* = wash-day, ⇨ wash-. '**~-machine** *n* power driven machine for washing clothes. '**~ soda** *n* sodium carbonate, used, dissolved in water, for washing clothes or dishes. **,~-'up** *n* ⇨ wash up at wash²(1).

washy /'wɒʃɪ US: 'wɔː-/ *adj* (of liquids) thin, watery; (of colours) faded-looking; pale; (of feeling, style) lacking in vigour.

wasp /wɒsp US: wɔːsp/ *n* kinds of flying insect of which the common kind has a narrow waist, black and yellow stripes and a powerful sting in the tail. ⇨ the illus at **insect**. **,~-'waisted** *adj* slender at the waist. **~-ish** /-ɪʃ/ *adj* irritable; ill tempered; sharp in making retorts.

was·sail /'wɒseɪl/ *n* (archaic) time of drinking and merry-making; spiced ale or other liquor drunk at such a time.

wast·age /'weɪstɪdʒ/ *n* [U] amount wasted; loss by waste.

waste /weɪst/ *adj* **1** (of land) that is not or cannot be used; no longer of use; barren: ~ *land,* not occupied or used for any purpose. '**~-land** /-lænd/ *n* **(a)** barren, desolate or unused land. **(b)** land ravaged by war, etc: *Vietnam reduced to ~land by bombing and shelling.* **(c)** (fig) life, society, looked upon as culturally and spiritually barren. **lay ~,** destroy the crops in, ravage (eg territory occupied in war). **2** useless; thrown away because not wanted: ~-*paper;* ~ *products,* unwanted after a manufacturing process. □ *vt,vi* **1** [VP6A,14,2A] ~ *sth (on sth),* make no use of; use without a good purpose; use more of (sth) than is necessary: ~ *one's time and money on paying bribes;* ~ *one's words/ breath,* talk without making any impression (on sb). *All his efforts were ~d,* had no result. **W~ not, want not,** (prov) If you do not ~ your money, etc you are unlikely to be in need. **2** [VP6A] make (land) waste; ravage. **3** [VP6A,2A,C] (cause to) lose strength by degrees: *He's wasting away. Consumption is a wasting disease. His body was ~d by long illness.* **4** [VP2A] be ~d: *Turn that tap off—the water is wasting.* □ *n* **1** [U] wasting or being ~d: *There's too much ~ in this house. It's a ~ of time to wait any longer. What a ~ of energy! go/run to ~,* be ~d: *What a pity to see all that water running to ~!* eg instead of being used for generating electric current. **2** [U] ~ material; refuse. '**~-basket/-bin** (US), **,~-'paper-basket** (GB) *nn* basket or other container for scraps of paper, etc. '**~-pipe** *n* pipe for carrying off used or superfluous water. **3** [U] area of ~ land: *the ~s of the Sahara;* dreary scene: *a ~ of waters.* **~r** *n* (colloq) wastrel. **~-ful** /-fl/ *adj* causing ~; using more than is needed: ~*ful habits/processes;* ~*ful expenditure.* **~-fully** /-fəlɪ/ *adv*

wast·rel /'weɪstrəl/ *n* good-for-nothing person; wasteful person.

watch¹ /wɒtʃ/ *n* **1** [U] act of watching, esp to see that all is well. **be on the ~ (for),** be watching for (sth or sb, or esp possible danger). **keep ~ (on/ over),** look out for danger, etc. '**~-dog** *n* dog kept to protect property, esp a house; (fig) sb or sth that protects. '**~-tower** *n* high tower from which to keep ~, eg in a forest, to look for forest fires, or a fortified observation post. **2 the ~,** (hist) body of men employed to go through the streets and protect people and their property, esp at night: *the constables of the ~; call out the ~.* **3** (in ships) period of duty (4 or 2 hours) for part of the crew (**the first ~,** 8pm to midnight. **the middle ~,** midnight to 4am; **the 'dog-~s,** 4pm to 6pm or 6pm to 8pm); either of the halves into which a ship's crew is divided for purposes of duty (called **the starboard** and **port ~es** from the positions of the men's bunks in former times). **on ~,** on duty in this way. **keep ~,** be on ~. **4** (old use) period of wakefulness in the night: *in the ~es of the night,* while one lies awake. '**~ night service,** church service at midnight, New Year's Eve. **~-ful** /-fl/ *adj* on the ~; wide-awake. **~-fully** /-fəlɪ/ *adv* **~-ful-ness** *n* **~-man** /-mən/ *n* (*pl* -men) **(a)** (hist) member of the ~(2). **(b)** man employed to guard a building (eg a bank, block of offices, factory) against thieves, esp at night. **~-word** /-wɜːd/ *n* **(a)** password. **(b)** slogan.

watch² /wɒtʃ/ *vt,vi* **1** [VP2A,B,C,3A,4,6A,8,10,15A,18A,19A] look at; keep the eyes on: *W~ me carefully. W~ what I do and how I do it. We sat there ~ing the cricket. Are*

you going to play or only ~? *He* ~ed *to see* (= ~ed in order to see) *what would happen. I* ~ed *her cross the street,* looked at and saw this action from start to finish. *I sat* ~ing *the shadows creep across the floor,* looked at and saw this happening (but not necessarily from start to finish). *My solicitor is* ~ing *the case for me/holds a* ~ing *brief for me,* is present in court during the case to protect my interests. ~ *one's step,* (a) be careful not to fall or stumble. (b) be careful not to make an error, let sb win an advantage, etc, eg in negotiations. ~ *one's time,* (more usu *bide*) wait for the right time. ~ *the time,* keep your eye on the time (eg to avoid being late for sth). ~ *(out) (for sth),* look out for: *There's a policeman* ~ing *outside,* ie for anything suspicious: *The doctor told her to* ~ *out* (= be on the look-out) *for symptoms of measles.* ~ *out,* be on one's guard. ~ *(over) sth,* guard; protect: *Will you* ~ *(over) my clothes while I have a swim?* 2 [VP2A] (old use) remain awake: ~ *all night at the bedside of a sick child.* ~er *n* person who ~es.
watch³ /wotʃ/ *n* small timepiece that can be carried in the pocket or worn on the wrist (cf *clock*): *What time is it by your* ~? *What does your* ~ *say?* '~-glass *n* disc covering the face of a ~. '~-guard/-chain *n* strap or chain for securing a ~ to the clothing. '~-key *n* separate key for winding a ~. '~-maker *n* person who makes or repairs ~es.
water¹ /'wɔːtə(r)/ *n* 1 [U] liquid (**H₂O**) as in rivers, lakes, seas and oceans: *W* ~ *is changed into steam by heat and into ice by cold. Fish live in (the)* ~. *by* ~, by boat, ship, barge, etc. *in deep* ~(s), experiencing or undergoing difficulty or misfortune. *in smooth* ~, making smooth or easy progress. *on the* ~, in a boat, etc. *under* ~, flooded: *The fields were under* ~ *after the heavy rain. be in/get into hot* ~, have/get into trouble (esp because of foolish behaviour, etc). *cast/throw one's bread upon the* ~(s), do a good action without requiring reward, although later some unexpected return may come. *drink the* ~s, go to a spa where there are mineral ~s and drink them for one's health. *go through fire and* ~ *(for sb/sth),* undergo severe hardship and trials. *hold* ~, (of a theory, etc) be sound when tested. *keep one's head above* ~, avoid (esp financial) troubles or misfortunes. *make* ~, (a) pass urine from the bladder. (b) (of a ship) have a leak. *spend money, etc like* ~, extravagantly. *throw cold* ~ *on* (a plan, etc), discourage (it). *tread* ~, ⇨ tread, *vi, vt*(4). *like a fish out of* ~, feeling uncomfortable, behaving awkwardly, because of unaccustomed surroundings, an unfamiliar situation, etc. *Still* ~s *run deep,* (prov) Beneath a quiet manner there may be depths of emotion, knowledge, cunning, etc. *written in* ~, (of a name, reputation, etc) soon forgotten; transient. ~ *on the brain/knee, etc,* morbid accumulation of fluid. *the* ~s *of forgetfulness,* oblivion. '*table*/'*mineral* ~s, with a mineral ingredient, bottled for use at table. '*back*~, ⇨ back⁴(3). 2 [U] the state of the tide: *at high/low* ~; *high/low* ~ *mark. in low* ~, (fig) short of money. 3 (*pl*) seas as indicated by a preceding word: *in Korean* ~s, on the seas near Korea; *a ship for service in Home* ~s, on the seas near the country to which the ship belongs. 4 (usu *pl*) mass of ~: *the* ('*head-*)~s *of the Nile,* the lake from which it flows. *The* ~s *of the lake flow out over a large waterfall.* 5 [U] solution of a substance in ~: '*lavender-*~; '*rose-*~, *etc.* 6 *of the first* ~, of the

finest quality: *a diamond of the first* ~. 7 (in compounds) '~-bird *n* kinds of bird that swim or wade in (esp fresh) ~. '~-biscuit *n* thin, hard biscuit made of flour and ~, usu eaten with butter and cheese. '~-blister *n* blister on the skin containing a colourless liquid, not blood. '~-borne *adj* (a) (of goods) carried by ~. (b) (of diseases) passed on by the use of contaminated drinking-~. '~-bottle *n* (a) glass container for ~ at table or in a bedroom. (b) metal flask (US = *canteen*) for use by a soldier, scout, etc. '~-buffalo *n* the common domestic buffalo of India, Indonesia, etc. ⇨ the illus at domestic. '~-butt, ⇨ butt¹(2). '~-cannon, high-pressure hose, for forcing a jet of ~, eg to disperse rioters. '~-cart *n* cart with a tank for ~, either for sale or for sprinkling on dusty roads, etc. '~-chute *n* sloping channel leading to ~, down which boats, toboggans, etc slide, eg at a fun fair. '~-closet *n* (common abbr **WC**) small room with a pan in which matter evacuated from the bowels may be flushed down a drain-pipe by ~ from a cistern. '~-colour (US = -color) *n* (a) (*pl*) paints (to be) mixed with ~, not oil. (b) picture painted with ~-colours. (c) (*pl* or *sing*) the art of painting such pictures. '~-course *n* (channel of a) brook or stream. '~-cress *n* [U] creeping plant that grows in running ~, with hot-tasting leaves used in salads. '~ diviner, ⇨ diviner. '~-fall *n* [C] fall of ~, esp where a river falls over rocks or a cliff. '~-finder *n* dowser, ⇨ dowsing. '~-fowl *n* (collective *pl*) ~birds, esp those that swim, considered as suitable for shooting by sportsmen. '~-front *n* land at the ~'s edge, esp the part of a town facing the sea, the harbour, a lake, etc. '~-glass *n* [U] thick liquid used for coating eggs to keep them in good condition. '~-hen *n* = *moorhen,* ⇨ moor¹. '~-hole *n* shallow depression in which ~ collects (esp in the bed of a river otherwise dry, and to which animals go to drink). '~-ice *n* [C] frozen ~ with sugar and fruit-juices or other flavouring. '~-jacket *n* case filled with ~ and fitted over part of a machine which is to be kept cool. '~ jump *n* obstacle (in show-jumping, steeplechases) of a ditch or water, usu with a fence, over which horses jump. '~-level *n* surface of ~ in a reservoir or other body of ~, esp as a datum for measurement. '~-lily *n* kinds of plant with broad, flat leaves floating on the surface of the ~, and white, blue or yellow flowers. '~-line *n* line along which the surface of the ~ touches a ship's side: *the load* ~-*line,* when the ship is loaded; *the light* ~-*line,* when the ship is empty of cargo. '~-logged /-lɒgd US: -lɔːgd/ *adj* (a) (of wood) so saturated with ~ that it will barely float. (b) (of a ship) so full of ~ that it will barely float. (c) (of land) thoroughly soaked with ~. '~-main *n* main pipe in a system of ~-supply. '~-man /-mən/ *n* (*pl* -men) boatman; man who manages a boat for hire; ferryman. '~-mark *n* (a) manufacturer's design in some kinds of paper, seen when the paper is held against light. (b) mark which shows how high ~ (eg the tide, a river) has risen or how low it has fallen. '~-melon *n* large, smooth-skinned melon with juicy pink or red flesh; trailing plant bearing such melons. '~-mill *n* mill whose machinery is turned by ~-power. '~-nymph *n* nymph associated with a river, lake, etc. '~-polo *n* [U] game played by two teams of swimmers who try to throw a ball into a goal. '~-power *n* [U] power obtained from flowing or falling ~, used to drive machinery or generate electric current. **'~·proof** adj which does not let ~ through: ~proof material. □ n ~proof coat; raincoat. □ vt make ~proof. **'~-rat/-vole** n rat-like animal frequenting ~. **'~-rate** n (GB) charge made (usu quarterly) for the use of ~ from a public ~-supply. **'~-shed** n line of high land separating river systems; (fig) dividing line between events which take different courses. **'~-side** n margin of the sea, a river, lake, etc: go for a stroll along the ~side. **'~-skiing** n the sport of skiing on ~ while being towed at speed by a fast motor-boat. **'~-skin** n skin bag for carrying ~. **'~-softener** n device or substance for removing the causes of hardness in ~. **'~-spaniel** n kind of spaniel that can be trained to swim out and bring back ~fowl, etc shot down by sportsmen. **'~-spout** n **(a)** pipe or spout from which ~ is discharged, eg rainwater from a roof. **(b)** whirlwind over the sea which draws up a whirling mass of ~ so as to look like a funnel-shaped column of ~ going up to the clouds. **'~-supply** n system of providing and storing ~, amount of ~ stored, for a district, town, building, etc. **'~-table** n level below which the ground is saturated with ~: The ~table has been lowered by drought. **'~-tight** adj **(a)** made, fastened, etc so that ~ cannot get in or out: ~tight boots/joints/ compartments in a ship. **(b)** (fig, of an agreement, etc) drawn up so that there can be no escape from any of the provisions; leaving no possibility of misunderstanding. **'~-tower** n one which supports a large tank which secures pressure for distributing a ~-supply. **'~-waggon** (US = **-wagon**) n = ~-cart: on the ~-waggon, ⇨ waggon(1). **'~-way** n navigable channel (eg a canal, channel up a river where the ~ is deep enough for ships). **'~-wheel** n one turned by a flow of ~, used to work machinery. **'~-wings** n pl floats worn on the shoulders by a person learning to swim. **'~-works** n (with sing or pl v) **(a)** system of reservoirs, pumping stations, ~-mains, etc for supplying ~. **(b)** ornamental fountains. **(c)** (colloq) (working of the) bladder: Are your ~works all right? Can you pass urine normally? **(d)** (colloq) tears: turn on the ~works, shed tears. **'~-worn** adj (of rocks, etc) made smooth by the action of ~.

water² /'wɔ:tə(r)/ vt,vi **1** [VP6A] put water on; sprinkle with water: ~ the lawn/the plants/the streets. ~-ing-can /'wɔ:tərɪŋ kæn/ n container with a long spout, used for ~ing plants. ~-ing-cart /'wɔ:tərɪŋ kɑ:t/ n one with a tank and a sprinkler for ~ing roads (to settle the dust, clean them). **2** [VP6A] give water to: ~ the horses. **3** [VP2A] (of the eyes or mouth) fill with water; have much liquid: The smoke made my eyes ~. The smell from the kitchen made my mouth ~, aroused my appetite. Hence, **'mouth-~ing** adj highly appetizing. **4** [VP15B] ~ sth down, add water to: This whisky has been ~ed (down). The story has been ~ed down, (fig) weakened, eg by making details less vivid. **5** [VP6A] (fin) increase (a company's debt or nominal capital) by issuing new shares without increasing the assets. **6** ~ed (pp as adj) supplied with water: a country ~ed by numerous rivers. ~ed silk, manufactured so that there are wavy markings on the surface. **7** ~-ing-place /'wɔ:tərɪŋ pleɪs/ n **(a)** water-hole; place to which animals go to drink. **(b)** spa. **(c)** seaside resort.

Wat·er·loo /ˌwɔ:tə'lu:/ n meet one's ~, be finally and crushingly defeated in a contest (esp after a period of success).

wat·ery /'wɔ:tərɪ/ adj (-ier, -iest) **1** of or like water; (esp of cooked vegetables) containing, cooked in, too much water: ~ soup/cabbage. **2** (of colour) pale. **3** (of the eyes or lips) running with, covere, with, water. **4** suggesting that there will be rain: a ~ moon/sky.

watt /wɒt/ n unit of electrical power: a 60 ~ light-bulb. **wat·tage** /'wɒtɪdʒ/ n [U] amount of electrical power expressed in ~s.

wattle¹ /'wɒtl/ n **1** structure of sticks or twigs woven over and under thicker upright sticks, used for fences, walls, etc. ~ and 'daub, this structure covered with clay, for walls and roofs. **2** kinds of Australian acacia supplying such twigs, with golden flowers adopted as the national emblem.

wattle² /'wɒtl/ n red flesh hanging down from the head or throat of a bird, esp a turkey. ⇨ the illus at fowl.

wave /weɪv/ vi,vt **1** [VP2A,3A] ~ (at/to/in), (of a fixed object, eg a hand, flag, branch) move regularly to and fro, up and down: flags/branches waving in the wind. Bill ~ed at me, ie his hand, eg as a signal. Bill ~ed to me, ie his hand, eg as a greeting (in meeting or parting). **2** [VP6A,15A,12A,13A] cause (sth) to move in this way (eg to make a signal or request, to give a greeting, etc): ~ one's hand at sb; ~ one's umbrella/a flag. She ~d (me) a greeting. She ~d goodbye to us. **3** [VP15B,16A] cause (sb) to move in a certain direction by waving: The officer ~d his men on/~d them to advance. He ~d us away. ~ sth aside, (fig) dismiss: My objections were ~d aside. **4** [VP2A] (of a line or surface, of hair) be in a series of curves (∿∿∿): Her hair ~s beautifully. **5** [VP6A] cause to be in a series of curves: She's had her hair ~d. ⇨ perm. □ n [C] **1** long ridge of water, esp on the sea, between two hollows (or troughs, furrows); such a ridge curling over and breaking on the shore. the ~s, (poet) the sea. in ~s, in successive lines like sea-~s: The infantry attacked in ~s. **2** act of waving(1) the hand; waving movement: with a ~ of his hand, eg as a signal. **3** curve like a ~ of the sea: the ~s in a girl's hair. She has a natural ~ in her hair. **4** steady increase and spread: a ~ of enthusiasm/indignation; a 'crime ~; a 'heat ~, a period of weather with temperatures much higher than usual and over a large area. **5** ~-like motion by which heat, sound, light, radio, magnetism, etc is spread or carried. **'~-length** n distance between the highest point (the crest) of one ~ and that of the next (esp with reference to radio telegraphy). **long/medium/short ~, ~** used in radio broadcasting: a short-~ transmitter. **wavy** adj (-ier, -iest) having ~-like curves: a wavy line; wavy hair.

wa·ver /'weɪvə(r)/ vi [VP2A,C] **1** move uncertainly or unsteadily: ~ing shadows/flames. **2** be or become unsteady; begin to give way: His courage ~ed. He ~ed in his resolution. The line of troops ~ed and then broke. **3** hesitate: ~ between two opinions. ~er n person who ~s.

wax¹ /wæks/ n [U] soft yellow substance produced by bees ('beeswax) and used for making honeycomb cells; kinds of substance similar to beeswax (eg as obtained from petroleum); such material bleached and purified, used for making candles, for modelling, etc: (attrib) a wax candle; a wax doll, one with the head made of wax; 'paraffin wax; 'cobblers'-wax, kind of resin used on thread; 'ear-wax, substance secreted in the ears. **'wax-**

chandler *n* maker or seller of candles. **'wax-paper** *n* paper that is waterproofed with a layer of wax. **'wax-work** *n* object modelled in wax, esp the form of a human being with face and hands in wax, coloured and clothed to look like life and to be exhibited: *go to see the waxworks at Madame Tussaud's*, a place in London famous for waxworks. **'sealing-wax,** ⇨ seal, *vt*(1). □ *vt* [VP6A] cover, polish or treat with wax: *wax furniture/a wooden floor/linoleum*. **waxen** /'wæksn/ *adj* **1** (old use; now usu *wax*) made of wax. **2** like wax: *a waxen complexion*. **waxy** *adj* like wax; having a smooth, pale surface; like wax in texture: *waxy potatoes*.

wax² /wæks/ *vi* **1** [VP2A] (esp of the moon, contrasted with *wane*) show a larger bright area. **2** [VP2D] (old use) become: *wax merry/lyrical/eloquent*.

wax³ /wæks/ *n* (sl) fit of anger: *be in/get into/put sb into a wax*. **waxy** *adj* angry.

way¹ /weɪ/ *n* **1** road, street, path, etc: (in compounds) **'highway; 'railway; 'byway;** *a way across the fields; a covered* (= roofed) *way; the Appian Way,* a Roman road in Italy. **'clear~,** ⇨ clear ¹(5). *There's no way through. My friend lives across-/over the way*, on the other side of the street (or road). **pave the way for,** prepare for, prepare people to accept, (reforms, etc). **the Way of the Cross,** a series of paintings, carvings, etc (usu in or near a church) illustrating the progress of Jesus to Calvary. **2** route, road (to be) used (*from* one place *to* another): *Which is the best/right/quickest/shortest, etc way there/from A to B? Can you find your way home? We lost the way/our way in the dark. Which is the way in/out? The longest/farthest way round/about is the nearest way home,* (prov) Short cuts are often delusive. *We'd better stop and ask someone the way. He made/pushed/fought/felt his way out/back, etc. We had to pick our way along the muddy path.* **go one's way(s),** depart. **go out of one's way (to do sth),** make a special effort: *He went out of his way to be rude to me/to help me.* **lead the way,** go in front as leader; show by example how sth may be done. **make one's way in life,** succeed. **make the best of one's way,** go as fast as one can. **make one's way (to/towards),** go. **pay one's way,** (a) keep out of debt. (b) pay one's share of expenses instead of letting others pay. **the parting of the ways,** (fig) the time when an important decision must be made as to future plans, etc. **by way of,** via; using a route through: *He came by way of Dover.* ⇨ also 14 below. **out of the way,** exceptional, uncommon: *He has done nothing out of the way yet.* **out-of-the-'way,** (attrib use) remote: *an out-of-the-way place/corner.* **3 by the way,** (a) during a journey. (b) (fig) incidentally; in passing (often used to introduce a remark not connected with the subject of conversation). **on the/one's way,** being

waterbirds and seabirds

FLAMINGO

PELICAN

BITTERN

crest

GUILLEMOT

CRANE

PETREL

MOORHEN

SANDPIPER

GULL

engaged in going or coming: *They're still on the way. I'll buy some on the/my way home. He's on the way to success. She's got another child on the way,* (colloq) is pregnant again. **on the way out,** (fig; colloq) about to become out of date, out of fashion. **4** [C] method or plan; course of action: *the right/wrong/best, etc way to do/of doing a thing. Is this the way to do it/the way you do it? Do it (in) your own way if you don't like my way. The work must be finished (in) one way or another.* **Where there's a will there's a way,** (prov) If we want to do sth, we will find a method of doing it. **ways and means,** methods, esp of providing money. **have/get one's own way,** get/do what one wants. **go/take one's own way,** act independently, esp contrary to the advice of others. **5** (*sing* only) distance between two points; distance (to be) traversed: *It's a long way off/a long way from here. The roots go a long way down. Your work is still a long way off perfection,* is far from being perfect. *Your work this week is better by a long way,* much better. *This will go a long way* (= will be very helpful) *in overcoming the difficulty.* **6** [C] direction: *He went this/that/the other way. Look this way, please. He couldn't look my way,* towards me. *Such opportunities never come/fall my way,* come to me. *You've got your hat on the wrong way,* eg back to front. *He's in a fair way to succeed,* is making progress in the right direction. **put**

sb in the way of (doing) sth, help him to make a start: *A kind friend put him in the way of earning a living.* **7** (colloq; *sing* only; not stressed) neighbourhood: *He lives somewhere Lincoln way,* near Lincoln. *The crops are looking very well our way,* in our part of the country. **8** [U] advance in some direction; progress (esp of a ship or boat). **be under way; have way 'on,** (of a ship) be moving through the water. **gather/lose way,** gain/lose speed: *The boat slowly gathered way.* **get under way,** start to move forward. **give way,** (of oarsmen) row hard. Also ⇨ give¹(10). **make way,** (lit or fig) advance. **9** [U] space for forward movement, for passing ahead; freedom to go forward: *Don't stand in the way. Tell that boy not to get in the way. Tell him to stand out of the/my way. Clear the way!* be/put sth out of harm's way, in a safe place. **get sth out of the way,** settle it, dispose of it. **give way (to sth/sb),** ⇨ give¹(10). **make way (for),** allow space or a free passage: *All traffic has to make way for a fire-engine.* **put sb out of the way,** put him in prison, kill him (secretly), or otherwise get rid of him. **put sb in the way of sth,** give him the opportunity of securing, eg a good bargain. **see one's way (clear) to doing sth,** see how to do it; (esp) feel justified in doing it: *I don't see my way clear to helping you. I don't see my way clear to recommending you for the job.* **right of way,** ⇨ right³(2). **10** [C] custom; manner

PUFFIN

CURLEW

PENGUIN

HERON

ALBATROSS

GREBE

SNIPE

SWAN

STORK

CORMORANT

of behaving; personal peculiarity: *the good old ways; English/Chinese, etc ways of life/living; the way of the world,* what appears to be justified by custom. *It's not his way to be mean,* Meanness is not in his nature. *It's disgraceful the way he drinks,* His habit of (excessive) drinking is disgraceful. *I don't like the way* (= manner in which) *he looks at me. Don't take offence—it's only his way,* a manner of behaving that has no special significance. **to 'my way of thinking,** in my opinion. **the way,** (colloq; adverbial use) as; in the manner that: *He doesn't do it the way I do.* **he/she has a way with him/her,** he/she is persuasive. **mend one's ways,** improve one's manners, behaviour, etc. **11** [C] respect; point or detail: *He's a clever man in some ways. Can I help you in any way? He is in no way* (= not at all) *to blame. They are in no way similar. The work was well done in one way,* to a limited extent but not on the whole. *He's an amusing man in his* (*own*) *way. What have we in the way of food,* What food is there (eg in the house, for the next meal, etc)? **no way,** (sl) in no way; not at all. **12** [C] condition, state, degree: *Things are in a bad way. She was in a terrible way,* much agitated. **'any way,** in either case; in any case or event. **each way/both ways,** (in backing horses) to win, to get a place in the first three. **in the 'family way,** (colloq) pregnant. **in a big/small way,** on a big/ small scale: *live in a small way,* simply, without ostentation; *a printer in a small way; advertise in a big way.* **have it both ways,** choose first one and then the other of alternatives in order to suit one's convenience, argument, etc. **13** ordinary course: *do sth in the way of business.* **14 by way of,** (a) as a substitute for or as a kind of: *say sth by way of apology/introduction.* (b) for the purpose of, with the intention of: *make inquiries by way of learning the facts of the case.* (c) in the course of: *by way of business.* ⇨ also **2** above. **15** (*pl*) structure of heavy timber on which a ship is built and down which it slides when launched. ⇨ *slipway* at **slip¹**(6). **16** (compounds) **'way-bill** *n* list of goods being conveyed by a carrier, with instructions about their destinations, etc. **'way-farer** /-feərə(r)/ *n* (liter) traveller, esp on foot. **'way-faring** /-feərɪŋ/ *adj* travelling: *a wayfaring man.* **'way-side** *n* side of a road: (attrib) *wayside flowers.*

way² /weɪ/ *adv* far; by a long way **¹**(5): *The discussion wandered way off the point. Bill finished way ahead of me in the 100 metres sprint. The wage-claim is way above what the firm can afford.* **,way-'out** *adj* (colloq) strange; eccentric: *way-out clothes/ideas.*

way·lay /ˌweɪ'leɪ/ *vt* (*pt,pp* -laid /-'leɪd/) [VP6A] (wait somewhere to) attack, rob (sb); accost (sb) unexpectedly (usu with a request): *He was waylaid by bandits. He waylaid me with a request for a loan.*

way·ward /'weɪwəd/ *adj* self-willed; not easily controlled or guided: *a ～ child; a child with a ～ disposition.*

we /wiː/ *pron* **1** used by a speaker or writer referring to himself and another or others (with object form *us*). **2** used by a King, Pope, etc in proclamations instead of *I,* and by the writer of an unsigned article in a newspaper, etc.

weak /wiːk/ *adj* (-er, -est) **1** (opp of *strong*) lacking in strength; easily broken; unable to resist hard wear or use, attack, etc: *too ～ to walk; ～ in the legs; a table with ～ legs; a ～ defence; a ～ team;*

the ～ points of an argument/plan. **,～-'kneed** *adj* (fig) lacking determination; ～ in character. **2** (of the senses, etc) below the usual standard: ～ (more usu *poor*) *sight and hearing; a ～ heart.* Hence, *～-eyed; ～-headed; ～-minded; ～-sighted.* **3** (of mixed liquids or solutions) watery; having little of some substance in relation to the water, etc: ～ *tea/beer; a ～ solution.* **4** not good; not efficient: ～ *in spelling/arithmetic/biology.* **5** (gram) ～ **verb,** one inflected by additions to the stem, not by vowel change (as *walk, walked,* contrasted with *run, ran* and *come, came*). ～ **form** (of the pronunciation of some common words), form occurring in an unstressed position, usu by the use of a different vowel sound or by the absence of a vowel sound or consonant (eg /ən/ or /n/ for /ænd/ *and,* as in *bread and butter* /ˌbred n 'bʌtə(r)/). *～-en* /'wiːkən/ *vt,vi* [VP6A,2A] make or become ～(er). *～-ling n ～* person or animal. *～-ly adv* in a ～ manner. □ *adj* delicate in health; not robust: *a ～ly child.* *～-ness n* **1** [U] state of being ～: *the ～ness of old age; the ～ness of a country's defences.* **2** [C] fault or defect of character: *We all have our little ～nesses.* **3 have a ～ness for,** a special or foolish liking for: *He has a ～ness for fish and chips/fast cars.*

weal¹ /wiːl/ *n* [U] (liter) well-being (chiefly in): ～ *and woe,* good and bad fortune; *for the public/ general ～,* the welfare of all.

weal² /wiːl/ *n* [C] mark on the skin made by a blow from a stick, whip, etc.

weald /wiːld/ *n* (GB) stretch of open country, formerly forest: *the ～ of Kent.*

wealth /welθ/ *n* **1** [U] (possession of a) great amount of property, money, etc; riches: *a man of ～; acquire great ～.* **2 a/the ～ of,** great amount or number of: *a book with a ～ of illustrations; the ～ of phrases and sentences to illustrate meanings in this dictionary.* *～-y adj* (-ier, -iest) having ～(1); rich. *～-ily* /-ɪlɪ/ *adv*

wean /wiːn/ *vt* **1** [VP6A] accustom (a baby, a young animal) to food other than its mother's milk. **2** [VP14] ～ *sb from sth,* cause (sb) to turn away (from a habit, companions, etc).

weapon /'wepən/ *n* sth designed for, or used in, fighting or struggling (eg swords, guns, fists, a strike by workmen): *Whether a gun is a ～ of offence or a ～ of defence depends upon which end of it you are at.* *～-less adj* without ～s.

wear¹ /weə(r)/ *n* [U] **1** wearing or being worn; use as clothing: *a suit for everyday ～; a coat that has been in constant ～. This carpet will stand any amount of hard ～. This coat is beginning to look the worse for ～,* shows signs of having been worn for a long time, so that it is no longer in a good or useful condition. **2** damage or loss of quality from use: *These shoes are showing* (*signs of*) ～. ～ **and tear,** damage, loss in value, from normal use. **3** capacity to endure: *There's not much ～ left in these shoes,* They cannot be worn much longer. **4** (chiefly in compounds or in terms used by tradesmen) things to wear: *'under～; 'foot～; 'ladies'/ 'men's ～; a shop that specializes in 'children's ～.*

wear² /weə(r)/ *vt,vi* (*pt* wore /wɔː(r)/, *pp* worn /wɔːn/) **1** [VP6A,22,15B] have on the body, carry on one's person or on some part of it; (of looks) have on the face: *He was ～ing a hat/spectacles/a beard/heavy shoes/a ring on his finger/a troubled look. This is a style that is much worn now,* that is in fashion now. *She never ～s green,* ie green clothes. *She used to* ~ *her hair long,* used to have long hair. *The house wore* (= had) *a neglected look.* ~ *the crown,* (a) be a monarch. (b) be a martyr. **2** [VP2C,D,4,22,15A,B] (cause to) become less useful or to be in a certain condition, by being used: *I have worn my socks into holes. This material has worn thin. The stones were worn by the constant flow of water. This old overcoat is much worn,* is much the worse for wear. ~ *away,* become impaired, thin, weak, as the result of constant use: *The inscription on the stone had worn away,* the words were difficult to read. ~ *sth away,* consume or impair sth by constant use, etc: *The footsteps of thousands of visitors had worn away the steps.* ~ *down,* become gradually smaller, thinner, weaker, etc: *The heels of these shoes are ~ing down.* ~ *sth down,* cause to ~ down. ~ *sb/sth down,* weaken by constant attack, nervous strain, etc: *These noisy children do* ~ *me down! We wore down the enemy's resistance.* ~ *off,* pass away: *The novelty will soon* ~ *off.* ~ *sth off,* cause to pass away by degrees; be rubbed off by friction: ~ *the nap off a piece of velvet.* ~ *(sth) out,* (cause to) become useless, threadbare, exhausted: *Cheap shoes soon* ~ *out. My shoes are worn out. His patience had/was at last worn out. He has worn out* (= outstayed) *his welcome.* ~ *sb out,* exhaust, tire out: *I'm worn out by all this hard work. That fellow ~s me out with his silly chatter.* Hence, ,worn-'out *attrib adj: a worn-out coat.* **3** [VP6A] make (a hole, groove, etc) in by rubbing or attrition: ~ *holes in a rug/one's socks. In time a path was worn across the field.* **4** [VP2B,2A,C] endure continued use; remain in a certain condition: *Good leather will* ~ *for years. This cloth has worn well/badly. Old Mr Smith is ~ing well,* still looks well in spite of his advanced age. **5** [VP2C] ~ *on/ away, etc,* (of time) go slowly or tediously; pass gradually: *as the evening wore on; as winter wore away; as his life wore towards its close.* ~er *n* person who is ~ing sth.. ~·able /-əbl/ *adj* that can be, or is fit to be, worn. ~·ing *adj* tiring: *a ~ing day.*

weary /'wɪərɪ/ *adj* (-ier, -iest) **1** tired: ~ *in body and mind; feel ~; be* ~ *of someone's constant grumbling.* **2** causing tiredness: *a* ~ *journey/wait; after walking ten* ~ *miles.* **3** showing tiredness: *a* ~ *sigh.* □ *vt,vi* [VP6A,14,2A,3A] ~ *sb (with sth);* ~ *of sth,* make or become ~: ~ *sb with requests;* ~ *of living all alone; wearied with marching and climbing.* wear·i·ly /-əlɪ/ *adv* wear·i·ness *n* wear·i·some /'wɪərɪsəm/ *adj* tiring; long and dull.

wea·sel /'wi:zl/ *n* small, fierce animal with red-brown fur, living on rats, rabbits, birds' eggs, etc.

weather¹ /'weðə(r)/ *n* **1** [U] conditions over a particular area and at a specific time with reference to sunshine, temperature, wind, rain, etc. (⇨ climate, used with reference to a long period of time, eg a season): *He stays indoors in wet* ~. *She goes out in all ~s* (pl here = all kinds of ~). *Many crops depend on the* ~. *be/feel under the* ~, (colloq) ill. *keep a/one's'*~ *eye open,* be on the alert; be on the look-out (for trouble, etc). *make good/bad* ~, (used by sailors) meet with good/ bad ~. *make heavy* ~ *of sth,* find it (unnecessarily) troublesome, difficult. *under stress of* ~, because of storms, etc. **2** (compounds) '~-**beaten** *adj* bearing marks or signs which come from exposure to the sun, wind, rain, etc: *a* ~-*beaten face.* '~-**boarding/-boards** *nn* horizontal boards each

of which overlaps the one below to cause rain to run off and so keep the wall, etc, from becoming damp. '~-**bound** *adj* unable to make or continue a journey because of bad ~. '~-**bureau** *n* office where the ~ is studied and where ~ forecasts are made; meteorological office. '~-**chart/-map** *n* diagram showing details of the ~ over a wide area. '~-**cock** *n* ~-vane in the shape of a cock. '~ **forecast** *n* ⇨ forecast. '~-**glass** *n* barometer. '~-**man** /-mæn/ *n* (pl -men) (colloq) man who reports and forecasts the ~. '~-**proof** *adj* able to stand exposure to the ~, to keep out rain, snow, wind, etc. '~-**ship** *n* one stationed at sea to make observations of the ~. '~-**station** *n* one where the ~ is observed. '~-**vane** *n* = vane(1).

weather² /'weðə(r)/ *vt,vi* **1** [VP6A] come through successfully; survive: ~ *a storm;* ~ *a crisis.* **2** [VP6A] sail to the windward of: ~ *an island.* **3** [VP6A] expose to the weather: ~ *wood,* leave it in the open air until it is properly shrunk and ready for use. ⇨ season, *vt,vi*(1). **4** [VP6A,2A] discolour, be discoloured, (cause to) become worn by the weather: *rocks ~ed by wind and water; ~ed limestone.*

weave /wi:v/ *vt,vi* (pt wove /wəʊv/, pp woven /'wəʊvn/) **1** [VP6A,15A,B,2A] ~ *sth (up) into sth;* ~ *sth (from sth),* make (by hand or by machine) (threads) into cloth, etc; make (cloth, etc) from threads; work at a loom: ~ *cotton yarn into cloth;* ~ *threads together; woven from/of silk;* make (garlands, baskets, etc) by a similar process: ~ *flowers into a wreath;* ~ *a garland of flowers.* **2** [VP6A,15A] (fig) put together, compose (a story, romance, etc): ~ *a story round an incident;* ~ *a plot. get weaving (on sth),* (sl) make an energetic start (on a task, etc). **3** [VP2C] twist and turn: *The driver was weaving* (his way) *through the traffic. The road ~s through the valleys.* □ *n* style of weaving: *a loose/tight/coarse/plain, etc* ~. ~r *n* person whose trade is weaving cloth at a loom. ~r-**bird** *n* tropical bird that makes its nest by tightly weaving together leaves, grass, twigs, etc.

web /web/ *n* [C] **1** network (usu fig): *a web of lies/deceit/intrigue.* **2** sth made of threads by a spider or other spinning creature: *a spider's web.* ⇨ cobweb. ⇨ the illus at arachnid. **3** skin joining the toes of some waterbird, eg ducks, geese, bats and some water-animals (eg frogs). Hence, ,web-'footed/-'toed *adjj* **webbed** *adj* having the toes joined by webs. ⇨ the illus at fowl.

web·bing /'webɪŋ/ *n* [U] strong fabric (usu coarse woven) used in belts, upholstery, binding the edges of rugs, etc.

wed /wed/ *vt,vi* (pt,pp wedded or wed) [VP6A,14,2A] **1** (journalism) marry. **2** (liter) unite: *simplicity wed to beauty.* **wedded to,** devoted to; unable to give up: *He is wedded to his own opinions and nothing can change him.*

we'd /wi:d/ = we had/would.

wed·ding /'wedɪŋ/ *n* marriage ceremony (and festivities connected with it): *invite one's friends to one's* ~; *a* ~ *dress.* '~ **breakfast** *n* meal for the bride and bridegroom, their relatives, friends, etc between the ~ ceremony and departure for the honeymoon. '~-**cake** *n* cake distributed to guests and sent in small portions to absent friends. '~-**ring** *n* ring placed on the bride's (and in some cases the groom's) finger and worn by her/him afterwards. **silver/golden/diamond** ~, 25th/50th/ 60th (or 75th) anniversary of a ~.

wedge /wedʒ/ *n* **1** V-shaped piece of wood or

metal, used to split wood or rock (by being hammered), to widen an opening, or to keep two things separate. **the thin end of the ~,** (fig) a small change or demand likely to lead to big changes or demands. **2** sth shaped like or used like a ~: *a ~ of cake*, eg cut from a large round cake; *seats arranged in a ~*, so as to form a triangle. □ *vt* [VP6A,15A,22] fix tightly (as) with a ~; keep in place with a ~: *~ packing into a crack; ~ a door open*, by placing a ~ under it. *I was so tightly ~d between two fat women that it was difficult for me to get up and leave the bus.*

wed-lock /'wedlɒk/ *n* [U] (legal) condition of being married: *born in lawful ~*, born of married parents; *born out of ~*, illegitimate.

Wed-nes-day /'wenzdɪ/ *n* fourth day of the week.

wee¹ /wiː/ *adj* very small: *just a wee drop of brandy in my coffee.* **a wee bit,** (adverbial) a little: *She's a wee bit jealous.* **the wee folk,** the fairies. **the wee hours,** (US) the hours after midnight. □ *n* (Scot) *bide a wee,* stay for a short time.

wee², **wee-wee** /('wiː) wiː/ *n* (used by and to small children) urine: *do a wee-wee.* □ *vi* urinate.

weed /wiːd/ *n* [C] **1** wild plant growing where it is not wanted (eg in a garden, or in a field of wheat): *My garden is running to ~s*, is overgrown with ~s. '**~-killer** *n* substance used to kill ~s. **2** (fig) thin, tall, weak-looking person or horse. **3** (dated sl) cigar; cigarette; tobacco; (modern sl) marijuana. □ *vt,vi* **1** [VP6A,2A] take ~s out of (the ground): *~ the garden; be busy ~ing.* **2** [VP15B] **~ sth/sb out,** sort or thin out; remove or get rid of (what is unwanted, or of lower value than the rest): *~ out the herd*, get rid of the inferior animals. **weedy** *adj* (-ier, -iest) **1** full of, overgrown with, ~s. **2** (sl) tall, thin and weak: *a ~y young man.*

weeds /wiːdz/ *n pl* **widow's ~,** black clothes as formerly worn by a widow for mourning.

week /wiːk/ *n* **1** any period of seven days; (esp) seven days from Saturday midnight to Saturday midnight: *this/last/next ~; this day ~*, one week from today; *this Monday ~*, one week from Monday next; *for the last/next six ~s; a six weeks' holiday; tomorrow ~*, eight days from today; *yesterday ~*, eight days ago; *three ~s ago yesterday*, twenty-two days ago; *the working ~*, (usu) Monday to Friday or Saturday. *What day of the ~ is it?* Cf What's the date? *~ in, ~ out*, for ~s in succession. ~·'**end** *n* Saturday and Sunday (as a period of rest or holiday): *a ~end visit to the country; spend the ~end with friends.* □ *vi* spend a ~end: *I'm ~ending at Brighton.* ,~·'**ender** *n* person spending the ~end away from home. ,**long** ~·'**end** *n* ~end, together with Friday or Monday as a public holiday. **2** the working days of the ~. '**~·day** /-deɪ/ *n* any day except Sunday: *I'm always busy on ~days.* (attrib) *There are only ~day trains from this station.* **~·ly** *adj, adv* (happening) once a ~, every ~; of, for a ~: *a ~ly wage of £50; ~ly visits.* □ *n* periodical published once a ~.

weeny /'wiːnɪ/ *adj* (-ier, -iest) (often ,**teeny**-'~) (colloq) tiny.

weep /wiːp/ *vi,vt* (*pt,pp* wept /wept/) [VP2A,B,C,4B,3A,6A] (liter) cry; let tears fall from the eyes: *~ for joy; ~ over one's misfortunes. She wept to see him in such a terrible state. She wept over her sad fate.* **~·ing** *adj* (of trees, eg the birch and willow) having drooping branches.

wee-vil /'wiːvl/ *n* small beetle with a hard shell, feeding on and infesting stores of grain, nuts and

otner seeds. ⇨ **boll.**

weft /weft/ *n* the ~, cross-threads taken over and under the warp in weaving. ⇨ the illus at **warp.**

weigh /weɪ/ *vt,vi* [VP6A] measure (by means of a scale, balance, etc) how heavy sth is: *He ~ed himself on the scales. He ~ed the stone* (= estimated how heavy it was) *in his hands. ~ sth out,* distribute in definite quantities; take a definite quantity of: *She ~ed out flour, sugar and butter for a cake. ~ (oneself) in,* (of a jockey, boxer, etc) be ~ed before a race or contest. *~ in (with),* produce (arguments, facts, etc) triumphantly; bring (them) to bear on a discussion. '**~-bridge** *n* ~ing-machine with a platform on to which vehicles, etc can be driven to be ~ed. '**~·ing-machine** *n* machine for ~ing objects that are too large for a simple balance or scale. **2** [VP2B] show a certain measure when put on a scale, etc: *~ 10 kilos/a ton/nothing, etc. How much do you ~*, How heavy are you? **3** [VP2C] (of a machine, etc) be capable of taking, designed to take, objects up to a specified weight: *This machine will ~ up to 5 tons.* **4** [VP6A,14,15B] *~ sth (with/against sth)*, compare the importance, value, etc of (one thing and another): *~ one plan against another. ~ sth (up)*, consider carefully, assess: *~ (up) the consequences of an action; ~ one's words*, consider/choose them carefully; *~ the pros and cons.* **5** [VP15B,3A] *~ sth down*, pull or bring down; depress: *The fruit ~ed the branches down. ~ sb down*, depress; make tired, troubled, etc: *~ed down with sorrow/cares/anxieties. ~ on sb/sth*, cause concern, anxiety (because of importance, seriousness): *The problem/responsibility ~s heavily on him/on his mind. ~ with sb*, influence: *evidence that did not ~ with the judges; the point that ~s with me.* **6** *~ anchor*, raise the anchor and start a voyage.

weight /weɪt/ *n* **1** [U] gravitational force with which a body tends towards the centre of the earth. **2** [U] how heavy a thing is; this expressed in some scale (eg tons, kilogrammes) as measured on a scale, weighing-machine, etc (⇨ App 5): *Are bananas sold by ~ or at so much a piece? That man is twice my ~. My ~ is 70 kilos. The two boys are (of) the same ~. He is your superior both in size and in ~. under/over ~*, weighing too little/too much. **pull one's ~**, ⇨ pull²(2). **put on ~**, (of a person) become heavier. **throw one's ~ about**, (colloq) be domineering or conceited; try to bully people. **3** *a/the ~ (of)*, load to be supported: *The pillars have a great ~ to bear/have to support the ~ of the roof. That's a great ~ off my mind. He has a great ~ of responsibility.* **4** [U] (degree of) importance or influence: *arguments of great ~; considerations that had great ~ with me.* **carry ~**, be important or influential: *a man/an opinion that carries ~.* **5** [C] piece of metal of known ~ used in scales for weighing things: *an ounce/100 grammes/2 lb, etc ~*; heavy object for various purposes: *a clock worked by ~s; keep papers down with a ~* ('**paper~**). *The doctor said he must not lift ~s.* '**~-lifting** *n* gymnastic feat of lifting great ~s. **6** [U] system of units, scale or notation, for expressing ~: *troy/avoirdupois ~.* □ *vt* **1** [VP6A] put a ~ or ~s(5) on; add ~ to; make heavy: *~ a walking-stick with lead*, eg to make it useful as a weapon. *Circumstances are ~ed in his favour*, (fig) give him an extra advantage. **2** *~ sb down*, burden with: *He was ~ed down with packages.* **3** [VP6A] treat (a fabric) with a mineral substance to make it seem stronger: ∼ed silk. ∼·less adj having no ∼, eg because of absence of gravity. ∼-less·ness n: become accustomed to ∼lessness in a spacecraft. ∼y adj (-ier, -iest) 1 of great ∼; burdensome. 2 influential; important: ∼y considerations/arguments. ∼·ily /-ɪlɪ/ adv ∼i-ness n

weir /wɪə(r)/ n [C] wall or barrier across a river to control the flow of water; fence of stakes or broken branches in a stream as a trap for catching fish.

a weir

weird /wɪəd/ adj 1 unnatural; unearthly; mysterious: ∼ shrieks from the darkness of the ruined castle. 2 (colloq) strange; difficult to understand or explain: What ∼ shoes women sometimes wear! ∼ie /'wɪədɪ/, ∼o /'wɪədəʊ/ nn (sl) eccentric person, esp one who is very unconventional in behaviour, dress and appearance. ∼·ly adv. ∼·ness n

wel·come /'welkəm/ adj 1 received with, giving, pleasure: a ∼ visitor/rest; ∼ news; make a friend ∼, show him that his coming is ∼. A loan would be very ∼ to me just now. 2 ∼ to do sth/to sth, (a) freely permitted: You are ∼ to borrow my bicycle. You are ∼ to the use of my car. Anyone is ∼ to my share, may have it. (b) (ironic) permitted to have sth burdensome or unwanted: If anyone thinks he can do this job any better, he's ∼ to it/∼ to try! I'll gladly let him do it. (c) absolved of the need to express thanks: You are ∼ to it (usu shortened to) You're ∼, = Don't mention it. 3 (as an interjection) W∼ home! W∼ to England! □ n [C] greeting, response by word or action, when sb arrives, when an offer is received, etc: They gave us/We received a warm/cold/enthusiastic, etc ∼. The heartiest of ∼s awaited us. □ vt [VP6A,15A] show pleasure or satisfaction at sth, at the arrival of sb or sth; greet (in the manner indicated): ∼ a friend to one's home; ∼ a suggestion warmly/coldly.

weld /weld/ vt,vi 1 [VP6A,15A,B] join (pieces of metal) by hammering or pressure (usu when the metal is softened by heat) or fusing by the use of an oxy-acetylene flame or an electric arc; make by doing this: ∼ the pieces of a broken axle; ∼ parts together; (fig) arguments that are closely ∼ed. ⇨ the illus at oxy-acetylene. 2 [VP2A] (of iron, etc) be capable of being ∼ed: Some metals ∼ better than others. □ n ∼ed joint. ∼er n workman who ∼s.

wel·fare /'welfeə(r)/ n [U] 1 condition of having good health, comfortable living and working conditions, etc: work for the ∼ of the nation; be concerned about sb's ∼; child/infant ∼. the W∼ State, name applied to a country with State-financed social services, eg health, insurance, pensions. 2 (US) social security. ∼ work(er), (US) social work(er).

wel·kin /'welkɪn/ n (poet) sky: make the ∼ ring, make the air re-echo with shouts.

well¹ /wel/ n 1 shaft, usu lined with brick or stone, for obtaining water from an underground source:

drive/sink a ∼. '∼-water n water from a ∼. 2 hole bored for mineral oil: the 'oil-∼s of Iran. 3 (old use, or in place-names) spring or fountain of water; (fig) source. '∼-head n source of a spring or fountain. 4 deep, enclosed space in a building, often from roof to basement, for a staircase or lift. 5 (GB) railed space for barristers, etc in a law court. 6 '∼-deck n space on the main deck of a ship, enclosed by bulwarks and higher decks. □ vi [VP2C] ∼ out (from/of), flow, like water from a ∼: The blood was ∼ing out (from the wound). ∼ over, overflow. ∼ up (in), rise, like water in a ∼: Tears ∼ed up in her eyes. Their anger ∼ed up.

well² /wel/ (comp better, superl best) adv 1 in a good, right or satisfactory manner (placed after the v, and after the direct object if the v is transitive): The children behaved ∼. They are ∼-behaved children. The house is ∼ situated. He speak English ∼. W∼ done! W∼ run! W∼ played! (cries indicating satisfaction, praise, etc). I hope everything is going ∼ (= satisfactorily) with you. Do these two colours go ∼ together, Do they harmonize, look satisfactory side by side? Does this colour go ∼ with that colour? do ∼, succeed; make progress; prosper: Simon has done ∼ at school this term. Peter is doing ∼ in Canada. be doing ∼, (progressive tenses only) making a good recovery (from illness, etc): Both mother and baby are doing ∼. do oneself ∼, provide oneself with good things, esp comforts and luxuries. do ∼ by sb, treat him with generosity. do ∼ out of, make a profit from sb or sth. wish sb ∼, hope that he has good fortune, success, etc. 2 with praise or approval: think/speak ∼ of sb. It speaks ∼ for your teaching that all your pupils passed the examination, This fact is evidence that your teaching was good. stand ∼ with sb, be in his favour: He stands ∼ with his employers, They like him, think highly of his abilities, etc. 3 fortunately. be ,∼ 'out of sth, be out of an affair without loss, etc: You are ∼ out of it, may consider yourself fortunate to be out of the affair. I wish I was ∼ out of this business, that I could free myself from it without misfortune. ∼ off, (a) fortunate: He doesn't know when he is ∼ off, does not realize how fortunate he is. (b) wealthy. ∼ 'off for, ∼ provided with: ∼ off for food/drink/bright ideas. come off ∼, (a) (of a person) have good fortune; be lucky. (b) (of an event) have a satisfactory outcome. do ∼ to + inf, used to suggest either good judgement or good luck: He did ∼ to leave the country before the revolution started. You would do ∼ (= It would be wise for you) to say nothing about what happened. You did ∼ to ask my advice. 4 (mid position) with good reason, justice or likelihood; advisably: You may ∼ be surprised. We might ∼ make the experiment. I couldn't very ∼ refuse to help them, It would have been difficult, unreasonable, etc, to have done so. You may quite ∼ (= with good reason) give illness as an excuse. We may as ∼ begin at once. It may ∼ be that..., It is likely or possible that.... 5 'may ('just) as ∼, ⇨ may(4). (a) with equal reason, advantage, justification, etc: You might just as ∼ say that white is black (as say that...). Our holidays were ruined by the weather—we might just as ∼ have stayed at home! (b) without worse consequences: You may as ∼ tell me the truth, ie because if you don't tell me, I shall certainly hear it from others. be just as ∼, with no loss of advantage, no need for regret:

It's just as ~ I didn't lend him the money. 6 (end position) thoroughly; completely: *Examine the account ~ before you pay it. Shake the bottle ~.* 7 to a considerable extent: *He was leaning ~ back/ forward in his chair. His name is ~ up in the list,* near the top. *He must be ~ past forty/~ over forty years of age. It's ~ worth trying.* '~ **away,** (a) making good progress: *We're ~ away,* have made a good start. (b) (colloq) on the way to being slightly drunk, to becoming hilarious, etc. *be ~ up in/on,* ⇨ up(8). *leave/let ~ alone,* leave it as it is; don't interfere. 8 *as ~ (as),* in addition (to): *He gave me money as ~ as advice. He gave me advice, and money as ~. We shall travel by night as ~ as by day,* both by night and by day. *Give me those as ~,* = those, too. 9 (with another *adv*) *pretty ~,* almost: *You're pretty ~ the only person who's willing to help.* □ *pred adj* 1 in good health: *be/look/feel/get ~. I'm quite ~,* thank you. Cf *I'm fine,* thank you. 2 in a satisfactory condition: *All's ~ that ends ~. We're very ~ where we are. All is not ~ in the world nowadays.* It's all very ~..., formula (used ironically) to indicate discontent, dissatisfaction, disagreement, etc: *It's all very ~ (for you) to suggest a holiday in Italy, but how am I to find the money?* 3 advisable; desirable: *It would be ~ to start early. It would be just as ~ for you to ask your employer's permission.* 4 lucky; fortunate: *It was ~ for you that nobody saw you.* □ *int* 1 (expressing astonishment): *W~, who would have thought it? W~, ~! I should never have guessed it!* 2 (expressing relief): *W~, here we are at last!* 3 (expressing resignation): *W~, it can't be helped. W~, there's nothing we can do about it.* 4 (expressing understanding or agreement): *Very ~, then, we'll talk it over again tomorrow.* 5 (expressing concession): *W~, you may be right.* 6 (used to resume a story, etc): *W~, as I was saying,.... W~, the next day....*

well- /wel/ 1 (*pref*) ,~-'**being** *n* [U] welfare; health, happiness and prosperity: *have a sense of ~-being,* good bodily health; *work for the ~-being of the nation.* ,~-'**doer** *n* (archaic) virtuous person. ,~-'**doing** *n* [U] (archaic) virtuous conduct; good deeds. '~-**nigh** *adv* (archaic) almost: *It's ~-nigh impossible. He was ~-nigh drowned.* ,~-**to-'do** *adj* wealthy. '~-**wisher** *n* person who wishes well to one, to a cause, etc. 2 (compounds with numerous participles and words in *-ed,* usu hyphened when attrib (before a *n*), but not hyphened when pred except when the compound has acquired a restricted sense) ,~-**ad'vised,** prudent; wise: *a ~-advised action.* ,~-**ap'pointed,** having all the necessary equipment, furniture, etc: *a ~-appointed expedition/hotel/ office/suite.* ,~-'**balanced,** sane, sensible. ,~-'**born,** of a family with high social position. ,~-'**bred,** of good upbringing. ,~-**con'ducted,** characterized by good organization and control: *a ~-conducted meeting.* ,~-**con'nected,** connected by blood or marriage with families of good social position or to rich or influential people. ,~-**dis'posed (towards),** having kind feelings (towards); ready to help. ,~-'**favoured,** (old use) good-looking. ,~-'**found,** = ~-appointed. ,~-'**founded,** based on facts, having a foundation in fact; *~-founded suspicions.* ,~-'**groomed,** carefully tended; neat; meticulously dressed. ,~-'**grounded, (a)** = ~-founded. (b) having a good training in or knowledge of the groundwork of a subject. ,~-'**heeled,**

(sl) rich. ,~-**in'formed, (a)** having wide knowledge. (b) having access to reliable information: *in ~-informed quarters.* ,~-**in'tentioned,** aimed or aiming (often or usu unsuccessfully) at good results. ,~-'**knit,** compact; firmly jointed, not loose-made (esp of a person or his body). ,~-'**known,** widely known. ,~-'**lined,** (of a purse, colloq) full of money. ,~-'**marked,** definite; distinct. ,~-'**meaning,** = ~-intentioned. ,~-'**meant,** done, said, etc, with good intentions. ,~-'**read,** having read much; having a mind well stored with information as the result of wide reading. ,~-'**rounded,** complete and symmetrical. ,~-'**set,** = ~-knit. ,~-'**spoken, (a)** speaking well, politely, in refined language. (b) spoken well. ,~-'**timed,** done, said, at the right or a suitable time. ,~-'**tried,** (of methods, remedies) tested and proved useful. ,~-'**turned,** (of a compliment, phrase, verse) gracefully expressed. ,~-'**worn,** much used; (esp) commonplace; trite.

we'll /wi:l/ = we shall, we will.

wel·ling·ton /'welɪŋtən/ *n* ~ (**boot**), waterproof boot reaching to the knee.

Welsh /welʃ/ *n, adj* (the language) of the people of Wales. ~ '**rabbit/'rarebit,** ⇨ rarebit.

welsh /welʃ/ *vi* [VP3A] ~ *on sth/sb,* 1 avoid payment of: ~ *on a debt.* 2 break one's word to: ~ *on a friend.* ~er *n*

welt /welt/ *n* [C] 1 strip of leather to which the sole and the upper part of a shoe are stitched. 2 = weal².

Welt·an·schau·ung /,velt,ɑːn'ʃaʊʊŋ/ *n* (G) philosophy of life; perception of the world.

wel·ter¹ /'weltə(r)/ *vi* [VP2C] roll; wallow; be soaked or steeped (in blood, etc). □ *n* (*sing* only) general confusion; disorderly mixture or aimless conflict: *the ~ of creeds/political beliefs; a ~ of meaningless verbiage.*

wel·ter² /'weltə(r)/ *adj* '~ **race** *n* race for horses with heavy-weight riders. '~-**weight** *n* (esp boxing) boxer weighing 135-147lb/61-66.6kg.

wen /wen/ *n* [C] harmless, usu permanent, tumour on the scalp or other part of the body; (fig) abnormally large or overgrown urban area.

wench /wentʃ/ *n* (archaic) 1 girl or young woman. 2 prostitute. □ *vi* [VP2A] associate with prostitutes.

wend /wend/ *vt* (old use, only in) ~ *one's way (home),* go, make one's way.

went /went/ *pt* of go¹.

wept /wept/ *pt,pp* of weep.

were /wɜː(r); *weak form:* wə(r)/ *pt* of be¹.

we're /wɪə(r)/ = we are.

weren't /wɜːnt/ = were not.

were·wolf /'wɪəwʊlf/ *n* (*pl* -wolves /-wʊlvz/) (myth) human being turned into a wolf.

wert /wɜːt/*thou ~,* (archaic) you were.

Wes·leyan /'wezliən/ *n, adj* (member) of the Methodist Church deriving from John Wesley /'wezli/ (1703-91).

west /west/ *n* 1 **the ~,** point of the horizon where the sun sets; that part of the world, of a country, etc, in this direction: *Bristol is in the ~ of England.* **the W~, (a)** Europe and the continent of America (contrasted with Asia). (b) (world politics) Western Europe and America (contrasted with Eastern Europe, the USSR and China). (c) the part of the US between the Mississippi River and the Pacific Ocean. (d) ~ern part of any country. ~ **north·'west,** ~-**south·'west,** ⇨ the illus at compass. 2 (attrib) coming from the ~: *a ~ wind;* towards, at, in the direction of the ∼: *on the* ∼ *coast;* ∼ *longitude.* **the W∼ End,** part of London with the largest and most fashionable shops, theatres, etc. Hence, ∼-'**end** *adj:* ∼**-end** *theatres/department stores.* **the** '∼ **country,** part of England ∼ of a line from the Isle of Wight to the mouth of the River Severn. Hence, '∼**-country** *adj* of, from, characteristic of the ∼ country. **W∼ Central,** (abbr **WC**) London postal district. □ *adv* towards the ∼: *sail/travel* ∼. **go** ∼, (sl) be lost, ruined, etc. ∼ *of,* farther ∼ than. '∼**-ward** /-wəd/ *adj* towards the ∼: *in a* ∼*ward direction.* ∼**-ward(s)** /-wəd(z)/ *adv: travel* ∼*ward*(*s*).

west·er·ly /'westəlɪ/ *attrib adj* towards the west; (of winds) from the west. □ *adv* towards the west.

west·ern /'westən/ *adj* of, in, from, characteristic of, the west. **the W∼ Hemisphere,** N and S America. **the W∼ Empire,** that part of the old Roman Empire with Rome as its capital. □ *n* [C] film or novel dealing with life in the ∼ part of the US in the times of the wars with the American Indians, or one with cowboys, rustlers, sheriffs, etc. ∼**er** *n* native of the West, esp of the ∼ US. ∼**·ize** /-aɪz/ *vt* [VP6A] introduce ideas, ways of living, working, etc of *the West*(b) into. ∼**·iz·ation** /ˌwestənaɪ'zeɪʃn *US:* -nɪ'z-/ *n* '∼**·most** /-məʊst/ *adj* farthest west.

wet /wet/ *adj* (wetter, wettest) **1** covered or soaked with water or other liquid: *wet clothes/ roads. Her cheeks were wet with tears. Did you get wet,* eg in the rain? *We got wet to the skin,* Our clothes were soaked through. *Your coat is wet through,* from one side to the other. ,**wet 'blanket,** ⇨ blanket(1). ,**wet 'dock** *n* one (that can be) filled with water, able to float a ship. '**wet–nurse** *n* woman employed to suckle another's child. ,**wet 'paint,** paint recently applied, not yet dry. **2** rainy: *wet weather; the wettest summer for 20 years.* **3** (US) not prohibiting or opposing the sale and use of alcoholic drinks: *a wet State.* **4** (sl, of a person) ineffectual; spiritless. □ *n* **1 the wet,** rain: *Come in out of the wet.* **2** [U] moisture. □ *vt* (*pt,pp* wetted or wet) (-tt-) [VP6A] make wet: *The baby has wet*(*ted*) *its bed again.* **wet one's whistle,** ⇨ whistle, *n*(3). **wet·ting** *n* becoming or being made wet: *get a wetting,* eg in heavy rain.

weth·er /'weðə(r)/ *n* castrated ram.

we've /wiːv/ = we have.

whack /wæk *US:* hwæk/ *vt* [VP6A] strike (sb or sth) with a hard blow; thwack. □ *n* **1** (sound of a) hard blow. **2** (sl) share: *Have you all had a fair* ∼? ∼**ed** *adj* (colloq) (of a person) worn out; tired. ∼**ing** *n* beating: *give a naughty child a* ∼*ing.* □ *adj* (colloq) big of its kind: *a* ∼*ing lie.* □ *adv* (colloq) very: *a* ∼*ing great lie.* ∼**er** *n* sth big of its kind.

whale /weɪl *US:* hweɪl/ *n* **1** kinds of large sea-animal some of which are hunted for their oil and flesh (used for pet foods). ⇨ the illus at sea. '∼**bone** *n* thin, horny springy substance from the upper jaw of some kinds of ∼. **2** (colloq) **a** '∼ **of a time,** an exceedingly (good time); no end of (a good time). □ *vi* [VP2A] hunt ∼s: *go whaling; the whaling industry.* '**whaling–gun** *n* one used for firing harpoons at ∼s. ∼**r** /'weɪlə(r) *US:* 'hw-/ *n* man or ship engaged in hunting ∼s.

whang /wæŋ *US:* hwæŋ/ *vt* (colloq) strike heavily and loudly. □ *n* ∼ing sound or blow. □ *adv* (colloq) exactly: *hit the target* ∼ *in the centre.*

wharf /wɔːf *US:* hwɔːrf/ *n* (*pl* ∼s or wharves /-vz/) wooden or stone structure at which ships are

moored for (un)loading cargo. '∼**·age** /-ɪdʒ/ *n* [U] (money paid for) accommodation at a ∼.

what /wɒt *US:* hwɒt/ *adj* **1** (interr) asking for a selection from an indefinite number (⇨ which): *W∼ books have you read on this subject? Tell me* ∼ *books you have read recently. W∼ time is it? Ask him* ∼ *time it is. W∼ size/colour/shape, etc do you want?* **2** (exclamatory): *W∼ a good idea! W∼ genius you have!* **3** the... that; any... that; as much/many... as: *Give me* ∼ *books* (= the books, any books, that) *you have on the subject. W∼ little* (= The little that) *he said on the subject was full of wisdom. W∼ few friends* (= The few friends that) *I have here have been very kind to me.* □ *pron* (interr) ∼ thing(s): *W∼ happened? Tell me* ∼ *happened. W∼ is he, W∼ is his occupation?* ∼... '**for,** for ∼ purpose: *W∼ is this tool used for? W∼ did you do that for,* (colloq) Why did you do that? ∼-'**for** *n* [U] (colloq) punishment: *give sb* ∼*-for.* ∼... '**like,** (used to ask for a description, for details, etc): *W∼'s the weather like this morning? W∼'s the new neighbour like?* '∼ **if,** ∼ will, would, be the result if: *W∼ if it rains while we are a long way from shelter? W∼ if the rumour is true?* '∼ **though,** (liter) ∼ does it matter if: *W∼ though we are poor, we still have each other.* ∼ **about/of,** (a) ∼ news is there about.... (b) ⇨ about³(4), of(10). ∼ '**of it?** (or, mod colloq) ,**So** '∼? (used to admit that sth is true, but questioning the inference (to be) made from it.) **and** '∼ **not,** and other things of the same kind. **and/or** ∼ '**have you,** used to indicate that there are other things, etc: *Then there are bills for gas and electricity and* ∼ *have you.* '∼**-not** *n* unnamed thing; piece of furniture with open shelves for small ornaments, odds and ends. ,**I know** '∼...,** I have an idea, a suggestion to make.... ,**I/I'll tell you** '∼...,** Here's a suggestion.... **know** ∼**'s** '∼, have common sense; know how to distinguish useful things from useless, good things from bad, etc. '∼**-d'you-call-him/-her/-it/-them** /'wɒt dʒʊ kɔːl ɪm *etc*/; '∼**'s-his/-her/-its/-their-name,** used as substitutes for a name that one cannot recall. □ *rel pron* that which; the thing(s) which: *W∼ he says is not important. Do* ∼ *you think is right. W∼ the country needs most is wise leadership. When people say that they know* ∼ *they like, they really mean that they like* ∼ *they know,* They like ∼ they are familiar with. *It's a useful book and,* ∼ *is more, not an expensive one.* '∼ **with... and** ('∼ **with),** between various causes: *W∼ with one thing and another,...,* as a result of many things,.... *W∼ with overwork and* (∼ *with) undernourishment he fell ill.*

what·e'er /wɒt'eə(r) *US:* hw-/ (poet for) whatever.

what·ever /wɒt'evə(r) *US:* hw-/ *adj* **1** (emphatic for *what*) of any sort, degree, etc: *W∼ nonsense the newspapers print, some people always believe it. Take* ∼ *measures you consider best.* **2** (placed after a *n* in a negative context, giving emphasis to the negative): *There can be no doubt* ∼ *about it. I have no intention* ∼ (= not the least intention) *of resigning.* □ *pron* **1** no matter what: *You are certainly right,* ∼ *others may say. Keep calm,* ∼ *happens.* **2** anything or everything that: *Do* ∼ *you like. W∼ I have is at your service.* **3 or** ∼, (colloq) (usu at the end of a list of similar *nn* or *adjj*) or anything at all: *He'd have difficulty in learning any language—Greek, Chinese, or* ∼.

what·so·e'er /ˌwɒtsəʊ'eə(r) *US:* ˌhw-/ (poet for)
what·so·ever /ˌwɒtsəʊ'evə(r) *US:* ˌhw-/ (emphatic for) whatever.

wheat /wiːt *US:* hw-/ *n* [U] (plant producing) grain from which flour (as used for bread and pastry products) is made: *a field of* ~. ⇨ the illus at cereal. ~**en** /'wiːtn *US:* 'hw-/ *adj* of ~: ~*en flour/bread.*

wheedle /'wiːdl *US:* 'hw-/ *vt* [VP6A,14] ~ *(into/out of),* make oneself pleasant to sb, flatter or coax, to get sth one wants: *The girl ~d a pound out of her father/~d her father into buying her a bicycle.*

wheel /wiːl *US:* hwiːl/ *n* 1 circular frame or disc which turns on an axle (as on carts, cars, bicycles, etc and for various purposes in machines). ⇨ the illus at bicycle. ~*s within* ~*s,* (fig) complicated motives and influences; indirect and secret agencies, all interacting. *put one's shoulder to the* ~, help a cause or undertaking. *the man at the* ~, the driver (at the steering~ of a car, etc). '~-**barrow** *n* small vehicle with one ~ and two handles for moving small loads. '~-**base** *n* distance between the axles of a motor-vehicle. '~-**chair** *n* chair with large ~s for the use of sb unable to walk. '~-**house** *n* small enclosed place on a ship (old style sailing-ship, a small river-launch, a tug, etc), to shelter the pilot or steersman. '~-**wright** *n* man who makes and repairs (esp waggon and cart) ~s. 2 potter's ~, ⇨ potter². '**paddle-**~, ⇨ paddle¹(3). 3 [C] motion like that of a ~; motion of a line of men as on a pivoted end, esp as a military movement: *a right/left* ~. □ *vt,vi* 1 [VP6A,15A,B] push or pull (a vehicle with ~s): ~ *a bike up a hill;* ~ *a barrow;* convey (sb or sth) in a vehicle with ~s: ~ *the rubbish out to the dump.* 2 [VP2A,C,6A,15B] (cause to) turn in a curve or circle: *The sails of the windmill were ~ing round. The seagulls were ~ing in the air above me. Right/Left ~!* (an order given to a column of men, esp troops, to change their line of route to the right (left)).

wheeze /wiːz *US:* hwiːz/ *vi,vt* 1 [VP2A,B,C] breathe noisily, esp with a whistling sound in the chest (as when suffering from asthma); (of a pump, etc) make a similar sound. 2 [VP15B] ~ *sth out,* utter with such sounds: *The asthmatic old man ~d out a few words. A barrel-organ was wheezing out an old tune.* □ *n* [C] 1 sound of wheezing. 2 (dated school sl) trick; bright idea. **wheezy** *adj* breathing, speaking, uttered, with ~s: *a fat and wheezy old dog; a wheezy old pump.* **wheez·ily** /-ɪlɪ/ *adv* **wheezi·ness** *n*

whelk /welk *US:* hwelk/ *n* kinds of marine mollusc (like a snail) with a spiral shell, some used as food. ⇨ the illus at mollusc.

whelp /welp *US:* hwelp/ *n* 1 young dog, lion, tiger, bear, wolf, fox, etc. 2 ill-bred boy or youth. □ *vi* give birth to ~s(1).

when /wen *US:* hwen/ *interr adv* 1 at what time; on what occasion: *W~ can you come? W~ did that happen? I don't know* ~ *that happened.* 2 (after a *prep*) what time: *Till* ~ *can you stay? Since* ~ *has he been missing?* □ *rel adv* (with *day, time,* etc as antecedent) at or on which: *Sunday is the day* ~ *I am least busy. There are times* ~ *joking is not permissible. It was one of those cold, wet evenings* ~ *most people stay indoors.* □ *conj* 1 at or during the time that: *It was raining* ~ *we arrived. He waved* ~ *he saw her. W~ speaking French, I often make mistakes.* 2 although: *He walks* ~ *he*

might take a taxi. 3 since; considering that: *How can I help them to understand* ~ *they won't listen to me?* 4 at or during which time: *The Queen will visit the town in May,* ~ *she will open the new hospital.*

whence /wens *US:* hwens/ *adv* (formal) 1 (in questions) from what place or cause: *Do you know* ~ *she came? W~ comes it that...,* How is it that...? 2 (in statements) from which place: *the land* ~ *they are come.* 3 to the place from which: *Return* ~ *you came.* ~·**so'ever** *adv, conj* from whatever place, cause or origin.

when·ever /wen'evə(r) *US:* hw-/ *adv, conj* 1 at whatever time; no matter when: *I'll discuss it with you* ~ *you like.* 2 on any occasion; as often as; every time that: *W~ that man says 'To tell the truth', I suspect that he's about to tell a lie.* 3 or ~, (colloq) or at any time: *He might turn up on Monday, or Friday, or* ~, *and expect to be given a meal.*

where /weə(r) *US:* hweə(r)/ *interr adv* 1 in or to what place or position; in what direction; in what respect: *W~ does he live? I wonder* ~ *he lives. W~ shall we be* (ie What will be our situation) *if another world war breaks out?* 2 (with a *prep* following the *v*) what place: *W~ does he come from? W~ are you going to? W~ did we get up to,* ie What point did we reach? □ *rel adv* 1 (with *place,* etc as antecedent) in or at which: *She would like to live in a country* ~ *it never snows. That's the place* ~ *the accident occurred.* 2 (with no antecedent) in, at or to the place in which; in the direction in which: *W~ there is no rain, farming is difficult or impossible. I found my books* ~ *I had left them. That's* ~ (ie the point in respect of which) *you are mistaken.* ~·**a'bouts** *adv* in or near what place: *W~abouts did you find it? I wonder ~abouts he put it.* □ '~-**abouts** *n* (with *sing* or *pl v*) place ~ sb or sth is: *Her present ~abouts is/are unknown.* ~·'**as** *conj* 1 (esp legal) considering that. 2 but in contrast; while on the other hand: *Some people like fatty meat, ~as others hate it.* ~·'**at** *adv* (old use) at or upon which. ~·'**by** *adv* by what; by which: *He devised a plan ~by he might escape.* '~·**fore** *adv* (old use) why. *the whys and the ~fores,* the reasons, causes. ~·'**in** *adv* (formal) in what; in which; in what respect: *W~in am I mistaken?* ~·'**of** *adv* (formal) of what; of which. ~·'**on** *adv* (old use) on which; on what. ~·**so·'ever** *adv* (emphatic for) ~ver. ~·'**to** *adv* (old use) to what; to which; to what end (= purpose). ~·'**unto** *adv* (old use) = ~to. ~·**u'pon** *adv* after which; and then.

wher·ever /ˌweər'evə(r) *US:* ˌhw-/ *adv* to, at, whatever place; at those places: *Sit ~ver you like. He comes from Boula, ~ver that may be,* from a place called Boula, and I have no idea where it is. ~·'**with** *adv* (old use) with that; with which. '~-**withal** /-wɪðɔːl/ *adv* (old use) = ~with. □ *n* the ~·**withal,** (colloq) money needed for a purpose: *I should like to buy a new car but haven't got the ~withal.*

wherry /'werɪ *US:* 'hw-/ *n* (*pl* -ries) light, shallow rowing-boat for carrying passengers and goods on rivers.

whet /wet *US:* hwet/ *vt* (-tt-) [VP6A] sharpen (a knife, axe, etc); (fig) sharpen or excite (the appetite, a desire). '~-**stone** *n* shaped stone used for sharpening tools, eg scythes.

whether /'weðə(r) *US:* 'hw-/ *conj* 1 (introducing an indirect question; ⇨ VP10,21; often replaced by *if* in colloq style except when there is possible confusion with a true conditional clause): *I don't know ∼/if she will be able to come. I wonder ∼/if it's large enough.* (Note that when there are two indirect questions with *or*, ∼ is repeated after *or*): *I wonder ∼ we shall be in time for the last bus or ∼ we shall have to walk home.* (Compare ∼ and *if* in these sentences): *Send me a telegram letting me know ∼ I am to come,* ie saying 'Come' or 'Don't come'. *Send me a telegram if I am to come,* ie only if I am to come, no telegram being needed if I am not to come. **2** (introducing an infinitive phrase; ⇨ VP8,20): *I don't know ∼ to accept or refuse. Would you advise me ∼ to accept the offer (or not)?* **3** (Clauses and infinitive phrases introduced by ∼ are used with preparatory *it*): *It's doubtful ∼ we shall be able to come.* (Such clauses and phrases may be subjects or complements): *The question was ∼ to take the children to the funeral or to leave them at home. W∼ to pay the price demanded was a question that worried him a long time.* (Such a clause may be the object of a *prep*): *Everything depends upon ∼ we have enough money. I am not interested in ∼ you like the plan or not.* (A clause introduced by ∼ may be used in opposition to a *n*): *I am in doubt ∼ I ought to give this plan my approval. The question ∼ we ought to call in a specialist was answered by the family doctor. ∼ **or no**,* (a) = ∼ or not. (b) in either case: *You may rely upon my help, ∼ or no,* eg ∼ others agree to help, or refuse to help. *∼* **or not,** (allowing the negative alternative): *W∼ or not it rains, I'm giving a party tomorrow. Tell me ∼ or not I should invite Nick and his wife.*

whew /fju: *or similar sounds roughly breathed out or whistled/ int* cry used (often in joke) to express consternation, dismay, fatigue or surprise.

whey /weɪ *US:* hweɪ/ *n* [U] liquid part of sour milk after separation of curds (for cheese).

which /wɪtʃ *US:* hwɪtʃ/ *interr adj* (asking for selection from two, or from a group, esp from possibilities thought of as limited in number; ⇨ what) **1** *W∼ way shall we go—up the hill or along the river bank? W∼ way* (= How) *shall we do it? W∼ Jones do you mean—Jones the baker or Jones the postman? W∼ foreign languages have you studied? Tell me ∼ ones you want.* **2** (*rel adj,* formal, and rare except after a *prep;* preceded by a comma) and this; and these: *I told him to go to a doctor, ∼ advice he took,* and this advice he took. *Don't call between 1 o'clock and 2 o'clock, at ∼ time I am usually having lunch.* □ *interr pron ∼* thing(s); ∼ person(s): *W∼ is taller, Mike or Steve? W∼ of the boys is the tallest? W∼ of you wish to go with me? Tell me ∼ of them is better. Please advise me ∼ to take. The twins are so much alike that I never know ∼ is ∼,* ie I cannot distinguish one from the other. □ *rel pron* (of things only, not of persons; ⇨ that) **1** (in defining or restrictive clauses, often replaced by *that;* used with no selective meaning; no pause before the clause and not set off by commas) **(a)** (with the *rel pron* as the subject of the *v* in the clause): *Take the book ∼ is lying on that table. The house ∼ is for sale is at the end of the street. The river ∼ flows through London is called the Thames.* **(b)** (with the *rel pron* as the object of the *v* in the clause; in spoken English usually suppressed): *Was the book (∼) you were reading a novel?* **(c)** (with the *rel pron* as the object of a *prep;* when replaced by *that,* the *prep* follows the

v; if ∼ is used, the *prep* should precede): *The photographs at ∼ you were looking/The photographs (that) you were looking at were all taken by my brother. The hotel at ∼ we stayed/The hotel we stayed at was both cheap and comfortable. The book to ∼ I wanted to refer/The book I wanted to refer to was not in the library. The shop opposite ∼ the car is parked is a grocer's.* **2** (in non-defining or non-restrictive clauses, rare in the spoken language but common in the written language; ∼ is not replaceable by *that;* the clause is preceded by a pause and is set off by commas) **(a)** (referring to an antecedent *n*): (*i*) (with the *rel pron* as the subject of the clause): *This house, ∼ is to be sold by auction next month, was built about fifty years ago. The meeting, ∼ was held in the park, was attended by five hundred people.* (*ii*) (with the *rel pron* as the object of the *v* in the clause): *These apple-trees, ∼ I planted three years ago, have not yet borne any fruit. This desk, ∼ I bought second-hand, is made of oak.* (*iii*) (with the *rel pron* as the object of a *prep*): *His car, for ∼ he paid £8000, is a five-seater saloon. Their house, at ∼ I have often stayed, is just outside Dorking.* **(b)** (in non-defining clauses that refer to a clause or sentence, not to a *n*): *It was raining hard, ∼* (= and this) *kept us indoors. He said he had lost the book, ∼* (= but this) *was untrue.* (The clause may occasionally precede the sentence to ∼ it refers): *Moreover, ∼ you may hardly believe, the examiners had decided in advance to fail half the candidates!*

which·ever /wɪtʃˈevə(r) *US:* hw-/ *adj, pron* **1** the one which: *Take ∼ you like best. W∼ (of you) comes in first will receive a prize.* **2** no matter which: *W∼ of the three sisters you choose to marry, you will have a good wife. Does British foreign policy remain the same, ∼ party is in power?* **which·so·ever**, (emphatic for) ∼.

whiff /wɪf *US:* hwɪf/ *n* [C] slight puff or breath (*of* sth): *a ∼ of fresh air; the ∼* (= smell) *of a cigar. The dentist gave her another ∼ of anaesthetic. He stopped work to have a few ∼s,* a short smoke (of a pipe, etc).

Whig /wɪg *US:* hwɪg/ *n* member of a political party in GB which upheld the authority of Parliament (against the sovereign) during the 17th and 18th cc, their place being taken in the 19th c by the Liberals.

while /waɪl *US:* hwaɪl/ *n* (*sing* only) (period of) time: *Where have you been all this ∼? I haven't seen him for a long ∼/for this long ∼ past. We're going away for a ∼. I'll be back in a little ∼,* soon. *He was here a short ∼ ago.* **once in a ∼,** occasionally. **worth (one's) ∼,** worth the time spent in doing it, etc: *It isn't worth ∼ going there now,* ie It would be a waste of time to go. *He will make it worth your ∼,* ie will pay or reward you in some way. □ *vt* [VP15B] (only in) *∼ sth away,* pass (the time) in a leisurely way: *∼ away the time; ∼ a few hours away.* □ *conj* **1** during the time that; for as long as; at the same time as: *He fell asleep ∼* (he was) *doing his English exercises. W∼ in London he studied music. W∼* (= As long as) *there is life there is hope.* **2** (implying a contrast) whereas: *Jane was dressed in brown ∼ Mary was dressed in blue.* **3** (implying a concession) although: *W∼ I admit that the problems are difficult, I don't agree that they cannot be solved.* **whilst** /waɪlst *US:* hwaɪlst/ *conj* = ∼.

whim /wɪm *US:* hwɪm/ *n* [C] sudden desire or idea,

often sth unusual or unreasonable: *only a passing* ~, an idea, a desire, that will soon pass; *full of* ~s. *His every* ~ *is complied with/catered for.*

whim·per /'wɪmpə(r) *US:* 'hw-/ *vi,vt* **1** [VP2A] utter weak, frightened or complaining sounds, eg a baby when ill, a dog when frightened of punishment. **2** [VP6A] utter in a ~ing voice. □ *n* [C] ~ing cry; low sobbing sound.

whimsy, whim·sey /'wɪmzɪ *US:* 'hw-/ *n* (*pl* -sies, -seys) **1** [C] whim; fanciful idea or wish. **2** [U] quaintness; odd or fanciful humour. **whim·si·cal** /'wɪmzɪkl *US:* 'hw-/ *adj* full of whimsies; quaint. **whim·si·cal·ly** /-klɪ/ *adv* **whim·si·cal·ity** /ˌwɪmzɪ'kælɪtɪ *US:* ˌhw-/ *n* [U] quality of being whimsical; [C] (*pl* -ties) caprice; quaint fancy ◊ **whin** /wɪn *US:* hw-/ *n* [U] = gorse.

whine /waɪn *US:* hwaɪn/ *n* [C] long complaining cry or high-pitched sound (eg as made by a miserable dog, a siren, a motor or a shell in flight). □ *vi,vt* **1** [VP2A,C,4A] make such cries; utter complaints, esp about trivial things: *The dog was whining outside the door/whining to come into the room. If that child doesn't stop whining, I'll clobber it!* **2** [VP6A,15B] utter with a ~ or ~s: *beggars whining (out) requests for alms.* ~**r** *n* animal or person that ~s.

whinny /'wɪnɪ *US:* 'hw-/ *n* (*pl* -nies) gentle neigh. □ *vi* (*pt,pp* -nied) make such a sound.

whip¹ /wɪp *US:* hwɪp/ *n* [C] **1** lash (length of cord, strip of leather, etc) fastened to a handle, used for urging a horse on, or for punishing. **have the ~ hand (over sb),** have mastery over; be in a position to control. '~**-cord** *n* [U] (**a**) tightly twisted cord used for the lashes of ~s. (**b**) kind of hardwearing worsted fabric. **2** (also ~**per-'in**) (foxhunting) person who controls the hounds. **3** organizing secretary of a political party (in GB and US) with authority over its members to maintain discipline and secure attendance at parliamentary debates and divisions(6); such authority; order given by such a secretary to members of his party to attend a debate and vote: *take the Liberal* ~. *The* ~*s are off,* Members may vote as they wish. **a** ,**three-line** '~, urgent order of this kind. **4** preparation of eggs, cream, etc beaten or whipped(2). ~**py** *adj* flexible; springy.

whip² /wɪp *US:* hwɪp/ *vt,vi* (-pp-) **1** [VP6A,15A,B] strike with a whip; beat or flog: ~ *a horse/a child;* ~ *a top,* ⇨ top³. *The rain was* ~*ping the window-panes,* beating against them. *The driver* ~*ped the horses on.* **2** [VP6A] beat (eggs, cream, etc) with a fork or other utensil to mix thoroughly or to make stiff: ~*ped cream.* **3** [VP6A] (colloq) defeat. **4** [VP15B,2C] take, be taken, move, be moved, suddenly: *He* ~*ped off his coat. He* ~*ped out a knife. The thief* ~*ped the jewels off the counter. The thief* ~*ped round the corner and disappeared in the crowd.* [VP6A] (GB colloq) steal: *Someone's* ~*ped my purse!* ~ **round for money, etc,** appeal to friends, members of a club, etc for money to buy a gift, etc. Hence, '~**-round** *n* such an appeal. **5** [VP6A] bind (a stick, a rope-end, etc) with a close, tight covering of thread or string; sew (a seam, the edge of a piece of cloth) with stitches that pass over and over. ~**-ping** *n* [C] beating with a whip as a punishment. '~**-ping-boy** *n* (hist) boy educated with a prince and ~ped when the prince deserved punishment; (hence) scapegoat. '~**-ping-post** *n* (hist) post to which persons were tied to be ~ped. '~**-ping-top** *n* = top³.

whip·per-in /ˌwɪpər 'ɪn *US:* 'hw-/ ⇨ whip¹(2).

whip·per-snap·per /'wɪpə snæpə(r) *US:* 'hw-/ *n* young insignificant person who intrudes upon people and behaves as if he were important.

whip·pet /'wɪpɪt *US:* 'hw-/ *n* dog that looks like a small greyhound, used for racing.

whip-poor-will /'wɪp pʊə wɪl *US:* 'hwɪp pər wɪl/ *n* small American bird whose call (made at night or twilight) is imitative of its name.

whir /wɜ:(r) *US:* hw-/ = whirr.

whirl /wɜ:l *US:* hw-/ *vt,vi* **1** [VP15A,B,2C] (cause to) move quickly round and round: *The wind* ~*ed the dead leaves about. The leaves came* ~*ing down in the autumn wind. The dancers* ~*ed round the room.* **2** [VP15A,B,2C] (cause to) move or travel rapidly (*off, away,* etc): *The telegraph poles* ~*ed past us as the train gathered speed. Our friends were* ~*ed away in Jack's sports-car.* **3** [VP2A,C] (of the brain, the senses) seem to go round and round; (of thoughts) be confused: *His head* ~*ed.* □ *n* (*sing* only) **1** ~ing movement: *a* ~ *of dust/of dead leaves. His brain was in a* ~, (fig) a confused state. **2** rapid succession of activities, etc: *the* ~ *of modern life in a big city; a* ~ *of social engagements,* eg parties, receptions. **3** (compounds) '~**-pool** *n* place where there are ~ing currents (circular eddies) in the sea, etc (usu drawing floating objects towards its centre). '~**-wind** *n* swift circling current of air in a funnel-shaped column. **Sow the wind and reap the** ~**wind,** (prov) Do wrong and, as a result, bring severe punishment upon oneself.

whirli·gig /'wɜ:lɪgɪg *US:* 'hw-/ *n* **1** kinds of spinning top, ⇨ top³. **2** revolving motion: *the* ~ *of time,* the changes of fortune that come with time.

whirr /wɜ:(r) *US:* hw-/ *n* (*sing* only) sound (as) of a bird's wings moving quickly, or of wheels, etc turning fast: *the* ~ *of an aircraft's propellers.* □ *vi* [VP2A,C] make such sounds: *A bird* ~*ed past.*

whisk /wɪsk *US:* hw-/ *n* **1** small brush for removing dust (from clothes, etc). ('**fly-**)~, brush made of hair for flapping flies away. **2** device (eg coiled wire) for whipping eggs, cream, etc. **3** light brushing movement (eg of a horse's tail). □ *vt,vi* **1** [VP15B] ~ *sb/sth off/away,* brush quickly and lightly: ~ *the flies off.* **2** [VP6A] move or sweep quickly through the air: *The cow* ~*ed her tail.* **3** [VP15B] take (sb) quickly and suddenly: *They* ~*ed him off to prison. I was* ~*ed up to the top floor in an express lift.* **4** [VP6A] = whip²(2): ~ *eggs.*

whisker /'wɪskə(r) *US:* 'hw-/ *n* **1** ~s, hair allowed to grow on the sides of a man's face. ⇨ beard(1), moustache. **2** one of the long, stiff hairs growing near the mouth of a cat, rat, etc. **cat's** ~**s,** (sl) fine thing or person: *He thinks he's the cat's* ~*s,* He thinks highly of himself. ~**ed** *adj* having ~s.

whis·key /'wɪskɪ *US:* 'hw-/ *n* (*pl* ~s) US and Irish spelling of whisky.

whisky /'wɪskɪ *US:* 'hw-/ *n* (*pl* -kies) (GB and Canadian spelling) [C,U] strong alcoholic drink distilled from malted grain (esp barley or rye); drink of this: *Two whiskies, please.*

whis·per /'wɪspə(r) *US:* 'hw-/ *vi,vt* **1** [VP2A,3A,6A,14,19] ~ *(to),* speak, say (sth), using the breath but no vibration of the vocal cords: ~ *(a word) to sb;* ~ *(to sb) that.* '~**-ing-gallery,** gallery in which a sound made at one point may be heard at another far off (owing to acoustic peculiarities). **2** [VP6A,15B] tell privately or secretly; (esp) put (a story, slander) into circulation: *The* story is being ~ed about the neighbourhood. It is ~ed that he is heavily in debt. '~·ing campaign, systematic attack on sb by passing from person to person malicious statements, etc. 3 [VP2A,C] (of leaves, the wind, etc) make soft sounds; rustle: The wind was ~ing in the pines. □ n 1 ~ing sound or speech: He answered in a ~. They were talking in ~s. 2 ~ed remark; sth ~ed secretly; rumour: W~s are going round that the firm is likely to go bankrupt. ~·er n

whist /wɪst US: hwɪst/ n card-game like bridge² for two pairs of players. '~·drive n series of games played by several sets of partners at different tables, certain players after each round passing to the next table.

whistle /'wɪsl US: 'hw-/ n 1 (usu steady) clear note made by forcing air or steam through a small opening, or made by the wind; tuneful sound made by some kinds of bird (eg the blackbird): We heard the ~ of a steam-engine. '~·stop n (US) short stop (during a journey made by a politician) for electioneering purposes (eg to speak to voters in a rural district): (attrib) a ~-stop tour. 2 instrument for producing such sounds: the referee's ~; a 'steam-~, sounded by a jet of steam. 3 wet one's ~, (sl) have a drink. □ vi,vt 1 [VP2A,C] make a ~(1) (eg by blowing through the rounded lips or by using a ~(2): The engine/The driver ~d before reaching the level-crossing. The wind ~d through the rigging/up the chimney, etc. ~ for sth, wish in vain for: I owe my butcher £10, but he can ~ for it, I shan't pay him. 2 [VP2A,C,6A] produce a tune in this way: ~ a tune. The boy was whistling (away) merrily. ~ down the wind, abandon sth. ~ in the dark, do sth to overcome one's fears. 3 [VP6A,15B,16A] ~ (up), make a signal (to) by whistling: He ~d his dog back/~d to his dog to come back to him/~d up his dog. 4 [VP2A,C] pass swiftly with a whistling sound: The bullets/arrows ~d past our ears.

whit /wɪt US: hwɪt/ n not a ~; no ~, not the least, not at all: There's not a ~ of truth in the statement. I don't care a ~.

Whit /wɪt US: hwɪt/ n⇨ Whitsun.

white¹ /waɪt US: hwaɪt/ adj 1 of the colour of fresh snow or common salt: His hair has turned ~. Her face went ~, pale. bleed (sb/sth) ~, (fig) drain (sb/sth) of wealth, strength, etc. 2 (special uses, compounds) ~ alloy, any of various alloys that are cheap imitations of silver. '~ ant, termite. '~· bait n [U] small fish, the young of several varieties, eaten fried when small (about 2 inches long). '~ bear, polar bear. '~·caps n pl waves at sea with ~ foam on their crests. ~-'collar, used as a symbol of non-manual labour: ~-collar jobs/ workers. ⇨ blue-collar at blue²(7). ~ coffee, with milk added. ~ 'elephant/'ensign/'feather, ⇨ these nouns. ~ flag, symbol of surrender. ~ heat, high temperature at which metals become ~; (fig) intense passion. Hence, ~-'hot adj. the 'W~ House, the official residence of the President of the US, in Washington, DC; (hence) US Government (policy). ~ lead n poisonous compound of lead carbonate, used in paints. ~ lie, lie considered to be harmless, esp one told for the sake of being polite: She tells enough ~ lies to ice a wedding-cake! ~-'lipped adj having ~ lips, esp with fear. ~-'livered adj cowardly. ~ magic, ⇨ magic. '~ man/woman, European person. ~ meat, poultry, veal, pork. ~ metal, ~ alloy. ~

paper, (GB) report issued by the Government to give information. ~d sepulchre, (from Matt 23: 27) person who appears to be righteous but is in fact wicked; hypocrite. ~ slave, ~ girl who is forced to be a prostitute, esp one who is tricked into going to a foreign country by promises of employment: the ,~-'slave traffic. '~·thorn n hawthorn. ~ tie, ~ bow tie worn with men's full evening dress; (short for) full evening dress: Is it dinner jacket or ~ tie? '~·wash n [U] mixture of powdered lime or chalk and water, used for coating walls, ceilings, etc; (fig) means used to cover or hide sb's errors, faults, etc. □ vt put ~wash on (a wall, etc); (fig) try to make (sb, his reputation, etc) appear blameless by covering up his faults, etc.

white² /waɪt US: hwaɪt/ n 1 [U] ~ colour: dressed in ~. 2 [C] ~ person. 3 [C,U] colourless part round the yolk of an egg: Take the ~s of two eggs. There's too much ~ of egg in this mixture. 4 [C] the ~ part of the eyeball: Don't fire until you see the ~s of their eyes, until they are very close. ~· ness n ~n /'waɪtn US: 'hw-/ vt,vi [VP6A,2A] make or become ~.

White·hall /waɪt'hɔːl US: hw-/ n (street in London where there are) Government offices; (hence) British Government (policy).

whit·en·ing /'waɪtnɪŋ US: 'hw-/ n [U] = whiting².

whither /'wɪðə(r) US: 'hw-/ adv (old use) to which place; (current use, rhet, or in journalism) what is the likely future of: W~ Ulster? W~ the pound sterling? ~so·'ever adv (old use) to whatever place; anywhere at all.

whit·ing¹ /'waɪtɪŋ US: 'hw-/ n (pl unchanged) kinds of small sea-fish used as food.

whit·ing² /'waɪtɪŋ US: 'hw-/ n [U] powdered white chalk used in whitewashing, and for polishing silver, etc.

whit·low /'wɪtləʊ US: 'hw-/ n small inflamed place on a finger or toe, esp near the nail.

Whit·sun /'wɪtsn US: 'hw-/ n (also ,Whit 'Sunday) 7th Sunday after Easter, the feast of the Pentecost. ~·tide /-taɪd/ n ~ and the weekend or the following week.

whittle /'wɪtl US: 'hw-/ vt,vi 1 [VP15B,2C,3A] ~ (sth) away, cut thin slices or strips off, eg wood; (fig) reduce. ~ (away) at sth, cut at sth in this way: He was whittling at a piece of wood. ~ sth down, reduce the size of by cutting away slices, etc; (fig) reduce the amount of: They won't dare to ~ down our salaries. 2 [VP6A,15A] make or shape by whittling: The boy ~d a whip handle from a branch/~d a branch into a whip handle.

whiz /wɪz US: hwɪz/ vi [VP2C] (-zz-), n [U] (make the) sound of sth rushing through the air: The arrows/shells ~zed past.

whizz-kid /'wɪz kɪd US: 'hw-/ n (sl) bright, inventive young person with progressive ideas who achieves rapid success.

who /huː/ interr pron (used as the subject, and only *Pers.* of persons; object form whom /huːm/) 1 Who is that man? Who are those men? I wonder who those people are. Who broke the window? Do you know who broke the window? Who do you think he is? (know) ,who's 'who, (know) who people are, what they do, etc. 2 (Whom is used in formal and literary style, but is usually replaced by who in ordinary colloq style): To whom did you give it? Who did you give it to? Who(m) did you see? Who(m) do you think I met in the post-office this morning?

I don't know to whom I ought to address the request. I don't know who I ought to address the request to. Who else did you see? □ **rel pron 1** (in defining, or restrictive, clauses; ⇨ that³, which sometimes replaces *who*): *This is the man who/ These are the men who wanted to see you.* (After *there* + *to be* the **rel pron** '*who*' may be omitted: *There's somebody (who) wants you on the telephone. There was a man (who) called to see you while you were out.*) **2** (*Whom* is often replaced by *that* except after a *prep*; the *prep* may be placed at the end and *that* used for *whom*): *That is the man (whom) I met in London last year. That is the man about whom we were speaking. That's the man (that) we were speaking about. I know the man (whom) you mean.* **3** (in non-defining clauses, not replaceable by *that*; clause set off by the use of commas or placed in parentheses): *My wife, who has been abroad recently, hopes to see you soon. My brother, whom you met the other day, has recently written a book on Indian art. Our new neighbours, to whom I was introduced yesterday, have come here from Yorkshire.* **4** (independent relative) **Whom** (= Those whom) **the gods love die young,** Those who are specially favoured by Providence die young.

whoa /wəʊ/ *int* ⇨ wo.

who'd /huːd/ = who had/would.

who·dun·it /ˌhuːˈdʌnɪt/ *n* (sl) (= *who done it*, sl for *who did it*) detective or mystery story.

who·ever /huːˈevə(r)/ *pron* any person who; the person who: *W∼ says that is wrong. W∼ else may object, I shall approve.*

whole /həʊl/ *adj* **1** not injured or damaged; unbroken: *You're lucky to escape with a ∼ skin. There isn't a ∼ plate* (= a plate that is not chipped, cracked, broken, etc) *in the house.* (Because ∼(3) means 'all', ∼(1) is sometimes placed after the *n.* Cf: *He swallowed the plum ∼,* without chewing it. *He ate the ∼ loaf,* all of it. *The ox was roasted ∼,* without being cut up into joints. *They ate the ∼ ox,* all of it. *Snakes swallow their victims ∼.*) **go the ∼ hog,** ⇨ hog. **2** entire; complete: *I waited for a ∼ hour.* '∼ **food** *n* [U] food that is nutritious and free of artificial substances: (attrib) *a ∼ food restaurant/shop.* ⁀ '**note** *n* [C] (US) semibreve. ⁀'**number** *n* [C] undivided quantity; integer. '∼·**meal;** ∼ '**wheat** *nn* [U] flour containing everything in the grain, with nothing extracted. **3** (attrib only, with a *sing n*) **the/one's ∼,** all that there is of; complete: *I want to know the ∼ truth about this matter. The ∼ country* (= Everyone in the country) *was anxious for peace. I didn't see him the ∼ evening. He gave his ∼ attention* (= all of his attention) *to the problem. You haven't eaten the ∼ lot* (= all of it, all of them), *have you?* **do sth with one's ∼ heart,** do it with concentrated efforts, undivided attention. Hence, ˌ**whole-**'**hearted(ly),** *adj, adv* **4** (attrib with a *pl n*) not less or fewer than; nothing less than: *It rained for three ∼ days. Give your ∼ energies to the task. W∼* (= Complete) *regiments surrendered to the enemy.* **5** (old use; biblical) in good health; well: *They that are ∼ need not a physician. His hand was made ∼.* □ *n* thing that is complete in itself; all that there is of something: *Four quarters make a ∼. A ∼ is greater than any of its parts. The ∼* (= All) *of my money was stolen. He spent the ∼ of that year in Pakistan. Is the land to be divided up or sold as a ∼?* **on the ∼,** taking everything into considera-

tion. **(taken) as a ∼,** (considered) all together, not separately. **wholly** /ˈhəʊllɪ/ *adv* completely; entirely: *Few men are wholly bad. I wholly agree.*

whole·sale /ˈhəʊlseɪl/ *n* (usu attrib) selling of goods (esp in large quantities) to shopkeepers, for resale to the public. ⇨ retail: *sell by ∼* (US *at ∼*); *∼ prices; a ∼ dealer.* □ *adj, adv* on the ∼ plan; (fig) on a large scale: *Our business is ∼ only. We buy goods ∼. There was a ∼ slaughter when the police opened fire.* ∼**r** *n* one who sells by ∼.

whole·some /ˈhəʊlsəm/ *adj* healthy; favourable to the health (bodily or moral); suggesting good health: *∼ food/exercise/surroundings; a ∼ appearance; ∼ advice.*

who'll /huːl/ = who will.

whom /huːm/ ⇨ who.

whoop /huːp/ *n* [C] **1** loud cry: *∼s of joy.* **2** gasping sound heard during a fit of coughing. '∼·**ing-cough** *n* [U] children's disease with gasping coughs and long, noisy indrawing of breath. □ *vi, vt* utter a loud cry or yell: *to ∼ with joy. ∼ it up* /wuːp US: hwʊp/, (sl) have a hilarious time.

whoopee /ˈwʊpɪ/ *n* **make ∼,** (sl) take part in noisy rejoicing.

whop /wɒp US: hwɒp/ *vt* (-pp-) [VP6A] (sl) beat; defeat. ∼·**per** *n* anything unusually big, esp a big lie. ∼·**ping** *adj* very large of its kind: *a ∼ping lie.* □ *adv* very: *a ∼ping big fish.*

who're /ˈhuːə(r)/ = who are.

whore /ˈhɔː(r)/ *n* △ (derog) prostitute.

whorl /wɜːl US: hw–/ *n* ring of leaves, petals, etc round a stem of a plant; one turn of a spiral, eg as seen on the shell of a mollusc or on a fingerprint: *identify a criminal by the ∼s of his fingerprints.* ∼**ed** *adj* having ∼s; arranged in ∼s.

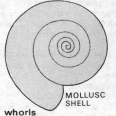
MOLLUSC SHELL
whorls

FINGERPRINT

who's /huːz/ = who is/has.

whose /huːz/ *poss pron* (⇨ who) of whom; of which. **1** *W∼ house is that? I wonder ∼ house that is.* **2** (in rel, defining clauses): *Is that the man ∼ house was broken into by burglars last week? The boy ∼ father complained to me is very stupid.* **4** (*W∼* is sometimes used in place of the usual *of which*, but it is often better to use a different construction, as shown below): *the house ∼ windows are broken,* the house with the broken windows; *that dictionary ∼/of which the cover has come off,* that dictionary without a cover. **4** (in rel, non-defining clauses): *Members of the Fire Service, ∼ work is often dangerous, are paid less than members of the Police Force. Mr Hamilton, ∼ car I borrowed for this journey, is a rich lawyer.*

who·so /ˈhuːsəʊ/, **who·so·ever** /ˌhuːsəʊˈevə(r)/ *pron* (old use) = whoever.

why /waɪ US: hwaɪ/ *adv* **1** (interr) for what reason; with what purpose: *Why was he late? Do you know why he was late? Tell me why. Why not let her do as she likes?* **2** (rel *adv*): *The reasons why he did it are obscure. This is (the reason) why I left early.*

Why you should always arrive late I don't know. □ *int* **1** (expressing surprise) *Why, it's quite easy! A child could do it!* **2** (expressing protest): *Why, what's the harm?* ie there's no harm in it, is there? □ *n* (*pl* whys) reason or cause. **the whys and the wherefores,** the reasons, causes.

wick /wɪk/ *n* [C,U] (length of) thread through a candle, the top end of which is lit, to burn with a light-giving flame; (strip of) woven material by which oil is drawn up in some cigarette lighters, an oil-lamp or oil-stove to burn: *trim the ~ of an oil-lamp.*

wicked /'wɪkɪd/ *adj* **1** (of a person, his acts) bad; wrong; immoral: *It was ~ of you to torment the poor cat.* **2** spiteful; intended to injure: *a ~ blow.* **3** roguish; mischievous: *She gave me a ~ look.* **~·ly** *adv* **~·ness** *n*

wicker /'wɪkə(r)/ *n* [U] (usu attrib) twigs or canes woven together, usu for baskets and furniture: *a ~ chair.* **'~·work** *n* [U] things made of ~.

wicket /'wɪkɪt/ *n* [C] **1** ~(-'door/-'gate), small door or gate, esp one at the side of, or made in, a larger one. **2** small opening (eg one with a sliding window) at which tickets are sold. **3** (cricket) either of the two pairs of three stumps (with crosspieces called *bails*) at which the ball is bowled, ⇨ the illus at cricket; stretch of grass between two ~s: *take a ~, defeat a batsman. A soft ~ (= soft ground between ~s) helps the bowler. Surrey were four ~s down, Four of their batsmen were out. We won by six ~s,* won with seven of our batsmen not out. *keep ~,* act as ~-keeper. **'~·keeper** *n* player who stands behind the ~ to stop balls not struck by the batsman, to catch batsmen out, etc. **3** (US) croquet hoop.

wide /waɪd/ *adj* (-r, -st) **1** measuring much from side to side or in comparison with length; broad: *a ~ river; a road twelve feet ~.* **2** of great extent; comprehensive: *a man with ~ interests,* interested in many subjects; *the ~ world; the ~ Atlantic; a ~ selection of new books.* **3** fully opened: *She stared at him with ~ eyes. Open your mouth ~.* **4** far from what is aimed at or from a specific point: *a ~ ball,* (in cricket) one judged by the umpire to be out of the batsman's reach. *Your answer was ~ of the mark.* **5** (sl) shrewdly aware of business chances; unscrupulous. *~ boy,* (sl) such a man. □ *adv* **1** far from the point aimed at: *The arrow fell ~ of the mark.* **2** fully: *He was ~ awake. The window was ~ open.* **,~-a'wake** *adj* (fig) alert, vigilant: *a ~-awake young woman,* one who realizes what is going on, etc and is not easily deceived. **3** over a large area: *travel far and ~.* **'~-spread** *adj* (esp) found, distributed, over a large area. **~·ly** *adv* **1** at ~ intervals: *~ly scattered.* Cf *scattered far and ~.* **2** to a large extent or degree: *~ly different; differing ~ly in opinions.* **3** over a large area: *It is ~ly known that....* **~n** /'waɪdn/ *vt,vi* [VP6A,2A] make or become ~(r): *'road-~ning in process.*

wid·geon /'wɪdʒən/ *n* kind of wild freshwater duck.

widow /'wɪdəʊ/ *n* woman who has not married again after her husband's death. **~er** *n* man who has not married again after his wife's death. **wid·owed** /'wɪdəʊd/ *adj* made into a ~ or ~er: *~ed by war.* **'~·hood** /-hʊd/ *n* state of, time of being, a ~.

width /wɪtθ/ *n* **1** [U] quality or state of being wide: *a road of great ~;* (fig) *~ of mind/intellect/views.* Cf *broadminded, broad views.* **2** measurement

from side to side: *a ~ of 10 metres; 10 metres in ~.* **3** [C] piece of material of a certain ~: *join two ~s of cloth; curtain material of various ~s.*

wield /wiːld/ *vt* [VP6A] have and use: *~ an axe; ~ power/authority/control.*

wife /waɪf/ *n* (*pl* wives /waɪvz/) married woman, esp in relation to her husband: *Smith and his ~; the baker's ~; a club for young wives.* **old wives' tale,** foolish or superstitious story, usu traditional. ⇨ also *fish~* at fish¹(2), *house~* at house¹(7). **'~·like, ~·ly** *adjj* of, like, suitable for, a ~: *~ly virtues/duties.*

wig /wɪg/ *n* head-covering of false hair (as worn to hide baldness, and by actors, barristers and judges, and formerly worn as a fashionable ornament in Europe during the 17th and 18th cc). ⇨ the illus at judge. **wig·ged** /wɪgd/ *adj* wearing a wig.

wig·ging /'wɪgɪŋ/ *n* (colloq) scolding: *get/give sb a good ~.*

wiggle /'wɪgl/ *vt,vi* [VP6A,2A] (cause to) move with quick, short, side-to-side movements: *The baby was wiggling its toes. Stop wiggling and sit still.* □ *n* wiggling movement.

wight /waɪt/ *n* (archaic) person; human being: *a luckless ~.*

wig·wam /'wɪgwæm US: -wɑːm/ *n* hut or tent made by fastening skins or mats over a framework of poles, as formerly used by N American Indians.

wild /waɪld/ *adj* (-er, -est) **1** ⇨ the illus at cat, large, small. (of animals) not tamed or domesticated; living in natural conditions (eg lions, giraffes, wolves); (of plants) growing in natural conditions; not cultivated: *~ flowers; a reserve for the preservation of ~ life,* area where ~ animals, birds, etc are protected and helped to survive; (attrib): *a ~-life sanctuary.* **'~·cat** *attrib adj* reckless, unsound, impracticable: *~cat schemes,* esp in finance and commerce; *a ~cat strike,* unofficial and irresponsible strike (by workers). **'~·fowl** *n* (esp) birds ordinarily shot or hunted as game, eg ~ ducks and geese, quail, pheasants. **,~-'goose chase,** foolishly useless enterprise. *sow one's ~ oats,* ⇨ oat(1). **2** (of horses, game birds, etc) easily startled; hard to get near: *The deer/pheasants are rather ~.* **3** (of persons, tribes, etc) uncivilized; savage. **4** (of scenery, areas of land, etc) desolate; waste; unsettled: *~ scenery; ~, mountainous areas.* **5** violent; uncontrolled; stormy: *You'd better stay indoors on a ~ night like this. What ~ weather we're having!* **6** excited; passionate; distracted: *There were sounds of ~ laughter. He was ~ with anger. It made her ~ (= filled her with anger) to see such cruelty. The anxiety drove them almost ~,* mad. **7** *be ~ about sth/sb,* (colloq) have a strong desire for; be madly enthusiastic about: *~ about strawberries/Prince Charles.* **8** disorderly; out of control: *a state of ~ confusion; a room in ~ disorder; settle down after a ~ youth. run ~,* be without check, restraint or training: *They allow their children to run ~,* allow them to amuse themselves in any way they like, with no control of any kind. **'~·fire** *n* [U] (chiefly in) *spread like ~fire,* (of reports, rumours, etc) very fast. **9** reckless; done or said without reflection or consideration: *a ~ guess/scheme; ~ shooting,* without taking aim. **10** (of a playing-card) having any value (as eg a *joker*): *a ~ card.* □ *adv* in a ~ manner: *shoot ~.* □ *n pl* **the ~s,** uncultivated (and often uninhabited) areas: *the ~s of Africa; go out into the ~s.* **~·ly** *adv* in a ~ manner:

rush about ~*ly; talk* ~*ly,* eg in an exaggerated way; *a* ~*ly exaggerated account.* ~**-ness** *n*

wilde·beest /'wɪldɪbi:st/ *n* = gnu. ⇨ the illus at large.

wil·der·ness /'wɪldənɪs/ *n* (rarely *pl*) **1** wild uncultivated waste land. **2** desolate expanse: *a* ~ *of waters. From his attic window he looked out over a* ~ *of roofs.*

wile /waɪl/ *n* (usu *pl*) trick; bit of cunning: *fall a victim to the* ~*s of an unscrupulous rogue; the* ~*s of the Devil.*

wil·ful (US also **will-**) /'wɪlfl/ *adj* **1** (of a person) obstinate; determined to have one's own way: *a* ~ *child.* **2** intentional; for which compulsion, ignorance or accident is no excuse: ~ *murder/ negligence/waste/disobedience.* ~**ly** /-fəlɪ/ *adv* ~**-ness** *n*

will¹ /*weak form:* l; *strong form:* wɪl/ *anom fin* (often shortened to *'ll; neg* ~ not or won't /wəʊnt/; *pt,* conditional *would* /*after* 'I, he, she, we, you, they': d, *elsewhere: weak form:* əd; *strong form:* wʊd/, *neg* would not or wouldn't /'wʊdnt/) [VP5] **1** (used as an auxiliary verb of the future tense): *If today is Monday, tomorrow* ~ *be Tuesday. You'll be in time if you hurry. You won't be in time unless you hurry.* (*Would* replaces ~ to show future in the past.) *I wonder whether it* ~ *be ready. I wondered whether it would be ready. You'll be in Oxford this time tomorrow. You would have been in Oxford this time yesterday.* **2** (used with the 1st person (*I, we*) to express willingness, consent, an offer or a promise): *All right, I'll come. I won't do it again. We'll pay back the money soon.* (*Would* replaces ~ to show future in the past): *I said I would do it. We said we would help them.* **3** (used with the 2nd person in questions, marking polite requests, and often equivalent to *please*): '*W*~ *you* (*please*) *come in?*' '*Would you* (*please*) *come back later?*' '*Pass the salt, would you?*' '*Would you* (*please*) *pass the salt?*' **4** (used in *affirm* sentences, always with stress (never '*ll* or '*d*), indicating insistence or inevitability): *He*'~ *have his own way,* insists on this. *Boys* '~ *be boys,* We cannot expect them to behave except as boys naturally behave. *Accidents* '~ *happen,* They are to be expected from time to time. *That's just what you* '*would say,* what you might be expected to say. *Of course it* '*would rain on the day we chose for a picnic,* We might expect such treatment from Fate. **5** (used in the neg to indicate refusal): *He won't/wouldn't help me. This window won't open,* cannot be opened. **6** (used to indicate that sth happens from time to time, that sb is in the habit of doing sth, that sth is natural or to be expected): *He'll sit there hour after hour looking at the traffic go by. Sometimes the boys would play a trick on their teacher. Occasionally the machine will go wrong without any apparent cause.* **7** (used to indicate probability or likelihood): *This'll be the book you're looking for, I think. She would be about 60 when she died.* '*I want someone to do a lot of typing for me*'—'*Will/Would I do?*' Am I likely to be suitable for the job? **8** (*Would* is used with the 2nd and 3rd persons to form conditional statements and questions): *They'd be killed if the car went over the cliff. They'd have been killed if the car had gone over the cliff.* **would rather,** ⇨ rather(1). **9** (*Would* is used with the 1st person to form conditional statements expressing the speaker's will or intention): *We would have come if it hadn't rained.*

will² /wɪl/ *vt* (*pt* would /wʊd/, no other forms used) (all old uses) **1** [VP6A] wish: *Let him do what he* ~. *What would you?* **2** [VP9] (the subject *I* is often omitted) used to express wishes: *Would* (*that*) *it were otherwise! Would* (= I would) *to God* (*that*) *I had not agreed! Would that they were safe home again!* **3** [VP5] choose; desire: *the place where he would be. Come whenever you* ~ (ie ~ or wish to come). (Cf will³ with which will² is closely connected.) '**would-be** *attrib adj* used to indicate what is desired, aspired to, or intended: *would-be authors,* persons who aspire to be authors.

will³ /wɪl/ *vt,vi* (*pt,pp* ~ed) **1** [VP6A] make use of one's mental powers in an attempt to do sth or get sth: *We cannot achieve success merely by* ~*ing it.* **2** [VP2A] exercise will-power: *W*~*ing and wishing are not the same thing.* **3** [VP6A,9] intend unconditionally: *God has* ~*ed it so. God* ~*s that man should be happy.* **4** [VP17,14,15A] influence, control or compel, by exercising the will: *Can you* ~ *yourself to keep awake/into keeping awake? It would be convenient if we could* ~ *ourselves across lands and oceans.* **5** [VP12A,13A] ~ **sth to sb;** ~ **sb sth,** leave (property, etc) (to sb) by means of a will and testament: *He* ~*ed most of his money to charities. I hope my uncle has* ~*ed me that fine painting.*

will⁴ /wɪl/ *n* **1** the ~, mental power by which a person can direct his thoughts and actions, and influence those of others: *the freedom of the* ~. **2** [U,C] (*sing* only) (also '~-**power**) control exercised over oneself, one's impulses: *He has no* ~ *of his own,* is easily influenced by others. *W*~ *can conquer habit. He has a strong/weak* ~. *He showed a strength of* ~ *that overcame all obstacles.* -**willed,** (in compound *adjj*) having the kind of ~ indicated: *,strong-'*~*ed; ,weak-'*~*ed.* **3** [U,C] (*sing* only) determination; desire or purpose: *The* ~ *to live helps a patient to recover. She has a boundless* ~ *to please,* is full of desire to please. **Where there's a** ~ **there's a way,** (prov) If one has the determination to achieve sth, a way of doing so will be found. **take the** ~ **for the deed,** understand and be grateful for the fact that one wants to help, etc although unable to do so. **of one's own free** ~, without being required or compelled: *I did it of my own free* ~. **at** ~, whenever and however one pleases: *You may come and go at* ~. **tenant at** ~, (legal) one who can be required to give up (land, a house, etc). **4 a** ~, energy; enthusiasm: *work with a* ~. **5** [U] (with a *possessive*) that which is desired or determined upon: *God's* ~ *be done. He has always had his* ~ (or, more colloq, *his own way*). *What is your* ~ (more usu, *What do you want*)? **6 good/ill** ~, kind/unkind disposition or feeling: *feel no ill will towards anybody.* '*Peace on earth and good* ~ *towards men.*' **7** [C] (also **last** ~ **and testament**), = testament. ~**·ful** /-fl/ *adj* (US spelling of) wilful.

wil·lies /'wɪlɪz/ *n pl* (sl) feeling of unease or nervousness: *This gloomy old house gives me the* ~.

will·ing /'wɪlɪŋ/ *adj* **1** ready to help, to do what is needed, asked, etc: ~ *workers. He's quite* ~ *to pay the price I ask.* **2** done, given, etc readily, without hesitation: ~ *obedience.* ~**·ly** *adv* ~**·ness** *n* [U].

will-o'-the-wisp /ˌwɪl ə ðə 'wɪsp/ *n* moving light seen at night over marshy ground; (more usu fig) sth or sb that one pursues unsuccessfully because it or he is difficult to grasp or reach.

wil·low /'wɪləʊ/ n [C] ⇨ the illus at tree. '∼(-tree), kinds of tree and shrub with thin, easily bent branches; [U] twigs of this tree used for weaving into baskets; its wood, used for making cricket bats, etc. '∼-pattern n Chinese design (with a ∼-tree, a river, etc) in blue upon white china (seen on plates, etc). ∼y adj (of persons) lithe and slender.

willy-nilly /ˌwɪlɪ 'nɪlɪ/ adv willingly or unwillingly; whether wanted or unwanted.

wilt[1] /wɪlt/ v (archaic form of will[2]) thou ∼, = you will.

wilt[2] /wɪlt/ vi,vt [VP6A,2A] (of plants, flowers) (cause to) droop, lose freshness; (of persons) become limp.

Wil·ton /'wɪltən/ n kind of carpet.

wily /'waɪlɪ/ adj (-ier, -iest) full of wiles; cunning: a ∼ old fox.

wimple /'wɪmpl/ n linen covering arranged in folds about the head, cheeks, chin and neck, worn by women in the Middle Ages, and still by some nuns.

win /wɪn/ vt,vi (pt,pp won /wʌn/) (-nn-) 1 [VP6A,12B,13B,15A,2A] get by means of hard work, perseverance, struggle, as the result of competition, gambling, etc; do best (in a fight, etc): win a race/a battle/a war/a scholarship/a prize; ∼ fame and fortune. Which side won? She has a nature that quickly won her the friendship of her colleagues. He soon won a reputation for himself. We've won! He won £5 from me at cards. **win the day/the field,** be victorious. **win free/clear/out/through,** make one's way through, out, etc; free oneself, get out of a difficult position, etc by effort. **win hands down,** (colloq) succeed easily. '**winning-post** n post marking the end of a race. 2 [VP6A,15B,17] **win sb over (to sth);** (less usu) **win sb to do sth,** persuade (sb) by argument; gain the favour of: We won him over to our view. 3 [VP6A] reach by effort: win the summit/the shore. □ n [C] success in a game, competition, etc: Our team has had five wins this summer. **win·ner** n person, animal, thing, that wins. **win·ning** adj 1 that wins: the winning horse. 2 persuasive; gaining confidence and friendship: a winning smile. **winnings** /'wɪnɪŋz/ n pl (esp) money won in betting, gambling, etc.

wince /wɪns/ vt [VP2A,C] show bodily or mental pain or distress (by a movement or by loss of composure): He ∼d under the blow/at the insult. He didn't ∼ when the knife slipped and cut his thumb. □ n wincing movement: without a ∼.

win·cey·ette /ˌwɪnsɪ'et/ n [U] strong material of wool and cotton, or wool, used for shirts, etc.

winch /wɪntʃ/ n windlass; stationary machine for hoisting or pulling. □ vt [VP6A,15B] move by using a ∼: The glider was ∼ed off the ground, pulled along by means of a ∼ until it rose into the air: We can ∼ out these big tree roots, get them out by using a ∼.

wind[1] /wɪnd/ n 1 [C,U] (often the ∼; with much, little, etc when the reference is to degree or force; with indef art or in pl when the reference is to the kind of ∼, etc; ⇨ the examples) air in motion as the result of natural forces: a north ∼, blowing from the north; warm ∼s from the south. The ∼ blew my hat off. He ran like the ∼, very fast. The ∼ is rising/falling, becoming stronger/weaker. There's no/not much/a lot of ∼ today. **fling/**

throw caution/prudence, etc to the ∼s, abandon it, take no thought of it. **get/have the** '∼ **up,** (sl) become/be frightened. **raise the ∼,** (sl) obtain the money needed. **put the** '∼ **up sb,** (sl) cause him to feel frightened. **see/find out how the** '∼ **blows,** what people are thinking, what is likely to happen. **sail close/near to the ∼,** ⇨ sail[2](1). **take the** '∼ **out of sb's sails,** prevent him from doing or saying sth by doing it or saying it before him; take away his advantage suddenly. **there is/was sth in the ∼,** being secretly prepared or plotted. 2 (pl) the cardinal points: The house stands on a hilltop, exposed to the four ∼s of heaven, ∼s from all directions. My papers were blown to the four ∼s, in all directions. 3 [U] breath needed for running or continuous exertion: The runner soon lost his ∼, became out of breath. He stopped to recover/get back his ∼. **get one's second ∼,** recover the ability to breathe regularly after a first period of breathlessness; (fig) get new energy for a task. **sound in ∼ and limb,** in excellent physical condition. 4 [U] scent carried by the ∼ (as indicating where sth is): **get ∼ of,** (fig) hear a rumour of, begin to suspect. 5 [U] empty words; meaningless or useless talk: Don't listen to the politicians—they're all ∼. 6 [U] gas formed in the bowels and causing discomfort: The baby is suffering from ∼. **break ∼,** expel ∼ from the bowels or stomach. 7 **the ∼,** orchestral ∼ instruments. 8 (compounds) '∼-bag n (colloq) person who talks a lot but says nothing important. '∼-break n hedge, fence, line of trees, etc to break the force of the ∼ and give protection. '∼-cheater (US = '∼-breaker) n close-fitting garment for the upper part of the body, designed to give protection against the ∼. '∼-fall n [C] (a) fruit (eg an apple) blown off a tree by the ∼. (b) (fig) unexpected piece of good fortune, esp money coming to sb. '∼-flower n anemone. '∼-gauge n instrument for measuring the force of the ∼. '∼ instrument n musical instrument in which sound is produced by a current of air (eg an organ, a flute, a cornet). ⇨ the illus at brass. '∼-jammer n (colloq) merchant sailing-ship. '∼-mill n mill worked by the action of the ∼

sail

a windmill

on sails which revolve. **fight/tilt at ∼mills,** (from the story of Don Quixote) fight imaginary enemies; try to put right imaginary wrongs. '∼-pipe n passage for air from the throat to the lungs. ⇨ the illus at respiratory. '∼-screen (US = '∼-shield) n screen of glass in front of a motor-vehicle, etc. ⇨ the illus at motor. '∼-screen-wiper n ⇨ wiper at wipe. '∼-sock n canvas sleeve flown at the top of a pole (eg on an airfield) to show the direction of the ∼. '∼-swept adj exposed to the ∼s; blown bare by strong ∼s: a ∼swept hillside. '∼-tunnel n structure through which air is forced (at controlled speeds) to study its effects on (models of) aircraft, etc. ~·**less** *adj* without ~: *a ~less day.* ~·**ward** /-wəd/ *n,adj* (side) in the direction from which the ~ blows; (side) exposed to the ~: *Let's get to ~ward of that tannery* (to avoid the bad smell). **windy** *adj* (-ier, -iest) **1** with much ~: *a ~y day; ~y weather; a ~y hilltop,* open to the ~. **2** wordy, ⇨ **5** above. **3** (sl) frightened. ~·**ily** /-ɪlɪ/ *adv* ~·**i-ness** *n*

wind² /wɪnd/ *vt* (from **wind¹**) (*pt,pp* ~ed /'wɪndɪd/) [VP6A] **1** detect the presence of by scent: *The hounds ~ed the fox. The deer ~ed the stalkers.* **2** exhaust the wind(3) of; cause to breathe fast: *He was quite ~ed by the long climb/by running to catch the bus.* **3** give an opportunity of recovering the breath to: *We stopped to ~ our horses.*

wind³ /waɪnd/ *vi,vt* (*pt,pp* wound /waʊnd/) **1** [VP2A,B,C,15A] go, (cause to) move, in a curving, spiral, or twisting manner: *The river ~s (its way) to the sea. We climbed the ~ing* (= spiral) *staircase. The path ~s up the hillside. She wound herself/her way into his affections,* won his affections by her clever ways. **2** [VP6A,15A,B] twist (string, wool yarn, etc) into a ball, or round or on to sth: ~ (*up*) *wool into a ball;* ~ *yarn;* ~ *thread on to a reel;* ~ *in the line,* eg a fishing-line on to a reel. ~ *sth off,* unwind it. ~ *sb round one's (little) finger,* make him do whatever one wants him to do. **3** [VP14,15A] ~ *sth round sb/sth;* ~ *sb/sth in sth,* fold or wrap closely; embrace: ~ *a shawl round a baby;* ~ *a baby in a shawl. She wound her arms round the child.* '~·**ing-sheet** *n* shroud; sheet (to be) wound round a corpse. **4** [VP6A,15B] ~ *sth (up),* turn (a handle, eg of a windlass); raise (sth) by doing this: ~ *a handle;* ~

up ore from a mine/a bucket from a well. **5** [VP6A,15B] ~ *sth (up),* tighten the spring of (a watch or clock); raise the weights that operate a clock (to put or keep the watch or clock in motion): *If you forget to ~ (up) your watch it will stop—unless it is a self-~ing watch,* ie one that is wound up automatically by movements of the wrist. **6 be wound up (to),** be (emotionally) excited (esp in passive), ⇨ unwind: *He was wound up to a high pitch of excitement. Expectation was wound up to a high pitch. She was wound up to a fury.* **7** [VP2C,15B] ~ *(sth) up,* come or bring to an end: *It's time for him to ~ up his speech,* come to a conclusion. *He wound up by declaring that his efforts would be continued. They wound up the evening by singing some folk-songs.* ~ *up a business company,* put everything in order before dissolving it. ~ *up one's affairs,* put them in order before bringing them to an end. □ *n* [C] single turn in ~ing string, ~ing up a clock, etc.

wind·lass /'wɪndləs/ *n* machine for pulling or lifting things (eg water from a well) by means of a rope or chain which is wound round an axle; winch.

win·dow /'wɪndəʊ/ *n* opening in a wall or roof of a building, the side of a ship, carriage, car, etc to let in light and air: *look out of the ~.* '~-**box** *n* long narrow box fixed to a ~-sill in which to grow plants. '~-**dressing** *n* art of arranging goods attractively in shop-~s; (fig) (art of) making an impressive display of one's work, abilities, qualities, etc. '~ **envelope** *n* one with a transparent part in the front through which an address on the paper inside may be read. '~-**pane** *n* pane of glass for or in a ~. **go** '~-**shopping,** look at goods displayed in

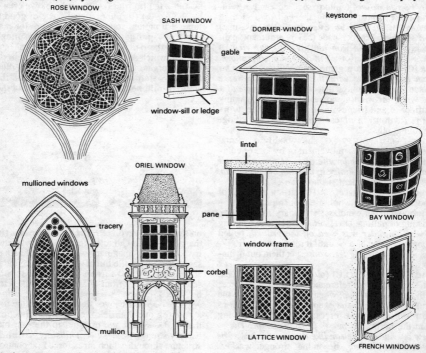

ROSE WINDOW

SASH WINDOW

DORMER-WINDOW

keystone

gable

window-sill or ledge

lintel

ORIEL WINDOW

mullioned windows

tracery

mullion

corbel

pane

window frame

BAY WINDOW

LATTICE WINDOW

FRENCH WINDOWS

windows

shop-~s (for interest, but not necessarily with the idea of buying anything). '~-sill *n* ⇨ sill. *a ~ on the world,* (fig) means of learning about, or coming into contact with, other countries: *The English language is a ~ on the world.*

windy /'wɪndɪ/ ⇨ wind¹.

wine /waɪn/ *n* [U] **1** alcoholic drink made from the fermented juice of grapes: *a barrel/bottle/glass of ~; French ~(s),* (*pl* for different kinds of ~). *new ~ in old bottles,* a new principle that is too strong to be held back by old forms. '~-glass *n* glass designed for drinking ~ from. '~-press *n* one in which grapes are pressed. '~-skin *n* whole skin of a goat, etc sewn up and used formerly for holding ~. **2** fermented drink resembling ~, made from other fruits or plants: *currant/cowslip/palm, etc ~.* □ *vt* (esp) *~ and dine sb,* entertain at a meal with ~: *We were ~d and dined at the firm's expense.*

wing /wɪŋ/ *n* **1** either of the two organs of a bird by which it flies; one of the similar organs of an insect; one of the surfaces by which an aircraft is supported in the air. ⇨ the illus at air, bird. *clip a person's ~s,* limit his movements, activities, expenditure, etc. *lend/add ~s to,* cause to go fast: *Fear lent him ~s,* made him run off fast. *take (to itself) ~s,* disappear, vanish: *As soon as we go on a holiday, our money seems to take ~s. take sb under one's ~,* take him under one's protection; give him care and guidance. '~-nut/-screw, = thumb-nut. '~-span/-spread *nn* measurement across ~s when these are extended. **2** part of an object, building, etc which projects or is extended from one of its sides (eg the part of a motor-vehicle covering a wheel, called a *fender* in US): *a '~ chair,* an upholstered chair with arms as high as the back; *add a new ~ to a hospital. The north ~ of the house was added 50 years ago.* **3** (mil) either of the flanks of an army or fleet; unit placed to guard a flank. **4** those members of a political party holding more extreme views than those of the majority: *the radical ~ of the Labour Party.* Hence, ,left-/ ,right-'~(er). **5** unseen areas to the right and left of the stage of a theatre; the scenery there: *We were allowed to watch the performance from the ~s.* **6** flying. *on the ~,* in flight: *shoot a bird on the ~. take ~,* start flying. **7** sth like a ~ in appearance or position, eg certain seeds (eg of the maple and sycamore). **8** (also ~er) (football, hockey) forward player whose place is either side of the centre. ⇨ the illus at football. **9** (GB; RAF) formation of two or more squadrons; (*pl*) pilot's badge: *get one's ~s.* '~-commander, RAF rank, next below Group Captain. □ *vt,vi* **1** [VP6A] give ~s to; lend speed to: (usu fig) *Fear ~ed his steps.* **2** [VP2C,15A] fly; travel on ~s: *The planes ~ed (their way) over the Alps.* **3** [VP6A] wound (a bird) in the ~; (colloq) wound (a person) in the arm. *~ed adj* having ~s: *the ~ed god,* Mercury; *a ~ed Victory,* a statue of the goddess of victory with ~s. *~-less adj* without ~s. *~er n* person who acts or plays in a position on the ~s. ⇨ 4 and 8 above.

wink /wɪŋk/ *vi,vt* **1** [VP2A,3A,15B] *~ (at),* close and open (one's eyes, or more usu one eye); get rid of (tears) by doing this: *She ~ed at me,* eg as a sign of secret amusement, or to call my attention to sth, or as a private signal of some kind. *He ~ed a tear away. ~ at sth,* purposely avoid seeing; deliberately ignore (a piece of misconduct, a trans-

gression). **2** [VP2A,C] (of a star, light, etc) shine or flash intermittently, at very short intervals: *A lighthouse was ~ing in the far distance.* □ *n* **1** act of ~ing, esp as a signal or hint. *tip sb the ~,* (colloq) give him special information; warn him secretly. *A ~ is as good as a nod,* A hint, etc given by a wink, etc is as effective as a more obvious signal. **2** very short time: *I didn't sleep a ~/ didn't have a ~ of sleep,* didn't sleep at all. *forty ~s,* a short sleep (esp during the day).

win-kle /'wɪŋkl/ *n* sea snail used as food; periwinkle. □ *vt* [VP15B] *~ sb/sth out,* extract, force or pull out (as a ~ is picked or pulled out of its shell with a pin).

win-ner, win-ning ⇨ win.

win-now /'wɪnəʊ/ *vt* [VP6A,14,15A,B] use a stream of air to separate dry outer coverings from (grain): *~ wheat;* blow (husks, chaff) away from grain in this way: *~ the chaff away/out;* (fig) *~ truth from falsehood.*

win-some /'wɪnsəm/ *adj* (of a person, his appearance) attractive; pleasing; bright: *a ~ smile/ manner. ~-ly adv~-ness n*

win-ter /'wɪntə(r)/ *n* [U,C] season between autumn and spring (Nov or Dec to Feb or March in the northern hemisphere): *many ~s* (liter, = years) *ago; ~ sports,* eg ice-skating, skiing; *~ wheat,* planted in the autumn and harvested in the following spring or summer; *~ quarters,* (esp) to which troops retired for the ~ (in former times). '~ garden, glass-enclosed area with plants, etc eg as the lounge of a hotel. □ *vi* [VP2C] pass the ~: *~ in the south; the ~ing quarters of wild geese. ~y,* wintry /'wɪntrɪ/ *adj* of or like ~; cold: *a wintry sky/ day; wintry weather;* (fig) *a wintry smile/greeting,* one lacking in warmth or liveliness.

wipe /waɪp/ *vt,vi* [VP6A,15A,B,22] clean or dry (sth) by rubbing with a cloth, paper, the hands, etc: *~ the dishes; ~ one's hands on a towel; ~ one's face; ~ sth dry; ~ one's eyes,* dry the tears. *Take this handkerchief and ~ your nose, David. ~ the floor with sb,* ⇨ floor¹(1). *~ the slate clean,* make a new start, with past errors, enmities, etc forgotten. *~ sth away,* remove (eg tears) by wiping. *~ sth off,* (a) remove by wiping: *~ off a drawing from the blackboard.* (b) get rid of: *~ off a debt. ~ sth out,* (a) clean the inside of: *~ out a jug; ~ out the bath.* (b) get rid of; remove: *~ out a disgrace; ~ out old scores,* forget old quarrels, etc; *~ out an insult* (esp by vengeance). (c) destroy completely: *a disease that almost ~d out the population of the island: ~ sth up,* take up (liquid, etc) by wiping: *~ up spilt milk; ~ up a mess.* □ *n* act of wiping: *Give this plate a ~. ~r n* sth that ~s or is used for wiping: *a 'windscreen-wiper,* for wiping rainwater from the windscreen. ⇨ the illus at motor.

wire /'waɪə(r)/ *n* **1** [C,U] (piece or length of) metal drawn out into the form of a thread: *'telephone ~(s); copper ~; barbed ~* (⇨ the illus at barb); *~ rope,* made by twisting strands of ~ together; *~ netting,* made by weaving ~ (used for fences, fruit cages, etc). *pull (the) ~s,* (fig) use secret or indirect influence to gain one's ends, manage a political party, etc; hence '~-puller *n.* *live ~,* (a) ~ charged with electric current. (b) (fig) active, vigorous person. '~-cutters *n pl* tool for cutting ~. *,~-'haired adj* (esp of a dog) with stiff or wiry hair. '~ tapping *n* [U] tapping of telephones, ⇨ tap¹, *vt*(2). *~ wool n* [C,U] (pad of) fine ~ for cleaning pots and pans. '∼-**worm** n kinds of worm-like larva destructive to plants. **2** [C] (colloq, esp US) telegram: send sb a ∼; send off a ∼. Let me know by ∼ what time to expect you. □ vt,vi **1** [VP6A,15A,B] fasten with ∼: ∼ two things together; put ∼(s) in or on; put (beads, pearls, etc) on fine ∼. **2** [VP6A] install electrical circuits (in a building, to provide lighting, power, etc): Has the house been ∼d for electricity yet? **3** [VP6A] catch, snare (birds, rabbits, etc) with ∼. **4** [VP6A,16,12A,13A,11] (colloq, esp US) telegraph: He ∼d (to) his brother to buy oil shares. He ∼d me that he would be delayed. **wir-ing** n [U] (esp) system of ∼s for electric current. **wiry** adj (-ier, -iest) like ∼; (of persons) lean and with strong sinews.

wire-less /'waɪəlɪs/ adj without the use of wire(s). □ n (dated word for) **1** [U] radio. **2** [C] radio set.

wis-dom /'wɪzdəm/ n [U] **1** quality of being wise. '∼-**tooth** n (pl -teeth) back tooth, usu coming through after 20 years of age: cut one's ∼-teeth, reach the age when one has discretion, etc. ⇨ the illus at mouth. **2** wise thoughts, sayings, etc: the ∼ of the ancients/our ancestors.

wise¹ /waɪz/ adj (-r, -st) having or showing experience, knowledge, good judgement, prudence, etc: ∼ men/acts. He was ∼ enough not to drive when he was feeling ill. 'I don't agree', he said, with a ∼ shake of the head, ie suggesting that he was ∼. It's easy to be ∼ after the event, to know, after sth has happened, what one failed to see in advance. **be none the** ∼r, be no better informed: He came away none the ∼r, knowing no more than before. **be/get** ∼ **to sb/sth,** (sl) be/become aware of: get ∼ to what's happening/to the ways of business men, etc. **put sb** ∼ **to sb/sth,** inform him of (what is happening, etc). '∼-**acre** n dull and boring person who pretends to be much ∼r than he is. '∼-**crack** n (sl) smart, witty saying or remark. □ vi make ∼cracks. ∼-**ly** adv

wise² /waɪz/ n (sing only; old use) way, manner: in no ∼; in this ∼.

wish /wɪʃ/ vt,vi **1** [VP9] ∼ **that...,** (that usu omitted; the that-clause usu in the pt) have as an unfulfilled desire or a desire that cannot be fulfilled: I ∼ I knew what is happening. I ∼ I were rich. I ∼ I were a bird. She ∼ed she'd stayed at home, was sorry that she had not stayed at home. **2** [VP15A] have as a desire: She ∼ed herself home (= ∼ed that she was at home) again. They ∼ed the voyage at an end. He began to ∼ himself (= ∼ that he was) out of the affair. **3** [VP22] ∼ **sb well/ill,** hope that he may have good/ill fortune, etc: He ∼ed me well. I ∼ nobody ill. **4** [VP12A,13A] say that one hopes for: ∼ sb a pleasant journey; ∼ happiness to all one's friends; express as a greeting: ∼ sb good morning/goodbye. **5** [VP7A,17, rarely VP6A with pron] want: She ∼es to be alone. Do you really ∼ me to go? I ∼ there to be no misunderstanding on this matter. What do you ∼? Well, if you ∼ it..., if that is what you want me to do, etc. **6** [VP3A] ∼ **for,** have a desire for, pray for (esp sth unlikely to be obtained or achieved, or sth that can be obtained only by good fortune or in exceptional circumstances): She has everything a woman can ∼ for, (suggesting unusual good fortune). How he ∼ed for an opportunity to go abroad!, (suggesting small likelihood of getting one). The weather was everything they could ∼ for, (suggesting unusual good fortune). What more can you ∼ for? (Cf He would

like a glass of cold water, and How he ∼ed for a glass of cold water, the second sentence suggesting that there was little likelihood of his getting one). **7** [VP2A] express a desire: Doing is better than ∼ing. '∼-**bone** n forked bone above the breastbone of a fowl, pulled in two by two persons, the person getting the longer part having the right to the magic fulfilment of any wish. '∼-**ing-cap** n (in fairy tales) cap which secures to the wearer the fulfilment of any wish. **8** ∼ **sb/sth on sb,** (colloq) transfer him/it to sb (esp with the idea of getting rid of sb/sth unwanted or disliked): I wouldn't ∼ my mother-in-law on anyone, suggesting that she is intolerable. We had the Jones children ∼ed on us for the weekend. □ n **1** [C,U] desire; longing: He has no/not much ∼ to go. She expressed a ∼ to be alone. He disregarded his father's ∼es. I hope you will grant my ∼. **If** ∼**es were horses, beggars might ride,** (prov) If things could be obtained merely by ∼ing for them, poor people would soon be rich. **The** ∼ **is father to the thought,** (prov) We are apt to believe sth because we ∼ it were true. **2** [C] that which is ∼ed for: She got her ∼. ∼-**ful** /-fl/ having or expressing a ∼; desiring. ∼-**ful thinking,** thinking or believing that sth is true because one ∼es it were true. ∼-**fully** /-fəlɪ/ adv

wishy-washy /'wɪʃɪ wɒʃɪ US: wɔːʃɪ/ adj (of soup, tea, etc) thin; weak; (of talk, persons) lacking in spirit or vigour; sloppy.

wisp /wɪsp/ n [C] small bundle, bunch or twist: a ∼ of straw/hay; a ∼ of hair; spiral or ribbon: a ∼ of smoke/steam. ∼-**y** adj like a ∼; slight.

wis-teria /wɪ'stɪərɪə/ n (kinds of) climbing plant with a woody stem and long drooping clusters of pale purple or white flowers and seeds in long pods, often grown on walls or over pergolas.

wist-ful /'wɪstfl/ adj sad and longing; having, showing, moved by, a rather unsatisfied and often vague desire: ∼ eyes; a ∼ expression; in a ∼ mood. ∼-**ly** /-fəlɪ/ adv in a ∼ manner: She looked ∼ly at the photographs of herself when she was young and beautiful.

wit¹ /wɪt/ n **1** (sing or pl) intelligence; understanding; quickness of mind: He hadn't the wits/hadn't wit enough to realize what to do in the emergency. **at one's wit's end,** not knowing what to do or say. **out of one's wits,** greatly upset; distracted; mad: You'll drive me out of my wits if you go on behaving in this way. **have a ready wit,** be quick to make clever and amusing remarks. **have/keep one's 'wits about one,** be quick to see what is happening, alert and ready to act. **live by one's wits,** live by clever, not always honest, methods (as opportunities arise). **2** [U] clever and humorous expression of ideas; liveliness of spirit: Our teacher/Our teacher's conversation is full of wit. His writings sparkle with wit. **3** [C] person noted for his wit(2). **witty** adj (-ier, -iest) full of humour: a witty girl/remark. **wit-tily** /-ɪlɪ/ adv **wit-ti-cism** /'wɪtɪsɪzəm/ n [C] witty remark. **wit-less** adj stupid.

wit² /wɪt/ v **to wit,** (legal) namely; that is to say.

witch /wɪtʃ/ n woman said to use magic, esp for evil purposes; (fig) fascinating or bewitching woman. '∼-**craft** n [U] sorcery; use of magic. '∼-**doctor** n male ∼; tribal magician (esp among primitive peoples). '∼-**hunt** n (fig) searching out and persecution (eg of persons said to be disloyal or untrustworthy). ∼-**ery** /'wɪtʃərɪ/ n [U] **1** ∼craft. **2**

fascination; charm. **~-ing** adj bewitching: the ~ing hour of night, the time when ~es are active; midnight.

witch-elm, witch-hazel ⇨ wych.

with /wɪð/ prep 1 (equivalent to constructions with the v 'have') having; carrying; characterized by: a cup ~ a broken handle; a coat ~ two pockets; a girl ~ blue eyes; a baby ~ no clothes on; a woman ~ an angry look in her eyes; ~ your permission. ~ child (of a woman); ~ young (of an animal), pregnant. 2 (to indicate what is used for filling, covering, etc): Fill the box ~ sand. The lorry was loaded ~ timber. The sack was stuffed ~ straw. The hills were covered ~ snow. 3 (to indicate the means or instrument): write ~ a pen; take sth ~ both hands; walk ~ a crutch; cut sth ~ a knife; see sth ~ your own eyes; ~ the help of your friends; ~ your help. 4 (to indicate accompaniment or relationship): live ~ your parents; go for a walk ~ a friend; discuss a problem ~ somebody; spend the day ~ one's uncle; mix one substance ~ another; put one thing ~ others. I shall be ~ you in a few minutes. Is there anyone ~ you or are you alone? The general, (together) ~ his staff officers, will inspect the camp. **in ~,** in association ~; mixed up ~: She's in ~ the wrong crowd, eg of a girl whose companions are criminals. 5 (to indicate antagonism, opposition): fight/argue/struggle/quarrel, etc ~ sb; have an argument ~ sb; in competition ~; a battle ~ savages; at war ~ the Romans. **fall out ~,** ⇨ fall²(14). **have it out ~ sb,** ⇨ have⁴(9). 6 (to indicate cause) because of; owing to: silent ~ shame; trembling ~ fear/rage; shaking ~ cold; a face wet ~ tears. 7 (to indicate manner): do sth ~ an effort/~ a light heart/~ one's whole heart/~ joy/~ pleasure; standing ~ his hands in his pockets; win ~ ease, easily; fight ~ courage, courageously; ~ a roar/a growl/a shout of triumph; receive sb ~ open arms. 8 in the same way or direction as; at the same time as: A tree's shadow moves ~ the sun. W~ the approach of sunset it becomes chilly. Do you rise ~ the sun, ie at dawn? 9 (to indicate care, charge or possession): Leave the child ~ (= in the care of) its aunt. I have no money ~ me. The next move is ~ you. It rests ~ you to decide/The decision rests ~ you, ie you must decide. 10 in regard to; concerning: be patient ~ them; ~mpathize ~ him; bear/put up ~ (= endure) sb or sth; have dealings/business ~ sb. What do you want ~ me? What's your business ~ him? It's a habit ~ some people. We can't do anything/can do nothing ~ him, cannot influence, control, make use of, him. It's holiday time ~ us now. The first object ~ him (= His first object) is always to make a profit. Away ~ him! Send or take him away! Out with you! Get out! Off with his head! (and many other exclamatory sentences in the pattern adv + ~ + n/pron). 11 (to indicate separation): Let us dispense ~ ceremony, ie not be ceremonious. I parted ~ her at the gate. He has broken ~ his best friend. 12 (to indicate agreement, harmony): He that is not ~ me (= on my side) is against me. I'm ~ you (= in agreement or sympathy ~ you) in what you say. I (dis)agree ~ you. I can't go along ~ you on that question, can't agree or co-operate with you. Does this blue go well ~ this green? **be/get '~ it,** (sl) become aware of what is popular and up to date: (attrib) '~-it clothes. 13 in spite of; notwithstanding (the possession of): W~ all her faults he still liked her. He failed ~ the best of intentions to win the sympathy of his pupils.

withal /wɪˈðɔːl/ adv (archaic) in addition.

with·draw /wɪðˈdrɔː/ vt,vi (pt -drew /-ˈdruː/, pp -drawn /-ˈdrɔːn/) 1 [VP6A,14] ~ sth/sb (from), pull or draw back; take out or away: ~ money from the Bank/dirty banknotes from circulation; ~ a boy from school, not allow him to attend. The workers threatened to ~ their labour, to go on strike. 2 [VP6A,2A] take back (a statement, an accusation, an offer): He refused to ~ (the offending expression), eg after calling sb a liar. 3 VP6A,14,2A,C] (cause to) move back or away: ~ troops from an exposed position; ~ from society. Our troops had to ~. (Cf The enemy had to retreat.) **~al** /-ˈdrɔːəl/ n [U] ~ing or being withdrawn; [C] instance of this. **'~al symptom,** physical or mental reaction when steadily deprived of sth to which one is addicted (in order to break the habit). **~n** adj (of persons, their looks) retiring; unsociable; abstracted.

withe /wɪθ/, **withy** /ˈwɪðɪ/ nn [C] tough but easily bent twig or branch, esp of willow or osier used for binding bundles, eg of firewood.

wither /ˈwɪðə(r)/ vt,vi [VP6A,15B,2A,C] ~ (sth) up; ~ (away), (cause to) become dry, faded or dead: The hot summer ~ed (up) the grass. Her hopes ~ed (away). 2 [VP6A] cause (sb) to be covered with shame or confusion: She ~ed him with a scornful look/gave him a ~ing look. **~-ing·ly** /ˈwɪðərɪŋlɪ/ adv

with·ers /ˈwɪðəz/ n pl highest part of the back of a horse, etc between the shoulder-blades (where the strain of the collar is taken). ⇨ the illus at dog, domestic.

with·hold /wɪðˈhəʊld/ vt (pt,pp -held /-ˈheld/) [VP6A,14] ~ sth (from), keep back; refuse to give: He tried to ~ the truth from us. I shall ~ my consent.

with·in /wɪˈðɪn/ prep inside; not beyond: remain ~ call/reach, near by; live ~ one's income, not spend more than one's income; ~ an hour, in less than an hour; ~ a mile of the station. □ adv (liter) inside.

with·out /wɪˈðaʊt/ prep 1 not having; not with; free from; lacking: You can't buy anything ~ money. Do you ever travel ~ a ticket? I once did it ~ being caught. The rumour was ~ foundation. He was working ~ any hope of reward. She went out ~ (= not wearing) a coat. Please don't leave ~ me, Don't leave until I have joined you. ~ **fail,** certainly. **do ~,** ⇨ do²(15). ~ **doubt,** admittedly; certainly. 2 (before gerunds) He can't speak German ~ making mistakes, He speaks German incorrectly. Can you make an omelette ~ breaking eggs? Can you do it ~ his knowing, so that he will not know? He passed ~ seeing me, and did not see me. He passed ~ my seeing him, and I did not see him. He left ~ so much as saying (= left and did not even say) that he was sorry/~ even a thankyou. **go ~ saying,** be too obvious, too well known, etc to need saying. 3 (old use) outside. □ adv (liter or old use) outside.

with·stand /wɪðˈstænd/ vt (pt,pp -stood /-ˈstʊd/) [VP6A] resist; hold out against (pressure, attack): ~ a siege; shoes that will ~ hard wear.

withy /ˈwɪðɪ/ n (pl -thies) ⇨ withe.

wit·less /ˈwɪtlɪs/ adj ⇨ wit¹.

wit·ness /ˈwɪtnɪs/ n 1 (often '**eye-~**) person who was actually present at an event and should, for this reason, be able to describe it; person who gives evidence under oath in a law court. **'~-box** (US also **'~-stand**) *n* enclosure in a law court in which ~es stand while giving evidence. **2** [U] evidence; testimony; what is said about sb, an event, etc: *give ~ on behalf of an accused person at his trial.* **bear ~ to sb/sth, (a)** speak in support of, eg sb's character. **(b)** be evidence of: *The tests bear ~ to the quality of this new car.* **3** person who adds his own signature to a document to testify that another person's signature on it is genuine. **4** sb or sth that is a sign or proof of sth: *My clothes are a ~ to my poverty.* □ *vt,vi* **1** [VP6A] be present at and see: *~ an accident.* **2** [VP3A] **~ to sth/doing sth,** give evidence (in a law court): *~ (__ testify) to the truth of a statement. Mr X ~ed to having seen the accused near the scene of the crime.* **3** [VP6A] be a ~(3) to the signing of (an agreement, a will, etc): *~ a signature.* **4** [VP6A] give evidence of; show: *Her pale face ~ed the agitation she felt.*

wit·ti·cism /'wɪtɪsɪzəm/ ⇨ wit¹.

wit·ting·ly /'wɪtɪŋlɪ/ *adv* knowingly; intentionally.

witty /'wɪtɪ/ *adj* (-ier, -iest) ⇨ wit¹.

wive /waɪv/ *vi,vt* [VP6A,2A] (archaic) marry.

wives /waɪvz/ *pl* of wife.

wiz·ard /'wɪzəd/ *n* **1** magician. **2** person with amazing abilities: *a financial ~,* person able to make money with amazing ease. □ *adj* (sl) excellent. **~ry** /-drɪ/ *n* [U] magic (which is more usu).

wiz·ened /'wɪznd/ *adj* having a dried-up appearance; shrivelled: *a ~ old man; an old man with a ~ face; ~ apples.*

wo, whoa /wəʊ/ *int* (used chiefly to a horse) stop.

woad /wəʊd/ *n* [U] (plant from which is obtained a) kind of blue dye.

wobble /'wɒbl/ *vi,vt* [VP2A,C,6A] (cause to) move unsteadily from side to side; (fig) be uncertain (in opinions, in making decisions, etc): *This table ~s. The front wheels of that car ~. Don't ~ the desk. He ~d between two opinions. Her voice sometimes ~s on high notes,* Her high notes are not always steady. **wob·bler** /'wɒblə(r)/ *n* sb or sth that ~s. **wob·bly** /'wɒblɪ/ *adj* not firm or steady; inclined to ~: *a wobbly chair. He's still a bit wobbly on his legs after his long illness.*

woe /wəʊ/ *n* (chiefly poet; sometimes hum) **1** [U] sorrow; grief; distress: *a tale of woe. Woe (be) to...,* A curse upon.... **2** (*pl*) causes of woe; troubles: *poverty, illness and other woes.* **woe·ful** /-fl/ *adj* sorrowful; causing woe; regrettable: *woeful ignorance.* **woe·fully** /-fəlɪ/ *adv* **woe·be·gone** /'wəʊbɪgɒn US: -gɔːn/ *adj* dismal(-looking): *What woebegone looks!*

woke, woken ⇨ wake¹.

wold /wəʊld/ *n* [C,U] (area of) open uncultivated country; down or moor.

wolf /wʊlf/ *n* (*pl* wolves /wʊlvz/) wild, flesh-eating animal of the dog family, hunting in packs. **cry ~,** raise false alarms: *You've cried ~ too often* (suggesting that genuine cries for help will in future be ignored). **a ~ in sheep's clothing,** person who appears friendly but is really an enemy. **keep the ~ from the door,** be able to buy enough food for oneself and one's family. **'~'s-bane** *n* aconite. **'~-cub** *n* (a) young ~. (b) (former name for) junior Boy Scout (now *Cub Scout*). **'~-hound** *n* large dog originally bred for hunting wolves. **'~ whistle** *n* whistle expressing sexual admiration. □ *vt* [VP6A,15A] eat quickly and greedily: *~ (down) one's food.* **~·ish** /-ɪʃ/ *adj* of or like a ~: *a ~ish appetite.*

wolf·ram /'wʊlfrəm/ *n* tungsten; tungsten ore.

woman /'wʊmən/ *n* (*pl* women /'wɪmɪn/) **1** adult female human being: *men, women and children; a single* (= unmarried) *~; a ~ of the world,* one with experience of society, not young and innocent: (attrib; to be preferred to *lady*) *a ~ 'doctor* (*pl* ˌwomen ˈdoctors); *a ˌ~ ˈdriver* (*pl* ˌwomen ˈdrivers); *a caˈreer-~,* with a career; *a ˈcountry-~,* who lives and works in the country; *a ˈneedle-~,* expert at sewing, etc. **2** [U] (without article) the female sex. **3** [U] feminine character: *All the ~ in her rebelled against the treatment she was receiving.* **'~-hood** /-hʊd/ *n* [U] **(a)** (collective) women in general. **(b)** the state of being a ~: *She had now grown to/reached ~hood.* **~·ish** /-ɪʃ/ *adj* of, like, for women. **~·ize** /-aɪz/ *vi* pursue women (esp for casual sexual intercourse). **~·izer** *n* man who does this. **'~·kind** *n* women in general. **'~-like, ~·ly** *adj* like a ~. **women·folk** /'wɪmɪnfəʊk/ *n pl* women; women of one's family.

womb /wuːm/ *n* (anat) organ in a female mammal in which offspring is carried and nourished while developing before birth: (fig) *It still lies in the ~ of time,* is sth which the passage of time will reveal. ⇨ the illus at reproduce.

wom·bat /'wɒmbæt/ *n* Australian animal (looking like a small bear), the female of which has a pouch for its young.

won /wʌn/ ⇨ win.

won·der /'wʌndə(r)/ *n* **1** [U] feeling caused by sth unusual, surprising or inexplicable; surprise combined with admiration, bewilderment, etc: *They were filled with ~. We looked at the conjurer in silent ~.* **no/little/small ~,** it is not/hardly surprising: *No ~ you were so late. He was taken ill, and no/little ~, considering that he had been overworking for years.* **'~-land** /-lænd/ *n* **(a)** fairyland. **(b)** [C] country that is remarkable in some way (eg because of abundant natural resources). **'~-struck** *adj* overcome with ~. **2** [C] thing or event that causes such feeling: *Walking on the moon is one of the ~s of our times.* **signs and ~s,** miracles. **work ~s,** work with remarkable results, perform miracles. **a nine days' ~,** sth which arouses great interest or admiration for a short time. **for a ~,** it is surprising (because unusual, unexpected, etc): *For a ~ he paid back the money he had borrowed.* **It is a ~ (that),** It is surprising (that): *It's a ~ (that) you didn't lose your way in the dark.* **What a ~,** How surprising! □ *vi,vt* **1** [VP2A,3A,B,4B] **~ (at sth),** be filled with ~(1); marvel; feel surprised: *Can you ~ at it,* Isn't it natural, to be expected, etc? *I don't ~ at her refusing to marry him. It's not to be ~ed at,* is sth one might expect. *I ~ (at the fact) (that) he wasn't killed,* am surprised that he wasn't killed. *I shouldn't ~ if...,* shouldn't be surprised if.... *I ~ed to hear her voice in the next room.* **2** [VP2A,3A] **~ (about sth),** feel curiosity; ask oneself: *I was ~ing about that. I was just ~ing.* **3** [VP8,10] ask oneself: *I ~ who he is/what he wants/why he is late/whether he will come/whose it is. I was ~ing how to get there quickly/where to spend the weekend, etc.* **~·ing·ly** /'wʌndrɪŋlɪ/ *adv* **~·ful** /-fl/ *adj* causing ~; surprising; remarkable; admirable: *We've been having ~ful weather recently. What a ~ful memory she has!* **~·fully** /-fəlɪ/ *adv* **~·ment** /-mənt/ *n* [U] surprise. **won·drous** /'wʌndrəs/ *adj* (archaic, or liter) ~ful. □

adv (only with *adjj*) ~fully: *wondrous kind.*

wonky /'woŋkɪ/ *adj* (GB sl) **1** infirm; unreliable: *a* ~ *chair,* one that might break. **2** tottery; in poor health: *She still feels a bit* ~ *after that attack of flu.*

wont /wəʊnt *US:* wɔːnt/ *n* (archaic or liter) (*sing* only) what sb is accustomed to doing: *He went to bed much earlier than was his* ~, than he usually did. **use and** ~, established custom. □ *pred adj* **be** ~ **to,** be accustomed to. ~**ed** *attrib adj* customary; usual.

won't /wəʊnt/ = will not. ⟹ will¹.

woo /wuː/ *vt* (*pt, pp* wooed) [VP6A] **1** (old use) try to win (a woman's) hand in marriage; court. **2** try to win (fame, fortune, success, sleep). **3** try to get the support of (voters, customers, businessmen). **wooer** *n* one who woos.

wood /wʊd/ *n* **1** [U] (with *indef art* and *pl* only when meaning *kind, sort, variety*) hard solid substance of a tree below the bark: *Tables are usually made of* ~. *Put some more* ~ *on the fire. He was chopping* ~ *for the fire. Teak is a hard* (*kind of*) ~ *and pine is a soft* (*kind of*) ~. (attrib): ~ *floors/ pavements,* made of blocks of ~. Cf *wooden,* used for articles made of ~. **2** [C] (often *pl*) area of land covered with growing trees (not so extensive as a forest): *a* ~ *of beech*(-*trees*); *a house in the middle of a* ~; *go for a walk in the* ~(*s*). **out of the** ~, (fig) free from troubles or difficulties: *We're not yet out of the* ~, still have difficulties to face. **be unable to see the** ~ **for the trees,** (fig) unable to get a clear view of the whole because of too many details. **3** *in/from the* ~, in/from the cask or barrel: *wine in the* ~; *drawn from the* ~. **4** (compounds, from 1 above) ~ **alcohol** *n* [U] kind of alcohol distilled from ~ (also called *methyl alcohol*) used as a fuel and a solvent. '~-**block** *n* block of ~ from which ~cuts are made. '~-**cut** *n* print from a design, drawing, picture, etc cut on a block of ~. '~-**louse** *n* (*pl* -lice) kinds of small, wingless, insect-like creature living in decaying ~, damp soil, etc. '~-**pecker** *n* kinds of bird that clings to the bark of trees and taps or pecks it to find insects. '~-**pile** *n* pile of ~, esp for fuel. '~-**shed** *n* shed for storing ~ (esp for fuel). '~-**pulp** *n* [U] ~ shredded to pulp as the material for making paper. '~-**wind** *n* musical wind instrument made (originally) of ~. '~-**work** *n* [U] (a) things made of ~, esp the ~en parts of a building (eg doors, stairs). (b) art of making things of ~; carpentry. '~-**worm** *n* (a) ~-eating larva that bores into ~. (b) [U] damage caused by ~worm. **5** (compounds, from 2 above) ~-**bine** *n* wild honeysuckle. '~-**cock** *n* (*pl* unchanged) kinds of game bird, brown with a long, straight bill, short legs and tail, found in ~land and valued as food. '~-**craft** *n* [U] knowledge of forest conditions, skill in finding one's way in ~s and forests, esp as used in hunting, etc. '~-**cutter** *n* man who cuts down trees. '~-**land** /-lənd/ *n* [U] land covered with trees; ~s: (attrib) ~*land scenery.* '~-**man** /-mən/ *n* (*pl* -men) forester; ~-cutter. '~s-**man** /-zmən/ *n* (*pl* -men) (esp US) = ~man. ~**ed** *adj* covered with growing trees: ~*ed country,* abounding in trees. ~**en** /'wʊdn/ *adj* **1** (attrib) made of ~: *a* ~*en leg;* ~*en walls* (fig, of the old ~en warships, thought of as a defence); *a* '~*en-head,* ⟹ blockhead. Hence, ~**en-'headed** *adj* stupid. **2** stiff, clumsy, awkward (as if made of ~): *a* ~*en* (= inexpressive) *smile. His manners were extremely* ~*en.* ~**y** *adj* (-ier, -iest) **1** ~ed: *a* ~*y hillside.* **2** of or like

~: *the* ~*y stems of a plant.*

wooer /'wuːə(r)/ *n* ⟹ woo.

woof /wuːf/ *n* = weft.

woofer /'wʊfə(r)/ *n* loudspeaker designed to produce low notes.

wool /wʊl/ *n* [U] **1** soft hair of sheep, goats and some other animals (eg the llama and alpaca); thread, yarn, cloth, clothing, made from this: *wear* ~ (ie clothing made of ~) *next to the skin; the* '~ *trade;* '~ *merchants; imports of* ~ *from Australia;* '*knitting-*~, ~ *yarn for knitting.* **dyed in the** ~, dyed before spinning and weaving; (fig) thorough; complete: *a dyed-in-the-*~ *Tory,* person who is strongly convinced that Tory principles, etc are the best. **much cry and little** ~, much talk with little result; fuss about trifles. **pull the** '~ *over sb's eyes,* deceive or trick him. '~-**gathering** *adj, n* absent-minded(ness). **the** '~-**sack,** ~-stuffed cushion on which the Lord Chancellor sits in the House of Lords: *reach the* ~*sack,* become Lord Chancellor. **2** material similar in appearance or texture to ~; *cotton-*~, raw cotton (US = *cotton-batting*). **3** (person's) thick curly hair. **lose one's** ~, (colloq) get angry. ~-**len** (US = ~en) /'wʊlən/ *attrib adj* made of ~: ~*len cloth/ blankets;* of ~ fabrics: ~*len manufacturers/ merchants.* ~-**lens** (US = ~ens) *n pl* ~len fabrics; cloth, flannel, blankets, etc, made of ~. ~**ly** (US also ~**y**) /'wʊlɪ/ *adj* (-ier, -iest) **1** covered with, made of, looking like, ~: ~*ly hair; a* ~*ly coat.* **2** (fig, of the mind, ideas, arguments) confused; not clear; not incisive. □ *n* (*pl* -lies) (colloq) ~len garment, esp a sweater: *Put an extra* ~*ly on when you go out.*

word /wɜːd/ *n* **1** [C] sound or combination of sounds (or the written or printed symbols) forming a unit of the grammar or vocabulary of a language: *When we speak we put our thoughts into* ~s. *I have no* ~s *to* (= cannot adequately) *express my gratitude. W*~s *failed him,* He could not express his thoughts, his emotion, etc in ~s. **a play on/ upon** ~s, a pun. **be not the** ~ **for it,** not an adequate or satisfactory description: *Warm's not the* ~ *for it* (ie *hot* is perhaps a better ~)! **not get a** ~ **in edgeways,** ⟹ edgeways. **(repeat sth)** ~ **for** ~, exactly, with no changes or omissions. **(trans- late sth)** ~ **for** ~, literally. Cf *a free translation.* **in a/one** ~, briefly; to sum up. **by** ~ **of mouth,** in spoken, not written, ~s. **2** [C] sth said; remark or statement: *He didn't say a* ~ *about it. I don't believe a* ~ *of the story. Mr A will now say a few* ~s, make a few remarks, give a short address. *Don't waste* ~s *on that fellow,* don't try to persuade, convince, warn, etc him. **eat one's** ~s, admit that one was wrong; take one's ~s back and apologize. **have a** ~ **with sb,** speak to him. **have** ~s **(with sb),** quarrel: *They've had* ~s, *I hear.* **have the last** ~, make the final remark in an argument, esp by making a retort to which there is no good answer. **put in/say a good** ~ **(for sb),** speak on his behalf (to support or defend). **suit the ac- tion to the** ~, do at once what one has said one will do (eg of a threat). **take sb at his** ~, act on the belief that he means what he says. **big** ~s, boasting. **on/with the** ~, as soon as sth has been said. **a** ~ **in/out of season,** a piece of advice given when it is welcome and helpful/unwelcome and interfering. **the last** ~ **on** (a subject), statement, etc which includes the latest views and information: *The last* ~ *has not yet been said on this* *subject*, There will be further facts, views, etc. *the last ~ (in sth)*, the latest, most up-to-date, etc, in: *Our coach tours of Scotland are the last ~ in comfort and convenience*. **3** (*sing*, without *def art*) news; information: *Please send me ~ of your safe arrival. Please leave ~ for me at work. W~ came that I was wanted at home*. **4** (*sing* only, with a possessive) promise; assurance. *be as good as one's ~*, do what one promises: *Don't worry—I'm sure he'll be as good as his ~*. *give sb¹ one's ~ (that...)*, promise: *The goods will arrive on time—I give you my ~*. *keep/break one's ~*, do/fail to do what one has promised to do. *take sb's '~ for it*, believe what he says: *I have no proof, but you may take my ~ for it*. *take sb at his ~*, believe that he is telling the truth, that he will keep a promise. *upon my ~*, **(a)** on my honour. **(b)** used as an exclamation of surprise. **5** (*sing* only) command; order; spoken signal: *The officer gave the ~ to fire. His ~ is law*, His orders must be obeyed. *You must give the ~ before you can pass*. ⇨ *password* at **pass¹**(10). **6** (in the Christian religion) **the W~ (of God); God's W~**, **(a)** the Scriptures, esp the Gospel: *preach the W~*. **(b)** title of Jesus Christ. **7** (compounds) **'~-book** *n* vocabulary; list of ~s with meanings, etc. **'~-division** *n* [U] dividing of the spelling of a ~, eg at the end of a line on a page. **'~-painter** *n* person who can describe vividly in ~s. **,~-'perfect** *adj* knowing, able to repeat, a poem, a part in a play, etc by heart. **'~-picture** *n* vivid description in ~s. **'~-splitting** *n* [U] sophistry; making of distinctions of meaning, that are subtle. □ *vt* [VP6A] express in ~s: *a well-~ed letter. The suggestion might be ~ed more politely*. **~-ing** *n* (*sing* only) way in which sth is expressed; choice of ~s to express meaning: *A different ~ing might make the meaning clearer*. **~-less** *adj* without ~s; not put into ~s: *~less grief*. **wordy** *adj* (-ier, -iest) using, expressed in, a large number of ~s, esp unnecessary ~s: *a ~y telegram; ~y warfare*, ie argument. **~-ily** /-ɪlɪ/ *adv* **~-i-ness** *n*

wore /wɔː(r)/ *pt* of **wear²**.

work¹ /wɜːk/ *n* **1** [U] use of bodily or mental powers with the purpose of doing or making sth (esp contrasted with play or recreation); use of energy supplied by steam, electric current, etc: *Are you fond of hard ~? The ~ of building the new bridge took six months. It was the ~ of a moment* (= Only a moment was needed) *to turn the key in the lock and make him a prisoner. It was very hard ~ getting to the top of the mountain. This is the ~ of an enemy*, An enemy has done this. *Machines now do much of the ~ formerly done by man*. *make hard ~ of sth*, make it seem more difficult than it is. *make short ~ of sth*, finish it quickly. *set/get to ~ (on sth/to do sth)*, begin; make a start. *set/go about one's ~*, start doing it: *You're not setting about your ~ in the right way*. *at ~ (on sth)*, busy or occupied with (indicating uncompleted ~, ~ in progress). *all in the day's ~*, (used to indicate that sth is) normal; what is usual or to be expected. **2** [U] what a person does to earn a living; employment: *What time do you get to (your) ~ every day? The men were on their way to ~. It is difficult to find ~ during a depression. at ~*, at one's place of employment: *He's at ~ now, but he'll be back at six. in/out of ~*, having/not having employment: *He has been out of ~ for a year. He'll be glad to be in regular ~ again*.

Hence, (attrib *adj*) **,out-of-'work**. **3** [U] sth to be done, not necessarily connected with a trade or occupation, not necessarily for payment: *I always find plenty of ~ that needs doing in my garden. I have some ~ for you to do*. **4** [U] things needed or used for ~: *She took her ~* (eg her sewing materials) *out on the verandah*. **'~-bag/-basket/ -box** *nn* bag, etc for holding such things, esp for sewing. **5** [U] that which is produced by ~: *The ~ of famous silversmiths and sculptors may be seen in museums. What a beautiful piece of ~! The villagers sell their ~* (eg needlework, wood-carvings, metal articles) *to tourists*. ⇨ also compounds such as *stone~, wood~* at **stone**(1), **wood**(4). **6** [C] product of the intellect or the imagination: *the ~s of Shakespeare; the ~s of Beethoven*. ⇨ **opus**; *~s of art; a new ~* (= musical composition) *by John Lewis; a new ~* (= book) *on modern art*. **7** (*pl*) moving parts of a machine: *the ~s of a clock or watch. There's something wrong with the ~s*. **8** (*pl*, with *sing* or *pl v*) building(s) where industrial or manufacturing processes are carried on: *a 'gas-~s; an 'iron-~s; a 'brick-~s. The 'steel-~s was/were closed for the Christmas holidays*. **'~s council/committee**, joint council of representatives of employers and employees to deal with problems of management, labour relations, etc. **9 public ~s**, the building of roads, dams, embankments; other engineering operations (by government departments, etc): *the Ministry of Public Building and W~*, (until 1971) government department (now part of the Department of the Environment) responsible for these operations. **10** (*pl v*) (cf *'earth~s, 'out~s*) defensive structures; fortifications: *The ~s were thought to be impregnable*. **11** (compounds) **'~-bench** *n* table at which a mechanic does his ~. **'~-book** *n* book with outlines of a subject of study, with questions to be answered (in blank spaces, in writing), for notes, etc. **'~-day** *n* day for ~; day which is not a Sunday or a holiday. **'~-force** *n* total number of men working in a particular factory, etc. **'~-house** *n* **(a)** (GB hist) public institution for homeless people. **(b)** (US) place where those who have committed small crimes are confined and made to work. **'~-man** /-mən/ *n* (*pl* -men) **(a)** man who earns a living by physical labour or at machines, etc. **(b)** person who works in a specified way: *a skilled/quick, etc ~man*. **'~-man-like** *adj* characteristic of a good ~man. **'~-man-ship** /-mənʃɪp/ *n* [U] quality as seen in sth made: *articles of poor/excellent ~manship*; person's skill in doing ~. **'~-room** *n* room in which ~ is done. **'~-shop** *n* room or building in which things (esp machines) are made or repaired. **'~-shy** *adj* disinclined to work; lazy. **'~-study** *n* (*pl* -dies) study of how ~ may be done efficiently and economically (eg by observing the sequence of movements in an operation, time needed, etc). **'~-table** *n* (esp) table with drawers for sewing materials, etc. **'~-a-day** /'wɜːkədeɪ/ *adj* commonplace; dull: *this ~aday world/life*.

work² /wɜːk/ *vi,vt* (*pt,pp* ~ed or wrought /rɔːt/) (For uses with *adverbial particles* and *preps*, ⇨ 10 below. For uses with *wrought*, ⇨ wrought). **1** [VP2A,B,C,3A,4A] do work; engage in physical or mental activity: *He's been ~ing hard all day. The men in this factory ~ 40 hours a week. Most people have to ~ in order to live*, ie to earn a living. *He isn't ~ing now*, eg because unemployed or retired. *Have British statesmen always ~ed for*

peace? He's ~*ing at* (= studying) *Physics and Chemistry. Green is* ~*ing on* (= writing) *a new novel. This man* ~*s in leather,* is a craftsman in leather. *He has always* ~*ed against* (= opposed) *reform.* ~ **to rule,** ⇨ rule(1). '~**-in** *n* occasion when workers continue to ~ in a factory to protest against proposed dismissal, closure of the factory, etc. **2** [VP2A,C] (of a machine, apparatus, bodily organ, plan, method, etc) do what it is designed to do; have the desired result; function; operate: *The lift/elevator/bell/telephone is not* ~*ing. The gears* ~ *smoothly. This machine* ~*s by electricity. My brain doesn't seem to be* ~*ing well today. Will this new plan/scheme/method* ~? *The charm* ~*ed. It* ~*ed like a charm.* **3** [VP6A,15A] cause to ~; set in motion: *He* ~*s his wife/himself too hard. Don't* ~ *yourself/your poor wife to death. She was* ~*ing the treadle of her sewing-machine. This machine is* ~*ed by steam/electricity.* **4** [VP6A] produce or obtain as the result of effort: ~ *wonders/a cure/harm/mischief.* ~ **one's passage,** earn it by ~*ing: He* ~*ed his passage from England to Australia,* by ~*ing on the ship.* ~ **one's way (through college, etc),** have a paid job, while studying to meet costs: *He's* ~*ing his way through medical school.* ~ **one's will (on sb),** make him do what one wants him to do. ~ *it,* (sl) bring sth about (by scheming, etc): *I'll* ~ *it if I can,* eg by using influence, cajolery, etc. **5** [VP6A] operate; control; be employed in the management of: ~ *a mine. This salesman* ~*s the North Wales area,* travels there as a salesman. **6** [VP2C,D,15A,B,22] (cause to) move into, reach, a new state or position, usu by degrees or with a succession of small movements: *Your shirt has* ~*ed out,* has come out from above the top of your trousers. *One of the screws has* ~*ed loose. The rain had* ~*ed through the roof,* had penetrated it slowly. *Can you* ~ *the stone into place,* eg when building a stone wall? *The men* ~*ed their way forward. Many months later the splinter* ~*ed out of her arm,* came out after travelling through the flesh from the point at which it had entered. *The wind has* ~*ed round to the south,* changed direction by degrees. **7** [VP6A] make or shape by hammering, kneading, pressure, etc: ~ *clay,* knead it with water; ~ *dough,* (when making bread). ⇨ **wrought** for *wrought iron.* **8** [VP2A] ferment; move in an agitated way: *The yeast began to* ~, to ferment, eg in dough. *His face/features began to* ~ *violently,* twitch, etc in a way showing agitation. **9** [VP6A,14] make by stitching; embroider: ~ *a design on a cushion-cover/one's initials on a handkerchief.* **10** [VP2C,3A,14,15B] (special uses with *adverbial particles* and *preps*):
work away (at sth), continue to ~: *He's been* ~*ing away at this job since breakfast.*
work 'in; ~ **into sth,** (⇨ 6 above) penetrate; find a way in/into: *The dust has* ~*ed in everywhere,* eg into a house during a sandstorm. ~ **sth in/into,** introduce; find a place for: *Can't you* ~ *in a few jokes/* ~ *a few jokes into your story?*
work sth off, get rid of; dispose of; deal with: ~ *off arrears of correspondence/superfluous energy/one's excess weight.*
work on/upon sb/sth, (⇨ 8 above) excite, influence: *Will the high figure for unemployment* ~ *on the conscience of the Government? The sufferings of the refugees* ~*ed upon our feelings so much that we gave them all the help we could.* ⇨ also **1**

above: ~ *on a new novel, etc.*
work out, (a) be capable of being solved: *This sum/problem will not* ~ *out.* (b) be, turn out, in the end: *How will things* ~ *out? The situation* ~*ed out quite well. The total* ~*s out at £10. How much does it* ~ *out at,* What's the total? (c) ⇨ **6** above. (d) exercise, train (for a contest): *The champion is* ~*ing out in the gym this morning.* Hence, '~**-out** *n* period, form, of training or exercise. ~ **sth out,** (a) calculate: *I've* ~*ed out your share of the expenses at £5.* (b) get results for: *I can't* ~ *out these algebra problems.* (c) devise; invent; develop in detail: *a well-*~*ed out scheme. They've* ~*ed out a method of sending a spacecraft to Mars. You must* ~ *out your own salvation,* find a way of saving yourself by your own efforts. (d) solve: *He was* ~*ing out some coded messages.* (e) (usu passive) exhaust by using, operating, etc: *That silver-mine is now* ~*ed out,* has no more ore.
work up to sth, advance steadily to a high level: *The orchestra was* ~*ing up to a crescendo.* ~ **sth up,** (a) make by degrees; bring to an efficient or satisfactory condition: ~ *up a business.* (b) excite; stir up: ~ *up the feelings of an audience.* ~ **sb/ oneself up (into),** rouse to a high point (of excitement, etc): *He* ~*ed himself/everyone up into a frenzy/rage/state of hysteria. The audience was really* ~*ed up by this time.*
work upon sb/sth, ⇨ ~ on sb/sth above.
work·able /'wɜːkəbl/ *adj* that can be worked; that will work; practicable: *The silver-mine is no longer* ~, It cannot be worked (eg because it is flooded, or because the ore is exhausted). *Is the proposed scheme* ~, feasible?
worker /'wɜːkə(r)/ *n* person who works; (attrib) ~ *bees* (contrasted with the drones).
work·ing /'wɜːkɪŋ/ *n* **1** [C] mine, quarry, etc or part of it, which is being, or has been, worked: *The boys went exploring in some disused* ~*s,* eg the shafts of an old tin-mine. **2** [C] the way sth works, or the result of this: *the* ~*s of conscience; the principles that guide the* ~*s of the human mind. in* ~ *order,* able to function properly, do what is required; going smoothly: *put a machine in* ~ *order.* **3** (attrib) (in various senses of the *v*): '~ *clothes,* worn while ~; *a* ~ *drawing/plan,* one made as a guide for building, construction, etc. *The Government has a* ~ *majority,* one that is sufficient. ~ **breakfast/lunch/dinner,** one at which persons discuss business, etc: *The Prime Minister and some of his colleagues had a* ~ *breakfast to discuss the crisis in the docks.* ~ **capital,** money needed for carrying on a business, etc. ~ **day,** (a) workday (as opposed to a day of rest). (b) number of hours worked on a normal day: *a* ~ *day of eight hours.* ~ **hypothesis,** one formulated for a theory, etc. ~ **knowledge,** knowledge that is sufficient for the purpose. ,~**-'out** (a) calculation of results; elaboration of details: *the* ~*-out of a plan.* (b) execution: *Don't interfere with them in the* ~*-out of their scheme.* '~ **party,** (esp) committee appointed to secure efficiency in an industry, or one appointed (eg by a government department) to study and report on a question. □ *part adj* engaged in work: *a hard-*~ *woman.* **the** ~ **class(es),** those engaged in manual work. Hence, '~**-class** *adj* of this class: *a* ~*-class family.*
world /wɜːld/ *n* **1 the** ~, the earth, its countries and people: *the Old W*~, Europe, Asia and Africa; *the New W*~, America; *the Roman W*~, that part

known to the ancient Romans; *the English-speaking* ∼, those parts where English is the mother tongue of the inhabitants; *make a journey round the* ∼; *to the* ∼'s *end*, to the farthest distance possible. *The whole* ∼/*All the* ∼ *knows...*, It is widely or generally known.... [C] heavenly body that may resemble our ∼: *Are there any other* ∼s *besides ours?* **make a 'noise in the** ∼, be widely talked of; become famous. *a citizen of the* ∼, a cosmopolitan person. *It's a small* ∼! (said when meeting someone in an unexpected place). **2** (as **1** above; used attrib) affecting, used by, intended for, extending over, the ∼: *a* ∼ *language*, one that is or will be used, or is designed for use, in all or most parts of the ∼: *English is a* ∼ *language now. Esperanto was designed as a* ∼ *language. Which countries today can be called* ∼ *powers*, countries whose policies, etc affect all parts of the ∼? *We've had two* ∼ *wars in this century.* **the W**∼ **Bank**, international bank established in 1945 for providing loans for development when private capital is not available (officially the *International Bank for Reconstruction and Development*). ∼-'**wide** *adj* found in, spread over, all parts of the ∼: ∼-*wide fame.* **3** time, state or scene of existence: *this* ∼ *and the next*, life on earth and existence after death; *the* ∼ *to come*, existence after death; *the lower* ∼, hell, Hades; *bring a child into the* ∼, beget one or give birth to one. ∼-'**weary** *adj* tired of living. **4** the universe; everything: *Is this the best of all possible* ∼s? *in the* ∼, at all, in existence: *Nothing in the* ∼ *would please me more. Who in the* ∼ (= Who ever, Who on earth) *is that strange man? for all the* ∼ *like sb/sth*, exactly like: *She's for all the* ∼ *like a woman I knew 20 years ago, in looks, behaviour, everything. be all the* ∼ *to sb*, be everything to: *She's all the* ∼ *to him*, He lives for her alone. *not for the* ∼, not on any account: *I wouldn't hurt her feelings for the* ∼. *be/feel on top of the* ∼, elated (because of success, good health, etc). *be out of this* ∼, (sl) (of sth) be sublime, magnificent. *carry the* ∼ *be'fore one*, have quick and complete success. *a* ∼ *of sth*, a great number or quantity of; very much/many: *My holiday did me a* ∼ *of good. There was a* ∼ *of meaning in the look she gave him. There's often a* ∼ *of difference between promise and achievement. think the* ∼ *of sb/sth*, admire him/it. **5** the material things and occupations of life (contrasted with the spiritual). *the* ∼, *the flesh, and the devil*, the various temptations that face us. *the best of 'both* ∼s, the best of what is offered from two different (perhaps conflicting) sources. *forsake/renounce the* ∼, devote one's life to spiritual things. **6** human affairs; active life: *know/see the* ∼, have experience of life; *a man of the* ∼, person who has had experience of life, knows the ways of men, is tolerant, etc; *take the* ∼ *as one finds it*, adapt oneself to things, not try to reform people, etc. *How goes the* ∼ *with you*, How are your affairs going? **7** persons, institutions, etc connected with a special social class or special interests: *the* ∼ *of sport/art; the 'racing/'scientific* ∼; all that concerns or belongs to a specified sphere: *the 'animal/'mineral/'vegetable* ∼. ⇨ **kingdom(3)**. **8** the ∼, society, its opinions, customs, etc: *the great* ∼, fashionable society. *All the* ∼ *and his wife were at the ball*, all those who claim positions in high society. *What will the* ∼ *say*, What about public opinion; can we defy it, etc?

∼·**ly** *adj* **1** material: *my* ∼*ly goods*, my property. **2** temporal; of the affairs of this life (esp the pursuit of pleasure, contrasted with spiritual): ∼*ly wisdom*, prudence, etc which enables one to obtain material gains and advantages. **3** (also ∼*ly-'minded*) concerned with, interested in, material things. ∼·**li·ness** *n*

worm /wɜːm/ *n* **1** kinds of small, boneless, limbless, creeping creature, esp ('**earth-**∼) the kind living in the ground, or the kinds living as parasites in the intestines, etc of animals. ⇨ the illus at silk. ⇨ *hookworm* at hook(1), *tapeworm* at tape. ∼-**cast** *n* tubular pile of earth pushed up by an earth∼ on the ground. *the* ∼ *of conscience*, remorse. **2** (in compounds) used as a name for larvae, insects, etc: '*silk-*∼; '*glow-*∼. '∼-**eaten** *adj* full of ∼ holes; (fig) antiquated. '∼-**hole** *n* hole left in wood, fruit, etc by ∼s. **3** (fig) insignificant or contemptible person. *Even a* ∼ *will turn*, (prov) There are limits to patience. **4** spiral part of a screw. '∼-**gear** *n* arrangement in which a wheel with teeth gears with the ∼(4) of a revolving spiral. □ *vt* **1** [VP15A,B] ∼ *oneself/one's way in/into/through*, move slowly, or by patience, or with difficulty: *He* ∼*ed himself/his way through the undergrowth. He* ∼*ed himself into favour/into her confidence.* ∼ *sth out (of sb)*, extract (by persistent questioning, etc): *He* ∼*ed the secret out of me.* **2** [VP6A] rid of parasitic ∼s: *I think we'd better* ∼ *the cat*, eg by giving it a powder or pill. ∼**y** *adj* having many ∼s; damaged by ∼s; like a ∼.

worm·wood /'wɜːmwʊd/ *n* [U] kinds of perennial plant with a bitter flavour, used in the preparation of vermouth and absinthe and in medicine; (fig) bitter mortification and its cause.

worn /wɔːn/ *pp* of wear².

worri·some /'wʌrɪsəm/ *adj* troublesome; worrying.

worry /'wʌrɪ/ *vt,vi* (*pt,pp* -ried) **1** [VP6A,14,15A,17,22] trouble; give (sb, oneself) no peace of mind; cause anxiety or discomfort to: ∼ *sb with foolish questions;* ∼ *oneself sick/be worried sick about sth*, be extremely anxious about it. *The noise of the traffic worried her. What's* ∼*ing you? Her child has a bad cough and it rather worries her. I have a bad tooth that is* ∼*ing me. Don't* ∼ *yourself about the children; they're old enough to take good care of themselves. He'll* ∼ *himself to death*, kill himself by ∼*ing. She was always* ∼*ing her husband for more money/*∼*ing him to give her more money.* **2** [VP2A,B,C,3A] ∼ *(about/over sth)*, be anxious, uneasy, troubled: *Don't* ∼ *about trifles. You have no cause to* ∼. *What's the use of* ∼*ing? Don't* ∼ *trying to find it—it'll turn up one day.* ∼ *along*, (colloq) manage to get along in spite of troubles. **3** [VP6A] (esp of dogs) seize with the teeth and shake: *The dog was* ∼*ing the rat.* **4** [VP15B] ∼ *a problem, etc out*, attack it again and again until one solves it. □ *n* (*pl* -ries) **1** [U] condition of being troubled: *show signs of* ∼. **2** [C] (usu *pl*) sth that worries; cause of anxiety: *Is your life full of worries? Money worries and little domestic worries have made him look old. What a little* ∼ *that child is!* **wor·ried** *adj* troubled; anxious: *He has a worried look.* ∼·**ing** *adj* full of ∼; causing ∼: *have a* ∼*ing time.* ∼·**ing·ly** *adv*

worse /wɜːs/ *adj* (independent comparative; ⇨ bad, worst) **1** *Your work is bad but mine is much* ∼. *We couldn't have had* ∼ *weather for our journey. Is there anything* ∼ *than war/a* ∼ *catastrophe* *than war/a catastrophe* ∼ *than war? You are making things* ∼*. He escaped with nothing* ∼ *than a few scratches.* **the** ∼ **for wear,** badly worn as the result of long wear; (fig) exhausted: *He looks the* ∼ *for wear after only a year as President.* **2** (*pred* only) having less good health or condition or circumstances: *The doctor says she is much* ∼ *to-day. I'm glad you don't feel any* ∼. **be none the** ∼ **(for sth),** be unharmed (by it): *He fell into the river but is none the* ∼ *for it.* □ *adv* (⇨ badly, worst) **1** *He is behaving* ∼ *than ever. He has been taken* ∼, has become more seriously ill. **none the** ∼, not less: *I like a man none the* ∼ *for being out-spoken.* ∼ **off,** (⇨ badly off at bad¹; better off at better²(1); well off at well²(3)) more badly situat-ed; in ∼ circumstances. **2** (used to intensify): *It's raining* ∼ (= more heavily) *than ever. She hates me* ∼ (= more strongly) *than before.* □ *n* [U] ∼ thing(s): *I have* ∼ *to tell. The first news was bad, but* ∼ *followed. There has been a change for the* ∼ *in the patient's condition. Things seem to be going from bad to* ∼ *nowadays.* ∼**n** /'wɜːsn/ *vt,vi* [VP6A,2A] make or become ∼.

wor·ship /'wɜːʃɪp/ *n* [U] **1** reverence and respect paid to God: *places of* ∼, churches, mosques, synagogues, temples, etc; *hours of* ∼; times of church etc services; *public* ∼, church etc ser-vice(s). **2** admiration and respect shown to or felt for sb or sth: *the* ∼ *of success; hero* ∼. *She gazed at the film star with* ∼ *in her eyes.* **3** *your/his* **W**∼, (GB) title of respect used to/of a magistrate or mayor: *his W*∼ *the Mayor of Chester.* □ *vt,vi* (-pp-; US -p-) [VP6A,2A,B] give ∼(1,2) to: ∼ *God;* attend church service: *the church where she had* ∼*ped for ten years.* ∼**·per** (US = ∼er) *n* ∼**-ful** /-fl/ *adj* (in GB titles of respect, eg to Justices of the Peace, aldermen) worthy of respect; honour-able.

worst /wɜːst/ *adj* (independent superlative; ⇨ bad, worse): *the* ∼ *storm for five years; the* ∼ *dinner I've ever eaten; the* ∼ (= most intense) *frost this winter.* □ *adv* (independent superlative; ⇨ badly, worse) most badly: *Tom played badly, Harry played worse and I played* ∼. □ *n* ∼ part, state, event, etc: *You must be prepared for the* ∼, the ∼ possible news, outcome, etc. *The* ∼ *of the storm is over. She keeps cheerful, even when things are at their* ∼. *If the* ∼ *comes to the '*∼, If the ∼ hap-pens. **get the** ∼ **of it** (in a fight etc), be defeated. **The** ∼ **of it is that**...,The most unfortunate part of the affair is that.... **at (the)** ∼, if the ∼ happens. **do your** ∼**/let him do his** ∼, used as expressions of defiance. □ *vt* [VP6A] defeat; get the better of: *He* ∼*ed his enemy.*

wor·sted /'wʊstɪd/ *n* [U] twisted woollen yarn or thread; cloth made from this.

worth /wɜːθ/ *pred adj* **1** having a certain value; of value equal to: *I paid only £300 for this used car but it's* ∼ *much more. It's not* ∼ *more than two pounds.* ∼ (one's) while, ⇨ while. **for what it is** ∼, without any guarantee or promise concerning it: *That's the news I heard—I pass it on to you for what it is* ∼. ∼**·'while** *adj* that is ∼ the time, etc needed: *a* ∼*while experiment.* ⇨ while. **2** possess-ing; having property to the value of: *What's the old man* ∼*? He died* ∼ *a million pounds.* **for all one is** ∼, (colloq) with all one's energy; making every effort: *He was running for all he was* ∼. **3** ∼ + *verb* in **-ing,** giving a satisfactory or rewarding re-turn for: *The book is well* ∼ *reading. It's hardly* ∼

troubling about. He says life wouldn't be ∼ *living without friendship.* □ *n* [U] **1** value; what sb or sth is ∼: *books/discoveries, etc of great/little/not much* ∼*; know a friend's* ∼. **2** quantity of sth of a specified value: *a pound's* ∼ *of apples; fifty pence* ∼ *of copper coins; a penny*∼ *of sweets. It's not* ∼ *the paper its printed on.* ∼**·less** *adj* having no value. ∼**·less·ly** *adv*∼**·less·ness** *n*

worthy /'wɜːðɪ/ *adj* (-ier, -iest) **1** ∼ **(of sth/to be sth),** deserving: *a cause* ∼ *of support; behaviour* ∼ *of praise; nothing* ∼ *of mention; a man who is* ∼ *to have a place in the team. He found a* ∼ *enemy/an enemy* ∼ *of his sword,* one brave or strong enough. **2** (often ironic or used with a patro-nizing effect) having merit; deserving respect: *a* ∼ *gentleman. She says she helps only the* ∼ *poor* (in contrast to those people who, she thinks, are poor through their own laziness, etc). □ *n* **1** person of some distinction (in his own country or during a certain period): *an Elizabethan* ∼, ie during the reign of Queen Elizabeth I. **2** (hum or ironic) per-son who appears to be distinguished: *Who's the* ∼ *who has just arrived? Who are the worthies on the platform?* **worth·ily** /-ɪlɪ/ *adv* **worthi·ness** *n*

wot /wɒt/ *God wot,* (archaic or hum) God knows.

wot·cher /'wɒtʃə(r)/ *int* (GB sl) (as a greeting) Hello!

would ⇨ will¹.

wouldst /wʊdst/ *v* old form used with *thou*: *Thou* ∼, You would.

wound¹ /wuːnd/ *n* [C] **1** hurt or injury to the living tissue of the body, caused by cutting, shooting, tearing, etc, esp as the result of attack (*injury* being more usu for the result of an accident): *a* '*knife* ∼ *in the arm; a* '*bullet* ∼. *The dog was licking its* ∼*s,* eg after a fight with another dog. **2** injury to a plant, tree, etc in which the bark is cut or torn. **3** pain given to a person's feelings: *a* ∼ *to his pride/ vanity.* □ *vt* [VP6A] give a ∼ to: *Ten soldiers were killed and thirty* ∼*ed.* Cf *hurt* or *injured* in an ac-cident. *He felt* ∼*ed in his honour/affections.*

wound² /waʊnd/ *pt,pp* of wind³.

wove, wo·ven ⇨ weave.

wow¹ /waʊ/ *n* (sl) tremendous success: *The new play at the National Theatre's a wow.* □ *int* ex-pressing wonder, admiration, etc.

wow² /waʊ/ *n* [U] varieties in the pitch of sound reproduced from a disc or tape, caused by fluctua-tions in speed (from the motor). ⇨ flutter, *n*(3).

wrack /ræk/ *n* [U] **1** seaweed thrown up on the shore by the waves (and used for manure, etc). **2** = rack⁴.

wraith /reɪθ/ *n* apparition of a person seen shortly before or after his death.

wrangle /'ræŋgl/ *vi* [VP2A,3A] ∼ **(with sb)** **(about/over sth),** take part in a noisy or angry ar-gument. □ *n* such an arguement.

wrap /ræp/ *vt,vi* (-pp-) **1** [VP6A,15A,B] ∼ **(up) (in sth),** cover or roll up (in): ∼ *a child in a shawl;* ∼ *up sth in tissue paper;* ∼ *oneself in a blanket. The mountain top was* ∼*ped in mist. You'd better* ∼ (*yourself*) *up well before you go out,* put on an overcoat, scarf, etc. *Why does he* ∼ *up his mean-ing in such obscure language,* Why doesn't he ex-press his meaning clearly? ∼ *sth up,* (sl) complete it: ∼ *up a business deal.* **2** [VP14] ∼ *sth round sth,* put round; wind or fold round as a covering or protection; pack: *W*∼ *plenty of paper round it. W*∼ *this shawl round your shoulders.* **3** **be** ∼*ped up in,* (a) be packed or enclosed in; (fig) be concealed in: *The affair is ~ped up in mystery.* (b) be deeply interested in: *He is ~ped up in his work/ studies.* (c) be deeply devoted to: *She is ~ped up in her children*, devotes all her time, care, attention, etc to them. □ *n* outer garment or covering (eg a scarf, cloak, fur or rug); outer covering. (trade uses): **keep sth under ~s**, conceal it. **take off the ~s**, place on public view (eg a new model of a car). **~·per** *n* (esp) **1** piece of paper (to be) ~ped round a newspaper or other periodical, a book etc (esp for sending by post); cover of loose paper, etc for a book. **2** light dressing-gown. **~·ping** *n* **1** [C] sth used for covering or packing: *the ~pings of a mummy.* **2** [U] material for covering or packing sth: *Put plenty of ~ping round the cups and saucers when you pack them.*

wrath /rɒθ *US:* ræθ/ *n* [U] (liter) great anger; indignation. **~·ful** /-fl/ *adj* **~·fully** /-fəlɪ/ *adv*

wreak /ri:k/ *vt* [VP6A,14] **~ sth (on sb)**, give expression to; give effect to: *~ one's fury upon sb; ~ havoc/vengeance upon sb.*

wreath /ri:θ/ *n* (*pl* ~s /ri:ðz/) **1** flowers or leaves twisted or woven together into a circle (worn on the head as a garland, or placed on a coffin, a grave, a memorial to the dead, etc). **2** ring, spiral or curling line (of smoke, mist, etc).

wreathe /ri:ð/ *vt,vi* **1** [VP6A] (esp in *pp*) cover, encircle: *~d with flowers; hills ~d in mist; a face ~d in smiles.* **2** [VP14] (reflex) **~ itself round**, wind: *The snake ~d itself round the branch.* **3** [VP14] **~ sth into**, make (flowers, etc) (into a wreath). **4** [VP2A,C] (of smoke, mist, etc) move in the shape of a wreath.

wreck /rek/ *n* **1** [U] ruin or destruction, esp of a ship by storms: *save a ship from ~*; (fig) *the ~ of one's hopes/plans;* [C] instance of this: *The storm caused ~s all along the coast.* **2** [C] ship that has suffered ~(1): *Robinson Crusoe obtained food and supplies from the ~.* **3** [C] vehicle, building, etc that has been badly damaged or fallen into ruin; person whose health has been destroyed: *The car was a worthless ~ after the collision. He is a mere ~ of his former self. If these anxieties continue she will become a nervous ~.* □ *vt* [VP6A] cause the ~ of: *The ship/train was ~ed.* **~·age** /'rekɪdʒ/ *n* [U] ~ed material, fragments: *The ~age of the aircraft was scattered over a wide area.* **~er** *n* (a) person employed to recover a ~ed ship or its contents. (b) (US) person employed to demolish old buildings. ⇨ *housebreaker* at house¹(7). (c) (hist) person who tried from the shore to bring about shipwreck (eg by showing false lights) in order to plunder the cargo, etc.

wren /ren/ *n* kinds of small short-winged songbird.

wrench /rentʃ/ *n* [C] **1** sudden and violent twist or pull: *He gave his ankle a ~*, twisted it by accident. *He pulled the handle off with a single ~.* **2** (pain caused by a) sad parting or separation: *Separation from her children was a terrible ~.* **3** tool for gripping and turning nuts, bolts, etc; spanner. ⇨ the illus at tool. □ *vt* **1** [VP6A,15A,22] twist or pull violently: *~ the door open; ~ sth from sb; ~ sth out of his hand; ~ a door off its hinges. She ~ed herself from the villain's clutches.* **2** [VP6A] injure (eg one's ankle) by twisting. **3** [VP6A] (fig) distort (facts, the meaning of a sentence, etc).

wrest /rest/ *vt* **1** [VP14] **~ sth from/out of**, take (sth) violently away: *~ a knife from sb/~ it out of his hands.* **2** [VP14] **~ sth from**, get by effort: *~ a confession of guilt from sb; ~ a living from poor*

farmland. **3** twist or pervert (facts, the meaning of sth).

wrestle /'resl/ *vi* [VP2A,C,3A] **~ (with sb)**, struggle with sb (as a sport) and try to throw him to the ground without hitting him: *~ with sb;* (fig) *~ with a problem/a temptation/one's conscience.* □ *n* [C] wrestling match; hard struggle. **wres·tler** /'reslə(r)/ *n* person who ~s.

wretch /retʃ/ *n* **1** unfortunate and miserable person. **2** contemptible, mean person. **3** (playfully or affectionately) rogue.

wretched /'retʃɪd/ *adj* **1** miserable: *lead a ~ existence in the slums; living in ~ poverty. This aching tooth makes me feel ~.* **2** causing misery: *~ houses.* **3** of poor quality; bad: *~ weather/food.* **4** (with *nn* implying blame) that causes dismay (because excessive): *the ~ stupidity of the nation's leaders.* **~·ly** *adv* **~·ness** *n*

wrick, rick /rɪk/ *vt* [VP6A] sprain or twist slightly: *~ one's ankle/a muscle in one's back.* □ *n* [C] sprain: *give one's back a ~; have a ~ in the neck.*

wriggle /'rɪgl/ *vi,vt* **1** [VP2A,C,3A] move with quick, short, twistings; move along in this way: *The worm ~d as Jim put it on the fish-hook. Small children ~ in their seats when they are bored. The eel ~d out of my fingers. He ~d out of* (= escaped from) *the difficulty. He ~d (his way) through the thick hedge. My criticism made him ~*, feel uncomfortable. **2** [VP6A,15B,22] move with a wriggling motion: *~ one's toes; ~ oneself free, get free (eg from ropes round the body); ~ one's way out.* □ *n* wriggling movement. **wrig·gler** /'rɪglə(r)/ *n* (esp) larva of a mosquito.

wright /raɪt/ *n* (rare except in compounds) workman, maker. ⇨ *play~* at play¹(5), *ship~* at ship¹(3), *wheel~* at wheel(1).

wring /rɪŋ/ *vt* (*pt,pp* wrung /rʌŋ/) **1** [VP6A] twist; squeeze: *~ a hen's neck*, to kill it; *~ a person's hand*, clasp it warmly. **~ one's hands**, squeeze them together (indicating despair, sorrow, etc). **2** [VP15B,14] **~ sth out; ~ sth out of/from sth**, twist and squeeze sth tightly; force out (esp water) by doing this: *~ out wet clothes; ~ out the water from one's swimming-trunks. They wrung a confession from her*, (fig) forced her to confess, by persuasion, threats, etc. **~ing wet**, (of clothes, etc) so wet that water can be wrung from them. □ *n* [C] squeeze: *Give it another ~.* **~er** /'rɪŋə(r)/ *n* = mangle¹.

wrinkle¹ /'rɪŋkl/ *n* small fold or line in the skin (esp of the kind produced by age) or on the surface of sth: *She's beginning to get ~s round her eyes. Her new dress fits without a ~. She ironed out the ~s in her dress.* □ *vt,vi* [VP6A,15B,2A,C] **~ (up)** make, get, have, ~s in: *~ up one's forehead*, eg in perplexity; *~d with age. The front of this dress ~s.* **wrinkly** /'rɪŋklɪ/ *adj*

wrinkle² /'rɪŋkl/ *n* [C] (colloq) useful hint or suggestion: *give sb a ~.*

wrist /rɪst/ *n* joint between the hand and the arm: *He took me by the ~.* ⇨ the illus at arm. **'~-band** *n* band of a shirt-sleeve fitting round the ~. **'~-watch** *n* one worn on the ~. **~·let** /'rɪstlɪt/ *n* band or ornament for the ~.

writ /rɪt/ *n* **1** written order issued in the name of a ruler or sb in authority to an official to do or not to do sth: *a ~ of habeas corpus; a ~ for the arrest of sb.* **2** Holy W~, the Bible. □ (*pp*) **~ large**, ⇨ write(6).

write /raɪt/ *vi,vt* (*pt* wrote /rəʊt/, *pp* written

/'rɪtn/) **1** [VP2A,B,C] make letters or other symbols (eg ideographs) on a surface, esp with a pen or pencil on paper: *learn to read and ∼; ∼ on both sides of the paper. I've been writing (for) three hours. Are we to ∼ in ink or in pencil?* **2** [VP6A] put down (on paper) by means of words, etc: *∼ words/Chinese characters/shorthand; ∼ one's name; ∼ a cheque/a certificate/an application* (by filling in the spaces with words, figures, etc); *∼* (= fill) *three sheets.* **3** [VP2C,15B] *∼ sth down,* (a) put down (on paper) in words: *You'd better ∼ down the address/∼ it down before you forget it.* (b) (more usu **mark down**) reduce the nominal value of (stock, goods, etc); reduce in value or price. *∼ sb down as,* describe as: *I'd ∼ him down as a fool. ∼ in for sth,* apply by letter for. *∼ off (for sth),* order by post: *∼ off for another dozen bottles of rum. ∼ sth off,* (a) compose quickly and easily: *∼ off an account of a sports meeting.* (b) cancel; recognize that sth is a loss or failure: *∼ off a debt; ∼ off £500 for depreciation of machinery. He has just written off a new car,* damaged it beyond repair, so that the insurers regard it as a loss. Hence, '∼-off *n* sth that no longer has any value: *The burnt-out airliner was a complete ∼-off,* had no value whatever. *∼ sth out, ∼* the whole of; *∼* in full: *∼ out a copy of an agreement; ∼ out a cheque. ∼ sth up,* (a) bring up to date; complete: *∼ up one's diary. I must ∼ up my notes of the lecture.* (b) overstate the value of (assets). (c) describe, *∼* about, (an event) elaborately: *The journalist wrote up the wedding for his paper.* (d) *∼* a description giving praise: *A friendly critic wrote up the acting of the leading players.* Hence, '∼-up *n* written account or record of an event. **4** [VP6A,2A] do the work of an author; compose for publication: *∼ a novel; ∼ for the newspapers; make a living by writing.* **5** [VP2A,B,C,12A,13A,4A] *∼* and send a letter (*to,* or colloq without *to*): *He promised to ∼ (to) me every week. He ∼s home/∼s to his parents regularly. He wrote me that he was staying with his brother in York. He wrote me an account of his visit. I wrote to let them know that I was coming.* **6** (usu passive) show clear signs of: *He had trouble/honesty written on his face.* **written** (also **writ,** archaic form of the *pp*) *large,* easily or clearly recognizable.

writer /'raɪtə(r)/ *n* **1** person who writes: *the ∼ of this letter. ∼'s cramp,* cramp of the muscles in the hand, causing difficulty in writing. **2** author. **3** (GB) clerk in some government offices; naval rating who does office work.

writhe /raɪð/ *vi* [VP2A,C] twist or roll about in pain; (fig) suffer mental agony: *∼ under insults.*

writ·ing /'raɪtɪŋ/ *n* **1** [U] (in the senses of the *v* 'write'): *busy with his ∼; put sth down in ∼. His ∼* (= 'hand∼) *is difficult to read.* '∼-desk *n* desk (usu with drawers) for *∼* at. '∼-ink *n* ink for *∼* (contrasted with printing-ink). '∼-paper *n* [U] (esp) paper cut to the size usual for letters. **2** (*pl*) literary work: *the ∼s of Swift.*

writ·ten /'rɪtn/ ⇨ write.

wrong /rɒŋ *US:* rɔːŋ/ *adj* (contrasted with **right**) **1** not morally right; unjust: *It is ∼ to steal. It was ∼*

of you/You were *∼* to borrow his bicycle without asking his permission. **2** mistaken; unsuitable; improper: *He has six ∼ answers in his arithmetic. Can you prove that I am/that my opinions are ∼? You're doing it the ∼ way. We got into the ∼ train. We came the ∼ way/took a ∼ turning. This is the ∼ side of the tablecloth,* not the side intended to be seen. *∼ side out,* with the *∼* side outside. *be caught on the ∼ foot,* be caught when one is not ready. *get out of bed on the ∼ side,* said of sb who is in a bad temper early in the day. *get hold of the ∼ end of the stick,* have a completely mistaken idea or impression. *in the ∼ box,* in an awkward position. *on the ∼ side of fifty, etc,* over fifty, etc years old. *∼-'headed adj* perverse and obstinate. *∼-'headedly adv.* **3** out of order; in a bad condition: *There's nothing ∼ with the engine—perhaps there's no petrol in the tank. There's something ∼ with my digestion. What's ∼ with that?* (colloq, as a rhetorical question, meaning 'That's quite all right, isn't it?') □ *adv* (usu end position) not correctly; in a *∼* manner: *guess ∼. You've spelt my name ∼.* Cf *∼ly spelt. They told me ∼.* Cf *∼ly informed. get sth ∼,* miscalculate or misunderstand it. *go ∼,* (a) take the *∼* path or road. (b) have a bad or poor result; fail: *All our plans went ∼.* (c) (colloq) (of a machine, etc) break down. □ *n* **1** [U] what is morally *∼*; [C] *∼* action: *know the difference between right and ∼; do ∼,* do what is *∼*; sin. *Two ∼s don't make a right.* '∼-doer *n* person who does *∼.* '∼-doing *n* [U] doing *∼*; crime; sin. **2** [U] injustice; unjust treatment; [C] instance of this; unjust action: *suffer ∼; do ∼ to sb. You do me ∼,* treat me unjustly. *They have done me a great ∼. She complained of the ∼s she had suffered.* **3** *in the ∼,* in the position of being responsible for an error, for having caused a quarrel, etc: *He admitted that he was in the ∼,* that the fault, etc was his. *They tried to put me in the ∼,* to make it seem that the fault, etc was mine. *You are both in the ∼.* Each of you is in error. □ *vt* [VP6A] treat unjustly; be unfair to: *He ∼ed me when he said that I was envious. His deeply ∼ed wife deserves our help and sympathy. ∼-ful /-fl/ adj* unjust; unlawful: *∼ful dismissal* (from employment). *∼-fully /-fəlɪ/ adv ∼-ly adv* in a *∼* manner (used esp before a *pp*): *∼ly informed/ directed/accused.*

wrote /rəʊt/ ⇨ write.

wroth /rəʊθ *US:* rɔːθ/ *adj* (pred only; poet, biblical, or in mod use hum) angry; indignant.

wrought /rɔːt/ *pt,pp* of **work** [2] **1** beaten into shape: *∼ iron.* ⇨ *cast iron* at cast [1](3). **2** (archaic or liter) *∼ on/upon sb/sth,* excited him/it: *Their sufferings ∼ upon our feelings.* ⇨ *work on/upon sb/sth* at work [2](10). *∼-'up adj* over-excited; extremely agitated.

wrung /rʌŋ/ ⇨ wring.

wry /raɪ/ *adj* (**wrier, wriest**) pulled or twisted out of shape: *make a wry face,* usu to show disappointment or disgust; *a wry smile,* a forced smile that indicates disappointment. **wry·ly** *adv*

wych- (also **wich-, witch-**) /wɪtʃ/ *pref* used in names of trees: '∼-elm; '∼-hazel.

Xx

X, x /eks/ *n* (*pl* X's, x's /'eksɪz/) **1** the 24th letter of the English alphabet. **2** symbol for the Roman numeral 10. ⇨ App 4. **3** (algebra) first unknown quantity; (fig) factor or influence about which there is uncertainty.
xeno·phobia /ˌzenəˈfəʊbɪə/ *n* [U] irrational hatred or fear of strangers or foreigners.
Xerox /'zɪərɒks/ *n, vt* [VP6A] (P) = photocopy.
Xhosa /'kɔːzɑː/ *n, adj* (member or language) of the people of *Transkei* /ˌtrænˈskaɪ/ in Southern Africa.
Xmas /'krɪsməs/ *n* (common abbr, in writing, for) Christmas.
X-ray /'eks reɪ/ *n* short-wave ray that penetrates solids and makes it possible to see into or through them; photograph taken by this means: (attrib) *have an X-ray* (*examination*); *an X-ray diagnosis; X-ray photography.* □ *vt* [VP6A] examine, treat, photograph, with X-rays.
xylo·phone /'zaɪləfəʊn/ *n* musical instrument of parallel wooden bars, graduated in length, which produce different notes when struck with small wooden hammers. ⇨ the illus at percussion.

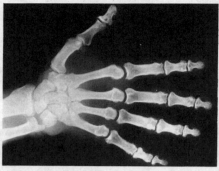

an X-ray photograph of the hand

Yy

Y, y /waɪ/ *n* (*pl* Y's, y's /waɪz/) the 25th letter of the English alphabet.
yacht /jɒt/ *n* **1** light sailing-boat built specially for racing. '∼-club *n* club for ∼-owners. '∼s-man /-smən/ *n* (*pl* -men) person who makes a hobby of sailing. **2** (usu privately-owned, usu motor-driven) vessel kept by a wealthy person for pleasure-cruising. □ *vi* [VP2A] travel or race in a ∼. ∼-ing *n* [U] the art, practice or sport of sailing ∼s.
yah /jɑː/ *int* used to express derision.
ya·hoo /jɑːˈhuː/ *n* name given by Swift (in *Gulliver's Travels*) to members of a race of inferior human beings with the habits of animals; hence, detestable person with bestial habits.
yak /jæk/ *n* long-haired ox, wild or domesticated, of Central Asia.
yam /jæm/ *n* [C] **1** (edible tuber of) kinds of tropical climbing plant. ⇨ the illus at vegetable. **2** (US) kind of sweet potato.
yam·mer /'jæmə(r)/ *vi* (colloq) **1** complain peevishly; whine. **2** talk volubly or foolishly.
yank /jæŋk/ (colloq) *vt* [VP6A,15A,B] give a sudden sharp pull to: ∼ *out a tooth. Tom ∼ed the bed-clothes off his young brother and told him to get up.* □ *n* sudden sharp pull.
Yank /jæŋk/ *n* (sl) (abbr of) Yankee.
Yan·kee /'jæŋkɪ/ *n* **1** native of New England (US). **2** (in the American Civil War) native of any of the Northern States. **3** (colloq, in GB, Europe) US citizen: (attrib) ∼ *inventions.*
yap /jæp/ *vi* (-pp-) [VP2A] **1** (esp of dogs) utter short, sharp barks. **2** (sl) talk noisily or foolishly: *Stop yapping!* □ *n* short, shrill bark.
yard¹ /jɑːd/ *n* **1** (usu unroofed) enclosed or partly enclosed space near or round a building or group of buildings, often paved: *a 'farm∼; a 'cattle-∼; the school* ∼, used as a playground; (US) area of land laid out as a garden round a house. **2** (usu in compounds) enclosure for a special purpose: *the 'railway* ∼s/'marshalling ∼s, area where trains are made up, where coaches, wagons, etc are stored; *a 'tan-∼* where tanning is carried on. ⇨ also *back* ∼ at back⁴(3), *dock∼* at dock¹, *ship∼* at ship¹(3), *vine∼* at vine(2). **3 the Y∼,** (colloq abbr for) *New Scotland Y∼.*
yard² /jɑːd/ *n* **1** (⇨ App 5) unit of length, 3 feet or 36 inches: *Can you still buy cloth by the* ∼ *in Britain?* ,∼-'measure *n* rod, tape, etc one ∼ long, marked in feet, inches, quarters, etc. '∼-stick *n* (fig) standard of comparison. **2** long, pole-like piece of wood fastened to a mast for supporting and spreading a sail. ⇨ the illus at barque. '∼-arm *n* either end of such a ∼. *man the ∼s,* place men along the ∼s, stand along the ∼s, as a form of salute.
yarn /jɑːn/ *n* **1** [U] fibres (esp of wool) which have been spun for knitting, weaving, etc. **2** [C] (colloq) story; traveller's tale. *spin a ∼,* tell a story; make up a story: *The beggar spun a long ∼ about his misfortunes.* □ *vi* [VP2A,C] tell ∼s: *We stayed up ∼ing until midnight.*
yar·row /'jærəʊ/ *n* common perennial herb with flat clusters of small flowers.
yash·mak /'jæʃmæk/ *n* veil worn in public by some Muslim women in some countries.
yaw /jɔː/ *vi* (of a ship or aircraft) turn unsteadily off the right course. □ *n* such a turn.
yawl /jɔːl/ *n* (naut) **1** sailing-boat with two masts, the second being a short one near the stern. **2** ship's boat with four or six oars.
yawn /jɔːn/ *vi* [VP2A,C] **1** take (usu involuntarily) a deep breath with the mouth wide open, as when sleepy or bored. **2** be wide open: *a ∼ing fissure. A gulf ∼ed at our feet.* □ *n* [C] act of ∼ing(1).
yaws /jɔːz/ *n pl* contagious tropical skin disease.
ye¹ /jiː/ *pron* (old form of) you: *Ye fools! How d'ye*

do /ˌhaʊ djɪ ˈduː/?

ye² /jiː/ *def art* = the (old written form, still seen on signboards over some shops and inns): *Ye Olde Bull and Bush.*

yea /jeɪ/ *adv, int* (archaic) yes. □ *n* aye: *Yeas and nays,* ayes and noes.

yeah /jeə/ *adv* (sl) yes.

year /jɜː(r) *US:* jɪər/ *n* **1** time taken by the earth in making one revolution round the sun, about 365¼ days. **2** period from 1 January to 31 December (also called the *calendar* ∼): *in the* ∼ *1865; last* ∼*; this* ∼*; next* ∼*; the* ∼ *after next; New Y*∼*'s Day,* 1 January. ∼ *in* ∼ *out,* ∼ after ∼. *all (the)* ∼ *round,* at all times of the ∼. ∼ *of grace...;* ∼ *of our Lord...,* any named ∼ after the birth of Jesus: *in the* ∼ *of our Lord, 1999. the* ∼ *dot,* (colloq) a very long time ago: *I've known her since the* ∼ *dot.* **3** any period of 365 consecutive days: *It is just a* ∼ *since I arrived here. He's twenty* ∼*s of age. He became blind in his twelfth* ∼, at the age of 11. '∼*-book n* book issued once a ∼ giving information (reports, statistics, etc) esp about trade or commerce. ∼*-'long adj* continuing for a ∼: *a* ∼*-long struggle.* **4** period of one ∼ associated with sth. *the academic* ∼, for schools, colleges and universities (beginning, in GB and US, in the autumn). *the financial/fiscal* ∼, (in GB, for making up accounts, etc from the beginning of April). **5** (*pl*) age; time of life: *a boy of ten* ∼*s; young for her* ∼*s,* looking young although not young in age; *reach the* ∼*s of discretion.* ∼·*ly adj, adv* (taking place) every ∼; once a ∼.

year·ling /ˈjɜːlɪŋ/ *n* animal between one and two years old: (attrib) *a* ∼ *colt.*

yearn /jɜːn/ *vi* [VP3A,4A] ∼ *(for sth/to do sth),* long for with tender feeling, affection, etc: *He* ∼*ed for a sight of the old, familiar faces. He* ∼*ed to return to his native land.* ∼·*ing n* strong desire; tender longing. ∼·*ing·ly adv*

yeast /jiːst/ *n* [U] substance used in brewing beer, and in the making of bread. ∼·*y adj* frothy like ∼.

yell /jel/ *vi,vt* **1** [VP2A,C] utter a loud sharp cry or cries as of pain, excitement, etc: ∼ *with fright/ laughter.* **2** [VP6A,15B] ∼ *sth (out),* say in a ∼ing voice: ∼ *(out) an order/oath;* ∼ *one's defiance.* □ *n* loud sharp cry: *a* ∼ *of terror; the college* ∼, (US) particular kind of shout or cheer used at a college to encourage a team, etc. *They greeted us with* ∼*s of hate.*

yel·low /ˈjeləʊ/ *n, adj* **1** the colour of gold or the yolk of a hen's egg. ∼ *fever,* infectious tropical disease causing the skin to turn ∼. '∼*-flag n* flag coloured ∼ displayed by a ship or hospital which is in quarantine. *the* ∼ *press,* newspapers which present news in a sensational way. **2** (often '∼*-bellied*) (colloq) cowardly: *He has a* ∼ *streak in him.* □ *vt,vi* [VP6A,2A] (cause to) become ∼: *The leaves of the book were* ∼*ed/had* ∼*ed with age. The leaves of the trees are* ∼*ing.* ∼·*ish* /-ɪʃ/ *adj* rather ∼. ∼·*ness n*

yelp /jelp/ *vi* [VP2A], *n* (utter a) short, sharp cry (of pain, anger, excitement, etc): *The dog* ∼*ed/gave a* ∼ *when I trod on its paw.*

yen¹ /jen/ *n* (*pl* unchanged) unit of currency in Japan.

yen² /jen/ *n* ∼ *(for),* (colloq) yearning (for sth). □ *vi* yearn (*to do* sth).

yeo·man /ˈjəʊmən/ *n* (*pl* -men) **1** (hist) working farmer who owned his land (contrasted with tenant farmers and those who owned large farms which

they did not work themselves). ∼ *service,* long and efficient service; help in time of need. **2** ∼ *of signals,* (GB) naval petty officer in the branch concerned with signalling by visual means (flags, etc); (US) petty officer with clerical duties. **3** *Y*∼ *of the Guard,* (GB) member of a royal bodyguard with ceremonial duties at the Tower of London, and elsewhere on special occasions. **4** member of the ∼ry. ∼·*ry* /-rɪ/ *n* (hist) (collective for) volunteer cavalry force raised from farmers, etc.

yes /jes/ *particle* (contrasted with *no*) expressing agreement, affirmation, consent, etc: *'Can you read this?' 'Yes.'* (Note that *yes* is used in answer to an interrogative-negative if the complete answer is affirmative: *'Don't you like it?'*—*'Yes'* (= 'Yes, I do like it') *'Isn't she beautiful!'*—*'Yes, isn't she?' 'Waiter!'*—*'Yes, sir.'* (= 'What do you want, sir?') □ *n* [C] affirmation; acceptance: *Answer with a plain 'Yes' or 'No'.*

yes·ter- /ˈjestə(r)/ *pref* (on) the day, year, etc before this, chiefly poet except in ∼*day* (⇨ below): *Where are the snows of* ∼*-year?*

yes·ter·day /ˈjestədɪ/ *adv, n* (on) the day just past; (on) the day before today: *He arrived* ∼. *Y*∼ *was Sunday. Where's* ∼*'s (news)paper? Why were you away from work the day before* ∼*? Where were you* ∼ *morning/afternoon/evening?* (Cf *last night.*) *She left home* ∼ *week,* eight days ago.

yet /jet/ *adv* **1** (in neg and conditional contexts and in contexts indicating ignorance or uncertainty; usu in end position, but also immediately after *not*; ⇨ *already*(2)) by this or that time; up to now; up to then: *They are not here yet/not yet here. We have had no news from him yet. We have not yet had news from him. At 2 o'clock they had not yet decided how to spend the afternoon. I wonder whether they have finished the work yet.* **2** (in interr and neg contexts; ⇨ *already* and *still*) so far; up to this/that time: *Has your brother arrived yet? Need you go yet? We needn't do it just yet.* **3** (in affirm sentences) still: *Be thankful you are yet alive* (*Still* is the more usu word). *Go at once while there is yet time,* while it is not too late. *This problem is yet* (= still) *more difficult. I have yet* (= still) *more exciting news for you.* **4** at some future time; before all is over: *The enemy may win yet/may yet win if we relax our efforts. He may surprise us all yet.* **5** *as yet,* up to now/then: *As yet we have/had not made any plans for the holidays. The scheme has worked well as yet. nor yet,* (liter) and not even: *The book is not well written—nor yet is it accurate.* □ *conj* but at the same time; nevertheless: *She's vain and foolish, and yet people like her. He worked hard, yet he failed. It is strange, yet* (*it is*) *true. He's a wealthy, yet honest, business-man.*

yeti /ˈjetɪ/ *n* name of a hairy, man-like animal reported to live in the highest part of the Himalayas.

yew /juː/ *n* [C] '*yew(-tree)*, evergreen, berry-bearing tree with dark-green leaves, often used for garden hedges; [U] wood of this tree (formerly used for making bows).

Yid·dish /ˈjɪdɪʃ/ *n* [U] international Jewish language, a form of old German with words borrowed from several modern languages, used by Jews in or from Eastern and Central Europe (*note:* the language used in Israel is modern Hebrew).

yield /jiːld/ *vt,vi* **1** [VP6A] give a natural product, a result or profit: *trees that* ∼ *fruit; investments* ∼*ing 10 per cent.* **2** [VP2A,3A,6A,15A,B] ∼ *(to sb/sth),* give way (to); cease opposition: *We will* never ∼ to force. The disease ∼ed to treatment. He ∼ed to temptation. ∼ (up) sth (to sb), give up; surrender: ∼ a fort; ∼ ground to the enemy. ∼ up the ghost, (liter or rhet) die. □ n [C,U] amount produced: a good ∼ of wheat. What is the ∼ per acre? The ∼s on his shares have decreased this year, The dividends are lower. ∼-ing adj easily giving way or bending; (fig) not obstinate. ∼-ing-ly adv

yip·pee /ˈjɪpɪ/ int cry of joy or elation.

yob /jɒb/, **yobo, yobbo** /ˈjɒbəʊ/ n (GB sl) idle, objectionable person.

yodel /ˈjəʊdl/ vt,vi (-ll-; US also -l-) sing (a song), utter a musical call, with frequent changes from the normal voice to high falsetto notes, in the manner of Swiss mountaineers. □ n ∼ling song or call. ∼-ler (US also ∼er) n person who ∼s.

yoga /ˈjəʊgə/ n [U] **1** Hindu system of meditation and self-control intended to produce mystical experience and the union of the individual soul with the universal spirit. **2** system of physical exercises and breathing-control. **yogi** /ˈjəʊgɪ/ n (pl ∼s) teacher of, expert in, ∼(1).

yo-gurt, yo-ghurt, yo-ghourt /ˈjɒgət US: ˈjəʊgərt/ n [U] thick fermented liquor made from milk.

yo-heave-ho /ˌjəʊ ˈhiːv həʊ/ int cry (formerly) used by sailors when pulling together (eg to raise a sail).

yoke /jəʊk/ n **1** shaped piece of wood placed across the necks of oxen pulling a cart, plough, etc. ⇨ harness. **2** (pl unchanged) two oxen working together: five ∼ of oxen. **3** (Roman history) arch of three spears (a symbol of the ∼ placed on oxen) under which defeated enemies were made to pass; hence, (fig) pass/come under the ∼, acknowledge and accept defeat; throw off the ∼ (of servitude, etc), rebel; refuse to obey; the ∼ of a tyrant. **4** shaped piece of wood to fit a person's shoulders and support a pail at each end. **5** (dressmaking) part of a garment fitting round the shoulders and from which the rest hangs; top part of a skirt, fitting the hips. □ vt,vi [VP6A, 15A] **1** put a ∼ on (oxen): ∼ oxen together; ∼ oxen to a plough. **2** unite: ∼d to an unwilling partner; ∼d in marriage.

yoked oxen

yokel /ˈjəʊkl/ n simple-minded countryman.

yolk /jəʊk/ n [C,U] yellow part of an egg: Beat up the ∼s of three eggs.

yon /jɒn/ adj, adv (archaic or dial) yonder.

yon·der /ˈjɒndə(r)/ adj, adv (liter) (that is, that can be seen) over there: ∼ group of trees.

yore /jɔː(r)/ n [U] of ∼, long ago: in days of ∼.

you /juː/ pron **1** the person(s) addressed: You are my friend(s). Does he know you? This is for you. **2** (colloq; used as an impers pron) one; anyone: It is much easier to cycle with the wind behind you. You never know, One can never be certain about things. **3** (preceding a n, esp in vocatives): You boys! You over there! (in exclamations): You bloody fool!

you'd /juːd/ = you had; you would.

you'll /juːl/ = you will.

young /jʌŋ/ adj (-nger, /-ŋgə(r)/, -ngest /-ŋgɪst/) **1** (contrasted with old) not far advanced in life, growth, development, etc; of recent birth or origin: a ∼ woman/tree/animal/nation, etc. **2** still near its beginning: The evening/century is still ∼. **3** the ∼er, (used before or after a person's name, to distinguish that person from another; contrasted with elder): the ∼er Pitt; Pliny the Y∼er. be sb's ∼er, be ∼er than him. **4** (used before a person's name to distinguish esp a son from his father): Y∼ Jones is always ready to help his old parents. **5** (as a familiar or condescending form of address): Now listen to me, ∼ man/my ∼ lady! **6** having little practice or experience (in sth): ∼ in crime. **7** ∼ and old, everyone. the ∼, ∼ people; children: books for the ∼. □ n [U] offspring; ∼ ones (of animals and birds): The cat fought fiercely to defend its ∼, its ∼ offspring. Some animals quickly desert their ∼. with ∼, (of an animal) pregnant. ∼-ish /ˈjʌnɪʃ/ adj fairly ∼; somewhat ∼. ∼-ster /ˈjʌŋstə(r)/ n child, youth.

your /jɔː(r) US: jʊər/ adj **1** belonging to, relating to, you: Show me ∼ hands. You'll see the post-office on ∼ right, ie ∼ right side. **2** (often indicating polite interest, or disapproval or contempt, or used to suggest that sth is not so good, remarkable, etc as is claimed): So this is what ∼ experts said, is it? This is ∼ famous English beer, is it?

you're /jʊə(r)/ = you are.

yours /jɔːz US: jʊərz/ pred adj, pron **1** of you: Is that book ∼? I borrowed a book of ∼. **2** (at the end of a letter): ∼ truly/sincerely/faithfully.

your·self /jɔːˈself US: jʊərˈself/ (pl -selves /-ˈselvz/) reflex pron: Did you hurt ∼? □ emphat pron: You ∼ said so. You said so ∼. (all) by ∼, (a) alone. (b) without help.

youth /juːθ/ n (pl ∼s /juːðz/) **1** [U] the state or time of being young: the enthusiasm of ∼; the friends of one's ∼; in my ∼, when I was young. **2** [C] young man: As a ∼ he showed no promise of becoming a great pianist. Half a dozen ∼s were standing at the street corner. **3** [U] (collective sing, with pl) young men and women: the ∼ of the nation; a '∼ hostel, ⇨ hostel; a '∼ centre/club, club (usu provided by a voluntary organization) for the leisure time activities of young people. ∼·ful /-fl/ adj young; having the qualities, etc, of young people: a ∼ful appearance. ∼·fully /-fəlɪ/ adv ∼·ful·ness n

you've /juːv/ = you have.

yowl /jaʊl/ vi howl; wail.

yo-yo /ˈjəʊjəʊ/ n toy in the shape of a top with a groove for string, the top moving up and down the string by movement of the fingers: The exchange rate is going up and down like a ∼.

yule /juːl/ n (also '∼-tide) (archaic) Christmas. '∼-log n log of wood burnt on Christmas Eve.

Zz

Z, z /zed *US:* ziː/ *n* (*pl* **Z's, z's** /zedz *US:* ziːz/) the last letter of the English alphabet.

zany /'zeɪnɪ/ *n* (*pl* -**nies**) half-witted person; foolish joker. □ *adj* foolish; mad.

zap /zæp/ *vt* (-pp-) [VP6A] (sl) attack; defeat.

zeal /ziːl/ *n* [U] energy and enthusiasm: *show* ∼ *for a cause; work with great* ∼. ∼**·ous** /'zeləs/ *adj* full of, acting with, showing, ∼: *∼ous to please one's employer; ∼ous for liberty and freedom.* ∼**·ous·ly** *adv*

zealot /'zelət/ *n* person who shows great and uncompromising enthusiasm for a religion, a party, a cause, etc; fanatic. ∼**ry** /-trɪ/ *n* [U].

zebra /'ziːbrə/ *n* horse-like wild animal of Africa, with dark stripes on its body. ⇨ the illus at large. ∼ **'crossing,** street-crossing marked with broad white stripes, at which pedestrians have priority over traffic. ⇨ **panda.**

zebu /'ziːbjuː/ *n* domestic animal like an ox, with a hump on its shoulders, used in Asia and E Africa.

zee /ziː/ *n* (US) name of the letter Z.

Zen /zen/ *n* [U] form of Buddhism asserting that enlightenment comes from meditation and intuition, with less dependence upon the scriptures.

zen·ith /'zenɪθ *US:* 'ziːnɪθ/ *n* part of the sky directly overhead; (fig) highest point (of one's fame, fortunes, etc): *at the* ∼ *of his career.* ∼**al** *adj:* ∼*al projection,* map obtained by projecting²(6). ⇨ **nadir.** ⇨ the illus at **projection.**

zephyr /'zefə(r)/ *n* west wind; (poet) soft, gentle breeze.

zep·pe·lin /'zepəlɪn/ *n* large dirigible used by the Germans in World War I.

zero /'zɪərəʊ/ *n* **1** the figure 0; nought. ⇨ App 4 (1, note 2). **2** the point between the positive (+) and negative (−) on a scale, esp on a thermometer (⇨ App 5): *The thermometer fell to* ∼ *last night. It was ten degrees below* ∼ (eg − 10°C or − 10°F). **absolute** ∼, ⇨ absolute(5). '∼ **hour,** (mil) time at which operations are to begin: *Z*∼ *hour was 3am.* □ *vi* [VP2C] ∼ *in (on),* (sl) fix attention (on).

zest /zest/ *n* [U] **1** great interest or pleasure; gusto:

He entered into our plans with ∼. **2** (often with *in-def art*) pleasing or stimulating quality or flavour: *The possibility of danger gave* (*a*) ∼ *to the adventure.*

zig·zag /'zɪgzæg/ *n* [C] line or path which turns right and left alternately at sharp (equal or unequal) angles: (attrib) *a* ∼ *path up the hillside.* □ *adv* in a ∼. □ *vi* (-gg-) go in a ∼: *The drunken man* ∼*ged down the street.*

zinc /zɪŋk/ *n* [U] hard, bluish-white metal (symbol **Zn**) used in alloys and in coating iron sheets and wire to give protection against rust.

zing /zɪŋ/ *n* [U] (sl) vigour; energy.

zin·nia /'zɪnɪə/ *n* kinds of garden plant with bright-coloured flowers.

Zion /'zaɪən/ *n* the Jewish homeland, esp as a symbol of Judaism; Israel. ∼**·ism** /-ɪzəm/ *n* (hist) political movement for the establishment of an independent state for the Jews; (mod use) movement concerned with the development of Israel as a Jewish political and religious State . ∼**·ist** /-ɪst/ *adj, n*

zip /zɪp/ *n* **1** sound as of a bullet going through the air, or of the sudden tearing of cloth. **2** (sl) vigour; energy. □ *vt* (-pp-) [VP6A,15B,22] open sth (*zip sth open*) or close sth (*zip sth up*) by means of a zip-fastener: *She zipped her bag open/up.* **zip·per,** **zip-fastener** *nn* device for locking together two toothed metal or plastic edges by means of a sliding tab, used for fastening articles of clothing, bags, etc.

zip code /'zɪp kəʊd/ *n* (US) = postcode.

zither /'zɪðə(r)/ *n* musical instrument with many strings on a flat sounding-board, played with a plectrum or the fingers.

zo·diac /'zəʊdɪæk/ *n* **1** belt of the heavens extending about 8° on each side of the path followed by the sun and containing the path of the principal planets, divided into 12 equal parts known as the *signs of the* ∼, named after 12 groups of stars. **2** diagram of the ∼, used in astrology.

zom·bie /'zɒmbɪ/ *n* (colloq) dull, slow, lifeless, mindless person.

Aries (the Ram)
21st March–20th April

Taurus (the Bull)
21st April–20th May

Gemini (the Twins)
21st May–20th June

Cancer (the Crab)
21st June–20th July

Leo (the Lion)
21st July–19th/22nd Aug

Virgo (the Virgin)
20th/23rd Aug–22nd Sept

Libra (the Scales)
23rd Sept–22nd Oct

Scorpio (the Scorpion)
23rd Oct–21st Nov

Sagittarius (the Archer)
22nd Nov–20th Dec

Capricorn (the Goat)
21st Dec–20th Jan

Aquarius (the Water Carrier)
21st Jan–19th Feb

Pisces (the Fishes)
20th Feb–20th March

the signs of the zodiac

zone /zəʊn/ n **1** belt, band or stripe going round, and distinguished by colour, appearance, etc. **2** one of the five parts into which the earth's surface is divided by imaginary lines parallel to the equator (the '*torrid*, N & S '*temperate*, and the '*frigid* ∼*s*). **3** area with particular features, purpose or use: *the war* ∼; *within the* ∼ *of submarine activity*, ie where, during a war, submarines are active; *the* '*danger* ∼; *a* '*parking* ∼; *smokeless* ∼*s*, (usu urban) areas in which only smokeless fuels may be used (in homes, factories, etc). **4** (US) particular area in which certain postal, telephone, etc rates are charged. □ *vt* [VP6A] encircle, mark, with, into, or as with a ∼ or ∼s; divide into ∼s. **zonal** /'zəʊnl/ *adj* relating to, arranged in, ∼s. **zon·ing** n [U] (in planning urban areas) designation of areas for various purposes, eg shopping, residential, industrial.

zonked /zɒŋkt/ *pred adj* ∼ *(out)*, (US sl) drugged; drunk.

zoo /zu:/ n zoological gardens: *take the children to the zoo*.

zo·ol·ogy /zəʊ'ɒlədʒɪ/ n [U] science of the structure, forms and distribution of animals. **zo·ol·ogi·cal** /ˌzəʊə'lɒdʒɪkl/ *adj* of ∼. **zoological gardens**, park (usu public) in which many kinds of animals are kept for exhibition. **zo·ol·ogist** /zəʊ'ɒlədʒɪst/ n expert in ∼.

zoom /zu:m/ n **1** [U] (low, deep humming sound of the) sudden upward flight of an aircraft. **2** ∼ **lens**, (on a camera), one with continuously variable focal length. ⇨ the illus at **camera**. □ *vi* [VP2A,C] **1** (of aircraft) move upwards at high speed: (fig, colloq) *Prices* ∼*ed*, rose sharply. **2** (of a camera with a ∼ lens): ∼ *in/out*, cause the object being photographed to appear nearer/further.

zo·ophyte /'zəʊəfaɪt/ n plant-like sea-animal (eg a sea anemone, coral).

zuc·chini /zʊ'ki:nɪ/ (*pl* ∼s or unchanged) (esp US) = **courgette**. ⇨ the illus at **vegetable**.

Zulu /'zu:lu:/ n, *adj* (member or language) of the people of *Kwazulu* /ˌkwɑ:'zu:lu:/ (formerly *Zululand*) in South Africa.

Appendix 1 IRREGULAR VERBS

Note: Full phonetic transcriptions of the irregular past tense and part participle forms are given in the entries on the infinitive forms in the dictionary.

Infinitive	Past Tense	Past Participle
abide	abode, abided	abode, abided
arise	arose	arisen
awake	awoke	awaked, awoken
be	was	been
bear	bore	borne
beat	beat	beaten
become	became	become
befall	befell	befallen
beget	begot	begotten
begin	began	begun
behold	beheld	beheld
bend	bent	bent
bereave	bereaved, bereft	bereaved, bereft
beseech	besought	besought
beset	beset	beset
bet	bet, betted	bet, betted
betake	betook	betaken
bethink	bethought	bethought
bid	bade, bid	bidden, bid
bind	bound	bound
bite	bit	bitten, bit
bleed	bled	bled
blend	blended, blent	blended, blent
bless	blessed, blest	blessed, blest
blow	blew	blown
break	broke	broken
breed	bred	bred
bring	brought	brought
broadcast	broadcast, broadcasted	broadcast, broadcasted
build	built	built
burn	burnt, burned	burnt, burned
burst	burst	burst
buy	bought	bought
cast	cast	cast
catch	caught	caught
chide	chided, chid	chided, chidden
choose	chose	chosen
cleave	clove, cleft	cloven, cleft
cling	clung	clung
clothe	clothed, clad	clothed, clad
come	came	come
cost	cost	cost
creep	crept	crept
crow	crowed, crew	crowed
cut	cut	cut
dare	dared, durst	dared
deal	dealt	dealt
dig	dug	dug
dive	dived; (US) dove	dived
do	did	done
draw	drew	drawn
dream	dreamt, dreamed	dreamt, dreamed
drink	drank	drunk
drive	drove	driven
dwell	dwelt	dwelt
eat	ate	eaten
fall	fell	fallen
feed	fed	fed
feel	felt	felt
fight	fought	fought
find	found	found
flee	fled	fled

fling	flung	flung
fly	flew	flown
forbear	forbore	forborne
forbid	forbade, forbad	forbidden
forecast	forecast, forecasted	forecast, forecasted
foreknow	foreknew	foreknown
foresee	foresaw	foreseen
foretell	foretold	foretold
forget	forgot	forgotten
forgive	forgave	forgiven
forsake	forsook	forsaken
forswear	forswore	forsworn
freeze	froze	frozen
gainsay	gainsaid	gainsaid
get	got	got; (US) gotten
gild	gilded, gilt	gilded
gird	girded, girt	girded, girt
give	gave	given
go	went	gone
grave	graved	graven, graved
grind	ground	ground
grow	grew	grown
hamstring	hamstringed, hamstrung	hamstringed, hamstrung
hang	hung, hanged	hung, hanged
have	had	had
hear	heard	heard
heave	heaved, hove	heaved, hove
hew	hewed	hewed, hewn
hide	hid	hidden
hit	hit	hit
hold	held	held
hurt	hurt	hurt
inlay	inlaid	inlaid
keep	kept	kept
kneel	knelt	knelt
knit	knitted, knit	knitted, knit
know	knew	known
lade	laded	laden
lay	laid	laid
lead	led	led
lean	leant, leaned	leant, leaned
leap	leapt, leaped	leapt, leaped
learn	learnt, learned	learnt, learned
leave	left	left
lend	lent	lent
let	let	let
lie	lay	lain
light	lit, lighted	lit, lighted
lose	lost	lost
make	made	made
mean	meant	meant
meet	met	met
melt	melted	melted, molten
miscast	miscast	miscast
misdeal	misdealt	misdealt
misgive	misgave	misgiven
mislay	mislaid	mislaid
mislead	misled	misled
misspell	misspelt	misspelt
misspend	misspent	misspent
mistake	mistook	mistaken
misunderstand	misunderstood	misunderstood
mow	mowed	mown; (US) mowed
outbid	outbid	outbid
outdo	outdid	outdone
outgo	outwent	outgone
outgrow	outgrew	outgrown
outride	outrode	outridden
outrun	outran	outrun
outshine	outshone	outshone

1004

overbear	overbore	overborne
overcast	overcast	overcast
overcome	overcame	overcome
overdo	overdid	overdone
overhang	overhung	overhung
overhear	overheard	overheard
overlay	overlaid	overlaid
overleap	overleapt, overleaped	overleapt, overleaped
overlie	overlay	overlain
override	overrode	overridden
overrun	overran	overrun
oversee	oversaw	overseen
overshoot	overshot	overshot
oversleep	overslept	overslept
overtake	overtook	overtaken
overthrow	overthrew	overthrown
partake	partook	partaken
pay	paid	paid
prove	proved	proved, proven
put	put	put
quit	quitted, quit	quitted, quit
read /riːd/	read /red/	read /red/
rebind	rebound	rebound
rebuild	rebuilt	rebuilt
recast	recast	recast
redo	redid	redone
relay	relaid	relaid
remake	remade	remade
rend	rent	rent
repay	repaid	repaid
rerun	reran	rerun
reset	reset	reset
retell	retold	retold
rewrite	rewrote	rewritten
rid	rid, ridded	rid, ridded
ride	rode	ridden
ring	rang	rung
rise	rose	risen
rive	rived	riven, rived
run	ran	run
saw	sawed	sawn, sawed
say	said	said
see	saw	seen
seek	sought	sought
sell	sold	sold
send	sent	sent
set	set	set
sew	sewed	sewn, sewed
shake	shook	shaken
shave	shaved	shaved, shaven
shear	sheared	sheared, shorn
shed	shed	shed
shine	shone /ʃɒn/; (US) /ʃəʊn/	shone /ʃɒn/; (US) /ʃəʊn/
shoe	shod	shod
shoot	shot	shot
show	showed	shown, showed
shrink	shrank, shrunk	shrunk, shrunken
shrive	shrove, shrived	shriven, shrived
shut	shut	shut
sing	sang	sung
sink	sank	sunk, sunken
sit	sat	sat
slay	slew	slain
sleep	slept	slept
slide	slid	slid
sling	slung	slung
slink	slunk	slunk
slit	slit	slit
smell	smelt, smelled	smelt, smelled
smite	smote	smitten

sow	sowed	sown, sowed
speak	spoke	spoken
speed	sped, speeded	sped, speeded
spell	spelt, spelled	spelt, spelled
spend	spent	spent
spill	spilt, spilled	spilt, spilled
spin	spun, span	spun
spit	spat	spat
split	split	split
spoil	spoilt, spoiled	spoilt, spoiled
spread	spread	spread
spring	sprang	sprung
stand	stood	stood
stave	staved, stove	staved, stove
steal	stole	stolen
stick	stuck	stuck
sting	stung	stung
stink	stank, stunk	stunk
strew	strewed	strewn, strewed
stride	strode	stridden
strike	struck	struck, stricken
string	strung	strung
strive	strove	striven
swear	swore	sworn
sweep	swept	swept
swell	swelled	swollen, swelled
swim	swam	swum
swing	swung	swung
take	took	taken
teach	taught	taught
tear	tore	torn
tell	told	told
think	thought	thought
thrive	throve, thrived	thriven, thrived
throw	threw	thrown
thrust	thrust	thrust
tread	trod	trodden, trod
unbend	unbent	unbent
unbind	unbound	unbound
underbid	underbid	underbid
undergo	underwent	undergone
understand	understood	understood
undertake	undertook	undertaken
undo	undid	undone
upset	upset	upset
wake	woke, waked	woken, waked
waylay	waylaid	waylaid
wear	wore	worn
weave	wove	woven
weep	wept	wept
win	won	won
wind	wound	wound
withdraw	withdrew	withdrawn
withhold	withheld	withheld
withstand	withstood	withstood
work	worked, wrought	worked, wrought
wring	wrung	wrung
write	wrote	written

Appendix 2 COMMON ABBREVIATIONS

Note: This list includes abbreviations that occur in newspapers, timetables, etc. For abbreviations of parts of speech etc used in the text of the dictionary, ⇨ the inside covers of this book.
The use of capital or lower case letters indicates the more common usage but some abbreviations can be written in either style. Full points are often used in abbreviations though they are usually omitted in modern style.
Those abbreviations and acronyms that may be spoken, usually in a colloquial context, are given with phonetic transcriptions or stress marks, e g ˌAG'M is pronounced /ˌeɪ dʒi: 'em/.

'A-bomb atomic bomb
'A-level advanced level (examination)
ˌA 'A Alcoholics Anonymous; Automobile Association
ˌA A 'A Amateur Athletics Association; American Automobile Association
ˌA 'B (GB) Able Seaman; (US) Bachelor of Arts
ˌA B 'C Australian Broadcasting Commission
ˌa 'c alternating current
a/c account
acc(t) account
ack(n) acknowledge(d)
ad(vt) advertisement
ˌA 'D *Anno Domini* in the year of the Lord
ˌA D 'C Aide-de-camp
add(r) address
Afr Africa(n)
ˌA G 'M Annual General Meeting
ˌA I 'D (US) Agency for International Development
ˌa 'm *ante meridiem* before noon
ˌA M 'A (US) American Medical Association
amp /æmp/ ampere(s)
anon anonymous
ˌA 'P Associated Press
ˌA P 'B (US) All Points Bulletin (for missing or wanted person)
appro /'æprəʊ/ approval
approx approximately
Apr April
arr arrival; arrives
asap as soon as possible
ASEAN Association of South-East Asian Nations
assoc associate; association
asst assistant
Aug August
ˌA 'V Audio-Visual; Authorised Version (of the Bible)
Av(e) Avenue
ˌA W O 'L absent without leave

b born; bowled
ˌb & 'b bed and breakfast
ˌB 'A (GB) Bachelor of Arts; British Airways
Barr Barrister
ˌB B 'C British Broadcasting Corporation
ˌB 'C Before Christ; British Council
ˌB 'D Bachelor of Divinity
bk book
Bldg(s) building(s)
Blvd Boulevard
ˌB 'M British Museum
ˌB M 'A British Medical Association
B Mus /ˌbi:'mʌs/ Bachelor of Music
ˌb 'o body odour; box office
Br Brother

Brig Brigadier
Brit Britain, British
Bro(s) brother(s)
ˌB 'S (US) Bachelor of Science
B Sc /ˌbi:es'si:/ (GB) Bachelor of Science
ˌB S 'T British Summer Time
Bt; Bart Baronet
ˌB Th 'U British Thermal Unit
ˌB V 'M *Beata Virgo Maria* Blessed Virgin Mary

C Centigrade; (Roman) 100
c cent(s); century; *circa* about; cubic
ca *circa* about, approximately
ˌC 'A Chartered Accountant
Cantab /'kæntæb/ *Cantabrigiensis* of Cambridge University
Capt Captain
CARE /keə(r)/ (US) Co-operative for American Relief Everywhere
Cath Catholic
ˌC B 'C Canadian Broadcasting Corporation
ˌC B 'I Confederation of British Industry
ˌC B 'S (US) Columbia Broadcasting System
ˌc 'c cubic centimetre(s)
cc *capita* chapters; centuries
ˌC 'D *Corps Diplomatique* Diplomatic Service
Cdr Commander
Cdre Commodore
cert certificate; certified
c 'f *confer* compare
cg centigram
c 'h central heating
ˌC 'H Companion of Honour
ch(ap) chapter
Ch B /ˌsi: eitʃ 'bi:/ Bachelor of Surgery
ˌC 'I Channel Islands
ˌC I 'A (US) Central Intelligence Agency
ˌC I 'D (GB) Criminal Investigation Department
c i 'f cost, insurance, freight
ˌC-in-'C Commander-in-Chief
cl class; centilitre(s)
cm centimetre(s)
Co (comm) Company
ˌC 'O Commanding Officer
c/o care of
ˌC O 'D Cash on Delivery
ˌC of 'E /ˌsi: əv 'i:/ Church of England
ˌC O 'I (GB) Central Office of Information
Col Colonel
Coll College
concl concluded; conclusion
Cons (GB) Conservative (political party)
cont contents; continued
Co-op /'kəʊ ɒp/ Co-operative (Society)
Corp Corporation
Coy (mil) Company
cp compare
ˌC 'P Cape Province; Communist Party

Cpl Corporal

c p 's cycles per second

Cres(c) Crescent

C 'S Civil Servant; Civil Service

C S 'E (GB) Certificate of Secondary Education

C S 'T (US) Central Standard Time

cu cubic

cwt hundredweight

D Roman 500

d *denarius* penny; died

D-day day on which a course of action is planned to start; ⇨ D-day in the dictionary

D 'A (US) District Attorney

dbl double

D 'C (US) District of Columbia

d 'c direct current

D 'D Doctor of Divinity

D D 'T *Dichloro-diphenyl-trichloroethane* insecticide

Dec December

dec deceased

deg degree(s)

Dem Democrat

dep departs; departure; deputy

Dept Department

D 'G *Dei Gratia* by the grace of God; Director General

diag diagram

diff difference; different

Dip Diploma

Dip Ed /ˌdɪp 'ed/ Diploma in Education

Dir Director

D I 'Y do it yourself

D 'J dinner jacket; disc jockey

D Litt /ˌdiː 'lɪt/ Doctor of Letters/Literature

DM *Deutschmark* /'dɔɪtʃmɑːk/ German currency

D N 'A *deoxyribonucleic acid* basic constituent of the gene

doz dozen

D Phil /ˌdiːˈfɪl/ Doctor of Philosophy

Dr Debtor; Doctor; Drive (i e small road)

dr dram(s)

D Sc /ˌdiː es 'siː/ Doctor of Science

D 'T; (the) d ts /ˌdiː 'tiːz/ *delirium tremens* 'trembling delirium' (extreme state of alcoholism)

dupl duplicate

D 'V *Deo Volente* God being willing

E east

Ed edited by; editor; edition; education; educated

E D 'P Electronic Data Processing

E E 'C European Economic Community (the Common Market)

E E 'G Electro-encephalo-gram/graph

EFTA /'eftə/ European Free Trade Association

e 'g *exempli gratia* for example, for instance

enc(l) enclosed

ENE east-northeast

Eng Engineer(ing); England; English

E 'P extended-playing (record)

E 'R *Elizabeth Regina* Queen Elizabeth

ESE east-southeast

E S 'P Extra-Sensory Perception

Esq Esquire

E S 'T (US) Eastern Standard Time

e t 'a estimated time of arrival

et al /ˌet 'æl/ *et alii* and other people; *et alia* and other things

etc; &c /ˌet 'setrə/ *et cetera* and the rest, and all the others

e t 'd estimated time of departure

et seq /ˌet 'sek/ *et sequens* and the following

eve evening

excl excluding; exclusive

ext exterior; external

F Fahrenheit; Fellow

f foot; feet; female; feminine

F 'A Football Association

F A 'O Food and Agricultural Organisation

F B 'A Fellow of the British Academy

F B 'I (US) Federal Bureau of Investigation

F 'D *Fidei Defensor* Defender of the Faith

Feb February

Fed Federal; Federated; Federation

fem female; feminine

fig figurative; figure

fl fluid; floor

fm fathom(s)

F 'M Frequency Modulation

F 'O (GB) Foreign Office

f o 'b free on board

fol(l) following

for foreign

Fr Father; Franc; France; French

Fri Friday

F R 'S Fellow of the Royal Society

ft foot; feet

fur furlong(s)

furn furnished

fwd forward

g acceleration due to gravity; gram(s)

gal(l) gallon(s)

GATT /gæt/ General Agreement on Tariffs and Trade

G 'B Great Britain

G 'C George Cross

G C 'E (GB) General Certificate of Education

Gdn(s) Garden(s)

Gen General

Ger German(y)

G H 'Q General Headquarters

G 'I (US) enlisted soldier

Gk Greek

G L 'C Greater London Council

gm gram(s)

G 'M General Manager

G M 'T Greenwich Mean Time

G N 'P Gross National Product

gov(t) government

Gov Governor

G 'P General Practitioner (Medical Doctor)

G P 'O General Post Office

gr grade; grain; gross; group

gt great

h height; hour

ha hectare(s)

h & 'c hot and cold (water)

'H-bomb Hydrogen bomb

H 'E high explosive; His/Her Excellency; His Eminence

H 'F High Frequency

H 'H His Holiness

H 'M His/Her Majesty
H M 'S His/Her Majesty's Ship
H M S 'O His/Her Majesty's Stationery Office
Hon Honorary; Honourable
hosp hospital
H 'P Hire Purchase; Horse Power
H 'Q Headquarters
hr hour(s)
H R 'H His/Her Royal Highness

I Island; Roman 1
ib; ibid *ibidem* in the same place
I B 'A (GB) Independent Broadcasting Authority
i/c in charge
I C B 'M Inter-Continental Ballistic Missile
i 'e *id est* which is to say, in other words
I H 'S *Iesous* (Greek for) Jesus (Christ)
I L 'O International Labour Organisation
I M 'F International Monetary Fund
in inch(es)
Inc Incorporated
incl including; inclusive
Ind India(n); Independent
inf *infra* below
info /'ɪnfəʊ/ information
infra dig /ˌɪnfrə 'dɪg/ *infra dignitatem* beneath
 one's social dignity
I N R 'I *Iesus Nazarenus Rex Iudaeorum* Jesus
 of Nazareth, King of the Jews
Inst Institute
int interior; internal; international
intro /'ɪntrəʊ/ introduction
I O 'U I owe you
I 'Q *Intelligence Quotient* comparative measure
 of intelligence
I R 'A Irish Republican Army
Ire Ireland
Is Islands
It(al) Italy, Italian
I T 'V (GB) independent television

Jan January
J 'C Jesus Christ
Jnr; Jr Junior
J 'P Justice of the Peace
Jul July
Jun June; Junior

kg kilogram(s)
K G 'B Intelligence Agency of the USSR
km kilometre(s)
K 'O knock-out
kw kilowatt(s)

L lake; little; Roman 50; (GB) Liberal (political
 party)
l left; length; line
L 'A Legislative Assembly; Los Angeles
Lab (GB) Labour (political party)
lang language
Lat Latin
lat latitude
lb pound(s) (weight)
l b 'w leg before wicket (cricket term)
Ld Lord
L E 'A Local Education Authority
l 'h left hand
Lib (GB) Liberal (political party); Liberation
lit literal(ly); literature; literary
ll lines

LL B /ˌel el 'biː/ Bachelor of Laws
L M 'T (US) Local Mean Time
loc cit /ˌlɒk 'sɪt/ *loco citato* in the place
 mentioned
long longitude
L 'P long-playing (record)
L S 'D *lysergic acid diethylamide* drug inducing
 hallucinations
£ s d /ˌel es 'diː/ *librae, solidi, denarii* pounds,
 shillings, pence (former G B currency system)
L S 'T (US) Local Standard Time
Lt Lieutenant
Ltd Limited
lux luxury

M Member
m male; married; metre(s); mile(s); million
M 'A Master of Arts
Maj Major
Mans Mansions
Mar March
masc masculine
math /mæθ/ (US) mathematics
maths /mæθs/ (GB) mathematics
max maximum
M 'B Bachelor of Medicine
M 'C (US) Marine Corps; Master of
 Ceremonies; (US) Member of Congress;
 (GB) Military Cross
M C 'C (GB) Marylebone Cricket Club (the
 governing body of English cricket)
Mc Megacycle(s)
M 'D Doctor of Medicine
Med(it) Mediterranean
mg milligram(s)
Mgr Monsignor
M I '5 (GB) National Security Division of
 Military Intelligence
min minimum
misc miscellaneous
mkt market
ml mile(s); millilitre(s)
mm millimetre(s)
M 'O Mail Order; Medical Officer; Money
 Order
mod moderate; modern
mod cons /ˌmɒd 'kɒnz/ modern conveniences
Mon Monday
M 'P Member of Parliament (House of
 Commons); Military Police
m p 'g miles per gallon
m p 'h miles per hour
Mr, Mrs, Ms ⇨ dictionary entries
MS(S) manuscript(s)
M Sc /ˌem es 'siː/ Master of Science
Mt Mount

N north
NAAFI /'næfɪ/ (GB) Navy, Army and Air
 Force Institute
nat national; native; natural
NATO /'neɪtəʊ/ North Atlantic Treaty
 Organisation
N 'B *nota bene* take special note of
N C 'O Non-Commissioned Officer
NE northeast
N H 'S (GB) National Health Service
NNE north-northeast
NNW north-northwest
no(s) number(s)

non-U /ˌnɒn ˈjuː/ not upper class; vulgar
Nov November
nr near
N S ͵P C ᐟC (GB) National Society for the Prevention of Cruelty to Children
N ᐟT New Testament
NW northwest
N ᐟY (ᐟC) New York (City)
N ᐟZ New Zealand

O A ᐟP (GB) old-age pensioner
O A ᐟS (US) Organisation of American States
O A ᐟU Organisation of African Unity
ob *obiit* died
Oct October
O E C ᐟD Organisation for Economic Co-operation and Development
O E ᐟD Oxford English Dictionary
O H M ᐟS (GB) On Her/His Majesty's Service
ᐟO-level (GB) Ordinary level (examination)
o n ᐟo or nearest offer
op opus; operation
op cit /ˌɒp ˈsɪt/ *opere citato* in the work mentioned
OPEC /ˈəʊpek/ Organisation of·Petroleum Exporting Countries
opp opposite
orch orchestra(l); orchestrated
O ᐟS Ordinary Seaman
O ᐟT Old Testament
Oxon /ˈɒksn/ *Oxoniensis* of Oxford University; Oxfordshire
oz ounce(s)

P Parking
p page; penny, pence; per
p ᐟa *per annum* per year
P ᐟA Personal Assistant; Press Association; Public Address (System)
para(s) paragraph(s)
P A Y ᐟE pay as you earn
P ᐟC (GB) Police Constable; (GB) Privy Councillor; (US) Peace Corps
pd paid
P D S ᐟA People's Dispensary for Sick Animals
P ᐟE physical education
PEN /pen/ International Association of Writers
P ᐟG Paying Guest
Ph D /ˌpiː eɪtʃ ˈdiː/ Doctor of Philosophy
Pk Park
pkt packet
Pl Place
P ᐟM Prime Minister
p ᐟm *post meridiem* after noon; per month
P ᐟO Personnel Officer; Petty Officer; Post Office; Postal Order
P ᐟO Box Post Office Box
P O ᐟE Port of Entry
pop popular; population
poss possible; possibly
P O ᐟW Prisoner of War
pp pages
p ᐟp *per procurationem* on behalf of (precedes name of person signed for)
P P ᐟS *post postscriptum* additional postscript
pr pair; price
P ᐟR Public Relations
Pres President

P R ᐟO Public Records Office; Public Relations Officer
pro /prəʊ/ professional
pro tem /ˌprəʊ ˈtem/ *pro tempore* for the time being; temporarily
Prof (*informally* /prɒf/) Professor
pron pronounced; pronunciation
Prot Protestant
Prov Province
Ps Psalm
P ᐟS Postscript
P S ᐟT (US) Pacific Standard Time
pt part; payment; pint; point
P ᐟT Physical Training
P T ᐟA Parent–Teacher Association
Pte (GB) Private (soldier)
P T ᐟO Please turn over
Pty Proprietary
Pvt (US) Private (soldier)
p ᐟw per week
P ᐟX post exchange (US equivalent of NAAFI)

Q ᐟC Queen's Counsel
Q E ᐟD *quod erat demonstrandum* which had to be proved
qt quart
q ᐟt ⇨ quiet (5)
Qu Queen; Question
q ᐟv *quod vide* which may be referred to

R River; Royal
r radius; right
R ᐟA Rear-Admiral; Royal Academy; Royal Academician
RADA /ˈrɑːdə/ Royal Academy of Dramatic Art
R A ᐟF (*also* /ræf/) Royal Air Force
R A ᐟM Royal Academy of Music
R ᐟC Red Cross; Roman Catholic
R C ᐟM Royal College of Music
Rd Road
rec(d) received
ref referee /ref/; reference; refer(red)
Rep Repertory /rep/; Representative /rep/; Republic(an)
res residence; resigned; reserved
resp respectively
ret(d) retired
rev revolution
Rev(d) Reverend
r ᐟh right hand
R I ᐟP *requiescat/requiescant in pace* may he/they rest in peace
rly railway
rm room
R ᐟM Royal Marines
R ᐟN Royal Navy
r p ᐟm revolutions per minute
R S ᐟM Regimental Sergeant Major; Royal School of Music
R S V ᐟP *répondez s'il vous plaît* please reply
R S ͵P C ᐟA Royal Society for the Prevention of Cruelty to Animals
rt right
Rt Hon Right Honourable
Rt Rev Right Reverend
R (S) ᐟV Revised (Standard) Version (of the Bible)
R ᐟU Rugby Union

S south
s second(s); shilling(s)
ˌ**S** ˈ**A** South Africa
ˌ**s a** ˈ**e** stamped addressed envelope
SALT /sɔːlt/ Strategic Arms Limitation Talks
Sat Saturday
ˌ**S A Y** ˈ**E** save as you earn
sc *scilicet* namely
s/c self-contained
Sch School
sci science
SE southeast
sec second(ary); secretary
Sen Senate; Senator; Senior
Sept September
ˌ**S** ˈ**F** Science Fiction
sgd signed
Sgt Sergeant
SHAPE /ʃeɪp/ Supreme Headquarters of
Allied Powers in Europe
Sn(r) Senior
Soc Society
Sol Solicitor
sp special; spelling
Sp Spain, Spanish
sp gr specific gravity
Sq Square
Sr Senior; Sister
ˌ**S R** ˈ**N** State Registered Nurse
ˌ**S** ˈ**S** Steamship
SSE south-southeast
SSW south-southwest
St Saint; Street
ˌ**S T** ˈ**D** subscriber trunk dialling (telephone)
Str Strait; Street
sub(s) subscription; substitute
Sun Sunday
Supt Superintendent
SW southwest

T temperature
t time; ton(s)
ˌ**T** ˈ**B** Tuberculosis
Tech /tek/ Technical (College)
tel telephone
temp temperature; temporary (secretary)
/temp/
Ter(r) Terrace; Territory
Thurs Thursday
ˌ**T K** ˈ**O** technical knock-out
ˌ**T N** ˈ**T** *Tri-nitro-toluene* explosive
trans translated
treas treasurer
ˌ**T** ˈ**U** Trade Union
ˌ**T U** ˈ**C** (GB) Trades Union Congress
Tues Tuesday
ˌ**T** ˈ**V** television

U Union; Upper; upper class, fashionable,
polite, ⇨ non-U above
ˌ**U D** ˈ**I** unilateral declaration of independence
ˌ**U F** ˈ**O** (*also* /ˈjuːfəʊ/) unidentified flying object
ˌ**U H** ˈ**F** ultra high frequency
ˌ**U** ˈ**K** United Kingdom
ˌ**U** ˈ**N** United Nations
UNCTAD /ˈʌŋktæd/ United Nations Conference
on Trade and Development
UNESCO /juːˈneskəʊ/ United Nations Educational, Scientific and Cultural Organisation

UNICEF /ˈjuːnɪsef/ United Nations Children's
Fund
Univ University
UNO /ˈjuːnəʊ/ United Nations Organisation
UNRWA /ˈʌnwə/ United Nations Relief and
Works Agency
ˌ**U P** ˈ**I** United Press International
ˌ**U** ˈ**S** United States
ˌ**U S** ˈ**A** United States of America; United
States Army
ˌ**U S A** ˈ**F** United States Air Force
ˌ**U S** ˈ**N** United States Navy
ˌ**U S** ˈ**S** United States Ship
ˌ**U S S** ˈ**R** Union of Soviet Socialist Republics

V Roman 5; Victory; Volt
v very; verse; versus; *vide* see, refer to
V & A /ˌviː ən ˈeɪ/ Victoria and Albert
(Museum in London)
vac /væk/ vacation
ˌ**V A** ˈ**T** (*also* /væt/) Value Added Tax,
⇨ value (3)
ˌ**V** ˈ**C** Vice Chairman; Vice Chancellor; Vice
Consul; Victoria Cross; Vietcong
ˌ**V** ˈ**D** Venereal Disease
ˌ**V** ˈ**E Day** Victory in Europe (end of Second
World War in Europe: 8.5.1945)
Ven Venerable
ˌ**V H** ˈ**F** very high frequency
ˌ**V I** ˈ**P** very important person
viz /vɪz/ *videlicet* namely
vol volume
ˌ**V** ˈ**P(res)** Vice-President
vs versus
ˌ**V** ˈ**S** (US) Veterinary Surgeon
ˌ**V S** ˈ**O** (GB) Voluntary Service Overseas

W west
w watt(s); week; width; with
WASP /wɒsp/ (US) White Anglo-Saxon
Protestant
ˌ**w** ˈ**c** water closet, ⇨ water¹(7)
ˌ**W C** ˈ**C** World Council of Churches
ˌ**w e** ˈ**f** with effect from
ˌ**W H** ˈ**O** (*also* /huː/) World Health
Organisation
ˌ**W** ˈ**I** West Indian; West Indies; Women's
Institute
wk week; work
WNW west-northwest
ˌ**W** ˈ**O** Warrant Officer
ˌ**w p** ˈ**b** waste paper basket
ˌ**w p** ˈ**m** words per minute
ˌ**W R A** ˈ**C** Women's Royal Army Corps
ˌ**W R A** ˈ**F** Women's Royal Air Force
ˌ**W R N** ˈ**S** (*also* /renz/) Women's Royal Naval
Service
WSW west-southwest
wt weight

X Roman 10; a kiss; an unknown number,
thing, name, etc
Xmas Christmas

Y Yen (Japanese currency)
ˌ**Y H** ˈ**A** Youth Hostels Association
ˌ**Y M C** ˈ**A** Young Men's Christian Association
yr year; your
ˌ**Y W C** ˈ**A** Young Women's Christian
Association

Appendix 3   AFFIXES

Note: Many affixes have more than one pronunciation form or stress pattern. This often depends on the form of the word to which it is attached. ⇨ the entries in the dictionary for full phonetic transcriptions of the words given as examples in this appendix.

a-[1] /eɪ-, ə-, æ-/ *pref* not, without: *amoral; aseptic; atheist.*

a-[2] /ə-/ *pref* **1** (∼ + *n* = *adv*) in: *abed;* on, at: *afield; ashore.* **2** (∼ + *v* = *adv*) in the state of, in the process of: *asleep; ablaze.* **3** (old use) (∼ + *gerund* = *adv*) in the act of: *a-running; a-singing.*

ab- /æb-, əb-/ *pref* from, away from: *absent; abduct.*

-able (also **-ible**) /-əbl/ *suff* **1** (*n* + ∼ = *adj*) showing qualities of: *fashionable; responsible.* **2** (*v* + ∼ = *adj*) that can be, fit to be: *eatable; reducible.* **-ably, -ibly** /-əblɪ/ *adv*

ad- /-əd-, æd-/ *pref* to, towards: *advance; adjoin.*

-ade /-eɪd, -ɑːd/ *suff* (used to form a *n*): *blockade; lemonade; façade.*

aer(o)- /eər(ə- *etc*)/ *pref* of aircraft: *aerodynamics; aeronaut.*

-age /-ɪdʒ, -ɑːʒ/ *suff* (used to form a *n*): *breakage; postage; sabotage.*

-al /-l, -əl/ *suff* **1** (*n* + ∼ = *adj*): *magical; verbal.* **-ally** /-lɪ, -əlɪ/ *adv* **2** (*v* + ∼ = *n*): *recital; survival; displayal.*

ambi- /æmbɪ- *etc*/ *pref* both, double, two: *ambiguous; ambidextrous.*

an- /æn-, ən-/ *pref* not, without: *anaesthetic; anonymous.*

-an /-ən, -n/ *suff* (*proper n* + ∼ = *n* or *adj*, ⇨ App 6): *Lutheran; Mexican.* ⇨ **-ian** below.

-ana ⇨ **-iana**

-ance (also **-ence**) /-əns, -ns/ *suff* (*v* + ∼ = *n*): *assistance; confidence.*

-ant (also **-ent**) /-ənt, -nt/ *suff* **1** (*v* + ∼ = *adj*): *significant; different.* **2** (*v* + ∼ = *n*): *assistant; deterrent.*

ante- /æntɪ-/ *pref* in front of: *anteroom;* before, previous to: *antenatal.*

anthrop(o)- /ænθrəp(ə- *etc*)/ *pref* of man, of mankind: *anthropoid; anthropology.*

anti-/æntɪ- *US*: æntaɪ-/ *pref* **1** opposed to, against: *anti-social; antiseptic.* **2** instead of: *anti-hero.*

arch- /ɑːk-, ɑːtʃ-/ *pref* first, chief, head: *archetype; archbishop.*

-arian /-eərɪən/ *suff* practiser of: *disciplinarian; vegetarian.*

-ary /-ərɪ, -rɪ *US*: -erɪ/ *suff* **1** (used to form an *adj*): *planetary; reactionary.* **2** (*pl* -aries) (used to form a *n*): *dictionary; functionary.*

astr(o)- /æstr(ə- *etc*)/ *pref* of the stars, of outer space: *astronomy; astronaut.*

-ate *suff* **1** /-ət, -ɪt/ (used to form an *adj*): *affectionate; passionate.* **-ately** /-ətlɪ, -ɪtlɪ/ *adv* **2** /-ət, -ɪt/ (used to form a *n*): *directorate; electorate.* **3** /-eɪt/ (used to form a *v*): *gyrate; stimulate.* **4** /-eɪt/ (chem) salt formed by the action of an acid on a base: *phosphate; nitrate.*

-ation ⇨ **-tion**

-ative /-ətɪv/ *suff* (used to form an *adj*, usu from an '-ate' *v*): *illustrative; quantitative.* **-atively** /-ətɪvlɪ/ *adv*

-ator /-eɪtə(r)/ *suff* object or person carrying out the action of an '-ate' *v*: *percolator; stimulator.*

audio- /ɔːdɪəʊ-/ *pref* of hearing, of sound: *audio-visual; audio-frequency.*

aut(o)- /ɔːt(ə- *etc*)/ *pref* **1** of oneself: *autobiography; autograph.* **2** without help, independent of others: *automatic; autocrat.*

be- /bɪ-/ *pref* **1** (∼ + *v* = *v*) all over, all around, in all directions: *bedeck; bespatter.* **2** (∼ + *n* or *adj* = *v*) make, become: *befriend; belittle.* **3** (∼ + *vi* = *vt*): *bemoan; bewail.*

bi- /baɪ-/ *pref* **1** occurring twice in one period: *bi-monthly; bi-annual.* **2** occurring once in a period of two: *bicentenary; biennial.* **3** having two: *bilingual; biped.*

bibl(i)- /bɪblɪ(ə- *etc*)/ *pref* of books: *bibliography; bibliophile.*

bio- /baɪ(ə- *etc*)/ *pref* of life, of living organisms: *biography; biology; biotic.*

by- (also **bye-**) /baɪ-/ *pref* of secondary importance, incidental: *by-election; bye-law; by-product.*

cent(i)- /sent(ɪ- *etc*)/ *pref* a hundred, a hundredth part: *Centigrade; centimetre.*

chron(o)- /krɒn(ə- *etc*)/ *pref* of time: *chronology; chronometer.*

-cide /-saɪd/ *suff* (used to form a *n*) killing, killer: *suicide; insecticide.*

co- /kəʊ- *etc*/ *pref* together, jointly, equally: *cohabit; co-operate; co-education.*

con- (also **col-, com-, cor-**) /kɒn-, kən-, *etc*/ *pref* with, together: *conduct; collaborate; combine; correlate.*

contra- /kɒntrə-/ *pref* against, opposite to: *contraception; contradict.*

-cracy /-krəsɪ/ *suff* (*pl* -cracies) (used to form a *n*) government or rule by, class characterised by: *democracy; aristocracy.*

-crat /-kræt/ *suff* (used to form a *n*) member or supporter of a '-cracy': *democrat; aristocrat.* **-cratic**/-krætɪk/ *adj*: *democratic; aristocratic.*

-cy (also **-acy**) /-(ə)sɪ/ *suff* (*pl* -(a)cies) (used to form a *n*) condition, quality: *accuracy; infancy; supremacy.*

-d ⇨ **-ed**

de- /diː-, dɪ-/ *pref* (used with a *v*) the negative, reverse, opposite of: *depopulate; defrost; defuse.*

demi- /demɪ-/ *pref* half, partly: *demimonde; demigod.*

di- /daɪ-, dɪ-/ *pref* twice, double: *dilemma; dioxide.*

dia- /daɪə-/ *pref* through, across: *diameter; diagonal; diaphragm.*

dis- /dɪs-/ *pref* (used with a *v*) the negative, reverse, opposite of: *disbelieve; disorder; disagree.*

-dom /-dəm/ *suff* (used to form a *n*) **1** a condition, state: *boredom; freedom.* **2** domain: *kingdom; officialdom.*

-ed (also **-d**) /*After* p, k, ʃ, f, θ, s *pronounced*

1012

-t; *after* t, d *pronounced* -ɪd; *otherwise pronounced* -d. *Exception* 'used', ⇨ use²/ *suff* **1** (used to form *pt* and *pp* of a *v*): *laughed; acted; washed.* **2** (*n*+∼=*adj*) having the characteristics of: *diseased; talented; cracked.*

-ee /-iː/ *suff* (*v*+∼=*n*) **1** person affected by the action of the *v*: *employee; payee.* **2** person acting: *absentee; refugee.* **3** (*n*+∼=*n*) diminutive: *bootee; coatee.*

-eer /-ɪə(r)/ *suff* (*n*+∼=*n*) person concerned with the *n*: *auctioneer; mountaineer.*

electr(o)- /ɪlektr(ə- etc)/ *pref* concerned with, caused by electricity: *electrocute; electromagnet.*

en-, en-/ (also **em-** /ɪm-, em-/ *pref* **1** (∼+*n* or *v*=*v*) put in, on: *encase; endanger; emplane.* **2** (∼+*n* or *adj*=*v*) make into, cause to be: *enlarge; enrich; empower.*

-en /-ən-, -n/ *suff* **1** (used to form the *pp* of some *vv*): *broken; eaten; hidden.* **2** (*n*+∼=*adj*) made of: *golden; wooden.* **3** (*adj*+∼=*v*) make, cause to be: *blacken; sadden.*

-ence ⇨ -ance

-ent ⇨ -ant

equi- /iːkwɪ- etc/ *pref* equal, the same: *equidistant; equivalent.*

-er /-ə(r)/ *suff* **1** (*v*+∼=*n*) person who carries out the action of the *v*: *runner; sleeper.* **2** (*n*+∼=*n*) practiser of: *astronomer; philosopher.* **3** (also -r) (used to form the *comp* of an *adj*): *stronger; rarer; thinner.* ⇨ also -ier.

-ery /-ərɪ, -rɪ/ (also **-ry** /-rɪ/ *suff* (*pl* -eries) (*n* or *v*+∼=*n*) **1** place where an action is carried out: *bakery; fishery.* **2** art of, practice of: *cookery; pottery.* **3** state, quality, character: *rivalry; snobbery.*

-es (also **-s**) /-ɪz/ *suff* **1** (used to form *pl* of a *n* ending in /s, z, ∫, ʒ/): *pieces; judges.* **2** (used to form *3rd pers sing pres t* of a *v* ending in /s, z, ∫, ʒ/): *washes; urges.*

-ese /iːz/ *suff* **1** (proper *n*+∼=*adj*) of a place or a country: *Burmese;* (the *adj* may also be used as a *n*, ⇨ App 6) person or language: *Japanese.* **2** (used to form a *n*) in the (literary) style of: *journalese.*

-esque /-esk/ *suff* (*n*+∼=*adj*) in the manner, style of: *statuesque; picturesque.*

-ess / -ɪs, -es/ *suff* (*n* or *v*+∼=*n*) female: *lioness; actress.*

-est (also **-st**) /-ɪst/ *suff* (used to form the *superl* of an *adj* or *adv*): *fastest; barest; wettest.*

-ette /-et/ *suff* (*n*+∼=*n*) **1** diminutive: *cigarette; kitchenette.* **2** female: *usherette; suffragette.* **3** imitation: *flannelette; leatherette.*

ex- *pref* **1** /ɪks-, eks-, ɪgz-, egz-/ out, out of, from: *exclaim; extract.* **2** /eks-/ former, at one time: *ex-wife; ex-president.*

extra- /ekstrə-/ *pref* **1** outside, beyond: *extramarital; extrasensory.* **2** very: *extra-thin.*

-fic /-fɪk/ *suff* (used with a '-fy' *v* to form an *adj*): *horrific; specific.*

-fied /-faɪd/ ⇨ -fy

-fold /-fəʊld/ *suff* (cardinal numeral+∼=*adj*) **1** multiplied by: *tenfold; hundredfold.* **2** of (so many) parts: *twofold.*

fore- /fɔː(r)-/ *pref* before, in front of: *foretell; foreground.*

-form /-fɔːm/ *suff* (used to form an *adj*) having the shape or character of: *uniform; cuneiform.*

-ful *suff* **1** /-fl/ (*n* or *v*+∼=*adj*) full of, having the quality of: *eventful; peaceful.* **2** /-fʊl/ (*n*+∼=*n*) amount that fills: *handful; mouthful.*

-gamy /-gəmɪ/ *suff* (used to form a *n*) of marriage: *monogamy; polygamy.* **-gamous** /-gəməs/ *adj.*

ge(o)- /dʒiː(ə- etc)/ *pref* (used to form a *n*) of the earth: *geography; geology.*

-gon /-gən, -gɒn/ angle, corner: *polygon; pentagon.*

-gram /-græm/ *suff* (used to form a *n*) sth written down or drawn: *telegram; monogram; diagram.*

-graph /grɑːf US: -græf/ *suff* (used to form a *n*) sth written down, of writing: *autograph; telegraph.* **-graphy** /-grəfɪ/ *n*: *calligraphy; orthography.*

hem(o)- (also **haem(o)-**) /hiːmə-, hemə-/ *pref* of the blood: *hemoglobin; hemorrhage.*

heter(o)- /hetər(ə- etc)/ *pref* the other, the opposite, different: *heterogeneous; heterosexual.*

hom(o)- /hɒm(ə- etc), həʊm-/ *pref* the same: *homogeneous; homosexual.*

-hood /-hʊd/ *suff* (*n*+∼=*n*) status, rank, condition of life: *boyhood; brotherhood.*

hydr(o)- /haɪdr(ə- etc)/ *pref* of water: *hydrant; hydro-electric.*

hyper- /haɪpə(r)-/ *pref* to a large or extreme degree: *hypercritical; hypersensitive.*

-ial /-ɪəl, -l/ *suff* (*n*+∼=*adj*) characteristic of: *dictatorial; palatial.* **-ially** /-ɪəlɪ, - l/ *adv*

-ian /-ɪən, -n/ *suff* **1** (proper *n*+∼=*n* or *adj*, ⇨ App 6): *Brazilian; Shakespearian.* **2** (used with an '-ics' *n* to form a *n* ending in -cian /-∫n/) specialist in: *optician; pediatrician.*

-(i)ana /-(ɪ)ɑːnə/ *suff* (used with words ending in '-ian' or '-an' to form a *collective n*) collection of facts, objects, etc relating to: *Victoriana; Africana.*

-ible ⇨ -able

-ic /-ɪk/ *suff* (*n*+∼=*adj*): *poetic; romantic.* **-ical** /-ɪkl/ *adj* **-ically** /-ɪklɪ/ *adv*

-ics /-ɪks/ *suff* (used to form a *n*) science or specific activity: *physics; politics; athletics.*

-ide /-aɪd/ *suff* (used to form a *n*) (chem) chemical compound: *chloride; sulphide.*

-ie ⇨ -y

-ier ⇨ -y

-ies ⇨ -y

-(i)fy /-(ɪ)faɪ/ *suff* (*pt* and *pp* -(i)fied /-(ɪ)faɪd/) (*n* or *adj*+∼=*v*) make into, cause to be, bring to a state of: *beautify; terrify; solidify.*

in- (also **il-, im-, ir-**) /ɪn-, ɪl-, ɪm-, ɪr-/ *pref* **1** (∼+*v*=*v* or *n*) in, on: *intake; imprint.* **1** (∼+*adj*=*adj*) not: *infinite; illicit; immoral; irrelevant.*

-ing /-ɪŋ/ *suff* (*v*+∼=*pres p* and *gerund*): *talking; thinking.*

inter- /ɪntə(r)-/ *pref* between, from one to another: *international; interplanetary.*

intra- (also **intro-**) /ɪntrə-/ *pref* inside: *intravenous; intra-uterine; introspection.*

-ise ⇨ -ize

-ish /-ɪ∫/ *suff* **1** (national name+∼=*adj*, ⇨ App 6): *Irish; Spanish.* **2** (*n*+∼=*adj*) resembling, in the manner of: *childish; devilish.* **3** (*adj*+∼=*adj*) somewhat, near to: *reddish; twentyish.*

-ism /-ɪzəm/ *suff* (used to form a *n*) **1** showing qualities typical of: *Americanism; heroism.* **2** specific doctrine, principle or movement: *Buddhism; Communism.*

-ist /-ɪst/ *suff* (*n* + ∼ = *n*) **1** agent of an '-ize' *v*: *dramatist; publicist.* **2** follower, practiser of an '-ism': *industrialist; fascist.* **3** person concerned with a specific activity or thing: *tobacconist; motorist.*

-ite /-aɪt/ *suff* **1** (*proper n* + ∼ = *n*) follower, devotee of a person or organisation: *Labourite.* **2** (chem) specific chemical substance: *anthracite; dynamite.*

-ities ⇨ -ity

-ition ⇨ -tion

-itis /-aɪtɪs/ *suff* (med) (used to form a *n*) inflammation of: *appendicitis; tonsillitis.*

-ity /-ɪtɪ/ *suff* (*pl* -ities) (used with an *adj* to form a *n*): *crudity; oddity.*

-ive /-ɪv/ *suff* (*v* + ∼ = *adj*) having a tendency towards, quality of: *active; constructive.*

-ize (also -**ise**, which is not used in this dictionary, but is equally acceptable) /-aɪz/ *suff* (used to form a *v*) **1** cause to be, make like, change into: *computerize; dramatize.* **2** act with the qualities of: *criticize; deputize.*

-less /-lɪs/ *suff* (*n* + ∼ = *adj*) without: *treeless; spiritless.* -**lessly** /-lɪslɪ/ *adv* -**lessness** /-lɪsnɪs/ *n*

-let /-lɪt/ *suff* (*n* + ∼ = *n*) diminutive: *piglet; booklet.*

-like /-laɪk/ *suff* (*n* + ∼ = *adj*) resembling, in the manner of a *n*: *childlike; godlike.*

-ling /-lɪŋ/ *suff* **1** (used to form a *n*) diminutive: *duckling; fledgeling.* **2** (used to form a *n*) person connected with (often used disparagingly): *hireling; underling.*

-logue /-lɒg *US:* -lɔːg/ *suff* (used to form a *n*) sth spoken: *dialogue; travelogue; monologue.*

-logy /-lədʒɪ/ *suff* (*pl* -logies) (used to form a *n*) branch of learning: *biology; sociology.*

-ly /-lɪ/ *suff* **1** (*n* + ∼ = *adj*) having the qualities of: *cowardly; scholarly.* **2** (*n* + ∼ = *adj* or *adv*) regular occurrence: *hourly; yearly.* **3** (*adj* + ∼ = *adv*) in the manner of the *adj*: *happily; stupidly.*

macro- /mækrə(ʊ)-/ *pref* relatively large, extending: *macrocosm; macrobiotic.*

mal- /mæl-/ *pref* bad, wrong, not: *maladjusted; malnutrition.*

-man *suff* **1** /-mən/ (used to form a *n*) dweller in: *Irishman; countryman.* **2** /-mən, -mæn/ (*n* + ∼ = *n*) sb connected by a specific activity to: *guardsman; doorman; businessman.*

-mania /-meɪnɪə/ *suff* (used to form a *n*) abnormal behaviour, excessive enthusiasm: *kleptomania; bibliomania.* -**maniac** /-meɪnɪæk/ sb affected by a '-mania': *kleptomaniac.*

matri- /meɪtrɪ-, mætrɪ-/ *pref* mother: *matriarch; matricide.*

mega- /megə-/ *pref* **1** large: *megalith.* **2** one million: *megaton.*

-ment /-mənt/ *suff* (*v* + ∼ = *n*) result or means of an action: *development; government.* -**mental** *adj* -**mentally** *adv*: *governmental(ly).*

-meter /-mɪtə(r)/ *suff* (used to form a *n*) a means of measuring: *speedometer.*

-metre /-miːtə(r)/ *suff* (used to form a *n*) a (specified) part of a metre: *centimetre.*

micro- /maɪkr(ə- *etc*)/ *pref* **1** relatively small: *microfilm; microwave.* **2** of examining or reproducing small quantities: *microscope; microphone.*

milli- /mɪlɪ-/ *pref* a thousandth part of: *milligram; millimetre.*

mis- /mɪs-/ *pref* bad, wrong, not: *misconduct; misdirect; mistrust.*

-monger /-mʌŋgə(r)/ *suff* (used to form a *n*) sb who deals in: *fishmonger; scandalmonger.*

mono- /mɒn(ə- *etc*)/ *pref* one, a single: *monosyllable; monotone.*

-most /-məʊst/ *suff* (*prep* or *adj* of position + ∼ = *superl adj*): *inmost; outermost.*

multi- /mʌltɪ-/ *pref* many: *multistage; multi-coloured.*

neo- /niː(ə- *etc*)/ *pref* new, revived, later: *neologism; neo-classical.*

-ness /-nɪs/ *suff* (*adj* + ∼ = *n*) a quality, state, character: *dryness; silliness.*

neur(o)- /njʊər(ə- *etc US:* nʊə-/ *pref* of the nervous system: *neuralgia; neurology.*

non- /nɒn-/ *pref* not: *nonsense; non-stop.*

-oid /-ɔɪd/ *suff* (used to form an *adj* or *n*) resembling in shape: *asteroid; rhomboid.*

-or /-ə(r), ɔː(r)/ *suff* (*v* + ∼ = *n*) sb or sth that carries out the action of the *v*: *governor; elevator; lessor.*

-ories ⇨ -ory

ortho- /ɔːθ(ə- *etc*)/ *pref* correct, standard: *orthodox; orthopaedic.*

-ory /-ərɪ, -rɪ *US:* -ɔːrɪ/ *suff* (*pl* -ories) **1** (used to form a *n*) place where specific activity is carried on: *laboratory; observatory.* **2** (used to form an *adj*): *compulsory; illusory.*

-osis /-əʊsɪs *etc*/ *suff* (used to form a *n*) a process, change: *hypnosis; metamorphosis.*

-ous /-əs/ *suff* (*n* + ∼ = *adj*) having the qualities of: *poisonous; zealous.* -**ously** /-əslɪ/ *adv* -**ousness** /-əsnɪs/ *n*

out- /aʊt-/ *pref* **1** located outside: *outhouse; outpost.* **2** surpassing, to a greater extent: *outnumber; outmanoeuvre.* **3** with the various senses of 'out' as defined in the dictionary: *outcry; outspoken.*

over- /əʊvə(r)-/ *pref* **1** across, above: *overland; overhead.* **2** to excess, too much: *overcharge; overwork.* **3** with the various senses of 'over' as defined in the dictionary: *overthrow; overpower.*

pale(o)- (also **palae(o)-** /pælɪ(ə- *etc*)/ *pref* of ancient times: *paleolithic; paleontology.*

pan- /pæn-/ *pref* all, throughout: *panchromatic; Pan-African.*

patri- /peɪtrɪ-, pætrɪ-/ *pref* father: *patriarch; patricide.*

-philia /-fɪlɪə/ *suff* (used to form a *n*) excessive love of: *Anglophilia; bibliophilia.* -**phile** /-faɪl/ *n* lover of.

-phobia /-fəʊbɪə/ *suff* (used to form a *n*) excessive fear of: *claustrophobia; xenophobia.* -**phobic** *adj* -**phobe** *n* fearer of.

-phone /-fəʊn/ *suff* (used to form a *n*) means of reproducing sound: *megaphone; telephone.* -**phonic** /-fɒnɪk/ *adj*: *stereophonic.*

phon(o)- /fə(ʊ)n(ə- *etc*)/ *pref* of sound: *phonetic; phonology.*

photo- /fəʊt(ə- *etc*)/ *pref* **1** of light: *photo-electric.* **2** of photography: *photocopy; photogenic.*

physi(o)- /fɪzɪ(ə- *etc*)/ *pref* of the body, of living things: *physiotherapy; physiology.*

poly- /pɒlɪ- *etc*/ *pref* many: *polygamy; polysyllabic.*

post- /pəʊst- *etc*/ *pref* after: *postscript; posthumous; post-graduate.*

pre- /priː- *etc*/ *pref* before: *prefabricate; premature; pre-recorded.*

pro- /prəʊ-/ *pref* **1** supporting, in favour of: *pro-Chinese; pro-revolutionary.* **2** acting as: *pro-Vice-Chancellor.*

proto- /prəʊt(ə- *etc*)/ *pref* first, original, basic: *prototype; protoplasm.*

pseud(o)- /sjuːd(ə- *etc*) US: suː-/ *pref* false, fake: *pseudonym; pseudo-intellectual.*

psych(o)- /saɪk(ə- *etc*)/ *pref* of the mind: *psychiatry; psycho-analysis.*

quasi- /kweɪsaɪ-/ *pref* almost, seemingly: *quasi-serious; quasi-explanation.*

re- /riː- *etc*/ *pref* again: *re-echo; reinstate.*

retro- /retr(ə- *etc*)/ *pref* backwards, behind: *retrospective; retro-rocket.*

-ry ⇨ -ery

-s /*After* p, t, k, f, θ *pronounced* s; *otherwise* z/ *suff* **1** (used to form the *pl* of a *n*): *pots; stars.* **2** (used to form *3rd pers sing pres t* of a *v*): *breaks; sees.*

-scape /-skeɪp/ *suff* (*n* + ∼ = *n*) a stretch of scenery: *landscape; moonscape.*

-scope /-skəʊp/ *suff* (used to form a *n*) means of observing or showing: *microscope; stroboscope.*

self- /self-/ *pref* of one's self, alone, independent: *self-taught; self-service.*

semi- /semɪ- US: semaɪ-/ *pref* half, partially, midway: *semi-circular; semi-detached; semi-final.*

-ship /-ʃɪp/ *suff* (*n* + ∼ = *n*) **1** state of being, status, office: *friendship; ownership; professorship.* **2** skill, proficiency as: *musicianship; scholarship.*

-sion ⇨ -tion

soci(o)- /səʊsɪ(ə- *etc*)/ *pref* of society: *sociology; socio-economic.*

-some /-səm/ *suff* (used to form an *adj*) likely to, productive of: *quarrelsome; meddlesome.*

-sphere /-sfɪə(r)/ *suff* (used to form a *n*) spherical, of a sphere: *hemisphere; atmosphere.*

-ster /-stə(r)/ *suff* **1** (*n* + ∼ = *n*) sb connected with the *n*: *songster; gangster.* **2** (*adj* + *n* = *n*) sb with the qualities of the *adj*: *youngster.*

sub- /sʌb- *etc*/ *pref* **1** under: *subway; subsoil.* **2** secondary, lower in rank: *sub-committee; sub-species.* **3** not quite: *sub-tropical; subnormal.* **4** (used with a *v*) secondary repetition: *sublet; subdivide.*

super- /suːpə(r)-/ *pref* **1** above, over: *superstructure; superimpose.* **2** superior to, more than: *superhuman; supernatural.*

sym- (also **syn-**) /sɪm-, sɪn- *etc*/ *pref* sharing with, together: *sympathy; synchronize.*

-t /-t/ *suff* (used to form the *pt* and *pp* of some *vv*): *burnt; lent; slept.*

techn(o)- /tekn(ɒ- *etc*)/ *pref* of applied science: *technocracy; technology.*

tele- /telɪ- *etc*/ *pref* of linking across distances: *telepathy; television.*

theo- /θiː(ɒ- *etc*)/ *pref* of God: *theocracy; theology.*

thermo- /θɜːm(ə- *etc*)/ *pref* of heat, of temperature: *thermostat; thermometer.*

-tion /-ʃn/ (also **-sion** /-ʃn, -ʒn/; **-ation** /-eɪʃn/; **-ition** /-ɪʃn/) *suff* (*v* + ∼ = *n*): *relation; confession; adhesion; hesitation; competition.* **-tional** /-ʃənl/ *adj* **-tionally** /-ʃnəlɪ/ *adv*

trans- /trænz- *etc*/ *pref* **1** across: *transatlantic; trans-continental.* **2** to a changed state: *transplant; transform.*

tri- /traɪ- *etc*/ *pref* three: *triangle; tricolour.*

-tude /-tjuːd US: -tuːd/ *suff* (used to form a *n*) condition: *magnitude; exactitude.*

-ule /-juːl/ *suff* (used to form a *n*) relative smallness: *capsule; globule.*

ultra- /ʌltrə-/ *pref* beyond, to excess: *ultraviolet; ultra-liberal.*

un- /ʌn-/ *pref* **1** (used with an *adj* or *n*) not: *unable; untruth.* **2** (used with a *v*) negative, reverse, opposite of: *uncover; unpack.*

under- /ʌndə(r)-/ *pref* **1** located beneath: *undercurrent; undergrowth.* **2** not enough: *underestimate; undersized.* **3** lower in rank, importance: *undersecretary; understudy.*

uni- /juːnɪ-/ *pref* one, the same: *uniform; unisex.*

up- /ʌp-/ *pref* to a higher or better state: *uphill; upgrade.*

-ure /-jʊə(r), -jə(r) *etc*/ *suff* (used to form a *n*) act, process, condition: *closure; legislature.*

vice- /vaɪs-/ *pref* sb who is next in rank to and may act for another: *vice-consul; vice-president.*

-ward /-wəd/ *suff* (used to form an *adj* or *adv*) in the direction of: *backward; eastward; homeward.* **-wards** /-wədz/ *adv*

well- /wel-/ *pref* (∼ + *pp* of a *v* = *adj*) **1** fortunately: *well-born.* **2** properly, thoroughly: *well-informed; well-worn.*

-wise /-waɪz/ *suff* (*n* or *adj* + ∼ = *adv*) **1** in the manner of: *crosswise; crabwise.* **2** (colloq) in connection with: *disciplinewise; accommodationwise.*

-worth /-wɜːθ, -wəθ/ *suff* (used to form a *n*) using the amount of: *poundsworth; daysworth.*

-worthy /-wɜːðɪ/ *suff* (*n* + ∼ = *adj*) deserving of: *praiseworthy; blameworthy.* **-worthily** *adv*

-y¹ (also **-ey**) /-ɪ/ *suff* (*n* + ∼ = *adj*): *dusty; bushy; clayey.* **-ier** /ɪə(r)/ *comp* **-iest** /-ɪɪst/ *superl* **-ily** /-ɪlɪ/ *adv*.

-y² (also **-ie**) /-ɪ/ *suff* (*n* + ∼ = *n*) pet name or familiar name: *piggy; doggie; daddy; Susie.* ⇨ also App 7.

Appendix 4 NUMERICAL EXPRESSIONS

The following section will give you help in the reading, speaking and writing of numbers and expressions which commonly contain numbers.

1 Numbers

Note. 'a /ə/ hundred' is a less formal usage than 'one /wʌn/ hundred'.

CARDINAL

1 one /wʌn/
2 two /tuː/
3 three /θriː/
4 four /fɔː(r)/
5 five /faɪv/
6 six /sɪks/
7 seven /'sevn/
8 eight /eɪt/
9 nine /naɪn/
10 ten /ten/
11 eleven /ɪ'levn/
12 twelve /twelv/
13 thirteen /ˌθɜː'tiːn/
14 fourteen /ˌfɔː'tiːn/
15 fifteen /ˌfɪf'tiːn/
16 sixteen /ˌsɪk'stiːn/
17 seventeen /ˌsevn'tiːn/
18 eighteen /ˌeɪ'tiːn/
19 nineteen /ˌnaɪn'tiːn/
20 twenty /'twentɪ/
21 twenty-one /ˌtwentɪ'wʌn/
22 twenty-two /ˌtwentɪ'tuː/
23 twenty-three /ˌtwentɪ'θriː/
30 thirty /'θɜːtɪ/
38 thirty-eight /ˌθɜːtɪ'eɪt/
40 forty /'fɔːtɪ/
50 fifty /'fɪftɪ/
60 sixty /'sɪkstɪ/
70 seventy /'sevntɪ/
80 eighty /'eɪtɪ/
90 ninety /'naɪntɪ/
100 a/one hundred /ə, wʌn 'hʌndrəd/
1000 a/one thousand /ə, wʌn 'θaʊznd/
10 000 ten thousand /ˌten 'θaʊznd/
100 000 a/one hundred thousand
/ə, wʌn ˌhʌndrəd 'θaʊznd/
1 000 000 a/one million
/ə, wʌn 'mɪlɪən/

ORDINAL

1st first /fɜːst/
2nd second /'sekənd/
3rd third /θɜːd/
4th fourth /fɔːθ/
5th fifth /fɪfθ/
6th sixth /sɪksθ/
7th seventh /'sevnθ/
8th eighth /eɪtθ/
9th ninth /naɪnθ/
10th tenth /tenθ/
11th eleventh /ɪ'levnθ/
12th twelfth /twelfθ/
13th thirteenth /ˌθɜː'tiːnθ/
14th fourteenth /ˌfɔː'tiːnθ/
15th fifteenth /ˌfɪf'tiːnθ/
16th sixteenth /ˌsɪk'stiːnθ/
17th seventeenth /ˌsevn'tiːnθ/
18th eighteenth /ˌeɪ'tiːnθ/
19th nineteenth /ˌnaɪn'tiːnθ/
20th twentieth /'twentɪəθ/
21st twenty-first /ˌtwentɪ'fɜːst/
22nd twenty-second /ˌtwentɪ'sekənd/
23rd twenty-third /ˌtwentɪ'θɜːd/
30th thirtieth /'θɜːtɪəθ/
38th thirty-eighth /ˌθɜːtɪ'eɪtθ/
40th fortieth /'fɔːtɪəθ/
50th fiftieth /'fɪftɪəθ/
60th sixtieth /'sɪkstɪəθ/
70th seventieth /'sevntɪəθ/
80th eightieth /'eɪtɪəθ/
90th ninetieth /'naɪntɪəθ/
100th a/one hundredth /ə, wʌn 'hʌndrədθ/
1000th a/one thousandth /ə, wʌn 'θaʊzndθ/
10 000th ten thousandth /ˌten 'θaʊzndθ/
100 000th a/one hundred thousandth
/ə, wʌn ˌhʌndrəd 'θaʊzndθ/
1 000 000th a/one millionth
/ə, wʌn 'mɪlɪənθ/

SOME MORE COMPLEX NUMBERS

101 a/one hundred and one /ə, wʌn ˌhʌndrəd n 'wʌn/
152 a/one hundred and fifty-two /ə, wʌn ˌhʌndrəd n ˌfɪftɪ 'tuː/
1 001 a/one thousand and one /ə, wʌn 'θaʊznd ən 'wʌn/
2 325 two thousand, three hundred and twenty-five /ˌtuː 'θaʊznd, ˌθriː hʌndrəd n ˌtwentɪ 'faɪv/
15 972 fifteen thousand, nine hundred and seventy-two /ˌfɪftiːn 'θaʊznd, ˌnaɪn hʌndrəd n ˌsevntɪ 'tuː/
234 753 two hundred and thirty-four thousand, seven hundred and fifty-three /ˌtuː ˌhʌndrəd n ˌθɜːtɪ fɔː: 'θaʊznd, ˌsevn ˌhʌndrəd n ˌfɪftɪ 'θriː/

		US	GB and other European countries
1 000 000 000	10⁹	a/one billion /ə, wʌn 'bɪlɪən/	a/one thousand million(s) /ə, wʌn 'θaʊznd 'mɪlɪən(z)/
1 000 000 000 000	10¹²	a/one trillion /ə, wʌn 'trɪlɪən/	a/one billion /ə, wʌn 'bɪlɪən/
1 000 000 000 000 000	10¹⁵	a/one quadrillion /ə, wʌn kwɒ'drɪlɪən/	a/one thousand billion(s) /ə, wʌn 'θaʊznd 'bɪlɪən(z)/
1 000 000 000 000 000 000	10¹⁸	a/one quintillion /ə, wʌn kwɪn'tɪlɪən/	a/one trillion /ə, wʌn 'trɪlɪən/

VULGAR FRACTIONS

⅛ an/one eighth /ən, wʌn 'eɪtθ/
¼ a/one quarter /ə, wʌn 'kwɔːtə(r)/

DECIMAL FRACTIONS

0·125 (nought) point one two five /(ˌnɔːt) pɔɪnt ˌwʌn tu: 'faɪv/
0·25 (nought) point two five /(ˌnɔːt) pɔɪnt ˌtuː: 'faɪv/

⅓ a/one third /ə, wʌn 'θɜːd/   0·33 (ˌnought) point ˌthree 'three
½ a/one half /ə, wʌn 'hɑːf *US:* 'hæf/ 0·5 (ˌnought) point 'five
¾ three quarters /ˌθriː 'kwɔːtəz/   0·75 (ˌnought) point ˌseven 'five

Notes. 1 In the spoken forms of vulgar fractions, the versions 'and a half/quarter/third' are preferred to 'and one half/quarter/third' whether the measurement is approximate or precise. With more obviously precise fractions like ⅛, 1/16, 'and one eighth/sixteenth' is normal. Complex fractions like 3/462, 20/83 are spoken as 'three over four-six-two; twenty over eighty-three', especially in mathematical expressions, e g 'twenty-two over seven' for 22/7.

2 When speaking ordinary numbers we can use 'zero', 'nought' or 'oh' /əʊ/ for the number 0; 'zero' is the most common US usage and the most technical or precise form, 'oh' is the least technical or precise. In using decimals, to say 'nought point five' for 0·5 is a more precise usage than 'point five'.

3 In most continental European countries a comma is used in place of the GB/US decimal point. Thus 6·014 is written 6,014 in France. A space is used to separate off the thousands in numbers larger than 9999, e g 10 000 or 875 380. GB/US usage can also have a comma in this place, e g 7,500,000. This comma is replaced by a full point in continental European countries, e g 7.500.000. Thus 23,500·75 (GB/US) will be written 23.500,75 in France.

COLLECTIVE NUMBERS

6	a half dozen/half a dozen	144	a/one gross /grəʊs/
12	a/one dozen (24 is two dozen *not* two dozens)		three score years and ten (Biblical) = 70 years,
20	a/one score		the traditional average life-span of man.

ROMAN		ARABIC	ROMAN		ARABIC	ROMAN	ARABIC	ROMAN	ARABIC
I	i	1	XVI	xvi	16	LX	60	DCC	700
II	ii	2	XVII	xvii	17	LXV	65	DCCC	800
III	iii	3	XVIII	xviii	18	LXX	70	CM	900
IV (IIII)	iv (iiii)	4	XIX	xix	19	LXXX	80	M	1000
V	v	5	XX	xx	20	XC	90	MC	1100
VI	vi	6	XXI	xxi	21	XCII	92	MCD	1400
VII	vii	7	XXV	xxv	25	XCV	95	MDC	1600
VIII	viii	8	XXIX	xxix	29	XCVIII	98	MDCLXVI	1666
IX	ix	9	XXX	xxx	30	IC	99	MDCCCLXXXVIII	
X	x	10	XXXI		31	C	100		1888
XI	xi	11	XXXIV		34	CC	200	MDCCCXCIX	1899
XII	xii	12	XXXIX		39	CCC	300	MCM	1900
XIII	xiii	13	XL		40	CD	400	MCMLXXVI	1976
XIV	xiv	14	L		50	D	500	MCMLXXXIV	1984
XV	xv	15	LV		55	DC	600	MM	2000

A letter placed after another letter of greater value adds, e g VI = 5+1 = 6. A letter placed before a letter of greater value subtracts, e g IV = 5−1 = 4. A dash placed over a letter multiplies the value by 1 000; thus X̄ = 10 000 and M̄ = 1 000 000. The alternative IIII is seen only on some clock faces (⇨ the illus at dial), and iiii is seen only in the preliminary pages of some books.

2 Mathematical Expressions

Below are some of the more common symbols and expressions used in mathematics, geometry and statistics; in the cases where alternative ways of saying the expressions are given, both are equally common but generally the first is more formal or technical and the second less formal or technical.

+ plus/and
− minus/take away
± plus or minus/approximately
× (is) multiplied by/times (*or when giving dimensions* by)
÷ (is) divided by
= is equal to/equals
≠ is not equal to/does not equal
≃ is approximately equal to
≡ is equivalent to/is identical with
< is less than
≮ is not less than
≤ is less than or equal to
> is more than
≯ is not more than
≥ is more than or equal to
% per cent
∞ infinity

∝ varies as/is proportional to
3:9::4:12 three is to nine, as four is to twelve, ⇨ proportion (5)
ε is an element of (a set)
∉ is not an element of (a set)
∅ *or* { } is an empty set
∩ intersection
∪ union
c is a subset of
⇒ implies
$\log_e$ natural logarithm *or* logarithm to the base e /iː/
√ (square) root
∛ cube root
x^2 x /eks/ squared
x^3 x /eks/ cubed
x^4 x /eks/ to the power four/to the fourth

π pi /paɪ/
r /ɑː(r)/ = radius of circle
πr^2 pi r squared /ˌpaɪ ɑː 'skweəd/ (formula for area of circle)
n! n /en/ factorial
∫ the integral of
∠ angle
∟ right angle
△ triangle
‖ is parallel to
⊥ is perpendicular to
° degree, ⇨ degree(1)
′ minute (of an arc), ⇨ minute[1](2); foot *or* feet (unit of length)
″ second (of an arc), ⇨ second[3](1); inch *or* inches (unit of length)

THE GREEK ALPHABET
Many letters of the Greek alphabet are commonly used in statistics and other branches of mathematics. Here is a complete list of the letters:

capitals	small letters	name		capitals	small letters	name
A	α	alpha /'ælfə/		N	ν	nu /nju: *US:* nu:/
B	β	beta /'bi:tə *US:* 'beɪtə/		Ξ	ξ	xi /ksaɪ/
Γ	γ	gamma /'gæmə/		O	o	omicron /əʊ'maɪkrən *US:* 'ɒmɪkrɒn/
Δ	δ	delta /'deltə/		Π	π	pi /paɪ/
E	ε	epsilon /ep'saɪlən *US:* 'epsɪlɒn/		P	ρ	rho /rəʊ/
Z	ζ	zeta /'zi:tə *US:* 'zeɪtə/		Σ	σ, ς	sigma /'sɪgmə/
H	η	eta /'i:tə *US:* 'eɪtə/		T	τ	tau /taʊ/
Θ	θ	theta /'θi:tə *US:* 'θeɪtə/		Y	υ	upsilon /ju:p'saɪlən *US:* 'ju:psɪlɒn/
I	ι	iota /aɪ'əʊtə/		Φ	φ	phi /faɪ/
K	κ	kappa /'kæpə/		X	χ	chi /kaɪ/
Λ	λ	lambda /'læmdə/		Ψ	ψ	psi /psaɪ/
M	μ	mu /mju:/		Ω	ω	omega /'əʊmɪgə *US:* əʊ'megə/

3 Computer Numbers

Cheque books, business accounts, etc have long strings of numerals. If such a number has to be read aloud, the numerals are spoken as separate digits (1–9, 0 = /əʊ/) grouped rhythmically into pairs. Doubled numerals may be read separately or as e g 'double six'. For example, '05216472' is ˌoh ˌfive/ˌtwo ˌone/ˌsix ˌfour/ˌseven 'two. As mentioned earlier, 0 can also be read as 'zero' (formal) or 'nought' (informal). ⇨ also binary.

4 Measurements (Inanimate)

Traditionally GB and US measurements have been made in inches, feet, yards, miles, etc, but there is now a gradual move towards the metric system of millimetres, metres, kilometres, etc. Examples of both are given below. (For tables of weight, measurement, etc and conversion tables, ⇨ App 5.) Even if the move towards metrication is completed in the near future, there will remain a vast amount of literature in which the other units are used.

in	inch(es)	sq in	square inch(es)	cu in	cubic inch(es)
ft	foot/feet	sq ft	square foot/feet	cu ft	cubic foot/feet
yd	yard(s)	sq yd	square yard(s)	cu yd	cubic yard(s)
—	mile(s)	—	square mile(s)	—	—
mm	millimetre(s)	mm²	square millimetre(s)	mm³	cubic millimetre(s)
cm	centimetre(s)	cm²	square centimetre(s)	cm³, cc	cubic centimetre(s)
m	metre(s)	m²	square metre(s)	m³	cubic metre(s)
km	kilometre(s)	km²	square kilometre(s)	—	—

(⇨ square¹(4) for the difference between e g 'four square feet' and 'four feet square')

DISTANCE
London to New York is three thousand, four hundred and forty-one miles. (3 441 miles)
London to New York is five thousand, five hundred and six kilometres. (5 506 km)
There is a speed limit of thirty miles per/an hour. (30 mph)
There is a speed limit of fifty kilometres per/an hour. (50 kph)
That ship has a top speed of fifteen knots. (1 knot = 1 nautical mile per hour)

HEIGHT/DEPTH
Mount Everest is twenty-nine thousand and twenty-eight feet high. (29 028 ft)
Mount Everest is eight thousand, eight hundred and forty-eight metres high. (8 848 m)
The airliner is flying at a height/an altitude of twenty thousand feet. (20 000 ft)
The airliner is flying at a height/an altitude of six thousand metres. (6 000 m)
The sea's average depth is twelve thousand feet or two and half miles. (12 000 ft)
The sea's average depth is three thousand seven hundred metres. (3 700 m)

DIMENSION
This room is sixteen foot/feet (wide) by twenty-five (foot/feet) (long). (16ft × 25ft or 16′ × 25′)
This room is three metres (wide) by eight and half (metres) (long). (3m × 8·5m)

AREA
We need five thousand square foot/feet of office space. (5 000 sq ft)
We need six hundred square metres of office space. (600 sq m)
Scotland has an area of thirty thousand, four hundred and five square miles. (30 405 sq miles) ⇨ square¹(4)
Scotland has an area of seventy-six thousand, two hundred and thirty-five square kilometres. (76 235 sq km)
The house is for sale with ten acres of grounds.
The house is for sale with four hectares of grounds.

VOLUME
You'll need thirty (cubic) feet/foot of sand to mix with the cement. (30 cu ft) ⇨ cubic
You'll need a (cubic) metre of sand to mix with the cement. (1 m³)

TEMPERATURE

The ordinary GB temperature scale for everyday use has been Fahrenheit. With metrication, the use of Centigrade (which has long been common in scientific usage) is becoming widespread.

FAHRENHEIT	CENTIGRADE
Water freezes at thirty-two degrees Fahrenheit. (32°F)	*Water freezes at nought degrees Centigrade.* (0°C)
Last night we had nine degrees of frost. (23°F)	*Last night the temperature was five degrees below zero.* (−5°C)
It was ninety-five in the shade this morning. (95°F)	*It was thirty-five in the shade this morning.* (35°C)

ATHLETICS

He holds the record for the fifteen hundred metres (colloq *'the metric mile').* (1 500 m)
She ran for her country in the two hundred metres women's hurdles. (200 m)
Our team was narrowly beaten in the four by four hundred metres relay. (4×400 m)
Our captain won the high jump with a jump of two point oh five metres (2·05 m), *and threw the javelin a national record of eighty-three point four four metres* (83·44 m).

SWIMMING

I swam for Britain in the eight hundred metres freestyle. (800 m)
She came second in the women's hundred metres back-stroke. (100 m)

5 Measurements (Human)

HEIGHT, ETC

i Note that 'tall', not 'high', is used. Feet and inches are used, or metres and centimetres if the metric system is employed.

My wife is five foot/feet six (inches) (tall). (5ft 6in/5'6″)	*My wife is one metre sixty-eight (centimetres) (tall).* (1m 68cm/1·68m)

ii Measurements round parts of the body are in inches or centimetres:

She is 36–24–36. (i e 36 inches round the bust, 24 round the waist, 36 round the hips)	*She is 91–61–91.* (i e 91 centimetres round the bust, 61 round the waist, 91 round the hips)

6 Time of Day

Note. When times are quoted, specified precisely or 'read' from a digital clock, the second form given below is more common.

GB

7.00 seven o'clock/a m/p m /əˈklɒk, ˌeɪˈem, ˌpiːˈem/
8.15 a quarter past eight/eight fifteen
9.45 a quarter to ten/nine forty-five
4.30 half past four/four thirty/(colloq) half four
5.10 ten (minutes) past five/five ten
6.25 twenty-five (minutes) past six/ six twenty-five
6.35 twenty-five (minutes) to seven/ six thirty-five
9.57 three minutes to ten/nine fifty-seven
2.03 three minutes past two/two oh three

TENNIS

Smith won the first set six four/by six games to four (6–4). *The scoring in the final game was:* *fifteen love* (15–0), *fifteen all* (15–15), *thirty fifteen* (30–15), *forty fifteen* (40–15), *forty thirty* (40–30), *deuce* (40–40), *advantage Smith, game to Smith. Smith went on to win the match by three sets to two* (3–2).

ASSOCIATION FOOTBALL (SOCCER)

In the first leg the half-time score was one all (1–1). *In the second half only Italy scored and won the match two one/by two goals to one* (2–1). *The full time score in the return match was nil all/a goalless draw/a no goal draw* (0–0), *but Brazil scored two magnificent goals in extra time to win the Cup two nil* (2–0).

RUGBY FOOTBALL (RUGGER)

Wales beat Scotland sixteen six/by sixteen points to six (16–6). *For Wales, Owen scored two tries* (8 points), *Price converted one* (2 points), *and kicked two penalty goals* (6 points). *Scotland's score came from a penalty* (3 points) *and a dropped goal* (3 points), *both kicked by Frazer.*

HORSE-RACING

The Derby is run over a distance of twelve furlongs/one mile four furlongs/one and a half miles/a mile and a half. (12 fur $= 1\frac{1}{2}$ miles)
The favourite in the Grand National was Never Say Die *at five to two.* (5–2, *betting stake; The odds on* Never Say Die *were five to two.*)

WEIGHT

In GB weight has traditionally been given in stones and pounds, and in the US in pounds only. The metric system uses kilos/kilograms.

I weigh twelve stone eleven (pounds)/a hundred and seventy-nine pounds. (12st 11lb/179lb)	*I weigh eighty-one kilos* (81 kg).

AGE

I have three children. The eldest is nine (years old), the middle one is five and a half and the youngest is four. I'm thirty-three. How old are you?

US

The system used is similar to that used in GB except that *after* is usual where GB has *past*:

5.10 ten after five
5.15 a quarter after five
9.30 'nine thirty' is more usual than 'half past nine'

of is common where GB has *to*:

7.45 a quarter of eight
7.55 five of eight

Appendix 4 NUMERICAL EXPRESSIONS

TWENTY-FOUR HOUR CLOCK
Used originally in military orders etc, but now increasingly used in travel timetables.

07.00 (͵oh) ͵seven 'hundred hours	=	7.00 a m	19.00 ͵nineteen 'hundred hours	=	7.00 p m
10.30 ͵ten 'thirty	=	10.30 a m	22.50 ͵twenty-͵two 'fifty	=	10.50 p m
12.00 ͵twelve 'hundred hours	=	midday/noon	23.05 ͵twenty-͵three ͵oh 'five	=	11.05 p m
13.45 ͵thirteen ͵forty-'five	=	1.45 p m	24.00 ͵twenty-͵four 'hundred hours	=	midnight
15.15 ͵fifteen ͵fif'teen	=	3.15 p m			

7 Dates

2000 BC 'two thousand /͵bi:'si:/
55 BC 'fifty-five /͵bi:'si:/

AD is usually reserved only for the earlier years:
AD 55 /͵eɪ'di:/ fifty-five'; but 1066, not AD
1066.

Queen Elizabeth I 1558–1603: 'Queen Elizabeth
the first reigned from fifteen (hundred and)
fifty-eight to sixteen (hundred and) three/sixteen
oh three.'

GB
3(rd) January 1985: 'the third of January
nineteen eighty-five', often abbreviated to 3 Jan
'85 (Feb, Mar, Apr, May, Jun, July, Aug, Sept,
Oct, Nov, Dec) or to numbers only e g 3/1/85.
Sometimes Roman numbers are used for the
month, e g 27 ii 40.

US
May 4, 1985: 'May fourth, nineteen eighty-
five.' In numbers only: 5.4.85 (GB = 4.5.85).

8 Money

For monetary tables ⇨ Appendix 5

GB
I paid a penny/
one p for it. (1p)
It's ten pence/ten p a
cup. (10p)
The cheapest seats are
fifty pence/fifty p
each. (50p)
They'll charge you a
pound/ (sl) *a quid*
membership fee. (£1)

US
I bought it for a cent.
(1¢)
It's ten cents a cup.
(10¢)
The cheapest seats are
half a dollar/(sl) *half*
a buck each. (50¢)
They'll charge you a
dollar/ (sl) *a buck*
membership fee. ($1)

I was given one
(pound) fifty (pence)
change. (£1.50)

The return ticket is
thirteen (pounds)
twenty-seven (pence).
(£13.27)

I was given a dollar
fifty/one fifty/ (sl)
one and a half bucks
change. ($1.50)

The return ticket is
thirteen (dollars)
twenty-seven (cents).
($13.17)

Note: The penny and cent signs (p, ¢) are *never*
shown with the pound and dollar signs (£, $)
when writing down a sum of money:
e g £6.25 and $6.25 are right
   £6.25p and $6.25¢ are wrong

9 Telephoning

Each digit is spoken separately, i e no figure
above nine is used. 0 is pronounced /əʊ/. In US
usage, 'zero' (and sometimes 'nought') may
replace 'oh'. The figures are usually grouped
rhythmically in pairs (pairing from the right),
though there is a tendency to use rhythmic
triplets, especially for six-figure numbers. If the
two digits of a pair are the same, it is usually
spoken as 'double three' etc. An exception is the
GB emergency call 999 which is always *͵nine*
͵nine 'nine.

6638 ͵double ͵six, ͵three 'eight
but
3668 ͵three ͵six, ͵six 'eight (or ͵three, ͵double
͵six, 'eight)
677 ͵six, ͵double 'seven
but
667 ͵six, ͵six 'seven (or ͵double ͵six, 'seven)
In numbers which include a code number,
the code is to be separated by a pause:
01-629 8495 ͵oh 'one‖ ͵six ͵two 'nine‖
͵eight ͵four, ͵nine 'five.

10 Chemical Formulae

In chemical formulae full-size and reduced-size
numbers, and capital and lower case letters
are not distinguished orally.

NaCl /͵en eɪ si: 'el/
$2H_2 + O_2 = 2H_2O$ /͵tu: eɪʃ ͵tu:‖ plʌs ͵əʊ 'tu:‖
͵i:kwəlz ͵tu: eɪʃ tu: 'əʊ/

Appendix 5 WEIGHTS AND MEASURES

The Metric System

METRIC		GB & US
	length	
10 millimetres (mm)	= 1 centimetre (cm)	= 0·3937 inches (in)
100 centimetres	= 1 metre (m)	= 39·37 inches or 1·094 yards (yd)
1000 metres	= 1 kilometre (km)	= 0·62137 miles or about ⅝ mile
	surface	
100 square metres (m²)	= 1 are (a)	= 0·0247 acres
100 ares	= 1 hectare (ha)	= 2·471 acres
100 hectares	= 1 square kilometre (km²)	= 0·386 square miles
	weight	
10 milligrams (mg)	= 1 centigram (cg)	= 0·1543 grains
100 centigrams	= 1 gram (g)	= 15·4323 grains
1000 grams	= 1 kilogram (kg)	= 2·2046 pounds
1000 kilograms	= 1 tonne	= 19·684 cwt
	capacity	
1000 millilitres (ml)	= 1 litre (l)	= 1·75 pints (2·101 US pints)
10 litres	= 1 decalitre (dl)	= 2·1997 gallons (2·63 US gallons)

Avoirdupois Weight

GB & US		METRIC
	1 grain (gr)	= 0·0648 grams (g)
437½ grains	= 1 ounce (oz)	= 28·35 grams
16 drams (dr)	= 1 ounce	= 28·35 grams
16 ounces	= 1 pound (lb)	= 0·454 kilograms (kg)
14 pounds	= 1 stone	= 6·356 kilograms
2 stone	= 1 quarter	= 12·7 kilograms
4 quarters	= 1 hundredweight (cwt)	= 50·8 kilograms
112 pounds	= 1 cwt	= 50·8 kilograms
100 pounds	= 1 short cwt	= 45·4 kilograms
20 cwt	= 1 ton	= 1016·04 kilograms
2000 pounds	= 1 short ton	= 0·907 metric tons
2240 pounds	= 1 long ton	= 1·016 metric tons

Troy Weight

*system of weights used in England for gold, silver
and precious stones*

GB & US		METRIC
24 grains	= 1 pennyweight (dwt)	= 1·555 grams
20 pennyweights	= 1 ounce	= 31·1 grams
12 ounces	= 1 pound (5760 grains)	= 0·373 kilograms

Apothecaries' Weight

*used by pharmacists for mixing their medicines;
they buy and sell drugs by Avoirdupois weight*

GB & US		METRIC
20 grains	= 1 scruple	= 1·296 grams
3 scruples	= 1 dram	= 3·888 grams
8 drams	= 1 ounce	= 31·1035 grams
12 ounces	= 1 pound	= 373·24 grams

Linear Measure

GB & US		METRIC
	1 inch (in)	= 25·3995 millimetres (mm)
12 inches	= 1 foot (ft)	= 30·479 centimetres (cm)
3 feet	= 1 yard (yd)	= 0·9144 metres (m)
5½ yards	= 1 rod, pole, or perch	= 5·0292 metres
22 yards	= 1 chain (ch)	= 20·1168 metres
220 yards	= 1 furlong (fur)	= 201·168 metres
8 furlongs	= 1 mile	= 1·6093 kilometres (km)
1760 yards	= 1 mile	= 1·6093 kilometres
3 miles	= 1 league	= 4·8279 kilometres

Square Measure

	GB & US		METRIC
	1 square inch	=	6·4516 sq centimetres
144 sq inches	= 1 sq foot	=	929·030 sq centimetres
9 sq feet	= 1 sq yard	=	0·836 sq metres
484 sq yards	= 1 sq chain	=	404·624 sq metres
4840 sq yards	= 1 acre	=	0·405 hectares
40 sq rods	= 1 rood	=	10·1168 ares
4 roods	= 1 acre	=	0·405 hectares
640 acres	= 1 sq mile	=	2·599 sq kilometres

Cubic Measure

	GB & US		METRIC
	1 cubic inch	=	16·387 cu centimetres
1728 cu inches	= 1 cu foot	=	0·028 cu metres
27 cu feet	= 1 cu yard	=	0·765 cu metres

Surveyors' Measure

	GB & US		METRIC
7·92 inches	= 1 link	=	20·1168 centimetres
100 links	= 1 chain	=	20·1168 metres
10 chains	= 1 furlong	=	201·168 metres
80 chains	= 1 mile	=	1·6093 kilometres
10 square chains	= 1 acre	=	0·405 hectares

Nautical Measure

used for measuring the depth and surface distance of seas, rivers, etc

	GB & US		METRIC
6 feet	= 1 fathom	=	1·8288 metres
608 feet	= 1 cable	=	185·313 metres
6080 feet	= sea (or nautical) mile	=	1·852 kilometres
	(1·151 statute miles)		
3 sea miles	= 1 sea league	=	5·550 kilometres
60 sea miles	= 1 degree		
360 degrees	= 1 circle		

The speed of one sea mile per hour is called a *knot*

Liquid Measure of Capacity

	GB		US		METRIC
4 gills	= 1 pint (pt)	=	1·201 pints	=	0·5679 litres
2 pints	= 1 quart (qt)	=	1·201 quarts	=	1·1359 litres
4 quarts	= 1 gallon (gal)	=	1·201 gallons	=	4·5435 litres

Apothecaries' Fluid Measure

used by pharmacists for measuring medicines

	GB & US		METRIC
60 minims	= 1 fluid dram	=	3·552 millilitres
8 fluid drams	= 1 fluid ounce	=	2·841 centilitres
20 fluid ounces	= 1 pint	=	0·568 litres
8 pints	= 1 gallon	=	4·546 litres

Dry Measure of Capacity

	GB & US		GB		US
	1 gallon	=	4·5435 litres	=	4·404 liters
2 gallons	= 1 peck	=	9·0870 litres	=	8·810 liters
4 pecks	= 1 bushel	=	36·3477 litres	=	35·238 liters
8 bushels	= 1 quarter	=	290·7816 litres	=	281·904 liters

Circular or Angular Measure

60 seconds (″)	= 1 minute (′)		90 degrees	=	1 quadrant or right angle (L)
60 minutes	= 1 degree (°)		360 degrees	=	1 circle or circumference

the diameter of a circle	=	the straight line passing through its centre
the radius of a circle	=	$\frac{1}{2}$ × the diameter
the circumference of a circle	=	22/7 × the diameter

Temperature Equivalents

	FAHRENHEIT (F)	CENTIGRADE (C)
Boiling Point	212°	100°
	194°	90°
	176°	80°
	158°	70°
	140°	60°
	122°	50°
	104°	40°
	86°	30°
	68°	20°
	50°	10°
Freezing Point	32°	0°
	14°	−10°
	0°	−17·8°
Absolute Zero	−459·67°	−273·15°

To convert Fahrenheit temperature into Centigrade: subtract 32 and multiply by 5/9 (five-ninths).
To convert Centigrade temperature into Fahrenheit: multiply by 9/5 (nine-fifths) and add 32.

Money

also ⇨ App 4(8)
GB: £ p (pounds and pence)
100 pence (100p) = 1 pound (£1)

	(amount)	(coin)
½p	a halfpenny /'heɪpnɪ/, half a penny	a halfpenny /'heɪpnɪ/
1p	a penny, (colloq) one p /piː/	a penny
2p	twopence /'tʌpəns/, two pence, (colloq) two p /piː/	a twopenny /'tʌpnɪ/ piece
5p	five pence /'faɪfpəns/	a fivepenny /'faɪfpənɪ/ piece
10p	ten pence /'tenpəns/	a tenpenny /'tenpənɪ/ piece
50p	fifty pence	a fifty pence piece
		(note)
£1	a pound, (sl) a quid	a pound note
£5, £10, £20	five/ten/twenty pounds, (sl) five/ten/twenty quid	a five/ten/twenty pound note, (sl) a fiver/tenner
£3·82	three pounds eighty-two (pence)	

us: $ ¢ (dollars and cents)
100 cents (100¢) = 1 dollar ($1)

	(amount)	(coin)
1¢	a cent	a penny
5¢	five cents	a nickel
10¢	ten cents	a dime
25¢	twenty-five cents	a quarter
50¢	half a dollar, (sl) half a buck	a half-dollar
		(note)
$1	a dollar, (sl) a buck	a dollar bill
$5, $10, $20	five/ten/twenty dollars, (sl) five/ten/twenty bucks	a five/ten/twenty dollar bill
$3·82	three dollars eighty-two (cents)	

Time

60 seconds	= 1 minute	4 weeks, or 28 days	= 1 lunar month
60 minutes	= 1 hour	52 weeks, 1 day; or 13	
24 hours	= 1 day	lunar months, 1 day	= 1 year
7 days	= 1 week	365 days, 6 hours	= 1 (Julian) year

Number of Days in the Month

30 days have September,
April, June and November;
All the rest have 31,
Excepting February alone,
Which has but 28 days clear
And 29 in each leap year.

Speed

Light travels at 186 300 miles per second; 300 000 kilometres per second.
Sound travels at 1130 feet per second; 330 metres per second; 770 miles per hour (the 'sound barrier').

Appendix 6 GEOGRAPHICAL NAMES

COUNTRIES OF THE WORLD

Notes

1 The list consists of both sovereign independent countries and dependent states forming such countries: e g *Malaysia*, a sovereign nation, is a federation of *Malaya*, *Sabah* and *Sarawak*; *England*, *Scotland* and *Wales* make up *Great Britain*; the *United Kingdom* is the union of *Great Britain* and *Northern Ireland*.

2 Some countries have different words for the *adjective* and the *person*; in these cases both are given, e g *Swedish*; *Swede*.

> Adjective: I admire *Swedish* architecture.
> He sang a *Japanese* song.
> Person: My mother is a *Swede*.
> A *Japanese* has joined our class.

3 Words for the *person* ending in '-ese', and *Swiss*, remain unchanged in the plural: I know many *Japanese*. The *Swiss* have arrived.

4 In some cases, the *adjective* is also the word for the country's language: I am learning to speak *Malay*.

COUNTRY	ADJECTIVE; PERSON
Afghanistan /æf₁gænɪˈstɑːn US: -ˈstæn/	Afghan /ˈæfgæn/; Afghanistani /-nɪ/
Albania /ælˈbeɪnɪə/	Albanian /-nɪən/
Algeria /ælˈdʒɪərɪə/	Algerian /-rɪən/
Andorra /ænˈdɔːrə/	Andorran /-rən/
Angola /æŋˈgəʊlə/	Angolan /-lən/
Anguilla /æŋˈgwɪlə/	Anguillan /-lən/
Antigua /ænˈtiːgə/	Antiguan /-gən/
Argentina /₁ɑːdʒənˈtiːnə/ (also *The Argentine* /ˈɑːdʒəntaɪn/)	Argentinian /-ˈtɪnɪən/ Argentine
Australia /ɒˈstreɪlɪə US: ɔːˈs-/	Australian /-lɪən/
Austria /ˈɒstrɪə US: ˈɔːs-/	Austrian /-strɪən/
(The) Bahamas /bəˈhɑːməz US: -ˈheɪm-/	Bahamian /bəˈheɪmɪən/
Bahrain /bɑːˈreɪn/	Bahraini /-reɪnɪ/
Bangladesh /₁bæŋgləˈdeʃ/	Bangladeshi /-ˈdeʃɪ/
Barbados /bɑːˈbeɪdəs/	Barbadian /-dɪən/
Belgium /ˈbeldʒəm/	Belgian /-dʒən/
Benin (formerly *Dahomey*) /beˈniːn/	Beninese /benɪˈniːz/
Bermuda /bəˈmjuːdə/	Bermudan /-dən/
Bhutan /buːˈtɑːn/	Bhutani /-nɪ/
Bolivia /bəˈlɪvɪə/	Bolivian /-vɪən/
Botswana /bɒˈtswɑːnə/	Tswana /ˈtswɑːnə/
Brazil /brəˈzɪl/	Brazilian /-lɪən/
Brunei /ˈbruːnaɪ/	Bruneian /bruːˈnaɪən/
Bulgaria /bʌlˈgeərɪə/	Bulgarian /-rɪən/
Burma /ˈbɜːmə/	Burmese /₁bɜːˈmiːz/
Burundi /bʊˈrʊndɪ/	Burundian /-dɪən/
Cambodia /kæmˈbəʊdɪə/	Cambodian /-dɪən/
Cameroon /₁kæməˈruːn/	Cameroonian /-nɪən/
Canada /ˈkænədə/	Canadian /kəˈneɪdɪən/
Chad /tʃæd/	Chadian /-dɪən/
Chile /ˈtʃɪlɪ/	Chilean /-lɪən/
China /ˈtʃaɪnə/	Chinese /₁tʃaɪˈniːz/
Colombia /kəˈlɒmbɪə/	Colombian /-bɪən/
Congo /ˈkɒŋgəʊ/	Congolese /₁kɒŋgəˈliːz/
Costa Rica /₁kɒstə ˈriːkə/	Costa Rican /-kən/
Cuba /ˈkjuːbə/	Cuban /-bən/
Cyprus /ˈsaɪprəs/	Cyprian /ˈsɪprɪən/; Cypriot /ˈsɪprɪət/
Czechoslovakia /₁tʃekəʊsləˈvækɪə/	Czech /tʃek/, Czechoslovak /₁tʃekəʊˈsləʊvæk/, Czechoslovakian /₁tʃekəʊsləˈvækɪən/
Denmark /ˈdenmɑːk/	Danish /ˈdeɪnɪʃ/; Dane /deɪn/
Djibouti /dʒɪˈbuːtɪ/	Djiboutian /-tɪən/
Dominica /dəˈmɪnɪkə/	Dominican /-kən/
Ecuador /ˈekwədɔː(r)/	Ecuadorian /₁ekwəˈdɔːrɪən/
Egypt /ˈiːdʒɪpt/	Egyptian /ɪˈdʒɪpʃn/
El Salvador /el ˈsælvədɔː(r)/	Salvadorean /₁sælvəˈdɔːrɪən/
Eritrea /₁erɪˈtreɪə/	Eritrean /-eɪən/
Ethiopia /₁iːθɪˈəʊpɪə/	Ethiopian /-pɪən/
Fiji /₁fiːˈdʒiː US: ˈfiːdʒiː/	Fijian /₁fiːˈdʒiːən US: ˈfiːdʒɪən/

1024

Finland /'fɪnlənd/ — Finnish /'fɪnɪʃ/; Finn /fɪn/
France /frɑːns/ — French /frentʃ/; Frenchman /'frentʃmən/
Gabon /gæ'bɒn/ — Gabonese /ˌgæbə'niːz/
(The) Gambia /'gæmbɪə/ — Gambian /-bɪən/
German Democratic Republic /ˌdʒɜːmən deməˌkrætɪk rɪ'pʌblɪk/ — (East) German /'dʒɜːmən/
(Federal Republic of) Germany /ˌfedərəl rɪˌpʌblɪk əv 'dʒɜːmənɪ/ — (West) German /'dʒɜːmən/
Ghana /'gɑːnə/ — Ghanaian /gɑː'neɪən/
Gibraltar /dʒɪ'brɔːltə(r)/ — Gibraltarian /ˌdʒɪbrɔːl'teərɪən/
Great Britain /ˌgreɪt 'brɪtn/ — British /'brɪtɪʃ/; Briton /'brɪtn/
Greece /griːs/ — Greek /griːk/
Grenada /grɪ'neɪdə/ — Grenadian /-dɪən/
Guatemala /ˌgwɑːtə'mɑːlə/ — Guatemalan /-lən/
Guinea /'gɪnɪ/ — Guinean /-nɪən/
Guyana /gaɪ'ænə/ — Guyanese /ˌgaɪə'niːz/
Haiti /'heɪtɪ/ — Haitian /'heɪʃn/
Holland /'hɒlənd/ (also The Netherlands /'neðələndz/) — Dutch /dʌtʃ/; Hollander /'hɒləndə(r)/, Dutchman /'dʌtʃmən/
Honduras /hɒn'djʊərəs US: -'dʊə-/ — Honduran /-rən/
Hong Kong /ˌhɒŋ 'kɒŋ/ — —
Hungary /'hʌŋgərɪ/ — Hungarian /hʌŋ'geərɪən/
Iceland /'aɪslənd/ — Icelandic /aɪs'lændɪk/; Icelander /'aɪsləndə(r)/
India /'ɪndɪə/ — Indian /-dɪən/
Indonesia /ˌɪndə'niːzɪə US: -'niːʒə/ — Indonesian /-zɪən US: -ʒn/
Iran (formerly Persia) /ɪ'rɑːn/ — Iranian /ɪ'reɪnɪən/
Iraq /ɪ'rɑːk/ — Iraqi /ɪ'rɑːkɪ/
(The Republic of) Ireland /'aɪələnd/ — Irish /'aɪərɪʃ/; Irishman /'aɪərɪʃmən/
Israel /'ɪzreɪl/ — Israeli /ɪz'reɪlɪ/
Italy /'ɪtəlɪ/ — Italian /ɪ'tælɪən/
Jamaica /dʒə'meɪkə/ — Jamaican /-kən/
Japan /dʒə'pæn/ — Japanese /ˌdʒæpə'niːz/
Java /'dʒɑːvə/ — Javanese /ˌdʒɑːvə'niːz/
Jordan /'dʒɔːdn/ — Jordanian /dʒɔː'deɪnɪən/
Kampuchea /ˌkæmpʊ'tʃɪə/ — Kampuchean /-'tʃɪən/
Kashmir /kæʃ'mɪə(r) US: 'kæʃmɪər/ — Kashmiri /kæʃ'mɪərɪ/
Kenya /'kenjə US: 'kiːnjə/ — Kenyan /-jən/
Korea /kə'rɪə/ — Korean /-'rɪən/
Kuwait /kʊ'weɪt US: -'waɪt/ — Kuwaiti /-tɪ/
Laos /'lɑːɒs/ — Laotian /'lɑːɒʃn US: leɪ'əʊʃn/
Lebanon /'lebənən/ — Lebanese /ˌlebə'niːz/
Lesotho /lə'suːtuː/ — Sotho /'suːtuː/
Liberia /laɪ'bɪərɪə/ — Liberian /-rɪən/
Libya /'lɪbɪə/ — Libyan /-bɪən/
Liechtenstein /'lɪktənstaɪn/ — Liechtenstein; Liechtensteiner /-nə(r)/
Luxemburg /'lʌksəmbɜːg/ — Luxemburg; Luxemburger /-gə(r)/
Madagascar /ˌmædə'gæskə(r)/ — Madagascan /-kən/
Malawi /mə'lɑːwɪ/ — Malawian /-wɪən/
Malaya /mə'leɪə/ — Malay /mə'leɪ/
Malaysia /mə'leɪzɪə US: -'leɪʒə/ — Malaysian /-zɪən US: -ʒn/
Mali /'mɑːlɪ/ — Malian /-lɪən/
Malta /'mɔːltə/ — Maltese /mɔːl'tiːz/
Mauritania /ˌmɒrɪ'teɪnɪə US: ˌmɔːr-/ — Mauritanian /-nɪən/
Mauritius /mə'rɪʃəs US: mɔː/ — Mauritian /-'rɪʃn/
Mexico /'meksɪkəʊ/ — Mexican /-kən/
Monaco /'mɒnəkəʊ/ — Monegasque /ˌmɒnə'gæsk/
Mongolia /mɒŋ'gəʊlɪə/ — Mongolian /-lɪən/; Mongol /'mɒŋgl/
Montserrat /ˌmɒntsə'ræt/ — Montserratian /-'ræʃn/
Morocco /mə'rɒkəʊ/ — Moroccan /-kən/
Mozambique /ˌməʊzæm'biːk/ — Mozambican /-'biːkən/
Namibia /nə'mɪbɪə/ — Namibian /-bɪən/
Nauru /ˌnaʊ'ruː/ — Nauruan /-'ruːən/
Nepal /nɪ'pɔːl/ — Nepalese /ˌnepə'liːz/
New Zealand /ˌnjuː 'ziːlənd US: ˌnuː/ — New Zealand; New Zealander /-də(r)/
Nicaragua /ˌnɪkə'rægjʊə US: -'rɑːgwə/ — Nicaraguan /-ən/
Niger /niː'ʒeə(r)/ — Nigerien /niː'ʒeərɪən/
Nigeria /naɪ'dʒɪərɪə/ — Nigerian /naɪ'dʒɪərɪən/
Norway /'nɔːweɪ/ — Norwegian /nɔː'wiːdʒən/
Oman /əʊ'mɑːn/ — Omani /əʊ'mɑːnɪ/
Pakistan /ˌpɑːkɪ'stɑːn US: 'pækɪstæn/ — Pakistani /-nɪ US: ˌpækɪ'stænɪ/

Palestine /'pæləstaɪn/
Palestinian /ˌpælə'stɪnɪən/
Panama /ˌpænə'mɑː US: 'pænəmɑː/
Panamanian /ˌpænə'meɪnɪən/
Papua /'pæpjʊə/
Papuan /-ən/
Paraguay /'pærəgwaɪ US: -gweɪ/
Paraguayan /ˌpærə'gwaɪən US: -'gweɪən/
Peru /pə'ruː/
Peruvian /-'ruːvɪən/
(The) Philippines /'fɪlɪpiːnz/
Philippine /'fɪlɪpiːn/; Filipino /ˌfɪlɪ'piːnəʊ/
Poland /'pəʊlənd/
Polish /'pəʊlɪʃ/; Pole /pəʊl/
Portugal /'pɔːtʃʊgl/
Portuguese /ˌpɔːtʃʊ'giːz/
Qatar /'kʌtɑː(r)/
Qatari /-ɑːrɪ/
Romania /rə'meɪnɪə/
Romanian /-nɪən/
Russia /'rʌʃə/
Russian /-ʃn/
Rwanda /rʊ'ændə/
Rwandan /-dən/
Sabah /'sʌbə/
Sabahan /'sʌbəhən/
Samoa /sə'məʊə/
Samoan /-ən/
San Marino /ˌsæn mə'riːnəʊ/
San Marinese /ˌsæn ˌmærɪ'niːz/
Sarawak /sə'rɑːwæk/
Sarawakian /ˌsærə'wækɪən/
Saudi Arabia /ˌsaʊdɪ ə'reɪbɪə/
Saudi Arabian /-bɪən/
Senegal /ˌsenɪ'gɔːl/
Senegalese /ˌsenɪgə'liːz/
(The) Seychelles /'seɪʃelz/
Seychellois /seɪ'ʃelwɑː/
Sierra Leone /sɪˌerə lɪ'əʊn/
Sierra Leonean /-nɪən/
Singapore /ˌsɪŋgə'pɔː(r) US: 'sɪŋəpɔːr/
Singaporean /ˌsɪŋgə'pɔːrɪən US: -ŋə-/
Somalia /sə'mɑːlɪə/
Somalian /-lɪən/; Somali /-lɪ/
South Africa /ˌsaʊθ 'æfrɪkə/
South African /-kən/
Spain /speɪn/
Spanish /'spænɪʃ/; Spaniard /'spænɪəd/
Sri Lanka (formerly Ceylon) /ˌsrɪ 'læŋkə/
Sri Lankan /ˌsrɪ 'læŋkən/
(The) Sudan /suː'dɑːn/
Sudanese /ˌsuːdə'niːz/
Sumatra /suː'mɑːtrə/
Sumatran /-trən/
Swaziland /'swɑːzɪlænd/
Swazi /'swɑːzɪ/
Sweden /'swiːdn/
Swedish /'swiːdɪʃ/; Swede /swiːd/
Switzerland /'swɪtsələnd/
Swiss /swɪs/
Syria /'sɪrɪə/
Syrian /-rɪən/
Tahiti /tɑː'hiːtɪ/
Tahitian /-'hiːʃn/
Taiwan (formerly Formosa) /taɪ'wɑːn/
Taiwanese /ˌtaɪwə'niːz/
Tanzania /ˌtænzə'nɪə/
Tanzanian /-nɪən/
Thailand (formerly Siam) /'taɪlænd/
Thai /taɪ/
Tibet /tɪ'bet/
Tibetan /-tn/
Tobago /tə'beɪgəʊ/
Tobagonian /ˌtəʊbə'gəʊnɪən/
Togo /'təʊgəʊ/
Togolese /ˌtəʊgə'liːz/
Tonga /'tɒŋə/
Tongan /-ən/
Trinidad /'trɪnɪdæd/
Trinidadian /ˌtrɪnɪ'deɪdɪən/
Tunisia /tjuː'nɪzɪə US: tuː'nɪʒə/
Tunisian /-ən/
Turkey /'tɜːkɪ/
Turkish /'tɜːkɪʃ/; Turk /tɜːk/
Uganda /juː'gændə/
Ugandan /-dən/
(The) Union of Soviet Socialist Republics /ˌjuːnɪən əv ˌsəʊvɪət ˌsəʊʃəlɪst rɪ'pʌblɪks/
Soviet /'səʊvɪət/; —
(The) United States of America /juːˌnaɪtɪd ˌsteɪts əv ə'merɪkə/
American /-kən/
Uruguay /'jʊərəgwaɪ US: -gweɪ/
Uruguayan /ˌjʊərə'gwaɪən US: -'gweɪən/
Venezuela /ˌvenɪ'zweɪlə/
Venezuelan /-lən/
Vietnam /ˌvɪet'næm US: -'nɑːm/
Vietnamese /ˌvɪetnə'miːz/
(The) West Indies /ˌwest 'ɪndɪz/
West Indian /-dɪən/
Yemen /'jemən/
Yemeni /-nɪ/
Yugoslavia /ˌjuːgəʊ'slɑːvɪə/
Yugoslavian /-vɪən/; Yugoslav /'juːgəʊslɑːv/
Zaire /zɑː'ɪə(r)/
Zairean /-rɪən/
Zambia /'zæmbɪə/
Zambian /-bɪən/
Zimbabwe /zɪm'bɑːbwɪ/
Zimbabwean /-wɪən/

THE UNITED KINGDOM OF GREAT BRITAIN (GB) AND NORTHERN IRELAND (NI)

COUNTIES AND SHIRES
The usual GB pronunciation of '-shire' is /-ʃə(r)/, the usual US pronunciation is /-ʃɪər/. Where the suffix '-shire' is usually omitted from the name of a county it is given in parentheses.
The common written abbreviations of the names of the counties are given in parentheses and transcribed in phonetics only when they are used in spoken English.

ENGLAND /'ɪŋglənd/
Note. By the Local Government Act of 1972, the boundaries of the English Counties were redrawn: those counties marked * ceased to function as official areas; those marked † were newly established.

†Avon /'eɪvən/
Bedfordshire (*Beds*) /'bedfədʃə(r)/
Berkshire (*Berks*) /'bɑːkʃə(r) US: 'bɜːrk-/
Buckinghamshire (*Bucks*) /'bʌkɪŋəmʃə(r)/
Cambridgeshire (*Cambs*) /'keɪmbrɪdʒʃə(r)/
Cheshire (*Ches*) /'tʃeʃə(r)/
†Cleveland /'kliːvlənd/
Cornwall (*Corn*) /'kɔːnwɔːl/
*Cumberland (*Cumb*) /'kʌmbələnd/
†Cumbria /'kʌmbrɪə/
Derbyshire /'dɑːbɪʃə(r) US: 'dɜːrbɪ-/
Devon(shire) /'devn(ʃə)(r)/
Dorset(shire) (*Dors*) /'dɔːsɪt(ʃə)(r)/
Durham (*Dur*) /'dʌrəm/
Essex (*Ess*) /'esɪks/
Gloucestershire (*Glos*) /'glɒstəʃə(r)/
Hampshire (*Hants* /hænts/) /'hæmpʃə(r)/
†Hereford and Worcester /ˌherɪfəd n 'wʊstə(r)/
*Herefordshire /'herɪfədʃə(r)/
Hertfordshire (*Herts* /hɑːts/) /'hɑː(t)fədʃə(r)/
†Humberside /'hʌmbəsaɪd/
*Huntingdonshire (*Hunts* /hʌnts/) /'hʌntɪŋdənʃə(r)/
†Isle of Wight (*I of W*) /ˌaɪl əv 'waɪt/
Kent /kent/
Lancashire (*Lancs* /læŋks/) /'læŋkəʃə(r)/
Leicestershire (*Leics*) /'lestəʃə(r)/

WALES /weɪlz/
Anglesey /'æŋglsɪ/
Brecknockshire /'breknɒkʃə(r)/
  (also Breconshire /'brekənʃə(r)/)
Caernarvonshire /kə'nɑːvənʃə(r)/
Cardiganshire /'kɑːdɪgənʃə(r)/
Carmarthenshire /kə'mɑːðnʃə(r)/
Denbighshire /'denbɪʃə(r)/
Flintshire /'flɪntʃə(r)/
Glamorgan(shire) /glə'mɔːgən(ʃə)(r)/
Merionethshire /ˌmerɪ'ɒnɪθ(r)/
Monmouthshire /'mɒnməθʃə(r)/
Montgomeryshire /mənt'gʌmrɪʃə(r)/

SCOTLAND /'skɒtlənd/
Aberdeenshire /ˌæbə'diːnʃə(r)/
Angus /'æŋgəs/
Argyllshire /ɑː'gaɪlʃə(r)/
Ayrshire /'eəʃə(r)/
Banffshire /'bænfʃə(r)/
Berwickshire /'berɪkʃə(r)/
Bute(shire) /'bjuːt(ʃə)(r)/
Caithness /'keɪθnes/
Clackmannanshire /klæk'mænənʃə(r)/
Dumbartonshire /dʌm'bɑːtnʃə(r)/
Dumfries-shire /dʌm'friːʃʃə(r)/
East Lothian /'ləʊðɪən/
Fifeshire /'faɪfʃə(r)/
Inverness-shire /ˌɪnvə'neʃʃə(r)/
Kincardineshire /kɪn'kɑːdɪnʃə(r)/
Kinross-shire /kɪn'rɒʃʃə(r)/
Kirkcudbrightshire /kɜː'kuːbrɪʃə(r)/
Lanarkshire /'lænəkʃə(r)/
Midlothian /mɪd'ləʊðɪən/
Morayshire /'mʌrɪʃə(r)/
Nairnshire /'neənʃə(r)/
Orkney /'ɔːknɪ/
Peebles-shire /'piːblʃə(r)/
Perthshire /'pɜːθʃə(r)/

NORTHERN IRELAND /ˌnɔːðən 'aɪələnd/
Antrim /'æntrɪm/
Armagh /ɑː'mɑː/
Down /daʊn/

Lincolnshire (*Lincs* /lɪŋks/) /'lɪŋkənʃə(r)/
London (County of) /'lʌndən/
†Manchester (County of) /'mæntʃɪstə(r)/
†Merseyside /'mɜːzɪsaɪd/
*Middlesex (*Middx*) /'mɪdlseks/
Norfolk (*Norf*) /'nɔːfək/
Northamptonshire (*Northants* /nɔː'θænts/) /nɔː'θæmptənʃə(r)/
Northumberland (*Northd*) /nɔː'θʌmbələnd/
Nottinghamshire (*Notts* /nɒts/) /'nɒtɪŋəmʃə(r)/
Oxfordshire (*Oxon* /'ɒksn/) /'ɒksfədʃə(r)/
*Rutland(shire) /'rʌtlənd(ʃə)(r)/
Shropshire (*Salop* /'sæləp/) /'ʃrɒpʃə(r)/
Somerset(shire) (*Som*) /'sʌməsət(ʃə)(r)/
Staffordshire (*Staffs* /stæfs/) /'stæfəd(ʃə)(r)/
Suffolk (*Suff*) /'sʌfək/
Surrey (*Sy*) /'sʌrɪ/
Sussex (*Sx*) /'sʌsɪks/
†Tyne and Wear /ˌtaɪn ən 'wɪə(r)/
Warwickshire (*Warks*) /'wɒrɪkʃə(r) US: 'wɔːr-/
†West Midlands /'mɪdləndz/
*Westmorland /'westmələnd/
Wiltshire (*Wilts* /wɪlts/) /'wɪltʃə(r)/
*Worcestershire (*Worcs*) /'wʊstəʃə(r)/
Yorkshire (*Yorks*) (North, South and West) /'jɔːkʃə(r)/

Pembrokeshire /'pembrʊkʃə(r)/
Radnorshire /'rædnəʃə(r)/

Note. By the Local Government Act of 1972,
  the above thirteen Welsh Counties were
  replaced by the following eight:

Clwyd /'kluːɪd/
Dyfed /'dʌvɪd/
Glamorgan (Mid, South and West) /glə'mɔːgən/
Gwent /gwent/
Gwynedd /'gwɪnəð/
Powys /'paʊɪs/

Renfrewshire /'renfruːʃə(r)/
Ross and Cromarty /ˌrɒs ən 'krɒmətɪ/
Roxburghshire /'rɒksbrəʃə(r)/
Selkirkshire /'selkɜːkʃə(r)/
Stirlingshire /'stɜːlɪŋʃə(r)/
Sutherland /'sʌðələnd/
West Lothian /'ləʊðɪən/
Wigtownshire /'wɪgtənʃə(r)/
Zetland /'zetlənd/

Note. From May 1975 the above counties were
  replaced by the following regions:

Borders /'bɔːdəz/
Central /'sentrəl/
Dumfries and Galloway /dʌmˌfriːs ən 'gæləweɪ/
Fife /faɪf/
Grampian /'græmpɪən/
Highland /'haɪlənd/
Lothian /'ləʊðɪən/
Orkney /'ɔːknɪ/
Shetland /'ʃetlənd/
Strathclyde /stræθ'klaɪd/
Tayside /'teɪsaɪd/
Western Isles /ˌwestən 'aɪlz/

Fermanagh /fə'mænə/
Londonderry /'lʌndəndərɪ/
Tyrone /tɪ'rəʊn/

THE REPUBLIC OF IRELAND

PROVINCES AND COUNTIES

THE PROVINCE OF LEINSTER /'lenstə(r)/
Carlow /'kɑ:ləʊ/
Dublin /'dʌblɪn/
Kildare /kɪl'deə(r)/
Kilkenny /kɪl'kenɪ/
Leix /li:ʃ/
Longford /'lɒŋfəd US: 'lɔ:ŋ-/
Louth /laʊð/
Meath /mi:θ/
Offaly /'ɒfəlɪ/
Westmeath /west'mi:θ/
Wexford /'weksfəd/
Wicklow /'wɪkləʊ/

THE PROVINCE OF MUNSTER /'mʌnstə(r)/
Clare /kleə(r)/
Cork /kɔ:k/
Kerry /'kerɪ/
Limerick /'lɪmərɪk/
Tipperary /ˌtɪpə'reərɪ/
Waterford /'wɔ:təfəd/

THE PROVINCE OF CONNAUGHT /'kɒnɔ:t/
Galway /'gɔ:lweɪ/
Leitrim /'li:trɪm/
Mayo /'meɪəʊ/
Roscommon /rɒs'kɒmən/
Sligo /'slaɪgəʊ/

PART OF THE PROVINCE OF ULSTER /'ʌlstə(r)/
Cavan /'kævən/
Donegal /'dɒnɪgɔ:l/
Monaghan /'mɒnəhən/

AUSTRALIA

STATES AND TERRITORIES
(*Australian Capital Territory:* Canberra
/'kænbərə/
New South Wales (*NSW*) /weɪlz/
Northern Territory (*NT*)
Queensland (*Qld*) /'kwi:nzlənd/
South Australia (*S Aus* or *S Austr*)
Tasmania (*Tas*) /tæz'meɪnɪə/
Victoria (*Vic*) /vɪk'tɔ:rɪə/
Western Australia (*W Aus* or *W Austr*)

NEW ZEALAND

PROVINCIAL DISTRICTS
Auckland /'ɔ:klənd/
Canterbury /'kæntəbrɪ US: -berɪ/
Hawke's Bay /ˌhɔ:ks 'beɪ/
Marlborough /'mɑ:lbrə/
Nelson /'nelsn/
Otago /əʊ'tɑ:gəʊ/
Taranaki /ˌtærə'nɑ:kɪ/
Wellington /'welɪŋtən/

CANADA

PROVINCES AND TERRITORIES
Alberta (*Alta*) /æl'bɜ:tə/
British Colombia (*BC*) /kə'lʌmbɪə/
Labrador (*Lab*) /'læbrədɔ:(r)/
Manitoba (*Man*) /ˌmænɪ'təʊbə/
New Brunswick (*NB*) /'brʌnzwɪk/
Newfoundland (*ND* or *Nfd*) /'nju:fənlənd/
 US: 'nu:-/

Nova Scotia (*NS*) /ˌnəʊvə 'skəʊʃə/
Ontario (*Ont*) /ɒn'teərɪəʊ/
Prince Edward Island (*PEI*) /prɪns ˌedwəd
 'aɪlənd/
Quebec (*Que*) /kwɪ'bek/
Saskatchewan (*Sask*) /sə'skætʃəwən/
Yukon Territory /'ju:kɒn/
North West Territories (*NWT*)

THE UNITED STATES OF AMERICA

STATES
Alabama (*AL*) /ˌælə'bæmə/
Alaska (*AK*) /ə'læskə/
Arizona (*AZ*) /ˌærɪ'zəʊnə/
Arkansas (*AR*) /'ɑ:kənsɔ:/
California (*CA*) /ˌkælɪ'fɔ:nɪə/
Colorado (*CO*) /ˌkɒlə'rɑ:dəʊ/
Connecticut (*CT*) /kə'netɪkət/
Delaware (*DE*) /'deləweə(r)/
District of Columbia (*DC*) /kə'lʌmbɪə/
Florida (*FL*) /'flɒrɪdə US: 'flɔ:r-/
Georgia (*GA*) /'dʒɔ:dʒə/
Hawaii (*HI*) /hə'waiɪ:/
Idaho (*ID*) /'aɪdəhəʊ/
Illinois (*IL*) /ˌɪlə'nɔɪ/
Indiana (*IN*) /ˌɪndɪ'ænə/
Iowa (*IA*) /'aɪəwə/
Kansas (*KS*) /'kænzəs/
Kentucky (*KY*) /ken'tʌkɪ/
Louisiana (*LA*) /lu:ˌi:zɪˌænə/
Maine (*ME*) /meɪn/
Maryland (*MD*) /'meərɪlənd/
Massachusetts (*MA*) /ˌmæsə'tʃu:sɪts/
Michigan (*MI*) /'mɪʃɪgən/
Minnesota (*MN*) /ˌmɪnɪ'səʊtə/
Mississippi (*MS*) /ˌmɪsɪ'sɪpɪ/

Missouri (*MO*) /mɪ'zʊərɪ/
Montana (*MT*) /mɒn'tænə/
Nebraska (*NE*) /nə'bræskə/
Nevada (*NV*) /nə'vɑ:də US: -'vædə/
New Hampshire (*NH*) /'hæmpʃə(r)/
New Jersey (*NJ*) /dʒɜ:zɪ/
New Mexico (*NM*) /'meksɪkəʊ/
New York (*NY*) /'jɔ:k/
North Carolina (*NC*) /ˌkærə'laɪnə/
North Dakota (*ND*) /də'kəʊtə/
Ohio (*OH*) /əʊ'haɪəʊ/
Oklahoma (*OK*) /ˌəʊklə'həʊmə/
Oregon (*OR*) /'ɒrɪgən US: 'ɔ:r-/
Pennsylvania (*PA*) /ˌpensl'veɪnɪə/
Rhode Island (*RI*) /ˌrəʊd 'aɪlənd/
South Carolina (*SC*) /ˌkærə'laɪnə/
South Dakota (*SD*) /də'kəʊtə/
Tennessee (*TN*) /ˌtenə'si:/
Texas (*TX*) /'teksəs/
Utah (*UT*) /'ju:tɔ:/
Vermont (*VT*) /və'mɒnt/
Virginia (*VA*) /və'dʒɪnɪə/
Washington (*WA*) /'wɒʃɪŋtən US: 'wɔ:ʃ-/
West Virginia (*WV*) /və'dʒɪnɪə/
Wisconsin (*WI*) /wɪs'kɒnsɪn/
Wyoming (*WY*) /waɪ'əʊmɪŋ/

Appendix 7 COMMON FORENAMES

Note. Pet-names are either shown after the name from which they are formed or listed separately with a note on their origins. Many of the names listed which consist of a single syllable have pet-name forms produced by adding /ɪ/ to the pronunciation and -y or -ie to the spelling, and doubling the final consonant if the preceding vowel is short:

> e g Fred, Freddy /'fredɪ/; Hugh, Hughie /'hjuːɪ/;
> Liz, Lizzie /'lɪzɪ/; Rose, Rosie /'rəʊzɪ/.

Men

Abraham /'eɪbrəhæm/
Adam /'ædəm/
Adrian /'eɪdrɪən/
Alan, Allan, Allen /'ælən/
Albert /'ælbət/; Al /æl/
Alexander /ˌælɪg'zɑːndə(r) *US:* -'zæn-/;
Alex /'ælɪks/
Alfred /'ælfrɪd/; Alf /ælf/
Andrew /'ændruː/; Andy /'ændɪ/
Angus /'æŋgəs/
Anthony, Antony /'æntənɪ/
Arnold /'ɑːnld/
Arthur /'ɑːθə(r)/
Barry /'bærɪ/
Bartholomew /bɑː'θɒləmjuː/; Bart /bɑːt/
Basil /'bæzl/
Benjamin /'bendʒəmɪn/; Ben /ben/
Bernard /'bɜːnəd *US:* bər'nɑːrd/; Bernie /'bɜːnɪ/
Bert /bɜːt/ (from *Albert, Gilbert, Herbert, Hubert*)
Bill /bɪl/ (from *William*)
Bob /bɒb/ (from *Robert*)
Boris /'bɒrɪs *US:* 'bɔːr-/
Brian, Bryan /'braɪən/
Bruce /bruːs/
Carl /kɑːl/
Cecil /'sesl *US:* 'siːsl/
Cedric /'sedrɪk/
Charles /tʃɑːlz/; Chas /tʃæz/
Christian /'krɪstʃən/
Christopher /'krɪstəfə(r)/; Chris /krɪs/
Claud(e) /klɔːd/
Clement /'klemənt/
Clifford /'klɪfəd/; Cliff /klɪf/
Clive /klaɪv/
Colin /'kɒlɪn/
Cyril /'sɪrəl/
Daniel /'dænɪəl/; Dan /dæn/
David /'deɪvɪd/; Dave /deɪv/
Dean /diːn/
Dennis, Denis /'denɪs/
Derek /'derɪk/
Desmond /'dezmənd/; Des /dez/
Dick /dɪk/ (from *Richard*)
Dominic /'dɒmɪnɪk/
Donald /'dɒnld/; Don /dɒn/
Douglas /'dʌgləs/; Doug /dʌg/
Duncan /'dʌŋkən/
Edgar /'edgə(r)/
Edmund /'edmənd/
Edward /'edwəd/; Ed /ed/
Enoch /'iːnɒk/
Eric /'erɪk/
Ernest /'ɜːnɪst/; Ernie /'ɜːnɪ/
Eugene /juː'dʒiːn/
Felix /'fiːlɪks/
Francis /'frɑːnsɪs *US:* 'fræn-/
Frank /fræŋk/
Frederick /'fredrɪk/; Fred /fred/
Gareth /'gærəθ/

Gary /'gærɪ/
Gavin /'gævɪn/
Gene /dʒiːn/ (from *Eugene*)
Geoffrey /'dʒefrɪ/; Geoff /dʒef/
George /dʒɔːdʒ/
Gerald /'dʒerəld/; Gerry /'dʒerɪ/
Gerard /'dʒerəd/
Gilbert /'gɪlbət/
Giles /dʒaɪlz/
Glen /glen/
Godfrey /'gɒdfrɪ/
Gordon /'gɔːdn/
Graham /'greɪəm/
Gregory /'gregərɪ/; Greg /greg/
Guy /gaɪ/
Harold /'hærəld/; Harry /'hærɪ/; Hal /hæl/
Harvey /'hɑːvɪ/
Henry /'henrɪ/
Herbert /'hɜːbət/
Hilary /'hɪlərɪ/
Horace /'hɒrɪs *US:* 'hɔːr-/
Howard /'haʊəd/
Hubert /'hjuːbət/
Hugh /hjuː/
Humphrey /'hʌmfrɪ/
Ian /'iːən/
Isaac /'aɪzək/
Ivan /'aɪvən/
Ivor /'aɪvə(r)/
Jack /dʒæk/ (from *John*)
Jacob /'dʒeɪkəb/
James /dʒeɪmz/
Jason /'dʒeɪsn/
Jeffrey /'dʒefrɪ/; Jeff /dʒef/
Jeremy /'dʒerəmɪ/; Jerry /'dʒerɪ/
Jerome /dʒə'rəʊm/
Jim /dʒɪm/ (from *James*)
John /dʒɒn/
Jonathan /'dʒɒnəθən/
Joseph /'dʒəʊzɪf/; Jo, Joe /dʒəʊ/
Joshua /'dʒɒʃʊə/
Julian /'dʒuːlɪən/
Justin /'dʒʌstɪn/
Keith /kiːθ/
Kenneth /'kenɪθ/; Ken /ken/
Kevin /'kevɪn/
Laurence, Lawrence /'lɒrəns *US:* 'lɔːrəns/;
Larry /'lærɪ/
Leo /'liːəʊ/
Leonard /'lenəd/; Len /len/
Leslie /'lezlɪ/; Les /lez/
Lewis /'luːɪs/
Lionel /'laɪənl/
Louis /'luːɪ *US:* 'luːɪs/; Lou /luː/
Luke /luːk/
Malcolm /'mælkəm/
Mark /mɑːk/
Martin /'mɑːtɪn *US:* -tn/
Matthew /'mæθjuː/; Matt /mæt/
Maurice /'mɒrɪs *US:* 'mɔːr-/
Max /mæks/
Michael /'maɪkl/; Mick /mɪk/; Mike /maɪk/

Miles /maɪlz/
Nathaniel /nəˈθænɪəl/; Nat /næt/
Neil /niːl/
Neville /ˈnevl/
Nicholas /ˈnɪkələs/; Nick /nɪk/
Ned /ned/ (from *Edward*)
Nigel /ˈnaɪdʒl/
Noel /ˈnəʊəl/
Norman /ˈnɔːmən/
Oliver /ˈɒlɪvə(r)/
Oscar /ˈɒskə(r)/
Oswald /ˈɒzwəld/
Patrick /ˈpætrɪk/; Pat /pæt/; Paddy /ˈpædɪ/
Paul /pɔːl/
Percy /ˈpɜːsɪ/
Peter /ˈpiːtə(r)/; Pete /piːt/
Philip /ˈfɪlɪp/; Phil /fɪl/
Quentin /ˈkwentɪn *US:* -tn/
Ralph /rælf/
Randolph /ˈrændɒlf/
Raymond /ˈreɪmənd/; Ray /reɪ/
Reginald /ˈredʒɪnld/; Reg /redʒ/
Rex /reks/
Richard /ˈrɪtʃəd/
Robert /ˈrɒbət/
Robin /ˈrɒbɪn/
Rodney /ˈrɒdnɪ/; Rod /rɒd/
Roger /ˈrɒdʒə(r)/
Ronald /ˈrɒnld/; Ron /rɒn/
Roy /rɔɪ/
Rudolf /ˈruːdɒlf/
Rupert /ˈruːpət/
Samuel /ˈsæmjʊəl/; Sam /sæm/
Sandy /ˈsændɪ/ (from *Alexander*)
Seamus /ˈʃeɪməs/
Sean /ʃɔːn/
Sidney /ˈsɪdnɪ/; Sid /sɪd/
Simon /ˈsaɪmən/
Stanley /ˈstænlɪ/; Stan /stæn/
Stephen, Steven /ˈstiːvn/; Steve /stiːv/
Stewart, Stuart /ˈstjuːət *US:* ˈstuː-/
Ted /ted/ (from *Edward*)
Terence /ˈterəns/; Terry /ˈterɪ/
Theodore /ˈθiːədɔː(r)/; Theo /ˈθiːəʊ/
Thomas /ˈtɒməs/; Tom /tɒm/
Timothy /ˈtɪməθɪ/; Tim /tɪm/
Toby /ˈtəʊbɪ/
Tony /ˈtəʊnɪ/ (from *Anthony*)
Trevor /ˈtrevə(r)/
Vernon /ˈvɜːnən/
Victor /ˈvɪktə(r)/; Vic /vɪk/
Vincent /ˈvɪnsnt/
Vivian /ˈvɪvɪən/
Walter /ˈwɔːltə(r)/
Wayne /weɪn/
Wilfred /ˈwɪlfrɪd/
William /ˈwɪlɪəm/; Will /wɪl/

Women

Ada /ˈeɪdə/
Agatha /ˈægəθə/
Agnes /ˈægnɪs/; Aggie /ˈægɪ/
Alexandra /ˌælɪgˈzɑːndrə *US:* -ˈzæn-/
Alice /ˈælɪs/
Alison /ˈælɪsn/
Amanda /əˈmændə/
Amy /ˈeɪmɪ/
Angela /ˈændʒələ/
Anita /əˈniːtə/
Ann, Anne /æn/

Annabel /ˈænəbel/
Anthea /ˈænθɪə/
Audrey /ˈɔːdrɪ/
Barbara /ˈbɑːbrə/; Babs /bæbz/
Beatrice /ˈbɪətrɪs/
Belinda /bəˈlɪndə/
Bella /ˈbelə/ (from *Isabella*)
Beryl /ˈberəl/
Bess /bes/ (from *Elizabeth*)
Betsy /ˈbetsɪ/ (from *Elizabeth*)
Betty /ˈbetɪ/ (from *Elizabeth*)
Brenda /ˈbrendə/
Bridget /ˈbrɪdʒɪt/
Carol, Carole /ˈkærəl/
Caroline /ˈkærəlaɪn/
Carolyn /ˈkærəlɪn/
Catherine /ˈkæθrɪn/; Cathy /ˈkæθɪ/
Cecilia /səˈsiːlɪə/
Cecily /ˈsesəlɪ/
Celia /ˈsiːlɪə/
Charlotte /ˈʃɑːlət/
Chloe /ˈkləʊɪ/
Christina /krɪˈstiːnə/
Christine /ˈkrɪstiːn/; Chris /krɪs/
Clare /kleə(r)/
Constance /ˈkɒnstəns/; Connie /ˈkɒnɪ/
Cynthia /ˈsɪnθɪə/
Daisy /ˈdeɪzɪ/
Daphne /ˈdæfnɪ/
Dawn /dɔːn/
Deborah /ˈdebərə/; Debby /ˈdebɪ/
Deirdre /ˈdɪədrɪ/
Denise /dəˈniːz/
Diana /daɪˈænə/
Dolly /ˈdɒlɪ/ (from *Dorothy*)
Dora /ˈdɔːrə/
Doreen /ˈdɔːriːn/
Doris /ˈdɒrɪs *US:* ˈdɔːr-/
Dorothy /ˈdɒrəθɪ *US:* ˈdɔːr-/
Edith /ˈiːdɪθ/
Eileen /ˈaɪliːn/
Elaine /ɪˈleɪn/
Eleanor /ˈelənə(r)/
Eliza /ɪˈlaɪzə/ (from *Elizabeth*)
Elizabeth /ɪˈlɪzəbəθ/
Ellen /ˈelən/
Elsie /ˈelsɪ/ (from *Elizabeth*)
Emily /ˈemɪlɪ/
Emma /ˈemə/
Erica /ˈerɪkə/
Ethel /ˈeθl/
Eunice /ˈjuːnɪs/
Eva /ˈiːvə/
Eve /iːv/
Evelyn /ˈiːvlɪn/
Fanny /ˈfænɪ/ (from *Frances*)
Felicity /fəˈlɪsətɪ/
Fiona /fɪˈəʊnə/
Flora /ˈflɔːrə/
Florence /ˈflɒrəns *US:* ˈflɔːr-/
Frances /ˈfrɑːnsɪs *US:* ˈfræn-/; Fran /fræn/
Freda /ˈfriːdə/
Geraldine /ˈdʒerəldiːn/
Gertrude /ˈgɜːtruːd/; Gertie /ˈgɜːtɪ/
Gillian /ˈdʒɪlɪən/; Gill /dʒɪl/
Gladys /ˈglædɪs/
Gloria /ˈglɔːrɪə/
Grace /greɪs/
Gwendoline /ˈgwendəlɪn/; Gwen /gwen/
Harriet /ˈhærɪət/

Hazel /'heɪzl/
Heather /'heðə(r)/
Helen /'helən/
Hilary /'hɪlərɪ/
Hilda /'hɪldə/
Ida /'aɪdə/
Ingrid /'ɪŋgrɪd/
Irene /aɪə'ri:nɪ US: 'aɪəri:n/
Iris /'aɪərɪs/
Isabel, Isobel /'ɪzəbel/
Isabella /ˌɪzə'belə/
Ivy /'aɪvɪ/
Jane /dʒeɪn/
Janet /'dʒænɪt/
Janice /'dʒænɪs/
Jacqueline /'dʒækəlɪn/; Jackie /'dʒækɪ/
Jean /dʒi:n/
Jennifer /'dʒenɪfə(r)/; Jenny /'dʒenɪ/
Jessica /'dʒesɪkə/; Jess /dʒes/
Jill /dʒɪl/ (from Gillian)
Joan /dʒəʊn/
Joanna /dʒəʊ'ænə/
Jocelyn /'dʒɒslɪn/
Josephine /'dʒəʊzəfi:n/; Jo /dʒəʊ/
Joy /dʒɔɪ/
Joyce /dʒɔɪs/
Judith /'dʒu:dɪθ/; Judy /'dʒu:dɪ/
Julia /'dʒu:lɪə/
Julie /'dʒu:lɪ/
Juliet /'dʒu:lɪət/
June /dʒu:n/
Karen /'kærən/
Katherine /'kæθrɪn/; Kate /keɪt/; Kathy /'kæθɪ/
Kay /keɪ/
Kitty /'kɪtɪ/ (from Katherine)
Laura /'lɔ:rə/
Lesley /'lezlɪ/
Lilian /'lɪlɪən/
Lily /'lɪlɪ/
Linda /'lɪndə/
Lisa /'li:sə/; Liza /'laɪzə/ (from Elizabeth)
Liz /lɪz/; (from Elizabeth)
Lois /'ləʊɪs/
Lorna /'lɔ:nə/
Louise /lu:'i:z/
Lucy /'lu:sɪ/
Lydia /'lɪdɪə/
Lynn /lɪn/
Mabel /'meɪbl/
Madeleine /'mædəlɪn/
Madge /mædʒ/ (from Margaret)
Maggie /'mægɪ/ (from Margaret)
Mamie /'meɪmɪ/ (from Mary)
Mandy /'mændɪ/ (from Amanda)
Margaret /'mɑ:grɪt/
Margery /'mɑ:dʒərɪ/; Margie /'mɑ:dʒɪ/
Marjorie /'mɑ:dʒərɪ/
Marlene /mɑ:'li:n/
Martha /'mɑ:θə/
Maria /mə'rɪə/
Marian, Marion /'mærɪən/
Marie /mə'ri:, 'mɑ:rɪ/
Marilyn /'mærəlɪn/
Mary /'meərɪ/
Maud /mɔ:d/
Maureen /'mɔ:ri:n/
Mavis /'meɪvɪs/
Maxine /'mæksi:n/
May /meɪ/ (from Mary)
Meg /meg/ (from Margaret)

Michelle /mɪ'ʃel/
Mildred /'mɪldrɪd/
Millicent /'mɪlɪsnt/; Milly /'mɪlɪ/
Miranda /mɪ'rændə/
Miriam /'mɪrɪəm/
Moira /'mɔɪrə/
Molly /'mɒlɪ/ (from Mary)
Monica /'mɒnɪkə/
Muriel /'mjʊərɪəl/
Myra /'maɪərə/
Nancy /'nænsɪ/
Naomi /'neɪəmɪ/
Natalie /'nætəlɪ/
Nelly /'nelɪ/ (from Eleanor or Helen)
Nora /'nɔ:rə/
Olive /'ɒlɪv/
Olivia /ə'lɪvɪə/
Pamela /'pæmələ/; Pam /pæm/
Patience /'peɪʃns/
Patricia /pə'trɪʃə/; Pat /pæt/
Paula /'pɔ:lə/
Pauline /'pɔ:li:n/
Pearl /pɜ:l/
Peg /peg/ (from Margaret)
Penelope /pə'neləpɪ/; Penny /'penɪ/
Philippa /'fɪlɪpə/
Phoebe /'fi:bɪ/
Phyllis /'fɪlɪs/
Polly /'pɒlɪ/
Priscilla /prɪ'sɪlə/
Prudence /'pru:dns/
Rachel /'reɪtʃl/
Rebecca /rə'bekə/
Rita /'ri:tə/
Rosalie /'rəʊzəlɪ/
Rosalind /'rɒzəlɪnd/
Rose /rəʊz/
Rosemary /'rəʊzmərɪ US: -merɪ/
Ruth /ru:θ/
Sally /'sælɪ/ (from Sarah)
Samantha /sə'mænθə/
Sandra /'sɑ:ndrə US: 'sæn-/
Sarah /'seərə/
Sharon /'ʃærən/
Shirley /'ʃɜ:lɪ/
Sheila /'ʃi:lə/
Sonia /'sɒnɪə/
Sophia /sə'faɪə/
Sophie /'səʊfɪ/
Stella /'stelə/
Stephanie /'stefənɪ/
Susan /'su:zn/; Sue /su:/; Susie /'su:zɪ/
Suzanne /su:'zæn/
Sylvia, Silvia /'sɪlvɪə/
Teresa, Theresa /tə'ri:zə/; Tess /tes/; Tessa /'tesə/
Tina /'ti:nə/ (from Christina)
Tracy /'treɪsɪ/
Ursula /'ɜ:sjʊlə/
Vanessa /və'nesə/
Vera /'vɪərə/
Veronica /və'rɒnɪkə/
Victoria /vɪk'tɔ:rɪə/; Vicky /'vɪkɪ/
Viola /'vaɪələ/
Violet /'vaɪələt/
Virginia /və'dʒɪnɪə/
Vivien(ne) /'vɪvɪən/
Wendy /'wendɪ/
Winifred /'wɪnɪfrɪd/; Winnie /'wɪnɪ/
Yvonne /ɪ'vɒn/
Zoe /'zəʊɪ/

Appendix 8 THE WORKS OF WILLIAM SHAKESPEARE (1564-1616)

Note. The list below includes the approximate date of composition, full title and common abbreviation; phonetic transcriptions are provided where necessary.

Plays

1590–1	The First Part of King Henry VI (*1 Hen VI*) The Second Part of King Henry VI (*2 Hen VI*) The Third Part of King Henry VI (*3 Hen VI*)
1592–3	The Tragedy of King Richard III (*Rich III*) The Comedy of Errors (*Com Err*)
1593–4	Titus Andronicus (*Titus A*) /ˌtaɪtəs æn'drɒnɪkəs/ The Taming of the Shrew (*Tam Shr*)
1594–5	The Two Gentlemen of Verona (*Two Gent*) /vəˈrəʊnə/ Love's Labour's Lost (*Love's L L*) Romeo and Juliet (*Rom & Jul*) /ˌrəʊmɪəʊ ən 'dʒuːlɪət/
1595–6	The Tragedy of King Richard II (*Rich II*) A Midsummer Night's Dream (*Mid N D*)
1596–7	The Life and Death of King John (*K John*) The Merchant of Venice (*Mer of Ven*) /'venɪs/
1597–8	The First Part of King Henry IV (*1 Hen IV*) The Second Part of King Henry IV (*2 Hen IV*)
1598–1600	Much Ado about Nothing (*M Ado*) As You Like It (*As You L It*) Twelfth Night, or, What You Will (*Tw N*) The Life of King Henry V (*Hen V*) Julius Caesar (*Jul Caes*) /'dʒuːlɪəs 'siːzə(r)/
1600–1	Hamlet, Prince of Denmark (*Haml*) /'hæmlɪt/ The Merry Wives of Windsor (*Merry W*) /'wɪnzə(r)/
1601–2	Troilus and Cressida (*Tro & Cr*) /ˌtrɔɪləs n 'kresɪdə/ All's Well that Ends Well (*All's Well*)
1604–5	Measure for Measure (*Meas for Meas*) Othello, the Moor of Venice (*Oth*) /ə'θeləʊ/
1605–6	King Lear (*K Lear*) /lɪə(r)/ Macbeth (*Macb*) /mæk'beθ/
1606–7	Antony and Cleopatra (*Ant & Cleop*) /ˌæntənɪ ən klɪə'pætrə/
1607–8	Coriolanus (*Cor*) /ˌkɒrɪə'leɪnəs US: ˌkɔːr-/ Timon of Athens (*Tim of Ath*) /ˌtaɪmən əv 'æθənz/
1608–10	Pericles, Prince of Tyre (*Per*) /'perɪkliːz/ Cymbeline (*Cymb*) /'sɪmbəliːn/ The Winter's Tale (*Wint T*)
1611–12	The Tempest (*Temp*)
1612–13	The Famous History of the Life of King Henry VIII (*Hen VIII*)

Poems

(Date given is that of first printing)

1593	Venus and Adonis (*Ven & Ad*) /ˌviːnəs n ə'dəʊnɪs US: ə'dɒnɪs/
1594	The Rape of Lucrece (*Lucr*) /luːkriːs/
1601	The Phoenix and the Turtle (*Phoen & T*)
1609	Sonnets (*Sonn*)
1609	A Lover's Complaint (*Lover's Comp*)

Appendix 9 PUNCTUATION

· Full Stop (US = Period)

Used to mark the end of a sentence:

Edward walked briskly into the hotel. The receptionist looked at him coldly.

Also ⇨ Letters and Abbreviations below.

? Question Mark

1 Used at the end of a *direct question*:

Who was the first to arrive?

(*Note*. It is not used at the end of an *indirect question*: *He asked who had been the first to arrive.*)

2 Used in parentheses to express doubt:

He was born in 1550(?) and died in 1613.

! Exclamation Mark (US also Exclamation Point)

Used at the end of a sentence or remark expressing a high degree of anger, amazement or other strong emotion:

'What a wonderful surprise!' she cried.
Get out of here and never come back!

(*Note*. Beware of over-using exclamation marks, or including them where the emotion is only mild.)

, Comma

1 Used to separate the items in lists of words, phrases or clauses:

Red, pink, yellow and white roses filled the huge vases.
If you take your time, stay calm, concentrate and think ahead, you'll pass your driving test.

2 Sometimes used after a subordinate adverbial clause or after a phrase which comes before the main clause. It is essential after longer clauses and phrases, and to avoid ambiguity:

When the sun is shining brightly above, the world seems a happier place.
In the summer of 1984, many trees died.

3 Used after a non-finite or verbless clause at the beginning of a sentence:

To get there on time, she left half an hour early.
Happy and contented, the cat fell asleep.

4 Used to separate an introductory or transitional word or phrase (e g *therefore, however, by the way, for instance*) from the rest of the sentence:

Yes, it certainly had been an eventful day.
In fact, I don't even know her name.
Driving on icy roads can be dangerous and one should, therefore, be very careful.

5 Used before and after any element (e g a dependent clause, a comment) which interrupts the sentence:

The fire, although it had been burning for several hours, was still blazing fiercely.
You should, indeed you must, report the matter to the police.

6 Used before and after a non-defining relative clause, or a phrase in apposition, which gives more information about the noun it follows:

The Pennine Hills, which have been a favourite with hikers for many years, are situated between Lancashire and Yorkshire.
Queen Elizabeth II, a very popular monarch, celebrated her Silver Jubilee in 1977.

(*Note*. No commas are used around a relative clause that *defines* the noun it follows:

The hills that separate Lancashire from Yorkshire are called The Pennines.)

7 Sometimes used to separate main clauses linked by a conjunction (e g *and, as, but, for, or*), especially when the first clause is long:

We had been looking forward to meeting Sarah's husband, but discovered that he was not as pleasant as we had hoped.

Also ⇨ Conversation and Letters below.

: Colon

1 (Formal) Used after a main clause where the following statement illustrates or explains the content of that clause. It may be replaced by a semicolon or a full stop:

The garden had been neglected for a long time: it was overgrown and full of weeds.

2 Used before a long list, and often introduced by phrases such as: *such as: for example: for instance: in the following examples: as follows:*

Your first aid kit should include the following items: cotton wool, lint, antiseptic lotion, sticking plaster, bandages and safety pins.

Also ⇨ Letters and Quotations below.

; Semicolon

1 (Formal) Used to separate main clauses, not (usually) joined by a conjunction, which are considered so closely connected as to belong to one sentence:

The sun was setting now; the shadows were long.
He had never been to Russia before; however, it had always been one of his life-long ambitions.

2 Used instead of a comma to separate from each other parts of a sentence that are already separated by commas:

There are two facts to consider: first, the weather; second, the expense.

— Dash

1 (Colloq) Used instead of a colon or a semicolon to make the writing more vivid or dramatic:

Sirens blared, men shouted, and people crowded in to witness the scene—it was chaos.
So you've been lying to me for years and years—how can I ever trust you again?

2 (Colloq) Used singly or in pairs to separate extra information, an after-thought or a comment, in a vivid or dramatic way, from the rest of the sentence:

Schooldays are the happiest days of our lives—or so we are told.
Schooldays—or so we are told—are the happiest days of our lives.

(*Note.* In more formal usage, parentheses or commas replace dashes.)

Also ⇨ Conversation below.

( ) Parentheses (GB also Brackets)

1 Used to separate extra information, an after-thought or a comment from the rest of the sentence:

Schooldays (so we are told) are the happiest days of our lives.
He said he'd never seen the sea before (but I think he was joking).

2 Used to enclose cross-references:

The abacus (see the picture on page 1) is used for teaching numbers to children.

' ' Quotation Marks (GB also Inverted Commas)

(*Note.* In GB usage they are usually single: *'Fire!'* In US usage they are usually double: *"Fire!"*)

Used around a slang or technical term when it is in a context in which it is not usually found, or around a word to which the writer wishes to draw particular attention:

Next, the clay pot had to be 'fired'.
He called himself a 'gentleman', but you would never have thought so from the way he behaved.

Also ⇨ Conversation and Quotations below.

- Hyphen

(*Note.* It must not be confused with the dash, which separates parts of a sentence. The hyphen is half the length of the dash.)

1 Sometimes used to form a compound word from two other words:

hard-hearted; radio-telescope; fork-lift truck.

2 Used to form a compound word from a prefix and a proper name:

pre-Raphaelite; pro-Soviet; anti-Nazi.

3 Used to form a compound word from two other words which are separated by a preposition:

mother-in-law; mother-to-be; mother-of-pearl; out-of-date.

4 (Esp GB) Sometimes used to separate a prefix ending in a vowel from a word beginning with that same vowel:

co-ordination; re-elect; pre-eminent.

Also ➪ Introduction: page xv (*A compound*); page xx (*How to divide a word*).

' Apostrophe

1 Used with 's' to indicate the possessive:

Singular noun: *the dog's* /dɒgz/ *bone.*
Singular noun ending in 's': *the princess's* /prɪnˈsesɪz/ *smile.*
Singular proper noun ending in 's' (two possible forms): *King Charles's* /ˈtʃɑːlzɪz/ *crown;*
King Charles' /ˈtʃɑːlzɪz/ *crown.*
Plural noun: *students'* /ˈstjuːdənts/ *books.*
Irregular plural: *men's* /menz/ *jackets.*

2 Used in a *contracted form* to indicate the omission of letters or figures:

I'm (= I am); *he's* (= he is/has); *they'd* (= they would/had). *In '87* (= 1987).

3 Used with 's' to form the plural of a letter, a figure or an abbreviation, when these are used as proper words. In modern usage it is often omitted after a figure or a capital letter:

in the 1960's or *in the 1960s. MP's* or *MPs. He can't pronounce his r's.*

4 Used with 's' to form the plural of a word (e g a preposition or a conjunction) that does not usually have a plural:

No if's or but's—just do as I say.

Abbreviations

1 A full stop may end an abbreviation or a person's initials, although this is becoming less common, especially in GB usage:

Mr. R. S. H. Smith or *Mr R S H Smith.*

2 When the abbreviation consists of capitals, it is common GB usage to omit the full stops:

UN WHO BBC

3 The omission of full stops in a lower case abbreviation is less common:

i.e. p.m. e.g. or *ie pm eg*

4 If the abbreviation includes the last letter of the word, it is usual in GB usage to omit the full stop:

Mr Dr St Rd

5 To form the plural of capital letter abbreviations, add a lower case *'s* or *s*:

MP's or *MPs   TV's* or *TVs*

Also ➪ Appendix 2 (*Abbreviations*).

Conversation

1 A new indented paragraph is begun with each new speaker.

2 Quotation marks enclose all words and punctuation in direct speech:

'What on earth did you do that for?' he asked.

3 Introductory words (e g *he said, she cried, they answered*) are separated from the actual words spoken by commas if no other punctuation mark (e g question mark, exclamation mark) is used:

John said, 'That's all I know.' 'That's all I know,' said John. 'That,' said John, 'is all I know.'
'Why?' asked John.

4 A comma separates a question tag from the rest of the sentence:

'You knew he'd come, didn't you?'

5 A mild interjection or the direct use of a name is separated from the rest of the sentence by a comma:

'Oh, so that's what he wanted.' (Cf *'Oh no! I don't believe you!'*)
'Well, Peter, I did my best.' (Cf *'Peter! Look out!'*)

6 Hesitant or interrupted speech can be indicated by dashes:

'Can I—I mean, would you mind if I came too?'
'You'll find it in—' were his dying words.

7 Speech within speech is shown by (GB usage) double quotation marks inside single marks, or (US usage) single quotation marks within double marks:

'When the judge said, "Not guilty," I could have hugged him.' (GB)
"When the judge said, 'Not guilty,' I could have hugged him." (US)

Letters

1 A business letter is set out as shown below. The punctuation marks are optional. The address of the person who is writing the letter is in the top right-hand corner; the address of the person to whom the letter is being written is in the top left-hand corner, but below the address of the sender:

> *3 Willow Street,*
> *Frambleton,*
> *Suffolk.*
> *SF5 9PK.*
> *6th June, 1984.*

Mr D. B. Taylor,
Metalwork Ltd,
Booth Street,
Ormton,
Lancashire.
LC14 3JQ.

Dear Mr Taylor,

Thank you for . . .

Yours faithfully/sincerely/(US) truly,

[signature]

Mary Burton.

2 In US usage, a colon is substituted for the comma in the salutation, except informally:

Dear Ms Burton: but   *Dear Mary,*

3 In an informal letter, only the address of the sender is necessary, the optional punctuation is more likely to be omitted, and *Yours sincerely* etc is replaced by a more friendly or personal phrase, e g *Yours, Yours affectionately, With best/warm wishes, With love.*

Quotations

1 The quotation is separated from its introduction by a colon and is enclosed by quotation marks:

It was Disraeli who said: 'Little things affect little minds.'

2 If a word or phrase is omitted from the quotation, this is indicated by a row of three dots (. . .):
'The condition of man . . . is a condition of war of everyone against everyone.' (Thomas Hobbes)

Also ⇨ Conversation above.

The Old Testament

Genesis (*Gen*) /'dʒenəsɪs/
Exodus (*Exod*) /'eksədəs/
Leviticus (*Lev*) /lɪ'vɪtɪkəs/
Numbers (*Num*) /'nʌmbəz/
Deuteronomy (*Deut*) /ˌdjuː:təˈrɒnəmɪ US: ˌduː:-/
Joshua (*Josh*) /'dʒɒʃʊə/
Judges (*Judg*) /'dʒʌdʒɪz/
Ruth /ruː:θ/
I Samuel (*I Sam*) /'sæmjʊəl/
II Samuel (*II Sam*) /'sæmjʊəl/
I Kings (*I Kgs*) /kɪŋz/
II Kings (*II Kgs*) /kɪŋz/
I Chronicles (*I Chron*) /'krɒnɪklz/
II Chronicles (*II Chron*) /'krɒnɪklz/
Ezra /'ezrə/
Nehemiah (*Neh*) /ˌniː:əˈmaɪə/
Esther /'estə(r)/
Job /dʒəʊb/
Psalms (*Ps*) /sɑ:mz/
Proverbs (*Prov*) /'prɒvɜ:bz/

Ecclesiastes (*Eccles*) /ɪˌkliː:zɪ'æstiː:z/
Song of Solomon /ˌsɒŋ əv 'sɒləmən US: ˌsɔ:ŋ/
  or Song of Songs (*S of S*)
Isaiah (*Isa*) /aɪ'zaɪə US: aɪ'zeɪə/
Jeremiah (*Jer*) /ˌdʒerɪ'maɪə/
Lamentations (*Lam*) /ˌlæmənˈteɪʃnz/
Ezekiel (*Ezek*) /ɪ'ziː:kɪəl/
Daniel (*Dan*) /'dænɪəl/
Hosea (*Hos*) /həʊ'ziː:ə/
Joel /'dʒəʊəl/
Amos /'eɪmɒs US: -məs/
Obadiah (*Obad*) /ˌəʊbə'daɪə/
Jonah /'dʒəʊnə/
Micah /'maɪkə/
Nahum /'neɪhəm/
Habakkuk (*Hab*) /'hæbəkək US: hə'bækək/
Zephaniah (*Zeph*) /ˌzefə'naɪə/
Haggai (*Hag*) /'hægeɪaɪ US: 'hægɪaɪ/
Zechariah (*Zech*) /ˌzekə'raɪə/
Malachi (*Mal*) /'mæləkaɪ/

The Apocrypha /ə'pɒkrɪfə/

Tobit /'təʊbɪt/
Judith /'dʒuː:dɪθ/
Wisdom /'wɪzdəm/
Ecclesiasticus /ɪˌkliː:zɪ'æstɪkəs/

Baruch /'beərək/
I Maccabees /'mækəbiː:z/
II Maccabees /'mækəbiː:z/

The New Testament

St Matthew (*Matt*) /'mæθjuː:/
St Mark /mɑ:k/
St Luke /luː:k/
St John /dʒɒn/
Acts /ækts/
Romans (*Rom*) /'rəʊmənz/
I Corinthians (*I Cor*) /kə'rɪnθɪənz/
II Corinthians (*II Cor*) /kə'rɪnθɪənz/
Galatians (*Gal*) /gə'leɪʃnz/
Ephesians (*Eph*) /ɪ'fiː:ʒnz/
Philippians (*Phil*) /fɪ'lɪpɪənz/
Colossians (*Col*) /kə'lɒʃnz/
I Thessalonians (*I Thess*) /ˌθesə'ləʊnɪənz/
II Thessalonians (*II Thess*) /ˌθesə'ləʊnɪənz/

I Timothy (*I Tim*) /'tɪməθɪ/
II Timothy (*II Tim*) /'tɪməθɪ/
Titus (*Tit*) /'taɪtəs/
Philemon (*Philem*) /fɪ'liː:mən/
Hebrews (*Heb*) /'hiː:bruz/
James (*Jas*) /dʒeɪmz/
I Peter (*I Pet*) /'piː:tə(r)/
II Peter (*II Pet*) /'piː:tə(r)/
I John /dʒɒn/
II John /dʒɒn/
III John /dʒɒn/
Jude /dʒuː:d/
Revelation (*Rev*) /ˌrevə'leɪʃn/
  or Apocalypse /ə'pɒkəlɪps/

NOTES

NOTES

NOTES

NOTES

NOTES

NOTES

NOTES

NOTES

Key to the verb patterns

Abbreviations used: S = Subject   vi = intransitive verb   vt = transitive verb
DO = Direct Object   IO = Indirect Object

[VP1]   S + BE + subject complement/adjunct
          This is a book/where I work.
[VP2A]   S + *vi*
          The moon rose.
[VP2B]   S + *vi* + (*for*) + adverbial adjunct
          We walked (for) five miles.
[VP2C]   S + *vi* + adverbial adjunct
          Go away/Come in.
[VP2D]   S + *vi* + adjective/noun/pronoun
          She married young.
[VP2E]   S + *vi* + present participle
          They've gone dancing.
[VP3A]   S + *vi* + preposition + noun/pronoun
          You can rely on me.
[VP3B]   S + *vi* + (preposition (+ *it*)) + clause
          Have you decided (on) what to do next?
[VP4A]   S + *vi* + *to*-infinitive
          We stopped to rest.
[VP4B]   S + *vi* + *to*-infinitive
          He awoke to find the house on fire.
[VP4C]   S + *vi* + *to*-infinitive
          He agreed to come at once.
[VP4D]   S + SEEM/APPEAR + (*to be*) + adjective/noun
          He seemed (to be) surprised at the news.
[VP4E]   S + SEEM/APPEAR/HAPPEN/CHANCE + *to*-infinitive
          She appears to have left already.
[VP4F]   S + BE + *to*-infinitive
          At what time am I to come?
[VP5]   S + anomalous finite + infinitive
          You needn't wait.
[VP6A]   S + *vt* + noun/pronoun
          Everyone likes her.
[VP6B]   S + *vt* + noun/pronoun
          She has green eyes.
[VP6C]   S + *vt* + gerund
          She enjoys playing tennis.
[VP6D]   S + *vt* + gerund
          He began talking about his family.
[VP6E]   S + NEED/WANT/BEAR + gerund
          He needs looking after.
[VP7A]   S + *vt* + (*not*) + *to*-infinitive
          I forgot to post your letter.
[VP7B]   S + HAVE/OUGHT + (*not*) + *to*-infinitive
          He often has to work overtime.
[VP8]   S + *vt* + interrogative pronoun/adverb + *to*-infinitive
          I couldn't decide what to do next.
[VP9]   S + *vt* + *that*-clause
          Do you think (that) it will rain?
[VP10]   S + *vt* + dependent clause/question
          Does anyone know how it happened?